COLLINS
CONCISE
DICTIONARY
Plus

COLLINS
CONCISE
DICTIONARY
Plus

COLLINS
London and Glasgow

First Published 1989
© William Collins Sons & Co. Ltd. 1989
ISBN 0 00 433252-0

Prepared in conjunction with
Market House Books Ltd., Aylesbury

Printed & Bound by
The Bath Press
for William Collins Sons & Co. Ltd.,
PO Box, Glasgow G4 0NB

British Library Cataloguing in Publication Data
Collins concise dictionary plus.
　1. English language, — Dictionaries
　423

CONTENTS

FOREWORD

The *Collins Concise Dictionary Plus* is a new book prepared using the full resources of the Collins Dictionaries database and compiled and edited with many special features to give the widest possible range of information both to the student and to the general user.

As its title implies, the *Collins Concise Dictionary Plus* is more than just a dictionary. It includes over 15,000 encyclopedic entries, covering people, places, geographical features, institutions, organizations, and movements, relating to all areas of human activity, past and present.

As a further dimension to this unique reference book, over fifty pages of supplementary encyclopedic information are included. These supplements cover a range of topics that are more readily comprehensible in chart or diagrammatic form and enable the user of the book to gain an overall view and to trace developments and interrelationships. They also serve in many cases as a quick reference source for information, study, or revision. Subjects covered are diverse, and include, for example, the development of the modern alphabet, symbols used in mathematics and science, anatomy, music, and statistical profiles of the past forty years. The final section of the dictionary comprises a chronology of the main events, developments, and discoveries in history, the arts, and the sciences, giving a 'bird's-eye' view of one thousand years of British history and the chronological relationship of different areas of human achievement.

The dictionary contains all the well-known features of the *Collins Concise Dictionary*. It is edited to ensure that it is easy to use. All entries which need a definition are entered as headwords, so the required item, whether it be a single word, a compound word, an encyclopedic entry, an abbreviation or acronym, or a foreign word, is entered in its alphabetical position. The meanings are written in clear, explanatory English, and numbered to make it easy to find the one required. The core modern meaning is the one given first, with older, rare, or specialized senses following. Meanings which are regional, technical, or otherwise restricted in their area of use are clearly labelled. Special attention has been given to the English of Commonwealth countries and the United States, so that the dictionary covers the language not just of the United Kingdom but of all the main English-speaking regions of the world. Help is given on many disputed or problematic points of usage, which are discussed in usage notes at the end of the relevant entries.

The *Collins Concise Dictionary Plus* thus provides for the user an up-to-date, comprehensive, and helpfully laid out dictionary text, together with modern, in-depth encyclopedic coverage. This unique general reference dictionary will prove equally helpful to home users and students, and to all who want clarity and exceptional coverage in a paperback format.

Finally, the editors would like to thank the many consultants, specialist editors, organizations, and individuals who have contributed to and advised on the material contained in this book, and to those members of the public who have written with suggestions.

Guide to the Use of the Dictionary

The Headword

The headwords are listed in strictly alphabetical order. This rule applies even if the headword consists of more than one word, or is an abbreviation, an acronym, or a symbol. Thus **bed** and the entries related to it are separated by intervening entries occurring in strict alphabetical order.

> **bed**
> **BEd**
> **bed and board**
> **bed and breakfast**
> **bedaub**
> **bedazzle**
> **bed bath**
> **bedbug**
> **bedchamber**
> **bedclothes**

Words that have the same spelling but are derived from different sources etymologically (homographs) are entered separately with superscript numbers after the headwords.

> **saw**[1] (sɔ:) n. **1.** any of various hand tools. . . .
> **saw**[2] (sɔ:) vb. the past tense of **see**[1].
> **saw**[3] (sɔ:) n. a wise saying, maxim, or proverb. . . .

Common acceptable variant spellings of English words are given as alternative forms of the headword.

> **characterize** or **-ise** ('kærɪktəˌraɪz) vb. . . .

Where it is different, the U.S. spelling of a word is also recorded in the headword.

> **centre** or U.S. **center** ('sɛntə) n. . . .

Prefixes (e.g. **in-**[1], **pre-**, **sub-**), suffixes (e.g. **-able**, **-ation**, **-ity**), and combining forms (e.g. **psycho-**, **-iatry**) have been entered as headwords if they are still used freely to produce new words in English.

The Pronunciation

Pronunciations of words in this dictionary represent those that are common in educated British English speech. They are transcribed in the International Phonetic Alphabet (IPA). A *Key to the Pronunciation Symbols* is printed at the end of this Guide.

When a headword has a common acceptable variant pronunciation or stress pattern, the variant is shown in full or by repeating only the syllable or syllables that change.

> **amok** (ə'mʌk, ə'mɒk) . . . . n
> **lactose** ('læktəʊs, -təʊz) n. . . .

When two or more parts of speech of a word have different pronunciations, the pronunciations are shown in parentheses before the relevant group of senses.

> **record** n. ('rɛkɔ:d). **1.** an account in permanent form. . . ~vb. (rɪ'kɔ:d). (mainly tr.) **18.** to set down in some permanent form. . . .

If one sense of a headword has a different pronunciation from that of the rest, that pronunciation is given in parentheses after the sense number.

> **conjure** ('kʌndʒə) vb. **1.** (intr.) to practise conjuring. . . . **3.** (kən'dʒʊə). (tr.) to appeal earnestly to: I conjure you to help me. . . .

Inflected Forms

Inflected forms are shown for the following:

Nouns and verbs whose inflections involve a change in internal spelling.

> **goose**[1] (gu:s) n., pl. **geese**. . . .
> **drive** (draɪv) vb. **driving, drove, driven.** . . .

Nouns, verbs, and adjectives that end in a consonant plus y, where y is changed to i before inflectional endings.

> **augury** ('ɔ:gjʊrɪ) n., pl. **-ries.** . . .

Nouns having identical singular and plural forms.

> **sheep** (ʃi:p) n., pl. **sheep.** . . .

Nouns that closely resemble others that form their plurals differently.

> **mongoose** ('mɒŋˌgu:s) n., pl. **-gooses.** . . .

Nouns that end in -ful, -o, and -us.

> **handful** ('hændfʊl) n., pl. **-fuls.** . . .
> **potato** (pə'teɪtəʊ) n., pl. **-toes.** . . .
> **prospectus** (prə'spɛktəs) n., pl. **-tuses.** . . .

Nouns whose plurals are not regular English inflections.

> **basis** ('beɪsɪs) n., pl. **-ses** (-si:z). . . .

Plural nouns whose singulars are not regular English forms.

> **bacteria** (bæk'tɪərɪə) pl. n., sing. **-rium.** . . .

Nouns whose plurals have regular spellings but involve a change in pronunciation.

> **house** n. (haʊs), pl. **houses** ('haʊzɪz). . . .

Multiword nouns when it is not obvious which word takes a plural inflection.

> **attorney-at-law** n., pl. **attorneys-at-law.** . . .

Adjectives that change their roots to form comparatives and superlatives.

> **good** (gʊd) adj. **better, best.** . . .

Adjectives and verbs that double their final consonant before adding endings.

> **fat** (fæt). . . . ~adj. **fatter, fattest.** . . .
> **control** (kən'trəʊl) vb. **-trolling, -trolled**

Verbs and adjectives that end in a vowel plus e.

> **canoe** (kə'nu:). . . ~vb. **-noeing, -noed.** . . .
> **free** (fri:) adj. **freer, freest.** . . . ~vb. **freeing, freed.** . . .

Parts of Speech

A part-of-speech label in italics precedes the account of the sense or senses relating to that part of speech.

Standard parts of speech

The following parts of speech, with abbreviations as shown, are standard and need no further explanation: adjective (adj.), adverb (adv.), conjunction (conj.), interjection (interj.), noun (n.), preposition (prep.), pronoun (pron.), verb (vb.).

Less traditional parts of speech

Certain other less traditional parts of speech have been adopted in this dictionary. They are as follows:

determiner. This denotes such words as the, a, some, any, that, this, possessives like my, his, and your, and the numerals. Many determiners can have a pronoun function without change of meaning, and this is shown thus:

> **some** (sʌm; unstressed səm) determiner. . . . **2. a.** an unknown or unspecified quantity or amount of: there's some rice on the table; he owns some horses. **b.** (as pron.; functioning as sing. or pl.): we'll buy some. . . .

sentence connector. This denotes words like however and therefore, which have been traditionally classed as adverbs but which function as conjunctions, linking sentences, without being restricted, as are conjunctions, to the initial position in their clause.

sentence substitute. Sentence substitutes comprise words such as *yes, no, perhaps, definitely,* and *maybe,* which can stand as meaningful utterances by themselves.

If a word can be used as more than one part of speech, the account of the senses of one part of speech is separated from the others by a swung dash (~).

lure (loə) *vb.* (*tr.*). . . . **2.** *Falconry.* to entice (a hawk or falcon) from the air to the falconer by a lure. ~*n.* **3.** a person or thing that lures. . . .

Headwords and senses that may take either a singular or a plural verb, etc., are marked "*functioning as sing. or pl.*"

bellows ('bɛləʊz) *n.* (*functioning as sing. or pl.*) **1.** Also: **pair of bellows.** an instrument consisting of an air chamber. . . .

Modifiers

A noun that is commonly used with adjectival force is labelled *modifier.*

If the sense of the modifier is strictly inferable from the sense of the noun, the modifier is shown without further explanation, with an example to illustrate its use; otherwise an account of its meaning and/or usage is given in a separate numbered definition.

key[1] (ki:) *n.* . . . **18.** (*modifier*) of great importance: *a key issue.* . . .

Grammatical Information

Adjectives and Determiners

Some adjectives and determiners are restricted by usage to a particular position relative to the nouns they qualify. This is indicated by the following labels:

postpositive (used predicatively or after the noun, but not before the noun):

ablaze (ə'bleɪz) *adj.* (*postpositive*), *adv.* **1.** on fire; burning. . . .

immediately postpositive (always used immediately following the noun qualified and never used predicatively):

galore (gə'lɔː) *determiner.* (*immediately postpositive*) in great numbers or quantity: *there were daffodils galore in the park.* . . .

prenominal (used before the noun, and never used predicatively):

chief (tʃi:f). . . . ~*adj.* **4.** (*prenominal*) **a.** most important; principal. **b.** highest in rank or authority. . . .

Intensifiers

Adjectives and adverbs that perform an exclusively intensifying function, with no addition of meaning, are described as (intensifier) without further explanation.

blooming ('blu:mɪŋ) *adv., adj. Brit. inf.* (intensifier): *a blooming genius; blooming painful.* . . .

Conjunctions

Conjunctions are divided into two classes, marked by the following labels placed in parentheses:

coordinating. Coordinating conjunctions connect words, phrases, or clauses that perform an identical function and are not dependent on each other. They include *and, but,* and *or.*

subordinating. Subordinating conjunctions introduce clauses that are dependent on a main clause in a complex sentence. Examples are *where, until,* and *before.*

Some conjunctions, such as *while* and *whether,* can function as either coordinating or subordinating conjunctions.

Singular and plural labelling

Headwords and senses that are apparently plural in form but that take a singular verb, etc., are marked "*functioning as sing.*"

physics ('fɪzɪks) *n.* (*functioning as sing.*) **1.** the branch of science. . . .

Headwords and senses that appear to be singular but take a plural verb, etc., are marked "*functioning as pl.*"

cattle ('kæt³l) *n.* (*functioning as pl.*) **1.** bovid mammals of the tribe *Bovini.* . . .

Verbs

The account of the meaning of a verb is given without subdivision into separate groupings for transitive and intransitive senses. Instead, each definition is worded so as to take account of transitivity or intransitivity. When a sense of a verb (*vb.*) is restricted to transitive use, it is labelled (*tr.*); if it is intransitive only, it is labelled (*intr.*). If all the senses of a verb are either transitive or intransitive, the appropriate label appears before the first numbered sense and is not repeated. Absence of a label indicates that the sense or verb may be used both transitively and intransitively. If nearly all the senses of a verb are transitive, the label (*mainly tr.*) appears immediately before the first numbered sense. This indicates that, unless otherwise labelled, any given sense of the verb is transitive.

Similarly, all the senses of a verb may be labelled (*mainly intr.*).

Copulas

A verb that takes a complement is labelled *copula.*

seem (si:m) *vb.* (*may take an infinitive*) **1.** (*copula*) to appear to the mind or eye; . . .

Phrasal verbs

Verbal constructions consisting of a verb and a preposition or a verb and an adverbial particle are given headword status if the meaning of the phrasal verb cannot be deduced from the separate meanings of the verb and the particle.

Phrasal verbs are labelled to show four possible distinctions:

a transitive verb with an adverbial particle (*tr., adv.*); a transitive verb with a preposition (*tr., prep.*); an intransitive verb with an adverbial particle (*intr., adv.*); an intransitive verb with a preposition (*intr., prep.*):

turn on. . . . **1.** (*tr., adv.*) to cause (something) to operate by turning a knob, etc.

take for. . . . (*tr., prep.*) **1.** . . . . to consider or suppose to be, esp. mistakenly: *the fake coins were taken for genuine; who do you take me for?*

play up. . . . (*adv.*). . . . **3.** (*intr.*) *Brit. inf.* (of a machine, etc.) to function erratically: *the car is playing up again.*

turn on. . . . **2.** (*intr., prep.*) to depend or hinge on: *the success of the party turns on you.*

As with the labelling of other verbs, the absence of a label is significant. If there is no label (*tr.*) or (*intr.*), the verb may be used either transitively or intransitively. If there is no label (*adv.*) or (*prep.*), the particle may be either adverbial or prepositional.

Any noun, adjective, or modifier formed from a phrasal verb is entered under the phrasal-verb headword. In some cases, where the noun or adjective is more common than the verb, the phrasal verb is entered after the noun/adjective form:

breakaway (ˈbreɪkəˌweɪ) *n.* **1. a.** loss or withdrawal of a group of members from an association, club, etc. **b.** (*as modifier*): *a breakaway faction.* . . . ~*vb.* **break away.** (*intr., adv.*). . . . **4.** to withdraw or secede.

Restrictive Labels

If a particular sense is restricted as to appropriateness, connotation, subject field, etc., an italicized label is placed immediately before the account of the relevant meaning.

hang on *vb.* (*intr.*). . . . **5.** (*adv.*) *Inf.* to wait: *hang on for a few minutes.*

If a label applies to all senses of one part of speech, it is placed immediately after the part-of-speech label.

assured (əˈʃʊəd) *adj.* . . . ~*n.* **4.** *Chiefly Brit.* **a.** the beneficiary. . . . **b.** the person whose life is insured.

If a label applies to all senses of a headword, it is placed immediately after the pronunciation (or inflections).

con[1] (kɒn) *Inf.* ~*n.* **1. a.** short for **confidence trick. b.** (*as modifier*): *con man.* ~*vb.* **conning, conned. 2.** (*tr.*) to swindle or defraud.

Arch. (*Archaic*). Denotes a word or sense that is no longer in common use but may be found in literary works or used to impart a historical colour to contemporary writing.

Obs. (*Obsolete*). Denotes a word or sense that is no longer in use. In specialist or technical fields the label often implies that the term has been superseded.

The word "formerly" is placed in parentheses before a sense or set of senses when the practice, concept, etc., being described, rather than the word itself, is obsolete or out-of-date.

Sl. (*Slang*). Refers to words or senses that are informal and restricted in context, for example, to members of a particular social or cultural group. Slang words are inappropriate in formal speech or writing.

Inf. (*Informal*). Applies to words or senses that may be widely used, especially in conversation, but are not common in formal writing. Such words are subject to fewer contextual restrictions than slang words.

Taboo. Indicates words that are not acceptable in polite use.

Not standard. Indicates words or senses that are frequently encountered but widely regarded as incorrect.

Derog. (*Derogatory*). Implies that the connotations of a word are unpleasant with intent on the part of the speaker or writer.

Offens. (*Offensive*). Indicates that a word may be regarded as offensive by the person described or referred to, even if the speaker uses the word without any malicious intention.

A number of other usage labels, such as *Facetious* and *Euphemistic,* are used where appropriate.

Various italicized labels are used to indicate that a word or sense is used in a particular specialist or technical field.

The Arrangement of Entries

As a general rule, where a headword has more than one sense, the first sense given is the one most common in current usage.

complexion (kəmˈplɛkʃən) *n.* **1.** the colour and general appearance of a person's skin, esp. of the face. **2.** aspect or nature: *the general complexion of a nation's finances.* **3.** *Obs.* temperament.

Where the editors consider that a current sense is the "core meaning", in that it illuminates the meaning of other senses, the core meaning may be placed first.

think (θɪŋk) *vb.* **thinking, thought. 1.** (*tr.; may take a clause as object*) to consider, judge, or believe: *he thinks my ideas impractical.* **2.** (*intr.; often foll. by about*) to exercise the mind as in order to make a decision; ponder. **3.** (*intr.*) to be capable of conscious thought: *man is the only animal that thinks.*

Subsequent senses are arranged so as to give a coherent account of the meaning of a headword. If a word is used as more than one part of speech, all the senses of each part of speech are grouped together in a single block. Within a part-of-speech block, closely related senses are grouped together; technical senses generally follow general senses; archaic and obsolete senses follow technical senses; idioms and fixed phrases are generally placed last.

Scientific definitions

Units, physical quantities, formulas, etc. In accordance with the recommendations of the International Standards Organization, all scientific measurements are expressed in SI units (*Système International d'Unités*). Measurements and quantities in more traditional units are often given as well as SI units. The entries for chemical compounds give the systematic names as well as the more familiar trivial names.

Place names

If a place has more than one name, the main entry is given at the name most common in present-day English-language contexts, with a cross-reference at other names. Thus, the main entry for the capital of Bavaria is at **Munich,** with a cross-reference at **München.** By contrast, the main entry for **Livorno** is given at that spelling rather than at **Leghorn,** an anglicized form that has now fallen into disuse. Historical names of importance are also given, with dates where these can be ascertained.

Paris[1] (ˈpærɪs; *French* pari) *n.* . . . Ancient name: **Lutetia.**

Volgograd (*Russian* vəlgaˈgrat; *English* ˈvɒlgəˌgræd) *n.* . . . Former names: **Tsaritsyn** (until 1925), **Stalingrad** (1925-61).

Statistical information about places has been obtained from the most up-to-date and reliable sources available. Population figures have been compiled from the most recent census available at the time of going to press. The date of the census is always given. Where no census figure is available, the most reliable recent estimate has been given, with a date.

Biographical entries

Biographical entries are entered separately from and immediately following place names of the same spelling. They are entered at the surname of the subject or at his title if that is the name by which he is better known and are grouped under one headword when the spelling of the surname (or title) is identical.

Cross-references

Cross-references refer the reader to additional information elsewhere in the dictionary. If the cross-reference is preceded by a swung dash (~), it applies to all the senses of the headword that have gone before it, unless otherwise stated. If there is no swung dash, the cross-reference applies only to the sense immediately preceding it. Many cross-references include a sense number for the sake of clarity.

Variant spellings are generally entered as cross-references if their place in the alphabetical list is more than ten entries distant from the main entry.

> **aether** ('i:θə) *n.* a variant spelling of **ether** (senses 3, 4).

Alternative names are printed in boldface type and introduced by the words "Also" or "Also called". If the alternative name is preceded by a swung dash (~), it applies to the entire entry.

Related adjectives

Certain nouns of Germanic origin have related adjectives that are derived from Greek, Latin, or French. For example, *mural* (from Latin) is an adjective related in meaning to *wall.* Such adjectives are shown in a number of cases after the sense (or part-of-speech block) to which they are related.

> **bishop** ('bɪʃəp) *n.* **1.** a clergyman having spiritual and administrative powers.... Related adj.: **episcopal.**

Idioms

Placement

Fixed noun phrases, such as **dark horse,** and certain other idioms are given full headword status. Other idioms are placed under the key word of the idiom, as a separate sense, generally at the end of the appropriate part-of-speech block.

> **ground**[1] (graʊnd) *n.*.... **17. break new ground.** to do something that has not been done before....

The Etymology

Placement and selection

Etymologies are placed in square brackets after the account of the meaning. They are given for most headwords except those that are derivative forms (consisting of a base word and a suffix or prefix), compound words, inflected forms, and some chemical compounds. Thus, the headword **manage** has been given an etymology but the related headwords **manageable** (equivalent to *manage* plus the suffix *-able*), **management** (*manage* plus *-ment*), **manager** (*manage* plus *-er*[1]), **manageress** (*manager* plus *-ess*), etc., do not have etymologies. Inflected forms such as **saw**[2] (the past tense of *see*[1]) and obvious compounds such as **mothball** are not given an etymology. Many headwords, such as **enlighten** and **prepossess**, consist of a prefix and a base word and are not accompanied by etymologies since the

essential etymological information is shown for the component parts, all of which are entered in the dictionary as headwords in their own right (in this instance, **en-**[1], **light**[1], **-en**[1] and **pre-, possess**).

Words printed in SMALL CAPITALS within etymologies refer the reader to other headwords where additional information, either in the definition text or in the etymology, may be found or to words that are etymologically related.

Dating

The etymology records the first known occurrence (a written citation) of a word in English. Words first appearing in the language during the Middle English period or later are dated by century, abbreviated C.

> **mantis.** . . . [C17: NL, from Gk: prophet, alluding to its praying posture]

This indicates that there is a written citation for *mantis* in the seventeenth century, when the word was in use as a New Latin term in the scientific vocabulary of the time. The absence of a New Latin or Greek form in the etymology means that the form of the word was the same in those languages as in English.

Native words from Old English are not dated, written records of Old English being comparatively scarce, but are simply identified as being of Old English origin.

Derived Words

Words derived from a base word by the addition of suffixes such as *-ly, -ness,* etc., are entered in boldface type at the end of the entry for the base word. The meanings of such words may be deduced from the meanings of the suffix and the headword. Where a derived word has developed a specialized or restricted meaning, it is entered as a headword and defined, e.g. **absolutely, arrangement.**

Abbreviations

Abbreviations and acronyms that are included as entries are styled in general without stops. Most abbreviations are, however, equally acceptable written with or without stops.

Listed Entries

In English many easily understood words are formed by adding productive prefixes such as *non-, over-, pre-, un-,* etc., to existing words. Such words are included, without definition, at the foot of the page on which they would occur in alphabetical sequence.

Usage Notes

A brief note introduced by the label **Usage** and the marginal sign ▷ has been added at the end of a number of entries in order to comment on matters of usage. These comments are based on the observed practice or preference of the majority of educated speakers and writers.

Pronunciation Key

The symbols used in the pronunciation transcriptions are those of the International Phonetic Alphabet. The following consonant symbols have their usual English values: *b, d, f, h, k, l, m, n, p, r, s, t, v, w, z*. The remaining symbols and their interpretations are listed below.

English Sounds

ɑː as in *father* ('fɑːðə), *alms* (ɑːmz), *clerk* (klɑːk), *heart* (hɑːt), *sergeant* ('sɑːdʒənt)

æ as in *act* (ækt), *Caedmon* ('kædmən), *plait* (plæt)

aɪ as in *dive* (daɪv), *aisle* (aɪl), *guy* (gaɪ), *might* (maɪt), *rye* (raɪ)

aɪə as in *fire* ('faɪə), *buyer* ('baɪə), *liar* ('laɪə), *tyre* ('taɪə)

aʊ as in *out* (aʊt), *bough* (baʊ), *crowd* (kraʊd), *slouch* (slaʊtʃ)

aʊə as in *flour* ('flaʊə), *cower* ('kaʊə), *flower* ('flaʊə), *sour* ('saʊə)

ɛ as in *bet* (bɛt), *ate* (ɛt), *bury* ('bɛrɪ), *heifer* ('hɛfə), *said* (sɛd), *says* (sɛz)

eɪ as in *paid* (peɪd), *day* (deɪ), *deign* (deɪn), *gauge* (geɪdʒ), *grey* (greɪ), *neigh* (neɪ)

ɛə as in *bear* (bɛə), *dare* (dɛə), *prayer* (prɛə), *stairs* (stɛəz), *where* (wɛə)

g as in *get* (gɛt), *give* (gɪv), *ghoul* (guːl), *guard* (gɑːd), *examine* (ɪg'zæmɪn)

I as in *pretty* ('prɪtɪ), *build* (bɪld), *busy* ('bɪzɪ), *nymph* (nɪmf), *pocket* ('pɒkɪt), *sieve* (sɪv), *women* ('wɪmɪn)

iː as in *see* (siː), *aesthete* ('iːsθiːt), *evil* ('iːvˀl), *magazine* (ˌmægə'ziːn), *receive* (rɪ'siːv), *siege* (siːdʒ)

Iə as in *fear* (fɪə), *beer* (bɪə), *mere* (mɪə), *tier* (tɪə)

j as in *yes* (jɛs), *onion* ('ʌnjən), *vignette* (vɪ'njɛt)

ɒ as in *pot* (pɒt), *botch* (bɒtʃ), *sorry* ('sɒrɪ)

əʊ as in *note* (nəʊt), *beau* (bəʊ), *dough* (dəʊ), *hoe* (həʊ), *slow* (sləʊ), *yeoman* ('jəʊmən)

ɔː as in *thaw* (θɔː), *broad* (brɔːd), *drawer* ('drɔːə), *fault* (fɔːlt), *halt* (hɔːlt), *organ* ('ɔːgən)

ɔɪ as in *void* (vɔɪd), *boy* (bɔɪ), *destroy* (dɪ'strɔɪ)

ʊ as in *pull* (pʊl), *good* (gʊd), *should* (ʃʊd), *woman* ('wʊmən)

uː as in *zoo* (zuː), *do* (duː), *queue* (kjuː), *shoe* (ʃuː), *spew* (spjuː), *true* (truː), *you* (juː)

ʊə as in *poor* (pʊə), *skewer* (skjʊə), *sure* (ʃʊə)

ə as in *potter* ('pɒtə), *alone* (ə'ləʊn), *furious* ('fjʊərɪəs), *nation* ('neɪʃən), *the* (ðə)

ɜː as in *fern* (fɜːn), *burn* (bɜːn), *fir* (fɜː), *learn* (lɜːn), *term* (tɜːm), *worm* (wɜːm)

ʌ as in *cut* (kʌt), *flood* (flʌd), *rough* (rʌf), *son* (sʌn)

ʃ as in *ship* (ʃɪp), *election* (ɪ'lɛkʃən), *machine* (mə'ʃiːn), *mission* ('mɪʃən), *pressure* ('prɛʃə), *schedule* ('ʃɛdjuːl), *sugar* ('ʃʊgə)

ʒ as in *treasure* ('trɛʒə), *azure* ('æʒə), *closure* ('kləʊʒə), *evasion* (ɪ'veɪʒən)

tʃ as in *chew* (tʃuː), *nature* ('neɪtʃə)

dʒ as in *jaw* (dʒɔː), *adjective* ('ædʒɪktɪv), *lodge* (lɒdʒ), *soldier* ('səʊldʒə), *usage* ('juːsɪdʒ)

θ as in *thin* (θɪn), *strength* (strɛŋθ), *three* (θriː)

ð as in *these* (ðiːz), *bathe* (beɪð), *lather* ('lɑːðə)

ŋ as in *sing* (sɪŋ), *finger* ('fɪŋgə), *sling* (slɪŋ)

ˀ indicates that the following consonant (*l* or *n*) is syllabic, as in *bundle* ('bʌndˀl), *button* ('bʌtˀn)

Foreign Sounds

The symbols above are also used to represent foreign sounds where these are similar to English sounds. However, certain common foreign sounds require symbols with markedly different values, as follows:

a *a* in French *ami*, German *Mann*, Italian *pasta*: a sound between English (æ) and (ɑː), similar to the vowel in Northern English *cat* or London *cut*.

ɑ *a* in French *bas*: a sound made with a tongue position similar to that of English (ɑː), but shorter.

e *é* in French *été, eh* in German *sehr, e* in Italian *che*: a sound similar to the first part of the English diphthong (eɪ) in *day* or to the Scottish vowel in *day*.

i *i* in French *il*, German *Idee*, Spanish *filo*, Italian *signor*: a sound made with a tongue position similar to that of English (iː), but shorter.

ɔ *o* in Italian *no*, French *bonne*, German *Sonne*: a vowel resembling English (ɒ), but with a higher tongue position and more rounding of the lips.

o *o* in French *rose*, German *so*, Italian *voce*: a sound between English (ɔː) and (uː) with closely rounded lips, similar to the Scottish vowel in *so*.

u *ou* in French *genou, u* in German *kulant*, Spanish *puna*: a sound made with a tongue position similar to that of English (uː), but shorter.

y *u* in French *tu, ü* in German *über* or *fünf*: a sound made with a tongue position similar to that of English (iː) but with closely rounded lips.

ø *eu* in French *deux, ö* in German *schön*: a sound made with the tongue position of (e) but with closely rounded lips.

œ *œu* in French *œuf, ö* in German *zwölf*: a sound made with a tongue position similar to that of English (ɛ) but with open rounded lips.

~ above a vowel indicates nasalization, as in French *un* (œ̃), *bon* (bɔ̃), *vin* (vɛ̃), *blanc* (blɑ̃).

x *ch* in Scottish *loch*, German *Buch, j* in Spanish *Juan*.

ç *ch* in German *ich*: a (j) sound as in *yes*, said without voice; similar to the first sound in *huge*.

β *b* in Spanish *Habana*: a voiced fricative sound similar to (v), but made by the two lips.

ʎ *ll* in Spanish *llamar, gl* in Italian *consiglio*: similar to the (lj) sequence in *million*, but with the tongue tip lowered and the sounds said simultaneously.

ɥ *u* in French *lui*: a short (y).

ɲ *gn* in French *vigne*, Italian *gnocchi, ñ* in Spanish *España*: similar to the (nj) sequence in *onion*, but with the tongue tip lowered and the two sounds said simultaneously.

ɣ *g* in Spanish *luego*: a weak (g) made with voiced friction.

Length

The symbol : denotes length and is shown together with certain vowel symbols when the vowels are typically long.

Pronunciation Key

Stress

Three grades of stress are shown in the transcriptions by the presence or absence of marks placed immediately *before* the affected syllable. Primary or strong stress is shown by ', while secondary or weak stress is shown by ˌ. Unstressed syllables are not marked. In *photographic* (ˌfəʊtəˈgræfɪk), for example, the first syllable carries secondary stress and the third primary stress, while the second and fourth are unstressed.

Notes

(i) Though words like *castle, path, fast* are shown as pronounced with an /ɑː/ sound, many speakers use an /æ/. Such variations are acceptable and are to be assumed by the reader.

(ii) The letter "r" in some positions is not sounded in the speech of Southern England and elsewhere. However, many speakers in other areas do sound the "r" in such positions with varying degrees of distinctness. Again, such variations are to be assumed, and in such words as *fern, fear, arm* the reader will sound or not sound the "r" according to his or her speech habits.

(iii) Though the widely received pronunciation of words like *which, why* is with a simple /w/ sound and is so shown in the dictionary, many speakers in Scotland and elsewhere preserve an aspirated sound: /hw/. Once again this variation is to be assumed.

Abbreviations and Symbols used in the Dictionary

abbrev. abbreviation
Abor. Aboriginal
adj. adjective
adv. adverb(ial)
Afrik. Afrikaans
Amerind American Indian
Anat. Anatomy
approx. approximate(ly)
Ar. Arabic
Arch. Archaic
Archaeol. Archaeology
Archit. Architecture
Astrol. Astrology
Astron. Astronomy
Austral. Australian

Biol. Biology
Bot. Botany
Brit. Britain; British

C century (e.g. C14=14th
century)
°C degrees Celsius
Canad. Canadian
cap. capital
cf. compare
Chem. Chemistry
comp. comparative
conj. conjunction

Derog. Derogatory
dim. diminutive
Du. Dutch

E east(ern): (in etymologies)
English
Econ. Economics
e.g. for example
esp. especially
est. estimate

F French
fem. feminine
foll. followed
ft. foot *or* feet

G German
Geog. Geography
Geol. Geology

Geom. Geometry
Gk Greek
Gmc Germanic

Heb. Hebrew

i.e. that is
imit. of imitative origin
in. inch(es)
Inf. Informal
infl. influence(d)
interj. interjection
intr. intransitive
It. Italian

km kilometre(s)

L Late; Latin
lit. literally
LL Late Latin

m metre(s)
M Middle
masc. masculine
Maths Mathematics
Med. Medicine; (in etymologies)
Medieval
MHG Middle High German
Mil. Military
Mod. Modern
Myth. Mythology

N North(ern)
n. noun
Naut. Nautical
NE Northeast(ern)
NL New Latin
no. number
NW Northwest(ern)
N.Z. New Zealand

O Old
Obs. Obsolete
Offens. Offensive
OHG Old High German
ON Old Norse
orig. originally

Photog. Photography
pl. plural
Pop. population

Port. Portuguese
p.p. past participle
prep. preposition(al)
prob. probably
pron. pronoun
Psychol. Psychology
pt. point
p.t. past tense

rel. related

S south(ern)
S. African South African
Sansk. Sanskrit
Scand. Scandinavian
Scot. Scottish; Scots
SE southeast(ern)
sing. singular
Sl. Slang
Sp. Spanish
sq. square
sup. superlative
SW southwest(ern)

Theol. Theology
tr. transitive

ult. ultimately
U.S. United States

var. variant
vb. verb
vol. volume

W west(ern)
wt. weight

Zool. Zoology

? in etymologies
indicates "query"

A

a *or* **A** (eɪ) *n., pl.* **a's, A's,** *or* **As. 1.** the first letter and first vowel of the English alphabet. **2.** any of several speech sounds represented by this letter, as in *take, bag,* or *calm.* **3.** Also called: **alpha.** the first in a series, esp. the highest mark. **4. from A to Z.** from start to finish.

a[1] (ə; *emphatic* eɪ) *determiner. (indefinite article;* used before an initial consonant. Cf. **an**[1]) **1.** used preceding a singular countable noun, not previously specified: *a dog; a great pity.* **2.** used preceding a noun or determiner of quantity: *a dozen eggs; a great many; to read a lot.* **3.** (preceded by *once, twice, several times,* etc.) each or every; per: *once a day.* **4.** a certain; one: *a Mr Jones called.* **5.** (preceded by *not*) any at all: *not a hope.* ~Cf. **the**[1].

a[2] *symbol for:* **1.** acceleration. **2.** are(s) (metric measure of area). **3.** atto-.

A *symbol for:* **1.** *Music.* **a.** the sixth note of the scale of C major. **b.** the major or minor key having this note as its tonic. **2.** a human blood type of the ABO group, containing the A antigen. **3.** (in Britain) a major arterial road. **4.** ampere(s). **5.** absolute (temperature). **6.** area. **7.** *(in combination)* atomic: *an A-bomb; an A-plant.*

Å *symbol for* angstrom unit.

a. *abbrev. for:* **1.** acre(s). **2.** Also **A.** alto.

A. *abbrev. for:* **1.** acre(s). **2.** America(n). **3.** answer.

a-[1] *or before a vowel* **an-** *prefix.* not; without; opposite to: *atonal; asocial.* [from Gk *a-, an-* not, without]

a-[2] *prefix.* **1.** on; in; towards: *aground; aback.* **2.** in the state of: *afloat; asleep.*

A1, A-1, *or* **A-one** ('eɪ'wʌn) *adj.* **1.** physically fit. **2.** *Inf.* first class; excellent. **3.** (of a vessel) in first-class condition.

A4 *n.* a standard paper size, 297 × 210 mm.

AA *abbrev. for:* **1.** Alcoholics Anonymous. **2.** anti-aircraft. **3.** (in Britain) Automobile Association.

AAA *abbrev. for:* **1.** *Brit.* Amateur Athletic Association. **2.** *U.S.* Automobile Association of America.

Aachen ('ɑːkən; *German* 'aːxən) *n.* a city and spa in West Germany, in North Rhine-Westphalia: the northern capital of Charlemagne's empire. Pop.: 238 600 (1986). French name: **Aix-la-Chapelle.**

Aalborg *or* **Ålborg** (*Danish* 'ɔlbɒr) *n.* a city and port in Denmark, in N Jutland. Pop.: 154 755 (1983 est.).

Aalesund (*Norwegian* 'ɔːləsun) *n.* a variant spelling of **Ålesund.**

Aalst (ɑːlst) *n.* the Flemish name for **Alost.**

Aalto (*Finnish* 'ɑːltɔ) *n.* **Alvar** ('alvar). 1898–1976, Finnish architect and furniture designer, noted particularly for his public and industrial buildings, in which wood is much used. He invented bent plywood furniture (1932).

A & R *abbrev. for* artists and repertoire.

AAP *abbrev. for* Australian Associated Press.

Aarau (*German* 'aːrau) *n.* a town in N Switzerland, capital of Aargau canton: capital of the Helvetic Republic from 1798 to 1803. Pop.: 15 788 (1980).

aardvark ('ɑːd,vɑːk) *n.* a nocturnal burrowing African mammal that has long ears and snout and feeds on termites. Also called: **ant bear.** [C19: from obs. Afrik., from *aarde* earth + *varken* pig]

aardwolf ('ɑːd,wulf) *n., pl.* **-wolves.** a nocturnal mammal of the hyena family that inhabits the plains of southern Africa and feeds on termites and insect larvae. [C19: from Afrik., from *aarde* earth + *wolf* wolf]

Aargau (*German* 'aːrgau) *n.* a canton in N Switzerland. Capital: Aarau. Pop.: 453 442 (1980). Area: 1404 sq. km (542 sq. miles). French name: **Argovie.**

Aarhus *or* **Århus** (*Danish* 'ɔrhuːs) *n.* a city and port in Denmark, in E Jutland. Pop.: 245 565 (1981 est.).

Aaron ('ɛərən) *n. Old Testament.* the first high priest of the Israelites, brother of Moses (Exodus 4:14).

Aaron's beard *n.* another name for **rose of Sharon.**

Aaron's rod *n.* a widespread Eurasian plant having tall erect spikes of yellow flowers.

A'asia *abbrev. for* Australasia.

ab-[1] *prefix.* away from; opposite to: *abnormal.* [from L *ab* away from]

ab-[2] *prefix.* a cgs unit of measurement in the electromagnetic system: *abampere, abwatt, abvolt.* [from ABSOLUTE]

AB *abbrev. for:* **1.** Also: **a.b.** able-bodied seaman. **2.** (in the U.S.) Bachelor of Arts. ~ **3.** *symbol for* a human blood type of the ABO group, containing both the A antigen and the B antigen.

aba ('æbə) *n.* **1.** a type of cloth from Syria, made of goat or camel hair. **2.** a sleeveless outer garment of such cloth. [from Ar.]

abaca ('æbəkə) *n.* **1.** a Philippine plant, the source of Manila hemp. **2.** another name for **Manila hemp.** [via Sp. from Tagalog *abaká*]

aback (ə'bæk) *adv.* **taken aback. a.** startled or disconcerted. **b.** *Naut.* (of a vessel or sail) having the wind against the forward side so as to prevent forward motion. [OE *on bæc* to the back]

abacus ('æbəkəs) *n., pl.* **-ci** (-,saɪ) *or* **-cuses. 1.** a counting device that consists of a frame holding rods on which a number of beads are free to move. **2.** *Archit.* the flat upper part of the capital of a column. [C16: from L, from Gk *abax* board covered with sand, from Heb. *ābhāq* dust]

Abadan (,æbə'dɑːn) *n.* a port in SW Iran, on an island in the Shatt-al-Arab delta. Pop.: 294 068 (1985 est.).

Abaddon (ə'bæd[ə]n) *n.* **1.** the Devil (Revelation 9:11). **2.** (in rabbinical literature) Hell. [Heb.: lit., destruction]

abaft (ə'bɑːft) *Naut.* ~*adv., adj. (postpositive)* **1.** closer to the stern than to another place on a vessel. ~*prep.* **2.** behind; aft of. [C13: *on baft; baft* from OE *beæftan,* from *be* by + *æftan* behind]

Abakan (*Russian* aba'kan) *n.* a city in the S Soviet Union, capital of the Khakass AR, at the confluence of the Yenisei and Abakan Rivers. Pop.: 143 000 (1983 est.).

abalone (,æbə'ləunɪ) *n.* an edible marine mollusc having an ear-shaped shell perforated with a row of respiratory holes and lined with mother-of-pearl. Also called: **ear shell.** [C19: from American Sp. *abulón*]

abandon (ə'bændən) *vb. (tr.)* **1.** to forsake completely; desert; leave behind. **2.** to give up completely: *to abandon hope.* **3.** to give up (something begun) before completion: *the game was abandoned.* **4.** to surrender (oneself) to emotion without restraint. **5.** to give (insured property that has suffered partial loss or damage) to the insurers in order that a claim for a total loss may be made. ~*n.* **6.** freedom from inhibitions, restraint, or worry: *she danced with abandon.* [C14: *abandounen* (vb.), from OF, from *a bandon* under one's control, from *a* at, to + *bandon* control] —**a'bandonment** *n.*

abandoned (ə'bændənd) *adj.* **1.** deserted: *an abandoned windmill.* **2.** forsaken: *an abandoned child.* **3.** uninhibited.

abase (ə'beɪs) *vb. (tr.)* **1.** to humble or belittle (oneself, etc.). **2.** to lower or reduce, as in rank. [C15 *abessen,* from OF *abaissier* to make low. See BASE[2]] —**a'basement** *n.*

abash (ə'bæʃ) *vb. (tr.; usually passive)* to cause to feel ill at ease, embarrassed, or confused. [C14: from OF *esbair* to be astonished, from *es-* out + *bair* to gape] —**a'bashed** *adj.*

abate (ə'beɪt) *vb.* **1.** to make or become less in amount, intensity, degree, etc. **2.** *(tr.) Law.* **a.** to suppress or terminate (a nuisance). **b.** to suspend or extinguish (a claim or action). **c.** to annul (a writ). **3.** *(intr.) Law.* (of a writ, etc.) to become null and void. [C14: from OF *abatre* to beat down] —**a'batement** *n.*

abatis *or* **abattis** ('æbətɪs) *n.* **1.** a rampart of felled trees with their branches outwards. **2.** a barbed-wire entanglement before a position. [C18: from F, from *abattre* to fell]

abattoir ('æbə,twɑː) *n.* another name for **slaughterhouse.** [C19: F, from *abattre* to fell]

Abba ('æbə) *n.* **1.** *New Testament.* father (used of God). **2.** a title given to bishops and patriarchs in the Syrian, Coptic, and Ethiopian Churches. [from Aramaic]

abbacy ('æbəsɪ) *n., pl.* **-cies.** the office, term of office, or jurisdiction of an abbot or abbess. [C15: from Church L *abbātia,* from *abbāt-* ABBOT]

Abbado (ə'bɑːdəʊ) *n.* **Claudio.** born 1933, Italian conductor; director of the London Symphony Orchestra from 1979 and the Vienna State Opera from 1986.

Abbasid ('æbə,sɪd, ə'bæsɪd) *n.* **a.** any caliph of the dynasty that ruled the Muslim empire from Baghdad (750–1258) and claimed descent from Abbas, uncle of Mohammed. **b.** (*as modifier*): *the Abbasid dynasty.*

abbatial (ə'beɪʃəl) *adj.* of an abbot, abbess, or abbey. [C17: from Church L *abbātiālis*, from *abbāt-* ABBOT]

abbé ('æbeɪ) *n.* **1.** a French abbot. **2.** a title used in addressing any other French cleric, such as a priest.

abbess ('æbɪs) *n.* the female superior of a convent. [C13: from OF, from Church L *abbātissa*]

Abbevillian (æb'vɪlɪən) *Archaeol.* ~*n.* **1.** the period represented by Lower Palaeolithic European sites containing the earliest hand axes. ~*adj.* **2.** of this period. [C20: after *Abbeville*, France, where the stone tools were discovered]

abbey ('æbɪ) *n.* **1.** a building inhabited by a community of monks or nuns. **2.** a church built in conjunction with such a building. **3.** a community of monks or nuns. [C13: via OF *abeie* from Church L *abbātia* ABBACY]

abbot ('æbət) *n.* the superior of an abbey of monks. [OE *abbod*, from Church L *abbāt-* (stem of *abbas*), ult. from Aramaic *abbā* father] —'**abbot,ship** *or* '**abbotcy** *n.*

abbreviate (ə'briːvɪ,eɪt) *vb.* (*tr.*) **1.** to shorten (a word or phrase) by contraction or omission of some letters or words. **2.** to cut short; curtail. [C15: from p.p. of LL *abbreviāre*, from L *brevis* brief]

abbreviation (ə,briːvɪ'eɪʃən) *n.* **1.** a shortened or contracted form of a word or phrase. **2.** the process or result of abbreviating.

ABC[1] *n.* **1.** (*pl. in U.S.*) the rudiments of a subject. **2.** an alphabetical guide. **3.** (*often pl. in U.S.*) the alphabet.

ABC[2] *abbrev. for:* **1.** Australian Broadcasting Corporation. **2.** American Broadcasting Company.

Abd-el-Krim (,æbdel'kriːm) *n.* 1882–1963, Moroccan chief who led revolts against Spain and France, surrendered before their combined forces in 1926, but later formed the North African independence movement.

Abdias (æb'daɪəs) *n. Bible.* the Douay form of **Obadiah.**

abdicate ('æbdɪ,keɪt) *vb.* to renounce (a throne, rights, etc.), esp. formally. [C16: from L *abdicāre* to disclaim] —,**abdi'cation** *n.* —'**abdi,cator** *n.*

abdomen ('æbdəmən) *n.* **1.** the region of the body of a vertebrate that contains the viscera other than the heart and lungs. **2.** the front or surface of this region; belly. **3.** (in arthropods) the posterior part of the body behind the thorax. [C16: from L; from ?] —**abdominal** (æb'dɒmɪnəl) *adj.*

abduct (æb'dʌkt) *vb.* (*tr.*) **1.** to remove (a person) by force or cunning; kidnap. **2.** (of certain muscles) to pull away (a leg, arm, etc.) from the median axis of the body. [C19: from L *abdūcere* to lead away] —**ab'duction** *n.* —**ab'ductor** *n.*

Abdul-Hamid II ('æbdul'hæmɪd) *n.* 1842–1918, sultan of Turkey (1876–1909), deposed by the Young Turks, noted for his brutal suppression of the Armenian revolt (1894–96).

abeam (ə'biːm) *adv., adj.* (*postpositive*) at right angles to the length of a vessel or aircraft. [C19: A-[2] + BEAM]

abed (ə'bed) *adv. Arch.* in bed.

Abednego (ə'bednɪ,gəʊ) *n. Old Testament.* one of Daniel's three companions who, together with Shadrach and Meshach, was miraculously saved from destruction in Nebuchadnezzar's fiery furnace (Daniel 3:12–30).

Abel ('eɪbəl) *n.* the second son of Adam and Eve, a shepherd, murdered by his brother Cain (Genesis 4:1–8).

Abelard ('æbə,lɑːd) *n.* **Peter.** French name *Pierre Abélard.* 1079–1142, French scholastic philosopher and theologian whose works include *Historia Calamitatum* and *Sic et Non* (1121). His love for Heloise is recorded in their correspondence.

Abeokuta (,æbɪəʊ'kuːtə) *n.* a town in W Nigeria, capital of Ogun state. Pop.: 308 800 (1983 est.).

Aberdare (,æbə'deə) *n.* a mining town in South Wales, in N Mid Glamorgan. Pop.: 38 000 (1982 est.).

Aberdeen[1] (,æbə'diːn) *n.* a city in NE Scotland, administrative centre of Grampian region on the North Sea: centre for processing North Sea oil and gas; university (1494). Pop.: 215 246 (1985 est.). —**Aberdonian** (,æbə'dəʊnɪən) *n., adj.*

Aberdeen[2] (,æbə'diːn) *n.* **George Hamilton-Gordon,** 4th Earl of. 1784–1860, British statesman. He was foreign

secretary under Wellington (1828) and Peel (1841–46); became prime minister of a coalition ministry in 1852 but was compelled to resign after mismanagement of the Crimean War (1855).

Aberdeen Angus *n.* a black hornless breed of beef cattle originating in Scotland.

Aberdeenshire (,æbə'diːn,ʃɪə, -ʃə) *n.* (until 1975) a county of N Scotland, now part of Grampian region.

Aberfan (,æbə'væn) *n.* a coal-mining village in S Wales, in Mid Glamorgan: scene of a disaster in 1966 when a slag heap collapsed onto part of the village killing 144 people (including 116 children).

aberrant (æ'berənt) *adj.* **1.** deviating from the normal or usual type. **2.** behaving in an abnormal or untypical way. **3.** deviating from morality. [rare before C19: from L *aberrāre* to wander away] —**ab'errance** *or* **ab'errancy** *n.*

aberration (,æbə'reɪʃən) *n.* **1.** deviation from what is normal, expected, or usual. **2.** departure from truth, morality, etc. **3.** a lapse in control of one's mental faculties. **4.** *Optics.* a defect in a lens or mirror that causes either a distorted image or one with coloured fringes. **5.** *Astron.* the apparent displacement of a celestial body due to the motion of the observer with the earth.

Aberystwyth (,æbə'rɪstwɪθ) *n.* a resort and university town in Wales, in Dyfed on Cardigan Bay. Pop.: 8666 (1981).

abet (ə'bet) *vb.* **abetting, abetted.** (*tr.*) to assist or encourage, esp. in wrongdoing. [C14: from OF *abeter* to lure on, from *beter* to bait] —**a'betment** *n.* —**a'better** *or* (*esp. Law*) **a'bettor** *n.*

abeyance (ə'beɪəns) *n.* **1.** (usually preceded by *in* or *into*) a state of being suspended or put aside temporarily. **2.** (usually preceded by *in*) *Law.* an indeterminate state of ownership. [C16–17: from Anglo-F, from OF *abeance* expectation, lit. a gaping after]

abhor (əb'hɔː) *vb.* **-horring, -horred.** (*tr.*) to detest vehemently; find repugnant. [C15: from L *abhorrēre*, from *ab-* away from + *horrēre* to shudder] —**ab'horrer** *n.*

abhorrence (əb'hɒrəns) *n.* **1.** a feeling of extreme loathing or aversion. **2.** a person or thing that is loathsome.

abhorrent (əb'hɒrənt) *adj.* **1.** repugnant; loathsome. **2.** (when *postpositive*, foll. by *of*) feeling extreme aversion (for): *abhorrent of vulgarity.* **3.** (usually *postpositive* and foll. by *to*) conflicting (with): *abhorrent to common sense.*

abide (ə'baɪd) *vb.* **abiding, abode** *or* **abided. 1.** (*tr.*) to tolerate; put up with. **2.** (*tr.*) to accept or submit to. **3.** (*intr.*; foll. by *by*) **a.** to comply (with): *to abide by the decision.* **b.** to remain faithful (to): *to abide by your promise.* **4.** (*intr.*) to remain or continue. **5.** (*intr.*) *Arch.* to dwell. **6.** (*tr.*) *Arch.* to await in expectation. [OE *ābīdan*, from *a-* (intensive) + *bīdan* to wait] —**a'bider** *n.*

abiding (ə'baɪdɪŋ) *adj.* permanent; enduring: *an abiding belief.*

Abidjan (,æbɪ'dʒɑːn; *French* abidʒɑ̃) *n.* a port in the Côte d'Ivoire, on the Gulf of Guinea: the former capital (until 1983). Pop.: 1 850 000 (1984).

Abigail ('æbɪ,geɪl) *n. Old Testament.* the woman who brought provisions to David and his followers and subsequently became his wife (I Samuel 25:1–42).

Abilene ('æbə,liːn) *n.* a city in central Texas. Pop.: 98 231 (1980).

ability (ə'bɪlɪtɪ) *n., pl.* **-ties. 1.** possession of necessary skill, competence, or power. **2.** considerable proficiency; natural capability: *a man of ability.* **3.** (*pl.*) special talents. [C14: from OF from L *habilitās* aptitude, from *habilis* ABLE]

Abingdon ('æbɪŋdən) *n.* a market town in S England, in Oxfordshire. Pop.: 22 686 (1981).

ab initio *Latin.* (æb ɪ'nɪʃɪ,əʊ) from the start.

abiogenesis (,eɪbaɪəʊ'dʒenɪsɪs) *n.* the hypothetical process by which living organisms arise from inanimate matter. Also called: **spontaneous generation.** [C19: NL, from A-[1] + BIO- + GENESIS]

abject ('æbdʒekt) *adj.* **1.** utterly wretched or hopeless. **2.** forlorn; dejected. **3.** submissive: *an abject apology.* **4.** contemptible; despicable: *an abject liar.* [C14 (in the sense: rejected, cast out): from L *abjectus* thrown away, from *abjicere*, from *ab-* away + *jacere* to throw] —**ab'jection** *n.* —'**abjectly** *adv.* —'**abjectness** *n.*

abjure (əb'dʒʊə) *vb.* (*tr.*) **1.** to renounce or retract, esp. formally or under oath. **2.** to abstain from. [C15: from OF *abjurer* or L *abjurāre* to deny on oath] —**abju'ration** *n.* —**ab'jurer** *n.*

Abkhaz Autonomous Soviet Socialist Republic *n.* an administrative division of the S Soviet Union, in the NW Georgian SSR between the Black Sea and the Caucasus Mountains: a subtropical region, with mountains rising over 3900 m (13 000 ft.). Capital: Sukhumi. Pop.: 530 000 (1986). Area: 8600 sq. km (3320 sq. miles). Also called: **Abkhazia** (æb'kɑːzɪə).

ablation (æb'leɪʃən) *n.* **1.** the surgical removal of an organ, structure, or part. **2.** the melting or wearing away of a part, such as the heat shield of a space re-entry vehicle on passing through the earth's atmosphere. **3.** the wearing away of a rock or glacier. [C15: from LL *ablatiōn-*, from L *auferre* to carry away] —**ablate** (æb'leɪt) *vb.*

ablative ('æblətɪv) *Grammar.* ~*adj.* **1.** (in certain inflected languages such as Latin) denoting a case of nouns, pronouns, and adjectives indicating the agent, or the instrument, manner, or place of the action. ~*n.* **2.** the ablative case or a speech element in it.

ablaut ('æblaʊt) *n. Linguistics.* vowel gradation, esp. in Indo-European languages. See **gradation** (sense 5). [G, coined 1819 by Jakob Grimm from *ab* off + *Laut* sound]

ablaze (ə'bleɪz) *adj.* (*postpositive*), *adv.* **1.** on fire; burning. **2.** brightly illuminated. **3.** emotionally aroused.

able ('eɪbªl) *adj.* **1.** (*postpositive*) having the necessary power, resources, skill, opportunity, etc., to do something. **2.** capable; talented. **3.** *Law.* competent or authorized. [C14: ult. from L *habilis* easy to hold, manageable, from *habēre* to have + -*ilis* -ILE]

-able *suffix forming adjectives.* **1.** capable of or deserving of (being acted upon as indicated): *enjoyable; washable.* **2.** inclined to; able to; causing: *comfortable; variable.* [via OF from L -*ābilis*, -*ībilis*, forms of -*bilis*, adjectival suffix] —**-ably** *suffix forming adverbs.* —**-ability** *suffix forming nouns.*

able-bodied *adj.* physically strong and healthy; robust.

able-bodied seaman *n.* a seaman, esp. one in the merchant navy, who has been trained in certain skills. Also: **able seaman.** Abbrev.: **AB, a.b.**

able rating *n.* (esp. in the Royal Navy) a rating who is qualified to perform certain duties of seamanship.

abloom (ə'bluːm) *adj.* (*postpositive*) in flower; blooming.

ablution (ə'bluːʃən) *n.* **1.** the ritual washing of a priest's hands or of sacred vessels. **2.** (*often pl.*) the act of washing: *perform one's ablutions.* **3.** (*pl.*) *Mil. inf.* a washing place. [C14: ult. from L *ablūere* to wash away] —**ab'lutionary** *adj.*

ably ('eɪblɪ) *adv.* in a competent or skilful manner.

ABM *abbrev. for* antiballistic missile.

abnegate ('æbnɪˌgeɪt) *vb.* (*tr.*) to deny to oneself; renounce. [C17: from L *abnegāre* to deny] —ˌ**abne'gation** *n.* —'**abneˌgator** *n.*

abnormal (æb'nɔːməl) *adj.* **1.** not normal; deviating from the usual or typical. **2.** concerned with abnormal behaviour: *abnormal psychology.* **3.** *Inf.* odd; strange. [C19: AB-[1] + NORMAL, replacing earlier *anormal* from Med. L *anormalus*, a blend of LL *anōmalus* ANOMALOUS + L *abnormis* departing from a rule] —**ab'normally** *adv.*

abnormality (ˌæbnɔː'mælɪtɪ) *n.*, *pl.* -**ties. 1.** an abnormal feature, event, etc. **2.** a physical malformation. **3.** deviation from the usual.

Abo ('æbəʊ) *n.*, *pl.* **Abos.** (*sometimes not cap.*) *Austral. inf.*, *often derog.* short for **Aborigine** (sense 1).

Åbo ('oːbuː) *n.* the Swedish name for **Turku.**

aboard (ə'bɔːd) *adv.*, *adj.* (*postpositive*), *prep.* **1.** on, in, onto, or into (a ship, train, etc.). **2.** *Naut.* alongside. **3. all aboard!** a warning to passengers to board a vehicle, ship, etc.

abode[1] (ə'bəʊd) *n.* a place in which one lives; one's home. [C17: *n.* formed from ABIDE]

abode[2] (ə'bəʊd) *vb.* a past tense and past participle of **abide.**

abolish (ə'bɒlɪʃ) *vb.* (*tr.*) to do away with (laws, regulations, customs, etc.). [C15: from OF, ult. from L *abolēre* to destroy] —**a'bolishable** *adj.* —**a'bolisher** *n.* —**a'bolishment** *n.*

abolition (ˌæbə'lɪʃən) *n.* **1.** the act of abolishing or the state of being abolished; annulment. **2.** (*often cap.*) (in British territories) the ending of the slave trade (1807) or of slavery (1833). **3.** (*often cap.*) (in the U.S.) the emancipation of slaves, by the Emancipation Proclamation (1863,

ratified 1865). [C16: from L *abolitio*, from *abolēre* to destroy] —ˌ**abo'litionary** *adj.* —ˌ**abo'litionism** *n.* —ˌ**abo'litionist** *n.*, *adj.*

abomasum (ˌæbə'meɪsəm) *n.* the fourth and last compartment of the stomach of ruminants. [C18: NL, from AB-[1] + *omāsum* bullock's tripe]

A-bomb *n.* short for **atom bomb.**

abominable (ə'bɒmɪnəbªl) *adj.* **1.** offensive; loathsome; detestable. **2.** *Inf.* very bad or inferior: *abominable workmanship.* [C14: from L, from *abōminārī* to ABOMINATE] —**a'bominably** *adv.*

abominable snowman *n.* a large manlike or apelike creature alleged to inhabit the Himalayas. Also called: **yeti.** [translation of Tibetan *metohkangmi*, from *metoh* foul + *kangmi* snowman]

abominate (ə'bɒmɪˌneɪt) *vb.* (*tr.*) to dislike intensely; detest. [C17: from L *abōminārī* to regard as an ill omen, from *ab-* away from + *ōmin-*, from OMEN] —**a'bomiˌnator** *n.*

abomination (əˌbɒmɪ'neɪʃən) *n.* **1.** a person or thing that is disgusting or loathsome. **2.** an action that is vicious, vile, etc. **3.** intense loathing or disgust.

aboriginal (ˌæbə'rɪdʒɪnªl) *adj.* existing in a place from the earliest known period; indigenous. —ˌ**abo'riginally** *adv.*

Aboriginal (ˌæbə'rɪdʒɪnªl) *adj.* **1.** of, relating to, or characteristic of the Aborigines of Australia. ~*n.* **2.** another word for **Aborigine** (sense 1).

aborigine (ˌæbə'rɪdʒɪnɪ) *n.* an original inhabitant of a country or region. [C16: back formation from *aborigines*, from L: inhabitants of Latium in pre-Roman times, associated in folk etymology with *ab origine* from the beginning]

Aborigine (ˌæbə'rɪdʒɪnɪ) *n.* **1.** Also called: **native Australian, Aboriginal.** a member of a dark-skinned hunting and gathering people who were living in Australia when European settlers arrived. Often shortened to **Abo. 2.** any of the languages of this people.

abort (ə'bɔːt) *vb.* **1.** to undergo or cause (a woman) to undergo the termination of pregnancy before the fetus is viable. **2.** (*tr.*) to cause (a fetus) to be expelled from the womb before it is viable. **3.** (*tr.*) to fail to come to completion. **4.** (*tr.*) to interrupt the development of. **5.** (*intr.*) to give birth to a dead or nonviable fetus. **6.** (of a space flight or other undertaking) to fail or terminate prematurely. **7.** (*intr.*) (of an organism or part of an organism) to fail to develop into the mature form. ~*n.* **8.** the premature termination or failure of (a space flight, etc.) [C16: from L *abortāre*, from *aborīrī* to miscarry, from *ab-* wrongly + *orīrī* to be born]

abortifacient (əˌbɔːtɪ'feɪʃənt) *adj.* **1.** causing abortion. ~*n.* **2.** a drug or agent that causes abortion.

abortion (ə'bɔːʃən) *n.* **1.** an operation or other procedure to terminate pregnancy before the fetus is viable. **2.** the premature termination of pregnancy by spontaneous or induced expulsion of a nonviable fetus from the uterus. **3.** an aborted fetus. **4.** a failure to develop to completion or maturity. **5.** a person or thing that is deformed.

abortionist (ə'bɔːʃənɪst) *n.* a person who performs abortions, esp. illegally.

abortive (ə'bɔːtɪv) *adj.* **1.** failing to achieve a purpose; fruitless. **2.** (of organisms) imperfectly developed. **3.** causing abortion.

ABO system *n.* a system for classifying human blood on the basis of the presence or absence of two antigens in the red cells: there are four such blood types (A, B, AB, and O).

Aboukir Bay or **Abukir Bay** (ˌæbuː'kɪə) *n.* a bay on the N coast of Egypt, where the Nile enters the Mediterranean: site of the Battle of the Nile (1798), in which Nelson defeated the French fleet. Arabic name: **Abu Qir** (abu'kiːr).

aboulia (ə'buːlɪə, -'bjuː-) *n.* a variant spelling of **abulia.**

abound (ə'baʊnd) *vb.* (*intr.*) **1.** to exist or occur in abundance. **2.** (foll. by *with* or *in*) to be plentifully supplied (with): *the fields abound in corn.* [C14: via OF from L *abundāre* to overflow, from *undāre* to flow, from *unda* wave]

about (ə'baʊt) *prep.* **1.** relating to; concerning. **2.** near or close to. **3.** carried on: *I haven't any money about me.* **4.** on every side of. **5.** active in or engaged in. ~*adv.* **6.** near in number, time, degree, etc.: *about 50 years old.* **7.** nearby. **8.** here and there: *walk about to keep warm.* **9.**

all around; on every side. **10.** in or to the opposite direction. **11.** in rotation or revolution: *turn and turn about.* **12.** used in informal phrases to indicate understatement: *it's about time you stopped.* **13.** *Arch.* around. **14. about to. a.** on the point of; intending to: *she was about to jump.* **b.** (*with a negative*) determined not to: *nobody is about to miss it.* ~*adj.* **15.** (*predicative*) active; astir after sleep: *up and about.* **16.** (*predicative*) in existence, current, or in circulation: *there aren't many about nowadays.* [OE *abūtan, onbūtan,* from ON + *būtan* outside]

about turn *or U.S.* **about face** *sentence substitute.* **1.** a military command to a formation of men to reverse the direction in which they are facing. ~*n.* **about-turn** *or U.S.* **about-face.** **2.** a complete change of opinion, direction, etc. ~*vb.* **about-turn** *or U.S.* **about-face.** **3.** (*intr.*) to perform an about-turn.

above (ə'bʌv) *prep.* **1.** on top of or higher than; over. **2.** greater than in quantity or degree: *above average.* **3.** superior to or prior to: *to place honour above wealth.* **4.** too high-minded or proud for: *above petty gossiping.* **5.** too respected for; beyond: *above suspicion.* **6.** too difficult to be understood by: *the talk was above me.* **7.** louder or higher than (other noise). **8.** in preference to. **9.** north of. **10.** upstream from. **11. above all.** most of all; especially. **12. above and beyond.** in addition to. ~*adv.* **13.** in or to a higher place: *the sky above.* **14. a.** in a previous place (in something written). **b.** (*in combination*): *the above-mentioned clause.* **15.** higher in rank or position. **16.** in or concerned with heaven. ~*n.* **17. the above.** something previously mentioned. ~*adj.* **18.** appearing in a previous place (in something written). [OE *abufan,* from *a-* on + *bufan* above]

above board *adj.* (**aboveboard** *when prenominal*), *adv.* in the open; without dishonesty, concealment, or fraud.

Abp *or* **abp** *abbrev. for* archbishop.

abracadabra (,æbrəkə'dæbrə) *interj.* **1.** a spoken formula, used esp. by conjurors. ~*n.* **2.** a word used in incantations, etc., considered to possess magic powers. **3.** gibberish. [C17: magical word used in certain Gnostic writings, ? rel. to Gk *Abraxas,* a Gnostic deity]

abrade (ə'breɪd) *vb.* (*tr.*) to scrape away or wear down by friction. [C17: from L *abrādere,* from AB- + *rādere* to scrape] —**a'brader** *n.*

Abraham ('eɪbrə,hæm, -həm) *n.* **1.** *Old Testament.* the first of the patriarchs, the father of Isaac and the founder of the Hebrew people (Genesis 11–25). **2. Abraham's bosom.** the place where the just repose after death (Luke 16:22).

abranchiate (ə'bræŋkɪɪt, -,eɪt) *or* **abranchial** *adj. Zool.* having no gills. [C19: A-¹ + BRANCHIATE]

abrasion (ə'breɪʒən) *n.* **1.** the process of scraping or wearing down by friction. **2.** a scraped area or spot; graze. **3.** *Geog.* the effect of mechanical erosion of rock, esp. a river bed, by rock fragments scratching and scraping it. [C17: from Med. L *abrāsiōn-,* from L *abrādere* to ABRADE]

abrasive (ə'breɪsɪv) *n.* **1.** a substance or material such as sandpaper, pumice, or emery, used for cleaning, smoothing, or polishing. ~*adj.* **2.** causing abrasion; rough. **3.** irritating in manner or personality.

abreaction (,æbrɪ'ækʃən) *n. Psychoanal.* the release and expression of emotional tension associated with repressed ideas by bringing those ideas into consciousness.

abreast (ə'brɛst) *adj.* (*postpositive*) **1.** alongside each other and facing in the same direction. **2.** (foll. by *of* or *with*) up to date (with).

abridge (ə'brɪdʒ) *vb.* (*tr.*) **1.** to reduce the length of (a written work) by condensing. **2.** to curtail. [C14: via OF *abregier* from LL *abbreviāre* to shorten] —**a'bridgable** *or* **a'bridgeable** *adj.* —**a'bridger** *n.*

abridgment *or* **abridgement** (ə'brɪdʒmənt) *n.* **1.** a shortened version of a written work. **2.** the act of abridging or state of being abridged.

abroad (ə'brɔːd) *adv.* **1.** to or in a foreign country or countries. ~*adj.* (*postpositive*) **2.** (of rumours, etc.) in general circulation. **3.** out in the open. **4.** over a wide area. [C13: from A-² + BROAD]

abrogate ('æbrəʊ,geɪt) *vb.* (*tr.*) to cancel or revoke formally or officially. [C16: from L *abrogātus* repealed, from AB-¹ + *rogāre* to propose (a law)] —,**abro'gation** *n.* —'**abro,gator** *n.*

abrupt (ə'brʌpt) *adj.* **1.** sudden; unexpected. **2.** brusque or brief in speech, manner, etc. **3.** (of a style of writing or

speaking) disconnected. **4.** precipitous; steep. **5.** *Bot.* truncate. **6.** *Geol.* (of strata) cropping out suddenly. [C16: from L *abruptus* broken off, from AB-¹ + *rumpere* to break] —**ab'ruptly** *adv.* —**ab'ruptness** *n.*

Abruzzi (*Italian* a'bruttsi) *n.* a region of S central Italy, between the Apennines and the Adriatic: separated from the former administrative region **Abruzzi e Molise** in 1965. Capital: Aquila. Pop.: 1 254 129 (1985 est.). Area: 10 794 sq. km (4210 sq. miles).

Absalom ('æbsələm) *n. Old Testament.* the third son of David, who rebelled against his father and was eventually killed by Joab (II Samuel 15–18).

abscess ('æbsɛs) *n.* **1.** a localized collection of pus formed as the product of inflammation. ~*vb.* **2.** (*intr.*) to form such a collection of pus. [C16: from L *abscessus,* from *abscēdere* to go away] —'**abscessed** *adj.*

abscissa (æb'sɪsə) *n., pl.* **-scissas** *or* **-scissae** (-'sɪsiː). the horizontal or *x*-coordinate of a point in a two-dimensional system of Cartesian coordinates. It is the distance from the *y*-axis measured parallel to the *x*-axis. Cf. **ordinate** (sense 1). [C17: NL, orig. *linea abscissa* a cut-off line]

abscission (æb'sɪʒən) *n.* **1.** the separation of leaves, branches, flowers, and bark from plants. **2.** the act of cutting off. [C17: from L *abscissiō* a cleaving]

abscond (əb'skɒnd) *vb.* (*intr.*) to run away secretly, esp. to avoid prosecution or punishment. [C16: from L *abscondere,* from *abs-* AB-¹ + *condere* to stow] —**ab'sconder** *n.*

abseil ('æbsaɪl) *Mountaineering.* ~*vb.* (*intr.*) **1.** to descend a steep slope or vertical drop by a rope secured from above and coiled around one's body. ~*n.* **2.** an instance or the technique of abseiling. [C20: from G *abseilen,* from *ab-* down + *Seil* rope]

absence ('æbsəns) *n.* **1.** the state of being away. **2.** the time during which a person or thing is away. **3.** the fact of being without something; lack. [C14: via OF from L *absentia,* from *absēns* a being away]

absent *adj.* ('æbsənt). **1.** away or not present. **2.** lacking. **3.** inattentive. ~*vb.* (æb'sɛnt). **4.** (*tr.*) to remove (oneself) or keep away. [C14: from L *absent-,* from *abesse* to be away] —**ab'senter** *n.*

absentee (,æbsən'tiː) *n.* **a.** a person who is absent. **b.** (*as modifier*): *an absentee landlord.*

absenteeism (,æbsən'tiːɪzəm) *n.* persistent absence from work, school, etc.

absent-minded *adj.* preoccupied; forgetful. —,**absent-'mindedly** *adv.* —,**absent-'mindedness** *n.*

absinthe *or* **absinth** ('æbsɪnθ) *n.* **1.** a potent green alcoholic drink, originally having high wormwood content. **2.** another name for **wormwood** (the plant). [C15: via F and L from Gk *apsinthion* wormwood]

absolute ('æbsə,luːt) *adj.* **1.** complete; perfect. **2.** free from limitations, restrictions, or exceptions. **3.** despotic: *an absolute ruler.* **4.** undoubted; certain: *the absolute truth.* **5.** not dependent on, conditioned by, or relative to anything else; independent: *absolute humidity; absolute units.* **6.** pure; unmixed: *absolute alcohol.* **7.** (of a grammatical construction) syntactically independent of the main clause, as for example the construction *Joking apart* in the sentence *Joking apart, we'd better leave now.* **8.** *Grammar.* (of a transitive verb) used without a direct object, as the verb *intimidate* in the sentence *His intentions are good, but his rough manner tends to intimidate.* **9.** *Grammar.* (of an adjective) used as a noun, as for instance *young* and *aged* in the sentence *The young care little for the aged.* ~*n.* **10.** something that is absolute. [C14: from L *absolūtus* unconditional, from *absolvere.* See ABSOLVE]

Absolute ('æbsə,luːt) *n.* (*sometimes not cap.*) *Philosophy.* **1.** the ultimate basis of reality. **2.** that which is totally unconditioned, unrestricted, pure, perfect, or complete.

absolutely (,æbsə'luːtlɪ) *adv.* **1.** in an absolute manner, esp. completely or perfectly. ~*sentence substitute.* **2.** yes; certainly.

absolute magnitude *n.* the magnitude a given star would have if it were 10 parsecs (32.6 light years) from earth.

absolute majority *n.* a number of votes totalling over 50 per cent, such as the total number of votes or seats obtained by a party that beats the combined opposition.

absolute pitch *n.* **1.** Also called: **perfect pitch.** the ability to identify exactly the pitch of a note without comparing it with another. **2.** the exact pitch of a note determined by vibration per second.

absolute temperature *n.* another name for **thermodynamic temperature.**

absolute value *n.* **1.** the positive real number equal to a given real but disregarding its sign: written |–x |. **2.** also called: **modulus.** a measure of the magnitude of a complex number.

absolute zero *n.* the lowest temperature theoretically attainable, at which the particles constituting matter would be at rest: equivalent to 0K, –273.15°C or –459.67°F.

absolution (ˌæbsəˈluːʃən) *n.* **1.** the act of absolving or the state of being absolved; release from guilt, obligation, or punishment. **2.** *Christianity.* **a.** a formal remission of sin pronounced by a priest in the sacrament of penance. **b.** the form of words granting such a remission. [C12: from L *absolūtiō*- acquittal, from *absolvere* to ABSOLVE]

absolutism (ˈæbsəluːˌtɪzəm) *n.* the principle or practice of a political system in which unrestricted power is vested in a monarch, dictator, etc.; despotism. —**'absolutist** *n.,* *adj.*

absolve (əbˈzɒlv) *vb.* (*tr.*) **1.** (usually foll. by *from*) to release from blame, sin, obligation, or responsibility. **2.** to pronounce not guilty. [C15: from L *absolvere,* from AB-[1] + *solvere* to make loose] —**ab'solver** *n.*

absorb (əbˈsɔːb) *vb.* (*tr.*) **1.** to soak or suck up (liquids). **2.** to engage or occupy (the interest or time) of (someone). **3.** to receive or take in (the energy of an impact). **4.** *Physics.* to take in (all or part of incident radiated energy) and retain it. **5.** to take in or assimilate; incorporate. **6.** to pay for as part of a commercial transaction: *the distributor absorbed the cost of transport.* **7.** *Chem.* to cause to undergo a process in which one substance permeates into or is dissolved by a liquid or solid: *porous solids absorb water.* [C15: via OF from L *absorbēre,* from AB-[1] + *sorbēre* to suck] —**ab,sorba'bility** *n.* —**ab'sorbable** *adj.*

absorbed (əbˈsɔːbd) *adj.* engrossed; deeply interested.

absorbed dose *n.* the amount of energy transferred by radiation to a unit mass of absorbing material.

absorbent (əbˈsɔːbənt) *adj.* **1.** able to absorb. ~*n.* **2.** a substance that absorbs. —**ab'sorbency** *n.*

absorbing (əbˈsɔːbɪŋ) *adj.* occupying one's interest or attention. —**ab'sorbingly** *adv.*

absorptance (əbˈsɔːptəns) *or* **absorption factor** *n.* *Physics.* the ability of an object to absorb radiation, measured as the ratio of absorbed flux to incident flux. [C20: from ABSORPTION + -ANCE]

absorption (əbˈsɔːpʃən) *n.* **1.** the process of absorbing or the state of being absorbed. **2.** *Physiol.* **a.** normal assimilation by the tissues of the products of digestion. **b.** the process of taking up various fluids, drugs, etc., through the mucous membranes or skin. [C16: from L *absorptiō*-, from *absorbēre* to ABSORB] —**ab'sorptive** *adj.*

absorption spectrum *n.* the characteristic pattern of dark lines or bands that occurs when electromagnetic radiation is passed through an absorbing medium into a spectroscope. See also **emission spectrum.**

abstain (əbˈsteɪn) *vb.* (*intr.; usually foll. by from*) **1.** to choose to refrain. **2.** to refrain from voting, esp. in a committee, legislature, etc. [C14: via OF from L *abstinēre,* from *abs-* AB-[1] + *tenēre* to hold] —**ab'stainer** *n.*

abstemious (əbˈstiːmɪəs) *adj.* sparing, esp. in the consumption of alcohol or food. [C17: from L *abstēmius,* from *abs-* AB-[1] + *tēm-,* from *tēmētum* intoxicating drink] —**ab'stemiously** *adv.* —**ab'stemiousness** *n.*

abstention (əbˈstɛnʃən) *n.* **1.** the act of refraining or abstaining. **2.** the act of withholding one's vote. [C16: from LL *abstentiō*; see ABSTAIN]

abstinence (ˈæbstɪnəns) *n.* the act or practice of refraining from some action or from the use of something, esp. alcohol. [C13: via OF from L *abstinentia,* from *abstinēre* to ABSTAIN] —'**abstinent** *adj.*

abstract *adj.* (ˈæbstrækt). **1.** having no reference to material objects or specific examples. **2.** not applied or practical; theoretical. **3.** hard to understand. **4.** denoting art characterized by geometric, formalized, or otherwise nonrepresentational qualities. ~*n.* (ˈæbstrækt). **5.** a condensed version of a piece of writing, speech, etc.; summary. **6.** an abstract term or idea. **7.** an abstract

painting, sculpture, etc. **8. in the abstract.** without reference to specific circumstances. ~*vb.* (æbˈstrækt). (*tr.*) **9.** to regard theoretically. **10.** to form a general idea of (something) by abstraction. **11.** (ˈæbstrækt). (*also intr.*) to summarize. **12.** to remove or extract. [C14 (in the sense: extracted): from L *abstractus* drawn off, from *abs-* AB-[1] + *trahere* to draw]

abstracted (æbˈstræktɪd) *adj.* **1.** lost in thought; preoccupied. **2.** taken out or separated. —**ab'stractedly** *adv.*

abstract expressionism *n.* a school of painting in the 1940s that combined the spontaneity of expressionism with abstract forms in apparently random compositions.

abstraction (æbˈstrækʃən) *n.* **1.** preoccupation. **2.** the process of formulating generalized concepts by extracting common qualities from specific examples. **3.** a concept formulated in this way: *good and evil are abstractions.* **4.** an abstract painting, sculpture, etc. —**ab'stractive** *adj.*

abstract noun *n.* a noun that refers to an abstract concept, as peace, joy, etc.

abstract term *n.* in traditional logic, the name of an attribute of many individuals: *humanity is an abstract term.*

abstruse (əbˈstruːs) *adj.* not easy to understand. [C16: from L *abstrūsus,* from *abs-* AB-[1] + *trūdere* to thrust] —**ab'strusely** *adv.* —**ab'struseness** *n.*

absurd (əbˈsɜːd) *adj.* **1.** incongruous; ridiculous. **2.** ludicrous. [C16: via F from L *absurdus,* from AB-[1] (intensive) + *surdus* dull-sounding, indistinct] —**ab'surdity** *or* **ab'surdness** *n.* —**ab'surdly** *adv.*

ABTA (ˈæbtə) *n.* acronym for Association of British Travel Agents.

Abu-Bekr (əˌbuːˈbɛkə) *or* **Abu-Bakr** (əˌbuːˈbækə) *n.* 573–634 A.D., father-in-law of Mohammed; the first caliph of Islam.

Abu Dhabi (ˈæbuː ˈdɑːbɪ) *n.* a sheikdom of SE Arabia, on the S coast of the Persian Gulf: the chief sheikdom and capital of the United Arab Emirates, consisting principally of the port of Abu Dhabi and a desert hinterland; contains major oilfields. Pop.: 449 000 (1980). Area: 67 350 sq. km (25 998 sq. miles).

Abuja (əˈbuːdʒə) *n.* the federal capital of Nigeria (from 1982), in the centre of the country. Pop.: 14 476 (1972 est.).

Abukir Bay (ˌæbuːˈkɪə) *n.* a variant spelling of **Aboukir Bay.**

abulia *or* **aboulia** (əˈbuːlɪə, -ˈbjuː-) *n.* *Psychiatry.* a pathological inability to take decisions. [C19: NL, from Gk *aboulia* lack of resolution, from A-[1] + *boulē* will]

abundance (əˈbʌndəns) *n.* **1.** a copious supply; great amount. **2.** fullness or benevolence: *from the abundance of my heart.* **3.** degree of plentifulness: *the abundance of uranium-235 in natural uranium.* **4.** Also: **abondance.** a call in solo whist undertaking to make nine tricks. **5.** affluence. [C14: via OF from L, from *abundāre* to ABOUND]

abundant (əˈbʌndənt) *adj.* **1.** existing in plentiful supply. **2.** (*postpositive; foll. by in*) having a plentiful supply (of). [C14: from L *abundant-,* p.p. of *abundāre* to ABOUND] —**a'bundantly** *adv.*

abuse *vb.* (əˈbjuːz). (*tr.*) **1.** to use incorrectly or improperly; misuse. **2.** to maltreat. **3.** to speak insultingly or cruelly to. ~*n.* (əˈbjuːs). **4.** improper, incorrect, or excessive use. **5.** maltreatment of a person; injury. **6.** insulting or coarse speech. **7.** an evil, unjust, or corrupt practice. **8.** *Arch.* a deception. [C14 (vb.): via OF from L *abūsus,* p.p. of *abūtī* to misuse, from AB-[1] + *ūtī* to USE] —**a'buser** *n.*

Abu Simbel (ˌæbuː ˈsɪmbəl) *n.* a former village in S Egypt: site of two temples of Rameses II, which were moved to higher ground (1966–67) before the area behind the Aswan High Dam was flooded. Also called: **Ipsambul.**

abusive (əˈbjuːsɪv) *adj.* **1.** characterized by insulting or coarse language. **2.** characterized by maltreatment. **3.** incorrectly used. —**a'busively** *adv.* —**a'busiveness** *n.*

abut (əˈbʌt) *vb.* **abutting, abutted.** (usually foll. by *on, upon,* or *against*) to adjoin, touch, or border on (something) at one end. [C15: from OF *abouter* to join at the ends; infl. by *abutter* to touch at an end]

abutment (əˈbʌtmənt) *or* **abuttal** *n.* **1.** the state or process of abutting. **2. a.** something that abuts. **b.** the thing on which something abuts. **c.** the point of junction between them. **3.** a construction that supports the end of a bridge.

abutter (əˈbʌtə) *n.* *Property law.* the owner of adjoining property.

abuzz (ə'bʌz) *adj.* (*postpositive*) humming, as with conversation, activity, etc.; buzzing.

Abydos (ə'baɪdɒs) *n.* **1.** an ancient town in central Egypt: site of many temples and tombs. **2.** an ancient Greek colony on the Asiatic side of the Dardanelles (Hellespont): scene of the legend of Hero and Leander.

abysm (ə'bɪzəm) *n.* an archaic word for **abyss**. [C13: via OF from Med. L *abysmus* ABYSS]

abysmal (ə'bɪzməl) *adj.* **1.** immeasurable; very great. **2.** *Inf.* extremely bad. —**a'bysmally** *adv.*

abyss (ə'bɪs) *n.* **1.** a very deep gorge or chasm. **2.** anything that appears to be endless or immeasurably deep, such as time, despair, or shame. **3.** hell. [C16: via LL from Gk *abussos* bottomless, from A-¹ + *bussos* depth] —**a'byssal** *adj.*

abyssal (ə'bɪsəl) *adj.* of or belonging to the ocean depths, esp. below 2000 metres (6500 ft): *abyssal zone.*

Abyssinia (ˌæbɪ'sɪnɪə) *n.* a former name for **Ethiopia**. —ˌAbys'sinian *adj., n.*

Ac *the chemical symbol for* actinium.

AC *abbrev. for:* **1.** Air Corps. **2.** alternating current. Cf. **DC.** **3.** ante Christum. [L: before Christ] **4.** athletic club. **5.** Companion of the Order of Australia.

a/c *Book-keeping. abbrev. for:* **1.** account. **2.** account current.

acacia (ə'keɪʃə) *n.* **1.** a tropical or subtropical shrub or tree, having small yellow or white flowers. In Australia the term is applied esp. to the wattle. **2. false acacia.** another name for **locust** (senses 2, 3). **3. gum acacia.** another name for **gum arabic.** [C16: from L, from Gk *akakia*, ? rel. to *akē* point]

academe ('ækəˌdiːm) *n. Literary.* any place of learning, such as a college or university. [C16: first used by Shakespeare in *Love's Labour's Lost* (1588); see ACADEMY]

academic (ˌækə'dɛmɪk) *adj.* **1.** belonging or relating to a place of learning, esp. a college, university, or academy. **2.** of purely theoretical or speculative interest. **3.** (esp. of pupils) having an aptitude for study. **4.** excessively concerned with intellectual matters. **5.** conforming to set rules and traditions: *an academic painter.* **6.** relating to studies such as languages and pure science rather than technical, applied, or professional studies. ∼*n.* **7.** a member of a college or university. —ˌaca'demically *adv.*

academician (əˌkædə'mɪʃən) *n.* a member of an academy (senses 1, 2).

academy (ə'kædəmɪ) *n., pl.* **-mies. 1.** an institution or society for the advancement of literature, art, or science. **2.** a school for training in a particular skill or profession: *a military academy.* **3.** a secondary school, esp. in Scotland: now only used as part of a name. [C16: via L from Gk *akadēmeia* the grove where Plato taught, named after the legendary hero *Akadēmos*] —ˌaca'demical *adj.*

Academy Award *n.* the official name for an **Oscar**.

Acadia (ə'keɪdɪə) *n.* **1. a.** the Maritime Provinces of Canada. **b.** the French-speaking areas of these provinces. **2.** (formerly) a French colony in the present-day Maritime Provinces: ceded to Britain in 1713. ∼French name: **Acadie** (akadi). —**A'cadian** *adj., n.*

acanthus (ə'kænθəs) *n., pl.* **-thuses** *or* **-thi** (-θaɪ). **1.** a shrub or herbaceous plant, native to the Mediterranean region but widely cultivated as an ornamental plant, having large spiny leaves and spikes of white or purplish flowers. **2.** a carved ornament based on the leaves of the acanthus plant, esp. as used on the capital of a Corinthian column. [C17: NL, from Gk *akanthos*, from *akantha* thorn, spine]

a cappella (ɑː kə'pɛlə) *adj., adv. Music.* without instrumental accompaniment. [It.: lit., according to (the style of the) chapel]

Acapulco (ˌækə'pʊlkəʊ; *Spanish* aka'pulko) *n.* a port and resort in SW Mexico, in Guerrero state. Pop.: 638 000 (1985 est.). Official name: **Acapulco de Juárez** (*Spanish* de 'xwares).

acariasis (ˌækə'raɪəsɪs) *n.* infestation with mites or ticks. [C19: NL: see ACARID, -IASIS]

acarid ('ækərɪd) *or* **acaridan** (ə'kærɪdᵊn) *n.* any of an order of small arachnids that includes the ticks and mites. [C19: from Gk *akari* a small thing, mite]

acarpous (eɪ'kɑːpəs) *adj.* (of plants) producing no fruit. [from Gk *akarpos*, from A-¹ + *karpos* fruit]

ACAS *or* **Acas** ('eɪkæs) *n.* (in Britain) *acronym for* Advisory Conciliation and Arbitration Service.

acc. *abbrev. for:* **1.** accompanied. **2.** according. **3.** *Bookkeeping.* account. **4.** *Grammar.* accusative.

Accad ('ækæd) *n.* a variant spelling of **Akkad.**

accede (æk'siːd) *vb.* (*intr.*; usually foll. by *to*) **1.** to assent or give one's consent. **2.** to enter upon or attain (an office, right, etc.): *the prince acceded to the throne.* **3.** *International law.* to become a party (to an agreement between nations, etc.). [C15: from L *accēdere*, from *ad-* to + *cēdere* to yield] —**ac'cedence** *n.*

accelerando (ækˌsɛlə'rændəʊ) *adj., adv. Music.* (to be performed) with increasing speed. [It.]

accelerate (æk'sɛləˌreɪt) *vb.* **1.** to go, occur, or cause to go or occur more quickly; speed up. **2.** (*tr.*) to cause to happen sooner than expected. **3.** (*tr.*) to increase the velocity of (a body, reaction, etc.). [C16: from L *accelerātus*, from *accelerāre*, from *ad-* (intensive) + *celerāre* to hasten, from *celer* swift] —**ac'celerative** *adj.*

acceleration (ækˌsɛlə'reɪʃən) *n.* **1.** the act of accelerating or the state of being accelerated. **2.** the rate of increase of speed or the rate of change of velocity. **3.** the power to accelerate.

acceleration of free fall *n.* the acceleration of a body falling freely in a vacuum in the earth's gravitational field. Symbol: *g* Also called: **acceleration due to gravity**.

accelerator (æk'sɛləˌreɪtə) *n.* **1.** a device for increasing speed, esp. a pedal for controlling the fuel intake in a motor vehicle; throttle. **2.** *Physics.* a machine for increasing the kinetic energy of subatomic particles or atomic nuclei. **3.** Also: **accelerant.** *Chem.* a substance that increases the speed of a chemical reaction; catalyst.

accelerometer (ækˌsɛlə'rɒmɪtə) *n.* an instrument for measuring acceleration, esp. of an aircraft or rocket.

accent *n.* ('æksənt). **1.** the characteristic mode of pronunciation of a person or group, esp. one that betrays social or geographical origin. **2.** the relative prominence of a spoken or sung syllable, esp. with regard to stress or pitch. **3.** a mark (such as ˈ , ˌ , ´ , or `) used in writing to indicate the stress or prominence of a syllable. **4.** any of various marks or symbols conventionally used in writing certain languages to indicate the quality of a vowel. See **acute** (sense 8), **grave**² (sense 5), **circumflex**. **5.** rhythmical stress in verse or prose. **6.** *Music.* **a.** stress placed on certain notes in a piece of music, indicated by a symbol printed over the note concerned. **b.** the rhythmical pulse of a piece or passage, usually represented as the stress on the first beat of each bar. **7.** a distinctive characteristic of anything, such as taste, pattern, style, etc. **8.** particular attention or emphasis: *an accent on learning.* **9.** a strongly contrasting detail. ∼*vb.* (æk'sɛnt). (*tr.*) **10.** to mark with an accent in writing, speech, music, etc. **11.** to lay particular emphasis or stress on. [C14: via OF from L *accentus*, from *ad-* to + *cantus* chant]

accentor (æk'sɛntə) *n.* a small sparrow-like songbird, which inhabits mainly mountainous regions of Europe and Asia. See also **hedge sparrow.**

accentual (æk'sɛntʃʊəl) *adj.* **1.** of, relating to, or having accents; rhythmical. **2.** *Prosody.* of or relating to verse based on the number of stresses in a line. —**ac'centually** *adv.*

accentuate (æk'sɛntʃʊˌeɪt) *vb.* (*tr.*) to stress or emphasize. —acˌcentu'ation *n.*

accept (ək'sɛpt) *vb.* (*mainly tr.*) **1.** to take or receive (something offered). **2.** to give an affirmative reply to. **3.** to take on the responsibilities, duties, etc., of: *he accepted office.* **4.** to tolerate. **5.** to consider as true or believe in (a philosophy, theory, etc.). **6.** (*may take a clause as object*) to be willing to believe: *you must accept that he lied.* **7.** to receive with approval or admit, as into a community, group, etc. **8.** *Commerce.* to agree to pay (a bill, draft, etc.). **9.** to receive as adequate or valid. [C14: from L *acceptāre*, from *ad-* to + *capere* to take] —**ac'cepter** *n.*

acceptable (ək'sɛptəbᵊl) *adj.* **1.** satisfactory; adequate. **2.** pleasing; welcome. **3.** tolerable. —acˌcepta'bility *or* **ac'ceptableness** *n.* —**ac'ceptably** *adv.*

acceptance (ək'sɛptəns) *n.* **1.** the act of accepting or the state of being accepted or acceptable. **2.** favourable reception. **3.** (often foll. by *of*) belief (in) or assent (to). **4.** *Commerce.* a formal agreement by a debtor to pay a draft, bill, etc. **5.** (*pl.*) *Austral. & N.Z.* a list of horses accepted as starters in a race.

acceptation (ˌæksɛp'teɪʃən) *n.* the accepted meaning, as of a word, phrase, etc.

accepted (ək'sɛptɪd) *adj.* commonly approved or recognized; customary; established.

acceptor (ək'sɛptə) *n.* **1.** *Commerce.* the person or organization on which a draft or bill of exchange is drawn. **2.** *Electronics.* an impurity, such as gallium, added to a semiconductor material to increase its p-type conductivity.

access ('æksɛs) *n.* **1.** the act of approaching or entering. **2.** the condition of allowing entry, esp. (of a building, etc.) entry by prams, wheelchairs, etc. **3.** the right or privilege to approach, enter, or make use of something. **4.** a way or means of approach or entry. **5.** (*modifier*) designating programmes made by the general public: *access television.* **6.** a sudden outburst or attack, as of rage or disease. ~*vb.* (*tr.*) **7.** *Computers.* **a.** to obtain or retrieve (information) from a storage device. **b.** to place (information) in a storage device. **8.** to gain access to; make accessible or available. [C14: from OF or from L *accessus*, from *accēdere* to ACCEDE]

accessary (ək'sɛsərɪ) *n., pl.* -ries. *Law.* a less common spelling of **accessory**.

accessible (ək'sɛsəb³l) *adj.* **1.** easy to approach, enter, or use. **2. accessible to.** likely to be affected by. **3.** obtainable; available. —**ac,cessi'bility** *n.*

accession (ək'sɛʃən) *n.* **1.** the act of attaining to an office, right, condition, etc. **2.** an increase due to an addition. **3.** an addition, as to a collection. **4.** *Property law.* an addition to land or property by natural increase or improvement. **5.** *International law.* the formal acceptance of a convention or treaty. **6.** agreement. ~*vb.* **7.** (*tr.*) to make a record of (additions to a collection). —**ac'cessional** *adj.*

accessory (ək'sɛsərɪ) *n., pl.* -ries. **1.** a supplementary part or object, as of a car, appliance, etc. **2.** (*often pl.*) a small accompanying item of dress, esp. of women's dress. **3.** (formerly) a person involved in a crime although absent during its commission. ~*adj.* **4.** supplementary; additional. **5.** assisting in or having knowledge of an act, esp. a crime. [C17: from LL *accessōrius*: see ACCESS] —**accessorial** (,æksɛ'sɔːrɪəl) *adj.* —**ac'cessorily** *adv.*

access road *n.* a road giving entry to a region or, esp., a motorway.

access time *n. Computers.* the time required to retrieve a piece of stored information.

acciaccatura (ə,tʃækə'tʊərə) *n., pl.* -ras *or* -re (-reɪ). a small grace note melodically adjacent to a principal note and played simultaneously with or immediately before it. [C18: It.: lit., a crushing sound]

accidence ('æksɪdəns) *n.* the part of grammar concerned with changes in the form of words for the expression of tense, person, case, number, etc. [C15: from L *accidentia* accidental matters, from *accidere* to happen. See ACCIDENT]

accident ('æksɪdənt) *n.* **1.** an unforeseen event or one without an apparent cause. **2.** anything that occurs unintentionally or by chance: *I met him by accident.* **3.** a misfortune or mishap, esp. one causing injury or death. **4.** *Geol.* a surface irregularity in a natural formation. [C14: via OF from L *accident-*, from the p.p. of *accidere* to happen, from *ad-* + *cadere* to fall]

accidental (,æksɪ'dɛnt³l) *adj.* **1.** occurring by chance, unexpectedly, or unintentionally. **2.** nonessential; incidental. **3.** *Music.* denoting sharps, flats, or naturals that are not in the key signature of a piece. ~*n.* **4.** an incidental or supplementary circumstance, factor, or attribute. **5.** *Music.* a symbol denoting that the following note is a sharp, flat, or natural that is not a part of the key signature. —,**acci'dentally** *adv.*

accident-prone *adj.* liable to become involved in accidents.

accidie ('æksɪdɪ) *or* **acedia** *n.* spiritual sloth; apathy; indifference. [in use C13 to C16 and revived C19: via LL from Gk *akēdia*, from A-¹ + *kēdos* care]

accipiter (æk'sɪpɪtə) *n.* any of a genus of hawks having short rounded wings and a long tail. [C19: NL, from L: hawk] —**ac'cipitrine** *adj.*

acclaim (ə'kleɪm) *vb.* **1.** (*tr.*) to acknowledge publicly the excellence of (a person, act, etc.). **2.** to applaud. **3.** (*tr.*) to acknowledge publicly: *they acclaimed him king.* ~*n.* **4.** an enthusiastic expression of approval, etc. [C17: from L *acclāmāre*, from *ad-* to + *clamāre* to shout] —**ac'claimer** *n.*

acclamation (,æklə'meɪʃən) *n.* **1.** an enthusiastic reception or exhibition of welcome, approval, etc. **2.** an expression of approval with shouts or applause. **3.** *Canad.* an instance of electing or being elected without opposition. —**acclamatory** (ə'klæmətərɪ) *adj.*

acclimatize *or* **-tise** (ə'klaɪmə,taɪz) *vb.* to adapt or become accustomed to a new climate or environment. —**ac'clima,tizable** *or* -,**tisable** *adj.* —**ac,climati'zation** *or* -**ti'sation** *n.*

acclivity (ə'klɪvɪtɪ) *n., pl.* -ties. an upward slope, esp. of the ground. Cf. **declivity**. [C17: from L, from *acclīvis* sloping up] —**ac'clivitous** *adj.*

accolade ('ækə,leɪd) *n.* **1.** strong praise or approval. **2.** an award or honour. **3.** the ceremonial gesture used to confer knighthood, a touch on the shoulder with a sword. **4.** a rare word for **brace** (sense 7). [C17: via F & It. from Vulgar L *accollāre* (unattested) to hug; rel. to L *collum* neck]

accommodate (ə'kɒmə,deɪt) *vb.* **1.** (*tr.*) to supply or provide, esp. with lodging. **2.** (*tr.*) to oblige or do a favour for. **3.** to adapt. **4.** (*tr.*) to bring into harmony. **5.** (*tr.*) to allow room for. **6.** (*tr.*) to lend money to. [C16: from L *accommodāre*, from *ad-* to + *commodus* having the proper measure]

accommodating (ə'kɒmə,deɪtɪŋ) *adj.* willing to help; kind; obliging.

accommodation (ə,kɒmə'deɪʃən) *n.* **1.** adjustment, as of differences or to new circumstances; settlement or reconciliation. **2.** lodging or board and lodging. **3.** something fulfilling a need, want, etc. **4.** *Physiol.* the automatic or voluntary adjustment of the thickness of the lens of the eye for far or near vision. **5.** willingness to help or oblige. **6.** *Commerce.* a loan.

accommodation address *n.* an address on letters, etc., to a person or business that does not wish or is not able to receive post at a permanent or actual address.

accommodation ladder *n. Naut.* a flight of stairs or a ladder for lowering over the side of a ship for access to and from a small boat, pier, etc.

accompaniment (ə'kʌmpənɪmənt) *n.* **1.** something that accompanies or is served or used with something else. **2.** *Music.* a subordinate or supporting part for an instrument, voices, or an orchestra.

accompanist (ə'kʌmpənɪst) *n.* a person who plays a musical accompaniment for another performer.

accompany (ə'kʌmpənɪ) *vb.* -nying, -nied. **1.** (*tr.*) to go along with, so as to be in company with. **2.** (*tr.; foll.* by *with*) to supplement. **3.** (*tr.*) to occur or be associated with. **4.** to provide a musical accompaniment for (a soloist, etc.). [C15: from OF *accompaignier*, from *compaing* COMPANION¹]

▷ **Usage.** *Accompany* is used with *by* for people, *with* for things: *she was accompanied by her husband; she accompanied her words with a broad wink.*

accomplice (ə'kɒmplɪs, ə'kʌm-) *n.* a person who has helped another in committing a crime. [C15: from *a complice*, interpreted as one word, from OF, from LL *complex* partner, from L *complicāre* to COMPLICATE]

accomplish (ə'kɒmplɪʃ, ə'kʌm-) *vb.* (*tr.*) **1.** to manage to do; achieve. **2.** to complete. [C14: from OF *acomplir*, ult. from L *complēre* to fill up. See COMPLETE]

accomplished (ə'kɒmplɪʃt, ə'kʌm-) *adj.* **1.** successfully completed; achieved. **2.** expert; proficient.

accomplishment (ə'kɒmplɪʃmənt, ə'kʌm-) *n.* **1.** the act of achieving. **2.** something successfully completed. **3.** (*often pl.*) skill or talent. **4.** (*often pl.*) social grace and poise.

accord (ə'kɔːd) *n.* **1.** agreement; accordance (esp. in **in accord with**). **2.** concurrence of opinion. **3. with one accord.** unanimously. **4.** pleasing relationship between sounds, colours, etc. **5. of one's own accord.** voluntarily. ~*vb.* **6.** to be or cause to be in harmony or agreement. **7.** (*tr.*) to grant; bestow. [C12: via OF from L *ad-* to + *cord-*, stem of *cor* heart]

accordance (ə'kɔːdəns) *n.* conformity; agreement; accord (esp. in **in accordance with**).

according (ə'kɔːdɪŋ) *adj.* **1.** (foll. by *to*) in proportion. **2.** (foll. by *to*) as stated (by). **3.** (foll. by *to*) in conformity (with). **4.** (foll. by *as*) depending (on whether).

accordingly (ə'kɔːdɪŋlɪ) *adv.* **1.** in an appropriate manner; suitably. ~*sentence connector.* **2.** consequently.

accordion (əˈkɔːdɪən) *n.* **1.** a portable box-shaped instrument consisting of metallic reeds that are made to vibrate by air from a set of bellows controlled by the player's hands. Notes are produced by means of studlike keys. **2.** short for **piano accordion.** [C19: from G, from *Akkord* harmony] —**acˈcordionist** *n.*

accordion pleats *pl. n.* tiny knife pleats.

accost (əˈkɒst) *vb.* (*tr.*) to approach, stop, and speak to (a person), as to ask a question, solicit sexually, etc. [C16: from LL *accostāre*, from L *costa* side, rib] —**acˈcostable** *adj.*

accouchement *French.* (akuʃmɑ̃) *n.* childbirth or the period of confinement. [C19: from *accoucher* to put to bed. See COUCH]

account (əˈkaʊnt) *n.* **1.** a verbal or written report, description, or narration of some occurrence, event, etc. **2.** an explanation of conduct, esp. one made to someone in authority. **3.** basis; consideration: *on this account.* **4.** importance, consequence, or value: *of little account.* **5.** assessment; judgment. **6.** profit or advantage: *to good account.* **7.** part or behalf (only in **on one's** *or* **someone's account**). **8.** *Finance.* **a.** a business relationship between a bank, department store, etc., and a depositor, customer, or client permitting the latter certain banking or credit services. **b.** the sum of money deposited at a bank. **c.** the amount of credit available to the holder of an account. **d.** a record of these. **9.** a statement of monetary transactions with the resulting balance. **10.** (on the London Stock Exchange) the period, ordinarily of a fortnight's duration, at the end of which settlements are made. **11.** *Chiefly U.S. & Canad.* **a.** a regular client or customer. **b.** an area of business assigned to another: *they transferred their publicity account to a new agent.* **12. call** (*or* **bring**) **to account. a.** to insist on explanation. **b.** to reprimand. **c.** to hold responsible. **13. give a good** (**bad**, etc.) **account of oneself.** to perform well (badly, etc.). **14. on account. a.** on credit. **b.** Also: **to account.** as partial payment. **15. on account of.** (*prep.*) because of. **16. take account of** *or* **take into account.** to take into consideration; allow for. **17. settle** *or* **square accounts with. a.** to pay or receive a balance due. **b.** to get revenge on (someone). **18. See bank account.** ~*vb.* **19.** (*tr.*) to consider or reckon: *he accounts himself poor.* [C13: from OF *acont*, from *conter* to COUNT[1]]

accountable (əˈkaʊntəbᵊl) *adj.* **1.** responsible to someone or for some action. **2.** able to be explained. —**acˌcountaˈbility** *n.* —**acˈcountably** *adv.*

accountancy (əˈkaʊntənsɪ) *n.* the profession or business of an accountant.

accountant (əˈkaʊntənt) *n.* a person concerned with the maintenance and audit of business accounts.

account for *vb.* (*intr., prep.*) **1.** to give reasons for (an event, act, etc.). **2.** to make or provide a reckoning of (expenditure, etc.). **3.** to be responsible for destroying or putting (people, aircraft, etc.) out of action.

accounting (əˈkaʊntɪŋ) *n.* the skill or practice of maintaining and auditing accounts and preparing reports on the assets, liabilities, etc., of a business.

accoutre *or U.S.* **accouter** (əˈkuːtə) *vb.* (*tr.; usually passive*) to provide with equipment or dress, esp. military. [C16: from OF *accoustrer*, ult. rel. to L *consuere* to sew together]

accoutrement (əˈkuːtrəmənt, əˈkuːtə-) *or U.S.* **accouterment** (əˈkuːtərmənt) *n.* **1.** equipment worn by soldiers in addition to their clothing and weapons. **2.** (*usually pl.*) clothing, equipment, etc.; trappings: *the correct accoutrements for any sport.*

Accra (əˈkrɑː) *n.* the capital of Ghana, a port on the Gulf of Guinea: built on the site of three 17th-century trading fortresses founded by the English, Dutch, and Danish. Pop.: 964 879 (1984).

accredit (əˈkrɛdɪt) *vb.* (*tr.*) **1.** to ascribe or attribute. **2.** to give official recognition to. **3.** to certify as meeting required standards. **4.** (often foll. by *at* or *to*) **a.** to send (an envoy, etc.) with official credentials. **b.** to appoint (someone) as an envoy, etc. **5.** to believe. **6.** *N.Z.* to pass a candidate for university entrance on school recommendation, without external examination. [C17: from F *accréditer*, from *mettre à crédit* to put to CREDIT] —**acˌcrediˈtation** *n.*

accredited (əˈkrɛdɪtɪd) *adj.* **1.** officially authorized; recognized. **2.** (of milk, cattle, etc.) certified as free from disease; meeting certain standards. **3.** *N.Z.* accepted for university entrance on school recommendation, without external examination.

accrete (əˈkriːt) *vb.* **1.** to grow or cause to grow together. **2.** to make or become bigger, as by addition. [C18: back formation from ACCRETION]

accretion (əˈkriːʃən) *n.* **1.** any gradual increase in size, as through growth or external addition. **2.** something added, esp. extraneously, to cause growth or an increase in size. **3.** the growing together of normally separate plant or animal parts. [C17: from L *accretiō* increase, from *accrēscere*. See ACCRUE] —**acˈcretive** *adj.*

Accrington (ˈækrɪŋtən) *n.* a town in NW England, in SE Lancashire. Pop.: 35 891 (1981).

accrue (əˈkruː) *vb.* **-cruing, -crued.** (*intr.*) **1.** to increase by growth or addition, esp. (of capital) to increase by periodic addition of interest. **2.** (often foll. by *to*) to fall naturally (to). [C15: from OF *accreue*, ult. from L *accrēscere*, from *ad-* to, in addition + *crēscere* to grow] —**acˈcrual** *n.*

acct *Book-keeping. abbrev. for* account.

acculturate (əˈkʌltʃəˌreɪt) *vb.* (of a cultural or social group) to assimilate the cultural traits of another group. [C20: from AD- + CULTURE + -ATE[1]] —**acˌculturˈation** *n.*

accumulate (əˈkjuːmjʊˌleɪt) *vb.* to gather or become gathered together in an increasing quantity; collect. [C16: from L *accumulāre* to heap up, from *cumulus* a heap] —**acˈcumulable** *adj.* —**acˈcumulative** *adj.*

accumulation (əˌkjuːmjʊˈleɪʃən) *n.* **1.** the act or process of collecting together or becoming collected. **2.** something that has been collected, gathered, heaped, etc. **3.** *Finance.* the continuous growth of capital by retention of interest or earnings.

accumulator (əˈkjuːmjʊˌleɪtə) *n.* **1.** Also called: **battery, storage battery.** a rechargeable device for storing electrical energy in the form of chemical energy. **2.** *Horse racing, Brit.* a collective bet on successive races, with both stake and winnings being carried forward to accumulate progressively. **3.** a register in a calculator or computer used for holding the results of a computation or data transfer.

accuracy (ˈækjʊrəsɪ) *n., pl.* **-cies.** faithful measurement or representation of the truth; correctness; precision.

accurate (ˈækjərɪt) *adj.* **1.** faithfully representing or describing the truth. **2.** showing a negligible or permissible deviation from a standard: *an accurate ruler.* **3.** without error; precise. **4.** *Maths.* (of a number) correctly represented to a specified number of decimal places or significant figures. [C16: from L *accūrāre* to perform with care, from *cūra* care] —**ˈaccurately** *adv.*

accursed (əˈkɜːsɪd, əˈkɜːst) *or* **accurst** (əˈkɜːst) *adj.* **1.** under or subject to a curse. **2.** (*prenominal*) hateful; detestable. [OE *ācursod*, p.p. of *ācursian* to put under a CURSE] —**accursedly** (əˈkɜːsɪdlɪ) *adv.* —**acˈcursedness** *n.*

accusation (ˌækjʊˈzeɪʃən) *n.* **1.** an allegation that a person is guilty of some fault or crime. **2.** a formal charge brought against a person.

accusative (əˈkjuːzətɪv) *adj.* **1.** *Grammar.* denoting a case of nouns, pronouns, and adjectives in inflected languages that is used to identify the direct object of a finite verb, of certain prepositions, and for certain other purposes. **2.** another word for **accusatorial.** ~*n.* **3.** *Grammar.* the accusative case or a speech element in it. [C15: from L; in grammar, from *cāsus accūsātīvus* accusative case, a mistaken translation of Gk *ptōsis aitiatikē* the case indicating causation. See ACCUSE] —**accusatival** (əˌkjuːzəˈtaɪvᵊl) *adj.* —**acˈcusatively** *adv.*

accusatorial (əˌkjuːzəˈtɔːrɪəl) *or* **accusatory** (əˈkjuːzətərɪ) *adj.* **1.** containing or implying blame or strong criticism. **2.** *Law.* denoting a legal system in which the defendant is prosecuted before a judge in public. Cf. **inquisitorial.**

accuse (əˈkjuːz) *vb.* to charge (a person or persons) with some fault, offence, crime, etc. [C13: via OF from L *accūsare* to call to account, from *ad-* to + *causa* lawsuit] —**acˈcuser** *n.* —**acˈcusing** *adj.* —**acˈcusingly** *adv.*

accused (əˈkjuːzd) *n.* (preceded by *the*) *Law.* the defendant or defendants on a criminal charge.

accustom (əˈkʌstəm) *vb.* (*tr.;* usually foll. by *to*) to make (oneself) familiar (with) or used (to), as by habit or experience. [C15: from OF *acostumer*, from *costume* CUSTOM]

accustomed (əˈkʌstəmd) *adj.* **1.** usual; customary. **2.** (*postpositive;* foll. by *to*) used (to). **3.** (*postpositive;* foll. by *to*) in the habit (of).

AC/DC *adj. Inf.* (of a person) bisexual. [C20: humorous reference to electrical apparatus that is adaptable for AL-TERNATING CURRENT and DIRECT CURRENT]

ace (eɪs) *n.* **1.** any die, domino, or any of four playing cards with one spot. **2.** a single spot or pip on a playing card, die, etc. **3.** *Tennis.* a winning serve that the opponent fails to reach. **4.** a fighter pilot accredited with destroying several enemy aircraft. **5.** *Inf.* an expert: *an ace at driving.* **6. an ace up one's sleeve.** a hidden and powerful advantage. ~*adj.* **7.** *Inf.* superb; excellent. [C13: via OF from L *as* a unit]

-acea *suffix forming plural proper nouns.* denoting animals belonging to a class or order: *Crustacea* (class); *Cetacea* (order). [NL, from L, neuter pl. of *-āceus* -ACEOUS]

-aceae *suffix forming plural proper nouns.* denoting plants belonging to a family: *Liliaceae.* [NL, from L, fem. pl. of *-āceus* -ACEOUS]

acedia (əˈsiːdɪə) *n.* another word for **accidie.**

Aceldama (əˈsɛldəmə) *n. New Testament.* the place near Jerusalem that was bought with the 30 pieces of silver paid to Judas for betraying Jesus (Matthew 27:8; Acts 1:19). [C14: from Aramaic *haqēl demā* field of blood]

-aceous *suffix forming adjectives.* relating to, having the nature of, or resembling: *herbaceous.* [NL, from L *-āceus* of a certain kind; rel. to *-āc, -āx,* adjectival suffix]

acephalous (əˈsɛfələs) *adj.* having no head or one that is reduced and indistinct, as certain insect larvae. [C18: via Med. L from Gk *akephalos.* See A-¹, -CEPHALIC]

acerbate (ˈæsəˌbeɪt) *vb.* (*tr.*) **1.** to embitter or exasperate. **2.** to make sour or bitter. [C18: from L *acerbāre* to make sour]

acerbic (əˈsɜːbɪk) *adj.* harsh, bitter, or astringent; sour. [C17: from L *acerbus* sour, bitter]

acerbity (əˈsɜːbɪtɪ) *n., pl.* **-ties. 1.** vitriolic or embittered speech, temper, etc. **2.** sourness or bitterness of taste.

acetabulum (ˌæsɪˈtæbjʊləm) *n., pl.* **-la** (-lə). the deep cuplike cavity on the side of the hipbone that receives the head of the thighbone. [L: vinegar cup, hence a cuplike cavity, from *acētum* vinegar + *-abulum,* suffix denoting a container]

acetal (ˈæsɪˌtæl) *n.* **1.** a type of organic compound formed by addition of an alcohol to an aldehyde or ketone. **2.** a colourless pleasant-smelling volatile liquid used in perfumes. Formula: CH₃CH(OC₂H₅)₂. Systematic name: **diethoxyethane.** [C19: from G *Azetal,* from ACETO- + ALCOHOL]

acetaldehyde (ˌæsɪˈtældɪˌhaɪd) *n.* a colourless volatile pungent liquid, used in the manufacture of organic compounds and as a solvent. Formula: CH₃CHO. Systematic name: **ethanal.**

acetanilide (ˌæsɪˈtænɪˌlaɪd) *n.* a white crystalline powder used in the manufacture of dyes and as an analgesic in medicine. Formula: C₆H₅NH(COCH₃). Systematic names: **N-phenylethanamide, phenylacetamide.** [C19: from ACETO- + ANILINE + -IDE]

acetate (ˈæsɪˌteɪt) *n.* **1.** any salt or ester of acetic acid. Systematic name: **ethanoate. 2.** short for **acetate rayon** *or* **cellulose acetate. 3.** an audio disc with an acetate lacquer coating; used for demonstration purposes, etc. [C19: from ACETIC + -ATE¹]

acetate rayon *n.* a synthetic textile fibre made from cellulose acetate.

acetic (əˈsiːtɪk) *adj.* of, containing, producing, or derived from acetic acid or vinegar. [C19: from L *acētum* vinegar]

acetic acid *n.* a colourless pungent liquid widely used in the manufacture of plastics, pharmaceuticals, dyes, etc. Formula: CH₃COOH. Systematic name: **ethanoic acid.** See also **vinegar.**

acetify (əˈsɛtɪˌfaɪ) *vb.* **-fying, -fied.** to become or cause to become acetic acid or vinegar. —**a,cetifiˈcation** *n.*

aceto- *or before a vowel* **acet-** *combining form.* containing an acetyl group or derived from acetic acid: *acetone.* [from L *acētum* vinegar]

acetone (ˈæsɪˌtəʊn) *n.* a colourless volatile pungent liquid used in the manufacture of chemicals and as a solvent for paints, varnishes, and lacquers. Formula: CH₃COCH₃. Systematic name: **propanone.** [C19: from G *Azeton,* from ACETO- + -ONE]

acetous (ˈæsɪtəs) *or* **acetose** (ˈæsɪˌtəʊs) *adj.* **1.** producing or resembling acetic acid or vinegar. **2.** tasting like

vinegar. [C18: from LL *acētōsus* vinegary, from *acētum* vinegar]

acetyl (ˈæsɪˌtaɪl, əˈsiːtaɪl) *n.* (*modifier*) of or containing the monovalent group CH₃CO-. [C19: from ACET(IC) + -YL]

acetylcholine (ˌæsɪtaɪlˈkəʊliːn, -lɪn) *n.* a chemical substance secreted at the ends of many nerve fibres, responsible for the transmission of nervous impulses.

acetylene (əˈsɛtɪˌliːn) *n.* **1.** a colourless soluble flammable gas used in the manufacture of organic chemicals and in cutting and welding metals. Formula: C₂H₂. Systematic name: **ethyne. 2.** another name for **alkyne.**

acetylene series another name for **alkyne series.**

acetylsalicylic acid (ˌæsɪtaɪlˌsælɪˈsɪlɪk) *n.* the chemical name for **aspirin.**

Achaea (əˈkiːə) *or* **Achaia** (əˈkaɪə) *n.* **1.** a department of Greece, in the N Peloponnese. Capital: Patras. Pop.: 275 193 (1981). Area: 3209 sq. km (1239 sq. miles). Modern Greek name: **Akhaia. 2.** a province of ancient Greece, in the N Peloponnese on the Gulf of Corinth: enlarged as a Roman province in 27 B.C.

Achaean (əˈkiːən) *or* **Achaian** (əˈkaɪən) *n.* **1.** a member of a principal Greek tribe in the Mycenaean era. ~*adj.* **2.** of or relating to the Achaeans.

Achates (əˈkeɪtiːz) *n.* **1.** *Classical myth.* Aeneas' faithful companion in Virgil's *Aeneid.* **2.** a loyal friend.

ache (eɪk) *vb.* (*intr.*) **1.** to feel, suffer, or be the source of a continuous dull pain. **2.** to suffer mental anguish. ~*n.* **3.** a continuous dull pain. [OE *ācan* (vb.), *œce* (n.), ME *aken* (vb.), *ache* (n.)] — **ˈaching** *adj.*

Achebe (əˈtʃeɪbɪ) *n.* **Chinua.** born 1930, Nigerian novelist. His works include *Things Fall Apart* (1958), *A Man of the People* (1966), and *Anthills of the Savannah* (1987).

Achelous (ˌækɪˈləʊəs) *n. Classical myth.* a river god who changed into a snake and a bull while fighting Hercules but was defeated when Hercules broke off one of his horns.

achene (əˈkiːn) *n.* a dry one-seeded indehiscent fruit with the seed distinct from the fruit wall. [C19: from NL *achaenium* that which does not open, from A-¹ + Gk *khainein* to yawn]

Acheron (ˈækəˌrɒn) *n. Greek myth.* **1.** one of the rivers in Hades over which the souls of the dead were ferried by Charon. Compare **Styx. 2.** the underworld or Hades.

Acheulian *or* **Acheulean** (əˈfuːlɪən) *Archaeol.* ~*n.* **1.** (in Europe) the period in the Lower Palaeolithic following the Abbevillian, represented by the use of soft hammerstones in hand-axe production. **2.** (in Africa) the period represented by every stage of hand-axe development. ~*adj.* **3.** of or relating to this period. [C20: after *St Acheul,* town in N France]

achieve (əˈtʃiːv) *vb.* (*tr.*) **1.** to bring to a successful conclusion. **2.** to gain as by hard work or effort: *to achieve success.* [C14: from OF *achever* to bring to an end, from *a chef* to a head] —**aˈchievable** *adj.* —**aˈchiever** *n.*

achievement (əˈtʃiːvmənt) *n.* **1.** something that has been accomplished, esp. by hard work, ability, or heroism. **2.** successful completion; accomplishment.

achillea (ˌækɪˈliːə) *n.* any of several cultivated varieties of yarrow. [NL, from Gk *akhilleios* plant used medicinally by *Achilles*]

Achilles (əˈkɪliːz) *n. Greek myth.* Greek hero, the son of Peleus and the sea goddess Thetis: in the *Iliad* the foremost of the Greek warriors at the siege of Troy. While he was a baby his mother plunged him into the river Styx making his body invulnerable except for the heel by which she held him. After slaying Hector, he was killed by Paris who wounded him in the heel. —**Achillean** (ˌækɪˈliːən) *adj.*

Achilles heel *n.* a small but fatal weakness.

Achilles tendon *n.* the fibrous cord that connects the muscles of the calf to the heelbone.

Achill Island (ˈækɪl) *n.* an island in Ireland, off the W coast of Co. Mayo. Area: 148 sq. km (57 sq. miles). Pop.: 3107 (1981).

Achitophel (əˈkɪtəˌfɛl) *n. Bible.* the Douay spelling of **Ahithophel.**

achromat (ˈækrəˌmæt) *or* **achromatic lens** *n.* a lens designed to reduce chromatic aberration.

achromatic (ˌækrəˈmætɪk) *adj.* **1.** without colour. **2.** capable of reflecting or refracting light without chromatic aberration. **3.** *Music.* involving no sharps or flats. —**ˌachroˈmatically** *adv.* —**achromatism** (əˈkrəʊməˌtɪzəm) *or* **achromaticity** (əˌkrəʊməˈtɪsɪtɪ) *n.*

acid ('æsɪd) n. 1. any substance that dissociates in water to yield a sour corrosive solution containing hydrogen ions, and turning litmus red. 2. a sour-tasting substance. 3. a slang name for LSD. 4. put the acid on (someone). *Austral. & N.Z. inf.* to apply pressure to someone, usually when seeking a favour. ~*adj.* 5. *Chem.* a. of, derived from, or containing acid. b. being or having the properties of an acid. 6. sharp or sour in taste. 7. cutting, sharp, or hurtful in speech, manner, etc. [C17: from F *acide* or L *acidus*, from *acēre* to be sour] — 'acidly *adv.* — 'acidness *n.*

acid-fast *adj.* (of bacteria and tissues) resistant to decolorization by mineral acids after staining.

Acid House *or* **Acid** *n.* a type of funk-based electronically edited disco music of the late 1980s, which has hypnotic sound effects and is associated with hippie culture and the use of the drug ecstasy. [C20: from ACID (LSD) + HOUSE (MUSIC)]

acidic (ə'sɪdɪk) *adj.* another word for acid.

acidify (ə'sɪdɪˌfaɪ) *vb.* -fying, -fied. to convert into or become acid. —a'cidiˌfiable *adj.* —aˌcidifi'cation *n.*

acidity (ə'sɪdɪtɪ) *n., pl.* -ties. 1. the quality or state of being acid. 2. the amount of acid present in a solution.

acidosis (ˌæsɪ'dəʊsɪs) *n.* a condition characterized by an abnormal increase in the acidity of the blood. —acidotic (ˌæsɪ'dɒtɪk) *adj.*

acid rain *n.* rain containing pollutants, chiefly sulphur dioxide and nitrogen oxide, released into the atmosphere by burning coal or oil.

acid rock *n.* rock music characterized by bizarre amplified instrumental effects. [C20: from ACID (LSD)]

acid test *n.* a rigorous and conclusive test to establish worth or value. [C19: from the testing of gold with nitric acid]

acidulate (ə'sɪdjʊˌleɪt) *vb.* (*tr.*) to make slightly acid or sour. [C18: ACIDULOUS + -ATE¹] —aˌcidu'lation *n.*

acidulous (ə'sɪdjʊləs) *or* **acidulent** *adj.* 1. rather sour. 2. sharp or sour in speech, manner, etc.; acid. [C18: from L *acidulus* sourish, dim. of *acidus* sour]

acinus ('æsɪnəs) *n., pl.* -ni (-ˌnaɪ). 1. *Anat.* any of the terminal saclike portions of a compound gland. 2. *Bot.* any of the small drupes that make up the fruit of the raspberry, etc. 3. *Bot., obs.* a collection of berries, such as a bunch of grapes. [C18: NL, from L: grape, berry]

Acis ('eɪsɪs) *n. Greek myth.* a Sicilian shepherd and the lover of the nymph Galatea. In jealousy, Polyphemus crushed him with a huge rock, and his blood was turned by Galatea into a river.

ack-ack ('ækˌæk) *n. Mil.* a. anti-aircraft fire. b. (*as modifier*): *ack-ack guns.* [C20: British Army World War I phonetic alphabet for AA, abbrev. of *anti-aircraft*]

acknowledge (ək'nɒlɪdʒ) *vb.* (*tr.*) 1. (*may take a clause as object*) to recognize or admit the existence, truth, or reality of. 2. to indicate recognition or awareness of, as by a greeting, glance, etc. 3. to express appreciation or thanks for. 4. to make the receipt of known: *to acknowledge a letter.* 5. to recognize, esp. in legal form, the authority, rights, or claims of. [C15: prob. from earlier *knowledge*, on the model of OE *oncnāwan*, ME *aknowen* to confess, recognize] —ac'knowledgeable *adj.*

acknowledgment *or* **acknowledgement** (ək'nɒlɪdʒmənt) *n.* 1. the act of acknowledging or state of being acknowledged. 2. something done or given as an expression of thanks. 3. (*pl.*) an author's statement acknowledging his use of the works of other authors.

aclinic line (ə'klɪnɪk) *n.* another name for magnetic equator. [C19 *aclinic*, from Gk *aklinēs* not bending, from A⁻¹ + *klinein* to bend]

acme ('ækmɪ) *n.* the culminating point, as of achievement or excellence. [C16: from Gk *akmē*]

acne ('æknɪ) *n.* a chronic skin disease common in adolescence, characterized by pustules on the face. [C19: NL, from a misreading of Gk *akmē* eruption on the face. See ACME]

acolyte ('ækəˌlaɪt) *n.* 1. a follower or attendant. 2. *Christianity.* an officer who assists a priest. [C16: via OF & Med. L from Gk *akolouthos* a follower]

Aconcagua (*Spanish* akon'kaywa) *n.* a mountain in W Argentina: the highest peak in the Andes and in the W Hemisphere. Height: 6960 m (22 835 ft.).

aconite ('ækəˌnaɪt) *n.* 1. any of a genus of N temperate plants, such as monkshood and wolfsbane, many of which

are poisonous. Cf. winter aconite. 2. the dried poisonous root of many of these plants, sometimes used as a narcotic. [C16: via OF or L from Gk *akoniton* aconite] —aconitic (ˌækə'nɪtɪk) *adj.*

Açôres (ə'soreʃ) *n.* the Portuguese name for (the) **Azores.**

acorn ('eɪkɔːn) *n.* the fruit of the oak tree, consisting of a smooth thick-walled nut in a woody scaly cuplike base. [C16: var. (infl. by *corn*) of OE *æcern* the fruit of a tree, acorn]

acoustic (ə'kuːstɪk) *or* **acoustical** *adj.* 1. of or related to sound, hearing, or acoustics. 2. designed to respond to or absorb sound: *an acoustic tile.* 3. (of a musical instrument or recording) without electronic amplification: *an acoustic guitar.* [C17: from Gk *akoustikos*, from *akouein* to hear] —a'coustically *adv.*

acoustics (ə'kuːstɪks) *n.* 1. (*functioning as sing.*) the scientific study of sound and sound waves. 2. (*functioning as pl.*) the characteristics of a room, auditorium, etc., that determine the fidelity with which sound can be heard within it.

acquaint (ə'kweɪnt) *vb.* (*tr.*) (foll. by *with* or *of*) to make (a person) familiar (with). [C13: via OF & Med. L from L *accognitus*, from *accognōscere* to know perfectly, from *ad-* (intensive) + *cognōscere* to know]

acquaintance (ə'kweɪntəns) *n.* 1. a person whom one knows but who is not a close friend. 2. knowledge of a person or thing, esp. when slight. 3. make the acquaintance of. to come into social contact with. 4. those persons collectively whom one knows. —ac'quaintance-ˌship *n.*

acquainted (ə'kweɪntɪd) *adj.* (*postpositive*) 1. (sometimes foll. by *with*) on terms of familiarity but not intimacy. 2. (foll. by *with*) familiar (with).

acquiesce (ˌækwɪ'ɛs) *vb.* (*intr.; often foll. by *in* or *to*) to comply (with); assent (to) without protest. [C17: from L *acquiēscere*, from *ad-* ad + *quiēscere* to rest, from *quiēs* QUIET] —ˌacqui'escence *n.* —ˌacqui'escent *adj.*

acquire (ə'kwaɪə) *vb.* (*tr.*) to get or gain (something, such as an object, trait, or ability). [C15: via OF from L *acquīrere*, from *ad-* in addition + *quaerere* to get, seek] —ac'quirable *adj.* —ac'quirement *n.*

acquired characteristic *n.* a characteristic of an organism resulting from the effects of the environment.

acquired taste *n.* 1. a liking for something at first considered unpleasant. 2. the thing liked.

acquisition (ˌækwɪ'zɪʃən) *n.* 1. the act of acquiring or gaining possession. 2. something acquired. 3. a person or thing of special merit added to a group. [C14: from L *acquīsītiōn-*, from *acquīrere* to ACQUIRE]

acquisitive (ə'kwɪzɪtɪv) *adj.* inclined or eager to acquire things, esp. material possessions. —ac'quisitively *adv.* —ac'quisitiveness *n.*

acquit (ə'kwɪt) *vb.* -quitting, -quitted. (*tr.*) 1. (foll. by *of*) a. to free or release (from a charge of crime). b. to pronounce not guilty. 2. (foll. by *of*) to free or relieve (from an obligation, duty, etc.). 3. to repay or settle (a debt or obligation). 4. to conduct (oneself). [C13: from OF *aquiter*, from *quiter* to release, QUIT] —ac'quittal *n.* —ac'quitter *n.*

acquittance (ə'kwɪtəns) *n.* 1. a release from or settlement of a debt, etc. 2. a record of this, such as a receipt.

acre ('eɪkə) *n.* 1. a unit of area used in certain English-speaking countries, equal to 4840 square yards or 4046.86 square metres. 2. (*pl.*) a. land, esp. a large area. b. *Inf.* a large amount. 3. farm the long acre. *N.Z.* to graze stock on the grass along a highway. [OE *æcer* field, acre]

Acre *n.* 1. ('aːkrə). a state of W Brazil: mostly unexplored tropical forests; acquired from Bolivia in 1903. Capital: Rio Branco. Pop.: 301 605 (1980). Area: 152 589 sq. km (58 899 sq. miles). 2. ('eɪkə, 'aːkə). a city and port in N Israel, strategically situated on the Bay of Acre in the E Mediterranean: taken and retaken during the Crusades (1104, 1187, 1191, 1291), taken by the Turks (1517), by Egypt (1832), and by the Turks again (1839). Pop.: 37 000 (1983). Old Testament name: **Accho** (aː'kəʊ). Arabic name: 'Akka (aː'kaː). Hebrew name: 'Akko (aː'kəʊ).

acreage ('eɪkərɪdʒ) *n.* land area in acres.

acrid ('ækrɪd) *adj.* 1. unpleasantly pungent or sharp to the smell or taste. 2. sharp or caustic, esp. in speech or nature. [C18: from L *ācer* sharp, sour; prob. infl. by ACID] —acridity (ə'krɪdɪtɪ) *n.* — 'acridly *adv.*

acridine ('ækrɪ,diːn) n. a colourless crystalline solid used in the manufacture of dyes.

acriflavine (,ækrɪ'fleɪvɪn) n. a brownish or orange-red powder used in medicine as an antiseptic. [C20: from ACRIDINE + FLAVIN]

acriflavine hydrochloride n. a red crystalline substance obtained from acriflavine and used as an antiseptic.

Acrilan ('ækrɪ,læn) n. Trademark. an acrylic fibre or fabric, characterized by strength and resistance to creasing and used for clothing, carpets, etc.

acrimony ('ækrɪmənɪ) n., pl. -nies. bitterness or sharpness of manner, speech, temper, etc. [C16: from L ācrimōnia, from ācer sharp, sour] —**acrimonious** (,ækrɪ'məʊnɪəs) adj.

acro- combining form. 1. denoting something at a height, top, beginning, or end: acropolis. 2. denoting an extremity of the human body: acromegaly. [from Gk akros extreme, topmost]

acrobat ('ækrə,bæt) n. 1. an entertainer who performs acts that require skill, agility, and coordination, such as swinging from a trapeze or walking a tightrope. 2. a person noted for his frequent and rapid changes of position or allegiance. [C19: via F from Gk akrobatēs, one who walks on tiptoe, from ACRO- + bat-, from bainein to walk] —**,acro'batic** adj. —**,acro'batically** adv.

acrobatics (,ækrə'bætɪks) pl. n. 1. the skills or feats of an acrobat. 2. any activity requiring agility and skill: mental acrobatics.

acrogen ('ækrədʒən) n. any flowerless plant, such as a fern or moss, in which growth occurs from the tip of the main stem. —**acrogenous** (ə'krɒdʒɪnəs) adj.

acromegaly (,ækrəʊ'mɛɡəlɪ) n. a chronic disease characterized by enlargement of the bones of the head, hands, and feet. It is caused by excessive secretion of growth hormone by the pituitary gland. [C19: from F acromégalie, from ACRO- + Gk megal-, stem of megas big] —**acromegalic** (,ækrəʊmɪ'ɡælɪk) adj., n.

acronym ('ækrənɪm) n. a pronounceable name made from a series of initial letters or parts of a group of words; for example, UNESCO for the United Nations Educational, Scientific, and Cultural Organization. [C20: from ACRO- + -ONYM]

acrophobia (,ækrə'fəʊbɪə) n. abnormal fear or dread of being at a great height. [C19: from ACRO- + -PHOBIA] —**,acro'phobic** adj., n.

acropolis (ə'krɒpəlɪs) n. the citadel of an ancient Greek city. [C17: from Gk, from ACRO- + polis city]

Acropolis (ə'krɒpəlɪs) n. the citadel of Athens on which the Parthenon stands.

across (ə'krɒs) prep. 1. from one side to the other side of. 2. on or at the other side of. 3. so as to transcend the boundaries or barriers of: across religious divisions. ~adv. 4. from one side to the other. 5. on or to the other side. [C13 on croice, acros, from OF a croix crosswise]

across-the-board adj. (of salary increases, taxation cuts, etc.) affecting all levels or classes equally.

acrostic (ə'krɒstɪk) n. a number of lines of writing, such as a poem, certain letters of which form a word, proverb, etc. A **single acrostic** is formed by the initial letters of the lines, a **double acrostic** by the initial and final letters, and a **triple acrostic** by the initial, middle, and final letters. [C16: via F from Gk, from ACRO- + stikhos line or verse] —**a'crostically** adv.

acrylic (ə'krɪlɪk) adj. 1. of, derived from, or concerned with acrylic acid. ~n. 2. short for **acrylic fibre, acrylic resin**. [C20: from L ācer sharp olēre to smell + -IC]

acrylic acid n. a colourless corrosive pungent liquid, used in the manufacture of acrylic resins. Formula: CH₂:CHCOOH. Systematic name: **propenoic acid**.

acrylic fibre n. a man-made fibre used in blankets, knitwear, etc.

acrylic resin n. any of a group of polymers of acrylic acid, its esters, or amides, used as synthetic rubbers, paints, and as plastics such as Perspex.

act (ækt) n. 1. something done or performed. 2. the performance of some physical or mental process; action. 3. (cap. when part of a name) the formally codified result of deliberation by a legislative body. 4. (often pl.) a formal written record of transactions, proceedings, etc., as of a society, committee, or legislative body. 5. a major division of a dramatic work. 6. a. a short performance of skill, a comic sketch, dance, etc. b. those giving such a performance. 7. an assumed attitude or pose, esp. one intended to impress. 8. **get in on the act**. Inf. to become involved in a profitable situation in order to share in the benefit. 9. **get one's act together**. Inf. to organize oneself. ~vb. 10. (intr.) to do something. 11. (intr.) to operate; react: his mind acted quickly. 12. to perform (a part or role) in a play, etc. 13. (tr.) to present (a play, etc.) on stage. 14. (intr.; usually foll. by for or as) to be a substitute (for). 15. (intr.; foll. by as) to serve the function or purpose (of). 16. (intr.) to conduct oneself or behave (as if one were): she usually acts like a lady. 17. (intr.) to behave in an unnatural or affected way. 18. (copula) to play the part of: to act the fool. 19. (copula) to behave in a manner appropriate to: to act one's age. ~See also **act on, act up**. [C14: from L actus a doing, & actum a thing done, from the p.p. of agere to do] —**'actable** adj. —**,acta'bility** n.

ACT abbrev. for Australian Capital Territory.

Actaeon (æk'tiːən, 'æktɪən) n. Greek myth. a hunter of Boeotia who, having accidentally seen Artemis bathing, was turned into a stag and torn apart by his own hounds.

ACTH n. adrenocorticotropic hormone; a hormone, secreted by the anterior lobe of the pituitary gland, that stimulates growth of the adrenal gland. It is used in treating rheumatoid arthritis, allergic and skin diseases, etc.

acting ('æktɪŋ) adj. (prenominal) 1. taking on duties temporarily, esp. as a substitute for another. 2. performing the duties of though not yet holding the rank of: acting lieutenant. 3. operating or functioning. 4. intended for stage performance; provided with directions for actors: an acting version of "Hedda Gabler". ~n. 5. the art or profession of an actor.

actinia (æk'tɪnɪə) n., pl. -tiniae (-'tɪnɪ,iː) or -tinias. a sea anemone common in rock pools. [C18: NL, lit.: things having a radial structure]

actinic (æk'tɪnɪk) adj. (of radiation) producing a photochemical effect. [C19: from ACTINO- + -IC] —**ac'tinically** adv. —**'actin,ism** n.

actinide series ('æktɪ,naɪd) n. a series of 15 radioactive elements with increasing atomic numbers from actinium to lawrencium.

actinium (æk'tɪnɪəm) n. a radioactive element of the actinide series, occurring as a decay product of uranium. It is used in neutron production. Symbol: Ac; atomic no.: 89; half-life of most stable isotope, ^{227}Ac: 22 years. [C19: NL, from ACTINO- + -IUM]

actino- or before a vowel **actin-** combining form. 1. indicating a radial structure: actinomorphic. 2. indicating radioactivity or radiation: actinometer. [from Gk, from aktis ray]

actinoid ('æktɪ,nɔɪd) adj. having a radiate form, as a sea anemone or starfish.

actinometer (,æktɪ'nɒmɪtə) n. an instrument for measuring the intensity of radiation, esp. of the sun's rays.

actinomycin (,æktɪnəʊ'maɪsɪn) n. any of several toxic antibiotics obtained from soil bacteria, used in treating some cancers.

actinozoan (,æktɪnəʊ'zəʊən) n., adj. another word for **anthozoan**.

action ('ækʃən) n. 1. the state or process of doing something or being active. 2. something done, such as an act or deed. 3. movement or posture during some physical activity. 4. activity, force, or energy: a man of action. 5. (usually pl.) conduct or behaviour. 6. Law. a legal proceeding brought by one party against another; lawsuit. 7. the operating mechanism, esp. in a piano, gun, watch, etc. 8. the force applied to a body. 9. the way in which something operates or works. 10. **out of action**. not functioning. 11. the events that form the plot of a story, play, or other composition. 12. Mil. a. a minor engagement. b. fighting at sea or on land: he saw action in the war. 13. Inf. the profits of an enterprise or transaction (esp. in a **piece of the action**). 14. Sl. the main activity, esp. social activity. 15. short for **industrial action**. ~vb. (tr.) 16. to put into effect; take action concerning. ~sentence substitute. 17. a command given by a film director to indicate that filming is to begin. [C14 accioun, ult. from L āctiōn-, from agere to do]

actionable ('ækʃənəb²l) adj. Law. affording grounds for legal action. —**'actionably** adv.

action committee or **group** n. a committee or group formed to pursue an end, usually political, using petitions, marches, etc.

action painting n. a development of abstract expressionism characterized by accidental effects of thrown, smeared, dripped, or spattered paint. Also called: **tachisme.**

action replay n. the rerunning of a small section of a television film or tape of a match or other sporting contest, often in slow motion.

action stations pl. n. **1.** Mil. the positions taken up by individuals in preparation for or during a battle. ~sentence substitute. **2.** a command to take up such positions. **3.** Inf. a warning to get ready for something.

Actium ('æktɪəm) n. a town of ancient Greece that overlooked the naval battle in 31 B.C. at which Octavian's fleet under Agrippa defeated that of Mark Antony and Cleopatra.

activate ('æktɪ,veɪt) vb. (tr.) **1.** to make active or capable of action. **2.** Physics. to make radioactive. **3.** Chem. to increase the rate of (a reaction). **4.** to purify (sewage) by aeration. **5.** U.S. mil. to mobilize or organize (a unit). —,acti'vation n. —'acti,vator n.

activated carbon n. a highly adsorptive form of carbon used to remove colour or impurities from liquids and gases.

activated sludge n. a mass of aerated precipitated sewage added to untreated sewage to bring about purification by hastening bacterial decomposition.

active ('æktɪv) adj. **1.** moving, working, or doing something. **2.** busy or involved: an active life. **3.** physically energetic. **4.** effective: an active ingredient. **5.** Grammar. denoting a voice of verbs used to indicate that the subject of a sentence is performing the action or causing the event or process described by the verb, as kicked in The boy kicked the football. **6.** being fully engaged in military service. **7.** (of a volcano) erupting periodically; not extinct. **8.** Astron. (of the sun) exhibiting a large number of sunspots, solar flares, etc., and a marked variation in intensity and frequency of radio emission. ~n. **9.** Grammar. **a.** the active voice. **b.** an active verb. [C14: from L āctīvus. See ACT, -IVE] —'actively adv. —'activeness n.

active list n. Mil. a list of officers available for full duty.

activism ('æktɪ,vɪzəm) n. a policy of taking direct and often militant action to achieve an end, esp. a political or social one. —'activist n.

activity (æk'tɪvɪtɪ) n., pl. -ties. **1.** the state or quality of being active. **2.** lively action or movement. **3.** any specific action, pursuit, etc.: recreational activities. **4.** the number of disintegrations of a radioactive substance in a given unit of time.

act of God n. Law. a sudden and inevitable occurrence caused by natural forces, such as a flood or earthquake.

act on or **upon** vb. (intr., prep.) **1.** to regulate one's behaviour in accordance with (advice, information, etc.). **2.** to have an effect on (illness, a part of the body, etc.).

Acton[1] ('æktən) n. a district of the London borough of Ealing.

Acton[2] ('æktən) n. **1. John Emerich Edward Dalberg,** 1st Baron Acton. 1834–1902, English historian: a proponent of Christian liberal ethics and adviser of Gladstone. **2.** his grandfather, Sir **John Francis Edward.** 1736-1811, European naval commander and statesman: admiral of Tuscany (1774–79) and Naples (1779 onwards) and chief minister of Naples (1779–1806).

actor ('æktə) or (fem.) **actress** ('æktrɪs) n. a person who acts in a play, film, broadcast, etc.

actual ('æktʃʊəl) adj. **1.** existing in reality or as a matter of fact. **2.** real or genuine. **3.** existing at the present time; current. [C14 actuel existing, from LL, from L āctus ACT]
▷ **Usage.** The excessive use of actual and actually should be avoided. They are unnecessary in sentences such as in actual fact, he is forty-two, and he did actually go to the play but did not enjoy it.

actuality (,æktʃʊ'ælɪtɪ) n., pl. -ties. **1.** true existence; reality. **2.** (sometimes pl.) a fact or condition that is real.

actualize or **-lise** ('æktʃʊə,laɪz) vb. (tr.) **1.** to make actual or real. **2.** to represent realistically. —,actuali'zation or -li'sation n.

actually ('æktʃʊəlɪ) adv. **1. a.** as an actual fact; really. **b.** (as sentence modifier): actually, I haven't seen him. **2.** at present.

actuarius ('æktʃʊ,ɛərɪəs) n. S. African history. an official of the synod of a Dutch Reformed Church. [from L; see ACTUARY]

actuary ('æktʃʊərɪ) n., pl. -aries. a statistician, esp. one employed by insurance companies to calculate risks, policy premiums, and dividends. [C16 (meaning: registrar): from L āctuārius one who keeps accounts, from actum public business, & acta documents] —**actuarial** (,æktʃʊ'ɛərɪəl) adj.

actuate ('æktʃʊ,eɪt) vb. (tr.) **1.** to put into action or mechanical motion. **2.** to motivate: actuated by unworthy desires. [C16: from Med. L actuātus, from actuāre to incite to action, from L āctus ACT] —,actu'ation n. —'actu,ator n.

act up vb. (intr., adv.) Inf. to behave in a troublesome way: the engine began to act up.

acuity (ə'kju:ɪtɪ) n. keenness or acuteness, esp. in vision or thought. [C15: from OF, from L acūtus ACUTE]

aculeus (ə'kju:lɪəs) n. **1.** a prickle, such as the thorn of a rose. **2.** a sting. [C19: from L, dim. of acus needle] —a'culeate adj.

acumen ('ækjʊ,mɛn, ə'kju:mən) n. the ability to judge well; insight. [C16: from L: sharpness, from acuere to sharpen] —a'cuminous adj.

acuminate adj. (ə'kju:mɪnɪt). **1.** narrowing to a sharp point, as some types of leaf. ~vb. (ə'kju:mɪ,neɪt). **2.** (tr.) to make pointed or sharp. [C17: from L acūmināre to sharpen] —a,cumi'nation n.

acupuncture ('ækjʊ,pʌŋktʃə) n. the insertion of the tips of needles into the skin at specific points for the purpose of treating various disorders by stimulating nerve impulses. [C17: from L acus needle + PUNCTURE] —'acu,puncturist n.

acute (ə'kju:t) adj. **1.** penetrating in perception or insight. **2.** sensitive to details; keen. **3.** of extreme importance; crucial. **4.** sharp or severe; intense. **5.** having a sharp end or point. **6.** Maths. (of an angle) less than 90°. **7.** (of a disease) **a.** arising suddenly and manifesting intense severity. **b.** of relatively short duration. **8.** Phonetics. of or relating to an accent (´) placed over vowels, denoting that the vowel is pronounced with higher musical pitch (as in ancient Greek) or with certain special quality (as in French). ~n. **9.** an acute accent. [C14: from L acūtus, p.p. of acuere to sharpen, from acus needle] —a'cutely adv. —a'cuteness n.

acute accent n. the diacritical mark (´), used in some languages to indicate that the vowel over which it is placed has a special quality (as in French été) or that it receives the strongest stress in the word (as in Spanish hablé).

acute dose n. a fatal dose of radiation.

ad (æd) n. Inf. short for **advertisement.**

A.D. or **AD** (indicating years numbered from the supposed year of the birth of Christ) abbrev. for anno Domini: 70 A.D. [L: in the year of the Lord]
▷ **Usage.** In strict usage, A.D. is only employed with specific years: he died in 1621 A.D., but he died in the 17th century. Formerly the practice was to write A.D. preceding the date (A.D. 1621), and it is also strictly correct to omit in when A.D. is used, since this is already contained in the meaning of the Latin anno Domini (in the year of Our Lord), but this is no longer general practice. B.C. is used with both specific dates and indications of the period: Heraclitus was born about 540 B.C.; the battle took place in the 4th century B.C.

ad- prefix. **1.** to; towards: adverb. **2.** near; next to: adrenal. [from L: to, towards. As a prefix in words of L origin, ad- became ac-, af-, ag-, al-, an-, acq-, ar-, as-, and at- before c, f, g, l, n, q, r, s, and t, and became a- before gn, sc, sp, st]

adage ('ædɪdʒ) n. a traditional saying that is accepted by many as true; proverb. [C16: via OF from L adagium; rel. to āio I say]

adagio (ə'dɑ:dʒɪ,əʊ) Music. ~adj., adv. **1.** (to be performed) slowly. ~n., pl. -gios. **2.** a movement or piece to be performed slowly. [C18: It., from at + agio ease]

Adam[1] ('ædəm) n. **1.** Bible. the first man, created by God (Genesis 2–3). **2. not know (someone) from Adam.** to have no knowledge of or acquaintance with someone. **3. Adam's ale** or **wine.** water.

Adam[2] ('ædəm) n. **1. Robert.** 1728–92, Scottish architect and furniture designer. Assisted by his brother, **James,** 1730–94, he emulated the harmony of classical and Italian Renaissance architecture. ~adj. **2.** in the neoclassical style made popular by Robert Adam.

adamant ('ædəmənt) *adj.* **1.** unshakable in determination, purpose, etc.; inflexible. **2.** unbreakable; impenetrable. ~*n.* **3.** any extremely hard substance. **4.** a legendary stone said to be impenetrable. [OE: from L *adamas*, from Gk, lit.: unconquerable, from A-[1] + *daman* to conquer] —,ada'mantine *adj.*

Adams[1] ('ædəmz) *n.* a mountain in SW Washington, in the Cascade Range. Height: 3751 m (12 307 ft.).

Adams[2] ('ædəmz) *n.* **1. John.** 1735–1826, second president of the U.S. (1797–1801); U.S. ambassador to Great Britain (1785–88); helped draft the Declaration of Independence (1776). **2. John Couch.** 1819–92, English astronomer who deduced the existence and position of the planet Neptune. **3. John Quincy,** son of John Adams. 1767–1848, sixth president of the U.S. (1825–29); secretary of state (1817–25). **4. Richard.** born 1920, British author, noted for his novels *Watership Down* (1972), *The Plague Dogs* (1977), and *The Girl in a Swing* (1980). **5. Samuel.** 1722–1803, American revolutionary leader; one of the organizers of the Boston Tea Party; a signatory of the Declaration of Independence.

Adam's apple *n.* the visible projection of the thyroid cartilage of the larynx at the front of the neck.

Adana ('ædənə) *n.* a city in S Turkey, capital of Adana province. Pop.: 776 000 (1985). Also called: **Seyhan.**

adapt (ə'dæpt) *vb.* **1.** (often foll. by *to*) to adjust (someone or something) to different conditions. **2.** (*tr.*) to fit, change, or modify to suit a new or different purpose. [C17: from L *adaptāre,* from *ad-* to + *aptāre* to fit] —a'daptable *adj.* —a,dapta'bility *n.* —a'daptive *adj.*

adaptation (,ædəp'teɪʃən) *n.* **1.** the act or process of adapting or the state of being adapted. **2.** something that is produced by adapting something else. **3.** something that is changed or modified to suit new conditions. **4.** *Biol.* a modification in organisms that makes them better suited to survive and reproduce in a particular environment.

adapter *or* **adaptor** (ə'dæptə) *n.* **1.** a person or thing that adapts. **2.** any device for connecting two parts, esp. ones that are of different sizes. **3. a.** a plug used to connect an electrical device to a mains supply when they have different types of terminals. **b.** a device used to connect several electrical appliances to a single socket.

ADC *abbrev. for:* **1.** aide-de-camp. **2.** analogue-digital converter.

add (æd) *vb.* **1.** to combine (two or more numbers or quantities) by addition. **2.** (*tr.;* foll. by *to*) to increase (a number or quantity) by another number or quantity using addition. **3.** (*tr.;* often foll. by *to*) to join (something) to something else in order to increase the size, effect, or scope: *to add insult to injury.* **4.** (*intr.;* foll. by *to*) to have an extra and increased effect (on). **5.** (*tr.*) to say or write further. **6.** (*tr.;* foll. by *in*) to include. ~See also **add up.** [C14: from L *addere,* from *ad-* to + *-dere, dare* to put]

Addams ('ædəmz) *n.* **Jane.** 1860–1935, U.S. social reformer, feminist, and pacifist, who founded Hull House, a social settlement in Chicago: Nobel peace prize 1931.

addax ('ædæks) *n.* a large light-coloured antelope having ribbed loosely spiralled horns and inhabiting desert regions in N Africa. [C17: L, from an unidentified ancient N African language]

addend ('ædɛnd) *n.* any of a set of numbers that is to be added. [C20: short for ADDENDUM]

addendum (ə'dɛndəm) *n., pl.* **-da** (-də). **1.** something added; an addition. **2.** a supplement or appendix to a book, magazine, etc. [C18: from L, gerundive of *addere* to ADD]

adder ('ædə) *n.* **1.** Also called: **viper.** a common viper that is widely distributed in Europe, including Britain, and Asia and is dark grey with a black zigzag pattern along the back. **2.** any of various similar venomous or nonvenomous snakes. ~See also **puff adder.** [OE *nædre* snake; in ME *a naddre* was mistaken for *an addre*]

adder's-tongue *n.* any of several ferns that grow in the N hemisphere and have a narrow spore-bearing body that sticks out like a spike from the leaf.

addict *vb.* (ə'dɪkt). **1.** (*tr.; usually passive;* often foll. by *to*) to cause (someone or oneself) to become dependent (on something, esp. a narcotic drug). ~*n.* ('ædɪkt). **2.** a person who is addicted, esp. to narcotic drugs. **3.** *Inf.* a person devoted to something: *a jazz addict.* [C16 (as adj. and as vb.; n. use C20): from L *addictus* given over, from

addīcere, from *ad-* to + *dīcere* to say] —ad'diction *n.* —ad'dictive *adj.*

Addington ('ædɪŋtən) *n.* **Henry,** 1st Viscount Sidmouth. 1757–1844, British statesman; prime minister (1801–04) and home secretary (1812–21).

Addis Ababa ('ædɪs 'æbəbə) *n.* the capital of Ethiopia, on a central plateau 2400 m (8000 ft.) above sea level: founded in 1887; became capital in 1896. Pop.: 1 412 575 (1984).

Addison ('ædɪsᵊn) *n.* **Joseph.** 1672–1719, English essayist and poet who, with Richard Steele, founded *The Spectator* (1711–14) and contributed most of its essays, including the *de Coverley Papers.*

Addison's disease *n.* a disease characterized by bronzing of the skin, anaemia, and extreme weakness, caused by underactivity of the adrenal glands. [C19: after Thomas *Addison* (1793–1860), E physician who identified it]

addition (ə'dɪʃən) *n.* **1.** the act, process, or result of adding. **2.** a person or thing that is added or acquired. **3.** a mathematical operation in which the sum of two numbers or quantities is calculated. Usually indicated by the symbol **+**. **4.** *Obs.* a title. **5. in addition.** (*adv.*) also; as well. **6. in addition to.** (*prep.*) besides; as well as. [C15: from L *additiōn-,* from *addere* to ADD] —ad'ditional *adj.*

additive ('ædɪtɪv) *adj.* **1.** characterized or produced by addition. ~*n.* **2.** any substance added to something to improve it, prevent deterioration, etc. **3.** short for **food additive.** [C17: from LL *additīvus,* from *addere* to ADD]

addle ('ædᵊl) *vb.* **1.** to make or become confused or muddled. **2.** to make or become rotten. ~*adj.* **3.** (*in combination*) indicating a confused or muddled state: *addlebrained.* [C18 (vb.), back formation from *addled,* from C13 *addle* rotten, from OE *adela* filth]

add-on *n.* *Computers.* a circuit, hardware, etc., that can be added to a computer to increase its capacity or performance.

address (ə'drɛs) *n.* **1.** the conventional form by which the location of a building is described. **2.** the written form of this, as on a letter or parcel. **3.** the place at which someone lives. **4.** a speech or written communication, esp. one of a formal nature. **5.** skilfulness or tact. **6.** *Arch.* manner of speaking. **7.** *Computers.* a number giving the location of a piece of stored information. **8.** (*usually pl.*) expressions of affection made by a man in courting a woman. ~*vb.* (*tr.*) **9.** to mark (a letter, parcel, etc.) with an address. **10.** to speak to, refer to in speaking, or deliver a speech to. **11.** (used reflexively; foll. by *to*) **a.** to speak or write to. **b.** to apply oneself to: *he addressed himself to the task.* **12.** to direct (a message, warning, etc.) to the attention of. **13.** to adopt a position facing (the ball in golf, etc.). [C14 (in the sense: to make right, adorn) and C15 (in the modern sense: to direct words): via OF from Vulgar L *addrictiāre* (unattested), from L *ad-* to + *dīrectus* DIRECT] —ad'dresser *or* ad'dressor *n.*

addressee (,ædrɛ'siː) *n.* a person or organization to whom a letter, etc., is addressed.

adduce (ə'djuːs) *vb.* (*tr.*) to cite (reasons, examples, etc.) as evidence or proof. [C15: from L *addūcere* to lead to] —ad'ducent *adj.* —ad'ducible *adj.* —adduction (ə'dʌkʃən) *n.*

adduct (ə'dʌkt) *vb.* (*tr.*) (of a muscle) to draw or pull (a leg, arm, etc.) towards the median axis of the body. [C19: from L *addūcere;* see ADDUCE] —ad'duction *n.* —ad'ductor *n.*

add up *vb.* (*adv.*) **1.** to find the sum (of). **2.** (*intr.*) to result in a correct total. **3.** (*intr.*) *Inf.* to make sense. **4.** (*intr.;* foll. by *to*) to amount to.

-ade *suffix forming nouns.* a sweetened drink made of various fruits: *lemonade.* [from F, from L *-āta* made of, fem. p.p. of verbs ending in *-āre*]

Adelaide ('ædɪ,leɪd) *n.* the capital of South Australia: **Port Adelaide,** 11 km (7 miles) away on St. Vincent Gulf, handles the bulk of exports. Pop.: 993 100 (1986).

Adélie Land ('ædɪlɪ; *French* adeli) *n.* a part of Antarctica, between Wilkes Land and George V Land: under French sovereignty. Also called: **Adélie Coast.** French name: **Terre Adélie.**

Aden ('eɪdᵊn) *n.* **1.** the main port and capital of South Yemen, on the N coast of the **Gulf of Aden,** an arm of the Indian Ocean at the entrance to the Red Sea: formerly an important port of call on shipping routes to the East. Pop.:

318 000 (1984). **2.** a former British colony and protectorate on the S coast of the Arabian Peninsula: became part of the People's Republic of Southern Yemen in 1967. Area: 195 sq. km (75 sq. miles).

Adenauer (*German* 'aːdənauər) *n.* **Konrad** ('kɔnraːt). 1876–1967, German statesman; chancellor of West Germany (1949–63).

adenine ('ædənɪn) *n.* a purine base present in animal and plant tissues as a constituent of the nucleic acids DNA and RNA.

adeno- *or before a vowel* **aden-** *combining form.* gland or glandular: *adenoid; adenology.* [NL, from Gk *adēn* gland]

adenoidal (ˌædɪ'nɔɪdəl) *adj.* **1.** having the nasal tones or impaired breathing of one with enlarged adenoids. **2.** of adenoids.

adenoids ('ædɪˌnɔɪdz) *pl. n.* a mass of lymphoid tissue at the back of the throat behind the uvula: when enlarged it often restricts nasal breathing, esp. in young children. [C19 : from Gk *adenoeidēs*. See ADENO-, -OID]

adenoma (ˌædɪ'nəumə) *n., pl.* **-mas** *or* **-mata** (-mətə). **1.** a tumour occurring in glandular tissue. **2.** a tumour having a glandlike structure.

adenosine (æ'denəˌsiːn) *n. Biochem.* a compound formed by the condensation of adenine and ribose. It is present in all living cells in a combined form. [C20: a blend of ADENINE + RIBOSE]

adept *adj.* (ə'dept). **1.** proficient in something requiring skill or manual dexterity. **2.** expert. ~*n.* ('ædept). **3.** a person who is skilled or proficient in something. [C17: from Med. L *adeptus*, from L *adipiscī*, from *ad-* to + *apiscī* to attain] —**a'deptness** *n.*

adequate ('ædɪkwɪt) *adj.* able to fulfil a need without being abundant, outstanding, etc. [C17: from L *adaequāre*, from *ad-* to + *aequus* EQUAL] —**adequacy** ('ædɪkwəsɪ) *n.* —'**adequately** *adv.*

à deux *French.* (a dø) *adj., adv.* of or for two persons.

adhere (əd'hɪə) *vb.* (*intr.*) **1.** (usually foll. by *to*) to stick or hold fast. **2.** (foll. by *to*) to be devoted (to a political party, religion, etc.). **3.** (foll. by *to*) to follow exactly. [C16: via Med. L, from L *adhaerēre* to stick to]

adherent (əd'hɪərənt) *n.* **1.** (usually foll. by *of*) a supporter or follower. ~*adj.* **2.** sticking, holding fast, or attached. —**ad'herence** *n.*

adhesion (əd'hiːʒən) *n.* **1.** the quality or condition of sticking together or holding fast. **2.** ability to make firm contact without slipping. **3.** attachment, as to a political party, cause, etc. **4.** an attraction or repulsion between the molecules of unlike substances in contact. **5.** *Pathol.* abnormal union of structures or parts. [C17: from L *adhaesiōn-* a sticking. See ADHERE]

adhesive (əd'hiːsɪv) *adj.* **1.** able or designed to adhere: *adhesive tape.* **2.** tenacious or clinging. ~*n.* **3.** a substance used for sticking, such as glue or paste. —**ad'hesively** *adv.* —**ad'hesiveness** *n.*

ad hoc (æd 'hɒk) *adj., adv.* for a particular purpose only: *an ad hoc committee.* [L, lit.: to this]

ad hominem *Latin.* (æd 'hɒmɪˌnɛm) *adj., adv.* directed against a person rather than his arguments. [lit.: to the man]

adiabatic (ˌædɪə'bætɪk) *adj.* **1.** (of a thermodynamic process) taking place without loss or gain of heat. ~*n.* **2.** a curve on a graph representing the changes in a system undergoing an adiabatic process. [C19: from Gk, from A-¹ + *diabatos* passable]

adieu (ə'djuː) *sentence substitute., n., pl.* **adieus** *or* **adieux** (ə'djuːz). goodbye. [C14: from OF, from *a* to + *dieu* God]

Adige (*Italian* 'aːdidʒe) *n.* a river in N Italy, flowing southeast to the Adriatic. Length: 354 km (220 miles).

ad infinitum (æd ˌɪnfɪ'naɪtəm) *adv.* without end; endlessly; to infinity. Abbrev.: **ad inf.** [L]

ad interim (æd 'ɪntərɪm) *adj., adv.* for the meantime: *ad interim measures.* Abbrev.: **ad int.** [L]

adipocere (ˌædɪpəu'sɪə) *n.* a waxlike fatty substance sometimes formed during the decomposition of corpses. [C19: from NL *adiposus* fat + F *cire* wax]

adipose ('ædɪˌpəus) *adj.* **1.** of, resembling, or containing fat; fatty. ~*n.* **2.** animal fat. [C18: from NL *adiposus*, from L *adeps* fat]

Adirondack Mountains (ˌædɪ'rɒndæk) *or* **Adirondacks** *pl. n.* a mountain range in NE New York State. Highest peak: Mount Marcy, 1629 m (5344 ft.).

adit ('ædɪt) *n.* an almost horizontal shaft into a mine, for access or drainage. [C17: from L *aditus*, from *adīre*, from *ad-* towards + *īre* to go]

adj. *abbrev. for:* **1.** adjective. **2.** adjunct. **3.** Also: **adjt.** adjutant.

adjacent (ə'dʒeɪsənt) *adj.* being near or close, esp. having a common boundary; contiguous. [C15: from L *adjacēre*, from *ad-* near + *jacēre* to lie] —**ad'jacency** *n.* —**ad'jacently** *adv.*

adjacent angles *pl. n.* two angles having the same vertex and a side in common.

adjective ('ædʒɪktɪv) *n.* **1. a.** a word imputing a characteristic to a noun or pronoun. **b.** (*as modifier*): *an adjective phrase.* Abbrev.: **adj.** ~*adj.* **2.** additional or dependent. [C14: from LL, from L from *adjicere*, from *ad-* to + *jacere* to throw] —**adjectival** (ˌædʒɪk'taɪvəl) *adj.*

adjoin (ə'dʒɔɪn) *vb.* **1.** to be next to (an area of land, etc.). **2.** (*tr.*; foll. by *to*) to join; attach. [C14: via OF from L, from *ad-* to + *jungere* to join] —**ad'joining** *adj.*

adjourn (ə'dʒɜːn) *vb.* **1.** (*intr.*) (of a court, etc.) to close at the end of a session. **2.** to postpone or be postponed, esp. temporarily. **3.** (*tr.*) to put off (a problem, discussion, etc.) for later consideration. **4.** (*intr.*) *Inf.* to move elsewhere: *let's adjourn to the kitchen.* [C14: from OF *ajourner* to defer to an arranged day, from *a-* to + *jour* day, from LL *diurnum*, from L *diēs* day] —**ad'journment** *n.*

adjudge (ə'dʒʌdʒ) *vb.* (*tr.*; *usually passive*) **1.** to pronounce formally; declare. **2. a.** to judge. **b.** to decree: *he was adjudged bankrupt.* **c.** to award (costs, damages, etc.). **3.** *Arch.* to condemn. [C14: via OF from L *adjūdicāre*. See ADJUDICATE]

adjudicate (ə'dʒuːdɪˌkeɪt) *vb.* **1.** (when *intr.*, usually foll. by *upon*) to give a decision (on), esp. a formal or binding one. **2.** (*intr.*) to serve as a judge or arbiter, as in a competition. [C18: from L *adjūdicāre*, from *ad-* to + *jūdicāre* to judge, from *jūdex* judge] —**ad,judi'cation** *n.* —**ad'judi,cator** *n.*

adjunct ('ædʒʌŋkt) *n.* **1.** something incidental or not essential that is added to something else. **2.** a person who is subordinate to another. **3.** *Grammar.* **a.** part of a sentence other than the subject or the predicate. **b.** a modifier. ~*adj.* **4.** added or connected in a secondary position. [C16: from L *adjunctus*, p.p. of *adjungere* to AD-JOIN] —**adjunctive** (ə'dʒʌŋktɪv) *adj.* —'**adjunctly** *adv.*

adjure (ə'dʒuə) *vb.* (*tr.*) **1.** to command, often by exacting an oath. **2.** to appeal earnestly to. [C14: from L *adjūrāre*, from *ad-* to + *jūrāre* to swear, from *jūs* oath] —**adjuration** (ˌædʒuə'reɪʃən) *n.* —**ad'juratory** *adj.* —**ad'jurer** *or* **ad'juror** *n.*

adjust (ə'dʒʌst) *vb.* **1.** (*tr.*) to alter slightly, esp. to achieve accuracy. **2.** to adapt, as to a new environment, etc. **3.** (*tr.*) to put into order. **4.** (*tr.*) *Insurance.* to determine the amount payable in settlement of a claim. [C17: from OF *adjuster*, from *ad-* to + *juste* right, JUST] —**ad'justable** *adj.* —**ad'juster** *n.*

adjustment (ə'dʒʌstmənt) *n.* **1.** the act of adjusting or state of being adjusted. **2.** a control for regulating.

adjutant ('ædʒətənt) *n.* an officer who acts as administrative assistant to a superior officer. [C17: from L *adjūtāre* to AID] —'**adjutancy** *n.*

adjutant bird *or* **stork** *n.* either of two large carrion-eating storks which are similar to the marabou and occur in S and SE Asia. [so called for its supposedly military gait]

adjutant general *n., pl.* **adjutants general.** **1.** *Brit. Army.* a member of the Army Board responsible for personnel and administrative functions. **2.** *U.S. Army.* the adjutant of a military unit with general staff.

Adler *n.* **1.** (*German* 'aːdlər). **Alfred** ('alfreːt). 1870–1937, Austrian psychiatrist, noted for his descriptions of overcompensation and inferiority feelings. **2.** ('ædlə). **Larry**, real name *Lawrence Cecil Adler.* born 1914, U.S. harmonica player. —**Adlerian** (æd'lɪərɪən) *adj.*

ad-lib (æd'lɪb) *vb.* **-libbing, -libbed.** **1.** to improvise and deliver spontaneously (a speech, etc.). ~*adj.* (**ad lib** when predicative) **2.** improvised. ~*adv.* **ad lib.** **3.** spontaneously; freely. ~*n.* **4.** an improvised performance, often humorous. [C18: short for L *ad libitum*, lit.: according to pleasure]

ad libitum (ˌæd 'lɪbɪtəm) *adv., adj. Music.* at the performer's discretion. [L.: see AD-LIB]

Adm. *abbrev. for:* **1.** Admiral. **2.** Admiralty.

adman (ˈædˌmæn) *n.*, *pl.* **-men.** *Inf.* a man who works in advertising.

admass (ˈædmæs) *n.* the section of the public that is susceptible to advertising, etc., and the processes involved in influencing them. [C20: from AD + MASS]

admeasure (ædˈmɛʒə) *vb.* to measure out (land, etc.) as a share; apportion. [C14 *amesuren*, from OF, from *mesurer* to MEASURE; the modern form derives from AD- + MEASURE]

Admetus (ædˈmiːtəs) *n.* *Greek myth.* a king of Thessaly, one of the Argonauts, who was married to Alcestis.

admin (ˈædmɪn) *n.* *Inf.* short for **administration.**

administer (ədˈmɪnɪstə) *vb.* (*mainly tr.*) **1.** (*also intr.*) to direct or control (the affairs of a business, etc.). **2.** to dispense: *administer justice.* **3.** (when *intr.*, foll. by *to*) to give or apply (medicine, etc.). **4.** to supervise the taking of (an oath, etc.). **5.** to manage (an estate, property, etc.). [C14 *amynistre* via OF from L, from *ad-* to + *ministrāre* to MINISTER]

administrate (ədˈmɪnɪˌstreɪt) *vb.* to manage or direct (the affairs of a business, institution, etc.).

administration (ədˌmɪnɪˈstreɪʃən) *n.* **1.** management of the affairs of an organization, such as a business or institution. **2.** the duties of an administrator. **3.** the body of people who administer an organization. **4.** the conduct of the affairs of government. **5.** term of office: used of governments, etc. **6.** the government as a whole. **7.** (*often cap.*) *Chiefly U.S.* the political executive, esp. of the U.S. **8.** *Property law.* **a.** the conduct or disposal of the estate of a deceased person. **b.** the management by a trustee of an estate. **9. a.** the administering of something, such as a sacrament or medical treatment. **b.** the thing that is administered. —**ad'ministrative** *adj.* —**ad'ministratively** *adv.*

administrator (ədˈmɪnɪˌstreɪtə) *n.* **1.** a person who administers the affairs of an organization, official body, etc. **2.** *Property law.* a person authorized to manage an estate.

admirable (ˈædmərəbəl) *adj.* deserving of inspiring admiration; excellent. — **'admirably** *adv.*

admiral (ˈædmərəl) *n.* **1.** the supreme commander of a fleet or navy. **2.** Also called: **admiral of the fleet, fleet admiral.** a naval officer of the highest rank. **3.** a senior naval officer entitled to fly his own flag. See also **rear admiral, vice admiral. 4.** *Chiefly Brit.* the master of a fishing fleet. **5.** any of various brightly coloured butterflies, esp. the red admiral or white admiral. [C13 *amyral*, from OF *amiral* emir, & from Med. L *admirālis* (spelling prob. infl. by *admīrābilis* admirable); both from Ar. *amīr* emir, commander, esp. in *amīr-al* commander of] — **'admiral,ship** *n.*

admiralty (ˈædmərəltɪ) *n.*, *pl.* **-ties. 1.** the office or jurisdiction of an admiral. **2.** jurisdiction over naval affairs.

Admiralty Board *n.* **the.** a department of the British Ministry of Defence, responsible for the administration of the Royal Navy.

Admiralty House *n.* the official residence of the governor general of Australia, in Sydney.

Admiralty Islands *pl. n.* a group of about 40 volcanic and coral islands in the SW Pacific, part of Papua New Guinea, in the Bismarck Archipelago: main island: Manus. Pop.: 25 844 (1980). Area: about 2000 sq. km (800 sq. miles). Also called: **Admiralties.**

Admiralty Range *n.* a mountain range in Antarctica, on the coast of Victoria Land, northwest of the Ross Sea.

admiration (ˌædməˈreɪʃən) *n.* **1.** pleasurable contemplation or surprise. **2.** a person or thing that is admired.

admire (ədˈmaɪə) *vb.* (*tr.*) **1.** to regard with esteem, approval, or pleased surprise. **2.** *Arch.* to wonder at. [C16: from L *admīrāri*, from *ad-* to, at + *mīrāri* to wonder] —**ad'mirer** *n.* —**ad'miring** *adj.* —**ad'miringly** *adv.*

admissible (ədˈmɪsəbəl) *adj.* **1.** able or deserving to be considered or allowed. **2.** deserving to be allowed to enter. **3.** *Law.* (of evidence) capable of being admitted in a court of law. —**ad,missi'bility** *n.*

admission (ədˈmɪʃən) *n.* **1.** permission to enter or the right to enter. **2.** the price charged for entrance. **3.** acceptance for a position, etc. **4.** a confession, as of a crime, etc. **5.** an acknowledgment of the truth of something. [C15: from L *admissiōn-*, from *admittere* to ADMIT] —**ad'missive** *adj.*

admit (ədˈmɪt) *vb.* **-mitting, -mitted.** (*mainly tr.*) **1.** (*may take a clause as object*) to confess or acknowledge

(a crime, mistake, etc.). **2.** (*may take a clause as object*) to concede (the truth of something). **3.** to allow to enter. **4.** (foll. by *to*) to allow participation (in) or the right to be part (of). **5.** (when *intr.*, foll. by *of*) to allow (of). [C14: from L *admittere*, from *ad-* to + *mittere* to send]

admittance (ədˈmɪtˀns) *n.* **1.** the right or authority to enter. **2.** the act of giving entrance. **3.** *Electricity.* the reciprocal of impedance.

admittedly (ədˈmɪtɪdlɪ) *adv.* (*sentence modifier*) willingly conceded: *admittedly I am afraid.*

admix (ədˈmɪks) *vb.* (*tr.*) *Rare.* to mix or blend. [C16: back formation from obs. *admixt*, from L *admīscēre* to mix with]

admixture (ədˈmɪkstʃə) *n.* **1.** a less common word for **mixture. 2.** an ingredient.

admonish (ədˈmɒnɪʃ) *vb.* (*tr.*) **1.** to reprove firmly but not harshly. **2.** to warn; caution. [C14: via OF from Vulgar L *admonestāre* (unattested), from L *admonēre*, from *monēre* to advise] —**admonition** (ˌædməˈnɪʃən) *n.* —**ad'monitory** *adj.*

ad nauseam (æd ˈnɔːzɪˌæm) *adv.* to a disgusting extent. [L: to (the point of) nausea]

ado (əˈduː) *n.* bustling activity; fuss; bother; delay (esp. in **without more ado, with much ado**). [C14: from *at do* a to-do, from ON *at* to (marking the infinitive) + DO[1]]

adobe (əˈdəʊbɪ) *n.* **1.** a sun-dried brick used for building. **2.** a building constructed of such bricks. **3.** the clayey material from which such bricks are made. [C19: from Sp.]

adolescence (ˌædəˈlɛsəns) *n.* the period in human development that occurs between the beginning of puberty and adulthood. [C15: via OF from L, from *adolēscere* to grow up]

adolescent (ˌædəˈlɛsˀnt) *adj.* **1.** of or relating to adolescence. **2.** *Inf.* behaving in an immature way. ~*n.* **3.** an adolescent person.

Adonis (əˈdəʊnɪs) *n.* **1.** *Greek myth.* a handsome youth loved by Aphrodite. **2.** a handsome young man. [C16: from L via Gk from Phoenician *adōni* my lord; rel. to Heb. *Adonai* Lord]

adopt (əˈdɒpt) *vb.* (*tr.*) **1.** *Law.* to take (another's child) as one's own child. **2.** to choose and follow (a plan, method, etc.). **3.** to take over (an idea, etc.) as if it were one's own. **4.** to assume: *to adopt a title.* **5.** to accept (a report, etc.). [C16: from L *adoptāre*, from *optāre* to choose] —**a'doption** *n.*

adopted (əˈdɒptɪd) *adj.* having been adopted.

adoptive (əˈdɒptɪv) *adj.* due to adoption: *an adoptive parent.*

adorable (əˈdɔːrəbəl) *adj.* **1.** very attractive; lovable. **2.** *Becoming rare.* deserving adoration. —**a'dorably** *adv.*

adoration (ˌædəˈreɪʃən) *n.* **1.** deep love or esteem. **2.** the act of worshipping.

adore (əˈdɔː) *vb.* **1.** (*tr.*) to love intensely or deeply. **2.** to worship (a god) with religious rites. **3.** (*tr.*) *Inf.* to like very much. [C15: via F from L *adōrāre*, from *ad-* to + *ōrāre* to pray] —**a'dorer** *n.* —**a'doring** *adj.* —**a'doringly** *adv.*

adorn (əˈdɔːn) *vb.* (*tr.*) **1.** to decorate. **2.** to increase the beauty, distinction, etc., of. [C14: via OF from L *adōrnāre*, from *ōrnāre* to furnish] —**a'dornment** *n.*

Adowa (ˈɑːdʊˌwɑː) *n.* a variant spelling of **Aduwa.**

ADP[1] *n. Biochem.* adenosine diphosphate; a substance derived from ATP with the liberation of energy that is then used in the performance of muscular work.

ADP[2], A.D.P., *or* **a.d.p.** *abbrev. for* automatic data processing.

Adrastus (əˈdræstəs) *n. Greek myth.* a king of Argos and leader of the Seven against Thebes of whom he was the sole survivor.

ad rem *Latin.* (æd ˈrɛm) *adj., adv.* to the point; without digression.

adrenal (əˈdriːnˀl) *adj.* **1.** on or near the kidneys. **2.** of or relating to the adrenal glands or their secretions. ~*n.* **3.** an adrenal gland. [C19: from AD- (near) + RENAL]

adrenal gland *n.* an endocrine gland at the anterior end of each kidney. It secretes adrenaline. Also called: **suprarenal gland.**

adrenaline *or* **adrenalin** (əˈdrɛnəlɪn) *n.* a hormone that is secreted by the adrenal medulla in response to stress and increases heart rate, pulse rate, and blood pressure. It is extracted from animals or synthesized for medical use. U.S. name: **epinephrine.**

Adrian ('eɪdrɪən) n. **Edgar Douglas,** Baron Adrian. 1889–1977, English physiologist, noted particularly for his research into the function of neurons: shared with Sherrington the Nobel prize for physiology and medicine 1932.

Adrian IV n. original name *Nicholas Breakspear.* ?1100–59, the only English pope (1154–59).

Adrianople (,eɪdrɪə'nəʊpəl) or **Adrianopolis** (,eɪdrɪə-'nɒpəlɪs) n. former names of **Edirne.**

Adriatic (,eɪdrɪ'ætɪk) adj. **1.** of or relating to the Adriatic Sea, or to the inhabitants of its coast or islands. ~n. **2. the.** short for the **Adriatic Sea.**

Adriatic Sea n. an arm of the Mediterranean between Italy and Yugoslavia.

adrift (ə'drɪft) adj. (postpositive), adv. **1.** floating without steering or mooring; drifting. **2.** without purpose; aimless. **3.** Inf. off course.

adroit (ə'drɔɪt) adj. **1.** skilful or dexterous. **2.** quick in thought or reaction. [C17: from F à droit rightly] —a'**droitly** adv. —a'**droitness** n.

adsorb (əd'sɔːb) vb. to undergo or cause to undergo a process in which a substance, usually a gas, accumulates on the surface of a solid forming a thin film. [C19: AD- + -sorb as in ABSORB] —ad'**sorbable** adj. —ad'**sorbent** adj. —ad'**sorption** n.

adsorbate (əd'sɔːbeɪt) n. a substance that has been or is to be adsorbed.

ADT (in the U.S. and Canada) abbrev. for Atlantic Daylight Time.

adulate ('ædjʊ,leɪt) vb. (tr.) to flatter or praise obsequiously. [C17: back formation from C15 adulation, from L adūlāri to flatter] —,adu'**lation** n. —'adu,**lator** n. —adulatory (,ædjʊ'leɪtərɪ) adj.

adult ('ædʌlt, ə'dʌlt) adj. **1.** having reached maturity; fully developed. **2.** of or intended for mature people: adult education. **3.** suitable only for adults because of being pornographic. ~n. **4.** a person who has attained maturity. **5.** a mature fully grown animal or plant. **6.** Law. a person who has attained the age of legal majority. [C16: from L adultus, from adolēscere to grow up] —a'**dulthood** n.

adulterant (ə'dʌltərənt) n. **1.** a substance that adulterates. ~adj. **2.** adulterating.

adulterate vb. (ə'dʌltə,reɪt). **1.** (tr.) to debase by adding inferior material: to adulterate milk with water. ~adj. (ə'dʌltərɪt). **2.** debased or impure. [C16: from L adulterāre to corrupt, commit adultery, prob. from alter another] —a,**dulter'ation** n. —a'**dulter,ator** n.

adulterer (ə'dʌltərə) or (fem.) **adulteress** n. a person who has committed adultery. [C16: orig. also adulter, from L adulter, back formation from adulterāre to ADULTERATE]

adulterous (ə'dʌltərəs) adj. of, characterized by, or inclined to adultery. —a'**dulterously** adv.

adultery (ə'dʌltərɪ) n., pl. -teries. voluntary sexual intercourse between a married man or woman and partner other than the legal spouse. [C15 adulterie, altered from C14 avoutrie, via OF from L adulterium, from adulter, back formation from adulterāre. See ADULTERATE]

adumbrate ('ædʌm,breɪt) vb. (tr.) **1.** to outline; give a faint indication of. **2.** to foreshadow. **3.** to obscure. [C16: from L adumbrāre to cast a shadow on, from umbra shadow] —,**adum'bration** n. —**adumbrative** (æd'ʌmbrətɪv) adj.

Aduwa or **Adowa** ('aːdʊ,waː) n. a town in N Ethiopia: Emperor Menelik II defeated the Italians here in 1896. Pop.: 26 782 (1982). Italian name: **Adua** (a'dua).

adv. abbrev. for: **1.** adverb. **2.** adverbial. **3.** adversus. [L: against] **4.** advertisement. **5.** advocate.

ad valorem (æd və'lɔːrəm) adj., adv. (of taxes) in proportion to the estimated value of the goods taxed. Abbrev.: **ad val., a.v., A/V.** [from L]

advance (əd'vaːns) vb. **1.** to go or bring forward in position. **2.** (foll. by on) to move (towards) in a threatening manner. **3.** (tr.) to present for consideration. **4.** to improve; further. **5.** (tr.) to cause (an event) to occur earlier. **6.** (tr.) to supply (money, goods, etc.) beforehand, either for a loan or as an initial payment. **7.** to increase (a price, etc.) or (of a price, etc.) to be increased. **8.** (intr.) to be promoted. ~n. **9.** forward movement; progress in time or space. **10.** improvement; progress in development. **11.** Commerce. **a.** the supplying of commodities or funds before receipt of an agreed consideration. **b.** the commodities or funds supplied in this manner. **12.** Also

called: **advance payment.** a money payment made before it is legally due. **13.** a loan of money. **14.** an increase in price, etc. **15. in advance. a.** beforehand: payment in advance. **b.** (foll. by of) ahead in time or development: ideas in advance of the time. **16.** (modifier) forward in position or time: advance booking. ~See also **advances.** [C15 advauncen, altered from C13 avauncen, via OF from L abante, from ab- away + ante before] —ad'**vancer** n.

advanced (əd'vaːnst) adj. **1.** being ahead in development, knowledge, progress, etc. **2.** having reached a comparatively late stage: a man of advanced age. **3.** ahead of the times.

advanced gas-cooled reactor n. a nuclear reactor using carbon dioxide as the coolant, and ceramic uranium dioxide cased in stainless steel as the fuel. Abbrev.: **AGR.**

Advanced level n. a formal name for **A level.**

advancement (əd'vaːnsmənt) n. **1.** promotion in rank, status, etc. **2.** a less common word for **advance** (senses 9, 10).

advances (əd'vaːnsɪz) pl. n. (sometimes sing.; often foll. by to or towards) overtures made in an attempt to become friendly, etc.

advantage (əd'vaːntɪdʒ) n. **1.** (often foll. by over or of) a more favourable position; superiority. **2.** benefit or profit (esp. in **to one's advantage**). **3.** Tennis. the point scored after deuce. **4. take advantage of. a.** to make good use of. **b.** to impose upon the weakness, good nature, etc., of. **c.** to seduce. **5. to advantage.** to good effect. ~vb. **6.** (tr.) to put in a better position; favour. [C14 avantage (later altered to advantage), from OF avant before, from L abante from before. See ADVANCE]

advantageous (,ædvən'teɪdʒəs) adj. producing advantage. —,**advan'tageously** adv.

advection (əd'vɛkʃən) n. the transference of heat energy in a horizontal stream of gas, esp. of air. [C20: from L advectiō, from advehere, from ad- to + vehere to carry]

advent ('ædvɛnt, -vənt) n. an arrival or coming, esp. one which is awaited. [C12: from L adventus, from advenīre, from ad- to + venīre to come]

Advent ('ædvɛnt) n. the season including the four Sundays preceding Christmas.

Advent calendar n. a large card with small numbered doors for children to open on each of the days of Advent, revealing pictures beneath them.

Adventist ('ædvɛntɪst) n. a member of a Christian group that holds that the Second Coming of Christ is imminent.

adventitious (,ædvɛn'tɪʃəs) adj. **1.** added or appearing accidentally. **2.** (of a plant or animal part) developing in an abnormal position. [C17: from L adventicius coming from outside, from adventus a coming] —,**adven'titiously** adv.

adventure (əd'vɛntʃə) n. **1.** a risky undertaking of unknown outcome. **2.** an exciting or unexpected event or course of events. **3.** a hazardous financial operation. ~vb. **4.** to take a risk or put at risk. **5.** (intr.; foll. by into, on, or upon) to dare to enter (into a place, dangerous activity, etc.). **6.** to dare to say (something): he adventured his opinion. [C13 aventure (later altered to adventure), via OF ult. from L advenīre to happen to (someone), arrive]

adventure playground n. Brit. a playground for children that contains building materials, etc., used to build with, climb on, etc.

adventurer (əd'vɛntʃərə) or (fem.) **adventuress** n. **1.** a person who seeks adventure, esp. one who seeks success or money through daring exploits. **2.** a person who seeks money or power by unscrupulous means. **3.** a speculator.

adventurism (əd'vɛntʃə,rɪzəm) n. recklessness, esp. in politics and finance. —ad'**venturist** n.

adventurous (əd'vɛntʃərəs) adj. **1.** Also: **adventuresome.** daring or enterprising. **2.** dangerous; involving risk.

adverb ('ædˌvɜːb) n. **a.** a word or group of words that serves to modify a whole sentence, a verb, another adverb, or an adjective; for example, easily, very, and happily respectively in the sentence They could easily envy the very happily married couple. **b.** (as modifier): an adverb marker. Abbrev.: **adv.** [C15–C16: from L adverbium adverb, lit.: added word] —ad'**verbial** adj.

adversarial (,ædvɜː'sɛərɪəl) adj. (of political parties) hostile to and opposing each other on party lines; antagonistic.

adversary ('ædvəsərı) *n.*, *pl.* **-saries.** **1.** a person or group that is hostile to someone. **2.** an opposing contestant in a sport. [C14: from L *adversārius*, from *adversus* against]

adversative (əd'vɜːsətɪv) *Grammar.* ~*adj.* **1.** (of a word, phrase, or clause) implying opposition. *But* and *although* are adversative conjunctions. ~*n.* **2.** an adversative word or speech element.

adverse ('ædvɜːs) *adj.* **1.** antagonistic; hostile: *adverse criticism.* **2.** unfavourable to one's interests: *adverse circumstances.* **3.** contrary or opposite: *adverse winds.* [C14: from L *adversus*, from *advertere*, from *ad-* towards + *vertere* to turn] —**ad'versely** *adv.* —**ad'verseness** *n.*

adversity (əd'vɜːsɪtɪ) *n.*, *pl.* **-ties.** **1.** distress; affliction; hardship. **2.** an unfortunate event.

advert[1] ('ædvɜːt) *vb.* (*intr.*; foll. by *to*) to draw attention (to). [C15: from L *advertere* to turn one's attention to]

advert[2] ('ædvɜːt) *n. Brit. inf.* short for **advertisement.**

advertise *or U.S.* (*sometimes*) **-tize** ('ædvə,taɪz) *vb.* **1.** to present or praise (goods, a service, etc.) to the public, esp. in order to encourage sales. **2.** to make (a vacancy, article for sale, etc.) publicly known: *to advertise a job.* **3.** (*intr.*; foll. by *for*) to make a public request (for): *she advertised for a cook.* [C15: from OF *avertir*, ult. from L *advertere* to turn one's attention to. See ADVERSE] —**'adver,tiser** *or U.S.* (*sometimes*) **'adver,tizer** *n.*

advertisement *or U.S.* (*sometimes*) **-tizement** (əd'vɜːtɪsmənt) *n.* any public notice, as a printed display in a newspaper, short film on television, etc., designed to sell goods, publicize an event, etc.

advertising *or U.S.* (*sometimes*) **-tizing** ('ædvə,taɪzɪŋ) *n.* **1.** the promotion of goods or services for sale through impersonal media such as television. **2.** the business that specializes in creating such publicity. **3.** advertisements collectively.

advertorial (,ædvɜː'tɔːrɪəl) *n.* **1.** advertising presented under the guise of editorial material. ~*adj.* **2.** presented in such a manner. [C20: from blend of ADVERT[2] + EDITORIAL]

advice (əd'vaɪs) *n.* **1.** recommendation as to appropriate choice of action. **2.** (*sometimes pl.*) formal notification of facts. [C13 *avis* (later *advise*), via OF from Vulgar L, from L *ad* to + *visum* view]

advisable (əd'vaɪzəbᵊl) *adj.* worthy of recommendation; prudent. —**ad'visably** *adv.*

advise (əd'vaɪz) *vb.* (*when tr., may take a clause as object or an infinitive*) **1.** to offer advice (to a person or persons): *he advised caution.* **2.** (*tr.*; sometimes foll. by *of*) to inform or notify. **3.** (*intr.*; foll. by *with*) *Chiefly U.S.*, *obs. in Britain.* to consult. [C14: via OF from Vulgar L *advīsāre* (unattested), from L *ad-* to + *vidēre* to see]

▷ *Usage. Advise* is often used in the same sense as *inform: as we advised you in our last communication, the order is being dealt with.* This use is common in business correspondence. Careful users of English prefer *inform*, *notify*, or *tell* in general English: *the police informed him that his car had been stolen.*

advised (əd'vaɪzd) *adj.* resulting from deliberation. See also **ill-advised, well-advised.** —**advisedly** (əd'vaɪzɪdlɪ) *adv.*

adviser *or* **advisor** (əd'vaɪzə) *n.* **1.** a person who advises. **2.** *Education.* a person responsible for advising students on career guidance, etc. **3.** *Brit. education.* a subject specialist who advises on current teaching methods and facilities.

advisory (əd'vaɪzərı) *adj.* empowered to make recommendations: *an advisory body.*

advocaat ('ædvəʊ,kɑː) *n.* a liqueur having a raw egg base. [C20: Du.]

advocacy ('ædvəkəsɪ) *n.*, *pl.* **-cies.** active support, esp. of a cause.

advocate *vb.* ('ædvə,keɪt). **1.** (*tr.*; *may take a clause as object*) to support or recommend publicly. ~*n.* ('ædvəkɪt). **2.** a person who upholds or defends a cause. **3.** a person who intercedes on behalf of another. **4.** a person who pleads his client's cause in a court of law. **5.** *Scots Law.* the usual word for **barrister.** [C14: via OF from L *advocātus* legal witness, from *advocāre*, from *vocāre* to call]

advowson (əd'vaʊzᵊn) *n. English ecclesiastical law.* the right of presentation to a vacant benefice. [C13: via OF from L *advocātiōn-*, from *advocāre* to summon]

advt *abbrev. for* advertisement.

Adygei Autonomous Region *n.* an administrative division of the SW Soviet Union, bordering on the Caucasus Mountains: chiefly agricultural. Capital: Maikop. Pop.: 423 000 (1986). Area: 7600 sq. km (2934 sq. miles).

adze *or U.S.* **adz** (ædz) *n.* a hand tool with a steel blade attached at right angles to a wooden handle, used for dressing timber. [OE *adesa*]

Adzhar Autonomous Soviet Socialist Republic (ə'dʒɑː) *n.* an administrative division of the S Soviet Union, in the SW Georgian SSR on the Black Sea: part of Turkey from the 17th century until 1878; mostly mountainous, reaching 2805 m (9350 ft.), with a subtropical coastal strip. Capital: Batumi. Pop.: 371 000 (1983 est.). Area: 3000 sq. km (1160 sq. miles). Also called: **Adzharia** (ə'dʒɑːrɪə).

AEA (in Britain) *abbrev. for* Atomic Energy Authority.

AEC (in the U.S.) *abbrev. for* Atomic Energy Commission.

aedes (eɪ'iːdiːz) *n.* a mosquito of tropical and subtropical regions which transmits yellow fever. [C20: NL, from Gk *aēdēs* unpleasant, from A-[1] + *ēdos* pleasant]

aedile *or U.S.* (*sometimes*) **edile** ('iːdaɪl) *n.* a magistrate of ancient Rome in charge of public works, games, buildings, and roads. [C16: from L *aedīlis*, from *aedēs* a building]

Aeëtes (iː'iːtiːz) *n. Greek myth.* a king of Colchis, father of Medea and keeper of the Golden Fleece.

Aegean (iː'dʒiːən) *adj.* of or relating to the Aegean Sea or Islands.

Aegean Islands *pl. n.* the islands of the Aegean Sea, including the Cyclades, Dodecanese, Euboea, and Sporades. The majority are under Greek administration.

Aegean Sea *n.* an arm of the Mediterranean between Greece and Turkey.

Aegeus (iː'dʒiːuːs, 'iːdʒiəs) *n. Greek myth.* an Athenian king and father of Theseus.

Aegina (iː'dʒaɪnə) *n.* **1.** an island in the Aegean Sea, in the Saronic Gulf. Area: 85 sq. km (33 sq. miles). **2.** a town on the coast of this island: a city-state of ancient Greece. **3. Gulf of.** another name for the **Saronic Gulf.** ~Greek name: **Aiyina.**

Aegir ('iːdʒɪə) *n. Norse myth.* the god of the sea.

aegis *or U.S.* (*sometimes*) **egis** ('iːdʒɪs) *n.* **1.** sponsorship or protection (esp. in **under the aegis of**). **2.** *Greek myth.* the shield of Zeus. [C18: from L, from Gk *aigis* shield of Zeus]

Aegisthus (iː'dʒɪsθəs) *n. Greek myth.* a cousin to and the murderer of Agamemnon, whose wife Clytemnestra he had seduced. He usurped the kingship of Mycenae until Orestes, Agamemnon's son, returned home and killed him.

Aegospotami (,iːgəs'pɒtə,maɪ) *n.* a river of ancient Thrace that flowed into the Hellespont. At its mouth the Spartan fleet under Lysander defeated the Athenians in 405 B.C., ending the Peloponnesian War.

aegrotat ('aɪgrəʊ,tæt, 'iː-) *n.* **1.** (in British and certain other universities, and, sometimes, schools) a certificate allowing a candidate to pass an examination although he has missed all or part of it through illness. **2.** a degree or other qualification obtained in such circumstances. [C19: L, lit.: he is ill]

Aegyptus (iː'dʒɪptəs) *n. Greek myth.* a king of Egypt and twin brother of Danaüs.

Ælfric ('ælfrɪk) *n.* called *Grammaticus.* ?955–?1020, English abbot, writer, and grammarian.

-aemia, -haemia, *or U.S.* **-emia, -hemia** *n. combining form.* denoting blood, esp. a specified condition of the blood in diseases: *leukaemia.* [NL, from Gk, from *haima* blood]

Aeneas (ɪ'niːəs) *n. Classical myth.* a Trojan prince, the son of Anchises and Aphrodite, who escaped the sack of Troy and sailed to Italy via Carthage and Sicily. After seven years, he and his followers established themselves near the site of the future Rome.

Aeneas Silvius *or* **Sylvius** ('sɪlvɪəs) *n.* the literary name of **Pius II.**

Aeneid (ɪ'niːɪd) *n.* an epic poem in Latin by Virgil relating the experiences of Aeneas after the fall of Troy.

aeolian harp (iː'əʊlɪən) *n.* a stringed instrument that produces a musical sound when wind passes over the strings. Also called: **wind harp.** [after AEOLUS]

Aeolian Islands *pl. n.* another name for the **Lipari Islands.**

Aeolis ('i:əlɪs) *or* **Aeolia** (i:'əʊlɪə) *n.* the ancient name for the coastal region of NW Asia Minor, including the island of Lesbos, settled by the Aeolian Greeks (about 1000 B.C.).

aeolotropic (,i:ələʊ'trɒpɪk) *adj.* a less common word for **anisotropic**. [C19: from Gk *aiolos* fickle + -TROPIC] —**aeolotropy** (,i:ə'lɒtrəpɪ) *n.*

Aeolus ('i:ələs, i:'əʊləs) *n. Greek myth.* **1.** the god of the winds. **2.** the founding king of the Aeolians in Thessaly.

aeon *or U.S.* **eon** ('i:ən, 'i:ɒn) *n.* **1.** an immeasurably long period of time. **2.** *Geol.* the longest division of geological time, comprising two or more eras. [C17: from Gk *aiōn* an infinitely long time]

aerate ('ɛəreɪt) *vb.* (*tr.*) **1.** to charge (a liquid) with a gas, as in the manufacture of effervescent drink. **2.** to expose to the action or circulation of the air. —**aer'ation** *n.* —'aer**ator** *n.*

aeri- *combining form.* a variant of **aero-**.

aerial ('ɛərɪəl) *adj.* **1.** of or resembling air. **2.** existing, moving, or operating in the air: *aerial cable car.* **3.** ethereal; light and delicate. **4.** imaginary. **5.** extending high into the air. **6.** of or relating to aircraft: *aerial combat.* ~*n.* **7.** Also called: **antenna.** the part of a radio or television system by means of which radio waves are transmitted or received. [C17: via L from Gk *aērios*, from *aēr* air]

aerialist ('ɛərɪəlɪst) *n.* a trapeze artist or tightrope walker.

aerie ('ɛərɪ) *n.* a variant spelling (esp. U.S.) of **eyrie**.

aeriform ('ɛərɪ,fɔːm) *adj.* **1.** having the form of air; gaseous. **2.** unsubstantial.

aero ('ɛərəʊ) *n.* (*modifier*) of or relating to aircraft or aeronautics: *an aero engine.*

aero-, aeri-, *or before a vowel* **aer-** *combining form.* **1.** denoting air, atmosphere, or gas: *aerodynamics.* **2.** denoting aircraft: *aeronautics.* [ult. from Gk *aēr* air]

aerobatics (,ɛərəʊ'bætɪks) *n.* (*functioning as sing. or pl.*) spectacular or dangerous manoeuvres, such as loops or rolls, performed in an aircraft or glider. [C20: from AERO-+ (ACRO)BATICS]

aerobe ('ɛərəʊb) *or* **aerobium** (ɛə'rəʊbɪəm) *n., pl.* **-obes** *or* **-obia** (-'əʊbɪə). an organism that requires free oxygen or air for respiration. [C19: from AERO-+ Gk *bios* life]

aerobic (ɛə'rəʊbɪk) *adj.* **1.** (of an organism or process) depending on free oxygen or air. **2.** of or relating to aerobes. **3.** designed for or relating to aerobics: *aerobic shoes; aerobic dances.*

aerobics (ɛə'rəʊbɪks) *n.* (*functioning as sing.*) any system of exercises designed to increase the amount of oxygen in the blood.

aerodrome ('ɛərə,drəʊm) *n.* a landing area that is smaller than an airport.

aerodynamics (,ɛərəʊdaɪ'næmɪks) *n.* (*functioning as sing.*) the study of the dynamics of gases, esp. of the forces acting on a body passing through air. —,**aerody'namic** *adj.* —,**aerody'namically** *adv.*

aeroembolism (,ɛərəʊ'embə,lɪzəm) *n.* the presence in the blood of nitrogen bubbles, caused by an abrupt reduction in atmospheric pressure. See **decompression sickness**.

aero engine *n.* an engine for powering an aircraft.

aerofoil ('ɛərəʊ,fɔɪl) *n.* a cross section of a wing, rotor blade, etc.

aerogram *or* **aerogramme** ('ɛərə,græm) *n.* an air-mail letter written on a single sheet of lightweight paper that folds and is sealed to form an envelope. Also called: **air letter**.

aerolite (ɛərə,laɪt) *n.* a stony meteorite consisting of silicate minerals.

aerology (ɛə'rɒlədʒɪ) *n.* the study of the atmosphere, including its upper layers. —**aerological** (,ɛərə'lɒdʒɪkəl) *adj.* —**aer'ologist** *n.*

aeromechanics (,ɛərəʊmɪ'kænɪks) *n.* (*functioning as sing.*) the mechanics of gases, esp. air. —,**aerome'chanical** *adj.*

aeronautics (,ɛərə'nɔːtɪks) *n.* (*functioning as sing.*) the study or practice of all aspects of flight through the air. —,**aero'nautical** *adj.*

aeropause ('ɛərə,pɔːz) *n.* the region of the upper atmosphere above which aircraft cannot fly.

aeroplane ('ɛərə,pleɪn) *or U.S.* **airplane** ('ɛə,pleɪn) *n.* a heavier-than-air powered flying vehicle with fixed wings. [C19: from F *aéroplane*, from AERO-+ Gk *-planos* wandering]

aerosol ('ɛərə,sɒl) *n.* **1.** a colloidal dispersion of solid or liquid particles in a gas. **2.** a substance, such as a paint or

insecticide, dispensed from a small metal container by a propellant under pressure. **3.** Also called: **air spray.** such a substance together with its container. [C20: from AERO-+ SOL(UTION)]

aerospace ('ɛərə,speɪs) *n.* **1.** the atmosphere and space beyond. **2.** (*modifier*) of rockets, missiles, space vehicles, etc.: *the aerospace industry.*

aerostat ('ɛərə,stæt) *n.* a lighter-than-air craft, such as a balloon. [C18: from F *aérostat*, from AERO-+ Gk *-statos* standing] —,**aero'static** *adj.*

aerostatics (,ɛərə'stætɪks) *n.* (*functioning as sing.*) **1.** the study of gases in equilibrium and bodies held in equilibrium in gases. Cf. **aerodynamics**. **2.** the study of lighter-than-air craft, such as balloons.

aerugo (ɪ'ruːgəʊ) *n.* (esp. of old bronze) another name for **verdigris**. [C18: from L, from *aes* copper, bronze] —**aeruginous** (ɪ'ruːdʒɪnəs) *adj.*

aery ('ɛərɪ) *n., pl.* **aeries.** a variant spelling of **eyrie**.

Aeschines ('i:skɪ,niːz) *n.* ?389–?314 B.C., Athenian orator; the main political opponent of Demosthenes.

Aeschylus ('i:skələs) *n.* ?525–?456 B.C., Greek dramatist, regarded as the father of Greek tragedy. Seven of his plays are extant, including *Seven Against Thebes, Prometheus Bound*, and the trilogy of the *Oresteia.* —**Aeschylean** (,i:skə'li:ən) *adj.*

Aesculapius (,i:skjʊ'leɪpɪəs) *n.* the Roman god of medicine or healing. Greek counterpart: **Asclepius.** —,**Aescu'lapian** *adj.*

Aesir ('eɪsɪə) *n.* the chief gods of Norse mythology dwelling in Asgard. [ON, lit.: gods]

Aesop ('i:sɒp) *n.* ?620–564 B.C., Greek author of fables in which animals are given human characters and used to satirize human failings. —**Ae'sopian** *or* **Ae'sopic** *adj.*

aesthesia *or U.S.* **esthesia** (i:s'θi:zɪə) *n.* the normal ability to experience sensation. [C20: back formation from ANAESTHESIA]

aesthete *or U.S.* **esthete** ('i:sθi:t) *n.* a person who has or who affects a highly developed appreciation of beauty. [C19: back formation from AESTHETICS]

aesthetic (i:s'θɛtɪk, ɪs-), **aesthetical** *or U.S.* (*sometimes*) **esthetic, esthetical** *adj.* **1.** connected with aesthetics. **2. a.** relating to pure beauty rather than to other considerations. **b.** artistic: *an aesthetic consideration.* [C19: from Gk *aisthētikos*, from *aisthanesthai* to perceive, feel] —**aes'thetically** *or U.S.* (*sometimes*) **es'thetically** *adv.* —**aes'theticism** *or U.S.* (*sometimes*) **es'theticism** *n.*

aesthetics *or U.S.* (*sometimes*) **esthetics** (i:s'θɛtɪks) *n.* (*functioning as sing.*) **1.** the branch of philosophy concerned with the study of such concepts as beauty, taste, etc. **2.** the study of the rules and principles of art.

aestival *or U.S.* **estival** (i:'staɪvəl) *adj. Rare.* of or occurring in summer. [C14: from F, from LL *aestīvālis*, from L *aestās* summer]

aestivate *or U.S.* **estivate** ('i:stɪ,veɪt) *vb.* (*intr.*) **1.** to pass the summer. **2.** (of animals) to pass the summer or dry season in a dormant condition. [C17: from L, from *aestīvāre*, from *aestās* summer] —,**aesti'vation** *or U.S.* ,**esti'vation** *n.*

aet. *or* **aetat.** *abbrev. for* aetatis. [L: at the age of]

Æthelbert ('æθəl,bɜːt) *n.* a variant spelling of **Ethelbert**.

Æthelred ('æθəl,rɛd) *n.* a variant spelling of **Ethelred**.

aether ('i:θə) *n.* a variant spelling of **ether** (senses 3, 4).

aetiology (,i:tɪ'ɒlədʒɪ) *n., pl.* **-gies.** a variant spelling of **etiology**.

Aetna ('ɛtnə) *n.* the Latin name for Mount **Etna**.

Aetolia (i:'təʊlɪə) *n.* a mountainous region forming a department of W central Greece, north of the Gulf of Patras: a powerful federal state in the 3rd century B.C. Chief city: Missolonghi. Pop. (with Acarnania): 219 764 (1981). Area: 5390 sq. km (2081 sq. miles).

AEU (in Britain) *abbrev. for* Amalgamated Engineering Union.

a.f. *abbrev. for* audio frequency.

afar (ə'fɑː) *adv.* **1.** at, from, or to a great distance. ~*n.* **2.** a great distance (esp. in **from afar**). [C14 *a fer*, altered from earlier *on fer & of fer*; see A-², FAR]

Afars and the Issas ('ɑːfɑːz; 'ɪsɑːs) *n.* **Territory of the.** a former name (1967–77) of Djibouti.

AFC *abbrev. for:* **1.** Air Force Cross. **2.** Association Football Club. **3.** automatic frequency control.

afeard *or* **afeared** (ə'fɪəd) *adj.* (*postpositive*) an archaic or dialect word for **afraid**. [OE *afǣred*, from *afǣran* to frighten]

affable ('æfəbªl) *adj.* **1.** showing warmth and friendliness. **2.** easy to converse with; approachable. [C16: from L *affābilis*, from *affāri*, from *ad-* to + *fāri* to speak] —,affa'bility *n.* —'affably *adv.*

affair (ə'fɛə) *n.* **1.** a thing to be done or attended to; matter. **2.** an event or happening: *a strange affair.* **3.** (*qualified by an adjective or descriptive phrase*) something previously specified: *our house is a tumbledown affair.* **4.** a sexual relationship between two people who are not married to each other. [C13: from OF, from *à faire* to do]

affairs (ə'fɛəz) *pl. n.* **1.** personal or business interests. **2.** matters of public interest: *current affairs.*

affect[1] *vb.* (ə'fɛkt). (*tr.*) **1.** to act upon or influence, esp. in an adverse way. **2.** to move or disturb emotionally or mentally. **3.** (of pain, disease, etc.) to attack. ~*n.* ('æfɛkt). *Psychol.* the emotion associated with an idea or set of ideas. [C17: from L *affectus*, p.p. of *afficere*, from *ad-* to + *facere* to do]

affect[2] (ə'fɛkt) *vb.* (*mainly tr.*) **1.** to put on an appearance or show of: *to affect ignorance.* **2.** to imitate or assume, esp. pretentiously. **3.** to have or use by preference. **4.** to adopt the character, manner, etc., of. **5.** to incline habitually towards. [C15: from L *affectāre* to strive after; rel. to *afficere* to AFFECT[1]]

affectation (,æfɛk'teɪʃən) *n.* **1.** an assumed manner of speech, dress, or behaviour, esp. one that is intended to impress others. **2.** (often foll. by *of*) deliberate pretence. [C16: from L *affectātiōn-*, from *affectāre*; see AFFECT[2]]

affected[1] (ə'fɛktɪd) *adj.* (*usually postpositive*) **1.** deeply moved, esp. by sorrow or grief. **2.** changed, esp. detrimentally. [C17: from AFFECT[1]]

affected[2] (ə'fɛktɪd) *adj.* **1.** behaving, speaking, etc., in an assumed way, esp. in order to impress others. **2.** feigned: *affected indifference.* [C16: from AFFECT[2]] —af'fectedly *adv.*

affecting (ə'fɛktɪŋ) *adj.* evoking feelings of pity; moving. —af'fectingly *adv.*

affection (ə'fɛkʃən) *n.* **1.** a feeling of fondness or tenderness for a person or thing. **2.** (*often pl.*) emotion, feeling, or sentiment: *to play on a person's affections.* **3.** *Pathol.* any disease or pathological condition. **4.** the act of affecting or the state of being affected. [C13: from L *affectiōn-*, from *afficere* to AFFECT[1]] —af'fectional *adj.*

affectionate (ə'fɛkʃənɪt) *adj.* having or displaying tender feelings, affection, or warmth. —af'fectionately *adv.*

affective (ə'fɛktɪv) *adj.* concerned with the emotions or affection. —**affectivity** (,æfɛk'tɪvɪtɪ) *n.*

afferent ('æfərənt) *adj.* bringing or directing inwards to a part or an organ of the body, esp. towards the brain or spinal cord. [C19: from L *afferre*, from *ad-* to + *ferre* to carry]

affiance (ə'faɪəns) *vb.* (*tr.*) to bind (a person or oneself) in a promise of marriage; betroth. [C14: via OF from Med. L *affīdāre* to trust (oneself) to, from *fīdāre* to trust]

affidavit (,æfɪ'deɪvɪt) *n.* *Law.* a declaration in writing made upon oath before a person authorized to administer oaths. [C17: from Med. L, lit.: he declares on oath, from *affīdāre;* see AFFIANCE]

affiliate (ə'fɪlɪ,eɪt). **1.** (*tr.; foll. by to or with*) to receive into close connection or association (with a larger body, group, organization, etc.). **2.** (foll. by *with*) to associate (oneself) or be associated, esp. as a subordinate or subsidiary. ~*n.* (ə'fɪlɪɪt). **3. a.** a person or organization that is affiliated with another. **b.** (*as modifier*): *an affiliate member.* [C18: from Med. L *affīliātus* adopted as a son, from *affīliāre*, from L *fīlius* son] —af,fili'ation *n.*

affiliation order *n.* *Law.* an order that a man adjudged to be the father of an illegitimate child shall contribute towards the child's maintenance.

affine ('æfaɪn) *adj.* *Maths.* denoting transformations which preserve collinearity, esp. those of translation, rotation, and reflection. [C16: from F: see AFFINITY]

affinity (ə'fɪnɪtɪ) *n., pl.* **-ties. 1.** a natural liking, taste, or inclination for a person or thing. **2.** the person or thing so liked. **3.** a close similarity in appearance or quality. **4.** relationship by marriage. **5.** similarity in structure, form, etc., between different animals, plants, or languages. **6.** *Chem.* chemical attraction. [C14: via OF from L *affīnitāt-*, from *affīnis* bordering on, related] —af'finitive *adj.*

affirm (ə'fɜːm) *vb.* (*mainly tr.*) **1.** (*may take a clause as object*) to declare to be true. **2.** to uphold, confirm, or ratify. **3.** (*intr.*) *Law.* to make an affirmation. [C14: via

OF from L *affirmāre*, from *ad-* to + *firmāre* to make FIRM[1]] —af'firmer *or* af'firmant *n.*

affirmation (,æfə'meɪʃən) *n.* **1.** the act of affirming or the state of being affirmed. **2.** a statement of the truth of something; assertion. **3.** *Law.* a solemn declaration permitted on grounds of conscientious objection to taking an oath.

affirmative (ə'fɜːmətɪv) *adj.* **1.** confirming or asserting something as true or valid. **2.** indicating agreement or assent. **3.** *Logic.* (of a categorical proposition) affirming the satisfaction by the subject of the predicate, as in the proposition *some men are married.* ~*n.* **4.** a positive assertion. **5.** a word or phrase stating agreement or assent, such as *yes: to answer in the affirmative.* ~*sentence substitute.* **6.** *Mil., etc.* a signal codeword used to express assent or confirmation. —af'firmatively *adv.*

affix *vb.* (ə'fɪks). (*tr.; usually foll. by to or on*) **1.** to attach, fasten, join, or stick. **2.** to add or append: *to affix a signature to a document.* **3.** to attach or attribute (guilt, blame, etc.). ~*n.* ('æfɪks). **4.** a linguistic element added to a word or root to produce a derived or inflected form, as *-ment* in *establishment.* See also **prefix, suffix, infix. 5.** something fastened or attached. [C15: from Med. L *affīxāre*, from *ad-* to + *fīxāre* to FIX] —**affixture** (ə'fɪkstʃə) *n.*

afflatus (ə'fleɪtəs) *n.* an impulse of creative power or inspiration considered to be of divine origin. [C17: L, from *afflātus*, from *afflāre*, from *flāre* to blow]

afflict (ə'flɪkt) *vb.* (*tr.*) to cause suffering or unhappiness to; distress greatly. [C14: from L *afflictus*, p.p. of *afflīgere* to knock against, from *flīgere* to strike] —af'flictive *adj.*

affliction (ə'flɪkʃən) *n.* **1.** a condition of great distress or suffering. **2.** something responsible for physical or mental suffering.

affluence ('æfluəns) *n.* **1.** an abundant supply of money, goods, or property; wealth. **2.** *Rare.* abundance or profusion.

affluent ('æfluənt) *adj.* **1.** rich; wealthy. **2.** abundant; copious. **3.** flowing freely. ~*n.* **4.** a tributary stream. [C15: from L *affluent-*, present participle of *affluere*, from *fluere* to flow]

affluent society *n.* a society in which the material benefits of prosperity are widely available.

afflux ('æflʌks) *n.* a flowing towards a point: *an afflux of blood to the head.* [C17: from L *affluxus*, from *fluxus* FLUX]

afford (ə'fɔːd) *vb.* **1.** (preceded by *can, could*, etc.) to be able to do or spare something, esp. without incurring financial difficulties or without risk of undesirable consequences. **2.** to give, yield, or supply. [OE *geforthian* to further, promote, from *forth* FORTH] —af'fordable *adj.*

afforest (ə'fɒrɪst) *vb.* (*tr.*) to plant trees on. [C15: from Med. L *afforestāre*, from *forestis* FOREST] —af,forest'a-tion *n.*

affranchise (ə'fræntʃaɪz) *vb.* (*tr.*) to release from servitude or an obligation. [C15: from OF *afranchir*] —af'franchisement *n.*

affray (ə'freɪ) *n.* a fight, noisy quarrel, or disturbance between two or more persons in a public place. [C14: via OF from Vulgar L *exfrīdāre* (unattested) to break the peace]

affricate ('æfrɪkɪt) *n.* a composite speech sound consisting of a stop and a fricative articulated at the same point, such as the sound written *ch*, as in *chair.* [C19: from L *affricāre*, from *fricāre* to rub]

affright (ə'fraɪt) *Arch. or poetic.* ~*vb.* **1.** (*tr.*) to frighten. ~*n.* **2.** a sudden terror. [OE *āfyrhtan*, from *a-* + *fyrhtan* to FRIGHT]

affront (ə'frʌnt) *n.* **1.** a deliberate insult. ~*vb.* (*tr.*) **2.** to insult, esp. openly. **3.** to offend the pride or dignity of. [C14: from OF *afronter* to strike in the face, from L *ad frontem* to the face]

afghan ('æfgæn, -gən) *n.* **1.** a knitted or crocheted wool blanket or shawl, esp. one with a geometric pattern. **2.** a sheepskin coat, often embroidered. [from AFGHANISTAN]

Afghan ('æfgæn) *or* **Afghani** (æf'gæni) *n.* **1.** a native, citizen, or inhabitant of Afghanistan. **2.** another name for **Pashto** (the language). ~*adj.* **3.** denoting Afghanistan, its people, or their language.

Afghan hound *n.* a tall graceful breed of hound with a long silky coat.

Afghanistan (æf'gænɪ,stɑːn, -,stæn) *n.* a republic in central Asia: became independent in 1919; invaded by Soviet troops in 1979; generally arid and mountainous, with the

Hindu Kush range rising over 7500 m (25 000 ft.) and fertile valleys of the Amu Darya, Helmand, and Kabul Rivers. Languages: Pashto and Tadzhik. Religion: Muslim. Currency: afghani. Capital: Kabul. Pop.: 9 000 000 (1986 est.). Area: 657 500 sq. km (250 000 sq. miles).

aficionado (ə,fɪʃjəˈnɑːdəʊ) *n.*, *pl.* **-dos.** **1.** an ardent supporter or devotee: *a jazz aficionado.* **2.** a devotee of bullfighting. [Sp., from *aficionar,* from *aficion* AFFECTION]

afield (əˈfiːld) *adv.*, *adj.* *(postpositive)* **1.** away from one's usual surroundings or home (esp. in **far afield). 2.** off the subject (esp. in **far afield). 3.** in or to the field.

afire (əˈfaɪə) *adv.*, *adj. (postpositive)* **1.** on fire. **2.** intensely interested or passionate: *he was afire with enthusiasm for the new plan.*

aflame (əˈfleɪm) *adv.*, *adj. (postpositive)* **1.** in flames. **2.** deeply aroused, as with passion: *he was aflame with desire.*

aflatoxin (,æfləˈtɒksɪn) *n.* a toxin produced by a fungus growing on peanuts, maize, etc., thought to cause liver disease (esp. cancer) in man. [C20: from L name of fungus *A(spergillus) fla(vus)* + TOXIN]

afloat (əˈfləʊt) *adj. (postpositive),* *adv.* **1.** floating. **2.** aboard ship; at sea. **3.** covered with water. **4.** aimlessly drifting. **5.** in circulation: *nasty rumours were afloat.* **6.** free of debt.

aflutter (əˈflʌtə) *adj. (postpositive),* *adv.* in or into a nervous or excited state.

AFM *abbrev. for* Air Force Medal.

afoot (əˈfʊt) *adj. (postpositive),* *adv.* **1.** in operation; astir: *mischief was afoot.* **2.** on or by foot.

afore (əˈfɔː) *adv.*, *prep.*, *conj.* an archaic or dialect word for **before.**

aforementioned (əˈfɔːˌmɛnʃənd) *adj. (usually prenominal)* (chiefly in legal documents) stated or mentioned before.

aforesaid (əˈfɔːˌsɛd) *adj. (usually prenominal)* (chiefly in legal documents) spoken of or referred to previously.

aforethought (əˈfɔːˌθɔːt) *adj. (immediately postpositive)* premeditated (esp. in **malice aforethought).**

a fortiori (eɪ,fɔːtɪˈɔːraɪ) *adv.* for similar but more convincing reasons. [L]

afp *abbrev. for* alpha-fetoprotein.

Afr. *abbrev. for* Africa(n).

afraid (əˈfreɪd) *adj. (postpositive)* **1.** (often foll. by *of*) feeling fear or apprehension. **2.** reluctant (to do something), as through fear or timidity. **3.** (often foll. by *that*; used to lessen the effect of an unpleasant statement) regretful: *I'm afraid that I shall have to tell you to go.* [C14 *affraied,* p.p. of AFFRAY *(obs.)* to frighten]

afreet *or* **afrit** (ˈæfriːt, əˈfriːt) *n. Arabian myth.* a powerful evil demon. [C19: from Ar. *'ifrīt*]

afresh (əˈfrɛʃ) *adv.* once more; again; anew.

Africa (ˈæfrɪkə) *n.* the second largest of the continents, on the Mediterranean in the north, the Atlantic in the west, and the Red Sea, Gulf of Aden, and Indian Ocean in the east. The Sahara desert divides the continent unequally into North Africa (an early centre of civilization, in close contact with Europe and W Asia, now inhabited chiefly by Arabs) and Africa south of the Sahara (relatively isolated from the rest of the world until the 19th century and inhabited chiefly by Negro peoples). It was colonized mainly in the 18th and 19th centuries by Europeans and now comprises chiefly independent nations. The largest lake is Lake Victoria and the chief rivers are the Nile, Niger, Congo, and Zambezi. Pop.: 537 000 000 (1984). Area: about 30 300 000 sq. km (11 700 000 sq. miles).

African (ˈæfrɪkən) *adj.* **1.** denoting or relating to Africa or any of its peoples, languages, nations, etc. ~*n.* **2.** a native or inhabitant of any of the countries of Africa. **3.** a member or descendant of any of the peoples of Africa, esp. a Negro.

Africana (,æfrɪˈkɑːnə, ,æf-) *n.* objects of cultural or historical interest of southern African origin.

Africander (,æfrɪˈkændə, ,æf-) *n.* a breed of hump-backed beef cattle originally raised in southern Africa. [C19: from South African Du., formed on the model of *Hollander*]

African National Congress *n.* an African nationalist movement founded in 1912 in South Africa and banned there in 1960: active in opposition to apartheid. Abbrev.: ANC.

African violet *n.* a tropical African plant cultivated as a house plant, with violet, white, or pink flowers and hairy leaves.

Afrikaans (,æfrɪˈkɑːns, -ˈkɑːnz, æf-) *n.* an official language of all the Republic of South Africa, closely related to Dutch and Flemish. [C20: from Du.: African]

Afrikaner (afriˈkɑːnə, ,æfrɪˈkɑːnə) *n.* a White native of the Republic of South Africa whose mother tongue is Afrikaans. See also **Boer.**

Afro (ˈæfrəʊ) *n.*, *pl.* **-ros.** a hairstyle in which the hair is shaped into a wide frizzy bush, popular esp. among Negroes. [C20: independent use of AFRO-]

Afro- *combining form.* indicating Africa or African: *Afro-Asiatic.*

Afro-American *n.* **1.** an American Negro. ~*adj.* **2.** denoting or relating to American Negroes, their history, or their culture.

afrormosia (,æfrɔːˈməʊzɪə) *n.* a hard teaklike wood obtained from a genus of tropical African trees. [C20: from AFRO- + *Ormosia* (genus name)]

aft (ɑːft) *adv.*, *adj. Chiefly naut.* towards or at the stern or rear: *the aft deck.* [C17: ? shortened from earlier ABAFT]

after (ˈɑːftə) *prep.* **1.** following in time; in succession to: *after dinner.* **2.** following; behind. **3.** in pursuit or search of: *he's only after money.* **4.** concerning: *to inquire after his health.* **5.** considering: *after what you have done, you shouldn't complain.* **6.** next in excellence or importance to. **7.** in imitation of; in the manner of. **8.** in accordance with or in conformity to: *a man after her own heart.* **9.** with a name derived from. **10.** *U.S.* past (the hour of): *twenty after three.* **11. after all. a.** in spite of everything: *it's only a game after all.* **b.** in spite of expectations, efforts, etc. **12. after you.** please go, enter, etc., before me. ~*adv.* **13.** at a later time; afterwards. **14.** coming afterwards. **15.** *Naut.* further aft. ~*conj.* **16.** *(subordinating)* at a time later than that at which. ~*adj.* **17.** *Naut.* further aft: *the after cabin.* [OE *æfter*]

afterbirth (ˈɑːftə,bɜːθ) *n.* the placenta and fetal membranes expelled from the uterus after the birth of offspring.

afterburner (ˈɑːftə,bɜːnə) *n.* **1.** a device in the exhaust system of an internal-combustion engine for removing dangerous exhaust gases. **2.** a device in an aircraft jet engine to produce extra thrust by igniting additional fuel.

aftercare (ˈɑːftə,kɛə) *n.* **1.** support services by a welfare agency for a person discharged from a hospital, prison, etc. **2.** *Med.* the care of a patient after a serious illness or operation.

afterdamp (ˈɑːftə,dæmp) *n.* a poisonous gas, consisting mainly of carbon monoxide, formed after the explosion of firedamp in coal mines.

aftereffect (ˈɑːftərɪ,fɛkt) *n.* any result occurring some time after its cause.

afterglow (ˈɑːftə,gləʊ) *n.* **1.** the glow left after a light has disappeared, such as that sometimes seen after sunset. **2.** the glow of an incandescent metal after the source of heat has been removed.

afterimage (ˈɑːftər,ɪmɪdʒ) *n.* a sustained or renewed sensation, esp. visual, after the original stimulus has ceased.

afterlife (ˈɑːftə,laɪf) *n.* life after death or at a later time in a person's lifetime.

aftermath (ˈɑːftə,mæθ) *n.* **1.** signs or results of an event or occurrence considered collectively: *the aftermath of war.* **2.** *Agriculture.* a second crop of grass from land that has already yielded one crop earlier in the same year. [C16: AFTER + *math* a mowing, from OE *mæth*]

aftermost (ˈɑːftə,məʊst) *adj.* closer or closest to the rear or (in a vessel) the stern; last.

afternoon (,ɑːftəˈnuːn) *n.* **1. a.** the period between noon and evening. **b.** *(as modifier): afternoon tea.* **2.** a later part: *the afternoon of life.*

afternoons (,ɑːftəˈnuːnz) *adv. Inf.* during the afternoon, esp. regularly.

afterpains (ˈɑːftə,peɪnz) *pl. n.* cramplike pains caused by contraction of the uterus after childbirth.

afters (ˈɑːftəz) *n. (functioning as sing. or pl.) Brit. inf.* dessert; sweet.

aftershave lotion (ˈɑːftə,ʃeɪv) *n.* a lotion, usually perfumed, for application to the face after shaving. Often shortened to **aftershave.**

aftertaste (ˈɑːftə,teɪst) *n.* **1.** a taste that lingers on after eating or drinking. **2.** a lingering impression or sensation.

afterthought (ˈɑːftə,θɔːt) *n.* **1.** a comment, reply, etc., that occurs to one after the opportunity to deliver it has passed. **2.** an addition to something already completed.

afterwards ('ɑːftəwədz) *or* **afterward** *adv.* after an earlier event or time. [OE *æfterweard*, *æfteweard*, from AFT + WARD]

Ag *the chemical symbol for* silver. [from L *argentum*]

AG *abbrev. for:* **1.** Adjutant General. **2.** Attorney General.

aga *or* **agha** ('ɑːgə) *n.* (in the Ottoman Empire) a title of respect, often used with the title of a senior position. [C17: Turkish, lit.: lord]

Agadir (,ægə'dɪə) *n.* a port in SW Morocco, which became the centre of an international crisis (1911), when a gunboat arrived to protect German interests. Britain issued a strong warning to Germany but the French negotiated and war was averted. In 1960 the town was virtually destroyed by an earthquake, about 10 000 people being killed. Pop.: 62 300 (1984).

again (ə'gɛn, ə'geɪn) *adv.* **1.** another or a second time: *he had to start again.* **2.** once more in a previously experienced state or condition: *he is ill again.* **3.** in addition to the original amount, quantity, etc. (esp. in **as much again; half as much again**). **4.** (*sentence modifier*) on the other hand. **5.** besides; also. **6.** *Arch.* in reply; back: *he answered again.* **7. again and again.** continuously; repeatedly. *~sentence connector.* **8.** moreover; furthermore. [OE *ongegn* opposite to, from A-² + *gegn* straight]

against (ə'gɛnst, ə'geɪnst) *prep.* **1.** opposed to; in conflict or disagreement with. **2.** standing or leaning beside: *a ladder against the wall.* **3.** coming in contact with. **4.** in contrast to: *silhouettes are outlines against a light background.* **5.** having an unfavourable effect on: *the system works against small companies.* **6.** as a protection from: *a safeguard against contaminated water.* **7.** in exchange for or in return for. **8.** *Now rare.* in preparation for: *he gave them warm clothing against their journey.* **9. as against.** as opposed to or as compared with. [C12 *ageines*, from *again*, *ageyn*, etc. AGAIN + *-es*, genitive ending]

Aga Khan ('ɑːgə 'kɑːn) *n.* the hereditary title of the head of the Ismaili Islamic sect.

Aga Khan IV *n.* Prince **Karim** (kə'riːm). born 1936, spiritual leader of the Ismaili sect of Muslims from 1957.

Agamemnon (,ægə'mɛmnɒn) *n. Greek myth.* a king of Mycenae who led the Greeks at the siege of Troy. On his return home he was murdered by his wife Clytemnestra and her lover Aegisthus. See also **Menelaus.**

agamic (ə'gæmɪk) *adj.* asexual; occurring or reproducing without fertilization. [C19: from Gk *agamos* unmarried, from A-¹ + *gamos* marriage]

agamogenesis (,ægəməʊ'dʒɛnɪsɪs) *n.* asexual reproduction, such as fission or parthenogenesis. [C19: AGAMIC + GENESIS]

Agaña (ə'gɑːnjə) *n.* the capital of the Pacific island of Guam, on its W coast. Pop.: 881 (1980).

agapanthus (,ægə'pænθəs) *n.* a South African plant with blue funnel-shaped flowers, widely cultivated for ornament. [C19: NL, from Gk *agape* love + *anthos* flower]

agape (ə'geɪp) *adj.* (*postpositive*) **1.** (esp. of the mouth) wide open. **2.** very surprised, expectant, or eager. [C17: A-² + GAPE]

Agape ('ægəpɪ) *n.* **1.** Christian love, esp. as contrasted with erotic love; charity. **2.** a communal meal in the early Church in commemoration of the Last Supper. [C17: Gk *agapē* love]

agar ('eɪgə) *n.* a gelatinous carbohydrate obtained from seaweeds, used as a culture medium for bacteria, as a laxative, a thickening agent (**E406**) in food, etc. Also called: **agar-agar.** [C19: Malay]

agaric ('ægərɪk) *n.* a fungus having gills on the underside of the cap. The group includes the edible mushrooms and poisonous forms such as the fly agaric. [C16: via L from Gk *agarikon*]

Agartala ('ʌgətə,lɑː) *n.* a city in NE India, capital of the state of Tripura. Pop.: 132 186 (1981).

Agassiz (*French* agasi) *n.* **Jean Louis Rodolphe** (ʒɑ̃ lwi rɔdɔlf). 1807–73, Swiss natural historian and geologist, settled in the U.S. after 1846.

agate ('ægɪt) *n.* **1.** an impure form of quartz consisting of a variegated, usually banded chalcedony, used as a gemstone and in making pestles and mortars. **2.** a playing marble of this quartz or resembling it. [C16: via F from L, from Gk *akhatēs*]

agave (ə'geɪvɪ) *n.* a plant native to tropical America with tall flower stalks rising from thick fleshy leaves. Some

species are the source of fibres such as sisal. [C18: NL, from Gk *agauē*, fem. of *agauos* illustrious]

age (eɪdʒ) *n.* **1.** the period of time that a person, animal, or plant has lived or is expected to live. **2.** the period of existence of an object, material, group, etc.: *the age of this table is 200 years.* **3. a.** a period or state of human life: *he should know better at his age.* **b.** (*as modifier*): *age group.* **4.** the latter part of life. **5. a.** a period of history marked by some feature or characteristic. **b.** (*cap. when part of a name*): *the Middle Ages.* **6.** generation: *the Edwardian age.* **7.** *Geol., palaeontol.* **a.** a period of the earth's history distinguished by special characteristics: *the age of reptiles.* **b.** a subdivision of an epoch. **8.** (*often pl.*) *Inf.* a relatively long time: *I've been waiting ages.* **9.** *Psychol.* the level in years that a person has reached in any area of development, compared with the normal level for his chronological age. **10. of age.** adult and legally responsible for one's actions (usually at 18 years). *~vb.* **ageing** *or* **aging, aged.** **11.** to become or cause to become old or aged. **12.** (*intr.*) to begin to seem older: *to have aged a lot in the past year.* **13.** *Brewing.* to mature or cause to mature. [C13: via OF from Vulgar L, from L *aetās*]

-age *suffix forming nouns.* **1.** indicating a collection, set, or group: *baggage.* **2.** indicating a process or action or the result of an action: *breakage.* **3.** indicating a state or relationship: *bondage.* **4.** indicating a house or place: *orphanage.* **5.** indicating a charge or fee: *postage.* **6.** indicating a rate: *dosage.* [from OF, from LL *-āticum* belonging to]

aged ('eɪdʒɪd) *adj.* **1. a.** advanced in years; old. **b.** (*as collective n.; preceded by the*): *the aged.* **2.** of, connected with, or characteristic of old age. **3.** (eɪdʒd). (*postpositive*) having the age of: *a woman aged twenty.*

ageing *or* **aging** ('eɪdʒɪŋ) *n.* **1.** the process of growing old or developing the appearance of old age. *~adj.* **2.** becoming or appearing older: *an ageing car.* **3.** giving the appearance of elderliness: *that dress is really ageing.*

ageism *or* **agism** ('eɪdʒɪzəm) *n.* discrimination against people on the grounds of age. — **'ageist** *or* **'agist** *adj.*

ageless ('eɪdʒlɪs) *adj.* **1.** apparently never growing old. **2.** timeless; eternal: *an ageless quality.*

Agen (*French* aʒɑ̃) *n.* a market town in SW France, on the Garonne river. Pop.: 33 784 (1983 est.).

agency ('eɪdʒənsɪ) *n., pl.* **-cies.** **1.** a business or other organization providing a specific service: *an employment agency.* **2.** the place where an agent conducts business. **3.** the business, duties, or functions of an agent. **4.** action, power, or operation: *the agency of fate.* [C17: from Med. L *agentia*, from L *agere* to do]

agenda (ə'dʒɛndə) *n.* **1.** (*functioning as sing.*) Also: **agendum.** a schedule or list of items to be attended to. **2.** (*functioning as pl.*) Also: **agendas, agendums.** matters to be attended to, as at a meeting. [C17: L, lit.: things to be done, from *agere* to do]

agent ('eɪdʒənt) *n.* **1.** a person who acts on behalf of another person, business, government, etc. **2.** a person or thing that acts or has the power to act. **3.** a substance or organism that exerts some force or effect: *a chemical agent.* **4.** the means by which something occurs or is achieved. **5.** a person representing a business concern, esp. a travelling salesman. [C15: from L *agent-*, noun use of the present participle of *agere* to do] —**agential** (eɪ'dʒɛnʃəl) *adj.*

agent-general *n., pl.* **agents-general.** a representative in London of a Canadian province or an Australian state.

Agent Orange *n.* a highly poisonous herbicide used as a spray for defoliation and crop destruction, esp. by U.S. forces during the Vietnam War. [C20: named after the identifying colour stripe on its container]

agent provocateur *French.* (aʒɑ̃ prɔvɔkatœr) *n., pl.* ***agents provocateurs*** (aʒɑ̃ prɔvɔkatœr) a secret agent employed to provoke suspected persons to commit illegal acts and so be discredited or liable to punishment.

age of consent *n.* the age at which a person, esp. a female, is considered legally competent to consent to marriage or sexual intercourse.

Age of Reason *n.* (usually preceded by *the*) the 18th century in W Europe. See also **Enlightenment.**

age-old *or* **age-long** *adj.* very old or of long duration; ancient.

ageratum (,ædʒə'reɪtəm) *n.* a tropical American plant with thick clusters of purplish-blue flowers. [C16: NL, via

L from Gk *agēraton* that does not age, from A-¹ + *gērat-*, stem of *gēras* old age]

agglomerate *vb.* (ə'glɒmə,reɪt). **1.** to form or be formed into a mass or cluster. ~*n.* (ə'glɒmərɪt, -,reɪt). **2.** a confused mass. **3.** a volcanic rock consisting of angular fragments within a groundmass of lava. ~*adj.* (ə'glɒmərɪt, -,reɪt). **4.** formed into a mass. [C17: from L *agglomerāre*, from *glomerāre* to wind into a ball] —**ag,glomer'ation** *n.* —**ag'glomerative** *adj.*

agglutinate (ə'gluːtɪ,neɪt) *vb.* **1.** to adhere or cause to adhere, as with glue. **2.** *Linguistics.* to combine or be combined by agglutination. **3.** (*tr.*) to cause (bacteria, red blood cells, etc.) to clump together. [C16: from L *agglūtināre* to glue to, from *gluten* glue] —**ag'glutinable** *adj.* —**ag'glutinant** *adj.*

agglutination (ə,gluːtɪ'neɪʃən) *n.* **1.** the act or process of agglutinating. **2.** a united mass of parts. **3.** *Linguistics.* the building up of words from component morphemes in such a way that these undergo little or no change of form or meaning.

aggrandize *or* **-dise** (ə'grændaɪz) *vb.* (*tr.*) **1.** to increase the power, wealth, prestige, scope, etc., of. **2.** to cause (something) to seem greater. [C17: from OF *aggrandiss-*, stem of *aggrandir*, from L *grandis* GRAND] —**aggrandizement** *or* **-disement** (ə'grændɪzmənt) *n.* —**'aggran,dizer** *or* -,**diser** *n.*

aggravate ('ægrə,veɪt) *vb.* (*tr.*) **1.** to make (a disease, situation, problem, etc.) worse. **2.** *Inf.* to annoy. [C16: from L *aggravāre* to make heavier, from *gravis* heavy] —**'aggra,vating** *adj.* —**,aggra'vation** *n.*

▷ **Usage.** The use of *aggravate*, *aggravating*, and *aggravation* for *annoy*, *annoying*, and *annoyance* is usually avoided in formal English.

aggregate *adj.* ('ægrɪgɪt). **1.** formed of separate units collected into a whole. **2.** (of fruits and flowers) composed of a dense cluster of florets. ~*n.* ('ægrɪgɪt, -,geɪt). **3.** a sum or assemblage of many separate units. **4.** *Geol.* a rock, such as granite, consisting of a mixture of minerals. **5.** the sand and stone mixed with cement and water to make concrete. **6. in the aggregate.** taken as a whole. ~*vb.* ('ægrɪ,geɪt). **7.** to combine or be combined into a body, etc. **8.** (*tr.*) to amount to (a number). [C16: from L *aggregāre* to add to a flock or herd, from *grex* flock] —**,aggre'gation** *n.* —**aggregative** ('ægrɪ,geɪtɪv) *adj.*

aggress (ə'grɛs) *vb.* (*intr.*) to attack first or begin a quarrel. [C16: from Med. L *aggressāre*, from L *aggredī* to attack] —**aggressor** (ə'grɛsə) *n.*

aggression (ə'grɛʃən) *n.* **1.** an attack or harmful action, esp. an unprovoked attack by one country against another. **2.** any offensive activity, practice, etc. **3.** *Psychol.* a hostile or destructive mental attitude. [C17: from L *aggression-*, from *aggrēdī* to attack]

aggressive (ə'grɛsɪv) *adj.* **1.** quarrelsome or belligerent. **2.** assertive; vigorous. —**ag'gressively** *adv.* —**ag'gressiveness** *n.*

aggrieve (ə'griːv) *vb.* (*tr.*) **1.** (*often impersonal or passive*) to grieve; distress; afflict. **2.** to injure unjustly, esp. by infringing a person's legal rights. [C14 *agreven*, via OF from L *aggravāre* to AGGRAVATE] —**ag'grieved** *adj.* —**ag'grievedly** (ə'griːvɪdlɪ) *adv.*

aggro ('ægrəʊ) *n. Brit. sl.* aggressive behaviour. [C20: from AGGRAVATION]

aghast (ə'ɡɑːst) *adj.* (*postpositive*) overcome with amazement or horror. [C13 *agast*, from OE *gæstan* to frighten]

agile ('ædʒaɪl) *adj.* **1.** quick in movement; nimble. **2.** mentally quick or acute. [C15: from L *agilis*, from *agere* to do, act] —**'agilely** *adv.* —**agility** (ə'dʒɪlɪtɪ) *n.*

agin (ə'ɡɪn) *prep. Inf. or dialect.* against. [C19: from obs. *again* AGAINST]

Agincourt ('ædʒɪn,kɔːt; *French* aʒɛ̃kur) *n.* a battle fought in 1415 near the village of Azincourt, N France: a decisive victory for English longbowmen under Henry V over French forces vastly superior in number.

agio ('ædʒɪəʊ) *n., pl.* **-ios. a.** the difference between the nominal and actual values of a currency. **b.** the charge payable for conversion of the less valuable currency. [C17: from It., lit.: ease]

agitate ('ædʒɪ,teɪt) *vb.* **1.** (*tr.*) to excite, disturb, or trouble (a person, the mind or feelings). **2.** (*tr.*) to shake, stir, or disturb. **3.** (*intr.*; often foll. by *for* or *against*) to attempt to stir up public opinion for or against something. [C16: from L *agitātus*, from *agitāre* to set into motion,

from *agere* to act] —**'agi,tated** *adj.* —**'agi,tatedly** *adv.* —**,agi'tation** *n.*

agitato (,ædʒɪ'tɑːtəʊ) *adj., adv. Music.* (to be performed) in an agitated manner.

agitator ('ædʒɪ,teɪtə) *n.* **1.** a person who agitates for or against a cause, etc. **2.** a device for mixing or shaking.

agitprop ('ædʒɪt,prɒp) *n.* **a.** any promotion, as in the arts, of political propaganda, esp. of a Communist nature. **b.** (*as modifier*): *agitprop theatre.* [C20: short for Russian *Agitpropbyuro*]

Aglaia (ə'glaɪə) *n. Greek myth.* one of the three Graces. [Gk: splendour, from *aglaos* splendid]

agleam (ə'gliːm) *adj.* (*postpositive*) glowing; gleaming.

aglet ('æglɪt) *or* **aiglet** *n.* **1.** a metal sheath or tag at the end of a shoelace, ribbon, etc. **2.** a variant spelling of **aiguillette.** [C15: from OF *aiguillette* a small needle]

agley (ə'gleɪ, ə'gliː; ə'glaɪ) *or* **aglee** (ə'gliː) *adv., adj. Scot.* awry; oblique(ly); askew. [from *gley* squint]

aglitter (ə'glɪtə) *adj.* (*postpositive*) sparkling; glittering.

aglow (ə'gləʊ) *adj.* (*postpositive*) glowing.

aglu *or* **agloo** ('æglu:) *n. Canad.* a breathing hole made in ice by a seal. [C19: from Eskimo]

AGM *abbrev. for* annual general meeting.

agnail ('æg,neɪl) *n.* another name for **hangnail.**

agnate ('ægneɪt) *adj.* **1.** related by descent from a common male ancestor. **2.** related in any way. ~*n.* **3.** a male or female descendant by male links from a common male ancestor. [C16: from L *agnātus* born in addition, from *agnāscī*, from *ad-* in addition + *gnāscī* to be born]

Agnes ('ægnɪs) *n.* **Saint.** ?292–?304 A.D., Christian child martyr under Diocletian. Feast day: Jan. 21.

Agni ('ʌgnɪ) *n. Hinduism.* the god of fire, one of the three chief deities of the Vedas. [Sansk.: fire]

agnostic (æg'nɒstɪk) *n.* **1.** a person who holds that knowledge of a Supreme Being, ultimate cause, etc., is impossible. **2.** a person who claims, with respect to any particular question, that the answer cannot be known with certainty. ~*adj.* **3.** of or relating to agnostics. [C19: coined 1869 by T. H. Huxley from A-¹ + GNOSTIC] —**ag'nosticism** *n.*

Agnus Dei ('ægnʊs 'deɪɪ) *n.* **1.** the figure of a lamb bearing a cross or banner, emblematic of Christ. **2.** a chant beginning with these words or a translation of them, forming part of the Roman Catholic Mass. [L: Lamb of God]

ago (ə'gəʊ) *adv.* in the past: *five years ago; long ago.* [C14 *ago*, from OE *āgān* to pass away]

▷ **Usage.** The use of *ago* with *since* (*it's ten years ago since he wrote the novel*) is redundant and is therefore avoided in careful English. *Ago* should be followed by *that: it was ten years ago that he wrote the novel.*

agog (ə'gɒg) *adj.* (*postpositive*) eager or curious. [C15: ?from OF *en gogues* in merriments]

-agogue *or esp. U.S.* **-agog** *n. combining form.* indicating a person or thing that leads or incites to action: *demagogue.* [via LL from Gk *agōgos*, from *agein* to lead] —**-agogic** *adj. combining form.* —**-agogy** *n. combining form.*

agonic (ə'gɒnɪk) *adj.* forming no angle. [C19: from Gk *agōnos*, from A-¹ + *gōnia* angle]

agonic line *n.* an imaginary line on the surface of the earth connecting points of zero magnetic declination.

agonize *or* **-nise** ('ægə,naɪz) *vb.* **1.** to suffer or cause to suffer agony. **2.** (*intr.*) to struggle; strive. [C16: via Med. L from Gk *agōnizesthai* to contend for a prize, from *agōn* contest] —**'ago,nizingly** *or* -,**nisingly** *adv.*

agony ('ægənɪ) *n., pl.* **-nies. 1.** acute physical or mental pain; anguish. **2.** the suffering or struggle preceding death. [C14: via LL from Gk *agōnia* struggle, from *agōn* contest]

agony aunt *n.* (*sometimes cap.*) a person who replies to readers' letters in an agony column.

agony column *n.* **1.** a newspaper or magazine feature offering sympathetic advice to readers on their personal problems. **2.** *Inf.* a newspaper or magazine column devoted to advertisements relating esp. to personal problems.

agora ('ægərə) *n., pl.* **-rae** (-riː, -raɪ) *or* **-ras.** (*often cap.*) **a.** the marketplace in Athens, used for popular meetings in ancient Greece. **b.** the meeting itself. [from Gk, from *agorein* to gather]

agoraphobia (,ægərə'fəʊbɪə) *n.* a pathological fear of open spaces. —**,agora'phobic** *adj., n.*

Agostini (*Italian* agos'ti:ni) *n.* **Giacomo** ('dʒa:komo). born 1944, Italian racing motorcyclist: world champion (500 cc. class) 1966–72, 1975; (350 cc. class) 1968–74.

agouti (ə'gu:tɪ) *n., pl.* **-tis** or **-ties**. a rodent of Central and South America and the West Indies. Agoutis are agile and long-legged, with hooflike claws, and are valued for their meat. [C18: via F & Sp. from Guarani]

AGR *abbrev. for* advanced gas-cooled reactor.

Agra ('a:grə) *n.* a city in N India, in W Uttar Pradesh on the Jumna River: a capital of the Mogul empire until 1658; famous for its Mogul architecture, esp. the Taj Mahal. Pop.: 723 676 (1981).

Agram ('a:gram) *n.* the German name for **Zagreb.**

agrarian (ə'grɛərɪən) *adj.* **1.** of or relating to land or its cultivation. **2.** of or relating to rural or agricultural matters. ~*n.* **3.** a person who favours the redistribution of landed property. [C16: from L *agrārius*, from *ager* field, land] —**a'grarianism** *n.*

agree (ə'gri:) *vb.* **agreeing, agreed.** (*mainly intr.*) **1.** (often foll. by *with*) to be of the same opinion. **2.** (*also tr.*; when *intr.*, often foll. by *to*; when *tr.*, *takes a clause as object or an infinitive*) to give assent; consent. **3.** (*also tr.*; when *intr.*, foll. by *on* or *about*; when *tr., may take a clause as object*) to come to terms (about). **4.** (foll. by *with*) to be similar or consistent; harmonize. **5.** (foll. by *with*) to be agreeable or suitable (to one's health, etc.). **6.** (*tr.*; *takes a clause as object*) to concede: *they agreed that the price was too high.* **7.** *Grammar.* to undergo agreement. [C14: from OF *agreer*, from *a gre* at will or pleasure]

agreeable (ə'gri:əb³l) *adj.* **1.** pleasing; pleasant. **2.** prepared to consent. **3.** (foll. by *to* or *with*) in keeping. **4.** (foll. by *to*) to one's liking. —**a'greeableness** *n.* —**a'greeably** *adv.*

agreed (ə'gri:d) *adj.* **1.** determined by common consent: *the agreed price.* ~*sentence substitute.* **2.** an expression of consent or agreement.

agreement (ə'gri:mənt) *n.* **1.** the act of agreeing. **2.** a settlement, esp. one that is legally enforceable. **3.** a contract or document containing such a settlement. **4.** the state of being of the same opinion. **5.** the state of being similar or consistent. **6.** *Grammar.* the determination of the inflectional form of one word by some grammatical feature, such as number or gender, of another word. [C14: from OF]

agribusiness ('ægrɪ,bɪznɪs) *n.* the various businesses that process and distribute farm products. [C20: from AGRI(CULTURE) + BUSINESS]

Agricola (ə'grɪkələ) *n.* **1. Georgius** ('dʒɔ:dʒɪəs), original name *Georg Bauer.* 1494–1555, German mineralogist, metallurgist, and author, commonly regarded as the father of mineralogy. **2. Gnaeus Julius** ('ni:əs 'dʒu:lɪəs) 40–93 A.D., Roman general; governor of Britain who advanced Roman rule north to the Firth of Forth.

agriculture ('ægrɪ,kʌltʃə) *n.* the science or occupation of cultivating land and rearing crops and livestock; farming. [C17: from L *agricultūra*, from *ager* field, land + *cultūra* CULTURE] —,**agri'cultural** *adj.* —,**agri'culturist** or ,**agri'culturalist** *n.*

Agrigento (*Italian* agri'dʒɛnto) *n.* a town in Italy, in SW Sicily: site of six Greek temples. Pop.: 51 325 (1981). Former name (until 1927): **Girgenti** (gɜ:'gɛntɪ).

agrimony ('ægrɪmənɪ) *n.* **1.** any of various plants of the rose family, which have compound leaves, long spikes of small yellow flowers, and bristly burlike fruits. **2.** any of several other plants, such as hemp agrimony. [C15: via OF from L, from Gk *argemōnē* poppy]

Agrippa (ə'grɪpə) *n.* **Marcus Vipsanius** ('ma:kəs vɪp'seɪnɪəs). 63–12 B.C., Roman general: chief adviser and later son-in-law of Augustus.

Agrippina (,ægrɪ'pi:nə) *n.* **1.** called *the Elder. c.* 14 B.C.–33 A.D., Roman matron: granddaughter of Augustus, wife of Germanicus, mother of Caligula and Agrippina the Younger. **2.** called *the Younger.* 15–59 A.D., mother of Nero, who put her to death after he became emperor.

agro- *combining form.* denoting fields, soil, or agriculture: *agrobiology.* [from Gk *agros* field]

agrobiology (,ægrəʊbaɪ'ɒlədʒɪ) *n.* the science of plant growth and nutrition in relation to agriculture.

agronomics (,ægrə'nɒmɪks) *n.* (*functioning as sing.*) the branch of economy dealing with the distribution, management, and productivity of land. —,**agro'nomic** *adj.*

agronomy (ə'grɒnəmɪ) *n.* the science of cultivation of land, soil management, and crop production. —**a'gronomist** *n.*

agrostemma (,ægrəʊ'stɛmə) *n.* any cultivated variety of corncockle. [NL, from Gk *agros* field + *stemma* wreath]

aground (ə'graʊnd) *adv., adj.* (*postpositive*) on or onto the ground or bottom, as in shallow water.

agterskot ('axtə,skɒt) *n.* (in South Africa) the final instalment of payment to a farmers' cooperative for a crop or wool clip. [from Afrik. *agter* afterwards + *skot* payment]

Aguascalientes (*Spanish* ,aɣwaska'ljentes) *n.* **1.** a state in central Mexico. Pop.: 503 410 (1980). Area: 5471 sq. km (2112 sq. miles). **2.** a city in central Mexico, capital of Aguascalientes state, about 1900 m (6200 ft.) above sea level, with hot springs. Pop.: 359 454 (1980).

ague ('eɪgju:) *n.* **1.** malarial fever with successive stages of fever and chills. **2.** a fit of shivering. [C14: from OF (*fievre*) *ague* acute fever; see ACUTE] —**'aguish** *adj.*

Agulhas (ə'gʌləs) *n.* **Cape.** a headland in South Africa, the southernmost point of the African continent.

ah (a:) *interj.* an exclamation expressing pleasure, pain, sympathy, etc., according to the intonation of the speaker.

AH (indicating years in the Muslim system of dating, numbered from the Hegira (622 A.D.)) *abbrev. for* anno Hegirae. [L]

aha (a:'ha:) *interj.* an exclamation expressing triumph, surprise, etc., according to the intonation of the speaker.

Ahab ('eɪhæb) *n. Old Testament.* the king of Israel from approximately 869 to 850 B.C. and husband of Jezebel: rebuked by Elijah (I Kings 16:29–22:40).

Ahasuerus (ə,hæzju:'ɪərəs) *n. Old Testament.* a king of ancient Persia and husband of Esther, generally identified with Xerxes.

ahead (ə'hɛd) *adj.* **1.** (*postpositive*) in front; in advance. ~*adv.* **2.** at or in the front; before. **3.** forwards: *go straight ahead.* **4. ahead of. a.** in front of; at a further advanced position than. **b.** *Stock Exchange.* in anticipation of: *the share price rose ahead of the annual figures.* **5.** *Inf.* **be ahead.** to have an advantage; be winning. **6. get ahead.** to attain success.

ahem (ə'hɛm) *interj.* a clearing of the throat, used to attract attention, express doubt, etc.

ahimsa (a:'hɪmsa:) *n.* (in Hindu, Buddhist, and Jainist philosophy) the law of reverence for, and nonviolence to, every form of life. [Sansk., from *a* without + *himsā* injury]

Ahithophel (ə'hɪθə,fel) or **Achitophel** *n. Old Testament.* a member of David's council, who became one of Absalom's advisers in his rebellion and hanged himself when his advice was overruled (II Samuel 15:12–17:23).

Ahmedabad or **Ahmadabad** ('a:mədə,ba:d) *n.* a city in W India, in Gujarat: famous for its mosque. Pop.: 2 024 917 (1981).

Ahmednagar or **Ahmadnagar** (,a:məd'nʌgə) *n.* a city in W India, in Maharashtra: formerly one of the kingdoms of Deccan. Pop.: 181 210 (1981 est.).

ahoy (ə'hɔɪ) *interj. Naut.* a hail used to call a ship or to attract attention.

Ahriman ('a:rɪmən) *n. Zoroastrianism.* the supreme evil spirit and diabolical opponent of Ormazd.

Ahura Mazda (ə'hʊərə 'mæzdə) *n. Zoroastrianism.* another name for **Ormazd.**

Ahvenanmaa ('ɑhvenɑmmɑ:) *n.* the Finnish name for the **Åland Islands.**

Ahwaz (a:'wa:z) or **Ahvaz** (a:'va:z) *n.* a town in SW Iran, on the Karun River. Pop.: 589 529 (1986).

ai ('a:i) *n., pl.* **ais.** another name for **three-toed sloth** (see **sloth** (sense 1)). [C17: from Port., from Tupi]

AI *abbrev. for:* **1.** Amnesty International. **2.** artificial insemination. **3.** artificial intelligence.

aid (eɪd) *vb.* **1.** to give support to (someone to do something); help or assist. **2.** (*tr.*) to assist financially. ~*n.* **3.** assistance; help; support. **4.** a person, device, etc., that helps or assists. **5.** *Mountaineering.* a device such as a piton when used as a direct help in the ascent. **6.** (in medieval Europe) a feudal payment made to the king or any lord by his vassals on certain occasions such as the knighting of an eldest son. [C15: via OF *aidier* from L *adjūtāre*, from *juvāre* to help] —**'aider** *n.*

Aid or **-aid** *n. combining form.* denoting a charitable organization or function that raises money for a cause: *Band Aid; Ferryaid.*

AID *abbrev. for:* **1.** *U.S.* Agency for International Development. **2.** artificial insemination (by) donor.

Aidan ('eɪdən) *n.* **Saint.** died 651 A.D., Irish missionary in Northumbria, who founded the monastery at Lindisfarne (635).

aide (eɪd) *n.* **1.** an assistant. **2.** short for **aide-de-camp.**

aide-de-camp *or* **aid-de-camp** ('eɪd də 'kɒŋ) *n., pl.* **aides-de-camp** *or* **aids-de-camp.** a military officer serving as personal assistant to a senior. Abbrev.: **ADC.** [C17: from F: camp assistant]

aide-mémoire ('eɪdmɛm'wɑː) *n., pl.* **aides-mémoire** ('eɪdzmɛm'wɑː). **1.** a note serving as a reminder. **2.** a summarized diplomatic communication. [F, from *aider* to help + *mémoire* memory]

Aidin ('aɪdɪn) *n.* a variant spelling of **Aydin.**

AIDS (eɪdz) *n. acronym for* acquired immune (*or* immuno-) deficiency syndrome: a condition in which the body loses its ability to resist infection.

AIDS-related complex *n.* See **ARC.**

AIF *abbrev. for* Australian Imperial Force.

aiglet ('eɪglɪt) *n.* a variant of **aglet.**

aigrette *or* **aigret** ('eɪgrɛt) *n.* **1.** a long plume worn on hats or as a headdress, esp. one of long egret feathers. **2.** an ornament in imitation of a plume of feathers. [C17: from F; see EGRET]

aiguille (eɪ'gwiːl) *n.* **1.** a rock mass or peak shaped like a needle. **2.** an instrument for boring holes in rocks or masonry. [C19: F, lit.: needle]

aiguillette (ˌeɪgwɪ'lɛt) *n.* **1.** an ornamentation worn by certain military officers, consisting of cords with metal tips. **2.** a variant of **aglet.** [C19: F; see AGLET]

AIH *abbrev. for* artificial insemination (by) husband.

ail (eɪl) *vb.* **1.** (*tr.*) to trouble; afflict. **2.** (*intr.*) to feel unwell. [OE *eglan*, from *egle* painful]

ailanthus (eɪ'lænθəs) *n., pl.* **-thuses.** an E Asian deciduous tree having pinnate leaves, small greenish flowers, and winged fruits. Also called: **tree of heaven.** [C19: NL, from native name in the Moluccas in the Indian and Pacific Oceans]

aileron ('eɪlərɒn) *n.* a flap hinged to the trailing edge of an aircraft wing to provide lateral control. [C20: from F, dim. of *aile* wing]

ailing ('eɪlɪŋ) *adj.* unwell, esp. over a long period.

ailment ('eɪlmənt) *n.* a slight but often persistent illness.

aim (eɪm) *vb.* **1.** to point (a weapon, missile, etc.) or direct (a blow) at a particular person or object. **2.** (*tr.*) to direct (satire, criticism, etc.) at a person, object, etc. **3.** (*intr.;* foll. by *at* or an infinitive) to propose or intend. **4.** (*intr.;* often foll. by *at* or *for*) to direct one's efforts or strive (towards). *~n.* **5.** the action of directing something at an object. **6.** the direction in which something is pointed: *to take aim.* **7.** the object at which something is aimed. **8.** intention; purpose. [C14: via OF *aesmer* from L *aestimāre* to ESTIMATE]

aimless ('eɪmlɪs) *adj.* having no purpose or direction. —**'aimlessly** *adv.* —**'aimlessness** *n.*

Ain (*French* ɛ̃) *n.* **1.** a department in E central France, in Rhône-Alpes region. Capital: Bourg. Pop.: 418 516 (1982). Area: 5785 sq. km (2256 sq. miles). **2.** a river in E France, rising in the Jura Mountains and flowing south to the Rhône. Length: 190 km (118 miles).

ain't (eɪnt) *Not standard.* contraction of am not, is not, are not, have not, or has not: *I ain't seen it.*

▷ **Usage.** Although the interrogative form *ain't I?* would be a natural contraction of *am not I?*, it is generally avoided in spoken English and never used in formal English.

Aintab (aɪn'tɑːb) *n.* the former name (until 1921) of **Gaziantep.**

Aintree ('eɪntrɪ) *n.* a suburb of Liverpool, in Merseyside: site of the racecourse over which the Grand National steeplechase has been run since 1839.

Ainu ('aɪnuː) *n.* **1.** (*pl.* **-nus** *or* **-nu**) a member of the aboriginal people of Japan. **2.** the language of this people, sometimes tentatively associated with Altaic, still spoken in parts of Hokkaido. [Ainu: man]

air (ɛə) *n.* **1.** the mixture of gases that forms the earth's atmosphere. It consists chiefly of nitrogen, oxygen, argon, and carbon dioxide. **2.** the space above and around the earth; sky. Related adj.: **aerial. 3.** breeze; slight wind. **4.** public expression; utterance. **5.** a distinctive quality: *an air of mystery.* **6.** a person's distinctive appearance, manner, or bearing. **7.** *Music.* a simple tune for either vocal or instrumental performance. **8.** transportation in aircraft (esp. in **by air**). **9.** an archaic word for **breath** (senses 1–3). **10. in the air. a.** in circulation; current. **b.** unsettled. **11. into thin air.** leaving no trace behind. **12. on** (*or* **off**) **the air.** (not) in the act of broadcasting or (not) being broadcast on radio or television. **13. take the air.** to go out of doors, as for a short walk. **14. up in the air. a.** uncertain. **b.** *Inf.* agitated or excited. **15.** (*modifier*) *Astrol.* of or relating to a group of three signs of the zodiac, Gemini, Libra, and Aquarius. *~vb.* **16.** to expose or be exposed to the air so as to cool or freshen. **17.** to expose or be exposed to warm or heated air so as to dry: *to air linen.* **18.** (*tr.*) to make known publicly: *to air one's opinions.* *~*See also **airs.** [C13: via OF & L from Gk *aēr* the lower atmosphere]

Aïr ('ɑːɪə) *n.* a mountainous region of N central Niger, in the Sahara, rising to 1500 m (5000 ft.): a former native kingdom. Area: about 77 700 sq. km (30 000 sq. miles). Also called: **Asben, Azbine.**

air bag *n.* a safety device in a car, consisting of a bag that inflates automatically in an accident and prevents the passengers from being thrown forwards.

air base *n.* a centre from which military aircraft operate.

air bladder *n.* **1.** an air-filled sac, lying above the alimentary canal in bony fishes, that regulates buoyancy at different depths by a variation in the pressure of the air. **2.** any air-filled sac, such as one in seaweeds.

airborne ('ɛəˌbɔːn) *adj.* **1.** conveyed by or through the air. **2.** (of aircraft) flying; in the air.

air brake *n.* **1.** a brake operated by compressed air, esp. in heavy vehicles and trains. **2.** an articulated flap or small parachute for reducing the speed of an aircraft.

airbrick ('ɛəˌbrɪk) *n. Chiefly Brit.* a brick with holes in it, put into the wall of a building for ventilation.

airbrush ('ɛəˌbrʌʃ) *n.* **1.** an atomizer for spraying paint or varnish by means of compressed air. *~vb.* (*tr.*) **2.** to paint or varnish (something) by using an airbrush.

airbus ('ɛəˌbʌs) *n.* an airliner operated over short distances.

air chief marshal *n.* a senior officer of the Royal Air Force and certain other air forces, of equivalent rank to admiral in the Royal Navy.

air commodore *n.* a senior officer of the Royal Air Force and certain other air forces, of equivalent rank to brigadier in the Army.

air conditioning *n.* a system or process for controlling the temperature and sometimes the humidity of the air in a house, etc. —**'air-conˌdition** *vb.* (*tr.*) —**air conditioner** *n.*

air-cool *vb.* (*tr.*) to cool (an engine) by a flow of air. Cf. **water-cool.**

aircraft ('ɛəˌkrɑːft) *n., pl.* **-craft.** any machine capable of flying by means of buoyancy or aerodynamic forces, such as a glider, helicopter, or aeroplane.

aircraft carrier *n.* a warship with an extensive flat deck for the launch of aircraft.

aircraftman ('ɛəˌkrɑːftmən) *n., pl.* **-men.** a serviceman of the most junior rank in the Royal Air Force. —**'aircraft,woman** *fem. n.*

air curtain *n.* an air stream across a doorway to exclude draughts, etc.

air cushion *n.* **1.** an inflatable cushion. **2.** the pocket of air that supports a hovercraft.

Airdrie ('ɛədrɪ; *Scot.* 'erdrɪ) *n.* a town in W central Scotland in Strathclyde region, E of Glasgow: coal and iron industries. Pop.: 45 643 (1981).

airdrop ('ɛəˌdrɒp) *n.* **1.** a delivery of supplies, troops, etc., from an aircraft by parachute. *~vb.* **-dropping, -dropped. 2.** (*tr.*) to deliver (supplies, etc.) by an airdrop.

Aire (ɛə) *n.* a river in N England rising in the Pennines and flowing southeast mainly through West Yorkshire to the Ouse. Length: 112 km (70 miles).

Airedale ('ɛəˌdeɪl) *n.* a large rough-haired tan-coloured breed of terrier with a black saddle-shaped patch covering most of the back. Also called: **Airedale terrier.** [C19: from district in Yorkshire]

airfield ('ɛəˌfiːld) *n.* a landing and taking-off area for aircraft.

airfoil ('ɛəˌfɔɪl) *n.* the U.S. and Canad. name for **aerofoil.**

air force *n.* **a.** the branch of a nation's armed services primarily responsible for air warfare. **b.** (*as modifier*): *an air-force base.*

airframe ('ɛə,freɪm) n. the body of an aircraft, excluding its engines.

air gun n. a gun discharged by means of compressed air.

air hole n. 1. a hole that allows the passage of air, esp. for ventilation. 2. a section of open water in a frozen surface.

air hostess n. a stewardess on an airliner.

airily ('ɛərɪlɪ) adv. 1. in a jaunty or high-spirited manner. 2. in a light or delicate manner.

airiness ('ɛərɪnɪs) n. 1. the quality or condition of being fresh, light, or breezy. 2. gaiety.

airing ('ɛərɪŋ) n. 1. a. exposure to air or warmth, as for drying or ventilation. b. (as modifier): airing cupboard. 2. an excursion in the open air. 3. exposure to public debate.

airless ('ɛəlɪs) adj. 1. lacking fresh air; stuffy or sultry. 2. devoid of air. —'**airlessness** n.

air letter n. another name for **aerogram**.

airlift ('ɛə,lɪft) n. 1. the transportation by air of passengers, troops, cargo, etc., esp. when other routes are blocked. ~vb. 2. (tr.) to transport by an airlift.

airline ('ɛə,laɪn) n. 1. a. a system or organization that provides scheduled flights for passengers or cargo. b. (as modifier): an airline pilot. 2. a hose or tube carrying air under pressure.

airliner ('ɛə,laɪnə) n. a large passenger aircraft.

airlock ('ɛə,lɒk) n. 1. a bubble in a pipe causing an obstruction. 2. an airtight chamber with regulated air pressure used to gain access to a space that has air under pressure.

air mail n. 1. the system of conveying mail by aircraft. 2. mail conveyed by aircraft. ~adj. **air-mail**. 3. of or for air mail.

airman ('ɛəmən) n., pl. -men. an aviator, esp. one serving in the armed forces.

air marshal n. 1. a senior Royal Air Force officer of equivalent rank to a vice admiral in the Royal Navy. 2. a Royal Australian Air Force officer of the highest rank. 3. a Royal New Zealand Air Force officer of the highest rank when chief of defence forces.

air mass n. a large body of air having characteristics of temperature, moisture, and pressure that are approximately uniform horizontally.

air miss n. a situation in which two aircraft pass very close to one another in the air; near miss.

airplane ('ɛə,pleɪn) n. the U.S. and Canad. name for **aeroplane**.

airplay ('ɛə,pleɪ) n. (of a gramophone record) radio exposure.

air pocket n. a localized region of low air density or a descending air current, causing an aircraft to suffer an abrupt decrease in height.

airport ('ɛə,pɔːt) n. a landing and taking-off area for civil aircraft, usually with runways and aircraft maintenance and passenger facilities.

air power n. the strength of a nation's air force.

air pump n. a device for pumping air into or out of something.

air raid n. a. an attack by hostile aircraft or missiles. b. (as modifier): an air-raid shelter.

air-raid warden n. a member of a civil defence organization responsible for enforcing regulations, etc., during an air attack.

air rifle n. a rifle discharged by compressed air.

airs (ɛəz) pl. n. affected manners intended to impress others: to give oneself airs; put on airs.

air sac n. any of the membranous air-filled extensions of the lungs of birds, which increase the efficiency of respiration.

airscrew ('ɛə,skruː) n. Brit. an aircraft propeller.

air-sea rescue n. an air rescue at sea.

air shaft n. a shaft for ventilation, esp. in a mine or tunnel.

airship ('ɛə,ʃɪp) n. a lighter-than-air self-propelled craft. Also called: **dirigible**.

airshow ('ɛə,ʃəʊ) n. an occasion when an air base is open to the public and a flying display and, usually, static exhibitions are held.

airsick ('ɛə,sɪk) adj. nauseated from travelling in an aircraft.

airspace ('ɛə,speɪs) n. the atmosphere above the earth or part of the earth, esp. the atmosphere above a particular country.

airspeed ('ɛə,spiːd) n. the speed of an aircraft relative to the air in which it moves.

airstrip ('ɛə,strɪp) n. a cleared area for the landing and taking-off of aircraft; runway. Also called: **landing strip**.

air terminal n. Brit. a building in a city from which air passengers are taken to an airport.

airtight ('ɛə,taɪt) adj. 1. not permitting the passage of air. 2. having no weak points; rigid or unassailable.

air-to-air adj. operating between aircraft in flight.

air-traffic control n. an organization that determines the altitude, speed, and direction at which planes fly in a given area, giving instructions to pilots by radio. —**air-traffic controller** n.

air vice-marshal n. 1. a senior Royal Air Force officer of equivalent rank to a rear admiral in the Royal Navy. 2. a Royal Australian Air Force officer of the second highest rank. 3. a Royal New Zealand Air Force officer of the highest rank.

airwaves ('ɛə,weɪvz) pl. n. Inf. radio waves used in radio and television broadcasting.

airway ('ɛə,weɪ) n. 1. an air route, esp. one that is fully equipped with navigational aids, etc. 2. a passage for ventilation, esp. in a mine. 3. the passage of air from the nose or mouth to the lungs. 4. Med. a tubelike device inserted via the throat to keep open the airway of an unconscious patient.

airworthy ('ɛə,wɜːðɪ) adj. (of an aircraft) safe to fly.

airy ('ɛərɪ) adj. **airier, airiest**. 1. abounding in fresh air. 2. spacious or uncluttered. 3. nonchalant. 4. visionary; fanciful: airy promises. 5. of or relating to air. 6. weightless and insubstantial. 7. light and graceful in movement. 8. buoyant and gay; lively. 9. high up in the air.

Aisha or **Ayesha** ('ɑːiː,ʃɑː) n. ?613–678 A.D., the favourite wife of Mohammed; daughter of Abu Bekr.

aisle (aɪl) n. 1. a passageway separating seating areas in a theatre, church, etc. 2. a lateral division in a church flanking the nave or chancel. [C14 ele (later aile, aisle, through confusion with isle), via OF from L āla wing] —**aisled** adj.

Aisne (eɪn; French ɛn) n. 1. a department of NE France, in Picardy region. Capital: Laon. Pop.: 533 970 (1982). Area: 7428 sq. km (2897 sq. miles). 2. a river in N France, rising in the Argonne Forest and flowing northwest and west to the River Oise: scene of a major Allied offensive in 1918 which turned the tide finally against Germany in World War I. Length: 282 km (175 miles).

aitch (eɪtʃ) n. the letter h or the sound represented by it. [C16: a phonetic spelling]

aitchbone ('eɪtʃ,bəʊn) n. 1. the rump bone in cattle. 2. a cut of beef from or including the rump bone. [C15 hachboon, altered from earlier nache-bone (a nache mistaken for an ache, an aitch); nache buttock, via OF from LL natica, from L natis buttock]

Aitken ('eɪtkɪn) n. 1. **Robert Grant**. 1864–1951, U.S. astronomer who discovered over three thousand double stars. 2. **William Maxwell**. See **Beaverbrook**.

Aix-en-Provence (French ɛksɑ̃prɔvɑ̃s) n. a city and spa in SE France: the medieval capital of Provence. Pop.: 109 183 (1983 est.). Also called: **Aix**.

Aix-la-Chapelle (French ɛkslaʃapɛl) n. the French name for **Aachen**.

Aíyina ('ɛjina) n. transliteration of the Modern Greek name for **Aegina**.

Ajaccio (ə'dʒætsɪ,əʊ, -'dʒeɪ-) n. the capital of Corsica, a port on the W coast. Pop.: 50 428 (1983 est.).

ajar (ə'dʒɑː) adj. (postpositive), adv. (esp. of a door) slightly open. [C18: altered form of obs. on char, lit.: on the turn; from OE cierran to turn]

Ajax ('eɪdʒæks) n. Greek myth. 1. the son of Telamon; a Greek hero of the Trojan War who killed himself in vexation when Achilles' armour was given to Odysseus. 2. called Ajax the Lesser, a Locrian king, a swift-footed Greek hero of the Trojan War.

Ajmer (ʌdʒ'mɪə) n. a city in NW India, in Rajasthan: textile centre. Pop.: 374 350 (1981).

a.k.a. or **AKA** abbrev. for also known as.

Akbar ('ækbɑː) n. called Akbar the Great. 1542–1605, Mogul emperor of India (1556–1605), who extended the Mogul empire to include N India.

akene (ə'kiːn) n. a variant spelling of **achene**.

Akhaïa (a'xaːja) n. transliteration of the modern Greek name for **Achaea**.

Akhenaten or **Akhenaton** (,ækə'nɑːt⁽ə⁾n) n. original name Amenhotep IV. died ?1358 B.C., king of Egypt, of the

18th dynasty; he moved his capital from Thebes to Tell El Amarna and introduced the cult of Aten.

Akhmatova (*Russian* ax'matəvə) *n.* **Anna** ('annə). pseudonym of *Anna Gorenko*. 1889–1966, Russian poet: noted for her concise and intensely personal lyrics.

Akihito (,ækɪ'hi:təʊ) *n.* born 1933, Emperor of Japan from 1989.

akimbo (ə'kɪmbəʊ) *adj.* (*postpositive*), *adv.* with hands on hips and elbows out. [C15 *in kenebowe*, lit.: in keen bow, that is, in a sharp curve]

akin (ə'kɪn) *adj.* (*postpositive*) **1.** related by blood. **2.** (often foll. by *to*) having similar characteristics, properties, etc.

Akkad *or* **Accad** ('ækæd) *n.* **1.** a city on the Euphrates in N Babylonia, the centre of a major empire and civilization (2360–2180 B.C.). Ancient name: **Agade** (ə'ɡɑːdɪ, ə'ɡeɪdɪ). **2.** an ancient region lying north of Babylon, from which the Akkadian language and culture is named.

Akkadian *or* **Accadian** (ə'keɪdɪən) *n.* **1.** a member of an ancient Semitic people who lived in central Mesopotamia in the third millennium B.C. **2.** the extinct language of this people.

Akkerman (*Russian* akɪr'man) *n.* the former name (until 1946) of **Byelgorod-Dnestrovski**.

Akmolinsk (*Russian* ak'mɔlinsk) *n.* the former name (until 1961) of **Tselinograd**.

Akron ('ækrən) *n.* a city in NE Ohio. Pop.: 222 060 (1986).

Aksum *or* **Axum** ('ɑːksʊm) *n.* an ancient town in N Ethiopia, in Tigré province: capital of the Aksumite Empire (1st to 6th centuries A.D.). According to tradition, the Ark of the Covenant was brought here from Jerusalem.

Aktyubinsk (*Russian* ak'tjubinsk) *n.* an industrial city in the Soviet Union, in the Kazakh SSR. Pop.: 248 000 (1987).

Akure (ə'kuːre) *n.* a city in SW Nigeria, capital of Ondo state: agricultural trade centre. Pop.: 117 300 (1983).

Al *the chemical symbol for* aluminium.

-al[1] *suffix forming adjectives.* of; related to: *functional; sectional; tonal.* [from L *-ālis*]

-al[2] *suffix forming nouns.* the act or process of doing what is indicated by the verb stem: *renewal.* [via OF *-aille, -ail*, from L *-ālia*, neuter pl. used as substantive, from *-ālis* -AL[1]]

-al[3] *suffix forming nouns.* **1.** (*not used systematically*) indicating any aldehyde: *ethanal.* **2.** indicating a pharmaceutical product: *phenobarbital.* [shortened from ALDEHYDE]

ala ('eɪlə) *n.*, *pl.* **alae** ('eɪliː). **1.** *Zool.* a wing or flat winglike process or structure. **2.** *Bot.* a winglike part, such as one of the wings of a sycamore seed. [C18: from L *āla* a wing]

à la (ɑː lɑː) *prep.* **1.** in the manner or style of. **2.** as prepared in (a particular place) or by or for (a particular person). [C17: from F, short for *à la mode de* in the style of]

Alabama (,ælə'bæmə) *n.* **1.** a state of the southeastern U.S., on the Gulf of Mexico: consists of coastal and W lowlands crossed by the Tombigbee, Black Warrior, and Alabama Rivers, with parts of the Tennessee Valley and Cumberland Plateau in the north; noted for producing cotton and white marble. Capital: Montgomery. Pop.: 4 053 000 (1986 est.). Area: 131 333 sq. km (50 708 sq. miles). Abbrevs.: **Ala.** or (with zip code) **AL 2.** a river in Alabama, flowing southwest to the Mobile and Tensaw Rivers. Length: 507 km (315 miles). —,**Ala'bamian** *adj.*

alabaster ('ælə,bɑːstə) *n.* **1.** a fine-grained usually white, opaque, or translucent variety of gypsum. **2.** a variety of hard semitranslucent calcite. ~*adj.* **3.** of or resembling alabaster. [C14: from OF *alabastre*, from L *alabaster*, from Gk *alabastros*] —,**alaba'strine** *adj.*

à la carte (ɑː lɑː 'kɑːt) *adj., adv.* (of a menu) having dishes listed separately and individually priced. Cf. **table d'hôte.** [C19: from F, lit.: according to the card]

alack (ə'læk) *or* **alackaday** (ə'lækə,deɪ) *interj.* an archaic or poetic word for **alas.** [C15: from *a* ah! *lack* loss, LACK]

alacrity (ə'lækrɪtɪ) *n.* liveliness or briskness. [C15: from L, from *alacer* lively]

Ala Dağ *or* **Ala Dagh** (*Turkish* a'lɑ dɑː) *n.* **1.** the E part of the Taurus Mountains, in SE Turkey, rising over 3600 m (12 000 ft.). **2.** a mountain range in E Turkey, rising over 3300 m (11 000 ft.). **3.** a mountain range in NE Turkey, rising over 3000 m (10 000 ft.).

Alagez *or* **Alagöz** (ɑlɑ'ɡœz) *n.* the Turkish name for (Mount) **Aragats**.

Alagoas (*Portuguese* ala'ɡoːaʃ) *n.* a state in NE Brazil, on the Atlantic coast. Capital: Maceió. Pop.: 1 987 581 (1980). Area: 30 776 sq. km (11 031 sq. miles).

Alai (ɑː'laɪ) *n.* a mountain range in the S Soviet Union, in the SW Kirghiz SSR, running from the Tian Shan range in China into the Tadzhik SSR. Average height: 4800 m (16 000 ft.), rising over 5850 m (19 500 ft.).

Alain-Fournier (*French* alɛ̃furnje) *n.* real name *Henri-Alban Fournier.* 1886–1914, French novelist; author of *Le Grand Meaulnes* (1913; translated as *The Lost Domain*, 1959).

Alamein ('ælə,meɪn) *n.* see **El Alamein.**

Alamo ('ælə,məʊ) *n.* **the.** a mission in San Antonio, Texas, the site of a siege and massacre in 1836 by Mexican forces under Santa Anna of a handful of American rebels fighting for Texan independence from Mexico.

à la mode (ɑː lɑː 'məʊd) *adj.* **1.** fashionable in style, design, etc. **2.** (of meats) braised with vegetables in wine. [C17: from F: according to the fashion]

Alanbrooke ('ælən,brʊk) *n.* **Alan Francis Brooke,** 1st Viscount. 1883–1963, British field marshal; chief of Imperial General Staff (1941–46).

Åland Islands ('ɑːlənd, 'ɔːlənd; *Swedish* 'oːland) *pl. n.* a group of over 6000 islands under Finnish administration, in the Gulf of Bothnia. Capital: Mariehamn. Pop.: 23 640 (1986). Finnish name: **Ahvenanmaa.**

alar ('eɪlə) *adj.* relating to, resembling, or having wings or alae. [C19: from L *āla* a wing]

Alarcón (*Spanish* alar'kon) *n.* **Pedro Antonio de** ('peðro an'tonjo de). 1833–91, Spanish novelist and short-story writer, noted for his humorous sketches of rural life, esp. in *The Three-Cornered Hat* (1874).

Alaric ('ælərɪk) *n.* ?370–410 A.D., king of the Visigoths, who served under the Roman emperor Theodosius I but later invaded Greece and Italy, capturing Rome in 410.

alarm (ə'lɑːm) *vb.* (*tr.*) **1.** to fill with apprehension, anxiety, or fear. **2.** to warn about danger; alert. ~*n.* **3.** fear or terror aroused by awareness of danger. **4.** apprehension or uneasiness. **5.** a noise, signal, etc., warning of danger. **6.** any device that transmits such a warning: *a burglar alarm.* **7. a.** the device in an alarm clock that triggers off the bell or buzzer. **b.** short for **alarm clock. 8.** *Arch.* a call to arms. [C14: from OF *alarme*, from OIt. *all'arme* to arms; see ARM[2]] —**a'larming** *adj.*

alarm clock *n.* a clock with a mechanism that sounds at a set time: used esp. for waking a person up.

alarmist (ə'lɑːmɪst) *n.* **1.** a person who alarms or attempts to alarm others needlessly. **2.** a person who is easily alarmed. ~*adj.* **3.** characteristic of an alarmist.

alarum (ə'lærəm, -'lɑːr-) *n.* **1.** *Arch.* an alarm, esp. a call to arms. **2.** (used as a stage direction, esp. in Elizabethan drama) a loud disturbance or conflict (esp. in **alarums and excursions**). [C15: var. of ALARM]

alas (ə'læs) *sentence connector.* **1.** unfortunately; regrettably: *there were, alas, none left.* ~*interj.* **2.** *Arch.* an exclamation of grief or alarm. [C13: from OF *ha las!* oh wretched!; *las* from L *lassus* weary]

Alaska (ə'læskə) *n.* **1.** the largest state of the U.S., in the extreme northwest of North America: the aboriginal inhabitants are Eskimos; the earliest White settlements were made by the Russians. It is mostly mountainous and volcanic, rising over 6000 m (20 000 ft.), with the Yukon basin in the central region; large areas are covered by tundra; it has important mineral resources (chiefly coal, oil, and natural gas). Capital: Juneau. Pop.: 534 000 (1986 est.). Area: 1 530 694 sq. km (591 004 sq. miles). Abbrevs.: **Alas.** or (with zip code) **AK 2. Gulf of.** the N part of the Pacific, between the Alaska Peninsula and the Alexander Archipelago. —**A'laskan** *adj., n.*

Alaska Highway *n.* a road extending from Dawson Creek, British Columbia, to Fairbanks, Alaska: built by the U.S. Army (1942). Length: 2452 km (1523 miles). Originally called: **Alcan Highway.**

Alaska Peninsula *n.* an extension of the mainland of SW Alaska between the Pacific and the Bering Sea, ending in the Aleutian Islands. Length: about 644 km (400 miles).

Alaska Range *n.* a mountain range in S central Alaska. Highest peak: Mount McKinley, 6194 m (20 320 ft.).

alate ('eɪleɪt) *adj.* having wings or winglike extensions. [C17: from L, from *āla* wing]

alb (ælb) *n. Christianity.* a long white linen vestment with sleeves worn by priests and others. [OE *albe*, from Med. L *alba* (*vestis*) white (clothing)]

Alba (*Spanish* 'alβa) *n.* See (Duke of) **Alva.**

Albacete (*Spanish* alβa'θete) *n.* a city in SE Spain. Pop.: 117 126 (1981).

albacore ('ælbəˌkɔː) *n.* a tunny occurring mainly in warm regions of the Atlantic and Pacific. It has very long pectoral fins and is a valued food fish. [C16: from Port., from Ar.]

Alba Longa ('ælbə 'lɒŋɡə) *n.* a city of ancient Latium, southeast of modern Rome: the legendary birthplace of Romulus and Remus.

Albania (æl'beɪnɪə) *n.* a republic in SE Europe, on the Balkan Peninsula: became independent in 1912 after more than four centuries of Turkish rule; established as a republic (1946) under Communist rule. It is generally mountainous, rising over 2700 m (9000 ft.), with extensive forests. Language: Albanian. Currency: lek. Capital: Tirana. Pop.: 3 020 000 (1986). Area: 28 749 sq. km (11 100 sq. miles). Official name: **Socialist People's Republic of Albania.** —**Al'banian** *adj., n.*

Albany ('ɔːlbənɪ) *n.* **1.** a city in E New York State, on the Hudson River: the state capital. Pop.: 101 727 (1980). **2.** a river in central Canada, flowing east and northeast to James Bay. Length: 982 km (610 miles).

albatross ('ælbəˌtrɒs) *n.* **1.** a large bird of cool southern oceans, with long narrow wings and a powerful gliding flight. See also **wandering albatross. 2.** a constant and inescapable burden or handicap. **3.** *Golf.* a score of three strokes under par for a hole. [C17: from Port. *alcatraz* pelican, from Ar., from *al* the + *ghattās* white-tailed sea eagle; infl. by L *albus* white: C20 in sense 2, from Coleridge's poem *The Rime of the Ancient Mariner* (1798)]

albedo (æl'biːdəʊ) *n.* the ratio of the intensity of light reflected from an object, such as a planet, to that of the light it receives from the sun. [C19: from Church L: whiteness, from L *albus* white]

Albee ('ɔːlbiː) *n.* **Edward.** born 1928, U.S. dramatist. His plays include *Who's Afraid of Virginia Woolf?* (1962), *A Delicate Balance* (1957), and *Seascape* (1975).

albeit (ɔːl'biːɪt) *conj.* even though. [C14 *al be it,* that is, although it be (that)]

Albemarle Sound ('ælbəˌmɑːl) *n.* an inlet of the Atlantic in NE North Carolina. Length: about 96 km (60 miles).

Albéniz (*Spanish* al'βeniθ) *n.* **Isaac** (is'ak). 1860–1909, Spanish composer; noted for piano pieces inspired by folk music, such as the suite *Iberia.*

Alberich (*German* 'albərıç) *n.* (in medieval German legend) the king of the dwarfs and guardian of the treasures of the Nibelungs.

albert ('ælbət) *n.* a kind of watch chain usually attached to a waistcoat. [C19: after Prince ALBERT]

Albert[1] ('ælbət) *n.* **Lake.** a former name for **Lake Mobutu.**

Albert[2] ('ælbət) *n.* **Prince.** full name *Albert Francis Charles Augustus Emmanuel of Saxe-Coburg-Gotha.* 1819–61, Prince Consort of Queen Victoria of Great Britain and Ireland.

Albert I *n.* **1.** *c.* 1255–1308, king of Germany (1298–1308). **2.** 1875–1934, king of the Belgians (1909–34). **3.** called *Albert the Bear. c.* 1100–70. German military leader: first margrave of Brandenburg.

Alberta (æl'bɜːtə) *n.* a province of W Canada: mostly prairie, with the Rocky Mountains in the southwest. Capital: Edmonton. Pop.: 2 365 825 (1986). Area: 661 188 sq. km (255 285 sq. miles). Abbrevs.: **Alta, AB** —**Al'bertan** *adj., n.*

Albert Edward *n.* a mountain in SE New Guinea, in the Owen Stanley Range. Height: 3993 m (13 100 ft.).

Alberti (*Italian* al'bɛrti) *n.* **Leon Battista** (le'ɔn bat'tista). 1404–72, Italian Renaissance architect, painter, writer, and musician; among his architectural designs are the façades of Sta. Maria Novella at Florence and S. Francesco at Rimini.

Albertus Magnus (æl'bɜːtəs 'mæɡnəs) *n.* **Saint.** original name *Albert, Count von Böllstadt.* ?1193–1280, German scholastic philosopher; teacher of Thomas Aquinas and commentator on Aristotle. Feast day: Nov. 15.

albescent (æl'bɛsᵊnt) *adj.* shading into or becoming white. [C19: from L *albēscere,* from *albus* white] —**al'bescence** *n.*

Albi (*French* albi) *n.* a town in S France: connected with the Albigensian heresy and the crusade against it. Pop.: 45 291 (1983 est.).

Albigenses (ˌælbɪ'dʒɛnsiːz) *pl. n.* members of a Manichean sect that flourished in S France from the 11th to the 13th century. [from Med. L: inhabitants of ALBI] —**Al'bigensian** *adj.* —ˌAlbi'gensianism *n.*

albino (æl'biːnəʊ) *n., pl.* **-nos. 1.** a person with congenital absence of pigmentation in the skin, eyes, and hair. **2.** any animal or plant that is deficient in pigment. [C18: via Port. & Sp. from L *albus* white] —**albinism** ('ælbɪˌnɪzəm) *n.* —**albinotic** (ˌælbɪ'nɒtɪk) *adj.*

Albinoni (*Italian* albi'noːni) *n.* **Tomaso** (to'maːzo). 1671–1750, Italian composer and violinist. He wrote concertos and over 50 operas.

Albinus (æl'biːnəs) *n.* another name for **Alcuin.**

Albion ('ælbɪən) *n. Arch. or poetic.* Britain or England. [C13: from L, of Celtic origin]

albite ('ælbaɪt) *n.* a white, bluish-green, or reddish-grey feldspar mineral used in the manufacture of glass and as a gemstone. [C19: from L *albus* white]

Alboin ('ælbɔɪn, -bʊɪn) *n.* died 573 A.D., king of the Lombards (565–73); conqueror of N Italy.

Ålborg (*Danish* 'ɔlbɔr) *n.* a variant spelling of **Aalborg.**

album ('ælbəm) *n.* **1.** a book or binder consisting of blank pages, for keeping photographs, stamps, autographs, etc. **2.** one or more long-playing records released as a single item. **3.** a booklike holder containing sleeves for gramophone records. **4.** *Chiefly Brit.* an anthology. [C17: from L: blank tablet, from *albus* white]

albumen ('ælbjʊmɪn) *n.* **1.** the white of an egg; the nutritive substance that surrounds the yolk. **2.** a variant spelling of **albumin.** [C16: from L: white of an egg, from *albus* white]

albumin *or* **albumen** ('ælbjʊmɪn) *n.* any of a group of simple water-soluble proteins that are found in blood plasma, egg white, etc. [C19: from ALBUMEN + -IN] —**al'buminous** *adj.*

albuminuria (æⱡˌbjuːmɪ'njʊərɪə) *n.* the presence of albumin in the urine. Also called: **proteinuria.**

albumose ('ælbjʊˌməʊs) *n.* the U.S. name for **proteose.** [C19: from ALBUMIN + -OSE²]

Albuquerque[1] ('ælbəˌkɜːkɪ) *n.* a city in central New Mexico, on the Rio Grande. Pop.: 366 750 (1986 est.).

Albuquerque[2] ('ælbəˌkɜːkɪ; *Portuguese* albu'kɛrkə) *n.* **Afonso de** (ə'fõsu dɑː). 1453–1515, Portuguese navigator who established Portuguese colonies in the East by conquering Goa, Ceylon, Malacca, and Ormuz.

alburnum (æl'bɜːnəm) *n.* a former name for **sapwood.** [C17: from L: sapwood, from *albus* white]

Albury ('ɔːlbərɪ, -brɪ) *n.* a city in SE Australia, in S central New South Wales, on the Murray River: commercial centre of an agricultural region. Pop.: 35 183 (1986).

Alcaeus (æl'sɪəs) *n.* 7th century B.C., Greek lyric poet who wrote hymns, love songs, and political odes.

Alcaic (æl'keɪɪk) *adj.* **1.** of a metre used by Alcaeus, consisting of a strophe of four lines each with four feet. ~*n.* **2.** (*usually pl.*) verse written in the Alcaic form. [C17: from LL *Alcaicus* of ALCAEUS]

alcalde (æl'kældɪ) *or* **alcade** (æl'keɪd) *n.* (in Spain and Spanish America) the mayor or chief magistrate in a town. [C17: from Sp., from Ar. *al-qādī* the judge]

Alcan Highway ('ælkæn) *n.* original name of the **Alaska Highway.**

Alcatraz ('ælkəˌtræz) *n.* an island in W California, in San Francisco Bay: a federal prison until 1963.

alcazar (ˌælkə'zɑː; *Spanish* al'kaθar) *n.* any of various palaces or fortresses built in Spain by the Moors. [C17: from Sp., from Ar. *al-qasr* the castle]

Alcazar de San Juan ('ælkəˌzɑː; *Spanish* al'kaθar) *n.* a town in S central Spain: associated with Cervantes and Don Quixote. Pop.: 25 185 (1981).

Alcestis (æl'sɛstɪs) *n. Greek myth.* the wife of king Admetus of Thessaly. To save his life, she died in his place, but was rescued from Hades by Hercules.

alchemist ('ælkəmɪst) *n.* a person who practises alchemy.

alchemize *or* **-mise** ('ælkəˌmaɪz) *vb.* (*tr.*) to alter (an element, metal, etc.) by alchemy.

alchemy ('ælkəmɪ) *n., pl.* **-mies. 1.** the pseudoscientific predecessor of chemistry that sought a method of transmuting base metals into gold, and an elixir to prolong life indefinitely. **2.** a power like that of alchemy: *her beauty had a potent alchemy.* [C14 *alkamye,* via OF from Med. L, from Ar., from *al* the + *kīmiyā'* transmutation, from LGk *khēmeia* the art of transmutation] —**alchemic** (æl'kɛmɪk) *or* **al'chemical** *adj.*

alcheringa (ˌæltʃə'rɪŋgə) *n.* (in the mythology of Australian Aboriginal peoples) a mythical Golden Age of the past, when the first men were created. Also called: **dream time.** [from Abor., lit.: dream time]

Alcibiades (ˌælsɪ'baɪəˌdiːz) *n.* 450–404 B.C., Athenian statesman and general in the Peloponnesian War: brilliant, courageous, and unstable, he defected to the Spartans in 415, but returned and led the Athenian victories at Abydos (411) and Cyzicus (410). — ˌAlci,bia'dean *adj.*

Alcides (æl'saɪdiːz) *n.* another name for **Hercules**[1] (sense 1).

Alcinoüs (æl'sɪnəʊəs) *n.* (in Homer's *Odyssey*) a Phaeacian king at whose court the shipwrecked Odysseus told of his wanderings. See also **Nausicaä.**

Alcman ('ælkmən) *n.* 7th century B.C., Greek lyric poet.

Alcmene (ælk'miːnɪ) *n. Greek myth.* the mother of Hercules by Zeus who visited her in the guise of her husband, Amphitryon.

Alcock ('ɔːlkɒk) *n.* Sir **John William.** 1892–1919, English aviator who with A.W. Brown made the first flight across the Atlantic (1919).

alcohol ('ælkəˌhɒl) *n.* **1.** a colourless flammable liquid, the active principle of intoxicating drinks, produced by the fermentation of sugars. Formula: C_2H_5OH. Also called: **ethanol, ethyl alcohol. 2.** a drink or drinks containing this substance. **3.** *Chem.* any one of a class of organic compounds that contain one or more hydroxyl groups bound to carbon atoms that are not part of an aromatic ring. Cf. **phenol** (sense 2). [C16: via NL from Med. L, from Ar. *al-kuhl* powdered antimony]

alcoholic (ˌælkə'hɒlɪk) *n.* **1.** a person affected by alcoholism. ~*adj.* **2.** of, relating to, containing, or resulting from alcohol.

Alcoholics Anonymous *n.* an association of alcoholics who try, esp. by mutual assistance, to overcome alcoholism.

alcoholism ('ælkəhɒˌlɪzəm) *n.* a condition in which dependence on alcohol harms a person's health, family life, etc.

alcoholize *or* **-lise** ('ælkəhɒˌlaɪz) *vb.* (*tr.*) to turn into alcoholic drink, as by fermenting or mixing with alcohol. — ˌalco,holi'zation *or* -li'sation *n.*

Alcoran *or* **Alkoran** (ˌælkɒ'rɑːn) *n.* another name for the **Koran.** — ˌAlco'ranic *or* ˌAlko'ranic *adj.*

Alcott ('ɔːlkət) *n.* **Louisa May.** 1832–88, U.S. novelist, noted for her children's books, esp. *Little Women* (1869).

alcove ('ælkəʊv) *n.* **1.** a recess or niche in the wall of a room, as for a bed, books, etc. **2.** any recessed usually vaulted area, as in a garden wall. **3.** any covered or secluded spot. [C17: from F, from Sp. *alcoba*, from Ar. *al-qubbah* the vault]

Alcuin ('ælkwɪn) *or* **Albinus** *n.* 735–804 A.D., English scholar and theologian; friend and adviser of Charlemagne.

Alcyone (æl'saɪənɪ) *n. Greek myth.* Also called: **Halcyone.** the daughter of Aeolus and wife of Ceyx, who drowned herself in grief for her husband's death. She was transformed into a kingfisher. See also **Ceyx.**

Aldabra (æl'dæbrə) *n.* an island group in the Indian Ocean: part of the British Indian Ocean Territory (1965–76); now administratively part of the Seychelles.

Aldan (*Russian* al'dan) *n.* a river in the Soviet Union in the SE Yakut ASSR, rising in the **Aldan Mountains** and flowing north and west to the Lena River. Length: about 2700 km (1700 miles).

Aldeburgh ('ɔːlbərə) *n.* a small resort in SE England, in Suffolk: site of an annual music festival established in 1948 by Benjamin Britten. Pop.: 3000 (1985 est.).

aldehyde ('ældɪˌhaɪd) *n.* **1.** any organic compound containing the group -CHO. Aldehydes are oxidized to carboxylic acids. **2.** (*modifier*) consisting of, containing, or concerned with the group -CHO. [C19: from NL *al(cohol) dehyd(rogenātum)* dehydrogenated alcohol] —**aldehydic** (ˌældə'hɪdɪk) *adj.*

al dente (æl 'dɛntə) *adj.* (of pasta) still firm after cooking. [It., lit: to the tooth]

alder ('ɔːldə) *n.* **1.** a shrub or tree of the birch family, having toothed leaves and conelike fruits. The wood is used for bridges, etc., because it resists underwater rot. **2.** any of several similar trees or shrubs. [OE *alor*]

alderman ('ɔːldəmən) *n., pl.* **-men. 1.** (in England and Wales until 1974) one of the senior members of a local council, elected by other councillors. **2.** (in the U.S., Canada, etc.) a member of the governing body of a municipality. **3.** *History.* a variant spelling of **ealdorman.** [OE *aldormann*, from *ealdor* chief (comp. of *eald* OLD) + *mann* MAN] —**aldermanic** (ˌɔːldə'mænɪk) *adj.*

Aldermaston ('ɔːldəˌmɑːstən) *n.* a village in S England, in Berkshire southwest of Reading: site of the Atomic Weapons Research Establishment and starting point of the Aldermaston marches (1958–63), organized by the Campaign for Nuclear Disarmament. Pop.: 2157 (1987 est.).

Alderney ('ɔːldənɪ) *n.* **1.** one of the Channel Islands, in the English Channel: separated from the French coast by a dangerous tidal channel (the **Race of Alderney**). Pop.: 2086 (1981 est.). Area: 8 sq. km (3 sq. miles). **2.** any of a breed of dairy cattle originating from the island of Alderney.

Aldershot ('ɔːldəˌʃɒt) *n.* a town in S England, in Hampshire: site of a large military camp. Pop.: 38 000 (1985 est.).

Aldington ('ɔːldɪŋtən) *n.* **Richard.** 1892–1962, English poet, novelist, and biographer. His novels include *Death of a Hero* (1929) and *The Colonel's Daughter* (1931), which reflect postwar disillusion following World War I.

Aldis lamp ('ɔːldɪs) *n.* a portable signalling lamp. [C20: after its inventor A.C.W. *Aldis*]

Aldridge-Brownhills ('ɔːldrɪdʒ'braʊnˌhɪlz) *n.* a town in central England, in N West Midlands: formed by the amalgamation of neighbouring towns in 1966; coalmining. Pop.: 87 219 (1981).

aldrin ('ɔːldrɪn) *n.* a poisonous crystalline solid, mostly $C_{12}H_8Cl_6$, used as an insecticide. [C20: after K. *Alder* (1902–58), G chemist]

Aldrin ('ɔːldrɪn) *n.* **Edwin Eugene Jr.,** known as *Buzz.* born 1930, U.S. astronaut; the second man to set foot on the moon on July 20, 1969, during the Apollo 11 flight.

Aldus Manutius ('ɔːldəs mə'njuːʃɪəs) *n.* 1450–1515, Italian printer, noted for his fine editions of the classics. He introduced italic type. —**Aldine** ('ɔːldaɪn, -diːn) *adj., n.*

ale (eɪl) *n.* **1.** an alcoholic drink made by fermenting a cereal, esp. barley, originally differing from beer by being unflavoured by hops. **2.** *Chiefly Brit.* another word for **beer.** [OE *alu, ealu*]

aleatory ('eɪlɪətərɪ) *or* **aleatoric** (ˌeɪlɪə'tɒrɪk) *adj.* **1.** dependent on chance. **2.** (esp. of a musical composition) involving elements chosen at random by the performer. [C17: from L, from *āleātor* gambler, from *ālea* game of chance]

alec *or* **aleck** ('ælɪk) *n.* **1.** *Austral. sl.* a fool. **2.** See **smart aleck.**

Alecto (ə'lɛktəʊ) *n. Greek myth.* one of the three Furies; the others are Megaera and Tisiphone.

alee (ə'liː) *adv., adj.* (*postpositive*) *Naut.* on or towards the lee: *with the helm alee.*

alehouse ('eɪlˌhaʊs) *n.* **1.** *Arch.* a place where ale was sold; tavern. **2.** *Inf.* a pub.

Alekhine ('ælɪˌkiːn; *Russian* a'ljɔxin) *n.* **Alexander.** 1892–1946, Russian-born chess player who lived in France; world champion (1927–35, 1937–46).

Aleksandropol (*Russian* alıksan'drɔpəlj) *n.* the former name (from 1837 until after the Revolution) of **Leninakan.**

Aleksandrovsk (*Russian* alık'sandrəfsk) *n.* the former name (until 1921) of **Zaporozhye.**

Alemán (*Spanish* ale'man) *n.* **Mateo** (ma'teo). 1547–?1614, Spanish novelist, author of the picaresque novel *Guzmán de Alfarache* (1599).

Alembert, d' (*French* dalɑ̃bɛr) *n.* **Jean Le Rond** (ʒɑ̃ lə rɔ̃). 1717–83, French mathematician, physicist, and rationalist philosopher, noted for his contribution to Newtonian physics in *Traité de dynamique* (1743) and for his collaboration with Diderot in editing the *Encyclopédie.*

alembic (ə'lɛmbɪk) *n.* **1.** an obsolete type of retort used for distillation. **2.** anything that distils or purifies. [C14: from Med. L, from Ar. *al-anbīq* the still, from Gk *ambix* cup]

Alençon (*French* alɑ̃sɔ̃) *n.* a town in NW France: early lace-manufacturing centre. Pop.: 32 939 (1983 est.).

aleph ('ɑːlɪf; *Hebrew* 'alɛf) *n.* the first letter in the Hebrew alphabet. [Heb.: ox]

aleph-null *or* **aleph-zero** *n.* the smallest infinite cardinal number; the cardinal number of the set of positive integers.

Aleppo (ə'lɛpəʊ) *n.* an ancient city in NW Syria: industrial and commercial centre. Pop.: 985 413 (1982 est.). French name: **Alep** (alɛp). Arabic name: **Haleb** ('halɛp).

alert (ə'lɜːt) *adj.* (*usually postpositive*) **1.** vigilantly attentive: *alert to the problems.* **2.** brisk, nimble, or lively. ~*n.* **3.** an alarm or warning. **4.** the period during which such a warning remains in effect. **5. on the alert. a.** on guard against danger, attack, etc. **b.** watchful; ready. ~*vb.* (*tr.*) **6.** to warn or signal (troops, police, etc.) to prepare for action. **7.** to warn of danger, an attack, etc. [C17: from It. *all'erta* on the watch, from *erta* lookout post] —**a'lertly** *adv.* —**a'lertness** *n.*

Alessandria (*Italian* ales'sandrja) *n.* a town in NW Italy, in Piedmont. Pop.: 100 523 (1981).

Ålesund *or* **Aalesund** (*Norwegian* 'ɔːləsun) *n.* a port and market town in W Norway, on an island between Bergen and Trondheim: fishing and sealing fleets. Pop.: 35 314 (1987).

alethic (ə'liːθɪk) *adj. Logic.* designating the branch of modal logic dealing with necessary, contingent, and impossible truths. [C20: from Gk *alētheia* truth]

aleurone (ə'lʊərən) *or* **aleuron** (ə'lʊərɒn) *n.* a protein that occurs in the form of storage granules in plant cells, esp. in seeds such as maize. [C19: from Gk *aleuron* flour]

Aleut (æ'luːt) *n.* **1.** a member of a people inhabiting the Aleutian Islands and SW Alaska, related to the Eskimos. **2.** the language of this people, related to Eskimo. [from Russian *aleút*, prob. of native origin] —**Aleutian** (ə'luːʃən) *n., adj.*

Aleutian Islands *n.* a chain of over 150 volcanic islands, extending southwestwards from the Alaska Peninsula between the N Pacific and the Bering Sea.

A level *n. Brit.* **1. a.** the advanced level of a subject taken for the General Certificate of Education. **b.** (*as modifier*): *A-level maths.* **2.** a pass in a subject at A level: *he has two A levels.*

alewife ('eɪl,waɪf) *n., pl.* **-wives.** a North American fish similar to the herring. [C19: ?from F *alose* shad]

Alexander (,ælɪg'zɑːndə) *n.* **Harold** (**Rupert Leofric George**), Earl Alexander of Tunis. 1891–1969, British field marshal in World War II, who organized the retreat from Dunkirk and commanded the victories of North Africa (1943) and Sicily and Italy (1944–45); governor general of Canada (1946–52); British minister of defence (1952–54).

Alexander I *n.* **1.** *c.* 1080–1124, king of Scotland (1107–24), son of Malcolm III. **2.** 1777–1825, tsar of Russia (1801–25), who helped defeat Napoleon and formed the Holy Alliance (1815).

Alexander II *n.* **1.** 1198–1249, king of Scotland (1214–49), son of William I. **2.** 1818–81, tsar of Russia (1855–81), son of Nicholas I, who emancipated the serfs (1861). He was assassinated by the Nihilists.

Alexander III *n.* **1.** 1241–86, king of Scotland (1249–86), son of Alexander II. **2.** original name *Orlando Bandinelli.* died 1181, pope (1159–81), who excommunicated Barbarossa. **3.** 1845–94, tsar of Russia (1881–94), son of Alexander II.

Alexander VI *n.* original name *Rodrigo Borgia.* 1431–1503, pope (1492–1503): noted for his extravagance and immorality as well as for his patronage of the arts; father of Cesare and Lucrezia Borgia, with whom he is said to have committed incest.

Alexander Archipelago *n.* a group of over 1000 islands along the coast of SE Alaska.

Alexander I Island *n.* an island of Antarctica, west of Palmer Land, in the Bellingshausen Sea. Length: about 378 km (235 miles).

Alexander Nevski ('nɛvskɪ, 'nɛf-; *Russian* 'njɛfskij) *n.* **Saint.** ?1220–63, Russian prince and military leader, who defeated the Swedes at the River Neva (1240) and the Teutonic knights at Lake Peipus (1242).

Alexander the Great *n.* 356–323 B.C., king of Macedon, who conquered Greece (336), Egypt (331), and the Persian Empire (328), and founded Alexandria.

Alexandra (,ælɪg'zɑːndrə) *n.* 1844–1925, queen consort of Edward VII of Great Britain and Ireland.

Alexandretta (,ælɪgzɑːn'drɛtə) *n.* the former name of **Iskenderun.**

Alexandria (,ælɪg'zændrɪə, -'zɑːn-) *n.* the chief port of Egypt, on the Nile Delta: cultural centre of ancient times, founded by Alexander the Great (332 B.C.). Pop.: 2 821 000 (1985). Arabic name: **El Iskandariyah.** —,**Alex'andrian** *adj., n.*

Alexandrine (,ælɪg'zændraɪn) *n.* **1.** a line of verse having six iambic feet, usually with a caesura after the third foot. ~*adj.* **2.** of or written in Alexandrines. [C16: from F, from *Alexandre,* 15th-cent. poem in this metre]

alexandrite (,ælɪg'zændraɪt) *n.* a green variety of chrysoberyl used as a gemstone. [C19: after ALEXANDER I of Russia; see -ITE[1]]

Alexandroúpolis (*Greek* alɛksan'ðrupɔlis) *n.* a port in NE Greece, in W Thrace. Pop.: 35 856 (1981). Former name (until the end of World War I): **Dedéagach.**

alexia (ə'lɛksɪə) *n.* a disorder of the central nervous system characterized by impaired ability to read. [C19: from NL, from A-[1] + Gk *lexis* speech]

Alexis Mikhailovich (ə'lɛksɪs mɪ'kaɪlə,vɪtʃ) *n.* 1629–76, tsar of Russia (1645–76); father of Peter the Great.

Alexius I Comnenus (ə'lɛksɪəs; kɒm'niːnəs) *n.* 1048–1118, ruler of the Byzantine Empire (1081–1118).

alfalfa (æl'fælfə) *n.* a leguminous plant of Europe and Asia, widely cultivated for forage. Also called: **lucerne.** [C19: from Sp., from Ar. *al-faṣfaṣah*]

Alfieri (*Italian* al'fjɛri) *n.* **Count Vittorio** (vit'tɔːrjo). 1749–1803, Italian dramatist and poet, noted for his classical tragedies and political satires.

Alfonso XIII (*Spanish* al'fonso) *n.* 1886–1941, king of Spain (1886–1931), who was forced to abdicate on the establishment of the republic in 1931.

Alfred the Great ('ælfrɪd) *n.* 849–99, king of Wessex (871–99) and overlord of England, who defeated the Danes and encouraged learning and writing in English.

alfresco (æl'frɛskəʊ) *adj., adv.* in the open air. [C18: from It.: in the cool]

Alfvén (al'ven) *n.* **Hannes Olaf Gösta** ('hanɛs 'uːlaf 'jøsta). born 1908, Swedish physicist, noted for his research on magnetohydrodynamics; shared the Nobel prize for physics in 1970.

alg. *abbrev. for* algebra *or* algebraic.

algae ('ældʒiː) *pl. n., sing.* **alga** ('ælgə). unicellular or multicellular plants, occurring in water or moist ground, that have chlorophyll but lack true stems, roots, and leaves. [C16: from L, pl. of *alga* seaweed, from ?] —**algal** ('ælgəl) *or* **algoid** ('ælgɔɪd) *adj.*

Algarve (æl'gɑːv) *n.* **the.** the southernmost province of Portugal, on the Atlantic; it corresponds to the administrative district of Faro: fishing and tourism important. Pop.: 322 900 (1981 est.). Area: 5071 sq. km (1957 sq. miles).

algebra ('ældʒɪbrə) *n.* **1.** a branch of mathematics in which arithmetical operations and relationships are generalized by using symbols to represent numbers. **2.** any abstract calculus, a formal language in which functions and operations can be defined and their properties studied. [C14: from Med. L, from Ar. *al-jabr* the bone-setting, mathematical reduction] —**algebraic** (,ældʒɪ'breɪɪk) *or* ,**alge'braical** *adj.* —**algebraist** (,ældʒɪ'breɪɪst) *n.*

Algeciras (,ældʒɪ'sɪrəs; *Spanish* alxe'θiras) *n.* a port and resort in SW Spain, on the Strait of Gibraltar: scene of a conference of the Great Powers in 1906. Pop.: 86 042 (1981).

Alger ('ældʒə) *n.* **Horatio.** 1834–99, U.S. author of adventure stories for boys, including *Ragged Dick* (1867).

Algeria (æl'dʒɪərɪə) *n.* a republic in NW Africa, on the Mediterranean: became independent in 1962, after more than a century of French rule; consists chiefly of the N Sahara, with the Atlas Mountains in the north, and contains rich deposits of oil and natural gas. Official language: Arabic; French also widely spoken. Religion: Muslim. Currency: dinar. Capital: Algiers. Pop.: 23 546 000 (1988 est.). Area: about 2 382 800 sq. km (920 000 sq. miles). French name: **Algérie** (alʒeri). —**Al'gerian** *or* **Algerine** ('ældʒə,riːn) *adj., n.*

-algia *n. combining form.* denoting pain in the part specified: *neuralgia; odontalgia.* [from Gk *algos* pain] —**algic** *adj. combining form.*

algid ('ældʒɪd) *adj. Med.* chilly or cold. [C17: from L *algidus,* from *algēre* to be cold] —**al'gidity** *n.*

Algiers (æl'dʒɪəz) *n.* the capital of Algeria, an ancient port on the Mediterranean; up to 1830 a centre of piracy. Pop.: 1 860 000 (1984 est.). Arabic name: **Al-Jezair** (,ældʒɛ-'zɑːɪə). French name: **Alger** (alʒe).

alginate ('ældʒɪ,neɪt) *n.* a salt or ester of alginic acid.

alginic acid (æl'dʒɪnɪk) *n.* a white or yellowish powdery substance having hydrophilic properties. Extracted from kelp, it is used mainly in the food and textile industries.

ALGOL ('ælgɒl) *n.* a computer programming language designed for mathematical and scientific purposes. [C20 *alg(orithmic) o(riented) l(anguage)*]

algolagnia (,ælgə'lægnɪə) *n.* sexual pleasure got from suffering or inflicting pain. [ML, from Gk *algos* pain + *lagneiā* lust]

Algonquian (æl'gɒŋkɪən, -kwɪ-) *or* **Algonkian** *n.* **1.** a widespread family of North American Indian languages. **2.** (*pl.* **-ans** *or* **-an**) a member of any of the North American Indian peoples that speak any of these languages. ~*adj.* **3.** denoting or relating to this linguistic family or its speakers.

Algonquin (æl'gɒŋkɪn, -kwɪn) *or* **Algonkin** (æl'gɒŋkɪn) *n.* **1.** (*pl.* **quins, quin** *or* **kins, kin**) a member of a North American Indian people formerly living along the St Lawrence and Ottawa Rivers in Canada. **2.** the language of this people, a dialect of Ojibwa. ~*n., adj.* **3.** a variant of **Algonquian.** [C17: from Canad. F., earlier written as *Algoumequin;* perhaps rel. to Micmac *algoomaking* at the fish-spearing place]

Algonquin Park *n.* a provincial park in S Canada, in E Ontario, containing over 1200 lakes. Area: 7100 sq. km (2741 sq. miles).

algorism ('ælgə,rɪzəm) *n.* **1.** the Arabic or decimal system of counting. **2.** the skill of computation. **3.** an algorithm. [C13: from OF, from Med. L, from Ar., from the name of abu-Ja'far Mohammed ibn-Mūsa *al-Khuwārizmi*, 9th-cent. Persian mathematician]

algorithm ('ælgə,rɪðəm) *n.* **1.** a logical arithmetical or computational procedure that if correctly applied ensures the solution of a problem. **2.** *Logic, maths.* a recursive procedure whereby an infinite sequence of terms can be generated. ~Also called: **algorism.** [C17: changed from ALGORISM, infl. by Gk *arithmos* number] —**algo'rithmic** *adj.*

Alhambra (æl'hæmbrə) *n.* a citadel and palace in Granada, Spain, built for the Moorish kings during the 13th and 14th centuries: noted for its rich ornamentation. —**Alhambresque** (,ælhæm'brɛsk) *adj.*

Al Hasa (ɑːl 'hɑːsə) *n.* the former name of the **Eastern Province.**

Al Hufuf *or* **Al Hofuf** (æl hʊ'fuːf) *n.* a town in E Saudi Arabia: a trading centre with nearby oilfields and oases. Pop.: 101 271 (1974).

Ali ('ɑːliː) *n.* **1.** ?600–661 A.D., fourth caliph of Islam (656–61 A.D.), considered the first caliph by the Shiites: cousin and son-in-law of Mohammed. **2. Mehemet.** See **Mehemet Ali. 3. Muhammad.** See **Muhammad Ali.**

alias ('eɪlɪəs) *adv.* **1.** at another time or place known as or named: *Dylan,* alias *Zimmerman.* ~*n., pl.* **-ases. 2.** an assumed name. [C16: from L *aliās* (adv.) otherwise, from *alius* other]

alibi ('ælɪ,baɪ) *n., pl.* **-bis. 1.** *Law.* **a.** a defence by an accused person that he was elsewhere at the time the crime was committed. **b.** the evidence given to prove this. **2.** *Inf.* an excuse. ~*vb.* **3.** (*tr.*) to provide with an alibi. [C18: from L *alibī* elsewhere, from *alius* other + *-bī* as in *ubī* where]

▷ **Usage.** The noun *alibi* is often used informally to mean an excuse: *he was late but, as always, had a good alibi.* In formal English, however, only the legal sense is acceptable.

Alicante (,ælɪ'kæntɪ) *n.* a port in SE Spain: commercial centre. Pop.: 245 963 (1981).

Alice-in-Wonderland *adj.* fantastic; irrational. [C20: alluding to the absurdities of Wonderland in Lewis Carroll's book]

Alice Springs *n.* a town in central Australia, in the Northern Territory, in the Macdonnell Ranges: capital of the former territory of Central Australia. Pop.: 22 759 (1986). Former name (until 1931): **Stuart.**

alicyclic (,ælɪ'saɪklɪk, -'sɪk-) *adj.* (of an organic compound) having essentially aliphatic properties, in spite of the presence of a ring of carbon atoms. [C19: from AL-I(PHATIC) + CYCLIC]

alidade ('ælɪ,deɪd) *or* **alidad** ('ælɪ,dæd) *n.* **1.** a surveying instrument used for drawing lines of sight on a distant object and taking angular measurements. **2.** the upper rotatable part of a theodolite. [C15: from F, from Med. L, from Ar. *al-'idāda* the revolving radius of a circle]

alien ('eɪlɪən) *n.* **1.** a person owing allegiance to a country other than that in which he lives. **2.** any being or thing foreign to its environment. **3.** (in science fiction) a being from another world. ~*adj.* **4.** unnaturalized; foreign. **5.** having foreign allegiance: *alien territory.* **6.** unfamiliar: *an alien quality.* **7.** (*postpositive;* foll. by *to*) repugnant or opposed (to): *war is alien to his philosophy.* **8.** (in science fiction) of or from another world. [C14: from L *aliēnus* foreign, from *alius* other]

alienable ('eɪlɪənəb²l) *adj. Law.* (of property) transferable to another owner. —**,aliena'bility** *n.*

alienate ('eɪlɪə,neɪt) *vb.* (*tr.*) **1.** to cause (a friend, etc.) to become unfriendly or hostile. **2.** to turn away: *to alienate the affections of a person.* **3.** *Law.* to transfer the ownership of (property, etc.) to another person. —**,alien'ation** *n.* —**'alien,ator** *n.*

alienee (,eɪlɪə'niː) *n. Law.* a person to whom a transfer of property is made.

alienist ('eɪlɪənɪst) *n. U.S.* a psychiatrist who specializes in the legal aspects of mental illness.

alienor ('eɪlɪənə) *n. Law.* a person who transfers property to another.

aliform ('ælɪ,fɔːm) *adj.* wing-shaped. [C19: from NL *āliformis,* from L *āla* a wing]

Aligarh (,ɑːlɪ'gɜː, ,ælɪ-) *n.* a city in N India, in W Uttar Pradesh, with a famous Muslim university (1920). Pop.: 319 981 (1981).

alight[1] (ə'laɪt) *vb.* **alighting, alighted** *or* **alit.** (*intr.*) **1.** (usually foll. by *from*) to step out (of): *to alight from a taxi.* **2.** to come to rest; land: *a thrush alighted on the wall.* [OE *ālihtan,* from A-[2] + *lihtan* to make less heavy]

alight[2] (ə'laɪt) *adj.* (*postpositive*), *adv.* **1.** burning; on fire. **2.** illuminated. [OE, from *ālihtan* to light up]

align (ə'laɪn) *vb.* **1.** to place or become placed in a line. **2.** to bring (components or parts) into proper coordination or relation. **3.** (*tr.;* usually foll. by *with*) to bring (a person, country, etc.) into agreement with the policy, etc., of another. [C17: from OF, from *à ligne* into line]

alignment (ə'laɪnmənt) *n.* **1.** arrangement in a straight line. **2.** the line or lines formed in this manner. **3.** alliance with a party, cause, etc. **4.** proper coordination or relation of components. **5.** a ground plan of a railway, road, etc.

alike (ə'laɪk) *adj.* (*postpositive*) **1.** possessing the same or similar characteristics: *they all look alike.* ~*adv.* **2.** in the same or a similar manner or degree: *they walk alike.* [OE *gelīc*]

aliment ('ælɪmənt) *n.* something that nourishes or sustains the body or mind. [C15: from L *alimentum* food, from *alere* to nourish] —**,ali'mental** *adj.*

alimentary (,ælɪ'mɛntərɪ) *adj.* **1.** of or relating to nutrition. **2.** providing sustenance or nourishment.

alimentary canal *n.* the tubular passage extending from the mouth to the anus, through which food is passed and digested.

alimentation (,ælɪmɛn'teɪʃən) *n.* **1.** nourishment. **2.** sustenance; support.

alimony ('ælɪmənɪ) *n. Law.* (formerly) an allowance paid under a court order by one spouse to another when they are separated but not divorced. See also **maintenance.** [C17: from L, from *alere* to nourish]

aline (ə'laɪn) *vb.* a rare spelling of **align.** —**a'linement** *n.*

A-line ('eɪ,laɪn) *adj.* (of garments) flaring out slightly from the waist or shoulders.

Ali Pasha ('ɑːliː 'pɑːʃə) *n.* known as *the Lion of Janina.* 1741–1822, Turkish pasha and ruler of Albania (1787–1820), who was deposed and assassinated after intriguing against Turkey.

aliphatic (,ælɪ'fætɪk) *adj.* (of an organic compound) not aromatic, esp. having an open chain structure. [C19: from Gk *aleiphar,* aleiphar- oil]

aliquant ('ælɪkwənt) *adj. Maths.* of or signifying a quantity or number that is not an exact divisor of a given quantity or number: *5 is an aliquant part of 12.* [C17: from NL, from L *aliquantus* somewhat, a certain quantity of]

aliquot ('ælɪ,kwɒt) *adj. Maths.* of or signifying an exact divisor of a quantity or number: *3 is an aliquot part of 12.* [C16: from L: several, a few]

alit (ə'lɪt) *vb.* a rare past tense and past participle of **alight**[1].

alive (ə'laɪv) *adj.* (*postpositive*) **1.** living; having life. **2.** in existence; active: *they kept hope alive*. **3.** (*immediately postpositive*) now living: *the happiest woman alive*. **4.** full of life; lively. **5.** (usually foll. by *with*) animated: *a face alive with emotion*. **6.** (foll. by *to*) aware (of); sensitive (to). **7.** (foll. by *with*) teeming (with): *the mattress was alive with fleas*. **8.** *Electronics.* another word for **live**[2] (sense 10). [OE *on līfe* in LIFE]

alizarin (ə'lɪzərɪn) *n.* a brownish-yellow powder or orange-red crystalline solid used as a dye. [C19: prob. from F, from Ar. *al-'asārah* the juice, from *'asara* to squeeze]

alkali ('ælkə,laɪ) *n.*, *pl.* **-lis** *or* **-lies**. **1.** *Chem.* a soluble base or a solution of a base. **2.** a soluble mineral salt that occurs in arid soils. [C14: from Med. L, from Ar. *al-qili* the ashes (of saltwort)]

alkali metal *n.* any of the monovalent metals lithium, sodium, potassium, rubidium, caesium, and francium.

alkaline ('ælkə,laɪn) *adj.* having the properties of or containing an alkali. —**alkalinity** (,ælkə'lɪnɪtɪ) *n.*

alkaline earth *n.* **1.** Also called: **alkaline earth metal.** any of the divalent electropositive metals beryllium, magnesium, calcium, strontium, barium, and radium. **2.** an oxide of one of the alkaline earth metals.

alkalize *or* **-lise** ('ælkə,laɪz) *vb.* (*tr.*) to make alkaline. —'**alka,lizable** *or* -,**lisable** *adj.*

alkaloid ('ælkə,lɔɪd) *n.* any of a group of nitrogenous compounds found in plants. Many are poisonous and some are used as drugs.

alkane ('ælkeɪn) *n.* any saturated aliphatic hydrocarbon with the general formula C_nH_{2n+2}. Former name: **paraffin.**

alkane series *n.* a homologous series of saturated hydrocarbons starting with methane and having the general formula C_nH_{2n+2}. Also called: **methane series.**

alkanet ('ælkə,nɛt) *n.* **1.** a European plant, the roots of which yield a red dye. **2.** the dye obtained. [C14: from Sp., from Med. L, from Ar. *al* the + *hinnā'* henna]

alkene ('ælki:n) *n.* any unsaturated aliphatic hydrocarbon with the general formula C_nH_{2n}. Former name: **olefine.**

alkene series *n.* a homologous series of unsaturated hydrocarbons starting with ethylene (ethene) and having the general formula C_2H_{2n}. Also called: **ethylene series, ethene series.**

Alkmaar (*Dutch* 'alkma:r) *n.* a city in the W Netherlands, in North Holland. Pop.: 87 034 (1987).

Alkoran *or* **Alcoran** (,ælkɒ'ra:n) *n.* a less common name for the **Koran.**

alkyd resin ('ælkɪd) *n.* any of several synthetic resins made from a dicarboxylic acid, used in paints and adhesives.

alkyl ('ælkɪl) *n.* (*modifier*) of or containing the monovalent group C_nH_{2n+1}: *alkyl radical*. [C19: from G, from *Alk(ohol)* ALCOHOL + -YL]

alkyne ('ælkaɪn) *n.* any unsaturated aliphatic hydrocarbon with the general formula C_nH_{2n-2}.

alkyne series *n.* a homologous series of unsaturated hydrocarbons starting with acetylene (ethyne) and having the general formula C_nH_{2n-2}. Also called: **acetylene series.**

all (ɔːl) *determiner.* **1. a.** the whole quantity or amount of: *all the rice*. **b.** (*as pronoun; functioning as sing. or pl.*): *all of it is nice; all are welcome.* **2.** every one of a class: *all men are mortal.* **3.** the greatest possible: *in all earnestness.* **4.** any whatever: *beyond all doubt.* **5. all along.** all the time. **6. all but.** nearly: *all but dead.* **7. all of.** no less or smaller than: *she's all of thirteen years.* **8. all over. a.** finished. **b.** everywhere (in, on, etc.): *all over England.* **c.** *Inf.* typically (in **that's me** (**him**, etc.) **all over**). **d.** unduly effusive towards. **9. all in all. a.** everything considered: *all in all, it was a great success.* **b.** the object of one's attention: *you are my all in all.* **10. all the.** (foll. by a comp. adj. or adv.) so much (more or less) than otherwise: *we must work all the faster now.* **11. at all. a.** (*used with a negative or in a question*) in any way or to any degree: *I didn't know that at all.* **b.** anyway: *I'm surprised you came at all.* **12. be all for.** *Inf.* to be strongly in favour of. **13. for all. a.** in so far as: *for all anyone knows, he was a baron.* **b.** notwithstanding: *for all my pushing, I still couldn't move it.* **14. for all that.** in spite of that: *he was a nice man for all that.* **15. in all.** altogether: *there were five in all.* ~*adv.* **16.** (in scores of games) apiece; each: *the score was three all.* ~*n.* **17.** (preceded by *my, his,* etc.) (one's) complete effort or interest: *to give your all.* **18.** totality or whole. [OE *eall*]

all- *combining form.* a variant of **allo-** before a vowel.

alla breve ('ælə 'breɪvɪ) *Music.* ~*adj., adv.* **1.** with two beats to the bar instead of four, i.e. twice as fast as written. ~*n.* **2.** (formerly) a time of two or four minims to the bar. Symbol: ¢ [C19: It., lit.: according to the breve]

Allah ('ælə) *n.* the name of God in Islam. [C16: from Ar., from *al* the + *Ilāh* god]

Allahabad (,æləhə'bæd, -'ba:d) *n.* a city in N India, in SE Uttar Pradesh at the confluence of the Ganges and Jumna Rivers: Hindu pilgrimage centre. Pop.: 609 232 (1981).

all-American *adj.* *U.S.* **1.** representative of the whole of the United States. **2.** composed exclusively of American members. **3.** (of a person) typically American.

allantois (,ælən'təʊɪs, ə'læntɔɪs) *n.* a membranous sac growing out of the ventral surface of the hind gut of embryonic reptiles, birds, and mammals. [C17: NL, from Gk *allantoeidēs* sausage-shaped] —**allantoic** (,ælən'təʊɪk) *adj.*

allay (ə'leɪ) *vb.* **1.** to relieve (pain, grief, etc.) or be relieved. **2.** (*tr.*) to reduce (fear, anger, etc.). [OE *ālecgan* to put down]

All Blacks *pl. n.* **the.** the international Rugby Union football team of New Zealand. [so named because of the players' black strip]

all clear *n.* **1.** a signal indicating that some danger, such as an air raid, is over. **2.** permission to proceed.

allegation (,ælɪ'geɪʃən) *n.* **1.** the act of alleging. **2.** an unproved assertion, esp. an accusation.

allege (ə'lɛdʒ) *vb.* (*tr.; may take a clause as object*) **1.** to state without or before proof: *he alleged malpractice.* **2.** to put forward (an argument or plea) for or against an accusation, claim, etc. [C14 *aleggen*, ult. from L *allēgāre* to dispatch on a mission, from *lēx* law]

alleged (ə'lɛdʒd) *adj.* (*prenominal*) **1.** stated to be such: *the alleged murderer.* **2.** dubious: *an alleged miracle.* —**allegedly** (ə'lɛdʒɪdlɪ) *adv.*

Allegheny Mountains (,ælɪ'geɪnɪ) *or* **Alleghenies** *pl. n.* a mountain range in Pennsylvania, Maryland, Virginia, and West Virginia: part of the Appalachian system; rising from 600 m (2000 ft.) to over 1440 m (4800 ft.).

allegiance (ə'liːdʒəns) *n.* **1.** loyalty, as of a subject to his sovereign. **2.** (in feudal society) the obligations of a vassal to his liege lord. [C14: from OF, from *lige* LIEGE]

allegorical (,ælɪ'gɒrɪk³l) *or* **allegoric** *adj.* used in, containing, or characteristic of allegory.

allegorize *or* **-ise** ('ælɪgə,raɪz) *vb.* **1.** to transform (a story, fable, etc.) into or compose in the form of allegory. **2.** (*tr.*) to interpret allegorically. —,**allegori'zation** *or* -**i'sation** *n.*

allegory ('ælɪgərɪ) *n.*, *pl.* **-ries.** **1.** a poem, play, picture, etc., in which the apparent meaning of the characters and events is used to symbolize a moral or spiritual meaning. **2.** use of such symbolism. **3.** anything used as a symbol. [C14: from OF, from L, from Gk, from *allēgorein* to speak figuratively, from *allos* other + *agoreuein* to make a speech in public] —'**allegorist** *n.*

allegretto (,ælɪ'grɛtəʊ) *Music.* ~*adj., adv.* **1.** (to be performed) fairly quickly or briskly. ~*n.*, *pl.* **-tos. 2.** a piece or passage to be performed in this manner. [C19: dim. of ALLEGRO]

allegro (ə'leɪgrəʊ, -'lɛg-) *Music.* ~*adj., adv.* **1.** (to be performed) in a brisk lively manner. ~*n.*, *pl.* **-gros. 2.** a piece or passage to be performed in this manner. [C17: from It.: cheerful, from L *alacer* brisk, lively]

allele (ə'liːl) *n.* any of two or more genes that are responsible for alternative characteristics, such as smooth or wrinkled seeds in peas. Also called: **allelomorph** (ə'liːlə,mɔːf). [C20: from G *Allel*, from *Allelomorph*, from Gk *allēl-* one another + *morphē* form]

alleluia (,ælɪ'luːjə) *interj.* praise the Lord! Used in liturgical contexts in place of *hallelujah*. [C14: via Med. L from Heb. *hallelūyāh*]

allemande ('ælɪmænd) *n.* **1.** the first movement of the classical suite, composed in a moderate tempo. **2.** any of several German dances. **3.** a figure in country dancing or square dancing by which couples change position in the set. [C17: from F *danse allemande* German dance]

Allen[1] ('ælən) *n.* **1. Bog of.** a region of peat bogs in central Ireland, west of Dublin. Area: over 10 sq. km (3.75 sq. miles). **2. Lough.** a lake in Ireland, in county Leitrim.

Allen[2] ('ælən) *n.* **1. Ethan.** 1738–89, American soldier during the War of Independence who led the Green Mountain Boys of Vermont. **2. Woody.** real name *Allen Stewart Konigsberg.* born 1935, U.S. film comedian, screenwriter, and director. His films as an actor include *Play it again, Sam* (1973), *Annie Hall* (1977), *Manhattan* (1979), and *Hannah and Her Sisters* (1986). He also directed *Annie Hall, Interiors* (1978), *Manhattan, Hannah and Her Sisters*, and *September* (1988).

Allenby ('ælənbɪ) *n.* **Edmund Henry Hynman,** 1st Viscount Allenby. 1861–1936, British field marshal who captured Palestine from the Turks in 1918; high commissioner in Egypt (1919–25).

Allende (*Spanish* a'ʎende) *n.* **Salvador** (salβa'ðor). 1908–73, Chilean Marxist politician; president of Chile from 1970 until 1973, when the army seized power and he was killed.

Allentown ('ælən,taun) *n.* a city in E Pennsylvania, on the Lehigh River. Pop.: 103 758 (1980).

Alleppey ('ʌləpɪ) *n.* a port in S India, in Kerala on the Malabar Coast. Pop.: 169 940 (1981).

allergen ('ælə,dʒɛn) *n.* any substance capable of inducing an allergy. —,**aller'genic** *adj.*

allergic (ə'lɜːdʒɪk) *adj.* **1.** of, having, or caused by an allergy. **2.** (*postpositive;* foll. *by to*) *Inf.* having an aversion (to): *allergic to work.*

allergist ('ælədʒɪst) *n.* a physician skilled in the treatment of allergies.

allergy ('ælədʒɪ) *n., pl.* **-gies. 1.** a hypersensitivity to a substance that causes the body to react to any contact with it. Hay fever is an allergic reaction to pollen. **2.** *Inf.* an aversion. [C20: from G *Allergie* (indicating a changed reaction), from Gk *allos* other + *ergon* activity]

alleviate (ə'liːvɪ,eɪt) *vb.* (*tr.*) to make (pain, sorrow, etc.) easier to bear; lessen. [C15: from LL, from L *levis* light] —**al,levi'ation** *n.* —**al'levi,ator** *n.*

alley[1] ('ælɪ) *n.* **1.** a narrow passage, esp. one between or behind buildings. **2.** See **bowling alley. 3.** *Tennis, chiefly U.S.* the space between the singles and doubles sidelines. **4.** a walk in a garden, esp. one lined with trees. **5. up** (*or* **down**) **one's alley.** *Sl.* suited to one's abilities or interests. [C14: from OF, from *aler* to go, ult. from L *ambulāre* to walk]

alley[2] ('ælɪ) *n.* a large playing marble. [C18: shortened and changed from ALABASTER]

alleyway ('ælɪ,weɪ) *n.* a narrow passage; alley.

All Fools' Day *n.* another name for **April Fools' Day** (see **April fool**).

all found *adj.* (of charges for accommodation) inclusive of meals, heating, etc.

all hail *sentence substitute.* an archaic greeting or salutation. [C14, lit.: all health (to someone)]

Allhallows (,ɔːl'hæləuz) *n.* a less common term for **All Saints' Day.**

alliaceous (,ælɪ'eɪʃəs) *adj.* **1.** of or relating to a genus of plants that have a strong smell and often have bulbs. The genus occurs in the N hemisphere and includes onion and garlic. **2.** tasting or smelling like garlic or onions. [C18: from L *allium* garlic]

alliance (ə'laɪəns) *n.* **1.** the act of allying or state of being allied; union. **2.** a formal agreement, esp. a military one, between two or more countries. **3.** the countries involved. **4.** a union between families through marriage. **5.** affinity or correspondence in characteristics. **6.** *Bot.* a taxonomic category consisting of a group of related families. [C13: from OF, from *alier* to ALLY]

allied (ə'laɪd, 'ælaɪd) *adj.* **1.** joined, as by treaty or marriage; united. **2.** of the same type or class.

Allied ('ælaɪd) *adj.* of or relating to the Allies.

Allier (*French* alje) *n.* **1.** a department of central France, in Auvergne region. Capital: Moulins. Pop.: 369 580 (1982). Area: 7382 sq. km (2879 sq. miles). **2.** a river in S central France, rising in the Cévennes and flowing north to the Loire. Length: over 403 km (250 miles).

Allies ('ælaɪz) *pl. n.* **1.** (in World War I) the powers of the Triple Entente (France, Russia, and Britain) together with the nations allied with them. **2.** (in World War II) the countries that fought against the Axis and Japan, esp. Britain and the Commonwealth countries, the U.S., the Soviet Union, China, Poland, and France.

alligator ('ælɪ,geɪtə) *n.* **1.** a large crocodilian of the southern U.S., having powerful jaws but differing from the crocodiles in having a shorter and broader snout. **2.** a

similar but smaller species occurring in China. **3.** any of various tools or machines having adjustable toothed jaws. [C17: from Sp. *el lagarto* the lizard, from L *lacerta*]

alligator pear *n.* another name for **avocado.**

all-important *adj.* crucial; vital.

all in *adj.* **1.** (*postpositive*) *Inf.* completely exhausted. ~*adv., adj.* (**all-in** *when prenominal*). **2.** with all expenses included: *twenty pounds a week all in.* **3.** (of wrestling) in freestyle.

Allingham ('ælɪŋəm) *n.* **Margery.** 1904–66, English author of detective stories, featuring Albert Campion. Her works include *Tiger in the Smoke* (1952) and *The Mind Readers* (1965).

alliterate (ə'lɪtə,reɪt) *vb.* **1.** to contain or cause to contain alliteration. **2.** (*intr.*) to speak or write using alliteration.

alliteration (ə,lɪtə'reɪʃən) *n.* the use of the same consonant (**consonantal alliteration**) or of a vowel (**vocalic alliteration**), at the beginning of each word or stressed syllable in a line of verse, as in *around the rock the ragged rascal ran.* [C17: from L *litera* letter] —**al'literative** *adj.*

allium ('ælɪəm) *n.* a genus of liliaceous plants that includes the onion, garlic, shallot, leek, and chive. [C19: from L: garlic]

allo- *or before a vowel* **all-** *combining form.* indicating difference, variation, or opposition: *allopathy; allomorph.* [from Gk *allos* other, different]

Alloa ('æləuə) *n.* a town in E central Scotland, in Central region. Pop.: 26 930 (1981).

allocate ('ælə,keɪt) *vb.* (*tr.*) **1.** to assign for a particular purpose. **2.** a less common word for **locate** (sense 2). [C17: from Med. L, from L *locus* a place] —'**allo,catable** *adj.* —,**allo'cation** *n.*

allocution (,ælə'kjuːʃən) *n. Rhetoric.* a formal or authoritative speech or address. [C17: from LL *allocūtiō*, from L *alloquī* to address]

allomerism (ə'lɒmə,rɪzəm) *n.* similarity of crystalline structure in substances of different chemical composition. —**al'lomerous** *adj.*

allomorph ('ælə,mɔːf) *n.* **1.** *Linguistics.* any of the representations of a single morpheme. For example, the final (s) and (z) sounds of *bets* and *beds* are allomorphs. **2.** any of the different crystalline forms of a chemical compound, such as a mineral. —,**allo'morphic** *adj.*

allopath ('ælə,pæθ) *or* **allopathist** (ə'lɒpəθɪst) *n.* a person who practises or is skilled in allopathy.

allopathy (ə'lɒpəθɪ) *n.* the usual method of treating disease, by inducing a condition different from the cause of the disease. Cf. **homeopathy.** —**allopathic** (,ælə'pæθɪk) *adj.*

allophone ('ælə,fəun) *n.* any of several speech sounds regarded as variants of the same phoneme. In English the aspirated initial (p) in *pot* and the unaspirated (p) in *spot* are allophones of the phoneme /p/. —**allophonic** (,ælə'fɒnɪk) *adj.*

allot (ə'lɒt) *vb.* **-lotting, -lotted.** (*tr.*) **1.** to assign or distribute (shares, etc.). **2.** to designate for a particular purpose; apportion: *we allotted two hours to the case.* [C16: from OF, from *lot* portion]

allotment (ə'lɒtmənt) *n.* **1.** the act of allotting. **2.** a portion or amount allotted. **3.** *Brit.* a small piece of land rented by an individual for cultivation.

allotrope ('ælə,trəup) *n.* any of two or more physical forms in which an element can exist: *diamond and graphite are allotropes of carbon.*

allotropy (ə'lɒtrəpɪ) *or* **allotropism** *n.* the existence of an element in two or more physical forms. —**allotropic** (,ælə'trɒpɪk) *adj.*

all-out *Inf.* ~*adj.* **1.** using one's maximum powers: *an all-out effort.* ~*adv.* **all out. 2.** to one's maximum capacity: *he went all out.*

allow (ə'lau) *vb.* **1.** (*tr.*) to permit (to do something). **2.** (*tr.*) to set aside: *five hours were allowed to do the job.* **3.** (*tr.*) to let enter or stay: *they don't allow dogs.* **4.** (*tr.*) to acknowledge (a point, claim, etc.). **5.** (*tr.*) to let have: *he was allowed few visitors.* **6.** (*intr.;* foll. *by for*) to take into account. **7.** (*intr.;* often foll. *by of*) to permit: *a question that allows of only one reply.* **8.** (*tr.; may take a clause as object*) *U.S. dialect.* to assert; maintain. [C14: from OF, from L *allaudāre* to extol, infl. by Med. L *allocāre* to assign] —**al'lowable** *adj.* —**al'lowably** *adv.*

allowance (ə'lauəns) *n.* **1.** an amount of something, esp. money or food, given at regular intervals. **2.** a discount, as in consideration for something given in part exchange;

rebate. **3.** (in Britain) an amount of a person's income that is not subject to income tax. **4.** a portion set aside to cover special expenses. **5.** admission; concession. **6.** the act of allowing; toleration. **7. make allowances** (*or* **allowance**). (usually foll. by *for*) **a.** to take mitigating circumstances into account. **b.** to allow (for). ~*vb.* (*tr.*) **8.** to supply (something) in limited amounts.

Alloway ('ælə,weɪ) *n.* a village in Scotland, in Strathclyde region south of Ayr: birthplace of Robert Burns.

allowedly (ə'laʊɪdlɪ) *adv.* (*sentence modifier*) by general admission or agreement; admittedly.

alloy *n.* ('ælɔɪ, ə'lɔɪ). **1.** a metallic material, such as steel, consisting of a mixture of two or more metals or of metallic with nonmetallic elements. **2.** something that impairs the quality of the thing to which it is added. ~*vb.* (ə'lɔɪ). (*tr.*) **3.** to add (one metal or element to another) to obtain a substance with a desired property. **4.** to debase (a pure substance) by mixing with an inferior element. **5.** to diminish or impair. [C16: from OF *aloi* a mixture, from *aloier* to combine, from L *alligāre*]

all-purpose *adj.* useful for many things.

all right *adj.* (*postpositive except in slang use*), *adv.* **1.** adequate; satisfactory. **2.** unharmed; safe. **3. all-right.** *U.S. sl.* acceptable; reliable. ~*sentence substitute.* **4.** very well: used to express assent. ~*adv.* **5.** satisfactorily: *the car goes all right.* **6.** without doubt. ~Also **alright.**
▷ **Usage.** See at **alright.**

all-round *adj.* **1.** efficient in all respects, esp. in sport: *an all-round player.* **2.** comprehensive; many-sided: *an all-round education.*

all-rounder *n.* a versatile person, esp. in a sport.

All Saints' Day *n.* a Christian festival celebrated on Nov. 1 to honour all the saints.

All Souls' Day *n. R.C. Church.* a day of prayer (Nov. 2) for the dead in purgatory.

allspice ('ɔːl,spaɪs) *n.* **1.** a tropical American tree, having small white flowers and aromatic berries. **2.** the seeds of this berry used as a spice, having a flavour said to resemble a mixture of cinnamon, cloves, and nutmeg. ~Also called: **pimento.**

all-star *adj.* (*prenominal*) consisting of star performers.

all-time *adj.* (*prenominal*) *Inf.* unsurpassed.
▷ **Usage.** *All-time* is an imprecise superlative and is avoided by careful writers as being superfluous: *his high jump was a record* (not *an all-time record*).

all told *adv.* (*sentence modifier*) in all: *we were seven all told.*

allude (ə'luːd) *vb.* (*intr.*; foll. by *to*) **1.** to refer indirectly. **2.** (loosely) to mention. [C16: from L *allūdere*, from *lūdere* to sport, from *lūdus* a game]

allure (ə'luə) *vb.* **1.** (*tr.*) to entice or tempt (someone); attract. ~*n.* **2.** attractiveness; appeal. [C15: from OF *alurer*, from *lure* bait] —**al'lurement** *n.* —**al'luring** *adj.*

allusion (ə'luːʒən) *n.* **1.** the act of alluding. **2.** a passing reference. [C16: from LL *allūsiō*, from L *allūdere* to sport with]

allusive (ə'luːsɪv) *adj.* containing or full of allusions. —**al'lusiveness** *n.*

alluvial (ə'luːvɪəl) *adj.* **1.** of or relating to alluvium. ~*n.* **2.** another name for **alluvium.**

alluvion (ə'luːvɪən) *n.* **1. a.** the wash of the sea or a river. **b.** a flood. **c.** sediment; alluvium. **2.** *Law.* the gradual formation of new land, as by the recession of the sea. [C16: from L *alluviō* an overflowing, from *luere* to wash]

alluvium (ə'luːvɪəm) *n.*, *pl.* **-viums** *or* **-via** (-vɪə). a fine-grained fertile soil consisting of mud, silt, and sand deposited by flowing water. [C17: from L; see ALLUVION]

ally *vb.* (ə'laɪ). **-lying, -lied.** (usually foll. by *to* or *with*) **1.** to unite or be united, esp. formally, as by treaty. **2.** (*tr.*; *usually passive*) to be related, as through being similar. ~*n.* ('ælaɪ), *pl.* **-lies. 3.** a country, person, or group allied with another. **4.** a plant, animal, etc., closely related to another in characteristics or form. [C14: from OF *alier* to join, from L *ligāre* to bind]

allyl resin ('ælɪl) *n.* any of several thermosetting synthetic resins, containing the CH_2:CHCH$_2$– group, used as adhesives. [C19: from L *allium* garlic + -YL]

Alma-Ata (*Russian* al'maa'ta) *n.* a city in the S Soviet Union, the capital of the Kazakh SSR. Pop.: 1 108 000 (1987). Former name (until 1927): **Verny.**

Almada (*Portuguese* al'mɑːdə) *n.* a town in S central Portugal, on the S bank of the Tagus estuary opposite Lisbon:

statue of Christ 110 m (360 ft.) high, erected 1959. Pop.: 42 607 (1981).

Almadén (*Spanish* alma'θen) *n.* a town in S Spain: rich cinnabar mines, worked since Roman times. Pop.: 9521 (1981).

Al Madinah (,æl mæ'diːnə) *n.* the Arabic name for **Medina.**

alma mater ('ælmə 'mɑːtə, 'meɪtə) *n.* (*often caps.*) one's school, college, or university. [C17: from L: bountiful mother]

almanac ('ɔːlmə,næk) *n.* a yearly calendar giving statistical information, such as the phases of the moon, tides, anniversaries, etc. Also (archaic): **almanack.** [C14: from Med. L *almanachus*, ?from LGk *almenikhiaka*]

almandine ('ælməndɪn) *n.* a deep violet-red garnet. [C17: from F, from Med. L, from *Alabanda*, ancient city of Asia Minor where these stones were cut]

Al Mansûrah (,æl mæn'suərə) *n.* a variant of **El Man-sûra.**

Al Marj (æl 'mɑːdʒ) *n.* an ancient town in N Libya: founded in about 550 B.C. Pop.: 10 645 (1969 est.). Italian name: **Barce.**

Alma-Tadema ('ælmə'tædɪmə) *n.* Sir **Lawrence.** 1836–1912, Dutch-English painter of studies of Greek and Roman life.

Almelo (*Dutch* 'almə,loː) *n.* a city in the E Netherlands, in Overijssel province. Pop.: 62 222 (1987).

Almería (*Spanish* alme'ria) *n.* a port in S Spain. Pop.: 124 925 (1982).

almighty (ɔːl'maɪtɪ) *adj.* **1.** omnipotent. **2.** *Inf.* (intensifier): *an almighty row.* ~*adv.* **3.** *Inf.* (intensifier): *an almighty loud bang.*

Almighty (ɔːl'maɪtɪ) *n.* **the.** another name for **God.**

almond ('ɑːmənd) *n.* **1.** a small widely cultivated rosaceous tree that is native to W Asia and has pink flowers and an edible nutlike seed. **2.** the seed, which has a yellowish-brown shell. **3.** (*modifier*) made of or containing almonds: *almond cake.* [C13: from OF *almande*, ult. from Gk *amugdalē*]

almond-eyed *adj.* having narrow oval eyes.

almoner ('ɑːmənə) *n.* **1.** *Brit.* a former name for a trained hospital social worker. **2.** (formerly) a person who distributes charity on behalf of a household or institution. [C13: from OF, from *almosne* alms, ult. from LL *eleēmosyna*]

almost ('ɔːlməʊst) *adv.* very nearly.

alms (ɑːmz) *pl. n.* charitable donations of money or goods to the poor or needy. [OE *ælmysse*, from LL, from Gk *eleēmosunē* pity]

almshouse ('ɑːmz,haʊs) *n. Brit.* a privately supported house offering accommodation to the aged or needy.

almucantar *or* **almacantar** (,ælmə'kæntə) *n.* **1.** a circle on the celestial sphere parallel to the horizon. **2.** an instrument for measuring altitudes. [C14: from F, from Ar. *almukantarāt* sundial]

aloe ('æləʊ) *n.*, *pl.* **-oes. 1.** any plant of the genus *Aloe*, chiefly native to southern Africa, with fleshy spiny-toothed leaves. **2. American aloe.** Also called: **century plant.** a tropical American agave which blooms only once in 10 to 30 years. [C14: from L *aloē*, from Gk]

aloes ('æləʊz) *n.* (*functioning as sing.*) a bitter purgative drug made from the leaves of several species of aloe. Also called: **bitter aloes.**

aloft (ə'lɒft) *adv.*, *adj.* (*postpositive*) **1.** in or into a high or higher place. **2.** *Naut.* in or into the rigging of a vessel. [C12: from ON *ā lopt* in the air]

alone (ə'ləʊn) *adj.* (*postpositive*), *adv.* **1.** apart from another or others. **2.** without anyone or anything else: *one man alone could lift it.* **3.** without equal: *he stands alone in the field of microbiology.* **4.** to the exclusion of others: *she alone believed him.* **5. leave *or* let alone.** to refrain from annoying or interfering with. **6. leave well alone.** to refrain from interfering with something that is satisfactory. **7. let alone.** not to mention; much less: *he can't afford beer, let alone whisky.* [OE *al one*, lit.: all (entirely) one]

along (ə'lɒŋ) *prep.* **1.** over or for the length of: *along the road.* ~*adv.* **2.** continuing over the length of some specified thing. **3.** together with some specified person or people: *he'd like to come along.* **4.** forward: *the horse trotted* *along.* **5.** to a more advanced state: *he got the work moving along.* **6. along with.** together with: *consider the advantages along with the disadvantages.* [OE *andlang,* from *and-* against + *lang* LONG[1]]

▷ **Usage.** See at **plus.**

alongshore (ə,lɒŋ'ʃɔː) *adv., adj. (postpositive)* close to, by, or along a shore.

alongside (ə'lɒŋ,saɪd) *prep.* **1.** (often foll. by *of*) close beside: *alongside the quay.* ~*adv.* **2.** near the side of something: *come alongside.*

aloof (ə'luːf) *adj.* distant, unsympathetic, or supercilious in manner. [C16: from A-[1] + *loof,* var. of LUFF] —**a'loofly** *adv.* —**a'loofness** *n.*

alopecia (,ælə'piːʃɪə) *n.* baldness. [C14: from L, from Gk *alópekia,* orig.: mange in foxes]

Alost (*French* alɔst) *n.* a town in central Belgium, in East Flanders province. Pop.: 77 113 (1987 est.). Flemish name: **Aalst.**

aloud (ə'laʊd) *adv., adj. (postpositive)* **1.** in a normal voice. **2.** in a spoken voice; not silently.

alp (ælp) *n.* **1.** (in Switzerland) a mountain pasture. **2.** a high mountain. **3. the Alps.** a high mountain range in S central Europe. [C16: from L *Alpes*]

ALP *abbrev. for* Australian Labor Party.

alpaca (æl'pækə) *n.* **1.** a domesticated South American mammal related to the llama, with dark shaggy hair. **2.** the wool or cloth obtained from this hair. **3.** a glossy fabric simulating this. [C18: via Sp. from Aymara *allpaca*]

alpenhorn ('ælpən,hɔːn) *n.* another name for **alphorn.**

alpenstock ('ælpən,stɒk) *n.* a stout stick with an iron tip used by hikers, mountain climbers, etc. [C19: from G, from *Alpen* Alps + *Stock* STICK[1]]

Alpes-de-Haute-Provence (*French* alpdəotprɔvɑ̃s) *n.* a department of SE France in Provence-Alpes-Côte-d'Azur region. Capital: Digne. Pop.: 119 068 (1982). Area: 6988 sq. km (2725 sq. miles). Former name: **Basses-Alpes.**

Alpes Maritimes (*French* alp maritim) *n.* a department of the SE corner of France in Provence-Alpes-Côte-d'Azur region. Capital: Nice. Pop.: 881 198 (1982). Area: 4298 sq. km (1676 sq. miles).

alpha ('ælfə) *n.* **1.** the first letter in the Greek alphabet (Α, α). **2.** *Brit.* the highest grade or mark, as in an examination. **3.** (*modifier*) **a.** involving helium nuclei. **b.** denoting an isomeric or allotropic form of a substance. [via L from Gk, of Phoenician origin]

alpha and omega *n.* the first and last, a phrase used in Revelation 1:8 to signify God's eternity.

alphabet ('ælfə,bɛt) *n.* **1.** a set of letters or other signs used in a writing system, each letter or sign being used to represent one or sometimes more than one phoneme in the language being transcribed. **2.** any set of characters, esp. one representing sounds of speech. **3.** basic principles or rudiments. [C15: from LL, from the first two letters of the Greek alphabet; see ALPHA, BETA]

alphabetical (,ælfə'bɛtɪk³l) *or* **alphabetic** *adj.* **1.** in the conventional order of the letters of an alphabet. **2.** of or expressed by an alphabet. —,**alpha'betically** *adv.*

alphabetize *or* **-ise** ('ælfəbə,taɪz) *vb. (tr.)* **1.** to arrange in conventional alphabetical order. **2.** to express by an alphabet. —,**alphabeti'zation** *or* **-i'sation** *n.*

alpha-fetoprotein (,ælfə,fiːtəʊ'prəʊtiːn) *n.* a protein that forms in the liver of the human fetus; excessive quantities in the amniotic fluid may indicate spina bifida in the fetus. Abbrev.: **afp**

alphanumeric (,ælfənju:'mɛrɪk) *or* **alphameric** *adj.* (of a character set or file of data) consisting of alphabetical and numerical symbols.

alpha particle *n.* a helium nucleus, containing two neutrons and two protons, emitted during some radioactive transformations.

alpha ray *n.* ionizing radiation consisting of a stream of alpha particles.

alpha rhythm *or* **wave** *n. Physiol.* the normal bursts of electrical activity from the cerebral cortex of a person at rest. See also **brain wave.**

Alpheus (,ælə'fiːəs) *n. Greek myth.* a river god, lover of the nymph Arethusa. She changed into a spring to evade him, but he changed into a river and mingled with her.

alphorn ('ælp,hɔːn) *or* **alpenhorn** *n.* a wind instrument used in the Swiss Alps, made from a very long tube of wood. [C19: from G: Alps horn]

alpine ('ælpaɪn) *adj.* **1.** of or relating to high mountains. **2.** (of plants) growing on mountains above the limit for

tree growth. **3.** connected with mountaineering. **4.** *Skiing.* of racing events on steep prepared slopes, such as the slalom and downhill. Compare **nordic.** ~*n.* **5.** a plant grown in or native to high altitudes.

Alpine ('ælpaɪn) *adj.* of or relating to the Alps or their inhabitants.

alpinist ('ælpɪnɪst) *n.* a mountain climber.

Alps (ælps) *pl. n.* **1.** a mountain range in S central Europe, extending over 1000 km (650 miles) from the Mediterranean coast of France and NW Italy through Switzerland, N Italy, and Austria to NW Yugoslavia. Highest peak: Mont Blanc, 4807 m (15 771 ft.). **2.** a range of mountains in the NW quadrant of the moon, which is cut in two by a straight fracture, the **Alpine Valley.**

already (ɔːl'rɛdɪ) *adv.* **1.** by or before a stated or implied time: *he is already here.* **2.** at a time earlier than expected: *is it ten o'clock already?*

alright (ɔːl'raɪt) *adv., sentence substitute, adj.* a variant spelling of **all right.**

▷ **Usage.** The form *alright,* though very commonly encountered, is still considered by many careful users of English to be wrong or less acceptable than *all right.*

Alsace (æl'sæs; *French* alzas) *n.* a region and former province of NE France, between the Vosges mountains and the Rhine: famous for its wines. Area: 8280 sq. km (3196 sq. miles). Ancient name: **Alsatia.** German name: **Elsass.**

Alsace-Lorraine *n.* an area of NE France, comprising the modern regions of Alsace and Lorraine: under German rule 1871–1919 and 1940–44. Area: 14 522 sq. km (5607 sq. miles). German name: **Elsass-Lothringen.**

Alsatia (æl'seɪʃə) *n.* **1.** the ancient name for **Alsace. 2.** an area around Whitefriars, London, in the 17th century, which was a sanctuary for criminals and debtors.

Alsatian (æl'seɪʃən) *n.* **1.** Also called: **German shepherd (dog).** a large wolflike breed of dog often used as a guard dog and by the police. **2.** a native or inhabitant of Alsace. ~*adj.* **3.** of or relating to Alsace or its inhabitants.

also ('ɔːlsəʊ) *adv.* **1.** (*sentence modifier*) in addition; as well; too. ~*sentence connector.* **2.** besides; moreover. [OE *alswā*; see ALL, SO[1]]

▷ **Usage.** Since *also* is not a conjunction, careful writers and speakers consider it poor style to use it alone as a connector in sentences like *he bought pens, paper, ink, also notebooks.* In such sentences, *and* or *and also* would be the appropriate words: *he bought pens, paper, ink, and notebooks.*

also-ran *n.* **1.** a contestant, horse, etc., failing to finish among the first three. **2.** a loser.

alstroemeria (,ælstrəʊ'mɪərɪə) *n.* any of several plants with fleshy roots and brightly coloured flowers in summer, esp. the Peruvian lily. [C18: NL, after Claude Alstroemer (1736–96), Swedish naturalist]

alt. *abbrev. for:* **1.** alternate. **2.** altitude. **3.** alto.

Alta. *abbrev. for* Alberta.

Altaic (æl'teɪɪk) *n.* **1.** a postulated family of languages of Asia and SE Europe, including the Turkic, Tungusic, and Mongolic subfamilies. See also **Ural-Altaic.** ~*adj.* **2.** denoting or relating to this linguistic family or its speakers.

Altai Mountains (ɑːl'taɪ) *pl. n.* a mountain system of central Asia, in W Mongolia, W China, and the S Soviet Union. Highest peak: Belukha, 4506 m (14 783 ft.).

Altamira (*Spanish* alta'mira) *n.* a cave in N Spain, SW of Santander, noted for Old Stone Age wall drawings.

altar ('ɔːltə) *n.* **1.** a raised place or structure where sacrifices are offered and religious rites performed. **2.** (in Christian churches) the communion table. **3.** a step in the wall of a dry dock. [OE, from L *altus* high]

altar boy *n. R.C. Church, Church of England.* a boy serving as an acolyte.

altarpiece ('ɔːltə,piːs) *n.* a work of art set above and behind an altar; a reredos.

altazimuth (æl'tæzɪməθ) *n.* an instrument for measuring the altitude and azimuth of a celestial body. [C19: from ALT(ITUDE) + AZIMUTH]

Altdorf (*German* 'altdɔrf) *n.* a town in central Switzerland, capital of Uri canton: setting of the William Tell legend. Pop.: 8200 (1980).

Altdorfer (*German* 'altdɔrfər) *n.* **Albrecht** ('albrɛçt). ?1480–?1538, German painter and engraver: one of the earliest landscape painters.

alter ('ɔːltə) vb. **1.** to make or become different in some respect; change. **2.** (tr.) Inf., chiefly U.S. a euphemistic word for **castrate** or **spay**. [C14: from OF, ult. from L *alter* other] — '**alterable** adj.

alteration (ˌɔːltə'reɪʃən) n. **1.** a change or modification. **2.** the act of altering.

alterative ('ɔːltərətɪv) adj. **1.** likely or able to produce alteration. **2.** (of a drug) able to restore health. ~n. **3.** such a drug.

altercate ('ɔːltəˌkeɪt) vb. (intr.) to argue, esp. heatedly; dispute. [C16: from L *altercāri* to quarrel with another, from *alter* other]

altercation (ˌɔːltə'keɪʃən) n. an angry or heated discussion or quarrel; argument.

alter ego ('æltər 'iːgəʊ, 'ɛgəʊ) n. **1.** a second self. **2.** a very close friend. [L: other self]

alternate vb. ('ɔːltəˌneɪt). **1.** (often foll. by *with*) to occur or cause to occur by turns: *day and night alternate*. **2.** (intr.; often foll. by *between*) to swing repeatedly from one condition, action, etc., to another. **3.** (tr.) to interchange regularly or in succession. **4.** (intr.) (of an electric current, voltage, etc.) to reverse direction or sign at regular intervals. ~adj. (ɔːl'tɜːnɪt). **5.** occurring by turns: *alternate feelings of love and hate*. **6.** every other or second one of a series: *he came on alternate days*. **7.** being a second choice; alternative. **8.** Bot. (of leaves, flowers, etc.) arranged singly at different heights on either side of the stem. ~n. ('ɔːltənɪt, ɔːl'tɜːnɪt). **9.** U.S. & Canad. a person who substitutes for another; stand-in. [C16: from L *alternāre* to do one thing and then another, ult. from *alter* other] — ,**alter'nation** n.

alternate angles pl. n. two angles at opposite ends and on opposite sides of a transversal cutting two lines.

alternately (ɔːl'tɜːnɪtlɪ) adv. in an alternating sequence or position.

alternating current n. an electric current that reverses direction with a frequency independent of the characteristics of the circuit through which it flows. Abbrev.: **AC**.

alternation of generations n. the occurrence in the life cycle of many plants and lower animals of alternating sexual and asexual reproductive forms.

alternative (ɔːl'tɜːnətɪv) n. **1.** a possibility of choice, esp. between two things. **2.** either of such choices: *we took the alternative of walking*. ~adj. **3.** presenting a choice, esp. between two possibilities only. **4.** (of two things) mutually exclusive. **5.** denoting a lifestyle, culture, art form, etc., that is regarded as preferable to that of contemporary society because it is less conventional, materialistic, or institutionalized. — **al'ternatively** adv.

▷ **Usage.** The use of *alternative* with reference to more than two possibilities is commonly encountered, but is regarded as unacceptable by some people. Careful writers and speakers of English may prefer to restrict its use to instances where two choices only are mentioned. The addition of *other* before *alternative* is redundant: *there is no alternative* not *there is no other alternative*.

alternative energy n. a form of energy derived from a natural source, such as the sun, wind, tides, or waves. Also called: **renewable energy.**

alternative medicine n. the treatment or alleviation of disease by techniques such as osteopathy and acupuncture, allied with attention to a person's general wellbeing. Also called: **complementary medicine.**

alternative society n. a group of people who agree in rejecting the traditional values of the society around them.

alternator ('ɔːltəˌneɪtə) n. an electrical machine that generates an alternating current.

althaea or U.S. **althea** (æl'θiːə) n. any Eurasian plant of the genus *Althaea*, such as the hollyhock, having tall spikes of showy flowers. [C17: from L, from Gk *althaia* marsh mallow]

althorn ('ælt,hɔːn) n. a valved brass musical instrument belonging to the saxhorn family.

although (ɔːl'ðəʊ) conj. (subordinating) even though: *although she was ill, she worked hard*.

altimeter (æl'tɪmɪtə, 'æltɪ,miːtə) n. an instrument that indicates height above sea level, esp. one based on an aneroid barometer and fitted to an aircraft. [C19: from L *altus* high + -METER]

Altiplano (Spanish alti'plano) n. a plateau of the Andes, covering two thirds of Bolivia and extending into S Peru:

contains Lake Titicaca. Height: 3000 m (10 000 ft.) to 3900 m (13 000 ft.).

altitude ('æltɪ,tjuːd) n. **1.** the vertical height of an object, esp. above sea level. **2.** Geom. the perpendicular distance from the apex to the base of a triangle. **3.** Also called: **elevation.** Astron., navigation. the angular distance of a celestial body from the horizon. **4.** Surveying. the angle of elevation of a point above the horizontal plane of the observer. **5.** (often pl.) a high place or region. [C14: from L *altus* high, deep]

alto ('æltəʊ) n., pl. **-tos.** **1.** (in choral singing) short for **contralto.** **2.** the highest adult male voice; countertenor. **3.** a singer with such a voice. **4.** a flute, saxophone, etc., that is the third or fourth highest instrument in its group. ~adj. **5.** denoting such an instrument. [C18: from It.: high, from L *altus*]

alto clef n. the clef that establishes middle C as being on the third line of the staff.

altocumulus (ˌæltəʊ'kjuːmjʊləs) n., pl. **-li** (-laɪ). a globular cloud at an intermediate height of about 2400 to 6000 metres (8000 to 20 000 feet).

altogether (ˌɔːltə'gɛðə, 'ɔːltəˌgɛðə) adv. **1.** with everything included: *altogether he owed me sixty pounds*. **2.** completely; utterly: *altogether mad*. **3.** on the whole: *altogether it was very good*. ~n. **4. in the altogether.** Inf. naked.

Altona (æl'təʊnə; German 'alto:na) n. a port in N West Germany: part of Hamburg since 1937.

altostratus (ˌæltəʊ'streɪtəs, -'strɑː-) n., pl. **-ti** (-taɪ). a layer cloud at an intermediate height of about 2400 to 6000 metres (8000 to 20 000 feet).

altricial (æl'trɪʃəl) adj. **1.** denoting birds whose young, after hatching, are naked, blind, and dependent on the parents for food. ~n. **2.** an altricial bird. ~Cf. **precocial**. [C19: from NL, from L *altrix* a nurse]

Altrincham ('ɔːltrɪŋəm) n. a residential town in NW England, in Greater Manchester. Pop.: 39 641 (1981).

altruism ('æltruː,ɪzəm) n. unselfish concern for the welfare of others. [C19: from F, from It. *altrui* others, from L] — '**altruist** n. — ,**altru'istic** adj. — ,**altru'istically** adv.

ALU Computers. abbrev. for arithmetical and logical unit.

alum ('æləm) n. **1.** a colourless soluble hydrated double sulphate of aluminium and potassium used in manufacturing and in medicine. Formula: $K_2SO_4.Al_2(SO_4)_3.24H_2O$. **2.** any of a group of similar hydrated double sulphates of a monovalent metal or group and a trivalent metal. [C14: from OF, from L *alūmen*]

alumina (ə'luːmɪnə) n. another name for **aluminium oxide.** [C18: from NL, pl. of L *alūmen* ALUM]

aluminium (ˌæljuː'mɪnɪəm) or U.S. & Canad. **aluminum** (ə'luːmɪnəm) n. a light malleable silvery-white metallic element that resists corrosion; the third most abundant element in the earth's crust, occurring as a compound, principally as bauxite. Symbol: Al; atomic no.: 13; atomic wt.: 26.981.

aluminium oxide n. a powder occurring naturally as corundum and used in the production of aluminium, abrasives, glass, and ceramics. Formula: Al_2O_3. Also called: **alumina.**

aluminize or **-ise** (ə'luːmɪ,naɪz) vb. (tr.) to cover with aluminium or aluminium paint.

aluminous (ə'luːmɪnəs) adj. resembling aluminium.

alumnus (ə'lʌmnəs) or (fem.) **alumna** (ə'lʌmnə) n., pl. **-ni** (-naɪ) or **-nae** (-niː). Chiefly U.S. & Canad. a graduate of a school, college, etc. [C17: from L: nursling, pupil, from *alere* to nourish]

Alva or **Alba** (Spanish 'alβa) n. **Duke of,** title of *Fernando Alvarez de Toledo*. 1508–82, Spanish general and statesman who suppressed the Protestant revolt in the Netherlands (1567–72) and conquered Portugal (1580).

alveolar (æl'vɪələ, ,ælvɪ'əʊlə) adj. **1.** Anat. of an alveolus. **2.** denoting the part of the jawbone containing the roots of the teeth. **3.** (of a consonant) articulated with the tongue in contact with the part of the jawbone immediately behind the upper teeth. ~n. **4.** an alveolar consonant, such as *t*, *d*, and *s* in English.

alveolate (æl'vɪəlɪt, -,leɪt) adj. having many small cavities. [C19: from LL *alveolātus* hollowed, from L: ALVEOLUS] — ,**alveo'lation** n.

alveolus (æl'vɪələs) n., pl. **-li** (-,laɪ). any small pit, cavity, or saclike dilation, such as a honeycomb cell, a tooth socket, or the tiny air sacs in the lungs. [C18: from L: a little hollow, dim. of *alveus*]

always ('ɔːlweɪz) *adv.* **1.** without exception; every time: *he always arrives on time.* **2.** continually; repeatedly. **3.** in any case: *you could always take a day off work.* ~Also (archaic): **alway.** [C13 *alles weiss*, from OE *ealne weg*, lit.: all the way]

alyssum ('ælɪsəm) *n.* a widely cultivated herbaceous garden plant, having clusters of small yellow or white flowers. [C16: from NL, from Gk *alusson*, from *alussos* (adj.) curing rabies]

Alzheimer's disease ('ælts,haɪməz) *n.* a disorder of the brain resulting in progressive decline and eventual senility. Often shortened to **Alzheimer's.** [C20: after A. *Alzheimer* (1864–1915), G physician who first identified it]

am (æm; *unstressed* əm) *vb.* (used with *I*) a form of the present tense of **be.** [OE *eam*]

Am *the chemical symbol for* americium.

AM *abbrev. for:* **1.** Also: **am.** amplitude modulation. **2.** U.S. Master of Arts. **3.** Member of the Order of Australia.

Am. *abbrev. for* America(n).

a.m., A.M., am, *or* **AM** (indicating the time period from midnight to midday) *abbrev. for* ante meridiem. [L: before noon]

Amadhlozi *or* **Amadlozi** (,æmæ'hlɔʒiː) *pl. n. S. African.* the ancestral spirits. [from Zulu. pl. *amadlozi*]

amadoda (,æmæ'dɒdə) *pl. n. S. African.* men, esp. Black men. [from Bantu *ama* (pl. prefix) + *doda* man]

amadou ('æmə,duː) *n.* a spongy substance got from some fungi, used (formerly) as tinder, a styptic, and by fishermen to dry flies. [C18: from F, from Provençal: lover, from L *amāre* to love (because easily set alight)]

Amagasaki (ə,mɑːɡə'sɑːkɪ) *n.* an industrial city in Japan, in W Honshu, on Osaka Bay. Pop.: 509 000 (1985).

amah ('ɑːmə) *n.* in the East, esp. formerly) a nurse or maidservant. [C19: from Port. *ama* nurse]

amain (ə'meɪn) *adv. Arch. or poetic.* with great strength or haste. [C16: from A-² + MAIN¹]

amalgam (ə'mælɡəm) *n.* **1.** an alloy of mercury with another metal, esp. silver: *dental amalgam.* **2.** a blend or combination. [C15: from Med. L *amalgama*, from ?]

amalgamate (ə'mælɡə,meɪt) *vb.* **1.** to combine or cause to combine; unite. **2.** to alloy (a metal) with mercury.

amalgamation (ə,mælɡə'meɪʃən) *n.* **1.** the process of amalgamating. **2.** the state of being amalgamated. **3.** a method of extracting precious metals by treatment with mercury. **4.** a merger.

Amalthea (,æmæl'θiːə) *n. Greek myth.* **a.** a nymph who brought up the infant Zeus on goat's milk. **b.** the goat itself. ~Also: **Amaltheia.**

amanuensis (ə,mænjʊ'ɛnsɪs) *n., pl.* **-ses** (-siːz). a person employed to take dictation or to copy manuscripts. [C17: from L, from *servus ā manū* slave at hand (that is, handwriting)]

Amapá (*Portuguese* ,əmə'pɑː) *n.* a territory of N Brazil, on the Amazon delta. Capital: Macapá. Pop.: 175 634 (1980). Area: 143 716 sq. km (55 489 sq. miles).

amaranth ('æmə,rænθ) *n.* **1.** *Poetic.* an imaginary flower that never fades. **2.** any of numerous plants having tassellike heads of small green, red, or purple flowers. **3.** a synthetic red food colouring (**E123**), used in packet soups, cake mixes, etc. [C17: from L *amarantus*, from Gk, from A-¹ + *marainein* to fade]

Amarillo (,æmə'rɪləʊ) *n.* an industrial city in NW Texas. Pop.: 149 230 (1980).

amaryllis (,æmə'rɪlɪs) *n.* **1.** a plant native to southern Africa having large lily-like reddish or white flowers. **2.** any of several related plants. [C18: from NL, from L: after *Amaryllis*, Gk conventional name for a shepherdess]

amass (ə'mæs) *vb.* **1.** (*tr.*) to accumulate or collect (esp. riches, etc.). **2.** to gather in a heap. [C15: from OF, from *masse* MASS] —**a'masser** *n.*

amateur ('æmətə) *n.* **1.** a person who engages in an activity, esp. a sport, as a pastime rather than for gain. **2.** a person unskilled in a subject or activity. **3.** a person who is fond of or admires something. **4.** (*modifier*) of or for amateurs: *an amateur event.* ~*adj.* **5.** not professional or expert: *an amateur approach.* [C18: from F, from L *amātor* lover, from *amāre* to love] —**'amateurism** *n.*

amateurish ('æmətərɪʃ) *adj.* lacking professional skill or expertise. —**'amateurishly** *adv.*

Amati *n.* **1.** (*Italian* a'mɑːti). a family of Italian violin makers, active in Cremona in the 16th and 17th centuries, esp. **Nicolò** (niko'lɔ), 1596–1684, who taught Guarneri

and Stradivari. **2.** (ə'mɑːti). (*pl.* **Amatis**) a violin or other stringed instrument made by any member of this family.

amative ('æmətɪv) *adj.* a rare word for **amorous.** [C17: from Med. L, from L *amāre* to love]

amatory ('æmətərɪ) *or* **amatorial** (,æmə'tɔːrɪəl) *adj.* of, relating to, or inciting sexual love or desire. [C16: from L *amātōrius*, from *amāre* to love]

amaurosis (,æmɔː'rəʊsɪs) *n.* blindness, esp. when occurring without observable damage to the eye. [C17: via NL from Gk: darkening, from *amauroun* to dim] —**amaurotic** (,æmɔː'rɒtɪk) *adj.*

amaze (ə'meɪz) *vb.* (*tr.*) **1.** to fill with incredulity or surprise; astonish. ~*n.* **2.** an archaic word for **amazement.** [OE *āmasian*] —**a'mazing** *adj.*

amazement (ə'meɪzmənt) *n.* incredulity or great astonishment; complete wonder.

Amazon¹ ('æməzⁿ) *n.* **1.** *Greek myth.* one of a race of women warriors of Scythia near the Black Sea. **2.** (*often not cap.*) any tall, strong, or aggressive woman. [C14: via L from Gk *Amazōn*, from ?] —**Amazonian** (,æmə'zəʊnɪən) *adj.*

Amazon² ('æməzⁿ) *n.* a river in South America, rising in the Peruvian Andes and flowing east through N Brazil to the Atlantic: in volume, the largest river in the world; navigable for 3700 km (2300 miles). Length: over 6440 km (4000 miles). Area of basin: over 5 827 500 sq. km (2 250 000 sq. miles). —**Amazonian** (,æmə'zəʊnɪən) *adj.*

Amazonas (,æmə'zəʊnəs) *n.* a state of W Brazil, consisting of the central Amazon basin: vast areas of unexplored tropical rainforest. Capital: Manaus. Pop.: 1 432 066 (1980). Area: 1 542 277 sq. km (595 474 sq. miles).

Ambala (əm'bɑːlə) *n.* a city in N India, in Haryana: site of archaeological remains of a prehistoric Indian civilization. Pop.: 121 203 (1981 est.).

ambassador (æm'bæsədə) *n.* **1.** a diplomat of the highest rank, accredited as permanent representative to another country. **2. ambassador extraordinary.** a diplomat of the highest rank sent on a special mission. **3. ambassador plenipotentiary.** a diplomat of the first rank with treaty-signing powers. **4. ambassador-at-large.** *U.S.* an ambassador with special duties who may be sent to more than one government. **5.** an authorized representative or messenger. [C14: from OF, from It., from OProvençal *ambaisador*, from *ambaisa* (unattested) mission, errand] —**am'bassadress** *fem. n.* —**ambassadorial** (æm,bæsə'dɔːrɪəl) *adj.* —**am'bassador,ship** *n.*

amber ('æmbə) *n.* **1.** a yellow translucent fossil resin derived from extinct coniferous trees and often containing trapped insects. **2. a.** a brownish-yellow colour. **b.** (*as adj.*): *an amber dress.* **3.** an amber traffic light used as a warning between red and green. [C14: from Med. L *ambar*, from Ar. *'anbar* ambergris]

ambergris ('æmbə,griːs, -grɪs) *n.* a waxy substance secreted by the intestinal tract of the sperm whale and often found floating in the sea: used in the manufacture of some perfumes. [C15: from OF *ambre gris* grey amber]

amberjack ('æmbə,dʒæk) *n.* any of several large fishes occurring in tropical and subtropical Atlantic waters. [C19: from AMBER + JACK]

ambi- *combining form.* indicating both: *ambidextrous; ambivalence.* [from L: round, on both sides, both, from *ambo* both]

ambidextrous (,æmbɪ'dɛkstrəs) *adj.* **1.** equally expert with each hand. **2.** *Inf.* skilled or adept. **3.** underhanded. —**ambidexterity** (,æmbɪdɛk'stɛrɪtɪ) *or* ,ambi'dextrousness *n.*

ambience *or* **ambiance** ('æmbɪəns) *n.* the atmosphere of a place. [C19: from F, from *ambiant* surrounding]

ambient ('æmbɪənt) *adj.* surrounding. [C16: from L *ambiēns* going round, from AMBI- + *īre* to go]

ambiguity (,æmbɪ'ɡjuːɪtɪ) *n., pl.* **-ties. 1.** the possibility of interpreting an expression in more than one way. **2.** an instance or example of this, as in the sentence *they are cooking apples.* **3.** vagueness or uncertainty of meaning.

ambiguous (æm'bɪɡjʊəs) *adj.* **1.** having more than one possible interpretation. **2.** difficult to understand; obscure. [C16: from L *ambiguus* going here and there; uncertain, from *ambigere* to go around] —**am'biguously** *adv.* —**am'biguousness** *n.*

ambit ('æmbɪt) *n.* **1.** scope or extent. **2.** limits or boundary. [C16: from L *ambitus* a going round, from *ambīre* to go round]

ambition (æm'bɪʃən) n. 1. strong desire for success or distinction. 2. something so desired; goal. [C14: from OF, from L ambitiō a going round (of candidates), from ambīre to go round]

ambitious (æm'bɪʃəs) adj. 1. having a strong desire for success or achievement. 2. necessitating extraordinary effort or ability: an ambitious project. 3. (often foll. by of) having a great desire (for something or to do something). —am'bitiousness n.

ambivalence (æm'bɪvələns) or **ambivalency** n. the coexistence of two opposed and conflicting emotions, etc. —am'bivalent adj.

amble ('æmb³l) vb. (intr.) 1. to walk at a leisurely relaxed pace. 2. (of a horse) to move, lifting both legs on one side together. 3. to ride a horse at an amble. ~n. 4. a leisurely motion in walking. 5. a leisurely walk. 6. the ambling gait of a horse. [C14: from OF, from L ambulāre to walk]

Ambler ('æmblə) n. Eric. 1909–86, English novelist. His thrillers include The Mask of Dimitrios (1939) and Journey into Fear (1940).

amblyopia (ˌæmblɪ'əʊpɪə) n. impaired vision with no discernible damage to the eye or optic nerve. [C18: NL, from Gk ambluōpia, from amblus dull, dim + ōps eye] —amblyopic (ˌæmblɪ'ɒpɪk) adj.

Amboina (æm'bɔɪnə) n. 1. an island in Indonesia, in the Moluccas. Capital: Amboina. Area: 1000 sq. km (386 sq. miles). 2. Also called: **Ambon** ('ɑːmbɔːn). a port in the Moluccas, the capital of Amboina island.

Amboise (French ɑ̃bwaz) n. a town in NW central France, on the River Loire: famous castle, a former royal residence. Pop.: 11 415 (1982).

amboyna or **amboina** (æm'bɔɪnə) n. the mottled curly-grained wood of an Indonesian tree, used in making furniture.

Ambrose ('æmbrəʊz) n. Saint. ?340–397 A.D., bishop of Milan; built up the secular power of the early Christian Church; also wrote music and Latin hymns. Feast day: Dec. 7. —Am'brosian adj.

ambrosia (æm'brəʊzɪə) n. 1. Classical myth. the food of the gods, said to bestow immortality. Cf. **nectar** (sense 2). 2. anything particularly delightful to taste or smell. 3. another name for **beebread**. [C16: via L from Gk: immortality, from A-¹ + brotos mortal] —am'brosial or am'brosian adj.

ambry ('æmbrɪ) or **aumbry** ('ɔːmbrɪ) n., pl. -bries. 1. a recessed cupboard in the wall of a church near the altar, used to store sacred vessels, etc. 2. Obs. a small cupboard. [C14: from OF almarie, ult. from L armārium chest for storage, from arma arms]

ambulance ('æmbjʊləns) n. a motor vehicle designed to carry sick or injured people. [C19: from F, based on (hôpital) ambulant mobile or field (hospital), from L ambulāre to walk]

ambulant ('æmbjʊlənt) adj. 1. moving about from place to place. 2. Med. another word for **ambulatory** (sense 3).

ambulate ('æmbjʊˌleɪt) vb. (intr.) to wander about or move from place to place. [C17: from L ambulāre to walk] —ˌambu'lation n.

ambulatory ('æmbjʊlətərɪ) adj. 1. of or designed for walking. 2. changing position; not fixed. 3. Also: **ambulant**. able to walk. ~n., pl. -ries. 4. a place for walking, such as an aisle or a cloister.

ambuscade (ˌæmbə'skeɪd) n., pl. -cades. ~vb. 2. to ambush or lie in ambush. [C16: from F, from OIt. imboscata, prob. of Gmc origin; cf. AMBUSH]

ambush ('æmbʊʃ) n. 1. the act of waiting in a concealed position in order to launch a surprise attack. 2. a surprise attack from such a position. 3. the concealed position from which such an attack is launched. 4. the person or persons waiting to launch such an attack. ~vb. 5. to lie in wait (for). 6. (tr.) to attack suddenly from a concealed position. [C14: from OF embuschier to position in ambush, from em- IM- + -buschier, from busche piece of firewood, prob. of Gmc origin]

ameba (ə'miːbə) n., pl. -bae (-biː) or -bas. the usual U.S. spelling of amoeba. —a'mebic adj.

ameer (ə'mɪə) n. a variant spelling of emir.

ameliorate (ə'miːljəˌreɪt) vb. to make or become better. [C18: from F améliorer to improve, from OF, from meillor better, from L melior] —aˌmelio'ration n. —a'meliorative adj. —a'melioˌrator n.

amen (ˌeɪ'mɛn, ˌɑː'mɛn) sentence substitute. 1. so be it!: a term used at the end of a prayer. ~n. 2. the use of the word amen. [C13: via LL via Gk from Heb. āmēn certainly]

Amen, Amon, or **Amūn** ('ɑːmən) n. Egyptian myth. a local Theban god, having a ram's head and symbolizing life and fertility, identified by the Egyptians with the national deity Amen-Ra.

amenable (ə'miːnəb³l) adj. 1. likely to listen, cooperate, etc. 2. accountable to some authority; answerable. 3. capable of being tested, judged, etc. [C16: from Anglo-F, from OF, from L mināre to drive (cattle), from minārī to threaten] —aˌmena'bility or a'menableness n. —a'menably adv.

amend (ə'mɛnd) vb. (tr.) 1. to improve; change for the better. 2. to correct. 3. to alter or revise (legislation, etc.) by formal procedure. [C13: from OF, from L ēmendāre to EMEND] —a'mendable adj. —a'mender n.

▷ **Usage.** Confusion sometimes arises between amend and emend. Amend means to improve, and can be used of a situation, character, etc., as well as of making improvements to the substance of written or spoken material: we will amend our lifestyle; they all participate in amending or adding to the text. Emend should be used only of correcting errors in a manuscript or text.

amendment (ə'mɛndmənt) n. 1. correction. 2. an addition or alteration to a document, etc.

amends (ə'mɛndz) n. (functioning as sing.) recompense or compensation for some injury, insult, etc.: to make amends. [C13: from OF, from amende compensation, from amender to EMEND]

Amenhotep III (ˌæmɛn'həʊtɛp) or **Amenhotpe III** (ˌæmɛn'hɒtpɪ) n. Greek name Amenophis. ?1411–?1375 B.C., Egyptian pharaoh who expanded Egypt's influence by peaceful diplomacy and erected many famous buildings.

Amenhotep IV or **Amenhotpe IV** n. the original name of **Akhenaten.**

amenity (ə'miːnɪtɪ) n., pl. -ties. 1. (often pl.) a useful or pleasant facility: a swimming pool was one of the amenities. 2. the fact or condition of being agreeable. 3. (usually pl.) a social courtesy. [C14: from L, from amoenus agreeable]

amenorrhoea or esp. U.S. **amenorrhea** (æˌmɛnə'rɪə, eɪ-) n. abnormal absence of menstruation. [C19: from A-¹ + MENO- + -RRHOEA]

Amen-Ra (ˌɑːmən'rɑː) n. Egyptian myth. the sun-god; the principle deity during the period of Theban hegemony.

ament ('æmənt) n. another name for **catkin**. Also called: **amentum** (ə'mɛntəm). [C18: from L āmentum thong] —ˌamen'taceous adj.

amentia (ə'mɛnʃə) n. severe mental deficiency, usually congenital. [C14: from L: insanity, from āmēns mad, from mēns mind]

amerce (ə'mɜːs) vb. (tr.) Obs. 1. Law. to punish by a fine. 2. to punish with any arbitrary penalty. [C14: from Anglo-F, from OF à merci at the mercy; see MERCY] —a'mercement n.

America (ə'mɛrɪkə) n. 1. short for the **United States of America.** 2. Also called: **the Americas.** the American continent, including North, South, and Central America. [C16: from Americus, L form of Amerigo; see VESPUCCI]

American (ə'mɛrɪkən) adj. 1. of or relating to the United States of America, its inhabitants, or their form of English. 2. of or relating to the American continent. ~n. 3. a native or citizen of the U.S. 4. a native or inhabitant of any country of North, Central, or South America. 5. the English language as spoken or written in the United States.

Americana (əˌmɛrɪ'kɑːnə) n. objects, such as documents, relics, etc., relating to America.

American aloe n. See **aloe** (sense 2).

American Dream n. **the.** the notion that the American social, economic, and political system makes success possible for every individual.

American football n. 1. a team game similar to rugby, with 11 players on each side. 2. the oval-shaped inflated ball used in this game.

American Indian n. 1. Also called: **Indian, Red Indian, Amerindian.** a member of any of the indigenous peoples of America, having straight black hair and a yellow-to-brown skin. ~adj. 2. Also called: **Amerindian.** of or relating to any of these peoples, their languages, or their cultures.

Americanism (ə'mɛrɪkə,nɪzəm) n. **1.** a custom, linguistic usage, or other feature peculiar to or characteristic of the United States. **2.** loyalty to the United States.

Americanize or **-ise** (ə'mɛrɪkə,naɪz) vb. to make or become American in outlook, attitudes, etc. —**A,merican-i'zation** or **-i'sation** n.

American Revolution n. the usual U.S. term for **War of American Independence.**

American Samoa n. the part of Samoa administered by the U.S. Capital: Pago Pago. Pop.: 32 395 (1980). Area: 197 sq. km (76 sq. miles).

americium (,æmə'rɪsɪəm) n. a white metallic transuranic element artificially produced from plutonium. It is used as an alpha-particle source. Symbol: Am; atomic no.: 95; half-life of most stable isotope, ^{243}Am: 7.4 × 10^3 years. [C20: from AMERICA (where it was first produced) + -IUM]

Amerigo Vespucci (Italian ame'riːgo ves'puttʃi) n. See **Vespucci.**

Amerindian (,æmə'rɪndɪən) n. also **Amerind** ('æmərɪnd). adj. another word for **American Indian.** — ,Amer'indic adj.

Amersfoort (Dutch 'aːmərsfoːrt) n. a town in the central Netherlands, in E Utrecht province. Pop.: 88 365 (1981 est.).

amethyst ('æmɪθɪst) n. **1.** a purple or violet variety of quartz used as a gemstone. **2.** a purple variety of sapphire. **3. a.** the purple colour of amethyst. **b.** (as adj.): amethyst shadow. [C13: from OF, from L, from Gk amethustos, lit.: not drunken, from A-^{1} + methuein to make drunk; from the belief that the stone could prevent intoxication] —**amethystine** (,æmɪ'θɪstaɪn) adj.

AMF abbrev. for Australian Military Forces.

Amhara (æm'hɑːrə) n. **1.** a region of NW Ethiopia: formerly a kingdom. **2.** an inhabitant of the former kingdom of Amhara.

Amharic (æm'hærɪk) n. **1.** the official language of Ethiopia. ~adj. **2.** denoting this language.

Amherst ('æmhɜːst) n. **Jeffrey,** 1st Baron Amherst. 1717–97, British general who defeated the French in Canada (1758–60): governor general of British North America (1761–63).

amiable ('eɪmɪəb°l) adj. having or displaying a pleasant or agreeable nature; friendly. [C14: from OF, from LL amīcābilis AMICABLE] —,amia'bility or 'amiableness n. —'amiably adv.

amianthus (,æmɪ'ænθəs) n. any of the fine silky varieties of asbestos. [C17: from L amiantus, from Gk amiantos unsullied, from A-^{1} + miainein to pollute]

amicable ('æmɪkəb°l) adj. characterized by friendliness: an amicable agreement. [C15: from LL amīcābilis, from L amīcus friend] —,amica'bility or 'amicableness n. —'amicably adv.

amice ('æmɪs) n. Christianity. a rectangular piece of white linen worn by priests around the neck and shoulders under the alb or, formerly, on the head. [C15: from OF, from L amictus cloak]

amicus curiae (æ'miːkʊs 'kjʊərɪ,iː) n., pl. **amici curiae** (æ'miːkaɪ) Law. a person, not directly engaged in a case, who advises the court. [L, lit.: friend of the court]

amid (ə'mɪd) or **amidst** prep. in the middle of; among. [OE on middan in the middle]

amide ('æmaɪd) n. **1.** any organic compound containing the group -CONH₂. **2.** (modifier) containing the group -CONH₂: amide group or radical. **3.** an inorganic compound containing the NH₂⁻ ion and having the general formula M(NH₂)ₓ, where M is a metal atom. [C19: from AM(MONIA) + -IDE]

amidships ('ə'mɪdʃɪps) adv., adj. (postpositive) Naut. at, near, or towards the centre of a vessel.

Amiens ('æmɪənz; French amjɛ̃) n. a city in N France: its Gothic cathedral is the largest church in France. Pop.: 130 358 (1983 est.).

amigo (æ'miːgəʊ, ə-) n., pl. **-gos.** a friend; comrade. [Sp., from L amicus]

Amin^1 (æ'miːn, ɑː-) n. **Lake.** a former official name for (Lake) **Edward.**

Amin^2 (æ'miːn, ɑː-) n. **Idi** ('iːdiː). born 1925, Ugandan soldier; dictator and head of state (1971–79).

amine (ə'miːn, 'æmɪn) n. an organic base formed by replacing one or more of the hydrogen atoms of ammonia by hydrocarbon groups. [C19: from AM(MONIUM) + -INE^2]

amino (ə'miːnəʊ) n. (modifier) of or containing the group of atoms -NH₂: amino radical.

amino acid n. **1.** any of a group of organic compounds containing one or more amino groups, -NH₂, and one or more carboxyl groups, -COOH. **2.** any of a group of organic nitrogenous compounds that form the component molecules of proteins.

amino resin n. a thermosetting synthetic resin used as an adhesive and coating for paper and textiles.

amir (ə'mɪə) n. a variant spelling of **emir.** [C19: from Ar., var. of EMIR] —a'mirate n.

Amis ('eɪmɪs) n. **Kingsley.** born 1922, English novelist and poet, noted for his novels Lucky Jim (1954), Jake's Thing (1978), Stanley and the Women (1984), The Old Devils (1986), and Difficulties with Girls (1988).

Amish ('æmɪʃ, 'ɑː-) adj. of a U.S. and Canadian Mennonite sect. [C19: from G Amisch, after Jakob Amman, 17th-cent. Swiss Mennonite bishop]

amiss (ə'mɪs) adv. **1.** in an incorrect or defective manner. **2. take (something) amiss.** to be annoyed or offended by (something). ~adj. **3.** (postpositive) wrong or faulty. [C13 a mis, from mis wrong]

amitosis (,æmɪ'təʊsɪs) n. a form of cell division in which the nucleus and cytoplasm divide without the formation of chromosomes. [C20: from A-^{1} + MITOSIS] —**amitotic** (,æmɪ'tɒtɪk) adj.

amity ('æmɪtɪ) n., pl. **-ties.** friendship; cordiality. [C15: from OF amité, ult. from L amīcus friend]

Amman (ə'mɑːn) n. the capital of Jordan, northeast of the Dead Sea: ancient capital of the Ammonites, rebuilt by Ptolemy in the 3rd century B.C. Pop.: 777 500 (1984 est.). Ancient names: **Rabbath Ammon, Philadelphia.**

ammeter ('æm,miːtə) n. an instrument for measuring an electric current in amperes. [C19: AM(PERE) + -METER]

ammo ('æməʊ) n. Inf. short for **ammunition.**

Ammon^1 ('æmən) n. Old Testament. the ancestor of the Ammonites.

Ammon^2 ('æmən) n. Myth. the classical name of the Egyptian god Amen, identified by the Greeks with Zeus and by the Romans with Jupiter.

ammonia (ə'məʊnɪə) n. **1.** a colourless pungent gas used in the manufacture of fertilizers and as a refrigerant and solvent. Formula: NH₃. **2.** a solution of ammonia in water, containing ammonium hydroxide. [C18: from NL, from L (sal) ammōniacus (sal) AMMONIAC]

ammoniac (ə'məʊnɪ,æk) n. a gum resin obtained from the stems of an Asian plant and formerly used as a stimulant, perfume, and in porcelain cement. Also called: **gum ammoniac.** [C14: from L, from Gk ammōniakos belonging to Ammon (apparently the gum resin was extracted from plants found in Libya near the temple of Ammon)]

ammoniacal (,æmə'naɪək°l) adj. of, containing, or resembling ammonia.

ammoniate (ə'məʊnɪ,eɪt) vb. to unite or treat with ammonia. —am,moni'ation n.

ammonify (ə'mɒnɪ,faɪ) vb. **-fying, -fied.** to treat or impregnate with ammonia or a compound of ammonia. —am,monifi'cation n.

ammonite ('æmə,naɪt) n. **1.** any extinct marine cephalopod mollusc of the order Ammonoidea, which were common in Mesozoic times and had a coiled partitioned shell. **2.** the shell of any of these animals, commonly occurring as a fossil. [C18: from L cornū Ammōnis, lit.: horn of Ammon]

ammonium (ə'məʊnɪəm) n. (modifier) of or containing the monovalent group NH₄- or the ion NH₄⁺: ammonium compounds.

ammonium chloride n. a white soluble crystalline solid used as an electrolyte in dry batteries. Formula: NH₄Cl. Also called: **sal ammoniac.**

ammonium hydroxide n. a compound existing in solution when ammonia is dissolved in water, used in the manufacture of rayon and plastics, in photography, and in pharmaceuticals. Formula: NH₄OH.

ammonium sulphate n. a white soluble crystalline solid used mainly as a fertilizer and in water purification. Formula: (NH₄)₂SO₄.

ammunition (,æmjʊ'nɪʃən) n. **1.** any projectiles, such as bullets, rockets, etc., that can be discharged from a weapon. **2.** bombs, missiles, chemicals, etc., capable of use as weapons. **3.** any means of defence or attack, as in an argument. [C17: from obs. F amunition, by mistaken division from earlier la munition; see MUNITION]

amnesia (æm'niːzjə, -ʒjə, -zɪə) n. a defect in memory, esp. one resulting from a pathological cause. [C19: via NL from

Gk: forgetfulness, prob. from *amnēstia* oblivion] —**amnesiac** (æm'niːzɪˌæk) *or* **amnesic** (æm'niːsɪk, -zɪk) *adj.*, *n.*

amnesty ('æmnɪstɪ) *n.*, *pl.* **-ties. 1.** a general pardon, esp. for offences against a government. **2.** a period during which a law is suspended to allow offenders to admit their crime without fear of prosecution. ~*vb.* **-tying, -tied. 3.** (*tr.*) to overlook or forget (an offence). [C16: from L, from Gk: oblivion, from A-¹ + *-mnēstos*, from *mnasthai* to remember]

Amnesty International *n.* an international organization that works to secure the release of people imprisoned for their beliefs, to ban the use of torture, and to abolish the death penalty. Abbrev.: **AI.**

amniocentesis (ˌæmnɪəʊsɛn'tiːsɪs) *n.*, *pl.* **-ses** (-siːz). removal of amniotic fluid for diagnostic purposes by the insertion into the womb of a hollow needle. [C20: from AMNION + *centesis* from Gk *kentēsis* from *kentein* to prick]

amnion ('æmnɪən) *n.*, *pl.* **-nions** *or* **-nia** (-nɪə). the innermost of two membranes enclosing an embryonic reptile, bird, or mammal. [C17: via NL from Gk: a little lamb, from *amnos* a lamb] —**amniotic** (ˌæmnɪ'ɒtɪk) *adj.*

amniotic fluid *n.* the fluid surrounding the fetus in the womb.

amoeba *or U.S.* **ameba** (ə'miːbə) *n.*, *pl.* **-bae** (-biː) *or* **-bas.** any of an order of protozoans able to change shape because of the movements of cell processes. They live in fresh water or soil or as parasites in man and animals. [C19: from NL, from Gk, from *ameibein* to change, exchange] —**a'moebic** *or U.S.* **a'mebic** *adj.*

amok (ə'mʌk, ə'mɒk) *or* **amuck** (ə'mʌk) *n.* **1.** a state of murderous frenzy. ~*adv.* **2. run amok.** to run about as with a frenzied desire to kill. [C17: from Malay *amoq* furious assault]

Amon ('ɑːmən) *n. Egyptian myth.* a variant spelling of **Amen.**

among (ə'mʌŋ) *or* **amongst** *prep.* **1.** in the midst of: *he lived among the Indians.* **2.** to each of: *divide the reward among yourselves.* **3.** in the group, class, or number of: *among the greatest writers.* **4.** taken out of (a group): *he is one among many.* **5.** with one another within a group: *decide it among yourselves.* **6.** in the general opinion or practice of: *accepted among experts.* [OE *amang*, contracted from *on gemang* in the group of, from ON + *gemang* crowd]
▷ **Usage.** See at **between.**

amontillado (əˌmɒntɪ'lɑːdəʊ) *n.* a medium-dry sherry. [C19: from Sp. *vino amontillado* wine of *Montilla*, town in Spain]

amoral (ˌeɪ'mɒrəl) *adj.* **1.** having no moral quality; nonmoral. **2.** without moral standards or principles. —**amorality** (ˌeɪmɒ'rælɪtɪ) *n.*
▷ **Usage.** *Amoral* is frequently and incorrectly used where *immoral* is meant. In careful usage, *immoral* is used of that which infringes moral rules and *amoral* only of that to which considerations of morality are irrelevant or of persons who lack any moral code.

amorist ('æmərɪst) *n.* a lover or a writer about love.

amoroso (ˌæmə'rəʊsəʊ) *adj.*, *adv.* **1.** *Music.* (to be played) tenderly. ~*n.* **2.** a rich sweet sherry. [from It. & Sp.: AMOROUS]

amorous ('æmərəs) *adj.* **1.** inclined towards or displaying love or desire. **2.** in love. **3.** of or relating to love. [C14: from OF, from Med. L, from L *amor* love] —**'amorously** *adv.* —**'amorousness** *n.*

amorphous (ə'mɔːfəs) *adj.* **1.** lacking a definite shape. **2.** of no recognizable character or type. **3.** (of rocks, etc.) not having a crystalline structure. [C18: from NL, from Gk, from A-¹ + *morphē* shape] —**a'morphism** *n.* —**a'morphousness** *n.*

amortize *or* **-tise** (ə'mɔːtaɪz) *vb.* (*tr.*) **1.** *Finance.* to liquidate (a debt, mortgage, etc.) by payments or by periodic transfers to a sinking fund. **2.** to write off (a wasting asset) by transfers to a sinking fund. **3.** *Property law.* (formerly) to transfer (lands, etc.) in mortmain. [C14: from Med. L, from OF *amortir* to reduce to the point of death, ult. from L *ad* to + *mors* death] —**aˌmorti'zation** *or* **-ti'sation** *n.*

Amos ('eɪmɒs) *n. Old Testament.* **1.** a Hebrew prophet of the 8th century B.C. **2.** the book containing his oracles.

amount (ə'maʊnt) *n.* **1.** extent; quantity. **2.** the total of two or more quantities. **3.** the full value or significance of

something. **4.** a principal sum plus the interest on it, as in a loan. ~*vb.* **5.** (*intr.*; usually foll. by *to*) to be equal or add up. [C13: from OF *amonter* to go up, from *amont* upwards, from *a* to + *mont* mountain (from L *mōns*)]

amount of substance *n.* a measure of the number of entities (atoms, molecules, ions, electrons, etc.) present in a substance, expressed in moles.

amour (ə'mʊə) *n.* a love affair, esp. a secret or illicit one. [C13: from OF, from L *amor* love]

amour-propre *French.* (amurprɔprə) *n.* self-respect.

Amoy (ə'mɔɪ) *n.* **1.** a port in SE China, in Fujian province on **Amoy Island,** at the mouth of the Jiu-long River opposite Taiwan: one of the first treaty ports opened to European trade (1842). Pop.: 588 000 (1980 est.). Modern Chinese name: **Xiamen. 2.** the dialect of Chinese spoken in Amoy, Taiwan, and elsewhere: a Min dialect.

amp (æmp) *n.* **1.** an ampere. **2.** *Inf.* an amplifier.

ampelopsis (ˌæmpɪ'lɒpsɪs) *n.* any of a genus of woody climbing plants of tropical and subtropical Asia and America. [C19: from NL, from Gk *ampelos* grapevine]

amperage ('æmpərɪdʒ) *n.* the strength of an electric current measured in amperes.

ampere ('æmpɛə) *n.* **1.** the basic SI unit of electric current; the constant current that, when maintained in two parallel conductors of infinite length and negligible cross section placed 1 metre apart in free space, produces a force of 2×10^{-7} newton per metre between them. **2.** a former unit of electric current (**international ampere**); the current that, when passed through a solution of silver nitrate, deposits silver at the rate of 0.001118 gram per second. ~Abbrev.: **amp.** Symbol: A [C19: after A. M. AMPÈRE]

Ampère ('æmpɛə; *French* ɑ̃pɛr) *n.* **André Marie** (ɑ̃dre mari). 1775–1836, French physicist and mathematician, who made major discoveries in the fields of magnetism and electricity.

ampere-turn *n.* a unit of magnetomotive force; the magnetomotive force produced by a current of 1 ampere passing through one complete turn of a coil.

ampersand ('æmpəˌsænd) *n.* the character (&), meaning *and: John Brown & Co.* [C19: shortened from *and per se and,* that is, the symbol & by itself (represents) *and*]

amphetamine (æm'fɛtəˌmiːn) *n.* a synthetic colourless liquid used medicinally, mainly for its stimulant action on the central nervous system. [C20: from A(LPHA) + M(ETHYL) + PH(ENYL) + ET(HYL) + -AMINE]

amphi- *prefix of nouns and adjectives.* **1.** on both sides; at both ends; of both kinds: *amphipod; amphibious.* **2.** around: *amphibole.* [from Gk]

amphibian (æm'fɪbɪən) *n.* **1.** any cold-blooded vertebrate of the class *Amphibia,* typically living on land but breeding in water. The class includes newts, frogs, and toads. **2.** an aircraft able to land and take off from both water and land. **3.** any vehicle able to travel on both water and land. ~*adj.* **4.** another word for **amphibious. 5.** of or belonging to the class *Amphibia.*

amphibious (æm'fɪbɪəs) *adj.* **1.** able to live both on land and in the water, as frogs, etc. **2.** designed for operation on or from both water and land. **3.** relating to military forces and operations launched from the sea against an enemy shore. **4.** having a dual or mixed nature. [C17: from Gk *amphibios,* having a double life, from AMPHI- + *bios* life] —**am'phibiousness** *n.*

amphibole ('æmfɪˌbəʊl) *n.* any of a large group of minerals consisting of the silicates of calcium, iron, magnesium, sodium, and aluminium, which are common constituents of igneous rocks. [C17: from F, from Gk *amphibolos* uncertain; so called from the large number of varieties in the group]

amphibology (ˌæmfɪ'bɒlədʒɪ) *or* **amphiboly** (æm'fɪbəlɪ) *n.*, *pl.* **-gies** *or* **-lies.** ambiguity of expression, esp. when due to a grammatical construction, as in *save rags and waste paper.* [C14: from LL, ult. from Gk *amphibolos* ambiguous]

amphimixis (ˌæmfɪ'mɪksɪs) *n.*, *pl.* **-mixes** (-'mɪksiːz). true sexual reproduction, esp. the fusion of gametes from two organisms. [C19: from AMPHI- + Gk *mixis* a blending] —**amphimictic** (ˌæmfɪ'mɪktɪk) *adj.*

amphioxus (ˌæmfɪ'ɒksəs) *n.*, *pl.* **-oxi** (-'ɒksaɪ) *or* **-oxuses.** another name for the **lancelet.** [C19: from NL, from AMPHI- + Gk *oxus* sharp]

amphipod ('æmfɪˌpɒd) *n.* **1.** any marine or freshwater crustacean of the order *Amphipoda,* such as the sand hoppers, in which the body is laterally compressed. ~*adj.* **2.** of or belonging to the *Amphipoda*.

amphiprostyle (æm'fɪprə,staɪl) *adj.* **1.** (esp. of a classical temple) having a set of columns at both ends but not at the sides. ~*n.* **2.** a temple of this kind.

amphisbaena (æmfɪs'biːnə) *n.*, *pl.* **-nae** (-niː) *or* **-nas. 1.** a genus of wormlike lizards of tropical America. **2.** *Classical myth.* a fabulous serpent with a head at each end. [C16: from L, from Gk *amphisbaina*, from *amphis* both ways + *bainein* to go]

amphitheatre *or U.S.* **amphitheater** ('æmfɪ,θɪətə) *n.* **1.** a building, usually circular or oval, in which tiers of seats rise from a central open arena. **2.** a place where contests are held. **3.** any level circular area of ground surrounded by higher ground. **4.** a gallery in a theatre. **5.** a lecture room in which seats are tiered away from a central area.

Amphitrite (,æmfɪ'traɪtɪ) *n. Greek myth.* a sea goddess, wife of Poseidon and mother of Triton.

Amphitryon (æm'fɪtrɪən) *n. Greek myth.* the grandson of Perseus and husband of Alcmene.

amphora ('æmfərə) *n.*, *pl.* **-phorae** (-fə,riː) *or* **-phoras.** a Greek or Roman two-handled narrow-necked jar for oil, etc. [C17: from L, from Gk, from AMPHI- + *phoreus* bearer, from *pherein* to bear]

amphoteric (,æmfə'tɛrɪk) *adj. Chem.* able to function as either a base or an acid. [C19: from Gk *amphoteros* each of two (from *amphō* both) + -IC]

ample ('æmpəl) *adj.* **1.** more than sufficient: *an ample helping.* **2.** large: *of ample proportions.* [C15: from OF, from L *amplus* spacious] —**'ampleness** *n.*

amplexicaul (æm'plɛksɪ,kɔːl) *adj.* (of some sessile leaves, stipules, etc.) having an enlarged base that encircles the stem. [C18: from NL, from L *amplecti* to embrace + *caulis* stalk]

amplification (,æmplɪfɪ'keɪʃən) *n.* **1.** the act or result of amplifying. **2.** material added to a statement, story, etc., to expand or clarify it. **3.** a statement, story, etc., with such additional material. **4.** *Electronics.* the increase in strength of an electrical signal by means of an amplifier.

amplifier ('æmplɪ,faɪə) *n.* **1.** an electronic device used to increase the strength of the current fed into it, esp. one for the amplification of sound signals in a radio, record player, etc. **2.** *Photog.* an additional lens for altering focal length. **3.** a person or thing that amplifies.

amplify ('æmplɪ,faɪ) *vb.* **-fying, -fied. 1.** (*tr.*) to increase in size, extent, effect, etc., as by the addition of extra material. **2.** *Electronics.* to produce amplification of (electrical signals). **3.** (*intr.*) to expand a speech, narrative, etc. [C15: from OF, ult. from L *amplificāre* to enlarge, from *amplus* spacious + *facere* to make]

amplitude ('æmplɪ,tjuːd) *n.* **1.** greatness of extent; magnitude. **2.** abundance. **3.** breadth or scope, as of the mind. **4.** *Astron.* the angular distance along the horizon measured from true east or west to the point of intersection of the vertical circle passing through a celestial body. **5.** *Physics.* the maximum displacement from the zero or mean position of a periodic motion. [C16: from L, from *amplus* spacious]

amplitude modulation *n.* one of the principal methods of transmitting information using radio waves, the relevant signal being superimposed onto a radio-frequency carrier wave. The frequency of the carrier wave remains unchanged but its amplitude is varied in accordance with the amplitude of the input signal. Cf. **frequency modulation.**

amply ('æmplɪ) *adv.* fully; generously.

ampoule ('æmpuːl, -pjuːl) *or esp. U.S.* **ampule** *n. Med.* a small glass vessel in which liquids for injection are hermetically sealed. [C19: from F, from L: see AMPULLA]

ampulla (æm'pulə) *n.*, *pl.* **-pullae** (-'puliː). **1.** *Anat.* the dilated end part of certain ducts or canals. **2.** *Christianity.* **a.** a vessel for the wine and water used at the Eucharist. **b.** a small flask for consecrated oil. **3.** a Roman two-handled bottle for oil, wine, or perfume. [C16: from L, dim. of AMPHORA]

amputate ('æmpju,teɪt) *vb. Surgery.* to remove (all or part of a limb). [C17: from L, from *am-* around + *putāre* to trim, prune] —**,ampu'tation** *n.*

amputee (,æmpju'tiː) *n.* a person who has had a limb amputated.

Amravati (æm'rɑːvətɪ) *n.* a town in central India, in NE Maharashtra: cotton centre. Pop.: 261 404 (1981 est.). Former name: **Amraoti** ('æm,rɑːətɪ, ,ʌm-).

Amritsar (æm'rɪtsə) *n.* a city in India, in NW Punjab: centre of the Sikh religion; site of a massacre in 1919 of unarmed supporters of Indian self-government by British troops; in 1984 the Golden Temple, fortified by Sikhs, was attacked by Indian troops with the loss of many Sikh lives. Pop.: 594 844 (1981).

Amsterdam (,æmstə'dæm; *Dutch* amstər'dam) *n.* the commercial capital of the Netherlands, a major industrial centre and port on the IJsselmeer, connected with the North Sea by canal: built on about 100 islands within a network of canals. Pop.: 682 702 (1987).

AMU *abbrev. for* atomic mass unit.

amuck (ə'mʌk) *n.*, *adv.* a variant spelling of **amok.**

Amu Darya (*Russian* a'mu darj'ja) *n.* a river in central Asia, rising in the Pamirs and flowing northwest through the Hindu Kush and across the Turkmen and Uzbek SSRs to its delta in the Aral Sea: forms much of the boundary between Afghanistan and the Soviet Union. Length: 2400 km (1500 miles). Ancient name: **Oxus.**

amulet ('æmjulɪt) *n.* a trinket or piece of jewellery worn as a protection against evil; charm. [C17: from L *amulētum*, from ?]

Amūn ('ɑːmən) *n. Egyptian myth.* a variant spelling of **Amen.**

Amundsen (*Norwegian* 'aːmunsən) *n.* **Roald** ('rɔald). 1872–1928, Norwegian explorer and navigator, who was the first man to reach the South Pole (1911).

Amundsen Sea ('ɑːmundsən) *n.* a part of the South Pacific Ocean, in Antarctica off Byrd Land.

Amur (ə'muə) *n.* a river in NE Asia, rising in N Mongolia as the Argun and flowing southeast, then northeast to the Sea of Okhotsk: forms the boundary between Manchuria and the Soviet Union. Length: about 4350 km (2700 miles). Modern Chinese name: **Heilong Jiang.**

amuse (ə'mjuːz) *vb.* (*tr.*) **1.** to entertain; divert. **2.** to cause to laugh or smile. [C15: from OF *amuser* to cause to be idle, from *muser* to MUSE[1]]

amusement (ə'mjuːzmənt) *n.* **1.** something that amuses, such as a game or pastime. **2.** a mechanical device used for entertainment, as at a fair. **3.** the act of amusing or the state or quality of being amused.

amusement arcade *n. Brit.* a covered area having coin-operated game machines.

amusing (ə'mjuːzɪŋ) *adj.* entertaining; causing a smile or laugh. —**a'musingly** *adv.*

amygdalin (ə'mɪgdəlɪn) *n.* a white soluble bitter-tasting glycoside extracted from bitter almonds. [C17: from Gk: ALMOND + -IN]

amyl ('æmɪl) *n.* (*modifier*) (no longer in technical usage) of or containing any of eight isomeric forms of the monovalent group $C_5H_{11}-$: *amyl group or radical.* [C19: from L: AMYLUM]

amylaceous (,æmɪ'leɪʃəs) *adj.* of or resembling starch.

amyl alcohol *n.* **1.** any of eight isomeric alcohols with the general formula $C_5H_{11}OH$. **2.** A mixture of these alcohols, used in preparing amyl nitrite.

amylase ('æmɪ,leɪz) *n.* any of several enzymes that hydrolyse starch and glycogen to simple sugars, such as glucose.

amyl nitrite *n.* an ester of amyl alcohol and nitrous acid used as a vasodilator, esp. to treat angina pectoris.

amyloid ('æmɪ,lɔɪd) *n.* **1.** any substance resembling starch. ~*adj.* **2.** starchlike.

amylopsin (,æmɪ'lɒpsɪn) *n.* an enzyme of the pancreatic juice that converts starch into sugar; pancreatic amylase. [C19: from AMYL + (PE)PSIN]

amylum ('æmɪləm) *n.* another name for **starch** (senses 1,2). [L, from Gk *amulon* fine meal, starch]

Amytal ('æmɪ,tæl) *n. Trademark.* sodium amytal, used as a sedative and hypnotic.

an[1] (æn; *unstressed* ən) *determiner.* (*indefinite article*) a form of **a**[1], used before an initial vowel sound: *an old car; an elf; an hour.* [OE *ān* ONE]

▷ **Usage.** *An* was formerly often used before words that begin with *h* and are unstressed on the first syllable: *an hotel; an historic meeting:* sometimes the initial *h* was not pronounced. In British English this usage is now obsolescent.

an[2] *or* **an'** (æn; *unstressed* ən) *conj.* (*subordinating*) an obsolete or dialect word for **if.** See **and** (sense 8).

An[1] (ɑːn) *n. Myth.* the Sumerian sky god. Babylonian counterpart: **Anu.**

An[2] *the chemical symbol for* actinon.

an. *abbrev. for* anno. [L: in the year]

an- *or before a consonant* **a-** *prefix.* not; without: *anaphrodisiac.* [from Gk]

-an, -ean, *or* **-ian** *suffix.* **1.** (*forming adjectives and nouns*) belonging to; coming from; typical of; adhering to: *European; Elizabethan; Christian.* **2.** (*forming nouns*) a person who specializes or is expert in: *dietitian.* [from L *-ānus,* suffix of adjectives]

ana- *or before a vowel* **an-** *prefix.* **1.** up; upwards: *anadromous.* **2.** again: *anagram.* **3.** back; backwards: *anapaest.* [from Gk *ana*]

-ana *or* **-iana** *suffix forming nouns.* denoting a collection of objects or information relating to a particular individual, subject or place: *Victoriana, Americana.* [NL, from L *-āna,* lit.: matters relating to, neuter pl. of *-ānus;* see -AN]

Anabaptist (ˌænəˈbæptɪst) *n.* **1.** a member of any of various Protestant movements, esp. of the 16th century, that rejected infant baptism, insisted that adults be rebaptized, and sought to establish Christian communism. *~adj.* **2.** of these sects or their doctrines. [C16: from Ecclesiastical L, from *anabaptīzāre* to baptize again, from LGk *anabaptizein*] —**Ana'baptism** *n.*

anabas (ˈænəˌbæs) *n.* any of several freshwater fishes, esp. the climbing perch, that can travel on land. [C19: from NL, from Gk *anabainein* to go up]

anabasis (əˈnæbəsɪs) *n., pl.* **-ses** (-ˌsiːz). **1.** the march of Cyrus the Younger from Sardis to Cunaxa in Babylonia in 401 B.C., described by Xenophon in his *Anabasis.* **2.** any military expedition, esp. one from the coast to the interior. [C18: from Gk: a going up, from *anabainein* to go up]

anabatic (ˌænəˈbætɪk) *adj. Meteorol.* (of air currents) rising upwards. [C19: from Gk *anabatikos* relating to ascents, from *anabainein* to go up]

anabiosis (ˌænəbaɪˈəʊsɪs) *n.* a return to life after apparent death. [C19: via NL from Gk, from *anabioein* to come back to life] —**anabiotic** (ˌænəbaɪˈɒtɪk) *adj.*

anabolic steroid *n.* any of a group of synthetic steroid hormones (androgens) used to stimulate muscle and bone growth for athletic or therapeutic purposes.

anabolism (əˈnæbəˌlɪzəm) *n.* a metabolic process in which complex molecules are synthesized from simpler ones with the storage of energy; constructive metabolism. [C19: from ANA- + (META)BOLISM] —**anabolic** (ˌænəˈbɒlɪk) *adj.*

anachronism (əˈnækrəˌnɪzəm) *n.* **1.** the representation of an event, person, or thing in a historical context in which it could not have occurred or existed. **2.** a person or thing that belongs or seems to belong to another time. [C17: from L, from Gk *anakhronismos* a mistake in chronology, from ANA- + *khronos* time] —**a,nachro'nistic** *adj.* —**a,nachro'nistically** *adv.*

anacoluthon (ˌænəkəˈluːθɒn) *n., pl.* **-tha** (-θə). a construction that involves the change from one grammatical sequence to another within a single sentence. [C18: from LL, from Gk, from *anakolouthos* not consistent, from AN- + *akolouthos* following]

anaconda (ˌænəˈkɒndə) *n.* a very large nonvenomous arboreal and semiaquatic snake of tropical South America, which kills its prey by constriction. [C18: prob. changed from Sinhalese *henakandayā* whip snake; orig. referring to a snake of Sri Lanka]

Anacreon (əˈnækrɪˌɒn, -ən) *n.* ?572–?488 B.C., Greek lyric poet, noted for his short songs celebrating love and wine. —**A,nacre'ontic** *adj., n.*

anacrusis (ˌænəˈkruːsɪs) *n., pl.* **-ses** (-siːz). **1.** *Prosody.* one or more unstressed syllables at the beginning of a line of verse. **2.** *Music.* an unstressed note or group of notes immediately preceding the strong first beat of the first bar. [C19: from Gk, from *anakrouein* to strike up, from ANA-+ *krouein* to strike]

anadromous (əˈnædrəməs) *adj.* (of fishes such as the salmon) migrating up rivers from the sea in order to breed. [C18: from Gk *anadromos* running upwards]

Anadyr (*Russian* ɑˈnadirj) *n.* **1.** a town in the Soviet Union, in NE Siberia at the mouth of the Anadyr River. Pop.: 7703 (1970). **2.** a mountain range in the Soviet Union, in NE Siberia, rising over 1500 m (5000 ft.). **3.** a river in the Soviet Union, rising in mountains on the Arctic Circle, south of the Anadyr Range, and flowing east to the Gulf of Anadyr. Length: 725 km (450 miles). **4.** **Gulf of.** an inlet of the Bering Sea, off the coast of the NE Soviet Union.

anaemia *or U.S.* **anemia** (əˈniːmɪə) *n.* a deficiency in the number of red blood cells or in their haemoglobin content, resulting in pallor and lack of energy. [C19: from NL, from Gk *anaimia* lack of blood, from AN- + *haima* blood]

anaemic *or U.S.* **anemic** (əˈniːmɪk) *adj.* **1.** relating to or suffering from anaemia. **2.** pale and sickly looking; lacking vitality.

anaerobe (æˈnɛərəʊb, ˈænərəʊb) *or* **anaerobium** (ˌænɛəˈrəʊbɪəm) *n., pl.* **-obes** *or* **-obia** (-ˈəʊbɪə). an organism that does not require, or requires the absence of, free oxygen or air. —**,anaer'obic** *adj.*

anaesthesia *or U.S.* **anesthesia** (ˌænɪsˈθiːzɪə) *n.* **1.** loss of bodily sensation, esp. of touch, as the result of nerve damage or other abnormality. **2.** loss of sensation, esp. of pain, induced by drugs: called **general anaesthesia** when consciousness is lost and **local anaesthesia** when only a specific area of the body is involved. [C19: from NL, from Gk *anaisthēsia* absence of sensation]

anaesthetic *or U.S.* **anesthetic** (ˌænɪsˈθɛtɪk) *n.* **1.** a substance that causes anaesthesia. *~adj.* **2.** causing or characterized by anaesthesia.

anaesthetics (ˌænɪsˈθɛtɪks) *n.* (*functioning as sing.*) the science of anaesthesia and its application. U.S. name: **anesthesiology.**

anaesthetist (əˈniːsθətɪst) *n.* **1.** *Brit.* a doctor specializing in the administration of anaesthetics. U.S. name: **anesthesiologist.** **2.** *U.S.* See **anesthetist.**

anaesthetize, anaesthetise, *or U.S.* **anesthetize** (əˈniːsθəˌtaɪz) *vb.* (*tr.*) to render insensible to pain by administering an anaesthetic. —**a,naestheti'zation, a,naestheti'sation,** *or U.S.* **a,nestheti'zation** *n.*

anaglyph (ˈænəˌglɪf) *n.* **1.** *Photog.* a stereoscopic picture consisting of two images of the same object, taken from slightly different angles, in two complementary colours. When viewed through coloured spectacles, the images merge to produce a stereoscopic sensation. **2.** anything cut to stand in low relief, such as a cameo. [C17: from Gk *anagluphē* carved in low relief, from ANA- + *gluphē* carving, from *gluphein* to carve] —**,ana'glyphic** *adj.*

Anaglypta (ˌænəˈglɪptə) *n. Trademark.* a type of thick embossed wallpaper designed to be painted. [C19: from Gk *anagluptos;* see ANAGLYPH]

anagram (ˈænəˌgræm) *n.* a word or phrase the letters of which can be rearranged into another word or phrase. [C16: from NL, from Gk, from *anagrammatizein* to transpose letters, from ANA-+ *gramma* a letter] —**anagrammatic** (ˌænəɡrəˈmætɪk) *or* **,anagram'matical** *adj.*

anagrammatize *or* **-tise** (ˌænəˈɡræməˌtaɪz) *vb.* to arrange into an anagram.

Anaheim (ˈænəˌhaɪm) *n.* a city in SW California: site of Disneyland. Pop.: 240 730 (1986).

anal (ˈeɪnəl) *adj.* **1.** of or near the anus. **2.** *Psychoanal.* relating to a stage of psychosexual development during which the child's interest is concentrated on the anal region and excremental functions. [C18: from NL *ānālis;* see ANUS] —**'anally** *adv.*

analects (ˈænəˌlɛkts) *or* **analecta** (ˌænəˈlɛktə) *pl. n.* selected literary passages from one or more works. [C17: via L from Gk, from *analegein* to collect up, from *legein* to gather]

analeptic (ˌænəˈlɛptɪk) *adj.* **1.** (of a drug, etc.) restorative or invigorating. *~n.* **2.** a restorative remedy or drug. [C17: from NL, from Gk *analēptikos* stimulating, from *analambanein* to take up]

anal fin *n.* an unpaired fin between the anus and tail fin in fishes that maintains equilibrium.

analgesia (ˌænəlˈdʒiːzɪə) *or* **analgia** (ænˈældʒɪə) *n.* inability to feel pain. [C18: via NL from Gk: insensibility, from AN- + *algēsis* sense of pain]

analgesic (ˌænəlˈdʒiːzɪk) *adj.* **1.** of or causing analgesia. *~n.* **2.** a substance that produces analgesia.

analog (ˈænəˌlɒɡ) *n.* a variant spelling of **analogue.** ▷ **Usage.** The spelling *analog* is a U.S. variant of *analogue* in all its senses, and is also the generally preferred spelling in the computer industry.

analog computer *n.* a computer that performs arithmetical operations by using some variable physical quantity, such as mechanical movement or voltage, to represent numbers.

analogize *or* **-gise** (əˈnæləˌdʒaɪz) *vb.* **1.** (*intr.*) to make use of analogy, as in argument. **2.** (*tr.*) to make analogous or reveal analogy in.

analogous (ə'næləgəs) *adj.* **1.** similar or corresponding in some respect. **2.** *Biol.* (of organs and parts) having the same function but different evolutionary origin. **3.** *Linguistics.* formed by analogy: *an analogous plural.* [C17: from L, from Gk *analogos* proportionate, from ANA- + *logos* speech, ratio]

analogue *or U.S.* (*sometimes*) **analog** ('ænˌlɒg) *n.* **1. a.** a physical object or quantity used to measure or represent another quantity. **b.** (*as modifier*): *analogue watch; analogue recording.* **2.** something analogous to something else. **3.** *Biol.* an analogous part or organ.

▷ **Usage.** See at **analog.**

analogy (ə'nælədʒɪ) *n., pl.* **-gies. 1.** agreement or similarity, esp. in a limited number of features. **2.** a comparison made to show such a similarity: *an analogy between an atom and the solar system.* **3.** *Biol.* the relationship between analogous organs or parts. **4.** *Logic, maths, philosophy.* a form of reasoning in which a similarity between two or more things is inferred from a known similarity between them in other respects. **5.** *Linguistics.* imitation of existing models or regular patterns in the formation of words, etc.: *a child may use "sheeps" as the plural of "sheep" by analogy with "cat," "cats," etc.* [C16: from Gk *analogia* correspondence, from *analogos* ANALOGOUS]

analysand (ə'nælɪˌsænd) *n.* any person who is undergoing psychoanalysis. [C20: from ANALYSE + -*and*, on the model of *multiplicand*]

analyse *or U.S.* **-lyze** ('ænˌlaɪz) *vb.* **1.** (*tr.*) to examine in detail in order to discover meaning, essential features, etc. **2.** (*tr.*) to break down into components or essential features. **3.** (*tr.*) to make a mathematical, chemical, grammatical, etc., analysis of. **4.** another word for **psychoanalyse.** [C17: back formation from ANALYSIS] —'**ana,lyser** *or U.S.* -,**lyzer** *n.*

analysis (ə'nælɪsɪs) *n., pl.* **-ses** (-,siːz). **1.** the division of a physical or abstract whole into its constituent parts to examine or determine their relationship. **2.** a statement of the results of this. **3.** short for **psychoanalysis. 4.** *Chem.* **a.** the decomposition of a substance in order to determine the kinds of constituents present (**qualitative analysis**) or the amount of each constituent (**quantitative analysis**). **b.** the result obtained by such a determination. **5.** *Linguistics.* the use of word order together with word function to express syntactic relations in a language, as opposed to the use of inflections. **6.** *Maths.* the branch of mathematics principally concerned with the properties of functions. **7. in the last, final,** *or* **ultimate analysis.** after everything has been given due consideration. [C16: from NL, from Gk *analusis*, lit.: a dissolving, from ANA- + *luein* to loosen]

analysis of variance *n. Statistics.* a technique for analysing the total variation of a set of observations as measured by the variance of the observations multiplied by their number.

analyst ('ænəlɪst) *n.* **1.** a person who analyses or is skilled in analysis. **2.** short for **psychoanalyst.**

analytic (ˌænə'lɪtɪk) *or* **analytical** *adj.* **1.** relating to analysis. **2.** capable of or given to analysing: *an analytic mind.* **3.** *Linguistics.* denoting languages characterized by analysis. **4.** *Logic.* (of a proposition) true or false by virtue of the meanings of the words alone: *all spinsters are unmarried is analytically true.* [C16: via LL from Gk *analutikos*, from *analuein* to dissolve, break down] —,**ana'lytically** *adv.* —**analyticity** (,ænəlɪ'tɪsɪtɪ) *n.*

analytical geometry *n.* the branch of geometry that uses algebraic notation to locate a point; coordinate geometry.

analytic philosophy *n.* See **philosophical analysis.**

Anam (æ'næm, 'ænæm) *n.* a variant spelling of **Annam.**

Anambra (ə'næmbrə) *n.* a state of S Nigeria, formed in 1976 from part of East-Central State. Capital: Enugu. Pop.: 6 029 500 (1984). Area: 19 233 sq. km (7424 sq. miles).

anandrous (æn'ændrəs) *adj.* (of flowers) having no stamens. [C19: from Gk *anandros* lacking males, from AN- + *anēr* man]

Ananias (,ænə'naɪəs) *n.* **1.** *New Testament.* a Jewish Christian of Jerusalem who was struck dead for lying (Acts 5). **2.** a liar.

anapaest *or* **anapest** ('ænəpɛst, -piːst) *n. Prosody.* a metrical foot of three syllables, the first two short, the last long (‿ ‿ ‒). [C17: via L from Gk *anapaistos* reversed, from *ana*- back + *paiein* to strike] —,**ana'paestic** *or* ,**ana'pestic** *adj.*

anaphora (ə'næfərə) *n.* **1.** *Grammar.* the use of a word such as a pronoun to avoid repetition, as for example *one* in *He offered me a drink but I didn't want one.* **2.** *Rhetoric.* the repetition of a word or phrase at the beginning of successive clauses. [C16: via L from Gk: repetition, from ANA- + *pherein* to bear]

anaphrodisiac (,ænæfrə'dɪzɪ,æk) *adj.* **1.** tending to lessen sexual desire. ~*n.* **2.** an anaphrodisiac drug.

anaphylaxis (,ænəfɪ'læksɪs) *n.* extreme sensitivity to an injected antigen following a previous injection. [C20: from ANA- + (PRO)PHYLAXIS]

anaptyxis (,ænæp'tɪksɪs) *n., pl.* **-tyxes** (-'tɪksiːz). the insertion of a short vowel between consonants in order to make a word more easily pronounceable. [C19: via NL from Gk *anaptuxis*, from *anaptussein* to unfold, from ANA- + *ptussein* to fold]

Anapurna (,ænə'puənə) *n.* a variant spelling of **Annapurna.**

anarchism ('ænəˌkɪzəm) *n.* **1.** *Political theory.* a doctrine advocating the abolition of government. **2.** the principles or practice of anarchists.

anarchist ('ænəkɪst) *n.* **1.** a person who advocates the abolition of government and a social system based on voluntary cooperation. **2.** a person who causes disorder or upheaval.

anarchy ('ænəkɪ) *n.* **1.** general lawlessness and disorder, esp. when thought to result from an absence or failure of government. **2.** the absence of government. **3.** the absence of any guiding or uniting principle; chaos. **4.** political anarchism. [C16: from Med. L, from Gk, from *anarkhos* without a ruler, from AN- + *arkh-* leader, from *arkhein* to rule] —**anarchic** (æn'ɑːkɪk) *or* **an'archical** *adj.*

Anastasia (,ænə'stɑːzɪə, -'steɪ-) *n.* **Grand Duchess.** 1901–?18, daughter of Tsar Nicholas II, believed to have been executed by the Bolsheviks in 1918, although several women subsequently claimed to be her.

anastigmat (æ'næstɪgmæt, ,ænə'stɪgmæt) *n.* a lens system designed to be free of astigmatism. [C19: from AN- + ASTIGMATIC] —,**anastig'matic** *adj.*

anastomose (ə'næstə,məuz) *vb.* to join (two parts of a blood vessel, etc.) by anastomosis.

anastomosis (ə,næstə'məusɪs) *n., pl.* **-ses** (-siːz). **1.** a natural connection between two tubular structures, such as blood vessels. **2.** the union of two hollow parts that are normally separate. [C16: via NL from Gk: opening, from *anastomoun* to equip with a mouth, from *stoma* mouth]

anastrophe (ə'næstrəfɪ) *n. Rhetoric.* another term for **inversion** (sense 3). [C16: from Gk, from *anastrephein* to invert]

anathema (ə'næθəmə) *n., pl.* **-mas. 1.** a detested person or thing: *he is anathema to me.* **2.** a formal ecclesiastical excommunication, or denunciation of a doctrine. **3.** the person or thing so cursed. **4.** a strong curse. [C16: via Church L from Gk: something accursed, from *anatithenai* to dedicate, from ANA-+ *tithenai* to set]

anathematize *or* **-tise** (ə'næθɪmə,taɪz) *vb.* to pronounce an anathema (upon a person, etc.); curse.

Anatolia (,ænə'təulɪə) *n.* the Asian part of Turkey, occupying the peninsula between the Black Sea, the Mediterranean, and the Aegean: consists of a plateau, largely mountainous, with salt lakes in the interior. Historical name: **Asia Minor.** —,**Ana'tolian** *adj., n.*

anatomical (,ænə'tɒmɪk⁹l) *adj.* of anatomy.

anatomist (ə'nætəmɪst) *n.* an expert in anatomy.

anatomize *or* **-mise** (ə'nætə,maɪz) *vb.* (*tr.*) **1.** to dissect (an animal or plant). **2.** to examine in minute detail.

anatomy (ə'nætəmɪ) *n., pl.* **-mies. 1.** the science concerned with the physical structure of animals and plants. **2.** the physical structure of an animal or plant or any of its parts. **3.** a book or treatise on this subject. **4.** dissection of an animal or plant. **5.** any detailed analysis: *the anatomy of a crime.* **6.** *Inf.* the human body. [C14: from L, from Gk *anatomē*, from ANA- + *temnein* to cut]

anatto (ə'nætəu) *n., pl.* **-tos.** a variant spelling of **annatto.**

Anaxagoras (,ænæk'sægərəs) *n.* ?500–428 B.C., Greek philosopher who maintained that all things were composed of minute particles arranged by an eternal intelligence.

Anaximander (ə,næksɪ'mændə) *n.* 611–547 B.C., Greek philosopher, astronomer, and mathematician who believed the first principle of the world to be the Infinite.

Anaximenes (ˌænæk'sɪmə,niːz) *n.* 6th century B.C., Greek philosopher who believed air to be the primary substance.

ANC *abbrev. for* African National Congress.

-ance *or* **-ancy** *suffix forming nouns.* indicating an action, state or condition, or quality: *resemblance; tenancy.* [via OF from L *-antia*]

ancestor ('ænsɛstə) *n.* **1.** a person from whom another is directly descended; forefather. **2.** an early animal or plant from which a later type has evolved. **3.** a person or thing regarded as a forerunner: *the ancestor of the modern camera.* [C13: from OF, from LL *antecēssor* one who goes before, from L *antecēdere*] — 'ancestress *fem. n.*

ancestral (æn'sɛstrəl) *adj.* of or inherited from ancestors.

ancestry ('ænsɛstrɪ) *n., pl.* **-tries. 1.** lineage or descent, esp. when noble or distinguished. **2.** ancestors collectively.

Anchises (æn'kaisiːz) *n. Classical myth.* a Trojan prince and father of Aeneas. In the *Aeneid*, he is rescued by his son at the fall of Troy and dies in Sicily.

anchor ('æŋkə) *n.* **1.** a device attached to a vessel by a cable and dropped overboard so as to grip the bottom and restrict movement. **2.** an object used to hold something else firmly in place: *the rock provided an anchor for the rope.* **3.** a source of stability or security. **4.** short for **anchor man. 5. cast, come to,** *or* **drop anchor.** to anchor a vessel. **6. ride at anchor.** to be anchored. ~*vb.* **7.** to use an anchor to hold (a vessel) in one place. **8.** to fasten or be fastened securely; fix or become fixed firmly. [OE *ancor*, from L, from Gk *ankura*]

anchorage ('æŋkərɪdʒ) *n.* **1.** the act of anchoring. **2.** any place where a vessel is anchored. **3.** a place designated for vessels to anchor. **4.** a fee imposed for anchoring. **5.** anything used as an anchor. **6.** a source of security or strength.

Anchorage ('æŋkərɪdʒ) *n.* the largest city in Alaska, a port in the south, at the head of Cook Inlet. Pop.: 244 030 (1984).

anchorite ('æŋkə,rait) *n.* a person who lives in seclusion, esp. a religious recluse; hermit. [C15: from Med. L, from LL, from Gk, from *anakhōrein* to retire, from *khōra* a space] — 'anchoress *fem. n.*

anchor man *n.* **1.** *Sport.* the last person in a team to compete, esp. in a relay race. **2.** (in broadcasting) a person in a central studio who links up and maintains contact with various outside camera units, reporters, etc.

anchovy ('æntʃəvɪ) *n., pl.* **-vies** *or* **-vy.** any of various small marine food fishes which have a salty taste and are often tinned or made into a paste or essence. [C16: from Sp. *anchova*, ? ult. from Gk *aphuē* small fish]

anchusa (æŋ'kjuːsə) *n.* any of several Eurasian plants having rough hairy stems and leaves and blue flowers. [C18: from L]

anchylose ('æŋkɪ,ləʊz) *vb.* a variant spelling of **ankylose.**

ancien régime French. (ɑ̃sjẽ reʒim) *n., pl.* **anciens régimes** (ɑ̃sjẽ reʒim). the political and social system of France before the Revolution of 1789. [lit.: old regime]

ancient ('einʃənt) *adj.* **1.** dating from very long ago: *ancient ruins.* **2.** very old. **3.** of the far past, esp. before the collapse of the Western Roman Empire (476 A.D.). ~*n.* **4.** (*often pl.*) a member of a civilized nation in the ancient world, esp. a Greek or Roman. **5.** (*often pl.*) one of the classical authors of Greek or Roman antiquity. **6.** *Arch.* an old man. [C14: from OF *ancien*, from Vulgar L *anteanus* (unattested), from L *ante* before] — 'ancientness *n.*

ancient lights *n.* (*usually functioning as sing.*) the legal right to receive, by a particular window or windows, adequate and unobstructed daylight.

anciently ('einʃəntlɪ) *adv.* in ancient times.

ancillary (æn'sɪlərɪ) *adj.* **1.** subsidiary. **2.** auxiliary; supplementary: *ancillary services.* ~*n., pl.* **-laries. 3.** a subsidiary or auxiliary thing or person. [C17: from L *ancillāris* concerning maidservants, ult. from *ancūla* female servant]

Ancohuma (ˌæŋkəʊ'uːmə) *n.* one of the two peaks of (Mount) **Sorata.**

ancon ('æŋkɒn) *or* **ancone** ('æŋkəʊn) *n., pl.* **ancones** (æŋ'kəʊniːz). *Architect.* a projecting bracket or console supporting a cornice. [C18: from Gk *ankōn* a bend]

Ancona (*Italian* aŋ'koːna) *n.* a port in Central Italy, on the Adriatic, capital of the Marches: founded by Greeks from Syracuse in about 390 B.C. Pop.: 104 409 (1986).

-ancy *suffix forming nouns.* a variant of **-ance,** indicating condition or quality: *poignancy.*

ancylostomiasis (ˌænsɪ,lɒstə'maɪəsɪs) *or* **ankylostomiasis** (ˌæŋkɪ,lɒstə'maɪəsɪs) *n.* infestation of the intestine with blood-sucking hookworms; hookworm disease. [from NL, ult. from Gk *ankulos* hooked + *stoma* mouth]

and (ænd; *unstressed* ənd, ən) *conj. (coordinating)* **1.** in addition to: *boys and girls.* **2.** as a consequence: *he fell down and cut his knee.* **3.** afterwards: *we pay and go through that door.* **4.** plus: *two and two equals four.* **5.** used to give emphasis or indicate repetition or continuity: *it rained and rained.* **6.** used to express a contrast between instances of what is named: *there are jobs and jobs.* **7.** *Inf.* used in place of *to* in infinitives after verbs such as *try, go,* and *come: try and see it my way.* **8.** an obsolete word for *if: and it please you.* [OE *and*] ▷ **Usage.** See at **to.**

-and *or* **-end** *suffix forming nouns.* indicating a person or thing that is to be dealt with in a specified way: *dividend; multiplicand.* [from L gerundives ending in *-andus, -endus*]

Andalusia (ˌændə'luːzɪə) *n.* a region of S Spain, on the Mediterranean and the Atlantic, with the Sierra Morena in the north, the Sierra Nevada in the southeast, and the Guadalquivir River flowing over fertile lands between them; a centre of Moorish civilization; it became an autonomous region in 1981. Area: about 87 280 sq. km (33 700 sq. miles). Spanish name: **Andalucía** (andalu'θia).

Andaman and Nicobar Islands ('ændəmən; 'nɪkəʊ,bɑː) *pl. n.* a territory of India, in the E Bay of Bengal, consisting of two groups of over 200 islands. Capital: Port Blair. Pop.: 188 254 (1981). Area: 8140 sq. km (3143 sq. miles).

Andaman Islands *pl. n.* a group of islands in the E Bay of Bengal, part of the Indian territory of the Andaman and Nicobar Islands. Area: 6475 sq. km (2500 sq. miles).

Andaman Sea *n.* part of the Bay of Bengal, between the Andaman and Nicobar Islands and the Malay Peninsula.

andante (æn'dæntɪ) *Music.* ~*adj., adv.* **1.** (to be performed) at a moderately slow tempo. ~*n.* **2.** a passage or piece to be performed in this manner. [C18: from It., from *andare* to walk, from L *ambulāre*]

andantino (ˌændæn'tiːnəʊ) *Music.* ~*adj., adv.* **1.** (to be performed) slightly faster or slower than andante. ~*n., pl.* **-nos. 2.** a passage or piece to be performed in this manner. [C19: dim. of ANDANTE]

AND circuit *or* **gate** (ænd) *n. Computers.* a logic circuit that has a high-voltage output signal if and only if all input signals are at a high voltage simultaneously. [C20: from similarity of operation of *and* in logical conjunctions]

Andean (æn'diːən, 'ændɪən) *adj.* of, relating to, or resembling the Andes.

Anderlecht (*Flemish* 'ɑndərlɛxt) *n.* a town in central Belgium, a suburb of Brussels. Pop.: 94 715 (1982).

Andersen ('ændəsᵊn) *n.* **Hans Christian.** 1805–75, Danish author of fairy tales, including *The Ugly Duckling, The Tin Soldier,* and *The Snow Queen.*

Andersen Nexø ('anərsen) *n.* See (Martin Andersen) **Nexø.**

Anderson[1] ('ændəsᵊn) *n.* a river in N Canada, in the Northwest Territories, rising in lakes north of Great Bear Lake and flowing west and north to the Beaufort Sea. Length: about 580 km (360 miles).

Anderson[2] ('ændəsᵊn) *n.* **1. Carl David.** born 1905, U.S. physicist, who discovered the positron in cosmic rays (1932): Nobel prize for physics 1936. **2. Elizabeth Garrett.** 1836–1917, English physician and feminist: a campaigner for the admission of women to the professions. **3.** Dame **Judith,** real name *Frances Margaret Anderson.* born 1898, stage and film actress. **4. Marian.** born 1902, U.S. contralto, the first Negro permanent member of the Metropolitan Opera Company, New York.

Anderssen ('ændəsᵊn) *n.* **Adolf** ('aːdɔlf). 1818–79, German chess player: noted for the incisiveness of his combination play.

Andes ('ændiːz) *pl. n.* a major mountain system of South America, extending for about 7250 km (4500 miles) along the entire W coast, with several parallel ranges or cordilleras and many volcanic peaks: rich in minerals, including gold, silver, copper, iron ore, and nitrates. Average height: 3900 m (13 000 ft.). Highest peak: Aconcagua, 6960 m (22 835 ft.).

Andhra Pradesh ('ændrə prɑː'deʃ) *n.* a state of SE India, on the Bay of Bengal: formed in 1953 from parts of Madras and Hyderabad states. Capital: Hyderabad. Pop.: 53 403 619 (1981). Area: about 275 068 sq. km (106 181 sq. miles).

andiron ('ænd,aɪən) *n.* either of a pair of metal stands for supporting logs in a hearth. [C14: from OF *andier*, from ?; infl. by IRON]

Andizhan (*Russian* andi'ʒan) *n.* a city in the SW Soviet Union, in the E Uzbek SSR. Pop.: 288 000 (1987).

Andong ('æn'dʊŋ) *or* **Antung** *n.* a port in E China, in Liaoning province at the mouth of the Yalu River. Pop.: 102 024 (1980).

and/or *conj.* (*coordinating*) used to join terms when either one or the other or both is indicated: *passports and/or other means of identification.*

▷ **Usage.** *And/or* is not universally accepted as being good usage outside legal and commercial contexts. It is never used by careful writers and speakers where *or* is meant: *he must bring his car or his bicycle* (not *his car and/or his bicycle*).

Andorra (æn'dɔːrə) *n.* a mountainous coprincipality in SW Europe, between France and Spain: according to tradition, given independence by Charlemagne in the 9th century for helping to fight the Moors; placed under the joint sovereignty of the Comte de Foix and the Spanish bishop of Urgel in 1278; under the joint overlordship of the French head of state and the bishop of Urgel from the 16th century. Languages: Catalan, French, and Spanish. Religion: Roman Catholic. Currency: French franc and Spanish peseta. Capital: Andorra la Vella. Pop.: 47 000 (1985). Area: 464 sq. km (179 sq. miles). Official name: **Principat d'Andorra. —An'dorran** *adj., n.*

Andorra la Vella (*Spanish* an'dɔrra la 'beʎa) *n.* the capital of Andorra, situated in the west of the principality. Pop.: 14 783 (1981). French name: **Andorre la Vieille** (ɑ̃dɔr la vjɛj).

Andrássy (æn'dræsɪ; *Hungarian* 'ɔndraːʃi) *n.* Count **Gyula** ('djulɔ). 1823–90, Hungarian statesman; the first prime minister of Hungary under the Dual Monarchy of Austria-Hungary (1867).

André ('ɑːndreɪ, 'ændrɪ) *n.* **John.** 1751–80, British major who was hanged as a spy for conspiring with Benedict Arnold during the War of American Independence.

Andrea del Sarto (*Italian* an'drea del 'sarto) *n.* See **Sarto.**

Andreanof Islands (,ændrɪ'ɑːnɒf) *pl. n.* a group of islands in the central Aleutian Islands, Alaska. Area: 3710 sq. km (1432 sq. miles).

Andrew ('ændruː) *n. New Testament.* one of the twelve apostles of Jesus; the brother of Peter; patron saint of Scotland. Feast day: Nov. 30.

Andrewes ('ændruːz) *n.* **Lancelot.** 1555–1626, English bishop and theologian.

Andrews ('ændruːz) *n.* **Thomas.** 1813–85, Irish physical chemist, noted for his work on the liquefaction of gases.

Andrić (*Serbo-Croat* 'andritʃ) *n.* **Ivo** ('iːvɔ). 1892–1975, Yugoslav novelist; author of *The Bridge on the Dvina* (1945): Nobel prize for literature 1961.

andro- *or before a vowel* **andr-** *combining form.* **1.** male; masculine: *androsterone.* **2.** (in botany) stamen or anther: *androecium.* [from Gk *anēr* (genitive *andros*) man]

Androcles ('ændrə,kliːz) *or* **Androclus** ('ændrəkləs) *n.* (in Roman legend) a slave whose life was spared in the arena by a lion from whose paw he had once extracted a thorn.

androecium (æn'driːsɪəm) *n., pl.* **-cia** (-sɪə). the stamens of a flowering plant collectively. [C19: from NL, from ANDRO- + Gk *oikion* a little house]

androgen ('ændrədʒən) *n.* any of several steroids that promote development of male sexual characteristics. **—androgenic** (,ændrə'dʒɛnɪk) *adj.*

androgyne ('ændrə,dʒaɪn) *n.* another word for **hermaphrodite.** [C17: from OF, via L from Gk *androgunos*, from *anēr* man + *gunē* woman]

androgynous (æn'drɒdʒɪnəs) *adj.* **1.** *Bot.* having male and female flowers in the same inflorescence. **2.** having male and female characteristics; hermaphrodite. **—an'drogyny** *n.*

android ('ændrɔɪd) *n.* **1.** (in science fiction) a robot resembling a human being. ~*adj.* **2.** resembling a human being. [C18: from LGk *androeidēs* manlike; see ANDRO-, -OID]

Andromache (æn'drɒməkɪ) *n. Greek myth.* the wife of Hector.

Andromeda (æn'drɒmɪdə) *n. Greek myth.* the daughter of Cassiopeia and wife of Perseus, who saved her from a sea monster.

Andropov[1] (æn'drɒpɒv; *Russian* ən'drɔːpəf) *n.* a city in the W central Soviet Union, on the River Volga: an important river port, terminal of the Mariinsk Waterway (between Leningrad and the Volga) at the SE end of the **Rybinsk Reservoir** (area: 4700 sq. km (1800 sq. miles)). Pop.: 254 000 (1987). Former names: (from the Revolution until 1957) **Shcherbakov**, (1957–84) **Rybinsk.**

Andropov[2] (æn'drɒpɒv; *Russian* ən'drɔːpəf) *n.* **Yuri Vladimirovich.** 1914–84, Soviet statesman; president of the Soviet Union (1983–84).

Andros ('ændrəs) *n.* **1.** an island in the Aegean Sea, the northernmost of the Cyclades: long famous for wine. Capital: Andros. Pop.: 10 457 (1971). Area: about 311 sq. km (120 sq. miles). **2.** an island in the N West Indies, the largest of the Bahamas. Pop.: 8397 (1980). Area: 4144 sq. km (1600 sq. miles).

androsterone (æn'drɒstə,rəʊn) *n.* an androgenic steroid hormone produced in the testes.

-androus *adj. combining form.* (in botany) indicating number or type of stamens: *diandrous.* [from NL, from Gk *-andros*, from *anēr* man]

Andvari (æn'dwaːrɪ) *n. Norse myth.* a dwarf who possessed a treasure hoard, which was robbed by Loki.

ane (eɪn) *determiner, pron., n.* a Scottish word for **one.**

-ane *suffix forming nouns.* indicating a hydrocarbon of the alkane series: *hexane.* [coined to replace *-ene*, *-ine*, and *-one*]

anecdotage ('ænɪk,dəʊtɪdʒ) *n.* (usually used humorously) garrulous old age. [from ANECDOTE + -AGE, with play on *dotage*]

anecdote ('ænɪk,dəʊt) *n.* a short usually amusing account of an incident. [C17: from Med. L, from Gk *anekdotos* unpublished, from AN- + *ekdotos* published] **—,anec'dotal** *or* ,**anec'dotic** *adj.* **—,anec'dotalist** *or* '**anec,dotist** *n.*

anechoic (,ænɪ'kəʊɪk) *adj.* having a low degree of reverberation: *an anechoic recording studio.*

anemia (ə'niːmɪə) *n.* the usual U.S. spelling of **anaemia. —anemic** (ə'niːmɪk) *adj.*

anemo- *combining form.* indicating wind: *anemometer; anemophilous.* [from Gk *anemos* wind]

anemograph (ə'nɛməʊ,grɑːf) *n.* a self-recording anemometer.

anemometer (,ænɪ'mɒmɪtə) *n.* an instrument for recording the speed and often the direction of winds. Also called: **wind gauge. —,ane'mometry** *n.* **—anemometric** (,ænɪməʊ'mɛtrɪk) *adj.*

anemone (ə'nɛmənɪ) *n.* any woodland plant of the genus *Anemone* of N temperate regions, such as the white-flowered **wood anemone** or **windflower.** Some cultivated anemones have coloured flowers. [C16: via L from Gk: windflower, from *anemos* wind]

anemophilous (,ænɪ'mɒfɪləs) *adj.* (of flowering plants such as grasses) pollinated by the wind.

anent (ə'nɛnt) *prep. Arch. or Scot.* **1.** lying against; alongside. **2.** concerning; about. [OE *on efen*, lit.: on even (ground)]

aneroid barometer ('ænə,rɔɪd) *n.* a device for measuring atmospheric pressure without the use of fluids. It consists of a partially evacuated chamber, the lid of which is displaced by variations in air pressure. This displacement is magnified by levers and made to operate a pointer. [C19 *aneroid*, from F, from AN- + Gk *nēros* wet + -OID]

anesthesia (,ænɪs'θiːzɪə) *n.* the usual U.S. spelling of **anaesthesia.**

anesthesiologist (,ænɪs,θiːzɪ'ɒlədʒɪst) *n.* the U.S. name for an **anaesthetist.**

anesthesiology (,ænɪs,θiːzɪ'ɒlədʒɪ) *n.* the U.S. name for **anaesthetics.**

anesthetic (,ænɪs'θɛtɪk) *n., adj.* the usual U.S. spelling of **anaesthetic.**

anesthetist (ə'nɛsθətɪst) *n.* (in the U.S.) a person qualified to administer anaesthesia, often a nurse or someone other than a physician.

Aneto (*Spanish* a'neto) *n.* **Pico de** ('piko de). a mountain in N Spain, near the French border: the highest in the Pyrenees. Height: 3404 m (11 168 ft.).

aneurysm *or* **aneurism** ('ænjə,rɪzəm) *n.* a sac formed by abnormal dilation of the weakened wall of a blood vessel. [C15: from Gk *aneurusma*, from *aneurunein* to dilate]

anew (ə'nju:) *adv.* **1.** once more. **2.** in a different way; afresh. [OE *of nīwe;* see OF, NEW]

Angara (*Russian* anga'ra) *n.* a river in the S Soviet Union, in Siberia, flowing from Lake Baikal north and west to the Yenisei River: important for hydroelectric power. Length: 1840 km (1150 miles).

Angarsk (*Russian* an'garsk) *n.* an industrial city in the SE Soviet Union, in the southern RSFSR northwest of Irkutsk. Pop.: 262 000 (1987).

angary ('æŋgəri) *n. Law.* the right of a belligerent state to use the property of a neutral state or to destroy it subject to payment of compensation to the owners. [C19: from F, from LL *angaria* enforced service, from Gk *angaros* courier]

angel ('eɪndʒəl) *n.* **1.** one of a class of spiritual beings attendant upon God. In medieval angelology they are divided by rank into nine orders. **2.** a divine messenger from God. **3.** a guardian spirit. **4.** a conventional representation of any of these beings, depicted in human form with wings. **5.** *Inf.* a person who is kind, pure, or beautiful. **6.** *Inf.* an investor, esp. in a theatrical production. **7.** Also called: **angel-noble.** a former English gold coin with a representation of the archangel Michael on it. **8.** *Inf.* an unexplained signal on a radar screen. [OE, from LL *angelus,* from Gk *angelos* messenger]

angel cake *or esp. U.S.* **angel food cake** *n.* a very light sponge cake made without egg yolks.

Angel Falls *n.* a waterfall in SE Venezuela, on the Caroní River. Height (probably the highest in the world): 979 m (3211 ft.).

angelfish ('eɪndʒəl,fɪʃ) *n., pl.* **-fish** *or* **-fishes. 1.** any of various small tropical marine fishes which have a deep flattened brightly coloured body. **2.** a South American freshwater fish having a compressed body and large dorsal and anal fins: a popular aquarium fish. **3.** a shark with flattened pectoral fins.

angelic (æn'dʒɛlɪk) *adj.* **1.** of or relating to angels. **2.** Also: **angelical.** resembling an angel in beauty, etc. — **an'gelically** *adv.*

angelica (æn'dʒɛlɪkə) *n.* **1.** an umbelliferous plant, the aromatic seeds, leaves, and stems of which are used in medicine and cookery. **2.** the candied stems of this plant, used for decorating and flavouring sweet dishes. [C16: from Med. L (*herba*) *angelica* angelic herb]

Angelico (*Italian* an'dʒɛ:liko) *n.* **Fra** (fra), original name *Guido di Pietro;* monastic name *Fra Giovanni da Fiesole.* ?1400–55, Italian fresco painter and Dominican friar.

Angell ('eɪndʒəl) *n.* Sir **Norman,** real name *Ralph Norman Angell Lane.* 1874–1967, English writer, pacifist, and economist, noted for his work on the economic futility of war, *The Great Illusion* (1910): Nobel peace prize 1933.

Angelou ('ændʒəlu:) *n.* **Maya,** real name *Marguerite Johnson.* born 1928, U.S. Black novelist, poet, and dramatist. Her works include the autobiographical novel *I Know Why the Caged Bird Sings* (1970) and its sequels.

Angelus ('ændʒɪləs) *n. R.C. Church.* **1.** a series of prayers recited in the morning, at midday, and in the evening. **2.** the bell (**Angelus bell**) signalling the times of these prayers. [C17: L, from *Angelus domini nuntiavit Mariae* the angel of the Lord brought tidings to Mary]

anger ('æŋgə) *n.* **1.** a feeling of great annoyance or antagonism as the result of some real or supposed grievance; rage; wrath. ~*vb.* (*tr.*) **2.** to make angry; enrage. [C12: from ON *angr* grief]

Angers (*French* ãʒe) *n.* a city in W France, on the River Maine. Pop.: 136 855 (1983 est.).

Angevin ('ændʒɪvɪn) *n.* **1.** a native or inhabitant of Anjou. **2.** *History.* a member of the Plantagenet royal line, esp. one of the kings of England from Henry II to Richard II (1154–1216). ~*adj.* **3.** of Anjou or its inhabitants. **4.** of the Plantagenet kings of England.

angina (æn'dʒaɪnə) *n.* **1.** any disease marked by painful attacks of spasmodic choking. **2.** short for **angina pectoris.** [C16: from L: quinsy, from Gk *ankhonē* a strangling]

angina pectoris ('pɛktərɪs) *n.* a sudden intense pain in the chest, caused by momentary lack of adequate blood supply to the heart muscle. Sometimes shortened to **angina.** [C18: NL: angina of the chest]

angioma (,ændʒɪ'əumə) *n., pl.* **-mas** *or* **-mata** (-mətə). a tumour consisting of a mass of blood vessels or a mass of lymphatic vessels.

angiosperm ('ændʒɪə,spɜ:m) *n.* any seed-bearing plant in which the ovules are enclosed in an ovary which develops into the fruit after fertilization; any flowering plant. Cf. **gymnosperm.**

Angkor ('æŋkɔ:) *n.* a large area of ruins in NW Kampuchea, containing **Angkor Thom** (tɔːm), the capital of the former Khmer Empire, and **Angkor Wat** (wɒt), a three-storey temple, which were overgrown with dense jungle from the 14th to 19th centuries.

angle[1] ('æŋg°l) *n.* **1.** the space between two straight lines or two planes that extend from a common point. **2.** the shape formed by two such lines or planes. **3.** the extent to which one such line or plane diverges from the other, measured in degrees or radians. **4.** a recess; corner. **5.** point of view: *look at the question from another angle.* **6.** See **angle iron.** ~*vb.* **7.** to move in or bend into angles or an angle. **8.** (*tr.*) to produce (an article, statement, etc.) with a particular point of view. **9.** (*tr.*) to present or place at an angle. **10.** (*intr.*) to turn in a different direction. [C14: from F, from OL *angulus* corner]

angle[2] ('æŋg°l) *vb.* (*intr.*) **1.** to fish with a hook and line. **2.** (often foll. by *for*) to attempt to get: *he angled for a compliment.* ~*n.* **3.** *Obs.* a fish-hook. [OE *angul* fish-hook]

Angle ('æŋg°l) *n.* a member of a people from N Germany who invaded and settled large parts of E and N England in the 5th and 6th centuries A.D. [from L *Anglus,* of Gmc origin, an inhabitant of *Angul,* a district in Schleswig, a name identical with OE *angul* hook, ANGLE[2], referring to its shape] — **'Anglian** *adj., n.*

angle iron *n.* an iron or a steel structural bar that has an L-shaped cross section. Also called: **angle, angle bar.**

angle of incidence *n.* **1.** the angle that a line or beam of radiation makes with a line perpendicular to the surface at the point of incidence. **2.** the angle between the chord line of an aircraft wing or tailplane and the aircraft's longitudinal axis.

angle of reflection *n.* the angle that a beam of reflected radiation makes with the normal to a surface at the point of reflection.

angle of refraction *n.* the angle that a refracted beam of radiation makes with the normal to the surface between two media at the point of refraction.

angle of repose *n.* the maximum angle to the horizontal at which rock, soil, etc., will remain without sliding.

angler ('æŋglə) *n.* **1.** a person who fishes with a hook and line. **2.** Also called: **angler fish.** any of various spiny-finned fishes which live at the bottom of the sea and typically have a long movable dorsal fin with which they lure their prey.

Anglesey ('æŋg°lsɪ) *n.* an island and, until 1974, a county of N Wales, now part of Gwynedd, separated from the mainland by the Menai Strait. Pop.: 68 500 (1984 est.). Area: 714 sq. km (276 sq. miles).

Anglican ('æŋglɪkən) *adj.* **1.** denoting or relating to the Church of England or one of the churches in communion with it. ~*n.* **2.** a member of the Anglican Church. [C17: from Med. L, from *Anglicus* English, from L *Anglī* the Angles] — **'Anglican,ism** *n.*

Anglicism ('æŋglɪ,sɪzəm) *n.* **1.** a word, or idiom peculiar to the English language, esp. as spoken in England. **2.** an English mannerism, custom, etc. **3.** the fact of being English.

anglicize *or* **-cise** ('æŋglɪ,saɪz) *vb.* **-cizing, -cized** *or* **-cising, -cised.** (*sometimes cap.*) to make or become English in outlook, form, etc.

angling ('æŋglɪŋ) *n.* the art or sport of catching fish with a baited hook or other lure, such as a fly; fishing.

Anglo ('æŋgləʊ) *n., pl.* **-glos. 1.** *U.S.* a White inhabitant of the U.S. who is not of Latin extraction. **2.** *Canad.* an English-speaking Canadian, esp. one of Anglo-Celtic origin; an Anglo-Canadian.

Anglo- *combining form.* denoting English or England: *Anglo-Saxon.* [from Med. L *Anglii*]

Anglo-American *adj.* **1.** of relations between England and the United States. ~*n.* **2.** *Chiefly U.S.* an inhabitant of the United States who was or whose ancestors were born in England.

Anglo-Catholic *adj.* **1.** of or relating to a group within the Anglican Church that emphasizes the Catholic elements in its teaching and practice. ~*n.* **2.** a member of this group. — **,Anglo-Ca'tholi,cism** *n.*

Anglo-Egyptian Sudan *n.* the former name (1899–1956) of the **Sudan.**

Anglo-French *adj.* **1.** of England and France. **2.** of Anglo-French. ~*n.* **3.** the Norman-French language of medieval England.

Anglo-Indian *adj.* **1.** of England and India. **2.** denoting or relating to Anglo-Indians. **3.** (of a word) introduced into English from an Indian language. ~*n.* **4.** a person of mixed English and Indian descent. **5.** an Englishman who lives or has lived for a long time in India.

Anglomania (ˌæŋɡləʊˈmeɪnɪə) *n.* excessive respect for English customs, etc. — ˌAngloˈmaniˌac *n.*

Anglo-Norman *adj.* **1.** relating to the Norman conquerors of England, their society, or their language. ~*n.* **2.** a Norman inhabitant of England after 1066. **3.** the Anglo-French language.

Anglophile (ˈæŋɡləʊfɪl, -ˌfaɪl) *or* **Anglophil** *n.* a person having admiration for England or the English.

Anglophobe (ˈæŋɡləʊˌfəʊb) *n.* a person who hates or fears England or its people.

Anglophone (ˈæŋɡləʊˌfəʊn) (*often not cap.*) ~*n.* **1.** a person who speaks English. ~*adj.* **2.** speaking English.

Anglo-Saxon *n.* **1.** a member of any of the West Germanic tribes that settled in Britain from the 5th century A.D. **2.** the language of these tribes. See **Old English. 3.** any White person whose native language is English. **4.** *Inf.* plain blunt English. ~*adj.* **5.** forming part of the Germanic element in Modern English: *"forget" is an Anglo-Saxon word.* **6.** of the Anglo-Saxons or the Old English language. **7.** of the White Protestant culture of Britain and the U.S.

Angola (æŋˈɡəʊlə) *n.* a republic in SW Africa, on the Atlantic: includes the enclave of Cabinda, north of the River Congo; a Portuguese possession from 1575 until its independence in 1975. It consists of a narrow coastal plain with a large fertile plateau in the east. Currency: kwanza. Capital: Luanda. Pop.: 8 164 000 (1986). Area: 1 246 693 sq. km (481 351 sq. miles). —**An'golan** *adj., n.*

angora (æŋˈɡɔːrə) *n.* (*sometimes cap.*) **1.** the long soft hair of the Angora goat or the fur of the Angora rabbit. **2.** yarn, cloth, or clothing made from this hair or fur. **3.** (*as modifier*): *an angora sweater.* ~See also **mohair.** [from *Angora,* former name of Ankara, in Turkey]

Angora goat (æŋˈɡɔːrə) *n.* a breed of domestic goat with long soft hair.

Angora rabbit *n.* a breed of rabbit with long silky fur.

Angostura (*Spanish* aŋɡɔsˈtura) *n.* the former name (1764–1846) for **Ciudad Bolívar.**

angostura bark (ˌæŋɡɒˈstjʊərə) *n.* the bitter aromatic bark of certain South American trees, formerly used to reduce fever. [C18: from ANGOSTURA]

angostura bitters *pl. n.* (*often cap.*) *Trademark.* a bitter aromatic tonic, used as a flavouring in alcoholic drinks.

Angra do Heroísmo (*Portuguese* ˈɔːŋɡrə duː iruˈiʃmu) *n.* a port in the Azores, on Terceira Island. Pop.: 75 010 (1981).

angry (ˈæŋɡrɪ) *adj.* **-grier, -griest. 1.** feeling or expressing annoyance, animosity, or resentment. **2.** suggestive of anger: *angry clouds.* **3.** severely inflamed: *an angry sore.* —ˈangrily *adv.*

angst (æŋst) *n.* an acute but nonspecific sense of anxiety or remorse. [G]

angstrom (ˈæŋstrəm) *n.* a unit of length equal to 10^{-10} metre, used principally to express the wavelengths of electromagnetic radiations. Symbol: Å or A Also called: **angstrom unit.** [C20: after Anders J. *Ångström* (1814–74), Swedish physicist]

Ångström (ˈæŋstrəm; *Swedish* ˈɔŋstrœm) *n.* **Anders Jonas** (ˈandərs ˈjuːnas). 1814–74, Swedish physicist, noted for his work on spectroscopy and solar physics.

Anguilla (æŋˈɡwɪlə) *n.* an island in the West Indies, in the Leeward Islands: part of the British associated state of St Kitts-Nevis-Anguilla from 1967 until 1980, when it reverted to the status of a British dependency. Pop.: 7000 (1985 est.). Area: 90 sq. km (35 sq. miles).

anguine (ˈæŋɡwɪn) *adj.* of or similar to a snake. [C17: from L *anguinus,* from *anguis* snake]

anguish (ˈæŋɡwɪʃ) *n.* **1.** extreme pain or misery; mental or physical torture; agony. ~*vb.* **2.** to afflict or be afflicted with anguish. [C13: from OF *angoisse* a strangling, from L, from *angustus* narrow] —ˈanguished *adj.*

angular (ˈæŋɡjʊlə) *adj.* **1.** lean or bony. **2.** awkward or stiff. **3.** having an angle or angles. **4.** placed at an angle.

5. measured by an angle or by the rate at which an angle changes; *angular momentum; angular velocity.* [C15: from L *angulāris,* from *angulus* ANGLE[1]]

angularity (ˌæŋɡjʊˈlærɪtɪ) *n., pl.* **-ties. 1.** the condition of being angular. **2.** an angular shape.

Angus (ˈæŋɡəs) *n.* (until 1975) a county of E Scotland, now part of Tayside region.

Angus Og (əʊɡ) *n. Irish myth.* the god of love and beauty.

Anhalt (*German* ˈanhalt) *n.* a former state of central Germany, now part of East Germany.

anhedral (ænˈhiːdrəl) *n.* the downward inclination of an aircraft wing in relation to the lateral axis.

Anhui *or* **Anhwei** (ˈænˈweɪ) *n.* a province of E China, crossed by the Yangtze River. Capital: Hefei. Pop.: 51 030 000 (1985). Area: 139 860 sq. km (54 000 sq. miles).

anhydride (ænˈhaɪdraɪd) *n.* **1.** a compound that has been formed from another compound by dehydration. **2.** a compound that forms an acid or base when added to water. [C19: from ANHYDR(OUS) + -IDE]

anhydrous (ænˈhaɪdrəs) *adj.* containing no water, esp. no water of crystallization. [C19: from Gk *anudros;* see AN-, HYDRO-]

Aniakchak (ˌænɪˈæktʃæk) *n.* an active volcanic crater in SW Alaska, on the Alaska Peninsula: the largest explosion crater in the world. Height: 1347 m (4420 ft.). Diameter: 9 km (6 miles).

anil (ˈænɪl) *n.* a leguminous West Indian shrub which is a source of indigo. Also called: **indigo.** [C16: from Port., from Ar. *an-nīl,* the indigo]

aniline (ˈænɪlɪn, -ˌliːn) *n.* a colourless oily poisonous liquid used in the manufacture of dyes, plastics, and explosives. Formula: $C_6H_5NH_2$.

aniline dye *n.* any synthetic dye originally made from aniline, obtained from coal tar.

anima (ˈænɪmə) *n.* (in Jungian psychology) **a.** the feminine principle as present in the male unconscious. **b.** the inner personality. [L: air, breath, spirit, fem. of ANIMUS]

animadversion (ˌænɪmædˈvɜːʃən) *n.* criticism or censure.

animadvert (ˌænɪmædˈvɜːt) *vb.* (*intr.*) **1.** (usually foll. by *on* or *upon*) to comment with strong criticism (upon); make censorious remarks (about). **2.** to make an observation or comment. [C16: from L *animadvertere* to notice, from *animus* mind + *advertere* to turn to]

animal (ˈænɪməl) *n.* **1.** *Zool.* any living organism characterized by voluntary movement, the possession of specialized sense organs enabling rapid response to stimuli, and the ingestion of complex organic substances. **2.** any mammal, esp. except man. **3.** a brutish person. **4.** *Facetious.* a person or thing (esp. in **no such animal**). ~*adj.* **5.** of, relating to, or derived from animals. **6.** of or relating to physical needs or desires; carnal; sensual. [C14: from L, from *animālis* (adj.) living, breathing; see ANIMA]

animalcule (ˌænɪˈmælkjuːl) *n.* a microscopic animal such as an amoeba or rotifer. [C16: from NL *animalculum* a small animal] —ˌaniˈmalcular *adj.*

animal husbandry *n.* the science of breeding, rearing, and caring for farm animals.

animalism (ˈænɪməˌlɪzəm) *n.* **1.** preoccupation with physical matters; sensuality. **2.** the doctrine that man lacks a spiritual nature. **3.** a mode of behaviour typical of animals.

animality (ˌænɪˈmælɪtɪ) *n.* **1.** the animal side of man, as opposed to the intellectual or spiritual. **2.** the characteristics of an animal.

animalize *or* **-ise** (ˈænɪməˌlaɪz) *vb.* (*tr.*) to rouse to brutality or sensuality or make brutal or sensual. —ˌanimalˈization *or* -iˈsation *n.*

animal magnetism *n.* **1.** the quality of being attractive, esp. to members of the opposite sex. **2.** *Obs.* hypnotism.

animal spirits *pl. n.* boisterous exuberance. [from a vital force once supposed to be dispatched by the brain to all points of the body]

animate *vb.* (ˈænɪˌmeɪt). (*tr.*) **1.** to give life to or cause to come alive. **2.** to make gay or lively. **3.** to encourage or inspire. **4.** to impart motion to. **5.** to record on film or video tape so as to give movement to. ~*adj.* (ˈænɪmɪt). **6.** having life. **7.** gay, spirited, or lively. [C16: from L *animāre* to make alive, from *anima* breath, spirit] —ˈaniˌmatedly *adv.*

animated cartoon n. a film produced by photographing a series of gradually changing drawings, etc., which give the illusion of movement when the series is projected rapidly.
animation (,ænɪ'meɪʃən) n. **1.** vivacity. **2.** the condition of being alive. **3.** the techniques used in the production of animated cartoons.
animato (,ænɪ'mɑːtəʊ) adj., adv. Music. lively; animated. [It.]
animé ('ænɪ,meɪ, -mɪ) n. any of various resins, esp. that obtained from a tropical American leguminous tree. [F: from ?]
animism ('ænɪ,mɪzəm) n. **1.** the belief that natural objects possess souls. **2.** (in the philosophies of Plato and Pythagoras) the hypothesis that there is an immaterial force that animates the universe. [C19: from L *anima* vital breath, spirit] **—animistic** (,ænɪ'mɪstɪk) adj.
animosity (,ænɪ'mɒsɪtɪ) n., pl. **-ties.** a powerful and active dislike or hostility. [C15: from LL *animósitás*, from ANIMUS]
animus ('ænɪməs) n. **1.** intense dislike; hatred; animosity. **2.** motive or purpose. **3.** (in Jungian psychology) the masculine principle present in the female unconscious. [C19: from L: mind, spirit]
anion ('æn,aɪən) n. a negatively charged ion; an ion that is attracted to the anode during electrolysis. [C19: from ANA- + ION] **—anionic** (,ænaɪ'ɒnɪk) adj.
anise ('ænɪs) n. a Mediterranean umbelliferous plant having clusters of small yellowish-white flowers and liquorice-flavoured seeds. [C13: from OF *anis*, via L from Gk *anison*]
aniseed ('ænɪ,siːd) n. the liquorice-flavoured aromatic seeds of the anise plant, used medicinally for expelling intestinal gas and in cookery.
anisette (,ænɪ'zɛt, -'sɛt) n. a liquorice-flavoured liqueur made from aniseed. [C19: from F]
anisotropic (æn,aɪsəʊ'trɒpɪk) adj. **1.** having different physical properties in different directions: *anisotropic crystals.* **2.** (of a plant) responding unequally to an external stimulus in different parts. **—an,iso'tropically** adv. **—anisotropy** (,ænaɪ'sɒtrəpɪ) n.
Anjou (French ɑ̃ʒu) n. a former province of W France, in the Loire valley: a medieval countship from the 10th century, belonging to the English crown from 1154 until 1204; annexed by France in 1480.
Ankara ('æŋkərə) n. the capital of Turkey: an ancient city in the Anatolian highlands: first a capital in the 3rd century B.C., in the Celtic kingdom of Galatia. Pop.: 2 251 533 (1985). Ancient name: **Ancyra.** Former name (until 1930): **Angora.**
ankh (æŋk) n. a tall cross with a loop on the top, symbolizing eternal life: often appearing in Egyptian personal names, such as Tutankhamen. [from Egyptian *'nh* life, soul]
Anking ('ɑːn'kɪŋ) n. a variant transliteration of the Chinese name for **Anqing.**
ankle ('æŋkəl) n. **1.** the joint connecting the leg and the foot. **2.** the part of the leg just above the foot. [C14: from ON]
ankle biter n. Austral. sl. a child.
anklebone ('æŋkəl,bəʊn) n. the nontechnical name for **talus**[1].
anklet ('æŋklɪt) n. an ornamental chain worn around the ankle.
ankylose or **anchylose** ('æŋkɪ,ləʊz) vb. (of bones in a joint, etc.) to fuse or stiffen by ankylosis.
ankylosis or **anchylosis** (,æŋkɪ'ləʊsɪs) n. abnormal adhesion or immobility of the bones in a joint, as by a fibrous growth of tissues within the joint. [C18: from NL, from Gk *ankuloun* to crook] **—ankylotic** or **anchylotic** (,æŋkɪ'lɒtɪk) adj.
anna ('ænə) n. a former Indian coin, worth one sixteenth of a rupee. [C18: from Hindi *ānā*]
Annaba ('ænəbə) n. a port in NE Algeria: site of the Roman city of Hippo Regius. Pop.: 348 322 (1983 est.). Former name: **Bône.**
annals ('ænəlz) pl. n. **1.** yearly records of events. **2.** history in general. **3.** regular reports of the work of a society, learned body, etc. [C16: from L (*librī*) *annálés* yearly (books), from *annus* year] **—'annalist** n. **—,annal'istic** adj.
Annam or **Anam** (æ'næm, 'ænæm) n. a former kingdom (3rd century–1428), empire (1428–1884), and French

protectorate (1884–1945) of E Indochina: now part of Vietnam. **—,Anna'mese** adj., n.
Annapolis (ə'næpəlɪs) n. the capital of Maryland, near the mouth of the Severn River on Chesapeake Bay: site of the U.S. Naval Academy. Pop.: 31 898 (1984 est.).
Annapolis Royal n. a town in SE Canada in W Nova Scotia on an arm of the Bay of Fundy: the first settlement in Canada (1605). Pop.: 600 (1984 est.). Former name (until 1710): **Port Royal.**
Annapurna or **Anapurna** (,ænə'pʊənə) n. a massif of the Himalayas, in Nepal. Highest peak: 8078 m (26 502 ft.).
Ann Arbor (æn 'ɑːbə) n. a city in SE Michigan: seat of the University of Michigan. Pop.: 107 316 (1980).
annates ('æneɪts, -əts) pl. n. R.C. Church. the first year's revenue of a see, etc., paid to the pope. [C16: from F, from Med. L *annáta*, from L *annus* year]
annatto or **anatto** (ə'nætəʊ) n., pl. **-tos. 1.** a small tropical American tree having pulpy seeds that yield a dye. **2.** the yellowish-red dye obtained from the seeds of this tree, used for colouring fabrics, butter, varnish, etc. [from Carib]
Anne (æn) n. **1. Princess,** the Princess Royal. Born 1950, daughter of Elizabeth II of Great Britain and Northern Ireland; a noted horsewoman and president of the Save the Children Fund. **2. Queen.** 1665–1714, queen of Great Britain and Ireland (1702–14), daughter of James II, and the last of the Stuart monarchs. **3. Saint.** (in Christian tradition) the mother of the Virgin Mary. Feast day: July 26.
anneal (ə'niːl) vb. **1.** to temper or toughen (something) by heat treatment to remove internal stress, crystal defects, and dislocations. **2.** (tr.) to toughen or strengthen (the will, determination, etc.). ~n. **3.** an act of annealing. [OE *onǽlan*, from ON + *ǽlan* to burn, from *ál* fire] **—an'nealer** n.
Anne Boleyn n. See (Anne) **Boleyn.**
Annecy (French ansi) n. **1.** a city and resort in E France, on Lake Annecy. Pop.: 53 147 (1983 est.). **2. Lake.** a lake in E France, in the Alps.
annelid ('ænəlɪd) n. **1.** a worm in which the body is divided into segments both externally and internally, as the earthworms. ~adj. **2.** of such worms. [C19: from NL *Annelida*, from OF, ult. from L *ānulus* ring] **—annelidan** (ə'nɛlɪdən) n., adj.
Anne of Austria n. 1601–66, wife of Louis XIII of France and daughter of Philip III of Spain: regent of France (1643–61) for her son Louis XIV.
Anne of Bohemia n. 1366–94, queen consort of Richard II of England.
Anne of Cleves (kliːvz) n. 1515–57, the fourth wife of Henry VIII of England, whose marriage (1540) was annulled after six months.
annex vb. (æ'nɛks). (tr.) **1.** to join or add, esp. to something larger. **2.** to add (territory) by conquest or occupation. **3.** to add or append as a condition, etc. **4.** to appropriate without permission. ~n. ('ænɛks). **5.** a variant spelling (esp. U.S.) of **annexe.** [C14: from Med. L, from L *annectere* to attach to, from *nectere* to join] **—an'nexable** adj. **—,annex'ation** n.
annexe or esp. U.S. **annex** ('ænɛks) n. **1. a.** an extension to a main building. **b.** a building used as an addition to a main one nearby. **2.** something added, esp. a supplement to a document.
Annigoni (Italian anni'goːni) n. **Pietro** ('pjɛːtro). 1910–88, Italian painter; noted esp. for his portraits of President Kennedy (1961) and Queen Elizabeth II (1955 and 1970).
annihilate (ə'naɪə,leɪt) vb. (tr.) **1.** to destroy completely; extinguish. **2.** Inf. to defeat totally, as in argument. [C16: from LL, from L *nihil* nothing] **—an,nihi'lation** n. **—an'nihi,lator** n.
anniversary (,ænɪ'vɜːsərɪ) n., pl. **-ries. 1.** the date on which an event occurred in some previous year: *a wedding anniversary.* **2.** the celebration of this. ~adj. **3.** of or relating to an anniversary. [C13: from L *anniversárius* returning every year, from *annus* year + *vertere* to turn]
anno Domini ('ænəʊ 'dɒmɪ,naɪ, -,niː) **1.** the full form of **A.D. 2.** Inf. advancing old age. [L: in the year of our Lord]
annotate ('ænəʊ,teɪt, 'ænə,teɪt) vb. to supply (a written work) with critical or explanatory notes. [C18: from L *annotáre*, from *nota* mark] **—'anno,tative** adj. **—'anno,tator** n.

annotation (ˌænəʊˈteɪʃən, ˌænəˈteɪʃən) n. **1.** the act of annotating. **2.** a note added in explanation, etc., esp. of some literary work.

announce (əˈnaʊns) vb. **1.** (tr.; may take a clause as object) to make known publicly. **2.** (tr.) to declare the arrival of: to announce a guest. **3.** (tr.; may take a clause as object) to presage: the dark clouds announced rain. **4.** (intr.) to work as an announcer, as on radio or television. [C15: from OF, from L annuntiāre, from nuntius messenger] —**an'nouncement** n.

announcer (əˈnaʊnsə) n. a person who announces, esp. one who reads the news, etc., on radio or television.

annoy (əˈnɔɪ) vb. **1.** to irritate or displease. **2.** to harass with repeated attacks. [C13: from OF, from LL inodiāre to make hateful, from L in odiō (esse) (to be) hated, from odium hatred] —**an'noyer** n. —**an'noying** adj. —**an'noyingly** adv.

annoyance (əˈnɔɪəns) n. **1.** the feeling of being annoyed. **2.** the act of annoying. **3.** a person or thing that annoys.

annual (ˈænjʊəl) adj. **1.** occurring, done, etc., once a year or every year; yearly: an annual income. **2.** lasting for a year: an annual subscription. ~n. **3.** a plant that completes its life cycle in one year. **4.** a book, magazine, etc., published once every year. [C14: from LL, from L annuus yearly, from annus year] —**'annually** adv.

annual general meeting n. the statutory meeting of the directors and shareholders of a company or of the members of a society, held once every financial year. Abbrev.: **AGM.**

annualize or **-ise** (ˈænjʊəˌlaɪz) vb. (tr.) to calculate for a shorter period as though on the basis of a full year: an annualized percentage rate.

annual ring n. a ring indicating one year's growth, seen in the transverse section of stems and roots of woody plants. Also called: **tree ring.**

annuitant (əˈnjuːɪtənt) n. a person in receipt of or entitled to an annuity.

annuity (əˈnjuːɪtɪ) n., pl. **-ties.** a fixed sum payable at specified intervals over a period, such as the recipient's life, or in perpetuity, in return for a premium paid either in instalments or in a single payment. [C15: from F, from Med. L annuitās, from L annuus ANNUAL]

annul (əˈnʌl) vb. **-nulling, -nulled.** (tr.) to make (something, esp. a law or marriage) void; abolish. [C14: from OF, from LL adnullāre to bring to nothing, from L nullus not any] —**an'nullable** adj.

annular (ˈænjʊlə) adj. ring-shaped. [C16: from L annulāris, from annulus, ānulus ring]

annular eclipse n. an eclipse of the sun in which the moon does not cover the entire disc of the sun, so that a ring of sunlight surrounds the shadow of the moon.

annular ligament n. Anat. any of various ligaments that encircle a part, such as the wrist.

annulate (ˈænjʊlɪt, -ˌleɪt) adj. having, composed of, or marked with rings. [C19: from L ānulātus, from ānulus a ring] —**ˌannu'lation** n.

annulet (ˈænjʊlɪt) n. **1.** Archit. a moulding in the form of a ring. **2.** Heraldry. a ring-shaped device on a shield. **3.** a little ring. [C16: from L ānulus ring -ET]

annulment (əˈnʌlmənt) n. **1.** a formal invalidation, as of a marriage, judicial proceeding, etc. **2.** the act of annulling.

annulus (ˈænjʊləs) n., pl. **-li** (-ˌlaɪ) or **-luses. 1.** the area between two concentric circles. **2.** a ring-shaped part. [C16: from L, var. of ānulus ring]

annunciate (əˈnʌnsɪˌeɪt, -ʃɪ-) vb. (tr.) a less common word for **announce.** [C16: from Med L from L annuntiāre; see ANNOUNCE]

Annunciation (əˌnʌnsɪˈeɪʃən) n. **1. the.** the announcement of the Incarnation by the angel Gabriel to the Virgin Mary (Luke 1:26–38). **2.** Also called: **Annunciation Day.** the festival commemorating this, on March 25 (Lady Day).

annunciator (əˈnʌnsɪˌeɪtə) n. **1.** a device that gives a visual indication as to which of a number of electric circuits has operated, such as an indicator showing in which room a bell has been rung. **2.** a device giving an audible signal indicating the position of a train. **3.** an announcer.

annus mirabilis Latin. (ˈænʊs mɪˈræbɪlɪs) n., pl. ***anni mirabiles*** (ˈænaɪ mɪˈræbɪliːz). a year of wonders, catastrophes, or other notable events.

anoa (əˈnəʊə) n. the smallest of the cattle tribe, having small straight horns and inhabiting the island of Celebes in Indonesia. [from a native name in Celebes]

anode (ˈænəʊd) n. **1.** the positive electrode in an electrolytic cell or in an electronic valve or tube. **2.** the negative terminal of a primary cell. Cf. **cathode.** [C19: from Gk anodos a way up, from hodos a way; alluding to the movement of the current] —**anodal** (eɪˈnəʊdəl) or **anodic** (əˈnɒdɪk) adj.

anodize or **-dise** (ˈænəˌdaɪz) vb. to coat (a metal, such as aluminium) with a protective oxide film by electrolysis.

anodyne (ˈænəˌdaɪn) n. **1.** a drug that relieves pain. **2.** anything that alleviates mental distress. ~adj. **3.** capable of relieving pain or distress. [C16: from L, from Gk anōdunos painless, from AN- + odunē pain]

anoint (əˈnɔɪnt) vb. (tr.) **1.** to smear or rub over with oil. **2.** to apply oil to as a sign of consecration or sanctification. [C14: from OF, from L inunguere, from IN-² + unguere to smear with oil] —**a'nointer** n. —**a'nointment** n.

anomalistic (əˌnɒməˈlɪstɪk) adj. **1.** Astron. **a.** (of a month) measured between successive perigees of the moon. **b.** (of a year) between successive perihelia of the earth. **2.** anomalous.

anomalous (əˈnɒmələs) adj. deviating from the normal or usual order, type, etc. [C17: from LL, from Gk anōmalos uneven, inconsistent, from AN- + homalos even, from homos one and the same] —**a'nomalousness** n.

anomaly (əˈnɒməlɪ) n., pl. **-lies. 1.** something anomalous. **2.** deviation from the normal; irregularity. **3.** Astron. the angle between a planet, the sun, and the previous perihelion of the planet.

anomie or **anomy** (ˈænəʊmɪ) n. Sociol. lack of social or moral standards in an individual or society. [from Gk anomia lawlessness, from A-¹ + nomos law] —**anomic** (əˈnɒmɪk) adj.

anon (əˈnɒn) adv. Arch. or literary. **1.** soon. **2. ever and anon.** now and then. [OE on āne, lit.: in one, that is, immediately]

anon. abbrev. for anonymous.

anonym (ˈænənɪm) n. **1.** a less common word for **pseudonym. 2.** an anonymous person or publication.

anonymous (əˈnɒnɪməs) adj. **1.** from or by a person, author, etc., whose name is unknown or withheld. **2.** having no known name. **3.** lacking individual characteristics. **4.** (often cap.) denoting an organization which provides help to applicants who remain anonymous: Alcoholics Anonymous. [C17: via LL from Gk anōnumos, from AN- + onoma name] —**anonymity** (ˌænəˈnɪmɪtɪ) n.

anopheles (əˈnɒfɪˌliːz) n., pl. **-les.** any of various mosquitoes constituting the genus Anopheles, some species of which transmit the malaria parasite to man. [C19: via NL from Gk anōphelēs useless, from AN- + ōphelein to help]

anorak (ˈænəˌræk) n. a warm waterproof hip-length jacket usually with a hood. [from Eskimo ánorâq]

anorexia (ˌænɒˈrɛksɪə) n. **1.** loss of appetite. **2.** Also called: **anorexia nervosa** (nɜːˈvəʊsə). a disorder characterized by fear of becoming fat and refusal of food, leading to debility and even death. [C17: via NL from Gk, from AN-+ orexis appetite] —**anorectic** or **anorexic** (ˌænɒˈrɛksɪk) adj., n.

anosmia (ænˈɒzmɪə, -ˈɒs-) n. loss of the sense of smell. [C19: from NL, from AN- + Gk osmē smell] —**anosmatic** (ˌænɒzˈmætɪk) or **an'osmic** adj.

another (əˈnʌðə) determiner. **1. a.** one more: another chance. **b.** (as pron.): help yourself to another. **2. a. a.** different: another era from ours. **b.** (as pron.): to try one, then another. **3. a.** a different example of the same sort. **b.** (as pron.): we got rid of one, but I think this is another. [C14: orig. an other]

A.N. Other n. Brit. an unnamed person: used in team lists, etc., to indicate a place that remains to be filled.

Anouilh (French anuj) n. **Jean** (ʒɑ̃). 1910–87, French dramatist, noted for his reinterpretations of Greek myths: his works include Eurydice (1942), Antigone (1944), and Becket (1959).

anoxia (ænˈɒksɪə) n. lack or deficiency of oxygen. [C20: from AN- + OX(YGEN) + -IA] —**an'oxic** adj.

Anqing (ˈɑːnˈtʃɪŋ) or **Anking** n. a city in E China, in SW Anhui province on the Yangtze River: famous seven-storeyed pagoda. Pop.: 207 200 (1985 est.).

Anschluss (ˈænʃlʊs) n. a political or economic union, esp. the annexation of Austria by Nazi Germany (1938). [G, from anschliessen to join]

Anselm (ˈænselm) n. **Saint.** 1033–1109, Italian Benedictine monk; archbishop of Canterbury (1093–1109): one of the founders of scholasticism; author of *Cur Deus Homo?* (*Why did God become Man?*). Feast day: Aug. 21.

anserine ('ænsə,raın) *adj.* of or resembling a goose. [C19: from L *anserīnus*, from *anser* goose]

Ansermet (*French* āsɛrmɛ) *n.* **Ernest** (ɛrnɛst). 1883–1969, Swiss orchestral conductor; principal conductor of Diaghilev's Ballet Russe.

Anshan (,æn'ʃæn) *n.* **1.** a city in NE China, in Liaoning province. Pop.: 1 280 000 (1986 est.). **2.** an ancient city and region in Persia, associated with Elam.

answer ('ɑ:nsə) *n.* **1.** a reply, either spoken or written, as to a question, request, letter, or article. **2.** a reaction or response: *drunkenness was his answer to disappointment.* **3.** a solution, esp. of a mathematical problem. ~*vb.* **4.** (when *tr.*, *may take a clause as object*) to reply or respond (to) by word or act: *to answer a question; to answer the door.* **5.** (*tr.*) to reply correctly to; solve: *I could answer only three questions.* **6.** (*intr.; usually foll. by* to) to respond or react: *the steering answers to the slightest touch.* **7. a.** (when *intr.*, often foll. by *for*) to meet the requirements (of); be satisfactory (for): *this will answer his needs.* **b.** to be responsible (to a person or for a thing). **8.** (when *intr.*, foll. by *to*) to match or correspond (esp. in **answer** (*or* **answer to**) **the description**). **9.** (*tr.*) to give a defence or refutation of (a charge) or in (an argument). [OE *andswaru* an answer; see SWEAR]

answerable ('ɑ:nsərəbəl) *adj.* **1.** (*postpositive; foll. by for or* to) responsible or accountable: *answerable to one's boss.* **2.** able to be answered.

answer back *vb.* (*adv.*) to reply rudely to (a person, esp. someone in authority) when one is expected to remain silent.

answering machine *n.* a device by which a telephone call is answered automatically and the caller leaves a recorded message. In full: **telephone answering machine.**

ant (ænt) *n.* **1.** a small social insect of a widely distributed hymenopterous family, typically living in highly organized colonies of winged males, wingless sterile females (workers), and fertile females (queens). Related adj.: **formic. 2. white ant.** another name for a **termite.** [OE *ǣmette*]

-ant *suffix forming adjectives and nouns.* causing or performing an action or existing in a certain condition: *pleasant; deodorant; servant.* [from L -*ant*, ending of present participles of the first conjugation]

antacid (ænt'æsɪd) *n.* **1.** a substance used to treat acidity, esp. in the stomach. ~*adj.* **2.** having the properties of this substance.

Antaeus (æn'ti:əs) *n. Greek myth.* an African giant who was invincible as long as he touched the ground, but was lifted into the air by Hercules and crushed to death.

antagonism (æn'tægə,nızəm) *n.* **1.** openly expressed and usually mutual opposition. **2.** the inhibiting or nullifying action of one substance or organism on another.

antagonist (æn'tægənɪst) *n.* **1.** an opponent or adversary. **2.** any muscle that opposes the action of another. **3.** a drug that counteracts the effects of another drug. —**an,tago'nistic** *adj.* —**an,tago'nistically** *adv.*

antagonize *or* **-nise** (æn'tægə,naɪz) *vb.* (*tr.*) **1.** to make hostile; annoy or irritate. **2.** to act in opposition to or counteract. [C17: from Gk, from ANTI- + *agōnizesthai* to strive, from *agōn* contest] —**an,tagoni'zation** *or* **-ni'sation** *n.*

Antakiya (,æntɑ:'ki:jə) *n.* the Arabic name for **Antioch.**

Antakya (ɑn'takja) *n.* the Turkish name for **Antioch.**

antalkali (ænt'ælkə,laɪ) *n., pl.* **-lis** *or* **-lies** a substance that neutralizes alkalis.

Antalya (*Turkish* ɑn'talja) *n.* a port in SW Turkey, on the **Gulf of Antalya.** Pop.: 258 139 (1985).

Antananarivo (,æntə,nænə'ri:vəʊ) *n.* the capital of Madagascar, on the central plateau: founded in the 17th century by a Hova chief; university (1961). Pop.: 600 000 (1982 est.). Former name: **Tananarive.**

Antarctic (ænt'ɑ:ktɪk) **1. the.** Also called: **Antarctic Zone.** Antarctica and the surrounding waters. ~*adj.* **2.** of or relating to the south polar regions. [C14: via L from Gk *antarktikos*; see ANTI-, ARCTIC]

Antarctica (ænt'ɑ:ktɪkə) *n.* a continent around the South Pole: consists of an ice-covered plateau, 1800–3000 m (6000 ft. to 10 000 ft.) above sea level, and mountain ranges rising to 4500 m (15 000 ft.) with some volcanic peaks; average temperatures all below freezing and human settlement is confined to research stations.

Antarctic Archipelago *n.* the former name of the **Palmer Archipelago.**

Antarctic Circle *n.* the imaginary circle around the earth, parallel to the equator, at latitude 66° 32′ S.

Antarctic Ocean *n.* the sea surrounding Antarctica, consisting of the most southerly parts of the Pacific, Atlantic, and Indian Oceans.

Antarctic Peninsula *n.* the largest peninsula of Antarctica, between the Weddell Sea and the Pacific: consists of Graham Land in the north and the Palmer Peninsula in the south. Former name (until 1964): **Palmer Peninsula.**

ant bear *n.* another name for **aardvark.**

ante ('æntɪ) *n.* **1.** the gaming stake put up before the deal in poker by the players. **2.** *Inf.* a sum of money representing a person's share, as in a syndicate. ~*vb.* **-teing, -ted** *or* **-teed. 3.** to place (one's stake) in poker. **4.** (usually foll. by *up*) *Inf.* to pay.

ante- *prefix.* before in time or position: *antedate; antechamber.* [from L]

anteater ('ænt,i:tə) *n.* any of several toothless mammals having a long tubular snout used for eating termites.

antebellum (,æntɪ'bɛləm) *adj.* of or during the period before a war, esp. the American Civil War. [L *ante bellum*, lit.: before the war]

antecede (,æntɪ'si:d) *vb.* (*tr.*) to go before; precede. [C17: from L *antecēdere*, from *cēdere* to go]

antecedent (,æntɪ'si:dənt) *n.* **1.** an event, etc., that happens before another. **2.** *Grammar.* a word or phrase to which a pronoun refers. In "People who live in glass houses shouldn't throw stones," *people* is the antecedent of *who.* **3.** *Logic.* the first hypothetical clause in a conditional statement. ~*adj.* **4.** preceding in time or order; prior. —,**ante'cedence** *n.*

antecedents (,æntɪ'si:dənts) *pl. n.* **1.** ancestry. **2.** a person's past history.

antechamber ('æntɪ,tʃeɪmbə) *n.* an anteroom. [C17: from OF, from It. *anticamera*; see ANTE-, CHAMBER]

antedate ('æntɪ,deɪt) *vb.* (*tr.*) **1.** to be or occur at an earlier date than. **2.** to affix or assign a date to (a document, event, etc.) that is earlier than the actual date. **3.** to cause to occur sooner. ~*n.* **4.** an earlier date.

antediluvian (,æntɪdɪ'lu:vɪən) *adj.* **1.** belonging to the ages before the biblical Flood. **2.** old-fashioned. ~*n.* **3.** an antediluvian person or thing. [C17: from ANTE- + L *dīluvium* flood]

antelope ('æntɪ,ləʊp) *n., pl.* **-lopes** *or* **-lope.** any of a group of mammals of Africa and Asia. They are typically graceful, having long legs and horns, and include the gazelles, springbok, impala, and dik-diks. [C15: from OF, from Med. L, from LGk *antholops* a legendary beast]

antemeridian (,æntɪmə'rɪdɪən) *adj.* before noon; in the morning. [C17: from L]

ante meridiem ('æntɪ mə'rɪdɪəm) the full form of **a.m.** [L, from ANTE- + *merīdiēs* midday]

antenatal (,æntɪ'neɪtəl) *adj.* occurring or present before birth; during pregnancy.

antenna (æn'tɛnə) *n.* **1.** (*pl.* **-nae** (-ni:)) one of a pair of mobile appendages on the heads of insects, crustaceans, etc., that often respond to touch and taste but may be specialized for swimming. **2.** (*pl.* **-nas**) an aerial. [C17: from L: sail yard, from ?] —**an'tennal** *or* **an'tennary** *adj.*

antenuptial contract (,æntɪ'nʌpʃəl) *n.* (in South Africa) a marriage contract effected prior to the wedding giving each partner control over his or her property.

antependium (,æntɪ'pɛndɪəm) *n., pl.* **-dia** (-dɪə). a covering hung over the front of an altar. [C17: from Med. L, from L ANTE- + *pendēre* to hang]

antepenult (,æntɪpɪ'nʌlt) *n.* the third last syllable in a word. [C16: shortened from L (*syllaba*) *antepaenultima*; see ANTE-, PENULT]

antepenultimate (,æntɪpɪ'nʌltɪmɪt) *adj.* **1.** third from last. ~*n.* **2.** anything that is third from last.

anterior (æn'tɪərɪə) *adj.* **1.** at or towards the front. **2.** earlier. **3.** *Zool.* of or near the head end. **4.** *Bot.* (of part of a flower or leaf) farthest away from the main stem. [C17: from L, comp. of *ante* before]

anteroom ('æntɪ,ru:m, -,rʊm) *n.* a room giving entrance to a larger room, often used as a waiting room.

anthelion (æn'θi:lɪən) *n., pl.* **-lia** (-lɪə). **1.** a faint halo sometimes seen in high altitude regions around a shadow cast onto fog. **2.** a white spot occasionally appearing at the same height as and opposite to the sun. [C17: from

LGk, from *anthēlios* opposite the sun, from ANTE- + *hē-lios* sun]

anthelmintic (ˌænθɛlˈmɪntɪk) *or* **anthelminthic** (ˌænθɛlˈmɪnθɪk) *n. Med.* another name for **vermifuge**.

anthem (ˈænθəm) *n.* **1.** a song of loyalty or devotion: *a national anthem.* **2.** a musical composition for a choir, usually set to words from the Bible. **3.** a religious chant sung antiphonally. [OE *antemne*, from LL *antiphōna* ANTIPHON]

anthemis (ænˈθiːmɪs) *n.* any of several cultivated varieties of camomile. [NL, from L, from Gk *anthos* flower]

anther (ˈænθə) *n.* the terminal part of a stamen consisting of two lobes each containing two sacs in which the pollen matures. [C18: from NL, from L, from Gk *anthēros* flowery, from *anthos* flower]

antheridium (ˌænθəˈrɪdɪəm) *n., pl.* **-ia** (-ɪə). the male sex organ of algae, fungi, mosses, etc. [C19: from NL, dim. of *anthēra* ANTHER]

ant hill *n.* a mound of soil, leaves, etc., near the entrance of an ants' nest, deposited there by the ants while constructing the nest.

anthologize *or* **-gise** (ænˈθɒləˌdʒaɪz) *vb.* to compile or put into an anthology.

anthology (ænˈθɒlədʒɪ) *n., pl.* **-gies.** **1.** a collection of literary passages, esp. poems, by various authors. **2.** any printed collection of literary pieces, songs, etc. [C17: from Med. L, from Gk, lit.: a flower gathering, from *anthos* flower + *legein* to collect] —**an'thologist** *n.*

Anthony (ˈæntənɪ) *n.* **Saint.** ?251–?356 A.D., Egyptian hermit, commonly regarded as the founder of Christian monasticism. Feast day: Jan. 17.

Anthony of Padua *n.* **Saint.** 1195–1231, Franciscan friar, who preached in France and Italy. Feast day: June 13.

anthozoan (ˌænθəˈzəʊən) *n.* **1.** any of the sessile marine coelenterates of the class *Anthozoa*, including corals and sea anemones, in which the body is in the form of a polyp. ~*adj.* **2.** Also: **actinozoan**. of or relating to these.

anthracene (ˈænθrəˌsiːn) *n.* a colourless crystalline solid, used in the manufacture of chemicals and as crystals in scintillation counters. [C19: from ANTHRAX + -ENE]

anthracite (ˈænθrəˌsaɪt) *n.* a hard coal that burns slowly with a nonluminous flame giving out intense heat. Also called: **hard coal**. [C19: from L, from Gk *anthrakitēs* coallike, from *anthrax* coal] —**anthracitic** (ˌænθrəˈsɪtɪk) *adj.*

anthrax (ˈænθræks) *n., pl.* **-thraces** (-θrəˌsiːz). **1.** a highly infectious bacterial disease of animals, esp. cattle and sheep, which can be transmitted to man. **2.** a pustule caused by this disease. [C19: from LL, from Gk: carbuncle]

anthropo- *combining form.* indicating man or human: *anthropology.* [from Gk *anthrōpos*]

anthropocentric (ˌænθrəpəʊˈsɛntrɪk) *adj.* regarding man as the central factor in the universe.

anthropogenesis (ˌænθrəpəʊˈdʒɛnɪsɪs) *or* **anthropogeny** (ˌænθrəˈpɒdʒɪnɪ) *n.* the study of the origins of man.

anthropoid (ˈænθrəˌpɔɪd) *adj.* **1.** resembling man. **2.** resembling an ape; apelike. ~*n.* **3.** any primate of the suborder *Anthropoidea*, including monkeys, apes, and man.

anthropoid ape *n.* any of a group of primates having no tail, elongated arms, and a highly developed brain, including gibbons, orang-utans, chimpanzees, and gorillas.

anthropology (ˌænθrəˈpɒlədʒɪ) *n.* the study of man, his origins, institutions, religious beliefs, social relationships, etc. —**anthropological** (ˌænθrəpəˈlɒdʒɪkᵊl) *adj.* —ˌanˈthroˈpologist *n.*

anthropometry (ˌænθrəˈpɒmɪtrɪ) *n.* the comparative study of sizes and proportions of the human body. —**anthropometric** (ˌænθrəpəˈmɛtrɪk) *or* ˌanthropoˈmetrical *adj.*

anthropomorphic (ˌænθrəpəˈmɔːfɪk) *adj.* **1.** of or relating to anthropomorphism. **2.** resembling the human form.

anthropomorphism (ˌænθrəpəˈmɔːfɪzəm) *n.* the attribution of human form or behaviour to a deity, animal, etc.

anthropomorphous (ˌænθrəpəˈmɔːfəs) *adj.* **1.** shaped like a human being. **2.** another word for **anthropomorphic**.

anthropophagi (ˌænθrəˈpɒfəˌgaɪ) *pl. n., sing.* **-gus** (-gəs). cannibals. [C16: from L, from Gk *anthrōpophagos;* see ANTHROPO-, -PHAGE]

anthurium (ænˈθjʊərɪəm) *n.* any of various tropical American plants, many of which are cultivated as house plants

for their showy foliage and their flowers. [C19: NL, from Gk *anthos* flower + *oura* a tail]

anti (ˈæntɪ) *Inf.* ~*adj.* **1.** opposed to a party, policy, attitude, etc.: *he won't join because he is rather anti.* ~*n.* **2.** an opponent.

anti- *prefix.* **1.** against; opposing: *anticlerical.* **2.** opposite to: *anticlimax.* **3.** rival; false: *antipope.* **4.** counteracting or neutralizing: *antifreeze; antihistamine.* **5.** designating the antiparticle of the particle specified: *antineutron.* [from Gk *anti*]

anti-aircraft (ˌæntɪˈɛəkrɑːft) *n. (modifier)* of or relating to defence against aircraft attack: *anti-aircraft batteries.*

antiar (ˈæntɪˌɑː) *n.* another name for **upas** (senses 1, 2). [from Javanese]

antiballistic missile (ˌæntɪbəˈlɪstɪk) *n.* a ballistic missile designed to destroy another ballistic missile in flight.

Antibes (*French* ɑ̃tib) *n.* a port and resort in SE France, on the Mediterranean: an important Roman town. Pop.: 55 684 (1983 est.).

antibiosis (ˌæntɪbaɪˈəʊsɪs) *n.* an association between two organisms, esp. microorganisms, that is harmful to one of them.

antibiotic (ˌæntɪbaɪˈɒtɪk) *n.* **1.** any of various chemical substances, such as penicillin, produced by microorganisms, esp. fungi, or made synthetically, and capable of destroying microorganisms, esp. bacteria. ~*adj.* **2.** of or relating to antibiotics.

antibody (ˈæntɪˌbɒdɪ) *n., pl.* **-bodies.** any of various proteins produced in the blood in response to an antigen. By becoming attached to antigens on infectious organisms antibodies can render them harmless.

antic (ˈæntɪk) *Arch.* ~*n.* **1.** an actor in a ludicrous or grotesque part; clown. ~*adj.* **2.** fantastic; grotesque. ~See also: **antics**. [C16: from It. *antico* something grotesque (from its application to fantastic carvings found in ruins of ancient Rome)]

anticathode (ˌæntɪˈkæθəʊd) *n.* the target electrode for the stream of electrons in a vacuum tube, esp. an x-ray tube.

Antichrist (ˈæntɪˌkraɪst) *n.* **1.** *Bible.* the antagonist of Christ, expected by early Christians to appear and reign over the world until overthrown at Christ's Second Coming. **2.** *(sometimes not cap.)* an enemy of Christ or Christianity.

anticipant (ænˈtɪsɪpənt) *adj.* **1.** operating in advance. ~*n.* **2.** a person who anticipates.

anticipate (ænˈtɪsɪˌpeɪt) *vb. (mainly tr.)* **1.** *(may take a clause as object)* to foresee and act in advance of; forestall: *I anticipated his punch.* **2.** *(also intr.)* to mention (something) before its proper time: *don't anticipate the climax of the story.* **3.** *(may take a clause as object)* to regard as likely; expect. **4.** to make use of in advance of possession: *he anticipated his salary in buying a leather jacket.* [C16: from L *anticipāre* to take before, from *anti-* ANTE- + *capere* to take] —**anˈticiˌpator** *n.* —**anˈticiˌpatory** *or* **anˈticipative** *adj.*

▷ **Usage.** The use of *anticipate* to mean *expect*, while very common, is avoided by careful writers and speakers of English.

anticipation (ænˌtɪsɪˈpeɪʃən) *n.* **1.** the act of anticipating; expectation, premonition, or foresight. **2.** *Music.* an unstressed, usually short note introduced before a downbeat.

anticlerical (ˌæntɪˈklɛrɪkᵊl) *adj.* opposed to the power and influence of the clergy, esp. in politics. ~*n.* **2.** a supporter of an anticlerical party. —ˌanti'clericalism *n.*

anticlimax (ˌæntɪˈklaɪmæks) *n.* **1.** a disappointing or ineffective conclusion to a series of events, etc. **2.** a sudden change from a serious subject to one that is disappointing or ludicrous. —**anticlimactic** (ˌæntɪklaɪˈmæktɪk) *adj.*

anticline (ˈæntɪˌklaɪn) *n.* a formation of stratified rock raised up, by folding, into a broad arch so that the strata slope down on both sides from a common crest. —ˌanti'clinal *adj.*

anticlockwise (ˌæntɪˈklɒkˌwaɪz) *adv., adj.* in the opposite direction to the rotation of the hands of a clock. U.S. equivalent: **counterclockwise**.

anticoagulant (ˌæntɪkəʊˈægjʊlənt) *adj.* **1.** acting to prevent or retard coagulation, esp. of blood. ~*n.* **2.** an agent that prevents or retards coagulation.

anticonvulsant (ˌæntɪkənˈvʌlsənt) *n.* any of a class of drugs used to relieve convulsions. ~*adj.* **2.** of or relating to such drugs.

Anticosti (ˌæntɪˈkɒstɪ) *n.* an island of E Canada, in the Gulf of St Lawrence; part of Quebec. Area: 7881 sq. km (3043 sq. miles).

antics (ˈæntɪks) *pl. n.* absurd acts or postures.

anticyclone (ˌæntɪˈsaɪkləʊn) *n. Meteorol.* a body of moving air of higher pressure than the surrounding air, in which the pressure decreases away from the centre. Also called: **high**. — **anticyclonic** (ˌæntɪsaɪˈklɒnɪk) *adj.*

antidepressant (ˌæntɪdɪˈprɛsᵊnt) *n.* 1. any of a class of drugs used to alleviate depression. ~*adj.* 2. of this class of drugs.

antidote (ˈæntɪˌdəʊt) *n.* 1. *Med.* a drug or agent that counteracts or neutralizes the effects of a poison. 2. anything that counteracts or relieves a harmful condition. [C15: from L, from Gk *antidoton* something given as a countermeasure, from ANTI- + *didonai* to give] — **antiˈdotal** *adj.*

Antietam (ænˈtiːtəm) *n.* a creek in NW Maryland, flowing into the Potomac: scene of a Civil War battle (1862), in which the Confederate forces of General Robert E. Lee were defeated.

antifreeze (ˈæntɪˌfriːz) *n.* a liquid, usually ethylene glycol (ethanediol), added to water to lower its freezing point, esp. for use in an internal-combustion engine.

antigen (ˈæntɪdʒən, -ˌdʒɛn) *n.* a substance, usually a toxin produced by a bacterium, that stimulates the production of antibodies. [C20: from ANTI(BODY) + -GEN]

Antigone (ænˈtɪɡənɪ) *n. Greek myth.* daughter of Oedipus and Jocasta, who was condemned to death for cremating the body of her brother Polynices in defiance of an edict of her uncle, King Creon of Thebes.

Antigonus I (ænˈtɪɡənəs) *n.* known as *Cyclops.* 382–301 B.C., Macedonian general under Alexander the Great; king of Macedon (306–301).

Antigua (ænˈtiːɡə) *n.* an island of the West Indies, one of the Leeward Islands: a British colony, with its dependency Barbuda, until 1967, when it became a British associated state; it became independent in 1981 as part of the state of Antigua and Barbuda. Area: 279 sq. km (108 sq. miles). — **Anˈtiguan** *adj., n.*

Antigua and Barbuda *n.* a state of the West Indies, comprising the islands of Antigua, Barbuda, and Redonda: gained independence in 1981: a member of the Commonwealth. Official language: English. Religion: Christian majority. Currency: East Caribbean dollar. Capital: St John's. Pop.: 81 600 (1986 est.). Area: 442 sq. km (171 sq. miles).

antihero (ˈæntɪˌhɪərəʊ) *n., pl.* **-roes.** a central character in a novel, play, etc., who lacks the traditional heroic virtues.

antihistamine (ˌæntɪˈhɪstəˌmiːn, -mɪn) *n.* any drug that neutralizes the effects of histamine, used esp. in the treatment of allergies.

antiknock (ˌæntɪˈnɒk) *n.* a compound, such as lead tetraethyl, added to petrol to reduce knocking in the engine.

Anti-Lebanon *n.* a mountain range running north and south between Syria and Lebanon, east of the Lebanon Mountains. Highest peak: Mount Hermon, 2814 m (9232 ft.).

Antilles (ænˈtɪliːz) *pl. n.* **the.** a group of islands in the West Indies consisting of the **Greater Antilles** and the **Lesser Antilles.**

antilogarithm (ˌæntɪˈlɒɡəˌrɪðəm) *n.* a number whose logarithm to a given base is a given number: *100 is the antilogarithm of 2 to base 10.* Often shortened to **antilog.** — **ˌantiˌlogaˈrithmic** *adj.*

antilogy (ænˈtɪlədʒɪ) *n., pl.* **-gies.** a contradiction in terms. [C17: from Gk *antilogia*]

antimacassar (ˌæntɪməˈkæsə) *n.* a cloth covering the back and arms of chairs, etc., to prevent soiling. [C19: from ANTI- + MACASSAR (OIL)]

antimagnetic (ˌæntɪmæɡˈnɛtɪk) *adj.* of a material that does not acquire permanent magnetism when exposed to a magnetic field.

antimalarial (ˌæntɪməˈlɛərɪəl) *adj.* 1. effective in the treatment of malaria. ~*n.* 2. an antimalarial drug or agent.

antimasque (ˈæntɪˌmɑːsk) *n.* a comic dance, presented between the acts of a masque.

antimatter (ˈæntɪˌmætə) *n.* a hypothetical form of matter composed of antiparticles.

antimissile (ˌæntɪˈmɪsaɪl) *adj.* 1. relating to defensive measures against missile attack: *an antimissile system.* ~*n.* 2. Also called: **antimissile missile.** a defensive missile used to intercept and destroy attacking missiles.

antimony (ˈæntɪmənɪ) *n.* a toxic metallic element that exists in two allotropic forms and is added to alloys to increase their strength and hardness. Symbol: Sb; atomic no.: 51; atomic wt.: 121.75. [C15: from Med. L *antimōnium*, from ?] — **antimonial** (ˌæntɪˈməʊnɪəl) *adj.*

antinomian (ˌæntɪˈnəʊmɪən) *adj.* 1. relating to the doctrine that by faith a Christian is released from the obligation of adhering to any moral law. ~*n.* 2. a member of a Christian sect holding such a doctrine. — **ˌantiˈnomianism** *n.*

antinomy (ænˈtɪnəmɪ) *n., pl.* **-mies.** 1. opposition of one law, principle, or rule to another. 2. *Philosophy.* contradiction existing between two apparently indubitable propositions. [C16: from L, from Gk: conflict between laws, from ANTI- + *nomos* law] — **antinomic** (ˌæntɪˈnɒmɪk) *adj.*

antinovel (ˈæntɪˌnɒvᵊl) *n.* a type of prose fiction in which conventional or traditional novelistic elements are rejected.

antinuclear (ˌæntɪˈnjuːklɪə) *adj.* opposed to nuclear weapons or nuclear power.

Antioch (ˈæntɪˌɒk) *n.* a city in S Turkey, on the Orantes River: ancient commercial centre and capital of Syria (300–64 B.C.); early centre of Christianity. Pop.: 94 942 (1980). Arabic name: **Antakiyah.** Turkish name: **Antakya.**

Antiochus III (ænˈtaɪəkəs) *n.* known as *Antiochus the Great.* 242–187 B.C., king of Syria (223–187), who greatly extended the Seleucid empire but was forced (190) to surrender most of Asia Minor to the Romans.

Antiochus IV *n.* ?215–164 B.C., Seleucid king of Syria (175–164), who attacked the Jews and provoked the revolt of the Maccabees.

antiparticle (ˈæntɪˌpɑːtɪkᵊl) *n.* any of a group of elementary particles that have the same mass as their corresponding particle but have a charge of equal magnitude but opposite sign. When a particle collides with its antiparticle mutual annihilation occurs.

antipasto (ˌæntɪˈpɑːstəʊ, -ˈpæs-) *n., pl.* **-tos.** a course of hors d'oeuvres in an Italian meal. [It.: before food]

Antipater (ænˈtɪpətə) *n.* ?398–319 B.C., Macedonian general under Alexander the Great: regent of Macedon (334–323).

antipathetic (ænˌtɪpəˈθɛtɪk, ˌæntɪpə-) *or* **antipathetical** *adj.* (often foll. by *to*) having or arousing a strong aversion.

antipathy (ænˈtɪpəθɪ) *n., pl.* **-thies.** 1. a feeling of dislike or hostility. 2. the object of such a feeling. [C17: from L, from Gk, from ANTI- + *patheia* feeling]

antipersonnel (ˌæntɪˌpɜːsəˈnɛl) *adj.* (of weapons, etc.) designed to cause casualties to personnel rather than to destroy equipment.

antiperspirant (ˌæntɪˈpɜːspərənt) *n.* 1. a substance applied to the skin to reduce or prevent perspiration. ~*adj.* 2. reducing perspiration.

antiphlogistic (ˌæntɪflɒˈdʒɪstɪk) *adj.* 1. of or relating to the prevention or alleviation of inflammation. ~*n.* 2. an antiphlogistic drug.

antiphon (ˈæntɪfən) *n.* 1. a short passage, usually from the Bible, recited or sung as a response after certain parts of a liturgical service. 2. a psalm, hymn, etc., chanted or sung in alternate parts. 3. any response. [C15: from LL *antiphōna* sung responses, from LGk, pl. of *antiphōnon* (something) responsive, from ANTI- + *phōnē* sound] — **antiphonal** (ænˈtɪfənəl) *adj.*

antiphonary (ænˈtɪfənərɪ) *n., pl.* **-naries.** a bound collection of antiphons.

antiphony (ænˈtɪfənɪ) *n., pl.* **-nies.** 1. antiphonal singing. 2. any musical or other sound effect that answers or echoes another.

antipode (ˈæntɪˌpəʊd) *n.* the exact or direct opposite. — **antipodal** (ænˈtɪpədᵊl) *adj.*

antipodes (ænˈtɪpəˌdiːz) *pl. n.* 1. either or both of two places that are situated diametrically opposite one another on the earth's surface. 2. the people who live there. 3. (*often cap.*) **the.** Australia and New Zealand. [C16: via LL from Gk, pl. of *antipous* having the feet opposite, from ANTI- + *pous* foot] — **antipodean** (ænˌtɪpəˈdiːən) *adj.*

Antipodes Islands *pl. n.* **the.** a group of small uninhabited islands in the South Pacific, southeast of and belonging to New Zealand. Area: 62 sq. km (24 sq. miles).

antipope (ˈæntɪˌpəʊp) *n.* a rival pope elected in opposition to one who has been canonically chosen.

antipyretic (ˌæntɪpaɪˈrɛtɪk) *adj.* **1.** preventing or alleviating fever. ~*n.* **2.** an antipyretic remedy or drug.

antiquarian (ˌæntɪˈkwɛərɪən) *adj.* **1.** concerned with the study of antiquities or antiques. ~*n.* **2.** a less common name for **antiquary.** — **anti'quarianism** *n.*

antiquary ('æntɪkwərɪ) *n., pl.* **-quaries.** a person who collects, deals in, or studies antiques or ancient works of art. Also called: **antiquarian.**

antiquate ('æntɪˌkweɪt) *vb.* (*tr.*) to make obsolete or old-fashioned. [C15: from L *antīquāre* to make old, from *antīquus* ancient] — **'anti,quated** *adj.*

antique (æn'tiːk) *n.* **1. a.** a decorative object, piece of furniture, or other work of art created in an earlier period, that is valued for its beauty, workmanship, and age. **b.** (*as modifier*): *an antique shop.* **2.** any object made in an earlier period. **3. the.** the style of ancient art, esp. Greek or Roman. ~*adj.* **4.** made in or in the style of an earlier period. **5.** of or belonging to the distant past, esp. of ancient Greece or Rome. **6.** *Inf.* old-fashioned. **7.** *Arch.* aged or venerable. ~*vb.* **8.** (*tr.*) to give an antique appearance to. [C16: from L *antīquus* ancient, from *ante* before]

antiquities (æn'tɪkwɪtɪz) *pl. n.* remains or relics, such as statues, buildings, or coins, that date from ancient times.

antiquity (æn'tɪkwɪtɪ) *n., pl.* **-ties.** **1.** the quality of being ancient: *a vase of great antiquity.* **2.** the far distant past, esp. preceding the Middle Ages. **3.** the people of ancient times collectively.

antiracism (ˌæntɪˈreɪsɪzəm) *n.* the policy of challenging racism and promoting racial tolerance. — ,anti'racist *n., adj.*

antirrhinum (ˌæntɪˈraɪnəm) *n.* any plant of the genus *Antirrhinum*, esp. the snapdragon, which has two-lipped flowers of various colours. [C16: via L from Gk *antirrhinon*, from ANTI- (imitating) + *rhis* nose]

Antisana (*Spanish* anti'sana) *n.* a volcano in N central Ecuador, in the Andes. Height: 5756 m (18 885 ft.).

antiscorbutic (ˌæntɪskɔːˈbjuːtɪk) *adj.* **1.** preventing or curing scurvy. ~*n.* **2.** an antiscorbutic agent.

anti-Semite *n.* a person who persecutes or discriminates against Jews. — ,anti-Se'mitic *adj.* — ,anti-'Semitism *n.*

antisepsis (ˌæntɪˈsɛpsɪs) *n.* **1.** destruction of undesirable microorganisms, such as those that cause disease or putrefaction. **2.** the state of being free from such microorganisms.

antiseptic (ˌæntɪˈsɛptɪk) *adj.* **1.** of or producing antisepsis. **2.** entirely free from contamination. **3.** *Inf.* lacking spirit or excitement. ~*n.* **4.** an antiseptic agent. — ,anti'septically *adv.*

antiserum (ˌæntɪˈsɪərəm) *n., pl.* **-rums** *or* **-ra** (-rə). blood serum containing antibodies against a specific antigen, used to treat or provide immunity to a disease.

antisocial (ˌæntɪˈsəʊʃəl) *adj.* **1.** avoiding the company of other people; unsociable. **2.** contrary or injurious to the interests of society in general.

antispasmodic (ˌæntɪspæzˈmɒdɪk) *adj.* **1.** preventing or arresting spasms. ~*n.* **2.** an antispasmodic drug.

antistatic (ˌæntɪˈstætɪk) *adj.* (of a substance, textile, etc.) retaining sufficient moisture to provide a conducting path, thus avoiding the effects of static electricity.

Antisthenes (æn'tɪsθəˌniːz) *n.* ?445–365 B.C., Greek philosopher, founder of the Cynic school, who taught that the only good was virtue, won by self-control and independence from worldly needs.

antistrophe (æn'tɪstrəfɪ) *n.* (in ancient Greek drama) **a.** the second of two movements made by a chorus during the performance of a choral ode. **b.** the second part of a choral ode sung during this movement. ~See **strophe.** [C17: via LL from Gk *antistrophē* an answering turn, from ANTI- + *strophē* a turning]

antitank (ˌæntɪˈtæŋk) *adj.* designed to immobilize or destroy armoured vehicles.

antithesis (æn'tɪθɪsɪs) *n., pl.* **-ses** (-ˌsiːz). **1.** the exact opposite. **2.** contrast or opposition. **3.** *Rhetoric.* the juxtaposition of contrasting ideas or words to produce an effect of balance, such as *my words fly up, my thoughts remain below.* [C15: via L from Gk: a setting against, from ANTI- + *tithenai* to place] — **antithetical** (ˌæntɪˈθɛtɪkəl) *adj.*

antitoxin (ˌæntɪˈtɒksɪn) *n.* **1.** an antibody that neutralizes a toxin. **2.** blood serum that contains a specific antibody. — ,anti'toxic *adj.*

antitrades ('æntɪˌtreɪdz) *pl. n.* winds in the upper atmosphere blowing in the opposite direction from and above the trade winds.

antitrust (ˌæntɪˈtrʌst) *n.* (*modifier*) *Chiefly U.S.* regulating or opposing trusts, monopolies, cartels, or similar organizations.

antitussive (ˌæntɪˈtʌsɪv) *n.* **1.** any of a class of drugs used to suppress or alleviate coughing. ~*adj.* **2.** of or relating to such drugs.

antitype ('æntɪˌtaɪp) *n.* **1.** a person or thing that is foreshadowed or represented by a type or symbol. **2.** an opposite type. — **antitypical** (ˌæntɪˈtɪpɪkəl) *adj.*

antivenin (ˌæntɪˈvɛnɪn) *or* **antivenene** (ˌæntɪvɪˈniːn) *n.* an antitoxin that counteracts a specific venom, esp. snake venom. [C19: from ANTI- + VEN(OM) + -IN]

antler ('æntlə) *n.* one of a pair of bony outgrowths on the heads of male deer and some related species of either sex. [C14: from OF *antoillier*] — **'antlered** *adj.*

antlion ('ænt,laɪən) *n.* **1.** any of various insects which resemble dragonflies and are most common in tropical regions. **2.** the larva of this insect, which buries itself in the sand to await its prey.

Antofagasta (ˌæntəfəˈɡæstə; *Spanish* antofaˈɣasta) *n.* a port in N Chile. Pop.: 175 486 (1985 est.).

Antoinette (*French* ātwanɛt) *n.* See **Marie Antoinette.**

Antonine Wall ('æntənaɪn) *n.* a Roman frontier defence work across S Scotland, extending between the River Clyde and the Firth of Forth. It was built in 142 A.D. on the orders of Antoninus Pius.

Antoninus (ˌæntəˈnaɪnəs) *n.* See **Marcus Aurelius Antoninus.**

Antoninus Pius *n.* 86–161 A.D., emperor of Rome (138–161); adopted son and successor of Hadrian.

Antonioni (ˌæntəʊnɪˈəʊnɪ) *n.* **Michelangelo** (mikeˈlandʒelo). born 1912, Italian film director; his films include *L'Avventura* (1959), *La Notte* (1961), *Blow-Up* (1966), and *Zabriskie Point* (1970).

Antonius (æn'təʊnɪəs) *n.* **Marcus** ('mɑːkəs). Latin name of (Mark) **Antony.**

antonomasia (ˌæntənəˈmeɪzɪə) *n.* **1.** the substitution of a title or epithet for a proper name, such as *his highness.* **2.** the use of a proper name for an idea: *he is a Daniel come to judgment.* [C16: via L from Gk, from *antonomazein* to name differently, from *onoma* name]

Antony ('æntənɪ) *n.* **Mark.** Latin name *Marcus Antonius.* ?83–30 B.C., Roman general who served under Julius Caesar in the Gallic wars and became a member of the second triumvirate (43). He defeated Brutus and Cassius at Philippi (42) but having repudiated his wife for Cleopatra, queen of Egypt, he was defeated by his brother-in-law Octavian (Augustus) at Actium (31).

antonym ('æntənɪm) *n.* a word that means the opposite of another. [C19: from Gk, from ANTI- + *onoma* name] — **antonymous** (æn'tɒnɪməs) *adj.*

Antrim ('æntrɪm) *n.* a district (former county) of NE Northern Ireland: famous for the Giant's Causeway on the N coast. Pop.: 45 900 (1986 est.). Area: 415 sq. km (160 sq. miles).

antrum ('æntrəm) *n., pl.* **-tra** (-trə). *Anat.* a natural cavity, hollow, or sinus, esp. in a bone. [C14: from L: cave, from Gk *antron*] — **'antral** *adj.*

Antseranana (ˌæntsɪˈrænənə) *n.* a port in N Madagascar: former French naval base. Pop.: 49 000 (1982). Former name: **Diégo-Suarez.**

Antung ('æn'tʊŋ) *n.* a variant transliteration of the Chinese name for **Andong.**

Antwerp ('æntwɜːp) *n.* **1.** a province of N Belgium. Pop.: 1 585 163 (1986 est.). Area: 2859 sq. km (1104 sq. miles). **2.** a port in N Belgium, capital of Antwerp province, on the River Scheldt: a major European port. Pop.: 479 748 (1987 est.). Flemish name: **Antwerpen** ('ɑntwɛrpə). French name: **Anvers.**

Anu ('ɑːnuː) *n. Babylonian myth.* the sky god.

ANU *abbrev. for* Australian National University.

Anubis (ə'njuːbɪs) *n. Egyptian myth.* a deity, a son of Osiris, who conducted the dead to judgment. He is represented as having a jackal's head and was identified by the Greeks with Hermes.

Anuradhapura (ə'nʊərədə,pʊərə, ˌʌnʊˈrɑːdə-) *n.* a town in Sri Lanka: ancient capital of Ceylon; site of the sacred bo tree and place of pilgrimage for Buddhists. Pop.: 36 248 (1981).

anuresis (,ænjʊ'riːsɪs) *n.* inability to urinate. [C20: NL, from AN- + Gk *ouresis* urination]

anus ('eɪnəs) *n.* the excretory opening at the end of the alimentary canal. [C16: from L]

Anvers (ãvɛr) *n.* the French name for **Antwerp**.

anvil ('ænvɪl) *n.* **1.** a heavy iron or steel block on which metals are hammered during forging. **2.** any part having a similar shape or function, such as the lower part of a telegraph key. **3.** *Anat.* the nontechnical name for **incus**. [OE *anfealt*]

anxiety (æŋ'zaɪɪtɪ) *n.*, *pl.* **-ties. 1.** a state of uneasiness or tension caused by apprehension of possible misfortune, danger, etc. **2.** intense desire; eagerness. **3.** *Psychol.* a state of intense apprehension, common in mental illness or after a very distressing experience. [C16: from L *anxietas*]

anxious ('æŋkʃəs, 'æŋʃəs) *adj.* **1.** worried and tense because of possible misfortune, danger, etc. **2.** causing anxiety; worrying; distressing: *an anxious time.* **3.** intensely desirous: *anxious for promotion.* [C17: from L *anxius*; rel. to L *angere* to torment] —**'anxiously** *adv.* — **'anxiousness** *n.*

any ('ɛnɪ) *determiner.* **1. a.** one, some, or several, as specified, no matter how much, what kind, etc.: *you may take any clothes you like.* **b.** (*as pron.; functioning as sing. or pl.*): *take any you like.* **2.** (*usually used with a negative*) **a.** even the smallest amount or even one: *I can't stand any noise.* **b.** (*as pron.; functioning as sing. or pl.*): *don't give her any.* **3.** whatever or whichever: *any dictionary will do.* **4.** an indefinite or unlimited (amount or number): *any number of friends.* ~*adv.* **5.** (*usually used with a negative*) (foll. by a comp. adj.) to even the smallest extent: *it isn't any worse.* [OE *ænig*]

▷ **Usage.** Educated speakers and writers avoid using *any* for *at all* in formal English: *a translation would not help at all* (not *would not help any*).

Anyang ('ɑːn'jɑːŋ) *n.* a town in E China, in Henan province: archaeological site and capital of the Shang dynasty. Pop.: 253 541 (1980).

anybody ('ɛnɪ,bɒdɪ) *pron.* **1.** any person; anyone. **2.** (*usually used with a negative or a question*) a person of any importance: *he isn't anybody.* ~*n.*, *pl.* **-bodies. 3.** (often preceded by *just*) any person at random.

anyhow ('ɛnɪ,haʊ) *adv.* **1.** in any case. **2.** by any means whatever. **3.** carelessly.

any more *or esp. U.S.* **anymore** (,ɛnɪ'mɔː) *adv.* any longer; still; nowadays.

anyone ('ɛnɪ,wʌn) *pron.* **1.** any person; anybody. **2.** (*used with a negative or a question*) a person of any importance: *is he anyone?* **3.** (often preceded by *just*) any person at random.

anyplace ('ɛnɪ,pleɪs) *adv. U.S. & Canad. inf.* anywhere.

anything ('ɛnɪ,θɪŋ) *pron.* **1.** any object, event, action, etc., whatever: *anything might happen.* ~*n.* **2.** a thing of any kind: *have you anything to declare?* ~*adv.* **3.** in any way: *he wasn't anything like his father.* **4. anything but.** not in the least: *she was anything but happy.* **5. like anything.** (intensifier): *he ran like anything.*

anyway ('ɛnɪ,weɪ) *adv.* **1.** in any case; at any rate; nevertheless. **2.** in a careless manner. **3.** Usually **any way.** in any manner.

anywhere ('ɛnɪ,wɛə) *adv.* **1.** in, at, or to any place. **2. get anywhere.** to be successful.

anywise ('ɛnɪ,waɪz) *adv. Chiefly U.S.* in any way.

ANZAAS ('ænzəs, -zæs) *n. acronym for* Australian and New Zealand Association for the Advancement of Science.

Anzac ('ænzæk) *n.* **1.** (in World War I) a soldier serving with the Australian and New Zealand Army Corps. **2.** (now) any Australian or New Zealand soldier. **3.** the Anzac landing at Gallipoli in 1915.

Anzac Day *n.* April 25, a public holiday in Australia and New Zealand commemorating the Anzac landing at Gallipoli in 1915.

Anzio ('ænzɪ,əʊ; *Italian* 'antsjo) *n.* a port and resort on the W coast of Italy: site of Allied landings in World War II. Pop.: 27 094 (1981).

ANZUS ('ænzəs) *n. acronym for* Australia, New Zealand, and the United States, with reference to the security alliance between them.

AO *abbrev. for* Officer of the Order of Australia.

A/O *or* **a/o** (accounting, etc.) *abbrev. for* account of.

AOB *or* **a.o.b.** *abbrev. for* any other business.

Aorangi (,eɪəʊ'ræŋɪ) *n.* another name for Mount **Cook**.

aorist ('eɪərɪst, 'ɛərɪst) *n. Grammar.* a tense of the verb, esp. in classical Greek, indicating past action without reference to whether the action involved was momentary or continuous. [C16: from Gk *aoristos* not limited, from A-¹ + *horistos*, from *horizein* to define]

aorta (eɪ'ɔːtə) *n.*, *pl.* **-tas** *or* **-tae** (-tiː). the main vessel in the arterial network, which conveys oxygen-rich blood from the heart. [C16: from NL, from Gk *aortē*: something lifted, from *aeirein* to raise] —**a'ortic** *or* **a'ortal** *adj.*

Aosta (*Italian* a'ɔsta) *n.* a town in NW Italy, capital of Valle d'Aosta region: Roman remains. Pop.: 37 194 (1981).

Aotearoa ('æɒ,tɪə,rɒːə) *n. N.Z.* the Maori name for New Zealand. [Maori: the long white cloud]

aoudad ('ɑːʊ,dæd) *n.* a wild mountain sheep of N Africa. Also called: **Barbary sheep**. [from F, from Berber *audad*]

Aouita (aʊ'iːtə) *n.* **Said** (saɪ'iːd). born 1960, Moroccan middle-distance runner: world record holder in the 2000 m, 5000 m, and 15 000 m events (1987).

apace (ə'peɪs) *adv.* quickly; rapidly. [C14: prob. from OF *à pas*, at a (good) pace]

apache (ə'pæʃ) *n.* a Parisian gangster or ruffian. [from F: APACHE]

Apache (ə'pætʃɪ) *n.* **1.** (*pl.* **Apaches** *or* **Apache**) a member of a North American Indian people inhabiting the southwestern U.S. and N Mexico. **2.** the language of this people. [from Mexican Sp.]

apanage ('æpənɪdʒ) *n.* a variant spelling of **appanage**.

apart (ə'pɑːt) *adj.* (*postpositive*), *adv.* **1.** to or in pieces: *he had the television apart.* **2.** placed or kept separately or for a particular purpose, etc.; aside (esp. in **set** *or* **put apart**). **3.** separate in time, place, or position: *he stood apart from the group.* **4.** not being taken into account: *these difficulties apart, the project ran smoothly.* **5.** individual; distinct: *a race apart.* **6.** separately or independently: *considered apart, his reasoning was faulty.* **7. apart from.** (*prep.*) besides. ~See also **take apart, tell apart.** [C14: from OF *a part* at (the) side]

apartheid (ə'pɑːthaɪt, -heɪt) *n.* (in South Africa) the official government policy of racial segregation. [C20: Afrik., from *apart* APART + -*heid* -HOOD]

apartment (ə'pɑːtmənt) *n.* **1.** (*often pl.*) any room in a building, usually one of several forming a suite, used as living accommodation, offices, etc. **2. a.** another name (esp. U.S. and Canad.) for **flat²** (sense 1). **b.** (*as modifier*): *apartment house.* [C17: from F *appartement*, from It., from *appartare* to separate]

apathetic (,æpə'θɛtɪk) *adj.* having or showing little or no emotion or interest. [C18: from APATHY + PATHETIC] —,apa'thetically *adv.*

apathy ('æpəθɪ) *n.* **1.** absence of interest in or enthusiasm for things generally considered interesting or moving. **2.** absence of emotion. [C17: from L, from Gk *apatheia*, from A-¹ + *pathos* feeling]

apatite ('æpə,taɪt) *n.* a common naturally occurring mineral consisting basically of calcium fluorophosphate. It is a source of phosphorus and is used in fertilizers. [C19: from G *Apatit*, from Gk *apatē* deceit; from its misleading similarity to other minerals]

ape (eɪp) *n.* **1.** any of various primates in which the tail is very short or absent. **2.** (not in technical use) any monkey. **3.** an imitator; mimic. ~*vb.* **4.** (*tr.*) to imitate. [OE *apa*] — **'ape,like** *adj.*

APEC *Canad. abbrev. for* Atlantic Provinces Economic Council.

Apeldoorn ('æpəl,dɔːn; *Dutch* 'aːpəldoːrn) *n.* a town in the Netherlands, in central Gelderland province: nearby is the summer residence of the Dutch royal family. Pop.: 140 769 (1981 est.).

Apelles (ə'pɛliːz) *n.* 4th century B.C., Greek painter of mythological subjects, none of whose work survives, his fame resting on the testimony of Pliny and other writers.

apeman ('eɪp,mæn) *n.*, *pl.* **-men.** any of various extinct apelike primates thought to have been the forerunners of modern man.

Apennines ('æpə,naɪnz) *pl. n.* **1.** a mountain range in Italy, extending over 1250 km (800 miles) from the northwest to the southernmost tip of the peninsula. Highest peak: Monte Corno, 2912 m (9554 ft.). **2.** a mountain range lying in the N quadrants of the moon, extending over 950 km along the SE border of the Mare Imbrium and rising to 6200 m.

aperçu *French.* (apɛrsy) *n.* **1.** an outline. **2.** an insight. [from *apercevoir* to PERCEIVE]

aperient (ə'pɪərɪənt) *Med.* ~*adj.* **1.** laxative. ~*n.* **2.** a mild laxative. [C17: from L *aperire* to open]

aperiodic (,eɪpɪərɪ'ɒdɪk) *adj.* **1.** not periodic; not occurring at regular intervals. **2.** *Physics.* **a.** (of a system or instrument) being damped sufficiently to reach equilibrium without oscillation. **b.** (of an oscillation or vibration) not having a regular period. **c.** (of an electrical circuit) not having a measurable resonant frequency. — **aperiodicity** (,eɪpɪərɪə'dɪsɪtɪ) *n.*

apéritif (ə,pɛrɪ'tiːf) *n.* an alcoholic drink before a meal to whet the appetite. [C19: from F, from Med. L, from L *aperire* to open]

aperture ('æpətʃə) *n.* **1.** a hole; opening. **2.** *Physics.* a usually circular and often variable opening in an optical instrument or device that controls the quantity of radiation entering or leaving it. [C15: from LL *apertūra* opening, from *aperire* to open]

apetalous (eɪ'pɛtələs) *adj.* (of flowering plants such as the wood anemone) having no petals. [C18: from NL; see A-[1], PETAL]

apex ('eɪpɛks) *n.*, *pl.* **apexes** *or* **apices.** **1.** the highest point; vertex. **2.** the pointed end or tip of something. **3.** a high point, as of a career. [C17: from L: point]

APEX ('eɪpɛks) *n. acronym for:* **1.** Advance Purchase Excursion, a reduced airline fare, paid for at least 30 days before departure. **2.** Association of Professional, Executive, Clerical, and Computer Staff.

Apex Club ('eɪpɛks) *n.* (in Australia) an association of business and professional men to promote community welfare. — **Apexian** (eɪ'pɛksɪən) *adj.*, *n.*

aphaeresis *or* **apheresis** (ə'fɪərɪsɪs) *n.* the omission of a letter or syllable at the beginning of a word. [C17: via LL from Gk, from *aphairein* to remove]

aphasia (ə'feɪzɪə) *n.* a disorder of the central nervous system characterized by loss of the ability to communicate, esp. in speech. [C19: via NL from Gk, from A-[1] + -*phasia*, from *phanai* to speak]

aphelandra (,æfɛl'ændrə) *n.* any of a genus of tropical American plants cultivated for their dark foliage and bright flowers or bracts. [NL, from Gk *aphelēs* simple + -*andra*, from the one-celled anthers]

aphelion (æp'hiːlɪən, ə'fiː-) *n.*, *pl.* -**lia** (-lɪə). the point in its orbit when a planet or comet is at its greatest distance from the sun. [C17: from NL *aphēlium*, from AP(O)- + Gk *hēlios* sun]

aphesis ('æfɪsɪs) *n.* the gradual disappearance of an unstressed vowel at the beginning of a word, as in *squire* from *esquire*. [C19: from Gk, from *aphienai* to set free] — **aphetic** (ə'fɛtɪk) *adj.*

aphid ('eɪfɪd) *n.* any of the small homopterous insects of the family Aphididae, which feed by sucking the juices from plants. [C19: from *aphides*, pl. of APHIS]

aphis ('eɪfɪs) *n.*, *pl.* **aphides** ('eɪfɪ,diːz). any of a genus of aphids, such as the blackfly. [C18: from NL (coined by Linnaeus for obscure reasons)]

aphonia (ə'fəʊnɪə) *or* **aphony** ('æfənɪ) *n.* loss of voice caused by damage to the vocal tract. [C18: NL, from Gk, from A-[1] + *phōnē* sound]

aphorism ('æfə,rɪzəm) *n.* a short pithy saying expressing a general truth; maxim. [C16: from LL, from Gk *aphorismos*, from *aphorizein* to define] — **aphorist** *n.* — ,aph-o'**ristic** *adj.*

aphrodisiac (,æfrə'dɪzɪæk) *n.* **1.** a drug, food, etc., that excites sexual desire. ~*adj.* **2.** exciting sexual desire. [C18: from Gk, from *aphrodisios* belonging to *Aphrodite*, goddess of love]

Aphrodite (,æfrə'daɪtɪ) *n. Greek myth.* the goddess of love and beauty, daughter of Zeus. Roman counterpart: **Venus.** Also called: **Cytherea.**

aphyllous (ə'fɪləs) *adj.* (of plants) having no leaves. [C19: from NL, from Gk A-[1] + *phullon* leaf]

Apia (æ'pɪə, 'æpɪə) *n.* the capital of Western Samoa: a port on the N coast of Upolu. Pop.: 36 000 (1981 est.).

apian ('eɪpɪən) *adj.* of, relating to, or resembling bees. [C19: from L *apiānus*, from *apis* bee]

apiarist ('eɪpɪərɪst) *n.* a person who studies or keeps bees.

apiary ('eɪpɪərɪ) *n.*, *pl.* -**aries.** a place where bees are kept. [C17: from L *apiārium*, from *apis* bee]

apical ('æpɪk⁽ə⁾l, 'eɪ-) *adj.* of, at, or being the apex. [C19: from NL *apicālis*] — '**apically** *adv.*

apices ('æpɪ,siːz, 'eɪ-) *n.* a plural of **apex.**

apiculture ('eɪpɪ,kʌltʃə) *n.* the breeding and care of bees. [C19: from L *apis* bee + CULTURE] — ,api'**cultural** *adj.* — ,api'**culturist** *n.*

apiece (ə'piːs) *adv.* for, to, or from each one: *they were given two apples apiece.*

Apis ('ɑːpɪs) *n.* (in ancient Egypt) a sacred bull worshipped at Memphis.

apish ('eɪpɪʃ) *adj.* **1.** stupid; foolish. **2.** resembling an ape. **3.** slavishly imitative. — '**apishly** *adv.* — '**apishness** *n.*

aplanatic (,æplə'nætɪk) *adj.* (of a lens or mirror) free from spherical aberration. [C18: from Gk *aplanetos* free from error, from A-[1] + *planaein* to wander]

aplenty (ə'plɛntɪ) *adj.* (*postpositive*), *adv.* in plenty.

aplomb (ə'plɒm) *n.* equanimity, self-confidence, or self-possession. [C18: from F: uprightness, from *à plomb* according to the plumb line]

apnoea *or U.S.* **apnea** (æp'nɪə) *n.* a temporary inability to breathe. [C18: from NL, from Gk *apnoia*, from A-[1] + *pnein* to breathe]

Apo ('ɑːpəʊ) *n.* the highest mountain in the Philippines, on SE Mindanao: active volcano with three peaks. Height: 2954 m (9690 ft.).

apo- *or* **ap-** *prefix.* **1.** away from; off: *apogee.* **2.** separation of: *apocarpous.* [from Gk *apo* away, off]

Apoc. *abbrev. for:* **1.** Apocalypse. **2.** Apocrypha *or* Apocryphal.

apocalypse (ə'pɒkəlɪps) *n.* **1.** a prophetic disclosure or revelation. **2.** an event of great importance, violence, etc., like the events described in the Apocalypse. [C13: from LL *apocalypsis*, from Gk, from APO- + *kaluptein* to hide] — a,poca'**lyptic** *adj.*

Apocalypse (ə'pɒkəlɪps) *n. Bible.* another name for the Book of Revelation.

apocarpous (,æpə'kɑːpəs) *adj.* (of the ovaries of flowering plants) consisting of separate carpels. [C19: from NL, from Gk APO- + *karpos* fruit]

apochromat (,æpə'krəʊmæt) *or* **apochromatic lens** (,æpəkrə'mætɪk) *n.* a lens system designed to bring trichromatic light to a single focus and reduce chromatic aberration.

apocope (ə'pɒkəpɪ) *n.* omission of the final sound or sounds of a word. [C16: via LL from Gk, from *apokoptein* to cut off]

apocrine ('æpəkraɪn, -krɪn) *adj.* losing cellular tissue in the process of secretion, as in mammary glands. Cf. **eccrine.** [C20: from APO- + -*crine*, from Gk *krinein* to separate]

Apocrypha (ə'pɒkrɪfə) *n.* **the.** (*functioning as sing. or pl.*) the 14 books included as an appendix to the Old Testament in the Septuagint and the Vulgate but not in the Hebrew canon. [C14: via LL *apocrypha* (*scripta*) hidden (writings), from Gk, from *apokruptein* to hide away]

apocryphal (ə'pɒkrɪfəl) *adj.* **1.** of questionable authenticity. **2.** (*sometimes cap.*) of or like the Apocrypha. **3.** untrue; counterfeit.

apodal ('æpəd⁽ə⁾l) *adj.* without feet; having no pelvic fins. [C18: from Gk A-[1] + *pous* foot]

apodosis (ə'pɒdəsɪs) *n.*, *pl.* -**ses** (-,siːz). *Logic, grammar.* the consequent of a conditional statement, as *I won't go in if it rains I won't go.* [C17: via LL from Gk, from *apodidonai* to give back]

apogee ('æpə,dʒiː) *n.* **1.** the point in its orbit around the earth when the moon or an artificial satellite is at its greatest distance from the earth. **2.** the highest point. [C17: from NL, from Gk, from *apogaios* away from the earth] — ,apo'**gean** *adj.*

apolitical (,eɪpə'lɪtɪk⁽ə⁾l) *adj.* politically neutral; without political attitudes, content, or bias.

Apollinaire (*French* apɔlinɛr) *n.* **Guillaume** (gijom), real name *Wilhelm Apollinaris de Kostrowitzki.* 1880–1918, French poet, novelist, and dramatist, regarded as a precursor of surrealism; author of *Alcoöls* (1913) and *Calligrammes* (1918).

Apollo (ə'pɒləʊ) *n. Classical myth.* the god of light, poetry, music, healing, and prophecy: son of Zeus and Leto.

Apollyon (ə'pɒljən) *n.* the destroyer, a name given to the Devil (Revelation 9:11). [C14: via LL from Gk, from *apollunai* to destroy totally]

apologetic (ə,pɒlə'dʒɛtɪk) *adj.* **1.** expressing or anxious to make apology; contrite. **2.** defending in speech or writing. —**a,polo'getically** *adv.*

apologetics (ə,pɒlə'dʒɛtɪks) *n.* (*functioning as sing.*) **1.** the branch of theology concerned with the rational justification of Christianity. **2.** a defensive method of argument.

apologia (,æpə'ləʊdʒɪə) *n.* a formal written defence of a cause or one's beliefs or conduct.

apologist (ə'pɒlədʒɪst) *n.* a person who offers a defence by argument.

apologize *or* **-gise** (ə'pɒlə,dʒaɪz) *vb.* (*intr.*) **1.** to express or make an apology; acknowledge faults. **2.** to make a formal defence.

apologue ('æpə,lɒg) *n.* an allegory or moral fable. [C17: from L, from Gk *apologos*]

apology (ə'pɒlədʒɪ) *n.*, *pl.* **-gies.** **1.** a verbal or written expression of regret or contrition for a fault or failing. **2.** a poor substitute. **3.** another word for **apologia.** [C16: from OF, from LL, from Gk: a verbal defence, from APO- + *logos* speech]

apophthegm *or* **apothegm** ('æpə,θɛm) *n.* a short remark containing some general or generally accepted truth; maxim. [C16: from Gk *apophthegma*, from *apophthengesthai* to speak frankly]

apoplectic (,æpə'plɛktɪk) *adj.* **1.** of apoplexy. **2.** *Inf.* furious. —**,apo'plectically** *adv.*

apoplexy ('æpə,plɛksɪ) *n.* sudden loss of consciousness, often followed by paralysis, caused by rupture or occlusion of a blood vessel in the brain. [C14: from OF *apoplexie*, from LL, from Gk, from *apoplēssein* to cripple by a stroke]

aport (ə'pɔːt) *adv.*, *adj.* (*postpositive*) *Naut.* on or towards the port side: *with the helm aport.*

apostasy (ə'pɒstəsɪ) *n.*, *pl.* **-sies.** abandonment of one's religious faith, party, a cause, etc. [C14: from Church L *apostasia*, from Gk *apostasis* desertion]

apostate (ə'pɒsteɪt, -tɪt) *n.* **1.** a person who abandons his religion, party, etc. ~*adj.* **2.** guilty of apostasy. —**apostatical** (,æpə'stætɪkəl) *adj.*

apostatize *or* **-tise** (ə'pɒstə,taɪz) *vb.* (*intr.*) to abandon one's belief, faith, or allegiance.

a posteriori (eɪ pɒs,tɛrɪ'ɔːraɪ, -rɪ; ɑː) *adj. Logic.* **1.** relating to inductive reasoning from particular facts to a general principle. **2.** derived from or requiring evidence for its validation; empirical. [C18: from L, lit.: from the latter]

apostle (ə'pɒsəl) *n.* **1.** (*often cap.*) one of the 12 disciples chosen by Christ to preach his gospel. **2.** any prominent Christian missionary, esp. one who first converts a people. **3.** an ardent early supporter of a cause, movement, etc. [OE *apostol*, from Church L, from Gk *apostolos* a messenger]

Apostles' Creed *n.* a concise statement of Christian beliefs dating from about 500 A.D., traditionally ascribed to the Apostles.

apostolate (ə'pɒstəlɪt, -,leɪt) *n.* the office, authority, or mission of an apostle.

apostolic (,æpə'stɒlɪk) *adj.* **1.** of or relating to the Apostles or their teachings or practice. **2.** of or relating to the pope as successor of the Apostles. —**,apos'tolical** *adj.*

Apostolic See (,æpə'stɒlɪk) *n.* the see of the pope.

Apostolic succession *n.* the doctrine that the authority of Christian bishops derives from the Apostles through an unbroken line of consecration.

apostrophe[1] (ə'pɒstrəfɪ) *n.* the punctuation mark ' used to indicate the omission of a letter or number, such as *he's* for *he has* or *he is*, also used in English to form the possessive, as in *John's father.* [C17: from LL, from Gk *apostrophos* mark of elision, from *apostrephein* to turn away]

apostrophe[2] (ə'pɒstrəfɪ) *n. Rhetoric.* a digression from a discourse, esp. an address to an imaginary or absent person or a personification. [C16: from L *apostrophē*, from Gk: a turning away]

apostrophize *or* **-phise** (ə'pɒstrə,faɪz) *vb.* (*tr.*) to address an apostrophe to.

apothecaries' measure *n.* a system of liquid volume measure used in pharmacy in which 20 fluid ounces equal 1 pint.

apothecaries' weight *n.* a system of weights formerly used in pharmacy based on the Troy ounce.

apothecary (ə'pɒθɪkərɪ) *n.*, *pl.* **-caries.** **1.** an archaic word for **chemist.** **2.** *Law.* a chemist licensed by the Society of Apothecaries of London to prescribe, prepare,

and sell drugs. [C14: from OF, from LL, from Gk *apothēkē* storehouse]

apothegm ('æpə,θɛm) *n.* a variant spelling of **apophthegm.**

apothem ('æpə,θɛm) *n.* the perpendicular from the centre of a regular polygon to any of its sides. [C20: from APO- + Gk *thema*, from *tithenai* to place]

apotheosis (ə,pɒθɪ'əʊsɪs) *n.*, *pl.* **-ses** (-siːz). **1.** elevation to the rank of a god; deification. **2.** glorification of a person or thing. **3.** a glorified ideal. [C17: via LL from Gk: deification]

apotheosize *or* **-ise** (ə'pɒθɪə,saɪz) *vb.* (*tr.*) **1.** to deify. **2.** to glorify or idealize.

app. *abbrev. for:* **1.** apparatus. **2.** appendix (of a book). **3.** applied. **4.** appointed. **5.** apprentice. **6.** approved. **7.** approximate.

appal *or U.S.* **appall** (ə'pɔːl) *vb.* **-palling, -palled.** (*tr.*) to fill with horror; shock or dismay. [C14: from OF *appalir* to turn pale]

Appalachia (,æpə'leɪtʃɪə) *n.* a highland region of the eastern U.S., containing the Appalachian Mountains, extending from Pennsylvania to Alabama. —**,Appa'lachian** *adj.*

Appalachian Mountains *or* **Appalachians** *pl. n.* a mountain system of E North America, extending from Quebec province in Canada to central Alabama: contains rich deposits of anthracite, bitumen, and iron ore. Highest peak: Mount Mitchell, 2038 m (6684 ft.).

appalling (ə'pɔːlɪŋ) *adj.* causing dismay, horror, or revulsion. —**ap'pallingly** *adv.*

Appaloosa (,æpə'luːsə) *n.* a breed of horse, originally from America, having a spotted rump. [C19: ?from *Palouse*, river in Idaho]

appanage *or* **apanage** ('æpənɪdʒ) *n.* **1.** land or other provision granted by a king for the support of esp. a younger son. **2.** a customary accompaniment or perquisite, as to a job or position. [C17: from OF, from Med. L, from *appānāre* to provide for, from L *pānis* bread]

apparatchik (,æpə'rɑːtʃɪk) *n.* **1.** a member of a Communist Party organization. **2.** a bureaucrat in any organization. [C20: from Russian, from *apparat* apparatus, instrument + -*ckik*, suffix denoting agent]

apparatus (,æpə'reɪtəs, -'rɑːtəs) *n.*, *pl.* **-ratus** *or* **-ratuses.** **1.** a collection of equipment used for a particular purpose. **2.** a machine having a specific function: *breathing apparatus.* **3.** the means by which something operates; organization. **4.** *Anat.* any group of organs having a specific function. [C17: from L, from *apparāre* to make ready]

apparel (ə'pærəl) *n.* **1.** garments or clothing. **2.** *Naut.* a vessel's gear and equipment. ~*vb.* **-elling, -elled** *or U.S.* **-eling, -eled.** **3.** (*tr.*) *Arch.* to clothe, adorn, etc. [C13: from OF *apareillier* to make ready, from Vulgar L *appariculāre* (unattested), from L *parāre* to prepare]

apparent (ə'pærənt) *adj.* **1.** readily seen or understood; obvious. **2.** (*usually prenominal*) seeming, as opposed to real: *his apparent innocence.* **3.** *Physics.* as observed but ignoring such factors as the motion of the observer, etc. [C14: from L *appārēns*, from *appārēre* to APPEAR] —**ap'parently** *adv.*

apparent magnitude *n.* See **magnitude** (sense 4).

apparition (,æpə'rɪʃən) *n.* **1.** an appearance, esp. of a ghost or ghostlike figure. **2.** the figure so appearing; spectre. **3.** the act of appearing. [C15: from LL *appāritiō*, from L *appārēre* to APPEAR]

appassionato (ə,pæsjə'nɑːtəʊ) *adj.*, *adv. Music.* (to be performed) with passion. [It.]

appeal (ə'piːl) *n.* **1.** a request for relief, aid, etc. **2.** the power to attract, please, stimulate, or interest. **3.** an application or resort to another authority, esp. a higher one, as for a decision. **4.** *Law.* **a.** the judicial review by a superior court of the decision of a lower tribunal. **b.** a request for such review. **5.** *Cricket.* a request to the umpire to declare a batsman out. ~*vb.* **6.** (*intr.*) to make an earnest request. **7.** (*intr.*) to attract, please, stimulate, or interest. **8.** *Law.* to apply to a superior court to review (a case or issue decided by a lower tribunal). **9.** (*intr.*) to resort (to), as for a decision. **10.** (*intr.*) *Cricket.* to ask the umpire to declare a batsman out. **11.** (*intr.*) to challenge the umpire's or referee's decision. [C14: from OF *appeler*, from L *appellāre* to entreat, from *pellere* to drive] —**ap'pealable** *adj.* —**ap'pealer** *n.* —**ap'pealing** *adj.* —**ap'pealingly** *adv.*

appear (ə'pɪə) *vb.* (*intr.*) **1.** to come into sight. **2.** (*copula; may take an infinitive*) to seem: *the evidence appears to support you.* **3.** to be plain or clear, as after further evidence, etc.: *it appears you were correct after all.* **4.** to develop; occur: *faults appeared during testing.* **5.** to be published: *his biography appeared last month.* **6.** to perform: *he has appeared in many London productions.* **7.** to be present in court before a magistrate or judge: *he appeared on two charges of theft.* [C13: from OF *aparoir*, from L *appārēre* to become visible, attend upon, from *pārēre* to appear]

appearance (ə'pɪərəns) *n.* **1.** the act or an instance of appearing. **2.** the outward aspect of a person or thing. **3.** an outward show; pretence: *he gave an appearance of working hard.* **4. keep up appearances.** to maintain the public impression of wellbeing or normality. **5. put in** *or* **make an appearance.** to attend briefly, as out of politeness. **6. to all appearances.** apparently.

appearance money *n.* money paid by a promoter of an event to a particular celebrity in order to ensure that the celebrity takes part in the event.

appease (ə'piːz) *vb.* (*tr.*) **1.** to calm or pacify, esp. by acceding to the demands of. **2.** to satisfy or quell (a thirst, etc.). [C16: from OF *apaisier*, from *pais* peace, from L *pax*] —**ap'peaser** *n.*

appeasement (ə'piːzmənt) *n.* **1.** the policy of acceding to the demands of a potentially hostile nation in the hope of maintaining peace. **2.** the act of appeasing.

Appel (*Dutch* 'apəl) *n.* **Karel** ('kɑːrəl). born 1921, Dutch abstract expressionist painter.

appellant (ə'pɛlənt) *n.* **1.** a person who appeals. **2.** *Law.* the party who appeals to a higher court from the decision of a lower tribunal. ~*adj.* **3.** *Law.* another word for **appellate.** [C14: from OF; see APPEAL]

appellate (ə'pɛlɪt) *adj. Law.* **1.** of appeals. **2.** (of a tribunal) having jurisdiction to review cases on appeal. [C18: from L *appellātus* summoned, from *appellāre* to APPEAL]

appellation (,æpɪ'leɪʃən) *n.* **1.** a name or title. **2.** the act of naming.

appellative (ə'pɛlətɪv) *n.* **1.** a name or title. **2.** *Grammar.* another word for **common noun.** ~*adj.* **3.** of or relating to a name. **4.** (of a proper noun) used as a common noun.

append (ə'pɛnd) *vb.* (*tr.*) **1.** to add as a supplement: *to append a footnote.* **2.** to attach; hang on. [C15: from LL *appendere* to hang (something) from, from L *pendere* to hang]

appendage (ə'pɛndɪdʒ) *n.* an ancillary or secondary part attached to a main part; adjunct, such as an organ that projects from the trunk of an animal.

appendant (ə'pɛndənt) *adj.* **1.** attached or added. **2.** attendant or associated as an accompaniment or result. ~*n.* **3.** a person or thing attached or added.

appendicectomy (ə,pɛndɪ'sɛktəmɪ) *or* **appendectomy** *U.S. & Canad.* **appendectomy** (,æpən'dɛktəmɪ) *n., pl.* **-mies.** surgical removal of any appendage, esp. the vermiform appendix.

appendicitis (ə,pɛndɪ'saɪtɪs) *n.* inflammation of the vermiform appendix.

appendix (ə'pɛndɪks) *n., pl.* **-dixes** *or* **-dices** (-dɪ,siːz). **1.** a body of separate additional material at the end of a book, etc. **2.** any part that is dependent or supplementary. **3.** *Anat.* See **vermiform appendix.** [C16: from L: an appendage, from *appendere* to APPEND]

Appenzell (*German* apən'tsɛl, 'apəntsɛl) *n.* **1.** a canton of NE Switzerland, divided in 1597 into the Protestant demicanton of **Appenzell Outer Rhodes** and the Catholic demicanton of **Appenzell Inner Rhodes.** Capitals: Herisau and Appenzell. Pop.: 49 300 and 13 100 (1986 est.) respectively. Areas: 243 sq. km (94 sq. miles) and 171 sq. km (66 sq. miles) respectively. **2.** a town in NE Switzerland, capital of Appenzell Inner Rhodes demicanton. Pop.: 5300 (1980).

apperceive (,æpə'siːv) *vb.* (*tr.*) **1.** to be aware of perceiving. **2.** *Psychol.* to comprehend by assimilating (a perception) to ideas already in the mind. [C19: from OF, from L *percipere* to PERCEIVE]

apperception (,æpə'sɛpʃən) *n.* **1.** *Psychol.* the attainment of full awareness of a sensation or idea. **2.** the act of apperceiving. —**,apper'ceptive** *adj.*

appertain (,æpə'teɪn) *vb.* (*intr.*; usually foll. by *to*) to belong (to) as a part, function, right, etc.; relate (to) or be

connected (with). [C14: from OF *apertenir*, from LL, from L AD- + *pertinēre* to PERTAIN]

appetence ('æpɪtəns) *or* **appetency** *n., pl.* **-tences** *or* **-tencies.** **1.** a craving or desire. **2.** an attraction or affinity. [C17: from L *appetentia*, from *appetere* to crave]

appetite ('æpɪ,taɪt) *n.* **1.** a desire for food or drink. **2.** a desire to satisfy a bodily craving, as for sexual pleasure. **3.** (usually foll. by *for*) a liking or willingness: *a great appetite for work.* [C14: from OF *apetit*, from L, from *appetere* to desire ardently] —**appetitive** (ə'pɛtɪtɪv) *adj.*

appetizer *or* **-iser** ('æpɪ,taɪzə) *n.* **1.** a small amount of food or drink taken to stimulate the appetite. **2.** any stimulating foretaste.

appetizing *or* **-ising** ('æpɪ,taɪzɪŋ) *adj.* pleasing or stimulating to the appetite; delicious; tasty.

Appian Way ('æpɪən) *n.* a Roman road in Italy, extending from Rome to Brindisi: begun in 312 B.C. by Appius Claudius Caecus. Length: about 560 km (350 miles).

applaud (ə'plɔːd) *vb.* **1.** to indicate approval of (a person, performance, etc.) by clapping the hands. **2.** (*usually tr.*) to express approval or praise of: *I applaud your decision.* [C15: from L *applaudere*, from *plaudere* to beat, applaud]

applause (ə'plɔːz) *n.* appreciation or praise, esp. as shown by clapping the hands.

apple ('æpəl) *n.* **1.** a rosaceous tree, widely cultivated in temperate regions in many varieties. **2.** the fruit of this tree, having red, yellow, or green skin and crisp whitish flesh. **3.** the wood of this tree. **4.** any of several unrelated trees that have fruit similar to the apple. **5. apple of one's eye.** a person or thing that is very much loved. [OE *æppel*]

apple green *n.* **a.** a bright light green. **b.** (*as adj.*): *an apple-green carpet.*

Apple Isle *n.* the. *Austral. informal.* Tasmania. —**Apple Islander** *n.*

apple-pie bed *n. Brit.* a way of making a bed so as to prevent the person from entering it.

apple-pie order *n. Inf.* perfect order or condition.

Appleton ('æpəltən) *n.* Sir **Edward** (**Victor**). 1892–1965, English physicist, noted particularly for his research on the ionosphere: Nobel prize for physics 1947.

appliance (ə'plaɪəns) *n.* **1.** a machine or device, esp. an electrical one used domestically. **2.** any piece of equipment having a specific function. **3.** another name for a **fire engine.**

applicable ('æplɪkəbəl, ə'plɪkə-) *adj.* being appropriate or relevant; able to be applied; fitting. —**,applica'bility** *n.* —**'applicably** *adv.*

applicant ('æplɪkənt) *n.* a person who applies, as for a job, grant, support, etc.; candidate. [C15: from L *applicāns*, from *applicāre* to APPLY]

application (,æplɪ'keɪʃən) *n.* **1.** the act of applying to a particular use. **2.** relevance or value: *the practical applications of space technology.* **3.** the act of asking for something. **4.** a written request, as for a job, etc. **5.** diligent effort: *a job requiring application.* **6.** something, such as a lotion, that is applied, esp. to the skin.

applicator ('æplɪ,keɪtə) *n.* a device, such as a spatula or rod, for applying a medicine, glue, etc.

applicatory ('æplɪkətərɪ) *adj.* suitable for application.

applied (ə'plaɪd) *adj.* put to practical use: *applied mathematics.* Cf. **pure** (sense 5).

appliqué (æ'pliːkeɪ) *n.* **1.** a decoration of one material sewn or fixed onto another. **2.** the practice of decorating in this way. ~*vb.* **-quéing, -quéd.** **3.** (*tr.*) to sew or fix (a decoration) on as an appliqué. [C18: from F, lit.: applied]

apply (ə'plaɪ) *vb.* **-plying, -plied.** **1.** (*tr.*) to put to practical use; employ. **2.** (*intr.*) to be relevant or appropriate. **3.** (*tr.*) to cause to come into contact with. **4.** (*intr.*; often foll. by *for*) to put in an application or request. **5.** (*tr.*; often foll. by *to*) to devote (oneself or one's efforts) with diligence. **6.** (*tr.*) to bring into use: *the police only applied the law to aliens.* [C14: from OF *aplier*, from L *applicāre* to attach to] —**ap'plier** *n.*

appoggiatura (ə,pɒdʒə'tʊərə) *n., pl.* **-ras** *or* **-re** (-reɪ). *Music.* an ornament consisting of a nonharmonic note preceding a harmonic one either before or on the stress. [C18: from It., lit.: a propping]

appoint (ə'pɔɪnt) *vb.* (*mainly tr.*) **1.** (*also intr.*) to assign officially, as for a position, responsibility, etc. **2.** to establish by agreement or decree. **3.** to prescribe: *laws appointed by tribunal.* **4.** *Property law.* to nominate (a person) to take an interest in property. **5.** to equip with

usual features; furnish: *a well-appointed hotel*. [C14: from OF *apointer* to put into a good state] —**appoin'tee** *n.*
—**ap'pointer** *n.*

appointive (ə'pɔɪntɪv) *adj. Chiefly U.S.* filled by appointment: *an appointive position.*

appointment (ə'pɔɪntmənt) *n.* **1.** an arrangement to meet a person or be at a place at a certain time. **2.** the act of placing in a job or position. **3.** the person who receives such a job. **4.** the job or position to which such a person is appointed. **5.** (*usually pl.*) a fixture or fitting.

Appomattox (,æpə'mætəks) *n.* a village in central Virginia where the Confederate army under Robert E. Lee surrendered to Ulysses S. Grant's Union forces on April 9, 1865, effectively ending the American Civil War.

apportion (ə'pɔːʃən) *vb.* (*tr.*) to divide, distribute, or assign shares of; allot proportionally. —**ap'portionable** *adj.* —**ap'portionment** *n.*

appose (ə'pəʊz) *vb.* (*tr.*) **1.** to place side by side. **2.** (usually foll. by *to*) to place (something) near or against another thing. [C16: from OF *apposer*, from *poser* to put, from L *pōnere*] —**ap'posable** *adj.*

apposite ('æpəzɪt) *adj.* appropriate; apt. [C17: from L *appositus*, from *appōnere*, from *pōnere* to put] —'**appositely** *adv.* —'**appositeness** *n.*

apposition (,æpə'zɪʃən) *n.* **1.** a putting into juxtaposition. **2.** a grammatical construction in which a word, esp. a noun, is placed after another to modify its meaning. —,**appo'sitional** *adj.*

appositive (ə'pɒzɪtɪv) *Grammar.* ~*adj.* **1.** in, of, or relating to apposition. ~*n.* **2.** an appositive word or phrase. —**ap'positively** *adv.*

appraisal (ə'preɪzəl) *or* **appraisement** *n.* **1.** an assessment of the worth or quality of a person or thing. **2.** a valuation.

appraise (ə'preɪz) *vb.* (*tr.*) **1.** to assess the worth, value, or quality of. **2.** to make a valuation of, as for taxation. [C15: from OF, from *prisier* to PRIZE[2]] —**ap'praisable** *adj.* —**ap'praiser** *n.*

appreciable (ə'priːʃəbəl) *adj.* sufficient to be easily measured or noticed. —**ap'preciably** *adv.*

appreciate (ə'priːʃɪ,eɪt, -sɪ-) *vb.* (*mainly tr.*) **1.** to feel thankful or grateful for. **2.** (*may take a clause as object*) to take sufficient account of: *to appreciate a problem.* **3.** to value highly. **4.** (*usually intr.*) to increase in value. [C17: from Med. L *appretiāre* to value, from L *pretium* PRICE] —**ap'preci,ator** *n.*

appreciation (ə,priːʃɪ'eɪʃən, -sɪ-) *n.* **1.** thanks or gratitude. **2.** assessment of the true worth of persons or things. **3.** perceptive recognition of qualities, as in art. **4.** an increase in value. **5.** a review of a book, etc., esp. when favourable.

appreciative (ə'priːʃɪətɪv) *or* **appreciatory** *adj.* feeling or expressing appreciation. —**ap'preciatively** *adv.* —**ap'preciativeness** *n.*

apprehend (,æprɪ'hɛnd) *vb.* **1.** (*tr.*) to arrest and escort into custody. **2.** to grasp mentally; understand. **3.** to await with fear or anxiety. [C14: from L *apprehendere* to lay hold of]

apprehensible (,æprɪ'hɛnsɪbəl) *adj.* capable of being comprehended or grasped mentally. —,**appre,hensi'bility** *n.*

apprehension (,æprɪ'hɛnʃən) *n.* **1.** anxiety over what may happen. **2.** the act of arresting. **3.** understanding. **4.** a notion or conception.

apprehensive (,æprɪ'hɛnsɪv) *adj.* **1.** fearful or anxious. **2.** (*usually postpositive* and foll. by *of*) *Arch.* intelligent, perceptive. —,**appre'hensively** *adv.* —,**appre'hensiveness** *n.*

apprentice (ə'prɛntɪs) *n.* **1.** someone who works for a skilled or qualified person in order to learn a trade, esp. for a recognized period. **2.** any beginner or novice. ~*vb.* **3.** (*tr.*) to take, place, or bind as an apprentice. [C14: from OF *aprentis*, from *aprendre* to learn, from L *apprehendere* to APPREHEND] —**ap'prentice,ship** *n.*

apprise *or* **-ize** (ə'praɪz) *vb.* (*tr.; often foll. by of*) to make aware; inform. [C17: from F *appris*, from *apprendre* to teach; learn]

appro ('æprəʊ) *n.* an informal shortening of **approval:** *on appro.*

approach (ə'prəʊtʃ) *vb.* **1.** to come nearer in position, time, quality, character, etc., to (someone or something). **2.** (*tr.*) to make a proposal or suggestion to. **3.** (*tr.*) to begin to deal with. ~*n.* **4.** the act of drawing close or

closer. **5.** a close approximation. **6.** the way or means of entering or leaving. **7.** (*often pl.*) an overture to a person. **8.** a means adopted in tackling a problem, job of work, etc. **9.** Also called: **approach path.** the course followed by an aircraft preparing for landing. **10.** Also called: **approach shot.** *Golf.* a shot made to or towards the green after a tee shot. [C14: from OF *aprochier*, from LL *appropiāre* to draw near, from L *prope* near] —**ap'proachable** *adj.* —**ap,proacha'bility** *n.*

approbation (,æprə'beɪʃən) *n.* **1.** commendation; praise. **2.** official recognition. —'**appro,bative** *or* '**appro,batory** *adj.*

appropriate *adj.* (ə'prəʊprɪɪt). **1.** right or suitable; fitting. ~*vb.* (ə'prəʊprɪeɪt). **2.** to take for one's own use, esp. illegally. **3.** to put aside (funds, etc.) for a particular purpose or person. [C15: from LL *appropriāre* to make one's own, from L *proprius* one's own] —**ap'propriately** *adv.* —**ap'propriateness** *n.* —**ap'propri,ator** *n.*

appropriation (ə,prəʊprɪ'eɪʃən) *n.* **1.** the act of setting apart or taking for one's own use. **2.** a sum of money set apart for a specific purpose.

approval (ə'pruːvəl) *n.* **1.** the act of approving. **2.** formal agreement. **3.** a favourable opinion. **4. on approval.** (of articles for sale) for examination with an option to buy or return.

approve (ə'pruːv) *vb.* **1.** (when *intr.*, often foll. by *of*) to consider fair, good, or right. **2.** (*tr.*) to authorize or sanction. [C14: from OF *aprover*, from L *approbāre* to approve, from *probāre* to test, PROVE]

approved school *n.* (in Britain) a former name for **community home.**

approx. *abbrev. for* approximate(ly).

approximate *adj.* (ə'prɒksɪmɪt). **1.** almost accurate or exact. **2.** inexact; rough; loose. **3.** much alike; almost the same. **4.** near; close together. ~*vb.* (ə'prɒksɪ,meɪt). **5.** (usually foll. by *to*) to come or bring near or close; be almost the same (as). **6.** *Maths.* to find an expression for (some quantity) accurate to a specified degree. [C15: from LL *approximāre*, from L *proximus* nearest] —**ap'proximately** *adv.*

approximation (ə,prɒksɪ'meɪʃən) *n.* **1.** the process or result of making a rough calculation, estimate, or guess. **2.** an imprecise or unreliable record or version. **3.** *Maths.* an inexact number, relationship, or theory that is sufficiently accurate for a specific purpose.

appurtenance (ə'pɜːtɪnəns) *n.* **1.** a less significant thing or part. **2.** (*pl.*) accessories. **3.** *Property law.* a minor right, interest, or privilege. [C14: from Anglo-F *apurtenance*, from OF *apartenance*, from *apartenir* to APPERTAIN]

Apr. *abbrev. for* April.

APR *abbrev. for:* **1.** annualized percentage rate. **2.** Annual Purchase Rate (in hire-purchase).

apraxia (ə'præksɪə) *n.* a disorder of the central nervous system characterized by impaired ability to carry out certain purposeful muscular movements. [C19: via NL from Gk: inactivity, from A-[1] + *praxis* action]

après-ski (,æpreɪ'skiː) *n.* **a.** social activity following a day's skiing. **b.** (*as modifier*): *an après-ski outfit.* [F, lit.: after ski]

apricot ('eɪprɪ,kɒt) *n.* **1.** a tree native to Africa and W Asia, but widely cultivated for its edible fruit. **2.** the yellow juicy fruit of this tree, which resembles a small peach. [C16: from Port., from Ar., from LGk, from L *praecox* early-ripening]

April ('eɪprəl) *n.* the fourth month of the year, consisting of 30 days. [C14: from L *Aprīlis*]

April fool *n.* a victim of a practical joke performed on the first of April (**April Fools' Day** *or* **All Fools' Day**).

a priori (eɪ praɪ'ɔːraɪ, ɑː prɪ'ɔːrɪ) *adj.* **1.** *Logic.* relating to or involving deductive reasoning from a general principle to the expected facts or effects. **2.** known to be true independently of experience of the subject matter. [C18: from L, lit.: from the previous] —**apriority** (,eɪpraɪ'ɒrɪtɪ) *n.*

apron ('eɪprən) *n.* **1.** a protective or sometimes decorative garment worn over the front of the body and tied around the waist. **2.** the part of a stage extending in front of the curtain. **3.** a hard-surfaced area in front of an aircraft hangar, terminal building, etc. **4.** a continuous conveyor belt composed of metal slats. **5.** a protective plate screening the operator of a machine, artillery piece, etc. **6.** *Geol.* a sheet of sand, gravel, etc., deposited at the front of a moraine. **7.** another name for **skirt** (sense 3). **8.**

tied to someone's apron strings. dominated by someone, esp. a mother or wife. ~*vb.* **9.** (*tr.*) to protect or provide with an apron. [C16: mistaken division of *a napron*, from OF, from L *mappa* napkin]

apron stage *n.* a stage that projects into the auditorium so that the audience sits on three sides of it.

apropos (ˌæprə'pəʊ) *adj.* **1.** appropriate. ~*adv.* **2.** appropriately. **3.** by the way; incidentally. **4. apropos of.** (*prep.*) in respect of. [C17: from F *à propos* to the purpose]

apse (æps) *n.* a domed or vaulted semicircular or polygonal recess, esp. at the east end of a church. Also called: **apsis.** [C19: from L *apsis*, from Gk: a fitting together, from *haptein* to fasten] —**apsidal** ('æpsɪdᵊl) *adj.*

apsis ('æpsɪs) *n., pl.* **apsides** (æp'saɪdiːz). either of two points lying at the extremities of an eccentric orbit of a planet, satellite, etc. Also called: **apse.** [C17: via L from Gk; see APSE] —**apsidal** ('æpsɪdᵊl) *adj.*

apt (æpt) *adj.* **1.** suitable; appropriate. **2.** (*postpositive; foll.* by an infinitive) having a tendency (to behave as specified). **3.** having the ability to learn and understand easily. [C14: from L *aptus* fitting, from *apere* to fasten] —**'aptly** *adv.* —**'aptness** *n.*

APT *abbrev. for* Advanced Passenger Train.

apterous ('æptərəs) *adj.* **1.** (of insects) without wings, as silverfish. **2.** without winglike expansions, as some seeds and fruits. [C18: from Gk, from A-¹ + *pteron* wing]

apteryx ('æptərɪks) *n.* another name for **kiwi** (the bird). [C19: from NL; see APTEROUS]

aptitude ('æptɪˌtjuːd) *n.* **1.** inherent or acquired ability. **2.** ease in learning or understanding. **3.** the quality of being apt. [C15: via OF from LL, from L *aptus* APT]

Apuleius (ˌæpjʊ'liːəs) *n.* **Lucius** ('luːsɪəs). 2nd century A.D., Roman writer, noted for his romance *The Golden Ass.*

Apulia (ə'pjuːljə) *n.* a region of SE Italy, on the Adriatic. Capital: Bari. Pop.: 3 908 484 (1982 est.). Area: 19 223 sq. km (7422 sq. miles). Italian name: **Puglia.**

Apure (*Spanish* a'pure) *n.* a river in W Venezuela, rising in the Andes and flowing east to the Orinoco. Length: about 676 km (420 miles).

Apurimac (ˌæpuː'riːmæk) *n.* a river in S Peru, rising in the Andes and flowing northwest into the Urubamba River. Length: about 885 km (550 miles).

Aqaba *or* **Akaba** ('ækəbə) *n.* the only port in Jordan, in the southwest, on the **Gulf of Aqaba.** Pop.: 40 000 (1983 est.).

aqua ('ækwə) *n., pl.* **aquae** ('ækwiː) *or* **aquas.** **1.** water: used in compound names of certain liquid substances or solutions of substances in water. ~*n., adj.* **2.** short for **aquamarine** (the colour). [L: water]

aquaculture ('ækwəˌkʌltʃə) *or* **aquiculture** *n.* the cultivation of freshwater and marine organisms for human consumption or use.

aqua fortis ('fɔːtɪs) *n.* an obsolete name for **nitric acid.** [C17: from L, lit.: strong water]

aqualung ('ækwəˌlʌŋ) *n.* breathing apparatus used by divers, etc., consisting of a mouthpiece attached to air cylinders strapped to the back.

aquamarine (ˌækwəmə'riːn) *n.* **1.** a pale greenish-blue transparent variety of beryl used as a gemstone. **2. a.** a pale blue to greenish-blue colour. **b.** (*as adj.*): *an aquamarine dress.* [C19: from NL, from L: sea water (referring to the gem's colour)]

aquanaut ('ækwənɔːt) *n.* a person who works, swims, or dives underwater. [C20: from AQUA + *-naut*, as in ASTRONAUT]

aquaplane ('ækwəˌpleɪn) *n.* **1.** a board on which a person stands and is towed by a motorboat. ~*vb.* (*intr.*) **2.** to ride on an aquaplane. **3.** (of a motor vehicle travelling at high speeds on wet roads) to rise up onto a thin film of water so that contact with the road is lost.

aqua regia ('riːdʒɪə) *n.* a mixture of nitric acid and hydrochloric acid. [C17: from NL: royal water; referring to its use in dissolving gold, the royal metal]

aquarist ('ækwərɪst) *n.* **1.** the curator of an aquarium. **2.** a person who studies aquatic life.

aquarium (ə'kwɛərɪəm) *n., pl.* **aquariums** *or* **aquaria** (ə'kwɛərɪə). **1.** a tank, bowl, or pool in which aquatic animals and plants are kept for pleasure, study, or exhibition. **2.** a building housing a collection of aquatic life, as for exhibition. [C19: from L *aquārius* relating to water, on the model of VIVARIUM]

Aquarius (ə'kwɛərɪəs) *n., Latin genitive* **Aquarii** (ə'kwɛərɪˌaɪ). **1.** *Astron.* a S constellation. **2.** *Astrol.* also called: the **Water Carrier.** the eleventh sign of the zodiac. The sun is in this sign between about Jan. 20 and Feb. 18. [L]

aquatic (ə'kwætɪk) *adj.* **1.** growing, living, or found in water. **2.** *Sport.* performed in or on water. ~*n.* **3.** a marine animal or plant. [C15: from L *aquāticus*, from *aqua* water]

aquatics (ə'kwætɪks) *pl. n.* sports or pastimes performed in or on the water.

aquatint ('ækwəˌtɪnt) *n.* **1.** a technique of etching copper with acid to produce an effect resembling watercolour. **2.** an etching made in this way. ~*vb.* **3.** (*tr.*) to etch (a block, etc.) in aquatint. [C18: from It. *acqua tinta* dyed water]

aquavit ('ækwəˌviːt) *n.* a grain- or potato-based spirit flavoured with aromatic seeds. Also called: **akvavit.** [of Scandinavian origin: see AQUA VITAE]

aqua vitae ('viːtaɪ, 'vaɪtiː) *n.* an archaic name for **brandy.** [Med. L: water of life]

aqueduct ('ækwɪˌdʌkt) *n.* **1.** a conduit used to convey water over a long distance. **2.** a structure, often a bridge, that carries such a conduit or a canal across a valley or river. **3.** a channel or conduit in the body. [C16: from L *aquaeductus*, from *aqua* water + *dūcere* to convey]

aqueous ('eɪkwɪəs) *adj.* **1.** of, like, or containing water. **2.** (of rocks, etc.) formed from material laid down in water. [C17: from Med. L *aqueus*, from L *aqua* water]

aqueous ammonia *n.* a solution of ammonia in water, containing ammonium hydroxide.

aqueous humour *n. Physiol.* the watery fluid within the eyeball between the cornea and the lens.

aquiculture ('eɪkwɪˌkʌltʃə, 'ækwɪ-) *n.* **1.** another name for **hydroponics.** **2.** a variant of **aquaculture.** —**'aqui,culturist** *n.* —**'aqui,cultural** *adj.*

aquifer ('ækwɪfə) *n.* a deposit or rock, such as a sandstone, containing water that can be used to supply wells.

Aquila ('ækwɪlə; *Italian* 'aːkwila) *or* **l'Aquila** *n.* a city in central Italy, capital of Abruzzi region. Pop.: 63 678 (1981). Official name: **Aquila degli Abruzzi** ('deʎʎi a'bruttsi).

aquilegia (ˌækwɪ'liːdʒɪə) *n.* another name for **columbine**¹. [C19: from Med. L, from ?]

Aquileia (ˌækwɪ'liːə) *n.* a town in NE Italy, at the head of the Adriatic: important Roman centre, founded in 181 B.C. Pop.: 3041 (1971).

aquiline ('ækwɪˌlaɪn) *adj.* **1.** (of a nose) having the curved shape of an eagle's beak. **2.** of or like an eagle. [C17: from L, from *aquila* eagle]

Aquinas (ə'kwaɪnəs) *n.* **Saint Thomas.** 1225–74, Italian theologian, scholastic philosopher, and Dominican friar, whose works include *Summa contra Gentiles* (1259–64) and *Summa Theologiae* (1267–73), the first attempt at a comprehensive theological system. See also **Thomism.**

Aquino (ə'kiːnəʊ) *n.* **Corazón,** known as *Cory.* born 1933, Philippine stateswoman: president from 1986.

Aquitaine (ˌækwɪ'teɪn; *French* akitɛn) *n.* a region of SW France, on the Bay of Biscay: a former Roman province and medieval duchy. It is generally flat in the west, rising to the slopes of the Massif Central in the northeast and the Pyrenees in the south; mainly agricultural. Ancient name: **Aquitania** (ˌækwɪ'teɪnɪə).

Ar *the chemical symbol for* argon.

ar. *abbrev. for:* **1.** arrival. **2.** arrive(s).

Ar. *abbrev. for:* **1.** Arabia(n). **2.** Also: **Ar** Arabic. **3.** Aramaic.

a.r. *abbrev. for* anno regni. [L: in the year of the reign]

-ar *suffix forming adjectives.* of; belonging to; like: *linear; polar.* [via OF *-er* from L *-āris*]

ARA *abbrev. for:* **1.** (in Britain) Associate of the Royal Academy. **2.** (in New Zealand) Auckland Regional Authority.

Arab ('ærəb) *n.* **1.** a member of a Semitic people originally inhabiting Arabia. **2.** a small breed of horse, used for riding. **3.** See **street Arab. 4.** (*modifier*) of or relating to the Arabs. [C14: from L, from Gk *Araps*, from Ar. '*Arab*]

arabesque (ˌærə'bɛsk) *n.* **1.** *Ballet.* a classical position in which the dancer has one leg raised behind. **2.** *Music.* a piece or movement with a highly ornamented melody. **3.** *Arts.* a type of curvilinear decoration in painting, metalwork, etc., with intricate intertwining designs. [C18: from F, from It. *arabesco* in the Arabic style]

Arabia (ə'reɪbɪə) *n.* a great peninsula of SW Asia, between the Red Sea and the Persian Gulf: consists chiefly of a desert plateau, with mountains rising over 3000 m (10 000 ft.) in the west and scattered oases; includes the present-day countries of Saudi Arabia, North Yemen, South Yemen, Oman, Bahrain, Qatar, Kuwait, and the United Arab Emirates. Area: about 2 600 000 sq. km (1 000 000 sq. miles).

Arabian (ə'reɪbɪən) *adj.* **1.** of or relating to Arabia or the Arabs. ~*n.* **2.** another word for **Arab.**

Arabian camel *n.* a domesticated camel with one hump on its back, used as a beast of burden in the deserts of N Africa and SW Asia.

Arabian Desert *n.* **1.** a desert in E Egypt, between the Nile, the Gulf of Suez, and the Red Sea: mountainous parts rise over 1800 m (6000 ft.). **2.** the desert area of the Arabian Peninsula, esp. in the north.

Arabian Sea *n.* the NW part of the Indian Ocean, between Arabia and India.

Arabic ('ærəbɪk) *n.* **1.** the Semitic language of the Arabs, which has its own alphabet and is spoken in Algeria, Egypt, Iraq, Jordan, Saudi Arabia, Syria, Tunisia, etc. ~*adj.* **2.** denoting or relating to this language, any of the peoples that speak it, or the countries in which it is spoken.

arabica bean (ə'ræbɪkə) *n.* a type of coffee bean obtained from the tree *Coffea arabica.*

Arabic numeral *n.* one of the numbers 1,2,3,4,5,6,7,8,9,0 (opposed to *Roman numerals*).

arabis ('ærəbɪs) *n.* any of several trailing plants having pink or white flowers in spring. Also called: **rock cress.** [C16: from Med. L, from Gk *arabis,* ult. from *Arābios* Arabian, prob. from growing in sandy or stony soil]

Arabist ('ærəbɪst) *n.* a student of Arabic culture, language, history, etc.

arable ('ærəbəl) *adj.* **1.** (of land) being or capable of being tilled for the production of crops. **2.** of, relating to, or using such land. [C15: from L *arābilis,* from *arāre* to plough]

Araby ('ærəbɪ) *n.* an archaic or poetic name for **Arabia.**

Aracajú (*Portuguese* ərəkə'ʒu) *n.* a port in E Brazil, capital of Sergipe state. Pop.: 288 106 (1980).

Arachne (ə'ræknɪ) *n. Greek myth.* a maiden changed into a spider for having presumptuously challenged Athena to a weaving contest. [from Gk *arakhnē* spider]

arachnid (ə'ræknɪd) *n.* any of a class of arthropods characterized by simple eyes and four pairs of legs, including the spiders, scorpions, and ticks. [C19: from NL *Arachnida,* from Gk *arakhnē* spider] —**a'rachnidan** *adj., n.*

arachnoid (ə'ræknɔɪd) *n.* **1.** the middle one of three membranes that cover the brain and spinal cord. ~*adj.* **2.** of or relating to this membrane. **3.** *Bot.* consisting of or covered with soft fine hairs or fibres.

Arad ('æræd) *n.* a city in W Romania, on the Mures River: became part of Romania after World War I, after belonging successively to Turkey, Austria, and Hungary. Pop.: 185 892 (1985).

Arafat ('ærəfæt) *n.* **Yasser** ('jæsə). born 1929, Palestinian leader; cofounder of Al Fatah (1956) and leader from 1968 of the Palestine Liberation Organization.

Arafura Sea (,ærə'fʊərə) *n.* a section of the W Pacific Ocean, between N Australia and SW New Guinea.

Aragats (*Russian* ,ara'gats) *n.* **Mount.** a volcanic mountain in the Soviet Union, in the NW Armenian SSR. Height: 4090 m (13 419 ft.). Turkish name: **Alagez.**

Aragon[1] ('ærəgən) *n.* a region of NE Spain: independent kingdom from the 11th century until 1479, when it was united with Castile to form modern Spain. Area: 47 609 sq. km (18 382 sq. miles). —**Aragonese** (,ærəgə'niːz) *n., adj.*

Aragon[2] (*French* aragɔ̃) *n.* **Louis** (lwi). 1897–1982, French poet, essayist, and novelist; an early surrealist, later a committed Communist. His works include the verse collections *Le Crève-Coeur* (1941) and *Les Yeux d'Elsa* (1942) and the series of novels *Le Monde réel* (1933–51).

Araguaia *or* **Araguaya** (,ɑːrə'gwaɪə) *n.* a river in central Brazil, rising in S central Mato Grosso state and flowing north to the Tocantins River. Length: over 1771 km (1100 miles).

arak ('ærək) *n.* a variant spelling of **arrack.**

Arakan Yoma (,ɑːrɑː'kɑːn 'jəʊmɑː) *n.* a mountain range in Burma, between the Irrawaddy River and the W coast: forms a barrier between Burma and India; teak forests.

Araks (a'raks) *n.* the Russian name for the **Aras.**

Araldite ('ærəldaɪt) *n. Trademark.* an epoxy resin used as a glue for mending glass, plastic, and china.

Aral Sea ('ærəl) *n.* the fourth largest lake in the world, in the SW Soviet Union east of the Caspian Sea: shallow and saline. Area: about 64 750 sq. km (25 000 sq. miles). Also called: **Lake Aral.**

Aram ('ɛəræm, -rəm) *n.* the biblical name for ancient Syria. —**Aramaean** *or* **Aramean** (,ærə'miːən) *adj., n.*

Aram. *abbrev. for* Aramaic.

Aramaic (,ærə'meɪɪk) *n.* **1.** an ancient Semitic language of the Middle East, still spoken in parts of Syria and the Lebanon. ~*adj.* **2.** of, relating to, or using this language.

Aran ('ærən) *adj.* **1.** of or relating to the Aran Islands. **2.** made of thick natural wool: *an Aran sweater.*

Aran Islands *pl. n.* a group of three islands in the Atlantic, off the W coast of Ireland: Aranmore or Inishmore (the largest), Inishmaan, and Inisheer. Pop.: 1612 (1966). Area: 46 km (18 sq. miles).

Arany (*Hungarian* 'ɔrɔnj) *n.* **János** ('jɑːnɔʃ). 1817–82, Hungarian epic poet, ballad writer, and scholar.

Ararat ('ærə,ræt) *n.* an extinct volcanic mountain massif in E Turkey: two main peaks; **Great Ararat** 5155 m (16 916 ft.), said to be the resting place of Noah's Ark after the Flood (Genesis 8:4), and **Little Ararat** 3914 m (12 843 ft.).

Aras (æ'ræs) *n.* a river rising in mountains in Turkish Armenia and flowing east to the Caspian Sea: forms part of the border between the Soviet Union and Turkey and Iran. Length: about 1100 km (660 miles). Ancient name: **Araxes.** Russian name: **Araks.**

Araucania (,ærɔː'keɪnɪə; *Spanish* arau'kanja) *n.* a region of central Chile, inhabited by Araucanian Indians. —**Arau'canian** *adj., n.*

araucaria (,ærɔː'kɛərɪə) *n.* any of a group of coniferous trees of South America, Australia, and Polynesia, such as the monkey puzzle. [C19: from NL (*arbor*) *Araucaria* (tree) from *Arauco,* a province in Chile]

Araxes (ə'ræksiːz) *n.* the ancient name for the **Aras.**

arbalest *or* **arbalist** ('ɑːbəlɪst) *n.* a large medieval crossbow, usually cocked by mechanical means. [C11: from OF, from LL *arcuballista,* from L *arcus* bow + BALLISTA]

Arbela (ɑː'biːlə) *n.* an ancient city in Assyria, near which the **Battle of Arbela** took place (331 B.C.), in which Alexander the Great defeated the Persians. Modern name: **Erbil.**

Arbil ('ɑːbɪl) *n.* a variant spelling of **Erbil.**

arbiter ('ɑːbɪtə) *n.* **1.** a person empowered to judge in a dispute; referee. **2.** a person having control of something. [C15: from L, from ?] —**'arbitress** *fem. n.*

arbitrament (ɑː'bɪtrəmənt) *n.* **1.** the decision or award made by an arbitrator upon a disputed matter. **2.** another word for **arbitration.**

arbitrary ('ɑːbɪtrərɪ) *adj.* **1.** founded on or subject to personal whims, prejudices, etc. **2.** not absolute. **3.** (of a government, ruler, etc.) despotic or dictatorial. **4.** *Law.* (esp. of a penalty) within the court's discretion. [C15: from L *arbitrārius* arranged through arbitration] —**'arbitrarily** *adv.* —**'arbitrariness** *n.*

arbitrate ('ɑːbɪ,treɪt) *vb.* **1.** to achieve a settlement between parties. **2.** to submit to or settle by arbitration. [C16: from L *arbitrāri* to give judgment] —**'arbi,trator** *n.*

arbitration (,ɑːbɪ'treɪʃən) *n.* the hearing and determination of a dispute, esp. an industrial one, by an impartial referee selected or agreed upon by the parties concerned.

Arblay, d' ('dɑːbleɪ; *French* darblɛ) *n.* **Madame.** the married name of (Fanny) **Burney.**

arbor[1] ('ɑːbə) *n.* the U.S. spelling of **arbour.**

arbor[2] ('ɑːbə) *n.* **1.** a rotating shaft in a machine on which a milling cutter or grinding wheel is fitted. **2.** a rotating shaft. [C17: from L: tree]

arboraceous (,ɑːbə'reɪʃəs) *adj. Literary.* **1.** resembling a tree. **2.** wooded.

arboreal (ɑː'bɔːrɪəl) *adj.* **1.** of or resembling a tree. **2.** living in or among trees.

arborescent (,ɑːbə'rɛsənt) *adj.* having the shape or characteristics of a tree. —**,arbo'rescence** *n.*

arboretum (,ɑːbə'riːtəm) *n., pl.* **-ta** (-tə) *or* **-tums.** a place where trees or shrubs are cultivated. [C19: from L, from *arbor* tree]

arboriculture ('ɑːbərɪ,kʌltʃə) *n.* the cultivation of trees or shrubs. —**,arbori'culturist** *n.*

arbor vitae ('ɑːbɔː 'viːtaɪ, 'vaɪtiː) *n.* any of several Asian and North American evergreen coniferous trees having tiny scalelike leaves and egglike cones. [C17: from NL, lit.: tree of life]

arbour ('ɑːbə) *n.* a leafy glade or bower shaded by trees, vines, shrubs, etc. [C14 *erber*, from OF, from L *herba* grass]

Arbroath (ɑː'brəʊθ) *n.* a port and resort in E Scotland, in Tayside region: scene of the barons of Scotland's declaration of independence to Pope John XXII in 1320. Pop.: 24 093 (1981).

Arbuthnot (ɑː'bʌθnɒt) *n.* **John.** 1667–1735, Scottish physician and satirist: author of *The History of John Bull* (1712) and, with others, of the *Memoirs of Martinus Scriblerus* (1741).

arbutus (ɑː'bjuːtəs) *n.*, *pl.* **-tuses.** any of a genus of shrubs having clusters of white or pinkish flowers, broad evergreen leaves, and strawberry-like berries. [C16: from L; rel. to *arbor* tree]

arc (ɑːk) *n.* **1.** something curved in shape. **2.** part of an unbroken curved line. **3.** a luminous discharge that occurs when an electric current flows between two electrodes separated by a small gap. **4.** *Maths.* a section of a curve, graph, or geometric figure. ~*vb.* **arcing, arced** *or* **arcking, arcked.** **5.** (*intr.*) to form an arc. ~*adj.* **6.** *Maths.* specifying an inverse trigonometric function: *arcsin, arccos, arctan.* [C14: from OF, from L *arcus* bow, arch]

ARC *abbrev. for* AIDS-related complex: a condition in which a person is infected with the AIDS virus at an early stage before the disease has reached its full development and may suffer from relatively mild symptoms such as loss of weight, fever, etc.

arcade (ɑː'keɪd) *n.* **1.** a set of arches and their supporting columns. **2.** a covered and sometimes arched passageway, usually with shops on one or both sides. [C18: from F, from It. *arcata*, from L *arcus* bow, arch]

Arcadia (ɑː'keɪdɪə) *n.* **1.** a department of Greece, in the central Peloponnese. Capital: Tripolis. Pop.: 107 932 (1981). Area: 4367 sq. km (1686 sq. miles). **2.** Also called (poetic): **Arcady** ('ɑːkədɪ). the traditional idealized rural setting of Greek and Roman bucolic poetry and later in the literature of the Renaissance.

Arcadian (ɑː'keɪdɪən) *adj.* **1.** of the idealized Arcadia of pastoral poetry. **2.** rustic or bucolic. ~*n.* **3.** a person who leads a quiet simple rural life. —**Ar'cadianism** *n.*

arcane (ɑː'keɪn) *adj.* requiring secret knowledge to be understood; esoteric. [C16: from L *arcānus* secret, from *arcēre* to keep safe]

arcanum (ɑː'keɪnəm) *n.*, *pl.* **-na** (-nə). (*sometimes pl.*) a secret or mystery. [C16: from L; see ARCANE]

arch[1] (ɑːtʃ) *n.* **1.** a curved structure that spans an opening. **2.** Also called: **archway.** a structure in the form of an arch that serves as a gateway. **3.** something curved like an arch. **4.** any of various parts or structures of the body having a curved or archlike outline, such as the raised instep vault formed by the tarsal and metatarsal bones (**arch of the foot**). ~*vb.* **5.** (*tr.*) to span (an opening) with an arch. **6.** to form or cause to form an arch or a curve resembling that of an arch. **7.** (*tr.*) to span or extend over. [C14: from OF *arche*, from L *arcus* bow, ARC]

arch[2] (ɑːtʃ) *adj.* **1.** (*prenominal*) chief; principal; leading. **2.** (*prenominal*) expert: *an arch criminal.* **3.** knowing or superior; coyly playful: *an arch look.* [C16: independent use of ARCH-] —**'archly** *adv.* —**'archness** *n.*

arch. *abbrev. for:* **1.** archaic. **2.** archaism. **3.** archipelago. **4.** architect. **5.** architectural. **6.** architecture.

arch- *or* **archi-** *combining form.* **1.** chief; principal: *archangel; archbishop.* **2.** eminent above all others of the same kind: *archenemy.* [ult. from Gk *arkhi-*, from *arkhein* to rule]

-arch *n. combining form.* leader; ruler; chief: *patriarch; monarch.* [from Gk *-arkhēs*, from *arkhein* to rule]

Archaean *or esp. U.S.* **Archean** (ɑː'kiːən) *adj.* of the metamorphosed rocks formed in the early Precambrian era.

archaeology *or* **archeology** (,ɑːkɪ'ɒlədʒɪ) *n.* the study of man's past by scientific analysis of the material remains of his cultures. [C17: from LL, from Gk *arkhaiologia* study of what is ancient, from *arkhē* beginning] —**archaeological** *or* **archeological** (,ɑːkɪə'lɒdʒɪk³l) *adj.* —,**archae'ologist** *or* ,**arche'ologist** *n.*

archaeopteryx (,ɑːkɪ'ɒptərɪks) *n.* any of several extinct primitive birds which occurred in Jurassic times and had teeth, a long tail, and well-developed wings. [C19: from Gk *arkhaios* ancient + *pterux* winged creature]

archaic (ɑː'keɪɪk) *adj.* **1.** belonging to or characteristic of a much earlier period. **2.** out of date; antiquated. **3.** (of vocabulary, etc.) characteristic of an earlier period of a language. [C19: from F, from Gk *arkhaïkos*, from *arkhaios* ancient, from *arkhē* beginning, from *arkhein* to begin] —**ar'chaically** *adv.*

archaism ('ɑːkeɪ,ɪzəm) *n.* **1.** the adoption or imitation of archaic words or style. **2.** an archaic word, style, etc. [C17: from NL, from Gk, from *arkhaizein* to model one's style upon that of ancient writers; see ARCHAIC] —**'archaist** *n.* —,**archa'istic** *adj.*

archangel ('ɑːk,eɪndʒəl) *n.* a principal angel. —**archangelic** (,ɑːkæn'dʒɛlɪk) *adj.*

Archangel ('ɑːk,eɪndʒəl) *n.* a port in the NW Soviet Union, on the Dvina River: major centre for the timber trade and White Sea fisheries. Pop.: 416 000 (1987). Russian name: **Arkhangelsk.**

archbishop (ɑːtʃ'bɪʃəp) *n.* a bishop of the highest rank. Abbrev.: **abp, Abp, Arch., Archbp.**

archbishopric (ɑːtʃ'bɪʃəprɪk) *n.* the rank, office, or jurisdiction of an archbishop.

archdeacon ('ɑːtʃ'diːkən) *n.* **1.** an Anglican clergyman ranking just below a bishop. **2.** a clergyman of similar rank in other Churches. —**'arch'deaconry** *n.*

archdiocese (,ɑːtʃ'daɪə,siːs) *n.* the diocese of an archbishop. —**archdiocesan** (,ɑːtʃdaɪ'ɒsɪs³n) *adj.*

archducal ('ɑːtʃ'djuːk³l) *adj.* of or relating to an archduke, archduchess, or archduchy.

archduchess ('ɑːtʃ'dʌtʃɪs) *n.* **1.** the wife or widow of an archduke. **2.** (since 1453) a princess of the Austrian imperial family.

archduchy ('ɑːtʃ'dʌtʃɪ) *n.*, *pl.* **-duchies.** the territory ruled by an archduke or archduchess.

archduke ('ɑːtʃ'djuːk) *n.* a chief duke, esp. (since 1453) a prince of the Austrian imperial dynasty.

Archean (ɑː'kiːən) *adj.* a variant spelling (esp. U.S.) of **Archaean.**

archegonium (,ɑːkɪ'gəʊnɪəm) *n.*, *pl.* **-nia** (-nɪə). a female sex organ, occurring in mosses, ferns, etc. [C19: from NL, from Gk, from *arkhe-* chief, first + *gonos* seed, race]

archenemy ('ɑːtʃ'ɛnɪmɪ) *n.*, *pl.* **-mies.** **1.** a chief enemy. **2.** (*often cap.;* preceded by *the*) the devil.

archeology (,ɑːkɪ'ɒlədʒɪ) *n.* a variant spelling of **archaeology.**

archer ('ɑːtʃə) *n.* a person skilled in the use of a bow and arrow. [C13: from OF, from LL, from L *arcus* bow]

Archer[1] ('ɑːtʃə) *n.* **the.** the constellation Sagittarius.

Archer[2] ('ɑːtʃə) *n.* **William.** 1856–1924, Scottish critic and dramatist: made the first English translations of Ibsen.

archerfish ('ɑːtʃə,fɪʃ) *n.*, *pl.* **-fish** *or* **-fishes.** a freshwater fish, related to the perch, of SE Asia and Australia, that catches insects by spitting water at them.

archery ('ɑːtʃərɪ) *n.* **1.** the art or sport of shooting with bows and arrows. **2.** archers or their weapons collectively.

archetype ('ɑːkɪ,taɪp) *n.* **1.** a perfect or typical specimen. **2.** an original model; prototype. **3.** *Psychoanal.* one of the inherited mental images postulated by Jung. **4.** a recurring symbol or motif in literature, etc. [C17: from L *archetypum* an original, from Gk, from *arkhetupos* first-moulded; see ARCH-, -TYPE] —,**arche'typal** *adj.*

archfiend (,ɑːtʃ'fiːnd) *n.* (*often cap.*) **the.** the devil; Satan.

archidiaconal (,ɑːkɪdaɪ'ækən³l) *adj.* of or relating to an archdeacon or his office. —,**archidi'aconate** *n.*

archiepiscopal (,ɑːkɪɪ'pɪskəp³l) *adj.* of or associated with an archbishop. —,**archie'piscopate** *n.*

archil ('ɑːtʃɪl) *n.* a variant of **orchil.**

Archilochus (ɑː'kɪləkəs) *n.* 7th century B.C., Greek poet of Paros, notable for using his own experience as subject matter. —,**Archi'lochian** *adj.*

archimandrite (,ɑːkɪ'mændraɪt) *n.* *Greek Orthodox Church.* the head of a monastery. [C16: from LL, from LGk *arkhimandritēs*, from ARCHI- + *mandra* monastery]

Archimedes (,ɑːkɪ'miːdiːz) *n.* ?287–212 B.C., Greek mathematician and physicist of Syracuse, noted for his work in geometry, hydrostatics, and mechanics. —**Archimedean** (,ɑːkɪ'miːdɪən, -mɪ'diːən) *adj.*

Archimedes' principle *n.* a law of physics stating that the apparent loss in weight of a body immersed in a fluid is equal to the weight of the displaced fluid.

Archimedes' screw *or* **Archimedean screw** *n.* an ancient water-lifting device using a spiral passage in an inclined cylinder.

archipelago (ˌɑːkɪˈpɛləˌgəʊ) *n.*, *pl.* **-gos** *or* **-goes. 1.** a group of islands. **2.** a sea studded with islands. [C16 (meaning: the Aegean Sea): from It., from L *pelagus*, from Gk, from ARCH- + *pelagos* sea] **—archipelagic** (ˌɑːkɪpəˈlædʒɪk) *adj.*

Archipenko (*Russian* arˈxipinkə) *n.* **Aleksandr Porfiryevich** (alɪkˈsandr parˈfirjɪvitʃ). 1887–1964, Russian sculptor and painter, in the U.S. after 1923, whose work is characterized by economy of form.

architect (ˈɑːkɪˌtɛkt) *n.* **1.** a person qualified to design buildings and to supervise their erection. **2.** a person similarly qualified in another form of construction: *a naval architect.* **3.** any planner or creator. [C16: from F, from L, from Gk *arkhitektōn* director of works, from ARCHI- + *tektōn* workman; rel. to *tekhnē* art, skill]

architectonic (ˌɑːkɪtɛkˈtɒnɪk) *adj.* **1.** denoting, relating to, or having architectural qualities. **2.** *Metaphysics.* of the systematic classification of knowledge. [C16: from LL *architectonicus* concerning architecture; see ARCHITECT]

architectonics (ˌɑːkɪtɛkˈtɒnɪks) *n.* (*functioning as sing.*) **1.** the science of architecture. **2.** *Metaphysics.* the scientific classification of knowledge.

architecture (ˈɑːkɪˌtɛktʃə) *n.* **1.** the art and science of designing and superintending the erection of buildings, etc. **2.** a style of building or structure. **3.** buildings or structures collectively. **4.** the structure or design of anything. **—ˌarchiˈtectural** *adj.*

architrave (ˈɑːkɪˌtreɪv) *n. Archit.* **1.** the lowest part of an entablature that bears on the columns. **2.** a moulding around a doorway, window opening, etc. [C16: via F from It., from ARCHI- + *trave* beam, from L *trabs*]

archive (ˈɑːkaɪv) *n.* (*often pl.*) **1.** a collection of records of an institution, family, etc. **2.** a place where such records are kept. [C17: from LL, from Gk *arkheion* repository of official records, from *arkhē* government] **—arˈchival** *adj.*

archivist (ˈɑːkɪvɪst) *n.* a person in charge of archives.

archon (ˈɑːkɒn) *n.* (in ancient Athens) one of the nine chief magistrates. [C17: from Gk *arkhōn* ruler, from *arkhein* to rule] **—ˈarchonˌship** *n.*

archpriest (ˈɑːtʃˈpriːst) *n.* **1.** (formerly) a chief assistant to a bishop. **2.** a senior priest.

archway (ˈɑːtʃˌweɪ) *n.* a passageway or entrance under an arch or arches.

-archy *n. combining form.* government; rule: *anarchy; monarchy.* [from Gk *-arkhia;* see -ARCH]

arc light *n.* a light source in which an arc between two electrodes produces intense white illumination. Also called: **arc lamp.**

arctic (ˈɑːktɪk) *adj.* **1.** of or relating to the Arctic. **2.** *Inf.* cold; freezing. *~n.* **3.** (*modifier*) suitable for conditions of extreme cold: *arctic clothing.* [C14: from L *arcticus*, from Gk *arktikos* northern, lit.: pertaining to (the constellation of) the Bear, from *arktos* bear]

Arctic (ˈɑːktɪk) *n.* **1. the.** Also called: **Arctic Zone.** the regions north of the Arctic Circle. *~adj.* **2.** of or relating to the regions north of the Arctic Circle.

Arctic Circle *n.* the imaginary circle round the earth, parallel to the equator, at latitude 66° 32′ N.

arctic hare *n.* a large hare of the Canadian Arctic whose fur is white in winter.

Arctic Ocean *n.* the ocean surrounding the North Pole, north of the Arctic Circle. Area: about 14 100 000 sq. km (5 440 000 sq. miles).

arctic willow *n.* a low-growing shrub of the Canadian tundra.

Arcturus (ɑːkˈtjʊərəs) *n.* the brightest star in the constellation Boötes: a red giant. [C14: from L, from Gk *Arktouros*, from *arktos* bear + *ouros* guard, keeper]

arcuate (ˈɑːkjʊɪt) *adj.* shaped or bent like an arc or bow. [C17: from L *arcuāre*, from *arcus* ARC]

arc welding *n.* a technique in which metal is welded by heat generated by an electric arc. **—arc welder** *n.*

-ard *or* **-art** *suffix forming nouns.* indicating a person who does something, esp. to excess: *braggart; drunkard.* [via OF, of Gmc origin]

Ardèche (*French* ardɛʃ) *n.* a department of S France, in Rhône-Alpes region. Capital: Privas. Pop.: 267 970 (1982). Area: 5556 sq. km (2167 sq. miles).

Arden[1] (ˈɑːdᵊn) *n.* **Forest of.** a region of N Warwickshire, part of a former forest: scene of Shakespeare's *As You Like It.*

Arden[2] (ˈɑːdᵊn) *n.* **John.** born 1930, English dramatist. His plays include *Serjeant Musgrave's Dance* (1959) and *The Workhouse Donkey* (1963).

Ardennes (ɑːˈdɛn; *French* ardɛn) *n.* **1.** a department of NE France, in Champagne-Ardenne region. Capital: Mézières. Pop.: 302 338 (1982). Area: 5253 sq. km (2049 sq. miles). **2. the.** a wooded plateau in SE Belgium, Luxembourg, and NE France: scene of heavy fighting in both World Wars.

ardent (ˈɑːdᵊnt) *adj.* **1.** expressive of or characterized by intense desire or emotion. **2.** intensely enthusiastic; eager. **3.** glowing or shining: *ardent eyes.* **4. ardent spirits.** alcoholic drinks. [C14: from L *ārdēre* to burn] **—ˈardency** *n.* **—ˈardently** *adv.*

ardour *or U.S.* **ardor** (ˈɑːdə) *n.* **1.** feelings of great intensity and warmth. **2.** eagerness; zeal. [C14: from OF, from L *ārdor*, from *ārdēre* to burn]

arduous (ˈɑːdjʊəs) *adj.* **1.** difficult to accomplish; strenuous. **2.** hard to endure; harsh. **3.** steep or difficult: *an arduous track.* [C16: from L *arduus* steep, difficult] **—ˈarduously** *adv.* **—ˈarduousness** *n.*

are[1] (ɑː; *unstressed* ə) *vb.* the plural form of the present tense of **be** and the singular form used with *you.* [OE *aron*, second person pl. of *bēon* to BE]

are[2] (ɑː) *n.* a unit of area equal to 100 square metres. [C19: from F, from L *ārea* piece of ground; see AREA]

area (ˈɛərɪə) *n.* **1.** any flat, curved, or irregular expanse of a surface. **2. a.** the extent of a two-dimensional surface: *the area of a triangle.* **b.** the two-dimensional extent of a plane or surface: *the area of a sphere.* **3.** a section or part. **4.** region; district. **5. a.** a geographical division of administrative responsibility. **b.** (*as modifier*): *area manager.* **6.** a part or section, as of a building, town, etc., having some specified function: *reception area; commercial area.* **7.** the range or scope of anything. **8.** a subject field or field of study. **9.** Also called: **areaway.** a sunken area, usually enclosed, giving light, air, and sometimes access to a cellar basement. [C16: from L: level ground, threshing-floor; rel. to *ārēre* to be dry] **—ˈareal** *adj.*

arena (əˈriːnə) *n.* **1.** an enclosure or platform, usually surrounded by seats, in which sports events, entertainments, etc., take place: *a boxing arena.* **2.** the central area of an ancient Roman amphitheatre, in which gladiatorial contests were held. **3.** a sphere of intense activity: *the political arena.* [C17: from L *harēna* sand, place where sand was strewn for the combats]

arenaceous (ˌærɪˈneɪʃəs) *adj.* **1.** (of sedimentary rocks) composed of sand. **2.** (of plants) growing in a sandy soil. [C17: from L *harēnāceus* sandy, from *harēna* sand]

aren't (ɑːnt) **1.** *contraction of* are not. **2.** *Inf., chiefly Brit.* (used in interrogative sentences) *contraction of* am not.

areola (əˈrɪələ) *n.*, *pl.* **-lae** (-ˌliː) *or* **-las. 1.** *Biol.* a space outlined on a surface, such as an area between veins on a leaf. **2.** *Anat.* any small circular area, such as the pigmented ring around the human nipple. [C17: from L: dim. of AREA] **—aˈreolar** *or* **areolate** (əˈrɪəlɪt, -ˌleɪt) *adj.*

Arequipa (ˌærɪˈkiːpə; *Spanish* areˈkipa) *n.* a city in S Peru, at an altitude of 2250 m (7500 ft.): founded in 1540 on the site of an Inca city. Pop.: 447 431 (1981).

Ares (ˈɛəriːz) *n. Greek myth.* the god of war, born of Zeus and Hera. Roman counterpart: **Mars.**

arête (əˈreɪt, əˈrɛt) *n.* a sharp ridge that separates glacial valleys. [C19: from F: fishbone, ridge, from L *arista* ear of corn, fishbone]

Arethusa (ˌærɪˈθjuːzə) *n. Greek myth.* a nymph who was changed into a spring on the island of Ortygia to escape the amorous advances of the river god Alpheus.

Aretino (*Italian* areˈtiːno) *n.* **Pietro** (ˈpjɛːtro). 1492–1556, Italian satirist, poet, and dramatist, noted for his satirical attacks on leading political figures.

Arezzo (əˈrɛtsəʊ; *Italian* aˈrettso) *n.* a city in central Italy, in E Tuscany. Pop.: 92 105 (1981). Ancient Latin name: **Arretium.**

argal ('ɑːgəl) *n.* another name for **argol.**

argali ('ɑːgəlɪ) *or* **argal** *n., pl.* **-gali** *or* **-gals.** a wild sheep, with massive horns in the male, inhabiting semidesert regions in central Asia. [C18: from Mongolian]

argent ('ɑːdʒənt) *n.* **a.** an archaic or poetic word for **silver. b.** (*as adj.; often postpositive, esp. in heraldry*): *a bend argent.* [C15: from OF, from L]

Argenteuil (*French* arʒãtœj) *n.* a suburb of Paris, with a convent (656) that became famous when Héloïse was abbess (12th century). Pop.: 102 446 (1983 est.).

argentiferous (,ɑːdʒən'tɪfərəs) *adj.* containing or bearing silver.

Argentina (,ɑːdʒən'tiːnə) *n.* a republic in southern South America: colonized by the Spanish from 1516 onwards; gained independence in 1816 and became a republic in 1852; consists chiefly of subtropical plains and forests (the Chaco) in the north, temperate plains (the pampas) in the central parts, the Andes in the west, and an infertile plain extending to Tierra del Fuego in the south (Patagonia); an important meat producer. Language: Spanish. Religion: Roman Catholic. Currency: austral. Capital: Buenos Aires. Pop.: 31 060 000 (1986 est.). Area: 2 776 653 sq. km (1 072 067 sq. miles). Also called: **the Argentine.**

argentine ('ɑːdʒən,taɪn) *adj.* **1.** of or resembling silver. ~*n.* **2.** a small marine fish characterized by a long silvery body.

Argentine ('ɑːdʒən,tiːn, -,taɪn) *n.* **1. the.** another name for **Argentina. 2.** a native or inhabitant of Argentina. ~*adj.* **3.** of or relating to Argentina. ~Also (for senses 2, 3): **Argentinian** (,ɑːdʒən'tɪnɪən).

argillaceous (,ɑːdʒɪ'leɪʃəs) *adj.* (of sedimentary rocks) composed of very fine-grained material, such as clay. [C18: from L *argilla* white clay, from Gk, from *argos* white]

Argive ('ɑːdʒaɪv, -gaɪv) *adj.* **1.** of or relating to Argos. **2.** a literary word for **Greek.** ~*n.* **3.** an ancient Greek, esp. one from Argos.

Argo ('ɑːgəʊ) *n. Greek myth.* the ship in which Jason sailed in search of the Golden Fleece.

argol ('ɑːgɒl) *or* **argal** ('ɑːgəl) *n.* crude potassium hydrogentartrate. [C14: from Anglo-F *argoil*, from ?]

Argolis ('ɑːgəlɪs) *n.* **1.** a department and ancient region of Greece, in the NE Peloponnese. Capital: Nauplion. Pop.: 93 020 (1981). Area: 2261 sq. km (873 sq. miles). **2. Gulf of.** an inlet of the Aegean Sea, in the E Peloponnese.

argon ('ɑːgɒn) *n.* an unreactive colourless odourless element of the rare gas series that forms almost 1 per cent of the atmosphere. It is used in electric lights. Symbol: Ar; atomic no.: 18; atomic wt.: 39.95. [C19: from Gk, from *argos* inactive, from A-[1] + *ergon* work]

Argonaut ('ɑːgə,nɔːt) *n.* **1.** *Greek myth.* one of the heroes who sailed with Jason in quest of the Golden Fleece. **2.** a person who took part in the Californian gold rush of 1849. [C16: from Gk *Argonautēs*, from *Argō* the name of Jason's ship + *nautēs* sailor] —,**Argo'nautic** *adj.*

Argonne ('ɑːgɒn; *French* argɔn) *n.* **the.** a wooded region of NE France: scene of major battles in both World Wars.

Argos ('ɑːgɒs, -gəs) *n.* an ancient city in SE Greece, in the NE Peloponnese: one of the oldest Greek cities, it dominated the Peloponnese in the 7th century B.C. Pop.: 20 702 (1981).

argosy ('ɑːgəsɪ) *n., pl.* **-sies.** *Arch. or poetic.* a large abundantly laden merchant ship, or a fleet of such ships. [C16: from It. *Ragusea* (*nave*) (ship) of Ragusa]

argot ('ɑːgəʊ) *n.* slang or jargon peculiar to a particular group, esp. (formerly) a group of thieves. [C19: from F, from ?]

Argovie (argɔvi) *n.* the French name for **Aargau.**

arguable ('ɑːgjʊəbʰl) *adj.* **1.** capable of being disputed. **2.** plausible; reasonable. —'**arguably** *adv.*

argue ('ɑːgjuː) *vb.* **-guing, -gued. 1.** (*intr.*) to quarrel; wrangle. **2.** (*intr.; often foll. by for or against*) to present supporting or opposing reasons or cases in a dispute. **3.** (*tr.; may take a clause as object*) to try to prove by presenting reasons. **4.** (*tr.; often passive*) to debate or discuss. **5.** (*tr.*) to persuade. **6.** (*tr.*) to suggest: *her looks argue despair.* [C14: from OF *arguer* to assert, from L *arguere* to make clear, accuse] —'**arguer** *n.*

argufy ('ɑːgjʊ,faɪ) *vb.* **-fying, -fied.** *Facetious or dialect.* to argue or quarrel, esp. over something trivial.

argument ('ɑːgjʊmənt) *n.* **1.** a quarrel; altercation. **2.** a discussion in which reasons are put forward; debate. **3.** (*sometimes pl.*) a point or series of reasons presented to

support or oppose a proposition. **4.** a summary of the plot or subject of a book, etc. **5.** *Logic.* **a.** a process of reasoning in which the conclusion can be shown to be true or false. **b.** the middle term of a syllogism. **6.** *Maths.* another name for **independent variable** of a function.

argumentation (,ɑːgjʊmɛn'teɪʃən) *n.* **1.** the process of reasoning methodically. **2.** argument; debate.

argumentative (,ɑːgjʊ'mɛntətɪv) *adj.* **1.** given to arguing. **2.** characterized by argument; controversial.

Argus ('ɑːgəs) *n.* **1.** *Greek myth.* a giant with a hundred eyes who was made guardian of the heifer Io. **2.** a vigilant person.

Argus-eyed *adj.* observant; vigilant.

argy-bargy *or* **argie-bargie** ('ɑːdʒɪ'bɑːdʒɪ) *n., pl.* **-bargies.** *Brit. inf.* a wrangling argument or verbal dispute. [C19: from Scot., from dialect *argle*, prob. from AR-GUE]

Argyllshire (ɑː'gaɪl,ʃɪə, -ʃə) *n.* (until 1975) a county of W Scotland, now part of Strathclyde region.

Århus (*Danish* 'ɔːhuːs) *n.* a variant spelling of **Aarhus.**

aria ('ɑːrɪə) *n.* an elaborate accompanied song for solo voice from a cantata, opera, or oratorio. [C18: from It.: tune, AIR]

Ariadne (,ærɪ'ædnɪ) *n. Greek myth.* daughter of Minos and Pasiphaë: she gave Theseus the thread with which he found his way out of the Minotaur's labyrinth.

Arian ('ɛərɪən) *adj.* **1.** of or relating to Arius or to Arianism. ~*n.* **2.** an adherent of Arianism.

-arian *suffix forming nouns.* indicating a person or thing that advocates, believes, or is associated with something: *vegetarian; librarian.* [from L *-ārius* -ARY + -AN]

Arianism ('ɛərɪə,nɪzəm) *n.* the doctrine of Arius, declared heretical, which asserted that Christ was not of one substance with the Father.

Arias ('ærɪæs) *n.* **Oscar.** born 1941, Costa Rican statesman; president from 1986; Nobel peace prize 1987.

Arica (ə'riːkə; *Spanish* a'rika) *n.* a port in extreme N Chile: awarded to Chile in 1929 after the lengthy Tacna-Arica dispute with Peru; outlet for Bolivian and Peruvian trade. Pop.: 127 925 (1985 est.). See also **Tacna-Arica.**

arid ('ærɪd) *adj.* **1.** having little or no rain; dry. **2.** devoid of interest. [C17: from L *āridus*, from *ārēre* to be dry] —**aridity** (ə'rɪdɪtɪ) *or* '**aridness** *n.*

Ariège (*French* arjɛʒ) *n.* a department of SW France, in Midi-Pyrénées region. Capital: Foix. Pop.: 135 725 (1982). Area: 4903 sq. km (1912 sq. miles).

Aries ('ɛəriːz) *n., Latin genitive* **Arietis** (ə'raɪɪtɪs). **1.** *Astron.* a N constellation. **2.** *Astrol.* Also called: **the Ram.** the first sign of the zodiac. The sun is in this sign between about March 21 and April 19. [C14: from L: ram]

aright (ə'raɪt) *adv.* correctly; rightly; properly.

aril ('ærɪl) *n.* an additional covering formed on certain seeds, such as those of the yew and nutmeg, after fertilization. [C18: from NL, from Med. L *arilli* raisins, pips of grapes] —'**aril,late** *adj.*

Arimathea *or* **Arimathaea** (,ærɪmə'θiːə) *n.* a town in ancient Palestine: location unknown.

Ariminum (ə'rɪmɪnəm) *n.* the ancient name of **Rimini.**

arioso (,ɑːrɪ'əʊzəʊ) *n., pl.* **-sos** *or* **-si** (-siː). *Music.* a recitative with the lyrical quality of an aria. [C18: from It., from ARIA]

Ariosto (*Italian* a'rjɔsto) *n.* **Ludovico** (ludo'viːko). 1474–1533, Italian poet, famous for his romantic epic *Orlando Furioso* (1516).

arise (ə'raɪz) *vb.* **arising, arose, arisen** (ə'rɪzʰn). (*intr.*) **1.** to come into being; originate. **2.** (foll. by *from*) to proceed as a consequence. **3.** to get or stand up, as from a sitting or lying position. **4.** to come into notice. **5.** to ascend. [OE *ārīsan*]

Aristaeus (,ærɪ'stiːəs) *n. Greek myth.* a son of Apollo and Cyrene: protector of herds and fields.

Aristarchus of Samos *n.* 3rd century B.C., Greek astronomer who anticipated Copernicus in advancing the theory that the earth revolves around the sun.

Aristarchus of Samothrace *n.* ?220–?150 B.C., Greek scholar: librarian at Alexandria, noted for his edition of Homer.

Aristides (,ærɪ'staɪdiːz) *n.* known as *Aristides the Just.* ?530–?468 B.C., Athenian general and statesman, who played a prominent part in the Greek victories over the Persians at Marathon (490), Salamis (480), and Plataea (479).

Aristippus (ˌærɪˈstɪpəs) n. ?435–?356 B.C., Greek philosopher, who believed pleasure to be the highest good and founded the Cyrenaic school.

aristo (ˈærɪstəʊ, əˈrɪstəʊ) n., pl. -tos. Inf. short for **aristocrat**.

aristocracy (ˌærɪˈstɒkrəsɪ) n., pl. -cies. **1.** government by the best citizens. **2.** a privileged class of people; the nobility. **3.** government by such a class. **4.** a state governed by such a class. **5.** a class of people considered to be outstanding in a sphere of activity. [C16: from LL, from Gk aristokratia rule by the best-born, from aristos best; see -CRACY]

aristocrat (ˈærɪstəˌkræt) n. **1.** a member of the aristocracy. **2.** a person who has the manners or qualities of a member of a privileged class. **3.** a supporter of aristocracy as a form of government.

aristocratic (ˌærɪstəˈkrætɪk) adj. **1.** relating to or characteristic of aristocracy or an aristocrat. **2.** elegant or stylish in appearance and behaviour. — **ˌaristoˈcratically** adv.

Aristophanes (ˌærɪˈstɒfəˌniːz) n. ?448–?380 B.C., Greek comic dramatist, who satirized leading contemporary figures such as Socrates and Euripides. Eleven of his plays are extant, including The Clouds, The Frogs, The Birds, and Lysistrata.

Aristotelian (ˌærɪstəˈtiːlɪən) adj. **1.** of or relating to Aristotle or to his philosophy. ~n. **2.** a follower of Aristotle.

Aristotelian logic n. **1.** traditional logic, esp. relying on the theory of syllogism. **2.** the logical method of Aristotle, esp. as developed in the Middle Ages.

Aristotle (ˈærɪˌstɒtəl) n. 384–322 B.C., Greek philosopher; pupil of Plato, tutor of Alexander the Great, and founder of the Peripatetic school at Athens; author of works on logic, ethics, politics, poetics, rhetoric, biology, zoology, and metaphysics. His works influenced Muslim philosophy and science and medieval scholastic philosophy.

arithmetic n. (əˈrɪθmətɪk). **1.** the branch of mathematics concerned with numerical calculations, such as addition, subtraction, multiplication, and division. **2.** calculations involving numerical operations. **3.** knowledge of or skill in using arithmetic. ~adj. (ˌærɪθˈmɛtɪk) also **arithmetical**. **4.** of, relating to, or using arithmetic. [C13: from L, from Gk arithmētikē, from arithmein to count, from arithmos number] — **ˌarithˈmetically** adv. — **aˌrithmeˈtician** n.

arithmetic mean n. the average value of a set of terms or quantities, expressed as their sum divided by their number: the arithmetic mean of 3, 4, and 8 is 5. Also called: **average**.

arithmetic progression n. a sequence, each term of which differs from the succeeding term by a constant amount, such as 3,6,9,12.

-arium suffix forming nouns. indicating a place for or associated with something: aquarium; solarium. [from L -ārium, neuter of -ārius -ARY]

Arius (ˈɛərɪəs) n. ?250–336 A.D., Greek Christian theologian, originator of the doctrine of Arianism.

Arizona (ˌærɪˈzəʊnə) n. a state of the southwestern U.S.: consists of the Colorado plateau in the northeast, including the Grand Canyon, divided from desert in the southwest by mountains rising over 3750 m (12 500 ft.). Capital: Phoenix. Pop.: 3 317 000 (1986 est.). Area: 293 750 sq. km (113 417 sq. miles). Abbrevs.: **Ariz.** or (with zip code) **AZ**

Arjuna (ˈɑːdʒʊnə) n. Hindu myth. the most important of the five princes in the Mahabharata. Krishna served as his charioteer in the battle with the Kauravas.

ark (ɑːk) n. **1.** the vessel that Noah built which survived the Flood (Genesis 6–9). **2.** a place or thing offering shelter or protection. **3.** Dialect. a box. [OE arc, from L arca box, chest]

Ark (ɑːk) n. Judaism. **1.** Also called: **Holy Ark.** the cupboard in a synagogue in which the Torah scrolls are kept. **2.** Also called: **Ark of the Covenant.** the most sacred symbol of God's presence among the Hebrew people, carried in their journey from Sinai to the Promised Land (Canaan).

Arkansas n. **1.** (ˈɑːkənˌsɔː) a state of the southern U.S.: mountainous in the north and west, with the alluvial plain of the Mississippi in the east; has the only diamond mine in the U.S.; the chief U.S. producer of bauxite. Capital: Little Rock. Pop.: 2 372 000 (1986 est.). Area: 134 537 sq. km (51 945 sq. miles). Abbrevs.: **Ark.** or (with zip code) **AR**

2. (ɑːˈkænzəs). a river in the S central U.S., rising in central Colorado and flowing east and southeast to join the Mississippi in Arkansas. Length: 2335 km (1450 miles).

Arkhangelsk (arˈxangɪljsk) n. the Russian name for **Archangel**.

Arkwright (ˈɑːkraɪt) n. Sir **Richard.** 1732–92, English cotton manufacturer: inventor of the spinning frame (1769) which produced cotton thread strong enough to be used as a warp.

Arlberg (German ˈarlbɛrk) n. a mountain pass in W Austria: a winter sports region. Height: 1802 m (5910 ft.).

Arles (ɑːlz; French arl) n. **1.** a city in SE France, on the Rhône: Roman amphitheatre. Pop.: 50 056 (1983 est.). **2. Kingdom of.** a kingdom in SE France which had dissolved by 1378: known as the Kingdom of Burgundy until about 1200.

Arlington (ˈɑːlɪŋtən) n. a county of N Virginia: site of **Arlington National Cemetery.**

Arlon (French arlɔ̃) n. a town in SE Belgium, capital of Luxembourg province. Pop.: 22 364 (1981 est.).

arm[1] (ɑːm) n. **1.** (in man) either of the upper limbs from the shoulder to the wrist. Related adj.: **brachial. 2.** the part of either of the upper limbs from the elbow to the wrist; forearm. **3. a.** the corresponding limb of any other vertebrate. **b.** an armlike appendage of some invertebrates. **4.** an object that covers or supports the human arm, esp. the sleeve of a garment or the side of a chair, etc. **5.** anything considered to resemble an arm in appearance, function, etc.: an arm of the sea; the arm of a record player. **6.** an administrative subdivision of an organization: an arm of the government. **7.** power; authority: the arm of the law. **8. arm in arm.** with arms linked. **9. at arm's length.** at a distance. **10. in the arms of Morpheus.** sleeping. **11. with open arms.** with great warmth and hospitality. [OE] — **ˈarmless** adj.

arm[2] (ɑːm) vb. **1.** to equip with weapons as a preparation for war. **2.** (tr.) to provide (a person or thing) with something that strengthens, protects, or increases efficiency. **3. a.** (tr.) to activate (a fuse) so that it will explode at the required time. **b.** to prepare (an explosive device) for use by introducing a detonator, etc. ~n. **4.** (usually pl.) a weapon, esp. a firearm. [C14: from OF armes, from L arma arms, equipment]

armada (ɑːˈmɑːdə) n. a large number of ships or aircraft. [C16: from Sp., from Med. L armāta fleet, armed forces, from L armāre to provide with arms]

Armada (ɑːˈmɑːdə) n. (usually preceded by the) See **Spanish Armada.**

armadillo (ˌɑːməˈdɪləʊ) n., pl. -los. a burrowing mammal of Central and South America with a covering of strong horny plates over most of the body. [C16: from Sp., dim. of armado armed (man), from L armātus armed; cf. ARMADA]

Armageddon (ˌɑːməˈɡɛdən) n. **1.** New Testament. the final battle between good and evil at the end of the world. **2.** a catastrophic and extremely destructive conflict. [C19: from LL, from Gk, from Heb. har megiddōn, mountain district of Megiddo (in N Palestine)]

Armagh (ɑːˈmɑː) n. **1.** a district (former county) of S Northern Ireland. Pop.: 51 200 (1986 est.). Area: 667 sq. km (258 sq. miles). **2.** a town in S Northern Ireland, in the district of Armagh: seat of Roman Catholic and Protestant archbishops. Pop.: 12 297 (1971).

armament (ˈɑːməmənt) n. **1.** the weapon equipment of a military vehicle, ship, or aircraft. **2.** a military force raised and armed ready for war. **3.** preparation for war. [C17: from L armāmenta utensils, from armāre to equip]

armature (ˈɑːmətjʊə) n. **1.** a revolving structure in an electric motor or generator, wound with the coils that carry the current. **2.** any part of an electric machine or device that vibrates under the influence of a magnetic field or within which an electromotive force is induced. **3.** Also called: **keeper.** a soft iron or steel bar placed across the poles of a magnet to close the magnetic circuit. **4.** Sculpture. a framework to support the clay or other material used in modelling. **5.** the protective outer covering of an animal or plant. [C15: from L armātūra armour, equipment, from armāre to furnish with equipment]

armchair (ˈɑːmˌtʃɛə) n. **1.** a chair, esp. an upholstered one, that has side supports for the arms or elbows. **2.** (modifier) taking or involving no active part: an armchair strategist.

armed[1] (ɑːmd) *adj.* **1.** equipped with or supported by arms, armour, etc. **2.** prepared for conflict or any difficulty. **3.** (of an explosive device) prepared for use.

armed[2] (ɑːmd) *adj.* **a.** having an arm or arms. **b.** (*in combination*): *long-armed; one-armed.*

armed forces *pl. n.* the military forces of a nation or nations, including the army, navy, air force, marines, etc.

Armenia (ɑːˈmiːnɪə) *n.* **1.** a former kingdom in W Asia, between the Black Sea and the Caspian Sea, south of Georgia. **2.** another name for *Armenian Soviet Socialist Republic.* **3.** a town in central Colombia: centre of a coffee-growing district. Pop.: 199 459 (1985). —**Arˈmenian** *adj., n.*

Armenian Soviet Socialist Republic *n.* an administrative division of the S Soviet Union, bordering on Iran in the south and Turkey in the west: mountainous, rising over 4000 m (13 000 ft.). Capital: Yerevan. Pop.: 3 400 000 (1987). Area: 229 800 sq. km (11 490 sq. miles).

Armentières (ˈɑːmənˌtɪəz; *French* armɑ̃tjɛr) *n.* a town in N France: site of battles in both World Wars. Pop.: 25 992 (1982 est.).

armful (ˈɑːmfʊl) *n., pl.* **-fuls.** the amount that can be held by one or both arms.

armhole (ˈɑːmˌhəʊl) *n.* the opening in an article of clothing through which the arm passes.

armillary sphere (ɑːˈmɪlərɪ) *n.* a model of the celestial sphere formerly used in fixing the positions of heavenly bodies.

Arminian (ɑːˈmɪnɪən) *adj.* denoting, relating to, or believing in the Protestant doctrines of Jacobus Arminius, which rejected absolute predestination and stressed free will in man. —**Arˈminianˌism** *n.*

Arminius (ɑːˈmɪnɪəs) *n.* **1.** Also called: **Hermann.** ?17 B.C.–?21 A.D., Germanic chieftain: organized a revolt against the Romans in 9 A.D. **2. Jacobus** (dʒəˈkəʊbəs), real name *Jacob Harmensen.* 1560–1609, Dutch Protestant theologian.

armistice (ˈɑːmɪstɪs) *n.* an agreement between opposing armies to suspend hostilities; truce. [C18: from NL, from L *arma* arms + *sistere* to stop]

Armistice Day (ˈɑːmɪstɪs) *n.* the anniversary of the signing of the armistice that ended World War I, on Nov. 11, 1918. See also **Remembrance Sunday.**

armlet (ˈɑːmlɪt) *n.* **1.** a small arm, as of a lake. **2.** a band or bracelet worn round the arm.

armoire (ɑːmˈwɑː) *n.* a large cabinet, originally used for storing weapons. [C16: from F, from OF *armaire,* from L *armārium* chest, closet; see AMBRY]

armorial (ɑːˈmɔːrɪəl) *adj.* of or relating to heraldry or heraldic arms.

Armorica (ɑːˈmɒrɪkə) *n.* an ancient name for Brittany. —**Arˈmorican** *n., adj.*

armour *or U.S.* **armor** (ˈɑːmə) *n.* **1.** any defensive covering, esp. that of metal, chain mail, etc., worn by medieval warriors. **2.** the protective metal plates on a tank, warship, etc. **3.** *Mil.* armoured fighting vehicles in general. **4.** any protective covering, such as the shell of certain animals. **5.** heraldic insignia; arms. ~*vb.* **6.** (*tr.*) to equip or cover with armour. [C13: from OF *armure,* from L *armātūra* armour, equipment]

armoured *or U.S.* **armored** (ˈɑːməd) *adj.* **1.** having a protective covering. **2.** comprising units making use of armoured vehicles: *an armoured brigade.*

armourer *or U.S.* **armorer** (ˈɑːmərə) *n.* **1.** a person who makes or mends arms and armour. **2.** a person employed in the maintenance of small arms and weapons in a military unit.

armour plate *n.* a tough heavy steel often hardened on the surface, used for protecting warships, tanks, etc.

armoury *or U.S.* **armory** (ˈɑːmərɪ) *n., pl.* **-mouries** *or* **-mories.** **1.** a secure place for the storage of weapons. **2.** armour generally; military supplies. **3.** resources, such as arguments, on which to draw: *a few choice terms from her armoury of invective.*

armpit (ˈɑːmˌpɪt) *n.* the small depression beneath the arm where it joins the shoulder. Technical name: **axilla.**

armrest (ˈɑːmˌrɛst) *n.* the part of a chair, sofa, etc., that supports the arm. Sometimes shortened to **arm.**

arms (ɑːmz) *pl. n.* **1.** weapons collectively. See also **small arms. 2.** military exploits: *prowess in arms.* **3.** the official heraldic symbols of a family, state, etc. **4. bear arms. a.** to carry weapons. **b.** to serve in the armed forces. **c.** to have a coat of arms. **5. in** *or* **under arms.**

armed and prepared for war. **6. lay down one's arms.** to stop fighting; surrender. **7. take (up) arms.** to prepare to fight. **8. up in arms.** indignant; prepared to protest strongly. [C13: from OF, from L *arma;* see ARM[2]]

Armstrong (ˈɑːmˌstrɒŋ) *n.* **1. (Daniel) Louis,** known as *Satchmo.* 1900–71, U.S. jazz trumpeter and bandleader. **2. Neil (Alden).** born 1930, U.S. astronaut; commanded Apollo 11 on the first manned lunar landing during which he became the first man to set foot on the moon on July 20, 1969.

arm wrestling *n.* a contest of strength in which two people rest the elbow of one arm on a flat surface, grasp each other's hand, and try to force their opponent's forearm down flat.

army (ˈɑːmɪ) *n., pl.* **-mies. 1.** the military land forces of a nation. **2.** a military unit usually consisting of two or more corps with supporting arms and services. **3.** (*modifier*) of or characteristic of an army. **4.** any large body of people united for some specific purpose. **5.** a large number of people, animals, etc. [C14: from OF, from Med. L *armāta* armed forces]

army ant *n.* any of various tropical American predatory ants which travel in vast hordes preying on other animals. Also called: **legionary ant.**

army worm *n.* a type of caterpillar which travels in vast hordes and is a serious pest of cereal crops.

Arne (ɑːn) *n.* **Thomas (Augustine).** 1710–78, English composer, noted for his setting of Shakespearean songs and for his song *Rule Britannia.*

Arnhem (ˈɑːnəm) *n.* a city in the E Netherlands, capital of Gelderland province, on the Rhine: site of a World War II battle. Pop.: 127 671 (1987).

Arnhem Land *n.* a region of N Australia, in the N Northern Territory: mainly a reserve for Aborigines.

arnica (ˈɑːnɪkə) *n.* **1.** any of a genus of N temperate or arctic plants having yellow flowers. **2.** the tincture of the dried flower heads of any of these plants, used in treating bruises. [C18: from NL, from ?]

Arnim (*German* ˈarnɪm) *n.* **Achim von** (ˈaxɪm fɔn). 1781–1831, German romantic poet. He published, with Clemens Brentano, the collection of folk songs, *Des Knaben Wunderhorn* (1805–08).

Arno (ˈɑːnəʊ) *n.* a river in central Italy, rising in the Apennines and flowing through Florence and Pisa to the Ligurian Sea. Length: about 240 km (150 miles).

Arnold[1] (ˈɑːnᵊld) *n.* a town in N central England, in S Nottinghamshire. Pop.: 37 242 (1981).

Arnold[2] (ˈɑːnᵊld) *n.* **1. Malcolm.** born 1921, English composer, esp. of orchestral works in a traditional idiom. **2. Matthew.** 1822–88, English poet, essayist, and literary critic, noted particularly for his poems *Sohrab and Rustum* (1853) and *Dover Beach* (1867), and for his *Essays in Criticism* (1865) and *Culture and Anarchy* (1869). **3.** his father, **Thomas.** 1795–1842, English historian and educationalist, headmaster of Rugby School, noted for his reforms in public-school education.

aroha (ˈɑːrəhə) *n. N.Z.* love, compassion, or affectionate regard. [Maori]

aroid (ˈærɔɪd, ˈɛər-) *adj.* of or relating to a plant family that includes the arum, calla, and anthurium. [C19: from ARUM + -OID]

aroint thee *or* **ye** (əˈrɔɪnt) *sentence substitute. Arch.* away! begone! [C17: from ?]

aroma (əˈrəʊmə) *n.* **1.** a distinctive usually pleasant smell, esp. of spices, wines, and plants. **2.** a subtle pervasive quality or atmosphere. [C18: via L from Gk: spice]

aromatherapy (əˌrəʊməˈθɛrəpɪ) *n.* the massaging of the skin with fragrant oils in order to relieve tension.

aromatic (ˌærəˈmætɪk) *adj.* **1.** having a distinctive, usually fragrant smell. **2.** (of an organic compound) having an unsaturated ring, esp. containing a benzene ring. Cf. **aliphatic.** ~*n.* **3.** something, such as a plant or drug, giving off a fragrant smell. —ˌaroˈmatically *adv.* —aˌroˈmaticity *n.*

aromatize *or* **-tise** (əˈrəʊməˌtaɪz) *vb.* (*tr.*) to make aromatic. —aˌromatiˈzation *or* -iˈsation *n.*

arose (əˈrəʊz) *vb.* the past tense of **arise.**

around (əˈraʊnd) *prep.* **1.** situated at various points in: *a lot of shelves around the house.* **2.** from place to place in: *driving around Ireland.* **3.** somewhere in or near. **4.** *Chiefly U.S.* approximately in: *it happened around 1957.* ~*adv.* **5.** in all directions from a point of reference: *he owns the land for ten miles around.* **6.** in the vicinity,

esp. restlessly but idly: *to stand around.* **7.** in no particular place or direction: *dotted around.* **8.** *Inf.* (of people) active and prominent in a particular area or profession. **9.** *Inf.* present in some place (the exact location being unknown or unspecified). **10.** *Inf.* in circulation; available: *that type of phone has been around for some years now.* **11.** *Inf.* to many places, so as to have gained considerable experience, often of a worldly or social nature: *I've been around.* [C17 (rare earlier): from A-² + ROUND]
▷ **Usage.** In American English, *around* is usually used instead of *round* in adverbial and prepositional senses, except in a few fixed phrases such as *all year round.* Such uses of *around* are less common in British English.

arouse (ə'rauz) *vb.* **1.** (*tr.*) to evoke or elicit (a reaction, emotion, or response). **2.** to awaken from sleep. —**a'rousal** *n.* —**a'rouser** *n.*

Arp (*French* arp) *n.* **Jean** (ʒɑ̃) or **Hans** (hans). 1887–1966, Alsatian sculptor, painter, and poet, cofounder of the Dada movement in Zürich, noted particularly for his abstract organic sculptures based on natural forms.

Arpád ('ɑːpɑːd) *n.* died 907 A.D., Magyar chieftain who conquered Hungary in the late 9th century.

arpeggio (ɑː'pɛdʒɪəu) *n., pl.* **-gios.** a chord whose notes are played or sung in rapid succession rather than simultaneously. [C18: from It., from *arpeggiare* to perform on the harp, from *arpa* HARP]

arquebus ('ɑːkwɪbəs) or **harquebus** *n.* a portable long-barrelled gun dating from the 15th century. [C16: via OF from MDu. *hakebusse,* lit.: hook gun, from the shape of the butt, from *hake* hook + *busse* box, gun, from LL *busis* box]

arr. *abbrev. for:* **1.** arranged (by). **2.** arrival. **3.** arrive(d).

arrack or **arak** ('ærək) *n.* a coarse spirit distilled in various Eastern countries from grain, rice, sugar cane, etc. [C17: from Ar. *'araq* sweat, sweet juice, liquor]

arraign (ə'reɪn) *vb.* (*tr.*) **1.** to bring (a prisoner) before a court to answer an indictment. **2.** to call to account; accuse. [C14: from OF, from Vulgar L *ratiōnāre* (unattested) to talk, argue, from L *ratiō* a reasoning] —**ar'raigner** *n.* —**ar'raignment** *n.*

Arran ('ærən) *n.* an island off the SW coast of Scotland, in the Firth of Clyde. Pop.: 4726 (1981). Area: 427 sq. km (165 sq. miles).

arrange (ə'reɪndʒ) *vb.* **1.** (*tr.*) to put into a proper or systematic order. **2.** (*tr.; may take a clause as object or an infinitive*) to arrive at an agreement about. **3.** (when *intr.,* often foll. by *for;* when *tr.,* may take a clause as object or an infinitive) to make plans or preparations in advance (for something): *we arranged for her to be met.* **4.** (*tr.*) to adapt (a musical composition) for performance in a different way, esp. on different instruments. **5.** (*intr.; often foll. by *with*) to come to an agreement. [C14: from OF *arangier,* from A-² + *rangier* to put in a row, RANGE] —**ar'rangeable** *adj.* —**ar'ranger** *n.*

arrangement (ə'reɪndʒmənt) *n.* **1.** the act of arranging or being arranged. **2.** the form in which things are arranged. **3.** a thing composed of various ordered parts: *a flower arrangement.* **4.** (*often pl.*) a preparation. **5.** an understanding. **6.** an adaptation of a piece of music for performance in a different way, esp. on different instruments.

arrant ('ærənt) *adj.* utter; out-and-out: *an arrant fool.* [C14: var. of ERRANT (wandering, vagabond)] —**'arrantly** *adv.*

arras ('ærəs) *n.* a wall hanging, esp. of tapestry.

Arras ('ærəs; *French* arɑs) *n.* a town in N France: formerly famous for tapestry; severely damaged in both World Wars. Pop.: 45 943 (1983 est.).

Arrau (ə'rau) *n.* **Claudio.** born 1903, Chilean pianist.

array (ə'reɪ) *n.* **1.** an impressive display or collection. **2.** an orderly arrangement, esp. of troops in battle order. **3.** *Poetic.* rich clothing. **4.** *Maths.* a set of numbers or symbols arranged in rows and columns, as in a determinant or matrix. **5.** *Law.* a panel of jurors. **6.** *Computers.* a regular data structure in which elements may be ordered by reference to index numbers. ~*vb.* (*tr.*) **7.** to dress in rich attire. **8.** to arrange in order (esp. troops for battle). **9.** *Law.* to draw up (a panel of jurors). [C13: from OF, from *arayer* to arrange, of Gmc origin] —**ar'rayal** *n.*

arrears (ə'rɪəz) *n.* (*sometimes sing.*) **1.** Also called: **arrearage.** something outstanding or owed. **2. in arrears** or **arrear.** late in paying a debt or meeting an obligation.

[C18: from obs. *arrear* (adv.) behindhand, from OF, from Med. L *adretrō,* from L *ad* to + *retrō* backwards]

arrest (ə'rɛst) *vb.* (*tr.*) **1.** to deprive (a person) of liberty by taking him into custody, esp. under lawful authority. **2.** to seize (a ship) under lawful authority. **3.** to slow or stop the development of (a disease, growth, etc.). **4.** to catch and hold (one's attention, etc.). ~*n.* **5.** the act of taking a person into custody, esp. under lawful authority. **6.** the act of seizing and holding a ship under lawful authority. **7.** the state of being held: *under arrest.* **8.** the slowing or stopping of something: *a cardiac arrest.* [C14: from OF, from Vulgar L *arrestāre* (unattested), from L *ad* at, to + *restāre* to stand firm, stop]

arresting (ə'rɛstɪŋ) *adj.* attracting attention; striking. —**ar'restingly** *adv.*

Arretium (æ'riːtɪəm, -'rɛt-) *n.* the ancient Latin name of **Arezzo.** —**Arretine** ('ærɪˌtaɪn) *adj.*

Arrhenius (*Swedish* a'reːnɪus) *n.* **Svante August** ('svantə 'august). 1859–1927, Swedish chemist and physicist, noted for his work on the theory of electrolytic dissociation: Nobel prize for chemistry 1903.

arrhythmia (ə'rɪðmɪə) *n.* any variation from the normal rhythm in the heartbeat. [C19: NL, from Gk *arrhuthmia,* from A-¹ + *rhuthmos* RHYTHM]

arrière-pensée *French.* (arjɛrpɑ̃se) *n.* an unrevealed thought or intention. [C19: lit.: behind thought]

Ar Rimal ('ɑːr rɪ'mɑːl) *n.* another name for **Rub' al Khali.**

arris ('ærɪs) *n., pl.* **-ris** or **-rises.** a sharp edge at the meeting of two surfaces at an angle with one another. [C17: from OF *areste* beard of grain, sharp ridge; see ARÊTE]

arrival (ə'raɪvəl) *n.* **1.** the act or time of arriving. **2.** a person or thing that arrives or has arrived.

arrive (ə'raɪv) *vb.* (*intr.*) **1.** to come to a certain place during or after a journey. **2.** to reach: *to arrive at a decision.* **3.** to occur eventually: *the moment arrived when pretence was useless.* **4.** *Inf.* (of a baby) to be born. **5.** *Inf.* to attain success. [C13: from OF, from Vulgar L *arripāre* (unattested) to land, reach the bank, from L *ad* to + *rīpa* river bank]

arrivederci *Italian.* (arrive'dertʃi) *sentence substitute.* goodbye.

arriviste (ˌæriː'viːst) *n.* a person who is unscrupulously ambitious. [F: see ARRIVE, -IST]

arrogant ('ærəgənt) *adj.* having or showing an exaggerated opinion of one's own importance, merit, ability, etc.: *an arrogant person.* [C14: from L *arrogāre* to claim as one's own; see ARROGATE] —**'arrogance** *n.* —**'arrogantly** *adv.*

arrogate ('ærəˌgeɪt) *vb.* (*tr.*) **1.** to claim or appropriate for oneself without justification. **2.** to attribute or assign to another without justification. [C16: from L *arrogāre,* from *rogāre* to ask] —**,arro'gation** *n.* —**arrogative** (ə'rɒgətɪv) *adj.*

arrondissement (*French* arɔ̃dismɑ̃) *n.* (in France) **1.** the largest subdivision of a department. **2.** a municipal district of large cities, esp. Paris. [C19: from *arrondir* to make round]

arrow ('ærəu) *n.* **1.** a long slender pointed weapon, usually having feathers fastened at the end as a balance, that is shot from a bow. **2.** any of various things that resemble an arrow in shape, function, or speed. [OE *arwe*]

arrowhead ('ærəuˌhɛd) *n.* **1.** the pointed tip of an arrow, often removable from the shaft. **2.** something that resembles the head of an arrow in shape. **3.** an aquatic herbaceous plant having arrow-shaped leaves.

arrowroot ('ærəuˌruːt) *n.* **1.** a white-flowered West Indian plant, whose rhizomes yield an easily digestible starch. **2.** the starch obtained from this plant.

arroyo (ə'rɔɪəu) *n., pl.* **-os.** *Chiefly southwestern U.S.* a stream or brook. [C19: from Sp., prob. rel. to L *arrūgia* shaft in a gold mine]

Arru Islands ('ɑːruː) *pl. n.* a variant spelling of **Aru Islands.**

arse (ɑːs) or *U.S. & Canad.* **ass** *n. Taboo.* **1.** the buttocks. **2.** the anus. **3.** a stupid person; fool. ~Also called (for senses 2, 3): **arsehole,** (U.S. & Canad.) **asshole.** [OE]

arsenal ('ɑːsənəl) *n.* **1.** a store for arms, ammunition, and other military items. **2.** a workshop that produces munitions. **3.** a store of anything regarded as weapons. [C16: from It. *arsenale* dockyard, from Ar., from *dār* house + *siñ'ah* manufacture]

arsenate ('ɑːsə,neɪt, -nɪt) n. a salt or ester of arsenic acid.

arsenic n. ('ɑːsnɪk). **1.** a toxic metalloid element used in transistors, lead-based alloys, and high-temperature brasses. Symbol: As; atomic no.: 33; atomic wt.: 74.92. **2.** a nontechnical name for **arsenic trioxide** (As$_2$O$_3$, used as rat poison and an insecticide. ~adj. (ɑː'sɛnɪk). **3.** of or containing arsenic, esp. in the pentavalent state; designating an arsenic(V) compound. [C14: from L, from Gk arsenikon yellow arsenic ore, from Syriac zarnīg (infl. by Gk arsenikos virile)]

arsenic acid n. a white poisonous soluble crystalline solid used in the manufacture of insecticides.

arsenical (ɑː'sɛnɪkəl) adj. **1.** of or containing arsenic. ~n. **2.** a drug or insecticide containing arsenic.

arsenious (ɑː'siːnɪəs) or **arsenous** ('ɑːsɪnəs) adj. of or containing arsenic in the trivalent state; designating an arsenic(III) compound.

arson ('ɑːsən) n. Criminal law. the act of intentionally or recklessly setting fire to property for some improper reason. [C17: from OF, from Med. L ārsiō, from L ārdēre to burn] —'**arsonist** n.

art[1] (ɑːt) n. **1. a.** the creation of works of beauty or other special significance. **b.** (as modifier): an art movement. **2.** the exercise of human skill (as distinguished from nature). **3.** imaginative skill as applied to representations of the natural world or figments of the imagination. **4. a.** works of art collectively, esp. of the visual arts. **b.** (as modifier): an art gallery. **5.** any branch of the visual arts, esp. painting. **6. a.** any field using the techniques of art to display artistic qualities. **b.** (as modifier): art film. **7.** method, facility, or knack: the art of threading a needle. **8.** skill governing a particular human activity: the art of government. **9.** cunning. **10. get something down to a fine art.** to become highly proficient at something through practice. ~See also **arts.** [C13: from OF, from L ars craftsmanship]

art[2] (ɑːt) vb. Arch. (used with the pronoun thou) a singular form of the present tense of **be.** [OE eart, part of bēon to BE]

art. abbrev. for: **1.** article. **2.** artificial. **3.** Also: **arty.** artillery.

-art suffix forming nouns. a variant of **-ard.**

Artaud (French arto) n. **Antonin** (ɑ̃tɔnɛ̃). 1896–1948, French stage director and dramatist, whose concept of the theatre of cruelty is expounded in Manifeste du théâtre de la cruauté (1932) and Le Théâtre et son double (1938).

Artaxerxes I (,ɑːtə'zɜːksiːz) n. died 425 B.C., king of Persia (465–425): son of Xerxes I.

Artaxerxes II n. died ?358 B.C., king of Persia (?404–?358). He defeated his brother Cyrus the Younger at Cunaxa (401).

Art Deco ('dɛkəʊ) n. a style of interior decoration, architecture, etc., at its height in the 1930s and characterized by geometrical shapes. [C20: from art décoratif, after the Exposition des arts décoratifs held in Paris in 1925]

artefact or **artifact** ('ɑːtɪ,fækt) n. **1.** something made or given shape by man, such as a tool or a work of art, esp. an object of archaeological interest. **2.** Cytology. a structure seen in dead tissue that is not normally present in the living tissue. [C19: from L arte factum, from ars skill + facere to make]

artel (ɑː'tɛl) n. (in the Soviet Union) a cooperative union or organization, esp. of producers, such as peasants. [from Russian artel', from It. artieri artisans, from arte work, from L ars ART[1]]

Artemis ('ɑːtɪmɪs) n. Greek myth. the virgin goddess of the hunt and the moon: the twin sister of Apollo. Roman counterpart: **Diana.** Also called: **Cynthia.**

arterial (ɑː'tɪərɪəl) adj. **1.** of or affecting an artery or arteries. **2.** denoting or relating to the bright red reoxygenated blood that circulates in the arteries. **3.** being a major route, esp. one with many minor branches. —**ar'terially** adv.

arterialize or **-lise** (ɑː'tɪərɪə,laɪz) vb. (tr.) **1.** to change (venous blood) into arterial blood by replenishing the depleted oxygen. **2.** to provide with arteries. —**ar,terial-i'zation** or **-li'sation** n.

arteriole (ɑː'tɪərɪ,əʊl) n. Anat. any of the small subdivisions of an artery that form thin-walled vessels ending in capillaries. [C19: from NL, from L artēria ARTERY]

arteriosclerosis (ɑː,tɪərɪəʊsklɪə'rəʊsɪs) n., pl. -ses (-siːz). a thickening and loss of elasticity of the walls of

the arteries. Nontechnical name: **hardening of the arteries.** —**arteriosclerotic** (ɑː,tɪərɪəʊsklɪə'rɒtɪk) adj.

artery ('ɑːtərɪ) n., pl. **-teries**. **1.** any of the tubular thick-walled muscular vessels that convey oxygenated blood from the heart to various parts of the body. Cf. **pulmonary artery, vein**. **2.** a major road or means of communication. [C14: from L artēria, rel. to Gk aortē the great artery, AORTA]

artesian well (ɑː'tiːzɪən) n. a well sunk through impermeable strata into strata receiving water from an area at a higher altitude than that of the well, so the water is forced to flow upwards. [C19: from F, from OF Arteis Artois, old province, where such wells were common]

Artex ('ɑːtɛks) n. Trademark. a textured coating for walls and ceilings.

art form n. **1.** an accepted mode of artistic composition, such as the sonnet, symphony, etc. **2.** a recognized medium of artistic expression.

artful ('ɑːtfʊl) adj. **1.** cunning or tricky. **2.** skilful in achieving a desired end. —'**artfully** adv. —'**artfulness** n.

arthralgia (ɑː'θrældʒə) n. Pathol. pain in a joint. —**ar'thralgic** adj.

arthritis (ɑː'θraɪtɪs) n. inflammation of a joint or joints characterized by pain and stiffness of the affected parts. [C16: via L from Gk arthron joint + -ITIS] —**arthritic** (ɑː'θrɪtɪk) adj., n.

arthropod ('ɑːθrə,pɒd) n. an invertebrate having jointed limbs, a segmented body, and an exoskeleton made of chitin, as the crustaceans, insects, arachnids, and centipedes. [C19: from NL, from Gk arthron joint + -podus footed, from pous foot]

Arthur ('ɑːθə) n. **1.** a legendary king of the Britons in the sixth century A.D., who led Celtic resistance against the Saxons: possibly based on a historical figure; represented as leader of the Knights of the Round Table at Camelot. **2. Chester Alan.** 1830–86, 21st president of the U.S. (1881–85).

Arthurian (ɑː'θjʊərɪən) adj. of or relating to King Arthur and his Knights of the Round Table.

artic (ɑː'tɪk) n. Inf. short for **articulated lorry.**

artichoke ('ɑːtɪ,tʃəʊk) n. **1.** Also called: **globe artichoke.** a thistle-like Eurasian plant, cultivated for its large edible flower head. **2.** the unopened flower head of this plant, which can be cooked and eaten. **3.** See **Jerusalem artichoke.** [C16: from It., from OSp., from Ar. al-kharshūf]

article ('ɑːtɪkəl) n. **1.** one of a class of objects; item. **2.** an unspecified or previously named thing, esp. a small object. **3.** a written composition on a subject, often being one of several found in a magazine, newspaper, etc. **4.** Grammar. a kind of determiner, occurring in many languages including English, that lacks independent meaning. See also **definite article, indefinite article**. **5.** a clause or section in a written document. **6.** (often cap.) Christianity. See **Thirty-nine Articles.** ~vb. (tr.) **7.** to bind by a written contract, esp. one that governs a period of training: an articled clerk. [C13: from OF, from L articulus small joint, from artus joint]

articular (ɑː'tɪkjʊlə) adj. of or relating to joints or to the structural components in a joint. [C15: from L articulāris concerning the joints, from articulus small joint]

articulate adj. (ɑː'tɪkjʊlɪt). **1.** able to express oneself fluently and coherently. **2.** having the power of speech. **3.** distinct, clear, or definite: an articulate document. **4.** Zool. (of arthropods and higher vertebrates) possessing joints or jointed segments. ~vb. (ɑː'tɪkjʊ,leɪt). **5.** to speak or enunciate (words, syllables, etc.) clearly and distinctly. **6.** (tr.) to express coherently in words. **7.** (intr.) Zool. to be jointed or form a joint. [C16: from L articulāre to divide into joints] —**ar'ticulately** adv. —**ar'ticulateness** n. —**ar'ticu,lator** n.

articulated lorry n. a large lorry made in two separate sections, a tractor and a trailer, connected by a pivoted bar.

articulation (ɑː,tɪkjʊ'leɪʃən) n. **1.** the act or process of speaking or expressing in words. **2. a.** the process of articulating a speech sound. **b.** the sound so produced, esp. a consonant. **3.** the act or state of being jointed together. **4.** Zool. **a.** a joint such as that between bones or arthropod segments. **b.** the way in which jointed parts are connected. **5.** Bot. the part of a plant at which natural separation occurs.

artifact ('ɑːtɪ,fækt) *n.* a variant spelling of **artefact.**

artifice ('ɑːtɪfɪs) *n.* **1.** a clever expedient. **2.** crafty or subtle deception. **3.** skill; cleverness. **4.** a skilfully contrived device. [C16: from OF, from L *artificium* skill, from *artifex* one possessed of a specific skill, from *ars* skill + *-fex,* from *facere* to make]

artificer (ɑː'tɪfɪsə) *n.* **1.** a skilled craftsman. **2.** a clever or inventive designer. **3.** a serviceman trained in mechanics.

artificial (,ɑːtɪ'fɪʃəl) *adj.* **1.** produced by man; not occurring naturally. **2.** made in imitation of a natural product: *artificial cream.* **3.** pretended; insincere. **4.** lacking in spontaneity; affected: *an artificial laugh.* [C14: from L *artificiālis* belonging to art, from *artificium* skill, ARTIFICE] —**artificiality** (,ɑːtɪ,fɪʃɪ'ælɪtɪ) *n.* —,**arti'ficially** *adv.*

artificial insemination *n.* introduction of spermatozoa into the vagina or uterus by means other than sexual union.

artificial intelligence *n.* the ability of a machine, such as a computer, to imitate intelligent human behaviour.

artificial respiration *n.* **1.** any of various methods of restarting breathing after it has stopped. **2.** any method of maintaining respiration, as by use of an iron lung.

artillery (ɑː'tɪlərɪ) *n.* **1.** guns, cannon, mortars, etc., of calibre greater than 20mm. **2.** troops or military units specializing in using such guns. **3.** the science dealing with the use of guns. [C14: from OF, from *artillier* to equip with weapons, from ?]

artiodactyl (,ɑːtɪəʊ'dæktɪl) *n.* an ungulate with an even number of toes, as pigs, camels, deer, cattle, etc. [C19: from Gk *artios* even-numbered + *daktulos* finger]

artisan ('ɑːtɪ,zæn, ,ɑːtɪ'zæn) *n.* a skilled workman; craftsman. [C16: from F, from OIt. *artigiano,* from *arte* ART[1]]

artist ('ɑːtɪst) *n.* **1.** a person who practises or is skilled in an art, esp. painting, drawing, or sculpture. **2.** a person who displays in his work qualities required in art, such as sensibility and imagination. **3.** a person whose profession requires artistic expertise. **4.** a person skilled in some task or occupation. **5.** *Sl.* a person devoted to or proficient in something: *a con artist; a booze artist.* —**ar'tistic** *adj.* —**ar'tistically** *adv.*

artiste (ɑː'tiːst) *n.* **1.** an entertainer, such as a singer or dancer. **2.** a person who is highly skilled in some occupation: *a hair artiste.* [F]

artistry ('ɑːtɪstrɪ) *n.* **1.** artistic workmanship, ability, or quality. **2.** artistic pursuits. **3.** great skill.

artless ('ɑːtlɪs) *adj.* **1.** free from deceit; ingenuous: *an artless remark.* **2.** natural; unpretentious. **3.** without art or skill. —'**artlessly** *adv.*

Art Nouveau (ɑː nuː'vəʊ; *French* ar nuvo) *n.* a style of art and architecture of the 1890s, characterized by sinuous outlines and stylized natural forms. [F, lit.: new art]

Artois (*French* artwa) *n.* a former province of N France.

art paper *n.* a high-quality type of paper having a smooth coating of china clay or similar substance on it.

arts (ɑːts) *pl. n.* **1. a. the.** imaginative, creative, and non-scientific branches of knowledge considered collectively, esp. as studied academically. **b.** (*as modifier*): *an arts degree.* **2.** See **fine art. 3.** cunning actions or schemes.

art union *n. Austral. & N.Z.* an officially approved lottery for prizes of cash or (formerly) works of art.

arty ('ɑːtɪ) *adj.* **artier, artiest.** *Inf.* having an affected interest in artists or art. —'**artiness** *n.*

Aruba (ə'ruːbə; *Dutch* a'ryːba:) *n.* an island in the West Indies, in the Netherlands Antilles off the NW coast of Venezuela. Chief town: Oranjestad. Pop.: 67 014 (1983 est.). Area: about 181 sq. km (70 sq. miles).

Aru Islands or **Arru Islands** ('ɑːruː) *pl. n.* a group of islands in Indonesia, in the SW Moluccas. Area: about 8500 sq. km (3300 sq. miles).

arum ('ɛərəm) *n.* **1.** any of various aroid plants of Europe and the Mediterranean region, having arrow-shaped leaves and a typically white spathe, such as the cuckoopint. **2. arum lily.** another name for **calla** (sense 1). [C16: from L, var. of *aros* wake-robin, from Gk *aron*]

Arunachal Pradesh (,ɑːrə'nɑːkəl prə'deʃ) *n.* a state in NE India, formed in 1986 from the former Union Territory. Capital: Itanagar. Pop.: 628 050 (1981). Area: 81 426 sq. km (31 756 sq. miles). Former name (until 1972): **North East Frontier Agency.**

Arundel ('ærəndəl) *n.* a town in S England, in West Sussex: 11th-century castle. Pop.: 2235 (1981).

Aruwimi (,ɑːruː'wiːmɪ) *n.* a river in NE Zaïre, rising near Lake Albert as the Ituri and flowing west into the River Congo (Zaire). Length: about 1288 km (800 miles).

arvo ('ɑːvəʊ) *n. Austral. inf.* afternoon.

-ary *suffix.* **1.** (*forming adjectives*) of; related to; belonging to: *cautionary.* **2.** (*forming nouns*) a person or thing connected with: *missionary; aviary.* [from L *-ārius, -āria, -ārium*]

Aryan ('ɛərɪən) *n.* **1.** (in Nazi ideology) a Caucasian of non-Jewish descent. **2.** a member of any of the peoples supposedly descended from the Indo-Europeans. ~*adj.* **3.** of or characteristic of an Aryan or Aryans. ~*adj.,* *n.* **4.** *Arch.* Indo-European. [C19: from Sansk. *ārya* of noble birth]

as[1] (æz; *unstressed* əz) *conj.* (*subordinating*) **1.** (often preceded by *just*) while; when: *he caught me as I was leaving.* **2.** in the way that: *dancing as only she can.* **3.** that which; what: *I did as I was told.* **4.** (of) which fact, event, etc. (referring to the previous statement): *to become wise, as we all know, is not easy.* **5. as it were.** in a way; as if it were really so. **6.** since; seeing that. **7.** in the same way that: *he died of cancer, as his father had done.* **8.** for instance: *capital cities, as London.* ~*adv., conj.* **9. a.** used to indicate identity of extent, amount, etc.: *she is as heavy as her sister.* **b.** used with this sense after a noun phrase introduced by *the same: the same height as her sister.* ~*prep.* **10.** in the role of; being: *his friend, my opinions are probably biased.* **11. as for** or **to.** with reference to: *as for my past, I'm not telling you anything.* **12. as if** or **though.** as it would be if: *he talked as if he knew all about it.* **13. as (it) is.** in the existing state of affairs. **14. as was.** in a previous state. [OE *alswā* likewise]

as[2] (æs) *n.* **1.** an ancient Roman unit of weight approximately equal to 1 pound troy (373 grams). **2.** a copper coin of ancient Rome. [C17: from L *ās* unity]

As *symbol for:* **1.** altostratus. **2.** *Chem.* arsenic.

AS *abbrev. for:* **1.** Also: **A.S.** Anglo-Saxon. **2.** antisubmarine.

ASA *abbrev. for:* **1.** (in Britain) Amateur Swimming Association. **2.** (in the U.S.) American Standards Association.

ASA/BS *abbrev.* an expression of the speed of a photographic film. [C20: from *American Standards Association/British Standard*]

asafoetida or **asafetida** (,æsə'fetɪdə) *n.* a bitter resin with an unpleasant onion-like smell, obtained from the roots of some umbelliferous plants: formerly used to treat flatulence, etc. [C14: from Med. L, from *asa* gum (cf. Persian *azā* mastic) + L *foetidus* evil-smelling]

a.s.a.p. *abbrev. for* as soon as possible.

Asben (æs'bɛn) *n.* another name for **Aïr** (region of the Sahara).

asbestos (æs'bɛstɒs) *n.* **a.** any of the fibrous amphibole minerals that are incombustible and resistant to chemicals. It was formerly widely used in the form of fabric or board as a heat-resistant structural material. **b.** (*as modifier*): *asbestos matting.* [C14: via L from Gk: from *asbestos* inextinguishable, from A-[1] + *shennunai* to extinguish]

asbestosis (,æsbɛs'təʊsɪs) *n.* inflammation of the lungs resulting from chronic inhalation of asbestos particles.

Ascanius (æ'skeɪnɪəs) *n. Roman myth.* the son of Aeneas and Creusa; founder of Alba Longa, mother city of Rome. Also called: **Iulus.**

ascarid ('æskərɪd) *n.* a parasitic nematode worm such as the common roundworm of man and pigs. [C14: from NL, from Gk *askarides,* pl. of *askaris*]

ascend (ə'sɛnd) *vb.* **1.** to go or move up (a ladder, hill, slope, etc.). **2.** (*intr.*) to slope or incline upwards. **3.** (*intr.*) to rise to a higher point, level, etc. **4.** to trace (a genealogy, etc.) back in time. **5.** to sing or play (a scale, etc.) from the lower to higher notes. **6. ascend the throne.** to become king or queen. [C14: from L *ascendere,* from *scandere*]

ascendancy, ascendency (ə'sɛndənsɪ) or **ascendance, ascendence** *n.* the condition of being dominant.

ascendant or **ascendent** (ə'sɛndənt) *adj.* **1.** proceeding upwards; rising. **2.** dominant or influential. ~*n.* **3.** a position or condition of dominance. **4.** *Astrol.* (*sometimes cap.*) **a.** a point on the ecliptic that rises on the eastern horizon at a particular moment. **b.** the sign of the zodiac containing this point. **5. in the ascendant.** increasing in influence, etc.

ascender (ə'sɛndə) *n.* **1.** *Printing.* **a.** the part of certain lower-case letters, such as *b* or *h*, that extends above the body of the letter. **b.** any letter having such a part. **2.** a person or thing that ascends.

ascension (ə'sɛnʃən) *n.* the act of ascending. —**as'censional** *adj.*

Ascension[1] (ə'sɛnʃən) *n. Bible.* the passing of Jesus Christ from earth into heaven (Acts 1:9).

Ascension[2] (ə'sɛnʃən) *n.* an island in the S Atlantic, northwest of St Helena: uninhabited until claimed by Britain in 1815. Pop.: 971 (1981). Area: 88 sq. km (34 sq. miles).

Ascension Day *n.* the 40th day after Easter, when the Ascension of Christ into heaven is celebrated.

ascent (ə'sɛnt) *n.* **1.** the act of ascending; upward movement. **2.** an upward slope. **3.** movement back through time (esp. in **line of ascent**).

ascertain (ˌæsə'teɪn) *vb.* (*tr.*) **1.** to determine definitely. **2.** *Arch.* to make certain. [C15: from OF *acertener* to make certain] —ˌascer'tainable *adj.* —ˌascer'tainment *n.*

ascetic (ə'sɛtɪk) *n.* **1.** a person who practises great self-denial and abstains from worldly comforts and pleasures, esp. for religious reasons. ~*adj. also* **ascetical.** **2.** rigidly abstinent or abstemious. **3.** of or relating to ascetics or asceticism. [C17: from Gk *askētikos*, from *askētēs*, from *askein* to exercise] —**as'cetically** *adv.*

Asch (æʃ) *n.* **Sholem** ('ʃəʊləm). 1880–1957, U.S. writer, born in Poland, who wrote in Yiddish. His works include biblical novels.

Aschaffenburg (*German* a'ʃafənbʊrk) *n.* a city in central West Germany, on the River Main in Bavaria: seat of the Imperial Diet (1447); ceded to Bavaria in 1814. Pop.: 55 100 (1970).

Ascham ('æskəm) *n.* **Roger.** ?1515–68, English humanist writer and classical scholar: tutor to Queen Elizabeth I.

ascidian (ə'sɪdɪən) *n.* any of a class of minute marine invertebrate animals, such as the sea squirt, the adults of which are degenerate and sedentary.

ascidium (ə'sɪdɪəm) *n., pl.* **-cidia** (-'sɪdɪə). part of a plant that is shaped like a pitcher, such as the modified leaf of the pitcher plant. [C18: from NL, from Gk *askidion* a little bag, from *askos* bag]

Asclepius (ə'skliːpɪəs) *n. Greek myth.* a god of healing; son of Apollo. Roman counterpart: **Aesculapius** (ˌiːskjʊ'leɪpɪəs).

Ascoli Piceno (*Italian* 'askoli pi'tʃɛːno) *n.* a town in E central Italy, in the Marches: capital of the Roman province of Picenum; site of the massacre of all its Roman citizens in the Social War in 90 B.C. Pop.: 54 298 (1981). Latin name: **Asculum Picenum** ('æskjʊləm paɪ'siːnəm).

ascomycete (ˌæskəmaɪ'siːt) *n.* any of a class of fungi in which the spores (ascospores) are formed inside a club-shaped cell (ascus). The group includes yeast, penicillium, and certain mildews. —ˌascomy'cetous *adj.*

ascorbic acid (ə'skɔːbɪk) *n.* a white crystalline vitamin present in plants, esp. citrus fruits, tomatoes, and green vegetables. A deficiency in the diet of man leads to scurvy. Also called: **vitamin C.**

ascribe (ə'skraɪb) *vb.* (*tr.*) **1.** to credit or assign, as to a particular origin or period. **2.** to consider as belonging to: *to ascribe beauty to youth.* [C15: from L *ascrībere* to enrol, from *ad* in addition + *scrībere* to write] —**as'cribable** *adj.*

ascription (ə'skrɪpʃən) *n.* **1.** the act of ascribing. **2.** a statement ascribing something to someone. [C16: from L *ascrīptiō*, from *ascrībere* to ASCRIBE]

asdic ('æzdɪk) *n.* an early form of **sonar.** [C20: from A(*nti*-)S(*ubmarine*) D(*etection*) I(*nvestigation*) C(*ommittee*)]

-ase *suffix forming nouns.* indicating an enzyme: *oxidase.* [from DIASTASE]

ASEAN ('æsiˌæn) *n. acronym for* Association of South-East Asian Nations.

asepsis (ə'sɛpsɪs, eɪ-) *n.* **1.** the state of being free from living pathogenic organisms. **2.** the methods of achieving a germ-free condition. —**a'septic** *adj.*

asexual (eɪ'sɛksjʊəl) *adj.* **1.** having no apparent sex or sex organs. **2.** (of reproduction) not involving the fusion of male and female gametes. —ˌasexu'ality *n.* —a'sexually *adv.*

Asgard ('æsgɑːd) *or* **Asgarth** ('æsgɑːθ) *n. Norse myth.* the dwelling place of the principal gods, the Aesir.

ash[1] (æʃ) *n.* **1.** the residue formed when matter is burnt. **2.** fine particles of lava thrown out by an erupting volcano. **3.** a light silvery-grey colour. ~See also **ashes.** [OE *æsce*]

ash[2] (æʃ) *n.* **1.** a tree having compound leaves, clusters of small greenish flowers, and winged seeds. **2.** the wood of this tree, used for tool handles, etc. **3.** any of several trees resembling the ash, such as the mountain ash. **4.** *Austral.* any of various eucalypts. [OE *æsc*]

ash[3] (æʃ) *n.* the digraph *æ*, as in Old English, representing a vowel approximately like that of the *a* in Modern English *hat.*

ASH (æʃ) *n.* (in Britain) *acronym for* Action on Smoking and Health.

ashamed (ə'ʃeɪmd) *adj.* (*usually postpositive*) **1.** overcome with shame or remorse. **2.** (foll. by *of*) suffering from feelings of shame in relation to (a person or deed). **3.** (foll. by *to*) unwilling through fear of humiliation, shame, etc. [OE *āscamod*, p.p. of *āscamian* to shame, from *scamu* SHAME] —**ashamedly** (ə'ʃeɪmɪdlɪ) *adv.*

Ashanti (ə'ʃæntɪ) *n.* **1.** an administrative region of central Ghana: former native kingdom, suppressed by the British in 1900 after four wars. Capital: Kumasi. Pop.: 2 089 683 (1984). Area: 24 390 sq. km (9417 sq. miles). **2.** (*pl.* **-ti** *or* **-tis**) a native or inhabitant of Ashanti.

A shares *pl. n.* ordinary shares in a company which carry restricted voting rights.

ash can *n.* a U.S. word for **dustbin.** Also called: **garbage can, ash bin, trash can.**

Ashcroft ('æʃkrɒft) *n.* Dame **Peggy.** born 1907, English stage and film actress.

Ashdown ('æʃdaʊn) *n.* **Paddy,** real name *Jeremy John Dunham Ashdown.* born 1941, British politician; leader of the Social and Liberal Democratic Party from 1988.

Ashe (æʃ) *n.* **Arthur** (**Robert**). born 1943, U.S. tennis player: U.S. champion 1968; Wimbledon champion 1975.

ashen[1] ('æʃən) *adj.* **1.** drained of colour. **2.** consisting of or resembling ashes. **3.** of a pale greyish colour.

ashen[2] ('æʃən) *adj.* of, relating to, or made from the ash tree or its timber.

Asher ('æʃə) *n.* the son of Jacob and ancestor of one of the 12 tribes of Israel.

ashes ('æʃɪz) *pl. n.* **1.** ruins or remains, as after burning. **2.** the remains of a human body after cremation.

Ashes ('æʃɪz) *pl. n.* **the.** a cremated cricket bail constituting a trophy competed for by England and Australia in test cricket since 1882. [from a mock obituary of English cricket after a great Australian victory]

Ashford ('æʃfəd) *n.* a market town in SE England, in central Kent. Pop.: 47 000 (1985).

Ashkenazi (ˌæʃkə'nɑːzɪ) *n., pl.* **-zim** (-zɪm). **1.** (*modifier*) of or relating to the Jews of Germany and E Europe. **2.** a Jew of German or E European descent. Cf. **Sephardi.** [C19: LHeb., from Heb. *Ashkenaz,* the son of Gomer (Genesis 10:3; I Chronicles 1:6)]

Ashkenazy (ˌæʃkə'nɑːzɪ) *n.* **Vladimir.** born 1937 in the Soviet Union, pianist and conductor.

Ashkhabad (*Russian* aʃxa'bat) *n.* a city in the SW Soviet Union, capital of the Turkmen SSR. Pop.: 382 000 (1987).

ashlar *or* **ashler** ('æʃlə) *n.* **1.** a square block of hewn stone for use in building. **2.** a thin dressed stone with straight edges, used to face a wall. **3.** masonry made of ashlar. [C14: from OF *aisselier* crossbeam, from *ais* board, from L *axis* axletree]

ashore (ə'ʃɔː) *adv.* **1.** towards or onto land from the water. ~*adj.* (*postpositive*), *adv.* **2.** on land: *a day ashore before sailing.*

ashram ('æʃrəm) *n.* a religious retreat or community where a Hindu holy man lives. [from Sansk. *āśrama,* from *ā-* near + *śrama* religious exertion]

Ashton ('æʃtən) *n.* Sir **Frederick.** 1906–88, British ballet dancer and choreographer. His ballets include *Façade* (1931), to music by Walton, *La Fille mal gardée* (1960), *The Dream* (1964), and *A Month in the Country* (1976).

Ashton-under-Lyne (laɪn) *n.* a town in NW England, in Greater Manchester. Pop.: 44 671 (1981).

Ashtoreth ('æʃtəˌrɛθ) *n. Old Testament.* an ancient Semitic fertility goddess, identified with Astarte and Ishtar.

ashtray ('æʃˌtreɪ) *n.* a receptacle for tobacco ash, cigarette butts, etc.

Ashur ('æʃʊə) *n.* a variant spelling of **Assur.**

Ashurbanipal (ˌæʃʊə'bɑːnɪˌpæl) *or* **Assurbanipal** *n.* died ?626 B.C., king of Assyria (?668–?626): son of Esarhaddon. He built the magnificent palace and library at Nineveh. Greek name: **Sardanapalus.**

Ash Wednesday *n.* the first day of Lent, named from the former Christian custom of sprinkling ashes on penitents' heads.

ashy ('æʃɪ) *adj.* **ashier, ashiest.** **1.** of a pale greyish colour; ashen. **2.** consisting of, covered with, or resembling ash.

'Asi ('æsɪ) *n.* the Arabic name for the **Orontes.**

Asia ('eɪʃə, 'eɪʒə) *n.* the largest of the continents, bordering on the Arctic Ocean, the Pacific Ocean, the Indian Ocean, and the Mediterranean and Red Seas in the west. It includes the large peninsulas of Asia Minor, India, Arabia, and Indochina and the island groups of Japan, Indonesia, the Philippines, and Ceylon; contains the mountain ranges of the Hindu Kush, Himalayas, Pamirs, Tian Shan, Urals, and Caucasus, the great plateaus of India, Iran, and Tibet, vast plains and deserts, and the valleys of many large rivers including the Mekong, Irrawaddy, Indus, Ganges, Tigris, and Euphrates. Pop.: 2 625 000 000 (1981 est.). Area: 44 391 162 sq. km (17 139 445 sq. miles).

Asia Minor *n.* the historical name for **Anatolia.**

Asian ('eɪʃən, 'eɪʒən) *adj.* **1.** of or relating to Asia or to any of its peoples or languages. ~*n.* **2.** a native or inhabitant of Asia or a descendant of one.

▷ **Usage.** *Asian* is used in formal writing as a noun indicating a person from Asia. The use of the word *Asiatic* in this sense is regarded by some people as offensive.

Asian flu *n.* a type of influenza caused by a virus which apparently originated in China in 1957.

Asiatic (ˌeɪʃɪ'ætɪk, -zɪ-) *n., adj.* another word for **Asian.**

Asiatic cholera *n.* another name for **cholera.**

aside (ə'saɪd) *adv.* **1.** on or to one side. **2.** out of hearing; in or into seclusion. **3.** away from oneself: *he threw the book aside.* **4.** out of mind or consideration: *he put aside all fears.* **5.** in or into reserve: *to put aside money for old age.* ~*n.* **6.** something spoken by an actor, intended to be heard by the audience, but not by the others on stage. **7.** any confidential statement spoken in undertones. **8.** an incidental remark, note, etc.

A-side *n.* the side of a gramophone record regarded as more important.

asinine ('æsɪˌnaɪn) *adj.* **1.** obstinate or stupid. **2.** resembling an ass. [C16: from L *asininus*, from *asinus* ASS[1]] —**'asiˌninely** *adv.* —**asininity** (ˌæsɪ'nɪnɪtɪ) *n.*

ASIO *abbrev. for* Australian Security Intelligence Organization.

Asir (æ'sɪə) *n.* a region of SW Saudi Arabia, in the Southern Province on the Red Sea: under Turkish rule until 1933. Pop.: about 1 000 000 (1970 est.). Area: 103 600 sq. km (40 000 sq. miles).

ask (ɑːsk) *vb.* **1.** (often foll. by *about*) to put a question (to); request an answer (from). **2.** (*tr.*) to inquire about: *she asked the way.* **3.** (*tr.*) to direct or put (a question). **4.** (*may take a clause as object or an infinitive;* often foll. by *for*) to make a request or demand: *they asked for a deposit.* **5.** (*tr.*) to demand or expect (esp. in **ask a lot of, ask too much of**). **6.** (*tr.*) Also: **ask out, ask over.** to request (a person) politely to come or go to a place: *he asked her to the party.* [OE *āscian*] —**'asker** *n.*

Ask (ɑːsk) *n. Norse myth.* the first man, created by the gods from an ash tree.

ask after *vb.* (*prep.*) to make inquiries about the health of (someone): *he asked after her mother.*

askance (ə'skæns) *or* **askant** (ə'skænt) *adv.* **1.** with an oblique glance. **2.** with doubt or mistrust. [C16: from ?]

askew (ə'skjuː) *adv., adj.* at an oblique angle; towards one side; awry.

ask for *vb.* (*prep.*) **1.** to try to obtain by requesting. **2.** (*intr.*) *Inf.* to behave in a provocative manner that is regarded as inviting (trouble, etc.): *you're asking for it.*

asking price *n.* the price suggested by a seller but usually considered to be subject to bargaining.

Askja ('ɑːskjə) *n.* a volcano in E central Iceland: active in 1961; largest crater in Iceland. Height: 1510 m (4954 ft.). Area of crater: 88 sq. km (34 sq. miles).

aslant (ə'slɑːnt) *adv.* **1.** at a slant. ~*prep.* **2.** at a slant across or athwart.

asleep (ə'sliːp) *adj.* (*postpositive*) **1.** in or into a state of sleep. **2.** in or into a dormant or inactive state. **3.** (of limbs) numb; lacking sensation. **4.** *Euphemistic.* dead.

ASLEF ('æzlɛf) *n.* (in Britain) *acronym for* Associated Society of Locomotive Engineers and Firemen.

ASM *abbrev. for* air-to-surface missile.

Asmara (æs'mɑːrə) *n.* a city in Ethiopia: capital of Eritrea. Pop.: 275 385 (1984 est.).

Asnières (*French* anjɛr) *n.* a suburb of Paris, on the Seine. Pop.: 75 365 (1983 est.).

Aso ('ɑːsəʊ) *n.* a group of five volcanic cones in Japan on central Kyushu, one of which, Naka-dake, has the largest crater in the world, between 16 km (10 miles) and 24 km (15 miles) in diameter. Highest cone: 1592 m (5223 ft.). Also called: **Asosan** (ˌɑːsəʊ'sɑːn).

asocial (eɪ'səʊʃəl) *adj.* **1.** avoiding contact. **2.** unconcerned about the welfare of others. **3.** hostile to society.

Asoka (ə'səʊkə, ə'ʃəʊ-) *n.* died 232 B.C., Indian emperor (?273–232 B.C.), who elevated Buddhism to the official state religion.

asp (æsp) *n.* **1.** the venomous snake that caused the death of Cleopatra. **2.** Also called: **asp viper.** a viper that occurs in S Europe and is very similar to but smaller than the adder. **3. horned asp.** another name for **horned viper.** [C15: from L *aspis*, from Gk]

asparagus (ə'spærəgəs) *n.* **1.** a plant of the lily family, having small scaly or needle-like leaves. **2.** the succulent young shoots, which may be cooked and eaten. **3. asparagus fern.** a fernlike species of asparagus, native to southern Africa. [C15: from L, from Gk *asparagos*, from ?]

aspartame (ə'spɑːˌteɪm) *n.* an artificial sweetener produced from a nonessential amino acid. [C20: from *aspart(ic acid)* + (*phenyl*)*a*(*lanine*) *m*(*ethyl*) *e*(*ster*)]

Aspasia (ə'speɪzɪə) *n.* 5th century B.C., Greek courtesan; mistress of Pericles.

aspect ('æspɛkt) *n.* **1.** appearance to the eye; visual effect. **2.** a distinct feature or element in a problem, situation, etc.; facet. **3.** the way in which a problem, idea, etc., may be considered. **4.** a facial expression: *a severe aspect.* **5.** a position facing a particular direction: *the southern aspect of a house.* **6.** a view in a certain direction. **7.** *Astrol.* any of several specific angular distances between two planets. **8.** *Grammar.* a category of verbal inflections that expresses such features as the continuity, repetition, or completedness of the action described. [C14: from L *aspectus* a sight, from *ad-* to, at + *specere* to look]

aspect ratio *n.* **1.** the ratio of width to height of a picture on a television or cinema screen. **2.** *Aeronautics.* the ratio of the span of a wing to its mean chord.

aspen ('æspən) *n.* a kind of poplar tree in which the leaves are attached to the stem by long flattened stalks so that they quiver in the wind. [OE *æspe*]

asperity (æ'spɛrɪtɪ) *n., pl.* **-ties.** **1.** roughness or sharpness of temper. **2.** roughness or harshness of a surface, sound, etc. [C16: from L *asperitās*, from *asper* rough]

asperse (ə'spɜːs) *vb.* (*tr.*) to spread false rumours about; defame. [C15: from L *aspersus*, from *aspergere* to sprinkle] —**as'perser** *n.* —**as'persive** *adj.*

aspersion (ə'spɜːʃən) *n.* **1.** a disparaging or malicious remark (esp. in **cast aspersions (on)**). **2.** the act of defaming.

asphalt ('æsfælt) *n.* **1.** any of several black semisolid substances composed of bitumen and inert mineral matter. They occur naturally and as a residue from petroleum distillation. **2.** a mixture of this substance with gravel, used in road-surfacing and roofing materials. **3.** (*modifier*) containing or surfaced with asphalt. ~*vb.* **4.** (*tr.*) to cover with asphalt. [C14: from LL *aspaltus*, from Gk *asphaltos*, prob. from A-[1] + *sphallein* to cause to fall; referring to its use as a binding agent] —**as'phaltic** *adj.*

asphodel ('æsfəˌdɛl) *n.* **1.** any of various S European plants of the lily family having clusters of white or yellow flowers. **2.** an unidentified flower of Greek legend said to cover the Elysian fields. [C16: from L *asphodelus*, from Gk *asphodelos*, from ?]

asphyxia (æs'fɪksɪə) *n.* lack of oxygen in the blood due to restricted respiration; suffocation. [C18: from NL, from Gk *asphuxia* a stopping of the pulse, from A-[1] + *sphuxis* pulse, from *sphuzein* to throb] —**as'phyxial** *adj.* —**as'phyxiant** *adj.*

asphyxiate (æs'fɪksɪˌeɪt) *vb.* to cause asphyxia in or undergo asphyxia; smother; suffocate. —**asˌphyxi'ation** *n.* —**as'phyxiˌator** *n.*

aspic ('æspɪk) n. a savoury jelly based on meat or fish stock, used as a relish or as a mould for meat, vegetables, etc. [C18: from F: aspic (jelly), asp]

aspidistra (ˌæspɪ'dɪstrə) n. a popular house plant of the lily family with long tough evergreen leaves. [C19: from NL, from Gk aspis shield, on the model of Tupistra, genus of liliaceous plants]

Aspinwall ('æspɪnˌwɔːl) n. the former name of **Colón**.

aspirant ('æspɪrənt) n. 1. a person who aspires, as to a high position. ~adj. 2. aspiring.

aspirate vb. ('æspɪˌreɪt). (tr.) 1. Phonetics. a. to articulate (a stop) with some force, so that breath escapes audibly. b. to pronounce (a word or syllable) with an initial h. 2. to remove by inhalation or suction, esp. to suck (air or fluid) from a body cavity. ~n. ('æspɪrɪt). 3. Phonetics. a. a stop pronounced with an audible release of breath. b. the glottal fricative represented in English and several other languages as h. ~adj. ('æspɪrɪt). 4. Phonetics. (of a stop) pronounced with a forceful expulsion of breath.

aspiration (ˌæspɪ'reɪʃən) n. 1. strong desire to achieve something, such as success. 2. the aim of such desire. 3. the act of breathing. 4. Phonetics. a. the pronunciation of an aspirated consonant. b. an aspirated consonant. 5. Med. the sucking of fluid or foreign matter into the air passages of the body. —ˌaspi'rational adj. —aspiratory (ə'spaɪrətərɪ) adj.

aspirator ('æspɪˌreɪtə) n. a device employing suction, such as a jet pump or one for removing fluids from a body cavity.

aspire (ə'spaɪə) vb. (intr.) 1. (usually foll. by to or after) to yearn (for), desire, or hope (to do or be something): to aspire to be a great leader. 2. to rise to a great height. [C15: from L aspīrāre to breathe upon, from spīrāre to breathe] —as'piring adj.

aspirin ('æsprɪn) n., pl. **-rin** or **-rins**. 1. a white crystalline compound widely used in the form of tablets to relieve pain, fever, and colds. Chemical name: **acetylsalicylic acid**. 2. a tablet of aspirin. [C19: from G, from A(cetyl) + Spir(säure) spiraeic acid (modern salicylic acid) + -IN]

Aspirin ('æsprɪn) n. (in Canada) a trademark for **aspirin**.

asquint (ə'skwɪnt) adv., adj. (postpositive) with a glance from the corner of the eye, esp. a furtive one. [C13: ?from Du. schuinte slant, from ?]

Asquith ('æskwɪθ) n. **Herbert Henry,** 1st Earl of Oxford and Asquith. 1852–1928, British statesman; prime minister (1908–16); leader of the Liberal Party (1908–26).

ass¹ (æs) n. 1. a mammal related to the horse. It is hardy and sure-footed, having longer ears than the horse. 2. (not in technical use) the donkey. 3. a foolish or ridiculously pompous person. [OE assa, prob. from OIrish asan, from L asinus; rel. to Gk onos ass]

ass² (æs) n. the usual U.S. and Canad. word for **arse**. [OE ærs]

Assad ('asat) n. **Hafezal** ('hafɛzal). born 1928, Syrian statesman and general; president of Syria from 1971.

assagai ('æsəˌgaɪ) n., pl. **-gais.** a variant spelling of **assegai**.

assai (æ'saɪ) adv. Music. (usually preceded by a musical direction) very: allegro assai. [It.: enough]

assail (ə'seɪl) vb. (tr.) 1. to attack violently; assault. 2. to criticize or ridicule vehemently. 3. to beset or disturb: his mind was assailed by doubts. 4. to encounter with the intention of mastering. [C13: from OF asalir, from L assilīre, from salīre to leap] —as'sailable adj. —as'sailer n.

assailant (ə'seɪlənt) n. a person who attacks another, either physically or verbally.

Assam (æ'sæm) n. a state of NE India, situated in the central Brahmaputra valley: tropical forest, with the heaviest rainfall in the world; produces large quantities of tea. Capital: Dispur. Pop.: 19 902 826 (1981). Area: about 220 150 sq. km (85 000 sq. miles). —ˌAssa'mese adj., n.

assassin (ə'sæsɪn) n. a murderer, esp. one who kills a prominent political figure. [C16: from Med. L assassīnus, from Ar. hashshāshin, pl. of hashshāsh one who eats HASHISH]

assassinate (ə'sæsɪˌneɪt) vb. (tr.) 1. to murder (a political figure). 2. to ruin or harm (a person's reputation, etc.) by slander. —asˌsassi'nation n.

assault (ə'sɔːlt) n. 1. a violent attack, either physical or verbal. 2. Law. an act that causes violence to another. 3. a. the culmination of a military attack. b. (as modifier):

assault troops. 4. rape. ~vb. (tr.) 5. to make an assault upon. 6. to rape or attempt to rape. [C13: from OF asaut, from Vulgar L, from assalīre (unattested) to leap upon; see ASSAIL] —as'saultive adj.

assault and battery n. Criminal law. a threat of attack to another person followed by actual attack.

assault course n. an obstacle course designed to give soldiers practice in negotiating hazards.

assay vb. (ə'seɪ). 1. to subject (a substance, such as silver or gold) to chemical analysis, as in the determination of the amount of impurity. ~n. (ə'seɪ, 'æseɪ). 2. (tr.) to attempt (something or to do something). 3. a. an analysis, esp. a determination of the amount of metal in an ore or the amounts of impurities in a precious metal. b. (as modifier): an assay office. 4. a substance undergoing an analysis. 5. a written report on the results of an analysis. 6. a test. [C14: from OF assai; see ESSAY] —as'sayer n.

assegai or **assagai** ('æsəˌgaɪ) n., pl. **-gais.** 1. a southern African tree, the wood of which is used for making spears. 2. a sharp light spear. [C17: from Port. azagaia, from Ar. az zaghāyah, from al the + zaghāyah assegai, from Berber]

assemblage (ə'sɛmblɪdʒ) n. 1. a number of things or persons assembled together. 2. the act of assembling or the state of being assembled. 3. (ˌæsəm'blɑːʒ). a three-dimensional work of art that combines various objects.

assemble (ə'sɛmbᵊl) vb. 1. to come or bring together; collect or congregate. 2. to fit or join together (the parts of something, such as a machine). [C13: from OF assembler, from Vulgar L assimulāre (unattested) to bring together, from L simul together]

assembler (ə'sɛmblə) n. 1. a person or thing that assembles. 2. a computer program that converts a set of low-level symbolic data into machine language. Cf. **compiler**. 3. In full: **assembler language**. a symbolic language that uses an assembler program to convert to machine language.

assembly (ə'sɛmblɪ) n., pl. **-blies.** 1. a number of people gathered together, esp. for a formal meeting held at regular intervals. 2. the act of assembling or the state of being assembled. 3. the process of putting together a number of parts to make a machine. 4. Mil. a signal for personnel to assemble.

Assembly (ə'sɛmblɪ) n., pl. **-blies.** 1. the lower chamber in various state legislatures, esp. in Australia and America. See also **House of Assembly, legislative assembly.** 2. N.Z. short for **General Assembly.**

assembly language n. Computers. a programming language that uses mnemonic instruction codes, labels, and names to refer directly to their machine code equivalents.

assembly line n. a sequence of machines, tools, operations, workers, etc., in a factory, arranged so that at each stage a further process is carried out.

Assen (Dutch 'asə) n. a city in the N Netherlands, capital of Drenthe province. Pop.: 48 131 (1987).

assent (ə'sɛnt) n. 1. agreement, as to a statement, proposal, etc. 2. compliance. ~vb. (intr.; usually foll. by to) 3. to agree or express agreement. [C13: from OF assenter, from L assentīrī, from sentīre to think]

assert (ə'sɜːt) vb. (tr.) 1. to insist upon (rights, etc.). 2. (may take a clause as object) to state to be true; declare. 3. to put (oneself) forward in an insistent manner. [C17: from L asserere to join to oneself, from serere to join] —as'serter or as'sertor n.

assertion (ə'sɜːʃən) n. 1. a positive statement, usually made without evidence. 2. the act of asserting.

assertion sign n. a sign ⊢ used in symbolic logic to introduce the conclusion of a valid argument: often read as "therefore."

assertive (ə'sɜːtɪv) adj. given to making assertions; dogmatic or aggressive. —as'sertively adv. —as'sertiveness n.

assess (ə'sɛs) vb. (tr.) 1. to evaluate. 2. (foll. by at) to estimate the value of (income, property, etc.) for taxation purposes. 3. to determine the amount of (a fine, tax, etc.). 4. to impose a tax, fine, etc., on (a person or property). [C15: from OF assesser, from L assidēre to sit beside, from sedēre to sit] —as'sessable adj.

assessment (ə'sɛsmənt) n. 1. the act of assessing. esp., (in Britain) the evaluation of a student's achievement on a course. 2. an amount determined as payable. 3. a valuation set on taxable property, etc. 4. evaluation.

assessor (ə'sɛsə) n. **1.** a person who evaluates the merits of something. **2.** a person who values property for taxation. **3.** a person who estimates the value of damage to property for insurance purposes. **4.** a person with technical expertise called in to advise a court. —**assessorial** (,æsɛ'sɔːrɪəl) adj.

asset ('æsɛt) n. anything valuable or useful. [C19: back formation from ASSETS]

assets ('æsɛts) pl. n. **1.** Accounting. the property and claims against debtors that are shown balanced against liabilities. **2.** Law. the property available to an executor for settling a deceased person's estate. **3.** any property owned by a person or firm. [C16: from OF asez enough, from Vulgar L ad satis (unattested) from L ad up to + satis enough]

asset-stripping n. Commerce. the practice of taking over a failing company at a low price and then selling the assets piecemeal. —'**asset-**,**stripper** n.

asseverate (ə'sɛvə,reɪt) vb. (tr.) to declare solemnly. [C18: from L assevērāre to do (something) earnestly, from sevērus SEVERE] —**as**,**sever'ation** n.

Asshur ('æʃʊə) n. a variant spelling of **Assur**.

assibilate (ə'sɪbɪ,leɪt) vb. (tr.) Phonetics. to pronounce (a speech sound) with or as a sibilant. [C19: from LL assibilāre to hiss at, from OF asez enough. [C16: from OF asez enough, from sibilāre to hiss] —**as**,**sibi'lation** n.

assiduity (,æsɪ'djuːɪtɪ) n., pl. -ties. **1.** constant and close application. **2.** (often pl.) devoted attention.

assiduous (ə'sɪdjʊəs) adj. **1.** hard-working; persevering. **2.** undertaken with perseverance and care. [C16: from L, from assidēre to sit beside, from sedēre to sit] —**as'siduousness** n.

assign (ə'saɪn) vb. (mainly tr.) **1.** to select for and appoint to a post, etc. **2.** to give out or allot (a task, problem, etc.). **3.** to set apart (a place, person, time, etc.) for a particular function or event: to assign a day for the meeting. **4.** to attribute to a specified cause, origin, or source. **5.** to transfer (one's right, interest, or title to property) to someone else. ~n. **6.** Law. a person to whom property is assigned; assignee. [C14: from OF, from L assignāre, from signāre to mark out] —**as'signable** adj. —**as'signer** or ,**assign'or** n.

assignation (,æsɪg'neɪʃən) n. **1.** a secret or forbidden arrangement to meet, esp. one between lovers. **2.** the act of assigning; assignment. [C14: from OF, from L assignātiō a marking out]

assignee (,æsaɪ'niː) n. Law. a person to whom some right, interest, or property is transferred.

assignment (ə'saɪnmənt) n. **1.** something that has been assigned, such as a mission or task. **2.** a position or post to which a person is assigned. **3.** the act of assigning or state of being assigned. **4.** Law. **a.** the transfer to another of a right, interest, or title to property. **b.** the document effecting such a transfer.

assimilate (ə'sɪmɪ,leɪt) vb. **1.** (tr.) to learn (information, etc.) and understand it thoroughly. **2.** (tr.) to absorb (food). **3.** (intr.) to become absorbed, incorporated, or learned and understood. **4.** (usually foll. by into or with) to adjust or become adjusted: the new immigrants assimilated easily. **5.** (usually foll. by to or with) to become or cause to become similar. **6.** (usually foll. by to) Phonetics. to change (a consonant) or (of a consonant) to be changed into another under the influence of one adjacent to it. [C15: from L assimilāre to make one thing like another, from similis like, SIMILAR] —**as'similable** adj. —**as**,**simi'lation** n. —**as'similative** or **as'similatory** adj. —**as'simi**,**lator** n.

Assiniboine (ə'sɪnɪ,bɔɪn) n. a river in W Canada, rising in E Saskatchewan and flowing southeast and east to the Red River at Winnipeg. Length: over 860 km (500 miles).

Assisi (Italian as'siːzi) n. a town in central Italy, in Umbria: birthplace of St Francis, who founded the Franciscan religious order here in 1208. Pop.: 24 440 (1981 est.).

assist (ə'sɪst) vb. **1.** to give help or support to (a person, cause, etc.). **2.** to work or act as an assistant or subordinate to (another). ~n. **3.** U.S. the act of helping. [C15: from F, from L assistere to stand by, from sistere to cause to stand, from stāre to stand] —**as'sister** n.

assistance (ə'sɪstəns) n. **1.** help; support. **2.** the act of assisting. **3.** Brit. inf. See **national assistance**.

assistant (ə'sɪstənt) n. **1.** a person who assists, esp. in a subordinate position. **b.** (as modifier): assistant manager. **2.** See **shop assistant**.

Assiut (æ'sjuːt) n. a variant spelling of **Asyut**.

assize (ə'saɪz) n. Scots Law. **a.** trial by a jury. **b.** a jury. [C13: from OF assise session, from asseoir to seat, from L assidēre to sit beside]

assizes (ə'saɪzɪz) pl. n. (formerly in England and Wales) the sessions of the principal court in each county, exercising civil and criminal jurisdiction: replaced in 1971 by crown courts.

assn abbrev. for association.

assoc. abbrev. for: **1.** associate(d). **2.** association.

associate vb. (ə'səʊʃɪ,eɪt, -sɪ-). (usually foll. by with) **1.** (tr.) to link or connect in the mind or imagination. **2.** (intr.) to mix socially: to associate with writers. **3.** (intr.) to form or join an association, group, etc. **4.** (tr.; usually passive) to consider in conjunction: rainfall is associated with humidity. **5.** (tr.) to bring (a person, esp. oneself) into friendship, partnership, etc. **6.** (tr.; often passive) to express agreement (with): Bertrand Russell was associated with the CND movement. ~n. (ə'səʊʃɪɪt, -sɪ-). **7.** a person joined with another or others in an enterprise, business, etc. **8.** a companion or friend. **9.** something that usually accompanies another thing. **10.** a person having a subordinate position in or admitted to only partial membership of an institution, association, etc. ~adj. (ə'səʊʃɪɪt, -sɪ-). (prenominal) **11.** joined with another or others in an enterprise, business, etc.: an associate director. **12.** having partial rights or subordinate status: an associate member. **13.** accompanying; concomitant. [C14: from L associāre to ally with, from sociāre to join, from socius an ally] —**as'sociable** adj. —**as'sociator** n. —**as'sociate**,**ship** n.

association (ə,səʊsɪ'eɪʃən, -ʃɪ-) n. **1.** a group of people having a common purpose or interest; a society or club. **2.** the act of associating or the state of being associated. **3.** friendship or companionship: their association will not last. **4.** a mental connection of ideas, feelings, or sensations. **5.** Chem. the formation of groups of molecules and ions held together by weak chemical bonds. **6.** Ecology. a group of similar plants that grow in a uniform environment.

association football n. **1.** a more formal name for **soccer**. **2.** (in Australia) Australian Rules played in a football association rather than a league.

associative (ə'səʊʃɪətɪv, -sɪ-) adj. **1.** of, relating to, or causing association or union. **2.** Maths, logic. **a.** of an operation, such as multiplication or division, in which the answer is the same regardless of the way in which the elements are grouped: $(2 \times 3) \times 4 = 2 \times (3 \times 4)$. **b.** referring to this property: the associative laws of arithmetic.

assonance ('æsənəns) n. **1.** the use of the same vowel sound with different consonants or the same consonant with different vowels, as in a line of verse. Examples are time and light or mystery and mastery. **2.** partial correspondence. [C18: from F, from L assonāre to sound, from sonāre to sound] —'**assonant** adj., n.

assort (ə'sɔːt) vb. **1.** (tr.) to arrange or distribute into groups of the same type; classify. **2.** (intr.; usually foll. by with) to fit or fall into a class or group. **3.** (tr.) to supply with an assortment of merchandise. **4.** (tr.) to put in the same category as others. [C15: from OF assorter, from sorte SORT] —**as'sortative** adj.

assorted (ə'sɔːtɪd) adj. **1.** consisting of various kinds mixed together. **2.** classified: assorted categories. **3.** matched (esp. in **well-assorted, ill-assorted**).

assortment (ə'sɔːtmənt) n. **1.** a collection or group of various things or sorts. **2.** the act of assorting.

ASSR abbrev. for Autonomous Soviet Socialist Republic.

asst abbrev. for assistant.

assuage (ə'sweɪdʒ) vb. (tr.) **1.** to soothe, moderate, or relieve (grief, pain, etc.). **2.** to give relief to (thirst, etc.). **3.** to pacify; calm. [C14: from OF, from Vulgar L assuāviāre (unattested) to sweeten, from L suāvis pleasant] —**as'suagement** n. —**as'suager** n.

Assuan or **Assouan** (ɑːs'wɑːn) n. variant spellings of **Aswan**.

assume (ə'sjuːm) vb. (tr.) **1.** (may take a clause as object) to take for granted; suppose. **2.** to undertake or take on or over (a position, responsibility, etc.): to assume office. **3.** to pretend to; feign: he assumed indifference. **4.** to take or put on; adopt: the problem assumed gigantic proportions. **5.** to appropriate or usurp (power, control, etc.). [C15: from L assūmere to take up, from sūmere to

take up, from SUB- + *emere* to take] —**as'sumable** *adj.*
—**as'sumer** *n.*

assumed (ə'sjuːmd) *adj.* **1.** false; fictitious: *an assumed name.* **2.** taken for granted. **3.** usurped.

assuming (ə'sjuːmɪŋ) *adj.* **1.** expecting too much; presumptuous. ~*conj.* **2.** (often foll. by *that*) if it is assumed or taken for granted.

assumption (ə'sʌmpʃən) *n.* **1.** the act of taking something for granted or something that is taken for granted. **2.** an assuming of power or possession. **3.** presumption. **4.** *Logic.* a statement that is used as the premise of a particular argument but may not be otherwise accepted. [C13: from L *assūmptiō* a taking up, from *assūmere* to ASSUME] —**as'sumptive** *adj.*

Assumption (ə'sʌmpʃən) *n. Christianity.* **1.** the taking up of the Virgin Mary (body and soul) into heaven when her earthly life was ended. **2.** the feast commemorating this.

Assur, Asur ('æsə), **Asshur,** *or* **Ashur** ('æʃʊə) *n.* **1.** the supreme national god of the ancient Assyrians, chiefly a war god, whose symbol was an archer within a winged disc. **2.** one of the chief cities of ancient Assyria, on the River Tigris about 100 km (60 miles) downstream from the present-day city of Mosul.

assurance (ə'ʃʊərəns) *n.* **1.** a statement, assertion, etc., intended to inspire confidence. **2.** a promise or pledge of support. **3.** freedom from doubt; certainty. **4.** forwardness; impudence. **5.** *Chiefly Brit.* insurance providing for certainties such as death as contrasted with fire.

Assurbanipal (,æsʊə'bɑːnɪ,pæl) *n.* a variant spelling of **Ashurbanipal.**

assure (ə'ʃʊə) *vb.* (*tr.; may take a clause as object*) **1.** to convince: *to assure a person of one's love.* **2.** to promise; guarantee. **3.** to state positively. **4.** to make (an event) certain. **5.** *Chiefly Brit.* to insure against loss, esp. of life. [C14: from OF, from Med. L *assēcūrāre* to secure or make sure, from *sēcūrus* SECURE] —**as'surable** *adj.* —**as'surer** *n.*

assured (ə'ʃʊəd) *adj.* **1.** sure; guaranteed. **2.** self-assured. **3.** *Chiefly Brit.* insured. ~*n.* **4.** *Chiefly Brit.* **a.** the beneficiary under a life assurance policy. **b.** the person whose life is insured. —**assuredly** (ə'ʃʊərɪdlɪ) *adv.*

Assyria (ə'sɪrɪə) *n.* an ancient kingdom of N Mesopotamia: it established an empire that stretched from Egypt to the Persian Gulf, reaching its greatest extent between 721 and 633 B.C. Its chief cities were Assur and Nineveh. —**A'ssyrian** *adj., n.*

AST *abbrev. for* Atlantic Standard Time.

Astaire (ə'stɛə) *n.* **Fred,** real name *Frederick Austerlitz.* 1899–1987, U.S. dancer, singer, and actor, whose films include *Top Hat* (1935), *Swing Time* (1936), and *The Band Wagon* (1953).

Astarte (æ'stɑːtɪ) *n.* a fertility goddess worshipped by the Phoenicians: identified with Ashtoreth of the Hebrews and Ishtar of the Babylonians and Assyrians.

astatic (æ'stætɪk, eɪ-) *adj.* **1.** not static; unstable. **2.** *Physics.* having no tendency to assume any particular position or orientation. [C19: from Gk *astatos* unsteady] —**a'statically** *adv.*

astatine ('æstə,tiːn) *n.* a radioactive element that occurs naturally in minute amounts and is artificially produced by bombarding bismuth with alpha particles. Symbol: At; atomic no.: 85; half-life of most stable isotope, ^{210}At: 8.3 hours. [C20: from Gk *astatos* unstable]

aster ('æstə) *n.* **1.** a plant having white, blue, purple, or pink daisy-like flowers. **2. China aster.** a related Chinese plant widely cultivated for its showy brightly coloured flowers. [C18: from NL, from L *aster* star, from Gk]

-aster *suffix forming nouns.* a person or thing that is inferior to what is specified: *poetaster.* [from L]

asterisk ('æstərɪsk) *n.* **1.** a star-shaped character (*) used in printing or writing to indicate a cross-reference to a footnote, an omission, etc. ~*vb.* **2.** (*tr.*) to mark with an asterisk. [C17: from LL *asteriscus* a small star, from Gk, from *astēr* star]

asterism ('æstə,rɪzəm) *n.* **1.** three asterisks arranged in a triangle (⁂ or ⁂), to draw attention to the text that follows. **2.** a cluster of stars or a constellation. [C16: from Gk *asterismos* arrangement of constellations, from *astēr* star]

astern (ə'stɜːn) *adv., adj. (postpositive) Naut.* **1.** at or towards the stern. **2.** with the stern first: *full speed astern!* **3.** aft of the stern of a vessel.

asteroid ('æstə,rɔɪd) *n.* **1.** Also called: **minor planet, planetoid.** any of numerous small celestial bodies that move around the sun mainly between the orbits of Mars and Jupiter. **2.** a starfish. ~*adj. also* ,**aste'roidal. 3.** of a starfish. **4.** shaped like a star. [C19: from Gk *asteroeidēs* starlike, from *astēr* a star]

asthenia (æs'θiːnɪə) *n. Pathol.* an abnormal loss of strength; debility. [C19: via NL from Gk *astheneia* weakness, from A-¹ + *sthenos* strength]

asthenic (æs'θɛnɪk) *adj.* **1.** of or having asthenia; weak. **2.** referring to a physique characterized by long limbs and a small trunk. ~*n.* **3.** a person with long limbs and a small trunk.

asthma ('æsmə) *n.* a respiratory disorder, often of allergic origin, characterized by difficulty in breathing. [C14: from Gk: laborious breathing, from *azein* to breathe hard]

asthmatic (æs'mætɪk) *adj.* **1.** of or having asthma. ~*n.* **2.** a person who has asthma. —**asth'matically** *adv.*

Asti ('æstɪ) *n.* a town in NW Italy: famous for its sparkling wine (**Asti spumante** (spuː'mæntɪ)). Pop.: 76 439 (1983).

astigmatic (,æstɪg'mætɪk) *adj.* of, having, correcting, or corrected for astigmatism. [C19: from A-¹ + Gk *stigmat-, stigma* spot, focus] —,**astig'matically** *adv.*

astigmatism (ə'stɪgmə,tɪzəm) *or* **astigmia** (ə'stɪgmɪə) *n.* **1.** a defect of a lens resulting in the formation of distorted images, caused by light rays not meeting at a single focal point. **2.** faulty vision resulting from astigmatism of the lens of the eye.

astilbe (ə'stɪlbɪ) *n.* any perennial plant of the genus *Astilbe,* cultivated for its spikes of ornamental pink or white flowers. [C19: NL, from Gk A-¹ + *stilbē,* from *stilbein* to glitter; referring to its inconspicuous individual flowers]

astir (ə'stɜː) *adj. (postpositive)* **1.** awake and out of bed. **2.** in motion; on the move.

ASTMS (in Britain) *abbrev. for* Association of Scientific, Technical, and Managerial Staffs.

Astolat ('æstəʊ,læt) *n.* a town in Arthurian legend: location unknown.

Aston ('æstən) *n.* **Francis William.** 1877–1945, English physicist and chemist, who developed the first mass spectrograph, using it to investigate the isotopic structures of elements: Nobel prize for chemistry 1922.

astonish (ə'stɒnɪʃ) *vb.* (*tr.*) to fill with amazement; surprise greatly. [C15: from earlier *astonyen,* from OF, from Vulgar L *extonāre* (unattested) to strike with thunder, from L *tonāre* to thunder] —**a'stonishing** *adj.*

astonishment (ə'stɒnɪʃmənt) *n.* **1.** extreme surprise; amazement. **2.** a cause of amazement.

Astor ('æstə) *n.* **1. John Jacob,** 1st Baron Astor of Hever. 1886–1971, British proprietor of *The Times* (1922–66). **2.** Viscountess **Nancy Witcher Langhorne** ('wɪtʃə'læŋ,hɔːn). 1879–1964, British politician, born in the U.S.; the first woman to sit in the British House of Commons.

Astoria (ə'stɔːrɪə) *n.* a port in NW Oregon, near the mouth of the Columbia River: founded as a fur-trading post in 1811 by John Jacob Astor. Pop.: 9998 (1980).

astound (ə'staʊnd) *vb.* (*tr.*) to overwhelm with amazement; bewilder. [C17: from *astoned* amazed, from OF, from *estoner* to ASTONISH] —**a'stounding** *adj.*

astraddle (ə'strædˀl) *adj. (postpositive)* with a leg on either side of something. ~*prep.* **2.** astride.

astragal ('æstrəgˀl) *n.* **1.** *Archit.* Also called: **bead.** a small convex moulding, usually with a semicircular cross section. **2.** *Anat.* the ankle or anklebone. [C17: from L, from Gk *astragalos* anklebone, hence, small round moulding]

astragalus (æ'strægələs) *n., pl.* **-li** (-,laɪ). *Anat.* another name for **talus**¹. [C16: via NL from L: ASTRAGAL]

astrakhan (,æstrə'kæn) *n.* **1.** a fur, usually black or grey, made of the closely curled wool of lambs from Astrakhan. **2.** a cloth with curled pile resembling this. **3.** (*modifier*) made of such fur or cloth.

Astrakhan (,æstrə'kæn, -'kɑːn; *Russian* 'astrəxənj) *n.* a city in the S Soviet Union, on the delta of the Volga River, 21 m (70 ft.) below sea level. Pop.: 509 000 (1987).

astral ('æstrəl) *adj.* **1.** relating to or resembling the stars. **2.** *Theosophy.* relating to a supposed supersensible substance taking the form of an aura discernible to certain gifted individuals. [C17: from LL *astrālis,* from L *astrum* star, from Gk *astron*]

astray (ə'streɪ) *adj.* *(postpositive)*, *adv.* **1.** out of the correct path or direction. **2.** out of the right or expected way. [C13: from OF, from *estraier* to STRAY]

astride (ə'straɪd) *adj.* *(postpositive)* **1.** with a leg on either side. **2.** with the legs far apart. ~*prep.* **3.** with a leg on either side of. **4.** with a part on both sides of; spanning.

astringent (ə'strɪndʒənt) *adj.* **1.** severe; harsh. **2.** sharp or invigorating. **3.** causing contraction of body tissues, checking blood flow; styptic. ~*n.* **4.** an astringent drug or lotion. [C16: from L *astringēns* drawing together] —**as'tringency** *n.* —**as'tringently** *adv.*

astro- *combining form.* indicating a star or star-shaped structure: *astrology.* [from Gk, from *astron* star]

astrobiology (,æstrəʊbaɪ'ɒlədʒɪ) *n.* the branch of biology that investigates the possibility of life on other planets.

astrodome ('æstrə,dəʊm) *n.* a transparent dome on the top of an aircraft, through which observations can be made.

astrol. *abbrev. for:* **1.** astrologer. **2.** astrological. **3.** astrology.

astrolabe ('æstrə,leɪb) *n.* an instrument used by early astronomers to measure the altitude of stars and planets and also as a navigational aid. [C13: via OF & Med. L from Gk, from *astrolabos*, from *astron* star + *lambanein* to take]

astrology (ə'strɒlədʒɪ) *n.* **1.** the study of the motions and relative positions of the planets, sun, and moon, interpreted in terms of human characteristics and activities. **2.** primitive astronomy. [C14: from OF, from L *astrologia*, from Gk, from *astrologos* (orig.: astronomer); see ASTRO-, -LOGY] —**as'trologer** *or* **as'trologist** *n.* —**astrological** (,æstrə'lɒdʒɪk⁹l) *adj.*

astron. *abbrev. for:* **1.** astronomer. **2.** astronomical. **3.** astronomy.

astronaut ('æstrə,nɔːt) *n.* a person trained for travelling in space. [C20: from ASTRO- + -naut, from Gk *nautēs* sailor, on the model of *aeronaut*]

astronautics (,æstrə'nɔːtɪks) *n.* *(functioning as sing.)* the science and technology of space flight. —,**astro'nautical** *adj.*

astronomical (,æstrə'nɒmɪk⁹l) *or* **astronomic** *adj.* **1.** enormously large. **2.** of or relating to astronomy. —,**astro'nomically** *adv.*

astronomical unit *n.* a unit of distance used in astronomy equal to the mean distance between the earth and the sun. 1 astronomical unit is equivalent to 1.495 × 10¹¹ metres.

astronomy (ə'strɒnəmɪ) *n.* the scientific study of the individual celestial bodies (excluding the earth) and of the universe as a whole. [C13: from OF, from L *astronomia*, from Gk; see ASTRO-, -NOMY] —**as'tronomer** *n.*

astrophysics (,æstrəʊ'fɪzɪks) *n.* *(functioning as sing.)* the branch of physics concerned with the physical and chemical properties of the celestial bodies. —,**astro'physicist** *n.*

Astroturf ('æstrəʊ,tɜːf) *n. Trademark.* a type of grasslike artificial surface used for playing fields and lawns. [C20: from *Astro*(*dome*) the baseball stadium in Texas where it was first used + *turf*]

Asturias (æ'stʊərɪ,æs) *n.* a region and former kingdom of NW Spain, consisting of a coastal plain and the Cantabrian Mountains: a Christian stronghold against the Moors (8th to 13th centuries); rich mineral resources.

astute (ə'stjuːt) *adj.* having insight or acumen; perceptive; shrewd. [C17: from L *astūtus* cunning, from *astus* (n.) cleverness] —**as'tutely** *adv.* —**as'tuteness** *n.*

Astyanax (æ'staɪə,næks) *n. Greek myth.* the young son of Hector and Andromache, who was hurled from the walls of Troy by the Greeks.

Asunción (Spanish asun'sjon) *n.* the capital and chief port of Paraguay, on the Paraguay River, 1530 km (950 miles) from the Atlantic. Pop.: 708 000 (1983 est.).

asunder (ə'sʌndə) *adv., adj.* *(postpositive)* in or into parts or pieces; apart: *to tear asunder.* [OE *on sundran* apart]

Asur ('æsə) *n.* a variant spelling of **Assur.**

Aswan, Assuan, *or* **Assouan** (ɑːs'wɑːn) *n.* an ancient town in SE Egypt, on the Nile, just below the First Cataract. Pop.: 182 700 (1985). Ancient name: **Syene.**

Aswan High Dam *n.* a dam on the Nile forming a reservoir (Lake Nasser) extending 480 km (300 miles) from the First to the Third Cataracts: opened in 1971, it was built 6 km (4 miles) upstream from the old **Aswan Dam** (built in 1902 and twice raised). Height of dam: 109 m (365 ft.).

asylum (ə'saɪləm) *n.* **1.** shelter; refuge; sanctuary. **2.** a safe or inviolable place of refuge, esp. as formerly offered by the Christian Church. **3.** *International law.* refuge afforded to a person whose extradition is sought by a foreign government: *political asylum.* **4.** an institution for the care or confinement of individuals, esp. (formerly) a mental hospital. [C15: via L from Gk *asulon* refuge, from A-¹ + *sulon* right of seizure]

asymmetric (,æsɪ'mɛtrɪk, ,eɪ-) *or* **asymmetrical** *adj.* **1.** not symmetrical; lacking symmetry; misproportioned. **2.** *Logic, maths.* (of a relation) never holding between a pair of values *x* and *y* when it holds between *y* and *x*, as in *John is the father of David.* —,**asym'metrically** *adv.*

asymmetry (æ'sɪmɪtrɪ, eɪ-) *n.* lack or absence of symmetry.

asymptomatic (,eɪsɪmptə'mætɪk) *adj.* not showing any symptoms of disease. .

asymptote ('æsɪm,təʊt) *n.* a straight line that is closely approached by a curve so that the distance between them decreases to zero as the distance from the origin increases to infinity. [C17: from Gk *asumptōtos* not falling together, from A-¹ + SYN- + *ptōtos* inclined to fall, from *piptein* to fall] —**asymptotic** (,æsɪm'tɒtɪk) *or* ,**asym'p'totical** *adj.*

Asyut *or* **Assiut** (æ'sjuːt) *n.* an ancient city in central Egypt, on the Nile. Pop.: 274 400 (1985). Ancient Greek name: **Lycopolis.**

at (æt) *prep.* **1.** used to indicate location or position: *are they at the table?* **2.** towards; in the direction of: *looking at television.* **3.** used to indicate position in time: *come at three o'clock.* **4.** engaged in; in a state of (being): *children at play.* **5.** (in expressions concerned with habitual activity) during the passing of: *he used to work at night.* **6.** for; in exchange for: *it's selling at four pounds.* **7.** used to indicate the object of an emotion: *shocked at his behaviour.* **8. where it's at.** *Sl.* the real place of action. [OE *æt*]

At *the chemical symbol for* astatine.

at. *abbrev. for:* **1.** atmosphere (unit of pressure). **2.** atomic.

Atacama Desert (Spanish ata'kama) *n.* a desert region along the W coast of South America, mainly in N Chile: a major source of nitrates.

Atahualpa (,ætə'wɑːlpə) *or* **Atabalipa** (,ætə'bɑːlipə) *n.* ?1500–33, the last Inca emperor of Peru (1525–33), who was put to death by the Spanish under Pizarro.

Atalanta (,ætə'læntə) *n. Greek myth.* a maiden who agreed to marry any man who could defeat her in a running race. She lost to Hippomenes when she paused to pick up three golden apples that he had deliberately dropped.

ataractic (,ætə'ræktɪk) *or* **ataraxic** (,ætə'ræksɪk) *adj.* **1.** able to calm or tranquillize. ~*n.* **2.** an ataractic drug.

ataraxia (,ætə'ræksɪə) *or* **ataraxy** ('ætə,ræksɪ) *n.* calmness or peace of mind; emotional tranquillity. [C17: from Gk: serenity, from A-¹ + *tarassein* to trouble]

Atatürk ('ætə,tɜːk) *n.* **Kemal** (kɛ'mɑːl), real name *Mustafa Kemal.* 1881–1938, Turkish general and statesman; founder of the Turkish republic and president of Turkey (1923–38), who westernized and secularized the country.

atavism ('ætə,vɪzəm) *n.* **1.** the recurrence in a plant or animal of certain primitive characteristics that were present in an ancestor but have not occurred in intermediate generations. **2.** reversion to a former type. [C19: from F, from L *atavus* strictly: great-grandfather's grandfather, prob. from *atta* daddy + *avus* grandfather] —,**ata'vistic** *adj.*

ataxia (ə'tæksɪə) *or* **ataxy** (ə'tæksɪ) *n. Pathol.* lack of muscular coordination. [C17: via NL from Gk: lack of coordination, from A-¹ + *-taxia*, from *tassein* to put in order] —**a'taxic** *adj.*

Atbara ('ætbərə, æt'bɑː-) *n.* **1.** a town in NE Sudan. Pop.: 73 009 (1983). **2.** a river in NE Africa, rising in N Ethiopia and flowing through E Sudan to the Nile at Atbara. Length: over 800 km (500 miles).

ATC *abbrev. for:* **1.** air-traffic control. **2.** (in Britain) Air Training Corps.

ate (ɛt, eɪt) *vb.* the past tense of **eat.**

Ate ('eɪtɪ, 'ɑːtɪ) *n. Greek myth.* a goddess who makes men blind so that they will blunder into guilty acts. [C16: via L from Gk *atē* a rash impulse]

-ate[1] *suffix.* **1.** (*forming adjectives*) having the appearance or characteristics of: *fortunate.* **2.** (*forming nouns*) a chemical compound, esp. a salt or ester of an acid: *carbonate.* **3.** (*forming nouns*) the product of a process: *condensate.* **4.** forming verbs from nouns and adjectives: *hyphenate.* [from L *-ātus*, p.p. ending of verbs ending in *-āre*]

-ate[2] *suffix forming nouns.* denoting office, rank, or a group having a certain function: *episcopate.* [from L *-ātus*, suffix of collective nouns]

atelier ('ætəlˌjeɪ) *n.* an artist's studio or workshop. [C17: from OF, from *astele* chip of wood, from L *astula* splinter, from *assis* board]

a tempo (ɑː 'tɛmpəʊ) *Music.* ~*adj.*, *adv.* **1.** to the original tempo. ~*n.* **2.** a passage thus marked. ~Also: **tempo primo.** [It.: in (the original) time]

Aten *or* **Aton** ('ɑːtˀn) *n.* (in ancient Egypt) the solar disc worshipped as the sole god in the reign of Akhenaten.

Athabaska *or* **Athabasca** (ˌæθəˈbæskə) *n.* **1. Lake.** a lake in W Canada, in NW Saskatchewan and NE Alberta. Area: about 7770 sq. km (3000 sq. miles). **2.** a river in W Canada, rising in the Rocky Mountains and flowing northeast to Lake Athabaska. Length: 1230 km (765 miles).

Athamas ('æθəˌmæs) *n. Greek myth.* a king of Orchomenus in Boeotia; the father of Phrixus and Helle by his first wife Nephele, whom he deserted for Ino.

Athanasian Creed (ˌæθəˈneɪʒən) *n. Christianity.* a profession of faith widely used in the Western Church which, though formerly attributed to Athanasius, probably originated in Gaul between 381 and 428 A.D.

Athanasius (ˌæθəˈneɪʃəs) *n. Saint.* ?296–373 A.D., patriarch of Alexandria who championed Christian orthodoxy against Arianism. Feast day: May 2. — ˌAtha'nasian *adj.*

Athapascan, Athapaskan (ˌæθəˈpæskən) *or* **Athabascan, Athabaskan** (ˌæθəˈbæskən) *n.* a group of North American Indian languages including Apache and Navaho. [from Cree *athapaskaaw* scattered grass]

atheism ('eɪθɪˌɪzəm) *n.* rejection of belief in God or gods. [C16: from F, from Gk *atheos* godless, from A-[1] + *theos* god] —'**atheist** *n., adj.* —ˌathe'istic *adj.*

Athelstan ('æθəlstən) *n.* ?895–939 A.D., king of Wessex and Mercia (924–939 A.D.), who extended his kingdom to include most of England.

athematic (ˌæθɪˈmætɪk) *adj.* **1.** *Music.* not based on themes. **2.** *Linguistics.* (of verbs) having a suffix attached with no intervening vowel.

Athena (əˈθiːnə) *or* **Athene** (əˈθiːnɪ) *n. Greek myth.* a virgin goddess of wisdom, practical skills, and prudent warfare. She was born, fully armed, from the head of Zeus. Also called: **Pallas Athena, Pallas.** Roman counterpart: **Minerva.**

athenaeum *or U.S.* **atheneum** (ˌæθɪˈniːəm) *n.* **1.** an institution for the promotion of learning. **2.** a building containing a reading room or library. [C18: from LL, from Gk *Athēnaion* temple of Athene, frequented by poets and teachers]

Athenian (əˈθiːnɪən) *n.* **1.** a native or inhabitant of Athens. ~*adj.* **2.** of or relating to Athens.

Athens ('æθɪnz) *n.* the capital of Greece, in the southeast near the Saronic Gulf: became capital after independence in 1834; ancient city-state, most powerful in the 5th century B.C.; contains the hill citadel of the Acropolis. Pop.: 885 136 (1981). Greek name: **Athinai** (aˈθinɛ).

atherosclerosis (ˌæθərəʊsklɪəˈrəʊsɪs) *n.*, *pl.* **-ses** (-siːz). a degenerative disease of the arteries characterized by thickening of the arterial walls, caused by deposits of fatty material. [C20: from NL, from Gk *athērōma* tumour full of grainy matter + SCLEROSIS] —**atherosclerotic** (ˌæθərəʊsklɪəˈrɒtɪk) *adj.*

athirst (əˈθɜːst) *adj.* (*postpositive*) **1.** (often foll. by *for*) having an eager desire; longing. **2.** *Arch.* thirsty.

athlete ('æθliːt) *n.* **1.** a person trained to compete in sports or exercises. **2.** a person who has a natural aptitude for physical activities. **3.** *Chiefly Brit.* a competitor in track and field events. [C18: from L via Gk, from *athlein* to compete for a prize, from *athlos* a contest]

athlete's foot *n.* a fungal infection of the skin of the foot, esp. between the toes and on the soles.

athletic (æθˈlɛtɪk) *adj.* **1.** physically fit or strong. **2.** of, relating to, or suitable for an athlete or for athletics. —ath'letically *adv.* —ath'leticism *n.*

athletics (æθˈlɛtɪks) *n.* (*functioning as pl. or sing.*) **1. a.** track and field events. **b.** (*as modifier*): *an athletics meeting.* **2.** sports or exercises engaged in by athletes.

athletic support *n.* a more formal term for **jockstrap.**

at-home *n.* **1.** a social gathering in a person's home. **2.** another name for **open day.**

-athon *suffix forming nouns.* a variant of **-thon.**

Athos ('æθɒs, 'eɪ-) *n.* **Mount.** a department of NE Greece, in Macedonia: autonomous since 1927; inhabited by Greek Orthodox Basilian monks in 20 monasteries founded in the 10th century. Administrative centre: Karyai. Pop.: 1472 (1981). Area: 336 sq. km (130 sq. miles).

athwart (əˈθwɔːt) *adv.* **1.** transversely; from one side to another. ~*prep.* **2.** across the path or line of (esp. a ship). **3.** in opposition to; against. [C15: from A-[2] + THWART]

-atic *suffix forming adjectives.* of the nature of the thing specified: *problematic.* [from F, from Gk *-atikos*]

atilt (əˈtɪlt) *adv.*, *adj.* (*postpositive*) **1.** in a tilted or inclined position. **2.** *Arch.* in or as if in a joust.

-ation *suffix forming nouns.* indicating an action, process, state, condition, or result: *arbitration; hibernation.* [from L *-ātiōn-*, suffix of abstract nouns]

-ative *suffix forming adjectives.* of, relating to, or tending to: *authoritative; informative.* [from L *-ātivus*]

Atkinson ('ætkɪnsən) *n.* Sir **Harry Albert.** 1831–92, New Zealand statesman, born in England: prime minister of New Zealand (1876–77; 1883–84; 1887–91).

Atlanta (ætˈlæntə) *n.* a city in N Georgia: the state capital. Pop.: 421 910 (1986).

Atlantean (ˌætlænˈtiːən) *adj. Literary.* of, relating to, or like Atlas; extremely strong.

atlantes (ətˈlæntiːz) *n.* the plural of **atlas** (sense 4).

Atlantic (ətˈlæntɪk) *n.* **1. the.** short for the **Atlantic Ocean.** ~*adj.* **2.** of, relating to, or bordering the Atlantic Ocean. **3.** of or relating to Atlas or the Atlas Mountains. [C15: from L, from Gk (*pelagos*) *Atlantikos* (the sea) of Atlas (so called because it lay beyond the Atlas Mountains)]

Atlantic City *n.* a resort in SE New Jersey on Absecon Beach, an island on the Atlantic coast. Pop.: 40 199 (1980).

Atlantic Intracoastal Waterway *n.* a system of inland and coastal waterways along the Atlantic coast of the U.S. from Cape Cod to Florida Bay. Length: 2495 km (1550 miles).

Atlantic Ocean *n.* the world's second largest ocean, bounded in the north by the Arctic, in the south by the Antarctic, in the west by North and South America, and in the east by Europe and Africa. Greatest depth: 9220 m (30 246 ft.). Area: about 81 585 000 sq. km (31 500 000 sq. miles).

Atlantic Provinces *pl. n.* **the.** certain of the Canadian provinces with coasts facing the Gulf of St Lawrence or the Atlantic: New Brunswick, Nova Scotia, Prince Edward Island, and Newfoundland.

Atlantis (ətˈlæntɪs) *n.* (in ancient legend) a continent said to have sunk beneath the Atlantic west of Gibraltar.

atlas ('ætləs) *n.* **1.** a collection of maps, usually in book form. **2.** a book of charts, graphs, etc.: *an anatomical atlas.* **3.** *Anat.* the first cervical vertebra, supporting the skull in man. **4.** (*pl.* **atlantes**) *Archit.* another name for **telamon.** [C16: via L from Gk; first applied to maps from depictions of Atlas supporting the heavens in 16th-cent. books of maps]

Atlas ('ætləs) *n. Greek myth.* a Titan compelled to support the sky on his shoulders as punishment for rebelling against Zeus.

Atlas Mountains *pl. n.* a mountain system of N Africa, between the Mediterranean and the Sahara. Highest peak: Mount Toubkal, 4165 m (13 664 ft.).

Atli ('ɑːtlɪ) *n. Norse legend.* a king of the Huns who married Gudrun for her inheritance and was slain by her after he killed her brothers.

atm. *abbrev. for:* **1.** atmosphere (unit of pressure). **2.** atmospheric.

atman ('ɑːtmən) *n. Hinduism.* **1.** the personal soul or self. **2.** Brahman considered as the Universal Soul. [from Sansk. *ātman* breath]

atmolysis (ætˈmɒlɪsɪs) *n.*, *pl.* **-ses** (-ˌsiːz). the separation of gases by differential diffusion through a porous substance.

atmosphere ('ætməsˌfɪə) *n.* **1.** the gaseous envelope surrounding the earth or any other celestial body. **2.** the air or climate in a particular place. **3.** a general pervasive feeling or mood. **4.** the prevailing tone or mood of a novel, symphony, painting, etc. **5.** any local gaseous environment or medium: *an inert atmosphere.* **6.** Abbrev: **at., atm.** a unit of pressure; the pressure that will support a column of mercury 760 mm high at 0°C at sea level. —**atmospheric** (ˌætməsˈfɛrɪk) *adj.* — ˌ**atmos'pherically** *adv.*

atmospheric pressure *n.* the pressure exerted by the atmosphere at the earth's surface. It has an average value of 1 atmosphere.

atmospherics (ˌætməsˈfɛrɪks) *pl. n.* radio interference, heard as crackling or hissing in receivers, caused by electrical disturbance.

at. no. *abbrev. for* atomic number.

atoll (ˈætɒl) *n.* a circular coral reef or string of coral islands surrounding a lagoon. [C17: from *atollon,* native name in the Maldive Islands]

atom (ˈætəm) *n.* **1. a.** the smallest quantity of an element that can take part in a chemical reaction. **b.** this entity as a source of nuclear energy: *the power of the atom.* **2.** the hypothetical indivisible particle of matter postulated by certain ancient philosophers. **3.** a very small amount or quantity: *to smash something to atoms.* [C16: via OF & L, from Gk, from *atomos* (adj.) that cannot be divided, from A-¹ + *temnein* to cut]

atom bomb *or* **atomic bomb** *n.* a type of bomb in which the energy is provided by nuclear fission. Also called: **A-bomb, fission bomb.** Cf. **fusion bomb.**

atomic (əˈtɒmɪk) *adj.* **1.** of, using, or characterized by atom bombs or atomic energy: *atomic warfare.* **2.** of or comprising atoms: *atomic hydrogen.* —**a'tomically** *adv.*

atomic clock *n.* an extremely accurate clock in which an electrical oscillator is controlled by the natural vibrations of an atomic or molecular system such as caesium or ammonia.

atomic energy *n.* another name for **nuclear energy.**

atomicity (ˌætəˈmɪsɪtɪ) *n.* **1.** the state of being made up of atoms. **2.** the number of atoms in the molecules of an element. **3.** a less common name for **valency.**

atomic mass unit *n.* a unit of mass used to express atomic and molecular weights that is equal to one twelfth of the mass of an atom of carbon-12. Abbrev.: **AMU.**

atomic number *n.* the number of protons in the nucleus of an atom of an element. Abbrev.: **at. no.**

atomic pile *n.* the original name for a **nuclear reactor.**

atomic sentence *n. Logic.* a sentence consisting of one predicate and a finite number of terms: *"it is raining" is an atomic sentence.*

atomic structure *n.* the concept of an atom as a central positively charged nucleus consisting of protons and neutrons surrounded by a number of electrons. The number of electrons is equal to the number of protons: the whole entity is thus electrically neutral.

atomic theory *n.* **1.** any theory in which matter is regarded as consisting of atoms. **2.** the current concept of the atom as an entity with a definite structure. See **atomic structure.**

atomic weight *n.* the ratio of the average mass per atom of an element to one-twelfth the mass of an atom of carbon-12. Abbrev.: **at. wt.** Also called: **relative atomic mass.**

▷ **Usage.** Until 1961 *atomic weights* were based on the mass of an atom of oxygen-16. The carbon-12 atom is now the usual basis of calculations and *relative atomic mass* is the preferred term for the new atomic weights.

atomize *or* **-ise** (ˈætəˌmaɪz) *vb.* **1.** to separate or be separated into free atoms. **2.** to reduce (a liquid or solid) to fine particles or spray or (of a liquid or solid) to be reduced in this way. **3.** (*tr.*) to destroy by weapons, esp. nuclear weapons.

atomizer *or* **-iser** (ˈætəˌmaɪzə) *n.* a device for reducing a liquid to a fine spray, such as a bottle with a fine outlet used to spray perfumes.

atom smasher *n. Physics.* the nontechnical name for **accelerator** (sense 2).

atomy (ˈætəmɪ) *n., pl.* **-mies.** *Arch.* a minute particle or creature. [C16: from L *atomi* atoms, used as sing.]

Aton (ˈɑːtɒn) *n.* a variant spelling of **Aten.**

atonal (eɪˈtəʊnəl) *adj. Music.* having no established key.

atonality (ˌeɪtəʊˈnælɪtɪ) *n.* **1.** absence of or disregard for an established musical key in a composition. **2.** the principles of composition embodying this.

atone (əˈtəʊn) *vb.* (*intr.;* foll. by *for*) to make amends or reparation (for a crime, sin, etc.). [C16: back formation from ATONEMENT] —**a'toner** *n.*

atonement (əˈtəʊnmənt) *n.* **1.** satisfaction, reparation, or expiation given for an injury or wrong. **2.** (*often cap.*) *Christian theology.* **a.** the reconciliation of man with God through the sacrificial death of Christ. **b.** the sufferings and death of Christ. [C16: from ME *at onement* in harmony]

atonic (eɪˈtɒnɪk, æ-) *adj.* **1.** (of a syllable, word, etc.) carrying no stress; unaccented. **2.** lacking body or muscle tone. ~*n.* **3.** an unaccented or unstressed syllable, word, etc. [C18: from L, from Gk *atonos* lacking tone]

atop (əˈtɒp) *adv.* **1.** on top; at the top. ~*prep.* **2.** on top of; at the top of.

-ator *suffix forming nouns.* a person or thing that performs a certain action: *agitator; radiator.* [from L *-ātor*]

-atory *suffix forming adjectives.* of, relating to, characterized by, or serving to: *circulatory; explanatory.* [from L *-ātōrius*]

ATP *n.* adenosine triphosphate; a substance found in all plant and animal cells. It is the major source of energy for cellular reactions.

Atreus (ˈeɪtrɪˌuːs, ˈeɪtrɪəs) *n. Greek myth.* a king of Mycenae, son of Pelops, father of Agamemnon and Menelaus, and member of the family known as the **Atreids** (ˈeɪtrɪɪdz).

atrium (ˈeɪtrɪəm, ˈɑː-) *n., pl.* **atria** (ˈeɪtrɪə, ˈɑː-). **1.** the open main court of a Roman house. **2.** a central often glass-roofed hall that extends through several storeys in a building, such as a shopping centre or hotel. **3.** a court in front of an early Christian or medieval church. **4.** *Anat.* a cavity or chamber in the body, esp. the upper chamber of each half of the heart. [C17: from L; rel. to *āter* black] —ˈ**atrial** *adj.*

atrocious (əˈtrəʊʃəs) *adj.* **1.** extremely cruel or wicked: *atrocious deeds.* **2.** horrifying or shocking. **3.** *Inf.* very bad: *atrocious writing.* [C17: from L *ātrōx* dreadful, from *āter* black] —**a'trociousness** *n.*

atrocity (əˈtrɒsɪtɪ) *n., pl.* **-ties. 1.** behaviour or an action that is wicked or ruthless. **2.** the fact or quality of being atrocious. **3.** (*usually pl.*) acts of extreme cruelty.

atrophy (ˈætrəfɪ) *n., pl.* **-phies. 1.** a wasting away of an organ or part, or a failure to grow to normal size. **2.** any degeneration or diminution. ~*vb.* **-phying, -phied. 3.** to waste away or cause to waste away. [C16: from LL, from Gk, from *atrophos* ill-fed, from A-¹ + *-trophos,* from *trephein* to feed] —**atrophic** (əˈtrɒfɪk) *adj.*

atropine (ˈætrəˌpiːn) *n.* a poisonous alkaloid obtained from the deadly nightshade, used to treat peptic ulcers, biliary and renal colic, etc. [C19: from NL *atropa* deadly nightshade, from Gk *atropos* unchangeable, inflexible]

Atropos (ˈætrəˌpɒs) *n. Greek myth.* the one of the three Fates who severs the thread of life. [Greek, from *atropos* that may not be turned, from A-¹ + *-tropos* from *trepein* to turn]

att. *abbrev. for:* **1.** attached. **2.** attorney.

attach (əˈtætʃ) *vb.* (*mainly tr.*) **1.** to join, fasten, or connect. **2.** (*reflexive or passive*) to become associated with or join. **3.** (*intr.;* foll. by *to*) to be connected (with): *responsibility attaches to the job.* **4.** to attribute or ascribe. **5.** to include or append: *a proviso is attached to the contract.* **6.** (*usually passive*) *Mil.* to place on temporary duty with another unit. **7.** to appoint officially. **8.** *Law.* to arrest or take (a person, property, etc.) with lawful authority. [C14: from OF *atachier* to fasten, changed from *estachier* to fasten with a stake] —**at'tachable** *adj.* —**at'tacher** *n.*

attaché (əˈtæʃeɪ) *n.* a specialist attached to a diplomatic mission: *military attaché.* [C19: from F: someone attached (to a mission)]

attaché case *n.* a small flat rectangular briefcase used for carrying documents, papers, etc.

attached (əˈtætʃt) *adj.* **1.** (foll. by *to*) fond (of). **2.** married, engaged, or associated in an exclusive sexual relationship.

attachment (əˈtætʃmənt) *n.* **1.** a fastening. **2.** (often foll. by *to*) affection or regard (for). **3.** an object to be attached: *an attachment for an electric drill.* **4.** the act of attaching or the state of being attached. **5. a.** the lawful seizure of property and placing of it under control of a court. **b.** a writ authorizing such seizure.

attack (ə'tæk) vb. **1.** to launch a physical assault (against) with or without weapons. **2.** (intr.) to take the initiative in a game, sport, etc. **3.** (tr.) to criticize or abuse vehemently. **4.** (tr.) to turn one's mind or energies to (a job, problem, etc.). **5.** (tr.) to begin to injure or affect adversely: *rust attacked the metal.* ~n. **6.** the act or an instance of attacking. **7.** strong criticism or abuse. **8.** an offensive move in a game, sport, etc. **9. the attack.** *Ball games.* the players in a team whose main role is to attack the opponents. **10.** commencement of a task, etc. **11.** any sudden and usually severe manifestation of a disease or disorder: *a heart attack.* **12.** *Music.* decisiveness in beginning a passage, movement, or piece. [C16: from F, from OIt. *attaccare* to attack, attach, from *estaccare* to attach] —**at'tacker** n.

attain (ə'teɪn) vb. **1.** (tr.) to achieve or accomplish (a task, aim, etc.). **2.** (tr.) to reach in space or time. **3.** (intr.; often foll. by to) to arrive (at) with effort or exertion. [C14: from OF, from L *attingere* to reach, from *tangere* to touch] —**at'tainable** adj. —**at,taina'bility** or **at'tainableness** n.

attainder (ə'teɪndə) n. (formerly) the extinction of a person's civil rights resulting from a sentence of death or outlawry on conviction for treason or felony. [C15: from Anglo-F *attaindre* to convict, from OF *ateindre* to ATTAIN]

attainment (ə'teɪnmənt) n. an achievement or the act of achieving; accomplishment.

attaint (ə'teɪnt) vb. (tr.) Arch. **1.** to pass judgment of death or outlawry upon (a person). **2.** (of sickness) to affect or strike (somebody). ~n. **3.** a less common word for **attainder**. [C14: from OF *ateint* convicted, from *ateindre* to ATTAIN]

attar ('ætə), **otto** ('ɒtəʊ), or **ottar** ('ɒtə) n. an essential oil from flowers, esp. the damask rose: *attar of roses.* [C18: from Persian, from *'itr* perfume, from Ar.]

attempt (ə'tɛmpt) vb. (tr.) **1.** to make an effort (to do something) or to achieve (something); try. **2.** to try to surmount (an obstacle). **3.** to try to climb. ~n. **4.** an endeavour to achieve something; effort. **5.** a result of an attempt or endeavour. **6.** an attack, esp. with the intention to kill. [C14: from OF, from L *attemptāre* to strive after, from *tentāre* to try] —**at'temptable** adj.

Attenborough ('ætⁿbⁿrə) n. **1.** Sir **David.** born 1926, English naturalist and broadcaster; noted esp. for his TV series *Life on Earth* (1978) and *The Living Planet* (1983). **2.** his brother Sir **Richard.** born 1923, English film actor, director, and producer; noted esp. for the films *Gandhi* (1982) and *Cry Freedom* (1987), which he directed.

attend (ə'tɛnd) vb. **1.** to be present at (an event, etc.). **2.** (when intr., foll. by to) to give care (to); minister (to). **3.** (when intr., foll. by to) to pay attention. **4.** (tr.; often passive) to accompany or follow: *a high temperature attended by a severe cough.* **5.** (intr.; foll. by on or upon) to follow as a consequence (of). **6.** (intr.; foll. by to) to apply oneself: *to attend to the garden.* **7.** (tr.) to escort or accompany. **8.** (intr.; foll. by on or upon) to provide for the needs (of): *to attend on a guest.* [C13: from OF, from L *attendere* to stretch towards, from *tendere* to extend]

attendance (ə'tɛndəns) n. **1.** the act or state of attending. **2.** the number of persons present.

attendant (ə'tɛndənt) n. **1.** a person who accompanies or waits upon another. **2.** a person employed to assist, guide, or provide a service for others. **3.** a person who is present. ~adj. **4.** being in attendance. **5.** associated: *attendant problems.*

attention (ə'tɛnʃən) n. **1.** concentrated direction of the mind, esp. to a problem or task. **2.** consideration, notice, or observation. **3.** detailed care or special treatment: *to pay attention to one's appearance.* **4.** (usually pl.) an act of courtesy or gallantry indicating affection or love. **5.** the motionless position of formal military alertness, an upright position with legs and heels together. ~sentence substitute. **6.** the order to be alert or to adopt a position of formal military alertness. [C14: from L, from *attendere* to apply the mind to]

attentive (ə'tɛntɪv) adj. **1.** paying attention; listening carefully. **2.** (postpositive; often foll. by to) careful to fulfil the needs or wants (of). —**at'tentively** adv. —**at'tentiveness** n.

attenuate vb. (ə'tɛnjʊˌeɪt). **1.** to weaken or become weak. **2.** to make or become thin or fine; extend. ~adj.

(ə'tɛnjʊɪt, -ˌeɪt). **3.** weakened or reduced. **4.** *Bot.* tapering. [C16: from L *attenuāre* to weaken, from *tenuis* thin] —**at,tenu'ation** n.

attest (ə'tɛst) vb. **1.** (tr.) to affirm the correctness or truth of. **2.** (when intr., usually foll. by to) to witness (an act, event, etc.) or bear witness (to an act, event, etc.). **3.** (tr.) to make evident; demonstrate. **4.** (tr.) to provide evidence for. [C16: from L, from *testārī* to bear witness, from *testis* a witness] —**at'testable** adj. —**at'testant, at'tester** or esp. in legal usage **at'testor** n. —**attestation** (ˌætɛ'steɪʃən) n.

attested (ə'tɛstɪd) adj. *Brit.* (of cattle, etc.) certified to be free from a disease, esp. from tuberculosis.

attic ('ætɪk) n. **1.** a space or room within the roof of a house. **2.** *Archit.* a storey or low wall above the cornice of a classical façade. [C18: special use of ATTIC, from use of Attic-style pilasters on façade of top storey]

Attic ('ætɪk) adj. **1.** of or relating to Attica, its inhabitants, or the dialect of Greek spoken there. **2.** (often not cap.) classically elegant, simple, or pure. ~n. **3.** the dialect of Ancient Greek spoken in Athens.

Attica ('ætɪkə) n. a department of E central Greece: in ancient times the territory of Athens. Capital: Athens. Pop.: 342 093 (1981). Area: 2496 sq. km (964 sq. miles).

Atticism ('ætɪˌsɪzəm) n. **1.** the idiom or character of the Attic dialect of Ancient Greek. **2.** an elegant, simple expression.

Attic salt or **wit** n. refined incisive wit.

Attila (ə'tɪlə) n. ?406–453 A.D., king of the Huns, who devastated much of the Roman Empire, invaded Gaul in 451 A.D., but was defeated by the Romans and Visigoths at Châlons-sur-Marne.

attire (ə'taɪə) vb. **1.** (tr.) to dress, esp. in fine elegant clothes; array. ~n. **2.** clothes or garments, esp. if fine or decorative. [C13: from OF *atirier* to put in order, from *tire* row]

Attis ('ætɪs) n. *Classical myth.* a youth of Phrygia, loved by the goddess Cybele. In a jealous passion she caused him to go mad, whereupon he castrated himself and died.

attitude ('ætɪˌtjuːd) n. **1.** the way a person views something or tends to behave towards it, often in an evaluative way. **2.** a theatrical pose created for effect (esp. in **strike an attitude**). **3.** a position of the body indicating mood or emotion. **4.** the orientation of an aircraft's axes or a spacecraft in relation to some plane or the direction of motion. [C17: from F, from It. *attitudine* disposition, from LL *aptitūdō* fitness, from L *aptus* APT] —**,atti'tudinal** adj.

attitudinize or **-nise** (ˌætɪ'tjuːdɪˌnaɪz) vb. (intr.) to adopt a pose or opinion for effect; strike an attitude.

Attlee ('ætlɪ) n. **Clement Richard,** 1st Earl Attlee. 1883–1967, British statesman; prime minister (1945–51); leader of the Labour party (1935–55). His government instituted the welfare state, with extensive nationalization.

attn abbrev. for attention.

atto- prefix. denoting 10^{-18}: *attotesla.* Symbol: a [from Norwegian & Danish *atten* eighteen]

attorney (ə'tɜːnɪ) n. **1.** a person legally appointed or empowered to act for another. **2.** *U.S.* a lawyer qualified to represent clients in legal proceedings. [C14: from OF, from *atourner* to direct to, from *tourner* to TURN] —**at'torney,ship** n.

attorney-at-law n., pl. **attorneys-at-law.** Law, now chiefly U.S. a lawyer.

attorney general n., pl. **attorneys general** or **attorney generals.** a chief law officer and senior legal adviser of some national and state governments.

attract (ə'trækt) vb. (mainly tr.) **1.** to draw (notice, a crowd of observers, etc.) to oneself (esp. in **attract attention**). **2.** (also intr.) to exert a force on (a body) that tends to oppose a separation: *the gravitational pull of the earth attracts objects to it.* **3.** to possess some property that pulls or draws (something) towards itself. **4.** (also intr.) to exert a pleasing or fascinating influence (upon). [C15: from L *attrahere* to draw towards, from *trahere* to pull] —**at'tractable** adj. —**at'tractor** n.

attraction (ə'trækʃən) n. **1.** the act or quality of attracting. **2.** a person or thing that attracts or is intended to attract. **3.** a force by which one object attracts another: *magnetic attraction.*

attractive (ə'træktɪv) *adj.* **1.** appealing to the senses or mind through beauty, form, character, etc. **2.** arousing interest: *an attractive opportunity.* **3.** possessing the ability to draw or pull: *an attractive force.* —**at'tractively** *adv.*

attrib. *abbrev. for:* **1.** attribute. **2.** attributive.

attribute *vb.* (ə'trɪbjuːt). **1.** (*tr.; usually foll. by to*) to regard as belonging (to), produced (by), or resulting (from): *to attribute a painting to Picasso.* ~*n.* ('ætrɪˌbjuːt). **2.** a property, quality, or feature belonging to or representative of a person or thing. **3.** an object accepted as belonging to a particular office or position. **4.** *Grammar.* **a.** an adjective or adjectival phrase. **b.** an attributive adjective. **5.** *Logic.* the property or feature that is affirmed or denied concerning the subject of a proposition. [C15: from L *attribuere* to associate with, from *tribuere* to give] —**at'tributable** *adj.* —**attribution** (ˌætrɪ'bjuːʃən) *n.*

attributive (ə'trɪbjutɪv) *adj.* **1.** relating to an attribute. **2.** *Grammar.* (of an adjective or adjectival phrase) preceding the noun modified. Cf. **predicative.**

attrition (ə'trɪʃən) *n.* **1.** the act of wearing away or the state of being worn away, as by friction. **2.** constant wearing down to weaken or destroy (often in **war of attrition**). **3.** *Geog.* the grinding down of rock particles by friction. **4.** *Theol.* sorrow for sin arising from fear of damnation, esp. as contrasted with contrition. [C14: from LL *attrītiō* a rubbing against something, from L *atterere* to weaken, from *terere* to rub]

Attu ('ætuː) *n.* the westernmost of the Aleutian Islands, off the coast of SW Alaska: largest of the Near Islands.

attune (ə'tjuːn) *vb.* (*tr.*) to adjust or accustom (a person or thing); acclimatize.

at. vol. *abbrev. for* atomic volume.

at. wt. *abbrev. for* atomic weight.

atypical (eɪ'tɪpɪkəl) *adj.* not typical; deviating from or not conforming to type. —**a'typically** *adv.*

Au *the chemical symbol for* gold. [from NL *aurum*]

aubade (əʊ'bɑːd) *n.* a poem or short musical piece to greet the dawn. [C19: F, from OProvençal *auba* dawn, ult. from L *albus* white]

Aube (*French* ob) *n.* **1.** a department of N central France, in Champagne-Ardenne region. Capital: Troyes. Pop.: 289 300 (1982). Area: 6026 sq. km (2350 sq. miles). **2.** a river in N central France, flowing northwest to the Seine. Length: about 225 km (140 miles).

Auber (*French* obɛr) *n.* **Daniel François Esprit** (danjɛl frɑ̃swa ɛspri). 1782–1871, French composer, who was prominent in development of opéra comique. His works include 48 operas.

aubergine ('əʊbəˌʒiːn) *n.* **1.** a tropical Old World plant widely cultivated for its egg-shaped typically dark purple fruit. U.S. and Canad. name: **eggplant. 2.** the fruit of this plant, which is cooked and eaten as a vegetable. **3. a.** a dark purple colour. **b.** (*as adj.*): *an aubergine dress.* [C18: from F, from Catalan *alberginia,* from Ar. *bādindjān,* ult. from Sansk. *vatin-ganah,* from ?]

Aubervilliers (*French* obɛrvilje) *n.* an industrial suburb of Paris, on the Seine. Pop.: 72 874 (1983 est.). Former name: **Notre-Dame-des-Vertus** (*French* nɔtrədam-devɛrty).

Aubrey ('ɔːbrɪ) *n.* **John.** 1626–97, English antiquary and author, noted for his vivid biographies of his contemporaries, *Brief Lives* (edited 1898).

aubrietia, aubrieta, *or* **aubretia** (ɔː'briːʃə) *n.* a trailing purple-flowered plant native to European mountains but widely planted in rock gardens. [C19: from NL, after Claude *Aubriet,* 18th-cent. F painter of flowers and animals]

auburn ('ɔːbən) *n.* **a.** a moderate reddish-brown colour. **b.** (*as adj.*): *auburn hair.* [C15 (orig. meaning: blond): from OF *alborne* blond, from Med. L, from L *albus* white]

Auckland ('ɔːklənd) *n.* the chief port of New Zealand, in the northern part of North Island: former capital of New Zealand (1840–65). Pop. (urban area): 889 200 (1987).

Auckland Islands *pl. n.* a group of six uninhabited islands, south of New Zealand. Area: 611 sq. km (234 sq. miles).

au courant **French.** (o kurɑ̃) *adj.* up-to-date, esp. in knowledge of current affairs. [lit.: in the current]

auction ('ɔːkʃən) *n.* **1.** a public sale of goods or property in which prospective purchasers bid until the highest price is reached. **2.** the competitive calls made in bridge before play begins. ~*vb.* **3.** (*tr.; often foll. by off*) to sell by auction. [C16: from L *auctiō* an increasing, from *augēre* to increase]

auction bridge *n.* a variety of bridge in which all the tricks made score towards game.

auctioneer (ˌɔːkʃə'nɪə) *n.* **1.** a person who conducts an auction. ~*vb.* **2.** (*tr.*) to sell by auction.

auctorial (ɔːk'tɔːrɪəl) *adj.* of or relating to an author. [C19: from L *auctor* AUTHOR]

audacious (ɔː'deɪʃəs) *adj.* **1.** recklessly bold or daring. **2.** impudent or presumptuous. [C16: from L *audāx* bold, from *audēre* to dare] —**au'daciousness** *or* **audacity** (ɔː'dæsɪtɪ) *n.*

Aude (*French* od) *n.* a department of S France on the Gulf of Lions, in Languedoc-Roussillon region. Capital: Carcassonne. Pop.: 280 686 (1982). Area: 6342 sq. km (2473 sq. miles).

Auden ('ɔːdən) *n.* **W(ystan) H(ugh).** 1907–73, U.S. poet, dramatist, critic, and librettist, born in Britain; noted for his lyric and satirical poems and for plays written in collaboration with Christopher Isherwood.

audible ('ɔːdɪbəl) *adj.* perceptible to the hearing; loud enough to be heard. [C16: from LL, from L *audīre* to hear] —**audi'bility** *or* **'audibleness** *n.* —**'audibly** *adv.*

audience ('ɔːdɪəns) *n.* **1.** a group of spectators or listeners, esp. at a concert or play. **2.** the people reached by a book, film, or radio or television programme. **3.** the devotees or followers of a public entertainer, etc. **4.** a formal interview with a monarch or head of state. [C14: from OF, from L *audientia* a hearing, from *audīre* to hear]

audio ('ɔːdɪəʊ) *n.* (*modifier*) **1.** of or relating to sound or hearing: *audio frequency.* **2.** relating to or employed in the transmission or reproduction of sound. [C20: from L *audīre* to hear]

audio frequency *n.* a frequency in the range 20 hertz to 20 000 hertz. A sound wave of this frequency would be audible to the human ear.

audiology (ˌɔːdɪ'ɒlədʒɪ) *n.* the scientific study of hearing, often including the treatment of persons with hearing defects. —ˌaudi'ologist *n.*

audiometer (ˌɔːdɪ'ɒmɪtə) *n.* an instrument for testing hearing. —ˌaudi'ometrist *n.* —ˌaudi'ometry *n.*

audiophile ('ɔːdɪəʊˌfaɪl) *n.* a person who has a great interest in high-fidelity sound reproduction.

audiotypist ('ɔːdɪəʊˌtaɪpɪst) *n.* a typist trained to type from a dictating machine. —'audio,typing *n.*

audiovisual (ˌɔːdɪəʊ'vɪʒʊəl) *adj.* (esp. of teaching aids) involving or directed at both hearing and sight. —ˌaudio'visually *adv.*

audit ('ɔːdɪt) *n.* **1. a.** an inspection, correction, and verification of business accounts by a qualified accountant. **b.** (*as modifier*): *audit report.* **2.** *U.S.* an audited account. **3.** any thoroughgoing examination or check. ~*vb.* **4.** to inspect, correct, and certify (accounts, etc.). [C15: from L *audītus* a hearing, from *audīre* to hear]

audition (ɔː'dɪʃən) *n.* **1.** a test at which a performer or musician is asked to demonstrate his ability for a particular role, etc. **2.** the act or power of hearing. ~*vb.* **3.** to judge by means of or be tested in an audition. [C16: from L *audītiō* a hearing, from *audīre* to hear]

auditor ('ɔːdɪtə) *n.* **1.** a person qualified to audit accounts. **2.** a person who hears or listens. [C14: from OF, from L *audītor* a hearer] —ˌaudi'torial *adj.*

Auditor General *n.* (in Canada) an officer appointed by the Governor General to audit the accounts of the Federal Government and report to Parliament.

auditorium (ˌɔːdɪ'tɔːrɪəm) *n., pl.* **-toriums** *or* **-toria** (-'tɔːrɪə). **1.** the area of a concert hall, theatre, etc., in which the audience sits. **2.** *U.S. & Canad.* a building for public meetings. [C17: L: a judicial examination]

auditory ('ɔːdɪtərɪ) *adj.* of or relating to hearing or the sense of hearing. [C14: from L *audītōrius* relating to hearing, from *audīre* to hear]

Audubon ('ɔːdəˌbɒn) *n.* **John James.** 1785–1851, U.S. naturalist and artist, noted particularly for his paintings of birds in *Birds of America* (1827–38).

Auer (*German* 'aʊər) *n.* **Karl** (karl), **Baron von Welsbach.** 1858–1929, Austrian chemist who discovered the cerium-iron alloy used for flints in cigarette lighters and invented the incandescent gas mantle.

AUEW (in Britain) *abbrev. for* Amalgamated Union of Engineering Workers: the former name of the AEU.

au fait **French.** (o fɛ) *adj.* fully informed; in touch or expert. [C18: lit.: to the point]

au fond *French.* (o fɔ̃) *adv.* fundamentally; essentially. [lit.: at the bottom]

auf Wiedersehen *German.* (auf 'viːdərzeːən) *sentence substitute.* goodbye, until we see each other again.

Aug. *abbrev. for* August.

Augean (ɔː'dʒiːən) *adj.* extremely dirty or corrupt. [C16: from *Augeas*, in Gk myth., king whose filthy stables Hercules cleaned in one day]

augend ('ɔːdʒɛnd, ɔː'dʒɛnd) *n.* a number to which another number, the addend, is added. [from L *augendum*, from *augēre* to increase]

auger ('ɔːgə) *n.* **1.** a hand tool with a bit shaped like a corkscrew, for boring holes in wood. **2.** a larger tool of the same kind for boring holes in the ground. [C15: *an augur*, mistaken division of *a nauger*, from OE *nafugār* nave (of a wheel) spear, from *nafu* NAVE² + *gār* spear]

aught *or* **ought** (ɔːt) (*used with a negative or in conditional or interrogative sentences or clauses*) *Arch. or literary.* ~*pron.* **1.** anything whatever (esp. in **for aught I know**). ~*adv.* **2.** *Dialect.* to any degree. [OE *āwiht*, from *ā* ever, + *wiht* thing]

augment (ɔːg'mɛnt) *vb.* to make or become greater in number, strength, etc. [C15: from LL, from *augmentum* growth, from L *augēre* to increase] —**aug'mentable** *adj.* —**aug'menter** *n.*

augmentation (ˌɔːgmɛn'teɪʃən) *n.* **1.** the act of augmenting or the state of being augmented. **2.** the amount by which something is increased.

augmentative (ɔːg'mɛntətɪv) *adj.* **1.** tending or able to augment. **2.** *Grammar.* denoting an affix that may be added to a word to convey the meaning *large* or *great*.

augmented (ɔːg'mɛntɪd) *adj.* **1.** *Music.* (of an interval) increased from being perfect or major by the raising of the higher note or the dropping of the lower note by one semitone: *C to G sharp is an augmented fifth.* **2.** having been increased, esp. in number: *an augmented orchestra.*

au gratin (*French* o gratɛ̃) *adj.* covered and cooked with browned breadcrumbs and sometimes cheese. [F, lit.: with the grating]

Augsburg (*German* 'auksburk) *n.* a city in S West Germany, in Bavaria: founded by the Romans in 14 B.C.; site of the diet that produced the **Peace of Augsburg** (1555), which ended the struggles between Lutherans and Catholics in the Holy Roman Empire and established the principle that each ruler should determine the form of worship in his lands. Pop.: 245 600 (1986). Roman name: **Augusta Vindelicorum** (aʊ'guːstə vɪn'dɛlɪˌkəʊrəm).

augur ('ɔːgə) *n.* **1.** (in ancient Rome) a religious official who observed and interpreted omens and signs. **2.** any prophet or soothsayer. ~*vb.* **3.** to predict (some future event), as from signs or omens. **4.** (*tr.; may take a clause as object*) to be an omen (of). **5.** (*intr.*) to foreshadow future events: *this augurs well for us.* [C14: from L: a diviner, ?from *augēre* to increase] —**augural** ('ɔːgjʊrəl) *adj.*

augury ('ɔːgjʊrɪ) *n., pl.* **-ries. 1.** the art of or a rite conducted by an augur. **2.** a sign or portent; omen.

august (ɔː'gʌst) *adj.* **1.** dignified or imposing. **2.** of noble birth or high rank: *an august lineage.* [C17: from L *augustus*; rel. to *augēre* to increase] —**au'gustness** *n.*

August ('ɔːgəst) *n.* the eighth month of the year, consisting of 31 days. [OE, from L, after the emperor AUGUSTUS]

Augusta (ɔː'gʌstə) *n.* a port in S Italy, in E Sicily. Pop.: 38 900 (1981 est.).

Augustan (ɔː'gʌstən) *adj.* **1.** characteristic of or relating to the Roman emperor Augustus Caesar, his period, or the poets writing during his reign. **2.** of or characteristic of any literary period noted for refinement and classicism, esp. the 18th century in England. ~*n.* **3.** an author in an Augustan Age.

Augustine (ɔː'gʌstɪn) *n.* **1. Saint.** 354–430 A.D., one of the Fathers of the Christian Church; bishop of Hippo in North Africa (396–430), who profoundly influenced both Catholic and Protestant theology. His most famous works are *Confessions*, a spiritual autobiography, and *De Civitate Dei*, a vindication of the Christian Church. Feast day: Aug. 28. **2. Saint.** died 604 A.D., Roman monk, sent to Britain (597 A.D.) to convert the Anglo-Saxons to Christianity and to establish the authority of the Roman See over the native Celtic Church; became the first archbishop of Canterbury (601–604). Feast day: May 26 or 27. **3.** a member of an Augustinian order.

Augustinian (ˌɔːgə'stɪnɪən) *adj.* **1.** of Saint Augustine of Hippo, his doctrines, or the Christian religious orders founded on his doctrines. ~*n.* **2.** a member of any of several religious orders which are governed by the rule of Saint Augustine. **3.** a person who follows the doctrines of Saint Augustine.

Augustus (ɔː'gʌstəs) *n.* original name *Gaius Octavianus;* after his adoption by Julius Caesar (44 B.C.) known as *Gaius Julius Caesar Octavianus.* 63 B.C.–14 A.D., Roman statesman, a member of the second triumvirate (43 B.C.). After defeating Mark Antony at Actium (31 B.C.), he became first emperor of Rome, adopting the title Augustus (27 B.C.).

auk (ɔːk) *n.* **1.** a diving bird of northern oceans having a heavy body, short tail, narrow wings, and a black-and-white plumage. See also **great auk, razorbill. 2. little auk.** a small short-billed auk, abundant in Arctic regions. [C17: from ON *ālka*]

auklet ('ɔːklɪt) *n.* any of various small auks.

au lait (əʊ 'leɪ) *adj.* prepared or served with milk. [F, lit.: with milk]

auld (ɔːld) *adj.* a Scottish word for **old.** [OE *āld*]

auld lang syne ('ɔːld læŋ 'saɪn) *n.* times past, esp. those remembered with nostalgia. [Scot., lit.: old long since]

Aulis ('ɔːlɪs) *n.* an ancient town in E central Greece, in Boeotia: traditionally the harbour from which the Greeks sailed at the beginning of the Trojan war.

au naturel *French.* (o natyrɛl) *adj., adv.* **1.** naked; nude. **2.** uncooked or plainly cooked. [lit.: in (a) natural (condition)]

aunt (ɑːnt) *n.* (*often cap., esp. as a term of address*) **1.** a sister of one's father or mother. **2.** the wife of one's uncle. **3.** a term of address used by children for a female friend of the parents. **4. my (sainted) aunt!** an exclamation of surprise. [C13: from OF, from L *amita* a father's sister]

auntie *or* **aunty** ('ɑːntɪ) *n., pl.* **-ies.** a familiar or diminutive word for **aunt.**

Auntie ('ɑːntɪ) *n. Brit. inf.* the BBC.

Aunt Sally ('sælɪ) *n., pl.* **-lies.** *Brit.* **1.** a figure of an old woman used in fairgrounds and fêtes as a target. **2.** any person who is a target for insults or criticism.

au pair (əʊ 'pɛə) *n.* **a.** a young foreigner, usually a girl, who undertakes housework in exchange for board and lodging, esp. in order to learn the language. **b.** (*as modifier*): *an au pair girl.* [C20: from F: on an equal footing]

aura ('ɔːrə) *n., pl.* **auras** *or* **aurae** ('ɔːriː). **1.** a distinctive air or quality considered to be characteristic of a person or thing. **2.** any invisible emanation, esp. surrounding a person or object. **3.** *Pathol.* strange sensations, such as noises in the ears or flashes of light, that immediately precede an attack, esp. of epilepsy. [C18: via L from Gk: breeze]

aural ('ɔːrəl) *adj.* of or relating to the sense or organs of hearing; auricular. [C19: from L *auris* ear] —**'aurally** *adv.*

Aurangzeb *or* **Aurungzeb** ('ɔːrəŋˌzɛb) *n.* 1618–1707, Mogul emperor of Hindustan (1658–1707), whose reign marked both the height of Mogul prosperity and the decline of its power through the revolts of the Marathas.

aureate ('ɔːrɪɪt) *adj.* **1.** covered with gold; gilded. **2.** (of a style of writing or speaking) excessively elaborate. [C15: from LL, from L *aureus* golden, from *aurum* gold]

Aurelian (ɔː'riːlɪən) *n.* Latin name *Lucius Domitius Aurelianus.* ?212–275 A.D., Roman emperor (270–275), who conquered Palmyra (273) and restored political unity to the Roman Empire.

Aurelius (ɔː'riːlɪəs) *n.* See **Marcus Aurelius Antoninus.**

aureole ('ɔːrɪˌəʊl) *or* **aureola** (ɔː'riːələ) *n.* **1.** a border of light or radiance enveloping the head of a figure represented as holy. **2.** a less common word for **halo. 3.** another name for **corona** (sense 2). [C13: from OF, from Med. L (*corōna*) *aureola* golden (crown), from L, from *aurum* gold]

au revoir *French.* (o rəvwar) *sentence substitute.* goodbye. [lit.: to the seeing again]

auric ('ɔːrɪk) *adj.* of or containing gold, esp. in the trivalent state; designating a gold(III) compound. [C19: from L *aurum* gold]

Auric (*French* ɔrik) *n.* **Georges** (ʒɔrʒ). 1899–1983, French composer; one of *les Six.* His works include ballet and film music.

auricle ('ɔːrɪkəl) *n.* **1.** the upper chamber of the heart; atrium. **2.** Also called: **pinna.** *Anat.* the external part of the ear. **3.** *Biol.* an ear-shaped part or appendage. [C17: from L *auricula* the external ear, from *auris* ear] —'**auricled** *adj.*

auricula (ɔːˈrɪkjʊlə) *n., pl.* **-lae** (-,liː) *or* **-las. 1.** Also called: **bear's-ear.** a widely cultivated alpine primrose with leaves shaped like a bear's ear. **2.** another word for **auricle** (sense 3). [C17: from NL, from L; see AURICLE]

auricular (ɔːˈrɪkjʊlə) *adj.* **1.** of, relating to, or received by the sense or organs of hearing; aural. **2.** shaped like an ear. **3.** of or relating to an auricle of the heart.

auriferous (ɔːˈrɪfərəs) *adj.* (of rock) containing gold; gold-bearing. [C18: from L, from *aurum* gold + *ferre* to bear]

Aurignacian (,ɔːrɪgˈneɪʃən) *adj.* of or produced during a flint culture of the Upper Palaeolithic type characterized by the use of bone and antler tools, and also by cave art. [C20: after *Aurignac,* France, near the cave where remains were discovered]

Auriol (*French* ɔrjɔl) *n.* **Vincent** (vɛ̃sã). 1884–1966, French statesman; president of the Fourth Republic (1947–54).

aurochs ('ɔːrɒks) *n., pl.* **-rochs.** a recently extinct member of the cattle tribe that inhabited forests in N Africa, Europe, and SW Asia. Also called: **urus.** [C18: from G, from OHG *ūrohso,* from *ūro* bison + *ohso* OX]

aurora (ɔːˈrɔːrə) *n., pl.* **-ras** *or* **-rae** (-riː). **1.** an atmospheric phenomenon consisting of bands, curtains, or streamers of light, that move across the sky in polar regions. **2.** *Poetic.* the dawn. [C14: from L: dawn] —**au'roral** *adj.*

Aurora[1] (ɔːˈrɔːrə) *n.* **1.** the Roman goddess of the dawn. Greek counterpart: **Eos. 2.** the dawn or rise of something.

Aurora[2] (ɔːˈrɔːrə) *n.* another name for **Maewo.**

aurora australis (ɒˈstreɪlɪs) *n.* (*sometimes cap.*) the aurora seen around the South Pole. Also called: **southern lights.** [NL: southern aurora]

aurora borealis (,bɔːrɪˈeɪlɪs) *n.* (*sometimes cap.*) the aurora seen around the North Pole. Also called: **northern lights.** [C17: NL: northern aurora]

aurous ('ɔːrəs) *adj.* of or containing gold, esp. in the monovalent state; designating a gold(I) compound. [C19: from F *aureux,* LL *aurōsus* gold-coloured, from L *aurum* gold]

Auschwitz (*German* 'aʊʃvɪts) *n.* an industrial town in S Poland; site of a Nazi concentration camp during World War II. Pop.: 45 200 (1982 est.). Polish name: **Oświęcim.**

auscultation (,ɔːskəlˈteɪʃən) *n.* **1.** the diagnostic technique in medicine of listening to the various internal sounds made by the body, usually with the aid of a stethoscope. **2.** the act of listening. [C19: from L, from *auscultāre* to listen attentively; rel. to L *auris* ear] —'**auscul,tate** *vb.* —**auscultatory** (ɔːˈskʌltətərɪ) *adj.*

Ausonius (ɔːˈsəʊnɪəs) *n.* **Decimus Magnus** ('dɛsɪməs 'mægnəs). ?310–?395 A.D., Latin poet, born in Gaul.

auspice ('ɔːspɪs) *n.* **1.** (*usually pl.*) patronage (esp. in **under the auspices of**). **2.** (*often pl.*) an omen, esp. one that is favourable. [C16: from L *auspicium* augury from birds]

auspicious (ɔːˈspɪʃəs) *adj.* **1.** favourable or propitious. **2.** *Arch.* fortunate. —**aus'piciously** *adv.* —**aus'piciousness** *n.*

Aussie ('ɒzɪ) *n., adj. Inf.* Australian.

Aust. *abbrev. for:* **1.** Australia(n). **2.** Austria(n).

Austen ('ɒstɪn, 'ɔː-) *n.* **Jane.** 1775–1817, English novelist, noted particularly for the insight and delicate irony of her portrayal of middle-class families. Her completed novels are *Sense and Sensibility* (1811), *Pride and Prejudice* (1813), *Mansfield Park* (1814), *Emma* (1816), *Northanger Abbey* (1818), and *Persuasion* (1818).

austere (ɒˈstɪə) *adj.* **1.** stern or severe in attitude or manner. **2.** grave, sober, or serious. **3.** self-disciplined, abstemious, or ascetic: *an austere life.* **4.** severely simple or plain: *an austere design.* [C14: from OF, from L *austērus* sour, from Gk *austēros* astringent; rel. to Gk *hauein* to dry] —**aus'terely** *adv.*

austerity (ɒˈstɛrɪtɪ) *n., pl.* **-ties. 1.** the state or quality of being austere. **2.** (*often pl.*) an austere habit, practice, or act. **3. a.** reduced availability of luxuries and consumer goods. **b.** (*as modifier*): *an austerity budget.*

Austerlitz ('ɔːstəlɪts) *n.* a town in central Czechoslovakia, in Moravia: site of Napoleon's victory over the Russian and Austrian armies in 1805. Pop.: 4747 (1972 est.). Czech name: **Slavkov.**

Austin[1] ('ɒstɪn) *n.* a city in central Texas, on the Colorado River: state capital since 1845. Pop.: 345 496 (1980).

Austin[2] ('ɒstɪn, 'ɔː-) *n.* **1. John.** 1790–1859, British jurist, whose book *The Province of Jurisprudence Determined* (1832) greatly influenced legal theory and the English legal system. **2. John Langshaw** ('læŋʃɔː). 1911–60, English philosopher, whose lectures *Sense and Sensibilia* and *How to do Things with Words* were published posthumously in 1962.

austral ('ɔːstrəl) *adj.* of or coming from the south: *austral winds.* [C14: from L *austrālis,* from *auster* the south wind]

Austral. *abbrev. for:* **1.** Australasia. **2.** Australia(n).

Australasia (,ɒstrəˈleɪzɪə) *n.* **1.** Australia, New Zealand, and neighbouring islands in the S Pacific Ocean. **2.** (loosely) the whole of Oceania. —,**Austra'lasian** *adj.*

Australia (ɒˈstreɪlɪə) *n.* the smallest continent, situated between the Indian Ocean and the Pacific: a former British colony, now an independent member of the Commonwealth; consists chiefly of a low plateau, mostly arid in the west, with the basin of the Murray River and the Great Dividing Range in the east and the Great Barrier Reef off the NE coast. Language: English. Currency: dollar. Capital: Canberra. Pop.: 16 102 000 (1987 est.). Area: 7 682 300 sq. km (2 966 150 sq. miles). —**Aus'tralian** *adj., n.*

Australiana (ɒ,streɪlɪ'ɑːnə) *n.* objects, books, documents, etc. relating to Australia and its history and culture.

Australian Alps *pl. n.* a mountain range in SE Australia, in E Victoria and SE New South Wales. Highest peak: Mount Kosciusko, 2195 m (7316 ft.).

Australian Antarctic Territory *n.* the area of Antarctica, other than Adélie Land, that is administered by Australia, lying south of latitude 60°S and between longitudes 45°E and 160°E.

Australian Capital Territory *n.* a territory of SE Australia, within New South Wales: consists of two exclaves, one containing Canberra, the capital of Australia, and one at Jervis Bay. Pop.: 263 085 (1985). Area: 2432 sq. km (939 sq. miles). Former name: **Federal Capital Territory.**

Australian Rules *n.* (*functioning as sing.*) a game resembling rugby, played in Australia between teams of 18 men each on an oval pitch, with a ball resembling a large rugby ball. Players attempt to kick the ball between posts (without crossbars) at either end of the pitch.

Australian terrier *n.* a small wire-haired breed of terrier *n.* a small wire-haired breed of terrier similar to the cairn.

Austral Islands ('ɔːstrəl) *pl. n.* another name for the **Tubuai Islands.**

Australoid ('ɒstrə,lɔɪd) *adj.* **1.** denoting, relating to, or belonging to a racial group that includes the Australian Aborigines and certain other peoples of southern Asia and the Pacific islands. ~*n.* **2.** any member of this racial group.

australopithecine (,ɒstrələʊ'pɪθɪ,siːn) *n.* any of various extinct apelike primates whose remains have been found in southern and E Africa. Some species are estimated to be over 4.5 million years old. [C20: from NL, from L *austrālis* southern + Gk *pithēkos* ape]

Australorp ('ɒstrə,lɔːp) *n.* a heavy black breed of domestic fowl laying brown eggs. [shortened from *Austral(ian Black) Orp(ington)*]

Austrasia (ɒˈstreɪʒə, -ʃə) *n.* the eastern region of the kingdom of the Merovingian Franks that had its capital at Metz and lasted from 511 A.D. until 814 A.D. It covered the area now comprising NE France, Belgium, and western Germany.

Austria ('ɒstrɪə) *n.* a republic in central Europe: ruled by the Hapsburgs from 1282 to 1918; formed a dual monarchy with Hungary in 1867 and became a republic in 1919; contains part of the Alps, the Danube basin in the east, and extensive forests. Language: German. Religion: chiefly Roman Catholic. Currency: schilling. Capital: Vienna. Pop.: 7 564 000 (1986). Area: 83 849 sq. km (32 374 sq. miles). German name: **Osterreich.** —'**Austrian** *adj., n.*

Austrian blind *n.* a window blind consisting of rows of vertically gathered fabric that may be drawn up to form a series of ruches.

Austro-[1] ('ɒstrəʊ) *combining form.* southern: *Austro-Asiatic.* [from L *auster* the south wind]

Austro-[2] ('ɒstrəʊ) *combining form.* Austrian: *Austro-Hungarian.*

Austronesia (,ɒstrəʊ'niːʒə, -ʃə) *n.* the islands of the central and S Pacific, including Indonesia, Melanesia, Micronesia, and Polynesia. — ,Austro'nesian *adj., n.*

AUT (in Britain) *abbrev. for* Association of University Teachers.

autarchy ('ɔːtɑːkɪ) *n., pl.* **-chies.** unlimited rule; autocracy. [C17: from Gk *autarkhia*, from *autarkhos* autocratic] — **au'tarchic** *or* **au'tarchical** *adj.*

autarky ('ɔːtɑːkɪ) *n., pl.* **-kies.** (esp. of a political unit) a system or policy of economic self-sufficiency. [C17: from Gk *autarkeia*, from *autarkēs* self-sufficient, from AUTO- + *arkein* to suffice] — **au'tarkic** *adj.* — 'autarkist *n.*

authentic (ɔː'θɛntɪk) *adj.* **1.** of undisputed origin or authorship; genuine. **2.** trustworthy; reliable: *an authentic account.* **3.** (of a deed, etc.) duly executed. **4.** *Music.* commencing on the final and ending an octave higher. Cf. **plagal.** [C14: from LL *authenticus* coming from the author, from Gk, from *authentēs* one who acts independently, from AUTO- + *hentēs* a doer] — **au'thentically** *adv.* —**authenticity** (,ɔːθɛn'tɪsɪtɪ) *n.*

authenticate (ɔː'θɛntɪ,keɪt) *vb.* (*tr.*) **1.** to establish as genuine or valid. **2.** to give authority or legal validity to. — **au,thenti'cation** *n.* — **au'thenti,cator** *n.*

author ('ɔːθə) *n.* **1.** a person who composes a book, article, or other written work. Related adj.: **auctorial.** **2.** a person who writes books as a profession; writer. **3.** an originator or creator: *the author of this plan.* ~*vb.* (*tr.*) **4.** to write or originate. [C14: from OF, from L *auctor* author, from *augēre* to increase] — **authorial** (ɔː'θɔːrɪəl) *adj.*

authoritarian (ɔː,θɒrɪ'tɛərɪən) *adj.* **1.** favouring or characterized by strict obedience to authority. **2.** favouring or relating to government by a small elite. **3.** dictatorial; domineering. ~*n.* **4.** a person who favours or practises authoritarian policies.

authoritative (ɔː'θɒrɪtətɪv) *adj.* **1.** recognized or accepted as being true or reliable. **2.** commanding: *an authoritative manner.* **3.** possessing or supported by authority; official. — **au'thoritatively** *adv.* — **au'thoritativeness** *n.*

authority (ɔː'θɒrɪtɪ) *n., pl.* **-ties.** **1.** the power or right to control, judge, or prohibit the actions of others. **2.** (*often pl.*) a person or group of people having this power, such as a government, police force, etc. **3.** a position that commands such a power or right (often in **in authority**). **4.** such a power or right delegated: *she has his authority.* **5.** the ability to influence or control others. **6.** an expert or an authoritative written work in a particular field. **7.** evidence or testimony. **8.** confidence resulting from great expertise. **9.** (*cap. when part of a name*) a public board or corporation exercising governmental authority: *Independent Broadcasting Authority.* [C14: from OF, from L, from *auctor* author]

authorize *or* **-rise** ('ɔːθə,raɪz) *vb.* (*tr.*) **1.** to confer authority upon (someone to do something). **2.** to permit (someone to do or be something) with official sanction. — ,authori'zation *or* -ri'sation *n.*

Authorized Version *n.* **the.** an English translation of the Bible published in 1611 under James I. Also called: **King James Version.**

authorship ('ɔːθə,ʃɪp) *n.* **1.** the origin or originator of a written work, plan, etc. **2.** the profession of writing books.

autism ('ɔːtɪzəm) *n. Psychiatry.* abnormal self-absorption, usually affecting children, characterized by lack of response to people and limited ability to communicate. [C20: from Gk *autos* self + -ISM] —**au'tistic** *adj.*

auto ('ɔːtəʊ) *n., pl.* **-tos.** *U.S. & Canad. inf.* **a.** short for **automobile.** **b.** (*as modifier*): *auto parts.*

auto. *abbrev. for:* **1.** automatic. **2.** automobile. **3.** automotive.

auto- *or sometimes before a vowel* **aut-** *combining form.* **1.** self; same; or of by the same one: *autobiography.* **2.** self-caused: *autohypnosis.* **3.** self-propelling: *automobile.* [from AUTO- + *hentēs* a doer]

autobahn ('ɔːtə,bɑːn) *n.* a German motorway. [C20: from G from *Auto* car + *Bahn* road, track]

autobiography (,ɔːtəbaɪ'ɒɡrəfɪ) *n., pl.* **-phies.** an account of a person's life written or otherwise recorded by that person. — ,autobi'ographer *n.* —**autobiographical** (,ɔːtə,baɪə'ɡræfɪkəl) *adj.*

autocephalous (,ɔːtəʊ'sɛfələs) *adj.* (of an Eastern Christian Church) governed by its own national synods and appointing its own patriarchs or prelates.

autochthon (ɔː'tɒkθən) *n., pl.* **-thons** *or* **-thones** (-θə,niːz). **1.** (*often pl.*) one of the earliest known inhabitants of any country. **2.** an animal or plant that is native to a particular region. [C17: from Gk *autokhthōn* from the earth itself, from AUTO- + *khthōn* the earth] —**au'tochthonous** *adj.*

autoclave ('ɔːtə,kleɪv) *n.* **1.** a strong sealed vessel used for chemical reactions at high pressure. **2.** an apparatus for sterilizing objects (esp. surgical instruments) by means of steam under pressure. [C19: from F AUTO- + -*clave*, from L *clāvis* key]

autocracy (ɔː'tɒkrəsɪ) *n., pl.* **-cies.** **1.** government by an individual with unrestricted authority. **2.** a country, society, etc., ruled by an autocrat.

autocrat ('ɔːtə,kræt) *n.* **1.** a ruler who possesses absolute and unrestricted authority. **2.** a domineering or dictatorial person. — ,auto'cratic *adj.* — ,auto'cratically *adv.*

autocross ('ɔːtəʊ,krɒs) *n.* a motor sport in which cars race over a half-mile circuit of rough grass.

Autocue ('ɔːtəʊ,kjuː) *n. Trademark.* an electronic television prompting device whereby a script, unseen by the audience, is displayed for the speaker.

auto-da-fé (,ɔːtəʊdə'feɪ) *n., pl.* **autos-da-fé.** **1.** *History.* a ceremony of the Spanish Inquisition including the pronouncement and execution of sentences passed on sinners or heretics. **2.** the burning to death of people condemned as heretics by the Inquisition. [C18: from Port., lit.: act of the faith]

autoeroticism (,ɔːtəʊɪ'rɒtɪ,sɪzəm) *or* **autoerotism** (,ɔːtəʊ'ɛrə,tɪzəm) *n. Psychol.* the arousal and use of one's own body as a sexual object. — ,autoe'rotic *adj.*

autogamy (ɔː'tɒɡəmɪ) *n.* self-fertilization. —**au'togamous** *adj.*

autogenous (ɔː'tɒdʒɪnəs) *adj.* **1.** originating within the body. **2.** self-produced. **3.** (of a joint between two parts) achieved without flux, adhesive, or solder: *autogenous welding.*

autogiro *or* **autogyro** (,ɔːtəʊ'dʒaɪrəʊ) *n., pl.* **-ros.** a self-propelled aircraft supported in flight mainly by unpowered rotating horizontal blades. [C20: orig. a trademark]

autograph ('ɔːtə,ɡrɑːf) *n.* **1. a.** a handwritten signature, esp. that of a famous person. **b.** (*as modifier*): *an autograph album.* **2.** a person's handwriting. **3. a.** a book, document, etc., handwritten by its author. **b.** (*as modifier*): *an autograph letter.* ~*vb.* (*tr.*) **4.** to write one's signature on or in; sign. **5.** to write with one's own hand. —**autographic** (,ɔːtə'ɡræfɪk) *adj.* — ,auto'graphically *adv.*

autohypnosis (,ɔːtəʊhɪp'nəʊsɪs) *n. Psychol.* the process or result of self-induced hypnosis.

autointoxication (,ɔːtəʊɪn,tɒksɪ'keɪʃən) *n.* self-poisoning caused by toxic products originating within the body.

Autolycus (ɔː'tɒlɪkəs) *n. Greek myth.* a thief who stole cattle from his neighbour Sisyphus and prevented him from recognizing them by making them invisible.

autolysis (ɔː'tɒlɪsɪs) *n.* the destruction of cells and tissues of an organism by enzymes produced by the cells themselves. —**autolytic** (,ɔːtə'lɪtɪk) *adj.*

automat ('ɔːtə,mæt) *n.* another name, esp. U.S., for **vending machine.**

automata (ɔː'tɒmətə) *n.* a plural of **automaton.**

automate ('ɔːtə,meɪt) *vb.* to make (a manufacturing process, factory, etc.) automatic, or (of a manufacturing process, etc.) to be made automatic.

automatic (,ɔːtə'mætɪk) *adj.* **1.** performed from force of habit or without conscious thought: *an automatic smile.* **2. a.** (of a device, mechanism, etc.) able to activate, move, or regulate itself. **b.** (of an act or process) performed by such automatic equipment. **3.** (of the action of a muscle, etc.) involuntary or reflex. **4.** occurring as a necessary consequence: *promotion is automatic after a year.* **5.** (of a firearm) utilizing some of the force of each explosion to eject the empty shell, replace it with a new one, and fire continuously until release of the trigger. ~*n.* **6.** an automatic firearm. **7.** a motor vehicle having automatic transmission. **8.** a machine that operates automatically. [C18: from Gk *automatos* acting independently] — ,auto'matically *adv.*

automatic data processing *n.* data processing performed by automatic electromechanical devices. Abbrev.: **ADP, A.D.P., a.d.p.** Cf. **electronic data processing.**

automatic gain control *n.* a control of a radio receiver which adjusts the magnitude of the input so that the output (or volume) remains approximately constant.

automatic pilot *n.* a device that automatically maintains an aircraft on a preset course. Also called: **autopilot.**

automatic transmission *n.* a transmission system in a motor vehicle in which the gears change automatically.

automation (,ɔːtə'meɪʃən) *n.* **1.** the use of methods for controlling industrial processes automatically, esp. by electronically controlled systems. **2.** the extent to which a process is so controlled.

automatism (ɔː'tɒmə,tɪzəm) *n.* **1.** the state or quality of being automatic; mechanical or involuntary action. **2.** *Psychol.* the performance of actions, such as sleepwalking, without conscious knowledge or control. —**au'tomatist** *n.*

automatize *or* **-tise** (ɔː'tɒmə,taɪz) *vb.* to make (a process, etc.) automatic or (of a process, etc.) to be made automatic. —**au,tomati'zation** *or* **-ti'sation** *n.*

automaton (ɔː'tɒmət³n) *n., pl.* **-tons** *or* **-ta. 1.** a mechanical device operating under its own hidden power. **2.** a person who acts mechanically. [C17: from L, from Gk, from *automatos* spontaneous]

autometer ('ɔːtəʊ,miːtə) *n.* a small device inserted in a photocopier to enable copying to begin and to record the number of copies made.

automobile ('ɔːtəmə,biːl) *n.* another word (esp. U.S.) for **car** (sense 1). —,**automo'bilist** *n.*

automotive (,ɔːtə'məʊtɪv) *adj.* **1.** relating to motor vehicles. **2.** self-propelling.

autonomic (,ɔːtə'nɒmɪk) *adj.* **1.** occurring spontaneously. **2.** of or relating to the autonomic nervous system. **3.** Also: **autonomous.** (of plant movements) occurring as a result of internal stimuli. —,**auto'nomically** *adv.*

autonomic nervous system *n.* the section of the nervous system of vertebrates that controls the involuntary actions of the smooth muscles, heart, and glands.

autonomous (ɔː'tɒnəməs) *adj.* **1.** (of a community, country, etc.) possessing a large degree of self-government. **2.** of or relating to an autonomous community. **3.** independent of others. **4.** *Biol.* existing as an organism independent of other organisms or parts. [C19: from Gk *autonomos* living under one's own laws, from AUTO- + *nomos* law] —**au'tonomously** *adv.*

autonomy (ɔː'tɒnəmɪ) *n., pl.* **-mies. 1.** the right or state of self-government, esp. when limited. **2.** a state or individual possessing autonomy. **3.** freedom to determine one's own actions, behaviour, etc. **4.** *Philosophy.* the doctrine that the individual human will is, or ought to be, governed only by its own principles and laws. [C17: from Gk *automonia* freedom to live by one's own laws]

autopilot ('ɔːtə'paɪlət) *n.* short for **automatic pilot.**

autopsy ('ɔːtəpsɪ, ɔː'tɒp-) *n., pl.* **-sies. 1.** Also called: **postmortem examination.** dissection and examination of a dead body to determine the cause of death. **2.** an eyewitness observation. **3.** any critical analysis. [C17: from NL, from Gk: seeing with one's own eyes, from AUTO- + *opsis* sight]

autoroute ('ɔːtəʊ,ruːt) *n.* a French motorway. [C20: from F from *auto* car + *route* road]

autostrada ('ɔːtəʊ,strɑːdə) *n.* an Italian motorway. [C20: from It. from *auto* car + *strada* road]

autosuggestion (,ɔːtəʊsə'dʒɛstʃən) *n.* a process of suggestion in which the person unconsciously supplies the means of influencing his own behaviour or beliefs.

autotelic (,ɔːtəʊ'tɛlɪk) *adj.* being or having an end or justification in itself. [C20: from AUTO- + Gk *telos* end]

auto-teller ('ɔːtəʊ,tɛlə) *n. Banking.* a computerized dispenser that can provide cash or account information at any time.

autotomy (ɔː'tɒtəmɪ) *n., pl.* **-mies.** the casting off by an animal of a part of its body, to facilitate escape when attacked. —**autotomic** (,ɔːtə'tɒmɪk) *adj.*

autotrophic (,ɔːtə'trɒfɪk) *adj.* (of organisms such as green plants) capable of manufacturing complex organic nutritive compounds from simple inorganic sources.

autumn ('ɔːtəm) *n.* **1.** (*sometimes cap.*) **a.** Also called (esp. U.S. and Canad.): **fall.** the season of the year between summer and winter, astronomically from the September equinox to the December solstice in the N

hemisphere and from the March equinox to the June solstice in the S hemisphere. **b.** (*as modifier*): *autumn leaves.* **2.** a period of late maturity, esp. one followed by a decline. [C14: from L *autumnus*] —**autumnal** (ɔː'tʌmn³l) *adj.*

autumn crocus *n.* a plant of the lily family having pink or purplish autumn flowers, found in Europe and N Africa.

Auvergne (əʊ'vɛən, əʊ'vɜːn; *French* ovɛrɲ) *n.* a region of S central France: largely mountainous, rising over 1800 m (6000 ft.).

aux. *abbrev. for* auxiliary.

auxanometer (,ɔːksə'nɒmɪtə) *n.* an instrument that measures the linear growth of plant shoots. [C19: from Gk *auxanein* to increase + -METER]

Aux Cayes (əʊ 'keɪ; *French* o kaj) *n.* the former name of **Les Cayes.**

auxiliaries (ɔːg'zɪljərɪz, -'zɪlə-) *pl. n.* foreign troops serving another nation; mercenaries.

auxiliary (ɔːg'zɪljərɪ, -'zɪlə-) *adj.* **1.** secondary or supplementary. **2.** supporting. ~*n., pl.* **-ries. 3.** a person or thing that supports or supplements. **4.** *Naut.* **a.** a sailing vessel with an engine. **b.** the engine of such a vessel. [C17: from L, from *auxilium* help, from *augēre* to increase, strengthen]

auxiliary verb *n.* a verb used to indicate the tense, voice, or mood of another verb where this is not indicated by inflection, such as English *will* in *he will go.*

auxin ('ɔːksɪn) *n.* a plant hormone that promotes growth. [C20: from Gk *auxein* to grow]

AV *abbrev. for* Authorized Version (of the Bible).

av. *abbrev. for:* **1.** average. **2.** avoirdupois.

Av. *or* **av.** *abbrev. for* avenue.

a.v. *or* **A/V** *abbrev. for* ad valorem.

avadavat (,ævədə'væt) *or* **amadavat** (,æmədə'væt) *n.* either of two Asian weaverbirds having a red plumage: often kept as cagebirds. [C18: from *Ahmadabad*, Indian city from which these birds were brought to Europe]

avail (ə'veɪl) *vb.* **1.** to be of use, advantage, profit, or assistance (to). **2. avail oneself of.** to make use of to one's advantage. ~*n.* **3.** use or advantage (esp. in **of no avail, to little avail**). [C13 *availen*, from OF *valoir*, from L *valēre* to be strong]

available (ə'veɪləb³l) *adj.* **1.** obtainable or accessible; capable of being made use of. **2.** *Arch.* advantageous. —**a,vaila'bility** *or* **a'vailableness** *n.* —**a'vailably** *adv.*

avalanche ('ævə,lɑːntʃ) *n.* **1. a.** a fall of large masses of snow and ice down a mountain. **b.** a fall of rocks, sand, etc. **2.** a sudden or overwhelming appearance of a large quantity of things. ~*vb.* **3.** to come down overwhelmingly (upon). [C18: from F, by mistaken division from *la valanche*, from *valanche*, from dialect *lavantse*]

Avalon ('ævə,lɒn) *n. Celtic myth.* an island paradise in the western seas: in Arthurian legend it is where King Arthur was taken after he was mortally wounded. [from Med L *insula avallonis* island of Avalon, from O Welsh *aballon* apple]

Avalon Peninsula *n.* a large peninsula of Newfoundland, between Trinity and Placentia Bays. Area: about 10 000 sq. km (4000 sq. miles).

avant-garde (,ævɒŋ'gɑːd) *n.* **1.** those artists, writers, musicians, etc., whose techniques and ideas are in advance of those generally accepted. ~*adj.* **2.** of such artists, etc., their ideas, or techniques. [from F: VANGUARD]

avarice ('ævərɪs) *n.* extreme greed for riches. [C13: from OF, from L, from *avārus* covetous, from *avēre* to crave] —**avaricious** (,ævə'rɪʃəs) *adj.*

avast (ə'vɑːst) *sentence substitute. Naut.* stop! cease! [C17: ?from Du. *hou'vast* hold fast]

avatar ('ævə,tɑː) *n.* **1.** *Hinduism.* the manifestation of a deity in human or animal form. **2.** a visible manifestation of an abstract concept. [C18: from Sansk. *avatāra* a going down, from *ava* down + *tarati* he passes over]

avaunt (ə'vɔːnt) *sentence substitute. Arch.* go away! depart! [C15: from OF *avant!* forward! from LL *ab ante* forward, from L *ab* from + *ante* before]

avdp. *abbrev. for* avoirdupois.

ave ('ɑːvɪ, 'ɑːveɪ) *sentence substitute.* welcome or farewell. [L]

Ave[1] ('ɑːvɪ) *n. R.C. Church.* short for **Ave Maria:** see **Hail Mary.** [C13: from L: hail!]

Ave[2] *or* **ave** *abbrev. for* avenue.

Avebury ('eɪvbərɪ) *n.* a village in Wiltshire, near Stonehenge: site of an extensive neolithic stone circle.

Aveiro (*Portuguese* ə'veːiru) *n.* a port in N central Portugal, on the **Aveiro lagoon:** ancient Roman town; linked by canal with the Atlantic Ocean. Pop.: 28 625 (1981 est.). Ancient name: **Talabriga** (ˌtælə'briːgə).

Avellaneda (*Spanish* aβeʎa'neða) *n.* a city in E Argentina, an industrial suburb of Buenos Aires. Pop.: 334 145 (1980).

avenge (ə'vɛndʒ) *vb.* (*usually tr.*) to inflict a punishment in retaliation for (harm, injury, etc.) done to (a person or persons): *to avenge a crime; to avenge a murdered friend.* [C14: from OF, from *vengier*, from L *vindicāre*; see VENGEANCE, VINDICATE] —**a'venger** *n.*

avens ('ævɪnz) *n.*, *pl.* **-ens.** (*functioning as sing.*) **1.** any of a genus of plants, such as **water avens,** which has a purple calyx and orange-pink flowers. **2. mountain avens.** a trailing evergreen white-flowered shrub that grows on mountains in N temperate regions. [C15: from OF, from Med. L *avencia* a variety of clover]

aventurine (ə'vɛntjurin) *or* **avanturine** (ə'væntjurin) *n.* **1.** a dark-coloured glass, usually green or brown, spangled with fine particles of gold, copper, or some other metal. **2.** a variety of quartz containing red or greenish particles of iron oxide or mica. [C19: from F, from It., from *avventura* chance; so named because usually found by accident]

avenue ('ævɪnjuː) *n.* **1. a.** a broad street, often lined with trees. **b.** (*cap. as part of a street name*) a road, esp. in a built-up area. **2.** a main approach road, as to a country house. **3.** a way bordered by two rows of trees. **4.** a line of approach: *explore every avenue.* [C17: from F, from *avenir* to come to, from L, from *venīre* to come]

aver (ə'vɜː) *vb.* **averring, averred.** (*tr.*) **1.** to state positively. **2.** *Law.* to allege as a fact or prove to be true. [C14: from OF, from Med. L *adverāre*, from L *vērus* true] —**a'verment** *n.*

average ('ævərɪdʒ, 'ævrɪdʒ) *n.* **1.** the typical or normal amount, quality, degree, etc.: *above average in intelligence.* **2.** Also called: **arithmetic mean.** the result obtained by adding the numbers or quantities in a set and dividing the total by the number of members in the set: *the average of 3, 4, and 8 is 5.* **3.** a similar mean for continuously variable ratios, such as speed. **4.** *Maritime law.* **a.** a loss incurred or damage suffered by a ship or its cargo at sea. **b.** the equitable apportionment of such loss among the interested parties. **5. on** (**the** *or* **an**) **average.** usually; typically. ~*adj.* **6.** usual or typical. **7.** mediocre or inferior: *his performance was only average.* **8.** constituting a numerical average: *an average speed.* **9.** approximately typical of a range of values: *the average contents of a matchbox.* ~*vb.* **10.** (*tr.*) to obtain or estimate a numerical average of. **11.** (*tr.*) to assess the general quality of. **12.** (*tr.*) to perform or receive a typical number of: *to average eight hours' work a day.* **13.** (*tr.*) to divide up proportionately. **14.** to amount to or be on average: *the children averaged 15 years of age.* [C15 *averay* loss arising from damage to ships, from OIt. *avaria*, ult. from Ar. *awār* damage, blemish] —**'averagely** *adv.*

Averno (*Italian* a'vɛrno) *n.* a crater lake in Italy, near Naples: in ancient times regarded as an entrance to hell. Latin name: **Avernus** (ə'vɜːnəs). [from L, from Gk *aornos* without birds, from A⁻¹ + *ornis* bird; referring to the legend that the lake's sulphurous exhalations killed birds]

Averroës (ə'vɛrəʊˌiːz) *n.* Arabic name *ibn-Rushd.* 1126– 88, Arab philosopher and physician in Spain, noted particularly for his attempts to reconcile Aristotelian philosophy with Islamic religion, which profoundly influenced Christian scholasticism.

averse (ə'vɜːs) *adj.* (*postpositive*; usually foll. by *to*) opposed, disinclined, or loath. [C16: from L, from *āvertere* to turn from, from *vertere* to turn] —**a'versely** *adv.* —**a'verseness** *n.*

▷ **Usage.** *To* is the preposition now normally used with *averse* (*he was averse to giving any assistance*), although *from* is often used with *averse* and *aversion* and was at one time considered to be grammatically correct.

aversion (ə'vɜːʃən) *n.* **1.** (usually foll. by *to* or *for*) extreme dislike or disinclination. **2.** a person or thing that arouses this: *he is my pet aversion.*

aversion therapy *n. Psychiatry.* a way of suppressing an undesirable habit, such as smoking, by associating an unpleasant effect, such as an electric shock, with the habit.

avert (ə'vɜːt) *vb.* (*tr.*) **1.** to turn away or aside: *to avert one's gaze.* **2.** to ward off: *to avert danger.* [C15: from OF, from L *āvertere*; see AVERSE] —**a'vertible** *or* **a'vertable** *adj.*

Avesta (ə'vɛstə) *n.* a collection of sacred writings of Zoroastrianism, including the Songs of Zoroaster.

Avestan (ə'vɛstən) *n.* **1.** the earliest recorded form of the Iranian language, formerly called **Zend.** ~*adj.* **2.** of the Avesta or its language.

Aveyron (*French* avɛrɔ̃) *n.* a department of S France in Midi-Pyrénées region. Capital: Rodez. Pop.: 278 654 (1982). Area: 8771 sq. km (3421 sq. miles).

avg. *abbrev. for* average.

avian ('eɪvɪən) *adj.* of, relating to, or resembling a bird. [C19: from L *avis* bird]

aviary ('eɪvjərɪ) *n.*, *pl.* **aviaries.** a large enclosure in which birds are kept. [C16: from L, from *aviārius* concerning birds, from *avis* bird]

aviation (ˌeɪvɪ'eɪʃən) *n.* **1.** the art or science of flying aircraft. **2.** the design, production, and maintenance of aircraft. [C19: from F, from L *avis* bird]

aviator ('eɪvɪˌeɪtə) *n. Old-fashioned.* the pilot of an aeroplane or airship; flier. —**'aviˌatrix** *or* **'aviˌatress** *fem. n.*

Avicenna (ˌævɪ'sɛnə) *n.* Arabic name *ibn-Sina.* 980– 1037, Arab philosopher and physician whose philosophical writings, which combined Aristotelianism with neo-Platonist ideas, greatly influenced scholasticism, and whose medical work *Qanun* was the greatest single influence on medieval medicine.

avid ('ævɪd) *adj.* **1.** very keen; enthusiastic: *an avid reader.* **2.** (*postpositive*; often foll. by *for* or *of*) eager (for): *avid for revenge.* [C18: from L, from *avēre* to long for] —**avidity** (ə'vɪdɪtɪ) *n.* —**'avidly** *adv.*

Aviemore (ˌævɪ'mɔː) *n.* a winter sports resort in Scotland, in Highland region between the Monadhliath and Cairngorm Mountains.

avifauna (ˌeɪvɪ'fɔːnə) *n.* all the birds in a particular region. —ˌavi'faunal *adj.*

Avignon (*French* aviɲɔ̃) *n.* a city in SE France, on the Rhône: seat of the papacy (1309–77); famous 12th-century bridge, now partly destroyed. Pop.: 88 661 (1983 est.).

Ávila (*Spanish* 'aβila) *n.* a city in central Spain: 11th-century granite walls and Romanesque cathedral. Pop.: 40 173 (1981).

avionics (ˌeɪvɪ'ɒnɪks) *n.* **1.** (*functioning as sing.*) the science and technology of electronics applied to aeronautics. **2.** (*functioning as pl.*) the electronic circuits and devices of an aerospace vehicle. [C20: from *avi(ation electr)onics*] —ˌavi'onic *adj.*

avitaminosis (æ,vɪtəmɪn'əʊsɪs) *n.*, *pl.* **-ses** (-siːz). any disease caused by a vitamin deficiency in the diet.

Avlona (æv'ləʊnə) *n.* the ancient name for **Vlorë.**

avocado (ˌævə'kɑːdəʊ) *n.*, *pl.* **-dos.** **1.** a pear-shaped fruit having a leathery green or blackish skin, a large stony seed, and a greenish-yellow edible pulp. **2.** the tropical American tree that bears this fruit. **3. a.** a dull greenish colour. **b.** (*as adj.*): *an avocado bathroom suite.* ~Also called (for senses 1 & 2): **avocado pear, alligator pear.** [C17: from Sp. *aguacate*, from Nahuatl *ahuacatl* testicle, alluding to the shape of the fruit]

avocation (ˌævə'keɪʃən) *n. Arch.* **1.** a minor occupation undertaken as a diversion. **2.** a person's regular job. [C17: from L, from *āvocāre* to distract, from *vocāre* to call]

avocet ('ævəˌsɛt) *n.* a long-legged shore bird having black-and-white plumage and a long slender upward-curving bill. [C18: from F, from It. *avocetta*, from ?]

Avogadro (ˌævə'gɑːdrəʊ; *Italian* avo'ɡaːdro) *n.* **Amedeo** (ame'dɛːo), *Conte di Quaregna.* 1776– 1856, Italian physicist, noted for his work on gases.

Avogadro constant *or* **number** *n.* the number of atoms or molecules in a mole of a substance, equal to 6.02252 × 10^{23} per mole.

Avogadro's law *or* **hypothesis** *n.* the principle that equal volumes of all gases contain the same number of molecules at the same temperature and pressure.

avoid (ə'vɔɪd) *vb.* (*tr.*) **1.** to keep out of the way of. **2.** to refrain from doing. **3.** to prevent from happening: *to avoid damage to machinery.* **4.** *Law.* to invalidate; quash. [C14: from Anglo-F, from OF *esvuidier*, from *vuidier* to empty] —**a'voidable** *adj.* —**a'voidably** *adv.* —**a'voidance** *n.* —**a'voider** *n.*

avoirdupois *or* **avoirdupois weight** (ˌævədə'pɔɪz) *n.* a system of weights used in many English-speaking countries. It is based on the pound, which contains 16 ounces or 7000 grains. [C14: from OF *aver de peis* goods of weight]

Avon¹ ('eɪvⁿn) *n.* **1.** (since 1974) a county of SW England, comprising areas that were formerly parts of N Somerset and Gloucestershire. Administrative centre: Bristol. Pop.:

909 408 (1981). Area: 1346 sq. km (520 sq. miles). **2.** a river in central England, rising in Northamptonshire and flowing southwest through Stratford-on-Avon to the River Severn at Tewkesbury. Length: 154 km (96 miles). **3.** a river in SW England, rising in Gloucestershire and flowing south and west through Bristol to the Severn estuary at **Avonmouth.** Length: 120 km (75 miles). **4.** a river in S England, rising in Wiltshire and flowing south to the English Channel. Length: about 96 km (60 miles).

Avon[2] ('eɪvᵊn) n. **Earl of.** title of (Anthony) **Eden.**

avouch (ə'vaʊtʃ) vb. (tr.) Arch. **1.** to vouch for; guarantee. **2.** to acknowledge. **3.** to assert. [C16: from OF avochier to summon, call on, from L advocāre; see ADVOCATE] —**a'vouchment** n.

avow (ə'vaʊ) vb. (tr.) **1.** to state or affirm. **2.** to admit openly. [C13: from OF avouer to confess, from L advocāre to appeal to, call upon] —**a'vowal** n. —**a'vowed** adj. —**avowedly** (ə'vaʊɪdlɪ) adv. —**a'vower** n.

avuncular (ə'vʌŋkjʊlə) adj. **1.** of or concerned with an uncle. **2.** resembling an uncle; friendly. [C19: from L avunculus (maternal) uncle, dim. of avus grandfather]

AWACS or **Awacs** ('eɪwæks) n. acronym for Airborne Warning and Control System.

await (ə'weɪt) vb. **1.** (tr.) to wait for. **2.** (tr.) to be in store for. **3.** (intr.) to wait, esp. with expectation.

awake (ə'weɪk) vb. **awaking; awoke** or **awaked; awoken** or **awaked. 1.** to emerge or rouse from sleep. **2.** to become or cause to become alert. **3.** (usually foll. by to) to become or make aware (of). **4.** Also: **awaken.** (tr.) to arouse (feelings, etc.) or cause to remember (memories, etc.). ~adj. (postpositive) **5.** not sleeping. **6.** (sometimes foll. by to) lively or alert. [OE awacian, awacan]

▷ **Usage.** See at **wake**[1].

award (ə'wɔːd) vb. (tr.) **1.** to give (something due), esp. as a reward for merit: to award prizes. **2.** Law. to declare to be entitled, as by decision of a court or an arbitrator. ~n. **3.** something awarded, such as a prize or medal. **4.** Austral. & N.Z. the amount of an **award wage** (esp. in **above award**). **5.** Law. **a.** the decision of an arbitrator. **b.** a grant made by a court of law. [C14: from Anglo-F awarder, from OF eswarder to decide after investigation, from es- EX-[1] + warder to observe] —**a'warder** n.

award wage n. (in Australia and New Zealand) statutory minimum pay for a particular group of workers. Sometimes shortened to **award.**

aware (ə'wɛə) adj. **1.** (postpositive; foll. by of) having knowledge: aware of his error. **2.** informed of current developments: politically aware. [OE gewær] —**a'wareness** n.

awash (ə'wɒʃ) adv., adj. (postpositive) Naut. **1.** at a level even with the surface of the sea. **2.** washed over by the waves.

away (ə'weɪ) adv. **1.** from a particular place: to swim away. **2.** in or to another, a usual, or a proper place: to put toys away. **3.** apart; at a distance: to keep away from strangers. **4.** out of existence: the music faded away. **5.** indicating motion, displacement, transfer, etc., from a normal or proper place: to turn one's head away. **6.** indicating activity that is wasteful or designed to get rid of something: to sleep away the hours. **7.** continuously: laughing away. **8. away with.** a command for a person to go or be removed: away with him to prison! ~adj. (usually postpositive) **9.** not present: away from school. **10.** distant: he is a good way away. **11.** having started; released: he was away before sunrise. **12.** (also prenominal) Sport. played on an opponent's ground. ~n. **13.** Sport. a game played or won at an opponent's ground. ~sentence substitute. **14.** an expression of dismissal. [OE on weg on way]

awayday (ə'weɪ,deɪ) n. a day trip taken for pleasure, relaxation, etc.; day excursion. [C20: from awayday ticket, name applied to some special-rate railway day returns]

awe (ɔː) n. **1.** overwhelming wonder, respect, or dread. **2.** Arch. power to inspire fear or reverence. ~vb. **3.** (tr.) to inspire with reverence or dread. [C13: from ON agi]

aweigh (ə'weɪ) adj. (postpositive) Naut. (of an anchor) no longer hooked into the bottom; hanging by its rope or chain.

awe-inspiring adj. causing or worthy of admiration or respect; amazing or magnificent.

awesome ('ɔːsəm) adj. inspiring or displaying awe. —**'awesomely** adv. —**'awesomeness** n.

awe-stricken or **awe-struck** adj. overcome or filled with awe.

awful ('ɔːfʊl) adj. **1.** very bad; unpleasant. **2.** Arch. inspiring reverence or dread. **3.** Arch. overcome with awe. ~adv. **4.** Not standard. (intensifier): an awful cold day. [C13: see AWE, -FUL] —**'awfulness** n.

awfully ('ɔːfəlɪ) adv. **1.** in an unpleasant, bad, or reprehensible manner. **2.** Inf. (intensifier): I'm awfully keen to come. **3.** Arch. so as to express or inspire awe.

awhile (ə'waɪl) adv. for a brief period.

awkward ('ɔːkwəd) adj. **1.** lacking dexterity, proficiency, or skill; clumsy. **2.** ungainly or inelegant in movements or posture. **3.** unwieldy; difficult to use. **4.** embarrassing: an awkward moment. **5.** embarrassed: he felt awkward about leaving. **6.** difficult to deal with; requiring tact: an awkward customer. **7.** deliberately unhelpful. **8.** dangerous or difficult. [C14: awk, from ON öfugr turned the wrong way round + -WARD] —**'awkwardly** adv. —**'awkwardness** n.

awl (ɔːl) n. a pointed hand tool with a fluted blade used for piercing wood, leather, etc. [OE æl]

awn (ɔːn) n. any of the bristles growing from the flowering parts of certain grasses and cereals. [OE agen ear of grain] —**awned** adj.

awning ('ɔːnɪŋ) n. a roof of canvas or other material supported by a frame to provide protection from the weather, esp. one placed over a doorway or part of a deck of a ship. [C17: from ?]

awoke (ə'wəʊk) vb. a past tense and (now rare or dialectal) past participle of **awake.**

AWOL ('eɪwɒl) or **A.W.O.L.** adj. Mil. absent without leave but without intending to desert.

awry (ə'raɪ) adv., adj. (postpositive) **1.** with a slant or twist to one side; askew. **2.** away from the appropriate or right course; amiss. [C14 on wry; see A-[2], WRY]

axe or U.S. **ax** (æks) n., pl. **axes. 1.** a hand tool with one side of its head forged and sharpened to a cutting edge, used for felling trees, splitting timber, etc. **2. an axe to grind. a.** an ulterior motive. **b.** a grievance. **c.** a pet subject. **3. the axe.** Inf. **a.** dismissal, esp. from employment (esp. in **get the axe**). **b.** Brit. severe cutting down of expenditure, esp. in a public service. ~vb. (tr.) **4.** to chop or trim with an axe. **5.** Inf. to dismiss (employees), restrict (expenditure or services), or terminate (a project, etc.). [OE æx]

axel ('æksəl) n. Skating. a jump of one and a half, two and a half, or three and a half turns, taking off from the forward outside edge of one skate and landing on the backward outside edge of the other. [C20: after Axel Paulsen (d. 1938), Norwegian skater]

axes[1] ('æksiːz) n. the plural of **axis**[1].

axes[2] ('æksɪz) n. the plural of **axe.**

axial ('æksɪəl) adj. **1.** forming or characteristic of an axis. **2.** situated in, on, or along an axis. —**,axi'ality** n. —**'axially** adv.

axil ('æksɪl) n. the upper angle between a branch or leafstalk and the stem from which it grows. [C18: from L axilla armpit]

axilla (æk'sɪlə) n., pl. **-lae** (-liː). **1.** the technical name for the **armpit. 2.** the area under a bird's wing corresponding to the armpit. [C17: from L: armpit]

axillary (æk'sɪlərɪ) adj. **1.** of, relating to, or near the armpit. **2.** Bot. growing in or relating to the axil. ~n., pl. **-laries. 3.** (usually pl.) Also called: **axillar** (æk'sɪlə). one of the feathers growing from the axilla of a bird's wing.

axiom ('æksɪəm) n. **1.** a generally accepted proposition or principle, sanctioned by experience. **2.** a universally established principle or law that is not a necessary truth. **3.** a self-evident statement. **4.** Logic, maths. a statement that is stipulated to be true for the purpose of a chain of reasoning. [C15: from L axiōma a principle, from Gk, from axioun to consider worthy, from axios worthy]

axiomatic (,æksɪə'mætɪk) adj. **1.** self-evident. **2.** containing maxims; aphoristic. —**,axio'matically** adv.

axis[1] ('æksɪs) n., pl. **axes. 1.** a real or imaginary line about which a body, such as an aircraft, can rotate or about which an object, form, composition, or geometrical construction is symmetrical. **2.** one of two or three reference lines used in coordinate geometry to locate a point in a plane or in space. **3.** Anat. the second cervical vertebra. **4.** Bot. the main central part of a plant, typically consisting of the stem and root. **5.** an alliance between a number of states to coordinate their foreign policy. **6.** Also called: **principal axis.** Optics. the line of symmetry of an optical system, such as the line passing through the centre of a lens. [C14: from L: axletree, earth's axis; rel. to Gk axōn axis]

axis[2] ('æksɪs) *n., pl.* **axises.** a S Asian deer with a reddish-brown white-spotted coat and slender antlers. [C18: from L: Indian wild animal, from ?]

Axis ('æksɪs) *n.* **a. the.** the alliance (1936) of Nazi Germany and Fascist Italy, later joined by Japan and other countries, and lasting until their defeat in World War II. **b.** (*as modifier*): *the Axis powers.*

axle ('æksəl) *n.* a bar or shaft on which a wheel, pair of wheels, or other rotating member revolves. [C17: from ON *öxull*]

axletree ('æksəl,triː) *n.* a bar fixed across the underpart of a wagon or carriage that has rounded ends on which the wheels revolve.

Axminster carpet ('æks,mɪnstə) *n.* a type of patterned carpet with a cut pile. Often shortened to **Axminster.** [after *Axminster* in Devon]

axolotl (,æksə'lɒt[ə]l) *n.* an aquatic salamander of N America, such as the **Mexican axolotl,** in which the larval form (including external gills) is retained throughout life under natural conditions. [C18: from Nahuatl, from *atl* water + *xolotl* servant, doll]

axon ('æksɒn) *n.* the long threadlike extension of a nerve cell that conducts nerve impulses from the cell body. [C19: via NL from Gk: axis, axle, vertebra]

Axum ('ɑːksʊm) *n.* a variant spelling of **Aksum.**

ay[1] *or* **aye** (eɪ) *adv. Arch., poetic* always.

ay[2] (aɪ) *sentence substitute.* a variant spelling of **aye.**

Ayacucho (*Spanish* aja'kutʃo) *n.* a city in SE Peru: nearby is the site of the battle (1824) that won independence for Peru. Pop.: 69 533 (1981).

ayah ('aɪə) *n.* (in parts of the former British Empire) a native maidservant or nursemaid. [C18: from Hindi *āyā,* from Port. *aia,* from L *avia* grandmother]

ayatollah (,aɪə'tɒlə) *n.* one of a class of Shiite religious leaders in Iran. [via Persian from Ar., from *aya* creation + ALLAH]

Ayckbourn ('eɪkbɔːn) *n.* **Alan.** born 1939, English dramatist. His plays include *Absurd Person Singular* (1973), the trilogy *The Norman Conquests* (1974), *Sisterly Feelings* (1980), and *Man of the Moment* (1988).

Aycliffe ('eɪklɪf) *n.* a town in Co. Durham: founded as a new town in 1947. Pop.: 36 826 (1981).

Aydin *or* **Aidin** ('aɪdɪn) *n.* a town in SW Turkey: an ancient city of Lydia. Pop.: 60 000 (1980 est.). Ancient name: **Tralles.**

aye *or* **ay** (aɪ) *sentence substitute.* **1.** yes: archaic or dialectal except in voting by voice. ~*n.* **2. a.** a person who votes in the affirmative. **b.** an affirmative vote. ~Cf. **nay.** [C16: prob. from pron. *I,* expressing assent]

aye-aye ('aɪ,aɪ) *n.* a rare nocturnal arboreal primate of Madagascar related to the lemurs. It has long bony fingers and rodent-like incisor teeth. [C18: from F, from Malagasy *aiay,* prob. imit.]

Ayer (ɛə) *n.* Sir **Alfred Jules.** born 1910, English positivist philosopher, noted particularly for his antimetaphysical work *Language, Truth, and Logic* (1936).

Ayers Rock (ɛəz) *n.* the world's largest monolith, in the Northern Territory of Australia. Height: 330 m (1100 ft.). Base circumference: 9 km (5.6 miles).

Ayesha ('ɑːɪ,ʃɑː) *n.* a variant spelling of **Aisha.**

Aylesbury ('eɪlzbərɪ, -brɪ) *n.* a town in SE central England, administrative centre of Buckinghamshire. Pop.: 50 000 (1985 est.).

Aylward ('eɪlwəd) *n.* **Gladys.** 1903–70, English missionary in China.

Aymara (,aɪmə'rɑː) *n.* **1.** (*pl.* **-ras** *or* **-ra**) a member of a S American Indian people of Bolivia and Peru. **2.** the language of this people. [from Sp. *aimará,* from Amerind]

Aymé (*French* ɛme) *n.* **Marcel** (marsɛl). 1902–67, French writer: noted for his light and witty narratives.

Ayr (ɛə) *n.* a port in SW Scotland, in Strathclyde region. Pop.: 49 481 (1985 est.).

Ayrshire ('ɛəʃə) *n.* any one of a hardy breed of brown-and-white dairy cattle. [from *Ayrshire,* former Scot. county]

Ayub Khan (aɪ'juːb 'kɑːn) *n.* **Mohammed.** 1907–74, Pakistani field marshal; president of Pakistan (1958–69).

Ayutthaya (ɑː'juːtəjə) *n.* a city in S Thailand, on the Chao Phraya River: capital of the country until 1767; noted for its canals and ruins. Pop.: 47 189 (1980). Also called: **Ayudhya** (ɑː'juːdjə), **Ayuthia** (ɑː'juːθɪə).

AZ *abbrev. for* Arizona.

azalea (ə'zeɪljə) *n.* an ericaceous plant cultivated for its showy pink or purple flowers. [C18: via NL from Gk, from

azaleos dry; from its supposed preference for a dry situation]

Azaña (*Spanish* a'θaɲa) *n.* **Manuel** (ma'nwel). 1880–1940, Spanish statesman; president of the Spanish Republic (1936–39) until overthrown by Franco.

Azbine (æz'biːn) *n.* another name for **Aïr.**

azeotrope (ə'ziː,trəʊp) *n.* a mixture of liquids that boils at a constant temperature, at a given pressure, without change of composition. [C20: from A-[1] + *zeo-,* from Gk *zein* to boil + -TROPE] —**azeotropic** (,eɪzɪə'trɒpɪk) *adj.*

Azerbaijan (,æzəbaɪ'dʒɑːn) *n.* a mountainous region of NW Iran, separated from Soviet Azerbaijan by the Aras River: divided administratively into **Eastern Azerbaijan** and **Western Azerbaijan.** Capitals: Tabriz and Rezaiyeh. Pop.: 6 200 000 (1981 est.). —**,Azerbai'jani.**

Azerbaijan Soviet Socialist Republic *n.* an administrative division of the S Soviet Union, on the Caspian Sea in the east: consists of dry subtropical steppes around the Aras and Kura Rivers, surrounded by the Caucasus; contains the extensive Baku oilfields. Capital: Baku. Pop.: 6 297 000 (1982 est.). Area: 86 600 sq. km (33 430 sq. miles).

azide ('eɪzaɪd) *n.* **a.** an acyl derivative or salt of hydrazoic acid, used as a coating to enhance electron emission. **b.** (*as modifier*): *an azide group or radical.*

Azikiwe (,ɑːziː'kiːweɪ) *n.* **Nnamdi** ([ə]n'næmdɪ). born 1904, Nigerian statesman; first president of Nigeria (1963–66).

Azilian (ə'zɪlɪən) *n.* **1.** a Palaeolithic culture of Spain and SW France that can be dated to the 10th millennium B.C., characterized by flat bone harpoons and schematically painted pebbles. ~*adj.* **2.** of or relating to this culture. [C19: after Mas d'*Azil,* France, where artefacts were found]

azimuth ('æzɪməθ) *n.* **1.** *Astron., navigation.* the angular distance usually measured clockwise from the south point of the horizon in astronomy or from the north point in navigation to the intersection with the horizon of the vertical circle passing through a celestial body. **2.** *Surveying.* the horizontal angle of a bearing clockwise from north. [C14: from OF *azimut,* from Ar. *as-sumūt,* pl. of *as-samt* the path, from L *semita* path] —**azimuthal** (,æzɪ'mʌθəl) *adj.*

azine ('eɪziːn) *n.* an organic compound having a six-membered ring with at least one nitrogen atom, the other atoms in the ring being carbon atoms.

azo ('eɪzəʊ, 'æ-) *adj.* of, consisting of, or containing the divalent group -N:N-: *an azo group or radical.* See also **diazo.** [from F *azote* nitrogen, from Gk *azöos* lifeless]

azoic (ə'zəʊɪk) *adj.* without life; characteristic of the ages that have left no evidence of life in the form of organic remains. [C19: from Gk *azöos* lifeless]

Azores (ə'zɔːz) *pl. n.* **the.** three groups of volcanic islands in the N Atlantic, forming the Portuguese districts of Angra do Heroísmo, Horta, and Ponta Delgada: achieved partial autonomy (1976). Capital: Ponta Delgada (on São Miguel). Pop.: 251 352 (1981). Area: 2335 sq. km (901 sq. miles). Portuguese name: **Açôres.**

Azorín (*Spanish* aθo'rin) *n.* real name *José Martínez Ruiz.* 1874–1967, Spanish writer: noted for his stories of the Spanish countryside.

Azov ('ɑːzɒv) *n.* **Sea of.** a shallow arm of the Black Sea, to which it is connected by the Kerch Strait: almost entirely landlocked; fed chiefly by the River Don. Area: about 37 500 sq. km (14 500 sq. miles).

AZT *abbrev. for* azidothymidine: a drug that prolongs life and alleviates symptoms among some AIDS sufferers.

Aztec ('æztɛk) *n.* **1.** a member of a Mexican Indian people who established a great empire, centred on the valley of Mexico, that was overthrown by Cortés in the early 16th century. **2.** the language of the Aztecs. See also **Nahuatl.** ~*adj. also* **Aztecan.** **3.** of, relating to, or characteristic of the Aztecs, their civilization, or their language. [C18: from Sp., from Nahuatl *Aztecatl,* from *Aztlan,* their traditional place of origin, lit.: near the cranes]

azure ('æʒə, 'eɪ-) *n.* **1.** a deep blue similar to the colour of a clear blue sky. **2.** *Poetic.* a clear blue sky. ~*adj.* **3.** of the colour azure. **4.** (*usually postpositive*) *Heraldry.* of the colour blue. [C14: from OF, from OSp., from Ar. *lāzaward* lapis lazuli, from Persian *lāzhuward*]

azurite ('æʒʊ,raɪt) *n.* a deep blue mineral consisting of hydrated basic copper carbonate. It is used as an ore of copper and as a gemstone.

azygous ('æzɪgəs) *adj. Biol.* developing or occurring singly. [C17: via NL from Gk *azugos,* from A-[1] + *zugon* YOKE]

B

b *or* **B** (bi:) *n.*, *pl.* **b's, B's,** *or* **Bs.** **1.** the second letter of the English alphabet. **2.** a speech sound represented by this letter, as in *bell.* **3.** Also: **beta.** the second in a series, class, or rank.

B *symbol for:* **1.** *Music.* **a.** the seventh note of the scale of C major. **b.** the major or minor key having this note as its tonic. **2.** the less important of two things. **3.** a human blood type of the ABO group, containing the B antigen. **4.** (in Britain) a secondary road. **5.** *Chem.* boron. **6.** magnetic flux density. **7.** *Chess.* bishop. **8.** (on Brit. pencils, signifying degree of softness of lead) black. **9.** Also: **b** *Physics.* bel. **10.** *Physics.* baryon number.

b. *abbrev. for:* **1.** born. **2.** *Cricket.* **a.** bowled. **b.** bye.

b. *or* **B.** *abbrev. for:* **1.** *Music.* bass *or* basso. **2.** billion. **3.** book. **4.** breadth.

B. *abbrev. for:* **1.** (on maps, etc.) bay. **2.** Bible.

B- (of U.S. military aircraft) *abbrev. for* bomber.

Ba[1] *the chemical symbol for* barium.

Ba[2] (ba:) *n. Egyptian myth.* the soul, represented as a bird with a human head.

BA *abbrev. for:* **1.** Bachelor of Arts. **2.** British Academy. **3.** British Airways. **4.** British Association (for the Advancement of Science).

baa (ba:) *vb.* **baaing, baaed. 1.** (*intr.*) to make the cry of a sheep; bleat. ~*n.* **2.** the cry made by sheep.

BAA *abbrev. for* British Airports Authority.

Baal (ba:l) *n.* **1.** any of several ancient Semitic fertility gods. **2.** *Phoenician myth.* the sun god and supreme national deity. **3.** (*sometimes not cap.*) any false god or idol. [from Heb. *bá'al* lord, master]

Baalbek ('ba:lbɛk) *n.* a town in E Lebanon: an important city in Phoenician and Roman times; extensive ruins. Pop. 14 000 (1982 est.). Ancient name: **Heliopolis.**

Baal Shem Tov *or* **Baal Shem Tob** (ba:l 'ʃɛm tɒv, 'ʃa:m) *n.* original name *Israel ben Eliezer.* ?1700–60, Jewish religious leader, teacher, and healer in Poland: founder of modern Hasidism.

baas (ba:s) *n.* a South African word for **boss**: used by Africans and Coloureds in addressing European managers or overseers. [C17: from Afrik., from MDu. *baes* master]

baaskap *or* **baasskap** ('ba:s,kap) *n.* (*sometimes cap.*) (in South Africa) control by Whites of non-Whites. [from Afrik., from BAAS + -*skap* -SHIP]

Bab (ba:b) *n.* **the.** title of *Mirza Ali Mohammed.* 1819–50, Persian religious leader: founded Babism; executed as a heretic of Islam. [from Persian *bāb* gate, from Ar.]

baba ('ba:ba:) *n.* a small cake, usually soaked in rum (**rum baba**). [C19: from F, from Polish, lit.: old woman]

babalas ('bæbə,læs) *n. S. African.* a hangover. [from Zulu *ibhabhalasi*]

Babar ('ba:bə) *n.* a variant spelling of **Baber.**

Babbage ('bæbɪdʒ) *n.* **Charles.** 1792–1871, English mathematician and inventor, who built a calculating machine that anticipated the modern electronic computer.

babbitt ('bæbɪt) *vb.* (*tr.*) to line (a bearing) or face (a surface) with Babbitt metal.

Babbitt ('bæbɪt) *n. U.S. derog.* a narrow-minded and complacent member of the middle class. [C20: after George *Babbitt,* central character in the novel *Babbitt* (1922) by Sinclair Lewis] —'**Babbittry** *n.*

Babbitt metal *n.* any of a number of alloys originally based on tin, antimony, and copper but now often including lead: used esp. in bearings. [C19: after Isaac *Babbitt* (1799–1862), U.S. inventor]

babble ('bæbᵊl) *vb.* **1.** to utter (words, sounds, etc.) in an incoherent jumble. **2.** (*intr.*) to talk foolishly, incessantly, or irrelevantly. **3.** (*tr.*) to disclose (secrets, etc.) carelessly. **4.** (*intr.*) (of streams, birds, etc.) to make a low murmuring sound. ~*n.* **5.** incoherent or foolish speech. **6.** a murmuring sound. [C13: prob. imit.]

babbler ('bæblə) *n.* **1.** a person or thing that babbles. **2.** any of various birds of the Old World tropics and subtropics having an incessant song.

babe (beɪb) *n.* **1.** a baby. **2.** *Inf.* a naive or gullible person. **3.** *Sl., chiefly U.S.* a girl.

Babel[1] ('beɪbᵊl) *n.* **1.** *Old Testament.* Also called: **Tower of Babel.** a tower presumptuously intended to reach from earth to heaven, the building of which was frustrated when Jehovah confused the language of the builders (Genesis 11:1–10). **2.** (*often not cap.*) **a.** a confusion of noises or voices. **b.** a scene of noise and confusion. [from Heb. *Bābhēl,* from Akkadian *Bāb-ilu,* lit.: gate of God]

Babel[2] (*Russian* 'babɪl) *n.* **Isaak Emmanuilovich** (i'sak imənu'iləvɪtʃ). 1894–1941, Russian short-story writer, whose works include *Stories from Odessa* (1924) and *Red Cavalry* (1926).

Bab el Mandeb ('bæb ɛl 'mændɛb) *n.* a strait between SW Arabia and E Africa, connecting the Red Sea with the Gulf of Aden.

Baber, Babar, *or* **Babur** ('ba:bə) *n.* original name *Zahir ud-Din Mohammed.* 1483–1530, founder of the Mogul Empire: conquered India in 1526.

Babeuf (*French* babœf) *n.* **François Noël** (frɑ̃swa nɔɛl). 1760–97, French political agitator: plotted unsuccessfully to destroy the Directory and establish a communistic system.

babirusa (,ba:bɪ'ru:sə) *n.* a wild pig of Indonesia. It has an almost hairless wrinkled skin and enormous curved canine teeth. [C17: from Malay, from *bābī* hog + *rūsa* deer]

Babism ('ba:bɪzəm) *n.* a pantheistic Persian religious sect, founded in 1844, forbidding polygamy, concubinage, begging, trading in slaves, and indulgence in alcohol and drugs. [C19: from the BAB]

baboon (bə'bu:n) *n.* any of several medium-sized Old World monkeys. They have an elongated muzzle, large teeth, and a fairly long tail. [C14 *babewyn* gargoyle, later, baboon, from OF]

babu ('ba:bu:) *n.* (in India) **1.** a form of address more or less equivalent to *Mr.* **2.** (formerly) an Indian clerk who could write English. [Hindi, lit.: father]

Babur ('ba:bə) *n.* a variant spelling of **Baber.**

babushka (bə'bu:ʃkə) *n.* **1.** a headscarf tied under the chin, worn by Russian peasant women. **2.** (in Russia) an old woman. [Russian: grandmother, from *baba* old woman]

baby ('beɪbɪ) *n.*, *pl.* **-bies. 1. a.** a newborn child; infant. **b.** (*as modifier*): *baby food.* **2.** an unborn child; fetus. **3.** the youngest or smallest of a family or group. **4.** a newborn or recently born animal. **5.** *Usually derog.* an immature person. **6.** *Sl.* a young woman or sweetheart. **7.** a project of personal concern. **8. be left holding the baby.** to be left with the responsibility. ~*adj.* **9.** (*prenominal*) comparatively small of its type: *a baby car.* ~*vb.* **-bying, -bied. 10.** (*tr.*) to treat with love and attention. **11.** to treat (someone) like a baby; pamper or overprotect. [C14: prob. childish reduplication] —'**babyhood** *n.* —'**babyish** *adj.*

baby bonus *n. Canad. inf.* Family Allowance.

baby boomer *n.* a person who was born during the **baby boom,** the years immediately after World War II when there was a sharp increase in the birth rate.

baby carriage *n.* the U.S. and Canad. name for **pram**[1].

Babylon ('bæbɪlɒn) *n.* **1.** the chief city of ancient Mesopotamia: first settled around 3000 B.C. See also **Hanging Gardens of Babylon. 2.** *Derog.* (in Protestant polemic) the Roman Catholic Church, regarded as the seat of luxury and corruption. **3.** *Derog.* any society or group in a society considered as corrupt or as a place of exile by another society or group, esp. White Britain as viewed by some West Indians. [via L and Gk from Heb. *Bābhel;* see BABEL[1]] —**Babylonian** (bæbɪ'ləʊnɪən) *adj., n.*

Babylonia (,bæbɪ'ləʊnɪə) *n.* the southern kingdom of ancient Mesopotamia: a great empire from about 2200–538 B.C., when it was conquered by the Persians.

baby's-breath *or* **babies'-breath** *n.* **1.** a tall Eurasian plant, bearing small white or pink fragrant flowers. **2.** any of several other plants that have small scented flowers.

baby-sit *vb.* **-sitting, -sat.** (*intr.*) to act or work as a baby-sitter. — '**baby-,sitting** *n., adj.*

baby-sitter n. a person who takes care of a child or children while the parents are out.

baby snatcher n. *Inf.* **1.** a person who steals a baby from its pram. **2.** someone who marries or has an affair with a much younger person.

baccalaureate (,bækə'lɔːrɪɪt) n. the university degree of Bachelor of Arts. [C17: from Med. L *baccalaureātus*, from *baccalaureus* advanced student from *baccalárius* BACHELOR]

baccarat ('bækə,rɑː, ,bækə'rɑː) n. a card game in which two or more punters gamble against the banker. [C19: from F *baccara* from ?]

baccate ('bækeɪt) adj. *Bot.* **1.** like a berry. **2.** bearing berries. [C19: from L *bāca* berry]

Bacchae ('bæki:) pl. n. the priestesses or female devotees of Bacchus. [L, from Gk *Bakkhai*, plural of *Bakkhē* priestess of BACCHUS]

bacchanal ('bækənəl) n. **1.** a follower of Bacchus. **2.** a drunken and riotous celebration. **3.** a participant in such a celebration. ~adj. **4.** of or relating to Bacchus. [C16: from L *Bacchānālis*]

bacchanalia (,bækə'neɪlɪə) pl. n. **1.** (often cap.) orgiastic rites associated with Bacchus. **2.** any drunken revelry. —,baccha'nalian adj., n.

bacchant ('bækənt) or (fem.) **bacchante** (bə'kæntɪ) n., pl. **bacchants** or **bacchantes** (bə'kæntɪz). **1.** a priest, priestess, or votary of Bacchus. **2.** a drunken reveller. [C17: from L *bacchāns*, from *bacchārī* to celebrate the BACCHANALIA]

Bacchic ('bækɪk) adj. **1.** of or relating to Bacchus. **2.** (often not cap.) riotously drunk.

Bacchus ('bækəs) n. (in ancient Greece and Rome) a god of wine and giver of ecstasy, identified with Dionysus. [C15: from L, from Gk *Bakkhos*; related to L *bāca* small round fruit, berry]

baccy ('bækɪ) n. a Brit. informal name for **tobacco**.

bach (bætʃ) n. *N.Z.* ~n. **1.** a seaside, bush, or country cottage. ~vb. **2.** a variant spelling of **batch**².

Bach (German bax) n. **1. Johann Christian** (jo'han 'krɪstjan), 11th son of J. S. Bach, called *the English Bach.* 1735–82, German composer, resident in London from 1762. **2. Johann Christoph** ('krɪstɔf). 1642–1705, German composer: wrote oratorios, cantatas, and motets, some of which were falsely attributed to J. S. Bach, of whom he was a distant relative. **3. Johann Sebastian** (ze'bastjan). 1685–1750, German composer: church organist at Arnstadt (1703–07) and Mühlhausen (1707–08); court organist at Weimar (1708–17); musical director for Prince Leopold of Köthen (1717–28); musical director for the city of Leipzig (1728–50). His output was enormous and displays great vigour and invention within the northern European polyphonic tradition. His works include nearly 200 cantatas and oratorios, settings of the *Passion according to St John* (1723) and *St Matthew* (1729), the six *Brandenburg Concertos* (1720–21), the 48 preludes and fugues of the *Well-tempered Clavier* (completed 1744), and the *Mass in B Minor* (1733–38). **4. Karl** (or **Carl**) **Philipp Emanuel** (karl 'fiːlɪp e'maːnuɛl), 3rd son of J. S. Bach. 1714–88, German composer, chiefly of symphonies, keyboard sonatas, and church music. **5. Wilhelm Friedemann** ('vɪlhɛlm 'friːdəman), eldest son of J. S. Bach. 1710–84, German composer: wrote nine symphonies and much keyboard and religious music.

Bacharach ('bækəræk) n. *Burt.* born 1928, U.S. composer of popular songs, usually with lyricist Hal David.

bachelor ('bætʃələ, 'bætʃlə) n. **1. a.** an unmarried man. **b.** (as modifier): a bachelor flat. **2.** a person who holds the degree of Bachelor of Arts, Bachelor of Science, etc. **3.** (in the Middle Ages) a young knight serving a great noble. **4. bachelor seal.** a young male seal that has not yet mated. [C13: from OF *bacheler* youth, squire, from Vulgar L *baccalāris* (unattested) farm worker] —**'bachelorhood** n.

bachelor girl n. a young unmarried woman, esp. one who is self-supporting.

Bachelor of Arts n. **1.** a degree conferred on a person who has successfully completed undergraduate studies in the liberal arts or humanities. **2.** a person who holds this degree.

Bachelor of Science n. **1.** a degree conferred on a person who has successfully completed undergraduate studies in a science. **2.** a person who holds this degree.

bachelor's-buttons n. (functioning as sing. or pl.) any of various plants with button-like flower heads, esp. a double-flowered buttercup.

bacillary (bə'sɪlərɪ) or **bacillar** (bə'sɪlə) adj. **1.** of, relating to, or caused by bacilli. **2.** Also: **bacilliform** (bə'sɪlɪ,fɔːm). shaped like a short rod.

bacillus (bə'sɪləs) n., pl. **-cilli** (-'sɪlaɪ). **1.** any rod-shaped bacterium. **2.** any of various rodlike spore-producing bacteria constituting the family Bacillaceae. [C19: from L, from *baculum* walking stick]

back (bæk) n. **1.** the posterior part of the human body, from the neck to the pelvis. **2.** the corresponding or upper part of an animal. **3.** the spinal column. **4.** the part or side of an object opposite the front. **5.** the part or side of anything less often seen or used. **6.** the part or side of anything that is furthest from the front or from a spectator: *the back of the stage.* **7.** something that supports, covers, or strengthens the rear of an object. **8.** *Ball games.* **a.** a mainly defensive player behind a forward. **b.** the position of such a player. **9.** the part of a book to which the pages are glued or that joins the covers. **10. at the back of one's mind.** not in one's conscious thoughts. **11. back of Bourke.** *Austral.* a remote or backward place. **12. behind one's back.** secretly or deceitfully. **13. break one's back.** to overwork or work very hard. **14. break the back of.** to complete the greatest or hardest part of (a task). **15. get off someone's back.** *Inf.* to stop criticizing or pestering someone. **16. put one's back into.** to devote all one's strength to (a task). **17. put** (or **get**) **someone's back up.** to annoy someone. **18. the back of beyond.** a very remote place. **19. turn one's back on. a.** to turn away from in anger or contempt. **b.** to refuse to help; abandon. ~vb. (mainly tr.) **20.** (also intr.) to move or cause to move backwards. **21. back water.** to reverse the direction of a boat, esp. to push the oars of a rowing boat. **22.** to provide support, money, or encouragement for (a person, enterprise, etc.). **23.** to bet on the success of: *to back a horse.* **24.** to provide with a back, backing, or lining. **25.** to provide with a musical accompaniment. **26.** to countersign or endorse. **27.** (intr.; foll. by on or onto) to have the back facing (towards): *the house backs onto a river.* **28.** (intr.) (of the wind) to change direction anticlockwise. Cf. **veer**¹ (sense 3). ~adj. (prenominal) **29.** situated behind: *a back lane.* **30.** of the past: *back issues of a magazine.* **31.** owing from an earlier date: *back rent.* **32.** remote: *a back road.* **33.** *Phonetics.* of or denoting a vowel articulated with the tongue retracted towards the soft palate, as for the vowels in English *hard, fall, hot, full, fool.* ~adv. **34.** at, to, or towards the rear; behind. **35.** in, to, or towards the original starting point, place, or condition: *to go back home; put the book back.* **36.** in or into the past: *to look back on one's childhood.* **37.** in reply, repayment, or retaliation: *to hit someone back.* **38.** in check: *the dam holds back the water.* **39.** in concealment; in reserve: *to keep something back.* **40. back and forth.** to and fro. **41. back to front. a.** in reverse. **b.** in disorder. ~See also **back down, back out, back up.** [OE *bæc*]

backbencher ('bæk'bentʃə) n. *Brit., Austral., N.Z., etc.* a Member of Parliament who does not hold office in the government or opposition.

backbite ('bæk,baɪt) vb. **-biting, bit; bitten** or **bit.** to talk spitefully about (an absent person). — **'back,biter** n.

backboard ('bæk,bɔːd) n. **1.** a board that is placed behind something to form or support its back. **2.** a board worn to straighten or support the back, as after surgery. **3.** (in basketball) a flat upright surface supported on a high frame, under which the basket is attached.

back boiler n. a tank or series of pipes at the back of a fireplace for heating water.

backbone ('bæk,bəʊn) n. **1.** a nontechnical name for **spinal column. 2.** something that resembles the spinal column in function, position, or appearance. **3.** strength of character; courage.

backbreaking ('bæk,breɪkɪŋ) adj. exhausting.

backburn ('bæk,bɜːn) vb. (tr.) *Austral. & N.Z.* **1.** to clear (an area of bush, etc.) by creating a new fire that burns in the opposite direction to the line of advancing fire. ~n. **2.** the act or result of backburning.

back-calculate vb. to estimate (the probable amount of alcohol in a person's blood) at an earlier time than that at which the blood test was taken, based on an average rate at which alcohol leaves the bloodstream: used to determine whether a driver had more than the legal limit of alcohol at the time of an accident. —'**back-,calcu'lation** *n.*

backchat ('bæk,tʃæt) *n. Inf.* the act of answering back, esp. impudently.

backcloth ('bæk,klɒθ) *n.* a painted curtain at the back of a stage set. Also called: **backdrop.**

backcomb ('bæk,kəʊm) *vb.* to comb the under layers of (the hair) towards the roots to give more bulk to a hairstyle. Also: **tease.**

back country *n. Austral. & N.Z.* land remote from settled areas.

backdate (,bæk'deɪt) *vb.* (*tr.*) to make effective from an earlier date.

back door *n.* **1.** a door at the rear or side of a building. **2.** a means of entry to a job, etc., that is secret or obtained through influence.

back down *vb.* **1.** (*intr., adv.*) to withdraw an earlier claim. ~*n.* **backdown. 2.** abandonment of an earlier claim.

backed (bækt) *adj.* **a.** having a back or backing. **b.** (*in combination*): *high-backed; black-backed.*

backer ('bækə) *n.* **1.** a person who gives financial or other support. **2.** a person who bets on a competitor or contestant.

backfill ('bæk,fɪl) *vb.* (*tr.*) to refill an excavated trench, esp. (in archaeology) at the end of an investigation.

backfire (,bæk'faɪə) *vb.* (*intr.*) **1.** (of an internal-combustion engine) to emit a loud noise as a result of an explosion in the exhaust system. **2.** to fail to have the desired effect, and, instead, recoil upon the originator. **3.** to start a controlled fire in order to halt an advancing forest or prairie fire by creating a barren area. ~*n.* **4.** (in an internal-combustion engine) an explosion of unburnt gases in the exhaust system. **5.** a controlled fire started to create a barren area that will halt an advancing forest or prairie fire.

back formation *n.* **1.** the unwitting invention of a new word on the assumption that a familiar word is derived from it. The verbs *edit* and *burgle* in English were so created from *editor* and *burglar.* **2.** a word formed by this process.

backgammon ('bæk,gæmən) *n.* **1.** a game for two people played on a board with pieces moved according to throws of the dice. **2.** the most complete form of win in this game. [C17: BACK + *gammon*, var. of GAME¹]

background ('bæk,graʊnd) *n.* **1.** the part of a scene furthest from the viewer. **2. a.** an inconspicuous or unobtrusive position (esp. in **in the background**). **b.** (*as modifier*): *a background influence.* **3.** the plane or ground in a picture upon which all other planes or forms appear superimposed. **4.** a person's social class, education, or experience. **5. a.** the circumstances that lead up to or help to explain something. **b.** (*as modifier*): *background information.* **6. a.** a low level of sound, lighting, etc., whose purpose is to be an unobtrusive accompaniment to something else. **b.** (*as modifier*): *background music.* **7.** Also called: **background radiation.** *Physics.* low-intensity radiation from small amounts of radioisotopes in soil, air, etc. **8.** *Electronics.* unwanted effects, such as noise, occurring in a measuring instrument, electronic device, etc.

backhand ('bæk,hænd) *n.* **1.** *Tennis, etc.* a stroke made across the body with the back of the hand facing the direction of the stroke. **2.** the side on which backhand strokes are made. **3.** handwriting slanting to the left. ~*adv.* **4.** with a backhand stroke.

backhanded (,bæk'hændɪd) *adj.* **1.** (of a blow, shot, etc.) performed with the arm moving across the body. **2.** double-edged; equivocal: *a backhanded compliment.* **3.** (of handwriting) slanting to the left. ~*adv.* **4.** in a backhanded manner.

backhander ('bæk,hændə) *n.* **1.** a backhanded stroke or blow. **2.** *Inf.* an indirect attack. **3.** *Sl.* a bribe.

backing ('bækɪŋ) *n.* **1.** support. **2.** a body of supporters. **3.** something that forms, protects, or strengthens the back of something. **4.** musical accompaniment, esp. for a pop singer.

backing dog *n. N.Z.* a dog that moves a flock of sheep by jumping on their backs.

backlash ('bæk,læʃ) *n.* **1.** a sudden and adverse reaction. **2.** a reaction or recoil between interacting worn or

badly fitting parts in a mechanism. **3.** the excessive play between such parts.

backlog ('bæk,lɒg) *n.* an accumulation of uncompleted work, unsold stock, etc., to be dealt with.

back marker *n.* a competitor who is at the back of a field in a race.

back matter *n.* the parts of a book, such as the index and appendixes, that follow the text.

backmost ('bæk,məʊst) *adj.* furthest back.

back number *n.* **1.** an issue of a newspaper, magazine, etc., that appeared on a previous date. **2.** *Inf.* a person or thing considered to be old-fashioned.

back out *vb.* (*intr., adv.; often foll. by of*) to withdraw (from an agreement, etc.).

backpack ('bæk,pæk) *n.* **1.** a rucksack. **2.** a pack carried on the back of an astronaut, containing oxygen cylinders, etc. ~*vb.* (*intr.*) **3.** to travel about or go hiking with a backpack.

back passage *n.* the rectum.

back-pedal *vb.* **-pedalling, -pedalled** *or U.S.* **-pedaling, -pedaled.** (*intr.*) **1.** to turn the pedals of a bicycle backwards. **2.** to retract or modify a previous opinion, principle, etc.

back projection *n.* a method of projecting pictures onto a translucent screen so that they are viewed from the opposite side, used esp. in films to create the illusion that the actors in the foreground are moving.

Back River *n.* a river in N Canada, rising in the Northwest Territories and flowing northeast to the Arctic Ocean. Length: about 966 km (600 miles).

back room *n.* **a.** a place where important and usually secret research or planning is done. **b.** (*as modifier*): *back-room boys.*

back seat *n.* **1.** a seat at the back, esp. of a vehicle. **2.** *Inf.* a subordinate or inconspicuous position (esp. in **take a back seat**).

back-seat driver *n. Inf.* **1.** a passenger in a car who offers unwanted advice to the driver. **2.** a person who offers advice on or tries to direct matters that are not his concern.

backsheesh ('bækʃiːʃ) *n.* a variant spelling of **baksheesh.**

backside (,bæk'saɪd) *n. Inf.* the buttocks.

backslide (,bæk'slaɪd) *vb.* **-sliding, -slid.** (*intr.*) to relapse into former bad habits or vices. —,**back'slider** *n.*

backspace ('bæk,speɪs) *vb.* to move (a typewriter carriage, etc.) backwards.

backspin ('bæk,spɪn) *n. Sport.* a backward spin imparted to a ball to reduce its speed at impact.

backstage (,bæk'steɪdʒ) *adv.* **1.** behind the part of the theatre in view of the audience. **2.** towards the rear of the stage. ~*adj.* **3.** situated backstage. **4.** *Inf.* away from public view.

backstairs (,bæk'steəz) *pl. n.* **1.** a secondary staircase in a house, esp. one originally for the use of servants. ~*adj. also* **backstair. 2.** underhand: *backstairs gossip.*

backstay ('bæk,steɪ) *n. Naut.* a stay leading aft from the upper mast to the deck or stern.

backstreet ('bæk,striːt) *n.* **1.** a street in a town remote from the main roads. **2.** (*modifier*) denoting illicit activities regarded as likely to take place in such a street: *a backstreet abortion.*

backstroke ('bæk,strəʊk) *n. Swimming.* a stroke performed on the back, using backward circular strokes of each arm and flipper movements of the feet. Also called: **back crawl.**

back-to-back *adj.* (*usually postpositive*) **1.** facing in opposite directions, often with the backs touching. **2.** *Chiefly Brit.* (of urban houses) built so that their backs are adjacent or separated only by a narrow alley.

backtrack ('bæk,træk) *vb.* (*intr.*) **1.** to return by the same route by which one has come. **2.** to retract or reverse one's opinion, policy, etc.

back up *vb.* (*adv.*) **1.** (*tr.*) to support. **2.** (*intr.*) *Cricket.* (of a nonstriking batsman) to move down the wicket in readiness for a run as a ball is bowled. **3.** (of water) to accumulate. **4.** *Computers.* to make a copy of (a data file), esp. as a security copy. **5.** (*intr.; usually foll. by on*) *Austral.* to repeat an action immediately. ~*n.* **backup. 6.** a support or reinforcement. **7. a** a reserve or substitute. **b.** (*as modifier*): *a backup copy.* **8.** the overflow from a blocked drain or pipe. **9.** *Austral.* a second helping.

backveld ('bæk,fɛlt, -,vɛlt) *n. S. African inf.* a remote sparsely populated rural area. [Afrik., from *back* BACK + *velt* field] —'**back,velder** *n.*

backward ('bækwəd) *adj.* **1.** (*usually prenominal*) directed towards the rear: *a backward glance.* **2.** retarded in physical, material, or intellectual development. **3. a.** conservative or reactionary. **b.** (*in combination*): *backward-looking.* **4.** reluctant or bashful: *a backward lover.* ~*adv.* **5.** a variant of **backwards.** —'**backwardness** *n.*

backwardation (,bækwə'deɪʃən) *n.* **1.** (on the London Stock Exchange) postponement of delivery by a seller of securities until the next settlement period. **2.** the fee paid for such postponement. ~Cf. **contango.**

backwards ('bækwədz) *or* **backward** *adv.* **1.** towards the rear. **2.** with the back foremost. **3.** in the reverse of usual order or direction. **4.** to or towards the past. **5.** into a worse state. **6.** towards the point of origin. **7. bend, lean,** *or* **fall over backwards.** *Inf.* to make a special effort, esp. in order to please.

backwash ('bæk,wɒʃ) *n.* **1.** water washed backwards by the motion of oars or other propelling devices. **2.** the backward flow of air set up by aircraft engines. **3.** a repercussion.

backwater ('bæk,wɔːtə) *n.* **1.** a body of stagnant water connected to a river. **2.** an isolated or backward place or condition.

backwoods ('bækwʊdz) *pl. n.* **1.** partially cleared, sparsely populated forests. **2.** any remote sparsely populated place. **3.** (*modifier*) of or like the backwoods. **4.** (*modifier*) uncouth; rustic. —'**back,woodsman** *n.*

back yard *n.* **1.** a yard at the back of a house, etc. **2. in one's own back yard. a.** close at hand. **b.** involving or implicating one.

baclava ('bɑːklə,vɑː) *n.* a variant spelling of **baklava.**

Bacolod (bə'kɒləd) *n.* a town in the Philippines, on the NW coast of Negros Island. Pop.: 266 604 (1980).

bacon ('beɪkən) *n.* **1.** meat from the back and sides of a pig, dried, salted, and usually smoked. **2. bring home the bacon.** *Inf.* **a.** to achieve success. **b.** to provide material support. **3. save (someone's) bacon.** *Brit. inf.* to help (someone) to escape from danger. [C12: from OF *bacon,* from OHG *bahho*]

Bacon ('beɪkən) *n.* **1. Francis,** Baron Verulam, Viscount St. Albans. 1561–1626, English philosopher, statesman, and essayist; described the inductive method of reasoning: his works include *Essays* (1625), *The Advancement of Learning* (1605), and *Novum Organum* (1620). **2. Francis.** born 1909, Irish painter, noted for his distorted, richly coloured human figures, dogs, and carcasses. **3. Roger.** ?1214–92, English Franciscan monk, scholar, and scientist: stressed the importance of experiment, demonstrated that air is required for combustion, and first used lenses to correct vision. His *Opus Majus* (1266) is a compendium of all the sciences of his age.

Baconian (beɪ'kəʊnɪən) *adj.* **1.** of or relating to Francis Bacon, the philosopher, or his inductive method of reasoning. ~*n.* **2.** a follower of Bacon's philosophy. **3.** one who believes that plays attributed to Shakespeare were written by Bacon.

bacteria (bæk'tɪərɪə) *pl. n., sing.* **-rium.** a large group of typically unicellular microorganisms, many of which cause disease. [C19: NL, from Gk *baktērion,* from *baktron* rod, staff] —**bac'terial** *adj.* —**bac'terially** *adv.*

bactericide (bæk'tɪərɪ,saɪd) *n.* a substance able to destroy bacteria. —**bac,teri'cidal** *adj.*

bacterio-, bacteri-, *or sometimes before a vowel* **bacter-** *combining form.* indicating bacteria or an action or condition relating to bacteria: *bacteriology; bactericide.*

bacteriology (bæk,tɪərɪ'ɒlədʒɪ) *n.* the study of bacteria. —**bacteriological** (bæk,tɪərɪə'lɒdʒɪk³l) *adj.* —**bac,teri'ologist** *n.*

bacteriophage (bæk'tɪərɪə,feɪdʒ) *n.* a virus that is parasitic in a bacterium and destroys its host. Often shortened to **phage.**

bacterium (bæk'tɪərɪəm) *n.* the singular of **bacteria.**

Bactria ('bæktrɪə) *n.* an ancient country of SW Asia, between the Hindu Kush mountains and the Oxus River: forms the present district of Balkh in N Afghanistan. —'**Bactrian** *adj., n.*

Bactrian camel *n.* a two-humped camel, used in the cold deserts of central Asia.

bad[1] (bæd) *adj.* **worse, worst. 1.** not good; of poor quality; inadequate. **2.** (often foll. by *at*) lacking skill or talent;

incompetent. **3.** (often foll. by *for*) harmful. **4.** immoral; evil. **5.** naughty; mischievous. **6.** rotten; decayed: *a bad egg.* **7.** severe; intense: *a bad headache.* **8.** incorrect; faulty: *bad pronunciation.* **9.** ill or in pain (esp. in **feel bad**). **10.** sorry or upset (esp. in **feel bad about**). **11.** unfavourable; distressing: *bad news.* **12.** offensive; unpleasant: *bad language; bad temper.* **13.** not valid or sound: *a bad cheque.* **14.** not recoverable: *a bad debt.* **15.** (**badder, baddest**) *sl.* good, excellent. **16. go bad.** to putrefy; spoil. **17. in a bad way.** *Inf.* **a.** seriously ill. **b.** in trouble. **18. make the best of a bad job.** to manage as well as possible in unfavourable circumstances. **19. not bad** *or* **not so bad.** *Inf.* passable; fairly good. **20. too bad.** *Inf.* (often used dismissively) regrettable. ~*n.* **21.** unfortunate or unpleasant events (often in **take the bad with the good**). **22.** an immoral or degenerate state (often in **go to the bad**). **23.** the debit side of an account: *£200 to the bad.* **24. go from bad to worse.** to deteriorate even more. ~*adv.* **25.** *Not standard.* badly: *to want something bad.* [C13: prob. from *bæd-,* as the first element of OE *bæddel* hermaphrodite] —'**baddish** *adj.* —'**badness** *n.*

▷ **Usage.** See at **good.**

bad[2] (bæd) *vb.* a variant spelling of **bade.**

Badajoz ('bædə,hɒz; *Spanish* ba'ðaxoθ) *n.* a city in SW Spain: strategically positioned near the frontier with Portugal. Pop.: 111 456 (1981).

Badalona (*Spanish* baða'lona) *n.* a port in NE Spain: an industrial suburb of Barcelona. Pop.: 229 780 (1981).

bad blood *n.* a feeling of intense hatred or hostility; enmity.

bade (bæd, beɪd) *or* **bad** *vb.* a past tense of **bid.**

Baden ('baːdən) *n.* a former state of West Germany, now part of Baden-Württemberg.

Baden-Baden *n.* a spa in SW West Germany, in Baden-Württemberg. Pop.: 49 000 (1984).

Baden-Powell ('beɪdⁿ'pəʊəl, -'paʊəl) *n.* **Robert Stephenson Smyth** (smɪθ, smaɪθ), 1st Baron Baden-Powell. 1857–1941, British general, noted for his defence of Mafeking (1899–1900) in the Boer War; founder of the Boy Scouts (1908) and (with his sister Agnes) the Girl Guides (1910).

Baden-Württemberg (*German* 'baːdən'vyrtəmbɛrk) *n.* a state of SW West Germany. Capital: Stuttgart. Pop.: 9 295 100 (1986). Area: 35 742 sq. km (13 800 sq. miles).

badge (bædʒ) *n.* **1.** a distinguishing emblem or mark worn to signify membership, employment, achievement, etc. **2.** any revealing feature or mark. [C14: from OF *bage*]

badger ('bædʒə) *n.* **1.** any of various stocky omnivorous mammals occurring in Europe, Asia, and N America. They are large burrowing animals, with strong claws and a thick coat striped black and white on the head. ~*vb.* **2.** (*tr.*) to pester or harass. [C16: var. of *badgeard,* prob. from BADGE (from the white mark on its forehead) + -ARD]

Bad Godesberg (*German* baːt 'goːdəsbɛrk) *n.* the official name for **Godesberg.**

badinage ('bædɪ,nɑːʒ) *n.* playful or frivolous repartee or banter. [C17: from F, from *badiner* to jest]

badlands ('bæd,lændz) *pl. n.* any deeply eroded barren area.

Bad Lands *pl. n.* a deeply eroded barren region of SW South Dakota and NW Nebraska.

badly ('bædlɪ) *adv.* **worse, worst. 1.** poorly; defectively; inadequately. **2.** unfavourably; unsuccessfully: *our scheme worked out badly.* **3.** severely; gravely: *badly hurt.* **4.** incorrectly or inaccurately: *to speak German badly.* **5.** improperly; wickedly: *to behave badly.* **6.** cruelly: *to treat badly.* **7.** very much (esp. in **need badly, want badly**). **8.** regretfully: *he felt badly about it.* **9. badly off.** poor; impoverished.

badminton ('bædmɪntən) *n.* **1.** a game played with rackets and a shuttlecock which is hit back and forth across a high net. **2.** Also called: **badminton cup.** a long drink of claret with soda water and sugar. [from *Badminton House,* Glos]

bad-mouth *vb.* (*tr.*) *Sl., chiefly U.S. & Canad.* to speak unfavourably about.

Badoglio (*Italian* ba'dɔʎʎo) *n.* **Pietro** ('pjetro). 1871–1956, Italian marshal; premier (1943–44) following Mussolini's downfall: arranged an armistice with the Allies (1943).

bad-tempered *adj.* angry; irritable.

BAe *abbrev. for* British Aerospace.

Baeda ('biːdə) *n.* the Latin name for (Saint) **Bede.**

Baedeker ('beɪdɪkə) *n.* any of a series of travel guidebooks issued by the German publisher Karl Baedeker (1801–59) or his firm.

Baeyer (*German* 'baɪər) *n.* **Johann Friedrich Wilhelm Adolf von** (joˈhan 'friːdrɪç 'vɪlhelm 'aːdɔlf fɔn). 1835–1917, German chemist, noted for the synthesis of indigo: Nobel prize for chemistry 1905.

Baez (baɪˈɛz) *n.* **Joan.** born 1941, U.S. rock and folk singer, guitarist, and songwriter, noted for the pure quality of her voice and for her committed pacifist and protest songs.

Baffin Bay ('bæfɪn) *n.* part of the Northwest Passage, situated between Baffin Island and Greenland. [after William *Baffin*, 17th-century English navigator]

Baffin Island *n.* the largest island of the Canadian Arctic, between Greenland and Hudson Bay. Area: 476 560 sq. km (184 000 sq. miles). [see BAFFIN BAY]

baffle ('bæfʰl) *vb.* (*tr.*) **1.** to perplex; bewilder; puzzle. **2.** to frustrate (plans, efforts, etc.). **3.** to check, restrain, or regulate (the flow of a fluid or the emission of sound or light). ~*n.* **4.** Also called: **baffle board, baffle plate.** a plate or mechanical device to restrain or regulate the flow of fluid, light, or sound, esp. in a loudspeaker or microphone. [C16: ?from Scot. dialect *bachlen* to condemn publicly] —'**bafflement** *n.* —'**baffler** *n.* —'**baffling** *adj.* —'**bafflingly** *adv.*

BAFTA ('bæftə) *n. acronym for* British Association of Film and Television Arts.

bag (bæg) *n.* **1.** a flexible container with an opening at one end. **2.** Also: **bagful.** the contents of or amount contained in such a container. **3.** a piece of portable luggage. **4.** short for **handbag. 5.** anything that sags, or is shaped like a bag, such as a loose fold of skin under the eyes. **6.** any pouch or sac forming part of the body of an animal. **7.** the quantity of quarry taken in a single hunting trip or by a single hunter. **8.** *Derog. sl.* an ugly or bad-tempered woman or girl (often in **old bag**). **9. bag and baggage.** *Inf.* **a.** with all one's belongings. **b.** entirely. **10. bag of bones.** a lean creature. **11. in the bag.** *Sl.* almost assured of succeeding or being obtained. **12. rough as bags.** *Austral. sl.* **a.** uncouth. **b.** shoddy. ~*vb.* **bagging, bagged. 13.** (*tr.*) to put into a bag. **14.** to bulge or cause to bulge. **15.** (*tr.*) to capture or kill, as in hunting. **16.** (*tr.*) to catch, seize, or steal. **17.** (*intr.*) to hang loosely; sag. **18.** (*tr.*) *Brit. inf.* to secure the right to do or to have: *he bagged the best chair.* ~ See also **bags.** [C13: prob. from ON *baggi*]

bagasse (bəˈgæs) *n.* the dry pulp remaining after the extraction of juice from sugar cane or similar plants: used as fuel, for making fibreboard, etc. [C19: from F, from Sp. *bagazo* dregs]

bagatelle (ˌbægəˈtɛl) *n.* **1.** something of little value; trifle. **2.** a board game in which balls are struck into holes, with pins as obstacles. **3.** a short light piece of music. [C17: from F, from It. *bagattella*, from (dialect) *bagatta* a little possession]

Bagdad (bægˈdæd) *n.* a variant spelling of **Baghdad.**

Bagehot ('bædʒət) *n.* **Walter.** 1826–77, English economist and journalist: editor of *The Economist*; author of *The English Constitution* (1867), *Physics and Politics* (1872), and *Lombard Street* (1873).

bagel *or* **beigel** ('beɪgʰl) *n.* a hard ring-shaped bread roll. [C20: from Yiddish *beygel*]

baggage ('bægɪdʒ) *n.* **1.** suitcases, bags, etc., packed for a journey; luggage. **2.** an army's portable equipment. **3.** *Inf., old-fashioned.* **a.** a pert young woman. **b.** an immoral woman. [C15: from OF *bagage*, from *bague* a bundle]

baggy ('bægɪ) *adj.* **-gier, -giest.** (of clothes) hanging loosely; puffed out. —'**baggily** *adv.* —'**bagginess** *n.*

Baghdad *or* **Bagdad** (bægˈdæd) *n.* the capital of Iraq, on the River Tigris: capital of the Abbasid Caliphate (762–1258). Pop.: 4 038 430 (1982 est.).

bag lady *n.* a homeless woman who wanders city streets with all her possessions in shopping bags.

bagman ('bægmən) *n., pl.* **-men. 1.** *Brit. inf.* a travelling salesman. **2.** *Sl., chiefly U.S.* a person who collects or distributes money for racketeers. **3.** *Austral.* a tramp or swagman, esp. one on horseback. **4.** *Inf., chiefly Canad.* a person who solicits money for a political party.

bagnio ('baːnjəʊ) *n., pl.* **-ios. 1.** a brothel. **2.** *Obs.* an oriental prison for slaves. **3.** *Obs.* an Italian or Turkish bathhouse. [C16: from It. *bagno*, from L *balneum* bath]

bagpipes ('bæg,paɪps) *pl. n.* any of a family of musical wind instruments in which sounds are produced in reed pipes by air from a bag inflated either by the player's mouth or by arm-operated bellows.

bags (bægz) *pl. n.* **1.** *Inf.* a lot. **2.** *Brit. inf.* trousers. ~*interj.* **3.** Also: **bags I.** *Children's sl., Brit.* an indication of the desire to do, be, or have something.

baguette *or* **baguet** (bæˈgɛt) *n.* **1.** a small gem cut as a long rectangle. **2.** *Archit.* a small moulding having a semicircular cross section. **3.** a narrow French stick loaf. [C18: from F, from It. *bacchetta* a little stick, from *bacchio* rod]

Baguio ('bægɪ,əʊ) *n.* a city in the N Philippines, on N Luzon: summer capital of the Republic. Pop.: 119 009 (1980).

bah (baː, bæ) *interj.* an expression of contempt or disgust.

Bahai (bəˈhaːɪ) *n.* **1.** an adherent of Bahaism. ~*adj.* **2.** of or relating to Bahaism. [from Persian *bahāʾī*, lit.: of glory]

Bahaism (bəˈhaː,ɪzəm) *n.* a religious system founded in 1863, based on Babism and emphasizing the value of all religions and the spiritual unity of mankind. —**Ba'haist** *or* **Ba'haite** *adj., n.*

Bahamas (bəˈhaːməz) *or* **Bahama Islands** *pl. n.* **the.** a group of over 700 coral islands (about 20 of which are inhabited) in the West Indies: a British colony from 1783 until 1964; an independent nation within the Commonwealth from 1973. Language: English. Currency: Bahamian dollar. Capital: Nassau. Pop.: 235 000 (1986). Area: 13 939 sq. km (5381 sq. miles). —**Bahamian** (bəˈheɪmɪən, -ˈhaː-) *adj., n.*

Baha'ullah (ˌbaːhaːˈʊlə) *n.* title of *Mirza Hosein Ali.* 1817–92, Persian religious leader: originally a Shiite Muslim, later a disciple of the Bab: founder of Bahaism.

Bahia (bəˈhiːə; *Portuguese* baˈiːə) *n.* **1.** a state of E Brazil, on the Atlantic coast. Capital: Salvador. Pop.: 9 474 263 (1980). Area: about 562 000 sq. km (217 000 sq. miles). **2.** the former name of **San Salvador.**

Bahía Blanca (*Spanish* baˈia 'blanka) *n.* a port in E Argentina. Pop.: 233 126 (1980).

Bahia de los Cochinos (baˈia de los koˈtʃinos) *n.* the Spanish name for the **Bay of Pigs.**

Bahrain *or* **Bahrein** (baːˈreɪn) *n.* an independent sheikdom on the Persian Gulf, consisting of several islands: under British protection until the declaration of independence in 1971. It has large oil reserves. Language: Arabic. Religion: Muslim. Currency: dinar. Capital: Manama. Pop.: 416 275 (1987). Area: 678 sq. km (262 sq. miles). —**Bah'raini** *or* **Bah'reini** *adj., n.*

Baikal (baɪˈkaːl, -ˈkæl) *n.* **Lake.** a lake in the S Soviet Union, in SE Siberia: the largest freshwater lake in Eurasia and the deepest in the world. Greatest depth: over 1500 m (5000 ft.). Area: about 33 670 sq. km (13 000 sq. miles).

bail¹ (beɪl) *Law.* ~*n.* **1.** a sum of money by which a person is bound to take responsibility for the appearance in court of another person or himself, forfeited if the person fails to appear. **2.** the person or persons so binding themselves; surety. **3.** the system permitting release of a person from custody where such security has been taken: *he was released on bail.* **4. jump bail** *or* (*formal*) **forfeit bail.** to fail to appear in court to answer to a charge. **5. stand** *or* **go bail.** to act as surety (for someone). ~*vb.* (*tr.*) **6.** (often foll. by *out*) to release or obtain the release of (a person) from custody, security having been made. [C14: from OF: custody, from *baillier* to hand over, from L *bāiulāre* to carry burdens]

bail² *or* **bale** (beɪl) *vb.* (often foll. by *out*) to remove (water) from (a boat). See also **bale out.** [C13: from OF *baille* bucket, from L *bāiulus* carrier] —'**bailer** *or* '**baler** *n.*

bail³ (beɪl) *n.* **1.** *Cricket.* either of two small wooden bars across the tops of the stumps. **2.** a partition between stalls in a stable or barn. **3.** *Austral. & N.Z.* a framework in a cowshed used to secure the head of a cow during milking. **4.** a movable bar on a typewriter that holds the paper against the platen. ~*vb.* **5.** See **bail up.** [C18: from OF *baile* stake, fortification, prob. from L *baculum* stick]

bail⁴ *or* **bale** (beɪl) *n.* the semicircular handle of a kettle, bucket, etc. [C15: prob. of Scand. origin]

Baile Átha Cliath (blɑːˈklɪə) *n.* the Irish Gaelic name for **Dublin**.

bailey ('beɪlɪ) *n.* the outermost wall or court of a castle. [C13: from OF *baille* enclosed court, from *bailler* to enclose]

Bailey ('beɪlɪ) *n.* **1. David.** born 1938, English photographer. **2. Nathan** *or* **Nathaniel.** died 1742, English lexicographer: compiler of *An Universal Etymological English Dictionary* (1721-27).

Bailey bridge ('beɪlɪ) *n.* a temporary bridge made of prefabricated steel parts that can be rapidly assembled. [C20: after Sir Donald Coleman *Bailey* (1901-85), its E designer]

bailie ('beɪlɪ) *n.* (in Scotland) a municipal magistrate. [C13: from OF *bailli*, from earlier *baillif* BAILIFF]

bailiff ('beɪlɪf) *n.* **1.** *Brit.* the agent of a landlord or landowner. **2.** a sheriff's officer who serves writs and summonses, makes arrests, and ensures that the sentences of the court are carried out. **3.** *Chiefly Brit.* (formerly) a high official having judicial powers. **4.** *Chiefly U.S.* an official having custody of prisoners appearing in court. [C13: from OF *baillif*, from *bail* custody; see BAIL[1]]

bailiwick ('beɪlɪwɪk) *n.* **1.** *Law.* the area over which a bailiff has jurisdiction. **2.** a person's special field of interest. [C15: from BAILIE + WICK[2]]

bail up *vb.* (*adv.*) **1.** *Austral. & N.Z.* to confine (a cow) or (of a cow) to be confined by the head in a bail. See **bail**[3]. **2.** (*tr.*) *Austral.* (of a bushranger) to tie up or hold under guard in order to rob. **3.** (*intr.*) *Austral.* to submit to robbery without offering resistance. **4.** (*tr.*) *Austral. inf.* to accost or detain, esp. in conversation.

Bainbridge ('beɪn,brɪdʒ) *n.* **Beryl.** born 1934, British novelist and playwright. Novels include *The Dressmaker* (1973) and *Injury Time* (1977); plays include *It's a Lovely Day Tomorrow* (1977).

bain-marie *French.* (bɛ̃mari) *n., pl.* ***bains-marie*** (bɛ̃mari). a vessel for holding hot water, in which sauces and other dishes are gently cooked or kept warm. [C19: from F, from Med. L *balneum Mariae*, lit.: bath of Mary, inaccurate translation of Med. Gk *kaminos Marios*, lit.: furnace of *Miriam*, alleged author of a treatise on alchemy]

Bairam (baɪˈræm, ˈbaɪræm) *n.* either of two Muslim festivals, one (**Lesser Bairam**) at the end of Ramadan, the other (**Greater Bairam**) at the end of the Islamic year. [from Turkish *bayrām*]

Baird (bɛəd) *n.* **John Logie** ('ləʊgɪ). 1888-1946, Scottish engineer: inventor of a 240-line mechanically scanned system of television, replaced in 1935 by a 405-line electrically scanned system.

bairn (bɛən) *n.* *Scot. & N English.* a child. [OE *bearn*]

Bairnsfather ('bɛənz,fɑːðə) *n.* **Bruce.** 1888-1959, English cartoonist, born in India: best known for his cartoons of the war in the trenches during World War I.

bait[1] (beɪt) *n.* **1.** something edible fixed to a hook or in a trap to attract fish or animals. **2.** an enticement; temptation. **3.** a variant spelling of **bate**[3]. **4.** *Arch.* a short stop for refreshment during a journey. ~*vb.* **5.** (*tr.*) to put a piece of food on or in (a hook or trap). **6.** (*tr.*) to persecute or tease. **7.** (*tr.*) to entice; tempt. **8.** (*tr.*) to set dogs upon (a bear, etc.). **9.** (*intr.*) *Arch.* to stop for rest and refreshment during a journey. [C13: from ON *beita* to hunt, persecute]

bait[2] (beɪt) *vb.* a variant spelling of **bate**[2].

baize (beɪz) *n.* a woollen fabric resembling felt, usually green, used mainly for the tops of billiard tables. [C16: from OF *baies*, pl. of *baie* baize, from *bai* reddish brown, BAY[5]]

Baja California ('bæhə) *n.* **1.** a state of NW Mexico, in the N part of the Lower California peninsula. Capital: Mexicali. Pop.: 1 225 436 (1980). Area: about 71 500 sq. km (27 600 sq. miles). **2.** the Spanish name for **Lower California**.

Baja California Sur *n.* a state of NW Mexico, in the S part of the Lower California peninsula. Capital: La Paz. Pop.: 221 389 (1980). Area: 73 475 sq. km (28 363 sq. miles).

bake (beɪk) *vb.* **1.** (*tr.*) to cook by dry heat as in an oven. **2.** (*intr.*) to cook bread, pastry, etc. **3.** to make or become hardened by heat. **4.** (*intr.*) *Inf.* to be extremely hot. ~*n.* **5.** a batch of things baked at one time. **6.** *Caribbean.* a small flat fried cake. [OE *bacan*]

baked Alaska (əˈlæskə) *n.* a dessert made of cake and ice cream covered with meringue and cooked very quickly.

baked beans *pl. n.* haricot beans, baked and tinned in tomato sauce.

Bakelite ('beɪkə,laɪt) *n. Trademark.* any one of a class of thermosetting resins used as electric insulators and for making plastic ware, etc. [C20: after L. H. *Baekeland* (1863-1944), Belgian-born U.S. inventor]

baker ('beɪkə) *n.* a person whose business or employment is to make or sell bread, cakes, etc.

Baker ('beɪkə) *n.* **1.** Sir **Benjamin.** 1840-1907, English engineer who, with Sir John Fowler, designed and constructed much of the London underground railway, the Forth Railway Bridge, and the first Aswan Dam. **2.** Dame **Janet.** born 1933, English mezzo-soprano. **3.** Sir **Samuel White.** 1821-93, English explorer: discovered Lake Albert (1864).

baker's dozen *n.* thirteen. [C16: from the bakers' former practice of giving thirteen rolls where twelve were requested, to protect themselves against accusations of giving light weight]

bakery ('beɪkərɪ) *n., pl.* **-eries. 1.** a room or building equipped for baking. **2.** a shop in which bread, cakes, etc., are sold.

Bakewell ('beɪkwɛl) *n.* **Robert.** 1725-95, English agriculturist; radically improved livestock breeding, esp. of cattle and sheep.

Bakhtaran (,bæktəˈrɑːn, -ˈræn) *n.* a city in W Iran, in the valley of the Qareh Su: oil refinery. Pop.: 565 544 (1986). Former name (until 1987): **Kermanshah**.

baking powder *n.* a powdered mixture that contains sodium bicarbonate and one or more acidic compounds, such as cream of tartar: used in baking as a substitute for yeast.

baklava *or* **baclava** ('bɑːklə,vɑː) *n.* a rich cake consisting of thin layers of pastry filled with nuts and honey. [from Turkish]

baksheesh *or* **backsheesh** ('bækʃiːʃ) *n.* (in some Eastern countries, esp. formerly) money given as a tip, a present, or alms. [C17: from Persian *bakhshish*, from *bakhshidan* to give]

Bakst (*Russian* bakst) *n.* **Leon Nikolayevich** (lɪˈɒn nikaˈlajɪvitʃ). 1866-1924, Russian painter and stage designer, noted particularly for his richly coloured sets for Diaghilev's *Ballet Russe* (1909-21).

Baku (*Russian* baˈku) *n.* a port in the S Soviet Union, on the Caspian Sea: the capital of the Azerbaijan SSR: important for its extensive oilfields. Pop.: 1 741 000 (1987).

Bakunin (*Russian* baˈkunin) *n.* **Mikhail** (mixaˈil). 1814-76, Russian anarchist and writer: a prominent member of the First International, expelled from it after conflicts with Marx.

bal. *Book-keeping. abbrev. for* balance.

Bala ('bælə) *n.* **Lake.** a narrow lake in Gwynedd: the largest natural lake in Wales. Length: 6 km (4 miles).

Balaam ('beɪləm) *n. Old Testament.* a Mesopotamian diviner who, when summoned to curse the Israelites, prophesied future glories for them instead, after being reproached by his ass (Numbers 22-23).

Balaclava helmet (,bæləˈklɑːvə) *n.* a close-fitting woollen hood that covers the ears and neck, as originally worn by soldiers in the Crimean War. [C19: from BALACLAVA]

Balakirev (*Russian* baˈlakirif) *n.* **Mily Alexeyevich** ('milij alɪkˈsjejɪvitʃ). 1837-1910, Russian composer, whose works include two symphonic poems, two symphonies, and many arrangements of Russian folk songs.

Balaklava *or* **Balaclava** (,bæləˈklɑːvə; *Russian* bələˈklavə) *n.* a small port in the SW Soviet Union, in S Crimea: scene of an inconclusive battle (1854), which included the charge of the Light Brigade, during the Crimean War.

balalaika (,bæləˈlaɪkə) *n.* a Russian plucked musical instrument, usually having a triangular body and three strings. [C18: from Russian]

balance ('bæləns) *n.* **1.** a weighing device, generally consisting of a horizontal beam pivoted at its centre, from the ends of which two pans are suspended. The substance to be weighed is placed in one pan and weights are placed in the other until the beam returns to the horizontal. **2.** a state of equilibrium. **3.** something that brings about such a state. **4.** equilibrium of the body; steadiness: *to lose one's balance.* **5.** emotional stability. **6.** harmony in the parts of a whole. **7.** the act of weighing factors, quantities, etc., against each other. **8.** the power to influence or control: *the balance of power.* **9.** something that remains:

the balance of what you owe. **10.** *Accounting.* **a.** equality of debit and credit totals in an account. **b.** a difference between such totals. **11. in the balance.** in an uncertain or undecided condition. **12. on balance.** after weighing up all the factors. **13. strike a balance.** to make a compromise. ~*vb.* **14.** (*tr.*) to weigh in or as if in a balance. **15.** (*intr.*) to be or come into equilibrium. **16.** (*tr.*) to bring into or hold in equilibrium. **17.** (*tr.*) to compare the relative weight, importance, etc., of. **18.** (*tr.*) to be equal to. **19.** (*tr.*) to arrange so as to create a state of harmony. **20.** (*tr.*) *Accounting.* **a.** to compare the credit and debit totals of (an account). **b.** to equalize the credit and debit totals of (an account) by making certain entries. **c.** to settle or adjust (an account) by paying any money due. **21.** (*intr.*) (of a balance sheet, etc.) to have the debit and credit totals equal. [C13: from OF, from Vulgar L *bilancia* (unattested), from LL *bilanx* having two scales, from BI- + *lanx* scale] — **'balanceable** *adj.* — **'balancer** *n.*

balance of payments *n.* the difference over a given time between total payments to foreign nations and total receipts from foreign nations.

balance of power *n.* the distribution of power among countries so that no one nation can seriously threaten another.

balance of trade *n.* the difference in value between total exports and total imports of goods.

balance sheet *n.* a statement that shows the financial position of a business by listing the asset balances and the claims on such assets.

balance wheel *n.* a wheel oscillating against the hairspring of a timepiece, regulating its beat.

Balanchine ('bælən,tʃiːn, ,bælən'tʃiːn) *n.* **George.** 1904–83, U.S. choreographer, born in Russia.

balata ('bælətə) *n.* **1.** a tropical American tree, yielding a latex-like sap. **2.** a rubber-like gum obtained from this sap: a substitute for gutta-percha. [from American Sp., of Carib origin]

Balaton (*Hungarian* 'bɔlɔton) *n.* **Lake.** a large shallow lake in W Hungary. Area: 689 sq. km (266 sq. miles).

Balbo (*Italian* 'balbo) *n.* **Italo** ('italo). 1896–1940, Italian Fascist politician and airman: minister of aviation (1929–33).

Balboa¹ (bæl'bəuə; *Spanish* bal'βoa) *n.* **Vasco Núñez de** ('basko 'nuɲeθ de). ?1475–1519, Spanish explorer, who discovered the Pacific Ocean in 1513.

Balboa² (bæl'bəuə; *Spanish* bal'βoa) *n.* a port in Panama at the Pacific end of the Panama Canal: the administrative centre of the former Canal Zone. Pop.: 1952 (1980).

balcony ('bælkənɪ) *n., pl.* **-nies. 1.** a platform projecting from a building with a balustrade along its outer edge, often with access from a door or window. **2.** a gallery in a theatre, above the dress circle. **3.** *U.S. & Canad.* any circle in a theatre. [C17: from It. *balcone*, prob. from OHG *balko* beam] — **'balconied** *adj.*

bald (bɔːld) *adj.* **1.** having no hair or fur, esp. (of a man) having no hair on the scalp. **2.** lacking natural growth or covering. **3.** plain or blunt: *a bald statement.* **4.** bare or unadorned. **5.** Also: **baldfaced.** (of birds and animals) having white markings on the head and face. **6.** (of a tyre) having a worn tread. [C14 *ballede* (lit.: having a white spot)] — **'baldish** *adj.* — **'baldly** *adv.* — **'baldness** *n.*

baldachin *or* **baldaquin** ('bɔːldəkɪn) *n.* **1.** a richly ornamented brocade. **2.** a canopy over an altar, shrine, or throne or carried in Christian religious processions over an object of veneration. [OE *baldekin*, from It. *baldacchino*, lit.: stuff from Baghdad]

bald eagle *n.* a large eagle of North America, having a white head and tail. It is the U.S. national bird.

Balder ('bɔːldə) *n.* *Norse myth.* a god, son of Odin and Frigg, noted for his beauty and sweet nature. He was killed by a bough of mistletoe thrown by the blind god Höd, misled by the malicious Loki.

balderdash ('bɔːldə,dæʃ) *n.* stupid or illogical talk; senseless rubbish. [C16: from ?]

balding ('bɔːldɪŋ) *adj.* somewhat bald or becoming bald.

baldric ('bɔːldrɪk) *n.* a sash or belt worn over the right shoulder to the left hip for carrying a sword, etc. [C13: from OF *baudrei*, of Frankish origin]

Baldwin ('bɔːldwɪn) *n.* **1. James (Arthur).** 1924–87, U.S. writer, whose works include the novel *Go Tell it on the Mountain* (1954). **2. Stanley,** 1st Earl Baldwin of Bewdley. 1867–1947, British Conservative statesman: prime minister (1923–24, 1924–29, 1935–37).

Baldwin I *n.* 1058–1118, crusader and first king of Jerusalem (1100–18), who captured Acre (1104), Beirut (1109), and Sidon (1110).

bale¹ (beɪl) *n.* **1.** a large bundle, package, or carton of goods bound by ropes, wires, etc., for storage or transportation. **2.** *U.S.* 500 pounds of cotton. ~*vb.* **3.** to make (hay, etc.) or put (goods) into a bale or bales. [C14: prob. from OF *bale,* from OHG *balla* BALL¹]

bale² (beɪl) *n. Arch.* **1.** evil; injury. **2.** woe; suffering; pain. [OE *bealu*]

bale³ (beɪl) *vb.* a variant spelling of **bail².**

bale⁴ (beɪl) *n.* a variant spelling of **bail⁴.**

Bâle (bal) *n.* the French name for **Basel.**

Balearic Islands (,bælɪ'ærɪk) *pl. n.* a group of islands in the W Mediterranean, consisting of Majorca, Minorca, Ibiza, Formentera, Cabrera, and 11 islets: a province of Spain. Capital: Palma, on Majorca. Pop.: 669 101 (1982). Area: 5012 sq. km (1935 sq. miles). Spanish name: **Baleares** (bale'ares).

baleen (bə'liːn) *n.* whalebone. [C14: from L *bālaena* whale]

baleen whale *n.* another name for **whalebone whale.**

baleful ('beɪlful) *adj.* harmful, menacing, or vindictive. — **'balefully** *adv.* — **'balefulness** *n.*

Balenciaga (*Spanish* balen'θjaɣa) *n.* **Cristóbal** (kris'to-βal). 1895–1972, Spanish couturier.

bale out *or* **bail out** *vb.* (*adv.*) **1.** (*intr.*) to make an emergency parachute jump from an aircraft. **2.** (*tr.*) *Inf.* to help (a person, organization, etc.) out of a predicament.

baler ('beɪlə) *n.* a machine for making bales of hay, etc. Also called: **baling machine.**

Balfour ('bælfɔː, -fə, -fuə) *n.* **Arthur James,** 1st Earl of Balfour. 1848–1930, British Conservative statesman: prime minister (1902–05); foreign secretary (1916–19).

Bali ('baːlɪ) *n.* an island in Indonesia, east of Java: mountainous, rising over 3000 m (10 000 ft.). Capital: Denpasar. Pop.: 2 469 930 (1981 est.). Area: 5558 sq. km (2146 sq. miles). — ,**Bali'nese** *adj., n.*

Balikpapan (,baːlɪk'paːpaːn) *n.* a city in Indonesia, on the SE coast of Borneo. Pop.: 280 875 (1980).

Baliol *or* **Balliol** ('beɪlɪɔl) *n.* **1. Edward de.** ?1283–1364, king of Scotland (1332, 1333–56). **2. John de.** 1249–1315, king of Scotland (1292–96): defeated and imprisoned by Edward I of England (1296).

balk *or* **baulk** (bɔːk, bɔːlk) *vb.* **1.** (*intr.;* usually foll. by *at*) to stop short; jib: *the horse balked at the jump.* **2.** (*intr.;* foll. by *at*) to recoil: *he balked at the idea of murder.* **3.** (*tr.*) to thwart, check, or foil: *he was balked in his plans.* ~*n.* **4.** a roughly squared heavy timber beam. **5.** a timber tie beam of a roof. **6.** an unploughed ridge between furrows. **7.** an obstacle; hindrance; disappointment. **8.** *Baseball.* an illegal motion by a pitcher. ~See also **baulk.** [OE *balca*]

Balkan ('bɔːlkən) *adj.* of, denoting, or relating to the Balkan States or their inhabitants, the Balkan Peninsula, or the Balkan Mountains.

Balkan Mountains *pl. n.* a mountain range extending across Bulgaria from the Black Sea to the Yugoslav border. Highest peak: Mount Botev, 2376 m (7793 ft.).

Balkan Peninsula *n.* a large peninsula in SE Europe, between the Adriatic and Aegean Seas.

Balkan States *pl. n.* the countries of the Balkan Peninsula: Yugoslavia, Romania, Bulgaria, Albania, Greece, and the European part of Turkey. Also called: **the Balkans.**

Balkh (baːlk) *n.* a district of N Afghanistan, corresponding to ancient Bactria. Chief town: Mazar-i-Sharif.

Balkhash (*Russian* bal'xaʃ) *n.* **Lake.** a salt lake in the SW Soviet Union, in SE Kazakhstan: fed by the Ili River. Area: about 1800 sq. km (7000 sq. miles).

Balkis ('bælkɪs) *n.* the name in the Koran of the queen of **Sheba.**

balky *or* **baulky** ('bɔːkɪ, 'bɔːlkɪ) *adj.* **balkier, balkiest** *or* **baulkier, baulkiest.** inclined to stop abruptly and unexpectedly: *a balky horse.*

ball¹ (bɔːl) *n.* **1.** a spherical or nearly spherical body or mass. **2.** a round or roundish body, of a size and composition suitable for any of various games. **3.** a ball propelled in a particular way: *a high ball.* **4.** any rudimentary game with a ball: *to play ball.* **5.** a single delivery of the ball in cricket and other games. **6. a.** a solid nonexplosive projectile for a firearm, cannon, etc. **b.** such projectiles collectively. **7.** any more or less rounded part: *the ball of the foot.* **8. ball of muscle.** *Austral.* a very strong, fit person.

9. have the ball at one's feet. to have the chance of doing something. **10. keep the ball rolling.** to maintain the progress of a project, plan, etc. **11. on the ball.** *Inf.* alert; informed. **12. play ball.** *Inf.* to cooperate. **13. start** *or* **set the ball rolling.** to initiate an action, discussion, etc. ~*vb.* **14.** to make, form, wind, gather, etc., into a ball or balls. ~ See also **balls, balls-up.** [C13: from ON *böllr*]

ball² (bɔ:l) *n.* **1.** a social function for dancing, esp. one that is lavish or formal. **2.** *Inf.* a very enjoyable time (esp. in **have a ball**). [C17: from F *bal* (n.), from OF *baller* (vb.), from LL *ballāre* to dance]

Ball (bɔ:l) *n.* **John.** died 1381, English priest: executed as one of the leaders of the Peasants' Revolt (1381).

ballad ('bæləd) *n.* **1.** a narrative song with a recurrent refrain. **2.** a narrative poem in short stanzas of popular origin. **3.** a slow sentimental song, esp. a pop song. [C15: from OF *balade*, from OProvençal *balada* song accompanying a dance]

ballade (bæ'lɑ:d) *n.* **1.** *Prosody.* a verse form consisting of three stanzas and an envoy, all ending with the same line. **2.** *Music.* an instrumental composition based on or intended to evoke a narrative.

balladeer (,bælə'dɪə) *n.* a singer of ballads.

Ballance ('bæləns) *n.* **John.** 1839–93, New Zealand statesman, born in Northern Ireland: prime minister of New Zealand (1891–93).

ball-and-socket joint *n. Anat.* a joint in which a rounded head fits into a rounded cavity, allowing a wide range of movement.

Ballarat ('bælə,ræt, ,bælə'ræt) *n.* a town in SE Australia, in S central Victoria: originally the centre of a gold-mining region. Pop.: 78 290 (1986 est.). See also **Eureka Stockade.**

ballast ('bæləst) *n.* **1.** any heavy material used to stabilize a vessel, esp. one that is not carrying cargo. **2.** crushed rock, broken stone, etc., used for the foundation of a road or railway track or in making concrete. **3.** anything that provides stability or weight. **4.** *Electronics.* a device for maintaining the current in a circuit. ~*vb.* (*tr.*) **5.** to give stability or weight to. [C16: prob. from Low G]

ball bearing *n.* **1.** a bearing consisting of steel balls rolling between a metal sleeve fitted over the rotating shaft and an outer sleeve held in the bearing housing, so reducing friction. **2.** a metal ball, esp. one used in such a bearing.

ball boy *or* (*fem.*) **ball girl** *n.* (esp. in tennis) a person who retrieves balls that go out of play.

ball cock *n.* a device for regulating the flow of a liquid into a tank, cistern, etc., consisting of a floating ball mounted at one end of an arm and a valve on the other end that opens and closes as the ball falls and rises.

ballerina (,bælə'ri:nə) *n.* a female ballet dancer. [C18: from It., fem. of *ballerino* dancing master, from *ballare* to dance]

Ballesteros (,bælɛ'stɛrɒs; *Spanish* baʎes'terɔs) *n.* **Severiano** (sevɛ'rjano). born 1957, Spanish professional golfer: won the British Open Championship (1979; 1984; 1988).

ballet ('bæleɪ, bæ'leɪ) *n.* **1.** a classical style of expressive dancing based on precise conventional steps. **2.** a theatrical representation of a story or theme performed by ballet dancers. **3.** a troupe of ballet dancers. **4.** music written for a ballet. [C17: from F, from It. *balletto*, lit.: a little dance, from *ballare* to dance] — **balletic** (bæ'lɛtɪk) *adj.*

balletomane ('bælɪtəʊ,meɪn) *n.* a ballet enthusiast.

balletomania (,bælɪtəʊ'meɪnɪə) *n.* passionate enthusiasm for ballet.

ball game *n.* **1.** any game played with a ball. **2.** *U.S. & Canad.* a game of baseball. **3.** *Inf.* a situation; state of affairs (esp. in **a whole new ball game**).

Balliol ('beɪlɪəl) *n.* See **Baliol.**

ballista (bə'lɪstə) *n., pl.* **-tae** (-ti:). an ancient catapult for hurling stones, etc. [C16: from L, ult. from Gk *ballein* to throw]

ballistic (bə'lɪstɪk) *adj.* **1.** of or relating to ballistics. **2.** denoting or relating to the flight of projectiles moving under their own momentum and the force of gravity. **3.** (of a measurement or measuring instrument) depending on a brief impulse or current that causes a movement related to the quantity to be measured: *a ballistic pendulum.* — **bal'listically** *adv.*

ballistic missile *n.* a missile that has no wings or fins and that follows a ballistic trajectory when its propulsive power is discontinued.

ballistics (bə'lɪstɪks) *n.* (*functioning as sing.*) **1.** the study of the flight dynamics of projectiles. **2.** the study of the effects of firing on firearms and their projectiles.

ballocks ('bɒləks) *pl. n., interj.* a variant spelling of **bollocks.**

ball of fire *n. Inf.* a very lively person.

balloon (bə'lu:n) *n.* **1.** an inflatable rubber bag used as a plaything or party decoration. **2.** a large bag inflated with a lighter-than-air gas, designed to rise and float in the atmosphere. It may have a basket or gondola for carrying passengers, etc. **3.** an outline containing the words or thoughts of a character in a cartoon. **4.** a large rounded brandy glass. **5. when the balloon goes up.** *Inf.* when the action starts. ~*vb.* **6.** (*intr.*) to go up or fly in a balloon. **7.** to inflate or be inflated: *the wind ballooned the sails.* **8.** (*tr.*) *Brit.* to propel (a ball) high into the air. [C16 (in the sense: ball, ball game): from It. dialect *ballone*] — **bal'loonist** *n.* — **bal'loon-,like** *adj.*

balloon loan *n.* a loan in respect of which interest and capital are paid off in instalments at regular intervals.

ballot ('bælət) *n.* **1.** the practice of selecting a representative, course of action, etc., by submitting the options to a vote of all qualified persons. **2.** an instance of voting, usually in secret. **3.** a list of candidates standing for office. **4.** the number of votes cast in an election. ~*vb.* **-loting,** **-loted.** **5.** to vote or elicit a vote from: *we balloted the members on this issue.* **6.** (*tr.*; usually foll. by *for*) to vote for or decide on by lot or ballot. [C16: from It. *ballotta*, lit.: a little ball]

ballot box *n.* a box into which ballot papers are dropped after voting.

ballot paper *n.* a paper used for voting.

ballpark ('bɔ:l,pɑ:k) *n.* **1.** *U.S. & Canad.* a stadium used for baseball games. **2.** *Inf.* approximate range: *in the right ballpark.*

ball-peen hammer *n.* a hammer with one end of the head rounded for beating metal.

ballpoint *or* **ballpoint pen** ('bɔ:l,pɔɪnt) *n.* a pen having a small ball bearing as a writing point.

ballroom ('bɔ:l,ru:m, -,rʊm) *n.* a large hall for dancing.

ballroom dancing *n.* social dancing, popular since the beginning of the 20th century, to dances in conventional rhythms (**ballroom dances**).

balls (bɔ:lz) *Taboo sl.* ~*pl. n.* **1.** the testicles. **2.** nonsense; rubbish. ~*interj.* **3.** an exclamation of disagreement, contempt, etc.

balls-up *Taboo sl.* ~*n.* **1.** something botched or muddled. ~*vb.* **balls up.** **2.** (*tr., adv.*) to muddle or botch.

bally ('bælɪ) *adj., adv.* (intensifier) *Brit. sl.* a euphemistic word for **bloody** (sense 5).

ballyhoo (,bælɪ'hu:) *Inf. n.* **1.** a noisy, confused, or nonsensical situation. **2.** sensational or blatant advertising or publicity. ~*vb.* **-hooing, -hooed.** **3.** (*tr.*) *Chiefly U.S.* to advertise by sensational or blatant methods. [C19: from ?]

balm (bɑ:m) *n.* **1.** any of various oily aromatic substances obtained from certain tropical trees and used for healing and soothing. See also **balsam** (sense 1). **2.** any plant yielding such a substance, esp. the balm of Gilead. **3.** something comforting or soothing. **4.** Also called: **lemon balm.** an aromatic Eurasian plant, having clusters of small fragrant white flowers. **5.** a pleasant odour. [C13: from OF *basme*, from L *balsamum* BALSAM]

Balmain (*French* balmɛ̃) *n.* **Pierre Alexandre** (pjɛr alɛksɑ̃drə). 1914–82, French couturier.

balm of Gilead ('gɪlɪ,æd) *n.* **1.** any of several trees of Africa and W Asia that yield a fragrant oily resin. **2.** the resin exuded by these trees. **3.** a North American poplar tree. **4.** a fragrant resin obtained from the balsam fir.

Balmoral¹ (bæl'mɒrəl) *n.* (*sometimes not cap.*) **1.** a laced walking shoe. **2.** a Scottish brimless hat usually with a cockade and plume. [from BALMORAL Castle]

Balmoral² (bæl'mɒrəl) *n.* a castle in NE Scotland, in Grampian region: a private residence of the British sovereign.

balmy ('bɑ:mɪ) *adj.* **balmier, balmiest.** **1.** (of weather) mild and pleasant. **2.** having the qualities of balm; fragrant or soothing. **3.** a variant spelling of **barmy.** — **'balmily** *adv.* — **'balminess** *n.*

balneology (,bælnɪ'ɒlədʒɪ) *n.* the branch of medical science concerned with the therapeutic value of baths, esp.

with natural mineral waters. [C19: from L *balneum* bath]
— **balneological** (ˌbælnɪəˈlɒdʒɪkⁿl) *adj.* —ˌ**balne'olo-gist** *n.*

baloney *or* **boloney** (bəˈləʊnɪ) *n. Inf.* foolish talk; nonsense. [C20: from *Bologna* (sausage)]

BALPA ('bælpə) *n. acronym for* British Airline Pilots' Association.

balsa ('bɔːlsə) *n.* **1.** a tree of tropical America. **2.** Also called: **balsawood.** the very light wood of this tree, used for making rafts, etc. **3.** a light raft. [C18: from Sp.: raft]

balsam ('bɔːlsəm) *n.* **1.** any of various fragrant oleoresins, such as balm, obtained from any of several trees and shrubs and used as a base for medicines and perfumes. **2.** any of various similar substances used as ointments. **3.** any of certain aromatic resinous turpentines. See **Canada balsam. 4.** any plant yielding balsam. **5.** Also called: **busy Lizzie.** any of several plants of the genus *Impatiens.* **6.** anything healing or soothing. [C15: from L *balsamum,* from Gk *balsamon,* from Heb. *bāśām* spice] — **balsamic** (bɔːl'sæmɪk) *adj.*

balsam fir *n.* a fir tree of NE North America, that yields Canada balsam.

Balthazar ('bælθə,zɑː, bæl'θæzə) *n.* one of the Magi, the others being Caspar and Melchior.

Baltic ('bɔːltɪk) *adj.* **1.** denoting or relating to the Baltic Sea or the Baltic states. **2.** of or characteristic of Baltic as a group of languages. ~*n.* **3.** a branch of the Indo-European family of languages consisting of Lithuanian, Latvian, and Old Prussian. **4.** Also called: **Baltic Exchange.** a commodities exchange in the City of London.

Baltic Sea *n.* a sea in N Europe, connected with the North Sea by the Skaggerak, Kattegat, and Oresund; shallow, with low salinity and small tides.

Baltic Shield *n.* the wide area of ancient rock in Scandinavia. Also called: **Scandinavian Shield.** See **shield** (sense 7).

Baltic States *pl. n.* the formerly independent republics of Estonia, Latvia, and Lithuania, which became constituent republics of the Soviet Union in 1940.

Baltimore[1] ('bɔːltɪˌmɔː) *n.* **Lord.** See (Sir George) **Calvert.**

Baltimore[2] ('bɔːltɪˌmɔː) *n.* a port in N Maryland, on Chesapeake Bay. Pop.: 752 800 (1986).

Baluchistan (bəˈluːtʃɪˌstɑːn, -ˌstæn) *n.* **1.** a mountainous region of SW Asia, in SW Pakistan and SE Iran. **2.** a province of SW Pakistan: a former territory of British India (until 1947). Capital: Quetta.

baluster ('bæləstə) *n.* any of a set of posts supporting a rail or coping. [C17: from F *balustre,* from It. *balaustro* pillar resembling a pomegranate flower, ult. from Gk *balaustion*]

balustrade ('bælə,streɪd) *n.* an ornamental rail or coping with its supporting set of balusters. [C17: from F, from *balustre* BALUSTER]

Balzac ('bælzæk; *French* balzak) *n.* **Honoré de** (ɔnɔre də). 1799–1850, French novelist: author of a collection of novels under the general title *La Comédie humaine,* including *Eugénie Grandet* (1833), *Le Père Goriot* (1834), and *La Cousine Bette* (1846).

Bamako (ˌbæməˈkəʊ) *n.* the capital of Mali, in the south, on the River Niger. Pop.: 620 000 (1981).

Bamberg ('bæmbɜːg; *German* 'bambɛrk) *n.* a town in S West Germany, in the north of present-day Bavaria: seat of independent prince-bishops of the Holy Roman Empire (1007–1802). Pop.: 72 500 (1982).

bambino (bæm'biːnəʊ) *n., pl.* **-nos** *or* **-ni** (-niː). *Inf.* a young child, esp. Italian. [C18: from It.]

bamboo (bæm'buː) *n.* **1.** a tall treelike tropical or semitropical grass having hollow stems with ringed joints. **2.** the stem, used for building, poles, and furniture. [C16: prob. from Malay *bambu*]

bamboozle (bæm'buːzⁿl) *vb. (tr.) Inf.* **1.** to cheat; mislead. **2.** to confuse. [C18: from ?] — **bam'boozlement** *n.* — **bam'boozler** *n.*

ban (bæn) *vb.* **banning, banned. 1.** *(tr.)* to prohibit, esp. officially, from action, display, entrance, sale, etc.; forbid. ~*n.* **2.** an official prohibition or interdiction. **3.** a public proclamation, esp. of outlawry. **4.** *Arch.* a curse; imprecation. [OE *bannan* to proclaim]

Banaba (bəˈnɑːbə) *n.* an island in the SW Pacific, in the Republic of Kiribati. Phosphates were mined by Britain (1900–79). Area: about 5 sq. km (2 sq. miles). Pop.: 189 (1985). Also called: **Ocean Island.** — **Ba'naban** *adj., n.*

banal (bə'nɑːl) *adj.* lacking force or originality; trite; commonplace. [C18: from OF: relating to compulsory feudal service, hence common to all, commonplace] — **banality** (bə'nælɪtɪ) *n.* —**ba'nally** *adv.*

banana (bə'nɑːnə) *n.* **1.** any of several tropical and subtropical treelike plants, esp. a widely cultivated species having hanging clusters of edible fruit. **2.** the crescent-shaped fruit of any of these plants. [C16: from Sp. or Port., of African origin]

banana republic *n. Inf. & derog.* a small country, esp. in Central America, that is politically unstable and has an economy dominated by foreign interest, usually dependent on one export.

banana skin *n.* **1.** the soft outer covering of a banana. **2.** *Inf.* something unforeseen that causes an obvious and embarrassing mistake. [sense 2 from the common slapstick joke of slipping on a banana skin]

Banaras (bə'nɑːrəz) *n.* a variant spelling of **Benares.**

Banat ('bænɪt, 'bɑːnɪt) *n.* a fertile plain extending through Hungary, Romania, and Yugoslavia.

Banbury ('bænbərɪ) *n.* a town in central England, in N Oxfordshire. Pop.: 35 796 (1981).

band[1] (bænd) *n.* **1.** a company of people having a common purpose; group: *a band of outlaws.* **2.** a group of musicians playing either brass and percussion instruments only (**brass band**) or brass, woodwind, and percussion instruments (**concert band** or **military band**). **3.** a group of musicians who play popular music, jazz, etc., often for dancing. ~*vb.* **4.** (usually foll. by *together*) to unite; assemble. [C15: from F *bande,* prob. from OProvençal *banda,* of Gmc origin]

band[2] (bænd) *n.* **1.** a thin flat strip of some material, used esp. to encircle objects and hold them together: *a rubber band.* **2. a.** a strip of fabric or other material used as an ornament or to reinforce clothing. **b.** *(in combination):* *waistband; hatband.* **3.** a stripe of contrasting colour or texture. **4.** a driving belt in machinery. **5.** a range of values that are close or related in number, degree, or quality. **6.** *Physics.* a range of frequencies or wavelengths between two limits. **7.** short for **energy band. 8.** *Computers.* one or more tracks on a magnetic disk or drum. **9.** *Anat.* any structure resembling a ribbon or cord that connects, encircles, or binds different parts. **10.** *Archit.* a strip of flat panelling, such as a fascia, usually attached to a wall. **11.** either of a pair of hanging extensions of the collar, forming part of academic, legal, or (formerly) clerical dress. **12.** (of a gramophone record) another word for **track** (sense 10). ~*vb. (tr.)* **13.** to fasten or mark with a band. [C15: from OF *bende,* of Gmc origin]

Banda ('bændə) *n.* **Hastings Kamuzu** (kæ'muːzuː). born 1906, Malawi statesman. As first prime minister of Nyasaland (from 1963), he led his country to independence (1964) as Malawi: president from 1966.

bandage ('bændɪdʒ) *n.* **1.** a piece of material used to dress a wound, bind a broken limb, etc. ~*vb.* **2.** to cover or bind with a bandage. [C16: from F, from *bande* strip, BAND[2]]

bandanna *or* **bandana** (bæn'dænə) *n.* a large silk or cotton handkerchief or neckerchief. [C18: from Hindi *bāndhnū* tie-dyeing]

Bandaranaike (ˌbændərə'naɪkə) *n.* **1.** Mrs **Sirimavo** (ˌsɪrɪ'mɑːvəʊ). born 1916, prime minister of Sri Lanka, formerly Ceylon (1960–65; 1970–77). **2.** her husband, **Solomon.** 1899–1959, prime minister of Ceylon (1956–59); assassinated.

Bandar Seri Begawan ('bɑːndɑː 'sɛrɪ bə'gɑːwən) *n.* the capital of Brunei. Pop.: 54 000 (1984). Former name: **Brunei.**

Banda Sea *n.* a part of the Pacific in Indonesia, between Sulawesi and New Guinea.

b. and b. *or* **B & B** *abbrev. for* bed and breakfast.

bandbox ('bænd,bɒks) *n.* a lightweight usually cylindrical box for small articles, esp. hats.

bandeau ('bændəʊ) *n., pl.* **-deaux** (-dəʊz). a narrow band of ribbon, velvet, etc., worn round the head. [C18: from F, from OF *bandel* a little BAND[2]]

banderole *or* **banderol** ('bændə,rəʊl) *n.* **1.** a long narrow flag, usually with forked ends, esp. one attached to the mast of a ship. **2.** a ribbon-like scroll or sculptured band bearing an inscription. [C16: from OF, from It. *banderuola,* lit.: a little banner]

bandicoot ('bændɪ,kuːt) n. 1. an agile terrestrial marsupial of Australia and New Guinea with a long pointed muzzle and a long tail. 2. **bandicoot rat**. Also called: **mole rat**. any of three burrowing rats of S and SE Asia. [C18: from Telugu *pandikokku*]

banding ('bændɪŋ) n. Brit. the practice of putting schoolchildren into ability groups to ensure a balanced intake to secondary school.

bandit ('bændɪt) n., pl. **bandits** or **banditti** (bæn'dɪtɪ). a robber, esp. a member of an armed gang. [C16: from It. *bandito*, from *bandire* to proscribe, from *bando* edict] — '**banditry** n.

Bandjarmasin or **Bandjermasin** (,bændʒə'mɑːsɪn) n. variant spellings of **Banjarmasin**.

bandmaster ('bænd,mɑːstə) n. the conductor of a band.

Band of Hope n. a society devoted to abstinence from alcohol.

bandoleer or **bandolier** (,bændə'lɪə) n. a soldier's broad shoulder belt having small pockets or loops for cartridges. [C16: from OF *bandouliere*]

band-pass filter n. 1. *Electronics*. a filter that transmits only currents having frequencies within specified limits. 2. an optical device for transmitting waves of predetermined wavelengths.

band saw n. a power-operated saw consisting of an endless toothed metal band running over and driven by two wheels.

bandsman ('bændzmən) n., pl. **-men**. a player in a musical band, esp. a brass or military band.

bandstand ('bænd,stænd) n. a platform for a band, usually out of doors and roofed.

band theory n. the theory that electrons in solids have a range of energies falling into allowed bands, between which are forbidden bands.

Bandung ('bændʊŋ) n. a city in Indonesia, in SW Java. Pop.: 1 400 000 (1981).

bandwagon ('bænd,wægən) n. 1. *U.S.* a wagon for the band in a parade. 2. **climb, jump,** or **get on the bandwagon**. to join or support a party or movement that seems assured of success.

bandwidth ('bænd,wɪdθ) n. the range of frequencies within a given waveband used for a particular radio transmission.

bandy ('bændɪ) adj. **-dier, -diest.** 1. Also: **bandy-legged**. having legs curved outwards at the knees. 2. (of legs) curved thus. ~vb. **-dying, -died.** (tr.) 3. to exchange (words) in a heated or hostile manner. 4. to give and receive (blows). 5. (often foll. by *about*) to circulate (a name, rumour, etc.). [C16: prob. from OF *bander* to hit the ball back and forth at tennis]

bane (beɪn) n. 1. a person or thing that causes misery or distress (esp. in **bane of one's life**). 2. something that causes death or destruction. 3. **a.** a fatal poison. **b.** (*in combination*): *ratsbane*. 4. Arch. ruin or distress. [OE *bana*] — '**baneful** adj.

baneberry ('beɪnbərɪ) n., pl. **-ries.** 1. Also called: **herb Christopher** (Brit.). a plant which has small white flowers and red or white poisonous berries. 2. the berry.

Banff n. 1. (bæmf). a town in NE Scotland, in Grampian region. Pop.: 4246 (1984 est.). 2. (bænf). a town in Canada, in SW Alberta, in the Rocky Mountains: surrounded by **Banff National Park**. Pop.: 4208 (1981).

Banffshire ('bæmf,ʃɪə, -ʃə) n. (until 1975) a county of NE Scotland, now part of Grampian region.

bang[1] (bæŋ) n. 1. a short loud explosive noise, as of the report of a gun. 2. a hard blow or knock, esp. a noisy one. 3. *Sl.* an injection of heroin or other narcotic. 4. *Taboo sl.* an act of sexual intercourse. 5. **with a bang**. successfully: *the party went with a bang*. ~vb. 6. to hit or knock, esp. with a loud noise. 7. to move noisily or clumsily: *to bang about the house*. 8. to close (a door, window, etc.) or (of a door, etc.) be closed noisily; slam. 9. (tr.) to cause to move by hitting vigorously: *he banged the ball over the fence*. 10. to make or cause to make a loud noise, as of an explosion. 11. *Taboo sl.* to have sexual intercourse (with). 12. (*intr.*) *Sl.* to inject heroin, etc. 13. **bang one's head against a brick wall**. to try to achieve something impossible. ~adv. 14. with a sudden impact or effect: *the car drove bang into a lamppost*. 15. precisely: *bang in the middle*. 16. **go bang**. to burst, shut, etc., with a loud noise. [C16: from ON *bang, banga* hammer]

bang[2] (bæŋ) n. 1. a fringe of hair cut straight across the forehead. ~vb. (tr.) 2. to cut (the hair) in such a style. 3. to dock (the tail of a horse, etc.). [C19: prob. short for *bangtail* short tail]

Bangalore (,bæŋgə'lɔː) n. a city in S India, capital of Karnataka state. Pop.: 2 914 000 (1983).

banger ('bæŋə) n. Brit. 1. Sl. a sausage. 2. Inf. an old decrepit car. 3. a firework that explodes loudly.

Bangka or **Banka** ('bæŋkə) n. an island in Indonesia, separated from Sumatra by the **Bangka Strait**. Chief town: Pangkalpinang. Area: about 11 914 sq. km (4600 sq. miles).

Bangkok ('bæŋkɒk, bæŋ'kɒk) n. the capital and chief port of Thailand, on the Chao Phraya River: became a royal city and the capital in 1782. Pop.: 6 446 708 (1986 est.). Thai name: **Krung Thep** ('krʊŋ 'teɪp).

Bangladesh (,bæːŋglə'dɛʃ, ,bæŋ-) n. a republic in S Asia: formerly the Eastern Province of Pakistan; became independent in 1971 after civil war and the defeat of Pakistan by India; consists of the plains and vast deltas of the Ganges and Brahmaputra Rivers: economy based on jute and jute products (over 80 per cent of world production). Language: Bengali. Religion: Muslim. Currency: taka. Capital: Dhaka. Pop.: 104 100 000 (1987). Area: 142 797 sq. km (55 126 sq. miles). —,**Bangla'deshi** adj., n.

bangle ('bæŋgəl) n. a bracelet, usually without a clasp, often worn round the arm or sometimes round the ankle. [C19: from Hindi *bangri*]

bang on adj., adv. Brit. inf. 1. with absolute accuracy. 2. excellent or excellently.

Bangor ('bæŋgɔː, -gə) n. 1. a university town in NW Wales, in Gwynedd, on the Menai Strait. Pop.: 12 174 (1981). 2. a town in SE Northern Ireland, in Co. Down, on Belfast Lough. Pop.: 46 585 (1981).

bangtail ('bæŋ,teɪl) n. 1. a horse's tail cut straight across but not through the bone. 2. a horse with a tail cut in this way. [C19: from *bangtail* short tail]

Bangui (French bɑ̃gi) n. the capital of the Central African Republic, in the south part, on the Ubangi River. Pop.: 473 817 (1984).

Bangweulu (,bæŋwɪ'uːlʊ) n. Lake. a shallow lake in NE Zambia, discovered by David Livingstone, who died there in 1873. Area: about 9850 sq. km (3800 sq. miles), including swamps.

banian ('bænjən) n. a variant spelling of **banyan**.

banish ('bænɪʃ) vb. (tr.) 1. to expel from a place, esp. by an official decree as a punishment. 2. to drive away: *to banish gloom*. [C14: from OF *banir*, of Gmc origin] — '**banishment** n.

banisters or **bannisters** ('bænɪstəz) pl. n. the railing and supporting balusters on a staircase; balustrade. [C17: altered from BALUSTER]

Banja Luka (Serbo-Croatian 'baːnja: ,luːka) n. a city in NW central Yugoslavia, on the Vrbas River in Bosnia and Herzegovina: scene of battles between the Austrians and Turks in 1527, 1688, and 1737. Pop.: 183 618 (1981).

Banjarmasin, Banjermasin, Bandjarmasin or **Bandjermasin** (,bændʒə'mɑːsɪn) n. a port in Indonesia, in SW Borneo. Pop.: 381 286 (1980).

banjo ('bændʒəʊ) n., pl. **-jos** or **-joes**. a stringed musical instrument with a long neck and a circular drumlike body overlaid with parchment, plucked with the fingers or a plectrum. [C18: var. (U.S. Southern pronunciation) of earlier *bandore*, ult. from Gk *pandora*] — '**banjoist** n.

Banjul (bæn'dʒuːl) n. the capital of The Gambia, a port at the mouth of the Gambia River. Pop.: 44 188 (1983). Former name (until 1973): **Bathurst**.

bank[1] (bæŋk) n. 1. an institution offering certain financial services, such as the safekeeping of money and lending of money at interest. 2. the building used by such an institution. 3. a small container used at home for keeping money. 4. the funds held by a banker or dealer in some gambling games. 5. (in various games) **a.** the stock, as of money, etc., on which players may draw. **b.** the player holding this stock. 6. any supply, store, or reserve: *a data bank*. ~vb. 7. to deposit (cash, cheques, etc.) in a bank. 8. (*intr.*) to transact business with a bank. 9. (*intr.*) to engage in banking. ~See also **bank on**. [C15: prob. from It. *banca* bench, moneychanger's table, of Gmc origin]

bank[2] (bæŋk) n. 1. a long raised mass, esp. of earth; ridge. 2. a slope, as of a hill. 3. the sloping side of any hollow in the ground, esp. when bordering a river. 4. the ground beside a river or canal. 5. **a.** an elevated section of the bed of a sea, lake, or river. **b.** (*in combination*): *sandbank.* **6.** the face of a body of ore in a mine. **7.** the lateral inclination of an aircraft about its longitudinal axis during a turn. **8.** a bend on a road, athletics track, etc., having the outside built higher than the inside to reduce the effects of centrifugal force on vehicles, runners, etc., rounding it at speed. ~*vb.* **9.** (when *tr.*, often foll. by *up*) to form into a bank or mound. **10.** (*tr.*) to border or enclose (a road, etc.) with a bank. **11.** (*tr.*; sometimes foll. by *up*) to cover (a fire) with ashes, fresh fuel, etc., so that it will burn slowly. **12.** to cause (an aircraft) to tip laterally about its longitudinal axis or (of an aircraft) to tip in this way, esp. while turning. [C12: of Scand. origin]

bank[3] (bæŋk) *n.* **1.** an arrangement of similar objects in a row or in tiers: *a bank of dials.* **2.** a tier of oars in a galley. ~*vb.* **3.** (*tr.*) to arrange in a bank. [C17: from OF *banc* bench, of Gmc origin]

Banka ('bæŋkə) *n.* a variant spelling of **Bangka.**

bank account *n.* **1.** an account created by the deposit of money at a bank by a customer. **2.** the amount credited to a depositor at a bank.

bank bill *n.* **1.** a bill of exchange drawn by one bank on another. **2.** *U.S.* a banknote.

bankbook ('bæŋk,bʊk) *n.* a book held by depositors at certain banks, in which the bank enters a record of deposits, withdrawals, and earned interest. Also called: **passbook.**

banker[1] ('bæŋkə) *n.* **1.** a person who owns or is an executive in a bank. **2.** an official or player in charge of the bank in various games. **3.** a result that has been forecast identically in a series of entries on a football pool coupon. **4.** a person whose performance can be relied on.

banker[2] ('bæŋkə) *n. Austral. & N.Z. inf.* a stream almost overflowing its banks (esp. in **run a banker**).

banker's order *n.* another name for **standing order** (sense 1).

bank holiday *n.* (in Britain) any of several weekdays on which banks are closed by law and which are observed as national holidays.

banking ('bæŋkɪŋ) *n.* the business engaged in by a bank.

bank manager *n.* a person who directs the business of a local branch of a bank.

banknote ('bæŋk,nəʊt) *n.* a promissory note, esp. one issued by a central bank, serving as money.

Bank of England *n.* the central bank of the United Kingdom, which acts as banker to the government and the commercial banks.

bank on *vb.* (*intr., prep.*) to expect or rely with confidence on: *you can bank on him.*

bankrupt ('bæŋkrʌpt, -rəpt) *n.* **1.** a person adjudged insolvent by a court, his property being administered for the benefit of his creditors. **2.** any person unable to discharge all his debts. **3.** a person whose resources in a certain field are exhausted: *a spiritual bankrupt.* ~*adj.* **4.** adjudged insolvent. **5.** financially ruined. **6.** depleted in resources: *spiritually bankrupt.* **7.** (foll. by *of*) *Brit.* lacking: *bankrupt of intelligence.* ~*vb.* **8.** (*tr.*) to make bankrupt. [C16: from OF *banqueroute*, from OIt. *bancarotta*, from *banca* BANK[1] + *rotta* broken, from L *rup-tus*] — **'bankruptcy** *n.*

Banks (bæŋks) *n.* Sir **Joseph.** 1743–1820, English botanist and explorer: circumnavigated the world with James Cook (1768–71).

banksia ('bæŋksɪə) *n.* any shrub or tree of the Australian genus *Banksia*, having dense cylindrical heads of flowers that are often yellowish. [C19: NL, after Sir Joseph BANKS]

Banks Island *n.* **1.** an island of N Canada, in the Northwest Territories: the westernmost island of the Arctic Archipelago. Area: about 67 340 sq. km (26 000 sq. miles). **2.** an island of W Canada, off British Columbia. Length: about 72 km (45 miles).

bank statement *n.* a statement of transactions in a bank account, esp. one of a series sent at regular intervals to the depositor.

banner ('bænə) *n.* **1.** a long strip of material displaying a slogan, advertisement, etc. **2.** a placard carried in a procession or demonstration. **3.** something that represents a belief or principle. **4.** the flag of a nation, army, etc. **5.** Also called: **banner headline.** a large headline in a newspaper, etc., extending across the page. [C13: from OF *baniere*, of Gmc origin] — **'bannered** *adj.*

Bannister ('bænɪstə) *n.* Sir **Roger (Gilbert).** born 1929, British athlete: first man to run a mile in under four minutes (1954).

bannisters ('bænɪstəz) *pl. n.* a variant spelling of **banisters.**

bannock ('bænək) *n.* a round flat cake originating in Scotland, made from oatmeal or barley and baked on a griddle. [OE *bannuc*]

Bannockburn ('bænək,bɜːn) *n.* a village in central Scotland, in Central region south of Stirling: site of a victory (1314) of the Scots, led by Robert the Bruce, over the English.

banns *or* **bans** (bænz) *pl. n.* **1.** the public declaration of an intended marriage, usually on three successive Sundays in the parish churches of the betrothed. **2. forbid the banns.** to raise an objection to a marriage announced in this way. [C14: pl. of *bann* proclamation]

banquet ('bæŋkwɪt) *n.* **1.** a sumptuous meal; feast. **2.** a ceremonial meal for many people. ~*vb.* **-queting, -queted. 3.** (*intr.*) to hold or take part in a banquet. **4.** (*tr.*) to entertain (a person) with a banquet. [C15: from OF, from It. *banchetto*, from *banco* a table, of Gmc origin] — **'banqueter** *n.*

banquette (bæŋ'kɛt) *n.* **1.** (formerly) a raised part behind a parapet. **2.** *Chiefly U.S. & Canad.* an upholstered bench. [C17: from F, from Provençal *banqueta*, lit.: a little bench]

banshee ('bænʃiː, bæn'ʃiː) *n.* (in Irish folklore) a female spirit whose wailing warns of impending death. [C18: from Irish Gaelic *bean sidhe*, lit.: woman of the fairy mound]

Banstead ('bæn,stɛd) *n.* a town in S England, in NE Surrey: a dormitory town for London. Pop.: 43 163 (1981).

bantam ('bæntəm) *n.* **1.** any of various very small breeds of domestic fowl. **2.** a small but aggressive person. **3.** *Boxing.* short for **bantamweight.** [C18: after *Bantam*, village in Java, said to be the original home of this fowl]

bantamweight ('bæntəm,weɪt) *n.* **1. a.** a professional boxer weighing 112–118 pounds (51–53.5 kg). **b.** an amateur boxer weighing 51–54 kg (112–119 pounds). **2.** an amateur wrestler weighing usually 52–57 kg (115–126 pounds).

banter ('bæntə) *vb.* **1.** to speak or tease lightly or jokingly. ~*n.* **2.** teasing or joking language or repartee. [C17: from ?] — **'banterer** *n.*

Banting ('bæntɪŋ) *n.* Sir **Frederick Grant.** 1891–1941, Canadian physiologist: discovered the insulin treatment for diabetes with Best and Macleod (1922) and shared the Nobel prize for physiology or medicine with Macleod (1923).

Bantock ('bæntɒk) *n.* Sir **Granville.** 1868–1946, British composer. His works include the *Hebridean Symphony* (1915), five ballets, and three operas.

Bantu ('bɑːntuː) *n.* **1.** a group of languages of Africa, including most of the principal languages spoken from the equator to the Cape of Good Hope. **2.** (*pl.* **-tu** *or* **-tus**) *Derog.* a Black speaker of a Bantu language. ~*adj.* **3.** of or relating to this group of peoples or their languages. [C19: from Bantu *Ba-ntu* people]

Bantu beer *n.* (in South Africa) a malted drink of partially fermented and germinated kaffir corn.

Bantustan ('bɑːntuː,stɑːn) *n. Derog.* (in South Africa) an area reserved for occupation by a Black African people, with limited self-government. Official name: **homeland.** [from BANTU + Hindi *-stan* country of]

Banville (*French* bɑvil) *n.* **Théodore de** (teɔdɔr də). 1823–91, French poet, who anticipated the Parnassian school in his perfection of form and command of rhythm.

banyan *or* **banian** ('bænjən) *n.* **1.** an Indian tree with aerial roots that grow down into the soil forming additional trunks. **2.** a member of the Hindu merchant caste of India. **3.** a loose-fitting shirt, jacket, or robe, worn originally in India. [C16: from Hindi *baniyā*, from Sansk. *vānija* merchant]

banzai ('bɑːnzai, bɑːn'zaɪ) *interj.* a patriotic cheer, battle cry, or salutation. [Japanese: lit.: (may you live for) ten thousand years]

baobab ('beɪəʊ,bæb) *n.* a tropical African tree that has a very thick trunk, angular branches, and a gourdlike fruit with an edible pulp. [C17: prob. from a native African word]

Baoding ('baʊ'dɪŋ), **Paoting,** *or* **Pao-ting** *n.* a city in NE China, in N Hebei province. Former name: **Tsingyuan.**

BAOR *abbrev. for* British Army of the Rhine.

Baotou ('bau'tu:) *or* **Paotow** *n.* an industrial city in N China, in the central Inner Mongolia AR on the Yellow River. Pop.: 1 100 000 (1986).

bap (bæp) *n. Brit.* a large soft bread roll. [from ?]

baptism ('bæp,tɪzəm) *n.* a Christian religious rite consisting of immersion in or sprinkling with water as a sign that the subject is cleansed from sin and constituted as a member of the Church. —**bap'tismal** *adj.* —**bap'tismally** *adv.*

baptism of fire *n.* **1.** a soldier's first experience of battle. **2.** any initiating ordeal.

Baptist ('bæptɪst) *n.* **1.** a member of any of various Christian sects that affirm the necessity of baptism (usually of adults and by immersion). **2. the Baptist.** John the Baptist, the cousin and forerunner of Jesus, whom he baptized. ~*adj.* **3.** denoting or characteristic of any Christian sect of Baptists.

baptistry *or* **baptistery** ('bæptɪstrɪ) *n., pl.* **-ries. 1.** a part of a Christian church in which baptisms are carried out. **2.** a tank in a Baptist church in which baptisms are carried out.

baptize *or* **-ise** (bæp'taɪz) *vb.* **1.** *Christianity.* to immerse (a person) in water or sprinkle water on (a person) as part of the rite of baptism. **2.** (*tr.*) to give a name to; christen. [C13: from LL *baptizāre*, from Gk, from *baptein* to bathe, dip]

bar[1] (bɑː) *n.* **1.** a rigid usually straight length of metal, wood, etc., used esp. as a barrier or as a structural part: *a bar of a gate.* **2.** a solid usually rectangular block of any material: *a bar of soap.* **3.** anything that obstructs or prevents. **4.** an offshore ridge of sand, mud, or shingle across the mouth of a river, bay, or harbour. **5.** a counter or room where alcoholic drinks are served. **6.** a counter, room, or establishment where a particular range of goods, food, services, etc., are sold: *a coffee bar; a heel bar.* **7.** a narrow band or stripe, as of colour or light. **8.** a heating element in an electric fire. **9.** See **Bar. 10.** the place in a court of law where the accused stands during his trial. **11.** a particular court of law. **12.** *Brit.* (in Parliament) the boundary where nonmembers wishing to address either House appear and where persons are arraigned. **13.** a plea showing that a plaintiff has no cause of action. **14.** anything referred to as an authority or tribunal: *the bar of decency.* **15.** *Music.* a group of beats that is repeated with a consistent rhythm throughout a piece of music. The number of beats in the bar is indicated by the time signature. **16. a.** *Brit.* insignia added to a decoration indicating a second award. **b.** *U.S.* a strip of metal worn with uniform, esp. to signify rank or as an award for service. **17.** *Football, etc.* See **crossbar. 18.** *Gymnastics.* See **horizontal bar. 19.** *Heraldry.* a narrow horizontal line across a shield. **20. behind bars.** in prison. **21. won't have a bar of.** *Austral. & N.Z. inf.* cannot tolerate; dislike. ~*vb.* **barring, barred.** (*tr.*) **22.** to secure with a bar: *to bar the door.* **23.** to shut in or out with or as if with barriers: *to bar the entrances.* **24.** to obstruct: *the fallen tree barred the road.* **25.** (usually foll. by *from*) to prohibit; forbid: *to bar a couple from meeting.* **26.** (usually foll. by *from*) to keep out; exclude: *to bar a person from membership.* **27.** to mark with a bar or bars. **28.** *Law.* to prevent or halt (an action) by showing that the plaintiff has no cause. ~*prep.* **29.** except for. **30. bar none.** without exception. [C12: from OF *barre*, from Vulgar L *barra* (unattested) bar, rod, from ?]

bar[2] (bɑː) *n.* a cgs unit of pressure equal to 10^6 dynes per square centimetre. [C20: from Gk *baros* weight]

Bar (bɑː) *n.* **the. 1.** (in England and elsewhere) barristers collectively. **2.** *U.S.* the legal profession collectively. **3. be called to the Bar.** *Brit.* to become a barrister. **4. be called within the Bar.** *Brit.* to be appointed as a Queen's Counsel.

bar. *abbrev. for:* **1.** barometric. **2.** barrel. **3.** barrister.

Barabbas (bə'ræbəs) *n. New Testament.* a condemned robber who was released at the Passover instead of Jesus (Matthew 27:16).

Baranof Island ('bærənɒf) *n.* an island off SE Alaska, in the western part of the Alexander Archipelago. Area: 4162 sq. km (1607 sq. miles).

barathea (,bærə'θɪə) *n.* a fabric made of silk and wool or cotton and rayon. [C19: from ?]

barb[1] (bɑːb) *n.* **1.** a point facing in the opposite direction to the main point of a fish-hook, harpoon, etc., intended to

make extraction difficult. **2.** any of various pointed parts. **3.** a cutting remark. **4.** any of the hairlike filaments that form the vane of a feather. **5.** a beardlike growth, hair, or projection. ~*vb.* **6.** (*tr.*) to provide with a barb or barbs. [C14: from OF *barbe* beard, point, from L *barba* beard] —**barbed** *adj.*

barb[2] (bɑːb) *n.* a breed of horse of North African origin, similar to the Arab but less spirited. [C17: from F *barbe*, from It. *barbero* a Barbary (horse)]

Barbados (bɑː'beɪdəus, -dəuz, -dɒs) *n.* an island in the West Indies, in the E Lesser Antilles: a British colony from 1628 to 1966, now an independent state within the Commonwealth. Language: English. Currency: Barbados dollar. Capital: Bridgetown. Pop.: 256 000 (1987 est.). Area: 430 sq. km (166 sq. miles). —**Bar'badian** *adj., n.*

barbarian (bɑː'bɛərɪən) *n.* **1.** a member of a primitive or uncivilized people. **2.** a coarse or uncultured person. **3.** a vicious person. ~*adj.* **4.** of an uncivilized culture. **5.** uncultured or brutal. [C16: see BARBAROUS]

barbaric (bɑː'bærɪk) *adj.* **1.** of or characteristic of barbarians. **2.** primitive; unrestrained. **3.** brutal. [C15: from L *barbaricus* outlandish; see BARBAROUS] —**bar'barically** *adv.*

barbarism ('bɑːbə,rɪzəm) *n.* **1.** a brutal, coarse, or ignorant act. **2.** the condition of being backward, coarse, or ignorant. **3.** a substandard word or expression; solecism. **4.** any act or object that offends against accepted taste. [C16: from L *barbarismus* error of speech, from Gk *barbarismos*, from *barbaros* BARBAROUS]

barbarity (bɑː'bærɪtɪ) *n., pl.* **-ties. 1.** the state of being barbaric or barbarous. **2.** a vicious act.

barbarize *or* **-ise** ('bɑːbə,raɪz) *vb.* **1.** to make or become barbarous. **2.** to use barbarisms in (language). — ,**barba-ri'zation** *or* **-i'sation** *n.*

Barbarossa (,bɑːbə'rɒsə) *n.* the nickname of the Holy Roman Emperor **Frederick I.** See **Frederick Barbarossa.**

barbarous ('bɑːbərəs) *adj.* **1.** uncivilized; primitive. **2.** brutal or cruel. **3.** lacking refinement. [C15: via L from Gk *barbaros* barbarian, non-Greek, imit. of incomprehensible speech] —'**barbarously** *adv.* —'**barbarousness** *n.*

Barbary ('bɑːbərɪ) *n.* a region of N Africa, extending from W Egypt to the Atlantic and including the former **Barbary States** of Tripolitania, Tunisia, Algeria, and Morocco.

Barbary ape *n.* a tailless macaque that inhabits NW Africa and Gibraltar.

Barbary Coast *n.* **the.** the Mediterranean coast of North Africa: a centre of piracy against European shipping from the 16th to the 19th centuries.

barbate ('bɑːbeɪt) *adj. Biol.* having tufts of long hairs; bearded. [C19: from L *barba* a beard]

barbecue ('bɑːbɪ,kjuː) *n.* **1.** a meal cooked out of doors over an open fire. **2.** a grill or fireplace used in barbecuing. **3.** the food so cooked. **4.** a party or picnic at which barbecued food is served. ~*vb.* **-cuing, -cued.** (*tr.*) **5.** to cook (meat, fish, etc.) on a grill, usually over charcoal and often with a highly seasoned sauce. [C17: from American Sp. *barbacoa:* frame made of sticks]

barbed wire *n.* strong wire with sharply pointed barbs at close intervals.

barbel ('bɑːbəl) *n.* **1.** any of several slender tactile spines or bristles that hang from the jaws of certain fishes, such as the carp. **2.** any of several European cyprinid fishes that resemble the carp. [C14: from OF, from LL from L *barba* beard]

barbell ('bɑː,bɛl) *n.* a metal rod to which heavy discs are attached at each end for weightlifting.

barber ('bɑːbə) *n.* **1.** a person whose business is cutting men's hair and shaving beards. ~*vb.* (*tr.*) **2.** to cut the hair of. [C13: from OF *barbeor*, from *barbe* beard, from L *barba*]

Barber ('bɑːbə) *n.* **Samuel.** 1910–81, U.S. composer: his works include an *Adagio for Strings*, adapted from the second movement of his string quartet No. 1 (1936) and the opera *Vanessa* (1958).

barberry ('bɑːbərɪ) *n., pl.* **-ries.** any spiny Asian shrub of the genus *Berberis*, having clusters of yellow flowers and orange or red berries. [C15: from OF *berberis*, from Ar. *barbāris*]

barbershop ('bɑːbə,ʃɒp) *n.* **1.** *Now chiefly U.S.* the premises of a barber. **2.** (*modifier*) denoting a type of close four-part harmony for male voices: *a barbershop quartet.*

barber's pole n. a barber's sign consisting of a pole painted with red-and-white spiral stripes.

barbican ('bɑːbɪkən) n. **1.** a walled outwork to protect a gate or drawbridge of a fortification. **2.** a watchtower projecting from a fortification. [C13: from OF *barbacane*, from Med. L, from ?]

Barbican ('bɑːbɪkən) n. **the.** a building complex in the City of London: includes residential developments and the Barbican Arts Centre (completed 1982) housing concert and exhibition halls, theatres, cinemas, etc.

barbicel ('bɑːbɪˌsɛl) n. *Ornithol.* any of the minute hooks on the barbules of feathers that interlock with those of adjacent barbules. [C19: from NL *barbicella*, lit.: a small beard]

Barbirolli (ˌbɑːbəˈrɒlɪ) n. Sir **John.** 1899–1970, English conductor of the Hallé Orchestra (1943–68).

barbitone ('bɑːbɪˌtəʊn) or *U.S.* **barbital** ('bɑːbɪˌtæl) n. a long-acting barbiturate. [C20: from BARBIT(URIC ACID) + -ONE]

barbiturate (bɑːˈbɪtjʊrɪt, -ˌreɪt) n. a derivative of barbituric acid, such as barbitone, used in medicine as a sedative or hypnotic.

barbituric acid (ˌbɑːbɪˈtjʊərɪk) n. a white crystalline solid used in the preparation of barbiturate drugs. [C19: partial translation of G *Barbitursäure*]

Barbuda (bɑːˈbuːdə) n. a coral island in the E West Indies, in the Leeward Islands: part of the independent state of Antigua and Barbuda. Area: 160 sq. km (62 sq. miles).

barbule ('bɑːbjuːl) n. *Ornithol.* any of the minute hairs that project from a barb and in some feathers interlock. [C19: from L *barbula* a little beard]

Barbusse (*French* barbys) n. **Henri** (ɑ̃ri). 1873–1935, French novelist and poet. His novels include *L'Enfer* (1908) and *Le Feu* (1916), reflecting the horror of World War I.

barcarole or **barcarolle** ('bɑːkəˌrəʊl, -ˌrɒl; ˌbɑːkəˈrəʊl) n. **1.** a Venetian boat song. **2.** an instrumental composition resembling this. [C18: from F, from It. *barcarola*, from *barcaruolo* boatman, from *barca* boat]

Barce ('bɑːtʃe) or **Barca** ('barka) n. the Italian name for **Al Marj.**

Barcelona (ˌbɑːsɪˈləʊnə) n. the chief port of Spain, on the NE Mediterranean coast: seat of the Republican government during the Civil War (1936–39); the commercial capital of Spain. Pop.: 1 752 627 (1981). Ancient name: **Barcino** (bɑːˈsiːnəʊ).

bar chart n. another term for **bar graph.**

Barclay de Tolly ('bɑːklɪ də 'tɒlɪ; *Russian* bar'klai də 'tɔlj) n. Prince **Mikhail** (mixa'il). 1761–1818, Russian field marshal: commander in chief against Napoleon in 1812.

bar code n. *Commerce.* a machine-readable arrangement of numbers and parallel lines printed on a package, which can be electronically scanned at a checkout to register the price of the goods and to activate computer stock checking and reordering.

Barcoo River (bɑːˈkuː) n. another name for **Cooper's Creek.**

bard¹ (bɑːd) n. **1. a.** (formerly) one of an ancient Celtic order of poets. **b.** a poet who wins a verse competition at a Welsh eisteddfod. **2.** *Arch.* or *literary.* any poet. [C14: from Scot. Gaelic] —'**bardic** adj.

bard² (bɑːd) n. **1.** a piece of bacon or pork fat placed on meat during roasting to prevent drying out. ~vb. (tr.) **2.** to place a bard on. [C15: from OF *barde*, from OIt. *barda*, from Ar. *barda'ah* packsaddle]

Bard (bɑːd) n. **the.** an epithet of (William) **Shakespeare.**

Bardeen (ˌbɑːˈdiːn) n. **John.** born 1908, U.S. physicist and electrical engineer, noted for his research on electrical conduction in solids; shared Nobel prize for physics 1956 for research on semiconductors leading to the invention of the transistor; shared Nobel prize for physics 1972 for contributions to the theory of superconductivity.

bardie ('bɑːdiː) n. **1.** an edible white wood-boring grub of Australia. **2. starve the bardies!** *Austral.* an exclamation of surprise or protest. [from a native Australian language]

Bardot (*French* bardo) n. **Brigitte** (briʒit). born 1934, French film actress.

bare¹ (bɛə) adj. **1.** unclothed: used esp. of a part of the body. **2.** without the natural, conventional, or usual covering. **3.** lacking appropriate furnishings, etc. **4.**
unembellished; simple: *the bare facts*. **5.** (*prenominal*) just sufficient: *the bare minimum*. **6. with one's bare hands.** without a weapon or tool. ~vb. **7.** (tr.) to make bare; uncover. [OE *bær*] —'**bareness** n.

bare² (bɛə) vb. *Arch.* a past tense of **bear**¹.

bareback ('bɛəˌbæk) or **barebacked** adj., adv. (of horse-riding) without a saddle.

barefaced ('bɛəˌfeɪst) adj. unconcealed or shameless: *a barefaced lie*. —**barefacedly** ('bɛəˌfeɪsɪdlɪ) adv. —'**bare,facedness** n.

barefoot ('bɛəˌfʊt) or **barefooted** adj., adv. **1.** with the feet uncovered. ~adj. **2.** denoting a worker with basic training sent to help people in remote rural areas, esp. of China: *barefoot doctor*.

bareheaded (ˌbɛəˈhɛdɪd) adj., adv. with the head uncovered.

Bareilly (bəˈreɪlɪ) n. a city in N India, in N central Uttar Pradesh. Pop.: 386 734 (1981).

barely ('bɛəlɪ) adv. **1.** only just: *barely enough*. **2.** *Inf.* not quite: *barely old enough*. **3.** scantily: *barely furnished*. **4.** *Arch.* openly.

Barenboim ('bærənˌbɔɪm) n. **Daniel.** born 1942, Israeli concert pianist and conductor, born in Argentina.

Barents Sea ('bærənts) n. a part of the Arctic Ocean, bounded by Norway, the Soviet Union, and the islands of Novaya Zemlya, Spitsbergen, and Franz Josef Land. [after Willem *Barents* (1550–97), Dutch navigator and explorer who discovered it in 1596]

barf (bɑːf) vb. (intr.) *Sl.* to vomit. [C20: prob. imit.]

bargain ('bɑːgɪn) n. **1.** an agreement establishing what each party will give, receive, or perform in a transaction. **2.** something acquired or received in such an agreement. **3. a.** something bought or offered at a low price. **b.** (*as modifier*): *a bargain price*. **4. into the bargain.** in excess; besides. **5. make** or **strike a bargain.** to agree on terms. ~vb. **6.** (intr.) to negotiate the terms of an agreement, transaction, etc. **7.** (tr.) to exchange, as in a bargain. **8.** to arrive at (an agreement or settlement). [C14: from OF *bargaigne*, from *bargaignier* to trade, of Gmc origin] —'**bargainer** n.

bargain away vb. (tr., adv.) to lose (rights, etc.) in return for something valueless.

bargain for vb. (intr., prep.) to expect; anticipate: *he got more than he bargained for*.

bargain on vb. (intr., prep.) to rely or depend on (something): *he bargained on her support*.

barge (bɑːdʒ) n. **1.** a vessel, usually flat-bottomed and with or without its own power, used for transporting freight, esp. on canals. **2.** a vessel, often decorated, used in pageants, etc. **3.** *Navy.* a boat allocated to a flag officer, used esp. for ceremonial occasions. ~vb. **4.** (intr.; foll. by *into*) *Inf.* to bump (into). **5.** *Inf.* to push (someone or one's way) violently. **6.** (intr.; foll. by *into* or *in*) *Inf.* to interrupt rudely or clumsily: *to barge into a conversation*. [C13: from OF, from Med. L *barga*, prob. from LL *barca* a small boat]

bargeboard ('bɑːdʒˌbɔːd) n. a board, often decorated, along the gable end of a roof.

bargee (bɑːˈdʒiː) n. a person employed on or in charge of a barge.

bargepole ('bɑːdʒˌpəʊl) n. **1.** a long pole used to propel a barge. **2. not touch with a bargepole.** *Inf.* to refuse to have anything to do with.

bar graph n. a graph consisting of vertical or horizontal bars whose lengths are proportional to amounts or quantities.

Bari ('bɑːrɪ) n. a port in SE Italy, capital of Apulia, on the Adriatic coast. Pop.: 362 524 (1986).

Baring ('bɛərɪŋ) n. **Evelyn,** 1st Earl of Cromer. 1841–1917, English administrator. As consul general in Egypt with plenipotentiary powers, he controlled the Egyptian government from 1883 to 1907.

barite ('bɛəraɪt) n. the usual U.S. and Canad. name for **barytes.** [C18: from BAR(IUM) + -ITE¹]

baritone ('bærɪˌtəʊn) n. **1.** the second lowest adult male voice. **2.** a singer with such a voice. **3.** the second lowest instrument in the families of the saxophone, horn, oboe, etc. ~adj. **4.** relating to or denoting a baritone. [C17: from It., from Gk, from *barus* heavy, low + *tonos* TONE]

barium ('bɛərɪəm) n. a soft silvery-white metallic element of the alkaline earth group. Symbol: Ba; atomic no.: 56; atomic wt.: 137.34. [C19: from BAR(YTA) + -IUM]

barium meal *n.* a preparation of barium sulphate, which is opaque to x-rays, swallowed by a patient before x-ray examination of the upper part of his alimentary canal.

bark[1] (ba:k) *n.* **1.** the loud abrupt usually harsh cry of a dog or certain other animals. **2.** a similar sound, such as one made by a person, gun, etc. **3. his bark is worse than his bite.** he is bad-tempered but harmless. ~*vb.* **4.** (*intr.*) (of a dog, etc.) to make its typical cry. **5.** (*intr.*) (of a person, gun, etc.) to make a similar loud harsh sound. **6.** to say or shout in a brusque or angry tone: *he barked an order.* **7. bark up the wrong tree.** *Inf.* to misdirect one's attention, efforts, etc.; be mistaken. [OE *beorcan*]

bark[2] (ba:k) *n.* **1.** a protective layer of dead corky cells on the outside of the stems of woody plants. **2.** any of several varieties of this, used in tanning, dyeing, or in medicine. ~*vb.* (*tr.*) **3.** to scrape or rub off skin, as in an injury. **4.** to remove the bark or a circle of bark from (a tree). **5.** to tan (leather), principally by the tannins in barks. [C13: from ON *börkr*]

bark[3] (ba:k) *n.* a variant spelling of **barque.**

barkeeper ('ba:,ki:pə) *n.* another name (esp. U.S.) for **barman** or **barmaid.**

barkentine ('ba:kən,ti:n) *n.* the usual U.S. and Canad. spelling of **barquentine.**

barker ('ba:kə) *n.* **1.** an animal or person that barks. **2.** a person at a fair booth, etc., who loudly addresses passers-by to attract customers.

Barking and Dagenham ('ba:kɪŋ) *n.* a borough of Greater London. Pop.: 148 100 (1986 est.).

Barletta (*Italian* bar'letta) *n.* a port in SE Italy, in Apulia. Pop.: 83 719 (1981).

barley ('ba:lɪ) *n.* **1.** any of various annual temperate grasses that have dense bristly flower spikes and are widely cultivated for grain and forage. **2.** the grain of any of these grasses, used in making beer and whisky and for soups, puddings, etc. [OE *bærlic* (adj.); rel. to *bere* barley]

barleycorn ('ba:lɪ,kɔ:n) *n.* **1.** a grain of barley, or barley itself. **2.** an obsolete unit of length equal to one third of an inch.

barley sugar *n.* a brittle clear amber-coloured sweet.

barley water *n.* a drink made from an infusion of barley.

barm (ba:m) *n.* **1.** the yeasty froth on fermenting malt liquors. **2.** an archaic or dialect word for **yeast.** [OE *bearm*]

barmaid ('ba:,meɪd) *n.* a woman who serves in a pub.

barman ('ba:mən) *n.*, *pl.* **-men.** a man who serves in a pub.

Barmecide ('ba:mɪ,saɪd) *adj.* lavish in imagination only; illusory; sham: *a Barmecide feast.* [C18: from a prince in the *Arabian Nights' Entertainment* who served empty plates to beggars, alleging that they held sumptuous food]

bar mitzvah (ba: 'mɪtsvə) (*sometimes caps.*) *Judaism.* ~*adj.* **1.** (of a Jewish boy) having assumed full religious obligations, being at least thirteen years old. ~*n.* **2.** the occasion or celebration of this. **3.** the boy himself. [Heb.: son of the law]

barmy ('ba:mɪ) *adj.* **-mier, -miest.** *Sl.* insane. [C16: orig., full of BARM, hence frothing, excited]

barn[1] (ba:n) *n.* **1.** a large farm outbuilding, chiefly for storing grain, etc., but also for livestock. **2.** *U.S. & Canad.* a large shed for railroad cars, trucks, etc. **3.** any large building, esp. an unattractive one. [OE *beren*, from *bere* barley + *ærn* room]

barn[2] (ba:n) *n.* a unit of nuclear cross section equal to 10⁻²⁸ square metres. Symbol: b [C20: from BARN[1]; so called because of the relatively large cross section]

Barnabas ('ba:nəbəs) *n. New Testament.* original name: *Joseph.* a Cypriot Levite who supported Saint Paul in his apostolic work (Acts 4:36,37).

barnacle ('ba:nək[ə]l) *n.* **1.** any of various marine crustaceans that, as adults, live attached to rocks, ship bottoms, etc. **2.** a person or thing that is difficult to get rid of. [C16: from earlier *bernak*, from OF *bernac*, from LL, from ?] — **'barnacled** *adj.*

barnacle goose *n.* a N European goose that has a black-and-white head and body. [C13 *bernekke:* it was formerly believed that the goose developed from a shellfish]

Barnard ('ba:na:d) *n.* **1. Christiaan (Neethling).** born 1923, South African surgeon, who performed the first human heart transplant (1967). **2. Edward Emerson.** 1857–1923, U.S. astronomer: noted for his discovery of the fifth satellite of Jupiter and his discovery of comets, nebulae, and a red dwarf (1916).

Barnardo (bə'na:dəʊ, ba:-) *n.* Dr **Thomas John.** 1845–1905, British philanthropist, who founded homes for destitute children.

Barnaul (*Russian* bərna'ul) *n.* a city in the S Soviet Union, in the RSFSR. Pop.: 596 000 (1987).

barn dance *n.* **1.** *Brit.* a progressive round country dance. **2.** *Brit.* a disco or party held in a barn. **3.** *U.S. & Canad.* a party with hoedown music and square-dancing.

Barnet ('ba:nɪt) *n.* a borough of Greater London: scene of a Yorkist victory (1471) in the Wars of the Roses. Pop.: 304 600 (1986 est.).

barney ('ba:nɪ) *Inf.* ~*n.* **1.** a noisy fight or argument. ~*vb.* (*intr.*) *Chiefly Austral. & N.Z.* **2.** to argue or quarrel. [C19: from ?]

barn owl *n.* an owl with a pale brown and white plumage and a heart-shaped face.

Barnsley ('ba:nzlɪ) *n.* an industrial town in N England, in South Yorkshire. Pop.: 73 646 (1981).

barnstorm ('ba:n,stɔ:m) *vb.* (*intr.*) **1.** to tour rural districts putting on shows. **2.** *Chiefly U.S. & Canad.* to tour rural districts making speeches in a political campaign. — **'barn,storming** *n.*, *adj.*

Barnum ('ba:nəm) *n.* **P(hineas) T(aylor).** 1810–91, U.S. showman, who created The Greatest Show on Earth (1871) and, with J. A. Bailey, founded the Barnum and Bailey Circus (1881).

barnyard ('ba:n,ja:d) *n.* **1.** a yard adjoining a barn. **2.** (*modifier*) characteristic of a barnyard. **3.** (*modifier*) crude or earthy.

baro- *combining form.* indicating weight or pressure: *barometer.* [from Gk *baros* weight]

Barocchio (*Italian* ba'rɔkkjo) *n.* **Giacomo** ('dʒakomo). See (Giacomo Barozzi da) **Vignola.**

Baroda (bə'rəʊdə) *n.* **1.** a former state of W India, part of Gujarat since 1960. **2.** the former name (until 1976) of **Vadodara.**

barogram ('bærə,græm) *n. Meteorol.* the record of atmospheric pressure traced by a barograph or similar instrument.

barograph ('bærə,gra:f) *n. Meteorol.* a self-recording aneroid barometer. — **barographic** (,bærə'græfɪk) *adj.*

Baroja (*Spanish* ba'roxa) *n.* **Pio** ('pio). 1872–1956, Spanish Basque novelist, who wrote nearly 100 novels, including a series of twenty-two under the general title *Memorias de un Hombre de Acción* (1944–49).

barometer (bə'rɒmɪtə) *n.* **1.** an instrument for measuring atmospheric pressure, usually to determine altitude or weather changes. **2.** anything that shows change. — **barometric** (,bærə'mɛtrɪk) *or* ,baro'metrical *adj.* — **ba'rometry** *n.*

baron ('bærən) *n.* **1.** a member of a specific rank of nobility, esp. the lowest rank in the British Isles. **2.** (in Europe from the Middle Ages) originally a tenant-in-chief of a king or other overlord. **3.** a powerful businessman or financier: *a press baron.* [C12: from OF, of Gmc origin]

baronage ('bærənɪdʒ) *n.* **1.** barons collectively. **2.** the rank or dignity of a baron.

baroness ('bærənɪs) *n.* **1.** the wife or widow of a baron. **2.** a woman holding the rank of baron.

baronet ('bærənɪt, -,nɛt) *n.* (in Britain) a commoner who holds the lowest hereditary title of honour, ranking below a baron. Abbrev.: **Bart, Bt.** — **'baronetage** *n.* — **'baronetcy** *n.*

baronial (bə'rəʊnɪəl) *adj.* of, relating to, or befitting a baron or barons.

baron of beef *n.* a cut of beef consisting of a double sirloin joined at the backbone.

barony ('bærənɪ) *n.*, *pl.* **-nies. 1. a.** the domain of a baron. **b.** (in Ireland) a division of a county. **c.** (in Scotland) a large estate or manor. **2.** the rank or dignity of a baron.

baroque (bə'rɒk, bə'rəʊk) *n.* (*often cap.*) **1.** a style of architecture and decorative art in Europe from the late 16th to the early 18th century, characterized by extensive ornamentation. **2.** a 17th-century style of music characterized by extensive use of ornamentation. **3.** any ornate or heavily ornamented style. ~*adj.* **4.** denoting, in, or relating to the baroque. **5.** (of pearls) irregularly shaped. [C18: from F, from It. *barroco*]

baroreceptor ('bærəʊrɪ,sɛptə) *n.* a collection of sensory nerve endings, principally in the carotid sinuses and the aortic arch, that monitor blood pressure changes in the body.

baroscope ('bærə,skəʊp) *n.* any instrument for measuring atmospheric pressure. —**baroscopic** (,bærə'skɒpɪk) *adj.*

barouche (bə'ru:ʃ) *n.* a four-wheeled horse-drawn carriage, popular in the 19th century, having a retractable hood over the rear half. [C19: from G (dialect) *Barutsche*, from It. *baroccio*, from LL *birotus*, from BI- + *rota* wheel]

Barozzi (*Italian* ba'rottsi) *n.* See (Giacomo Barozzi da) **Vignola**.

barperson ('bɑː,pɜːsən) *n., pl.* -persons. a person who serves in a pub: used esp. in advertisements.

barque (bɑːk) *n.* **1.** a sailing ship of three or more masts having the foremasts rigged square and the aftermast rigged fore-and-aft. **2.** *Poetic.* any boat. [C15: from OF, from OProvençal *barca*]

barquentine *or* **barquantine** ('bɑːkən,ti:n) *n.* a sailing ship of three or more masts rigged square on the foremast and fore-and-aft on the others. [C17: from BARQUE + (BRIG)ANTINE]

Barquisimeto (*Spanish* barkisi'meto) *n.* a city in NW Venezuela. Pop.: 459 000 (1984 est.).

barrack[1] ('bærək) *vb.* to house (soldiers, etc.) in barracks.

barrack[2] ('bærək) *vb. Brit., Austral.,* & *N.Z. inf.* **1.** to criticize loudly or shout against (a team, speaker, etc.); jeer. **2.** (*intr.;* foll. by *for*) to shout support (for). [C19: from Irish: to boast]

barrack-room lawyer *n.* a person who freely offers opinions, esp. in legal matters, that he is unqualified to give.

barracks ('bærəks) *pl. n.* (*sometimes sing.; when pl., sometimes functions as sing.*) **1.** a building or group of buildings used to accommodate military personnel. **2.** any large building used for housing people, esp. temporarily. **3.** a large and bleak building. [C17: from F *baraque*, from OCatalan *barraca* hut, from ?]

barracouta (,bærə'ku:tə) *n.* a large predatory Pacific fish. [C17: var. of BARRACUDA]

barracuda (,bærə'kju:də) *n., pl.* -da *or* -das. a predatory marine mostly tropical fish, which attacks man. [C17: from American Sp., from ?]

barrage ('bærɑːʒ) *n.* **1.** *Mil.* the firing of artillery to saturate an area, either to protect against an attack or to support an advance. **2.** an overwhelming and continuous delivery of something, as questions. **3.** a construction across a watercourse, esp. one to increase the depth. [C19: from F, from *barrer* to obstruct; see BAR[1]]

barrage balloon *n.* one of a number of tethered balloons with cables or net suspended from them, used to deter low-flying air attack.

barramundi (,bærə'mʌndɪ) *n., pl.* -dis, -dies, -di. an Australian estuary fish of the perch family. [from Abor.]

Barranquilla (*Spanish* barran'kiʎa) *n.* a port in N Colombia, on the Magdalena River. Pop.: 920 695 (1985).

barrator ('bærətə) *n.* a person guilty of barratry. [C14: from OF *barateor*]

barratry *or* **barretry** ('bærətrɪ) *n.* **1.** *Criminal law.* (formerly) the vexatious stirring up of quarrels or bringing of lawsuits. **2.** *Maritime law.* a fraudulent practice committed by the master or crew of a ship to the prejudice of the owner. **3.** the purchase or sale of public or Church offices. [C15: from OF *baraterie* deception, from *barater* to BARTER] —**barratrous** *or* **barretrous** *adj.*

Barrault (*French* baro) *n.* **Jean-Louis** (ʒɑ̃lwi). born 1910, French actor and director, noted particularly as a mime.

barre *French.* (bar) *n.* a rail at hip height used for ballet practice. [lit.: bar]

barrel ('bærəl) *n.* **1.** a cylindrical container usually bulging outwards in the middle and held together by metal hoops. **2.** Also called: **barrelful.** the amount that a barrel can hold. **3.** a unit of capacity of varying amount in different industries. **4.** a thing shaped like a barrel, esp. a tubular part of a machine. **5.** the tube through which the projectile of a firearm is discharged. **6.** the trunk of a four-legged animal: *the barrel of a horse*. **7. over a barrel.** *Inf.* powerless. **8. scrape the barrel.** *Inf.* to be forced to use one's last and weakest resource. ~*vb.* -rel-ling, -relled *or U.S.* -reling, -reled. **9.** (*tr.*) to put into a barrel or barrels. [C14: from OF *baril*, ?from *barre* BAR[1]]

barrel-chested *adj.* having a large rounded chest.

barrel organ *n.* an instrument consisting of a cylinder turned by a handle and having pins on it that interrupt the

air flow to certain pipes or pluck strings, thereby playing tunes.

barrel roll *n.* a flight manoeuvre in which an aircraft rolls about its longitudinal axis while following a spiral course in line with the direction of flight.

barrel vault *n. Archit.* a vault in the form of a half cylinder.

barren ('bærən) *adj.* **1.** incapable of producing offspring, seed, or fruit; sterile. **2.** unable to support the growth of crops, etc.: *barren land*. **3.** lacking in stimulation; dull. **4.** not producing worthwhile results; unprofitable: *a barren period*. **5.** (foll. by *of*) devoid (of): *barren of wit*. [C13: from OF *brahain*, from ?] —'**barrenness** *n.*

Barren Grounds *pl. n.* **the.** a sparsely inhabited region of tundras in N Canada, extending westwards from Hudson Bay. Also called: **Barren Lands.**

Barrès (*French* barɛs) *n.* **Maurice** (mɔris). 1862–1923, French novelist, essayist, and politician: a fervent nationalist and individualist.

barricade (,bærɪ'keɪd, 'bærɪ,keɪd) *n.* **1.** a barrier for defence, esp. one erected hastily, as during street fighting. ~*vb.* (*tr.*) **2.** to erect a barricade across (an entrance, etc.) or at points of access to (a room, district, etc.). [C17: from OF, from *barriquer* to barricade, from *barrique* a barrel, from Sp. *barrica*, from *barril* BARREL]

Barrie ('bærɪ) *n.* **Sir James Matthew.** 1860–1937, Scottish dramatist and novelist, noted particularly for his popular children's play *Peter Pan* (1904).

barrier ('bærɪə) *n.* **1.** anything serving to obstruct passage or to maintain separation, such as a fence or gate. **2.** anything that prevents progress. **3.** anything that separates or hinders union: *a language barrier*. [C14: from OF *barriere*, from *barre* BAR[1]]

barrier cream *n.* a cream used to protect the skin, esp. the hands.

barrier reef *n.* a long narrow coral reef near the shore, separated from it by deep water.

barring ('bɑːrɪŋ) *prep.* unless (something) occurs; except for.

barrister ('bærɪstə) *n.* **1.** Also called: **barrister-at-law.** (in England) a lawyer who has been called to the bar and is qualified to plead in the higher courts. Cf. **solicitor. 2.** (in Canada) a lawyer who pleads in court **3.** *U.S.* a less common word for **lawyer.** [C16: from BAR[1]]

Barros (*Portuguese* 'bɑːrruʃ) *n.* **João de** (ʒuɐu' də:). 1496–1570, Portuguese historian: noted for his history of the Portuguese in the East Indies, *Décadas da Ásia* (1552–1615).

barrow[1] ('bærəʊ) *n.* **1.** See **wheelbarrow, handbarrow. 2.** Also called: **barrowful.** the amount contained in or on a barrow. **3.** *Chiefly Brit.* a handcart with a canvas roof, used esp. by street vendors. [OE *bearwe*]

barrow[2] ('bærəʊ) *n.* a heap of earth placed over one or more prehistoric tombs, often surrounded by ditches. [OE *beorg*]

Barrow ('bærəʊ) *n.* **1.** a river in SE Ireland, rising in the Slieve Bloom Mountains and flowing south to Waterford Harbour. Length: about 193 km (120 miles). **2.** See **Barrow-in-Furness** and **Barrow Point.**

barrow boy *n. Brit.* a man who sells his wares from a barrow; street vendor.

Barrow-in-Furness *n.* an industrial town in NW England, in S Cumbria. Pop.: 72 560 (1985 est.).

Barrow Point *n.* the northernmost tip of Alaska, on the Arctic Ocean.

Barry[1] ('bærɪ) *n.* a port in SE Wales, in South Glamorgan on the Bristol Channel. Pop.: 43 828 (1981).

Barry[2] *n.* **1.** ('bærɪ). Sir **Charles.** 1795–1860, English architect: designer of the Houses of Parliament in London. **2.** (*French* bari). **Comtesse du.** See **du Barry.**

Barrymore ('bærɪ,mɔː) *n.* a U.S. family of actors, esp. **Ethel** (1879–1959), **John** (1882–1942), and **Lionel** (1878–1954).

Barry Mountains *pl. n.* a mountain range in SE Australia, in E Victoria: part of the Australian Alps.

bar sinister *n.* **1.** (not in heraldic usage) another name for **bend sinister. 2.** the condition or stigma of being of illegitimate birth.

Bart (bɑːt) *n.* **Lionel.** born 1930, British composer and playwright. His musicals include *Oliver* (1960).

Bart. *abbrev. for* Baronet.

bartender ('bɑː,tɛndə) *n.* another name (esp. U.S. and Canad.) for **barman** or **barmaid.**

barter ('bɑːtə) vb. **1.** to trade (goods, services, etc.) in exchange for other goods, services, etc., rather than for money. **2.** (intr.) to haggle over such an exchange; bargain. ~n. **3.** trade by the exchange of goods. [C15: from OF barater to cheat]

Barth (German bart) n. **Karl** (karl). 1886–1968, Swiss Protestant theologian, who stressed man's dependence on divine grace and was a champion of tolerance and ecumenicalism. —**Barthian** ('bɑːtɪən, -θɪən) adj., n.

Bartholomew (bɑːˈθɒləˌmjuː) n. New Testament. one of the twelve apostles (Matthew 10:3). Feast day: Aug. 24.

bartizan ('bɑːtɪzən, ˌbɑːtɪˈzæn) n. a small turret projecting from a wall, parapet, or tower. [C19: var. of bertisene, erroneously for bretising, from bretasce parapet; see BRATTICE] —**bartizaned** ('bɑːtɪzənd, ˌbɑːtɪˈzænd) adj.

Bartók ('bɑːtɒk; Hungarian 'bortoːk) n. **Béla** ('beːlɒ). 1881–1945, Hungarian composer, pianist, and collector of folk songs, by which his music was deeply influenced. His works include six string quartets, several piano pieces including Mikrokosmos (1926–37), ballets (including The Miraculous Mandarin, 1919), and the opera Bluebeard's Castle (produced 1918).

Bartolommeo (Italian bartolom'meo) n. **Fra.** original name Baccio della Porta. 1472–1517, Italian painter of the Florentine school, noted for his austere religious works.

Barton ('bɑːtᵊn) n. Sir **Edmund.** 1849–1920, Australian statesman; first prime minister of Australia (1901–03).

Baruch n. **1.** (bəˈruːk). **Bernard Mannes** ('mænəs). 1870–1965, U.S. financier and statesman; economic adviser to Presidents Wilson and Roosevelt. **2.** ('bɛəruk, 'bɑː-). Bible. **a.** a disciple of Jeremiah (Jeremiah 32–36). **b.** the book of the Apocrypha said to have been written by him.

baryon ('bærɪ,ɒn) n. any of a class of elementary particles that have a mass greater than or equal to that of the proton. Baryons are either nucleons or hyperons. The **baryon number** is the number of baryons in a system minus the number of antibaryons. [C20: from Gk barus heavy + -ON] —ˌbary'onic adj.

Baryshnikov (bəˈrɪʃnɪkɒf) n. **Mikhail.** born 1948, Soviet-born ballet dancer, who defected (1974) to the West while on tour with the Kirov Ballet and is director (1980–) of the American Ballet Theatre.

baryta (bəˈraɪtə) n. another name for barium oxide or barium hydroxide. [C19: NL, from Gk barutēs weight, from barus heavy]

barytes (bəˈraɪtiːz) n. a colourless or white mineral occurring in sedimentary rocks and with sulphide ores: a source of barium. [C18: from Gk barus heavy + -itēs -ITE[1]]

basal ('beɪsᵊl) adj. **1.** at, of, or constituting a base. **2.** of or constituting a basis; fundamental.

basal metabolism n. the amount of energy required by an individual in the resting state, for such functions as breathing and blood circulation.

basalt ('bæsɔːlt) n. **1.** a dark basic igneous rock: the most common volcanic rock. **2.** a form of black unglazed pottery resembling basalt. [C18: from LL basaltēs, var. of basanitēs, from Gk basanitēs touchstone] —ba'saltic adj.

bascule ('bæskjuːl) n. **1.** a bridge with a movable section hinged about a horizontal axis and counterbalanced by a weight. **2.** a movable roadway forming part of such a bridge. [C17: from F: seesaw, from bas low + cul rump]

base[1] (beɪs) n. **1.** the bottom or supporting part of anything. **2.** the fundamental principle or part. **3. a.** a centre of operations, organization, or supply. **b.** (as modifier): base camp. **4.** starting point: the new discovery became the base for further research. **5.** the main ingredient of a mixture: to use rice as a base in cookery. **6.** a chemical compound that combines with an acid to form a salt and water. A solution of a base in water turns litmus paper blue and produces hydroxyl ions. **7.** a medium such as oil or water in which the pigment is dispersed in paints, inks, etc. **8.** Biol. the point of attachment of an organ or part. **9.** the bottommost layer or part of anything. **10.** Archit. the part of a column between the pedestal and the shaft. **11.** the lower side or face of a geometric construction. **12.** Maths. the number of units in a counting system that is equivalent to one in the next higher counting place: 10 is the base of the decimal system. **13.** Maths. the number that when raised to a certain power has a logarithm

(based on that number) equal to that power: the logarithm to the base 10 of 1000 is 3. **14.** Linguistics. a root or stem. **15.** Electronics. the region in a transistor between the emitter and collector. **16.** a starting or finishing point in any of various games. ~vb. **17.** (tr.; foll. by on or upon) to use as a basis (for); found (on). **18.** (often foll. by at or in) to station, post, or place (a person or oneself). [C14: from OF, from L basis pedestal; see BASIS]

base[2] (beɪs) adj. **1.** devoid of honour or morality; contemptible. **2.** of inferior quality or value. **3.** debased; alloyed; counterfeit: base currency. **4.** English history. (of land tenure) held by villein or other ignoble service. **5.** Arch. born of humble parents. **6.** Arch. illegitimate. [C14: from OF bas, from LL bassus of low height] —'baseness n.

baseball ('beɪs,bɔːl) n. **1.** a team game with nine players on each side, played on a field with four bases connected to form a diamond. The object is to score runs by batting the ball and running round the bases. **2.** the hard rawhide-covered ball used in this game.

baseborn ('beɪs,bɔːn) adj. Arch. **1.** born of humble parents. **2.** illegitimate.

base hospital n. Austral. a hospital serving a large rural area.

Basel ('bɑːzᵊl) or **Basle** (bɑːl) n. **1.** a canton of NW Switzerland, divided into the demicantons of **Basel-Land** and **Basel-Stadt.** Pops.: 225 800 and 194 300 (1986 est.). Areas: 427 sq. km (165 sq. miles) and 36 sq. km (14 sq. miles) respectively. **2.** a city in NW Switzerland, capital of Basel canton, on the Rhine: oldest university in Switzerland. Pop.: 174 600 (1985). French name: **Bâle.**

baseless ('beɪslɪs) adj. not based on fact; unfounded. —'baselessness n.

baseline ('beɪs,laɪn) n. **1.** Surveying. a measured line through a survey area from which triangulations are made. **2.** a line at each end of a tennis court that marks the limit of play.

basement ('beɪsmənt) n. **1. a.** a partly or wholly underground storey of a building, esp. one used for habitation rather than storage. **b.** (as modifier): a basement flat. **2.** the foundation of a wall or building.

base metal n. any of certain common metals, such as copper and lead, as distinct from precious metals.

basenji (bəˈsɛndʒɪ) n. a small African breed of dog having an inability to bark. [C20: from Bantu]

base rate n. Brit. the rate of interest used by individual commercial banks as a basis for their lending rates.

bases[1] ('beɪsiːz) n. the plural of **basis.**

bases[2] ('beɪsɪz) n. the plural of **base.**

bash (bæʃ) vb. **1.** (tr.) to strike violently or crushingly. **2.** (tr.; often foll. by in, down, etc.) to smash, break, etc., with a crashing blow. **3.** (intr.; foll. by into) to crash (into); collide (with). **4.** to dent or be dented. ~n. **5.** a heavy blow. **6.** a party. **7. have a bash.** Inf. to make an attempt. [C17: from ?]

Bashan ('beɪʃæn) n. Old Testament. a region to the east of the Jordan, renowned for its rich pasture (Deuteronomy 32:14).

bashful ('bæʃful) adj. **1.** shy or modest; diffident. **2.** indicating or characterized by shyness or modesty. [C16: from bash, short for ABASH + -FUL] —'bashfully adv. —'bashfulness n.

-bashing n. and adj. combining form. Inf. or sl. **a.** indicating a malicious attack on members of a group: union-bashing. **b.** indicating various other activities: Bible-bashing. —-**basher** n. combining form.

Bashkir Autonomous Soviet Socialist Republic n. an administrative division of the E central Soviet Union, in the S Urals: established as the first Soviet autonomous republic in 1919; rich mineral resources. Capital: Ufa. Pop.: 3 870 000 (1986). Area: 143 600 sq. km (55 430 sq. miles). Also called: **Bashkiria** (bæʃˈkɪərɪə).

Bashkirtseff or **Bashkirtsev** (bəʃˈkjɪrtsəf) n. **Marie,** original name Marya Konstantinovna Bashkirtseva. 1858–84, Russian painter and diarist who wrote in French, noted esp. for her Journal (1887).

basic ('beɪsɪk; Austral. also 'bæsɪk) adj. **1.** of, relating to, or forming a base or basis; fundamental. **2.** elementary or simple: a few basic facts. **3.** excluding additions or extras: basic pay. **4.** Chem. of, denoting, or containing a base; alkaline. **5.** Metallurgy. of or made by a process in which the furnace or converter is made of a basic material, such as magnesium oxide. **6.** (of such igneous rocks as basalt) containing between 52 and 45 per cent silica. ~*n.* **7.** (*usually pl.*) a fundamental principle, fact, etc. —'**basically** *adv.*

BASIC ('beɪsɪk) *n.* a computer programming language that uses common English terms. [C20: *b*(*eginner's*) *a*(*ll-purpose*) *s*(*ymbolic*) *i*(*nstruction*) *c*(*ode*)]

basic English *n.* a simplified form of English with a vocabulary of approximately 850 common words, intended as an international language.

basic industry *n.* an industry which is highly important in a nation's economy.

basicity (beɪ'sɪsɪtɪ) *n. Chem.* **a.** the state of being a base. **b.** the extent to which a substance is basic.

basic slag *n.* a slag produced in steel-making, containing calcium phosphate.

basic wage *n.* **1.** a person's wage excluding overtime, bonuses, etc. **2.** *Austral.* the statutory minimum wage for any worker.

basidiomycete (bæ,sɪdɪəʊmaɪ'siːt) *n.* any of a class of fungi, including puffballs and rusts, which produce spores at the tips of slender projecting stalks. [C19: see BASIS, -MYCETE] —**ba,sidiomy'cetous** *adj.*

Basie ('beɪsɪ) *n.* **William,** known as *Count Basie.* 1904–84, U.S. jazz pianist, bandleader, and composer: associated particularly with the polished phrasing and style of big-band jazz.

basil ('bæzᵊl) *n.* a Eurasian plant having spikes of small white flowers and aromatic leaves used as herbs for seasoning. Also called: **sweet basil.** [C15: from OF *basile,* from LL, from Gk *basilikos* royal]

Basil ('bæzᵊl) *n.* **Saint,** called *the Great.* ?329–379 A.D., Greek patriarch: an opponent of Arianism and one of the founders of monasticism. Feast Day: June 14.

Basilan (bə'siːlɑːn, bæ'siːlæn) *n.* **1.** a group of islands in the Philippines, SW of Mindanao. **2.** the main island of this group, separated from Mindanao by the **Basilan Strait.** Area: 1282 sq. km (495 sq. miles). **3.** a city on Basilan Island. Pop.: 125 304 (1975 est.).

basilar ('bæsɪlə) *adj. Chiefly anat.* of or at a base. Also: **basilary** ('bæsɪlərɪ, -sɪlrɪ). [C16: from NL *basilaris*]

Basildon ('bæzɪldən) *n.* a town in SE England, in S Essex: designated a new town in 1955. Pop.: 152 301 (1981).

basilica (bə'zɪlɪkə) *n.* **1.** a Roman building, used for public administration, having a large rectangular central nave with an aisle on each side and an apse at the end. **2.** a Christian church of similar design. **3.** a Roman Catholic church having special ceremonial rights. [C16: from L, from Gk, from *basilikē oikia* the king's house] —**ba'silican** *or* **ba'silic** *adj.*

Basilicata (*Italian* bazili'kata) *n.* a region of S Italy, between the Tyrrhenian Sea and the Gulf of Taranto. Capital: Potenza. Pop.: 620 260 (1985 est.). Area: 9985 sq. km (3855 sq. miles).

basilisk ('bæzɪ,lɪsk) *n.* **1.** (in classical legend) a serpent that could kill by its breath or glance. **2.** a small semi-aquatic lizard of tropical America. The males have an inflatable head crest, used in display. [C14: from L *basiliscus,* from Gk *basiliskos* royal child]

basin ('beɪsᵊn) *n.* **1.** a round container open and wide at the top with sides sloping inwards towards the bottom. **2.** Also called: **basinful.** the amount a basin will hold. **3.** a washbasin or sink. **4.** any partially enclosed or sheltered area where vessels may be moored. **5.** the catchment area of a particular river and its tributaries. **6.** a depression in the earth's surface. **7.** *Geol.* a part of the earth's surface consisting of rock strata that slope down to a common centre. [C13: from OF *bacin,* from LL *bacchinon*]

Basingstoke ('beɪzɪŋ,stəʊk) *n.* a town in S England, in N Hampshire. Pop.: 80 000 (1984 est.).

basis ('beɪsɪs) *n., pl.* **-ses** (-siːz). **1.** something that underlies, supports, or is essential to something else, esp. an idea. **2.** a principle on which something depends or from which something has issued. [C14: via L from Gk: step]

▷ **Usage.** The phrase *on the basis of* is inappropriate in contexts where *because* can be used: *he agreed to come because of your promise to protect him,* not *he agreed to come on the basis of your promise to protect him. On the basis of* is correctly used of a criterion of choice: *the players were chosen on the basis of their weight.*

bask (bɑːsk) *vb.* (*intr.*; usually foll. by *in*) **1.** to lie in or be exposed to pleasant warmth, esp. that of the sun. **2.** to

flourish or feel secure under some benevolent influence or favourable condition. [C14: from ON *bathask* to BATHE]

basket ('bɑːskɪt) *n.* **1.** a container made of interwoven strips of pliable materials, such as cane, and often carried by a handle. **2.** Also called: **basketful.** the amount a basket will hold. **3.** something resembling such a container, such as the structure suspended from a balloon. **4.** *Basketball.* **a.** the hoop fixed to the backboard, through which a player must throw the ball to score points. **b.** a point or points scored in this way. **5.** a group of similar or related things: *a basket of currencies.* **6.** *Inf.* a euphemism for **bastard** (senses 2, 3). [C13: prob. from OF *baskot* (unattested), from L *bascauda* wickerwork holder] —'**basketry** *n.*

basketball ('bɑːskɪt,bɔːl) *n.* **1.** a game played by two teams of five men (or six women), usually on an indoor court. Points are scored by throwing the ball through an elevated horizontal hoop. **2.** the ball used in this game.

basket chair *n.* a chair made of wickerwork.

basketry ('bɑːskɪtrɪ) *n.* **1.** the art or practice of making baskets. **2.** baskets collectively.

basket weave *n.* a weave of yarns, resembling that of a basket.

basketwork ('bɑːskɪt,wɜːk) *n.* another word for **wickerwork.**

basking shark *n.* a very large plankton-eating shark, often floating at the sea surface.

Basle (bɑːl) *n.* a variant spelling of **Basel.**

basophil ('beɪsəfɪl) *or* **basophile** *adj. also* **basophilic** (,beɪsə'fɪlɪk). **1.** (of cells or cell contents) easily stained by basic dyes. ~*n.* **2.** a basophil cell, esp. a leucocyte. [C19: from Gk; see BASIS, -PHILE]

Basotho-Qwaqwa (bə'suːtuː'kwɑːkwə, -'səʊtəʊ-) *n.* a Bantustan in South Africa, in the Orange Free State; the only Bantustan without exclaves. Also called: **Qwaqwa.** Former name (until 1972): **Basotho-Ba-Borwa.**

basque (bæsk) *n.* a type of tight-fitting bodice for women. [from F, from BASQUE]

Basque (bæsk, bɑːsk) *n.* **1.** a member of a people living around the W Pyrenees in France and Spain. **2.** the language of this people, of no known relationship with any other language. ~*adj.* **3.** of or relating to this people or their language. [C19: from F, from L *Vascō* a Basque]

Basque Provinces *n.* an autonomous region of N Spain, comprising the provinces of Álava, Guipúzcoa, and Viscaya: inhabited mainly by Basques, who retained virtual autonomy from the 9th to the 19th century. Pop.: 2 141 809 (1981). Area: about 7250 sq. km (2800 sq. miles).

Basra, Basrah ('bæzrə), **Busra,** *or* **Busrah** ('bʌsrə) *n.* a port in SE Iraq, on the Shatt-al-Arab. Pop.: 333 684 (1970 est.).

bas-relief (,bɑːrɪ'liːf, 'bæsrɪ,liːf) *n.* sculpture in low relief, in which the forms project slightly from the background. [C17: from F, from It. *basso rilievo* low relief]

Bas-Rhin (*French* barɛ̃) *n.* a department of NE France in Alsace region. Capital: Strasbourg. Pop.: 915 676 (1982). Area: 4793 sq. km (1869 sq. miles).

bass[1] (beɪs) *n.* **1.** the lowest adult male voice. **2.** a singer with such a voice. **3. the bass.** the lowest part in a piece of harmony. **4.** *Inf.* short for **bass guitar, double bass. 5. a.** the low-frequency component of an electrical audio signal, esp. in a record player or tape recorder. **b.** the knob controlling this. ~*adj.* **6.** relating to or denoting the bass. [C15 *bas* BASE[1]; modern spelling infl. by BASSO]

bass[2] (bæs) *n.* **1.** any of various sea perches. **2.** a European spiny-finned freshwater fish. **3.** any of various predatory North American freshwater fishes. [C15: from BASE[2], infl. by It. *basso* low]

bass clef (beɪs) *n.* the clef that establishes F a fifth below middle C on the fourth line of the staff.

bass drum (beɪs) *n.* a large drum of low pitch.

Bassein (bɑː'seɪn) *n.* a city in Burma, on the Irrawaddy delta: a port on the **Bassein River** (the westernmost distributary of the Irrawaddy). Pop.: 144 092 (1983).

Basse-Normandie (*French* basnɔrmɑ̃di) *n.* a region of NW France, on the English Channel: consists of the Cherbourg peninsula in the west rising to the Normandy hills in the east; mainly agricultural.

Bassenthwaite ('bæsᵊn,θweɪt) *n.* a lake in NW England, in Cumbria near Keswick. Length: 6 km (4 miles).

Basses-Alpes (*French* basalp) *n.* the former name for **Alpes-de-Haute-Provence.**

Basses-Pyrénées (*French* baspirene) *pl. n.* the former name for **Pyrénées-Atlantiques.**

basset ('bæsɪt) *n.* a smooth-haired breed of hound with short legs and long ears. Also: **basset hound.** [C17: from F, from *basset* short, from *bas* low]

Basseterre (bæs'tɛə; *French* bastɛr) *n.* a port in the West Indies, on St Kitts in the Leeward Islands: the capital of St Kitts-Nevis. Pop.: 14 725 (1980).

Basse-Terre ('bæs'tɛə; *French* bastɛr) *n.* **1.** a mountainous island in the West Indies, in the Leeward Islands, comprising part of Guadeloupe. Area: 848 sq. km (327 sq. miles). **2.** a port in W Guadeloupe, on Basse-Terre Island: the capital of the French Overseas Department of Guadeloupe. Pop.: 16 000 (1980 est.).

basset horn *n.* an obsolete woodwind instrument. [C19: prob. from G *Bassetthorn,* from It. *bassetto,* dim. of BASSO + HORN]

bass guitar (beɪs) *n.* an electrically amplified guitar that has the same pitch and tuning as a double bass.

bassinet (,bæsɪ'nɛt) *n.* a wickerwork or wooden cradle or pram, usually hooded. [C19: from F: little basin; associated in folk etymology with F *barcelonnette* a little cradle]

bassist ('beɪsɪst) *n.* a player of a double bass or bass guitar.

basso ('bæsəʊ) *n., pl.* **-sos** *or* **-si** (-sɪ). (esp. in operatic or solo singing) a singer with a bass voice. [C19: from It., from It. *bassus* low; see BASE²]

bassoon (bə'suːn) *n.* **1.** a woodwind instrument, the tenor of the oboe family. **2.** an orchestral musician who plays a bassoon. [C18: from F *basson,* from It., from *basso* deep] —**bas'soonist** *n.*

basso rilievo (*Italian* 'basso ri'ljɛːvo) *n., pl.* **-vos.** Italian name for **bas-relief.**

Bass Strait (bæs) *n.* a channel between mainland Australia and Tasmania, linking the Indian Ocean and the Tasman Sea.

bass viol (beɪs) *n.* **1.** another name for **viola da gamba. 2.** *U.S.* a less common name for **double bass** (sense 1).

bast (bæst) *n.* **1.** *Bot.* another name for **phloem. 2.** fibrous material obtained from the phloem of jute, flax, etc., used for making rope, matting, etc. [OE *bæst*]

bastard ('bɑːstəd, 'bæs-) *n.* **1.** a person born of parents not married to each other. **2.** *Inf., offens.* an obnoxious or despicable person. **3.** *Inf.* a person, esp. a man: *lucky bastard.* **4.** *Inf.* something extremely difficult or unpleasant. **5.** something irregular, abnormal, or inferior. **6.** a hybrid, esp. an accidental or inferior one. ~*adj. (prenominal)* **7.** illegitimate by birth. **8.** irregular, abnormal, or inferior. **9.** resembling a specified thing, but not actually being such: *a bastard cedar.* **10.** counterfeit; spurious. **11.** hybrid. [C13: from OF *bastart,* ?from *fils de bast* son of the packsaddle] —**'bastardy** *n.*

bastardize *or* **-ise** (bɑːstə,daɪz, 'bæs-) *vb. (tr.)* **1.** to debase. **2.** to declare illegitimate.

baste¹ (beɪst) *vb. (tr.)* to sew with loose temporary stitches. [C14: from OF *bastir* to build, of Gmc origin] —**'basting** *n.*

baste² (beɪst) *vb.* to moisten (meat) during cooking with hot fat and the juices produced. [C15: from ?]

baste³ (beɪst) *vb. (tr.)* to beat thoroughly; thrash. [C16: prob. from ON *beysta*]

Bastia ('bɑːstjə) *n.* a port in NE Corsica: the main commercial and industrial town of the island: capital of Haute-Corse department. Pop.: 50 500 (1983).

Bastille (bæ'stiːl) *n.* a fortress in Paris: a prison until its destruction in 1789, at the beginning of the French Revolution. [C14: from OF *bastile* fortress, from OProvençal *bastida,* from *bastir* to build]

bastinado (,bæstɪ'neɪdəʊ) *n., pl.* **-does. 1.** punishment or torture in which the soles of the feet are beaten with a stick. ~*vb.* **-doing, -doed. 2.** *(tr.)* to beat (a person) thus. [C16: from Sp. *bastonada,* from *baston* stick]

bastion ('bæstɪən) *n.* **1.** a projecting part of a fortification, designed to permit fire to the flanks along the face of the wall. **2.** any fortified place. **3.** a thing or person regarded as defending a principle, etc. [C16: from F, from earlier *bastillon* bastion, from *bastille* BASTILLE]

Bastogne (bæ'stəʊn; *French* bastɔɲ) *n.* a town in SE Belgium: of strategic importance to Allied defences during the Battle of the Bulge; besieged by the Germans during the winter of 1944–45. Pop.: 6816 (1970).

Basutoland (bə'suːtəʊ,lænd) *n.* the former name (until 1966) of **Lesotho.**

bat¹ (bæt) *n.* **1.** any of various types of club with a handle, used to hit the ball in certain sports, such as cricket. **2.** a flat round club with a short handle used by a man on the ground to guide the pilot of an aircraft when taxiing. **3.** *Cricket.* short for **batsman. 4.** *Inf.* a blow from a stick. **5.** *Sl.* speed; pace: *they went at a fair bat.* **6. carry one's bat.** *Cricket.* (of a batsman) to reach the end of an innings without being dismissed. **7. off one's own bat. a.** of one's own accord. **b.** by one's own unaided efforts. ~*vb.* **batting, batted. 8.** *(tr.)* to strike with or as if with a bat. **9.** *(intr.) Cricket, etc.* (of a player or a team) to take a turn at batting. [OE *batt* club, prob. of Celtic origin]

bat² (bæt) *n.* **1.** a nocturnal mouselike animal flying with a pair of membranous wings. **2. blind as a bat.** having extremely poor eyesight. **3. have bats in the** (*or* **one's) belfry.** *Inf.* to be mad or eccentric. [C14 *bakke,* prob. of Scand. origin]

bat³ (bæt) *vb.* **batting, batted.** *(tr.)* **1.** to wink or flutter (one's eyelids). **2. not bat an eye** (*or* **eyelid**). *Inf.* to show no surprise or concern. [C17: prob. var. of BATE²]

Bataan (bə'tæn, -'tɑːn) *n.* a peninsula in the Philippines, in W Luzon: scene of the surrender of U.S. and Philippine forces to the Japanese during World War II, later retaken by American forces.

Batangas (bə'tæŋgæs) *n.* a port in the Philippines, in SW Luzon. Pop.: 143 570 (1980).

Batan Islands (bə'tɑːn) *pl. n.* a group of islands in the Philippines, north of Luzon. Capital: Basco. Pop.: 11 398 (1970). Area: 197 sq. km (76 sq. miles).

Batavia (bə'teɪvɪə) *n.* **1.** an ancient district of the Netherlands, on an island at the mouth of the Rhine. **2.** an archaic or literary name for **Holland. 3.** a former name for **Jakarta.** —**Ba'tavian** *adj., n.*

batch¹ (bætʃ) *n.* **1.** a group or set of usually similar objects or people, esp. if sent off, handled, or arriving at the same time. **2.** the bread, cakes, etc., produced at one baking. **3.** the amount of a material needed for an operation. ~*vb.* **4.** to group (items) for efficient processing. **5.** to handle by batch processing. [C15 *bache;* rel. to OE *bacan* to BAKE]

batch² (bætʃ) *vb. (intr.) Austral. & N.Z.* to live as a bachelor. Also (N.Z.): **bach.**

batch processing *n.* a system by which the computer programs of a number of individual users are submitted as a single batch.

bate¹ (beɪt) *vb.* **1.** another word for **abate. 2. with bated breath.** in suspense or fear.

bate² (beɪt) *vb. (intr.)* (of a hawk) to jump violently from a perch or the falconer's fist, often hanging from the leash while struggling to escape. [C13: from OF *batre* to beat]

bate³ (beɪt) *n. Brit. Sl.* a bad temper or rage. [C19: from BAIT¹, alluding to the mood of a person who is being baited]

bateau (bæ'təʊ) *n., pl.* **-teaux** (-'təʊz). a light flat-bottomed boat used on rivers in Canada and the northern U.S. [C18: from F: boat]

bateleur eagle ('bætələ:) *n.* an African short-tailed bird of prey. [C19: from F *bateleur* juggler].

Bates (beɪts) *n.* **H(erbert) E(rnest).** 1905–74, English writer of short stories and novels, which include *The Darling Buds of May* (1958), *A Moment in Time* (1964), and *The Triple Echo* (1970).

bath (bɑːθ) *n., pl.* **baths** (bɑːðz). **1.** a large container used for washing the body. **2.** the act or an instance of washing in a bath. **3.** the amount of liquid contained in a bath. **4.** (*usually pl.*) a place having baths or a swimming pool for public use. **5. a.** a vessel in which something is immersed to maintain it at a constant temperature, to process it photographically, etc., or to lubricate it. **b.** the liquid used in such a vessel. ~*vb.* **6.** *Brit.* to wash in a bath. [OE *bæth*]

Bath (bɑːθ) *n.* a city in SW England, in Avon county on the River Avon: famous for its hot springs; a fashionable spa in the 18th century; Roman remains, notably the baths. Pop.: 79 965 (1981). Latin name: **Aquae Sulis** ('ækwiː-'suːlɪs).

Bath bun (bɑːθ) *n. Brit.* a sweet bun containing spices and dried fruit.

Bath chair *n.* a wheelchair for invalids.

bath cube *n.* a cube of soluble scented material for use in a bath.

bathe (beɪð) *vb.* **1.** *(intr.)* to swim in a body of open water, esp. for pleasure. **2.** *(tr.)* to apply liquid to (skin, a wound, etc.) in order to cleanse or soothe. **3.** to immerse or be immersed in a liquid. **4.** *Chiefly U.S. & Canad.* to wash in a bath. **5.** (*tr.; often passive*) to suffuse. ~*n.* **6.** *Brit.* a swim in a body of open water. [OE *bathian*] — '**bather** *n.*

bathers ('beiðəz) *pl. n. Austral.* a swimming costume.

bathhouse ('ba:θ,haus) *n.* a building containing baths, esp. for public use.

bathing cap ('beiðiŋ) *n.* a tight rubber cap worn by a swimmer to keep the hair dry.

bathing costume ('beiðiŋ) *n.* another name for **swimming costume**.

bathing machine ('beiðiŋ) *n.* a small hut, on wheels so that it could be pulled to the sea, used in the 18th and 19th centuries for bathers to change their clothes.

bathing suit ('beiðiŋ) *n.* a garment worn for bathing, esp. an old-fashioned one that covers much of the body.

batho- *combining form.* a variant of **bathy-**.

batholith (,bæθəlɪθ) *or* **batholite** ('bæθə,lait) *n.* a very large irregular-shaped mass of igneous rock, esp. granite, formed from an intrusion of magma at great depth, esp. one exposed after erosion of less resistant overlying rocks. — ,**batho'lithic** *or* **batholitic** (,bæθə'lɪtɪk) *adj.*

Bath Oliver ('ɒlivə) *n. Brit.* a kind of unsweetened biscuit [C19: after William *Oliver* (1695–1764), a physician at Bath]

bathometer (bə'θɒmitə) *n.* an instrument for measuring the depth of water. —**bathometric** (,bæθə'mɛtrɪk) *adj.* — ba'thometry *n.*

bathos ('beiθɒs) *n.* **1.** a sudden ludicrous descent from exalted to ordinary matters or style in speech or writing. **2.** insincere or excessive pathos. [C18: from Gk: depth] — ba'thetic *adj.*

bathrobe ('ba:θ,rəub) *n.* **1.** a loose-fitting garment of towelling, for wear before or after a bath or swimming. **2.** *U.S. & Canad.* a dressing gown.

bathroom ('ba:θ,ru:m, -,rum) *n.* **1.** a room containing a bath or shower and usually a washbasin and lavatory. **2.** *U.S. & Canad.* another name for **lavatory**.

bath salts *pl. n.* soluble scented salts for use in a bath.

Bathsheba (bæθ'ʃi:bə, 'bæθʃibə) *n. Old Testament.* the wife of Uriah, who committed adultery with David and later married him and became the mother of his son Solomon (II Samuel 11–12).

bathtub ('ba:θ,tʌb) *n.* a bath, esp. one not permanently fixed.

Bathurst ('bæθəst) *n.* **1.** a city in SE Australia, in E New South Wales: scene of a gold rush in 1851. Pop.: 25 700 (1984). **2.** a port in E Canada, in NE New Brunswick: rich mineral resources discovered in 1953. Pop.: 14 683 (1986). **3.** the former name (until 1973) of **Banjul**.

bathy- *or* **batho-** *combining form.* indicating depth: *bathysphere*. [from Gk *bathus* deep]

bathyscaph ('bæθɪ,skæf), **bathyscaphe** ('bæθɪ,skeif, -,skæf), *or* **bathyscape** *n.* a submersible vessel with an observation capsule underneath, capable of reaching ocean depths of over 10 000 metres. [C20: from BATHY- + Gk *skaphē* light boat]

bathysphere ('bæθɪ,sfɪə) *n.* a strong steel deep-sea diving sphere, lowered by cable.

batik ('bætɪk) *n.* **a.** a process of printing fabric in which parts not to be dyed are covered by wax. **b.** fabric printed in this way. [C19: via Malay from Javanese: painted]

Batista (*Spanish* ba'tista) *n.* **Fulgencio** (ful'xenθjo), full name *Batista y Zaldívar.* 1901–73, Cuban military leader and dictator: president of Cuba (1940–44, 1952–59); overthrown by Fidel Castro.

batiste (bæ'ti:st) *n.* a fine plain-weave cotton. [C17: from F, prob. after *Baptiste* of Cambrai, 13th-cent. F weaver, its reputed inventor]

Batley ('bætlɪ) *n.* a town in N England, in West Yorkshire. Pop.: 42 572 (1981).

batman ('bætmən) *n., pl.* **-men.** an officer's servant in the armed forces. [C18: from OF *bat, bast,* from Med. L *bastum* packsaddle]

Batman ('bætmən) *n.* **John.** 1801–39, a pioneer who selected the site of the city of Melbourne.

baton ('bætən) *n.* **1.** a thin stick used by the conductor of an orchestra, choir, etc. **2.** *Athletics.* a short bar carried by a competitor in a relay race and transferred to the next runner at the end of each stage. **3.** a long stick with a knob on one end, carried, twirled, and thrown up and down by a drum major or majorette, esp. at the head of a parade. **4.** a police truncheon (esp. in **baton charge**). **5.** a staff or club carried as a symbol of authority. [C16: from F *bâton,* from LL *bastum* rod]

Baton Rouge ('bæt²n ru:ʒ) *n.* the capital of Louisiana, in the SE part on the Mississippi River. Pop.: 241 130 (1986).

baton round *n.* the official name for **plastic bullet**.

batrachian (bə'treikiən) *n.* **1.** any amphibian, esp. a frog or toad. ~*adj.* **2.** of or relating to the frogs and toads. [C19: from NL *Batrachia,* from Gk *batrakhos* frog]

bats (bæts) *adj. Inf.* mad or eccentric.

batsman ('bætsmən) *n., pl.* **-men.** **1.** *Cricket, etc.* **a.** a person who bats or whose turn it is to bat. **b.** a player who specializes in batting. **2.** a person on the ground who uses bats to guide the pilot of an aircraft when taxiing. —'**batsman,ship** *n.*

battalion (bə'tæljən) *n.* **1.** a military unit comprised of three or more companies or formations of similar size. **2.** (*usually pl.*) any large array. [C16: from F *bataillon,* from OIt., from *battaglia* company of soldiers, BATTLE]

batten[1] ('bæt²n) *n.* **1.** a sawn strip of wood used in building to cover joints, support lathing, etc. **2.** a long narrow board used for flooring. **3.** a lath used for holding a tarpaulin along the side of a hatch on a ship. **4.** *Theatre.* **a.** a row of lights. **b.** the bar supporting them. ~*vb.* **5.** (*tr.*) to furnish or strengthen with battens. **6. batten down the hatches. a.** to use battens in securing a tarpaulin over a hatch on a ship. **b.** to prepare for action, a crisis, etc. [C15: from F *bâton* stick; see BATON]

batten[2] ('bæt²n) *vb.* (*intr.*) (usually foll. by *on*) to thrive, esp. at the expense of someone else. [C16: prob. from ON *batna* to improve]

batter[1] ('bætə) *vb.* **1.** to hit (someone or something) repeatedly using heavy blows, as with a club. **2.** (*tr.; often passive*) to damage or injure, as by blows, heavy wear, etc. **3.** (*tr.*) to subject (a person, esp. a close relative) to repeated physical violence. [C14 *bateren,* prob. from *batten* to BAT[1]] —'**batterer** *n.* —'**battering** *n.*

batter[2] ('bætə) *n.* a mixture of flour, eggs, and milk, used to make cakes, pancakes, etc., and to coat certain foods before frying. [C15 *bater,* prob. from *bateren* to BATTER[1]]

batter[3] ('bætə) *n. Baseball, etc.* a player who bats.

batter[4] ('bætə) *n.* **1.** the slope of the face of a wall that recedes gradually backwards and upwards. ~*vb.* **2.** (*intr.*) to have such a slope. [C16 (vb.: to incline): from ?]

battering ram *n.* (esp. formerly) a large beam used to break down fortifications.

Battersea ('bætəsɪ) *n.* a district in London, in Wandsworth: noted for its dogs' home, power station (being developed into a leisure centre), and park.

battery ('bætərɪ) *n., pl.* **-teries.** **1.** two or more primary cells connected, usually in series, to provide a source of electric current. **2.** another name for **accumulator** (sense 1). **3.** a number of similar things occurring together: *a battery of questions.* **4.** *Criminal law.* unlawful beating or wounding of a person or mere touching in a hostile or offensive manner. **5.** a fortified structure on which artillery is mounted. **6.** a group of guns, missile launchers, etc, operated as a single entity. **7.** a small unit of artillery. **8.** *Chiefly Brit.* **a.** a large group of cages for intensive rearing of poultry and other farm animals. **b.** (*as modifier*): *battery hens.* **9.** *Baseball.* the pitcher and the catcher considered together. [C16: from OF *batterie* beating, from *battre* to beat, from L *battuere*]

batting ('bætɪŋ) *n.* **1.** cotton or woollen wadding used in quilts, etc. **2.** the action of a person or team that hits with a bat.

battle ('bæt²l) *n.* **1.** a fight between large armed forces; military or naval engagement. **2.** conflict; struggle. **3. do, give,** *or* **join battle.** to engage in conflict or competition. ~*vb.* **4.** (*intr.;* often foll. by *against, for,* or *with*) to fight in or as if in military combat. **5.** to struggle: *he battled through the crowd.* **6.** (*intr.*) *Austral.* to scrape a living. [C13: from OF *bataile,* from LL *battālia* exercises performed by soldiers, from *battuere* to beat] —'**battler** *n.*

battle-axe *n.* **1.** (formerly) a large broad-headed axe. **2.** *Inf.* an argumentative domineering woman.

battle cruiser *n.* a high-speed warship of battleship size but with lighter armour.

battle cry *n.* **1.** a shout uttered by soldiers going into battle. **2.** a slogan used to rally the supporters of a campaign, movement, etc.

battledore ('bæt³l,dɔː) *n.* **1.** Also called: **battledore and shuttlecock.** an ancient racket game. **2.** a light racket used in this game. **3.** (formerly) a wooden utensil used for beating clothes, in baking, etc. [C15 *batyldoure*, ?from OProvençal *batedor* beater, from OF *battre* to beat]

battledress ('bæt³l,drɛs) *n.* the ordinary uniform of a soldier.

battle fatigue *n. Psychol.* mental disorder, characterized by anxiety and depression, caused by the stress of warfare. Also: **combat fatigue.**

battlefield ('bæt³l,fiːld) *or* **battleground** *n.* the place where a battle is fought.

battlement ('bæt³lmənt) *n.* a parapet or wall with indentations or embrasures, originally for shooting through. [C14: from OF *batailles*, pl. of *bataille* BATTLE] —'**battlemented** *adj.*

battle royal *n.* **1.** a fight, esp. with fists or cudgels, involving more than two combatants; melee. **2.** a long violent argument.

battleship ('bæt³l,ʃɪp) *n.* a heavily armoured warship of the largest type.

batty ('bætɪ) *adj.* **-tier, -tiest.** *Sl.* **1.** insane; crazy. **2.** odd; eccentric. [C20: from BAT²]

Batum (baː'tuːm) *or* **Batumi** (baː'tuːmɪ) *n.* a city in the S Soviet Union, in the Georgian SSR: capital of the Adzhar ASSR; a major Black Sea port. Pop.: 111 000 (1984 est.).

batwoman ('bætwʊmən) *n., pl.* **-women.** a female servant in any of the armed forces.

bauble ('bɔːb³l) *n.* **1.** a trinket of little value. **2.** (formerly) a mock staff of office carried by a jester. [C14: from OF *baubel* plaything, from ?]

Bauchi ('bautʃɪ) *n.* **1.** a state of N Nigeria: formed in 1976 from part of North-Eastern State; tin mining. Capital: Bauchi. Pop.: 4 075 800 (1984). Area: 67 647 sq. km (26 113 sq. miles). **2.** a town in N central Nigeria, capital of Bauchi state. Pop.: 47 200 (1973 est.).

Baucis ('bɔːsɪs) *n. Greek myth.* a poor peasant woman who, with her husband Philemon, was rewarded for hospitality to the disguised gods Zeus and Hermes.

baud (bɔːd) *n.* a unit used to measure the speed of electronic code transmissions. [after J. M. E. *Baudot* (1845–1903), F inventor]

Baudelaire (*French* bodlɛr) *n.* **Charles Pierre** (ʃarl pjɛr). 1821–67, French poet, noted for his macabre imagery; author of *Les fleurs du mal* (1857).

Baudouin I (*French* bodwɛ̃) *n.* born 1930, king of Belgium from 1951.

bauera ('bauərə) *n.* a small evergreen Australian shrub with pink or purple flowers. [C19: after Franz & Ferdinand *Bauer*, 19th-cent. Austrian botanical artists]

Bauhaus ('bau,haus) *n.* a German school of architecture and applied arts founded in 1919 on experimental principles of functionalism and truth to materials. [G, lit.: building house]

bauhinia (bɔː'hɪnɪə, bəʊ-) *n.* a climbing leguminous plant of tropical and warm regions, cultivated for ornament. [C18: NL, after Jean & Gaspard *Bauhin*, 16th-cent. F herbalists]

baulk (bɔːk; *usually for sense 1* bɔːlk) *n.* **1.** Also: **balk.** *Billiards.* the space between the baulk line and the bottom cushion. **2.** *Archaeol.* a strip of earth left between excavation trenches for the study of the complete stratigraphy of a site. ~*vb.*, *n.* **3.** a variant spelling of **balk.**

baulk line *or* **balk line** *n. Billiards.* a straight line across a billiard table behind which the cue balls are placed at the start of a game. Also: **string line.**

baulky ('bɔːkɪ, 'bɔːlkɪ) *adj.* a variant of **balky.**

Bautzen ('bautsən) *n.* a city in SE East Germany: site of an indecisive battle in 1813 between Napoleon's army and an allied army of Russians and Prussians. Pop.: 49 767 (1983).

bauxite ('bɔːksaɪt) *n.* an amorphous claylike substance consisting of hydrated alumina with iron and other impurities: the chief source of alumina and aluminium and also used as an abrasive and catalyst. [C19: from F, from (*Les*) *Baux* in southern France, where orig. found]

Bavaria (bə'vɛərɪə) *n.* a state of S West Germany: a former duchy and kingdom; mainly wooded highland, with the Alps in the south. Capital: Munich. Pop.: 10 993 400 (1986) Area: 70 531 sq. km (27 232 sq. miles). German name: **Bayern.** —**Ba'varian** *adj.*, *n.*

bawd (bɔːd) *n. Arch.* **1.** a person who runs a brothel, esp. a woman. **2.** a prostitute. [C14: from OF *baude*, fem. of *baud* merry]

bawdy ('bɔːdɪ) *adj.* **bawdier, bawdiest. 1.** (of language, plays, etc.) containing references to sex, esp. to be humorous. ~*n.* **2.** obscenity or eroticism, esp. in writing or drama. —'**bawdily** *adv.* —'**bawdiness** *n.* —**bawdry** ('bɔːdrɪ) *n.*

bawdyhouse ('bɔːdɪ,haus) *n.* an archaic word for **brothel.**

bawl (bɔːl) *vb.* **1.** (*intr.*) to utter long loud cries, as from pain or frustration; wail. **2.** to shout loudly, as in anger. ~*n.* **3.** a loud shout or cry. [C15: imit.] —'**bawler** *n.* —'**bawling** *n.*

bawl out *vb.* (*tr., adv.*) *Inf.* to scold loudly.

Bax (bæks) *n.* **Sir Arnold (Edward Trevor).** 1883–1953, English composer of romantic works, often based on Celtic legends, including the tone poem *Tintagel* (1917).

Baxter ('bækstə) *n.* **James.** 1926–72, New Zealand lyric poet. His works include *The Fallen House* (1953) and *In Fires of No Return* (1958).

bay¹ (beɪ) *n.* **1.** a wide semicircular indentation of a shoreline, esp. between two headlands. **2.** an extension of lowland into hills that partly surround it. [C14: from OF *baie*, ?from OF *baer* to gape, from Med. L *batāre* to yawn]

bay² (beɪ) *n.* **1.** an alcove or recess in a wall. **2.** any partly enclosed compartment. **3.** See **bay window. 4.** an area off a road in which vehicles may park or unload. **5.** a compartment in an aircraft: *the bomb bay.* **6.** *Naut.* a compartment in the forward part of a ship between decks, often used as the ship's hospital. **7.** *Brit.* a tracked recess in the platform of a railway station, esp. one forming the terminus of a branch line. [C14: from OF *baee* gap, from *baer* to gape; see BAY¹]

bay³ (beɪ) *n.* **1.** a deep howl, esp. of a hound on the scent. **2. at bay. a.** forced to turn and face attackers: *the dogs held the deer at bay.* **b.** at a distance. **3. bring to bay.** to force into a position from which retreat is impossible. ~*vb.* **4.** (*intr.*) to howl (at) in deep prolonged tones. **5.** (*tr.*) to utter in a loud prolonged tone. **6.** (*tr.*) to hold at bay. [C13: from OF, imit.]

bay⁴ (beɪ) *n.* **1.** a Mediterranean laurel. See **laurel** (sense 1). **2.** any of certain other trees or shrubs, esp. bayberry. **3.** (*pl.*) a wreath of bay leaves. [C14: from OF *baie* laurel berry, from L *bāca* berry]

bay⁵ (beɪ) *n., adj.* **1.** (of) a reddish-brown colour. ~*n.* **2.** an animal of this colour. [C14: from OF *bai*, from L *badius*]

Bayamón (*Spanish* baja'mon) *n.* a city in NE central Puerto Rico, south of San Juan. Pop.: 195 965 (1980).

Bayard ('beɪəd; *French* bajar) *n.* **Chevalier de** (ʃəvalje də), original name *Pierre de Terrail.* ?1473–1524, French soldier, known as *le chevalier sans peur et sans reproche* (the fearless and irreproachable knight).

bayberry ('beɪbərɪ) *or* **bay** *n., pl.* **-ries. 1.** any of several North American aromatic shrubs or small trees that bear grey waxy berries. **2.** a tropical American tree that yields an oil used in making bay rum. **3.** the fruit of any of these plants.

Bayern ('baɪərn) *n.* the German name for **Bavaria.**

Bayle (*French* bɛl) *n.* **Pierre** (pjɛr). 1647–1706, French philosopher and critic, noted for his *Dictionnaire historique et critique* (1697), which profoundly influenced Voltaire and the French Encyclopedists.

bay leaf *n.* a leaf, usually dried, of the Mediterranean laurel, used in cooking to flavour soups and stews.

Bay of Pigs *n.* a bay on the SW coast of Cuba: scene of an unsuccessful invasion of Cuba by U.S.-backed troops (April 17, 1961). Spanish name: **Bahía de los Cochinos.**

bayonet ('beɪənɪt) *n.* **1.** a blade for stabbing that can be attached to the muzzle of a firearm. **2.** a type of fastening in which a cylindrical member is inserted into a socket against spring pressure and turned so that pins on its side engage in slots in the socket. ~*vb.* **-neting, -neted** *or* **-netting, -netted. 3.** (*tr.*) to stab or kill with a bayonet. [C17: from F *baïonnette*, from BAYONNE]

Bayonne (*French* bajɔn) *n.* a port in SW France: a commercial centre for the Basque region. Pop.: 42 587 (1983 est.).

bayou ('baɪjuː) *n.* (in the southern U.S.) a sluggish marshy tributary of a lake or river. [C18: from Louisiana F, from Amerind *bayuk*]

Bayreuth (*German* bai'rɔyt) *n.* a city in SE West Germany, in NE Bavaria: home and burial place of Richard Wagner; annual festivals of his music. Pop.: 71 800 (1984 est.).

bay rum *n.* an aromatic liquid, used in medicines and cosmetics, originally obtained by distilling the leaves of the bayberry tree with rum: now also synthesized.

bay window *n.* a window projecting from a wall and forming an alcove of a room.

bazaar *or* **bazar** (bə'zɑː) *n.* **1.** (esp. in the Orient) a market area, esp. a street of small stalls. **2.** a sale in aid of charity, esp. of second-hand or handmade articles. **3.** a shop where a variety of goods is sold. [C16: from Persian *bāzār*]

bazooka (bə'zuːkə) *n.* a portable tubular rocket-launcher, used by infantrymen as a short-range antitank weapon. [C20: after a comic pipe instrument]

BB *abbrev. for:* **1.** Boys' Brigade. **2.** (on British pencils, signifying degrees of softness of lead) double black.

BBC *abbrev. for* British Broadcasting Corporation.

bbl. *abbrev. for* barrel (container or measure).

BC *abbrev. for* British Columbia.

B.C. *or* **BC** *abbrev. for* (indicating years numbered back from the supposed year of the birth of Christ) before Christ.

▷ **Usage.** See at **A.D.**

BCE *abbrev. for:* **1.** Before Common Era (used, esp. by non-Christians, in numbering years B.C.). **2.** *Brit.* Board of Customs and Excise.

BCG *abbrev. for* Bacillus Calmette-Guérin (anti-tuberculosis vaccine).

BCNZ *abbrev. for* Broadcasting Corporation of New Zealand.

BD *abbrev. for* Bachelor of Divinity.

bdellium ('dɛlɪəm) *n.* **1.** any of several African or W Asian trees that yield a gum resin. **2.** the aromatic gum resin produced by any of these trees. [C16: from L, from Gk *bdellion*, ?from Heb. *bĕdhōlah*]

BDS *abbrev. for* Bachelor of Dental Surgery.

be (biː; *unstressed* bɪ) *vb. present sing. 1st person* **am;** *2nd person* **are;** *3rd person* **is.** *present pl.* **are.** *past sing. 1st person* **was;** *2nd person* **were;** *3rd person* **was.** *past pl.* **were.** *past participle* **being.** *past participle* **been.** (*intr.*) **1.** to have presence in perceived reality; exist; live: *I think, therefore I am.* **2.** (*used in the perfect tenses only*) to pay a visit; go: *have you been to Spain?* **3.** to take place: *my birthday was last Thursday.* **4.** (*copula*) used as a linking verb between the subject of a sentence and its noun or adjective complement. *Be* has no intrinsic meaning of its own but rather expresses relationship of equivalence or identity (*John is a man; John is a musician*) or specifies an attribute (*honey is sweet; Susan is angry*). It is also used with an adverbial complement to indicate a relationship in space or time (*Bill is at the office; the dance is on Saturday*). **5.** (*takes a present participle*) forms the progressive present tense: *the man is running.* **6.** (*takes a past participle*) forms the passive voice of all transitive verbs: *a good film is being shown on television tonight.* **7.** (*takes an infinitive*) expresses intention, expectation, or obligation: *the president is to arrive at 9.30.* [OE *bēon*]

Be *the chemical symbol for* beryllium.

BE *abbrev. for:* **1.** bill of exchange. **2.** Bachelor of Education. **3.** Bachelor of Engineering.

be- *prefix forming transitive verbs.* **1.** (*from nouns*) to surround or cover: *befog.* **2.** (*from nouns*) to affect completely: *bedazzle.* **3.** (*from nouns*) to consider as or cause to be: *befriend.* **4.** (*from nouns*) to provide or cover with: *bejewel.* **5.** (*from nouns*) at, for, against, on, or over: *bewail; berate.* [OE *be-, bi-,* unstressed var. of *bī* BY]

beach (biːtʃ) *n.* **1.** an area of sand or shingle sloping down to a sea or lake, esp. the area between the high- and low-water marks on a seacoast. ~*vb.* **2.** to run or haul (a boat) onto a beach. [C16: perhaps rel. to OE *bæce* river]

beachcomber ('biːtʃˌkəʊmə) *n.* **1.** a person who searches shore debris for anything of worth. **2.** a long, high wave rolling onto a beach.

beachhead ('biːtʃˌhɛd) *n. Mil.* an area on a beach that has been captured from the enemy and on which troops and equipment are landed.

Beachy Head ('biːtʃɪ) *n.* a headland in East Sussex, on the English Channel, consisting of chalk cliffs 171 m (570 ft.) high.

beacon ('biːkən) *n.* **1.** a signal fire or light on a hill, tower, etc., esp. formerly as a warning of invasion. **2.** a hill on which such fires were lit. **3.** a lighthouse, signalling buoy, etc. **4.** short for **radio beacon. 5.** a radio or other signal marking a flight course in air navigation. **6.** short for **Belisha beacon. 7.** a person or thing that serves as a guide, inspiration, or warning. [OE *beacen* sign]

Beaconsfield ('biːkənz,fiːld, 'bɛk-) *n.* **1st Earl of.** title of (Benjamin) **Disraeli.**

bead (biːd) *n.* **1.** a small pierced usually spherical piece of glass, wood, plastic, etc., which may be strung with others to form a necklace, etc. **2. tell one's beads.** to pray with a rosary. **3.** a small drop of moisture. **4.** a small bubble in or on a liquid. **5.** a small metallic knob acting as the sight of a firearm. **6. to draw** *or* **hold a bead on.** to aim a rifle or pistol at. **7.** *Archit., furniture.* a small convex moulding having a semicircular cross section. ~*vb.* **8.** (*tr.*) to decorate with beads. **9.** to form into beads or drops. [OE *bed* prayer] —'**beaded** *adj.*

beading ('biːdɪŋ) *n.* **1.** another name for **bead** (sense 7). **2.** Also called: **beadwork** ('biːd,wɜːk). a narrow strip of some material used for edging or ornamentation.

beadle ('biːdᵊl) *n.* **1.** *Brit.* (formerly) a minor parish official who acted as an usher and kept order. **2.** *Judaism.* a synagogue attendant. **3.** *Scot.* a church official who attends the minister. **4.** an official in certain British institutions. [OE *bydel*] —'**beadleship** *n.*

Beadle ('biːdᵊl) *n.* **George Wells.** born 1903, U.S. biologist, who shared the Nobel prize for physiology or medicine in 1958 for his work in genetics.

beadsman *or* **bedesman** ('biːdzmən) *n., pl.* **-men.** *Arch.* **1.** a person who prays for another's soul, esp. one paid or fed for doing so. **2.** a person kept in an almshouse.

beady ('biːdɪ) *adj.* **beadier, beadiest. 1.** small, round, and glittering (esp. in **beady eyes**). **2.** resembling or covered with beads. —'**beadiness** *n.*

beagle ('biːgᵊl) *n.* **1.** a small sturdy breed of hound. **2.** *Arch.* a spy. ~*vb.* **3.** (*intr.*) to hunt with beagles. [C15: from ?]

Beaglehole ('biːgᵊl,həʊl) *n.* **John.** 1901–71, New Zealand historian and author. His works include *Exploration of the Pacific* (1934) and *The Journals of James Cook* (1955).

beak[1] (biːk) *n.* **1.** the projecting jaws of a bird, covered with a horny sheath. **2.** any beaklike mouthpart in other animals. **3.** *Sl.* a person's nose. **4.** any projecting part, such as the pouring lip of a bucket. **5.** *Naut.* another word for **ram** (sense 5). [C13: from OF *bec,* from L *beccus,* of Gaulish origin] —**beaked** *adj.* —'**beaky** *adj.*

beak[2] (biːk) *n.* a Brit. slang word for **judge, magistrate, headmaster,** or **schoolmaster.** [C19: orig. thieves' jargon]

beaker ('biːkə) *n.* **1.** a cup usually having a wide mouth. **2.** a cylindrical flat-bottomed container used in laboratories, usually made of glass and having a pouring lip. [C14: from ON *bikarr*]

Beaker folk ('biːkə) *n.* a prehistoric people inhabiting Europe and Britain during the second millennium B.C. [after beakers found among their remains]

be-all and end-all *n. Inf.* the ultimate aim or justification.

beam (biːm) *n.* **1.** a long thick piece of wood, metal, etc., esp. one used as a horizontal structural member. **2.** the breadth of a ship or boat taken at its widest part. **3.** a ray or column of light, as from a beacon. **4.** a broad smile. **5.** one of two cylindrical rollers on a loom, which hold the warp threads and the finished work. **6.** the main stem of a deer's antler. **7.** the central shaft of a plough to which all the main parts are attached. **8.** a narrow unidirectional flow of electromagnetic radiation or particles: *an electron beam.* **9.** the horizontal centrally pivoted bar in a balance. **10. beam in one's eye.** a fault or grave error greater in oneself than in another person. **11. broad in the beam.** *Inf.* having wide hips. **12. off (the) beam. a.** not following a radio beam to maintain a course. **b.** *Inf.* mistaken or irrelevant. **13. on the beam. a.** following a radio beam to maintain a course. **b.** *Inf.* correct, relevant, or appropriate. ~*vb.* **14.** to send out or radiate. **15.** (*tr.*) to divert or aim (a radio signal, light, etc.) in a certain direction: *to beam a programme to Tokyo.* **16.** (*intr.*) to smile broadly. [OE] —'**beaming** *adj.*

beam-ends *pl. n.* **1. on her beam-ends.** (of a vessel) heeled over through an angle of 90°. **2. on one's beam-ends.** out of resources; destitute.

bean (bi:n) *n.* **1.** any of various leguminous plants producing edible seeds in pods. **2.** any of various other plants whose seeds are produced in pods or podlike fruits. **3.** the seed or pod of any of these plants. **4.** any of various beanlike seeds, as coffee. **5.** *U.S. & Canad. sl.* another word for **head. 6. full of beans.** *Inf.* full of energy and vitality. **7. not have a bean.** *Sl.* to be without money. [OE *bēan*]

beanbag ('bi:n,bæg) *n.* **1.** a small cloth bag filled with dried beans and thrown in games. **2.** a very large cushion filled with foam rubber or polystyrene granules and used as a seat.

beanfeast ('bi:n,fi:st) *n. Brit. inf.* **1.** an annual dinner given by employers to employees. **2.** any festive or merry occasion.

beano ('bi:nəʊ) *n., pl.* **beanos.** *Brit. sl.* a celebration, party, or other enjoyable time.

beanpole ('bi:n,pəʊl) *n.* **1.** a tall stick used to support bean plants. **2.** *Sl.* a tall thin person.

bean sprout *n.* the sprout of a newly germinated mung bean, eaten esp. in Chinese dishes.

beanstalk ('bi:n,stɔ:k) *n.* the stem of a bean plant.

bear[1] (bɛə) *vb.* **bearing, bore, borne.** (*mainly tr.*) **1.** to support or hold up. **2.** to bring: *to bear gifts.* **3.** to accept or assume the responsibility of: *to bear an expense.* **4.** (**born** in passive use except when followed by *by*) to give birth to: *to bear children.* **5.** (*also intr.*) to produce as by natural growth: *to bear fruit.* **6.** to tolerate or endure. **7.** to admit of; sustain: *his story does not bear scrutiny.* **8.** to hold in the mind: *to bear a grudge.* **9.** to show or be marked with: *he still bears the scars.* **10.** to render or supply (esp. in **bear witness**). **11.** to conduct (oneself, the body, etc.). **12.** to have, be, or stand in (relation or comparison): *his account bears no relation to the facts.* **13.** (*intr.*) to move or lie in a specified direction. **14. bear a hand.** to give assistance. **15. bring to bear.** to bring into operation or effect. ~See also **bear down, bear on,** etc. [OE *beran*]

bear[2] (bɛə) *n., pl.* **bears** *or* **bear. 1.** a plantigrade mammal typically having a large head, a long shaggy coat, and strong claws. **2.** any of various bearlike animals, such as the koala. **3.** a clumsy, churlish, or ill-mannered person. **4.** a teddy bear. **5.** *Stock Exchange.* **a.** a speculator who sells in anticipation of falling prices to make a profit on repurchase. **b.** (*as modifier*): *a bear market.* Cf. **bull**[1] (sense 4). ~*vb.* **bearing, beared. 6.** (*tr.*) to lower or attempt to lower the price or prices of (a stock market or a security) by speculative selling. [OE *bera*]

Bear (bɛə) *n.* **the. 1.** the English name for either Ursa Major (Great Bear) or Ursa Minor (Little Bear). **2.** an informal name for Russia.

bearable ('bɛərəb²l) *adj.* endurable; tolerable.

bear-baiting *n.* (formerly) an entertainment in which dogs attacked a chained bear.

beard (bɪəd) *n.* **1.** the hair growing on the lower parts of a man's face. **2.** any similar growth in animals. **3.** a tuft of long hairs in plants such as barley; awn. **4.** a barb, as on a fish-hook. ~*vb.* (*tr.*) **5.** to oppose boldly or impertinently. [OE *beard*] —'**bearded** *adj.*

beardless ('bɪədlɪs) *adj.* **1.** without a beard. **2.** too young to grow a beard; immature.

bear down *vb.* (*intr., adv.; often foll. by on or upon*) **1.** to press or weigh down. **2.** to approach in a determined or threatening manner.

Beardsley ('bɪədzlɪ) *n.* **Aubrey (Vincent).** 1872–98, English illustrator: noted for his stylized black-and-white illustrations, esp. those for Oscar Wilde's *Salome* and Pope's *Rape of the Lock.*

bearer ('bɛərə) *n.* **1.** a person or thing that bears, presents, or upholds. **2.** a person who presents a note or bill for payment. **3.** (in Africa, India, etc., formerly) a native porter or servant. **4.** (*modifier*) *Finance.* payable to the person in possession: *bearer bonds.*

bear garden *n.* **1.** (formerly) a place where bear-baiting took place. **2.** a scene of tumult.

bear hug *n.* **1.** a wrestling hold in which the arms are locked tightly round an opponent's chest and arms. **2.** any similar tight embrace.

bearing ('bɛərɪŋ) *n.* **1.** a support for a rotating or reciprocating mechanical part. **2.** (foll. by *on or upon*) relevance

(to): *it has no bearing on this problem.* **3.** a person's general social conduct. **4.** the act, period, or capability of producing fruit or young. **5.** anything that carries weight or acts as a support. **6.** the angular direction of a point or course measured from a known position. **7.** (*usually pl.*) the position, as of a ship, fixed with reference to two or more known points. **8.** (*usually pl.*) a sense of one's relative position; orientation (esp. in **lose, get,** *or* **take one's bearings**). **9.** *Heraldry.* **a.** a device on a heraldic shield. **b.** another name for **coat of arms.**

bearing rein *n. Chiefly Brit.* a rein from the bit to the saddle, designed to keep the horse's head in the desired position.

bearish ('bɛərɪʃ) *adj.* **1.** like a bear; rough; clumsy; churlish. **2.** *Stock Exchange.* causing, expecting, or characterized by a fall in prices: *a bearish market.* —'**bearishness** *n.*

bear on *vb.* (*intr., prep.*) **1.** to be relevant to; relate to. **2.** to be burdensome to or afflict.

bear out *vb.* (*tr., adv.*) to show to be true or truthful; confirm: *the witness will bear me out.*

bearskin ('bɛə,skɪn) *n.* **1.** the pelt of a bear, esp. when used as a rug. **2.** a tall helmet of black fur worn by certain British Army regiments.

bear up *vb.* (*intr., adv.*) to endure cheerfully.

bear with *vb.* (*intr., prep.*) to be patient with.

beast (bi:st) *n.* **1.** any animal other than man, esp. a large wild quadruped. **2.** savage nature or characteristics: *the beast in man.* **3.** a brutal, uncivilized, or filthy person. [C13: from OF *beste,* from L *bestia,* from ?]

beastly ('bi:stlɪ) *adj.* **-lier, -liest. 1.** *Inf.* unpleasant; disagreeable. **2.** *Obs.* of or like a beast; bestial. ~*adv.* **3.** *Inf.* (intensifier): *the weather is so beastly hot.* —'**beastliness** *n.*

beast of burden *n.* an animal, such as a donkey or ox, used for carrying loads.

beast of prey *n.* any animal that hunts other animals for food.

beat (bi:t) *vb.* **beating, beat; beaten** *or* **beat. 1.** (when *intr.,* often foll. by *against, on,* etc.) to strike with or as if with a series of violent blows. **2.** (*tr.*) to punish by striking; flog. **3.** to move up and down; flap: *the bird beat its wings heavily.* **4.** (*intr.*) to throb rhythmically; pulsate. **5.** (*tr.; sometimes foll. by up*) *Cookery.* to stir or whisk vigorously. **6.** (*tr.; sometimes foll. by out*) to shape, thin, or flatten (metal) by repeated blows. **7.** (*tr.*) *Music.* to indicate (time) by one's hand, baton, etc., or by a metronome. **8.** (when *tr.,* sometimes foll. by *out*) to produce (a sound or signal) by or as if by striking a drum. **9.** to overcome; defeat. **10.** (*tr.*) to form (a path, track, etc.) by repeatedly walking or riding over it. **11.** (*tr.*) to arrive, achieve, or finish before (someone or something). **12.** (*tr.; often foll. by back, down, off,* etc.) to drive, push, or thrust. **13.** to scour (woodlands or undergrowth) so as to rouse game for shooting. **14.** (*tr.*) *Sl.* to puzzle or baffle: *it beats me.* **15.** (*intr.*) *Naut.* to steer a sailing vessel as close as possible to the direction from which the wind is blowing. **16. beat a retreat.** to withdraw in haste. **17. beat it.** *Sl.* (*often imperative*) to go away. **18. beat the bounds.** *Brit.* (formerly) to define the boundaries of a parish by making a procession around them and hitting the ground with rods. **19. can you beat it** *or* **that?** *Sl.* an expression of surprise. ~*n.* **20.** a stroke or blow. **21.** the sound made by a stroke or blow. **22.** a regular throb. **23.** an assigned or habitual round or route, as of a policeman. **24.** the basic rhythmic unit in a piece of music. **25. a.** a pop or rock music characterized by a heavy rhythmic beat. **b.** (*as modifier*): *a beat group.* **26.** *Physics.* one of the regular pulses produced by combining two sounds or electrical signals that have similar frequencies. **27.** *Prosody.* the accent or stress in a metrical foot. **28.** (*modifier*) (*often cap.*) of, characterized by, or relating to the Beat Generation. ~*adj.* **29.** (*postpositive*) *Sl.* totally exhausted. ~See also **beat down, beat up.** [OE *bēatan*] —'**beatable** *adj.*

beatbox ('bi:t,bɒks) *n.* another name for **drum machine.**

beat down *vb.* (*adv.*) **1.** (*tr.*) *Inf.* to force or persuade (a seller) to accept a lower price. **2.** (*intr.*) (of the sun) to shine intensely.

beaten ('bi:t²n) *adj.* **1.** defeated or baffled. **2.** shaped or made thin by hammering: *beaten gold.* **3.** much travelled; well trodden. **4. off the beaten track. a.** in unfamiliar territory. **b.** out of the ordinary; unusual. **5.** (of food) mixed by beating; whipped. **6.** tired out; exhausted.

beater ('bi:tə) *n.* **1.** a person who beats or hammers: *a panel beater.* **2.** a device used for beating: *a carpet beater.* **3.** a person who rouses wild game.

Beat Generation *n. (functioning as sing. or pl.)* members of the generation that came to maturity in the 1950s, whose rejection of the social and political systems of the West was expressed through contempt for regular work, possessions, traditional dress, etc.

beatific (,bi:ə'tɪfɪk) *adj.* **1.** displaying great happiness, calmness, etc. **2.** of or conferring a state of celestial happiness. [C17: from LL *beātificus*, from L *beātus*, from *beāre* to bless + *facere* to make] —,bea'tifically *adv.*

beatify (bɪ'ætɪ,faɪ) *vb.* **-fying, -fied.** (*tr.*) **1.** *R.C. Church.* (of the pope) to declare formally that (a deceased person) showed a heroic degree of holiness in life and is worthy of veneration: the first step towards canonization. **2.** to make extremely happy. [C16: from OF *beatifier;* see BEATIFIC] —**beatification** (bɪ,ætɪfɪ'keɪʃən) *n.*

beating ('bi:tɪŋ) *n.* **1.** a whipping or thrashing. **2.** a defeat or setback. **3. take some** *or* **a lot of beating.** to be difficult to improve upon.

beatitude (bɪ'ætɪ,tju:d) *n.* **1.** supreme blessedness or happiness. **2.** an honorific title of the Eastern Christian Church, applied to those of patriarchal rank. [C15: from L *beātitūdō*, from *beātus* blessed; see BEATIFIC]

Beatitude (bɪ'ætɪ,tju:d) *n. Christianity.* any of eight sayings of Jesus in the Sermon on the Mount (Matthew 5:1-8) in which he declares that the poor, the meek, etc., will, in various ways, receive the blessings of heaven.

Beatles ('bi:təlz) *pl. n.* **the.** English rock group (1961–70): comprised John Lennon (guitar, vocals), Paul McCartney (bass guitar, vocals), George Harrison (born 1943; guitar, vocals), and Ringo Starr (real name *Richard Starkey*, born 1940; drums, vocals). See also (John Winston Ono) **Lennon,** (Paul) **McCartney.**

beatnik ('bi:tnɪk) *n.* **1.** a member of the Beat Generation. **2.** *Inf.* any person with long hair and shabby clothes. [C20: from BEAT (n.) + -NIK]

Beaton ('bi:tⁿn) *n.* Sir **Cecil** (**Walter Hardy**). 1904–80, English photographer, noted esp. for his society portraits.

Beatrix ('bi:ətrɪks) *n.* full name *Beatrix Wilhelmina Armgard.* born 1938, queen of the Netherlands from 1980.

Beatty ('bi:tɪ) *n.* **David,** 1st Earl Beatty. 1871–1936, British admiral of the fleet in World War I.

beat up *Inf.* ~*vb.* **1.** (*tr., adv.*) to strike or kick repeatedly, so as to inflict severe physical damage. ~*adj.* **beat-up.** **2.** worn-out; dilapidated.

beau (bəʊ) *n., pl.* **beaus** (bəʊz) *or* **beaux. 1.** a man who is greatly concerned with his clothes and appearance; dandy. **2.** *Chiefly U.S.* a boyfriend; sweetheart. [C17: from F, from OF *biau*, from L *bellus* handsome]

Beaufort scale ('bəʊfət) *n. Meteorol.* an international scale of wind velocities from 0 (calm) to 12 (hurricane) (0 to 17 in the U.S.). [C19: after Sir Francis *Beaufort* (1774–1857), E admiral who devised it]

Beaufort Sea *n.* part of the Arctic Ocean off the N coast of North America.

beau geste *French.* (bo ʒɛst) *n., pl.* **beaux gestes** (bo ʒɛst) a noble or gracious gesture or act. [lit.: beautiful gesture]

Beauharnais (*French* boarnɛ) *n.* **1. Eugène de** (øʒɛn də), son of Joséphine. 1781–1824, viceroy of Italy (1805–14) for his stepfather Napoleon I. **2.** (**Eugénie**) **Hortense de** (ɔrtɑ̃s də), daughter of Joséphine. 1783–1837, queen of Holland (1806–10) as wife of Louis Bonaparte. **3. Joséphine de** (ʒozefin də). See (Empress) **Joséphine.**

beaujolais ('bəʊʒə,leɪ) *n. (sometimes cap.)* a popular fresh-tasting red or white wine from southern Burgundy in France.

Beaumarchais (*French* bomarʃɛ) *n.* **Pierre Augustin Caron de** (pjɛr ogystɛ̃ karɔ̃ də). 1732–99, French dramatist, noted for his comedies *The Barber of Seville* (1775) and *The Marriage of Figaro* (1784).

beau monde ('bəʊ 'mɒnd) *n.* the world of fashion and society. [C18: F, lit.: fine world]

Beaumont[1] ('bəʊmɒnt) *n.* a city in SE Texas. Pop.: 118 102 (1980).

Beaumont[2] ('bəʊmɒnt) *n.* **1. Francis.** 1584–1616, English dramatist, who collaborated with John Fletcher in plays including *The Knights of the Burning Pestle* (1607)

and *The Maid's Tragedy* (1611). **2. William.** 1785–1853, U.S. surgeon, noted for his pioneering work on digestion.

Beaune (bəʊn) *n.* **1.** a city in E France, near Dijon: an important trading centre for Burgundy wines. Pop.: 21 127 (1982 est.). **2.** a wine produced in this district.

beaut (bju:t) *Sl., chiefly Austral. & N.Z.* ~*n.* **1.** an outstanding person or thing. ~*adj., interj.* **2.** good or excellent.

beauteous ('bju:tɪəs) *adj.* a poetic word for **beautiful.** —'**beauteousness** *n.*

beautician (bju:'tɪʃən) *n.* a person who works in or manages a beauty salon.

beautiful ('bju:tɪfʊl) *adj.* **1.** possessing beauty; aesthetically pleasing. **2.** highly enjoyable; very pleasant. —'**beautifully** *adv.*

beautify ('bju:tɪ,faɪ) *vb.* **-fying, -fied.** to make or become beautiful. —**beautification** (,bju:tɪfɪ'keɪʃən) *n.* —'**beauti,fier** *n.*

beauty ('bju:tɪ) *n., pl.* **-ties. 1.** the combination of all the qualities of a person or thing that delight the senses and mind. **2.** a very attractive woman. **3.** *Inf.* an outstanding example of its kind. **4.** *Inf.* an advantageous feature: *one beauty of the job is the short hours.* ~*interj.* **5.** (*N.Z.* 'bju:dɪ). *Austral. & N.Z. sl.* an expression of approval or agreement. [C13: from OF *biauté*, from *biau* beautiful; see BEAU]

beauty queen *n.* an attractive young woman, esp. one who has won a beauty contest.

beauty salon *or* **parlour** *n.* an establishment providing services such as hairdressing, facial treatment, and massage.

beauty sleep *n. Inf.* sleep, esp. sleep before midnight.

beauty spot *n.* **1.** a small dark-coloured patch or spot worn on a lady's face as an adornment. **2.** a mole or other similar natural mark on the skin. **3.** a place of outstanding beauty.

Beauvais (*French* bovɛ) *n.* a market town in N France, 64 km (40 miles) northwest of Paris. Pop.: 53 783 (1983 est.).

Beauvoir (*French* bovwar) *n.* **Simone de** (simɔn də). 1908–86, French existentialist novelist and feminist, whose works include *Le sang des autres* (1944), *Le deuxième sexe* (1949), and *Les mandarins* (1954).

beaux (bəʊ, bəʊz) *n.* a plural of **beau.**

beaux-arts (bəʊ'za:) *pl. n.* **1.** another word for **fine art. 2.** (*modifier*) relating to the classical decorative style, esp. that of the École des Beaux-Arts in Paris: *beaux-arts influences.* [F]

beaver[1] ('bi:və) *n.* **1.** a large amphibious rodent of Europe, Asia, and North America. It has soft brown fur, a broad flat hairless tail, and webbed hind feet, and constructs complex dams and houses (lodges) in rivers. **2.** its fur. **3.** a tall hat of beaver fur worn during the 19th century. **4.** a woollen napped cloth resembling beaver fur. **5.** *Obs.* a full beard. **6.** a bearded man. **7.** (*modifier*) made of beaver fur or similar material. ~*vb.* **8.** (*intr.; usually foll. by away*) to work industriously or steadily. [OE *beofor*]

beaver[2] ('bi:və) *n.* a movable piece on a medieval helmet used to protect the lower face. [C15: from OF *baviere*, from *baver* to dribble]

Beaverbrook ('bi:və,brʊk) *n.* **1st Baron,** title of *William Maxwell Aitken.* 1879–1964, British newspaper proprietor and Conservative politician, born in Canada, whose newspapers included the *Daily Express;* minister of information (1918); minister of aircraft production (1940–41).

Bebel (*German* 'be:bəl) *n.* **August** ('aʊgʊst). 1840–1913, German socialist leader: one of the founders of the Social Democratic Party (1869).

Bebington ('bɛbɪŋtən) *n.* a town in NW England, in Merseyside: docks and chemical works. Pop.: 64 174 (1981).

bebop ('bi:bɒp) *n.* the full name for **bop** (sense 1). [C20: imit. of the rhythm] —'**bebopper** *n.*

becalmed (bɪ'ka:md) *adj.* (of a sailing boat or ship) motionless through lack of wind.

became (bɪ'keɪm) *vb.* the past tense of **become.**

because (bɪ'kɒz, -'kəz) *conj.* **1.** (*subordinating*) on account of the fact that; since: *because it's so cold we'll go home.* **2. because of.** (*prep.*) on account of: *I lost my job because of her.* [C14 *bi cause*, from *bi* BY + CAUSE]
▷ **Usage.** See at **reason.**

béchamel sauce (,beɪʃə'mɛl) *n.* a thick white sauce flavoured with onion and seasonings. [C18: after the Marquis of *Béchamel*, its F inventor]

Béchar (*French* beʃar) *n.* a city in NW Algeria: an oasis. Pop.: 72 790 (1977 est.). Former name: **Colomb-Béchar.**

bêche-de-mer (ˌbɛʃdə'mɛə) *n.*, *pl.* **bêches-de-mer** (ˌbɛʃdə'mɛə) *or* **bêche-de-mer.** another name for **trepang.** [C19: quasi-F, from earlier E *biche de mer*, from Port. *bicho do mar* worm of the sea]

Bechet ('bɛʃeɪ) *n.* **Sidney.** 1897–1959, U.S. jazz soprano saxophonist and clarinetist.

Bechuana (bɛ'tʃwɑːnə; ˌbɛkjʊ'ɑːnə) *n.*, *pl.* **-na** *or* **-nas.** a former name for a Bantu of Botswana.

Bechuanaland (bɛ'tʃwɑːnəˌlænd; ˌbɛtʃʊ'ɑːnəˌlænd, ˌbɛkjʊ-) *n.* the former name (until 1966) of **Botswana.**

beck¹ (bɛk) *n.* **1.** a nod, wave, or other gesture. **2. at (someone's) beck and call.** subject to (someone's) slightest whim. [C14: short for *becnen* to BECKON]

beck² (bɛk) *n.* (in N England) a stream. [OE *becc*]

Becker ('bɛkə) *n.* **Boris.** born 1967, West German tennis player: Wimbledon champion 1985 and 1986: the youngest man ever to win Wimbledon.

Becket ('bɛkɪt) *n.* **Saint Thomas à.** 1118–70, English prelate; chancellor (1155–62) to Henry II; archbishop of Canterbury (1162–70): murdered following his opposition to Henry's attempts to control the clergy.

Beckett ('bɛkɪt) *n.* **Samuel.** born 1906, Irish dramatist and novelist writing in French and English, whose works portray the human condition as insignificant or absurd in a bleak universe. They include the plays *En attendant Godot* (*Waiting for Godot*, 1952), *Fin de partie* (*Endgame*, 1957), and *Not I* (1973) and the novel *Malone meurt* (*Malone Dies*, 1951): Nobel prize for literature 1969.

Beckford ('bɛkfəd) *n.* **William.** 1759–1844, English writer and dilettante; author of the oriental romance *Vathek* (1787).

Beckmann (*German* 'bɛkman) *n.* **Max** (maks). 1884–1950, German expressionist painter.

beckon ('bɛkən) *vb.* **1.** to summon with a gesture of the hand or head. **2.** to entice or lure. ~*n.* **3.** a summoning gesture. [OE *bīecnan*, from *bēacen* sign] —'**beckoner** *n.* —'**beckoning** *adj.*, *n.*

becloud (bɪ'klaʊd) *vb.* (*tr.*) **1.** to cover or obscure with a cloud. **2.** to confuse or muddle.

become (bɪ'kʌm) *vb.* **-coming, -came, -come.** (*mainly intr.*) **1.** (*copula*) to come to be; develop or grow into: *he became a monster.* **2.** (foll. by *of; usually used in a question*) to happen (to): *what became of him?* **3.** (*tr.*) to suit: *that dress becomes you.* **4.** (*tr.*) to be appropriate; to befit: *it ill becomes you to complain.* [OE *becuman* to happen]

becoming (bɪ'kʌmɪŋ) *adj.* suitable; appropriate. —be'comingly *adv.* —be'comingness *n.*

becquerel (ˌbɛkə'rɛl) *n.* the SI unit of activity of a radioactive source. [after A. H. BECQUEREL]

Becquerel (*French* bɛkrɛl) *n.* **Antoine Henri** (ātwan āri). 1852–1908, French physicist, who discovered the photographic action of the rays emitted by uranium salts and so instigated the study of radioactivity: Nobel prize for physics 1903.

bed (bɛd) *n.* **1.** a piece of furniture on which to sleep. **2.** the mattress and bedclothes: *an unmade bed.* **3.** sleep or rest: *time for bed.* **4.** any place in which a person or animal sleeps or rests. **5.** *Med.* a unit of potential occupancy in a hospital or residential institution. **6.** *Inf.* sexual intercourse. **7.** a plot of ground in which plants are grown. **8.** the bottom of a river, lake, or sea. **9.** a part of this used for cultivation of a plant or animal: *oyster beds.* **10.** any underlying structure or part. **11.** a layer of rock, esp. sedimentary rock. **12. go to bed. a.** (often foll. by *with*) to have sexual intercourse (with). **b.** *Journalism, printing.* (of a newspaper, etc.) to go to press; start printing. **13. put to bed.** *Journalism.* to finalize work on (a newspaper, etc.) so that it is ready to go to press. **14. take to one's bed.** to remain in bed, esp. because of illness. ~*vb.* **bedding, bedded. 15.** (usually foll. by *down*) to go to or put into a place to sleep or rest. **16.** (*tr.*) to have sexual intercourse with. **17.** (*tr.*) to place firmly into position; embed. **18.** *Geol.* to form or be arranged in a distinct layer; stratify. **19.** (*tr.; often foll. by *out*) to plant in a bed of soil. [OE *bedd*]

BEd *abbrev. for* Bachelor of Education.

bed and board *n.* sleeping accommodation and meals.

bed and breakfast *n.* *Chiefly Brit.* **1.** (in a hotel, boarding house, etc.) overnight accommodation and breakfast. **2.** the selling of shares after hours one evening on a stock exchange and buying them back the next morning, in order to establish a loss for capital-gains tax purposes.

bedaub (bɪ'dɔːb) *vb.* (*tr.*) **1.** to smear all over with something thick, sticky, or dirty. **2.** to ornament in a gaudy or vulgar fashion.

bedazzle (bɪ'dæzˀl) *vb.* (*tr.*) to dazzle or confuse, as with brilliance. —be'**dazzlement** *n.*

bed bath *n.* another name for **blanket bath.**

bedbug ('bɛdˌbʌg) *n.* any of several bloodsucking wingless insects of temperate regions, infesting dirty houses.

bedchamber ('bɛdˌtʃeɪmbə) *n.* an archaic word for **bedroom.**

bedclothes ('bɛdˌkləʊðz) *pl. n.* sheets, blankets, and other coverings for a bed.

beddable ('bɛdəbˀl) *adj.* sexually attractive.

bedding ('bɛdɪŋ) *n.* **1.** bedclothes, sometimes considered with a mattress. **2.** litter, such as straw, for animals. **3.** a foundation, such as mortar under a brick. **4.** the stratification of rocks.

bedding plant *n.* an immature plant that may be planted out in a garden bed.

Bede (biːd) *n.* **Saint,** known as *the Venerable Bede.* ?673–735 A.D., English monk, scholar, historian, and theologian, noted for his Latin *Ecclesiastical History of the English People* (731). Feast day: May 27. Latin name: **Baeda.**

bedeck (bɪ'dɛk) *vb.* (*tr.*) to cover with decorations; adorn.

bedevil (bɪ'dɛvˀl) *vb.* **-illing, -illed** *or U.S.* **-iling, -iled.** (*tr.*) **1.** to harass or torment. **2.** to throw into confusion. **3.** to possess, as with a devil. —be'**devilment** *n.*

bedew (bɪ'djuː) *vb.* (*tr.*) to wet as with dew.

bedfellow ('bɛdˌfɛləʊ) *n.* **1.** a person with whom one shares a bed. **2.** a temporary ally or associate.

Bedford¹ ('bɛdfəd) *n.* **1.** a town in SE central England, administrative centre of Bedfordshire, on the River Ouse. Pop.: 89 200 (1983 est.). **2.** short for **Bedfordshire.**

Bedford² ('bɛdfəd) *n.* **Duke of,** title of *John of Lancaster.* 1389–1435, son of Henry IV of England: protector of England and regent of France (1422–35).

Bedfordshire ('bɛdfədˌʃɪə, -fə) *n.* a county of S central England: mainly low-lying, with the Chiltern Hills in the south. Administrative centre: Bedford. Pop.: 504 986 (1981). Area: 1235 sq. km (477 sq. miles). Abbrev.: **Beds.**

bedight (bɪ'daɪt) *Arch.* ~*vb.* **-dighting, -dight** *or* **-dighted. 1.** (*tr.*) to array or adorn. ~*adj.* **2.** (*p.p.*) adorned or bedecked. [C14: from DIGHT]

bedim (bɪ'dɪm) *vb.* **-dimming, -dimmed.** (*tr.*) to make dim or obscure.

Bedivere ('bɛdɪˌvɪə) *n.* **Sir.** (in Arthurian legend) a knight who took the dying King Arthur to the barge in which he was carried to Avalon.

bedizen (bɪ'daɪzˀn, -'dɪzˀn) *vb.* (*tr.*) *Arch.* to dress or decorate gaudily or tastelessly. [C17: from BE- + obs. *dizen* to dress up, from ?] —be'**dizenment** *n.*

bed jacket *n.* a woman's short upper garment worn over a nightgown when sitting up in bed.

bedlam ('bɛdləm) *n.* **1.** a noisy confused situation. **2.** *Arch.* a madhouse. [C13 *bedlem, bethlem,* from Hospital of St Mary of *Bethlehem* in London]

bed linen *n.* sheets, pillowcases, etc., for a bed.

Bedloe's Island ('bɛdləʊz) *or* **Bedloe Island** *n.* the former name (until 1956) of **Liberty Island.**

Bedouin *or* **Beduin** ('bɛdʊɪn) *n.* **1.** (*pl.* **-ins** *or* **-in**) a nomadic Arab tribesman of the deserts of Arabia, Jordan, and Syria. **2.** a wanderer. ~*adj.* **3.** of or relating to the Bedouins. **4.** wandering. [C14: from OF *beduin,* from Ar. *badāwi,* pl. of *badwi,* from *badw* desert]

bedpan ('bɛdˌpæn) *n.* a vessel used by a bedridden patient to collect his faeces and urine.

bedraggle (bɪ'drægˀl) *vb.* (*tr.*) to make (hair, clothing, etc.) limp, untidy, or dirty, as with rain or mud. —be'**draggled** *adj.*

bedridden ('bɛdˌrɪdˀn) *adj.* confined to bed because of illness, esp. for a long or indefinite period. [OE *bedreda*]

bedrock ('bɛdˌrɒk) *n.* **1.** the solid rock beneath the surface soil, etc. **2.** basic principles or facts. **3.** the lowest point, level, or layer.

bedroll ('bɛdˌrəʊl) *n.* a portable roll of bedding.

bedroom ('bɛdˌruːm, -ˌrʊm) *n.* **1.** a room used for sleeping. **2.** (*modifier*) containing references to sex: *a bedroom comedy.*

bedside ('bɛdˌsaɪd) *n.* **a.** the space beside a bed, esp. a sickbed. **b.** (*as modifier*): *a bedside lamp.*

bedsitter (ˌbɛd'sɪtə) n. a furnished sitting room containing sleeping accommodation. Also called: **bedsitting room, bedsit.**

bedsore ('bɛd,sɔː) n. a chronic ulcer on the skin of a bedridden person, caused by prolonged pressure.

bedspread ('bɛd,sprɛd) n. a top cover on a bed.

bedstead ('bɛd,stɛd) n. the framework of a bed.

bedstraw ('bɛd,strɔː) n. any of numerous plants which have small white or yellow flowers and prickly or hairy fruits: formerly used as straw for beds.

bedtime ('bɛd,taɪm) n. **a.** the time when one usually goes to bed. **b.** (as modifier): a bedtime story.

bed-wetting n. the act of urinating in bed.

Bedworth ('bɛdwəθ) n. a town in central England, in N Warwickshire. Pop.: 41 991 (1981).

bee[1] (biː) n. **1.** any of various four-winged insects that collect nectar and pollen and make honey and wax. **2. busy bee.** a person who is industrious or has many things to do. **3. have a bee in one's bonnet.** to be obsessed with an idea. [OE bīo]

bee[2] (biː) n. Chiefly U.S. a social gathering for a specific purpose, as to carry out a communal task: quilting bee. [?from dialect bean neighbourly help, from OE bēn boon]

Beeb (biːb) n. the. an informal name for the BBC.

beebread ('biː,brɛd) n. a mixture of pollen and nectar prepared by worker bees and fed to the larvae. Also called: **ambrosia.**

beech (biːtʃ) n. **1.** a European tree having smooth greyish bark. **2.** a similar tree of temperate Australasia and South America. **3.** the hard wood of either of these trees. **4.** See **copper beech.** [OE bēce] — '**beechen** or '**beechy** adj.

Beecham ('biːtʃəm) n. Sir **Thomas.** 1879–1961, English conductor who did much to promote the works of Delius, Sibelius, and Richard Strauss.

Beecher ('biːtʃə) n. **Henry Ward.** 1813–87, U.S. clergyman: a leader in the movement for the abolition of slavery.

Beecher Stowe n. See (Harriet Elizabeth Beecher) **Stowe.**

beechnut ('biːtʃ,nʌt) n. the small brown triangular edible nut of the beech tree, collectively often termed **beech mast.**

bee-eater n. any of various insectivorous birds of the Old World tropics and subtropics.

beef (biːf) n. **1.** the flesh of various bovine animals, esp. the cow, when killed for eating. **2.** (pl. **beeves**) an adult ox, etc., reared for its meat. **3.** Inf. human flesh, esp. when muscular. **4.** (pl. **beefs**) Sl. a complaint. ~vb. **5.** (intr.) Sl. to complain, esp. repeatedly. **6.** (tr.; often foll. by up) Inf. to strengthen; reinforce. [C13: from OF boef, from L bōs ox]

beefburger ('biːf,bɜːgə) n. a flat fried cake of minced beef; hamburger.

beefcake ('biːf,keɪk) n. Sl. men displayed for their muscular bodies, esp. in photographs.

beefeater ('biːf,iːtə) n. a yeoman warder of the Tower of London.

beef road n. Austral. a road used for transporting cattle.

beefsteak ('biːf,steɪk) n. a lean piece of beef that can be grilled, fried, etc.

beef tea n. a drink made by boiling pieces of lean beef.

beefy ('biːfɪ) adj. **beefier, beefiest. 1.** like beef. **2.** Inf. muscular; brawny. — '**beefiness** n.

beehive ('biː,haɪv) n. **1.** a man-made receptacle used to house a swarm of bees. **2.** a dome-shaped structure. **3.** a place where busy people are assembled. **4. the Beehive.** the dome-shaped building which houses Parliament in Wellington, New Zealand.

beekeeper ('biː,kiːpə) n. a person who keeps bees for their honey. — '**bee,keeping** n.

beeline ('biː,laɪn) n. the most direct route between two places (esp. in **make a beeline for**).

Beelzebub (bɪ'ɛlzɪ,bʌb) n. Satan or any devil. [OE Belzebub, ult. from Heb. bá'al zebūb, lit.: lord of flies]

bee moth n. any of various moths whose larvae live in the nests of bees or wasps, feeding on nest materials and host larvae.

been (biːn, bɪn) vb. the past participle of **be.**

beep (biːp) n. **1.** a short high-pitched sound, as made by a car horn or by electronic apparatus. ~vb. **2.** to make or cause to make such a noise. [C20: imit.] — '**beeper** n.

beer (bɪə) n. **1.** an alcoholic drink brewed from malt, sugar, hops, and water. **2.** a slightly fermented drink

made from the roots or leaves of certain plants: ginger beer. **3.** (modifier) relating to beer: beer glass. **4.** (modifier) in which beer is drunk, esp. (of licensed premises) having a licence to sell beer but not spirits: beer house; beer garden. [OE beor]

beer and skittles n. (functioning as sing.) Inf. enjoyment or pleasure.

Beerbohm ('bɪəbəʊm) n. Sir **Max.** 1872–1956, English critic, wit, and caricaturist, whose works include Zuleika Dobson (1911), a satire on Oxford undergraduates.

beer parlour n. Canad. a licensed place in which beer is sold to the public.

Beersheba (bɪə'ʃiːbə) n. a town in S Israel: commercial centre of the Negev. In biblical times it marked the southern limit of Palestine. Pop.: 115 000 (1986).

beery ('bɪərɪ) adj. **beerier, beeriest. 1.** smelling or tasting of beer. **2.** given to drinking beer. — '**beerily** adv. — '**beeriness** n.

bee's knees n. the (functioning as sing.) Inf. an excellent or ideally suitable person or thing.

beestings, biestings, or U.S. **beastings** ('biːstɪŋz) n. (functioning as sing.) the first milk secreted by a cow or similar animal after giving birth; colostrum. [OE bȳsting]

beeswax ('biːz,wæks) n. **1.** a wax secreted by honeybees for constructing honeycombs. **2.** this wax after refining, used in polishes, etc.

beeswing ('biːz,wɪŋ) n. a light filmy crust of tartar that forms in some wines after long keeping in the bottle.

beet (biːt) n. **1.** a plant of a genus widely cultivated in such varieties as the sugar beet, mangelwurzel, and beetroot. **2.** the leaves of any of several varieties of this plant, cooked and eaten as a vegetable. **3. red beet.** the U.S. name for **beetroot.** [OE bēte, from L bēta]

Beethoven ('beɪt,həʊvⁿn) n. **Ludwig van** ('luːtvɪç fan). 1770–1827, German composer, who greatly extended the form and scope of symphonic and chamber music, bridging the classical and romantic traditions. His works include nine symphonies, 32 piano sonatas, 16 string quartets, five piano concertos, a violin concerto, two masses, the opera Fidelio (1805), and choral music.

beetle[1] ('biːtⁿl) n. **1.** an insect having biting mouthparts and forewings modified to form shell-like protective casings. **2.** a game in which the players draw or assemble a beetle-shaped form. ~vb. (intr.; foll. by along, off, etc.) **3.** Inf. to scuttle or scurry; hurry. [OE bitela]

beetle[2] ('biːtⁿl) n. **1.** a heavy hand tool for pounding or beating. **2.** a machine used to finish cloth by stamping it with wooden hammers. [OE bīetel, from bēatan to BEAT]

beetle[3] ('biːtⁿl) vb. **1.** (intr.) to overhang; jut. ~adj. **2.** overhanging; prominent. [C14: ? rel. to BEETLE[1]] — '**beetling** adj.

beetle-browed adj. having bushy or overhanging eyebrows.

beetroot ('biːt,ruːt) n. a variety of the beet plant that has a bulbous dark red root that may be eaten as a vegetable, in salads, or pickled.

beet sugar n. the sucrose obtained from sugar beet, identical in composition to cane sugar.

beeves (biːvz) n. the plural of **beef** (sense 2).

BEF abbrev. for British Expeditionary Force, the British army that served in France 1939-40.

befall (bɪ'fɔːl) vb. **-falling, -fell, -fallen.** Arch. or literary. **1.** (intr.) to take place. **2.** (tr.) to happen to. **3.** (intr.; usually foll. by to) to be due, as by right. [OE befeallan; see BE-, FALL]

befit (bɪ'fɪt) vb. **-fitting, -fitted.** (tr.) to be appropriate to or suitable for. [C15: from BE- + FIT[1]] — **be'fitting** adj. — **be'fittingly** adv.

befog (bɪ'fɒg) vb. **-fogging, -fogged.** (tr.) **1.** to surround with fog. **2.** to make confused.

before (bɪ'fɔː) conj. (subordinating) **1.** earlier than the time when. **2.** rather than: he'll resign before he agrees to it. ~prep. **3.** preceding in space or time; in front of; ahead of: standing before the altar. **4.** in the presence of: to be brought before a judge. **5.** in preference to: to put friendship before money. ~adv. **6.** at an earlier time; previously. **7.** in front. [OE beforan]

beforehand (bɪ'fɔː,hænd) adj. (postpositive), adv. early; in advance; in anticipation.

befoul (bɪ'faʊl) vb. (tr.) to make dirty or foul.

befriend (bɪ'frɛnd) vb. (tr.) to be a friend to; assist; favour.

befuddle (bɪˈfʌdᵊl) vb. (tr.) **1.** to confuse. **2.** to make stupid with drink. —**be'fuddlement** n.

beg (bɛg) vb. **begging, begged. 1.** (when intr., often foll. by for) to solicit (for money, food, etc.), esp. in the street. **2.** to ask formally, humbly, or earnestly: I beg forgiveness; I beg to differ. **3.** (intr.) (of a dog) to sit up with forepaws raised expectantly. **4. beg the question. a.** to evade the issue. **b.** to assume the thing under examination as proved. **5. go begging.** to be unwanted or unused. ~See also **beg off.** [C13: prob. from OE bedecian]

began (bɪˈgæn) vb. the past tense of **begin.**

beget (bɪˈgɛt) vb. **-getting, -got** or **-gat; -gotten** or **-got.** (tr.) **1.** to father. **2.** to cause or create. [OE begietan; see BE-, GET] —**be'getter** n.

beggar (ˈbɛgə) n. **1.** a person who begs, esp. one who lives by begging. **2.** a person who has no money or resources; pauper. **3.** Chiefly Brit. a fellow: lucky beggar! ~vb. (tr.) **4.** to be beyond the resources of (esp. in to **beggar description). 5.** to impoverish. —**'beggardom** n.

beggarly (ˈbɛgəlɪ) adj. meanly inadequate; very poor. —**'beggarliness** n.

beggar-my-neighbour n. a card game in which one player tries to win all the cards of the other player.

beggary (ˈbɛgərɪ) n. extreme poverty or need.

begin (bɪˈgɪn) vb. **-ginning, -gan, -gun. 1.** to start or cause to start (something or to do something). **2.** to bring or come into being; arise or originate. **3.** to start to say or speak. **4.** (with a negative) to have the least capacity (to do something): he couldn't begin to compete. **5. to begin with,** in the first place. [OE beginnan]

Begin (ˈbeɪgɪn) n. **Menachem** (məˈnɑːkɪm). born 1913, Israeli statesman, born in Poland. In Palestine after 1942, he became a leader of the militant Zionists; prime minister of Israel (1977–83).

beginner (bɪˈgɪnə) n. a person who has just started to do or learn something; novice.

beginning (bɪˈgɪnɪŋ) n. **1.** a start; commencement. **2.** (often pl.) a first or early part or stage. **3.** the place where or time when something starts. **4.** an origin; source.

begird (bɪˈgɜːd) vb. **-girding, -girt** or **-girded.** (tr.) Poetic. **1.** to surround; gird around. **2.** to bind. [OE begierdan; see BE-, GIRD¹]

beg off vb. (intr., adv.) to ask to be released from an engagement, obligation, etc.

begone (bɪˈgɒn) sentence substitute. go away! [C14: from BE (imperative) + GONE]

begonia (bɪˈgəʊnjə) n. a plant of warm and tropical regions, having ornamental leaves and waxy flowers. [C18: NL, after Michel Bégon (1638–1710), F patron of science]

begorra (bɪˈgɒrə) interj. an emphatic exclamation, regarded as characteristic of Irishmen. [C19: from by God!]

begot (bɪˈgɒt) vb. a past tense and past participle of **beget.**

begotten (bɪˈgɒtᵊn) vb. a past participle of **beget.**

begrime (bɪˈgraɪm) vb. (tr.) to make dirty; soil.

begrudge (bɪˈgrʌdʒ) vb. (tr.) **1.** to give, admit, or allow unwillingly or with a bad grace. **2.** to envy (someone) the possession of (something). —**be'grudgingly** adv.

beguile (bɪˈgaɪl) vb. **-guiling, -guiled.** (tr.) **1.** to charm; fascinate. **2.** to delude; influence by slyness. **3.** (often foll. by of or out of) to cheat (someone) of. **4.** to pass pleasantly; while away. —**be'guilement** n. —**be'guiler** n. —**be'guilingly** adv.

beguine (bɪˈgiːn) n. **1.** a dance of South American origin in bolero rhythm. **2.** a piece of music in the rhythm of this dance. [C20: from Louisiana F, from F béguin flirtation]

begum (ˈbeɪgəm) n. (in certain Muslim countries) a woman of high rank. [C18: from Urdu begam, from Turkish begim; see BEY]

begun (bɪˈgʌn) vb. the past participle of **begin.**

behalf (bɪˈhɑːf) n. interest, part, benefit, or respect (only in **on (someone's) behalf, on** or U.S. & Canad. **in behalf of, in this** (or that) **behalf**). [OE be halfe, from be by + halfe side]

Behan (ˈbiːən) n. **Brendan.** 1923–64, Irish writer, noted esp. for his plays The Quare Fellow (1954) and The Hostage (1958) and for an account of his detention as a member of the Irish Republican Army, Borstal Boy (1958).

behave (bɪˈheɪv) vb. **1.** (intr.) to act or function in a specified or usual way. **2.** to conduct (oneself) in a specified way: he behaved badly. **3.** to conduct (oneself) properly or as desired. [C15: see BE-, HAVE]

behaviour or U.S. **behavior** (bɪˈheɪvjə) n. **1.** manner of behaving. **2. on one's best behaviour.** behaving with careful good manners. **3.** Psychol. the response of an organism to a stimulus. **4.** the reaction or functioning of a machine, etc., under normal or specified circumstances. [C15: from BEHAVE; infl. by ME havior, from OF havoir, from L habēre to have] —**be'havioural** or U.S. **be'havioral** adj.

behavioural science n. the scientific study of the behaviour of organisms.

behaviourism or U.S. **behaviorism** (bɪˈheɪvjəˌrɪzəm) n. a school of psychology that regards objective observation of the behaviour of organisms as the only valid subject for study. —**be'haviourist** or U.S. **be'haviorist** adj., n. —**be,haviour'istic** or U.S. **be,havior'istic** adj.

behaviour therapy n. any of various means of treating psychological disorders, such as aversion therapy, that depend on the patient systematically learning new behaviour.

behead (bɪˈhɛd) vb. (tr.) to remove the head from. [OE behēafdian, from BE- + heafod HEAD]

beheld (bɪˈhɛld) vb. the past tense and past participle of **behold.**

behemoth (bɪˈhiːmɒθ) n. **1.** Bible. a gigantic beast described in Job 40:15. **2.** a huge or monstrous person or thing. [C14: from Heb. behēmōth, pl. of bēhēmāh beast]

behest (bɪˈhɛst) n. an order or earnest request. [OE behǣs, from behātan; see BE-, HEST]

behind (bɪˈhaɪnd) prep. **1.** in or to a position further back than. **2.** in the past in relation to: I've got the exams behind me now. **3.** late according to: running behind schedule. **4.** concerning the circumstances surrounding: the reasons behind his departure. **5.** supporting: I'm right behind you in your application. ~adv. **6.** in or to a position further back; following. **7.** remaining after someone's departure: he left his books behind. **8.** in debt; in arrears: to fall behind with payments. ~adj. **9.** (postpositive) in a position further back. ~n. **10.** Inf. the buttocks. **11.** Australian Rules football. a score of one point made by kicking the ball over the **behind line** between a goalpost and one of the smaller outer posts (**behind posts**). [OE behindan]

behindhand (bɪˈhaɪndˌhænd) adj. (postpositive), adv. **1.** remiss in fulfilling an obligation. **2.** in arrears. **3.** backward. **4.** late.

Behistun (ˌbeɪhɪˈstuːn), **Bisitun,** or **Bisutun** n. a village in W Iran by the ancient road from Ecbatana to Babylon. On a nearby cliff is an inscription by Darius in Old Persian, Elamite, and Babylonian describing his enthronement.

behold (bɪˈhəʊld) vb. **-holding, -held.** (often imperative) Arch. or literary. to look (at); observe. [OE bihealdan; see BE-, HOLD¹] —**be'holder** n.

beholden (bɪˈhəʊldᵊn) adj. indebted; obliged. [OE behealden, p.p. of behealdan to BEHOLD]

behoof (bɪˈhuːf) n., pl. **-hooves.** Rare. advantage or profit. [OE behōf; see BEHOVE]

behove (bɪˈhəʊv) vb. (tr.; impersonal) Arch. to be necessary or fitting for: it behoves me to arrest you. [OE behōfian]

Behrens (ˈbeərənz; German ˈbeːrəns) n. **Peter.** 1868–1940, German architect.

Behring n. **1.** (German ˈbeːrɪŋ), **Emil von** (ˈeːmiːl fɔn). 1854–1917, German bacteriologist, who discovered diphtheria and tetanus antitoxins: Nobel prize for physiology or medicine 1901. **2.** (ˈbɛrɪŋ, ˈbɛər-). See (Vitus) **Bering.**

Beiderbecke (ˈbaɪdəˌbɛk) n. **Leon Bismarcke,** known as Bix. 1903–31, U.S. jazz cornettist, composer, and pianist.

beige (beɪʒ) n. **1. a.** a very light brown, sometimes with a yellowish tinge. **b.** (as adj.): beige gloves. **2.** a fabric made of undyed or unbleached wool. [C19: from OF, from ?]

Beijing (ˈbeɪˈdʒɪŋ) n. the official transliteration of the Chinese name for **Peking.**

being (ˈbiːɪŋ) n. **1.** the state or fact of existing; existence. **2.** essential nature; self. **3.** something that exists or is thought to exist: a being from outer space. **4.** a person; human being.

Beira ('baɪərə) n. a port in E Mozambique: terminus of a transcontinental railway from Lobito, Angola, through Zaïre, Zambia, and Zimbabwe. Pop.: 269 700 (1986).

Beirut or **Beyrouth** (beɪ'ruːt, 'beɪruːt) n. the capital of Lebanon, a port on the Mediterranean: part of the Ottoman Empire from the 16th century until 1918; four universities (Lebanese, American, French, and Arab). Pop.: 1 100 000 (1982 est.).

bejabers (bɪ'dʒeɪbəz) or **bejabbers** (bɪ'dʒæbəz) interj. an exclamation of surprise, emphasis, etc., regarded as characteristic of Irishmen. [C19: from by Jesus!]

Béjart (French beʒar) n. **Maurice** (mɔris). born 1928, French dancer and choreographer. His choreography is characterized by a combination of classic and modern dance and acrobatics.

bejewel (bɪ'dʒuːəl) vb. **-elling, -elled** or U.S. **-eling, -eled.** (tr.) to decorate as with jewels.

Bekaa or **Beqaa** (bɪ'kɑː) n. a broad valley in central Lebanon, between the Lebanon and Anti-Lebanon Mountains. Ancient name: **Coelesyria** (ˌsiːliː'sɪrɪə).

bel (bɛl) n. a unit for comparing two power levels, equal to the logarithm to the base ten of the ratio of the two powers. [C20: after A. G. BELL]

Bel (beɪl) n. (in Babylonian and Assyrian mythology) the god of the earth.

belabour or U.S. **belabor** (bɪ'leɪbə) vb. (tr.) **1.** to beat severely; thrash. **2.** to attack verbally.

belated (bɪ'leɪtɪd) adj. late or too late: belated greetings. **—be'latedly** adv. **—be'latedness** n.

Belau (bə'laʊ) n. **Republic of.** a republic comprising a group of islands in the W Pacific, in the W Caroline Islands; administratively part of the U.N. Trust Territory of the Pacific Islands 1947–87; entered into an agreement of free association with the U.S. (1980). Chief island: Babelthuap. Capital: Koror. Pop.: 15 000 (1987 est.). Area: 476 sq. km (184 sq. miles). Former names: **Pelew Islands,** (until 1981) **Palau Islands.**

belay (bɪ'leɪ) vb. **-laying, -layed. 1.** Naut. to secure (a line) to a pin, cleat, or bitt. **2.** (usually imperative) Naut. to stop. **3.** ('biː,leɪ). Mountaineering. to secure (a climber) by means of a belay. ~n. ('biːl,eɪ). **4.** Mountaineering. the attachment of a climber to a mountain by securing a rope round a rock, piton, etc., to safeguard the party in the event of a fall. [OE belecgan]

belaying pin n. Naut. a cylindrical metal or wooden pin used for belaying.

bel canto ('bɛl 'kæntəʊ) n. Music. a style of singing characterized by beauty of tone rather than dramatic power. [It., lit.: beautiful singing]

belch (bɛltʃ) vb. **1.** (usually intr.) to expel wind from the stomach noisily through the mouth. **2.** to expel or be expelled forcefully from inside: smoke belching from factory chimneys. ~n. **3.** an act of belching. [OE bialcan]

beldam or **beldame** ('bɛldəm) n. Arch. an old woman. [C15: from bel- grand (as in grandmother), from OF bel beautiful, + dam mother]

beleaguer (bɪ'liːgə) vb. (tr.) **1.** to lay siege to. **2.** to harass. [C16: from BE- + obs. leaguer a siege]

Belém (Portuguese bə'lẽi) n. a port in N Brazil, the capital of Pará state, on the Pará River: major trading centre for the Amazon basin. Pop.: 758 117 (1980 est.).

belemnite ('bɛləm,naɪt) n. **1.** an extinct marine mollusc related to the cuttlefish. **2.** its long pointed conical internal shell: a common fossil. [C17: from Gk belemnon dart]

Belfast ('bɛlfɑːst, bɛl'fɑːst) n. the capital of Northern Ireland, a port on Belfast Lough: became the centre of Irish Protestantism and of the linen industry in the 17th century. Pop.: 300 000 (1985).

Belfort (French bɛlfɔr) n. **1. Territoire de** (tɛritwar də). a department of E France: the only part of Alsace remaining to France after 1871. Capital: Belfort. Pop.: 131 999 (1982). Area: 608 sq. km (237 sq. miles). **2.** a fortress town in E France: strategically situated in the **Belfort Gap** between the Vosges and the Jura mountains. Pop.: 54 514 (1983 est.).

belfry ('bɛlfrɪ) n., pl. **-fries. 1.** the part of a tower or steeple in which bells are hung. **2.** a tower or steeple. [C13: from OF berfrei, of Gmc origin]

Belg. or **Bel.** abbrev. for: **1.** Belgian. **2.** Belgium.

Belgian ('bɛldʒən) n. **1.** a native or inhabitant of Belgium. ~adj. **2.** of or relating to Belgium, the Belgians, or their languages.

Belgian Congo n. a former name (1908–60) of **Zaïre.**

Belgian hare n. a large red domestic rabbit.

Belgium ('bɛldʒəm) n. a kingdom in NW Europe: at various times under the rulers of Burgundy, Spain, Austria, France, and the Netherlands before becoming an independent kingdom in 1830. It formed the Benelux customs union with the Netherlands and Luxembourg in 1947 and is now a member of the European Economic Community. It consists chiefly of a low-lying region of sand, woods, and heath (the Campine) in the north and west, and a fertile undulating central plain rising to the Ardennes Mountains in the southeast. Languages: French and Flemish. Religion: chiefly Roman Catholic. Currency: franc. Capital: Brussels. Pop.: 9 888 000 (1988 est.). Area: 30 513 sq. km (11 778 sq. miles).

Belgorod-Dnestrovski (Russian 'bjɛlgərətdnjɪ'strɔfskij) n. a variant spelling of **Byelgorod-Dnestrovski.**

Belgrade (bɛl'greɪd, 'bɛlgreɪd) n. the capital of Yugoslavia, in the E part at the confluence of the Danube and Sava Rivers: became the capital of Serbia in 1878 and of Yugoslavia in 1929. Pop.: 1 407 073 (1981). Serbo-Croatian name: **Beograd.**

Belgravia (bɛl'greɪvɪə) n. a fashionable residential district of W central London, around Belgrave Square.

Belial ('biːlɪəl) n. the devil or Satan. [C13: from Heb. bəlīyya'al, from bəlīy without + ya'al worth]

belie (bɪ'laɪ) vb. **-lying, -lied.** (tr.) **1.** to show to be untrue; contradict. **2.** to misrepresent; disguise the nature of. **3.** to fail to justify; disappoint. [OE beléogan; see BE-, LIE[1]]

belief (bɪ'liːf) n. **1.** a principle, etc., accepted as true, esp. without proof. **2.** opinion; conviction. **3.** religious faith. **4.** trust or confidence, as in a person's abilities, etc.

believe (bɪ'liːv) vb. **1.** (tr.; may take a clause as object) to accept (a statement or opinion) as true or real: I believe God exists. **2.** (tr.) to accept the statement or opinion of (a person) as true. **3.** (intr.; foll. by in) to be convinced of the truth or existence (of): to believe in fairies. **4.** (intr.) to have religious faith. **5.** (when tr., takes a clause as object) to think, assume, or suppose. **6.** (tr.) to think that someone is able to do (a particular action): I wouldn't have believed it of him. [OE beliefan] **—be'lievable** adj. **—be'liever** n.

belike (bɪ'laɪk) adv. Arch. perhaps; maybe.

Belisarius (ˌbɛlɪ'sɑːrɪəs) n. ?505–565 A.D., Byzantine general under Justinian I. He recovered North Africa from the Vandals and Italy from the Ostrogoths and led forces against the Persians.

Belisha beacon (bə'liːʃə) n. Brit. a flashing orange globe mounted on a post, indicating a pedestrian crossing on a road. [C20: after L. Hore-Belisha (1893-1957), Brit. politician]

belittle (bɪ'lɪt²l) vb. (tr.) **1.** to consider or speak of (something) as less valuable or important than it really is; disparage. **2.** to make small; dwarf. **—be'littlement** n. **—be'littler** n.

Belitung (bɪ'liːtʊŋ) n. another name for **Billiton.**

Belize (bɛ'liːz) n. a state in Central America, on the Caribbean: site of a Mayan civilization until the 9th century A.D.; colonized by the British from 1638; granted internal self-government in 1964; became an independent state within the Commonwealth in 1981. Official language: English; Carib and Spanish are also spoken. Currency: Belize dollar. Capital: Belmopan. Pop.: 171 000 (1986 est.). Area: 22 965 sq. km (8867 sq. miles). Former name (until 1973): **British Honduras. —Be'lizean** adj., n.

Belize City n. a port and the largest city in Belize, on the Caribbean coast: capital until 1973, when it was abandoned as hurricane-prone. Pop.: 47 000 (1986 est.).

bell[1] (bɛl) n. **1.** a hollow, usually metal, cup-shaped instrument that emits a ringing sound when struck. **2.** the sound made by such an instrument, as for marking the beginning or end of a period of time. **3.** an electrical device that rings or buzzes as a signal. **4.** something shaped like a bell, as the tube of certain musical wind instruments, or the corolla of certain flowers. **5.** Naut. a signal rung on a ship's bell to count the number of half-hour intervals during each of six four-hour watches reckoned from midnight. **6.** Brit. sl. a telephone call **7. bell, book, and candle.** instruments used formerly in excommunications. **8. ring a bell.** to sound familiar; recall something previously experienced. **9. sound as a bell.** in perfect condition. ~*vb.* **10.** to be or cause to be shaped like a bell. **11.** (*tr.*) to attach a bell or bells to. [OE *belle*]

bell² (bɛl) *n.* **1.** a bellowing or baying cry, esp. that of a stag in rut. ~*vb.* **2.** to utter (such a cry). [OE *bellan*]

Bell (bɛl) *n.* **1. Acton, Currer** ('kʌrə), and **Ellis.** pen names of the sisters Anne, Charlotte, and Emily **Brontë.** **2. Alexander Graham.** 1847–1922, U.S. scientist, born in Scotland, who invented the telephone (1876). **3.** Sir **Francis Henry Dillon.** 1851–1936, New Zealand statesman; prime minister of New Zealand (1925).

belladonna (ˌbɛlə'dɒnə) *n.* **1.** either of two alkaloid drugs obtained from the leaves and roots of the deadly nightshade. **2.** another name for **deadly nightshade.** [C16: from It., lit.: beautiful lady; supposed to refer to its use as a cosmetic]

Bellay (*French* bɛlɛ) *n.* **Joachim du** (ʒɔaʃɛ̃ dy). 1522–60, French poet, a member of the Pléiade.

bellbird ('bɛl,bɜːd) *n.* **1.** any of several tropical American birds having a bell-like call. **2.** either of two other birds with a bell-like call: an Australian flycatcher (**crested bellbird**) or a New Zealand honeyeater.

bell-bottoms *pl. n.* trousers that flare from the knee. — '**bell-ˌbottomed** *adj.*

bellboy ('bɛl,bɔɪ) *n. Chiefly U.S. & Canad.* a porter or page in a hotel, club, etc. Also called: **bellhop.**

bell buoy *n.* a navigational buoy with a bell which strikes when the waves move the buoy.

belle (bɛl) *n.* **1.** a beautiful woman. **2.** the most attractive woman at a function, etc. (esp. in **belle of the ball**). [C17: from F, fem. of BEAU]

Belleau Wood ('bɛləʊ; *French* bɛlo) *n.* a forest in N France: site of a battle (1918) in which the U.S. Marines halted a German advance on Paris.

belle époque French. (bɛl epɔk) *n.* the period of comfortable well-established life before World War I. [lit.: fine period]

Belle Isle *n.* an island in the Atlantic, at the N entrance to the **Strait of Belle Isle,** between Labrador and Newfoundland. Area: about 39 sq. km (15 sq. miles).

Bellerophon (bə'lɛrəˌfɒn) *n. Greek myth.* a hero of Corinth who performed many deeds with the help of the winged horse Pegasus, notably the killing of the monster Chimera.

belles-lettres (*French* bɛllɛtrə) *n.* (*functioning as sing.*) literary works, esp. essays and poetry, valued for their aesthetic content. [C17: from F: fine letters] —**bel'letrist** *n.*

bellflower ('bɛl,flaʊə) *n.* another name for **campanula.**

bellfounder ('bɛl,faʊndə) *n.* a foundry worker who casts bells.

bellicose ('bɛlɪˌkəʊs, -ˌkəʊz) *adj.* warlike; aggressive; ready to fight. [C15: from L *bellicōsus,* from *bellum* war] —**bellicosity** (ˌbɛlɪ'kɒsɪtɪ) *n.*

belligerence (bɪ'lɪdʒərəns) *n.* the act or quality of being belligerent or warlike; aggressiveness.

belligerency (bɪ'lɪdʒərənsɪ) *n.* the state of being at war.

belligerent (bɪ'lɪdʒərənt) *adj.* **1.** marked by readiness to fight or argue; aggressive. **2.** relating to or engaged in a war. ~*n.* **3.** a person or country engaged in war. [C16: from L *belliger,* from *bellum* war + *gerere* to wage]

Bellingshausen Sea ('bɛlɪŋz,haʊzən) *n.* an area of the S Pacific Ocean off the coast of Antarctica.

Bellini (*Italian* bel'lini) *n.* **1. Giovanni** (dʒo'vanni). ?1430–1516, Italian painter of the Venetian school, noted for his altarpieces, landscapes, and Madonnas. His father **Jacopo** (?1400–70) and his brother **Gentile** (?1429–1507) were also painters. **2. Vincenzo** (vin'tʃɛntso). 1801–35, Italian composer of operas, esp. *La Sonnambula* (1831) and *Norma* (1831).

Bellinzona (*Italian* bellin'tsona) *n.* a town in SE central Switzerland, capital of Ticino canton. Pop.: 16 743 (1983).

bell jar *n.* a bell-shaped glass cover to protect flower arrangements, etc., or to cover apparatus in experiments. Also called: **bell glass.**

bellman ('bɛlmən) *n., pl.* **-men.** a man who rings a bell; (formerly) a town crier.

bell metal *n.* an alloy of copper and tin, with some zinc and lead, used in casting bells.

Belloc ('bɛlɒk) *n.* **Hilaire** ('hɪlɛə, hɪ'lɛə). 1870–1953, British poet, essayist, and historian, born in France, noted particularly for his verse for children in *The Bad Child's Book of Beasts* (1896) and *Cautionary Tales* (1907).

Bellona (bə'ləʊnə) *n.* the Roman goddess of war.

bellow ('bɛləʊ) *vb.* **1.** (*intr.*) to make a loud deep cry like that of a bull; roar. **2.** to shout (something) unrestrainedly, as in anger or pain. ~*n.* **3.** the characteristic noise of a bull. **4.** a loud deep sound, as of pain or anger. [C14: prob. from OE *bylgan*]

Bellow ('bɛləʊ) *n.* **Saul.** born 1915, U.S. novelist, born in Canada. His works include *Dangling Man* (1944), *The Adventures of Augie March* (1953), *Herzog* (1964), *Humboldt's Gift* (1975), *Him with his Foot in his Mouth* (1986), and *More Die of Heartbreak* (1987): Nobel prize for literature 1976.

bellows ('bɛləʊz) *n.* (*functioning as sing. or pl.*) **1.** Also: **pair of bellows.** an instrument consisting of an air chamber with flexible sides that is used to create a stream of air, as for producing a draught for a fire or for sounding organ pipes. **2.** a flexible corrugated part, as that connecting the lens system of some cameras to the body. [C16: from pl. of OE *belig* BELLY]

bell pull *n.* a handle, rope, or cord pulled to operate a doorbell or servant's bell.

bell push *n.* a button pressed to operate an electric bell.

bell-ringer *n.* a person who rings church bells or musical handbells. — '**bell-ˌringing** *n.*

bell tent *n.* a cone-shaped tent having a single central supporting pole.

bellwether ('bɛl,wɛðə) *n.* **1.** a sheep that leads the herd, often bearing a bell. **2.** a leader, esp. one followed blindly.

belly ('bɛlɪ) *n., pl.* **-lies.** **1.** the lower or front part of the body of a vertebrate, containing the intestines and other organs; abdomen. **2.** the stomach, esp. when regarded as the seat of gluttony. **3.** a part that bulges deeply: *the belly of a sail.* **4.** the inside or interior cavity of something. **5.** the front, lower, or inner part of something. **6.** the surface of a stringed musical instrument over which the strings are stretched. **7.** *Austral. & N.Z.* **a.** the wool from a sheep's belly. **b.** (*as modifier*): *belly wool.* **8.** an archaic word for **womb** (sense 1). ~*vb.* **-lying, -lied. 9.** to swell out or cause to swell out; bulge. [OE *belig*]

bellyache ('bɛlɪˌeɪk) *n.* **1.** an informal term for **stomachache.** ~*vb.* **2.** (*intr.*) *Sl.* to complain repeatedly. — '**belly,acher** *n.*

bellyband ('bɛlɪˌbænd) *n.* a strap around the belly of a draught animal, holding the shafts of a vehicle.

bellybutton ('bɛlɪˌbʌtᵊn) *n.* an informal name for the **navel.** Also called: **tummy button.**

belly dance *n.* **1.** a sensuous dance of Middle Eastern origin, performed by women, with undulating movements of the abdomen. ~*vb.* **belly-dance. 2.** (*intr.*) to dance thus. — **belly dancer** *n.*

belly flop *n.* **1.** a dive into water in which the body lands horizontally. ~*vb.* **belly-flop, -flopping, -flopped. 2.** (*intr.*) to perform a belly flop.

bellyful ('bɛlɪˌfʊl) *n.* **1.** as much as one wants or can eat. **2.** *Sl.* more than one can tolerate.

belly landing *n.* the landing of an aircraft on its fuselage without use of its landing gear.

belly laugh *n.* a loud deep hearty laugh.

Belmondo (bɛl'mɒndəʊ; *French* bɛlmɔ̃do) *n.* **Jean-Paul** (ʒãpol). born 1933, French film actor.

Belmopan (ˌbɛlmə'pæn) *n.* (since 1973) the capital of Belize, about 50 miles inland: founded in 1970. Pop.: 3500 (1986).

Belo Horizonte (*Portuguese* 'bɛːlori'zõːntə) *n.* a city in SE Brazil, the capital of Minas Gerais state. Pop.: 1 442 483 (1980).

belong (bɪ'lɒŋ) *vb.* (*intr.*) **1.** (foll. by *to*) to be the property or possession (of). **2.** (foll. by *to*) to be bound (to) by ties of affection, allegiance, etc. **3.** (foll. by *to, under, with,* etc.) to be classified (with): *this plant belongs to the daisy family.* **4.** (foll. by *to*) to be a part or adjunct (of). **5.** to have a proper or usual place. **6.** *Inf.* to be acceptable, esp. socially. [C14 *belongen,* from BE- (intensive) + *longen,* from OE *langian* to belong]

belonging (bɪ'lɒŋɪŋ) *n.* secure relationship; affinity (esp. in **a sense of belonging**).

belongings (bɪ'lɒŋɪŋz) *pl. n.* (*sometimes sing.*) the things that a person owns or has with him.

Belorussian (ˌbɛləʊ'rʌʃən) *adj., n.* a variant spelling of **Byelorussian.**

Belostok (bjɪlɐ'stɔk) *n.* transliteration of the Russian name for **Bialystok.**

beloved (bɪˈlʌvɪd, -ˈlʌvd) *adj.* **1.** dearly loved. ~*n.* **2.** a person who is dearly loved.

Belovo (*Russian* ˈbjɛləvə) *n.* a variant spelling of **Byelovo.**

below (bɪˈləʊ) *prep.* **1.** at or to a position lower than; under. **2.** less than. **3.** south of. **4.** downstream of. **5.** unworthy of; beneath. ~*adv.* **6.** at or to a lower position. **7.** at a later place (in something written). **8.** *Arch.* on earth or in hell. [C14 *bilooghe*, from *bi* BY + *looghe* LOW[1]]

Bel Paese (ˈbɛl paːˈeɪzɪ) *n.* a mild creamy Italian cheese. [from It., lit.: beautiful country]

Belsen (ˈbɛlsən; *German* ˈbɛlzən) *n.* a village in N West Germany: with Bergen, the site of a Nazi concentration camp (1943–45).

Belshazzar (bɛlˈʃæzə) *n.* the son of Nabonidus; coregent of Babylon with his father for eight years: referred to as king and son of Nebuchadnezzar in the Old Testament (Daniel 5:1, 17; 8:1); described as having received a divine message of doom written on a wall at a banquet (**Belshazzar's Feast**).

belt (bɛlt) *n.* **1.** a band of cloth, leather, etc., worn, usually around the waist, to support clothing, carry weapons, etc., or as decoration. **2.** a belt worn to show rank (as by a knight), to mark expertise (as in judo), or awarded as a prize (as in boxing). **3.** a narrow band, circle, or stripe, as of colour. **4.** an area where a specific thing is found; zone: *a belt of high pressure.* **5.** See **seat belt. 6.** a band of flexible material between rotating shafts or pulleys to transfer motion or transmit goods: *a fan belt; a conveyer belt.* **7.** *Inf.* a sharp blow. **8. below the belt. a.** *Boxing.* below the waist. **b.** *Inf.* in an unscrupulous or cowardly way. **9. tighten one's belt.** to take measures to reduce expenditure. **10. under one's belt. a.** in one's stomach. **b.** as part of one's experience: *he had a degree under his belt.* ~*vb.* **11.** (*tr.*) to fasten or attach with or as if with a belt. **12.** (*tr.*) to hit with a belt. **13.** (*tr.*) *Sl.* to give a sharp blow; punch. **14.** (*intr.;* often foll. by *along*) *Sl.* to move very fast, esp. in a car. **15.** (*tr.*) *Rare.* to encircle. [OE, from L *balteus*] —ˈbelted *adj.*

Beltane (ˈbɛlteɪn, -tən) *n.* an ancient Celtic festival with a sacrificial bonfire on May Day. [C15: from Scot. Gaelic *bealltainn*]

belting (ˈbɛltɪŋ) *n.* **1.** material for belts. **2.** belts collectively. **3.** *Inf.* a beating.

belt man *n. Austral. & N.Z.* the member of a beach lifesaving team who swims out wearing a belt with a line attached.

belt out *vb.* (*tr., adv.*) *Inf.* to sing or emit sound loudly.

belt up *vb.* (*adv.*) **1.** *Sl.* to stop talking: often imperative. **2.** to fasten with a belt.

beluga (bɪˈluːgə) *n.* **1.** a large white sturgeon of the Black and Caspian Seas: a source of caviar and isinglass. **2.** another name for **white whale.** [C18: from Russian *byeluga*, from *byely* white]

belvedere (ˈbɛlvɪˌdɪə, ˌbɛlvɪˈdɪə) *n.* a building, such as a summerhouse, sited to command a fine view. [C16: from It.: beautiful sight]

BEM *abbrev. for* British Empire Medal.

bemire (bɪˈmaɪə) *vb.* (*tr.*) **1.** to soil as with mire. **2.** (*usually passive*) to stick fast in mire.

bemoan (bɪˈməʊn) *vb.* to mourn; lament (esp. in **bemoan one's fate**). [OE *bemǣnan*; see BE-, MOAN]

bemuse (bɪˈmjuːz) *vb.* (*tr.*) to confuse; bewilder.

bemused (bɪˈmjuːzd) *adj.* preoccupied; lost in thought.

ben[1] (bɛn) *Scot.* ~*n.* **1.** an inner room in a cottage. ~*prep., adv.* **2.** in; within; inside. ~Cf. **but**[2]. [OE *binnan*, from BE- + *innan* inside]

ben[2] (bɛn) *n. Scot., Irish.* a mountain peak: *Ben Lomond.* [C18: from Gaelic *beinn*, from *beann*]

Benares (bɪˈnɑːrɪz) *or* **Banaras** *n.* the former name of Varanasi.

Ben Bella (ˈbɛn ˈbɛlə) *n.* **Ahmed** (ˈɑːmɪd). born 1916, Algerian statesman: first prime minister (1962–65) and president (1963–65) of independent Algeria.

bench (bɛntʃ) *n.* **1.** a long seat for more than one person, usually lacking a back. **2.** a plain stout worktable. **3. the bench.** (*sometimes cap.*) **a.** a judge or magistrate sitting in court. **b.** judges or magistrates collectively. **4.** a ledge in a mine or quarry from which work is carried out. **5.** (in a gymnasium) a low table, which may be inclined, used for various exercises. **6.** a platform on which dogs, etc., are exhibited at shows. **7.** *N.Z.* a hollow formed by sheep

on a hillside. ~*vb.* (*tr.*) **8.** to provide with benches. **9.** to exhibit (a dog, etc.) at a show. [OE *benc*]

bencher (ˈbɛntʃə) *n.* (*often pl.*) *Brit.* **1.** a member of the governing body of one of the Inns of Court. **2.** See **backbencher.**

bench mark *n.* **1.** a mark on a stone post or other permanent feature, used as a reference point in surveying. **2.** a criterion by which to measure something; reference point.

bench warrant *n.* a warrant issued by a judge or court directing that an offender be apprehended.

bend[1] (bɛnd) *vb.* **bending, bent. 1.** to form or cause to form a curve. **2.** to turn or cause to turn from a particular direction: *the road bends left.* **3.** (*intr.;* often foll. by *down,* etc.) to incline the body; stoop; bow. **4.** to submit or cause to submit: *to bend before superior force.* **5.** (*tr.*) to turn or direct (one's eyes, steps, attention, etc.). **6.** (*tr.*) *Naut.* to attach or fasten, as a sail to a boom. **7. bend the rules.** *Inf.* to ignore rules or change them to suit one's own convenience. ~*n.* **8.** a curved part. **9.** *Naut.* a knot in a line for joining it to another or to an object. **10.** the act of bending. **11. round the bend.** *Brit. sl.* mad. [OE *bendan*] —ˈbendable *adj.* —ˈbendy *adj.*

bend[2] (bɛnd) *n. Heraldry.* a diagonal line traversing a shield. [OE *bend* BAND[2]]

Bendel (ˈbɛndɛl) *n.* a state of S Nigeria, on the Gulf of Guinea: mainly tropical rain forest. Capital: Benin City. Pop.: 4 125 500 (1984). Area: 39 737 sq. km (15 339 sq. miles). Former name (until 1976): **Mid-Western State.**

bender (ˈbɛndə) *n. Inf.* a drinking bout.

Bendigo (ˈbɛndɪˌgəʊ) *n.* a city in SE Australia, in central Victoria: founded in 1851 after the discovery of gold. Pop.: 62 380 (1986).

bends (bɛndz) *pl. n.* (*functioning as sing. or pl.*) **the.** a nontechnical name for **decompression sickness.**

bend sinister *n. Heraldry.* a diagonal line bisecting a shield from the top right to the bottom left, typically indicating a bastard line.

beneath (bɪˈniːθ) *prep.* **1.** below, esp. if covered, protected, or obscured by. **2.** not as great or good as would be demanded by: *beneath his dignity.* ~*adv.* **3.** below; underneath. [OE *beneothan,* from BE- + *neothan* low]

benedicite (ˌbɛnɪˈdaɪsɪtɪ) *n.* (esp. in Christian religious orders) a blessing or grace. [C13: from L, from *benedicere,* from *bene* well + *dicere* to speak]

Benedict (ˈbɛnɪˌdɪkt) *n.* **Saint.** ?480–?547 A.D., Italian monk: founded the Benedictine order at Monte Cassino in Italy in about 540 A.D. His *Regula Monachorum* became the basis of all Western Christian monastic orders. Feast day: March 21.

Benedict XV *n.* original name *Giacomo della Chiesa.* 1854–1922, pope (1914–22); noted for his repeated attempts to end World War I and for his organization of war relief.

Benedictine *n.* **1.** (ˌbɛnɪˈdɪktɪn, -taɪn). a monk or nun who is a member of the order of Saint Benedict. **2.** (ˌbɛnɪˈdɪktiːn). a greenish-yellow liqueur first made at the Benedictine monastery at Fécamp in France in about 1510. ~*adj.* (ˌbɛnɪˈdɪktɪn, -taɪn). **3.** of or relating to Saint Benedict or his order.

benediction (ˌbɛnɪˈdɪkʃən) *n.* **1.** an invocation of divine blessing. **2.** a Roman Catholic service in which the congregation is blessed with the sacrament. **3.** the state of being blessed. [C15: from L *benedictio,* from *benedicere* to bless; see BENEDICITE] —**bene'dictory** *adj.*

Benedictus (ˌbɛnɪˈdɪktəs) *n.* (*sometimes not cap.*) *Christianity.* **1.** a canticle beginning *Benedictus qui venit in nomine Domini* in Latin and *Blessed is he that cometh in the name of the Lord* in English. **2.** a canticle beginning *Benedictus Dominus Deus Israel* in Latin and *Blessed be the Lord God of Israel* in English.

benefaction (ˌbɛnɪˈfækʃən) *n.* **1.** the act of doing good, esp. by giving a donation to charity. **2.** the donation or help given. [C17: from LL *benefactiō,* from L *bene* well + *facere* to do]

benefactor (ˈbɛnɪˌfæktə, ˌbɛnɪˈfæk-) *n.* a person who supports or helps a person, institution, etc., esp. by giving money. —ˈbene,factress *fem. n.*

benefice (ˈbɛnɪfɪs) *n.* **1.** *Christianity.* an endowed Church office yielding an income to its holder; a Church living. **2.** the property or revenue attached to such an office. [C14: from OF, from L *beneficium* benefit, from *bene* well + *facere* to do] —ˈbeneficed *adj.*

beneficent (bɪˈnɛfɪsᵊnt) *adj.* charitable; generous. [C17: from L *beneficus;* see BENEFICE] —**beˈneficence** *n.*

beneficial (ˌbɛnɪˈfɪʃəl) *adj.* **1.** (sometimes foll. by *to*) advantageous. **2.** *Law.* entitling a person to receive the profits or proceeds of property. [C15: from LL *beneficiālis,* from L *beneficium* kindness]

beneficiary (ˌbɛnɪˈfɪʃərɪ) *n., pl.* -**ciaries. 1.** a person who gains or benefits. **2.** *Law.* a person entitled to receive funds or other property under a trust, will, etc. **3.** the holder of a benefice. **4.** *N.Z.* a person who receives government assistance: *social security beneficiary.* ~*adj.* **5.** of or relating to a benefice.

benefit (ˈbɛnɪfɪt) *n.* **1.** something that improves or promotes. **2.** advantage or sake. **3.** (*sometimes pl.*) a payment or series of payments made by an institution or government to a person who is ill, unemployed, etc. **4.** a theatrical performance, sports event, etc., to raise money for a charity. ~*vb.* -**fiting, -fited** or *U.S.* -**fitting, -fitted. 5.** to do or receive good; profit. [C14: from Anglo-F *benfet,* from L *benefactum,* from *bene facere* to do well]

benefit of clergy *n. Christianity.* **1.** sanction by the church: *marriage without benefit of clergy.* **2.** (in the Middle Ages) a privilege that placed the clergy outside the jurisdiction of secular courts.

benefit society *n.* a U.S. term for **friendly society.**

Benelux (ˈbɛnɪˌlʌks) *n.* **1.** the customs union formed by Belgium, the Netherlands, and Luxembourg in 1948; became an economic union in 1960. **2.** these countries collectively.

Beneš (*Czech* ˈbɛnɛʃ) *n.* **Eduard** (ˈeːduart). 1884–1948, Czech statesman; president of Czechoslovakia (1935–38; 1946–48) and of its government in exile (1939–45).

Benét (bəˈneɪ) *n.* **Stephen Vincent.** 1898–1943, U.S. poet and novelist, best known for his poem on the American Civil War *John Brown's Body* (1928).

Benevento (ˌbɛnəˈvɛntəʊ) *n.* a city in S Italy, in N Campania: at various times under Samnite, Roman, Lombard, Saracen, Norman, and papal rule. Pop.: 62 636 (1981). Ancient name: **Beneventum** (ˌbɛnəˈvɛntʊm).

benevolence (bɪˈnɛvələns) *n.* **1.** inclination to do good; charity. **2.** an act of kindness.

benevolent (bɪˈnɛvələnt) *adj.* **1.** intending or showing goodwill; kindly; friendly. **2.** doing good rather than making profit; charitable: *a benevolent organization.* [C15: from L *benevolēns,* from *bene* well + *velle* to wish]

Benfleet (ˈbɛnˌfliːt) *n.* a town in SE England, in S Essex on an inlet of the Thames estuary. Pop.: 50 240 (1981).

BEng *abbrev. for* Bachelor of Engineering.

Bengal (bɛŋˈgɔːl, bɛŋ-) *n.* **1.** a former province of NE India, in the great deltas of the Ganges and Brahmaputra Rivers: in 1947 divided into West Bengal (belonging to India) and East Bengal (Bangladesh). **2. Bay of.** a wide arm of the Indian Ocean, between India and Burma.

Bengali (bɛŋˈgɔːlɪ, bɛŋ-) *n.* **1.** a member of a people living chiefly in Bangladesh and in West Bengal. **2.** their language. ~*adj.* **3.** of or relating to Bengal, the Bengalis, or their language.

Bengal light *n.* a firework or flare that burns with a bright blue light, formerly used as a signal.

Bengbu (ˈbɛŋˈbuː), **Pengpu** or **Pang-fou** *n.* a city in E China, in Anhui province.

Benghazi or **Bengasi** (bɛnˈgɑːzɪ) *n.* a port in N Libya, on the Gulf of Sidra: centre of Italian colonization (1911–42); scene of much fighting in World War II. Pop.: 650 000 (1984 est.). Ancient names: **Hesperides, Berenice** (bɛrəˈnaɪsɪ).

Benguela (bɛŋˈgwɛlə) *n.* a port in W Angola: founded in 1617; a terminus (with Lobito) of the railway that runs from Beira in Mozambique through the Copper Belt of Zambia and Zimbabwe. Pop.: 41 000 (1975).

Ben-Gurion (bɛnˈguərɪən) *n.* **David,** original name *David Gruen.* 1886–1973, Israeli socialist statesman, born in Poland; first prime minister of Israel (1948–53, 1955–63).

Beni (*Spanish* ˈbeni) *n.* a river in N Bolivia, rising in the E Cordillera of the Andes and flowing north to the Marmoré River. Length: over 1600 km (1000 miles).

benighted (bɪˈnaɪtɪd) *adj.* **1.** lacking cultural, moral, or intellectual enlightenment. **2.** *Arch.* overtaken by night. —**beˈnightedness** *n.*

benign (bɪˈnaɪn) *adj.* **1.** showing kindliness; genial. **2.** (of soil, climate, etc.) mild; gentle. **3.** favourable; propitious. **4.** *Pathol.* (of a tumour, etc.) not malignant. [C14:

from OF *benigne,* from L *benignus,* from *bene* well + *gignere* to produce] —**beˈnignly** *adv.*

benignant (bɪˈnɪgnənt) *adj.* **1.** kind; gracious. **2.** a less common word for **benign** (senses 3, 4). —**beˈnignancy** *n.*

benignity (bɪˈnɪgnɪtɪ) *n., pl.* -**ties. 1.** the quality of being benign. **2.** a kind or gracious act.

Beni Hasan (ˈbɛnɪ hæˈsɑːn) *n.* a village in central Egypt, on the Nile, with cliff-cut tombs dating from 2000 B.C.

Benin (bɛˈniːn) *n.* **1.** a republic in W Africa, on the **Bight of Benin,** a section of the Gulf of Guinea: in the early 19th century a powerful Negro kingdom, famed for its women warriors; became a French colony in 1893, gaining independence in 1960. It consists chiefly of coastal lagoons and swamps in the south, a fertile plain and marshes in the centre, and the Atakora Mountains in the northwest. Official language: French. Currency: franc. Capital: Porto Novo. Pop.: 4 153 000 (1987 est.). Area: 112 622 sq. km (43 474 sq. miles). Official name: **People's Republic of Benin.** Former name (until 1975): **Dahomey. 2.** a former kingdom of W Africa, powerful from the 14th to the 17th centuries: now a province of S Nigeria: noted for its bronzes. —**Beˌniˈnese** *adj., n.*

Benin City *n.* a city in S Nigeria, capital of Bendel state: former capital of the kingdom of Benin. Pop.: 231 976 (1984).

benison (ˈbɛnɪzᵊn, -sᵊn) *n. Arch.* a blessing. [C13: from OF *beneison,* from L *benedictiō* BENEDICTION]

Benjamin[1] (ˈbɛndʒəmɪn) *n.* **1.** *Old Testament.* **a.** the youngest and best-loved son of Jacob and Rachel (Genesis 35:16–18; 42:4). **b.** the tribe descended from this patriarch. **c.** the territory of this tribe, northwest of the Dead Sea. **2.** *Archaic.* a youngest and favourite son.

Benjamin[2] (ˈbɛndʒəmɪn) *n.* **Arthur.** 1893–1960, Australian composer. In addition to *Jamaican Rumba* (1938), he wrote five operas and a harmonica concerto (1953).

Ben Lomond (bɛn ˈləʊmənd) *n.* **1.** a mountain in W central Scotland, on the E side of Loch Lomond. Height: 973 m (3192 ft.). **2.** a mountain in NE Tasmania. Height: 1527 m (5010 ft.). **3.** a mountain in SE Australia, in NE New South Wales. Height: 1520 m (4986 ft.).

Bennett (ˈbɛnɪt) *n.* **1. Alan.** born 1934, British actor and playwright. His plays include *Forty Years On* (1968), *The Old Country* (1977), and many television productions. **2. (Enoch) Arnold.** 1867–1931, English novelist, noted for *The Old Wives' Tale* (1908), *Clayhanger* (1910), and other works set in the Staffordshire Potteries. **3. Richard Rodney.** born 1936, English composer, noted for his operas *The Mines of Sulphur* (1965) and *Victory* (1970). **4.** Sir **William Sterndale.** 1816–75, English composer.

Ben Nevis (bɛn ˈnɛvɪs) *n.* a mountain in W Scotland, in the Grampian mountains: highest peak in Great Britain. Height: 1343 m (4406 ft.).

Bennington (ˈbɛnɪŋtən) *n.* a town in SW Vermont: the site of a British defeat (1777) in the War of American Independence. Pop.: 15 815 (1980).

Benoît de Sainte-Maure (*French* bənwa də sɛ̃t mɔr) *n.* 12th-century French trouvère: author of the *Roman de Troie,* which contains the episode of Troilus and Cressida.

Benoni (bɪˈnəʊnɪ) *n.* a city in NE South Africa, in S Transvaal: gold mines. Pop.: 206 810 (1980 est.).

bent[1] (bɛnt) *adj.* **1.** not straight; curved. **2.** (foll. by *on*) resolved (to); determined (to). **3.** *Sl.* **a.** dishonest; corrupt. **b.** (of goods) stolen. **c.** crazy. **d.** sexually deviant. ~*n.* **4.** personal inclination or aptitude. **5.** capacity of endurance (esp. in **to the top of one's bent**).

bent[2] (bɛnt) *n.* **1.** short for **bent grass. 2.** *Arch.* any stiff grass or sedge. **3.** *Arch. or dialect.* heath or moorland. [OE *bionot*]

bent grass *n.* a perennial grass which has a spreading panicle of tiny flowers sometimes planted for hay or in lawns.

Bentham (ˈbɛnθəm) *n.* **Jeremy.** 1748–1832, English philosopher and jurist: a founder of utilitarianism. His works include *A Fragment on Government* (1776) and *Introduction to the Principles of Morals and Legislation* (1789). —**ˈBenthamism** *n.* —**ˈBenthamite** *n., adj.*

benthos (ˈbɛnθɒs) *n.* the animals and plants living at the bottom of a sea or lake. [C19: from Gk: depth; rel. to *bathus* deep] —**ˈbenthic** *adj.*

Bentinck ('bɛntɪŋk) n. Lord **William Cavendish**. 1774–1839, British statesman, first governor general of India (1828–35).

Bentley ('bɛntlɪ) n. **1. Edmund Clerihew**. 1875–1956, English journalist, noted for his invention of the clerihew. **2. Richard.** 1662–1742, English classical scholar, noted for his imaginative textual emendations.

bentonite ('bɛntə‚naɪt) n. a clay that swells as it absorbs water: used as a filler in various industries. [after Fort *Benton*, Montana, U.S.A., where found]

bentwood ('bɛnt‚wʊd) n. **a.** wood bent in moulds after being heated by steaming, used mainly for furniture. **b.** (*as modifier): a bentwood chair.*

Benue ('bɛnʊ‚eɪ) n. **1.** a state of SE Nigeria, formed in 1976 from part of Benue-Plateau state. Capital: Makurdi. Pop.: 3 968 200 (1983 est.). Area: 19 200 sq. km (7412 sq. miles). **2.** a river in W Africa, rising in N Cameroon and flowing west across Nigeria: chief tributary of the River Niger. Length: 1400 km (870 miles).

benumb (bɪ'nʌm) vb. (tr.) **1.** to make numb or powerless; deaden, as by cold. **2.** (usually passive) to stupefy (the mind, senses, will, etc.).

Benxi ('bɛn'ʃiː), **Penchi,** or **Penki** n. an industrial city in SE China, in S Liaoning province. Pop.: 810 500 (1985 est.).

Benz (bɛnz; German bɛnts) n. **Karl** (**Friedrich**) (karl). 1844–1929, German engineer; designed and built the first car to be driven by an internal-combustion engine (1885).

Benzedrine ('bɛnzɪ‚driːn, -drɪn) n. a trademark for **amphetamine.**

benzene ('bɛnziːn) n. a colourless flammable poisonous liquid used in the manufacture of styrene, phenol, etc., as a solvent for fats, resins, etc., and as an insecticide. Formula: C_6H_6.

benzene ring n. the hexagonal ring of bonded carbon atoms in the benzene molecule.

benzine ('bɛnziːn, bɛn'ziːn) or **benzin** ('bɛnzɪn) n. **1.** a volatile mixture of the lighter hydrocarbon constituents of petroleum. **2.** Austral. & N.Z. a rare name for **petrol.**

benzo- or **benz-** combining form. **1.** indicating a fused benzene ring. **2.** indicating derivation from benzene or benzoic acid or the presence of phenyl groups. [from BENZOIN]

benzoate ('bɛnzəʊ‚eɪt, -ɪt) n. a salt or ester of benzoic acid.

benzocaine ('bɛnzəʊ‚keɪn) n. a white crystalline ester used as a local anaesthetic.

benzoic (bɛn'zəʊɪk) adj. of, containing, or derived from benzoic acid or benzoin.

benzoic acid n. a white crystalline solid occurring in many natural resins, used in plasticizers and dyes and as a food preservative (**E210**).

benzoin ('bɛnzɔɪn, -zəʊɪn) n. a gum resin containing benzoic acid, obtained from various tropical Asian trees and used in ointments, perfume, etc. [C16: from F benjoin, from OCatalan benjui, from Ar. lubān jāwī, lit.: frankincense of Java]

benzol or **benzole** ('bɛnzɒl) n. **1.** a crude form of benzene obtained from coal tar or coal gas and used as a fuel. **2.** an obsolete name for **benzene.**

Ben-Zvi (bɛn'zviː; Hebrew bɛn'tsviː) n. **Itzhak** ('ɪtsxak). 1884–1963, Israeli statesman; president (1952–63).

Beograd (bɛ'ɔgrad) n. the Serbo-Croatian name for **Belgrade.**

bequeath (bɪ'kwiːð, -'kwiːθ) vb. (tr.) **1.** Law. to dispose of (property) by will. **2.** to hand down; pass on. [OE becwethan] —**be'queathal** n.

bequest (bɪ'kwɛst) n. **1.** the act of bequeathing. **2.** something that is bequeathed. [C14: BE- + OE -cwiss degree]

Béranger (French berɑ̃ʒe) n. **Pierre Jean de** (pjɛr ʒɑ̃ də). 1780–1857, French lyric and satirical poet.

Berar (bɛ'rɑː) n. a region of W central India: part of Madhya Pradesh state since 1950; important for cotton growing.

berate (bɪ'reɪt) vb. (tr.) to scold harshly.

Berber ('bɜːbə) n. **1.** a member of a Caucasoid Muslim people of N Africa. **2.** the language of this people. ~adj. **3.** of or relating to this people or their language.

Berbera ('bɜːbərə) n. a port in N Somalia, on the Gulf of Aden. Pop.: 65 000 (1980 est.).

berberis ('bɜːbərɪs) n. any of a genus of mainly N temperate shrubs. See **barberry.** [C19: from Med. L, from ?]

berceuse (French bɛrsøz) n. **1.** a lullaby. **2.** an instrumental piece suggestive of this. [C19: from F: lullaby]

Berchtesgaden (German 'bɛrçtəsgaːdən) n. a town in West Germany, in SE Bavaria: site of the fortified mountain retreat of Adolf Hitler. Pop.: 8186 (1983).

Berdyayev (Russian bɪr'djajɪf) n. **Nikolai Aleksandrovich** (nika'laj alɪk'sandrəvɪtʃ). 1874–1948, Russian philosopher. Although he was a Marxist, his Christian views led him to criticize Soviet communism and he was forced into exile (1922).

bereave (bɪ'riːv) vb. (tr.) (usually foll. by of) to deprive (of) something or someone valued, esp. through death. [OE bereafian] —**be'reaved** adj. —**be'reavement** n.

bereft (bɪ'rɛft) adj. (usually foll. by of) deprived; parted (from): bereft of hope.

Berenson ('bɛrənsən) n. **Bernard.** 1865–1959, U.S. art historian, born in Lithuania: an authority on art of the Italian Renaissance.

beret ('bɛreɪ) n. a round close-fitting brimless cap. [C19: from F béret, from OProvençal berret]

Berezina (Russian bɪrɪzi'na) n. a river in the W Soviet Union, in the Byelorussian SSR, rising in the north and flowing south to the River Dnieper: linked with the River Dvina and the Baltic Sea by the **Berezina Canal.** Length: 563 km (350 miles).

Berezniki (Russian bɪrɪzni'ki) n. a city in the E Soviet Union: chemical industries. Pop.: 200 000 (1987).

berg[1] (bɜːg) n. short for **iceberg.**

berg[2] (bɜːg) n. a South African word for **mountain.**

Berg (bɜːg; German bɛrk) n. **Alban** ('albaːn). 1885–1935, Austrian composer: a pupil of Schoenberg. His works include the operas Wozzeck (1921) and Lulu (1935), chamber works, and songs.

Bergamo (Italian 'bergamo) n. a walled city in N Italy, in Lombardy. Pop.: 118 959 (1986).

bergamot ('bɜːgə‚mɒt) n. **1.** a small Asian tree having sour pear-shaped fruit. **2. essence of bergamot.** a fragrant essential oil from the fruit rind of this plant, used in perfumery. **3.** a Mediterranean mint that yields a similar oil. [C17: from F bergamote, from It. bergamotta, of Turkic origin]

Bergen n. **1.** (Norwegian 'bærgən) a port in SW Norway: chief city in medieval times. Pop.: 208 809 (1987). **2.** ('bɛrxən). the Flemish name for **Mons.**

Bergerac (French bɛrʒərak) n. See **Cyrano de Bergerac.**

Bergie ('bɜːgiː) n. S. African inf. a vagabond, esp. one living on the slopes of Table Mountain in SW South Africa. [from Afrik. berg mountain]

Bergius (German 'bɛrgjʊs) n. **Friedrich** ('friːdrɪç). 1884–1949, German chemist, who invented a process for producing oil by high-pressure hydrogenation of coal: Nobel prize for chemistry 1931.

Bergman ('bɜːgmən) n. **1. Ingmar** ('ɪŋmar). born 1918, Swedish film and stage director, whose films include The Seventh Seal (1956), Wild Strawberries (1957), Persona (1966), Scenes from a Marriage (1974), Autumn Sonata (1978), and Fanny and Alexander (1982). **2. Ingrid.** 1915–82, Swedish film and stage actress, working in Hollywood 1938–48; noted for her leading roles in many films, including Casablanca (1942), For Whom the Bell Tolls (1943), Anastasia (1956), and The Inn of the Sixth Happiness (1958).

bergschrund ('bɛrkʃrʊnt) n. a crevasse at the head of a glacier. [C19: G: mountain crack]

Bergson ('bɜːgsən; French bɛrksɔn) n. **Henri Louis** (ɑ̃ri lwi). 1859–1941, French philosopher, who sought to bridge the gap between metaphysics and science. His main works are Memory and Matter (1896, trans. 1911) and Creative Evolution (1907, trans. 1911): Nobel prize for literature 1927. —**Bergsonian** (bɜːg'səʊnɪən) adj., n. —'**Bergson‚ism** n.

bergwind ('bɜːxvənt) n. a hot dry wind in South Africa blowing from the plateau down to the coast.

Beria ('bɛrɪə; Russian 'bjerɪjə) n. **Lavrenti Pavlovich** (la'vrjentɪj 'pavləvɪtʃ). 1899–1953, Soviet chief of secret police; killed by his associates shortly after Stalin's death.

beriberi (‚bɛrɪ'bɛrɪ) n. a disease, endemic in E and S Asia, caused by dietary deficiency of thiamine (vitamin B_1). [C19: from Sinhalese, by reduplication from beri weakness]

Bering or **Behring** ('bɛrɪŋ, 'bɛər-; *Danish* 'be:reŋ) *n.* **Vitus** ('vi:tʊs). 1681–1741, Danish navigator, who explored the N Pacific for the Russians and discovered Bering Island and the Bering Strait.

Bering Sea *n.* a part of the N Pacific Ocean, between NE Siberia and Alaska. Area: about 2 275 000 sq. km (878 000 sq. miles).

Bering Strait *n.* a strait between Alaska and the Soviet Union, connecting the Bering Sea and the Arctic Ocean.

Berio (*Italian* 'berjo) *n.* **Luciano** (lu'tʃano). born 1925, Italian composer, noted esp. for works that exploit instrumental and vocal timbre and technique.

Beriosova (bɛrɪ'əʊsəvə) *n.* **Svetlana** (svɪt'lanə). born 1932, British ballet dancer, born in Russia.

berk (bɜːk) *n. Brit. sl.* a variant spelling of **burk.**

Berkeley[1] ('bɑːklɪ) *n.* a city in W California, on San Francisco Bay: seat of the University of California. Pop.: 103 328 (1980).

Berkeley[2] *n.* **1.** ('bɑːklɪ). **Busby.** real name *William Berkeley Enos.* 1895–1976, U.S. dance director, noted esp. for his elaborate choreography in film musicals. **2.** ('bɑːklɪ). **George.** 1685–1753, Irish philosopher and Anglican bishop, whose system of subjective idealism was expounded in his works *A Treatise concerning the Principles of Human Knowledge* (1710) and *Three Dialogues between Hylas and Philonous* (1713). He also wrote *Essay towards a New Theory of Vision* (1709). **3.** ('bɑːklɪ). Sir **Lennox** (**Randal Francis**). born 1903, English composer.

berkelium (bɜː'kiːlɪəm, 'bɜːklɪəm) *n.* a radioactive transuranic element produced by bombardment of americium. Symbol: Bk; atomic no.: 97; half-life of most stable isotope, [247]Bk: 1400 years. [C20: after BERKELEY[1], where it was discovered]

Berks (bɑːks) *abbrev. for* Berkshire.

Berkshire ('bɑːkʃɪə, -ʃə) *n.* a county of S England: the River Thames marks the N boundary and the **Berkshire Downs** occupy central parts. Administrative centre: Reading. Pop.: 734 100 (1986 est.). Area: 1259 sq. km (486 sq. miles). Abbrev.: **Berks.**

berley or **burley** ('bɜːlɪ) *Austral.* ~*n.* **1.** groundbait. **2.** *Sl.* rubbish, nonsense. ~*vb.* **3.** (*tr.*) to scatter groundbait over. **4.** (*tr.*) to hurry (someone); urge on. [from ?]

Berlichingen (*German* 'bɛrlɪçɪŋən) *n.* **Götz von** (gœts fɔn), called *the Iron Hand.* 1480–1562, German warrior knight, who robbed merchants and kidnapped nobles for ransom.

berlin (bə'lɪn, 'bɜːlɪn) *n.* **1.** (*sometimes cap.*) Also called: **berlin wool.** a fine wool yarn used for tapestry work, etc. **2.** a four-wheeled two-seated covered carriage, popular in the 18th century. [after BERLIN[1]]

Berlin[1] (bɜː'lɪn; *German* bɛr'liːn) *n.* a city in N Germany, divided since 1945 into the eastern sector, capital of East Germany, and the western sectors, which form an exclave in East German territory closely affiliated politically and economically with West Germany: a wall dividing the sectors was built in 1961 by the East German authorities to stop the flow of refugees from east to west; formerly the capital of Brandenburg, Prussia, and Germany. Pop.: (East Berlin) 1 223 309 (1986); (West Berlin) 1 867 700 (1986). —**Ber'liner** *n.*

Berlin[2] (bɜː'lɪn) *n.* **1.** **Irving.** original name *Israel Baline,* born 1888, U.S. composer and writer of lyrics, born in Russia. His musical comedies include *Annie Get Your Gun* (1946); his most popular song is *White Christmas.* **2.** Sir **Isaiah.** born 1909, British philosopher, historian, and diplomat. His books include *The Inevitability of History* (1954).

Berlioz ('bɛəlɪˌəʊz; *French* bɛrljoz) *n.* **Hector** (ɛktər). 1803–69, French composer, regarded as a pioneer of modern orchestration. His works include the cantata *La Damnation de Faust* (1846), the operas *Les Troyens* (1856–59) and *Béatrice et Bénédict* (1860–62), the *Symphonie fantastique* (1830), and the oratorio *L'Enfance du Christ* (1854).

berm or **berme** (bɜːm) *n.* **1.** a narrow path or ledge as at the edge of a slope, road, or canal. **2.** *N.Z.* the grass verge of a suburban street, usually kept mown. [C18: from F *berme,* from Du. *berm*]

Bermejo (*Spanish* ber'mexo) *n.* a river in Argentina, rising in the northwest and flowing southeast to the Paraguay River. Length: about 1600 km (1000 miles).

Bermuda (bə'mjuːdə) *n.* a British colony consisting of a group of over 300 coral islands (**the Bermudas**) in the NW Atlantic: discovered in 1515, first colonized by the British in 1684. Capital: Hamilton. Pop.: 59 000 (1986). Area: 53 sq. km (20 sq. miles). —**Ber'mudan** or **Ber'mudian** *n., adj.*

Bermuda shorts *pl. n.* close-fitting shorts that come down to the knees.

Bermuda Triangle *n.* an area in the Atlantic Ocean bounded by Bermuda, Puerto Rico, and Florida where ships and aeroplanes are alleged to have disappeared mysteriously.

Bern (bɜːn; *German* bɛrn) *n.* **1.** the capital of Switzerland, in the W part, on the Aar River: entered the Swiss confederation in 1353 and became the capital in 1848. Pop.: 138 600 (1985). **2.** a canton of Switzerland, between the French frontier and the Bernese Alps. Capital: Bern. Pop.: 925 600 (1986 est.). Area: 6884 sq. km (2658 sq. miles). French name: **Berne** (bɛrn).

Bernadette (ˌbɜːnə'dɛt) *n.* **Saint.** original name *Marie Bernarde Soubirous.* 1844–79, French peasant girl born in Lourdes, whose visions of the Virgin Mary led to the establishment of Lourdes as a centre of pilgrimage, esp. for the sick or crippled. Feast day: Feb. 18.

Bernadotte ('bɜːnəˌdɒt; *French* bɛrnadɔt) *n.* **Jean Baptiste Jules** (ʒɑ̃ batist ʒyl). 1764–1844, French marshal under Napoleon; king of Norway and Sweden (1818–44) as Charles XIV.

Bernard *n.* **1.** (*French* bɛrnar). **Claude** (klod). 1813–78, French physiologist, noted for his research on the action of secretions of the alimentary canal and the glycogenic function of the liver. **2.** ('bɜːnəd) **Saint,** known as *Bernard of Menthon* and the *Apostle of the Alps.* 923–1008, French monk who founded hospices in the Alpine passes.

Bernard of Clairvaux *n.* **Saint.** ?1090–1153, French abbot and theologian, who founded the stricter branch of the Cistercians in 1115.

Bernese Alps or **Oberland** ('bɜːniːz) *n.* a mountain range in SW Switzerland, the N central part of the Alps. Highest peak: Finsteraarhorn, 4274 m (14 022 ft.).

Bernhardt ('bɜːnhɑːt; *French* bɛrnar) *n.* **Sarah.** original name *Rosine Bernard.* 1844–1923, French actress, regarded as one of the greatest tragic actresses of all time.

Bernina (bə'niːnə; *Italian* ber'nina) *n.* **Piz.** a mountain in SE Switzerland, the highest peak of the **Bernina Alps,** in the S Rhaetian Alps. Height: 4049 m (13 284 ft.).

Bernina Pass *n.* a pass in the Alps between SE Switzerland and N Italy, east of Piz Bernina. Height: 2323 m (7622 ft.).

Bernini (*Italian* bernini) *n.* **Giovanni Lorenzo** (dʒo'vanni lo'rɛntso). 1598–1680, Italian painter, architect, and sculptor: the greatest exponent of the Italian baroque.

Bernoulli or **Bernouilli** (*French* bɛrnuji; *German* bɛr'nʊli) *n.* **1.** **Daniel** (danjɛl), son of Jean Bernoulli. 1700–82, Swiss mathematician and physicist, who developed an early form of the kinetic theory of gases and stated the principle of conservation of energy in fluid dynamics. **2.** **Jacques** (ʒɑk) or **Jakob** ('jɑːkɔp). 1654–1705, Swiss mathematician, noted for his work on calculus and the theory of probability. **3.** his brother, **Jean** (ʒɑ̃) or **Johann** (jo'han). 1667–1748, Swiss mathematician who developed the calculus of variations.

Bernstein ('bɜːnstaɪn, -stiːn) *n.* **Leonard.** born 1918, U.S. conductor and composer, whose works include *The Age of Anxiety* (1949), the score of the musical *West Side Story* (1957), and *Mass* (1971).

berretta (bɪ'rɛtə) *n.* a variant spelling of **biretta.**

berry ('bɛrɪ) *n., pl.* **-ries. 1.** any of various small edible fruits such as the blackberry and strawberry. **2.** *Bot.* a fruit with two or more seeds and a fleshy pericarp, such as the grape or gooseberry. **3.** any of various seeds or dried kernels, such as a coffee bean. **4.** the egg of a lobster, crayfish, or similar animal. ~*vb.* **-rying, -ried.** (*intr.*) **5.** to bear or produce berries. **6.** to gather or look for berries. [OE *berie*]

Berry ('bɛrɪ) *n.* **Chuck,** full name *Charles Edward Berry.* born 1926, U.S. rock-and-roll guitarist, singer, and songwriter. His frequently-covered songs include "Maybellene" (1955), "Roll over Beethoven" (1956), "Johnny B. Goode" (1958), "Memphis, Tennessee" (1959), and "Promised Land" (1964).

berserk (bə'zɜːk, -'sɜːk) *adj.* **1.** frenziedly violent or destructive (esp. in **go berserk**). ~*n.* **2.** Also called: **berserker.** one of a class of ancient Norse warriors who fought frenziedly. [C19: Icelandic *berserkr*, from *björn* bear + *serkr* shirt]

berth (bɜːθ) *n.* **1.** a bed or bunk in a vessel or train. **2.** *Naut.* a place assigned to a ship at a mooring. **3.** *Naut.* sufficient room for a ship to manoeuvre. **4. give a wide berth to.** to keep clear of. **5.** *Inf.* a job, esp. as a member of a ship's crew. ~*vb.* **6.** (*tr.*) *Naut.* to assign a berth to (a vessel). **7.** *Naut.* to dock (a vessel). **8.** (*tr.*) to provide with a sleeping place. **9.** (*intr.*) *Naut.* to pick up a mooring in an anchorage. [C17: prob. from BEAR¹ + -TH¹]

bertha ('bɜːθə) *n.* a wide deep collar, often of lace, usually to cover a low neckline. [C19: from F *berthe*, from *Berthe*, 8th-cent. Frankish queen]

Bertolucci (*Italian* berto'luttʃi) *n.* **Bernardo** (ber'nardo). born 1940, Italian film director: his films include *The Spider's Stratagem* (1970), *The Conformist* (1970), *1900* (1976), and *The Last Emperor* (1987).

Berwickshire ('bɛrɪk,ʃɪə, -ʃə) *n.* (until 1975) a county of SE Scotland, now part of the Borders region.

Berwick-upon-Tweed (twiːd) *n.* a town in N England, in N Northumberland at the mouth of the Tweed: much involved in border disputes between England and Scotland between the 12th and 16th centuries; neutral territory 1551–1885. Pop.: 12 169 (1981). Also called: **Berwick.**

beryl ('bɛrɪl) *n.* a green, blue, yellow, pink, or white hard mineral consisting of beryllium aluminium silicate in hexagonal crystalline form. Emerald and aquamarine are transparent varieties. [C13: from OF, from L, from Gk *bērullos*] —'**beryline** *adj.*

beryllium (bɛ'rɪlɪəm) *n.* a corrosion-resistant toxic silvery-white metallic element used mainly in x-ray windows and alloys. Symbol: Be; atomic no.: 4; atomic wt.: 9.012. [C19: from L, from Gk *bērullos*]

Berzelius (bə'ziːlɪəs; *Swedish* bær'seːlius) *n.* Baron **Jöns Jakob** ('jœns 'jɑːkɔp). 1779–1848, Swedish chemist, who invented the present system of chemical symbols and formulas, discovered several elements, and determined the atomic and molecular weight of many substances.

Bes (bɛs) *n.* an ancient Egyptian god represented as a grotesque hairy dwarf: the patron of music and pleasure.

Besançon (*French* bəzɑ̃sɔ̃) *n.* a city in E France, on the Doubs River: university (1422). Pop.: 119 901 (1983 est.).

Besant ('bɛzənt, bɪ'zænt) *n.* **Annie,** *née* **Wood.** 1847–1933, British theosophist, writer, and political reformer in England and India.

beseech (bɪ'siːtʃ) *vb.* **-seeching, -sought** *or* **-seeched.** (*tr.*) to ask (someone) earnestly (to do something or for something); beg. [C12: see BE-, SEEK]

beseem (bɪ'siːm) *vb.* *Arch.* to be suitable for or worthy of; befit.

beset (bɪ'sɛt) *vb.* **-setting, -set.** (*tr.*) **1.** (esp. of dangers or temptations) to trouble or harass constantly. **2.** to surround or attack from all sides. **3.** *Arch.* to cover with, esp. with jewels.

besetting (bɪ'sɛtɪŋ) *adj.* tempting, harassing, or assailing (esp. in **besetting sin**).

beshrew (bɪ'ʃruː) *vb.* (*tr.*) *Arch.* to wish evil on; curse (used in mild oaths). [C14: see BE-, SHREW]

beside (bɪ'saɪd) *prep.* **1.** next to; at, by, or to the side of. **2.** as compared with. **3.** away from; wide of. **4.** *Arch.* besides. **5. beside oneself.** (*postpositive*; often foll. by *with*) overwhelmed; overwrought: *beside oneself with grief.* ~*adv.* **6.** at, by, to, or along the side of something or someone. [OE *be sīdan*; see BY, SIDE]

besides (bɪ'saɪdz) *prep.* **1.** apart from; even considering. ~ *sentence connector.* **2.** anyway; moreover. ~*adv.* **3.** as well.

besiege (bɪ'siːdʒ) *vb.* (*tr.*) **1.** to surround (a fortified area) with military forces to bring about its surrender. **2.** to crowd round; hem in. **3.** to overwhelm, as with requests. —be'**sieger** *n.*

besmear (bɪ'smɪə) *vb.* (*tr.*) **1.** to smear over; daub. **2.** to sully; defile (often in **besmear (a person's) reputation**).

besmirch (bɪ'smɜːtʃ) *vb.* (*tr.*) **1.** to make dirty; soil. **2.** to reduce the brightness of. **3.** to sully (often in **besmirch (a person's) name**).

besom¹ ('biːzəm) *n.* a broom, esp. one made of a bundle of twigs tied to a handle. [OE *besma*]

besom² ('bɪzəm) *n. Scot. & N English dialect.* a derogatory term for a **woman.** [?from OE *bysen* example; rel. to ON *bysn* wonder]

besotted (bɪ'sɒtɪd) *adj.* **1.** stupefied with drink. **2.** infatuated; doting. **3.** foolish; muddled.

besought (bɪ'sɔːt) *vb.* the past tense and past participle of **beseech.**

bespangle (bɪ'spæŋgəl) *vb.* (*tr.*) to cover or adorn with or as if with spangles.

bespatter (bɪ'spætə) *vb.* (*tr.*) **1.** to splash, as with dirty water. **2.** to defile; besmirch.

bespeak (bɪ'spiːk) *vb.* **-speaking, -spoke; -spoken** *or* **-spoke.** (*tr.*) **1.** to engage or ask for in advance. **2.** to indicate or suggest: *this act bespeaks kindness.* **3.** *Poetic.* to address.

bespectacled (bɪ'spɛktəkəld) *adj.* wearing spectacles.

bespoke (bɪ'spəuk) *adj. Chiefly Brit.* **1.** (esp. of a suit, jacket, etc.) made to the customer's specifications. **2.** making or selling such suits, jackets, etc.: *a bespoke tailor.*

besprinkle (bɪ'sprɪŋkəl) *vb.* (*tr.*) to sprinkle all over with liquid, powder, etc.

Bessarabia (,bɛsə'reɪbɪə) *n.* a region of the SW Soviet Union, mostly in the Moldavian SSR: long disputed by the Turks and Russians; a province of Romania from 1918 until 1940. Area: about 44 300 sq. km (17 100 sq. miles).

Bessel ('bɛsəl) *n.* **Friedrich Wilhelm** ('friːdrɪç 'vɪlhɛlm). 1784–1846, German astronomer and mathematician. He made the first authenticated measurement of a star's distance from the earth (1841) and systematized a series of mathematical functions used in physics.

Bessemer process ('bɛsɪmə) *n.* (formerly) a process for producing steel by blowing air through molten pig iron in a **Bessemer converter** (a refractory-lined furnace): impurities are removed and the carbon content is controlled. [C19: after Sir Henry *Bessemer* (1813–98), E engineer]

best (bɛst) *adj.* **1.** the superlative of **good. 2.** most excellent of a particular group, category, etc. **3.** most suitable, desirable, etc. **4. the best part of.** most of. ~*adv.* **5.** the superlative of **well**¹. **6** in a manner surpassing all others; most excellently, attractively, etc. ~*n.* **7. the best.** the most outstanding or excellent person, thing, or group in a category. **8.** the utmost effort. **9.** a winning majority. **10.** Also: **all the best.** best wishes. **11.** a person's smartest outfit of clothing. **12. at best. a.** in the most favourable interpretation. **b.** under the most favourable conditions. **13. for the best. a.** for an ultimately good outcome. **b.** with good intentions. **14. get** *or* **have the best of.** to defeat or outwit. **15. give (someone) the best.** to concede (someone's) superiority. **16. make the best of.** to cope as well as possible with. ~*vb.* **17.** (*tr.*) to gain the advantage over or defeat. [OE *betst*]

Best (bɛst) *n.* **1. Charles Herbert.** 1899–1978, Canadian physiologist: associated with Banting and Macleod in their discovery of insulin in 1922. **2. George.** born 1946, Northern Ireland footballer.

bestead (bɪ'stɛd) *Arch.* ~*vb.* **-steading, -steaded; -steaded** *or* **-stead. 1.** (*tr.*) to help; avail. ~*adj. also* **bested. 2.** placed; situated. [C13: see BE-, STEAD]

bestial ('bɛstɪəl) *adj.* **1.** brutal or savage. **2.** sexually depraved. **3.** lacking in refinement; brutish. **4.** of or relating to a beast. [C14: from LL *bestiālis*, from L *bestia* BEAST]

bestiality (,bɛstɪ'ælɪtɪ) *n., pl.* **-ties. 1.** bestial behaviour. **2.** sexual activity between a person and an animal.

bestialize *or* **-ise** ('bɛstɪə,laɪz) *vb.* (*tr.*) to make bestial or brutal.

bestiary ('bɛstɪərɪ) *n., pl.* **-aries.** a moralizing medieval collection of descriptions of real and mythical animals.

bestir (bɪ'stɜː) *vb.* **-stirring, -stirred.** (*tr.*) to cause (oneself) to become active; rouse.

best man *n.* the male attendant of the bridegroom at a wedding.

bestow (bɪ'stəu) *vb.* (*tr.*) **1.** to present (a gift) or confer (an honour). **2.** *Arch.* to apply (energy, resources, etc.). **3.** *Arch.* to house (a person) or store (goods). —be'**stowal** *n.*

bestrew (bɪ'struː) *vb.* **-strewing, -strewed; -strewn** *or* **-strewed.** (*tr.*) to scatter or lie scattered over (a surface).

bestride (bɪ'straɪd) *vb.* **-striding, -strode** *or* (*Arch.*) **-strid; -stridden** *or* (*Arch.*) **-strid.** (*tr.*) **1.** to have or put a leg on either side of. **2.** to extend across; span. **3.** to stride over or across.

best seller n. **1.** a book or other product that has sold in great numbers. **2.** the author of one or more such books, etc. — ˌbest-ˈselling adj.

bet (bɛt) n. **1.** an agreement between two parties that a sum of money or other stake will be paid by the loser to the party who correctly predicts the outcome of an event. **2.** the stake risked. **3.** the predicted result in such an agreement. **4.** a person, event, etc., considered as likely to succeed or occur. **5.** a course of action (esp. in **one's best bet**). **6.** Inf. an opinion: my bet is that you've been up to no good. ~vb. **betting, bet** or **betted. 7.** (when intr. foll. by on or against) to make or place a bet with (a person or persons). **8.** (tr.) to stake (money, etc.) in a bet. **9.** (tr.; may take a clause as object) Inf. to predict (a certain outcome). **10. you bet.** Inf. of course; naturally. [C16: prob. short for ABET]

beta (ˈbiːtə) n. **1.** the second letter in the Greek alphabet (Β or β). **2.** the second in a group or series. [from Gk bēta, from Heb.; see BETH]

beta-blocker n. any of a class of drugs, such as propranolol, that decrease the activity of the heart: used in the treatment of high blood pressure and angina pectoris.

beta decay n. the radioactive change in an atomic nucleus accompanying the emission of an electron.

betake (bɪˈteɪk) vb. **-taking, -took, -taken.** (tr.) **1. betake oneself.** to go; move. **2.** Arch. to apply (oneself) to.

beta particle n. a high-speed electron or positron emitted by a nucleus during radioactive decay or nuclear fission.

beta ray n. a stream of beta particles.

beta rhythm or **wave** n. Physiol. the normal electrical activity of the cerebral cortex.

betatron (ˈbiːtəˌtrɒn) n. a type of particle accelerator for producing high-energy beams of electrons by magnetic induction.

betel (ˈbiːtᵊl) n. an Asian climbing plant, the leaves of which are chewed by the peoples of SE Asia. [C16: from Port., from Malayalam vettila]

betel nut n. the seed of the betel palm, chewed with betel leaves and lime by people in S and SE Asia as a digestive stimulant and narcotic.

betel palm n. a tropical Asian feather palm.

bête noire French. (bɛt nwar) n., pl. **bêtes noires** (bɛt nwar). a person or thing that one particularly dislikes or dreads. [lit.: black beast]

beth (bɛt) n. the second letter of the Hebrew alphabet. [from Heb. bēth-, bayith house]

Bethany (ˈbɛθənɪ) n. a village on the west bank of the River Jordan, near Jerusalem at the foot of the Mount of Olives: in the New Testament, the home of Lazarus and the lodging place of Jesus during Holy Week.

Bethe (ˈbeɪtə) n. **Hans Albrecht** (hans ˈalbrɛçt). born 1906, U.S. physicist, born in Germany; noted for his research on astrophysics and nuclear physics: Nobel prize for physics 1967.

Bethel (ˈbɛθəl) n. **1.** an ancient town on the west bank of the River Jordan, near Jerusalem: in the Old Testament, the place where the dream of Jacob occurred (Genesis 28:19). **2.** a chapel of any of certain Nonconformist Christian sects. **3.** a seamen's chapel. [C17: from Heb. bēth 'El house of God]

Bethesda (bəˈθɛzdə) n. **1.** New Testament. a pool in Jerusalem reputed to have healing powers, where a paralytic was healed by Jesus (John 5:2). **2.** a chapel of any certain Nonconformist Christian sects.

bethink (bɪˈθɪŋk) vb. **-thinking, -thought.** Arch. or dialect. **1.** to cause (oneself) to consider or meditate. **2.** (tr.; often foll. by of) to remind (oneself).

Bethlehem (ˈbɛθlɪˌhɛm, -lɪəm) n. a town on the west bank of the River Jordan, near Jerusalem: birthplace of Jesus and early home of King David.

Bethmann Hollweg (German ˈbeːtman ˈhɔlveːk) n. **Theobald** von (ˈteːobalt fɔn). 1856–1921, chancellor of Germany (1909–17).

Bethsaida (bɛθˈseɪdə) n. a ruined town in N Israel, near the N shore of the Sea of Galilee.

betide (bɪˈtaɪd) vb. to happen or happen to (often in **woe betide** (someone)). [C13: from BE- + obs. tide to happen]

betimes (bɪˈtaɪmz) adv. Arch. **1.** in good time; early. **2.** soon. [C14 bitimes; see BY, TIME]

Betjeman (ˈbɛtʃəmən) n. **Sir John.** 1906–84, English poet, noted for his nostalgic and humorous verse and essays and for his concern for the preservation of historic buildings, esp. of the Victorian era. Poet laureate (1972–84).

betoken (bɪˈtəʊkən) vb. (tr.) **1.** to indicate; signify. **2.** to portend; augur.

betony (ˈbɛtənɪ) n., pl. **-nies. 1.** a Eurasian plant with a spike of reddish-purple flowers, formerly used in medicine and dyeing. **2.** any of several related plants. [C14: from OF, from L]

betray (bɪˈtreɪ) vb. (tr.) **1.** to hand over or expose (one's nation, friend, etc.) treacherously to an enemy. **2.** to disclose (a secret, confidence, etc.) treacherously. **3.** to break (a promise) or be disloyal to (a person's trust). **4.** to show signs of; indicate. **5.** to reveal unintentionally: his grin betrayed his satisfaction. [C13: from BE- + trayen, from OF, from L trādere to hand over] —beˈtrayal n. —beˈtrayer n.

betroth (bɪˈtrəʊð) vb. (tr.) Arch. to promise to marry or to give in marriage. [C14 betreuthen, from BE- + treuthe TROTH, TRUTH]

betrothal (bɪˈtrəʊðəl) n. **1.** engagement to be married. **2.** a mutual promise to marry.

betrothed (bɪˈtrəʊðd) adj. **1.** engaged to be married: he was betrothed to her. ~n. **2.** the person to whom one is engaged; fiancé or fiancée.

better (ˈbɛtə) adj. **1.** the comparative of **good. 2.** more excellent than others. **3.** more suitable, advantageous, attractive, etc. **4.** improved or fully recovered in health. **5. better off.** in more favourable circumstances, esp. financially. **6. the better part of.** a large part of. ~adv. **7.** the comparative of **well**[1]. **8.** in a more excellent manner; more advantageously, attractively, etc. **9.** in or to a greater degree or extent; more. **10. had better.** would be wise, sensible, etc., to: I had better be off. **11. think better of. a.** to change one's mind about (a course of action, etc.) after reconsideration. **b.** to rate more highly. ~n. **12. the better.** something that is the more excellent, useful, etc., of two such things. **13.** (usually pl.) a person who is superior, esp. in social standing or ability. **14. for the better.** by way of improvement. **15. get the better of.** to defeat, outwit, or surpass. ~vb. **16.** to make or become better. **17.** (tr.) to improve upon; surpass. [OE betera]

better half n. Humorous. one's spouse.

betterment (ˈbɛtəmənt) n. **1.** a change for the better; improvement. **2.** Property law. an improvement effected on real property that enhances the value of the property.

Betti (Italian ˈbetti) n. **Ugo** (ˈugo). 1892–1953, Italian writer, noted esp. for his plays, including La Padrona (1927), Corruzione al palazzo di giustizia (1949), and La Regina e gli insorte (1951).

betting shop n. (in Britain) a licensed bookmaker's premises not on a racecourse.

between (bɪˈtwiːn) prep. **1.** at a point or in a region intermediate to two other points in space, times, degrees, etc. **2.** in combination; together: between them, they saved enough money to buy a car. **3.** confined or restricted to: between you and me. **4.** indicating a reciprocal relation or comparison. **5.** indicating two or more alternatives. ~adv. also **in between. 6.** between one specified thing and another. [OE betwēonum; see TWO, TWAIN]
▷**Usage.** In careful usage, between is restricted to cases where only two people, objects, possibilities, etc., are concerned. Grammatically, between you and I is incorrect. The proper construction is between you and me.

betweentimes (bɪˈtwiːnˌtaɪmz) or **betweenwhiles** adv. between other activities; during intervals.

betwixt (bɪˈtwɪkst) prep., adv. **1.** Arch. another word for **between. 2. betwixt and between.** in an intermediate or indecisive position. [OE betwix]

Beuthen (ˈbɔytən) n. the German name for **Bytom.**

BeV (in the U.S.) abbrev. for gigaelectronvolts (GeV). [C20: from b(illion) e(lectron) v(olts)]

Bevan (ˈbɛvən) n. **Aneurin** (əˈnaɪᵊrɪn), known as **Nye.** 1897–1960, British Labour statesman, born in Wales: noted for his oratory. As minister of health (1945–51) he introduced the National Health Service (1948). —ˈBevanˌite n., adj.

bevatron (ˈbɛvəˌtrɒn) n. a synchrotron used to accelerate protons. [C20: from BEV + -TRON]

bevel (ˈbɛvᵊl) n. **1.** Also called: **cant.** a surface that meets another at an angle other than a right angle. ~vb. **-elling, -elled** or U.S. **-eling, -eled. 2.** (intr.) to be inclined;

slope. **3.** (*tr.*) to cut a bevel on (a piece of timber, etc.). [C16: from OF, from *baer* to gape; see BAY[1]]

bevel gear *n.* a gear having teeth cut into a conical surface. Two such gears mesh together to transmit power between two shafts at an angle.

bevel square *n.* a tool with an adjustable arm that can be set to mark out an angle.

beverage ('bɛvərɪdʒ, 'bɛvrɪdʒ) *n.* any drink, usually other than water. [C13: from OF *bevrage*, from *beivre* to drink, from L *bibere*]

beverage room *n.* *Canad.* another name for **beer parlour.**

Beveridge ('bɛvərɪdʒ) *n.* **William Henry,** 1st Baron Beveridge. 1879–1963, British economist, whose *Report on Social Insurance and Allied Services* (1942) formed the basis of social-security legislation in Britain.

Beverley ('bɛvəlɪ) *n.* a market town in NE England; administrative centre of Humberside. Pop.: 16 433 (1981).

Beverly Hills ('bɛvəlɪ) *n.* a city in SW California, near Los Angeles: famous as the home of film stars. Pop.: 32 367 (1980).

Bevin ('bɛvɪn) *n.* **Ernest.** 1881–1951, British Labour statesman and trade unionist, who was largely responsible for the creation of the Transport and General Workers' Union (1922): minister of labour (1940–45); foreign secretary (1945–51).

bevvy ('bɛvɪ) *n.*, *pl.* **-vies.** *Dialect.* **1.** a drink, esp. an alcoholic one. **2.** a night of drinking. [prob. from OF *bevee, buvee* drinking]

bevy ('bɛvɪ) *n.*, *pl.* **bevies. 1.** a flock of quails. **2.** a group, esp. of girls. [C15: from ?]

bewail (bɪ'weɪl) *vb.* to express great sorrow over (a person or thing); lament. **—be'wailer** *n.*

beware (bɪ'wɛə) *vb.* (*usually used in the imperative or infinitive*; often foll. by *of*) to be cautious or wary (of); be on one's guard (against). [C13 *be war,* from BE (imperative) + *war* WARY]

Bewick ('bjuːɪk) *n.* **Thomas.** 1753–1828, English wood engraver; his best-known works are *Chillingham Bull* (1789), a large woodcut, *Aesop's Fables* (1818), and his *History of British Birds* (1797–1804).

bewilder (bɪ'wɪldə) *vb.* (*tr.*) to confuse utterly; puzzle. [C17: see BE-, WILDER] **—be'wildering** *adj.* **—be'wilderingly** *adv.* **—be'wilderment** *n.*

bewitch (bɪ'wɪtʃ) *vb.* (*tr.*) **1.** to attract and fascinate. **2.** to cast a spell over. [C13 *bewicchen;* see BE-, WITCH[1]] **—be'witching** *adj.*

bewray (bɪ'reɪ) *vb.* (*tr.*) an obsolete word for **betray.** [C13: from BE- + OE *wrēgan* to accuse]

Bexhill(-on-Sea) (ˌbɛks'hɪl) *n.* a resort in S England, in East Sussex on the English Channel. Pop.: 37 000 (1985 est.).

Bexley ('bɛkslɪ) *n.* a borough of Greater London. Pop.: 220 100 (1986 est.).

bey (beɪ) *n.* **1.** (in the Ottoman Empire) a title given to provincial governors. **2.** (in modern Turkey) a title of address, corresponding to *Mr.* ~Also called: **beg.** [C16: Turkish: lord]

Beyoğlu ('beɪɔːluː) *n.* a district of Istanbul, north of the Golden Horn: the European quarter. Former name: **Pera.**

beyond (bɪ'jɒnd) *prep.* **1.** at or to a point on the other side of; at or to the further side of: *beyond those hills.* **2.** outside the limits or scope of. ~*adv.* **3.** at or to the other or far side of something. **4.** outside the limits of something. ~*n.* **5. the beyond.** the unknown, esp. life after death in certain religious beliefs. [OE *begeondan;* see BY, YONDER]

Beyrouth (beɪ'ruːt, 'beɪruːt) *n.* a variant spelling of **Beirut.**

bezel ('bɛzᵊl) *n.* **1.** the sloping face adjacent to the working edge of a cutting tool. **2.** the upper oblique faces of a cut gem. **3.** a grooved ring or part holding a gem, watch crystal, etc. [C17: prob. from F *biseau*]

Béziers (*French* bezje) *n.* a city in S France: scene of a massacre (1209) during the Albigensian Crusade. It is a centre of the wine trade. Pop.: 84 000 (1983).

bezique (bɪ'ziːk) *n.* **1.** a card game for two or more players using two packs with nothing below a seven. **2.** (in this game) the queen of spades and jack of diamonds declared together. [C19: from F *bésigue,* from ?]

Bezwada ('beɪzˌwɑːdə) *n.* the former name of **Vijayawada.**

bf *abbrev. for:* **1.** *Brit. inf.* bloody fool. **2.** *Printing.* bold face.

B/F or **b/f** *Book-keeping. abbrev. for* brought forward.

BFPO *abbrev. for* British Forces Post Office.

bhang or **bang** (bæŋ) *n.* a preparation of the leaves and flower tops of Indian hemp having psychoactive properties: much used in India. [C16: from Hindi *bhāng*]

bhangra ('bæŋgrə) *n.* a type of Asian pop music that combines elements of traditional Punjabi music with Western pop. [C20: from Hindi]

bharal or **burhel** ('bʌrəl) *n.* a wild Himalayan sheep with a bluish-grey coat. [Hindi]

Bharat ('bʌrʌt) *n.* transliteration of the Hindi name for **India.**

Bhatpara (bɑːt'pɑːrə) *n.* a city in NE India, in West Bengal on the Hooghly River: jute and cotton mills. Pop.: 260 761 (1982 est.).

Bhavnagar ('bɑːvnəgə) *n.* a port in W India, in S Gujarat. Pop.: 308 000 (1981).

bhindi ('bɪndɪ) *n.* the okra as used in Indian cooking. [Hindi]

Bhopal (bəʊ'pɑːl) *n.* a city in central India, the capital of Madhya Pradesh state and of the former state of Bhopal. Pop.: 672 329 (1981).

bhp *abbrev. for* brake horsepower.

BHP *Austral. abbrev. for* Broken Hill Proprietary.

Bhubaneswar (ˌbubə'neɪʃwə) *n.* an ancient city in E India, the capital of Orissa state: many temples built between the 7th and 16th centuries. Pop.: 219 211 (1981).

Bhutan (buː'tɑːn) *n.* a kingdom in central Asia: disputed by Tibet, China, India, and Britain since the 18th century, the conflict now being chiefly between China and India (which is responsible for Bhutan's external affairs); contains inaccessible stretches of the E Himalayas in the north. Official language: Dzongka; Nepali is also spoken. Religion: mostly Mahayana Buddhist. Currencies: Ngultrum and Indian rupee. Capital: Thimphu. Pop.: 1 286 000 (1985). Area: about 46 600 sq. km (18 000 sq. miles). **—ˌBhutan'ese** *n., adj.*

Bhutto ('buːtəʊ) *n.* **1. Benazir** ('bɛnəzɪə). born 1953, Pakistani stateswoman; prime minister of Pakistan from 1988. **2.** her father, **Zulfikar Ali** ('zʊlfɪkɑː 'ɑːlɪ). 1928–79, Pakistani statesman; president (1971–73) and prime minister (1973–77) of Pakistan: executed for the murder of a political rival.

Bi *the chemical symbol for* bismuth.

bi- or *sometimes before a vowel* **bin-** *combining form.* **1.** two; having two: *bifocal.* **2.** occurring every two; lasting for two: *biennial.* **3.** on both sides, directions, etc.: *bilateral.* **4.** occurring twice during: *biweekly.* **5. a.** denoting a compound containing two identical cyclic hydrocarbon systems: *biphenyl.* **b.** (rare in technical usage) indicating an acid salt of a dibasic acid: *sodium bicarbonate.* **c.** (not in technical usage) equivalent of **di-[1]** (sense 2). [from L, from *bis* TWICE]·

▷**Usage.** In order to avoid ambiguity, care should be taken in observing the distinction between *bi-* and *semi-* in *biweekly, bimonthly, biyearly* (once in two weeks, months, years) and *semiweekly, semimonthly, semiyearly* (twice during one week, month, year). In strict usage, *biennial* (lasting or occurring once in two years) is distinguished from *biannual* (occurring twice in one year).

Biafra (bɪ'æfrə) *n.* **1.** a region of E Nigeria: seceded as an independent republic (1967–70) during the Civil War, but defeated by Nigerian government forces. **2. Bight of.** former name (until 1975) of (the Bight of) **Bonny.** **—Bi'afran** *adj., n.*

Biak (biː'jɑːk) *n.* an island in Indonesia, north of West Irian: the largest of the Schouten Islands. Area: 2455 sq. km (948 sq. miles).

Białystok (*Polish* bja'uisɔk) *n.* a city in E Poland: belonged to Prussia (1795–1807) and to Russia (1807–1919). Pop.: 245 000 (1985). Russian name: **Belostock.**

biannual (baɪ'ænjʊəl) *adj.* occurring twice a year. Cf. **biennial. —bi'annually** *adv.*

Biarritz ('bɪərɪts, bɪə'rɪts; *French* bjarits) *n.* a town in SW France, on the Bay of Biscay: famous resort, patronized by Napoleon III and by Queen Victoria and Edward VII of Great Britain and Ireland. Pop.: 26 647 (1982 est.).

bias ('baɪəs) *n.* **1.** mental tendency or inclination, esp. irrational preference or prejudice. **2.** a diagonal line or cut across the weave of a fabric. **3.** *Electronics.* the voltage applied to an electrode of a transistor or valve to establish suitable working conditions. **4.** *Bowls.* **a.** a bulge or weight inside one side of a bowl. **b.** the curved course of such a bowl. **5.** *Statistics.* a latent influence that disturbs an analysis. ~*adv.* **6.** obliquely; diagonally. ~*vb.* **-asing, -ased** *or* **-assing, -assed. 7.** (*tr.; usually passive*) to cause to have a bias; prejudice; influence. [C16: from OF *biais*] —**'biased** *or* **'biassed** *adj.*

bias binding *n.* a strip of material cut on the bias, used for binding hems or for decoration.

biathlon (baɪ'æθlɒn, -lɒn) *n. Sport.* a contest in which skiers with rifles shoot at four targets along a 20-kilometre (12.5-mile) cross-country course.

biaxial (baɪ'æksɪəl) *adj.* (esp. of a crystal) having two axes.

bib (bɪb) *n.* **1.** a piece of cloth or plastic worn, esp. by babies, to protect their clothes while eating. **2.** the upper front part of some aprons, dungarees, etc. **3.** Also called: **pout, whiting pout.** a light brown European marine gadoid food fish with a barbel on its lower jaw. **4. stick one's bib in.** *Austral. inf.* to interfere. ~*vb.* **bibbing, bibbed. 5.** *Arch.* to drink (something). [C14 *bibben* to drink, prob. from L *bibere*]

Bib. *abbrev. for:* **1.** Bible. **2.** Biblical.

bib and tucker *n. Inf.* an outfit of clothes.

bibcock ('bɪb,kɒk) *or* **bib** *n.* a tap with a nozzle bent downwards fed from a horizontal pipe.

bibelot ('bɪbləʊ) *n.* an attractive or curious trinket. [C19: from F, from OF *beubelet*]

bibl. *abbrev. for:* **1.** bibliographical. **2.** bibliography.

Bibl. *abbrev. for* Biblical.

Bible ('baɪbəl) *n.* **1. a. the.** the sacred writings of the Christian religion, comprising the Old and New Testaments. **b.** (*as modifier*): *a Bible reading.* **2.** (*usually not cap.*) the sacred writings of a religion. **3.** (*usually not cap.*) a book regarded as authoritative. [C13: from OF, from Med. L *biblia* books, from Gk, dim. of *biblos* papyrus]

▷ **Usage.** The Bible is written with a capital initial but should not be put in inverted commas. The adjective *biblical* is written without a capital initial: *a new translation of the Bible; life in biblical times.*

Bible-thumper *n. Sl.* an enthusiastic or aggressive exponent of the Bible. Also: **Bible-basher.** —**'Bible-,thumping** *n.*, *adj.*

biblical ('bɪblɪkəl) *adj.* **1.** of or referring to the Bible. **2.** resembling the Bible in written style.

▷ **Usage.** See at Bible.

Biblicist ('bɪblɪsɪst) *or* **Biblist** *n.* **1.** a biblical scholar. **2.** a person who takes the Bible literally.

biblio- *combining form.* indicating book or books: *bibliography.* [from Gk *biblion* book]

bibliography (,bɪblɪ'ɒgrəfɪ) *n.*, *pl.* **-phies. 1.** a list of books on a subject or by a particular author. **2.** a list of sources used in a book, thesis, etc. **3. a.** the study of the history, classification, etc., of literary material. **b.** a work on this subject. —**,bibli'ographer** *n.* —**bibliographic** (,bɪblɪəʊ'græfɪk) *or* **,biblio'graphical** *adj.*

bibliomancy ('bɪblɪəʊ,mænsɪ) *n.* prediction of the future by interpreting a passage chosen at random from a book, esp. the Bible.

bibliomania (,bɪblɪəʊ'meɪnɪə) *n.* extreme fondness for books. —**,biblio'mani,ac** *n.*, *adj.*

bibliophile ('bɪblɪə,faɪl) *or* **bibliophil** ('bɪblɪəfɪl) *n.* a person who collects or is fond of books. —**bibliophilism** (,bɪblɪ'ɒfɪ,lɪzəm) *n.* —**,bibli'ophily** *n.*

bibliopole ('bɪblɪəʊ,pəʊl) *or* **bibliopolist** (,bɪblɪ'ɒpəlɪst) *n.* a dealer in books, esp. rare or decorative ones. [C18: from L, from Gk, from BIBLIO- + *pōlein* to sell] —,bibli'opoly *n.*

bibulous ('bɪbjʊləs) *adj.* addicted to alcohol. [C17: from L *bibulus*, from *bibere* to drink] —**'bibulously** *adv.* —**'bibulousness** *n.*

bicameral (baɪ'kæmərəl) *adj.* (of a legislature) consisting of two chambers. [C19: from BI- + L *camera* CHAMBER] —**bi'cameral,ism** *n.*

bicarb ('baɪkɑːb) *n.* short for **bicarbonate of soda.**

bicarbonate (baɪ'kɑːbənɪt, -,neɪt) *n.* a salt of carbonic acid.

bicarbonate of soda *n.* sodium bicarbonate, esp. as medicine or a raising agent in baking.

bice (baɪs) *n.* **1.** Also called: **bice blue.** medium blue. **2.** Also called: **bice green.** a yellowish green. [C14: from OF *bis* dark grey, from ?]

bicentenary (,baɪsɛn'tiːnərɪ) *or U.S.* **bicentennial** (,baɪsɛn'tɛnɪəl) *adj.* **1.** marking a 200th anniversary. **2.** occurring every 200 years. **3.** lasting 200 years. ~*n.*, *pl.* **-naries. 4.** a 200th anniversary.

bicephalous (baɪ'sɛfələs) *adj.* **1.** *Biol.* having two heads. **2.** crescent-shaped.

biceps ('baɪsɛps) *n.*, *pl.* **-ceps.** *Anat.* any muscle having two heads or origins, esp. the muscle that flexes the forearm. [C17: from L, from BI- + *caput* head]

bichloride (baɪ'klɔːraɪd) *n.* another name for **dichloride.**

bichloride of mercury *n.* another name for **mercuric chloride.**

bichromate (baɪ'krəʊ,meɪt, -mɪt) *n.* another name for **dichromate.**

bicker ('bɪkə) *vb.* (*intr.*) **1.** to argue over petty matters; squabble. **2.** *Poetic.* **a.** (esp. of a stream) to run quickly. **b.** to flicker; glitter. ~*n.* **3.** a squabble. [C13: from ?] —**'bickerer** *n.*

bicolour ('baɪ,kʌlə), **bicoloured** *or U.S.* **bicolor, bicolored** *adj.* two-coloured.

biconcave (baɪ'kɒnkeɪv, ,baɪkɒn'keɪv) *adj.* (of a lens) having concave faces on both sides.

biconditional (,baɪkən'dɪʃənəl) *n.* **1.** *Logic, maths.* a relation, taken as meaning *if and only if*, between two propositions which are either both true or both false and such that each implies the other. **2.** *Logic.* a logical connective between two propositions whose truth table is true only if both propositions are true or both false. ~Also called (esp. sense 1): **equivalence.**

biconvex (baɪ'kɒnvɛks, ,baɪkɒn'vɛks) *adj.* (of a lens) having convex faces on both sides.

bicuspid (baɪ'kʌspɪd) *or* **bicuspidate** (baɪ'kʌspɪ,deɪt) *adj.* **1.** having two cusps or points. ~*n.* **2.** a bicuspid tooth; premolar.

bicycle ('baɪsɪkəl) *n.* **1.** a vehicle with a tubular metal frame mounted on two spoked wheels, one behind the other. The rider sits on a saddle, propels the vehicle by means of pedals, and steers with handlebars on the front wheel. Often shortened to **bike** (inf.), **cycle.** ~*vb.* **2.** (*intr.*) to ride a bicycle. —**'bicyclist** *or* **'bicycler** *n.*

bicycle clip *n.* one of a pair of clips worn around the ankles by cyclists to keep the trousers tight and out of the chain.

bid (bɪd) *vb.* **bidding; bad, bade,** *or* (esp. for senses 1, 4, 5) **bid; bidden** *or* (esp. for senses 1, 4, 5) **bid. 1.** (often foll. by *for* or *against*) to offer (an amount) in attempting to buy something. **2.** (*tr.*) to say (a greeting, etc.): *to bid farewell.* **3.** to order; command: *do as you are bid!* **4.** (*intr.; usually foll. by for*) to attempt to attain power, etc. **5.** *Bridge, etc.* to declare before play how many tricks one expects to make. **6. bid defiance.** to resist boldly. **7. bid fair.** to seem probable. ~*n.* **8. a.** an offer of a specified amount. **b.** the price offered. **9. a.** the quoting by a seller of a price. **b.** the price quoted. **10.** an attempt, esp. to attain power. **11.** *Bridge, etc.* **a.** the number of tricks a player undertakes to make. **b.** a player's turn to make a bid. ~See also **bid up.** [OE *biddan*] —**'bidder** *n.*

▷ **Usage.** *Bid* in journalistic usage has become a noun used to refer to any kind of attempt to achieve something: *bid to climb Everest; doctor makes bid to save life.* This use of *bid* is avoided by careful writers, however, and the word is restricted to the sense of an offer of a price: *the auctioneer accepted a bid of £3000.*

Bida ('baɪdɑː) *or* **El Beda** (ɛl 'beɪdɑː) *n.* the former name of Doha.

biddable ('bɪdəbəl) *adj.* **1.** having sufficient value to be bid on, as a hand at bridge. **2.** docile; obedient. —**'biddableness** *n.*

bidding ('bɪdɪŋ) *n.* **1.** an order; command. **2.** an invitation; summons. **3.** bids or the act of making bids.

Biddle ('bɪdəl) *n.* **John.** 1615–62, English theologian; founder of Unitarianism in England.

biddy¹ ('bɪdɪ) *n.*, *pl.* **-dies.** a dialect word for **chicken** or **hen.** [C17: ? imit. of calling chickens]

biddy² ('bɪdɪ) *n.*, *pl.* **-dies.** *Inf.* a woman, esp. an old gossipy one. [C18: from pet form of *Bridget*]

biddy-biddy ('bɪdɪ,bɪdɪ) *n.*, *pl.* **-biddies. 1.** a low-growing rosaceous plant of New Zealand, having prickly burs. **2.** the burs of this plant. ~Also: **bidgee-widgee** ('bɪdʒɪ,wɪdʒɪ). [from Maori *piripiri*]

bide (baɪd) *vb.* **biding, bided** *or* **bode, bided. 1.** (*intr.*) *Arch. or dialect.* to continue in a certain place or state; stay. **2.** (*tr.*) *Arch. or dialect.* to tolerate; endure. **3. bide**

one's time. to wait patiently for an opportunity. [OE *bīdan*]

bidentate (bar'dɛn,teɪt) *adj.* having two teeth or toothlike parts or processes.

bidet ('biːdeɪ) *n.* a small low basin for washing the genital area. [C17: from F: small horse]

bid up *vb.* (*adv.*) to increase the market price of (a commodity) by making artificial bids.

Biel (biːl) *n.* **1.** a town in NW Switzerland, on Lake Biel. Pop.: 52 000 (1985). French name: **Bienne.** **2.** **Lake.** a lake in NW Switzerland: remains of lake dwellings were discovered here in the 19th century. Area: 39 sq. km (15 sq. miles). German name: **Bielersee** ('biːlǝzeː).

Bielefeld (*German* 'biːlǝfɛlt) *n.* a city in West Germany, in NE North Rhine-Westphalia. Pop.: 229 200 (1986).

Bielsko-Biała (*Polish* 'bjɛlskɔ'bjaua) *n.* a town in S Poland: created in 1951 by the union of Bielsko and Biala Krakowska; a leading textile centre since the 16th century. Pop.: 174 000 (1985).

Bien Hoa ('bjɛn 'hǝuǝ) *n.* a town in S Vietnam: a former capital of Cambodia. Pop.: 190 086 (1979).

Bienne (bjɛn) *n.* the French name for **Biel.**

biennial (baɪ'ɛnɪǝl) *adj.* **1.** occurring every two years. **2.** lasting two years. Cf. **biannual.** ~*n.* **3.** a plant that completes its life cycle in two years. **4.** an event that takes place every two years. —**bi'ennially** *adv.*

bier (bɪǝ) *n.* a platform or stand on which a corpse or a coffin containing a corpse rests before burial. [OE *bēr*; rel. to *beran* to BEAR[1]]

Bierce (bɪǝs) *n.* **Ambrose (Gwinett).** 1842–?1914, U.S. journalist and author of humorous sketches, horror stories, and tales of the supernatural: he disappeared during a mission in Mexico (1913).

biestings ('biːstɪŋz) *n.* a variant spelling of **beestings.**

biff (bɪf) *Sl.* ~*n.* **1.** a blow with the fist. ~*vb.* **2.** (*tr.*) to give (someone) such a blow. [C20: prob. imit.]

bifid ('baɪfɪd) *adj.* divided into two lobes by a median cleft. [C17: from L, from BI- + -*fidus*, from *findere* to split] —**bi'fidity** *n.* —**'bifidly** *adv.*

bifocal (baɪ'fǝukǝl) *adj.* **1.** *Optics.* having two different focuses. **2.** relating to a compound lens permitting near and distant vision.

bifocals (baɪ'fǝukǝlz) *pl. n.* a pair of spectacles with bifocal lenses.

BIFU (in Britain) *abbrev. for* Banking, Insurance and Finance Union.

bifurcate *vb.* ('baɪfǝ,keɪt). **1.** to fork or divide into two branches. ~*adj.* ('baɪfǝ,keɪt, -kɪt). **2.** forked or divided into two branches. [C17: from Med. L, from L, from BI- + *furca* fork] —**,bifur'cation** *n.*

big (bɪg) *adj.* **bigger, biggest. 1.** of great or considerable size, height, weight, number, power, or capacity. **2.** having great significance; important. **3.** important through having power, influence, wealth, authority, etc. **4.** *Inf.* considerable in extent or intensity (esp. in **in a big way**). **5. a.** elder: *my big brother.* **b.** grown-up. **6. a.** generous; magnanimous: *that's very big of you.* **b.** (*in combination*): *big-hearted.* **7.** extravagant; boastful: *big talk.* **8. too big for one's boots** or **breeches.** conceited; unduly self-confident. **9.** in an advanced stage of pregnancy (esp. in **big with child**). ~*adv. Inf.* **10.** boastfully; pretentiously (esp. in **talk big**). **11.** in an exceptional way; well: *his talk went over big.* **12.** on a grand scale (esp. in **think big**). [C13: ?from ON] —**'bigness** *n.*

bigamy ('bɪgǝmɪ) *n., pl.* -**mies.** the crime of marrying a person while still legally married to someone else. [C13: via F from Med. L; see BI-, -GAMY] —**'bigamist** *n.* —**'bigamous** *adj.*

Big Apple *n.* **the** *inf.* New York City. [C20: prob. from U.S. jazzmen's earlier use to mean any big, esp. northern, city; from ?]

Big Bang *n.* the reorganization of the London Stock Exchange that took effect in October 1986 when operations became fully computerized, fixed commissions were abolished, and the functions of jobbers and brokers were merged.

big-bang theory *n.* a cosmological theory postulating that all the matter of the universe was hurled in all directions by a cataclysmic explosion and that the universe is still expanding. Cf. **steady-state theory.**

Big Brother *n.* a person, organization, etc., that exercises total dictatorial control. [C20: from George Orwell's novel *1984* (1949)]

big business *n.* large commercial organizations collectively, esp. when considered as exploitative or socially harmful.

big deal *interj. Sl.* an exclamation of scorn, derision, etc., used esp. to belittle a claim or offer.

big dipper *n.* (in amusement parks) a narrow railway with open carriages that run swiftly over a route of sharp curves and steep inclines.

big end *n. Brit.* the larger end of a connecting rod in an internal-combustion engine.

big game *n.* large animals that are hunted or fished for sport.

big gun *n. Inf.* an important person.

bighead ('bɪg,hɛd) *n. Inf.* a conceited person. —**,big'headed** *adj.* —**,big'headedness** *n.*

bighorn ('bɪg,hɔːn) *n., pl.* -**horns** or -**horn.** a large wild sheep inhabiting mountainous regions in North America.

bight (baɪt) *n.* **1.** a wide indentation of a shoreline, or the body of water bounded by such a curve. **2.** the slack middle part or loop in a rope. [OE *byht*; see BOW[2]]

Bight (baɪt) *n.* **the.** the major indentation of the S coast of Australia. In full: **the Great Australian Bight.**

bigmouth ('bɪg,maʊθ) *n. Sl.* a noisy, indiscreet, or boastful person. —**'big-,mouthed** *adj.*

big noise *n. Brit. inf.* an important person.

bignonia (bɪg'nǝunɪǝ) *n.* a tropical American climbing shrub cultivated for its trumpet-shaped yellow or reddish flowers. [C19: from NL, after the Abbé Jean-Paul *Bignon* (1662–1743)]

big-note *vb.* (*tr.*) *Austral. inf.* to boast about (oneself).

bigot ('bɪgǝt) *n.* a person who is intolerant, esp. regarding religion, politics, or race. [C16: from OF: name applied contemptuously to the Normans by the French, from ?] —**'bigoted** *adj.* —**'bigotry** *n.*

big shot *n. Inf.* an important person.

big smoke *n.* **the.** *Inf.* a large city, esp. London.

big stick *n. Inf.* force or the threat of force.

big time *n. Inf.* **a.** **the.** the highest level of a profession, esp. entertainment. **b.** (*as modifier*): *a big-time comedian.* —**'big-'timer** *n.*

big top *n. Inf.* **1.** the main tent of a circus. **2.** the circus itself.

bigwig ('bɪg,wɪg) *n. Inf.* an important person.

Bihar (bɪ'hɑː) *n.* a state of NE India: hilly in the south, with the Ganges plain in the north; important for rice and mineral resources, esp. coal. Capital: Patna. Pop.: 69 823 154 (1981). Area: 174 038 sq. km (67 875 sq. miles).

Biisk (*Russian* bijsk) *n.* a variant spelling of **Biysk.**

Bijapur (bɪ'dʒɑːpʊǝ) *n.* an ancient city in W India, in N Mysore: capital of a former kingdom, which fell at the end of the 17th century. Pop.: 147 313 (1981).

bijou ('biːʒuː) *n., pl.* -**joux** (-ʒuːz). **1.** something small and delicately worked. **2.** (*modifier*) *Often ironic.* small but tasteful: *a bijou residence.* [C19: from F, from Breton *bizou* finger ring, from *biz* finger]

bijugate ('baɪdʒu,geɪt, baɪ'dʒuː,geɪt) or **bijugous** *adj.* (of compound leaves) having two pairs of leaflets.

Bikaner ('biːkǝ,nɪǝ) *n.* a walled city in NW India, in Rajasthan: capital of the former state of Bikaner, on the edge of the Thar Desert. Pop.: 280 000 (1981).

bike (baɪk) *n.* **1.** *Inf.* short for **bicycle** or **motorcycle.** **2.** *Sl.* a promiscuous woman. **3. get off one's bike.** *Austral. & N.Z. sl.* to lose one's self-control. ~*vb.* **4.** (*intr.*) to ride a bike.

biker ('baɪkǝ) *n.* a member of a motorcycle gang. Also called (*Austral. & N.Z.*): **bikie.**

Bikila (bɪ'kiːlǝ) *n.* **Abebe** (ǝ'beɪbeɪ). 1932–73, Ethiopian long-distance runner: winner of the Marathon at the Olympic Games in Rome (1960) and Tokyo (1964).

bikini (bɪ'kiːnɪ) *n.* a woman's very brief two-piece swimming costume. [C20: after *Bikini* atoll, from a comparison between the devastating effect of the atom-bomb test and the effect caused by women wearing bikinis]

Bikini (bɪ'kiːnɪ) *n.* an atoll in the N Pacific; one of the Marshall Islands: site of a U.S. atom-bomb test in 1946.

Biko ('biːkǝu) *n.* **Stephan,** known as **Steve.** 1946–77, Black South African civil rights leader: founder of the South African Students Organization. His death in police custody caused worldwide concern.

bilabial (baɪ'leɪbɪǝl) *adj.* **1.** of or denoting a speech sound articulated using both lips: (*p*) *is a bilabial stop.* ~*n.* **2.** a bilabial speech sound.

bilabiate (bar'leɪbɪ,eɪt, -ɪt) *adj. Bot.* divided into two lips: *the snapdragon has a bilabiate corolla.*

bilateral (bar'lætərəl) *adj.* **1.** having or involving two sides. **2.** affecting or undertaken by two parties; mutual. **3.** having identical sides or parts on each side of an axis; symmetrical.

bilateral symmetry *n.* symmetry in one plane only. Cf. **radial symmetry.**

Bilbao (bɪl'baːəʊ; *Spanish* bil'βau) *n.* a port in N Spain, on the Bay of Biscay: famous since medieval times for the production of iron and steel goods, esp. swords; still contains the country's largest iron and steel works and exports iron ore. Pop.: 433 115 (1981).

bilberry ('bɪlbərɪ) *n., pl.* **-ries. 1.** any of several shrubs, such as the whortleberry, having edible blue or blackish berries. **2.** the fruit of any of these plants. [C16: prob. of Scand. origin]

bilboes ('bɪlbəʊz) *pl. n.* a long iron bar with sliding shackles, for the ankles of a prisoner. [C16: ?from *Bilbao*, Spain]

Bildungsroman *German.* ('bɪldʊŋsromaːn) *n.* a novel about a person's formative years.

bile (baɪl) *n.* **1.** a bitter greenish to golden brown alkaline fluid secreted by the liver and stored in the gall bladder. It aids digestion of fats. **2.** a health disorder due to faulty secretion of bile. **3.** irritability or peevishness. [C17: from F, from L *bīlis*]

bilge (bɪldʒ) *n.* **1.** *Naut.* the parts of a vessel's hull where the sides curve inwards to form the bottom. **2.** (*often pl.*) the parts of a vessel between the lowermost floorboards and the bottom. **3.** Also called: **bilge water.** the dirty water that collects in a vessel's bilge. **4.** *Inf.* silly rubbish; nonsense. **5.** the widest part of a cask. ~*vb.* **6.** (*intr.*) *Naut.* (of a vessel) to take in water at the bilge. **7.** (*tr.*) *Naut.* to damage (a vessel) in the bilge. [C16: prob. var. of BULGE]

bilharzia (bɪl'haːtsɪə) *n.* **1.** another name for a **schistosome. 2.** another name for **schistosomiasis.** [C19: NL, after Theodor *Bilharz* (1825–62), G parasitologist who discovered schistosomes]

bilharziasis (,bɪlhaː'tsaɪəsɪs) *or* **bilharziosis** (bɪl,-haːtsɪ'əʊsɪs) *n.* another name for **schistosomiasis.**

biliary ('bɪlɪərɪ) *adj.* of or relating to bile, to the ducts that convey bile, or to the gall bladder.

bilingual (bar'lɪŋgwəl) *adj.* **1.** able to speak two languages, esp. with fluency. **2.** expressed in two languages. ~*n.* **3.** a bilingual person. —**bi'lingual,ism** *n.*

bilious ('bɪlɪəs) *adj.* **1.** of or relating to bile. **2.** affected with or denoting any disorder related to secretion of bile. **3.** *Inf.* bad-tempered; irritable. [C16: from L *bīliōsus* full of BILE] —**'biliousness** *n.*

bilk (bɪlk) *vb.* (*tr.*) **1.** to balk; thwart. **2.** (often foll. by *of*) to cheat or deceive, esp. to avoid making payment to. **3.** to escape from; elude. ~*n.* **4.** a swindle or cheat. **5.** a person who swindles or cheats. [C17: ? var. of BALK] —**'bilker** *n.*

bill¹ (bɪl) *n.* **1.** money owed for goods or services supplied. **2.** a statement of money owed. **3.** *Chiefly Brit.* such an account for food and drink in a restaurant, hotel, etc. **4.** any list of items, events, etc., such as a theatre programme. **5.** a statute in draft, before it becomes law. **6.** a printed notice or advertisement. **7.** *U.S. & Canad.* a piece of paper money; note. **8.** an obsolete name for **promissory note. 9.** See **bill of exchange, bill of fare.** ~*vb.* (*tr.*) **10.** to send or present an account for payment to (a person). **11.** to enter (items, goods, etc.) on an account or statement. **12.** to advertise by posters. **13.** to schedule as a future programme. [C14: from Anglo-L *billa*, alteration of LL *bulla* document, BULL³]

bill² (bɪl) *n.* **1.** the projecting jaws of a bird, covered with a horny sheath; beak. **2.** any beaklike mouthpart in other animals. **3.** a narrow promontory. ~*vb.* (*intr.*) (esp. in **bill and coo**). **4.** (of birds, esp. doves) to touch bills together. **5.** (of lovers) to kiss and whisper amorously. [OE *bile*]

bill³ (bɪl) *n.* **1.** a pike or halberd with a narrow hooked blade. **2.** short for **billhook.** [OE *bill* sword]

billabong ('bɪlə,bɒŋ) *n. Austral.* **1.** a stagnant pool in the bed of an intermittent stream. **2.** a branch of a river running to a dead end. [C19: from Abor., from *billa* river + *bong* dead]

billboard ('bɪl,bɔːd) *n. Chiefly U.S. & Canad.* another name for **hoarding.** [C19: from BILL¹ BOARD]

billet¹ ('bɪlɪt) *n.* **1.** accommodation, esp. for a soldier, in civilian lodgings. **2.** the official requisition for such lodgings. **3.** a space or berth in a ship. **4.** *Inf.* a job. ~*vb.* **5.** (*tr.*) to assign a lodging to (a soldier). **6.** to lodge or be lodged. [C15: from OF *billette*, from *bulle* a document; see BULL³]

billet² ('bɪlɪt) *n.* **1.** a chunk of wood, esp. for fuel. **2.** a small bar of iron or steel. [C15: from OF *billette* a little log, from *bille* log]

billet-doux (,bɪlɪ'duː) *n., pl.* **billets-doux** (,bɪlɪ'duːz). *Old-fashioned or jocular.* a love letter. [C17: from F, lit.: a sweet letter]

billhook ('bɪl,hʊk) *n.* a tool with a curved blade terminating in a hook, used for pruning, chopping, etc. Also called: **bill.**

billiard ('bɪljəd) *n.* (*modifier*) of or relating to billiards: *a billiard table; a billiard cue.*

billiards ('bɪljədz) *n.* (*functioning as sing.*) any of various games in which long cues are used to drive balls on a rectangular table covered with a smooth cloth and having raised cushioned edges. [C16: from OF *billard* curved stick, from *bille* log; see BILLET²]

billing ('bɪlɪŋ) *n.* **1.** *Theatre.* the relative importance of a performer or act as reflected in the prominence given in programmes, advertisements, etc. **2.** *Chiefly U.S. & Canad.* public notice or advertising.

billingsgate ('bɪlɪŋz,geɪt) *n.* obscene or abusive language. [C17: after BILLINGSGATE, notorious for such language]

Billingsgate ('bɪlɪŋz,geɪt) *n.* the largest fish market in London, on the N bank of the River Thames; moved to new site on the Isle of Dogs in 1982.

billion ('bɪljən) *n., pl.* **-lions** *or* **-lion. 1.** (in Britain, orig.) one million million: written as 1 000 000 000 000 or 10^{12}. U.S. word: **trillion. 2.** (in the U.S., Canada, and increasingly in Britain and elsewhere) one thousand million: written as 1 000 000 000 or 10^9. **3.** (*often pl.*) any exceptionally large number. ~*determiner.* **4.** (preceded by *a* or a cardinal number) amounting to a billion. [C17: from F, from BI- + *-llion* as in *million*] —**'billionth** *adj., n.*

billionaire (,bɪljə'nɛə) *n.* a person whose wealth exceeds a billion monetary units of his country.

Billiton ('bɪlɪtɒn, bɪ'liːtɒn) *n.* an island of Indonesia, in the Java Sea between Borneo and Sumatra. Chief town: Tandjungpandan. Area: 4833 sq. km (1866 sq. miles). Also called: **Belitung.**

bill of attainder *n.* (formerly) a legislative act finding a person guilty without trial of treason or felony and declaring him attainted.

bill of exchange *n.* (now chiefly in foreign transactions) a document, usually negotiable, instructing a third party to pay a stated sum at a designated future date or on demand.

bill of fare *n.* another name for **menu.**

bill of health *n.* **1.** a certificate that attests to the health of a ship's company. **2. clean bill of health.** *Inf.* **a.** a good report of one's physical condition. **b.** a favourable account of a person's or a company's financial position.

bill of lading *n.* (in foreign trade) a document containing full particulars of goods shipped.

Bill of Rights *n.* **1.** an English statute of 1689 guaranteeing the rights and liberty of the individual subject. **2.** the first ten amendments to the U.S. Constitution which guarantee the liberty of the individual. **3.** (*usually not caps.*) any charter of basic human rights.

bill of sale *n. Law.* a deed transferring personal property.

billow ('bɪləʊ) *n.* **1.** a large sea wave. **2.** a swelling or surging mass, as of smoke or sound. ~*vb.* **3.** to rise up, swell out, or cause to rise up or swell out. [C16: from ON *bylgja*] —**'billowing** *adj., n.* —**'billowy** *adj.* —**'billowiness** *n.*

billposter ('bɪl,pəʊstə) *or* **billsticker** *n.* a person who sticks advertising posters to walls, etc. —**'bill,posting** *or* **'bill,sticking** *n.*

billy ('bɪlɪ) *or* **billycan** ('bɪlɪ,kæn) *n., pl.* **-lies** *or* **-lycans. 1.** a metal can or pot for boiling water, etc., over a campfire. **2.** *Austral. & N.Z.* (*as modifier*): *billy-tea.* **3. boil the billy.** *Austral. & N.Z. inf.* to make tea. [C19: from Scot. *billypot* cooking vessel]

billy goat *n.* a male goat.

Billy the Kid *n.* nickname of *William H. Bonney.* 1859–81, U.S. outlaw.

bilobate (baɪˈləʊˌbeɪt) *or* **bilobed** (ˈbaɪˌləʊbd) *adj.* divided into or having two lobes.

biltong (ˈbɪlˌtɒŋ) *n. S. African.* strips of meat dried and cured in the sun. [C19: Afrik., from Du. *bil* buttock + *tong* TONGUE]

BIM *abbrev. for* British Institute of Management.

bimanous (ˈbɪmənəs, baɪˈmeɪ-) *adj.* (of man and the higher primates) having two hands distinct in form and function from the feet. [C19: from NL, from BI- + L *manus* hand]

bimanual (ˌbaɪˈmænjʊəl) *adj.* using both hands.

bimbo (ˈbɪmbəʊ) *n., pl.* **-bos.** *Sl.* an attractive but empty-headed young woman.

bimetallic (ˌbaɪmɪˈtælɪk) *adj.* **1.** consisting of two metals. **2.** of or based on bimetallism.

bimetallic strip *n.* strips of two metals that expand differently welded together for use in a thermostat.

bimetallism (baɪˈmɛtəˌlɪzəm) *n.* the use of two metals, esp. gold and silver, in fixed relative values as the standard of value and currency. —**biˈmetallist** *n.*

bimonthly (baɪˈmʌnθlɪ) *adj., adv.* **1.** every two months. **2.** twice a month. ~*n., pl.* **-lies.** **3.** a periodical published every two months.

bimorph (ˈbaɪmɔːf) *or* **bimorph cell** *n. Electron.* two piezoelectric crystals cemented together so that their movement converts electrical signals into mechanical energy or vice versa: used in record-player pick-ups and loudspeakers.

bin (bɪn) *n.* **1.** a large container for storing something in bulk, such as coal, grain, or bottled wine. **2.** Also called: **bread bin.** a small container for bread. **3.** Also called: **dustbin, rubbish bin.** a container for rubbish, etc. ~*vb.* **binning, binned.** (*tr.*) **4.** to store in a bin. **5.** to put in a wastepaper bin. [OE *binne* basket]

binary (ˈbaɪnərɪ) *adj.* **1.** composed of or involving two; dual. **2.** *Maths, computers.* of or expressed in binary notation or binary code. **3.** (of a compound or molecule) containing atoms of two different elements. ~*n., pl.* **-ries.** **4.** something composed of two parts. **5.** *Astron.* See **binary star.** [C16: from LL *bīnārius;* see BI-]

binary code *n. Computers.* the representation of each one of a set of numbers, letters, etc., as a unique group of bits.

binary notation *or* **system** *n.* a number system having a base of two, numbers being expressed by sequences of the digits 0 and 1: used in computing, as 0 and 1 can be represented electrically as *off* and *on.*

binary number *n.* a number expressed in binary notation.

binary star *n.* a double star system containing two associated stars revolving around a common centre of gravity in different orbits.

binary weapon *n.* a chemical weapon containing two substances separately that mix to produce a nerve gas when the projectile is fired.

binate (ˈbaɪˌneɪt) *adj. Bot.* occurring in two parts or in pairs: *binate leaves.* [C19: from NL *bīnātus,* prob. from L *combīnātus* united] —ˈ**biˌnately** *adv.*

binaural (baɪˈnɔːrəl, bɪnˈɔːrəl) *adj.* **1.** relating to, having, or hearing with both ears. **2.** employing two separate channels for recording or transmitting sound.

bind (baɪnd) *vb.* **binding, bound.** **1.** to make or become fast or secure with or as if with a tie or band. **2.** (*tr.;* often foll. by *up*) to encircle or enclose with a band: *to bind the hair.* **3.** (*tr.*) to place (someone) under obligation; oblige. **4.** (*tr.*) to impose legal obligations or duties upon (a person). **5.** (*tr.*) to make (a bargain, agreement, etc.) irrevocable; seal. **6.** (*tr.*) to restrain or confine with or as if with ties, as of responsibility or loyalty. **7.** (*tr.*) to place under certain constraints; govern. **8.** (*tr.;* often foll. by *up*) to bandage. **9.** to cohere or cause to cohere: *egg binds fat and flour.* **10.** to make or become compact, stiff, or hard: *frost binds the earth.* **11.** (*tr.*) to enclose and fasten (the pages of a book) between covers. **12.** (*tr.*) to provide (a garment, hem, etc.) with a border or edging. **13.** (*tr.;* sometimes foll. by *out* or *over*) to employ as an apprentice; indenture. **14.** (*intr.*) *Sl.* to complain. ~*n.* **15.** something that binds. **16.** *Inf.* a difficult or annoying situation. **17.** a situation in which freedom of action is restricted. ~See also **bind over.** [OE *bindan*]

binder (ˈbaɪndə) *n.* **1.** a firm cover or folder for holding loose sheets of paper together. **2.** a material used to bind separate particles together. **3.** a person who binds books; bookbinder. **4.** something used to fasten or tie, such as rope or twine. **5.** Also called: **reaper binder.** *Obs.* a machine for cutting grain and binding it into sheaves. **6.** an informal agreement giving insurance coverage pending formal issue of a policy.

bindery (ˈbaɪndərɪ) *n., pl.* **-eries.** a place in which books are bound.

bindi-eye (ˈbɪndɪˌaɪ) *n. Austral.* **1.** any of various small weedy Australian herbaceous plants with burlike fruits. **2.** any bur or prickle. [C20: ?from Abor.]

binding (ˈbaɪndɪŋ) *n.* **1.** anything that binds or fastens. **2.** the covering within which the pages of a book are bound. **3.** the tape used for binding hems, etc. ~*adj.* **4.** imposing an obligation or duty. **5.** causing hindrance; restrictive.

bind over *vb.* (*tr., adv.*) to place (a person) under a legal obligation, such as one to keep the peace.

bindweed (ˈbaɪndˌwiːd) *n.* any of various plants that twine around a support. See also **convolvulus.**

bine (baɪn) *n.* the climbing or twining stem of any of various plants, such as the woodbine or bindweed. [C19: var. of BIND]

Binet-Simon scale (ˈbiːneɪˈsaɪmən) *n. Psychol.* a test used to determine the mental age of subjects, usually children. Also called: **Binet scale** *or* **test.** [C20: after Alfred *Binet* (1857–1911) + Théodore *Simon* (1873–1961), F psychologists]

binge (bɪndʒ) *Inf.* ~*n.* **1.** a bout of excessive drinking. **2.** excessive indulgence in anything. ~*vb.* **bingeing** *or* **binging, binged.** **3.** (*intr.*) to indulge in a binge. [C19: prob. dial. *binge* to soak]

Bingen (ˈbɪŋən) *n.* a town in W West Germany on the Rhine: wine trade and tourist centre. Pop.: 22 700 (1984 est.).

bingo (ˈbɪŋgəʊ) *n.* a gambling game, usually played with several people, in which random numbers are called out and the players cover the numbers on their individual cards. The first to cover a given arrangement of numbers is the winner. [C19: ?from *bing,* imit. of a bell ringing to mark the win]

binman (ˈbɪnˌmæn, ˈbɪnmən) *n., pl.* **-men.** another name for **dustman.**

binnacle (ˈbɪnəkᵊl) *n.* a housing for a ship's compass. [C17: changed from C15 *bitakle,* from Port. from LL *habitāculum* dwelling-place, from L *habitāre* to inhabit]

binocular (bɪˈnɒkjʊlə, baɪ-) *adj.* involving, relating to, seeing with or intended for both eyes: *binocular vision.* [C18: from BI- + L *oculus* eye]

binoculars (bɪˈnɒkjʊləz, baɪ-) *pl. n.* an optical instrument for use with both eyes, consisting of two small telescopes joined together.

binomial (baɪˈnəʊmɪəl) *n.* **1.** a mathematical expression consisting of two terms, such as $3x + 2y$. **2.** a two-part taxonomic name for an animal or plant indicating genus and species. ~*adj.* **3.** referring to two names or terms. [C16: from Med. L, from BI- + L *nōmen* name] —**biˈnomially** *adv.*

binomial distribution *n.* a statistical distribution giving the probability of obtaining a specified number of independent trials of an experiment, with a constant probability of success in each.

binomial theorem *n.* a general mathematical formula that expresses any power of a binomial without multiplying out, as in $(a+b)^2 = a^2 + 2ab + b^2$.

bint (bɪnt) *n. Sl.* a derogatory term for **girl** or **woman.** [C19: from Ar., lit.: daughter]

binturong (ˈbɪntjʊˌrɒŋ, bɪnˈtjʊərɒŋ) *n.* a long-bodied short-legged arboreal SE Asian mammal having shaggy black hair. [from Malay]

bio- *or before a vowel* **bi-** *combining form.* **1.** indicating or involving life or living organisms: *biogenesis.* **2.** indicating a human life or career: *biography.* [from Gk *bios* life]

bioassay (ˌbaɪəʊˈæseɪ) *n.* **1.** a method of determining the concentration or effect of a drug, etc., by comparing its effect on living organisms with that of a standard preparation. ~*vb.* (*tr.*) **2.** to subject to a bioassay.

bioastronautics (ˌbaɪəʊˌæstrəˈnɔːtɪks) *n.* (*functioning as sing.*) the study of the effects of space flight on living organisms.

Bío-Bío (*Spanish* ˈbiːoˈbiːo) *n.* a river in central Chile, rising in the Andes and flowing northwest to the Pacific. Length: about 390 km (240 miles).

biochemical oxygen demand *n.* a measure of the organic pollution of water; the number of milligrams of oxygen per litre of water absorbed in a given period. Abbrev.: **BOD**

biochemistry (ˌbaɪəʊˈkɛmɪstrɪ) *n.* the study of the chemical compounds, reactions, etc., occurring in living organisms. —**biochemical** (ˌbaɪəʊˈkɛmɪkəl) *adj.* —**bio-ˈchemist** *n.*

biocide (ˈbaɪəˌsaɪd) *n.* a chemical capable of killing living organisms. —**bioˈcidal** *adj.*

biocoenosis (ˌbaɪəʊsiːˈnəʊsɪs) *n.* the relationships between animals and plants subsisting together. [C19: NL from BIO-+ Gk *koinōsis* sharing]

biodegradable (ˌbaɪəʊdɪˈgreɪdəbəl) *adj.* (of sewage, packaging, etc.) capable of being decomposed by bacteria or other biological means.

bioengineering (ˌbaɪəʊˌɛndʒɪˈnɪərɪŋ) *n.* **1.** the design and manufacture of aids, such as artificial limbs, to rectify defective body functions. **2.** the design, manufacture, and maintenance of engineering equipment used in biosynthetic processes. —**bioˌengiˈneer** *n.*

bioethics (ˌbaɪəʊˈɛθɪks) *n.* (*functioning as sing.*) the study of ethical problems arising from scientific advances, esp. in biology and medicine.

biofeedback (ˌbaɪəʊˈfiːdˌbæk) *n. Physiol., psychol.* the technique of recording and presenting (usually visually) the activity of an autonomic function, such as the rate of heartbeat, in order to teach control of it.

biog. *abbrev. for:* **1.** biographical. **2.** biography.

biogenesis (ˌbaɪəʊˈdʒɛnɪsɪs) *n.* the principle that a living organism must originate from a parent organism similar to itself. —**bioˈgeˈnetic** *or* ˌbioˈgeˈnetical *adj.*

biography (baɪˈɒgrəfɪ) *n., pl.* **-phies. 1.** an account of a person's life by another. **2.** such accounts collectively. —**biˈographer** *n.* —**biographical** (ˌbaɪəˈgræfɪkəl) *adj.*

Bioko (baɪˈəʊkəʊ) *n.* an island in the Gulf of Guinea, off the coast of Cameroon: part of Equatorial Guinea. Capital: Malabo. Area: 2017 sq. km (786 sq. miles). Former names: **Fernando Po** (until 1973), **Macías Nguema** (1973–79).

biol. *abbrev. for:* **1.** biological. **2.** biology.

biological (ˌbaɪəˈlɒdʒɪkəl) *adj.* **1.** of or relating to biology. ~*n.* **2.** (*usually pl.*) a drug derived from a living organism.

biological clock *n.* **1.** an inherent periodicity in the physiological processes of living organisms that is independent of external periodicity. **2.** the hypothetical mechanism responsible for this. ~See also **circadian.**

biological control *n.* the control of destructive organisms by nonchemical means, such as introducing the natural enemy of a pest.

biological warfare *n.* the use of living organisms or their toxic products to induce death or incapacity in humans.

biology (baɪˈɒlədʒɪ) *n.* **1.** the study of living organisms. **2.** the animal and plant life of a particular region. —**biˈologist** *n.*

bioluminescence (ˌbaɪəʊˌluːmɪˈnɛsəns) *n.* the production of light by living organisms, such as the firefly. —**bioˌlumiˈnescent** *adj.*

biomass (ˈbaɪəʊˌmæs) *n.* the total number of living organisms in a given area, expressed in terms of living or dry weight per unit area.

biomedicine (ˌbaɪəʊˈmɛdɪsɪn) *n.* the medical and biological study of the effects of unusual environmental stress, esp. in connection with space travel.

biometry (baɪˈɒmɪtrɪ) *or* **biometrics** (ˌbaɪəˈmɛtrɪks) *n.* (*functioning as sing.*) the study of biological data by means of statistical analysis. —**bioˈmetric** *adj.*

bionic (baɪˈɒnɪk) *adj.* **1.** of or relating to bionics. **2.** (in science fiction) having physiological functions augmented by electronic equipment.

bionics (baɪˈɒnɪks) *n.* (*functioning as sing.*) **1.** the study of certain biological functions that are applicable to the development of electronic equipment designed to operate similarly. **2.** the replacement of limbs or body parts by artificial limbs or parts that are electronically or mechanically powered.

bionomics (ˌbaɪəˈnɒmɪks) *n.* (*functioning as sing.*) a less common name for **ecology.** [C19: from BIO- *nomics* on pattern of ECONOMICS] —**bioˈnomic** *adj.* —**bionomist** (baɪˈɒnəmɪst) *n.*

biophysics (ˌbaɪəʊˈfɪzɪks) *n.* (*functioning as sing.*) the physics of biological processes and the application of methods used in physics to biology. —**bioˈphysical** *adj.*

—ˌbioˈphysically *adv.* —**biophysicist** (ˌbaɪəʊˈfɪzɪsɪst) *n.*

biopic (ˈbaɪəʊˌpɪk) *n. Inf.* a film based on the life of a famous person. [C20: from *bio(graphical)* + *pic(ture)*]

biopsy (ˈbaɪɒpsɪ) *n., pl.* **-sies.** examination, esp. under a microscope, of tissue from a living body to determine the cause or extent of a disease. [C20: from BIO- + Gk *opsis* sight]

biorhythm (ˈbaɪəʊˌrɪðəm) *n.* a cyclically recurring pattern of physiological states, believed by some to affect a person's physical, emotional, and mental states and behaviour.

bioscope (ˈbaɪəˌskəʊp) *n.* **1.** a kind of early film projector. **2.** a South African word for **cinema.**

bioscopy (baɪˈɒskəpɪ) *n., pl.* **-pies.** examination of a body to determine whether it is alive.

-biosis *n. combining form.* indicating a specified mode of life. [NL, from Gk *biōsis*; see BIO-, -OSIS] —**biotic** *adj. combining form.*

biosphere (ˈbaɪəˌsfɪə) *n.* the part of the earth's surface and atmosphere inhabited by living things.

biosynthesis (ˌbaɪəʊˈsɪnθɪsɪs) *n.* the formation of complex compounds from simple substances by living organisms. —**biosynthetic** (ˌbaɪəʊsɪnˈθɛtɪk) *adj.*

biotechnology (ˌbaɪəʊtɛkˈnɒlədʒɪ) *n.* the use of microorganisms for beneficial effect, as to process waste matter.

biotic (baɪˈɒtɪk) *adj.* of or relating to living organisms. [C17: from Gk *biotikos*, from *bios* life]

biotin (ˈbaɪətɪn) *n.* a vitamin of the B complex, abundant in egg yolk and liver. [C20: from Gk *biotē* life, way of life + -IN]

bipartisan (ˌbaɪpɑːtɪˈzæn, baɪˈpɑːtɪˌzæn) *adj.* consisting of or supported by two political parties. —**bipartiˈsanship** *n.*

bipartite (baɪˈpɑːtaɪt) *adj.* **1.** consisting of or having two parts. **2.** affecting or made by two parties. **3.** *Bot.* (esp. of some leaves) divided into two parts almost to the base. —**biˈpartitely** *adv.* —**bipartition** (ˌbaɪpɑːˈtɪʃən) *n.*

biped (ˈbaɪpɛd) *n.* **1.** any animal with two feet. ~*adj. also* **bipedal** (baɪˈpiːdəl, -ˈpɛdəl). **2.** having two feet.

bipinnate (baɪˈpɪneɪt) *adj.* (of compound leaves) having both the leaflets and the stems bearing them arranged pinnately. —**biˈpinnately** *adv.*

biplane (ˈbaɪˌpleɪn) *n.* a type of aeroplane having two sets of wings, one above the other.

bipolar (baɪˈpəʊlə) *adj.* **1.** having two poles: *a bipolar dynamo.* **2.** of or relating to the North and South Poles. **3.** having or characterized by two opposed opinions, etc. **4.** (of a transistor) utilizing both majority and minority charge carriers. —**bipoˈlarity** *n.*

biquadratic (ˌbaɪkwɒˈdrætɪk) *Maths.* ~*adj.* **1.** of or relating to the fourth power. ~*n.* **2.** a biquadratic equation, such as $x^4 + x + 6 = 0$.

biracial (baɪˈreɪʃəl) *adj.* of or for members of two races. —**biˈracialism** *n.*

birch (bɜːtʃ) *n.* **1.** any catkin-bearing tree or shrub having thin peeling bark. See also **silver birch. 2.** the hard close-grained wood of any of these trees. **3. the birch.** a bundle of birch twigs or a birch rod used, esp. formerly, for flogging offenders. ~*adj.* **4.** consisting or made of birch. ~*vb.* **5.** (*tr.*) to flog with a birch. [OE *bierce*] —**ˈbirchen** *adj.*

bird (bɜːd) *n.* **1.** any warm-blooded egg-laying vertebrate, characterized by a body covering of feathers and forelimbs modified as wings. **2.** *Inf.* a person, as in **rare bird, odd bird, clever bird. 3.** *Sl., chiefly Brit.* a girl or young woman. **4.** *Sl.* prison or a term in prison (esp. in **do bird**). **5. a bird in the hand.** something definite or certain. **6. birds of a feather.** people with the same characteristics, ideas, interests, etc. **7. get the bird.** *Inf.* **a.** to be fired or dismissed. **b.** (esp. of a public performer) to be hissed at. **8. kill two birds with one stone.** to accomplish two things with one action. **9.** (strictly) **for the birds.** *Inf.* deserving of disdain or contempt; not important. [OE *bridd*, from ?]

Bird (bɜːd) *n.* nickname of (Charlie) **Parker.**

birdbath (ˈbɜːdˌbɑːθ) *n.* a small basin or trough for birds to bathe in, usually in a garden.

bird-brained *adj. Inf.* silly; stupid.

birdcage (ˈbɜːdˌkeɪdʒ) *n.* **1.** a wire or wicker cage for captive birds. **2.** *Austral. & N.Z.* an area on a racecourse where horses parade before a race. **3.** *N.Z. inf.* a secondhand car dealer's yard.

bird call *n.* **1.** the characteristic call or song of a bird. **2.** an imitation of this.

birdie ('bɜːdɪ) *n.* **1.** *Golf.* a score of one stroke under par for a hole. **2.** *Inf.* a bird, esp. a small bird.

birdlime ('bɜːd,laɪm) *n.* **1.** a sticky substance smeared on twigs to catch small birds. ~*vb.* **2.** (*tr.*) to smear (twigs) with birdlime to catch (small birds).

bird-nesting *or* **birds'-nesting** *n.* searching for birds' nests as a hobby, often to steal the eggs.

bird of paradise *n.* **1.** any of various songbirds of New Guinea and neighbouring regions, the males having brilliantly coloured plumage. **2. bird-of-paradise flower.** any of various plants native to tropical southern Africa and South America that have purple bracts and large orange or yellow flowers resembling birds' heads.

bird of passage *n.* **1.** a bird that migrates seasonally. **2.** a transient person.

bird of prey *n.* a bird, such as a hawk or owl, that hunts other animals for food.

birdseed ('bɜːd,siːd) *n.* a mixture of various kinds of seeds for feeding cagebirds.

bird's-eye *adj.* **1. a.** seen or photographed from high above. **b.** summarizing (esp. in **bird's-eye view**). **2.** having markings resembling birds' eyes.

bird's-foot *or* **bird-foot** *n., pl.* **-foots.** any of various plants whose flowers, leaves, or pods resemble a bird's foot or claw.

birdshot ('bɜːd,ʃɒt) *n.* small pellets designed for shooting birds.

bird strike *n.* a collision of an aircraft with a bird.

bird table *n.* a table or platform in the open on which food for birds may be placed.

bird-watcher *n.* a person who identifies and studies wild birds in their natural surroundings. — '**bird-,watching** *n.*

birefringence (,baɪrɪ'frɪndʒəns) *n.* another name for **double refraction.** — ,bire'fringent *adj.*

bireme ('baɪriːm) *n.* an ancient galley having two banks of oars. [C17: from L, from BI- + *-rēmus* oar]

Birendra Bir Bikram Shah Dev (bɪ'rendra: bɪə 'bɪkræm ʃɑː dev) *n.* born 1945, king of Nepal from 1972.

biretta *or* **berretta** (bɪ'rɛtə) *n. R.C. Church.* a stiff square clerical cap. [C16: from It. *berretta*, from OProvençal, from LL *birrus* hooded cape]

Birgitta (bɪə'gɪtə) *n.* **Saint.** See (Saint) **Bridget** (sense 2).

Birkenhead[1] (,bɜːkən'hɛd) *n.* a port in NW England, in Merseyside: former shipbuilding centre. Pop.: 123 907 (1981).

Birkenhead[2] ('bɜːkən,hɛd) *n.* **Frederick Edwin Smith,** 1st Earl of, known as *F. E. Smith.* 1872–1930, British Conservative statesman, lawyer, and orator.

birl (bɜːl) *vb.* **1.** *Scot.* to spin; twirl. **2.** *U.S. & Canad.* to cause (a floating log) to spin using the feet, esp. as a sport among lumberjacks. ~*n.* **3.** a variant spelling of **burl**[2]. [C18: prob. imit. & infl. by WHIRL & HURL]

Birmingham *n.* **1.** ('bɜːmɪŋəm) an industrial city in central England, in West Midlands: the second largest city in Great Britain. Pop.: 1 008 000 (1985). **2.** ('bɜːmɪŋ,hæm) an industrial city in N central Alabama: rich local deposits of coal, iron ore, and other minerals. Pop.: 277 510 (1986).

Biro ('baɪrəʊ) *n., pl.* **-ros.** *Trademark, Brit.* a kind of ballpoint.

Birobidzhan (*Russian* birəbid'ʒan) *n.* **1.** a city in the Soviet Union, in SE Siberia: capital of the Jewish Autonomous Region. Pop.: 72 000 (1981 est.). **2.** another name for the **Jewish Autonomous Region.**

birth (bɜːθ) *n.* **1.** the process of bearing young; childbirth. **2.** the act or fact of being born; nativity. **3.** the coming into existence of something; origin. **4.** ancestry; lineage: *of high birth.* **5.** natural or inherited talent: *an artist by birth.* **6. give birth (to). a.** to bear (offspring). **b.** to produce or originate (an idea, plan, etc.). ~*vb.* (*tr.*). **7.** *Rare.* to bear or bring forth (a child). [C12: from ON *byrth*]

birth certificate *n.* an official form giving details of the time and place of a person's birth.

birth control *n.* limitation of child-bearing by means of contraception.

birthday ('bɜːθ,deɪ) *n.* **1. a.** an anniversary of the day of one's birth. **b.** (*as modifier*): *birthday present.* **2.** the day on which a person was born.

birthmark ('bɜːθ,mɑːk) *n.* a blemish on the skin formed before birth; naevus.

birthplace ('bɜːθ,pleɪs) *n.* the place where someone was born or where something originated.

birth rate *n.* the ratio of live births in a specified area, group, etc., to population, usually expressed per 1000 population per year.

birthright ('bɜːθ,raɪt) *n.* **1.** privileges or possessions that a person has or is believed to be entitled to as soon as he is born. **2.** the privileges or possessions of a first-born son. **3.** inheritance.

birthstone ('bɜːθ,stəʊn) *n.* a precious or semiprecious stone associated with a month or sign of the zodiac and thought to bring luck if worn by a person born in that month or under that sign.

Birtwhistle ('bɜːt,wɪsəl) *n.* **Harrison.** born 1934, English composer, whose works include the opera *Punch and Judy* (1967).

biryani *or* **biriani** (,bɪrɪ'ɑːnɪ) *n.* an Indian dish made with rice, flavoured and coloured, mixed with meat or fish. [from Urdu]

Bisayas (bi'sajas) *pl.n.* the Spanish name for the **Visayan Islands.**

Biscay ('bɪskeɪ, -kɪ) *n.* **Bay of.** a large bay of the Atlantic Ocean between W France and N Spain: notorious for storms.

biscuit ('bɪskɪt) *n.* **1.** *Brit.* a small flat dry sweet or plain cake of many varieties. U.S. and Canad. word: **cookie. 2. a.** a pale brown or yellowish-grey colour. **b.** (*as adj.*): *biscuit gloves* **3.** Also called: **bisque.** earthenware or porcelain that has been fired but not glazed. **4. take the biscuit.** *Brit.* to be regarded (by the speaker) as most surprising. [C14: from OF, from (*pain*) *bescuit* twice-cooked (bread), from *bes* twice + *cuire* to cook]

bise (biːz) *n.* a cold dry northerly wind in Switzerland and the neighbouring parts of France and Italy. [C14: from OF, of Gmc origin]

bisect (baɪ'sɛkt) *vb.* **1.** (*tr.*) *Maths.* to divide into two equal parts. **2.** to cut or split into two. [C17: BI- + *-sect*, from L *secāre* to cut] —**bisection** (baɪ'sɛkʃən) *n.*

bisector (baɪ'sɛktə) *n. Maths.* a straight line or plane that bisects an angle, etc.

bisexual (baɪ'sɛksjʊəl) *adj.* **1.** sexually attracted by both men and women. **2.** showing characteristics of both sexes. **3.** of or relating to both sexes. ~*n.* **4.** a bisexual organism; a hermaphrodite. **5.** a bisexual person. **bisexuality** (baɪ,sɛksjʊ'ælɪtɪ) *n.*

bishop ('bɪʃəp) *n.* **1.** a clergyman having spiritual and administrative powers over a diocese. See also **suffragan.** Related adj.: **episcopal. 2.** a chesspiece, capable of moving diagonally. **3.** mulled wine, usually port, spiced with oranges, cloves, etc. [OE *biscop*, from LL, from Gk *episkopos*, from EPI- + *skopos* watcher]

Bishop Auckland *n.* a town in N England, in central Durham: seat of the bishops of Durham since the 12th century. Pop.: 32 572 (1981).

bishopric ('bɪʃəprɪk) *n.* the see, diocese, or office of a bishop.

Bisitun (,biːsɪ'tuːn) *n.* another name for **Behistun.**

Bisk (*Russian* bijsk) *n.* a variant spelling of **Biysk.**

Biskra ('bɪskrɑː) *n.* a town and oasis in NE Algeria, in the Sahara. Pop.: 90 471 (1977).

Bismarck[1] ('bɪzmɑːk) *n.* a city in North Dakota, on the Missouri River: the state capital. Pop.: 44 485 (1980).

Bismarck[2] (*German* 'bɪsmark) *n.* **Prince Otto (Eduard Leopold) von** ('ɔto fɔn), called *the Iron Chancellor.* 1815–98, German statesman; prime minister of Prussia (1862–90). Under his leadership Prussia defeated Austria and France, and Germany was united. In 1871 he became the first chancellor of the German Reich.

Bismarck Archipelago *n.* a group of over 200 islands in the SW Pacific, northeast of New Guinea: part of Papua New Guinea. Main islands: New Britain, New Ireland, Lavongai, and the Admiralty Islands. Chief town: Rabaul, on New Britain. Pop.: 314 308 (1980 est.). Area: 49 658 sq. km (19 173 sq. miles).

bismuth ('bɪzməθ) *n.* a brittle pinkish-white crystalline metallic element. It is widely used in alloys; its compounds are used in medicines. Symbol: Bi; atomic no.: 83; atomic wt.: 208.98. [C17: from NL *bisemūtum*, from G *Wismut*, from ?]

bison ('baɪs'n) *n., pl.* **-son. 1.** Also called: **American bison, buffalo.** a member of the cattle tribe, formerly widely distributed over the prairies of W North America, with a massive head, shaggy forequarters, and a humped back. **2.** Also called: **wisent, European bison.** a closely related and similar animal formerly widespread in Europe. [C14: from L *bisōn*, of Gmc origin]

bisque[1] (bisk) *n.* a thick rich soup made from shellfish. [C17: from F]

bisque[2] (bisk) *n.* **1. a.** a pink to yellowish tan colour. **b.** (*as adj.*): *a bisque tablecloth.* **2.** *Ceramics.* another name for **biscuit** (sense 3). [C20: shortened from BISCUIT]

bisque[3] (bisk) *n.* *Tennis, golf, croquet.* an extra point, stroke, or turn allowed to an inferior player, usually taken when desired. [C17: from F, from ?]

Bissau (bɪ'saʊ) *or* **Bissão** (*Portuguese* bi'sɔu) *n.* a port in W Guinea-Bissau, on the Atlantic: until 1974 the capital of Portuguese Guinea. Pop.: 109 486 (1979).

bistable (ˌbaɪ'steɪbᵊl) *adj.* (of an electrical circuit switch, etc.) having two stable states.

bistort ('bɪstɔːt) *n.* **1.** Also called: **snakeweed.** a Eurasian plant having leaf stipules fused to form a tube around the stem and a spike of small pink flowers. **2.** Also called: **snakeroot.** a related plant of W North America, with oval clusters of pink or white flowers. **3.** any of several similar plants. [C16: from F, from L *bis* twice + *tortus* from *torquēre* to twist]

bistoury ('bɪstərɪ) *n., pl.* **-ies.** a long narrow-bladed surgical knife. [C15: from OF *bistorie* dagger, from ?]

bistre *or U.S.* **bister** ('bɪstə) *n.* **1.** a transparent water-soluble brownish-yellow pigment made by boiling the soot of wood. **2. a.** a yellowish-brown to dark brown colour. **b.** (*as adj.*): *bistre paint.* [C18: from F, from ?]

bistro ('biːstrəʊ) *n., pl.* **-tros.** a small restaurant. [F: from ?]

bisulphate (baɪ'sʌlˌfeɪt) *n.* a salt or ester of sulphuric acid containing the monovalent group -HSO$_4$ or the ion HSO$_4^-$. Also called: **hydrogen sulphate.**

bisulphide (baɪ'sʌlfaɪd) *n.* another name for **disulphide.**

Bisutun (ˌbiːsuː'tuːn) *n.* another name for **Behistun.**

bit[1] (bɪt) *n.* **1.** a small piece, portion, or quantity. **2.** a short time or distance. **3.** *U.S. & Canad. inf.* the value of an eighth of a dollar: spoken of only in units of two: *two bits.* **4.** any small coin. **5.** short for **bit part. 6. a bit.** rather; somewhat: *a bit dreary.* **7. a bit of. a.** rather: *a bit of a dope.* **b.** a considerable amount: *that must take quite a bit of courage.* **8. bit by bit.** gradually. **9. do one's bit.** to make one's expected contribution. [OE *bite* action of biting; see BITE]

bit[2] (bɪt) *n.* **1.** a metal mouthpiece on a bridle for controlling a horse. **2.** anything that restrains or curbs. **3.** a cutting or drilling tool, part, or head in a brace, drill, etc. **4.** the part of a key that engages the levers of a lock. ~*vb.* **bitting, bitted.** (*tr.*) **5.** to put a bit in the mouth of (a horse). **6.** to restrain; curb. [OE *bita*; rel. to OE *bītan* to BITE]

bit[3] (bɪt) *vb.* the past tense of **bite.**

bit[4] (bɪt) *n.* *Maths, computers.* **1.** a single digit of binary notation, represented either by 0 or by 1. **2.** the smallest unit of information, indicating the presence or absence of a single feature. [C20: from B(INARY + DIG)IT]

bitch (bɪtʃ) *n.* **1.** a female dog or other female canine animal, such as a wolf. **2.** *Sl., derog.* a malicious, spiteful, or coarse woman. **3.** *Inf.* a difficult situation or problem. ~*vb. Inf.* **4.** (*intr.*) to complain; grumble. **5.** to behave (towards) in a spiteful manner. **6.** (*tr.*; often foll. by *up*) to botch; bungle. [OE *bicce*]

bitchy ('bɪtʃɪ) *adj.* **-ier, -iest.** *Sl.* of or like a bitch; malicious; snide. —'**bitchiness** *n.*

bite (baɪt) *vb.* **biting, bit, bitten. 1.** to grip, cut off, or tear as with the teeth or jaws. **2.** (of animals, insects, etc.) to injure by puncturing or tearing (the skin or flesh) with the teeth, fangs, etc. **3.** (*tr.*) to cut or penetrate, as with a knife. **4.** (of corrosive material such as acid) to eat away or into. **5.** to smart or cause to smart; sting. **6.** (*intr.*) *Angling.* (of a fish) to take or attempt to take the bait or lure. **7.** (*tr.*) *Sl.* to annoy or worry: *what's biting her?* **9.** (*tr.*; often foll. by *for*) *Austral. & N.Z. sl.* to ask (for); scrounge from. **10. bite the dust. a.** to fall down dead. **b.** to be rejected: *another good idea bites the dust.* ~*n.* **11.** the act of biting. **12.** a thing or amount bitten off. **13.** a wound, bruise, or sting inflicted by biting. **14.** *Angling.* an attempt by a fish to take the bait or lure. **15.** a light meal; snack. **16.** a cutting, stinging, or smarting sensation. **17.** *Dentistry.* the angle or manner of contact between the upper and lower teeth. **18. put the bite on.** *Sl.* to cadge or borrow from. [OE *bītan*] —'**biter** *n.*

Bithynia (bɪ'θɪnɪə) *n.* an ancient country on the Black Sea in NW Asia Minor.

biting ('baɪtɪŋ) *adj.* **1.** piercing; keen: *a biting wind.* **2.** sarcastic; incisive. —'**bitingly** *adv.*

Bitolj (*Serbo-Croatian* 'bitolj) *n.* a city in S Yugoslavia, in Macedonia: under Turkish rule from 1382 until 1913. Pop.: 137 835 (1981).

bit part *n.* a very small acting role with few lines to speak.

bitt (bɪt) *Naut.* ~*n.* **1.** one of a pair of strong posts on the deck of a ship for securing mooring and other lines. **2.** another word for **bollard** (sense 1). ~*vb.* **3.** (*tr.*) to secure (a line) by means of a bitt. [C14: prob. from ON]

bitten ('bɪtᵊn) *vb.* the past participle of **bite.**

bitter ('bɪtə) *adj.* **1.** having or denoting an unpalatable harsh taste, as the peel of an orange. **2.** showing or caused by strong unrelenting hostility or resentment. **3.** difficult or unpleasant to accept or admit: *a bitter blow.* **4.** cutting; sarcastic: *bitter words.* **5.** bitingly cold: *a bitter night.* ~*adv.* **6.** very; extremely (esp. in **bitter cold**). ~*n.* **7.** a thing that is bitter. **8.** *Brit.* draught beer with a slightly bitter taste. [OE *biter*; rel. to *bītan* to BITE] —'**bitterly** *adv.* —'**bitterness** *n.*

bitter end *n.* **1.** *Naut.* the end of a line, chain, or cable. **2. to the bitter end. a.** until the finish of a task, etc., however unpleasant or difficult. **b.** until final defeat or death. [C19: ?from BITT]

Bitter Lakes *pl. n.* two lakes, the **Great Bitter Lake** and **Little Bitter Lake,** in NE Egypt: part of the Suez Canal.

bittern ('bɪtən) *n.* a wading bird related and similar to the herons but with shorter legs and neck and a booming call. [C14: from OF *butor*, ?from L *būtiō* bittern + *taurus* bull]

bitters ('bɪtəz) *pl. n.* **1.** bitter-tasting spirits of varying alcoholic content flavoured with plant extracts. **2.** a similar liquid containing a bitter-tasting substance, used as a tonic.

bittersweet ('bɪtəˌswiːt) *n.* **1.** any of several North American woody climbing plants having orange capsules that open to expose scarlet-coated seeds. **2.** another name for **woody nightshade.** ~*adj.* **3.** tasting of or being a mixture of bitterness and sweetness. **4.** pleasant but tinged with sadness.

bitty ('bɪtɪ) *adj.* **-tier, -tiest. 1.** lacking unity; disjointed. **2.** containing bits, sediment, etc.

bitumen ('bɪtjʊmɪn) *n.* **1.** any of various viscous or solid impure mixtures of hydrocarbons that occur naturally in asphalt, tar, mineral waxes, etc.: used as a road surfacing and roofing material. **2. the bitumen.** *Austral. & N.Z. inf.* any road with a bitumen surface. [C15: from L *bitūmen*] —**bituminous** (bɪ'tjuːmɪnəs) *adj.*

bituminize *or* **-ise** (bɪ'tjuːmɪˌnaɪz) *vb.* (*tr.*) to treat with or convert into bitumen.

bituminous coal *n.* a soft black coal that burns with a smoky yellow flame.

bivalent (baɪ'veɪlənt, 'bɪvə-) *adj.* **1.** *Chem.* another word for **divalent. 2.** (of homologous chromosomes) associated together in pairs. —**bi'valency** *n.*

bivalve ('baɪˌvælv) *n.* **1.** a marine or freshwater mollusc, having a laterally compressed body, a shell consisting of two hinged valves, and gills for respiration. The group includes clams, cockles, oysters, and mussels. ~*adj.* **2.** of or relating to these molluscs. ~ Also: **lamellibranch.**

bivouac ('bɪvʊˌæk, 'bɪvwæk) *n.* **1.** a temporary encampment, as used by soldiers, mountaineers, etc. ~*vb.* **-acking, -acked. 2.** (*intr.*) to make such an encampment. [C18: from F *bivouac*, prob. from Swiss G *Beiwacht*, lit.: BY + WATCH]

biweekly (baɪ'wiːklɪ) *adj., adv.* **1.** every two weeks. **2.** twice a week. ~*n., pl.* **-lies. 3.** a periodical published every two weeks.

biyearly (baɪ'jɪəlɪ) *adj., adv.* **1.** every two years; biennial or biennially. **2.** twice a year; biannual or biannually. See **bi-.**

Biysk, Biisk, *or* **Bisk** (*Russian* bijsk) *n.* a city in the SW Soviet Union, at the foot of the Altai Mountains. Pop: 231 000 (1987).

biz (bɪz) *n.* *Inf.* short for **business.**

bizarre (bɪ'zɑː) *adj.* odd or unusual, esp. in an interesting or amusing way. [C17: from F, from It. *bizzarro* capricious, from ?] —**bi'zarreness** *n.*

Bizerte (bɪ'zɜːt; *French* bizɛrt) *or* **Bizerta** *n.* a port in N Tunisia, on the Mediterranean at the canalized outlet of Lake Bizerte. Pop.: 94 509 (1984).

Bizet ('biːzeɪ; *French* bizɛ) *n.* **Georges** (ʒɔrʒ). 1838–75, French composer, whose works include the opera *Carmen* (1875) and incidental music to Daudet's *L'Arlésienne* (1872).

Björneborg (bjœrnəˈborj) *n.* the Swedish name for **Pori**.

bk *abbrev. for:* **1.** bank. **2.** book.

Bk *the chemical symbol for* berkelium.

bkg *abbrev. for* banking.

BL *abbrev. for:* **1.** Bachelor of Law. **2.** Bachelor of Letters. **3.** Barrister-at-Law. **4.** British Library.

B/L, b/l, *or* **b.l.** *pl.* **Bs/L, bs/l,** *or* **bs.l.** *abbrev. for* bill of lading.

blab (blæb) *vb.* **blabbing, blabbed. 1.** to divulge (secrets, etc.) indiscreetly. **2.** (*intr.*) to chatter thoughtlessly; prattle. ~*n.* **3.** a less common word for **blabber.** [C14: of Gmc origin]

blabber ('blæbə) *n.* **1.** a person who blabs. **2.** idle chatter. ~*vb.* **3.** (*intr.*) to talk without thinking; chatter. [C15 *blabberen*, prob. imit.]

black (blæk) *adj.* **1.** of the colour of jet or carbon black, having no hue due to the absorption of all or nearly all incident light. **2.** without light; completely dark. **3.** without hope of alleviation; gloomy: *the future looked black.* **4.** very dirty or soiled. **5.** angry or resentful: *black looks.* **6.** (of a play or other work) dealing with the unpleasant realities of life, esp. in a cynical or macabre manner: *black comedy.* **7.** (of coffee or tea) without milk or cream. **8. a.** wicked or harmful: *a black lie.* **b.** (*in combination*): *black-hearted.* **9.** *Brit.* (of goods, jobs, works, etc.) being subject to boycott by trade unionists. ~*n.* **10.** a black colour. **11.** a dye or pigment of or producing this colour. **12.** black clothing, worn esp. as a sign of mourning. **13.** *Chess, draughts.* a black or dark-coloured piece or square. **14.** complete darkness: *the black of the night.* **15. in the black.** in credit or without debt. ~*vb.* **16.** another word for **blacken.** **17.** (*tr.*) to polish (shoes, etc.) with blacking. **18.** (*tr.*) *Brit., Austral., & N.Z.* (of trade unionists) to organize a boycott of (specified goods, jobs, work, etc.). ~See also **blackout.** [OE *blæc*] —'**blackness** *n.*

Black[1] (blæk) *n.* **1.** a member of a dark-skinned race, esp. a Negro or an Australian Aborigine. ~*adj.* **2.** of or relating to a Black or Blacks.

Black[2] (blæk) *n.* Sir **James** (**Whyte**). born 1924, British biochemist. He discovered beta-blockers and drugs for peptic ulcers. He was awarded a Nobel Prize in 1988.

blackamoor ('blækə,muə, -,mɔː) *n.* a Negro or other person with dark skin. [C16: see BLACK, MOOR]

black-and-blue *adj.* **1.** (of the skin) discoloured, as from a bruise. **2.** feeling pain or soreness, as from a beating.

Black and Tan *n.* a member of the armed force sent to Ireland in 1921 by the British Government to combat Sinn Fein. [named after the colour of their uniforms]

black-and-white *n.* **1. a.** a photograph, picture, sketch, etc., in black, white, and shades of grey rather than in colour. **b.** (*as modifier*): *black-and-white film.* **2. in black and white. a.** in print or writing. **b.** in extremes: *he always saw things in black and white.*

black art *n.* **the.** another name for **black magic.**

black-backed gull *n.* either of two common black-and-white European coastal gulls, **lesser black-backed gull** and **great black-backed gull.**

blackball ('blæk,bɔːl) *n.* **1.** a negative vote or veto. **2.** a black wooden ball used to indicate disapproval or to veto in a vote. ~*vb.* (*tr.*) **3.** to vote against. **4.** to exclude (someone) from a group, profession, etc.; ostracize. [C18: from *black ball* used to veto]

black bean *n.* an Australian leguminous tree: used in furniture manufacture. Also called: **Moreton Bay chestnut.**

black bear *n.* **1. American black bear.** a bear inhabiting forests of North America. It is smaller and less ferocious than the brown bear. **2. Asiatic black bear.** a bear of central and E Asia, black with a pale V-shaped mark on the chest.

Blackbeard ('blæk,bɪəd) *n.* nickname of (Edward) **Teach.**

black belt *n. Judo, karate, etc.* **a.** a black belt worn by an instructor or expert. **b.** a person entitled to wear this.

blackberry ('blækbərɪ) *n., pl.* **-ries. 1.** Also called: **bramble.** any of several woody rosaceous plants that have thorny stems and black or purple edible berry-like fruits. **2.** the fruit of any of these plants. ~*vb.* **-rying, -ried. 3.** (*intr.*) to gather blackberries.

blackbird ('blæk,bɜːd) *n.* **1.** a common European thrush in which the male has black plumage and a yellow bill. **2.** any of various American orioles having dark plumage. **3.** (formerly) a person, esp. a South Sea Islander, who was kidnapped and sold as a slave, esp. in Australia. ~*vb.* **4.** (*tr.*) (formerly) to kidnap and sell into slavery.

blackboard ('blæk,bɔːd) *n.* a hard or rigid surface made of a smooth usually dark substance, used for writing or drawing on with chalk, esp. in teaching.

black body *n. Physics.* a hypothetical body capable of absorbing all the electromagnetic radiation falling on it. Also called: **full radiator.**

black book *n.* **1.** a book containing the names of people to be punished, blacklisted, etc. **2. in someone's black books.** *Inf.* out of favour with someone.

black box *n.* **1.** a self-contained unit in an electronic or computer system whose circuitry need not be known to understand its function. **2.** an informal name for **flight recorder.**

blackboy ('blæk,bɔɪ) *n.* another name for **grass tree** (sense 1).

blackbuck ('blæk,bʌk) *n.* an Indian antelope, the male of which has a dark back.

Blackburn ('blækbɜːn) *n.* **1.** a city in NW England, in central Lancashire: textile industries. Pop: 88 236 (1981). **2. Mount.** a mountain in SE Alaska, the highest peak in the Wrangell Mountains. Height: 5037 m (16 523 ft.).

blackbutt ('blæk,bʌt) *n.* any of various Australian eucalyptus trees having rough fibrous bark and hard wood used as timber.

blackcap ('blæk,kæp) *n.* a brownish-grey Old World warbler, the male of which has a black crown.

blackcock ('blæk,kɒk) *n.* the male of the black grouse.

Black Country *n.* **the.** the heavily industrialized West Midlands of England.

blackcurrant (,blæk'kʌrənt) *n.* **1.** a N temperate shrub having red or white flowers and small edible black berries. **2.** its fruit.

blackdamp ('blæk,dæmp) *n.* air that is low in oxygen content and high in carbon dioxide as a result of an explosion in a mine. Also called: **chokedamp.**

Black Death *n.* **the.** a form of bubonic plague pandemic in Europe and Asia during the 14th century. See **bubonic plague.**

black disc *n.* a conventional black vinyl gramophone record as opposed to a compact disc.

black earth *n.* another name for **chernozem.**

black economy *n.* that portion of the income of a nation that remains illegally undeclared.

blacken ('blækən) *vb.* **1.** to make or become black or dirty. **2.** (*tr.*) to defame; slander (esp. in **blacken someone's name**).

Blackett ('blækɪt) *n.* **Patrick Maynard Stuart,** Baron. 1897–1974, English physicist, noted for his work on cosmic radiation and his discovery of the positron. Nobel prize for physics 1948.

black eye *n.* bruising round the eye.

black-eyed Susan ('suːzᵊn) *n.* any of several North American plants having flower heads of orange-yellow rays and brown-black centres.

blackface ('blæk,feɪs) *n.* **1.** a variety of sheep with a black face. **2.** the make-up used by a performer imitating a Negro.

blackfish ('blæk,fɪʃ) *n., pl.* **-fish** *or* **-fishes. 1.** any of various dark fishes, esp. a common edible Australian estuary fish. **2.** a female salmon that has recently spawned. Cf. **redfish** (sense 1).

black flag *n.* another name for the **Jolly Roger.**

blackfly ('blæk,flaɪ) *n., pl.* **-flies.** a black aphid that infests beans, sugar beet, and other plants. Also called: **bean aphid.**

Black Forest *n.* **the.** a hilly wooded region of SW West Germany, in Baden-Württemberg: a popular resort area. German name: **Schwarzwald.**

Black Friar *n.* a Dominican friar.

black grouse *n.* **1.** a large N European grouse, the male of which has a bluish-black plumage. **2.** a related and similar species of W Asia.

blackguard ('blægɑːd, -gəd) *n.* **1.** an unprincipled contemptible person; scoundrel. ~*vb.* **2.** (*tr.*) to ridicule or denounce with abusive language. **3.** (*intr.*) to behave like a blackguard. [C16: see BLACK, GUARD] —'**blackguardism** *n.* —'**blackguardly** *adj.*

blackhead ('blæk,hɛd) *n.* **1.** a black-tipped plug of fatty matter clogging a pore of the skin. **2.** any of various birds with black plumage on the head.

Black Hills *pl. n.* a group of mountains in W South Dakota and NE Wyoming: famous for the gigantic sculptures of U.S. presidents on the side of Mount Rushmore. Highest peak: Harney Peak, 2207 m (7242 ft.).

black hole *n. Astron.* a hypothetical region of space resulting from the gravitational collapse of a star and surrounded by a gravitational field so high that neither matter nor radiation could escape from it.

black ice *n.* a thin transparent layer of new ice on a road or similar surface.

blacking ('blækɪŋ) *n.* any preparation for giving a black finish to shoes, metals, etc.

Black Isle *n.* **the.** a peninsula in NE Scotland, in the Highland Region, between the Cromarty and Moray Firths. [so called because until the late 18th century much of it was uncultivated black moor]

blackjack[1] ('blæk,dʒæk) *Chiefly U.S. & Canad.* ~*n.* **1.** a truncheon of leather-covered lead with a flexible shaft. ~*vb.* (*tr.*) **2.** to hit as with a blackjack. **3.** to compel (a person) by threats. [C19: from BLACK + JACK (implement)]

blackjack[2] ('blæk,dʒæk) *n.* pontoon or any similar card game. [C20: from BLACK + JACK (the knave)]

black lead (lɛd) *n.* another name for **graphite**.

blackleg ('blækleɡ) *n.* **1.** Also called: **scab.** *Brit.* a person who acts against the interests of a trade union, as by continuing to work during a strike or taking over a striker's job. ~*vb.* **-legging, -legged.** **2.** (*intr.*) *Brit.* to act against the interests of a trade union, esp. by refusing to join a strike.

black light *n.* the invisible electromagnetic radiation in the ultraviolet and infrared regions of the spectrum.

blacklist ('blæk,lɪst) *n.* **1.** a list of persons or organizations under suspicion, or considered untrustworthy, disloyal, etc. ~*vb.* **2.** (*tr.*) to put on a blacklist.

black magic *n.* magic used for evil purposes.

blackmail ('blæk,meɪl) *n.* **1.** the act of attempting to obtain money by intimidation, as by threats to disclose discreditable information. **2.** the exertion of pressure, esp. unfairly, in an attempt to influence someone. ~*vb.* (*tr.*) **3.** to exact or attempt to exact (money or anything of value) from (a person) by threats or intimidation; extort. **4.** to attempt to influence (a person), esp. by unfair pressure. [C16: from BLACK + OE *māl* terms] —**'black,mailer** *n.*

Black Maria (mə'raɪə) *n.* a police van for transporting prisoners.

black mark *n.* an indication of disapproval, failure, etc.

black market *n.* **1.** any system in which goods or currencies are sold and bought illegally, esp. in violation of controls or rationing. **2.** the place where such a system operates. ~*vb.* **black-market.** **3.** to sell (goods) on the black market. —**black marketeer** *n.*

black mass *n.* (*sometimes cap.*) a blasphemous travesty of the Christian Mass, performed by practitioners of black magic.

Blackmore ('blæk,mɔː) *n.* **R(ichard) D(oddridge).** 1825–1900, English novelist; author of *Lorna Doone* (1869).

Black Mountains *pl. n.* **1.** a mountain range in S Wales, in E Dyfed and W Powys. Highest peak: Carmarthen Van, 802 m (2632 ft.). **2.** a mountain range in S Wales, in E Gwent. Highest peak: Waun Fach, 811 m (2660 ft.).

Black Muslim *n.* (esp. in the U.S.) a member of an Islamic political movement of Black people who seek to establish a new Black nation.

black nightshade *n.* a common poisonous weed in cultivated land, having small white flowers and black berrylike fruits.

blackout ('blækaʊt) *n.* **1.** the extinguishing or hiding of all artificial light, esp. in a city visible to an air attack. **2.** a momentary loss of consciousness, vision, or memory. **3.** a temporary electrical power failure or cut. **4.** the suspension of broadcasting, as by a strike or for political reasons. ~*vb.* **black out.** (*adv.*) **5.** (*tr.*) to obliterate or extinguish (lights). **6.** (*tr.*) to create a blackout in (a city, etc.). **7.** (*intr.*) to lose vision, consciousness, or memory temporarily. **8.** (*tr.*) to stop (news, a television programme, etc.) from being broadcast.

black pepper *n.* a pungent condiment made by grinding the dried unripe berries and husks of the pepper plant.

Blackpool ('blæk,puːl) *n.* a town and resort in NW England, in Lancashire on the Irish Sea: famous for its tower, 158 m (520 ft.) high, and its illuminations. Pop.: 147 000 (1983).

Black Power *n.* a social, economic, and political movement of Black people, esp. in the U.S. and Australia, to obtain equality with Whites.

Black Prince *n.* **the.** See **Edward** (Prince of Wales).

black pudding *n.* a kind of black sausage made from minced pork fat, pig's blood, and other ingredients. Also called: **blood pudding.**

Black Rod *n.* (in Britain) an officer of the House of Lords and of the Order of the Garter, whose main duty is summoning the Commons at the opening and proroguing of Parliament.

Black Sea *n.* an inland sea between SE Europe and Asia: connected to the Aegean Sea by the Bosporus, the Sea of Marmara, and the Dardanelles, and to the Sea of Azov by the Kerch Strait. Area: about 415 000 sq. km (160 000 sq. miles). Also called: **Euxine Sea.** Ancient name: **Pontus Euxinus.**

black section *n.* (in Britain) an unofficial group within the Labour Party in any constituency which represents the interests of local Black people.

black sheep *n.* a person who is regarded as a disgrace or failure by his family or peer group.

Blackshirt ('blæk,ʃɜːt) *n.* (in Europe) a member of a fascist organization, esp. the Italian Fascist party before and during World War II.

blacksmith ('blæk,smɪθ) *n.* an artisan who works iron with a furnace, anvil, hammer, etc. [C14: see BLACK, SMITH]

black snake *n.* **1.** any of several Old World black venomous snakes, esp. the **Australian black snake. 2.** any of various dark nonvenomous snakes.

black spot *n.* **1.** a place on a road where accidents frequently occur. **2.** any dangerous or difficult place. **3.** a disease of roses that causes black blotches on the leaves.

Blackstone ('blæk,stəʊn, -stən) *n.* Sir **William.** 1723–80, English jurist noted particularly for his *Commentaries on the Laws of England* (1865–69), which had a profound influence on jurisprudence in the U.S.

black stump *n.* **the.** *Austral.* an imaginary marker of the extent of civilization (esp. in **beyond the black stump**).

black tea *n.* tea made from fermented tea leaves.

blackthorn ('blæk,θɔːn) *n.* a thorny Eurasian shrub with black twigs, white flowers, and small sour plumlike fruits. Also called: **sloe.**

black tie *n.* **1.** a black bow tie worn with a dinner jacket. **2.** (*modifier*) denoting an occasion when a dinner jacket should be worn.

blacktop ('blæk,tɒp) *n. Chiefly U.S. & Canad.* a bituminous mixture used for paving.

Black tracker *n. Austral.* an Aboriginal tracker working for the police.

black velvet *n.* a mixture of stout and champagne in equal proportions.

Black Volta *n.* a river in W Africa, rising in SW Burkina-Faso and flowing northeast, then south into Lake Volta: forms part of the border of Ghana with Burkina-Faso and with the Ivory Coast. Length: about 800 km (500 miles).

Black Watch *n.* **the.** the Royal Highland Regiment in the British Army.

blackwater fever ('blæk,wɔːtə) *n.* a rare and serious complication of malaria, characterized by massive destruction of red blood cells, producing dark red or blackish urine.

black widow *n.* an American spider, the female of which is highly venomous, and commonly eats its mate.

Blackwood ('blæk,wʊd) *n. Bridge.* a conventional bidding sequence of four and five no-trumps, which are requests to the partner to show aces and kings respectively. [C20: after E. F. *Blackwood*, its U.S. inventor]

bladder ('blædə) *n.* **1.** *Anat.* a distensible membranous sac, usually containing liquid or gas, esp. the urinary bladder. **2.** an inflatable part of something. **3.** a hollow sac-like part in certain plants, such as the bladderwrack. [OE *blǣdre*] —**'bladdery** *adj.*

bladderwort ('blædə,wɜːt) *n.* an aquatic plant some of whose leaves are modified as small bladders to trap minute aquatic animals.

bladderwrack ('blædə,ræk) *n.* any of several seaweeds that grow in the intertidal regions of rocky shores and have branched brown fronds with air bladders.

blade (bleɪd) n. **1.** the part of a sharp weapon, tool, etc., that forms the cutting edge. **2.** the thin flattish part of various tools, implements, etc., as of a propeller. **3.** the flattened expanded part of a leaf, sepal, or petal. **4.** the long narrow leaf of a grass or related plant. **5.** the striking surface of a bat, club, stick, or oar. **6.** the metal runner on an ice skate. **7.** the upper part of the tongue lying directly behind the tip. **8.** *Arch.* a dashing or swaggering young man. **9.** short for **shoulder blade. 10.** a poetic word for a **sword** or **swordsman.** [OE *blæd*] — **'bladed** *adj.*

blaeberry ('bleɪbərɪ) n., pl. **-ries.** *Brit.* another name for **whortleberry** (senses 1, 2). [C15: from dialect *blae* bluish + BERRY]

blag (blæg) *Sl.* ~n. **1.** a robbery, esp. with violence. ~vb. **blagging, blagged.** (*tr.*) **2.** to snatch (wages, someone's handbag, etc.); steal. **3.** to rob (esp. a bank or post office). [C19: from ?] — **'blagger** n.

Blagoveshchensk (*Russian* bləga'vjeʃtʃɪnsk) n. a city and port in the SE Soviet Union, in Siberia on the Amur River. Pop.: 202 000 (1987).

blah *or* **blah blah** (blɑː) n. *Sl.* worthless or silly talk. [C20: imit.]

blain (bleɪn) n. a blister, blotch, or sore on the skin. [OE *blegen*]

Blake (bleɪk) n. **1. Robert.** 1599–1657, English admiral, who commanded Cromwell's fleet against the Royalists, the Dutch, and the Spanish. **2. William.** 1757–1827, English poet, painter, engraver, and mystic. His literary works include *Songs of Innocence* (1789) and *Songs of Experience* (1794), *The Marriage of Heaven and Hell* (1793), and *Jerusalem* (1820). His chief works in the visual arts include engravings of a visionary nature, such as the illustrations for *The Book of Job* (1826), for Dante's poems, and for his own *Prophetic Books* (1783–1804).

blame (bleɪm) n. **1.** responsibility for something that is wrong; culpability. **2.** an expression of condemnation. ~vb. (*tr.*) **3.** (usually foll. by *for*) to attribute responsibility to: *I blame him for the failure.* **4.** (usually foll. by *on*) to ascribe responsibility for (something) to: *I blame the failure on him.* **5.** to find fault with. **6. be to blame.** to be at fault. [C12: from OF *blasmer,* ult. from LL *blasphēmāre* to blaspheme] — **'blamable** *or* **'blameable** *adj.* — **'blamably** *or* **'blameably** *adv.*

blameful ('bleɪmfʊl) *adj.* deserving blame; guilty. — **'blamefully** *adv.* — **'blamefulness** n.

blameless ('bleɪmlɪs) *adj.* free from blame; innocent. — **'blamelessness** n.

blameworthy ('bleɪm,wɜːðɪ) *adj.* deserving censure. — **'blame,worthiness** n.

Blanc[1] (*French* blɑ̃) n. **1. Mont.** See **Mont Blanc. 2. Cape.** a headland in N Tunisia: the northernmost point of Africa. **3. Cape.** Also called: **Cape Blanco** ('blæŋkəʊ). a peninsula in Mauritania, on the Atlantic coast.

Blanc[2] (*French* blɑ̃) n. (**Jean Joseph Charles**) **Louis** (lwi). 1811–82, French socialist and historian: author of *L'Organisation du travail* (1840), in which he advocated the establishment of cooperative workshops subsidized by the state.

blanch (blɑːntʃ) vb. (*mainly tr.*) **1.** to remove colour from; whiten. **2.** (*usually intr.*) to become or cause to become pale, as with sickness or fear. **3.** to prepare (meat, green vegetables, nuts, etc.) by plunging them in boiling water. **4.** to cause (celery, chicory, etc.) to grow free of chlorophyll by the exclusion of sunlight. [C14: from OF *blanchir,* from *blanc* white; see BLANK]

blancmange (blə'mɒnʒ) n. a jelly-like dessert of milk, stiffened usually with cornflour. [C14: from OF *blanc manger,* lit.: white food]

bland (blænd) *adj.* **1.** devoid of distinctive or stimulating characteristics; uninteresting. **2.** gentle and agreeable; suave. **3.** mild and soothing. [C15: from L *blandus* flattering] — **'blandly** *adv.* — **'blandness** n.

blandish ('blændɪʃ) vb. (*tr.*) to seek to persuade or influence by mild flattery; coax. [C14: from OF *blandir,* from L *blandīrī*]

blandishments ('blændɪʃmənts) pl. n. (*rarely sing.*) flattery intended to coax or cajole.

blank (blæŋk) *adj.* **1.** (of a writing surface) bearing no marks; not written on. **2.** (of a form, etc.) with spaces left for details to be filled in. **3.** without ornament or break. **4.** not filled in; empty. **5.** exhibiting no interest or expression: *a blank look.* **6.** lacking understanding; confused: *he looked blank.* **7.** absolute; complete: *blank rejection.* **8.** devoid of ideas or inspiration: *his mind went blank.* ~n. **9.** an emptiness; void; blank space. **10.** an empty space for writing in. **11.** a printed form containing such empty spaces. **12.** something characterized by incomprehension or confusion: *my mind went a complete blank.* **13.** a mark, often a dash, in place of a word, esp. a taboo word. **14.** short for **blank cartridge. 15.** a piece of material prepared for stamping, punching, forging, or some other operation. **16. draw a blank.** to get no results from something. ~vb. (*tr.*) **17.** (usually foll. by *out*) to cross out, blot, or obscure. [C15: from OF *blanc* white, of Gmc origin] — **'blankness** n.

blank cartridge n. a cartridge containing powder but no bullet.

blank cheque n. **1.** a cheque that has been signed but on which the amount payable has not been specified. **2.** complete freedom of action.

blanket ('blæŋkɪt) n. **1.** a large piece of thick cloth for use as a bed covering, animal covering, etc. **2.** a concealing cover, as of smoke, leaves, or snow. **3.** (*modifier*) applying to or covering a wide group or variety of people, conditions, situations, etc.: *blanket insurance against loss, injury, and theft.* **4. (born) on the wrong side of the blanket.** *Inf.* illegitimate. ~vb. (*tr.*) **5.** to cover as with a blanket; overlie. **6.** to cover a wide area; give blanket coverage. **7.** (usually foll. by *out*) to obscure or suppress. [C13: from OF *blancquete,* from *blanc;* see BLANK]

blanket bath n. an all-over wash given to a person confined to bed.

blanket stitch n. a strong reinforcing stitch for the edges of blankets and other thick material.

blankety ('blæŋkɪtɪ) *adj., adv.* a euphemism for any taboo word. [C20: from BLANK]

blank verse n. *Prosody.* unrhymed verse, esp. in iambic pentameters.

Blantyre-Limbe (blæn'taɪə'lɪmbeɪ) n. a city in S Malawi: largest city in the country; formed in 1956 from the adjoining towns of Blantyre and Limbe. Pop.: 355 200 (1985 est.).

blare (blɛə) vb. **1.** to sound loudly and harshly. **2.** to proclaim loudly and sensationally. ~n. **3.** a loud harsh noise. [C14: from MDu. *bleren;* imit.]

blarney ('blɑːnɪ) n. **1.** flattering talk. ~vb. **2.** to cajole with flattery; wheedle. [C19: after the *Blarney* Stone in SW Ireland, said to endow whoever kisses it with skill in flattery]

Blasco Ibáñez (*Spanish* 'blasko i'βaɲeθ) n. **Vicente** (bi-'θente). 1867–1928, Spanish novelist, whose books include *Blood and Sand* (1909) and *The Four Horsemen of the Apocalypse* (1916).

blasé (blɑː'zeɪ) *adj.* **1.** indifferent to something because of familiarity. **2.** lacking enthusiasm; bored. [C19: from F, p.p. of *blaser* to cloy]

blaspheme (blæs'fiːm) vb. **1.** (*tr.*) to show contempt or disrespect for (God or sacred things), esp. in speech. **2.** (*intr.*) to utter profanities or curses. [C14: from LL, from Gk, from *blasphēmos* BLASPHEMOUS] — **blas'phemer** n.

blasphemous ('blæsfɪməs) *adj.* involving impiousness or gross irreverence towards God or something sacred. [C15: via LL, from Gk *blas-phēmos* evil-speaking, from *blapsis* evil + *phēmē* speech]

blasphemy ('blæsfɪmɪ) n., pl. **-mies.** blasphemous behaviour or language.

blast (blɑːst) n. **1.** an explosion, as of dynamite. **2.** the rapid movement of air away from the centre of an explosion; shock wave. **3.** the charge used in a single explosion. **4.** a sudden strong gust of wind or air. **5.** a sudden loud sound, as of a trumpet. **6.** a violent verbal outburst, as of criticism. **7.** a forcible jet of air, esp. one used to intensify the heating effect of a furnace. **8.** any of several diseases of plants and animals. **9. (at) full blast.** at maximum speed, volume, etc. ~interj. **10.** *Sl.* an exclamation of annoyance. ~vb. **11.** (*tr.*) to destroy or blow up with explosives, shells, etc. **12.** to make or cause to make a loud harsh noise. **13.** to wither or cause to wither; blight or be blighted. **14.** (*tr.*) to criticize severely. [OE *blæst*] — **'blaster** n.

-blast n. *combining form.* (in biology) indicating an embryonic cell or formative layer: *mesoblast.* [from Gk *blastos* bud]

blasted ('blɑːstɪd) *adj.* **1.** blighted or withered. ~adj. (*prenominal*), adv. **2.** *Sl.* (intensifier): *a blasted idiot.*

blast furnace *n.* a vertical cylindrical furnace for smelting into which a blast of preheated air is forced.

blasto- *combining form.* indicating an embryo or bud. [see BLAST]

blastoff ('bla:st,ɒf) *n.* **1.** the launching of a rocket under its own power. **2.** the time at which this occurs. ~*vb.* **blast off. 3.** (*adv.; when tr., usually passive*) to be launched.

blastula ('blæstjʊlə) *n., pl.* **-las** *or* **-lae** (-li:). an early form of an animal embryo that develops a sphere of cells with a central cavity. Also called: **blastosphere.** [C19: NL from Gk, from dim. of *blastos* bud] — **'blastular** *adj.*

blatant ('bleɪt³nt) *adj.* **1.** glaringly conspicuous or obvious: *a blatant lie.* **2.** offensively noticeable; obtrusive. **3.** offensively noisy. [C16: coined by Edmund Spenser; prob. infl. by L *blatīre* to babble] — **'blatancy** *n.*

blather ('blæðə) *vb., n.* a variant of **blether.**

blatherskite ('blæðə,skaɪt) *n.* **1.** a talkative silly person. **2.** foolish talk; nonsense. [C17: from BLATHER + Scot & N English dialect *skate* fellow]

Blavatsky (blə'vætskɪ) *n.* **Elena Petrovna** (jɪ'ljɛnə pɪ-'trɒvnə), called *Madame Blavatsky.* 1831–91, Russian theosophist; author of *Isis Unveiled* (1877).

Blaydon ('bleɪd³n) *n.* an industrial town in NE England, in Tyne and Wear. Pop: 30 563 (1981).

blaze[1] (bleɪz) *n.* **1.** a strong fire or flame. **2.** a very bright light or glare. **3.** an outburst (of passion, acclaim, patriotism, etc.). **4.** brilliance; brightness. ~*vb.* (*intr.*) **5.** to burn fiercely. **6.** to shine brightly. **7.** (often foll. by *up*) to become stirred, as with anger or excitement. **8.** (usually foll. by *away*) to shoot continuously. ~See also **blazes.** [OE *blǣse*]

blaze[2] (bleɪz) *n.* **1.** a mark, usually indicating a path, made on a tree. **2.** a light-coloured marking on the face of a domestic animal. ~*vb.* (*tr.*) **3.** to mark (a tree, path, etc.) with a blaze. **4. blaze a trail.** to explore new territories, areas of knowledge, etc., so that others can follow. [C17: prob. from MLow G *bles* white marking]

blaze[3] (bleɪz) *vb.* (*tr; often foll. by abroad*) to make widely known; proclaim. [C14: from MDu. *blāsen*, from OHG *blāsan*]

blazer ('bleɪzə) *n.* a fairly lightweight jacket, often in the colours of a sports club, school, etc.

blazes ('bleɪzɪz) *pl. n.* **1.** *Sl.* a euphemistic word for **hell.** **2.** *Inf.* (intensifier): *to run like blazes.*

blazon ('bleɪz³n) *vb.* (*tr.*) **1.** (often foll. by *abroad*) to proclaim publicly. **2.** *Heraldry.* to describe (heraldic arms) in proper terms. **3.** to draw and colour (heraldic arms) conventionally. ~*n.* **4.** *Heraldry.* a conventional description or depiction of heraldic arms. [C13: from OF *blason* coat of arms] — **'blazoner** *n.*

blazonry ('bleɪz³nrɪ) *n., pl.* **-ries. 1.** the art or process of describing heraldic arms in proper form. **2.** heraldic arms collectively. **3.** colourful or ostentatious display.

bldg *abbrev. for* building.

bleach (bli:tʃ) *vb.* **1.** to make or become white or colourless, as by exposure to sunlight, by the action of chemical agents, etc. ~*n.* **2.** a bleaching agent. **3.** the act of bleaching. [OE *blǣcan*] — **'bleacher** *n.*

bleaching powder *n.* a white powder consisting of chlorinated calcium hydroxide. Also called: **chloride of lime, chlorinated lime.**

bleak[1] (bli:k) *adj.* **1.** exposed and barren. **2.** cold and raw. **3.** offering little hope; dismal: *a bleak future.* [OE *blāc* bright, pale] — **'bleakness** *n.*

bleak[2] (bli:k) *n.* any of various European cyprinid fishes occurring in slow-flowing rivers. [C15: prob. from ON *bleikja* white colour]

blear (blɪə) *Arch.* ~*vb.* **1.** (*tr.*) to make (eyes or sight) dim as with tears; blur. ~*adj.* **2.** a less common word for **bleary.** [C13: *blere* to make dim]

bleary ('blɪərɪ) *adj.* **blearier, bleariest. 1.** (of eyes or vision) dimmed or blurred, as by tears or tiredness. **2.** indistinct or unclear. — **'bleariness** *n.*

bleary-eyed *or* **blear-eyed** *adj.* with eyes blurred, as with old age or after waking.

bleat (bli:t) *vb.* **1.** (*intr.*) (of a sheep, goat, or calf) to utter its characteristic plaintive cry. **2.** (*intr.*) to speak with any similar sound. **3.** to whine; whimper. ~*n.* **4.** the characteristic cry of sheep, goats, and calves. **5.** any sound similar to this. **6.** a weak complaint or whine. [OE *blǣtan*] — **'bleater** *n.* — **'bleating** *n., adj.*

bleb (blɛb) *n.* **1.** a fluid-filled blister on the skin. **2.** a small air bubble. [C17: var. of BLOB]

bleed (bli:d) *vb.* **bleeding, bled** (blɛd). **1.** (*intr.*) to lose or emit blood. **2.** (*tr.*) to remove or draw blood from (a person or animal). **3.** (*intr.*) to be injured or die, as for a cause. **4.** (of plants) to exude (sap or resin), esp. from a cut. **5.** (*tr.*) *Inf.* to obtain money, etc., from, esp. by extortion. **6.** (*tr.*) to draw liquid or gas from (a container or enclosed system): *to bleed the hydraulic brakes.* **7.** (*intr.*) (of dye or paint) to run or become mixed, as when wet. **8.** to print or be printed so that text, illustrations, etc., run off the trimmed page. **9. one's heart bleeds.** used to express sympathetic grief, often ironically. [OE *blēdan*]

bleeder ('bli:də) *n.* **1.** *Sl.* **a.** *Derog.* a despicable person. **b.** any person. **2.** *Pathol.* a nontechnical name for a **haemophiliac.**

bleeding ('bli:dɪŋ) *adj., adv. Brit. sl.* (intensifier): *a bleeding fool.*

bleeding heart *n.* **1.** any of several plants, esp. a widely cultivated Japanese species which has heart-shaped nodding pink flowers. **2.** *Inf.* **a.** an excessively softhearted person. **b.** (*as modifier*): *bleeding-heart liberals.*

bleep (bli:p) *n.* **1.** a single short high-pitched signal made by an electronic apparatus; beep. **2.** Also called: **bleeper.** a small portable radio receiver that makes a bleeping signal. ~*vb.* **3.** (*intr.*) to make such a noise. **4.** (*tr.*) to call (somebody) by means of a bleep. [C20: imit.]

blemish ('blɛmɪʃ) *n.* **1.** a defect; flaw; stain. ~*vb.* **2.** (*tr.*) to flaw the perfection of; spoil; tarnish. [C14: from OF *blemir* to make pale]

blench (blɛntʃ) *vb.* (*intr.*) to shy away, as in fear; quail. [OE *blencan* to deceive]

blend (blɛnd) *vb.* **1.** to mix or mingle (components) together thoroughly. **2.** (*tr.*) to mix (different grades or varieties of tea, whisky, etc.). **3.** (*intr.*) to look good together; harmonize. **4.** (*intr.*) (esp. of colours) to shade imperceptibly into each other. ~*n.* **5.** a mixture or type produced by blending. **6.** the act of blending. **7.** Also called: **portmanteau word.** a word formed by joining together the beginning and the end of two other words: *"brunch"* is a blend of *"breakfast"* and *"lunch."* [OE *blandan*]

blende (blɛnd) *n.* **1.** another name for **sphalerite. 2.** any of several sulphide ores. [C17: G, from *blenden* to deceive, BLIND; so called because it is easily mistaken for galena]

blender ('blɛndə) *n.* **1.** a person or thing that blends. **2.** Also called: **liquidizer.** a kitchen appliance with blades used for puréeing vegetables, blending liquids, etc.

Blenheim ('blɛnɪm) *n.* a village in SW Germany, site of a victory of Anglo-Austrian forces under the Duke of Marlborough and Prince Eugène of Savoy that saved Vienna from the French and Bavarians (1704) during the War of the Spanish Succession. Modern name: **Blindheim.**

blenny ('blɛnɪ) *n., pl.* **-nies.** any of various small fishes of coastal waters having a tapering scaleless body, a long dorsal fin, and long raylike pelvic fins. [C18: from L, from Gk *blennos* slime]

blent (blɛnt) *vb. Arch. or literary.* a past participle of **blend.**

blepharitis (,blɛfə'raɪtɪs) *n.* inflammation of the eyelids. [C19: from Gk *blephar(on)* eyelid + -ITIS]

Blériot (*French* blerjo) *n.* **Louis** (lwi). 1872–1936, French aviator and aeronautical engineer: made the first flight across the English Channel (1909).

blesbok *or* **blesbuck** ('blɛs,bʌk) *n., pl.* **-boks, -bok** *or* **-buck, -buck.** an antelope of southern Africa. The coat is reddish brown with a white blaze between the eyes; the horns are lyre-shaped. [C19: Afrik., from Du. *bles* BLAZE[2] + *bok* BUCK[1]]

bless (blɛs) *vb.* **blessing, blessed** *or* **blest.** (*tr.*) **1.** to consecrate or render holy by means of a religious rite. **2.** to give honour or glory to (a person or thing) as holy. **3.** to call upon God to protect; give a benediction to. **4.** to worship or adore (God). **5.** (*often passive*) to grant happiness, health, or prosperity to. **6.** (*usually passive*) to endow with a talent, beauty, etc. **7.** *Rare.* to protect against evil or harm. **8. bless you!** (*interj.*) **a.** a traditional phrase said to a person who has just sneezed. **b.** an exclamation of well-wishing or surprise. **9. bless me!** *or* **(God) bless my soul!** (*interj.*) an exclamation of surprise. [OE *blǣdsian* to sprinkle with sacrificial blood]

blessed ('blɛsɪd, blɛst) *adj.* **1.** made holy; consecrated. **2.** worthy of deep reverence or respect. **3.** *R.C. Church.* (of a person) beatified by the pope. **4.** characterized by happiness or good fortune. **5.** bringing great happiness or good fortune. **6.** a euphemistic word for **damned,** used in mild oaths: *I'm blessed if I know.* — **'blessedly** *adv.* — **'blessedness** *n.*

Blessed Sacrament *n. Chiefly R.C. Church.* the consecrated elements of the Eucharist.

Blessed Virgin *n. Chiefly R.C. Church.* another name for the **Virgin Mary.**

blessing ('blɛsɪŋ) *n.* **1.** the act of invoking divine protection or aid. **2.** the words or ceremony used for this. **3.** a short prayer before or after a meal; grace. **4.** approval; good wishes. **5.** the bestowal of a divine gift or favour. **6.** a happy event.

blest (blɛst) *vb.* a past tense and past participle of **bless.**

blether ('blɛðə) *Scot.* ~*vb.* **1.** (*intr.*) to speak foolishly. ~*n.* **2.** foolish talk; nonsense. [C16: from ON *blathr* nonsense]

blew (blu:) *vb.* the past tense of **blow**[1] and **blow**[3].

Blida ('bli:də) *n.* a city in N Algeria, on the edge of the Mitidja Plain. Pop.: 191 314 (1983).

Bligh (blaɪ) *n.* **William.** 1754–1817, British admiral; Governor of New South Wales (1806–9), deposed by the New South Wales Corps: as a captain, commander of *H.M.S. Bounty* when the crew mutinied in 1789.

blight (blaɪt) *n.* **1.** any plant disease characterized by withering and shrivelling without rotting. **2.** any factor that causes the symptoms of blight in plants. **3.** a person or thing that mars or prevents growth. **4.** an ugly urban district. ~*vb.* **5.** to cause or suffer a blight. **6.** (*tr.*) to frustrate or disappoint. **7.** (*tr.*) to spoil; destroy. [C17: ? rel. to OE *blǣce* rash]

blighter ('blaɪtə) *n. Brit. inf.* **1.** a fellow. **2.** a despicable or irritating person or thing.

Blighty ('blaɪtɪ) *n.* (*sometimes not cap.*) *Brit. sl.* (used esp. by troops serving abroad) **1.** England; home. **2.** (*pl.* **Blighties**) Also called: **a blighty one.** (esp. in World War I) a wound that causes the recipient to be sent home to England. [C20: from Hindi *bilāyatī* foreign land, England, from Ar. *wilāyat* country]

blimey ('blaɪmɪ) *interj. Brit. sl.* an exclamation of surprise or annoyance. [C19: short for *gorblimey* God blind me]

blimp[1] (blɪmp) *n.* **1.** a small nonrigid airship. **2.** *Films.* a soundproof cover fixed over a camera during shooting. [C20: prob. from (*type*) *B-limp*]

blimp[2] (blɪmp) *n.* (*often cap.*) *Chiefly Brit.* a person, esp. a military officer, who is stupidly complacent and reactionary. Also called: **Colonel Blimp.** [C20: from a character created by David Lᴏw] — **'blimpish** *adj.*

blind (blaɪnd) *adj.* **1. a.** unable to see; sightless. **b.** (*as collective n.; preceded by the*): *the blind.* **2.** (usually foll. by *to*) unable or unwilling to understand or discern. **3.** not determined by reason: *blind hatred.* **4.** acting or performed without control or preparation. **5.** done without being able to see, relying on instruments for information. **6.** hidden from sight: *a blind corner.* **7.** closed at one end: *a blind alley.* **8.** completely lacking awareness or consciousness: *a blind stupor.* **9.** *Inf.* very drunk. **10.** having no openings or outlets: *a blind wall.* **11.** (intensifier): *not a blind bit of notice.* ~*adv.* **12.** without being able to see ahead or using only instruments: *to drive blind; flying blind.* **13.** without adequate knowledge or information; carelessly: *to buy a house blind.* **14. bake blind.** to bake (an empty pastry case) by half filling with dried peas, crusts, etc., to keep it in shape. ~*vb.* (*mainly tr.*) **15.** to deprive of sight permanently or temporarily. **16.** to deprive of good sense, reason, or judgment. **17.** to darken; conceal. **18.** (foll. by *with*) to overwhelm by showing detailed knowledge: *to blind somebody with science.* ~*n.* **19.** (*modifier*) for or intended to help the blind: *a blind school.* **20.** a shade for a window, usually on a roller. **21.** any obstruction or hindrance to sight, light, or air. **22.** a person, action, or thing that serves to deceive or conceal the truth. [OE *blind*] — **'blindly** *adv.* — **'blindness** *n.*

blind alley *n.* **1.** an alley open at one end only; cul-de-sac. **2.** *Inf.* a situation in which no further progress can be made.

blind date *n. Inf.* a social meeting between a man and a woman who have not met before.

blinders ('blaɪndəz) *pl. n.* the usual U.S. & Canad. word for **blinkers.**

blindfold ('blaɪnd,fəʊld) *vb.* (*tr.*) **1.** to prevent (a person or animal) from seeing by covering (the eyes). ~*n.* **2.** a piece of cloth, bandage, etc., used to cover the eyes. ~*adj., adv.* **3.** having the eyes covered with a cloth or bandage. **4.** rash; inconsiderate. [changed (C16) through association with FOLD[1] from OE *blindfellian* to strike blind; see BLIND, FELL[2]]

Blindheim ('blɪnt,haɪm) *n.* the German name for **Blenheim.**

blind man's buff *n.* a game in which a blindfolded person tries to catch and identify the other players. [C16: *buff,* ?from OF *buffe* a blow; see BUFFET[2]]

blind spot *n.* **1.** a small oval-shaped area of the retina, where the optic nerve enters, in which vision is not experienced. **2.** a place or area where vision is obscured. **3.** a subject about which a person is ignorant or prejudiced.

blindworm ('blaɪnd,wɜ:m) *n.* another name for **slow-worm.**

blink (blɪŋk) *vb.* **1.** to close and immediately reopen (the eyes or an eye), usually involuntarily. **2.** (*intr.*) to look with the eyes partially closed. **3.** to shine intermittently or unsteadily. **4.** (*tr.*; foll. by *away, from,* etc.) to clear the eyes of (dust, tears, etc.). **5.** (when *tr.*, usually foll. by *at*) to be surprised or amazed. **6.** (when *intr.*, foll. by *at*) to pretend not to know or see (a fault, injustice, etc.). ~*n.* **7.** the act or an instance of blinking. **8.** a glance; glimpse. **9.** short for **iceblink** (sense 1). **10. on the blink.** *Sl.* not working properly. [C14: var. of BLENCH]

blinker[1] ('blɪŋkə) *n.* **1.** a flashing light for sending messages, as a warning device, etc., such as a direction indicator on a road vehicle. **2.** (*often pl.*) a slang word for **eye.**

blinker[2] ('blɪŋkə) *vb.* (*tr.*) **1.** to provide (a horse) with blinkers. **2.** to obscure or be obscured with or as with blinkers. — **'blinkered** *adj.*

blinkers ('blɪŋkəz) *pl. n.* (*sometimes sing.*) *Chiefly Brit.* leather sidepieces attached to a horse's bridle to prevent sideways vision.

blinking ('blɪŋkɪŋ) *adj., adv. Inf.* (intensifier): *a blinking fool; a blinking good film.*

blip (blɪp) *n.* **1.** a repetitive sound, such as that produced by an electronic device. **2.** Also called: **pip.** the spot of light on a radar screen indicating the position of an object. ~*vb.* **blipping, blipped. 3.** (*intr.*) to produce such a noise. [C20: imit.]

bliss (blɪs) *n.* **1.** perfect happiness; serene joy. **2.** the ecstatic joy of heaven. [OE *blīths;* rel. to *blithe* BLITHE]

Bliss (blɪs) *n.* Sir **Arthur.** 1891–1975, English composer; Master of the Queen's Musick (1953–75). His works include the *Colour Symphony* (1922), film and ballet music, and a cello concerto (1970).

blissful ('blɪsfʊl) *adj.* **1.** serenely joyful or glad. **2. blissful ignorance.** unawareness or inexperience of something unpleasant. — **'blissfully** *adv.* — **'blissfulness** *n.*

blister ('blɪstə) *n.* **1.** a small bubble-like elevation of the skin filled with serum, produced as a reaction to a burn, mechanical irritation, etc. **2.** a swelling containing air or liquid, as on a painted surface. **3. a.** *N.Z. sl.* a rebuke. **b.** *N.Z. & Austral. sl.* a summons to court. ~*vb.* **4.** to have or cause to have blisters. **5.** (*tr.*) to attack verbally with great scorn or sarcasm. [C13: from OF *blestre*] — **'blistered** *adj.* — **'blistery** *adj.*

blister pack *n.* a type of pack for small goods, consisting of a transparent dome on a firm backing. Also called: **bubble pack.**

BLit *abbrev. for* Bachelor of Literature.

blithe (blaɪð) *adj.* **1.** very happy or cheerful; gay. **2.** heedless; casual and indifferent. [OE *blithe*] — **'blithely** *adv.* — **'blitheness** *n.*

blithering ('blɪðərɪŋ) *adj.* **1.** talking foolishly; jabbering. **2.** *Inf.* stupid; foolish: *you blithering idiot.* [C19: var. of BLETHER + -ING[2]]

blithesome ('blaɪðsəm) *adj. Literary.* cheery; merry.

BLitt *abbrev. for* Bachelor of Letters. [L *Baccalaureus Litterarum*]

blitz (blɪts) *n.* **1.** a violent and sustained attack, esp. with intensive aerial bombardment. **2.** any sudden intensive attack or concerted effort. ~*vb.* **3.** (*tr.*) to attack suddenly and intensively. [C20: shortened from G *Blitzkrieg* lightning war]

Blitz (blɪts) *n.* **the.** the systematic bombing of Britain in 1940–41 by the German Luftwaffe.

blitzkrieg ('blɪts,kriːg) *n.* a swift intensive military attack designed to defeat the opposition quickly. [C20: from G: lightning war]

blizzard ('blɪzəd) *n.* a strong cold wind accompanied by widespread heavy snowfall. [C19: from ?]

bloat (bləʊt) *vb.* **1.** to swell or cause to swell, as with a liquid or air. **2.** to become or cause to be puffed up, as with conceit. **3.** (*tr.*) to cure (fish, esp. herring) by half drying in smoke. [C17: prob. rel. to ON *blautr* soaked] —'**bloated** *adj.*

bloater ('bləʊtə) *n.* a herring that has been salted in brine, smoked, and cured.

blob (blɒb) *n.* **1.** a soft mass or drop. **2.** a spot, dab, or blotch of colour, ink, etc. **3.** an indistinct or shapeless form or object. [C15: ? imit.]

bloc (blɒk) *n.* a group of people or countries combined by a common interest. [from F: BLOCK]

Bloch (blɒk) *n.* **1. Ernest.** 1880–1959, U.S. composer, born in Switzerland, who found inspiration in Jewish liturgical and folk music: his works include the symphonies *Israel* (1916) and *America* (1926). **2. Felix.** 1905–83, U.S. physicist, born in Switzerland: Nobel prize for physics (1952) for his work on the magnetic moments of atomic particles. **3. Konrad Emil.** born 1912, U.S. biochemist, born in Germany: shared the Nobel prize for physiology or medicine in 1964 for his work on fatty-acid metabolism.

block (blɒk) *n.* **1.** a large solid piece of wood, stone, or other material usually having at least one face fairly flat. **2.** such a piece on which particular tasks may be done, as chopping, cutting, or beheading. **3.** Also called: **building block.** one of a set of wooden or plastic cubes as a child's toy. **4.** a form on which things are shaped: *a wig block.* **5.** *Sl.* a person's head. **6. do one's block.** *Austral. & N.Z. sl.* to become angry. **7.** a dull, unemotional, or hardhearted person. **8.** a large building of offices, flats, etc. **9. a.** a group of buildings in a city bounded by intersecting streets on each side. **b.** the area or distance between such intersecting streets. **10.** *Austral. & N.Z.* an area of land, usually extensive, taken up for farming, settlement, etc. **11.** *N.Z.* an area of bush reserved by licence for a trapper or hunter. **12.** a piece of wood, metal, or other material having a design in relief, used for printing. **13.** *Austral. & N.Z.* a log, usually of willow, fastened to a timber base and used in a wood-chopping competition. **14.** a casing housing one or more freely rotating pulleys. See also **block and tackle.** **15.** an obstruction or hindrance. **16.** *Pathol.* **a.** interference in the normal physiological functioning of an organ or part. **b.** See **heart block.** **17.** *Psychol.* a short interruption of perceptual or thought processes. **18.** obstruction of an opponent in a sport. **19. a.** a quantity handled or considered as a single unit. **b.** (*as modifier*): *a block booking.* **20.** *Athletics.* short for **starting block.** ~*vb.* (*mainly tr.*) **21.** (often foll. by *up*) to obstruct (a passage, channel, etc.) or prevent or impede the motion or flow of (something or someone) by introducing an obstacle: *to block the traffic; to block up a pipe.* **22.** to impede, retard, or prevent (an action, procedure, etc.). **23.** to stamp (a title, design, etc.) on (a book cover, etc.) esp. using gold leaf. **24.** to shape by use of a block: *to block a hat.* **25.** (*also intr.*) *Sports.* to obstruct or impede movement by (an opponent). **26.** to interrupt a physiological function, as by use of an anaesthetic. **27.** (*also intr.*) *Cricket.* to play (a ball) defensively. ~See also **block in, block out.** [C14: from OF *bloc*, from Du. *blok*] —'**blocker** *n.*

blockade (blɒ'keɪd) *n.* **1.** *Mil.* the interdiction of a nation's sea lines of communications, esp. of an individual port by the use of sea power. **2.** something that prevents access or progress. ~*vb.* (*tr.*) **3.** to impose a blockade on. **4.** to obstruct the way to. [C17: from BLOCK + -*ade*, as in AMBUSCADE] —**block'ader** *n.*

blockage ('blɒkɪdʒ) *n.* **1.** the act of blocking or state of being blocked. **2.** an object causing an obstruction.

block and tackle *n.* a hoisting device in which a rope or chain is passed around a pair of blocks containing one or more pulleys.

blockboard ('blɒk,bɔːd) *n.* a bonded board in which strips of soft wood are sandwiched between two layers of veneer.

blockbuster ('blɒk,bʌstə) *n. Inf.* **1.** a large bomb used to demolish extensive areas. **2.** a very successful, effective, or forceful person, thing, etc.

block diagram *n.* a diagram showing the interconnections between the parts of an industrial process or the components of an electronic or electrical system.

blockhead ('blɒk,hɛd) *n. Derog.* a stupid person. —'**block,headed** *adj.*

blockhouse ('blɒk,haʊs) *n.* **1.** (formerly) a wooden fortification with ports for defensive fire, observation, etc. **2.** a concrete structure strengthened to give protection against enemy fire, with apertures to allow defensive gunfire. **3.** a building constructed of logs or squared timber.

block in *vb.* (*tr., adv.*) to sketch or outline with little detail.

blockish ('blɒkɪʃ) *adj.* lacking vivacity or imagination; stupid. —'**blockishly** *adv.*

block letter *n.* **1.** *Printing.* a less common name for **sans serif.** **2.** Also called: **block capital.** a plain capital letter.

block out *vb.* (*tr., adv.*) **1.** to plan or describe (something) in a general fashion. **2.** to prevent the entry or consideration of (something).

block release *n. Brit.* the release of industrial trainees from work for study at a college for several weeks.

block vote *n. Brit.* (at a trade-union conference) the system whereby each delegate's vote has a value in proportion to the number of people he represents.

Bloemfontein ('bluːmfɒn,teɪn) *n.* a city in central South Africa: capital of the Orange Free State and judicial capital of the Republic. Pop.: 204 000 (1985).

Blois (*French* blwa) *n.* a city in N central France, on the Loire: 13th-century castle. Pop.: 49 379 (1983 est.).

Blok (blɒk) *n.* **Aleksandr Aleksandrovich** (alɪk'sandr alɪk'sandrəvitʃ). 1880–1921, Russian poet whose poems, which include *Verses about the Beautiful Lady* (1901–2) and *Rasput'ya* (1902–4), contain a mixture of symbolism, romanticism, tragedy, and irony.

bloke (bləʊk) *n. Brit.* an informal word for **man.** [C19: from Shelta]

blonde *or* (*masc.*) **blond** (blɒnd) *adj.* **1.** (of hair) of a light colour; fair. **2.** (of people or a race) having fair hair, a light complexion, and, typically, blue or grey eyes. ~*n.* **3.** a person having light-coloured hair and skin. [C15: from OF *blond* (fem. *blonde*), prob. of Gmc origin] —'**blondeness** *or* '**blondness** *n.*

blood (blʌd) *n.* **1.** a reddish fluid in vertebrates that is pumped by the heart through the arteries and veins. **2.** a similar fluid in invertebrates. **3.** bloodshed, esp. when resulting in murder. **4.** life itself; lifeblood. **5.** relationship through being of the same family, race, or kind; kinship. **6. flesh and blood. a.** near kindred or kinship, esp. that between a parent and child. **b.** human nature (esp. in **it's more than flesh and blood can stand**). **7. in one's blood.** as a natural or inherited characteristic or talent. **8. the blood.** royal or noble descent: *a prince of the blood.* **9.** temperament; disposition; temper. **10. a.** good or pure breeding; pedigree. **b.** (*as modifier*): *blood horses.* **11.** people viewed as members of a group, esp. as an invigorating force (**new blood, young blood**). **12.** *Chiefly Brit., rare.* a dashing young man. **13. in cold blood.** showing no passion; deliberately; ruthlessly. **14. make one's blood boil.** to cause to be angry or indignant. **15. make one's blood run cold.** to fill with horror. ~*vb.* (*tr.*) **16.** *Hunting.* to cause (young hounds) to taste the blood of a freshly killed quarry. **17.** to initiate (a person) to war or hunting. [OE *blōd*]

blood-and-thunder *adj.* denoting or relating to a melodramatic adventure story.

blood bank *n.* a place where whole blood or blood plasma is stored until required in transfusion.

blood bath *n.* indiscriminate slaughter; a massacre.

blood brother *n.* **1.** a brother by birth. **2.** a man or boy who has sworn to treat another as his brother, often in a ceremony in which their blood is mingled.

blood count *n.* determination of the number of red and white blood corpuscles in a specific sample of blood.

bloodcurdling ('blʌd,kɜːdlɪŋ) *adj.* terrifying; horrifying. —'**blood,curdlingly** *adv.*

blood donor *n.* a person who gives his blood to be used for transfusion.

blood doping *n.* the illegal practice of removing a quantity of blood from an athlete long before a race and re-injecting it shortly before a race, so boosting oxygenation of the blood.

blooded ('blʌdɪd) *adj.* **1.** (of horses, cattle, etc.) of good breeding. **2.** (*in combination*) having blood or temperament as specified: *hot-blooded, cold-blooded, warm-blooded, red-blooded.*

blood group *n.* any one of the various groups into which human blood is classified on the basis of its specific agglutinating properties. Also called: **blood type.**

blood heat *n.* the normal temperature of the human body, 98.4°F. or 37°C.

bloodhound ('blʌd,haʊnd) *n.* a large breed of hound, formerly used in tracking and police work.

bloodless ('blʌdlɪs) *adj.* **1.** without blood. **2.** conducted without violence (esp. in **bloodless revolution**). **3.** anaemic-looking; pale. **4.** lacking vitality; lifeless. **5.** lacking in emotion; unfeeling. —'**bloodlessly** *adv.* — '**bloodlessness** *n.*

blood-letting ('blʌd,lɛtɪŋ) *n.* **1.** the therapeutic removal of blood. See also **phlebotomy**. **2.** bloodshed, esp. in a feud.

blood money *n.* **1.** compensation paid to the relatives of a murdered person. **2.** money paid to a hired murderer. **3.** a reward for information about a criminal, esp. a murderer.

blood orange *n.* a variety of orange all or part of the pulp of which is dark red when ripe.

blood poisoning *n.* a nontechnical term for **septicaemia.**

blood pressure *n.* the pressure exerted by the blood on the inner walls of the arteries, being relative to the elasticity and diameter of the vessels and the force of the heartbeat.

blood pudding *n.* another name for **black pudding.**

blood relation *or* **relative** *n.* a person related to another by birth, as distinct from one related by marriage.

bloodshed ('blʌd,ʃɛd) *n.* slaughter; killing.

bloodshot ('blʌd,ʃɒt) *adj.* (of an eye) inflamed.

blood sport *n.* any sport involving the killing of an animal, esp. hunting.

bloodstain ('blʌd,steɪn) *n.* a dark discoloration caused by blood, esp. dried blood. — '**blood,stained** *adj.*

bloodstock ('blʌd,stɒk) *n.* thoroughbred horses.

bloodstone ('blʌd,stəʊn) *n.* a dark green variety of chalcedony with red spots: used as a gemstone. Also called: **heliotrope.**

bloodstream ('blʌd,striːm) *n.* the flow of blood through the vessels of a living body.

bloodsucker ('blʌd,sʌkə) *n.* **1.** an animal that sucks blood, esp. a leech or mosquito. **2.** *Inf.* a person or thing that preys upon another person, esp. by extorting money. — '**blood,sucking** *adj.*

bloodthirsty ('blʌd,θɜːstɪ) *adj.* **-thirstier, -thirstiest.** **1.** murderous; cruel. **2.** taking pleasure in bloodshed or violence. **3.** describing or depicting killing and violence; gruesome. —'**blood,thirstily** *adv.* —'**blood,thirstiness** *n.*

blood type *n.* another name for **blood group.**

blood vessel *n.* an artery, capillary, or vein.

bloodwood ('blʌd,wʊd) *n.* any of several species of Australian eucalyptus with red sap.

bloody ('blʌdɪ) *adj.* **bloodier, bloodiest. 1.** covered or stained with blood. **2.** resembling or composed of blood. **3.** marked by much killing and bloodshed: *a bloody war.* **4.** cruel or murderous: *a bloody tyrant.* ~*adv., adj.* **5.** *Sl.* (intensifier): *a bloody fool.* ~*vb.* **bloodying, bloodied.** **6.** (*tr.*) to stain with blood. —'**bloodily** *adv.* — '**bloodiness** *n.*

Bloody Mary *n.* a drink consisting of tomato juice and vodka.

bloody-minded *adj. Brit. inf.* deliberately obstructive and unhelpful.

bloom[1] (bluːm) *n.* **1.** a blossom on a flowering plant; a flower. **2.** the state, time, or period when flowers open. **3.** open flowers collectively. **4.** a healthy, vigorous, or flourishing condition; prime. **5.** youthful or healthy rosiness in the cheeks or face; glow. **6.** a fine whitish coating on the surface of fruits, leaves, etc. **7.** Also called: **chill.** a dull area on the surface of old gloss paint, lacquer, or varnish. ~*vb.* (*intr.*) **8.** (of flowers) to open; come into flower. **9.** to bear flowers; blossom. **10.** to flourish or

grow. **11.** to be in a healthy, glowing, or flourishing condition. [C13: of Gmc origin; cf. ON *blōm* flower]

bloom[2] (bluːm) *n.* a rectangular mass of metal obtained by rolling or forging a cast ingot. [OE *blōma* lump of metal]

bloomer[1] ('bluːmə) *n.* a plant that flowers, esp. in a specified way: *a night bloomer.*

bloomer[2] ('bluːmə) *n. Brit. inf.* a stupid mistake; blunder. [C20: from BLOOMING]

bloomer[3] ('bluːmə) *n. Brit.* a medium-sized loaf, glazed and notched on top. [C20: from?]

bloomers ('bluːməz) *pl. n.* **1.** *Inf.* women's baggy knickers. **2.** (formerly) loose trousers gathered at the knee worn by women for cycling, etc. **3.** *History.* loose trousers gathered at the ankle and worn under a shorter skirt. [after Mrs A. *Bloomer* (1818–94), U.S. social reformer]

Bloomfield ('bluːm,fiːld) *n.* **Leonard.** 1887–1949, U.S. linguist, influential for his strictly scientific and descriptive approach to comparative linguistics; author of *Language* (1933).

blooming ('bluːmɪŋ) *adv., adj. Brit. inf.* (intensifier): *a blooming genius; blooming painful.* [C19: euphemistic for BLOODY]

Bloomington ('bluːmɪŋtən) *n.* a city in central Indiana: seat of the University of Indiana (1820). Pop.: 52 044 (1980).

Bloomsbury ('bluːmzbərɪ, -brɪ) *n.* a district of central London in the borough of Camden: contains the British Museum, part of the University of London, and many publishers' offices.

blossom ('blɒsəm) *n.* **1.** the flower or flowers of a plant, esp. producing edible fruit. **2.** the time or period of flowering. ~*vb.* (*intr.*) **3.** (of plants) to come into flower. **4.** to develop or come to a promising stage. [OE *blōstm*] —'**blossomy** *adj.*

blot (blɒt) *n.* **1.** a stain or spot of ink, paint, dirt, etc. **2.** something that spoils. **3.** a blemish or stain on one's character or reputation. **4.** *Austral. sl.* the anus ~*vb.* **blotting, blotted.** **5.** (of ink, dye, etc.) to form spots or blobs on (a material) or (of a person) to cause such spots or blobs to form on (a material). **6.** (*intr.*) to stain or become stained or spotted. **7.** (*tr.*) to cause a blemish in or on; disgrace. **8.** to soak up (excess ink, etc.) by using blotting paper. **9.** (of blotting paper) to absorb (excess ink, etc.). **10.** (*tr.*; often foll. by *out*) **a.** to darken or hide completely; obscure; obliterate. **b.** to destroy; annihilate. [C14: prob. of Gmc origin]

blotch (blɒtʃ) *n.* **1.** an irregular spot or discoloration, esp. a dark and relatively large one. ~*vb.* **2.** to become or cause to become marked by such discoloration. [C17: prob. from BOTCH, infl. by BLOT] —'**blotchy** *adj.*

blotter ('blɒtə) *n.* something used to absorb excess ink, esp. a sheet of blotting paper.

blotting paper *n.* a soft absorbent unsized paper, used esp. for soaking up surplus ink.

blotto ('blɒtəʊ) *adj. Sl.* unconscious, esp. through drunkenness. [C20: from BLOT (vb.)]

blouse (blaʊz) *n.* **1.** a woman's shirtlike garment. **2.** a waist-length belted jacket worn by soldiers. ~*vb.* **3.** to hang or make so as to hang in full loose folds. [C19: from F, from ?]

blouson ('bluːzɒn) *n.* a tight-waisted jacket or top that blouses out. [C20: from F]

blow[1] (bləʊ) *vb.* **blowing, blew, blown. 1.** (of a current of air, the wind, etc.) to be or cause to be in motion. **2.** (*intr.*) to move or be carried by or as if by wind. **3.** to expel (air, cigarette smoke, etc.) through the mouth or nose. **4.** to force or cause (air, dust, etc.) to move (into, in, over, etc.) by using an instrument or by expelling breath. **5.** (*intr.*) to breathe hard; pant. **6.** (sometimes foll. by *up*) to inflate with air or the breath. **7.** (*intr.*) (of wind, a storm, etc.) to make a roaring sound. **8.** to cause (a whistle, siren, etc.) to sound by forcing air into it or (of a whistle, etc.) to sound thus. **9.** (*tr.*) to force air from the lungs through (the nose) to clear out mucus. **10.** (often foll. by *up, down, in,* etc.) to explode, break, or disintegrate completely. **11.** *Electronics.* to burn out (a fuse, valve, etc.) because of excessive current or (of a fuse, valve, etc.) to burn out. **12.** (*tr.*) to wind (a horse) by making it run excessively. **13.** to cause (a wind instrument) to sound by forcing one's breath into the mouthpiece or (of such an instrument) to sound in this way. **14.**

(*intr.*) (of flies) to lay eggs (in). **15.** to shape (glass, ornaments, etc.) by forcing air or gas through the material when molten. **16.** (*tr.*) *Sl.* to spend (money) freely. **17.** (*tr.*) *Sl.* to use (an opportunity) ineffectively. **18.** *Sl.* to go suddenly away (from). **19.** (*tr.*) *Sl.* to expose or betray (a secret). **20.** (p.p. **blowed**). *Inf.* another word for **damn**. **21. blow hot and cold.** *Inf.* to vacillate. **22. blow one's top.** *Inf.* to lose one's temper. ~*n.* **23.** the act or an instance of blowing. **24.** the sound produced by blowing. **25.** a blast of air or wind. **26.** *Austral. sl.* a brief rest; a breather. ~See also **blow in, blow out,** etc. [OE *blāwan*]

blow² (bləʊ) *n.* **1.** a powerful or heavy stroke with the fist, a weapon, etc. **2. at one** *or* **a blow.** by or with only one action. **3.** a sudden setback. **4. come to blows. a.** to fight. **b.** to result in a fight. **5.** an attacking action: *a blow for freedom.* **6.** *Austral. & N.Z.* a stroke of the shears in sheep-shearing. [C15: prob. of Gmc origin]

blow³ (bləʊ) *vb.* **blowing, blew, blown. 1.** (*intr.*) (of a plant or flower) to blossom or open out. ~*n.* **2.** a mass of blossoms. **3.** the state or period of blossoming. [OE *blōwan*]

blow-by-blow *adj.* (*prenominal*) explained in great detail: *a blow-by-blow account.*

blow-dry *vb.* **-drying, -dried. 1.** (*tr.*) to style (the hair) while drying it with a hand-held hair dryer. ~*n.* **2.** this method of styling hair.

blower ('bləʊə) *n.* **1.** a mechanical device, such as a fan, that blows. **2.** a low-pressure compressor, esp. in a furnace or internal-combustion engine. **3.** an informal name for **telephone**.

blowfish ('bləʊˌfɪʃ) *n.,* *pl.* **-fish** *or* **-fishes.** a popular name for **puffer** (sense 2).

blowfly ('bləʊˌflaɪ) *n.,* *pl.* **-flies.** any of various flies that lay their eggs in rotting meat, dung, carrion, and open wounds. Also called: **bluebottle.**

blowgun ('bləʊˌgʌn) *n.* the U.S. word for **blowpipe** (sense 1).

blowhard ('bləʊˌhɑːd) *Inf.* ~*n.* **1.** a boastful person. ~*adj.* **2.** blustering or boastful.

blowhole ('bləʊˌhəʊl) *n.* **1.** the nostril of whales, situated far back on the skull. **2.** a hole in ice through which whales, seals, etc., breathe. **3.** a vent in a cliff connecting with a cave below, through which spray is forced. **4. a.** a vent for air or gas. **b.** *N.Z.* a hole emitting gas or steam in a volcanic region.

blow in *Inf.* ~*vb.* **1.** (*intr., adv.*) to arrive or enter suddenly. ~*n.* **blow-in. 2.** *Austral.* a newcomer.

blow job *Taboo.* a slang term for **fellatio.**

blowlamp ('bləʊˌlæmp) *n.* a small burner that produces a very hot flame, used to remove old paint, melt soft metal, etc. U.S. and Canad. name: **blowtorch.**

blown (bləʊn) *vb.* the past participle of **blow¹** and **blow³**.

blow out *vb.* (*adv.*) **1.** to extinguish (a flame, candle, etc.) or (of a flame, etc.) to become extinguished. **2.** (*intr.*) (of a tyre) to puncture suddenly, esp. at high speed. **3.** (*intr.*) (of a fuse) to melt suddenly. **4.** (*tr.; often reflexive*) to diminish or use up the energy of: *the storm blew itself out.* **5.** (*intr.*) (of an oil or gas well) to lose oil or gas in an uncontrolled manner. ~*n.* **blowout. 6.** the sudden melting of an electrical fuse. **7.** a sudden burst in a tyre. **8.** the uncontrolled escape of oil or gas from an oil or gas well. **9.** *Sl.* a large filling meal or lavish entertainment.

blow over *vb.* (*intr., adv.*) **1.** to cease or be finished: *the storm blew over.* **2.** to be forgotten.

blowpipe ('bləʊˌpaɪp) *n.* **1.** a long tube from which pellets, poisoned darts, etc., are shot by blowing. **2.** Also called: **blow tube.** a tube for blowing air or oxygen into a flame to intensify its heat. **3.** a long narrow iron pipe used to gather molten glass and blow it into shape.

blow through *vb.* (*intr., adv.*) *Austral. inf.* to leave; make off.

blowtorch ('bləʊˌtɔːtʃ) *n.* the U.S. and Canad. name for **blowlamp.**

blow up *vb.* (*adv.*) **1.** to explode or cause to explode. **2.** (*tr.*) to increase the importance of (something): *they blew the whole affair up.* **3.** (*intr.*) to arise: *we lived very quietly before this affair blew up.* **4.** (*intr.*) to come into existence with sudden force: *a storm had blown up.* **5.** (*intr.*) *Inf.* to lose one's temper (with a person). **6.** (*tr.*) *Inf.* to reprimand. **7.** (*tr.*) *Inf.* to enlarge the size of (a photograph). ~*n.* **blow-up. 8.** an explosion. **9.** *Inf.* an enlarged photograph or part of a photograph. **10.** *Inf.* a fit of temper.

blowy ('bləʊɪ) *adj.* **blowier, blowiest.** another word for **windy** (sense 1).

blowzy *or* **blowsy** ('blaʊzɪ) *adj.* **blowzier, blowziest** *or* **blowsier, blowsiest. 1.** (esp. of a woman) untidy in appearance; slovenly or sluttish. **2.** (of a woman) ruddy in complexion. [C18: from dialect *blowze* beggar girl, from ?]

blub (blʌb) *vb.* **blubbing, blubbed.** *Brit.* a slang word for **blubber** (senses 1-3).

blubber ('blʌbə) *vb.* **1.** to sob without restraint. **2.** to utter while sobbing. **3.** (*tr.*) to make (the face) wet and swollen by crying. ~*n.* **4.** the fatty tissue of aquatic mammals such as the whale. **5.** *Inf.* flabby body fat. **6.** the act or an instance of weeping without restraint. ~*adj.* **7.** (*often in combination*) swollen or fleshy: *blubber-faced.* [C12: ?from Low G *blubbern* to BUBBLE, imit.] —'**blubberer** *n.* —'**blubbery** *adj.*

Blücher (*German* 'blyçər) *n.* **Gebhard Leberecht von** ('gephart 'leːbəreçt fɔn). 1742–1819, Prussian field marshal, who commanded the Prussian army against Napoleon at Waterloo (1815).

bludge (blʌdʒ) *Austral. & N.Z. inf.* ~*vb.* **1.** (when *intr.,* often foll. by *on*) to scrounge from (someone). **2.** (*intr.*) to skive. ~*n.* **3.** a very easy task. [C19: back formation from *bludger* pimp, from BLUDGEON]

bludgeon ('blʌdʒən) *n.* **1.** a stout heavy club, typically thicker at one end. **2.** a person, line of argument, etc., that is effective but unsubtle. ~*vb.* (*tr.*) **3.** to hit as with a bludgeon. **4.** (often foll. by *into*) to force; bully; coerce. [C18: from ?]

bludger ('blʌdʒə) *n. Austral. & N.Z. inf.* **1.** a person who scrounges. **2.** a person who avoids work. **3.** a person in authority regarded as ineffectual by those working under him.

blue (bluː) *n.* **1.** any of a group of colours, such as that of a clear unclouded sky or the deep sea. **2.** a dye or pigment of any of these colours. **3.** blue cloth or clothing: *dressed in blue.* **4.** a sportsman who represents or has represented Oxford or Cambridge University and has the right to wear the university colour. **5.** *Brit.* an informal name for **Tory. 6.** any of numerous small blue-winged butterflies. **7.** a blue substance used in laundering. **8.** *Austral. & N.Z. sl.* an argument or fight: *he had a blue with a taxi driver.* **9.** Also: **bluey.** *Austral. & N.Z. inf.* a court summons. **10.** *Austral. & N.Z. inf.* a mistake; error. **11. out of the blue.** apparently from nowhere; unexpectedly. ~*adj.* **bluer, bluest. 12.** of the colour blue. **13.** (of the flesh) having a purple tinge, as from cold or contusion. **14.** depressed, moody, or unhappy. **15.** indecent, titillating, or pornographic: *blue films.* ~*vb.* **blueing** *or* **bluing, blued. 16.** to make, dye, or become blue. **17.** (*tr.*) to treat (laundry) with blue. **18.** (*tr.*) *Sl.* to spend extravagantly or wastefully; squander. ~ See also **blues** [C13: from OF *bleu*, of Gmc origin] —'**blueness** *n.*

Blue (bluː) *n. Austral. inf.* a person with red hair.

blue baby *n.* a baby born with a bluish tinge to the skin because of lack of oxygen in the blood.

Bluebeard ('bluːˌbɪəd) *n.* **1.** a villain in European folk tales who marries several wives and murders them in turn. **2.** a man who has had several wives.

bluebell ('bluːˌbɛl) *n.* **1.** Also called: **wild** *or* **wood hyacinth.** a European woodland plant having a one-sided cluster of blue bell-shaped flowers. **2.** a Scottish name for **harebell. 3.** any of various other plants with blue bell-shaped flowers.

blueberry ('bluːbərɪ, -brɪ) *n.,* *pl.* **-ries. 1.** Also called: **huckleberry.** any of several North American ericaceous shrubs that have blue-black edible berries with tiny seeds. See also **bilberry. 2.** the fruit of any of these plants.

bluebird ('bluːˌbɜːd) *n.* **1.** a North American songbird of the thrush family having a blue or partly blue plumage. **2.** any of various other birds having a blue plumage.

blue blood *n.* royal or aristocratic descent. [C19: translation of Sp. *sangre azul*] —,**blue-'blooded** *adj.*

bluebook ('bluːˌbʊk) *n.* **1.** (in Britain) a government publication bound in a stiff blue paper cover: usually the report of a royal commission or a committee. **2.** (in Canada) an annual statement of government accounts.

bluebottle ('bluːˌbɒt²l) *n.* **1.** another name for the **blowfly. 2.** any of various blue-flowered plants, esp. the cornflower. **3.** *Brit.* an informal word for a **policeman. 4.** *Austral. & N.Z.* an informal name for **Portuguese man-of-war.**

blue cheese *n.* cheese containing a blue mould, esp. Stilton, Roquefort, or Danish blue.

blue chip *n.* **1.** a gambling chip with the highest value. **2.** *Finance.* a stock considered reliable with respect to both dividend income and capital value. **3.** (*modifier*) denoting something considered to be a valuable asset.

blue-collar *adj.* of or designating manual industrial workers. Cf. **white-collar.**

blue-eyed boy *n. Inf., chiefly Brit.* the favourite or darling of a person or group.

bluefish ('blu:,fɪʃ) *n., pl.* **-fish** *or* **-fishes. 1.** Also called: **snapper.** a bluish marine food and game fish, related to the horse mackerel. **2.** any of various other bluish fishes.

blue fox *n.* **1.** a variety of the arctic fox that has a pale grey winter coat. **2.** the fur of this animal.

blue funk *n. Sl.* a state of great terror.

bluegill ('blu:,gɪl) *n.* a common North American freshwater sunfish: an important food and game fish.

bluegrass ('blu:,grɑːs) *n.* **1.** any of several North American bluish-green grasses, esp. **Kentucky bluegrass,** grown for forage. **2.** a type of folk music originating in Kentucky.

blue-green algae *pl. n.* a family of algae that contain a blue pigment as well as chlorophyll.

blue ground *n. Mineralogy.* another name for **kimberlite.**

blue gum *n.* a tall fast-growing widely cultivated Australian eucalyptus, having bluish aromatic leaves containing a medicinal oil, bark that peels off in shreds, and hard timber.

blue heeler *n. Austral.* a type of dog with dark speckled markings: used for herding cattle.

bluejacket ('blu:,dʒækɪt) *n.* a sailor in the Navy.

blue jay *n.* a common North American jay having bright blue plumage.

blue moon *n.* **once in a blue moon.** *Inf.* very rarely; almost never.

blue mould *n.* any fungus that forms a bluish mass on decaying food, leather, etc. Also called: **green mould.**

Blue Mountains *pl. n.* **1.** a mountain range in NE Oregon and SE Washington. Highest peak: Rock Creek Butte, 2773 m (9097 ft.). **2.** a mountain range in the West Indies, in E Jamaica: Blue Mountain coffee is grown on its slopes. Highest peak: Blue Mountain Peak, 2256 m (7402 ft.). **3.** a plateau in SE Australia, in E New South Wales: part of the Great Dividing Range. Highest part: about 1134 m (3871 ft.).

Blue Nile *n.* a river in E Africa, rising in central Ethiopia as the Abbai and flowing southeast, then northwest to join the White Nile. Length: about 1530 km (950 miles).

blue pencil *n.* **1.** deletion, alteration, or censorship of the contents of a book or other work. ~*vb.* **blue-pencil, -cilling, -cilled** *or U.S.* **-ciling, -ciled. 2.** (*tr.*) to alter or delete parts of (a book, film, etc.), esp. to censor.

blue peter *n.* a signal flag of blue with a white square at the centre, displayed by a vessel about to leave port. [C19:from the name *Peter*]

blue pointer *n.* a large shark of Australian coastal waters, having a blue back and pointed snout.

blueprint ('blu:,prɪnt) *n.* **1.** Also called: **cyanotype.** a photographic print of plans, technical drawings, etc., consisting of white lines on a blue background. **2.** an original plan or prototype. ~*vb.* **3.** (*tr.*) to make a blueprint of (a plan, etc.).

blue ribbon *n.* **1.** (in Britain) a badge of blue silk worn by members of the Order of the Garter. **2.** a badge awarded as the first prize in a competition.

Blue Ridge Mountains *pl. n.* a mountain range in the eastern U.S., extending from West Virginia into Georgia: part of the Appalachian mountains. Highest peak: Mount Mitchell, 2038 m (6684 ft.).

blues (blu:z) *pl. n.* (*sometimes functioning as sing.*) **the. 1.** a feeling of depression or deep unhappiness. **2.** a type of folk song originating among Black Americans, usually employing a basic 12-bar chorus and frequent minor intervals.

bluestocking ('blu:,stɒkɪŋ) *n. Usually disparaging.* a scholarly or intellectual woman. [from the blue worsted stockings worn by members of an 18th-cent. literary society]

bluestone ('blu:,stəʊn) *n.* **1.** a blue-grey sandstone containing much clay, used for building and paving. **2.** the blue crystalline form of copper sulphate.

bluetit ('blu:,tɪt) *n.* a common European tit having a blue crown, wings, and tail, yellow underparts, and a black-and-grey head.

blue whale *n.* the largest mammal: a widely distributed bluish-grey whalebone whale, closely related and similar to the rorquals.

bluey ('blu:ɪ) *n. Austral. inf.* **1.** a blanket. **2.** a swagman's bundle. **3. hump (one's) bluey.** to carry one's bundle; tramp. **4.** a variant of **blue** (sense 9). **5.** a cattle dog. **6.** a variant of **blue** (sense 11). [(for senses 1, 2, 4) C19: from BLUE (on account of their colour) + -y²]

bluff¹ (blʌf) *vb.* **1.** to pretend to be confident about an uncertain issue in order to influence (someone). ~*n.* **2.** deliberate deception intended to create the impression of a stronger position than one actually has. **3. call someone's bluff.** to challenge someone to give proof of his claims. [C19: orig. U.S. poker-playing term, from Du. *bluffen* to boast] —**'bluffer** *n.*

bluff² (blʌf) *n.* **1.** a steep promontory, bank, or cliff. **2.** *Canad.* a clump of trees on the prairie; copse. ~*adj.* **3.** good-naturedly frank and hearty. **4.** (of a bank, cliff, etc.) presenting a steep broad face. [C17 (in the sense: nearly perpendicular): ?from MDu. *blaf* broad] —**'bluffly** *adv.* —**'bluffness** *n.*

bluish *or* **blueish** ('blu:ɪʃ) *adj.* somewhat blue.

Blum (blu:m) *n.* **Léon** (leõ). 1872–1950, French socialist statesman; premier of France (1936–37; 1938; 1946–47).

blunder ('blʌndə) *n.* **1.** a stupid or clumsy mistake. **2.** a foolish tactless remark. ~*vb.* (*mainly intr.*) **3.** to make stupid or clumsy mistakes. **4.** to make foolish tactless remarks. **5.** (often foll. by *about, into,* etc.) to act clumsily; stumble. **6.** (*tr.*) to mismanage; botch. [C14: of Scand. origin; cf. ON *blunda* to close one's eyes] —**'blunderer** *n.* —**'blundering** *n., adj.*

blunderbuss ('blʌndə,bʌs) *n.* an obsolete short musket with large bore and flared muzzle. [C17: changed (infl. by BLUNDER) from Du. *donderbus;* from *donder* THUNDER + obs. *bus* gun]

blunge (blʌndʒ) *vb.* (*tr.*) to mix (clay or a similar substance) with water in order to form a suspension for use in ceramics. [C19: prob. from BLEND + PLUNGE] —**'blunger** *n.*

blunt (blʌnt) *adj.* **1.** (esp. of a knife or blade) lacking sharpness or keenness; dull. **2.** not having a sharp edge or point: *a blunt instrument.* **3.** (of people, manner of speaking, etc.) straightforward and uncomplicated. ~*vb.* (*tr.*) **4.** to make less sharp. **5.** to diminish the sensitivity or perception of; make dull. [C12: prob. of Scand. origin] —**'bluntly** *adv.* —**'bluntness** *n.*

Blunt (blʌnt) *n.* **Anthony.** 1907–83, British art historian and Soviet spy.

blur (blɜ:) *vb.* **blurring, blurred. 1.** to make or become vague or less distinct. **2.** to smear or smudge. **3.** (*tr.*) to make (the judgment, memory, or perception) less clear; dim. ~*n.* **4.** something vague, hazy, or indistinct. **5.** a smear or smudge. [C16: ? var. of BLEAR] —**blurred** *adj.* —**'blurry** *adj.*

blurb (blɜ:b) *n.* a promotional description, as on the jackets of books. [C20: coined by G. Burgess (1866–1951), U.S. humorist & illustrator]

blurt (blɜ:t) *vb.* (*tr.;* often foll. by *out*) to utter suddenly and involuntarily. [C16: prob. imit.]

blush (blʌʃ) *vb.* **1.** (*intr.*) to become suddenly red in the face from embarrassment, shame, modesty, or guilt; redden. **2.** to make or become reddish or rosy. ~*n.* **3.** a sudden reddening of the face from embarrassment, shame, modesty, or guilt. **4.** a rosy glow. **5. at first blush.** when first seen; as first impression. [OE *blȳscan*]

blusher ('blʌʃə) *n.* a cosmetic applied to the cheeks to give a rosy colour.

bluster ('blʌstə) *vb.* **1.** to speak or say loudly or boastfully. **2.** to act in a bullying way. **3.** (*tr.;* foll. by *into*) to force or attempt to force (a person) into doing something by behaving thus. **4.** (*intr.*) (of the wind) to be noisy or gusty. ~*n.* **5.** boisterous talk or action; swagger. **6.** empty threats or protests. **7.** a strong wind; gale. [C15: prob. from MLow G *blüsteren* to storm, blow violently] —**'blusterer** *n.* —**'blustery** *adj.*

Blvd *abbrev. for* Boulevard.

Blyth¹ (blaɪð) *n.* a port in N England, in SE Northumberland, on the North Sea. Pop.: 36 466 (1981).

Blyth[2] (blaɪð) *n.* **Chay** (tʃeɪ). born 1940, British yachtsman. He sailed round the world alone (1970–71) and has won many races.

BM *abbrev. for:* **1.** Bachelor of Medicine. **2.** *Surveying.* bench mark. **3.** British Museum.

BMA *abbrev. for* British Medical Association.

BMC *abbrev. for* British Medical Council.

B-movie *n.* a film originally made (esp. in the 1940s and 50s) as a supporting film, now often considered as a genre in its own right.

BMus *abbrev. for* Bachelor of Music.

BMX **1.** *abbrev. for* bicycle motocross: stunt riding over an obstacle course on a bicycle. ~*n.* **2.** a bicycle designed for bicycle motocross.

Bn *abbrev. for:* **1.** Baron. **2.** Battalion.

BNFL *abbrev. for* British Nuclear Fuels Limited.

bo *or* **boh** (bəʊ) *interj.* an exclamation to startle or surprise someone, esp. a child in a game.

BO *abbrev. for:* **1.** *Inf.* body odour. **2.** box office.

b.o. *abbrev. for:* **1.** back order. **2.** branch office. **3.** broker's order. **4.** buyer's option.

boa ('bəʊə) *n.* **1.** any of various large nonvenomous snakes of Central and South America and the West Indies. They kill their prey by constriction. **2.** a woman's long thin scarf, usually of feathers or fur. [C19: from NL, from L]

Boabdil (*Spanish* boaβ'ðil) *n.* original name *Abu-Abdullah*, called *El Chico*, ruled as *Mohammed XI.* died ?1538, last Moorish king of Granada (1482–83; 1486–92).

boa constrictor *n.* a very large snake of tropical America and the West Indies that kills its prey by constriction.

Boadicea (ˌbəʊədɪ'siːə) *n.* another name for **Boudicca.**

boar (bɔː) *n.* **1.** an uncastrated male pig. **2.** See **wild boar.** [OE *bār*]

board (bɔːd) *n.* **1.** a long wide flat piece of sawn timber. **2. a.** a smaller flat piece of rigid material for a specific purpose: *ironing board.* **b.** (*in combination*): *breadboard.* **3.** a person's meals, provided regularly for money. **4.** *Arch.* a table, esp. when laden with food. **5. a.** (*sometimes functioning as pl.*) a group of people who officially administer a company, trust, etc. **b.** (*as modifier*): *a board meeting.* **6.** any other committee or council: *a board of interviewers.* **7.** stiff cardboard or similar material, used for the outside covers of a book. **8.** a flat thin rectangular sheet of composite material, such as plasterboard or chipboard. **9.** *Chiefly U.S.* a list of stock-exchange prices. **b.** *Inf.* the stock exchange itself. **10.** *Naut.* the side of a ship. **11.** *Austral. & N.Z.* the part of the floor of a sheep-shearing shed where the shearers work. **12.** any of various portable surfaces specially designed for indoor games such as chess, backgammon, etc. **13. go by the board.** *Inf.* to be in disuse, neglected, or lost: *in these days courtesy goes by the board.* **14. on board.** on or in a ship, boat, aeroplane, or other vehicle. **15. the boards.** the stage. ~*vb.* **16.** to go aboard (a vessel, train, aircraft, or other vehicle). **17.** to attack (a ship) by forcing one's way aboard. **18.** (*tr.*; often foll. by *up, in,* etc.) to cover or shut with boards. **19.** (*intr.*) to receive meals or meals and lodging in return for money. **20.** (sometimes foll. by *out*) to arrange for (someone, esp. a child) to receive food and lodging away from home. **21.** (in ice hockey and box lacrosse) to bodycheck an opponent against the boards. ~See also **boards.** [OE *bord*]

boarder ('bɔːdə) *n.* **1.** a pupil who lives at school during term time. **2.** another word for **lodger.** **3.** a person who boards a ship, esp. in an attack.

boarding ('bɔːdɪŋ) *n.* **1.** a structure of boards. **2.** timber boards collectively. **3. a.** the act of embarking on an aircraft, train, ship, etc. **b.** (*as modifier*): *a boarding pass.* **4.** (in ice hockey and box lacrosse) an act of bodychecking an opponent against the boards.

boarding house *n.* a private house in which accommodation and meals are provided for paying guests.

boarding school *n.* a school providing living accommodation for some or all of its pupils.

Board of Trade *n.* (in the United Kingdom) a ministry responsible for the supervision of commerce and the promotion of export trade.

boardroom ('bɔːdˌruːm, -ˌrʊm) *n.* a room where the board of directors of a company meets.

boards (bɔːdz) *pl. n.* a wooden wall about one metre high forming the enclosure in which ice hockey or box lacrosse is played.

board school *n.* (formerly) a school managed by a board of local ratepayers.

boardwalk ('bɔːdˌwɔːk) *n.* *U.S. & Canad.* a promenade, esp. along a beach, usually made of planks.

Boas ('bəʊæz; *German* 'boːas) *n.* **Franz** (frants). 1858–1942, U.S. anthropologist, born in Germany. He made major contributions to cultural and linguistic anthropology in studies of North American Indians, including *The Mind of Primitive Man* (1911; 1938).

boast (bəʊst) *vb.* **1.** (*intr.*; sometimes foll. by *of* or *about*) to speak in excessively proud terms of one's possessions, skills, or superior qualities; brag. **2.** (*tr.*) to possess (something to be proud of): *the city boasts a fine cathedral.* ~*n.* **3.** a bragging statement. **4.** a possession, attribute, etc., that is or may be bragged about. [C13: from ?] —'**boaster** *n.* —'**boasting** *n., adj.*

boastful ('bəʊstfʊl) *adj.* tending to boast; characterized by boasting. —'**boastfully** *adv.* —'**boastfulness** *n.*

boat (bəʊt) *n.* **1.** a small vessel propelled by oars, paddle, sails, or motor. **2.** (not in technical use) another word for **ship.** **3.** a container for gravy, sauce, etc. **4. in the same boat.** sharing the same problems. **5. miss the boat.** to lose an opportunity. **6. rock the boat.** *Inf.* to cause a disturbance in the existing situation. ~*vb.* **7.** (*intr.*) to travel or go in a boat, esp. as a form of recreation. **8.** (*tr.*) to transport or carry in a boat. [OE *bāt*]

boater ('bəʊtə) *n.* a stiff straw hat with a straight brim and flat crown.

boathook ('bəʊtˌhʊk) *n.* a pole with a hook at one end, used aboard a vessel for fending off other vessels or for catching a mooring buoy.

boathouse ('bəʊtˌhaʊs) *n.* a shelter by the edge of a river, lake, etc., for housing boats.

boatie ('bəʊtɪ) *n.* *Austral. & N.Z. inf.* a boating enthusiast.

boating ('bəʊtɪŋ) *n.* rowing, sailing, or cruising in boats as a form of recreation.

boatload ('bəʊtˌləʊd) *n.* the amount of cargo or number of people held by a boat or ship.

boatman ('bəʊtmən) *n., pl.* **-men.** a man who works on, hires out, or repairs a boat or boats.

boatswain, bo's'n, *or* **bosun** ('bəʊsᵊn) *n.* a petty officer or a warrant officer who is responsible for the maintenance of a ship and its equipment. [OE *bātswegen;* see BOAT, SWAIN]

boat train *n.* a train scheduled to take passengers to or from a particular ship.

Boa Vista (*Portuguese* 'boːə 'viʃtə) *n.* a town in N Brazil, capital of the federal territory of Roraima, on the Rio Branco. Pop.: 43 131 (1980).

Boaz ('bəʊæz) *n.* *Old Testament.* a kinsman of Naomi, who married her daughter-in-law Ruth (Ruth 2–4); one of David's ancestors.

bob[1] (bɒb) *vb.* **bobbing, bobbed.** **1.** to move or cause to move up and down repeatedly, as while floating in water. **2.** to move or cause to move with a short abrupt movement, as of the head. **3.** (*intr.*; usually foll. by *up*) to appear or emerge suddenly. **4.** (*intr.*; usually foll. by *for*) to attempt to get hold (of a floating or hanging object, esp. an apple) in the teeth as a game. ~*n.* **5.** a short abrupt movement, as of the head. [C14: from ?]

bob[2] (bɒb) *n.* **1.** a hairstyle for women and children in which the hair is cut short evenly all round the head. **2.** a dangling or hanging object, such as the weight on a pendulum or on a plumb line. **3.** short for **bobsleigh.** **4.** a docked tail, esp. of a horse. ~*vb.* **bobbing, bobbed.** **5.** (*tr.*) to cut (the hair) in a bob. **6.** (*tr.*) to cut short (something, esp. the tail of an animal); dock or crop. **7.** (*intr.*) to ride on a bobsleigh. [C14 *bobbe* bunch of flowers]

bob[3] (bɒb) *n., pl.* **bob.** *Brit.* (formerly) an informal word for a **shilling.** [C19: from ?]

bobbejaan ('bɒbəˌjɑːn) *n.* *S. African.* a baboon. [from Afrik., from MDu. *babiaen*]

bobbejaan spanner *n.* *S. African.* a monkey wrench.

bobbin ('bɒbɪn) *n.* a spool or reel on which thread or yarn is wound. [C16: from OF *bobine,* from ?]

bobble ('bɒbᵊl) *n.* a tufted ball, usually for ornament, as on a knitted hat. [C19: from BOB[1] (vb.)]

bobby ('bɒbɪ) *n., pl.* **-bies.** *Inf.* a British policeman. [C19: from *Bobby,* after *Robert* PEEL, who set up the Metropolitan Police Force in 1828]

bobby calf *n.* an unweaned calf culled for slaughter.

bobby-dazzler *n. Dialect.* anything outstanding, striking, or showy. [C19: expanded from *dazzle* something striking or attractive]

bobby pin *n. U.S., Canad., Austral., & N.Z.* a metal hairpin bent in order to hold the hair in place.

bobby socks *pl. n.* ankle-length socks worn by teenage girls, esp. in the U.S. in the 1940s.

bobcat ('bɒb,kæt) *n.* a North American feline mammal, closely related to but smaller than the lynx, having reddish-brown fur with dark spots or stripes, tufted ears, and a short tail. Also called: **bay lynx.** [C19: from BOB² + CAT]

Bobo-Dioulasso ('bəʊbəʊdjuː'læsəʊ) *n.* a city in W Burkina-Faso. Pop.: 231 162 (1985).

bobolink ('bɒbə,lɪŋk) *n.* an American songbird, the male of which has a white back and black underparts. [C18: imit.]

bobotie (bʊ'bʊtɪ) *n.* a South African dish consisting of curried mincemeat with a topping of beaten egg baked to a crust. [C19: from Afrik., prob. from Malay]

bobsleigh ('bɒb,sleɪ) *n.* **1.** a racing sledge for two or more people, with a steering mechanism enabling the driver to direct it down a steeply banked ice-covered run. ~*vb.* **2.** (*intr.*) to ride on a bobsleigh. ~Also called (esp. U.S. and Canad.): **bobsled** ('bɒb,slɛd). [C19: BOB² + SLEIGH]

bobstay ('bɒb,steɪ) *n.* a strong stay between a bowsprit and the stem of a vessel for holding down the bowsprit. [C18: ?from BOB¹ + STAY³]

bobsy-die ('bɒbzɪ,daɪ) *n. N.Z. inf.* fuss; confusion (esp. in **kick up bobsy-die**). [from C19 *Bob's a-dying*]

bobtail ('bɒb,teɪl) *n.* **1.** a docked or diminutive tail. **2.** an animal with such a tail. ~*adj. also* **bobtailed. 3.** having the tail cut short. ~*vb.* (*tr.*) **4.** to dock the tail of. **5.** to cut short; curtail.

bobwhite ('bɒb,waɪt) *n.* a brown North American quail: the male has white markings on the head. [C19: imit.]

Boccaccio (*Italian* bok'kattʃo) *n.* **Giovanni** (dʒo'vani). 1313–75, Italian poet and writer, noted particularly for his *Decameron* (1353), a collection of 100 short stories. His other works include *Filostrato* (?1338) and *Teseida* (1341).

Boccherini (*Italian* bokke'rini) *n.* **Luigi** (lu'idʒi). 1743–1805, Italian composer and cellist.

Boccioni (*Italian* bot'tʃoni) *n.* **Umberto** (um'berto). 1882–1916, Italian painter and sculptor: principal theorist of the futurist movement.

Boche (bɒʃ) *n. Derog. sl.* (esp. in World Wars I and II) **1.** a German, esp. a German soldier. **2. the.** (*usually functioning as pl.*) Germans collectively, esp. German soldiers regarded as the enemy. [C20: from F, prob. shortened from *alboche* German, from *allemand* German + *caboche* pate]

Bochum (*German* 'boːxʊm) *n.* an industrial city in West Germany, in W North Rhine-Westphalia, in the Ruhr Valley. Pop.: 381 000 (1986).

bod (bɒd) *n. Inf.* a fellow; chap: *he's a queer bod.* [C18: short for BODY]

BOD *abbrev. for:* biochemical oxygen demand.

bode¹ (bəʊd) *vb.* **1.** to be an omen of (good or ill, esp. of ill); portend; presage. **2.** (*tr.*) *Arch.* to predict; foretell. [OE *bodian*] —'**bodement** *n.*

bode² (bəʊd) *vb.* a past tense of **bide.**

bodega (bəʊ'diːgə) *n.* a shop selling wine and sometimes groceries, esp. in a Spanish-speaking country. [C19: from Sp., ult. from Gk *apothēkē* storehouse]

Bodensee ('boːdənzeː) *n.* the German name for (Lake) **Constance.**

bodge (bɒdʒ) *vb. Inf.* to make a mess of; botch. [C16: changed from BOTCH]

bodgie ('bɒdʒi) *Austral. & N.Z. sl.* ~*n.* **1.** an unruly or uncouth young man, esp. in the 1950s. ~*adj.* **2.** false, fraudulent. [C20: from BODGE]

Bodh Gaya ('bɒd gə'jɑː) *n.* a variant spelling of **Buddh Gaya.**

Bodhisattva (,bəʊdɪ'sætvə, -wə, ,bɒd-) *n.* (in Buddhism) a divine being worthy of nirvana who remains on the human plane to help men to salvation. [Sansk., from *bodhi* enlightenment + *sattva* essence]

bodice ('bɒdɪs) *n.* **1.** the upper part of a woman's dress, from the shoulder to the waist. **2.** a tight-fitting corset worn laced over a blouse, or (formerly) as a woman's undergarment. [C16: orig. Scot. *bodies*, pl. of BODY]

bodice ripper *n. Inf.* a romantic novel, usually on a historical theme, that involves some sex and violence.

-bodied *adj.* (*in combination*) having a body or bodies as specified: *able-bodied; long-bodied.*

bodiless ('bɒdɪlɪs) *adj.* having no body or substance; incorporeal or insubstantial.

bodily ('bɒdɪlɪ) *adj.* **1.** relating to or being a part of the human body. ~*adv.* **2.** by taking hold of the body: *he threw him bodily from the platform.* **3.** in person; in the flesh.

bodkin ('bɒdkɪn) *n.* **1.** a blunt large-eyed needle. **2.** *Arch.* a dagger. **3.** *Arch.* a long ornamental hairpin. [C14: prob. of Celtic origin]

Bodmin ('bɒdmɪn) *n.* a market town in SW England, administrative centre of Cornwall, near **Bodmin Moor,** a granite upland rising to 420 m (1375 ft.). Pop.: 15 000 (1984).

body ('bɒdɪ) *n., pl.* **bodies. 1. a.** the entire physical structure of an animal or human being. Related adj.: **corporeal. b.** (*as modifier*): *body odour.* **2.** the trunk or torso. **3.** a dead human or animal; corpse. **4.** the flesh as opposed to the spirit. **5.** the largest or main part of anything: *the body of a vehicle; the body of a plant.* **6.** a separate or distinct mass of water or land. **7.** a number of individuals regarded as a single entity; group. **8.** the characteristic full quality of certain wines. **9.** firmness, esp. of cloth. **10. a.** the pigment contained in or added to paint, dye, etc. **b.** the opacity of a paint. **c.** (*as modifier*): *body colour.* **11.** an informal or dialect word for a **person. 12. keep body and soul together.** to manage to keep alive; survive. ~*vb.* **bodying, bodied.** (*tr.*) **13.** (usually foll. by *forth*) to give a body or shape to. [OE *bodig*]

body blow *n.* **1.** *Boxing.* a blow to an opponent's body **2.** a severe disappointment or setback.

body building *n.* the practice of exercises to make the muscles of the body conspicuous.

bodycheck ('bɒdɪ,tʃɛk) *Ice hockey, etc.* ~*n.* **1.** obstruction of another player. ~*vb.* **2.** (*tr.*) to deliver a bodycheck to (an opponent).

bodyguard ('bɒdɪ,gɑːd) *n.* a man or group of men who escort and protect someone.

body language *n.* the nonverbal imparting of information by means of conscious or subconscious bodily gestures, posture, etc.

body-line *adj. Cricket.* denoting or relating to fast bowling aimed at the batsman's body.

body politic *n.* **the.** the people of a nation or the nation itself considered as a political entity.

body popping *n.* a dance of the 1980s, characterized by schematic, rhythmic movements. —**body popper** *n.*

body shop *n.* a repair yard for vehicle bodywork.

body snatcher *n.* (formerly) a person who robbed graves and sold the corpses for dissection.

body stocking *n.* a one-piece undergarment for women, usually of nylon, covering the torso.

bodysuit ('bɒdɪ,suːt, -,sjuːt) *n.* a woman's close-fitting one-piece garment for the torso. Sometimes shortened to **body.**

body warmer *n.* a sleeveless type of jerkin, usually quilted, worn as an outer garment.

bodywork ('bɒdɪ,wɜːk) *n.* the external shell of a motor vehicle.

Boeotia (bɪ'əʊʃɪə) *n.* **1.** a region of ancient Greece, northwest of Athens. It consisted of ten city-states, which formed the Boeotian League, led by Thebes: at its height in the 4th century B.C. **2.** transliteration of the Modern Greek name for **Voiotia.** —**Boe'otian** *n., adj.*

Boer (bʊə) *n.* **a.** a descendant of any of the Dutch or Huguenot colonists who settled in South Africa. **b.** (*as modifier*): *a Boer farmer.* [C19: from Du. *Boer;* see BOOR]

boerbul ('bʊəbəl) *n. S. African.* a crossbred mastiff used esp. as a watchdog. [from Afrik. *boerboel,* from *boel* large dog]

boeremusiek ('bʊərə,mœsik) *n. S. African.* light music associated with the culture of the Afrikaners. [from Afrik. *boere* country, folk + *musiek* music]

boer-goat ('bʊə,gəʊt) *n. S. African.* a hardy indigenous breed of goat. [from Afrik from *boer* + GOAT]

boerperd ('bʊə,pɜːt) *n.* a S. African breed of rugged horse, often palomino. [from Afrik. *boer* Afrikaner, indigenous + *perd,* from Du. *paard* horse]

boet (bʊt) *or* **boetie** *n. S. African inf.* a friend. [from Afrik.: brother]

Boethius (bəʊˈiːθɪəs) n. **Anicius Manlius Severinus** (əˈnɪsɪəs ˈmænlɪəs ˌsɛvəˈraɪnəs). ?480–?524 A.D., Roman philosopher and statesman, noted particularly for his work *De Consolatione Philosophiae*. He was accused of treason and executed by Theodoric.

boffin (ˈbɒfɪn) n. *Brit. inf.* a scientist, esp. one carrying out military research. [C20: from ?]

Bofors gun (ˈbəʊfəz) n. an automatic double-barrelled anti-aircraft gun. [C20: after *Bofors*, Sweden, where it was first made]

bog (bɒg) n. **1.** wet spongy ground consisting of decomposing vegetation. **2.** an area of such ground. **3.** a slang word for **lavatory**. [C13: from Gaelic *bogach* swamp, from *bog* soft] —ˈ**boggy** adj. —ˈ**bogginess** n.

bogan (ˈbəʊgən) n. *Canad.* (esp. in the Maritime Provinces) a sluggish side stream. Also called: **logan, pokelogan**. [of Algonquian origin]

Bogarde (ˈbəʊgɑːd) n. **Dirk**, real name *Derek Jules Gaspard Ulric Niven van den Bogaerde*. born 1920, British film actor and writer: his films include *The Servant* (1963), *Accident* (1967), and *Death in Venice* (1970). His writings include the autobiographical *A Postillion Struck by Lightning* (1977) and *Snakes and Ladders* (1978) and the novels *A Gentle Occupation* (1980) and *Voices in the Garden* (1981).

Bogart (ˈbəʊgɑːt) n. **Humphrey** (**DeForest**). nicknamed *Bogie*. 1899–1957, U.S. film actor: his films include *High Sierra* (1941), *Casablanca* (1942), *The Big Sleep* (1946), *The African Queen* (1951), and *The Caine Mutiny* (1954).

Boğazköy (*Turkish* bɔːˈɑzkœi) n. a village in central Asia Minor: site of the ancient Hittite capital.

bogbean (ˈbɒɡˌbiːn) n. another name for **buckbean**.

bog down vb. **bogging, bogged.** (*adv.;* when *tr.,* often *passive*) to impede or be impeded physically or mentally.

bogey or **bogy** (ˈbəʊgɪ) n. **1.** an evil or mischievous spirit. **2.** something that worries or annoys. **3.** *Golf.* **a.** a standard score for a hole or course, regarded as one that a good player should make. **b.** *U.S.* a score of one stroke over par on a hole. Cf. **par** (sense 5). **4.** *Sl.* a piece of dried mucus discharged from the nose. [C19: prob. rel. to obs. *bug* an evil spirit & BOGLE]

bogeyman (ˈbəʊgɪˌmæn) n., *pl.* **-men.** a person, real or imaginary, used as a threat, esp. to children.

boggle (ˈbɒgᵊl) vb. (*intr.;* often foll. by *at*) **1.** to be surprised, confused, or alarmed (esp. in the **mind boggles**). **2.** to hesitate or be evasive when confronted with a problem. [C16: prob. var. of BOGLE]

bogie or **bogy** (ˈbəʊgɪ) n. **1.** an assembly of four or six wheels forming a pivoted support at either end of a railway coach. **2.** *Chiefly Brit.* a small railway truck of short wheelbase, used for conveying coal, ores, etc. [C19: from ?]

bogle (ˈbəʊgᵊl, ˈbɒg-) n. a dialect or archaic word for **bogey** (sense 1). [C16: from Scot. *bogill*]

bog myrtle n. another name for **sweet gale**.

Bognor Regis (ˈbɒgnə ˈriːdʒɪs) n. a resort in S England, in West Sussex on the English Channel. *Regis* was added to the name after King George V's convalescence there in 1929. Pop.: 39 530 (1981).

bog oak n. oak found preserved in peat bogs.

bogong (ˈbəʊˌgɒŋ) or **bugong** (ˈbuːˌgɒŋ) n. an edible dark-coloured Australian noctuid moth.

Bogor (ˈbəʊgɔː) n. a city in Indonesia, in W Java: botanical gardens and research institutions. Pop.: 246 000 (1980). Former name: **Buitenzorg**.

Bogotá (ˌbəʊgəˈtɑː; *Spanish* boɣoˈta) n. the capital of Colombia, on a central plateau of the E Andes: originally the centre of Chibcha civilization; founded as a city in 1538 by the Spaniards. Pop.: 4 185 174 (1985).

bogtrotter (ˈbɒgˌtrɒtə) n. a derogatory term for an Irishman, esp. an Irish peasant.

bogus (ˈbəʊgəs) adj. spurious or counterfeit; not genuine. [C19: from *bogus* apparatus for making counterfeit money] —ˈ**bogusly** adv. —ˈ**bogusness** n.

bogy (ˈbəʊgɪ) n., *pl.* **-gies.** a variant spelling of **bogey** or **bogie**.

Bohai (ˈbɔːˈhaɪ) or **Pohai** n. a large inlet of the Yellow Sea on the coast of NE China. Also called: (Gulf of) **Chihli**.

bohea (bəʊˈhiː) n. a black Chinese tea, once regarded as the choicest, but now as an inferior grade. [C18: from Chinese *Wu-i Shan*, range of hills on which this tea was grown]

Bohemia (bəʊˈhiːmɪə) n. **1.** a former kingdom of central Europe, surrounded by mountains: independent from the 9th to the 13th century; belonged to the Hapsburgs from 1526 until 1918. **2.** the Czech-speaking part of W Czechoslovakia, formerly a province (1918–49). From 1939 until 1945 it formed part of the German protectorate of **Bohemia-Moravia**. Czech name: **Čechy**. German name: **Böhmen** (ˈbøːmən). **3.** a district frequented by unconventional people, esp. artists or writers.

Bohemian (bəʊˈhiːmɪən) n. **1.** a native or inhabitant of Bohemia; a Czech. **2.** (*often not cap.*) a person, esp. an artist or writer, who lives an unconventional life. **3.** the Czech language. ~adj. **4.** of, relating to, or characteristic of Bohemia, its people, or their language. **5.** unconventional in appearance, behaviour, etc.

Bohemian Forest n. a mountain range between SW Czechoslovakia and SE West Germany. Highest peak: Arber, 1457 m (4780 ft.). Czech name: **Český Les** (ˈtʃɛskiː ˈlɛs). German name: **Böhmerwald** (ˈbøːmər‚valt).

Bohemianism (bəʊˈhiːmɪə‚nɪzəm) n. unconventional behaviour or appearance, esp. of an artist.

Böhm (*German* bøːm) n. **Karl** (karl). 1894–1981, Austrian orchestral conductor.

Böhme, Boehme (*German* ˈbøːmə), or **Böhm** n. **Jakob** (ˈjaːkɔp). 1575–1624, German mystic.

Bohol (bəʊˈhɔːl) n. an island of the central Philippines. Chief town: Tagbilaran. Pop.: 763 330 (1980). Area: about 3900 sq. km (1500 sq. miles).

Bohr (bɔː; *Danish* boːr) n. **Niels** (**Henrik David**) (neːls). 1885–1962, Danish physicist, who applied the quantum theory to Rutherford's model of the atom to explain spectral lines: Nobel prize for physics 1922.

Boiardo (*Italian* boˈjardo) n. **Matteo Maria** (matˈtɛːo maˈria). 1434–94, Italian poet; author of the historical epic *Orlando Innamorato* (1487).

boil[1] (bɔɪl) vb. **1.** to change or cause to change from a liquid to a vapour so rapidly that bubbles of vapour are formed in the liquid. **2.** to reach or cause to reach boiling point. **3.** to cook or be cooked by the process of boiling. **4.** (*intr.*) to bubble and be agitated like something boiling; seethe: *the ocean was boiling.* **5.** (*intr.*) to be extremely angry or indignant. ~n. **6.** the state or action of boiling. ~See also **boil away, boil down, boil over.** [C13: from OF, from L, from *bulla* a bubble]

boil[2] (bɔɪl) n. a red painful swelling with a hard pus-filled core caused by bacterial infection of the skin. Technical name: **furuncle**. [OE *bȳle*]

boil away vb. (*adv.*) to cause (liquid) to evaporate completely by boiling or (of liquid) to evaporate completely.

boil down vb. (*adv.*) **1.** to reduce or be reduced in quantity by boiling. **2. boil down to. a.** (*intr.*) to be the essential element in something. **b.** (*tr.*) to summarize; reduce to essentials.

Boileau (*French* bwalo) n. **Nicolas** (nikɔla). full name *Nicolas Boileau-Despréaux*. 1636–1711, French poet and critic; author of satires, epistles, and *L'Art poétique* (1674), in which he laid down the basic principles of French classical literature.

boiled shirt n. *Inf.* a dress shirt with a stiff front.

boiler (ˈbɔɪlə) n. **1.** a closed vessel in which water is heated to supply steam or provide heat. **2.** a domestic device to provide hot water, esp. for central heating. **3.** a large tub for boiling laundry.

boilermaker (ˈbɔɪlə‚meɪkə) n. a person who works with metal in heavy industry; plater or welder.

boiler suit n. *Brit.* a one-piece overall work garment.

boiling point n. **1.** the temperature at which a liquid boils at sea level. **2.** *Inf.* the condition of being angered or highly excited.

boiling-water reactor n. a nuclear reactor using water as coolant and moderator, steam being produced in the reactor itself. Abbrev.: **BWR**.

boil over vb. (*adv.*) **1.** to overflow or cause to overflow while boiling. **2.** (*intr.*) to burst out in anger or excitement.

Bois de Boulogne (*French* bwa də bulɔɲ) n. a large park in W Paris, formerly a forest: includes the racecourses of Auteuil and Longchamp.

Boise or **Boise City** (ˈbɔɪzɪ, -sɪ) n. a city in SW Idaho: the state capital. Pop.: 107 188 (1984 est.).

Bois-le-Duc (bwa lə dyk) n. the French name for **'s Hertogenbosch**.

boisterous ('bɔɪstərəs, -strəs) adj. **1.** noisy and lively; unruly. **2.** (of the wind, sea, etc.) turbulent or stormy. [C13 boistuous, from ?] —**'boisterously** adv. —**'boisterousness** n.

Boito (Italian 'bɔːito) n. **Arrigo** (ar'rigo). 1842–1918, Italian operatic composer and librettist, whose works include the opera Mefistofele (1868) and the librettos for Verdi's Otello and Falstaff.

Bokassa I (bə'kæsə) n. original name Jean Bedel Bokassa. born 1921, president of the Central African Republic (1972–76); emperor of the renamed Central African Empire from 1976 until overthrown in 1979.

Bokhara (bʊ'xɑːrə) n. a variant spelling of **Bukhara**.

bola ('bəʊlə) or **bolas** ('bəʊləs) n., pl. **-las** or **-lases**. a missile used by gauchos and Indians of South America, consisting of heavy balls on a cord. It is hurled at a running quarry, so as to entangle its legs. [Sp.: ball, from L bulla knob]

Boland ('bʊələnt) n. an area of high altitude in the SW Cape Province of South Africa.

Bolan Pass (bəʊ'lɑːn) n. a mountain pass in W central Pakistan through the Brahui Range, between Sibi and Quetta, rising to 1800 m (5900 ft.).

bold (bəʊld) adj. **1.** courageous, confident, and fearless; ready to take risks. **2.** showing or requiring courage: a bold plan. **3.** immodest or impudent: she gave him a bold look. **4.** standing out distinctly; conspicuous: a figure carved in bold relief. **5.** very steep: the bold face of the cliff. **6.** imaginative in thought or expression. [OE beald] —**'boldly** adv. —**'boldness** n.

bold face Printing. ~n. **1.** a weight of type characterized by thick heavy lines, as the entry words in this dictionary. ~adj. **boldface**. **2.** (of type) having this weight.

Boldrewood ('bəʊldɪ,wʊd) n. **Rolf**, real name Thomas Alexander Browne. 1826–1915, noted for his novels of the Australian outback, esp. Robbery Under Arms (1882–3).

bole (bəʊl) n. the trunk of a tree. [C14: from ON bolr]

bolero (bə'lɛərəʊ) n., pl. **-ros. 1.** a Spanish dance, usually in triple time. **2.** a piece of music for or in the rhythm of this dance. **3.** (also 'bɒlərəʊ) a short open bodice-like jacket not reaching the waist. [C18: from Sp.]

Boleyn (bʊ'lɪn, 'bʊlɪn) n. **Anne**. 1507–36, second wife of Henry VIII of England; mother of Elizabeth I. She was executed on a charge of adultery.

Bolingbroke ('bɒlɪŋ,brʊk) n. **1.** the surname of **Henry IV** of England. **2. Henry St John,** 1st Viscount Bolingbroke. 1678–1751, English politician; fled to France in 1714 and acted as secretary of state to the Old Pretender; returned to England in 1723. His writings include A Dissertation on Parties (1733–34) and Idea of a Patriot King (1738).

Bolivar ('bɒlɪ,vɑː; Spanish bo'liβar) n. **Simon** (si'mon). 1783–1830, South American soldier and liberator. He drove the Spaniards from Venezuela, Colombia, Ecuador, and Peru and hoped to set up a republican confederation, but was prevented by separatist movements in Venezuela and Colombia (1829–30). Upper Peru became a separate state and was called Bolivia in his honour.

Bolivia (bə'lɪvɪə) n. an inland republic in central S America: original Aymará Indian population conquered by the Incas in the 13th century; colonized by Spain from 1538; became a republic in 1825; consists of low plains in the east, with ranges of the Andes rising to over 6400 m (21 000 ft.) and the Altiplano, a plateau averaging 3900 m (13 000 ft.) in the west; contains some of the world's highest inhabited regions; important producer of tin and other minerals. Official languages: Spanish, Quechua, and Aymara. Religion: Roman Catholic. Currency: boliviano. Capital: La Paz. Pop.: 6 730 000 (1987 est.). Area: 1 098 580 sq. km (424 260 sq. miles). —**Bo'livian** adj., n.

boll (bəʊl) n. the fruit of such plants as flax and cotton, consisting of a rounded capsule containing the seeds. [C13: from Du. bolle; rel. to OE bolla BOWL[1]]

Böll (German bœl) n. **Heinrich** ('haɪnrɪç). 1917–85, German novelist and short-story writer; his novels include Gruppenbild mit Dame (1971): Nobel prize for literature 1972.

bollard ('bɒlɑːd, 'bɒləd) n. **1.** a strong wooden or metal post on a wharf, quay, etc., used for securing mooring lines. **2.** Brit. a small post placed on a kerb or traffic island to make it conspicuous to motorists. [C14: ?from BOLE + -ARD]

bollocking ('bɒləkɪŋ) n. Sl. a severe telling-off. [from bollock (vb.) in the sense "to reprimand"]

bollocks ('bɒləks) or **ballocks** Taboo sl. ~pl. n. **1.** another word for **testicles**. ~interj. **2.** an exclamation of annoyance, disbelief, etc. [OE beallucas; see BALL[1]]

boll weevil n. a greyish weevil of the southern U.S. and Mexico, whose larvae live in and destroy cotton bolls.

Bologna (bə'lɒnjə; Italian bo'loɲɲa) n. a city in N Italy, at the foot of the Apennines: became a free city in the Middle Ages; university (1088). Pop.: 432 406 (1986). Ancient name: **Bononia** (bə'nəʊnɪə). —**Bolognese** (,bɒlə'niːz, -'neɪz) adj., n.

bologna sausage (bə'ləʊnjə) n. Chiefly U.S. & Canad. a large smoked sausage made of seasoned mixed meats. Also called: **baloney, boloney,** (esp. Brit.) **polony**.

bolometer (bəʊ'lɒmɪtə) n. a sensitive instrument for measuring radiant energy. [C19: from Gk bolē ray of light, from ballein to throw + -METER] —**bolometric** (,bəʊlə-'mɛtrɪk) adj.

boloney (bə'ləʊnɪ) n. **1.** a variant of **baloney**. **2.** another name for **bologna sausage**.

Bolshevik ('bɒlʃɪvɪk) n., pl. **-viks** or **-viki** (,bɒlʃɪ'viːkɪ). **1.** (formerly) a Russian Communist. Cf **Menshevik**. **2.** any Communist. **3.** (often not cap.) Inf. & derog. any political radical, esp. a revolutionary. [C20: from Russian Bol'shevik majority, from bol'shoi great] —**'Bolshe,vism** n. —**'Bolshevist** adj., n.

bolshie or **bolshy** ('bɒlʃɪ) (sometimes cap.) Brit. inf. ~adj. **1.** difficult to manage; rebellious. **2.** politically radical or left-wing. ~n., pl. **-shies**. **3.** Derog. any political radical. [C20: shortened from BOLSHEVIK]

bolster ('bəʊlstə) vb. (tr.) **1.** (often foll. by up) to support or reinforce; strengthen: to bolster morale. **2.** to prop up with a pillow or cushion. ~n. **3.** a long narrow pillow or cushion. **4.** any pad or padded support. **5.** a cold chisel used for cutting stone slabs, etc. [OE bolster]

bolt[1] (bəʊlt) n. **1.** a bar that can be slid into a socket to lock a door, gate, etc. **2.** a bar or rod that forms part of a locking mechanism and is moved by a key or a knob. **3.** a metal rod or pin that has a head and a screw thread to take a nut. **4.** a sliding bar in a breech-loading firearm that ejects the empty cartridge, replaces it with a new one, and closes the breech. **5.** a flash of lightning. **6. a bolt from the blue.** a sudden, unexpected, and usually unwelcome event. **7.** a sudden start or movement, esp. in order to escape. **8.** a roll of something, such as cloth, wallpaper, etc. **9.** an arrow, esp. for a crossbow. **10. shoot one's bolt.** to exhaust one's efforts. ~vb. **11.** (tr.) to secure or lock with or as with a bolt. **12.** (tr.) to eat hurriedly. **13.** (intr.; usually foll. by from or out) to move or jump suddenly: he bolted from the chair. **14.** (intr.) (esp. of a horse) to start hurriedly and run away without warning. **15.** (tr.) to roll (cloth, wallpaper, etc.) into bolts. **16.** (intr.) (of cultivated plants) to produce flowers and seeds prematurely. ~adv. **17.** stiffly, firmly, or rigidly (archaic except in **bolt upright**). [OE bolt arrow] —**'bolter** n.

bolt[2] or **boult** (bəʊlt) vb. (tr.) **1.** to pass (flour, a powder, etc.) through a sieve. **2.** to examine and separate. [C13: from OF bulter, prob. of Gmc origin] —**'bolter** or **'boulter** n.

Bolt (bəʊlt) n. **Robert Oxton**. born 1924, British playwright. His plays include A Man for All Seasons (1960) and he has written a number of screenplays.

bolt hole n. a place of escape from danger.

Bolton ('bəʊltən) n. a metropolitan district in NW England, in Greater Manchester: centre of the woollen trade since the 14th century; later important for cotton. Pop.: 261 000 (1985).

boltrope ('bəʊlt,rəʊp) n. Naut. a rope sewn to the foot or luff of a sail to strengthen it.

Boltzmann (German 'bɒltsman) n. **Ludwig** ('luːtvɪç). 1844–1906, Austrian physicist. He established the principle of the equipartition of energy and developed the kinetic theory of gases with J. C. Maxwell.

bolus ('bəʊləs) n., pl. **-luses. 1.** a small round soft mass, esp. of chewed food. **2.** a large pill or tablet used in veterinary and clinical medicine. [C17: from NL, from Gk bōlos clod, lump]

Bolzano (Italian bol'tsano) n. a city in NE Italy, in Trentino-Alto Adige: belonged to Austria until 1919. Pop.: 101 515 (1986). German name: **Bozen**.

bomb (bɒm) n. **1. a.** a hollow projectile containing explosive, incendiary, or other destructive substance. **b.** (as

modifier): *bomb disposal; a bomb bay.* **c.** (*in combination*): *bombproof.* **2.** an object in which an explosive device has been planted: *a car bomb; a letter bomb.* **3.** a round mass of volcanic rock, solidified from molten lava that has been thrown into the air. **4.** *Med.* a container for radioactive material, applied therapeutically to any part of the body: *a cobalt bomb.* **5.** *Brit. sl.* a large sum of money. **6.** *U.S. & Canad. sl.* a disastrous failure: *the new play was a total bomb.* **7.** *Austral. & N.Z. sl.* an old or dilapidated motorcar. **8. like a bomb.** *Brit. & N.Z. inf.* with great speed or success; very well. **9. the bomb.** a hydrogen or an atom bomb considered as the ultimate destructive weapon. ~*vb.* **10.** to attack with or as if with a bomb or bombs; drop bombs (on). **11.** (*intr.; often foll. by off, along,* etc.) *Inf.* to move or drive very quickly. **12.** (*intr.*) *U.S. sl.* to fail disastrously. [C17: from F, from It., from L, from Gk *bombos*, imit.]
bombard *vb.* (bɒmˈbɑːd). (*tr.*) **1.** to attack with concentrated artillery fire or bombs. **2.** to attack with vigour and persistence. **3.** to attack verbally, esp. with questions. **4.** *Physics.* to direct high-energy particles or photons against (atoms, nuclei, etc.). ~*n.* (ˈbɒmbɑːd). **5.** an ancient type of cannon that threw stone balls. [C15: from OF, from *bombarde* stone-throwing part. prob. from L *bombus* booming sound; see BOMB] —**bomˈbardment** *n.*
bombardier (ˌbɒmbəˈdɪə) *n.* **1.** the member of a bomber aircrew responsible for aiming and releasing the bombs. **2.** *Brit.* a noncommissioned rank, below the rank of sergeant, in the Royal Artillery. **3.** *Canad. trademark.* a snow tractor, usually having caterpillar tracks at the rear and skis at the front. [C16: from OF; see BOMBARD]
bombast (ˈbɒmbæst) *n.* pompous and grandiloquent language. [C16: from OF, from Med. L *bombāx* cotton] —**bomˈbastic** *adj.* —**bomˈbastically** *adv.*
Bombay (bɒmˈbeɪ) *n.* a port in W India, capital of Maharashtra state, on the Arabian Sea: ceded by Portugal to England in 1661 and of major importance in British India; commercial and industrial centre, esp. for cotton. Pop.: 8 202 759 (1981).
Bombay duck *n.* a fish that is eaten dried with curry dishes as a savoury. Also called: **bummalo.** [C19: changed from *bombil* through association with Bombay, from which it was exported]
bombazine *or* **bombasine** (ˌbɒmbəˈziːn, ˈbɒmbəˌziːn) *n.* a twilled fabric, esp. one of silk and worsted, formerly worn dyed black for mourning. [C16: from OF, from L, from *bombyx* silk]
bomber (ˈbɒmə) *n.* **1.** a military aircraft designed to carry out bombing missions. **2.** a person who plants bombs.
bomber jacket *n.* a short jacket finishing at the waist with an elasticated band, usually having a zip front.
bombora (bɒmˈbɔːrə) *n. Austral.* **1.** a submerged reef. **2.** a turbulent area of sea over such a reef. [from Abor.]
bombshell (ˈbɒmˌʃɛl) *n.* **1.** (esp. formerly) a bomb or artillery shell. **2.** a shocking or unwelcome surprise.
bombsight (ˈbɒmˌsaɪt) *n.* a mechanical or electronic device in an aircraft for aiming bombs.
Bomu (ˈbəʊmuː) *or* **Mbomu** (ᵊmˈbəʊmuː) *n.* a river in central Africa, rising in the SE Central African Republic and flowing west into the Uele River, forming the Ubangi River. Length: about 800 km (500 miles).
Bon (bɒn) *n.* **Cape.** a peninsula of NE Tunisia.
Bona (ˈbəʊnə) *n.* **Mount.** a mountain in S Alaska, in the Wrangell Mountains. Height: 5005 m (16 420 ft.).
bona fide (ˈbəʊnə ˈfaɪdɪ) *adj.* **1.** real or genuine: *a bona fide manuscript.* **2.** undertaken in good faith: *a bona fide agreement.* [C16: from L]
bona fides (ˈbəʊnə ˈfaɪdiːz) *n. Law.* good faith; honest intention. [L]
Bonaire (bɒnˈɛə) *n.* an island in the S West Indies, in the E Netherlands Antilles: one of the Leeward Islands. Chief town: Kralendijk. Pop.: 8753 (1981). Area: about 288 sq. km (111 sq. miles).
bonanza (bəˈnænzə) *n.* **1.** a source, usually sudden and unexpected, of luck or wealth. **2.** *U.S. & Canad.* a mine or vein rich in ore. [C19: from Sp., lit.: calm sea, hence, good luck, from Med. L, from L *bonus* good + *malacia* calm, from Gk *malakia* softness]
Bonaparte (ˈbəʊnəˌpɑːt; *French* bɔnapart) *n.* **1.** See **Napoleon I.** **2. Jérôme** (ʒerom), brother of Napoleon I. 1784–1860, king of Westphalia (1807–13). **3. Joseph** (ʒozɛf), brother of Napoleon I. 1768–1844, king of Naples

(1806–08) and of Spain (1808–13). **4. Louis** (lwi), brother of Napoleon I. 1778–1846, king of Holland (1806–10). **5. Lucien** (lysjɛ̃), brother of Napoleon I. 1775–1840, prince of Canino.
Bonaventura (ˌbɒnəvɛnˈtjʊərə) *or* **Bonaventure** (ˈbɒnəˌvɛntʃə) *n.* **Saint,** called *the Seraphic Doctor.* 1221–74, Italian Franciscan monk, mystic, theologian, and philosopher; author of a *Life of St Francis* and *Journey of the Soul to God.* Feast day: July 14.
bonbon (ˈbɒnbɒn) *n.* a sweet. [C19: from F, orig. a children's word from *bon* good]
bonce (bɒns) *n. Brit. sl.* the head. [C19 (orig.: a large playing marble): from ?]
bond (bɒnd) *n.* **1.** something that binds, fastens, or holds together, such as a chain or rope. **2.** (*often pl.*) something that brings or holds people together; tie: *a bond of friendship.* **3.** (*pl.*) something that restrains or imprisons; captivity or imprisonment. **4.** a written or spoken agreement, esp. a promise. **5.** *Finance.* a certificate of debt issued in order to raise funds. It is repayable with or without security at a specified future date. **6.** *Law.* a written acknowledgment of an obligation to pay a sum or to perform a contract. **7.** any of various arrangements of bricks or stones in a wall in which they overlap so as to provide strength. **8. chemical bond.** a mutual attraction between two atoms resulting from a redistribution of their outer electrons, determining chemical properties; shown in some formulae by a dot (.) or score (—). **9.** See **bond paper.** **10. in bond.** *Commerce.* deposited in a bonded warehouse. ~*vb.* (*mainly tr.*) **11.** (*also intr.*) to hold or be held together, as by a rope or an adhesive; bind; connect. **12.** (*intr.*) to become emotionally attached. **13.** to put or hold (goods) in bond. **14.** *Law.* to place under bond. **15.** *Finance.* to issue bonds on; mortgage. [C13: from ON *band;* see BAND²]
bondage (ˈbɒndɪdʒ) *n.* **1.** slavery or serfdom; servitude. **2.** subjection to some influence or duty. **3.** a sexual practice in which one participant is physically bound.
bonded (ˈbɒndɪd) *adj.* **1.** *Finance.* consisting of, secured by, or operating under a bond or bonds. **2.** *Commerce.* deposited in a bonded warehouse.
bonded warehouse *n.* a warehouse in which goods are deposited until duty is paid.
bondholder (ˈbɒndˌhəʊldə) *n.* an owner of bonds issued by a company or other institution.
bonding (ˈbɒndɪŋ) *n.* the process by which individuals become emotionally attached to one another.
bondmaid (ˈbɒndˌmeɪd) *n.* an unmarried female serf or slave.
bond paper *n.* a superior quality of strong white paper, used esp. for writing and typing.
bondservant (ˈbɒndˌsɜːvənt) *n.* a serf or slave.
bondsman (ˈbɒndzmən) *n., pl.* **-men. 1.** *Law.* a person bound by bond to act as surety for another. **2.** another word for **bondservant.**
bond washing *n.* a series of illegal deals in bonds made with the intention of avoiding taxation.
bone (bəʊn) *n.* **1.** any of the various structures that make up the skeleton in most vertebrates. **2.** the porous rigid tissue of which these parts are made. **3.** something consisting of bone or a bonelike substance. **4.** (*pl.*) the human skeleton or body. **5.** a thin strip of whalebone, plastic, etc., used to stiffen corsets and brassieres. **6.** (*pl.*) the essentials (esp. in **the bare bones**). **7.** (*pl.*) dice. **8. feel in one's bones.** to have an intuition of. **9. have a bone to pick.** to have grounds for a quarrel. **10. make no bones about. a.** to be direct and candid about. **b.** to have no scruples about. **11. near** *or* **close to the bone. a.** risqué or indecent. **b.** in poverty; destitute. **12. point the bone.** (often foll. by *at*) *Austral.* **a.** to wish bad luck (on). **b.** to cast a spell (on) in order to kill. ~*vb.* (*mainly tr.*) **13.** to remove the bones from (meat for cooking, etc.). **14.** to stiffen (a corset, etc.) by inserting bones. **15.** *Brit.* a slang word for **steal.** ~See also **bone up.** [OE *bān*] —**ˈboneless** *adj.*
Bône (*French* bon) *n.* a former name of **Annaba.**
bone ash *n.* ash obtained when bones are burnt in air, consisting mainly of calcium phosphate.
bone china *n.* porcelain containing bone ash.
bone-dry *adj. Inf.* **a.** completely dry: *a bone-dry well.* **b.** (*postpositive*): *the well was bone dry.*
bonehead (ˈbəʊnˌhɛd) *n. Sl.* a stupid or obstinate person. —**ˈboneˌheaded** *adj.*

bone idle *adj.* very idle; extremely lazy.

bone meal *n.* dried and ground animal bones, used as a fertilizer or in stock feeds.

boner ('bəʊnə) *n. Sl.* a blunder.

bonesetter ('bəʊn,sɛtə) *n.* a person who sets broken or dislocated bones, esp. one who has no formal medical qualifications.

boneshaker ('bəʊn,ʃeɪkə) *n.* **1.** an early type of bicycle having solid tyres and no springs. **2.** *Sl.* any decrepit or rickety vehicle.

bone up *vb.* (*adv.*; when *intr.*, usually foll. by *on*) *Inf.* to study intensively.

bonfire ('bɒn,faɪə) *n.* a large outdoor fire. [C15: alteration (infl. by F *bon* good) of *bone-fire;* from the use of bones as fuel]

bong (bɒŋ) *n.* **1.** a deep reverberating sound, as of a large bell. ~*vb.* **2.** to make a deep reverberating sound. [C20: imit.]

bongo[1] ('bɒŋgəʊ) *n., pl.* **-go** *or* **-gos.** a rare spiral-horned antelope inhabiting forests of central Africa. The coat is bright red-brown with narrow vertical stripes. [of African origin]

bongo[2] ('bɒŋgəʊ) *n., pl.* **-gos** *or* **-goes.** a small bucket-shaped drum, usually one of a pair, played by beating with the fingers. [American Sp., prob. imit.]

Bongo ('bɒŋgəʊ) *n.* **Omar.** real name *Albert Bernard Bongo.* born 1935, Gabonese statesman; president of Gabon from 1967.

Bonheur (*French* bɔnœr) *n.* **Rosa** (roza). 1822–99, French painter of animals.

Bonhoeffer (*German* 'bɔ:nhœfər) *n.* **Dietrich** ('di:trɪç). 1906–45, German Lutheran theologian: executed by the Nazis.

bonhomie ('bɒnəmi:) *n.* exuberant friendliness. [C18: from F, from *bon* good + *homme* man]

Boniface ('bɒnɪ,feɪs) *n.* **Saint.** original name *Wynfrith.* ?680–?755 A.D. Anglo-saxon missionary: archbishop of Mainz (746–755). Feast day: June 5.

Boniface VIII *n.* original name *Benedict Caetano.* ?1234–1303, pope (1294–1303).

Bonington ('bɒnɪŋtən) *n.* **Chris(tian).** born 1934, English mountaineer and writer; led 1970 Annapurna I and 1975 Everest expeditions.

Bonin Islands ('bəʊnɪn) *pl. n.* a group of 27 volcanic islands in the W Pacific: occupied by the U.S. after World War II; returned to Japan in 1968. Largest island: Chichijima. Area: 103 sq. km (40 sq. miles). Japanese name: **Ogasawara Gunto.**

bonito (bə'ni:təʊ) *n., pl.* **-tos.** any of various small tunny-like marine food fishes of warm Atlantic and Pacific waters. [C16: from Sp., from L *bonus* good]

bonk (bɒŋk) *vb. Inf.* **1.** (*tr.*) to hit. **2.** to have sexual intercourse (with). [C20: prob. imit.] —'**bonking** *n.*

bonkers ('bɒŋkəz) *adj. Sl., chiefly Brit.* mad; crazy. [C20: from ?]

bon mot (*French* bɔ̃ mo) *n., pl.* **bons mots** (bɔ̃mo). a clever and fitting remark. [F, lit.: good word]

Bonn (bɒn; *German* bɔn) *n.* the capital of West Germany, in North Rhine-Westphalia on the Rhine: became the capital in 1949; university (1786). Pop.: 290 800 (1986 est.).

Bonnard (*French* bɔnar) *n.* **Pierre** (pjɛr). 1867–1947, French painter and lithographer, noted for the effects of light and colour in his landscapes and sunlit interiors.

bonnet ('bɒnɪt) *n.* **1.** any of various hats worn, esp. formerly, by women and girls, and tied with ribbons under the chin. **2.** (in Scotland) Also: **bunnet. a.** a soft cloth cap. **b.** (formerly) a flat brimless cap worn by men. **3.** the hinged metal part of a motor vehicle body that provides access to the engine. U.S. name: **hood. 4.** a cowl on a chimney. **5.** *Naut.* a piece of sail laced to the foot of a foresail to give it greater area in light winds. **6.** (in the U.S. and Canada) a headdress of feathers worn by some tribes of American Indians. [C14: from OF *bonet,* from ?]

bonny ('bɒnɪ) *adj.* **-nier, -niest. 1.** *Scot. & N English dialect.* beautiful or handsome: *a bonny lass.* **2.** good or fine. **3.** (esp. of babies) plump. [C15: from OF *bon* good, from L *bonus*]

Bonny ('bɒnɪ) *n.* **Bight of.** a wide bay at the E end of the Gulf of Guinea off the coasts of Nigeria and Cameroon. Former name (until 1975): **Bight of Biafra.**

bonsai ('bɒnsaɪ) *n., pl.* **-sai. 1.** the art of growing dwarfed ornamental varieties of trees or shrubs in small shallow pots by selective pruning, etc. **2.** a tree or shrub

grown by this method. [C20: from Japanese, from *bon* bowl + *sai* to plant]

bontebok ('bɒntɪ,bʌk) *n., pl.* **-boks** *or* **-bok.** an antelope of southern Africa, having a deep reddish-brown coat with a white blaze, tail, and rump patch. [C18: Afrik. from *bont* pied + *bok* BUCK[1]]

bonus ('bəʊnəs) *n.* **1.** something given, paid, or received above what is due or expected. **2.** *Chiefly Brit.* an extra dividend allotted to shareholders out of profits. **3.** *Insurance, Brit.* a dividend, esp. a percentage of net profits, distributed to policyholders. [C18: from L *bonus* (adj.) good]

bonus issue *n. Brit.* a free issue of shares distributed among shareholders pro rata with their holdings.

bon vivant *French.* (bɔ̃ vivɑ̃) *n., pl.* **bons vivants** (bɔ̃ vivɑ̃). a person who enjoys luxuries, esp. good food and drink. Also called (but not in French): **bon viveur** (,bɒn vi:'vɜ:). [lit.: good-living (man)]

bon voyage (*French* bɔ̃ vwajaʒ) *sentence substitute.* a phrase used to wish a traveller a pleasant journey. [F, lit.: good journey]

bony ('bəʊnɪ) *adj.* **bonier, boniest. 1.** resembling or consisting of bone. **2.** having many bones. **3.** having prominent bones. **4.** thin or emaciated.

bony fish *n.* any of a class of fishes, including most of the extant species, having a skeleton of bone rather than cartilage.

bonze (bɒnz) *n.* a Chinese or Japanese Buddhist priest or monk. [C16: from F, from Port. *bonzo,* from Chinese *fan sēng,* from *fan* Buddhist + *sēng* MONK]

bonzer ('bɒnzə) *adj. Austral & N.Z. sl.,* *arch.* very good; excellent. [C20: ?from BONANZA]

boo (bu:) *interj.* **1.** an exclamation uttered to startle or surprise someone, esp. a child. **2.** a shout uttered to express disgust, dissatisfaction, or contempt. ~*vb.* **booing, booed. 3.** to shout "boo" at (someone or something), esp. as an expression of disapproval.

boob (bu:b) *Sl.* ~*n.* **1.** an ignorant or foolish person. **2.** *Brit.* an embarrassing mistake; blunder. **3.** a female breast. ~*vb.* **4.** (*intr.*) *Brit.* to make a blunder. [C20: back formation from BOOBY]

boobialla (,bu:bɪ'ælə) *n. Austral.* **1.** another name for **golden wattle** (sense 2). **2.** any of various trees or shrubs of the genus *Myoporum.*

boo-boo *n., pl.* **-boos.** an embarrassing mistake; blunder. [C20: ?from nursery talk]

boob tube *n. Sl.* **1.** a close-fitting strapless top, worn by women. **2.** *Chiefly U.S. & Canad.* a television receiver.

booby ('bu:bɪ) *n., pl.* **-bies. 1.** an ignorant or foolish person. **2.** *Brit.* the losing player in a game. **3.** any of several tropical marine birds related to the gannet. They have a straight stout bill and the plumage is white with darker markings. [C17: from Sp. *bobo,* from L *balbus* stammering]

booby prize *n.* a mock prize given to the person having the lowest score.

booby trap *n.* **1.** a hidden explosive device primed in such a way as to be set off by an unsuspecting victim. **2.** a trap for an unsuspecting person, esp. one intended as a practical joke. ~*vb.* **booby-trap, -trapping, -trapped. 3.** (*tr.*) to set a booby trap in or on (a building or object) or for (a person).

boodle ('bu:dəl) *n. Sl.* money or valuables, esp. when stolen, counterfeit, or used as a bribe. [C19: from Du. *boedel* possessions]

boogie ('bu:gɪ) *vb.* **-gieing, -gied.** (*intr.*) *Sl.* **1.** to dance to pop music. **2.** to make love. [C20: orig. American Negro slang, ?from Bantu *mbugi* devilishly good]

boogie-woogie ('bʊgɪ'wʊgɪ, 'bu:gɪ'wu:gɪ) *n.* a style of piano jazz using a dotted bass pattern, usually with eight notes in a bar and the harmonies of the 12-bar blues. [C20: ? imit.]

boohai (bu:'haɪ) *n. N.Z. inf.* **up the boohai.** thoroughly lost. [from remote township of *Puhoi*]

boohoo (,bu:'hu:) *vb.* **-hooing, -hooed. 1.** to sob or pretend to sob noisily. ~*n., pl.* **-hoos. 2.** (*sometimes pl.*) distressed or pretended sobbing. [C20: nursery talk]

book (bʊk) *n.* **1.** a number of printed or written pages bound together along one edge and usually protected by covers. **2. a.** a written work or composition, such as a novel, technical manual, or dictionary. **b.** (*as modifier*): *book reviews.* **c.** (*in combination*): *bookseller; bookshop; bookshelf.* **3.** a number of blank or ruled sheets of paper bound together, used to record lessons, keep accounts, etc. **4.** (*pl.*) a record of the transactions of a business or society. **5.** the libretto of an opera, musical, etc. **6.** a major division of a written composition, as of a long novel or of the Bible. **7.** a number of tickets, stamps, etc., fastened together along one edge. **8.** a record of betting transactions. **9.** (in card games) the number of tricks that must be taken by a side or player before any trick has a scoring value. **10.** strict or rigid rules or standards (esp. in **by the book**). **11.** a source of knowledge or authority: *the book of life*. **12. a closed book.** a person or subject that is unknown or beyond comprehension: *chemistry is a closed book to him.* **13. an open book.** a person or subject that is thoroughly understood. **14. bring to book.** to reprimand or require (someone) to give an explanation of his conduct. **15. close the books.** *Book-keeping.* to balance accounts in order to prepare a statement or report. **16. in someone's good** (*or* **bad**) **books.** regarded by someone with favour (*or* disfavour). **17. keep the books.** to keep written records of the finances of a business. **18. on the books. a.** enrolled as a member. **b.** recorded. **19. the book.** (*sometimes cap.*) the Bible. **20. throw the book at. a.** to charge with every relevant offence. **b.** to inflict the most severe punishment on. ~*vb.* **21.** to reserve (a place, passage, etc.) or engage the services of (a performer, driver, etc.) in advance. **22.** (*tr.*) to take the name and address of (a person guilty of a minor offence) with a view to bringing a prosecution. **23.** (*tr.*) (of a football referee) to take the name of (a player) who grossly infringes the rules. **24.** (*tr.*) *Arch.* to record in a book. ~See also **book in.** [OE *bōc*; see BEECH (its bark was used as a writing surface)]

bookbinder ('bʊk,baɪndə) *n.* a person whose business is binding books. —'**book,binding** *n.*

bookbindery ('bʊk,baɪndərɪ) *n., pl.* -eries. a place in which books are bound. Often shortened to **bindery.**

bookcase ('bʊk,keɪs) *n.* a piece of furniture containing shelves for books.

book club *n.* a club that sells books at low prices to members, usually by mail order.

book end *n.* one of a pair of usually ornamental supports for holding a row of books upright.

Booker Prize ('bʊkə) *n.* An annual prize for a work of British fiction of £15,000, awarded since 1969 by the Booker McConnell engineering company.

bookie ('bʊkɪ) *n. Inf.* short for **bookmaker.**

book in *vb.* (*adv.*) **1.** to reserve a room at a hotel. **2.** *Chiefly Brit.* to register, esp. one's arrival at a hotel.

booking ('bʊkɪŋ) *n.* **1.** *Chiefly Brit.* a reservation, as of a table, room, or seat. **2.** *Theatre.* an engagement of an actor or company.

bookish ('bʊkɪʃ) *adj.* **1.** fond of reading; studious. **2.** consisting of or forming opinions through reading rather than experience; academic. **3.** of or relating to books. —'**bookishness** *n.*

book-keeping *n.* the skill or occupation of systematically recording business transactions. —'**book-,keeper** *n.*

book-learning *n.* knowledge gained from books rather than from experience.

booklet ('bʊklɪt) *n.* a thin book, esp. one having paper covers; pamphlet.

bookmaker ('bʊk,meɪkə) *n.* a person who as an occupation accepts bets, esp. on horseraces, and pays out to winning betters. —'**book,making** *n.*

bookmark ('bʊk,mɑːk) *or* **bookmarker** *n.* a strip of some material put between the pages of a book to mark a place.

Book of Common Prayer *n.* the official book of church services of the Church of England until 1980, when the Alternative Service Book was sanctioned.

bookplate ('bʊk,pleɪt) *n.* a label bearing the owner's name and a design, pasted into a book.

bookstall ('bʊk,stɔːl) *n.* a stall or stand where periodicals, newspapers, or books are sold.

book token *n. Brit.* a gift token to be exchanged for books.

book value *n.* **1.** the value of an asset of a business according to its books. **2.** the net capital value of an enterprise as shown by the excess of book assets over book liabilities.

bookworm ('bʊk,wɜːm) *n.* **1.** any of various small insects that feed on the binding paste of books. **2.** a person devoted to reading.

Boole (buːl) *n.* **George.** 1815–64, English mathematician. In *Mathematical Analysis of Logic* (1847) and *An Investigation of the Laws of Thought* (1854), he applied mathematical formulae to logic, creating Boolean algebra.

boom[1] (buːm) *vb.* **1.** to make a deep prolonged resonant sound. **2.** to prosper or cause to prosper vigorously and rapidly: *business boomed.* ~*n.* **3.** a deep prolonged resonant sound. **4.** a period of high economic growth. [C15: ?from Du. *bommen*, imit.]

boom[2] (buːm) *n.* **1.** *Naut.* a spar to which a sail is fastened to control its position relative to the wind. **2.** a pole carrying an overhead microphone and projected over a film or television set. **3.** a barrier across a waterway, usually consisting of a chain of logs, to confine free-floating logs, protect a harbour from attack, etc. [C16: from Du. *boom* tree, BEAM]

boomer ('buːmə) *n.* **1.** *Austral.* a large male kangaroo. **2.** *Austral. & N.Z. inf.* anything exceptionally large.

boomerang ('buːmə,ræŋ) *n.* **1.** a curved flat wooden missile of Australian Aborigines, which can be made to return to the thrower. **2.** an action or statement that recoils on its originator. ~*vb.* **3.** (*intr.*) to recoil or return unexpectedly, causing harm to its originator. [C19: from Abor.]

boomslang ('buːm,slæŋ) *n.* a large greenish venomous arboreal snake of southern Africa. [C18: from Afrik., from *boom* tree + *slang* snake]

boon[1] (buːn) *n.* **1.** something extremely useful, helpful, or beneficial; a blessing or benefit. **2.** *Arch.* a favour; request. [C12: from ON *bón* request]

boon[2] (buːn) *adj.* **1.** close, special, or intimate (in **boon companion**). **2.** *Arch.* jolly or convivial. [C14: from OF *bon*, from L *bonus* good]

boondocks ('buːn,dɒks) *pl. n.* **the.** *U.S. & Canad. sl.* **1.** wild, desolate, or uninhabitable country. **2.** a remote rural or provincial area. [C20: from Tagalog *bundok* mountain]

Boone (buːn) *n.* **Daniel.** 1734–1820, American pioneer, explorer, and guide, esp. in Kentucky.

boong (buːŋ) *n. Austral. offens.* a Black person. [C20: from Abor.]

boor (buə) *n.* an ill-mannered, clumsy, or insensitive person. [OE *gebūr* dweller, farmer; see NEIGHBOUR] —'**boorish** *adj.* —'**boorishly** *adv.* —'**boorishness** *n.*

boost (buːst) *n.* **1.** encouragement, improvement, or help: *a boost to morale.* **2.** an upward thrust or push. **3.** an increase or rise. **4.** the amount by which the induction pressure of a supercharged internal-combustion engine is increased. ~*vb.* (*tr.*) **5.** to encourage, assist, or improve: *to boost morale.* **6.** to lift by giving a push from below or behind. **7.** to increase or raise: *to boost the voltage in an electrical circuit.* **8.** to cause to rise; increase: *to boost sales.* **9.** to advertise on a big scale. **10.** to increase the induction pressure of (an internal-combustion engine); supercharge. [C19: from ?]

▷**Usage.** Except in the terminology of rocketry, the word *boost* is regarded as slightly informal, esp. in a figurative sense: *a boost to the economy.*

booster ('buːstə) *n.* **1.** a person or thing that supports, assists, or increases power. **2.** Also called: **launching vehicle.** the first stage of a multistage rocket. **3.** a radio-frequency amplifier to strengthen signals. **4.** another name for **supercharger.** **5.** short for **booster shot.**

booster shot *n. Inf.* a supplementary injection of a vaccine given to maintain the immunization provided by an earlier dose.

boot[1] (buːt) *n.* **1.** a strong outer covering for the foot; shoe that extends above the ankle, often to the knee. **2.** *Brit.* an enclosed compartment of a car for holding luggage, etc., usually at the rear. U.S. and Canad. name: **trunk.** **3.** an instrument of torture used to crush the foot and lower leg. **4.** *Inf.* a kick: *he gave the door a boot.* **5. boots and all.** *Austral. & N.Z.* making every effort. **6. die with one's boots on.** to die while still active. **7. lick the boots of.** to be servile towards. **8. put the boot in.** *Sl.* **a.** to kick a person, esp. when he is already down. **b.** to harass someone. **c.** to finish off (something) with unnecessary brutality. **9. the boot.** *Sl.* dismissal from employment; the sack. **10. the boot is on the other foot** *or* **leg.** the situation is or has now reversed. ~*vb.* **11.** to kick. **12.** to equip with boots. **13.** *Inf.* **a.** (often foll. by *out*) to eject forcibly. **b.** to dismiss from employment.

14. to bootstrap (a computer system). [C14 *bote*, from OF, from ?]

boot² (buːt) *vb.* (*usually impersonal*) **1.** *Arch.* to be of advantage or use to (a person): *what boots it to complain?* ~*n.* **2.** *Obs.* an advantage. **3. to boot.** as well; in addition. [OE *bōt* compensation]

bootblack ('buːt,blæk) *n.* (esp. formerly) a person who shines boots and shoes.

bootee ('buːtiː, buːˈtiː) *n.* **1.** a soft shoe for a baby, esp. a knitted one. **2.** a boot for women and children, esp. an ankle-length one.

Boötes (bəʊˈəʊtiːz) *n.*, *Latin genitive* **Boötis** (bəʊˈəʊtɪs). a constellation in the N hemisphere containing the star Arcturus. [C17: via L from Gk: ploughman]

booth (buːð, buːθ) *n.*, *pl.* **booths** (buːðz). **1.** a stall, esp. a temporary one at a fair or market. **2.** a small partially enclosed cubicle, such as one for telephoning (**telephone booth**) or for voting (**polling booth**). **3.** *Chiefly U.S. & Canad.* two high-backed benches with a table between, used esp. in bars and restaurants. **4.** (formerly) a temporary structure for shelter, dwelling, storage, etc. [C12: of Scand. origin]

Booth (buːð) *n.* **1. Edwin Thomas,** son of Junius Brutus Booth. 1833–93, U.S. actor. **2. John Wilkes,** son of Junius Brutus Booth. 1838–65, U.S. actor; assassin of Abraham Lincoln. **3. Junius Brutus** ('dʒuːnɪəs 'bruːtəs). 1796–1852, U.S. actor, born in England. **4. William.** 1829–1912, English religious leader; founder and first general of the Salvation Army (1878).

Boothia Peninsula ('buːθɪə) *n.* a peninsula of N Canada: the northernmost part of the mainland of North America, lying west of the **Gulf of Boothia,** an arm of the Arctic Ocean.

bootjack ('buːt,dʒæk) *n.* a device that grips the heel of a boot to enable the foot to be withdrawn easily.

Bootle ('buːtᵊl) *n.* a port in NW England, in Merseyside, on the River Mersey adjoining Liverpool. Pop.: 62 463 (1981).

bootleg ('buːt,lɛg) *vb.* **-legging, -legged.** **1.** to make, carry, or sell (illicit goods, esp. alcohol). ~*n.* **2.** something made or sold illicitly, such as alcohol. ~*adj.* **3.** produced, distributed, or sold illicitly. [C17: see BOOT¹, LEG; from smugglers carrying bottles of liquor concealed in their boots] —'**boot,legger** *n.*

bootless ('buːtlɪs) *adj.* of little or no use; vain; fruitless. [OE *bōtlēas*, from *bōt* compensation]

bootlicker ('buːt,lɪkə) *n.* *Inf.* one who seeks favour by servile or ingratiating behaviour towards (someone, esp. in authority); toady.

boot sale *n.* a sale of goods from car boots in a car park hired for the occasion. Also called: **car-boot sale.**

bootstrap ('buːt,stræp) *n.* **1.** a loop on a boot for pulling it on. **2. by one's (own) bootstraps.** by one's own efforts; unaided. **3. a.** a technique for loading the first few program instructions into a computer main store to enable the rest of the program to be introduced from an input device. **b.** (*as modifier*): *a bootstrap loader.* ~*vb.* (*tr.*) **4.** to initiate (a computer system) by executing a bootstrap; boot.

booty ('buːtɪ) *n.*, *pl.* **-ties.** any valuable article or articles, esp. when obtained as plunder. [C15: from OF, from MLow G *buite* exchange]

booze (buːz) *Inf.* ~*n.* **1.** alcoholic drink. **2.** a drinking bout. ~*vb.* **3.** (*usually intr.*) to drink (alcohol), esp. in excess. [C13: from MDu. *būsen*]

boozer ('buːzə) *n.* *Inf.* **1.** a person who is fond of drinking. **2.** *Brit., Austral., & N.Z.* a bar or pub.

booze-up *n. Brit., Austral., & N.Z. sl.* a drinking spree.

boozy ('buːzɪ) *adj.* **boozier, booziest.** *Inf.* inclined to or involving excessive drinking of alcohol; drunken: *a boozy lecturer; a boozy party.*

bop (bɒp) *n.* **1.** a form of jazz originating in the 1940s, characterized by rhythmic and harmonic complexity and instrumental virtuosity. Originally called: **bebop.** ~*vb.* **bopping, bopped.** **2.** (*intr.*) *Inf.* to dance to pop music. [C20: shortened from BEBOP] —'**bopper** *n.*

bo-peep (,bəʊ'piːp) *n.* a game for very young children, in which one hides (esp. hiding one's face in one's hands) and reappears suddenly.

Bophuthatswana (,bɒʊpʊtɑːt'swɑːnə) *n.* a Bantustan in N South Africa: consists of six separate areas, the smallest (in the Orange Free State) being about 201 km (125 miles) from the nearest other area in the Bantustan; became an

autonomous state in 1977. Capital: Mmabatho. Pop.: 1 420 000 (1984 est.). Area: 40 330 sq. km (15 571 sq. miles).

bora¹ ('bɔːrə) *n.* (*sometimes cap.*) a violent cold north wind blowing from the Adriatic. [C19: from It. dialect., from L *boréas* the north wind]

bora² ('bɔːrə) *n.* an initiation ceremony of Australian Aborigines, introducing youths to manhood. [from Abor.]

Bora Bora ('bɔːrə 'bɔːrə) *n.* an island in the S Pacific, in the Society Islands: one of the Leeward Islands. Area: 39 sq. km (15 sq. miles).

boracic (bə'ræsɪk) *adj.* another word for **boric.**

borage ('bɒrɪdʒ, 'bʌrɪdʒ) *n.* a Mediterranean plant with star-shaped blue flowers. The young leaves are sometimes used in salads. [C13: from OF, ?from Ar. *abū 'āraq*, lit.: father of sweat]

Borås (*Swedish* bu'roːs) *n.* a city in SW Sweden, chiefly producing textiles. Pop.: 100 054 (1986).

borate *n.* ('bɔːreɪt, -ɪt). **1.** a salt or ester of boric acid. ~*vb.* ('bɔːreɪt). **2.** (*tr.*) to treat with borax, boric acid, or borate.

borax ('bɔːræks) *n.*, *pl.* **-raxes** *or* **-races** (-rə,siːz). a soluble readily fusible white mineral in monoclinic crystalline form, occurring in alkaline soils and salt deposits. Formula: $Na_2B_4O_7.10H_2O$. [C14: from OF, from Med. L, from Ar., from Persian *būrah*]

borazon ('bɔːrə,zɒn) *n.* an extremely hard form of boron nitride. [C20: from BOR(ON) + AZO + -ON]

borborygmus (,bɔːbə'rɪgməs) *n.*, *pl.* **-mi** (-maɪ). rumbling of the stomach. [C18: from Gk]

Bordeaux (bɔː'dəʊ; *French* bɔrdo) *n.* **1.** a port in SW France, on the River Garonne: a major centre of the wine trade. Pop.: 221 334 (1983 est.). **2.** any of several red, white, or rosé wines produced around Bordeaux.

Bordeaux mixture *n. Horticulture.* a fungicide consisting of a solution of equal quantities of copper sulphate and quicklime.

border ('bɔːdə) *n.* **1.** a band or margin around or along the edge of something. **2.** the dividing line or frontier between political or geographic regions. **3.** a region straddling such a boundary. **4.** a design around the edge of something. **5.** a long narrow strip of ground planted with flowers, shrubs, etc.: *a herbaceous border.* ~*vb.* **6.** (*tr.*) to provide with a border. **7.** (when *intr.*, foll. by *on* or *upon*) **a.** to be adjacent (to); lie along the boundary (of). **b.** to be nearly the same (as); verge (on): *his stupidity borders on madness.* [C14: from OF, from *bort* side of a ship, of Gmc origin]

Border ('bɔːdə) *n.* **the.** (*often pl.*) the area straddling the border between England and Scotland.

borderer ('bɔːdərə) *n.* a person who lives in a border area.

borderland ('bɔːdə,lænd) *n.* **1.** land located on or near a frontier or boundary. **2.** an indeterminate state or condition.

borderline ('bɔːdə,laɪn) *n.* **1.** a border; dividing line. **2.** an indeterminate position between two conditions: *the borderline between friendship and love.* ~*adj.* **3.** on the edge of one category and verging on another: *a borderline failure in the exam.*

Borders Region *n.* a local government region in S Scotland, formed in 1975 from Berwick, Peebles, Roxburgh, Selkirk, and part of Midlothian: generally hilly with the Merse (fertile lowlands) in the southeast. Administrative centre: Newtown St Boswells. Pop.: 101 800 (1986 est.). Area: 4700 sq. km (1800 sq. miles).

bore¹ (bɔː) *vb.* **1.** to produce (a hole) in (a material) by use of a drill, auger, or rotary cutting tool. **2.** to increase the diameter of (a hole), as by turning. **3.** (*tr.*) to produce (a hole in the ground, tunnel, mine shaft, etc.) by digging, drilling, etc. **4.** (*intr.*) *Inf.* (of a horse or athlete in a race) to push other competitors out of the way. ~*n.* **5.** a hole or tunnel in the ground, esp. one drilled in search of minerals, oil, etc. **6.** *Austral.* an artesian well. **7. a.** the hollow part of a tube or cylinder, esp. of a gun barrel. **b.** the diameter of such a hollow part; calibre. [OE *borian*]

bore² (bɔː) *vb.* **1.** (*tr.*) to tire or make weary by being dull, repetitious, or uninteresting. ~*n.* **2.** a dull or repetitious person, activity, or state. [C18: from ?] —**bored** *adj.* —'**boring** *adj.*

bore³ (bɔː) *n.* a high steep-fronted wave moving up a narrow estuary, caused by the tide. [C17: from ON *bára* wave, billow]

bore[4] (bɔː) *vb.* the past tense of **bear**[1].

boreal ('bɔːrɪəl) *adj.* of or relating to the north or the north wind. [C15: from L *boreās* the north wind]

Boreal ('bɔːrɪəl) *adj.* of or denoting the coniferous forests in the north of the N hemisphere.

Boreas ('bɔːrɪəs) *n. Greek myth.* the god personifying the north wind. [C14: via L from Gk]

boredom ('bɔːdəm) *n.* the state of being bored.

boree ('bɔːriː) *n. Austral.* another name for **myall**. [from Abor.]

borer ('bɔːrə) *n.* **1.** a tool for boring holes. **2.** any of various insects, insect larvae, molluscs, or crustaceans, that bore into plant material, esp. wood.

Borg (bɔːg; *Swedish* bɔrj) *n.* **Björn** (bjœrn). born 1956, Swedish tennis player: Wimbledon champion 1976–80.

Borgerhout (*Flemish* bɔrxər'hɔut) *n.* a city in N Belgium, near Antwerp. Pop.: 43 556 (1982 est.).

Borges (*Spanish* 'bɔrxes) *n.* **Jorge Luis** ('xɔrxe lwis). 1899–1986, Argentinian poet, short-story writer, and literary scholar. The short stories collected in *Ficciones* (1944) he described as "games with infinity".

Borghese (*Italian* bor'geze) *n.* a noble Italian family whose members were influential in Italian art and politics from the 16th to the 19th century.

Borgia (*Italian* 'bordʒa) *n.* **1. Cesare** ('tʃezare), son of Rodrigo Borgia (Pope Alexander VI). 1475–1507, Italian cardinal, politician, and military leader; model for Machiavelli's *The Prince*. **2.** his sister, **Lucrezia** (lu'krɛttsja), daughter of Rodrigo Borgia. 1480–1519, Italian noblewoman. Her first marriage (1493) was annulled; her second husband was murdered (1500); she was also said to have committed incest with her father and brother. Her third marriage (1501), to the Duke of Ferrara, was more normal, and she became a patron of the arts and science. **3. Rodrigo** (rod'rigo). See **Alexander VI.**

Borglum ('bɔːgləm) *n.* **Gutzon** ('gʌtsən). 1867–1941, U.S. sculptor, noted for his monumental busts of U.S. presidents carved in the mountainside of Mount Rushmore.

boric ('bɔːrɪk) *adj.* of or containing boron. Also: **boracic.**

boric acid *n.* a white soluble weakly acid crystalline solid used in the manufacture of heat-resistant glass and porcelain enamels, as a fireproofing material, and as a mild antiseptic. Formula: H_3BO_3. Also called: **orthoboric acid.**

born (bɔːn) *vb.* **1.** the past participle (in most passive uses) of **bear**[1] (sense 4). **2. not born yesterday.** not gullible or foolish. ~*adj.* **3.** possessing certain qualities from birth: *a born musician.* **4. a.** being at birth in a particular social status or other condition as specified: *ignobly born.* **b.** (*in combination*): *lowborn.* **5. in all one's born days.** *Inf.* so far in one's life.

Born (bɔːn) *n.* **Max.** 1882–1970, British nuclear physicist, born in Germany, noted for his fundamental contribution to quantum mechanics: Nobel prize for physics 1954.

born-again ('bɔːnə,gɛn) *adj.* **1.** having experienced conversion, esp. to evangelical Christianity. **2.** showing the enthusiasm of one newly converted to any cause: *a born-again monetarist.*

borne (bɔːn) *vb.* **1.** the past participle of **bear**[1](for all active uses of the verb; also for all passive uses except sense 4 unless foll. by *by*). **2. be borne in on** *or* **upon.** (of a fact, etc.) to be realized by (someone).

Borneo ('bɔːnɪ,əʊ) *n.* an island in the W Pacific, between the Sulu and Java Seas, part of the Malay Archipelago: divided into Kalimantan (**Indonesian Borneo**), the Malaysian states of Sarawak and Sabah, and the British-protected sultanate of Brunei; mountainous and densely forested. Area: about 750 000 sq. km (290 000 sq. miles). — **Bornean** *adj., n.*

Bornholm (*Danish* bɔrn'hɔlm) *n.* an island in the Baltic Sea, south of Sweden: administratively part of Denmark. Chief town: Rønne. Pop.: 46 839 (1987). Area: 588 sq. km (227 sq. miles).

Borno ('bɔːnəʊ) *n.* a state of NE Nigeria, on Lake Chad: the second largest state, formed in 1976 from part of North-Eastern State. Capital: Maiduguri. Pop.: 5 025 000 (1984). Area: 116 589 sq. km (45 006 sq. miles).

Borodin ('bɒrədɪn; *Russian* bərʌ'din) *n.* **Aleksandr Porfirevich** (alɪk'sandr pərfi'rjevitʃ). 1834–87, Russian composer, whose works include the unfinished opera *Prince Igor*, symphonies, songs, and chamber music.

Borodino (,bɒrə'diːnəʊ; *Russian* bərədi'nɔ) *n.* a village in the W Soviet Union, about 110 km (70 miles) west of Moscow: scene of a battle (1812) in which Napoleon defeated the Russians but irreparably weakened his army.

boron ('bɔːrɒn) *n.* a very hard almost colourless crystalline metalloid element that in impure form exists as a brown amorphous powder. It occurs principally in borax and is used in hardening steel. Symbol: B; atomic no.: 5; atomic wt.: 10.81. [C19: from BOR(AX) + (CARB)ON]

boron carbide *n.* a black extremely hard inert substance used as an abrasive and in control rods in nuclear reactors. Formula: B_4C.

boronia (bə'rəʊnɪə) *n.* any aromatic shrub of the Australian genus *Boronia*.

boron nitride *n.* a white inert crystalline solid, used as a refractory, high-temperature lubricant and insulator, and heat shield.

Borotra (bɔrɔtra) *n.* **Jean** (**Robert**) (ʒã). born 1898, French tennis player: secretary general of physical education under the Vichy government (1940).

borough ('bʌrə) *n.* **1.** a town, esp. (in Britain) one that forms the constituency of an MP or that was originally incorporated by royal charter. See also **burgh. 2.** any of the 32 constituent divisions of Greater London. **3.** any of the five constituent divisions of New York City. **4.** (in the U.S.) a self-governing incorporated municipality. [OE *burg*]

borrow ('bɒrəʊ) *vb.* **1.** to obtain or receive (something, such as money) on loan for temporary use, intending to give it, or something equivalent, back to the lender. **2.** to adopt (ideas, words, etc.) from another source; appropriate. **3.** *Not standard.* to lend. **4.** (*intr.*) *Golf.* to putt the ball uphill of the direct path to the hole: *make sure you borrow enough.* [OE *borgian*] — **'borrower** *n.*

▷ **Usage.** See at **lend.**

Borrow ('bɒrəʊ) *n.* **George.** 1803–81, English traveller and writer. His best-known works are the semiautobiographical novels of Gypsy life and language, *Lavengro* (1851) and its sequel *The Romany Rye* (1857).

Bors (bɔːs) *n.* **Sir.** (in Arthurian legend) **1.** one the knights of the Round Table, nephew of Lancelot. **2.** an illegitimate son of King Arthur.

borsch, borsh (bɔːʃ), **borscht** (bɔːʃt), *or* **borshch** (bɔːʃtʃ) *n.* a Russian and Polish soup based on beetroot. [from Russian *borshch*]

borstal ('bɔːstəl) *n.* (in Britain) an informal name for an establishment in which offenders aged 15 to 21 may be detained for corrective training. Official name: **youth custody centre.** [C20: after *Borstal*, village in Kent where the first institution was founded]

bort, boart (bɔːt), *or* **bortz** (bɔːts) *n.* an inferior grade of diamond used for cutting and drilling or, in powdered form, as an industrial abrasive. [OE *gebrot* fragment]

borzoi ('bɔːzɔɪ) *n.,* *pl.* **-zois.** a tall fast-moving breed of dog with a long coat. Also called: **Russian wolfhound.** [C19: Russian, lit.: swift]

boscage *or* **boskage** ('bɒskɪdʒ) *n. Literary.* a mass of trees and shrubs; thicket. [C14: from OF *bosc*, prob. of Gmc origin; see BUSH[1], -AGE]

Bosch (bɒʃ) *n.* **Hieronymus** (hɪ'rɒnɪməs), original name probably *Jerome van Aken* (or *Aeken*). ?1450–1516, Dutch painter, noted for his macabre allegorical representations of biblical subjects in brilliant transparent colours, esp. the triptych *The Garden of Earthly Delights.*

Bose (bəʊs) *n.* **1.** Sir **Jagadis Chandra** (dʒəgə'diːs 'tʃʌndrə). 1858–1937, Indian physicist and plant physiologist. **2. Satyendra Nath** (sə'tjɛndrə 'nɑːθ). 1894–1974, Indian physicist, who collaborated with Einstein in devising Bose-Einstein statistics. **3. Subhas Chandra** (sub'haːʃ 'tʃʌndrə), known as *Netaji*. 1897–1945, Indian nationalist leader; president of the Indian National Congress (1938–39); organized the Indian National Army, with Japanese support, in Singapore to free India from British Rule.

bosh (bɒʃ) *n. Inf.* empty or meaningless talk or opinions; nonsense. [C19: from Turkish *boş* empty]

bosk (bɒsk) *n. Literary.* a small wood of bushes and small trees. [C13: var. of *busk* BUSH[1]]

bosky ('bɒskɪ) *adj.* **boskier, boskiest.** *Literary.* containing or consisting of bushes or thickets.

bo's'n ('bəʊsⁿn) *n. Naut.* a variant spelling of **boatswain.**

Bosnia ('bɒznɪə) *n.* a region of central Yugoslavia: belonged to Turkey (1463–1878), then to Austria-Hungary

(1879–1918); now part of Bosnia and Herzegovina. —'**Bosnian** adj.

Bosnia and Herzegovina or **Hercegovina** n. a constituent republic of Yugoslavia, in the W central part: mostly barren and mountainous, with forests in the east. Capital: Sarajevo. Pop.: 4 310 000 (1985). Area: 51 129 sq. km (19 737 sq. miles).

bosom ('buzəm) n. **1.** the chest or breast of a person, esp. the female breasts. **2.** the part of a woman's dress, coat, etc., that covers the chest. **3.** a protective centre or part: *the bosom of the family*. **4.** the breast considered as the seat of emotions. **5.** (*modifier*) very dear; intimate: *a bosom friend*. ~*vb.* (*tr.*) **6.** to embrace. **7.** to conceal or carry in the bosom. [OE *bōsm*]

bosomy ('buzəmɪ) adj. (of a woman) having large breasts.

boson ('bəʊzɒn) n. any of a group of elementary particles, such as a photon or pion, that has zero or integral spin and does not obey the Pauli exclusion principle. Cf. **fermion**. [C20: after S. N. BOSE (1894-1974), Indian physicist]

Bosporus ('bɒspərəs) or **Bosphorus** ('bɒsfərəs) n. **the.** a strait between European and Asian Turkey, linking the Black Sea and the Sea of Marmara.

boss[1] (bɒs) *Inf.* ~*n.* **1.** a person in charge of or employing others. **2.** *Chiefly U.S.* a professional politician who controls a political organization, often using devious or illegal methods. ~*vb.* (*tr.*) **3.** to employ, supervise, or be in charge of. **4.** (usually foll. by *around* or *about*) to be domineering or overbearing towards (others). ~*adj.* **5.** *Sl.* excellent; fine: *a boss hand at carpentry; that's boss!* [C19: from Du. *baas* master]

boss[2] (bɒs) n. **1.** a knob, stud, or other circular rounded protuberance, esp. an ornamental one on a vault, a ceiling, or a shield. **2.** an area of increased thickness, usually cylindrical, that strengthens or provides room for a locating device on a shaft, hub of a wheel, etc. **3.** a rounded mass of igneous rock. ~*vb.* (*tr.*) **4.** to ornament with bosses; emboss. [C13: from OF *boce*; rel. to It. *bozza* metal knob, swelling]

bossa nova ('bɒsə 'nəʊvə) n. **1.** a dance similar to the samba, originating in Brazil. **2.** a piece of music composed for or in the rhythm of this dance. [C20: from Port., lit.: new voice]

Bossuet (*French* bɔsɥɛ) n. **Jacques Bénigne** (ʒɑk beniɲ). 1627–1704, French bishop: noted for his funeral orations.

bossy ('bɒsɪ) adj. **bossier, bossiest.** *Inf.* domineering, overbearing, or authoritarian. —'**bossily** adv. —'**bossiness** n.

Boston ('bɒstən) n. **1.** a port in E Massachusetts, the state capital. Pop.: 573 600 (1986). **2.** a port in E England, in SE Lincolnshire. Pop.: 27 000 (1985 est.).

bosun ('bəʊsᵊn) n. *Naut.* a variant spelling of **boatswain**.

Boswell ('bɒzwəl) n. **James.** 1740–95, Scottish author and lawyer, noted particularly for his *Life of Samuel Johnson* (1791). —**Boswellian** (bɒz'welɪən) adj.

Bosworth Field ('bɒzwɜːθ, -wəθ) n. *English history.* the site, two miles south of Market Bosworth in Leicestershire, of the battle that ended the Wars of the Roses (August, 1485). Richard III was killed and Henry Tudor was crowned king as Henry VII.

bot[1] or **bott** (bɒt) n. **1.** the larva of a botfly, which typically develops inside the body of a horse, sheep, or man. **2.** any similar larva. [C15: prob. from Low G; rel. to Du. *bot*, from ?]

bot[2] (bɒt) *Austral. inf.* ~*vb.* **botting, botted. 1.** to scrounge or borrow. ~*n.* **2.** a scrounger. **3. on the bot (for).** wanting to scrounge. [C20: ?from BOTFLY, alluding to its bite; see BITE (sense 9)]

bot. *abbrev. for:* **1.** botanical. **2.** botany. **3.** bottle.

botanical (bə'tænɪkᵊl) or **botanic** adj. **1.** of or relating to botany or plants. ~*n.* **2.** any drug that is made from parts of a plant. [C17: from Med. L, from Gk *botanē* plant, pasture] —**bo'tanically** adv.

botanize or **-ise** ('bɒtəˌnaɪz) vb. **1.** (*intr.*) to collect or study plants. **2.** (*tr.*) to explore and study the plants in (an area or region).

botany ('bɒtənɪ) n., pl. **-nies. 1.** the study of plants, including their classification, structure, physiology, ecology, and economic importance. **2.** the plant life of a particular region or time. **3.** the biological characteristics of a particular group of plants. [C17: from BOTANICAL; cf. ASTRONOMY, ASTRONOMICAL] —'**botanist** n.

Botany Bay n. **1.** an inlet of the Tasman Sea, on the SE coast of Australia: surrounded by the suburbs of Sydney. **2.** (in the 19th century) a British penal settlement that was in fact at Port Jackson, New South Wales.

Botany wool n. a fine wool from the merino sheep. [C19: from BOTANY BAY, where the wool came from originally]

botch (bɒtʃ) vb. (*tr.*; often foll. by *up*) **1.** to spoil through clumsiness or ineptitude. **2.** to repair badly or clumsily. ~*n.* **3.** a badly done piece of work or repair (esp. in **make a botch of**). [C14: from ?] —'**botcher** n. —'**botchy** adj.

botfly ('bɒt,flaɪ) n., pl. **-flies.** any of various stout-bodied hairy dipterous flies, the larvae of which are parasites of man, sheep, and horses.

both (bəʊθ) determiner. **1. a.** the two; two considered together: *both dogs were dirty.* **b.** (*as pron.*): *both are to blame.* ~*conj.* **2.** (*coordinating*) used preceding words, phrases, or clauses joined by *and*: *both Ellen and Keith enjoyed the play; both new and exciting.* [C12: from ON *bāthir*]

Botha ('bəʊtə) n. **1. Louis.** 1862–1919, South African statesman and general; first prime minister of the Union of South Africa (1910–19). **2. P(ieter) W(illem)** born 1916, South African politician; defence minister (1965); prime minister (1978); state president from 1984.

Botham ('bəʊθəm) n. **Ian (Terence).** born 1955, English cricketer: played for Somerset (1973–86); captained England (1980–81); joined Worcestershire 1987.

bother ('bɒðə) vb. **1.** (*tr.*) to give annoyance, pain, or trouble to. **2.** (*tr.*) to trouble (a person) by repeatedly disturbing; pester. **3.** (*intr.*) to take the time or trouble; concern oneself: *don't bother to come with me.* **4.** (*tr.*) to make (a person) alarmed or confused. ~*n.* **5.** a state of worry, trouble, or confusion. **6.** a person or thing that causes fuss, trouble, or annoyance. **7.** *Inf.* a disturbance or fight; trouble (esp. in **a spot of bother**). ~*interj.* **8.** *Chiefly Brit.* an exclamation of slight annoyance. [C18: ?from Irish Gaelic *bodhar* deaf, vexed]

botheration (,bɒðə'reɪʃən) n., interj. *Inf.* another word for **bother** (senses 5, 8).

bothersome ('bɒðəsəm) adj. causing bother; troublesome.

Bothnia ('bɒθnɪə) n. **Gulf of.** an arm of the Baltic Sea, extending north between Sweden and Finland.

Bothwell ('bɒθwəl, 'bɒð-) n. **Earl of,** title of *James Hepburn.* 1535–78, Scottish nobleman; third husband of Mary Queen of Scots. He is generally considered to have instigated the murder of Darnley (1567).

bothy ('bɒθɪ) n., pl. **bothies.** *Chiefly Scot.* **1.** a cottage or hut. **2.** a farmworker's summer quarters. [C18: ? rel. to BOOTH]

bo tree (bəʊ) n. another name for the **peepul.** [C19: from Sinhalese, from Pali *bodhitaru* tree of wisdom]

Botswana (bu'tʃwɑːnə; bʊt'swɑːnə, bɒt-) n. a republic in southern Africa: established as the British protectorate of Bechuanaland in 1885 as a defence against the Boers; became an independent state within the Commonwealth in 1966; consists mostly of a plateau averaging 1000 m (3300 ft.), with the extensive Okavango swamps in the northwest and the Kalahari Desert in the southwest. Languages: English and Tswana. Religion: mostly animist. Currency: pula. Capital: Gaborone. Pop.: 1 131 700 (1986 est.). Area: about 570 000 sq. km (220 000 sq. miles).

bott (bɒt) n. a variant spelling of **bot**[1].

Botticelli (*Italian* botti'tʃɛlli) n. **Sandro** ('sandro). 1444–1510, Italian (Florentine) painter, illustrator, and engraver, noted for the graceful outlines and delicate details of his mythological and religious paintings.

bottle ('bɒtᵊl) n. **1. a.** a vessel, often of glass and typically cylindrical with a narrow neck, for containing liquids. **b.** (*as modifier*): *a bottle rack.* **2.** Also called: **bottleful.** the amount such a vessel will hold. **3.** *Brit. sl.* courage; nerve; initiative. **4. the bottle.** *Inf.* drinking of alcohol, esp. to excess. ~*vb.* (*tr.*) **5.** to put or place in a bottle or bottles. **6.** to store (gas) in a portable container under pressure. ~See also **bottle up.** [C14: from OF *botaille*, from Med. L *butticula*, from LL *buttis* cask]

bottle bank n. a large container into which the public may throw glass bottles for recycling.

bottlebrush ('bɒtᵊl‚brʌʃ) n. **1.** any of various Australian shrubs or trees having dense spikes of large red flowers with protruding brushlike stamens. **2.** a cylindrical brush on a thin shaft, used for cleaning bottles.

bottled (*or* **bottle**) **gas** n. butane or propane liquefied under pressure in portable metal containers for use in camping stoves, blowlamps, etc.

bottle-feed vb. **-feeding, -fed.** to feed (a baby) with milk from a bottle.

bottle green n., adj. (of) a dark green colour.

bottle-jack n. N.Z. a large jack used for heavy lifts.

bottleneck ('bɒtᵊl‚nɛk) n. **1. a.** a narrow stretch of road or a junction at which traffic is or may be held up. **b.** the hold-up. **2.** something that holds up progress.

bottlenose dolphin ('bɒtᵊl‚nəʊz) n. a type of dolphin with a bottle-shaped snout.

bottle party n. a party to which guests bring drink.

bottler ('bɒtᵊlə) n. Austral. & N.Z. inf. an exceptional or outstanding person or thing.

bottle shop n. Austral. a shop where alcohol is sold in unopened containers for consumption elsewhere.

bottle store n. S. African & N.Z. an off-licence.

bottle tree n. any of several Australian trees that have a bottle-shaped swollen trunk.

bottle up vb. (tr., adv.) **1.** to restrain (powerful emotion). **2.** to keep (an army or other force) contained or trapped.

bottom ('bɒtəm) n. **1.** the lowest, deepest, or farthest removed part of a thing: *the bottom of a hill.* **2.** the least important or successful position: *the bottom of a class.* **3.** the ground underneath a sea, lake, or river. **4.** the inner depths of a person's true feelings (esp. in **from the bottom of one's heart**). **5.** the underneath part of a thing. **6.** Naut. the parts of a vessel's hull that are under water. **7.** (in literary or commercial contexts) a boat or ship. **8.** (esp. of horses) staying power; stamina. **9.** Inf. the buttocks. **10. at bottom.** in reality; basically. **11. be at the bottom of.** to be the ultimate cause of. **12. get to the bottom of.** to discover the real truth about. ~adj. (prenominal) **13.** lowest or last. **14. bet** (*or* **put**) **one's bottom dollar on.** to be absolutely sure of. **15.** of, relating to, or situated at the bottom. **16.** fundamental; basic. ~vb. **17.** (tr.) to provide (a chair, etc.) with a bottom or seat. **18.** (tr.) to discover the full facts or truth of; fathom. **19.** (usually foll. by *on* or *upon*) to base or be founded (on an idea, etc.). [OE *botm*]

bottom drawer n. Brit. a young woman's collection of linen, cutlery, etc., made in anticipation of marriage. U.S., Canad., and N.Z. equivalent: **hope chest.**

bottomless ('bɒtəmlɪs) adj. **1.** having no bottom. **2.** unlimited; inexhaustible. **3.** very deep.

bottom line n. **1.** the last line of a financial statement that shows the net profit or loss of a company or organization. **2.** the conclusion or main point of a process, discussion, etc.

bottom out vb. (intr., adv.) to reach the lowest point and level out.

bottomry ('bɒtəmrɪ) n., pl. **-ries.** Maritime law. a contract whereby the owner of a ship borrows money to enable the vessel to complete the voyage and pledges the ship as security for the loan. [C16: from Du. *bodemerij*, from *bodem* BOTTOM (hull of a ship) + *-erij* -RY]

Bottrop (German 'bɔtrɔp) n. an industrial city in West Germany, in North Rhine-Westphalia in the Ruhr. Pop.: 112 100 (1986).

botulism ('bɒtjʊ‚lɪzəm) n. severe, often fatal, poisoning resulting from the potent bacterial toxin, **botulin,** produced in imperfectly preserved food, etc. [C19: from G *Botulismus,* lit.: sausage poisoning, from L *botulus* sausage]

Botvinnik ('bɒtvɪnɪk) n. **Mikhail Moiseivich** (mixa'il məi'sjejɪvɪtʃ). born 1911, Soviet chess player; world champion (1948–57, 1958–60, 1961–63).

Bouaké (French bwake) n. a market town in S central Côte d'Ivoire. Pop.: 220 000 (1984).

Boucher (French buʃe) n. **François** (frɑ̃swa). 1703–70, French rococo artist, noted for his delicate ornamental paintings of pastoral scenes and mythological subjects.

Bouches-du-Rhône (French buʃdyrɔn) n. a department of S central France, in Provence-Alpes-Côte d'Azur region. Capital: Marseille. Pop.: 1 724 199 (1982). Area: 5284 sq. km (2047 sq. miles).

Boucicault ('buːsɪ‚kəʊ) n. **Dion** ('daɪɒn). real name *Dionysius Lardner Boursiquot.* 1822–90, Irish dramatist

and actor. His plays include *London Assurance* (1841), *The Corsican Brothers* (1852), and *The Poor of New York* (1857).

bouclé ('buːkleɪ) n. **1.** a curled or looped yarn or fabric giving a thick knobbly effect. ~adj. **2.** of or designating such a yarn or fabric. [C19: from F *bouclé* curly, from *boucle* a curl]

Boudicca (bəʊ'dɪkə) n. died 62 A.D., a queen of the Iceni, who led a revolt against Roman rule in Britain; after being defeated she poisoned herself. Also called: **Boadicea.**

Boudin (French budɛ̃) n. **Eugène** (øʒɛn). 1824–98, French painter: one of the first French landscape painters to paint in the open air; a forerunner of impressionism.

boudoir ('buːdwɑː, -dwɔː) n. a woman's bedroom or private sitting room. [C18: from F, lit.: room for sulking in, from *bouder* to sulk]

bouffant ('buːfɔːŋ) adj. **1.** (of a hairstyle) having extra height and width through backcombing; puffed out. **2.** (of sleeves, skirts, etc.) puffed out. [C20: from F, from *bouffer* to puff up]

Bougainville[1] ('buːgən‚vɪl) n. an island in the W Pacific, in Papua New Guinea: the largest of the Solomon Islands. Chief town: Kieta. Area: 10 049 sq. km (3880 sq. miles).

Bougainville[2] (French bugɛ̃vil) n. **Louis Antoine de** (lwi ɑ̃twan də). 1729–1811, French navigator.

bougainvillea (‚buːgən'vɪlɪə) n. a tropical woody climbing plant having inconspicuous flowers surrounded by showy red or purple bracts. [C19: NL, after L. A. de BOUGAINVILLE]

bough (baʊ) n. any of the main branches of a tree. [OE *bōg* arm, twig]

bought (bɔːt) vb. the past tense and past participle of **buy.**

bougie ('buːʒiː, buːʒiː) n. Med. a slender semiflexible instrument for inserting into body passages such as the rectum or urethra to dilate structures, introduce medication, etc. [C18: from F, orig. a wax candle from *Bougie* (Bujiya), Algeria]

bouillabaisse (‚buːjə'bɛs) n. a rich stew or soup of fish and vegetables. [C19: from F, from Provençal *bouiabaisso,* lit.: boil down]

bouillon ('buːjɒn) n. a plain unclarified broth or stock. [C18: from F, from *bouillir* to BOIL[1]]

Boulanger (French bulɑ̃ʒe) n. **1. Georges** (ʒɔrʒ). 1837–91, French general and minister of war (1886–87). Accused of attempting a coup d'état, he fled to Belgium, where he committed suicide. **2. Nadia** (nadʒa). 1887–1979, French teacher of musical composition: her pupils included Elliott Carter, Aaron Copland, Darius Milhaud, and Virgil Thomson. She is noted also for her work in reviving the works of Monteverdi.

boulder ('bəʊldə) n. a smooth rounded mass of rock that has been shaped by erosion. [C13: prob. from ON; cf. OSwedish *bulder* rumbling + *sten* STONE]

boulder clay n. an unstratified glacial deposit consisting of fine clay, boulders, and pebbles.

Boulder Dam n. the former name (1933–47) of **Hoover Dam.**

boule ('buːliː) n. **1.** the senate of an ancient Greek city-state. **2.** the parliament in modern Greece. [C19: from Gk *boulē* senate]

boules French. (bul) n. (functioning as sing.) a game, popular in France, in which metal bowls are thrown to land as near as possible to a target ball. [pl. of *boule* BALL[1]; see BOWL[2]]

boulevard ('buːlvɑː, -vɑːd) n. a wide usually tree-lined road in a city. [C18: from F, from MDu. *bolwerc* BULWARK; so called because orig. often built on the ruins of an old rampart]

Boulez (French bulɛz; French bulɛ) n. **Pierre** (pjɛr). born 1925, French composer and conductor, whose works employ total serialization.

boulle, boule, *or* **buhl** (buːl) adj. **1.** denoting or relating to a type of marquetry of patterned inlays of brass and tortoiseshell, etc. ~n. **2.** something ornamented with such marquetry. [C18: after A. C. *Boulle* (1642–1732), F cabinet-maker]

Boulogne (bʊ'lɔɪn; French bulɔn) n. a port in N France, on the English Channel. Pop.: 48 406 (1983 est.). Official name: **Boulogne-sur-Mer** (French bulɔ̃syrmɛr).

Boulogne-Billancourt (French bulɔ̃pbijɑ̃kur) n. an industrial suburb of SW Paris. Pop.: 103 527 (1983 est.). Also called: **Boulogne-sur-Seine** (French bulɔ̃syrsɛn).

boult (bəʊlt) *vb.* a variant spelling of **bolt**[2].

Boult (bəʊlt) *n.* Sir **Adrian** (**Cedric**). 1889–1983, English conductor.

Boumédienne (bu:ˌmeɪdɪˈɛn) *n.* **Houari** (ˈhaʊərɪ). 1927–78, Algerian statesman and soldier: prime minister of Algeria since overthrowing Ben Bella in a coup (1965).

bounce (baʊns) *vb.* **1.** (*intr.*) (of a ball, etc.) to rebound from an impact. **2.** (*tr.*) to cause (a ball, etc.) to hit a solid surface and spring back. **3.** to move or cause to move suddenly, excitedly, or violently; spring: *she bounced up from her chair.* **4.** *Sl.* (of a bank) to send (a cheque) back or (of a cheque) to be sent back by a bank to a payee unredeemed because of lack of funds in the drawer's account. **5.** (*tr.*) *Sl.* to force (a person) to leave a place or job; throw out; eject. ~*n.* **6.** the action of rebounding from an impact. **7.** a leap; jump; bound. **8.** the quality of being able to rebound; springiness. **9.** *Inf.* vitality; vigour; resilience. **10.** *Brit.* swagger or impudence. [C13: prob. imit.; cf. Low G *bunsen* to beat, Du. *bonken* to thump]

bounce back *vb.* (*intr., adv.*) to recover one's health, good spirits, confidence, etc., easily.

bouncer (ˈbaʊnsə) *n. Sl.* a man employed at a club, disco, etc., to eject drunks or troublemakers.

bouncing (ˈbaʊnsɪŋ) *adj.* (when *postpositive*, foll. by *with*) vigorous and robust (esp. in **a bouncing baby**).

bouncy (ˈbaʊnsɪ) *adj.* **bouncier, bounciest.** **1.** lively, exuberant, or self-confident. **2.** having the capability or quality of bouncing: *a bouncy ball.* **3.** responsive to bouncing; springy: *a bouncy bed.*

bound[1] (baʊnd) *vb.* **1.** the past tense and past participle of **bind.** ~*adj.* **2.** in bonds or chains; tied as with a rope. **3.** (*in combination*) restricted; confined: *housebound.* **4.** (*postpositive;* foll. by an infinitive) destined; sure; certain: *it's bound to happen.* **5.** (*postpositive;* often foll. by *by*) compelled or obliged. **6.** *Rare.* constipated. **7.** (of a book) secured within a cover or binding. **8.** *Logic.* (of a variable) occurring within the scope of a quantifier. Cf. **free** (sense 18). **9. bound up with.** closely or inextricably linked with.

bound[2] (baʊnd) *vb.* **1.** to move forwards by leaps or jumps. **2.** to bounce; spring away from an impact. ~*n.* **3.** a jump upwards or forwards. **4.** a bounce, as of a ball. [C16: from OF *bond* a leap]

bound[3] (baʊnd) *vb.* **1.** (*tr.*) to place restrictions on; limit. **2.** (when *intr.*, foll. by *on*) to form a boundary of. ~*n.* **3.** See **bounds.** [C13: from OF *bonde,* from Med. L *bodina*]

bound[4] (baʊnd) *adj.* **a.** (*postpositive;* often foll. by *for*) going or intending to go so somewhere: *bound for Jamaica; homeward bound.* **b.** (*in combination*): *northbound traffic.* [C13: from ON *buinn,* p.p. of *búa* to prepare]

boundary (ˈbaʊndərɪ, -drɪ) *n., pl.* **-ries.** **1.** something that indicates the farthest limit, as of an area; border. **2.** *Cricket.* **a.** the marked limit of the playing area. **b.** a stroke that hits the ball beyond this limit. **c.** the four or six runs scored with such a stroke.

boundary rider *n. Austral.* an employee on a sheep or cattle station whose job is to maintain fences in good repair.

bounden (ˈbaʊndən) *adj.* morally obligatory (arch. except in **bounden duty**). [arch. p.p. of BIND]

bounder (ˈbaʊndə) *n. Old-fashioned Brit. sl.* a morally reprehensible person; cad.

boundless (ˈbaʊndlɪs) *adj.* unlimited; vast: *boundless energy.* —**ˈboundlessly** *adv.*

bounds (baʊndz) *pl. n.* **1.** (*sometimes sing.*) a limit; boundary (esp. in **know no bounds**). **2.** something that restrains or confines, esp. the standards of a society: *within the bounds of modesty.* ~See also **out of bounds.**

bounteous (ˈbaʊntɪəs) *adj. Literary.* **1.** giving freely; generous. **2.** plentiful; abundant. —**ˈbounteously** *adv.* —**ˈbounteousness** *n.*

bountiful (ˈbaʊntɪfʊl) *adj.* **1.** plentiful; ample (esp. in **a bountiful supply**). **2.** giving freely; generous. —**ˈbountifully** *adv.*

bounty (ˈbaʊntɪ) *n., pl.* **-ties.** **1.** generosity; liberality. **2.** a generous gift. **3.** a payment made by a government, as, formerly, to a sailor on enlisting or to a soldier after a campaign. **4.** any reward or premium. [C13 (in the sense: goodness): from OF, from L, from *bonus* good]

bouquet (bu:ˈkeɪ) *n.* **1.** a bunch of flowers, esp. a large carefully arranged one. **2.** the characteristic aroma or fragrance of a wine or liqueur. **3.** a compliment or expression of praise. [C18: from F: thicket, from OF *bosc* forest]

bouquet garni (ˈbu:keɪ gɑ:ˈni:) *n., pl.* **bouquets garnis** (ˈbu:keɪz gɑ:ˈni:). a bunch of herbs tied together and used for flavouring soups, stews, etc. [C19: from F, lit.: garnished bouquet]

bourbon (ˈbɜ:bən) *n.* a whiskey distilled, chiefly in the U.S., from maize, esp. one containing at least 51 per cent maize. [C19: after *Bourbon* county, Kentucky, where it was first made]

Bourbon (ˈbʊəbən; *French* burbɔ̃) *n.* **a.** a member of the European royal line that ruled in France from 1589 to 1793 (when Louis XVI was executed by the revolutionaries) and was restored in 1815, continuing to rule in its Orleans branch from 1830 until 1848. Bourbon dynasties also ruled in Spain (1700–1808; 1813–1931) and Naples and Sicily (1734–1806; 1815–1860). **b.** (*as modifier*): *the Bourbon kings.*

bourdon (ˈbʊədən, ˈbɔ:dən) *n.* **1.** a bass organ stop. **2.** the drone of a bagpipe. [C14: from OF: drone (of a musical instrument), imit.]

bourgeois (ˈbʊəʒwɑ:) *Often disparaging.* ~*n., pl.* **-geois.** **1.** a member of the middle class, esp. one regarded as being conservative and materialistic or capitalistic. **2.** a mediocre, unimaginative, or materialistic person. ~*adj.* **3.** characteristic of, relating to, or comprising the middle class. **4.** conservative or materialistic in outlook. **5.** (in Marxist thought) dominated by capitalists or capitalist interests. [C16: from OF *borjois, burgeis* burgher, citizen; see BURGESS] —**bourgeoise** (ˈbʊəʒwɑ:z, bʊəˈʒwɑ:z) *fem. n.*

Bourgeois (*French* burʒwa) *n.* **Léon Victor Auguste** (leɔ̃ viktɔr ogyst). 1851–1925, French statesman; first chairman of the League of Nations: Nobel peace prize 1920.

bourgeoisie (ˌbʊəʒwɑ:ˈzi:) *n.* **the. 1.** the middle classes. **2.** (in Marxist thought) the capitalist ruling class. The bourgeoisie owns the means of production, through which it exploits the working class.

bourgeon (ˈbɜ:dʒən) *n., vb.* a variant spelling of **burgeon.**

Bourges (*French* burʒ) *n.* a city in central France. Pop.: 76 152 (1983 est.).

Bourgogne (burgɔɲ) *n.* the French name for **Burgundy.**

Bourguiba (bʊəˈgi:bə) *n.* **Habib ben Ali** (hæˈbɪb bɛn ˈɑ:li:). born 1903, Tunisian statesman: president of Tunisia (1957–87); a moderate and an advocate of gradual social change. He was deposed in a bloodless coup.

bourn[1] *or* **bourne** (bɔ:n) *n. Arch.* **1.** a destination; goal. **2.** a boundary. [C16: from OF *borne;* see BOUND[3]]

bourn[2] (bɔ:n) *n. Chiefly southern Brit.* a stream. [C16: from OF *bodne* limit; see BOUND[3]]

Bournemouth (ˈbɔ:nməθ) *n.* a resort in S England, in SE Dorset on the English Channel. Pop.: 145 000 (1985 est.).

bourrée (ˈbʊəreɪ) *n.* **1.** a traditional French dance in fast duple time. **2.** a piece of music in the rhythm of this dance. [C18: from F]

Bourse (bʊəs) *n.* a stock exchange of continental Europe, esp. Paris. [C19: from F, lit.: purse, from Med. L *bursa,* ult. from Gk: leather]

boustrophedon (ˌbaʊstrəˈfi:dən) *adj.* having alternate lines written from right to left and from left to right. [C17: from Gk, lit.: turning as in ploughing with oxen, from *bous* ox + *strephein* to turn]

bout (baʊt) *n.* **1. a.** a period of time spent doing something, such as drinking. **b.** a period of illness. **2.** a contest or fight, esp. a boxing or wrestling match. [C16: var. of obs. *bought* turn]

boutique (bu:ˈti:k) *n.* a shop, esp. a small one selling fashionable clothes and other items. [C18: from F, ult. from Gk *apothēkē* storehouse]

boutonniere (ˌbutɒnɪˈɛə) *n.* another name for **buttonhole** (sense 2). [C19: from F: buttonhole]

bouzouki (bu:ˈzu:kɪ) *n.* a Greek long-necked stringed musical instrument related to the mandolin. [C20: from Mod. Gk, ?from Turkish *büjük* large]

bovine (ˈbəʊvaɪn) *adj.* **1.** of or relating to cattle. **2.** (of people) dull; sluggish; stolid. [C19: from LL *bovinus,* from L *bōs* ox, cow] —**ˈbovinely** *adv.*

Bovril (ˈbɒvrɪl) *n. Trademark.* a concentrated beef extract, used for flavouring, as a stock, etc.

bovver ('bɒvə) *n. Brit. sl.* **a.** rowdiness, esp. caused by gangs of teenage youths. **b.** (*as modifier*): *a bovver boy.* [C20: sl. pronunciation of BOTHER]

bow[1] (baʊ) *vb.* **1.** to lower (one's head) or bend (one's knee or body) as a sign of respect, greeting, assent, or shame. **2.** to bend or cause to bend. **3.** (*intr.*; usually foll. by *to* or *before*) to comply or accept: *bow to the inevitable.* **4.** (*tr.*; foll. by *in, out, to,* etc.) to usher (someone) in or out with bows and deference. **5.** (*tr.*; usually foll. by *down*) to bring (a person, nation, etc.) to a state of submission. **6. bow and scrape.** to behave in an excessively deferential or obsequious way. ~*n.* **7.** a lowering or inclination of the head or body as a mark of respect, greeting, or assent. **8. take a bow.** to acknowledge or receive applause or praise. ~See also **bow out.** [OE *būgan*]

bow[2] (bəʊ) *n.* **1.** a weapon for shooting arrows, consisting of an arch of flexible wood, plastic, etc., bent by a string fastened at each end. **2. a.** a long stick across which are stretched strands of horsehair, used for playing the strings of a violin, viola, cello, etc. **b.** a stroke with such a stick. **3. a.** a decorative interlacing of ribbon or other fabrics, usually having two loops and two loose ends. **b.** the knot forming such an interlacing. **4.** something that is curved, bent, or arched. ~*vb.* **5.** to form or cause to form a curve or curves. **6.** to make strokes of a bow across (violin strings). [OE *boga* arch, bow]

bow[3] (baʊ) *n.* **1.** *Chiefly Naut.* **a.** (*often pl.*) the forward end or part of a vessel. **b.** (*as modifier*): *the bow mooring line.* **2.** *Rowing.* the oarsman at the bow. [C15: prob. from Low G *boog*]

bow compass (bəʊ) *n. Geom.* a compass in which the legs are joined by a flexible metal bow-shaped spring rather than a hinge.

bowdlerize *or* **-ise** ('baʊdlə,raɪz) *vb.* (*tr.*) to remove passages or words regarded as indecent from (a play, novel, etc.); expurgate. [C19: after Thomas *Bowdler* (1754–1825), E editor who expurgated Shakespeare] —,**bowdleri'zation** *or* **-i'sation** *n.* —'**bowdlerism** *n.*

bowel ('baʊəl) *n.* **1.** an intestine, esp. the large intestine in man. **2.** (*pl.*) innards; entrails. **3.** (*pl.*) the deep or innermost part (esp. in **the bowels of the earth**). [C13: from OF *bouel,* from L *botellus* a little sausage]

bowel movement *n.* **1.** the discharge of faeces; defecation. **2.** the waste matter discharged; faeces.

bower[1] ('baʊə) *n.* **1.** a shady leafy shelter or recess, as in a wood or garden; arbour. **2.** *Literary.* a lady's bedroom or apartments; boudoir. [OE *būr* dwelling]

bower[2] ('baʊə) *n. Naut.* a vessel's bow anchor. [C18: from BOW[3] + -ER[1]]

bowerbird ('baʊə,bɜːd) *n.* **1.** any of various songbirds of Australia and New Guinea. The males build bower-like display grounds to attract the females. **2.** *Inf., chiefly Austral.* a collector of unconsidered trifles.

bowfin ('bəʊ,fɪn) *n.* a primitive North American freshwater bony fish with an elongated body and a very long dorsal fin.

bowhead ('bəʊ,hɛd) *n.* a large-mouthed arctic whale.

Bowie ('baʊɪ, 'bəʊɪ) *n.* **David,** real name *David Jones.* born 1947, English rock singer, songwriter, and film actor, noted for his protean image. His recordings include "Space Oddity" (1969), *The Rise and Fall of Ziggy Stardust and the Spiders from Mars* (1972), *Aladdin Sane* (1973), "Fame", and *Let's Dance* (1983).

bowie knife ('bəʊɪ) *n.* a stout hunting knife with a short hilt and a guard for the hand. [C19: after Jim *Bowie* (1796–1836), Texan adventurer]

bowl[1] (bəʊl) *n.* **1.** a round container open at the top, used for holding liquid, serving food, etc. **2.** Also: **bowlful.** the amount a bowl will hold. **3.** the rounded or hollow part of an object, esp. of a spoon or tobacco pipe. **4.** any container shaped like a bowl, such as a sink or lavatory. **5.** a bowl-shaped building or other structure, such as an amphitheatre. **6.** *Chiefly U.S.* a bowl-shaped depression of the land surface. **7.** *Literary.* a drinking cup. [OE *bolla*]

bowl[2] (bəʊl) *n.* **1.** a wooden ball used in the game of bowls, having one flattened side in order to make it run on a curved course. **2.** a large heavy ball with holes for gripping, used in tenpin bowling. ~*vb.* **3.** to roll smoothly or cause to roll smoothly along the ground. **4.** (*intr.*; usually foll. by *along*) to move easily and rapidly, as in a car. **5.** *Cricket.* **a.** to send (a ball) from one's hand towards the batsman. **b.** Also: **bowl out.** to dismiss (a batsman) by

delivering a ball that breaks his wicket. **6.** (*intr.*) to play bowls or tenpin bowling. ~See also **bowl over, bowls.** [C15: from F *boule,* ult. from L *bulla* bubble]

bow legs (bəʊ) *pl. n.* a condition in which the legs curve outwards like a bow between the ankle and the thigh. Also called: **bandy legs.** —**bow-legged** (bəʊ'lɛgɪd, bəʊ'lɛgd) *adj.*

bowler[1] ('bəʊlə) *n.* **1.** one who bowls in cricket. **2.** a player at the game of bowls.

bowler[2] ('bəʊlə) *n.* a stiff felt hat with a rounded crown and narrow curved brim. U.S. and Canad. name: **derby.** [C19: after John *Bowler,* 19th-cent. London hatter]

bowline ('bəʊlɪn) *n. Naut.* **1.** a line for controlling the weather leech of a square sail when a vessel is closehauled. **2.** a knot used for securing a loop that will not slip at the end of a piece of rope. [C14: prob. from MLow G *bōline,* equivalent to BOW[3] + LINE[1]]

bowling ('bəʊlɪŋ) *n.* **1.** any of various games in which a heavy ball is rolled down a special alley at a group of wooden pins. **2.** the game of bowls. **3.** *Cricket.* the act of delivering the ball to the batsman.

bowling alley *n.* **1. a.** a long narrow wooden lane down which the ball is rolled in tenpin bowling. **b.** a similar lane or alley for playing skittles. **2.** a building having lanes for tenpin bowling.

bowling green *n.* an area of closely mown turf on which the game of bowls is played.

bowl over *vb.* (*tr., adv.*) **1.** *Inf.* to surprise (a person) greatly, esp. in a pleasant way; astound; amaze. **2.** to knock down.

bowls (bəʊlz) *n.* (*functioning as sing.*) **1.** a game played on a bowling green in which a small bowl (the jack) is pitched from a mark and two opponents take turns to roll biased wooden bowls as near the jack as possible. **2.** skittles or tenpin bowling.

bowman ('bəʊmən) *n., pl.* **-men.** *Arch.* an archer.

bow out (baʊ) *vb.* (*adv.; usually tr.;* often foll. by *of*) to retire or withdraw gracefully.

bowser ('baʊzə) *n.* **1.** a tanker containing fuel for aircraft, military vehicles, etc. **2.** *Austral. & N.Z.* a petrol pump at a filling station. [orig. a U.S. proprietary name]

bowshot ('bəʊ,ʃɒt) *n.* the distance an arrow travels from the bow.

bowsprit ('bəʊsprɪt) *n. Naut.* a spar projecting from the bow of a vessel, esp. a sailing vessel. [C13: from MLow G, from *bōch* BOW[3] + *sprēt* pole]

bowstring ('bəʊ,strɪŋ) *n.* the string of an archer's bow.

bow tie (bəʊ) *n.* a man's tie tied in a bow, now chiefly in plain black for formal evening wear.

bow window (bəʊ) *n.* a bay window in the shape of a curve.

bow-wow ('baʊ,waʊ, -'waʊ) *n.* **1.** a child's word for **dog.** **2.** an imitation of the bark of a dog. ~*vb.* **3.** (*intr.*) to bark or imitate a dog's bark.

bowyangs ('bəʊjæŋz) *pl. n. Austral. & N.Z. sl.* a pair of strings or straps worn around the trouser leg below the knee, orig. esp. by agricultural workers. [C19: from E dialect *bowy-yanks* leggings]

box[1] (bɒks) *n.* **1.** a receptacle or container made of wood, cardboard, etc., usually rectangular and having a removable or hinged lid. **2.** Also called: **boxful.** the contents of such a receptacle. **3.** (*often in combination*) any of various small cubicles, kiosks, or shelters: *a telephone box; a signal box.* **4.** a separate compartment in a public place for a small group of people, as in a theatre. **5.** an enclosure within a courtroom: *witness box.* **6.** a compartment for a horse in a stable or a vehicle. **7.** *Brit.* a small country house occupied by sportsmen when following a field sport, esp. shooting. **8. a.** a protective housing for machinery or mechanical parts. **b.** (*in combination*): *a gearbox.* **9.** a shaped device of light tough material worn by sportsmen to protect the genitals, esp. in cricket. **10.** a section of printed matter on a page, enclosed by lines, a border, etc. **11.** a central agency to which mail is addressed and from which it is collected or redistributed: *a post-office box; a box number in a newspaper advertisement.* **12.** short for **penalty box. 13.** the raised seat on which the driver sits in a horse-drawn coach. **14.** *Austral. & N.Z.* an accidental mixing of herds or flocks. **15.** *Brit.* (esp. formerly) a present, esp. of money, given at Christmas to tradesmen, etc. **16.** *Austral. taboo sl.* the female genitals. **17. out of the box.** *Austral. inf.* outstanding or excellent. **18. the box.** *Brit. inf.* television.

box 149 **brace**

~*vb.* **19.** (*tr.*) to put into a box. **20.** (*tr.;* usually foll. by *in* or *up*) to prevent from moving freely; confine. **21.** *Austral. & N.Z.* to mix (flocks or herds) or (of flocks) to become mixed accidentally. **22. box the compass.** *Naut.* to name the compass points in order. [OE *box*, from L *buxus*, from Gk *puxos* BOX³] —'**box,like** *adj.*

box² (bɒks) *vb.* **1.** (*tr.*) to fight (an opponent) in a boxing match. **2.** (*intr.*) to engage in boxing. **3.** (*tr.*) to hit (a person) with the fist. ~*n.* **4.** a punch with the fist, esp. on the ear. [C14: from ?]

box³ (bɒks) *n.* **1.** a slow-growing evergreen tree or shrub with small shiny leaves: used for hedges. **2.** the wood of this tree. **3.** any of several trees the timber or foliage of which resembles this tree, esp. species of *Eucalyptus.* [OE, from L *buxus*]

box camera *n.* a simple box-shaped camera having an elementary lens, shutter, and viewfinder.

boxer ('bɒksə) *n.* **1.** a man who boxes; pugilist. **2.** a medium-sized smooth-haired breed of dog with a short nose and a docked tail.

Boxer ('bɒksə) *n.* a member of a nationalistic Chinese secret society that led an unsuccessful rebellion in 1900 against foreign interests in China. [C18: rough translation of Chinese *I Ho Ch'üan*, lit.: virtuous harmonious fist]

boxer shorts *pl. n.* men's underpants shaped like shorts but having a front opening.

box girder *n.* a girder that is hollow and square or rectangular in shape.

boxing ('bɒksɪŋ) *n.* **a.** the act, art, or profession of fighting with the fists. **b.** (*as modifier*): *a boxing enthusiast.*

Boxing Day *n. Brit.* the first weekday after Christmas, observed as a holiday. [C19: from the custom of giving Christmas boxes to tradesmen and staff on this day]

boxing glove *n.* one of a pair of thickly padded mittens worn for boxing.

box junction *n.* (in Britain) a road junction having yellow cross-hatching painted on the road surface. Vehicles may only enter the hatched area when their exit is clear.

box kite *n.* a kite with a boxlike frame open at both ends.

box lacrosse *n. Canad.* lacrosse played indoors. Also called: **boxla.**

box number *n.* **1.** the number of an individual pigeonhole at a newspaper to which replies to an advertisement may be addressed. **2.** the number of an individual pigeonhole at a post office from which mail may be collected.

box office *n.* **1.** an office at a theatre, cinema, etc., where tickets are sold. **2. a.** the public appeal of an actor or production. **b.** (*as modifier*): *a box-office success.*

box pleat *n.* a flat double pleat made by folding under the fabric on either side of it.

boxroom ('bɒks,ruːm, -,rʊm) *n.* a small room or large cupboard in which boxes, cases, etc., may be stored.

box seat *n.* **1.** a seat in a theatre box. **2. in the box seat.** *Austral. & N.Z.* in the best position.

box spanner *n.* a spanner consisting of a steel cylinder with a hexagonal end that fits over a nut.

box spring *n.* a coiled spring contained in a boxlike frame, used for mattresses, chairs, etc.

boxwood ('bɒks,wʊd) *n.* **1.** the hard close-grained yellow wood of the box tree, used to make tool handles, etc. **2.** the box tree.

boy (bɔɪ) *n.* **1.** a male child; lad; youth. **2.** a man regarded as immature or inexperienced. **3. the boys.** *Inf.* a group of men, esp. a group of friends. **4.** *S. African derog.* a Black male servant. ~*interj.* **5.** an exclamation of surprise, pleasure, contempt, etc. [C13 (in the sense: male servant; C14: young male): ?from Anglo-F *abuié* fettered (unattested), from L *boia* fetter] —'**boyish** *adj.*

Boyce (bɔɪs) *n.* **William.** ?1710–79, English composer, noted esp. for his church music and symphonies.

boycott ('bɔɪkɒt) *vb.* **1.** (*tr.*) to refuse to have dealings with (a person, organization, etc.) or refuse to buy (a product) as a protest or means of coercion. ~*n.* **2.** an instance or the use of boycotting. [C19: after Captain C. C. *Boycott* (1832–97), Irish land agent, a victim of such practices for refusing to reduce rents]

Boycott ('bɔɪkɒt) *n.* **Geoff(rey).** born 1940, English cricketer: captained Yorkshire (1970–78); played for England (1964–74, 1977–81).

Boyd (bɔɪd) *n.* **1. Arthur.** born 1920, Australian painter and sculptor, noted for his large ceramic sculptures and his series of engravings. **2. Martin.** 1893–1972, Australian novelist, author of *Lucinda Brayford* (1946) and of

the Langton tetralogy *The Cardboard Crown* (1952), *A Difficult Young Man* (1955), *Outbreak of Love* (1957), and *When Blackbirds Sing* (1962). **3. William (Andrew Murray).** born 1953, British writer born in Ghana. His novels include *A Good Man in Africa* (1981), *An Ice-Cream War* (1982), *Stars and Bars* (1984), and *The New Confessions* (1987). His TV plays include *Scoop* (1987).

Boyd Orr (ɔː) *n.* **John,** 1st Baron Boyd Orr. 1880–1971, Scottish biologist; director general of the United Nations Food and Agriculture Organization: Nobel peace prize 1949.

Boyer (*French* bwaje) *n.* **Charles** (ʃarl), known as *the Great Lover.* 1899–1978, French film actor.

boyfriend ('bɔɪ,frɛnd) *n.* a male friend with whom a person is romantically or sexually involved; sweetheart or lover.

boyhood ('bɔɪhʊd) *n.* the state or time of being a boy.

Boyle (bɔɪl) *n.* **Robert.** 1627–91, Irish scientist who helped to dissociate chemistry from alchemy. He established that air has weight and studied the behaviour of gases; author of *The Sceptical Chymist* (1661).

Boyle's law *n.* the principle that the pressure of a gas varies inversely with its volume at constant temperature. [C18: after Robert BOYLE]

Boyne (bɔɪn) *n.* a river in the E Republic of Ireland, rising in the Bog of Allen and flowing northeast to the Irish Sea: William III of England defeated the deposed James II in a battle (**Battle of the Boyne**) on its banks in 1690, completing the overthrow of the Stuart cause in Ireland. Length: about 112 km (70 miles).

Boyoma Falls (bɔɪ'əʊmə) *pl. n.* a series of seven cataracts in NE Zaïre, on the upper River Congo: forms an unnavigable stretch of 90 km (56 miles), which falls 60 m (200 ft.). Former name: **Stanley Falls.**

Boys' Brigade *n.* (in Britain) an organization for boys, founded in 1883, with the aim of promoting discipline and self-respect.

boy scout *n.* See **Scout.**

boysenberry ('bɔɪzᵊnbərɪ) *n., pl.* -**ries. 1.** a type of bramble: a hybrid of the loganberry and various blackberries and raspberries. **2.** the large red edible fruit of this plant. [C20: after Rudolph *Boysen*, American botanist]

Boz (bɒz) *n.* pen name of (Charles) **Dickens.**

Bozcaada (,bɒzdʒaaˈda) *n.* the Turkish name for **Tenedos.**

Bozen ('boːtsən) *n.* the German name for **Bolzano.**

bp *abbrev. for:* **1.** (of alcoholic density) below proof. **2.** boiling point. **3.** bishop. **4.** Also: **B/P.** bills payable.

BP *abbrev. for:* **1.** British Petroleum. **2.** British Pharmacopoeia.

bp. *abbrev. for:* **1.** baptized. **2.** birthplace.

B/P *or* **bp** *abbrev. for* bills payable.

BPC *abbrev. for* British Pharmaceutical Codex.

BPhil *abbrev. for* Bachelor of Philosophy.

bpi *abbrev. for* bits per inch (used of a computer tape).

b.pt. *abbrev. for* boiling point.

Bq *Physics. symbol for* becquerel.

br *abbrev. for* brother.

Br 1. *abbrev. for* (in a religious order) Brother. ~ **2.** *the chemical symbol for* bromine.

BR *abbrev. for* British Rail (British Railways).

br. *abbrev. for:* **1.** branch. **2.** bronze.

Br. *abbrev. for:* **1.** Breton. **2.** Britain. **3.** British.

bra (brɑː) *n.* a woman's undergarment for covering and supporting the breasts. [C20: from BRASSIERE]

braai (braɪ) *n.* short for **braaivleis.**

braaivleis ('braɪ,fleɪs) *n. S. African.* a barbecue. [from Afrik. *braai* grill + *vleis* meat]

Brabant (brə'bænt) *n.* **1.** a former duchy of W Europe: divided when Belgium became independent (1830), the south forming the Belgian provinces of Antwerp and Brabant and the north forming the province of North Brabant in the Netherlands. **2.** a province of central Belgium: densely populated and intensively farmed, with large industrial centres. Capital: Brussels. Pop.: 2 219 272 (1986). Area: 3284 sq. km (1268 sq. miles).

Brabham ('bræbəm) *n.* **John Arthur,** known as *Jack.* born 1926, Australian motor-racing driver. He was world champion 1959, 1960, and 1966.

brace (breɪs) *n.* **1.** a hand tool for drilling holes, with a socket to hold the drill at one end and a cranked handle by which the tool can be turned. See also **brace and bit. 2.** something that steadies, binds, or holds up another thing. **3.** a structural member, such as a beam or prop, used to stiffen a framework. **4.** a pair, esp. of game birds. **5.** either of a pair of characters, { }, used for connecting lines of printing or writing. **6.** Also called: **accolade.** a line or bracket connecting two or more staves of music. **7.** (*often pl.*) an appliance of metal bands and wires for correcting uneven alignment of teeth. **8.** *Med.* any of various appliances for supporting the trunk or a limb. **9.** See **braces.** ~*vb.* (*mainly tr.*) **10.** to provide, strengthen, or fit with a brace. **11.** to steady or prepare (oneself or something) as before an impact. **12.** (*also intr.*) to stimulate; freshen; invigorate: *sea air is bracing.* [C14: from OF, from L *bracchia* arms]

brace and bit *n.* a hand tool for boring holes, consisting of a cranked handle into which a drilling bit is inserted.

bracelet ('breɪslɪt) *n.* an ornamental chain worn around the arm or wrist. [C15: from OF, from L *bracchium* arm]

bracelets ('breɪslɪts) *pl. n.* a slang name for **handcuffs.**

bracer ('breɪsə) *n.* **1.** a person or thing that braces. **2.** *Inf.* a tonic, esp. an alcoholic drink taken as a tonic.

braces ('breɪsɪz) *pl. n. Brit.* a pair of straps worn over the shoulders by men for holding up the trousers. U.S. and Canad. word: **suspenders.**

brachial ('breɪkɪəl, 'bræk-) *adj.* of or relating to the arm or to an armlike part or structure.

brachiate *adj.* ('breɪkɪɪt, -ˌeɪt, 'bræk-). **1.** *Bot.* having widely divergent paired branches. ~*vb.* ('breɪkɪˌeɪt, 'bræk-). **2.** (*intr.*) (of some arboreal apes and monkeys) to swing by the arms from one hold to the next. [C19: from L *bracchiātus* with armlike branches] — **brachi'ation** *n.*

brachio- *or before a vowel* **brachi-** *combining form.* indicating a brachium: *brachiopod.*

brachiopod ('breɪkɪəˌpɒd, 'bræk-) *n.* any marine invertebrate animal having a ciliated feeding organ and a shell consisting of dorsal and ventral valves. [C19: from NL *Brachiopoda*; see BRACHIUM, -POD]

brachiosaurus (ˌbreɪkɪə'sɔːrəs, ˌbræk-) *n.* a dinosaur up to 30 metres long: the largest land animal ever known.

brachium ('breɪkɪəm, 'bræk-) *n., pl.* **-chia** (-kɪə). **1.** *Anat.* the arm, esp. the upper part. **2.** a corresponding part in an animal. **3.** *Biol.* a branching or armlike part. [C18: NL, from L *bracchium* arm]

brachy- *combining form.* indicating something short: *brachycephalic.* [from Gk *brakhus* short]

brachycephalic (ˌbrækɪsɪ'fælɪk) *adj.* having a head nearly as broad from side to side as from front to back. Also: **brachycephalous** (ˌbrækɪ'sɛfələs). — ˌbrachy'cephaly *n.*

bracing ('breɪsɪŋ) *adj.* **1.** refreshing; stimulating; invigorating. ~*n.* **2.** a system of braces used to strengthen or support.

bracken ('brækən) *n.* **1.** Also called: **brake.** any of various large coarse ferns having large fronds with spore cases along the undersides. **2.** a clump of any of these ferns. [C14: from ON]

bracket ('brækɪt) *n.* **1.** an L-shaped or other support fixed to a wall to hold a shelf, etc. **2.** one or more wall shelves carried on brackets. **3.** *Archit.* a support projecting from the side of a wall or other structure. **4.** Also called: **square bracket.** either of a pair of characters, [ ], used to enclose a section of writing or printing. **5.** a general name for **parenthesis** (sense 2), **square bracket,** and **brace** (sense 5). **6.** a group or category falling within certain defined limits: *the lower income bracket.* **7.** the distance between two preliminary shots of artillery fire in range-finding. ~*vb.* (*tr.*) **8.** to fix or support by means of brackets. **9.** to put (written or printed matter) in brackets. **10.** to couple or join (two lines of text, etc.) with a brace. **11.** (often foll. by *with*) to group or class together. **12.** to adjust (artillery fire) until the target is hit. [C16: from OF *braguette* codpiece, from OProvençal *braga,* from L *brāca* breeches]

brackish ('brækɪʃ) *adj.* (of water) slightly briny or salty. [C16: from MDu. *brac* salty; see -ISH] — **'brackishness** *n.*

Bracknell ('bræknəl) *n.* a new town in E Berkshire, founded in 1949. Pop.: 51 552 (1985 est.).

bract (brækt) *n.* a specialized leaf with a single flower or inflorescence growing in its axil. [C18: from L *bractea* thin metal plate, gold leaf, from ?] — **'bracteal** *adj.* — **bracteate** ('bræktɪɪt) *adj.*

bracteole ('bræktɪˌəʊl) *n.* a secondary or small bract. Also called: **bractlet.** [C19: from NL *bracteola;* see BRACT]

brad (bræd) *n.* a small tapered nail with a small head. [OE *brord* point, prick]

bradawl ('brædˌɔːl) *n.* an awl used to pierce wood, leather, etc.

Bradford ('brædfəd) *n.* an industrial city in N England, in West Yorkshire: a centre of the woollen industry from the 14th century and of the worsted trade from the 18th century. Pop.: 464 400 (1985).

Bradbury ('brædbrɪ) *n.* **1. Malcolm (Stanley).** born 1932, British novelist. His books include *The History Man* (1975), *Rates of Exchange* (1983), and *Cuts* (1988). **2. Ray.** born 1920, U.S. science-fiction writer. His novels include *Fahrenheit 451* (1953) and *Death is a Lonely Business* (1986).

Bradley ('brædlɪ) *n.* **1. Andrew Cecil.** 1851–1935, English critic; author of *Shakespearian Tragedy* (1904). **2. Francis Herbert.** 1846–1924, English idealist philosopher and metaphysical thinker; author of *Ethical Studies* (1876), *Principles of Logic* (1883), and *Appearance and Reality* (1893). **3. Henry.** 1845–1923, English lexicographer; one of the editors of the *Oxford English Dictionary.* **4. James.** 1693–1762, English astronomer, who discovered the aberration of light and the nutation of the earth's axis.

Bradman ('brædmən) *n.* (Sir) **Don(ald George).** born 1908, Australian cricketer: an outstanding batsman.

Bradshaw ('bræd.ʃɔː) *n.* a British railway timetable, published annually from 1839 to 1961. [C19: after its original publisher, George *Bradshaw* (1801–53)]

bradycardia (ˌbrædɪ'kɑːdɪə) *n. Pathol.* an abnormally slow heartbeat. [C19: from Gk *bradus* slow + *kardia* heart]

brae (breɪ) *n. Scot.* **1.** a hill or hillside **2.** (*pl.*) an upland area. [C14 *bra;* rel to ON *brā* eyelash]

brag (bræg) *vb.* **bragging, bragged. 1.** to speak arrogantly and boastfully. ~*n.* **2.** boastful talk or behaviour. **3.** something boasted of. **4.** a braggart; boaster. **5.** a card game: an old form of poker. [C13: from ?] — **'bragger** *n.*

Braga (*Portuguese* 'brɑːgə) *n.* a city in N Portugal: capital of the Roman province of Lusitania; 12th-century cathedral, seat of the Primate of Portugal. Pop.: 63 033 (1984). Ancient name: **Bracara Augusta.**

Bragg (bræg) *n.* Sir **William Henry,** 1862–1942, and his son, Sir (**William**) **Lawrence,** 1890–1971, English physicists, who shared a Nobel prize for physics (1915) for their study of crystal structures by means of x-rays.

braggadocio (ˌbrægə'dəʊtʃɪˌəʊ) *n., pl.* **-os. 1.** vain empty boasting. **2.** a person who boasts; braggart. [C16: from *Braggadocchio,* a boastful character in Spenser's *Faerie Queene;* prob. from BRAGGART + It. *-occhio* (augmentative suffix)]

braggart ('brægət) *n.* **1.** a person who boasts loudly or exaggeratedly; bragger. ~*adj.* **2.** boastful. [C16: see BRAG]

Bragi ('brɑːgɪ) *or* **Brage** ('brɑːgə) *n. Norse myth.* the god of poetry and music, son of Odin.

Brahe (brɑː, 'brɑːhɪ; *Danish* 'brɑːə) *n.* **Tycho** ('tyːço). 1546–1601, Danish astronomer, who designed and constructed instruments that he used to plot accurately the positions of the planets, sun, moon, and stars.

Brahma ('brɑːmə) *n.* **1.** a Hindu god, the Creator. **2.** another name for **Brahman** (sense 2). [from Sansk., from *brahman* praise]

Brahman ('brɑːmən) *n., pl.* **-mans. 1.** (*sometimes not cap.*) Also (esp. formerly): **Brahmin.** a member of the highest or priestly caste in the Hindu caste system. **2.** *Hinduism.* the ultimate and impersonal divine reality of the universe. **3.** another name for **Brahma.** [C14: from Sansk. *brahman* prayer] — **Brahmanic** (brɑːˈmænɪk) *or* **Brah'manical** *adj.*

Brahmanism ('brɑːməˌnɪzəm) *or* **Brahminism** *n.* (*sometimes not cap.*) the religious and social system of orthodox Hinduism. — **'Brahmanist** *or* **'Brahminist** *n.*

Brahmaputra (ˌbrɑːmə'puːtrə) *n.* a river in S Asia, rising in SW Tibet as the Tsangpo and flowing through the Himalayas and NE India to join the Ganges at its delta in Bangladesh. Length: about 2900 km (1800 miles).

Brahmin ('brɑːmɪn) *n., pl.* **-min** *or* **-mins. 1.** the older spelling of **Brahman** (a Hindu priest). **2.** *U.S.* a highly intelligent or socially exclusive person.

Brahms (brɑːmz) *n.* **Johannes** (joˈhanəs). 1833–97, German composer, whose music, though classical in form, exhibits a strong lyrical romanticism. His works include four symphonies, four concertos, chamber music, and *A German Requiem* (1868).

braid (breɪd) *vb.* (*tr.*) **1.** to interweave (hair, thread, etc.); plait. **2.** to decorate with an ornamental trim or border. ~*n.* **3.** a length of hair, fabric, etc., that has been braided; plait. **4.** narrow ornamental tape of woven silk, wool, etc. [OE *bregdan* to move suddenly, weave together] —'**braider** *n.* —'**braiding** *n.*

Brǎila (*Romanian* bra'ila) *n.* a port in E Romania: belonged to Turkey (1544–1828). Pop.: 234 600 (1985).

Braille[1] (breɪl) *n.* **1.** a system of writing for the blind consisting of raised dots interpreted by touch. **2.** any writing produced by this method. ~*vb.* **3.** (*tr.*) to print or write using this method.

Braille[2] (*French* braj) *n.* **Louis** (lwi). 1809–52, French inventor, musician, and teacher of the blind, who himself was blind from the age of three and who devised the Braille system of raised writing.

brain (breɪn) *n.* **1.** the soft convoluted mass of nervous tissue within the skull of vertebrates that is the controlling and coordinating centre of the nervous system and the seat of thought, memory, and emotion. Related adj.: **cerebral. 2.** (*often pl.*) *Inf.* intellectual ability: *he's got brains.* **3.** *Inf.* shrewdness or cunning. **4.** *Inf.* an intellectual or intelligent person. **5.** (*usually pl.; functioning as sing.*) *Inf.* a person who plans and organizes. **6.** an electronic device, such as a computer, that performs similar functions to those of the human brain. **7. on the brain.** *Inf.* constantly in mind: *I had that song on the brain.* ~*vb.* (*tr.*) **8.** to smash the skull of. **9.** *Sl.* to hit hard on the head. [OE *brægen*]

brainchild ('breɪn,tʃaɪld) *n., pl.* **-children.** *Inf.* an idea or plan produced by creative thought.

brain death *n.* irreversible cessation of respiration due to irreparable brain damage: widely considered as the criterion of death. —**brain dead** *adj.*

brain drain *n.* *Inf.* the emigration of scientists, technologists, academics, etc.

Braine (breɪn) *n.* **John.** 1922–86, English novelist, whose works include *Room at the Top* (1957) and *Life at the Top* (1962).

brain fever *n.* inflammation of the brain.

brainless ('breɪnlɪs) *adj.* stupid or foolish.

brainpan ('breɪn,pæn) *n.* *Inf.* the skull.

brainstem ('breɪn,stɛm) *n.* the part of the brain that controls such reflex actions as breathing and is continuous with the spinal cord.

brainstorm ('breɪn,stɔːm) *n.* **1.** a severe outburst of excitement, often as the result of a transitory disturbance of cerebral activity. **2.** *Brit. inf.* a sudden mental aberration. **3.** *U.S. & Canad. inf.* another word for **brain wave** (sense 2).

brainstorming ('breɪn,stɔːmɪŋ) *n.* intensive discussion to solve problems or generate ideas.

brains trust *n.* a group of knowledgeable people who discuss topics in public or on radio or television.

brain-teaser *or* **brain-twister** *n.* *Inf.* a difficult problem.

brainwash ('breɪn,wɒʃ) *vb.* (*tr.*) to effect a radical change in the ideas and beliefs of (a person), esp. by methods based on isolation, sleeplessness, etc. —'**brain,washing** *n.*

brain wave *n.* **1.** any of the fluctuations of electrical potential in the brain. **2.** *Inf.* a sudden idea or inspiration.

brainy ('breɪnɪ) *adj.* **brainier, brainiest.** *Inf.* clever; intelligent. —'**braininess** *n.*

braise (breɪz) *vb.* to cook (meat, vegetables, etc.) by lightly browning in fat and then cooking slowly in a closed pan with a small amount of liquid. [C18: from F *braiser*, from OF *brese* live coals]

brak (bræk) *n. S. African.* a crossbred dog; mongrel. [from Du. *brak* setter]

brake[1] (breɪk) *n.* **1.** (*often pl.*) a device for slowing or stopping a vehicle, wheel, shaft, etc., or for keeping it stationary, esp. by means of friction. **2.** a machine or tool for crushing or breaking flax or hemp to separate the fibres. **3.** Also called: **brake harrow.** a heavy harrow for breaking up clods. **4.** short for **shooting brake.** ~*vb.* **5.** to slow down or cause to slow down, by or as if by using a brake. **6.** (*tr.*) to crush or break up using a brake. [C18: from MDu. *braeke*; rel. to *breken* to BREAK] —'**brakeless** *adj.*

brake[2] (breɪk) *n.* an area of dense undergrowth, shrubs, brushwood, etc.; thicket. [OE *bracu*]

brake[3] (breɪk) *n.* another name for **bracken** (sense 1).

brake[4] (breɪk) *vb. Arch., chiefly biblical.* a past tense of **break.**

brake horsepower *n.* the rate at which an engine does work, expressed in horsepower. It is measured by the resistance of an applied brake. Abbrev.: **bhp.**

brake light *n.* a red light at the rear of a motor vehicle that lights up when the brakes are applied.

brake lining *n.* a renewable strip of asbestos riveted to a brake shoe.

brake shoe *n.* the curved metal casting to which the brake lining is riveted in a drum brake.

brakesman ('breɪksmən) *n., pl.* **-men. 1.** a pithead winch operator. **2.** a brake operator on railway rolling stock.

brake van *n. Railways, Brit.* the coach or vehicle from which the guard applies the brakes; guard's van.

Brakpan ('bræk,pæn) *n.* a city in E South Africa, in S Transvaal: gold-mining centre. Pop.: 79 732 (1980).

Bramante (*Italian* bra'mante) *n.* **Donato** (do'nato). ?1444–1514, Italian architect and artist of the High Renaissance. He modelled his designs for domed centrally planned churches on classical Roman architecture.

bramble ('bræmb³l) *n.* **1.** any of various prickly rosaceous plants or shrubs, esp. the blackberry. **2.** any of several similar and related shrubs, such as the dog rose. **3.** *Scot. & N English.* a blackberry. [OE *brǣmbel*] —'**brambly** *adj.*

brambling ('bræmblɪŋ) *n.* a Eurasian finch with a speckled head and back and, in the male, a reddish-brown breast.

bran (bræn) *n.* **1.** husks of cereal grain separated from the flour. **2.** food prepared from these husks. [C13: from OF, prob. of Gaulish origin]

Branagh ('brænə) *n.* **Kenneth.** born 1961, British actor and director, born in Ireland. He founded the Renaissance Theatre Company in 1986.

branch (brɑːntʃ) *n.* **1.** a secondary woody stem arising from the trunk or bough of a tree or the main stem of a shrub. **2.** an offshoot or secondary part: *a branch of a deer's antlers.* **3. a.** a subdivision or subsidiary section of something larger or more complex: *branches of learning; branch of the family.* **b.** (*as modifier*): *a branch office.* **4.** *U.S.* any small stream. ~*vb.* **5.** (*intr.*) (of a tree or other plant) to produce or possess branches. **6.** (*intr.;* usually foll. by *from*) (of stems, roots, etc.) to grow and diverge (from another part). **7.** to divide or be divided into subsidiaries or offshoots. **8.** (*intr.;* often foll. by *off*) to diverge from the main way, road, topic, etc. [C13: from OF *branche*, from LL *branca* paw, foot] —'**branch,like** *adj.*

branchia ('bræŋkɪə) *n., pl.* **-chiae** (-kɪ,iː). a gill in aquatic animals. —'**branchial** *or* '**branchiate** *adj.*

branch out *vb.* (*intr., adv.;* often foll. by *into*) to expand or extend one's interests.

Brancusi (bræŋ'kuːzɪ; *Romanian* briŋ'kuʃj) *n.* **Constantin** (konstan'tin). 1876–1957, Romanian sculptor, noted for his streamlined abstractions of animal forms.

brand (brænd) *n.* **1.** a particular product or a characteristic that identifies a particular producer. **2.** a particular kind or variety. **3.** an identifying mark made, usually by burning, on the skin of animals or (formerly) slaves or criminals, esp. as a proof of ownership. **4.** an iron heated and used for branding animals, etc. **5.** a mark of disgrace or infamy; stigma. **6.** a burning or burnt piece of wood, as in a fire. **7.** *Arch. or poetic.* **a.** a flaming torch. **b.** a sword. **8.** a fungal disease of garden plants characterized by brown spots on the leaves. ~*vb.* (*tr.*) **9.** to label, burn, or mark with or as with a brand. **10.** to place indelibly in the memory: *the scene was branded in their minds.* **11.** to denounce; stigmatize: *they branded him a traitor.* [OE *brand-*; see BURN[1]] —'**brander** *n.*

Brandenburg ('brændən,bɜːg; *German* 'brandənburk) *n.* **1.** a former electorate in NE Germany that expanded under the Hohenzollerns to become the kingdom of Prussia (1701). The district east of the Oder River became Polish in 1945, the remainder being part of East Germany. **2.** a city in central East Germany: former capital of the Prussian province of Brandenburg. Pop.: 95 052 (1983).

brandish ('brændɪʃ) *vb.* **1.** (*tr.*) to wave or flourish (a weapon, etc.) in a triumphant, threatening, or ostentatious way. ~*n.* **2.** a threatening or defiant flourish. [C14: from OF *brandir*, of Gmc origin] —'**brandisher** *n.*

brand leader n. the most widely sold brand of a particular product.

brandling ('brændlɪŋ) n. a small red earthworm, found in manure and used as bait by anglers. [C17: from BRAND (n.) + -LING¹]

brand name n. the name used for a particular make of a commodity.

brand-new adj. absolutely new. [C16: from BRAND (n.) + NEW, likened to newly forged iron]

Brando ('brændəʊ) n. **Marlon**. born 1924, U.S. actor; his films include *A Streetcar named Desire* (1951), *On the Waterfront* (1954) and *The Godfather* (1972), for both of which he won Oscars, *Last Tango in Paris* (1972), and *Apocalypse Now* (1979).

Brandt (*German* brant) n. **Willy** ('vɪli). born 1913, German statesman; socialist chancellor of West Germany (1969–74); chairman of the Social Democratic party (1964–87). His policy of détente and reconciliation with E Europe brought him international acclaim. Nobel prize for peace 1971.

brandy ('brændɪ) n., pl. **-dies**. 1. an alcoholic spirit distilled from grape wine. 2. a distillation of wines made from other fruits: *plum brandy*. [C17: from earlier *brandewine*, from Du. *brandewijn*, burnt (or distilled) wine]

brandy butter n. butter and sugar creamed together with brandy and served with Christmas pudding, etc.

brandy snap n. a crisp sweet biscuit, rolled into a cylinder and filled with whipped cream.

Branson ('brænsən) n. **Richard**. born 1950, British entrepreneur. In 1969 he founded the Virgin record company, adding the Virgin airline later.

brant (brænt) n., pl. **brants** or **brant**. another name (esp. U.S. and Canad.) for **brent** (the goose).

Brantford ('bræntfəd) n. a city in central Canada, in SW Ontario. Pop.: 74 315 (1981).

bran tub n. *Brit.* a tub containing bran in which small wrapped gifts are hidden.

Braque (*French* brak) n. **Georges** (ʒɔrʒ). 1882–1963, French painter who developed cubism with Picasso (1908–14).

brash¹ (bræʃ) adj. 1. tastelessly or offensively loud, showy, or bold. 2. hasty; rash. 3. impudent. [C19: ? infl. by RASH¹] —**'brashly** adv. —**'brashness** n.

brash² (bræʃ) n. loose rubbish, such as broken rock, hedge clippings, etc. [C18: from ?] —**'brashy** adj.

brasier ('breɪzɪə) n. a less common spelling of **brazier**.

Brasil (brə'ziːl) n. the Portuguese spelling of **Brazil**.

Brasília (brə'zɪljə; *Portuguese* brəzi'liːə) n. the capital of Brazil (since 1960), on the central plateau: the former capital was Rio de Janeiro. Pop.: 411 305 (1980).

Braşov (*Romanian* bra'ʃov) n. an industrial city in central Romania: formerly a centre for expatriate Germans; ceded by Hungary to Romania in 1920. Pop.: 346 640 (1985). Former name (1950–61): **Stalin**. German name: **Kronstadt**. Hungarian name: **Brassó**.

brass (brɑːs) n. 1. an alloy of copper and zinc containing more than 50 per cent of copper. Cf. **bronze** (sense 1). 2. an object, ornament, or utensil made of brass. 3. a. the large family of wind instruments including the trumpet, trombone, French horn, etc., made of brass. b. (*sometimes functioning as pl.*) instruments of this family forming a section in an orchestra. 4. (*functioning as pl.*) *Inf.* important or high-ranking officials, esp. military officers: *the top brass*. See also **brass hat**. 5. *N English dialect.* money. 6. *Brit.* an engraved brass memorial tablet or plaque in a church. 7. *Inf.* bold self-confidence; cheek; nerve. 8. (*modifier*) of, consisting of, or relating to brass or brass instruments: *a brass ornament; a brass band*. [OE *bræs*]

brassard ('bræsɑːd) or **brassart** ('bræsət) n. an identifying armband or badge. [C19: from F, from *bras* arm]

brass band n. See **band¹** (sense 2).

brasserie ('bræsərɪ) n. 1. a bar in which drinks and often food are served. 2. a small and usually cheap restaurant. [C19: from F, from *brasser* to stir]

brass hat n. *Brit. inf.* a top-ranking official, esp. a military officer. [C20: from the gold decoration on the caps of officers of high rank]

brassica ('bræsɪkə) n. any plant of the genus *Brassica*, such as cabbage, rape, swede, turnip, and mustard. [C19: from L: cabbage]

brassie or **brassy** ('bræsɪ, 'brɑː-) n., pl. **brassies**. *Golf.* a former name for a club, a No. 2 wood, originally having a brass-plated sole.

brassiere ('bræsɪə, 'bræz-) n. the full name for **bra**. [C20: from 17th-cent. F: bodice, from OF *braciere* a protector for the arm]

Brassó ('brɒʃʃoː) n. the Hungarian name for **Braşov**.

brass rubbing n. 1. the taking of an impression of an engraved brass tablet or plaque by rubbing a paper placed over it with heelball, chalk, etc. 2. an impression made in this way.

brass tacks pl. n. *Inf.* basic realities; hard facts (esp. in **get down to brass tacks**).

brassy ('brɑːsɪ) adj. **brassier, brassiest**. 1. insolent; brazen. 2. flashy; showy. 3. (of sound) harsh and strident. 4. like brass, esp. in colour. 5. decorated with or made of brass. —**'brassily** adv. —**'brassiness** n.

brat (bræt) n. a child, esp. one who is dirty or unruly. [C16: ?from earlier *brat* rag, from OE *bratt* cloak]

Bratislava (,brætɪ'slɑːvə) n. a port in S Czechoslovakia on the River Danube: capital of Slovakia since 1918; capital of Hungary (1541–1784) and seat of the Hungarian parliament until 1848. Pop.: 417 000 (1986). German name: **Pressburg**. Hungarian name: **Pozsony**.

brattice ('brætɪs) n. 1. a partition of wood or treated cloth used to control ventilation in a mine. 2. *Medieval fortifications*. a fixed wooden tower or parapet. [C13: from OF *bretesche* wooden tower]

Braun (*German* braun) n. 1. **Eva** ('eːfa). 1910–45, Adolf Hitler's mistress, whom he married shortly before their suicides in 1945. 2. See (Wernher) **von Braun**.

Braunschweig ('braunʃvaik) n. the German name for **Brunswick**.

bravado (brə'vɑːdəʊ) n., pl. **-does** or **-dos**. vaunted display of courage or self-confidence; swagger. [C16: from Sp. *bravada*; see BRAVE]

brave (breɪv) adj. 1. a. having or displaying courage, resolution, or daring; not cowardly or timid. b. (*as collective n.*; preceded by *the*): *the brave*. 2. fine; splendid: *a brave sight*. ~n. 3. a warrior of a North American Indian tribe. ~vb. (*tr.*) 4. to dare or defy: *to brave the odds*. 5. to confront with resolution or courage: *to brave the storm*. [C15: from F, from It. *bravo* courageous, wild, ? ult. from L *barbarus* BARBAROUS] —**'bravely** adv. —**'braveness** n. —**'bravery** n.

bravo (interj. 1. (brɑː'vəʊ). well done! ~n. 2. (brɑː'vəʊ) pl. **-vos**. a cry of "bravo." 3. ('brɑːvəʊ) pl. **-voes** or **-vos**. a hired killer or assassin. [C18: from It.: splendid! see BRAVE]

bravura (brə'vjʊərə, -'vʊərə) n. 1. a display of boldness or daring. 2. *Music*. brilliance of execution. [C18: from It.: spirit, courage; see BRAVE]

braw (brɔː, brɑː) adj. *Chiefly Scot.* fine or excellent, esp. in appearance or dress. [C16: Scot. var. of BRAVE]

brawl (brɔːl) n. 1. a loud disagreement or fight. 2. *U.S. & Canad. sl.* an uproarious party. ~vb. (*intr.*) 3. to quarrel or fight noisily; squabble. 4. (esp. of water) to flow noisily. [C14: prob. rel. to Du. *brallen* to boast, behave aggressively] —**'brawler** n.

brawn (brɔːn) n. 1. strong well-developed muscles. 2. physical strength, esp. as opposed to intelligence. 3. *Brit.* a seasoned jellied loaf made from the head of a pig or calf. [C14: from OF *braon* slice of meat, of Gmc origin]

brawny ('brɔːnɪ) adj. **brawnier, brawniest**. muscular and strong. —**'brawniness** n.

bray (breɪ) vb. 1. (*intr.*) (of a donkey) to utter its characteristic loud harsh sound; heehaw. 2. (*intr.*) to make a similar sound, as in laughing. 3. (*tr.*) to utter with a loud harsh sound. ~n. 4. the loud harsh sound uttered by a donkey. 5. a similar loud cry or uproar. [C13: from OF *braire*, prob. of Celtic origin]

braze¹ (breɪz) vb. (*tr.*) 1. to decorate with or make of brass. 2. to make like brass, as in hardness. [OE *bræsen*, from *bræs* BRASS]

braze² (breɪz) vb. (*tr.*) to make a joint between (two metal surfaces) by fusing a layer of brass or high-melting solder between them. [C16: from OF: to burn, of Gmc origin; see BRAISE] —**'brazer** n.

brazen ('breɪzªn) adj. 1. shameless and bold. 2. made of or resembling brass. 3. having a ringing metallic sound. ~vb. (*tr.*) 4. (usually foll. by *out* or *through*) to face and overcome boldly or shamelessly. [OE *bræsen*, from *bræs* BRASS] —**'brazenly** adv. —**'brazenness** n.

brazier[1] *or* **brasier** ('breɪzɪə) *n.* a person engaged in brass-working or brass-founding. [C14: from OE *bræsian* to work in brass + -ER[1]] —'**braziery** *n.*

brazier[2] *or* **brasier** ('breɪzɪə) *n.* a portable metal receptacle for burning charcoal or coal. [C17: from F *brasier*, from *braise* live coals; see BRAISE]

brazil (brə'zɪl) *n.* **1.** Also called: **brazil wood.** the red wood obtained from various tropical trees of America: used for cabinetwork. **2.** the red or purple dye extracted from these woods. **3.** short for **brazil nut.** [C14: from OSp., from *brasa* glowing coals, of Gmc origin; referring to the redness of the wood]

Brazil (brə'zɪl) *n.* a republic in South America, comprising about half the area and half the population of South America: colonized by the Portuguese from 1500 onwards; became independent in 1822 and a republic in 1889; consists chiefly of the tropical Amazon basin in the north, semiarid scrub in the northeast, and a vast central tableland; an important producer of coffee and minerals, esp. iron ore. Official language: Portuguese. Religion: chiefly Roman Catholic. Currency: cruzado. Capital: Brasília. Pop.: 141 459 000 (1987). Area: 8 511 957 sq. km (3 286 470 sq. miles). —**Bra'zilian** *adj., n.*

brazil nut *n.* **1.** a tropical South American tree producing large globular capsules, each containing several closely packed triangular nuts. **2.** the nut, having an edible oily kernel and a woody shell. ~Often shortened to **brazil.**

Brazzaville (*French* brazavil) *n.* the capital of the Congo Republic, in the south on the River Congo. Pop.: 422 402 (1980 est.).

BRCS *abbrev. for* British Red Cross Society.

breach (bri:tʃ) *n.* **1.** a crack, break, or rupture. **2.** a breaking, infringement, or violation of a promise, obligation, etc. **3.** any severance or separation. ~*vb.* (*tr.*) **4.** to break through or make an opening, hole, or incursion in. **5.** to break a promise, law, etc. [OE *bræc*]

breach of promise *n. Law.* (formerly) failure to carry out one's promise to marry.

breach of the peace *n. Law.* an offence against public order causing an unnecessary disturbance of the peace.

bread (brɛd) *n.* **1.** a food made from a dough of flour or meal mixed with water or milk, usually raised with yeast or baking powder and then baked. **2.** necessary food; nourishment. **3.** *Sl.* money. **4. cast one's bread upon the waters.** to do good without expectation of advantage or return. **5. know which side one's bread is buttered.** to know what to do in order to keep one's advantages. **6. take the bread out of (someone's) mouth.** to deprive of a livelihood. ~*vb.* **7.** (*tr.*) to cover with bread-crumbs before cooking. [OE *brēad*]

bread and butter *Inf.* ~*n.* **1.** a means of support or subsistence; livelihood. ~*modifier.* **bread-and-butter 2. a.** providing a basic means of subsistence. **b.** expressing gratitude, as for hospitality (esp. in **bread-and-butter letter**).

breadbasket ('brɛd,bɑːskɪt) *n.* **1.** a basket for carrying bread or rolls. **2.** *Sl.* stomach.

breadboard ('brɛd,bɔːd) *n.* **1.** a wooden board on which bread is sliced. **2.** an experimental arrangement of electronic circuits.

breadfruit ('brɛd,fruːt) *n., pl.* **-fruits** *or* **-fruit. 1.** a tree of the Pacific Islands, having edible round, usually seedless, fruit. **2.** the fruit, which is eaten baked or roasted and has a texture like bread.

breadline ('brɛd,laɪn) *n.* **1.** a queue of people waiting for free food. **2. on the breadline.** impoverished; living at subsistence level.

breadth (brɛdθ, brɛtθ) *n.* **1.** the linear extent or measurement of something from side to side; width. **2.** a piece of fabric, etc., having a standard or definite width. **3.** distance, extent, size, or dimension. **4.** openness and lack of restriction, esp. of viewpoint or interest; liberality. [C16: from obs. *brēde* (from OE *brǣdu*, from *brād* BROAD) + -TH[1]]

breadthways ('brɛdθ,weɪz, 'brɛtθ-) *or esp. U.S.* **breadthwise** ('brɛdθ,waɪz, 'brɛtθ-) *adv.* from side to side.

breadwinner ('brɛd,wɪnə) *n.* a person supporting a family with his or her earnings.

break (breɪk) *vb.* **breaking, broke, broken. 1.** to separate or become separated into two or more pieces. **2.** to damage or become damaged so as to be inoperative: *my radio is broken.* **3.** to crack or become cracked without separating. **4.** to burst or cut the surface of (skin, etc.)

5. to discontinue or become discontinued: *to break a journey.* **6.** to disperse or become dispersed: *the clouds broke.* **7.** (*tr.*) to fail to observe (an agreement, promise, law, etc.): *to break one's word.* **8.** (foll. by *with*) to discontinue an association (with). **9.** to disclose or be disclosed: *he broke the news gently.* **10.** (*tr.*) to fracture (a bone) in (a limb, etc.). **11.** (*tr.*) to divide (something complete or perfect): *to break a set of books.* **12.** to bring or come to an end: *the summer weather broke at last.* **13.** (*tr.*) to bring to an end as by force: *to break a strike.* **14.** (when *intr.*, often foll. by *out*) to escape (from): *he broke out of jail.* **15.** to weaken or overwhelm or be weakened or overwhelmed, as in spirit. **16.** (*tr.*) to cut through or penetrate: *a cry broke the silence.* **17.** (*tr.*) to improve on or surpass: *to break a record.* **18.** (*tr.*; often foll. by *in*) to accustom (a horse) to the bridle and saddle, to being ridden, etc. **19.** (*tr.*; often foll. by *of*) to cause (a person) to give up (a habit): *this cure will break you of smoking.* **20.** (*tr.*) to weaken the impact or force of: *this net will break his fall.* **21.** (*tr.*) to decipher: *to break a code.* **22.** (*tr.*) to lose the order of: *to break ranks.* **23.** (*tr.*) to reduce to poverty or the state of bankruptcy. **24.** (when *intr.*, foll. by *into*) to obtain, give, or receive smaller units in exchange for; change: *to break a pound note.* **25.** (*tr.*) *Chiefly mil.* to demote to a lower rank. **26.** (*intr.*; often foll. by *from* or *out of*) to proceed suddenly. **27.** (*intr.*) to come into being: *light broke over the mountains.* **28.** (*intr.*; foll. by *into* or *out into*) **a.** to burst into song, laughter, etc. **b.** to change to a faster pace. **29.** (*tr.*) to open with explosives: *to break a safe.* **30.** (*intr.*) (of waves) **a.** (often foll. by *against*) to strike violently. **b.** to collapse into foam or surf. **31.** (*intr.*) (of prices, esp. stock exchange quotations) to fall sharply. **32.** (*intr.*) to make a sudden effort, as in running, horse racing, etc. **33.** (*intr.*) *Cricket.* (of a ball) to change direction on bouncing. **34.** (*intr.*) *Billiards.* to scatter the balls at the start of a game. **35.** (*intr.*) *Boxing, wrestling.* (of two fighters) to separate from a clinch. **36.** (*intr.*) (of the male voice) to undergo a change in register, quality, and range at puberty. **37.** (*tr.*) to open the breech of (certain firearms) by snapping the barrel away from the butt on its hinge. **38.** (*tr.*) to interrupt the flow of current in (an electrical circuit). **39.** *Inf., chiefly U.S.* to become successful. **40. break camp.** to pack up and leave a camp. **41. break the bank.** to ruin financially or deplete the resources of a bank (as in gambling). **42. break service.** *Tennis.* to win a game in which an opponent is serving. ~*n.* **43.** the act or result of breaking; fracture. **44.** a crack formed as the result of breaking. **45.** a brief respite. **46.** a sudden rush, esp. to escape: *to make a break for freedom.* **47.** a breach in a relationship. **48.** any sudden interruption in a continuous action. **49.** *Brit.* a short period between classes at school. **50.** *Inf.* a fortunate opportunity, esp. to prove oneself. **51.** *Inf.* a piece of good or bad luck. **52.** (esp. in a stock exchange) a sudden and substantial decline in prices. **53.** *Billiards, snooker.* a series of successful shots during one turn. **54.** *Billiards, snooker.* the opening shot that scatters the placed balls. **55.** Also called: **service break, break of serve.** *Tennis.* the act or an instance of breaking an opponent's service. **56. a.** *Jazz.* a short usually improvised solo passage. **b.** an instrumental passage in a pop song. **57.** a discontinuity in an electrical circuit. **58.** access to a radio channel by a citizens' band radio operator. **59. break of day.** the dawn. ~*interj.* **60.** *Boxing, wrestling.* a command by a referee for two opponents to separate. ~See also **breakaway, break down,** etc. [OE *brecan*]

breakable ('breɪkəb²l) *adj.* **1.** capable of being broken. ~*n.* **2.** (*usually pl.*) a fragile easily broken article.

breakage ('breɪkɪdʒ) *n.* **1.** the act or result of breaking. **2.** the quantity or amount broken. **3.** compensation or allowance for goods damaged while in use, transit, etc.

breakaway ('breɪkə,weɪ) *n.* **1. a.** loss or withdrawal of a group of members from an association, club, etc. **b.** (*as modifier*): *a breakaway faction.* **2.** *Austral.* a stampede of animals, esp. at the smell of water. ~*vb.* **break away.** (*intr., adv.*) **3.** (often foll. by *from*) to leave hastily or escape. **4.** to withdraw or secede.

break dance *n.* **1.** an acrobatic dance style of the 1980s. ~*vb.* **break-dance.** (*intr.*) **2.** to perform a break dance. —**break dancer** *n.* —**break dancing** *n.*

break down *vb.* (*adv.*) **1.** (*intr.*) to cease to function; become ineffective. **2.** to yield or cause to yield, esp. to strong emotion or tears. **3.** (*tr.*) to crush or destroy. **4.** (*intr.*) to have a nervous breakdown. **5.** to analyse or be subjected to analysis. **6. break it down.** *Austral. & N.Z. inf.* **a.** stop it. **b.** don't expect me to believe that; come off it. ~*n.* **breakdown. 7.** an act or instance of breaking down; collapse. **8.** short for **nervous breakdown. 9.** an analysis or classification of something into its component parts: *he prepared a breakdown of the report.*

breaker ('breɪkə) *n.* **1.** a person or thing that breaks something, such as a person or firm that breaks up old cars, etc. **2.** a large wave with a white crest on the open sea or one that breaks into foam on the shore. **3.** a citizens' band radio operator.

break even *vb.* **1.** (*intr., adv.*) to attain a level of activity, as in commerce, or a point of operation, as in gambling, at which there is neither profit nor loss. ~*n.* **breakeven. 2.** *Accounting.* the level of commercial activity at which the total cost and total revenue of a business enterprise are equal.

breakfast ('brɛkfəst) *n.* **1.** the first meal of the day. **2.** the food at this meal. ~*vb.* **3.** to eat or supply with breakfast. [C15: from BREAK + FAST²] —**'breakfaster** *n.*

break in *vb.* (*adv.*) **1.** (sometimes foll. by *on*) to interrupt. **2.** (*intr.*) to enter a house, etc., illegally, esp. by force. **3.** (*tr.*) to accustom (a person or animal) to normal duties or practice. **4.** (*tr.*) to use or wear (shoes, new equipment, etc.) until comfortable or running smoothly. **5.** *Austral.* to bring new land under cultivation. ~*n.* **break-in. 6.** the illegal entering of a building, esp. by thieves.

breaking and entering *n.* (formerly) the gaining of unauthorized access to a building with intent to commit a crime.

breaking point *n.* the point at which something or someone gives way under strain.

breakneck ('breɪk,nɛk) *adj.* (*prenominal*) (of speed, pace, etc.) excessive and dangerous.

break off *vb.* **1.** to sever or detach or be severed or detached. **2.** (*adv.*) to end (a relationship, association, etc.) or (of a relationship, etc.) to be ended. **3.** (*intr., adv.*) to stop abruptly: *he broke off in the middle of his speech.*

break out *vb.* (*intr., adv.*) **1.** to begin or arise suddenly. **2.** to make an escape, esp. from prison or confinement. **3.** (foll. by *in*) (of the skin) to erupt (in a rash, pimples, etc.). ~*n.* **break-out. 4.** an escape, esp. from prison or confinement.

break through *vb.* **1.** (*intr.*) to penetrate. **2.** (*intr., adv.*) to achieve success, make a discovery, etc., esp. after lengthy efforts. ~*n.* **breakthrough. 3.** a significant development or discovery, esp. in science. **4.** the penetration of an enemy's defensive position.

break up *vb.* (*adv.*) **1.** to separate or cause to separate. **2.** to put an end to (a relationship) or (of a relationship) to come to an end. **3.** to dissolve or cause to dissolve; disrupt or be disrupted: *the meeting broke up at noon.* **4.** (*intr.*) *Brit.* (of a school) to close for the holidays. **5.** *Inf.* to lose or cause to lose control of the emotions. **6.** *Sl.* to be or cause to be overcome with laughter. ~*n.* **break-up. 7.** a separation or disintegration. **8. a.** in the Canadian north, the breaking up of the ice on a body of water that marks the beginning of spring. **b.** this season.

breakwater ('breɪk,wɔːtə) *n.* **1.** Also called: **mole.** a massive wall built out into the sea to protect a shore or harbour from the force of waves. **2.** another name for **groyne.**

bream¹ (briːm; *Austral.* brɪm) *or Austral.* **brim** (brɪm) *n., pl.* **bream** *or* **brim. 1.** any of several Eurasian freshwater cyprinid fishes having a deep compressed body covered with silvery scales. **2.** short for **sea bream. 3.** *Austral.* any of various marine fishes. [C14: from OF *bresme*, of Gmc origin]

bream² (briːm) *vb. Naut.* (formerly) to clean debris from (the bottom of a vessel) by heating to soften the pitch. [C15: prob. from MDu. *bremme* broom; from burning broom as a source of heat]

Bream (briːm) *n.* **Julian (Alexander).** born 1933, English guitarist and lutenist.

breast (brɛst) *n.* **1.** the front part of the body from the neck to the abdomen; chest. **2.** either of the two soft fleshy milk-secreting glands on the chest in sexually mature human females. **3.** a similar organ in certain other mammals. **4.** anything that resembles a breast in shape or position: *the breast of the hill.* **5.** a source of nourishment. **6.** the source of human emotions. **7.** the part of a garment that covers the breast. **8.** a projection from the side of a wall, esp. that formed by a chimney. **9. beat one's breast.** to display guilt and remorse publicly or ostentatiously. **10. make a clean breast of.** to make a confession of. ~*vb.* (*tr.*) **11.** to confront boldly; face: *breast the storm.* **12.** to oppose with the breast or meet at breast level: *breasting the waves.* **13.** to reach the summit of: *breasting the mountain top.* [OE *brēost*]

breastbone ('brɛst,bəʊn) *n.* the nontechnical name for **sternum.**

breast-feed *vb.* **-feeding, -fed.** to feed (a baby) with milk from the breast; suckle.

breastpin ('brɛst,pɪn) *n.* a brooch worn on the breast, esp. to close a garment.

breastplate ('brɛst,pleɪt) *n.* a piece of armour covering the chest.

breaststroke ('brɛst,strəʊk) *n.* a swimming stroke in which the arms are extended in front of the head and swept back on either side while the legs are drawn up beneath the body and thrust back together.

breastwork ('brɛst,wɜːk) *n. Fortifications.* a temporary defensive work, usually breast-high.

breath (brɛθ) *n.* **1.** the intake and expulsion of air during respiration. **2.** the air inhaled or exhaled during respiration. **3.** a single respiration or inhalation of air, etc. **4.** the vapour, heat, or odour of exhaled air. **5.** a slight gust of air. **6.** a short pause or rest. **7.** a brief time. **8.** a suggestion or slight evidence; suspicion: *a breath of scandal.* **9.** a whisper or soft sound. **10.** life, energy, or vitality: *the breath of new industry.* **11.** *Phonetics.* the exhalation of air without vibration of the vocal cords, as in pronouncing fricatives such as (f) or (h) or stops such as (p) or (k). **12. catch one's breath. a.** to rest until breathing is normal, esp. after exertion. **b.** to stop breathing momentarily from excitement, fear, etc. **13. in the same breath.** done or said at the same time. **14. out of breath.** gasping for air after exertion. **15. save one's breath.** to refrain from useless talk. **16. take one's breath away.** to overwhelm with surprise, etc. **17. under** *or* **below one's breath.** in a quiet voice or whisper. [OE *brǣth*]

Breathalyser *or* **-lyzer** ('brɛθə,laɪzə) *n. Brit., trademark.* a device for estimating the amount of alcohol in the breath: used in testing people suspected of driving under the influence of alcohol. [C20: BREATH + (AN)ALYSER] —**'breatha,lyse** *or* **-,lyze** *vb.* (*tr.*)

breathe (briːð) *vb.* **1.** to take in oxygen and give out carbon dioxide; respire. **2.** (*intr.*) to exist; be alive. **3.** (*intr.*) to rest to regain breath, composure, etc. **4.** (*intr.*) (esp. of air) to blow lightly. **5.** (*intr.*) *Machinery.* to take in air, esp. for combustion. **6.** (*tr.*) *Phonetics.* to articulate (a speech sound) without vibration of the vocal cords. **7.** to exhale or emit: *the dragon breathed fire.* **8.** (*tr.*) to impart; instil: *to breathe confidence into the actors.* **9.** (*tr.*) to speak softly; whisper. **10.** (*tr.*) to permit to rest: *to breathe a horse.* **11. breathe again, freely,** *or* **easily.** to feel relief. **12. breathe one's last.** to die or be finished or defeated. [C13: from BREATH]

breather ('briːðə) *n.* **1.** *Inf.* a short pause for rest. **2.** a person who breathes in a specified way: *a deep breather.* **3.** a vent in a container to equalize internal and external pressure.

breathing ('briːðɪŋ) *n.* **1.** the passage of air into and out of the lungs to supply the body with oxygen. **2.** a single breath: *a breathing between words.* **3.** *Phonetics.* **a.** expulsion of breath (**rough breathing**) or absence of such expulsion (**smooth breathing**) preceding the pronunciation of an initial vowel or rho in ancient Greek. **b.** either of two symbols indicating this.

breathless ('brɛθlɪs) *adj.* **1.** out of breath; gasping, etc. **2.** holding one's breath or having it taken away by excitement, etc. **3.** (esp. of the atmosphere) motionless and stifling. **4.** *Rare.* lifeless; dead. —**'breathlessly** *adv.* —**'breathlessness** *n.*

breathtaking ('brɛθ,teɪkɪŋ) *adj.* causing awe or excitement. —**'breath,takingly** *adv.*

breath test *n. Brit.* a chemical test of a driver's breath to determine the amount of alcohol he has consumed.

breathy ('brɛθɪ) *adj.* **breathier, breathiest. 1.** (of the speaking voice) accompanied by an audible emission of breath. **2.** (of the singing voice) lacking resonance. —**'breathily** *adv.* —**'breathiness** *n.*

breccia ('brɛtʃɪə) n. a rock consisting of angular fragments embedded in a finer matrix. [C18: from It.] —'**brecci,ated** adj.

Brecht (German brɛçt) n. **Bertolt** ('bɛrtɔlt). 1898–1956, German dramatist, theatrical producer, and poet, who developed a new style of "epic" theatre and a new theory of theatrical alienation, notable also for his wit and compassion. His early works include *The Threepenny Opera* (1928) and *Rise and Fall of the City of Mahagonny* (1930) (both with music by Kurt Weill). His later plays are concerned with moral and political dilemmas and include *Mother Courage and her Children* (1941), *The Good Woman of Setzuan* (1943), and *The Caucasian Chalk Circle* (1955). —'**Brechtian** adj., n.

Brecon ('brɛkən) or **Brecknock** ('brɛknɒk) n. **1.** a town in SE Wales, in Powys: textile and leather industries. Pop.: 7422 (1981). **2.** short for **Breconshire.**

Breconshire ('brɛkən,ʃɪə, -ʃə) or **Brecknockshire** ('brɛknɒk,ʃɪə, -ʃə) n. (until 1974) a county of SE Wales, now part of Powys: over half its area forms the **Brecon Beacons National Park.**

bred (brɛd) vb. the past tense and past participle of **breed.**

Breda ('bri:də; Dutch bre'da:) n. a city in the S Netherlands, in North Brabant province: residence of Charles II of England during his exile. Pop.: 119 427 (1987).

breech n. (bri:tʃ). **1.** the buttocks; rump. **2.** the lower part or bottom of something. **3.** the part of a firearm behind the barrel or bore. ~vb. (bri:tʃ, brɪtʃ). (tr.) **4.** to fit (a gun) with a breech. **5.** Arch. to clothe in breeches or any other clothing. [OE brēc, pl. of brōc leg covering]

breechblock ('bri:tʃ,blɒk) n. a metal block in breech-loading firearms that is withdrawn to insert the cartridge and replaced before firing.

breech delivery n. birth of a baby with the feet or buttocks appearing first.

breeches ('brɪtʃɪz, 'bri:-) pl. n. **1.** trousers extending to the knee or just below, worn for riding, etc. **2.** Inf. or dialect. any trousers or pants, esp. extending to the knee.

breeches buoy n. a ring-shaped life buoy with a support in the form of a pair of short breeches, in which a person is suspended for safe transfer from a ship.

breeching ('brɪtʃɪŋ, 'bri:-) n. the strap of a harness that passes behind a horse's haunches.

breechloader ('bri:tʃ,ləudə) n. a firearm that is loaded at the breech. —'**breech-,loading** adj.

breed (bri:d) vb. **breeding, bred. 1.** to bear (offspring). **2.** (tr.) to bring up; raise. **3.** to produce or cause to produce by mating; propagate. **4.** to produce new or improved strains of (domestic animals and plants). **5.** to produce or be produced; generate: *to breed trouble.* ~n. **6.** a group of organisms within a species, esp. domestic animals, having clearly defined characteristics. **7.** a lineage or race. **8.** a kind, sort, or group. [OE brēdan, of Gmc origin; rel. to BROOD]

breeder ('bri:də) n. **1.** a person who breeds plants or animals. **2.** something that reproduces. **3.** an animal kept for breeding purposes. **4.** a source or cause: *a breeder of discontent.* **5.** short for **breeder reactor.**

breeder reactor n. a type of nuclear reactor that produces more fissionable material than it consumes.

breeding ('bri:dɪŋ) n. **1.** the process of bearing offspring; reproduction. **2.** the process of producing plants or animals by hybridization, inbreeding, or other methods of reproduction. **3.** the result of good training, esp. the knowledge of correct social behaviour; refinement.

Breed's Hill (bri:dz) n. a hill in E Massachusetts, adjoining Bunker Hill: site of the Battle of Bunker Hill (1775).

breeze[1] (bri:z) n. **1.** a gentle or light wind. **2.** Meteorol. a wind of force two to six (4–31 mph) inclusive on the Beaufort scale. **3.** U.S. & Canad. inf. an easy task or state of ease. **4.** Inf., chiefly Brit. a disturbance, esp. a lively quarrel. ~vb. (intr.) **5.** to move quickly or casually: *he breezed into the room.* [C16: prob. from OSp. briza northeast wind]

breeze[2] (bri:z) n. ashes of coal, coke, or charcoal used to make breeze blocks. [C18: from F braise live coals; see BRAISE]

breeze block n. a light building brick made from the ashes of coal, coke, etc., bonded together by cement.

breezeway ('bri:z,weɪ) n. a roofed passageway connecting two buildings.

breezy ('bri:zɪ) adj. **breezier, breeziest. 1.** fresh; windy. **2.** casual or carefree; lively; light-hearted. —'**breezily** adv. —'**breeziness** n.

Bregenz (German bre':gɛnts) n. a resort in W Austria, the capital of Vorarlberg province. Pop.: 24 624 (1981).

Brel (brɛl) n. **Jacques** (ʒak). 1929–78, Belgian-born composer and singer, based in Paris. His songs include "Ne me quitte pas" ("If you Go away").

Bremen ('breɪmən) n. **1.** a state of N West Germany, centred on the city of Bremen and its outport Bremerhaven. Pop.: 657 500 (1986). Area: 404 sq. km (156 sq. miles). **2.** an industrial city and port in N West Germany, on the Weser estuary. Pop.: 524 700 (1986).

Bremerhaven (German bre:mər'ha:fən) n. a port in N West Germany: an outport for Bremen. Pop.: 132 800 (1986). Former name (until 1947): **Wesermünde.**

bremsstrahlung ('brɛmz,ʃtraːlʊŋ) n. the xradiation produced when an electrically charged particle, such as an electron, is slowed down by the electric field of an atomic nucleus. [G: braking radiation]

Brendel (German 'brɛndəl) n. **Alfred.** born 1931, Austrian pianist.

Bren gun (brɛn) n. an air-cooled gas-operated light machine gun: used by the British in World War II. [C20: after Br(no), Czechoslovakia, where it was first made and En(field), England, where manufacture was continued]

Brennan ('brɛnən) n. **Christopher John.** 1870–1932, poet and classical scholar, disciple of Mallarmé and exponent of French symbolism in Australian verse.

Brenner Pass ('brɛnə) n. a pass over the E Alps, between Austria and Italy. Highest point: 1372 m (4501 ft.).

Brent (brɛnt) n. a borough of Greater London, in the northwestern part. Pop.: 255 700 (1986 est.).

Brentano (German brɛn'ta:no) n. **Clemens (Maria)** ('kle:mənz). 1778–1842, German romantic poet and compiler of fairy stories and folk songs esp. (with Achim von Arnim) the collection *Des Knaben Wunderhorn* (1805–08).

brent goose (brɛnt) n. a small goose that has a dark grey plumage and short neck and occurs in most northern coastal regions. Also called: **brent,** (esp. U.S. and Canad.) **brant.** [C16: ? of Scand. origin]

Brentwood ('brɛnt,wʊd) n. a residential town in SE England, in SW Essex near London. Pop.: 55 762 (1981).

Brescia (Italian 'brɛʃʃa) n. a city in N Italy, in Lombardy: at its height in the 16th century. Pop.: 119 286 (1986). Ancient name: **Brixia** ('brɪksɪə).

Breslau ('brɛzlau) n. the German name for **Wroclaw.**

Bresson (French brɛsɔ̃) n. **Robert** (rɔbɛr). born 1907, French film director: his films include *Le Journal d'un curé de campagne* (1951), *Une Femme douce* (1970), and *L'Argent* (1983).

Brest (brɛst) n. **1.** a port in NW France, in Brittany: chief naval station of the country, planned by Richelieu in 1631 and fortified by Vauban. Pop.: 166 558 (1983 est.). **2.** a city in the W Soviet Union, in SW Byelorussia: Polish until 1795 and from 1921 to 1945. Pop.: 238 000 (1987). Former name (until 1921): **Brest Litovsk** (brɛst li'tɔfsk). Polish name: **Brześć nad Bugiem.**

Bretagne (brətaɲ) n. the French name for **Brittany.**

brethren ('brɛðrɪn) pl. n. Arch. except when referring to *fellow members of a religion, society, etc.* a plural of **brother.**

Breton[1] ('brɛt'n) adj. **1.** of, relating to, or characteristic of Brittany, its people, or their language. ~n. **2.** a native or inhabitant of Brittany. **3.** the Celtic language of Brittany.

Breton[2] (French brətɔ̃) n. **André** (ãdre). 1896–1966, French poet and art critic: founder and chief theorist of surrealism, publishing the first surrealist manifesto in 1924.

Breuer ('brɔɪə) n. **1. Josef** ('jo:zɛf). 1842–1925, Austrian physician: treated the mentally ill by hypnosis. **2. Marcel Lajos** (mɑ:'sɛl 'lɔjoʃ). 1902–81, U.S. architect and furniture designer, born in Hungary. He developed bent plywood and tubular metal furniture and designed the UNESCO building in Paris (1953–58).

Breughel ('brɔɪgl) n. a variant spelling of **Brueghel.**

breve (bri:v) n. **1.** an accent, ˘ placed over a vowel to indicate that it is short or is pronounced in a specified way. **2.** Music. a note, now rarely used, equivalent to two semibreves. **3.** R.C. Church. a less common word for

brief (papal letter). [C13: from Med. L, from L *brevis* short]

brevet ('brɛvɪt) *n.* **1.** a document entitling a commissioned officer to hold temporarily a higher military rank without the appropriate pay and allowances. ~*vb.* **-vetting, -vetted** *or* **-veting, -veted. 2.** (*tr.*) to promote by brevet. [C14: from OF, from *brief* letter; see BRIEF] —'**brevetcy** *n.*

breviary ('briːvjərɪ) *n., pl.* **-ries.** *R.C. Church.* a book of psalms, hymns, prayers, etc., to be recited daily by clerics and certain members of religious orders as part of the divine office. [C16: from L *breviārium* an abridged version, from *brevis* short]

brevity ('brɛvɪtɪ) *n., pl.* **-ties. 1.** conciseness of expression; lack of verbosity. **2.** a short duration; brief time. [C16: from L, from *brevis* BRIEF]

brew (bruː) *vb.* **1.** to make (beer, ale, etc.) from malt and other ingredients by steeping, boiling, and fermentation. **2.** to prepare (a drink, such as tea) by boiling or infusing. **3.** (*tr.*) to devise or plan: *to brew a plot.* **4.** (*intr.*) to be in the process of being brewed. **5.** (*intr.*) to be impending or forming: *there's a storm brewing.* ~*n.* **6.** a beverage produced by brewing, esp. beer or beer. **7.** an instance or time of brewing: *last year's brew.* [OE *brēowan*] —'**brewer** *n.*

brewery ('bruərɪ) *n., pl.* **-eries.** a place where beer, ale, etc., is brewed.

brewing ('bruːɪŋ) *n.* a quantity of a beverage brewed at one time.

Brewster ('bruːstə) *n.* Sir **David.** 1781–1868, Scottish physicist, noted for his studies of the polarization of light.

Brezhnev ('brɛʒnɛf; *Russian* 'brjɛʒnɪf) *n.* **Leonid Ilyich** (lɪa'nit 'ilitʃ). 1906–82, Soviet statesman; president of the Soviet Union (1977–82); general secretary of the Soviet Communist Party (1964–82).

Brian ('braɪən) *n.* **Havergal** ('hævəgəl). 1876–1972, English composer, who wrote 32 symphonies, including the large-scale *Gothic Symphony* (1919–27).

Brian Boru (bə'ruː) *n.* ?941–1014, king of Ireland (1002–14): killed during the defeat of the Danes at the battle of Clontarf.

Briand (*French* briɑ̃) *n.* **Aristide** (aristid). 1862–1932, French socialist statesman: prime minister of France 11 times. He was responsible for the separation of Church and State (1905) and he advocated a United States of Europe. Nobel peace prize 1926.

briar[1] *or* **brier** ('braɪə) *n.* **1.** Also called: **tree heath.** a shrub of S Europe, having a hard woody root (briarroot). **2.** a tobacco pipe made from the root of this plant. [C19: from F *bruyère* heath] —'**briary** *or* '**briery** *adj.*

briar[2] ('braɪə) *n.* a variant spelling of **brier**[1].

Briareus (braɪ'ɛərɪəs) *n. Greek myth.* a giant with a hundred arms and fifty heads who aided Zeus and the Olympians against the Titans. —**Bri'arean** *adj.*

briarroot *or* **brierroot** ('braɪə,ruːt) *n.* the hard woody root of the briar, used for making tobacco pipes. Also called: **briarwood, brierwood.**

bribe (braɪb) *vb.* **1.** to promise, offer, or give something, often illegally, to (a person) to procure services or gain influence. ~*n.* **2.** a reward, such as money or favour, given or offered for this purpose. **3.** any persuasion or lure. [C14: from OF *briber* to beg, from ?] —'**bribery** *n.*

bric-a-brac ('brɪkə,bræk) *n.* miscellaneous small objects, esp. furniture and curios, kept because they are ornamental or rare. [C19: from F]

brick (brɪk) *n.* **1. a.** a rectangular block of clay mixed with sand and fired in a kiln or baked by the sun, used in building construction. **b.** (*as modifier*): *a brick house.* **2.** the material used to make such blocks. **3.** any rectangular block: *a brick of ice.* **4.** bricks collectively. **5.** *Inf.* a reliable, trustworthy, or helpful person. **6.** *Brit.* a child's building block. **7. drop a brick.** *Brit. inf.* to make a tactless or indiscreet remark. **8. like a ton of bricks.** *Inf.* with great force; severely. ~*vb.* **9.** (*tr.; usually foll. by in, up, or over*) to construct, line, pave, fill, or wall up with bricks: *to brick up a window.* [C15: from OF *brique,* from MDu. *bricke*] —'**bricky** *adj.*

brickbat ('brɪk,bæt) *n.* **1.** a piece of brick or similar material, esp. one used as a weapon. **2.** blunt criticism.

brickie ('brɪkɪ) *n. Inf.* a bricklayer.

bricklayer ('brɪk,leɪə) *n.* a person trained or skilled in laying bricks. —'**brick,laying** *n.*

brick red *n., adj.* (of) a reddish-brown colour.

brickwork ('brɪk,wɜːk) *n.* **1.** a structure built of bricks. **2.** construction using bricks.

brickyard ('brɪk,jɑːd) *n.* a place in which bricks are made, stored, or sold.

bridal ('braɪdəl) *adj.* of or relating to a bride or a wedding; nuptial. [OE *brydealu,* lit.: "bride ale", that is, wedding feast]

bride (braɪd) *n.* a woman who has just been or is about to be married. [OE *bryd*]

Bride (braɪd) *n.* See (Saint) **Bridget.**

bridegroom ('braɪd,gruːm, -,grʊm) *n.* a man who has just been or is about to be married. [C14: changed (through infl. of GROOM) from OE *brydguma,* from *bryd* BRIDE + *guma* man]

bride price *or* **wealth** *n.* (in some societies) money, property, or services given by a bridegroom to the kinsmen of his bride.

bridesmaid ('braɪdz,meɪd) *n.* a girl or young unmarried woman who attends a bride at her wedding.

bridge[1] (brɪdʒ) *n.* **1.** a structure that spans and provides a passage over a road, railway, river, or some other obstacle. **2.** something that resembles this in shape or function. **3.** the hard ridge at the upper part of the nose, formed by the underlying nasal bones. **4.** the part of a pair of glasses that rests on the nose. **5.** Also called: **bridgework.** a dental plate containing one or more artificial teeth that is secured to the surrounding natural teeth. **6.** a platform from which a ship is piloted and navigated. **7.** a piece of wood, usually fixed, supporting the strings of a violin, guitar, etc., and transmitting their vibrations to the sounding board. **8.** Also called: **bridge passage.** a passage in a musical, literary, or dramatic work linking two or more important sections. **9.** Also called: **bridge circuit.** *Electronics.* any of several networks across which a device is connected for measuring resistance, capacitance, etc. **10.** *Billiards, snooker.* a support for a cue. **11. cross a bridge when (one) comes to it.** to deal with a problem only when it arises. ~*vb.* (*tr.*) **12.** to build or provide a bridge over something; span: *to bridge a river.* **13.** to connect or reduce the distance between: *let us bridge our differences.* [OE *brycg*] —'**bridgeable** *adj.*

bridge[2] (brɪdʒ) *n.* a card game for four players, based on whist, in which one hand (the dummy) is exposed and the trump suit decided by bidding between the players. See also **contract bridge, auction bridge.** [C19: from ?]

Bridge (brɪdʒ) *n.* **Frank.** 1879–1941, English composer, esp. of chamber music. He taught Benjamin Britten.

bridgehead ('brɪdʒ,hɛd) *n.* **1.** *Mil.* an area of ground secured or to be taken on the enemy's side of an obstacle. **2.** *Mil.* a fortified or defensive position at the end of a bridge nearest to the enemy. **3.** an advantageous position gained for future expansion.

Bridge of Sighs *n.* a covered 16th-century bridge in Venice, between the Doge's Palace and the prisons, through which prisoners were formerly led to trial or execution.

Bridgeport ('brɪdʒ,pɔːt) *n.* a port in SW Connecticut, on Long Island Sound. Pop.: 142 546 (1980).

bridge roll *n.* a soft bread roll in a long thin shape. [C20: from BRIDGE[2] *or* ? BRIDGE[1]]

Bridges ('brɪdʒɪz) *n.* **Robert (Seymour).** 1844–1930, English poet: poet laureate (1913–30).

Bridget ('brɪdʒɪt) *n.* **Saint. 1.** Also called: **Bride, Brigid.** 453–523 A.D., Irish abbess; a patron saint of Ireland. Feast day: Feb. 1. **2.** Also called: **Birgitta.** ?1303–73, Swedish nun and visionary; patron saint of Sweden. Feast day: Oct. 8.

Bridgetown ('brɪdʒ,taʊn) *n.* the capital of Barbados, a port on the SW coast. Pop.: 7517 (1980).

bridgework ('brɪdʒ,wɜːk) *n.* a partial denture attached to the surrounding teeth.

bridging loan *n.* a loan made to cover the period between two transactions, such as the buying of another house before the sale of the first is completed.

Bridgman ('brɪdʒmən) *n.* **Percy Williams.** 1882–1961, U.S. physicist: Nobel prize for physics (1946) for his work on high-pressure physics and thermodynamics.

Bridgwater ('brɪdʒ,wɔːtə) *n.* a town in SW England, in central Somerset. Pop.: 26 132 (1981).

bridle ('braɪdəl) *n.* **1.** a headgear for a horse, etc., consisting of a series of buckled straps and a metal mouthpiece (bit) by which the animal is controlled through the reins. **2.** something that curbs or restrains; check. **3.** a Y-shaped

cable, rope, or chain, used for holding, towing, etc. ~*vb.*
4. (*tr.*) to put a bridle on (a horse, mule, etc.). **5.** (*tr.*) to restrain; curb: *he bridled his rage.* **6.** (*intr.*; often foll. by *at*) to show anger, scorn, or indignation. [OE *brigdels*]
bridle path *n.* a path suitable for riding or leading horses.
Brie (bri:) *n.* a soft creamy white cheese. [C19: F, after *Brie*, region in N France where it originated]
brief (bri:f) *adj.* **1.** short in duration. **2.** short in length or extent; scanty: *a brief bikini.* **3.** abrupt in manner; brusque: *the professor was brief with me.* **4.** terse or concise. ~*n.* **5.** a condensed statement or written synopsis; abstract. **6.** *Law.* a document containing all the facts and points of law of a case by which a solicitor instructs a barrister to represent a client. **7.** *R.C. Church.* a letter issuing from the Roman court written in modern characters, as contrasted with a papal bull; papal brief. **8.** Also called: **briefing.** instructions. **9. hold a brief for.** to argue for; champion. **10. in brief.** in short; to sum up. ~*vb.* (*tr.*) **11.** to prepare or instruct by giving a summary of relevant facts. **12.** to make a summary or synopsis of. **13.** *English law.* **a.** to instruct (a barrister) by brief. **b.** to retain (a barrister) as counsel. [C14: from OF *bref*, from L *brevis*] —'**briefly** *adv.* —'**briefness** *n.*
briefcase ('bri:f,keɪs) *n.* a flat portable case, often of leather, for carrying papers, books, etc.
briefing ('bri:fɪŋ) *n.* **1.** a meeting at which information and instructions are given. **2.** the facts presented at such a meeting.
briefless ('bri:flɪs) *adj.* (said of a barrister) without clients.
briefs (bri:fs) *pl. n.* men's underpants or women's pants without legs.
brier[1] *or* **briar** ('braɪə) *n.* any of various thorny shrubs or other plants, such as the sweetbrier. [OE *brēr*, *brǣr*, from ?] —'**briery** *or* '**briary** *adj.*
brier[2] ('braɪə) *n.* a variant spelling of **briar**[1].
brierroot ('braɪə,ru:t) *n.* a variant spelling of **briarroot**. Also called: **brierwood.**
brig[1] (brɪg) *n.* **1.** *Naut.* a two-masted square-rigger. **2.** *Chiefly U.S.* a prison, esp. in a navy ship. [C18: shortened from BRIGANTINE]
brig[2] (brɪg) *n.* a Scot. and N English word for a **bridge**[1].
Brig. *abbrev. for* Brigadier.
brigade (brɪ'geɪd) *n.* **1.** a military formation smaller than a division and usually commanded by a brigadier. **2.** a group of people organized for a certain task: *a rescue brigade.* ~*vb.* (*tr.*) **3.** to organize into a brigade. [C17: from OF, from OIt., from *brigare* to fight; see BRIGAND]
brigadier (,brɪgə'dɪə) *n.* **1.** an officer of the British Army or Royal Marines junior to a major general but senior to a colonel, usually commanding a brigade. **2.** an equivalent rank in other armed forces. [C17: from F, from BRIGADE]
brigalow ('brɪgələʊ) *n. Austral.* **a.** any of various acacia trees, forming dense scrub. **b.** (*as modifier*): *brigalow country.* [C19: from Abor.]
brigand ('brɪgənd) *n.* a bandit, esp. a member of a gang operating in mountainous areas. [C14: from OF, from OIt. *brigante* fighter, from *briga* strife] —'**brigandage** *or* '**brigandry** *n.*
brigantine ('brɪgən,ti:n, -,taɪn) *n.* a two-masted sailing ship, rigged square on the foremast and fore-and-aft on the mainmast. [C16: from OIt. *brigantino* pirate ship, from *brigante* BRIGAND]
Briggs (brɪgz) *n.* **Henry.** 1561–1631, English mathematician: introduced common logarithms.
Brighouse ('brɪg,haʊs) *n.* a town in N England, in West Yorkshire. Pop.: 35 241 (1981).
bright (braɪt) *adj.* **1.** emitting or reflecting much light; shining. **2.** (of colours) intense or vivid. **3.** full of promise: *a bright future.* **4.** full of animation; cheerful: *a bright face.* **5.** *Inf.* quick-witted or clever: *a bright child.* **6.** magnificent; glorious. **7.** polished; glistening. **8.** (of a liquid) translucent and clear. **9. bright and early.** very early in the morning. ~*adv.* **10.** brightly: *the fire was burning bright.* [OE *beorht*] —'**brightly** *adv.* —'**brightness** *n.*
Bright (braɪt) *n.* **John.** 1811–89, British liberal statesman, economist, and advocate of free trade: with Richard Cobden he led the Anti-Corn-Law League (1838–46).
brighten ('braɪtⁿn) *vb.* **1.** to make or become bright or brighter. **2.** to make or become cheerful.
Brighton ('braɪtⁿn) *n.* a resort in S England, in East Sussex: patronized by the Prince Regent, who had the Royal

Pavilion built (1782); seat of the University of Sussex. Pop.: 146 134 (1981).
Bright's disease (braɪts) *n.* chronic inflammation of the kidneys; chronic nephritis. [C19: after Richard *Bright* (1789–1858), E physician]
brightwork ('braɪt,wɜ:k) *n.* shiny metal trimmings or fittings on ships, cars, etc.
Brigid ('brɪdʒɪd) *n.* See (Saint) **Bridget.**
brill (brɪl) *n.*, *pl.* **brill** *or* **brills.** a European flatfish similar to the turbot. [C15: prob. from Cornish *brÿthel* mackerel, from OCornish *brÿth* speckled]
Brillat-Savarin (*French* brijasavarɛ̃) *n.* **Anthelme** (ãtɛlm). 1755–1826, French politician and gourmet; author of *Physiologie du Goût* (1825).
brilliance ('brɪljəns) *or* **brilliancy** *n.* **1.** great brightness; radiance. **2.** excellence or distinction in physical or mental ability; exceptional talent. **3.** splendour; magnificence.
brilliant ('brɪljənt) *adj.* **1.** shining with light; sparkling. **2.** (of a colour) reflecting a considerable amount of light; vivid. **3.** outstanding; exceptional: *a brilliant success.* **4.** splendid; magnificent: *a brilliant show.* **5.** of outstanding intelligence or intellect: *a brilliant mind.* ~*n.* **6.** Also called: **brilliant cut. a.** a cut for diamonds and other gemstones in the form of two many-faceted pyramids joined at their bases. **b.** a diamond of this cut. [C17: from F *brillant* shining, from It., from *brillo* BERYL] —'**brilliantly** *adv.*
brilliantine ('brɪljən,ti:n) *n.* a perfumed oil used to make the hair smooth and shiny. [C19: from F, from *brillant* shining]
brim (brɪm) *n.* **1.** the upper rim of a vessel: *the brim of a cup.* **2.** a projecting rim or edge: *the brim of a hat.* **3.** the brink or edge of something. ~*vb.* **brimming, brimmed. 4.** to fill or be full to the brim: *eyes brimming with tears.* [C13: from MHG *brem*] —'**brimless** *adj.*
brimful *or* **brimfull** (,brɪm'fʊl) *adj.* (*postpositive;* foll. by *of*) filled up to the brim (with).
brimstone ('brɪm,stəʊn) *n.* **1.** an obsolete name for **sulphur. 2.** a common yellow butterfly of N temperate regions of the Old World. [OE *brynstān;* see BURN[1], STONE]
Brindisi (*Italian* 'brindizi) *n.* a port in SE Italy, in SE Apulia: important naval base in Roman times and a centre of the Crusades in the Middle Ages. Pop.: 89 786 (1981). Ancient name: **Brundisium.**
brindle ('brɪndⁿl) *n.* **1.** a brindled animal. **2.** a brindled colouring. [C17: back formation from BRINDLED]
brindled ('brɪndⁿld) *adj.* brown or grey streaked or patched with a darker colour: *a brindled dog.* [C17: changed from C15 *brended*, lit.: branded]
brine (braɪn) *n.* **1.** a strong solution of salt and water, used for salting and pickling meats, etc. **2.** the sea or its water. ~*vb.* **3.** (*tr.*) to soak in or treat with brine. [OE *brīne*] —'**brinish** *adj.*
bring (brɪŋ) *vb.* **bringing, brought.** (*tr.*) **1.** to carry, convey, or take (something or someone) to a designated place or person: *bring that book to me.* **2.** to cause to happen or occur to (oneself or another): *to bring disrespect on oneself.* **3.** to cause to happen as a consequence: *responsibility brings maturity.* **4.** to cause to come to mind: *it brought back memories.* **5.** to cause to be in a certain state, position, etc.: *the punch brought him to his knees.* **6.** to force, persuade, or make (oneself): *I couldn't bring myself to do it.* **7.** to sell for; fetch: *the painting brought 20 pounds.* **8.** *Law.* **a.** to institute (proceedings, charges, etc.). **b.** to put (evidence, etc.) before a tribunal. **9. bring forth.** to give birth to. ~See also **bring about, bring down,** etc. [OE *bringan*] —'**bringer** *n.*
bring about *vb.* (*tr.*, *adv.*) **1.** to cause to happen. **2.** to turn (a ship) around.
bring-and-buy sale *n. Brit. & N.Z.* an informal sale, often for charity, to which people bring items for sale and buy those that others have brought.
bring down *vb.* (*tr.*, *adv.*) to cause to fall.
bring forward *vb.* (*tr.*, *adv.*) **1.** to present or introduce (a subject) for discussion. **2.** *Book-keeping.* to transfer (a sum) to the top of the next page or column.
bring in *vb.* (*tr.*, *adv.*) **1.** to yield (income, profit, or cash). **2.** to produce or return (a verdict). **3.** to introduce (a legislative bill, etc.).
bring off *vb.* (*tr.*, *adv.*) to succeed in achieving (something), esp. with difficulty.

bring out vb. (tr., adv.) **1.** to produce or publish or have published. **2.** to expose, reveal, or cause to be seen: *she brought out the best in me.* **3.** (foll. by *in*) to cause (a person) to become covered (with spots, a rash, etc.). **4.** *Brit.* to introduce (a girl) formally into society as a debutante.

bring over vb. (tr., adv.) to cause (a person) to change allegiances.

bring round or **around** vb. (tr., adv.) **1.** to restore (a person) to consciousness, esp. after a faint. **2.** to convince (another person, usually an opponent) of an opinion or point of view.

bring to vb. (tr., adv.) **1.** to restore (a person) to consciousness. **2.** to cause (a ship) to turn into the wind and reduce her headway.

bring up vb. (tr., adv.) **1.** to care for and train (a child); rear. **2.** to raise (a subject) for discussion; mention. **3.** to vomit (food).

brinjal ('brɪndʒəl) n. (in India and Africa) another name for the **aubergine**. [C17: from Port. *berinjela*, from Ar.]

brink (brɪŋk) n. **1.** the edge, border, or verge of a steep place. **2.** the land at the edge of a body of water. **3.** the verge of an event or state: *the brink of disaster.* [C13: from MDu. *brinc*, of Gmc origin]

brinkmanship ('brɪŋkmən,ʃɪp) n. the art or practice of pressing a dangerous situation, esp. in international affairs, to the limit of safety and peace in order to win an advantage.

briny ('braɪnɪ) adj. **brinier, briniest. 1.** of or resembling brine; salty. ~n. **2.** (preceded by *the*) *Inf.* the sea. —'**brininess** n.

brio ('briːəʊ) n. liveliness or vigour; spirit. See also **con brio**. [C19: from It., of Celtic origin]

brioche ('briːəʊʃ, -ɒʃ) n. a soft roll made from a very light yeast dough. [C19: from Norman dialect, from *brier* to knead, of Gmc origin]

briquette or **briquet** (brɪ'kɛt) n. a small brick made of compressed coal dust, sawdust, charcoal, etc., used for fuel. [C19: from F: a little brick, from *brique* BRICK]

Brisbane ('brɪzbən) n. a port in E Australia, the capital of Queensland: founded in 1824 as a penal settlement; vast agricultural hinterland. Pop.: 1 180 400 (1988).

brisk (brɪsk) adj. **1.** lively and quick; vigorous: *a brisk walk.* **2.** invigorating or sharp: *brisk weather.* ~vb. **3.** (often foll. by *up*) to enliven; make or become brisk. [C16: prob. var. of BRUSQUE] —'**briskly** adv. —'**briskness** n.

brisket ('brɪskɪt) n. **1.** the breast of a four-legged animal. **2.** the meat from this part, esp. of beef. [C14: prob. from ON]

brisling ('brɪslɪŋ) n. another name for a **sprat**. [C20: from Norwegian; rel. to obs. Danish *bretling*]

bristle ('brɪsəl) n. **1.** any short stiff hair of an animal or plant, such as on a pig's back. **2.** something resembling these hairs: *toothbrush bristle.* ~vb. **3.** (when *intr.*, often foll. by *up*) to stand up or cause to stand up like bristles. **4.** (intr.) sometimes foll. by *up*) to show anger, indignation, etc.: *she bristled at the suggestion.* **5.** (intr.) to be thickly covered or set: *the target bristled with arrows.* [C13 *bristil, brustel*, from earlier *brust*, from OE *byrst*] —'**bristly** adj.

Bristol ('brɪstəl) n. a port and industrial city in SW England, administrative centre of the county of Avon, on the River Avon seven miles from its mouth on the Bristol Channel: a major port, trading with America, in the 17th and 18th centuries; the modern port consists chiefly of docks at Avonmouth and Portishead; noted for the **Clifton Suspension Bridge** (designed by I. K. Brunel, 1834) over the Avon gorge; university (1909). Pop.: 394 000 (1985).

Bristol board n. a heavy smooth cardboard of fine quality, used for drawing.

Bristol Channel n. an inlet of the Atlantic, between S Wales and SW England, merging into the Severn estuary. Length: about 137 km (85 miles).

Bristol fashion adv., adj. (postpositive) in good order; efficiently arranged.

bristols ('brɪstəlz) pl. n. Brit. sl. a woman's breasts. [C20: short for *Bristol Cities*, rhyming slang for *titties*]

Bristow ('brɪstəʊ) n. **Eric.** born 1957, British darts player.

Brit (brɪt) n. Inf. a British person.

Brit. abbrev. for: **1.** Britain. **2.** British.

Britain ('brɪtən) n. another name for **Great Britain** or the **United Kingdom**.

Britannia (brɪ'tænɪə) n. **1.** a female warrior carrying a trident and wearing a helmet, personifying Great Britain or the British Empire. **2.** (in the ancient Roman Empire) the S part of Great Britain.

Britannia metal n. an alloy of tin with antimony and copper: used for decorative purposes and for bearings.

Britannic (brɪ'tænɪk) adj. of Britain; British (esp. in **His** or **Her Britannic Majesty**).

britches ('brɪtʃɪz) pl. n. a variant spelling of **breeches**.

Briticism ('brɪtɪ,sɪzəm) n. a custom, linguistic usage, or other feature peculiar to Britain or its people. Also: **Britishism**.

British ('brɪtɪʃ) adj. **1.** of or denoting Britain. **2.** relating to, denoting, or characteristic of the inhabitants of Britain. **3.** relating to or denoting the English language as spoken and written in Britain. **4.** of or relating to the Commonwealth: *British subjects.* ~n. **5. the British.** (functioning as pl.) the natives or inhabitants of Britain. —'**Britishness** n.

▷ **Usage.** See at **English**.

British Antarctic Territory n. a British colony in the S Atlantic: created in 1962 and consisting of the South Shetland Islands, the South Orkney Islands, and Graham Land; formerly part of the Falkland Islands Dependencies.

British Cameroons pl. n. a former British trust territory of West Africa. See **Cameroon**.

British Columbia n. a province of W Canada, on the Pacific coast: largely mountainous with extensive forests, rich mineral resources, and important fisheries. Capital: Victoria. Pop.: 2 883 367 (1986). Area: 930 532 sq. km (359 279 sq. miles). Abbrev.: **BC.** —**British Columbian** n., adj.

British East Africa n. the former British possessions of Uganda, Kenya, Tanganyika, and Zanzibar, before their independence in the 1960s.

British Empire n. (formerly) the United Kingdom and the territories under its control, which reached its greatest extent at the end of World War I when it embraced over a quarter of the world's population and more than a quarter of the world's land surface.

Britisher ('brɪtɪʃə) n. (not used by the British) **1.** a native or inhabitant of Great Britain. **2.** any British subject.

British Guiana n. the former name (until 1966) of **Guyana**.

British Honduras n. the former name of **Belize**.

British India n. the 17 provinces of India formerly governed by the British under the British sovereign: ceased to exist in 1947 when the independent states of India and Pakistan were created.

British Indian Ocean Territory n. a British colony in the Indian Ocean: consists of the Chagos Archipelago (formerly a dependency of Mauritius) and formerly included (until 1976) Aldabra, Farquhar, and Des Roches, now administratively part of the Seychelles.

British Isles pl. n. a group of islands in W Europe, consisting of Great Britain, Ireland, the Isle of Man, Orkney, the Shetland Islands, the Channel Islands belonging to Great Britain, and the islands adjacent to these.

Britishism ('brɪtɪ,ʃɪzəm) n. a variant of **Briticism**.

British Legion n. Brit. an organization founded in 1921 to provide services and assistance for former members of the armed forces.

British North America n. (formerly) Canada or its constituent regions or provinces that formed part of the British Empire.

British Somaliland n. a former British protectorate (1884–1960) in E Africa, on the Gulf of Aden: united with Italian Somaliland in 1960 to form the Somali Republic.

British thermal unit n. a unit of heat in the fps system equal to the quantity of heat required to raise the temperature of 1 pound of water by 1°F. 1 British thermal unit is equivalent to 1055.06 joules. Abbrev.: **btu, BThU.**

British Virgin Islands pl. n. a British colony in the West Indies, consisting of 36 islands in the E Virgin Islands: formerly part of the Federation of the Leeward Islands (1871–1956). Capital: Road Town, on Tortola. Pop.: 11 152 (1980). Area: 153 sq. km (59 sq. miles).

British West Africa n. the former British possessions of Nigeria, The Gambia, Sierra Leone, and the Gold Coast, and the former trust territories of Togoland and Cameroons.

British West Indies *pl. n.* the states in the Caribbean that are members of the Commonwealth: the Bahamas, Barbados, Jamaica, Trinidad and Tobago, the Leeward Islands, and the Windward Islands.

Briton ('brɪtªn) *n.* **1.** a native or inhabitant of Britain. **2.** *History.* any of the early Celtic inhabitants of S Britain. [C13: from OF *Breton*, of Celtic origin]

Brittany ('brɪtənɪ) *n.* a region of NW France, the peninsula between the English Channel and the Bay of Biscay: settled by Celtic refugees from Wales and Cornwall during the Anglo-Saxon invasions; disputed between England and France until 1364. Breton name: **Breiz** (braɪz). French name: **Bretagne**.

Britten ('brɪtªn) *n.* **(Edward) Benjamin,** Baron Britten. 1913–76, English composer, pianist, and conductor. His works include the operas *Peter Grimes* (1945) and *Billy Budd* (1951), the choral works *Hymn to St Cecilia* (1942) and *A War Requiem* (1962), and numerous orchestral pieces.

brittle ('brɪtªl) *adj.* **1.** easily cracked, snapped, or broken; fragile. **2.** curt or irritable. **3.** hard or sharp in quality. ~*n.* **4.** a crunchy sweet made with treacle and nuts: *peanut brittle.* [C14: ult. from OE *brēotan* to break] — **'brittleness** *n.*

brittle-star *n.* an echinoderm occurring on the sea bottom and having long slender arms radiating from a small central disc.

Brno ('bɜːnəʊ; *Czech* 'brnɔ) *n.* a city in central Czechoslovakia, capital of Moravia: the country's second largest city. Pop.: 385 000 (1986). German name: **Brünn.**

bro. *abbrev. for* brother.

broach (brəʊtʃ) *vb.* (*tr.*) **1.** to initiate (a topic) for discussion. **2.** to tap or pierce (a container) to draw off (a liquid): *to broach a cask.* **3.** to open in order to begin to use. ~*n.* **4.** a long tapered toothed cutting tool for enlarging holes. **5.** a spit for roasting meat, etc. [C14: from OF *broche*, from L *brochus* projecting]

broad (brɔːd) *adj.* **1.** having relatively great breadth or width. **2.** of vast extent; spacious: *a broad plain.* **3.** (*postpositive*) from one side to the other: *four miles broad.* **4.** of great scope or potential: *that invention had broad applications.* **5.** not detailed; general: *broad plans.* **6.** clear and open; full (esp. in **broad daylight**). **7.** obvious or plain: *broad hints.* **8.** liberal; tolerant: *a broad political stance.* **9.** widely spread; extensive: *broad support.* **10.** vulgar; coarse; indecent: *a broad joke.* **11.** (of a dialect or pronunciation) consisting of a large number of speech sounds characteristic of a particular geographic area: *a broad Yorkshire accent.* **12.** *Finance.* denoting an assessment of liquidity as including notes and coin in circulation with the public, banks' till money and balances, most private-sector bank deposits, and sterling bank-deposit certificates: *broad money.* Cf. **narrow** (sense 7). **13.** *Phonetics.* the long vowel in English words such as *father, half,* as represented in Received Pronunciation. ~*n.* **14.** the broad part of something. **15.** *Sl., chiefly U.S. & Canad.* **a.** a girl or woman. **b.** a prostitute. **16.** See **Broads.** [OE *brād*] — **'broadly** *adv.*

B-road *n.* a secondary road in Britain.

broad arrow *n.* **1.** a mark shaped like a broad arrowhead designating British government property and formerly used on prison clothing. **2.** an arrow with a broad head.

broad bean *n.* **1.** an erect annual Eurasian bean plant cultivated for its large edible flattened seeds. **2.** the seed of this plant.

broadcast ('brɔːd,kɑːst) *vb.* **-casting, -cast** *or* **-casted. 1.** to transmit (announcements or programmes) on radio or television. **2.** (*intr.*) to take part in a radio or television programme. **3.** (*tr.*) to make widely known throughout an area: *to broadcast news.* **4.** (*tr.*) to scatter (seed, etc.) over an area, esp. by hand. ~*n.* **5. a.** a transmission or programme on radio or television. **b.** (*as modifier*): *a broadcast signal.* **6.** the act of scattering seeds. ~*adj.* **7.** dispersed over a wide area. ~*adv.* **8.** far and wide. — **'broad,caster** *n.* — **'broad,casting** *n.*

Broad Church *n.* **1.** a party within the Church of England which favours a broad and liberal interpretation of Anglican doctrine. ~*adj.* **Broad-Church. 2.** of or relating to this party.

broadcloth ('brɔːd,klɒθ) *n.* **1.** fabric woven on a wide loom. **2.** a closely woven fabric of wool, worsted, cotton, or rayon with lustrous finish, used for clothing.

broaden ('brɔːdªn) *vb.* to make or become broad or broader; widen.

broad gauge *n.* **1.** a railway track with a greater distance between the lines than the standard gauge of 56½ inches. ~*adj.* **broad-gauge. 2.** of or denoting a railway having this track.

broad-leaved *adj.* denoting trees other than conifers; having broad rather than needle-shaped leaves.

broadloom ('brɔːd,luːm) *n.* (*modifier*) of or designating carpets woven on a wide loom.

broad-minded *adj.* **1.** tolerant of opposing viewpoints; not prejudiced; liberal. **2.** not easily shocked by permissive sexual habits, pornography, etc. — ,**broad-'mindedly** *adv.* — ,**broad'mindedness** *n.*

Broads (brɔːdz) *pl. n.* **the.** a group of shallow navigable lakes, connected by a network of rivers, in E England, in Norfolk and Suffolk.

broadsheet ('brɔːd,ʃiːt) *n.* **1.** a newspaper having a large format, approximately 15 by 24 inches (38 by 61 centimetres). **2.** another word for **broadside** (sense 4).

broadside ('brɔːd,saɪd) *n.* **1.** *Naut.* the entire side of a vessel. **2.** *Naval.* **a.** all the armament fired from one side of a warship. **b.** the simultaneous discharge of such armament. **3.** a strong or abusive verbal or written attack. **4.** Also called: **broadside ballad.** a ballad or popular song printed on one side of a sheet of paper, esp. in 16th-century England. ~*adv.* **5.** with a broader side facing an object; sideways.

broad-spectrum *n.* (*modifier*) effective against a wide variety of diseases or microorganisms: *a broad-spectrum antibiotic.*

broadsword ('brɔːd,sɔːd) *n.* a broad-bladed sword used for cutting rather than stabbing.

broadtail ('brɔːd,teɪl) *n.* **1.** the highly valued black wavy fur obtained from the skins of newly born karakul lambs; caracul. **2.** another name for **karakul.**

Broadway ('brɔːd,weɪ) *n.* **1.** a thoroughfare in New York City: the centre of the commercial theatre in the U.S. ~*adj.* **2.** of, relating to, or suitable for the commercial theatre, esp. on Broadway.

Broca (*French* brɔka) *n.* **Paul** (pɔl). 1824–80, French surgeon and anthropologist who discovered the motor speech centre of the brain and did pioneering work in brain surgery.

brocade (brəʊ'keɪd) *n.* **1.** a rich fabric woven with a raised design, often using gold or silver threads. ~*vb.* **2.** (*tr.*) to weave with such a design. [C17: from Sp. *brocado*, from It. *broccato* embossed fabric, from L *brochus* projecting]

broccoli ('brɒkəlɪ) *n.* **1.** a cultivated variety of cabbage having branched greenish flower heads. **2.** the flower head, eaten as a vegetable before the buds have opened. [C17: from It., pl. of *broccolo* a little sprout, from *brocco* sprout]

broch (brɒk, brɒx) *n.* (in Scotland) a prehistoric circular dry-stone tower large enough to serve as a fortified home. [C17: from ON *borg*; rel. to OE *burh* settlement, burgh]

brochette (brɒ'ʃɛt) *n.* a skewer or small spit, used for holding pieces of meat, etc., while roasting or grilling. [C19: from OF *brochete* small pointed tool; see BROACH]

brochure ('brəʊʃjʊə, -ʃə) *n.* a pamphlet or booklet, esp. one containing summarized or introductory information or advertising. [C18: from F, from *brocher* to stitch (a book)]

brock (brɒk) *n.* a Brit. name for **badger** (sense 1). [OE *broc*, of Celtic origin]

Brocken (*German* 'brɔkən) *n.* a mountain in East Germany: the highest peak of the Harz Mountains; important in German folklore. Height: 1142 m (3747 ft.). The **Brocken Bow** or **Brocken Spectre** is an atmospheric phenomenon in which an observer, when the sun is low, may see his enlarged shadow against the clouds, often surrounded by coloured lights.

brocket ('brɒkɪt) *n.* a small deer of tropical America, having small unbranched antlers. [C15: from Anglo-F *broquet*, from *broque* horn]

broderie anglaise ('brəʊdərɪ ɑːŋ'glɛz) *n.* open embroidery on white cotton, fine linen, etc. [C19: from F: English embroidery]

Broederbond ('brudə,bɒnt, 'bruːdə,bɒnt) *n.* (in South Africa) a secret society of Afrikaner Nationalists. [Afrik.: band of brothers]

Broglie (brɔj) n. **1.** Prince **Louis Victor de** (lwi viktɔr də). 1892–1987, French physicist, noted for his research in quantum mechanics and his development of wave mechanics: Nobel prize for physics 1929. **2.** his brother, **Maurice** (mɔris), Duc de Broglie. 1875–1960, French physicist, noted for his research into x-ray spectra.

brogue[1] (brəʊg) n. a broad gentle-sounding dialectal accent, esp. that used by the Irish in speaking English. [C18: from ?]

brogue[2] (brəʊg) n. **1.** a sturdy walking shoe, often with ornamental perforations. **2.** an untanned shoe worn formerly in Ireland and Scotland. [C16: from Irish Gaelic bróg shoe]

broil[1] (brɔɪl) vb. **1.** the usual U.S. & Canad. word for **grill** (sense 1). **2.** to become or cause to become extremely hot. **3.** (intr.) to be furious. [C14: from OF bruillir to burn, from ?]

broil[2] (brɔɪl) Arch. ~n. **1.** a loud quarrel or disturbance; brawl. ~vb. **2.** (intr.) to brawl; quarrel. [C16: from OF brouiller to mix]

broiler ('brɔɪlə) n. **1.** a young tender chicken suitable for roasting. **2.** a pan, grate, etc., for broiling food. **3.** a very hot day.

broke (brəʊk) vb. **1.** the past tense of **break.** ~adj. **2.** Inf. having no money; bankrupt. **3. go for broke.** Sl. to risk everything in a gambling or other venture.

broken ('brəʊkən) vb. **1.** the past participle of **break.** ~adj. **2.** fractured, smashed, or splintered: a broken vase. **3.** interrupted; disturbed; disconnected: broken sleep. **4.** intermittent or discontinuous: broken sunshine. **5.** not functioning. **6.** spoilt or ruined by divorce (esp. in **broken home, broken marriage). 7.** (of a trust, promise, contract, etc.) violated; infringed. **8.** (of the speech of a foreigner) imperfect in grammar, vocabulary, and pronunciation: broken English. **9.** Also: **broken-in.** made tame or disciplined by training. **10.** exhausted or weakened, as through ill-health or misfortune. **11.** irregular or rough; uneven: broken ground. **12.** bankrupt. —'**brokenly** adv.

broken chord n. another term for **arpeggio.**

broken-down adj. **1.** worn out, as by age or long use; dilapidated. **2.** not in working order.

brokenhearted (,brəʊkən'hɑːtɪd) adj. overwhelmed by grief or disappointment. —,**broken'heartedly** adv.

Broken Hill n. a city in SE Australia, in W New South Wales: mining centre for lead, silver, and zinc. Pop.: 26 913 (1981 est.).

broken wind (wɪnd) n. Vet. science. another name for **heaves.** —,**broken'winded** adj.

broker ('brəʊkə) n. **1.** an agent who, acting on behalf of a principal, buys or sells goods, securities, etc.: insurance broker. **2.** short for **stockbroker. 3.** a person who deals in second-hand goods. [C14: from Anglo-F brocour broacher of casks, hence, one who sells, agent), from OF broquier to tap a cask]

brokerage ('brəʊkərɪdʒ) n. **1.** commission charged by a broker. **2.** a broker's business or office.

brolga ('brɒlgə) n. a large grey Australian crane having a red-and-green head and a trumpeting call. Also called: **native companion.** [C19: from Abor.]

brolly ('brɒlɪ) n., pl. **-lies.** an informal Brit. name for **umbrella** (sense 1).

Bromberg ('brɒmbɛrk) n. the German name for **Bydgoszcz.**

bromeliad (brəʊ'miːlɪˌæd) n. any of a family of tropical American plants, typically epiphytes with a rosette of fleshy leaves, such as the pineapple and Spanish moss. [C19: from NL, after Olaf Bromelius (1639-1705), Swedish botanist]

bromide ('brəʊmaɪd) n. **1.** any salt of hydrobromic acid. **2.** any compound containing a bromine atom. **3.** a dose of sodium or potassium bromide given as a sedative. **4. a.** a platitude. **b.** a boring person.

bromide paper n. a type of photographic paper coated with an emulsion of silver bromide.

bromine ('brəʊmiːn, -mɪn) n. a pungent dark red volatile liquid element that occurs in brine and is used in the production of chemicals. Symbol: Br; atomic no.: 35; atomic wt.: 79.91. [C19: from F brome bromine, from Gk brōmos bad smell, from ?]

Bromley ('brɒmlɪ) n. a SE borough of Greater London. Pop.: 297 000 (1986 est.).

Bromsgrove ('brɒmz,grəʊv) n. a town in W central England, in NE Hereford and Worcester. Pop.: 46 673 (1981).

bronchi ('brɒŋkaɪ) n. the plural of **bronchus.**

bronchial ('brɒŋkɪəl) adj. of or relating to the bronchi or the bronchial tubes. —'**bronchially** adv.

bronchial tubes pl. n. the bronchi or their smaller divisions.

bronchiectasis (,brɒŋkɪ'ɛktəsɪs) n. chronic dilation and usually infection of the bronchi. [C19: from BRONCHO- + Gk ektasis a stretching]

bronchiole ('brɒŋkɪˌəʊl) n. any of the smallest bronchial tubes. [C19: from NL; see BRONCHUS] —,**bronchi'olar** adj.

bronchitis (brɒŋ'kaɪtɪs) n. inflammation of the bronchial tubes, characterized by coughing, difficulty in breathing, etc. —**bronchitic** (brɒŋ'kɪtɪk) adj., n.

broncho- or before a vowel **bronch-** combining form. indicating or relating to the bronchi: bronchitis. [from Gk: BRONCHUS]

bronchopneumonia (,brɒŋkəʊnjuː'məʊnɪə) n. inflammation of the lungs, starting in the bronchioles.

bronchoscope ('brɒŋkəˌskəʊp) n. an instrument for examining and providing access to the interior of the bronchial tubes.

bronchus ('brɒŋkəs) n., pl. **-chi.** either of the two main branches of the trachea. [C18: from NL, from Gk bronkhos windpipe]

bronco or **broncho** ('brɒŋkəʊ) n., pl. **-cos** or **-chos.** (in the U.S. and Canada) a wild or partially tamed pony or mustang of the western plains. [C19: from Mexican Sp., from Sp.: rough, wild]

Brontë ('brɒntɪ) n. **1. Anne,** pen name Acton Bell. 1820–49, English novelist; author of The Tenant of Wildfell Hall (1847). **2.** her sister, **Charlotte,** pen name Currer Bell. 1816–55, English novelist, author of Jane Eyre (1847), Villette (1853), and The Professor (1857). **3.** her sister, **Emily (Jane),** pen name Ellis Bell. 1818–48, English novelist and poet; author of Wuthering Heights (1847).

brontosaurus (,brɒntə'sɔːrəs) or **brontosaur** ('brɒntəˌsɔː) n. a very large herbivorous quadrupedal dinosaur, common in N America during late Jurassic times, having a long neck and long tail. [C19: from NL, from Gk brontë thunder + sauros lizard]

Bronx (brɒŋks) n. **the.** a borough of New York City, on the mainland, separated from Manhattan by the Harlem River. Pop.: 1 168 972 (1980).

bronze (brɒnz) n. **1.** any hard water-resistant alloy consisting of copper and smaller proportions of tin and sometimes zinc and lead. **2.** a yellowish-brown colour or pigment. **3.** a statue, medal, or other object made of bronze. ~adj. **4.** made of or resembling bronze. **5.** of a yellowish-brown colour. ~vb. **6.** (esp. of the skin) to make or become brown; tan. **7.** (tr.) to give the appearance of bronze to. [C18: from F, from It. bronzo] —'**bronzy** adj.

Bronze Age n. **a.** a technological stage between the Stone and Iron Ages, beginning in the Middle East about 4500 B.C. and lasting in Britain from about 2000 to 500 B.C., during which weapons and tools were made of bronze. **b.** (as modifier): a Bronze-Age tool.

bronze medal n. a medal awarded to a competitor who comes third in a contest or race.

Bronzino II (bron'dziːno) n. real name Agnolo di Cosimo. 1503–72, Florentine mannerist painter.

brooch (brəʊtʃ) n. an ornament with a hinged pin and catch, worn fastened to clothing. [C13: from OF broche; see BROACH]

brood (bruːd) n. **1.** a number of young animals, esp. birds, produced at one hatching. **2.** all the offspring in one family: often used jokingly or contemptuously. **3.** a group of a particular kind; breed. **4.** (modifier) kept for breeding: a brood mare. ~vb. **5.** (of a bird) **a.** to sit on or hatch (eggs). **b.** (tr.) to cover (young birds) protectively with the wings. **6.** (when intr., often foll. by on, over, or upon) to ponder morbidly or persistently. [OE brōd] —'**brooding** n., adj.

brooder ('bruːdə) n. **1.** a structure, usually heated, used for rearing young chickens or other fowl. **2.** a person or thing that broods.

broody ('bruːdɪ) adj. **broodier, broodiest. 1.** moody; introspective. **2.** (of poultry) wishing to sit on or hatch eggs. **3.** Inf. (of a woman) wishing to have a baby. —'**broodiness** n.

brook[1] (brʊk) n. a natural freshwater stream smaller than a river. [OE brōc]

brook[2] (brʊk) vb. (tr.) (usually used with a negative) to bear; tolerate. [OE brūcan]

Brook (brʊk) n. **Peter** (**Paul Stephen**). born 1925, British stage and film director, noted esp. for his experimental work in the theatre.

Brooke (brʊk) n. **1. Alan Francis.** See (1st Viscount) **Alanbrooke. 2.** Sir **James.** 1803–68, English soldier; first rajah of Sarawak (1841–63). **3. Rupert.** 1887–1915, English lyric poet, noted for his idealistic war poetry, which made him a national hero.

brooklet ('brʊklɪt) n. a small brook.

brooklime ('brʊk,laɪm) n. either of two blue-flowered trailing plants, Veronica americana of North America or V. beccabunga of Europe and Asia, growing in moist places. See also **speedwell.** [C16: from BROOK[1] + -lemk, from OE hleomoce]

Brooklyn ('brʊklɪn) n. a borough of New York City, on the SW end of Long Island. Pop.: 2 230 936 (1980).

Brookner ('brʊknə) n. **Anita.** born 1938, British writer and art historian. Her novels include Hotel du Lac (1984) and Latecomers (1988).

Brooks Range n. a mountain range in N Alaska. Highest peak: Mount Isto, 2761 m (9058 ft.).

brook trout n. a North American trout, valued as a food and game fish.

broom (bruːm, brʊm) n. **1.** an implement for sweeping consisting of a long handle to which is attached either a brush of straw or twigs, bound together, or a solid head into which are set tufts of bristles or fibres. **2.** any of various yellow-flowered Eurasian leguminous shrubs. **3. new broom.** a newly appointed official, etc., eager to make radical changes. ~vb. **4.** (tr.) to sweep with a broom. [OE brōm]

Broome (bruːm) n. **David.** born 1940, English show-jumping rider.

broomrape ('bruːm,reɪp, 'brʊm-) n. any of a genus of leafless fleshy parasitic plants growing on the roots of other plants, esp. on broom. [C16: adaptation & partial translation of Med. L rāpum genistae tuber (hence: root nodule) of Genista (a type of broom plant)]

broomstick ('bruːm,stɪk, 'brʊm-) n. the long handle of a broom.

Broonzy ('bruːnzɪ) n. **William Lee Conley,** called Big Bill. 1893–1958, U.S. blues singer and guitarist.

bros. or **Bros.** abbrev. for brothers.

brose (brəʊz) n. Scot. a porridge made by adding a boiling liquid to meal, esp. oatmeal. [C13 broys, from OF broez, from breu broth, of Gmc origin]

broth (brɒθ) n. **1.** a soup made by boiling meat, fish, vegetables, etc., in water. **2.** another name for **stock** (sense 19). [OE broth]

brothel ('brɒθəl) n. **1.** a house where men pay to have sexual intercourse with prostitutes. **2.** Austral. inf. any untidy or messy place. [C16: short for brothel-house, from C14 brothel useless person, from OE brēothan to deteriorate]

brother ('brʌðə) n. **1.** a male person having the same parents as another person. **2. a.** a male person belonging to the same group, profession, nationality, trade union, etc., as another or others; fellow member. **b.** (as modifier): brother workers. **3.** comrade; friend: used as a form of address. **4.** Christianity. a member of a male religious order. ~Related adj.: **fraternal.** [OE brōthor]

brotherhood ('brʌðə,hʊd) n. **1.** the state of being related as a brother or brothers. **2.** an association or fellowship, such as a trade union. **3.** all persons engaged in a particular profession, trade, etc. **4.** the belief, feeling, or hope that all men should treat one another as brothers.

brother-in-law n., pl. **brothers-in-law. 1.** the brother of one's wife or husband. **2.** the husband of one's sister. **3.** the husband of the sister of one's husband or wife.

brotherly ('brʌðəlɪ) adj. of, resembling, or suitable to a brother, esp. in showing loyalty and affection; fraternal. —'brotherliness n.

brougham ('bruːəm, bruːm) n. **1.** a four-wheeled horse-drawn closed carriage having a raised open driver's seat in front. **2.** Obs. a large car with an open compartment at the front for the driver. **3.** Obs. an early electric car. [C19: after Lord Brougham (1778–1868)]

brought (brɔːt) vb. the past tense and past participle of **bring.**

brouhaha ('bruːhɑːˌhɑː) n. a loud confused noise; commotion; uproar. [F, imit.]

brow (braʊ) n. **1.** the part of the face from the eyes to the hairline; forehead. **2.** short for **eyebrow. 3.** the expression of the face; countenance: a troubled brow. **4.** the jutting top of a hill, etc. [OE brū]

browbeat ('braʊ,biːt) vb. **-beating, -beat, -beaten.** (tr.) to discourage or frighten with threats or a domineering manner; intimidate.

brown (braʊn) n. **1.** any of various dark colours, such as those of wood or earth. **2.** a dye or pigment producing these colours. ~adj. **3.** of the .colour brown. **4.** (of bread) made from a flour that has not been bleached or bolted, such as wheatmeal or wholemeal flour. **5.** deeply tanned or sunburnt. ~vb. **6.** to make (esp. food as a result of cooking) brown or (esp. of food) to become brown. [OE brūn] —'brownish or 'browny adj. —'brownness n.

Brown (braʊn) n. **1.** Sir **Arthur Whitten** ('wɪtⁿn). 1886–1948, English aviator who with J. W. Alcock made the first flight across the Atlantic (1919). **2. George** (**Alfred**), Lord George-Brown. 1914–85, British Labour leader; vice-chairman and deputy leader of the Labour party (1960–70); foreign secretary 1966–68. **3. James.** born 1928, U.S. soul singer and songwriter, noted for his dynamic stage performances and for his commitment to Black rights. **4. John.** 1800–59, U.S. abolitionist leader, hanged after leading an unsuccessful rebellion of slaves at Harper's Ferry, Virginia. **5. Lancelot,** called Capability Brown. 1716–83, English landscape gardener. **6. Robert.** 1773–1858, Scottish botanist who was the first to observe the Brownian movement in fluids.

brown bear n. a large ferocious brownish bear inhabiting temperate forests of North America, Europe, and Asia.

brown coal n. another name for **lignite.**

Browne (braʊn) n. Sir **Thomas.** 1605–82, English physician and author, noted for his magniloquent prose style. His works include Religio Medici (1642) and Hydriotaphia or Urn Burial (1658).

browned-off adj. Inf., chiefly Brit. thoroughly discouraged or disheartened; fed up.

brown fat n. a dark form of adipose tissue that is readily converted into energy.

Brownian movement ('braʊnɪən) n. random movement of microscopic particles suspended in a fluid, caused by bombardment of the particles by molecules of the fluid. [C19: after Robert Brown]

brownie ('braʊnɪ) n. **1.** (in folklore) an elf said to do helpful work at night, esp. household chores. **2.** a small square nutty chocolate cake. [C16: dim. of BROWN (that is, a small brown man)]

Brownie Guide or **Brownie** ('braʊnɪ) n. a member of the junior branch of the Guides.

Brownie point n. a notional mark to one's credit for being seen to do the right thing. [C20: ?from the mistaken notion that Brownie Guides earn points for good deeds]

browning ('braʊnɪŋ) n. Brit. a substance used to darken soups, gravies, etc.

Browning ('braʊnɪŋ) n. **1. Elizabeth Barrett.** 1806–61, English poet and critic; author of the Sonnets from the Portuguese (1850). **2.** her husband, **Robert.** 1812–89, English poet, noted for his dramatic monologues and The Ring and the Book (1868–69).

brown paper n. a kind of coarse unbleached paper used for wrapping.

brown rice n. unpolished rice, in which the grains retain the outer yellowish-brown layer (bran).

Brown Shirt n. **1.** (in Nazi Germany) a storm trooper. **2.** a member of any fascist party or group.

brownstone ('braʊn,stəʊn) n. U.S. a reddish-brown ironrich sandstone used for building.

brown sugar n. sugar that is unrefined or only partially refined.

brown trout n. a common brownish variety of the trout that occurs in the rivers of N Europe.

browse (braʊz) vb. **1.** to look through (a book, articles for sale in a shop, etc.) in a casual leisurely manner. **2.** (of deer, goats, etc.) to feed upon (vegetation) by continual nibbling. ~n. **3.** the act or an instance of browsing. **4.** the young twigs, shoots, leaves, etc., on which certain animals feed. [C15: from F broust, brost bud, of Gmc origin] —'browser n.

Broz (*Serbo-Croatian* brɔːz) *n.* **Josip** ('jɔsip). original name of (Marshal) **Tito.**

BRS *abbrev. for* British Road Services.

Brubeck ('bruːbɛk) *n.* **Dave.** born 1920, U.S. modern jazz pianist and composer. He studied composition with Darius Milhaud and Arnold Schoenberg; formed his own quartet in 1951.

Bruce (bruːs) *n.* **1. Lenny.** 1925–66, U.S. comedian, whose satirical sketches, esp. of the sexual attitudes of his contemporaries, brought him prosecutions for obscenity, but are now regarded as full of insight as well as wit. **2. Robert the.** See **Robert I. 3. Stanley Melbourne,** 1st Viscount Bruce of Melbourne. 1883–1967, Australian statesman; prime minister, in coalition with Sir Earle Page's Country Party, of Australia (1923–29). **4.** an informal name for an Australian man.

brucellosis (ˌbruːsɪˈləʊsɪs) *n.* an infectious disease of cattle, goats, and pigs, caused by bacteria and transmittable to man. Also called: **undulant fever.** [C20: from NL *Brucella*, after Sir David *Bruce* (1855–1931), Australian bacteriologist & physician]

Bruch (*German* brʊx) *n.* **Max** (maks). 1838–1920, German composer, noted chiefly for his three violin concertos.

Bruckner (*German* 'brʊknər) *n.* **Anton** ('antoːn). 1824–96, Austrian composer and organist in the Romantic tradition. His works include nine symphonies, four masses, and a Te Deum.

Brueghel, Bruegel, or **Breughel** ('brɔɪɡ°l; *Flemish* 'brøːxəl) *n.* **1. Jan** (jɑn). 1568–1625, Flemish painter, noted for his detailed still lifes and landscapes. **2.** his father, **Pieter** ('piːtər), called *the Elder.* ?1525–69, Flemish painter, noted for his landscapes, his satirical paintings of peasant life, and his allegorical biblical scenes. **3.** his son, **Pieter,** called *the Younger.* ?1564–1637, Flemish painter, noted for his gruesome pictures of hell.

Bruges (bruːʒ; *French* bryʒ) *n.* a city in NW Belgium, capital of West Flanders province: centre of the medieval European wool and cloth trade. Pop.: 117 755 (1987 est.). Flemish name: **Brugge** ('bryxə).

bruin ('bruːɪn) *n.* a name for a bear, used in children's tales, etc. [C17: from Du. *bruin* brown]

bruise (bruːz) *vb. (mainly tr.)* **1.** (*also intr.*) to injure (tissues) without breaking the skin, usually with discoloration, or (of tissues) to be injured in this way. **2.** to offend or injure (someone's feelings). **3.** to damage the surface of (something). **4.** to crush (food, etc.) by pounding. ~*n.* **5.** a bodily injury without a break in the skin, usually with discoloration; contusion. [OE *brȳsan*]

bruiser ('bruːzə) *n.* a strong tough person, esp. a boxer or a bully.

bruit (bruːt) *vb.* **1.** (*tr.; often passive; usually foll. by about*) to report; rumour. ~*n.* **2.** *Arch.* **a.** a rumour. **b.** a loud outcry; clamour. [C15: via F from Med. L *brūgītus*, prob. from L *rugīre* to roar]

brumby ('brʌmbɪ) *n., pl.* **-bies.** *Austral.* **1.** a wild horse, esp. one descended from runaway stock. **2.** a disorderly person. [C19: from ?]

brume (bruːm) *n.* *Poetic* heavy mist or fog. [C19: from F: mist, winter, from L *brūma*, contracted from *brevissima diēs* the shortest day]

Brummell ('brʌməl) *n.* **George Bryan,** called *Beau Brummell.* 1778–1840, English dandy: leader of fashion in the Regency period.

brunch (brʌntʃ) *n.* a meal eaten late in the morning, combining breakfast with lunch. [C20: from BR(EAKFAST) + (L)UNCH]

Brundisium (brʌnˈdɪzɪəm) *n.* the ancient name for **Brindisi.**

Brunei (bruːˈnaɪ, ˈbruːnaɪ) *n.* **1.** a sultanate in NW Borneo, consisting of two separate areas on the South China Sea, otherwise bounded by Sarawak: controlled all of Borneo and parts of the Philippines and the Sulu Islands in the 16th century; under British protection since 1888; internally self-governing since 1971; became independent in 1984. The economy depends chiefly on oil and natural gas. Official language: Malay; English is also widely spoken. Religion: Muslim. Currency: Brunei dollar. Capital: Bandar Seri Begawan. Pop.: 240 000 (1986). Area: 5765 sq. km (2226 sq. miles). **2.** the former name of **Bandar Seri Begawan.**

Brunel (bruːˈnɛl) *n.* **1. Isambard Kingdom** ('ɪzəmˌbɑːd). 1806–59, English engineer: designer of the Clifton Suspension Bridge (1828), many railway lines, tunnels, bridges, etc., and the steamships *Great Western* (1838), *Great Britain* (1845), and *Great Eastern* (1858). **2.** his father, Sir **Marc Isambard.** 1769–1849, French engineer in England.

Brunelleschi (*Italian* brunelˈleski) *n.* **Filippo** (fiˈlippo). 1377–1446, Italian architect, whose works in Florence include the dome of the cathedral, the Pazzi chapel of Santa Croce, and the church of San Lorenzo.

brunette (bruːˈnɛt) *n.* **1.** a girl or woman with dark brown hair. ~*adj.* **2.** dark brown: *brunette hair.* [C17: from F, fem. of *brunet* dark, brownish, from *brun* brown]

Brunhild ('brʊnhɪld, -hɪlt) or **Brünnhilde** (*German* brynˈhɪldə) *n.* (in the *Nibelungenlied*) a legendary queen won for King Gunther by the magic of Siegfried: corresponds to Brynhild in Norse mythology.

Brüning (*German* 'bryːnɪŋ) *n.* **Heinrich** ('hainrɪç). 1885–1970, German statesman; chancellor (1930–32). He was forced to resign in 1932, making way for the Nazis.

Brünn (bryn) *n.* the German name for **Brno.**

Bruno ('bruːnəʊ) *n.* **1. Franklyn Roy,** known as *Frank.* born 1961, British heavyweight boxer. **2.** (*Italian* 'bruno) **Giordano** (dʒorˈdano). 1548–1600, Italian philosopher, who developed a pantheistic monistic philosophy: he was burnt at the stake for heresy.

Brunswick ('brʌnzwɪk) *n.* **1.** a former duchy (1635–1918) and state (1918–46) of central Germany: now part of Lower Saxony in West Germany. **2.** a city in E West Germany: formerly capital of the duchy and state of Brunswick. Pop.: 253 478 (1985 est.). German name: **Braunschweig.**

brunt (brʌnt) *n.* the main force or shock of a blow, attack, etc. (esp. in **bear the brunt of**). [C14: from ?]

Brusa (*Turkish* 'bruːsɑː) *n.* the former name of **Bursa.**

brush[1] (brʌʃ) *n.* **1.** a device made of bristles, hairs, wires, etc., set into a firm back or handle: used to apply paint, clean or polish surfaces, groom the hair, etc. **2.** the act or an instance of brushing. **3.** a light stroke made in passing; graze. **4.** a brief encounter or contact, esp. an unfriendly one; skirmish. **5.** the bushy tail of a fox. **6.** an electric conductor, esp. one made of carbon, that conveys current between stationary and rotating parts of a generator, motor, etc. ~*vb.* **7.** (*tr.*) to clean, polish, scrub, paint, etc., with a brush. **8.** (*tr.*) to apply or remove with a brush or brushing movement. **9.** (*tr.*) to touch lightly and briefly. **10.** (*intr.*) to move so as to graze or touch something lightly. ~See also **brush aside, brush off, brush up.** [C14: from OF *broisse,* ?from *broce* BRUSH[2]] —'**brusher** *n.*

brush[2] (brʌʃ) *n.* **1.** a thick growth of shrubs and small trees; scrub. **2.** land covered with scrub. **3.** broken or cut branches or twigs; brushwood. **4.** wooded sparsely populated country; backwoods. [C16 (dense undergrowth), C14 (cuttings of trees): from OF *broce,* from Vulgar L *bruscia* (unattested) brushwood] —'**brushy** *adj.*

brush aside or **away** *vb.* (*tr., adv.*) to dismiss without consideration; disregard.

brush discharge *n.* a slightly luminous brushlike electrical discharge.

brushed (brʌʃt) *adj.* *Textiles.* treated with a brushing process to raise the nap and give a softer and warmer finish: *brushed nylon.*

brush off *Sl.* ~*vb.* (*tr., adv.*) **1.** to dismiss and ignore (a person), esp. curtly. ~*n.* **brushoff. 2.** an abrupt dismissal or rejection.

brush turkey *n.* any of several gallinaceous flightless birds of New Guinea and Australia, having a black plumage.

brush up *vb.* (*adv.*) **1.** (*tr.; often foll. by on*) to refresh one's knowledge, skill, or memory of (a task). **2.** to make (a person or oneself) clean or neat as after a journey. ~*n.* **brush-up. 3.** *Brit.* the act or an instance of tidying one's appearance (esp. in **wash and brush-up**).

brushwood ('brʌʃˌwʊd) *n.* **1.** cut or broken-off tree branches, twigs, etc. **2.** another word for **brush**[2] (sense 1).

brushwork ('brʌʃˌwɜːk) *n.* **1.** a characteristic manner of applying paint with a brush: *Rembrandt's brushwork.* **2.** work done with a brush.

brusque (bruːsk, brʊsk) *adj.* blunt or curt in manner or speech. [C17: from F, from It. *brusco* sour, rough, from

Med. L *bruscus* butcher's broom] —**'brusquely** *adv.*
—**'brusqueness** *n.*

Brussels ('brʌsªlz) *n.* the capital of Belgium, in the central part: became capital of Belgium in 1830; seat of the Common Market Commission. Pop.: 973 499 (1987 est.). Flemish name: **Brussel** ('brysəl). French name: **Brux-elles**.

Brussels carpet *n.* a worsted carpet with a heavy pile formed by uncut loops of wool on a linen warp.

Brussels lace *n.* a fine lace with a raised or appliqué design.

Brussels sprout *n.* **1.** a variety of cabbage, having a stout stem studded with budlike heads resembling tiny cabbages. **2.** the head of this plant, eaten as a vegetable.

brutal ('bru:tªl) *adj.* **1.** cruel; vicious; savage. **2.** extremely honest or coarse in speech or manner. **3.** harsh; severe; extreme: *brutal cold.* —**bru'tality** *n.* —**'brutally** *adv.*

brutalize *or* **-ise** ('bru:tə,laɪz) *vb.* **1.** to make or become brutal. **2.** (*tr.*) to treat brutally. —**,brutali'zation** *or* **-i'sation** *n.*

brute (bru:t) *n.* **1. a.** any animal except man; beast; lower animal. **b.** (*as modifier*): *brute nature.* **2.** a brutal person. ~*adj.* (*prenominal*) **3.** wholly instinctive or physical (esp. in **brute strength, brute force**). **4.** without reason or intelligence. **5.** coarse and grossly sensual. [C15: from L *brūtus* heavy, irrational]

brutish ('bru:tɪʃ) *adj.* **1.** of, relating to, or resembling a brute; animal. **2.** coarse; cruel; stupid. —**'brutishly** *adv.* —**'brutishness** *n.*

Brutus ('bru:təs) *n.* **1. Lucius Junius** ('lu:ʃəs 'dʒu:nɪəs). late 6th century B.C., Roman statesman who ousted the tyrant Tarquin (509) and helped found the Roman republic. **2. Marcus Junius** ('mɑːkəs 'dʒu:nɪəs) ?85–42 B.C., Roman statesman who, with Cassius, led the conspiracy to assassinate Caesar (44): committed suicide after being defeated by Antony and Octavian (Augustus) at Philippi (42).

Bruxelles (brysɛl) *n.* the French name for **Brussels**.

Bryansk (brɪ'ænsk; *Russian* brjansk) *n.* a city in the W Soviet Union. Pop.: 445 000 (1987).

Brynhild ('brɪnhɪld) *n. Norse myth.* a Valkyrie won as the wife of Gunnar by Sigurd who wakes her from an enchanted sleep: corresponds to Brunhild in the *Nibelungenlied*.

bryology (braɪ'ɒlədʒɪ) *n.* the branch of botany concerned with the study of bryophytes. —**bryological** (,braɪə-'lɒdʒɪkªl) *adj.* —**bry'ologist** *n.*

bryony *or* **briony** ('braɪənɪ) *n., pl.* **-nies.** any of several herbaceous climbing plants of Europe and N Africa. [OE *bryōnia*, from L, from Gk *bruōnia*]

bryophyte ('braɪə,faɪt) *n.* any plant of the division *Bryophyta*, esp. mosses and liverworts. [C19: from Gk *bruon* moss + -PHYTE] —**bryophytic** (,braɪə'fɪtɪk) *adj.*

bryozoan (,braɪə'zəʊən) *n.* any aquatic invertebrate animal forming colonies of polyps each having a ciliated feeding organ. Popular name: **sea mat.** [C19: from Gk *bruon* moss + *zōion* animal]

Brythonic (brɪ'θɒnɪk) *n.* **1.** the S group of Celtic languages, consisting of Welsh, Cornish, and Breton. ~*adj.* **2.** of or relating to this group of languages. [C19: from Welsh; see BRITON]

Brześć nad Bugiem (bʒɛʃtʃ nad 'bugjɛm) *n.* the Polish name for **Brest** (sense 2).

bs *abbrev. for:* **1.** balance sheet. **2.** bill of sale.

BS *abbrev. for* British Standard(s).

BSc *abbrev. for* Bachelor of Science.

BSI *abbrev. for* British Standards Institution.

B-side *n.* the less important side of a gramophone record.

BST *abbrev. for:* **1.** British Standard Time. **2.** British Summer Time.

Bt *abbrev. for* Baronet.

BT *abbrev. for* British Telecom. [C20: shortened from TELE-COMMUNICATIONS]

btu *or* **BThU** *abbrev. for* British thermal unit. U.S. abbrev.: **BTU.**

bu. *abbrev. for* bushel.

bubble ('bʌbªl) *n.* **1.** a thin film of liquid forming a hollow globule around air or a gas: *a soap bubble.* **2.** a small globule of air or a gas in a liquid or a solid. **3.** the sound made by a bubbling liquid. **4.** something lacking substance, stability, or seriousness. **5.** an unreliable scheme or enterprise. **6.** a dome, esp. a transparent glass or

plastic one. ~*vb.* **7.** to form or cause to form bubbles. **8.** (*intr.*) to move or flow with a gurgling sound. **9.** (*intr.*; often foll. by *over*) to overflow (with excitement, anger, etc.). [C14: prob. from ON; imit.]

bubble and squeak *n. Brit.* a dish of leftover boiled cabbage and potatoes fried together.

bubble bath *n.* **1.** a powder, liquid, or crystals used to scent, soften, and foam in bath water. **2.** a bath to which such a substance has been added.

bubble car *n. Brit.* a small car with a transparent bubble-shaped top.

bubble chamber *n.* a device that enables the tracks of ionizing particles to be photographed as a row of bubbles in a superheated liquid.

bubble gum *n.* a type of chewing gum that can be blown into large bubbles.

bubble memory *n. Computers.* a method of storing high volumes of data by using minute pockets of magnetism (bubbles) in a semiconducting material.

bubbly ('bʌblɪ) *adj.* **-blier, -bliest. 1.** full of or resembling bubbles. **2.** lively; animated; excited. ~*n.* **3.** *Inf.* champagne.

Buber ('bu:bə) *n.* **Martin.** 1878–1965, Jewish theologian, existentialist philosopher, and scholar of Hasidism, born in Austria, whose works include *I and Thou* (1923), *Between Man and Man* (1946), and *Eclipse of God* (1952).

bubo ('bju:bəʊ) *n., pl.* **-boes.** *Pathol.* inflammation and swelling of a lymph node, esp. in the armpit or groin. [C14: from Med. L *bubō*, from Gk *boubōn* groin] —**bubonic** (bju:'bɒnɪk) *adj.*

bubonic plague *n.* an acute infectious febrile disease characterized by chills, prostration, delirium, and formation of buboes: caused by the bite of an infected rat flea.

Bucaramanga (*Spanish* bukara'manga) *n.* a city in N central Colombia, in the Cordillera Oriental: centre of a district growing coffee, tobacco, and cotton. Pop.: 363 909 (1985).

buccal ('bʌkªl) *adj.* **1.** of or relating to the cheek. **2.** of or relating to the mouth; oral. [C19: from L *bucca* cheek]

buccaneer (,bʌkə'nɪə) *n.* **1.** a pirate, esp. one who preyed on Spanish shipping in the Caribbean in the 17th and 18th centuries. ~*vb.* (*intr.*) **2.** to be or act like a buccaneer. [C17: from F *boucanier*, from *boucaner* to smoke meat]

buccinator ('bʌksɪ,neɪtə) *n.* either of two flat cheek muscles used in chewing. [C17: from L, from *buccina* a trumpet]

Buchan ('bʌkən) *n.* **John,** 1st Baron Tweedsmuir. 1875–1940, Scottish statesman, historian, and writer of adventure stories, esp. *The Thirty-Nine Steps* (1915) and *Greenmantle* (1916); governor general of Canada (1935–40).

Buchanan (bju:'kænən) *n.* **James.** 1791–1868, 15th president of the U.S. (1857–61).

Bucharest (,bu:kə'rɛst, ,bju:-) *n.* the capital of Romania, in the southeast. Pop.: 1 861 007 (1980 est.). Romanian name: **Bucureşti.**

Buchenwald (*German* 'bu:xənvalt) *n.* a village in SW East Germany, near Weimar: site of a Nazi concentration camp (1937–45).

Buchner (*German* 'bu:xnər) *n.* **Eduard** ('e:duart). 1860–1917, German chemist who demonstrated that alcoholic fermentation is due to the action of enzymes in the yeast: Nobel prize for chemistry 1907.

Büchner (*German* 'by:çnər) *n.* **Georg** ('ge:ɔrk). 1813–37, German dramatist; regarded as a forerunner of the Expressionists: author of *Danton's Death* (1835) and *Woyzeck* (1837).

buck[1] (bʌk) *n.* **1. a.** the male of various animals including the goat, hare, kangaroo, rabbit, and reindeer. **b.** (*as modifier*): *a buck antelope.* **2.** *S. African.* an antelope or deer of either sex. **3.** *Arch.* a robust spirited young man. **4.** the act of bucking. ~*vb.* **5.** (*intr.*) (of a horse or other animal) to jump vertically, with legs stiff and back arched. **6.** (*tr.*) (of a horse, etc.) to throw (its rider) by bucking. **7.** (when *intr.*, often foll. by *against* or *at*) *Chiefly U.S., Canad., & Austral. inf.* to resist or oppose obstinately. **8.** (*tr.; usually passive*) *Inf.* to cheer or encourage: *I was very bucked at passing the exam.* ~See also **buck up.** [OE *bucca* he-goat] —**'bucker** *n.*

buck[2] (bʌk) *n. U.S., Canad., & Austral. sl.* a dollar. [C19: from ?]

buck[3] (bʌk) *n.* **1.** *Poker.* a marker in the jackpot to remind the winner of some obligation when his turn comes to deal. **2. pass the buck.** *Inf.* to shift blame or responsibility onto another. [C19: prob. from *buckhorn knife*, placed before a player in poker to indicate that he was the next dealer]

Buck (bʌk) *n.* **Pearl S(ydenstricker).** 1892–1973, U.S. novelist, noted particularly for her novel of Chinese life *The Good Earth* (1931): Nobel prize for literature 1938.

buckbean ('bʌk,biːn) *n.* a marsh plant with white or pink flowers. Also called: **bogbean.**

buckboard ('bʌk,bɔːd) *n. U.S. & Canad.* an open four-wheeled horse-drawn carriage with the seat attached to a flexible board between the front and rear axles.

bucket ('bʌkɪt) *n.* **1.** an open-topped roughly cylindrical container; pail. **2.** Also called: **bucketful.** the amount a bucket will hold. **3.** any of various bucket-like parts of a machine, such as the scoop on a mechanical shovel. **4.** *Austral.* a small container for ice cream. **5. kick the bucket.** *Sl.* to die. ~*vb.* **6.** (*tr.*) to carry in or put into a bucket. **7.** (*intr.; often foll. by along*) *Chiefly Brit.* to travel or drive fast. **8.** (*tr.*) *Austral. sl.* to criticize severely. [C13: from Anglo-F *buket*, from OE *būc*]

bucket down *vb.* (*intr.*) (of rain) to fall very heavily.

bucket seat *n.* a seat in a car, aircraft, etc., having curved sides.

bucket shop *n.* **1.** an unregistered firm of stockbrokers that engages in fraudulent speculation. **2.** *Chiefly Brit.* a firm specializing in cheap airline tickets.

buckeye ('bʌk,aɪ) *n.* any of several North American trees of the horse chestnut family having erect clusters of white or red flowers and prickly fruits.

buckhorn ('bʌk,hɔːn) *n.* **a.** horn from a buck, used for knife handles, etc. **b.** (*as modifier*): *a buckhorn knife.*

Buckingham[1] ('bʌkɪŋəm) *n.* a town in S central England, in Buckinghamshire; university (1975). Pop.: 6627 (1981).

Buckingham[2] ('bʌkɪŋəm) *n.* **1. George Villiers, 1st Duke of.** 1592–1628, English courtier and statesman; favourite of James I and Charles I: his arrogance, military incompetence, and greed increased the tensions between the King and Parliament that eventually led to the Civil War. **2.** his son, **George Villiers, 2nd Duke of.** 1628–87, English courtier and writer; chief minister of Charles II and member of the Cabal (1667–73).

Buckingham Palace *n.* the London residence of the British sovereign: built in 1703, rebuilt by John Nash in 1821–36 and partially redesigned in the early 20th century.

Buckinghamshire ('bʌkɪŋəm,ʃɪə, -ʃə) *n.* a county in SE central England, containing the Vale of Aylesbury and parts of the Chiltern Hills. Administrative centre: Aylesbury. Pop.: 612 900 (1986 est.). Area: 1883 sq. km (727 sq. miles). Abbrev.: **Bucks.**

buckjumper ('bʌk,dʒʌmpə) *n. Austral.* an untamed horse.

Buckland ('bʌklənd) *n.* **William.** 1784–1856, English geologist; he became a proponent of the idea of catastrophic ice ages.

buckle ('bʌkᵊl) *n.* **1.** a clasp for fastening together two loose ends, esp. of a belt or strap, usually consisting of a frame with an attached movable prong. **2.** an ornamental representation of a buckle, as on a shoe. **3.** a kink, bulge, or other distortion. ~*vb.* **4.** to fasten or be fastened with a buckle. **5.** to bend or cause to bend out of shape, esp. as a result of pressure or heat. [C14: from OF, from L *buccula* a little cheek, hence, cheek strap of a helmet]

buckle down *vb.* (*intr., adv.*) *Inf.* to apply oneself with determination.

buckler ('bʌklə) *n.* **1.** a small round shield worn on the forearm. **2.** a means of protection; defence. [C13: from OF *bocler*, from *bocle* shield boss]

Buckley's chance ('bʌklɪz) *n. Austral. & N.Z. sl.* no chance at all. Often shortened to **Buckley's.** [C19: from ?]

bucko ('bʌkəʊ) *n., pl.* **buckoes.** *Irish.* a young fellow: often a term of address.

buckram ('bʌkrəm) *n.* **a.** cotton or linen cloth stiffened with size, etc., used in lining or stiffening clothes, bookbinding, etc. **b.** (*as modifier*): *a buckram cover.* [C14: from OF *boquerant*, ult. from BUKHARA, once important for textiles]

Bucks (bʌks) *abbrev. for* Buckinghamshire.

buckshee (,bʌk'ʃiː) *adj. Brit. sl.* without charge; free. [C20: from BAKSHEESH]

buckshot ('bʌk,ʃɒt) *n.* lead shot of large size used in shotgun shells, esp. for hunting game.

buckskin ('bʌk,skɪn) *n.* **1.** the skin of a male deer. **2. a.** a strong greyish-yellow suede leather, originally made from deerskin but now usually made from sheepskin. **b.** (*as modifier*): *buckskin boots.* **3.** a stiffly starched cotton cloth. **4.** a strong and heavy satin-woven woollen fabric.

buckthorn ('bʌk,θɔːn) *n.* any of several thorny small-flowered shrubs whose berries were formerly used as a purgative. [C16: from BUCK[1] (from the spiny branches resembling antlers) + THORN]

bucktooth ('bʌk,tuːθ) *n., pl.* **-teeth.** *Derog.* a projecting upper front tooth. [C18: from BUCK[1] (deer) + TOOTH]

buck up *vb.* (*adv.*) *Inf.* **1.** to make or cause to make haste. **2.** to make or become more cheerful, confident, etc.

buckwheat ('bʌk,wiːt) *n.* **1.** a cereal plant with fragrant white flowers, cultivated, esp. in the U.S., for its seeds. **2.** the edible seeds of this plant, ground into flour or used as animal fodder. **3.** the flour obtained from these seeds. [C16: from MDu. *boecweite*, from *boeke* BEECH + *weite* WHEAT, from the resemblance of the seeds to beechnuts]

bucolic (bjuː'kɒlɪk) *adj. also* **bucolical. 1.** of the countryside or country life; rustic. **2.** of or relating to shepherds; pastoral. ~*n.* **3.** (*sometimes pl.*) a pastoral poem. [C16: from L, from Gk, from *boukolos* cowherd, from *bous* ox] —**bu'colically** *adv.*

Bucovina (,buːkə'viːnə) *n.* a variant spelling of Bukovina.

Bucureşti (buku'reʃtj) *n.* the Romanian name for Bucharest.

bud (bʌd) *n.* **1.** a swelling on a plant stem consisting of overlapping immature leaves or petals. **2. a.** a partially opened flower. **b.** (*in combination*): *rosebud.* **3.** any small budlike outgrowth: *taste buds.* **4.** something small or immature. **5.** an asexually produced outgrowth in simple organisms such as yeasts that develops into a new individual. **6. nip in the bud.** to put an end to (an idea, movement, etc.) in its initial stages. ~*vb.* **budding, budded. 7.** (*intr.*) (of plants and some animals) to produce buds. **8.** (*intr.*) to begin to develop or grow. **9.** (*tr.*) *Horticulture.* to graft (a bud) from one plant onto another. [C14 *budde*, of Gmc origin]

Budapest (,bjuː'dəˈpɛst; *Hungarian* 'budɒpɛʃt) *n.* the capital of Hungary, in the central part, on the River Danube: formed in 1873 from the towns of Buda and Pest. Traditionally Buda, the old Magyar capital, was the administrative and Pest the trade centre: suffered severely in the Russian siege of 1945 and in the unsuccessful revolt against the Communist regime (1956). Pop.: 2 089 000 (1985).

Buddha ('budə) *n.* **the.** ?563–483 B.C., a title applied to Gautama Siddhartha, a nobleman and religious teacher of N India regarded by his followers as the most recent rediscoverer of the path to enlightenment: the founder of Buddhism.

Buddh Gaya ('bud gə'jaː), **Buddha Gaya,** *or* **Bodh Gaya** *n.* a village in NE India, in central Bihar: site of the sacred bo tree under which Gautama Siddhartha attained enlightenment and became the Buddha; pilgrimage centre. Pop.: 15 724 (1981).

Buddhism ('budɪzəm) *n.* a religious teaching propagated by the Buddha and his followers, which declares that by destroying greed, hatred, and delusion, which are the causes of all suffering, man can attain perfect enlightenment. —**'Buddhist** *n., adj.*

buddleia ('bʌdlɪə) *n.* an ornamental shrub which has long spikes of mauve flowers. Also called: **butterfly bush.** [C19: after A. *Buddle* (died 1715), Brit. botanist]

buddy ('bʌdɪ) *n., pl.* **-dies. 1.** (as a term of address): **bud.** *Chiefly U.S. & Canad.* an informal word for **friend. 2.** a volunteer who visits and gives help and support to a person suffering from AIDS. ~*vb.* **-dying, -died. 3.** (*intr.*) to act as a buddy to a person suffering from AIDS. [C19: prob. baby-talk var. (U.S.) of BROTHER]

buddy movie *or* **film** *n.* a genre of film dealing with the relationship and adventures of two friends.

budge (bʌdʒ) *vb.* (*usually used with a negative*) **1.** to move, however slightly. **2.** to change or cause to change opinions, etc. [C16: from OF *bouger*, from L *bullīre* to boil]

Budge (bʌdʒ) *n.* **Don(ald).** born 1915, U.S. tennis player, the first man to win the singles championships of Australia, France, and the U.S. in one year (1938).

budgerigar ('bʌdʒərɪˌgɑː) n. a small green Australian parrot: a popular cagebird bred in many different-coloured varieties. [C19: from Abor., from *budgeri* good + *gar* cockatoo]

budget ('bʌdʒɪt) n. **1.** an itemized summary of expected income and expenditure over a specified period. **2.** (*modifier*) economical; inexpensive: *budget meals for a family*. **3.** the total amount of money allocated for a specific purpose during a specified period. ~vb. **4.** (*tr.*) to enter or provide for in a budget. **5.** to plan the expenditure of (money, time, etc.). **6.** (*intr.*) to make a budget. [C15 (meaning: leather pouch, wallet): from OF *bougette*, dim. of *bouge*, from L *bulga*] —**'budgetary** adj.

Budget ('bʌdʒɪt) n. **the.** an estimate of British government expenditures and revenues and the financial plans for the ensuing fiscal year presented annually to the House of Commons by the Chancellor of the Exchequer.

budget account n. **1.** an account with a department store, etc., enabling a customer to make monthly payments to cover his past and future purchases. **2.** a bank account that allows the holder credit to pay certain bills in return for regular deposits.

budgie ('bʌdʒɪ) n. *Inf.* short for **budgerigar.**

Budweis ('buːtvais) n. the German name for **České Budějovice.**

Buenaventura (*Spanish* bwenaβen'tura) n. a major port in W Colombia, on the Pacific coast. Pop.: 122 500 (1984 est.).

Buena Vista (*Spanish* 'bwena 'vista) n. a village in NE Mexico, near Saltillo: site of the defeat of the Mexicans by U.S. forces (1847).

Bueno (*Portuguese* 'bwɛːnu) n. **Maria.** (mə'riːə). born 1939, Brazilian tennis player.

Buenos Aires ('bweɪnɒs 'aɪrɪz; *Spanish* 'bwenos 'aires) n. the capital of Argentina, a major port and industrial city on the Rio de la Plata estuary: became capital in 1880; university (1821). Pop.: 2 908 000 (1980).

buff¹ (bʌf) n. **1. a.** a soft thick flexible undyed leather made chiefly from the skins of buffalo, oxen, and elk. **b.** (*as modifier*): *a buff coat.* **2. a.** a dull yellow or yellowish-brown colour. **b.** (*as adj.*): *a buff envelope.* **3.** Also called: **buffer. a.** a cloth or pad of material used for polishing an object. **b.** a disc or wheel impregnated with a fine abrasive for polishing metals, etc. **4.** *Inf.* one's bare skin (esp. in **in the buff**). ~vb. **5.** to clean or polish (a metal, floor, shoes, etc.) with a buff. **6.** to remove the grain surface of (a leather). [C16: from OF, from OIt. *bufalo*, from LL *būfalus* BUFFALO]

buff² (bʌf) n. *Arch.* a blow or buffet (now only in **blind man's buff**). [C15: back formation from BUFFET²]

buff³ (bʌf) n. *Inf.* an expert on or devotee of a given subject. [C20: orig. U.S.: an enthusiastic fire-watcher, from the buff-coloured uniforms worn by volunteer firemen in New York City]

buffalo ('bʌfəˌləʊ) n., pl. **-loes** or **-lo. 1.** a type of cattle, mostly found in game reserves in southern and eastern Africa and having upward-curving horns. **2.** short for **water buffalo. 3.** a U.S. & Canad. name for **bison** (sense 1). [C16: from It. *bufalo*, from LL *būfalus*, ult. from Gk *bous* ox]

Buffalo ('bʌfəˌləʊ) n. a port in W New York State, at the E end of Lake Erie. Pop.: 324 820 (1986).

Buffalo Bill n. nickname of *William Frederick Cody.* 1846–1917, U.S. showman who toured Europe and the U.S. with his famous *Wild West Show.*

buffalo grass n. **1.** a short grass growing on the dry plains of the central U.S. **2.** *Austral.* a grass, *Stenotaphrum americanum*, introduced from North America.

buffel grass ('bʌfəl) n. (in Australia) any of various grasses used for grazing or fodder, originally introduced from Africa.

buffer¹ ('bʌfə) n. **1.** one of a pair of spring-loaded steel pads attached at both ends of railway vehicles and at the end of a railway track to reduce shock due to contact. **2.** a person or thing that lessens shock or protects from damaging impact, circumstances, etc. **3.** *Chem.* **a.** an ionic compound added to a solution to resist changes in its acidity or alkalinity and thus stabilize its pH. **b.** Also called: **buffer solution.** a solution containing such a compound. **4.** *Computers.* a memory device for temporarily storing data. ~vb. (*tr.*) **5.** *Chem.* to add a buffer to (a

solution). **6.** to insulate against or protect from shock. [C19: from BUFF²]

buffer² ('bʌfə) n. **1.** any device used to shine, polish, etc.; buff. **2.** a person who uses such a device.

buffer³ ('bʌfə) n. *Brit. inf.* a stupid or bumbling man (esp. in **old buffer**). [C18: ?from ME *buffer* stammerer]

buffer state n. a small and usually neutral state between two rival powers.

buffet¹ n. **1.** ('bufeɪ). a counter where light refreshments are served. **2.** ('bufeɪ). **a.** a meal at which guests help themselves from a number of dishes. **b.** (*as modifier*): *a buffet lunch.* **3.** ('bʌfɪt, 'bufeɪ). (formerly) a piece of furniture used for displaying plate, etc., and typically comprising cupboards and some open shelves. [C18: from F, from ?]

buffet² ('bʌfɪt) vb. **-feting, -feted. 1.** (*tr.*) to knock against or about; batter. **2.** (*tr.*) to hit, esp. with the fist; cuff. **3.** to force (one's way), as through a crowd. **4.** (*intr.*) to struggle; battle. ~n. **5.** a blow, esp. with a fist or hand. [C13: from OF *buffet* a light blow, from *buffe*, imit.]

Buffet (*French* byfɛ) n. **Bernard** (bɛrnar). born 1928, French painter and engraver. His works are characterized by sombre tones and thin angular forms.

buffet car ('bufeɪ) n. *Brit.* a railway coach where light refreshments are served.

bufflehead ('bʌfəlˌhɛd) n. a small North American diving duck: the male has black-and-white plumage and a fluffy head. [C17 *buffle*, from obs. *buffle* wild ox, referring to the duck's head]

buffo ('bufəʊ) n., pl. **-fi** (-fɪ) or **-fos. 1.** (in Italian opera of the 18th century) a comic part, esp. one for a bass. **2.** Also called: **buffo bass, basso buffo.** a bass singer who performs such a part. [C18: from It. (adj.): comic, from *buffo* (n.) BUFFOON]

Buffon (*French* byfɔ̃) n. **Georges Louis Leclerc** (ʒɔrʒ lwi ləklɛr), **Comte de.** 1707–88, French encyclopedist of natural history; principal author of *Histoire naturelle* (36 vols., 1749–89), containing the *Époques de la nature* (1777), which foreshadowed later theories of evolution.

buffoon (bə'fuːn) n. **1.** a person who amuses others by ridiculous or odd behaviour, jokes, etc. **2.** a foolish person. [C16: from F *bouffon*, from It. *buffone*, from Med. L *būfō*, from L: toad] —**buf'foonery** n.

bug (bʌg) n. **1.** an insect having piercing and sucking mouthparts specialized as a beak. **2.** *Chiefly U.S. & Canad.* any insect. **3.** *Inf.* **a.** a microorganism, esp. a bacterium, that produces disease. **b.** a disease, esp. a stomach infection, caused by a microorganism. **4.** *Inf.* an obsessive idea, hobby, etc.; craze. **5.** *Inf.* a person having such a craze. **6.** (*often pl.*) *Inf.* a fault, as in a machine. **7.** *Inf.* a concealed microphone used for recording conversations, as in spying. ~vb. **bugging, bugged.** *Inf.* **8.** (*tr.*) to irritate; bother. **9.** (*tr.*) to conceal a microphone in (a room, etc.). **10.** (*intr.*) *U.S.* (of eyes) to protrude. [C16: from ?]

Bug (*Russian* buk) n. **1.** Also called: **Southern Bug.** a river in the SW Soviet Union, rising in the W Ukraine and flowing southeast to the Dnieper estuary and the Black Sea. Length: 853 km (530 miles). **2.** Also called: **Western Bug.** a river in E central Europe, rising in the Soviet Union in the SW Ukraine and flowing northwest to the River Vistula in Poland, forming part of the border between Poland and the Soviet Union. Length: 724 km (450 miles).

bugaboo ('bʌgəˌbuː) n., pl. **-boos.** an imaginary source of fear; bugbear; bogey. [C18: prob. of Celtic origin; cf. Cornish *buccaboo* the devil]

Buganda (bʊ'gændə) n. an administrative region of Uganda: a powerful Bantu kingdom from the 17th century.

bugbear ('bʌgˌbɛə) n. **1.** a thing that causes obsessive anxiety. **2.** (in English folklore) a goblin in the form of a bear. [C16: from obs. *bug* an evil spirit + BEAR²]

bugger ('bʌgə) n. **1.** a person who practises buggery. **2.** *Taboo sl.* a person or thing considered to be contemptible, unpleasant, or difficult. **3.** *Sl.* a humorous or affectionate term for a man or child: *a friendly little bugger.* **4. bugger all.** *Sl.* nothing. ~vb. **5.** to practise buggery (with). **6.** (*tr.*) *Sl.*, *chiefly Brit.* to ruin, complicate, or frustrate. **7.** (*tr.*) *Sl.* to tire; weary. ~*interj.* **8.** *Taboo sl.* an exclamation of annoyance or disappointment. [C16: from OF *bougre*, from Med. L *Bulgarus* Bulgarian; from the condemnation of the Eastern Orthodox Bulgarians as heretics]

bugger about or **around** vb. (adv.) Sl. **1.** (intr.) to fool about and waste time. **2.** (tr.) to create difficulties or complications for (a person).

bugger off vb. (intr., adv.) Taboo sl. to go away; depart.

buggery ('bʌgərɪ) n. anal intercourse between a man and another man, a woman, or an animal.

buggy[1] ('bʌgɪ) n., pl. **-gies. 1.** a light horse-drawn carriage having either four wheels (esp. in the U.S. and Canada) or two wheels (esp. in Britain and India). **2.** any small light cart or vehicle, such as a baby buggy or beach buggy. [C18: from ?]

buggy[2] ('bʌgɪ) adj. **-gier, -giest.** infested with bugs.

bugle[1] ('bju:gəl) n. **1.** Music. a brass instrument similar to the cornet but usually without valves: used for military fanfares, signal calls, etc. ~vb. **2.** (intr.) to play or sound (on) a bugle. [C14: short for bugle horn ox horn, from OF bugle, from L būculus young bullock, from bōs ox] —**'bugler** n.

bugle[2] ('bju:gəl) n. any of several Eurasian plants having small blue or white flowers. [C13: from LL bugula, from ?]

bugle[3] ('bju:gəl) n. a tubular glass or plastic bead sewn onto clothes for decoration. [C16: from ?]

bugloss ('bju:glɒs) n. any of various hairy Eurasian plants having clusters of blue flowers. [C15: from L, from Gk bouglōssos ox-tongued]

bugong ('bu:gɒŋ) n. another name for **bogong.**

buhl (bu:l) adj., n. a variant spelling of **boulle.**

build (bɪld) vb. **building, built. 1.** to make, construct, or form by joining parts or materials: to build a house. **2.** (tr.) to order the building of: the government builds most of our hospitals. **3.** (foll. by on or upon) to base; found: his theory was not built on facts. **4.** (tr.) to establish and develop: it took ten years to build a business. **5.** (tr.) to make in a particular way or for a particular purpose: the car was not built for speed. **6.** (intr.; often foll. by up) to increase in intensity. ~n. **7.** physical form, figure, or proportions: a man with an athletic build. [OE byldan]

builder ('bɪldə) n. a person who builds, esp. one who contracts for and supervises the construction or repair of buildings.

building ('bɪldɪŋ) n. **1.** something built with a roof and walls. **2.** the act, business, occupation, or art of building houses, boats, etc.

building society n. a cooperative banking enterprise financed by deposits on which interest is paid and from which mortgage loans are advanced on homes and real property.

build up vb. (adv.) **1.** (tr.) to construct gradually, systematically, and in stages. **2.** to increase, accumulate, or strengthen, esp. by degrees: the murmur built up to a roar. **3.** (tr.) to improve the health or physique of (a person). **4.** (intr.) to prepare for or gradually approach a climax. ~n. **build-up. 5.** progressive increase in number, size, etc.: the build-up of industry. **6.** a gradual approach to a climax. **7.** extravagant publicity or praise, esp. in the form of a campaign. **8.** Mil. the process of attaining the required strength of forces and equipment.

built (bɪlt) vb. the past tense and past participle of **build.**

built-in adj. **1.** made or incorporated as an integral part: a built-in cupboard. **2.** essential; inherent. ~n. **3.** Austral. a built-in cupboard.

built-up adj. **1.** having many buildings (esp. in **built-up area**). **2.** increased by the addition of parts: built-up heels.

Buitenzorg (Dutch 'bœitənzɔrx) n. the former name of **Bogor.**

Bujumbura (ˌbu:dʒəm'buərə) n. the capital of Burundi, a port at the NE end of Lake Tanganyika. Pop.: 272 600 (1986). Former name: **Usumbura.**

Bukavu (bu:'kɑːvu:) n. a port in E Zaïre, on Kivu: commercial and industrial centre. Pop.: 171 064 (1984). Former name (until 1966): **Costermansville.**

Bukhara or **Bokhara** (bʊ'xɑːrə) n. **1.** a city in the SW Soviet Union, in W Uzbekistan: capital of the former emirate of Bukhara. Pop.: 220 000 (1987). **2.** a former emirate of central Asia: a powerful kingdom and centre of Islam; became a territory of the Soviet Union (1920) and was divided between the Uzbek, Tadzhik, and Turkmen SSRs.

Bukharin (Russian bu'xarin) n. **Nikolai Ivanovich** (nika'laj i'vanəvitʃ). 1888–1938, Soviet Bolshevik leader: executed in one of Stalin's purges.

Bukovina or **Bucovina** (ˌbu:kə'vi:nə) n. a region of E central Europe, part of the NE Carpathians: the north was seized by the Soviet Union (1940) and later became part of the Ukrainian SSR; the south remained Romanian.

Bulawayo (ˌbʊlə'weɪəʊ) n. a city in SW Zimbabwe founded (1893) on the site of the kraal of Lobengula, the last Matabele king; the country's main industrial centre. Pop.: 414 800 (1982).

bulb (bʌlb) n. **1.** a rounded organ of vegetative reproduction in plants such as the tulip and onion: a flattened stem bearing a central shoot surrounded by fleshy nutritive inner leaves and thin brown outer leaves. **2.** a plant, such as a hyacinth or daffodil, that grows from a bulb. **3.** See **light bulb. 4.** any bulb-shaped thing. [C16: from L bulbus, from Gk bolbos onion] —**'bulbous** adj.

bulbil ('bʌlbɪl) n. **1.** a small bulb produced from a parent bulb. **2.** a bulblike reproductive organ in a leaf axil of certain plants. [C19: from NL bulbillus BULB]

bulbul ('bʊlbʊl) n. a songbird of tropical Africa and Asia having brown plumage and, in many species, a distinct crest. [C18: via Persian from Ar.]

Bulganin (Russian bul'ganin) n. **Nikolai Aleksandrovich** (nika'laj alɪk'sandrəvitʃ). 1895–1975, Soviet statesman and military leader; chairman of the council of ministers (1955–58).

Bulgaria (bʌl'gɛərɪə, bʊl-) n. a republic in SE Europe, on the Balkan Peninsula on the Black Sea: under Turkish rule from 1395 until 1878; became an independent kingdom in 1908 and a republic in 1946; consists chiefly of the Danube valley in the north, the Balkan Mountains in the central part, separated from the Rhodope Mountains of the south by the valley of the Maritsa River. Language: Bulgarian. Currency: lev. Capital: Sofia. Pop.: 8 949 600 (1987). Area: 110 911 sq. km (42 823 sq. miles). —**Bul'garian** adj., n.

bulge (bʌldʒ) n. **1.** a swelling or an outward curve. **2.** a sudden increase in number, esp. of population. ~vb. **3.** to swell outwards. [C13: from OF bouge, from L bulga bag, prob. of Gaulish origin] —**'bulging** adj. — **'bulgy** adj.

bulimia (bju:'lɪmɪə) n. **1.** pathologically insatiable hunger. **2.** Also called: **bulimia nervosa.** a disorder characterized by compulsive overeating followed by vomiting. [C17: from NL, from Gk bous ox + limos hunger]

bulk (bʌlk) n. **1.** volume, size, or magnitude, esp. when great. **2.** the main part: the bulk of the work is repetitious. **3.** a large body, esp. of a person. **4.** the part of food which passes unabsorbed through the digestive system. **5. in bulk. a.** in large quantities. **b.** (of a cargo, etc.) unpackaged. ~vb. **6.** to cohere or cause to cohere in a mass. **7. bulk large.** to be or seem important or prominent. [C15: from ON bulki cargo]

bulk buying n. the purchase of goods in large amounts, often at reduced prices.

bulkhead ('bʌlk,hɛd) n. any upright wall-like partition in a ship, aircraft, etc. [C15: prob. from bulk projecting framework from ON bálkr + HEAD]

bulk modulus n. a coefficient of elasticity of a substance equal to the ratio of the applied stress to the resulting fractional change in volume.

bulky ('bʌlkɪ) adj. **bulkier, bulkiest.** very large and massive, esp. so as to be unwieldy. —**'bulkily** adv. —**'bulkiness** n.

bull[1] (bʊl) n. **1.** any male bovine animal, esp. one that is sexually mature. Related adj.: **taurine. 2.** the male of various other animals including the elephant and whale. **3.** a very large, strong, or aggressive person. **4.** Stock Exchange. **a.** a speculator who buys in anticipation of rising prices in order to make a profit on resale. **b.** (as modifier): a bull market. Cf. bear[2] (sense 5). **5.** Chiefly Brit. short for **bull's-eye** (senses 1, 2). **6.** Sl. short for **bullshit. 7.** a bull in a china shop. a clumsy person. **8. take the bull by the horns.** to face and tackle a difficulty without shirking. ~adj. **9.** male; masculine: a bull elephant. **10.** large; strong. [OE bula]

bull[2] (bʊl) n. a ludicrously self-contradictory or inconsistent statement. [C17: from ?]

bull[3] (bʊl) n. a formal document issued by the pope. [C13: from Med. L bulla seal attached to a bull, from L: round object]

Bull[1] (bʊl) n. the. the constellation Taurus, the second sign of the zodiac.

Bull[2] (bʊl) n. **John.** 1563–1628, English composer and organist.

Bullamakanka (ˌbu:ləmə'kæŋkə) n. Austral. an imaginary very remote place.

bulldog ('bʊl,dɒg) *n.* a sturdy thickset breed of dog with an undershot jaw, broad head, and a muscular body.

bulldog clip *n.* a clip for holding papers together, consisting of two T-shaped metal clamps held in place by a cylindrical spring.

bulldoze ('bʊl,dəʊz) *vb.* (*tr.*) **1.** to move, demolish, flatten, etc., with a bulldozer. **2.** *Inf.* to force; push. **3.** *Inf.* to intimidate or coerce. [C19: prob. from BULL[1] + DOSE]

bulldozer ('bʊl,dəʊzə) *n.* **1.** a powerful tractor fitted with caterpillar tracks and a blade at the front, used for moving earth, rocks, etc. **2.** *Inf.* a person who bulldozes.

bull dust *n. Austral.* **1.** fine dust, as on roads in outback Australia. **2.** *Sl.* nonsense.

bullet ('bʊlɪt) *n.* **1. a.** a small metallic missile enclosed in a cartridge, used as the projectile of a gun, rifle, etc. **b.** the entire cartridge. **2.** something resembling a bullet, esp. in shape or effect. [C16: from F *boulette*, dim. of *boule* ball; see BOWL[2]] —'**bullet-,like** *adj.*

bulletin ('bʊlɪtɪn) *n.* **1.** an official statement on a matter of public interest. **2.** a broadcast summary of the news. **3.** a periodical publication of an association, etc. ~*vb.* **4.** (*tr.*) to make known by bulletin. [C17: from F, from It., from *bulletta*, dim. of *bulla* papal edict, BULL[3]]

bulletin board *n.* the U.S. and Canad. name for **notice board.**

bullet loan *n.* a loan which is repaid with interest in a single payment at the end of a fixed term.

bulletproof ('bʊlɪt,pruːf) *adj.* **1.** not penetrable by bullets. ~*vb.* **2.** (*tr.*) to make bulletproof.

bullfight ('bʊl,faɪt) *n.* a traditional Spanish, Portuguese, and Latin American spectacle in which a matador baits and usually kills a bull in an arena. —'**bull,fighter** *n.* —'**bull,fighting** *n.*

bullfinch ('bʊl,fɪntʃ) *n.* **1.** a common European finch: the male has a bright red throat and breast. **2.** any of various similar finches. [C14: see BULL[1], FINCH]

bullfrog ('bʊl,frɒg) *n.* any of various large American frogs having a loud deep croak.

bullhead ('bʊl,hɛd) *n.* any of various small northern mainly marine fishes that have a large head covered with bony plates and spines.

bull-headed *adj.* blindly obstinate; stupid. —,**bull-'headedly** *adv.* —,**bull-'headedness** *n.*

bullhorn ('bʊl,hɔːn) *n.* the U.S. and Canad. name for **loudhailer.**

bullion ('bʊljən) *n.* **1.** gold or silver in mass. **2.** gold or silver in the form of bars and ingots, suitable for further processing. [C14: from Anglo-F: mint, prob. from OF *bouillir* to boil, from L *bullire*]

bullish ('bʊlɪʃ) *adj.* **1.** like a bull. **2.** *Stock Exchange.* causing, expecting, or characterized by a rise in prices. **3.** *Inf.* cheerful and optimistic.

bull-necked *adj.* having a short thick neck.

bullock ('bʊlək) *n.* **1.** a gelded bull; steer. ~*vb.* **2.** (*intr.*) *Austral. & N.Z. inf.* to work hard and long. [OE *bulluc*; see BULL[1], -OCK]

bullocky ('bʊləkɪ) *n.*, *pl.* **-ockies.** *Austral. & N.Z.* a bullock driver; teamster.

bullring ('bʊl,rɪŋ) *n.* an arena for bullfighting.

bullroarer ('bʊl,rɔːrə) *n.* a wooden slat attached to a thong that makes a roaring sound when the thong is whirled: used esp. by Australian Aborigines in religious rites.

bull's-eye *n.* **1.** the small central disc of a target, usually the highest valued area. **2.** a shot hitting this. **3.** *Inf.* something that exactly achieves its aim. **4.** a small circular or oval window or opening. **5.** a thick disc of glass set into a ship's deck, etc., to admit light. **6.** the glass boss at the centre of a sheet of blown glass. **7. a.** a small thick plano-convex lens used as a condenser. **b.** a lamp or lantern containing such a lens. **8.** a peppermint-flavoured boiled sweet.

bullshit ('bʊl,ʃɪt) *Taboo sl.* ~*n.* **1.** exaggerated or foolish talk; nonsense. **2.** deceitful or pretentious talk. **3.** (in the British Army) exaggerated zeal, esp. for ceremonial drill, cleaning, polishing, etc. Usually shortened to **bull.** ~*vb.* **-shitting, -shitted. 4.** (*intr.*) to talk in an exaggerated or foolish manner. **5.** (*tr.*) to talk bullshit to.

bull terrier *n.* a breed of terrier having a muscular body and thick neck, with a short smooth coat.

bully ('bʊlɪ) *n.*, *pl.* **-lies. 1.** a person who hurts, persecutes, or intimidates weaker people. **2.** a small New Zealand freshwater fish. ~*vb.* **-lying, -lied. 3.** (when *tr.*,

often foll. by *into*) to hurt, intimidate, or persecute (a weaker or smaller person), esp. to make him do something. ~*adj.* **4.** dashing; jolly: *my bully boy.* **5.** *Inf.* very good; fine. ~*interj.* **6.** Also: **bully for you, him,** etc. *Inf.* well done! bravo! [C16 (in the sense: sweetheart, hence fine fellow, hence swaggering coward): prob. from MDu. *boele* lover, from MHG *buole*]

bully beef *n.* canned corned beef. Often shortened to **bully.** [C19 *bully,* anglicized version of F *bouilli,* from *boeuf bouilli* boiled beef]

bully-off *Hockey.* ~*n.* **1.** the method by which a game is started. Two opposing players stand with the ball between them and alternately strike their sticks together and against the ground three times before trying to hit the ball. ~*vb.* **bully off. 2.** (*intr.*, *adv.*) to start play with a bully-off. ~Often shortened to **bully.** [C19: from ?]

bullyrag ('bʊlɪ,ræg) *vb.* **-ragging, -ragged.** (*tr.*) to bully, esp. by means of cruel practical jokes. Also: **ballyrag.** [C18: from ?]

Bülow (*German* 'byːlɔv) *n.* Prince **Bernhard von** ('bɛrnhart fɔn). 1849–1929, chancellor of Germany (1900–09).

bulrush ('bʊl,rʌʃ) *n.* **1.** a popular name for **reed mace. 2.** a grasslike marsh plant used for making mats, chair seats, etc. **3.** a biblical word for **papyrus** (the plant). [C15 *bulrish, bul-* ?from BULL[1] + *rish* RUSH[2]]

bulwark ('bʊlwək) *n.* **1.** a wall or similar structure used as a fortification; rampart. **2.** a person or thing acting as a defence. **3.** (*often pl.*) *Naut.* a solid vertical fencelike structure along the outward sides of a deck. **4.** a breakwater or mole. ~*vb.* **5.** (*tr.*) to defend or fortify with or as if with a bulwark. [C15: via Du. from MHG *bolwerk,* from *bol* plank, BOLE + *werk* WORK]

Bulwer-Lytton ('bʊlwə'lɪtən) *n.* See (1st Baron) Lytton.

bum[1] (bʌm) *n. Brit. sl.* the buttocks or anus. [C14: from ?]

bum[2] (bʌm) *Inf.*, *chiefly U.S. & Canad.* ~*n.* **1.** a disreputable loafer or other. **2.** a tramp; hobo. ~*vb.* **bumming, bummed. 3.** (*tr.*) to get by begging; cadge: *to bum a lift.* **4.** (*intr.*; often foll. by *around*) to live by begging or as a vagrant or loafer. **5.** (*intr.*; usually foll. by *around*) to spend time to no good purpose; loaf; idle. ~*adj.* **6.** (*prenominal*) of poor quality; useless. [C19: prob. shortened from earlier *bummer* a loafer, prob. from G *bummeln* to loaf]

bumbailiff (,bʌm'beɪlɪf) *n. Brit. derog.* (formerly) an officer employed to collect debts and arrest debtors. [C17: from BUM[1] + *bailiff,* so called because he follows hard behind debtors]

bumble ('bʌmbəl) *vb.* **1.** to speak or do in a clumsy, muddled, or inefficient way. **2.** (*intr.*) to proceed unsteadily. [C16: ? a blend of BUNGLE + STUMBLE] —'**bumbler** *n.* —'**bumbling** *adj.*, *n.*

bumblebee ('bʌmbəl,biː) *or* **humblebee** *n.* any large hairy social bee of temperate regions. [C16: from *bumble* to buzz + BEE]

bumf (bʌmf) *n.* a variant spelling of **bumph.**

bump (bʌmp) *vb.* **1.** (when *intr.*, usually foll. by *against* or *into*) to knock or strike with a jolt. **2.** (*intr.*; often foll. by *along*) to travel or proceed in jerks and jolts. **3.** (*tr.*) to hurt by knocking. **4.** *Cricket.* to bowl (a ball) so that it bounces high on pitching or (of a ball) to bounce high when bowled. ~*n.* **5.** an impact; knock; jolt; collision. **6.** a dull thud or other noise from an impact or collision. **7.** the shock of a blow or collision. **8.** a lump on the body caused by a blow. **9.** a protuberance, as on a road surface. **10.** any of the natural protuberances of the human skull, said by phrenologists to indicate underlying faculties and character. ~See also **bump into, bump off, bump up.** [C16: prob. imit.]

bumper[1] ('bʌmpə) *n.* **1.** a horizontal usually metal bar attached to the front or rear end of a car, lorry, etc., to protect against damage from impact. **2.** *Cricket.* a ball bowled so that it bounces high on pitching; bouncer.

bumper[2] ('bʌmpə) *n.* **1.** a glass, tankard, etc., filled to the brim, esp. as a toast. **2.** an unusually large or fine example of something. ~*adj.* **3.** unusually large, fine, or abundant: *a bumper crop.* [C17 (in the sense: a brimming glass): prob. from *bump* (obs. vb.) to bulge; see BUMP]

bumph *or* **bumf** (bʌmf) *n. Inf., derog.* **1.** *Inf., derog.* official documents, forms, etc. **2.** *Sl.* toilet paper. [C19: short for earlier *bumfodder*; see BUM[1]]

bump into *vb.* (*intr.*, *prep.*) *Inf.* to meet by chance; encounter unexpectedly.

bumpkin ('bʌmpkɪn) n. an awkward simple rustic person (esp. in **country bumpkin**). [C16: ?from Du. *boomken* small tree, or from MDu. *boomekijn* small barrel]

bump off vb. (tr., adv.) Sl. to murder; kill.

bumptious ('bʌmpʃəs) adj. offensively self-assertive or conceited. [C19: ?from BUMP + FRACTIOUS] —'**bumptiously** adv. —'**bumptiousness** n.

bump up vb. (tr., adv.) Inf. to raise or increase.

bumpy ('bʌmpɪ) adj. **bumpier, bumpiest. 1.** having an uneven surface. **2.** full of jolts; rough. —'**bumpily** adv. —'**bumpiness** n.

bun (bʌn) n. **1.** a small roll, similar to bread but usually containing sweetening, currants, etc. **2.** Chiefly Scot. & N English. any of various small round cakes. **3.** a hairstyle in which long hair is gathered into a bun shape at the back of the head. [C14: from ?]

bunch (bʌntʃ) n. **1.** a number of things growing, fastened, or grouped together: *a bunch of grapes; a bunch of keys.* **2.** a collection; group: *a bunch of queries.* **3.** Inf. a group or company: *a bunch of boys.* ~vb. **4.** (sometimes foll. by *up*) to group or be grouped into a bunch. [C14: from ?]

Bunche (bʌntʃ) n. **Ralph Johnson.** 1904–71, U.S. diplomat and United Nations official: awarded the Nobel peace prize in 1950 for his work as UN mediator in Palestine (1948–49); UN undersecretary (1954–71).

bunchy ('bʌntʃɪ) adj. **bunchier, bunchiest. 1.** composed of or resembling bunches. **2.** bulging.

buncombe ('bʌŋkəm) n. a variant spelling (esp. U.S.) of **bunkum.**

Bundaberg ('bʌndə,bɜːg) n. a city in E Australia, near the E coast of Queensland: centre of a sugar-growing area, with a nearby deep-water port. Pop.: 42 550 (1986).

Bundelkhand (,bʌndəl'kʌnd, -'xʌnd) n. a region of central India: formerly native states, now mainly part of Madhya Pradesh.

bundle ('bʌndəl) n. **1.** a number of things or a quantity of material gathered or loosely bound together: *a bundle of sticks.* Related adj.: **fascicular. 2.** something wrapped or tied for carrying; package. **3.** Sl. a large sum of money. **4. go a bundle on.** Sl. to be extremely fond of. **5.** Biol. a collection of strands of specialized tissue such as nerve fibres. **6.** Bot. short for **vascular bundle. 7. drop one's bundle.** Austral. & N.Z. sl. to panic or give up hope. ~vb. **8.** (tr.; often foll. by *up*) to make into a bundle. **9.** (foll. by *out, off, into,* etc.) to go or cause to go, esp. roughly or unceremoniously. **10.** (tr.; usually foll. by *into*) to push or throw, esp. quickly and untidily. **11.** (intr.) to sleep or lie in one's clothes on the same bed as one's betrothed: formerly a custom in New England, Wales, and elsewhere. [C14: prob. from MDu. *bundel;* rel. to OE *bindele* bandage; see BIND, BOND] —'**bundler** n.

bundle up vb. (adv.) **1.** to dress (somebody) warmly and snugly. **2.** (tr.) to make (something) into a bundle or bundles, esp. by tying.

bundu ('bundu) n. S. African & Zimbabwean sl. a largely uninhabited wild region far from towns. [C20: from a Bantu language]

bun fight n. Brit. sl. **1.** a tea party. **2.** Ironic. an official function.

bung[1] (bʌŋ) n. **1.** a stopper, esp. of cork or rubber, for a cask, etc. **2.** short for **bunghole.** ~vb. (tr.) **3.** (often foll. by *up*) Inf. to close or seal with or as with a bung. **4.** Brit. sl. to throw; sling. **5. bung it on.** Austral. sl. to behave in a pretentious manner. [C15: from MDu. *bonghe*]

bung[2] (bʌŋ) adj. Austral. & N.Z. sl. **1.** dead. **2.** destroyed. **3.** useless. **4. go bung. a.** to fail or collapse. **b.** to die. [C19: from Abor.]

bungalow ('bʌŋgə,ləʊ) n. a one-storey house, sometimes with an attic. [C17: from Hindi *banglā* (house) of the Bengal type]

bunghole ('bʌŋ,həʊl) n. a hole in a cask, barrel, etc., through which liquid can be drained.

bungle ('bʌŋgəl) vb. **1.** (tr.) to spoil (an operation) through clumsiness, incompetence, etc.; botch. ~n. **2.** a clumsy or unsuccessful performance; mistake; botch. [C16: ? of Scand. origin] —'**bungler** n. —'**bungling** adj., n.

Bunin (Russian 'bunin) n. **Ivan Alekseyevich** (i'van alɪk'sjejivitʃ). 1870–1953, Russian novelist and poet; author of *The Gentleman from San Francisco* (1922).

bunion ('bʌnjən) n. an inflamed swelling of the first joint of the big toe. [C18: ?from obs. *bunny* a swelling, from ?]

bunk[1] (bʌŋk) n. **1.** a narrow shelflike bed fixed along a wall. **2.** short for **bunk bed. 3.** Inf. any place where one sleeps. ~vb. **4.** (intr.; often foll. by *down*) to prepare to sleep: *he bunked down on the floor.* **5.** (intr.) to occupy a bunk or bed. [C19: prob. short for BUNKER]

bunk[2] (bʌŋk) n. Inf. short for **bunkum** (sense 1).

bunk[3] (bʌŋk) n. Brit. sl. a hurried departure, usually under suspicious circumstances (esp. in **do a bunk**). [C19: ?from BUNK[1] (in the sense: to occupy a bunk, hence a hurried departure)]

bunk bed n. one of a pair of beds constructed one above the other to save space.

bunker ('bʌŋkə) n. **1.** a large storage container or tank, as for coal. **2.** Also called (esp. U.S. and Canad.): **sand trap.** an obstacle on a golf course, usually a sand-filled hollow bordered by a ridge. **3.** an underground shelter with a bank and embrasures for guns above ground. ~vb. **4.** (tr.) Golf. **a.** to drive (the ball) into a bunker. **b.** (passive) to have one's ball trapped in a bunker. [C16 (in the sense: chest, box): from Scot. *bonkar,* from ?]

bunkhouse ('bʌŋk,haʊs) n. (in the U.S. and Canada) a building containing the sleeping quarters of workers on a ranch.

bunkum or **buncombe** ('bʌŋkəm) n. **1.** empty talk; nonsense. **2.** Chiefly U.S. empty or insincere speechmaking by a politician. [C19: after *Buncombe,* a county in North Carolina, alluded to in an inane speech by its Congressional representative Felix Walker (about 1820)]

bunny ('bʌnɪ) n., pl. **-nies. 1.** Also called: **bunny rabbit.** a child's word for **rabbit** (sense 1). **2.** Also called: **bunny girl.** a night-club hostess whose costume includes rabbit-like tail and ears. **3.** Austral. sl. a mug; dupe. [C17: from Scot. Gaelic *bun* scut of a rabbit]

Bunsen ('bʌnsᵊn; German 'bʊnzən) n. **Robert Wilhelm** ('roːbɛrt 'vɪlhɛlm). 1811–99, German chemist who with Kirchhoff developed spectrum analysis and discovered the elements caesium and rubidium. He invented the Bunsen burner and the ice calorimeter.

Bunsen burner n. a gas burner consisting of a metal tube with an adjustable air valve at the base. [C19: after R. W. BUNSEN]

bunting[1] ('bʌntɪŋ) n. **1.** a coarse, loosely woven cotton fabric used for flags, etc. **2.** decorative flags, pennants, and streamers. [C18: from ?]

bunting[2] ('bʌntɪŋ) n. any of numerous seed-eating songbirds of the Old World and North America having short stout bills. [C13: from ?]

buntline ('bʌntlɪn, -,laɪn) n. Naut. one of several lines fastened to the foot of a square sail for hauling it up to the yard when furling. [C17: from *bunt* centre of a sail + LINE[1](sense 11)]

Buñuel (Spanish bu'ɲwel) n. **Luis** (lwis). 1900–83, Spanish film director. He collaborated with Salvador Dali on the first surrealist films, *Un Chien andalou* (1929) and *L'Age d'or* (1930). His later films include *Viridiana* (1961), *Belle de jour* (1966), *The Discreet Charm of the Bourgeoisie* (1972), and *That Obscure Object of Desire* (1977).

bunya-bunya ('bʌnjə'bʌnjə) or **bunya** n. a tall dome-shaped Australian coniferous tree having edible seeds and thickish flattened needles. [C19: from Abor.]

Bunyan ('bʌnjən) n. **John.** 1628–88, English preacher and writer, noted particularly for his allegory *The Pilgrim's Progress* (1678).

bunyip ('bʌnjip) n. Austral. a legendary monster said to inhabit swamps and lagoons. [C19: from Abor.]

Buonaparte (bwona'parte) n. the Italian spelling of **Bonaparte.**

Buonarroti (Italian bwonar'roti) n. See **Michelangelo.**

buoy (bɔɪ; U.S. 'buːɪ) n. **1.** a distinctively shaped and coloured float, anchored to the bottom, for designating moorings, navigable channels, or obstructions in a body of water. See also **life buoy.** ~vb. **2.** (tr.; usually foll. by *up*) to prevent from sinking: *the life belt buoyed him up.* **3.** (tr.; usually foll. by *up*) to raise the spirits of; hearten. **4.** (tr.) Naut. to mark (a channel or obstruction) with a buoy or buoys. **5.** (intr.) to rise to the surface; float. [C13: prob. of Gmc origin]

buoyancy ('bɔɪənsɪ) n. **1.** the ability to float in a liquid or to rise in liquid, air, or other gas. **2.** the tendency of a fluid to keep a body afloat. **3.** the ability to recover quickly after setbacks; resilience. **4.** cheerfulness.

buoyant ('bɔɪənt) *adj.* **1.** able to float in or rise to the surface of a liquid. **2.** (of a liquid or gas) able to keep a body afloat. **3.** cheerful or resilient. [C16: prob. from Sp. *boyante*, from *boyar* to float]

BUPA ('bjuːpə, 'buːpə) *n. acronym for* British United Provident Association.

bur (bɜː) *n.* **1.** a seed vessel or flower head having hooks or prickles. **2.** any plant that produces burs. **3.** a person or thing that clings like a bur. **4.** a small surgical or dental drill. ~*vb.* **burring, burred. 5.** (*tr.*) to remove burs from. ~Also: **burr.** [C14: prob. from ON]

Buraydah *or* **Buraida** (buˈraɪdə) *n.* a town and oasis in central Saudi Arabia. Pop.: 69 940 (1974).

Burbage ('bɜːbɪdʒ) *n.* **Richard.** ?1567–1619, English actor, closely associated with Shakespeare.

burble ('bɜːbəl) *vb.* **1.** to make or utter with a bubbling sound; gurgle. **2.** (*intr.; often foll. by away or on*) to talk quickly and excitedly. ~*n.* **3.** a bubbling or gurgling sound. **4.** a flow of excited speech. [C14: prob. imit.] —**'burbler** *n.*

burbot ('bɜːbət) *n., pl.* **-bots** *or* **-bot.** a freshwater gadoid food fish that has barbels around its mouth and occurs in Europe, Asia, and North America. [C14: from OF *bourbotte*, from *bourbeter* to wallow in mud, from *bourbe* mud]

burden[1] ('bɜːdən) *n.* **1.** something that is carried; load. **2.** something that is exacting, oppressive, or difficult to bear. Related adj.: **onerous. 3.** *Naut.* **a.** the cargo capacity of a ship. **b.** the weight of a ship's cargo. ~*vb.* (*tr.*) **4.** (sometimes foll. by *up*) to put or impose a burden on; load. **5.** to weigh down; oppress. [OE *byrthen*]

burden[2] ('bɜːdən) *n.* **1.** a line of words recurring at the end of each verse of a song; chorus or refrain. **2.** the theme of a speech, book, etc. **3.** another word for **bourdon.** [C16: from OF *bourdon* bass horn, droning sound, imit.]

burden of proof *n. Law.* the obligation to provide evidence that will convince the court or jury of the truth of one's contention.

burdensome ('bɜːdənsəm) *adj.* hard to bear.

burdock ('bɜː,dɒk) *n.* a coarse weedy Eurasian plant having large heart-shaped leaves, tiny purple flowers surrounded by hooked bristles, and burlike fruits. [C16: from BUR + DOCK[4]]

bureau ('bjuərəu) *n., pl.* **-reaus** *or* **-reaux. 1.** *Chiefly Brit.* a writing desk with pigeonholes, drawers, etc., against which the writing surface can be closed when not in use. **2.** *U.S.* a chest of drawers. **3.** an office or agency, esp. one providing services for the public. **4.** a government department. [C17: from F, orig.: type of cloth used for covering desks, from OF *burel*]

bureaucracy (bjuəˈrɒkrəsɪ) *n., pl.* **-cies. 1.** a system of administration based upon organization into bureaus, division of labour, a hierarchy of authority, etc. **2.** government by such a system. **3.** government or other officials collectively. **4.** any administration in which action is impeded by unnecessary official procedures.

bureaucrat ('bjuərə,kræt) *n.* **1.** an official in a bureaucracy. **2.** an official who adheres to bureaucracy, esp. rigidly. —,**bureau'cratic** *adj.* —,**bureau'cratically** *adv.*

bureaucratize *or* **-tise** (bjuəˈrɒkrə,taɪz) *vb.* (*tr.*) to administer by or transform into a bureaucracy. —**bu,reaucrati'zation** *or* **-ti'sation** *n.*

bureaux ('bjuərəuz) *n.* a plural of **bureau.**

burette *or U.S.* **buret** (bjuˈret) *n.* a graduated glass tube with a stopcock on one end for dispensing and transferring known volumes of fluids, esp. liquids. [C15: from F, from OF *buire* ewer]

burg (bɜːg) *n.* **1.** *History.* a fortified town. **2.** *U.S. inf.* a town or city. [C18 (in the sense: fortress): from OHG *burg*]

burgage ('bɜːgɪdʒ) *n. History.* **1.** (in England) tenure of land or tenement in a town or city, which originally involved a fixed money rent. **2.** (in Scotland) the tenure of land direct from the crown in Scottish royal burghs in return for watching and warding. [C14: from Med. L *burgāgium*, from OE *burg*]

Burgas (*Bulgarian* burˈgas) *n.* a port in SE Bulgaria on an inlet of the Black Sea. Pop.: 182 570 (1985).

Burgenland (*German* 'burgən,lant) *n.* a province of E Austria. Capital: Eisenstadt. Pop.: 267 279 (1986). Area: 3965 sq. km (1531 sq. miles).

burgeon *or* **bourgeon** ('bɜːdʒən) *vb.* **1.** (often foll. by *forth* or *out*) (of a plant) to sprout (buds). **2.** (*intr.; often*

foll. by *forth* or *out*) to develop or grow rapidly; flourish. [C13: from OF *burjon*]

burger ('bɜːgə) *n. Inf.* **a.** short for **hamburger. b.** (*in combination*): *a cheeseburger.*

Bürger (*German* 'byrgər) *n.* **Gottfried August** ('gɔtfriːt 'august). 1747–94, German lyric poet, noted particularly for his ballad *Lenore* (1773).

burgess ('bɜːdʒɪs) *n.* **1.** (in England) a citizen, freeman, or inhabitant of a borough. **2.** *English history.* a Member of Parliament from a borough, corporate town, or university. [C13: from OF *burgeis;* see BOROUGH]

Burgess ('bɜːdʒɪs) *n.* **1. Anthony.** born 1917, English novelist and critic: author of satirical novels, such as *A Clockwork Orange* (1962), *Tremor of Intent* (1966), *Earthly Powers* (1980), and *Little Wilson and Big God* (1988). **2. Guy.** 1911–63, British spy, who fled to the Soviet Union (with Donald Maclean) in 1951.

burgh ('bʌrə) *n.* **1.** (in Scotland until 1975) a town, esp. one incorporated by charter, that enjoyed a degree of self-government. **2.** an archaic form of **borough.** [C14: Scot. form of BOROUGH] —**burghal** ('bɜːgəl) *adj.*

burgher ('bɜːgə) *n.* **1.** a member of the trading or mercantile class of a medieval city. **2.** a respectable citizen; bourgeois. **3.** *Arch.* a citizen or inhabitant of a corporate town, esp on the Continent. **4.** *S. African history.* a citizen of the Cape Colony or of one of the Transvaal and Free State republics. [C16: from G *Bürger* or Du. *burger* freeman of a BOROUGH]

Burghley *or* **Burleigh** ('bɜːlɪ) *n.* **William Cecil,** 1st Baron Burghley. 1520–98, English statesman: chief adviser to Elizabeth I; secretary of state (1558–72) and Lord High Treasurer (1572–98).

burglar ('bɜːglə) *n.* a person who commits burglary; housebreaker. [C15: from Anglo-F, from Med. L *burglātor*, prob. from *burgāre* to thieve]

burglary ('bɜːglərɪ) *n., pl.* **-ries.** the crime of entering a building as a trespasser to commit theft or another offence. —**burglarious** (bɜːˈglɛərɪəs) *adj.* —'**burgla,rize** *or* **-ise** *vb.* (*tr.*)

burgle ('bɜːgəl) *vb.* to commit burglary upon (a house, etc.).

burgomaster ('bɜːgə,mɑːstə) *n.* the chief magistrate of a town in Austria, Belgium, Germany, or the Netherlands; mayor. [C16: partial translation of Du. *burgemeester;* see BOROUGH, MASTER]

Burgoyne (bɜːˈgɔɪn) *n.* **John.** 1722–92, British general in the War of American Independence who was forced to surrender at Saratoga (1777).

Burgundy ('bɜːgəndɪ) *n., pl.* **-dies. 1.** a region of E France famous for its wines, lying west of the Saône: formerly a semi-independent duchy; annexed to France in 1482. French name: **Bourgogne. 2. Free County of.** another name for **Franche-Comté. 3.** a monarchy (1384–1477) of medieval Europe, at its height including the Low Countries, the duchy of Burgundy, and Franche-Comté. **4. Kingdom of.** a kingdom in E France, established in the early 6th century A.D., eventually including the later duchy of Burgundy, Franche-Comté, and the Kingdom of Provence: known as the Kingdom of Arles from the 13th century. **5. a.** any red or white wine produced in the region of Burgundy, around Dijon. **b.** any heavy red table wine. **6.** (*often not cap.*) a blackish-purple to purplish-red colour. —**Burgundian** (bɜːˈgʌndɪən) *adj., n.*

burial ('berɪəl) *n.* the act of burying, esp. the interment of a dead body. [OE *byrgels* burial place, tomb; see BURY, -AL[2]]

burial ground *n.* a graveyard or cemetery.

burin ('bjuərɪn) *n.* **1.** a chisel of tempered steel used for engraving metal, wood, or marble. **2.** *Archaeol.* a prehistoric flint tool. [C17: from F, ?from It. *burino*, of Gmc origin]

burk *or* **berk** (bɜːk) *n. Brit. sl.* a stupid person; fool. [C20: shortened from *Berkeley* or *Berkshire Hunt*, rhyming slang for *cunt*]

Burke (bɜːk) *n.* **1. Edmund.** 1729–97, British Whig statesman, conservative political theorist, and orator, born in Ireland: defended parliamentary government and campaigned for a more liberal treatment of the American colonies. **2. Robert O'Hara.** 1820–61, Irish explorer, who led the first expedition (1860–61) across Australia from South to North. He was accompanied by W. J. Wills, George Grey, and John King; King alone survived the return journey.

Burkina-Faso (bɜː'kiːnə'fæsəʊ) *n.* an inland republic in W Africa: dominated by Mossi kingdoms (10th–19th centuries); French protectorate established in 1896; became an independent republic in 1960; consists mainly of a flat savanna plateau. Languages: French, Mossi, and African languages. Religion: mostly animist, with a Muslim minority. Currency: franc. Capital: Ouagadougou. Pop.: 8 334 000 (1987 est.). Area: 273 200 sq. km (105 900 sq. miles). Former name (until 1984): **Upper Volta.**

burl[1] (bɜːl) *n.* **1.** a small knot or lump in wool. **2.** a roundish warty outgrowth from certain trees. ~*vb.* **3.** (*tr.*) to remove the burls from (cloth). [C15: from OF *burle* tuft of wool, prob. ult. from LL *burra* shaggy cloth] —'**burler** *n.*

burl[2] *or* **birl** (bɜːl) *n. Inf.* **1.** *Scot., Austral., & N.Z.* an attempt; try (esp. in **give it a burl**). **2.** *Austral, & N.Z.* a ride in a car. [C20: ?from BIRL in Scots sense: to spin or turn]

burlap ('bɜːlæp) *n.* a coarse fabric woven from jute, hemp, or the like. [C17: from *borel* coarse cloth, from OF *burel* (see BUREAU) + LAP[1]]

Burleigh ('bɜːlɪ) *n.* a variant spelling of **Burghley.**

burlesque (bɜː'lɛsk) *n.* **1.** an artistic work, esp. literary or dramatic, satirizing a subject by caricaturing it. **2.** a ludicrous imitation or caricature. **3.** Also: **burlesk.** *U.S. & Canad. theatre.* a bawdy comedy show of the late 19th and early 20th centuries: the striptease eventually became one of its chief elements. ~*adj.* **4.** of, relating to, or characteristic of a burlesque. ~*vb.* **-lesquing, -lesqued. 5.** to represent or imitate (a person or thing) in a ludicrous way; caricature. [C17: from F, from It., from *burla* a jest, piece of nonsense] —**bur'lesquer** *n.*

burley ('bɜːlɪ) *n.* a variant spelling of **berley.**

Burlington ('bɜːlɪŋtən) *n.* **1.** a city in S Canada on Lake Ontario, northeast of Hamilton. Pop.: 114 853 (1981). **2.** a city in NW Vermont on Lake Champlain: largest city in the state; University of Vermont (1791). Pop.: 37 712 (1980).

burly ('bɜːlɪ) *adj.* **-lier, -liest.** large and thick of build; sturdy. [C13: of Gmc origin] —'**burliness** *n.*

Burma ('bɜːmə) *n.* a republic in SE Asia, on the Bay of Bengal and the Andaman Sea: unified from small states in 1752; annexed by Britain (1823–85) and made a province of India in 1886; became independent in 1948. It is generally mountainous, with the basins of the Chindwin and Irrawaddy Rivers in the central part and the Irrawaddy delta in the south. Language: Burmese. Religion: chiefly Buddhist. Currency: kyat. Capital: Rangoon. Pop.: 37 850 000 (1987 est.). Area: 678 000 sq. km (261 789 sq. miles). Official name: **Socialist Republic of the Union of Burma.**

Burmese (bɜː'miːz) *adj.* also **Burman. 1.** of or denoting Burma, or its inhabitants, their customs, etc. ~*n.* **2.** (*pl.* **-mese**) a native or inhabitant of Burma. **3.** the language of the Burmese.

burn[1] (bɜːn) *vb.* **burning, burnt** *or* **burned. 1.** to undergo or cause to undergo combustion. **2.** to destroy or be destroyed by fire. **3.** (*tr.*) to damage, injure, or mark by heat: *he burnt his hand; she was burnt by the sun.* **4.** to die or put to death by fire. **5.** (*intr.*) to be or feel hot: *my forehead burns.* **6.** to smart or cause to smart: *brandy burns one's throat.* **7.** (*intr.*) to feel strong emotion, esp. anger or passion. **8.** (*tr.*) to use for the purposes of light, heat, or power: *to burn coal.* **9.** (*tr.*) to form by or as if by fire: *to burn a hole.* **10.** to char or become charred: *the potatoes are burning.* **11.** (*tr.*) to brand or cauterize. **12.** to produce by or subject to heat as part of a process: *to burn charcoal.* **13. burn one's boats** *or* **bridges.** to commit oneself to a particular course of action with no possibility of turning back. **14. burn one's fingers.** to suffer from having meddled or interfered. ~*n.* **15.** an injury caused by exposure to heat, electrical, chemical, or radioactive agents. **16.** a mark, e.g. on wood, caused by burning. **17.** a controlled use of rocket propellant, esp. for a course correction. **18.** a hot painful sensation in a muscle, experienced during vigorous exercise. **19.** *Sl.* tobacco or a cigarette. ~See also **burn out.** [OE *beornan* (intr.), *bœrnan* (tr.)]

burn[2] (bɜːn) *n. Scot.* a small stream; brook. [OE *burna*; rel. to ON *brunnr* spring]

Burne-Jones (bɜːn'dʒəʊnz) *n.* Sir **Edward.** 1833–98, English Pre-Raphaelite painter and designer of stained-glass windows and tapestries.

burner ('bɜːnə) *n.* **1.** the part of a stove, lamp, etc., that produces flame or heat. **2.** an apparatus for burning something, as fuel or refuse.

burnet ('bɜːnɪt) *n.* **1.** a plant of the rose family which has purple-tinged green flowers and leaves. **2. burnet rose.** a very prickly Eurasian rose with white flowers and purplish-black fruits. **3.** a moth with red-spotted dark green wings and antennae with enlarged tips. [C14: from OF *burnete,* var. of *brunete* BRUNETTE]

Burnet (bə'nɛt, 'bɜːnɪt) *n.* **1.** Sir **Macfarlane** (mək'fɑːlən). 1899–1985, Australian physician and virologist, who shared a Nobel prize for medicine or physiology in 1960 with P. B. Medawar for their work in immunology. **2. Thomas.** 1635–1715, English theologian who tried to reconcile science and religion in his *Sacred theory of the Earth* (1680–89).

Burnett (bɜː'nɛt) *n.* **Frances Hodgson** ('hɒdʒsən). 1849–1924, U.S. novelist, born in England; author of *Little Lord Fauntleroy* (1886) and *The Secret Garden* (1911).

Burney ('bɜːnɪ) *n.* **1. Charles.** 1726–1814, English composer and music historian, whose books include *A General History of Music* (1776–89). **2.** his daughter, **Frances.** known as *Fanny;* married name *Madame D'Arblay.* 1752–1840, English novelist and diarist: author of *Evelina* (1778). Her *Diaries and Letters* (1768–1840) are of historical interest.

burning ('bɜːnɪŋ) *adj.* **1.** intense; passionate. **2.** urgent; crucial: *a burning problem.*

burning bush *n.* **1.** any of several shrubs or trees that have bright red fruits or seeds. **2.** any of several plants with a bright red autumn foliage. **3.** *Bible.* the bush that burned without being consumed, from which God spoke to Moses (Exodus 3:2–4).

burning glass *n.* a convex lens for concentrating the sun's rays to produce fire.

burnish ('bɜːnɪʃ) *vb.* **1.** to make or become shiny or smooth by friction; polish. ~*n.* **2.** a shiny finish; lustre. [C14 *burnischen,* from OF *brunir* to make brown, from *brun* BROWN] —'**burnisher** *n.*

Burnley ('bɜːnlɪ) *n.* an industrial town in NW England, in E Lancashire. Pop.: 92 200 (1983 est.).

burnoose, burnous, *or* **burnouse** (bɜː'nuːs, -'nuːz) *n.* a long circular cloak with a hood attached, worn esp. by Arabs. [C20: via F *burnous* from Ar. *burnus,* from Gk *birros* cloak]

burn out *vb.* (*adv.*) **1.** to become or cause to become inoperative as a result of heat or friction: *the clutch burnt out.* **2.** (*intr.*) (of a rocket, jet engine, etc.) to cease functioning as a result of exhaustion of the fuel supply. **3.** (*tr.; usually passive*) to destroy by fire. **4.** to become or cause to become exhausted through overwork or dissipation.

Burns (bɜːnz) *n.* **Robert.** 1759–96, Scottish lyric poet. His verse, written mostly in dialect, includes love songs, nature poetry, and satires, of which *Auld Lang Syne* and *Tam o' Shanter* are among the best known.

burnt (bɜːnt) *vb.* **1.** a past tense and past participle of **burn**[1]. ~*adj.* **2.** affected by or as if by burning; charred.

burnt offering *n.* a sacrificial offering burnt, usually on an altar, to honour, propitiate, or supplicate a deity.

burnt sienna *n.* **1.** a reddish-brown pigment obtained by roasting raw sienna. ~*n., adj.* **2.** (of) a reddish-brown colour.

burnt umber *n.* **1.** a brown pigment obtained by heating umber. ~*n., adj.* **2.** (of) a dark brown colour.

burp (bɜːp) *n. Inf.* **1.** a belch. ~*vb.* **2.** (*intr.*) *Inf.* to belch. **3.** (*tr.*) to cause (a baby) to burp. [C20: imit.]

burr[1] (bɜː) *n.* **1.** a small power-driven hand-operated rotary file, esp. for removing burrs or for machining recesses. **2.** a rough edge left on a workpiece after cutting, drilling, etc. **3.** a rough or irregular protuberance, such as a burl on a tree. **4.** a variant spelling of **bur.** [C14: var. of BUR]

burr[2] (bɜː) *n.* **1.** an articulation of (r) characteristic of certain English dialects, esp. the uvular fricative trill of Northumberland or the retroflex *r* of the West of England. **2.** a whirring sound. ~*vb.* **3.** to pronounce (words) with a burr. **4.** (*intr.*) to make a whirring sound. [C18: either special use of BUR (in the sense: rough sound) or imit.]

Burren ('bʌrən) *n.* **the.** a limestone area on the North Clare coast in the Irish Republic, famous for its wild flowers, caves, and dolmens.

burro ('bʊrəʊ) n., pl. **-ros.** a donkey, esp. one used as a pack animal. [C19: Sp., from Port., from *burrico*]

Burroughs ('bʌrəʊz) n. **1. Edgar Rice.** 1875–1950, U.S. novelist, author of the *Tarzan* stories. **2. William.** born 1914, U.S. novelist, noted for his works portraying the life of drug addicts, esp. *The Naked Lunch* (1959). Other works include *The Ticket that Exploded* (1962), *Nova Express* (1964), and *The Western Lands* (1988).

burrow ('bʌrəʊ) n. **1.** a hole dug in the ground by a rabbit or other small animal. **2.** a small snug place affording shelter or retreat. ~vb. **3.** to dig (a burrow) in, through, or under (ground). **4.** (*intr.; often foll. by through*) to move through by or as by digging. **5.** (*intr.*) to hide or live in a burrow. **6.** (*intr.*) to delve deeply: *he burrowed into his pockets.* **7.** to hide (oneself). [C13: prob. var. of BOROUGH] —'**burrower** n.

burry ('bɜːrɪ) adj. **-rier, -riest. 1.** full of or covered in burs. **2.** resembling burs; prickly.

bursa ('bɜːsə) n., pl. **-sae** (-siː) or **-sas.** Anat. a small fluid-filled sac that reduces friction, esp. at joints. [C19: from Med. L: bag, pouch, from Gk: skin, hide; see PURSE] —'**bursal** adj.

Bursa ('bɜːsə) n. a city in NW Turkey: founded in the 2nd century B.C.; seat of Bithynian kings. Pop.: 614 133 (1985). Former name: **Brusa.**

bursar ('bɜːsə) n. **1.** a treasurer of a school, college, or university. **2.** Chiefly Scot. & N.Z. a student holding a bursary. [C13: from Med. L *bursārius* keeper of the purse, from *bursa* purse]

bursary ('bɜːsərɪ) n., pl. **-ries. 1.** Also called: '**bursar,ship.** a scholarship awarded esp. in Scottish and New Zealand schools and universities. **2.** Brit. the treasury of a college, etc. —**bursarial** (bɜː'sɛərɪəl) adj.

bursitis (bɜː'saɪtɪs) n. inflammation of a bursa.

burst (bɜːst) vb. **bursting, burst. 1.** to break or cause to break open or apart suddenly and noisily; explode. **2.** (*intr.*) to come, go, etc., suddenly and forcibly: *he burst into the room.* **3.** (*intr.*) to be full to the point of breaking open. **4.** (*intr.*) to give vent (to) suddenly or loudly: *to burst into song.* **5.** (*tr.*) to cause or suffer the rupture of: *to burst a blood vessel.* ~n. **6.** a sudden breaking open; explosion. **7.** a break; breach; rupture. **8.** a sudden display or increase of effort; spurt: *a burst of speed.* **9.** a sudden and violent emission, occurrence, or outbreak: *a burst of applause.* **10.** a volley of fire from a weapon. [OE *berstan*]

burthen ('bɜːðən) n., vb. an archaic word for **burden**[1]. —'**burthensome** adj.

burton ('bɜːtⁿn) n. **go for a burton.** Brit. sl. **a.** to be broken, useless, or lost. **b.** to die. [C20: from ?]

Burton ('bɜːtⁿn) n. **1.** Sir **Richard Francis.** 1821–90, English explorer, Orientalist, and writer who discovered Lake Tanganyika with John Speke (1858); produced the first unabridged translation of *The Thousand Nights and a Night* (1885–88). **2. Richard**, real name *Richard Jenkins.* 1925–84, Welsh stage and film actor: films include *Becket* (1964), *Who's Afraid of Virginia Woolf?* (1966), and *Equus* (1977). **3. Robert**, pen name *Democritus Junior.* 1577–1640, English clergyman, scholar, and writer, noted for his *Anatomy of Melancholy* (1621).

Burton-upon-Trent n. a town in W central England, in E Staffordshire: famous for brewing. Pop.: 57 725 (1983).

Burundi (bə'rʊndɪ) n. a republic in E central Africa: inhabited chiefly by the Bahutu, Watutsi, and Batwa; made part of German East Africa in 1899; part of the Belgian territory of Ruanda-Urundi from 1923 until it became independent in 1962; consists mainly of high plateaus along the main Nile-Congo dividing range, dropping rapidly to the Great Rift Valley in the west. Languages: Kirundi and French. Currency: Burundi franc. Capital: Bujumbura. Pop.: 4 927 000 (1987 est.). Area: 27 731 sq. km (10 707 sq. miles). Former name (until 1962): **Urundi.**

bury ('bɛrɪ) vb. **burying, buried.** (*tr.*) **1.** to place (a corpse) in a grave; inter. **2.** to place in the earth and cover with soil. **3.** to cover from sight; hide. **4.** to embed; sink: *to bury a nail in plaster.* **5.** to occupy (oneself) with deep concentration; engross: *to be buried in a book.* **6.** to dismiss from the mind; abandon: *to bury old hatreds.* [OE *byrgan*]

Bury ('bɛrɪ) n. a town in NW England, part of Greater Manchester: an early textile centre. Pop.: 67 529 (1981).

Buryat Autonomous Soviet Socialist Republic n. an administrative division of the SE central Soviet Union, in the RSFSR, on Lake Baikal: mountainous, with forests covering over half the total area. Capital: Ulan-Ude. Pop.: 941 000 (1982 est.). Area: 351 300 sq. km (135 608 sq. miles).

Bury St Edmunds ('bɛrɪ sənt 'ɛdməndz) n. a market town in E England, in Suffolk. Pop.: 29 500 (1985).

bus (bʌs) n., pl. **buses** or **busses. 1.** a large motor vehicle designed to carry passengers between stopping places along a regular route. More formal name: **omnibus. 2.** (*modifier*) of or relating to a bus or buses: *a bus driver; a bus station.* **3.** Inf. a car or aircraft, esp. one that is old and shaky. **4.** Electronics, computers. short for **busbar. 5. miss the bus.** to miss an opportunity. ~vb. **busing, bused** or **bussing, bussed. 6.** to travel or transport by bus. **7.** Chiefly U.S. & Canad. to transport (children) by bus from one area to another in order to create racially integrated schools. [C19: short for OMNIBUS]

bus. abbrev. for business.

busbar ('bʌz,bɑː) n. **1.** an electrical conductor usually used to make a common connection between several circuits. **2.** a group of such electrical conductors maintained at a low voltage, used for carrying data in binary form between the various parts of a computer or its peripherals.

busby ('bʌzbɪ) n., pl. **-bies. 1.** a tall fur helmet worn by hussars. **2.** (not in official usage) another name for **bearskin** (the hat). [C18: ?from a proper name]

Busby ('bʌzbɪ) n. Sir **Matthew**, known as *Matt.* British footballer. He managed Manchester United (1946–69).

bush[1] (bʊʃ) n. **1.** a dense woody plant, smaller than a tree, with many branches arising from the lower part of the stem; shrub. **2.** a dense cluster of such shrubs; thicket. **3.** something resembling a bush, esp. in density: *a bush of hair.* **4.** (often preceded by *the*) an uncultivated or sparsely settled area, covered with trees or shrubs, which can vary from open, shrubby country to dense rainforest. **5.** a forested area; woodland. **6.** Canad. Also called: **bush lot, woodlot.** an area on a farm on which timber is grown and cut. **7.** (often preceded by *the*) Inf. the countryside, as opposed to the city: *out in the bush.* **8.** Obs. a bunch of ivy hung as a vintner's sign in front of a tavern. **9. beat about the bush.** to avoid the point at issue; prevaricate. ~adj. **10.** Austral. & N.Z. inf. rough-and-ready. **11. go bush.** Inf. **a.** Austral. to go off into the bush. **b.** Austral. to go into hiding. **c.** N.Z. to abandon city amenities and live rough. ~vb. **12.** (*intr.*) to grow thick and bushy. **13.** (*tr.*) to cover, decorate, support, etc., with bushes. **14. bush it.** Austral. to camp out in the bush. [C13: of Gmc origin]

bush[2] (bʊʃ) n. **1.** a thin metal sleeve or tubular lining serving as a bearing. ~vb. **2.** to fit a bush to (a casing, bearing, etc.). [C15: from MDu. *busse* box, bush; rel. to LL *buxis* BOX[1]]

Bush (bʊʃ) n. **George.** born 1924, U.S. Republican politician; vice president of the U.S. (1981–88): president of the US from 1989.

bushbaby ('bʊʃ,beɪbɪ) n., pl. **-babies.** an agile nocturnal arboreal primate occurring in Africa south of the Sahara. It has large eyes and ears and a long tail. Also called: **galago.**

bushbuck ('bʊʃ,bʌk) or **boschbok** ('bɒʃ,bʌk) n., pl. **-bucks, -buck** or **-boks, -bok.** a small nocturnal spiral-horned antelope of the bush and tropical forest of Africa.

bush carpenter n. Austral. & N.Z. a rough-and-ready unskilled workman.

bushed (bʊʃt) adj. Inf. **1.** (*postpositive*) extremely tired; exhausted. **2.** Canad. mentally disturbed from living in isolation. **3.** Austral. & N.Z. lost or bewildered, as in the bush.

bushel ('bʊʃəl) n. **1.** a British unit of dry or liquid measure equal to 8 Imperial gallons. 1 Imperial bushel is equivalent to 0.036 37 cubic metres. **2.** a U.S. unit of dry measure equal to 64 U.S. pints. 1 U.S. bushel is equivalent to 0.035 24 cubic metres. **3.** a container with a capacity equal to either of these quantities. **4.** U.S. inf. a large amount. **5. hide one's light under a bushel.** to conceal one's abilities or good qualities. [C14: from OF *boissel*]

bushfire ('bʊʃ,faɪə) n. a wild fire in the bush; a scrub or forest fire.

bushfly ('bʊʃ,flaɪ) n. pl. **-flies.** any of various small black dipterous flies of Australia that breed in faeces and dung.

bush house n. Chiefly Austral. a shed or hut in the bush or a garden.

Bushido (ˌbuːʃɪˈdəu) n. (sometimes not cap.) the feudal code of the Japanese samurai. [C19: from Japanese *bushi* warrior + *dō* way]

bushie ('buʃɪ) n. a variant spelling of **bushy**².

bushing ('buʃɪŋ) n. 1. another word for **bush**². 2. an adapter used to connect pipes of different sizes. 3. a layer of electrical insulation enabling a live conductor to pass through an earthed wall, etc.

Bushire (bjuːˈʃaɪə) n. a port in SW Iran, on the Persian Gulf. Pop.: 57 681 (1976). Persian name: **Bushehr** (buˈʃehr).

bush jacket or **shirt** n. a casual jacket or shirt having four patch pockets and a belt.

bush lawyer n. *Austral. & N.Z.* 1. a trailing plant with sharp hooks. 2. *Inf.* a person who gives legal opinions but is not qualified to do so.

bush line n. an airline operating in the bush country of Canada's northern regions.

bushman ('buʃmən) n., pl. **-men.** *Austral. & N.Z.* a person who lives or travels in the bush, esp. one versed in bush lore.

Bushman ('buʃmən) n., pl. **-men.** a member of a hunting and gathering people of southern Africa. [C18: from Afrik. *boschjesman*] from Afrikaans *boschjesman*]

bushmaster ('buʃˌmɑːstə) n. a large greyish-brown highly venomous snake inhabiting wooded regions of tropical America.

bush pilot n. *Canad.* a pilot who operates in the bush country.

bushranger ('buʃˌreɪndʒə) n. 1. *Austral.* (formerly) an outlaw living in the bush. 2. *U.S.* a person who lives away from civilization.

bush sickness n. *N.Z.* an animal disease caused by mineral deficiency in old bush country. —**'bush-ˌsick** adj.

bush tea n. 1. a leguminous shrub of southern Africa. 2. a beverage prepared from the dried leaves of such a plant.

bush telegraph n. a means of spreading rumour, gossip, etc.

bushveld ('buʃˌfɛlt) n. *S. African.* bushy countryside. [from Afrik. *bosveld*]

bushwhack ('buʃˌwæk) vb. 1. (*tr.*) *U.S. & Canad.* to ambush. 2. (*intr.*) *U.S. & Canad.* to cut or beat one's way through thick woods. 3. (*intr.*) *U.S., Canad., & Austral.* to range or move around in woods or the bush. 4. (*intr.*) *N.Z.* to work in the wild. 5. (*intr.*) *U.S. & Canad.* to fight as a guerrilla in wild regions.

bushwhacker ('buʃˌwækə) n. 1. *U.S., Canad., & Austral.* a person who travels around or lives in thinly populated woodlands. 2. *Austral. sl.* an unsophisticated person. 3. *N.Z.* a person who works in the bush. 4. a Confederate guerrilla in the American Civil War. 5. *U.S.* any guerrilla.

bushy¹ ('buʃɪ) adj. **bushier, bushiest.** 1. covered or overgrown with bushes. 2. thick and shaggy. — **'bushily** adv. — **'bushiness** n.

bushy² or **bushie** ('buʃɪ) n., pl. **bushies.** *Austral. inf.* 1. a person who lives in the bush. 2. an unsophisticated uncouth person.

business ('bɪznɪs) n. 1. a trade or profession. 2. the purchase and sale of goods and services. 3. a commercial or industrial establishment. 4. commercial activity; dealings (esp. in **do business**). 5. volume of commercial activity: *business is poor today.* 6. commercial policy: *overcharging is bad business.* 7. proper or rightful concern or responsibility (often in **mind one's own business**). 8. a special task; assignment. 9. an affair; matter. 10. serious work or activity: *get down to business.* 11. a difficult or complicated matter. 12. *Theatre.* an incidental action performed by an actor for dramatic effect. 13. **mean business.** to be in earnest. [OE *bisignis* solicitude, from *bisig* BUSY + *-nis* -NESS]

business college n. a college providing courses in secretarial studies, business management, accounting, commerce, etc.

businesslike ('bɪznɪsˌlaɪk) adj. efficient and methodical.

businessman ('bɪznɪsˌmæn, -mən) or (fem.) **businesswoman** n., pl. **-men** or **-women.** a person engaged in commercial or industrial business, esp. as an owner or executive.

business park n. an area specially designated and landscaped to accommodate business offices, warehouses, light industry, etc.

business school n. an institution that offers courses in aspects of business, such as marketing, finance, and law, designed to train managers in industry and commerce to do their jobs effectively.

busker ('bʌskə) n. a person who entertains for money in public places, as in front of theatre queues. [C20: from ?]
—**busk** vb. (*intr.*)

buskin ('bʌskɪn) n. 1. (formerly) a sandal-like covering for the foot and leg, reaching the calf. 2. a thick-soled laced half-boot worn esp. by actors of ancient Greece. 3. (usually preceded by *the*) *Chiefly literary.* tragic drama. [C16: ?from Sp. *borzegui*; rel. to OF *bouzequin*]

busman's holiday ('bʌsmənz) n. *Inf.* a holiday spent doing the same as one does at work. [C20: from a bus driver having a driving holiday]

Busoni (*Italian* buˈzoni) n. **Ferruccio Benvenuto** (ferˈruttʃo benveˈnuto). 1866–1924, Italian pianist and composer, esp. of works for piano.

Busra or **Busrah** ('bʌsrə) n. variant spellings of **Basra.**

buss (bʌs) n., vb. an archaic or dialect word for **kiss.** [C16: prob. imit.]

bust¹ (bʌst) n. 1. the chest of a human being, esp. a woman's bosom. 2. a sculpture of the head, shoulders, and upper chest of a person. [C17: from F, from It. *busto* a sculpture, from ?]

bust² (bʌst) *Inf.* ~vb. **busting, busted** or **bust.** 1. to burst or break. 2. to make or become bankrupt. 3. (*tr.*) (of the police) to raid, search, or arrest. 4. (*tr.*) *U.S. & Canad.* to demote, esp. in military rank. ~n. 5. a raid, search, or arrest by the police. 6. *Chiefly U.S.* a punch. 7. *U.S. & Canad.* a failure, esp. bankruptcy. 8. a drunken party. ~adj. 9. broken. 10. bankrupt. 11. **go bust.** to become bankrupt.

bustard ('bʌstəd) n. a large terrestrial bird inhabiting open regions of the Old World. It has long strong legs, a heavy body, a long neck, and speckled plumage. [C15: from OF *bistarde*, from L *avis tarda* slow bird]

bustier ('buːstɪeɪ) n. a type of close-fitting usually strapless top worn by women, esp. with a puffball skirt.

bustle¹ ('bʌsʲl) vb. 1. (when *intr.,* often foll. by *about*) to hurry or cause to hurry with a great show of energy or activity. ~n. 2. energetic and noisy activity. [C16: prob. from obs. *buskle* to make energetic preparation] — **'bustling** adj.

bustle² ('bʌsʲl) n. a cushion or framework worn by women in the late 19th century at the back in order to expand the skirt. [C18: from ?]

bust-up *Inf.* ~n. 1. a quarrel, esp. a serious one ending a friendship, etc. 2. *Brit.* a disturbance or brawl. ~vb. **bust up** (adv.) 3. (*intr.*) to quarrel and part. 4. (*tr.*) to disrupt (a meeting), esp. violently.

busy ('bɪzɪ) adj. **busier, busiest.** 1. actively or fully engaged; occupied. 2. crowded with or characterized by activity. 3. *Chiefly U.S. & Canad.* (of a room, telephone line, etc.) in use; engaged. 4. overcrowded with detail: *a busy painting.* 5. meddlesome; inquisitive. ~vb. **busying, busied.** 6. (*tr.*) to make or keep (someone, esp. oneself) busy; occupy. [OE *bisig*] — **'busily** adv. — **'busyness** n.

busybody ('bɪzɪˌbɒdɪ) n., pl. **-bodies.** a meddlesome, prying, or officious person.

busy Lizzie ('lɪzɪ) n. a flowering plant that has pink, red, or white flowers and is often grown as a pot plant.

but¹ (bʌt; unstressed bət) conj. (coordinating) 1. contrary to expectation: *he cut his knee but didn't cry.* 2. in contrast; on the contrary: *I like opera but my husband doesn't.* 3. (usually used after a negative) other than: *we can't do anything but wait.* 4. only: *I can but try.* ~conj. (subordinating) 5. (usually used after a negative) without it happening: *we never go out but it rains.* 6. (foll. by *that*) except that: *nothing is impossible but that we live forever.* 7. *Arch.* if not; unless. ~prep. 8. except; save: *they saved all but one.* 9. **but for.** were it not for: *but for you, we couldn't have managed.* ~adv. 10. just; merely: *he was but a child.* 11. *Dialect & Austral.* though; however: *it's a rainy day; warm, but.* ~n. 12. an objection (esp. in **ifs and buts**). [OE *būtan* without, outside, except, from *be* BY + *ūtan* OUT]

but² (bʌt) n. *Scot.* the outer room of a two-roomed cottage. Cf. **ben**¹. [C18: from *but* (adv.) outside; see BUT¹]

butadiene (ˌbjuːtəˈdaɪiːn) n. a colourless flammable gas used mainly in the manufacture of synthetic rubbers.

Formula: CH$_2$:CHCH:CH$_2$. [C20: from BUTA(NE) + DI-^{1} + -ENE]

butane ('bju:teɪn, bju:'teɪn) *n.* a colourless flammable gaseous alkane used mainly in the manufacture of rubber and fuels. Formula: C$_4$H$_{10}$. [C20: from BUT(YL) + -ANE]

butanol ('bju:tə,nɒl) *n.* a colourless substance existing in four isomeric forms. The three liquid isomers are used as solvents and in the manufacture of organic compounds. Formula: C$_4$H$_9$OH. Also called: **butyl alcohol.**

butanone ('bju:tə,nəʊn) *n.* a colourless flammable liquid used as a resin solvent, and paint remover, and in lacquers, adhesives, etc. Formula: CH$_3$COC$_2$H$_5$.

butch (bʊtʃ) *Sl.* ~*adj.* **1.** (of a woman or man) markedly or aggressively masculine. ~*n.* **2.** a lesbian who is noticeably masculine. **3.** a strong rugged man. [C18: back formation from BUTCHER]

butcher ('bʊtʃə) *n.* **1.** a retailer of meat. **2.** a person who slaughters or dresses meat. **3.** an indiscriminate or brutal murderer. ~*vb.* **4.** to slaughter or dress (animals) for meat. **5.** to kill indiscriminately or brutally. **6.** to make a mess of; botch. [C13: from OF *bouchier*, from *bouc* he-goat]

butcherbird ('bʊtʃə,bɜːd) *n.* **1.** a shrike, esp. of the genus *Lanius.* **2.** any of several Australian magpies that impale their prey on thorns.

butcher's-broom *n.* an evergreen shrub with stiff prickle-tipped flattened green stems, formerly used for making brooms.

butchery ('bʊtʃərɪ) *n., pl.* **-eries. 1.** the business of a butcher. **2.** wanton and indiscriminate slaughter. **3.** a slaughterhouse.

Bute^1 (bju:t) *n.* an island off the coast of SW Scotland, in the Firth of Clyde, separated from the Cowal peninsula by the **Kyles of Bute.** Chief town: Rothesay. Pop.: 7733 (1981). Area: 121 sq. km (47 sq. miles).

Bute^2 (bju:t) *n.* **John Stuart,** 3rd Earl of Bute. 1713–92, British Tory statesman; prime minister (1762–63).

Buteshire ('bju:t,ʃɪə, -ʃə) *n.* (until 1975) a county of SW Scotland, now part of Strathclyde region, that consisted of islands in the Firth of Clyde and Kilbrannan Sound.

butler ('bʌtlə) *n.* the male servant of a household in charge of the wines, table, etc.: usually the head servant. [C13: from OF, from *bouteille* BOTTLE]

Butler ('bʌtlə) *n.* **1. Joseph.** 1692–1752, English theologian and author. **2. R(ichard) A(usten),** Baron Butler of Saffron Walden. 1902–82, British Conservative politician: Chancellor of the Exchequer (1951–55); Home Secretary (1957–62); Foreign Secretary (1963–64). **3. Samuel.** 1612–80, English poet and satirist; author of *Hudibras* (1663–78). **4. Samuel.** 1835–1902, English novelist, noted for his satirical work *Erewhon* (1872) and his autobiographical novel *The Way of All Flesh* (1903).

butlery ('bʌtlərɪ) *n., pl.* **-leries. 1.** a butler's room. **2.** another name for **buttery**^{2}.

butt^1 (bʌt) *n.* **1.** the thicker or blunt end of something, such as the end of the stock of a rifle. **2.** the unused end of something, esp. of a cigarette; stub. **3.** *U.S.* a slang word for **cigarette. 4.** *Building.* short for **butt joint.** [C15 (in the sense: thick end of something, buttock): rel. to OE *buttuc* end, ridge]

butt^2 (bʌt) *n.* **1.** a person or thing that is the target of ridicule, wit, etc. **2.** *Shooting, archery.* **a.** a mound of earth behind the target that stops bullets or wide shots. **b.** the target itself. **c.** (*pl.*) the target range. **3.** a low barrier behind which sportsmen shoot game birds, esp. grouse. ~*vb.* **4.** (usually foll. by *on* or *against*) to lie or be placed end on to; abut. [C14 (in the sense: mark for archery practice): from OF *but*]

butt^3 (bʌt) *vb.* **1.** to strike or push (something) with the head or horns. **2.** (*intr.*) to project; jut. **3.** (*intr.*; foll. by *in* or *into*) to intrude, esp. into a conversation; interfere. ~*n.* **4.** a blow with the head or horns. [C12: from OF *boter*, of Gmc origin]

butt^4 (bʌt) *n.* a large cask for storing wine or beer. [C14: from OF *botte*, from LL *buttis* cask]

Butt (bʌt) *n.* Dame **Clara.** 1872–1936, English contralto.

butte (bju:t) *n.* *U.S. & Canad.* an isolated steep flat-topped hill. [C19: F, from OF *bute* mound behind a target; see BUTT^2]

butter ('bʌtə) *n.* **1.** an edible fatty whitish-yellow solid made from cream by churning. **2.** any substance with a butter-like consistency, such as peanut butter. **3. look as**

if butter wouldn't melt in one's mouth. to look innocent, although probably not so. ~*vb.* (*tr.*) **4.** to put butter on or in. **5.** to flatter. ~See also **butter up.** [OE *butere*, from L, from Gk *bouturon*, from *bous* cow + *turos* cheese]

butter bean *n.* a variety of lima bean that has large pale flat edible seeds.

butterbur ('bʌtə,bɜː) *n.* a plant of the composite family with fragrant whitish or purple flowers, and large leaves formerly used to wrap butter.

buttercup ('bʌtə,kʌp) *n.* any of various yellow-flowered plants of the genus *Ranunculus* of Europe, Asia, and North America.

butterfat ('bʌtə,fæt) *n.* the fatty substance of milk from which butter is made, consisting of a mixture of glycerides.

butterfingers ('bʌtə,fɪŋɡəz) *n.* (*functioning as sing.*) *Inf.* a person who drops things inadvertently or fails to catch things. —'**butter,fingered** *adj.*

butterfish ('bʌtə,fɪʃ) *n., pl.* **-fish** *or* **-fishes.** any of several species of fishes having a slippery skin.

butterflies ('bʌtə,flaɪz) *pl. n. Inf.* tremors in the stomach region due to nervousness.

butterfly ('bʌtə,flaɪ) *n., pl.* **-flies. 1.** any diurnal insect that has a slender body with clubbed antennae and typically rests with the wings (often brightly coloured) closed over the back. **2.** a person who never settles with one interest or occupation for long. **3.** a swimming stroke in which the arms are plunged forward together in large circular movements. [OE *buttorfléoge*]

butterfly nut *n.* another name for **wing nut.**

Buttermere ('bʌtə,mɪə) *n.* a lake in NW England, in Cumbria, in the Lake District, southwest of Keswick. Length: 2 km (1.25 miles).

buttermilk ('bʌtə,mɪlk) *n.* the sourish liquid remaining after the butter has been separated from milk.

butter muslin *n.* a fine loosely woven cotton material originally used for wrapping butter.

butternut ('bʌtə,nʌt) *n.* **1.** *Austral. & N.Z.* a type of small edible pumpkin. **2. a.** a walnut tree of North America. **b.** its oily edible nut.

butterscotch ('bʌtə,skɒtʃ) *n.* **1.** a kind of hard brittle toffee made with butter, brown sugar, etc. **2.** a flavouring made from these ingredients. [C19: ? first made in Scotland]

butter up *vb.* (*tr., adv.*) to flatter.

butterwort ('bʌtə,wɜːt) *n.* a plant that grows in wet places and has violet-blue spurred flowers and fleshy greasy glandular leaves on which insects are trapped and digested.

buttery^1 ('bʌtərɪ) *adj.* containing, like, or coated with butter. —'**butteriness** *n.*

buttery^2 ('bʌtərɪ) *n., pl.* **-teries. 1.** a room for storing foods or wines. **2.** *Brit.* (in some universities) a room in which food and drink are supplied or sold to students. [C14: from Anglo-F *boterie*, prob. from L *butta* cask, BUTT^4]

butt joint *n.* a joint between two plates, planks, etc., fastened end to end without overlapping or interlocking. Sometimes shortened to **butt.**

buttock ('bʌtək) *n.* **1.** either of the two large fleshy masses of thick muscular tissue that form the human rump. See also **gluteus.** Related adj.: **gluteal. 2.** the analogous part in some mammals. [C13: ?from OE *buttuc* round slope]

button ('bʌt³n) *n.* **1.** a disc or knob of plastic, wood, etc., attached to a garment, etc., usually for fastening two surfaces together by passing it through a buttonhole or loop. **2.** a small round object, such as any of various sweets, decorations, or badges. **3.** a small disc that completes an electric circuit when pushed, as one that operates a doorbell or machine. **4.** *Biol.* any rounded knoblike part or organ, such as an unripe mushroom. **5.** *Fencing.* the protective knob fixed to the point of a foil. **6.** *Brit.* an object of no value (esp. in **not worth a button**). ~*vb.* **7.** to fasten with a button or buttons. **8.** (*tr.*) to provide with buttons. [C14: from OF *boton*, from *boter* to thrust, butt; see BUTT^3] —'**buttoner** *n.* —'**buttonless** *adj.*

buttonhole ('bʌt³n,həʊl) *n.* **1.** a slit in a garment, etc., through which a button is passed to fasten two surfaces together. **2.** a flower or small bunch of flowers worn pinned to the lapel or in the buttonhole, esp. at weddings.

U.S. name: **boutonniere.** ~*vb.* (*tr.*) **3.** to detain (a person) in conversation. **4.** to make buttonholes in.

buttonhook ('bʌtⁿn,hʊk) *n.* a thin tapering hooked instrument formerly used for pulling buttons through the buttonholes of shoes.

button up *vb.* (*tr., adv.*) **1.** to fasten (a garment) with a button or buttons. **2.** *Inf.* to conclude (business) satisfactorily. **3. button up one's lip** *or* **mouth.** *Sl.* to be silent.

buttress ('bʌtrɪs) *n.* **1.** Also called: **pier.** a construction, usually of brick or stone, built to support a wall. **2.** any support or prop. **3.** something shaped like a buttress, such as a projection from a mountainside. ~*vb.* (*tr.*) **4.** to support (a wall) with a buttress. **5.** to support or sustain. [C13: from OF *bouterez*, from *bouter* to thrust, BUTT³]

butty¹ ('bʌtɪ) *n., pl.* **-ties.** *Chiefly N English dialect.* a sandwich: *a jam butty.* [C19: from *buttered* (bread)]

butty² ('bʌtɪ) *n., pl.* **-ties.** *English dialect.* (esp. in mining parlance) a friend or workmate. [C19: ?from obs. *booty* sharing, from BOOT²]

Butung ('buːtʊŋ) *n.* an island of Indonesia, southeast of Sulawesi: hilly and forested. Chief town: Baubau. Pop.: 317 124 (1980). Area: 4555 sq. km (1759 sq. miles).

butyl ('bjuː,taɪl, -tɪl) *n.* (*modifier*) of or containing any of four isomeric forms of the group C₄H₉–: *butyl rubber.* [C19: from BUT(YRIC ACID) + -YL]

butyl alcohol *n.* another name for **butanol.**

butyric acid (bjuː'tɪrɪk) *n.* a carboxylic acid which produces the smell in rancid butter. Formula: CH₃(CH₂)₂COOH. [C19 *butyric*, from L *būtyrum* BUTTER]

buxom ('bʌksəm) *adj.* **1.** (esp. of a woman) healthily plump, attractive, and vigorous. **2.** (of a woman) full-bosomed. [C12: *buhsum* compliant, pliant, from OE *būgan* to bend, BOW¹] —'**buxomness** *n.*

Buxtehude (*German* bʊkstə'huːdə) *n.* **Dietrich** ('diːtrɪç). 1637–1707, Danish composer and organist, resident in Germany from 1668, who influenced Bach and Handel.

Buxton ('bʌkstən) *n.* a town in N England, in NW Derbyshire in the Peak District: thermal springs. Pop.: 20 797 (1981).

buy (baɪ) *vb.* **buying, bought.** (*mainly tr.*) **1.** to acquire by paying or promising to pay a sum of money; purchase. **2.** to be capable of purchasing: *money can't buy love.* **3.** to acquire by any exchange or sacrifice: *to buy time by equivocation.* **4.** to bribe or corrupt; hire by or as by bribery. **5.** *Sl.* to accept as true, practical, etc. **6.** (*intr.;* foll. by *into*) to purchase shares of (a company). ~*n.* **7.** a purchase (often in **good** or **bad buy**). ~See also **buy in, buy into,** etc. [OE *bycgan*]

buyer ('baɪə) *n.* **1.** a person who buys; customer. **2.** a person employed to buy merchandise, materials, etc., as for a shop or factory.

buy in *vb.* (*adv.*) **1.** (*tr.*) to buy back for the owner (an item in an auction) at or below the reserve price. **2.** (*intr.*) to purchase shares in a company. **3.** (*tr.*) Also: **buy into.** *U.S. inf.* to pay money to secure a position or place for (someone, esp. oneself) in some organization, esp. a business or club. **4.** to purchase (goods, etc.) in large quantities.

buy into *vb.* (*intr., prep.*) *Austral. & N.Z.* to get involved in (an argument, fight, etc.)

buy off *vb.* (*tr., adv.*) to pay (a person or group) to drop a charge, end opposition, etc.

buy out *vb.* (*tr., adv.*) **1.** to purchase the ownership, controlling interest, shares, etc., of (a company, etc.). **2.** to gain the release of (a person) from the armed forces by payment. **3.** to pay (a person) to give up ownership of (property, etc.). ~*n.* **buy-out. 4.** the purchase of a company, esp. by its former workers.

buy up *vb.* (*tr., adv.*) **1.** to purchase all, or all that is available, of (something). **2.** to purchase a controlling interest in (a company, etc.).

buzz (bʌz) *n.* **1.** a rapidly vibrating humming sound, as of a bee. **2.** a low sound, as of many voices in conversation. **3.** a rumour; report; gossip. **4.** *Inf.* a telephone call. **5.** *Inf.* **a.** a pleasant sensation. **b.** a sense of excitement; kick. **6.** (*modifier*) fashionable, trendy. ~*vb.* **7.** (*intr.*) to make a vibrating sound like that of a prolonged *z.* **8.** (*intr.*) to talk or gossip with an air of excitement: *the town buzzed with the news.* **9.** (*tr.*) to utter or spread (a rumour). **10.** (*intr.;* often foll. by *about*) to move around quickly and busily. **11.** (*tr.*) to signal or summon with a buzzer. **12.** (*tr.*) *Inf.* to call by telephone. **13.** (*tr.*) *Inf.* to fly an aircraft very low over (an object). **14.** (*tr.*) (esp. of

insects) to make a buzzing sound with (wings, etc.). [C16: imit.]

buzzard ('bʌzəd) *n.* a diurnal bird of prey of the hawk family, typically having broad wings and tail and a soaring flight. [C13: from OF *buisard*, from L *būteō* hawk]

buzzer ('bʌzə) *n.* **1.** a device that produces a buzzing sound, esp. one similar to an electric bell. **2.** *N.Z.* a wood-planing machine.

buzz off *vb.* (*intr., adv.; often imperative*) *Inf., chiefly Brit.* to go away; leave; depart.

buzz word *n.* *Inf.* a word, originally from a particular jargon, which becomes a popular vogue word. [C20: from ?]

BVM *abbrev. for* Beata Virgo Maria. [L: Blessed Virgin Mary]

bwana ('bwɑːnə) *n.* (in E Africa) a master, often used as a form of address corresponding to *sir.* [Swahili, from Ar. *abūna* our father]

by (baɪ) *prep.* **1.** used to indicate the agent after a passive verb: *seeds eaten by the birds.* **2.** used to indicate the person responsible for a creative work: *this song is by Schubert.* **3.** via; through: *enter by the back door.* **4.** foll. by a gerund to indicate a means used: *he frightened her by hiding behind the door.* **5.** beside; next to; near: *a tree by the house.* **6.** passing the position of; past: *he drove by the old cottage.* **7.** not later than; before: *return the books by Tuesday.* **8.** used to indicate extent, after a comparative: *it is hotter by five degrees.* **9.** (esp. in oaths) invoking the name of: *I swear by all the gods.* **10.** multiplied by: *four by three equals twelve.* **11.** during the passing of (esp. in **by day, by night**). **12.** placed between measurements of the various dimensions of something: *a plank fourteen inches by seven.* ~*adv.* **13.** near: *the house is close by.* **14.** away; aside: *he put some money by each week.* **15.** passing a point near something; past: *he drove by.* ~*n., pl.* **byes. 16.** a variant spelling of **bye.** [OE *bī*]

by- *or* **bye-** *prefix.* **1.** near: *bystander.* **2.** secondary or incidental: *by-election; by-product.* [from BY]

by and by *adv.* presently or eventually.

by and large *adv.* in general; on the whole. [C17: orig. nautical: to the wind and off it]

Bydgoszcz (*Polish* 'bidgɔʃtʃ) *n.* an industrial city and port in N Poland: under Prussian rule from 1772 to 1919. Pop.: 361 000 (1985). German name: **Bromberg.**

bye (baɪ) *n.* **1.** *Sport.* the situation in which a player or team wins a preliminary round by virtue of having no opponent. **2.** *Golf.* one or more holes that are left unplayed after the match has been decided. **3.** *Cricket.* a run scored off a ball not struck by the batsman. **4.** something incidental or secondary. **5. by the bye.** incidentally; by the way. [C16: var. of BY]

bye-bye *sentence substitute. Brit. inf.* goodbye.

bye-byes *n.* (*functioning as sing.*) an informal word for **sleep,** used esp. to children (as in **go to bye-byes**).

by-election *or* **bye-election** *n.* (in Great Britain and other countries of the Commonwealth) an election held during the life of a parliament to fill a vacant seat.

Byelgorod-Dnestrovski *or* **Belgorod-Dnestrovski** (*Russian* 'bjɛlgərətdnjɪ'strɔfskij) *n.* a port in the SW Soviet Union, in the SW Ukrainian SSR, on the Dniester estuary: belonged to Romania from 1918 until 1940; ceded to the Soviet Union in 1944. Pop.: 293 000 (1987). Romanian name: **Cetatea Albă.** Former name (until 1946): **Akkerman.**

Byelorussian *or* **Belorussian** (,bjɛləʊ'rʌʃən, ,bɛl-) *adj.* **1.** of, relating to, or characteristic of Byelorussia, its people, or their language. ~*n.* **2.** the official language of the Byelorussian SSR. **3.** a native or inhabitant of Byelorussia. ~Also called: **White Russian.**

Byelorussian Soviet Socialist Republic *n.* an administrative division of the W Soviet Union: mainly low-lying and forested. Capital: Minsk. Pop.: 9 744 000 (1982 est.). Area: 207 600 sq. km (80 134 sq. miles). Also: **Belorussian Soviet Socialist Republic,** or **Byelorussia, Belorussia** (,bjɛləʊ'rʌʃə, ,bɛl-). Also called: **White Russia.**

Byelostok (bjɪla'stɔk) *n.* a Russian name for **Bialystok.**

Byelovo *or* **Belovo** (*Russian* 'bjɛlavə) *n.* a city in the S Soviet Union, in the southwestern RSFSR. Pop.: 113 000 (1981 est.).

bygone ('baɪ,gɒn) *adj.* **1.** (*usually prenominal*) past; former. ~*n.* **2.** (*often pl.*) a past occurrence. **3.** an artefact, implement, etc., of former domestic or industrial use. **4. let bygones be bygones.** to agree to forget past quarrels.

bylaw *or* **bye-law** ('baɪˌlɔː) *n.* **1.** a rule made by a local authority. **2.** a regulation of a company, society, etc. [C13: prob. of Scand. origin; cf. ON *bẏr* dwelling, town]

by-line *n.* **1.** a line under the title of a newspaper or magazine article giving the author's name. **2.** another word for **touchline.**

Byng (bɪŋ) *n.* **1. George,** Viscount Torrington. 1663–1733, British admiral: defeated fleet of James Edward Stuart, the Old Pretender, off Scotland (1708); defeated Spanish fleet off Messina (1717). **2.** his son **John.** 1704–57, English admiral: executed after failing to relieve Minorca. **3. Julian Hedworth George,** 1st Viscount Byng of Vimy. 1862–1935, British general in World War I; governor general of Canada (1921–26).

BYO(G) *n. Austral. & N.Z.* an unlicensed restaurant at which diners may drink their own wine, etc. [C20: from *bring your own (grog)*]

bypass ('baɪˌpɑːs) *n.* **1.** a main road built to avoid a city or other congested area. **2.** a means of redirecting the flow of a substance around an appliance through which it would otherwise pass. **3.** *Electronics.* an electrical circuit connected in parallel around one or more components, providing an alternative path for certain frequencies. ~*vb.* (*tr.*) **4.** to go around or avoid (a city, obstruction, problem, etc.). **5.** to cause (traffic, fluid, etc.) to go through a bypass. **6.** to proceed without reference to (regulations, a superior, etc.); get round; avoid.

bypass engine *n.* a gas turbine in which part of the compressor delivery bypasses the combustion zone, flowing directly into or around the exhaust to provide additional thrust.

bypath ('baɪˌpɑːθ) *n.* a little-used path or track.

by-play *n.* secondary action or talking carried on apart while the main action proceeds, esp. in a play.

by-product *n.* **1.** a secondary or incidental product of a manufacturing process. **2.** a side effect.

Byrd (bɜːd) *n.* **1. Richard Evelyn.** 1888–1957, U.S. rear admiral, aviator, and polar explorer. **2. William.** 1543–1623, English composer and organist, noted for his madrigals, masses, and music for virginals.

Byrd Land *n.* a part of Antarctica, east of the Ross Ice Shelf and the Ross Sea: claimed for the U.S. by Richard E. Byrd in 1929. Former name: **Marie Byrd Land.**

byre ('baɪə) *n. Brit.* a shelter for cows. [OE *bẏre;* rel. to *būr* hut, cottage]

byroad ('baɪˌrəʊd) *n.* a secondary or side road.

Byron ('baɪərən) *n.* **George Gordon,** 6th Baron. 1788–1824, English Romantic poet, noted also for his passionate and disastrous love affairs. His major works include *Childe Harold's Pilgrimage* (1812–18), and *Don Juan* (1819–24). He spent much of his life abroad and died while fighting for Greek independence. —**Byronic** (baɪˈrɒnɪk) *adj.* —**By'ronically** *adv.* —'**Byronˌism** *n.*

byssinosis (ˌbɪsɪˈnəʊsɪs) *n.* a lung disease caused by prolonged inhalation of fibre dust. [C19: from NL, from Gk *bussinos* of linen + -OSIS]

bystander ('baɪˌstændə) *n.* a person present but not involved; onlooker; spectator.

byte (baɪt) *n. Computers.* **1.** a group of bits processed as one unit of data. **2.** the storage space allocated to such a group of bits. **3.** a subdivision of a word. [C20: prob. a blend of BIT⁴ + BITE]

Bytom (*Polish* 'bitɔm) *n.* an industrial city in SW Poland, in Upper Silesia: under Prussian and German rule from 1742 to 1945. Pop.: 239 000 (1985). German name: **Beuthen.**

byway ('baɪˌweɪ) *n.* **1.** a secondary or side road, esp. in the country. **2.** an area, field of study, etc., that is very obscure or of secondary importance.

byword ('baɪˌwɜːd) *n.* **1.** a person or thing regarded as a perfect or proverbial example of something: *their name is a byword for good service.* **2.** an object of scorn or derision. **3.** a common saying; proverb. [OE *biwyrde;* see BY, WORD]

Byzantine (bɪˈzænˌtaɪn, -ˌtiːn, baɪ-; 'bɪzənˌtiːn, -ˌtaɪn) *adj.* **1.** of, characteristic of, or relating to Byzantium or the Byzantine Empire. **2.** of, relating to, or characterizing the Orthodox Church or its rites and liturgy. **3.** of or relating to the highly coloured stylized form of religious art developed in the Byzantine Empire. **4.** of or relating to the style of architecture developed in the Byzantine Empire, characterized by massive domes with square bases, rounded arches, spires and minarets, and the extensive use of mosaics. **5.** denoting the Medieval Greek spoken in the Byzantine Empire. **6.** (of attitudes, etc.) inflexible or complicated. ~*n.* **7.** an inhabitant of Byzantium. —**Byzantinism** (bɪˈzæntaɪˌnɪzəm, -tiː, baɪ-; 'bɪzəntiːˌnɪzəm, -taɪ-) *n.*

Byzantine Empire *n.* the continuation of the Roman Empire in the East, esp. after the deposition of the last emperor in Rome (476 A.D.). It was finally extinguished by the fall of Constantinople, its capital, in 1453. See also **Eastern Roman Empire.**

Byzantium (bɪˈzæntɪəm, baɪ-) *n.* an ancient Greek city on the Bosphorus: founded about 660 B.C.; rebuilt by Constantine I in 330 A.D. and called Constantinople; present-day Istanbul.

Bz *or* **bz.** *abbrev. for* benzene.

C

c *or* **C** (siː) *n., pl.* **c's, C's,** *or* **Cs. 1.** the third letter of the English alphabet. **2.** a speech sound represented by this letter, usually either as in *cigar* or as in *case*. **3.** the third in a series, esp. the third highest grade in an examination. **4.** something shaped like a C.

c *symbol for:* **1.** centi-. **2.** *Maths.* constant. **3.** cubic. **4.** cycle. **5.** specific heat capacity. **6.** the speed of light and other types of electromagnetic radiation in free space.

C *symbol for:* **1.** *Music.* **a.** the first degree of a major scale containing no sharps or flats (**C major**). **b.** the major or minor key having this note as its tonic. **c.** a time signature denoting four crotchet beats to the bar. See also **alla breve** (sense 2), **common time. 2.** *Chem.* carbon. **3.** capacitance. **4.** heat capacity. **5.** cold (water). **6.** *Physics.* compliance. **7.** Celsius. **8.** centigrade. **9.** century: *C20.* **10.** coulomb. ~ **11.** *the Roman numeral for* 100.

c. *abbrev. for:* **1.** carat. **2.** carbon (paper). **3.** *Cricket.* caught. **4.** cent(s). **5.** century *or* centuries. **6.** *(pl.* **cc.**) chapter. **7.** (used esp. preceding a date) circa: *c. 1800.* [L: about] **8.** colt. **9.** contralto. **10.** copyright. **11.** coulomb.

C. *abbrev. for:* **1.** (on maps as part of name) Cape. **2.** Catholic. **3.** Celtic. **4.** Conservative. **5.** Corps.

c/- (in Australia) *abbrev. for* care for.

Ca *the chemical symbol for* calcium.

CA *abbrev. for:* **1.** Central America. **2.** chartered accountant. **3.** Civil Aviation. **4.** (in Britain) Consumers' Association.

ca. *abbrev. for* circa. [L: about]

CAA (in Britain) *abbrev. for* Civil Aviation Authority.

Caaba ('kɑːbə) *n.* a variant spelling of **Kaaba.**

cab (kæb) *n.* **1. a.** a taxi. **b.** *(as modifier): a cab rank.* **2.** the enclosed compartment of a lorry, crane, etc., from which it is driven. **3.** (formerly) a horse-drawn vehicle used for public hire. [C19: from CABRIOLET]

cabal (kə'bæl) *n.* **1.** a small group of intriguers, esp. one formed for political purposes. **2.** a secret plot; conspiracy. **3.** a clique. *~vb.* **-balling, -balled. 4.** *(intr.)* to form a cabal; plot. [C17: from F *cabale,* from Med. L *cabala*]

cabala (kə'bɑːlə) *n.* a variant spelling of **cabbala.**

Caballé *(Spanish* kaβa'ʎe) *n.* **Montserrat** (monser'rat). born 1933, Spanish operatic soprano.

caballero (,kæbə'ljɛərəʊ) *n., pl.* **-ros** (-rəʊz). a Spanish gentleman. [C19: from Sp.: gentleman, from LL *caballārius* rider, from *caballus* horse]

cabana (kə'bɑːnə) *n. Chiefly U.S.* a tent used as a dressing room by the sea. [from Sp. *cabaña:* CABIN]

cabaret ('kæbə,reɪ) *n.* **1.** a floor show of dancing, singing, etc., at a nightclub or restaurant. **2.** *Chiefly U.S.* a nightclub or restaurant providing such entertainment. [C17: from Norman F: tavern, prob. from LL *camera* an arched roof]

cabbage ('kæbɪdʒ) *n.* **1.** Also called: **cole.** any of various cultivated varieties of a plant of the genus *Brassica* having a short thick stalk and a large head of green or reddish edible leaves. See also **brassica. 2. a.** the head of a cabbage. **b.** the edible leaf bud of the cabbage palm. **3.** *Inf.* a dull or unimaginative person. **4.** *Inf.* a person who has no mental faculties and is dependent on others. [C14: from Norman F *caboche* head]

cabbage palm *n.* **1.** a West Indian palm whose leaf buds are eaten like cabbage. **2.** a similar Brazilian palm.

cabbage rose *n.* a rose with a round compact full-petalled head.

cabbage tree *n.* **1.** a tall palmlike ornamental New Zealand tree. **2.** a palm tree of Eastern Australia.

cabbage white *n.* a large white butterfly, the larvae of which feed on the leaves of cabbages and related vegetables.

cabbala, cabala, kabbala, *or* **kabala** (kə'bɑːlə) *n.* **1.** an ancient Jewish mystical tradition. **2.** any secret or occult doctrine. [C16: from Med. L, from Heb. *qabbālāh* tradition, from *qābal* to receive] **—cabbalism, cabalism, kabbalism,** *or* **kabalism** ('kæbə,lɪzəm) *n.* **—'cabbalist,**

'cabalist, 'kabbalist, *or* **'kabalist** *n.* **—,cabba'listic, ,caba'listic, ,kabba'listic,** *or* **,kaba'listic** *adj.*

cabby *or* **cabbie** ('kæbɪ) *n., pl.* **-bies.** *Inf.* a cab driver.

caber ('keɪbə) *n. Scot.* a heavy section of trimmed tree trunk thrown in competition at Highland games (**tossing the caber**). [C16: from Gaelic *cabar* pole]

Cabimas *(Spanish* ka'βimas) *n.* a town in NW Venezuela, on the NE shore of Lake Maracaibo. Pop.: 162 300 (1981 est.).

cabin ('kæbɪn) *n.* **1.** a small simple dwelling; hut. **2.** a simple house providing accommodation for travellers or holiday-makers. **3.** a room used as an office or living quarters in a ship. **4.** a covered compartment used for shelter in a small boat. **5.** *Brit.* another name for **signal box. 6. a.** the enclosed part of a light aircraft in which the pilot and passengers sit. **b.** the part of an aircraft for passengers or cargo. *~vb.* **7.** *(tr.)* to confine in a small space. [C14: from OF *cabane,* from OProvençal *cabana,* from LL *capanna* hut]

cabin boy *n.* a boy who waits on the officers and passengers of a ship.

cabin cruiser *n.* a power boat fitted with a cabin for pleasure cruising or racing.

Cabinda (kə'biːndə) *n.* an exclave of Angola, separated from the rest of the country by part of Zaïre. Pop.: 108 000 (1985 est.). Area: 7270 sq. km (2807 sq. miles).

cabinet ('kæbɪnɪt) *n.* **1.** a piece of furniture containing shelves, cupboards, or drawers for storage or display. **2.** the outer case of a television, radio, etc. **3. a.** *(often cap.)* the executive and policy-making body of a country, consisting of senior government ministers. **b.** *(sometimes cap.)* an advisory council to a president, governor, etc. **c.** *(as modifier): a cabinet reshuffle.* **4. a.** a standard size of paper, 6 × 4 inches (15 × 10 cm), for mounted photographs. **b.** *(as modifier): a cabinet photograph.* **5.** *Arch.* a private room. [C16: from OF, dim. of *cabine,* from ?]

cabinet-maker *n.* a craftsman specializing in making fine furniture. **—'cabinet-,making** *n.*

cabinetwork ('kæbɪnɪt,wɜːk) *n.* **1.** the making of furniture, esp. of fine quality. **2.** an article made by a cabinet-maker.

cabin fever *n. Canad.* acute depression resulting from being isolated or sharing cramped quarters in the wilderness.

cable ('keɪbᵊl) *n.* **1.** a strong thick rope, usually of twisted hemp or steel wire. **2.** *Naut.* an anchor chain or rope. **3.** Also called: **cable length, cable's length.** a unit of length in nautical use that has various values. It is most commonly taken as 120 fathoms (720 feet) in the U.S. and one tenth of a nautical mile (608 feet) in Britain. **4.** a wire or bundle of wires that conducts electricity: *a submarine cable.* **5.** Also called: **cablegram.** a telegram sent abroad by submarine cable, telephone line, etc. **6.** Also called: **cable stitch.** a knitting pattern resembling a twisted rope. *~vb.* **7.** to send (a message) to (someone) by cable. **8.** *(tr.)* to fasten or provide with a cable or cables. **9.** *(tr.)* to supply (a place) with cable television. [C13: from OF, from LL *capulum* halter]

cable car *n.* **1.** a cabin suspended from and moved by an overhead cable in a mountain area. **2.** the passenger car on a **cable railway,** drawn along by a strong cable operated by a motor.

cablegram ('keɪbᵊl,græm) *n.* a more formal name for **cable** (sense 5).

cable television *n.* a television service in which the subscriber's television is connected to the supplier by cable, enabling a much greater choice of channels to be provided.

cabochon ('kæbə,ʃɒn) *n.* a smooth domed gem, polished but unfaceted. [C16: from OF, from *caboche* head]

caboodle (kə'buːdᵊl) *n. Inf.* a lot, bunch, or group (esp. in **the whole caboodle**). [C19: prob. contraction of KIT & BOODLE]

caboose (kə'buːs) *n.* **1.** *U.S. inf.* short for **calaboose. 2.** *Railways. U.S. & Canad.* a guard's van. **3.** *Naut.* **a.** a deckhouse for a galley aboard ship. **b.** *Chiefly Brit.* the galley itself. **4.** *Canad.* **a.** a mobile bunkhouse used by lumbermen, etc. **b.** an insulated cabin on runners, equipped with a stove. [C18: from Du. *cabūse*, from ?]

Cabora Bassa (kə'bɔːrə 'bæsə) *n.* the site on the Zambezi River in N Mozambique of the largest dam in southern Africa.

Cabot ('kæbət) *n.* **1. John,** Italian name *Giovanni Caboto.* 1450–98, Italian explorer, who landed in North America in 1497, under patent from Henry VII of England, and explored the coast from Nova Scotia to Newfoundland. **2.** his son, **Sebastian.** ?1476–1557, English navigator and cartographer who explored the La Plata region of Brazil (1526–30).

cabotage ('kæbə,tɑːʒ) *n.* **1.** *Naut.* coastal navigation or shipping. **2.** reservation to a country's carriers of its internal traffic, esp. air traffic. [C19: from F, from *caboter* to sail near the coast, apparently from Sp. *cabo* CAPE²]

Cabral (*Portuguese* kə'brɑl) *n.* **Pedro Álvarez** ('pɛːdru 'ɑlvərəʃ). ?1460–?1526, Portuguese navigator: discovered and took possession of Brazil for Portugal in 1500.

cabriole ('kæbrɪ,əʊl) *n.* a type of curved furniture leg, popular in the first half of the 18th century. Also called: **cabriole leg.** [C18: from F, from *cabrioler* to caper; from its being based on the leg of a capering animal]

cabriolet (,kæbrɪəʊ'leɪ) *n.* **1.** a small two-wheeled horse-drawn carriage with two seats and a folding hood. **2.** a type of motorcar with a folding top. [C18: from F, lit.: a little skip, from L, from *caper* goat; referring to the lightness of movement]

cacao (kə'kɑːəʊ, -'keɪəʊ) *n.* **1.** a small tropical American evergreen tree having reddish-brown seed pods from which cocoa and chocolate are prepared. **2. cacao bean.** the seed pod; cocoa bean. **3. cacao butter.** another name for **cocoa butter.** [C16: from Sp., from Nahuatl *cacauatl* cacao beans]

Cáceres (*Spanish* 'kaθeres) *n.* a city in W Spain: held by the Moors (1142–1229). Pop.: 65 758 (1981).

cachalot ('kæʃə,lɒt) *n.* another name for **sperm whale.** [C18: from F, from Port., *cachalote*, from ?]

cache (kæʃ) *n.* **1.** a hidden store of provisions, weapons, treasure, etc. **2.** the place where such a store is hidden. ~*vb.* **3.** (*tr.*) to store in a cache. [C19: from F, from *cacher* to hide]

cachepot ('kæʃ,pɒt, kæʃ'pəʊ) *n.* an ornamental container for a flowerpot. [F: pot-hider]

cachet ('kæʃeɪ) *n.* **1.** an official seal on a document, letter, etc. **2.** a distinguishing mark. **3.** prestige; distinction. **4.** *Philately.* a mark stamped by hand on mail for commemorative purposes. **5.** a hollow wafer, formerly used for enclosing an unpleasant-tasting medicine. [C17: from OF, from *cacher* to hide]

cachexia (kə'kɛksɪə) *or* **cachexy** *n.* a weakened condition of body or mind resulting from any debilitating disease. [C16: from LL, from Gk, from *kakos* bad + *hexis* condition]

cachinnate ('kækɪ,neɪt) *vb.* (*intr.*) to laugh loudly. [C19: from L *cacchināre*, prob. imit.] —,cachin'nation *n.* —,cachin'natory *adj.*

cachou ('kæʃuː, kæ'ʃuː) *n.* **1.** a lozenge eaten to sweeten the breath. **2.** another name for **catechu.** [C18: via F from Port., from Malay *kāchu*]

cacique (kə'siːk) *or* **cazique** (kə'ziːk) *n.* **1.** an American Indian chief in a Spanish-speaking region. **2.** (esp. in Spanish America) a local political boss. [C16: from Sp., of Amerind origin]

cack-handed (,kæk'hændɪd) *adj. Inf.* **1.** left-handed. **2.** clumsy. [from dialect *cack* excrement]

cackle ('kækəl) *vb.* **1.** (*intr.*) (esp. of a hen) to squawk with shrill broken notes. **2.** (*intr.*) to laugh or chatter raucously. **3.** (*tr.*) to utter in a cackling manner. ~*n.* **4.** the noise or act of cackling. **5.** noisy chatter. **6. cut the cackle.** *Inf.* to be quiet. [C13: prob. from MLow G *kākelen,* imit.]

caco- *combining form.* bad, unpleasant, or incorrect: *cacophony.* [from Gk *kakos* bad]

cacodyl ('kækə,daɪl) *n.* an oily poisonous liquid with a strong garlic smell; tetramethyldiarsine. [C19: fromGk, from *kakos* CACO- + *ozein* to smell + -YL]

cacoethes (,kækəʊ'iːθiːz) *n.* an uncontrollable urge or desire: *a cacoethes for smoking.* [C16: from L *cacoēthes* malignant disease, from Gk, from *kakos* CACO- + *ēthos* character]

cacography (kæ'kɒgrəfɪ) *n.* **1.** bad handwriting. **2.** incorrect spelling. —**cacographic** (,kækə'græfɪk) *adj.*

cacophony (kə'kɒfənɪ) *n., pl.* -**nies.** harsh discordant sound. —**ca'cophonous** *adj.*

cactus ('kæktəs) *n., pl.* -**tuses** *or* -**ti** (-taɪ). **1.** any of a family of spiny succulent plants of the arid regions of America with swollen tough stems and leaves reduced to spines. **2. cactus dahlia.** a double-flowered variety of dahlia. [C17: from L: prickly plant, from Gk *kaktos* cardoon] —**cactaceous** (kæk'teɪʃəs) *adj.*

cacuminal (kæ'kjuːmɪnəl) *Phonetics.* ~*adj.* **1.** denoting a consonant articulated with the tip of the tongue turned back towards the hard palate. ~*n.* **2.** a consonant articulated in this manner. [C19: from L *cacūmen* point]

cad (kæd) *n. Brit. inf. old-fashioned.* a man who does not behave in a gentlemanly manner towards others. [C18: from CADDIE] —**'caddish** *adj.*

CAD (kæd) *acronym for* computer-aided design.

cadaver (kə'deɪvə, -'dɑːv-) *n. Med.* a corpse. [C16: from L, from *cadere* to fall] —**cadaveric** (kə'dævərɪk) *adj.*

cadaverous (kə'dævərəs) *adj.* **1.** of or like a corpse, esp. in being deathly pale. **2.** thin and haggard. —**ca'daverousness** *n.*

caddie *or* **caddy** ('kædɪ) *Golf.* ~*n., pl.* -**dies. 1.** an attendant who carries clubs, etc., for a player. ~*vb.* -**dying, -died. 2.** (*intr.*) to act as a caddie. [C17 (C18 (Scot.): an errand-boy): from F CADET]

caddis fly *n.* a small mothlike insect having two pairs of hairy wings and aquatic larvae (caddis worms). [C17: from ?]

caddis worm *or* **caddis** ('kædɪs) *n.* the aquatic larva of a caddis fly, which constructs a protective case around itself made of silk, sand, stones, etc. Also called: **case-worm, strawworm.**

caddy¹ ('kædɪ) *n., pl.* -**dies.** *Chiefly Brit.* a small container, esp. for tea. [C18: from Malay *kati*]

caddy² ('kædɪ) *n., pl.* -**dies,** *vb.* -**dying, -died.** a variant spelling of **caddie.**

Cade (keɪd) *n.* **Jack.** died 1450, English leader of the Kentish rebellion against the misgovernment of Henry VI (1450).

cadence ('keɪdəns) *or* **cadency** *n., pl.* -**dences** *or* -**dencies. 1.** the beat or measure of something rhythmic. **2.** a fall in the pitch of the voice, as at the end of a sentence. **3.** intonation. **4.** rhythm in verse or prose. **5.** the close of a musical phrase. [C14: from OF, from OIt. *cadenza*, lit.: a falling, from L *cadere* to fall]

cadenza (kə'dɛnzə) *n.* a virtuoso solo passage occurring near the end of a piece of music, formerly improvised by the soloist. [C19: from It.; see CADENCE]

cadet (kə'dɛt) *n.* **1.** a young person undergoing preliminary training, usually before full entry to the uniformed services, police, etc. **2.** (in England and in France before 1789) a gentleman who entered the army to prepare for a commission. **3.** a younger son. **4. cadet branch.** the family of a younger son. **5.** (in New Zealand, formerly) a person learning sheep farming on a sheep station. [C17: from F, from dialect *capdet* captain, ult. from L *caput* head] —**ca'detship** *n.*

cadge (kædʒ) *vb.* **1.** to get (food, money, etc.) by sponging or begging. ~*n.* **2.** *Brit.* a person who cadges. [C17: from ?] —**'cadger** *n.*

cadi *or* **kadi** ('kɑːdɪ, 'keɪdɪ) *n., pl.* -**dis.** a judge in a Muslim community. [C16: from Ar. *qādī* judge]

Cádiz (kə'dɪz; *Spanish* 'kaðiθ) *n.* a port in SW Spain, on a narrow peninsula that forms the **Bay of Cádiz** at the E end of the **Gulf of Cádiz:** founded about 1100 B.C. as a Phoenician trading colony; centre of trade with America from the 16th to 18th centuries. Pop.: 156 711 (1981).

Cadmean victory ('kædmɪən) *n.* another name for **Pyrrhic victory.**

cadmium ('kædmɪəm) *n.* a malleable bluish-white metallic element that occurs in association with zinc ores. It is used in electroplating and alloys. Symbol: Cd; atomic no.: 48; atomic wt.: 112.4. [C19: from NL, from L *cadmīa* zinc ore, CALAMINE: both calamine and cadmium are found in the ore]

cadmium yellow *n.* an orange or yellow insoluble solid (cadmium sulphide) used as a pigment in paints, etc.

Cadmus ('kædməs) *n. Greek myth.* a Phoenician prince who killed a dragon and planted its teeth, from which sprang a multitude of warriors who fought among themselves until only five remained, who joined Cadmus to found Thebes. —'**Cadmean** *adj.*

cadre ('ka:də) *n.* **1.** the nucleus of trained professional servicemen forming the basis for military expansion. **2.** a group of activists, esp. in the Communist Party. **3.** a basic unit or structure; nucleus. **4.** a member of a cadre. [C19: from F, from It. *quadro*, from L *quadrum* square]

caduceus (kə'dju:sɪəs) *n., pl.* **-cei** (-sɪ,aɪ). **1.** *Classical myth.* a winged staff entwined with two serpents carried by Hermes (Mercury) as messenger of the gods. **2.** an insignia resembling this staff used as an emblem of the medical profession. [C16: from L, from Doric Gk *karukeion*, from *karux* herald]

caducous (kə'dju:kəs) *adj. Biol.* (of parts of a plant or animal) shed during the life of the organism. [C17: from L, from *cadere* to fall]

CAE (in Australia) *abbrev. for* College of Advanced Education.

caecilian (si:'sɪlɪən) *n.* a tropical limbless cylindrical amphibian resembling the earthworm and inhabiting moist soil. [C19: from *caecus* blind]

caecum *or U.S.* **cecum** ('si:kəm) *n., pl.* **-ca** (-kə). *Anat.* any structure that ends in a blind sac or pouch, esp. that at the beginning of the large intestine. [C18: short for L *intestinum caecum* blind intestine, translation of Gk *tuphlon enteron*] —'**caecal** *or U.S.* '**cecal** *adj.*

Cædmon ('kædmən) *n.* 7th century A.D., Anglo-Saxon poet and monk, the earliest English poet whose name survives.

Caelian ('si:lɪən) *n.* the southeasternmost of the Seven Hills of Rome.

Caen (kɒŋ; *French* kɑ̃) *n.* an industrial city in NW France. Pop.: 117 453 (1983 est.).

Caenozoic (,si:nə'zəʊɪk) *adj.* a variant spelling of **Cenozoic.**

Caerleon (ka:'lɪən) *n.* a town in SE Wales, in Gwent on the River Usk: traditionally the seat of King Arthur's court. Pop.: 6711 (1981).

Caernarfon, Caernarvon, *or* **Carnarvon** (ka:'nɑ:vⁿn) *n.* a port and resort in NW Wales, in Gwynedd on the Menai Strait: 13th-century castle. Pop.: 9506 (1981).

Caernarvonshire (ka:'nɑ:vⁿn,ʃɪə, -ʃə) *n.* (until 1974) a county of NW Wales, now part of Gwynedd.

Caerphilly (kɛə'fɪlɪ) *n.* **1.** a market town in SE Wales, in SE Mid Glamorgan: site of a large castle in Wales (13th–14th centuries). Pop.: 42 736 (1981). **2.** a creamy white mild-flavoured cheese.

Caesar ('si:zə) *n.* **1. Gaius Julius** ('gaɪəs 'dʒu:lɪəs). 100–44 B.C., Roman general, statesman, and historian. He formed the first triumvirate with Pompey and Crassus (60), conquered Gaul (58–50), invaded Britain (55–54), mastered Italy (49), and defeated Pompey (46). As dictator of the Roman Empire (49–44) he destroyed the power of the corrupt Roman nobility. He also introduced the Julian calendar and planned further reforms, but fear of his sovereign power led to his assassination (44) by conspirators led by Marcus Brutus and Cassius Longinus. **2.** any Roman emperor. **3.** (*sometimes not cap.*) any emperor, autocrat, dictator, or other powerful ruler. **4.** a title of the Roman emperors from Augustus to Hadrian.

Caesaraugusta (,si:zərɔ:'gʌstə) *n.* the Latin name for **Zaragoza.**

Caesarea (,si:zə'rɪə) *n.* an ancient port in NW Israel, capital of Roman Palestine: founded by Herod the Great.

Caesarea Mazaca ('mæzəkə) *n.* the ancient name of **Kayseri.**

Caesarean, Caesarian, *or U.S.* **Cesarean, Cesarian** (sɪ'zɛərɪən) *adj.* **1.** of or relating to any of the Caesars, esp. Julius Caesar. ~*n.* **2.** (*sometimes not cap.*) *Surgery.* **a.** a Caesarean section. **b.** (*as modifier*): *Caesarean operation.*

Caesarean section *n.* surgical incision through the abdominal and uterine walls in order to deliver a baby. [C17: from the belief that Julius Caesar was so delivered, the name allegedly being derived from *caedere* to cut]

caesium *or U.S.* **cesium** ('si:zɪəm) *n.* a ductile silvery-white element of the alkali metal group. It is used in photocells and in an atomic clock (**caesium clock**) that uses the frequency of radiation from changing the spin of electrons. The radioisotope **caesium-137**, with a half-life of 30.2 years, is used in radiotherapy. Symbol: Cs; atomic no.: 55; atomic wt.: 132.905.

caesura (sɪ'zjʊərə) *n., pl.* **-ras** *or* **-rae** (-ri:). **1.** (in modern prosody) a pause, esp. for sense, usually near the middle of a verse line. **2.** (in classical prosody) a break between words within a metrical foot. [C16: from L, lit.: a cutting, from *caedere* to cut] —**cae'sural** *adj.*

Caetano (kaɪ'tɑ:nəʊ; *Portuguese* kɑi'tɐnu) *n.* **Marcello** (mar'selu). 1906–80, prime minister of Portugal from 1968 until he was replaced by an army coup in 1974.

café ('kæfeɪ, 'kæfɪ) *n.* a small or inexpensive restaurant serving light or easily prepared meals and refreshments. [C19: from F: COFFEE]

café au lait *French.* (kafe o lɛ) *n.* **1.** coffee with milk. **2. a.** a light brown colour. **b.** (*as adj.*): *café au lait brocade.*

café noir *French.* (kafe nwar) *n.* black coffee.

cafeteria (,kæfɪ'tɪərɪə) *n.* a self-service restaurant. [C20: from American Sp.: coffee shop]

caff (kæf) *n.* a slang word for **café.**

caffeine *or* **caffein** ('kæfi:n) *n.* a white crystalline bitter alkaloid responsible for the stimulant action of tea, coffee, and cocoa. [C19: from G *Kaffein*, from *Kaffee* COFFEE]

caftan ('kæf,tæn, -,tɑ:n) *n.* a variant spelling of **kaftan.**

cage (keɪdʒ) *n.* **1. a.** an enclosure, usually made with bars or wire, for keeping birds, monkeys, etc. **b.** (*as modifier*): *cagebird.* **2.** a thing or place that confines. **3.** something resembling a cage in function or structure: *the rib cage.* **4.** the enclosed platform of a lift, esp. as used in a mine. ~*vb.* **5.** (*tr.*) to confine in or as in a cage. [C13: from OF, from L *cavea* enclosure, from *cavus* hollow]

Cage (keɪdʒ) *n.* **John.** born 1912, U.S. composer of experimental music for a variety of conventional, modified, or invented instruments. He evolved a type of music apparently undetermined by the composer, such as in *Imaginary Landscape* (1951) for 12 radio sets. Other works include *Reunion* (1968) and *Apartment Building 1776* (1976).

cagey *or* **cagy** ('keɪdʒɪ) *adj.* **cagier, cagiest.** *Inf.* not frank; wary. [C20: from ?] —'**caginess** *n.*

Cagliari[1] (kæl'jɑ:rɪ; *Italian* kaʎ'ʎari) *n.* a port in Italy, the capital of Sardinia, on the S coast. Pop.: 222 574 (1986).

Cagliari[2] (*Italian* kaʎ'ʎari) *n.* **Paolo** ('pa:olo), original name of (Paolo) **Veronese.**

Cagliostro (*Italian* kaʎ'ʎostro) *n.* Count **Alessandro di** (ales'sandro di), original name *Giuseppe Balsamo.* 1743–95, Italian adventurer and magician, who was imprisoned for life by the Inquisition for his association with freemasonry.

Cagney ('kægnɪ) *n.* **James.** 1899–1986, U.S. film actor, esp. in gangster roles; his films include *The Public Enemy* (1931), *Angels with Dirty Faces* (1938), *The Roaring Twenties* (1939), and *Yankee Doodle Dandy* (1942) for which he won an Oscar.

cagoule (kə'gu:l) *n.* a lightweight usually knee-length type of anorak. [C20: from F]

Cahokia Mounds (kə'həʊkɪə) *pl. n.* the largest group of prehistoric Indian earthworks in the U.S., located northeast of East St Louis.

cahoots (kə'hu:ts) *pl. n.* (*sometimes sing.*) *Inf.* **1.** *U.S.* partnership; league. **2. in cahoots.** in collusion. [C19: from ?]

Caiaphas ('kaɪə,fæs) *n. New Testament.* the high priest at the beginning of John the Baptist's preaching and during the trial of Jesus (Luke 3:2; Matthew 26).

Caicos Islands ('keɪkəs) *pl. n.* a group of islands in the West Indies: part of the British colony of the **Turks and Caicos Islands.**

caiman ('keɪmən) *n., pl.* **-mans.** a variant spelling of **cayman.**

Cain (keɪn) *n.* **1.** the first son of Adam and Eve, who killed his brother Abel (Genesis 4:1–16). **2. raise Cain. a.** to cause a commotion. **b.** to react or protest heatedly.

Caine (keɪn) *n.* **Michael.** real name *Maurice Micklewhite.* born 1933, British film actor. His films include *The Ipcress File* (1965), *Educating Rita* (1983), and *Hannah and Her Sisters* (1986).

Cainozoic (,kaɪnəʊ'zəʊɪk, ,keɪ-) *adj.* a variant spelling of **Cenozoic.**

caïque (kaɪ'i:k) *n.* **1.** a long rowing skiff used on the Bosporus. **2.** a sailing vessel of the E Mediterranean with a square topsail. [C17: from F, from It. *caicco*, from Turkish *kayik*]

Caird Coast (kɛəd) *n.* a region of Antarctica: a part of Coats Land on the SE coast of the Weddell Sea; now included in the British Antarctic Territory.

cairn (kɛən) *n.* **1.** a mound of stones erected as a memorial or marker. **2.** Also called: **cairn terrier.** a small rough-haired breed of terrier orig. from Scotland. [C15: from Gaelic *carn*]

cairngorm (ˌkɛən'gɔːm) *n.* a smoky yellow or brown variety of quartz, used as a gemstone. Also called: **smoky quartz.** [C18: from *Cairn Gorm* (lit.: blue cairn), mountain in Scotland]

Cairngorm Mountains *pl. n.* a mountain range of NE Scotland: part of the Grampians. Highest peak: Ben Macdhui, 1309 m (4296 ft.). Also called: **the Cairngorms.**

Cairns (kɛənz) *n.* a port in NE Australia, in Queensland. Pop.: 69 500 (1986).

Cairo ('kaɪrəu) *n.* the capital of Egypt, on the Nile: the largest city in Africa and in the Middle East; industrial centre; site of the university and mosque of Al Azhar (founded in 972). Pop.: 6 205 000 (1985). Arabic name: **El Qahira** (ɛl 'kahiːrə). — **'Cairene** *n., adj.*

caisson (kə'suːn, 'keɪsⁿn) *n.* **1.** a watertight chamber open at the bottom and containing air under pressure, used to carry out construction work under water. **2.** a watertight float filled with air, used to raise sunken ships. **3.** a watertight structure placed across the entrance of a dry dock, etc., to exclude water. **4. a.** a box containing explosives formerly used as a mine. **b.** an ammunition chest. [C18: from F, assimilated to *caisse* CASE²]

caisson disease *n.* another name for **decompression sickness.**

Caithness (keɪθ'nɛs, 'keɪθnɛs) *n.* (until 1975) a county of NE Scotland, now part of the Highland region.

caitiff ('keɪtɪf) *Arch. or poetic.* ~*n.* **1.** a cowardly or base person. ~*adj.* **2.** cowardly. [C13: from OF, from L *captīvus* CAPTIVE]

Caius ('kaɪəs) *n.* a variant of **Gaius.**

cajole (kə'dʒəul) *vb.* to persuade (someone) by flattery to do what one wants; wheedle; coax. [C17: from F *cajoler* to coax, from ?] — **ca'jolement** *n.* — **ca'joler** *n.* — **ca'jolery** *n.*

cake (keɪk) *n.* **1.** a baked food, usually in loaf or layer form, made from a mixture of flour, sugar, and eggs. **2.** a flat thin mass of bread, esp. unleavened bread. **3.** a shaped mass of dough or other food: *a fish cake.* **4.** a mass, slab, or crust of a solidified substance, as of soap. **5. go** *or* **sell like hot cakes.** *Inf.* to be sold very quickly. **6. have one's cake and eat it.** to enjoy both of two desirable but incompatible alternatives. **7. piece of cake.** *Inf.* something that is easily achieved or obtained. **8. take the cake.** *Inf.* to surpass all others, esp. in stupidity, folly, etc. **9.** *Inf.* the whole of something that is to be shared or divided: *a larger slice of the cake.* ~*vb.* **10.** (*tr.*) to encrust: *the hull was caked with salt.* **11.** to form or be formed into a hardened mass. [C13: from ON *kaka*]

cakewalk ('keɪk,wɔːk) *n.* **1.** a dance based on a march with intricate steps, orig. performed by American Negroes for the prize of a cake. **2.** a piece of music for this dance. **3.** *Inf.* an easy task.

cal. *abbrev. for:* **1.** calendar. **2.** calibre. **3.** calorie (small).

Cal. *abbrev. for* Calorie (large).

CAL (kæl) *acronym for* computer-aided learning.

Calabar ('kælə,bɑː) *n.* a port in SE Nigeria, capital of Cross River state. Pop.: 126 000 (1983 est.).

calabash ('kælə,bæʃ) *n.* **1.** Also called: **calabash tree.** a tropical American evergreen tree that produces large round gourds. **2.** the gourd. **3.** the dried hollow shell of a gourd used as the bowl of a tobacco pipe, a bottle, etc. **4. calabash nutmeg.** a tropical African shrub whose seeds can be used as nutmegs. [C17: from obs. F *calabasse*, from Sp., ?from Ar., from *qar'ah* gourd + *yábisah* dry]

calaboose ('kælə,buːs) *n. U.S. inf.* a prison. [C18: from Creole F, from Sp. *calabozo* dungeon, from ?]

calabrese (ˌkælə'breɪzɪ) *n.* a variety of green sprouting broccoli. [C20: from It.: Calabrian]

Calabria (kə'læbrɪə) *n.* **1.** a region of SW Italy: mostly mountainous and subject to earthquakes. Chief town: Reggio di Calabria. Pop.: 2 139 301 (1985 est.). Area: 15 080 sq. km (5822 sq. miles). **2.** an ancient region of extreme SE Italy (3rd century B.C. to about 668 A.D.); now part of Apulia. — **Ca'labrian** *adj., n.*

Calais ('kæleɪ, 'kælɪ; *French* kalɛ) *n.* a port in N France, on the Strait of Dover: the nearest French port to England; belonged to England 1347 – 1558. Pop.: 78 819 (1983 est.).

calamander ('kælə,mændə) *n.* the hard black-and-brown striped wood of several trees of India and Ceylon, used in making furniture. See also **ebony** (sense 2). [C19: metathetic var. of COROMANDEL]

calamine ('kælə,maɪn) *n.* a pink powder consisting of zinc oxide and iron(III) oxide, used medicinally in the form of soothing lotions or ointments. [C17: from OF, from Med. L *calamīna*, from L *cadmīa*; see CADMIUM]

calamint ('kæləmɪnt) *n.* an aromatic Eurasian plant having clusters of purple or pink flowers. [C14: from OF *calament*, from Med. L *calamentum*, from Gk *kalaminthē*]

calamitous (kə'læmɪtəs) *adj.* causing, involving, or resulting in a calamity; disastrous.

calamity (kə'læmɪtɪ) *n., pl.* **-ties.** **1.** a disaster or misfortune, esp. one causing distress or misery. **2.** a state or feeling of deep distress or misery. [C15: from F *calamité*, from L *calamitās*]

calamus ('kæləməs) *n., pl.* **-mi** (-ˌmaɪ). **1.** any of a genus of tropical Asian palms, some of which are a source of rattan and canes. **2.** another name for **sweet flag.** **3.** *Ornithol.* a quill. [C14: from L, from Gk *kalamos* reed, stem]

calandria (kə'lændrɪə) *n.* a cylindrical vessel through which vertical tubes pass, esp. one forming part of a heat exchanger or nuclear reactor. [C20: arbitrarily named, from Sp., lit.: lark]

calash (kə'læʃ) *or* **calèche** *n.* **1.** a horse-drawn carriage with low wheels and a folding top. **2.** a woman's folding hooped hood worn in the 18th century. [C17: from F, from G, from Czech *kolesa* wheels]

calcaneus (kæl'keɪnɪəs) *or* **calcaneum** *n., pl.* **-nei** (-nɪˌaɪ). the largest tarsal bone, forming the heel in man. Nontechnical name: **heel bone.** [C19: from LL: heel, from L *calx* heel]

calcareous (kæl'kɛərɪəs) *adj.* of, containing, or resembling calcium carbonate; chalky. [C17: from L *calcārius*, from *calx* lime]

calceolaria (ˌkælsɪə'lɛərɪə) *n.* a tropical American plant cultivated for its speckled slipper-shaped flowers. Also called: **slipperwort.** [C18: from L *calceolus* small shoe, from *calceus*]

calces ('kælsiːz) *n.* a plural of **calx.**

Calchas ('kælkæs) *n. Greek myth.* a soothsayer who assisted the Greeks in the Trojan War.

calci- *or before a vowel* **calc-** *combining form.* indicating lime or calcium: *calcify.* [from L *calx, calc-* limestone]

calciferol (kæl'sɪfərɒl) *n.* a fat-soluble steroid, found esp. in fish-liver oils and used in the treatment of rickets. Also called: **vitamin D₂.** [C20: from CALCIF(EROUS ERGOST)EROL]

calciferous (kæl'sɪfərəs) *adj.* producing salts of calcium, esp. calcium carbonate.

calcify ('kælsɪ,faɪ) *vb.* **-fying, -fied.** **1.** to convert or be converted into lime. **2.** to harden or become hardened by impregnation with calcium salts. — **calcifi'cation** *n.*

calcimine ('kælsɪ,maɪn) *n.* **1.** a white or tinted wash for walls. ~*vb.* **2.** (*tr.*) to cover with calcimine. [C19: from *Kalsomine*, a trademark]

calcine ('kælsaɪn, -sɪn) *vb.* **1.** (*tr.*) to heat (a substance) so that it is oxidized, is reduced, or loses water. **2.** (*intr.*) to oxidize as a result of heating. [C14: from Med. L *calcināre* to heat, from L *calx* lime] — **calcination** (ˌkælsɪ'neɪʃən) *n.*

calcite ('kælsaɪt) *n.* a colourless or white mineral consisting of crystalline calcium carbonate: the transparent variety is Iceland spar. Formula: $CaCO_3$.

calcium ('kælsɪəm) *n.* a malleable silvery-white metallic element of the alkaline earth group, occurring esp. as forms of calcium carbonate. It is an essential constituent of bones and teeth. Symbol: Ca; atomic no.: 20; atomic wt.: 40.08. [C19: from NL, from L *calx* lime]

calcium carbide *n.* a grey salt of calcium used in the production of acetylene. Formula: CaC_2. Sometimes shortened to **carbide.**

calcium carbonate *n.* a white crystalline salt occurring in limestone, chalk, and pearl: used in the production of lime. Formula: $CaCO_3$.

calcium chloride *n.* a white deliquescent salt occurring naturally in seawater and used in the de-icing of roads. Formula: $CaCl_2$.

calcium hydroxide *n.* a white crystalline slightly soluble alkali with many uses, esp. in cement, water softening, and the neutralization of acid soils. Formula: Ca(OH)$_2$. Also called: **lime, slaked lime, caustic lime.**

calcium oxide *n.* a white crystalline base used in the production of calcium hydroxide and in the manufacture of glass and steel. Formula: CaO. Also called: **lime, quicklime, calx.**

calcium phosphate *n.* an insoluble nonacid calcium salt that occurs in bones and is the main constituent of bone ash. Formula: Ca$_3$(PO$_4$)$_2$

calcspar ('kælk,spɑː) *n.* another name for **calcite.** [C19: from Swedish *kalkspat*, from *kalk* lime (ult. from L *calx*) + *spat* SPAR^3]

calculable ('kælkjʊləb³l) *adj.* **1.** that may be computed or estimated. **2.** predictable. — ,calcula'bility *n.* — 'calculably *adv.*

calculate ('kælkjʊ,leɪt) *vb.* **1.** to solve (one or more problems) by a mathematical procedure. **2.** (*tr.; may take a clause as object*) to determine beforehand by judgment, etc.; estimate. **3.** (*tr.; usually passive*) to aim: *the car was calculated to appeal to women.* **4.** (*intr.; foll. by on or upon*) to rely. **5.** (*tr.; may take a clause as object*) *U.S. dialect.* to suppose. [C16: from LL *calculāre*, from *calculus* pebble used as a counter] — **calculative** ('kælkjʊlətɪv) *adj.*

calculated ('kælkjʊ,leɪtɪd) *adj.* (*usually prenominal*) **1.** undertaken after considering the likelihood of success or failure. **2.** premeditated: *a calculated insult.*

calculating ('kælkjʊ,leɪtɪŋ) *adj.* **1.** selfishly scheming. **2.** shrewd. — 'calcu,latingly *adv.*

calculation (,kælkjʊ'leɪʃən) *n.* **1.** the act, process, or result of calculating. **2.** a forecast. **3.** careful planning, esp. for selfish motives.

calculator ('kælkjʊ,leɪtə) *n.* **1.** a device for performing mathematical calculations, esp. an electronic device that can be held in the hand. **2.** a person or thing that calculates. **3.** a set of tables used as an aid to calculations.

calculous ('kælkjʊləs) *adj. Pathol.* of or suffering from a calculus.

calculus ('kælkjʊləs) *n., pl.* **-luses. 1.** a branch of mathematics, developed independently by Newton and Leibnitz. Both **differential calculus** and **integral calculus** are concerned with the effect on a function of an infinitesimal change in the independent variable. **2.** any mathematical system of calculation involving the use of symbols. **3.** (*pl.* -li (-,laɪ)). *Pathol.* a stonelike concretion of minerals found in organs of the body. [C17: from L: pebble, from *calx* small stone, counter]

Calcutta (kæl'kʌtə) *n.* a port in E India, capital of West Bengal state, on the Hooghly River: former capital of the country (1833–1912); major commercial and industrial centre; three universities. Pop.: 3 291 655 (1981).

Calder ('kɔːldə) *n.* **Alexander.** 1898–1976, U.S. sculptor, who originated mobiles and stabiles (moving or static abstract sculptures, generally suspended from wire).

caldera (kæl'dɛərə) *n.* a large basin-shaped crater at the top of a volcano, formed by the collapse of the cone. [C19: from Sp. *caldera*, lit.: CAULDRON]

Calderón de la Barca (*Spanish* kalde'ron de la 'barka) *n.* **Pedro** (peðro). 1600–81, Spanish dramatist, whose best-known work is *La Vida es Sueño.* He also wrote *autos sacramentales,* outdoor plays for the feast of Corpus Christi, 76 of which survive.

caldron ('kɔːldrən) *n.* a variant spelling of **cauldron.**

Caldwell ('kɔːldwel, -wəl) *n.* **Erskine** ('ɜːskɪn). 1903–87, U.S. novelist whose works include *Tobacco Road* (1932).

calèche (*French* kalɛʃ) *n.* a variant of **calash.**

Caledonia (,kælɪ'dəʊnɪə) *n.* the Roman name for **Scotland.**

Caledonian (,kælɪ'dəʊnɪən) *adj.* **1.** relating to Scotland. **2.** of a period of mountain building in NW Europe in the Palaeozoic era. ~*n.* **3.** *Literary.* a native or inhabitant of Scotland.

Caledonian Canal *n.* a canal in N Scotland, linking the Atlantic with the North Sea through the Great Glen: built 1803–47; now little used.

calefacient (,kælɪ'feɪʃənt) *adj.* **1.** causing warmth. ~*n.* **2.** *Med.* an agent that warms, such as a mustard plaster. [C17: from L, from *calefacere* to heat]

calendar ('kælɪndə) *n.* **1.** a system for determining the beginning, length, and order of years and their divisions.

2. a table showing any such arrangement, esp. as applied to one or more successive years. **3.** a list or schedule of pending court cases, appointments, etc. ~*vb.* **4.** (*tr.*) to enter in a calendar; schedule. [C13: via Norman F from Med. L *kalendārium* account book, from *Kalendae* the CALENDS] —**calendrical** (kæ'lendrɪk³l) *or* ca'lendric *adj.*

calendar month *n.* See **month** (sense 1).

calendar year *n.* See **year** (sense 1).

calender ('kælɪndə) *n.* **1.** a machine in which paper or cloth is smoothed by passing between rollers. ~*vb.* **2.** (*tr.*) to subject (material) to such a process. [C17: from F *calandre,* from ?]

calends *or* **kalends** ('kælɪndz) *pl. n.* the first day of each month in the ancient Roman calendar. [C14: from L *kalendae*]

calendula (kæ'lendjʊlə) *n.* any of a genus of Eurasian plants, esp. the pot marigold, having orange-and-yellow rayed flowers. [C19: from Med. L, from L *kalendae* CALENDS]

calf[1] (kɑːf) *n., pl.* **calves. 1.** the young of cattle, esp. domestic cattle. **2.** the young of certain other mammals, such as the buffalo and whale. **3.** a large piece of ice detached from an iceberg, etc. **4. kill the fatted calf.** to celebrate lavishly, esp. as a welcome. [OE *cealf*]

calf[2] (kɑːf) *n., pl.* **calves.** the thick fleshy part of the back of the leg between the ankle and the knee. [C14: from ON *kalfi*]

calf love *n.* temporary infatuation of an adolescent for a member of the opposite sex.

calf's-foot jelly *n.* a jelly made from the stock of boiled calves' feet and flavourings.

calfskin ('kɑːf,skɪn) *n.* **1.** the skin or hide of a calf. **2.** Also called: **calf. a.** fine leather made from this skin. **b.** (*as modifier*): *calfskin boots.*

Calgary ('kælgərɪ) *n.* a city in Canada, in S Alberta: centre of a large agricultural region; oilfields. Pop.: 636 104 (1986).

Cali (*Spanish* 'kali) *n.* a city in SW Colombia: commercial centre in a rich agricultural region. Pop.: 1 397 433 (1985).

calibrate ('kælɪ,breɪt) *vb.* (*tr.*) **1.** to measure the calibre of (a gun, etc.). **2.** to mark (the scale of a measuring instrument) so that readings can be made in appropriate units. **3.** to determine the accuracy of (a measuring instrument, etc.). — ,cali'bration *n.* — 'cali,brator *n.*

calibre *or U.S.* **caliber** ('kælɪbə) *n.* **1.** the diameter of a cylindrical body, esp. the internal diameter of a tube or the bore of a firearm. **2.** the diameter of a shell or bullet. **3.** ability; distinction. **4.** personal character: *a man of high calibre.* [C16: from OF, from It. *calibro,* from Ar. *qālib* shoemaker's last] — 'calibred *or U.S.* 'calibered *adj.*

calices ('kælɪ,siːz) *n.* the plural of **calix.**

calico ('kælɪ,kəʊ) *n., pl.* **-coes** *or* **-cos. 1.** a white or unbleached cotton fabric. **2.** *Chiefly U.S.* a coarse printed cotton fabric. [C16: based on *Calicut,* town in India]

Calicut ('kælɪ,kʌt) *n.* the former name for **Kozhikode.**

calif ('keɪlɪf, 'kæl-) *n.* a variant spelling of **caliph.**

California (,kælɪ'fɔːnɪə) *n.* a state on the W coast of the U.S.: the third largest state in area and the largest in population; consists of a narrow, warm coastal plain rising to the Coast Range, deserts in the south, the fertile central valleys of the Sacramento and San Joaquin Rivers, and the mountains of the Sierra Nevada in the east; major industries include the growing of citrus fruits and grapes, fishing, oil production, electronics, and films. Capital: Sacramento. Pop.: 27 662 900 (1987 est.). Area: 411 015 sq. km (158 693 sq. miles). Abbrevs.: **Cal., Calif.** or (with zip code) **CA 2. Gulf of.** an arm of the Pacific Ocean, between Sonora and Lower California. — ,Cali'fornian *adj., n.*

californium (,kælɪ'fɔːnɪəm) *n.* a transuranic element artificially produced from curium. Symbol: Cf; atomic no.: 98; half-life of most stable isotope, ^{251}Cf: 800 years (approx.). [C20: NL; discovered at the University of *California*]

Caligula (kə'lɪgjʊlə) *n.* original name *Gaius Caesar,* son of Germanicus. 12–41 A.D., Roman emperor (37–41), noted for his cruelty and tyranny; assassinated.

Calimere ('kælɪmɪə) *n.* **Point.** a cape on the SE coast of India, on the Palk Strait.

calipash *or* **callipash** ('kælɪ,pæʃ) *n.* the greenish glutinous edible part of the turtle found next to the upper shell. [C17: ? changed from Sp. *carapacho* CARAPACE]

calipee ('kælɪ,piː) *n.* the yellow glutinous edible part of the turtle found next to the lower shell. [C17: ? a var. of CALIPASH]

caliper ('kælɪpə) *n.* the usual U.S. spelling of **calliper**.

caliph, calif, *or* **khalif** ('keɪlɪf, 'kæl-) *n. Islam.* the title of the successors of Mohammed as rulers of the Islamic world. [C14: from OF, from Ar. *khalīfa* successor]

caliphate, califate, *or* **khalifate** ('keɪlɪ,feɪt) *n.* the office, jurisdiction, or reign of a caliph.

calisthenics (,kælɪs'θɛnɪks) *n.* a variant spelling of **callisthenics**. U.S.) of **callisthenics**.

calix ('keɪlɪks, 'kæ-) *n., pl.* **calices.** a cup; chalice. [C18: from L: CHALICE]

calk[1] (kɔːk) *vb.* a variant spelling of **caulk**.

calk[2] (kɔːk) *or* **calkin** ('kɔːkɪn, 'kæl-) *n.* **1.** a metal projection on a horse's shoe to prevent slipping. ~*vb.* (*tr.*) **2.** to provide with calks. [C17: from L *calx* heel]

call (kɔːl) *vb.* **1.** (often foll. by *out*) to speak or utter (words, sounds, etc.) loudly so as to attract attention: *he called out her name.* **2.** (*tr.*) to ask or order to come: *to call a policeman.* **3.** (*intr.;* sometimes foll. by *on*) to make a visit (to): *she called on him.* **4.** (often foll. by *up*) to telephone (a person). **5.** (*tr.*) to summon to a specific office, profession, etc. **6.** (of animals or birds) to utter (a characteristic sound or cry). **7.** (*tr.*) to summon (a bird or animal), as by imitating its cry. **8.** (*tr.*) to name or style: *they called the dog Rover.* **9.** (*tr.*) to designate: *they called him a coward.* **10.** (*tr.*) to regard in a specific way: *I call it a foolish waste of time.* **11.** (*tr.*) to attract (attention). **12.** (*tr.*) to read (a list, etc.) aloud to check for omissions or absentees. **13.** (when *tr.,* usually foll. by *for*) to give an order (for): *to call a strike.* **14.** (*intr.*) to try to predict the result of tossing a coin. **15.** (*tr.*) to awaken: *I was called early this morning.* **16.** (*tr.*) to cause to assemble. **17.** (*tr.*) *Sport.* (of an umpire, etc.) to pass judgment upon (a shot, etc.) with a call. **18.** (*tr.*) *Austral. & N.Z.* to broadcast a commentary on (a horse race, etc.). **19.** (*tr.*) to demand repayment of (a loan, security, etc.). **20.** (*tr.*) *Brit.* to award (a student at an Inn of Court) the degree of barrister (esp. in **call to the bar**). **21.** (*tr.*) *Poker.* to demand that (a player) expose his hand, after equalling his bet. **22.** (*intr.*) *Bridge.* to make a bid. **23.** (*tr.*) to expose (a person's misleading statements, etc.): *I called his bluff.* **24.** (in square-dancing) to call out (instructions) to the dancers. **25.** (*intr.;* foll. by *for*) **a.** to require: *this problem calls for study.* **b.** to come or go (for) in order to fetch. **26.** (*intr.;* foll. by *on* or *upon*) to make an appeal or request (to): *they called upon him to reply.* **27. call into being.** to create. **28. call to mind.** to remember or cause to be remembered. ~*n.* **29.** a cry or shout. **30.** the characteristic cry of a bird or animal. **31.** a device, such as a whistle, intended to imitate the cry of a bird or animal. **32.** a summons or invitation. **33.** a summons or signal sounded on a horn, bugle, etc. **34.** a short visit: *the doctor made six calls this morning.* **35.** an inner urge to some task or profession; vocation. **36.** allure or fascination, esp. of a place: *the call of the forest.* **37.** need, demand, or occasion: *there is no call to shout.* **38.** demand or claim (esp. in **the call of duty**). **39.** *Theatre.* a notice to actors informing them of times of rehearsals. **40.** a conversation or a request for a connection by telephone. **41.** *Commerce.* **a.** a demand for repayment of a loan. **b.** (*as modifier*): *call money.* **42.** *Finance.* a demand for redeemable bonds or shares to be presented for repayment. **43.** *Poker.* a demand for a hand or hands to be exposed. **44.** *Bridge.* a bid or a player's turn to bid. **45.** *Sport.* a decision of an umpire or referee regarding a shot, pitch, etc. **46.** *Austral.* a broadcast commentary on a horse race, etc. **47.** Also called: **call option.** *Stock Exchange.* an option to buy a stated amount of securities at a specified price during a specified period. **48. on call. a.** (of a loan, etc.) repayable on demand. **b.** (of a doctor, etc.) available for duty. **49. within call.** accessible. ~See also **call down, call forth,** etc. [OE *ceallian*]

calla ('kælə) *n.* **1.** Also called: **calla lily, arum lily.** a southern African plant which has a white funnel-shaped spathe enclosing a yellow spadix. **2.** a plant that grows in wet places and has a white spathe and red berries. [C19: from NL, prob. from Gk *kalleia* wattles on a cock, prob. from *kallos* beauty]

Callaghan ('kælə,hæn) *n.* **(Leonard) James,** Baron Callaghan of Cardiff. born 1912, British Labour statesman; prime minister (1976–79).

Callao (*Spanish* ka'ʎao) *n.* a port in W Peru, near Lima, on **Callao Bay:** chief import centre of Peru. Pop.: 545 000 (1987).

Callas ('kæləs) *n.* **Maria.** 1923–77, Greek operatic soprano, born in the U.S.

call box *n.* a soundproof enclosure for a public telephone. Also called: **telephone kiosk.**

callboy ('kɔː,bɔɪ) *n.* a person who notifies actors when it is time to go on stage.

call down *vb.* (*tr., adv.*) to request or invoke: *to call down God's anger.*

caller ('kɔːlə) *n.* **1.** a person or thing that calls, esp. a person who makes a brief visit. **2.** *Austral.* a racing commentator.

call forth *vb.* (*tr., adv.*) to cause (something) to come into action or existence.

call girl *n.* a prostitute with whom appointments are made by telephone.

Callicrates (kə'lɪkrə,tiːz) *n.* 5th century B.C., Greek architect: with Ictinus, designed the Parthenon.

calligraphy (kə'lɪgrəfɪ) *n.* handwriting, esp. beautiful handwriting. — **cal'ligrapher** *or* **cal'ligraphist** *n.* — **calligraphic** (,kælɪ'græfɪk) *adj.*

call in *vb.* (*adv.*) **1.** (*intr.;* often foll. by *on*) to pay a visit, esp. a brief one: *call in if you are in the neighbourhood.* **2.** (*tr.*) to demand payment of: *to call in a loan.* **3.** (*tr.*) to take (something) out of circulation, because it is defective. **4.** to summon to one's assistance: *to call in a specialist.*

calling ('kɔːlɪŋ) *n.* **1.** a strong inner urge to follow an occupation, etc.; vocation. **2.** an occupation, profession, or trade.

calling card *n.* the usual U.S. and Canad. term for **visiting card.**

calliope (kə'laɪəpɪ) *n. U.S. & Canad.* a steam organ. [after CALLIOPE (lit.: beautiful-voiced)]

Calliope (kə'laɪəpɪ) *n. Greek myth.* the Muse of epic poetry.

calliper *or U.S.* **caliper** ('kælɪpə) *n.* **1.** (*often pl.*) Also called: **calliper compasses.** an instrument for measuring internal or external dimensions, consisting of two steel legs hinged together. **2.** Also called: **calliper splint.** *Med.* a metal splint for supporting the leg. ~*vb.* **3.** (*tr.*) to measure with callipers. [C16: var. of CALIBRE]

calliper rule *n.* a measuring instrument having two parallel jaws, one fixed and the other sliding.

callisthenics *or* **calisthenics** (,kælɪs'θɛnɪks) *n.* **1.** (*functioning as pl.*) light exercises designed to promote general fitness. **2.** (*functioning as sing.*) the practice of callisthenic exercises. [C19: from Gk *kalli-* beautiful + Gk *sthenos* strength] — **,callis'thenic** *or* **,calis'thenic** *adj.*

Callisto (kə'lɪstəʊ) *n. Greek myth.* a nymph who attracted the love of Zeus and was changed into a bear by Hera. Zeus then set her in the sky as the constellation Ursa Major.

call loan *n.* a loan that is repayable on demand. Also called: **demand loan.**

call off *vb.* (*tr., adv.*) **1.** to cancel or abandon: *the game was called off.* **2.** to order (an animal or person) to desist: *the man called off his dog.* **3.** to stop (something).

callosity (kə'lɒsɪtɪ) *n., pl.* **-ties. 1.** hard-heartedness. **2.** a callus.

callous ('kæləs) *adj.* **1.** insensitive. **2.** (of skin) hardened and thickened. ~*vb.* **3.** *Pathol.* to make or become callous. [C16: from L *callōsus;* see CALLUS] — **'callously** *adv.* — **'callousness** *n.*

call out *vb.* (*adv.*) **1.** to utter aloud, esp. loudly. **2.** (*tr.*) to summon: *call out the troops.* **3.** (*tr.*) to order (workers) to strike. **4.** (*tr.*) to challenge to a duel.

callow ('kæləʊ) *adj.* lacking experience of life; immature. [OE *calu*] — **'callowness** *n.*

call sign *n.* a group of letters and numbers identifying a radio transmitting station.

call up *vb.* (*tr., adv.*) **1.** to summon to report for active military service, as in time of war. **2.** to recall (something); evoke. **3.** to bring or summon (people, etc.) into action. **4.** to telephone. ~*n.* **call-up. 5. a.** a general order to report for military service. **b.** the number of men so summoned.

callus ('kæləs) *n., pl.* **-luses. 1.** Also called: **callosity.** an area of skin that is hard or thick, esp. on the sole of the foot. **2.** an area of bony tissue formed during the healing of a fractured bone. **3.** *Bot.* a mass of hard protective tissue produced in woody plants at the site of an injury. [C16: from L, var. of *callum* hardened skin]

calm (kɑːm) *adj.* **1.** still: *a calm sea.* **2.** *Meteorol.* without wind, or with wind of less than 1 mph. **3.** not disturbed, agitated, or excited. **4.** tranquil; serene: *a calm voice.* ~*n.* **5.** an absence of disturbance or rough motion. **6.** absence of wind. **7.** tranquillity. ~*vb.* **8.** (often foll. by *down*) to make or become calm. [C14: from OF *calme*, from OIt., from LL *cauma* heat, hence a rest during the heat of the day, from Gk, from *kaiein* to burn] —'**calmly** *adv.* —'**calmness** *n.*

calmative ('kælmətɪv, 'kɑːmə-) *adj.* (of a remedy or agent) sedative.

calomel ('kælə,mɛl, -məl) *n.* a colourless tasteless powder consisting chiefly of mercurous chloride, used medicinally, esp. as a cathartic. [C17: ?from NL *calomelas* (untested), lit.: beautiful black, from Gk *kalos* beautiful + *melas* black]

Calor Gas ('kælə) *n. Trademark.* butane gas liquefied under pressure in portable containers for domestic use.

caloric (kə'lɒrɪk) *adj.* **1.** of or concerned with heat or calories. ~*n.* **2.** *Obs.* a hypothetical elastic fluid, the embodiment of heat.

calorie or **calory** ('kælərɪ) *n., pl.* **-ries.** a unit of heat, equal to 4.1868 joules (**International Table calorie**): formerly defined as the quantity of heat required to raise the temperature of 1 gram of water by 1°C. Abbrev.: **cal.** Also called: **small calorie.** [C19: from F, from L *calor* heat]

Calorie ('kælərɪ) *n.* **1.** Also called: **kilogram calorie, large calorie.** a unit of heat, equal to one thousand calories. Abbrev.: **Cal.** **2.** the amount of a specific food capable of producing one thousand calories of energy.

calorific (,kælə'rɪfɪk) *adj.* of, concerning, or generating heat. —,**calo'rifically** *adv.*

calorific value *n.* the quantity of heat produced by the complete combustion of a given mass of a fuel.

calorimeter (,kælə'rɪmɪtə) *n.* an apparatus for measuring amounts of heat, esp. to find calorific values, etc. —**calorimetric** (,kælərɪ'mɛtrɪk) *adj.* —,**calo'rimetry** *n.*

Calpe ('kælpɪ) *n.* the ancient name for the (Rock of) Gibraltar.

calque (kælk) *n.* another word for **loan translation.** [C20: from F: a tracing, from L *calcāre* to tread]

Caltanissetta (*Italian* kaltanis'sɛtta) *n.* a city in central Sicily: sulphur mines. Pop.: 61 146 (1981).

calumet ('kæljʊ,mɛt) *n.* the peace pipe. [C18: from Canad. F, from F: straw, from LL *calamellus* a little reed, from L: CALAMUS]

calumniate (kə'lʌmnɪ,eɪt) *vb.* (*tr.*) to slander. —**ca,lumni'ation** *n.* —**ca'lumni,ator** *n.*

calumny ('kæləmnɪ) *n., pl.* **-nies.** **1.** the malicious utterance of false charges or misrepresentation. **2.** such a false charge or misrepresentation. [C15: from L *calumnia* deception, slander] —**calumnious** (kə'lʌmnɪəs) or **ca'lumniatory** *adj.*

Calvados ('kælvə,dɒs) *n.* **1.** a department of N France in the Basse-Normandie region. Capital: Caen. Pop.: 589 559 (1982). Area: 5693 sq. km (2198 sq. miles). **2.** an apple brandy distilled from cider in this region.

Calvary ('kælvərɪ) *n.* the place just outside the walls of Jerusalem where Jesus was crucified. Also called: **Golgotha.** [from LL *Calvāria*, translation of Gk *kranion* skull, translation of Aramaic *gulgulta* Golgotha]

calve (kɑːv) *vb.* **1.** to give birth to (a calf). **2.** (of a glacier or iceberg) to release (masses of ice) in breaking up.

Calvert ('kælvət) *n.* **1.** Sir **George,** 1st Baron Baltimore. ?1580–1632, English statesman; founder of the colony of Maryland. **2.** his son, **Leonard.** 1606–47, English statesman; first colonial governor of Maryland (1634–47).

calves (kɑːvz) *n.* the plural of **calf**[1] and **calf**[2].

Calvin ('kælvɪn) *n.* **1. John,** original name *Jean Cauvin, Caulvin,* or *Chauvin.* 1509–64, French theologian: a leader of the Protestant Reformation in France and Switzerland, establishing the first presbyterian government in Geneva. His theological system is described in his *Institutes of the Christian Religion* (1536). **2. Melvin.** born 1911, U.S. chemist, noted particularly for his research on photosynthesis: Nobel prize for chemistry 1961.

Calvinism ('kælvɪ,nɪzəm) *n.* the theological system of John Calvin and his followers, characterized by emphasis on predestination and justification by faith. —'**Calvinist** *n., adj.* —,**Calvin'istic** or ,**Calvin'istical** *adj.*

calx (kælks) *n., pl.* **calxes** or **calces.** **1.** the powdery metallic oxide formed when an ore or mineral is roasted. **2.** calcium oxide. [C15: from L: lime, from Gk *khalix* pebble]

Calydonian boar (,kælɪ'dəʊnɪən) *n. Greek myth.* a savage boar sent by Artemis to destroy Calydon, a city in Aetolia, because its king had neglected to sacrifice to her. It was killed by Meleager, the king's son.

calypso (kə'lɪpsəʊ) *n., pl.* **-sos.** a popular type of satirical West Indian ballad, esp. from Trinidad, usually extemporized to a syncopated accompaniment. [C20: prob. from CALYPSO]

Calypso (kə'lɪpsəʊ) *n. Greek myth.* (in Homer's *Odyssey*) a sea nymph who detained Odysseus on the island of Ogygia for seven years.

calyx ('keɪlɪks, 'kælɪks) *n., pl.* **calyxes** or **calyces** ('kælɪ,siːz, 'keɪlɪ-). **1.** the sepals of a flower collectively that protect the developing flower bud. **2.** any cup-shaped cavity or structure. [C17: from L, from Gk *kalux* shell, from *kaluptein* to cover]

cam (kæm) *n.* a rotating cylinder attached to a revolving shaft to give a reciprocating motion to a part in contact with it. [C16: from Du. *kam* comb]

Cam (kæm) *n.* a river in E England, in Cambridgeshire, flowing through Cambridge to the River Ouse. Length: about 64 km (40 miles).

CAM (kæm) *acronym for* computer-aided manufacture.

Camagüey ('kæmə,gweɪ; *Spanish* kama'ɣwej) *n.* a city in E central Cuba. Pop.: 260 800 (1986 est.).

camaraderie (,kæmə'rɑːdərɪ) *n.* a spirit of familiarity and trust existing between friends. [C19: from F, from *camarade* COMRADE]

Camargue (kæ'mɑːg) *n.* **la** (la). a delta region in S France, between the channels of the Grand and Petit Rhône: cattle, esp. bulls for the Spanish bullrings, and horses are reared.

camarilla (,kæmə'rɪlə) *n.* a group of confidential advisers, esp. formerly, to the Spanish kings. [C19: from Sp., lit.: a little room]

Cambay (kæm'beɪ) *n.* **Gulf of.** an inlet of the Arabian Sea on the W coast of India, southeast of the Kathiawar Peninsula.

camber ('kæmbə) *n.* **1.** a slight upward curve to the centre of the surface of a road, ship's deck, etc. **2.** another name for **bank**[2] (sense 8). **3.** an outward inclination of the front wheels of a road vehicle so that they are slightly closer together at the bottom. **4.** aerofoil curvature expressed by the ratio of the maximum height of the aerofoil mean line to its chord. ~*vb.* **5.** to form or be formed with a surface that curves upwards to its centre. [C17: from OF *cambre* curved, from L *camurus*]

cambium ('kæmbɪəm) *n., pl.* **-biums** or **-bia** (-bɪə). *Bot.* a layer of cells that increases the girth of stems and roots. [C17: from Med. L: exchange, from LL *cambiāre* to exchange] —'**cambial** *adj.*

Cambodia (kæm'bəʊdɪə) *n.* a former name for **Kampuchea.** —**Cam'bodian** *adj., n.*

Camborne-Redruth ('kæmbɔːn'rɛd,ruːθ) *n.* a town in SW England, in Cornwall: formed in 1934 by the amalgamation of neighbouring towns. Pop.: 46 482 (1981).

Cambrai (*French* kɑ̃brɛ) *n.* a town in NE France: textile industry: scene of a battle in which massed tanks were first used and broke through the German line (November, 1917). Pop.: 38 941 (1983 est.).

Cambria ('kæmbrɪə) *n.* the Medieval Latin name for **Wales.**

Cambrian ('kæmbrɪən) *adj.* **1.** of or formed in the first 100 million years of the Palaeozoic era. **2.** of or relating to Wales. ~*n.* **3. the.** the Cambrian period or rock system. **4.** a Welshman.

Cambrian Mountains *pl. n.* a mountain range in Wales, extending from S Dyfed to Clwyd. Highest peak: Aran Fawddwy 891 m (2970 ft.).

cambric ('keɪmbrɪk) *n.* a fine white linen fabric. [C16: from Flemish *Kamerijk* CAMBRAI]

Cambridge ('keɪmbrɪdʒ) *n.* **1.** a city in E England, administrative centre of Cambridgeshire, on the River Cam: centred around the university, founded in the 12th century. Pop.: 100 500 (1983). Medieval Latin name: **Cantabrigia.** **2.** short for **Cambridgeshire.** **3.** a city in E Massachusetts: educational centre, with Harvard University (1636) and the Massachusetts Institute of Technology. Pop.: 95 322 (1980).

Cambridgeshire ('keimbridʒ,ʃiə, -ʃə) n. a county of E England, in East Anglia: includes the former counties of the Isle of Ely and Huntingdon and lies largely in the Fens. Administrative centre: Cambridge. Pop.: 635 200 (1986 est.). Area: 3409 sq. km (1350 sq. miles).

Cambs abbrev. for Cambridgeshire.

Cambyses (kæm'baisiːz) n. died ?522 B.C., king of Persia (529–522 B.C.), who conquered Egypt (525); son of Cyrus the Great.

camcorder ('kæm,kɔːdə) n. a video camera and recorder combined in a portable unit.

Camden[1] ('kæmdən) n. a borough of N Greater London. Pop.: 183 300 (1986 est.).

Camden[2] ('kæmdən) n. **William**. 1551–1623, English antiquary and historian; author of Britannia (1586).

came (keim) vb. the past tense of **come**.

camel ('kæməl) n. 1. either of two cud-chewing, humped mammals (see **Arabian camel**, **Bactrian camel**) that are adapted for surviving long periods without food or water in desert regions. 2. a float attached to a vessel to increase its buoyancy. 3. a. a fawn colour. b. (as adj.): a camel coat. [OE, from L, from Gk kamēlos, of Semitic origin]

cameleer (,kæmɪ'lɪə) n. a camel driver.

camellia (kə'miːlɪə) n. any of a genus of ornamental shrubs having glossy evergreen leaves and showy white, pink, or red flowers. Also called: **japonica**. [C18: NL, after Georg Josef Kamel (1661–1706), Moravian Jesuit missionary]

camelopard ('kæmɪlə,pɑːd, kə'mɛl-) n. an obsolete word for **giraffe**. [C14: from Med. L, from Gk, from kamēlos CAMEL + pardalis LEOPARD, because the giraffe was thought to have a head like a camel's and spots like a leopard's]

Camelot ('kæmɪ,lɒt) n. (in Arthurian legend) the English town where King Arthur's palace and court were situated.

camel's hair or **camelhair** ('kæməl,hɛə) n. 1. the hair of a camel, used in rugs, etc. 2. soft cloth made of this hair, usually tan in colour. 3. (modifier) (of a painter's brush) made from the tail hairs of squirrels.

Camembert ('kæməm,bɛə) n. a soft creamy cheese. [F, from Camembert, a village in Normandy]

Camenae (kə'miːniː) pl. n. Roman myth. a group of nymphs originally associated with a sacred spring in Rome, later identified with the Greek Muses.

cameo ('kæmɪ,əʊ) n., pl. **cameos**. 1. a medallion, as on a brooch or ring, with a profile head carved in relief. 2. an engraving upon a gem or other stone so that the background is of a different colour from the raised design. 3. a stone with such an engraving. 4. a. a brief dramatic scene played by a well-known actor or actress in a film or television play. b. (as modifier): a cameo performance. 5. a short literary work. [C15: from It. cammeo, from ?]

camera ('kæmərə) n. 1. an optical device consisting of a lens system set in a light-proof construction inside which a light-sensitive film or plate can be positioned. 2. Television. the equipment used to convert the optical image of a scene into the corresponding electrical signals. 3. (pl. -erae (-ə,riː)). a judge's private room. 4. **in camera. a.** Law. relating to a hearing from which members of the public are excluded. **b.** in private. [C18: from L: vault, from Gk kamara]

cameraman ('kæmərə,mæn) n., pl. **-men**. a person who operates a film or television camera.

camera obscura (ɒb'skjʊərə) n. a darkened chamber with an aperture, in which images of outside objects are projected onto a flat surface. [NL: dark chamber]

camera-shy adj. having an aversion to being photographed or filmed.

Cameroon (,kæmə'ruːn, 'kæmə,ruːn) n. 1. a republic in West Africa, on the Gulf of Guinea: became a German colony in 1884; divided in 1919 into the **Cameroons** (administered by Britain) and **Cameroun** (administered by France); Cameroun and the S part of the Cameroons formed a republic in 1961 (the N part joined Nigeria). Official languages: French and English. Religions: Christian, Muslim, and animist. Currency: franc. Capital: Yaoundé. Pop.: 9 880 000 (1986 est.). Area: 475 500 sq. km (183 591 sq. miles). French name: **Cameroun**. German name: **Kamerun**. 2. an active volcano in W Cameroon: the highest peak on the West African coast. Height: 4070 m (13 352 ft.).

Cameroun (kamrun) n. the French name for **Cameroon**.

camiknickers ('kæmɪ,nikəz) pl. n. women's knickers attached to a camisole top.

camisole ('kæmɪ,səʊl) n. 1. a woman's underbodice with shoulder straps, originally designed as a cover for a corset. 2. a woman's short negligee. [C19: from F, from Provençal camisola, from camisa shirt, from LL camisia]

Camoëns ('kæməʊ,ɛns) or **Camões** (Portuguese kə'mõəʃ) n. **Luis Vaz de** (lwiʃ vaʃ 'dɔ:). 1524–80, Portuguese epic poet; author of The Lusiads (1572).

camomile or **chamomile** ('kæmə,maɪl) n. 1. any of a genus of aromatic plants whose finely dissected leaves and daisy-like flowers are used medicinally. 2. any plant of a related genus as **German** or **wild camomile**. 3. **camomile tea**. a medicinal beverage made from the fragrant leaves and flowers of any of these plants. [C14: from OF, from Med. L, from Gk khamaimēlon lit., earth-apple (referring to the scent of the flowers)]

camouflage ('kæmə,flɑːʒ) n. 1. the exploitation of natural surroundings or artificial aids to conceal or disguise the presence of military units, etc. 2. the means by which animals escape the notice of predators. 3. a device or expedient designed to conceal or deceive. ~vb. 4. (tr.) to conceal by camouflage. [C20: from F, from camoufler, from It. camuffare to disguise, from ?]

camp[1] (kæmp) n. 1. a place where tents, cabins, etc., are erected for the use of military troops, etc. 2. tents, cabins, etc., used as temporary lodgings by holiday-makers, Scouts, Gypsies, etc. 3. the group of people living in such lodgings. 4. a group supporting a given doctrine: the socialist camp. 5. (modifier) suitable for use in temporary quarters, on holiday, etc.: a camp bed; a camp chair. 6. S. African. a field or pasture. 7. Austral. a place where sheep or cattle gather to rest. ~vb. (intr.) 8. (often foll. by down) to establish or set up a camp. 9. (often foll. by out) to live temporarily in or as if in a tent. [C16: from OF, ult. from L campus field] —'camping n.

camp[2] (kæmp) Inf. ~adj. 1. effeminate; affected. 2. homosexual. 3. consciously artificial, vulgar, or mannered. ~vb. 4. (tr.) to perform or invest with a camp quality. 5. **camp it up. a.** to overact. **b.** to flaunt one's homosexuality. [C20: from ?] —'campy adj.

Campagna (kæm'pɑːnjə) n. a low-lying plain surrounding Rome, Italy: once fertile, it deteriorated to malarial marshes; recently reclaimed. Area: about 2000 sq. km (800 sq. miles). Also called: **Campagna di Roma** (dɪ 'rəʊmə).

campaign (kæm'pein) n. 1. a series of coordinated activities, such as public speaking, designed to achieve a social, political, or commercial goal: a presidential campaign. 2. Mil. a number of operations aimed at achieving a single objective. ~vb. 3. (intr.; often foll. by for) to conduct, serve in, or go on a campaign. [C17: from F campagne open country, from It., from LL, from L campus field] —cam'paigner n.

Campania (kæm'peiniə, Italian kam'panjna) n. a region of SW Italy: includes the islands of Capri and Ischia. Chief town: Naples. Pop.: 5 690 431 (1985 est.). Area: 13 595 sq. km (5248 sq. miles).

campanile (,kæmpə'niːli) n. (esp. in Italy) a bell tower, not usually attached to another building. [C17: from It., from campana bell]

campanology (,kæmpə'nɒlədʒi) n. the art or skill of ringing bells. [C19: from NL, from LL campāna bell] —**campanological** (,kæmpənə'lɒdʒik°l) adj. —,**campa'nologist** or ,**campa'nologer** n.

campanula (kæm'pænjʊlə) n. any of a genus of N temperate plants having blue or white bell-shaped flowers. Also called: **bellflower**. [C17: from NL: a little bell, from LL campāna bell]

Campbell ('kæmb°l) n. 1. Sir **Colin**, Baron Clyde. 1792–1863, British field marshal who relieved Lucknow for the second time (1857) and commanded in Oudh, suppressing the Indian Mutiny. 2. **Donald**. 1921–67, English water speed record-holder. 3. his father, Sir **Malcolm**. 1885–1948, English racing driver and land speed record-holder. 4. **Mrs Patrick**, original name Beatrice Stella Tanner. 1865–1940, English actress. 5. **Roy**. 1901–57, South African poet. His poetry is often satirical and includes The Flaming Terrapin (1924). 6. **Thomas**. 1777–1844, Scottish poet and critic, noted particularly for his war poems Hohenlinden and Ye Mariners of England.

Campbell-Bannerman ('kæmb°l'bænəmən) n. Sir **Henry**. 1836–1908, British statesman and leader of the

Liberal Party (1899–1908); prime minister (1905–8), who granted self-government to the Transvaal and the Orange River Colony.

camp drafting *n. Austral.* a competitive test of horsemen's skill in drafting cattle.

Campeche (*Spanish* kam'petʃe) *n.* **1.** a state of SE Mexico, on the SW of the Yucatán peninsula: forestry and fishing. Capital: Campeche. Pop.: 372 277 (1980). Area: 56 114 sq. km (21 666 sq. miles). **2.** a port in SE Mexico, capital of Campeche state. Pop.: 120 000 (1984 est.). **3.** Also called: **Gulf of Campeche. Bay of.** the SW part of the Gulf of Mexico.

camper ('kæmpə) *n.* **1.** a person who lives or temporarily stays in a tent, cabin, etc. **2.** *U.S. & Canad.* a vehicle equipped for camping out.

camp follower *n.* **1.** any civilian, esp. a prostitute, who unofficially provides services to military personnel. **2.** a nonmember who is sympathetic to a particular group, theory, etc.

camphor ('kæmfə) *n.* a whitish crystalline aromatic ketone obtained from the wood of an Asian or Australian laurel (**camphor tree**): used in medicine as a liniment. [C15: from OF *camphre*, from Med. L *camphora*, from Ar. *kāfūr*, from Malay *kāpūr* chalk] —**camphoric** (kæm'fɒrɪk) *adj.*

camphorate ('kæmfə,reɪt) *vb.* (*tr.*) to apply, treat with, or impregnate with camphor.

camphor ball *n.* another name for **mothball** (sense 1).

camphor ice *n.* an ointment consisting of camphor, white wax, spermaceti, and castor oil, used to treat skin ailments, esp. chapped skin.

camphor wood *n. Austral.* a popular name for any of several trees with pungent smelling wood.

Campina Grande (*Portuguese* kəm'piːnə 'grəːndə) *n.* a city in NE Brazil, in E Paraíba state. Pop.: 222 229 (1980).

Campinas (kæm'piːnəs; *Portuguese* kəm'piːnəʃ) *n.* a city in SE Brazil, in São Paulo state: centre of a rich agricultural region, producing esp. coffee. Pop.: 566 517 (1980).

campion ('kæmpɪən) *n.* any of various plants related to the pink, having red, pink, or white flowers. [C16: prob. from *campion*, obs. var. of CHAMPION]

Campion ('kæmpɪən) *n.* **1. Edmund.** 1540–81, English Jesuit martyr. He joined the Jesuits in 1573 and returned to England (1580) as a missionary. He was charged with treason and hanged. **2. Thomas.** 1567–1620, English poet and musician, noted particularly for his songs for the lute.

Campobello (,kæmpə'bɛləʊ) *n.* an island in the Bay of Fundy, off the coast of SE Canada: part of New Brunswick province. Area: about 52 sq. km (20 sq. miles). Pop.: 1424 (1981).

Campo Formio (*Italian* 'kampo 'fɔrmjo) *n.* a village in NE Italy, in Friuli-Venezia Giulia: scene of the signing of a treaty in 1797 that ended the war between revolutionary France and Austria. Modern name: **Campoformido** (kampo'fɔrmido).

Campo Grande (*Portuguese* 'kəːmpu 'grəːndə) *n.* a city in SW Brazil, capital of Mato Grosso do Sul state on the São Paulo–Corumbá railway: market centre. Pop.: 282 844 (1980).

Campos (*Portuguese* 'kəːmpuʃ) *n.* a city in E Brazil, in E Rio de Janeiro state on the Paraíba River. Pop.: 174 000 (1984 est.).

camp oven *n. Austral. & N.Z.* a metal pot or box with a heavy lid, used for baking over an open fire.

camp site *n.* an area on which holiday-makers may pitch a tent, etc. Also called: **camping site.**

campus ('kæmpəs) *n., pl.* **-puses. 1.** the grounds and buildings of a university. **2.** *Chiefly U.S.* the outside area of a college, etc. [C18: from L: field]

campylobacter ('kæmpɪləʊ,bæktə) *n.* a rod-shaped bacterium that causes infections in animals and man; a common cause of gastroenteritis. [from Gk *kampulos* bent + BACTER(IUM)]

Cam Ranh ('kæm 'ræn) *n.* a port in SE Vietnam: large natural harbour, in recent years used as a naval base by French, Japanese, U.S., and Soviet forces successively. Pop.: 118 111 (1973 est.).

camshaft ('kæm,ʃɑːft) *n.* a shaft having one or more cams attached to it.

Camus (*French* kamy) *n.* **Albert** (albɛr). 1913–60, French novelist, dramatist, and essayist, noted for his pessimistic portrayal of man's condition of isolation in an absurd world: author of the novels *L'Etranger* (1942) and *La Peste* (1947), the plays *Le Malentendu* (1945) and *Caligula* (1946), and the essays *Le Mythe de Sisyphe* (1942) and *L'Homme révolté* (1951): Nobel prize for literature 1957.

can[1] (kæn; *unstressed* kən) *vb. past* **could.** (takes an infinitive without *to* or an implied infinitive) used as an auxiliary: **1.** to indicate ability, skill, or fitness to perform a task: *I can run.* **2.** to indicate permission or the right to something: *can I have a drink?* **3.** to indicate knowledge of how to do something: *he can speak three languages.* **4.** to indicate the possibility, opportunity, or likelihood: *my trainer says I can win the race.* [OE *cunnan*]
▷ **Usage.** See at **may**[1].

can[2] (kæn) *n.* **1.** a container, esp. for liquids, usually of thin metal: *a petrol can.* **2.** a tin (metal container): *a beer can.* **3.** Also: **canful.** the contents of a can or the amount a can will hold. **4.** a slang word for **prison. 5.** *U.S. & Canad.* a slang word for **toilet. 6.** a shallow cylindrical metal container used for storing and handling film. **7. can of worms.** *Inf.* a complicated problem. **8. in the can. a.** (of a film, piece of music, etc.) having been recorded, edited, etc. **b.** *Inf.* agreed: *the contract is in the can.* ~*vb.* **canning, canned. 9.** to put (food, etc.) into a can or cans. [OE *canne*] —**'canner** *n.*

Can. *abbrev. for:* **1.** Canada. **2.** Canadian.

Cana ('keɪnə) *n. New Testament.* the town in Galilee, north of Nazareth, where Jesus performed his first miracle by changing water into wine (John 2:1, 11).

Canaan ('keɪnən) *n.* an ancient region between the River Jordan and the Mediterranean: the Promised Land of the Israelites.

Canaanite ('keɪnə,naɪt) *n.* a member of an ancient Semitic people who occupied the land of Canaan before the Israelite conquest.

Canada ('kænədə) *n.* a country in North America: the second largest country in the world; first permanent settlements made by the French from 1605; ceded to Britain in 1763 after a series of colonial wars; established as the Dominion of Canada in 1867; member of the Commonwealth. It consists generally of sparsely inhabited tundra regions, rich in natural resources, in the north, the Rocky Mountains in the west, the Canadian Shield in the east, and vast central prairies; the bulk of the population is concentrated along the U.S. border and the Great Lakes in the south. Languages: English and French. Currency: Canadian dollar. Capital: Ottawa. Pop.: 25 963 000 (1987). Area: 9 976 185 sq. km (3 851 809 sq. miles).

Canada balsam *n.* **1.** a yellow transparent resin obtained from the balsam fir. Because its refractive index is similar to that of glass, it is used as a mounting medium for microscope specimens. **2.** another name for **balsam fir.**

Canada Day *n.* (in Canada) July 1, the anniversary of the day in 1867 when Canada received dominion status: a public holiday.

Canada goose *n.* a large common greyish-brown North American goose with a black neck and head and a white throat patch.

Canada jay *n.* a grey crestless jay, notorious in northern parts of N America for its stealing. Also called: **camp robber, whisky-jack.**

Canadian (kə'neɪdɪən) *adj.* **1.** of or relating to Canada or its people. ~*n.* **2.** a native, citizen, or inhabitant of Canada.

Canadiana (kə,neɪdɪ'ɑːnə; *Canad.* -'ænə) *n.* objects, such as books, furniture, and antiques, relating to Canadian history and culture.

Canadian football *n.* a game like American football played on a grass pitch between teams of 12 players.

Canadianism (kə'neɪdɪə,nɪzəm) *n.* **1.** the Canadian national character or spirit. **2.** a linguistic usage, custom, or other feature peculiar to Canada, its people, or their culture.

Canadianize *or* **-ise** (kə'neɪdɪə,naɪz) *vb.* to make or become Canadian by changing customs, ownership, character, content, etc.

Canadian River *n.* a river in the southern U.S., rising in NE New Mexico and flowing east to the Arkansas River in E Oklahoma. Length: 1458 km (906 miles).

Canadian Shield *n.* the wide area of Precambrian rock extending over most of E and central Canada: rich in minerals. Also called: **Laurentian Shield.**

Canadien (*French* kanadjɛ̃; *English* kə,nædɪ'ɛn) *or* (*fem.*) **Canadienne** (*French* kanadjɛn; *English* kə,nædɪ'ɛn) *n.* a French Canadian.

canaille *French.* (kanɑj) *n.* the masses; mob; rabble. [C17: from F, from It. *canaglia* pack of dogs]

canakin ('kænɪkɪn) *n.* a variant spelling of **cannikin.**

canal (kə'næl) *n.* **1.** an artificial waterway constructed for navigation, irrigation, etc. **2.** any of various passages or ducts: *the alimentary canal.* **3.** any of various intercellular spaces in plants. **4.** *Astron.* any of the indistinct surface features of Mars orig. thought to be a network of channels. ~*vb.* **-nalling, -nalled** *or U.S.* **-naling, -naled.** (*tr.*) **5.** to dig a canal through. **6.** to provide with a canal or canals. [C15 (in the sense: pipe, tube): from L *canālis* channel, from *canna* reed]

canal boat *n.* a long narrow boat used on canals, esp. for carrying freight.

Canaletto (*Italian* kana'lɛtto) *n.* original name *Giovanni Antonio Canale.* 1697–1768, Italian painter and etcher, noted particularly for his highly detailed paintings of cities, esp. Venice, which are marked by strong contrasts of light and shade.

canaliculus (,kænə'lɪkjuləs) *n., pl.* **-li** (-,laɪ). a small channel or groove, as in some bones. [C16: from L: a little channel, from *canālis* CANAL] —,**cana'licular** *or* ,**cana'liculate** *adj.*

canalize *or* **-lise** ('kænə,laɪz) *vb.* (*tr.*) **1.** to provide with or convert into a canal or canals. **2.** to give a particular direction to or provide an outlet for. —,**canali'zation** *or* **-li'sation** *n.*

canal ray *n. Physics.* a stream of positive ions produced in a discharge tube by allowing them to pass through holes in the cathode.

Canal Zone *n.* a former administrative region of the U.S., on the Isthmus of Panama around the Panama Canal: bordered on each side by the Republic of Panama, into which it was incorporated in 1979. Also called: **Panama Canal Zone.**

canapé ('kænəpɪ, -,peɪ) *n.* a small piece of bread, toast, etc., spread with a savoury topping. [C19: from F: sofa]

Canara (kə'nɑːrə) *n.* a variant spelling of **Kanara.**

canard (kæ'nɑːd) *n.* **1.** a false report; rumour or hoax. **2.** an aircraft in which the tailplane is mounted in front of the wing. [C19: from F: a duck, from OF *caner* to quack, imit.]

canary (kə'nɛərɪ) *n., pl.* **-naries. 1.** a small finch of the Canary Islands and Azores: a popular cage-bird noted for its singing. **2. canary yellow. a.** a light yellow. **b.** (*as adj.*): *a canary-yellow car.* **3.** a sweet wine similar to Madeira. **4.** *Arch.* a sweet wine from the Canary Islands. [C16: from OSp. *canario* of or from the Canary Islands]

Canary Islands *or* **Canaries** *pl. n.* a group of mountainous islands in the Atlantic off the NW coast of Africa, forming the Spanish provinces of Las Palmas and Santa Cruz de Tenerife. Pop.: 1 442 500 (1986 est.).

canasta (kə'næstə) *n.* **1.** a card game for two to six players who seek to amass points by declaring sets of cards. **2.** Also called: **meld.** a declared set in this game, containing seven or more like cards. [C20: from Sp.: basket (because two packs of cards are required), from L *canistrum*; see CANISTER]

canaster ('kænəstə) *n.* coarsely broken dried tobacco leaves. [C19: (meaning: basket in which tobacco was packed): from Sp.; see CANISTER]

Canaveral (kə'nævərəl) *n.* **Cape.** a cape on the E coast of Florida: site of the U.S. Air Force Missile Test Centre, from which the majority of U.S. space missions have been launched. Former name (1963–73): Cape **Kennedy.**

Canberra ('kænbərə, -brə) *n.* the capital of Australia, in Australian Capital Territory: founded in 1913 as a planned capital. Pop.: 285 800 (1986 est.).

cancan ('kæn,kæn) *n.* a high-kicking dance performed by a female chorus, originating in the music halls of 19th-century Paris. [C19: from F, from ?]

cancel ('kænsəl) *vb.* **-celling, -celled** *or U.S.* **-celing, -celed.** (*mainly tr.*) **1.** to order (something already arranged, such as a meeting or event) to be postponed indefinitely; call off. **2.** to revoke or annul: *the order was cancelled.* **3.** to delete (writing, numbers, etc.); cross out.

4. to mark (a cheque, stamp, etc.) with an official stamp to prevent further use. **5.** (*also intr.*; usually foll. by *out*) to counterbalance: *his generosity cancelled out his past unkindness.* **6.** *Maths.* to eliminate (numbers or terms) as common factors from both the numerator and denominator of a fraction or as equal terms from opposite sides of an equation. ~*n.* **7.** a new leaf or section of a book replacing one containing errors, or one that has been omitted. **8.** a cancellation. **9.** *Music.* a U.S. word for **natural** (sense 15). [C14: from OF *canceller*, from Med. L, from LL: to make like a lattice, from L *cancellī* lattice] —'**canceller** *or U.S.* '**canceler** *n.*

cancellate ('kænsɪ,leɪt) *or* **cancellated** *adj.* **1.** *Anat.* having a spongy internal structure: *cancellate bones.* **2.** *Bot.* forming a network. [C17: from L *cancellāre* to make like a lattice]

cancellation (,kænsɪ'leɪʃən) *n.* **1.** the fact or an instance of cancelling. **2.** something that has been cancelled, such as a theatre ticket: *we have a cancellation in the balcony.* **3.** the marks made by cancelling.

cancer ('kænsə) *n.* **1.** any type of malignant growth or tumour, caused by abnormal and uncontrolled cell division. **2.** the condition resulting from this. **3.** an evil influence that spreads dangerously. [C14: from L: crab, a creeping tumour] —'**cancerous** *adj.*

Cancer ('kænsə) *n., Latin genitive* **Cancri** ('kænkriː). **1.** *Astron.* Also called: the **Crab.** a small N constellation. **2.** *Astrol.* the fourth sign of the zodiac. The sun is in this sign between about June 21 and July 22. **3. tropic of Cancer.** See **tropic** (sense 1).

cancroid ('kæŋkrɔɪd) *adj.* **1.** resembling a cancerous growth. **2.** resembling a crab. ~*n.* **3.** a skin cancer.

candela (kæn'diːlə, -'deɪlə) *n.* the basic SI unit of luminous intensity; the intensity, in a perpendicular direction, of a surface of 1/600 000 square metre of a black body at the temperature of freezing platinum under a pressure of 101 325 newtons per square metre. Symbol: cd [C20: from L: CANDLE]

Candela (kæn'diːlə) *n.* **Felix.** born 1910, Mexican architect, noted for his naturalistic modern style and thin prestressed concrete roofs.

candelabrum (,kændɪ'lɑːbrəm) *or* **candelabra** *n., pl.* **-bra** (-brə), **-brums,** *or* **-bras.** a large, branched table candleholder. [C19: from L, from *candēla* CANDLE]

candescent (kæn'dɛsənt) *adj. Rare.* glowing or starting to glow with heat. [C19: from L, from *candēre* to be white, shine] —**can'descence** *n.*

c & f *abbrev. for* cost and freight.

C & G *abbrev. for* City and Guilds.

Candia ('kandja) *n.* the Italian name for **Iráklion.**

candid ('kændɪd) *adj.* **1.** frank and outspoken. **2.** without partiality; unbiased. **3.** unposed or informal: *a candid photograph.* [C17: from L, from *candēre* to be white] —'**candidly** *adv.* —'**candidness** *n.*

candida ('kændɪdə) *n.* any of a genus of yeastlike parasitic fungi, esp. one that causes thrush (**candidiasis**).

candidate ('kændɪ,deɪt) *n.* **1.** a person seeking or nominated for election to a position of authority or selection for a job, etc. **2.** a person taking an examination or test. **3.** a person or thing regarded as suitable or likely for a particular fate or position. [C17: from L *candidātus* clothed in white (because the candidate wore a white toga), from *candidus* white] —**candidacy** ('kændɪdəsɪ) *or* **candidature** ('kændɪdətʃə) *n.*

candid camera *n.* a small camera that may be used to take informal photographs of people.

candied ('kændɪd) *adj.* impregnated or encrusted with or as if with sugar: *candied peel.*

candle ('kændəl) *n.* **1.** a cylindrical piece of wax, tallow, or other fatty substance surrounding a wick, which is burned to produce light. **2.** *Physics.* another name for **candela. 3. burn the candle at both ends.** to exhaust oneself by doing too much, esp. by being up late and getting up early to work. **4. not hold a candle to.** *Inf.* to be inferior or contemptible in comparison with. **5. not worth the candle.** *Inf.* not worth the price or trouble entailed. ~*vb.* **6.** (*tr.*) to examine (eggs) for freshness or the likelihood of being hatched by viewing them against a bright light. [OE *candel*, from L *candēla*, from *candēre* to glitter] —'**candler** *n.*

candleberry ('kændəl,bɛrɪ) *n., pl.* **-ries.** another name for **wax myrtle.**

candlelight ('kænd^əl,laɪt) n. **1. a.** the light from a candle or candles. **b.** (as modifier): a candlelight dinner. **2.** dusk; evening.

Candlemas ('kænd^əlməs) n. Christianity. Feb. 2, the Feast of the Purification of the Virgin Mary and the presentation of Christ in the Temple.

candlenut ('kænd^əl,nʌt) n. **1.** a tree of tropical Asia and Polynesia. **2.** the nut of this tree, which yields an oil used in paints. In their native regions the nuts are burned as candles.

candlepower ('kænd^əl,paʊə) n. the luminous intensity of a source of light in a given direction: now expressed in candelas.

candlestick ('kænd^əl,stɪk) or **candleholder** ('kænd^əl-,həʊldə) n. a holder, usually ornamental, with a spike or socket for a candle.

candlewick ('kænd^əl,wɪk) n. **1.** unbleached cotton or muslin into which loops of yarn are hooked and then cut to give a tufted pattern. **2.** (modifier) being or made of candlewick fabric.

candour or U.S. **candor** ('kændə) n. **1.** the quality of being open and honest; frankness. **2.** fairness; impartiality. [C17: from L candor, from candēre to be white]

C & W abbrev. for country and western.

candy ('kændɪ) n., pl. **-dies. 1.** Chiefly U.S. & Canad. sweets, chocolate, etc. ~vb. **-dying, -died. 2.** to cause (sugar, etc.) to become crystalline or (of sugar) to become crystalline. **3.** (tr.) to preserve (fruit peel, ginger, etc.) by boiling in sugar. **4.** (tr.) to cover with any crystalline substance, such as ice or sugar. [C18: from OF sucre candi candied sugar, from Ar. qandi candied, from qand cane sugar]

candyfloss ('kændɪ,flɒs) n. Brit. a very light fluffy confection made from coloured spun sugar, usually held on a stick. U.S. and Canad. name: **cotton candy.**

candy-striped adj. (esp. of clothing fabric) having narrow coloured stripes on a white background. —**candy stripe** n.

candytuft ('kændɪ,tʌft) n. either of two species of Iberis having clusters of white, red, or purplish flowers. [C17 Candy, obs. var. of CANDIA (Crete) + TUFT]

cane (keɪn) n. **1. a.** the long jointed pithy or hollow flexible stem of the bamboo, rattan, or any similar plant. **b.** any plant having such a stem. **2. a.** strips of such stems, woven or interlaced to make wickerwork, etc. **b.** (as modifier): a cane chair. **3.** the woody stem of a reed, blackberry, or loganberry. **4.** a flexible rod with which to administer a beating. **5.** a slender rod used as a walking stick. **6.** see **sugar cane.** ~vb. (tr.) **7.** to whip or beat with or as if with a cane. **8.** to make or repair with cane. **9.** Inf. to defeat: we got well caned in the match. [C14: from OF, from L canna, from Gk kanna, of Semitic origin] —**'caner** n.

Canea (kæ'nɪə) n. the capital and chief port of Crete, on the NW coast. Pop.: 47 451 (1981). Greek name: **Khaniá.**

canebrake ('keɪn,breɪk) n. U.S. a thicket of canes.

cane sugar n. **1.** the sucrose obtained from sugar cane. **2.** another name for **sucrose.**

cangue or **cang** ('kæŋ) n. (formerly in China) a large wooden collar worn by petty criminals as a punishment. [C18: from F, from Port. canga yoke]

canikin ('kænɪkɪn) n. a variant spelling of **cannikin.**

canine ('keɪnaɪn, 'kæn-) adj. **1.** of or resembling a dog. **2.** of or belonging to the Canidae, a family of mammals, including dogs, wolves, and foxes, typically having a bushy tail, erect ears, and a long muzzle. **3.** of or relating to any of the four teeth, two in each jaw, situated between the incisors and the premolars. ~n. **4.** any animal of the family Canidae. **5.** a canine tooth. [C17: from L canīnus, from canis dog]

caning ('keɪnɪŋ) n. Inf. a severe defeat or punishment.

Canis Major ('keɪnɪs) n., Latin genitive **Canis Majoris** (mə'dʒɔːrɪs). a S constellation containing Sirius, the brightest star in the sky. Also called: the **Great Dog.** [L: the greater dog]

Canis Minor n., Latin genitive **Canis Minoris** (maɪ'nɔːrɪs). a small N constellation. Also called: the **Little Dog.** [L: the lesser dog]

canister ('kænɪstə) n. **1.** a container, usually made of metal, in which dry food, such as tea or coffee, is stored. **2.** (formerly) **a.** a type of shrapnel shell for firing from a

cannon. **b.** Also called: **canister shot.** the shot or shrapnel packed inside this. [C17: from L canistrum basket woven from reeds, from Gk, from kanna reed]

canker ('kæŋkə) n. **1.** an ulceration, esp. of the lips. **2.** Vet. science. **a.** a disease of horses in which the horn of the hoofs becomes spongy. **b.** an ulcerative disease of the lining of the external ear, esp. in dogs and cats. **3.** an open wound in the stem of a tree or shrub. **4.** something evil that spreads and corrupts. ~vb. **5.** to infect or become infected with or as if with canker. [OE cancer, from L cancer cancerous sore] —**'cankerous** adj.

cankerworm ('kæŋkə,wɜːm) n. the larva of either of two moths, which feed on and destroy fruit and shade trees in North America.

canna ('kænə) n. any of a genus of tropical plants having broad leaves and red or yellow showy flowers. [C17: from NL CANE]

cannabis ('kænəbɪs) n. **1.** another name for **hemp** (the plant), esp. Indian hemp. **2.** the drug obtained from the dried leaves and flowers of the hemp plant, which is smoked or chewed for its psychoactive properties. See also **hashish, marijuana. 3. cannabis resin.** a poisonous resin obtained from the hemp plant. [C18: from L, from Gk kannabis]

Cannae ('kæniː) n. an ancient city in SE Italy: scene of a victory by Hannibal over the Romans (216 B.C.).

canned (kænd) adj. **1.** preserved and stored in airtight cans or tins. **2.** Inf. prepared or recorded in advance: canned music. **3.** Sl. drunk.

cannel coal or **cannel** ('kæn^əl) n. a dull coal burning with a smoky luminous flame. [C16: from N English dialect cannel candle]

cannelloni or **cannelloni** (,kænɪ'ləʊnɪ) pl. n. tubular pieces of pasta filled with meat or cheese. [It., pl. of cannellone, from cannello stalk]

cannery ('kænərɪ) n., pl. **-neries.** a place where foods are canned.

Cannes (kæn, kænz; French kan) n. a port and resort in SE France: developed in the 19th century from a fishing village; annual film festival. Pop.: 70 302 (1983 est.).

cannibal ('kænɪb^əl) n. **1.** a person who eats the flesh of other human beings. **2.** an animal that feeds on the flesh of others of its kind. [C16: from Sp. Canibales, the name used by Columbus to designate the Caribs of Cuba and Haiti] —**'canniba,lism** n.

cannibalize or **-lise** ('kænɪbə,laɪz) vb. (tr.) to use (serviceable parts from one machine or vehicle) to repair another. —,**cannibali'zation** or **-li'sation** n.

cannikin, canakin, or **canikin** ('kænɪkɪn) n. a small can, esp. one used as a drinking vessel. [C16: from MDu. kanneken; see CAN[2], -KIN]

canning ('kænɪŋ) n. the process or business of sealing food in cans or tins to preserve it.

Canning ('kænɪŋ) n. **1. Charles John,** 1st Earl Canning. 1812–62, British statesman; governor general of India (1856–58) and first viceroy (1858–62). **2.** his father, **George.** 1770–1827, British Tory statesman; foreign secretary (1822–27) and prime minister (1827).

Canning Basin n. an arid basin in NW Western Australia, largely unexplored. Area: about 400 000 sq. km (150 000 sq. miles).

Cannock ('kænək) n. a town in W central England, in S Staffordshire: **Cannock Chase** (a public area of heathland, once a royal preserve) is just to the E. Pop.: 59 235 (1981).

cannon ('kænən) n., pl. **-nons** or **-non. 1.** an automatic aircraft gun. **2.** History. a heavy artillery piece consisting of a metal tube mounted on a carriage. **3.** a heavy tube or drum, esp. one that can rotate freely. **4.** See **cannon bone. 5.** Billiards. a shot in which the cue ball is caused to contact one object ball after another. Usual U.S. and Canad. word: **carom.** ~vb. **6.** (intr.) to rebound; collide (with into). **7.** (intr.) Billiards. to make a cannon. [C16: from OF canon, from It. cannone cannon, from canna tube]

cannonade (,kænə'neɪd) n. **1.** an intense and continuous artillery bombardment. ~vb. **2.** to attack (a target) with cannon.

cannonball ('kænən,bɔːl) n. **1.** a projectile fired from a cannon: usually a solid round metal shot. ~vb. (intr.) **2.** (often foll. by along, etc.) to rush along. ~adj. **3.** very fast or powerful.

cannon bone *n.* a bone in the legs of horses and other hoofed animals consisting of greatly elongated fused metatarsals or metacarpals.

cannoneer (ˌkænəˈnɪə) *n.* (formerly) a soldier who served and fired a cannon; artilleryman.

cannon fodder *n.* men regarded as expendable in war because they are part of a huge army.

cannonry (ˈkænənrɪ) *n., pl.* **-ries.** *Rare* **1.** a volley of artillery fire. **2.** artillery in general.

cannot (ˈkænɒt, kæˈnɒt) an auxiliary verb expressing incapacity, inability, withholding permission, etc.; can not.

cannula *or* **canula** (ˈkænjulə) *n., pl.* **-las** *or* **-lae** (-ˌliː). *Surgery.* a narrow tube for draining fluid from or introducing medication into the body. [C17: from L: a small reed, from *canna* a reed]

canny (ˈkænɪ) *adj.* **-nier, -niest. 1.** shrewd, esp. in business. **2.** *Scot. & NE English dialect.* good or nice: used as a general term of approval. **3.** *Scot.* lucky or fortunate. [C16: from CAN¹ (in the sense: to know how) + -Y¹] —**'cannily** *adv.* —**'canniness** *n.*

canoe (kəˈnuː) *n.* **1.** a light narrow open boat, propelled by one or more paddles. ~*vb.* **-noeing, -noed. 2.** to go in or transport by canoe. [C16: from Sp. *canoa*, of Carib origin] —**ca'noeist** *n.*

canon¹ (ˈkænən) *n.* **1.** *Christianity.* a Church decree enacted to regulate morals or religious practices. **2.** (*often pl.*) a general rule or standard, as of judgment, morals, etc. **3.** (*often pl.*) a principle or criterion applied in a branch of learning or art. **4.** *R.C. Church.* the list of the canonized saints. **5.** *R.C. Church.* Also called: **Eucharistic Prayer.** the prayer in the Mass in which the Host is consecrated. **6.** a list of writings, esp. sacred writings, recognized as genuine. **7.** a piece of music in which an extended melody in one part is imitated successively in one or more other parts. **8.** a list of the works of an author that are accepted as authentic. [OE, from L, from Gk *kanōn* rule, rod for measuring]

canon² (ˈkænən) *n.* **1.** a priest who is a member of a cathedral chapter. **2.** *R.C. Church.* Also called: **canon regular.** a member of either of two religious orders living communally as monks but performing clerical duties.. [C13: from Anglo-F, from LL *canonicus* one living under a rule, from CANON¹]

canonical (kəˈnɒnɪkəl) *or* **canonic** *adj.* **1.** included in a canon of sacred or other officially recognized writings. **2.** in conformity with canon law. **3.** accepted; authoritative. **4.** *Music.* in the form of a canon. **5.** of or relating to a cathedral chapter. **6.** of a canon (clergyman). —**ca'noni-cally** *adv.*

canonical hour *n.* **1.** *R.C. Church.* one of the seven prayer times appointed for each day by canon law. **2.** *Church of England.* any time at which marriages may lawfully be celebrated.

canonicals (kəˈnɒnɪkəlz) *pl. n.* the vestments worn by clergy when officiating.

canonicity (ˌkænəˈnɪsɪtɪ) *n.* the fact or quality of being canonical.

canonist (ˈkænənɪst) *n.* a specialist in canon law.

canonize *or* **-ise** (ˈkænəˌnaɪz) *vb.* (*tr.*) **1.** *R.C. Church.* to declare (a person) to be a saint. **2.** to regard as a saint. **3.** to sanction by canon law. —ˌcanoni'zation *or* -i'sation *n.*

canon law *n.* the codified body of laws enacted by the supreme authorities of a Christian Church.

canonry (ˈkænənrɪ) *n., pl.* **-ries. 1.** the office, benefice, or status of a canon. **2.** canons collectively. [C15: from CANON² + -RY]

canoodle (kəˈnuːdəl) *vb.* (*intr.; often foll. by with*) *Sl.* to kiss and cuddle. [C19: from ?]

Canopic jar, urn, *or* **vase** (kəˈnəʊpɪk) *n.* (in ancient Egypt) one of four containers for holding the entrails of a mummy.

Canopus (kəˈnəʊpəs) *n.* a port in ancient Egypt east of Alexandria where granite monuments have been found inscribed with the name of Rameses II and written in languages similar to those of the Rosetta stone. —**Ca'nopic** *adj.*

canopy (ˈkænəpɪ) *n., pl.* **-pies. 1.** an ornamental awning above a throne, bed, person, etc. **2.** a rooflike covering over an altar, niche, etc. **3.** a roofed structure serving as a sheltered passageway. **4.** a large or wide covering: *the sky was a grey canopy.* **5.** the hemisphere that forms the supporting surface of a parachute. **6.** the transparent

cover of an aircraft cockpit. **7.** the highest level of foliage in a forest, formed by the crowns of the trees. ~*vb.* **-py-ing, -pied. 8.** (*tr.*) to cover with or as with a canopy. [C14: from Med. L *canōpeum* mosquito net, from L, from Gk *kōnōpeion* bed with protective net]

Canossa (kəˈnɒsə; *Italian* kaˈnɔssa) *n.* a ruined castle in N Italy, in Emilia near Reggio nell'Emilia: scene of the penance done by the Holy Roman Emperor Henry IV before Pope Gregory VII.

Canova (*Italian* kaˈnɔːva) *n.* **Antonio** (anˈtɔːnjo). 1757–1822, Italian neoclassical sculptor.

Canso (ˈkænsəʊ) *n.* **1. Cape.** a cape in Canada, at the NE tip of Nova Scotia. **2. Strait of.** Also called: **Gut of Canso.** a channel in Canada, between the Nova Scotia mainland and S Cape Breton Island.

canst (kænst) *vb. Arch.* the form of **can**¹ used with the pronoun *thou* or its relative form.

cant¹ (kænt) *n.* **1.** insincere talk, esp. concerning religion or morals. **2.** phrases that have become meaningless through repetition. **3.** specialized vocabulary of a particular group, such as thieves, journalists, or lawyers. ~*vb.* **4.** (*intr.*) to speak in or use cant. [C16: prob. via Norman F *canter* to sing, from L *cantāre;* used disparagingly, from the 12th cent., of chanting in religious services] —**'cant-ingly** *adv.*

cant² (kænt) *n.* **1.** inclination from a vertical or horizontal plane. **2.** a sudden movement that tilts or turns something. **3.** the angle or tilt thus caused. **4.** a corner or outer angle. **5.** an oblique or slanting surface, edge, or line. ~*vb.* (*tr.*) **6.** to tip, tilt, or overturn. **7.** to set in an oblique position. **8.** another word for **bevel** (sense 1). ~*adj.* **9.** oblique; slanting. **10.** having flat surfaces. [C14 (in the sense: edge): ?from L *canthus* iron hoop round a wheel, from ?]

can't (kɑːnt) *contraction of* cannot.

Cantab. (ˈkæntæb) *abbrev. for* Cantabrigiensis. [L: of Cambridge]

cantabile (kænˈtɑːbɪlɪ) *Music.* ~*adj., adv.* **1.** (to be performed) flowingly and melodiously. ~*n.* **2.** a piece or passage performed in this way. [It., from LL, from L *cantāre* to sing]

Cantabrian Mountains *pl. n.* a mountain chain along the N coast of Spain, consisting of a series of high ridges that rise over 2400 m (8000 ft.): rich in minerals (esp. coal and iron).

Cantabrigian (ˌkæntəˈbrɪdʒɪən) *adj.* **1.** of or characteristic of Cambridge or Cambridge University. ~*n.* **2.** a member or graduate of Cambridge University. **3.** an inhabitant or native of Cambridge. [C17: from Med. L *Cantabrigia*]

Cantal (*French* kɑtal) *n.* **1.** a department of S central France, in the Auvergne region. Capital: Aurillac. Pop.: 162 838 (1982). Area: 5779 sq. km (2254 sq. miles). **2.** a hard strong cheese made in this area.

cantaloupe *or* **cantaloup** (ˈkæntəˌluːp) *n.* **1.** a cultivated variety of muskmelon with ribbed warty rind and orange flesh. **2.** any of several other muskmelons. [C18: from F, from *Cantaluppi*, near Rome, where first cultivated in Europe]

cantankerous (kænˈtæŋkərəs) *adj.* quarrelsome; irascible. [C18: ?from C14 (obs.) *conteckour* a contentious person, from Anglo-F *contek* strife, from ?] —**can'tanker-ously** *adv.* —**can'tankerousness** *n.*

cantata (kænˈtɑːtə) *n.* a musical setting of a text, esp. a religious text, consisting of arias, duets, and choruses. [C18: from It., from *cantare* to sing, from L]

canteen (kænˈtiːn) *n.* **1.** a restaurant attached to a factory, school, etc., providing meals for large numbers. **2. a.** a small shop that provides a limited range of items to a military unit. **b.** a recreation centre for military personnel. **3.** a temporary or mobile stand at which food is provided. **4. a.** a box in which a set of cutlery is laid out. **b.** the cutlery itself. **5.** a flask for carrying water or other liquids. [C18: from F, from It. *cantina* wine cellar, from *canto* corner, from L *canthus* iron hoop encircling chariot wheel]

Canteloube (ˈkæntəˌluːb; *French* kɑtlub) *n.* (**Marie**) **Joseph** (*French* ʒɔzɛf). 1879–1957, French composer.

canter (ˈkæntə) *n.* **1.** a gait of horses, etc., between a trot and a gallop in speed. **2. at a canter.** easily; without effort. ~*vb.* **3.** to move or cause to move at a canter. [C18: short for *Canterbury trot*, the supposed pace at which pilgrims rode to Canterbury]

Canterbury ('kæntəbərɪ, -brɪ) *n.* **1.** a city in SE England, in E Kent: starting point for St Augustine's mission to England (597 A.D.); cathedral where St Thomas à Becket was martyred (1170); seat of the archbishop and primate of England; seat of the University of Kent. Pop.: 39 000 (1984). Latin name: **Durovernum** (ˌduːrəʊ'vɜːnəm, ˌdjʊə-). **2.** a statistical area of New Zealand, on E central South Island on **Canterbury Bight**: mountainous with coastal lowlands; agricultural. Chief town: Christchurch. Pop.: 424 280 (1981). Area: 43 371 sq. km (16 742 sq. miles).

Canterbury bell *n.* a biennial European plant related to the campanula and widely cultivated for its blue, violet, or white flowers.

cantharides (kæn'θærɪˌdiːz) *pl. n., sing.* **cantharis** ('kænθərɪs). a diuretic and urogenital stimulant prepared from the dried bodies of Spanish fly. Also called: **Spanish fly**. [C15: from L, pl. of *cantharis*, from Gk *kantharis* Spanish fly]

Can Tho ('kʌn 'təʊ, 'kæn) *n.* a town in S Vietnam, on the River Mekong. Pop.: 182 856 (1979).

cant hook *or* **dog** *n. Forestry.* a wooden pole with an adjustable hook at one end, used for handling logs.

canthus ('kænθəs) *n., pl.* **-thi** (-ˌθaɪ). the inner or outer corner of the eye, formed by the natural junction of the eyelids. [C17: from NL, from L: iron tyre]

canticle ('kæntɪkˀl) *n.* a nonmetrical hymn, derived from the Bible and used in the liturgy of certain Christian churches. [C13: from L *canticulum*, dim. of *canticus* a song, from *canere* to sing]

cantilena (ˌkæntɪ'leɪnə) *n.* a smooth flowing style in the writing of vocal music. [C18: It.]

cantilever ('kæntɪˌliːvə) *n.* **1.** a beam, girder, or structural framework that is fixed at one end only. **2.** a part of a beam or a structure projecting outwards beyond its support. [C17: ?from CANT² + LEVER]

cantilever bridge *n.* a bridge having spans that are constructed as cantilevers.

cantillate ('kæntɪˌleɪt) *vb.* **1.** to chant (passages of the Hebrew Scriptures) according to the traditional Jewish melody. **2.** to intone or chant. [C19: from LL *cantillāre* to sing softly, from L *cantāre* to sing] — ˌcantil'lation *n.*

cantle ('kæntˀl) *n.* **1.** the back part of a saddle that slopes upwards. **2.** a broken-off piece. [C14: from OF *cantel*, from *cant* corner]

canto ('kæntəʊ) *n., pl.* **-tos.** a main division of a long poem. [C16: from It.: song, from L, from *canere* to sing]

canto fermo ('kæntəʊ 'fɜːməʊ) *or* **cantus firmus** ('kæntəs 'fɜːməs) *n.* **1.** a melody that is the basis to which other parts are added in polyphonic music. **2.** the traditional Church plainchant as prescribed by use and regulation. [It., from Med L: fixed song]

canton *n.* **1.** ('kæntɒn, kæn'tɒn). a political division of Switzerland. **2.** ('kæntən). *Heraldry.* a small square charge on a shield, usually in the top left corner. ~*vb.* **3.** (kæn'tɒn). (*tr.*) to divide into cantons. **4.** (kən'tuːn). (esp. formerly) to allocate accommodation to (military personnel, etc.). [C16: from OF: corner, from It., from *canto* corner, from L *canthus* iron rim] — 'cantonal *adj.*

Canton *n.* **1.** (kæn'tɒn). a port in SE China, capital of Guangdong province, on the Zhu Jiang (Pearl River): the first Chinese port open to European trade. Pop.: 3 290 000 (1986). Chinese names: **Guangzhou, Kwangchow. 2.** ('kæntən). a city in NE Ohio. Pop.: 93 077 (1980).

Cantonese (ˌkæntə'niːz) *n.* **1.** the Chinese language spoken in Canton, and elsewhere inside and outside China. **2.** (*pl.* **-ese**) a native or inhabitant of Canton. ~*adj.* **3.** of or relating to Canton or the Chinese language spoken there.

cantonment (kən'tuːnmənt) *n. Mil.* (esp. formerly) **1.** a large training camp. **2.** the winter quarters of a campaigning army. **3.** *History.* a permanent military camp in British India.

Canton River (kæn'tɒn) *n.* another name for the **Zhu Jiang**.

cantor ('kæntɔː) *n.* **1.** *Judaism.* a man employed to lead synagogue services. **2.** *Christianity.* the leader of the singing in a church choir. [C16: from L: singer, from *canere* to sing]

cantorial (kæn'tɔːrɪəl) *adj.* **1.** of a precentor. **2.** (of part of a choir) on the same side of a cathedral, etc., as the precentor.

cantoris (kæn'tɔːrɪs) *adj.* (in antiphonal music) to be sung by the cantorial side of a choir. Cf. **decani.** [L: genitive of *cantor* precentor]

Canuck (kə'nʌk) *n., adj. U.S. & Canad. inf.* Canadian. [C19: from ?]

Canute, Cnut, *or* **Knut** (kə'njuːt) *n.* died 1035, Danish king of England (1016–35), Denmark (1018–35), and Norway (1028–35). He defeated Edmund II of England (1016), but divided the kingdom with him until Edmund's death. An able ruler, he invaded Scotland (1027) and drove Olaf II from Norway (1028).

canvas ('kænvəs) *n.* **1. a.** a heavy cloth made of cotton, hemp, or jute, used for sails, tents, etc. **b.** (*as modifier*): *a canvas bag.* **2. a.** a piece of canvas, etc., on which a painting is done, usually in oils. **b.** an oil painting. **3.** a tent or tents collectively. **4.** *Naut.* the sails of a vessel collectively. **5.** any coarse loosely woven cloth on which tapestry, etc., is done. **6.** (preceded by *the*) the floor of a boxing or wrestling ring. **7.** *Rowing.* the covered part at either end of a racing boat: *to win by a canvas.* **8. under canvas. a.** in tents. **b.** *Naut.* with sails unfurled. [C14: from Norman F *canevas*, ult. from L *cannabis* hemp]

canvasback ('kænvəsˌbæk) *n., pl.* **-backs** *or* **-back.** a North American diving duck, the male of which has a reddish-brown head.

canvass ('kænvəs) *vb.* **1.** to solicit votes, orders, etc., (from). **2.** to determine the opinions of (voters before an election, etc.), esp. by conducting a survey. **3.** to investigate (something) thoroughly, esp. by discussion. **4.** *Chiefly U.S.* to inspect (votes) to determine their validity. ~*n.* **5.** a solicitation of opinions, votes, etc. [C16: prob. from obs. sense of CANVAS (to toss someone in a canvas sheet, hence, to criticize)] — 'canvasser *n.*

canyon *or* **cañon** ('kænjən) *n.* a gorge or ravine, esp. in North America, usually formed by a river. [C19: from Sp., from *caña* tube, from L *canna* cane]

canzonetta (ˌkænzə'nɛtə) *or* **canzonet** (ˌkænzə'nɛt) *n.* a short, lively song, typically of the 16th to 18th centuries. [C16: It.: dim. of *canzone*, from L *canere* to sing]

caoutchouc ('kaʊtʃʊk) *n.* another name for **rubber¹** (sense 1). [C18: from F, from obs. Sp., from Quechua]

cap (kæp) *n.* **1.** a covering for the head, esp. a small close-fitting one. **2.** such a covering serving to identify the wearer's rank, occupation, etc.: *a nurse's cap.* **3.** something that protects or covers: *lens cap.* **4.** an uppermost surface or part: *the cap of a wave.* **5. a.** See **percussion cap. b.** a small amount of explosive enclosed in paper and used in a toy gun. **6.** *Sport, chiefly Brit.* **a.** an emblematic hat or beret given to someone chosen for a representative team. **b.** a player chosen for such a team. **7.** any part like a cap in shape. **8.** *Bot.* the pileus of a mushroom or toadstool. **9.** *Hunting.* money contributed to the funds of a hunt by a follower who is neither a subscriber nor a farmer, in return for a day's hunting. **10.** *Anat.* **a.** the natural enamel covering of a tooth. **b.** an artificial protective covering for a tooth. **11.** Also: **Dutch cap, diaphragm.** a contraceptive membrane placed over the mouth of the cervix. **12.** a mortarboard worn at an academic ceremony (esp. in **cap and gown**). **13. set one's cap at.** (of a woman) to be determined to win as a husband or lover. **14. cap in hand.** humbly, as when asking a favour. ~*vb.* **capping, capped.** (*tr.*) **15.** to cover, as with a cap: *snow capped the mountain tops.* **16.** to seal off (an oil or gas well). **17.** to impose an upper level on the rate of increase of (a tax): *rate-capping.* **18.** *Inf.* to outdo; excel. **19. cap it all.** to provide the finishing touch. **20.** *Sport, Brit.* to select (a player) for a representative team. **21.** *Chiefly Scot. & N.Z.* to award a degree to. [OE *cæppe*, from LL *cappa* hood, ?from L *caput* head]

cap. *abbrev. for:* **1.** capacity. **2.** capital. **3.** capitalize. **4.** capital letter.

capability (ˌkeɪpə'bɪlɪtɪ) *n., pl.* **-ties. 1.** the quality of being capable; ability. **2.** the quality of being susceptible to the use or treatment indicated: *the capability of a metal to be fused.* **3.** (*usually pl.*) potential aptitude.

Capablanca (*Spanish* kapa'βlaŋka) *n.* José Raúl (xo'se ra'ul), called *Capa* or *Chess Machine.* 1888–1942, Cuban chess player; world champion 1921–27.

capable ('keɪpəbˀl) *adj.* **1.** having ability; competent. **2.** (*postpositive*; foll. by *of*) able or having the ability (to do something): *she is capable of hard work.* **3.** (*postpositive*; foll. by *of*) having the temperament or inclination (to do something): *he seemed capable of murder.* [C16: from

F, from LL *capābilis* able to take in, from L *capere* to take] —'**capableness** *n.* —'**capably** *adv.*

capacious (kə'peɪʃəs) *adj.* capable of holding much; roomy. [C17: from L, from *capere* to take] —**ca'paciously** *adv.* —**ca'paciousness** *n.*

capacitance (kə'pæsɪtəns) *n.* 1. the property of a system that enables it to store electric charge. 2. a measure of this, equal to the charge that must be added to such a system to raise its electrical potential by one unit. Former name: **capacity**. [C20: from CAPACIT(Y) + -ANCE] —**ca'pacitive** *adj.*

capacitor (kə'pæsɪtə) *n.* a device for accumulating electric charge, usually consisting of two conducting surfaces separated by a dielectric. Former name: **condenser**.

capacity (kə'pæsɪtɪ) *n., pl.* -**ties.** 1. the ability or power to contain, absorb, or hold. 2. the amount that can be contained: *a capacity of six gallons.* 3. a. the maximum amount something can contain or absorb (esp. in **filled to capacity**). b. (*as modifier*): *a capacity crowd.* 4. the ability to understand or learn: *he has a great capacity for Greek.* 5. the ability to do or produce: *the factory's output was not at capacity.* 6. a specified position or function. 7. a measure of the electrical output of a piece of apparatus such as a generator or accumulator. 8. *Electronics.* a former name for **capacitance**. 9. *Computers.* a. the number of words or characters that can be stored in a storage device. b. the range of numbers that can be processed in a register. 10. legal competence: *the capacity to make a will.* [C15: from OF *capacite*, from L, from *capāx* spacious, from *capere* to take]

cap and bells *n.* the traditional garb of a court jester, including a cap with bells.

cap-a-pie (ˌkæpə'piː) *adv.* (dressed, armed, etc.) from head to foot. [C16: from OF]

caparison (kə'pærɪsᵊn) *n.* 1. a decorated covering for a horse. 2. rich or elaborate clothing and ornaments. ~*vb.* 3. (*tr.*) to put a caparison on. [C16: via obs. F from OSp. *caparazón* saddle-cloth, prob. from *capa* CAPE¹]

cape¹ (keɪp) *n.* a sleeveless garment like a cloak but usually shorter. [C16: from F, from Provençal *capa*, from LL *cappa*; see CAP]

cape² (keɪp) *n.* a headland or promontory. [C14: from OF *cap*, from OProvençal, from L *caput* head]

Cape (keɪp) *n.* **the.** 1. the SW region of the Cape Province of South Africa. 2. See **Cape of Good Hope.**

Cape Breton Island *n.* an island off SE Canada, in NE Nova Scotia, separated from the mainland by the Strait of Canso: its easternmost point is **Cape Breton.** Pop.: 170 088 (1981). Area: 10 280 sq. km (3970 sq. miles).

Cape Cod *n.* a long sandy peninsula in SE Massachusetts, between **Cape Cod Bay** and the Atlantic.

Cape Colony *n.* the former name (until 1910) of the **Cape Province** of South Africa.

Cape Coloured *n.* (in South Africa) another name for a **Coloured** (sense 2).

Cape doctor *n. S. African inf.* a strong fresh SE wind blowing in the vicinity of Cape Town, esp. in the summer.

Cape Dutch *n.* 1. (in South Africa) a distinctive style of furniture or buildings. 2. an obsolete name for **Afrikaans.**

Cape Flats *pl. n.* the strip of low-lying land in South Africa joining the Cape Peninsula proper to the African mainland.

Cape gooseberry *n.* another name for **strawberry tomato.**

Cape Horn *n.* a rocky headland on an island at the extreme S tip of South America, belonging to Chile. It is notorious for gales and heavy seas; until the building of the Panama Canal it lay on the only sea route between the Atlantic and the Pacific. Also called: **the Horn.**

capelin ('kæpəlɪn) *or* **caplin** ('kæplɪn) *n.* a small marine food fish of northern and Arctic seas. [C17: from F *capelan*, from OProvençal, lit.: chaplain]

capellmeister *or* **kapellmeister** (kæ'pɛl,maɪstə) *n.* a person in charge of an orchestra, esp. in an 18th-century princely household. [from G, from *Kapelle* chapel + *Meister* MASTER]

Cape of Good Hope *n.* a cape in SW South Africa south of Cape Town.

Cape Peninsula *n.* (in South Africa) the peninsula and the part of the mainland on which Cape Town and most of its suburbs are located.

Cape pigeon *n.* a kind of petrel common in S Africa.

Cape Province *n.* a province occupying the southern tip of South Africa: mainly a high plateau, rising over 2700 m (9000 ft.). Capital: Cape Town. Pop.: 4 901 261. (1986). Area: 646 332 sq. km (243 424 sq. miles). Official name: **Cape of Good Hope Province.** Former name (until 1910): **Cape Colony.**

caper¹ ('keɪpə) *n.* 1. a playful skip or leap. 2. a high-spirited escapade. 3. **cut a caper** *or* **capers.** to skip, leap, or frolic. 4. *U.S & Canad. sl.* a crime. ~*vb.* 5. (*intr.*) to leap or dance about in a light-hearted manner. [C16: prob. from CAPRIOLE]

caper² ('keɪpə) *n.* 1. a spiny trailing Mediterranean shrub with edible flower buds. 2. its pickled flower buds, used in sauces. [C15: from earlier *capers, capres* (assumed to be pl.), from L, from Gk *kapparis*]

capercaillie *or* **capercailzie** (ˌkæpə'keɪljɪ) *n.* a large European woodland grouse having a black plumage. [C16: from Scot. Gaelic *capull coille* horse of the woods]

Capernaum (kə'pɜːnɪəm) *n.* a ruined town in N Israel, on the NW shore of the Sea of Galilee: closely associated with Jesus Christ during his ministry.

Cape sparrow *n.* a sparrow very common in southern Africa. Also called (esp. S. African): **mossie.**

Capet ('kæpɪt, kæ'pɛt; *French* kapɛ) *n.* **Hugh** *or* **Hugues** (yg). ?938–996 A.D., king of France (987–96); founder of the Capetian dynasty. —**Capetian** (kə'piːʃən) *adj., n.*

Cape Town *n.* the legislative capital of South Africa and capital of Cape Province, situated in the southwest on Table Bay: founded in 1652, the first White settlement in southern Africa; important port. Pop.: 1 911 521 (1985).

Cape Verde (vɜːd) *n.* a republic in the Atlantic off the coast of West Africa, consisting of a group of ten islands and five islets: an overseas territory of Portugal until 1975, when the islands became independent. Official language: Portuguese. Religions: Roman Catholic and animist. Currency: Cape Verdean escudo. Capital: Praia. Pop.: 331 000 (1988 est.). Area: 4033 sq. km (1557 sq. miles). —**Cape Verdean** ('vɜːdɪən) *adj., n.*

Cape York *n.* the northernmost point of the Australian mainland, in N Queensland on the Torres Strait at the tip of **Cape York Peninsula** (a peninsula between the Coral Sea and the Gulf of Carpentaria).

Cap-Haitien (*French* kapaisjɛ̃, -tjɛ̃) *n.* a port in N Haiti: capital during the French colonial period. Pop.: 72 161 (1987). Also called: **le Cap** (lə kap).

capias ('keɪpɪˌæs, 'kæp-) *n. Law.* a writ directing a sheriff or other officer to arrest a named person. [C15: from L, lit.: you must take, from *capere*]

capillarity (ˌkæpɪ'lærɪtɪ) *n.* a phenomenon caused by surface tension and resulting in the elevation or depression of the surface of a liquid in contact with a solid. Also called: **capillary action.**

capillary (kə'pɪlərɪ) *adj.* 1. resembling a hair; slender. 2. (of tubes) having a fine bore. 3. *Anat.* of the delicate thin-walled blood vessels that interconnect between the arterioles and the venules. 4. *Physics.* of or relating to capillarity. ~*n., pl.* -**laries.** 5. *Anat.* any of the capillary blood vessels. [C17: from L *capillāris*, from *capillus* hair]

capital¹ ('kæpɪtᵊl) *n.* 1. a. the seat of government of a country. b. (*as modifier*): *a capital city.* 2. material wealth owned by an individual or business enterprise. 3. wealth available for or capable of use in the production of further wealth, as by industrial investment. 4. **make capital (out) of.** to get advantage from. 5. (*sometimes cap.*) the capitalist class or their interests: *capital versus labour.* 6. *Accounting.* a. the ownership interests of a business as represented by the excess of assets over liabilities. b. the nominal value of the issued shares. 7. any assets or resources. 8. a. a capital letter. Abbrev.: **cap.** b. (*as modifier*): *capital B.* ~*adj.* 9. (*prenominal*) *Law.* involving or punishable by death: *a capital offence.* 10. very serious: *a capital error.* 11. primary, chief, or principal: *our capital concern.* 12. of, relating to, or designating the large letter used chiefly as the initial letter in personal names and place names and often for abbreviations and acronyms. See also **upper case.** 13. *Chiefly Brit.* excellent; first-rate: *a capital idea.* [C13: from L *capitālis* (adj.) concerning the head, from *caput* head]

capital² ('kæpɪtᵊl) *n.* the upper part of a column or pier that supports the entablature. [C14: from OF, from LL *capitellum*, dim. of *caput* head]

capital account n. **1.** Econ. that part of a balance of payments composed of movements of capital. **2.** Accounting. a financial statement showing the net value of a company at a specified date.

capital expenditure n. expenditure to increase fixed assets.

capital gain n. the amount by which the selling price of a financial asset exceeds its cost.

capital gains tax n. a tax on the profit made from sale of an asset.

capital goods pl. n. Econ. goods that are themselves utilized in the production of other goods.

capitalism ('kæpɪtə,lɪzəm) n. an economic system based on the private ownership of the means of production, distribution, and exchange. Also called: **free enterprise, private enterprise.** Cf. **socialism** (sense 1).

capitalist ('kæpɪtəlɪst) n. **1.** a person who owns capital, esp. capital invested in a business. **2.** Politics. a supporter of capitalism. ~adj. **3.** relating to capital, capitalists, or capitalism. —,**capital'istic** adj.

capitalization or **-isation** (,kæpɪtəlaɪ'zeɪʃən) n. **1. a.** the act of capitalizing. **b.** the sum so derived. **2.** Accounting. the par value of the total share capital issued by a company. **3.** the act of estimating the present value of future payments, etc.

capitalize or **-ise** ('kæpɪtə,laɪz) vb. (mainly tr.) **1.** (intr.; foll. by on) to take advantage (of). **2.** to write or print (text) in capital letters. **3.** to convert (debt or earnings) into capital stock. **4.** to authorize (a business enterprise) to issue a specified amount of capital stock. **5.** to provide with capital. **6.** Accounting. to treat (expenditures) as assets. **7. a.** to estimate the present value of (a periodical income). **b.** to compute the present value of (a business) from actual or potential earnings.

capital levy n. a tax on capital or property as contrasted with a tax on income.

capitally ('kæpɪtəlɪ) adv. Chiefly Brit. in an excellent manner; admirably.

capital punishment n. the punishment of death for a crime; death penalty.

capital ship n. one of the largest and most heavily armed ships in a naval fleet.

capital stock n. **1.** the par value of the total share capital that a company is authorized to issue. **2.** the total physical capital existing in an economy at any moment of time.

capital transfer tax n. (in Britain) a tax payable on the cumulative total of gifts of money or property made during the donor's lifetime or after his death.

capitation (,kæpɪ'teɪʃən) n. **1.** a tax levied on the basis of a fixed amount per head. **2. capitation grant.** a grant of money given to every person who qualifies under certain conditions. [C17: from LL, from L caput head]

Capitol ('kæpɪtəl) n. **1. a.** another name for the **Capitoline. b.** the temple on the Capitoline. **2. the.** the main building of the U.S. Congress. [C14: from Latin Capitōlium, from caput head]

Capitoline ('kæpɪtə,laɪn, kə'pɪtəʊ-) n. **1. the.** the most important of the Seven Hills of Rome. The temple of Jupiter was on the southern summit and the ancient citadel on the northern summit. ~adj. **2.** of or relating to the Capitoline or the temple of Jupiter.

capitulate (kə'pɪtjʊ,leɪt) vb. (intr.) to surrender, esp. under agreed conditions. [C16 (meaning: to draw up in order): from Med. L capitulare to draw up under heads, from capitulum CHAPTER] —**ca'pitu,lator** n.

capitulation (kə,pɪtjʊ'leɪʃən) n. **1.** the act of capitulating. **2.** a document containing terms of surrender. **3.** a statement summarizing the main divisions of a subject. —**ca'pitulatory** adj.

capitulum (kə'pɪtjʊləm) n., pl. **-la** (-lə). an inflorescence in the form of a disc, the youngest at the centre. It occurs in the daisy and related plants. [C18: from L, lit.: a little head, from caput head]

capo ('kæpəʊ) n., pl. **-pos.** a device fitted across all the strings of a guitar, lute, etc., so as to raise the pitch of each string simultaneously. Also called: **capo tasto** ('tæstəʊ). [from It. capo tasto head stop]

capon ('keɪpən) n. a castrated cock fowl fattened for eating. [OE capun, from L cāpō capon] —'**capon,ize** or -,**ise** vb.

Capone (kə'pəʊn) n. **Alphonse,** called Al. 1899–1947, U.S. gangster in Chicago during Prohibition.

Caporetto (kapo'retto) n. the Italian name for **Kobarid.**

capote (kə'pəʊt) n. a long cloak or soldier's coat, usually with a hood. [C19: from F: cloak, from cape]

Capote (kə'pəʊtɪ) n. **Truman.** 1924–84, U.S. writer; his novels include Other Voices, Other Rooms (1948) and In Cold Blood (1964), based on an actual multiple murder.

Cappadocia (,kæpə'dəʊsɪə) n. an ancient region of E Asia Minor famous for its horses. —,**Cappa'docian** adj., n.

capping ('kæpɪŋ) n. **a.** Scot. & N.Z. the act of conferring an academic degree. **b.** (as modifier): Capping Day.

cappuccino (,kæpʊ'tʃiːnəʊ) n., pl. **-nos.** coffee with steamed milk, usually sprinkled with powdered chocolate. [It.: CAPUCHIN]

Capra ('kæprə) n. **Frank.** born 1896, U.S. film director born in Italy. His films include It Happened One Night (1934), It's a Wonderful Life (1946), and a number of propaganda films during World War II.

Capri (kə'priː; Italian 'kapri) n. an island off W Italy, in the Bay of Naples: resort since Roman times. Pop.: 7489 (1981 est.). Area: about 13 sq. km (5 sq. miles).

capriccio (kə'prɪtʃɪ,əʊ) or **caprice** n., pl. **-priccios, -pricci** (-'priːtʃɪ), or **-prices.** Music. a lively piece of irregular musical form. [C17: from It.: CAPRICE]

capriccioso (kə,prɪtʃɪ'əʊzəʊ) adv. Music. to be played in a free and lively style. [It.: from capriccio CAPRICE]

caprice (kə'priːs) n. **1.** a sudden change of attitude, behaviour, etc. **2.** a tendency to such changes. **3.** another word for **capriccio.** [C17: from F, from It. capriccio a shiver, caprice, from capo head + riccio lit.: hedgehog]

capricious (kə'prɪʃəs) adj. characterized by or liable to sudden unpredictable changes in attitude or behaviour. —**ca'priciously** adv.

Capricorn ('kæprɪ,kɔːn) n. **1.** Astrol. Also called: the **Goat, Capricornus.** the tenth sign of the zodiac. The sun is in this sign between about Dec. 22 and Jan. 19. **2.** Astron. a S constellation. **3. tropic of Capricorn.** See **tropic** (sense 1). [C14: from L Capricornus, from caper goat + cornū horn]

Capricornia (,kæprɪ'kɔːnɪə) n. the regions of Australia in the tropic of Capricorn.

caprine ('kæpraɪn) adj. of or resembling a goat. [C17: from L caprīnus, from caper goat]

capriole ('kæprɪ,əʊl) n. **1.** Dressage. a high upward but not forward leap made by a horse with all four feet off the ground. ~vb. **2.** (intr.) to perform a capriole. [C16: from F, from OIt., from capriolo roebuck, from L capreolus, caper goat]

caps. abbrev. for: **1.** capital letters. **2.** capsule.

capsicum ('kæpsɪkəm) n. **1.** any of a genus of tropical American plants related to the potato, having mild or pungent seeds enclosed in a bell-shaped fruit. **2.** the fruit of any of these plants, used as a vegetable or ground to produce a condiment. ~See also **pepper** (sense 4). [C18: from NL, from L capsa box]

capsid[1] ('kæpsɪd) n. a bug related to the water bug that feeds on plant tissues, causing damage to crops. [C19: from NL Capsus (genus)]

capsid[2] ('kæpsɪd) n. the outer protein coat of a mature virus. [C20: from F capside, from L capsa box]

capsize (kæp'saɪz) vb. to overturn accidentally; upset. [C18: from ?] —**cap'sizal** n.

capstan ('kæpstən) n. **1.** a windlass with a drum equipped with a ratchet, used on ships for hauling in ropes, etc. **2.** the rotating shaft in a tape recorder that pulls the tape past the head. [C14: from OProvençal cabestan, from L capistrum a halter, from capere to seize]

capstan lathe n. a lathe for repetitive work, having a rotatable turret to hold tools for successive operations. Also called: **turret lathe.**

capstone ('kæp,stəʊn) n. another word for **copestone** (sense 2).

capsule ('kæpsjuːl) n. **1.** a soluble case of gelatin enclosing a dose of medicine. **2.** a thin metal cap, seal, or cover. **3.** Bot. **a.** a dry fruit that liberates its seeds by splitting, as in the violet, or through pores, as in the poppy. **b.** the spore-producing organ of mosses and liverworts. **4.** Anat. a membranous envelope surrounding any of certain organs or parts. **5.** See **space capsule. 6.** an aeroplane cockpit that can be ejected in a flight emergency, complete with crew, instruments, etc. **7.** (modifier) in a highly concise form: a capsule summary. [C17: from F, from L capsula, dim. of capsa box] —'**capsu,late** adj.

capsulize *or* **-ise** ('kæpsjʊ,laɪz) *vb.* (*tr.*) **1.** to state (information, etc.) in a highly condensed form. **2.** to enclose in a capsule.

Capt. *abbrev. for* Captain.

captain ('kæptɪn) *n.* **1.** the person in charge of a vessel. **2.** an officer of the navy who holds a rank junior to a rear admiral. **3.** an officer of the army, certain air forces, and the marines who holds a rank junior to a major. **4.** the officer in command of a civil aircraft. **5.** the leader of a team in games. **6.** a person in command over a group, organization, etc.: *a captain of industry.* **7.** *U.S.* a policeman in charge of a precinct. **8.** *U.S. & Canad.* a head waiter. ~*vb.* **9.** (*tr.*) to be captain of. [C14: from OF, from LL *capitāneus* chief, from L *caput* head] — '**captaincy** *or* '**captain,ship** *n.*

Captain Cooker ('kʊkə) *n. N.Z.* a wild pig. [from Captain James COOK, who first released pigs in the New Zealand bush]

caption ('kæpʃən) *n.* **1.** a title, brief explanation, or comment accompanying an illustration. **2.** a heading or title of a chapter, article, etc. **3.** graphic material used in television presentation. **4.** another name for **subtitle** (sense 2). **5.** the formal heading of a legal document. ~*vb.* **6.** to provide with a caption or captions. [C14 (meaning: seizure): from L *captiō* a seizing, from *capere* to take]

captious ('kæpʃəs) *adj.* apt to make trivial criticisms. [C14 (meaning: catching in error): from L *captiōsus*, from *captiō* a seizing] — '**captiously** *adv.* — '**captiousness** *n.*

captivate ('kæptɪ,veɪt) *vb.* (*tr.*) to hold the attention of by fascinating; enchant. [C16: from LL *captivāre*, from *captīvus* CAPTIVE] — '**capti,vating** *adj.* — ,**capti'vation** *n.*

captive ('kæptɪv) *n.* **1.** a person or animal that is confined or restrained. **2.** a person whose behaviour is dominated by some emotion: *a captive of love.* ~*adj.* **3.** held as prisoner. **4.** held under restriction or control; confined. **5.** captivated. **6.** unable to avoid speeches, advertisements, etc.: *a captive audience.* [C14: from L *captivus*, from *capere* to take]

captivity (kæp'tɪvɪtɪ) *n., pl.* **-ties. 1.** imprisonment. **2.** the period of imprisonment.

captor ('kæptə) *n.* a person or animal that holds another captive. [C17: from L, from *capere* to take]

capture ('kæptʃə) *vb.* (*tr.*) **1.** to take prisoner or gain control over: *to capture a town.* **2.** (in a game) to win possession of: *to capture a pawn in chess.* **3.** to succeed in representing (something elusive): *the artist captured her likeness.* **4.** *Physics.* (of an atom, etc.) to acquire (an additional particle). ~*n.* **5.** the act of taking by force. **6.** the person or thing captured. **7.** *Physics.* a process by which an atom, etc., acquires an additional particle. **8.** *Geog.* the process by which the headwaters of one river are diverted into another. **9.** *Computers.* the collection of data for processing. [C16: from L *captūra* a catching, that which is caught, from *capere* to take] — '**capturer** *n.*

Capua ('kæpjʊə; *Italian* 'kapua) *n.* a town in S Italy, in NW Campania: strategically important in ancient times, situated on the Appian Way. Pop.: 18 053 (1981 est.).

capuchin ('kæpjutʃɪn, -jʊʃɪn) *n.* **1.** an agile intelligent S American monkey having a cowl of thick hair on the top of the head. **2.** a woman's hooded cloak. **3.** (*sometimes cap.*) a variety of domestic fancy pigeon. [C16: from F, from It., from *cappuccio* hood]

Capuchin ('kæpjutʃɪn, -jʊʃɪn) *n.* **1.** a friar belonging to a branch of the Franciscan Order founded in 1525. ~*adj.* **2.** of or relating to this order. [C16: from F, from It. *cappuccio* hood]

capybara (,kæpɪ'bɑːrə) *n.* the largest rodent, resembling a guinea pig and native to Central and South America. [C18: from Port. *capibara*, from Tupi]

Caquetá (*Spanish* kake'ta) *n.* the Japurá River from its source in Colombia to the border with Brazil.

car (kɑː) *n.* **1. a.** Also called: **motorcar, automobile.** a self-propelled road vehicle designed to carry passengers, that is powered by an internal-combustion engine. **b.** (*as modifier*): *car coat.* **2.** a conveyance for passengers, freight, etc., such as a cable car or the carrier of an airship or balloon. **3.** *Brit.* a railway vehicle for passengers only. **4.** *Chiefly U.S. & Canad.* a railway carriage or van. **5.** a poetic word for **chariot.** [C14: from Anglo-F *carre*, ult. rel. to L *carra*, *carrum* two-wheeled wagon, prob. of Celtic origin]

carabineer *or* **carabinier** (,kærəbɪ'nɪə) *n.* variants of **carabineer.**

carabiner (,kærə'biːnə) *n.* a variant of **karabiner.**

caracal ('kærə,kæl) *n.* **1.** a lynxlike feline mammal inhabiting deserts of N Africa and S Asia, having a smooth coat of reddish fur. **2.** this fur. [C18: from F, from Turkish *kara kūlāk*, lit.: black ear]

Caracalla (,kærə'kælə) *n.* real name *Marcus Aurelius Antoninus*, original name *Bassianus*. 188–217 A.D., Roman emperor (211–17): ruled with cruelty and extravagance; assassinated.

caracara (,kɑːrə'kɑːrə) *n.* a large carrion-eating bird of prey of Central and South America, having long legs. [C19: from Sp. or Port., from Tupi; imit.]

Caracas (kə'ræks, -'rɑː-; *Spanish* ka'rakas) *n.* the capital of Venezuela, in the north: founded in 1567; major industrial and commercial centre, notably for oil companies. Pop.: 1 246 677 (1987).

caracole ('kærə,kəʊl) *or* **caracol** ('kærə,kɒl) *Dressage.* ~*n.* **1.** a half turn to the right or left. ~*vb.* (*intr.*) **2.** to execute a half turn. [C17: from F, from Sp. *caracol* snail, spiral staircase]

Caractacus (kə'ræktəkəs) *n.* a variant of **Caratacus.**

caracul ('kærə,kʌl) *n.* **1.** Also called: **Persian lamb.** the black loosely curled fur obtained from the skins of newly born lambs of the karakul sheep. **2.** a variant spelling of **karakul.**

carafe (kə'ræf, -'rɑːf) *n.* an open-topped glass container for serving water or wine at table [C18: from F, from It., from Sp., from Ar. *gharrāfah* vessel]

carageen ('kærə,giːn) *n.* a variant spelling of **carrageen.**

carambola (,kærəm'bəʊlə) *n.* the yellow edible star-shaped fruit of a Brazilian tree. Also called: **star fruit.** [Sp., from Port.]

caramel ('kærəməl) *n.* **1.** burnt sugar, used for colouring and flavouring food. **2.** a chewy sweet made from sugar, milk, etc. [C18: from F, from Sp. *caramelo*, from ?]

caramelize *or* **-ise** ('kærəmə,laɪz) *vb.* to convert or be converted into caramel.

carapace ('kærə,peɪs) *n.* the thick hard shield that covers part of the body of crabs, tortoises, etc. [C19: from F, from Sp. *carapacho*, from ?]

carat ('kærət) *n.* **1.** a measure of the weight of precious stones, esp. diamonds, now standardized as 0.20 grams. **2.** Usual U.S. spelling: **karat.** a measure of the gold in an alloy, expressed as the number of parts of gold in 24 parts of the alloy. [C16: from OF, from Med. L, from Ar. *qīrāt* weight of four grains, from Gk, from *keras* horn]

Caratacus (kə'rætəkəs), **Caractacus,** *or* **Caradoc** (kə'rædək) *n.* died ?54 A.D., British chieftain: led an unsuccessful resistance against the Romans (43–50).

Caravaggio (*Italian* kara'vaddʒo) *n.* **Michelangelo Merisi da** (mike'landʒelo me'riːzi da). 1573–1610, Italian painter, noted for his realistic depiction of religious subjects and for his dramatic use of chiaroscuro.

caravan ('kærə,væn) *n.* **1. a.** a large enclosed vehicle capable of being pulled by a car and equipped to be lived in. U.S. and Canad. name: **trailer. b.** (*as modifier*): *a caravan site.* **2.** (esp. in some parts of Asia and Africa) a company of traders or other travellers journeying together. **3.** a large covered vehicle, esp. a gaily coloured one used by Gypsies, circuses, etc. ~*vb.* **-vanning, -vanned. 4.** (*intr.*) *Brit.* to travel or have a holiday in a caravan. [C16: from It. *caravana*, from Persian *kārwān*]

caravanserai (,kærə'vænsə,raɪ) *or* **caravansary** (,kærə'vænsərɪ) *n., pl.* **-rais** *or* **-ries.** (in some Eastern countries) a large inn enclosing a courtyard, providing accommodation for caravans. [C16: from Persian *kārwān-sarāī* caravan inn]

caravel ('kærə,vɛl) *or* **carvel** *n.* a two- or three-masted sailing ship used by the Spanish and Portuguese in the 15th and 16th centuries. [C16: from Port. *caravela*, dim. of *caravo* ship, ult. from Gk *karabos* crab]

caraway ('kærə,weɪ) *n.* **1.** an umbelliferous Eurasian plant having finely divided leaves and clusters of small whitish flowers. **2. caraway seed.** the pungent aromatic fruit of this plant, used in cooking. [C14: prob. from Med. L *carvi*, from Ar. *karawyā*, from Gk *karon*]

carbide ('kɑːbaɪd) *n.* **1.** a binary compound of carbon with a metal. **2.** See **calcium carbide.**

carbine ('kɑːbaɪn) *n.* **1.** a light automatic or semiautomatic rifle. **2.** a light short-barrelled rifle formerly used by cavalry. [C17: from F *carabine*, from OF *carabin* carabineer]

carbineer (ˌkɑːbɪˈnɪə), **carabineer**, *or* **carabinier** (ˌkærəbɪˈnɪə) *n.* (formerly) a soldier equipped with a carbine.

carbo- *or before a vowel* **carb-** *combining form.* carbon: *carbohydrate; carbonate.*

carbohydrate (ˌkɑːbəʊˈhaɪdreɪt) *n.* any of a large group of organic compounds, including sugars and starch, that contain carbon, hydrogen, and oxygen, with the general formula $C_m(H_2O)_n$: a source of food and energy for animals.

carbolic acid (kɑːˈbɒlɪk) *n.* another name for **phenol,** esp. when it is used as a disinfectant. [C19: from CARBO-+ -OL[1] + -IC]

carbon (ˈkɑːbᵊn) *n.* **1. a.** a nonmetallic element existing in the three allotropic forms: amorphous carbon, graphite, and diamond: occurring in all organic compounds. The isotope **carbon-12** is the standard for atomic wt.; **carbon-14** is used in radiocarbon dating and as a tracer. Symbol: C; atomic no.: 6; atomic wt.: 12.011 15. **b.** *(as modifier): a carbon compound.* **2.** short for **carbon paper** or **carbon copy. 3.** a carbon electrode used in a carbon-arc light. **4.** a rod or plate, made of carbon, used in some types of battery. [C18: from F, from L *carbō* charcoal]

carbon-14 dating *n.* another name for **carbon dating.**

carbonaceous (ˌkɑːbəˈneɪʃəs) *adj.* of, resembling, or containing carbon.

carbonade (ˌkɑːbəˈneɪd, -ˈnɑːd) *n.* beef and onions stewed in beer. [C20: F]

carbonado (ˌkɑːbəˈneɪdəʊ) *n., pl.* **-dos** *or* **-does.** an inferior variety of diamond used in industry. Also called: **black diamond.** [Port., lit.: carbonated]

carbon arc *n.* an electric arc between two carbon electrodes or between a carbon electrode and materials to be welded.

carbonate *n.* (ˈkɑːbə‚neɪt, -nɪt). **1.** a salt or ester of carbonic acid. ~*vb.* (ˈkɑːbə‚neɪt). **2.** to turn into a carbonate. **3.** *(tr.)* to treat with carbon dioxide, as in the manufacture of soft drinks. [C18: from F, from *carbone* CARBON]

carbon black *n.* a finely divided form of carbon produced by incomplete combustion of natural gas or petroleum: used in pigments and ink.

carbon copy *n.* **1.** a duplicate copy of writing, typewriting, or drawing obtained by using carbon paper. **2.** *Inf.* a person or thing that is identical to another.

carbon dating *n.* a technique for determining the age of organic materials, such as wood, based on their content of the radioisotope ^{14}C acquired from the atmosphere when they formed part of a living plant.

carbon dioxide *n.* a colourless odourless incombustible gas present in the atmosphere and formed during respiration, etc.: used in fire extinguishers, and as dry ice for refrigeration. Formula: CO_2. Also called: **carbonic-acid gas.**

carbonette (ˌkɑːbəˈnɛt) *n. N.Z.* a ball of compressed coal dust used as fuel.

carbon fibre *n.* a thread of pure carbon used because of its lightness and strength at high temperatures for reinforcing resins, ceramics, and metals, and for fishing rods.

carbonic (kɑːˈbɒnɪk) *adj.* (of a compound) containing carbon, esp. tetravalent carbon.

carbonic acid *n.* a weak acid formed when carbon dioxide combines with water. Formula: H_2CO_3.

carboniferous (ˌkɑːbəˈnɪfərəs) *adj.* yielding coal or carbon.

Carboniferous (ˌkɑːbəˈnɪfərəs) *adj.* **1.** of, denoting, or formed in the fifth period of the Palaeozoic era during which coal measures were formed. ~*n.* **2. the.** the Carboniferous period or rock system divided into the Upper **Carboniferous** period and the Lower **Carboniferous** period.

carbonize *or* **-ise** (ˈkɑːbə‚naɪz) *vb.* **1.** to turn into carbon as a result of heating. **2.** *(tr.)* to coat (a substance) with carbon. — ‚carboni'zation *or* -i'sation *n.*

carbon monoxide *n.* a colourless odourless poisonous gas formed when carbon compounds burn in insufficient air. Formula: CO.

carbon paper *n.* a thin sheet of paper coated on one side with a dark waxy pigment, often containing carbon, that is transferred by pressure onto the copying surface below.

carbon tetrachloride *n.* a colourless volatile nonflammable liquid made from chlorine and used as a solvent, cleaning fluid, and insecticide. Formula: CCl_4.

car-boot sale *n.* another name for **boot sale.**

Carborundum (ˌkɑːbəˈrʌndəm) *n. Trademark.* any of various abrasive materials, esp. one consisting of silicon carbide.

carboxyl group *or* **radical** (kɑːˈbɒksaɪl) *n.* the monovalent group -COOH: the functional group in organic acids. [C19 *carboxyl*, from CARBO- + OXY-[2] + -YL]

carboxylic acid (ˌkɑːbɒkˈsɪlɪk) *n.* any of a class of organic acids containing the carboxyl group. See also **fatty acid.**

carboy (ˈkɑː‚bɔɪ) *n.* a large bottle, usually protected by a basket or box, used for containing corrosive liquids. [C18: from Persian *qarāba*]

carbuncle (ˈkɑː‚bʌŋkᵊl) *n.* **1.** an extensive skin eruption, similar to a boil, with several openings. **2.** a rounded gemstone, esp. a garnet cut without facets. [C13: from L *carbunculus,* dim. of *carbō* coal] —**carbuncular** (kɑːˈbʌŋkjʊlə) *adj.*

carburation (ˌkɑːbjʊˈreɪʃən) *n.* the process of mixing a hydrocarbon fuel with air to make an explosive mixture for an internal-combustion engine.

carburet (ˈkɑːbjʊ‚rɛt, ˌkɑːbjʊˈrɛt) *vb.* **-retting, -retted** *or U.S.* **-reting, -reted.** *(tr.)* to combine or mix (a gas, etc.) with carbon or carbon compounds. [C18: from CARB(ON) + -URET]

carburettor, carburetter (ˌkɑːbjʊˈrɛtə, ˈkɑːbjʊ‚rɛtə), *or U.S.* **carburetor** (ˈkɑːbjʊ‚reɪtə) *n.* a device used in petrol engines for mixing atomized petrol with air, and regulating the intake of the mixture into the engine.

carcajou (ˈkɑːkə‚dʒuː, -kə‚ʒuː) *n.* a North American name for **wolverine.** [C18: from Canad. F, from Algonquian *karkajou*]

carcass *or* **carcase** (ˈkɑːkəs) *n.* **1.** the dead body of an animal, esp. one that has been slaughtered for food. **2.** *Inf., usually facetious or derog.* a person's body. **3.** the skeleton or framework of a structure. **4.** the remains of anything when its life or vitality is gone. [C14: from OF *carcasse,* from ?]

Carcassonne (*French* karkasɔn) *n.* a city in SW France: extensive remains of medieval fortifications. Pop.: 41 951 (1983 est.).

Carchemish (ˈkɑːkəmɪʃ, kɑːˈkiː-) *n.* an ancient city in Syria on the Euphrates, lying on major trade routes; site of a victory of the Babylonians over the Egyptians (605 B.C.).

carcinogen (kɑːˈsɪnədʒən) *n. Pathol.* any substance that produces cancer. [C20: from Gk *karkinos* CANCER + -GEN] —‚carcino'genic *adj.*

carcinoma (ˌkɑːsɪˈnəʊmə) *n., pl.* **-mas** *or* **-mata** (-mətə). *Pathol.* any malignant tumour derived from epithelial tissue, esp. a cancer. [C18: from L, from Gk, from *karkinos* CANCER]

card[1] (kɑːd) *n.* **1.** a piece of stiff paper or thin cardboard, usually rectangular, with varied uses, as for bearing a written notice for display, etc. **2.** such a card used for identification, reference, proof of membership, etc.: *identity card.* **3.** such a card used for sending greetings, messages, or invitations: *birthday card.* **4. a.** one of a set of small pieces of cardboard, marked with figures, symbols, etc., used for playing games or for fortune-telling. See also **playing card. b.** *(as modifier): a card game.* **5.** a small rectangle of stiff plastic with identifying numbers, issued by banks and other organizations, and signed by the holder, for use as a credit card, banker's card, etc. **6.** *Inf.* a witty or eccentric person. **7.** See **compass card. 8.** Also called: **racecard.** *Horse racing.* a daily programme of all the races at a meeting. **9. a card up one's sleeve.** a thing or action used in order to gain an advantage, esp. one kept in reserve until needed. **10.** *Computers.* See **punched card.** ~See also **cards.** [C15: from OF *carte,* from L *charta* leaf of papyrus, from Gk *khartēs,* prob. of Egyptian origin]

card[2] (kɑːd) *n.* **1.** a machine for combing fibres of cotton, wool, etc., to remove small unwanted fibres before spinning. **2.** a comblike tool for raising the nap on cloth. ~*vb.* **3.** *(tr.)* to process with such a machine or tool. [C15: from OF *carde* card, teasel, from L *carduus* thistle] —'**carder** *n.*

cardamom *or* **cardamum** (ˈkɑːdəməm) *n.* **1.** a tropical Asian plant that has large hairy leaves. **2.** the seeds of this plant, used esp. as a spice or condiment. [C15: from L,

from Gk, from *kardamon* cress + *amōmon* an Indian spice]
cardboard ('kɑːd,bɔːd) *n.* **1. a.** a thin stiff board made from paper pulp. **b.** (*as modifier*): *cardboard boxes.* ~*adj.* **2.** (*prenominal*) without substance.
card-carrying *adj.* being an official member of an organization: *a card-carrying Communist.*
Cárdenas (*Spanish* 'karðenas) *n.* **Lázaro** ('laθaro). 1895–1970, Mexican statesman and general; president of Mexico (1934–40).
cardiac ('kɑːdɪ,æk) *adj.* **1.** of or relating to the heart. **2.** of or relating to the portion of the stomach connected to the oesophagus. ~*n.* **3.** a person with a heart disorder. [C17: from L *cardiacus*, from Gk, from *kardia* heart]
cardie *or* **cardy** ('kɑːdɪ) *n., pl.* **-dies.** *Inf.* short for **cardigan.**
Cardiff ('kɑːdɪf) *n.* the capital of Wales, situated in the southeast: administrative centre of South Glamorgan: an important port. Pop.: 279 800 (1983).
cardigan ('kɑːdɪgən) *n.* a knitted jacket or sweater with buttons up the front. [C19: after 7th Earl of *Cardigan* (1797–1868)]
Cardigan Bay *n.* an inlet of St. George's Channel, on the W coast of Wales.
Cardiganshire ('kɑːdɪgən,ʃɪə, -ʃə) *n.* (until 1974) a county of W Wales, now part of Dyfed.
Cardin (*French* kardɛ̃) *n.* **Pierre** (pjɛr). born 1922, French couturier, noted esp. for his collections for men.
cardinal ('kɑːdɪnᵊl) *n.* **1.** *R.C. Church.* any of the members of the Sacred College who elect the pope and act as his chief counsellors. **2.** Also called: **cardinal red.** a deep red colour. **3.** See **cardinal number. 4.** Also called (U.S.): **redbird.** a crested North American bunting, the male of which has a bright red plumage. **5.** a woman's hooded shoulder cape worn in the 17th and 18th centuries. ~*adj.* **6.** (*usually prenominal*) fundamentally important; principal. **7.** of a deep red. [C13: from L *cardinālis*, lit.: relating to a hinge, from *cardō* hinge] —'**cardinally** *adv.*
cardinalate ('kɑːdɪnᵊ,leɪt) *or* **cardinalship** *n.* **1.** the rank, office, or term of office of a cardinal. **2.** the cardinals collectively.
cardinal flower *n.* a lobelia of E North America that has brilliant scarlet flowers.
cardinal number *or* **numeral** *n.* a number denoting quantity but not order in a group. Sometimes shortened to **cardinal.** Cf. **ordinal number.**
cardinal points *pl. n.* the four main points of the compass: north, south, east, and west.
cardinal virtues *pl. n.* the most important moral qualities, traditionally justice, prudence, temperance, and fortitude.
card index *or* **file** *n.* **1.** an index in which each item is separately listed on systematically arranged cards. ~*vb.* **card-index.** (*tr.*) **2.** to make such an index of (a book, etc.).
cardio- *or before a vowel* **cardi-** *combining form.* heart: *cardiogram.* [from Gk *kardia* heart]
cardiogram ('kɑːdɪəʊ,græm) *n.* short for **electrocardiogram.** See **electrocardiograph.**
cardiograph ('kɑːdɪəʊ,grɑːf) *n.* **1.** an instrument for recording heart movements. **2.** short for **electrocardiograph.** —**cardiographer** (,kɑːdɪ'ɒgrəfə) *n.* —,**cardi'ography** *n.*
cardiology (,kɑːdɪ'ɒlədʒɪ) *n.* the branch of medical science concerned with the heart and its diseases. —,**cardi'ologist** *n.*
cardiovascular (,kɑːdɪəʊ'væskjʊlə) *adj.* of or relating to the heart and the blood vessels.
cardoon (kɑː'duːn) *n.* a thistle-like relative of the artichoke with an edible leafstalk. [C17: from F, from L *carduus* thistle, artichoke]
card punch *n.* a device, controlled by a computer, for transferring information from the central processing unit onto punched cards which can then be read by a **card reader.**
cards (kɑːdz) *n.* **1.** (*usually functioning as sing.*) **a.** any game played with cards, esp. playing cards. **b.** the playing of such a game. **2.** an employee's tax and national insurance documents or information held by the employer. **3. ask for** *or* **get one's cards.** to ask *or* be told to terminate one's employment. **4. on the cards.** possible. **5. play one's cards (right).** to manoeuvre (cleverly). **6. put** *or* **lay one's cards on the table.** to declare one's intentions, etc.
cardsharp ('kɑːd,ʃɑːp) *or* **cardsharper** *n.* a professional card player who cheats.
Carducci (*Italian* kar'duttʃi) *n.* **Giosuè** (dʒozu'ɛ). 1835–1907, Italian poet: Nobel prize for literature 1906.
card vote *n. Brit.* a vote by delegates, esp. at a trade-union conference, in which each delegate's vote counts as a vote by all his constituents.
care (kɛə) *vb.* **1.** (when *tr.*, *may take a clause as object*) to be troubled or concerned: *he is dying, and she doesn't care.* **2.** (*intr.;* foll. by *for* or *about*) to have regard or consideration (for): *he cares more for his hobby than his job.* **3.** (*intr.;* foll. by *for*) to have a desire or taste (for): *would you care for tea?* **4.** (*intr.;* foll. by *for*) to provide physical needs, help, or comfort (for). **5.** (*tr.*) to agree or like (to do something): *would you care to sit down?* **6. for all I care** *or* **I couldn't care less.** I am completely indifferent. ~*n.* **7.** careful or serious attention: *he does his work with care.* **8.** protective or supervisory control: *in the care of a doctor.* **9.** (*often pl.*) trouble; worry. **10.** an object of or cause for concern. **11.** caution: *handle with care.* **12. care of.** at the address of: written on envelopes. Usual abbrev.: **c/o. 13. in** (*or* **into**) **care.** *Brit.* made the legal responsibility of a local authority by order of a court. [OE *cearu* (n.), *cearian* (vb.), of Gmc origin] —'**carer** *n.*
CARE (kɛə) *n. acronym for:* **1.** *N.Z.* Citizens' Association for Racial Equality. **2.** Cooperative for American Relief Everywhere.
careen (kə'riːn) *vb.* **1.** to sway or cause to sway over to one side. **2.** (*tr.*) *Naut.* to cause (a vessel) to keel over to one side, esp. in order to clean its bottom. **3.** (*intr.*) *Naut.* (of a vessel) to keel over to one side. [C17: from F, from It., from L *carīna* keel] —**ca'reenage** *n.*
career (kə'rɪə) *n.* **1.** a path through life or history. **2. a.** a profession or occupation chosen as one's life's work. **b.** (*as modifier*): *a career diplomat.* **3.** a course or path, esp. a headlong one. ~*vb.* **4.** (*intr.*) to rush in an uncontrolled way. [C16: from F, from LL *carrāria* carriage road, from L *carrus* two-wheeled wagon]
career girl *or* **woman** *n.* a woman, often unmarried, who follows a profession.
careerist (kə'rɪərɪst) *n.* a person who seeks to advance his career by any possible means.
carefree ('kɛə,friː) *adj.* without worry or responsibility. —'**care,freeness** *n.*
careful ('kɛəfʊl) *adj.* **1.** cautious in attitude or action. **2.** painstaking in one's work; exact and thorough. **3.** (*usually postpositive;* foll. by *of, in,* or *about*) solicitous; protective. **4.** *Brit.* mean or miserly. —'**carefully** *adv.* —'**carefulness** *n.*
careless ('kɛəlɪs) *adj.* **1.** done with or acting with insufficient attention. **2.** (often foll. by *in, of,* or *about*) unconcerned in attitude or action. **3.** (*usually prenominal*) carefree. **4.** (*usually prenominal*) unstudied: *careless elegance.* —'**carelessly** *adv.* —'**carelessness** *n.*
caress (kə'rɛs) *n.* **1.** a gentle touch or embrace, esp. one given to show affection. ~*vb.* **2.** (*tr.*) to touch or stroke gently with or as with affection. [C17: from F, from It., from L *cārus* dear]
caret ('kærɪt) *n.* a symbol (ʎ) used to indicate the place in written or printed matter at which something is to be inserted. [C17: from L, lit.: there is missing, from *carēre* to lack]
caretaker ('kɛə,teɪkə) *n.* **1.** a person who is in charge of a place or thing, esp. in the owner's absence. **2.** (*modifier*) interim: *a caretaker government.*
Carew (kə'ruː) *n.* **Thomas.** ?1595–?1639, English Cavalier poet.
careworn ('kɛə,wɔːn) *adj.* showing signs of care, stress, worry, etc.: *a careworn face.*
Carey ('kɛərɪ) *n.* **William.** 1761–1834, English orientalist and pioneer Baptist missionary in India.
cargo ('kɑːgəʊ) *n., pl.* **-goes** *or esp. U.S.* **-gos. 1. a.** goods carried by a ship, aircraft, or other vehicle; freight. **b.** (*as modifier*): *a cargo vessel.* **2.** any load: *a cargo of new arrivals.* [C17: from Sp.: from *cargar* to load, from LL, from L *carrus* CAR]
Caria ('kɛərɪə) *n.* an ancient region of SW Asia Minor, on the Aegean Sea: chief cities were Halicarnassus and Cnidus: corresponds to the present-day Turkish districts of S Aydin and W Muğla.

Carib ('kærɪb) *n.* **1.** (*pl.* **-ibs** *or* **-ib**) a member of a group of American Indian peoples of NE South America and the Lesser Antilles. **2.** the family of languages spoken by these peoples. [C16: from Sp. *Caribe*, from Amerind]

Caribbean (,kærɪ'bɪən; *U.S.* kə'rɪbɪən) *adj.* **1.** of or relating to the Caribbean Sea and its islands. **2.** of or relating to the Carib or any of their languages. ~*n.* **3. the.** short for the **Caribbean Sea. 4.** a member of any of the peoples inhabiting the islands of the Caribbean Sea, such as a West Indian or a Carib.

Caribbean Sea *n.* an almost landlocked sea, part of the Atlantic Ocean, bounded by the West Indies, Central America, and the N coast of South America. Area: 2 718 200 sq. km (1 049 500 sq. miles).

Caribbees ('kærɪ,biːz) *pl. n.* **the.** another name for the **Lesser Antilles.**

Cariboo ('kærɪ,buː) *n.* **the.** *Canad.* a region in the W foothills of the Cariboo Mountains, scene of a gold rush beginning in 1860.

Cariboo Mountains *pl. n.* a mountain range in SW Canada, in SE British Columbia. Highest peak: Mount Sir Wilfrid Laurier, 3582 m (11 750 ft.).

caribou ('kærɪ,buː) *n.*, *pl.* **-bous** *or* **-bou.** a large North American reindeer. [C18: from Canad. F, of Algonquian origin]

caricature ('kærɪkə,tjʊə) *n.* **1.** a pictorial, written, or acted representation of a person, which exaggerates his characteristic traits for comic effect. **2.** an inadequate or inaccurate imitation. ~*vb.* **3.** (*tr.*) to represent in caricature or produce a caricature of. [C18: from It. *caricatura* a distortion, from *caricare* to load, exaggerate] —'**cari-ca,turist** *n.*

caries ('kɛəriːz) *n.*, *pl.* **-ies.** progressive decay of a bone or a tooth. [C17: from L: decay]

carillon (kə'rɪljən) *n. Music.* **1.** a set of bells usually hung in a tower. **2.** a tune played on such bells. **3.** a mixture stop on an organ giving the effect of a bell. [C18: from F: set of bells, from OF *quarregnon*, ult. from L *quattuor* four]

carina (kə'riːnə, -'raɪ-) *n.*, *pl.* **-nae** (-niː) *or* **-nas.** a keel-like part or ridge, as in the breastbone of birds. [C18: from L: keel]

carinate ('kærɪ,neɪt) *or* **carinated** *adj. Biol.* having a keel or ridge. [C17: from L *carināre*, from *carina* keel]

caring (kɛərɪŋ) *adj.* **1.** showing care and compassion: *a caring attitude.* **2.** of or relating to professional social or medical care: *nursing is a caring job.* ~*n.* **3.** the practice of providing care.

Carinthia (kə'rɪnθɪə) *n.* a province of S Austria: an independent duchy from 976 to 1276; mainly mountainous, with many lakes and resorts. Capital: Klagenfurt. Pop.: 541 526 (1986). Area: 9533 sq. km (3681 sq. miles). German name: **Kärnten.**

carioca (,kærɪ'əʊkə) *n.* **1.** a Brazilian dance similar to the samba. **2.** a piece of music for this dance. [C19: from Brazilian Port.]

cariole *or* **carriole** ('kærɪ,əʊl) *n.* **1.** a small open two-wheeled horse-drawn vehicle. **2.** a covered cart. [C19: from F, ult. from L *carrus;* see CAR]

carious ('kɛərɪəs) *adj.* (of teeth or bone) affected with caries; decayed.

carl *or* **carle** (kaːl) *n. Arch. or Scot.* another word for **churl.** [OE, from ON *karl*]

Carl XVI Gustaf (*Swedish* kaːrl 'gʊstav) *n.* born 1946, king of Sweden from 1973.

Carlisle (kaː'laɪl) *n.* a city in NW England, administrative centre of Cumbria: railway and industrial centre. Pop.: 71 503 (1981). Latin name: **Luguvallum** (,luːguː'væləm).

Carlos ('kaːlɒs) *n.* **Don.** full name *Carlos María Isidro de Borbón.* 1788–1855, second son of Charles IV: pretender to the Spanish throne and leader of the Carlists.

Carlota (*Spanish* kar'lota) *n.* original name *Marie Charlotte Amélie Augustine Victoire Clémentine Léopoldine.* 1840–1927, wife of Maximilian; empress of Mexico (1864–67).

Carlovingian (,kaːləʊ'vɪndʒɪən) *adj.*, *n. History.* a variant of **Carolingian.**

Carlow ('kaːləʊ) *n.* **1.** a county of SE Ireland, in Leinster: mostly flat, with barren mountains in the southeast. County town: Carlow. Pop.: 40 948 (1986). Area: 896 sq. km (346 sq. miles). **2.** a town in SE Ireland, county town of Co. Carlow. Pop.: 10 000 (1985 est.).

Carlsbad (*German* 'karlsbaːt) *n.* a variant spelling of **Karlsbad.**

Carlton ('kaːltən) *n.* a town in N central England, in S Nottinghamshire. Pop.: 46 456 (1981).

Carlyle (kaː'laɪl) *n.* **Thomas.** 1795–1881, Scottish essayist and historian. His works include *Sartor Resartus* (1833–34), a spiritual autobiography, *The French Revolution* (1837), and lectures *On Heroes, Hero-Worship, and the Heroic in History* (1841).

carmagnole (,kaːmən'jəʊl) *n.* **1.** a dance and song popular during the French Revolution. **2.** the costume worn by many French Revolutionaries. [C18: from F, prob. after *Carmagnola*, Italy]

Carmarthen (kaː'maːðən) *n.* a market town in S Wales, in S Dyfed: Norman castle. Pop.: 12 302 (1981).

Carmarthenshire (kaː'maːðən,ʃɪə, -ʃə) *n.* (until 1974) a county of S Wales, now part of Dyfed.

Carmel ('kaːməl) *n.* **Mount.** a mountain ridge in NW Israel, extending from the Samarian Hills to the Mediterranean. Highest point: about 540 m (1800 ft.).

Carmelite ('kaːmə,laɪt) *n. R.C. Church.* **1.** a member of an order of mendicant friars founded about 1154. **2.** a member of a corresponding order of nuns founded in 1452. ~*adj.* **3.** of or relating to either of these orders. [C14: from F, after Mount CARMEL, where the order was founded]

Carmichael (kaː'maɪkəl) *n.* **Hoagland Howard** ('həʊglənd), known as *Hoagy.* 1899–1981, U.S. pianist, singer, and composer of such standards as "Star Dust" (1929).

carminative ('kaːmɪnətɪv) *adj.* **1.** able to relieve flatulence. ~*n.* **2.** a carminative drug. [C15: from F, from L *carmināre* to card wool]

carmine ('kaːmaɪn) *n.* **1. a.** a vivid red colour. **b.** (*as adj.*): *carmine paint.* **2.** a pigment of this colour obtained from cochineal. [C18: from Med. L *carmīnus*, from Ar. *qirmiz* KERMES]

Carnac ('kaːnæk) *n.* a village in NW France: noted for its many megalithic monuments, including alignments of stone menhirs.

carnage ('kaːnɪdʒ) *n.* extensive slaughter. [C16: from F, from It., from Med. L, from L *carō* flesh]

carnal ('kaːnəl) *adj.* relating to the appetites and passions of the body. [C15: from LL, from L *carō* flesh] —**car'nality** *n.* —'**carnally** *adv.*

carnal knowledge *n. Chiefly law.* sexual intercourse.

Carnap ('kaːnæp) *n.* **Rudolf.** 1891–1970, U.S. logical positivist philosopher, born in Germany: attempted to construct a formal language for the empirical sciences that would eliminate ambiguity.

Carnarvon (kaː'naːvᵊn) *n.* a variant spelling of **Caernarfon.**

Carnatic (kaː'nætɪk) *n.* a region of S India, between the Eastern Ghats and the Coromandel Coast: originally the country of the Kanarese; historically important as a rich and powerful trading centre; now part of Madras state.

carnation (kaː'neɪʃən) *n.* **1.** Also called: **clove pink.** a Eurasian plant cultivated in many varieties for its white, pink, or red flowers, which have a fragrant scent of cloves. **2.** the flower of this plant. **3. a.** a pink or reddish-pink colour. **b.** (*as adj.*): *a carnation dress.* [C16: from F: flesh colour, from LL, from L *carō* flesh]

carnauba (kaː'naʊbə) *n.* **1.** Also called: **wax palm.** a Brazilian fan palm. **2.** Also called: **carnauba wax.** the wax obtained from the young leaves of this tree. [from Brazilian Port., prob. of Tupi origin]

Carné (kar'ne) *n.* **Marcel** (mar'sɛl). born 1903, French film director. His films include *Le Jour se lève* (1939) and *Les Portes de la nuit* (1946).

Carnegie (kaː'nəgɪ, kaː'neɪ-) *n.* **Andrew.** 1835–1919, U.S. steel manufacturer and philanthropist, born in Scotland: endowed public libraries, education, and research trusts.

carnelian (kaː'niːljən) *n.* a reddish-yellow translucent variety of chalcedony, used as a gemstone. [C17: var. of *cornelian*, from OF, from ?]

carnet ('kaːneɪ) *n.* **1.** a customs licence authorizing the temporary importation of a motor vehicle. **2.** an official document permitting motorists to cross certain frontiers. [F: notebook, from OF, ult. from L *quaternī* four at a time]

Carniola (,kaːnɪ'əʊlə) *n.* a region of NW Yugoslavia: a former duchy and crownland of Austria (1335–1919); divided between Yugoslavia and Italy in 1919; became part of Yugoslavia in 1947. German name: **Krain** (krain). Slovene name: **Kranj.**

carnival ('kɑːnɪvəl) n. **1. a.** a festive period marked by merrymaking, etc.: esp. in some Roman Catholic countries, the period just before Lent. **b.** (as modifier): a carnival atmosphere. **2.** a travelling fair having sideshows, merry-go-rounds, etc. **3.** a show or display arranged as an amusement. **4.** Austral. a sports meeting. [C16: from It., from OIt. carnelevare a removing of meat (referring to the Lenten fast)]

carnivore ('kɑːnɪˌvɔː) n. **1.** any of an order of mammals having large pointed canine teeth specialized for eating flesh. The order includes cats, dogs, bears, and weasels. **2.** any other animal or any plant that feeds on animals. [C19: prob. back formation from CARNIVOROUS]

carnivorous (kɑːˈnɪvərəs) adj. **1.** (esp. of animals) feeding on flesh. **2.** (of plants such as the pitcher plant and sundew) able to trap and digest insects. **3.** of or relating to the carnivores. [C17: from L, from carō flesh + vorāre to consume] —**car'nivorousness** n.

Carnot ('kɑːnəʊ; French karno) n. **Nicolas Léonard Sadi** (nikɔla leɔnar sadi). 1796–1832, French physicist, whose work on a cycle for an ideal heat engine formed the basis for the second law of thermodynamics, enunciated in 1850; author of Réflexions sur la puissance motrice du feu (1824).

carob ('kærəb) n. **1.** an evergreen Mediterranean tree with compound leaves and edible pods. **2.** the long blackish sugary pod of this tree, used for animal fodder and sometimes for human food. [C16: from OF, from Med. L carrūbium, from Ar. al kharrūbah]

carol ('kærəl) n. **1.** a joyful hymn or religious song, esp. one (a **Christmas carol**) celebrating the birth of Christ. ~vb. **-olling, -olled** or U.S. **-oling, -oled. 2.** (intr.) to sing carols at Christmas. **3.** to sing (something) in a joyful manner. [C13: from OF, from ?]

Carol II ('kærəl) n. 1893–1953, king of Romania (1930–40), who was deposed by the Iron Guard, a Romanian fascist party.

Carolina (ˌkærəˈlaɪnə) n. a former English colony on the E coast of North America, first established in 1663: divided in 1729 into North and South Carolina, which are often referred to as **the Carolinas.**

Caroline ('kærəˌlaɪn) or **Carolean** (ˌkærəˈliːən) adj. characteristic of or relating to Charles I or Charles II (kings of England, Scotland, and Ireland), the society over which they ruled, or their government. Also called: **Carolinian.**

Caroline Islands pl. n. an archipelago of over 500 islands and islets in Micronesia, in the W Pacific Ocean east of the Philippines: formerly part of the U.S. Trust Territory of the Pacific Islands; centre of a typhoon zone. Area: (land) 1183 sq. km (457 sq. miles).

Carolingian (ˌkærəˈlɪndʒɪən) adj. **1.** of or relating to the Frankish dynasty founded by Pepin the Short which ruled in France from 751–987 A.D. and in Germany until 911 A.D. ~n. **2.** a member of the dynasty of the Carolingian Franks. ~Also: **Carlovingian, Carolinian.**

Carolinian (ˌkærəˈlɪnɪən) adj., n. a variant of **Caroline** or **Carolingian.**

carom ('kærəm) n. Billiards. another word (esp. U.S. and Canad.) for **cannon** (sense 5). [C18: from earlier carambole (taken as carom ball), from Sp. carambola a CARAMBOLA]

carotene ('kærəˌtiːn) or **carotin** ('kærətɪn) n. any of four orange-red isomers of a hydrocarbon present in many plants and converted to vitamin A in the liver. [C19 carotin, from L carōta CARROT]

carotenoid or **carotinoid** (kəˈrɒtɪˌnɔɪd) n. any of a group of red or yellow pigments, including carotenes, found in plants and certain animal tissues.

carotid (kəˈrɒtɪd) n. **1.** either of the two principal arteries that supply blood to the head and neck. ~adj. **2.** of either of these arteries. [C17: from F, from Gk, from karoun to stupefy; so named because pressure on them produced unconsciousness]

carousal (kəˈraʊzəl) n. a merry drinking party.

carouse (kəˈraʊz) vb. **1.** (intr.) to have a merry drinking spree. ~n. **2.** another word for **carousal.** [C16: via F carrousser from G (trinken) gar aus (to drink) right out] —**ca'rouser** n.

carousel (ˌkærəˈsɛl, -ˈzɛl) n. **1.** a circular tray in which slides for a projector are held in slots from which they can be released in turn. **2.** a revolving luggage conveyor, as at an airport. **3.** U.S. and Canad. a merry-go-round. **4.** History. a tournament in which horsemen took part in races. [C17: from F, from It. carosello, from ?]

carp[1] (kɑːp) n., pl. **carp** or **carps. 1.** a freshwater food fish having one long dorsal fin, and two barbels on each side of the mouth. **2.** a cyprinid. [C14: from OF carpe, of Gmc origin]

carp[2] (kɑːp) vb. (intr.; often foll. by at) to complain or find fault. [C13: from ON karpa to boast] —**'carper** n. —**'carping** adj., n.

-carp n. combining form. (in botany) fruit or a reproductive structure that develops into a particular part of the fruit: epicarp. [from NL -carpium, from Gk -karpion, from karpos fruit]

Carpaccio (ˌkɑːˈpætʃɪəʊ, -tʃəʊ; Italian karˈpattʃo) n. **Vittore** (vitˈtoːre). ?1460–?1525, Italian painter of the Venetian school.

carpal ('kɑːpəl) n. **a.** any bone of the wrist. **b.** (as modifier): carpal bones. [C18: from NL carpālis, from Gk karpos wrist]

car park n. an area or building reserved for parking cars. Usual U.S. and Canad. term: **parking lot.**

Carpathian Mountains (kɑːˈpeɪθɪən) or **Carpathians** pl. n. a mountain system of central and E Europe, extending from N Czechoslovakia to central Romania: mainly forested, with rich iron ore resources. Highest peak: Gerlachovka, 2663 m (8788 ft.).

Carpatho-Ukraine (kɑːˈpeɪθəʊjuːˈkreɪn) n. another name for **Ruthenia.**

carpe diem Latin. ('kɑːpɪ 'diːɛm) sentence substitute. enjoy the pleasures of the moment, without concern for the future. [lit.: seize the day!]

carpel ('kɑːpəl) n. the female reproductive organ of flowering plants, consisting of an ovary, style, and stigma. [C19: from NL carpellum, from Gk karpos fruit] —**'carpellary** adj.

Carpentaria (ˌkɑːpənˈtɛərɪə) n. **Gulf of.** a shallow inlet of the Arafura Sea, in N Australia between Arnhem Land and Cape York Peninsula.

carpenter ('kɑːpɪntə) n. **1.** a person skilled in woodwork, esp. in buildings, ships, etc. ~vb. **2.** (intr.) to do the work of a carpenter. **3.** (tr.) to make or fit together by or as if by carpentry. [C14: from Anglo-F, from L, from carpentum wagon]

Carpenter ('kɑːpɪntə) n. **John Alden.** 1876–1951, U.S. composer, who used jazz rhythms in orchestral music: his works include the ballet Skyscrapers (1926) and the orchestral suite Adventures in a Perambulator (1915).

Carpentier (French karpɑtje) n. **Georges** (ʒɔrʒ), known as Gorgeous Georges. 1894–1975, French boxer: world light-heavyweight champion (1920–22).

carpentry ('kɑːpɪntrɪ) n. **1.** the art or technique of working wood. **2.** the work produced by a carpenter; woodwork.

carpet ('kɑːpɪt) n. **1.** a heavy fabric for covering floors. **2.** a covering like a carpet: a carpet of leaves. **3. on the carpet.** Inf. **a.** before authority to be reproved. **b.** under consideration. ~vb. (tr.) **4.** to cover with or as if with a carpet. **5.** Inf. to reprimand. [C14: from OF, from OIt., from LL carpeta, from L carpere to pluck, card]

carpetbag ('kɑːpɪtˌbæg) n. a travelling bag originally made of carpeting.

carpetbagger ('kɑːpɪtˌbægə) n. a politician who seeks public office in a locality where he has no real connections.

carpet beetle or U.S. **carpet bug** n. any of various beetles, the larvae of which feed on carpets, furnishing fabrics, etc.

carpeting ('kɑːpɪtɪŋ) n. carpet material or carpets in general.

carpet slipper n. one of a pair of slippers, originally one made with woollen uppers resembling carpeting.

carpet snake or **python** n. a large nonvenomous Australian snake having a carpet-like pattern on its back.

carpet-sweeper n. a household device with a revolving brush for sweeping carpets.

car phone n. a telephone that operates by cellular radio for use in a car.

carpo- combining form. (in botany) indicating fruit or a seed. [from Gk karpos fruit]

carport ('kɑː,pɔːt) *n.* a shelter for a car usually consisting of a roof built out from the side of a building and supported by posts.

-carpous *or* **-carpic** *adj. combining form.* (in botany) indicating a certain kind or number of fruit: *apocarpous.* [from NL, from Gk *karpos* fruit]

carpus ('kɑːpəs) *n., pl.* **-pi** (-paɪ). **1.** the technical name for **wrist**. **2.** the eight small bones of the human wrist. [C17: NL, from Gk *karpos*]

Carracci (kəˈrɑːtʃɪ; *Italian* karˈrattʃi) *n.* a family of Italian painters, born in Bologna: **Agostino** (agosˈtiːno) (1557–1602); his brother, **Annibale** (anˈniːbale) (1560–1609); and their cousin, **Ludovico** (ludoˈviːko) (1555–1619). They were influential in reviving the classical tradition of the Renaissance and founded a teaching academy (1582) in Bologna.

carrack ('kærək) *n.* a galleon sailed in the Mediterranean as a merchantman in the 15th and 16th centuries. [C14: from OF *caraque*, from OSp. *carraca*, from Ar. *qarāqīr* merchant ships]

carrageen, carragheen, *or* **carageen** ('kærə,giːn) *n.* an edible red seaweed, of rocky shores of North America and N Europe, used to make a beverage, medicine, and jelly, and as an emulsifying and gelling agent (**E407**). Also called: **Irish moss**. [C19: from *Carragheen*, near Waterford, Ireland]

Carrara (kəˈrɑːrə; *Italian* karˈraːra) *n.* a town in NW Italy, in NW Tuscany: famous for its marble. Pop.: 65 687 (1981).

carrel *or* **carrell** ('kærəl) *n.* a small individual study room or private desk, often in a library. [C20: from obs. *carrel* study area, var. of CAROL]

Carrel (kəˈrɛl, 'kærəl; *French* karɛl) *n.* **Alexis** (əˈlɛksɪs; *French* alɛksi). 1873–1944, French surgeon and biologist, active in the U.S. (1905–39): developed a method of suturing blood vessels, making the transplantation of arteries and organs possible: Nobel prize for physiology or medicine 1912.

carriage ('kærɪdʒ) *n.* **1.** *Brit.* a railway coach for passengers. **2.** the manner in which a person holds and moves his head and body. **3.** a four-wheeled horse-drawn vehicle for persons. **4.** the moving part of a machine that bears another part: *a typewriter carriage.* **5.** ('kærɪdʒ, 'kærɪɪdʒ). **a.** the act of conveying. **b.** the charge made for conveying (esp. in **carriage forward,** when the charge is to be paid by the receiver, and **carriage paid**). [C14: from OF *cariage*, from *carier* to CARRY]

carriage clock *n.* a portable clock, usually in a rectangular case, originally used by travellers.

carriage trade *n.* trade from the wealthy part of society.

carriageway ('kærɪdʒ,weɪ) *n. Brit.* the part of a road along which traffic passes in a single line moving in one direction only: *a dual carriageway.*

Carrickfergus (,kærɪkˈfɜːgəs) *n.* a town in NE Northern Ireland, on Belfast Lough; historic settlement of Scottish Protestants; Norman castle. Pop.: 29 000 (1981).

carrier ('kærɪə) *n.* **1.** a person, thing, or organization employed to carry goods, etc. **2.** a mechanism by which something is carried or moved, such as a device for transmitting rotation from the faceplate of a lathe to the workpiece. **3.** *Pathol.* another name for **vector** (sense 2). **4.** *Pathol.* a person or animal that, without having any symptoms of a disease, is capable of transmitting it to others. **5.** Also called: **charge carrier**. *Physics.* an electron or hole that carries the charge in a conductor or semiconductor. **6.** short for **carrier wave**. **7.** *Chem.* **a.** an inert substance used to absorb a dyestuff, transport a sample through a gas chromatography column, contain a radioisotope for radioactive tracing, etc. **b.** a substance used to support a catalyst. **8.** See **aircraft carrier**.

carrier bag *n. Brit.* a large paper or plastic bag for carrying shopping, etc.

carrier pigeon *n.* any homing pigeon, esp. one used for carrying messages.

carrier wave *n. Radio.* a wave of fixed amplitude and frequency that is modulated in order to carry a signal in radio transmission, etc.

Carrington ('kærɪŋtən) *n.* **Peter (Alexander Rupert)**, 6th Baron. born 1919, British Conservative politician: secretary of state for defence (1970–74); foreign secretary (1979–82); secretary general of NATO from 1984.

carriole ('kærɪ,əʊl) *n.* a variant spelling of **cariole**.

carrion ('kærɪən) *n.* **1.** dead and rotting flesh. **2.** (*modifier*) eating carrion. **3.** something rotten. [C13: from Anglo-F *caroine*, ult. from L *carō* flesh]

carrion crow *n.* a common predatory and scavenging European crow similar to the rook but having a pure black bill.

Carroll ('kærəl) *n.* **Lewis.** real name *the Reverend Charles Lutwidge Dodgson.* 1832–98, English writer; an Oxford mathematics don who wrote *Alice's Adventures in Wonderland* (1865) and *Through the Looking-Glass* (1872) and the nonsense poem *The Hunting of the Snark* (1876).

carrot ('kærət) *n.* **1.** an umbelliferous plant with finely divided leaves. **2.** the long tapering orange root of this plant, eaten as a vegetable. **3.** something offered as a lure or incentive. [C16: from OF *carotte*, from LL *carōta*, from Gk *karōton*]

carroty ('kærətɪ) *adj.* **1.** of a reddish or yellowish-orange colour. **2.** having red hair.

carrousel (,kærəˈsɛl, -ˈzɛl) *n.* a variant spelling of **carousel**.

carry ('kærɪ) *vb.* **-rying, -ried.** (*mainly tr.*) **1.** (*also intr.*) to take or bear (something) from one place to another. **2.** to transfer for consideration: *he carried his complaints to her superior.* **3.** to have on one's person: *he carries a watch.* **4.** (*also intr.*) to be transmitted or serve as a medium for transmitting: *sound carries over water.* **5.** to bear or be able to bear the weight, pressure, or responsibility of: *her efforts carry the whole production.* **6.** to have as an attribute or result: *this crime carries a heavy penalty.* **7.** to bring or communicate: *to carry news.* **8.** (*also intr.*) to be pregnant with (young). **9.** to bear (the head, body, etc.) in a specified manner: *she carried her head high.* **10.** to conduct or bear (oneself) in a specified manner: *she carried herself well.* **11.** to continue or extend: *the war was carried into enemy territory.* **12.** to cause to move or go: *desire for riches carried him to the city.* **13.** to influence, esp. by emotional appeal: *his words carried the crowd.* **14.** to secure the passage of (a bill, motion, etc.). **15.** to win (an election). **16.** to obtain victory for (a candidate). **17.** *Chiefly U.S.* to win a majority of votes in (a district, etc.): *the candidate carried 40 states.* **18.** to capture: *our troops carried the town.* **19.** (of communications media) to include as the content: *this newspaper carries no book reviews.* **20.** Also (esp. U.S.): **carry over.** *Book-keeping.* to transfer (an item) to another account, esp. to transfer to the following year's account: *to carry a loss.* **21.** *Maths.* to transfer (a number) from one column of figures to the next. **22.** (of a shop, trader, etc.) to keep in stock: *to carry confectionery.* **23.** to support (a musical part or melody) against the other parts. **24.** (*intr.*) (of a ball, projectile, etc.) to travel through the air or reach a specified point: *his first drive carried to the green.* **25.** *Inf.* to imbibe (alcoholic drink) without showing ill effects. **26.** (*intr.*) *Sl.* to have drugs on one's person. **27. carry all before (one).** to win unanimous support or approval for (oneself). **28. carry the can (for).** *Inf.* to take responsibility for some misdemeanour, etc. (on behalf of). **29. carry the day.** to be successful. ~*n., pl.* **-ries.** **30.** the act of carrying. **31.** *U.S. & Canad.* a portion of land over which a boat must be portaged. **32.** the range of a firearm or its projectile. **33.** *Golf.* the distance from where the ball is struck to where it first touches the ground. ~See also **carry away, carry forward,** etc. [C14 *carien*, from OF *carier* to move by vehicle, from *car*, from L *carrum* transport wagon]

carryall ('kærɪ,ɔːl) *n.* the usual U.S. and Canad. name for a **holdall**.

carry away *vb.* (*tr., adv.*) **1.** to remove forcefully. **2.** (*usually passive*) to cause (a person) to lose self-control. **3.** (*usually passive*) to delight: *he was carried away by the music.*

carrycot ('kærɪ,kɒt) *n.* a light cot with handles, similar to but smaller than the body of a pram.

carry forward *vb.* (*tr., adv.*) **1.** *Book-keeping.* to transfer (a balance) to the next column, etc. **2.** *Tax accounting.* to apply (a legally permitted credit, esp. an operating loss) to the taxable income of following years. ~Also: **carry over.**

carrying-on *n., pl.* **carryings-on.** *Inf.* **1.** unconventional behaviour. **2.** excited or flirtatious behaviour.

carry off *vb.* (*tr., adv.*) **1.** to remove forcefully. **2.** to win. **3.** to handle (a situation) successfully: *he carried off the* *introductions well.* **4.** to cause to die: *he was carried off by pneumonia.*

carry on *vb. (adv.)* **1.** *(intr.)* to continue or persevere. **2.** *(tr.)* to conduct: *to carry on a business.* **3.** *(intr.; often foll. by with) Inf.* to have an affair. **4.** *(intr.) Inf.* to cause a fuss or commotion. ~*n.* **carry-on.** **5.** *Inf., chiefly Brit.* a fuss.

carry out *vb. (tr., adv.)* **1.** to perform or cause to be implemented: *I wish he could afford to carry out his plan.* **2.** to accomplish. ~*n.* **carry-out.** *Chiefly Scot.* **3.** alcohol bought at an off-licence, etc., for consumption elsewhere. **4. a.** a shop which sells hot cooked food for consumption away from the premises. **b.** *(as modifier): a carry-out shop.*

carry over *vb. (tr., adv.)* **1.** to postpone or defer. **2.** *Book-keeping, tax accounting.* another term for **carry forward.** ~*n.* **carry-over.** **3.** something left over for future use; esp. goods to be sold. **4.** *Book-keeping.* a sum or balance carried forward.

carry through *vb. (tr., adv.)* **1.** to bring to completion. **2.** to enable to endure (hardship, trouble, etc.); support.

carse (kɑːs) *n. Scot.* a riverside area of flat fertile alluvium. [C14: from ?]

carsick ('kɑː,sɪk) *adj.* nauseated from riding in a car or other vehicle. ~*'car,sickness n.*

Carson ('kɑːs⁰n) *n.* **1. Christopher,** known as *Kit Carson.* 1809–68, U.S. frontiersman, trapper, scout, and Indian agent. **2. Edward Henry,** Baron. 1854–1935, Irish politician and lawyer; led northern Irish resistance to the British government's home rule for Ireland. **3. Rachel (Louise).** 1907–64, U.S. marine biologist and science writer; author of *Silent Spring* (1962).

Carson City *n.* a city in W Nevada, capital of the state. Pop.: 35 000 (1985).

Carstensz ('kɑːstənz) *n.* **Mount.** a former name of (Mount) **Jaya.**

cart (kɑːt) *n.* **1.** a heavy open vehicle, usually having two wheels and drawn by horses. **2.** a light open horse-drawn vehicle for business or pleasure. **3.** any small vehicle drawn or pushed by hand, such as a trolley. **4. in the cart. a.** in an awkward situation. **b.** in the lurch. **5. put the cart before the horse.** to reverse the usual order of things. ~*vb.* **6.** *(usually tr.)* to use or draw a cart to convey (goods, etc.). **7.** *(tr.)* to carry with effort: *to cart wood home.* [C13: from ON *kartr*] —*'carter n.*

cartage ('kɑːtɪdʒ) *n.* the process or cost of carting.

Cartagena (,kɑːtə'dʒiːnə; *Spanish* karta'xena) *n.* **1.** a port in NW Colombia, on the Caribbean: centre for the Inquisition and the slave trade in the 16th century; chief oil port of Colombia. Pop.: 559 581 (1985). **2.** a port in SE Spain, on the Mediterranean: important since Carthaginian and Roman times for its minerals. Pop.: 167 936 (1981).

Carte (kɑːt) *n.* See (Richard) **D'Oyly Carte.**

carte blanche ('kɑːt 'blɑːntʃ) *n., pl.* **cartes blanches** ('kɑːts 'blɑːntʃ).** complete discretion or authority: *the government gave their negotiator carte blanche.* [C18: from F: blank paper]

cartel (kɑː'tɛl) *n.* **1.** Also called: **trust.** a collusive association of independent enterprises formed to monopolize production and distribution of a product or service. **2.** *Politics.* an alliance of parties to further common aims. [C20: from G *Kartell,* from F, from It. *cartello* public notice, dim. of *carta* CARD¹]

Carter ('kɑːtə) *n.* **1. Elliot (Cook).** born 1908, U.S. composer. His works include the *Piano Sonata* (1945–46), three string quartets, and orchestral pieces: Pulitzer Prize 1960. **2. Howard.** 1873–1939, English Egyptologist: discovered and excavated the tomb of the Pharaoh Tutankhamen. **3. James Earl,** known as *Jimmy.* born 1924, U.S. Democratic statesman; 39th president of the U.S. (1977–81).

Carteret ('kɑːtərɪt) *n.* **John,** 1st Earl Granville. 1690–1763, British statesman, diplomat, and orator who led the opposition to Walpole (1730–42), after whose fall he became a leading minister as secretary of state (1742–44).

Cartesian (kɑː'tiːzɪən) *adj.* **1.** of or relating to the works of Descartes. **2.** of or used in Descartes' mathematical system. —**Car'tesian,ism** *n.*

Cartesian coordinates *pl. n.* a system of coordinates that defines the location of a point in space in terms of its perpendicular distance from each of a set of mutually perpendicular axes.

Carthage ('kɑːθɪdʒ) *n.* an ancient city state, on the N African coast near present-day Tunis. Founded about 800 B.C. by Phoenician traders, it grew into an empire dominating N Africa and the Mediterranean. Destroyed and then rebuilt by Rome, it was finally razed by the Arabs in 697 A.D. See also **Punic Wars.** —**Carthaginian** (,kɑːθə'dʒɪnɪən) *adj., n.*

carthorse ('kɑːt,hɔːs) *n.* a large heavily built horse kept for pulling carts or carriages.

Carthusian (kɑː'θjuːzɪən) *R.C. Church.* ~*n.* **1.** a member of a monastic order founded by Saint Bruno in 1084 near Grenoble, France. ~*adj.* **2.** of or relating to this order. [C14: from Med. L, from L *Carthusia* Chartreuse, near Grenoble]

Cartier (*French* kartje) *n.* **Jacques** (ʒak). 1491–1557, French navigator and explorer in Canada, who discovered the St. Lawrence River (1535).

Cartier-Bresson (*French* kartjebrɛsɔ̃) *n.* **Henri** (ɑ̃ri). born 1908, French photographer.

cartilage ('kɑːtɪlɪdʒ) *n.* a tough elastic tissue composing most of the embryonic skeleton of vertebrates. In the adults of higher vertebrates it is mostly converted into bone. Nontechnical name: **gristle.** [C16: from L *cartilāgō*] —**cartilaginous** (,kɑːtɪ'lædʒɪnəs) *adj.*

cartilaginous fish *n.* any of a class of fish including the sharks and rays, having a skeleton composed entirely of cartilage.

cartload ('kɑːt,ləʊd) *n.* the amount a cart can hold.

cart off, away, *or* **out** *vb. (tr., adv.) Inf.* to carry or remove brusquely or by force.

cartogram ('kɑːtə,græm) *n.* a map showing statistical information in diagrammatic form. [C20: from F *cartogramme,* from *carte* map, CHART]

cartography (kɑː'tɒgrəfɪ) *n.* the art, technique, or practice of compiling or drawing maps or charts. [C19: from F *cartographie,* from *carte* map, CHART] —**car'tographer** *n.* —**cartographic** (,kɑːtə'græfɪk) *or* ,**carto'graphical** *adj.*

carton ('kɑːt⁰n) *n.* **1.** a cardboard box for containing goods. **2.** a container of waxed paper in which liquids, such as milk, are sold. [C19: from F, from It. *cartone* pasteboard, from *carta* CARD¹]

cartoon (kɑː'tuːn) *n.* **1.** a humorous or satirical drawing, esp. one in a newspaper or magazine. **2.** Also called: **comic strip.** a sequence of drawings in a newspaper, magazine, etc. **3.** See **animated cartoon.** **4.** a full-size preparatory sketch for a fresco, tapestry, mosaic, etc. [C17: from It. *cartone* pasteboard] —**car'toonist** *n.*

cartouche *or* **cartouch** (kɑː'tuːʃ) *n.* **1.** a carved or cast ornamental tablet or panel in the form of a scroll. **2.** an oblong figure enclosing characters expressing royal or divine names in Egyptian hieroglyphics. [C17: from F: scroll, cartridge, from It., from *carta* paper]

cartridge ('kɑːtrɪdʒ) *n.* **1.** a metal casing containing an explosive charge and often a bullet, for a rifle or other small arms. **2.** a stylus unit in the pick-up of a record player, either containing a piezoelectric crystal (**crystal cartridge**) or an electromagnet (**magnetic cartridge**). **3.** an enclosed container of magnetic tape, photographic film, ink, etc., for insertion into a tape deck, camera, pen, etc. [C16: from earlier *cartage,* var. of CARTOUCHE (cartridge)]

cartridge belt *n.* a belt with pockets for cartridge clips or loops for cartridges.

cartridge clip *n.* a metallic container holding cartridges for an automatic firearm.

cartridge paper *n.* **1.** an uncoated type of drawing or printing paper. **2.** a heavy paper used in making cartridges or as drawing or printing paper.

cartwheel ('kɑːt,wiːl) *n.* **1.** the wheel of a cart, usually having wooden spokes. **2.** an acrobatic movement in which the body makes a revolution supported by the hands with legs outstretched.

Cartwright ('kɑːt,raɪt) *n.* **Edmund.** 1743–1823, English clergyman, who invented the power loom.

caruncle ('kærəŋk⁰l, kə'rʌŋ-) *n.* **1.** a fleshy outgrowth on the heads of certain birds, such as a cock's comb. **2.** an outgrowth near the hilum on the seeds of some plants. [C17: from obs. F *caruncule,* from L *caruncula* a small piece of flesh, from *carō* flesh] —**caruncular** (kə'rʌŋkjʊlə) *or* **ca'runculous** *adj.*

Caruso (*Italian* ka'ru:so) *n.* **Enrico** (en'ri:ko). 1873–1921, an outstanding Italian operatic tenor; one of the first to make gramophone records.

carve (kɑ:v) *vb.* **1.** (*tr.*) to cut or chip in order to form something: *to carve wood.* **2.** to form (something) by cutting or chipping: *to carve statues.* **3.** to slice (meat) into pieces. ~See also **carve out, carve up.** [OE *ceorfan*]

carvel ('kɑ:vᵊl) *n.* another word for **caravel.**

carvel-built *adj.* (of a vessel) having a hull with planks made flush at the seams. Cf. **clinker-built.**

carven ('kɑ:vᵊn) *vb.* an archaic or literary past participle of **carve.**

carve out *vb.* (*tr., adv.*) *Inf.* to make or create (a career): *he carved out his own future.*

carver ('kɑ:və) *n.* **1.** a carving knife. **2.** (*pl.*) a large matched knife and fork for carving meat. **3.** *Brit.* a chair having arms that forms part of a set of dining chairs.

Carver ('kɑ:və) *n.* **George Washington.** ?1864–1943, U.S. agricultural chemist and botanist.

carvery ('kɑ:vərɪ) *n., pl.* **-veries.** an eating establishment at which customers pay a set price for unrestricted helpings from a variety of meats, salads, etc.

carve up *vb.* (*tr., adv.*) **1.** to cut (something) into pieces. **2.** to divide (land, etc.). ~*n.* **carve-up. 3.** *Inf.* an act or instance of dishonestly prearranging the result of a competition. **4.** *Sl.* the distribution of something.

carving ('kɑ:vɪŋ) *n.* a figure or design produced by carving stone, wood, etc.

carving knife *n.* a long-bladed knife for carving cooked meat for serving.

Cary ('kɛərɪ, 'kærɪ) *n.* (**Arthur**) **Joyce** (**Lunel**). 1888–1957, English novelist; author of *Mister Johnson* (1939), *A House of Children* (1941), and *The Horse's Mouth* (1944).

caryatid (,kærɪ'ætɪd) *n., pl.* **-ids** *or* **-ides** (-ɪ,di:z). a column, used to support an entablature, in the form of a draped female figure. [C16: from L, from Gk *Karuatides* priestesses of Artemis at *Karuai* (Caryae), in Laconia]

Casablanca (,kæsə'blæŋkə) *n.* a port in NW Morocco, on the Atlantic: largest city in the country; industrial centre. Pop.: 2 600 000 (1984).

Casals (*Spanish* ka'sals) *n.* **Pablo** ('paβlo). 1876–1973, Spanish cellist and composer, noted for his interpretation of J. S. Bach's cello suites.

Casanova (,kæsə'nəʊvə) *n.* **1. Giovanni Jacopo** (dʒo-'vanni 'ja:kopo). 1725–98, Italian adventurer noted for his *Mémoires,* a vivid account of his sexual adventures and of contemporary society. **2.** any man noted for his amorous adventures; a rake.

Casaubon (kə'sɔ:bᵊn; *French* kazobɔ̃) *n.* **Isaac** (izaak). 1559–1614, French Protestant theologian and classical scholar.

casbah ('kæzbɑ:) *n.* (*sometimes cap.*) a variant spelling of **kasbah.**

cascade (kæs'keɪd) *n.* **1.** a waterfall or series of waterfalls over rocks. **2.** something resembling this, such as folds of lace. **3.** a consecutive sequence of chemical or physical processes. **4.** a series of stages in the processing chain of an electrical signal where each operates the next in turn. ~*vb.* **5.** (*intr.*) to flow or fall in or like a cascade. [C17: from F, from It., ult. from L *cadere* to fall]

Cascade Range *n.* a chain of mountains in the U.S. and Canada: a continuation of the Sierra Nevada range from N California through Oregon and Washington to British Columbia. Highest peak: Mount Rainier, 4392 m (14 408 ft.).

cascara (kæs'kɑ:rə) *n.* **1.** Also called: **cascara sagrada.** the dried bark of the cascara buckthorn, used as a laxative and stimulant. **2.** Also called: **cascara buckthorn.** a shrub or small tree of NW North America. [C19: from Sp.: bark]

case[1] (keɪs) *n.* **1.** a single instance or example of something. **2.** an instance of disease, injury, etc. **3.** a question or matter for discussion. **4.** a specific condition or state of affairs; situation. **5.** a set of arguments supporting a particular action, cause, etc. **6. a.** a person attended or served by a doctor, social worker, solicitor, etc. **b.** (*as modifier*): *a case study.* **7. a.** an action or suit at law: *he has a good case.* **b.** the evidence offered in court to support a claim. **8.** *Grammar.* **a.** a set of grammatical categories of nouns, pronouns, and adjectives indicating the relation of the noun, adjective, or pronoun to other words in the sentence. **b.** any one of these categories: *the nominative case.* **9.** *Inf.* an eccentric. **10. in any case.** (*adv.*) no matter what. **11. in case.** (*adv.*) **a.** in order to allow for eventualities. **b.** (*conj.*) in order to allow for the possibility that: *take your coat in case it rains.* **12. in case of.** (*prep.*) in the event of. **13. in no case.** (*adv.*) under no circumstances. [OE *casus* (grammatical) case, associated also with OF *cas* a happening; both from L *cāsus,* a befalling, from *cadere* to fall]

case[2] (keɪs) *n.* **1. a.** a container, such as a box or chest. **b.** (*in combination*): *suitcase.* **2.** an outer cover, esp. for a watch. **3.** a receptacle and its contents: *a case of ammunition.* **4.** *Archit.* another word for **casing** (sense 3). **5.** a cover ready to be fastened to a book to form its binding. **6.** *Printing.* a tray in which a compositor keeps individual metal types of a particular size and style. Cases were originally used in pairs, one (the **upper case**) for capitals, the other (the **lower case**) for small letters. ~*vb.* (*tr.*) **7.** to put into or cover with a case. **8.** *Sl.* to inspect carefully (esp. a place to be robbed). [C13: from OF *casse,* from L, from *capere* to take, hold]

case-harden *vb.* (*tr.*) **1.** *Metallurgy.* to form a hard surface layer of high carbon content on (a steel component). **2.** to make callous: *experience had case-hardened the judge.*

case history *n.* a record of a person's background, medical history, etc.

casein ('keɪsɪɪn, -si:n) *n.* a protein, precipitated from milk by the action of rennin, forming the basis of cheese. [C19: from L *cāseus* cheese + -IN]

case law *n.* law established by following judicial decisions given in earlier cases. Cf. **statute law.**

casemate ('keɪs,meɪt) *n.* an armoured compartment in a ship or fortification in which guns are mounted. [C16: from F, from It. *casamatta,* ?from Gk *khasmata* apertures]

casement ('keɪsmənt) *n.* **1.** a window frame that is hinged on one side. **2.** a window containing frames hinged at the side. **3.** a poetic word for **window.** [C15: prob. from OF *encassement* frame, from *encasser* to encase, from *casse* framework]

Casement ('keɪsmənt) *n.* Sir **Roger** (**David**). 1864–1916, British diplomat and Irish nationalist: hanged by the British for treason in attempting to gain German support for Irish independence.

caseous ('keɪsɪəs) *adj.* of or like cheese. [C17: from L *cāseus* CHEESE]

casern *or* **caserne** (kə'zɜ:n) *n.* (formerly) a billet or accommodation for soldiers in a town. [C17: from F *caserne,* from OProvençal *cazerna* group of four men, ult. from L *quattuor* four]

Caserta (*Italian* ka'zɛrta) *n.* a town in S Italy, in Campania: centre of Garibaldi's campaigns for the unification of Italy (1860); Allied headquarters in World War II. Pop.: 66 318 (1981).

casework ('keɪs,wɜ:k) *n.* social work based on close study of the personal histories and circumstances of individuals and families. —'**case,worker** *n.*

cash[1] (kæʃ) *n.* **1.** banknotes and coins, esp. in hand or readily available. **2.** immediate payment for goods or services (esp. in **cash down**). **3.** (*modifier*) of, for, or paid by cash: *a cash transaction.* ~*vb.* **4.** (*tr.*) to obtain or pay ready money for. ~See also **cash in, cash up.** [C16: from Olt. *cassa* money box, from L *capsa* CASE[2]] —'**cashable** *adj.*

cash[2] (kæʃ) *n., pl.* **cash.** any of various Chinese or Indian coins of low value. [C16: from Port. *caixa,* from Tamil *kāsu,* from Sansk. *karsa* weight of gold]

Cash (kæʃ) *n.* **1. Johnny.** born 1932, U.S. country-and-western singer, guitarist, and songwriter. His hits include "I Walk the Line" (1956), "Ring of Fire" (1963), and "A Boy named Sue" (1969). **2. Pat.** born 1965, Australian tennis player: Wimbledon champion 1987.

cash-and-carry *adj., adv.* sold or operated on a basis of cash payment for merchandise that is not delivered but removed by the purchaser.

cash-book *n. Book-keeping.* a journal in which all receipts and disbursements are recorded.

cash card *n.* a plastic card issued by a bank or building society enabling the holder to obtain cash from a cash dispenser.

cash crop *n.* a crop grown for sale rather than for subsistence.

cash desk *n.* a counter or till in a shop where purchases are paid for.

cash discount *n.* a discount granted to a purchaser who pays before a stipulated date.

cash dispenser *n.* a computerized device outside a bank that supplies cash when the user inserts his cash card and keys in his identification number.

cashew ('kæʃuː, kæ'ʃuː) *n.* **1.** a tropical American evergreen tree, bearing kidney-shaped nuts. **2.** Also called: **cashew nut.** the nut of this tree, edible only when roasted. [C18: from Port. *cajú*, from Tupi *acajú*]

cash flow *n.* the movement of money into and out of a business.

cashier[1] (kæ'ʃɪə) *n.* **1.** a person responsible for receiving payments for goods, services, etc., as in a shop. **2.** an employee of a bank responsible for receiving deposits, cashing cheques, etc.: bank clerk. **3.** any person responsible for handling cash in a business. [C16: ?from Du. or F, from *casse* money chest]

cashier[2] (kæ'ʃɪə) *vb.* (*tr.*) to dismiss with dishonour, esp. from the armed forces. [C16: from MDu., from OF, from L *quassāre* to QUASH]

cash in *vb.* (*adv.*) **1.** (*tr.*) to give (something) in exchange. **2.** (*intr.; often foll. by on*) *Inf.* **a.** to profit (from). **b.** to take advantage (of).

cashmere ('kæʃmɪə) *n.* **1.** a fine soft wool from goats of the Kashmir area. **2. a.** cloth or knitted material made from this or similar wool. **b.** (*as modifier*): *a cashmere sweater.*

Cashmere (kæʃ'mɪə) *n.* a variant spelling of **Kashmir.**

cash on delivery *n.* a service entailing cash payment to the carrier on delivery of merchandise.

cash point *n.* **1.** any retail outlet at which goods are bought for cash. **2.** a cash dispenser.

cash register *n.* a till with a keyboard that operates a mechanism for displaying and adding the amounts of cash received in individual sales.

cash up *vb.* (*intr., adv.*) *Brit.* (of cashiers, shopkeepers, etc.) to add up the money taken, esp. at the end of a working day.

casing ('keɪsɪŋ) *n.* **1.** a protective case or cover. **2.** material for a case or cover. **3.** Also called: **case.** a frame containing a door or window.

casino (kə'siːnəʊ) *n., pl.* **-nos. 1.** a public building or room in which gaming takes place. **2.** a variant spelling of **cassino.** [C18: from It., dim. of *casa* house, from L]

cask (kɑːsk) *n.* **1.** a strong wooden barrel used mainly to hold alcoholic drink: *a wine cask.* **2.** any barrel. **3.** the quantity contained in a cask. [C15: from Sp. *casco* helmet]

casket ('kɑːskɪt) *n.* **1.** a small box or chest for valuables, esp. jewels. **2.** another word for **coffin.** (sense 1). [C15: prob. from OF *cassette* little box]

Caslon ('kæzlən) *n.* a style of type designed by William Caslon, English type-founder (1692–1766).

Caspar ('kæspə, 'kæspɑː) *or* **Gaspar** *n.* (in Christian tradition) one of the Magi, the other two being Melchior and Balthazar.

Caspian Sea ('kæspɪən) *n.* a salt lake between SE Europe and Asia: the largest inland sea in the world; fed mainly by the River Volga. Area: 394 299 sq. km (152 239 sq. miles).

casque (kæsk) *n. Zool.* a helmet or a helmet-like structure, as on the head of most hornbills. [C17: from F, from Sp. *casco*] **—casqued** *adj.*

Cassandra (kə'sændrə) *n.* **1.** *Greek myth.* a daughter of Priam and Hecuba, endowed with the gift of prophecy but fated never to be believed. **2.** anyone whose prophecies of doom are unheeded.

Cassatt (kə'sæt) *n.* **Mary.** 1845–1926, U.S. impressionist painter.

cassava (kə'sɑːvə) *n.* **1.** Also called: **manioc.** any of various tropical plants, esp. the widely cultivated American species (**bitter cassava, sweet cassava**). **2.** a starch derived from the root of this plant: a source of tapioca. [C16: from Sp. *cazabe* cassava bread, from Taino *caçábi*]

Cassel (*German* 'kasəl) *n.* a variant spelling of **Kassel.**

casserole ('kæsə,rəʊl) *n.* **1.** a covered dish of earthenware, glass, etc., in which food is cooked and served. **2.** any food cooked and served in such a dish: *chicken casserole.* ~*vb.* **3.** to cook or be cooked in a casserole. [C18: from F, from OF *casse* ladle, from OProvençal, from LL *cattia* dipper, from Gk *kuathion*, dim. of *kuathos* cup]

cassette (kæ'sɛt) *n.* **1. a.** a plastic container for magnetic tape, inserted into a tape deck to be played or used.

b. (*as modifier*): *a cassette recorder.* **2.** *Photog.* another term for **cartridge** (sense 3). [C18: from F: little box]

cassia ('kæsɪə) *n.* **1.** any of a genus of tropical plants whose pods yield **cassia pulp,** a mild laxative. See also **senna. 2.** a lauraceous tree of tropical Asia. **3. cassia bark.** the cinnamon-like bark of this tree, used as a spice. [OE, from L *casia,* from Gk *kasia,* of Semitic origin]

cassino *or* **casino** (kə'siːnəʊ) *n.* a card game for two to four players in which players pair cards with those exposed on the table.

Cassino (*Italian* kas'siːno) *n.* a town in central Italy, in Latium at the foot of Monte Cassino: an ancient Volscian (and later Roman) town and citadel. Pop.: 31 139 (1981). Latin name: **Casinum.**

Cassiodorus (,kæsɪəʊ'dɔːrəs) *n.* **Flavius Magnus Aurelius** ('fleɪvɪəs 'mæɡnəs ɔː'riːlɪəs). ?490–?585 A.D., Roman statesman, writer, and monk; author of *Variae,* a collection of official documents written for the Ostrogoths.

Cassiopeia[1] (,kæsɪə'piːə) *n., Latin genitive* **Cassiopeiae** (,kæsɪə'piːiː). a very conspicuous W-shaped constellation near the Pole Star.

Cassiopeia[2] (,kæsɪə'piːə) *n. Greek myth.* the wife of Cepheus and mother of Andromeda.

Cassirer (*German* ka'siːrər) *n.* **Ernst** (ɛrnst). 1874–1945, German neo-Kantian philosopher. *The Philosophy of Symbolic Forms* (1923–29) analyses the symbols that underlie all manifestations, including myths and language, of human culture.

cassis (ka:'siːs) *n.* a blackcurrant cordial. [C19: from F]

cassiterite (kə'sɪtə,raɪt) *n.* a hard heavy brownish-black mineral, the chief ore of tin. Formula: SnO_2. Also called: **tinstone.** [C19: from Gk *kassiteros* tin]

Cassius Longinus ('kæsɪəs lɒn'dʒaɪnəs) *n.* **Gaius** ('ɡaɪəs). died 42 B.C., Roman general: led the conspiracy against Julius Caesar (44); defeated at Philippi by Anthony (42).

cassock ('kæsək) *n.* an ankle-length garment, usually black, worn by Christian priests. [C16: from OF, from It. *casacca* a long coat, from ?]

Casson ('kæsᵊn) *n.* Sir **Hugh** (**Maxwell**). born 1910, British architect; president of the Royal Academy of Arts (1976–84).

cassowary ('kæsə,wɛərɪ) *n., pl.* **-waries.** a large flightless bird inhabiting forests in NE Australia, New Guinea, and adjacent islands, having a horny head crest, black plumage, and brightly coloured neck. [C17: from Malay *kěsuari*]

cast (kɑːst) *vb.* **casting, cast.** (*mainly tr.*) **1.** to throw or expel with force. **2.** to throw off or away: *she cast her clothes to the ground.* **3.** to reject: *he cast the idea from his mind.* **4.** to shed or drop: *the horse cast a shoe.* **5.** to cause to appear: *to cast a shadow.* **6.** to express (doubts, etc.) or cause (them) to be felt. **7.** to direct (a glance, etc.): *cast your eye over this.* **8.** to place, esp. violently: *he was cast into prison.* **9.** (*also intr.*) *Angling.* to throw (a line) into the water. **10.** to draw or choose (lots). **11.** to give or deposit (a vote). **12.** to select (actors) to play parts in (a play, etc.). **13. a.** to shape (molten metal, glass, etc.) by pouring into a mould. **b.** to make (an object) by such a process. **14.** (*also intr.;* often foll. by *up*) to compute (figures or a total). **15.** *Astrol.* to draw on (a horoscope) details concerning the positions of the planets in the signs of the zodiac at a particular time for interpretation. **16.** to contrive (esp. in **cast a spell**). **17.** to formulate: *he cast his work in the form of a chart.* **18.** (*also intr.*) to twist or cause to twist. **19.** (*intr.*) (of birds or prey) to eject from the crop and bill a pellet consisting of the indigestible parts of birds or animals previously eaten. **20.** *Printing.* to stereotype or electrotype. **21. be cast.** *N.Z.* (of sheep) to have fallen and been unable to rise. ~*n.* **22.** the act of casting or throwing. **23. a.** Also called: **casting.** something that is shed, dropped, or egested, such as the coil of earth left by an earthworm. **b.** another name for **pellet** (sense 4). **24.** the distance an object is or may be thrown. **25. a.** a throw at dice. **b.** the resulting number shown. **26.** *Angling.* the act or an instance of casting a line. **27.** the wide sweep made by a sheepdog to get behind a flock of sheep or by a hunting dog in search of a scent. **28. a.** the actors in a play collectively. **b.** (*as modifier*): *a cast list.* **29. a.** an object made of metal, glass, etc., that has been shaped in a molten state by being poured or pressed into a mould. **b.** the mould used to shape such an object. **30.** form or appearance. **31.** a sort, kind, or style. **32.** a fixed twist or defect, esp. in the eye. **33.** a distortion of shape. **34.** *Surgery.* a rigid encircling casing, often made of plaster of Paris, **plaster cast,** for immobilizing broken bones while they heal. **35.** a slight tinge or trace, as of colour. **36.** fortune or stroke of fate. ~See also **cast about, castaway,** etc. [C13: from ON *kasta*]

cast about *vb.* (*intr., adv.*) to make a mental or visual search: *to cast about for a plot.*

Castalia (kæ'steɪlɪə) *n.* a spring on Mount Parnassus: in ancient Greece sacred to Apollo and the Muses and believed to be a source of inspiration. —**Cas'talian** *adj.*

castanets (,kæstə'nɛts) *pl. n.* curved pieces of hollow wood, usually held between the fingers and thumb and made to click together: used esp. by Spanish dancers. [C17 *castanet*, from Sp. *castañeta*, dim. of *castaña* CHESTNUT]

castaway ('kɑːstə,weɪ) *n.* **1.** a person who has been shipwrecked. ~*adj.* (*prenominal*) **2.** shipwrecked. **3.** thrown away or rejected. ~*vb.* **cast away. 4.** (*tr., adv.; often passive*) to cause (a ship, person, etc.) to be shipwrecked.

cast back *vb.* (*adv.*) to turn (the mind) to the past.

cast down *vb.* (*tr., adv.*) to make (a person) discouraged or dejected.

caste (kɑːst) *n.* **1. a.** any of the four major hereditary classes, namely the **Brahman, Kshatriya, Vaisya,** and **Sudra,** into which Hindu society is divided. **b.** Also called: **caste system.** the system or basis of such classes. **2.** any social class or system based on such distinctions as heredity, rank, wealth, etc. **3.** the position conferred by such a system. **4. lose caste.** *Inf.* to lose one's social position. **5.** *Entomol.* any of various types of individual, such as the worker, in social insects. [C16: from Port. *casta* race, from *casto* pure, chaste, from L *castus*]

Castellammare di Stabia (*Italian* kastellam'maːre di 'stabja) *n.* a port and resort in SW Italy, in Campania on the Bay of Naples: site of the Roman resort of Stabiae, which was destroyed by the eruption of Vesuvius in 79 A.D. Pop.: 70 317 (1981).

castellan ('kæstɪlən) *n. Rare.* a keeper or governor of a castle. Also called: **chatelain.** [C14: from L *castellānus*, from *castellum* CASTLE]

castellated ('kæstɪ,leɪtɪd) *adj.* **1.** having turrets and battlements, like a castle. **2.** having indentations similar to battlements: *a castellated nut.* [C17: from Med. L *castellātus*, from *castellāre* to fortify as a CASTLE] —,castel'lation *n.*

Castellón de la Plana (*Spanish* kaste'ʎon de la 'plana) *n.* a port in E Spain. Pop.: 124 487 (1981).

caster ('kɑːstə) *n.* **1.** a person or thing that casts. **2.** a bottle with a perforated top for sprinkling sugar, etc. **3.** a small wheel mounted on a swivel so that the wheel turns to turn into its plane of rotation. ~ Also (for senses 2, 3): **castor.**

caster sugar ('kɑːstə) *n.* finely ground white sugar.

castigate ('kæstɪ,geɪt) *vb.* (*tr.*) to rebuke or criticize in a severe manner. [C17: from L *castīgāre* to correct, from *castum* pure + *agere* to compel (to be)] —,casti'gation *n.* —'casti,gator *n.*

Castiglione (,kæstɪl'jəʊnɪ) *n.* Count **Baldassare** (baldas'saːre). 1478–1529, Italian diplomat and writer, noted particularly for his dialogue on ideal courtly life, *Il Libro del Cortegiano* (The Courtier) (1528).

Castile (kæ'stiːl) *or* **Castilla** (*Spanish* kas'tiʎa) *n.* a former kingdom comprising most of modern Spain: originally part of León, it became an independent kingdom in the 10th century and united with Aragon (1469), the first step in the formation of the Spanish state.

Castile soap *n.* a hard soap made from olive oil and sodium hydroxide.

Castilian (kæ'stɪljən) *n.* **1.** the Spanish dialect of Castile; the standard form of European Spanish. **2.** a native or inhabitant of Castile. ~*adj.* **3.** denoting or of Castile, its inhabitants, or the standard form of European Spanish.

Castilla la Vieja (kas'tiʎa la 'bjexa) *n.* the Spanish name for **Old Castile.**

casting ('kɑːstɪŋ) *n.* **1.** an object that has been cast, esp. in metal from a mould. **2.** the process of transferring molten steel to a mould. **3.** the choosing of actors for a production. **4.** *Zool.* another word for **cast** (sense 23) or **pellet** (sense 4).

casting couch *n. Inf.* a couch on which a casting director is said to seduce girls seeking a part in a film or play.

casting vote *n.* the deciding vote used by the presiding officer of an assembly when votes cast on both sides are equal in number.

cast iron *n.* **1.** iron containing so much carbon that it cannot be wrought and must be cast into shape. ~*adj.* **cast-iron.** **2.** made of cast iron. **3.** rigid or unyielding: *a cast-iron decision.*

castle ('kɑːsˀl) *n.* **1.** a fortified building or set of buildings as in medieval Europe. **2.** any fortified place or structure. **3.** a large magnificent house, esp. when the present or former home of a nobleman or prince. **4.** *Chess.* another name for **rook**². ~*vb.* **5.** *Chess.* to move (the king) two squares laterally on the first rank and place the nearest rook on the square passed over by the king. [C11: from L *castellum*, dim. of *castrum* fort]

Castleford ('kɑːsˀlfəd) *n.* a town in N England, in West Yorkshire on the River Aire. Pop.: 36 032 (1981).

castle in the air *or* **in Spain** *n.* a hope or desire unlikely to be realized; daydream.

Castlereagh ('kɑːsˀl,reɪ) *n.* **Viscount.** title of *Robert Stewart,* Marquis of Londonderry. 1769–1822, British statesman: as foreign secretary (1812–22) led the Grand Alliance against Napoleon and attended the Congress of Vienna (1815).

cast-off *adj.* **1.** (*prenominal*) abandoned: *cast-off shoes.* ~*n.* **castoff.** **2.** a person or thing that has been discarded or abandoned. **3.** *Printing.* an estimate of the amount of space that a piece of copy will occupy. ~*vb.* **cast off.** (*adv.*) **4.** to remove (mooring lines) that hold (a vessel) to a dock. **5.** to knot (a row of stitches, esp. the final row) in finishing off knitted or woven material. **6.** *Printing.* to estimate the amount of space that will be taken up by (a book, piece of copy, etc.).

cast on *vb.* (*adv.*) to form (the first row of stitches) in knitting and weaving.

castor¹ ('kɑːstə) *n.* **1.** the aromatic secretion of a beaver, used in perfumery and medicine. **2.** the fur of the beaver. **3.** a hat made of beaver or similar fur. [C14: from L, from Gk *kastōr* beaver]

castor² ('kɑːstə) *n.* a variant spelling of **caster** (senses 2, 3).

Castor and Pollux ('kɑːstə) *n. Classical myth.* the twin sons of Leda: Pollux was fathered by Zeus, Castor by the mortal Tyndareus. After Castor's death, Pollux spent half his days with his half-brother in Hades and half with the gods in Olympus.

castor oil *n.* an oil obtained from the seeds of the castor-oil plant and used as a lubricant and cathartic.

castor-oil plant *n.* a tall Indian plant cultivated for its poisonous seeds, from which castor oil is extracted.

castrate (kæ'streɪt) *vb.* (*tr.*) **1.** to remove the testicles of. **2.** to deprive of vigour, masculinity, etc. **3.** to remove the ovaries of; spay. [C17: from L *castrāre* to emasculate, geld] —**cas'tration** *n.*

castrato (kæ'strɑːtəʊ) *n., pl.* **-ti** (-tɪ) *or* **-tos.** (in 17th- and 18th-century opera, etc.) a male singer whose testicles were removed before puberty, allowing the retention of a soprano or alto voice. [C18: from It., from L *castrātus* castrated]

Castries (kæs'triːs) *n.* the capital and chief port of St Lucia. Pop.: 52 868 (1986).

Castro ('kæstrəʊ) *n.* **Fidel** (fɪ'ðɛl). full name *Fidel Castro Ruz.* born 1927, Cuban statesman: prime minister from 1959, when he led the Communist overthrow of Batista. —'Castro,ism *n.* —'Castroist *adj., n.*

Castrop-Rauxel *or* **Kastrop-Rauxel** (*German* 'kastrɔp-'rauksəl) *n.* an industrial city in W West Germany, in North Rhine-Westphalia. Pop.: 77 659 (1983 est.).

cast steel *n.* steel containing varying amounts of carbon, manganese, etc., that is cast into shape rather than wrought.

casual ('kæʒjʊəl) *adj.* **1.** happening by accident or chance. **2.** offhand: *a casual remark.* **3.** shallow or superficial: *a casual affair.* **4.** being or seeming unconcerned or apathetic: *he assumed a casual attitude.* **5.** (esp. of dress) for informal wear: *a casual coat.* **6.** occasional or irregular: *a casual labourer.* ~*n.* **7.** (*usually pl.*) an informal article of clothing or footwear. **8.** an occasional worker. **9.** (*usually pl.*) a young man dressed in expensive casual clothes who goes to football matches in order to start fights. [C14: from LL *cāsuālis* happening by chance, from L *cāsus* event, from *cadere* to fall] —'**casually** *adv.* —'**casualness** *n.*

casualty ('kæ3juəltɪ) *n., pl.* **-ties.** **1.** a serviceman who is killed, wounded, captured, or missing as a result of enemy action. **2.** a person who is injured or killed in an accident. **3.** the hospital department treating victims of accidents. **4.** anything that is lost, damaged, or destroyed as the result of an accident, etc.

casuarina (,kæsjuə'raɪnə) *n.* any of a genus of trees of Australia and the East Indies, having jointed leafless branches. [C19: from NL, from Malay *kěsuari* CASSOWARY, referring to the resemblance of the branches to the feathers of the cassowary]

casuist ('kæzjuɪst) *n.* **1.** a person, esp. a theologian, who attempts to resolve moral dilemmas by the application of general rules and the careful distinction of special cases. **2.** a sophist. [C17: from F, from Sp. *casuista*, from L *cāsus* CASE[1]] —,**casu'istic** *or* ,**casu'istical** *adj.*

casuistry ('kæzjuɪstrɪ) *n., pl.* **-ries.** **1.** *Philosophy.* the resolution of particular moral dilemmas, esp. those arising from conflicting general moral rules, by the careful distinction of the cases to which these rules apply. **2.** reasoning that is specious or oversubtle.

cat (kæt) *n.* **1.** Also called: **domestic cat.** a small domesticated feline mammal having thick soft fur and occurring in many breeds in which the colour of the fur varies greatly: kept as a pet or to catch rats and mice. **2.** Also called: **big cat.** any of the larger felines, such as a lion or tiger. **3.** any wild feline mammal such as the lynx or serval, resembling the domestic cat. **4.** *Inf.* a woman who gossips maliciously. **5.** *Sl.* a man. **6.** *Naut.* a heavy tackle for hoisting an anchor to the cathead. **7.** *Austral. sl.* a coward. **8.** *Inf.* short for **caterpillar** (the vehicle). **9.** short for **cat-o'-nine-tails.** **10. fight like Kilkenny cats.** to fight until both parties are destroyed. **11. let the cat out of the bag.** to disclose a secret, often by mistake. **12. like a cat on a hot tin roof** *or* **on hot bricks.** in an uneasy or agitated state. **13. put, set,** etc., **the cat among the pigeons.** to introduce some violently disturbing new element. **14. rain cats and dogs.** to rain very heavily. *~vb.* **catting, catted.** **15.** (*tr.*) *Naut.* to hoist (an anchor) to the cathead. **16.** (*intr.*) *Sl.* to vomit. [OE *catte*, from L *cattus*] —'**cat,like** *adj.* —'**cattish** *adj.*

cat. *abbrev. for:* **1.** catalogue. **2.** catamaran.

cata-, kata-, *before an aspirate* **cath-,** *or before a vowel* **cat-** *prefix.* **1.** down; downwards; lower in position: *catadromous.* **2.** indicating reversal, opposition, degeneration, etc.: *catatonia.* [from Gk *kata-*, from *kata.* In compound words borrowed from Gk *kata-* means: down, away, off, against, according to, and thoroughly]

catabolism *or* **katabolism** (kə'tæbə,lɪzəm) *n.* a metabolic process in which complex molecules are broken down into simple ones with the release of energy; destructive metabolism. [C19: from Gk *katabolē* a throwing down, from *kata-* down + *ballein* to throw] —**catabolic** *or* **katabolic** (,kætə'bɒlɪk) *adj.*

catachresis (,kætə'kriːsɪs) *n.* the incorrect use of words, as *luxuriant* for *luxurious.* [C16: from L, from Gk *katakhrēsis* a misusing, from *khrēsthai* to use] —**catachrestic** (,kætə'krɛstɪk) *adj.*

cataclysm ('kætə,klɪzəm) *n.* **1.** a violent upheaval, esp. of a political, military, or social nature. **2.** a disastrous flood. [C17: via F from L, from Gk, from *katakluzein* to flood, from *kluzein* to wash] —,**cata'clysmic** *or* ,**cata'clysmal** *adj.* —,**cata'clysmically** *adv.*

catacomb ('kætə,kəʊm) *n.* **1.** (*usually pl.*) an underground burial place, esp. in Rome, consisting of tunnels with niches leading off them for tombs. **2.** a series of underground tunnels or caves. [OE *catacumbe*, from LL *catacumbas* (sing.), name of the cemetery under the Basilica of St Sebastian, near Rome; from ?]

catadromous (kə'tædrəməs) *adj.* (of fishes such as the eel) migrating down rivers to the sea in order to breed. Cf. **anadromous.** [C19: from Gk, from *kata-* down + *dromos*, from *dremein* to run]

catafalque ('kætə,fælk) *n.* a temporary raised platform on which a body lies in state before or during a funeral. [C17: from F, from It. *catafalco*, from ?]

Catalan ('kætə,læn) *n.* **1.** a language of Catalonia, closely related to Spanish and Provençal. **2.** a native or inhabitant of Catalonia. *~adj.* **3.** denoting or characteristic of Catalonia, its inhabitants, or their language.

catalepsy ('kætə,lɛpsɪ) *n.* a state of prolonged rigid posture, occurring for example in schizophrenia. [C16: from LL *catalēpsis*, from Gk *katalēpsis*, lit.: a seizing, from *kata-* down + *lambanein* to grasp] —,**cata'leptic** *adj.*

Catalina Island (,kætə'liːnə) *n.* another name for **Santa Catalina.**

catalogue *or U.S.* **catalog** ('kætə,lɒg) *n.* **1.** a complete, usually alphabetical, list of items. **2.** a book, usually illustrated, containing details of items for sale. **3.** a list of all the books of a library. **4.** *U.S. and Canad.* a list of courses offered by a university, etc. *~vb.* **5.** to compile a catalogue of (a library, etc.). **6.** to add (books, items, etc.) to an existing catalogue. [C15: from LL *catalogus*, from Gk, from *katalegein* to list, from *kata-* completely + *legein* to collect] —'**cata,loguer** *n.*

Catalonia (,kætə'ləʊnɪə) *n.* a region of NE Spain, with a strong separatist tradition: became an autonomous region with its own parliament in 1979; an important agricultural and industrial region, with many resorts. Pop.: 6 057 200 (1986 est.). Area: 31 929 sq. km (12 328 sq. miles). Catalan name: **Catalunya** (,katə'luːnɪə). Spanish name: **Cataluña** (katə'luɲa).

catalpa (kə'tælpə) *n.* any of a genus of trees of North America and Asia, having large leaves, bell-shaped whitish flowers, and long slender pods. [C18: NL, from Carolina Creek *kutuhlpa*, lit.: winged head]

catalyse *or U.S.* **catalyze** ('kætə,laɪz) *vb.* (*tr.*) to influence (a chemical reaction) by catalysis.

catalysis (kə'tælɪsɪs) *n., pl.* **-ses** (-,siːz). acceleration of a chemical reaction by the action of a catalyst. [C17: from NL, from Gk, from *kataluein* to dissolve] —**catalytic** (,kætə'lɪtɪk) *adj.*

catalyst ('kætəlɪst) *n.* **1.** a substance that increases the rate of a chemical reaction without itself suffering any permanent chemical change. **2.** a person or thing that causes a change.

catalytic cracker *n.* a unit in an oil refinery in which mineral oils with high boiling points are converted to fuels with lower boiling points by a catalytic process.

catamaran (,kætəmə'ræn) *n.* **1.** a sailing vessel with twin hulls held parallel by a rigid framework. **2.** a primitive raft made of logs lashed together. **3.** *Inf.* a quarrelsome woman. [C17: from Tamil *kattumaram* tied timber]

catamite ('kætə,maɪt) *n.* a boy kept for homosexual purposes. [C16: from L *Catamītus*, var. of *Ganymēdēs* GANYMEDE]

catamount ('kætə,maʊnt) *or* **catamountain** *n.* any of various felines, such as the puma or lynx. [C17: short for *cat of the mountain*]

catananche (kætən'æŋkɪ) *n.* any herb of the genus *Catananche*, having blue or yellow flowers. [C18: NL, from L, from Gk *kata* down + *anagkē* compulsion (from its use by ancient Greeks as a philtre)]

Catania (*Italian* ka'taːnja) *n.* a port in E Sicily, near Mount Etna. Pop.: 372 486 (1986).

Catanzaro (*Italian* katan'dzaːro) *n.* a city in S Italy, in Calabria. Pop.: 102 558 (1986).

cataplexy ('kætə,plɛksɪ) *n.* **1.** sudden temporary paralysis, brought on by severe shock. **2.** a state assumed by animals while shamming death. [C19: from Gk *kataplēxis* amazement, from *kataplēssein*, from *kata-* down + *plēssein* to strike] —,**cata'plectic** *adj.*

catapult ('kætə,pʌlt) *n.* **1.** a Y-shaped implement with a loop of elastic fastened to the ends of the prongs, used mainly by children for shooting stones, etc. U.S. and Canad. name: **slingshot.** **2.** a war engine used formerly for hurling stones, etc. **3.** a device installed in warships to launch aircraft. *~vb.* **4.** (*tr.*) to shoot forth from or as if from a catapult. **5.** (foll. by *over, into,* etc.) to move precipitately. [C16: from L, from Gk *katapeltēs*, from *kata-* down + *pallein* to hurl]

cataract ('kætə,rækt) *n.* **1.** a large waterfall or rapids. **2.** a downpour. **3.** *Pathol.* **a.** partial or total opacity of the lens of the eye. **b.** the opaque area. [C15: from L, from Gk, from *katarassein* to dash down, from *arassein* to strike]

catarrh (kə'tɑː) *n.* inflammation of a mucous membrane with increased production of mucus, esp. affecting the nose and throat. [C16: via F from LL, from Gk, from *katarrhein* to flow down, from *kata-* down + *rhein* to flow] —**ca'tarrhal** *adj.*

catarrhine ('kætə,raɪn) *adj.* **1.** (of apes and Old World monkeys) having the nostrils set close together and opening to the front of the face. *~n.* **2.** an animal with this characteristic. [C19: ult. from Gk *katarrhin* having a hooked nose, from *kata*-down + *rhis* nose]

catastrophe (kə'tæstrəfɪ) *n.* **1.** a sudden, extensive disaster or misfortune. **2.** the denouement of a play. **3.** a final decisive event, usually causing a disastrous end. [C16: from Gk, from *katastrephein* to overturn, from *strephein* to turn] —**catastrophic** (,kætə'strɒfɪk) *adj.* —,**cata'strophically** *adv.*

catastrophism (kə'tæstrə,fɪzəm) *n.* **1.** a former doctrine that the earth was formed by sudden divine acts rather than by evolutionary processes. **2.** a modern doctrine that the evolutionary processes shaping the earth have in the past been supplemented by the effects of huge natural catastrophes.

catatonia (,kætə'təʊnɪə) *n.* a form of schizophrenia characterized by stupor, with outbreaks of excitement. [C20: NL, from G *Katatonie*, from CATA- + Gk *tonos* tension] —**catatonic** (,kætə'tɒnɪk) *adj., n.*

catbird ('kæt,bɜːd) *n.* **1.** any of several North American songbirds whose call resembles the mewing of a cat. **2.** any of several Australian bowerbirds having a catlike call.

catboat ('kæt,bəʊt) *n.* a sailing vessel with a single mast, set well forward, and a large sail. Shortened form: **cat.**

cat burglar *n.* a burglar who enters buildings by climbing through upper windows, etc.

catcall ('kæt,kɔːl) *n.* **1.** a shrill whistle or cry expressing disapproval, as at a public meeting, etc. ~*vb.* **2.** to utter such a call (at).

catch (kætʃ) *vb.* **catching, caught. 1.** (*tr.*) to take hold of so as to retain or restrain. **2.** (*tr.*) to take or capture, esp. after pursuit. **3.** (*tr.*) to ensnare or deceive. **4.** (*tr.*) to surprise or detect in an act: *he caught the dog rifling the larder.* **5.** (*tr.*) to reach with a blow: *the stone caught him on the side of the head.* **6.** (*tr.*) to overtake or reach in time to board. **7.** (*tr.*) to see or hear; attend. **8.** (*tr.*) to be infected with: *to catch a cold.* **9.** to hook or entangle or become hooked or entangled. **10.** to fasten or be fastened with or as if with a latch or other device. **11.** (*tr.*) to attract: *she tried to catch his eye.* **12.** (*tr.*) to comprehend: *I didn't catch his meaning.* **13.** (*tr.*) to hear accurately: *I didn't catch what you said.* **14.** (*tr.*) to captivate or charm. **15.** (*tr.*) to reproduce accurately: *the painter managed to catch his model's beauty.* **16.** (*tr.*) to hold back or restrain: *he caught his breath in surprise.* **17.** (*intr.*) to become alight: *the fire won't catch.* **18.** (*tr.*) *Cricket.* to dismiss (a batsman) by intercepting and holding a ball struck by him before it touches the ground. **19.** (*intr.*; often foll. by *at*) **a.** to grasp or attempt to grasp. **b.** to take advantage (of): *he caught at the chance.* **20. catch it.** *Inf.* to be scolded or reprimanded. ~*n.* **21.** the act of catching or grasping. **22.** a device that catches and fastens, such as a latch. **23.** anything that is caught. **24.** the amount or number caught. **25.** *Inf.* an eligible matrimonial prospect. **26.** a check or break in the voice. **27.** *Inf.* **a.** a concealed, unexpected, or unforeseen drawback. **b.** (*as modifier*): *a catch question.* **28.** *Cricket.* the catching of a ball struck by a batsman before it touches the ground, resulting in him being out. **29.** *Music.* a type of round having a humorous text that is often indecent or bawdy and hard to articulate. ~See also **catch on, catch out, catch up.** [C13 *cacchen* to pursue, from OF *cachier*, from L *captāre* to snatch, from *capere* to seize] —'**catchable** *adj.*

catch-22 *n.* a situation in which a person is frustrated by a set of circumstances that preclude any attempt to escape from them. [C20: from the title of a novel (1961) by J. Heller]

catch-as-catch-can *n.* a style of wrestling in which trips, holds below the waist, etc., are allowed.

catchfly ('kætʃ,flaɪ) *n., pl.* **-flies.** any of various plants that have sticky calyxes and stems on which insects are sometimes trapped.

catching ('kætʃɪŋ) *adj.* **1.** infectious. **2.** attractive; captivating.

catching pen *n. Austral. & N.Z.* a pen adjacent to a shearer's stand containing the sheep ready for shearing.

catchment ('kætʃmənt) *n.* **1.** the act of catching or collecting water. **2.** a structure in which water is collected. **3.** the water so collected. **4.** *Brit.* the intake of a school from one catchment area.

catchment area *n.* **1.** the area of land bounded by watersheds draining into a river, basin, or reservoir. **2.** the area

from which people are allocated to a particular school, hospital, etc.

catch on *vb.* (*intr., adv.*) *Inf.* **1.** to become popular or fashionable. **2.** to understand.

catch out *vb.* (*tr., adv.*) *Inf., chiefly Brit.* to trap (a person), esp. in an error.

catchpenny ('kætʃ,pɛnɪ) *adj.* (*prenominal*) designed to have instant appeal, esp. in order to sell quickly: *catchpenny ornaments.*

catch phrase *n.* a well-known frequently used phrase, esp. one associated with a particular group, etc.

catch up *vb.* (*adv.*) **1.** (*tr.*) to seize and take up (something) quickly. **2.** (when *intr.*, often foll. by *with*) to reach or pass (someone or something): *he caught him up.* **3.** (*intr.*; usually foll. by *on* or *with*) to make up for lost ground or deal with a backlog. **4.** (*tr.*; *often passive*) to absorb or involve: *she was caught up in her reading.* **5.** (*tr.*) to raise by or as if by fastening.

catchweight ('kætʃ,weɪt) *adj. Wrestling.* of or relating to a contest in which normal weight categories have been waived by agreement.

catchword ('kætʃ,wɜːd) *n.* **1.** a word or phrase made temporarily popular; slogan. **2.** a word printed as a running head in a book. **3.** *Theatre.* an actor's cue to speak or enter. **4.** the first word of a page repeated at the bottom of the page preceding.

catchy ('kætʃɪ) *adj.* **catchier, catchiest. 1.** (of a tune, etc.) pleasant and easily remembered. **2.** deceptive: *a catchy question.* **3.** irregular: *a catchy breeze.*

cat cracker *n.* an informal name for **catalytic cracker.**

catechetical (,kætɪ'kɛtɪkəl) *or* **catechetic** *adj.* of or relating to teaching by question and answer. —,**cate'chetically** *adv.*

catechism ('kætɪ,kɪzəm) *n.* instruction by a series of questions and answers, esp. a book containing such instruction on the religious doctrine of a Christian Church. [C16: from LL, ult. from Gk *katēkhizein* to CATECHIZE] —,**cate'chismal** *adj.*

catechize *or* **-ise** ('kætɪ,kaɪz) *vb.* (*tr.*) **1.** to teach or examine by means of questions and answers. **2.** to give oral instruction in Christianity, esp. by using a catechism. **3.** to put questions to (someone). [C15: from LL, from Gk *katēkhizein*, from *katēkhein* to instruct orally, from *kata*-down + *ēkhein* to sound] —'**catechist, 'cate,chizer** *or* **-iser** *n.*

catechu ('kætɪ,tʃuː) *or* **cachou** *n.* an astringent resinous substance obtained from certain tropical plants, and used in medicine, tanning, and dyeing. [C17: prob. from Malay *kachu*]

catechumen (,kætɪ'kjuːmɛn) *n. Christianity.* a person, esp. in the early Church, undergoing instruction prior to baptism. [C15: via OF, from LL, from Gk *katēkhoumenos* one being instructed verbally]

categorial (,kætɪ'gɔːrɪəl) *adj.* **1.** of or relating to a category. **2.** *Logic.* (of a statement) consisting of a subject, S, and a predicate, P, each of which denote a class, as in: *all S are P.*

categorical (,kætɪ'gɒrɪkəl) *or* **categoric** *adj.* **1.** unqualified; unconditional: *a categorical statement.* **2.** relating to or included in a category. **3.** another word for **categorial** (sense 2). —,**cate'gorically** *adv.*

categorize *or* **-ise** ('kætɪgə,raɪz) *vb.* (*tr.*) to place in a category. —,**categori'zation** *or* **-i'sation** *n.*

category ('kætɪgərɪ) *n., pl.* **-ries. 1.** a class or group of things, people, etc., possessing some quality or qualities in common. **2.** *Metaphysics.* one of the most basic classes into which objects and concepts can be analysed. **3. a.** (in the philosophy of Aristotle) any one of ten most fundamental modes of being, such as quantity, quality, and substance. **b.** (in the philosophy of Kant) one of twelve concepts required by human beings to interpret the empirical world. [C15: from LL, from Gk *katēgoria*, from *katēgorein* to accuse, assert]

catena (kə'tiːnə) *n., pl.* **-nae** (-niː). a connected series, esp. of patristic comments on the Bible. [C17: from L: chain]

catenary (kə'tiːnərɪ) *n., pl.* **-ries. 1.** the curve formed by a heavy uniform flexible cord hanging freely from two points. **2.** the hanging cable between pylons along a railway track, from which the trolley wire is suspended. ~*adj.* **3.** of, resembling, relating to, or constructed using a catenary or suspended chain. [C18: from L *catēnārius* relating to a chain]

catenate ('kætɪˌneɪt) vb. Biol. to arrange or be arranged in a series of chains or rings. [C17: from L catēnāre to bind with chains] —ˌcate'nation n.

cater ('keɪtə) vb. 1. (intr.; foll. by for or to) to provide what is required or desired (for). 2. (when intr., foll. by for) to provide food, services, etc. (for): we cater for parties. [C16: from earlier catour purchaser, var. of acatour, from Anglo-Norman acater to buy] —'catering n.

cater-cornered ('kætəˌkɔːnəd) adj., adv. U.S. & Canad. inf. diagonal. Also: **catty-cornered**. [C16: from dialect cater (adv.) diagonally, from obs. cater (n.) four-spot of dice, from OF quatre four, from L quattuor]

caterer ('keɪtərə) n. one who as a profession provides food for large social events, etc.

caterpillar ('kætəˌpɪlə) n. 1. the wormlike larva of butterflies and moths, having numerous pairs of legs and powerful biting jaws. 2. an endless track, driven by sprockets or wheels, used to propel a heavy vehicle. 3. a vehicle, such as a tractor, tank, etc., driven by such tracks. [C15 catyrpel, prob. from OF catepelose, lit.: hairy cat]

caterwaul ('kætəˌwɔːl) vb. (intr.) 1. to make a yowling noise, as a cat on heat. ~n. 2. a yell made by or sounding like a cat on heat. [C14: imit.]

catfish ('kætˌfɪʃ) n., pl. -fish or -fishes. 1. any of numerous mainly freshwater fishes having whisker-like barbels around the mouth. 2. another name for **wolffish**.

cat flap or **door** n. a small flap or door in a larger door through which a cat can pass.

catgut ('kætˌgʌt) n. a strong cord made from the dried intestines of sheep and other animals that is used for stringing certain musical instruments and sports rackets.

Cath. abbrev. for: 1. Cathedral. 2. Catholic.

cath- prefix. a variant of **cata-** before an aspirate: cathode.

Cathar ('kæθə) or **Catharist** ('kæθərɪst) n., pl. -ars, -ari (-əri) or -arists. a member of a Christian sect in Provence in the 12th and 13th centuries who believed the material world was evil and only the spiritual was good. [from Med. L, from Gk katharoi the pure] —'Cathar,ism n.

catharsis (kə'θɑːsɪs) n. 1. the purging or purification of the emotions through the evocation of pity and fear, as in tragedy. 2. Psychoanal. the bringing of repressed ideas or experiences into consciousness, thus relieving tensions. 3. purgation, esp. of the bowels. [C19: NL, from Gk katharsis, from kathairein to purge, purify]

cathartic (kə'θɑːtɪk) adj. 1. purgative. 2. effecting catharsis. ~n. 3. a purgative drug or agent. —ca'thartically adv.

Cathay (kæ'θeɪ) n. a literary or archaic name for **China**. [C14: from Med. L Cataya]

cathead ('kætˌhɛd) n. a fitting at the bow of a vessel for securing the anchor when raised.

cathedral (kə'θiːdrəl) n. a. the principal church of a diocese, containing the bishop's official throne. b. (as modifier): a cathedral city. [C13: from LL (ecclesia) cathedrālis cathedral (church), from Gk kathedra seat]

Catherine ('kæθrɪn) n. Saint. died 307 A.D., legendary Christian martyr of Alexandria, who was tortured on a spiked wheel and beheaded. Feast day: Nov. 25.

Catherine I n. ?1684–1727, second wife of Peter the Great, whom she succeeded as empress of Russia (1725–27).

Catherine II n. known as Catherine the Great. 1729–96, empress of Russia (1762–96), during whose reign Russia extended her boundaries at the expense of Turkey, Sweden, and Poland: she was a patron of literature and the arts.

Catherine de' Medici or **de Médicis** n. 1519–89, queen of Henry II of France; mother of Francis II, Charles IX, and Henry III of France; regent of France (1560–74). She was largely responsible for the massacre of Protestants on Saint Bartholomew's Day (1572).

Catherine of Aragon n. 1485–1536, first wife of Henry VIII of England and mother of Mary I. The annulment of Henry's marriage to her (1533) against papal authority marked an initial stage in the English Reformation.

Catherine of Siena n. Saint. 1347–80, Italian mystic and ascetic; patron saint of the Dominican order. Feast day: April 30.

Catherine wheel n. 1. a firework which rotates, producing sparks and coloured flame. 2. a circular window having ribs radiating from the centre. [C16: after St CATHERINE of Alexandria]

catheter ('kæθɪtə) n. Med. a long slender flexible tube for inserting into a bodily cavity for introducing or withdrawing fluid. [C17: from LL, from Gk kathetēr, from kathienai to insert]

catheterize or **-ise** ('kæθɪtəˌraɪz) vb. (tr.) to insert a catheter into.

cathexis (kə'θɛksɪs) n., pl. -thexes (-'θɛksiːz). Psychoanal. concentration of psychic energy on a single goal. [C20: from NL, from Gk kathexis, from katekhein to hold fast]

cathode ('kæθəʊd) n. 1. the negative electrode in an electrolytic cell. 2. the negatively charged electron source in an electronic valve. 3. the positive terminal of a primary cell. ~Cf. **anode**. [C19: from Gk kathodos a descent, from kata- down + hodos way] —**cathodal** (kæ'θəʊdəl) or **cathodic** (kæ'θɒdɪk, -'θəʊ-) adj.

cathode rays pl. n. a stream of electrons emitted from the surface of a cathode in a vacuum tube.

cathode-ray tube n. a vacuum tube in which a beam of electrons is focused onto a fluorescent screen to give a visible spot of light. The device is used in television receivers, visual display units, etc.

catholic ('kæθəlɪk, 'kæθlɪk) adj. 1. universal; relating to all men. 2. broad-minded; liberal. [C14: from L, from Gk katholikos universal, from kata- according to + holos whole] —**catholically** or **catholicly** (kə'θɒlɪklɪ) adv.

Catholic ('kæθəlɪk, 'kæθlɪk) Christianity. ~adj. 1. denoting or relating to the entire body of Christians, esp. to the Church before separation into the Eastern and Western Churches. 2. denoting or relating to the Latin or Western Church after this separation. 3. denoting or relating to the Roman Catholic Church. ~n. 4. a member of the Roman Catholic Church.

Catholicism (kə'θɒlɪˌsɪzəm) n. 1. short for **Roman Catholicism**. 2. the beliefs, practices, etc., of any Catholic Church.

catholicity (ˌkæθə'lɪsɪtɪ) n. 1. a wide range of interests, tastes, etc. 2. comprehensiveness.

catholicize or **-cise** (kə'θɒlɪˌsaɪz) vb. 1. to make or become catholic. 2. (often cap.) to convert to or become converted to Catholicism.

Catiline ('kætɪˌlaɪn) n. Latin name Lucius Sergius Catilina. ?108–62 B.C., Roman politician: organized an unsuccessful conspiracy against Cicero (63–62). —**Catilinarian** (ˌkætɪlɪ'nɛərɪən) adj.

cation ('kætaɪən) n. a positively charged ion; an ion that is attracted to the cathode during electrolysis. Cf. **anion**. [C19: from CATA- + ION] —**cationic** (ˌkætaɪ'ɒnɪk) adj.

catkin ('kætkɪn) n. an inflorescence consisting of a hanging spike of much reduced flowers of either sex: occurs in birch, hazel, etc. [C16: from obs. katteken kitten]

cat litter n. absorbent material used to line a receptacle in which a domestic cat can urinate and defecate.

catmint ('kætˌmɪnt) n. a Eurasian plant having spikes of purple-spotted white flowers and scented leaves of which cats are fond. Also called: **catnip**.

catnap ('kætˌnæp) n. 1. a short sleep or doze. ~vb. -napping, -napped. 2. (intr.) to sleep or doze for a short time or intermittently.

Cato ('keɪtəʊ) n. 1. **Marcus Porcius** ('mɑːkəs 'pɔːʃɪəs), known as Cato the Elder or the Censor. 234–149 B.C., Roman statesman and writer, noted for his relentless opposition to Carthage. 2. his great-grandson, **Marcus Porcius**, known as Cato the Younger or Uticensis. 95–46 B.C., Roman statesman, general, and Stoic philosopher; opponent of Catiline and Caesar.

cat-o'-nine-tails n., pl. -tails. a rope whip consisting of nine knotted thongs, used formerly to flog prisoners. Often shortened to **cat**.

CAT scanner (kæt) n. former name for **CT scanner**. [C20: from Computerized Axial Tomography]

cat's cradle n. a game played by making patterns with a loop of string between the fingers.

cat's-eye n. any of a group of gemstones that reflect a streak of light when cut in a rounded unfaceted shape.

Catseye ('kætsaɪ) n. Trademark, Brit. a glass reflector set into a small fixture, placed at intervals along roads to indicate traffic lanes at night.

Catskill Mountains ('kætskɪl) pl. n. a mountain range in SE New York State: resort. Highest peak: Slide Mountain, 1261 m (4204 ft.). Also called: **Catskills**.

cat's-paw n. 1. a person used by another as a tool; dupe. 2. a pattern of ripples on the surface of water caused by a light wind. [(sense 1) C18: so called from the tale of the monkey who used a cat's paw to draw chestnuts out of a fire]

catsup ('kætsəp) *n.* a variant spelling (esp. U.S.) of **ketchup.**

cat's whisker *n.* a pointed wire formerly used to make contact with a crystal in a crystal radio receiver.

cat's whiskers *or* **cat's pyjamas** *n.* **the.** *Sl.* a person or thing that is excellent or superior.

Cattegat ('kætɪˌgæt) *n.* a variant spelling of **Kattegat.**

cattery ('kætərɪ) *n.*, *pl.* **-teries.** a place where cats are bred or looked after.

cattle ('kætəl) *n.* (*functioning as pl.*) **1.** bovid mammals of the tribe *Bovini* (bovines). **2.** Also called: **domestic cattle.** any domesticated bovine mammals. [C13: from OF *chatel* CHATTEL]

cattle-stop *n.* the New Zealand name for a **cattle-grid.**

cattle-cake *n.* concentrated food for cattle in the form of cakes.

cattle-grid *n.* a grid of metal bars covering a hole dug in a roadway intended to prevent the passage of livestock while allowing vehicles, etc., to pass unhindered.

cattleman ('kætəlmən) *n.*, *pl.* **-men.** **1.** a person who breeds, rears, or tends cattle. **2.** *Chiefly U.S. & Canad.* a person who rears cattle on a large scale.

catty ('kætɪ) *or* **cattish** *adj.* **-tier, -tiest.** **1.** *Inf.* spiteful: *a catty remark.* **2.** of or resembling a cat. — '**cattily** *or* '**cattishly** *adv.* — '**cattiness** *or* '**cattishness** *n.*

Catullus (kə'tʌləs) *n.* **Gaius Valerius** ('gaɪəs və'lɪərɪəs). ?84–?54 B.C., Roman lyric poet, noted particularly for his love poems. —**Catullan** (kə'tʌlən) *adj.*

catwalk ('kætˌwɔːk) *n.* a narrow pathway over the stage of a theatre, along a bridge, etc.

Cauca (*Spanish* 'kauka) *n.* a river in W Colombia, rising in the northwest and flowing north to the Magdalena River. Length: about 1350 km (840 miles).

Caucasia (kɔː'keɪzɪə, -ʒə) *n.* a region of the SW Soviet Union, between the Caspian Sea and the Black Sea: contains the Caucasus Mountains, dividing it into Ciscaucasia in the north and Transcaucasia in the south; one of the most complex ethnic areas in the world, with over 50 different peoples. Also called: the **Caucasus.**

Caucasian (kɔː'keɪzɪən) *adj.* **1.** another word for **Caucasoid.** **2.** of or relating to the Caucasus. ∼*n.* **3.** a member of the Caucasoid race; a White person. **4.** a native or inhabitant of the Caucasus.

Caucasoid ('kɔːkəˌzɔɪd) *adj.* **1.** denoting or belonging to the light-complexioned racial group of mankind, which includes the peoples indigenous to Europe, N Africa, SW Asia, and the Indian subcontinent. ∼*n.* **2.** a member of this racial group.

Caucasus ('kɔːkəsəs) *n.* **the.** **1.** a mountain range in the SW Soviet Union, in Caucasia between the Black Sea and the Caspian Sea: mostly over 2700 m (9000 ft.). Highest peak: Mount Elbrus, 5642 m (18 510 ft.). Also called: **Caucasus Mountains.** **2.** another name for **Caucasia.**

Cauchy ('kauʃɪ; *French* koʃi) *n.* **Augustin Louis** (ogystɛ̃ lwi), Baron Cauchy. 1789–1857, French mathematician, noted for his work on the theory of functions and the wave theory of light.

caucus ('kɔːkəs) *n.*, *pl.* **-cuses.** **1.** *Chiefly U.S. & Canad.* a closed meeting of the members of one party in a legislative chamber, etc., to coordinate policy, choose candidates, etc. **2.** *Chiefly U.S.* a local meeting of party members. **3.** *Brit.* a group or faction within a larger group, esp. a political party, who discuss tactics, choose candidates, etc. **4.** *N.Z.* a formal meeting of all MPs of one party. **5.** *Austral.* a group of MPs from one party who meet to discuss tactics, etc. ∼*vb.* **6.** (*intr.*) to hold a caucus. [C18: prob. of Algonquian origin]

caudal ('kɔːdəl) *adj.* **1.** *Anat.* of the posterior part of the body. **2.** *Zool.* resembling or in the position of the tail. [C17: from NL, from L *cauda* tail] — '**caudally** *adv.*

caudal fin *n.* the tail fin of fishes and some other aquatic vertebrates, used for propulsion.

caudate ('kɔːdeɪt) *adj.* having a tail or a tail-like appendage. [C17: from NL *caudātus*, from L *cauda* tail] —**cau'dation** *n.*

caudillo (kɔː'diːljəʊ) *n.*, *pl.* **-los** (-ljəʊz). (in Spanish-speaking countries) a military or political leader. [Sp., from LL *capitellum*, dim. of L *caput* head]

Caudine Forks ('kɔːdaɪn) *pl. n.* a narrow pass in the Apennines, in S Italy, between Capua and Benevento: scene of the defeat of the Romans by the Samnites (321 B.C.).

caudle ('kɔːdəl) *n.* a hot spiced wine drink made with gruel, formerly used medicinally. [C13: from OF *caudel*, from Med. L, from L *calidus* warm]

caught (kɔːt) *vb.* the past tense and past participle of **catch.**

caul (kɔːl) *n. Anat.* a portion of the amniotic sac sometimes covering a child's head at birth. [C13: from OF *cale*, back formation from *calotte* close-fitting cap, of Gmc origin]

cauldron *or* **caldron** ('kɔːldrən) *n.* a large pot used for boiling, esp. one with handles. [C13: from Anglo-F, from L *caldārium* hot bath, from *calidus* warm]

cauliflower ('kɒlɪˌflaʊə) *n.* **1.** a variety of cabbage having a large edible head of crowded white flowers on a very short thick stem. **2.** the flower head of this plant, used as a vegetable. [C16: from It. *caoli fiori*, lit.: cabbage flowers]

cauliflower ear *n.* permanent swelling and distortion of the external ear as the result of ruptures of the blood vessels: usually caused by blows received in boxing.

caulk *or* **calk** (kɔːk) *vb.* **1.** to stop up (cracks, crevices, etc.) with a filler. **2.** *Naut.* to pack (the seams) between the planks of the bottom of (a vessel) with waterproof material to prevent leakage. [C15: from OF *cauquer* to press down, from L *calcāre* to trample, from *calx* heel]

causal ('kɔːzəl) *adj.* **1.** acting as or being a cause. **2.** stating, involving, or implying a cause: *the causal part of the argument.* — '**causally** *adv.*

causality (kɔː'zælɪtɪ) *n.*, *pl.* **-ties.** **1. a.** the relationship of cause and effect. **b.** the principle that nothing can happen without being caused. **2.** causal agency or quality.

causation (kɔː'zeɪʃən) *n.* **1.** the production of an effect by a cause. **2.** the relationship of cause and effect. —**cau'sational** *adj.*

causative ('kɔːzətɪv) *adj.* **1.** *Grammar.* relating to a form or class of verbs, such as *persuade*, that express causation. **2.** (*often postpositive and foll. by of*) producing an effect. ∼*n.* **3.** the causative form or class of verbs. — '**causatively** *adv.*

cause (kɔːz) *n.* **1.** a person, thing, event, state, or action that produces an effect. **2.** grounds for action; justification: *she had good cause to shout like that.* **3.** the ideals, etc., of a group or movement: *the Communist cause.* **4.** the welfare or interests of a person or group in a dispute: *they fought for the miners' cause.* **5. a.** a ground for legal action; matter giving rise to a lawsuit. **b.** the lawsuit itself. **6.** *Arch.* a subject of debate or discussion. **7. make common cause with.** to join with (a person, group, etc.) for a common objective. ∼*vb.* **8.** (*tr.*) to be the cause of; bring about. [C13: from L *causa* cause, reason, motive] — '**causeless** *adj.*

cause célèbre ('kɔːz sə'lɛbrə) *n.*, *pl.* **causes célèbres** ('kɔːz sə'lɛbrəz). a famous lawsuit, trial, or controversy. [C19: from F: famous case]

causerie ('kəʊzərɪ) *n.* an informal talk or conversational piece of writing. [C19: from F, from *causer* to chat]

causeway ('kɔːzˌweɪ) *n.* **1.** a raised path or road crossing water, marshland, etc. **2.** a paved footpath. [C15 *cauciwey* (from *cauci* + WAY); *cauci* paved road, from Med. L, from L *calx* limestone]

caustic ('kɔːstɪk) *adj.* **1.** capable of burning or corroding by chemical action: *caustic soda.* **2.** sarcastic; cutting: *a caustic reply.* ∼*n.* **3.** Also called: **caustic surface.** a surface that envelops the light rays reflected or refracted by a curved surface. **4.** Also called: **caustic curve.** a curve formed by the intersection of a caustic surface with a plane. **5.** *Chem.* a caustic substance, esp. an alkali. [C14: from L, from Gk *kaustikos*, from *kaiein* to burn] — '**caustically** *adv.* —**causticity** (kɔː'stɪsɪtɪ) *n.*

caustic potash *n.* another name for **potassium hydroxide.**

caustic soda *n.* another name for **sodium hydroxide.**

cauterize *or* **-ise** ('kɔːtəˌraɪz) *vb.* (*tr.*) (esp. in the treatment of a wound) to burn or sear (body tissue) with a hot iron or caustic agent. [C14: from OF, from LL, from *cautērium* branding iron, from Gk *kautērion*, from *kaiein* to burn] —ˌ**cauteri'zation** *or* **-i'sation** *n.*

cautery ('kɔːtərɪ) *n.*, *pl.* **-teries.** **1.** the coagulation of blood or destruction of body tissue by cauterizing. **2.** an instrument or agent for cauterizing. [C14: from OF *cautère*, from L *cautērium*]

caution ('kɔːʃən) n. **1.** care, forethought, or prudence, esp. in the face of danger. **2.** something intended or serving as a warning. **3.** *Law, chiefly Brit.* a formal warning given to a person suspected of an offence that his words will be taken down and may be used in evidence. **4.** *Inf.* an amusing or surprising person or thing. ~*vb.* **5.** (*tr.*) to warn (a person) to be careful. **6.** (*tr.*) *Law, chiefly Brit.* to give a caution to (a person). **7.** (*intr.*) to warn, urge, or advise: *he cautioned against optimism.* [C13: from OF, from L *cautiō*, from *cavēre* to beware]

cautionary ('kɔːʃənərɪ) adj. serving as a warning; intended to warn: *a cautionary tale.*

cautious ('kɔːʃəs) adj. showing or having caution. — **'cautiously** adv. — **'cautiousness** n.

Cauvery or **Kaveri** ('kɔːvərɪ) n. a river in S India, rising in the Western Ghats and flowing southeast to the Bay of Bengal. Length: 765 km (475 miles).

Cavaco Silva ('kavaku 'silvə) n. **Anibal** (a'nibal). born 1939, Portuguese statesman; prime minister of Portugal from 1985.

Cavafy (kə'vɑːfɪ) n. **Constantine.** Greek name *Kavafis.* 1863–1933, Greek poet of Alexandria in Egypt.

cavalcade (ˌkævəl'keɪd) n. **1.** a procession of people on horseback, in cars, etc. **2.** any procession. [C16: from F, from It., from *cavalcare* to ride on horseback, from LL, from *caballus* horse]

cavalier (ˌkævə'lɪə) adj. **1.** supercilious; offhand. ~n. **2.** a courtly gentleman, esp. one acting as a lady's escort. **3.** *Arch.* a horseman, esp. one who is armed. [C16: from It., from OProvençal, from LL *caballārius* rider, from *caballus* horse, from F] — ˌcava'lierly adv.

Cavalier (ˌkævə'lɪə) n. a supporter of Charles I during the English Civil War.

cavalry ('kævəlrɪ) n., pl. **-ries. 1.** (esp. formerly) the part of an army composed of mounted troops. **2.** the armoured element of a modern army. **3.** (*as modifier*): *a cavalry unit.* [C16: from F *cavallerie*, from It., from *cavaliere* horseman] — **'cavalryman** n.

Cavan ('kævən) n. **1.** a county of N Ireland: hilly, with many small lakes and bogs. County town: Cavan. Pop.: 53 855 (1981). Area: 1890 sq. km (730 sq. miles). **2.** a market town in N Ireland, county town of Co. Cavan. Pop.: 5035 (1981).

cavatina (ˌkævə'tiːnə) n., pl. **-ne** (-nɪ). **1.** a simple solo song. **2.** an instrumental composition reminiscent of this. [C19: from It.]

cave[1] (keɪv) n. **1.** an underground hollow with access from the ground surface or from the sea. **2.** *Brit. history.* a secession or a group seceding from a political party on some issue. **3.** (*modifier*) living in caves. ~*vb.* **4.** (*tr.*) to hollow out. [C13: from OF, from L *cava*, pl. of *cavum* cavity, from *cavus* hollow]

cave[2] ('keɪvɪ) *Brit. school sl.* ~n. **1.** lookout: *keep cave.* ~*sentence substitute.* **2.** watch out! [from L *cavē* beware!]

caveat ('keɪvɪˌæt, 'kæv-) n. **1.** *Law.* a formal notice requesting the court not to take a certain action without warning the person lodging the caveat. **2.** a caution. [C16: from L, lit.: let him beware]

caveat emptor ('ɛmptɔː) n. the principle that the buyer must bear the risk for the quality of goods purchased. [L: let the buyer beware]

cave in vb. (*intr., adv.*) **1.** to collapse; subside. **2.** *Inf.* to yield completely, esp. under pressure. ~n. **cave-in. 3.** the sudden collapse of a roof, piece of ground, etc. **4.** the site of such a collapse, as at a mine or tunnel.

cavel ('keɪvᵊl) n. *N.Z.* a drawing of lots among miners for an easy and profitable place at the coalface. [C19: from E dialect *cavel* to cast lots, apportion]

Cavell ('kævᵊl) n. **Edith Louisa.** 1865–1915, English nurse: executed by the Germans in World War I for helping Allied prisoners to escape.

caveman ('keɪvˌmæn) n., pl. **-men. 1.** a man of the Palaeolithic age; cave dweller. **2.** *Inf.* a man who is primitive or brutal in behaviour, etc.

cavendish ('kævəndɪʃ) n. tobacco that has been sweetened and pressed into moulds to form bars. [C19: ?from the name of the first maker]

Cavendish ('kævəndɪʃ) n. **Henry.** 1731–1810, English physicist and chemist: recognized hydrogen, determined the composition of water, and calculated the density of the earth by an experiment named after him.

cavern ('kævᵊn) n. **1.** a cave, esp. when large. ~*vb.* (*tr.*) **2.** to shut in or as if in a cavern. **3.** to hollow out. [C14: from OF *caverne*, from L *caverna*, from *cavus* hollow]

cavernous ('kævənəs) adj. **1.** suggestive of a cavern in vastness, etc.: *cavernous eyes.* **2.** filled with small cavities. **3.** (of rocks) containing caverns.

caviar or **caviare** ('kævɪˌɑː, ˌkævɪ'ɑː) n. the salted roe of sturgeon, usually served as an hors d'oeuvre. [C16: from earlier *cavery*, from OIt. *caviari*, pl. of *caviaro* caviar, from Turkish *havyār*]

cavil ('kævɪl) vb. **-illing, -illed** or *U.S.* **-iling, -iled. 1.** (*intr.*; foll. by *at* or *about*) to raise annoying petty objections. ~n. **2.** a trifling objection. [C16: from OF, from L *cavillārī* to jeer, from *cavilla* raillery] — **'caviller** n.

caving ('keɪvɪŋ) n. the sport of climbing in and exploring caves. — **'caver** n.

Cavite (kə'viːtɪ, -teɪ) n. a port in the N Philippines, in S Luzon on Manila Bay: U.S. naval base. Pop.: 87 666 (1980).

cavity ('kævɪtɪ) n., pl. **-ties. 1.** a hollow space. **2.** *Dentistry.* a decayed area on a tooth. **3.** any empty or hollow space within the body. [C16: from F, from LL *cavitās*, from L *cavus* hollow]

cavity wall n. a wall that consists of two separate walls with an airspace between them.

cavort (kə'vɔːt) vb. (*intr.*) to prance; caper. [C19: ?from CURVET] — **ca'vorter** n.

Cavour (*Italian* ka'vur) n. **Conte Camillo Benso di** (ka'millo 'bɛnzo di). 1810–61, Italian statesman and premier of Piedmont-Sardinia (1852–59; 1860–61): a leader of the movement for the unification of Italy.

cavy ('keɪvɪ) n., pl. **-vies.** a small South American rodent having a thickset body and very small tail. See also **guinea pig.** [C18: from NL *Cavia*, from Carib *cabiai*]

caw (kɔː) n. **1.** the cry of a crow, rook, or raven. ~*vb.* **2.** (*intr.*) to make this cry. [C16: imit.]

Cawdrey ('kɔːdrɪ) n. **Robert.** 16th–17th-century English schoolmaster and lexicographer: compiled the first English dictionary (*A Table Alphabeticall*) in 1604.

Cawley ('kɔːlɪ) n. **Evonne** (née *Goolagong*). born 1951, Australian tennis player: Wimbledon champion 1971 and 1980; Australian champion 1974–76.

Cawnpore (ˌkɔːn'pɔː) or **Cawnpur** (ˌkɔːn'puə) n. the former name of **Kanpur.**

CAWU *abbrev. for* Clerical and Administrative Workers' Union.

Caxton ('kækstən) n. **William.** ?1422–91, English printer and translator: published, in Bruges, the first book printed in English (1475) and established the first printing press in England (1477).

cay (keɪ, kiː) n. a small low island or bank composed of sand and coral fragments. [C18: from Sp. *cayo*, prob. from OF *quai* QUAY]

Cayenne (keɪ'ɛn) n. the capital of French Guiana, on an island at the mouth of the Cayenne River: French penal settlement from 1854 to 1938. Pop.: 38 091 (1982).

cayenne pepper (keɪ'ɛn) n. a very hot red condiment made from the dried seeds of various capsicums. Often shortened to **cayenne.** Also called: **red pepper.** [C18: ult. from Tupi *quiynha*]

Cayes (keɪ; *French* kaj) n. short for **Les Cayes.**

cayman or **caiman** ('keɪmən) n., pl. **-mans.** a tropical American crocodilian similar to alligators but with a more heavily armoured belly. [C16: from Sp. *caimán*, from Carib *cayman*]

Cayman Islands ('keɪmən) pl. n. three coral islands in the Caribbean Sea northwest of Jamaica: a dependency of Jamaica until 1962, now a British crown colony. Capital: George Town. Pop.: 22 900 (1987 est.). Area: about 260 sq. km (100 sq. miles).

CB *abbrev. for:* **1.** Citizens' Band. **2.** Companion of the (Order of the) Bath (a Brit. title). **3.** County Borough.

CBC *abbrev. for* Canadian Broadcasting Corporation.

CBE *abbrev. for* Commander of the (Order of the) British Empire.

CBI *abbrev. for:* **1.** *U.S.* Central Bureau of Investigation. **2.** Confederation of British Industry.

cc or **c.c.** *abbrev. for:* **1.** carbon copy or copies. **2.** cubic centimetre(s).

CC *abbrev. for:* **1.** City Council. **2.** County Council. **3.** Cricket Club.

cc. *abbrev. for* chapters.

C clef *n. Music.* a symbol (𝄡), placed at the beginning of the staff, establishing the position of middle C: see **alto clef, soprano clef, tenor clef.**

CCTV *abbrev. for* closed-circuit television.

cd *symbol for* candela.

Cd *the chemical symbol for* cadmium.

CD *abbrev. for:* **1.** Civil Defence (Corps). **2.** compact disc. **3.** Corps Diplomatique (Diplomatic Corps).

CDI *abbrev. for* compact disc interactive.

Cdn *abbrev. for* Canadian.

Cdr *Mil. abbrev. for* Commander.

CD player *n.* a device for playing compact discs. In full: **compact-disc player.**

CD-ROM (-rɒm) *abbrev. for* compact disc read only memory; a compact disc used for storing written information to be displayed on a visual-display unit.

CDT (in the U.S. and Canada) *abbrev. for* Central Daylight Time.

CD-video *n.* a compact-disc player that, when connected to a television and hi-fi, produces high-quality stereo sound and synchronized pictures from a disc resembling a compact audio disc. In full **compact-disc video.**

CDV *abbrev. for* compact disc video.

Ce *the chemical symbol for* cerium.

CE *abbrev. for:* **1.** Church of England. **2.** civil engineer. **3.** Common Era.

Ceará (*Portuguese* sia'ra) *n.* **1.** a state of NE Brazil: sandy coastal plain, rising to a high plateau. Capital: Fortaleza. Pop.: 5 294 876 (1980). Area: 150 630 sq. km (58 746 sq. miles). **2.** another name for **Fortaleza.**

cease (si:s) *vb.* **1.** (when *tr.*, may take a gerund or an infinitive as object) to bring or come to an end. ~*n.* **2.** **without cease.** without stopping. [C14: from OF, from L *cessāre,* frequentative of *cēdere* to yield]

cease-fire *Chiefly mil.* ~*n.* **1.** a period of truce, esp. one that is temporary. ~*sentence substitute, n.* **2.** the order to stop firing.

ceaseless ('si:slɪs) *adj.* without stop or pause; incessant. — **'ceaselessly** *adv.*

Ceauşescu (tʃaʊ'ʃesku:) *n.* **Nicolae** (ˌnɪkɒ'laɪ). born 1918, Romanian statesman; chairman of the state council from 1967 and president of Romania from 1974.

Cebú (sɪ'bu:) *n.* **1.** an island in the central Philippines. Pop.: 2 091 602 (1980). Area: 4422 sq. km (1707 sq. miles). **2.** a port in the Philippines, on E Cebú island. Pop.: 552 250 (1984).

Cechy ('tʃexi) *n.* the Czech name for **Bohemia.**

Cecil ('sɛsᵊl, 'sɪs-) *n.* **1.** Lord **David.** 1902–86, English literary critic and biographer. **2.** **Robert.** See (3rd Marquess of) **Salisbury. 3.** **William.** See (William Cecil) **Burghley.**

Cecilia (sɪ'si:ljə) *n.* **Saint.** died ?230 A.D., Roman martyr; patron saint of music. Feast day: Nov. 22.

Cecrops ('si:krɒps) *n.* (in ancient Greek tradition) the first king of Attica, represented as half-human, half-dragon.

cecum ('si:kəm) *n., pl.* -**ca** (-kə). *U.S.* a variant spelling of **caecum.** — **'cecal** *adj.*

cedar ('si:də) *n.* **1.** any of a genus of Old World coniferous trees having needle-like evergreen leaves, and erect barrel-shaped cones. See also **cedar of Lebanon, deodar. 2.** of various other conifers, such as the red cedars and white cedars. **3.** the wood of any of these trees. ~*adj.* **4.** made of the wood of a cedar tree. [C13: from OF, from L *cedrus,* from Gk *kedros*]

cedar of Lebanon ('lɛbənən) *n.* a cedar of SW Asia with level spreading branches and fragrant wood.

Cedar Rapids *n.* a city in E Iowa. Pop.: 110 243 (1980).

cede (si:d) *vb.* **1.** (when *intr.*, often foll. by *to*) to transfer, make over, or surrender (something, esp. territory or legal rights). **2.** (*tr.*) to allow or concede (a point in an argument, etc.). [C17: from L *cēdere* to yield] — '**ceder** *n.*

cedilla (sɪ'dɪlə) *n.* a character (͵) placed underneath a *c* before *a, o,* or *u,* esp. in French and Portuguese, denoting that it is to be pronounced (s), not (k). [C16: from Sp.: little *z,* from *ceda* zed, from LL *zeta*]

Ceefax ('si:fæks) *n. Trademark.* the BBC teletext service.

CEGB (in Britain) *abbrev. for* Central Electricity Generating Board.

ceil (si:l) *vb.* (*tr.*) **1.** to line (a ceiling) with plaster, etc. **2.** to provide with a ceiling. [C15 *celen,* ? back formation from CEILING]

ceilidh ('keɪlɪ) *n.* (esp. in Scotland and Ireland) an informal social gathering with singing, dancing, and storytelling. [C19: from Gaelic]

ceiling ('si:lɪŋ) *n.* **1.** the inner upper surface of a room. **2.** an upper limit, such as one set by regulation on prices or wages. **3.** the upper altitude to which an aircraft can climb measured under specified conditions. **4.** *Meteorol.* the highest level in the atmosphere from which the earth's surface is visible at a particular time, usually the base of a cloud layer. [C14: from ?]

celadon ('sɛlə,dɒn) *n.* **1.** a type of porcelain having a greyish-green glaze: mainly Chinese. **2. a.** a pale greyish-green colour. **b.** (*as adj.*): *a celadon jar.* [C18: from F, from the name of the shepherd hero of *L'Astrée* (1610), a romance by Honoré d'Urfé]

celandine ('sɛlən,daɪn) *n.* either of two unrelated plants, **greater celandine** or **lesser celandine,** with yellow flowers. [C13: earlier *celydon,* from L, from Gk *khelidōn* swallow; the plant's season was believed to parallel the migration of swallows]

Celaya (*Spanish* θe'laja) *n.* a city in central Mexico, in Guanajuato state: market town, famous for its sweetmeats; textile-manufacturing. Pop.: 219 010 (1980).

-cele *n. combining form.* tumour or hernia: *hydrocele.* [from Gk *kēlē* tumour]

celeb (sɪ'lɛb) *n. Inf.* a celebrity.

Celebes ('sɛlɪbi:z, sɛ'li:bɪz) *n.* the English name for **Sulawesi.**

Celebes Sea *n.* the part of the Pacific Ocean between Sulawesi, Borneo, and Mindanao.

celebrant ('sɛlɪbrənt) *n.* a person participating in a religious ceremony, esp. at the Eucharist.

celebrate ('sɛlɪ,breɪt) *vb.* **1.** to rejoice in or have special festivities to mark (a happy day, event, etc.). **2.** (*tr.*) to observe (a birthday, anniversary, etc.). **3.** (*tr.*) to perform (a solemn or religious ceremony), esp. to officiate at (Mass). **4.** (*tr.*) to praise publicly; proclaim. [C15: from L, from *celeber* numerous, renowned] — ,**cele'bration** *n.* — '**cele,brator** *n.* — '**cele,bratory** *adj.*

celebrated ('sɛlɪ,breɪtɪd) *adj.* (*usually prenominal*) famous: *a celebrated pianist.*

celebrity (sɪ'lɛbrɪtɪ) *n., pl.* -**ties. 1.** a famous person. **2.** fame or notoriety.

celeriac (sɪ'lɛrɪ,æk) *n.* a variety of celery with a large turnip-like root, used as a vegetable. [C18: from CELERY + -*ac,* from ?]

celerity (sɪ'lɛrɪtɪ) *n.* rapidity; swiftness; speed. [C15: from OF *celerite,* from L *celeritās,* from *celer* swift]

celery ('sɛlərɪ) *n.* **1.** an umbelliferous Eurasian plant whose blanched leafstalks are used in salads or cooked as a vegetable. **2. wild celery.** a related and similar plant. [C17: from F *céleri,* from It. (Lombardy) dialect *selleri* (pl.), from Gk *selinon* parsley]

celesta (sɪ'lɛstə) *or* **celeste** (sɪ'lɛst) *n. Music.* a keyboard percussion instrument consisting of a set of steel plates of graduated length that are struck with key-operated hammers. [C19: from F, Latinized var. of *céleste* heavenly]

celestial (sɪ'lɛstɪəl) *adj.* **1.** heavenly; divine: *celestial peace.* **2.** of or relating to the sky: *celestial bodies.* **3.** of or connected with the celestial sphere: *celestial pole.* [C14: from Med. L, from L *caelestis,* from *caelum* heaven] — ce'**lestially** *adv.*

Celestial Empire *n.* an archaic or literary name for the **Chinese Empire.**

celestial equator *n.* the great circle lying on the celestial sphere the plane of which is perpendicular to the line joining the north and south celestial poles. Also called: **equinoctial, equinoctial circle.**

celestial sphere *n.* an imaginary sphere of infinitely large radius enclosing the universe so that all celestial bodies appear to be projected onto its surface.

celiac ('si:lɪ,æk) *adj. Anat.* the usual U.S. spelling of **coeliac.**

celibate ('sɛlɪbɪt) *n.* **1.** a person who is unmarried, esp. one who has taken a religious vow of chastity. ~*adj.* **2.** unmarried. [C17: from L, from *caelebs* unmarried, from ?] — '**celibacy** *n.*

Céline (seɪ'li:n) *n.* **Louis-Ferdinand** (lwifɛrdinā). 1894–1961, French novelist and physician; become famous with his controversial first novel *Journey to the End of the Night* (1932).

cell (sɛl) *n.* **1.** a small simple room, as in a prison, convent, etc. **2.** any small compartment: *the cells of a honeycomb.* **3.** *Biol.* the smallest unit of an organism that is able to function independently. It consists of a nucleus, containing the genetic material, surrounded by the cytoplasm. **4.** *Biol.* any small cavity, such as the cavity containing pollen in an anther. **5.** a device for converting chemical energy into electrical energy, usually consisting of a container with two electrodes immersed in an electrolyte. See also **dry cell, fuel cell. 6.** in full **electrolytic cell.** a device in which electrolysis occurs. **7.** a small religious house dependent upon a larger one. **8.** a small group of persons operating as a nucleus of a larger organization: *Communist cell.* [C12: from Med. L *cella* monk's cell, from L: room, storeroom]

cellar ('sɛlə) *n.* **1.** an underground room, or storey of a building, usually used for storage. **2.** a place where wine is stored. **3.** a stock of bottled wines. ~*vb.* **4.** (*tr.*) to store in a cellar. [C13: from Anglo-F, from L *cellārium* foodstore, from *cella* cell]

cellarage ('sɛlərɪdʒ) *n.* **1.** an area of a cellar. **2.** a charge for storing goods in a cellar, etc.

cellarer ('sɛlərə) *n.* a monastic official responsible for food, drink, etc.

cellaret (,sɛlə'rɛt) *n.* a cabinet or sideboard with compartments for holding wine bottles.

Celle (*German* 'tsɛlə) *n.* a city in NE West Germany, on the Aller River in Lower Saxony: from 1378 to 1705 the residence of the Dukes of Brunswick-Lüneburg. Pop.: 71 200 (1984 est.).

Cellini (tʃɪ'liːnɪ) *n.* **Benvenuto** (benve'nuːto). 1500–71, Italian sculptor, goldsmith, and engraver, noted also for his autobiography.

Cellnet ('sɛl,nɛt) *n. Trademark.* a British Telecom car phone.

cello ('tʃɛləʊ) *n., pl.* **-los.** *Music.* a bowed stringed instrument of the violin family. It has four strings, is held between the knees, and has a metal spike at the lower end, which acts as a support. Full name: **violoncello.** — **'cellist** *n.*

cellophane ('sɛlə,feɪn) *n.* a flexible thin transparent sheeting made from wood pulp and used as a moistureproof wrapping. [C20: orig. a trademark, from CELLULOSE + -PHANE]

cellphone ('sɛl,fəʊn) *n.* a portable telephone operated by cellular radio. In full: **cellular telephone.**

cellular ('sɛljʊlə) *adj.* **1.** of, relating to, or resembling a cell. **2.** consisting of or having cells or small cavities; porous. **3.** *Textiles.* woven with an open texture: *a cellular blanket.* **4** designed for or involving cellular radio.

cellular radio *n.* radio communication based on a network of transmitters each serving a small area known as a 'cell': used esp. in car phones in which the receiver switches frequencies automatically as it passes from one cell to another.

cellule ('sɛljuːl) *n.* a very small cell. [C17: from L *cellula*, dim. of *cella* CELL]

cellulite ('sɛljʊ,laɪt) *n.* subcutaneous fat alleged to resist dieting.

cellulitis (,sɛljʊ'laɪtɪs) *n.* inflammation of body tissue, with fever, pain, and swelling. [C19: from L *cellula* CELLULE + -ITIS]

celluloid ('sɛljʊ,lɔɪd) *n.* **1.** a flammable material consisting of cellulose nitrate and camphor: used in sheets, rods, etc. **2. a.** a cellulose derivative used for coating film. **b.** cinema film.

cellulose ('sɛljʊ,ləʊz, -,ləʊs) *n.* a substance which is the main constituent of plant cell walls and used in making paper, rayon, and film. [C18: from F *cellule* cell (see CELLULE) + -OSE²]

cellulose acetate *n.* nonflammable material used in the manufacture of film, dopes, lacquers, and artificial fibres.

cellulose nitrate *n.* cellulose treated with nitric and sulphuric acids, used in plastics, lacquers, and explosives. See also **guncotton.**

Celsius ('sɛlsɪəs) *adj.* denoting a measurement on the Celsius scale. Symbol: C [C18: after Anders *Celsius* (1701–44), Swedish astronomer who invented it]

Celsius scale *n.* a scale of temperature in which 0° represents the melting point of ice and 100° represents the boiling point of water. See also: **centigrade scale.** Cf. **Fahrenheit scale.**

celt (sɛlt) *n. Archaeol.* a stone or metal axelike instrument. [C18: from LL *celtes* chisel, from ?]

Celt (kɛlt, sɛlt) *or* **Kelt** *n.* **1.** a person who speaks a Celtic language. **2.** a member of an Indo-European people who in pre-Roman times inhabited Britain, Gaul, and Spain.

Celtic ('kɛltɪk, 'sɛl-) *or* **Keltic** *n.* **1.** a branch of the Indo-European family of languages that includes Gaelic, Welsh, and Breton. Modern Celtic is divided into the Brythonic (southern) and Goidelic (northern) groups. ~*adj.* **2.** of, relating to, or characteristic of the Celts or the Celtic languages. — **Celticism** ('kɛltɪ,sɪzəm, 'sɛl-) *or* **'Kelti,cism** *n.*

Celtic cross *n.* a Latin cross with a broad ring surrounding the point of intersection.

cembalo ('tʃɛmbələʊ) *n., pl.* **-li** (-lɪ) *or* **-los.** another word for **harpsichord.** [C19: from It. *clavicembalo* from Med. L *clāvis* key + *cymbalum* CYMBAL]

cement (sɪ'mɛnt) *n.* **1.** a fine grey powder made of a mixture of limestone and clay, used with water and sand to make mortar, or with water, sand, and aggregate, to make concrete. **2.** a binder, glue, or adhesive. **3.** something that unites or joins. **4.** *Dentistry.* any of various materials used in filling teeth. **5.** another word for **cementum.** ~*vb.* (*tr.*) **6.** to join, bind, or glue together with or as if with cement. **7.** to coat or cover with cement. [C13: from OF, from L *caementum* stone from the quarry, from *caedere* to hew]

cementum (sɪ'mɛntəm) *n.* a thin bonelike tissue that covers the dentine in the root of a tooth. [C19: NL, from L: CEMENT]

cemetery ('sɛmɪtrɪ) *n., pl.* **-teries.** a place where the dead are buried, esp. one not attached to a church. [C14: from LL, from Gk *koimētērion*, from *koiman* to put to sleep]

-cene *n. and adj. combining form.* denoting a recent geological period. [from Gk *kainos* new]

Cenis (*French* sənɪ) *n.* **Mont.** a pass over the Graian Alps in SE France, between Lanslebourg (France) and Susa (Italy): nearby tunnel, opened in 1871. Highest point: 2082 m (6831 ft.). Italian name: **Monte Cenisio** ('monte tʃe'niːzjo).

cenobite ('siːnəʊ,baɪt) *n.* a variant spelling of **coenobite.**

cenotaph ('sɛnə,tɑːf) *n.* a monument honouring a dead person or persons buried elsewhere. [C17: from L, from Gk, from *kenos* empty + *taphos* tomb]

Cenotaph ('sɛnə,tɑːf) *n.* **the.** the monument in Whitehall, London, honouring the dead of both World Wars: designed by Sir Edwin Lutyens: erected in 1920.

Cenozoic, Caenozoic (,siːnəʊ'zəʊɪk), *or* **Cainozoic** *adj.* **1.** of, denoting, or relating to the most recent geological era characterized by the development and increase of the mammals. ~*n.* **2. the.** the Cenozoic era. [C19: from Gk *kainos* recent + *zōikos*, from *zōion* animal]

censer ('sɛnsə) *n.* a container for burning incense. Also called: **thurible.**

censor ('sɛnsə) *n.* **1.** a person authorized to examine publications, films, letters, etc., in order to suppress in whole or part those considered obscene, politically unacceptable, etc. **2.** any person who controls or suppresses the behaviour of others, usually on moral grounds. **3.** (in republican Rome) either of two senior magistrates elected to keep the list of citizens up to date, and supervise public morals. **4.** *Psychoanal.* the postulated factor responsible for regulating the translation of ideas and desires from the unconscious to the conscious mind. ~*vb.* (*tr.*) **5.** to ban or cut portions of (a film, letter, etc.). **6.** to act as a censor of (behaviour, etc.). [C16: from L, from *cēnsēre* to consider] — **censorial** (sɛn'sɔːrɪəl) *adj.*

censorious (sɛn'sɔːrɪəs) *adj.* harshly critical; fault-finding. — **cen'soriously** *adv.*

censorship ('sɛnsə,ʃɪp) *n.* **1.** a policy or programme of censoring. **2.** the act or system of censoring.

censure ('sɛnʃə) *n.* **1.** severe disapproval. ~*vb.* **2.** to criticize (someone or something) severely. [C14: from L *cēnsūra*, from *cēnsēre*: see CENSOR] — **'censurable** *adj.*

census ('sɛnsəs) *n., pl.* **-suses. 1.** an official periodic count of a population including such information as sex, age, occupation, etc. **2.** any official count: *a traffic census.* **3.** (in ancient Rome) a registration of the population and a property evaluation for taxation. [C17: from L, from *cēnsēre* to assess]

cent (sɛnt) *n.* a monetary unit of Australia, Barbados, Botswana, Canada, Hong Kong, Kenya, Malaysia, New Zealand, Singapore, South Africa, Tanzania, Trinidad and Tobago, Uganda, the United States, etc. It is worth one hundredth of their respective standard units. [C16: from L *centēsimus* hundredth, from *centum* hundred]

cent. *abbrev. for:* **1.** centigrade. **2.** central. **3.** century.

centaur ('sɛntɔː) *n. Greek myth.* one of a race of creatures with the head, arms, and torso of a man, and the lower body and legs of a horse. [C14: from L, from Gk *kentauros*, from ?]

centaurea (sɛntɔː'rɪə, sɛn'tɔːrɪə) *n.* any plant of the genus *Centaurea* which includes the cornflower and knapweed. [C19: ult. from Gk *Kentauros* the Centaur; see CENTAURY]

centaury ('sɛntɔːrɪ) *n., pl.* **-ries.** **1.** any of a genus of Eurasian plants having purplish-pink flowers and formerly believed to have medicinal properties. **2.** another name for **centaurea**. [C14: ult. from Gk *Kentauros* the Centaur; from the legend that Chiron the Centaur divulged its healing properties]

centavo (sɛn'tɑːvəʊ) *n., pl.* **-vos.** a monetary unit of Argentina, Brazil, Colombia, Ecuador, El Salvador, Mexico, Nicaragua, Peru, the Philippines, Portugal, etc. It is worth one hundredth of their respective standard units. [Sp.: one hundredth part]

centenarian (ˌsɛntɪ'nɛərɪən) *n.* **1.** a person who is at least 100 years old. ~*adj.* **2.** being at least 100 years old. **3.** of or relating to a centenarian.

centenary (sɛn'tiːnərɪ) *adj.* **1.** of or relating to a period of 100 years. **2.** occurring once every 100 years. ~*n., pl.* **-naries.** **3.** a 100th anniversary or its celebration. [C17: from L, from *centēnī* a hundred each, from *centum* hundred]

centennial (sɛn'tɛnɪəl) *adj.* **1.** relating to or completing a period of 100 years. **2.** occurring every 100 years. ~*n.* **3.** *U.S. & Canad.* another name for **centenary**. [C18: from L *centum* hundred, on the model of BIENNIAL]

center ('sɛntə) *n., vb.* the U.S. spelling of **centre**.

centesimal (sɛn'tɛsɪməl) *n.* **1.** hundredth. ~*adj.* **2.** relating to division into hundredths. [C17: from L, from *centum* hundred] —**cen'tesimally** *adv.*

centesimo (sɛn'tɛsɪˌməʊ) *n., pl.* **-mos.** a monetary unit of Chile, Italy, etc. It is worth one hundredth of their respective standard units. [C19: from Sp. & It., from L, from *centum* hundred]

centi- *or before a vowel* **cent-** *prefix.* **1.** denoting one hundredth: *centimetre.* Symbol: c **2.** *Rare.* denoting a hundred: *centipede.* [from F, from L *centum* hundred]

centiare ('sɛntɪˌɛə) *or* **centare** ('sɛntɛə) *n.* a unit of area equal to one square metre. [F, from CENTI- + *are* from L *ārea*]

centigrade ('sɛntɪˌgreɪd) *adj.* **1.** another name for **Celsius.** ~*n.* **2.** a unit of angle equal to one hundredth of a grade.
▷ **Usage.** *Centigrade*, when indicating the Celsius scale of temperature, is now usually avoided in scientific contexts because of possible confusion with the hundredth part of a grade.

centigram *or* **centigramme** ('sɛntɪˌgræm) *n.* one hundredth of a gram.

centilitre *or U.S.* **centiliter** ('sɛntɪˌliːtə) *n.* one hundredth of a litre.

centime ('sɒnˌtiːm; *French* sãtim) *n.* a monetary unit of Algeria, Belgium, the Central African Republic, France, Guinea, Haiti, Liechtenstein, Luxembourg, Mali, Mauritania, Switzerland, Tahiti, Togo, etc. It is worth one hundredth of their respective standard units. [C18: from F, from OF, from L, from *centum* hundred]

centimetre *or U.S.* **centimeter** ('sɛntɪˌmiːtə) *n.* one hundredth of a metre.

centimetre-gram-second *n.* See **cgs units.**

céntimo ('sɛntɪˌməʊ) *n., pl.* **-mos.** a monetary unit of Costa Rica, Spain, Venezuela, etc. It is worth one hundredth of their respective standard currency units. [from Sp.; see CENTIME]

centipede ('sɛntɪˌpiːd) *n.* a carnivorous arthropod having a body of between 15 and 190 segments, each bearing one pair of legs.

cento ('sɛntəʊ) *n., pl.* **-tos.** a piece of writing, esp. a poem, composed of quotations from other authors. [C17: from L, lit.: patchwork garment]

CENTO ('sɛntəʊ) *n. acronym for* Central Treaty Organization; an organization for military and economic cooperation formed in 1959 by the U.K., Iran, Pakistan, and Turkey: disbanded 1979.

central ('sɛntrəl) *adj.* **1.** in, at, of, from, containing, or forming the centre of something: *the central street in a*

city. **2.** main, principal, or chief: *the central cause of a problem.* —**centrality** (sɛn'trælɪtɪ) *n.* —'**centrally** *adv.*

Central African Federation *n.* another name for the **Federation of Rhodesia and Nyasaland** or the **Rhodesia and Nyasaland Federation.**

Central African Republic *n.* a landlocked country of central Africa: joined with Chad as a territory of French Equatorial Africa in 1910; became an independent republic in 1960; a parliamentary monarchy (1976–79); consists of a huge plateau, mostly savanna, with dense forests in the south; drained chiefly by the Shari and Ubangi Rivers. Languages: French and Sangho. Religion: chiefly animist. Currency: franc. Capital: Bangui. Pop.: 2 775 000 (1987 est.). Area: 622 577 sq. km (240 376 sq. miles). Former names: (until 1958) **Ubangi-Shari;** (1976-79) **Central African Empire.** French name: **République Centrafricaine** (repyblik sãtrafrikɛn)

Central America *n.* an isthmus joining the continents of North and South America, extending from the S border of Mexico to the NW border of Colombia and consisting of Belize, Guatemala, Honduras, El Salvador, Nicaragua, Costa Rica, and Panama. Area: about 518 000 sq. km (200 000 sq. miles). —**Central American** *adj.*

central bank *n.* a national bank that does business mainly with a government and with other banks: it regulates the volume of credit.

central heating *n.* a system for heating the rooms of a building by means of radiators or air vents connected to a central source of heat.

Centralia (sɛn'treɪlɪə) *n.* an archaic name for **Centre** (sense 1).

Central India Agency *n.* a former group of 89 states in India, under the supervision of a British political agent until 1947: most important were Indore, Bhopal, and Rewa.

centralism ('sɛntrəˌlɪzəm) *n.* the principle or act of bringing something under central control. —'**centralist** *n., adj.*

centralize *or* **-lise** ('sɛntrəˌlaɪz) *vb.* **1.** to draw or move (something) to or towards a centre. **2.** to bring or come under central, esp. governmental, control. —ˌcentrali'zation *or* -li'sation *n.*

central limit theorem *n. Statistics.* the fundamental result that the sum of independent identically distributed random variables with finite variance approaches a normally distributed random variable as their number increases.

central locking *n.* a system by which all the doors of a motor vehicle can be locked simultaneously.

central nervous system *n.* the mass of nerve tissue that controls and coordinates the activities of an animal. In vertebrates it consists of the brain and spinal cord.

central processing unit *n.* the part of a computer that performs logical and arithmetical operations on the data. Abbrev.: **CPU.**

Central Provinces and Berar (bɛ'rɑː) *n.* a former province of central India: reorganized and renamed Madhya Pradesh in 1950.

Central Region *n.* a local government region in central Scotland, formed in 1975 from Clackmannanshire, most of Stirlingshire, and parts of Perthshire, West Lothian, Fife, and Kinross-shire. Administrative centre: Stirling. Pop.: 271 819 (1986 est.). Area: 2629 sq. km (1015 sq. miles).

central reserve *or* **reservation** *n. Brit.* the strip, often covered with grass, that separates the two sides of a motorway or dual carriageway.

central tendency *n. Statistics.* the tendency of the values of a random variable to cluster around the mean, median, and mode.

centre *or U.S.* **center** ('sɛntə) *n.* **1.** *Geom.* **a.** the midpoint of any line or figure, esp. the point within a circle or sphere that is equidistant from any point on the circumference or surface. **b.** the point within a body through which a specified force may be considered to act, such as the centre of gravity. **2.** the point, axis, or pivot about which a body rotates. **3.** a point, area, or part that is approximately in the middle of a larger area or volume. **4.** a place at which some specified activity is concentrated: *a shopping centre.* **5.** a person or thing that is a focus of interest. **6.** a place of activity or influence: *a centre of power.* **7.** a person, group, or thing in the middle. **8.** (*usually cap.*) *Politics.* a political party or group favouring moderation. **9.** a bar with a conical point upon which a workpiece or part may be turned or ground. **10.** *Football, hockey, etc.* **a.** a player who plays in the middle of the forward line. **b.** an instance of passing the ball from a wing to the middle of the field, etc. ~*vb.* **11.** to move towards, mark, put, or be at a centre. **12.** (*tr.*) to focus or bring together: *to centre one's thoughts.* **13.** (*intr.*; often foll. by *on*) to have as a main theme: *the novel centred on crime.* **14.** (*intr.*; foll. by *on* or *round*) to have as a centre. **15.** (*tr.*) *Football, hockey, etc.* to pass (the ball) into the middle of the field or court. [C14: from L *centrum* the stationary point of a compass, from Gk *kentron* needle, from *kentein* to prick]

▷ **Usage.** *To centre round* is considered illogical by many writers and speakers, who prefer the more precise phrase *to centre on.*

Centre ('sɛntə) *n.* **the.** the sparsely inhabited central region of Australia. Also called: **Centralia** (arch.), **the Red Centre.**

centre bit *n.* a drilling bit with a central point and two side cutters.

centreboard ('sɛntə,bɔːd) *n.* a supplementary keel for a sailing vessel.

centrefold *or U.S.* **centerfold** ('sɛntə,fəʊld) *n.* a large coloured illustration folded so that it forms the central spread of a magazine.

centre forward *n. Soccer, hockey, etc.* the central forward in the attack.

centre half *or* **centre back** *n. Soccer.* a defender who plays in the middle of the defence.

centre of gravity *n.* the point through which the resultant of the gravitational forces on a body always acts.

centrepiece ('sɛntə,piːs) *n.* an object used as the centre of something, esp. for decoration.

centre spread *n.* the pair of two facing pages in the middle of a magazine, newspaper, etc.

centri- *combining form.* a variant of **centro-.**

centric ('sɛntrɪk) *or* **centrical** *adj.* **1.** being central or having a centre. **2.** relating to a nerve centre. —**centricity** (sɛn'trɪsɪtɪ) *n.*

-centric *suffix forming adjectives.* having a centre as specified: *heliocentric.* [abstracted from ECCENTRIC, CONCENTRIC, etc.]

centrifugal (sɛn'trɪfjʊgəl, 'sɛntrɪ,fjuːgəl) *adj.* **1.** acting, moving, or tending to move away from a centre. Cf. **centripetal.** **2.** of, concerned with, or operated by centrifugal force: *centrifugal pump.* [C18: from NL, from CENTRI- + L *fugere* to flee] —**cen'trifugally** *adv.*

centrifugal force *n.* a fictitious force that can be thought of as acting outwards on any body that rotates or moves along a curved path.

centrifuge ('sɛntrɪ,fjuːdʒ) *n.* **1.** any of various rotating machines that separate liquids from solids or other liquids by the action of centrifugal force. **2.** any of various rotating devices for subjecting human beings or animals to varying accelerations. ~*vb.* **3.** (*tr.*) to subject to the action of a centrifuge. —**centrifugation** (,sɛntrɪfjuˈgeɪʃən) *n.*

centring ('sɛntrɪŋ) *or U.S.* **centering** ('sɛntərɪŋ) *n.* a temporary structure, esp. one made of timber, used to support an arch during construction.

centripetal (sɛn'trɪpɪtəl, 'sɛntrɪ,piːtəl) *adj.* **1.** acting, moving, or tending to move towards a centre. Cf. **centrifugal.** **2.** of, concerned with, or operated by centripetal force. [C17: from NL *centripetus* seeking the centre] —**cen'tripetally** *adv.*

centripetal force *n.* a force that acts inwards on any body that rotates or moves along a curved path.

centrist ('sɛntrɪst) *n.* a person holding moderate political views. —**'centrism** *n.*

centro-, centri-, *or before a vowel* **centr-** *combining form.* denoting a centre: *centrosome; centrist.* [from Gk *kentron* CENTRE]

centrosome ('sɛntrə,səʊm) *n.* a small protoplasmic body found near the cell nucleus.

centuplicate *vb.* (sɛn'tjuːplɪ,keɪt). **1.** (*tr.*) to increase 100 times. ~*adj.* (sɛn'tjuːplɪkɪt). **2.** increased a hundredfold. ~*n.* (sɛn'tjuːplɪkɪt). **3.** one hundredfold. ~Also **centuple** ('sɛntjʊpəl). [C17: from LL, from *centuplex* hundredfold, from L *centum* hundred + *-plex* -fold]

centurion (sɛn'tjʊərɪən) *n.* the officer commanding a Roman century. [C14: from L *centuriō*, from *centuria* CENTURY]

century ('sɛntʃərɪ) *n., pl.* **-ries. 1.** a period of 100 years. **2.** one of the successive periods of 100 years dated before

or after an epoch or event, esp. the birth of Christ. **3.** a score or grouping of 100: *to score a century in cricket.* **4.** (in ancient Rome) a unit of foot soldiers, originally consisting of 100 men. **5.** (in ancient Rome) a division of the people for purposes of voting. [C16: from L *centuria*, from *centum* hundred]

▷ **Usage.** In strict usage, the dating of any century begins with a year ending -01 and ends with a year ending -00: *the nineteenth century covers the years 1801 to 1900.* This is because the system of dating by A.D. is based on the supposed year in which Christ was born, so that it begins with A.D. 1. In popular practice, however, the dating of a century is often moved back by one year so that it includes all the years starting with the same number: *the nineteenth century covers the years 1800 to 1899.*

cep (sɛp) *n.* an edible woodland fungus with a brown shining cap and a rich nutty flavour. [C19: from F, from Gascon dialect *cep*, from L *cippus* stake]

cephalic (sɪ'fælɪk) *adj.* **1.** of or relating to the head. **2.** situated in, on, or near the head.

-cephalic *or* **-cephalous** *adj. combining form.* indicating skull or head; -headed: *brachycephalic.* [from Gk *-kephalos*] —**-cephaly** *or* **-cephalism** *n. combining form.*

cephalic index *n.* the ratio of the greatest width of the human head to its greatest length, multiplied by 100.

cephalo- *or before a vowel* **cephal-** *combining form.* indicating the head: *cephalopod.* [via L from Gk, from *kephale* head]

Cephalonia (,sɛfə'ləʊnɪə) *n.* a mountainous island in the Ionian Sea, the largest of the Ionian Islands, off the W coast of Greece. Pop.: 31 297 (1981). Area: 935 sq. km (365 sq. miles). Modern Greek name: **Kephallinía.**

cephalopod ('sɛfələ,pɒd) *n.* any of various marine molluscs, characterized by well-developed head and eyes and a ring of sucker-bearing tentacles, including the octopuses, squids, and cuttlefish. —,**cepha'lopodan** *adj., n.*

cephalothorax (,sɛfələʊ'θɔːræks) *n., pl.* **-raxes** *or* **-races** (-rə,siːz). the anterior part of many crustaceans and some other arthropods consisting of a united head and thorax.

-cephalus *n. combining form.* denoting a cephalic abnormality: *hydrocephalus.* [NL *-cephalus*; see -CEPHALIC]

Cepheid variable ('siːfiɪd) *n. Astron.* any of a class of variable stars with regular cycles of variations in luminosity, which are used for measuring distances.

Cepheus ('siːfjuːs) *n. Greek myth.* a king of Ethiopia, father of Andromeda and husband of Cassiopeia.

Ceram (sɪ'ræm) *n.* a variant spelling of **Seram.**

ceramic (sɪ'ræmɪk) *n.* **1.** a hard brittle material made by firing clay and similar substances. **2.** an object made from such a material. ~*adj.* **3.** of or made from a ceramic. **4.** of or relating to ceramics: *ceramic arts.* [C19: from Gk, from *keramos* potter's clay]

ceramic hob *n.* (on an electric cooker) a flat ceramic cooking surface having heating elements fitted on the underside.

ceramic oxide *n.* a compound of oxygen with nonorganic material: recently discovered to act as a high-temperature superconductor.

ceramics (sɪ'ræmɪks) *n.* (*functioning as sing.*) the art and techniques of producing articles of clay, porcelain, etc. —**ceramist** ('sɛrəmɪst) *n.*

Cerberus ('sɜːbərəs) *n.* **1.** *Greek myth.* a dog, usually represented as having three heads, that guarded the entrance to Hades. **2. a sop to Cerberus.** a bribe or something given to propitiate a potential source of danger or problems. —**Cerberean** (sə'bɪərɪən) *adj.*

cere (sɪə) *n.* a soft waxy swelling, containing the nostrils, at the base of the upper beak, as in the parrot. [C15: from OF *cire* wax, from L *cēra*]

cereal ('sɪərɪəl) *n.* **1.** any grass that produces an edible grain, such as oat, wheat, rice, maize, and millet. **2.** the grain produced by such a plant. **3.** any food made from this grain, esp. breakfast food. **4.** (*modifier*) of or relating to any of these plants or their products. [C19: from L *cereālis* concerning agriculture]

cerebellum (,sɛrɪ'bɛləm) *n., pl.* **-lums** *or* **-la** (-lə). one of the major divisions of the vertebrate brain whose function is coordination of voluntary movements. [C16: from L, dim. of CEREBRUM]

cerebral ('sɛrɪbrəl; *U.S. also* sə'riːbrəl) *adj.* **1.** of or relating to the cerebrum or to the entire brain. **2.** involving intelligence rather than emotions or instinct. **3.** *Phonetics.* another word for **cacuminal.** —**'cerebrally** *adv.*

cerebral haemorrhage *n.* bleeding from an artery in the brain, which in severe cases causes a stroke.

cerebral palsy *n.* an impairment of muscular function and weakness of the limbs, caused by lack of oxygen to the brain before, during, or immediately after birth, brain injury during birth, or viral infection.

cerebrate ('sɛrɪ,breɪt) *vb.* (*intr.*) *Usually facetious.* to use the mind; think; ponder; consider. —**cere'bration** *n.*

cerebro- *or before a vowel* **cerebr-** *combining form.* indicating the brain: *cerebrospinal.* [from CEREBRUM]

cerebrospinal (,sɛrɪbrəʊ'spaɪnəl) *adj.* of or relating to the brain and spinal cord: *cerebrospinal fluid.*

cerebrovascular (,sɛrɪbrəʊ'væskjʊlə) *adj.* of or relating to the blood vessels and the blood supply of the brain.

cerebrum ('sɛrɪbrəm) *n., pl.* **-brums** *or* **-bra** (-brə). **1.** the anterior portion of the brain of vertebrates, consisting of two lateral hemispheres: the dominant part of the brain in man, associated with intellectual function, emotion, and personality. **2.** the brain considered as a whole. [C17: from L: the brain] —'**cerebric** *adj.*

cerecloth ('sɪə,klɒθ) *n.* waxed waterproof cloth of a kind formerly used as a shroud. [C15: from earlier *cered cloth,* from L *cērāre* to wax]

cerement ('sɪəmənt) *n.* **1.** cerecloth. **2.** any burial clothes. [C17: from F, from *cirer* to wax]

ceremonial (,sɛrɪ'məʊnɪəl) *adj.* **1.** involving or relating to ceremony or ritual. ~*n.* **2.** the observance of formality, esp. in etiquette. **3.** a plan for formal observances; ritual. **4.** *Christianity.* **a.** the prescribed order of rites and ceremonies. **b.** a book containing this. —,**cere-e'monialism** *n.* —,**cere'monialist** *n.* —,**cere'monially** *adv.*

ceremonious (,sɛrɪ'məʊnɪəs) *adj.* **1.** especially or excessively polite or formal. **2.** involving formalities. —,**cere'moniously** *adv.*

ceremony ('sɛrɪmənɪ) *n., pl.* **-nies. 1.** a formal act or ritual, often set by custom or tradition, performed in observation of an event or anniversary. **2.** a religious rite or series of rites. **3.** a courteous gesture or act: *the ceremony of toasting the Queen.* **4.** ceremonial observances or gestures collectively. **5. stand on ceremony.** to insist on or act with excessive formality. [C14: from Med. L, from L *caerimōnia* what is sacred]

Cerenkov (*Russian* tʃɪ'rjɛnkəf) *n.* See (Pavel Alekseyevich) **Cherenkov.**

Ceres ('sɪəri:z) *n.* the Roman goddess of agriculture. Greek counterpart: **Demeter.**

cerise (sə'ri:z, -'ri:s) *n., adj.* (of) a moderate to dark red colour. [C19: from F: CHERRY]

cerium ('sɪərɪəm) *n.* a malleable ductile steel-grey element of the lanthanide series of metals, used in lighter flints. Symbol: Ce; atomic no.: 58; atomic wt.: 140.12. [C19: NL, from *Ceres* (the asteroid) + -IUM]

cermet ('sɜ:mɪt) *n.* any of several materials consisting of a metal and ceramic particles. They are hard and resistant to high temperatures. [C20: from CER(AMIC) + MET(AL)]

CERN (sɜ:n) *n. acronym for* Conseil Européen pour la Recherche Nucléaire; an organization of European states with a centre in Geneva, for research in high-energy particle physics.

Cernăuţi (tʃɛrnə'utsj) *n.* the Romanian name for **Chernovtsy.**

cerography (sɪə'rɒgrəfɪ) *n.* the art of engraving on a waxed plate on which a printing surface is created by electrotyping.

ceroplastic (,sɪərəʊ'plæstɪk) *adj.* **1.** relating to wax modelling. **2.** modelled in wax.

Cerro de Pasco (*Spanish* 'θɛrrɔ ðe 'pasko) *n.* a town in central Peru, in the Andes: one of the highest towns in the world, 4400 m (14 436 ft.) above sea level; mining centre. Pop.: 71 558 (1981).

Cerro Gordo (*Spanish* 'θɛrrɔ 'gorðo) *n.* a mountain pass in E Mexico, between Veracruz and Jalapa: site of a battle in the Mexican War (1847) in which American forces under General Scott decisively defeated the Mexicans.

cert (sɜ:t) *n. Inf.* something that is a certainty, esp. a horse that is certain to win a race.

cert. *abbrev. for:* **1.** certificate. **2.** certification. **3.** certified.

certain ('sɜ:tən) *adj.* **1.** (*postpositive*) positive and confident about the truth of something; convinced: *I am certain that he wrote a book.* **2.** (*usually postpositive*) definitely known: *it is certain that they were on the bus.*

3. (*usually postpositive*) sure; bound: *he was certain to fail.* **4.** fixed: *the date is already certain for the invasion.* **5.** reliable: *his judgment is certain.* **6.** moderate or minimum: *to a certain extent.* **7. for certain.** without a doubt. ~*determiner.* **8. a.** known but not specified or named: *certain people.* **b.** (*as pron.; functioning as pl.*): *certain of the members have not paid.* **9.** named but not known: *he had written to a certain Mrs Smith.* [C13: from OF, from L *certus* sure, from *cernere* to decide]

certainly ('sɜ:tənlɪ) *adv.* **1.** without doubt: *he certainly rides very well.* ~ *sentence substitute.* **2.** by all means; definitely.

certainty ('sɜ:təntɪ) *n., pl.* **-ties. 1.** the condition of being certain. **2.** something established as inevitable. **3. for a certainty.** without doubt.

CertEd (in Britain) *abbrev. for* Certificate in Education.

certes ('sɜ:tɪz) *adv. Arch.* with certainty; truly. [C13: from OF, ult. from L *certus* CERTAIN]

certificate *n.* (sə'tɪfɪkɪt). **1.** an official document attesting the truth of the facts stated, as of birth, death, completion of an academic course, etc. **2.** short for **share certificate.** ~*vb.* (sə'tɪfɪ,keɪt). **3.** (*tr.*) to authorize by or present with an official document. [C15: from OF, from *certifier* to CERTIFY] —**cer'tificatory** *adj.*

Certificate of Secondary Education *n.* the full name for CSE.

certification (,sɜ:tɪfɪ'keɪʃən) *n.* **1.** the act of certifying or state of being certified. **2.** *Law.* a document attesting the truth of a fact or statement.

certified ('sɜ:tɪ,faɪd) *adj.* **1.** holding or guaranteed by a certificate. **2.** endorsed or guaranteed: *a certified cheque.* **3.** (of a person) declared legally insane.

certify ('sɜ:tɪ,faɪ) *vb.* **-fying, -fied. 1.** to confirm or attest (to), usually in writing. **2.** (*tr.*) to endorse or guarantee that certain required standards have been met. **3.** to give reliable information or assurances: *he certified that it was Walter's handwriting.* **4.** (*tr.*) to declare legally insane. [C14: from OF, from Med. L, from L *certus* CERTAIN + *facere* to make] —'**certi,fiable** *adj.*

certiorari (,sɜ:tɪɔ:'rɛəraɪ) *n. Law.* an order of a superior court directing that a record of proceedings in a lower court be sent up for review. [C15: from legal L: to be informed]

certitude ('sɜ:tɪ,tju:d) *n.* confidence; certainty. [C15: from Church L *certitūdō,* from L *certus* CERTAIN]

cerulean (sɪ'ru:lɪən) *n., adj.* (of) a deep blue colour. [C17: from L *caeruleus,* prob. from *caelum* sky]

cerumen (sɪ'ru:mɛn) *n.* the soft brownish-yellow wax secreted by glands in the external ear. Nontechnical name: **earwax.** [C18: from NL, from L *cēra* wax + ALBUMEN] —**ce'ruminous** *adj.*

Cervantes (sə'væntiːz; *Spanish* θɛr'βantes) *n.* **Miguel de** (mi'γɛl ðe), full surname *Cervantes Saavedra.* 1547–1616, Spanish dramatist, poet, and prose writer, most famous for *Don Quixote* (1605), which satirizes the chivalric romances and greatly influenced the development of the novel.

cervelat ('sɜ:və,læt, -,lɑ:) *n.* a smoked sausage made from pork and beef. [C17: via obs. F from It. *cervellata*]

cervical (sə'vaɪkəl, 'sɜ:vɪkəl) *adj.* of or relating to the neck or cervix. [C17: from NL, from L *cervix* neck]

cervical smear *n. Med.* a smear taken from the neck (cervix) of the uterus for detection of cancer. See also **Pap test.**

Cervin (sɛrvɛ̃) *n. Mont.* the French name for the **Matterhorn.**

cervine ('sɜ:vaɪn) *adj.* resembling or relating to a deer. [C19: from L *cervīnus,* from *cervus* a deer]

cervix ('sɜ:vɪks) *n., pl.* **cervixes** *or* **cervices** (sə'vaɪsiːz). **1.** the technical name for **neck. 2.** any necklike part, esp. the lower part of the uterus that extends into the vagina. [C18: from L]

Cesena (*Italian* tʃe'zɛːna) *n.* a city in N Italy, in Emilia-Romagna. Pop.: 89 620 (1981).

cesium ('siːzɪəm) *n.* the usual U.S. spelling of **caesium.**

cess[1] (sɛs) *n. Brit.* any of several special taxes, such as a land tax in Scotland. [C16: short for ASSESSMENT]

cess[2] (sɛs) *n.* an Irish slang word for **luck** (esp. in **bad cess to you!**). [C19: prob. from CESS[1]]

cessation (sɛ'seɪʃən) *n.* a ceasing or stopping; pause: *temporary cessation of hostilities.* [C14: from L, from *cessāre* to be idle, from *cēdere* to yield]

cession ('sɛʃən) *n.* **1.** the act of ceding. **2.** something that is ceded, esp. land or territory. [C14: from L *cessiō*, from *cēdere* to yield]

cessionary ('sɛʃənərɪ) *n., pl.* **-aries.** *Law.* a person to whom something is transferred.

cesspit ('sɛs,pɪt) *n.* a pit for the disposal of refuse, esp. sewage. [C19: see CESSPOOL]

cesspool ('sɛs,puːl) *n.* **1.** Also called: **sink, sump.** a covered cistern, etc., for collecting and storing sewage or waste water. **2.** a filthy or corrupt place: *a cesspool of iniquity.* [C17:? changed from earlier *cesperalle*, from OF *souspirail* vent, air, from *soupirer* to sigh]

cestoid ('sɛstɔɪd) *adj.* (esp. of tapeworms and similar animals) ribbon-like in form.

cesura (sɪ'zjʊərə) *n., pl.* **-ras** *or* **-rae** (-riː). *Prosody.* a variant spelling of **caesura.**

cetacean (sɪ'teɪʃən) *adj. also* **cetaceous. 1.** of or belonging to an order of aquatic placental mammals having no hind limbs and a blowhole for breathing: includes toothed whales (dolphins, porpoises, etc.) and whalebone whales (rorquals, etc.). ~*n.* **2.** a whale. [C19: from NL, ult. from L *cētus* whale, from Gk *kētos*]

cetane ('siːteɪn) *n.* a colourless insoluble liquid hydrocarbon used in the determination of the cetane number of diesel fuel. Also called: **hexadecane.** [C19: from L *cētus* whale -ANE]

cetane number *n.* a measure of the quality of a diesel fuel expressed as the percentage of cetane. Also called: **cetane rating.** Cf. **octane number.**

Cetatea Albă (tʃe'tatea 'albə) *n.* the Romanian name for **Byelgorod-Dnestrovski.**

Cetinje (*Serbo-Croatian* 'tsɛtinje) *n.* a city in S Yugoslavia, in SW Montenegro: former capital of Montenegro (until 1945); palace and fortified monastery, residences of Montenegrin prince-bishops. Pop.: 20 213 (1981).

Cetshwayo *or* **Cetewayo** (*Zulu* kɛ'tʃwaːjɔ) *n.* ?1826–84, king of the Zulus (1873–79): defeated the British at Isandhlwana (1879) but was overwhelmed by them at Ulundi (1879); captured, he stated his case in London, and was reinstated as ruler of part of Zululand (1883).

Ceuta (*Spanish* 'θeuta) *n.* an enclave in Morocco on the Strait of Gibraltar, consisting of a port and military station: held by Spain since 1580. Pop.: 70 864 (1981).

Cévennes (*French* sevɛn) *n.* a mountain range in S central France, on the SE edge of the Massif Central. Highest peak: 1754 m (5755 ft.).

Ceylon (sɪ'lɒn) *n.* **1.** the former name (until 1972) of **Sri Lanka. 2.** an island in the Indian Ocean, off the SE coast of India: consists politically of the republic of Sri Lanka. Area: 64 644 sq. km (24 959 sq. miles). —**Ceylonese** (,sɛlə'niːz, ,siːlə-) *adj.*

Ceyx ('siːɪks) *n. Greek myth.* a king of Trachis in Thessaly and the husband of Alcyone. He died in a shipwreck and his wife drowned herself in grief. Compare **Alcyone**[1] (sense 1).

Cézanne (*French* sezan) *n.* **Paul** (pɔl). 1839–1906, French postimpressionist painter, who was a major influence on modern art, esp. cubism, in stressing the structural elements latent in nature, such as the sphere and the cone.

Cf *the chemical symbol for* californium.

CF *abbrev. for* Canadian Forces.

cf. *abbrev. for:* **1.** (in bookbinding, etc.) calfskin. **2.** confer. [L: compare]

CFB *abbrev. for* Canadian Forces Base.

CFC *abbrev. for* chlorofluorocarbon.

CFL *abbrev. for* Canadian Football League.

cg *abbrev. for* centigram.

cgs units *pl. n.* a metric system of units based on the centimetre, gram, and second. For scientific and technical purposes these units have been replaced by SI units.

CGT *abbrev. for* Capital Gains Tax.

CH *abbrev. for* Companion of Honour (a Brit. title).

ch. *abbrev. for:* **1.** chain (unit of measure). **2.** chapter. **3.** *Chess.* check. **4.** chief. **5.** church.

chablis ('ʃæblɪ) *n.* (*sometimes cap.*) a dry white wine made around Chablis, France.

Chabrier (ʃaː'briːeɪ; *French* ʃabrie) *n.* **Alexis Emmanuel** (alɛksi emanɥel). 1841–94, French composer; noted esp. for the orchestral rhapsody *España* (1883).

Chabrol (*French* ʃabrɔl) *n.* **Claude** (klod). born 1930, French film director, whose films, such as *Les Biches*

(1968), *Le Boucher* (1969), and *Une Affaire des femmes* (1988), show a penchant for the bizarre.

cha-cha-cha (,tʃaːtʃaː'tʃaː) *or* **cha-cha** *n.* **1.** a modern ballroom dance from Latin America with small steps and swaying hip movements. **2.** a piece of music composed for this dance. ~*vb.* (*intr.*) **3.** to perform this dance. [C20: from American (Cuban) Sp.]

Chaco (*Spanish* 'tʃako) *n.* See **Gran Chaco.**

chaconne (ʃə'kɒn) *n.* **1.** a musical form consisting of a set of continuous variations upon a ground bass. **2.** *Arch.* a dance in slow triple time probably originating in Spain. [C17: from F, from Sp. *chacona*]

Chad (tʃæd) *n.* **1.** a republic in N central Africa: made a territory of French Equatorial Africa in 1910; became independent in 1960; contains much desert and the Tibesti Mountains, with Lake Chad in the west; produces chiefly cotton and livestock; has suffered intermittent civil war from 1963 and prolonged drought. Official language: French. Religion: chiefly Muslim, also animist. Currency: franc. Capital: Ndjamena. Pop.: 5 241 000 (1987 est.). Area: 1 284 000 sq. km (495 750 sq. miles). French name: **Tchad. 2. Lake.** a lake in N central Africa: fed chiefly by the Shari River, it has no apparent outlet. Area: 10 000 to 26 000 sq. km (4000 to 10 000 sq. miles), varying seasonally.

Chadderton ('tʃædətən) *n.* a town in NW England, in Greater Manchester. Pop.: 34 013 (1981).

Chadwick ('tʃædwɪk) *n.* Sir **James.** 1891–1974, English physicist: discovered the neutron (1932): Nobel prize for physics 1935.

Chaeronea (,kɛrə'niːə) *n.* an ancient Greek town in W Boeotia: site of the victory of Philip of Macedon over the Athenians and Thebans (338 B.C.) and of Sulla over Mithridates (86 B.C.).

chafe (tʃeɪf) *vb.* **1.** to make or become sore or worn by rubbing. **2.** (*tr.*) to warm (the hands, etc.) by rubbing. **3.** to irritate or be irritated or impatient. **4.** (*intr.;* often foll. by *on, against,* etc.) to rub. ~*n.* **5.** a soreness or irritation caused by friction. [C14: from OF *chaufer* to warm, ult. from L, from *calēre* to be warm + *facere* to make]

chafer ('tʃeɪfə) *n.* any of various beetles, such as the cockchafer. [OE *ceafor*]

chaff[1] (tʃɑːf) *n.* **1.** the mass of husks, etc., separated from the seeds during threshing. **2.** finely cut straw and hay used to feed cattle. **3.** something of little worth; rubbish: *to separate the wheat from the chaff.* **4.** thin strips of metallic foil released into the earth's atmosphere to deflect radar signals and prevent detection. [OE *ceaf*] —'**chaffy** *adj.*

chaff[2] (tʃɑːf) *n.* **1.** light-hearted teasing or joking; banter. ~*vb.* **2.** to tease good-naturedly. [C19: prob. slang var. of CHAFE] —'**chaffer** *n.*

chaffer ('tʃæfə) *vb.* **1.** (*intr.*) to haggle or bargain. **2.** to chatter, talk, or say idly. ~*n.* **3.** haggling or bargaining. [C13 *chaffare,* from *chep* bargain + *fare* journey] —'**chafferer** *n.*

chaffinch ('tʃæfɪntʃ) *n.* a common European finch with black-and-white wings and, in the male, a reddish body and blue-grey head. [OE *ceaffinc,* from *ceaf* CHAFF[1] + *finc* FINCH]

chafing dish *n.* a vessel with a heating apparatus beneath it, for cooking or keeping food warm at the table.

Chagall (*French* ʃagal) *n.* **Marc** (mark). 1887–1985, French painter and illustrator, born in Russia, noted for his richly coloured pictures of men, animals, and objects in fantastic combinations and often suspended in space: his work includes 12 stained glass windows for a synagogue in Jerusalem (1961) and the decorations for the ceiling of the Paris Opera House (1964).

Chagres (*Spanish* 'tʃaɣres) *n.* a river in Panama, flowing southwest through Gatún Lake, then northwest to the Caribbean Sea.

chagrin ('ʃægrɪn) *n.* **1.** a feeling of annoyance or mortification. ~*vb.* **2.** to embarrass and annoy. [C17: from F *chagrin, chagriner,* from ?]

chain (tʃeɪn) *n.* **1.** a flexible length of metal links, used for confining, connecting, etc., or in jewellery. **2.** (*usually pl.*) anything that confines or restrains: *the chains of poverty.* **3.** (*usually pl.*) a set of metal links that fit over the tyre of a motor vehicle to reduce skidding on an icy surface. **4.** a series of related or connected facts, events, etc. **5. a.** a number of establishments such as hotels, shops, etc., having the same owner or management. **b.** (*as modifier*): *a chain store.* **6.** Also called: **Gunter's**

chain. a unit of length equal to 22 yards. **7.** Also called: **engineer's chain.** a unit of length equal to 100 feet. **8.** Also called: **nautical chain.** a unit of length equal to 15 feet. **9.** *Austral. & N.Z.* **a.** the rail along which carcasses are moved in a slaughterhouse. **b.** the team of workers who slaughter, skin, and otherwise process carcasses in a slaughterhouse. **10.** *Chem.* two or more atoms or groups bonded together so that the resulting molecule, ion, or radical resembles a chain. **11.** *Geog.* a series of natural features, esp. mountain ranges. ~*vb.* **12.** (*tr.; often foll. by up*) to confine, tie, or make fast with or as if with a chain. [C13: from OF, ult. from L; see CATENA]

Chain (tʃeɪn) *n.* **Ernst Boris.** 1906–79, British biochemist, born in Germany: purified and adapted penicillin for clinical use; with Fleming and Florey shared the Nobel prize for physiology or medicine 1945.

chain gang *n.* *U.S.* a group of convicted prisoners chained together.

chain letter *n.* a letter, often with a request for and promise of money, that is sent to many people who add to or recopy it and send it on.

chain mail *n.* **a.** another term for **mail²** (sense 1). **b.** (*as modifier*): *a chain-mail hood.*

chain printer *n.* a line printer in which the type is on a continuous chain.

chain reaction *n.* **1.** a process in which a neutron colliding with an atomic nucleus causes fission and the ejection of one or more other neutrons. **2.** a chemical reaction in which the product of one step is a reactant in the following step. **3.** a series of events, each of which precipitates the next. —,**chain-re'act** *vb.* (*intr.*).

chain saw *n.* a motor-driven saw in which the cutting teeth form links in a continuous chain.

chain-smoke *vb.* to smoke (cigarettes, etc.) continually, esp. lighting one from the preceding one. —**chain smoker** *n.*

chain stitch *n.* **1.** a looped embroidery stitch resembling the links of a chain. ~*vb.* **chain-stitch.** **2.** to sew (something) with this stitch.

chainwheel ('tʃeɪn,wiːl) *n.* (esp. on a bicycle) a toothed wheel that transmits drive via the chain.

chair (tʃɛə) *n.* **1.** a seat with a back on which one person sits, typically having four legs and often having arms. **2.** an official position of authority. **3.** a person holding an office of authority: *questions are to be addressed to the chair.* **4.** a professorship. **5.** *Railways.* an iron or steel cradle bolted to a sleeper in which the rail is locked in position. **6.** short for **sedan chair. 7. take the chair.** to preside as chairman for a meeting, etc. **8. the chair.** *Inf.* the electric chair. ~*vb.* (*tr.*) **9.** to preside over (a meeting). **10.** *Brit.* to carry aloft in a sitting position after a triumph. **11.** to provide with a chair of office. **12.** to install in a chair. [C13: from OF, from L *cathedra*, from Gk *kathedra*, from *kata-* down + *hedra* seat]

chair lift *n.* a series of chairs suspended from a power-driven cable for conveying people, esp. skiers, up a mountain.

chairman ('tʃɛəmən) *n., pl.* **-men.** a person who presides over a company's board of directors, a committee, a debate, etc. Also: **chairperson** or (*fem.*) **chairwoman.**

chaise (ʃeɪz) *n.* **1.** a light open horse-drawn carriage, esp. one with two wheels. **2.** short for **post chaise** and **chaise longue.** [C18: from F, var. of OF *chaiere* CHAIR]

chaise longue (ʃeɪz 'lɒŋ) *n., pl.* **chaise longues** or **chaises longues** (ʃeɪz 'lɒŋ) *n.* a long low chair with a back and single armrest. [C19: from F: long chair]

Chaka ('ʃaka) *n.* a variant spelling of **Shaka.**

chalaza (kə'leɪzə) *n., pl.* **-zas** or **-zae** (-ziː). one of a pair of spiral threads holding the yolk of a bird's egg in position. [C18: NL, from Gk: hailstone]

chalcedony (kæl'sɛdənɪ) *n., pl.* **-nies.** a form of quartz with crystals arranged in parallel fibres: a gemstone. [C15: from LL, from Gk *khalkēdōn* a precious stone, ? after *Khalkēdōn* Chalcedon, town in Asia Minor] —**chalcedonic** (,kælsɪ'dɒnɪk) *adj.*

Chalcidice (kæl'sɪdɪsɪ) *n.* a peninsula of N central Greece, in Macedonia, ending in the three promontories of Kassandra, Sithonia, and Akti. Area: 2945 sq. km (1149 sq. miles). Modern Greek name: **Khalkidiki.**

Chalcis ('kælsɪs) *n.* a city in SE Greece, at the narrowest point of the Euripus strait: important since the 7th century B.C., founding many colonies in ancient times. Pop.:

44 774 (1981). Modern Greek name: **Khalkís.** Medieval English name: **Negropont.**

chalcolithic (,kælkə'lɪθɪk) *adj. Archaeol.* of or relating to the period in which both stone and bronze tools were used. [C19: from Gk *khalkos* copper + *lithos* stone]

chalcopyrite (,kælkə'paɪraɪt) *n.* a common ore of copper, a crystalline sulphide of copper and iron. Formula: CuFeS₂. Also called: **copper pyrites.**

Chaldea or **Chaldaea** (kæl'diːə) *n.* **1.** an ancient region of Babylonia; the land lying between the Euphrates delta, the Persian Gulf, and the Arabian desert. **2.** another name for **Babylonia.**

chaldron ('tʃɔːldrən) *n.* a unit of capacity equal to 36 bushels. [C17: from OF *chauderon* CAULDRON]

chalet ('ʃæleɪ) *n.* **1.** a type of wooden house of Swiss origin, with wide projecting eaves. **2.** a similar house used as a ski lodge, etc. [C19: from F (Swiss dialect)]

Chaliapin (*Russian* ʃa'ljapin) *n.* **Fyodor Ivanovich** ('fjɔdər i'vanəvitʃ). 1873–1938, Russian operatic bass singer.

chalice ('tʃælɪs) *n.* **1.** *Poetic.* a drinking cup; goblet. **2.** *Christianity.* a gold or silver cup containing the wine at Mass. **3.** a cup-shaped flower. [C13: from OF, from L *calix* cup]

chalk (tʃɔːk) *n.* **1.** a soft fine-grained white sedimentary rock consisting of nearly pure calcium carbonate, containing minute fossil fragments of marine organisms. **2.** a piece of chalk, or substance like chalk, often coloured, used for writing and drawing on blackboards. **3. as alike** (*or* **different**) **as chalk and cheese.** *Inf.* totally different in essentials. **4. by a long chalk.** *Brit. inf.* by far. **5. not by a long chalk.** *Brit. inf.* by no means. **6.** (*modifier*) made of chalk. ~*vb.* **7.** to draw or mark (something) with chalk. **8.** (*tr.*) to mark, rub, or whiten with or as with chalk. [OE *cealc*, from L *calx* limestone, from Gk *khalix* pebble] —'**chalk,like** *adj.* —'**chalky** *adj.* —'**chalkiness** *n.*

chalk out *vb.* (*tr., adv.*) to outline (a plan, scheme, etc.); sketch.

chalkpit ('tʃɔːk,pɪt) *n.* a quarry for chalk.

chalk up *vb.* (*tr., adv.*) *Inf.* **1.** to score or register (something). **2.** to credit (money) to an account, etc. (esp. in **chalk it up**).

challenge ('tʃælɪndʒ) *vb.* (*mainly tr.*) **1.** to invite or summon (someone to do something, esp. to take part in a contest). **2.** (*also intr.*) to call (something) into question. **3.** to make demands on; stimulate: *the job challenges his ingenuity.* **4.** to order (a person) to halt and be identified. **5.** *Law.* to make formal objection to (a juror or jury). **6.** to lay claim to (attention, etc.). **7.** to inject (an experimental animal immunized with a test substance) with disease microorganisms to test for immunity to the disease. ~*n.* **8.** a call to engage in a fight, argument, or contest. **9.** a questioning of a statement or fact. **10.** a demanding or stimulating situation, career, etc. **11.** a demand by a sentry, police, etc., for identification or a password. **12.** *Law.* a formal objection to a person selected to serve on a jury or to the whole body of jurors. [C13: from OF *chalenge*, from L *calumnia* CALUMNY] —'**challengeable** *adj.* —'**challenger** *n.* —'**challenging** *adj.*

challis ('ʃælɪ, -lɪs) or **challie** ('ʃælɪ) *n.* a lightweight fabric of wool, cotton, etc., usually with a printed design. [C19: prob. from a surname]

Châlons-sur-Marne (*French* ʃalɔ̃syrmarn) *n.* a city in NE France, on the River Marne: scene of Attila's defeat by the Romans (451 A.D.). Pop.: 51 027 (1983 est.). Shortened form: **Châlons.**

Chalon-sur-Saône (*French* ʃalɔ̃syrson) *n.* an industrial city in E central France, on the Saône River. Pop.: 58 061 (1983 est.). Shortened form: **Chalon.**

chalybeate (kə'lɪbɪɪt) *adj.* containing or impregnated with iron salts. [C17: from NL *chalybeātus*, ult. from Gk *khalups* iron]

chamber ('tʃeɪmbə) *n.* **1.** a meeting hall, esp. one used for a legislative or judicial assembly. **2.** a reception room in an official residence, palace, etc. **3.** *Arch. or poetic.* a room in a private house, esp. a bedroom. **4. a.** a legislative, judicial, or administrative assembly. **b.** any of the houses of a legislature. **5.** an enclosed space; compartment; cavity. **6.** an enclosure for a cartridge in the cylinder of a revolver or for a shell in the breech of a cannon. **7.** short for **chamber pot. 8.** (*modifier*) of, relating to, or suitable for chamber music: *a chamber concert.* **9.** (*modifier*) on a small, quasi-domestic scale. ~ See also **chambers.** [C13: from OF, from LL *camera* room, L: vault, from Gk *kamara*]

chamberlain ('tʃeɪmbəlɪn) *n.* **1.** an officer who manages the household of a king. **2.** the steward of a nobleman or landowner. **3.** the treasurer of a municipal corporation. [C13: from OF *chamberlayn*, of Frankish origin]

Chamberlain ('tʃeɪmbəlɪn) *n.* **1.** (**Arthur**) **Neville.** 1869–1940, British statesman; Conservative prime minister (1937–40): pursued a policy of appeasement towards Germany; following the German invasion of Poland, he declared war on Germany on Sept. 3, 1939. **2.** his father, **Joseph.** 1836–1914, British statesman; originally a Liberal, he resigned in 1886 over Home Rule for Ireland and became leader of the Liberal Unionists; a leading advocate of preferential trading agreements with members of the British Empire. **3.** his son, Sir **Joseph Austen.** 1863–1937, British Conservative statesman; foreign secretary (1924–29); awarded a Nobel peace prize for his negotiation of the Locarno Pact (1925).

chambermaid ('tʃeɪmbə,meɪd) *n.* a woman employed to clean bedrooms, esp. in hotels.

chamber music *n.* music for performance by a small group of instrumentalists.

chamber of commerce *n.* (*sometimes cap.*) an organization composed mainly of local businessmen to promote, regulate, and protect their interests.

chamber orchestra *n.* a small orchestra of about 25 players, used for the authentic performance of baroque and early classical music as well as modern music.

chamber organ *n. Music.* a small compact organ used esp. for the authentic performance of preclassical music.

chamber pot *n.* a vessel for urine, used in bedrooms.

chambers ('tʃeɪmbəz) *pl. n.* **1.** a judge's room for hearing private cases not taken in open court. **2.** (in England) the set of rooms occupied by barristers where clients are interviewed.

Chambéry (*French* ʃãberi) *n.* a city in SE France, in the Alps: skiing centre; former capital of the duchy of Savoy. Pop.: 54 054 (1983 est.).

Chambord (*French* ʃãbɔr) *n.* a village in N central France: site of a famous Renaissance chateau.

chambray ('ʃæmbreɪ) *n.* a smooth light fabric of cotton, linen, etc., with a white weft and a coloured warp. [C19: after CAMBRAI]

chameleon (kə'miːlɪən) *n.* **1.** a lizard of Africa and Madagascar, having long slender legs, a prehensile tail and tongue, and the ability to change colour. **2.** a changeable or fickle person. [C14: from L, from Gk *khamaileōn*, from *khamai* on the ground + *leōn* LION] —**chameleonic** (kə,miːlɪ'ɒnɪk) *adj.*

chamfer ('tʃæmfə) *n.* **1.** a narrow flat surface at the corner of a beam, post, etc. ~*vb.* (*tr.*) **2.** to cut such a surface on (a beam, etc.). [C16: back formation from *chamfering*, from OF, from *chant* edge (see CANT²) + *fraindre* to break, from L *frangere*]

chamois ('ʃæmɪ; *for senses 1 and 4* 'ʃæmwɑː) *n., pl.* **-ois.** **1.** a sure-footed goat antelope of Europe and SW Asia, having vertical horns with backward-pointing tips. **2.** a soft suede leather formerly made from this animal, now obtained from the skins of sheep and goats. **3.** Also called: **chamois leather, shammy** (**leather**), **chammy** (**leather**). a piece of such leather or similar material used for polishing, etc. **4. a.** a greyish-yellow colour. **b.** (*as adj.*): *a chamois stamp.* ~*vb.* (*tr.*) **5.** to dress (leather or skin) like chamois. **6.** to polish with a chamois. [C16: from OF, from LL *camox*, from ?]

chamomile ('kæmə,maɪl) *n.* a variant spelling of **camomile.**

Chamonix ('ʃæmənɪ; *French* ʃamɔni) *n.* a town in SE France, in the Alps at the foot of Mont Blanc: skiing and tourist centre. Pop.: 9255 (1982 est.).

champ¹ (tʃæmp) *vb.* **1.** to munch (food) noisily like a horse. **2.** (when *intr.*, often foll. by *on, at*, etc.) to bite (something) nervously or impatiently. **3. champ** (*or* **chafe**) **at the bit.** *Inf.* to be impatient to start work, a journey, etc. ~*n.* **4.** the act or noise of champing. [C16: prob. imit.]

champ² (tʃæmp) *n. Inf.* short for **champion.**

champagne (ʃæm'peɪn) *n.* **1.** (*sometimes cap.*) a white sparkling wine produced around Reims and Épernay,

France. **2.** (loosely) any effervescent white wine. **3. a.** a pale tawny colour. **b.** (*as adj.*): *champagne tights.*

Champagne-Ardenne (ʃæm'peɪnɑː'dɛn; *French* ʃãpaɲardɛn) *n.* a region of NE France: a countship and commercial centre in medieval times; it consists of a great plain, with sheep and dairy farms and many vineyards.

Champaigne (ʃæm'peɪn; *French* ʃãpɛɲ) *n.* **Philippe de** (filip də). 1602–74, French painter, born in Brussels: noted particularly for his portraits and historical and religious scenes.

champers ('ʃæmpəz) *n.* (*functioning as sing.*) *Sl.* champagne.

champerty ('tʃæmpətɪ) *n., pl.* **-ties.** *Law.* (formerly) an illegal bargain between a party to litigation and an outsider whereby the latter agrees to pay for the action and thereby share in any proceeds recovered. [C14: from Anglo-F *champartie*, from OF *champart* share of produce, from *champ* field + *part* share]

Champigny-sur-Marne (*French* ʃãpiɲisyrmarn) *n.* a suburb of Paris, on the River Marne. Pop.: 80 290 (1983 est.).

champion ('tʃæmpɪən) *n.* **1. a.** a person, plant, or animal that has defeated all others in a competition: *a chess champion.* **b.** (*as modifier*): *a champion team; a champion marrow.* **2.** a person who defends a person or cause: *champion of the underprivileged.* **3.** (formerly) a knight who did battle for another, esp. a king or queen. ~*adj.* **4.** *N English dialect.* excellent. ~*adv.* **5.** *N English dialect.* very well. ~*vb.* (*tr.*) **6.** to support: *we champion the cause of liberty.* [C13: from OF, from LL *campiō*, from L *campus* field]

championship ('tʃæmpɪən,ʃɪp) *n.* **1.** (*sometimes pl.*) any of various contests held to determine a champion. **2.** the title of being a champion. **3.** support for a cause, person, etc.

Champlain¹ (ʃæm'pleɪn) *n.* **Lake.** a lake in the northeastern U.S., between the Green Mountains and the Adirondack Mountains: linked by the **Champlain Canal** to the Hudson River and by the Richelieu River to the St Lawrence; a major communications route in colonial times.

Champlain² (ʃæm'pleɪn; *French* ʃãplē) *n.* **Samuel de** (samɥɛl də). ?1567–1635, French explorer; founder of Quebec (1608) and governor of New France (1633–35).

champlevé *French.* (ʃãlve) *adj.* **1.** of a process of enamelling by which grooves are cut into a metal base and filled with enamel colours. ~*n.* **2.** an object enamelled by this process. [C19: from *champ* field (level surface) + *levé* raised]

Champollion (*French* ʃãpɔljɔ̃) *n.* **Jean François** (ʒã frãswa). 1790–1832, French Egyptologist, who deciphered the hieroglyphics on the Rosetta stone.

Champs Elysées (ʃɒnz e'liːzeɪ; *French* ʃãz elize) *n.* a major boulevard in Paris, leading from the Arc de Triomphe: site of the Elysées Palace and government offices.

Chanc. *abbrev. for:* **1.** Chancellor. **2.** Chancery.

chance (tʃɑːns) *n.* **1. a.** the unknown and unpredictable element that causes an event to result in a certain way rather than another, spoken of as a real force. **b.** (*as modifier*): *a chance meeting.* Related *adj.*: **fortuitous.** **2.** fortune; luck; fate. **3.** an opportunity or occasion. **4.** a risk; gamble. **5.** the extent to which an event is likely to occur; probability. **6.** an unpredicted event, esp. a fortunate one. **7. by chance.** accidentally: *he slipped by chance.* **8. on the** (**off**) **chance.** acting on the (remote) possibility. ~*vb.* **9.** (*tr.*) to risk; hazard. **10.** (*intr.*) to happen by chance: *I chanced to catch sight of her.* **11. chance on** (*or* **upon**). to come upon by accident. **12. chance one's arm.** to attempt to do something although the chance of success may be slight. [C13: from OF, from *cheoir* to occur, from L *cadere*] —'**chanceful** *adj.*

chancel ('tʃɑːnsəl) *n.* the part of a church containing the altar, sanctuary, and choir. [C14: from OF, from L *cancellī* (pl.) lattice]

chancellery *or* **chancellory** ('tʃɑːnsələrɪ) *n., pl.* **-leries** *or* **-lories.** **1.** the building or room occupied by a chancellor's office. **2.** the position or office of a chancellor. **3.** *U.S.* the office of an embassy or legation. [C14: from Anglo-F *chancellerie*, from OF *chancelier* CHANCELLOR]

chancellor ('tʃɑːnsələ) *n.* **1.** the head of the government in several European countries. **2.** *U.S.* the president of a university. **3.** *Brit. & Canad.* the honorary head of a university. Cf. **vice chancellor. 4.** *Christianity.* a clergyman acting as the law officer of a bishop. [C11: from Anglo-F *chanceler*, from LL *cancellārius* porter, from L *cancelli* lattice] —'**chancellor,ship** *n.*

Chancellor of the Exchequer *n. Brit.* the cabinet minister responsible for finance.

chance-medley *n. Law.* a sudden quarrel in which one party kills another. [C15: from Anglo-F *chance medlee* mixed chance]

chancer ('tʃɑːnsə) *n. Sl.* an unscrupulous or dishonest opportunist. [C19: from CHANCE + -ER¹]

chancery ('tʃɑːnsərɪ) *n., pl.* **-ceries.** (*usually cap.*) **1.** Also called: **Chancery Division.** (in England) the Lord Chancellor's court, now a division of the High Court of Justice. **2.** Also called: **court of chancery.** (in the U.S.) a court of equity. **3.** *Brit.* the political section or offices of an embassy or legation. **4.** another name for **chancellery. 5.** a court of public records. **6.** *Christianity.* a diocesan office under the supervision of a bishop's chancellor. **7. in chancery. a.** *Law.* (of a suit) pending in a court of equity. **b.** in an awkward situation. [C14: shortened from CHANCELLERY]

chancre ('ʃæŋkə) *n. Pathol.* a small hard growth, which is the first sign of syphilis. [C16: from F, from L: CANCER] —'**chancrous** *adj.*

chancroid ('ʃæŋkrɔɪd) *n.* **1.** a soft venereal ulcer, esp. of the male genitals. ~*adj.* **2.** relating to or resembling a chancroid or chancre.

chancy *or* **chancey** ('tʃɑːnsɪ) *adj.* **chancier, chanciest.** *Inf.* uncertain; risky.

chandelier (,ʃændɪ'lɪə) *n.* an ornamental hanging light with branches and holders for several candles or bulbs. [C17: from F: candleholder, from L CANDELABRUM]

Chandernagore (,tʃʌndənə'gɔː) *n.* a port in E India, in S West Bengal on the Hooghly River: a former French settlement (1686–1950). Pop.: 101 925 (1981 est.).

Chandigarh (,tʃʌndɪ'gɑː) *n.* a city and Union Territory of N India, joint capital of the Punjab and Haryana: modern city planned in the 1950s by Le Corbusier. Pop.: 371 992 (1981), of city; 450 061 (1981), of union territory. Area (of union territory): 114 sq. km (44 sq. miles).

chandler ('tʃɑːndlə) *n.* **1.** a dealer in a specified trade or merchandise: *ship's chandler.* **2.** a person who makes or sells candles. [C14: from OF *chandelier* one who makes or deals in candles, from *chandelle* CANDLE] —'**chandlery** *n.*

Chandler ('tʃɑːndlə) *n.* **Raymond (Thornton).** 1888–1959, U.S. thriller writer: created Philip Marlowe, one of the first detective heroes in fiction.

Chandragupta (,tʃʌndrə'guptə) *n.* Greek name *Sandracottos.* died ?297 B.C., ruler of N India, who founded the Maurya dynasty (325) and defeated Seleucus (?305).

Chandrasekhar (,tʃændrə'siːkə) *n.* **Subrahmanyan** (,subrə'mænjən). born 1910, U.S. astronomer born in Lahore, India (now Pakistan). His work on stellar evolution led to an understanding of white dwarfs.

Chanel (*French* ʃanɛl) *n.* **Gabrielle** (gabriɛl), known as *Coco.* 1883–1971, French couturière and perfumer, who created "the little black dress" and the perfume Chanel No. 5.

Chang (tʃæŋ) *n.* another name for the **Yangtze.**

Changan ('tʃæŋ'ɑːn) *n.* a former name of **Xi An.**

Changchiakow *or* **Changchiak'ou** ('tʃæŋ'tʃjɑː'kəʊ) *n.* a variant transliteration of the Chinese name for **Zhangjiakou.**

Changchow *or* **Ch'ang-chou** ('tʃæŋ'tʃaʊ) *n.* **1.** a variant transliteration of the Chinese name for **Changzhou. 2.** a variant transliteration of the Chinese name for **Zhangzhou.**

Changchun *or* **Ch'ang Ch'un** ('tʃæŋ'tʃʊn) *n.* a city in NE China, capital of Jilin province: as **Hsinking,** capital of the Japanese state of Manchukuo (1932–45). Pop.: 1 860 000 (1986).

Changde ('tʃæŋ'deɪ), **Changteh,** *or* **Ch'ang-te** *n.* a port in SE central China, in N Hunan province, near the mouth of the Yuan River: severely damaged by the Japanese in World War II. Pop.: 213 890 (1982).

change (tʃeɪndʒ) *vb.* **1.** to make or become different; alter. **2.** (*tr.*) to replace with or exchange for another: *to change one's name.* **3.** (sometimes foll. by *to* or *into*) to transform or convert or be transformed or converted. **4.** to give and receive (something) in return: *to change places.* **5.** (*tr.*) to give or receive (money) in exchange for

the equivalent sum in a smaller denomination or different currency. **6.** (*tr.*) to remove or replace the coverings of: *to change a baby.* **7.** (when *intr.*, may be foll. by *into* or *out of*) to put on other clothes. **8.** to operate (the gear lever of a motor vehicle): *to change gear.* **9.** to alight from (one bus, train, etc.) and board another. ~*n.* **10.** the act or fact of changing or being changed. **11.** a variation or modification. **12.** the substitution of one thing for another. **13.** anything that is or may be substituted for something else. **14.** variety or novelty (esp. in **for a change**). **15.** a different set, esp. of clothes. **16.** money given or received in return for its equivalent in a larger denomination or in a different currency. **17.** the balance of money when the amount tendered is larger than the amount due. **18.** coins of a small denomination. **19.** (*often cap.*) *Arch.* a place where merchants meet to transact business. **20.** the act of passing from one state or phase to another. **21.** the transition from one phase of the moon to the next. **22.** the order in which a peal of bells may be rung. **23. get no change out of** (someone). *Sl.* not to be successful in attempts to exploit (someone). **24. ring the changes.** to vary the manner or performance of an action that is often repeated. ~See also **change down, changeover, change up.** [C13: from OF, from L *cambire* to exchange, barter] —'**changeful** *adj.* —'**changeless** *adj.* —'**changer** *n.*

changeable ('tʃeɪndʒəbəl) *adj.* **1.** able to change or be changed: *changeable weather.* **2.** varying in colour as when viewed from different angles. —,**changea'bility** *n.* —'**changeably** *adv.*

change down *vb.* (*intr., adv.*) to select a lower gear when driving.

changeling ('tʃeɪndʒlɪŋ) *n.* a child believed to have been exchanged by fairies for the parents' true child.

change of life *n.* a nontechnical name for **menopause.**

changeover ('tʃeɪndʒ,əʊvə) *n.* **1.** an alteration or complete reversal from one method, system, or product to another. **2.** a reversal of a situation, attitude, etc. **3.** *Sport.* the act of transferring to or being relieved by a team-mate in a relay race, as by handing over a baton, etc. ~*vb.* **change over.** (*adv.*) **4.** to adopt (a different position or attitude): *the driver and navigator changed over.*

change-ringing *n.* the art of bell-ringing in which a set of bells is rung in an established order which is then changed.

change up *vb.* (*intr., adv.*) to select a higher gear when driving.

Changsha *or* **Ch'ang-sha** ('tʃæŋ'ʃɑː) *n.* a port in SE China, capital of Hunan province, on the Xiang River. Pop.: 1 160 000 (1986).

Changteh *or* **Ch'ang-te** ('tʃæŋ'teɪ) *n.* a variant transliteration of the Chinese name for **Changde.**

channel ('tʃænəl) *n.* **1.** a broad strait connecting two areas of sea. **2.** the bed or course of a river, stream, or canal. **3.** a navigable course through a body of water. **4.** (*often pl.*) a means or agency of access, communication, etc.: *through official channels.* **5.** a course into which something can be directed or moved. **6.** *Electronics.* **a.** band of radio frequencies assigned for a particular purpose, esp. the broadcasting of a television signal. **b.** a path for an electrical signal: *a stereo set has two channels.* **7.** a tubular passage for fluids. **8.** a groove, as in the shaft of a column. **9.** *Computers.* **a.** a path along which data can be transmitted. **b.** one of the lines along the length of a paper tape on which information can be stored in the form of punched holes. ~*vb.* **-nelling, -nelled** *or U.S.* **-neling, -neled. 10.** to make or cut channels in (something). **11.** (*tr.*) to guide into or convey through a channel or channels: *information was channelled through to them.* [C13: from OF, from L *canālis* pipe, groove, conduit]

Channel ('tʃænəl) *n.* **the.** short for **English Channel.**

Channel Country *n.* **the.** an area of E central Australia, in SW Queensland: crossed by intermittent rivers and subject to both flooding and long periods of drought.

Channel Islands *pl. n.* a group of islands in the English Channel, off the NW coast of France, consisting of Jersey, Guernsey, Alderney, Brechou, Great Sark, Little Sark, Herm, Jethou, and Lihou (British crown dependencies), and the Roches Douvres and the Îles Chausey (which belong to France): the only part of the duchy of Normandy remaining to Britain. Pop.: 144 494 (1986). Area: 194 sq. km (75 sq. miles).

chanson de geste *French.* (ʃɑ̃sɔ̃ də ʒɛst) *n.* one of a genre of Old French epic poems, the most famous of which is the *Chanson de Roland*. [lit.: song of exploits]

chant (tʃɑːnt) *n.* **1.** a simple song. **2.** a short simple melody in which several words or syllables are assigned to one note. **3.** a psalm or canticle performed by using such a melody. **4.** a rhythmic or repetitious slogan, usually spoken or sung, as by sports supporters, etc. ~*vb.* **5.** to sing or recite (a psalm, etc.) as a chant. **6.** to intone (a slogan). [C14: from OF *chanter* to sing, from L *cantāre*, frequentative of *canere* to sing] —'**chanting** *n.*, *adj.*

chanter ('tʃɑːntə) *n.* the pipe on a set of bagpipes on which the melody is played.

chanterelle (ˌtʃæntə'rɛl) *n.* any of a genus of fungi having an edible yellow funnel-shaped mushroom. [C18: from F, from L *cantharus* drinking vessel, from Gk *kantharos*]

chanteuse (*French* ʃɑ̃tøz) *n.* a female singer, esp. in a nightclub or cabaret. [F: singer]

chanticleer (ˌtʃæntɪ'klɪə) *n.* a name for a cock, used esp. in fables. [C13: from OF, from *chanter cler* to sing clearly]

Chantilly (ʃæn'tɪlɪ; *French* ʃɑ̃tiji) *n.* **1.** a town in N France, near the **Forest of Chantilly:** formerly famous for lace and porcelain. Pop.: 10 208 (1982 est.). ~*adj.* **2.** (of cream) lightly sweetened and whipped.

chantry ('tʃɑːntrɪ) *n.*, *pl.* **-tries.** *Christianity.* **1.** an endowment for the singing of Masses for the soul of the founder. **2.** a chapel or altar so endowed. [C14: from OF, from *chanter* to sing; see CHANT]

chanty ('ʃæntɪ, 'tʃæn-) *n.*, *pl.* **-ties.** a variant of **shanty**[2].

Chanukah *or* **Hanukkah** ('hɑːnəkə, -nʊˌkɑː) *n.* the eight-day Jewish festival of lights commemorating the rededication of the temple by Judas Maccabeus in 165 B.C. Also called: **Feast of Dedication, Feast of Lights.** [from Heb., lit.: a dedication]

Chaoan ('tʃaʊ'ɑːn) *n.* a city in SE China, in E Guangdong province, on the Han River: river port. Pop.: 1 202 800 (1984 est.). Former name: **Chaochow.**

Chaochow ('tʃaʊ'tʃəʊ) *n.* the former name of **Chaoan.**

Chao Phraya ('tʃaʊ prə'jɑː) *n.* a river in N Thailand, rising in the N highlands and flowing south to the Gulf of Siam. Length: (including the headstreams Nan and Ping) 1200 km (750 miles). Also called: **Menam.**

chaos ('keɪɒs) *n.* **1.** (*usually cap.*) the disordered formless matter supposed to have existed before the ordered universe. **2.** complete disorder; utter confusion. [C15: from L, from Gk *khaos*] —**chaotic** (keɪ'ɒtɪk) *adj.* —**cha'otically** *adv.*

chap[1] (tʃæp) *vb.* **chapping, chapped. 1.** (of the skin) to make or become raw and cracked, esp. by exposure to cold. ~*n.* **2.** (*usually pl.*) a cracked patch on the skin. [C14: prob. of Gmc origin]

chap[2] (tʃæp) *n. Inf.* a man or boy; fellow. [C16 (in the sense: buyer): shortened from CHAPMAN]

chap[3] (tʃɒp, tʃæp) *n.* a less common word for **chop**[3].

chaparejos *or* **chaparajos** (ˌʃæpə'reɪəʊs) *pl. n.* another name for **chaps.** [from Mexican Sp.]

chaparral (ˌtʃæpə'ræl, ˌʃæp-) *n.* (in the southwestern U.S.) a dense growth of shrubs and trees. [C19: from Sp., from *chaparra* evergreen oak]

chapatti *or* **chapati** (tʃə'pætɪ, -'pɑːtɪ) *n.*, *pl.* **-ti, -tis,** *or* **-ties.** (in Indian cookery) a flat unleavened bread resembling a pancake. [from Hindi]

chapbook ('tʃæp,bʊk) *n.* a book of popular ballads, stories, etc., formerly sold by chapmen.

chapel ('tʃæpᵊl) *n.* **1.** a place of Christian worship, esp. with a separate altar, in a church or cathedral. **2.** a similar place of worship in a large house or institution, such as a college. **3.** a church subordinate to a parish church. **4.** (in Britain) **a.** a Nonconformist place of worship. **b.** Nonconformist religious practices or doctrine. **5. a.** the members of a trade union in a particular newspaper office, printing house, etc. **b.** a meeting of these members. [C13: from OF, from LL *cappella*, dim. of *cappa* (see CAP); orig. the sanctuary where the cloak of St Martin was kept]

chaperon *or* **chaperone** ('ʃæpə,rəʊn) *n.* **1.** (esp. formerly) an older or married woman who accompanies or supervises a young unmarried woman on social occasions. ~*vb.* **2.** to act as a chaperon to. [C14: from OF, from *chape* hood; see CAP] —**chaperonage** ('ʃæpərənɪdʒ) *n.*

chapfallen ('tʃæp,fɔːlən) *or* **chopfallen** *adj.* dejected; downhearted. [C16: from CHOPS + FALLEN]

chaplain ('tʃæplɪn) *n.* a Christian clergyman attached to a chapel of an institution or ministering to a military body, etc. [C12: from OF, from LL, from *cappella* CHAPEL] —'**chaplaincy** *n.*

chaplet ('tʃæplɪt) *n.* **1.** an ornamental wreath of flowers worn on the head. **2.** a string of beads. **3.** *R.C. Church.* **a.** a string of prayer beads constituting one third of the rosary. **b.** the prayers counted on this string. **4.** a narrow moulding in the form of a string of beads; astragal. [C14: from OF, from *chapel* hat] —'**chapleted** *adj.*

Chaplin ('tʃæplɪn) *n.* Sir **Charles Spencer,** known as *Charlie Chaplin.* 1889–1977, English comedian, film actor, and director. He is renowned for his portrayal of a downtrodden little man with baggy trousers, bowler hat, and cane. His films, most of which were made in Hollywood, include *The Gold Rush* (1924), *Modern Times* (1936), and *The Great Dictator* (1940). —ˌ**Chaplin'esque** *adj.*

chapman ('tʃæpmən) *n.*, *pl.* **-men.** *Arch.* a trader, esp. an itinerant pedlar. [OE *cēapman*, from *cēap* buying and selling]

Chapman ('tʃæpmən) *n.* **George.** 1559–1634, English dramatist and poet, noted for his translation of Homer.

Chappell ('tʃæpᵊl) *n.* **Greg(ory Stephen)** born 1948, Australian cricketer: first Australian to score over 7000 test runs.

chappie ('tʃæpɪ) *n. Inf.* another word for **chap**[2].

chaps (tʃæps, ʃæps) *pl. n.* leather overleggings without a seat, worn by cowboys. Also called: **chaparajos, chaparejos.** [C19: shortened from CHAPAREJOS]

chapter ('tʃæptə) *n.* **1.** a division of a written work. **2.** a sequence of events: *a chapter of disasters.* **3.** a period in a life, history, etc. **4.** a numbered reference to that part of a Parliamentary session which relates to a specified Act of Parliament. **5.** a branch of some societies, clubs, etc. **6.** the collective body or a meeting of the canons of a cathedral or of the members of a monastic or knightly order. **7. chapter and verse.** exact authority for an action or statement. ~*vb.* **8.** (*tr.*) to divide into chapters. [C13: from OF *chapitre*, from L *capitulum*, lit.: little head, hence, section of writing, from *caput* head]

chapterhouse ('tʃæptə,haʊs) *n.* **1.** the building in which a chapter meets. See **chapter** (sense 6). **2.** *U.S.* the meeting place of a college fraternity or sorority.

char[1] (tʃɑː) *vb.* **charring, charred. 1.** to burn or be burned partially; scorch. **2.** (*tr.*) to reduce (wood) to charcoal by partial combustion. [C17: short for CHARCOAL]

char[2] *or* **charr** (tʃɑː) *n.*, *pl.* **char, chars** *or* **charr, charrs.** any of various troutlike fishes occurring in cold lakes and northern seas. [C17: from ?]

char[3] (tʃɑː) *n.* **1.** *Inf.* short for **charwoman.** ~*vb.* **charring, charred. 2.** (*intr.*) *Brit. inf.* to do cleaning as a job. [C18: from OE *cerran*]

char[4] (tʃɑː) *n.* a slang word for **tea.** [from Chinese *ch'a*]

charabanc ('ʃærə,bæŋ) *n. Brit.* a coach, esp. for sightseeing. [C19: from F: wagon with seats]

character ('kærɪktə) *n.* **1.** the combination of traits and qualities distinguishing the individual nature of a person or thing. **2.** one such distinguishing quality; characteristic. **3.** moral force: *a man of character.* **4. a.** reputation, esp. a good reputation. **b.** (*as modifier*): *character assassination.* **5.** a person represented in a play, film, story, etc.; role. **6.** an outstanding person: *one of the great characters of the century.* **7.** *Inf.* an odd, eccentric, or unusual person: *he's quite a character.* **8.** an informal word for **person:** *a shady character.* **9.** a symbol used in a writing system, such as a letter of the alphabet. **10.** Also called: **sort.** *Printing.* any single letter, numeral, etc., cast as a type. **11.** *Computers.* any such letter, numeral, etc., which can be represented uniquely by a binary pattern. **12.** a style of writing or printing. **13.** *Genetics.* any structure, function, attribute, etc., in an organism that is determined by a gene or group of genes. **14.** a short prose sketch of a distinctive type of person. **15. in** (*out of*) **character.** typical (*or* not typical) of the apparent character of a person. [C14: from L: distinguishing mark, from Gk *kharaktēr* engraver's tool] —'**characterful** *adj.* —'**characterless** *adj.*

character actor *n.* an actor who specializes in playing odd or eccentric characters.

characteristic (ˌkærɪktə'rɪstɪk) *n.* **1.** a distinguishing quality, attribute, or trait. **2.** *Maths.* **a.** the integral part of a common logarithm: *the characteristic of 2.4771 is 2.* **b.** another name for **exponent** (sense 4). ~*adj.* **3.** indicative of a distinctive quality, etc.; typical. —,**character'istically** *adv.*

characterize *or* **-ise** ('kærɪktə,raɪz) *vb.* (*tr.*) **1.** to be a characteristic of. **2.** to distinguish or mark as a characteristic. **3.** to describe or portray the character of. —,**characteri'zation** *or* **-i'sation** *n.*

charade (ʃə'rɑːd) *n.* **1.** an act in the game of charades. **2.** *Chiefly Brit.* an absurd act; travesty.

charades (ʃə'rɑːdz) *n.* (*functioning as sing.*) a parlour game in which one team acts out each syllable of a word, the other team having to guess the word. [C18: from F, from Provençal *charrado* chat, from *charra* chatter]

charcoal ('tʃɑː,kəʊl) *n.* **1.** a black amorphous form of carbon made by heating wood or other organic matter in the absence of air. **2.** a stick of this for drawing. **3.** a drawing done in charcoal. **4.** Also: **charcoal grey. a.** a dark grey colour. **b.** (*as adj.*): *a charcoal suit.* ~*vb.* **5.** (*tr.*) to write, draw, or blacken with charcoal. [C14: from *char* (from ?) + COAL]

Charcot (*French* ʃarko) *n.* **Jean Martin** (ʒã martɛ̃). 1825–93, French neurologist, noted for his attempt using hypnotism to find an organic cause for hysteria, which influenced Freud.

chard (tʃɑːd) *n.* a variety of beet with large succulent leaves and thick stalks, used as a vegetable. Also called: **Swiss chard.** [C17: prob. from F *carde*, ult. from L *carduus* thistle]

Chardin (*French* ʃardɛ̃) *n.* **Jean-Baptiste Siméon** (ʒɑ̃batist simeɔ̃). 1699–1779, French still-life and genre painter, noted for his subtle use of scumbled colour.

Charente (*French* ʃarɑ̃t) *n.* **1.** a department of W central France, in Poitou-Charentes region. Capital: Angoulême. Pop.: 340 770 (1982). Area: 5972 sq. km (2329 sq. miles). **2.** a river in W France, flowing west to the Bay of Biscay. Length: 362 km (225 miles).

Charente-Maritime (*French* ʃarɑ̃tmaritim) *n.* a department of W France, in Poitou-Charentes region. Capital: La Rochelle. Pop.: 513 220 (1982). Area: 7232 sq. km (2820 sq. miles).

charge (tʃɑːdʒ) *vb.* **1.** to set or demand (a price). **2.** (*tr.*) to enter a debit against a person or his account. **3.** (*tr.*) to accuse or impute a fault to (a person, etc.), as formally in a court of law. **4.** (*tr.*) to command; place a burden upon or assign responsibility to: *I was charged to take the message to headquarters.* **5.** to make a rush at or sudden attack upon (a person or thing). **6.** (*tr.*) to fill (a receptacle) with the proper quantity. **7.** (often foll. by *up*) to cause (an accumulator, capacitor, etc.) to take or store electricity (or of an accumulator) to have electricity fed into it. **8.** to fill or be filled with matter by dispersion, solution, or absorption: *to charge water with carbon dioxide.* **9.** (*tr.*) to fill or suffuse with feeling, emotion, etc.: *the atmosphere was charged with excitement.* **10.** (*tr.*) *Law.* (of a judge) to address (a jury) authoritatively. **11.** (*tr.*) to load (a firearm). **12.** (*tr.*) *Heraldry.* to paint (a shield, banner, etc.) with a charge. ~*n.* **13.** a price charged for some article or service; cost. **14.** a financial liability, such as a tax. **15.** a debt or a book entry recording it. **16.** an accusation or allegation, such as a formal accusation of a crime in law. **17. a.** an onrush, attack, or assault. **b.** the call to such an attack in battle. **18.** custody or guardianship. **19.** a person or thing committed to someone's care. **20. a.** a cartridge or shell. **b.** the explosive required to discharge a firearm. **c.** an amount of explosive to be detonated at any one time. **21.** the quantity of anything that a receptacle is intended to hold. **22.** *Physics.* **a.** the attribute of matter responsible for all electrical phenomena, existing in two forms: *negative charge; positive charge.* **b.** an excess or deficiency of electrons in a system. **c.** a quantity of electricity determined by the product of an electric current and the time for which it flows, measured in coulombs. **d.** the total amount of electricity stored in a capacitor or an accumulator. **23.** a load or burden. **24.** a duty or responsibility; control. **25.** a command, injunction, or order. **26.** *Heraldry.* a design depicted on heraldic arms. **27. in charge.** in command. **28. in charge of. a.** having responsibility for. **b.** *U.S.* under the care of. [C13: from OF *chargier* to load, from LL *carricāre*; see CARRY]

chargeable ('tʃɑːdʒəbᵊl) *adj.* **1.** liable to be charged. **2.** liable to result in a legal charge.

charge account *n.* another term for **credit account.**

charge card *n.* a card issued by a chain store, shop, or organization, that enables customers to obtain goods and services for which they pay at a later date.

charge carrier *n.* an electron, hole, or ion that transports the electric charge in an electric current.

chargé d'affaires ('ʃɑːʒeɪ dæ'fɛə) *n., pl.* **chargés d'affaires** ('ʃɑːʒeɪ, -ʒeɪz). **1.** the temporary head of a diplomatic mission in the absence of the ambassador or minister. **2.** the head of a diplomatic mission of the lowest level. [C18: from F: (one) charged with affairs]

charge hand *n. Brit.* a workman whose grade of responsibility is just below that of a foreman.

charge nurse *n. Brit.* a nurse in charge of a ward in a hospital. Male equivalent of **sister.**

charger¹ ('tʃɑːdʒə) *n.* **1.** a person or thing that charges. **2.** a horse formerly ridden into battle. **3.** a device for charging an accumulator.

charger² ('tʃɑːdʒə) *n. Antiques.* a large dish. [C14 *chargeour*, from *chargen* to CHARGE]

charge sheet *n. Brit.* a document on which a police officer enters details of the charge against a prisoner and the court in which he will appear.

Chari ('tʃɑːrɪ) *or* **Shari** *n.* a river in N central Africa, rising in the N Central African Republic and flowing north to Lake Chad. Length: about 2250 km (1400 miles).

charily ('tʃɛərɪlɪ) *adv.* **1.** cautiously; carefully. **2.** sparingly.

chariness ('tʃɛərɪnɪs) *n.* the state of being chary.

Charing Cross ('tʃærɪŋ) *n.* a district of London, in the city of Westminster: the modern cross (1863) in front of Charing Cross railway station replaces the one erected by Edward I (1290), the last of twelve marking the route of the funeral procession of his queen, Eleanor.

chariot ('tʃærɪət) *n.* **1.** a two-wheeled horse-drawn vehicle used in ancient wars, races, etc. **2.** a light four-wheeled horse-drawn ceremonial carriage. **3.** *Poetic.* any stately vehicle. [C14: from OF, augmentative of *char* CAR]

charioteer (,tʃærɪə'tɪə) *n.* the driver of a chariot.

charisma (kə'rɪzmə) *or* **charism** ('kærɪzəm) *n.* **1.** a special personal quality or power of an individual making him capable of influencing or inspiring large numbers of people. **2.** a quality inherent in a thing, such as a particular type of car, which inspires great enthusiasm and devotion. **3.** *Christianity.* a divinely bestowed power or talent. [C17: from Church L, from Gk *kharisma*, from *kharis* grace, favour] —**charismatic** (,kærɪz'mætɪk) *adj.*

charismatic movement *n. Christianity.* any of various groups, within existing denominations, emphasizing the charismatic gifts of speaking in tongues, healing, etc.

charitable ('tʃærɪtəbᵊl) *adj.* **1.** generous in giving to the needy. **2.** kind or lenient in one's attitude towards others. **3.** of or for charity. —'**charitableness** *n.* —'**charitably** *adv.*

charity ('tʃærɪtɪ) *n., pl.* **-ties. 1. a.** the giving of help, money, food, etc., to those in need. **b.** (*as modifier*): *a charity show.* **2.** an institution or organization set up to provide help, money, etc., to those in need. **3.** the help, money, etc., given to the needy; alms. **4.** a kindly attitude towards people. **5.** love of one's fellow men. [C13: from OF, from L *cāritās* affection, from *cārus* dear]

charivari (,ʃɑːrɪ'vɑːrɪ), **shivaree**, *or esp. U.S.* **chivaree** *n.* **1.** a discordant mock serenade to newlyweds, made with pans, kettles, etc. **2.** a confused noise; din. [C17: from F, from LL, from Gk *karēbaria*, from *karē* head + *barus* heavy]

charlady ('tʃɑː,leɪdɪ) *n., pl.* **-dies.** another name for **charwoman.**

charlatan ('ʃɑːlətᵊn) *n.* someone who professes expertise, esp. in medicine, that he does not have; quack. [C17: from F, from It., from *ciarlare* to chatter] —'**charlatan,ism** *or* '**charlatanry** *n.*

Charlemagne ('ʃɑːlə,meɪn) *n.* ?742–814 A.D., king of the Franks (768–814) and, as Charles I, Holy Roman Emperor (800–814). He conquered the Lombards (774), the Saxons (772–804), and the Avars (791–799). He instituted many judicial and ecclesiastical reforms, and promoted commerce and agriculture throughout his empire, which extended from the Ebro to the Elbe. Under Alcuin his court at Aachen became the centre of a revival of learning.

Charleroi (*French* ʃarlərwa) *n.* a town in SW Belgium, in Hainaut province: centre of an industrial region. Pop.: 209 395 (1987 est.).

Charles (tʃɑːlz) *n.* **1.** *Prince of Wales.* born 1948, son of Elizabeth II; heir apparent to the throne of Great Britain and Northern Ireland. He married (1981) Lady Diana Spencer; their son, Prince William of Wales, was born in 1982 and their second son, Prince Henry, in 1984. **2. Ray,** real name *Ray Charles Robinson.* born 1930, U.S. singer, pianist, and songwriter, whose work spans jazz, blues, gospel, pop, and country music.

Charles I *n.* **1.** title as Holy Roman Emperor of **Charlemagne. 2.** title as king of France of **Charles II** (Holy Roman Emperor). **3.** title as king of Spain of **Charles V** (Holy Roman Emperor). **4.** title of **Charles Stuart.** 1600–49, king of England, Scotland, and Ireland (1625–49); son of James I. He ruled for 11 years (1629–40) without parliament, advised by his minister Strafford, until rebellion broke out in Scotland. Conflict with the Long Parliament led to the Civil War and after his defeat at Naseby (1645) he sought refuge with the Scots (1646). He was handed over to the English army under Cromwell (1647) and executed. **5.** 1887–1922, emperor of Austria, and, as Charles IV, king of Hungary (1916–18). The last ruler of the Austro-Hungarian monarchy, he was forced to abdicate at the end of World War I.

Charles II *n.* **1.** known as *Charles the Bald.* 823–877 A.D., Holy Roman Emperor (875–877) and, as Charles I, king of France (843–877). **2.** 1630–85, king of England, Scotland, and Ireland (1660–85) following the Restoration (1660); son of Charles I. He did much to promote commerce, science, and the Navy, but his Roman Catholic sympathies caused widespread distrust.

Charles IV *n.* title as king of Hungary of **Charles I** (sense 5).

Charles V *n.* 1500–58, Holy Roman Emperor (1519–56), king of Burgundy and the Netherlands (1506–55) and, as Charles I, king of Spain (1516–56): his reign saw the empire threatened by Francis I of France, the Turks, and the spread of Protestantism; abdicated.

Charles VI *n.* known as *Charles the Mad* or *Charles the Well-Beloved.* 1368–1422, king of France (1380–1422): defeated by Henry V of England at Agincourt (1415), he was forced by the Treaty of Troyes (1420) to recognize Henry as his successor.

Charles VII *n.* 1403–61, king of France (1422–61), son of Charles VI. He was excluded from the French throne by the Treaty of Troyes, but following Joan of Arc's victory over the English at Orléans (1429), was crowned.

Charles IX *n.* 1550–74, king of France (1560–74), son of Catherine de' Medici and Henry II: his reign was marked by war between Huguenots and Catholics.

Charles X *n.* 1757–1836, king of France (1824–30): his attempt to restore absolutism led to his enforced exile.

Charles XIV *n.* the title as king of Sweden and Norway of (Jean Baptiste Jules) **Bernadotte.**

Charles Edward Stuart *n.* See (Charles Edward) **Stuart.**

Charles Martel (mɑːˈtɛl) *n.* grandfather of Charlemagne. ?688–741 A.D., Frankish ruler of Austrasia (715–41), who checked the Muslim invasion of Europe by defeating the Moors at Poitiers (732).

Charles's Wain (weɪn) *n.* another name for the **Plough.** [OE *Carles wægn,* from *Carl* CHARLEMAGNE + *wægn* WAIN]

Charles the Great *n.* another name for **Charlemagne.**

charleston (ˈtʃɑːlstən) *n.* a fast rhythmic dance of the 1920s, characterized by kicking and by twisting of the legs from the knee down. [named after *Charleston,* South Carolina]

Charleston (ˈtʃɑːlstən) *n.* **1.** a city in central West Virginia: the state capital. Pop.: 59 371 (1985 est.). **2.** a port in SE South Carolina, on the Atlantic: scene of the first action in the Civil War. Pop.: 68 900 (1986).

Charleville-Mézières (*French* ʃarləvilmezjɛr) *n.* twin towns on opposite sides of the River Meuse in NE France. Pop.: 59 577 (1983 est.). See **Mézières.**

charley horse (ˈtʃɑːlɪ) *n. U.S. & Canad. inf.* cramp following strenuous athletic exercise. [C19: from ?]

charlie (ˈtʃɑːlɪ) *n. Brit. inf.* a silly person; fool.

charlock (ˈtʃɑːlɒk) *n.* a weedy Eurasian plant with hairy stems and foliage and yellow flowers. Also called: **wild mustard.** [OE *cerlic,* from ?]

charlotte (ˈʃɑːlət) *n.* **1.** a dessert made with fruit and layers or a casing of bread or cake crumbs, sponge cake, etc.: *apple charlotte.* **2.** short for **charlotte russe.** [C19: from F, from the name *Charlotte*]

Charlotte (ˈʃɑːlət) *n.* a city in S North Carolina: the largest city in the state. Pop.: 314 447 (1980).

Charlotte Amalie (ˈʃɑːlət əˈmɑːlɪə) *n.* the capital of the Virgin Islands of the United States, a port on St Thomas Island. Pop.: 52 660 (1985). Former name (1921–37): **Saint Thomas.**

Charlottenburg (*German* ʃarˈlɔtənburk) *n.* a district of West Berlin, formerly an independent city.

charlotte russe (ruːs) *n.* a cold dessert made with sponge fingers enclosing a mixture of cream, custard, etc. [F.: Russian charlotte]

Charlottetown (ˈʃɑːlətˌtaʊn) *n.* a port in SE Canada, capital of the province of Prince Edward Island. Pop.: 15 282 (1981).

Charlton (ˈtʃɑːltən) *n.* **Robert,** known as *Bobby.* born 1937, English footballer; played for England over 100 times.

charm (tʃɑːm) *n.* **1.** the quality of pleasing, fascinating, or attracting people. **2.** a pleasing or attractive feature. **3.** a small object worn for supposed magical powers; amulet. **4.** a trinket worn on a bracelet. **5.** a magic spell. **6.** a formula used in casting such a spell. **7.** *Physics.* a property of certain elementary particles, used to explain some scattering experiments. **8. like a charm.** perfectly; successfully. ~*vb.* **9.** to attract or fascinate; delight greatly. **10.** to cast a magic spell on. **11.** to protect, influence, or heal, supposedly by magic. **12.** (*tr.*) to influence or obtain by personal charm. [C13: from OF, from L *carmen* song] —'**charmer** *n.*

charming (ˈtʃɑːmɪŋ) *adj.* delightful; pleasant; attractive. —'**charmingly** *adv.*

charnel (ˈtʃɑːnˠl) *n.* **1.** short for **charnel house.** ~*adj.* **2.** ghastly; sepulchral; deathly. [C14: from OF: burial place, from L *carnālis* fleshly, CARNAL]

charnel house *n.* (esp. formerly) a building or vault where corpses or bones are deposited.

Charnley (ˈtʃɑːnlɪ) *n.* Sir **John.** 1911–82, British surgeon noted for his invention of an artificial hip joint and his development of hip-replacement surgery.

Charon (ˈkɛərən) *n. Greek myth.* the ferryman who brought the dead across the rivers Styx or Acheron to Hades.

Charpentier (*French* ʃarpɑ̃tje) *n.* **Gustave** (gystav). 1860–1956, French composer, whose best-known work is the opera *Louise* (1900).

chart (tʃɑːt) *n.* **1.** a map designed to aid navigation by sea or air. **2.** an outline map, esp. one on which weather information is plotted. **3.** a sheet giving graphical, tabular, or diagrammatical information. **4. the charts.** *Inf.* the lists produced weekly of the best-selling pop singles and albums. ~*vb.* **5.** (*tr.*) to make a chart of. **6.** (*tr.*) to plot or outline the course of. **7.** (*intr.*) (of a record) to appear in the charts. [C16: from L, from Gk *khartēs* papyrus] —'**chartless** *adj.*

charter (ˈtʃɑːtə) *n.* **1.** a formal document from the sovereign or state incorporating a city, bank, college, etc., and specifying its purposes and rights. **2.** (*sometimes cap.*) a formal document granting or demanding certain rights or liberties. **3.** a document issued by a society or an organization authorizing the establishment of a local branch or chapter. **4.** a special privilege or exemption. **5.** (*often cap.*) the fundamental principles of an organization; constitution. **6. a.** the hire or lease of transportation. **b.** (*as modifier*): *a charter flight.* ~*vb.* (*tr.*) **7.** to lease or hire by charter. **8.** to hire (a vehicle, etc.). **9.** to grant a charter to (a group or person). [C13: from OF, from L *chartula,* dim. of *charta* leaf of papyrus; see CHART] —'**charterer** *n.*

chartered accountant *n.* (in Britain) an accountant who has passed the examinations of the Institute of Chartered Accountants.

chartered bank *n. Canad.* a privately owned bank that has been incorporated by Parliament to operate in the commercial banking system.

Chartism (ˈtʃɑːtɪzəm) *n. English history.* a movement (1838–48) to achieve certain political reforms, demand for which was embodied in charters presented to Parliament. —'**Chartist** *n., adj.*

Chartres (ˈʃɑːtrə, ʃɑːt; *French* ʃartrə) *n.* a city in NW France: Gothic cathedral; market town. Pop.: 38 715 (1983 est.).

chartreuse (ʃaː'trɜːz; French ʃartrøz) n. **1.** either of two liqueurs, green or yellow, made from herbs. **2. a.** a yellowish-green colour. **b.** (as adj.): a chartreuse dress. [C19: from F, after La Grande Chartreuse, monastery near Grenoble, where the liqueur is produced]

charwoman ('tʃɑː,wʊmən) n., pl. **-women.** Brit. a woman who is hired to clean a house.

chary ('tʃɛərɪ) adj. **charier, chariest. 1.** wary; careful. **2.** choosy; finicky. **3.** shy. **4.** sparing; mean. [OE cearig; rel. to caru CARE]

Charybdis (kə'rɪbdɪs) n. a ship-devouring monster in classical mythology, identified with a whirlpool off the coast of Sicily. Cf. **Scylla.**

chase[1] (tʃeɪs) vb. **1.** to follow or run after (a person, animal, or goal) persistently or quickly. **2.** (tr.; often foll. by out, away, or off) to force to run (away); drive (out). **3.** (tr.) Inf. to court (a member of the opposite sex) in an unsubtle manner. **4.** (tr.; often foll. by up) Inf. to pursue persistently and energetically in order to obtain results, information, etc. **5.** (intr.) Inf. to hurry; rush. ~n. **6.** the act of chasing; pursuit. **7.** any quarry that is pursued. **8.** Brit. an unenclosed area of land where wild animals are preserved to be hunted. **9.** Brit. the right to hunt a particular quarry over the land of others. **10. the chase.** the act or sport of hunting. **11.** short for **steeplechase. 12. give chase.** to pursue (a person, animal, or thing) actively. [C13: from OF chacier, from Vulgar L captiāre (unattested), from L, from capere to take; see CATCH]

chase[2] (tʃeɪs) n. **1.** Letterpress printing. a rectangular steel frame into which metal type and blocks are locked for printing. **2.** the part of a gun barrel from the trunnions to the muzzle. **3.** a groove or channel, esp. to take a pipe, cable, etc. ~vb. (tr.) **4.** Also: **chamfer.** to cut a groove, furrow, or flute in (a surface, column, etc.). [C17: prob. from F châsse frame, from OF chas enclosure, from LL capsus pen for animals; both from L capsa CASE[2]]

chase[3] (tʃeɪs) vb. (tr.) to ornament (metal) by engraving or embossing. Also: **enchase.** [C14: from OF enchasser ENCHASE]

chaser ('tʃeɪsə) n. **1.** a person or thing that chases. **2.** a drink drunk after another of a different kind, as beer after spirits.

chasm ('kæzəm) n. **1.** a deep cleft in the ground; abyss. **2.** a break in continuity; gap. **3.** a wide difference in interests, feelings, etc. [C17: from L, from Gk khasma; rel. to khainein to gape] —**chasmal** ('kæzməl) or '**chasmic** adj.

chasseur (ʃæ'sɜː) n. **1.** French Army. a member of a unit specially trained for swift deployment. **2.** a uniformed attendant. ~adj. **3.** (often postpositive) designating or cooked in a sauce consisting of white wine and mushrooms. [C18: from F: huntsman]

Chassid or **Hassid** ('hæsɪd) n., pl. **Chassidim** or **Hassidim** ('hæsɪ,diːm, -dɪm). **1.** a sect of Jewish mystics founded in Poland about 1750, characterized by religious zeal and a spirit of prayer, joy, and charity. **2.** a Jewish sect of the 2nd century B.C., formed to combat Hellenistic influences. —**Chassidic** or **Hassidic** (hə'sɪdɪk) adj.

chassis ('ʃæsɪ) n., pl. **-sis** (-sɪz). **1.** the steel frame, wheels, and mechanical parts of a motor vehicle. **2.** Electronics. a mounting for the circuit components of an electrical or electronic device, such as a radio or television. **3.** the landing gear of an aircraft. **4.** the frame on which a cannon carriage moves. [C17 (meaning: window frame): from F châssis, from Vulgar L capsicum (unattested), ult. from L capsa CASE[2]]

chaste (tʃeɪst) adj. **1.** not having experienced sexual intercourse; virginal. **2.** abstaining from unlawful sexual intercourse. **3.** abstaining from all sexual intercourse. **4.** (of conduct, speech, etc.) pure; decent; modest. **5.** (of style) simple; restrained. [C13: from OF, from L castus pure] —'**chastely** adv. —'**chasteness** n.

chasten ('tʃeɪsᵊn) vb. (tr.) **1.** to bring to submission; subdue. **2.** to discipline or correct by punishment. **3.** to moderate; restrain. [C16: from OF, from L castigāre; see CASTIGATE] —'**chastener** n.

chastise (tʃæs'taɪz) vb. (tr.) **1.** to punish, esp. by beating. **2.** to scold severely. [C14 chastisen, irregularly from chastien to CHASTEN] —**chastisement** ('tʃæstɪzmənt, tʃæs'taɪz-) n. —**chas'tiser** n.

chastity ('tʃæstɪtɪ) n. **1.** the state of being chaste; purity. **2.** abstention from sexual intercourse; virginity or celibacy. [C13: from OF, from L, from castus CHASTE]

chasuble ('tʃæzjʊbᵊl) n. Christianity. a long sleeveless outer vestment worn by a priest when celebrating Mass. [C13: from F, from LL casubla garment with a hood]

chat (tʃæt) n. **1.** informal conversation or talk in an easy familiar manner. **2.** an Old World songbird of the thrush family, having a harsh chattering cry. **3.** any of various North American warblers. **4.** any of various Australian wrens. ~vb. **chatting, chatted. 5.** (intr.) to talk in an easy familiar way. ~See also **chat up.** [C16: short for CHATTER]

chateau or **château** ('ʃætəʊ) n., pl. **-teaux** (-təʊ, -təʊz) or **-teaus. 1.** a country house or castle, esp. in France. **2.** (in the name of a wine) estate or vineyard. [C18: from F, from OF, from L castellum CASTLE]

Chateaubriand (French ʃatobrijã) n. **1. François René** (frãswa rəne), Vicomte de Chateaubriand. 1768–1848, French writer and statesman: a precursor of the romantic movement in France; his works include Le Génie du Christianisme (1802) and Mémoires d'outre-tombe (1849–50). **2.** a thick steak cut from the fillet of beef.

Châteauroux (French ʃatoru) n. a city in central France: tenth-century castle (**Château-Raoul**). Pop.: 53 284 (1983 est.).

Château-Thierry ('ʃætəʊ'tɪərɪ; French ʃatotjeri) n. a town in N central France, on the River Marne: scene of the second battle of the Marne (1918) during World War I. Pop.: 14 920 (1982 est.).

chatelaine ('ʃætə,leɪn) n. **1.** (esp. formerly) the mistress of a castle or large household. **2.** a chain or clasp worn at the waist by women in the 16th to the 19th centuries, with handkerchief, keys, etc., attached. [from F, from OF, ult. from L castellum CASTLE]

Chatham[1] ('tʃætəm) n. **1.** a town in SE England, in N Kent on the River Medway: formerly royal naval dockyard. Pop.: 61 909 (1981). **2.** a city in SE Canada, in SE Ontario on the Thames River. Pop.: 40 952 (1981).

Chatham[2] ('tʃætəm) n. **1st Earl of.** title of the elder (William) **Pitt.**

Chatham Island n. another name for **San Cristóbal** (sense 1).

Chatham Islands pl. n. a group of islands in the S Pacific Ocean, forming a county of South Island, New Zealand: consists of the main islands of Chatham, Pitt, and several rocky islets. Chief settlement: Waitangi. Pop.: 770 (1983). Area: 963 sq. km (372 sq. miles).

chat show n. Brit. a television or radio show in which guests are interviewed informally.

Chattanooga (,tʃætə'nuːgə) n. a city in SE Tennessee, on the Tennessee River: scene of two battles during the Civil War, in which the North defeated the Confederates, cleared Tennessee, and opened the way to Georgia (1863). Pop.: 169 558 (1980).

chattel ('tʃætᵊl) n. **1.** (often pl.) Property law. **a. chattel personal.** an item of movable personal property, such as furniture, etc. **b. chattel real.** an interest in land less than a freehold. **2. goods and chattels.** personal property. [C13: from OF chatel personal property, from Med. L capitāle wealth]

chatter ('tʃætə) vb. **1.** to speak (about unimportant matters) rapidly and incessantly. **2.** (intr.) (of birds, monkeys, etc.) to make rapid repetitive high-pitched noises. **3.** (intr.) (of the teeth) to click together rapidly through cold or fear. **4.** (intr.) to make rapid intermittent contact with a component, as in machining. ~n. **5.** idle or foolish talk; gossip. **6.** the high-pitched repetitive noise made by a bird, monkey, etc. **7.** the rattling of objects, such as parts of a machine. [C13: imit.] —'**chatterer** n.

chatterbox ('tʃætə,bɒks) n. Inf. a person who talks constantly, esp. about trivial matters.

Chatterton ('tʃætətən) n. **Thomas.** 1752–70, English poet; author of spurious medieval verse and prose: he committed suicide at the age of 17.

chatty ('tʃætɪ) adj. **-tier, -tiest. 1.** full of trivial conversation; talkative. **2.** informal and friendly; gossipy. —'**chattily** adv. —'**chattiness** n.

chat up vb. (tr., adv.) Brit. inf. **1.** to talk persuasively to (a person), esp. with an ulterior motive. **2.** to talk flirtatiously to (a person of the opposite sex).

Chaucer ('tʃɔːsə) n. **Geoffrey.** ?1340–1400, English poet, noted for his narrative skill, humour, and insight, particularly in his most famous work, The Canterbury Tales. He was influenced by the continental tradition of rhyming verse. His other works include *Troilus and Criseyde, The Legende of Good Women,* and *The Parlement of Foules.* —**Chaucerian** (tʃɔːˈsɪərɪən) *adj., n.*

chauffeur (ˈʃəʊfə, ʃəʊˈfɜː) *n.* **1.** a person employed to drive a car. ~*vb.* **2.** to act as driver for (a person, etc.): *he chauffeured me to the stadium.* [C20: from F, lit.: stoker, from *chauffer* to heat] —**chauffeuse** (ʃəʊˈfɜːz) *fem. n.*

chaunt (tʃɔːnt) *n.* a less common variant of **chant.** —ˈ**chaunter** *n.*

chauvinism (ˈʃəʊvɪˌnɪzəm) *n.* **1.** aggressive or fanatical patriotism; jingoism. **2.** enthusiastic devotion to a cause. **3.** smug irrational belief in the superiority of one's own race, party, sex, etc.: *male chauvinism.* [C19: from F, after Nicolas *Chauvin,* F soldier under Napoleon, noted for his unthinking patriotism] —ˈ**chauvinist** *n., adj.* —ˌ**chauvin'istic** *adj.* —ˌ**chauvin'istically** *adv.*

cheap (tʃiːp) *adj.* **1.** costing relatively little; inexpensive; of good value. **2.** charging low prices: *a cheap hairdresser.* **3.** of poor quality; shoddy: *cheap furniture.* **4.** worth relatively little: *promises are cheap.* **5.** not worthy of respect; vulgar. **6.** ashamed; embarrassed: *to feel cheap.* **7.** stingy; miserly. **8.** *Inf.* mean; despicable: *a cheap liar.* ~*n.* **9. on the cheap.** *Brit. inf.* at a low cost. ~*adv.* **10.** at very little cost. [OE *ceap* barter, bargain, price, property] —ˈ**cheaply** *adv.* —ˈ**cheapness** *n.*

cheapen (ˈtʃiːpən) *vb.* **1.** to make or become lower in reputation, quality, etc. **2.** to make or become cheap or cheaper. —ˈ**cheapener** *n.*

cheap-jack *Inf.* ~*n.* **1.** a person who sells cheap and shoddy goods. ~*adj.* **2.** shoddy or inferior. [C19: from CHEAP + JACK]

cheapo (ˈtʃiːpəʊ) *adj. Inf.* very cheap and possibly shoddy.

cheapskate (ˈtʃiːpˌskeɪt) *n. Inf.* a miserly person.

cheat (tʃiːt) *vb.* **1.** to deceive or practise deceit, esp. for one's own gain; trick or swindle (someone). **2.** (*intr.*) to obtain unfair advantage by trickery, as in a game of cards. **3.** (*tr.*) to escape or avoid (something unpleasant) by luck or cunning: *to cheat death.* **4.** (when *intr.,* usually foll. by *on*) *Inf.* to be sexually unfaithful to (one's wife, husband, or lover). ~*n.* **5.** a person who cheats. **6.** a deliberately dishonest transaction, esp. for gain; fraud. **7.** *Inf.* sham. **8.** *Law.* the obtaining of another's property by fraudulent means. [C14: short for ESCHEAT] —ˈ**cheater** *n.*

Cheb (*Czech* xɛp) *n.* a town in W Czechoslovakia, in W Bohemia on the Ohře River: 12th-century castle where Wallenstein was murdered (1634); a centre of the Sudeten-German movement after World War I. Pop.: 31 239 (1983). German name: **Eger.**

Cheboksary (*Russian* tʃɪbakˈsari) *n.* a port in the central Soviet Union on the River Volga: capital of the Chuvash ASSR. Pop.: 414 000 (1987).

Checheno-Ingush Autonomous Soviet Socialist Republic (tʃɪˈtʃɛnəʊɪnˌguːʃ) *n.* an administrative division of the S Soviet Union, in the RSFSR on the N slopes of the Caucasus Mountains: major oil and natural gas resources. Capital: Grozny. Pop.: 1 230 000 (1986). Area: 19 300 sq. km (7450 sq. miles).

check (tʃɛk) *vb.* **1.** to pause or cause to pause, esp. abruptly. **2.** (*tr.*) to restrain or control: *to check one's tears.* **3.** (*tr.*) to slow the growth or progress of; retard. **4.** (*tr.*) to rebuke or rebuff. **5.** (when *intr.,* often foll. by *on* or *up on*) to examine, investigate, or make an inquiry into (facts, a product, etc.) for accuracy, quality, or progress. **6.** (*tr.*) *Chiefly U.S. & Canad.* to mark off so as to indicate approval, correctness, or preference. **7.** (*intr.;* often foll. by *with*) *Chiefly U.S. & Canad.* to correspond or agree: *this report checks with the other.* **8.** (*tr.*) *Chiefly U.S., Canad., & N.Z.* to leave in or accept for temporary custody. **9.** *Chess.* to place (an opponent's king) in check. **10.** (*tr.*) to mark with a pattern of squares or crossed lines. **11.** to crack or cause to crack. **12.** (*tr.*) *Ice hockey.* to impede (an opponent). **13.** (*intr.*) *Hunting.* (of hounds) to pause while relocating a lost scent. ~*n.* **14.** a break in progress; stoppage. **15.** a restraint or rebuff. **16.** a person or thing that restrains, halts, etc. **17.** a control, esp. a rapid or informal one, to ensure accuracy, progress, etc. **18.** a means or standard to ensure against fraud or error. **19.** the U.S. word for **tick**[1]. **20.** the U.S. spelling of **cheque.** **21.** *U.S. & Canad.* the bill in a restaurant. **22.** *Chiefly U.S. & Canad.* a tag used to identify property deposited for custody. **23.** a pattern of squares or crossed lines. **24.** a single square in such a pattern.

25. fabric with a pattern of squares or crossed lines. **26.** *Chess.* the state or position of a king under direct attack. **27.** a small crack, as one that occurs in timber during drying. **28.** a chip or counter used in some card and gambling games. **29.** *Hunting.* a pause by the hounds owing to loss of the scent. **30.** *Ice hockey.* the act of impeding an opponent with one's body or stick. **31. in check.** under control or restraint. ~*sentence substitute.* **32.** *Chess.* a call made to an opponent indicating that his king is in check. **33.** *Chiefly U.S. & Canad.* an expression of agreement. ~See also **check in, check out, checkup.** [C14: from OF *eschec* a check at chess, via Ar. from Persian *shāh* the king] —ˈ**checkable** *adj.*

checked (tʃɛkt) *adj.* having a pattern of squares.

checker[1] (ˈtʃɛkə) *n., vb.* **1.** the usual U.S. spelling of **chequer.** ~*n.* **2.** *Textiles.* a variant spelling of **chequer** (sense 2). **3.** the U.S. name for **draughtsman** (sense 3).

checker[2] (ˈtʃɛkə) *n. Chiefly U.S.* **1.** a cashier, esp. in a supermarket. **2.** an attendant in a cloakroom, left-luggage office, etc.

checkerboard (ˈtʃɛkəˌbɔːd) *n.* the U.S. and Canad. name for a **draughtboard.**

checkers (ˈtʃɛkəz) *n.* (*functioning as sing.*) the U.S. and Canad. name for **draughts.**

check in *vb.* (*adv.*) **1.** (*intr.*) to record one's arrival, as at a hotel or for work; sign in or report. **2.** (*tr.*) to register the arrival of (passengers, etc.). ~*n.* **check-in. 3.** the formal registration of arrival, as at an airport or a hotel. **4.** the place where one registers arrival at an airport, etc.

check list *n.* a list of items, names, etc., to be referred to for identification or verification.

checkmate (ˈtʃɛkˌmeɪt) *n.* **1.** *Chess.* **a.** the winning position in which an opponent's king is under attack and unable to escape. **b.** the move by which this position is achieved. **2.** utter defeat. ~*vb.* (*tr.*) **3.** *Chess.* to place (an opponent's king) in checkmate. **4.** to thwart or render powerless. ~*sentence substitute.* **5.** *Chess.* a call made when placing an opponent's king in checkmate. [C14: from OF, from Ar. *shāh māt* the king is dead; see CHECK]

check out *vb.* (*adv.*) **1.** (*intr.*) to pay the bill and depart, esp. from a hotel. **2.** (*intr.*) to depart from a place; record one's departure from work. **3.** (*tr.*) to investigate or prove to be in order after investigation: *the police checked out all the statements.* **4.** (*tr.*) *Inf.* to have a look at; inspect: *check out the wally in the pink shirt.* ~*n.* **checkout. 5.** the latest time for vacating a room in a hotel, etc. **6.** a counter, esp. in a supermarket, where customers pay.

checkpoint (ˈtʃɛkˌpɔɪnt) *n.* a place, as at a frontier, where vehicles or travellers are stopped for official identification, inspection, etc.

checkup (ˈtʃɛkˌʌp) *n.* **1.** an examination to see if something is in order. **2.** *Med.* a medical examination, esp. one taken at regular intervals. ~*vb.* **check up. 3.** (*intr., adv.;* sometimes foll. by *on*) to investigate or make an inquiry into (a person's character, evidence, etc.).

Cheddar (ˈtʃɛdə) *n.* **1.** (*sometimes not cap.*) any of several types of smooth hard yellow or whitish cheese. **2.** a village in SW England, in N Somerset: situated near **Cheddar Gorge,** a pass through the Mendip Hills renowned for its stalactitic caverns and rare limestone flora.

cheek (tʃiːk) *n.* **1.** either side of the face, esp. that part below the eye. **2.** *Inf.* impudence; effrontery. **3.** (*often pl.*) *Inf.* either side of the buttocks. **4.** (*often pl.*) a side of a door jamb. **5.** one of the jaws of a vice. **6. cheek by jowl.** close together; intimately linked. **7. turn the other cheek.** to be submissive and refuse to retaliate. ~*vb.* **8.** (*tr.*) *Inf.* to speak or behave disrespectfully to. [OE *ceace*]

cheekbone (ˈtʃiːkˌbəʊn) *n.* the nontechnical name for **zygomatic bone.**

cheeky (ˈtʃiːkɪ) *adj.* **cheekier, cheekiest.** disrespectful in speech or behaviour; impudent. —ˈ**cheekily** *adv.* —ˈ**cheekiness** *n.*

cheep (tʃiːp) *n.* **1.** the short weak high-pitched cry of a young bird; chirp. ~*vb.* **2.** (*intr.*) (of young birds) to utter such sounds. —ˈ**cheeper** *n.*

cheer (tʃɪə) *vb.* **1.** (usually foll. by *up*) to make or become happy or hopeful; comfort or be comforted. **2.** to applaud with shouts. **3.** (when *tr.,* sometimes foll. by *on*) to encourage (a team, etc.) with shouts. ~*n.* **4.** a shout or cry of approval, encouragement, etc., often using **hurrah! 5. three cheers.** three shouts of hurrah given in unison to honour someone or celebrate something. **6.** happiness;

good spirits. **7.** state of mind; spirits (archaic, except in **be of good cheer, with good cheer**). **8.** *Arch.* provisions for a feast; fare. [C13 (in the sense: face, welcoming aspect): from OF *chere*, from LL *cara* face, from Gk *kara* head]

cheerful ('tʃɪəfʊl) *adj.* **1.** having a happy disposition; in good spirits. **2.** pleasantly bright: *a cheerful room.* **3.** ungrudging: *cheerful help.* —'**cheerfully** *adv.* —'**cheerfulness** *n.*

cheerio (,tʃɪərɪ'əʊ) *Inf.* ~*sentence substitute.* **1.** *Chiefly Brit.* a farewell greeting. **2.** *Chiefly Brit.* a drinking toast. ~*n., pl.* **cheerios. 3.** *N.Z.* a type of small sausage.

cheerleader ('tʃɪə,liːdə) *n. U.S. & Canad.* a person who leads a crowd in cheers, esp. at sports events.

cheerless ('tʃɪəlɪs) *adj.* dreary or gloomy. —'**cheerlessly** *adv.* —'**cheerlessness** *n.*

cheers (tʃɪəz) *sentence substitute. Inf., chiefly Brit.* **1.** a drinking toast. **2.** goodbye! cheerio! **3.** thanks!

cheery ('tʃɪərɪ) *adj.* **cheerier, cheeriest.** showing or inspiring cheerfulness; gay. —'**cheerily** *adv.* —'**cheeriness** *n.*

cheese (tʃiːz) *n.* **1.** the curd of milk separated from the whey and variously prepared as a food. **2.** a mass or cake of this substance. **3.** any of various substances of similar consistency, etc.: *lemon cheese.* **4.** *Sl.* an important person (esp. in **big cheese**). [OE *cēse*, from L *cāseus* cheese]

cheeseburger ('tʃiːz,bɜːgə) *n.* a hamburger cooked with a slice of cheese on top of it.

cheesecake ('tʃiːz,keɪk) *n.* **1.** a rich tart filled with cheese, esp. cream cheese, cream, sugar, etc. **2.** *Sl.* women displayed for their sex appeal, as in photographs in magazines or films.

cheesecloth ('tʃiːz,klɒθ) *n.* a loosely woven cotton cloth formerly used for wrapping cheese.

cheesed off *adj.* (*usually postpositive*) *Brit. sl.* bored, disgusted, or angry. [C20: from ?]

cheeseparing ('tʃiːz,pɛərɪŋ) *adj.* **1.** penny-pinching. ~*n.* **2. a.** a paring of cheese rind. **b.** anything similarly worthless. **3.** stinginess.

cheesy ('tʃiːzɪ) *adj.* **cheesier, cheesiest.** **1.** like cheese in flavour, smell, or consistency. **2.** *Inf.* (of a smile) broad but possibly insincere: *a big cheesy grin.* —'**cheesiness** *n.*

cheetah *or* **chetah** ('tʃiːtə) *n.* a large feline of Africa and SW Asia: the swiftest mammal, having very long legs, and a black-spotted coat. [C18: from Hindi *citā*, from Sansk. *citra* speckled]

chef (ʃɛf) *n.* a cook, esp. the principal cook in a restaurant. [C19: from F, from OF *chief* head, CHIEF]

chef-d'œuvre *French.* (ʃɛdœvrə) *n., pl.* **chefs-d'œuvre** (ʃɛdœvrə). a masterpiece.

Chefoo ('tʃiː'fuː) *n.* another name for **Yantai.**

Che Guevara (tʃeɪ ɡə'vɑːrə; *Spanish* tʃe ɡe'βara) *n.* See **Guevara.**

Cheiron ('kaɪrɒn, -rən) *n.* a variant spelling of **Chiron.**

Cheju ('tʃɛ'dʒuː) *n.* a volcanic island in the N East China Sea, southwest of Korea: constitutes a province of South Korea. Capital: Cheju. Pop.: 463 000 (1980). Area: 1792 sq. km (692 sq. miles). Also called: **Quelpart.**

Chekhov *or* **Chekov** ('tʃɛkɒf; *Russian* 'tʃexəf) *n.* **Anton Pavlovich** (an'tɔn 'pavləvitʃ). 1860–1904, Russian dramatist and short-story writer. His plays include *The Seagull* (1896), *Uncle Vanya* (1900), *The Three Sisters* (1901), and *The Cherry Orchard* (1904). —**Chekhovian** *or* **Chekovian** (tʃɛ'kəʊvɪən) *adj.*

Chekiang ('tʃɛ'kjæŋ, -kaɪ'æŋ) *n.* a variant transliteration of the Chinese name for **Zhejiang.**

chela[1] ('kiːlə) *n., pl.* **-lae** (-liː). a large pincer-like claw of such arthropods as the crab and scorpion. [C17: NL, from Gk *khēlē* claw]

chela[2] ('tʃeɪlə) *n. Hinduism.* a disciple of a religious teacher. [C19: from Hindi *celā*, from Sansk. *ceta* servant, slave]

chelate ('kiːleɪt) *n.* **1.** *Chem.* a chemical compound whose molecules contain a closed ring of atoms of which one is a metal atom. ~*adj.* **2.** *Zool.* of or possessing chelae. **3.** *Chem.* of a chelate. ~*vb.* **4.** (*intr.*) *Chem.* to form a chelate. [C20: from CHELA[1]] —**che'lation** *n.*

chelicera (kɪ'lɪsərə) *n., pl.* **-erae** (-ə,riː). one of a pair of appendages on the head of spiders and other arachnids: often modified as food-catching claws. [C19: from NL, from Gk *khēlē* claw + *keras* horn]

Chelmsford ('tʃɛlmzfəd) *n.* a town in SE England, administrative centre of Essex: market town. Pop.: 144 000 (1985 est.).

cheloid ('kiːlɔɪd) *n. Pathol.* a variant spelling of **keloid.** —**che'loidal** *adj.*

chelonian (kɪ'ləʊnɪən) *n.* **1.** any reptile of the order *Chelonia*, including the tortoises and turtles, in which most of the body is enclosed in a bony capsule. ~*adj.* **2.** of or belonging to the *Chelonia*. [C19: from NL, from Gk *khelōnē* tortoise]

Chelsea ('tʃɛlsɪ) *n.* a residential district of SW London, in the Royal Borough of Kensington and Chelsea: site of the Chelsea Royal Hospital for old and invalid soldiers (**Chelsea Pensioners**).

Cheltenham ('tʃɛltnəm) *n.* **1.** a town in W England, in central Gloucestershire: famous for its schools, racecourse, and saline springs (discovered in 1716). Pop.: 86 000 (1983 est.). **2.** a style of type.

Chelyabinsk (*Russian* tʃɪ'ljabinsk) *n.* an industrial city in the W central Soviet Union, in the southern RSFSR. Pop.: 1 119 000 (1987).

Chelyuskin (*Russian* tʃɪ'ljuskin) *n.* **Cape.** a cape in the NW Soviet Union, in N Siberia at the end of the Taimyr Peninsula: the northernmost point of Asia.

chem. *abbrev. for:* **1.** chemical. **2.** chemist. **3.** chemistry.

chem- *combining form.* a variant of **chemo-** before a vowel.

chemical ('kɛmɪkəl) *n.* **1.** any substance used in or resulting from a reaction involving changes to atoms or molecules. ~*adj.* **2.** of or used in chemistry. **3.** of, made from, or using chemicals: *chemical fertilizer.* —'**chemically** *adv.*

chemical engineering *n.* the branch of engineering concerned with the design and manufacture of the plant used in industrial chemical processes. —**chemical engineer** *n.*

chemical warfare *n.* warfare using asphyxiating or nerve gases, poisons, defoliants, etc.

chemiluminescence (,kɛmɪ,luːmɪ'nɛsəns) *n.* the phenomenon in which a chemical reaction leads to the emission of light without incandescence. —,**chemi,lumi'nescent** *adj.*

chemin de fer (ʃə'mæn də 'fɛə) *n.* a gambling game, a variation of baccarat. [F: railway, referring to the fast tempo of the game]

chemise (ʃə'miːz) *n.* **1.** an unwaisted loose-fitting dress hanging straight from the shoulders. **2.** a loose shirtlike undergarment. ~Also called: **shift.** [C14: from OF: shirt, from LL *camisa*]

chemist ('kɛmɪst) *n.* **1.** *Brit.* a shop selling medicines, cosmetics, etc. **2.** *Brit.* a qualified dispenser of prescribed medicines. **3.** a person studying, trained in, or engaged in chemistry. [C16: from earlier *chimist*, from NL, shortened from Med. L *alchimista* ALCHEMIST]

chemistry ('kɛmɪstrɪ) *n., pl.* **-tries. 1.** the branch of physical science concerned with the composition, properties, and reactions of substances. **2.** the composition, properties, and reactions of a particular substance. **3.** the nature and effects of any complex phenomenon: *the chemistry of humour.* [C17: from earlier *chimistrie*, from *chimist* CHEMIST]

Chemnitz (*German* 'kɛmnɪts) *n.* the former name (until 1953) of **Karl-Marx-Stadt.**

chemo-, chemi-, *or before a vowel* **chem-** *combining form.* indicating that chemicals or chemical reactions are involved: *chemotherapy.* [NL, from LGk *khēmeia*; see ALCHEMY]

chemoreceptor (,kɛməʊrɪ'sɛptə) *or* **chemoceptor** *n.* a sensory receptor in a biological cell membrane to which an external molecule binds to generate a smell or taste sensation.

chemosynthesis (,kɛməʊ'sɪnθɪsɪs) *n.* the formation of organic material by some bacteria using energy from simple chemical reactions.

chemotherapy (,kɛməʊ'θɛrəpɪ) *n.* treatment of disease by means of chemical agents. —,**chemo'therapist** *n.*

Chemulpo (,tʃɛmʊl'pəʊ) *n.* a former name of **Inchon.**

chemurgy ('kɛmɜːdʒɪ) *n.* the branch of chemistry concerned with the industrial use of organic raw materials, esp. of agricultural origin. —**chem'urgic** *or* **chem'urgical** *adj.*

Chenab (tʃɪ'næb) *n.* a river rising in the Himalayas and flowing southwest to the Sutlej River in Pakistan. Length: 1087 km (675 miles).

Cheng-chiang ('tʃɛŋ'tʃæŋ) *n.* a variant transliteration of the Chinese name for **Jinjiang**.

Chengchow *or* **Cheng-chou** ('tʃɛŋ'tʃaʊ) *n.* a variant transliteration of the Chinese name for **Zhengzhou**.

Chengde, Chengteh, *or* **Ch'eng-te** ('tʃɛŋ'teɪ) *n.* a city in NE China, in Hebei on the Luan River: summer residence of the Manchu emperors. Pop.: 150 000 (1982).

Chengdu, Chengtu, *or* **Ch'eng-tu** ('tʃɛŋ'tu:) *n.* a city in S central China, capital of Sichuan province. Pop.: 2 580 000 (1986).

Chénier (*French* ʃenje) *n.* **André** (**Marie de**) (ɑ̃dre). 1762–94, French poet; his work was influenced by the ancient Greek elegiac poets. He was guillotined during the French Revolution.

chenille (ʃə'ni:l) *n.* **1.** a thick soft tufty silk or worsted velvet cord or yarn used in embroidery and for trimmings, etc. **2.** a fabric of such yarn. **3.** a carpet of such fabric. [C18: from F, lit.: hairy caterpillar, from L *canicula*, dim. of *canis* dog]

cheongsam ('tʃɔ:ŋ'sæm) *n.* a straight dress with a stand-up collar and a slit in one side of the skirt, worn by Chinese women. [from Chinese *ch'ang shan* long jacket]

Cheops ('ki:ɒps) *n.* original name *Khufu.* Egyptian king of the fourth dynasty (?2613–?2494 B.C.), who built the largest pyramid at El Giza.

cheque *or U.S.* **check** (tʃɛk) *n.* **1.** a bill of exchange drawn on a bank by the holder of a current account. **2.** *Austral. & N.Z.* the total sum of money received for contract work or a crop. [C18: from CHECK, in the sense: means of verification]

cheque account *n.* an account at a bank or a building society upon which cheques can be drawn.

chequebook *or U.S.* **checkbook** ('tʃɛk,bʊk) *n.* a book of detachable blank cheques issued by a bank or building society to holders of cheque accounts.

chequebook journalism *n.* the practice of securing exclusive rights to material for newspaper stories by paying a high price, regardless of any moral implications.

cheque card *n.* a card issued by a bank or building society, guaranteeing payment of a customer's cheques up to a stated value.

chequer *or U.S.* **checker** ('tʃɛkə) *n.* **1.** any of the marbles, pegs, or other pieces used in the game of Chinese chequers. **2. a.** a pattern of squares. **b.** one of the squares in such a pattern. ~*vb.* (*tr.*) **3.** to make irregular in colour or character; variegate. **4.** to mark off with alternating squares of colour. ~See also **chequers**. [C13: chessboard, from Anglo-F *escheker*, from *eschec* CHECK]

chequered *or esp. U.S.* **checkered** ('tʃɛkəd) *adj.* marked by fluctuations of fortune (esp. in **a chequered career**).

chequers ('tʃɛkəz) *n.* (*functioning as sing.*) another name for **draughts**.

Chequers ('tʃɛkəz) *n.* an estate and country house in S England, in central Buckinghamshire: the official country residence of the Prime Minister.

Cher (*French* ʃɛr) *n.* **1.** a department of central France, in E Centre region. Capital: Bourges. Pop.: 320 174 (1982). Area: 7304 sq. km (2849 sq. miles). **2.** a river in central France, rising in the Massif Central and flowing northwest to the Loire. Length: 354 km (220 miles).

Cherbourg ('ʃɛəbʊəg; *French* ʃɛrbur) *n.* a port in NW France, on the English Channel. Pop.: 32 415 (1983 est.).

Cherenkov *or* **Cerenkov** (tʃɪ'rɛŋkɒf; *Russian* tʃɪ'rjɛnkəf) *n.* **Pavel Alekseyevich** ('pavɪl alɪk'sjejɪvitʃ). born 1904, Soviet physicist: noted for work on the effects produced by high-energy particles: shared Nobel prize for physics 1958.

Cheribon ('tʃɪərə,bɒn) *n.* a variant spelling of **Tjirebon**.

cherish ('tʃɛrɪʃ) *vb.* (*tr.*) **1.** to feel or show great tenderness or care for. **2.** to cling fondly to (a hope, idea, etc.); nurse: *to cherish ambitions.* [C14: from OF, from *cher* dear, from L *cārus*]

Chernenko (tʃə:'nɛŋkəʊ) *n.* **Konstantin** (**Ustinovich**) (kənstan'tin). 1911–85, Soviet statesman; general secretary of the Soviet Communist Party (1984–85).

Chernobyl (tʃə:'nɒbəl, -nɒbɪl) *n.* a town in the SW Soviet Union, in the Ukrainian SSR; site of a nuclear power station accident in 1986.

Chernovtsy (*Russian* tʃɪrnaf'tsi) *n.* a city in the SW Soviet Union, in the W Ukrainian SSR on the Prut River: formerly under Polish, Austro-Hungarian, and Romanian rule; ceded to the Soviet Union in 1947. Pop.: 254 000 (1987). German name: **Czernowitz**. Romanian name: **Cernăuţi**.

chernozem ('tʃɜ:nəʊ,zɛm) *n.* a rich black soil found in temperate semiarid regions, such as the grasslands of Russia. [from Russian *chernaya zemlya* black earth]

Cherokee ('tʃɛrə,ki:) *n.* **1.** (*pl.* -**kees** *or* -**kee**) a member of a North American Indian people formerly living in the Appalachian Mountains. **2.** the Iroquois language of this people.

cheroot (ʃə'ru:t) *n.* a cigar with both ends cut off squarely. [C17: from Tamil *curuttu* curl, roll]

cherry ('tʃɛrɪ) *n.,* *pl.* -**ries.** **1.** any of several trees of the genus *Prunus,* having a small fleshy rounded fruit containing a hard stone. **2.** the fruit or wood of any of these trees. **3.** any of various unrelated plants, such as the ground cherry and Jerusalem cherry. **4. a.** a bright red colour; cerise. **b.** (*as adj.*): *a cherry coat.* **5.** *Taboo sl.* virginity or the hymen as its symbol. [C14: back formation from OE *ciris* (mistakenly thought to be pl.), ult. from LL *ceresia*, ?from L *cerasus* cherry tree, from Gk *kerasios*]

cherry tomato *n.* a miniature tomato not much bigger than a cherry.

chert (tʃɜ:t) *n.* an impure black or grey microcrystalline variety of quartz that resembles flint. [C17: from ?] —'**cherty** *adj.*

Chertsey ('tʃɜ:tsɪ) *n.* a town in S England, in N Surrey on the River Thames. Pop.: 43 265 (1981).

cherub ('tʃɛrəb) *n.,* *pl.* **cherubs** *or* (*for sense 1*) **cherubim** ('tʃɛrəbɪm, -ʊbɪm). **1.** a member of the second order of angels, often represented as a winged child. **2.** an innocent or sweet child. [OE, from Heb. *kĕrūbh*] —**cherubic** (tʃə'ru:bɪk) *or* **che'rubical** *adj.* —**che'rubically** *adv.*

Cherubini (,kɛru'bi:nɪ) *n.* (**Maria**) **Luigi** (**Carlo Zenobio Salvatore**) (lu'i:dʒi). 1760–1842, Italian composer, noted particularly for his church music and his operas.

chervil ('tʃɜ:vɪl) *n.* an aromatic umbelliferous Eurasian plant with small white flowers and aniseed-flavoured leaves used as herbs in soups and salads. [OE *cerfelle*, from L, from Gk, from *khairein* to enjoy + *phullon* leaf]

Cherwell ('tʃɜ:wəl) *n.* **Frederick Alexander Lindemann** ('lɪndəmən), Baron. 1886–1957, British physicist, born in Germany, noted for his research on heat capacity, aeronautics, and atomic physics. He was scientific adviser to Winston Churchill during World War II.

Chesapeake Bay ('tʃɛsə,pi:k) *n.* the largest inlet of the Atlantic in the coast of the U.S.: bordered by Maryland and Virginia.

Cheshire[1] ('tʃɛʃə, 'tʃɛʃɪə) *n.* a county of NW England: low-lying and undulating, bordering on the Pennines in the east; mainly agricultural. Administrative centre: Chester. Pop.: 946 500 (1986 est.). Area: 2328 sq. km (899 sq. miles). Abbrev.: **Ches.**

Cheshire[2] ('tʃɛʃə) *n.* **Group Captain** (**Geoffrey**) **Leonard**. born 1917, English philanthropist: awarded the Victoria Cross in World War II; founded the Leonard Cheshire Foundation Homes for the Disabled.

Cheshire cheese *n.* a mild-flavoured cheese with a crumbly texture, originally made in Cheshire.

Cheshunt ('tʃɛʃənt) *n.* a town in SE England, in SE Hertfordshire: a dormitory town of London. Pop.: 49 670 (1981).

chess (tʃɛs) *n.* a game of skill for two players using a chessboard on which chessmen are moved. The object is to checkmate the opponent's king. [C13: from OF *esches*, pl. of *eschec* CHECK]

chessboard ('tʃɛs,bɔ:d) *n.* a square board divided into 64 squares of two alternating colours, used for playing chess or draughts.

chessman ('tʃɛs,mæn, -mən) *n.,* *pl.* -**men.** any of the pieces and pawns used in a game of chess. [C17: from *chessmen*, from ME *chessemeyne* chess company]

chest (tʃɛst) *n.* **1. a.** the front part of the trunk from the neck to the belly. Related adj.: **pectoral.** **b.** (*as modifier*): *a chest cold.* **2. get** (*something*) **off one's chest.** *Inf.* to unburden oneself of troubles, worries, etc., by talking about them. **3.** a box used for storage or shipping: *a tea chest.* [OE *cest*, from L, from Gk *kistē* box] —'**chested** *adj.*

Chester ('tʃɛstə) *n.* a city in NW England, administrative centre of Cheshire, on the River Dee: intact surrounding walls; 16th-and 17th-century double-tier shops. Pop.: 116 657 (1984). Latin name: **Deva**.

chesterfield ('tʃɛstə,fiːld) *n.* **1.** a man's overcoat, usually with a velvet collar. **2.** a large tightly stuffed sofa, with straight upholstered arms of the same height as the back. [C19: after a 19th-cent. Earl of *Chesterfield*]

Chesterfield[1] ('tʃɛstə,fiːld) *n.* an industrial town in N central England, in Derbyshire: famous 14th-century church with twisted spire. Pop.: 70 546 (1981).

Chesterfield[2] ('tʃɛstə,fiːld) *n.* **Philip Dormer Stanhope**, 4th Earl of Chesterfield. 1694–1773, English statesman and writer, noted for his elegance, suavity, and wit; author of *Letters to His Son* (1774).

Chesterton ('tʃɛstət³n) *n.* **G(ilbert) K(eith)**. 1874–1936, English essayist, novelist, poet, and critic.

chestnut ('tʃɛs,nʌt) *n.* **1.** a N temperate tree such as the **sweet** or **Spanish chestnut**, which produces flowers in long catkins and nuts in a prickly bur. Cf. **horse chestnut**. **2.** the edible nut of any of these trees. **3.** the hard wood of any of these trees, used in making furniture, etc. **4. a.** a reddish-brown colour. **b.** (*as adj.*): *chestnut hair*. **5.** a horse of a golden-brown colour. **6.** *Inf.* an old or stale joke. [C16: from earlier *chesten nut*: *chesten*, from OF, from L, from Gk *kastanea*]

chest of drawers *n.* a piece of furniture consisting of a set of drawers in a frame.

chesty ('tʃɛstɪ) *adj.* **chestier, chestiest.** *Inf.* **1.** *Brit.* suffering from or symptomatic of chest disease: *a chesty cough.* **2.** having a large well-developed chest or bosom. —**'chestiness** *n.*

cheval glass (ʃə'væl) *n.* a full-length mirror mounted so as to swivel within a frame. [C19: from F *cheval* support (lit.: horse)]

chevalier (,ʃevə'lɪə) *n.* **1.** a member of certain orders of merit, such as the French Legion of Honour. **2.** the lowest title of rank in the old French nobility. **3.** an archaic word for **knight**. **4.** a chivalrous man; gallant. [C14: from OF, from Med. L *caballārius* horseman, CAVALIER]

Chevalier (*French* ʃavalje) *n.* **Maurice** (mɔris). 1888–1972, French singer and film actor.

Cheviot ('tʃiːvɪət, 'tʃɛv-) *n.* **1.** a large British breed of sheep reared for its wool. **2.** (*often not cap.*) a rough twill-weave woollen suiting fabric.

Cheviot Hills *pl. n.* a range of hills on the border between England and Scotland, mainly in Northumberland.

chevron ('ʃevrən) *n.* **1.** *Mil.* a badge or insignia consisting of one or more V-shaped stripes to indicate a noncommissioned rank or length of service. **2.** *Heraldry.* an inverted V-shaped charge on a shield. **3.** any V-shaped pattern or device. [C14: from OF, ult. from L *caper* goat; cf. L *capreoli* pair of rafters (lit.: little goats)]

chevrotain ('ʃevrə,teɪn, -tɪn) *n.* a small timid ruminant mammal of S and SE Asia. Also called: **mouse deer**. [C18: from F, from OF *chevrot* kid, from *chèvre* goat, ult. from L *caper* goat]

chevy ('tʃevɪ) *n.*, *vb.* a variant spelling of **chivy**.

chew (tʃuː) *vb.* **1.** to work the jaws and teeth in order to grind (food); masticate. **2.** to bite repeatedly: *she chewed her nails anxiously.* **3.** (*intr.*) to use chewing tobacco. **4. chew the fat** or **rag.** *Sl.* **a.** to argue over a point. **b.** to talk idly; gossip. ~*n.* **5.** the act of chewing. **6.** something that is chewed. [OE *ceowan*] —**'chewable** *adj.* —**'chewer** *n.*

chewing gum *n.* a preparation for chewing, usually made of flavoured and sweetened chicle.

chew over *vb.* (*tr.*, *adv.*) to consider carefully.

chewy ('tʃuːɪ) *adj.* **chewier, chewiest.** of a consistency requiring chewing.

Cheyenne (ʃaɪ'æn, -'ɛn) *n.* a city in SE Wyoming, capital of the state. Pop.: 47 283 (1980).

chez *French.* (ʃe) *prep.* **1.** at the home of. **2.** with, among, or in the manner of.

chi (kaɪ) *n.* the 22nd letter of the Greek alphabet (X, χ).

chiack or **chyack** ('tʃaɪæk) *Austral. inf.* ~*vb.* **1.** (*tr.*) to tease or banter. ~*n.* **2.** Also called: **chiacking.** good-humoured banter. [C19: from *chi-hike*, a shout of greeting]

Chiang Ch'ing ('tʃæŋ 'tʃɪŋ) *n.* a variant transliteration of the Chinese name for **Jiang Qing**.

Chiang Ching-kuo ('tʃæŋ tʃɪŋ'kwəʊ) or **Jiang Jing Guo** *n.* 1910–88, Chinese statesman; the son of Chiang

Kai-shek. He was prime minister of Taiwan (1971–78); president (1978–88).

Chiang Kai-shek ('tʃæŋ kaɪ'ʃɛk) or **Jiang Jie Shi** *n.* original name *Chiang Chung-cheng*, 1887–1975, Chinese general: president of China (1928–31; 1943–49) and of the Republic of China (Taiwan) (1950–75). As chairman of the Kuomintang, he allied with the Communists against the Japanese (1937–45), but in the Civil War that followed was forced to withdraw to Taiwan after his defeat by the Communists (1949).

chianti (kɪ'æntɪ) *n.* (*sometimes cap.*) a dry red or white wine produced in Tuscany, Italy.

Chianti (*Italian* 'kjanti) *pl. n.* a mountain range in central Italy, in Tuscany, rising over 870 m (2900 ft.): part of the Apennines.

Chiapas (*Spanish* 'tʃjapas) *n.* a state of S Mexico: mountainous and forested; Maya ruins in the northeast; rich mineral resources. Capital: Tuxtla Gutiérrez. Pop.: 2 096 812 (1980). Area: 73 887 sq. km (28 816 sq. miles).

chiaroscuro (kɪ,ɑːrə'skʊərəʊ) *n.*, *pl.* **-ros.** **1.** the artistic distribution of light and dark masses in a picture. **2.** monochrome painting using light and dark only. [C17: from It., from *chiaro* CLEAR + *oscuro* OBSCURE]

chiasma (kaɪ'æzmə) *n.*, *pl.* **-mas, -mata** (-mətə) **1.** *Cytology.* the cross-shaped connection produced by the crossing over of pairing chromosomes during meiosis. **2.** *Anat.* the crossing over of two parts or structures. [C19: from Gk *khiasma*, from *khi* CHI]

chiasmus (kaɪ'æzməs) *n.*, *pl.* **-mi** (-maɪ). *Rhetoric.* reversal of word order in the second of two parallel phrases: *he came in triumph and in defeat departs.* [NL from Gk: see CHIASMA] —**chiastic** (kaɪ'æstɪk) *adj.*

Chiba ('tʃiːba) *n.* an industrial city in central Japan, in SE Honshu on Tokyo Bay. Pop.: 789 000 (1985).

chic (ʃiːk, ʃɪk) *adj.* **1.** (esp. of fashionable clothes, women, etc.) stylish or elegant. ~*n.* **2.** stylishness, esp. in dress; modishness; fashionable good taste. [C19: from F, from ?] —**'chicly** *adv.*

Chicago (ʃɪ'kɑːgəʊ) *n.* a port in NE Illinois, on Lake Michigan: the second largest city in the U.S.; it is a major railway and air traffic centre. Pop.: 3 009 530 (1986).

chicane (ʃɪ'keɪn) *n.* **1.** a bridge or whist hand without trumps. **2.** *Motor racing.* a short section of sharp narrow bends formed by barriers placed on a motor-racing circuit. **3.** a less common word for **chicanery**. ~*vb.* **4.** (*tr.*) to deceive or trick by chicanery. **5.** (*intr.*) to use tricks or chicanery. [C17: from F *chicaner* to quibble, from ?] —**chi'caner** *n.*

chicanery (ʃɪ'keɪnərɪ) *n.*, *pl.* **-eries.** **1.** verbal deception or trickery, dishonest or sharp practice. **2.** a trick, deception, or quibble.

chicano (tʃɪ'kɑːnəʊ) *n.*, *pl.* **-nos.** *U.S.* an American citizen of Mexican origin. [C20: from Sp. *mejicano* Mexican]

Chichagof Island ('tʃɪtʃə,gɔːf) *n.* an island of Alaska, in the Alexander Archipelago. Area: 5439 sq. km (2100 sq. miles).

Chichen Itzá (*Spanish* tʃi'tʃen it'sa) *n.* a village in Yucatán state in Mexico: site of important Mayan ruins.

Chichester[1] ('tʃɪtʃɪstə) *n.* a town in S England, administrative centre of West Sussex: Roman ruins; 11th-century cathedral; Festival Theatre. Pop.: 24 189 (1981).

Chichester[2] ('tʃɪtʃɪstə) *n.* **Sir Francis**. 1901–72, English yachtsman, who sailed alone round the world in *Gipsy Moth IV* (1966–67).

chichi ('ʃiː,ʃiː) *adj.* **1.** affectedly pretty or stylish. ~*n.* **2.** the quality of being affectedly pretty or stylish. [C20: from F]

Chichihaerh or **Ch'i-ch'i-haerh** ('tʃiː,tʃiː'hɑː) *n.* a variant transliteration of the Chinese name for **Qiqihar**.

chick (tʃɪk) *n.* **1.** the young of a bird, esp. of a domestic fowl. **2.** *Sl.* a girl or young woman, esp. an attractive one. **3.** a young child: used as a term of endearment. [C14: short for CHICKEN]

chickadee ('tʃɪkə,diː) *n.* any of various small North American songbirds, typically having grey-and-black plumage. [C19: imit.]

chicken ('tʃɪkɪn) *n.* **1.** a domestic fowl bred for its flesh or eggs. **2.** the flesh of such a bird used for food. **3.** any of various similar birds, such as a prairie chicken. **4.** *Sl.* a cowardly person. **5.** *Sl.* a young inexperienced person. **6. count one's chickens before they are hatched.** to be over-optimistic in acting on expectations which are not yet fulfilled. ~*adj.* **7.** *Sl.* easily scared; cowardly; timid. [OE *ciecen*]

chicken feed *n. Sl.* a trifling amount of money.

chicken-hearted *or* **chicken-livered** *adj.* easily frightened; cowardly.

chicken out *vb.* (*intr., adv.*) *Inf.* to fail to do something through fear or lack of conviction.

chickenpox ('tʃɪkɪn,pɒks) *n.* a highly communicable viral disease most commonly affecting children, characterized by slight fever and the eruption of a rash.

chicken wire *n.* wire netting with a hexagonal mesh.

chickpea ('tʃɪk,piː) *n.* **1.** a bushy leguminous plant, cultivated for its edible pealike seeds. **2.** the seed of this plant. [C16 *ciche peasen*, from *ciche* (from F, from L *cicer* chickpea) + *peasen;* see PEA]

chickweed ('tʃɪk,wiːd) *n.* any of various plants of the pink family, esp. a common garden weed with small white flowers.

Chiclayo (*Spanish* tʃi'klajo) *n.* a city in NW Peru. Pop.: 379 000 (1987).

chicle ('tʃɪkᵊl) *n.* a gumlike substance obtained from the sapodilla; the main ingredient of chewing gum. [from Sp., from Nahuatl *chictli*]

chicory ('tʃɪkərɪ) *n., pl.* **-ries. 1.** a blue-flowered plant, cultivated for its leaves, which are used in salads, and for its roots. **2.** the root of this plant, roasted, dried, and used as a coffee substitute. ~Cf. **endive.** [C15: from OF, from L *cichorium*, from Gk *kikhōrion*]

chide (tʃaɪd) *vb.* **chiding, chided** *or* **chid** (tʃɪd); **chided, chid** *or* **chidden** ('tʃɪdᵊn). **1.** to rebuke or scold. **2.** (*tr.*) to goad into action. [OE *cidan*] — **'chider** *n.* — **'chidingly** *adv.*

chief (tʃiːf) *n.* **1.** the head or leader of a group or body of people. **2.** *Heraldry.* the upper third of a shield. **3. in chief.** primarily; especially. ~*adj.* **4.** (*prenominal*) **a.** most important; principal. **b.** highest in rank or authority. ~*adv.* **5.** *Arch.* principally. [C13: from OF, from L *caput* head]

chief justice *n.* **1.** (in any of several Commonwealth countries) the judge presiding over a supreme court. **2.** (in the U.S.) the presiding judge of a court composed of a number of members. ~See also **Lord Chief Justice.**

chiefly ('tʃiːflɪ) *adv.* **1.** especially or essentially; above all. **2.** in general; mainly; mostly. ~*adj.* **3.** of or relating to a chief or chieftain.

Chief of Staff *n.* **1.** the senior staff officer under the commander of a major military formation or organization. **2.** the senior officer of each service of the armed forces.

chief petty officer *n.* the senior naval rank for personnel without commissioned or warrant rank.

chieftain ('tʃiːftən, -tɪn) *n.* the head or leader of a tribe or clan. [C14: from OF, from LL *capitāneus* commander; see CAPTAIN] — **'chieftaincy** *or* **'chieftain,ship** *n.*

chief technician *n.* a noncommissioned officer in the Royal Air Force, junior to a flight sergeant.

chiffchaff ('tʃɪf,tʃæf) *n.* a common European warbler with a yellowish-brown plumage. [C18: imit.]

chiffon (ʃɪ'fɒn, 'ʃɪfɒn) *n.* **1.** a fine almost transparent fabric of silk, nylon, etc. **2.** (*often pl.*) *Now rare.* feminine finery. ~*adj.* **3.** made of chiffon. **4.** (of soufflés, pies, cakes, etc.) having a very light fluffy texture. [C18: from F, from *chiffe* rag]

chiffonier *or* **chiffonnier** (,ʃɪfə'nɪə) *n.* **1.** a tall, elegant chest of drawers. **2.** a wide low open-fronted cabinet. [C19: from F, from *chiffon* rag]

Chifley ('tʃɪflɪ) *n.* **Joseph Benedict.** 1885–1951, Australian statesman; prime minister of Australia (1945–49).

chigetai (,tʃɪgɪ'taɪ) *n.* a variety of the Asiatic wild ass of Mongolia. Also spelled: **dziggetai.** [from Mongolian *tchikhitei* long-eared, from *tchikhi* ear]

chigger ('tʃɪgə) *n.* **1.** *U.S. & Canad.* the parasitic larva of a mite, which causes intense itching. **2.** another name for **chigoe.**

chignon ('ʃiːnjɒn) *n.* an arrangement of long hair in a roll or knot at the back of the head. [C18: from F, from OF *chaignon* link, from *chaine* CHAIN; infl. also by OF *tignon* coil of hair]

chigoe ('tʃɪgəʊ) *n.* **1.** a tropical flea, the female of which burrows into the skin of its host, which includes man. **2.** another name for **chigger.** [C17: from Carib *chigo*]

Chigwell ('tʃɪgwəl) *n.* a town in S England, in W Essex. Pop.: 51 290 (1981).

Chihli ('tʃiːliː) *n.* **Gulf of.** another name for the **Bohai.**

Chihuahua (tʃɪ'wɑːwɑː, -wə) *n.* **1.** a state of N Mexico: mostly high plateau; important mineral resources, with many silver mines. Capital: Chihuahua. Pop.: 1 933 856 (1980). Area: 247 087 sq. km (153 194 sq. miles). **2.** a city in N Mexico, capital of Chihuahua state. Pop.: 375 000 (1984). **3.** a breed of tiny dog originally from Mexico, having short smooth hair, large erect ears, and protruding eyes.

chilblain ('tʃɪl,bleɪn) *n.* (*usually pl.*) an inflammation of the fingers or toes, caused by exposure to cold. [C16: from CHILL (n.) + BLAIN] — **'chil,blained** *adj.*

child (tʃaɪld) *n., pl.* **children. 1. a.** a boy or girl between birth and puberty. **b.** (*as modifier*): *child labour.* **2.** a baby or infant. **3.** an unborn baby. **4. with child.** an old-fashioned term for **pregnant. 5.** a human offspring; a son or daughter. Related adj.: **filial. 6.** a childish or immature person. **7.** a member of a family or tribe; descendant: *a child of Israel.* **8.** a person or thing regarded as the product of an influence or environment: *a child of nature.* [OE *cild*] — **'childless** *adj.* — **'childlessness** *n.*

child abuse *n.* physical, sexual, or emotional ill-treatment of a child by its parents or other adults responsible for its welfare.

child-bearing *n.* **a.** the act or process of carrying and giving birth to a child. **b.** (*as modifier*): *of child-bearing age.*

childbed ('tʃaɪld,bed) *n.* (often preceded by *in*) the condition of giving birth to a child.

child benefit *n.* (in Britain and New Zealand) a regular government payment to parents of children up to a certain age. In New Zealand more commonly called: **family benefit.** Austral. equivalent: **child endowment.**

childbirth ('tʃaɪld,bɜːθ) *n.* the act of giving birth to a child.

childhood ('tʃaɪldhʊd) *n.* the condition of being a child; the period of life before puberty.

childish ('tʃaɪldɪʃ) *adj.* **1.** in the manner of or suitable to a child. **2.** foolish or petty: *childish fears.* — **'childishly** *adv.* — **'childishness** *n.*

childlike ('tʃaɪld,laɪk) *adj.* like or befitting a child, as in being innocent, trustful, etc.

child minder *n.* a person who looks after children, esp. those whose parents are working.

children ('tʃɪldrən) *n.* the plural of **child.**

Children of Israel *pl. n.* the Jewish people or nation.

child's play *n. Inf.* something easy to do.

chile ('tʃɪlɪ) *n.* a variant spelling of **chilli.**

Chile ('tʃɪlɪ) *n.* a republic in South America, on the Pacific, with a total length of about 4090 km (2650 miles) and an average width of only 177 km (110 miles): gained independence from Spain in 1818; the government of President Allende (elected 1970) attempted the implementation of Marxist policies within a democratic system until overthrown by a military coup (1973). Chile consists chiefly of the Andes in the east, the Atacama Desert in the north, a central fertile region, and a huge S region of almost uninhabitable mountains, glaciers, fjords, and islands; an important producer of copper, iron ore, nitrates, etc. Language: Spanish. Religion: Roman Catholic. Currency: peso. Capital: Santiago. Pop.: 12 416 000 (1987). Area: 756 945 sq. km (292 256 sq. miles). — **'Chilean** *adj., n.*

Chile pine *n.* another name for the **monkey puzzle.**

Chile saltpetre *or* **nitre** *n.* a naturally occurring form of sodium nitrate.

chiliad ('kɪlɪ,æd) *n.* **1.** a group of one thousand. **2.** one thousand years. [C16: from Gk, from *khilioi* a thousand]

Chilkoot Pass ('tʃɪlkuːt) *n.* a mountain pass in North America between SE Alaska and NW British Columbia, over the Coast Range.

chill (tʃɪl) *n.* **1.** a moderate coldness. **2.** a sensation of coldness resulting from a cold or damp environment, or from a sudden emotional reaction. **3.** a feverish cold. **4.** a check on enthusiasm or joy. ~*adj.* **5.** another word for **chilly.** ~*vb.* **6.** to make or become cold. **7.** (*tr.*) to cool or freeze (food, drinks, etc.). **8.** (*tr.*) **a.** to depress (enthusiasm, etc.). **b.** to discourage. ~See also **chill out.** [OE *ciele*] — **'chilling** *adj.* — **'chillingly** *adv.* — **'chillness** *n.*

Chillán (*Spanish* tʃi'ʎan) *n.* a city in central Chile. Pop.: 128 920 (1985 est.).

chiller ('tʃɪlə) *n.* **1.** short for **spine-chiller. 2.** *N.Z.* a refrigerated storage area for meat.

chilli or **chili** ('tʃɪlɪ) n., pl. **chillies** or **chilies**. the small red hot-tasting pod of a type of capsicum used for flavouring sauces, etc. [C17: from Sp., from Nahuatl *chilli*]

chilli con carne ('tʃɪlɪ kɒn 'kɑːnɪ) n. a highly seasoned Mexican dish of meat, onions, beans, and chilli powder. [from Sp.: chilli with meat]

chilli powder n. ground chilli blended with other spices.

chilli sauce n. a highly seasoned sauce made of tomatoes cooked with chilli and other spices.

chill out vb. (intr., adv.) Sl., chiefly U.S. to relax.

chilly ('tʃɪlɪ) adj. **-lier, -liest. 1.** causing or feeling cool or moderately cold. **2.** without warmth; unfriendly. **3.** (of people) sensitive to cold. — '**chilliness** n.

chilly bin n. N.Z. inf. a portable insulated container with provision for packing food and drink in ice.

Chilpancingo (Spanish tʃilpan'θingo) n. a town in S Mexico, capital of Guerrero state, in the Sierra Madre del Sur. Pop.: 56 904 (1970).

Chiltern Hills ('tʃɪltən) pl. n. a range of low chalk hills in SE England extending northwards from the Thames valley. Highest point: 260 m (852 ft.).

Chiltern Hundreds ('tʃɪltən) pl. n. (in Britain) short for **Stewardship of the Chiltern Hundreds**; a nominal office that an MP applies for in order to resign his seat.

Chilung or **Chi-lung** ('tʃiː'lʊŋ) n. a port in N Taiwan: fishing and industrial centre. Pop.: 347 828 (1982 est.). Also called: **Keelung, Kilung.**

Chimborazo (,tʃɪmbə'rɑːzəʊ, -'reɪ-; Spanish tʃimbo'raθo) n. an extinct volcano in central Ecuador, in the Andes: the highest peak in Ecuador. Height: 6267 m (20 561 ft.).

Chimbote (Spanish tʃim'bote) n. a port in N central Peru: contains Peru's first steelworks (1958), using hydroelectric power from the Santa River. Pop.: 185 000 (1984 est.).

chime[1] (tʃaɪm) n. **1.** an individual bell or the sound it makes when struck. **2.** (often pl.) the machinery employed to sound a bell in this way. **3.** Also called: **bell.** a percussion instrument consisting of a set of vertical metal tubes of graduated length, suspended in a frame and struck with a hammer. **4.** agreement; concord. ~vb. **5. a.** to sound (a bell) or (of a bell) to be sounded by a clapper or hammer. **b.** to produce (music or sounds) by chiming. **6.** (tr.) to indicate or show (time or the hours) by chiming. **7.** (intr.; foll. by with) to agree or harmonize. [C13: prob. shortened from earlier chymbe bell, ult. from L cymbalum CYMBAL] —'**chimer** n.

chime[2], **chimb** (tʃaɪm), or **chine** n. the projecting rim of a cask or barrel. [OE cimb-]

chime in vb. (intr., adv.) Inf. **1.** to join in or interrupt (a conversation), esp. repeatedly and unwelcomely. **2.** to voice agreement.

chimera or **chimaera** (kaɪ'mɪərə, kɪ-) n. **1.** (often cap.) Greek myth. a fire-breathing monster with the head of a lion, body of a goat, and tail of a serpent. **2.** a fabulous beast made up of parts taken from various animals. **3.** a grotesque product of the imagination. **4.** Biol. an organism consisting of at least two genetically different kinds of tissue as a result of mutation, grafting, etc. [C16: from L, from Gk khimaira she-goat]

chimerical or **chimeric** (kaɪ'mɛrɪk³l, kɪ-) or **chimeric** adj. **1.** wildly fanciful; imaginary. **2.** given to or indulging in fantasies. — chi'**merically** adv.

Chimkent (tʃim'kɛnt) n. a city in the SW Soviet Union, in the S Kazakh SSR. Pop.: 389 000 (1987).

chimney ('tʃɪmnɪ) n. **1.** a vertical structure of brick, masonry, or steel that carries smoke or steam away from a fire, engine, etc. **2.** another name for **flue**[1] (sense 1). **3.** short for **chimney stack. 4.** an open-ended glass tube fitting around the flame of an oil or gas lamp in order to exclude draughts. **5.** Brit. a fireplace, esp. an old and large one. **6.** the vent of a volcano. **7.** Mountaineering. a vertical fissure large enough for a person's body to enter. [C14: from OF cheminée, from LL camināta, from L camīnus furnace, from Gk kaminos oven]

chimney breast n. the wall or walls that surround the base of a chimney or fireplace.

chimneypot ('tʃɪmnɪ,pɒt) n. a short pipe on the top of a chimney.

chimney stack n. the part of a chimney that rises above the roof of a building.

chimney sweep or **sweeper** n. a person who cleans soot from chimneys.

chimp (tʃɪmp) n. Inf. short for **chimpanzee.**

chimpanzee (,tʃɪmpæn'ziː) n. a gregarious and intelligent anthropoid ape, inhabiting forests in central W Africa. [C18: from Central African dialect]

chin (tʃɪn) n. **1.** the protruding part of the lower jaw. **2.** the front part of the face below the lips. **3. keep one's chin up.** Inf. to keep cheerful under difficult circumstances. **4. take it on the chin.** Inf. to face squarely up to a defeat, adversity, etc. ~vb. **chinning, chinned. 5.** Gymnastics. to raise one's chin to (a horizontal bar, etc.) when hanging by the arms. [OE cinn]

Chin. abbrev. for: **1.** China. **2.** Chinese.

china ('tʃaɪnə) n. **1.** ceramic ware of a type originally from China. **2.** any porcelain or similar ware. **3.** cups, saucers, etc., collectively. **4.** (modifier) made of china. [C16 chiny, from Persian chīnī]

China ('tʃaɪnə) n. **1. People's Republic of.** Also called: **Communist China, Red China.** a republic in E Asia: the third largest and the most populous country in the world; the oldest continuing civilization (beginning over 2000 years B.C.); republic established in 1911 after the overthrow of the Manchu dynasty by Sun Yat-sen; People's Republic formed in 1949; contains vast deserts, steppes, great mountain ranges (Himalayas, Kunlun, Tian Shan, and Nan Shan), a central rugged plateau, and intensively cultivated E plains. Language: Chinese in various dialects, the chief of which is Mandarin. Currency: yuan. Capital: Peking. Pop.: 1 072 200 000 (1988). Area: 9 560 990 sq. km (3 691 502 sq. miles). **2. Republic of.** Also called: **Nationalist China, Taiwan.** a republic in E Asia occupying the island of Taiwan, 13 nearby islands, and 64 islands of the Penghu (Pescadores) group: established in 1949 by the Nationalist government of China under Chiang Kai-shek after its expulsion by the Communists from the mainland; under U.S. protection 1954–79. Language: Mandarin Chinese. Religion: predominantly Buddhist and Taoist. Currency: New Taiwan dollar. Capital: Taipei. Pop.: 18 135 508 (1981 est.). Area: 35 981 sq. km (13 892 sq. miles). Former name: **Formosa.** ~Related adj.: **Sinitic.**

china clay n. another name for **kaolin.**

Chinagraph ('tʃaɪnə,grɑːf) n. Trademark. a coloured pencil used for writing on china, glass, etc.

Chinaman ('tʃaɪnəmən) n., pl. **-men. 1.** Arch. or derog. a native or inhabitant of China. **2.** (often not cap.) Cricket. a ball bowled by a left-handed bowler to a right-handed batsman that spins from off to leg.

Chinan or **Chi-nan** ('tʃiː'næn) n. a variant transliteration of the Chinese name for **Jinan.**

China Sea n. part of the Pacific Ocean off the coast of China: divided by Taiwan into the East China Sea in the north and the South China Sea in the south.

Chinatown ('tʃaɪnə,taʊn) n. a quarter of any city or town outside China with a predominantly Chinese population.

chinaware ('tʃaɪnə,wɛə) n. articles made of china, esp. those made for domestic use.

chincherinchee (,tʃɪntʃərɪn'tʃiː, -'rɪntʃɪ) n. a bulbous South African liliaceous plant having long spikes of white or yellow long-lasting flowers. [from ?]

chinchilla (tʃɪn'tʃɪlə) n. **1.** a small squirrel-like rodent inhabiting mountainous regions of South America. It is bred in captivity for its soft silvery grey fur. **2.** the highly valued fur of this animal. **3.** a thick napped woollen cloth used for coats. [C17: from Sp., ?from Aymara]

chin-chin sentence substitute. Inf. a greeting or toast. [C18: from Chinese (Peking) ch'ing-ch'ing, please-please]

Chin-Chou or **Chinchow** ('tʃin'tʃaʊ) n. a variant transliteration of the Chinese name for **Jinzhou.**

Chindit ('tʃɪndɪt) n. a member of the Allied forces fighting behind the Japanese lines in Burma (1943–45). [C20: from Burmese chinthé a fabulous lion]

Chindwin ('tʃɪn'dwɪn) n. a river in N Burma, rising in the Kumôn Range and flowing northwest then south to the Irrawaddy, of which it is the main tributary. Length: about 966 km (600 miles).

chine[1] (tʃaɪn) n. **1.** the backbone. **2.** the backbone of an animal with adjoining meat, cut for cooking. **3.** a ridge or crest of land. ~vb. **4.** (tr.) to cut (meat) along or across the backbone. [C14: from OF eschine, of Gmc origin; see SHIN]

chine[2] (tʃaɪn) n. S English dialect. a deep fissure in the wall of a cliff. [OE cinan to crack]

Chinese (tʃaɪ'niːz) adj. **1.** of, relating to, or characteristic of China, its people, or their languages. ~n. **2.** (pl.

-nese) a native or inhabitant of China or a descendant of one. **3.** any of the languages of China.

Chinese cabbage *n.* a Chinese plant that is related to the cabbage and has crisp edible leaves growing in a loose cylindrical head.

Chinese chequers *n.* (*functioning as sing.*) a board game played with marbles or pegs.

Chinese Empire *n.* China as ruled by the emperors until the establishment of the republic in 1911–12.

Chinese gooseberry *n.* another name for **kiwi fruit.**

Chinese lantern *n.* **1.** a collapsible lantern made of thin coloured paper. **2.** an Asian plant, cultivated for its attractive orange-red inflated calyx.

Chinese leaves *pl. n.* the edible leaves of a Chinese cabbage.

Chinese puzzle *n.* **1.** an intricate puzzle, esp. one consisting of boxes within boxes. **2.** a complicated problem.

Chinese Turkestan *n.* the E part of the central Asian region of Turkestan: corresponds generally to the present-day Xinjiang Uygur Autonomous Region of China.

Chinese wall *n.* (esp. in financial institutions) a notional barrier between departments in the same company in order to avoid conflicts of interest between them.

Chinghai *or* **Ch'ing-hai** ('tʃɪŋ'haɪ) *n.* a variant transliteration of the Chinese name for **Qinghai.**

Chingtao *or* **Ch'ing-tao** ('tʃɪŋ'taʊ) *n.* a variant transliteration of the Chinese name for **Qingdao.**

Ch'ing-yüan ('tʃɪŋ'juːɑːn) *n.* a former name of **Baoding.**

Chin Hills (tʃɪn) *pl. n.* a mountainous region of W Burma: part of the Arakan Yoma system. Highest peak: Mount Victoria, 3053 m (10 075 ft.).

Chin-Hsien ('tʃɪn'ʃjɛn) *n.* the former name (1913–47) of **Jinzhou.**

chink[1] (tʃɪŋk) *n.* **1.** a small narrow opening, such as a fissure or crack. **2. chink in one's armour.** a small but fatal weakness. [C16: ? var. of earlier *chine*, from OE *cine* crack]

chink[2] (tʃɪŋk) *vb.* **1.** to make or cause to make a light ringing sound, as by the striking of glasses or coins. ~*n.* **2.** such a sound. [C16: imit.]

Chinkiang ('tʃɪn'kjæŋ, -kaɪ'æŋ) *n.* a variant transliteration of the Chinese name for **Jinjiang.**

chinless wonder ('tʃɪnlɪs) *n. Brit. inf.* a person, esp. upper-class, lacking strength of character.

chinoiserie (ʃiːn,wɑːzə'riː, -'wɑːzərɪ) *n.* **1.** a style of decorative or fine art based on imitations of Chinese motifs. **2.** an object or objects in this style. [F, from *chinois* CHINESE; see -ERY]

chinook (tʃɪ'nuːk, -'nʊk) *n.* **1.** a warm dry southwesterly wind blowing down the eastern slopes of the Rocky Mountains. **2.** a warm moist wind blowing onto the Washington and Oregon coasts from the sea. [C19: from Amerind]

Chinook (tʃɪ'nuːk, -'nʊk) *n.* **1.** (*pl.* **-nook** *or* **-nooks**) a North American Indian people of the Pacific coast near the Columbia River. **2.** the language of this people.

Chinook Jargon *n.* a pidgin language containing elements of North American Indian languages, English, and French: formerly used among fur traders and Indians on the NW coast of North America.

Chinook salmon *n.* a Pacific salmon valued as a food fish.

chinos ('tʃiːnəʊz) *pl. n.* trousers made of a durable cotton twill cloth. [C20: from *chino*, the cloth, from ?]

chintz (tʃɪnts) *n.* a printed, patterned cotton fabric, with glazed finish. [C17: from Hindi *chint*, from Sansk. *citra* gaily-coloured]

chintzy ('tʃɪntsɪ) *adj.* **chintzier, chintziest. 1.** of, resembling, or covered with chintz. **2.** *Brit. inf.* typical of the décor associated with the use of chintz soft furnishings.

chinwag ('tʃɪn,wæg) *n. Brit. inf.* a chat.

Chios ('kaɪɒs, -ɒs, 'kiː-) *n.* **1.** an island in the Aegean Sea, off the coast of Turkey: belongs to Greece. Capital: Chios. Pop.: 49 865 (1981). Area: 904 sq. km (353 sq. miles). **2.** a port on the island of Chios: in ancient times, one of the 12 Ionian city-states. Pop.: 24 115 (1981). Modern Greek name: **Khíos.**

chip (tʃɪp) *n.* **1.** a small piece removed by chopping, cutting, or breaking. **2.** a mark left after a small piece has been broken off something. **3.** (in some games) a counter used to represent money. **4.** a thin strip of potato fried in deep fat. **5.** the U.S. and Canad. name for **crisp** (sense 10). **6.** *Sport.* a shot, kick, etc., lofted into the air, and

travelling only a short distance. **7.** *Electronics.* a tiny wafer of semiconductor material, such as silicon, processed to form a type of integrated circuit or component such as a transistor. **8.** a thin strip of wood or straw used for making woven hats, baskets, etc. **9.** *N.Z.* a container for soft fruit, made of thin sheets of wood; punnet. **10. chip off the old block.** *Inf.* a person who resembles one of his or her parents in behaviour. **11. have a chip on one's shoulder.** *Inf.* to be aggressive or bear a grudge. **12. have had one's chips.** *Brit. inf.* to be defeated, condemned to die, killed, etc. **13. when the chips are down.** *Inf.* at a time of crisis. ~*vb.* **chipping, chipped. 14.** to break small pieces from or become broken off in small pieces: *will the paint chip?* **15.** (*tr.*) to break or cut into small pieces: *to chip ice.* **16.** (*tr.*) to shape by chipping. **17.** *Austral.* to dig or weed (a crop) with a hoe. **18.** *Sport.* to strike or kick (a ball) in a high arc. [OE *cipp* (n.), *cippian* (vb.), from ?]

chip-based *adj.* using or incorporating microchips in electronic equipment.

chipboard ('tʃɪp,bɔːd) *n.* a thin rigid sheet made of compressed wood particles.

chip heater *n. Austral. & N.Z.* a domestic water heater that burns chips of wood.

chip in *vb.* (*adv.*) *Inf.* **1.** to contribute (money, time, etc.) to a cause or fund. **2.** (*intr.*) to interpose a remark or interrupt with a remark.

chipmunk ('tʃɪp,mʌŋk) *n.* a burrowing rodent of North America and Asia, typically having black-striped yellowish fur and cheek pouches for storing food. [C19: of Algonquian origin]

chipolata (,tʃɪpə'lɑːtə) *n. Chiefly Brit.* a small sausage. [via F from It., from *cipolla* onion]

Chippendale ('tʃɪpən,deɪl) *n.* **1. Thomas.** ?1718–79, English cabinet-maker and furniture designer. ~*adj.* **2.** (of furniture) designed by, made by, or in the style of Thomas Chippendale, characterized by the use of Chinese and Gothic motifs, cabriole legs, and massive carving.

chipper ('tʃɪpə) *adj. Inf.* **1.** cheerful; lively. **2.** smartly dressed.

chippy ('tʃɪpɪ) *n., pl.* **-pies. 1.** *Brit. inf.* a fish-and-chip shop. **2.** *N.Z.* a potato crisp.

chip shot *n. Golf.* a short approach shot to the green, esp. one that is lofted.

Chirac (*French* ʃirak) *n.* **Jacques** (**René**) (ʒak). born 1932, French Gaullist politician: prime minister of France (1974–76 and 1986–88); mayor of Paris from 1977.

chiral ('kaɪrəl) *adj.* relating to chirality. [C20: from CHIRO- + AL[1]]

chirality (kaɪ'rælɪtɪ) *n.* right- or left-handedness in an asymmetric molecule.

Chirico (*Italian* 'kiːriko) *n.* **Giorgio de** ('dʒɔrdʒo de). 1888–1978, Italian artist born in Greece: profoundly influenced the surrealist movement.

chiro- *or* **cheiro-** *combining form.* of or by means of the hand: *chiromancy; chiropractic.* [via L from Gk *kheir* hand]

chirography (kaɪ'rɒgrəfɪ) *n.* another name for **calligraphy.** —**chi'rographer** *n.* —**chirographic** (,kaɪrə'græfɪk) *or* ,**chiro'graphical** *adj.*

chiromancy ('kaɪrə,mænsɪ) *n.* another word for **palmistry.** —'**chiro,mancer** *n.*

Chiron *or* **Cheiron** ('kaɪrɒn, -rən) *n.* **1.** *Greek myth.* a wise and kind centaur who taught many great heroes in their youth, including Achilles, Actaeon, and Jason. **2.** a minor planet, discovered by Charles Kowal in 1977, revolving round the sun between the orbits of Saturn and Uranus.

chiropody (kɪ'rɒpədɪ) *n.* the treatment of the feet, esp. corns, verrucas, etc. —**chi'ropodist** *n.*

chiropractic (,kaɪrə'præktɪk) *n.* a system of treating bodily disorders by manipulation of the spine and other parts. [C20: from CHIRO- + Gk *praktikos* PRACTICAL] —'**chiro,practor** *n.*

chirp (tʃɜːp) *vb.* (*intr.*) **1.** (esp. of some birds and insects) to make a short high-pitched sound. **2.** to speak in a lively fashion. ~*n.* **3.** a chirping sound. [C15 (as *chirpinge*, gerund): imit.] —'**chirper** *n.*

chirpy ('tʃɜːpɪ) *adj.* **chirpier, chirpiest.** *Inf.* cheerful; lively. —'**chirpily** *adv.* —'**chirpiness** *n.*

chirr *or* **churr** (tʃɜː) *vb.* **1.** (*intr.*) (esp. of certain insects, such as crickets) to make a shrill trilled sound. ~*n.* **2.** such a sound. [C17: imit.]

chirrup ('tʃɪrəp) *vb.* (*intr.*) **1.** (esp. of some birds) to chirp repeatedly. **2.** to make clucking sounds with the lips. ~*n.* **3.** such a sound. [C16: var. of CHIRP] —'**chirruper** *n.* —'**chirrupy** *adj.*

chisel ('tʃɪzəl) *n.* **1. a.** a hand tool for working wood, consisting of a flat steel blade with a handle. **b.** a similar tool without a handle for working stone or metal. ~*vb.* -**elling**, -**elled** *or U.S.* -**eling**, -**eled.** **2.** to carve (wood, stone, metal, etc.) or form (an engraving, statue, etc.) with or as with a chisel. **3.** *Sl.* to cheat or obtain by cheating. [C14: via OF, from Vulgar L *cīsellus* (unattested), from L *caesus* cut] —'**chiseller** *n.*

Chishima (ˌtʃiːʃiːˈmɑ) *n.* the Japanese name for the **Kuril Islands.**

Chisimaio (ˌkiːziˈmɑːjəʊ) *n.* a port in S Somalia, on the Indian Ocean. Pop.: 70 000 (1981 est.). Also called: **Kismayu.**

Chişinău (kiʃiˈnəu) *n.* the Romanian name for **Kishinev.**

chi-square distribution *n. Statistics.* a continuous single-parameter distribution used esp. to measure goodness of fit and to test hypotheses.

chi-square test *n. Statistics.* a test derived from the chi-square distribution to compare the goodness of fit of theoretical and observed frequency distributions.

chit[1] (tʃɪt) *n.* **1.** a voucher for a sum of money owed, esp. for food or drink. **2.** Also called: **chitty.** *Chiefly Brit.* **a.** a note or memorandum. **b.** a requisition or receipt. [C18: from earlier *chitty*, from Hindi *cittha* note, from Sansk. *citra* marked]

chit[2] (tʃɪt) *n. Facetious or derog.* a pert, impudent, or self-confident girl or child. [C14 (in the sense: young of an animal, kitten): from ?]

Chita (*Russian* tʃiˈta) *n.* an industrial city in the SE central Soviet Union, on the Trans-Siberian railway. Pop.: 349 000 (1987).

chital ('tʃiːtəl) *n.* another name for **axis**[2] (the deer). [from Hindi]

chitchat ('tʃɪtˌtʃæt) *n.* **1.** gossip. ~*vb.* -**chatting,** -**chatted.** **2.** (*intr.*) to gossip.

chitin ('kaɪtɪn) *n.* a polysaccharide that is the principal component of the exoskeletons of arthropods and of the bodies of fungi. [C19: from F, from Gk *khitōn* CHITON + -IN] —'**chitinous** *adj.*

chiton ('kaɪtən, -tɒn) *n.* **1.** (in ancient Greece) a loose woollen tunic worn by men and women. **2.** any small primitive marine mollusc having an elongated body covered with eight overlapping shell plates. [C19: from Gk *khitōn* coat of mail]

Chittagong ('tʃɪtəˌgɒŋ) *n.* a port in E Bangladesh, on the Bay of Bengal: industrial centre. Pop.: 1 750 000 (1986).

chitterlings ('tʃɪtəlɪŋz) *or* **chitlings** ('tʃɪtlɪŋz) *pl. n.* (*sometimes sing.*) the intestines of a pig or other animal prepared as a dish. [C13: from ?]

chiv (tʃɪv, ʃɪv) *or* **shiv** (ʃɪv) *Sl.* ~*n.* **1.** a knife. ~*vb.* **chiving, chivved** *or* **shivving, shivved.** **2.** to stab (someone). [C17: ?from Romany *chiv* blade]

chivalrous ('ʃɪvəlrəs) *adj.* **1.** gallant; courteous. **2.** involving chivalry. [C14: from OF, from CHEVALIER] —'**chivalrously** *adv.* —'**chivalrousness** *n.*

chivalry ('ʃɪvəlrɪ) *n., pl.* -**ries.** **1.** the combination of qualities expected of an ideal knight, esp. courage, honour, justice, and a readiness to help the weak. **2.** courteous behaviour, esp. towards women. **3.** the medieval system and principles of knighthood. **4.** knights, noblemen, etc., collectively. [C13: from OF *chevalerie*, from CHEVALIER] —'**chivalric** *adj.*

chive (tʃaɪv) *n.* a small Eurasian purple-flowered alliaceous plant, whose long slender hollow leaves are used in cooking. Also called: **chives.** [C14: from OF *cive*, ult. from L *caepa* onion]

chivy, chivvy, ('tʃɪvɪ), *or* **chevy** *Brit.* ~*vb.* **chivying, chivied, chivvying, chivvied,** *or* **chevying, chevied.** **1.** (*tr.*) to harass or nag. **2.** (*tr.*) to hunt. **3.** (*intr.*) to run about. ~*n., pl.* **chivies, chivvies,** *or* **chevies.** **4.** a hunt. **5.** *Obs.* a hunting cry. [C19: var. of *chevy*, prob. from *Chevy Chase*, a Scottish border ballad]

Chkalov (*Russian* 'tʃkaləf) *n.* the former name (1938–57) of Orenburg.

chlamydia (kləˈmɪdɪə) *n.* a microorganism of a type midway between a virus and a bacterium that causes trachoma and inflammation of the genital organs in women and of the urinary passage in men. [C20: from NL, from Gk *khlamus* mantle + -IA]

Chlodwig ('klɔːtvɪç) *n.* the German name for **Clovis I.**

Chloe ('kləuɪ) *n.* See **Daphnis and Chloe.**

chloral ('klɔːrəl) *n.* **1.** a colourless oily liquid with a pungent odour, made from chlorine and acetaldehyde and used in preparing chloral hydrate and DDT. Formula: CCl_3CHO. **2.** short for **chloral hydrate.**

chloral hydrate *n.* a colourless crystalline soluble solid produced by the reaction of chloral with water and used as a sedative and hypnotic. Formula: $CCl_3C(OH)_3$.

chloramphenicol (ˌklɔːræmˈfɛnɪˌkɒl) *n.* a broad-spectrum antibiotic used esp. in treating typhoid fever and rickettsial infections. [C20: from CHLORO- + AM(IDE) + PHE(NO)- + NI(TRO)- + (GLY)COL]

chlorate ('klɔːreɪt, -rɪt) *n.* any salt of chloric acid, containing the monovalent ion ClO_3–.

chlordane ('klɔːdeɪn) *or* **chlordan** *n.* a white insoluble toxic solid used as an insecticide. [C20: from CHLORO- + (IN)D(OLE + -ENE) + -ANE]

chloric ('klɔːrɪk) *adj.* of or containing chlorine in the pentavalent state.

chloric acid *n.* a strong acid with a pungent smell, known only in solution and in the form of chlorate salts. Formula: $HClO_3$.

chloride ('klɔːraɪd) *n.* **1.** any salt of hydrochloric acid, containing the chloride ion Gl– **2.** any compound containing a chlorine atom, such as methyl chloride (chloromethane), CH_3Cl.

chloride of lime *or* **chlorinated lime** *n.* another name for **bleaching powder.**

chlorinate ('klɔːrɪˌneɪt) *vb.* (*tr.*) **1.** to combine or treat (a substance) with chlorine. **2.** to disinfect (water) with chlorine. —ˌchlorin'ation *n.* —'chlorinˌator *n.*

chlorine ('klɔːriːn) *or* **chlorin** ('klɔːrɪn) *n.* a toxic pungent greenish-yellow gas of the halogen group; occurring only in the combined state, mainly in common salt: used in the manufacture of many organic chemicals, in water purification, and as a disinfectant and bleaching agent. Symbol: Cl; atomic no.: 17; atomic wt.: 35.453. [C19 (coined by Sir Humphrey Davy): from CHLORO- + -INE[2], referring to its colour]

chlorite[1] ('klɔːraɪt) *n.* any of a group of green soft secondary minerals consisting of the hydrated silicates of aluminium, iron, and magnesium. [C18: from L, from Gk, from *khlōros* greenish yellow] —**chloritic** (klɔːˈrɪtɪk) *adj.*

chlorite[2] ('klɔːraɪt) *n.* any salt of chlorous acid.

chloro- *or before a vowel* **chlor-** *combining form.* **1.** indicating the colour green: *chlorophyll.* **2.** chlorine: *chloroform.*

chlorofluorocarbon (ˌklɔːrəˌfluərəʊˈkɑːbən) *n.* any of various gaseous compounds of carbon, hydrogen, chlorine, and fluorine, used as refrigerants, aerosol propellants, solvents, and in foam: some cause a breakdown of ozone in the earth's atmosphere.

chloroform ('klɔːrəˌfɔːm) *n.* a heavy volatile liquid with a sweet taste and odour, used as a solvent and cleansing agent and in refrigerants: formerly used as an inhalation anaesthetic. Formula: $CHCl_3$. Systematic name: **trichloromethane.** [C19: from CHLORO- + *formyl* from FORMIC]

Chloromycetin (ˌklɔːrəʊmaɪˈsiːtɪn) *n. Trademark.* a brand of **chloramphenicol.**

chlorophyll *or U.S.* **chlorophyl** ('klɔːrəfɪl) *n.* the green pigment of plants, occurring in chloroplasts, that traps the energy of sunlight for photosynthesis: used as a colouring agent (E140) in medicines and food. —'chloroˌphylloid *adj.* —ˌchloro'phyllous *adv.*

chloroplast ('klɔːrəʊˌplæst) *n.* a plastid containing chlorophyll and other pigments, occurring in plants that carry out photosynthesis.

chlorosis (kləˈrəʊsɪs) *n.* a once-common iron-deficiency disease of adolescent girls, characterized by greenish-yellow skin colour, weakness, and palpitation. Also called: **greensickness.** [C17: from CHLORO- + -OSIS]

chlorous ('klɔːrəs) *adj.* **1.** of or containing chlorine in the trivalent state. **2.** of or containing chlorous acid.

chlorous acid *n.* an unstable acid that is a strong oxidizing agent. Formula: $HClO_2$.

chlorpromazine (klɔːˈprɒməˌziːn) *n.* a drug used as a sedative and tranquillizer. [C20: from CHLORO- + PRO(PYL + A)M(INE) + AZINE]

chlortetracycline (klɔːˌtɛtrəˈsaɪkliːn) *n.* an antibiotic used in treating many bacterial and rickettsial infections and some viral infections.

chock (tʃɒk) n. **1.** a block or wedge of wood used to prevent the sliding or rolling of a heavy object. **2.** *Naut.* **a.** a ringlike device with an opening at the top through which a rope is placed. **b.** a cradle-like support for a boat, barrel, etc. ~vb. (tr.) **3.** (usually foll. by up) *Brit.* to cram full. **4.** to fit with or secure by a chock. **5.** to support (a boat, barrel, etc.) on chocks. ~adv. **6.** as closely or tightly as possible: *chock against the wall.* [C17: from ?; ? rel. to OF *çoche* log]

chock-a-block adj., adv. **1.** filled to capacity; in a crammed state. **2.** *Naut.* with the blocks brought close together, as when a tackle is pulled as tight as possible.

chocker ('tʃɒkə) adj. **1.** *Austral. & N.Z. inf.* full up; packed. **2.** *Brit. sl.* irritated; fed up. [C20: from CHOCK-A-BLOCK]

chock-full or **choke-full** adj. (postpositive) completely full. [C17 *choke-full*; see CHOKE, FULL[1]]

choco or **chocko** ('tʃɒkəu) n., pl. **chocos** or **chockos.** *Austral. sl.* a conscript or militiaman. [from *chocolate soldier*]

chocolate ('tʃɒkəlɪt, 'tʃɒklɪt, -lət) n. **1.** a food preparation made from roasted ground cacao seeds, usually sweetened and flavoured. **2.** a drink or sweetmeat made from this. **3. a.** a deep brown colour. **b.** (as adj.): a *chocolate carpet.* [C17: from Sp., from Aztec *xocolatl*, from *xococ* sour + *atl* water] — **'chocolaty** adj.

chocolate-box n. (modifier) *Inf.* sentimentally pretty or appealing.

Choctaw ('tʃɒktɔ:) n. **1.** (pl. **-taws** or **-taw**) a member of a N American people originally of Alabama. **2.** their language. [C18: from Choctaw *Chahta*]

choice (tʃɔɪs) n. **1.** the act or an instance of choosing or selecting. **2.** the opportunity or power of choosing. **3.** a person or thing chosen or that may be chosen: *he was a possible choice.* **4.** an alternative action or possibility: *what choice did I have?* **5.** a supply from which to select. ~adj. **6.** of superior quality; excellent: *choice wine.* [C13: from OF, from *choisir* to CHOOSE] — **'choicely** adv. — **'choiceness** n.

choir ('kwaɪə) n. **1.** an organized group of singers, esp. for singing in church services. **2.** the part of a cathedral, abbey, or church in front of the altar and used by the choir and clergy. **3.** a number of instruments of the same family playing together: *a brass choir.* **4.** Also called: **choir organ.** one of the manuals on an organ controlling a set of soft sweet-toned pipes. [C13 *quer*, from OF *cuer*, from L CHORUS]

choirboy ('kwaɪə‚bɔɪ) n. a young boy who sings the treble part in a church choir.

choir school n. (in Britain) a school attached to a cathedral, college, etc., offering general education to boys whose singing ability is good.

Choiseul (French ʃwazœl) n. an island in the SW Pacific Ocean, in the Solomon Islands: hilly and densely forested. Area: 3885 sq. km (1500 sq. miles).

choke (tʃəuk) vb. **1.** (tr.) to hinder or stop the breathing of (a person or animal), esp. by constricting the windpipe or by asphyxiation. **2.** (intr.) to have trouble or fail in breathing, swallowing, or speaking. **3.** (tr.) to block or clog up (a passage, pipe, street, etc.). **4.** (tr.) to retard the growth or action of: *the weeds are choking my plants.* **5.** (tr.) to enrich the petrol-air mixture by reducing the air supply to (a carburettor, petrol engine, etc.). ~n. **6.** the act or sound of choking. **7.** a device in the carburettor of a petrol engine that enriches the petrol-air mixture by reducing the air supply. **8.** any mechanism for reducing the flow of a fluid in a pipe, tube, etc. **9.** Also called: **choke coil.** *Electronics.* an inductor having a relatively high impedance, used to prevent the passage of high frequencies or to smooth the output of a rectifier. [OE *ācēocian*] — **'choky** or **'chokey** adj.

choke back or **down** vb. (tr., adv.) to suppress (anger, tears, etc.).

choke chain n. a collar and lead for a dog so designed that if the dog drags on the lead the collar tightens round its neck.

choked (tʃəukt) adj. *Brit. inf.* annoyed or disappointed.

choker ('tʃəukə) n. **1.** a woman's high collar. **2.** any neckband or necklace worn tightly around the throat. **3.** a high clerical collar; stock. **4.** a person or thing that chokes.

choke up vb. (tr., adv.) **1.** to block (a drain, pipe, etc.) completely. **2.** *Inf.* (usually passive) to overcome (a person) with emotion.

chokey or **choky** ('tʃəukɪ) n. *Brit. sl.* prison. [C17: from Anglo-Indian, from Hindi *caukī* a lockup]

choko ('tʃəukəu) n., pl. **-kos.** *Austral. & N.Z.* the cucumber-like fruit of a tropical American vine. [C18: from Brazilian Indian]

chole- or before a vowel **chol-** combining form. bile or gall: *cholesterol.* [from Gk *kholē*]

choler ('kɒlə) n. **1.** anger or ill humour. **2.** *Arch.* one of the four bodily humours; yellow bile. [C14: from OF, from Med. L, from L: jaundice, CHOLERA]

cholera ('kɒlərə) n. an acute intestinal infection characterized by severe diarrhoea, cramp, etc.: caused by ingestion of water or food contaminated with the bacterium *Vibrio comma.* [C14: from L, from Gk *kholera* jaundice, from *kholē* bile] — **choleraic** (‚kɒlə'reɪk) adj.

choleric ('kɒlərɪk) adj. **1.** bad-tempered. **2.** *Obs.* bilious or causing biliousness. — **'cholerically** adv.

cholesterol (kə'lɛstə‚rɒl) or **cholesterin** (kə'lɛstərɪn) n. a sterol found in all animal tissues, blood, bile, and animal fats. A high level of cholesterol is implicated in some cases of atherosclerosis. [C19: from CHOLE- + Gk *stereos* solid]

choline ('kəuli:n, -ɪn, 'kɒl-) n. a colourless viscous soluble alkaline substance present in animal tissues, esp. as a constituent of lecithin. [C19: from CHOLE- + -INE[2]]

Cholon (tʃə'lʌn; French ʃɔlɔ̃) n. a city in S Vietnam: a suburb of Ho Chi Minh City.

Cholula (Spanish tʃo'lula) n. a town in S Mexico, in Puebla state: ancient ruins, notably a pyramid, 53 m (177 ft.) high. Pop.: 15 399 (1970).

chomp (tʃɒmp) or **chump** vb. **1.** to chew (food) noisily; champ. ~n. **2.** the act or sound of chewing in this manner. [var. of CHAMP[1]]

Chomsky ('tʃɒmskɪ) n. **Noam** ('nəuəm). born 1928, U.S. linguist and political critic. His theory of language structure, transformational generative grammar, superseded the behaviourist view of Bloomfield. — **'Chomskyan** or **'Chomsky‚ite** n., adj.

chondrite ('kɒndraɪt) n. a stony meteorite consisting mainly of silicate minerals in small spherical masses.

Chŏngjin or **Chungjin** ('tʃʌŋ'dʒɪn) n. a port in W North Korea, on the Sea of Japan. Pop.: 490 000 (1981).

Chongqing ('tʃuŋ'tʃɪŋ), **Chungking**, or **Ch'ung-ch'ing** n. a port in SW China, in Sichuan province at the confluence of the Yangtze and Jialing rivers: site of a city since the 3rd millennium B.C.; wartime capital of China (1938–45); major trade centre for W China. Pop.: 2 780 000 (1986). Also called: **Pahsien.**

Chŏnju ('tʃʌn'dʒu:) n. a city in SW South Korea: centre of large rice-growing region. Pop.: 366 997 (1980).

choof off (tʃuf) vb. (intr., adv.) *Austral. sl.* to go away; make off.

chook (tʃuk) n. *Inf., chiefly Austral. & N.Z.* a hen or chicken. Also called: **chookie.**

choose (tʃu:z) vb. **choosing, chose, chosen. 1.** to select (a person, thing, course of action, etc.) from a number of alternatives. **2.** (tr.; takes a clause as object or an infinitive) to consider it desirable or proper: *I don't choose to read that book.* **3.** (intr.) to like; please: *you may stand if you choose.* [OE *ceosan*] — **'chooser** n.

choosy ('tʃu:zɪ) adj. **choosier, choosiest.** *Inf.* particular in making a choice; difficult to please.

chop[1] (tʃɒp) vb. **chopping, chopped. 1.** (often foll. by *down* or *off*) to cut (something) with a blow from an axe or other sharp tool. **2.** (tr.; often foll. by *up*) to cut into pieces. **3.** (tr.) *Brit. inf.* to dispense with or reduce. **4.** (intr.) to move quickly or violently. **5.** *Tennis, cricket, etc.* to hit (a ball) sharply downwards. **6.** *Boxing, karate, etc.* to punch or strike (an opponent) with a short sharp blow. ~n. **7.** a cutting blow. **8.** the act or an instance of chopping. **9.** a piece chopped off. **10.** a slice of mutton, lamb, or pork, generally including a rib. **11.** *Austral. & N.Z. sl.* a share (esp. in **get** or **hop in for one's chop**). **12.** *Austral. & N.Z.* a competition of skill and speed in chopping logs. **13.** *Sport.* a sharp downward blow or stroke. **14. not much chop.** *Austral. & N.Z. inf.* not much good; poor. **15. the chop.** *Sl., chiefly Brit.* dismissal from employment. [C16: var. of CHAP[1]]

chop[2] (tʃɒp) vb. **chopping, chopped. 1.** (intr.) to change direction suddenly; vacillate (esp. in **chop and change**).

2. chop logic. use excessively subtle or involved argument. [OE *ceapian* to barter]

chop[3] (tʃɒp) *n.* a design stamped on goods as a trademark, esp. in the Far East. [C17: from Hindi *chhāp*]

chop chop *adv.* pidgin English for **quickly.** [C19: from Chinese dialect]

chophouse ('tʃɒp,haʊs) *n.* a restaurant specializing in steaks, grills, chops, etc.

Chopin ('ʃɒpæn; *French* ʃɔpɛ̃) *n.* **Frédéric François** (frederik frãswa). 1810–49, Polish composer and pianist active in France, who wrote chiefly for the piano: noted for his harmonic imagination and his lyrical and melancholy qualities.

choplogic ('tʃɒp,lɒdʒɪk) *n.* fallacious reasoning. [C16: from CHOP[2] + LOGIC]

chopper ('tʃɒpə) *n.* **1.** *Chiefly Brit.* a small hand axe. **2.** a butcher's cleaver. **3.** a person or thing that cuts or chops. **4.** an informal name for a **helicopter. 5.** a device for periodically interrupting an electric current or beam of radiation to produce a pulsed current or beam. **6.** a type of bicycle or motorcycle with very high handlebars. **7.** *N.Z.* a child's bicycle. **8.** *Sl., chiefly U.S.* a submachine-gun.

choppy ('tʃɒpɪ) *adj.* **-pier, -piest.** (of the sea, weather, etc.) fairly rough. —'**choppily** *adv.* —'**choppiness** *n.*

chops (tʃɒps) *pl. n.* **1.** the jaws or cheeks; jowls. **2.** the mouth. **3. lick one's chops.** *Inf.* to anticipate with pleasure. [C16: from ?]

chopsticks ('tʃɒpstɪks) *pl. n.* a pair of thin sticks, of ivory, wood, etc., used as eating utensils by the Chinese, Japanese, etc. [C17: from pidgin E, from *chop* quick, from Chinese dialect + STICK[1]]

chop suey ('suːɪ) *n.* a Chinese-style dish originating in the U.S., consisting of meat, bean sprouts, etc., stewed and served with rice. [C19: from Chinese *tsap sui* odds and ends]

choral ('kɔːrəl) *adj.* relating to, sung by, or designed for a chorus or choir. —'**chorally** *adv.*

chorale *or* **choral** (kɒ'rɑːl) *n.* **1.** a slow stately hymn tune. **2.** *Chiefly U.S.* a choir or chorus. [C19: from G *Choralgesang,* translation of L *cantus chorālis* choral song]

chord[1] (kɔːd) *n.* **1.** *Maths.* a straight line connecting two points on a curve or curved surface. **2.** *Engineering.* one of the principal members of a truss, esp. one that lies along the top or the bottom. **3.** *Anat.* a variant spelling of **cord. 4.** an emotional response, esp. one of sympathy: *the story struck the right chord.* [C16: from L, from Gk *khordē* gut, string; see CORD]

chord[2] (kɔːd) *n.* **1.** the simultaneous sounding of a group of musical notes, usually three or more in number. ~*vb.* **2.** (*tr.*) to provide (a melodic line) with chords. [C15: short for ACCORD; spelling infl. by CHORD[1]] —'**chordal** *adj.*

chordate ('kɔːdeɪt) *n.* **1.** an animal with a backbone or notochord. ~*adj.* **2.** of or relating to the chordates. [C19: from Med. L *chordata:* see CHORD[1] & -ATE[1]]

chore (tʃɔː) *n.* **1.** a small routine task, esp. a domestic one. **2.** an unpleasant task. [C19: from ME *chare,* from OE *cierr* a job]

-chore *n. combining form.* (in botany) indicating a plant that is distributed by a certain means: *anemochore.* [from Gk *khōrein* to move] —**-chorous** *or* **-choric** *adj. combining form.*

chorea (kɒ'rɪə) *n.* a disorder of the central nervous system characterized by uncontrollable irregular brief jerky movements. See **Huntington's chorea, Sydenham's chorea.** [C19: from NL, from L: dance, from Gk *khoreia;* see CHORUS]

choreograph ('kɒrɪə,grɑːf) *vb.* (*tr.*) to compose the steps and dances for (a ballet, etc.)

choreography (,kɒrɪ'ɒgrəfɪ) *or* **choregraphy** (kɒ-'rɛgrəfɪ) *n.* **1.** the composition of dance steps and sequences for ballet and stage and film dancing. **2.** the steps and sequences of a ballet or dance. **3.** the notation representing such steps. **4.** the art of dancing. [C18: from Gk *khoreia* dance + -GRAPHY] —,**chore'ographer** *or* **cho'regrapher** *n.* —**choreographic** (,kɒrɪə'græfɪk) *or* **choregraphic** (,kɒrə'græfɪk) *adj.* —,**choreo'graphically** *or* ,**chore'graphically** *adv.*

choric ('kɒrɪk) *adj.* of, like, or for a chorus, esp. of singing, dancing, or the speaking of verse.

chorion ('kɔːrɪən) *n.* the outer membrane surrounding an embryo. [C16: from Gk *khorion* afterbirth] —**chorionic** (,kɔːrɪ'ɒnɪk) *adj.*

chorionic villus sampling *n.* a method of diagnosing genetic disorders early in pregnancy by the removal by catheter through the cervix of a tiny sample of tissue from the chorionic villi. Abbrev.: **CVS**

chorister ('kɒrɪstə) *n.* a singer in a choir, esp. a choirboy. [C14: from Med. L *chorista*]

Chorley ('tʃɔːlɪ) *n.* a town in NW England, in S Lancashire: cotton textiles. Pop.: 54 775 (1981).

choroid ('kɔːrɔɪd) *or* **chorioid** ('kɔːrɪ,ɔɪd) *adj.* **1.** resembling the chorion, esp. in being vascular. ~*n.* **2.** the vascular membrane of the eyeball between the sclera and the retina. [C18: from Gk *khoroeidēs,* erroneously for *khorioeidēs,* from CHORION]

chortle ('tʃɔːt^əl) *vb.* **1.** (*intr.*) to chuckle gleefully. ~*n.* **2.** a gleeful chuckle. [C19: coined (1871) by Lewis Carroll; prob. a blend of CHUCKLE + SNORT] —'**chortler** *n.*

chorus ('kɔːrəs) *n., pl.* **-ruses. 1.** a large choir of singers or a piece of music composed for such a choir. **2.** a body of singers or dancers who perform together. **3.** a section of a song in which a soloist is joined by a group of singers, esp. in a recurring refrain. **4.** an intermediate section of a pop song, blues, etc., as distinct from the verse. **5.** *Jazz.* any of a series of variations on a theme. **6.** (in ancient Greece) **a.** a lyric poem sung by a group of dancers, originally as a religious rite. **b.** an ode or series of odes sung by a group of actors. **c.** the actors who sang the chorus and commented on the action of the play. **7. a.** (esp. in Elizabethan drama) the actor who spoke the prologue, etc. **b.** the part spoken by this actor. **8.** a group of people or animals producing words or sounds simultaneously. **9.** any speech, song, or utterance produced by a group of people or animals simultaneously: *the dawn chorus.* **10. in chorus.** in unison. ~*vb.* **11.** to speak, sing, or utter (words, sounds, etc.) in unison. [C16: from L, from Gk *khoros*]

chorus girl *n.* a girl who dances or sings in the chorus of a musical comedy, revue, etc.

Chorzów (*Polish* 'xɔʒuf) *n.* an industrial city in SW Poland: under German administration from 1794 to 1921. Pop.: 158 000 (1982). German name: **Königshütte.**

chose (tʃəʊz) *vb.* the past tense of **choose.**

chosen ('tʃəʊz^ən) *vb.* **1.** the past participle of **choose.** ~*adj.* **2.** selected or picked out, esp. for some special quality.

Chosen ('tʃəʊ'sɛn) *n.* the official name for **Korea** as a Japanese province (1910–45).

Chosŏn ('tʃəʊ'sɒn) *n.* the Korean name for **North Korea.**

Chota Nagpur ('tʃəʊtə 'nɑːgpʊə) *n.* a plateau in E India, in Bihar state: forested, with rich mineral resources and much heavy industry; produces chiefly lac (world's leading supplier), coal (half India's total output), and mica.

Chou En-lai (ɛn'laɪ) *or* **Zhou En Lai** *n.* 1898–1976, Chinese Communist statesman; foreign minister of the People's Republic of China (1949–58) and premier (1949–76).

chough (tʃʌf) *n.* a large black passerine bird of parts of Europe, Asia, and Africa, with a long downward-curving red bill: family Corvidae (crows). [C14: from ?]

choux pastry (ʃuː) *n.* a very light pastry made with eggs, used for éclairs, etc. [partial translation of F *pâte choux* cabbage dough]

chow (tʃaʊ) *n.* **1.** *Inf.* food. **2.** short for **chow-chow** (sense 1). **3. Chow.** *Austral. & N.Z. obs.* a derogatory term for **Chinese** (sense 2).

chow-chow *n.* **1.** a thick-coated breed of dog with a curled tail, originally from China. Often shortened to **chow. 2.** a Chinese preserve of ginger, orange peel, etc., in syrup. **3.** a mixed vegetable pickle. [C19: from pidgin E, prob. based on Chinese *cha* miscellaneous]

chowder ('tʃaʊdə) *n. Chiefly U.S. & Canad.* a thick soup or stew containing clams or fish. [C18: from F *chaudière* kettle, from LL *caldāria;* see CAULDRON]

chow mein (meɪn) *n.* a Chinese-American dish, consisting of mushrooms, meat, shrimps, etc., served with fried noodles. [from Chinese *ch'ao mien* fried noodles]

Chr. *abbrev. for:* **1.** Christ. **2.** Christian.

Chrétien de Troyes (*French* kretjɛ̃ də trwa) *n.* 12th century, French poet, who wrote the five Arthurian romances *Erec; Cligès; Lancelot, le chevalier de la charette; Yvain,* *le chevalier au lion;* and *Perceval, le conte del Graal* (?1155–?1190), the first courtly romances.

chrism *or* **chrisom** ('krɪzəm) *n.* a mixture of olive oil and balsam used for sacramental anointing in the Greek Orthodox and Roman Catholic Churches. [OE, from Med. L, from Gk, from *khriein* to anoint] —**chrismal** ('krɪzməl) *adj.*

Christ (kraɪst) *n.* **1.** Jesus of Nazareth (Jesus Christ), regarded by Christians as fulfilling Old Testament prophecies of the Messiah. **2.** the Messiah or anointed one of God as the subject of Old Testament prophecies. **3.** an image or picture of Christ. *~interj.* **4.** *Taboo sl.* an oath expressing annoyance, surprise, etc. *~See also* **Jesus.** [OE *Crist,* from L *Christus,* from Gk *khristos* anointed one (from *khriein* to anoint), translating Heb. *māshiah* MESSIAH] —**'Christly** *adj.*

Christadelphian (,krɪstə'dɛlfɪən) *n.* **1.** a member of a Christian millenarian sect founded in the U.S. about 1848, holding that only the just will enter eternal life, and that the ignorant and unconverted will not be raised from the dead. *~adj.* **2.** of or relating to this body or its beliefs and practices. [C19: from LGk *khristadelphos, khristos* CHRIST + *adelpos* brother]

Christchurch ('kraɪst,tʃɜːtʃ) *n.* **1.** the second largest city in New Zealand, on E South Island: manufacturing centre of a rich agricultural region. Pop. (urban area): 333 200 (1987). **2.** a town and resort in S England, in SE Dorset. Pop.: 40 300 (1983).

christen ('krɪsᵊn) *vb.* (*tr.*) **1.** to give a Christian name to in baptism as a sign of incorporation into a Christian Church. **2.** another word for **baptize. 3.** to give a name to anything, esp. with some ceremony. **4.** *Inf.* to use for the first time. [OE *cristnian,* from *Crist* CHRIST] —**'christening** *n.*

Christendom ('krɪsᵊndəm) *n.* the collective body of Christians throughout the world.

Christian¹ ('krɪstʃən) *n.* **1. a.** a person who believes in and follows Jesus Christ. **b.** a member of a Christian Church or denomination. **2.** *Inf.* a person who possesses Christian virtues. *~adj.* **3.** of, relating to, or derived from Jesus Christ, his teachings, example, or followers. **4.** (*sometimes not cap.*) exhibiting kindness or goodness. —**'christianly** *adj., adv.*

Christian² ('krɪstʃən) *n.* **Charlie.** 1919–42, U.S. modern-jazz guitarist.

Christian X ('krɪstʃən; *Danish* 'kresdjan) *n.* 1890–1947, king of Denmark (1912–47) and Iceland (1918–44).

Christian Era *n.* the period beginning with the year of Christ's birth.

Christiania (,krɪstɪ'ɑːnɪə) *n.* a former name (1624–1877) of **Oslo.**

Christianity (,krɪstɪ'ænɪtɪ) *n.* **1.** the Christian religion. **2.** Christian beliefs or practices. **3.** a less common word for **Christendom.**

Christianize *or* **-ise** ('krɪstʃə,naɪz) *vb.* (*tr.*) **1.** to make Christian or convert to Christianity. **2.** to imbue with Christian principles, spirit, or outlook. —,**Christiani'zation** *or* **-i'sation** *n.* —'**Christian,izer** *or* **-,iser** *n.*

Christian name *n.* *Brit.* a personal name formally given to Christians at christening: loosely used to mean any person's first name.

Christiansand ('krɪstʃən,sænd; *Norwegian* kristian'san) *n.* a variant spelling of **Kristiansand.**

Christian Science *n.* the religious system of the Church of Christ, Scientist, founded by Mary Baker Eddy (1866), and emphasizing spiritual healing. —**Christian Scientist** *n.*

Christie ('krɪstɪ) *n.* **1. Dame Agatha (Mary Clarissa).** 1890–1976, English author of detective stories, many featuring Hercule Poirot: also several plays, including *The Mousetrap* (1952). **2. John Reginald Halliday.** 1898–1953, English murderer. His trial influenced legislation regarding the death penalty after he had been found guilty of a murder for which Timothy Evans had been hanged.

Christina (krɪ'stiːnə) *n.* 1626–89, queen of Sweden (1632–54), daughter of Gustavus Adolphus, noted particularly for her patronage of literature.

Christlike ('kraɪst,laɪk) *adj.* resembling the spirit of Jesus Christ. —'**Christ,likeness** *n.*

Christmas ('krɪsməs) *n.* **1. a.** the annual commemoration by Christians of the birth of Jesus Christ, on Dec. 25. **b.** Also called: **Christmas Day.** Dec. 25, observed as a day of secular celebrations when gifts and greetings are exchanged. **c.** (*as modifier*): *Christmas celebrations.* **2.** another name for **Christmastide.** [OE *Crīstes mæsse* MASS of CHRIST] —'**Christmassy** *adj.*

Christmas box *n.* a tip or present given at Christmas, esp. to postmen, tradesmen, etc.

Christmas Eve *n.* the evening or the whole day before Christmas Day.

Christmas Island *n.* **1.** the former name (until 1981) of Kiritimati. **2.** an island in the Indian Ocean, south of Java: administered by Singapore (1900–58), now by Australia; phosphate mining. Pop.: 2000 (1986 est.). Area: 135 sq. km (52 sq. miles).

Christmas pudding *n.* *Brit.* a rich steamed pudding containing suet, dried fruit, spices, etc. Also called: **plum pudding.**

Christmas rose *n.* an evergreen plant of S Europe and W Asia with white or pinkish winter-blooming flowers. Also called: **hellebore, winter rose.**

Christmastide ('krɪsməs,taɪd) *n.* the season of Christmas, extending from Dec. 24 (Christmas Eve) to Jan. 6 (the festival of the Epiphany or Twelfth Night).

Christmas tree *n.* **1.** an evergreen tree or an imitation of one, decorated as part of Christmas celebrations. **2.** Also called: **Christmas bush.** *Austral.* any of various trees or shrubs flowering at Christmas and used for decoration. **3.** *N.Z.* another name for the **pohutukawa.**

Christoff ('krɪstɒf) *n.* **Boris.** born 1919, Bulgarian bass-baritone, noted esp. for his performance in the title role of Mussorgsky's *Boris Godunov.*

Christophe (*French* kristɔf) *n.* **Henri** (ɑ̃ri). 1767–1820, Haitian revolutionary leader; king of Haiti (1811–20).

Christopher ('krɪstəfə) *n.* **Saint.** 3rd century A.D., Christian martyr; patron saint of travellers. Feast day: July 25.

Christy *or* **Christie** ('krɪstɪ) *n., pl.* **-ties.** *Skiing.* a turn in which the body is swung sharply round with the skis parallel: used for stopping or changing direction quickly. [C20: from CHRISTIANIA]

chroma ('krəʊmə) *n.* the attribute of a colour that enables an observer to judge how much chromatic colour it contains. See also **saturation** (sense 4). [C19: from Gk *khrōma* colour]

chromate ('krəʊmeɪt) *n.* any salt or ester of chromic acid.

chromatic (krə'mætɪk) *adj.* **1.** of, relating to, or characterized by a colour or colours. **2.** *Music.* **a.** involving the sharpening or flattening of notes or the use of such notes in chords and harmonic progressions. **b.** of or relating to the chromatic scale or an instrument capable of producing it. [C17: from Gk, from *khrōma* colour] —**chro'matically** *adv.* —**chro'maticism** *n.* —**chromaticity** (,krəʊmə'tɪsɪtɪ) *n.*

chromatic aberration *n.* a defect in a lens system in which different wavelengths of light are focused at different distances because they are refracted through different angles. It produces a blurred image with coloured fringes.

chromatics (krəʊ'mætɪks) *n.* (*functioning as sing.*) the science of colour.

chromatic scale *n.* a twelve-note scale including all the semitones of the octave.

chromatin ('krəʊmətɪn) *n.* the part of the nucleus that consists of DNA, RNA, and proteins, forms the chromosomes, and stains with basic dyes.

chromato- *or before a vowel* **chromat-** *combining form.* **1.** indicating colour or coloured: *chromatophore.* **2.** indicating chromatin: *chromatolysis.* [from Gk *khrōma, khrōmat-* colour]

chromatography (,krəʊmə'tɒɡrəfɪ) *n.* the technique of separating and analysing the components of a mixture of liquids or gases by selective adsorption.

chrome (krəʊm) *n.* **1. a.** another word for **chromium,** esp. when present in a pigment or dye. **b.** (*as modifier*): *a chrome dye.* **2.** anything plated with chromium. **3.** a pigment or dye that contains chromium. *~vb.* **4.** to plate or be plated with chromium. **5.** to treat or be treated with a chromium compound, as in dyeing or tanning. [C19: via F from Gk *khrōma* colour]

-chrome *n. and adj. combining form.* colour, coloured, or pigment: *monochrome.* [from Gk *khrōma* colour]

chrome dioxide *n.* a chemical compound, chromium dioxide, which is used as the sensitive coating on some cassette tapes. Formula: CrO_2.

chrome steel *n.* any of various hard rust-resistant steels containing chromium.

chrome yellow *n.* any yellow pigment consisting of lead chromate.

chromic ('krəʊmɪk) *adj.* **1.** of or containing chromium in the trivalent state. **2.** of or derived from chromic acid.

chromic acid *n.* an unstable dibasic oxidizing acid known only in solution and in the form of chromate salts. Formula: H_2CrO_4.

chromite ('krəʊmaɪt) *n.* a brownish-black mineral consisting of a ferrous chromic oxide in crystalline form: the only commercial source of chromium. Formula: $FeCr_2O_4$.

chromium ('krəʊmɪəm) *n.* a hard grey metallic element, used in steel alloys and electroplating to increase hardness and corrosion-resistance. Symbol: Cr; atomic no.: 24; atomic wt.: 51.996. [C19: from NL, from F: CHROME]

chromium steel *n.* another name for **chrome steel**.

chromo ('krəʊməʊ) *n., pl.* **-mos.** short for **chromolithograph.**

chromo- *or before a vowel* **chrom-** *combining form.* **1.** indicating colour, coloured, or pigment: *chromogen.* **2.** indicating chromium: *chromyl.* [from Gk *khrōma* colour]

chromolithograph (,krəʊməʊ'lɪθə,grɑːf) *n.* a picture produced by chromolithography.

chromolithography (,krəʊməʊlɪ'θɒɡrəfɪ) *n.* the process of making coloured prints by lithography. —**chromoli'thographer** *n.* —**chromolithographic** (,krəʊməʊlɪθə'ɡræfɪk) *adj.*

chromosome ('krəʊmə,səʊm) *n.* any of the microscopic rod-shaped structures that appear in a cell nucleus during cell division, consisting of nucleoprotein arranged into units (genes) that are responsible for the transmission of hereditary characteristics. —,**chromo'somal** *adj.*

chromosphere ('krəʊmə,sfɪə) *n.* a gaseous layer of the sun's atmosphere extending from the photosphere to the corona. —**chromospheric** (,krəʊmə'sfɛrɪk) *adj.*

chromous ('krəʊməs) *adj.* of or containing chromium in the divalent state.

chron. *or* **chronol.** *abbrev. for:* **1.** chronological. **2.** chronology.

Chron. *Bible. abbrev. for* Chronicles.

chronic ('krɒnɪk) *adj.* **1.** continuing for a long time; constantly recurring. **2.** (of a disease) developing slowly, or of long duration. Cf. **acute** (sense 7). **3.** inveterate; habitual: *a chronic smoker.* **4.** *Inf.* **a.** very bad: *the play was chronic.* **b.** very serious: *he left her in a chronic condition.* [C15: from L, from Gk, from *khronos* time] —'**chronically** *adv.* —**chronicity** (krɒ'nɪsɪtɪ) *n.*

chronicle ('krɒnɪk°l) *n.* **1.** a record or register of events in chronological order. ~*vb.* **2.** (*tr.*) to record in or as if in a chronicle. [C14: from Anglo-F, via L *chronica* (pl.), from Gk *khronika* annals; see CHRONIC] —'**chronicler** *n.*

chrono- *or before a vowel* **chron-** *combining form.* time: *chronology.* [from Gk *khronos* time]

chronograph ('krɒnə,grɑːf, 'krəʊnə-) *n.* an accurate instrument for recording small intervals of time. —**chronographic** (,krɒnə'ɡræfɪk) *adj.*

chronological (,krɒnə'lɒdʒɪk°l, ,krəʊ-) *or* **chronologic** *adj.* **1.** (esp. of a sequence of events) arranged in order of occurrence. **2.** relating to or in accordance with chronology. —,**chrono'logically** *adv.*

chronology (krə'nɒlədʒɪ) *n., pl.* **-gies.** **1.** the determination of the proper sequence of past events. **2.** the arrangement of dates, events, etc., in order of occurrence. **3.** a table of events arranged in order of occurrence. —'**chro'nologist** *n.*

chronometer (krə'nɒmɪtə) *n.* a timepiece designed to be accurate in all conditions of temperature, pressure, etc., used esp. at sea. —**chronometric** (,krɒnə'mɛtrɪk) *or* ,**chrono'metrical** *adj.* —,**chrono'metrically** *adv.*

chronometry (krə'nɒmɪtrɪ) *n.* the science of measuring time with extreme accuracy.

chronon ('krəʊnɒn) *n.* a unit of time equal to the time that a photon would take to traverse the diameter of an electron: about 10^{-24} seconds.

chrysalid ('krɪsəlɪd) *n.* **1.** another name for **chrysalis.** ~*adj.* **2.** of or relating to a chrysalis.

chrysalis ('krɪsəlɪs) *n., pl.* **chrysalises** *or* **chrysalides** (krɪ'sælɪ,diːz). **1.** the pupa of a moth or butterfly, in a case or cocoon. **2.** anything in the process of developing. [C17: from L, from Gk *khrusallis*, from *khrusos* gold]

chrysanthemum (krɪ'sænθəməm) *n.* **1.** any of various widely cultivated plants of the composite family, having brightly coloured showy flower heads in autumn. **2.** any

other plant of the genus *Chrysanthemum*, such as the ox-eye daisy. [C16: from L: marigold, from Gk, from *khrusos* gold + *anthemon* flower]

chryselephantine (,krɪsɛlɪ'fæntɪn) *adj.* (of ancient Greek statues, etc.) made of or overlaid with gold and ivory. [C19: from Gk, from *khrusos* gold + *elephas* ivory]

chrysoberyl ('krɪsə,bɛrɪl) *n.* a rare very hard greenish-yellow mineral consisting of beryllium aluminate: used as a gemstone. Formula: $BeAl_2O_4$. [C17: from L, from Gk, from *khrusos* gold + *bērullos* beryl]

chrysolite ('krɪsə,laɪt) *n.* a brown or yellowish-green olivine: used as a gemstone. [C14 *crisolite*, from OF, from L, from Gk, from *khrusos* gold + *lithos* stone]

chrysoprase ('krɪsə,preɪz) *n.* an apple-green variety of chalcedony: used as a gemstone. [C13 *crisopace*, from OF, from L, from Gk, from *khrusos* gold + *prason* leek]

Chrysostom ('krɪsəstəm) *n.* Saint **John.** ?345–407 A.D., Greek patriarch; archbishop of Constantinople (398–404). Feast day: Jan. 27.

chthonian ('θəʊnɪən) *or* **chthonic** ('θɒnɪk) *adj.* of or relating to the underworld. [C19: from Gk *khthonios* in or under the earth, from *khthōn* earth]

chub (tʃʌb) *n., pl.* **chub** *or* **chubs.** **1.** a common European freshwater cyprinid game fish, having a cylindrical dark greenish body. **2.** any of various North American fishes, esp. certain whitefishes and minnows. [C15: from ?]

chubby ('tʃʌbɪ) *adj.* **-bier, -biest.** (esp. of the human form) plump and round. [C17: ?from CHUB] —'**chubbiness** *n.*

Chu Chiang ('tʃu: 'kjæŋ, kaɪ'æŋ) *n.* a variant transliteration of the Chinese name for the **Zhu Jiang.**

chuck[1] (tʃʌk) *vb.* (*mainly tr.*) **1.** *Inf.* to throw. **2.** to pat affectionately, esp. under the chin. **3.** *Inf.* (sometimes foll. by *in* or *up*) to give up; reject: *he chucked up his job.* ~*n.* **4.** a throw or toss. **5.** a pat under the chin. **6.** **the chuck.** *Inf.* dismissal. ~See also **chuck in, chuck off, chuck out.** [C16: from ?]

chuck[2] (tʃʌk) *n.* **1.** Also called: **chuck steak.** a cut of beef from the neck to the shoulder blade. **2.** a device that holds a workpiece in a lathe or tool in a drill. [C17: var. of CHOCK]

chuck[3] (tʃʌk) *n. W Canad.* **1.** a large body of water. **2.** In full: **saltchuck.** the sea. [C19: from Chinook Jargon, of Amerind origin, from *chauk*]

chuck in *vb.* (*adv.*) **1.** (*tr.*) *Brit inf.* to abandon or give up: *to chuck in a hopeless attempt.* **2.** (*intr.*) *Austral. inf.* to contribute to the cost of something. ~*n.* **chuck-in.** **3.** *Austral. inf.* a contribution to the cost of something.

chuckle ('tʃʌk°l) *vb.* (*intr.*) **1.** to laugh softly or to oneself. **2.** (of animals, esp. hens) to make a clucking sound. ~*n.* **3.** a partly suppressed laugh. [C16: prob. from *chuck* cluck + *le*]

chucklehead ('tʃʌk°l,hɛd) *n. Inf.* a stupid person; blockhead; dolt.

chuck off *vb.* (*intr., adv.;* often foll. by *at*) *Austral. & N.Z. inf.* to sneer.

chuck out *vb.* (*tr., adv.;* often foll. by *of*) *Inf.* to eject forcibly (from); throw out (of).

chuddy ('tʃʌdɪ) *n. Austral. & N.Z. inf.* chewing gum.

Chudskoye Ozero (*Russian* 'tʃutskəjɪ 'ɒzɪrə) *n.* the Russian name for Lake **Peipus.**

chuff[1] (tʃʌf) *n.* **1.** a puffing sound as of a steam engine. ~*vb.* **2.** (*intr.*) to move while emitting such sounds. [C20: imit.]

chuff[2] (tʃʌf) *vb.* (*tr.; usually passive*) *Brit. sl.* to please or delight: *he was chuffed by his pay rise.* [prob. from *chuff* (adj.) pleased, happy]

chug (tʃʌg) *n.* **1.** a short dull sound, such as that made by an engine. ~*vb.* **chugging, chugged.** **2.** (*intr.*) (of an engine, etc.) to operate while making such sounds. [C19: imit.]

chukar (tʃʌ'kɑː) *n.* a common Indian partridge having a red bill and black-barred sandy plumage. [from Hindi *cakor*, from Sansk. *cakora*, prob. imit.]

Chukchi Peninsula ('tʃʊktʃɪ) *n.* a peninsula in the extreme NE Soviet Union, in NE Siberia: mainly tundra. Also called: **Chukots Peninsula** ('tʃʊkɒts).

Chukchi Sea *n.* part of the Arctic Ocean, north of the Bering Strait between Asia and North America. Russian name: **Chukotskoye More** (tʃʊ'kɒtskəjɪ 'mɔrjɪ). Also called: **Chukots Sea** ('tʃʊkɒts).

Chu Kiang ('tʃu: 'kjæŋ, kaɪ'æŋ) n. a variant transliteration of the Chinese name for the **Zhu Jiang.**

chukka boot ('tʃʌkə) or **chukka** n. an ankle-high boot worn for playing polo. [C19: from CHUKKER]

chukker or **chukka** ('tʃʌkə) n. Polo. a period of continuous play, generally lasting 7½ minutes. [C20: from Hindi cakkar, from Sansk. cakra wheel]

chum (tʃʌm) n. 1. Inf. a close friend. ~vb. **chumming, chummed.** 2. (intr.; usually foll. by up with) to be or become an intimate friend (of). [C17 (meaning: a person sharing rooms with another): prob. shortened from chamber fellow]

chummy ('tʃʌmɪ) adj. **-mier, -miest.** Inf. friendly. — 'chummily adv. — 'chumminess n.

chump (tʃʌmp) n. 1. Inf. a stupid person. 2. a thick heavy block of wood. 3. the thick blunt end of anything, esp. of a piece of meat. 4. Brit. sl. the head (esp. in **off one's chump**). [C18: ? a blend of CHUNK LUMP[1]]

chunder ('tʃʌndə) Sl., chiefly Austral. ~vb. (intr.) 1. to vomit. ~n. 2. vomit. [C20: from ?]

Chungjin ('tʃʌŋ'dʒɪn) n. a variant spelling of **Chŏngjin.**

Chungking ('tʃʊŋ'kɪŋ, 'tʃʌŋ-) or **Ch'ung-ch'ing** ('tʃʊŋ'tʃɪŋ, 'tʃʌŋ-) n. a variant transliteration of the Chinese name for **Chongqing.**

chunk (tʃʌŋk) n. 1. a thick solid piece, as of meat, wood, etc. 2. a considerable amount. [C17: var. of CHUCK[2]]

chunky ('tʃʌŋkɪ) adj. **chunkier, chunkiest.** 1. thick and short. 2. containing thick pieces. 3. Chiefly Brit. (of clothes, esp. knitwear) made of thick bulky material. — 'chunkiness n.

Chunnel ('tʃʌnᵊl) n. Inf. the tunnel to be built under the English Channel, linking England and France. [C20: from CH(ANNEL) + T(UNNEL)]

chunter ('tʃʌntə) vb. (intr.) Brit. inf. to mutter or grumble. [C16: prob. imit.]

Chuquisaca (Spanish tʃuki'saka) n. the former name (until 1839) of **Sucre**[1].

Chur (German ku:r) n. a city in E Switzerland, capital of Grisons canton. Pop.: 33 000 (1985 est.). Ancient name: **Curia Rhaetorum** ('ku:rɪə ri:'tʊərəm, 'kju:-). French name: **Coire.**

church (tʃɜːtʃ) n. 1. a building for public worship, esp. Christian worship. 2. an occasion of public worship. 3. the clergy as distinguished from the laity. 4. (usually cap.) institutionalized forms of religion as a political or social force: conflict between Church and State. 5. (usually cap.) the collective body of all Christians. 6. (often cap.) a particular Christian denomination or group. 7. (often cap.) the Christian religion. ~Related adj.: **ecclesiastical.** ~vb. (tr.) 8. Church of England. to bring (someone, esp. a woman after childbirth) to church for special ceremonies. [OE cirice, from LGk, from Gk kuriakon (dōma) the Lord's (house), from kurios master, from kuros power]

Church Army n. a voluntary Anglican organization founded to assist the parish clergy.

Church Commissioners pl. n. Brit. a group of representatives of Church and State that administers the property of the Church of England.

churchgoer ('tʃɜːtʃˌgəʊə) n. a person who attends church regularly. — 'church,going adj., n.

Churchill[1] ('tʃɜːtʃɪl) n. 1. a river in E Canada, rising in SE Labrador and flowing north and southeast over Churchill Falls, then east to the Atlantic. Length: about 1000 km (600 miles). Former name: **Hamilton River.** 2. a river in central Canada, rising in NW Saskatchewan and flowing east through several lakes to Hudson Bay. Length: about 1600 km (1000 miles).

Churchill[2] ('tʃɜːtʃɪl) n. 1. **John.** See (1st Duke of) **Marlborough.** 2. Lord **Randolph.** 1849–95, British Conservative politician: secretary of state for India (1885–86) and chancellor of the Exchequer and leader of the House of Commons (1886). 3. his son, Sir **Winston (Leonard Spencer).** 1874–1965, British Conservative statesman, orator, and writer, noted for his leadership during World War II. He held various posts under both Conservative and Liberal governments, including 1st Lord of the Admiralty (1911–15), before becoming prime minister (1940–45; 1951–55). His writings include The World Crisis (1923–29), Marlborough (1933–38), The Second World War (1948–54), and History of the English-Speaking Peoples (1956–58): Nobel prize for literature 1953.

Churchill Falls pl. n. a waterfall in E Canada, in SW Labrador on the Churchill River: site of one of the largest hydroelectric power projects in the world. Height: 75 m (245 ft.). Former name: **Grand Falls.**

churchly ('tʃɜːtʃlɪ) adj. appropriate to or associated with the church. — 'churchliness n.

churchman ('tʃɜːtʃmən) n., pl. **-men.** 1. a clergyman. 2. a male member of a church.

Church of Christ, Scientist n. the official name for the **Christian Scientists.**

Church of England n. the reformed established state Church in England, with the Sovereign as its temporal head.

Church of Jesus Christ of Latter-Day Saints n. the official name for the Mormon Church.

churchwarden (ˌtʃɜːtʃ'wɔːdᵊn) n. 1. Church of England, Episcopal Church. one of two assistants of a parish priest who administer the secular affairs of the church. 2. a long-stemmed tobacco pipe made of clay.

churchwoman ('tʃɜːtʃˌwʊmən) n., pl. **-women.** a female member of a church.

churchyard ('tʃɜːtʃˌjɑːd) n. the grounds round a church, used as a graveyard.

churinga (tʃə'rɪŋgə) n., pl. **-ga** or **-gas.** a sacred amulet of the Australian Aborigines. [from Abor.]

churl (tʃɜːl) n. 1. a surly ill-bred person. 2. Arch. a farm labourer. 3. Arch. a miserly person. [OE ceorl] — 'churlish adj.

churn (tʃɜːn) n. 1. Brit. a large container for milk. 2. a vessel or machine in which cream or whole milk is vigorously agitated to produce butter. ~vb. 3. a. to agitate (milk or cream) to make butter. b. to make (butter) by this process. 4. (sometimes foll. by up) to move or cause to move with agitation. [OE ciern]

churn out vb. (tr., adv.) Inf. 1. to produce (something) at a rapid rate: to churn out ideas. 2. to perform (something) mechanically: to churn out a song.

churr (tʃɜː) vb., n. a variant spelling of **chirr.**

chute[1] (ʃuːt) n. 1. an inclined channel or vertical passage down which water, parcels, coal, etc., may be dropped. 2. a steep slope, used as a slide as for toboggans. 3. a slide into a swimming pool. 4. a rapid or waterfall. [C19: from OF cheoite, fem. p.p. of cheoir to fall, from L cadere; in some senses, var. spelling of SHOOT]

chute[2] (ʃuːt) n., vb. Inf. short for **parachute.** — 'chutist n.

Chu Teh ('tʃu: 'teɪ) or **Zhu De** n. 1886–1976, Chinese military leader and politician; he became commander in chief of the Red Army (1931) and was chairman of the Standing Committee of the National People's Congress of the People's Republic of China (1959–76).

chutney ('tʃʌtnɪ) n. a pickle of Indian origin, made from fruit, vinegar, spices, sugar, etc.: mango chutney. [C19: from Hindi catni, from ?]

chutzpah ('xʊtspə) n. U.S. & Canad. inf. shameless audacity; impudence. [C20: from Yiddish]

Chuvash Autonomous Soviet Socialist Republic n. an administrative division of the W central Soviet Union, in the middle Volga valley: generally low and undulating, with large areas of forest. Capital: Cheboksary. Pop.: 1 320 000 (1986). Area: 18 300 sq. km (7064 sq. miles).

chyack ('tʃaɪæk) vb., n. a variant spelling of **chiack.**

chyle (kaɪl) n. a milky fluid composed of lymph and emulsified fat globules, formed in the small intestine during digestion. [C17: from LL, from Gk khulos juice] —**chylaceous** (kaɪ'leɪʃəs) or **'chylous** adj.

chyme (kaɪm) n. the thick fluid mass of partially digested food that leaves the stomach. [C17: from LL, from Gk khumos juice] — 'chymous adj.

chypre French. (ʃiprə) n. a perfume made from sandalwood. [lit.: Cyprus, ? where it originated]

Ci symbol for curie.

CI abbrev. for Channel Islands.

CIA abbrev. for Central Intelligence Agency; a federal U.S. bureau created in 1947 to coordinate and conduct espionage and intelligence activities.

CIB abbrev. for Criminal Investigation Branch (of the New Zealand and Australian police).

Cibber ('sɪbə) n. **Colley** ('kɒlɪ). 1671–1757, English actor and dramatist; poet laureate (1730–57).

ciborium (sɪ'bɔːrɪəm) n., pl. **-ria** (-rɪə). Christianity. 1. a goblet-shaped lidded vessel used to hold consecrated wafers in Holy Communion. 2. a canopy fixed over an altar. [C17: from Med. L, from L, from Gk *kibōrion* cup-shaped seed vessel of the Egyptian lotus]

cicada (sɪ'kɑːdə) *or* **cicala** *n.*, *pl.* **-das, -dae** (-diː) *or* **-las, -le** (-leɪ). any large broad insect, most common in warm regions, having membranous wings: the males produce a high-pitched drone by vibration of a pair of drumlike abdominal organs. [C19: from L]

cicatrix ('sɪkətrɪks) *n.*, *pl.* **cicatrices** (,sɪkə'traɪsiːz). **1.** the tissue that forms in a wound during healing; scar. **2.** a scar on a plant indicating the former point of attachment of a part, esp. a leaf. [C17: from L: scar, from ?] —**cicatricial** (,sɪkə'trɪʃəl) *adj.*

cicatrize *or* **-trise** ('sɪkə,traɪz) *vb.* (of a wound or defect in tissue) to be closed by scar formation; heal. —**,cicatri'zation** *or* **-tri'sation** *n.*

cicely ('sɪsəlɪ) *n.*, *pl.* **-lies.** short for **sweet cicely.** [C16: from L *seselis*, from Gk, from ?]

Cicero ('sɪsə,rəʊ) *n.* **Marcus Tullius** ('mɑːkəs 'tʌlɪəs). 106–43 B.C., Roman consul, orator, and writer. He foiled Catiline's conspiracy (63) and was killed by Mark Antony's agents after he denounced Antony in the *Philippics*. His writings are regarded as a model of Latin prose. Formerly known in English as **Tully.**

cicerone (,sɪsə'rəʊnɪ, ,tʃɪtʃ-) *n.*, *pl.* **-nes** *or* **-ni** (-nɪ). a person who conducts and informs sightseers. [C18: from It.: antiquarian scholar, guide, after CICERO]

Cid (sɪd; *Spanish* θið) *n.* **El** *or* **the.** original name *Rodrigo Diaz de Vivar.* ?1043–99, Spanish soldier and hero of the wars against the Moors.

CID (in Britain) *abbrev. for* Criminal Investigation Department; the detective division of a police force.

-cide *n. combining form.* **1.** indicating a person or thing that kills: *insecticide.* **2.** indicating a killing; murder: *homicide.* [from L *-cīda* (agent), *-cīdium* (act), from *caedere* to kill] —**cidal** *adj. combining form.*

cider *or* **cyder** ('saɪdə) *n.* **1.** an alcoholic drink made from the fermented juice of apples. **2.** Also called: **sweet cider.** *U.S. & Canad.* an unfermented drink made from apple juice. [C14: from OF, via Med. L, from LGk *sikera* strong drink, from Heb. *shēkhār*]

Cienfuegos (*Spanish* θien'fueɣɒs) *n.* a port in S Cuba, on **Cienfuegos Bay.** Pop.: 109 300 (1986 est.).

c.i.f. *or* **CIF** *abbrev. for* cost, insurance, and freight (included in the price quoted).

cig (sɪg) *or* **ciggy** ('sɪgɪ) *n.*, *pl.* **cigs** *or* **ciggies.** *Inf.* a cigarette.

cigar (sɪ'gɑː) *n.* a cylindrical roll of cured tobacco leaves, for smoking. [C18: from Sp. *cigarro*]

cigarette *or U.S.* (*sometimes*) **cigaret** (,sɪgə'rɛt) *n.* a short tightly rolled cylinder of tobacco, wrapped in thin paper for smoking. [C19: from F, lit.: a little CIGAR]

cigarette card *n.* a small picture card, formerly given away with cigarettes, now collected as a hobby.

cigarillo (,sɪgə'rɪləʊ) *n.*, *pl.* **-los.** a small cigar, often only slightly larger than a cigarette.

ciliary ('sɪlɪərɪ) *adj.* of or relating to cilia.

ciliary body *n.* the part of the eye that joins the choroid to the iris.

Cilicia (sɪ'lɪʃɪə) *n.* an ancient region and former kingdom of SE Asia Minor, between the Taurus Mountains and the Mediterranean: corresponds to the region around present-day Adana. —**Ci'lician** *adj., n.*

Cilician Gates *pl. n.* a pass in S Turkey, over the Taurus Mountains. Turkish name: **Gülek Bogaz.**

cilium ('sɪlɪəm) *n.*, *pl.* **cilia** ('sɪlɪə). **1.** any of the short threads projecting from the surface of a cell, organism, etc., whose rhythmic beating causes movement. **2.** the technical name for **eyelash.** [C18: NL, from L: (lower) eyelid, eyelash] —**ciliate** ('sɪlɪɪt, -eɪt) *or* **'cili,ated** *adj.*

Cimabue (*Italian* tʃima'buːe) *n.* **Giovanni** (dʒo'vanni). ?1240–?1302, Italian painter of the Florentine school, who anticipated the movement, led by Giotto, away from the Byzantine tradition in art towards a greater naturalism.

Cimon ('saɪmən) *n.* died 449 B.C., Athenian military and naval commander: defeated the Persians at Eurymedon (?466).

C in C *or* **C.-in-C.** *Mil. abbrev. for* Commander in Chief.

cinch (sɪntʃ) *n.* **1.** *Sl.* an easy task. **2.** *Sl.* a certainty. **3.** a U.S. and Canad. name for **girth** (sense 2). **4.** *U.S. inf.* a firm grip. ~*vb.* **5.** (often foll. by *up*) *U.S. & Canad.* to fasten a girth around (a horse). **6.** (*tr.*) *Inf.* to make sure of. **7.** (*tr.*) *Inf., chiefly U.S.* to get a firm grip on. [C19: from Sp., from L, from *cingere* to encircle]

cinchona (sɪŋ'kəʊnə) *n.* **1.** any tree or shrub of the South American genus *Cinchona*, having medicinal bark. **2.** the dried bark of any of these trees, which yields quinine. **3.** any of the drugs derived from cinchona bark. [C18: NL, after the Countess of *Chinchón* (1576–1639), vicereine of Peru] —**cinchonic** (sɪŋ'kɒnɪk) *adj.*

Cincinnati (,sɪnsɪ'nætɪ) *n.* a city in SW Ohio, on the Ohio River. Pop.: 369 750 (1986).

Cincinnatus (,sɪnsɪ'nɑːtəs) *n.* **Lucius Quinctius** ('luːsɪəs 'kwɪŋktɪəs). ?519–438 B.C., Roman general and statesman, regarded as a model of simple virtue; dictator of Rome during two crises (458; 439), retiring to his farm after each one.

cincture ('sɪŋktʃə) *n.* something that encircles, esp. a belt or girdle. [C16: from L, from *cingere* to gird]

cinder ('sɪndə) *n.* **1.** a piece of incombustible material left after the combustion of coal, coke, etc.; clinker. **2.** a piece of charred material that burns without flames; ember. **3.** any solid waste from smelting or refining. **4.** (*pl.*) fragments of volcanic lava; scoriae. [OE *sinder*] —**'cindery** *adj.*

Cinderella (,sɪndə'rɛlə) *n.* **1.** a girl who achieves fame after being obscure. **2.** a poor, neglected, or unsuccessful person or thing. [C19: after *Cinderella*, the heroine of a fairy tale]

cine- *combining form.* indicating motion picture or cinema: *cine camera; cinephotography.*

cineaste ('sɪnɪ,æst) *n.* an enthusiast for films. [C20: F]

cinema ('sɪnɪmə) *n.* **1.** *Chiefly Brit.* a place designed for the exhibition of films. **2. the cinema. a.** the art or business of making films. **b.** films collectively. [C19 (earlier spelling: *kinema*): shortened from CINEMATOGRAPH] —**cinematic** (,sɪnɪ'mætɪk) *adj.* —**,cine'matically** *adv.*

cinematograph (,sɪnɪ'mætə,grɑːf) *Chiefly Brit.* ~*n.* **1.** a combined camera, printer, and projector. ~*vb.* **2.** to take (pictures) with a film camera. [C19 (earlier spelling: *kinematograph*): from Gk *kinēma* motion + -GRAPH] —**cinematographer** (,sɪnɪmə'tɒgrəfə) *n.* —**cinematographic** (,sɪnɪ,mætə'græfɪk) *adj.* —**,cine,mato'graphically** *adv.* —**,cinema'tography** *n.*

cinéma vérité (*French* sinema verite) *n.* films characterized by subjects, actions, etc., that have the appearance of real life. [F, lit.: truth cinema]

cineraria (,sɪnə'rɛərɪə) *n.* a plant of the Canary Islands, widely cultivated for its blue, purple, red, or variegated daisy-like flowers. [C16: from NL, from L, from *cinis* ashes; from its downy leaves]

cinerarium (,sɪnə'rɛərɪəm) *n.*, *pl.* **-raria** (-'rɛərɪə). a place for keeping the ashes of the dead after cremation. [C19: from L, from *cinerārius* relating to ashes] —**cinerary** ('sɪnərərɪ) *adj.*

cinerator ('sɪnə,reɪtə) *n. Chiefly U.S.* a furnace for cremating corpses. —**,cine'ration** *n.*

Cinna ('sɪnə) *n.* **Lucius Cornelius** ('luːsɪəs kɔː'niːlɪəs). died 84 B.C., Roman patrician; an opponent of Sulla.

cinnabar ('sɪnə,bɑː) *n.* **1.** a heavy red mineral consisting of mercury(II) sulphide: the chief ore of mercury. Formula: HgS. **2.** the red form of mercury(II) sulphide, esp. when used as a pigment. **3. a.** a bright red; vermilion. **b.** (*as adj.*): *a cinnabar tint.* **4.** a large red-and-black European moth. [C15: from OF, from L, from Gk *kinnabari*, of Oriental origin]

cinnamon ('sɪnəmən) *n.* **1.** a tropical Asian tree, having aromatic yellowish-brown bark. **2.** the spice obtained from the bark of this tree, used for flavouring food and drink. **3. a.** a light yellowish brown. **b.** (*as adj.*): *a cinnamon coat.* [C15: from OF, via L & Gk, from Heb. *qinnamown*]

cinque (sɪŋk) *n.* the number five in cards, dice, etc. [C14: from OF *cinq* five]

cinquecento (,tʃɪŋkwɪ'tʃɛntəʊ) *n.* the 16th century, esp. in reference to Italian art, architecture, or literature. [C18: It., shortened from *milcinquecento* 1500]

cinquefoil ('sɪŋk,fɔɪl) *n.* **1.** any plant of the N temperate rosaceous genus *Potentilla*, typically having five-lobed compound leaves. **2.** an ornamental carving in the form of five arcs arranged in a circle and separated by cusps. [C13 *sink foil*, from OF, from L *quinquefolium* plant with five leaves]

Cinque Ports (sɪŋk) *pl. n.* an association of ports on the SE coast of England, which from late Anglo-Saxon times until 1685 provided ships for the king's service in return for the profits of justice in their courts.

Cipango (sɪˈpæŋɡəʊ) n. (in medieval legend) an island E of Asia: called Zipangu by Marco Polo and sought by Columbus; identified with Japan.

cipher or **cypher** (ˈsaɪfə) n. **1.** a method of secret writing using substitution of letters according to a key. **2.** a secret message. **3.** the key to a secret message. **4.** an obsolete name for **zero** (sense 1). **5.** any of the Arabic numerals or the Arabic system of numbering. **6.** a person or thing of no importance; nonentity. **7.** a design consisting of interwoven letters; monogram. ~vb. **8.** to put (a message) into secret writing. **9.** Rare. to perform (a calculation) arithmetically. [C14: from OF cifre zero, from Med. L, from Ar. sifr zero]

circa (ˈsɜːkə) prep. (used with a date) at the approximate time of: circa 1182 B.C. Abbrev.: **c, ca.** [L: about]

circadian (sɜːˈkeɪdɪən) adj. of or relating to biological processes that occur regularly at 24-hour intervals. See also **biological clock.** [C20: from L circa about + diēs day]

Circassia (sɜːˈkæsɪə) n. a region of the S Soviet Union, on the Black Sea north of the Caucasus Mountains.

Circe (ˈsɜːsɪ) n. Greek myth. an enchantress who detained Odysseus on her island and turned his men into swine. —**Circean** (sɜːˈsɪən) adj.

circle (ˈsɜːkᵊl) n. **1.** a closed plane curve every point of which is equidistant from a given fixed point, the centre. **2.** the figure enclosed by such a curve. **3.** Theatre. the section of seats above the main level of the auditorium, usually comprising the dress circle and the upper circle. **4.** something formed or arranged in the shape of a circle. **5.** a group of people sharing an interest, activity, upbringing, etc.; set: golf circles; a family circle. **6.** a domain or area of activity, interest, or influence. **7.** a circuit. **8.** a process or chain of events or parts that forms a connected whole; cycle. **9.** a parallel of latitude. See also **great circle, small circle. 10.** one of a number of Neolithic or Bronze Age rings of standing stones, such as Stonehenge. **11. come full circle.** to arrive back at one's starting point. See also **vicious circle.** ~vb. **12.** to move in a circle (around). **13.** (tr.) to enclose in a circle; encircle. [C14: from L circulus, from circus ring, circle] — **'circler** n.

circlet (ˈsɜːklɪt) n. a small circle or ring, esp. a circular ornament worn on the head. [C15: from OF cerclet a little CIRCLE]

circuit (ˈsɜːkɪt) n. **1. a.** a complete route or course, esp. one that is curved or circular or that lies around an object. **b.** the area enclosed within such a route. **2.** the act of following such a route: we made three circuits of the course. **3. a.** a complete path through which an electric current can flow. **b.** (as modifier): a circuit diagram. **4. a.** a periodical journey around an area, as made by judges, salesmen, etc. **b.** the places visited on such a journey. **c.** the persons making such a journey. **5.** an administrative division of the Methodist Church comprising a number of neighbouring churches. **6.** a number of theatres, cinemas, etc., under one management. **7.** Sport. **a.** a series of tournaments in which the same players regularly take part: the international tennis circuit. **b.** (usually preceded by the) the contestants who take part in such a series. **8.** Chiefly Brit. a motor-racing track, usually of irregular shape. ~vb. **9.** to make or travel in a circuit around (something). [C14: from L circuitus, from circum around + īre to go] — **'circuital** adj.

circuit breaker n. a device that under abnormal conditions, such as a short circuit, stops the flow of current in an electrical circuit.

circuitous (sɜːˈkjuːɪtəs) adj. indirect and lengthy; roundabout: a circuitous route. —**cir'cuitously** adv. —**cir'cuitousness** n.

circuitry (ˈsɜːkɪtrɪ) n. **1.** the design of an electrical circuit. **2.** the system of circuits used in an electronic device.

circuity (sɜːˈkjuːɪtɪ) n., pl. **-ties.** (of speech, reasoning, etc.) a roundabout or devious quality.

circular (ˈsɜːkjʊlə) adj. **1.** of, involving, resembling, or shaped like a circle. **2.** circuitous. **3.** (of arguments) futile because the truth of the premises cannot be established independently of the conclusion. **4.** travelling or occurring in a cycle. **5.** (of letters, announcements, etc.) intended for general distribution. ~n. **6.** a printed advertisement or notice for mass distribution. —**circularity** (ˌsɜːkjʊˈlærɪtɪ) n. —**'circularly** adv.

circularize or **-ise** (ˈsɜːkjʊləˌraɪz) vb. (tr.) **1.** to distribute circulars to. **2.** to canvass or petition (people), as for support, votes, etc., by distributing letters, etc. **3.** to make circular. —**circulari'zation** or **-i'sation** n.

circular saw n. a power-driven saw in which a circular disc with a toothed edge is rotated at high speed.

circulate (ˈsɜːkjʊˌleɪt) vb. **1.** to send, go, or pass from place to place or person to person: don't circulate the news. **2.** to distribute or be distributed over a wide area. **3.** to move or cause to move through a circuit, system, etc., returning to the starting point: blood circulates through the body. **4.** to move in a circle. [C17: from L circulāri, from circulus CIRCLE] —**'circu,lative** adj. —**'circu,lator** n. —**'circulatory** adj.

circulating library n. **1.** another word (esp. U.S.) for **lending library. 2.** a small library circulated in turn to a group of institutions.

circulation (ˌsɜːkjʊˈleɪʃən) n. **1.** the transport of oxygenated blood through the arteries, and the return of oxygen-depleted blood through the veins to the heart, where the cycle is renewed. **2.** the flow of sap through a plant. **3.** any movement through a closed circuit. **4.** the spreading or transmission of something to a wider group of people or area. **5.** (of air and water) free movement within an area or volume. **6. a.** the distribution of newspapers, magazines, etc. **b.** the number of copies of an issue that are distributed. **7. in circulation. a.** (of currency) serving as a medium of exchange. **b.** (of people) active in a social or business context.

circum- prefix. around; surrounding; on all sides: circumlocution; circumpolar. [from L circum around, from circus circle]

circumambient (ˌsɜːkəmˈæmbɪənt) adj. surrounding. [C17: from LL, from L CIRCUM- + ambīre to go round] —**circum'ambience** or **circum'ambiency** n.

circumambulate (ˌsɜːkəmˈæmbjʊˌleɪt) vb. **1.** to walk around (something). **2.** (intr.) to avoid the point. [C17: from LL, from L CIRCUM- + ambulāre to walk] —**circum,ambu'lation** n.

circumcise (ˈsɜːkəmˌsaɪz) vb. (tr.) **1.** to remove the foreskin of (a male). **2.** to incise surgically the skin over the clitoris of (a female). **3.** to remove the clitoris of (a female). **4.** to perform such an operation as a religious rite on (someone). [C13: from L from CIRCUM- + caedere to cut] —**circumcision** (ˌsɜːkəmˈsɪʒən) n.

circumference (səˈkʌmfərəns) n. **1.** the boundary of a specific area or figure, esp. of a circle. **2.** the length of a closed geometric curve, esp. of a circle. [C14: from OF, from L from CIRCUM- + ferre to bear] —**circumferential** (sə,kʌmfəˈrɛnʃəl) adj. —**cir,cumfer'entially** adv.

circumflex (ˈsɜːkəmˌflɛks) n. **1.** a mark (ˆ) placed over a vowel to show that it is pronounced with rising and falling pitch, as in ancient Greek, or as a long vowel, as in French. ~adj. **2.** (of nerves, arteries, etc.) bending or curving around. [C16: from L, from CIRCUM- + flectere to bend] —**circum'flexion** n.

circumfluous (səˈkʌmflʊəs) adj. flowing all around. Also: **circumfluent.** [C17: from L CIRCUM- fluere to flow] —**cir'cumfluence** n.

circumfuse (ˌsɜːkəmˈfjuːz) vb. (tr.) **1.** to pour or spread (a liquid, powder, etc.) around. **2.** to surround with a substance, such as a liquid. [C16: from L circumfūsus, from CIRCUM- + fundere to pour] —**circumfusion** (ˌsɜːkəmˈfjuːʒən) n.

circumlocution (ˌsɜːkəmləˈkjuːʃən) n. **1.** an indirect way of expressing something. **2.** an indirect expression. —**circumlocutory** (ˌsɜːkəmˈlɒkjətərɪ, -trɪ) adj.

circumnavigate (ˌsɜːkəmˈnævɪˌɡeɪt) vb. (tr.) to sail or fly completely around. —**circum,navi'gation** n. —**circum'navi,gator** n.

circumscribe (ˌsɜːkəmˈskraɪb, ˈsɜːkəmˌskraɪb) vb. (tr.) **1.** to restrict within limits. **2.** to mark or set the bounds of. **3.** to draw a geometric construction around (another construction) so that the two are in contact but do not intersect. **4.** to draw a line round. [C15: from L from CIRCUM- scribere to write] —**circum'scribable** adj. —**circum'scriber** n. —**circumscription** (ˌsɜːkəmˈskrɪpʃən) n.

circumspect (ˈsɜːkəmˌspɛkt) adj. cautious, prudent, or discreet. [C15: from L, from CIRCUM- + specere to look] —**circum'spection** n. —**'circum,spectly** adv.

circumstance (ˈsɜːkəmstəns) n. **1.** (usually pl.) a condition of time, place, etc., that accompanies or influences an event or condition. **2.** an incident or occurrence, esp. a chance one. **3.** accessory information or detail. **4.** formal display or ceremony (archaic except in **pomp and circumstance**). **5. under** *or* **in no circumstances.** in no case; never. **6. under the circumstances.** because of conditions; this being the case. ~*vb.* (*tr.*) **7.** to place in a particular condition or situation. [C13: from OF, from L *circumstantia*, from CIRCUM- + *stāre* to stand]

circumstantial (ˌsɜːkəmˈstænʃəl) *adj.* **1.** of or dependent on circumstances. **2.** fully detailed. **3.** incidental. —**circumstantiality** (ˌsɜːkəmˌstænʃɪˈælɪtɪ) *n.* —ˌcircum'stantially *adv.*

circumstantial evidence *n.* indirect evidence that tends to establish a conclusion by inference.

circumstantiate (ˌsɜːkəmˈstænʃɪˌeɪt) *vb.* (*tr.*) to support by giving particulars. —ˌcircumˌstanti'ation *n.*

circumvallate (ˌsɜːkəmˈvæleɪt) *vb.* (*tr.*) to surround with a defensive fortification. [C19: from L, from CIRCUM-+ *vallum* rampart] —ˌcircumval'lation *n.*

circumvent (ˌsɜːkəmˈvɛnt) *vb.* (*tr.*) **1.** to evade or go around. **2.** to outwit. **3.** to encircle (an enemy) so as to intercept or capture. [C15: from L, from CIRCUM- + *venire* to come] —ˌcircum'vention *n.*

circus (ˈsɜːkəs) *n., pl.* **-cuses. 1.** a travelling company of entertainers such as acrobats, clowns, trapeze artists, and trained animals. **2.** a public performance given by such a company. **3.** an arena, usually tented, in which such a performance is held. **4.** a travelling group of professional sportsmen: *a cricket circus.* **5.** (in ancient Rome) **a.** an open-air stadium, usually oval or oblong, for chariot races or public games. **b.** the games themselves. **6.** *Brit.* **a.** an open place, usually circular, where several streets converge. **b.** (*cap. when part of a name*): *Piccadilly Circus.* **7.** *Inf.* noisy or rowdy behaviour. **8.** *Inf.* a group of people travelling together and putting on a display. [C16: from L, from Gk *kirkos* ring]

ciré (ˈsɪəreɪ) *adj.* **1.** (of fabric) treated with a heat or wax process to make it smooth. ~*n.* **2.** such a surface on a fabric. **3.** a fabric having such a surface. [C20: F, from L *cēra* wax]

Cirenaica (ˌsaɪrəˈneɪɪkə, ˌsɪrə-) *n.* a variant spelling of **Cyrenaica.**

Cirencester (ˈsaɪrənˌsɛstə) *n.* a market town in S England, in Gloucestershire: Roman amphitheatre. Pop.: 15 622 (1981). Latin name: **Corinium.**

cirque (sɜːk) *n.* a steep-sided semicircular or crescent-shaped depression found in mountainous regions. [C17: from F, from L *circus* ring]

cirrhosis (sɪˈrəʊsɪs) *n.* any of various chronic progressive diseases of the liver, characterized by death of liver cells, irreversible fibrosis, etc. [C19: NL, from Gk *kirrhos* orange-coloured + -OSIS; referring to the appearance of the diseased liver] —**cirrhotic** (sɪˈrɒtɪk) *adj.*

cirripede (ˈsɪrɪˌpiːd) *or* **cirriped** (ˈsɪrɪˌpɛd) *n.* **1.** any marine crustacean of the subclass *Cirripedia*, including the barnacles. ~*adj.* **2.** of, relating to, or belonging to the *Cirripedia.*

cirrocumulus (ˌsɪrəʊˈkjuːmjʊləs) *n., pl.* **-li** (-ˌlaɪ). a high cloud of ice crystals grouped into small separate globular masses.

cirrostratus (ˌsɪrəʊˈstrɑːtəs) *n., pl.* **-ti** (-taɪ). a uniform layer of cloud above about 6000 metres.

cirrus (ˈsɪrəs) *n., pl.* **-ri** (-raɪ). **1.** a thin wispy fibrous cloud at high altitudes, composed of ice particles. **2.** a plant tendril or similar part. **3.** a slender tentacle or filament in barnacles and other marine invertebrates. [C18: from L: curl]

cis- *prefix.* on this side of, as in **cismontane** on this side of the mountains. Often retains the original Latin sense of 'side nearest Rome', as in **cispadane** on this (the southern) side of the Po. [from L]

cisalpine (sɪsˈælpaɪn) *adj.* on this (the southern) side of the Alps, as viewed from Rome.

Cisalpine Gaul *n.* (in the ancient world) that part of Gaul between the Alps and the Apennines.

Ciscaucasia (ˌsɪskɔːˈkeɪzɪə, -ʒə) *n.* the part of Caucasia north of the Caucasus Mountains.

cisco (ˈsɪskəʊ) *n., pl.* **-coes** *or* **-cos.** any of various whitefish, esp. the lake herring of cold deep lakes of North America. [C19: short for Canad. F *ciscoette*, of Algonquian origin]

Ciskei (ˈsɪskaɪ) *n.* a Bantu homeland in South Africa, consisting of a wedge-shaped territory in E Cape Province;

granted independence in 1981 but this is not recognized outside South Africa. Capital: Bisho. Pop.: 2 100 000 (1981 est.). Area: 8500 sq. km (3280 sq. miles).

cislunar (sɪsˈluːnə) *adj.* of or relating to the space between the earth and the moon.

cissy (ˈsɪsɪ) *n.* a variant spelling of **sissy.**

cist¹ (sɪst) *n.* a wooden box for holding ritual objects used in ancient Rome and Greece. [C19: from L *cista* box, from Gk *kistē*]

cist² (sɪst) *or* **kist** *n.* a box-shaped burial chamber made from stone slabs or a hollowed tree trunk. [C19: from Welsh: chest, from L; see CIST¹]

Cistercian (sɪˈstɜːʃən) *n.* **1.** Also called: **White Monk.** a member of a Christian order of monks and nuns founded in 1098, which follows an especially strict form of the Benedictine rule. ~*adj.* **2.** of or relating to this order [C17: from F, from Med. L, from *Cistercium* (modern *Cîteaux*), original home of the order]

cistern (ˈsɪstən) *n.* **1.** a tank for the storage of water, esp. on or within the roof of a house or connected to a WC. **2.** an underground reservoir for the storage of a liquid, esp. rainwater. **3.** Also called: **cisterna.** *Anat.* a sac or partially enclosed space containing body fluid. [C13: from OF, from L *cisterna* underground tank, from *cista* box]

cistus (ˈsɪstəs) *n.* any plant of the genus *Cistus*. See **rock-rose.** [C16: NL, from Gk *kistos*]

citadel (ˈsɪtəd²l, -ˌdɛl) *n.* **1.** a stronghold within or close to a city. **2.** any strongly fortified building or place of safety; refuge. [C16: from OF, from OIt. *cittadella* a little city, from L *civitās*]

citation (saɪˈteɪʃən) *n.* **1.** the quoting of a book or author. **2.** a passage or source cited. **3. a.** an official commendation or award, esp. for bravery or outstanding service. **b.** a formal public statement of this. **4.** *Law.* **a.** an official summons to appear in court. **b.** the document containing such a summons. —**citatory** (ˈsaɪtətərɪ) *adj.*

cite (saɪt) *vb.* (*tr.*) **1.** to quote or refer to (a passage, book, or author). **2.** to mention or commend (a soldier, etc.) for outstanding bravery or meritorious action. **3.** to summon or appear before a court of law. **4.** to enumerate: *he cited the king's virtues.* [C15: from OF *citer* to summon, ult. from L *ciēre* to excite] —**'citable** *or* **'citeable** *adj.*

cithara (ˈsɪθərə) *or* **kithara** (ˈkɪθərə) *n.* a stringed musical instrument of ancient Greece, similar to the lyre. [C18: from Gk *kithara*]

cither (ˈsɪθə) *or* **cithern** (ˈsɪθən) *n.* a variant spelling of **cittern.** [C17: from L, from Gk *kithara*]

citified *or* **cityfied** (ˈsɪtɪˌfaɪd) *adj. Often derog.* having the customs, manners, or dress of city people.

citizen (ˈsɪtɪz²n) *n.* **1.** a native registered or naturalized member of a state, nation, or other political community. **2.** an inhabitant of a city or town. **3.** a civilian, as opposed to a soldier, public official, etc. [C14: from Anglo-F *citesein*, from OF *citeien*, from *cité* CITY]

citizenry (ˈsɪtɪzənrɪ) *n., pl.* **-ries.** citizens collectively.

Citizens' Band *n.* a range of radio frequencies assigned officially for use by the public for private communication. Abbrev.: **CB**

citizenship (ˈsɪtɪzənˌʃɪp) *n.* **1.** the condition or status of a citizen, with its rights and duties. **2.** a person's conduct as a citizen.

Citlaltépetl (ˌsiːtlɑːlˈteɪpɛt²l) *n.* a volcano in SE Mexico, in central Veracruz state: the highest peak in the country. Height: 5699 m (18 698 ft.). Spanish name: **Pico de Orizaba** (piko de ori'saba).

citrate (ˈsɪtreɪt, -rɪt; ˈsaɪtreɪt) *n.* any salt or ester of citric acid. [C18: from CITR(US) + -ATE¹]

citric (ˈsɪtrɪk) *adj.* of or derived from citrus fruits or citric acid.

citric acid *n.* a water-soluble weak tribasic acid found in many fruits, esp. citrus fruits, and used in pharmaceuticals and as a flavouring (**E330**). Formula: $CH_2(COOH)C(OH)(COOH)CH_2COOH$.

citrine (ˈsɪtrɪn) *n.* **1.** a brownish-yellow variety of quartz: a gemstone; false topaz. **2. a.** the yellow colour of a lemon. **b.** (*as adj.*): *citrine hair.*

citron (ˈsɪtrən) *n.* **1.** a small Asian tree, having lemon-like fruit with a thick aromatic rind. **2.** the fruit of this tree. **3.** the rind of this fruit candied and used for decoration and flavouring of foods. [C16: from OF, from L *citrus* citrus tree]

citronella (,sɪtrə'nɛlə) n. **1.** a tropical Asian grass with bluish-green lemon-scented leaves. **2.** Also called: **citronella oil.** the yellow aromatic oil obtained from this grass, used in insect repellents, soaps, perfumes, etc. [C19: NL, from F, from *citron* lemon]

citrus ('sɪtrəs) n., pl. **-ruses. 1.** any tree or shrub of the tropical and subtropical genus *Citrus*, which includes the orange, lemon, and lime. ~*adj. also* **citrous. 2.** of or relating to the genus *Citrus* or to the fruits of plants of this genus. [C19: from L: citrus tree]

Città del Vaticano (tʃit'ta del vati'ka:no) n. the Italian name for **Vatican City.**

cittern ('sɪtɜːn), **cither,** *or* **cithern** n. a medieval stringed instrument resembling a lute but having wire strings and a flat back. [C16: ? a blend of CITHER + GITTERN]

city ('sɪtɪ) n., pl. **cities. 1.** any large town or populous place. **2.** (in Britain) a large town that has received this title from the Crown: usually the seat of a bishop. **3.** (in the U.S.) an incorporated urban centre with its own government and administration established by state charter. **4.** (in Canada) a similar municipality incorporated by the provincial government **5.** the people of a city collectively. **6.** (*modifier*) in or characteristic of a city: *city habits.* ~Related adjs.: **civic, urban, municipal.** [C13: from OF *cité*, from L *cīvitās* state, from *cīvis* citizen]

City ('sɪtɪ) n. **the. 1.** short for **City of London:** the original settlement of London on the N bank of the Thames; a municipality governed by the Lord Mayor and Corporation. Resident pop.: 5893 (1981). **2.** the area in central London in which the United Kingdom's major financial business is transacted. **3.** the various financial institutions located in this area.

City and Guilds Institute n. (in Britain) an examining body for technical and craft skills.

city chambers n. (*functioning as sing.*) (in Scotland) the municipal buildings of a city; town hall.

city desk n. the editorial section of a newspaper dealing in Britain with financial news, in the U.S. and Canada with local news.

city editor n. (on a newspaper) **1.** *Brit.* the editor in charge of financial and commercial news. **2.** *U.S. & Canad.* the editor in charge of local news.

city father n. a person who is active or prominent in the public affairs of a city.

cityscape ('sɪtɪskeɪp) n. an urban landscape; view of a city.

city-state n. *Ancient history.* a state consisting of a sovereign city and its dependencies.

city technology college n. (in Britain) a type of senior secondary school specializing in technological subjects, set up in inner-city areas with funding from industry.

Ciudad Bolívar (*Spanish* θiu'ðað bo'liβar) n. a port in E Venezuela, on the Orinoco River: accessible to ocean-going vessels. Pop.: 153 900 (1981 est.). Former name (1764–1846): **Angostura.**

Ciudad Juárez (*Spanish* θiu'ðað 'xwarɛθ) n. a city in N Mexico, in Chihuahua state on the Río Grande, opposite El Paso, Texas. Pop.: 567 365 (1980). Former name (until 1888): **El Paso del Norte** (ɛl 'paso del 'nɔrte).

Ciudad Real (*Spanish* θiu'ðað rɛ'al) n. a market town in S central Spain. Pop.: 48 656 (1982).

Ciudad Trujillo (*Spanish* θiu'ðað tru'xiʎo) n. the former name (1936–61) of **Santo Domingo.**

Ciudad Victoria (*Spanish* θiu'ðað bik'torja) n. a city in E central Mexico, capital of Tamaulipas state. Pop.: 153 206 (1980 est.).

civet ('sɪvɪt) n. **1.** a catlike mammal of Africa and S Asia, typically having spotted fur and secreting a powerfully smelling fluid from anal glands. **2.** the yellowish fatty secretion of such an animal, used as a fixative in the manufacture of perfumes. **3.** the fur of such an animal. [C16: from OF, from It., from Ar. *zabād* civet perfume]

civic ('sɪvɪk) adj. of or relating to a city, citizens, or citizenship. [C16: from L, from *cīvis* citizen] —'**civically** adv.

civic centre n. *Brit.* the public buildings of a town, including recreational facilities and offices of local administration.

civics ('sɪvɪks) n. (*functioning as sing.*) the study of the rights and responsibilities of citizenship.

civies ('sɪvɪz) pl. n. *Inf.* a variant spelling of **civvies.**

civil ('sɪvəl) adj. **1.** of the ordinary life of citizens as distinguished from military, legal, or ecclesiastical affairs. **2.** of or relating to the citizen as an individual: *civil rights.* **3.** of or occurring within the state or between citizens: *civil strife.* **4.** polite or courteous: *a civil manner.* **5.** of or in accordance with Roman law. [C14: from OF, from L *cīvīlis*, from *cīvis* citizen] —'**civilly** adv.

civil defence n. the organizing of civilians to deal with enemy attacks.

civil disobedience n. a refusal to obey laws, pay taxes, etc.: a nonviolent means of protesting.

civil engineer n. a person qualified to design and construct public works, such as roads, bridges, harbours, etc. —**civil engineering** n.

civilian (sɪ'vɪljən) n. **a.** a person whose occupation is civil or nonmilitary. **b.** (*as modifier*): *civilian life.* [C14 (orig.: a practitioner of civil law): from *civile* (from L *jūs cīvīle* civil law) + -IAN]

civility (sɪ'vɪlɪtɪ) n., pl. **-ties. 1.** politeness or courtesy. **2.** (*often pl.*) an act of politeness.

civilization *or* **-isation** (,sɪvɪlaɪ'zeɪʃən) n. **1.** a human society that has a complex cultural, political, and legal organization; an advanced state in social development. **2.** the peoples or nations collectively who have achieved such a state. **3.** the total culture and way of life of a particular people, nation, region, or period. **4.** the process of bringing or achieving civilization. **5.** intellectual, cultural, and moral refinement. **6.** cities or populated areas, as contrasted with sparsely inhabited areas, deserts, etc.

civilize *or* **-ise** ('sɪvɪ,laɪz) vb. (*tr.*) **1.** to bring out of savagery or barbarism into a state characteristic of civilization. **2.** to refine, educate, or enlighten. —'**civi,lizable** *or* **-isable** adj. —'**civi,lized** *or* **-ised** adj.

civil law n. **1.** the law of a state relating to private and civilian affairs. **2.** the body of law in ancient Rome, esp. as applicable to private citizens. **3.** law based on the Roman system as distinguished from common law and canon law.

civil liberty n. the right of an individual to certain freedoms of speech and action.

civil list n. (in Britain) the annuities voted by Parliament for the support of the royal household and the royal family.

civil marriage n. *Law.* a marriage performed by an official other than a clergyman.

civil rights pl. n. **1.** the personal rights of the individual citizen. **2.** (*modifier*) of, relating to, or promoting equality in social, economic, and political rights.

civil servant n. a member of the civil service.

civil service n. **1.** the service responsible for the public administration of the government of a country. It excludes the legislative, judicial, and military branches. **2.** the members of the civil service collectively.

civil war n. war between parties or factions within the same nation.

civvy ('sɪvɪ) n., pl. **civvies** *or* **civies.** *Sl.* **1.** a civilian. **2.** (*pl.*) civilian dress as opposed to uniform. **3. civvy street.** civilian life.

CJ *abbrev. for* Chief Justice.

Cl *the chemical symbol for* chlorine.

clachan (*Gaelic* 'klaxən; *English* 'klæ-) n. *Scot. & Irish dialect.* a small village; hamlet. [C15: from Scot. Gaelic: prob. from *clach* stone]

clack (klæk) vb. **1.** to make or cause to make a sound like that of two pieces of wood hitting each other. **2.** (*intr.*) to jabber. ~n. **3.** a short sharp sound. **4.** chatter. **5.** Also called: **clack valve.** a simple nonreturn valve using a hinged flap or a ball. [C13: prob. from ON *klaka* to twitter, imit.] —'**clacker** n.

Clackmannan (klæk'mænən) n. a town in E central Scotland, in Central region: former county town of Clackmannanshire. Pop.: 3597 (1981 est.).

Clackmannanshire (klæk'mænən,ʃɪə, -ʃə) n. (until 1975) a county of central Scotland, now part of the Central region.

Clacton *or* **Clacton-on-Sea** ('klæktən) n. a town and resort in SE England, in E Essex. Pop.: 43 571 (1981).

clad[1] (klæd) vb. a past tense and past participle of **clothe.** [OE *clāthode* clothed, from *clāthian* to CLOTHE]

clad[2] (klæd) vb. **cladding, clad.** (*tr.*) to bond a metal to (another metal), esp. to form a protective coating. [C14: special use of CLAD[1]]

cladding ('klædɪŋ) n. **1.** the process of protecting one metal by bonding a second metal to its surface. **2.** the protective coating so bonded to metal. **3.** the material used for the outside facing of a building, etc.

cladistics (kləˈdɪstɪks) *n.* (*functioning as sing.*) a method of grouping animals by measurable likenesses or homologues. [C20: NL from Gk *kládos* branch, shoot] —**cladism** (ˈklædɪzəm) *n.* —**cladist** (ˈklædɪst) *n.*

claim (kleɪm) *vb.* (*mainly tr.*) **1.** to demand as being due or as one's property; assert one's title or right to: *he claimed the record.* **2.** (*takes a clause as object or an infinitive*) to assert as a fact; maintain against denial: *he claimed to be telling the truth.* **3.** to call for or need; deserve: *this problem claims our attention.* **4.** to take: *the accident claimed four lives.* ~*n.* **5.** an assertion of a right; a demand for something as due. **6.** an assertion of something as true, real, or factual. **7.** a right or just title to something; basis for demand: *a claim to fame.* **8.** anything that is claimed, such as a piece of land staked out by a miner. **9. a.** a demand for payment in connection with an insurance policy, etc. **b.** the sum of money demanded. [C13: from OF *claimer* to call, from L *clāmāre* to shout] —**ˈclaimable** *adj.* —**ˈclaimant** *or* **ˈclaimer** *n.*

▷ **Usage.** It is sometimes maintained that *claim* should be used only in the sense of asserting or declaring one's right to something: *he claimed his share of the profits.* Nevertheless, even the most careful users of English do not hesitate to employ the verb in the sense of asserting something to be true or declaring something to be a fact: *he claimed that he had seen the man before; she claimed that the witness had lied.*

Clair (*French* klɛr) *n.* **René** (rəne), real name *René Chomette.* 1898–1981, French film director; noted for his comedies including *An Italian Straw Hat* (1928) and pioneering sound films such as *Sous les toits de Paris* (1930); later films include *Les Belles de nuit* (1952).

clairvoyance (klɛəˈvɔɪəns) *n.* **1.** the alleged power of perceiving things beyond the natural range of the senses. **2.** keen intuitive understanding. [C19: from F: clear-seeing, from *clair* clear + *voyance*, from *voir* to see]

clairvoyant (klɛəˈvɔɪənt) *adj.* **1.** of or possessing clairvoyance. **2.** having great insight. ~*n.* **3.** a person claiming to have the power to foretell future events. —**clairˈvoyantly** *adv.*

clam (klæm) *n.* **1.** any of various burrowing bivalve molluscs. **2.** the edible flesh of such a mollusc. **3.** *Inf.* a reticent person. ~*vb.* **clamming, clammed.** **4.** (*intr.*) *Chiefly U.S.* to gather clams. ~See also **clam up.** [C16: from earlier *clamshell*, that is, shell that clamps]

clamant (ˈkleɪmənt) *adj.* **1.** noisy. **2.** calling urgently. [C17: from L, from *clāmāre* to shout]

clamber (ˈklæmbə) *vb.* **1.** (usually foll. by *up, over,* etc.) to climb (something) awkwardly, esp. by using both hands and feet. ~*n.* **2.** a climb performed in this manner. [C15: prob. var. of CLIMB] —**ˈclamberer** *n.*

clammy (ˈklæmɪ) *adj.* **-mier, -miest.** **1.** unpleasantly sticky; moist. **2.** (of the weather) close; humid. [C14: from OE *clǣman* to smear] —**ˈclammily** *adv.* —**ˈclamminess** *n.*

clamour *or U.S.* **clamor** (ˈklæmə) *n.* **1.** a loud persistent outcry. **2.** a vehement expression of collective feeling or outrage: *a clamour against higher prices.* **3.** a loud and persistent noise: *the clamour of traffic.* ~*vb.* **4.** (*intr.;* often foll. by *for* or *against*) to make a loud noise or outcry; make a public demand. **5.** (*tr.*) to move or force by outcry. [C14: from OF, from L, from *clāmāre* to cry out] —**ˈclamorous** *adj.* —**ˈclamorously** *adv.* —**ˈclamorousness** *n.*

clamp[1] (klæmp) *n.* **1.** a mechanical device with movable jaws with which an object can be secured to a bench or with which two objects may be secured together. **2.** See **wheel clamp.** ~*vb.* (*tr.*) **3.** to fix or fasten with or as if with a clamp **4.** to immobilize (a car) by means of a wheel clamp. **5.** to inflict or impose forcefully: *they clamped a curfew on the town.* [C14: from Du. or Low G *klamp*]

clamp[2] (klæmp) *n.* **1.** a mound of a harvested root crop, covered with straw and earth to protect it from winter weather. ~*vb.* **2.** (*tr.*) to enclose (a harvested root crop) in a mound. [C16: from MDu. *klamp* heap]

clamp down *vb.* (*intr., adv.;* often foll. by *on*) **1.** to behave repressively; attempt to suppress something regarded as undesirable. ~*n.* **clampdown. 2.** a sudden restrictive measure.

clam up *vb.* (*intr., adv.*) *Inf.* to keep or become silent or withhold information.

clan (klæn) *n.* **1.** a group of people interrelated by ancestry or marriage. **2.** a group of families with a common surname and a common ancestor, esp. among the Scots and the Irish. **3.** a group of people united by common characteristics, aims, or interests. [C14: from Scot. Gaelic *clann* family, descendants, from L *planta* sprout]

clandestine (klænˈdɛstɪn) *adj.* secret and concealed, often for illicit reasons; furtive. [C16: from L, from *clam* secretly] —**clanˈdestinely** *adv.*

clang (klæŋ) *vb.* **1.** to make or cause to make a loud resounding noise, as metal when struck. **2.** (*intr.*) to move or operate making such a sound. ~*n.* **3.** a resounding metallic noise. **4.** the harsh cry of certain birds. [C16: from L *clangere*]

clanger (ˈklæŋə) *n.* **1.** *Inf.* a conspicuous mistake (esp. in **drop a clanger**). **2.** something that clangs or causes a clang. [C20: from CLANG]

clangour *or U.S.* **clangor** (ˈklæŋgə, ˈklæŋə) *n.* **1.** a loud resonant often-repeated noise. **2.** an uproar. ~*vb.* **3.** (*intr.*) to make or produce a loud resonant noise. —**ˈclangorous** *adj.* —**ˈclangorously** *adv.*

clank (klæŋk) *n.* **1.** an abrupt harsh metallic sound. ~*vb.* **2.** to make or cause to make such a sound. **3.** (*intr.*) to move or operate making such a sound. [C17: imit.] —**ˈclankingly** *adv.*

clannish (ˈklænɪʃ) *adj.* **1.** of or characteristic of a clan. **2.** tending to associate closely within a group to the exclusion of outsiders; cliquish. —**ˈclannishly** *adv.* —**ˈclannishness** *n.*

clansman (ˈklænzmən) *or* (*fem.*) **clanswoman** *n., pl.* **-men** *or* **-women.** a person belonging to a clan.

clap[1] (klæp) *vb.* **clapping, clapped.** **1.** to make or cause to make a sharp abrupt sound, as of two nonmetallic objects struck together. **2.** to applaud (someone or something) by striking the palms of the hands together sharply. **3.** (*tr.*) to strike (a person) lightly with an open hand, in greeting, etc. **4.** (*tr.*) to place or put quickly or forcibly: *they clapped him into jail.* **5.** (of certain birds) to flap (the wings) noisily. **6.** (*intr.;* foll. by *up* or *together*) to contrive or put together hastily. **7. clap eyes on.** *Inf.* to catch sight of. **8. clap hold of.** *Inf.* to grasp suddenly or forcibly. ~*n.* **9.** the sharp abrupt sound produced by striking the hands together. **10.** the act of clapping, esp. in applause. **11.** a sudden sharp sound, esp. of thunder. **12.** a light blow. **13.** *Arch.* a sudden action or mishap. [OE *clæppan;* imit.]

clap[2] (klæp) *n.* (usually preceded by *the*) a slang word for **gonorrhoea.** [C16: from OF *clapoir* venereal sore, from *clapier* brothel, from ?]

clapboard (ˈklæp,bɔːd, ˈklæbəd) *n.* **1.** a long thin timber board, used esp. in the U.S. and Canada in wood-frame construction by lapping each board over the one below. ~*vb.* **2.** (*tr.*) to cover with such boards. [C16: partial translation of Low G *klappholt,* from *klappen* to crack + *holt* wood]

clapped out *adj.* (**clapped-out** *when prenominal*). *Inf.* **1.** *Brit., Austral. & N.Z.* worn out; dilapidated. **2.** *Austral. & N.Z.* extremely tired; exhausted.

clapper (ˈklæpə) *n.* **1.** a person or thing that claps. **2.** Also called: **tongue.** a small piece of metal suspended within a bell that causes it to sound when made to strike against its side. **3. go** (**run, move**) **like the clappers.** *Brit. inf.* to move extremely fast.

clapperboard (ˈklæpə,bɔːd) *n.* a pair of hinged boards clapped together during film shooting to aid in synchronizing sound and picture prints.

Clapton (ˈklæptən) *n.* **Eric.** born 1945, English rock guitarist, noted for his virtuoso style, his work with the Yardbirds (1963–65), Cream (1966–68), and, with Derek and the Dominos, the album *Layla* (1970).

claptrap (ˈklæp,træp) *n.* *Inf.* **1.** contrived but foolish talk. **2.** insincere and pretentious talk: *politicians' claptrap.* [C18: from CLAP[1] + TRAP[1]]

claque (klæk) *n.* **1.** a group of people hired to applaud. **2.** a group of fawning admirers. [C19: from F, from *claquer* to clap, imit.]

Clare[1] (klɛə) *n.* a county of W Ireland, in Munster between Galway Bay and the Shannon estuary. County town: Ennis. Pop.: 91 343 (1986). Area: 3188 sq. km (1231 sq. miles).

Clare[2] (klɛə) n. **John.** 1793–1864, English poet, noted for his descriptions of country life, particularly in *The Shepherd's Calendar* (1827) and *The Rural Muse* (1835). He was confined in a lunatic asylum from 1837.

Clarendon[1] ('klærəndən) n. a village near Salisbury in S England: site of a council held by Henry II in 1164 that produced a code of laws (the **Constitutions of Clarendon**) defining relations between church and state.

Clarendon[2] ('klærəndən) n. **1st Earl of,** title of *Edward Hyde.* 1609–74, English statesman and historian; chief adviser to Charles II (1660–67); author of *History of the Rebellion and Civil Wars in England* (1704–07).

Clare of Assisi n. **Saint.** 1194–1253, Italian nun; founder of the Franciscan Order of Poor Clares. Feast day: Aug. 12.

claret ('klærət) n. **1.** a red wine, esp. one from the Bordeaux district of France. **2. a.** a purplish-red colour. **b.** (*as adj.*): *a claret football strip.* [C14: from OF (*vin*) *claret* clear (wine), from Med. L *clārātum*, from L *clārus* clear]

clarify ('klærɪ,faɪ) vb. **-fying, -fied. 1.** to make or become clear or easy to understand. **2.** to make or become free of impurities. **3.** to make (fat, butter, etc.) clear by heating, etc., or (of fat, etc.) to become clear as a result of such a process. [C14: from OF, from LL, from L *clārus* clear + *facere* to make] —,**clarifi'cation** n. —'**clari,fier** n.

clarinet (,klærɪ'nɛt) n. *Music.* **1.** a keyed woodwind instrument with a cylindrical bore and a single reed. **2.** an orchestral musician who plays the clarinet. [C18: from F, prob. from It., from *clarino* trumpet] —,**clari'nettist** *or U.S. sometimes* ,**clari'netist** n.

clarion ('klærɪən) n. **1.** a stop of trumpet quality on an organ. **2.** an obsolete, high-pitched, small-bore trumpet. **3.** the sound of such an instrument or any similar sound. ~*adj.* **4.** (*prenominal*) clear and ringing; inspiring: *a clarion call to action.* ~*vb.* **5.** to proclaim loudly. [C14: from Med. L *clāriō* trumpet, from L *clārus* clear]

clarity ('klærɪtɪ) n. **1.** clearness, as of expression. **2.** clearness, as of water. [C16: from L *clāritās*, from *clārus* clear]

Clark (klɑːk) n. **1. James,** known as *Jim.* 1936–68, Scottish racing driver; World Champion (1963, 1965). **2. (Charles) Joseph,** known as *Joe.* born 1939, Canadian politician; prime minister (1979–80). **3. Kenneth,** Baron Clark of Saltwood. 1903–83, English art historian: his books include *Civilization* (1969), which he first presented as a television series.

Clarke (klɑːk) n. **Marcus (Andrew Hislop).** 1846–81, Australian novelist born in England, noted for his novel *For the Term of His Natural Life* which was published in serial form as *His Natural Life* (1870–72). His other works include *Twixt Shadow and Shine* (1875) and *Old Tales of a Young Country* (1871).

clarkia ('klɑːkɪə) n. any North American plant of the genus *Clarkia:* cultivated for their red, purple, or pink flowers. [C19: NL, after William *Clark* (1770–1838), American explorer]

clary ('klɛərɪ) n., pl. **claries.** any of several European plants having aromatic leaves and blue flowers. [C14: from earlier *sclarreye*, from Med. L *sclareia*, from ?]

-clase n. *combining form.* (in mineralogy) indicating a particular type of cleavage: *plagioclase.* [via F from Gk *klasis* a breaking]

clash (klæʃ) vb. **1.** to make or cause to make a loud harsh sound, esp. by striking together. **2.** (*intr.*) to be incompatible. **3.** (*intr.*) to engage together in conflict. **4.** (*intr.*) (of dates or events) to coincide. **5.** (*intr.*) (of colours) to look inharmonious together. ~*n.* **6.** a loud harsh noise. **7.** a collision or conflict. [C16: imit.] —'**clasher** n.

clasp (klɑːsp) n. **1.** a fastening, such as a catch or hook, for holding things together. **2.** a firm grasp or embrace. **3.** *Mil.* a bar on a medal ribbon, to indicate either a second award on the battle, campaign, or reason for its award. ~*vb.* (*tr.*) **4.** to hold in a firm grasp. **5.** to grasp firmly with the hand. **6.** to fasten together with or as if with a clasp. [C14: from ?] —'**clasper** n.

clasp knife n. a large knife with one or more blades or other devices folding into the handle.

class (klɑːs) n. **1.** a collection or division of people or things sharing a common characteristic. **2.** a group of persons sharing a similar social and economic position. **3. a.** the pattern of divisions that exist within a society on the basis of rank, economic status, etc. **b.** (*as modifier*):

the class struggle; class distinctions. **4. a.** a group of pupils or students who are taught together. **b.** a meeting of a group of students for tuition. **5.** *U.S.* a group of students who graduated in a specified year: *the class of '53.* **6.** (*in combination and as modifier*) *Brit.* a grade of attainment in a university honours degree: *second-class honours.* **7.** one of several standards of accommodation in public transport. **8.** *Inf.* excellence or elegance, esp. in dress, design, or behaviour. **9.** *Biol.* any of the taxonomic groups into which a phylum is divided and which contains one or more orders. **10.** *Maths.* another name for **set**[2] (sense 3). **11. in a class by oneself** *or* **in a class of its own.** unequalled; unparalleled. ~*vb.* **12.** to have or assign a place within a group, grade, or class. [C17: from L *classis* class, rank, fleet]

class. *abbrev. for:* **1.** classic(al). **2.** classification. **3.** classified.

class-conscious *adj.* aware of belonging to a particular social rank. —,**class-'consciousness** n.

classic ('klæsɪk) *adj.* **1.** of the highest class, esp. in art or literature. **2.** serving as a standard or model of its kind. **3.** adhering to an established set of principles in the arts or sciences: *a classic proof.* **4.** characterized by simplicity, balance, regularity, and purity of form; classical. **5.** of lasting interest or significance. **6.** continuously in fashion because of its simple style: *a classic dress.* ~*n.* **7.** an author, artist, or work of art of the highest excellence. **8.** a creation or work considered as definitive. **9.** *Horse racing.* any of the five principal races for three-year-old horses in Britain, namely the One Thousand Guineas, Two Thousand Guineas, Derby, Oaks, and Saint Leger. [C17: from L *classicus* of the first rank, from *classis* division, rank, class]

▷ **Usage.** The adjectives *classic* and *classical* can often be treated as synonyms, but there are two contexts in which they should be carefully distinguished. *Classic* is applied to that which is of the first rank, esp. in art and literature, as in: *Lewis Carroll's classic works for children. Classical* is used to refer to Greek and Roman culture.

classical ('klæsɪk[ə]l) *adj.* **1.** of, relating to, or characteristic of the ancient Greeks and Romans or their civilization. **2.** designating, following, or influenced by the art or culture of ancient Greece or Rome: *classical architecture.* **3.** *Music.* **a.** of, relating to, or denoting any music or its period of composition marked by stability of form, intellectualism, and restraint. Cf. **romantic** (sense 5). **b.** accepted as a standard: *the classical suite.* **c.** denoting serious art music in general. Cf. **pop**[2]. **4.** denoting or relating to a style in any of the arts characterized by emotional restraint and conservatism: *a classical style of painting.* **5.** (of an education) based on the humanities and the study of Latin and Greek. **6.** *Physics.* not involving the quantum theory or the theory of relativity: *classical mechanics.* —,**classi'cality** *or* '**classicalness** n. —'**classically** *adv.*

▷ **Usage.** See at **classic.**

classicism ('klæsɪ,sɪzəm) *or* **classicalism** ('klæsɪkə,lɪzəm) n. **1.** a style based on the study of Greek and Roman models, characterized by emotional restraint and regularity of form; the antithesis of romanticism. **2.** knowledge of the culture of ancient Greece and Rome. **3. a.** a Greek or Latin expression. **b.** an expression in a modern language that is modelled on a Greek or Latin form. —'**classicist** n.

classicize *or* **-cise** ('klæsɪ,saɪz) vb. **1.** (*tr.*) to make classic. **2.** (*intr.*) to imitate classical style.

classics ('klæsɪks) n. **1. the.** a body of literature regarded as great or lasting, esp. that of ancient Greece or Rome. **2. the.** the ancient Greek and Latin languages. **3.** (*functioning as sing.*) ancient Greek and Roman culture as a subject for academic study.

classification (,klæsɪfɪ'keɪʃən) n. **1.** systematic placement in categories. **2.** one of the divisions in a system of classifying. **3.** *Biol.* **a.** the placing of animals and plants in a series of increasingly specialized groups because of similarities in structure, origin, etc., that indicate a common relationship. **b.** the study of the principles and practice of this process; taxonomy. [C18: from F; see CLASS, -IFY, -ATION] —,**classifi'catory** *adj.*

classified ('klæsɪ,faɪd) *adj.* **1.** arranged according to some system of classification. **2.** *Government.* (of information) not available to people outside a restricted group, esp. for reasons of national security. **3.** *U.S. & Canad.*

inf. (of information) closely concealed or secret. **4.** (of advertisements in newspapers, etc.) arranged according to type. **5.** *Brit.* (of newspapers) containing sports results. **6.** (of British roads) having a number in the national road system.

classify ('klæsɪ,faɪ) *vb.* **-fying, -fied.** (*tr.*) **1.** to arrange or order by classes; categorize. **2.** *Government.* to declare (information, documents, etc.) of possible aid to an enemy and therefore not available to people outside a restricted group. [C18: back formation from CLASSIFICATION] — 'classi,fiable *adj.* — 'classi,fier *n.*

classless ('klɑːslɪs) *adj.* **1.** not belonging to a class. **2.** characterized by the absence of economic and social distinctions. — 'classlessness *n.*

class list *n.* (in Britain) a list categorizing students according to the class of honours they have obtained in their degree examination.

classmate ('klɑːs,meɪt) *n.* a friend or contemporary of the same class in a school.

classroom ('klɑːs,ruːm, -,rʊm) *n.* a room in which classes are conducted, esp. in a school.

class struggle *n.* the. *Marxism.* the continual conflict between the capitalist and working classes for economic and political power.

classy ('klɑːsɪ) *adj.* **classier, classiest.** *Sl.* elegant; stylish. — 'classiness *n.*

clatter ('klætə) *vb.* **1.** to make or cause to make a rattling noise, esp. as a result of movement. **2.** (*intr.*) to chatter. ~*n.* **3.** a rattling sound or noise. **4.** a noisy commotion, such as loud chatter. [OE *clatrung* clattering (gerund)] — 'clatterer *n.* — 'clatteringly *adv.*

Claudel (*French* klodɛl) *n.* **Paul (Louis Charles)** (pɔl). 1868–1955, French dramatist, poet, and diplomat, whose works testify to his commitment to the Roman Catholic faith. His plays include *L'Annonce faite à Marie* (1912) and *Le Soulier de satin* (1919–24).

Claude Lorrain (*French* klod lɔrɛ̃) *n.* real name *Claude Gelée.* 1600–82, French painter, esp. of idealized landscapes, noted for his subtle depiction of light.

Claudius ('klɔːdɪəs) *n.* full name *Tiberius Claudius Drusus Nero Germanicus.* 10 B.C.–54 A.D., Roman emperor (41–54); invaded Britain (43); poisoned by his fourth wife, Agrippina.

Claudius II *n.* full name *Marcus Aurelius Claudius,* called *Gothicus.* 214–270 A.D., Roman emperor (268–270).

clause (klɔːz) *n.* **1.** *Grammar.* a group of words, consisting of a subject and a predicate including a finite verb, that does not necessarily constitute a sentence. See also **main clause, subordinate clause. 2.** a section of a legal document such as a contract, will, or draft statute. [C13: from OF, from Med. L *clausa* a closing (of a rhetorical period), from L, from *claudere* to close] — 'clausal *adj.*

Clausewitz (*German* 'klauzəvɪts) *n.* **Karl von** (karl fɔn). 1780–1831, Prussian general, noted for his works on military strategy, esp. *Vom Kriege* (1833).

Clausius (*German* 'klauziʊs) *n.* **Rudolf Julius** ('ruːdɔlf 'juːlɪʊs). 1822–88, German physicist and mathematician. He enunciated the second law of thermodynamics (1850) and developed the kinetic theory of gases.

claustrophobia (,klɔːstrə'fəʊbɪə, ,klɒs-) *n.* an abnormal fear of being in a confined space. [C19: NL from L *claustrum* CLOISTER + -PHOBIA] — 'claustro,phobe *n.* — ,claustro'phobic *adj.*

clavate ('kleɪveɪt, -vɪt) *or* **claviform** ('klævɪ,fɔːm) *adj. Biol.* shaped like a club. [C19: from L *clāva* club] — 'clavately *adv.*

clave[1] (kleɪv, klɑːv) *n. Music.* one of a pair of hardwood sticks struck together to make a hollow sound. [C20: from American Sp., from L *clavis* key]

clave[2] (kleɪv) *vb. Arch.* a past tense of **cleave.**

clavichord ('klævɪ,kɔːd) *n.* a keyboard instrument consisting of a number of thin wire strings struck from below by brass tangents. [C15: from Med. L, from L *clāvis* key + *chorda* CHORD[1]]

clavicle ('klævɪk³l) *n.* **1.** either of the two bones connecting the shoulder blades with the upper part of the breastbone. Nontechnical name: **collarbone. 2.** the corresponding structure in other vertebrates. [C17: from Med. L *clāvicula,* from L *clāvis* key] —**clavicular** (klə'vɪkjʊlə) *adj.*

clavier (klə'vɪə, 'klævɪə) *n.* **a.** any keyboard instrument. **b.** the keyboard itself. [C18: from F: keyboard, from L *clāvis* key]

claw (klɔː) *n.* **1.** a curved pointed horny process on the end of each digit in birds, some reptiles, and certain mammals. **2.** a corresponding structure in some invertebrates, such as the pincer of a crab. **3.** a part or member like a claw in function or appearance. ~*vb.* **4.** to scrape, tear, or dig (something or someone) with claws, etc. **5.** (*tr.*) to create by scratching as with claws: *to claw an opening.* [OE *clawu*] — 'clawer *n.*

claw back *vb.* (*tr., adv.*) **1.** to get back (something) with difficulty. **2.** to recover (a part of a tax, duty, etc.) in the form of an allowance. ~*n.* **clawback. 3.** the recovery of part of a tax, etc., in the form of an allowance. **4.** the sum so recovered.

claw hammer *n.* a hammer with a cleft at one end of the head for extracting nails.

clay (kleɪ) *n.* **1.** a very fine-grained material that occurs as sedimentary rocks, soils, and other deposits. It becomes plastic when moist but hardens on heating and is used in the manufacture of bricks, ceramics, etc. **2.** earth or mud. **3.** *Poetic.* the material of the human body. [OE *clǣg*] — 'clayey, 'clayish, *or* 'clay,like *adj.*

Clay (kleɪ) *n.* **1.** See **Muhammad Ali. 2. Henry.** 1777–1852, U.S. statesman and orator; secretary of state (1825–29).

claymore ('kleɪ,mɔː) *n.* a large two-edged broadsword used formerly by Scottish Highlanders. [C18: from Gaelic *claidheamh mòr* great sword]

clay pigeon *n.* a disc of baked clay hurled into the air from a machine as a target to be shot at.

clay road *n. N.Z.* an unmetalled road in a rural area.

CLC *abbrev. for* Canadian Labour Congress.

-cle *suffix forming nouns.* indicating smallness: *cubicle; particle.* [via OF from L *-culus.* See -CULE]

clean (kliːn) *adj.* **1.** without dirt or other impurities; unsoiled. **2.** without anything in it or on it: *a clean page.* **3.** recently washed; fresh. **4.** without extraneous or foreign materials. **5.** without defect, difficulties, or problems. **6.** (of a nuclear weapon) producing little or no radioactive fallout or contamination. **7.** (of a wound, etc.) having no pus or other sign of infection. **8.** pure; morally sound. **9.** without objectionable language or obscenity. **10.** thorough or complete: *a clean break.* **11.** dexterous or adroit: *a clean throw.* **12.** *Sport.* played fairly and without fouls. **13.** simple in design: *a ship's clean lines.* **14.** *Aeronautics.* causing little turbulence; streamlined. **15.** honourable or respectable. **16.** habitually neat. **17.** (esp. of a driving licence) showing or having no record of offences. **18.** *Sl.* **a.** innocent; not guilty. **b.** not carrying illegal drugs, weapons, etc. ~*vb.* **19.** to make or become free of dirt, filth, etc.: *the stove cleans easily.* **20.** (*tr.*) to remove in making clean: *to clean marks off the wall.* **21.** (*tr.*) to prepare (fish, poultry, etc.) for cooking: *to clean a chicken.* ~*adv.* **22.** in a clean way; cleanly. **23.** *Not standard.* (intensifier): *clean forgotten.* **24. come clean.** *Inf.* to make a revelation or confession. ~*n.* **25.** the act or an instance of cleaning: *he gave his shoes a clean.* ~ See also **clean out, clean up.** [OE *clǣne*] — 'cleanable *adj.* — 'cleanness *n.*

clean-cut *adj.* **1.** clearly outlined; neat: *clean-cut lines of a ship.* **2.** definite.

cleaner ('kliːnə) *n.* **1.** a person, device, chemical agent, etc., that removes dirt, as from clothes or carpets. **2.** (*usually pl.*) a shop, etc., that provides a dry-cleaning service. **3. take (a person) to the cleaners.** *Inf.* to rob or defraud (a person).

cleanly *adv.* ('kliːnlɪ). **1.** in a fair manner. **2.** easily or smoothly. ~*adj.* ('klɛnlɪ), **-lier, -liest. 3.** habitually clean or neat. —**cleanlily** ('klɛnlɪlɪ) *adv.* —**cleanliness** ('klɛnlɪnɪs) *n.*

clean out *vb.* (*tr., adv.*) **1.** (foll. by *of* or *from*) *Sl.* to remove (something) (from or away from). **2.** *Sl.* to leave (someone) with no money. **3.** *Inf.* to exhaust (stocks, goods, etc.) completely.

cleanse (klɛnz) *vb.* (*tr.*) **1.** to remove dirt, filth, etc., from. **2.** to remove guilt from. **3.** *Arch.* to cure. [OE *clǣnsian;* see CLEAN]

cleanser ('klɛnzə) *n.* a cleansing agent.

clean-shaven *adj.* (of men) having the facial hair shaved off.

Cleanthes (klɪ'ænθiːz) n. ?300–?232 B.C., Greek philosopher: succeeded Zeno as head of the Stoic school.

clean up vb. (adv.) **1.** to rid (something) of dirt, filth, or other impurities. **2.** to make (someone or something) orderly or presentable. **3.** (tr.) to rid (a place) of undesirable people or conditions. **4.** Inf., chiefly U.S. & Canad. to make (a great profit). ~n. **cleanup. 5.** the process of cleaning up. **6.** Inf., chiefly U.S. a great profit.

clear (klɪə) adj. **1.** free from darkness or obscurity; bright. **2.** (of weather) free from dullness or clouds. **3.** transparent: clear water. **4.** even and pure in tone or colour. **5.** without blemish, or defect: a clear skin. **6.** easy to see or hear; distinct. **7.** free from doubt or confusion. **8.** (postpositive) certain in the mind; sure: are you clear? **9.** (in combination) perceptive, alert: clear-eyed; clear-headed; clear-sighted. **10.** evident or obvious: it is clear that he won't come now. **11.** (of sounds or the voice) not harsh or hoarse. **12.** serene; calm. **13.** without qualification or limitation; complete: a clear victory. **14.** free of suspicion, guilt, or blame: a clear conscience. **15.** free of obstruction; open: a clear passage. **16.** free from debt or obligation. **17.** (of money, profits, etc.) without deduction; net. **18.** emptied of freight or cargo. **19.** Showjumping. (of a round) ridden without any points being lost. ~adv. **20.** in a clear or distinct manner. **21.** completely or utterly. **22.** (postpositive; often foll. by of) not in contact (with); free: stand clear of the gates. ~n. **23.** a clear space. **24. in the clear. a.** free of suspicion, guilt, or blame. **b.** Sport. able to receive a pass without being tackled. ~vb. **25.** to make or become free from darkness, obscurity, etc. **26.** (intr.) **a.** (of the weather) to become free from dullness, fog, rain, etc. **b.** (of mist, fog, etc.) to disappear. **27.** (tr.) to free from impurity or blemish. **28.** (tr.) to free from doubt or confusion. **29.** (tr.) to rid of objects, obstructions, etc. **30.** (tr.) to make or form (a path, way, etc.) by removing obstructions. **31.** (tr.) to free or remove (a person or thing) from something, as of suspicion, blame, or guilt. **32.** (tr.) to move or pass by or over without contact: he cleared the wall easily. **33.** (tr.) to rid (the throat) of phlegm. **34.** (tr.) to make or gain (money) as profit. **35.** (tr.; often foll. by off) to discharge or settle (a debt). **36.** (tr.) to free (a debtor) from obligation. **37.** (intr.) (of a cheque) to pass through one's bank and be charged against one's account. **38.** Banking. to settle accounts by exchanging (commercial documents) in a clearing house. **39.** to permit (ships, aircraft, cargo, passengers, etc.) to unload, disembark, depart, etc., or (of ships, etc.) to be permitted to unload, etc. **40.** to obtain or give (clearance). **41.** (tr.) to obtain clearance from. **42.** (tr.) to permit (a person, company, etc.) to see or handle classified information. **43.** (tr.) Mil., etc. to decode (a message, etc.). **44.** (tr.) Computers. to remove data from a storage device and revert to zero. **45. clear the air.** to dispel tension, confusion, etc., by settling misunderstandings, etc. ~See also **clear away, clear off,** etc. [C13: clere, from OF cler, from L clārus clear] —'**clearer** n. —'**clearness** n.

clearance ('klɪərəns) n. **1. a.** the process or an instance of clearing: slum clearance. **b.** (as modifier): a clearance order. **2.** space between two parts in motion or in relative motion. **3.** permission for an aircraft, ship, passengers, etc., to proceed. **4.** official permission to have access to secret information, projects, areas, etc. **5.** Banking. the exchange of commercial documents drawn on the members of a clearing house. **6. a.** the disposal of merchandise at reduced prices. **b.** (as modifier): a clearance sale. **7.** the act of clearing an area of land by mass eviction: the Highland Clearances.

clear away vb. (adv.) to remove (objects) from (the table) after a meal.

clear-cut adj. (**clear cut** when postpositive). **1.** definite; not vague: a clear-cut proposal. **2.** clearly outlined.

clearing ('klɪərɪŋ) n. an area with few or no trees or shrubs in wooded or overgrown land.

clearing bank n. (in Britain) any bank that makes use of the central clearing house in London.

clearing house n. **1.** Banking. an institution where cheques and other commercial papers drawn on member banks are cancelled against each other so that only net balances are payable. **2.** a central agency for the collection and distribution of information or materials.

clear off vb. (intr., adv.) Inf. to go away: often used imperatively.

clear out vb. (adv.) **1.** (intr.) Inf. to go away: often used imperatively. **2.** (tr.) to remove and sort the contents of (a room, container, etc.). **3.** (tr.) Sl. to leave (someone) with no money. **4.** (tr.) Sl. to exhaust (stocks, goods, etc.) completely.

clearstory ('klɪə,stɔːrɪ) n. a variant of **clerestory**.

clear up vb. (adv.) **1.** (tr.) to explain or solve (a mystery, misunderstanding, etc.). **2.** to put (a place or thing that is disordered) in order. **3.** (intr.) (of the weather) to become brighter.

clearway ('klɪə,weɪ) n. **1.** Brit. a stretch of road on which motorists may stop only in an emergency. **2.** an area at the end of a runway over which an aircraft taking off makes its initial climb.

cleat (kliːt) n. **1.** a wedge-shaped block attached to a structure to act as a support. **2.** a device consisting of two hornlike prongs projecting horizontally in opposite directions from a central base, used for securing lines on vessels, wharves, etc. ~vb. (tr.) **3.** to supply or support with a cleat or cleats. **4.** to secure (a line) on a cleat. [C14: of Gmc origin]

cleavage ('kliːvɪdʒ) n. **1.** Inf. the separation between a woman's breasts, esp. as revealed by a low-cut dress. **2.** a division or split. **3.** (of crystals) the act of splitting or the tendency to split along definite planes so as to yield smooth surfaces. **4.** (in animals) the repeated division of a fertilized ovum into a solid ball of cells. **5.** the breaking of a chemical bond in a molecule to give smaller molecules or radicals.

cleave[1] (kliːv) vb. **cleaving; cleft, cleaved,** or **clove; cleft, cleaved,** or **cloven. 1.** to split or cause to split, esp. along a natural weakness. **2.** (tr.) to make by or as if by cutting: to cleave a path. **3.** (when intr., foll. by through) to penetrate or traverse. [OE clēofan] —'**cleavable** adj.

cleave[2] (kliːv) vb. (intr.; foll. by to) to cling or adhere. [OE cleofian]

cleaver ('kliːvə) n. a heavy knife or long-bladed hatchet, esp. one used by butchers.

cleavers ('kliːvəz) n. (functioning as sing.) a Eurasian plant, having small white flowers and prickly stems and fruits. Also called: **goosegrass, hairif.** [OE clīfe; see CLEAVE[2]]

Cleethorpes ('kliːθɔːps) n. a resort in E England, in SE Humberside. Pop.: 35 544 (1981).

clef (klɛf) n. one of several symbols placed on the left-hand side beginning of each stave indicating the pitch of the music written after it. [C16: from F: key, clef, from L clāvis]

cleft (klɛft) vb. **1.** a past tense and past participle of **cleave**[1]. ~n. **2.** a fissure or crevice. **3.** an indentation or split in something, such as the chin, palate, etc. ~adj. **4.** split; divided. [OE geclyft (n.); see CLEAVE[1]]

cleft palate n. a congenital crack or fissure in the midline of the hard palate, often associated with a harelip.

cleg (klɛg) n. another name for a **horsefly.** [C15: from ON kleggi]

Cleisthenes ('klaɪsθə,niːz) n. 6th century B.C., Athenian statesman: democratized the political structure of Athens.

clematis ('klɛmətɪs, klə'meɪtɪs) n. any N temperate climbing plant of the genus Clematis. Many species are cultivated for their large colourful flowers. [C16: from L, from Gk, from klēma vine twig]

Clemenceau (French klemɑ̃so) n. **Georges Eugène Benjamin** (ʒɔrʒ œʒɛn bɛʒamɛ̃). 1841–1929, French statesman; prime minister of France (1906–09; 1917–20); negotiated the Treaty of Versailles (1919).

clemency ('klɛmənsɪ) n., pl. -cies. **1.** mercy or leniency. **2.** mildness, esp. of the weather. [C15: from L, from clēmēns gentle]

Clemens ('klɛmənz) n. **Samuel Langhorne** ('læŋ,hɔːn). See (Mark) **Twain.**

clement ('klɛmənt) adj. **1.** merciful. **2.** (of the weather) mild. [C15: from L clēmēns mild]

Clement I ('klɛmənt) n. **Saint,** called Clement of Rome. pope (?88–?97 A.D.). Feast day: Nov. 23.

Clement V n. original name Bertrand de Got. ?1264–1314, pope (1305–14): removed the papal seat from Rome to Avignon in France (1309).

Clement VII n. original name Giulio de' Medici. 1478–1534, pope (1523–34): refused to authorize the annulment of the marriage of Henry VIII of England to Catherine of Aragon (1533).

clementine ('klɛmən,tiːn, -,taɪn) n. a citrus fruit thought to be either a variety of tangerine or a hybrid between a tangerine and sweet orange. [C20: from F *clémentine*]

Clement of Alexandria n. original name *Titus Flavius Clemens.* ?150–?215 A.D., Greek Christian theologian: head of the catechetical school at Alexandria; teacher of Origen.

clench (klɛntʃ) vb. (tr.) **1.** to close or squeeze together (the teeth, a fist, etc.) tightly. **2.** to grasp or grip firmly. ~n. **3.** a firm grasp or grip. **4.** a device that grasps or grips. ~n., vb. **5.** another word for **clinch.** [OE *beclencan*]

Cleon ('kliːɒn) n. died 422 B.C., Athenian demagogue and military leader.

Cleopatra (,kliːə'pætrə, -'pɑː-) n. ?69–30 B.C., queen of Egypt (51–30), renowned for her beauty: the mistress of Julius Caesar and later of Mark Antony. She killed herself with an asp to avoid capture by Octavian (Augustus).

Cleopatra's Needle n. either of two Egyptian obelisks, originally set up at Heliopolis about 1500 B.C.: one was moved to the Thames Embankment, London, in 1878, the other to Central Park, New York, in 1880.

clepsydra ('klɛpsɪdrə) n., pl. **-dras** or **-drae** (-,driː). an ancient device for measuring time by the flow of water or mercury through a small aperture. Also called: **water clock.** [C17: from L, from Gk, from *kleptein* to steal + *hudōr* water]

cleptomania (,klɛptəʊ'meɪnɪə) n. a variant spelling of **kleptomania.**

clerestory or **clearstory** ('klɪə,stɔːrɪ) n., pl. **-ries. 1.** a row of windows in the upper part of the wall of a church that divides the nave from the aisle. **2.** the part of the wall in which these windows are set. [C15: from CLEAR + STOREY] —'**clere,storied** or '**clear,storied** adj.

clergy ('klɜːdʒɪ) n., pl. **-gies.** the collective body of men and women ordained as ministers of the Christian Church. [C13: from OF; see CLERK]

clergyman ('klɜːdʒɪmən) n., pl. **-men.** a member of the clergy.

cleric ('klɛrɪk) n. a member of the clergy. [C17: from Church L *clēricus* priest, CLERK]

clerical ('klɛrɪkᵊl) adj. **1.** relating to or associated with the clergy: *clerical dress.* **2.** of or relating to office clerks or their work: *a clerical error.* **3.** supporting or advocating clericalism. —'**clerically** adv.

clerical collar n. a stiff white collar with no opening at the front that buttons at the back of the neck; the distinctive mark of the clergy in certain Churches. Informal name: **dog collar.**

clericalism ('klɛrɪkᵊ,lɪzəm) n. **1.** a policy of upholding the power of the clergy. **2.** the power of the clergy. —'**clericalist** n.

clericals ('klɛrɪkᵊlz) pl. n. the distinctive dress of a clergyman.

clerihew ('klɛrɪ,hjuː) n. a form of comic or satiric verse, consisting of two couplets of metrically irregular lines, containing the name of a well-known person. [C20: after E. *Clerihew* Bentley (1875–1956), E writer who invented it]

clerk (klɑːk; U.S. klɜːrk) n. **1.** a worker, esp. in an office, who keeps records, files, etc. **2.** an employee of a court, legislature, board, corporation, etc., who keeps records and accounts, etc.: *a town clerk.* Also called: **clerk in holy orders.** a cleric. **4.** U.S. & Canad. short for **sales-clerk. 5.** Also called: **desk clerk.** U.S. & Canad. a hotel receptionist. **6.** Arch. a scholar. ~vb. **7.** (intr.) to serve as a clerk. [OE *clerc*, from Church L *clēricus*, from Gk *klērikos* cleric, from *klēros* heritage] —'**clerkess** n. (chiefly Scot.) —'**clerkish** adj. —'**clerkship** n.

clerk of the works n. an employee who supervises building work in progress.

Clermont-Ferrand (French klɛrmɔ̃fɛrɑ̃) n. a city in S central France: capital of Puy-de-Dôme department; industrial centre. Pop.: 155 010 (1983 est.).

Cleveland[1] ('kliːvlənd) n. **1.** a county of NE England formed in 1974 from parts of E Durham and N Yorkshire. Administrative centre: Middlesbrough. Pop.: 565 775 (1981). Area: 583 sq. km (225 sq. miles). **2.** a port in NE Ohio, on Lake Erie: major heavy industries. Pop.: 535 830 (1986). **3.** a hilly region of NE England, extending from the **Cleveland Hills** to the River Tees.

Cleveland[2] ('kliːvlənd) n. **Stephen Grover.** 1837–1908, U.S. Democratic politician; the 22nd and 24th president of the U.S. (1885–89; 1893–97).

clever ('klɛvə) adj. **1.** displaying sharp intelligence or mental alertness. **2.** adroit or dexterous, esp. with the hands. **3.** smart in a superficial way. **4.** Brit. inf. sly; cunning. [C13 *cliver* (in the sense: quick to seize, adroit), from ?] —'**cleverly** adv. —'**cleverness** n.

clevis ('klɛvɪs) n. the U-shaped component of a shackle. [C16: rel. to CLEAVE[1]]

clew (kluː) n. **1.** a ball of thread, yarn, or twine. **2.** Naut. either of the lower corners of a square sail or the after lower corner of a fore-and-aft sail. ~vb. **3.** (tr.) to coil into a ball. [OE *cliewen* (vb.)]

clianthus (klɪ'ænθəs) n. a leguminous plant of Australia and New Zealand with ornamental clusters of slender flowers. [C19: NL, prob. from Gk *klei-, kleos* glory + *anthos* flower]

cliché ('kliːʃeɪ) n. **1.** a word or expression that has lost much of its force through overexposure. **2.** an idea, action, or habit that has become trite from overuse. **3.** Printing, chiefly Brit. a stereotype or electrotype plate. [C19: from F, from *clicher* to stereotype; imit.] —'**clichéd** or '**cliché'd** adj.

Clichy (kliː'ʃi) n. an industrial suburb of NW Paris: residence of the Merovingian kings (7th century). Pop.: 47 750 (1983 est.). Official name: **Clichy-la-Garenne** (French kliʃilagarɛn).

click (klɪk) n. **1.** a short light often metallic sound. **2.** the locking member of a ratchet mechanism, such as a pawl or detent. **3.** Phonetics. any of various stop consonants that are produced by the suction of air into the mouth. ~vb. **4.** to make or cause to make a clicking sound: *to click one's heels.* **5.** (intr.) Sl. to be a great success: *that idea really clicked.* **6.** (intr.) Inf. to become suddenly clear: *it finally clicked when her name was mentioned.* **7.** (intr.) Sl. to go or fit together with ease: *they clicked from their first meeting.* [C17: imit.] —'**clicker** n.

client ('klaɪənt) n. **1.** a person, company, etc., that seeks the advice of a professional man or woman. **2.** a customer. **3.** a person for whom a social worker, etc., is responsible. [C14: from L *cliēns* retainer, dependent] —'**cliental** (klaɪ'ɛntᵊl) adj.

clientele (,kliːɒn'tɛl) or **clientage** ('klaɪəntɪdʒ) n. customers or clients collectively. [C16: from L, from *cliēns* CLIENT]

cliff (klɪf) n. a steep high rock face, esp. one that runs along the seashore. [OE *clif*] —'**cliffy** adj.

cliffhanger ('klɪf,hæŋə) n. **1. a.** a situation of imminent disaster usually occurring at the end of each episode of a serialized film. **b.** the serialized film itself. **2.** a situation that is dramatic or uncertain. —'**cliff,hanging** adj.

climacteric (klaɪ'mæktərɪk, ,klaɪmæk'tɛrɪk) n. **1.** a critical event or period. **2.** another name for **menopause. 3.** the period in the life of a man corresponding to the menopause, chiefly characterized by diminished sexual activity. ~adj. also **climacterical** (,klaɪmæk'tɛrɪkᵊl). **4.** involving a crucial event or period. [C16: from L, from Gk, from *klimakter* rung of a ladder from *klimax* ladder]

climactic (klaɪ'mæktɪk) or **climactical** adj. consisting of, involving, or causing a climax. —'**cli'mactically** adv.

climate ('klaɪmɪt) n. **1.** the long-term prevalent weather conditions of an area, determined by latitude, altitude, etc. **2.** an area having a particular kind of climate. **3.** a prevailing trend: *the political climate.* [C14: from LL, from Gk *klima* inclination, region] —**climatic** (klaɪ'mætɪk), **cli'matical,** or '**climatal** adj. —**cli'matically** adv.

climatology (,klaɪmə'tɒlədʒɪ) n. the study of climates. —**climatologic** (,klaɪmətə'lɒdʒɪk) or ,**climato'logical** adj. —,**clima'tologist** n.

climax ('klaɪmæks) n. **1.** the most intense or highest point of an experience or of a series of events: *the party was the climax of the week.* **2.** a decisive moment in a dramatic or other work. **3.** a rhetorical device by which a series of sentences, clauses, or phrases are arranged in order of increasing intensity. **4.** Ecology. the stage in the development of a community during which it remains stable under the prevailing environmental conditions. **5.** another word for **orgasm.** ~vb. **6.** to reach or bring to a climax. [C16: from LL, from Gk *klimax* ladder]
▷**Usage.** In formal English careful writers avoid the use of *climax* as a verb. The phrase *reach a climax* is preferred.

climb (klaɪm) vb. (mainly intr.) **1.** (also tr.; often foll. by up) to go up or ascend (stairs, a mountain, etc.). **2.** (often foll. by along) to progress with difficulty: to climb along a ledge. **3.** to rise to a higher point or intensity: the temperature climbed. **4.** to incline or slope upwards: the road began to climb. **5.** to ascend in social position. **6.** (of plants) to grow upwards by twining, using tendrils or suckers, etc. **7.** Inf. (foll. by into) to put (on) or get (into). **8.** to be a climber or mountaineer. ~n. **9.** the act or an instance of climbing. **10.** a place or thing to be climbed, esp. a route in mountaineering. [OE climban] —'**climbable** adj.

climb down vb. (intr., adv.) **1.** to descend. **2.** (often foll. by from) to retreat (from an opinion, position, etc.). ~n. **climb-down.** a retreat from an opinion, etc.

climber ('klaɪmə) n. **1.** a person or thing that climbs, esp. a mountaineer. **2.** a plant that grows upwards by twining or clinging with tendrils and suckers. **3.** Chiefly Brit. short for **social climber.**

clime (klaɪm) n. Poetic. a region or its climate. [C16: from LL clima; see CLIMATE]

clinch (klɪntʃ) vb. **1.** (tr.) to secure (a driven nail), by bending the protruding point over. **2.** (tr.) to hold together in such a manner. **3.** (tr.) to settle (something, such as an argument, bargain, etc.) in a definite way. **4.** (tr.) Naut. to fasten by means of a clinch. **5.** (intr.) to engage in a clinch, as in boxing or wrestling. ~n. **6.** the act of clinching. **7. a.** a nail with its point bent over. **b.** the part of such a nail, etc., that has been bent over. **8.** Boxing, wrestling, etc. an act or an instance in which one or both competitors hold on to the other to avoid punches, regain wind, etc. **9.** Sl. a lovers' embrace. **10.** Naut. a loop or eye formed in a line. ~Also (for senses 1, 2, 4, 7, 8, 10): **clench.** [C16: var. of CLENCH]

clincher ('klɪntʃə) n. **1.** Inf. something decisive, such as fact, score, etc. **2.** a person or thing that clinches.

cline (klaɪn) n. the range of variation of form displayed within a species. [C20: from Gk klinein to lean] —'**clinal** adj.

-cline n. combining form. indicating a slope: anticline. [back formation from INCLINE] —**clinal** adj. combining form.

cling (klɪŋ) vb. **clinging, clung.** (intr.) **1.** (often foll. by to) to hold fast or adhere closely (to something), as by gripping or sticking. **2.** (foll. by together) to remain in contact (with each other). **3.** to be or remain physically or emotionally close. ~n. **4.** short for **clingstone.** [OE clingan] —'**clinging** adj. —'**clingingly** adv. —'**clingy** adj. —'**clinginess** or '**clingingness** n.

clingfilm ('klɪŋ,fɪlm) n. a thin polythene material having the power to adhere closely: used for wrapping food.

clingstone ('klɪŋ,stəʊn) n. **a.** a fruit, such as certain peaches, in which the flesh adheres to the stone. **b.** (as modifier): a clingstone peach.

clinic ('klɪnɪk) n. **1.** a place in which outpatients are given medical treatment or advice. **2.** a similar place staffed by specialist physicians or surgeons: eye clinic. **3.** Brit. a private hospital or nursing home. **4.** the teaching of medicine to students at the bedside. **5.** Chiefly U.S. & Canad. a group or centre that offers advice or instruction. [C17: from L clīnicus one on a sickbed, from Gk, from klinē bed]

clinical ('klɪnɪk^əl) adj. **1.** of or relating to a clinic. **2.** of or relating to the observation and treatment of patients directly: clinical medicine. **3.** scientifically detached; strictly objective: a clinical attitude to life. **4.** plain, simple, and usually unattractive. —'**clinically** adv.

clinical thermometer n. a thermometer for determining the temperature of the body.

clinician (klɪ'nɪʃən) n. a physician, psychiatrist, etc., who specializes in clinical work as opposed to one engaged in experimental studies.

clink[1] (klɪŋk) vb. **1.** to make or cause to make a light and sharply ringing sound. ~n. **2.** such a sound. [C14: ?from MDu. klinken]

clink[2] (klɪŋk) n. a slang word for **prison.** [C16: after Clink, a prison in Southwark, London]

clinker ('klɪŋkə) n. **1.** the ash and partially fused residues from a coal-fired furnace or fire. **2.** a partially vitrified brick or mass of brick. **3.** U.S. sl. a mistake or fault, esp. a wrong note in music. ~vb. **4.** (intr.) to form clinker during burning. [C17: from Du. klinker a type of brick, from klinken to CLINK[1]]

clinker-built or **clincher-built** adj. having a hull-constructed with each that below. [C18 clinker a nailing tog. CLINCH]

clinometer (klaɪ'nɒmɪtə) n. an instrument ... ing for measuring an angle of inclination. — (,klaɪnə'mɛtrɪk) or ,**clino'metrical** adj. —c... .ary n.

Clio ('klaɪəʊ) n. Greek myth. the Muse of history. [C19: from L, from Gk Kleiō, from kleein to celebrate]

clip[1] (klɪp) vb. **clipping, clipped.** (mainly tr.) **1.** (also intr.) to cut, snip, or trim with or as if with scissors or shears, esp. in order to shorten or remove a part. **2.** Brit. to punch (a hole) in something, esp. a ticket. **3.** to curtail or cut short. **4.** to move a short section from (a film, etc.). **5.** to shorten (a word). **6.** Inf. to strike with a sharp, often slanting, blow. **7.** Sl. to defraud or swindle, esp. by overcharging. ~n. **8.** the act or process of clipping. **9.** something clipped off. **10.** a short extract from a film, newspaper, etc. **11.** Inf. a sharp, often slanting, blow. **12.** Inf. speed: a rapid clip. **13.** Austral. & N.Z. the total quantity of wool shorn, as in one place, season, etc. **14.** another word for **clipped form.** [C12: from ON klippa to cut]

clip[2] (klɪp) n. **1.** any of various small implements used to hold loose articles together or to attach one article to another. **2.** an article of jewellery that can be clipped onto a dress, hat, etc. **3.** short for **paperclip** or **cartridge clip.** ~vb. **clipping, clipped.** (tr.) **4.** to hold together tightly, as with a clip. [OE clyppan to embrace]

clipboard ('klɪp,bɔːd) n. a portable writing board with a clip at the top for holding paper.

clip joint n. Sl. a place, such as a nightclub or restaurant, in which customers are overcharged.

clipped (klɪpt) adj. (of speech or tone of voice) abrupt, terse, and distinct.

clipped form n. a shortened form of a word.

clipper ('klɪpə) n. **1.** any fast sailing ship. **2.** a person or thing that cuts or clips.

clippers ('klɪpəz) or **clips** pl. n. **1.** a hand tool for clipping fingernails, veneers, etc. **2.** a hairdresser's tool for cutting short hair.

clippie ('klɪpɪ) n. Brit. inf. a bus conductress.

clipping ('klɪpɪŋ) n. something cut out, esp. an article from a newspaper; cutting.

clique (kliːk, klɪk) n. a small exclusive group of friends or associates. [C18: from F, ?from OF: latch, from cliquer to click] —'**cliquey** or '**cliquy** adj. —'**cliquish** adj. —'cliquishly adv. —'**cliquishness** n.

Clisthenes ('klaɪsθə,niːz) n. a variant spelling of **Cleisthenes.**

clitoris ('klɪtərɪs, 'klaɪ-) n. a part of the female genitalia consisting of a small elongated highly sensitive erectile organ at the front of the vulva: homologous with the penis. [C17: from NL, from Gk kleitoris] —'**clitoral** adj.

Clive (klaɪv) n. **Robert,** Baron Clive of Plassey. 1725–74, British general and statesman, whose victory at Plassey (1757) strengthened British control in India.

Cllr abbrev. for Councillor.

cloaca (kləʊ'eɪkə) n., pl. **-cae** (-kiː). **1.** a cavity in most vertebrates, except higher mammals, and certain invertebrates, into which the alimentary canal and the genital and urinary ducts open. **2.** a sewer. [C18: from L: sewer] —**clo'acal** adj.

cloak (kləʊk) n. **1.** a wraplike outer garment fastened at the throat and falling straight from the shoulders. **2.** something that covers or conceals. ~vb. (tr.) **3.** to cover with or as if with a cloak. **4.** to hide or disguise. [C13: from OF cloque, from Med. L clocca cloak, bell]

cloak-and-dagger n. (modifier) characteristic of or concerned with intrigue and espionage.

cloakroom ('kləʊk,ruːm, -rʊm) n. **1.** a room in which hats, coats, etc., may be temporarily deposited. **2.** Brit. a euphemistic word for **lavatory.**

clobber[1] ('klɒbə) vb. (tr.) Sl. **1.** to batter. **2.** to defeat utterly. **3.** to criticize severely. [C20: from ?]

clobber[2] ('klɒbə) n. Brit. sl. personal belongings, such as clothes. [C19: from ?]

clobbering machine n. N.Z. inf. pressure to conform with accepted standards.

cloche (klɒʃ) n. **1.** a bell-shaped cover used to protect young plants. **2.** a woman's close-fitting hat. [C19: from F: bell, from Med. L clocca]

ᵃ (klɒk) *n.* **1.** a timepiece having mechanically or electrically driven pointers that move constantly over a dial showing the numbers of the hours. Cf. **watch** (sense 7). **2.** any clocklike device for recording or measuring, such as a taximeter or pressure gauge. **3.** the downy head of a dandelion that has gone to seed. **4.** short for **time clock**. **5.** (usually preceded by *the*) an informal word for **speedometer** or **mileometer**. **6.** *Brit.* a slang word for **face**. **7. around** *or* **round the clock.** all day and all night. ~*vb.* (*tr.*) **8.** *Brit., Austral., & N.Z. sl.* to strike, esp. on the face or head. **9.** to record time as with a stopwatch, esp. in the calculation of speed. **10.** *Inf.* to turn back the mileometer on (a car) illegally so that its mileage appears less. [C14: from MDu. *clocke* clock, from Med. L *clocca* bell, ult. of Celtic origin]

clock² (klɒk) *n.* an ornamental design on the side of a stocking. [C16: see CLOCK¹]

clock off *or* **out** *vb.* (*intr., adv.*) to depart from work, esp. when it involves registering the time of departure on a card.

clock on *or* **in** *vb.* (*intr., adv.*) to arrive at work, esp. when it involves registering the time of arrival on a card.

clock up *vb.* (*tr., adv.*) to record or register: *this car has clocked up 80 000 miles.*

clock-watcher *n.* an employee who frequently checks the time in anticipation of a break or of the end of the working day.

clockwise ('klɒk,waɪz) *adv., adj.* in the direction that the hands of a clock rotate; from top to bottom towards the right when seen from the front.

clockwork ('klɒk,wɜːk) *n.* **1.** the mechanism of a clock. **2.** any similar mechanism, as in a wind-up toy. **3. like clockwork.** with complete regularity and precision; smoothly.

clod (klɒd) *n.* **1.** a lump of earth or clay. **2.** earth, esp. when heavy or in hard lumps. **3.** Also called: **clod poll, clodpate.** a dull or stupid person. [OE *clod-* (occurring in compound words) lump] —'**cloddy** *adj.* —'**cloddish** *adj.* —'**cloddishly** *adv.* —'**cloddishness** *n.*

clodhopper ('klɒd,hɒpə) *n. Inf.* **1.** a clumsy person; lout. **2.** (*usually pl.*) a large heavy shoe.

clog (klɒg) *vb.* **clogging, clogged. 1.** to obstruct or become obstructed with thick or sticky matter. **2.** (*tr.*) to encumber; hinder; impede. **3.** (*intr.*) to adhere or stick in a mass. ~*n.* **4. a.** any of various wooden or woodensoled shoes. **b.** (*as modifier*): *clog dance.* **5.** a heavy block, esp. of wood, fastened to the leg of a person or animal to impede motion. **6.** something that impedes motion or action; hindrance. [C14 (in the sense: block of wood): from ?] —'**cloggy** *adj.*

cloisonné (klwɑː'zɒneɪ) *n.* **1. a.** a design made by filling in with coloured enamel an outline of flattened wire put on edge. **b.** the method of doing this. ~*adj.* **2.** of or made by cloisonné. [C19: from F, from *cloisonner* to divide into compartments, ult. from L *claudere* to close]

cloister ('klɔɪstə) *n.* **1.** a covered walk, usually around a quadrangle in a religious institution, having an open colonnade on the inside. **2.** (*sometimes pl.*) a place of religious seclusion, such as a monastery. **3.** life in a monastery or convent. ~*vb.* **4.** (*tr.*) to confine or seclude in or as if in a monastery. [C13: from OF *cloistre*, from Med. L *claustrum* monastic cell, from L *claudere* to close] —'**cloistered** *adj.* —'**cloistral** *adj.*

clomb (kləʊm) *vb. Arch.* a past tense and past participle of **climb.**

clomp (klɒmp) *n., vb.* a less common word for **clump** (senses 2, 7).

clone (kləʊn) *n.* **1.** a group of organisms or cells of the same genetic constitution that are descended from a common ancestor by asexual reproduction, as by cuttings, grafting, etc. **2.** a segment of DNA that has been isolated and replicated by laboratory manipulation. **3.** *Inf.* a person or thing that closely resembles another. ~*vb.* **4.** to produce or cause to produce a clone. **5.** *Inf.* to produce near copies of (a person or thing). [C20: from Gk *klōn* twig, shoot] —'**cloning** *n.*

clonk (klɒŋk) *vb.* (*intr.*) **1.** to make a loud dull thud. **2.** (*tr.*) *Inf.* to hit. ~*n.* **3.** a loud thud. [C20: imit.]

clonus ('kləʊnəs) *n.* a type of convulsion characterized by rapid contraction and relaxation of a muscle. [C19: from NL, from Gk *klonos* turmoil] —**clonic** ('klɒnɪk) *adj.* —**clonicity** (klɒ'nɪsɪtɪ) *n.*

clop (klɒp) *vb.* **clopping, clopped. 1.** (*intr.*) to make or move along with a sound as of a horse's hooves striking the ground. ~*n.* **2.** a sound of this nature. [C20: imit.]

close¹ (kləʊs) *adj.* **1.** near in space or time; in proximity. **2.** having the parts near together; dense: *a close formation.* **3.** near to the surface; short: *a close haircut.* **4.** near in relationship: *a close relative.* **5.** intimate: *a close friend.* **6.** almost equal: *a close contest.* **7.** not deviating or varying greatly from a model or standard: *a close resemblance; a close translation.* **8.** careful, strict, or searching: *a close study.* **9.** confined or enclosed. **10.** shut or shut tight. **11.** oppressive, heavy, or airless: *a close atmosphere.* **12.** strictly guarded: *a close prisoner.* **13.** neat or tight in fit. **14.** secretive or reticent. **15.** miserly; not generous, esp. with money. **16.** (of money or credit) hard to obtain. **17.** restricted as to public admission or membership. **18.** hidden or secluded. **19** Also: **closed.** restricted or prohibited as to the type of game or fish able to be taken. ~*adv.* **20.** closely; tightly. **21.** near or in proximity. **22. close to the wind.** *Naut.* sailing as nearly as possible towards the direction from which the wind is blowing. See also **wind¹**(sense 23). [C13: from OF *clos*, from L *clausus*, from *claudere* to close] —'**closely** *adv.* —'**closeness** *n.*

close² (kləʊz) *vb.* **1.** to put or be put in such a position as to cover an opening; shut: *the door closed behind him.* **2.** (*tr.*) to bar, obstruct, or fill up (an entrance, a hole, etc.): *to close a road.* **3.** to bring the parts or edges of (a wound, etc.) together or (of a wound, etc.) to be brought together. **4.** (*intr.; foll. by on, over, etc.*) to take hold: *his hand closed over the money.* **5.** to bring or be brought to an end; terminate. **6.** (of agreements, deals, etc.) to complete or be completed successfully. **7.** to cease or cause to cease to render service: *the shop closed at six.* **8.** (*intr.*) *Stock Exchange.* to have a value at the end of a day's trading, as specified: *steels closed two points down.* **9.** (*tr.*) *Arch.* to enclose or shut in. ~*n.* **10.** the act of closing. **11.** the end or conclusion: *the close of the day.* **12.** (kləʊs). *Brit.* a courtyard or quadrangle enclosed by buildings or an entry leading to such a courtyard. **13.** (kləʊs). *Brit.* (*cap. when part of a street name*) a small quiet residential road: *Hillside Close.* **14.** (kləʊs). the precincts of a cathedral or similar building. **15.** (kləʊs). *Scot.* the entry from the street to a tenement building. ~See also **close down, close in**, etc. [C13: from OF *clos*, from L *clausus*, from *claudere* to close] —'**closer** *n.*

close company *n.* a company that is controlled by its directors or by five or fewer participants.

closed (kləʊzd) *adj.* **1.** blocked against entry; shut. **2.** restricted; exclusive. **3.** not open to question or debate. **4.** (of a hunting season, etc.) close. **5.** *Maths.* **a.** (of a curve or surface) completely enclosing an area or volume. **b.** (of a set) having members that can be produced by a specific operation on other members of the same set. **6.** *Phonetics.* denoting a syllable that ends in a consonant. **7.** not open to public entry or membership: *a closed society.*

closed chain *n. Chem.* another name for **ring¹** (sense 17).

closed circuit *n.* a complete electrical circuit through which current can flow.

closed-circuit television *n.* a television system in which signals are transmitted from the television camera to the receivers by cables or telephone links.

close down (kləʊz) *vb.* **1.** to cease or cause to cease operations. ~*n.* **close-down. 2.** a closure or stoppage, esp. in a factory. **3.** *Brit. radio, television.* the end of a period of broadcasting, esp. late at night.

closed shop *n.* an industrial establishment in which there exists a contract between a trade union and the employer permitting the employment of the union's members only.

close-fisted (,kləʊs'fɪstɪd) *adj.* very careful with money; mean. —,**close-'fistedness** *n.*

close harmony (kləʊs) *n.* a type of singing in which all the parts except the bass lie close together.

close-hauled (,kləʊs'hɔːld) *adj. Naut.* with the sails flat, so as to sail as close to the wind as possible.

close in (kləʊz) *vb.* (*intr., adv.*) **1.** (of days) to become shorter with the approach of winter. **2.** (foll. by *on* or *upon*) to advance (on) so as to encircle or surround.

close out (kləʊz) *vb.* (*adv.*) to terminate (a client's or other account) usually by sale of securities to realize cash.

close punctuation (kləʊs) *n.* punctuation in which many commas, full stops, etc., are used. Cf. **open punctuation.**

close quarters (kləʊs) *pl. n.* **1.** a narrow cramped space or position. **2. at close quarters. a.** engaged in hand-to-hand combat. **b.** in close proximity; very near together.

close season (kləʊs) *or* **closed season** *n.* the period of the year when it is prohibited to kill certain game or fish.

close shave (kləʊs) *n. Inf.* a narrow escape.

closet ('klɒzɪt) *n.* **1.** a small cupboard or recess. **2.** a small private room. **3.** short for **water closet. 4.** (*modifier*) private or secret. ~*vb.* **5.** (*tr.*) to shut up or confine in a small private room, esp. for conference or meditation. [C14: from OF, from *clos* enclosure; see CLOSE[1]]

close-up ('kləʊs,ʌp) *n.* **1.** a photograph or film or television shot taken at close range. **2.** a detailed or intimate view or examination. ~*vb.* **close up** (kləʊz). (*adv.*) **3.** to shut entirely. **4.** (*intr.*) to draw together: *the ranks closed up.* **5.** (*intr.*) (of wounds) to heal completely.

close with (kləʊz) *vb.* (*intr., prep.*) to engage in battle with (an enemy).

closure ('kləʊʒə) *n.* **1.** the act of closing or the state of being closed. **2.** an end or conclusion. **3.** something that closes or shuts, such as a cap or seal for a container. **4.** (in a deliberative body) a procedure by which debate may be halted and an immediate vote taken. ~*vb.* **5.** (*tr.*) (in a deliberative body) to end (debate) by closure. [C14: from OF, from LL, from L *claudere* to close]

clot (klɒt) *n.* **1.** a soft thick lump or mass. **2.** *Brit. inf.* a stupid person; fool. ~*vb.* **clotting, clotted. 3.** to form or cause to form into a soft thick lump or lumps. [OE *clott*, of Gmc origin]

cloth (klɒθ) *n.*, *pl.* **cloths** (klɒθs, klɒðz). **1. a.** a fabric formed by weaving, felting or knitting wool, cotton, etc. **b.** (*as modifier*): *a cloth bag.* **2.** a piece of such fabric used for a particular purpose, as for a dishcloth. **3.** (usually preceded by *the*) the clergy. [OE *clāth*]

clothe (kləʊð) *vb.* **clothing, clothed** *or* **clad.** (*tr.*) **1.** to dress or attire (a person). **2.** to provide with clothing. **3.** to conceal or disguise. **4.** to endow or invest. [OE *clāthian*, from *clāth* cloth]

clothes (kləʊðz) *pl. n.* **1.** articles of dress. **2.** *Chiefly Brit.* short for **bedclothes.** [OE *clāthas*, pl. of *clāth* cloth]

clotheshorse ('kləʊðz,hɔːs) *n.* **1.** a frame on which to hang laundry for drying or airing. **2.** *Inf.* an excessively fashionable person.

clothesline ('kləʊðz,laɪn) *n.* a piece of rope or wire on which clean washing is hung to dry.

clothes peg *n.* a small wooden or plastic clip for attaching washing to a clothesline.

clothes pole *n.* a post to which a clothesline is attached. Also called: **clothes post.**

clothes-press *n.* a piece of furniture for storing clothes, usually containing wide drawers.

clothes prop *n.* a long wooden pole with a forked end used to raise a line of washing to enable it to catch the breeze.

clothier ('kləʊðɪə) *n.* a person who makes, sells, or deals in clothes or cloth.

clothing ('kləʊðɪŋ) *n.* **1.** garments collectively. **2.** something that covers or clothes.

Clotho ('kləʊθəʊ) *n. Greek myth.* one of the three Fates, spinner of the thread of life. [L, from Gk *Klōthō*, one who spins, from *klōthein* to spin]

cloth of gold *n.* cloth woven from silk threads interspersed with gold.

clotted cream *n. Brit.* a thick cream made from scalded milk, esp. in SW England.

cloture ('kləʊtʃə) *n.* **1.** closure in the U.S. Senate. ~*vb.* **2.** (*tr.*) to end (debate) by cloture. [C19: from F *clôture,* from OF CLOSURE]

cloud (klaʊd) *n.* **1.** a mass of water or ice particles visible in the sky. **2.** any collection of particles visible in the air, esp. of smoke or dust. **3.** a large number of insects or other small animals in flight. **4.** something that darkens, threatens, or carries gloom. **5.** *Jewellery.* a cloudlike blemish in a transparent stone. **6. in the clouds.** not in contact with reality. **7. on cloud nine.** *Inf.* elated; very happy. **8. under a cloud. a.** under reproach or suspicion. **b.** in a state of gloom or bad temper. ~*vb.* **9.** (when *intr.*,

often foll. by *over* or *up*) to make or become cloudy, overcast, or indistinct. **10.** (*tr.*) to make obscure; darken. **11.** to make or become gloomy or depressed. **12.** (*tr.*) to place under or render liable to suspicion or disgrace. **13.** to render (liquids) milky or dull or (of liquids) to become milky or dull. [C13 (in the sense: a mass of vapour): from OE *clūd* rock, hill] —'**cloudless** *adj.* —'**cloudlessly** *adv.* —'**cloudlessness** *n.*

cloudburst ('klaʊd,bɜːst) *n.* a heavy downpour.

cloud chamber *n. Physics.* an apparatus for detecting high-energy particles by observing their tracks through a chamber containing a supersaturated vapour.

cloud-cuckoo-land *n.* a realm of fantasy, dreams, or impractical notions.

cloudy ('klaʊdɪ) *adj.* **cloudier, cloudiest. 1.** covered with cloud or clouds. **2.** of or like clouds. **3.** streaked or mottled like a cloud. **4.** opaque or muddy. **5.** obscure or unclear. **6.** troubled or gloomy. —'**cloudily** *adv.* —'**cloudiness** *n.*

Clouet (*French* kluɛ) *n.* **François** (frɑ̃swa), ?1515–72, and his father, **Jean** (ʒɑ̃), ?1485–?1540, French portrait painters.

clough (klʌf) *n. Dialect.* a ravine. [OE *clōh*]

Clough (klʌf) *n.* **Arthur Hugh.** 1819–61, English poet.

clout (klaʊt) *n.* **1.** *Inf.* a blow with the hand or a hard object. **2.** power or influence, esp. political. **3.** Also called: **clout nail.** a short, flat-headed nail. **4.** *Dialect.* **a.** a piece of cloth: *a dish clout.* **b.** a garment. ~*vb.* (*tr.*) **5.** *Inf.* to give a hard blow to, esp. with the hand. [OE *clūt* piece of metal or cloth, *clūtian* to patch (C14: to strike with the hand)]

clove[1] (kləʊv) *n.* **1.** a tropical evergreen tree of the myrtle family. **2.** the dried unopened flower buds of this tree, used as a pungent fragrant spice. [C14: from OF, lit.: nail of clove, *clou* from L *clāvus* nail + *girofle* clove tree]

clove[2] (kləʊv) *n.* any of the segments of a compound bulb that arise from the axils of the scales of a large bulb. [OE *clufu* bulb; see CLEAVE[1]]

clove[3] (kləʊv) *vb.* a past tense of **cleave**[1].

clove hitch *n.* a knot or hitch used for securing a rope to a spar, post, or larger rope.

cloven ('kləʊvᵊn) *vb.* **1.** a past participle of **cleave**[1]. ~*adj.* **2.** split; cleft; divided.

cloven hoof *or* **foot** *n.* **1.** the divided hoof of a pig, goat, cow, deer, or related animal. **2.** the mark or symbol of Satan. —,**cloven-'hoofed** *or* ,**cloven-'footed** *adj.*

clover ('kləʊvə) *n.* **1.** a leguminous fodder plant having trifoliate leaves and dense flower heads. **2.** any of various similar or related plants. **3. in clover.** *Inf.* in a state of ease or luxury. [OE *clǣfre*]

cloverleaf ('kləʊvə,liːf) *n., pl.* **-leaves. 1.** an arrangement of connecting roads, resembling a four-leaf clover in form, that joins two intersecting main roads. **2.** (*modifier*) in the shape or pattern of a leaf of clover.

Clovis I ('kləʊvɪs) *n.* German name *Chlodwig.* ?466–511 A.D., king of the Franks (481–511), who extended the Merovingian kingdom to include most of Gaul and SW Germany.

clown (klaʊn) *n.* **1.** a comic entertainer, usually grotesquely costumed and made up, appearing in the circus. **2.** a person who acts in a comic or buffoon-like manner. **3.** a clumsy rude person; boor. **4.** *Arch.* a countryman or rustic. ~*vb.* (*intr.*) **5.** to perform as a clown. **6.** to play jokes or tricks. **7.** to act foolishly. [C16: ?from Low G] —'**clownery** *n.* —'**clownish** *adj.* —'**clownishly** *adv.* —'**clownishness** *n.*

cloy (klɔɪ) *vb.* to make weary or cause weariness through an excess of something initially pleasurable or sweet. [C14 (orig.: to nail, hence, to obstruct): from earlier *acloyen,* from OF, from Med. L *inclavāre,* from L, from *clāvus* a nail] —'**cloyingly** *adv.*

cloze test (kləʊz) *n.* a test of the ability to comprehend text in which the reader has to supply the missing words that have been removed from the text. [altered from *close* to complete a pattern (in Gestalt theory)]

club (klʌb) *n.* **1.** a stout stick, usually with one end thicker than the other, esp. one used as a weapon. **2.** a stick or bat used to strike the ball in various sports, esp. golf. See **golf club. 3.** short for **Indian club. 4.** a group or association of people with common aims or interests. **5.** the room, building, or facilities used by such a group. **6.** a building in which elected, fee-paying members go to meet, dine, read, etc. **7.** a commercial establishment providing drinks, food, etc. See also **nightclub. 8.** *Chiefly Brit.* an organization, esp. in a shop, set up as a means of saving. **9.** *Brit.* an informal word for **friendly society. 10. a.** the black trefoil symbol on a playing card. **b.** a card with one or more of these symbols or (*when pl.*) the suit of cards so marked. **11. in the club.** *Brit. sl.* pregnant. ~*vb.* **clubbing, clubbed. 12.** (*tr.*) to beat with or as if with a club. **13.** (often foll. by *together*) to gather or become gathered into a group. **14.** (often foll. by *together*) to unite or combine (resources, efforts, etc.) for a common purpose. [C13: from ON *klubba*, rel. to CLUMP] —'**clubber** *n.*

club foot *n.* **1.** a congenital deformity of the foot, esp. one in which the foot is twisted so that most of the weight rests on the heel. Technical name: **talipes. 2.** a foot so deformed. —,**club·'footed** *adj.*

clubhouse ('klʌb,haʊs) *n.* the premises of a sports or other club, esp. a golf club.

clubman ('klʌbmən) *or* (*fem.*) **clubwoman** *n.*, *pl.* **-men** *or* **-women.** a person who is an enthusiastic member of a club or clubs.

club root *n.* a fungal disease of cabbages and related plants, in which the roots become thickened and distorted.

cluck (klʌk) *n.* **1.** the low clicking sound made by a hen or any similar sound. ~*vb.* **2.** (*intr.*) (of a hen) to make a clicking sound. **3.** (*tr.*) to call or express (a feeling) by making a similar sound. [C17: imit.]

clucky ('klʌkɪ) *adj. Austral. sl.* **1.** pregnant. **2.** preoccupied with the idea of having children.

clue (klu:) *n.* **1.** something that helps to solve a problem or unravel a mystery. **2. not have a clue. a.** to be completely baffled. **b.** to be ignorant or incompetent. ~*vb.* **cluing, clued. 3.** (*tr.*; usually foll. by *in* or *up*) to provide with helpful information. [C15: var. of CLEW]

clueless ('klu:lɪs) *adj. Sl.* helpless; stupid.

Cluj (kluʒ, klu:ʒ) *n.* an industrial city in NW Romania, on the Someşul-Mic River: former capital of Transylvania. Pop.: 309 843 (1985). German name: **Klausenburg.** Hungarian name: **Kolozsvár.**

clump (klʌmp) *n.* **1.** a cluster, as of trees or plants. **2.** a dull heavy tread or any similar sound. **3.** an irregular mass. **4.** an inactive mass of microorganisms, esp. a mass of bacteria produced as a result of agglutination. **5.** an extra sole on a shoe. **6.** *Sl.* a blow. ~*vb.* **7.** (*intr.*) to walk or tread heavily. **8.** to gather or be gathered into clumps, clusters, clots, etc. **9.** to cause (bacteria, blood cells, etc.) to collect together or (of bacteria, etc.) to collect together. See also **agglutination** (sense 3). **10.** (*tr.*) *Sl.* to punch (someone). [OE *clympe*] —'**clumpy** *adj.*

clumsy ('klʌmzɪ) *adj.* **-sier, -siest. 1.** lacking in skill or physical coordination. **2.** awkwardly constructed or contrived. [C16 (in obs. sense: benumbed with cold; hence, awkward): ?from C13 dialect *clumse* to benumb, prob. of Scand. origin] —'**clumsily** *adv.* —'**clumsiness** *n.*

clung (klʌŋ) *vb.* the past tense and past participle of **cling.**

clunk (klʌŋk) *n.* **1.** a blow or the sound of a blow. **2.** a dull metallic sound. ~*vb.* **3.** to make or cause to make such a sound. [C19: imit.]

Cluny ('klu:nɪ; *French* klyni) *n.* a town in E central France: reformed Benedictine order founded here in 910; important religious and cultural centre in the Middle Ages. Pop.: 4734 (1982 est.). —'**Cluniac** *adj.*

cluster ('klʌstə) *n.* **1.** a number of things growing, fastened, or occurring close together. **2.** a number of persons or things grouped together. ~*vb.* **3.** to gather or be gathered in clusters. [OE *clyster*] —'**clustered** *adj.* —'**clustery** *adj.*

clutch[1] (klʌtʃ) *vb.* **1.** (*tr.*) to seize with or as if with hands or claws. **2.** (*tr.*) to grasp or hold firmly. **3.** (*intr.*; usually foll. by *at*) to attempt to get hold or possession (of). ~*n.* **4.** a device that enables two revolving shafts to be joined or disconnected, esp. one that transmits the drive from the engine to the gearbox in a vehicle. **5.** a device for holding fast. **6.** a firm grasp. **7.** a hand, claw, or talon in the act of clutching: *in the clutches of a bear.* **8.** (*often pl.*) power or control: *in the clutches of the Mafia.* [OE *clyccan*]

clutch[2] (klʌtʃ) *n.* **1.** a hatch of eggs laid by a particular bird or laid in a single nest. **2.** a brood of chickens. **3.**

Inf. a group or cluster. ~*vb.* **4.** (*tr.*) to hatch (chickens). [C17 (N English dialect) *cletch*, from ON *klekja* to hatch]

Clutha ('klu:θə) *n.* a river in New Zealand, the longest river in South Island; rising in the Southern Alps it flows southeast to the Pacific. Length: 338 km (210 miles).

clutter ('klʌtə) *vb.* **1.** (*usually tr.;* often foll. by *up*) to strew or amass (objects) in a disorderly manner. **2.** (*intr.*) to move about in a bustling manner. ~*n.* **3.** a disordered heap or mass of objects. **4.** a state of disorder. **5.** unwanted echoes that confuse the observation of signals on a radar screen. [C15 *clotter*, from *clotteren* to CLOT]

Clwyd ('klu:ɪd) *n.* a county in NE Wales, formed in 1974 from Flintshire, most of Denbighshire, and part of Merionethshire: generally hilly or mountainous. Administrative centre: Mold. Pop.: 399 600 (1986 est.). Area: 2426 sq. km (936 sq. miles).

Clyde (klaɪd) *n.* **1. Firth of.** an inlet of the Atlantic in SW Scotland. Length: 103 km (64 miles). **2.** a river in S Scotland, rising in SE Strathclyde and flowing northwest to the Firth of Clyde: formerly extensive shipyards. Length: 170 km (106 miles).

Clydebank (,klaɪd'bæŋk, 'klaɪd,bæŋk) *n.* a town in W Scotland, in Strathclyde region on the north bank of the River Clyde. Pop.: 51 656 (1981).

Clydesdale ('klaɪdz,deɪl) *n.* a heavy powerful breed of carthorse, originally from Scotland.

clypeus ('klɪpɪəs) *n.*, *pl.* **clypei** ('klɪpɪ,aɪ). a cuticular plate on the head of some insects. [C19: from NL, from L *clipeus* round shield] —'**clypeal** *adj.* —**clypeate** ('klɪpɪ,eɪt) *adj.*

clyster ('klɪstə) *n. Med.* a former name for **enema.** [C14: from Gk *klustēr*, from *kluzein* to rinse]

Clytemnestra *or* **Clytaemnestra** (,klaɪtɪm'nɛstrə) *n. Greek myth.* the wife of Agamemnon, whom she killed on his return from the Trojan War.

cm *symbol for* centimetre.

Cm *the chemical symbol for* curium.

Cmdr *Mil. abbrev. for* Commander.

CMG *abbrev. for* Companion of St Michael and St George (a Brit. title).

CNAA *abbrev. for* Council for National Academic Awards.

CND (in Britain) *abbrev. for* Campaign for Nuclear Disarmament.

Cnidus ('naɪdəs, 'knaɪ-) *n.* an ancient Greek city in SW Asia Minor: famous for its school of medicine.

Cnossus ('nɒsəs, 'knɒs-) *n.* a variant spelling of **Knossos.**

Cnut (kə'nju:t) *n.* a variant spelling of **Canute.**

Co *the chemical symbol for* cobalt.

CO *abbrev. for:* **1.** Commanding Officer. **2.** conscientious objector.

Co. *or* **co.** *abbrev. for:* **1.** (esp. in names of business organizations) Company. **2. and co.** (kəʊ) *Inf.* and the rest of them: *Harold and co.*

Co. *abbrev. for* County.

co- *prefix.* **1.** together; joint or jointly; mutual or mutually: *coproduction.* **2.** indicating partnership or equality: *costar; copilot.* **3.** to the same or a similar degree: *coextend.* **4.** (in mathematics and astronomy) of the complement of an angle: *cosecant.* [from L, reduced form of COM-]

c/o *abbrev. for:* **1.** care of. **2.** *Book-keeping.* carried over.

coach (kəʊtʃ) *n.* **1.** a vehicle for several passengers, used for transport over long distances, sightseeing, etc. **2.** a large four-wheeled enclosed carriage, usually horse-drawn. **3.** a railway carriage. **4.** a trainer or instructor: *a drama coach.* **5.** a tutor who prepares students for examinations. ~*vb.* **6.** to give tuition or instruction to (a pupil). **7.** (*tr.*) to transport in a bus or coach. [C16: from F *coche,* from Hungarian *kocsi szekér* wagon of Kocs, village in Hungary where coaches were first made] —'**coacher** *n.*

coach-built *adj.* (of a vehicle) having specially built bodywork. —'**coach-,builder** *n.*

coach dog *n.* a former name for **Dalmatian.**

coachman ('kəʊtʃmən) *n.*, *pl.* **-men.** the driver of a coach or carriage.

coachwork ('kəʊtʃ,wɜ:k) *n.* **1.** the design and manufacture of car bodies. **2.** the body of a car.

coadjutor (kəʊ'ædʒʊtə) *n.* **1.** a bishop appointed as assistant to a diocesan bishop. **2.** *Rare.* an assistant. [C15:

via OF from L *co-* together + *adjūtor* helper, from *adjūtāre* to assist]

coagulate *vb.* (kəʊˈægjʊˌleɪt). **1.** to cause (a fluid, such as blood) to change into a soft semisolid mass or (of such a fluid) to change into such a mass; clot; curdle. ~*n.* (kəʊˈægjʊlɪt, -ˌleɪt). **2.** the solid or semisolid substance produced by coagulation. [C16: from L *coāgulāre*, from *coāgulum* rennet, from *cōgere* to drive together] —**co'agulant** *or* **co'aguˌlator** *n.* —**coˌaguˈlation** *n.* —**coagulative** (kəʊˈægjʊlətɪv) *adj.*

Coahuila (*Spanish* koaˈuila) *n.* a state of N Mexico: mainly plateau, crossed by several mountain ranges that contain rich mineral resources. Capital: Saltillo. Pop.: 1 735 586 (1983 est.). Area: 151 571 sq. km (59 112 sq. miles).

coal (kəʊl) *n.* **1. a.** a compact black or dark brown carbonaceous rock consisting of layers of partially decomposed vegetation deposited in the Carboniferous period: a fuel and a source of coke, coal gas, and coal tar. **b.** (*as modifier*): *coal cellar; coal mine; coal dust.* **2.** one or more lumps of coal. **3.** short for **charcoal. 4. coals to Newcastle.** something supplied where it is already plentiful. ~*vb.* **5.** to take in, provide with, or turn into coal. [OE *col*] —**'coaly** *adj.*

coaler ('kəʊlə) *n.* a ship, train, etc., used to carry or supply coal.

coalesce (ˌkəʊəˈlɛs) *vb.* (*intr.*) to unite or come together in one body or mass; merge; fuse; blend. [C16: from L co- + *alēscere* to increase, from *alere* to nourish] —ˌcoa'lescence *n.* —ˌcoa'lescent *adj.*

coalface ('kəʊlˌfeɪs) *n.* the exposed seam of coal in a mine.

coalfield ('kəʊlˌfiːld) *n.* an area rich in deposits of coal.

coalfish ('kəʊlˌfɪʃ) *n.*, *pl.* **-fish** *or* **-fishes.** a dark-coloured gadoid food fish occurring in northern seas. Also called (Brit.): **saithe, coley.**

coal gas *n.* a mixture of gases produced by the distillation of bituminous coal and used for heating and lighting.

coalition (ˌkəʊəˈlɪʃən) *n.* **1. a.** an alliance between groups or parties, esp. for some temporary and specific reason. **b.** (*as modifier*): *a coalition government.* **2.** a fusion or merging into one body or mass. [C17: from Med. L *coalitiō*, from L *coalēscere* to COALESCE] —ˌcoa'litionist *n.*

Coal Measures *pl. n.* **the.** a series of coal-bearing rocks formed in the upper Carboniferous period.

coal scuttle *n.* a container to supply coal to a domestic fire.

coal tar *n.* a black tar, produced by the distillation of bituminous coal, that can be further distilled to yield benzene, toluene, etc.

coal tit *n.* a small European songbird having a black head with a white patch on the nape.

coaming ('kəʊmɪŋ) *n.* a raised frame round a ship's hatchway for keeping out water. [C17: from ?]

coarse (kɔːs) *adj.* **1.** rough in texture, structure, etc.; not fine: *coarse sand.* **2.** lacking refinement or taste; indelicate; vulgar: *coarse jokes.* **3.** of inferior quality. **4.** (of a metal) not refined. [C14: from ?] —**'coarsely** *adv.* —**'coarseness** *n.*

coarse fish *n.* a freshwater fish that is not of the salmon family. —**coarse fishing** *n.*

coarsen ('kɔːsᵊn) *vb.* to make or become coarse.

coast (kəʊst) *n.* **1.** the line or zone where the land meets the sea. Related adj.: **littoral. 2.** *Brit.* the seaside. **3.** *U.S.* **a.** a slope down which a sledge may slide. **b.** the act or an instance of sliding down a slope. **4. the coast is clear.** *Inf.* the obstacles or dangers are gone. ~*vb.* **5.** to move or cause to move by momentum or force of gravity. **6.** (*intr.*) to proceed without great effort: *to coast to victory.* **7.** to sail along (a coast). [C13: from OF *coste*, from L *costa* side, rib] —**'coastal** *adj.*

coaster ('kəʊstə) *n.* **1.** *Brit.* a vessel engaged in coastal commerce. **2.** a small tray for holding a decanter, wine bottle, etc. **3.** a person or thing that coasts. **4.** a protective mat for glasses. **5.** *U.S.* short for **roller coaster.**

Coaster ('kəʊstə) *n.* *N.Z.* a person from the West Coast of the South Island, New Zealand.

coastguard ('kəʊstˌgɑːd) *n.* **1.** a maritime force which aids shipping, saves lives at sea, prevents smuggling, etc. **2.** Also called: **coastguardsman.** a member of such a force.

coastline ('kəʊstˌlaɪn) *n.* the outline of a coast.

Coast Mountains *pl. n.* a mountain range in Canada, on the Pacific coast of British Columbia. Highest peak: Mount Waddington, 4043 m (13 266 ft.).

coat (kəʊt) *n.* **1.** an outdoor garment with sleeves, covering the body from the shoulders to waist, knees, or feet. **2.** any similar garment, esp. one forming the top to a suit. **3.** a layer that covers or conceals a surface: *a coat of dust.* **4.** the hair, wool, or fur of an animal. ~*vb.* (*tr.*) **5.** (often foll. by *with*) to cover (with) a layer or covering. **6.** to provide with a coat. [C16: from OF *cote*, of Gmc origin]

Coatbridge ('kəʊtˌbrɪdʒ; *Scot.* ˌkəʊt'brɪdʒ) *n.* an industrial town in central Scotland, in Strathclyde region. Pop.: 50 866 (1981).

Coates (kəʊts) *n.* **Joseph Gordon.** 1878–1943, New Zealand statesman; prime minister of New Zealand (1925–28).

coat hanger *n.* a curved piece of wood, wire, etc., with a hook, used to hang up clothes.

coati (kəʊˈɑːtɪ), **coati-mondi,** *or* **coati-mundi** (kəʊˌɑːtɪˈmʌndɪ) *n.*, *pl.* **-tis** *or* **-dis.** an omnivorous mammal of Central and South America, related to but larger than the raccoons, having a long flexible snout and a brindled coat. [C17: from Port., from Tupi, lit.: belt-nosed, from *cua* belt + *tim* nose]

coating ('kəʊtɪŋ) *n.* **1.** a layer or film spread over a surface. **2.** fabric suitable for coats.

coat of arms *n.* the heraldic bearings of a person, family, or corporation.

coat of mail *n.* a protective garment made of linked metal rings or overlapping metal plates.

coat-tail *n.* the long tapering tails at the back of a man's tailed coat.

coauthor (kəʊˈɔːθə) *n.* **1.** a person who shares the writing of a book, etc., with another. ~*vb.* **2.** (*tr.*) to be the joint author of (a book, etc.).

coax (kəʊks) *vb.* **1.** to seek to manipulate or persuade (someone) by tenderness, flattery, pleading, etc. **2.** (*tr.*) to obtain by persistent coaxing. **3.** (*tr.*) to work on (something) carefully and patiently so as to make it function as desired: *he coaxed the engine into starting.* [C16: verb formed from obs. noun *cokes* fool, from ?] —**'coaxer** *n.* —**'coaxingly** *adv.*

coaxial (kəʊˈæksɪəl) *or* **coaxal** (kəʊˈæksᵊl) *adj.* **1.** having or mounted on a common axis. **2.** *Geom.* (of a set of circles) having the same radical axis. **3.** *Electronics.* formed from, using, or connected to a coaxial cable.

coaxial cable *n.* a cable consisting of an inner insulated core of stranded or solid wire surrounded by an outer insulated flexible wire braid, used esp. as a transmission line for radio-frequency signals. Often shortened to **coax** ('kəʊæks).

cob (kɒb) *n.* **1.** a male swan. **2.** a thickset type of riding and draught horse. **3.** short for **corncob** or **cobnut. 4.** *Brit.* another name for **hazel** (sense 1). **5.** a small rounded lump or heap of coal, ore, etc. **6.** *Brit. & N.Z.* a building material consisting of a mixture of clay and chopped straw. **7.** *Brit.* a round loaf of bread. [C15: from ?]

cobalt ('kəʊbɔːlt) *n.* a brittle hard silvery-white element that is a ferromagnetic metal: used in alloys. The radioisotope **cobalt-60** is used in radiotherapy and as a tracer. Symbol: Co; atomic no.: 27; atomic wt.: 58.933. [C17: G *Kobalt*, from MHG *kobolt* goblin; from the miners' belief that goblins placed it in the silver ore]

cobalt blue *n.* **1.** any greenish-blue pigment containing cobalt aluminate. **2. a.** a deep blue colour. **b.** (*as adj.*): *a cobalt-blue car.*

cobalt bomb *n.* **1.** a cobalt-60 device used in radiotherapy. **2.** a nuclear weapon consisting of a hydrogen bomb encased in cobalt, which releases large quantities of radioactive cobalt-60 into the atmosphere.

cobber ('kɒbə) *n.* *Austral. arch. & N.Z.* a friend; mate: used as a term of address to males. [C19: from E dialect *cob* to take a liking to someone]

Cobbett ('kɒbɪt) *n.* **William.** 1763–1835, English journalist and social reformer; founded *The Political Register* (1802); author of *Rural Rides* (1830).

cobble[1] ('kɒbᵊl) *n.* **1.** short for **cobblestone.** ~*vb.* **2.** (*tr.*) to pave (a road, etc.) with cobblestones. [C15 (in *cobblestone*): from COB]

cobble[2] ('kɒbəl) *vb.* (*tr.*) **1.** to make or mend (shoes). **2.** to put together clumsily. [C15: back formation from COBBLER[1]]

cobbler[1] ('kɒblə) *n.* a person who makes or mends shoes. [C13 (as surname): from ?]

cobbler[2] ('kɒblə) *n.* **1.** a sweetened iced drink, usually made from fruit and wine. **2.** *Chiefly U.S.* a hot dessert made of fruit covered with a rich cakelike crust. [C19: (for sense 1) ? shortened from *cobbler's punch*]

cobblers ('kɒbləz) *pl. n. Brit. taboo sl.* **1.** another word for **testicles. 2. (a load of old) cobblers.** rubbish; nonsense. [C20: from rhyming sl. *cobblers' awls* balls]

cobblestone ('kɒbəl,stəʊn) *n.* a rounded stone used for paving. Sometimes shortened to **cobble.**

Cobden ('kɒbdən) *n.* **Richard.** 1804–65, English economist and statesman: a leader of the successful campaign to abolish the Corn Laws (1846).

cobelligerent (,kəʊbɪ'lɪdʒərənt) *n.* a country fighting in a war on the side of another country.

Cóbh (kəʊv) *n.* a port in S Ireland, in SE Co. Cork: port of call for Atlantic liners. Pop.: 6587 (1981). Former name (1849–1922): **Queenstown.**

Cobham ('kɒbəm) *n.* **Lord,** title of (Sir John) **Oldcastle.**

cobia ('kəʊbɪə) *n.* a large striped percoid game fish of tropical and subtropical seas. [from ?]

Coblenz (*German* 'ko:blɛnts) *n.* a variant spelling of **Koblenz.**

cobnut ('kɒb,nʌt) *or* **cob** *n.* other names for a **hazelnut.** [C16: from earlier *cobylle nut*]

Cobol ('kəʊ,bɒl) *n.* a high-level computer programming language designed for general commercial use. [C20: *co(mmon) b(usiness) o(riented) l(anguage)*]

cobra ('kəʊbrə) *n.* any of several highly venomous snakes of tropical Africa and Asia. When alarmed they spread the skin of the neck region into a hood. [C19: from Port. *cobra (de capello)* snake (with a hood), from L *colubra* snake]

Coburg ('kəʊbɜ:g; *German* 'ko:burk) *n.* a city in E West Germany, in N Bavaria. Pop.: 44 500 (1984 est.).

cobweb ('kɒb,wɛb) *n.* **1.** a web spun by certain spiders. **2.** a single thread of such a web. **3.** something like a cobweb, as in its flimsiness or ability to trap. [C14: *cob,* from OE *(ātor)coppe* spider] —'**cob,webbed** *adj.* —'**cob,webby** *adj.*

cobwebs ('kɒb,wɛbz) *pl. n.* **1.** mustiness, confusion, or obscurity. **2.** *Inf.* stickiness of the eyelids experienced upon first awakening.

coca ('kəʊkə) *n.* either of two shrubs, native to the Andes, the dried leaves of which contain cocaine and are chewed for their stimulating effects. [C17: from Sp., from Quechuan *kúka*]

Coca-Cola (,kəʊkə'kəʊlə) *n. Trademark.* a carbonated soft drink flavoured with coca leaves, cola nuts, caramel, etc.

cocaine *or* **cocain** (kə'keɪn) *n.* an addictive narcotic drug derived from coca leaves or synthesized, used medicinally as a topical anaesthetic. [C19: from COCA + -INE[1]]

coccus ('kɒkəs) *n., pl.* **-ci** (-kaɪ, -saɪ). any spherical or nearly spherical bacterium, such as a staphylococcus. [C18: from NL, from Gk *kokkos* berry, grain] —'**coccoid** *or* '**coccal** *adj.*

coccyx ('kɒksɪks) *n., pl.* **coccyges** (kɒk'saɪdʒi:z). a small triangular bone at the end of the spinal column in man and some apes. [C17: from NL, from Gk *kokkux* cuckoo, imit.; from its likeness to a cuckoo's beak] —**coccygeal** (kɒk'sɪdʒɪəl) *adj.*

Cochabamba (*Spanish* kotʃa'βamba) *n.* a city in central Bolivia. Pop.: 317 251 (1985).

Cochin ('kəʊtʃɪn, 'kɒtʃ-) *n.* **1.** a region and former state of SW India: part of Kerala state since 1956. **2.** a port in SW India, on the Malabar Coast: the first European settlement in India, founded by Vasco da Gama in 1502. Pop.: 513 081 (1981).

Cochin China *n.* a former French colony of Indochina (1862–1948): now the part of Vietnam that lies south of Phan Thiet.

cochineal (,kɒtʃɪ'ni:l, 'kɒtʃɪ,ni:l) *n.* **1.** a Mexican insect that feeds on cacti. **2.** a crimson substance obtained from the crushed bodies of these insects, used for colouring food and for dyeing. **3.** the colour of this dye. [C16: from OSp. *cochinilla,* from L *coccineus* scarlet-coloured, from Gk *kokkos* kermes berry]

Cochise (kəʊ'tʃi:s, -'tʃi:z) *n.* died 1874, Apache Indian chief.

cochlea ('kɒklɪə) *n., pl.* **-leae** (-lɪ,i:). the spiral tube that forms part of the internal ear, converting sound vibrations into nerve impulses. [C16: from L: snail, spiral, from Gk *kokhlias*] —'**cochlear** *adj.*

cochleate ('kɒklɪ,eɪt, -lɪɪt) *or* **cochleated** *adj. Biol.* shaped like a snail's shell.

cock[1] (kɒk) *n.* **1.** the male of the domestic fowl. **2. a.** any other male bird. **b.** the male of certain other animals, such as the lobster. **c.** (*as modifier*): *a cock sparrow.* **3.** short for **stopcock** or **weathercock. 4.** a taboo slang word for **penis. 5. a.** the hammer of a firearm. **b.** its position when the firearm is ready to be discharged. **6.** *Brit. inf.* a friend, mate, or fellow. **7.** a jaunty or significant tilting upwards: *a cock of the head.* ~*vb.* **8.** (*tr.*) to set the firing pin, hammer, or breech block of (a firearm) so that a pull on the trigger will release it and thus fire the weapon. **9.** (*tr.;* sometimes foll. by *up*) to raise in an alert or jaunty manner. **10.** (*intr.*) to stick or stand up conspicuously. ~See also **cockup.** [OE *cocc,* ult. imit.]

cock[2] (kɒk) *n.* **1.** a small, cone-shaped heap of hay, straw, etc. ~*vb.* **2.** (*tr.*) to stack (hay, etc.) in such heaps. [C14: ? of Scand. origin]

cockabully (,kɒkə'bʊlɪ) *n., pl.* **-lies.** any of several small freshwater fish of New Zealand. [Maori *kokopu*]

cockade (kɒ'keɪd) *n.* a feather or ribbon worn on military headwear. [C18: changed from earlier *cockard,* from F, from *coq* COCK[1]] —**cock'aded** *adj.*

cock-a-doodle-doo (,kɒkə,du:dəl'du:) *interj.* an imitation or representation of a cock crowing.

cock-a-hoop *adj.* (*usually postpositive*) **1.** in very high spirits. **2.** boastful. **3.** askew; confused. [C16: ?from *set the cock a hoop*: to put a cock on a *hoop,* a full measure of grain]

cockalorum (,kɒkə'lɔ:rəm) *n.* **1.** a self-important little man. **2.** bragging talk. [C18: from COCK[1] -*alorum,* var. of L genitive pl. ending; ? intended to suggest: the cock of all cocks]

cock-and-bull story *n. Inf.* an obviously improbable story, esp. one used as an excuse.

cockatoo (,kɒkə'tu:, 'kɒkə,tu:) *n., pl.* **-toos. 1.** any of a genus of parrots having an erectile crest and light-coloured plumage. **2.** *Austral. & N.Z.* a small farmer or settler. **3.** *Austral. inf.* a lookout during some illegal activity. [C17: from Du., from Malay *kakatua*]

cockatrice ('kɒkətrɪs, -,traɪs) *n.* **1.** a legendary monster, part snake and part cock, that could kill with a glance. **2.** another name for **basilisk** (sense 1). [C14: from OF, ult. from L *calcāre* to tread, from *calx* heel]

cockboat ('kɒk,bəʊt) *or* **cockleboat** *n.* any small boat. [C15 *cokbote,* ? ult. from LL *caudica* dugout canoe, from L *caudex* tree trunk]

cockchafer ('kɒk,tʃeɪfə) *n.* any of various Old World beetles, whose larvae feed on crops and grasses. Also called: **May beetle, May bug.** [C18: from COCK[1] + CHAFER]

Cockcroft ('kɒk,krɒft) *n.* **Sir John Douglas.** 1897–1967, English nuclear physicist. With E. T. S. Walton, he produced the first artificial transmutation of an atomic nucleus (1932) and shared the Nobel prize for physics 1951.

cockcrow ('kɒk,krəʊ) *n.* daybreak.

cocked hat *n.* **1.** a hat with brims turned up and caught together in order to give two points (bicorn) or three points (tricorn). **2. knock into a cocked hat.** *Sl.* to outdo or defeat.

Cocker ('kɒkə) *n.* **1. Edward.** 1631–75, English arithmetician. **2. according to Cocker.** reliable or reliably; correct or correctly.

cockerel ('kɒkərəl, 'kɒkrəl) *n.* a young domestic cock, less than a year old. [C15: dim. of COCK[1]]

Cockerell ('kɒkərəl) *n.* **Sir Christopher Sydney.** born 1910, British engineer noted for his invention of the hovercraft.

cocker spaniel ('kɒkə) *n.* a small compact breed of spaniel. [C19: from *cocking* hunting woodcocks]

cockeyed ('kɒk,aɪd) *adj. Inf.* **1.** afflicted with strabismus or squint. **2.** physically or logically abnormal, absurd, etc.; crooked; askew: *cockeyed ideas.* **3.** drunk.

cockfight ('kɒk,faɪt) *n.* a fight between two gamecocks fitted with sharp metal spurs. —'**cock,fighting** *n.*

cockhorse (,kɒk'hɔ:s) *n.* another name for **rocking horse** or **hobbyhorse.**

cockieleekie, cockyleeky, or **cock-a-leekie** ('kɒk-ə'liːkɪ) n. Scot. a soup made from a fowl boiled with leeks.

cockle[1] ('kɒkəl) n. **1.** any edible sand-burrowing bivalve mollusc of Europe, typically having a rounded shell with radiating ribs. **2.** any of certain similar or related molluscs. **3.** short for **cockleshell** (sense 1). **4.** a wrinkle or puckering. **5.** one's deepest feelings (esp. in **warm the cockles of one's heart**). ~vb. **6.** to contract or cause to contract into wrinkles. [C14: from OF coquille shell, from L conchȳlium shellfish, from Gk konkhule mussel; see CONCH]

cockle[2] ('kɒkəl) n. any of several plants, esp. the corn cockle, that grow as weeds in cornfields.

cocklebur ('kɒkəl,bɜː) n. **1.** a coarse weed of the composite family having spiny burs. **2.** the bur of this plant.

cockleshell ('kɒkəl,ʃɛl) n. **1.** the shell of the cockle. **2.** any of the shells of certain other molluscs. **3.** any small light boat.

cockney ('kɒknɪ) (often cap.) ~n. **1.** a native of London, esp. of the East End, speaking a characteristic dialect of English. Traditionally defined as someone born within the sound of the bells of St Mary-le-Bow church. **2.** the urban dialect of London or its East End. ~adj. **3.** characteristic of cockneys or their dialect of English. [C14: from cokeney, lit.: cock's egg, later applied contemptuously to townsmen, from cokene, genitive pl. of cok COCK[1] + ey EGG[1]] —'**cockneyish** adj. —'**cockney,ism** n.

cock of the walk n. Inf. a person who asserts himself in a strutting pompous way.

cockpit ('kɒk,pɪt) n. **1.** the compartment in a small aircraft in which the pilot, crew, and sometimes the passengers sit. Cf. **flight deck** (sense 1). **2.** the driver's compartment in a racing car. **3.** Naut. an enclosed area towards the stern of a small vessel containing the wheel and tiller. **4.** the site of numerous battles or campaigns. **5.** an enclosure used for cockfights.

cockroach ('kɒk,rəutʃ) n. an insect having an oval flattened body with long antennae and biting mouthparts: a household pest. [C17: from Sp. cucaracha, from ?]

cockscomb or **coxcomb** ('kɒks,kəum) n. **1.** the comb of a domestic cock. **2.** a garden plant with yellow, crimson, or purple feathery plumelike flowers in a broad spike resembling the comb of a cock. **3.** Inf. a conceited dandy.

cockshy ('kɒk,ʃaɪ) n., pl. **-shies.** Brit. **1.** a target aimed at in throwing games. **2.** the throw itself. ~Often shortened to **shy.** [C18: from shying at a cock, the prize for the person who hit it]

cocksure (,kɒk'ʃuə, -'ʃɔː) adj. overconfident; arrogant. [C16: from ?] —,**cock'sureness** n.

cocktail ('kɒk,teɪl) n. **1. a.** any mixed drink with a spirit base. **b.** (as modifier): the cocktail hour. **2.** an appetizer of seafood, mixed fruits, etc. **3.** any combination of diverse elements, esp. one considered potent. **4.** (modifier) appropriate for formal occasions: a cocktail dress. [C19: from ?]

cockup ('kɒk,ʌp) n. **1.** Brit. sl. something done badly. ~vb. **cock up.** (tr., adv.) **2.** (of an animal) to raise (its ears etc.), esp. in an alert manner. **3.** Brit. sl. to botch.

cocky[1] ('kɒkɪ) adj. **cockier, cockiest.** excessively proud of oneself. —'**cockily** adv. —'**cockiness** n.

cocky[2] ('kɒkɪ) n., pl **cockies.** Austral. & N.Z. inf. short for **cockatoo** (sense 2).

coco ('kəukəu) n., pl. **-cos.** short for **coconut** or **coconut palm.** [C16: from Port. coco grimace; from the likeness of the three holes of the nut to a face]

cocoa ('kəukəu) or **cacao** n. **1.** a powder made from cocoa beans after they have been roasted and ground. **2.** a hot or cold drink made from cocoa and milk or water. **3. a.** a light to moderate brown colour. **b.** (as adj.): cocoa paint. [C18: altered from CACAO]

cocoa bean n. the seed of the cacao.

cocoa butter n. a yellowish-white waxy solid that is obtained from cocoa beans and used for confectionery, soap, etc.

coconut or **cocoanut** ('kəukə,nʌt) n. **1.** the fruit of the coconut palm, consisting of a thick fibrous oval husk inside which is a thin hard shell enclosing edible white meat. The hollow centre is filled with a milky fluid (**coconut milk**). **2.** the meat of the coconut, often shredded and used in cakes, curries, etc. [C18: see COCO]

coconut matting n. a form of coarse matting made from the fibrous husk of the coconut.

coconut oil n. the oil obtained from the meat of the coconut and used for making soap, etc.

coconut palm n. a tall palm tree, widely planted throughout the tropics, having coconuts as fruits. Also called: **coco palm, coconut tree.**

cocoon (kə'kuːn) n. **1.** a silky protective envelope secreted by silkworms and certain other insect larvae, in which the pupae develop. **2.** a protective spray covering used as a seal on machinery. **3.** a cosy warm covering. ~vb. **4.** (tr.) to wrap in a cocoon. [C17: from F, from Provençal coucoun eggshell, from coco shell]

cocopan ('kəukəu,pæn) n. (in South Africa) a small wagon running on narrow-gauge railway lines used in mines. Also called: **hopper.** [C20: from Zulu 'ngkumbana short truck]

Cocos Islands ('kəukɒs, 'kəukəs) pl. n. a group of 27 coral islands in the Indian Ocean, southwest of Java: a Territory of Australia since 1955. Pop.: 616 (1986). Area: 13 sq. km (5 sq. miles). Also called: **Keeling Islands.**

cocotte (kəu'kɒt, kɒ-) n. **1.** a small fireproof dish in which individual portions of food are cooked and served. **2.** a prostitute or promiscuous woman. [C19: from F, from fem. of coq COCK[1]]

Cocteau (French kɔkto) n. **Jean** (ʒɑ̃). 1889–1963, French dramatist, novelist, poet, critic, designer, and film director. His works include the novel Les Enfants terribles (1929) and the play La Machine infernale (1934).

cod[1] (kɒd) n., pl. **cod** or **cods. 1.** any of the gadoid food fishes which occur in the North Atlantic and have a long body with three rounded dorsal fins. **2.** any of various Australian fishes of fresh or salt water, such as the Murray cod or the red cod. [C13: prob. of Gmc origin]

cod[2] (kɒd) n. **1.** Brit. & U.S. dialect. a pod or husk. **2.** Taboo. an obsolete word for **scrotum.** [OE codd husk, bag]

cod[3] (kɒd) Brit. sl. ~vb. **codding, codded.** (tr.) **1.** to make fun of/tease. **2.** to play a trick on; befool. ~n. **3.** a hoax or trick. [C19: ?from earlier cod a fool]

Cod n. Cape. See **Cape Cod.**

COD abbrev. for: **1.** cash on delivery. **2.** (in the U.S.) collect on delivery.

coda ('kəudə) n. **1.** Music. the final part of a musical structure. **2.** a concluding part of a literary work that rounds off the main work but is independent of it. [C18: from It.: tail, from L cauda]

coddle ('kɒdəl) vb. (tr.) **1.** to treat with indulgence. **2.** to cook (something, esp. eggs) in water just below the boiling point. [C16: from ?; ? rel. to CAUDLE] —'**coddler** n.

code (kəud) n. **1.** a system of letters or symbols, by which information can be communicated secretly, briefly, etc.: binary code; Morse code. See also **genetic code. 2.** a message in code. **3.** a symbol used in a code. **4.** a conventionalized set of principles or rules: a code of behaviour. **5.** a system of letters or digits used for identification purposes. ~vb. (tr.) **6.** to translate or arrange into a code. [C14: from F, from L cōdex book, CODEX] —'**coder** n.

codeine ('kəudiːn) n. a white crystalline alkaloid prepared mainly from morphine. It is used as an analgesic, a sedative, and to relieve coughing. [C19: from Gk kōdeia head of a poppy, from kōos hollow place + -INE[2]]

codex ('kəudɛks) n., pl. **codices** ('kəudɪ,siːz, 'kɒdɪ-). **1.** a volume of manuscripts of an ancient text. **2.** Obs. a legal code. [C16: from L: tree trunk, wooden block, book]

codfish ('kɒd,fɪʃ) n., pl. **-fish** or **-fishes.** a cod.

codger ('kɒdʒə) n. Inf. a man, esp. an old or eccentric one: often in **old codger.** [C18: prob. var. of CADGER]

codicil ('kɒdɪsɪl) n. **1.** Law. a supplement modifying a will or revoking some provision of it. **2.** an additional provision; appendix. [C15: from LL dim. of CODEX] —,**codi'cillary** adj.

codify ('kəudɪ,faɪ, 'kɒd-) vb. **-fying, -fied.** (tr.) to organize or collect together (laws, rules, procedures, etc.) into a system or code. —'**codi,fier** n. —,**codifi'cation** n.

codling[1] ('kɒdlɪŋ) or **codlin** ('kɒdlɪn) n. **1.** any of several varieties of long tapering apples. **2.** any unripe apple. [C15 querdlyng, from ?]

codling[2] ('kɒdlɪŋ) n. a codfish, esp. a young one.

cod-liver oil n. an oil extracted from the livers of cod and related fish, rich in vitamins A and D.

codpiece ('kɒd,piːs) n. a bag covering the male genitals, attached to breeches: worn in the 15th and 16th centuries. [C15: from COD[2] + PIECE]

codswallop ('kɒdz,wɒləp) *n. Brit. sl.* nonsense. [C20: from ?]

Cody ('kəʊdɪ) *n.* **William Frederick.** the real name of **Buffalo Bill.**

Coe (kəʊ) *n.* **Sebastian.** born 1956, English middle-distance runner: winner of the 1500 metres in the 1980 and 1984 Olympic Games.

co-ed (,kəʊ'ɛd) *adj.* 1. coeducational. ~*n.* 2. *U.S.* a female student in a coeducational college or university. 3. *Brit.* a school or college providing coeducation.

coeducation (,kəʊɛdju'keɪʃən) *n.* instruction in schools, colleges, etc., attended by both sexes. —**,coedu'cational** *adj.* —**,coedu'cationally** *adv.*

coefficient (,kəʊɪ'fɪʃənt) *n.* 1. *Maths.* a numerical or constant factor in an algebraic term: *the coefficient of the term 3xyz is 3.* 2. *Physics.* a number that is the value of a given substance under specified conditions. [C17: from NL, from L *co-* together + *efficere* to EFFECT]

coefficient of variation *n. Statistics.* a measure of the relative variation of distributions independent of the units of measurement; the standard deviation divided by the mean, sometimes expressed as a percentage.

coel- *prefix.* indicating a cavity within a body or a hollow organ or part: *coelacanth; coelenterate.* [NL, from Gk *koilos* hollow]

coelacanth ('siːlə,kænθ) *n.* a primitive marine bony fish, having fleshy limblike pectoral fins: thought to be extinct until a living specimen was discovered in 1938. [C19: from NL, from COEL- + Gk *akanthos* spine]

coelenterate (sɪ'lɛntə,reɪt, -rɪt) *n.* any of various invertebrates having a saclike body with a single opening (mouth), such as jellyfishes, sea anemones, and corals. [C19: from NL *Coelenterata*, hollow-intestined (creatures)]

coeliac *or U.S.* **celiac** ('siːlɪ,æk) *adj.* of the abdomen. [C17: from L, from Gk, from *koilia* belly]

coeliac disease *n.* an illness, esp. of children, in which the lining of the small intestine is sensitive to gluten in the diet, causing an impairment of food absorption.

coelom *or esp. U.S.* **celom** ('siːləʊm, -ləm) *n.* the body cavity of many multicellular animals, containing the digestive tract and other visceral organs. [C19: from Gk, from *koilos* hollow]

coeno- *or before a vowel* **coen-** *combining form.* common: *coenobite.* [NL, from Gk *koinos*]

coenobite *or* **cenobite** ('siːnəʊ,baɪt) *n.* a member of a religious order following a communal rule of life. [C17: from OF or ecclesiastical L, from Gk *koinobion* convent, from *koinos* common + *bios* life] —**coenobitic** (,siːnəʊ'bɪtɪk), **,coeno'bitical** *or* **,ceno'bitic**, **,ceno'bitical** *adj.*

coequal (kəʊ'iːkwəl) *adj.* 1. of the same size, rank, etc. ~*n.* 2. a person or thing equal with another. —**coequality** (,kəʊɪ'kwɒlɪtɪ) *n.*

coerce (kəʊ'ɜːs) *vb. (tr.)* to compel or restrain by force or authority without regard to individual wishes or desires. [C17: from L, from *co-* together + *arcēre* to enclose] —**co'ercer** *n.* —**co'ercible** *adj.*

coercion (kəʊ'ɜːʃən) *n.* 1. the act or power of coercing. 2. government by force. —**coercive** (kəʊ'ɜːsɪv) *adj.* —**co'ercively** *adv.*

coeval (kəʊ'iːvəl) *adj.* 1. of or belonging to the same age or generation. ~*n.* 2. a contemporary. [C17: from LL, from L *co-* + *aevum* age] —**coevality** (,kəʊɪ'vælɪtɪ) *n.* —**co'evally** *adv.*

coexecutor (,kəʊɪg'zɛkjʊtə) *n. Law.* a person acting jointly with another or others as executor.

coexist (,kəʊɪg'zɪst) *vb. (intr.)* 1. to exist together at the same time or in the same place. 2. to exist together in peace. —**,coex'istence** *n.* —**,coex'istent** *adj.*

coextend (,kəʊɪk'stɛnd) *vb.* to extend or cause to extend equally in space or time. —**,coex'tension** *n.* —**,co-ex'tensive** *adj.*

C of C *abbrev. for* Chamber of Commerce.

C of E *abbrev. for* Church of England.

coffee ('kɒfɪ) *n.* 1. a. a drink consisting of an infusion of the roasted and ground seeds of the coffee tree. b. *(as modifier): coffee grounds.* 2. Also called: **coffee beans.** the beanlike seeds of the coffee tree, used to make this beverage. 3. the tree yielding these seeds. 4. a. a light brown colour. b. *(as adj.): a coffee carpet.* [C16: from It. *caffè*, from Turkish *kahve*, from Ar. *qahwah* coffee, wine]

coffee bar *n.* a café; snack bar.

coffee cup *n.* a small cup for serving coffee.

coffee house *n.* a place where coffee is served, esp. one that was a fashionable meeting place in 18th-century London.

coffee mill *n.* a machine for grinding roasted coffee beans.

coffeepot ('kɒfɪ,pɒt) *n.* a pot in which coffee is brewed or served.

coffee shop *n.* a shop where coffee is sold or drunk.

coffee table *n.* a low table on which coffee may be served.

coffee-table book *n.* a book, usually glossily illustrated, designed chiefly to be looked at, rather than read.

coffer ('kɒfə) *n.* 1. a chest, esp. for storing valuables. 2. *(usually pl.)* a store of money. 3. an ornamental sunken panel in a ceiling, dome, etc. 4. a watertight box or chamber. 5. short for **cofferdam.** ~*vb (tr.)* 6. to store, as in a coffer. 7. to decorate (a ceiling, dome, etc.) with coffers. [C13: from OF *coffre*, from L, from Gk *kophinos* basket]

cofferdam ('kɒfə,dæm) *n.* 1. a watertight structure that encloses an area under water, pumped dry to enable construction work to be carried out. 2. (on a ship) a compartment separating two bulkheads, as for insulation or to serve as a barrier against the escape of gas, etc. ~Often shortened to **coffer.**

coffin ('kɒfɪn) *n.* 1. a box in which a corpse is buried or cremated. 2. the bony part of a horse's foot. ~*vb.* 3. *(tr.)* to place in or as in a coffin. [C14: from OF *cofin*, from L *cophinus* basket]

coffin nail *n.* a slang term for **cigarette.**

coffle ('kɒfˤl) *n.* a line of slaves, beasts, etc., fastened together. [C18: from Ar. *qāfilah* caravan]

C of S *abbrev. for* Church of Scotland.

cog[1] (kɒg) *n.* 1. any of the teeth or projections on the rim of a gearwheel. 2. a gearwheel, esp. a small one. 3. a person or thing playing a small part in a large organization or process. [C13: of Scand. origin]

cog[2] (kɒg) *n.* 1. a tenon that projects from the end of a timber beam for fitting into a mortise. ~*vb.* **cogging, cogged.** 2. *(tr.)* to join (pieces of wood) with cogs. [C19: from ?]

cogent ('kəʊdʒənt) *adj.* compelling belief or assent; forcefully convincing. [C17: from L *cōgent-, cōgēns*, from *co-* together + *agere* to drive] —**'cogency** (-dʒənsɪ) *n.* —**'cogently** *adv.*

cogitate ('kɒdʒɪ,teɪt) *vb.* to think deeply about (a problem, possibility, etc.); ponder. [C16: from L, from *co-* (intensive) + *agitāre* to turn over] —**,cogi'tation** *n.* —**'cogitative** *adj.* —**'cogi,tator** *n.*

Cognac ('kɒnjæk; *French* kɔɲak) *n.* 1. a town in SW France: centre of the district famed for its brandy. Pop.: 20 995 (1982 est.). 2. *(sometimes not cap.)* a high-quality grape brandy.

cognate ('kɒgneɪt) *adj.* 1. akin; related: *cognate languages.* 2. related by blood or descended from a common maternal ancestor. ~*n.* 3. something that is cognate with something else. [C17: from L, from *co-* same + *gnātus* born, var. of *nātus*, p.p. of *nāscī* to be born] —**'cognately** *adv.* —**'cognateness** *n.* —**cog'nation** *n.*

cognition (kɒg'nɪʃən) *n.* 1. the mental act or process by which knowledge is acquired, including perception, intuition, and reasoning. 2. the knowledge that results from such an act or process. [C15: from L, from *co-* (intensive) + *nōscere* to learn] —**cog'nitional** *adj.* —**cognitive** ('kɒgnɪtɪv) *adj.*

cognizable *or* **cognisable** ('kɒgnɪzəbˤl, 'kɒnɪ-) *adj.* 1. perceptible. 2. *Law.* susceptible to the jurisdiction of a court.

cognizance *or* **cognisance** ('kɒgnɪzəns, 'kɒnɪ-) *n.* 1. knowledge; acknowledgment. 2. **take cognizance of.** to take notice of; acknowledge, esp. officially. 3. the range or scope of knowledge or perception. 4. *Law.* the right of a court to hear and determine a cause or matter. 5. *Heraldry.* a distinguishing badge or bearing. [C14: from OF, from L *cognōscere* to learn; see COGNITION]

cognizant *or* **cognisant** ('kɒgnɪzənt, 'kɒnɪ-) *adj.* (usually foll. by *of*) aware; having knowledge.

cognomen (kɒg'nəʊmen) *n., pl.* **-nomens** *or* **-nomina** (-'nɒmɪnə, -'nəʊ-). (originally) an ancient Roman's third name or nickname, which later became his family name. [C19: from L: additional name, from *co-* together + *nōmen* name] —**cognominal** (kɒg'nɒmɪnˤl, -'nəʊ-) *adj.*

cognoscenti (ˌkɒnjəʊˈʃɛntɪ, ˌkɒgnəʊ-) *or* **conoscenti** (ˌkɒnəʊˈʃɛntɪ) *pl. n., sing.* **-te** (-tiː). (*sometimes sing.*) people with informed appreciation of a particular field, esp. in the fine arts; connoisseurs. [C18: from obs. It., from L *cognōscere* to learn]

cogwheel (ˈkɒgˌwiːl) *n.* another name for **gearwheel**.

cohabit (kəʊˈhæbɪt) *vb.* (*intr.*) to live together as husband and wife, esp. without being married. [C16: from L *co-* together + *habitāre* to live] —**coˈhabitant** *or* **coˈhabiter** *n.*

cohabitation (kəʊˌhæbɪˈteɪʃən) *n.* **1.** the state or condition of living together as husband and wife without being married. **2.** (of political parties) the state or condition of cooperating for specific purposes without forming a coalition.

coheir (kəʊˈɛə) *n.* a person who inherits jointly with others. —**coˈheiress** *fem. n.*

cohere (kəʊˈhɪə) *vb.* (*intr.*) **1.** to hold or stick firmly together. **2.** to be connected logically; be consistent. **3.** *Physics.* to be held together by the action of molecular forces. [C16: from L *co-* together + *haerēre* to cling]

coherence (kəʊˈhɪərəns) *or* **coherency** *n.* **1.** logical or natural connection or consistency. **2.** another word for **cohesion** (sense 1).

coherent (kəʊˈhɪərənt) *adj.* **1.** capable of intelligible speech. **2.** logical; consistent and orderly. **3.** cohering or sticking together. **4.** *Physics.* (of two or more waves) having the same frequency and the same phase or a fixed phase difference: *coherent light.* —**coˈherently** *adv.*

cohesion (kəʊˈhiːʒən) *n.* **1.** the act or state of cohering; tendency to unite. **2.** *Physics.* the force that holds together the atoms or molecules in a solid or liquid, as distinguished from adhesion. **3.** *Bot.* the fusion in some plants of flower parts, such as petals, that are usually separate. [C17: from L *cohaesus*, p.p. of *cohaerēre* to COHERE] —**coˈhesive** *adj.*

coho (ˈkəʊhəʊ) *n., pl.* **-ho** *or* **-hos.** a Pacific salmon. Also called: **silver salmon.** [from ?]

cohort (ˈkəʊhɔːt) *n.* **1.** one of the ten units of an ancient Roman Legion. **2.** any band of warriors or associates: *the cohorts of Satan.* **3.** *Chiefly U.S.* an associate or follower. [C15: from L *cohors* yard, company of soldiers]

COHSE (ˈkəʊzɪ) *n.* (in Britain) *acronym for* Confederation of Health Service Employees.

COI (in Britain) *abbrev. for* Central Office of Information.

coif (kɔɪf) *n.* **1.** a close-fitting cap worn under a veil in the Middle Ages. **2.** a leather cap worn under a chain-mail hood. **3.** (kwaːf). a less common word for **coiffure** (sense 1). ~*vb.* **coiffing, coiffed.** (*tr.*) **4.** to cover with or as if with a coif. **5.** (kwaːf). to arrange (the hair). [C14: from OF *coiffe*, from LL *cofea* helmet, cap, from ?]

coiffeur (kwaːˈfɜː) *n.* a hairdresser. —**coiffeuse** (kwaːˈfɜːz) *fem. n.*

coiffure (kwaːˈfjʊə) *n.* **1.** a hairstyle. **2.** an obsolete word for **headdress.** ~*vb.* **3.** (*tr.*) to dress or arrange (the hair).

coign of vantage (kɔɪn) *n.* an advantageous position for observation or action.

coil[1] (kɔɪl) *vb.* **1.** to wind or gather (ropes, hair, etc.) into loops or (of ropes, hair, etc.) to be formed in such loops. **2.** (*intr.*) to move in a winding course. ~*n.* **3.** something wound in a connected series of loops. **4.** a single loop of such a series. **5.** an arrangement of pipes in a spiral or loop, as in a condenser. **6.** an electrical conductor wound into the form of a spiral, to provide inductance or a magnetic field. **7.** an intrauterine contraceptive device in the shape of a coil. **8.** the transformer in a petrol engine that supplies the high voltage to the sparking plugs. [C16: from OF *coillir* to collect together; see CULL]

coil[2] (kɔɪl) *n.* the troubles of the world (in Shakespeare's phrase **this mortal coil**). [C16: from ?]

Coimbatore (ˌkɔːɪmbəˈtɔː) *n.* an industrial city in SW India, in W Tamil Nadu. Pop.: 700 923 (1981).

Coimbra (*Portuguese* ˈkuɪmbrɐ) *n.* a city in central Portugal: capital of Portugal from 1190 to 1260; seat of the country's oldest university. Pop.: 74 616 (1984).

coin (kɔɪn) *n.* **1.** a metal disc or piece used as money. **2.** metal currency, as opposed to paper currency, etc. **3.** *Archit.* a variant spelling of **quoin. 4. pay (a person) back in (his) own coin.** to treat (a person) in the way that he has treated others. ~*vb.* (*tr.*) **5.** to make or stamp (coins). **6.** to make into a coin. **7.** to fabricate or invent (words, etc.). **8.** *Inf.* to make (money) rapidly (esp. in

coin it in). [C14: from OF: stamping die, from L *cuneus* wedge]

coinage (ˈkɔɪnɪdʒ) *n.* **1.** coins collectively. **2.** the act of striking coins. **3.** the currency of a country. **4.** the act of inventing something, esp. a word or phrase. **5.** a newly invented word, phrase, usage, etc.

coincide (ˌkəʊɪnˈsaɪd) *vb.* (*intr.*) **1.** to occur or exist simultaneously. **2.** to be identical in nature, character, etc. **3.** to agree. [C18: from Med. L, from L *co-*together + *incidere* to occur, befall, from *cadere* to fall]

coincidence (kəʊˈɪnsɪdəns) *n.* **1.** a chance occurrence of events remarkable either for being simultaneous or for apparently being connected. **2.** the fact, condition, or state of coinciding. **3.** (*modifier*) *Electronics.* of or relating to a circuit that produces an output pulse only when both its input terminals receive pulses within a specified interval: *coincidence gate.*

coincident (kəʊˈɪnsɪdənt) *adj.* **1.** having the same position in space or time. **2.** (usually *postpositive* and foll. by *with*) in exact agreement. —**coˌinciˈdental** *adj.* —**coˌinciˈdentally** *adv.*

coin-op (ˈkɔɪnˌɒp) *n.* a launderette or other installation in which the machines are operated by insertion of a coin. —**ˈcoin-ˌoperˌated** *adj.*

Cointreau (ˈkwaːntrəʊ) *n. Trademark.* a colourless liqueur with orange flavouring.

coir (ˈkɔɪə) *n.* the fibre from the husk of the coconut, used in making rope and matting. [C16: from Malayalam *kāyar* rope, from *kāyaru* to be twisted]

Coire (kwar) *n.* the French name for **Chur.**

coitus (ˈkəʊɪtəs) *or* **coition** (kəʊˈɪʃən) *n.* a technical term for **sexual intercourse.** [C18: from L, from *coīre* to meet, from *īre* to go] —**ˈcoital** *adj.*

coke[1] (kəʊk) *n.* **1.** a solid-fuel product produced by distillation of coal to drive off its volatile constituents: used as a fuel. **2.** the layer formed in the cylinders of a car engine by incomplete combustion of the fuel. ~*vb.* **3.** to become or convert into coke. [C17: prob. var. of C14 N English dialect *colk* core, from ?]

coke[2] (kəʊk) *n. Sl.* short for **cocaine.**

Coke[1] (kəʊk) *n. Trademark.* short for **Coca-Cola.**

Coke[2] (kuk, kəʊk) *n.* **1.** Sir **Edward.** 1552–1634, English jurist, noted for his defence of the common law against encroachment from the Crown: the Petition of Right (1628) was largely his work. **2.** (kuk) **Thomas William,** 1st Earl of Leicester, known as *Coke of Holkham.* 1752–1842, English agriculturist: pioneered agricultural improvement and considerably improved productivity at his Holkham estate in Norfolk.

col (kɒl) *n.* **1.** the lowest point of a ridge connecting two mountain peaks. **2.** *Meteorol.* a low-pressure region between two anticyclones. [C19: from F: neck, col, from L *collum* neck]

Col. *abbrev. for:* **1.** Colombia(n). **2.** Colonel. **3.** *Bible.* Colossians.

col- *prefix.* a variant of **com-** before *l: collateral.*

cola *or* **kola** (ˈkəʊlə) *n.* **1.** either of two trees widely cultivated in tropical regions for their seeds (see **cola nut**). **2.** a sweet carbonated drink flavoured with cola nuts. [C18: from *kola*, prob. var. of W African *kolo* nut]

colander (ˈkɒləndə, ˈkʌl-) *or* **cullender** *n.* a pan with a perforated bottom for straining or rinsing foods. [C14 *colyndore*, prob. from OProvençal *colador*, from LL, from L *cōlum* sieve]

cola nut *n.* any of the seeds of the cola tree, which contain caffeine and theobromine and are used medicinally and in soft drinks.

Colbert (*French* kɔlbɛr) *n.* **1. Claudette** (klɔːˈdɛt). real name *Lily Claudette Chauchoin.* born 1905, U.S. film actress, born in France. Her Hollywood comedies include *Three-Cornered Moon* (1933) and *It Happened One Night* (1934). **2. Jean Baptiste** (ʒɑ̃ batist). 1619–83, French statesman; chief minister to Louis XIV: reformed the taille and pursued a mercantilist policy, creating a powerful navy and merchant fleet and building roads and canals.

Colchester (ˈkəʊltʃɪstə) *n.* a town in E England, in NE Essex. Pop.: 81 945 (1981). Latin name: **Camulodunum** (ˌkæmjʊləʊˈdjuːnəm, ˌkæmʊləʊˈduːnəm).

colchicine (ˈkɒltʃɪˌsiːn, -sɪn, ˈkɒlkɪ-) *n.* a pale yellow crystalline alkaloid extracted from seeds or corms of the autumn crocus and used in the treatment of gout. [C19: from COLCHICUM + -INE[2]]

colchicum ('kɒltʃɪkəm, 'kɒlkɪ-) *n.* **1.** any Eurasian plant of the lily family, such as the autumn crocus. **2.** the dried seeds or corms of the autumn crocus. [C16: from L, from Gk, from *kolkhikos* of COLCHIS]

Colchis ('kɒlkɪs) *n.* an ancient country on the Black Sea south of the Caucasus; the land of Medea and the Golden Fleece in Greek mythology.

cold (kəʊld) *adj.* **1.** having relatively little warmth; of a rather low temperature: *cold weather; cold hands.* **2.** without proper warmth: *this meal is cold.* **3.** lacking in affection or enthusiasm: *a cold manner.* **4.** not affected by emotion: *cold logic.* **5.** dead. **6.** sexually unresponsive or frigid. **7.** lacking in freshness: *a cold scent; cold news.* **8.** chilling to the spirit; depressing. **9.** (of a colour) having violet, blue, or green predominating; giving no sensation of warmth. **10.** *Sl.* unconscious. **11.** *Inf.* (of a seeker) far from the object of a search. **12. cold comfort.** little or no comfort. **13. leave (someone) cold.** *Inf.* to fail to excite: *the performance left me cold.* **14. throw cold water on.** *Inf.* to be unenthusiastic about or discourage. ~*n.* **15.** the absence of heat regarded as a positive force: *the cold took away our breath.* **16.** the sensation caused by loss or lack of heat. **17. (out) in the cold.** *Inf.* neglected; ignored. **18.** an acute viral infection of the upper respiratory passages characterized by discharge of watery mucus from the nose, sneezing, etc. **19. catch a cold.** *Inf.* to make a financial loss. ~*adv.* **20.** *Inf.* without preparation: *he played his part cold.* [OE *ceald*] —'**coldish** *adj.* —'**coldly** *adv.* —'**coldness** *n.*

cold-blooded *adj.* **1.** having or showing a lack of feeling or pity. **2.** *Inf.* particularly sensitive to cold. **3.** (of all animals except birds and mammals) having a body temperature that varies with that of the surroundings. —,**cold-'bloodedly** *adv.* —,**cold-'bloodedness** *n.*

cold cathode *n. Electronics.* a cathode from which electrons are emitted at an ambient temperature.

cold chisel *n.* a toughened steel chisel.

cold cream *n.* an emulsion of water and fat used for softening and cleansing the skin.

cold cuts *pl. n.* cooked meats sliced and served cold.

cold feet *n. Inf.* loss or lack of confidence.

cold frame *n.* an unheated wooden frame with a glass top, used to protect young plants.

cold front *n. Meteorol.* the boundary line between a warm air mass and the cold air pushing it from beneath and behind as it moves.

cold-hearted *adj.* lacking in feeling or warmth; unkind. —,**cold-'heartedly** *adv.* —,**cold-'heartedness** *n.*

Colditz ('kəʊldɪts) *n.* a town in S East Germany, on the River Mulde; during World War II its castle was used as a top-security camp for Allied prisoners of war; many daring escape attempts, some successful, were made.

cold pack *n.* a tinning process in which raw food is packed in cans or jars and then heated.

cold shoulder *Inf.* ~*n.* **1.** (often preceded by *the*) a show of indifference; a slight. ~*vb.* **cold-shoulder.** (*tr.*) **2.** to treat with indifference.

cold sore *n.* a cluster of blisters at the margin of the lips, caused by a viral infection. Technical name: **herpes labialis.**

cold storage *n.* **1.** the storage of things in an artificially cooled place for preservation. **2.** *Inf.* a state of temporary suspension: *to put an idea into cold storage.*

cold sweat *n. Inf.* a bodily reaction to fear or nervousness, characterized by chill and moist skin.

cold turkey *n. Sl.* **1.** a method of curing drug addiction by abrupt withdrawal of all doses. **2.** the withdrawal symptoms, esp. nausea and shivering, brought on by this method.

cold war *n.* a state of political hostility and military tension between two countries or power blocs, involving propaganda, threats, etc.

cold wave *n.* **1.** *Meteorol.* a sudden spell of low temperatures over a wide area. **2.** *Hairdressing.* a permanent wave made by chemical agents applied at normal temperatures.

cole (kəʊl) *n.* any of various plants such as the cabbage and rape. Also called: **colewort.** [OE *cāl*, from L *caulis* cabbage]

Coleman ('kəʊlmən) *n.* **Ornette** (ɔː'nɛt). born 1930, U.S. avant-garde jazz alto saxophonist and multi-instrumentalist.

coleopteran (,kɒlɪ'ɒptərən) *n. also* **coleopteron. 1.** any of the order of insects in which the forewings are modified to form shell-like protective elytra. It includes the beetles and weevils. ~*adj. also* **coleopterous. 2.** of, relating to, or belonging to this order. [C18: from NL, from Gk, from *koleon* sheath + *pteron* wing]

Coleridge ('kəʊlərɪdʒ) *n.* **Samuel Taylor.** 1772–1834, English Romantic poet and critic, noted for poems such as *The Rime of the Ancient Mariner* (1798), *Kubla Khan* (1816), and *Christabel* (1816), and for his critical work *Biographia Literaria* (1817).

coleslaw ('kəʊl,slɔː) *n.* a salad of shredded cabbage, mayonnaise, carrots, onions, etc. [C19: from Du. *koolsla*, from *koolsalade*, lit.: cabbage salad]

Colet ('kɒlɪt) *n.* **John.** ?1467–1519, English humanist and theologian; founder of St. Paul's School, London (1509).

coletit ('kəʊltɪt) *n.* another name for **coal tit.**

Colette (kɒ'lɛt) *n.* full name *Sidonie Gabrielle Claudine Colette.* 1873–1954, French novelist; her works include *Chéri* (1920), *Gigi* (1944), and the series of *Claudine* books.

coleus ('kəʊlɪəs) *n., pl.* **-uses.** any plant of the Old World genus *Coleus:* cultivated for their variegated leaves. [C19: from NL, from Gk, var. of *koleon* sheath]

coley ('kəʊlɪ, 'kɒlɪ) *n. Brit.* any of various edible fishes, esp. the coalfish.

colic ('kɒlɪk) *n.* a condition characterized by acute spasmodic abdominal pain, esp. that caused by inflammation, distention, etc., of the gastrointestinal tract. [C15: from OF, from LL, from Gk *kōlon*, var. of *kolon* COLON[2]] —'**colicky** *adj.*

coliform bacteria ('kɒlɪfɔːm) *pl. n.* a large group of bacteria that inhabit the intestinal tract of man.

Coligny or **Coligni** (*French* kɔliɲi) *n.* **Gaspard de** (gaspar də). 1519–72, French Huguenot leader.

Colima (*Spanish* ko'lima) *n.* **1.** a state of SW Mexico, on the Pacific coast: mainly a coastal plain, rising to the foothills of the Sierra Madre, with important mineral resources. Capital: Colima. Pop.: 383 621 (1983 est.). Area: 5455 sq. km (2106 sq. miles). **2.** a city in SW Mexico, capital of Colima state, on the Colima River. Pop.: 58 000 (1984 est.). **3. Nevado de.** a volcano in SW Mexico, in Jalisco state. Height: 4339 m (14 235 ft.).

coliseum (,kɒlɪ'sɪəm) or **colosseum** (,kɒlə'sɪəm) *n.* a large building, such as a stadium, used for entertainments, sports, etc. [C18: from Med. L, var. of COLOSSEUM]

colitis (kɒ'laɪtɪs) *n.* inflammation of the colon.

collaborate (kə'læbə,reɪt) *vb.* (*intr.*) **1.** (often foll. by *on, with,* etc.) to work with another or others on a joint project. **2.** to cooperate as a traitor, esp. with an enemy occupying one's own country. [C19: from LL, from L *com-* together + *labōrāre* to work] —**col,labo'ration** *n.* —**col'laborative** *adj.* —**col'labo,rator** *n.*

collage (kə'lɑːʒ, kɒ-) *n.* **1.** an art form in which compositions are made out of pieces of paper, cloth, photographs, etc., pasted on a dry ground. **2.** a composition made in this way. **3.** any collection of unrelated things. [C20: F, from *colle* glue, from Gk *kolla*] —**col'lagist** *n.*

collagen ('kɒlədʒən) *n.* a fibrous protein of connective tissue and bones that yields gelatin on boiling. [C19: from Gk *kolla* glue + -GEN]

collapsar (kɒ'læpsɑː) *n. Astron.* another name for **black hole.**

collapse (kə'læps) *vb.* **1.** (*intr.*) to fall down or cave in suddenly: *the whole building collapsed.* **2.** (*intr.*) to fail completely. **3.** (*intr.*) to break down or fall down from lack of strength. **4.** to fold (furniture, etc.) compactly or (of furniture, etc.) to be designed to fold compactly. ~*n.* **5.** the act or instance of suddenly falling down, caving in, or crumbling. **6.** a sudden failure or breakdown. [C18: from L, from *collābī* to fall in ruins, from *lābī* to fall] —**col'lapsible** or **col'lapsable** *adj.* —**col,lapsi'bility** *n.*

collar ('kɒlə) *n.* **1.** the part of a garment around the neck and shoulders, often detachable or folded over. **2.** any band, necklace, garland, etc., encircling the neck. **3.** a band or chain of leather, rope, or metal placed around an animal's neck. **4.** *Biol.* a marking resembling a collar, such as that found around the necks of some birds. **5.** a section of a shaft or rod having a locally increased diameter to provide a bearing seat or a locating ring. **6.** a cut of meat, esp. bacon, taken from around the neck of an animal. ~*vb.* (*tr.*) **7.** to put a collar on; furnish with a collar. **8.** to seize by the collar. **9.** *Inf.* to seize; arrest; detain. [C13: from L *collāre* neckband, from *collum* neck]

collarbone ('kɒlə,bəʊn) *n.* the nontechnical name for **clavicle.**

collard ('kɒləd) *n.* a variety of the cabbage, having a crown of edible leaves. See also **kale.** [C18: var. of *colewort*, from COLE + WORT]

collate (kɒ'leɪt, kə-) *vb.* (*tr.*) **1.** to examine and compare (texts, statements, etc.) in order to note points of agreement and disagreement. **2.** to check the number and order of (the pages of a book). **3.** *Bookbinding.* **a.** to check the sequence of (the sections of a book) after gathering. **b.** a nontechnical word for **gather** (sense 8). **4.** (often foll. by *to*) *Christianity.* to appoint (an incumbent) to a benefice. [C16: from L, from *com-* together + *lātus*, p.p. of *ferre* to bring] —**col'lator** *n.*

collateral (kɒ'lætərəl, kə-) *n.* **1. a.** security pledged for the repayment of a loan. **b.** (*as modifier*): *a collateral loan.* **2.** a person, animal, or plant descended from the same ancestor as another but through a different line. ~*adj.* **3.** situated or running side by side. **4.** descended from a common ancestor but through different lines. **5.** serving to support or corroborate. [C14: from ML, from L *com-* together + *laterālis* of the side, from *latus* side] —**col'laterally** *adv.*

collation (kɒ'leɪʃən, kə-) *n.* **1.** the act or process of collating. **2.** a description of the technical features of a book. **3.** *R.C. Church.* a light meal permitted on fast days. **4.** any light informal meal.

colleague ('kɒliːg) *n.* a fellow worker or member of a staff, department, profession, etc. [C16: from F, from L *collēga*, from *com-* together + *lēgāre* to choose]

collect[1] (kə'lɛkt) *vb.* **1.** to gather together or be gathered together. **2.** to accumulate (stamps, books, etc.) as a hobby or for study. **3.** (*tr.*) to call for or receive payment of (taxes, dues, etc.). **4.** (*tr.*) to regain control of (oneself, one's emotions, etc.) as after a shock or surprise: *he collected his wits.* **5.** (*tr.*) to fetch: *collect your own post.* **6.** (*intr.*; sometimes foll. by *on*) *Sl.* to receive large sums of money. **7.** (*tr.*) *Austral. & N.Z. inf.* to collide with; be hit by. ~*adv., adj.* **8.** *U.S.* (of telephone calls, etc.) on a reverse-charge basis. [C16: from L, from *com-* together + *legere* to gather]

collect[2] ('kɒlɛkt) *n. Christianity.* a short Church prayer in Communion and other services. [C13: from Med. L *collecta* (from *ōrātiō ad collēctam* prayer at the assembly), from L *colligere* to COLLECT[1]]

collectable *or* **collectible** (kə'lɛktəb³l) *adj.* **1.** (of antiques) of interest to a collector. ~*n.* **2.** (*often pl.*) any object regarded as being of interest to a collector.

collected (kə'lɛktɪd) *adj.* **1.** in full control of one's faculties; composed. **2.** assembled in totality or brought together into one volume or a set of volumes: *the collected works of Dickens.* —**col'lectedly** *adv.* —**col'lectedness** *n.*

collection (kə'lɛkʃən) *n.* **1.** the act or process of collecting. **2.** a number of things collected or assembled together. **3.** something gathered into a mass or pile; accumulation: *a collection of rubbish.* **4.** a sum of money collected or solicited, as in church. **5.** removal, esp. regular removal of letters from a postbox. **6.** (*often pl.*) (at Oxford University) a college examination or an oral report by a tutor.

collective (kə'lɛktɪv) *adj.* **1.** formed or assembled by collection. **2.** forming a whole or aggregate. **3.** of, done by, or characteristic of individuals acting in cooperation. ~*n.* **4. a.** a cooperative enterprise or unit, such as a collective farm. **b.** the members of such a cooperative. **5.** short for **collective noun.** —**col'lectively** *adv.* —**col'lectiveness** *n.* —,**collec'tivity** *n.*

collective bargaining *n.* negotiation between a trade union and an employer or an employers' organization on the incomes and working conditions of the employees.

collective noun *n.* a noun that is singular in form but that refers to a group of people or things.

▷ **Usage.** Collective nouns are usually used with singular verbs: *the family is on holiday; General Motors is mounting a big sales campaign.* In British usage, however, plural verbs are sometimes employed in this context, esp. where reference is being made to a collection of individual objects or persons rather than to the group as a unit: *the family are all on holiday.* Care should be taken

that the same collective noun is not treated as both singular and plural in the same sentence: *the family is well and sends its best wishes* or *the family are all well and send their best wishes,* but not *the family is well and send their best wishes.*

collective ownership *n.* ownership by a group for the benefit of members of that group.

collective unconscious *n.* (in Jungian psychological theory) a part of the unconscious mind incorporating patterns of memories, instincts, and experiences common to all mankind.

collectivism (kə'lɛktɪ,vɪzəm) *n.* the principle of ownership of the means of production by the state or the people. —**col'lectivist** *n.* —**col,lectiv'istic** *adj.*

collectivize *or* **-vise** (kə'lɛktɪ,vaɪz) *vb.* (*tr.*) to organize according to the principles of collectivism. —**col,lectivi'zation** *or* **-vi'sation** *n.*

collector (kə'lɛktə) *n.* **1.** a person or thing that collects. **2.** a person employed to collect debts, rents, etc. **3.** a person who collects objects as a hobby. **4.** (in India, formerly) the head of a district administration. **5.** *Electronics.* the region in a transistor into which charge carriers flow from the base.

colleen ('kɒliːn, kɒ'liːn) *n.* an Irish word for **girl.** [C19: from Irish Gaelic *cailīn*]

college ('kɒlɪdʒ) *n.* **1.** an institution of higher education; part of a university. **2.** a school or an institution providing specialized courses: *a college of music.* **3.** the buildings in which a college is housed. **4.** the staff and students of a college. **5.** an organized body of persons with specific rights and duties: *an electoral college.* **6.** a body organized within a particular profession, concerned with regulating standards. **7.** *Brit.* a name given to some secondary schools. [C14: from L, from *collēga*; see COLLEAGUE]

College of Cardinals *n. R.C. Church.* the collective body of cardinals having the function of electing and advising the pope.

college of education *n. Brit.* a professional training college for teachers.

collegian (kə'liːdʒɪən) *n.* a member of a college.

collegiate (kə'liːdʒɪɪt) *adj.* **1.** Also: **col'legial.** of or relating to a college or college students. **2.** (of a university) composed of various colleges of equal standing.

collegiate church *n.* **1.** *R.C. Church, Church of England.* a church that has an endowed chapter of canons and prebendaries attached to it but that is not a cathedral. **2.** *U.S. Protestantism.* one of a group of churches presided over by a body of pastors. **3.** *Scot. Protestantism.* a church served by two or more ministers.

col legno ('kɒl 'lɛgnəʊ, 'leɪnjəʊ) *adv. Music.* to be played (on a stringed instrument) with the back of the bow. [It.: with the wood]

Colles' fracture ('kɒlɪs) *n.* a fracture of the radius just above the wrist with backward and outward displacement of the hand. [C19: after Abraham *Colles* (d. 1843), Irish surgeon]

collet ('kɒlɪt) *n.* **1.** (in a jewellery setting) a band or coronet-shaped claw that holds an individual stone. **2.** *Mechanical engineering.* an externally tapered sleeve made in two or more segments and used to grip a shaft passed through its centre. **3.** *Horology.* a small metal collar that supports the inner end of the hairspring. [C16: from OF: a little collar, from *col*, from L *collum* neck]

collide (kə'laɪd) *vb.* (*intr.*) **1.** to crash together with a violent impact. **2.** to conflict; clash; disagree. [C17: from L, from *com-* together + *laedere* to strike]

collie ('kɒlɪ) *n.* any of several silky-coated breeds of dog developed for herding sheep and cattle. [C17: Scot., prob. from earlier *colie* black from *cole* coal]

collier ('kɒlɪə) *n. Chiefly Brit.* **1.** a coal miner. **2. a.** a ship designed to transport coal. **b.** a member of its crew. [C14: from COAL + -IER]

colliery ('kɒljərɪ) *n., pl.* **-lieries.** *Chiefly Brit.* a coal mine.

collimate ('kɒlɪ,meɪt) *vb.* (*tr.*) **1.** to adjust the line of sight of (an optical instrument). **2.** to use a collimator on (a beam of radiation). **3.** to make parallel or bring into line. [C17: from NL *collimāre,* erroneously for L *collīneāre* to aim, from *com-* (intensive) + *līneāre,* from *līnea* line] —,**colli'mation** *n.*

collimator ('kɒlɪ,meɪtə) *n.* **1.** a small telescope attached to a larger optical instrument as an aid in fixing its line of sight. **2.** an optical system of lenses and slits producing a nondivergent beam of light. **3.** any device for limiting the size and angle of spread of a beam of radiation or particles.

collinear (kɒ'lɪnɪə) *adj.* lying on the same straight line. —**collinearity** (ˌkɒlɪnɪ'ærɪtɪ) *n.*

collins ('kɒlɪnz) *n.* (*functioning as sing.*) an iced drink made with gin, vodka, rum, etc., mixed with fruit juice, soda water, and sugar. [C20: prob. from the name *Collins*]

Collins ('kɒlɪnz) *n.* **1. Michael.** 1890–1922, Irish republican revolutionary: a leader of Sinn Féin; member of the Irish delegation that negotiated the treaty with Great Britain (1921) that established the Irish Free State. **2. William.** 1721–59, English poet, a precursor of romanticism, noted for his odes. **3. (William) Wilkie.** 1824–89, English author, noted particularly for his suspense novel *The Moonstone* (1868).

collision (kə'lɪʒən) *n.* **1.** a violent impact of moving objects; crash. **2.** the conflict of opposed ideas, wishes, attitudes, etc. [C15: from LL, from L *collīdere* to COLLIDE]

collocate ('kɒlə,keɪt) *vb.* (*tr.*) to group or place together in some system or order. [C16: from L, from *com-* together + *locāre* to place] —**,collo'cation** *n.*

collocutor ('kɒlə,kjuːtə) *n.* a person who talks or engages in conversation with another.

collodion (kə'ləʊdɪən) *or* **collodium** (kə'ləʊdɪəm) *n.* a syrupy liquid that consists of a solution of pyroxylin in ether and alcohol: used in medicine and in the manufacture of photographic plates, lacquers, etc. [C19: from NL, from Gk *kollōdēs* glutinous, from *kolla* glue]

collogue (kɒ'ləʊg) *vb.* **colloguing, collogued.** (*intr.*; usually foll. by *with*) to confer confidentially; conspire. [C16: ?from obs. *colleague* (vb.) to conspire, infl. by L *colloquī* to talk with]

colloid ('kɒlɔɪd) *n.* **1.** a mixture having particles of one component suspended in a continuous phase of another component. The mixture has properties between those of a solution and a fine suspension. **2.** *Physiol.* a gelatinous substance of the thyroid follicles that holds the hormonal secretions of the thyroid gland. [C19: from Gk *kolla* glue + -OID] —**col'loidal** *adj.*

collop ('kɒləp) *n. Dialect.* **1.** a slice of meat. **2.** a small piece of anything. [C14: of Scand. origin]

colloq. *abbrev. for* colloquial(ly).

colloquial (kə'ləʊkwɪəl) *adj.* **1.** of or relating to conversation. **2.** denoting or characterized by informal or conversational idiom or vocabulary. —**col'loquially** *adv.* —**col'loquialness** *n.*

colloquialism (kə'ləʊkwɪə,lɪzəm) *n.* **1.** a word or phrase appropriate to conversation and other informal situations. **2.** the use of colloquial words and phrases.

colloquium (kə'ləʊkwɪəm) *n., pl.* **-quiums** *or* **-quia** (-kwɪə). **1.** a gathering for discussion. **2.** an academic seminar. [C17: from L: COLLOQUY]

colloquy ('kɒləkwɪ) *n., pl.* **-quies. 1.** a formal conversation or conference. **2.** an informal conference on religious or theological matters. [C16: from L *colloquium*, from *com-*together + *loquī* to speak] —**'colloquist** *n.*

collotype ('kɒləʊ,taɪp) *n.* **1.** a method of lithographic printing (usually of high-quality reproductions) from a plate of hardened gelatin. **2.** a print so made.

collude (kə'luːd) *vb.* (*intr.*) to conspire together, esp. in planning a fraud. [C16: from L, from *com-* together + *lūdere* to play] —**col'luder** *n.*

collusion (kə'luːʒən) *n.* **1.** secret agreement for a fraudulent purpose; conspiracy. **2.** a secret agreement between opponents at law for some improper purpose. [C14: from L, from *collūdere* to COLLUDE] —**col'lusive** *adj.*

collywobbles ('kɒlɪ,wɒbəlz) *pl. n.* (usually preceded by *the*) *Sl.* **1.** an upset stomach. **2.** an intense feeling of nervousness. [C19: prob. from NL *cholera morbus*, infl. through folk etymology by COLIC and WOBBLE]

Colmar (*French* kɒlmar) *n.* a city in NE France: annexed to Germany 1871–1919 and 1940–45; textile industry. Pop.: 64 200 (1983). German name: **Kolmar.**

colobus ('kɒləbəs) *n.* any leaf-eating arboreal Old World monkey of W and central Africa, having long silky fur and reduced or absent thumbs. [C19: NL, from Gk *kolobos* cut short; referring to its thumb]

cologarithm (kəʊ'lɒgə,rɪðəm) *n.* the logarithm of the reciprocal of a number; the negative value of the logarithm: *the cologarithm of 4 is log ¹⁄₄* Abbrev.: **colog.**

cologne (kə'ləʊn) *n.* a perfumed liquid or solid made of fragrant essential oils and alcohol. Also called: **Cologne**

water, eau de cologne. [C18 *Cologne water* from CO-LOGNE, where it was first manufactured (1709)]

Cologne (kə'ləʊn) *n.* an industrial city and river port in West Germany, in North Rhine-Westphalia on the Rhine: important commercially since ancient times; university (1388). Pop.: 914 000 (1986). German name: **Köln.**

Colomb-Béchar (*French* kɔlɔ̃beʃar) *n.* the former name of **Béchar.**

Colombes (*French* kɔlɔ̃b) *n.* an industrial and residential suburb of NW Paris. Pop.: 83 260 (1983 est.).

Colombia (kə'lɒmbɪə) *n.* a republic in NW South America: inhabited by Chibchas and other Indians before Spanish colonization in the 16th century; independence won by Bolívar in 1819; became the Republic of Colombia in 1886. It consists chiefly of a hot swampy coastal plain, separated by ranges of the Andes from the pampas and the equatorial forests of the Amazon basin in the east. Language: Spanish. Religion: Roman Catholic. Currency: peso. Capital: Bogotá. Pop.: 29 956 000 (1986). Area: 1 138 908 sq. km (439 735 sq. miles). —**Co'lombian** *adj., n.*

Colombo (kə'lʌmbəʊ) *n.* the capital and chief port of Sri Lanka, on the W coast, with one of the largest artificial harbours in the world. Pop.: 585 776 (1981).

colon[1] ('kəʊlən) *n., pl.* **-lons. 1.** the punctuation mark : , usually preceding an explanation or an example, a list, or an extended quotation. **2.** this mark used for certain other purposes, such as when a ratio is given in figures, as in *5:3.* [C16: from L, from Gk *kōlon* limb, clause]

colon[2] ('kəʊlən) *n., pl.* **-lons** *or* **-la** (-lə). the part of the large intestine between the caecum and the rectum. [C16: from L: large intestine, from Gk *kolon*] —**colonic** (kə'lɒnɪk) *adj.*

colón (kə'lɒnɪn; *Spanish* ko'lon) *n., pl.* **-lons** *or* **-lones** (*Spanish* -'lones). **1.** the standard monetary unit of Costa Rica, divided into 100 céntimos. **2.** the standard monetary unit of El Salvador, divided into 100 centavos. [C19: American Sp., from Sp., after Cristóbal *Colón* Christopher Columbus]

Colón (kɒ'lɒn; *Spanish* ko'lon) *n.* **1.** a port in Panama, at the Caribbean entrance to the Panama Canal. Chief Caribbean port. Pop.: 68 688 (1987). Former name: **Aspinwall.** **2. Archipiélago de** (ˌartʃi'pjelaɣo ðe). the official name of the **Galápagos Islands.**

colonel ('kɜːnəl) *n.* an officer of land or air forces junior to a brigadier but senior to a lieutenant colonel. [C16: via OF, from OIt. *colonnello* column of soldiers, from *colonna* COLUMN] —**'colonelcy** *or* **'colonel,ship** *n.*

colonial (kə'ləʊnɪəl) *adj.* **1.** of, characteristic of, relating to, possessing, or inhabiting a colony or colonies. **2.** (*often cap.*) characteristic of or relating to the 13 British colonies that became the United States of America (1776). **3.** (*often cap.*) of or relating to the colonies of the British Empire. **4.** denoting or having the style of Neoclassical architecture used in the British colonies in America in the 17th and 18th centuries. **5.** (of animals and plants) having become established in a community in a new environment. ~*n.* **6.** a native of a colony. —**co'lonially** *adv.*

colonial goose *n. N.Z.* an old-fashioned name for stuffed roast mutton.

colonialism (kə'ləʊnɪə,lɪzəm) *n.* the policy and practice of a power in extending control over weaker peoples or areas. Also called: **imperialism.** —**co'lonialist** *n., adj.*

Colonies ('kɒlənɪz) *pl. n.* **the. 1.** *Brit.* the subject territories formerly in the British Empire. **2.** *U.S. history.* the 13 states forming the original United States of America when they declared their independence (1776).

colonist ('kɒlənɪst) *n.* **1.** a person who settles in or colonizes an area. **2.** an inhabitant of a colony.

colonize *or* **-ise** ('kɒlə,naɪz) *vb.* **1.** to send colonists to or establish a colony in (an area). **2.** to settle in (an area) as colonists. **3.** (*tr.*) to transform (a community, etc.) into a colony. **4.** (of plants and animals) to become established in (a new environment). —**,coloni'zation** *or* **-i'sation** *n.* —**'colo,nizer** *or* **-iser** *n.*

colonnade (ˌkɒlə'neɪd) *n.* **1.** a set of evenly spaced columns. **2.** a row of regularly spaced trees. [C18: from F, from *colonne* COLUMN; on the model of It. *colonnato*] —**,colon'naded** *adj.*

Colonsay ('kɒlənseɪ, -zeɪ) *n.* an island in W Scotland, in the Inner Hebrides. Area: about 41 sq. km (16 sq. miles).

colony ('kɒlənɪ) n., pl. **-nies.** **1.** a body of people who settle in a country distant from their homeland but maintain ties with it. **2.** the community formed by such settlers. **3.** a subject territory occupied by a settlement from the ruling state. **4. a.** a community of people who form a national, racial, or cultural minority concentrated in a particular place: *an artists' colony.* **b.** the area itself. **5.** *Zool.* a group of the same type of animal or plant living or growing together. **6.** *Bacteriol.* a group of bacteria, fungi, etc., derived from one or a few spores, esp. when grown on a culture medium. [C16: from L, from *colere* to cultivate, inhabit]

colophon ('kɒlə,fɒn, -fən) n. **1.** a publisher's emblem on a book. **2.** (formerly) an inscription at the end of a book showing the title, printer, date, etc. [C17: via LL, from Gk *kolophōn* a finishing stroke]

colophony (kə'lɒfənɪ) n. another name for **rosin** (sense 1). [C14: from L: resin from Colophon]

color ('kʌlə) n., vb. the U.S. spelling of **colour.**

Colorado (,kɒlə'rɑːdəʊ) n. **1.** a state of the central U.S.: consists of the Great Plains in the east and the Rockies in the west; drained chiefly by the Colorado, Arkansas, South Platte, and Rio Grande Rivers. Capital: Denver. Pop.: 3 267 118 (1986 est.). Area: 269 998 sq. km (104 247 sq. miles). Abbrevs.: **Colo.** or (with zip code) **CO 2.** a river in SW North America, rising in the Rocky Mountains and flowing southwest to the Gulf of California: famous for the 1600 km (1000 miles) of canyons along its course. Length: about 2320 km (1440 miles). **3.** a river in central Texas, flowing southeast to the Gulf of Mexico. Length: about 1450 km (900 miles). **4.** a river in central Argentina, flowing southeast to the Atlantic. Length: about 850 km (530 miles). [Sp., lit.: red, from L *colōrātus* coloured, tinted red; see COLOUR]

Colorado beetle n. a black-and-yellow beetle that is a serious pest of potatoes, feeding on the leaves.

Colorado Desert n. an arid region of SE California and NW Mexico, West of the Colorado River. Area: over 5000 sq. km (2000 sq. miles).

Colorado Springs n. a city and resort in central Colorado. Pop.: 270 724 (1986 est.).

colorant ('kʌlərənt) n. any substance that imparts colour, such as a pigment, dye, or ink.

coloration or **colouration** (,kʌlə'reɪʃən) n. **1.** arrangement of colour; colouring. **2.** the colouring or markings of insects, birds, etc.

coloratura (,kɒlərə'tʊərə) n. *Music.* **1.** (in 18th- and 19th-century arias) a florid virtuoso passage. **2.** Also called: **coloratura soprano.** a soprano who specializes in such music. [C19: from obs. It., lit.: colouring.]

colorific (,kʌlə'rɪfɪk) adj. producing, imparting, or relating to colour.

colorimeter (,kʌlə'rɪmɪtə) n. apparatus for measuring the quality of a colour by comparison with standard colours or combinations of colours. —**colorimetric** (,kʌlərɪ-'mɛtrɪk) adj. —,**color'imetry** n.

Colossae (kə'lɒsiː) n. an ancient city in SW Phrygia in Asia Minor: seat of an early Christian Church.

colossal (kə'lɒsəl) adj. **1.** of immense size; huge; gigantic. **2.** (in figure sculpture) approximately twice life-size. **3.** *Archit.* of the order of columns that extend more than one storey in a façade. —**co'lossally** adv.

Colosseum (,kɒlə'sɪəm) n. an amphitheatre in Rome built about 75–80 A.D.

colossus (kə'lɒsəs) n., pl. **-si** (-saɪ) or **-suses.** something very large, esp. a statue. [C14: from L, from Gk *kolossos*]

Colossus of Rhodes n. a giant bronze statue of Apollo built on Rhodes in about 292–280 B.C.; destroyed by an earthquake in 225 B.C.; one of the Seven Wonders of the World.

colostomy (kə'lɒstəmɪ) n., pl. **-mies.** the surgical formation of an opening from the colon onto the surface of the body, which functions as an anus.

colostrum (kə'lɒstrəm) n. the thin milky secretion from the nipples that precedes and follows true lactation. [C16: from L, from ?]

colotomy (kə'lɒtəmɪ) n., pl. **-mies.** a colonic incision. [C19: COLON[2] + -TOMY]

colour or U.S. **color** ('kʌlə) n. **1. a.** an attribute of things that results from the light they reflect or emit in so far as this causes a visual sensation that depends on its wavelengths. **b.** the aspect of visual perception by which an observer recognizes this attribute. **c.** the quality of the

light producing this visual perception. **2.** Also called: **chromatic colour. a.** a colour, such as red or green, that possesses hue, as opposed to achromatic colours such as white or black. **b.** (*as modifier*): *colour television.* **3.** a substance, such as a dye or paint, that imparts colour. **4. a.** the skin complexion of a person, esp. as determined by his race. **b.** (*as modifier*): *colour prejudice.* **5.** the use of all the hues in painting as distinct from composition, form, and light and shade. **6.** the quantity and quality of ink used in a printing process. **7.** the distinctive tone of a musical sound. **8.** vividness or authenticity: *period colour.* **9.** semblance or pretext: *under colour of.* **10.** *Physics.* one of three characteristics of quarks, designated red, blue, or green, but having only a remote formal relationship with the physical sensation. ~vb. **11.** (tr.) to apply colour to (something). **12.** (tr.) to give a convincing appearance to: *to colour an alibi.* **13.** (tr.) to influence or distort: *anger coloured her judgment.* **14.** (*intr.*; often foll. by *up*) to become red in the face, esp. when embarrassed or annoyed. ~See also **colours.** [C13 from OF *colour* from L *color* tint, hue]

colourable ('kʌlərəb³l) adj. **1.** capable of being coloured. **2.** appearing to be true; plausible. **3.** pretended; feigned.

colour bar n. discrimination against people of a different race, esp. as practised by Whites against Blacks.

colour-blind adj. of or relating to any defect in the normal ability to distinguish certain colours. —**colour blindness** n.

colour code n. a system of easily distinguishable colours, as for the identification of electrical wires or resistors.

coloured ('kʌləd) adj. **1.** possessing colour. **2.** having a strong element of fiction or fantasy; distorted (esp. in **highly coloured**).

Coloured ('kʌləd) n. **1.** an individual who is not a White, esp. a Negro. **2.** Also called: **Cape Coloured.** (in South Africa) a person of racially mixed parentage or descent. ~adj. **3.** designating or relating to a Coloured or Coloureds.

colourfast ('kʌlə,fɑːst) adj. (of a fabric) having a colour that does not run or change when washed or worn. —'**colour,fastness** n.

colourful ('kʌləful) adj. **1.** having intense colour or richly varied colours. **2.** vivid, rich, or distinctive in character. —'**colourfully** adv.

colour guard n. a military guard in a parade, ceremony, etc., that carries and escorts the flag.

colouring ('kʌlərɪŋ) n. **1.** the process or art of applying colour. **2.** anything used to give colour, such as paint. **3.** appearance with regard to shade and colour. **4.** arrangements of colours, as in the markings of birds. **5.** the colour of a person's complexion. **6.** a false or misleading appearance.

colourist ('kʌlərɪst) n. a person who uses colour, esp. an artist.

colourize, colourise, or U.S. **colorize** ('kʌlə,raɪz) vb. (tr.) to add colour electronically to (an old black-and-white film). —,**colouri'zation, -i'sation** or U.S. **colori'zation** n.

colourless ('kʌləlɪs) adj. **1.** without colour. **2.** lacking in interest: *a colourless individual.* **3.** grey or pallid in tone or hue. **4.** without prejudice; neutral. —'**colourlessly** adv.

colours ('kʌləz) pl. n. **1. a.** the flag that indicates nationality. **b.** *Mil.* the ceremony of hoisting or lowering the colours. **2.** a pair of silk flags borne by a military unit and showing its crest and battle honours. **3.** true nature or character (esp. in **show one's colours**). **4.** a distinguishing badge or flag. **5.** *Sport, Brit.* a badge or other symbol denoting membership of a team, esp. at a school or college. **6. nail one's colours to the mast. a.** to commit oneself publicly and irrevocably to some party, course of action, etc. **b.** to refuse to admit defeat.

colour sergeant n. a sergeant who carries the regimental, battalion, or national colours.

colour supplement n. *Brit.* an illustrated magazine accompanying a newspaper.

colourway ('kʌlə,weɪ) n. one of several different combinations of colours in which a given pattern is printed on fabrics or wallpapers, etc.

colposcope ('kɒlpə,skəʊp) n. an instrument for examining the cervix. [C20: from Gk *kolpos* womb + -SCOPE]

colt (kəʊlt) *n.* **1.** a male horse or pony under the age of four. **2.** *Sport.* **a.** a young and inexperienced player. **b.** a member of a junior team. [OE *colt* young ass]

colter ('kəʊltə) *n.* a variant spelling (esp. U.S.) of **coulter.**

coltish ('kəʊltɪʃ) *adj.* **1.** inexperienced; unruly. **2.** playful and lively. — **'coltishness** *n.*

Coltrane (kɒl'treɪn) *n.* **John.** 1926–67, U.S. jazz tenor and soprano saxophonist.

coltsfoot ('kəʊlts,fʊt) *n., pl.* **-foots.** a European plant with yellow daisy-like flowers and heart-shaped leaves: a common weed.

colubrine ('kɒlju,braɪn) *adj.* **1.** of or resembling a snake. **2.** of or belonging to the Colubrinae, a subfamily of harmless snakes. [C16: from L *colubrinus*, from *coluber* snake]

Colum ('kɒləm) *n.* **Padraic** ('pɑ:drɪk). 1881–1972, Irish lyric poet, resident in the U.S. (1914–72).

Columba (kə'lʌmbə) *n.* **Saint.** ?521–597 A.D., Irish missionary: founded the monastery at Iona (563) from which the Picts were converted to Christianity. Feast day: June 9.

Columbia (kə'lʌmbɪə) *n.* **1.** a river in NW North America, rising in the Rocky Mountains and flowing through British Columbia, then west to the Pacific. Length: about 1930 km (1200 miles). **2.** a city in central South Carolina, on the Congaree River: the state capital. Pop.: 93 020 (1986).

columbine ('kɒləm,baɪn) *n.* any plant of the genus *Aquilegia*, having flowers with five spurred petals. Also called: **aquilegia.** [C13: from Med. L *columbina herba* dovelike plant]

Columbine ('kɒləm,baɪn) *n.* the sweetheart of Harlequin in English pantomime.

Columbus¹ (kə'lʌmbəs) *n.* **1.** a city in central Ohio: the state capital. Pop.: 566 030 (1986). **2.** a city in W Georgia, on the Chattahoochee River. Pop.: 169 441 (1980).

Columbus² (kə'lʌmbəs) *n.* **Christopher.** Spanish name *Cristóbal Colón*, Italian name *Cristoforo Colombo*. 1451–1506, Italian navigator and explorer in the service of Spain, who discovered the New World (1492).

column ('kɒləm) *n.* **1.** an upright pillar usually having a cylindrical shaft, a base, and a capital. **2. a.** a form or structure in the shape of a column: *a column of air.* **b.** a monument. **3.** a line, as of people in a queue. **4.** *Mil.* a narrow formation in which individuals or units follow one behind the other. **5.** *Journalism.* **a.** a single row of type on a newspaper. **b.** a regular feature in a paper: *the fashion column.* **6.** a vertical array of numbers. [C15: from L *columna*, from *columen* top, peak] — **columnar** (kə'lʌmnə) *adj.* — **'columned** *adj.*

columniation (kə,lʌmnɪ'eɪʃən) *n.* the arrangement of architectural columns.

column inch *n.* a unit of measurement for advertising space, one inch deep and one column wide.

columnist ('kɒləmnɪst, -əmɪst) *n.* a journalist who writes a regular feature in a newspaper.

colure (kə'lʊə, 'kəʊlʊə) *n.* either of two great circles on the celestial sphere, one passing through the poles and the equinoxes, the other through the poles and the solstices. [C16: from LL, from Gk *kolourai*, dock-tailed, from *kolos* docked + *oura* tail (because the lower portion is not visible)]

Colwyn Bay ('kɒlwɪn) *n.* a town and resort in N Wales, in NW Clwyd. Pop.: 26 000 (1985 est.).

colza ('kɒlzə) *n.* another name for **rape².** [C18: via F (Walloon) from Du., from *kool* cabbage, COLE + *zaad* SEED]

COM (kɒm) *n.* direct conversion of computer output to microfiche or film. [C20: *C*(*omputer*) *O*(*utput on*) *M*(*icrofilm*)]

Com. *abbrev. for:* **1.** Commander. **2.** Committee. **3.** Commodore. **4.** Communist.

com- *or* **con-** *prefix.* together; with; jointly: *commingle.* [from L *com-*; rel. to *cum* with. In compound words of L origin, *com-* becomes *col-* and *cor-* before *l* and *r*, *co-* before *gn*, *h*, and most vowels, and *con-* before consonants other than *b*, *p*, and *m*]

coma¹ ('kəʊmə) *n., pl.* **-mas.** a state of unconsciousness from which a person cannot be aroused, caused by injury, narcotics, poisons, etc. [C17: from medical L, from Gk *kōma* heavy sleep]

coma² ('kəʊmə) *n., pl.* **-mae** (-mi:). **1.** *Astron.* the luminous cloud surrounding the nucleus in the head of a comet. **2.** *Bot.* **a.** a tuft of hairs attached to the seed coat of some seeds. **b.** the terminal crown of leaves of palms

and moss stems. [C17: from L: hair of the head, from Gk *komē*]

comanche (kə'mæntʃɪ) *n.* **1.** (*pl.* **-ches** *or* **-che**) a member of a North American Indian people formerly inhabiting the W plains of the U.S. **2.** the language of this people.

comatose ('kəʊmə,təʊs) *adj.* **1.** in a state of coma. **2.** torpid; lethargic.

comb (kəʊm) *n.* **1.** a toothed device for disentangling or arranging hair. **2.** a tool or machine that cleans and straightens wool, cotton, etc. **3.** *Austral. & N.Z.* the fixed cutter on a sheep-shearing machine. **4.** anything resembling a comb in form or function. **5.** the fleshy serrated outgrowth on the heads of certain birds, esp. the domestic fowl. **6.** a honeycomb. ~*vb.* **7.** (*tr.*) to use a comb on. **8.** (when *tr.*, often foll. *by through*) to search with great care: *the police combed the woods.* ~See also **comb out.** [OE *camb*]

combat *n.* ('kɒmbæt, -bət, 'kʌm-). **1.** a fight, conflict, or struggle. **2. a.** an action fought between two military forces. **b.** (*as modifier*): *a combat jacket.* **3. single combat.** a duel. ~*vb.* (kəm'bæt; 'kɒmbæt, 'kʌm-). **4.** (*tr.*) to fight. **5.** (*intr.*; often foll. *by with or against*) to struggle or strive (against): *to combat against disease.* [C16: from F, from OF *combattre*, from Vulgar L *combattere* (unattested), from L *com-* with + *battuere* to beat]

combatant ('kɒmbət°nt, 'kʌm-) *n.* **1.** a person or group engaged in or prepared for a fight. ~*adj.* **2.** engaged in or ready for combat.

combat fatigue *n.* another term for **battle fatigue.**

combative ('kɒmbətɪv, 'kʌm-) *adj.* eager or ready to fight, argue, etc. — '**combativeness** *n.*

combe *or* **comb** (ku:m) *n.* variant spellings of **coomb.**

comber ('kəʊmə) *n.* **1.** a person, tool, or machine that combs wool, flax, etc. **2.** a long curling wave; roller.

combination (,kɒmbɪ'neɪʃən) *n.* **1.** the act of combining or state of being combined. **2.** a union of separate parts, qualities, etc. **3.** an alliance of people or parties. **4.** the set of numbers that opens a combination lock. **5.** *Brit.* a motorcycle with a sidecar attached. **6.** *Maths.* an arrangement of the numbers, terms, etc., of a set into specified groups without regard to order in the group. **7.** the chemical reaction of two or more compounds, usually to form one other compound. **8.** *Chess.* a tactical manoeuvre involving a sequence of moves and more than one piece. — ,**combi'national** *adj.*

combination lock *n.* a type of lock that can only be opened when a set of dials is turned to show a specific sequence of numbers.

combinations (,kɒmbɪ'neɪʃənz) *pl. n. Brit.* a one-piece undergarment with long sleeves and legs. Often shortened to **combs** or **coms.**

combine *vb.* (kəm'baɪn). **1.** to join together. **2.** to unite or cause to unite to form a chemical compound. ~*n.* ('kɒmbaɪn). **3.** short for **combine harvester. 4.** an association of enterprises, esp. in order to gain a monopoly of a market. **5.** an association of related bodies, such as business corporations or sports clubs, for a common purpose. [C15: from LL *combīnāre*, from L *com-* together + *bīnī* two by two] — **com'binable** *adj.* — **com,bina'bility** *n.* — **combinative** ('kɒmbɪ,neɪtɪv) *or* **combinatory** ('kɒmbɪ,neɪtərɪ) *adj.*

combine harvester ('kɒmbaɪn) *n.* a machine that simultaneously cuts, threshes, and cleans a standing crop of grain.

combings ('kəʊmɪŋz) *pl. n.* **1.** the loose hair removed by combing. **2.** the unwanted fibres removed in combing cotton, etc.

combining form *n.* a linguistic element that occurs only as part of a compound word, such as *anthropo-* in *anthropology* and *anthropomorph.*

combo ('kɒmbəʊ) *n., pl.* **-bos. 1.** a small group of jazz musicians. **2.** *Inf.* any combination.

comb out *vb.* (*tr., adv.*) **1.** to remove (tangles) from (the hair) with a comb. **2.** to remove for a purpose. **3.** to examine systematically.

combustible (kəm'bʌstɪb°l) *adj.* **1.** capable of igniting and burning. **2.** easily annoyed; excitable. ~*n.* **3.** a combustible substance. — **com,busti'bility** *or* **com'bustibleness** *n.*

combustion (kəm'bʌstʃən) *n.* **1.** the process of burning. **2.** any process in which a substance reacts to produce a significant rise in temperature and the emission of light.

3. a process in which a compound reacts slowly with oxygen to produce little heat and no light. [C15: from OF, from L *comburere* to burn up] —**com'bustive** *n.*, *adj.*

combustion chamber *n.* an enclosed space in which combustion takes place, such as the space above the piston in the cylinder head of an internal-combustion engine.

combustor (kəm'bʌstə) *n.* the combustion system of a jet engine or ramjet.

Comdr *Mil. abbrev. for* Commander.

Comdt *Mil. abbrev. for* Commandant.

come (kʌm) *vb.* **coming, came, come.** (*mainly intr.*) **1.** to move towards a specified person or place. **2.** to arrive by movement or by making progress. **3.** to become perceptible: *light came into the sky.* **4.** to occur: *Christmas comes but once a year.* **5.** to happen as a result: *no good will come of this.* **6.** to be derived: *good may come of evil.* **7.** to occur to the mind: *the truth suddenly came to me.* **8.** to reach: *she comes up to my shoulder.* **9.** to be produced: *that dress comes in red.* **10.** to arrive at or be brought into a particular state: *you will soon come to grief.* **11.** (foll. by *from*) to be or have been a resident or native (of): *I come from London.* **12.** to become: *your wishes will come true.* **13.** (*tr.*) (used with *an infinitive*) to be given awareness: *I came to realize its value.* **14.** *Taboo sl.* to have an orgasm. **15.** (*tr.*) *Brit. inf.* to play the part of: *don't come the fine gentleman with me.* **16.** (*tr.*) *Brit. inf.* to cause or produce: *don't come that nonsense.* **17.** (*subjunctive use*): *come next August, he will be fifty years old:* when next August arrives. **18. as . . . as they come.** the most characteristic example of a type. **19. come again?** *Inf.* what did you say? **20. come good.** to recover and perform well after a setback or poor start. **21. come to light.** to be revealed. **22. come to light with.** *Austral. & N.Z. inf.* to find or produce. ~*interj.* **23.** an exclamation expressing annoyance, etc.: *come now!* ~See also **come about, come across**, etc. [OE *cuman*]

come about *vb.* (*intr.*, *adv.*) **1.** to take place; happen. **2.** *Naut.* to change tacks.

come across *vb.* (*intr.*) **1.** (*prep.*) to meet or find by accident. **2.** (*adv.*) to communicate the intended meaning or impression. **3.** (often foll. by *with*) to provide what is expected.

come at *vb.* (*intr.*, *prep.*) **1.** to discover (facts, the truth, etc.). **2.** to attack: *he came at me with an axe.* **3.** (*usually used with a negative*) *Austral. sl.* to agree to do (something).

comeback ('kʌm,bæk) *n. Inf.* **1.** a return to a former position, status, etc. **2.** a response, esp. recriminatory. **3.** a quick retort. ~*vb.* **come back.** (*intr.*, *adv.*) **4.** to return, esp. to the memory. **5.** to become fashionable again.

come between *vb.* (*intr.*, *prep.*) to cause the estrangement or separation of (two people).

come by *vb.* (*intr.*, *prep.*) to find or obtain, esp. accidentally: *do you ever come by any old books?*

Comecon ('kɒmɪ,kɒn) *n.* an association of Soviet-oriented Communist nations, founded in 1949 to coordinate economic development, etc. [C20: *Co(uncil for) M(utual) Econ(omic Aid)*]

comedian (kə'miːdɪən) *n.* **1.** an entertainer who specializes in jokes, comic skits, etc. **2.** an actor in comedy. **3.** an amusing person: sometimes used ironically.

comedienne (kə,miːdɪ'ɛn) *n.* a female comedian.

comedo ('kɒmɪ,dəʊ) *n.*, *pl.* **comedos** *or* **comedones** (,kɒmɪ'dəʊniːz). *Pathol.* the technical name for **blackhead.** [C19: from NL, from L: glutton]

comedown ('kʌm,daʊn) *n.* **1.** a decline in status or prosperity. **2.** *Inf.* a disappointment. ~*vb.* **come down.** (*intr.*, *adv.*) **3.** to come to a place regarded as lower. **4.** to lose status, etc. (esp. in **come down in the world**). **5.** (of prices) to become lower. **6.** to reach a decision: *the report came down in favour of a pay increase.* **7.** (often foll. by *to*) to be handed down by tradition or inheritance. **8.** *Brit.* to leave university. **9.** (foll. by *with*) to succumb (to illness). **10.** (foll. by *on*) to rebuke harshly. **11.** (foll. by *to*) to amount in essence (to): *it comes down to two choices.*

comedy ('kɒmɪdɪ) *n.*, *pl.* **-dies. 1.** a dramatic or other work of light and amusing character. **2.** the genre of drama represented by works of this type. **3.** (in classical literature) a play in which the main characters triumph over adversity. **4.** the humorous aspect of life or of events. **5.** an amusing event or sequence of events. **6.**

humour: *the comedy of Chaplin.* [C14: from OF, from L, from Gk *kōmōidia*, from *kōmos* village festival + *aeidein* to sing] —**comedic** (kə'miːdɪk) *adj.*

comedy of manners *n.* a comedy dealing with the way of life and foibles of a social group.

come forward *vb.* (*intr.*, *adv.*) **1.** to offer one's services; volunteer. **2.** to present oneself.

come-hither *adj.* (*usually prenominal*) *Inf.* alluring; seductive: *a come-hither look.*

come in *vb.* (*intr.*, *mainly adv.*) **1.** to enter. **2.** to prove to be: *it came in useful.* **3.** to become fashionable or seasonable. **4.** *Cricket.* to begin an innings. **5.** to finish a race (in a certain position). **6.** to be received: *news is coming in of a big fire in Glasgow.* **7.** (of money) to be received as income. **8.** to play a role: *where do I come in?* **9.** (foll. by *for*) to be the object of: *the Chancellor came in for a lot of criticism.*

come into *vb.* (*intr.*, *prep.*) **1.** to enter. **2.** to inherit.

comely ('kʌmlɪ) *adj.* **-lier, -liest. 1.** good-looking; attractive. **2.** *Arch.* suitable; fitting. [OE *cӯmlīc* beautiful] —**'comeliness** *n.*

Comenius (kə'meɪnɪəs) *n.* **John Amos,** Czech name *Jan Amos Komensky.* 1592–1670, Czech educational reformer.

come of *vb.* (*intr.*, *prep.*) **1.** to be descended from. **2.** to result from: *nothing came of it.*

come off *vb.* (*intr.*, *mainly adv.*) **1.** (*also prep.*) to fall (from). **2.** to become detached. **3.** (*prep.*) to be removed from (a price, tax, etc.): *will anything come off income tax in the budget?* **4.** (*copula*) to emerge from or as if from a contest: *he came off the winner.* **5.** *Inf.* to happen. **6.** *Inf.* to have the intended effect: *his jokes did not come off.* **7.** *Taboo sl.* to have an orgasm.

come-on *n.* **1.** *Inf.* anything that serves as a lure. ~*vb.* **come on** (*intr.*, *mainly adv.*) **2.** (of power, water, etc.) to start running or functioning. **3.** to progress: *my plants are coming on nicely.* **4.** to advance, esp. in battle. **5.** to begin: *a new bowler has come on.* **6.** to make an entrance on stage.

come out *vb.* (*intr.*, *adv.*) **1.** to be made public or revealed: *the news of her death came out last week.* **2.** to make a debut in society. **3.** *Also:* **come out of the closet. a.** to declare openly that one is a homosexual. **b.** to reveal or declare any practice or habit formerly concealed. **4.** *Chiefly Brit.* to go on strike. **5.** to declare oneself: *the government came out in favour of scrapping the project.* **6.** to be shown clearly: *you came out very well in the photos.* **7.** to yield a satisfactory solution: *these sums just won't come out.* **8.** to be published: *the paper comes out on Fridays.* **9.** (foll. by *in*) to become covered (with). **10.** (foll. by *with*) to declare openly: *you can rely on him to come out with the facts.*

come over *vb.* (*intr.*, *adv.*) **1.** to communicate the intended meaning or impression: *he came over very well.* **2.** to change allegiances. **3.** *Inf.* to feel a particular sensation: *I came over funny.*

comer ('kʌmə) *n.* **1.** (*in combination*) a person who comes: *all-comers; newcomers.* **2.** *Inf.* a potential success.

come round *vb.* (*intr.*, *adv.*) **1.** to be restored to consciousness. **2.** to modify one's opinion.

comestible (kə'mɛstɪbəl) *n.* (*usually pl.*) food. [C15: from LL *comestibilis*, from *comedere* to eat up]

comet ('kɒmɪt) *n.* a celestial body that travels around the sun, usually in a highly elliptical orbit: thought to consist of a frozen nucleus, part of which vaporizes on approaching the sun to form a long luminous tail. [C13: from OF, from L, from Gk *kōmētēs* long-haired] —**'cometary** *or* **cometic** (kə'mɛtɪk) *adj.*

come through *vb.* (*intr.*) **1.** (*adv.*) to emerge successfully. **2.** (*prep.*) to survive (an illness, etc.).

come to *vb.* (*intr.*) **1.** (*adv. or prep. and reflexive*) to regain consciousness. **2.** (*adv.*) *Naut.* to slow a vessel or bring her to a stop. **3.** (*prep.*) to amount to (a sum of money). **4.** (*prep.*) to arrive at: *what is the world coming to?*

come up *vb.* (*intr.*, *adv.*) **1.** to come to a place regarded as higher. **2.** (of the sun) to rise. **3.** to present itself: *that question will come up again.* **4.** *Brit.* to begin a term at a university. **5.** to appear from out of the ground: *my beans have come up early.* **6.** *Inf.* to win: *have your premium bonds ever come up?* **7. come up against.** to come into conflict with. **8. come up to.** to meet a standard. **9. come up with.** to produce.

come upon vb. (intr., prep.) to meet or encounter unexpectedly.

comeuppance (,kʌm'ʌpəns) n. Inf. just retribution. [C19: from come up (in the sense): to appear before a court]

comfit ('kʌmfɪt, 'kɒm-) n. a sugar-coated sweet containing a nut or seed. [C15: from OF, from L confectum something prepared]

comfort ('kʌmfət) n. **1.** a state of ease or well-being. **2.** relief from affliction, grief, etc. **3.** a person, thing, or event that brings solace or ease. **4.** (usually pl.) something that affords physical ease and relaxation. ~vb. (tr.) **5.** to soothe; cheer. **6.** to bring physical ease to. [C13: from OF confort, from LL confortāre to strengthen, from L con-(intensive) + fortis strong] —'**comforting** adj. —'**comfortless** adj.

comfortable ('kʌmftəb³l) adj. **1.** giving comfort. **2.** at ease. **3.** free from affliction or pain. **4.** (of a person or situation) relaxing. **5.** Inf. having adequate income. **6.** Inf. (of income, etc.) adequate to provide comfort. —'**comfortably** adv.

comforter ('kʌmfətə) n. **1.** a person or thing that comforts. **2.** Chiefly Brit. a woollen scarf. **3.** a baby's dummy. **4.** U.S. a quilted bed covering.

Comforter ('kʌmfətə) n. Christianity. an epithet of the Holy Spirit. [C14: translation of L consolātor, representing Gk paraklētos advocate]

comfrey ('kʌmfrɪ) n. a hairy Eurasian plant having blue, purplish-pink, or white flowers. [C15: from OF cunfirie, from L conferva water plant]

comfy ('kʌmfɪ) adj. **-fier, -fiest.** Inf. short for **comfortable.**

comic ('kɒmɪk) adj. **1.** of, characterized by, or characteristic of comedy. **2.** (prenominal) acting in or composing comedy: a comic writer. **3.** humorous; funny. ~n. **4.** a person who is comic; comedian. **5.** a book or magazine containing comic strips. [C16: from L cōmicus, from Gk kōmikos]

comical ('kɒmɪk³l) adj. **1.** causing laughter. **2.** ludicrous; laughable. —'**comically** adv.

comic opera n. a play largely set to music, employing comic effects or situations.

comic strip n. a sequence of drawings in a newspaper, magazine, etc., relating a humorous story or an adventure.

Comines or **Commines** (French kɔmin) n. **Philippe de** (filip də). ?1447–?1511, French diplomat and historian, noted for his Mémoires (1489–98).

coming ('kʌmɪŋ) adj. **1.** (prenominal) (of time, events, etc.) approaching or next. **2.** promising (esp. in **up and coming**). **3.** of future importance: this is the coming thing. **4. have it coming to one.** Inf. to deserve what one is about to suffer. ~n. **5.** arrival or approach.

Comintern or **Komintern** ('kɒmɪn,tɜːn) n. short for **Communist International;** an international Communist organization founded by Lenin in 1919 and dissolved in 1943; it degenerated under Stalin into an instrument of Soviet politics. Also called: **Third International.**

comity ('kɒmɪtɪ) n., pl. **-ties. 1.** mutual civility; courtesy. **2.** short for **comity of nations.** [C16: from L cōmitās, from cōmis affable]

comity of nations n. the friendly recognition accorded by one nation to the laws and usages of another.

comm. abbrev. for: **1.** commerce. **2.** commercial. **3.** committee. **4.** commonwealth.

comma ('kɒmə) n. **1.** the punctuation mark , indicating a slight pause and used where there is a listing of items or to separate a nonrestrictive clause from a main clause. **2.** Music. a minute interval. [C16: from L, from Gk komma clause, from koptein to cut]

comma bacillus n. a comma-shaped bacterium that causes cholera in man.

command (kə'mɑːnd) vb. **1.** (when tr., may take a clause as object or an infinitive) to order or compel. **2.** to have or be in control or authority over. **3.** (tr.) to receive as due: his nature commands respect. **4.** to dominate (a view, etc.) as from a height. ~n. **5.** an order. **6.** the act of commanding. **7.** the right to command. **8.** the exercise of the power to command. **9.** knowledge; control: a command of French. **10.** Chiefly mil. the jurisdiction of a commander. **11.** a military unit or units commanding a specific function, as in the RAF. **12.** Brit. **a.** an invitation

from the monarch. **b.** (as modifier): a command performance. **13.** Computers. another name for **instruction** (sense 3). [C13: from OF commander, from L com- (intensive) + mandāre to enjoin]

commandant ('kɒmən,dænt, -,dɑːnt) n. an officer commanding a group or establishment.

commandeer (,kɒmən'dɪə) vb. (tr.) **1.** to seize for public or military use. **2.** to seize arbitrarily. [C19: from Afrik. kommandeer, from F commander to COMMAND]

commander (kə'mɑːndə) n. **1.** an officer in command of a military formation or operation. **2.** a naval commissioned rank junior to captain but senior to lieutenant commander. **3.** the second in command of larger British warships. **4.** someone who holds authority. **5.** a high-ranking member of some knightly orders. **6.** an officer responsible for a district of the Metropolitan Police in London. —**com'mander,ship** n.

commander in chief n., pl. **commanders in chief.** the officer holding supreme command of the forces in an area or operation.

commanding (kə'mɑːndɪŋ) adj. (usually prenominal) **1.** being in command. **2.** having the air of authority: a commanding voice. **3.** (of a situation) exerting control. **4.** (of a viewpoint, etc.) overlooking; advantageous. —**com'mandingly** adv.

commanding officer n. an officer in command of a military unit.

commandment (kə'mɑːndmənt) n. **1.** a divine command, esp. one of the Ten Commandments of the Old Testament. **2.** Literary. any command.

command module n. the module used as the living quarters in an Apollo spacecraft and functioning as the splashdown vehicle.

commando (kə'mɑːndəʊ) n., pl. **-dos** or **-does. 1. a.** an amphibious military unit trained for raiding. **b.** a member of such a unit. **2.** the basic unit of the Royal Marine Corps. **3.** (originally) an armed force raised by Boers during the Boer War. **4.** (modifier) denoting or relating to commandos: a commando unit. [C19: from Afrik. kommando, from Du. commando command]

command paper n. (in Britain) a government document that is presented to Parliament, in theory by royal command.

command post n. Mil. the position from which a commander exercises command.

commedia dell'arte (Italian kɔm'me:dia del'larte) n. a form of popular improvised comedy in Italy during the 16th to 18th centuries, with stock characters such as Punchinello, Harlequin, and Columbine. [It., lit.: comedy of art]

comme il faut French. (kɔm il fo) correct or correctly.

commemorate (kə'mɛmə,reɪt) vb. (tr.) to honour or keep alive the memory of. [C16: from L commemorāre, from com- (intensive) + memorāre to remind] —**com,mem-o'ration** n. —**com'memorative** adj. —**com'memo,ra-tor** n.

commence (kə'mɛns) vb. to begin; come or cause to come into being, operation, etc. [C14: from OF comencer, from Vulgar L cominitiāre (unattested), from L com- (intensive) + initiāre to begin]

commencement (kə'mɛnsmənt) n. **1.** the beginning; start. **2.** U.S. a ceremony for the conferment of academic degrees. **3.** U.S. & Canad. a ceremony for the presentation of awards at secondary schools.

commend (kə'mɛnd) vb. (tr.) **1.** to represent as being worthy of regard, confidence, etc.; recommend. **2.** to give in charge; entrust. **3.** to praise. **4.** to give the regards of: commend me to your aunt. [C14: from L commendāre, from com- (intensive) + mandāre to entrust] —**com-'mendable** adj. —**com'mendably** adv. —**com'menda-tory** adj.

commendation (,kɒmɛn'deɪʃən) n. **1.** the act of commending; praise. **2.** U.S. an award.

commensal (kə'mɛnsəl) adj. **1.** (of two different species of plant or animal) living in close association without being interdependent. **2.** Rare. of or relating to eating together, esp. at the same table. ~n. **3.** a commensal plant or animal. **4.** Rare. a companion at table. [C14: from Med. L commensālis, from L com- together + mensa table] —**com'mensalism** n. —**commensality** (,kɒmɛn'sælɪtɪ) n.

commensurable (kə'mɛnsərəbəl, -ʃə-) *adj.* **1.** *Maths.* **a.** having a common factor. **b.** having units of the same dimensions and being related by whole numbers. **2.** proportionate. —**com,mensura'bility** *n.* —**com'mensurably** *adv.*

commensurate (kə'mɛnsərɪt, -ʃə-) *adj.* **1.** having the same extent or duration. **2.** corresponding in degree, amount, or size; proportionate. **3.** commensurable. [C17: from LL *commēnsūrātus*, from L *com-* same + *mēnsurāre* to MEASURE] —**com'mensurately** *adv.*

comment ('kɒmɛnt) *n.* **1.** a remark, criticism, or observation. **2.** talk or gossip. **3.** a note explaining or criticizing a passage in a text. **4.** explanatory or critical matter added to a text. ~*vb.* **5.** (when *intr.*, often foll. by *on;* when *tr.*, takes a clause as object) to remark or express an opinion. **6.** (*intr.*) to write notes explaining or criticizing a text. [C15: from L *commentum* invention, from *comminiscī* to contrive] —'**commenter** *n.*

commentary ('kɒməntərɪ) *n.*, *pl.* **-taries. 1.** an explanatory series of notes. **2.** a spoken accompaniment to a broadcast, film, etc. **3.** an explanatory treatise on a text. **4.** (*usually pl.*) a personal record of events: *the commentaries of Caesar.*

commentate ('kɒmən,teɪt) *vb.* **1.** (*intr.*) to serve as a commentator. **2.** (*tr.*) *U.S.* to make a commentary on.

▷ **Usage.** The verb *commentate*, derived from *commentator*, is sometimes used as a synonym for *comment on* or *provide a commentary for*. It is not yet fully accepted as standard, though widespread in sports reporting and journalism.

commentator ('kɒmən,teɪtə) *n.* **1.** a person who provides a spoken commentary for a broadcast, film, etc., esp. of a sporting event. **2.** a person who writes notes on a text, etc.

commerce ('kɒmɜːs) *n.* **1.** the activity embracing all forms of the purchase and sale of goods and services. **2.** social relations. **3.** *Arch.* sexual intercourse. [C16: from L *commercium*, from *commercārī*, from *mercārī* to trade, from *merx* merchandise]

commercial (kə'mɜːʃəl) *adj.* **1.** of or engaged in commerce. **2.** sponsored or paid for by an advertiser: *commercial television.* **3.** having profit as the main aim: *commercial music.* **4.** (of chemicals, etc.) unrefined and produced in bulk for use in industry. ~*n.* **5.** a commercially sponsored advertisement on radio or television. —**commerciality** (kə,mɜːʃɪ'ælɪtɪ) *n.* —**com'mercially** *adv.*

commercial art *n.* graphic art for commercial uses such as advertising, packaging, etc.

commercial bank *n.* a bank primarily engaged in making short-term loans from funds deposited in current accounts.

commercial break *n.* an interruption in a radio or television programme for the broadcasting of advertisements.

commercialism (kə'mɜːʃə,lɪzəm) *n.* **1.** the spirit, principles, or procedure of commerce. **2.** exclusive or inappropriate emphasis on profit.

commercialize *or* **-lise** (kə'mɜːʃə,laɪz) *vb.* (*tr.*) **1.** to make commercial. **2.** to exploit for profit, esp. at the expense of quality. —**com,merciali'zation** *or* **-li'sation** *n.*

commercial paper *n. Chiefly U.S.* a short-term negotiable document, such as a bill of exchange, calling for the transference of a specified sum of money at a designated date.

commercial traveller *n.* another name for a **travelling salesman.**

commercial vehicle *n.* a vehicle for carrying goods or (less commonly) passengers.

commie *or* **commy** ('kɒmɪ) *n.*, *pl.* **-mies,** *adj. Inf. & derog.* short for **communist.**

commination (,kɒmɪ'neɪʃən) *n.* **1.** the act of threatening punishment or vengeance. **2.** *Church of England.* a recital of prayers, including a list of God's judgments against sinners, in the office for Ash Wednesday. [C15: from L *comminātiō*, from *com-* (intensive) + *minārī* to threaten] —**comminatory** ('kɒmɪnətərɪ) *adj.*

Commines (*French* kɔmin) *n.* a variant spelling of (Philippe de) **Comines.**

commingle (kɒ'mɪŋɡəl) *vb.* to mix or be mixed.

comminute ('kɒmɪ,njuːt) *vb.* **1.** to break (a bone) into small fragments. **2.** to divide (property) into small lots. [C17: from L *comminuere*, from *com-* (intensive) + *minuere* to reduce] —,**commi'nution** *n.*

commis ('kɒmɪs, 'kɒmɪ) *n.*, *pl.* **-mis. 1.** an agent or deputy. **2.** an apprentice waiter or chef. [C16 (meaning: deputy): from F, from *commettre* to employ]

commiserate (kə'mɪzə,reɪt) *vb.* (when *intr.*, usually foll. by *with*) to feel or express sympathy or compassion (for). [C17: from L *commiserārī*, from *com-* together + *miserārī* to bewail] —**com,miser'ation** *n.* —**com'miser,ator** *n.*

commissar ('kɒmɪ,sɑː, ,kɒmɪ'sɑː) *n.* (in the Soviet Union) **1.** an official of the Communist Party responsible for political education. **2.** (before 1946) the head of a government department. [C20: from Russian *kommissar*]

commissariat (,kɒmɪ'sɛərɪət) *n.* **1.** (in the Soviet Union) a government department before 1946. **2.** a military department in charge of food supplies, etc. [C17: from NL *commissāriātus*, from Med. L *commissārius* COMMISSARY]

commissary ('kɒmɪsərɪ) *n.*, *pl.* **-saries. 1.** *U.S.* a shop supplying food or equipment, as in a military camp. **2.** *U.S. army.* an officer responsible for supplies. **3.** *U.S.* a restaurant in a film studio. **4.** a representative or deputy, esp. of a bishop. [C14: from Med. L *commissārius* official in charge, from L *committere* to COMMIT] —**commissarial** (,kɒmɪ'sɛərɪəl) *adj.*

commission (kə'mɪʃən) *n.* **1.** a duty committed to a person or group to perform. **2.** authority to perform certain duties. **3.** a document granting such authority. **4.** *Mil.* **a.** a document conferring a rank on an officer. **b.** the rank granted. **5.** a group charged with certain duties: *a commission of inquiry.* **6.** a government board empowered to exercise administrative, judicial, or legislative authority. See also **Royal Commission. 7. a.** the authority given to a person or organization to act as an agent to a principal in commercial transactions. **b.** the fee allotted to an agent for services rendered. **8.** the state of being charged with specific responsibilities. **9.** the act of committing a sin, crime, etc. **10.** good working condition or (esp. of a ship) active service (esp. in **in commission, out of commission**). ~*vb.* (*mainly tr.*) **11.** to grant authority to. **12.** *Mil.* to confer a rank on. **13.** to equip and test (a ship) for active service. **14.** to place an order for (something): *to commission a portrait.* **15.** to make or become operative or operable: *the plant is due to commission next year.* [C14: from OF, from L *commissiō* bringing together, from *committere* to COMMIT]

commissionaire (kə,mɪʃə'nɛə) *n. Chiefly Brit.* a uniformed doorman at a hotel, theatre, etc. [C18: from F, from COMMISSION]

commissioned officer *n.* a military officer holding a commission, such as Second Lieutenant in the British Army, Acting Sub-Lieutenant in the Royal Navy, Pilot Officer in the Royal Air Force, and officers of all ranks senior to these.

commissioner (kə'mɪʃənə) *n.* **1.** a person endowed with certain powers. **2.** any of several types of civil servant. **3.** a member of a commission. —**com'missioner,ship** *n.*

commissioner for oaths *n.* a solicitor authorized to authenticate oaths on sworn statements.

commit (kə'mɪt) *vb.* **-mitting, -mitted.** (*tr.*) **1.** to hand over, as for safekeeping; entrust. **2. commit to memory.** to memorize. **3.** to take into custody: *to commit someone to prison.* **4.** (*usually passive*) to pledge or align (oneself), as to a particular cause: *a committed radical.* **5.** to order (forces) into action. **6.** to perform (a crime, error, etc.). **7.** to surrender, esp. for destruction: *she committed the letter to the fire.* **8.** to refer (a bill, etc.) to a committee. [C14: from L *committere* to join, from *com-* together + *mittere* to send] —**com'mittable** *adj.* —**com'mitter** *n.*

commitment (kə'mɪtmənt) *n.* **1.** the act of committing or pledging. **2.** the state of being committed or pledged. **3.** an obligation, promise, etc., that restricts freedom of action. **4.** Also called (esp. formerly): **mittimus.** *Law.* a written order of a court directing that a person be imprisoned. **5.** a future financial obligation or contingent liability. ~Also called (esp. for sense 4): **committal** (kə'mɪtəl).

committee *n.* **1.** (kə'mɪtɪ). a group of people appointed to perform a specified service or function. **2.** (,kɒmɪ'tiː). (formerly) a person to whom the care of a mentally incompetent person or his property was entrusted by a court. [C15: from *committen* to entrust + -EE]

committeeman (kə'mɪtɪmən, -,mæn) n., pl. **-men.** Chiefly U.S. a member of one or more committees. —com'mittee,woman fem. n.

Committee of the Whole House n. (in Britain) an informal sitting of the House of Commons to discuss and amend a bill.

commode (kə'məud) n. **1.** a piece of furniture, usually highly ornamented, containing drawers or shelves. **2.** a bedside table with a cabinet for a chamber pot or washbasin. **3.** a chair with a hinged flap concealing a chamber pot. [C17: from F, from L commodus COMMODIOUS]

commodious (kə'məudɪəs) adj. **1.** roomy; spacious. **2.** Arch. convenient. [C15: from Med. L, from L commodus convenient, from com- with + modus measure] —com'modiousness n.

commodity (kə'mɒdɪtɪ) n., pl. **-ties. 1.** an article of commerce. **2.** something of use or profit. **3.** Econ. an exchangeable unit of economic wealth, such as a primary product. [C14: from OF commodité, from L commoditās suitability; see COMMODIOUS]

commodo (kə'məudəu) adv. a variant spelling of comodo.

commodore ('kɒmə,dɔ:) n. **1.** Brit. a naval rank junior to rear admiral and senior to captain. **2.** the captain of a shipping line. **3.** the officer in command of a merchant convoy. **4.** the titular head of a yacht club. [C17: prob. from Du. commandeur, from F, from OF commander from COMMAND]

Commodus (kə'məudəs, 'kɒmədəs) n. **Lucius Aelius Aurelius** ('luːsɪəs 'iːlɪəs ɔː'riːlɪəs), son of Marcus Aurelius. 161–192 A.D., Roman emperor (180–192), noted for his tyrannical reign.

common ('kɒmən) adj. **1.** belonging to two or more people: common property. **2.** belonging to one or more communities; public: a common culture. **3.** of ordinary standard; average. **4.** prevailing; widespread: common opinion. **5.** frequently encountered; ordinary: a common brand of soap. **6.** notorious: a common nuisance. **7.** Derog. considered by the speaker to be low-class, vulgar, or coarse. **8.** (prenominal) having no special distinction: the common man. **9.** Maths. having a specified relationship with a group of numbers or quantities: common denominator. **10.** Prosody. (of a syllable) able to be long or short. **11.** Grammar. (in certain languages) denoting or belonging to a gender of nouns that includes both masculine and feminine referents. **12. common or garden.** Inf. ordinary; unexceptional. ~n. **13.** a tract of open public land. **14.** Law. the right to go onto someone else's property and remove natural products, as by pasturing cattle (esp. in **right of common**). **15.** Christianity. **a.** a form of the proper of the Mass used on festivals that have no special proper of their own. **b.** the ordinary of the Mass. **16. in common.** mutually held or used. ~See also **commons.** [C13: from OF commun, from L commūnis general] —'commonly adv. —'commonness n.

commonage ('kɒmənɪdʒ) n. Chiefly law. **a.** the use of something, esp. a pasture, in common with others. **b.** the right to such use. **2.** the state of being held in common. **3.** another word for **commonalty** (sense 1).

commonality (,kɒmə'nælɪtɪ) n., pl. **-ties. 1.** the fact of being common. **2.** another word for **commonalty** (sense 1).

commonalty ('kɒmənəltɪ) n., pl. **-ties. 1.** the ordinary people as distinct from those with rank or title. **2.** the members of an incorporated society. [C13: from OF comunalte, from comunal communal]

common carrier n. a person or firm engaged in the business of transporting goods or passengers.

common chord n. Music. a chord consisting of the keynote, a major or minor third, and a perfect fifth.

common cold n. a mild viral infection of the upper respiratory tract, characterized by sneezing, coughing, etc.

commoner ('kɒmənə) n. **1.** a person who does not belong to the nobility. **2.** a person who has a right in or over common land. **3.** Brit. a student at a university who is not on a scholarship.

common fraction n. another name for **simple fraction.**

common knowledge n. something widely or generally known.

common law n. **1.** the body of law based on judicial decisions and custom, as distinct from statute law. **2.** (modifier) of or denoting a marriage that is deemed to exist

after a man and a woman have cohabited for a number of years: common-law marriage; common-law wife; common-law husband.

Common Market n. **the.** a European economic association, originally composed (1958) of Belgium, France, West Germany, Italy, Luxembourg, and the Netherlands, joined in 1973 by the United Kingdom, the Irish Republic, and Denmark, in 1981 by Greece, and in 1986 by Spain and Portugal. Officially called: **European Economic Community.**

common noun n. Grammar. a noun that refers to each member of a whole class sharing the features connoted by the noun, as for example orange and drum. Cf. **proper noun.**

commonplace ('kɒmən,pleɪs) adj. **1.** ordinary; everyday. **2.** dull; trite: commonplace prose. ~n. **3.** a platitude; truism. **4.** a passage in a book marked for inclusion in a commonplace book, etc. **5.** an ordinary thing. [C16: translation of L locus commūnis argument of wide application] —'common,placeness n.

commonplace book n. a notebook in which quotations, poems, etc., that catch the owner's attention are entered.

common room n. Chiefly Brit. a sitting room in schools, colleges, etc.

commons ('kɒmənz) n. **1.** (functioning as pl.) the lower classes as contrasted with the ruling or noble classes of society. **2.** (functioning as sing.) Brit. a hall for dining, recreation, etc., usually attached to a college, etc. **3.** (usually functioning as pl.) Brit. food or rations (esp. in **short commons**).

Commons ('kɒmənz) n. **the.** See **House of Commons.**

common sense n. **1.** sound practical sense. ~adj. **common-sense;** also **common-sensical. 2.** inspired by or displaying this.

common time n. Music. a time signature indicating four crotchet beats to the bar; four-four time. Symbol: **C**

commonweal ('kɒmən,wiːl) n. Arch. **1.** the public good. **2.** another name for **commonwealth.**

commonwealth ('kɒmən,wɛlθ) n. **1.** the people of a state or nation viewed politically; body politic. **2.** a state in which the people possess sovereignty; republic. **3.** a group of persons united by some common interest.

Commonwealth ('kɒmən,wɛlθ) n. **the. 1.** Official name: **the Commonwealth of Nations.** an association of sovereign states that are or at some time have been ruled by Britain. **2.** the republic that existed in Britain from 1649 to 1660. **3.** the official designation of Australia, four states of the U.S., and Puerto Rico.

Commonwealth Day n. the anniversary of Queen Victoria's birth, May 24, celebrated (now on the second Monday in March) in many parts of the Commonwealth. Former name: **Empire Day.**

commotion (kə'məuʃən) n. **1.** violent disturbance; upheaval. **2.** political insurrection. **3.** a confused noise; din. [C15: from L commōtiō, from commovēre, from com- (intensive) + movēre to MOVE]

communal ('kɒmjunəl) adj. **1.** belonging to a community as a whole. **2.** of a commune or a religious community. —**communality** (,kɒmju'nælɪtɪ) n. —'**communally** adv.

communalism ('kɒmjunə,lɪzəm) n. **1.** a system or theory of government in which the state is seen as a loose federation of self-governing communities. **2.** the practice or advocacy of communal living or ownership. —'**communalist** n. —,**communal'istic** adj.

communalize or **-lise** ('kɒmjunə,laɪz) vb. (tr.) to render (something) the property of a commune or community. —,**communali'zation** or **-li'sation** n.

commune[1] vb. (kə'mjuːn). (intr.; usually foll. by with) **1.** to talk intimately. **2.** to experience strong emotion (for): to commune with nature. ~n. ('kɒmjuːn). **3.** intimate conversation; communion. [C13: from OF comuner to hold in common, from comun COMMON]

commune[2] ('kɒmjuːn) n. **1.** a group of families or individuals living together and sharing possessions and responsibilities. **2.** any small group of people having common interests or responsibilities. **3.** the smallest administrative unit in Belgium, France, Italy, and Switzerland. **4.** a medieval town enjoying a large degree of autonomy. [C18: from F, from Med. L commūnia, from L: things held in common]

Commune ('kɒmjuːn) n. French history. **1.** See **Paris Commune. 2.** a committee that governed Paris during the French Revolution: suppressed 1794.

communicable (kə'mju:nɪkəbᵊl) *adj.* **1.** capable of being communicated. **2.** (of a disease) capable of being passed on readily. —**com,munica'bility** *n.* —**com'municably** *adv.*

communicant (kə'mju:nɪkənt) *n.* **1.** *Christianity.* a person who receives Communion. **2.** a person who communicates or informs.

communicate (kə'mju:nɪ,keɪt) *vb.* **1.** to impart (knowledge) or exchange (thoughts) by speech, writing, gestures, etc. **2.** (*tr.*; usually foll. by *to*) to transmit (to): *the dog communicated his fear to the other animals.* **3.** (*intr.*) to have a sympathetic mutual understanding. **4.** (*intr.*; usually foll. by *with*) to make or have a connecting passage: *the kitchen communicates with the dining room.* **5.** (*tr.*) to transmit (a disease). **6.** (*intr.*) *Christianity.* to receive Communion. [C16: from L *commūnicāre* to share, from *commūnis* COMMON] —**com'muni,cator** *n.* —**com'municatory** *adj.*

communication (kə,mju:nɪ'keɪʃən) *n.* **1.** the imparting or exchange of information, ideas, or feelings. **2.** something communicated, such as a message. **3.** (*usually pl.*; *sometimes functioning as sing.*) the study of ways in which human beings communicate. **4.** a connecting route or link. **5.** (*pl.*) *Mil.* the system of routes by which forces, supplies, etc., are moved within an area of operations.

communication cord *n. Brit.* a cord or chain in a train which may be pulled by a passenger to stop the train in an emergency.

communications satellite *n.* an artificial satellite used to relay radio, television, and telephone signals around the earth's surface.

communicative (kə'mju:nɪkətɪv) *adj.* **1.** inclined or able to communicate readily; talkative. **2.** of or relating to communication.

communion (kə'mju:njən) *n.* **1.** an exchange of thoughts, emotions, etc. **2.** sharing in common; participation. **3.** (foll. by *with*) strong feelings (for): *communion with nature.* **4.** a religious group or denomination having common beliefs and practices. **5.** spiritual union. [C14: from L *commūniō*, from *commūnis* COMMON]

Communion (kə'mju:njən) *n. Christianity.* **1.** the act of participating in the Eucharist. **2.** the celebration of the Eucharist. **3.** the consecrated elements of the Eucharist. ~Also called: **Holy Communion.**

communiqué (kə'mju:nɪ,keɪ) *n.* an official communication or announcement, esp. to the press or public. [C19: from F]

communism ('kɒmjʊ,nɪzəm) *n.* **1.** advocacy of a classless society in which private ownership has been abolished and the means of production belong to the community. **2.** any movement or doctrine aimed at achieving such a society. **3.** (*usually cap.*) a political movement based upon the writings of Marx that considers history in terms of class conflict and revolutionary struggle. **4.** (*usually cap.*) a system of government established by a ruling Communist Party, esp. in the Soviet Union. **5.** communal living. [C19: from F *communisme*, from *commun* COMMON]

communist ('kɒmjʊnɪst) *n.* **1.** a supporter of communism. **2.** (*often cap.*) a supporter of a Communist movement or state. **3.** (*often cap.*) a member of a Communist party. **4.** (*often cap.*) *Chiefly U.S.* any person holding left-wing views, esp. when considered subversive. **5.** a person who practises communal living. ~*adj.* **6.** of, favouring, or relating to communism. —,**commu'nistic** *adj.*

Communist China *n.* another name for the People's Republic of) **China.**

community (kə'mju:nɪtɪ) *n., pl.* **-ties. 1. a.** the people living in one locality. **b.** the locality in which they live. **c.** (*as modifier*): *community spirit.* **2.** a group of people having cultural, religious, or other characteristics in common: *the Protestant community.* **3.** a group of nations having certain interests in common. **4.** the public; society. **5.** common ownership. **6.** similarity or agreement: *community of interests.* **7.** (in Wales and Scotland) the smallest unit of local government. **8.** *Ecology.* a group of interdependent plants and animals inhabiting the same region. [C14: from L *commūnitās*, from *commūnis* COMMON]

community centre *n.* a building used by a community for social gatherings, etc.

community charge *n.* the formal name for **poll tax.**

community chest *n. U.S.* a fund raised by voluntary contribution for local welfare activities.

community council *n.* (in Scotland and Wales) an independent voluntary local body set up to attend to local interests and organize community activities.

community home *n.* (in Britain) **1.** a home provided by a local authority for children who cannot remain with their parents. **2.** a boarding school for young offenders.

community policing *n.* the assigning of the same one or two policemen to a particular area so that they become familiar with the residents and they with them, as a way of reducing crime.

community service *n.* work undertaken for the community by an offender without pay, by the order of a court.

communize *or* **-ise** ('kɒmju,naɪz) *vb.* (*tr.*) (*sometimes cap.*) **1.** to make (property) public; nationalize. **2.** to make (a person or country) communist. —,**communi'zation** *or* **-i'sation** *n.*

commutate ('kɒmju,teɪt) *vb.* (*tr.*) **1.** to reverse the direction of (an electric current). **2.** to convert (an alternating current) into a direct current.

commutation (,kɒmju'teɪʃən) *n.* **1.** a substitution or exchange. **2.** the replacement of one method of payment by another. **3.** the reduction in severity of a penalty imposed by law. **4.** the process of commutating an electric current.

commutative (kə'mju:tətɪv, 'kɒmju,teɪtɪv) *adj.* **1.** relating to or involving substitution. **2.** *Maths, logic.* **a.** giving the same result irrespective of the order of the arguments; thus addition is commutative but subtraction is not. **b.** relating to this property: *the commutative law of addition.*

commutator ('kɒmju,teɪtə) *n.* **1.** a device used to reverse the direction of flow of an electric current. **2.** the segmented metal cylinder or disc of an electric motor, generator, etc., used to make electrical contact with the rotating coils.

commute (kə'mju:t) *vb.* **1.** (*intr.*) to travel some distance regularly between one's home and one's place of work. **2.** (*tr.*) to substitute. **3.** (*tr.*) *Law.* to reduce (a sentence) to one less severe. **4.** to pay (an annuity, etc.) at one time, instead of in instalments. **5.** to change: *to commute base metal into gold.* [C17: from L *commutāre*, from *com*-mutually + *mutāre* to change] —**com'mutable** *adj.* —**com,muta'bility** *n.*

commuter (kə'mju:tə) *n.* a person who travels to work over an appreciable distance, usually from the suburbs to the centre of a city.

Como ('kəʊməʊ; *Italian* 'kɔ:mo) *n.* a city in N Italy, in Lombardy at the SW end of **Lake Como:** tourist centre. Pop.: 95 571 (1981). Latin name: **Comum** ('kəʊmʊm).

comodo *or* **commodo** (kə'məʊdəʊ) *adv. Music.* in a convenient tempo. [It.: comfortable, from L *commodus* convenient: see COMMODIOUS]

Comorin ('kɒmərɪn) *n.* **Cape.** a headland at the southernmost point of India, in Tamil Nadu state.

Comoros ('kɒmə,rəʊz) *pl. n.* a republic consisting of three volcanic islands in the Indian Ocean, off the NW coast of Madagascar; a French territory from 1947; became independent in 1976 except for Mayotte, the fourth island in the group, which chose to remain French. Official languages: French and Arabic. Religion: Islam. Currency: franc. Capital: Moroni. Pop.: 422 500 (1987 est.). Area: 1862 sq. km (719 sq. miles). Official name: **Federal and Islamic Republic of the Comoros.**

comose ('kəʊməʊs, kəʊ'məʊs) *adj. Bot.* having tufts of hair; hairy. Also: **comate.** [C18: from L *comōsus* hairy]

comp (kɒmp) *Inf.* ~*n.* **1.** an accompaniment. **2.** a compositor. **2.** an accompaniment. **3.** a competition. ~*vb.* **4.** (*intr.*) to work as a compositor in the printing industry. **5.** to play an accompaniment (to).

comp. *abbrev. for:* **1.** companion. **2.** comparative. **3.** compare. **4.** compiled. **5.** composer. **6.** composition. **7.** compositor. **8.** compound. **9.** comprehensive. **10.** comprising.

compact¹ *adj.* (kəm'pækt). **1.** closely packed together. **2.** neatly fitted into a restricted space. **3.** concise; brief. **4.** well constructed; solid; firm. **5.** (foll. by *of*) composed (of). ~*vb.* (kəm'pækt). (*tr.*) **6.** to pack closely together; compress. **7.** (foll. by *of*) to form by pressing together:

sediment compacted of three types of clay. **8.** Metallurgy. to compress (a metal powder) to form a stable product suitable for sintering. ~n. ('kɒmpækt). **9.** a small flat case containing a mirror, face powder, etc., designed to be carried in a woman's handbag. **10.** U.S. & Canad. a small and economical car. [C16: from L compactus, from compingere, from com- together + pangere to fasten] —**com'pactly** adv. —**com'pactness** n.

compact[2] ('kɒmpækt) n. an official contract or agreement. [C16: from L compactum, from compacisci, from com- together + pacisci to contract]

compact disc ('kɒmpækt) n. a small digital audio disc on which sound is recorded as a series of metallic pits enclosed in PVC and read by an optical laser system. Also called: **compact audio disc**. Abbrev.: **CD, CAD.**

compages (kəm'peɪdʒiːz) n. (functioning as sing.) a structure or framework. [C17: from L: from com- together + pangēre to fasten]

companion[1] (kəm'pænjən) n. **1.** a person who is an associate of another or others; comrade. **2.** (esp. formerly) an employee, usually a woman, who provides company for an employer. **3. a.** one of a pair. **b.** (as modifier): a companion volume. **4.** a guidebook or handbook. **5.** a member of the lowest rank of certain orders of knighthood. **6.** Astron. the fainter of the two components of a double star. ~vb. **7.** (tr.) to accompany. [C13: from LL compāniō, lit.: one who eats bread with another, from L com- with + pānis bread] —**com'panion,ship** n.

companion[2] (kəm'pænjən) n. Naut. a raised frame on an upper deck with windows to give light to the deck below. [C18: from Du. kompanje quarterdeck, from OF compagne, from OIt. compagna pantry, ? ult. from L pānis bread]

companionable (kəm'pænjənəb[ə]l) adj. sociable. —**com'panionableness** n. —**com'panionably** adv.

companionate (kəm'pænjənɪt) adj. **1.** resembling, appropriate to, or acting as a companion. **2.** harmoniously suited.

companionway (kəm'pænjən,weɪ) n. a ladder from one deck to another in a ship.

company ('kʌmpənɪ) n., pl. -nies. **1.** a number of people gathered together; assembly. **2.** the fact of being with someone; companionship: I enjoy her company. **3.** a guest or guests. **4.** a business enterprise. **5.** the members of an enterprise not specifically mentioned in the enterprise's title. Abbrev.: **Co., co. 6.** a group of actors. **7.** a small unit of troops. **8.** the officers and crew of a ship. **9.** a unit of Girl Guides. **10.** English history. a medieval guild. **11. keep company. a.** to accompany (someone). **b.** (esp. of lovers) to spend time together. ~vb. -nying, -nied. **12.** Arch. to associate (with someone). [C13: from OF compaignie, from LL compāniō; see COMPANION[1]]

company sergeant-major n. Mil. the senior noncommissioned officer in a company.

compar. abbrev. for comparative.

comparable ('kɒmpərəb[ə]l) adj. **1.** worthy of comparison. **2.** able to be compared (with). —,**compara'bility** or '**comparableness** n.

comparative (kəm'pærətɪv) adj. **1.** denoting or involving comparison: comparative literature. **2.** relative: a comparative loss of prestige. **3.** Grammar. denoting the form of an adjective that indicates that the quality denoted is possessed to a greater extent. In English the comparative is marked by the suffix -er or the word more. ~n. **4.** the comparative form of an adjective. —**com'paratively** adv. —**com'parativeness** n.

compare (kəm'pɛə) vb. **1.** (tr.; foll. by to) to regard as similar; liken: the general has been compared to Napoleon. **2.** (tr.) to examine in order to observe resemblances or differences: to compare rum and gin. **3.** (intr.; usually foll. by with) to be the same or similar: gin compares with rum in alcoholic content. **4.** (intr.) to bear a specified relation when examined: this car compares badly with the other. **5.** (tr.) Grammar. to give the positive, comparative, and superlative forms of (an adjective). **6. compare notes.** to exchange opinions. ~n. **7.** comparison (esp. in **beyond compare**). [C15: from OF, from L comparāre, from compar, from com- together + par equal]

▷ **Usage.** In careful usage, compare is followed by to when it is used in the sense of "liken, point out a resemblance": I don't know how to describe it — I haven't anything to compare it to; and by with when some account of points of resemblance is meant: in my next lecture I shall compare seventeenth-century French drama with classical Greek theatre.

comparison (kəm'pærɪs[ə]n) n. **1.** the act of comparing. **2.** the state of being compared. **3.** likeness: there was no comparison between them. **4.** a rhetorical device involving comparison, such as a simile. **5.** Also called: **degrees of comparison.** Grammar. the listing of the positive, comparative, and superlative forms of an adjective or adverb. **6. bear** or **stand comparison (with).** to be sufficiently similar to be compared with (something else), esp. favourably.

compartment (kəm'pɑːtmənt) n. **1.** one of the sections into which an area, esp. an enclosed space, is partitioned. **2.** any separate section: a compartment of the mind. **3.** a small storage space. [C16: from F compartiment, ult. from LL compartīrī to share] —**compartmental** (,kɒmpɑːt-'mɛnt[ə]l) adj. —,**compart'mentally** adv.

compartmentalize or **-lise** (,kɒmpɑːt'mɛnt[ə],laɪz) vb. (usually tr.) to put into categories, etc., esp. to an excessive degree. —,**compart,mentali'zation** or **-li'sation** n.

compass ('kʌmpəs) n. **1.** Also called: **magnetic compass.** an instrument for finding direction, having a magnetized needle which points to magnetic north. **2.** (often pl.) Also called: **pair of compasses.** an instrument used for drawing circles, measuring distances, etc., that consists of two arms, joined at one end. **3.** limits or range: within the compass of education. **4.** Music. the interval between the lowest and highest note attainable. ~vb. (tr.) **5.** to surround; hem in. **6.** to grasp mentally. **7.** to achieve; accomplish. **8.** Obs. to plot. [C13: from OF compas, from Vulgar L compassāre (unattested) to pace out, ult. from L passus step] —'**compassable** adj.

compass card n. a compass in the form of a card that rotates so that "0°" or "North" points to magnetic north.

compassion (kəm'pæʃ[ə]n) n. a feeling of distress and pity for the suffering or misfortune of another. [C14: from OF, from LL compassiō, from L com- with + patī to suffer]

compassionate (kəm'pæʃənɪt) adj. showing or having compassion. —**com'passionately** adv.

compassionate leave n. leave granted on the grounds of bereavement, family illness, etc.

compass rose n. a circle or decorative device printed on a map or chart showing the points of the compass.

compass saw n. a hand saw with a narrow tapered blade for making a curved cut.

compatible (kəm'pætɪb[ə]l) adj. **1.** (usually foll. by with) able to exist together harmoniously. **2.** (usually foll. by with) consistent: her deeds were not compatible with her ideology. **3.** (of pieces of machinery, etc.) capable of being used together without modification or adaptation. [C15: from Med. L compatibilis, from LL compatī; see COMPASSION] —**com,pati'bility** n. —**com'patibly** adv.

compatriot (kəm'pætrɪət) n. a fellow countryman. [C17: from F compatriote, from LL; see PATRIOT] —**com-,patri'otic** adj.

compeer ('kɒmpɪə) n. **1.** a person of equal rank, status, or ability. **2.** a comrade. [C13: from OF comper, from Med. L compater godfather]

compel (kəm'pɛl) vb. **-pelling, -pelled.** (tr.) **1.** to cause (someone) by force (to be or do something). **2.** to obtain by force; exact: to compel obedience. [C14: from L compellere, from com- together + pellere to drive] —**com'pellable** adj.

compelling (kəm'pɛlɪŋ) adj. arousing or denoting strong interest, esp. admiring interest.

compendious (kəm'pɛndɪəs) adj. stating the essentials of a subject in a concise form. —**com'pendiously** adv. —**com'pendiousness** n.

compendium (kəm'pɛndɪəm) n., pl. **-diums** or **-dia** (-dɪə). **1.** Brit. a book containing a collection of useful hints. **2.** Brit. a selection, esp. of different games in one container. **3.** a summary. [C16: from L: a saving, lit.: something weighed]

compensate ('kɒmpɛn,seɪt) vb. **1.** to make amends to (someone), esp. for loss or injury. **2.** (tr.) to serve as compensation or damages for (injury, loss, etc.). **3.** to counterbalance the effects of (a force, weight, etc.) so as to produce equilibrium. **4.** (intr.) to attempt to conceal one's shortcomings by the exaggerated exhibition of qualities regarded as desirable. [C17: from L compēnsāre, from *pendere* to weigh] —**compensative** ('kɒmpɛn-ˌseɪtɪv, kəm'pɛnsə-) *or* **compensatory** ('kɒmpɛnˌseɪtərɪ, kəm'pɛnsətərɪ) *adj.*

compensation (ˌkɒmpɛn'seɪʃən) *n.* **1.** the act of making amends for something. **2.** something given as reparation for loss, injury, etc. **3.** the attempt to conceal one's shortcomings by the exaggerated exhibition of qualities regarded as desirable. —ˌcompen'sational *adj.*

compere ('kɒmpɛə) *Brit.* ~*n.* **1.** a master of ceremonies who introduces cabaret, television acts, etc. ~*vb.* **2.** to act as a compere (for). [C20: from F, lit.: godfather]

compete (kəm'piːt) *vb.* (*intr.*; often foll. by *with*) to contend (against) for profit, an award, etc. [C17: from LL *competere*, from L, from *com-* together + *petere* to seek]

competence ('kɒmpɪtəns) *or* **competency** *n.* **1.** the condition of being capable; ability. **2.** a sufficient income to live on. **3.** the state of being legally competent or qualified.

competent ('kɒmpɪtənt) *adj.* **1.** having sufficient skill, knowledge, etc.; capable. **2.** suitable or sufficient for the purpose: *a competent answer.* **3.** *Law.* (of a witness, etc.) qualified to testify, etc. [C14: from L *competēns*, from *competere*; see COMPETE] —'**competently** *adv.*

competition (ˌkɒmpɪ'tɪʃən) *n.* **1.** the act of competing. **2.** a contest in which a winner is selected from among two or more entrants. **3.** a series of games, sports events, etc. **4.** the opposition offered by competitors. **5.** competitors offering opposition.

competitive (kəm'pɛtɪtɪv) *adj.* **1.** involving rivalry: *competitive sports.* **2.** sufficiently low in price or high in quality to be successful against commercial rivals. **3.** characterized by an urge to compete: *a competitive personality.* —**com'petitiveness** *n.*

competitor (kəm'pɛtɪtə) *n.* a person, group, team, firm, etc., that vies or competes; rival.

Compiègne (*French* kɔ̃pjɛɲ) *n.* a city in N France, on the Oise River: scene of the armistices of both World Wars. Pop.: 37 250 (1983).

compile (kəm'paɪl) *vb.* (*tr.*) **1.** to make or compose from other sources: *to compile a list of names.* **2.** to collect for a book, hobby, etc. **3.** *Computers.* to create (a set of machine instructions) from a high-level programming language, using a compiler. [C14: from L *compīlāre*, from *com-* together + *pīlāre* to thrust down, pack] —**compilation** (ˌkɒmpɪ'leɪʃən) *n.*

compiler (kəm'paɪlə) *n.* **1.** a person who compiles something. **2.** a computer program by which a high-level programming language is converted into machine language that can be acted upon by a computer. Cf. **assembler.**

complacency (kəm'pleɪsənsɪ) *or* **complacence** *n.* extreme self-satisfaction; smugness.

complacent (kəm'pleɪs³nt) *adj.* extremely self-satisfied. [C17: from L *complacēns* very pleasing, from *complacēre*, from *com-* (intensive) + *placēre* to please] —**com'placently** *adv.*

complain (kəm'pleɪn) *vb.* (*intr.*) **1.** to express resentment, displeasure, etc.; grumble. **2.** (foll. by *of*) to state the presence of pain, illness, etc.: *she complained of a headache.* [C14: from OF *complaindre*, from Vulgar L *complangere* (unattested), from L *com-* (intensive) + *plangere* to bewail] —**com'plainer** *n.* —**com'plainingly** *adv.*

complainant (kəm'pleɪnənt) *n. Law.* a plaintiff.

complaint (kəm'pleɪnt) *n.* **1.** the act of complaining. **2.** a cause for complaining; grievance. **3.** a mild ailment.

complaisant (kəm'pleɪz³nt) *adj.* showing a desire to comply or oblige; polite. [C17: from F *complaire*, from L *complacēre* to please greatly; cf. COMPLACENT] —**com'plaisance** *n.*

complement *n.* ('kɒmplɪmənt). **1.** a person or thing that completes something. **2.** a complete amount, number, etc. (often in **full complement**). **3.** the officers and crew needed to man a ship. **4.** *Grammar.* a word, phrase, or clause that completes the meaning of the predicate, as *an idiot* in *He is an idiot* or *that he would be early* in *I hoped that he would be early.* **5.** *Maths.* the angle that when added to a specified angle produces a right angle. **6.** *Logic.* the class of all the things that are not members of a given class. **7.** a group of proteins in the blood serum that, when activated by antibodies, destroys alien cells, such as bacteria. ~*vb.* ('kɒmplɪˌmɛnt). **8.** (*tr.*) to complete or form a complement to. [C14: from L *complēmentum*, from *complēre*, from *com-* (intensive) + *plēre* to fill]

complementary (ˌkɒmplɪ'mɛntərɪ) *adj.* **1.** forming a complement. **2.** forming a satisfactory or balanced whole. —ˌcomple'mentarily *adv.* —ˌcomple'mentariness *n.*

complementary angle *n.* either of two angles whose sum is 90°.

complementary colour *n.* one of any pair of colours, such as yellow and blue, that give white or grey when mixed in the correct proportions.

complementary medicine *n.* another name for **alternative medicine.**

complete (kəm'pliːt) *adj.* **1.** having every necessary part; entire. **2.** finished. **3.** (*prenominal*) thorough: *he is a complete rogue.* **4.** perfect in quality or kind: *he is a complete scholar.* **5.** (of a logical system) constituted such that a contradiction or inconsistency arises on the addition of an axiom that cannot be deduced from the axioms of the system. **6.** *Arch.* skilled; accomplished. ~*vb.* (*tr.*) **7.** to make perfect. **8.** to finish. [C14: from L *complētus*, p.p. of *complēre* to fill up; see COMPLEMENT] —**com'pletely** *adv.* —**com'pleteness** *n.* —**com'pletion** *n.*

complex ('kɒmplɛks) *adj.* **1.** made up of interconnected parts. **2.** (of thoughts, writing, etc.) intricate. **3.** *Maths.* **a.** of or involving complex numbers. **b.** consisting of a real and an imaginary part, either of which can be zero. ~*n.* **4.** a whole made up of related parts: *a building complex.* **5.** *Psychoanal.* a group of emotional impulses that have been banished from the conscious mind but continue to influence a person's behaviour. **6.** *Inf.* an obsession: *he's got a complex about cats.* **7.** any chemical compound in which one molecule is linked to another by a coordinate bond. [C17: from L *complexus*, from *complectī*, from *com-* together + *plectere* to braid] —'**complexness** *n.*

complex fraction *n. Maths.* a fraction in which the numerator or denominator or both contain fractions. Also called: **compound fraction.**

complexion (kəm'plɛkʃən) *n.* **1.** the colour and general appearance of a person's skin, esp. of the face. **2.** aspect or nature: *the general complexion of a nation's finances.* **3.** *Obs.* temperament. [C14: from L *complexiō* a combination, from *complectī* to embrace; see COMPLEX] —**com'plexional** *adj.*

complexioned (kəm'plɛkʃənd) *adj.* of a specified complexion: *light-complexioned.*

complexity (kəm'plɛksɪtɪ) *n., pl.* **-ties. 1.** the state or quality of being intricate or complex. **2.** something intricate or complex; complication.

complex number *n.* any number of the form $a + bi$, where a and b are real numbers and $i = \sqrt{-1}$.

complex sentence *n. Grammar.* a sentence containing at least one main clause and one subordinate clause.

compliance (kəm'plaɪəns) *or* **compliancy** *n.* **1.** acquiescence. **2.** a disposition to yield to others. **3.** a measure of the ability of a mechanical system to respond to an applied vibrating force.

compliance officer *or* **lawyer** *n.* a specialist, usually a lawyer, employed by a financial group operating in a variety of fields and for multiple clients to ensure that no conflict of interest arises and that all obligations and regulations are complied with.

compliant (kəm'plaɪənt) *adj.* complying, obliging, or yielding. —**com'pliantly** *adv.*

complicate *vb.* ('kɒmplɪˌkeɪt). **1.** to make or become complex, etc. ~*adj.* ('kɒmplɪkɪt). **2.** *Biol.* folded on itself: *a complicate leaf.* [C17: from L *complicāre* to fold together]

complicated ('kɒmplɪˌkeɪtɪd) *adj.* made up of intricate parts or aspects that are difficult to understand or analyse. —'**compli,catedly** *adv.*

complication (ˌkɒmplɪ'keɪʃən) *n.* **1.** a condition, event, etc., that is complex or confused. **2.** the act of complicating. **3.** an event or condition that complicates or frustrates: *her coming was a serious complication.* **4.** a disease arising as a consequence of another.

complicity (kəm'plɪsɪtɪ) *n., pl.* **-ties. 1.** the fact of being an accomplice, esp. in a criminal act. **2.** a less common word for **complexity.**

compliment *n.* ('kɒmplɪmənt). **1.** a remark or act expressing respect, admiration, etc. **2.** (*usually pl.*) a greeting of respect or regard. ~*vb.* ('kɒmplɪˌmɛnt). (*tr.*) **3.** to express admiration for; congratulate. **4.** to express or show regard for, esp. by a gift. [C17: from F, from It. *complimento*, from Sp. *cumplimiento*, from *cumplir* to complete]

complimentary (,kɒmplɪ'mɛntərɪ) *adj.* **1.** conveying a compliment. **2.** flattering. **3.** given free, esp. as a courtesy or for publicity purposes. — ,compli'mentarily *adv.*

compline ('kɒmplɪn, -plaɪn) *or* **complin** ('kɒmplɪn) *n.* R.C. Church. the last of the seven canonical hours of the divine office. [C13: from OF *complie*, from Med. L *hōra complēta*, lit.: the completed hour]

comply (kəm'plaɪ) *vb.* **-plying, -plied.** (*intr.*) (usually foll. by *with*) to act in accordance with rules, wishes, etc.; be obedient (to). [C17: from It. *complire*, from Sp. *cumplir* to complete]

compo ('kɒmpəʊ) *n., pl.* **-pos.** **1.** a mixture of materials, such as mortar, plaster, etc. **2.** *Austral. & N.Z. inf.* compensation, esp. for injury or loss of work. ~*adj.* **3.** *Mil.* intended to last for several days: *a compo pack.* [short for *composition, compensation, composite*]

component (kəm'pəʊnənt) *n.* **1.** a constituent part or aspect of something more complex. **2.** any electrical device that has distinct electrical characteristics and may be connected to other devices to form a circuit. **3.** *Maths.* one of a set of two or more vectors whose resultant is a given vector. **4.** See **phase rule.** ~*adj.* **5.** forming or functioning as a part or aspect; constituent. [C17: from L *compōnere* to put together] —**componential** (,kɒmpə-'nɛnʃəl) *adj.*

comport (kəm'pɔːt) *vb.* **1.** (*tr.*) to conduct or bear (oneself) in a specified way. **2.** (*intr.; foll. by with*) to agree (with). [C16: from L *comportāre* collect, from *com-* together + *portāre* to carry] — **com'portment** *n.*

compose (kəm'pəʊz) *vb.* (*mainly tr.*) **1.** to put together or make up. **2.** to be the component elements of. **3.** to create (a musical or literary work). **4.** (*intr.*) to write music. **5.** to calm (someone, esp. oneself); make quiet. **6.** to adjust or settle (a quarrel, etc.). **7.** to order the elements of (a painting, sculpture, etc.); design. **8.** *Printing.* to set up (type). [C15: from OF *composer*, from L *compōnere* to put in place]

composed (kəm'pəʊzd) *adj.* (of people) calm; tranquil. —**composedly** (kəm'pəʊzɪdlɪ) *adv.*

composer (kəm'pəʊzə) *n.* **1.** a person who composes music. **2.** a person or machine that composes anything, esp. type for printing.

composite *adj.* ('kɒmpəzɪt). **1.** composed of separate parts; compound. **2.** of or belonging to the plant family Compositae. **3.** *Maths.* capable of being factorized: *a composite function.* **4.** (*sometimes cap.*) denoting one of the five classical orders of architecture: characterized by a combination of the Ionic and Corinthian styles. ~*n.* ('kɒmpəzɪt). **5.** something composed of separate parts; compound. **6.** any plant of the family Compositae, having flower heads composed of many small flowers (e.g. dandelion, daisy). **7.** a material, such as reinforced concrete, made of two or more distinct materials. **8.** a proposal that has been composited. ~*vb.* (*tr.*) ('kɒmpə,zaɪt). **9.** to merge related motions from local branches (of a political party, trade union, etc.) so as to produce a manageable number of proposals for discussion at national level. [C16: from L *compositus* well arranged, from *compōnere* to arrange] —'**compositely** *adv.* —'**compositeness** *n.*

composite photograph *n.* a photograph formed by superimposing two or more separate photographs.

composite school *n.* *Canad.* a secondary school offering both academic and nonacademic courses.

composition (,kɒmpə'zɪʃən) *n.* **1.** the act of putting together or making up by combining parts. **2.** something formed in this manner; a mixture. **3.** the parts of which something is composed; constitution. **4.** a work of music, art, or literature. **5.** the harmonious arrangement of the parts of a work of art in relation to each other. **6.** a piece of writing undertaken as an academic exercise; an essay. **7.** *Printing.* the act or technique of setting up type. **8.** a settlement by mutual consent, esp. a legal agreement whereby the creditors agree to accept partial payment of a debt in full settlement. [C14: from OF, from L *compositus; see* COMPOSITE, -ION]

compositor (kəm'pɒzɪtə) *n.* *Printing.* a person who sets and corrects type.

compos mentis *Latin.* ('kɒmpəs 'mɛntɪs) *adj.* (*postpositive*) of sound mind; sane.

compost ('kɒmpɒst) *n.* **1.** a mixture of organic residues such as decomposed vegetation, manure, etc., used as a fertilizer. **2.** *Rare.* a mixture. ~*vb.* (*tr.*) **3.** to make (vegetable matter) into compost. **4.** to fertilize with compost. [C14: from OF *compost*, from L *compositus* put together]

Compostela (*Spanish* kɔmpɔs'tela) *n.* See **Santiago de Compostela.**

composure (kəm'pəʊʒə) *n.* calmness, esp. of the mind; tranquillity; serenity.

compote ('kɒmpəʊt) *n.* a dish of fruit stewed with sugar or in a syrup. [C17: from F *composte*, from L *compositus* put in place]

compound[1] *n.* ('kɒmpaʊnd). **1.** a substance that contains atoms of two or more chemical elements held together by chemical bonds. **2.** any combination of two or more parts, aspects, etc. **3.** a word formed from two existing words or combining forms. ~*vb.* (kəm'paʊnd). (*mainly tr.*) **4.** to combine so as to create a compound. **5.** to make by combining parts, aspects, etc.: *to compound a new plastic.* **6.** to intensify by an added element: *his anxiety was compounded by her crying.* **7.** (*also intr.*) to come to an agreement in (a dispute, etc.) or to settle (a debt, etc.) for less than what is owed; compromise. **8.** *Law.* to agree not to prosecute in return for a consideration: *to compound a crime.* ~*adj.* ('kɒmpaʊnd). **9.** composed of two or more parts, elements, etc. **10.** (of a word) consisting of elements that are also words or combining forms. **11.** *Grammar.* (of tense, mood, etc.) formed by using an auxiliary verb in addition to the main verb. **12.** *Music.* **a.** denoting a time in which the number of beats per bar is a multiple of three: *six-four is an example of compound time.* **b.** (of an interval) greater than an octave. **13.** (of a steam engine, etc.) having multiple stages in which the steam or working fluid from one stage is used in a subsequent stage. **14.** (of a piston engine) having a supercharger powered by a turbine in the exhaust stream. [C14: from earlier *compounen*, from OF *compondre* to set in order, from L *compōnere*] —**com'poundable** *adj.*

compound[2] ('kɒmpaʊnd) *n.* **1.** (esp. in South Africa) an enclosure, esp. on the mines, containing the living quarters for Black workers. **2.** any similar enclosure, such as a camp for prisoners of war. [C17: from Malay *kampong* village]

compound eye *n.* the convex eye of insects and some crustaceans, consisting of numerous separate light-sensitive units (ommatidia).

compound fraction *n.* another name for **complex fraction.**

compound fracture *n.* a fracture in which the broken bone pierces the skin.

compound interest *n.* interest calculated on both the principal and its accrued interest.

compound leaf *n.* a leaf consisting of two or more leaflets borne on the same leafstalk.

compound number *n.* a quantity expressed in two or more different but related units: *3 hours 10 seconds is a compound number.*

compound sentence *n.* a sentence containing at least two coordinate clauses.

compound time *n.* See **compound**[1] (sense 12).

comprehend (,kɒmprɪ'hɛnd) *vb.* **1.** to understand. **2.** (*tr.*) to comprise; include. [C14: from L *comprehendere*, from *prehendere* to seize]

comprehensible (,kɒmprɪ'hɛnsəb³l) *adj.* capable of being comprehended. — ,compre'hensi'bility *n.* — ,compre'hensibly *adv.*

comprehension (,kɒmprɪ'hɛnʃən) *n.* **1.** the act or capacity of understanding. **2.** the state of including; comprehensiveness.

comprehensive (,kɒmprɪ'hɛnsɪv) *adj.* **1.** of broad scope or content. **2.** (of a car insurance policy) providing protection against most risks, including third-party liability, fire, theft, and damage. **3.** of or being a comprehensive school. ~*n.* **4.** short for **comprehensive school.** — ,compre'hensively *adv.* — ,compre'hensiveness *n.*

comprehensive school *n.* *Chiefly Brit.* a secondary school for children of all abilities from the same district.

compress *vb.* (kəm'prɛs). **1.** (*tr.*) to squeeze together; condense. ~*n.* ('kɒmprɛs). **2.** a cloth or gauze pad applied firmly to some part of the body to relieve discomfort, reduce fever, etc. [C14: from LL *compressāre*, from L *comprimere*, from *premere* to press] —**com'pressible** *adj.* —**com,pressi'bility** *n.* —**com'pressive** *adj.*

compressed air *n.* air at a higher pressure than atmospheric pressure: used esp. as a source of power for machines.

compression (kəm'prɛʃən) *n.* **1.** the act of compressing or the condition of being compressed. **2.** an increase in pressure of the charge in an engine or compressor obtained by reducing its volume.

compressor (kəm'prɛsə) *n.* **1.** any device that compresses a gas. **2.** the part of a gas turbine that compresses the air before it enters the combustion chambers. **3.** any muscle that causes compression. **4.** an electronic device for reducing the variation in signal amplitude in a transmission system.

comprise (kəm'praɪz) *vb.* (*tr.*) **1.** to be made up of. **2.** to constitute the whole of; consist of: *her singing comprised the entertainment.* [C15: from F *compris* included, from *comprendre* to COMPREHEND] —**com'prisable** *adj.*
▷ **Usage.** *Comprise* in the sense "to consist of" is not itself followed by *of: the work comprises the following duties.* It differs from *include* in being comprehensive; the above example means that all the duties are about to be mentioned, whereas *the work includes the following duties* implies that there may be others in addition to those about to be mentioned.

compromise ('kɒmprə,maɪz) *n.* **1.** settlement of a dispute by concessions on both or all sides. **2.** the terms of such a settlement. **3.** something midway between different things. ~*vb.* **4.** to settle (a dispute) by making concessions. **5.** (*tr.*) to expose (oneself or another) to disrepute. [C15: from OF *compromis*, from L, from *compromittere*, from *promittere* to promise] —**'compro,miser** *n.* —**'compro,misingly** *adv.*

compte rendu French. (kɔ̃t rɑ̃dy) *n.*, *pl.* *comptes rendus* (kɔ̃t rɑ̃dy). **1.** a review or notice. **2.** an account. [lit.: account rendered]

Comptometer (kɒmp'tɒmɪtə) *n.* *Trademark.* a high-speed calculating machine.

Compton *n.* **1.** ('kɒmptən). **Arthur Holly.** 1892–1962, U.S. physicist, noted for his research on x-rays, gamma rays, and nuclear energy: Nobel prize for physics 1927. **2.** ('kʌmptən). **Denis.** born 1918, English cricketer, who played for Middlesex and England (1937–57); broke two records in 1947 scoring 3816 runs and 18 centuries in one season.

Compton-Burnett ('kɒmptənbə:'nɛt, -'bɜːnɪt) *n.* **Ivy.** 1892–1969, English novelist. Her novels include *Men and Wives* (1931) and *Mother and Son* (1955).

comptroller (kən'trəʊlə) *n.* a variant spelling of **controller** (sense 2), esp. as a title of any of various financial executives.

compulsion (kəm'pʌlʃən) *n.* **1.** the act of compelling or the state of being compelled. **2.** something that compels. **3.** *Psychiatry.* an inner drive that causes a person to perform actions, often repetitive, against his will. See also **obsession.** [C15: from OF, from L *compellere* to COMPEL]

compulsive (kəm'pʌlsɪv) *adj.* relating to or involving compulsion. —**com'pulsively** *adv.*

compulsory (kəm'pʌlsərɪ) *adj.* **1.** required by regulations or laws; obligatory. **2.** involving or employing compulsion; compelling; essential. —**com'pulsorily** *adv.* —**com'pulsoriness** *n.*

compulsory purchase *n.* purchase of a property by a local authority or government department for public use or development, regardless of whether or not the owner wishes to sell.

compunction (kəm'pʌŋkʃən) *n.* a feeling of remorse, guilt, or regret. [C14: from Church L *compunctio*, from L *compungere* to sting] —**com'punctious** *adj.* —**com-'punctiously** *adv.*

computation (,kɒmpjʊ'teɪʃən) *n.* a calculation involving numbers or quantities. —,**compu'tational** *adj.*

compute (kəm'pju:t) *vb.* to calculate (an answer, result, etc.), often with the aid of a computer. [C17: from L *computare*, from *putare* to think] —**com'putable** *adj.* —**com,puta'bility** *n.*

computer (kəm'pju:tə) *n.* **1. a.** a device, usually electronic, that processes data according to a set of instructions. The **digital computer** stores data in discrete units and performs operations at very high speed. The **analog computer** has no memory and is slower than the digital

computer but has a continuous rather than a discrete input. **b.** (*as modifier*): *computer technology.* **2.** a person who computes or calculates.

computer dating *n.* a meeting between a man and a woman arranged by an agency that claims to match its clients by computer.

computerize *or* **-ise** (kəm'pju:tə,raɪz) *vb.* **1.** (*tr.*) to cause (certain operations) to be performed by a computer, esp. as a replacement for human labour. **2.** (*intr.*) to install a computer. **3.** (*tr.*) to control or perform (operations) by means of a computer. **4.** (*tr.*) to process or store (information) by or in a computer. —**com,puter-i'zation** *or* **-i'sation** *n.*

computer language *n.* another term for **programming language.**

comrade ('kɒmreɪd, -rɪd) *n.* **1.** a companion. **2.** a fellow member of a political party, esp. a fellow Communist. [C16: from F *camarade*, from Sp. *camarada* group of soldiers sharing a billet, from *cámara* room, from L] —**'comradely** *adj.* —**'comrade,ship** *n.*

comsat ('kɒmsæt) *n.* short for **communications satellite.**

Comte (*French* kɔ̃t) *n.* **(Isidore) Auguste (Marie François)** (ɔgyst). 1798–1857, French mathematician and philosopher; the founder of positivism. —**Comtism** ('kɔ:n,tɪzəm) *n.* —**'Comtist** *or* **'Comtian** *adj.*, *n.*

Comus ('kəʊməs) *n.* (in late Roman mythology) a god of revelry. [C17: from L, from Gk *kōmos* a revel]

con[1] (kɒn) *Inf.* ~*n.* **1. a.** short for **confidence trick. b.** (*as modifier*): *con man.* ~*vb.* **conning, conned. 2.** (*tr.*) to swindle or defraud. [C19: from CONFIDENCE]

con[2] (kɒn) *n.* (*usually pl.*) an argument or vote against a proposal, motion, etc. See also **pros and cons.** [from L *contra* against]

con[3] *or esp. U.S.* **conn** (kɒn) *vb.* **conning, conned.** (*tr.*) *Naut.* to direct the steering of (a vessel). [C17 *cun*, from earlier *condien* to guide, from OF *conduire*, from L *conducere*; see CONDUCT]

con[4] (kɒn) *vb.* **conning, conned.** (*tr.*) *Arch.* to study attentively or learn. [C15: var. of CAN[1] in the sense: to come to know]

con[5] (kɒn) *prep. Music.* with. [It.]

con. *abbrev. for:* **1.** concerto. **2.** conclusion. **3.** connection. **4.** consolidated. **5.** continued.

con- *prefix.* a variant of **com-.**

Conakry *or* **Konakri** (*French* kɔnakri) *n.* the capital of Guinea, a port on the island of Tombo. Pop.: 705 280 (1983).

con amore (kɒn æ'mɔːrɪ) *adj., adv. Music.* (to be performed) lovingly. [C19: from It.: with love]

Conan Doyle ('kəʊnən 'dɔɪl, 'kɒnən) *n.* Sir **Arthur.** 1859–1930, British author of detective stories and historical romances and the creator of *Sherlock Holmes.*

con brio (kɒn 'bri:əʊ) *adj., adv. Music.* (to be performed) with liveliness or spirit. [It.: with energy]

concatenate (kɒn'kætɪ,neɪt) *vb.* (*tr.*) to link or join together, esp. in a chain or series. [C16: from LL *concatēnāre*, from L *com-* together + *catēna* CHAIN] —,**concate'nation** *n.*

concave ('kɒnkeɪv) *adj.* **1.** curving inwards; having the shape of a section of the interior of a sphere, paraboloid, etc.: *a concave lens.* ~*vb.* **2.** (*tr.*) to make concave. [C15: from L *concavus* arched, from *cavus* hollow] —**'concavely** *adv.* —**'concaveness** *n.*

concavity (kɒn'kævɪtɪ) *n.*, *pl.* **-ties. 1.** the state of being concave. **2.** a concave surface or thing.

concavo-concave (kɒn,keɪvəʊkɒn'keɪv) *adj.* (esp. of a lens) having both sides concave.

concavo-convex *adj.* **1.** having one side concave and the other side convex. **2.** (of a lens) having a concave face with greater curvature than the convex face.

conceal (kən'si:l) *vb.* (*tr.*) **1.** to keep from discovery; hide. **2.** to keep secret. [C14: from OF *conceler*, from L *concēlāre*, from *com-* (intensive) + *cēlāre* to hide] —**con'cealer** *n.* —**con'cealment** *n.*

concede (kən'si:d) *vb.* **1.** (when *tr.*, *may take a clause as object*) to admit or acknowledge (something) as true or correct. **2.** to yield or allow (something, such as a right). **3.** (*tr.*) to admit as certain in outcome: *to concede an election.* [C17: from L *concēdere*, from *cēdere* to give way] —**con'ceder** *n.*

conceit (kən'si:t) *n.* **1.** a high, often exaggerated, opinion of oneself or one's accomplishments. **2.** *Literary.* an elaborate image or far-fetched comparison. **3.** *Arch.* **a.** a witty expression. **b.** fancy; imagination. **c.** an idea. ~*vb.* (*tr.*) **4.** *Obs.* to think. [C14: from CONCEIVE]

conceited (kən'siːtɪd) *adj.* having an exaggerated opinion of oneself or one's accomplishments. —**con'ceitedly** *adv.* —**con'ceitedness** *n.*

conceivable (kən'siːvəbʲl) *adj.* capable of being understood, believed, or imagined; possible. —**con,ceiva'bility** *n.* —**con'ceivably** *adv.*

conceive (kən'siːv) *vb.* **1.** (when *intr.*, foll. by *of;* when *tr.*, *often takes a clause as object*) to have an idea (of); imagine; think. **2.** (*tr.*; *takes a clause as object or an infinitive*) to believe. **3.** (*tr.*) to develop: *she conceived a passion for music.* **4.** to become pregnant with (a child). **5.** (*tr.*) *Rare.* to express in words. [C13: from OF *conceivre*, from L *concipere* to take in, from *capere* to take]

concelebrate (kən'sɛlɪˌbreɪt) *vb. Christianity.* to celebrate (the Eucharist or Mass) jointly with one or more other priests. [C16: from L *concelebrāre*] —**con,cele'bration** *n.*

concentrate ('kɒnsənˌtreɪt) *vb.* **1.** to come or cause to come to a single purpose or aim: *to concentrate one's hopes on winning.* **2.** to make or become denser or purer by the removal of certain elements. **3.** (*intr.*; often foll. by *on*) to think intensely (about). ~*n.* **4.** a concentrated material or solution. [C17: back formation from CONCENTRATION, ult. from L *com-* same + *centrum* CENTRE] —**'concen,trative** *adj.* —**'concen,trator** *n.*

concentration (ˌkɒnsən'treɪʃən) *n.* **1.** intense mental application. **2.** the act of concentrating. **3.** something that is concentrated. **4.** the strength of a solution, esp. the amount of dissolved substance in a given volume of solvent. **5.** *Mil.* **a.** the act of bringing together military forces. **b.** the application of fire from a number of weapons against a target.

concentration camp *n.* a guarded prison camp for nonmilitary prisoners, esp. one in Nazi Germany.

concentre (kɒn'sɛntə) *vb.* to converge or cause to converge on a common centre; concentrate. [C16: from F *concentrer*]

concentric (kən'sɛntrɪk) *adj.* having a common centre: *concentric circles.* [C14: from Med. L *concentricus*, from L *com-* same + *centrum* CENTRE] —**con'centrically** *adv.*

Concepción (*Spanish* konθep'θjon) *n.* an industrial city in S central Chile. Pop.: 292 700 (1986).

concept ('kɒnsɛpt) *n.* **1.** an idea, esp. an abstract idea: *the concepts of biology.* **2.** *Philosophy.* a general idea that corresponds to some class of entities and consists of the essential features of the class. **3.** a new idea; invention. [C16: from L *conceptum*, from *concipere* to CONCEIVE]

conception (kən'sɛpʃən) *n.* **1.** something conceived; notion, idea, or plan. **2.** the description under which someone considers something: *a strange conception of freedom.* **3.** the state of an ovum being fertilized by a sperm in the womb. **4.** origin or beginning. [C13: from L *conceptiō*, from *concipere* to CONCEIVE] —**con'ceptional** or **con'ceptive** *adj.*

conceptual (kən'sɛptjʊəl) *adj.* of or characterized by concepts. —**con'ceptually** *adv.*

conceptualize or **-lise** (kən'sɛptjʊəˌlaɪz) *vb.* to form (a concept or concepts) out of observations, experience, data, etc. —**con,ceptuali'zation** or **-li'sation** *n.*

concern (kən'sɜːn) *vb.* (*tr.*) **1.** to relate to; affect. **2.** (usually foll. by *with* or *in*) to involve or interest (oneself): *he concerns himself with other people's affairs.* ~*n.* **3.** something that affects a person; affair; business. **4.** regard or interest: *he felt a strong concern for her.* **5.** anxiety or solicitude. **6.** important relation: *his news has great concern for us.* **7.** a commercial company. **8.** *Inf.* a material thing, esp. one of which one has a low opinion. [C15: from LL *concernere*, from L *com-* together + *cernere* to sift]

concerned (kən'sɜːnd) *adj.* **1.** (*postpositive*) interested, guilty, or involved: *I shall find the boy concerned and punish him.* **2.** worried or solicitous. —**concernedly** (kən'sɜːnɪdlɪ) *adv.*

concerning (kən'sɜːnɪŋ) *prep.* **1.** about; regarding. ~*adj.* **2.** worrying or troublesome.

concernment (kən'sɜːnmənt) *n. Rare.* affair or business; concern.

concert *n.* ('kɒnsɜːt). **1. a.** a performance of music by players or singers that does not involve theatrical staging.

b. (*as modifier*): *a concert version of an opera.* **2.** agreement in design, plan, or action. **3. in concert. a.** acting with a common purpose. **b.** (of musicians, etc.) performing live. ~*vb.* (kən'sɜːt). **4.** to arrange or contrive (a plan) by mutual agreement. [C16: from F *concerter* to bring into agreement, from It., from LL *concertāre* to work together, from L *certāre* to contend]

concertante (ˌkɒntʃəˈtænti) *adj. Music.* characterized by contrasting alternating tutti and solo passages. [It.: from *concertare* to perform a CONCERT]

concerted (kən'sɜːtɪd) *adj.* **1.** mutually contrived, planned, or arranged; combined: *a concerted effort.* **2.** *Music.* arranged in parts for a group of singers or players.

concert grand *n.* a grand piano of the largest size.

concertina (ˌkɒnsə'tiːnə) *n.* **1.** a hexagonal musical instrument similar to the accordion, in which metallic reeds are vibrated by air from a set of bellows operated by the player's hands. ~*vb.* **-naing, -naed.** **2.** (*intr.*) to collapse or fold up like the bellows of a concertina. [C19: CONCERT + *-ina*] —**,concer'tinist** *n.*

concertino (ˌkɒntʃə'tiːnəʊ) *n.*, *pl.* **-ni** (-nɪ). *Music.* **1.** the solo group in a concerto grosso. **2.** a short concerto. [It.: a little CONCERTO]

concertmaster ('kɒnsətˌmɑːstə) *n.* a U.S. and Canad. word for **leader** (of an orchestra).

concerto (kən'tʃɛətəʊ) *n.*, *pl.* **-tos** or **-ti** (-tɪ). a composition for an orchestra and one or more soloists. [C18: from It.: CONCERT]

concerto grosso ('grɒsəʊ) *n.*, *pl.* **concerti grossi** ('grɒsɪ) or **concerto grossos.** a composition for an orchestra and a group of soloists. [It., lit.: big concerto]

concert party *n.* **1.** esp. formerly, a social gathering for music-making. **2.** *Stock Exchange inf.* a group of individuals or companies who secretly agree together to purchase shares separately in a particular company which they plan to amalgamate later into a single holding: a malpractice which is illegal in some countries.

concert pitch *n.* **1.** the frequency of 440 hertz assigned to the A above middle C. **2.** *Inf.* a state of extreme readiness.

concession (kən'sɛʃən) *n.* **1.** the act of yielding or conceding. **2.** something conceded. **3.** any grant of rights, land, or property by a government, local authority, corporation, or individual. **4.** the right, esp. an exclusive right, to market a particular product in a given area. **5.** *Canad.* **a.** a land subdivision in a township survey. **b.** another name for a **concession road.** [C16: from L *concessiō*, from *concēdere* to CONCEDE] —**con'cessible** *adj.* —**con'cessive** *adj.*

concessionaire (kənˌsɛʃə'nɛə), **concessioner** (kən-'sɛʃənə), or **concessionary** *n.* someone who holds or operates a concession.

concessionary (kən'sɛʃənərɪ) *adj.* **1.** of, granted, or obtained by a concession. ~*n.*, *pl.* **-aries. 2.** another word for **concessionaire.**

concession road *n. Canad.* one of a series of roads separating concessions in a township.

conch (kɒŋk, kɒntʃ) *n.*, *pl.* **conchs** (kɒŋks) or **conches** ('kɒntʃɪz). **1.** any of various tropical marine gastropod molluscs characterized by a large brightly coloured spiral shell. **2.** the shell of such a mollusc, used as a trumpet. [C16: from L *concha*, from Gk *konkhē* shellfish]

conchie or **conchy** ('kɒntʃɪ) *n.*, *pl.* **-chies.** *Inf.* short for **conscientious objector.**

Conchobar ('kɒŋkəʊwə, 'kɒnʊə) *n.* (in Irish legend) a king of Ulster at about the beginning of the Christian era. See also **Deirdre.**

conchology (kɒŋ'kɒlədʒɪ) *n.* the study of mollusc shells. —**con'chologist** *n.*

concierge (ˌkɒnsɪ'ɛəʒ) *n.* (esp. in France) a caretaker of a block of flats, hotel, etc., esp. one who lives on the premises. [C17: from F, ult. from L *conservus*, from *servus* slave]

conciliar (kən'sɪlɪə) *adj.* of, from, or by means of a council, esp. an ecclesiastical one.

conciliate (kən'sɪlɪˌeɪt) *vb.* (*tr.*) **1.** to overcome the hostility of; win over. **2.** to gain (favour, regard, etc.), esp. by making friendly overtures. [C16: from L *conciliāre* to bring together, from *concilium* COUNCIL] —**con'ciliable** *adj.* —**con,cili'ation** *n.* —**con'cili,ator** *n.*

conciliatory (kən'sɪljətərɪ) or **conciliative** (kən'sɪljətɪv) *adj.* intended to placate or reconcile. —**con'ciliatorily** *adv.*

concise (kən'saɪs) *adj.* brief and to the point. [C16: from L *concīsus* cut short, from *concīdere*, from *caedere* to cut, strike down] —**con'cisely** *adv.* —**con'ciseness** *or* **concision** (kən'sɪʒən) *n.*

conclave ('kɒnkleɪv) *n.* **1.** a secret meeting. **2.** *R.C. Church.* **a.** the closed apartments where the college of cardinals elects a new pope. **b.** a meeting of the college of cardinals for this purpose. [C14: from Med. L *conclāve*, from L: place that may be locked, from *clāvis* key]

conclude (kən'kluːd) *vb.* (*mainly tr.*) **1.** (*also intr.*) to come or cause to come to an end. **2.** (*takes a clause as object*) to decide by reasoning; deduce: *the judge concluded that the witness had told the truth.* **3.** to settle: *to conclude a treaty.* **4.** *Obs.* to confine. [C14: from L *conclūdere*, from *claudere* to close]

conclusion (kən'kluːʒən) *n.* **1.** end or termination. **2.** the last main division of a speech, essay, etc. **3.** outcome or result (esp. in **a foregone conclusion**). **4.** a final decision or judgment (esp. in **come to a conclusion**). **5.** *Logic.* **a.** a statement that purports to follow from another or others (the **premises**) by means of an argument. **b.** a statement that does validly follow from given premises. **6.** *Law.* **a.** an admission or statement binding on the party making it; estoppel. **b.** the close of a pleading or of a conveyance. **7. in conclusion.** lastly; to sum up. **8. jump to conclusions.** to come to a conclusion prematurely, without sufficient thought or on incomplete evidence. [C14: via OF from L; see CONCLUDE, -ION]

conclusive (kən'kluːsɪv) *adj.* **1.** putting an end to doubt; decisive; final. **2.** approaching or involving an end. —**con'clusively** *adv.*

concoct (kən'kɒkt) *vb.* (*tr.*) **1.** to make by combining different ingredients. **2.** to invent; make up; contrive. [C16: from L *concoctus* cooked together, from *coquere* to cook] —**con'cocter** *or* **con'coctor** *n.* —**con'coction** *n.*

concomitance (kən'kɒmɪtəns) *n.* **1.** existence together. **2.** *Christianity.* the doctrine that the body and blood of Christ are present in the Eucharist.

concomitant (kən'kɒmɪtənt) *adj.* **1.** existing or occurring together. ~*n.* **2.** a concomitant act, person, etc. [C17: from LL *concomitārī* to accompany, from *com-* with + *comes* companion]

concord ('kɒnkɔːd) *n.* **1.** agreement or harmony. **2.** a treaty establishing peaceful relations between nations. **3.** *Music.* a combination of musical notes, esp. one containing a series of consonant intervals. **4.** *Grammar.* another word for **agreement** (sense 6). [C13: from OF *concorde*, from L *concordia*, from *com-* same + *cors* heart]

Concord ('kɒnkəd) *n.* a town in NE Massachusetts: scene of one of the opening military actions (1775) of the War of American Independence. Pop.: 16 293 (1980).

concordance (kən'kɔːdəns) *n.* **1.** a state of harmony. **2.** a book that indexes the principal words in a literary work, often with the immediate context and an account of the meaning. **3.** an index produced by computer or machine.

concordant (kən'kɔːdənt) *adj.* being in agreement; harmonious. —**con'cordantly** *adv.*

concordat (kən'kɔːdæt) *n.* a pact or treaty, esp. one between the Vatican and another state concerning the interests of religion in that state. [C17: via F, from Med. L *concordātum*, from L *concordāre* something agreed; see CONCORD]

concourse ('kɒnkɔːs) *n.* **1.** a crowd; throng. **2.** a coming together; confluence. **3.** a large open space for the gathering of people in a public place. [C14: from OF *concours*, ult. from L *concurrere* to run together]

concrete ('kɒnkriːt) *n.* **1.** a construction material made of cement, sand, stone and water that hardens to a stonelike mass. ~*adj.* **2.** relating to a particular instance; specific as opposed to general. **3.** relating to things capable of being perceived by the senses, as opposed to abstractions. **4.** formed by the coalescence of particles; condensed; solid. ~*vb.* **5.** (*tr.*) to construct in or cover with concrete. **6.** (*intr.*) to become or cause to become solid; coalesce. [C14: from L *concrētus*, from *concrēscere* to grow together] —'**concretely** *adv.* —'**concreteness** *n.*

concrete music *n.* music consisting of an electronically modified montage of tape-recorded sounds.

concrete noun *n.* a noun that refers to a material object.

concrete poetry *n.* poetry in which the visual form of the poem is used to convey meaning.

concretion (kən'kriːʃən) *n.* **1.** the act of growing together; coalescence. **2.** a solidified mass. **3.** something

made real, tangible, or specific. **4.** a rounded or irregular mineral mass different in composition from the sedimentary rock that surrounds it. **5.** *Pathol.* another word for **calculus.** —**con'cretionary** *adj.*

concretize *or* **-tise** ('kɒnkrɪˌtaɪz) *vb.* (*tr.*) to render concrete; make real or specific.

concubine ('kɒŋkjʊˌbaɪn, 'kɒŋ-) *n.* **1.** (in polygamous societies) a secondary wife. **2.** a woman who cohabits with a man, esp. (formerly) the mistress of a king, nobleman, etc. [C13: from OF, from L *concubīna*, from *concumbere* to lie together] —**concubinage** (kɒn'kjuːbɪnɪdʒ) *n.* —**con'cubinary** *n.*, *adj.*

concupiscence (kən'kjuːpɪsəns) *n.* strong desire, esp. sexual desire. [C14: from Church L *concupiscentia*, from L *concupiscere* to covet] —**con'cupiscent** *adj.*

concur (kən'kɜː) *vb.* **-curring, -curred.** (*intr.*) **1.** to agree; be in accord. **2.** to combine or cooperate. **3.** to occur simultaneously; coincide. [C15: from L *concurrere* to run together]

concurrence (kən'kʌrəns) *n.* **1.** the act of concurring. **2.** agreement; accord. **3.** cooperation or combination. **4.** simultaneous occurrence.

concurrent (kən'kʌrənt) *adj.* **1.** taking place at the same time or in the same location. **2.** cooperating. **3.** meeting at, approaching, or having a common point: *concurrent lines.* **4.** in agreement; harmonious. —**con'currently** *adv.*

concuss (kən'kʌs) *vb.* (*tr.*) **1.** to injure (the brain) by a violent blow, fall, etc. **2.** to shake violently. [C16: from L *concussus*, from *concutere* to disturb greatly, from *quatere* to shake]

concussion (kən'kʌʃən) *n.* **1.** a jarring of the brain, caused by a blow or a fall, usually resulting in loss of consciousness. **2.** any violent shaking.

Condé (*French* kɔ̃de) *n.* **Prince de** (prɛs də), title of *Louis II de Bourbon, Duc d'Enghien,* called the *Great Condé.* 1621–86, French general, who led Louis XIV's armies against the Fronde (1649) but joined the Fronde in a new revolt (1650–52). He later fought for both France and Spain.

condemn (kən'dɛm) *vb.* (*tr.*) **1.** to express strong disapproval of. **2.** to pronounce judicial sentence on. **3.** to demonstrate the guilt of: *his secretive behaviour condemned him.* **4.** to judge or pronounce unfit for use. **5.** to force into a particular state: *his disposition condemned him to boredom.* [C13: from OF *condempner*, from L *condemnāre*, from *damnāre* to condemn] —**con'demnable** *adj.* —ˌ**condem'nation** *n.* —ˌ**condem'natory** *adj.*

condensate (kən'dɛnseɪt) *n.* a substance formed by condensation.

condensation (ˌkɒndɛn'seɪʃən) *n.* **1.** the act or process of condensing, or the state of being condensed. **2.** anything that has condensed from a vapour, esp. on a window. **3.** *Chem.* a type of reaction in which two organic molecules combine to form a larger molecule as well as a simple molecule such as water, etc. **4.** an abridged version of a book. —ˌ**conden'sational** *adj.*

condensation trail *n.* another name for **vapour trail.**

condense (kən'dɛns) *vb.* **1.** (*tr.*) to increase the density of; compress. **2.** to reduce or be reduced in volume or size. **3.** to change or cause to change from a gaseous to a liquid or solid state. **4.** *Chem.* to undergo or cause to undergo condensation. [C15: from L *condēnsāre*, from *dēnsāre* to make thick, from *dēnsus* DENSE] —**con'densable** *or* **con'densible** *adj.*

condensed matter *n.* solids and liquids.

condensed milk *n.* milk reduced by evaporation to a thick concentration, with sugar added.

condenser (kən'dɛnsə) *n.* **1. a.** an apparatus for reducing gases to their liquid or solid form by the abstraction of heat. **b.** a device for abstracting heat, as in a refrigeration unit. **2.** a lens that concentrates light. **3.** another name for **capacitor.** **4.** a person or device that condenses.

condescend (ˌkɒndɪ'sɛnd) *vb.* (*intr.*) **1.** to act graciously towards another or others regarded as being on a lower level; behave patronizingly. **2.** to do something that one regards as below one's dignity. [C14: from Church L *condēscendere*, from L *dēscendere* to DESCEND] —ˌ**conde'scending** *adj.* —ˌ**conde'scendingly** *adv.* —ˌ**conde'scension** *n.*

condign (kən'daɪn) *adj.* (esp. of a punishment) fitting; deserved. [C15: from OF *condigne*, from L *condignus*, from *dignus* worthy] —**con'dignly** *adv.*

Condillac (*French* kɔ̃dijak) *n.* **Étienne Bonnot de** (etjɛn bɔno də). 1715–80, French philosopher. He developed Locke's view that all knowledge derives from the senses in his *Traité des sensations* (1754).

condiment ('kɒndɪmənt) *n.* any spice or sauce such as salt, pepper, mustard, etc. [C15: from L *condimentum* seasoning, from *condīre* to pickle]

condition (kən'dɪʃən) *n.* **1.** a particular state of being or existence: *the human condition.* **2.** something that limits or restricts; a qualification. **3.** (*pl.*) circumstances: *conditions were right for a takeover.* **4.** state of physical fitness, esp. good health: *out of condition.* **5.** an ailment: *a heart condition.* **6.** something indispensable: *your happiness is a condition of mine.* **7.** something required as part of an agreement; term: *the conditions of the lease are set out.* **8.** *Law.* **a.** a provision in a will, contract, etc., that makes some right or liability contingent upon the happening of some event. **b.** the event itself. **9.** *Logic.* a statement whose truth is either required for the truth of a given statement (a **necessary condition**) or sufficient to guarantee the truth of the given statement (a **sufficient condition**). **10.** rank, status, or position. **11. on condition that.** (*conj.*) provided that. ~*vb.* (*mainly tr.*) **12.** *Psychol.* **a.** to alter the response of (a person or animal) to a particular stimulus or situation. **b.** to establish a conditioned response in. **13.** to put into a fit condition. **14.** to improve the condition of (one's hair) by use of special cosmetics. **15.** to accustom or inure. **16.** to subject to a condition. [C14: from L *conditiō*, from *condīcere* to discuss, from *con*-together + *dīcere* to say] —**con'ditioner** *n.* —**con'ditioning** *n., adj.*

conditional (kən'dɪʃənəl) *adj.* **1.** depending on other factors. **2.** *Grammar.* expressing a condition on which something else is contingent: *"If he comes" is a conditional clause in the sentence "If he comes I shall go".* **3.** *Logic.* (of a proposition) consisting of two component propositions associated by the words *if . . . then* so that the proposition is false only when the antecedent is true and the consequent false. ~*n.* **4.** a conditional verb form, clause, sentence, etc. —**con,dition'ality** *n.* —**con'ditionally** *adv.*

conditioned response *n. Psychol.* a response that is transferred from the second to the first of a pair of stimuli. A well-known Pavlovian example is salivation by a dog when it hears a bell ring, because food has always been presented when the bell has been rung previously. Also called (esp. formerly): **conditioned reflex.**

condo ('kɒndəʊ) *n., pl.* **-dos.** *U.S. & Canad. inf.* a condominium building or apartment.

condole (kən'dəʊl) *vb.* (*intr.; foll. by with*) to express sympathy with someone in grief, pain, etc. [C16: from Church L *condolēre*, from L *com-* together + *dolēre* to grieve] —**con'dolence** *n.*

condom ('kɒndəm) *n.* a rubber sheath worn on the penis during sexual intercourse to prevent conception or infection. [C18: from ?]

condominium (,kɒndə'mɪnɪəm) *n., pl.* **-ums.** **1.** joint rule or sovereignty. **2.** a country ruled by two or more foreign powers. **3.** *U.S. & Canad.* an apartment building in which each apartment is individually owned and the common areas are jointly owned. [C18: from NL, from L *com-* together + *dominium* ownership]

condone (kən'dəʊn) *vb.* (*tr.*) **1.** to overlook or forgive (an offence, etc.). **2.** *Law.* (esp. of a spouse) to pardon or overlook (an offence, usually adultery). [C19: from L *condōnāre*, from *com-* (intensive) + *dōnāre* to donate] —**condonation** (,kɒndəʊ'neɪʃən) *n.* —**con'doner** *n.*

condor ('kɒndɔː) *n.* either of two very large rare New World vultures, the **Andean condor**, which has black plumage with white around the neck, and the **California condor**, which is nearly extinct. [C17: from Sp. *cóndor*, from Quechuan *kuntur*]

condottiere (,kɒndɒ'tjɛərɪ) *n., pl.* **-ri** (-riː). a commander or soldier in a professional mercenary company in Europe from the 13th to the 16th centuries. [C18: from It., from *condotto* leadership, from *condurre* to lead, from L *condūcere*]

conduce (kən'djuːs) *vb.* (*intr.; foll. by to*) to lead or contribute (to a result). [C15: from L *condūcere*, from *com-* together + *dūcere* to lead]

conducive (kən'djuːsɪv) *adj.* (when *postpositive*, foll. by *to*) contributing, leading, or tending.

conduct *n.* ('kɒndʌkt). **1.** behaviour. **2.** the way of managing a business, affair, etc.; handling. **3.** *Rare.* the act of leading. ~*vb.* (kən'dʌkt). **1.** (*tr.*) to accompany and guide (people, a party, etc.) (esp. in **conducted tour**). **5.** (*tr.*) to direct (affairs, business, etc.); control. **6.** (*tr.*) to carry out; organize: *conduct a survey.* **7.** (*tr.*) to behave (oneself). **8.** to control (an orchestra, etc.) by the movements of the hands or a baton. **9.** to transmit (heat, electricity, etc.). [C15: from Med. L *conductus* escorted, from L, from *condūcere* to CONDUCE] —**con'ductible** *adj.* —**con,duct-i'bility** *n.*

conductance (kən'dʌktəns) *n.* the ability of a system to conduct electricity, measured by the ratio of the current flowing through the system to the potential difference across it. Symbol: G

conduction (kən'dʌkʃən) *n.* **1.** the transfer of heat or electricity through a medium. **2.** the transmission of an impulse along a nerve fibre. **3.** the act of conveying or conducting, as through a pipe. **4.** *Physics.* another name for **conductivity** (sense 1). —**con'ductional** *adj.*

conductive (kən'dʌktɪv) *adj.* of, denoting, or having the property of conduction.

conductivity (,kɒndʌk'tɪvɪtɪ) *n., pl.* **-ties.** **1.** the property of transmitting heat, electricity, or sound. **2.** a measure of the ability of a substance to conduct electricity. Symbol: κ

conductivity water *n.* water that has a conductivity of less than 0.043×10^{-6} S cm^{-1}.

conductor (kən'dʌktə) *n.* **1.** an official on a bus who collects fares. **2.** a person who conducts an orchestra, choir, etc. **3.** a person who leads or guides. **4.** *U.S. & Canad.* a railway official in charge of a train. **5.** a substance, body, or system that conducts electricity, heat, etc. **6.** See **lightning conductor.** —**con'ductor,ship** *n.* —**conductress** (kən'dʌktrɪs) *fem. n.*

conduit ('kɒndɪt, -djʊɪt) *n.* **1.** a pipe or channel for carrying a fluid. **2.** a rigid tube for carrying electrical cables. [C14: from OF, from Med. L *conductus* channel, from L *condūcere* to lead]

condyle ('kɒndɪl) *n.* the rounded projection on the articulating end of a bone. [C17: from L *condylus*, from Gk *kondulos*] —**'condylar** *adj.*

cone (kəʊn) *n.* **1.** a geometric solid consisting of a plane base bounded by a closed curve, usually a circle or an ellipse, every point of which is joined to a fixed point lying outside the plane of the base. **2.** anything that tapers from a circular section to a point, such as a wafer shell used to contain ice cream. **3. a.** the reproductive body of conifers and related plants, made up of overlapping scales. **b.** a similar structure in horsetails, club mosses, etc. **4.** a small cone used as a temporary traffic marker on roads. **5.** any one of the cone-shaped cells in the retina of the eye, sensitive to colour and bright light. ~*vb.* **6.** (*tr.*) to shape like a cone. [C16: from L *cōnus*, from Gk *kōnus* pine cone, geometrical cone]

cone off *vb.* (*tr., adv.*) *Brit.* to close one carriageway of a motorway by placing warning cones across it.

coney ('kəʊnɪ) *n.* a variant spelling of **cony.**

Coney Island ('kəʊnɪ) *n.* an island off the S shore of Long Island, New York: site of a large amusement park.

confab ('kɒnfæb) *Inf.* ~*n.* **1.** a conversation. ~*vb.* **-fabbing, -fabbed. 2.** (*intr.*) to converse.

confabulate (kən'fæbjʊ,leɪt) *vb.* (*intr.*) **1.** to talk together; chat. **2.** *Psychiatry.* to replace the gaps left by a disorder of the memory with imaginary remembered experiences consistently believed to be true. [C17: from L *confābulārī*, from *fābulārī* to talk, from *fābula* a story] —**con,fabu'lation** *n.*

confect (kən'fɛkt) *vb.* (*tr.*) **1.** to prepare by combining ingredients. **2.** to make; construct. [C16: from L *confectus* prepared, from *conficere*, from *com-* (intensive) + *facere* to make]

confection (kən'fɛkʃən) *n.* **1.** the act of compounding or mixing. **2.** any sweet preparation, such as a preserve or a sweet. **3.** *Old-fashioned.* an elaborate article of clothing, esp. for women. [C14: from OF, from L *confectiō* a preparing, from *conficere*; see CONFECT]

confectioner (kən'fɛkʃənə) *n.* a person who makes or sells sweets or confections.

confectionery (kən'fɛkʃənərɪ) n., pl. -eries. 1. sweets and other confections collectively. 2. the art or business of a confectioner.

confederacy (kən'fɛdərəsɪ) n., pl. -cies. 1. a union of states, etc.; alliance; league. 2. a combination of groups or individuals for unlawful purposes. [C14: from OF *confederacie*, from LL *confoederātiō* agreement]

Confederacy (kən'fɛdərəsɪ, -'fɛdrəsɪ) n. the. another name for the **Confederate States of America.**

confederate n. (kən'fɛdərɪt). 1. a nation, state, or individual that is part of a confederacy. 2. someone who is part of a conspiracy. ~adj. (kən'fɛdərɪt). 3. united; allied. ~vb. (kən'fɛdə,reɪt). 4. to form into or become part of a confederacy. [C14: from LL *confoederātus*, from *confoederāre* to unite by a league]

Confederate (kən'fɛdərɪt) adj. 1. of or supporting the Confederate States of America. ~n. 2. a supporter of the Confederate States.

Confederate States of America pl. n. U.S. history. the 11 Southern states (Alabama, Arkansas, Florida, Georgia, North Carolina, South Carolina, Texas, Virginia, Tennessee, Louisiana, and Mississippi) that seceded from the Union in 1861, precipitating a civil war with the North. The Confederacy was defeated in 1865 and the South reincorporated into the U.S.

confederation (kən,fɛdə'reɪʃən) n. 1. the act of confederating or the state of being confederated. 2. a loose alliance of political units. 3. (esp. in Canada) another name for a **federation.** —con,feder'ationist n.

Confederation (kən,fɛdə'reɪʃən) n. 1. the. U.S. history. the original 13 states of the United States of America constituted under the Articles of Confederation and superseded by the more formal union established in 1789. 2. the federation of Canada, formed with four original provinces in 1867 and since joined by eight more.

confer (kən'fɜː) vb. **-ferring, -ferred.** 1. (tr.; foll. by on or upon) to grant or bestow (an honour, gift, etc.). 2. (intr.) to consult together. [C16: from L *conferre*, from *com-* together + *ferre* to bring] —con'ferment or con'ferral n. —con'ferrable adj.

conferee or **conferree** (,kɒnfɜː'riː) n. 1. a person who takes part in a conference. 2. a person on whom an honour or gift is conferred.

conference ('kɒnfərəns) n. 1. a meeting for consultation or discussion, esp. one with a formal agenda. 2. an assembly of the clergy or of clergy and laity of any of certain Protestant Churches acting as representatives of their denomination. 3. Sport, U.S. & Canad. a league of clubs or teams. [C16: from Med. L *conferentia*, from *conferre* to bring together] —conferential (,kɒnfə'rɛnʃəl) adj.

conference call n. a special telephone facility by which three or more people using conventional or cellular phones can be linked up to speak to one another.

conferencing ('kɒnfərənsɪŋ) n. a telephone facility enabling geographically separated groups of people to hold a meeting via the telephone network.

confess (kən'fɛs) vb. (when tr., may take a clause as object) 1. (when intr., often foll. by to) to make an admission (of faults, crimes, etc.). 2. (tr.) to admit to be true; concede. 3. Christianity. to declare (one's sins) to God or to a priest as his representative, so as to obtain pardon and absolution. [C14: from OF *confesser*, from LL, from L *confessus* confessed, from *confitērī* to admit]

confessedly (kən'fɛsɪdlɪ) adv. (sentence modifier) by admission or confession; avowedly.

confession (kən'fɛʃən) n. 1. the act of confessing. 2. something confessed. 3. an acknowledgment, esp. of one's faults or crimes. 4. Christianity. the act of a penitent accusing himself of his sins. 5. **confession of faith.** a formal public avowal of religious beliefs. 6. a religious sect united by common beliefs. —con'fessionary adj.

confessional (kən'fɛʃənəl) adj. 1. of or suited to a confession. ~n. 2. Christianity. a small stall where a priest hears confessions.

confessor (kən'fɛsə) n. 1. Christianity. a priest who hears confessions and sometimes acts as a spiritual counsellor. 2. History. a person who bears witness to his Christian religious faith by the holiness of his life, but does not suffer martyrdom. 3. a person who makes a confession.

confetti (kən'fɛtɪ) n. small pieces of coloured paper thrown on festive occasions, esp. at weddings. [C19: from It., pl. of *confetto*, orig., a bonbon]

confidant or (fem.) **confidante** (,kɒnfɪ'dænt, 'kɒnfɪ,dænt) n. a person to whom private matters are confided. [C17: from F *confident*, from It. *confidente*, n. use of adj.: trustworthy]

confide (kən'faɪd) vb. 1. (usually foll. by in; when tr., may take a clause as object) to disclose (secret or personal matters) in confidence (to). 2. (intr.; foll. by in) to have complete trust. 3. (tr.) to entrust into another's keeping. [C15: from L *confidere*, from *fidere* to trust] —con'fider n.

confidence ('kɒnfɪdəns) n. 1. trust in a person or thing. 2. belief in one's own abilities; self-assurance. 3. trust or a trustful relationship: take me into your confidence. 4. something confided; secret. 5. **in confidence.** as a secret.

confidence trick or U.S. & Canad. **confidence game** n. a swindle involving money in which the victim's trust is won by the swindler.

confident ('kɒnfɪdənt) adj. 1. (postpositive; foll. by of) having or showing certainty; sure: confident of success. 2. sure of oneself. 3. presumptuous. [C16: from L *confidens*, from *confidere* to have complete trust in] —'confidently adv.

confidential (,kɒnfɪ'dɛnʃəl) adj. 1. spoken or given in confidence; private. 2. entrusted with another's secret affairs: a confidential secretary. 3. suggestive of intimacy: a confidential approach. —,confi,denti'ality n. —,confi'dentially adv.

confiding (kən'faɪdɪŋ) adj. unsuspicious; trustful. —con'fidingly adv. —con'fidingness n.

configuration (kən,fɪgjʊ'reɪʃən) n. 1. the arrangement of the parts of something. 2. the external form or outline achieved by such an arrangement. 3. Psychol. the unit or pattern in perception studied by Gestalt psychologists. [C16: from LL *configūrātiō*, from *configūrāre* to model on something, from *figūrāre* to shape, fashion] —con,figu'rational or con'figurative adj.

confine vb. (kən'faɪn). (tr.) 1. to keep within bounds; limit; restrict. 2. to restrict the free movement of: arthritis confined him to bed. ~n. ('kɒnfaɪn). 3. (often pl.) a limit; boundary. [C16: from Med. L *confīnāre*, from L *confīnis* adjacent, from *finis* boundary] —con'finer n.

confined (kən'faɪnd) adj. 1. enclosed; limited. 2. in childbed; undergoing childbirth.

confinement (kən'faɪnmənt) n. 1. the act of confining or the state of being confined. 2. the period of the birth of a child.

confirm (kən'fɜːm) vb. (tr.) 1. (may take a clause as object) to prove to be true or valid; corroborate. 2. (may take a clause as object) to assert for a further time, so as to make more definite: he confirmed that he would appear in court. 3. to strengthen: his story confirmed my doubts. 4. to make valid by a formal act; ratify. 5. to administer the rite of confirmation to. [C13: from OF *confermer*, from L *confirmāre*, from *firmus* FIRM¹] —con'firmatory or con'firmative adj.

confirmation (,kɒnfə'meɪʃən) n. 1. the act of confirming. 2. something that confirms. 3. a rite in several Christian churches that confirms a baptized person in his faith and admits him to full participation in the church.

confirmed (kən'fɜːmd) adj. 1. (prenominal) long-established in a habit, way of life, etc. 2. having received the rite of confirmation.

confiscate ('kɒnfɪ,skeɪt) vb. (tr.) 1. to seize (property), esp. for public use and esp. by way of a penalty. ~adj. 2. confiscated; forfeit. [C16: from L *confiscāre* to seize for the public treasury, from *fiscus* treasury] —,confis'cation n. —'confis,cator n. —confiscatory (kən'fɪskətərɪ) adj.

Confiteor (kən'fɪtɪ,ɔː) n. R.C. Church. a prayer consisting of a general confession of sinfulness and an entreaty for forgiveness. [C13: from L: I confess]

conflagration (,kɒnflə'greɪʃən) n. a large destructive fire. [C16: from L *conflagrātiō*, from *conflagrāre*, from *com-* (intensive) + *flagrāre* to burn]

conflate (kən'fleɪt) vb. (tr.) to combine or blend (two things, esp. two versions of a text) so as to form a whole. [C16: from L *conflāre* to blow together, from *flāre* to blow] —con'flation n.

conflict n. ('kɒnflɪkt). 1. a struggle between opposing forces; battle. 2. opposition between ideas, interests, etc.; controversy. 3. Psychol. opposition between two simultaneous but incompatible wishes or drives, sometimes leading to emotional tension. ~*vb.* (kən'flɪkt). (*intr.*) **4.** to come into opposition; clash. **5.** to fight. [C15: from L *conflictus*, from *confligere* to combat, from *fligere* to strike] —**con'flicting** *adj.* —**con'flictingly** *adv.* —**con'fliction** *n.*

confluence ('kɒnfluəns) *or* **conflux** ('kɒnflʌks) *n.* **1.** a flowing together, esp. of rivers. **2.** a gathering. —'**confluent** *adj.*

conform (kən'fɔːm) *vb.* **1.** (*intr.*; usually foll. by *to*) to comply in actions, behaviour, etc., with accepted standards. **2.** (*intr.*; usually foll. by *with*) to be in accordance: *he conforms with my idea of a teacher.* **3.** to make or become similar. **4.** (*intr.*) to comply with the practices of an established church, esp. the Church of England. [C14: from OF *conformer*, from L *confirmāre* to strengthen, from *firmāre* to make firm] —**con'former** *n.* —**con'formist** *n., adj.*

conformable (kən'fɔːməb³l) *adj.* **1.** corresponding in character; similar. **2.** obedient; submissive. **3.** (foll. by *to*) consistent (with). **4.** (of rock strata) lying in a parallel arrangement so that their original relative positions have remained undisturbed. —**con,forma'bility** *n.* —**con-'formably** *adv.*

conformal (kən'fɔːməl) *adj.* (of a map projection) maintaining true shape over a small area and scale in every direction. [C17: from LL *conformālis*, from L *com-* same + *forma* shape]

conformation (,kɒnfɔː'meɪʃən) *n.* **1.** the general shape of an object; configuration. **2.** the arrangement of the parts of an object. **3.** the three-dimensional arrangement of the atoms in a molecule.

conformity (kən'fɔːmɪtɪ) *or* **conformance** *n., pl.* **-ities** *or* **-ances.** **1.** compliance in actions, behaviour, etc., with certain accepted standards. **2.** likeness; congruity; agreement. **3.** compliance with the practices of an established church.

confound (kən'faʊnd) *vb.* (*tr.*) **1.** to astound; bewilder. **2.** to confuse. **3.** to treat mistakenly as similar to or identical with. **4.** (kɒn'faʊnd). to curse (usually in **confound it!**). **5.** to contradict or refute (an argument, etc.). **6.** to rout or defeat (an enemy). [C13: from OF *confondre*, from L *confundere* to mingle, pour together] —**con'founder** *n.*

confounded (kən'faʊndɪd) *adj.* **1.** bewildered; confused. **2.** (*prenominal*) *Inf.* execrable; damned. —**con'foundedly** *adv.*

confraternity (,kɒnfrə'tɜːnɪtɪ) *n., pl.* **-ties.** a group of men united for some particular purpose, esp. Christian laymen organized for religious or charitable service; brotherhood. [C15: from Med. L *confrāternitās*, ult. from L *frāter* brother]

confrère ('kɒnfreə) *n.* a fellow member of a profession, etc. [C15: from OF, from Med. L *confrāter*]

confront (kən'frʌnt) *vb.* (*tr.*) **1.** (usually foll. by *with*) to present (with something), esp. in order to accuse or criticize. **2.** to face boldly; oppose in hostility. **3.** to be face to face with. [C16: from Med. L *confrontāri*, from *frons* forehead] —**confrontation** (,kɒnfrʌn'teɪʃən) *n.* —,con-**fron'tational** *adj.*

Confucian (kən'fjuːʃən) *adj.* **1.** of or relating to the doctrines of Confucius. ~*n.* **2.** a follower of Confucius.

Confucianism (kən'fjuːʃə,nɪzəm) *n.* the ethical system of Confucius, emphasizing moral order, the virtue of China's ancient rules, and gentlemanly education. —**Con-'fucianist** *n.*

Confucius (kən'fjuːʃəs) *n.* Chinese name *Kong Zi* or *K'ung Fu-tse.* 551–479 B.C., Chinese philosopher and teacher of ethics (see **Confucianism**). His doctrines were compiled after his death under the title *The Analects of Confucius.*

confuse (kən'fjuːz) *vb.* (*tr.*) **1.** to bewilder; perplex. **2.** to mix up (things, ideas, etc.). **3.** to make unclear: *he confused his talk with irrelevant details.* **4.** to mistake (one thing) for another. **5.** to disconcert; embarrass. **6.** to cause to become disordered: *the enemy ranks were confused by gas.* [C18: back formation from *confused*, from L *confūsus*, from *confundere* to pour together] —**con'fusable** *adj.* —**confusedly** (kən'fjuːzɪdlɪ, -'fjuːzd-) *adv.* —**con'fusing** *adj.* —**con'fusingly** *adv.*

confusion (kən'fjuːʒən) *n.* **1.** the act of confusing or the state of being confused. **2.** disorder. **3.** bewilderment; perplexity. **4.** lack of clarity. **5.** embarrassment; abashment.

confute (kən'fjuːt) *vb.* (*tr.*) to prove (a person or thing) wrong, invalid, or mistaken; disprove. [C16: from L *confūtāre* to check, silence] —**con'futable** *adj.* —**confutation** (,kɒnfjʊ'teɪʃən) *n.*

conga ('kɒŋɡə) *n.* **1.** a Latin American dance of three steps and a kick to each bar, performed by a number of people in single file. **2.** Also called: **conga drum.** a large tubular bass drum, usually played with the hands. ~*vb.* **-gaing, -gaed. 3.** (*intr.*) to perform this dance. [C20: from American Sp., fem. of *congo* belonging to the *Congo*]

congé ('kɒnʒeɪ) *n.* **1.** permission to depart or dismissal, esp. when formal. **2.** a farewell. [C16: from OF *congié*, from L *commeātus* leave of absence, from *meāre* to go]

congeal (kən'dʒiːl) *vb.* **1.** to change or cause to change from a soft or fluid state to a firm state. **2.** to form or cause to form into a coagulated mass; jell. [C14: from OF *congeler*, from L *congelāre*, from *com-* together + *gelāre* to freeze] —**con'gealable** *adj.* —**con'gealment** *n.*

congelation (,kɒndʒɪ'leɪʃən) *n.* **1.** the process of congealing. **2.** something formed by this process.

congener (kən'dʒiːnə, 'kɒndʒɪnə) *n.* a member of a class, group, or other category, esp. any animal of a specified genus. [C18: from L, from *com-* same + *genus* kind]

congenial (kən'dʒiːnjəl) *adj.* **1.** friendly, pleasant, or agreeable: *a congenial atmosphere to work in.* **2.** having a similar disposition, tastes, etc.; compatible. [C17: from CON- (same) + GENIAL¹] —**congeniality** (kən,dʒiːnɪ'ælɪtɪ) *n.*

congenital (kən'dʒɛnɪt³l) *adj.* **1.** denoting any nonhereditary condition, esp. an abnormal condition, existing at birth: *congenital blindness.* **2.** *Inf.* complete, as if from birth: *a congenital idiot.* [C18: from L *congenitus*, from *genitus* born, from *gignere* to bear] —**con'genitally** *adv.*

conger ('kɒŋɡə) *n.* a large marine eel occurring in temperate and tropical coastal waters. [C14: from OF *congre*, from L *conger*, from Gk *gongros*]

congeries (kɒn'dʒɪəriːz) *n.* (*functioning as sing. or pl.*) a collection; mass; heap. [C17: from L, from *congerere* to pile up, from *gerere* to carry]

congest (kən'dʒɛst) *vb.* **1.** to crowd or become crowded to excess; overfill. **2.** to clog (an organ) with blood or (of an organ) to become clogged with blood. **3.** (*tr.; usually passive*) to block (the nose) with mucus. [C16: from L *congestus*, from *congerere*; see CONGERIES] —**con'gestion** *n.*

conglomerate *n.* (kən'glɒmərɪt). **1.** a thing composed of heterogeneous elements. **2.** any coarse-grained sedimentary rock consisting of rounded fragments of rock embedded in a finer matrix. **3.** a large corporation consisting of a group of companies dealing in widely diversified goods, services, etc. ~*vb.* (kən'glɒmə,reɪt). **4.** to form into a mass. ~*adj.* (kən'glɒmərɪt). **5.** made up of heterogeneous elements. **6.** (of sedimentary rocks) consisting of rounded fragments within a finer matrix. [C16: from L *conglomerāre* to roll up, from *glomerāre*, from *glomus* ball of thread] —**con,glomer'ation** *n.*

Congo ('kɒŋɡəʊ) *n.* **1. Republic of the.** a republic in W Central Africa: formerly the French colony of Middle Congo, part of French Equatorial Africa, it became independent in 1960; consists mostly of equatorial forest, with savanna and extensive swamps; drained chiefly by the Rivers Congo and Ubangi. Official language: French. Religion: animist and Christian. Currency: franc. Capital: Brazzaville. Pop.: 2 180 000 (1987). Area: 342 000 sq. km (132 018 sq. miles). Former names: **Middle Congo** (until 1958), **Congo-Brazzaville. 2. Democratic Republic of the.** a former name (1960–71) of **Zaïre.** **3.** the second longest river in Africa, rising as the Lualaba on the Katanga plateau in Zaïre and flowing in a wide northerly curve to the Atlantic: forms the border between the Congo Republic and Zaïre. Length: about 4800 km (3000 miles). Area of basin: about 3 000 000 sq. km (1 425 000 sq. miles). Zaïrese name (since 1971): **Zaïre. 4.** a variant spelling of **Kongo** (the people and language). —**Congolese** (,kɒŋɡə'liːz) *adj., n.*

Congo Free State *n.* a former name (1885–1908) of Zaïre.

congrats (kən'græts) *pl. n., sentence substitute.* informal shortened form of **congratulations.**

congratulate (kən'grætjʊ,leɪt) *vb.* (*tr.*) **1.** (usually foll. by *on*) to communicate pleasure, approval, or praise to; compliment. **2.** (often foll. by *on*) to consider (oneself) clever or fortunate (as a result of): *she congratulated herself on her tact.* **3.** *Obs.* to greet; salute. [C16: from L *grātulārī*, from *grātulārī* to rejoice, from *grātus* pleasing] —**con₂gratu'lation** *n.* —**con'gratulatory** *or* **con'gratulative** *adj.*

congratulations (kən₂grætjʊ'leɪʃənz) *pl. n., sentence substitute.* expressions of pleasure or joy on another's success, good fortune, etc.

congregate ('kɒŋgrɪ₂geɪt) *vb.* to collect together in a body or crowd; assemble. [C15: from L *congregāre* to collect into a flock, from *grex* flock]

congregation (₂kɒŋgrɪ'geɪʃən) *n.* **1.** a group of persons gathered for worship, prayer, etc., esp. in a church. **2.** the act of congregating together. **3.** a group collected together; assemblage. **4.** the group of persons habitually attending a given church, chapel, etc. **5.** *R.C. Church.* **a.** a society of persons who follow a common rule of life but who are bound only by simple vows. **b.** an administrative subdivision of the papal curia. **6.** *Chiefly Brit.* an assembly of senior members of a university.

congregational (₂kɒŋgrɪ'geɪʃənᵊl) *adj.* **1.** of or relating to a congregation. **2.** (*usually cap.*) of or denoting Congregationalism.

Congregationalism (₂kɒŋgrɪ'geɪʃənə₂lɪzəm) *n.* a system of Christian doctrines and ecclesiastical government in which each congregation is self-governing. —₂**Congre'gationalist** *adj., n.*

congress ('kɒŋgrɛs) *n.* **1.** a meeting or conference, esp. of representatives of sovereign states. **2.** a national legislative assembly. **3.** a society or association. [C16: from L *congressus*, from *congredī*, from *com-* together + *gradī* to walk]

Congress ('kɒŋgrɛs) *n.* **1.** the bicameral federal legislature of the U.S., consisting of the House of Representatives and the Senate. **2.** Also called: **Congress Party.** (in India) a major political party. —**Con'gressional** *adj.*

congressional (kən'grɛʃənᵊl) *adj.* of or relating to a congress. —**con'gressionalist** *n.*

Congressman ('kɒŋgrɛsmən) *or* (*fem.*) **Congresswoman** *n., pl.* **-men** *or* **-women.** (in the U.S.) a member of Congress, esp. of the House of Representatives.

Congreve ('kɒŋgriːv) *n.* **William.** 1670–1729, English dramatist, a major exponent of Restoration comedy; author of *Love for Love* (1695) and *The Way of the World* (1700).

congruence ('kɒŋgrʊəns) *or* **congruency** *n.* **1.** the quality or state of corresponding, agreeing, or being congruent. **2.** *Maths.* the relationship between two integers, *x* and *y*, such that their difference, with respect to another integer called the modulus, *n*, is a multiple of the modulus.

congruent ('kɒŋgrʊənt) *adj.* **1.** agreeing; corresponding. **2.** having identical shapes so that all parts correspond: *congruent triangles.* **3.** of or concerning two integers related by a congruence. [C15: from L *congruere* to agree]

congruous ('kɒŋgrʊəs) *adj.* **1.** corresponding or agreeing. **2.** appropriate. [C16: from L *congruus*; see CONGRUENT] —**congruity** (kən'gruːɪtɪ) *n.*

conic ('kɒnɪk) *adj. also* **conical. 1. a.** having the shape of a cone. **b.** of a cone. ~*n.* **2.** another name for **conic section.** —**'conically** *adv.*

conics ('kɒnɪks) *n.* (*functioning as sing.*) the geometry of the parabola, ellipse, and hyperbola.

conic section *n.* one of a group of curves formed by the intersection of a plane and a right circular cone. It is either a circle, ellipse, parabola, or hyperbola.

conidium (kəʊ'nɪdɪəm) *n., pl.* **-nidia** (-'nɪdɪə). an asexual spore formed at the tip of a specialized hypha in fungi such as *Penicillium.* [C19: from NL, from Gk *konis* dust + -IUM]

conifer ('kəʊnɪfə, 'kɒn-) *n.* any tree or shrub of the group *Coniferae*, typically bearing cones and evergreen leaves. The group includes the pines, spruces, firs, larches, etc. [C19: from L, from *cōnus* CONE + *ferre* to bear] —**co'niferous** *adj.*

Coniston Water ('kɒnɪstən) *n.* a lake in NW England, in Cumbria: scene of the establishment of world water speed records by Sir Malcolm Campbell (1939) and his son Donald Campbell (1959). Length: 8 km (5 miles).

conj. *abbrev. for:* **1.** conjugation. **2.** conjunction.

conjectural (kən'dʒɛktʃərəl) *adj.* involving or inclined to ⁀onjecture. —**con'jecturally** *adv.*

conjecture (kən'dʒɛktʃə) *n.* **1.** the formation of conclusions from incomplete evidence; guess. **2.** the conclusion so formed. ~*vb.* **3.** to infer or arrive at (an opinion, conclusion, etc.) from incomplete evidence. [C14: from L *conjectūra*, from *conjicere* to throw together, from *jacere* to throw] —**con'jecturable** *adj.*

conjoin (kən'dʒɔɪn) *vb.* to join or become joined. [C14: from OF *conjoindre*, from L *conjungere*, from *jungere* to JOIN] —**con'joiner** *n.*

conjoint (kən'dʒɔɪnt) *adj.* united, joint, or associated. —**con'jointly** *adv.*

conjugal ('kɒndʒʊgᵊl) *adj.* of or relating to marriage or the relationship between husband and wife: *conjugal rights.* [C16: from L *conjugālis*, from *conjunx* wife or husband] —**conjugality** (₂kɒndʒʊ'gælɪtɪ) *n.* —**'conjugally** *adv.*

conjugate *vb.* ('kɒndʒʊ₂geɪt). **1.** (*tr.*) *Grammar.* to state or set out the conjugation of (a verb). **2.** (*intr.*) (of a verb) to undergo inflection according to a specific set of rules. **3.** (*intr.*) *Biol.* to undergo conjugation. **4.** (*tr.*) *Obs.* to join together, esp. in marriage. ~*adj.* ('kɒndʒʊgɪt, -₂geɪt). **5.** joined together in pairs. **6.** *Maths.* **a.** (of two angles) having a sum of 360°. **b.** (of two complex numbers) differing only in the sign of the imaginary part as 4 + 3*i* and 4 – 3*i*. **7.** *Chem.* of the state of equilibrium in which two liquids can exist as separate phases that are both solutions. **8.** *Chem.* (of acids and bases) related by loss or gain of a proton. **9.** (of a compound leaf) having one pair of leaflets. **10.** (of words) cognate; related in origin. ~*n.* ('kɒndʒʊgɪt). **11.** one of a pair or set of conjugate substances, values, quantities, words, etc. [C15: from L *conjugāre*, from *com-* together + *jugāre* to connect, from *jugum* a yoke] —**'conju₂gative** *adj.* —**'conju₂gator** *n.*

conjugation (₂kɒndʒʊ'geɪʃən) *n.* **1.** *Grammar.* **a.** inflection of a verb for person, number, tense, voice, mood, etc. **b.** the complete set of the inflections of a given verb. **2.** a joining. **3.** a type of sexual reproduction in ciliate protozoans involving the temporary union of two individuals and the subsequent migration and fusion of the gametic nuclei. **4.** the union of gametes, as in some fungi. **5.** the pairing of chromosomes in the early phase of a meiotic division. —₂**conju'gational** *adj.*

conjunct ('kɒndʒʌŋkt, kən'dʒʌŋkt) *n.* *Logic.* one of the propositions or formulas in a conjunction.

conjunction (kən'dʒʌŋkʃən) *n.* **1.** the act of joining together; union. **2.** simultaneous occurrence of events; coincidence. **3.** any word or group of words, other than a relative pronoun, that connects words, phrases, or clauses; for example *and* and *while.* **4.** *Astron.* **a.** the position of a planet when it is in line with the sun as seen from the earth. **b.** the apparent proximity or coincidence of two celestial bodies on the celestial sphere. **5.** *Logic.* **a.** the operator that forms a compound sentence from two given sentences, and corresponds to the English *and.* **b.** a sentence so formed: it is true only when both the component sentences are true. **c.** the relation between such sentences. —**con'junctional** *adj.*

conjunctiva (₂kɒndʒʌŋk'taɪvə) *n., pl.* **-vas** *or* **-vae** (-viː). the delicate mucous membrane that covers the eyeball and the under surface of the eyelid. [C16: from NL *membrāna conjunctīva* the conjunctive membrane] —₂**conjunc'tival** *adj.*

conjunctive (kən'dʒʌŋktɪv) *adj.* **1.** joining; connective. **2.** joined. **3.** of or relating to conjunctions. ~*n.* **4.** a less common word for **conjunction** (sense 3). [C15: from LL *conjunctīvus*, from L *conjungere* to CONJOIN]

conjunctivitis (kən₂dʒʌŋktɪ'vaɪtɪs) *n.* inflammation of the conjunctiva.

conjuncture (kən'dʒʌŋktʃə) *n.* a combination of events, esp. a critical one.

conjuration (₂kɒndʒʊ'reɪʃən) *n.* **1.** a magic spell; incantation. **2.** a less common word for **conjuring.** **3.** *Arch.* supplication; entreaty.

conjure ('kʌndʒə) *vb.* **1.** (*intr.*) to practise conjuring. **2.** (*intr.*) to call upon supposed supernatural forces by spells and incantations. **3.** (kən'dʒʊə). (*tr.*) to appeal earnestly to: *I conjure you to help me.* **4. a name to conjure with.** **a.** a person thought to have great power or influence. **b.** any name that excites the imagination. [C13: from OF *conjurer* to plot, from L *conjūrāre* to swear together]

conjurer or **conjuror** ('kʌndʒərə) n. **1.** a person who practises conjuring, esp. for people's entertainment. **2.** a sorcerer.

conjure up vb. (tr., adv.) **1.** to present to the mind; evoke or imagine: he conjured up a picture of his childhood. **2.** to call up or command (a spirit or devil) by an incantation.

conjuring ('kʌndʒərɪŋ) n. **1.** the performance of tricks that appear to defy natural laws. ~adj. **2.** denoting or of such tricks or entertainment.

conk (kɒŋk) Sl. ~vb. **1.** to strike (someone) a blow, esp. on the head or nose. ~n. **2.** a punch or blow, esp. on the head or nose. **3.** the head or nose. [C19: prob. changed from CONCH]

conker ('kɒŋkə) n. an informal name for the **horse chestnut** (sense 2).

conkers ('kɒŋkəz) n. (functioning as sing.) Brit. a game in which a player swings a horse chestnut (conker), threaded onto a string, against that of another player to try to break it. [C19: from dialect conker snail shell, orig. used in the game]

conk out vb. (intr., adv.) Inf. **1.** (of machines, cars, etc.) to fail suddenly. **2.** to tire suddenly or collapse. [C20: from ?]

con man n. Inf. a person who swindles another by means of a confidence trick. More formal term: **confidence man.**

con moto (kɒn 'məʊtəʊ) adj., adv. Music. (to be performed) in a brisk or lively manner. [It., lit.: with movement]

conn (kɒn) vb., n. a variant spelling (esp. U.S.) of **con**³.

Connacht ('kɒnət) n. a province and ancient kingdom of NW Ireland: consists of the counties of Galway, Leitrim, Mayo, Roscommon, and Sligo. Pop.: 430 726 (1986). Area: 17 122 sq. km (6611 sq. miles). Former name: **Connaught.**

connate ('kɒneɪt) adj. **1.** existing from birth; congenital or innate. **2.** allied in nature or origin. **3.** Biol. (of similar parts or organs) closely joined or united by growth. **4.** Geol. (of fluids) produced at the same time as the rocks surrounding them; connate water. [C17: from LL connātus born at the same time]

Connaught ('kɒnɔːt) n. the former name of **Connacht.**

connect (kə'nɛkt) vb. **1.** to link or be linked. **2.** (tr.) to associate: I connect him with my childhood. **3.** (tr.) to establish telephone communications with or between. **4.** (intr.) to be meaningful or meaningfully related. **5.** (intr.) (of two public vehicles, such as trains or buses) to have the arrival of one timed to occur just before the departure of the other, for the convenient transfer of passengers. **6.** (intr.) Inf. to hit, punch, kick, etc., solidly. [C17: from L connectere to bind together, from nectere to tie] —**con'nectible** or **con'nectable** adj. —**con'nector** or **con'necter** n.

Connecticut (kə'nɛtɪkət) n. **1.** a state of the northeastern U.S., in New England. Capital: Hartford. Pop.: 3 107 576 (1980). Area: 12 973 sq. km (5009 sq. miles). Abbrevs.: **Conn.** or (with zip code) **CT 2.** a river in the northeastern U.S., rising in N New Hampshire and flowing south to Long Island Sound. Length: 651 km (407 miles).

connecting rod n. **1.** a rod or bar for transmitting motion, esp. one that connects a rotating part to a reciprocating part. **2.** such a rod that connects the piston to the crankshaft in an internal-combustion engine.

connection or **connexion** (kə'nɛkʃən) n. **1.** the act of connecting; union. **2.** something that connects or relates; link or bond. **3.** a relationship or association. **4.** logical sequence in thought or expression; coherence. **5.** the relation of a word or phrase to its context: in this connection the word has no political significance. **6.** (often pl.) an acquaintance, esp. one who is influential. **7.** a relative, esp. if distant and related by marriage. **8. a.** an opportunity to transfer from one train, bus, etc., to another. **b.** the vehicle scheduled to provide such an opportunity. **9.** a link, usually a wire or metallic strip, between two components in an electric circuit. **10.** a communications link, esp. by telephone. **11.** Sl. a supplier of illegal drugs, such as heroin. **12.** Rare. sexual intercourse. —**con'nectional** or **con'nexional** adj.

connective (kə'nɛktɪv) adj. **1.** connecting. ~n. **2.** a thing that connects. **3.** Grammar, logic. **a.** any word that connects phrases, clauses, or individual words. **b.** a symbol used in a formal language in the construction of compound sentences, corresponding to terms such as or, and,

etc., in ordinary speech. **4.** Bot. the tissue of a stamen that connects the two lobes of the anther.

connective tissue n. an animal tissue that supports organs, fills the spaces between them, and forms tendons and ligaments.

Connemara (ˌkɒnɪ'mɑːrə) n. a barren coastal region of W Ireland, in Co. Galway: consists of quartzite mountains, peat bogs, and many lakes.

conning tower ('kɒnɪŋ) n. **1.** a superstructure of a submarine, used as the bridge when the vessel is on the surface. **2.** the armoured pilot house of a warship. [C19: see CON³]

connivance (kə'naɪvəns) n. **1.** the act or fact of conniving. **2.** Law. the tacit encouragement of or assent to another's wrongdoing.

connive (kə'naɪv) vb. (intr.) **1.** to plot together; conspire. **2.** (foll. by at) Law. to give assent or encouragement (to the commission of a wrong). [C17: from F conniver, from L connivēre to blink, hence, leave uncensured] —**con'niver** n.

connoisseur (ˌkɒnɪ'sɜː) n. a person with special knowledge or appreciation of a field, esp. in the arts. [C18: from F, from OF conoiseor, from connoistre to know, from L cognōscere] —**connois'seurship** n.

Connors ('kɒnəz) n. **Jimmy.** born 1952, U.S. tennis player: Wimbledon champion 1974 and 1982; U.S. champion 1974, 1976, 1978, 1982, and 1983.

connotation (ˌkɒnə'teɪʃən) n. **1.** an association or idea suggested by a word or phrase. **2.** the act of connoting. **3.** Logic. the characteristic or set of characteristics that determines to which object the common name properly applies. In traditional logic synonymous with **intension.** —**connotative** ('kɒnə,teɪtɪv, kə'nəʊtə-) or **con'notive** adj.

connote (kɒ'nəʊt) vb. (tr.; often takes a clause as object) **1.** (of a word, phrase, etc.) to imply or suggest (associations or ideas) other than the literal meaning: the word "maiden" connotes modesty. **2.** to involve as a consequence or condition. [C17: from Med. L connotāre, from L notāre to mark, note, from nota sign, note]

connubial (kə'njuːbɪəl) adj. of or relating to marriage: connubial bliss. [C17: from L cōnūbiālis, from cōnūbium marriage] —**con,nubi'ality** n.

conoid ('kəʊnɔɪd) n. **1.** a cone-shaped object. ~adj. also **conoidal** (kəʊ'nɔɪdˀl). **2.** cone-shaped. [C17: from Gk kōnoeidēs, from kōnos CONE] —**co'noidally** adv.

conquer ('kɒŋkə) vb. **1.** to overcome (an enemy, army, etc.); defeat. **2.** to overcome (an obstacle, desire, etc.); surmount. **3.** (tr.) to gain possession or control of as by force or war; win. [C13: from OF conquerre, from Vulgar L conquērere (unattested) to obtain, from L conquīrere to search for, from quaerere to seek] —**'conquerable** adj. —**'conquering** adj. —**'conqueror** n.

Conqueror ('kɒŋkərə) n. **William the.** epithet of William I, duke of Normandy, and king of England (1066–87).

conquest ('kɒŋkwɛst) n. **1.** the act of conquering or the state of having been conquered; victory. **2.** a person, thing, etc., that has been conquered. **3.** a person, whose compliance, love, etc., has been won. [C13: from OF conqueste, from Vulgar L conquēsta (unattested), from L conquīsīta, fem. p.p. of conquīrere; see CONQUER]

Conquest ('kɒŋkwɛst) n. **the.** See **Norman Conquest.**

conquistador (kɒn'kwɪstə,dɔː) n., pl. **-dors** or **conquistadores** (kɒn,kwɪstə'dɔːrɛs) an adventurer or conqueror, esp. one of the Spanish conquerors of the New World in the 16th century. [C19: from Sp., from conquistar to conquer]

Conrad ('kɒnræd) n. **Joseph.** real name Teodor Josef Konrad Korzeniowski. 1857–1924, British novelist born in Poland, noted for sea stories such as The Nigger of the Narcissus (1897) and Lord Jim (1900) and novels of politics and revolution such as Nostromo (1904) and Under Western Eyes (1911).

cons. abbrev. for: **1.** consecrated. **2.** consigned. **3.** consignment. **4.** consolidated. **5.** consonant. **6.** constitutional. **7.** construction.

Cons. abbrev. for Conservative.

consanguinity (ˌkɒnsæŋ'gwɪnɪtɪ) n. **1.** relationship by blood; kinship. **2.** close affinity or connection. [C14: see CON-, SANGUINE] —**,consan'guineous** or **con'sanguine** adj.

conscience ('kɒnʃəns) n. **1.** the sense of right and wrong that governs a person's thoughts and actions. **2.**

conscientiousness; diligence. **3.** a feeling of guilt or anxiety: *he has a conscience about his unkind action.* **4. in (all) conscience. a.** with regard to truth and justice. **b.** certainly. **5. on one's conscience.** causing feelings of guilt or remorse. [C13: from OF, from L *conscientia* knowledge, from *conscīre* to know; see CONSCIOUS]

conscience clause *n.* a clause in a law or contract exempting persons with moral scruples.

conscience money *n.* money paid voluntarily to compensate for dishonesty, esp. for taxes formerly evaded.

conscience-stricken *adj.* feeling anxious or guilty. Also: **conscience-smitten.**

conscientious (ˌkɒnʃɪ'ɛnʃəs) *adj.* **1.** involving or taking great care; painstaking. **2.** governed by or done according to conscience. —ˌconsci'entiously *adv.* —ˌconsci'entiousness *n.*

conscientious objector *n.* a person who refuses to serve in the armed forces on the grounds of conscience.

conscious ('kɒnʃəs) *adj.* **1.** alert and awake. **2.** aware of one's surroundings, one's own motivations and thoughts, etc. **3. a.** aware (of) and giving value and emphasis (to a particular fact): *I am conscious of your great kindness to me.* **b.** *(in combination):* clothes-conscious. **4.** deliberate or intended: *a conscious effort; conscious rudeness.* **5. a.** denoting a part of the human mind that is aware of a person's self, environment, and mental activity and that to a certain extent determines his choices of action. **b.** *(as n.):* the conscious is only a small part of the mind. [C17: from L *conscius* sharing knowledge, from *com-* with + *scīre* to know] —'consciously *adv.* —'consciousness *n.*

conscript *n.* ('kɒnskrɪpt). **1. a.** a person who is enrolled for compulsory military service. **b.** *(as modifier):* a conscript army. ~*vb.* (kən'skrɪpt). **2.** *(tr.)* to enrol (youths, civilians, etc.) for compulsory military service. [C15: from L *conscrīptus,* p.p. of *conscrībere* to enrol, from *scrībere* to write]

conscription (kən'skrɪpʃən) *n.* compulsory military service.

consecrate ('kɒnsɪˌkreɪt) *vb.* *(tr.)* **1.** to make or declare sacred or holy. **2.** to dedicate (one's life, time, etc.) to a specific purpose. **3.** *Christianity.* to sanctify (bread and wine) for the Eucharist to be received as the body and blood of Christ. **4.** to cause to be respected or revered: *time has consecrated this custom.* [C15: from L *consecrāre,* from *com-* (intensive) + *sacrāre* to devote, from *sacer* sacred] —ˌconse'cration *n.* —'conseˌcrator *n.* —ˌconse'cratory *adj.*

Consecration (ˌkɒnsɪ'kreɪʃən) *n.* *R.C. Church.* the part of the Mass after the sermon during which the bread and wine are believed to change into the Body and Blood of Christ.

consecutive (kən'sɛkjʊtɪv) *adj.* **1.** (of a narrative, account, etc.) following chronological sequence. **2.** following one another without interruption; successive. **3.** characterized by logical sequence. **4.** *Grammar.* expressing consequence or result: *consecutive clauses.* **5.** *Music.* another word for **parallel** (sense 3). [C17: from F *consécutif,* from L *consecūtus,* from *consequī* to pursue] —con'secutively *adv.* —con'secutiveness *n.*

consensual (kən'sɛnsjʊəl) *adj.* **1.** *Law.* (of a contract, etc.) existing by consent. **2.** (of reflex actions of the body) responding to stimulation of another part. —con'sensually *adv.*

consensus (kən'sɛnsəs) *n.* general or widespread agreement (esp. in **consensus of opinion**). [C19: from L, from *consentīre;* see CONSENT]

▷ **Usage.** Since *consensus* refers to a collective opinion, the words of *opinion* in the phrase *consensus of opinion* are redundant and are therefore avoided in careful usage.

consent (kən'sɛnt) *vb.* **1.** to give assent or permission; agree. ~*n.* **2.** acquiescence to or acceptance of something done or planned by another. **3.** harmony in opinion; agreement (esp. in **with one consent**). [C13: from OF *consentir,* from L *consentīre* to agree, from *sentīre* to feel] —con'senting *adj.*

consequence ('kɒnsɪkwəns) *n.* **1.** a result or effect. **2.** an unpleasant result (esp. in **take the consequences**). **3.** an inference reached by reasoning; conclusion. **4.** significance or importance: *it's of no consequence; a man of consequence.* **5. in consequence.** as a result.

consequent ('kɒnsɪkwənt) *adj.* **1.** following as an effect. **2.** following as a logical conclusion. **3.** (of a river) flowing in the direction of the original slope of the land. ~*n.* **4.** something that follows something else, esp. as a result. **5.** *Logic.* the resultant clause in a conditional sentence. [C15: from L *consequēns* following closely, from *consequī* to pursue]

▷ **Usage.** See at **consequential.**

consequential (ˌkɒnsɪ'kwɛnʃəl) *adj.* **1.** important or significant. **2.** self-important. **3.** following as a consequence, esp. indirectly: *consequential loss.* —ˌconseˌquenti'ality *n.* —ˌconse'quentially *adv.*

▷ **Usage.** Although both *consequential* and *consequent* can refer to that which follows as a result, *consequent* is more frequently used in this sense in general contexts, while *consequential* is often used in commercial or legal contexts.

consequently ('kɒnsɪkwəntlɪ) *adv., sentence connector.* as a result or effect; therefore; hence.

conservancy (kən'sɜːvənsɪ) *n., pl.* **-cies. 1.** (in Britain) a court or commission with jurisdiction over a river, port, area of countryside, etc. **2.** another word for **conservation** (sense 2).

conservation (ˌkɒnsə'veɪʃən) *n.* **1.** the act of conserving or keeping from change, loss, injury, etc. **2. a.** protection, preservation, and careful management of natural resources. **b.** *(as modifier):* a conservation area. **3.** *Physics, etc.* the preservation of a specified aspect or value of a system, as in **conservation of charge, conservation of momentum, conservation of parity.** —ˌconser'vational *adj.* —ˌconser'vationist *n.*

conservation of energy *n.* the principle that the total energy of any isolated system is constant and independent of any changes occurring within the system.

conservation of mass *n.* the principle that the total mass of any isolated system is constant and is independent of any chemical and physical changes taking place within the system.

conservatism (kən'sɜːvəˌtɪzəm) *n.* **1.** opposition to change and innovation. **2.** a political philosophy advocating the preservation of the best of the established order in society.

conservative (kən'sɜːvətɪv) *adj.* **1.** favouring the preservation of established customs, values, etc., and opposing innovation. **2.** of conservatism. **3.** moderate or cautious: *a conservative estimate.* **4.** conventional in style: *a conservative suit.* ~*n.* **5.** a person who is reluctant to change or consider new ideas; conformist. **6.** a supporter of conservatism. —con'servatively *adv.* —con'servativeness *n.*

Conservative (kən'sɜːvətɪv) (in Britain and elsewhere) ~*adj.* **1.** of, supporting, or relating to a Conservative Party. **2.** (in Canada) of, supporting, or relating to the Progressive Conservative Party. **3.** of, relating to, or characterizing Conservative Judaism. ~*n.* **4.** a supporter or member of a Conservative Party, or, (in Canada) of the Progressive Conservative Party.

Conservative Judaism *n.* a movement rejecting extreme change and advocating moderate relaxations of traditional Jewish law.

Conservative Party *n.* **1.** (in Britain) the major rightwing party, which developed from the Tories in the 1830s. It advocates a mixed economy, and encourages property owning and free enterprise. **2.** (in Canada) short for Progressive Conservative Party. **3.** (in other countries) any of various political parties generally opposing change.

conservatoire (kən'sɜːvəˌtwɑː) *n.* an institution or school for instruction in music. Also called: **conservatory.** [C18: from F: CONSERVATORY]

conservator ('kɒnsəˌveɪtə, kən'sɜːvə-) *n.* a custodian, guardian, or protector.

conservatorium (kənˌsɜːvə'tɔːrɪəm) *n. Austral.* the usual term for **conservatoire.**

conservatory (kən'sɜːvətrɪ) *n., pl.* **-tories. 1.** a greenhouse, esp. one attached to a house. **2.** another word for **conservatoire.**

conserve *vb.* (kən'sɜːv). *(tr.)* **1.** to keep or protect from harm, decay, loss, etc. **2.** to preserve (a foodstuff, esp. fruit) with sugar. ~*n.* ('kɒnsɜːv, kən'sɜːv). **3.** a preparation similar to jam but containing whole pieces of fruit. [(vb.) C14: from L *conservāre* to keep safe, from *servāre* to save; (n.) C14: from Med. L *conserva,* from L *conservāre*]

Consett ('kɒnsɪt) *n.* a town in N England, in N Durham. Pop.: 33 433 (1981).

consider (kən'sɪdə) *vb.* (*mainly tr.*) **1.** (*also intr.*) to think carefully about (a problem, decision, etc.). **2.** (*may take a clause as object*) to judge; deem: *I consider him a fool.* **3.** to have regard for: *consider your mother's feelings.* **4.** to look at: *he considered her face.* **5.** (*may take a clause as object*) to bear in mind: *when buying a car consider this make.* **6.** to describe or discuss. [C14: from L *considerāre* to inspect closely]

considerable (kən'sɪdərəb³l) *adj.* **1.** large enough to reckon with: *a considerable quantity.* **2.** a lot of; much: *he had considerable courage.* **3.** worthy of respect: *a considerable man in the scientific world.* —**con'siderably** *adv.*

considerate (kən'sɪdərɪt) *adj.* **1.** thoughtful towards other people; kind. **2.** *Rare.* carefully thought out; considered. —**con'siderately** *adv.*

consideration (kən,sɪdə'reɪʃən) *n.* **1.** deliberation; contemplation. **2. take into consideration.** to bear in mind; consider. **3. under consideration.** being currently discussed. **4.** a fact to be taken into account when making a judgment or decision. **5.** thoughtfulness for other people; kindness. **6.** payment for a service. **7.** thought resulting from deliberation; opinion. **8.** *Law.* the promise, object, etc., given by one party to persuade another to enter into a contract. **9.** esteem. **10. in consideration of. a.** because of. **b.** in return for.

considered (kən'sɪdəd) *adj.* **1.** presented or thought out with care: *a considered opinion.* **2.** (*qualified by a preceding adverb*) esteemed: *highly considered.*

considering (kən'sɪdərɪŋ) *prep.* **1.** in view of. ~*adv.* **2.** *Inf.* all in all; taking into account the circumstances: *it's not bad considering.* ~*conj.* **3.** (*subordinating*) in view of the fact that.

consign (kən'saɪn) *vb.* (*mainly tr.*) **1.** to give into the care or charge of; entrust. **2.** to commit irrevocably: *he consigned the papers to the flames.* **3.** to commit: *to consign someone to jail.* **4.** to address or deliver (goods): *it was consigned to his London address.* [C15: from OF *consigner*, from L *consignāre* to put one's seal to, sign, from *signum* mark] —**con'signable** *adj.* —,**consign'ee** *n.* —**con'signor** *or* **con'signer** *n.*

consignment (kən'saɪnmənt) *n.* **1.** the act of consigning; commitment. **2.** a shipment of goods consigned. **3. on consignment.** for payment by the consignee after sale.

consist (kən'sɪst) *vb.* (*intr.*) **1.** (foll. by *of* or *in*) to be composed (of). **2.** (foll. by *in* or *of*) to have its existence (in): *his religion consists only in going to church.* **3.** to be consistent; accord. [C16: from L *consistere* to stand firm, from *sistere* to stand]

consistency (kən'sɪstənsɪ) *or* **consistence** *n., pl.* **-encies** *or* **-ences**. **1.** agreement or accordance. **2.** degree of viscosity or firmness. **3.** the state or quality of holding or sticking together and retaining shape. **4.** conformity with previous attitudes, behaviour, practice, etc.

consistent (kən'sɪstənt) *adj.* **1.** (usually foll. by *with*) showing consistency or harmony. **2.** steady; even: *consistent growth.* **3.** *Logic.* (of a logical system) constituted so that the propositions deduced from different axioms of the system do not contradict each other. —**con'sistently** *adv.*

consistory (kən'sɪstərɪ) *n., pl.* **-ries. 1.** *Church of England.* the court of a diocese (other than Canterbury) administering ecclesiastical law. **2.** *R.C. Church.* an assembly of the cardinals and the pope. **3.** (in certain Reformed Churches) the governing body of a local congregation. **4.** *Arch.* a council. [C14: from OF, from Med. L *consistōrium* ecclesiastical tribunal, ult. from L *consistere* to stand still] —**consistorial** (,kɒnsɪ'stɔːrɪəl) *adj.*

consolation (,kɒnsə'leɪʃən) *n.* **1.** the act of consoling or state of being consoled. **2.** a person or thing that is a comfort in a time of grief, disappointment, etc. —**consolatory** (kən'sɒlətərɪ) *adj.*

consolation prize *n.* a prize given to console a loser of a game.

console[1] (kən'səʊl) *vb.* to serve as a comfort to (someone) in disappointment, sadness, etc. [C17: from L *consōlārī*, from *sōlārī* to comfort] —**con'solable** *adj.* —**con'soler** *n.* —**con'solingly** *adv.*

console[2] ('kɒnsəʊl) *n.* **1.** an ornamental bracket used to support a wall fixture, etc. **2.** the part of an organ comprising the manuals, pedals, stops, etc. **3.** a desk or table

on which the controls of an electronic system are mounted. **4.** a cabinet for a television, etc., designed to stand on the floor. **5.** See **console table.** [C18: from F, from OF *consolateur* one that provides support; see CONSOLE[1]]

console table ('kɒnsəʊl) *n.* a table with one or more curved legs of bracket-like construction, designed to stand against a wall.

consolidate (kən'sɒlɪ,deɪt) *vb.* **1.** to form or cause to form into a whole. **2.** to make or become stronger or more stable. **3.** *Mil.* to strengthen one's control over (a situation, area, etc.). [C16: from L *consolidāre* to make firm, from *solidus* strong] —**con,soli'dation** *n.* —**con'soli,dator** *n.*

consolidated fund *n.* *Brit.* a fund maintained from tax revenue to meet standing charges, esp. national debt interest.

consols ('kɒnsɒlz, kən'sɒlz) *pl. n.* irredeemable British government securities carrying annual interest. [short for *consolidated stock*]

consommé (kən'sɒmeɪ) *n.* a clear soup made from meat stock. [C19: from F, from *consommer* to use up]

consonance ('kɒnsənəns) *n.* **1.** agreement, harmony, or accord. **2.** *Prosody.* similarity between consonants, but not between vowels, as between the *s* and *t* sounds in *sweet silent thought.* **3.** *Music.* a combination of notes which can sound together without harshness.

consonant ('kɒnsənənt) *n.* **1.** a speech sound or letter of the alphabet other than a vowel. ~*adj.* **2.** (*postpositive; foll. by with* or *to*) consistent; in agreement. **3.** harmonious. **4.** *Music.* characterized by the presence of a consonance. [C14: from L *consonāns*, from *consonāre* to sound at the same time, from *sonāre* to sound] —**'consonantly** *adv.*

consonantal (,kɒnsə'nænt³l) *adj.* relating to, functioning as, or characterized by consonants.

consort *vb.* (kən'sɔːt). (*intr.*) **1.** (usually foll. by *with*) to keep company (with undesirable people); associate. **2.** to harmonize. ~*n.* ('kɒnsɔːt). **3.** (esp. formerly) a small group of instruments, either of the same type (**a whole consort**) or of different types (**a broken consort**). **4.** the husband or wife of a reigning monarch. **5.** a husband or wife. **6.** a ship that escorts another. [C15: from OF, from L *consors* partner, from *sors* lot, portion]

consortium (kən'sɔːtɪəm) *n., pl.* **-tia** (-tɪə). **1.** an association of financiers, companies, etc., esp. for a particular purpose. **2.** *Law.* the right of husband or wife to the company and affection of the other. [C19: from L: partnership; see CONSORT]

conspectus (kən'spɛktəs) *n.* **1.** an overall view; survey. **2.** a summary; résumé. [C19: from L: a viewing, from *conspicere*, from *specere* to look]

conspicuous (kən'spɪkjʊəs) *adj.* **1.** clearly visible. **2.** attracting attention because of a striking feature: *conspicuous stupidity.* [C16: from L *conspicuus*, from *conspicere* to perceive; see CONSPECTUS] —**con'spicuously** *adv.* —**con'spicuousness** *n.*

conspiracy (kən'spɪrəsɪ) *n., pl.* **-cies. 1.** a secret plan to carry out an illegal or harmful act, esp. with political motivation; plot. **2.** the act of making such plans in secret. —**con'spirator** *n.* —**con,spira'torial** *adj.*

conspire (kən'spaɪə) *vb.* (when *intr.*, sometimes foll. by *against*) **1.** to plan (a crime) together in secret. **2.** (*intr.*) to act together as if by design: *the elements conspired to spoil our picnic.* [C14: from OF, from L *conspīrāre* to plot together, lit.: to breathe together, from *spīrāre* to breathe]

con spirito (kɒn 'spɪrɪtəʊ) *adj., adv. Music.* (to be performed) in a spirited or lively manner. [It.: with spirit]

constable ('kʌnstəb³l, 'kɒn-) *n.* **1.** (in Britain, Australia, New Zealand, Canada, etc.) a police officer of the lowest rank. **2.** any of various officers of the peace, esp. one who arrests offenders, serves writs, etc. **3.** the keeper of a royal castle. **4.** (in medieval Europe) the chief military officer and functionary of a royal household. **5.** an officer of a hundred in medieval England. [C13: from OF, from LL *comes stabulī* officer in charge of the stable] —'**consta-ble,ship** *n.*

Constable ('kʌnstəb³l) *n.* **John.** 1776–1837, English landscape painter, noted particularly for his skill in rendering atmospheric effects of changing light.

constabulary (kən'stæbjʊlərɪ) *Chiefly Brit.* ~*n.*, *pl.* **-laries.** **1.** the police force of a town or district. ~*adj.* **2.** of or relating to constables.

Constance ('kɒnstəns) *n.* **1.** a city in S West Germany, in Baden-Württemberg at the outlet of the Rhine from Lake Constance: tourist centre. Pop.: 69 510 (1983 est.). German name: **Konstanz.** **2. Lake.** a lake in W Europe, bounded by West Germany, W Austria, and N Switzerland, through which the Rhine flows. Area: 536 sq. km. (207 sq. miles). German name: **Bodensee.**

constant ('kɒnstənt) *adj.* **1.** unchanging. **2.** incessant: *constant interruptions.* **3.** resolute; loyal. ~*n.* **4.** something that is unchanging. **5.** a specific quantity that is invariable: *the velocity of light is a constant.* **6. a.** *Maths.* a symbol representing an unspecified number that remains invariable throughout a particular series of operations. **b.** *Physics.* a quantity or property that is considered invariable throughout a particular series of experiments. [C14: from OF, from L *constāns*, from *constāre* to be steadfast, from *stāre* to stand] —**'constancy** *n.* —**'constantly** *adv.*

Constant (*French* kɔ̃stɑ̃) *n.* **Benjamin** (bɛ̃ʒamɛ̃). real name *Henri Benjamin Constant de Rebecque.* 1767–1830, French writer and politician: author of the psychological novel *Adolphe* (1816).

Constanţa (*Romanian* kon'stantsa) *n.* a port and resort in SE Romania, on the Black Sea: founded by the Greeks in the 6th century B.C. and rebuilt by Constantine the Great (4th century); exports petroleum. Pop.: 323 236 (1985).

Constantia (kɒn'stænʃə) *n. S. African.* **1.** a district of the Cape Peninsula. **2.** any of several red or white wines produced around Constantia.

Constantine ('kɒnstən,taɪn; *French* kɔ̃stɑ̃tin) *n.* a walled city in NE Algeria: built on an isolated rock; military and trading centre. Pop.: 438 000 (1987).

Constantine I ('kɒnstən,taɪn, -,tiːn) *n.* **1.** known as *Constantine the Great.* Latin name *Flavius Valerius Aurelius Constantinus.* ?280–337 A.D., first Christian Roman emperor (306–337): moved his capital to Byzantium, which he renamed Constantinople (330). **2.** 1868–1923, king of Greece (1913–17; 1920–22): deposed (1917), recalled by a plebiscite (1920), but forced to abdicate again (1922) after defeat by the Turks.

Constantine II *n.* official title *Constantine XIII.* born 1940, king of Greece (1964–73): went into exile when the army seized power in 1967. He was officially deposed in 1973 and Greece became a republic.

Constantine XI *n.* 1404–53, last Byzantine emperor (1448–53): killed when Constantinople was captured by the Turks.

Constantinople (,kɒnstæntɪ'nəʊpəl) *n.* the former name (330–1926) of **Istanbul.**

constellate ('kɒnstɪ,leɪt) *vb.* to form into clusters in or as if in constellations.

constellation (,kɒnstɪ'leɪʃən) *n.* **1.** any of the 88 groups of stars as seen from the earth, many of which were named by the ancient Greeks after animals, objects, or mythological persons. **2.** a gathering of brilliant people or things. **3.** *Psychoanalysis.* a group of ideas felt to be related. [C14: from LL *constellātiō*, from L *com-* together + *stella* star] —**constellatory** (kən'stɛlətərɪ) *adj.*

consternate ('kɒnstə,neɪt) *vb.* (*tr.; usually passive*) to fill with anxiety, dismay, dread, or confusion. [C17: from L *consternāre*, from *sternere* to lay low]

consternation (,kɒnstə'neɪʃən) *n.* a feeling of anxiety, dismay, dread, or confusion.

constipate ('kɒnstɪ,peɪt) *vb.* (*tr.*) to cause constipation in. [C16: from L *constipāre* to press closely together] —**'consti,pated** *adj.*

constipation (,kɒnstɪ'peɪʃən) *n.* infrequent or difficult evacuation of the bowels.

constituency (kən'stɪtjʊənsɪ) *n.*, *pl.* **-cies. 1.** the whole body of voters who elect one representative to a legislature or all the residents represented by one deputy. **2.** a district that sends one representative to a legislature.

constituent (kən'stɪtjʊənt) *adj.* (*prenominal*) **1.** forming part of a whole; component. **2.** having the power to frame a constitution or to constitute a government: *constituent assembly.* ~*n.* **3.** a component part; ingredient. **4.** a resident of a constituency, esp. one entitled to vote. **5.** *Chiefly law.* a person who appoints another to act for him. [C17: from L *constituēns*, from *constituere* to establish, CONSTITUTE] —**con'stituently** *adv.*

constitute ('kɒnstɪ,tjuːt) *vb.* (*tr.*) **1.** to form; compose: *the people who constitute a jury.* **2.** to appoint to an office: *a legally constituted officer.* **3.** to set up (an institution) formally; found. **4.** *Law.* to give legal form to (a court, assembly, etc.). [C15: from L *constituere*, from *com-* (intensive) + *statuere* to place] —**'consti,tutor** *n.*

constitution (,kɒnstɪ'tjuːʃən) *n.* **1.** the act of constituting or state of being constituted. **2.** physical make-up; structure. **3.** the fundamental principles on which a state is governed, esp. when considered as embodying the rights of the subjects. **4.** (*often cap.*) (in certain countries, esp. the U.S.) a statute embodying such principles. **5.** a person's state of health. **6.** a person's temperament.

constitutional (,kɒnstɪ'tjuːʃənəl) *adj.* **1.** of a constitution. **2.** authorized by or subject to a constitution: *constitutional monarchy.* **3.** inherent in the nature of a person or thing: *a constitutional weakness.* **4.** beneficial to one's physical wellbeing. ~*n.* **5.** a regular walk taken for the benefit of one's health. —**,consti,tution'ality** *n.* —**,consti'tutionally** *adv.*

constitutionalism (,kɒnstɪ'tjuːʃənə,lɪzəm) *n.* **1.** the principles or system of government in accord with a constitution. **2.** adherence to or advocacy of such a system. —**,consti'tutionalist** *n.*

constitutive ('kɒnstɪ,tjuːtɪv) *adj.* **1.** having power to enact or establish. **2.** another word for **constituent** (sense 1). —**'consti,tutively** *adv.*

constrain (kən'streɪn) *vb.* (*tr.*) **1.** to compel, esp. by circumstances, etc. **2.** to restrain as by force. [C14: from OF, from L *constringere* to bind together] —**con'strainer** *n.*

constrained (kən'streɪnd) *adj.* embarrassed, unnatural, or forced: *a constrained smile.*

constraint (kən'streɪnt) *n.* **1.** compulsion or restraint. **2.** repression of natural feelings. **3.** a forced unnatural manner. **4.** something that serves to constrain; restrictive condition.

constrict (kən'strɪkt) *vb.* (*tr.*) **1.** to make smaller or narrower, esp. by contracting at one place. **2.** to hold in or inhibit; limit. [C18: from L *constrictus*, from *constringere* to tie up together]

constriction (kən'strɪkʃən) *n.* **1.** a feeling of tightness in some part of the body, such as the chest. **2.** the act of constricting or condition of being constricted. **3.** something that is constricted. —**con'strictive** *adj.*

constrictor (kən'strɪktə) *n.* **1.** any of various very large nonvenomous snakes, such as the boas, that coil around and squeeze their prey to kill it. **2.** any muscle that constricts; sphincter.

construct *vb.* (kən'strʌkt). (*tr.*) **1.** to put together substances or parts systematically; build; assemble. **2.** to frame mentally (an argument, sentence, etc.). **3.** *Geom.* to draw (a line, angle, or figure) so that certain requirements are satisfied. ~*n.* ('kɒnstrʌkt). **4.** something formulated or built systematically. **5.** a complex idea resulting from a synthesis of simpler ideas. [C17: from L *constructus*, from *construere* to build, from *struere* to arrange, erect] —**con'structor** *or* **con'structer** *n.*

construction (kən'strʌkʃən) *n.* **1.** the act of constructing or manner in which a thing is constructed. **2.** a structure. **3. a.** the business or work of building dwellings, offices, etc. **b.** (*as modifier*): *a construction site.* **4.** an interpretation: *they put a sympathetic construction on her behaviour.* **5.** *Grammar.* a group of words that make up one of the constituents into which a sentence may be analysed; a phrase or clause. **6.** an abstract work of art in three dimensions. —**con'structional** *adj.* —**con'structionally** *adv.*

constructive (kən'strʌktɪv) *adj.* **1.** serving to improve; positive: *constructive criticism.* **2.** *Law.* deduced by inference; not expressed. **3.** another word for **structural.** —**con'structively** *adv.*

constructivism (kən'strʌktɪ,vɪzəm) *n.* a movement in abstract art evolved after World War I, which explored the use of movement and machine-age materials in sculpture. —**con'structivist** *adj.*, *n.*

construe (kən'struː) *vb.* **-struing, -strued.** (*mainly tr.*) **1.** to interpret the meaning of (something): *you can construe that in different ways.* **2.** (*may take a clause as object*) to infer; deduce. **3.** to analyse the grammatical structure of; parse (esp. a Latin or Greek text as a preliminary to translation). **4.** to combine words syntactically. **5.** (*also intr.*) *Old-fashioned.* to translate literally, esp.

aloud. [C14: from L *construere*; see CONSTRUCT] —**con'struable** *adj.*

consubstantial (ˌkɒnsəb'stænʃəl) *adj. Christian theol.* (esp. of the three persons of the Trinity) regarded as identical in essence though different in aspect. [C15: from Church L, from L *com-* COM- + *substantia* SUBSTANCE] —ˌconsubˌstanti'ality *n.*

consubstantiation (ˌkɒnsəbˌstænʃɪ'eɪʃən) *n. Christian theol.* (in the Lutheran branch of Protestantism) the doctrine that after the consecration of the Eucharist the substance of the body and blood of Christ coexists within the substance of the consecrated bread and wine. Cf. **transubstantiation.**

consuetude ('kɒnswɪˌtjuːd) *n.* an established custom or usage, esp. one having legal force. [C14: from L *consuētūdō*, from *consuēscere*, from CON- + *suēscere* to be wont]

consul ('kɒnsəl) *n.* **1.** an official appointed by a sovereign state to protect its commercial interests and aid its citizens in a foreign city. **2.** (in ancient Rome) either of two annually elected magistrates who jointly exercised the highest authority in the republic. **3.** (in France from 1799 to 1804) any of the three chief magistrates of the First Republic. [C14: from L, from *consulere* to CONSULT] —**consular** ('kɒnsjʊlə) *adj.* —'consulˌship *n.*

consulate ('kɒnsjʊlɪt) *n.* **1.** the premises of a consul. **2.** government by consuls. **3.** the office or period of office of a consul. **4.** (*often cap.*) **a.** the government of France by the three consuls from 1799 to 1804. **b.** this period. **5.** (*often cap.*) the consular government of the Roman republic.

consul general *n., pl.* **consuls general.** a consul of the highest grade, usually stationed in a city of considerable commercial importance.

consult (kən'sʌlt) *vb.* **1.** (when *intr.*, often foll. by *with*) to ask advice from (someone). **2.** (*tr.*) to refer to for information: *to consult a map.* **3.** (*tr.*) to have regard for (a person's feelings, interests, etc.); consider. [C17: from F, from L *consultāre*, from *consulere* to consult]

consultant (kən'sʌltᵊnt) *n.* **1. a.** a specialist physician who is asked to confirm a diagnosis. **b.** a physician or surgeon holding the highest appointment in a particular branch of medicine or surgery in a hospital. **2.** a specialist who gives expert advice or information. **3.** a person who asks advice in a consultation. —**con'sultancy** *n.*

consultation (ˌkɒnsᵊl'teɪʃən) *n.* **1.** the act of consulting. **2.** a conference for discussion or the seeking of advice. —**consultative** (kən'sʌltətɪv) *adj.*

consulting (kən'sʌltɪŋ) *adj.* (*prenominal*) acting in an advisory capacity on professional matters: *a consulting engineer.*

consulting room *n.* a room in which a doctor sees his patients.

consume (kən'sjuːm) *vb.* **1.** (*tr.*) to eat or drink. **2.** (*tr.; often passive*) to obsess. **3.** (*tr.*) to use up; expend. **4.** to destroy or be destroyed by: *fire consumed the forest.* **5.** (*tr.*) to waste. **6.** (*tr.; passive*) to waste away. [C14: from L *consūmere*, from *com-* (intensive) + *sūmere* to take up] —**con'sumable** *adj.* —**con'suming** *adj.*

consumedly (kən'sjuːmɪdlɪ) *adv. Old-fashioned.* (intensifier): *consumedly fascinating.*

consumer (kən'sjuːmə) *n.* **1.** a person who purchases goods and services for his own personal needs. Cf. **producer** (sense 5). **2.** a person or thing that consumes.

consumer durable *n.* a manufactured product that has a relatively long useful life, such as a car or a television.

consumer goods *pl. n.* goods that satisfy personal needs rather than those required for the production of other goods or services.

consumerism (kən'sjuːməˌrɪzəm) *n.* **1.** protection of the interests of consumers. **2.** advocacy of a high rate of consumption as a basis for a sound economy. —**con'sumerist** *n., adj.*

consummate *vb.* ('kɒnsəˌmeɪt). (*tr.*) **1.** to bring to completion; fulfil. **2.** to complete (a marriage) legally by sexual intercourse. ~*adj.* (kən'sʌmɪt, 'kɒnsəmɪt). **3.** supremely skilled: *a consummate artist.* **4.** (*prenominal*) (intensifier): *a consummate fool.* [C15: from L *consummāre* to complete, from *summus* utmost] —**con'summately** *adv.* —ˌconsum'mation *n.*

consumption (kən'sʌmpʃən) *n.* **1.** the act of consuming or the state of being consumed, esp. by eating, burning, etc. **2.** *Econ.* expenditure on goods and services for final

personal use. **3.** the quantity consumed. **4.** a wasting away of the tissues of the body, esp. in tuberculosis of the lungs. [C14: from L *consumptiō*, from *consūmere* to CONSUME]

consumptive (kən'sʌmptɪv) *adj.* **1.** causing consumption; wasteful; destructive. **2.** relating to or affected with tuberculosis of the lungs. ~*n.* **3.** *Pathol.* a person who suffers from consumption. —**con'sumptively** *adv.* —**con'sumptiveness** *n.*

cont. *abbrev. for:* **1.** contents. **2.** continued.

contact *n.* ('kɒntækt). **1.** the act or state of touching. **2.** the state or fact of communication (esp. in **in contact, make contact**). **3. a.** a junction of electrical conductors. **b.** the part of the conductors that makes the junction. **c.** the part of an electrical device to which such connections are made. **4.** an acquaintance, esp. one who might be useful in business, etc. **5.** any person who has been exposed to a contagious disease. **6.** (*modifier*) caused by touching the causative agent: *contact dermatitis.* **7.** (*modifier*) of or maintaining contact. ~*vb.* ('kɒntækt, kən'tækt). **8.** (when *intr.*, often foll. by *with*) to put, come, or be in association, touch, or communication. [C17: from L *contactus*, from *contingere* to touch on all sides, from *tangere* to touch] —**contactual** (kɒn'tæktjʊəl) *adj.*

contact lens *n.* a lens placed directly on the surface of the eye to correct defects of vision.

contact print *n.* a photographic print made by exposing the printing paper through a negative placed directly on to it.

contagion (kən'teɪdʒən) *n.* **1.** the transmission of disease from one person to another by contact. **2.** a contagious disease. **3.** a corrupting influence that tends to spread. **4.** the spreading of an emotional or mental state among a number of people: *the contagion of mirth.* [C14: from L *contāgiō* infection, from *contingere*; see CONTACT]

contagious (kən'teɪdʒəs) *adj.* **1.** (of a disease) capable of being passed on by direct contact with a diseased individual or by handling his clothing, etc. **2.** (of an organism) harbouring the causative agent of a transmissible disease. **3.** causing or likely to cause the same reaction in several people: *her laughter was contagious.*

contain (kən'teɪn) *vb.* (*tr.*) **1.** to hold or be capable of holding: *this contains five pints.* **2.** to restrain (feelings, behaviour, etc.). **3.** to consist of: *the book contains three sections.* **4.** *Mil.* to prevent (enemy forces) from operating beyond a certain area. **5.** to be a multiple of, leaving no remainder: *6 contains 2 and 3.* [C13: from OF, from L *continēre*, from *com-* together + *tenēre* to hold] —**con'tainable** *adj.*

container (kən'teɪnə) *n.* **1.** an object used for or capable of holding, esp. for transport or storage. **2. a.** a large cargo-carrying standard-sized container that can be loaded from one mode of transport to another. **b.** (*as modifier*): *a container ship.*

containerize *or* **-ise** (kən'teɪnəˌraɪz) *vb.* (*tr.*) **1.** to convey (cargo) in standard-sized containers. **2.** to adapt (a port or transportation system) to the use of standard-sized containers. —conˌtaineri'zation *or* -i'sation *n.*

containment (kən'teɪnmənt) *n.* the act of containing, esp. of restraining the power of a hostile country or the operations of a hostile military force.

contaminate (kən'tæmɪˌneɪt) *vb.* (*tr.*) **1.** to make impure; pollute. **2.** to make radioactive by the addition of radioactive material. [C15: from L *contamināre* to defile] —**con'taminable** *adj.* —**con'taminant** *n.* —conˌtami'nation *n.* —**con'tamiˌnator** *n.*

contango (kən'tæŋgəʊ) *n., pl.* **-gos. 1.** (on the London Stock Exchange) postponement of payment for and delivery of stock from one account day to the next. **2.** the fee paid for such a postponement. ~Also called: **carry-over, continuation.** Cf. **backwardation.** [C19: apparently an arbitrary coinage]

conte French. (kɔt) *n.* a tale or short story.

contemn (kən'tɛm) *vb.* (*tr.*) *Formal.* to regard with contempt; scorn. [C15: from L *contemnere*, from *temnere* to slight] —**contemner** (kən'tɛmnə, -'tɛmə) *n.*

contemplate ('kɒntɛmˌpleɪt) *vb.* (*mainly tr.*) **1.** to think about intently and at length. **2.** (*intr.*) to think intently and at length, esp. for spiritual reasons; meditate. **3.** to look at thoughtfully. **4.** to have in mind as a possibility. [C16: from L *contemplāre*, from *templum* TEMPLE[1]] —ˌcontem'plation *n.* —'contemˌplator *n.*

contemplative ('kɒntɛm,pleɪtɪv, -təm-; kən'tɛmplə-) *adj.*
1. denoting, concerned with, or inclined to contemplation;
meditative. ~*n.* **2.** a person dedicated to religious contemplation.
contemporaneous (kən,tɛmpə'reɪnɪəs) *adj.* existing, beginning, or occurring in the same period of time. —**contemporaneity** (kən,tɛmpərə'niːɪtɪ) *or* **con,tempo'raneousness** *n.*
contemporary (kən'tɛmprərɪ) *adj.* **1.** living or occurring
in the same period. **2.** existing or occurring at the present
time. **3.** conforming to modern ideas in style, fashion, etc.
4. having approximately the same age as one another.
~*n., pl.* **-raries.** **5.** a person living at the same time or of
approximately the same age as another. **6.** something
that is contemporary. [C17: from Med. L *contemporārius,*
from L *com-* together + *temporārius* relating to time,
from *tempus* time] —**con'temporarily** *adv.*
—**con'temporariness** *n.*
▷ **Usage.** *Contemporary* is most acceptable when used to
mean of the same period, in a sentence like *it is useful to
compare Shakespeare's plays with those of contemporary*
(that is, other Elizabethan) *playwrights.* The word is,
however, often used to mean modern or up-to-date in contexts such as *the furniture was of a contemporary design.* The second use should be avoided where ambiguity
is likely to arise, as in *a production of* Othello *in contemporary dress.*
contemporize *or* **-ise** (kən'tɛmpə,raɪz) *vb.* to be or make
contemporary.
contempt (kən'tɛmpt) *n.* **1.** the feeling of a person towards a person or thing that he considers despicable;
scorn. **2.** the state of being scorned; disgrace (esp. in
hold in contempt). **3.** wilful disregard of the authority
of a court of law or legislative body: *contempt of court.*
[C14: from L *contemptus,* from *contemnere* to CONTEMN]
contemptible (kən'tɛmptɪbᵊl) *adj.* deserving or worthy of
contempt. —**con,tempti'bility** *or* **con'temptibleness** *n.*
—**con'temptibly** *adv.*
contemptuous (kən'tɛmptjʊəs) *adj.* (when *predicative,*
often foll. by *of*) showing or feeling contempt; disdainful.
—**con'temptuously** *adv.*
contend (kən'tɛnd) *vb.* **1.** (*intr.;* often foll. by *with*) to
struggle in rivalry, battle, etc.; vie. **2.** to argue earnestly.
3. (*tr.; may take a clause as object*) to assert. [C15: from L
contendere to strive, from *com-* with + *tendere* to stretch]
—**con'tender** *n.*
content[1] ('kɒntɛnt) *n.* **1.** (*often pl.*) everything inside a
container. **2.** (*usually pl.*) **a.** the chapters or divisions of
a book. **b.** a list of these printed at the front of a book. **3.**
the meaning or significance of a work of art, as distinguished from its style or form. **4.** all that is contained or
dealt with in a piece of writing, etc.; substance. **5.** the
capacity or size of a thing. **6.** the proportion of a substance contained in an alloy, mixture, etc.: *the lead content of petrol.* [C15: from L *contentus* contained, from
continēre to CONTAIN]
content[2] (kən'tɛnt) *adj.* (*postpositive*) **1.** satisfied with
things as they are. **2.** assenting to or willing to accept
circumstances, a proposed course of action, etc. ~*vb.* **3.**
(*tr.*) to make (oneself or another person) satisfied. ~*n.*
4. peace of mind. [C14: from OF, from L *contentus* contented, having restrained desires, from *continēre* to restrain] —**con'tentment** *n.*
contented (kən'tɛntɪd) *adj.* accepting one's situation or
life with equanimity and satisfaction. —**con'tentedly**
adv. —**con'tentedness** *n.*
contention (kən'tɛnʃən) *n.* **1.** a struggling between opponents; competition. **2.** a point of dispute (esp. in **bone
of contention**). **3.** a point asserted in argument. [C14:
from L *contentiō,* from *contendere* to CONTEND]
contentious (kən'tɛnʃəs) *adj.* **1.** tending to quarrel. **2.**
causing or characterized by dispute; controversial.
—**con'tentiousness** *n.*
conterminous (kən'tɜːmɪnəs) *or* **coterminous** (kəʊ-
'tɜːmɪnəs) *adj.* **1.** enclosed within a common boundary.
2. without a break or interruption. [C17: from L *conterminus,* from CON- + *terminus* boundary]
contest *n.* ('kɒntɛst). **1.** a formal game or match in which
people, teams, etc., compete. **2.** a struggle for victory between opposing forces. ~*vb.* (kən'tɛst). **3.** (*tr.*) to try to
disprove; call in question. **4.** (when *intr.,* foll. by *with* or

against) to dispute or contend (with): *to contest an election.* [C16: from L *contestārī* to introduce a lawsuit, from
testis witness] —**con'testable** *adj.* —**con'tester** *n.*
contestant (kən'tɛstənt) *n.* a person who takes part in a
contest; competitor.
context ('kɒntɛkst) *n.* **1.** the parts of a piece of writing,
speech, etc., that precede and follow a word or passage
and contribute to its full meaning: *it is unfair to quote out
of context.* **2.** the circumstances that are relevant to an
event, fact, etc. [C15: from L *contextus* a putting together,
from *contexere,* from *com-* together + *texere* to weave]
—**con'textual** *adj.*
contiguous (kən'tɪgjʊəs) *adj.* **1.** touching along the side
or boundary; in contact. **2.** neighbouring. **3.** preceding
or following in time. [C17: from L *contiguus,* from *contingere* to touch; see CONTACT] —**con'tiguously** *adv.*
continent[1] ('kɒntɪnənt) *n.* **1.** one of the earth's large land
masses (Asia, Australia, Africa, Europe, North and South
America, and Antarctica). **2.** *Obs.* **a.** mainland. **b.** a continuous extent of land. [C16: from the L phrase *terra continens* continuous land] —**continental** (,kɒntɪ'nɛntᵊl)
adj. —**,conti'nentally** *adv.*
continent[2] ('kɒntɪnənt) *adj.* **1.** able to control urination
and defecation. **2.** exercising self-restraint, esp. from sexual activity; chaste. [C14: from L *continēre;* see CONTAIN]
—'**continence** *n.*
Continent ('kɒntɪnənt) *n.* **the.** the mainland of Europe as
distinguished from the British Isles.
Continental (,kɒntɪ'nɛntᵊl) *adj.* **1.** of or characteristic of
Europe, excluding the British Isles. **2.** of or relating to
the 13 original British North American colonies during the
War of American Independence. ~*n.* **3.** (*sometimes not
cap.*) an inhabitant of Europe, excluding the British Isles.
4. a regular soldier of the rebel army during the War of
American Independence.
continental breakfast *n.* a light breakfast of coffee and
rolls.
continental climate *n.* a climate characterized by hot
summers, cold winters, and little rainfall, typical of the interior of a continent.
continental drift *n. Geol.* the theory that the earth's continents move gradually over the surface of the planet on a
substratum of magma.
continental quilt *n. Brit.* a quilt, usually stuffed with
down, used as a bed cover in place of the top sheet and
blankets. Also called: **duvet.**
continental shelf *n.* the sea bed surrounding a continent
at depths of up to about 200 metres (100 fathoms), at the
edge of which the **continental slope** drops steeply.
contingency (kən'tɪndʒənsɪ) *or* **contingence** (kən-
'tɪndʒəns) *n., pl.* **-cies** *or* **-ces.** **1. a.** a possible but not
very likely future event or condition. **b.** (*as modifier): a
contingency plan.* **2.** something dependent on a possible
future event. **3.** a fact, event, etc., incidental to something
else. **4.** *Logic.* the state of being contingent. **5.** uncertainty. **6.** *Statistics.* **a.** the degree of association between
theoretical and observed common frequencies of two
graded or classified variables. **b.** (*as modifier): a contingency table.*
contingent (kən'tɪndʒənt) *adj.* **1.** (when *postpositive,*
often foll. by *on* or *upon*) dependent on events, conditions, etc., not yet known; conditional. **2.** *Logic.* (of a
proposition) true under certain conditions, false under
others; not logically necessary. **3.** happening by chance;
accidental. **4.** uncertain. ~*n.* **5.** a part of a military force,
parade, etc. **6.** a group distinguished by common interests, etc., that is part of a larger group. **7.** a chance occurrence. [C14: from L *contingere* to touch, befall]
continual (kən'tɪnjʊəl) *adj.* **1.** recurring frequently, esp.
at regular intervals. **2.** occurring without interruption;
continuous in time. [C14: from OF *continuel,* from L *continuus* uninterrupted, from *continēre* to CONTAIN]
—**con'tinually** *adv.*
continuance (kən'tɪnjʊəns) *n.* **1.** the act of continuing.
2. the duration of an action, etc. **3.** *U.S.* the adjournment
of a legal proceeding.
continuant (kən'tɪnjʊənt) *Phonetics.* ~*n.* **1.** a speech
sound, such as (l), (r), (f), or (s), in which the closure of
the vocal tract is incomplete, allowing the continuous passage of the breath. ~*adj.* **2.** relating to or denoting a continuant.
continuation (kən,tɪnjʊ'eɪʃən) *n.* **1.** a part or thing
added, esp. to a book or play; sequel. **2.** a renewal of an

interrupted action, process, etc.; resumption. **3.** the act of continuing; prolongation. **4.** another word for **contango**.

continue (kən'tɪnjuː) vb. **-uing, -ued. 1.** (when tr., may take an infinitive) to remain or cause to remain in a particular condition or place. **2.** (when tr., may take an infinitive) to carry on uninterruptedly (a course of action): he continued running. **3.** (when tr., may take an infinitive) to resume after an interruption: we'll continue after lunch. **4.** to prolong or be prolonged: continue the chord until it meets the tangent. **5.** (tr.) Law, chiefly Scots. to adjourn (legal proceedings). [C14: from OF continuer, from L continuāre to join together] —**con'tinuer** n.

continuity (ˌkɒntɪ'njuːɪtɪ) n., pl. **-ties. 1.** logical sequence. **2.** a continuous or connected whole. **3.** the comprehensive script or scenario of detail in a film or broadcast. **4.** the continuous projection of a film.

continuity girl or **man** n. a woman or man whose job is to ensure continuity and consistency in successive shots of a film.

continuo (kən'tɪnjuːəʊ) n., pl. **-os. 1.** Music. **a.** a shortened form of **basso continuo** (see **thorough bass**). **b.** (as modifier): a continuo accompaniment. **2.** the thorough-bass part as played on a keyboard instrument. [It., lit.: continuous]

continuous (kən'tɪnjuːəs) adj. **1.** unceasing: a continuous noise. **2.** in an unbroken series or pattern. **3.** Statistics. (of a variable) having a continuum of possible values so that its distribution requires integration rather than summation to determine its cumulative probability. **4.** Grammar. another word for **progressive** (sense 7). [C17: from L continuus, from continēre to CONTAIN] —**con'tinuously** adv.

continuous assessment n. the assessment of a pupil's progress throughout a course of study rather than exclusively by examination at the end of it.

continuous creation n. the theory that matter is created continuously in the universe. See **steady-state theory**.

continuum (kən'tɪnjuːəm) n., pl. **-tinua** (-'tɪnjuːə) or **-tinuums.** a continuous series or whole, no part of which is perceptibly different from the adjacent parts. [C17: from L, neuter of continuus CONTINUOUS]

contort (kən'tɔːt) vb. to twist or bend out of place or shape. [C15: from L contortus intricate, from contorquēre to whirl around, from torquēre to twist] —**con'tortion** n. —**con'tortive** adj.

contortionist (kən'tɔːʃənɪst) n. **1.** a performer who contorts his body for the entertainment of others. **2.** a person who twists or warps meaning.

contour ('kɒntʊə) n. **1.** the outline of a mass of land, figure, or body; a defining line. **2. a.** See **contour line**. **b.** (as modifier): a contour map. **3.** (often pl.) the shape of a curving form: the contours of her body were full and round. ~vb. (tr.) **4.** to shape so as to form the contour of something. **5.** to mark contour lines on. **6.** to construct (a road, railway, etc.) to follow the outline of the land. [C17: from F, from It. contorno, from contornare to sketch, from tornare to TURN]

contour line n. a line on a map or chart joining points of equal height or depth.

contour ploughing n. ploughing along the contours of the land to minimize erosion.

Contra ('kɒntrə) n. a member of a U.S.-backed guerrilla army, founded in 1979, whose aim is to overthrow the Sandinista government in Nicaragua.

contra- prefix. **1.** against; contrary; opposing; contrasting: contraceptive. **2.** (in music) pitched below: contrabass. [from L, from contrā against]

contraband ('kɒntrəˌbænd) n. **1. a.** goods that are prohibited by law from being exported or imported. **b.** illegally imported or exported goods. **2.** illegal traffic in such goods; smuggling. **3.** Also called: **contraband of war.** goods that a neutral country may not supply to a belligerent. ~adj. **4.** (of goods) **a.** forbidden by law from being imported or exported. **b.** illegally imported or exported. [C16: from Sp. contrabanda, from It., from Med. L, from CONTRA- + bannum ban] —'**contra,bandist** n.

contrabass ('kɒntrə'beɪs) n. **1.** another name for **double bass**. ~adj. **2.** denoting the instrument of a family that is lower than the bass.

contrabassoon (ˌkɒntrəbə'suːn) n. the largest instrument in the oboe family, pitched an octave below the bassoon; double bassoon.

contraception (ˌkɒntrə'sɛpʃən) n. the intentional prevention of conception by artificial or natural means. [C19: from CONTRA- + CONCEPTION] —,**contra'ceptive** adj., n.

contract vb. (kən'trækt). **1.** to make or become smaller, narrower, shorter, etc. **2.** ('kɒntrækt). (when intr., sometimes foll. by for; when tr., may take an infinitive) to enter into an agreement with (a person, company, etc.) to deliver (goods or services) or to do (something) on mutually agreed terms. **3.** to draw or be drawn together. **4.** (tr.) to incur or become affected by (a disease, debt, etc.). **5.** (tr.) to shorten (a word or phrase) by the omission of letters or syllables, usually indicated in writing by an apostrophe. **6.** (tr.) to wrinkle (the brow or a muscle). **7.** (tr.) to arrange (a marriage) for; betroth. ~n. ('kɒntrækt). **8.** a formal agreement between two or more parties. **9.** a document that states the terms of such an agreement. **10.** the branch of law treating of contracts. **11.** marriage considered as a formal agreement. **12.** See **contract bridge. 13.** Bridge. **a.** the highest bid, which determines trumps and the number of tricks one side must make. **b.** the number and suit of these tricks. [C16: from L contractus agreement, from contrahere to draw together, from trahere to draw] —**con'tractible** adj.

contract bridge ('kɒntrækt) n. the most common variety of bridge, in which the declarer receives points counting towards game and rubber only for tricks he bids as well as makes. Cf. **auction bridge.**

contractile (kən'træktaɪl) adj. having the power to contract or to cause contraction.

contraction (kən'trækʃən) n. **1.** an instance of contracting or the state of being contracted. **2.** a shortening of a word or group of words, often marked by an apostrophe: I've come for I have come. —**con'tractive** adj.

contractor (kən'træktə) n. **1.** a person or firm that contracts to supply materials or labour, esp. for building. **2.** something that contracts.

contract out ('kɒntrækt) vb. (intr., adv.) Brit. to agree not to participate in something, esp. the state pension scheme.

contractual (kən'træktjuəl) adj. of the nature of or assured by a contract.

contradance ('kɒntrəˌdɑːns) n. a variant spelling of **contredanse.**

contradict (ˌkɒntrə'dɪkt) vb. **1.** (tr.) to affirm the opposite of (a statement, etc.). **2.** (tr.) to declare (a statement, etc.) to be false or incorrect; deny. **3.** (tr.) to be inconsistent with: the facts contradicted his theory. **4.** (intr.) to be at variance; be in contradiction. [C16: from L contrādīcere, from CONTRA- + dīcere to speak] —,**contra'dictor** n.

contradiction (ˌkɒntrə'dɪkʃən) n. **1.** opposition; denial. **2.** a declaration of opposition. **3.** a statement that is at variance with itself (often in **a contradiction in terms**). **4.** conflict or inconsistency, as between events, qualities, etc. **5.** a person or thing containing conflicting qualities. **6.** Logic. a statement that is false under all circumstances; necessary falsehood.

contradictory (ˌkɒntrə'dɪktərɪ) adj. **1.** inconsistent; incompatible. **2.** given to argument and contention: a contradictory person. **3.** Logic. (of a pair of statements) unable both to be true or both to be false under the same circumstances. —,**contra'dictorily** adv. —,**contra'dictoriness** n.

contradistinction (ˌkɒntrədɪ'stɪŋkʃən) n. a distinction made by contrasting different qualities. —,**contradis'tinctive** adj.

contraflow ('kɒntrəˌfləʊ) n. Brit. two-way traffic on one carriageway of a motorway.

contrail ('kɒntreɪl) n. another name for **vapour trail**. [C20: from CON(DENSATION) + TRAIL]

contralto (kən'træltəʊ) n., pl. **-tos** or **-ti** (-tɪ). **1.** the lowest female voice: in the context of a choir often shortened to **alto. 2.** a singer with such a voice. ~adj. **3.** of or denoting a contralto: the contralto part. [C18: from It.; see CONTRA-, ALTO]

contraposition (ˌkɒntrəpə'zɪʃən) n. **1.** the act of placing opposite or against. **2.** Logic. (esp. in traditional logic) the conclusion drawn from a subject-predicate proposition by negating its terms and changing their order.

contraption (kən'træpʃən) n. Inf., often facetious or derog. a device or contrivance, esp. one considered strange, unnecessarily intricate, or improvised. [C19: ?from CON(TRIVANCE) + TRAP[1] + (INVEN)TION]

contrapuntal (ˌkɒntrəˈpʌntᵊl) *adj. Music.* characterized by counterpoint. [C19: from It. *contrappunto*] —**ˌcontraˈpuntally** *adv.* —**ˌcontraˈpuntist** *or* **ˌcontraˈpuntalist** *n.*

contrariety (ˌkɒntrəˈraɪətɪ) *n., pl.* **-ties. 1.** opposition between one thing and another; disagreement. **2.** an instance of such opposition; inconsistency; discrepancy.

contrariwise (ˈkɒntrərɪˌwaɪz) *adv.* **1.** from a contrasting point of view. **2.** in the reverse way. **3.** (kənˈtrɛərɪˌwaɪz). in a contrary manner.

contrary (ˈkɒntrərɪ) *adj.* **1.** opposed in nature, position, etc.: *contrary ideas.* **2.** (kənˈtrɛərɪ). perverse; obstinate. **3.** (esp. of wind) adverse; unfavourable. **4.** (of plant parts) situated at right angles to each other. **5.** *Logic.* (of a pair of propositions) related so they cannot both be true, although they may both be false. ~*n., pl.* **-ries. 6.** the exact opposite (esp. in **to the contrary**). **7. on the contrary.** quite the reverse. **8.** either of two exactly opposite objects, facts, or qualities. ~*adv.* (usually foll. by *to*) **9.** in an opposite or unexpected way: *contrary to usual belief.* **10.** in conflict (with): *contrary to nature.* [C14: from L *contrārius* opposite, from *contrā* against] —**conˈtrarily** *adv.* —**conˈtrariness** *n.*

contrast *vb.* (kənˈtrɑːst) **1.** (often foll. by *with*) to distinguish or be distinguished by comparison of unlike or opposite qualities. ~*n.* (ˈkɒntrɑːst). **2.** distinction by comparison of opposite or dissimilar things, qualities, etc. (esp. in **by contrast, in contrast to** *or* **with**). **3.** a person or thing showing differences when compared with another. **4.** the effect of the juxtaposition of different colours, tones, etc. **5.** the extent to which adjacent areas of an optical image, esp. on a television screen or in a photograph, differ in brightness. [C16: (n.): via F from It., from *contrastare* (vb.), from L *contra-* against + *stare* to stand] —**conˈtrasting** *adj.* —**conˈtrastive** *adj.*

contravene (ˌkɒntrəˈviːn) *vb.* (*tr.*) **1.** to infringe (rules, laws, etc.). **2.** to dispute or contradict (a statement, proposition, etc.). [C16: from LL *contrāvenīre*, from L CONTRA- + *venīre* to come] —**ˌcontraˈvener** *n.* —**contravention** (ˌkɒntrəˈvɛnʃən) *n.*

contredanse *or* **contradance** (ˈkɒntrəˌdɑːns) *n.* **1.** a courtly Continental version of the English country dance, similar to the quadrille. **2.** music for this. [C19: from F, changed from E *country dance; country* altered to F *contre* (opposite) (because the dancers face each other)]

contretemps (ˈkɒntrəˌtɑːn) *n., pl.* **-temps.** an awkward or difficult situation or mishap. [C17: from F, from *contre* against + *temps* time]

contribute (kənˈtrɪbjuːt) *vb.* (often foll. by *to*) **1.** to give (support, money, etc.) for a common purpose or fund. **2.** to supply (ideas, opinions, etc.). **3.** (*intr.*) to be partly responsible (for): *drink contributed to the accident.* **4.** to write (articles, etc.) for a publication. [C16: from L *contribuere* to collect, from *tribuere* to grant] —**conˈtributive** *adj.* —**conˈtributor** *n.*

contribution (ˌkɒntrɪˈbjuːʃən) *n.* **1.** the act of contributing. **2.** something contributed, such as money. **3.** an article, etc., contributed to a newspaper or other publication. **4.** *Arch.* a levy.

contributory (kənˈtrɪbjʊtərɪ, -trɪ) *adj.* **1.** (often foll. by *to*) being partly responsible: *a contributory factor.* **2.** giving to a common purpose or fund. **3.** of or designating an insurance or pension scheme in which the premiums are paid partly by the employer and partly by the employees who benefit from it. ~*n., pl.* **-ries. 4.** a person or thing that contributes. **5.** *Company law.* a member or former member of a company liable to contribute to the assets on the winding-up of the company.

contrite (kənˈtraɪt, ˈkɒntraɪt) *adj.* **1.** full of guilt or regret; remorseful. **2.** arising from a sense of shame or guilt: *contrite promises.* [C14: from L *contrītus* worn out, from *conterere* to bruise, from *terere* to grind] —**conˈtritely** *adv.* —**conˈtriteness** *or* **contrition** (kənˈtrɪʃən) *n.*

contrivance (kənˈtraɪvəns) *n.* **1.** something contrived, esp. an ingenious device; contraption. **2.** inventive skill or ability. **3.** an artificial rather than natural arrangement of details, parts, etc. **4.** an elaborate or deceitful plan; stratagem.

contrive (kənˈtraɪv) *vb.* **1.** (*tr.*) to manage (something or to do something), esp. by a trick: *he contrived to make them meet.* **2.** (*tr.*) to think up or adapt ingeniously: *he contrived a new mast for the boat.* **3.** to plot or scheme.

[C14: from OF *controver*, from LL *contropāre* to represent by figures of speech, compare] —**conˈtriver** *n.*

contrived (kənˈtraɪvd) *adj.* obviously planned; artificial; forced; unnatural.

control (kənˈtrəʊl) *vb.* **-trolling, -trolled.** (*tr.*) **1.** to command, direct, or rule. **2.** to check, limit, or restrain: *to control one's emotions.* **3.** to regulate or operate (a machine). **4.** to verify (a scientific experiment) by conducting a parallel experiment in which the variable being investigated is held constant or is compared with a standard. **5. a.** to regulate (financial affairs). **b.** to examine (financial accounts). ~*n.* **6.** power to direct: *under control.* **7.** a curb; check: *a frontier control.* **8.** (*often pl.*) a mechanism for operating a car, aircraft, etc. **9. a.** a standard of comparison used in a statistical analysis, etc. **b.** (*as modifier*): *a control group.* **10. a.** a device that regulates the operation of a machine. **b.** (*as modifier*): *control room.* [C15: from OF *conteroller* to regulate, from *contrerolle* duplicate register, from *contre*-COUNTER- + *rolle* ROLL] —**conˈtrollable** *adj.* —**conˌtrollaˈbility** *n.* —**conˈtrollably** *adv.*

control experiment *n.* an experiment designed to check or correct the results of another experiment by removing the variable or variables operating in that other experiment.

controller (kənˈtrəʊlə) *n.* **1.** a person who directs. **2.** Also called: **comptroller.** a business executive or government officer responsible for financial planning, control, etc. **3.** the equipment concerned with controlling the operation of an electrical device. —**conˈtrollerˌship** *n.*

controlling interest *n.* a quantity of shares in a business that is sufficient to ensure control over its direction.

control tower *n.* a tower at an airport from which air traffic is controlled.

controversy (ˈkɒntrəˌvɜːsɪ, kənˈtrɒvəsɪ) *n., pl.* **-sies.** dispute, argument, or debate, esp. one concerning a matter about which there is strong disagreement and only one carried on in public or in the press. [C14: from L *contrōversia*, from *contrōversus*, from CONTRA- + *vertere* to turn] —**controversial** (ˌkɒntrəˈvɜːʃəl) *adj.* —**ˌcontroˈversialˌism** *n.* —**ˌcontroˈversialist** *n.*

controvert (ˈkɒntrəˌvɜːt, ˌkɒntrəˈvɜːt) *vb.* (*tr.*) **1.** to deny, refute, or oppose (argument or opinion). **2.** to argue about. [C17: from L *contrōversus;* see CONTROVERSY] —**ˌcontroˈvertible** *adj.*

contumacious (ˌkɒntjʊˈmeɪʃəs) *adj.* stubbornly resistant to authority. —**ˌcontuˈmaciously** *adv.*

contumacy (ˈkɒntjʊməsɪ) *n., pl.* **-cies.** obstinate and wilful resistance to authority, esp. refusal to comply with a court order. [C14: from L *contumācia*, from *contumāx* obstinate]

contumely (ˈkɒntjʊmɪlɪ) *n., pl.* **-lies. 1.** scornful or insulting language or behaviour. **2.** a humiliating insult. [C14: from L *contumēlia*, from *tumēre* to swell, as with wrath] —**contumelious** (ˌkɒntjʊˈmiːlɪəs) *adj.* —**ˌcontuˈmeliously** *adv.*

contuse (kənˈtjuːz) *vb.* (*tr.*) to injure (the body) without breaking the skin; bruise. [C15: from L *contūsus* bruised, from *contundere* to grind, from *tundere* to beat] —**conˈtusion** *n.*

conundrum (kəˈnʌndrəm) *n.* **1.** a riddle, esp. one whose answer makes a play on words. **2.** a puzzling question or problem. [C16: from ?]

conurbation (ˌkɒnɜːˈbeɪʃən) *n.* a large densely populated urban sprawl formed by the growth and coalescence of individual towns or cities. [C20: from CON- + *-urbation*, from L *urbs* city]

convalesce (ˌkɒnvəˈlɛs) *vb.* (*intr.*) to recover from illness, injury, or the aftereffects of a surgical operation. [C15: from L *convalēscere*, from *com-* (intensive) + *valēscere* to grow strong]

convalescence (ˌkɒnvəˈlɛsəns) *n.* **1.** gradual return to health after illness, injury, or an operation. **2.** the period during which such recovery occurs. —**ˌconvaˈlescent** *n., adj.*

convection (kənˈvɛkʃən) *n.* **1.** the process of heat transfer caused by movement of molecules from cool regions to warmer regions of lower density. **2.** *Meteorol.* the process by which masses of relatively warm air are raised into the atmosphere, often cooling and forming clouds, with compensatory downward movements of cooler air.

[C19: from LL *convectiō*, from L *convehere* to bring together, from *vehere* to carry] —**con'vectional** *adj.* —**con'vective** *adj.*

convector (kən'vɛktə) *n.* a space-heating device from which heat is transferred to the surrounding air by convection.

convene (kən'viːn) *vb.* **1.** to gather, call together or summon, esp. for a formal meeting. **2.** (*tr.*) to order to appear before a court of law, judge, tribunal, etc. [C15: from L *convenīre* to assemble, from *venīre* to come] —**con'venable** *adj.*

convener *or* **convenor** (kən'viːnə) *n.* a person who convenes or chairs a meeting, committee, etc., esp. one who is specifically elected to do so: *a convener of shop stewards.*

convenience (kən'viːnɪəns) *n.* **1.** the quality of being suitable or opportune. **2.** a convenient time or situation. **3. at your convenience.** at a time suitable to you. **4.** usefulness, comfort, or facility. **5.** an object that is useful, esp. a labour-saving device. **6.** *Euphemistic, chiefly Brit.* a lavatory, esp. a public one. **7. make a convenience of.** to take advantage of; impose upon.

convenience food *n.* food that needs little preparation and can be used at any time.

convenient (kən'viːnɪənt) *adj.* **1.** suitable; opportune. **2.** easy to use. **3.** close by; handy. [C14: from L *conveniēns*, from *convenīre* to be in accord with, from *venīre* to come] —**con'veniently** *adv.*

convent ('kɒnvənt) *n.* **1.** a building inhabited by a religious community, usually such a building. **2.** the religious community inhabiting such a building. **3.** Also called: **convent school.** a school in which the teachers are nuns. [C13: from OF, from L *conventus* meeting, from *convenīre*; see CONVENE]

conventicle (kən'vɛntɪk³l) *n.* **1.** a secret or unauthorized assembly for worship. **2.** a small meeting house or chapel, esp. of Dissenters. [C14: from L *conventiculum*, from *conventus*; see CONVENT]

convention (kən'vɛnʃən) *n.* **1.** a large formal assembly of a group with common interests, such as a trade union. **2.** *U.S. politics.* an assembly of delegates of one party to select candidates for office. **3.** an international agreement second only to a treaty in formality. **4.** any agreement or contract. **5.** the established view of what is thought to be proper behaviour, good taste, etc. **6.** an accepted rule, usage, etc.: *a convention used by printers.* **7.** *Bridge.* a bid or play not to be taken at its face value, which one's partner can interpret according to a prearranged bidding system. [C15: from L *conventiō* an assembling]

conventional (kən'vɛnʃən³l) *adj.* **1.** following the accepted customs and proprieties, esp. in a way that lacks originality. **2.** established by accepted usage or general agreement. **3.** of a convention or assembly. **4.** *Visual arts.* conventionalized. **5.** (of weapons, warfare, etc.) not nuclear. —**con'ventionalism** *n.* —**con'ventionally** *adv.*

conventionality (kən,vɛnʃə'nælɪtɪ) *n., pl.* **-ties.** **1.** the quality of being conventional. **2.** (*often pl.*) something conventional.

conventionalize *or* **-lise** (kən'vɛnʃənə,laɪz) *vb.* (*tr.*) **1.** to make conventional. **2.** to simplify or stylize (a design, decorative device, etc.). —**con,ventionali'zation** *or* **-li'sation** *n.*

conventual (kən'vɛntjʊəl) *adj.* **1.** of, belonging to, or characteristic of a convent. ~*n.* **2.** a member of a convent. —**con'ventually** *adv.*

converge (kən'vɜːdʒ) *vb.* **1.** to move or cause to move towards the same point. **2.** to meet or join. **3.** (*intr.*) (of opinions, effects, etc.) to tend towards a common conclusion or result. **4.** (*intr.*) *Maths.* (of an infinite series) to approach a finite limit as the number of terms increases. **5.** (*intr.*) (of animals and plants) to undergo convergence. [C17: from LL *convergere*, from L *com-* together + *vergere* to incline] —**con'vergent** *adj.*

convergence (kən'vɜːdʒəns) *n.* **1.** Also: **convergency.** the act, degree, or a point of converging. **2.** Also called: **convergent evolution.** the evolutionary development of a superficial resemblance between unrelated animals that occupy a similar environment, as in the evolution of wings in birds and bats.

convergent thinking *n. Psychol.* analytical, usually deductive, thinking in which ideas are examined for their logical validity or in which a set of rules is followed, for example in arithmetic.

conversable (kən'vɜːsəb³l) *adj.* **1.** easy or pleasant to talk to. **2.** able or inclined to talk.

conversant (kən'vɜːs³nt) *adj.* (*usually postpositive* and foll. by *with*) experienced (in), familiar (with), or acquainted (with). —**con'versance** *or* **con'versancy** *n.* —**con'versantly** *adv.*

conversation (,kɒnvə'seɪʃən) *n.* the interchange through speech of information, ideas, etc.; spoken communication.

conversational (,kɒnvə'seɪʃən³l) *adj.* **1.** of, using, or in the manner of conversation; conversable. —,**conver'sationalist** *n.* —,**conver'sationally** *adv.*

conversation piece *n.* **1.** something, esp. an unusual object, that provokes conversation. **2.** (esp. in 18th-century Britain) a group portrait in a landscape or domestic setting.

converse¹ *vb.* (kən'vɜːs). (*intr.; often foll. by with*) **1.** to engage in conversation (with). **2.** to commune spiritually (with). ~*n.* (kɒnvɜːs). **3.** conversation (often in **hold converse with**). [C16: from OF *converser*, from L *conversārī* to keep company with, from *conversāre* to turn constantly, from *vertere* to turn]

converse² ('kɒnvɜːs) *adj.* **1.** (*prenominal*) reversed; opposite; contrary. ~*n.* **2.** something that is opposite or contrary. **3.** *Logic.* a categorial proposition obtained from another by the transposition of the subject and predicate, as *all bald men are bad* from *all bad men are bald*. [C16: from L *conversus* turned around; see CONVERSE¹] —**con'versely** *adv.*

conversion (kən'vɜːʃən) *n.* **1. a.** a change or adaptation in form, character, or function. **b.** something changed in one of these respects. **2.** a change to another belief, as in a change of religion. **3.** alteration to the structure or fittings of a building undergoing a change in function or legal status. **4.** *Maths.* a change in the units or form of a number or expression: *the conversion of miles to kilometres.* **5.** *Rugby.* a score made after a try by kicking the ball over the crossbar from a place kick. **6.** *Physics.* a change of fertile material to fissile material in a reactor. **7.** an alteration to a car engine to improve its performance. [C14: from L *conversiō* a turning around; see CONVERT]

convert *vb.* (kən'vɜːt). (*mainly tr.*) **1.** to change or adapt the form, character, or function of. **2.** to cause (someone) to change in opinion, belief, etc. **3.** (*intr.*) to admit of being changed (into): *the table converts into a tray.* **4.** (*also intr.*) to change or be changed into another state: *to convert water into ice.* **5.** *Law.* to assume unlawful proprietary rights over (personal property). **6.** (*also intr.*) *Rugby.* to make a conversion after (a try). **7.** *Logic.* to transpose the subject and predicate of (a proposition). **8.** to change (a value or measurement) from one system of units to another. **9.** to exchange (a security or bond) for something of equivalent value. ~*n.* ('kɒnvɜːt). **10.** a person who has been converted to another belief, religion, etc. [C13: from OF, from L *convertere* to turn around, alter, from *vertere* to turn]

converter *or* **convertor** (kən'vɜːtə) *n.* **1.** a person or thing that converts. **2.** *Physics.* **a.** a device for converting alternating current to direct current or vice versa. **b.** a device for converting a signal from one frequency to another. **3.** a vessel in which molten metal is refined, using a blast of air or oxygen.

converter reactor *n.* a nuclear reactor for converting one fuel into another, esp. fertile material into fissionable material.

convertible (kən'vɜːtɪb³l) *adj.* **1.** capable of being converted. **2.** (of a car) having a folding or removable roof. **3.** *Finance.* **a.** (of a currency) freely exchangeable into other currencies. **b.** (of a paper currency) exchangeable on demand for precious metal to an equivalent value. ~*n.* **4.** a car with a folding or removable roof. —**con,verti'bility** *n.* —**con'vertibly** *adv.*

convex ('kɒnvɛks, kɒn'vɛks) *adj.* **1.** curving outwards. **2.** having one or two surfaces curved or ground in the shape of a section of the exterior of a sphere, ellipsoid, etc.: *a convex lens.* [C16: from L *convexus* vaulted, rounded] —**con'vexity** *n.* —**'convexly** *adv.*

convexo-concave (kɒn,vɛksəʊkɒn'keɪv) *adj.* **1.** having one side convex and the other side concave. **2.** (of a lens) having a convex face with greater curvature than the concave face.

convexo-convex *adj.* (esp. of a lens) having both sides convex; biconvex.

convey (kən'veɪ) *vb.* (*tr.*) **1.** to take, carry, or transport from one place to another. **2.** to communicate (a message, information, etc.). **3.** (of a channel, path, etc.) to conduct or transfer. **4.** *Law.* to transfer (the title to property). [C13: from OF *conveier*, from Med. L *conviāre* to escort, from L *com-* with + *via* way] —**con'veyable** *adj.*

conveyance (kən'veɪəns) *n.* **1.** the act of conveying. **2.** a means of transport. **3.** *Law.* **a.** a transfer of the legal title to property. **b.** the document effecting such a transfer. —**con'veyancer** *n.* —**con'veyancing** *n.*

conveyor *or* **conveyer** (kən'veɪə) *n.* **1.** a person or thing that conveys. **2.** short for **conveyor belt.**

conveyor belt *n.* a flexible endless strip of fabric or linked plates driven by rollers and used to transport objects, esp. in a factory.

convict *vb.* (kən'vɪkt). (*tr.*) **1.** to pronounce (someone) guilty of an offence. ~*n.* ('kɒnvɪkt). **2.** a person found guilty of an offence against the law. **3.** a person serving a prison sentence. [C14: from L *convictus* convicted, from *convincere* to prove guilty, CONVINCE]

conviction (kən'vɪkʃən) *n.* **1.** the state of being convinced. **2.** a firmly held belief, opinion, etc. **3.** the act of convincing. **4.** the act of convicting or the state of being convicted. **5.** **carry conviction,** to be convincing. —**con'victional** *adj.* —**con'victive** *adj.*

convince (kən'vɪns) *vb.* (*tr.*) (*may take a clause as object*) to make (someone) agree, understand, or realize the truth or validity of something; persuade. [C16: from L *convincere* to demonstrate incontrovertibly, from *com-* (intensive) + *vincere* to overcome] —**con'vincer** *n.* —**con'vincible** *adj.* —**con'vincing** *adj.* —**con'vincingly** *adv.*

convivial (kən'vɪvɪəl) *adj.* sociable; jovial or festive: *a convivial atmosphere.* [C17: from LL *convīviālis*, from L *convīvium*, a living together, banquet, from *vīvere* to live] —**con,vivi'ality** *n.*

convocation (,kɒnvə'keɪʃən) *n.* **1.** a large formal assembly. **2.** the act of convoking or state of being convoked. **3.** *Church of England.* either of the synods of the provinces of Canterbury or York. **4.** *Episcopal Church.* an assembly of the clergy and part of the laity of a diocese. **5.** (*sometimes cap.*) (in some British universities) a legislative assembly. **6.** (in Australia and New Zealand) the graduate membership of a university. —**,convo'cational** *adj.*

convoke (kən'vəʊk) *vb.* (*tr.*) to call (a meeting, assembly, etc.) together; summon. [C16: from L *convocāre*, from *vocāre* to call] —**con'voker** *n.*

convolute ('kɒnvə,luːt) *vb.* (*tr.*) **1.** to form into a twisted, coiled, or rolled shape. ~*adj.* **2.** *Bot.* rolled longitudinally upon itself: *a convolute petal.* [C18: from L *convolūtus*, from *convolvere* to roll together, from *volvere* to turn]

convoluted ('kɒnvə,luːtɪd) *adj.* **1.** (esp. of meaning, style, etc.) difficult to comprehend; involved. **2.** coiled. —**'convo,lutedly** *adv.*

convolution (,kɒnvə'luːʃən) *n.* **1.** a turn, twist, or coil. **2.** an intricate or confused matter or condition. **3.** any of the numerous convex folds of the surface of the brain. —**,convo'lutional** *or* **,convo'lutionary** *adj.*

convolve (kən'vɒlv) *vb.* to wind or roll together; coil; twist. [C16: from L *convolvere*; see CONVOLUTE]

convolvulus (kən'vɒlvjʊləs) *n.*, *pl.* **-luses** *or* **-li** (-,laɪ). a twining herbaceous plant having funnel-shaped flowers and triangular leaves. [C16: from L: bindweed; see CONVOLUTE]

convoy ('kɒnvɔɪ) *n.* **1.** a group of merchant ships with an escort of warships. **2.** a group of land vehicles assembled to travel together. **3.** the act of travelling or escorting by convoy (esp. in **in convoy**). ~*vb.* **4.** (*tr.*) to escort while in transit. [C14: from OF *convoier* to CONVEY]

convulse (kən'vʌls) *vb.* **1.** (*tr.*) to shake or agitate violently. **2.** (*tr.*) to cause (muscles) to undergo violent spasms or contractions. **3.** (*intr.*; often foll. by *with*) *Inf.* to shake or be overcome (with violent emotion, esp. laughter). [C17: from L *convulsus*, from *convellere*, from *vellere* to pluck, pull] —**con'vulsive** *adj.* —**con'vulsively** *adv.*

convulsion (kən'vʌlʃən) *n.* **1.** a violent involuntary muscular contraction. **2.** a violent upheaval, esp. a social one. **3.** (*usually pl.*) *Inf.* uncontrollable laughter: *I was in convulsions.*

cony *or* **coney** ('kəʊnɪ) *n.*, *pl.* **-nies** *or* **-neys.** **1.** a rabbit or fur made from the skin of a rabbit. **2.** (in the Bible) another name for the **hyrax.** [C13: back formation from *conies*, from OF *conis*, pl. of *conil*, from L *cunīculus* rabbit]

Conybeare ('kɒnɪ,bɪə, 'kʌn-) *n.* **William David.** 1787–1857, English geologist. He summarized all that was known about rocks at the time in *Outlines of the Geology of England and Wales.*

coo (kuː) *vb.* **cooing, cooed.** **1.** (*intr.*) (of doves, pigeons, etc.) to make a characteristic soft throaty call. **2.** (*tr.*) to speak in a soft murmur. **3.** (*intr.*) to murmur lovingly (esp. in **bill and coo**). ~*n.* **4.** the sound of cooing. ~*interj.* **5.** *Brit. sl.* an exclamation of surprise, awe, etc. —**'cooing** *adj.*, *n.* —**'cooingly** *adv.*

Cooch Behar *or* **Kuch Bihar** (kuːtʃ bɪ'hɑː) *n.* **1.** a former state of NE India: part of West Bengal since 1950. **2.** a city in India, in NE West Bengal: capital of the former state of Cooch Behar. Pop.: 53 684 (1971).

cooee *or* **cooey** ('kuːiː) *interj.* **1.** a call used to attract attention, esp. a long loud high-pitched call on two notes. ~*vb.* **cooeeing, cooeed** *or* **cooeying, cooeyed.** **2.** (*intr.*) to utter this call. ~*n.* **3.** *Austral. & N.Z. inf.* calling distance (esp. in **within (a) cooee (of)**). [C19: from Abor.]

cook (kʊk) *vb.* **1.** to prepare (food) by the action of heat, or (of food) to become ready for eating through such a process. Related adj.: **culinary.** **2.** to subject or be subjected to intense heat: *the town cooked in the sun.* **3.** (*tr.*) *Sl.* to alter or falsify (figures, accounts, etc.): *to cook the books.* **4.** (*tr.*) *Sl.* to spoil (something). **5.** (*intr.*) *Sl.* to happen (esp. in **what's cooking?**). ~*n.* **6.** a person who prepares food for eating. ~See also **cook up.** [OE *cōc* (n.), from L *coquus* a cook, from *coquere* to cook] —**'cookable** *adj.*

Cook[1] (kʊk) *n.* **Mount. 1.** Also called: **Aorangi.** a mountain in New Zealand, in the South Island, in the Southern Alps: the highest peak in New Zealand. Height: 3764 m (12 349 ft.). **2.** a mountain in SE Alaska, in the St. Elias Mountains. Height: 4194 m (13 760 ft.).

Cook[2] (kʊk) *n.* **1.** Captain **James.** 1728–79, English navigator and explorer: claimed the E coast of Australia for Britain, circumnavigated New Zealand, and discovered several Pacific and Atlantic islands (1768–79). **2.** Sir **Joseph.** 1860–1947, Australian statesman, born in England: prime minister of Australia (1913–14).

cook-chill *n.* a method of food preparation used by caterers, in which cooked dishes are chilled rapidly and reheated as required.

cooker ('kʊkə) *n.* **1.** an apparatus heated by gas, electricity, oil, or solid fuel, for cooking food. **2.** *Brit.* another name for **cooking apple.**

cookery ('kʊkərɪ) *n.* **1.** the art, study, or practice of cooking. **2.** *U.S.* a place for cooking.

cookery book *or* **cookbook** ('kʊk,bʊk) *n.* a book containing recipes.

cook-general *n.*, *pl.* **cooks-general.** *Brit.* (formerly, esp. in the 1920s and 30s) a domestic servant who did cooking and housework.

cookie *or* **cooky** ('kʊkɪ) *n.*, *pl.* **cookies. 1.** the U.S. and Canad. word for **biscuit. 2.** *Inf., chiefly U.S. & Canad.* a person: *smart cookie.* **3. that's the way the cookie crumbles.** *Inf., chiefly U.S. & Canad.* matters are inevitably so. [C18: from Du. *koekje*, dim. of *koek* cake]

cooking apple *n.* any large sour apple used in cooking.

Cook Inlet *n.* an inlet of the Pacific on the coast of S Alaska: part of the Gulf of Alaska.

Cook Islands *pl. n.* a group of islands in the SW Pacific, an overseas territory of New Zealand: consists of the **Lower Cooks** and the **Northern Cooks.** Capital: Avarua, on Rarotonga. Pop.: 17 695 (1981). Area: 234 sq. km (90 sq. miles).

Cook's tour (kʊks) *n. Inf.* a rapid but extensive tour or survey of anything. [C19: after Thomas *Cook* (1808–92), travel agent]

Cook Strait *n.* the strait between North and South Islands, New Zealand. Width: 26 km (16 miles).

cook up *vb.* (*tr., adv.*) **1.** *Inf.* to concoct or invent (a story, alibi, etc.). **2.** to prepare (a meal), esp. quickly. **3.** *Sl.* to prepare (a drug) for use by heating, as by dissolving heroin in a spoon.

cool (kuːl) *adj.* **1.** moderately cold: *a cool day.* **2.** comfortably free of heat: *a cool room.* **3.** calm: *a cool head.*

4. lacking in enthusiasm, cordiality, etc.: *a cool welcome.* **5.** calmly impudent. **6.** *Inf.* (of sums of money, etc.) without exaggeration; actual: *a cool ten thousand.* **7.** (of a colour) having violet, blue, or green predominating; cold. **8.** (of jazz) economical and rhythmically relaxed. **9.** *Inf.* sophisticated or elegant; unruffled. **10.** *Inf., chiefly U.S. & Canad.* marvellous. ~*n.* **11.** coolness: *the cool of the evening.* **12.** *Sl.* calmness; composure (esp. in **keep or lose one's cool**). **13.** *Sl.* unruffled elegance or sophistication. ~*vb.* **14.** (usually foll. by *down* or *off*) to make or become cooler. **15.** (usually foll. by *down* or *off*) to lessen the intensity of (anger or excitement) or (of anger or excitement) to become less intense; calm down. **16. cool it.** *(usually imperative) Sl.* to calm down. [OE *cōl*] —'**coolly** *adv.* —'**coolness** *n.*

coolabah *or* **coolibar** ('ku:lǝ,ba:) *n.* an Australian eucalyptus that grows along rivers and has smooth bark and long narrow leaves. [from Abor.]

coolant ('ku:lǝnt) *n.* **1.** a fluid used to cool a system or to transfer heat from one part of it to another. **2.** a liquid used to lubricate and cool the workpiece and cutting tool during machining.

cool bag *or* **box** *n.* an insulated container for keeping food cool.

cool drink *n. S. African.* a soft drink.

cooler ('ku:lǝ) *n.* **1.** a container, vessel, or apparatus for cooling, such as a heat exchanger. **2.** a slang word for **prison. 3.** a drink consisting of wine, fruit juice, and carbonated water.

Coolidge ('ku:lɪdʒ) *n.* **(John) Calvin.** 1872–1933, 30th president of the U.S. (1923–29).

coolie *or* **cooly** ('ku:lɪ) *n., pl.* **-ies.** an unskilled Oriental labourer. [C17: from Hindi *kulī*]

cooling tower *n.* a tall, hollow structure, designed to permit free passage of air, inside which hot water trickles down, becoming cool as it does so: the water is normally reused as part of an industrial process.

coomb, combe, coombe, *or* **comb** (ku:m) *n.* **1.** *Chiefly southeastern English.* a short valley or deep hollow. **2.** *Chiefly northern English.* another name for a **cirque.** [OE *cumb*]

coon (ku:n) *n.* **1.** *Inf.* short for **raccoon. 2.** *Derog. sl.* a Negro or Australian Aborigine.

coonskin ('ku:n,skɪn) *n.* **1.** the pelt of a raccoon. **2.** a raccoon cap with the tail hanging at the back. **3.** *U.S.* an overcoat made of raccoon.

coop[1] (ku:p) *n.* **1.** a cage or small enclosure for poultry or small animals. **2.** a small narrow place of confinement, esp. a prison cell. **3.** a wicker basket for catching fish. ~*vb.* **4.** *(tr.; often foll. by up or in)* to confine in a restricted area. [C15: prob. from MLow G *kūpe* basket]

coop[2] *or* **co-op** ('kǝʊ,ɒp) *n.* a cooperative society or a shop run by a cooperative society.

cooper ('ku:pǝ) *n.* **1.** a person skilled in making and repairing barrels, casks, etc. ~*vb.* **2.** *(tr.)* to make or mend (barrels, casks, etc.). [C13: from MDu. *cūper* or MLow G *kūper*; see COOP[1]]

Cooper ('ku:pǝ) *n.* **1. Anthony Ashley.** See (Earl of) **Shaftesbury. 2. Gary,** real name *Frank James Cooper.* 1901–61, U.S. film actor; his many films include *Sergeant York* (1941) and *High Noon* (1952), for both of which he won Oscars. **3. James Fenimore.** 1789–1851, U.S. novelist, noted for his stories of American Indians, esp. *The Last of the Mohicans* (1826). **4. Samuel.** 1609–72, English miniaturist.

cooperage ('ku:pǝrɪdʒ) *n.* **1.** Also called: **coopery.** the craft, place of work, or products of a cooper. **2.** the labour fee charged by a cooper.

cooperate *or* **co-operate** (kǝʊ'ɒpǝ,reɪt) *vb. (intr.)* **1.** to work or act together. **2.** to be of assistance or be willing to assist. **3.** *Econ.* to engage in economic cooperation. [C17: from LL *cooperārī* to combine, from L *operārī* to work] —**co'oper,ator** *or* **co-'oper,ator** *n.*

cooperation *or* **co-operation** (kǝʊ,ɒpǝ'reɪʃǝn) *n.* **1.** joint operation or action. **2.** assistance or willingness to assist. **3.** *Econ.* the combination of consumers, workers, etc., in activities usually embracing production, distribution, or trade. —**co,oper'ationist** *or* **co-,oper'ationist** *n.*

cooperative *or* **co-operative** (kǝʊ'ɒpǝrǝtɪv, -'ɒprǝ-) *adj.* **1.** willing to cooperate; helpful. **2.** acting in conjunction with others; cooperating. **3. a.** (of an enterprise, farm,

etc.) owned collectively and managed for joint economic benefit. **b.** (of an economy) based on collective ownership and cooperative use of the means of production and distribution. ~*n.* **4.** a cooperative organization, such as a farm.

cooperative society *n.* a commercial enterprise owned and managed by and for the benefit of customers or workers.

Cooper's Creek *n.* an intermittent river in E central Australia, in the Channel Country: rises in central Queensland and flows generally southwest, reaching Lake Eyre only during wet-year floods; scene of the death of the explorers Burke and Wills in 1861; the surrounding basin provides cattle pastures after the floods subside. Total length: 1420 km (880 miles). Also called: **Barcoo River.**

coopt *or* **co-opt** (kǝʊ'ɒpt) *vb. (tr.)* to add (someone) to a committee, board, etc., by the agreement of the existing members. [C17: from L *cooptāre*, from *optāre* to choose] —**co'option, co-'option** *or* ,**coop'tation,** ,**co-op'tation** *n.*

coordinate *or* **co-ordinate** *vb.* (kǝʊ'ɔːdɪ,neɪt). **1.** *(tr.)* to integrate (diverse elements) in a harmonious operation. **2.** to place (things) in the same class, or (of things) to be placed in the same class, etc. **3.** *(intr.)* to work together harmoniously. **4.** *(intr.)* to take or be in the form of a harmonious order. ~*n.* (kǝʊ'ɔːdɪnɪt). **5.** *Maths.* any of a set of numbers that defines the location of a point with reference to a system of axes. **6.** a person or thing equal in rank, type, etc. ~*adj.* (kǝʊ'ɔːdɪnɪt). **7.** of or involving coordination. **8.** of the same rank, type, etc. **9.** of or involving the use of coordinates: *coordinate geometry.* **10.** *Chem.* denoting a type of covalent bond in which both the shared electrons are provided by one of the atoms. —**co'ordinative** *or* **co-'ordinative** *adj.* —**co'ordi,nator** *or* **co-'ordi,nator** *n.*

coordinate clause *n.* one of two or more clauses in a sentence having the same status and introduced by coordinating conjunctions.

coordinates (kǝʊ'ɔːdɪnɪts) *pl. n.* clothes of matching or harmonious colours and design, suitable for wearing together.

coordinating conjunction *n.* a conjunction that introduces coordinate clauses, such as *and*, *but*, and *or.*

coordination *or* **co-ordination** (kǝʊ,ɔːdɪ'neɪʃǝn) *n.* balanced and effective interaction of movement, actions, etc. [C17: from LL *coordinātiō*, from L *ordinātiō* an arranging]

Coorg (kʊǝg) *n.* a former province of SW India: since 1956 part of Karnataka state.

coot (ku:t) *n.* **1.** an aquatic bird of Europe and Asia, having dark plumage, and a white bill with a frontal shield: family Rallidae (rails, etc.). **2.** a foolish person, esp. an old man. [C14: prob. from Low G]

cootie ('ku:tɪ) *n. U.S. & N.Z.* a slang name for the body louse. [C20: from Maori & ? (for U.S.) Malay *kutu* louse]

cop[1] (kɒp) *Sl.* ~*n.* **1.** another name for **policeman. 2.** *Brit.* an arrest (esp. in **a fair cop**). ~*vb.* **copping, copped.** *(tr.)* **3.** to catch. **4.** to steal. **5.** to suffer (a punishment): *you'll cop a clout if you do that!* **6.** *Sl.* **cop this!** just look at this! ~See also **cop out.** [C18: (vb.) ?from obs. *cap* to arrest, from OF *caper* to seize]

cop[2] (kɒp) *n.* **1.** a conical roll of thread wound on a spindle. **2.** *Now chiefly dialect.* the top or crest, as of a hill. [OE *cop, copp* top, summit]

cop[3] (kɒp) *n. Brit. sl. (usually used with a negative)* value: *not much cop.* [C19: n. use of COP[1]]

copal ('kǝʊpǝl, -pæl) *n.* a hard aromatic resin obtained from various tropical trees and used in making varnishes and lacquers. [C16: from Sp., from Nahuatl *copalli*]

Copán (*Spanish* ko'pan) *n.* a village in W Honduras: site of a ruined Mayan city.

copartner (kǝʊ'pɑːtnǝ) *n.* a partner or associate, esp. an equal partner in business. —**co'partnership** *n.*

cope[1] (kǝʊp) *vb. (intr.)* **1.** (foll. by *with*) to contend (against). **2.** to deal successfully (with); manage: *she coped well with the problem.* [C14: from OF *coper* to strike, cut, from *coup* blow]

cope[2] (kǝʊp) *n.* **1.** a large ceremonial cloak worn at liturgical functions by priests of certain Christian sects. **2.** any covering shaped like a cope. ~*vb.* **3.** *(tr.)* to dress (someone) in a cope. [OE *cāp*, from Med. L *cāpa*, from LL *cappa* hooded cloak]

cope[3] (kəʊp) *vb.* (*tr.*) **1.** to provide (a wall, etc.) with a coping. ~*n.* **2.** another name for **coping**. [C17: prob. from F *couper* to cut]

copeck ('kəʊpɛk) *n.* a variant spelling of **kopeck**.

Copenhagen (,kəʊpən'heɪgən, -'hɑ:-; 'kəʊpən,heɪ-, -,hɑ:-) *n.* the capital of Denmark, a port on Zealand and Amager Islands on a site inhabited for some 6000 years: exports chiefly agricultural products; iron and steel works; university (1479). Pop.: 622 275 (1987). Danish name: **København**.

copepod ('kəʊpɪ,pɒd) *n.* a minute marine or freshwater crustacean, an important constituent of plankton. [C19: from NL *copepoda*, from Gk *kōpē* oar + *pous* foot]

coper ('kəʊpə) *n.* a horse dealer. [C17 (a dealer): from dialect *cope* to buy, barter, from Low G]

Copernican system (kə'pɜːnɪkən) *n.* the theory published in 1543 by Copernicus which stated that the earth and the planets rotated round the sun.

Copernicus (kə'pɜːnɪkəs) *n.* **Nicolaus** (,nɪkə'leɪəs). Polish name *Mikolaj Kopernik*. 1473–1543, Polish astronomer, whose theory of the solar system (the **Copernican system**) was published in 1543. —**Co'pernican** *adj.*

copestone ('kəʊp,stəʊn) *n.* **1.** Also called: **coping stone**. a stone used to form a coping. **2.** the stone at the top of a building, wall, etc.

copier ('kɒpɪə) *n.* a person or device that copies.

copilot ('kəʊ,paɪlət) *n.* a second or relief pilot of an aircraft.

coping ('kəʊpɪŋ) *n.* the sloping top course of a wall, usually made of masonry or brick.

coping saw *n.* a handsaw with a U-shaped frame used for cutting curves in a material too thick for a fret saw.

copious ('kəʊpɪəs) *adj.* **1.** abundant; extensive. **2.** having an abundant supply. **3.** full of words, ideas, etc.; profuse. [C14: from L *cōpiōsus*, from *cōpia* abundance] —**'copiously** *adv.* —**'copiousness** *n.*

coplanar (kəʊ'pleɪnə) *adj.* lying in the same plane: *coplanar lines*. —**copla'narity** *n.*

Copland ('kəʊplənd) *n.* **Aaron**. born 1900, U.S. composer of orchestral and chamber music, ballets, and film music.

Copley ('kɒplɪ) *n.* **John Singleton**. 1738–1815, U.S. painter.

copolymer (kəʊ'pɒlɪmə) *n.* a chemical compound of high molecular weight formed by uniting the molecules of two or more different compounds (monomers).

cop out *Sl.* ~ *vb.* **1.** (*intr., adv.*) to fail to assume responsibility or fail to perform. ~*n.* **cop-out. 2.** a way or an instance of avoiding responsibility or commitment. [C20: prob. from COP[1]]

copper[1] ('kɒpə) *n.* **1.** a malleable reddish metallic element occurring as the free metal, copper glance, and copper pyrites: used in such alloys as brass and bronze. Symbol: Cu; atomic no.: 29; atomic wt.: 63.54. Related adjs.: **cupric, cuprous. 2. a.** the reddish-brown colour of copper. **b.** (*as adj.*) *copper hair.* **3.** *Inf.* any copper or bronze coin. **4.** *Chiefly Brit.* a large vessel, formerly of copper, used for boiling or washing. **5.** any of various small widely distributed butterflies having reddish-brown wings. ~*vb.* **6.** (*tr.*) to coat or cover with copper. [OE *coper*, from L *Cyprium aes* Cyprian metal, from Gk *Kupris* Cyprus]

copper[2] ('kɒpə) *n.* a slang word for **policeman**. Often shortened to **cop**. [C19: from COP[1] (vb.)]

copperas ('kɒpərəs) *n.* a less common name for **ferrous sulphate**. [C14 *coperose*, via OF from Med. L *cuperosa*, ? orig. in *aqua cuprosa* copper water]

copper beech *n.* a cultivated variety of European beech that has reddish leaves.

Copper Belt *n.* a region of Central Africa, along the Zambia-Zaïre border: rich in deposits of copper.

copper-bottomed *adj.* reliable, esp. financially reliable. [from the practice of coating bottom of ships with copper to prevent the timbers rotting]

copperhead ('kɒpə,hɛd) *n.* **1.** a venomous pit viper of the U.S., with a reddish-brown head. **2.** a venomous marsh snake of Australia, with a reddish band behind the head.

copperplate ('kɒpə,pleɪt) *n.* **1.** a polished copper plate on which a design has been etched or engraved. **2.** a print taken from such a plate. **3.** a fine handwriting based upon that used on copperplate engravings.

copper pyrites ('paɪraɪts) *n.* (*functioning as sing.*) another name for **chalcopyrite**.

coppersmith ('kɒpə,smɪθ) *n.* a person who works in copper.

copper sulphate *n.* a copper salt found naturally and made by the action of sulphuric acid on copper oxide: used as a mordant, in electroplating, and in plant sprays. Formula: $CuSO_4$.

coppice ('kɒpɪs) *n.* **1.** a dense growth of small trees or bushes, esp. one regularly trimmed back so that a continual supply of small poles and firewood is obtained. ~*vb.* **2.** (*tr.*) to trim back (trees or bushes) to form a coppice. [C14: from OF *copeiz*] —**'coppiced** *adj.*

Coppola ('kɒpələ) *n.* **Francis Ford**. born 1939, U.S. film director. His films include *The Godfather* (1972), *Apocalypse Now* (1979), and *Tucker* (1988).

copra ('kɒprə) *n.* the dried, oil-yielding kernel of the coconut. [C16: from Port., from Malayalam *koppara* coconut]

copro- *or before a vowel* **copr-** *combining form.* indicating dung or obscenity, as in **cop'rology** *n.* preoccupation with excrement, **cop'rophagous** *adj.* feeding on dung. [from Gk *kopros* dung]

copse (kɒps) *n.* another word for **coppice** (sense 1). [C16: from COPPICE]

Copt (kɒpt) *n.* **1.** a member of the Coptic Church. **2.** an Egyptian descended from the ancient Egyptians. [C17: from Ar., from Coptic *kyptios* Egyptian, from Gk *Aiguptios*, from *Aiguptos* Egypt]

Coptic ('kɒptɪk) *n.* **1.** an Afro-Asiatic language, written in the Greek alphabet but descended from ancient Egyptian. Extinct as a spoken language, it survives in the Coptic Church. ~*adj.* **2.** of this language. **3.** of the Copts.

Coptic Church *n.* the ancient Christian Church of Egypt.

copula ('kɒpjʊlə) *n., pl.* **-las** *or* **-lae** (-,liː). **1.** a verb, such as *be, seem*, or *taste*, that is used to identify or link the subject with the complement of a sentence, as in *he became king, sugar tastes sweet.* **2.** anything that serves as a link. [C17: from L: bond, from *co-* together + *apere* to fasten] —**'copular** *adj.*

copulate ('kɒpjʊ,leɪt) *vb.* (*intr.*) to perform sexual intercourse. [C17: from L *copulāre* to join together; see COPULA] —**,copu'lation** *n.* —**'copulatory** *adj.*

copulative ('kɒpjʊlətɪv) *adj.* **1.** serving to join or unite. **2.** of copulation. **3.** *Grammar.* (of a verb) having the nature of a copula.

copy ('kɒpɪ) *n., pl.* **copies. 1.** an imitation or reproduction of an original. **2.** a single specimen of something that occurs in a multiple edition, such as a book. **3. a.** matter to be reproduced in print. **b.** written matter or text as distinct from graphic material in books, etc. **4.** the words used to present a promotional message in an advertisement. **5.** *Journalism, inf.* suitable material for an article: *disasters are always good copy.* **6.** *Arch.* a model to be copied, esp. an example of penmanship. ~*vb.* **copying, copied. 7.** (when *tr.*, often foll. by *out*) to make a copy (of). **8.** (*tr.*) to imitate as a model. **9.** to imitate unfairly. [C14: from Med. L *cōpia* an imitation, from L: abundance]

copybook ('kɒpɪ,bʊk) *n.* **1.** a book of specimens, esp. of penmanship, for imitation. **2.** *Chiefly U.S.* a book for or containing documents. **3. blot one's copybook**. *Inf.* to spoil one's reputation by a mistake or indiscretion. **4.** (*modifier*) trite or unoriginal.

copycat ('kɒpɪ,kæt) *n. Inf.* **a.** a person, esp. a child, who imitates or copies another. **b.** (*as modifier*): *copycat murders.*

copyhold ('kɒpɪ,həʊld) *n. Law.* (formerly) a tenure less than freehold of land in England evidenced by a copy of the Court roll.

copyist ('kɒpɪɪst) *n.* **1.** a person who makes written copies. **2.** a person who imitates.

copyreader ('kɒpɪ,riːdə) *n. U.S.* a person who edits and prepares newspaper copy for publication; subeditor.

copyright ('kɒpɪ,raɪt) *n.* **1.** the exclusive right to produce copies and to control an original literary, musical, or artistic work, granted by law for a specified number of years. ~*adj.* **2.** (of a work, etc.) subject to copyright. ~*vb.* **3.** (*tr.*) to take out a copyright on.

copy typist *n.* a typist whose job is to type from written or typed drafts rather than dictation.

copywriter ('kɒpɪ,raɪtə) *n.* a person employed to write advertising copy. —**'copy,writing** *n.*

coquet (kəʊ'kɛt, kɒ-) *vb.* **-quetting, -quetted.** (*intr.*) **1.** to behave flirtatiously. **2.** to dally or trifle. [C17: from F: a gallant, lit.: a little cock, from *coq* cock] —**'coquetry** *n.*

coquette (kəʊ'kɛt, kɒ'kɛt) *n.* **1.** a woman who flirts. **2.** any hummingbird of the genus *Lophornis*. [C17: from F, fem. of COQUET] —**co'quettish** *adj.* —**co'quettishness** *n.*

Cor. *Bible. abbrev. for* Corinthians.

coracle ('kɒrəkəl) *n.* a small roundish boat made of water-proofed hides stretched over a wicker frame. [C16: from Welsh *corwgl*]

coracoid ('kɒrə,kɔɪd) *n.* a paired ventral bone of the pec-toral girdle in vertebrates. In mammals it is reduced to a peg (the **coracoid process**) on the scapula. [C18: from NL *coracoīdēs*, from Gk *korakoeidēs* like a raven, from *korax* raven]

coral ('kɒrəl) *n.* **1.** any of a class of marine colonial coe-lenterates having a calcareous, horny, or soft skeleton. **2. a.** the calcareous or horny material forming the skeleton of certain of these animals. **b.** (*as modifier*): *a coral reef.* **3.** a rocklike aggregation of certain of these animals or their skeletons, forming an island or reef. **4. a.** something made of coral. **b.** (*as modifier*): *a coral necklace.* **5. a.** a yellowish-pink colour. **b.** (*as adj.*): *coral lipstick.* **6.** the roe of a lobster or crab, which becomes pink when cooked. [C14: from OF, from L *corāllium*, from Gk *koral-lion*, prob. of Semitic origin]

coral reef *n.* a marine reef consisting of coral consoli-dated into limestone.

coralroot ('kɒrəl,ruːt) *n.* a N temperate leafless orchid with branched roots resembling coral.

Coral Sea *n.* the SW arm of the Pacific, between Australia, New Guinea, and Vanuatu.

coral snake *n.* **1.** a venomous snake of tropical and sub-tropical America, marked with red, black, yellow, and white transverse bands. **2.** any of various other brightly coloured snakes of Africa and SE Asia.

cor anglais ('kɔːr 'ɑːŋgleɪ) *n., pl.* **cors anglais** ('kɔːz 'ɑːŋgleɪ). *Music.* a woodwind instrument, the alto of the oboe family. Also called: **English horn.** [C19: from F: Eng-lish horn]

Corantijn ('kɒrən,tɛɪn) *n.* the Dutch name of **Couran-tyne.**

corbel ('kɔːbəl) *Archit.* ~*n.* **1.** a bracket, usually of stone or brick. ~*vb.* **-belling, -belled** *or U.S.* **-beling, -beled.** **2.** (*tr.*) to lay (a stone) so that it forms a corbel. [C15: from OF, lit.: a little raven, from Med. L *corvellus*, from L *corvus* raven]

corbie ('kɔːbɪ) *n.* a Scot. name for **raven**[1] or **crow**[1]. [C15: from OF *corbin*, from L *corvinus* CORVINE]

corbie-step *or* **corbel step** *n. Archit.* any of a set of steps on the top of a gable. Also called: **crow step.**

Corbusier (*French* kɔrbyzje) *n.* **Le.** See **Le Corbusier.**

Corby ('kɔːbɪ) *n.* a town in central England, in N North-amptonshire: designated a new town in 1950. Pop.: 51 500 (1985 est.).

Corcovado *n.* **1.** (*Spanish* korko'βaðo). a volcano in S Chile, in the Andes. Height: 2300 m (7546 ft.). **2.** (*Portu-guese* korku'vaːdu). a mountain in SE Brazil, in SW Rio de Janeiro city. Height: 704 m (2310 ft.).

Corcyra (kɔː'saɪərə) *n.* the ancient name for **Corfu.**

cord (kɔːd) *n.* **1.** string or thin rope made of twisted strands. **2.** a length of woven or twisted strands of silk, etc., used as a belt, etc. **3.** a ribbed fabric, esp. corduroy. **4.** the U.S. and Canad. name for **flex** (sense 1). **5.** *Anat.* any part resembling a rope: *the spinal cord.* **6.** a unit for measuring cut wood, equal to 128 cubic feet. ~*vb.* (*tr.*) **7.** to bind or furnish with a cord or cords. ~See also **cords.** [C13: from OF *corde*, from L *chorda*, from Gk *khordē*] —**'cord,like** *adj.*

cordage ('kɔːdɪdʒ) *n.* **1.** *Naut.* the lines and rigging of a vessel. **2.** an amount of wood measured in cords.

cordate ('kɔːdeɪt) *adj.* heart-shaped.

Corday (*French* kɔrdɛ) *n.* **Charlotte** (ʃarlɔt), full name *Marie Anne Charlotte Corday d'Armont.* 1768–93, French Girondist revolutionary, who assassinated Marat.

corded ('kɔːdɪd) *adj.* **1.** bound or fastened with cord. **2.** (of a fabric) ribbed. **3.** (of muscles) standing out like cords.

cordial ('kɔːdɪəl) *adj.* **1.** warm and friendly: *a cordial greeting.* **2.** stimulating. ~*n.* **3.** a drink with a fruit base: *lime cordial.* **4.** another word for **liqueur.** [C14: from Med. L *cordiālis*, from L *cor* heart] —**'cordially** *adv.*

cordiality (,kɔːdɪ'ælɪtɪ) *n., pl.* **-ties.** warmth of feeling.

cordillera (,kɔːdɪl'jɛərə) *n.* a series of parallel ranges of mountains, esp. in the northwestern U.S. [C18: from Sp., from *cordilla*, lit.: a little cord]

Cordilleras (,kɔːdɪl'jɛərəz; *Spanish* korðiˈʎeras) *pl. n.* **the.** the complex of mountain ranges on the W side of the Americas, extending from Alaska to Cape Horn and in-cluding the Andes and the Rocky Mountains.

cordite ('kɔːdaɪt) *n.* any of various explosive materials containing cellulose nitrate, sometimes mixed with nitro-glycerin. [C19: from CORD + -ITE[1], from its stringy appear-ance]

cordless ('kɔːdlɪs) *adj.* (of an electrical device) operated by an internal battery so that no connection to mains sup-ply is needed.

Córdoba[1] (*Spanish* 'korðoβa) *n.* **1.** a city in central Ar-gentina: university (1613). Pop.: 982 018 (1980). **2.** a city in S Spain, on the Guadalquivir River: centre of Moorish Spain (711–1236). Pop.: 279 386 (1981). English name: **Cordova.** — **'Cordovan** *adj., n.*

Córdoba[2] *or* **Córdova** (*Spanish* 'korðoβa) *n.* **Francisco Fernández de** (fran'θisko fɛr'nandeθ de). died 1518, Spanish soldier and explorer, who discovered Yucatán.

cordon ('kɔːdᵊn) *n.* **1.** a chain of police, soldiers, ships, etc., stationed around an area. **2.** a ribbon worn as insig-nia of honour. **3.** a cord or ribbon worn as an ornament. **4.** *Archit.* another name for **string course. 5.** *Horticul-ture.* a fruit tree consisting of a single stem bearing fruit-ing spurs, produced by cutting back all lateral branches. ~*vb.* **6.** (*tr.;* often foll. by *off*) to put or form a cordon (around); close (off). [C16: from OF, lit.: a little cord, from *corde* CORD]

cordon bleu (*French* kɔrdɔ̃ blø) *n.* **1.** *French history.* the sky-blue ribbon worn by members of the highest order of knighthood under the Bourbon monarchy. **2.** any very high distinction. ~*adj.* **3.** of or denoting food prepared to a very high standard. [F, lit.: blue ribbon]

cordon sanitaire *French.* (kɔrdɔ̃ sanitɛr) *n.* **1.** a guarded line isolating an infected area. **2.** a line of buffer states shielding a country. [C19: lit.: sanitary line]

Cordova ('kɔːdəvə) *n.* the English name for **Córdoba**[1] (sense 2).

cordovan ('kɔːdəvᵊn) *n.* a fine leather now made mainly from horsehide. [C16: from Sp. *cordobán* of CÓRDOBA[1]]

cords (kɔːdz) *pl. n.* trousers made of corduroy.

corduroy ('kɔːdə,rɔɪ, ,kɔːdə'rɔɪ) *n.* a heavy cotton pile fabric with lengthways ribs. [C18: ?from the proper name *Corderoy*]

corduroys (,kɔːdə'rɔɪz, 'kɔːdə,rɔɪz) *pl. n.* trousers or breeches of corduroy.

cordwainer ('kɔːd,weɪnə) *n. Arch.* a shoemaker or worker in leather. [C12: *cordwaner*, from OF, from OSp. *cordován* CORDOVAN]

cordwood ('kɔːd,wʊd) *n.* wood that has been cut into lengths of four feet so that it can be stacked in cords.

core (kɔː) *n.* **1.** the central part of certain fleshy fruits, such as the apple, consisting of the seeds. **2.** the central or essential part of something: *the core of the argument.* **3.** a piece of magnetic material, such as soft iron, inside an electromagnet or transformer. **4.** *Geol.* the central part of the earth. **5.** a cylindrical sample of rock, soil, etc., ob-tained by the use of a hollow drill. **6.** *Physics.* the region of a nuclear reactor in which the reaction takes place. **7.** *Computers.* **a.** a ferrite ring used in a computer memory to store one bit of information. **b.** the whole memory of a computer when made up of such rings. **c.** (*as modifier*): *core memory.* **8.** *Archaeol.* a stone or flint from which flakes have been removed. ~*vb.* **9.** (*tr.*) to remove the core from (fruit). [C14: from ?]

coreligionist (,kəʊrɪ'lɪdʒənɪst) *n.* an adherent of the same religion as another.

Corelli (*Italian* ko'rɛlli) *n.* **Arcangelo** (ar'kandʒelo). 1653–1713, Italian violinist and composer of sonatas and concerti grossi.

coreopsis (,kɒrɪ'ɒpsɪs) *n.* a plant of America and Africa, with yellow, brown, or yellow-and-red daisy-like flowers. [C18: from NL, from Gk *koris* bedbug + -OPSIS; so called from the appearance of the seed]

co-respondent (,kəʊrɪ'spɒndənt) *n. Law.* a person cited in divorce proceedings, alleged to have committed adul-tery with the respondent.

core time *n.* See **flexitime.**

corf (kɔːf) *n., pl.* **corves.** *Brit.* a wagon or basket used formerly in mines. [C14: from MDu. *corf* or MLow G *korf*, prob. from L *corbis* basket]

Corfu (kɔːˈfuː) *n.* **1.** an island in the Ionian Sea, in the Ionian Islands: forms, with neighbouring islands, a department of Greece. Pop.: 99 477 (1981). Area: 641 sq. km (247 sq. miles). **2.** a port on E Corfu island. Pop.: 35 787 (1981). Modern Greek name: **Kérkyra.** ~Ancient name: **Corcyra.**

corgi (ˈkɔːgɪ) *n.* either of two short-legged sturdy breeds of dog, the Cardigan and the Pembroke. [C20: from Welsh, from *cor* dwarf + *ci* dog]

coriander (ˌkɒrɪˈændə) *n.* **1.** a European umbelliferous plant, cultivated for its aromatic seeds. **2.** the dried seeds of this plant used in flavouring food, etc. [C14: from OF *coriandre*, from L *coriandrum*, from Gk *koriannon*, from ?]

Corinth (ˈkɒrɪnθ) *n.* **1.** a port in S Greece, in the NE Peloponnese: the modern town is near the site of the ancient city, the largest and richest of the city-states after Athens. Pop.: 22 495 (1981). Modern Greek name: **Kórinthos. 2.** a region of ancient Greece, occupying most of the Isthmus of Corinth and part of the NE Peloponnese. **3. Gulf of.** Also called: Gulf of **Lepanto.** an inlet of the Ionian Sea between the Peloponnese and central Greece. **4. Isthmus of.** a narrow strip of land between the Gulf of Corinth and the Saronic Gulf: crossed by the **Corinth Canal,** making navigation possible between the gulfs.

Corinthian (kəˈrɪnθɪən) *adj.* **1.** of Corinth. **2.** denoting one of the five classical orders of architecture: characterized by a bell-shaped capital having carved ornaments based on acanthus leaves. **3.** *Obs.* given to luxury; dissolute. ~*n.* **4.** a native or inhabitant of Corinth.

Coriolanus (ˌkɒrɪəˈleɪnəs) *n.* **Gaius Marcius** (ˈgaɪəs ˈmɑːsɪəs). 5th century B.C., a legendary Roman general, who allegedly led an army against Rome but was dissuaded from conquering it by his mother and wife.

Coriolis force (ˌkɒrɪˈəʊlɪs) *n.* a hypothetical force postulated to explain a deflection in the path of a body moving relative to the earth: it is due to the earth's rotation and is to the left in the S hemisphere and to the right in the N hemisphere. [C19: after Gaspard G. *Coriolis* (1792–1843), F civil engineer]

corium (ˈkɔːrɪəm) *n., pl.* **-ria** (-rɪə). the deep inner layer of the skin, beneath the epidermis, containing connective tissue, blood vessels, and fat. Also called: **derma, dermis.** [C19: from L: rind, skin]

cork (kɔːk) *n.* **1.** the thick light porous outer bark of the cork oak. **2.** a piece of cork used as a stopper. **3.** an angling float. **4.** Also called: **phellem.** *Bot.* a protective layer of dead impermeable cells on the outside of the stems and roots of woody plants. ~*vb.* (*tr.*) **5.** to stop up (a bottle, etc.) with or as with a cork. **6.** (often foll. by *up*) to restrain. **7.** to black (the face, hands, etc.) with burnt cork. [C14: prob. from Ar. *qurq*, from L *cortex* bark] —**ˈcorkˌlike** *adj.*

Cork (kɔːk) *n.* **1.** a county of SW Ireland, in Munster province: crossed by ridges of low mountains; scenic coastline. County town: Cork. Pop.: 279 427 (1986). Area: 7459 sq. km (2880 sq. miles). **2.** a port in S Ireland, county town of Co. Cork, at the mouth of the River Lee: seat of the University College of Cork (1849). Pop.: 133 196 (1986).

corkage (ˈkɔːkɪdʒ) *n.* a charge made at a restaurant for serving wine, etc., bought off the premises.

corked (kɔːkt) *adj.* tainted through having a cork containing excess tannin.

corker (ˈkɔːkə) *n. Old-fashioned sl.* **1.** something or somebody striking or outstanding. **2.** an irrefutable remark that puts an end to discussion.

cork oak *n.* an evergreen Mediterranean oak whose porous bark yields cork.

corkscrew (ˈkɔːkˌskruː) *n.* **1.** a device for drawing corks from bottles, typically consisting of a pointed metal spiral attached to a handle or screw mechanism. **2.** (*modifier*) resembling a corkscrew in shape. ~*vb.* **3.** to move or cause to move in a spiral or zigzag course.

corm (kɔːm) *n.* an organ of vegetative reproduction in plants such as the crocus, consisting of a globular stem base swollen with food and surrounded by papery scale leaves. [C19: from NL *cormus,* from Gk *kormos* tree trunk from which the branches have been lopped]

cormorant (ˈkɔːmərənt) *n.* an aquatic bird having a dark plumage, a long neck and body, and a slender hooked beak. [C13: from OF *cormareng,* from *corp* raven + *-mareng* of the sea]

corn[1] (kɔːn) *n.* **1.** *Brit.* **a.** any of various cereal plants, esp. the predominant crop of a region, such as wheat in England and oats in Scotland. **b.** the seeds of such plants, esp. after harvesting. **c.** a single seed of such plants; a grain. **2.** the usual U.S., Canad., & N.Z. name for **maize. 3.** *Sl.* an idea, song, etc., regarded as banal or sentimental. ~*vb.* (*tr.*) **4. a.** to preserve in brine. **b.** to salt. [OE *corn*]

corn[2] (kɔːn) *n.* **1.** a hardening of the skin, esp. of the toes, caused by pressure. **2. tread on (someone's) corns.** *Brit. inf.* to offend or hurt (someone) by touching on a sensitive subject. [C15: from OF *corne* horn, from L *cornū*]

corn borer *n.* the larva of a moth native to Europe: in E North America a serious pest of maize.

corn bread *n. Chiefly U.S.* bread made from maize meal. Also called: **Indian bread.**

corn bunting *n.* a heavily built European songbird with a streaked brown plumage.

corncob (ˈkɔːnˌkɒb) *n.* the core of an ear of maize, to which kernels are attached.

corncob pipe *n.* a pipe made from a dried corncob.

corncockle (ˈkɔːnˌkɒkəl) *n.* a European plant that has reddish-purple flowers and grows in cornfields and by roadsides.

corncrake (ˈkɔːnˌkreɪk) *n.* a common Eurasian rail with a buff speckled plumage and reddish wings.

corn dolly *n.* a decorative figure made by plaiting straw.

cornea (ˈkɔːnɪə) *n., pl.* **-neas** or **-neae** (-nɪˌiː). the convex transparent membrane that forms the anterior covering of the eyeball. [C14: from Med. L *cornea tēla* horny web, from L *cornū* HORN] —**ˈcorneal** *adj.*

corned (kɔːnd) *adj.* (esp. of beef) cooked and then preserved or pickled in salt or brine.

Corneille (*French* kɔrnɛj) *n.* **Pierre** (pjɛr). 1606–84, French tragic dramatist often regarded as the founder of French classical drama. His plays include *Médée* (1635), *Le Cid* (1636), *Horace* (1640), and *Polyeucte* (1642).

cornel (ˈkɔːnəl) *n.* any shrub of the genus *Cornus,* such as the dogwood. [C16: prob. from MLow G *kornelle,* ult. from L *cornus*]

cornelian (kɔːˈniːlɪən) *n.* a variant spelling of **carnelian.**

corner (ˈkɔːnə) *n.* **1.** the place or angle formed by the meeting of two converging lines or surfaces. **2.** a projecting angle of a solid object. **3.** the place where two streets meet. **4.** any small, secluded, or private place. **5.** a dangerous position from which escape is difficult: *a tight corner.* **6.** any region, esp. a remote place. **7.** something used to protect or mark a corner, as of the hard cover of a book. **8.** *Commerce.* a monopoly over the supply of a commodity so that its market price can be controlled. **9.** *Soccer, hockey, etc.* a free kick or shot from the corner of the field, taken against a defending team when the ball goes out of play over their goal line after last touching one of their players. **10.** either of two opposite angles of a boxing ring in which the opponents take their rests. **11. cut corners.** to take the shortest or easiest way, esp. at the expense of high standards. **12. turn the corner.** to pass the critical point (in an illness, etc.). **13.** (*modifier*) on a corner: *a corner shop.* ~*vb.* **14.** (*tr.*) to manoeuvre (a person or animal) into a position from which escape is difficult or impossible. **15.** (*tr.*) **a.** to acquire enough of (a commodity) to attain control of the market. **b.** Also: **engross.** to attain control of (a market) in such a manner. **16.** (*intr.*) (of vehicles, etc.) to turn a corner. **17.** (*intr.*) (in soccer, etc.) to take a corner. [C13: from OF *corniere,* from L *cornū* point, HORN]

cornerstone (ˈkɔːnəˌstəʊn) *n.* **1.** a stone at the corner of a wall, uniting two intersecting walls. **2.** a stone placed at the corner of a building during a ceremony to mark the start of construction. **3.** a person or thing of prime importance: *the cornerstone of the whole argument.*

cornerwise (ˈkɔːnəˌwaɪz) or **cornerways** (ˈkɔːnəˌweɪz) *adv., adj.* with a corner in front; diagonally.

cornet (ˈkɔːnɪt) *n.* **1.** a three-valved brass instrument of the trumpet family. **2.** a person who plays the cornet. **3.** a cone-shaped paper container for sweets, etc. **4.** *Brit.* a cone-shaped wafer container for ice cream. **5.** (formerly) the lowest rank of commissioned cavalry officer in the British Army. **6.** the large white headdress of some nuns.

[C14: from OF, from L *cornū* HORN] —**cor'netist** *or* **cor'nettist** *n.*

corn exchange *n.* a building where corn is bought and sold.

cornfield ('kɔːn,fiːld) *n.* a field planted with cereal crops.

cornflakes ('kɔːn,fleɪks) *pl. n.* a breakfast cereal made from toasted maize.

cornflour ('kɔːn,flaʊə) *n.* a fine maize flour, used for thickening sauces. U.S. and Canad. name: **cornstarch.**

cornflower ('kɔːn,flaʊə) *n.* a herbaceous plant, with blue, purple, pink, or white flowers, formerly a common weed in cornfields.

cornice ('kɔːnɪs) *n.* **1.** *Archit.* **a.** the top projecting mouldings of an entablature. **b.** a continuous horizontal projecting course or moulding at the top of a wall, building, etc. **2.** an overhanging ledge of snow. [C16: from OF, from It., ?from L *cornix* crow, but infl. also by L *corōnis* decorative flourish]

corniche ('kɔːnɪʃ) *n.* a coastal road, esp. one built into the face of a cliff. [C19: from *corniche road;* see CORNICE]

Cornish ('kɔːnɪʃ) *adj.* **1.** of Cornwall or its inhabitants. ~*n.* **2.** a former language of Cornwall: extinct by 1800. **3. the.** (*functioning as pl.*) the natives or inhabitants of Cornwall. —**'Cornishman** *n.*

Cornish pasty ('pæstɪ) *n. Cookery.* a pastry case with a filling of meat and vegetables.

corn meal *n.* meal made from maize. Also called: **Indian meal.**

Corno (*Italian* 'kɔrno) *n.* **Monte** ('monte). a mountain in central Italy: the highest peak in the Apennines. Height: 2912 m (9554 ft.).

corn salad *n.* a plant which often grows in cornfields and whose leaves are sometimes used in salads. Also called: **lamb's lettuce.**

cornstarch ('kɔːn,staːtʃ) *n.* the U.S. and Canad. name for **cornflour.**

cornucopia (,kɔːnjʊ'kəʊpɪə) *n.* **1.** a representation of a horn in painting, sculpture, etc., overflowing with fruit, vegetables, etc.; horn of plenty. **2.** a great abundance. **3.** a horn-shaped container. [C16: from LL, from L *cornū cōpiae* horn of plenty] —**,cornu'copian** *adj.*

Cornwall ('kɔːn,wɔːl, -wəl) *n.* a county of SW England, including the Scilly Isles: hilly, with a deeply indented coastline. Administrative centre: Truro. Pop.: 448 200 (1986 est.). Area: 3564 sq. km (1376 sq. miles).

Cornwallis (kɔːn'wɒlɪs) *n.* **Charles,** 1st Marquis Cornwallis. 1738–1805, British general in the War of American Independence: commanded forces defeated at Yorktown (1781): defeated Tipu Sahib (1791): governor general of India (1786–93, 1805): negotiated the Treaty of Amiens (1801).

corn whisky *n.* whisky made from maize.

corny ('kɔːnɪ) *adj.* **cornier, corniest.** *Sl.* **1.** trite or banal. **2.** sentimental or mawkish. **3.** abounding in corn. [C16 (C20 in the sense banal): from CORN[1] + -Y[1]]

corolla (kə'rɒlə) *n.* the petals of a flower collectively, forming an inner floral envelope. [C17: dim. of L *corōna* crown]

corollary (kə'rɒlərɪ) *n., pl.* **-laries. 1.** a proposition that follows directly from the proof of another proposition. **2.** an obvious deduction. **3.** a natural consequence. [C14: from L *corollārium* money paid for a garland, from L *corolla* garland]

Coromandel Coast (,kɒrə'mændəl) *n.* the SE coast of India, along the Bay of Bengal, extending from Point Calimere to the mouth of the Krishna River.

corona (kə'rəʊnə) *n., pl.* **-nas** *or* **-nae** (-niː). **1.** a circle of light around a luminous body, usually the moon. **2.** Also called: **aureole.** the outermost region of the sun's atmosphere, visible as a faint halo during a solar eclipse. **3.** *Archit.* the flat vertical face of a cornice. **4.** a circular chandelier. **5.** *Bot.* **a.** the trumpet-shaped part of the corolla of daffodils and similar plants. **b.** a crown of leafy outgrowths from inside the petals of some flowers. **6.** *Anat.* a crownlike structure. **7.** a long cigar with blunt ends. **8.** *Physics.* an electrical discharge appearing around the surface of a charged conductor. [C16: from L: crown]

coronach ('kɒrənəx) *n. Scot. & Irish.* a dirge or lamentation for the dead. [C16: from Scot. Gaelic *corranach*]

coronary ('kɒrənərɪ) *adj.* **1.** *Anat.* designating blood vessels, nerves, ligaments, etc., that encircle a part or structure. ~*n., pl.* **-naries. 2.** short for **coronary**

thrombosis. [C17: from L *corōnārius* belonging to a wreath or crown]

coronary thrombosis *n.* a condition of interrupted blood flow to the heart due to a blood clot in a coronary artery.

coronation (,kɒrə'neɪʃən) *n.* the act or ceremony of crowning a monarch. [C14: from OF, from *coroner* to crown, from L *corōnāre*]

coroner ('kɒrənə) *n.* a public official responsible for the investigation of violent, sudden, or suspicious deaths. [C14: from Anglo-F *corouner,* from OF *corone* CROWN] —**'coroner,ship** *n.*

coronet ('kɒrənɪt) *n.* **1.** any small crown, esp. one worn by princes or peers. **2.** a woman's jewelled circlet for the head. **3.** the margin between the skin of a horse's pastern and the horn of the hoof. [C15: from OF *coronete*]

Corot (*French* kɔro) *n.* **Jean Baptiste Camille** (ʒɑ̃ batist kamij). 1796–1875, French landscape painter.

corp. *abbrev. for:* **1.** corporation. **2.** corporal.

corporal[1] ('kɔːpərəl, 'kɔːprəl) *adj.* of or relating to the body. [C14: from L *corporālis,* from *corpus* body] —**,corpo'rality** *n.* —**'corporally** *adv.*

corporal[2] ('kɔːpərəl) *n.* **1.** a noncommissioned officer junior to a sergeant in the army, air force, or marines. **2.** (in the Royal Navy) a petty officer who assists the master-at-arms. [C16: from OF, via It., from L *caput* head; ? also infl. in OF by *corps* body (of men)]

corporal[3] ('kɔːpərəl) *or* **corporale** (,kɔːpə'reɪlɪ) *n.* a white linen cloth on which the bread and wine are placed during the Eucharist. [C14: from Med. L *corporāle pallium* eucharistic altar cloth, from L *corporālis,* from *corpus* body (of Christ)]

Corporal of Horse *n.* a noncommissioned rank in the British Army, above that of sergeant and below that of staff sergeant.

corporal punishment *n.* punishment of a physical nature, such as caning.

corporate ('kɔːpərɪt) *adj.* **1.** forming a corporation; incorporated. **2.** of a corporation or corporations: *corporate finance.* **3.** of or belonging to a united group; joint. [C15: from L *corporātus,* from *corpus* body] —**'corporatism** *n.*

corporation (,kɔːpə'reɪʃən) *n.* **1.** a group of people authorized by law to act as an individual and having its own powers, duties, and liabilities. **2.** Also called: **municipal corporation.** the municipal authorities of a city or town. **3.** a group of people acting as one body. **4.** See **public corporation. 5.** *Brit. inf.* a large paunch. —**'corporative** *adj.*

corporeal (kɔː'pɔːrɪəl) *adj.* **1.** of the nature of the physical body; not spiritual. **2.** of a material nature; physical. [C17: from L *corporeus,* from *corpus* body] —**cor,po-re'ality** *or* **corporeity** (,kɒːpə'riːɪtɪ) *n.* —**cor'poreally** *adv.*

corps (kɔː) *n., pl.* **corps** (kɔːz). **1.** a military formation that comprises two or more divisions. **2.** a military body with a specific function: *medical corps.* **3.** a body of people associated together: *the diplomatic corps.* [C18: from F, from L *corpus* body]

corps de ballet ('kɔː də 'bæleɪ) *n.* the members of a ballet company who dance together in a group.

corps diplomatique (,dɪpləʊmæ'tiːk) *n.* another name for **diplomatic corps.**

corpse (kɔːps) *n.* a dead body, esp. of a human being. [C14: from OF *corps,* from L *corpus*]

corpulent ('kɔːpjʊlənt) *adj.* physically bulky; fat. [C14: from L *corpulentus*] —**'corpulence** *n.*

corpus ('kɔːpəs) *n., pl.* **-pora** (-pərə). **1.** a body of writings, esp. by a single author or on a specific topic: *the corpus of Dickens' works.* **2.** the main body or substance of something. **3.** *Anat.* **a.** any distinct mass or body. **b.** the main part of an organ or structure. **4.** *Obs.* a corpse. [C14: from L: body]

Corpus Christi[1] ('krɪstɪ) *n. Chiefly R.C. Church.* a festival in honour of the Eucharist, observed on the Thursday after Trinity Sunday. [C14: from L: body of Christ]

Corpus Christi[2] ('krɪstɪ) *n.* a port in S Texas, on **Corpus Christi Bay,** an inlet of the Gulf of Mexico. Pop.: 263 900 (1986).

corpuscle ('kɔːpʌsəl) *n.* **1.** any cell or similar minute body that is suspended in a fluid, esp. any of the **red blood corpuscles** (see **erythrocyte**) or **white blood corpuscles** (see **leucocyte**). **2.** Also: **corpuscule**

(kɔː'pʌskjuːl). any minute particle. [C17: from L *corpusculum* a little body, from *corpus* body] —**corpuscular** (kɔː'pʌskjʊlə) *adj.*

corpuscular theory *n.* the theory, originally proposed by Newton, that light consists of a stream of particles. Cf. **wave theory.**

corpus delicti (dɪ'lɪktaɪ) *n. Law.* the body of facts that constitute an offence. [NL, lit.: the body of the crime]

corpus juris ('dʒʊərɪs) *n.* a body of law, esp. of a nation or state. [from LL, lit.: a body of law]

corpus luteum ('luːtɪəm) *n., pl.* **corpora lutea** ('luːtɪə). a mass of tissue that forms in a Graafian follicle following release of an ovum. [NL, lit.: yellow body]

corral (kɒ'rɑːl) *n.* **1.** *Chiefly U.S. & Canad.* an enclosure for cattle or horses. **2.** *Chiefly U.S.* (formerly) a defensive enclosure formed by a ring of covered wagons. ~*vb.* **-ralling, -ralled.** (*tr.*) *U.S. & Canad.* **3.** to drive into a corral. **4.** *Inf.* to capture. [C16: from Sp., ult. from L *currere* to run]

corrasion (kə'reɪʒən) *n.* erosion of a rock surface by rock fragments transported over it by water, wind, or ice. [C17: from L *corrādere* to scrape together]

correa ('kɒrɪə, kɒ'riːə) *n.* an Australian evergreen shrub with large showy tubular flowers. [C19: after Jose Francesco *Correa* da Serra (1750-1823), Portuguese botanist]

correct (kə'rɛkt) *vb.* (*tr.*) **1.** to make free from errors. **2.** to indicate the errors in. **3.** to rebuke or punish in order to improve: *to stand corrected.* **4.** to rectify (a malfunction, ailment, etc.). **5.** to adjust or make conform, esp. to a standard. ~*adj.* **6.** true; accurate: *the correct version.* **7.** in conformity with accepted standards: *correct behaviour.* [C14: from L *corrigere* to make straight, from *com-* (intensive) + *regere* to rule] —**cor'rectly** *adv.* —**cor'rectness** *n.*

correction (kə'rɛkʃən) *n.* **1.** the act of correcting. **2.** something substituted for an error; an improvement. **3.** a reproof. **4.** a quantity added to or subtracted from a scientific calculation or observation to increase its accuracy. —**cor'rectional** *adj.*

corrective (kə'rɛktɪv) *adj.* **1.** tending or intended to correct. ~*n.* **2.** something that tends or is intended to correct.

Correggio (*Italian* kor'reddʒo) *n.* **Antonio Allegri da** (an'tɔːnjo al'leːgri da). 1494–1534, Italian painter, noted for his striking use of perspective and foreshortening.

Corregidor (kə'rɛgɪˌdɔː) *n.* an island at the entrance to Manila Bay, in the Philippines: site of the defeat of American forces by the Japanese (1942) in World War II.

correlate ('kɒrɪˌleɪt) *vb.* **1.** to place or be placed in a complementary or reciprocal relationship. **2.** (*tr.*) to establish or show a correlation between. ~*n.* **3.** either of two things mutually related.

correlation (ˌkɒrɪ'leɪʃən) *n.* **1.** a mutual relationship between two or more things. **2.** the act of correlating or the state of being correlated. **3.** *Statistics.* the extent of correspondence between the ordering of two variables. [C16: from Med. L *correlātiō*, from *com-* together + *relātiō* RELATION] —**ˌcorre'lational** *adj.*

correlation coefficient *n. Statistics.* a statistic measuring the degree of correlation between two variables.

correlative (kɒ'rɛlətɪv) *adj.* **1.** in complementary or reciprocal relationship; corresponding. **2.** denoting words, usually conjunctions, occurring together though not adjacently in certain grammatical constructions, as *neither* and *nor.* ~*n.* **3.** either of two things that are correlative. **4.** a correlative word. —**cor'relatively** *adv.* —**corˌrela'tivity** *n.*

correspond (ˌkɒrɪ'spɒnd) *vb.* (*intr.*) **1.** (usually foll. by *with* or *to*) to be consistent or compatible (with); tally (with). **2.** (usually foll. by *to*) to be similar in character or function. **3.** (usually foll. by *with*) to communicate by letter. [C16: from Med. L *corrēspondēre*, from L *respondēre* to RESPOND] —**ˌcorre'sponding** *adj.* —**ˌcorre'spondingly** *adv.*

▷ **Usage.** See at **similar.**

correspondence (ˌkɒrɪ'spɒndəns) *n.* **1.** the condition of agreeing or corresponding. **2.** similarity. **3.** agreement or conformity. **4. a.** communication by letters. **b.** the letters so exchanged.

correspondence school *n.* an educational institution that offers tuition (**correspondence courses**) by post.

correspondent (ˌkɒrɪ'spɒndənt) *n.* **1.** a person who communicates by letter. **2.** a person employed by a newspaper, etc., to report on a special subject or from a foreign country. **3.** a person or firm that has regular business relations with another, esp. one abroad. ~*adj.* **4.** similar or analogous.

Corrèze (*French* kɔrɛz) *n.* a department of central France, in Limousin region. Capital: Tulle. Pop.: 241 448 (1982). Area: 5888 sq. km (2296 sq. miles).

corrida (kɒ'rriða) *n.* the Spanish word for **bullfight.** [Sp., from *corrida de toros,* lit.: a running of bulls]

corridor ('kɒrɪˌdɔː) *n.* **1.** a passage connecting parts of a building. **2.** a strip of land or airspace that affords access, either from a landlocked country to the sea or from a state to an exclave. **3.** a passageway connecting the compartments of a railway coach. **4. corridors of power.** the higher echelons of government, the Civil Service, etc., considered as the location of power and influence. [C16: from OF, from OIt. *corridore,* lit.: place for running]

corrie ('kɒrɪ) *n.* **1.** (in Scotland) a circular hollow on a hillside. **2.** *Geol.* another name for **cirque.** [C18: from Gaelic *coire* cauldron]

Corrientes (*Spanish* ko'rrjentes) *n.* a port in NE Argentina, on the Paraná River. Pop.: 186 130 (1980).

corrigendum (ˌkɒrɪ'dʒɛndəm) *n., pl.* **-da** (-də). **1.** an error to be corrected. **2.** (*sometimes pl.*) Also called: **erratum.** a slip of paper inserted into a book after printing, listing corrections. [C19: from L: that which is to be corrected]

corrigible ('kɒrɪdʒɪbᵊl) *adj.* **1.** capable of being corrected. **2.** submissive. [C15: from OF, from Med. L *corrigibilis,* from L *corrigere* to CORRECT]

corroborate (kə'rɒbəˌreɪt) *vb.* (*tr.*) to confirm or support (facts, opinions, etc.), esp. by providing fresh evidence. [C16: from L *corrōborāre,* from *rōborāre* to make strong, from *rōbur* strength] —**corˌroboˈration** *n.* —**corroborative** (kə'rɒbərətɪv) *adj.* —**cor'roboˌrator** *n.*

corroboree (kə'rɒbərɪ) *n. Austral.* **1.** a native assembly of sacred, festive, or warlike character. **2.** any noisy gathering. [C19: from Abor.]

corrode (kə'rəʊd) *vb.* **1.** to eat away or be eaten away, esp. as in the oxidation or rusting of a metal. **2.** (*tr.*) to destroy gradually: *his jealousy corroded his happiness.* [C14: from L *corrōdere* to gnaw to pieces, from *rōdere* to gnaw] —**cor'rodible** *adj.*

corrosion (kə'rəʊʒən) *n.* **1.** a process in which a solid, esp. a metal, is eaten away and changed by a chemical action, as in the oxidation of iron. **2.** slow deterioration by being eaten or worn away. **3.** the product of corrosion.

corrosive (kə'rəʊsɪv) *adj.* **1.** tending to eat away or consume. ~*n.* **2.** a corrosive substance, such as a strong acid. —**cor'rosively** *adv.* —**cor'rosiveness** *n.*

corrosive sublimate *n.* another name for **mercuric chloride.**

corrugate ('kɒrʊˌgeɪt) *vb.* (*usually tr.*) to fold or be folded into alternate furrows and ridges. [C18: from L *corrūgāre,* from *rūga* a wrinkle] —**'corruˌgated** *adj.* —**ˌcorru'gation** *n.*

corrugated iron *n.* a thin sheet of iron or steel, formed with alternating ridges and troughs.

corrupt (kə'rʌpt) *adj.* **1.** open to or involving bribery or other dishonest practices: *a corrupt official; corrupt practices.* **2.** morally depraved. **3.** putrid or rotten. **4.** (of a text or manuscript) made meaningless or different in meaning by scribal errors or alterations. ~*vb.* **5.** to become or cause to become dishonest or disloyal. **6.** (*tr.*) to deprave. **7.** (*tr.*) to infect or contaminate. **8.** (*tr.*) to cause to become rotten. **9.** (*tr.*) to alter (a text, etc.) from the original. [C14: from L *corruptus* spoiled, from *corrumpere* to ruin, from *rumpere* to break] —**cor'rupter** or **cor'ruptor** *n.* —**cor'ruptly** *adv.* —**cor'ruptness** *n.*

corruptible (kə'rʌptɪbᵊl) *adj.* capable of being corrupted. —**cor'ruptibly** *adv.*

corruption (kə'rʌpʃən) *n.* **1.** the act of corrupting or state of being corrupt. **2.** depravity. **3.** dishonesty, esp. bribery. **4.** decay. **5.** alteration, as of a manuscript. **6.** an altered form of a word.

corsage (kɔː'sɑːʒ) *n.* **1.** a small bunch of flowers worn pinned to the lapel, bosom, etc. **2.** the bodice of a dress. [C15: from OF, from *cors* body, from L *corpus*]

corsair ('kɔ:sɛə) n. **1.** a pirate. **2.** a privateer, esp. of the Barbary Coast. [C15: from OF *corsaire*, from Med. L *cursārius*, from L *cursus* a running]

corse (kɔ:s) n. an archaic word for **corpse**.

Corse (kɔrs) n. the French name for **Corsica**.

corselet ('kɔ:slɪt) n. **1.** Also spelt: **corslet**. a piece of armour for the top part of the body. **2.** a one-piece foundation garment. [C15: from OF, from *cors* bodice, from L *corpus* body]

corset ('kɔ:sɪt) n. **1. a.** a stiffened, elasticated, or laced foundation garment, worn esp. by women. **b.** a similar garment worn because of injury, weakness, etc., by either sex. **2.** *Inf.* a restriction or limitation, esp. government control of bank lending. ∼*vb.* **3.** (*tr.*) to dress or enclose in, or as in, a corset. [C14: from OF, lit.: a little bodice] —**corsetière** (ˌkɔ:sɛti'ɛə) n. —'**corsetry** n.

Corsica ('kɔ:sɪkə) n. an island in the Mediterranean, west of N Italy: forms, with 43 islets, a region of France; mountainous; settled by Greeks in about 560 B.C.; sold by Genoa to France in 1768. Capital: Ajaccio. Pop.: 244 600 (1984). Area: 8682 sq. km (3367 sq. miles). French name: **Corse**. —'**Corsican** adj., n.

cortege or **cortège** (kɔ:'teɪʒ) n. **1.** a formal procession, esp. a funeral procession. **2.** a train of attendants; retinue. [C17: from F, from It. *corteggio*, from *corteggiare* to attend]

Cortés ('kɔ:tɛz; *Spanish* kor'tes) or **Cortez** (kɔ:'tɛz) n. **Hernando** (ɛr'nando) or **Hernán** (ɛr'nan). 1485–1547, Spanish conquistador: defeated the Aztecs and conquered Mexico (1523).

cortex ('kɔ:tɛks) n., pl. **-tices** (-tɪˌsi:z). **1.** *Anat.* the outer layer of any organ or part, such as the grey matter in the brain that covers the cerebrum (**cerebral cortex**). **2.** *Bot.* **a.** the tissue in plant stems and roots between the vascular bundles and the epidermis. **b.** the outer layer of a part such as the bark of a stem. [C17: from L: bark, outer layer] —**cortical** ('kɔ:tɪkəl) adj.

corticate ('kɔ:tɪkɪt, -ˌkeɪt) or **corticated** adj. (of plants, seeds, etc.) having a bark, husk, or rind. [C19: from L *corticātus*]

cortisone ('kɔ:tɪˌzəʊn) n. a steroid hormone, the synthetic form of which has been used in treating rheumatoid arthritis, allergic and skin diseases, leukaemia, etc. [C20: from *corticosterone*, a hormone]

Cortot (*French* kɔrto) n. **Alfred** (alfrɛd). 1877–1962, French pianist, born in Switzerland.

corundum (kə'rʌndəm) n. a hard mineral consisting of aluminium oxide: used as an abrasive. Precious varieties include ruby and sapphire. Formula: Al_2O_3. [C18: from Tamil *kuruntam*; rel. to Sansk. *kuruvinda* ruby]

Corunna (kə'rʌnə) n. the English name for **La Coruña**.

coruscate ('kɒrəˌskeɪt) vb. (*intr.*) to emit flashes of light; sparkle. [C18: from L *coruscāre* to flash] —ˌ**corus'cation** n.

corvée ('kɔ:veɪ) n. **1.** *European history.* a day's unpaid labour owed by a feudal vassal to his lord. **2.** the practice or an instance of forced labour. [C14: from OF, from LL *corrogāta* contribution, from L *corrogāre* to collect, from *rogāre* to ask]

corvette (kɔ:'vɛt) n. a lightly armed escort warship. [C17: from OF, ?from MDu. *corf*]

corvine ('kɔ:vaɪn) adj. **1.** of or resembling a crow. **2.** of the passerine bird family Corvidae, which includes the crows, ravens, rooks, jackdaws, magpies, and jays. [C17: from L *corvīnus*, from *corvus* a raven]

Corybant ('kɒrɪˌbænt) n., pl. **Corybants** or **Corybantes** (ˌkɒrɪ'bænti:z). *Classical myth.* a wild attendant of the goddess Cybele. [C14: from L *Corybās*, from Gk *Korubas*] —ˌ**Cory'bantic** adj.

corymb ('kɒrɪmb, -rɪm) n. an inflorescence in the form of a flat-topped flower cluster with the oldest flowers at the periphery. [C18: from L *corymbus*, from Gk *korumbos* cluster]

coryza (kə'raɪzə) n. acute inflammation of the mucous membrane of the nose, with discharge of mucus; a head cold. [C17: from LL: catarrh, from Gk *koruza*]

cos[1] or **cos lettuce** (kɒs) n. a variety of lettuce with a long slender head and crisp leaves. Usual U.S. and Canad. name: **romaine**. [C17: after *Kos*, the Aegean island of its origin]

cos[2] (kɒz) abbrev. for cosine.

Cos (kɒs) n. a variant spelling of **Kos**.

Cos. or **cos.** abbrev. for: **1.** Companies. **2.** Counties.

Cosa Nostra ('kəʊzə 'nɒstrə) n. the branch of the Mafia that operates in the U.S. [It.: our thing]

cosec ('kəʊsɛk) abbrev. for cosecant.

cosecant (kəʊ'si:kənt) n. (of an angle) a trigonometric function that in a right-angled triangle is the ratio of the length of the hypotenuse to that of the opposite side.

Cosenza (*Italian* ko'zentsa) n. a city in S Italy, in Calabria. Pop.: 106 026 (1988).

coset ('kəʊˌsɛt) n. *Maths.* a set that produces a specified larger set when added to another set.

Cosgrave ('kɒzgreɪv) n. **Liam** ('li:əm). born 1920, Irish politician; prime minister of the Republic of Ireland (1973–77).

cosh[1] (kɒʃ) *Brit.* ∼*n.* **1.** a blunt weapon, often made of hard rubber; bludgeon. **2.** an attack with such a weapon. ∼*vb.* **3.** to hit with such a weapon, esp. on the head. [C19: from Romany *kosh*]

cosh[2] (kɒʃ, kɒs'eɪtʃ) n. hyperbolic cosine. [C19: from COS(INE) + H(YPERBOLIC)]

cosignatory (kəʊ'sɪgnətərɪ, -trɪ) n., pl. **-ries.** **1.** a person, country, etc., that signs a document jointly with others. ∼*adj.* **2.** signing jointly.

cosine ('kəʊˌsaɪn) n. (of an angle) a trigonometric function that in a right-angled triangle is the ratio of the length of the adjacent side to that of the hypotenuse. [C17: from NL *cosinus*; see CO-, SINE[1]]

cosmetic (kɒz'mɛtɪk) n. **1.** any preparation applied to the body, esp. the face, with the intention of beautifying it. ∼*adj.* **2.** serving or designed to beautify the body, esp. the face. **3.** having no other function than to beautify: *cosmetic illustrations in a book.* [C17: from Gk *kosmētikos*, from *kosmein* to arrange, from *kosmos* order] —**cos'metically** adv.

cosmic ('kɒzmɪk) adj. **1.** of or relating to the whole universe: *cosmic laws.* **2.** occurring or originating in outer space, esp. as opposed to the vicinity of the earth: *cosmic rays.* **3.** immeasurably extended; vast. —'**cosmically** adv.

cosmic dust n. fine particles of solid matter occurring throughout interstellar space and often collecting into clouds of extremely low density.

cosmic rays pl. n. radiation consisting of atomic nuclei, esp. protons, of very high energy, that reach the earth from outer space. Also called: **cosmic radiation**.

cosmo- or before a vowel **cosm-** combining form. indicating the world or universe: *cosmology; cosmonaut.* [from Gk: COSMOS]

cosmogony (kɒz'mɒgənɪ) n., pl. **-nies.** the study of the origin and development of the universe or of a particular system in the universe, such as the solar system. [C17: from Gk *kosmogonia*, from COSMO- + *gonos* creation] —**cosmogonic** (ˌkɒzmə'gɒnɪk) or ˌ**cosmo'gonical** adj. —**cos'mogonist** n.

cosmography (kɒz'mɒgrəfɪ) n. **1.** a representation of the world or the universe. **2.** the science dealing with the whole order of nature. —**cos'mographer** n. —**cosmographic** (ˌkɒzmə'græfɪk) or ˌ**cosmo'graphical** adj.

cosmology (kɒz'mɒlədʒɪ) n. **1.** the study of the origin and nature of the universe. **2.** a particular account of the origin or structure of the universe. —**cosmological** (ˌkɒzmə'lɒdʒɪkəl) or ˌ**cosmo'logic** adj. —**cos'mologist** n.

cosmonaut ('kɒzməˌnɔ:t) n. a Soviet astronaut. [C20: from Russian *kosmonavt*, from COSMO- + Gk *nautēs* sailor]

cosmopolitan (ˌkɒzmə'pɒlɪt³n) n. **1.** a person who has lived and travelled in many countries, esp. one who is free of national prejudices. ∼*adj.* **2.** familiar with many parts of the world. **3.** sophisticated or urbane. **4.** composed of people or elements from all parts of the world or from many different spheres. [C17: from F, ult. from Gk *kosmopolitēs*, from *kosmo*-COSMO- + *politēs* citizen] —ˌ**cosmo'politanism** n.

cosmopolite (kɒz'mɒpəˌlaɪt) n. **1.** a less common word for **cosmopolitan** (sense 1). **2.** an animal or plant that occurs in most parts of the world. —**cos'mopol**iˌtism n.

cosmos ('kɒzmɒs) n. **1.** the universe considered as an ordered system. **2.** any ordered system. **3.** (pl. **-mos** or **-moses**) any tropical American plant of the genus *Cosmos* cultivated as garden plants for their brightly coloured flowers. [C17: from Gk *kosmos* order]

Cossack ('kɒsæk) *n.* **1.** (formerly) any of the free warrior-peasants of chiefly East Slavonic descent who served as cavalry under the tsars. ~*adj.* **2.** of, relating to, or characteristic of the Cossacks: *a Cossack dance.* [C16: from Russian *kazak* vagabond, of Turkic origin]

cosset ('kɒsɪt) *vb.* **1.** (*tr.*) to pamper; pet. ~*n.* **2.** any pet animal, esp. a lamb. [C16: from ?]

cost (kɒst) *n.* **1.** the price paid or required for acquiring, producing, or maintaining something, measured in money, time, or energy; outlay. **2.** suffering or sacrifice: *I know to my cost.* **3. a.** the amount paid for a commodity by its seller: *to sell at cost.* **b.** (*as modifier*): *the cost price.* **4.** (*pl.*) *Law.* the expenses of judicial proceedings. **5. at all costs.** regardless of sacrifice involved. **6. at the cost of.** at the expense of losing. ~*vb.* **costing, cost.** **7.** (*tr.*) to be obtained or obtainable in exchange for: *the ride cost one pound.* **8.** to cause or require the loss or sacrifice (of): *the accident cost him dearly.* **9.** to estimate the cost of (a product, process, etc.) for the purposes of pricing, budgeting, control, etc. [C13: from OF (*n.*), from *coster* to cost, from L *constāre* to stand at, cost, from *stāre* to stand]

costa ('kɒstə) *n., pl.* **-tae** (-tiː). **1.** the technical name for **rib**[1] (sense 1). **2.** a riblike part. [C19: from L: rib, side] —'**costal** *adj.*

Costa Brava ('kɒstə 'brɑːvə) *n.* a coastal region of NE Spain along the Mediterranean, extending from Barcelona to the French border: many resorts.

cost accounting *n.* the recording and controlling of all the expenditures of an enterprise in order to facilitate control of separate activities. Also called: **management accounting.** —**cost accountant** *n.*

Costa Rica ('kɒstə 'riːkə) *n.* a republic in Central America: gained independence from Spain in 1821; mostly mountainous and volcanic, with extensive forests. Language: Spanish. Religion: Roman Catholic. Currency: colón. Capital: San José. Pop.: 2 714 000 (1986). Area: 50 900 sq. km (19 652 sq. miles). —**Costa Rican** *adj.*, *n.*

cost-benefit analysis *n.* an accounting method of evaluating the benefits of a project that includes not only the money involved but also the social benefits and disadvantages.

Costermansville ('kɒstəmənz,vɪl) *n.* the former name (until 1966) of **Bukavu.**

costermonger ('kɒstə,mʌŋgə) *or* **coster** *n. Brit., rare.* a person who sells fruit, vegetables, etc., from a barrow. [C16: from *costard* a kind of apple + MONGER]

costive ('kɒstɪv) *adj.* **1.** constipated. **2.** niggardly. [C14: from OF *costivé*, from L *constipātus*; see CONSTIPATE] —'**costiveness** *n.*

costly ('kɒstlɪ) *adj.* **-lier, -liest. 1.** expensive. **2.** entailing great loss or sacrifice: *a costly victory.* **3.** splendid; lavish. —'**costliness** *n.*

cost of living *n.* **a.** the basic cost of the food, clothing, shelter, and fuel necessary to maintain life, esp. at a standard of living regarded as basic. **b.** (*as modifier*): *the cost-of-living index.*

cost-plus *n.* a method of establishing a selling price in which an agreed percentage is added to the cost price to cover profit.

costume ('kɒstjuːm) *n.* **1.** a style of dressing, including all the clothes, accessories, etc., worn at one time, as in a particular country or period. **2.** *Old-fashioned.* a woman's suit. **3.** a set of clothes, esp. unusual or period clothes: *a jester's costume.* **4.** short for **swimming costume.** ~*vb.* (*tr.*) **5.** to furnish the costumes for (a show, film, etc.). **6.** to dress (someone) in a costume. [C18: from F, from It.: dress, habit, CUSTOM]

costumier (kɒ'stjuːmɪə) *or* **costumer** *n.* a person or firm that makes or supplies theatrical or fancy costumes.

cosy *or U.S.* **cozy** ('kəʊzɪ) *adj.* **-sier, -siest** *or U.S.* **-zier, -ziest. 1.** warm and snug. **2.** intimate; friendly. ~*n., pl.* **-sies** *or U.S.* **-zies. 3.** a cover for keeping things warm: *egg cosy.* [C18: from Scot., from ?] —'**cosily** *or U.S.* '**cozily** *adv.* —'**cosiness** *or U.S.* '**coziness** *n.*

cot[1] (kɒt) *n.* **1.** a child's boxlike bed, usually incorporating vertical bars. **2.** a portable bed. **3.** a light bedstead. **4.** *Naut.* a hammock-like bed. [C17: from Hindi *khāt* bedstead]

cot[2] (kɒt) *n.* **1.** *Literary or arch.* a small cottage. **2.** Also called: **cote. a.** a small shelter, esp. one for pigeons, sheep, etc. **b.** (*in combination*): *dovecot.* [OE *cot*]

cot[3] (kɒt) *abbrev. for* cotangent.

cotangent (kəʊ'tændʒənt) *n.* (of an angle) a trigonometric function that in a right-angled triangle is the ratio of the length of the adjacent side to that of the opposite side.

COTC *abbrev. for* Canadian Officers Training Corps.

cot death *n.* the unexplained sudden death of an infant during sleep.

cote (kəʊt) *or* **cot** *n.* **1.** a small shelter for pigeons, sheep, etc. **2.** (*in combination*): *dovecote.* [OE *cote*]

Côte d'Azur (*French* kot dazyr) *n.* the Mediterranean coast of France, including the French Riviera: forms an administrative region with Provence.

Côte d'Ivoire (*French* kot divwar) *n.* a republic in West Africa, on the Gulf of Guinea: Portuguese trading for ivory and slaves began in the 16th century; made a French protectorate in 1842 and became independent in 1960; third largest producer of coffee in the world. Official language: French. Religion: animist majority, with Muslim and Roman Catholic minorities. Currency: franc. Capital: Yamoussoukro. Pop.: 10 595 000 (1986 est.). Area: 319 820 sq. km (123 483 sq. miles). Former name (until 1986): **the Ivory Coast.**

Côte-d'Or (*French* kotdɔr) *n.* a department of E central France, in NE Burgundy. Capital: Dijon. Pop.: 473 548 (1982). Area: 8787 sq. km (3427 sq. miles).

cotenant (kəʊ'tɛnənt) *n.* a person who holds property jointly or in common with others. —**co'tenancy** *n.*

coterie ('kəʊtərɪ) *n.* a small exclusive group of friends or people with common interests; clique. [C18: from F, from OF: association of tenants, from *cotier* (unattested) cottager]

coterminous (kəʊ'tɜːmɪnəs) *or* **conterminous** *adj.* **1.** having a common boundary. **2.** coextensive or coincident in range, time, etc.

Côtes-du-Nord (*French* kotdynɔr) *n.* a department of W France, on the N coast of Brittany. Capital: St Brieuc. Pop.: 538 869 (1982). Area: 7218 sq. km (2815 sq. miles).

coth (kɒθ, 'kɒt'eɪtʃ) *n.* hyperbolic cotangent. [C20: from COT(ANGENT) + H(YPERBOLIC)]

cotillion *or* **cotillon** (kə'tɪljən, kəʊ-) *n.* **1.** a French formation dance of the 18th century. **2.** *U.S.* a quadrille. **3.** *U.S.* a formal ball. [C18: from F *cotillon* dance, from OF: petticoat]

cotinga (kə'tɪŋgə) *n.* a tropical American passerine bird having a broad slightly hooked bill.

Cotman ('kɒtmən) *n.* **John Sell.** 1782–1842, English landscape watercolourist and etcher.

cotoneaster (kə,təʊnɪ'æstə) *n.* any Old World shrub of the rosaceous genus *Cotoneaster*: cultivated for their ornamental flowers and red or black berries. [C18: from NL, from L *cotōneum* QUINCE]

Cotonou (,kəʊtə'nuː) *n.* the chief port of Benin, on the Bight of Benin. Pop.: 487 020 (1982 est.).

Cotopaxi (*Spanish* koto'paksi) *n.* a volcano in central Ecuador, in the Andes: the world's highest active volcano. Height: 5896 m (19 344 ft.).

Cotswolds ('kɒts,wəʊldz, -wəldz) *pl. n.* a range of low hills in SW England, mainly in Gloucestershire: formerly a centre of the wool industry.

cotta ('kɒtə) *n. R.C. Church.* a short form of surplice. [C19: from It.: tunic]

cottage ('kɒtɪdʒ) *n.* a small simple house, esp. in a rural area. [C14: from COT[2]]

cottage cheese *n.* a mild loose soft white cheese made from skimmed milk curds.

cottage hospital *n. Brit.* a small rural hospital.

cottage industry *n.* an industry in which employees work in their own homes, often using their own equipment.

cottage pie *n. Brit.* another term for **shepherd's pie.**

cottager ('kɒtɪdʒə) *n.* **1.** a person who lives in a cottage. **2.** a rural labourer.

Cottbus (*German* 'kɔtbʊs) *n.* an industrial city in East Germany, on the Spree River. Pop.: 125 784 (1986).

cotter[1] ('kɒtə) *n. Machinery.* **1.** any part, such as a pin, wedge, key, etc., that is used to secure two other parts so that relative motion between them is prevented. **2.** short for **cotter pin.** [C14: shortened from *cotterel*, from ?]

cotter[2] ('kɒtə) *n.* **1.** *English history.* a villein in late Anglo-Saxon and early Norman times occupying a cottage and land in return for labour. **2.** Also called: **cottar.** a peasant occupying a cottage and land in the Scottish Highlands. [C14: from Med. L *cotārius*, from ME *cote* COT²]

cotter pin *n. Machinery.* a split pin secured, after passing through holes in the parts to be attached, by spreading the ends.

Cottian Alps ('kɒtɪən) *pl. n.* a mountain range in SW Europe, between NW Italy and SE France: part of the Alps. Highest peak: Monte Viso, 3841 m (12 600 ft.).

cotton ('kɒt²n) *n.* **1.** any of various herbaceous plants and shrubs cultivated in warm climates for the fibre surrounding the seeds and the oil within the seeds. **2.** the soft white downy fibre of these plants, used to manufacture textiles. **3.** cotton plants collectively, as a cultivated crop. **4.** a cloth or thread made from cotton fibres. [C14: from OF *coton*, from Ar. *qutn*] — **'cottony** *adj.*

cotton grass *n.* any of various N temperate and arctic grasslike bog plants whose clusters of long silky hairs resemble cotton tufts.

cotton on *vb.* (*intr., adv.; often foll. by to*) *Inf.* to perceive the meaning (of).

cotton-picking *adj. U.S. & Canad. sl.* (intensifier qualifying something undesirable): *you cotton-picking layabout!*

cottonseed ('kɒt²n,si:d) *n., pl.* **-seeds** *or* **-seed.** the seed of the cotton plant: a source of oil and fodder.

cottontail ('kɒt²n,teɪl) *n.* any of several common rabbits of American woodlands.

cottonwood ('kɒt²n,wʊd) *n.* any of several North American poplars, whose leaves are covered with cottony hairs.

cotton wool *n.* **1.** *Chiefly Brit.* bleached and sterilized cotton from which the impurities, such as the seeds, have been removed. Usual U.S. term: **absorbent cotton. 2.** cotton in the natural state. **3.** *Brit. inf.* a state of pampered comfort and protection.

cotyledon (,kɒtɪ'li:d²n) *n.* a simple embryonic leaf in seed-bearing plants, which, in some species, forms the first green leaf after germination. [C16: from L: a plant, navelwort, from Gk *kotulēdōn*, from *kotulē* cup, hollow] — **,coty'ledonous** *adj.* — **,coty'ledonal** *adj.*

coucal ('ku:kæl) *n.* any ground-living bird of the genus *Centropus* of Africa, S Asia, and Australia. [C19: from F, ?from *couc(ou)* cuckoo + *al(ouette)* lark]

couch (kautʃ) *n.* **1.** a piece of upholstered furniture, usually having a back and armrests, for seating more than one person. **2.** a bed, esp. one used in the daytime by the patients of a doctor or a psychoanalyst. ~*vb.* **3.** (*tr.*) to express in a particular style of language: *couched in an archaic style.* **4.** (when *tr., usually reflexive or passive*) to lie down or cause to lie down for or as for sleep. **5.** (*intr.*) *Arch.* to crouch. **6.** (*intr.*) *Arch.* to lie in ambush; lurk. **7.** (*tr.*) *Surgery.* to remove (a cataract) by downward displacement of the lens of the eye. **8.** (*tr.*) *Arch.* to lower (a lance) into a horizontal position. [C14: from OF *couche* a bed, lair, from *coucher* to lay down, from L *collocāre* to arrange, from *locāre* to place]

couchant ('kautʃənt) *adj.* (*usually postpositive*) *Heraldry.* in a lying position: *a lion couchant.* [C15: from F: lying]

couchette (ku:'ʃɛt) *n.* a bed or berth in a railway carriage, esp. one converted from seats. [C20: from F, dim. of *couche* bed]

couch grass (kautʃ, ku:tʃ) *n.* a grass with a yellowish-white creeping underground stem by which it spreads quickly: a troublesome weed. Also called: **twitch grass, quitch grass.**

couch potato *n. Sl., chiefly U.S.* a lazy person whose recreation consists chiefly of watching television and videos.

Coué (*French* kwe) *n.* **Émile** (emil). 1857–1926, French psychologist and pharmacist: advocated psychotherapy by autosuggestion. — **Couéism** ('ku:eɪ,ɪzəm) *n.*

cougar ('ku:gə) *n.* another name for **puma.** [C18: from F *couguar,* from Port., from Tupi]

cough (kɒf) *vb.* **1.** (*intr.*) to expel air abruptly and explosively through the partially closed vocal chords. **2.** (*intr.*) to make a sound similar to this. **3.** (*tr.*) to utter or express with a cough or coughs. ~*n.* **4.** an act or sound of coughing. **5.** a condition of the lungs or throat which causes frequent coughing. [OE *cohhetten*] — **'cougher** *n.*

cough drop *n.* a lozenge to relieve a cough.

cough mixture *n.* any medicine that relieves coughing.

cough up *vb.* (*adv.*) **1.** *Inf.* to surrender (money, information, etc.), esp. reluctantly. **2.** (*tr.*) to bring into the mouth or eject (phlegm, food, etc.) by coughing.

could (kʊd) *vb.* (takes an infinitive without *to* or an implied infinitive) used as an auxiliary: **1.** to make the past tense of **can¹. 2.** to make the subjunctive mood of **can¹,** esp. used in polite requests or in conditional sentences: *could I see you tonight?* **3.** to indicate suggestion of a course of action: *you could take the car if it's raining.* **4.** (often foll. by *well*) to indicate a possibility: *he could well be a spy.* [OE *cūthe*]

couldn't ('kʊd²nt) *contraction of* could not.

couldst (kʊdst) *vb. Arch.* the form of **could** used with the pronoun *thou* or its relative form.

coulee ('ku:leɪ, -lɪ) *n.* **1. a.** a flow of molten lava. **b.** such lava when solidified. **2.** *Western U.S. & Canad.* a steep-sided ravine. [C19: from Canad. F *coulée* a flow, from F, from *couler* to flow, from L *cōlāre* to sift]

coulomb ('ku:lɒm) *n.* the derived SI unit of electric charge; the quantity of electricity transported in one second by a current of 1 ampere. Symbol: C [C19: after C.A. de COULOMB]

Coulomb ('ku:lɒm; *French* kulɔ̃) *n.* **Charles Augustin de** (ʃarl ogystɛ̃ də). 1736–1806, French physicist: made many discoveries in the field of electricity and magnetism.

coulter ('kəultə) *n.* a blade or sharp-edged disc attached to a plough so that it cuts through the soil vertically in advance of the ploughshare. Also (*esp. U.S.*): **colter.** [OE *culter*, from L: ploughshare, knife]

coumarin *or* **cumarin** ('ku:mərɪn) *n.* a white vanilla-scented crystalline ester, used in perfumes and flavouring. [C19: from F, from *coumarou* tonka-bean tree, from Sp., from Tupi]

council ('kaunsəl) *n.* **1.** an assembly of people meeting for discussion, consultation, etc. **2. a.** a body of people elected or appointed to serve in an administrative, legislative, or advisory capacity: *a student council.* **b.** short for **legislative council. 3.** (*sometimes cap.; often preceded by the*) *Brit.* the local governing authority of a town, county, etc. **4.** a meeting of a council. **5.** (*modifier*) of, provided for, or used by a local council: *a council chamber; council offices.* **6.** (*modifier*) *Brit.* provided by a local council, esp. (of housing) at a subsidized rent: *a council house; a council estate; a council school.* **7.** *Christianity.* an assembly of bishops, etc., convened for regulating matters of doctrine or discipline. [C12: from OF *concile*, from L *concilium* assembly, from *com-* together + *calāre* to call]

councillor *or U.S.* **councilor** ('kaunsələ) *n.* a member of a council.

councilman ('kaunsəlmən) *n., pl.* **-men.** *Chiefly U.S.* a councillor.

counsel ('kaunsəl) *n.* **1.** advice or guidance on conduct, behaviour, etc. **2.** discussion; consultation: *to take counsel with a friend.* **3.** a person whose advice is sought. **4.** a barrister or group of barristers engaged in conducting cases in court and advising on legal matters. **5.** *Christianity.* any of the **counsels of perfection,** namely poverty, chastity, and obedience. **6. counsel of perfection.** excellent but unrealizable advice. **7.** private opinions (esp. in **keep one's own counsel**). **8.** *Arch.* wisdom; prudence. ~*vb.* **-selling, -selled** *or U.S.* **-seling, -seled. 9.** (*tr.*) to give advice or guidance to. **10.** (*tr.; often takes a clause as object*) to recommend; urge. **11.** (*intr.*) *Arch.* to take counsel; consult. [C13: from OF *counseil*, from L *consilium* deliberating body; rel. to CONSULT]

counselling *or U.S.* **counseling** ('kaunsəlɪŋ) *n.* systematic guidance offered by social workers, doctors, etc., in which a person's problems are discussed and advice is given.

counsellor *or U.S.* **counselor** ('kaunsələ) *n.* **1.** a person who gives counsel; adviser. **2.** Also called: **counselor-at-law.** *U.S.* a lawyer, esp. one who conducts cases in court. **3.** a senior diplomatic officer.

count¹ (kaunt) *vb.* **1.** to add up or check (each unit in a collection) in order to ascertain the sum: *count your change.* **2.** (*tr.*) to recite numbers in ascending order up to and including. **3.** (*tr.; often foll. by in*) to take into account or include: *we must count him in.* **4. not counting.** excluding. **5.** (*tr.*) to consider; deem: *count* *yourself lucky.* **6.** (*intr.*) to have importance: *this picture counts as a rarity.* **7.** (*intr.*) *Music.* to keep time by counting beats. ~*n.* **8.** the act of counting. **9.** the number reached by counting; sum: *a blood count.* **10.** *Law.* a paragraph in an indictment containing a separate charge. **11. keep** *or* **lose count.** to keep or fail to keep an accurate record of items, events, etc. **12.** *Boxing, wrestling.* the act of telling off a number of seconds by the referee, as when a boxer has been knocked down by his opponent. **13. out for the count.** *Boxing.* knocked out and unable to continue after a count of ten by the referee. ~See also **count against, countdown,** etc. [C14: from Anglo-F *counter,* from OF *conter,* from L *computāre* to calculate] — **'countable** *adj.*

count² (kaʊnt) *n.* **1.** a nobleman in any of various European countries having a rank corresponding to that of a British earl. **2.** any of various officials in the late Roman Empire and in the early Middle Ages. [C16: from OF *conte,* from L *comes* associate, from COM- with + *īre* to go]

count against *vb.* (*intr., prep.*) to have influence to the disadvantage of.

countdown ('kaʊnt,daʊn) *n.* **1.** the act of counting backwards to time a critical operation exactly, such as the launching of a rocket. ~*vb.* **count down.** (*intr., adv.*) **2.** to count thus.

countenance ('kaʊntɪnəns) *n.* **1.** the face, esp. when considered as expressing a person's character or mood. **2.** support or encouragement; sanction. **3.** composure; self-control (esp. in **keep** *or* **lose one's countenance**). ~*vb.* (*tr.*) **4.** to support or encourage; sanction. **5.** to tolerate; endure. [C13: from OF *contenance* mien, behaviour, from L *continentia* restraint, control; see CONTAIN]

counter¹ ('kaʊntə) *n.* **1.** a horizontal surface, as in a shop or bank, over which business is transacted. **2.** (in some cafeterias) a long table on which food is served. **3. a.** a small flat disc of wood, metal, or plastic, used in various board games. **b.** a similar disc or token used as an imitation coin. **4.** a person or thing that may be used or manipulated. **5. under the counter. (under-the-counter** *when prenominal*) (of the sale of goods) clandestine or illegal. **6. over the counter. (over-the-counter** *when prenominal*) (of security transactions) through a broker rather than on a stock exchange. [C14: from OF *comptouer,* ult. from L *computāre* to COMPUTE]

counter² ('kaʊntə) *n.* **1.** a person who counts. **2.** an apparatus that records the number of occurrences of events. [C14: from OF *conteor,* from L *computātor;* see COUNT¹]

counter³ ('kaʊntə) *adv.* **1.** in a contrary direction or manner. **2.** in a wrong or reverse direction. **3. run counter to.** to have a contrary effect or action to. ~*adj.* **4.** opposing; opposite; contrary. ~*n.* **5.** something that is contrary or opposite to some other thing. **6.** an act, effect, or force that opposes another. **7.** a return attack, such as a blow in boxing. **8.** *Fencing.* a parry in which the foils move in a circular fashion. **9.** the portion of the stern of a boat or ship that overhangs the water aft of the rudder. **10.** a piece of leather forming the back of a shoe. ~*vb.* **11.** to say or do (something) in retaliation or response. **12.** (*tr.*) to move, act, or perform in a manner or direction opposite to (a person or thing). **13.** to return the attack of (an opponent). [C15: from OF *contre,* from L *contrā* against]

counter- *prefix.* **1.** against; opposite; contrary: *counterattack.* **2.** complementary; corresponding: *counterfoil.* **3.** duplicate or substitute: *counterfeit.* [via OF from L *contrā* against; see CONTRA-]

counteract (,kaʊntər'ækt) *vb.* (*tr.*) to oppose or neutralize by contrary action; check. — **counter'action** *n.* — **counter'active** *adj.*

counterattack ('kaʊntərə,tæk) *n.* **1.** an attack in response to an attack. ~*vb.* **2.** to make a counterattack (against).

counterbalance *n.* ('kaʊntə,bæləns). **1.** a weight or force that balances or offsets another. ~*vb.* (,kaʊntə'bæləns). (*tr.*) **2.** to act as a counterbalance to. ~Also: **counterpoise.**

counterblast ('kaʊntə,blɑːst) *n.* an aggressive response to a verbal attack.

countercheck *n.* ('kaʊntə,tʃɛk). **1.** a check or restraint, esp. one that acts in opposition to another. **2.** a double check, as for accuracy. ~*vb.* (,kaʊntə'tʃɛk). (*tr.*) **3.** to oppose by counteraction. **4.** to double-check.

counterclaim ('kaʊntə,kleɪm) *Chiefly law.* ~*n.* **1.** a claim set up in opposition to another. ~*vb.* **2.** to set up (a

claim) in opposition to another claim. — **,counter'claimant** *n.*

counterclockwise (,kaʊntə'klɒk,waɪz) *adv., adj.* the U.S. and Canad. equivalent of **anticlockwise.**

counterculture ('kaʊntə,kʌltʃə) *n.* an alternative culture, deliberately at variance with the social norm.

counterespionage (,kaʊntər'ɛspɪə,nɑːʒ) *n.* activities to counteract enemy espionage.

counterfeit ('kaʊntəfɪt) *adj.* **1.** made in imitation of something genuine with the intent to deceive or defraud; forged. **2.** simulated; sham: *counterfeit affection.* ~*n.* **3.** an imitation designed to deceive or defraud. ~*vb.* **4.** (*tr.*) to make a fraudulent imitation of. **5.** (*intr.*) to make counterfeits. **6.** to feign; simulate. [C13: from OF *contrefait,* from *contrefaire* to copy, from *contre-* COUNTER- + *faire* to make] — **'counter,feiter** *n.*

counterfoil ('kaʊntə,fɔɪl) *n. Brit.* the part of a cheque, receipt, etc., retained as a record. Also called (esp. in the U.S. and Canada): **stub.**

counterinsurgency (,kaʊntərɪn's3ːdʒənsɪ) *n.* action taken by a government against rebels, guerrillas, etc.

counterintelligence (,kaʊntərɪn'tɛlɪdʒəns) *n.* activities designed to frustrate enemy espionage.

counterirritant (,kaʊntər'ɪrɪt²nt) *n.* **1.** an agent that causes a superficial irritation of the skin and thereby relieves inflammation of deep structures. ~*adj.* **2.** producing a counterirritation. ~**counterirritation** *n.*

countermand *vb.* (,kaʊntə'mɑːnd). (*tr.*) **1.** to revoke or cancel (a command, order, etc.). **2.** to order (forces, etc.) to retreat; recall. ~*n.* ('kaʊntə,mɑːnd). **3.** a command revoking another. [C15: from OF *contremander,* from *contre-* COUNTER- + *mander* to command, from L *mandāre*]

countermarch ('kaʊntə,mɑːtʃ) *Chiefly mil.* ~*vb.* **1.** to march or cause to march back or in the opposite direction. ~*n.* **2.** the act or an instance of countermarching.

countermeasure ('kaʊntə,mɛʒə) *n.* action taken to oppose, neutralize, or retaliate against some other action.

countermove ('kaʊntə,muːv) *n.* **1.** an opposing move. ~*vb.* **2.** to make or do (something) as an opposing move. — **'counter,movement** *n.*

counteroffensive ('kaʊntərə,fɛnsɪv) *n.* a series of attacks by a defending force against an attacking enemy.

counterpane ('kaʊntə,peɪn) *n.* another word for **bedspread.** [C17: from obs. *counterpoint* (infl. by *pane* coverlet), changed from OF *coutepointe* quilt, from Med. L *culcita puncta* quilted mattress]

counterpart ('kaʊntə,pɑːt) *n.* **1.** a person or thing identical to or closely resembling another. **2.** one of two parts that complement or correspond to each other. **3.** a duplicate, esp. of a legal document; copy.

counterplot ('kaʊntə,plɒt) *n.* **1.** a plot designed to frustrate another plot. ~*vb.* **-plotting, -plotted. 2.** (*tr.*) to oppose with a counterplot.

counterpoint ('kaʊntə,pɔɪnt) *n.* **1.** the technique involving the simultaneous sounding of two or more parts or melodies. **2.** a melody or part combined with another melody or part. **3.** the musical texture resulting from the simultaneous sounding of two or more melodies or parts. ~*vb.* **4.** (*tr.*) to set in contrast. ~Related adj.: **contrapuntal.** [C15: from OF *contrepoint,* from *contre-* COUNTER- + *point* dot, note in musical notation, i.e. an accompaniment set against the notes of a melody]

counterpoise ('kaʊntə,pɔɪz) *n.* **1.** a force, influence, etc., that counterbalances another. **2.** a state of balance; equilibrium. **3.** a weight that balances another. ~*vb.* (*tr.*) **4.** to oppose with something of equal effect, weight, or force; offset. **5.** to bring into equilibrium.

counterproductive (,kaʊntəprə'dʌktɪv) *adj.* tending to hinder the achievement of an aim; having effects contrary to those intended.

counterproposal ('kaʊntəprə,pəʊz²l) *n.* a proposal offered as an alternative to a previous proposal.

Counter-Reformation (,kaʊntə,rɛfə'meɪʃən) *n.* the reform movement of the Roman Catholic Church in the 16th and early 17th centuries considered as a reaction to the Reformation.

counter-revolution (,kaʊntə,rɛvə'luːʃən) *n.* a revolution opposed to a previous revolution. — **,counter-,revo'lutionist** *n.* — **counter-,revo'lutionary** *n., adj.*

countershaft ('kaʊntə,ʃɑːft) *n.* an intermediate shaft driven by a main shaft, esp. in a gear train.

countersign vb. ('kaʊntə,saɪn, ,kaʊntə'saɪn). **1.** (tr.) to sign (a document already signed by another). ~n. ('kaʊntə,saɪn). **2.** Also called: **countersignature.** the signature so written. **3.** a secret sign given in response to another sign. **4.** Chiefly mil. a password.

countersink ('kaʊntə,sɪŋk) vb. **-sinking, -sank, -sunk.** (tr.) **1.** to enlarge the upper part of (a hole) in timber, metal, etc., so that the head of a bolt or screw can be sunk below the surface. **2.** to drive (a screw) or sink (a bolt) into such a hole. ~n. **3.** Also called: **countersink bit.** a tool for countersinking. **4.** a countersunk hole.

counterspy ('kaʊntə,spaɪ) n., pl. **-spies.** a spy working against enemy espionage.

countertenor (,kaʊntə'tɛnə) n. **1.** an adult male voice with an alto range. **2.** a singer with such a voice.

countervail (,kaʊntə'veɪl, 'kaʊntə,veɪl) vb. **1.** (when intr., usually foll. by against) to act or act against with equal power or force. **2.** (tr.) to make up for; compensate; offset. [C14: from OF contrevaloir, from L contrā valēre, from contrā against + valēre to be strong]

counterweigh (,kaʊntə'weɪ) vb. another word for **counterbalance** (sense 2).

counterweight ('kaʊntə,weɪt) n. a counterbalancing weight, influence, or force.

countess ('kaʊntɪs) n. **1.** the wife or widow of a count or earl. **2.** a woman of the rank of count or earl.

counting house n. Rare, chiefly Brit. a room or building used by the accountants of a business.

countless ('kaʊntlɪs) adj. innumerable; myriad.

count noun n. a noun that can be qualified by the indefinite article and may be used in the plural, as telephone and thing but not airs and graces or bravery. Cf. **mass noun.**

count on vb. (intr., prep.) to rely or depend on.

count out vb. (tr., adv.) **1.** Inf. to leave out; exclude. **2.** (of a boxing referee) to judge (a floored boxer) to have failed to recover within the specified time.

count palatine n., pl. **counts palatine.** History. **1.** (in the Holy Roman Empire) a count who exercised royal authority in his own domain. **2.** (in England and Ireland) the lord of a county palatine.

countrified or **countryfied** ('kʌntrɪ,faɪd) adj. in the style, manners, etc., of the country; rural.

country ('kʌntrɪ) n., pl. **-tries. 1.** a territory distinguished by its people, culture, geography, etc. **2.** an area of land distinguished by its political autonomy; state. **3.** the people of a territory or state. **4. a.** the part of the land that is away from cities or industrial areas; rural districts. **b.** (as modifier): country cottage. Related adj.: **pastoral, rural. 5.** short for **country music. 6. across country.** not keeping to roads, etc. **7. go** or **appeal to the country.** Chiefly Brit. to dissolve Parliament and hold an election. **8. up country.** away from the coast or the capital. **9.** one's native land or land of citizenship. [C13: from OF contrée, from Med. L contrāta, lit.: that which lies opposite, from L contrā opposite]

country and western n. another name for **country music.**

country club n. a club in the country, having sporting and social facilities.

country dance n. a type of folk dance in which couples face one another in a line.

country house n. a large house in the country, esp. belonging to a wealthy family.

countryman ('kʌntrɪmən) n., pl. **-men. 1.** a person who lives in the country. **2.** a person from a particular country or from one's own country. —'**country,woman** fem. n.

country music n. a type of 20th-century popular music based on White folk music of the southeastern US.

country park n. Brit. an area of countryside set aside for public recreation.

country seat n. a large estate or property in the country.

countryside ('kʌntrɪ,saɪd) n. a rural area or its population.

county ('kaʊntɪ) n., pl. **-ties. 1. a.** any of various administrative, political, or judicial subdivisions of certain English-speaking countries or states. **b.** (as modifier): county cricket. ~adj. **2.** Brit. inf. upper class; of or like the landed gentry. [C14: from OF conté land belonging to a count, from LL comes COUNT²]

county palatine n., pl. **counties palatine. 1.** the lands of a count palatine. **2.** (in England and Ireland) a county in which the earl (or other lord) exercised many royal powers, esp. judicial authority.

county town n. the town in which a county's affairs are or were administered.

coup (kuː) n. **1.** a brilliant and successful stroke or action. **2.** short for **coup d'état.** [C18: from F: blow, from L colaphus blow with the fist, from Gk kolaphos]

coup de grâce French. (ku də grɑs) n., pl. **coups de grâce** (ku də grɑs). **1.** a mortal or finishing blow, esp. one delivered as an act of mercy to a sufferer. **2.** a final or decisive stroke. [lit.: blow of mercy]

coup d'état ('kuː deɪ'tɑː) n., pl. **coups d'état** ('kuːz deɪ'tɑː). a sudden violent or illegal seizure of government. [F, lit.: stroke of state]

coupe (kuːp) n. **1.** a dessert of fruit and ice cream. **2.** a dish or stemmed glass bowl designed for this dessert. [C19: from F: goblet, CUP]

coupé ('kuːpeɪ) n. **1.** a four-seater car with a sloping back, and usually two doors. **2.** a four-wheeled horse-drawn carriage with two seats inside and one outside for the driver. [C19: from F, short for carrosse coupé, lit.: cut-off carriage]

Couperin (French kuprɛ̃) n. **François** (frɑ̃swa). 1668–1733, French composer, noted for his harpsichord suites and organ music.

couple ('kʌpᵊl) n. **1.** two people who regularly associate with each other or live together: an engaged couple. **2.** (functioning as sing. or pl.) two people considered as a pair, for or as if for dancing, games, etc. **3.** a pair of equal and opposite parallel forces that have a tendency to produce rotation. **4.** a connector or link between two members, such as a tie connecting a pair of rafters in a roof. **5. a couple of.** (functioning as sing. or pl.) **a.** a combination of two; a pair of: a couple of men. **b.** Inf. a small number of; a few: a couple of days. ~pron. **6.** (usually preceded by a; functioning as sing. or pl.) two; a pair: give him a couple. ~vb. **7.** (tr.) to connect (two things) together or to connect (one thing) to (another): to couple railway carriages. **8.** to form or be formed into a pair or pairs. **9.** to associate, put, or connect together. **10.** (intr.) to have sexual intercourse. [C13: from OF: a pair, from L cōpula a bond; see COPULA]

coupler ('kʌplə) n. Music. a device on an organ or harpsichord connecting two keys, two manuals, etc., so that both may be played at once.

couplet ('kʌplɪt) n. two successive lines of verse, usually rhymed and of the same metre. [C16: from F, lit.: a little pair; see COUPLE]

coupling ('kʌplɪŋ) n. **1.** a mechanical device that connects two things. **2.** a device for connecting railway cars or trucks together.

coupon ('kuːpɒn) n. **1. a.** a detachable part of a ticket or advertisement entitling the holder to a discount, free gift, etc. **b.** a detachable slip usable as a commercial order form. **c.** a voucher given away with certain goods, a certain number of which are exchangeable for goods offered by the manufacturers. **2.** one of a number of detachable certificates attached to a bond, the surrender of which entitles the bearer to receive interest payments. **3.** Brit. a detachable entry form for any of certain competitions, esp. football pools. [C19: from F, from OF colpon piece cut off, from colper to cut, var. of couper]

courage ('kʌrɪdʒ) n. **1.** the power or quality of dealing with or facing danger, fear, pain, etc. **2. the courage of one's convictions.** the confidence to act in accordance with one's beliefs. [C13: from OF corage, from cuer heart, from L cor]

courageous (kə'reɪdʒəs) adj. possessing or expressing courage. —**cou'rageously** adv. —**cou'rageousness** n.

courante (kʊ'rɑːnt) n. Music. **1.** an old dance in quick triple time. **2.** a movement of a (mostly) 16th- to 18th-century suite based on this. [C16: from F, lit.: running, from courir to run, from L currere]

Courantyne ('kɔːrən,taɪn) n. a river in N South America, rising in S Guyana and flowing north to the Atlantic, forming the boundary between Guyana and Surinam. Length: 765 km (475 miles). Dutch name: **Corantijn.**

Courbet (French kurbɛ) n. **Gustave** (gystav). 1819–77, French painter, a leader of the realist movement; noted for his depiction of contemporary life.

Courbevoie (French kurbəvwa) n. an industrial suburb of Paris, on the Seine. Pop.: 54 410 (1983 est.).

coureur de bois (*French* kurœr də bwa) *n., pl.* **coureurs de bois** (kurœr də bwa). *Canad. history.* a French Canadian woodsman or Métis who traded with Indians for furs. [Canad. F: trapper (lit.: wood-runner)]

courgette (kuə'ʒɛt) *n.* a small variety of vegetable marrow. U.S. and Canad. name: **zucchini.** [from F, dim. of *courge* marrow, gourd]

courier ('kuərɪə) *n.* **1.** a special messenger, esp. one carrying diplomatic correspondence. **2.** a person who makes arrangements for or accompanies a group of travellers on a journey or tour. [C16: from OF *courrier*, from OIt. *correre* to run, from L *currere*]

Courland *or* **Kurland** ('kuələnd) *n.* a region of the W Soviet Union, between the Gulf of Riga and the Lithuanian border: part of the Latvian SSR. Latvian name: **Kurzeme.**

Courrèges (*French* kurɛʒ) *n.* **André** (ɑ̃dre). born 1923, French couturier: helped to launch unisex fashion in the mid-1960s.

course (kɔːs) *n.* **1.** a continuous progression in time or space; onward movement. **2.** a route or direction followed. **3.** the path or channel along which something moves: *the course of a river.* **4.** an area or stretch of land or water on which a sport is played or a race is run: *a golf course.* **5.** a period of time; duration: *in the course of the next hour.* **6.** the usual order of and time required for a sequence of events; regular procedure: *the illness ran its course.* **7.** a mode of conduct or action: *if you follow that course, you will fail.* **8.** a connected series of events, actions, etc. **9. a.** a prescribed number of lessons, lectures, etc., in an educational curriculum. **b.** the material covered in such a curriculum. **10.** a regimen prescribed for a specific period of time: *a course of treatment.* **11.** a part of a meal served at one time. **12.** a continuous, usually horizontal, layer of building material, such as a row of bricks, tiles, etc. **13. as a matter of course.** as a natural or normal consequence, mode of action, or event. **14. in course of.** in the process of. **15. in due course.** at some future time, esp. the natural or appropriate time. **16. of course. a.** (*adv.*) as expected; naturally. **b.** (*sentence substitute*) certainly; definitely. **17. the course of nature.** the ordinary course of events. ~*vb.* **18.** (*intr.*) to run, race, or flow. **19.** to cause (hounds) to hunt by sight rather than scent or (of hounds) to hunt (a quarry) thus. [C13: from OF *cours*, from L *cursus* a running, from *currere* to run]

courser[1] ('kɔːsə) *n.* **1.** a person who courses hounds or dogs, esp. greyhounds. **2.** a hound or dog trained for coursing.

courser[2] ('kɔːsə) *n. Literary.* a swift horse; steed. [C13: from OF *coursier*, from *cours* COURSE]

courser[3] ('kɔːsə) *n.* a terrestrial plover-like shore bird of desert and semidesert regions of the Old World.

coursing ('kɔːsɪŋ) *n.* **1.** hunting with hounds or dogs that follow their quarry by sight. **2.** a sport in which hounds are matched against one another in pairs for the hunting of hares by sight.

court (kɔːt) *n.* **1.** an area of ground wholly or partly surrounded by walls or buildings. **2.** *Brit.* **a.** a block of flats. **b.** a mansion or country house. **c.** a short street, sometimes closed at one end. **3. a.** the residence, retinue, or household of a sovereign or nobleman. **b.** (*as modifier*): *a court ball.* **4.** a sovereign or prince and his retinue, advisers, etc. **5.** any formal assembly held by a sovereign or nobleman. **6.** homage, flattering attention, or amorous approaches (esp. in **pay court to someone**). **7.** *Law.* **a.** a tribunal having power to adjudicate in civil, criminal, military, or ecclesiastical matters. **b.** the regular sitting of such a judicial tribunal. **c.** the room or building in which such a tribunal sits. **8. a.** a marked outdoor or enclosed area used for any of various ball games, such as tennis, squash, etc. **b.** a marked section of such an area. **9. go to court.** to take legal action. **10. hold court.** to preside over admirers, attendants, etc. **11. out of court.** without a trial or legal case. **12. the ball is in your court.** you are obliged to make the next move. ~*vb.* **13.** to attempt to gain the love of; woo. **14.** (*tr.*) to pay attention to (someone) in order to gain favour. **15.** (*tr.*) to try to obtain (fame, honour, etc.). **16.** (*tr.*) to invite, usually foolishly, as by taking risks. [C12: from OF, from L *cohors* COHORT]

Court (kɔːt) *n.* **Margaret** (née *Smith*). born 1942, Australian tennis player: Australian champion 1960–66, 1969–

71, and 1973; U.S. champion 1962, 1965, 1969–70, and 1973; Wimbledon champion 1963, 1965, and 1970.

court-bouillon ('kuət'buːjɒn) *n.* a stock made from root vegetables, water, and wine or vinegar, used primarily for poaching fish. [from F, from *court* short, + *bouillon* broth, from *bouillir* to BOIL[1]]

court card *n.* (in a pack of playing cards) a king, queen, or jack of any suit. [C17: altered from earlier *coat-card*, from the decorative coats worn by the figures depicted]

court circular *n.* a daily report of the activities, engagements, etc., of the sovereign, published in a national newspaper.

Courtelle (kɔː'tɛl) *n. Trademark.* a synthetic acrylic fibre resembling wool.

courteous ('kɜːtɪəs) *adj.* polite and considerate in manner. [C13 *corteis,* lit.: with courtly manners, from OF; see COURT] —**'courteously** *adv.* —**'courteousness** *n.*

courtesan *or* **courtezan** (,kɔːtɪ'zæn) *n.* (esp. formerly) a prostitute, or the mistress of a man of rank. [C16: from OF *courtisane,* from It. *cortigiana* female courtier, from *corte* COURT]

courtesy ('kɜːtɪsɪ) *n., pl.* **-sies.** **1.** politeness; good manners. **2.** a courteous gesture or remark. **3.** favour or consent (esp. in **by courtesy of**). **4.** common consent as opposed to right (esp. in **by courtesy**). [C13 *curteisie,* from OF, from *corteis* COURTEOUS]

courtesy light *n.* the interior light in a motor vehicle.

courtesy title *n.* any of several titles having no legal significance, such as those borne by the children of peers.

courthouse ('kɔːt,haus) *n.* a public building in which courts of law are held.

courtier ('kɔːtɪə) *n.* **1.** an attendant at a court. **2.** a person who seeks favour in an ingratiating manner. [C13: from Anglo-F *courteour* (unattested), from OF *corteier* to attend at court]

courtly ('kɔːtlɪ) *adj.* **-lier, -liest.** **1.** of or suitable for a royal court. **2.** refined in manner. **3.** ingratiating. —**'courtliness** *n.*

court martial *n., pl.* **court martials** *or* **courts martial.** **1.** a military court that tries persons subject to military law. ~*vb.* **court-martial, -tialling, -tialled** *or U.S.* **-tialing, -tialed.** **2.** (*tr.*) to try by court martial.

Court of Appeal *n.* a court that hears appeals from the High Court and from the county and crown courts.

Court of St James's *n.* the official name of the royal court of Britain.

court plaster *n.* a plaster, composed of isinglass on silk, formerly used to cover superficial wounds. [C18: so called because formerly used by court ladies for beauty spots]

Courtrai (*French* kurtrɛ) *n.* a town in W Belgium, in West Flanders on the Lys River: the largest producer of linen in W Europe. Pop.: 76 110 (1985). Flemish name: **Kortrijk.**

courtroom ('kɔːt,ruːm, -,rum) *n.* a room in which the sittings of a law court are held.

courtship ('kɔːtʃɪp) *n.* **1.** the act, period, or art of seeking the love of someone with intent to marry. **2.** the seeking or soliciting of favours.

court shoe *n.* a low-cut shoe for women, without any laces or straps.

courtyard ('kɔːt,jɑːd) *n.* an open area of ground surrounded by walls or buildings; court.

couscous ('kuːskuːs) *n.* a spicy dish, originating in North Africa, consisting of steamed semolina served with a meat stew. [C17: via F from Ar. *kouskous,* from *kaskasa* to pound until fine]

cousin ('kʌz²n) *n.* **1.** Also called: **first cousin, cousin-german, full cousin.** the child of one's aunt or uncle. **2.** a relative descended from one of one's common ancestors. **3.** a title used by a sovereign when addressing another sovereign or a nobleman. [C13: from OF *cosin,* from L *consōbrīnus,* from *sōbrīnus* cousin on the mother's side] —**'cousin,hood** *or* **'cousin,ship** *n.* —**'cousinly** *adj., adv.*

Cousin (*French* kuzɛ̃) *n.* **Victor** (viktɔr). 1792–1867, French philosopher and educational reformer.

Cousteau (*French* kusto) *n.* **Jacques Yves** (ʒɑk iv). born 1910, French underwater explorer.

couture (kuː'tuə) *n.* high-fashion designing and dressmaking. [from F: sewing, from OF *cousture* seam, from L *consuere* to stitch together]

couturier (kuː'tuərɪ,eɪ) *n.* a person who designs, makes, and sells fashion clothes for women. [from F: dressmaker; see COUTURE] —**couturière** (ku,tuːrɪ'ɛə) *fem. n.*

couvade (kuː'vɑːd) *n. Anthropol.* the custom in certain cultures of treating the husband of a woman giving birth as if he were bearing the child. [C19: from F, from *couver* to hatch, from L *cubāre* to lie down]

covalency (kəʊ'veɪlənsɪ) *or U.S.* **covalence** *n.* **1.** the formation and nature of covalent bonds, that is, chemical bonds involving the sharing of electrons between atoms in a molecule. **2.** the number of covalent bonds that a particular atom can make with other atoms in forming a molecule. — **co'valent** *adj.* —**co'valently** *adv.*

cove[1] (kəʊv) *n.* **1.** a small bay or inlet. **2.** a narrow cavern in the side of a cliff, mountain, etc. **3.** Also called: **coving.** *Archit.* a concave curved surface between the wall and ceiling of a room. [OE *cofa*]

cove[2] (kəʊv) *n. Sl., Brit. old-fashioned & Austral.* a fellow; chap. [C16: prob. from Romany *kova* thing, person]

coven ('kʌvⁿn) *n.* a meeting of witches. [C16: prob. from OF *covin* group, ult. from L *convenīre* to come together]

covenant ('kʌvənənt) *n.* **1.** a binding agreement; contract. **2.** *Law.* an agreement in writing under seal, as to pay a stated annual sum to a charity. **3.** *Bible.* God's promise to the Israelites and their commitment to worship him alone. ~*vb.* **4.** to agree to a covenant (concerning). [C13: from OF, from *covenir* to agree, from L *convenīre* to come together, make an agreement; see CONVENE] —**covenantal** (ˌkʌvə'næntⁿl) *adj.* —**'covenantor** *or* **'covenanter** *n.*

Covenanter ('kʌvənəntə, ˌkʌvə'næntə) *n. Scot. history.* a person upholding either of two 17th-century covenants to establish and defend Presbyterianism.

Covent Garden ('kɒvənt, 'kʌv-) *n.* **1.** a district of central London: famous for its former fruit, vegetable, and flower market, now rebuilt as a shopping precinct. **2.** the Royal Opera House (built 1858) in Covent Garden.

Coventry ('kɒvəntrɪ) *n.* **1.** a city in central England, in the West Midlands: devastated in World War II; modern cathedral (1954–62); industrial centre, esp. for motor vehicles. Pop.: 314 100 (1984 est.). **2. send to Coventry.** to ostracize or ignore.

cover ('kʌvə) *vb. (mainly tr.)* **1.** to place or spread something over so as to protect or conceal. **2.** to provide with a covering; clothe. **3.** to put a garment, esp. a hat, on (the body or head). **4.** to extend over or lie thickly on the surface of: *snow covered the fields.* **5.** to bring upon (oneself); invest (oneself) as if with a covering: *covered with shame.* **6.** (sometimes foll. by *up*) to act as a screen or concealment for; hide from view. **7.** *Mil.* to protect (an individual, formation, or place) by taking up a position from which fire may be returned if those being protected are fired upon. **8.** (*also intr.,* sometimes foll. by *for*) to assume responsibility for (a person or thing). **9.** (*intr.;* foll. by *for* or *up for*) to provide an alibi (for). **10.** to have as one's territory: *this salesman covers your area.* **11.** to travel over. **12.** to have or place in the aim and within the range of (a firearm). **13.** to include or deal with. **14.** (of an asset or income) to be sufficient to meet (a liability or expense). **15. a.** to insure against loss, risk, etc. **b.** to provide for (loss, risk, etc.) by insurance. **16.** to deposit (an equivalent stake) in a bet. **17.** to act as reporter or photographer on (a news event, etc.) for a newspaper or magazine: *to cover sports events.* **18.** *Music.* to record a cover version of. **19.** *Sport.* to guard or protect (an opponent, team-mate, or area). **20.** (of a male animal, esp. a horse) to copulate with (a female animal). ~*n.* **21.** anything that covers, spreads over, protects, or conceals. **22. a.** a blanket used on a bed for warmth. **b.** another word for **bedspread.** **23.** a pretext, disguise, or false identity: *the thief sold brushes as a cover.* **24.** an envelope or package for sending through the post: *under plain cover.* **25. a.** an individual table setting, esp. in a restaurant. **b.** (*as modifier*): *a cover charge.* **26.** Also called: **cover version.** a version by a different artist of a previously recorded musical item. **27.** *Cricket.* a. (*often pl.*) the area more or less at right angles to the pitch on the off side and usually about halfway to the boundary. **b.** (*as modifier*): *a cover drive.* **28.** *Philately.* an entire envelope that has been postmarked. **29. break cover.** to come out from a shelter or hiding place. **30. take cover.** to make for a place of safety or shelter. **31. under cover.** protected, concealed, or in secret. ~ See also **cover-up.** [C13: from OF *covrir,* from L *cooperīre* to cover completely, from *operīre* to cover over] — **'coverable** *adj.* — **'coverer** *n.*

coverage ('kʌvərɪdʒ) *n.* **1.** the amount or extent to which something is covered. **2.** *Journalism.* the amount and quality of reporting or analysis given to a particular subject or event. **3.** the extent of the protection provided by insurance.

cover crop *n.* a crop planted between main crops to prevent leaching or soil erosion or to provide green manure.

Coverdale ('kʌvə,deɪl) *n.* **Miles.** 1488–1568, the first translator of the complete Bible into English (1535).

covered wagon *n. U.S. & Canad.* a large horse-drawn wagon with an arched canvas top, used formerly for prairie travel.

cover girl *n.* a glamorous girl whose picture appears on the cover of a magazine.

covering letter *n.* an accompanying letter sent as an explanation, introduction, or record.

coverlet ('kʌvəlɪt) *n.* another word for **bedspread.**

cover note *n. Brit.* a certificate issued by an insurance company stating that a policy is operative: used as a temporary measure between the commencement of cover and the issue of the policy.

cover point *n. Cricket.* **a.** a fielding position in the covers. **b.** a fielder in this position.

covert ('kʌvət) *adj.* **1.** concealed or secret. ~*n.* **2.** a shelter or disguise. **3.** a thicket or woodland providing shelter for game. **4.** short for **covert cloth. 5.** *Ornithol.* any of the small feathers on the wings and tail of a bird that surround the bases of the larger feathers. [C14: from OF: covered, from *covrir* to COVER] —**'covertly** *adv.*

covert cloth *n.* a twill-weave cotton or worsted suiting fabric.

coverture ('kʌvətʃə) *n. Rare.* shelter, concealment, or disguise. [C13: from OF, from *covert* covered; see COVERT]

cover-up *n.* **1.** concealment or attempted concealment of a mistake, crime, etc. ~*vb.* **cover up.** (*adv.*) **2.** (*tr.*) to cover completely. **3.** (when *intr.,* often foll. by *for*) to attempt to conceal (a mistake or crime).

cover version *n.* another name for **cover** (sense 26).

covet ('kʌvɪt) *vb. (tr.)* to wish, long, or crave for (something, esp. the property of another person). [C13: from OF *coveitier,* from *coveitié* eager desire, ult. from L *cupiditās* CUPIDITY] —**'covetable** *adj.*

covetous ('kʌvɪtəs) *adj. (usually postpositive and foll. by of)* jealously eager for the possession of something (esp. the property of another person). —**'covetously** *adv.* —**'covetousness** *n.*

covey ('kʌvɪ) *n.* **1.** a small flock of grouse or partridge. **2.** a small group, as of people. [C14: from OF *covee,* from *cover* to sit on, hatch]

cow[1] (kaʊ) *n.* **1.** the mature female of any species of cattle, esp. domesticated cattle. **2.** the mature female of various other mammals, such as the elephant, whale, and seal. **3.** (not in technical use) any domestic species of cattle. **4.** *Inf.* a disagreeable woman. **5.** *Austral. & N.Z. sl.* something objectionable (esp. in **a fair cow**). [OE *cū*]

cow[2] (kaʊ) *vb. (tr.)* to frighten or overawe, as with threats. [C17: from ON *kūga* to oppress]

coward ('kaʊəd) *n.* a person who shrinks from or avoids danger, pain, or difficulty. [C13: from OF *cuard,* from *coue* tail, from L *cauda;* ? suggestive of a frightened animal with its tail between its legs]

Coward ('kaʊəd) *n.* Sir **Noël** (**Pierce**). 1899–1973, English dramatist, actor, and composer, noted for his sophisticated comedies, which include *Private Lives* (1930) and *Blithe Spirit* (1941).

cowardice ('kaʊədɪs) *n.* lack of courage in facing danger, pain, or difficulty.

cowardly ('kaʊədlɪ) *adj.* of or characteristic of a coward; lacking courage. —**'cowardliness** *n.*

cowbell ('kaʊ,bɛl) *n.* a bell hung around a cow's neck so that the cow can be easily located.

cowberry ('kaʊbərɪ, -brɪ) *n., pl.* **-ries. 1.** a creeping evergreen shrub of N temperate and arctic regions, with pink or red flowers and edible slightly acid berries. **2.** the berry of this plant.

cowbird ('kaʊ,bɜːd) *n.* any of various American orioles, having dark plumage and a short bill.

cowboy ('kaʊ,bɔɪ) *n.* **1.** Also called: **cowhand,** a hired man who herds and tends cattle, usually on horseback, esp. in the western U.S. **2.** a conventional character of Wild West folklore, films, etc., esp. one involved in fighting Indians. **3.** *Inf.* an irresponsible or unscrupulous operator in business, etc. —**'cow,girl** *fem. n.*

cowcatcher ('kaʊ,kætʃə) n. U.S. & Canad. a metal frame on the front of a locomotive to clear the track of animals or other obstructions.

cow-cocky n., pl. **-cockies.** Austral. & N.Z. a one-man dairy farmer.

Cowdrey ('kaʊdrɪ) n. **(Michael) Colin.** born 1932, English cricketer. He played for Kent and in a record number of 114 Test matches (captaining England 27 times).

cower ('kaʊə) vb. (intr.) to crouch or cringe, as in fear. [C13: from MLow G kūren to lie in wait; rel. to Swedish kura]

Cowes (kaʊz) n. a town in S England, on the Isle of Wight: famous for its annual regatta. Pop.: 19 663 (1981).

cowherd ('kaʊ,hɜːd) n. a person employed to tend cattle.

cowhide ('kaʊ,haɪd) n. **1.** the hide of a cow. **2.** the leather made from such a hide.

cowl (kaʊl) n. **1.** a hood, esp. a loose one. **2.** the hooded habit of a monk. **3.** a cover fitted to a chimney to increase ventilation and prevent draughts. **4.** the part of a car body that supports the windscreen and the bonnet. ~vb. (tr.) **5.** to cover or provide with a cowl. [OE cugele, from LL cuculla cowl, from L cucullus hood]

Cowley ('kaʊlɪ) n. **Abraham.** 1618–67, English poet and essayist, influenced by the Metaphysical poets.

cowlick ('kaʊ,lɪk) n. a tuft of hair over the forehead.

cowling ('kaʊlɪŋ) n. a streamlined metal covering, esp. around an aircraft engine.

cowman ('kaʊmən) n., pl. **-men. 1.** Brit. another name for **cowherd. 2.** U.S. & Canad. a man who owns cattle; rancher.

co-worker n. a fellow worker; associate.

cow parsley n. a common Eurasian umbelliferous hedgerow plant having umbrella-shaped clusters of white flowers.

cowpat ('kaʊ,pæt) n. a single dropping of cow dung.

cowpea ('kaʊ,piː) n. **1.** a leguminous tropical climbing plant producing pods containing edible pealike seeds. **2.** the seed of this plant.

Cowper ('kuːpə, 'kaʊ-) n. **William.** 1731–1800, English poet, noted for his nature poetry, such as in The Task (1785), and his hymns.

cowpox ('kaʊ,pɒks) n. a contagious viral disease of cows characterized by vesicles, esp. on the teats and udder. Inoculation of humans with this virus provides temporary immunity to smallpox.

cowpuncher ('kaʊ,pʌntʃə) or **cowpoke** ('kaʊ,pəʊk) n. U.S. & Canad. an informal word for **cowboy.**

cowrie or **cowry** ('kaʊrɪ) n., pl. **-ries. 1.** any marine gastropod mollusc of a mostly tropical family having a glossy brightly marked shell. **2.** the shell of any of these molluscs, esp. the money cowrie, used as money in parts of Africa and S Asia. [C17: from Hindi kaurī, from Sansk. kaparda]

cowslip ('kaʊ,slɪp) n. **1.** a primrose native to temperate regions of the Old World, having yellow flowers. **2.** U.S. & Canad. another name for **marsh marigold.** [OE cūslyppe; see COW[1], SLIP[3]]

cox (kɒks) n. **1.** a coxswain. ~vb. **2.** to act as coxswain of (a boat). —'**coxless** adj.

Cox (kɒks) n. **David.** 1783–1859, English landscape painter.

coxa ('kɒksə) n., pl. **coxae** ('kɒksiː). **1.** a technical name for the hipbone or hip joint. **2.** the basal segment of the leg of an insect. [C18: from L: hip] —'**coxal** adj.

coxalgia (kɒk'sældʒɪə) n. **1.** pain in the hip joint. **2.** disease of the hip joint causing pain. [C19: from COXA + -ALGIA] —**cox'algic** adj.

coxcomb ('kɒks,kəʊm) n. **1.** a variant spelling of **cockscomb. 2.** Obs. the cap, resembling the cock's comb, worn by a jester. —'**cox,combry** n.

coxswain ('kɒksən, -,sweɪn) n. the helmsman of a lifeboat, racing shell, etc. Also called: **cockswain.** [C15: from cock a ship's boat + SWAIN]

coy (kɔɪ) adj. **1.** affectedly demure, esp. in a playful or provocative manner. **2.** shy; modest. **3.** evasive, esp. in an annoying way. [C14: from OF coi reserved, from L quiētus QUIET] —'**coyly** adv. —'**coyness** n.

Coy. Mil. abbrev. for company.

coyote ('kɔɪəʊt, kɔɪ'əʊtɪ; esp. U.S. 'kaɪəʊt, kaɪ'əʊtɪ) n., pl. **-otes** or **-ote.** a predatory canine mammal of the deserts and prairies of North America. Also called: **prairie wolf.** [C19: from Mexican Sp., from Nahuatl coyotl]

coypu ('kɔɪpuː) n., pl. **-pus** or **-pu. 1.** an aquatic South American rodent, naturalized in Europe. It resembles a small beaver and is bred for its fur. **2.** the fur of this animal. ~Also called: **nutria.** [C18: from American Sp. coipú, from Amerind kóypu]

coz (kʌz) n. an archaic word for **cousin.**

cozen ('kʌzᵊn) vb. to cheat or trick (someone). [C16: cant term ? rel. to COUSIN] —'**cozenage** n.

cozy ('kəʊzɪ) adj., n. the usual U.S. spelling of **cosy.**

cp abbrev. for candle power.

CP abbrev. for: **1.** Canadian Pacific Ltd. **2.** Common Prayer. **3.** Communist Party. **4.** (in Australia) Country Party.

cp. abbrev. for compare.

CPAG abbrev. for Child Poverty Action Group.

cpd abbrev. for compound.

Cpl abbrev. for Corporal.

CPO abbrev. for Chief Petty Officer.

cps Physics. abbrev. for cycles per second.

CPSA abbrev. for Civil and Public Services Association.

CQ a symbol transmitted by an amateur radio operator requesting communication with any other amateur radio operator.

Cr 1. abbrev. for Councillor. **2.** the chemical symbol for chromium.

cr. abbrev. for: **1.** credit. **2.** creditor.

crab[1] (kræb) n. **1.** any chiefly marine decapod crustacean having a broad flattened carapace covering the cephalothorax, beneath which is folded the abdomen. The first pair of limbs are pincers. **2.** any of various similar or related arthropods. **3.** short for **crab louse. 4.** a mechanical lifting device, esp. the travelling hoist of a gantry crane. **5. catch a crab.** Rowing. to make a stroke in which the oar either misses the water or digs too deeply, causing the rower to fall backwards. ~vb. **crabbing, crabbed. 6.** (intr.) to hunt or catch crabs. [OE crabba]

crab[2] (kræb) Inf. ~vb. **crabbing, crabbed. 1.** (intr.) to find fault; grumble. ~n. **2.** an irritable person. [C16: prob. back formation from CRABBED]

crab[3] (kræb) n. short for **crab apple.** [C15: ? of Scand. origin; cf. Swedish skrabbe crab apple]

Crab (kræb) n. **the.** the constellation Cancer, the fourth sign of the zodiac.

crab apple n. **1.** any of several rosaceous trees that have white, pink, or red flowers and small sour apple-like fruits. **2.** the fruit of any of these trees, used to make jam.

Crabbe (kræb) n. **George.** 1754–1832, English narrative poet, noted for his depiction of impoverished rural life in The Village (1783) and The Borough (1810).

crabbed ('kræbɪd) adj. **1.** surly; irritable; perverse. **2.** (esp. of handwriting) cramped and hard to decipher. **3.** Rare. abstruse. [C13: prob. from CRAB[1] (from its wayward gait), infl. by CRAB (APPLE) (from its tartness)] —'**crabbedly** adv. —'**crabbedness** n.

crabby ('kræbɪ) adj. **-bier, -biest.** bad-tempered.

crab louse n. a parasitic louse that infests the pubic region in man.

crabwise ('kræb,waɪz) adj., adv. (of motion) sideways; like a crab.

crack (kræk) vb. **1.** to break or cause to break without complete separation of the parts. **2.** to break or cause to break with a sudden sharp sound; snap. **3.** to make or cause to make a sudden sharp sound: to crack a whip. **4.** to cause (the voice) to change tone or become harsh or (of the voice) to change tone, esp. to a higher register; break. **5.** Inf. to fail or cause to fail. **6.** to yield or cause to yield. **7.** (tr.) to hit with a forceful or resounding blow. **8.** (tr.) to break into or force open: to crack a safe. **9.** (tr.) to solve or decipher (a code, problem, etc.). **10.** (tr.) Inf. to tell (a joke, etc.). **11.** to break (a molecule) into smaller molecules or radicals by the action of heat, as in the distillation of petroleum. **12.** (tr.) to open (a bottle) for drinking. **13.** (intr.) Scot. & N English dialect. to chat; gossip. **14.** (tr.) Inf. to achieve (esp. in **crack it**). **15. crack a smile.** Inf. to break into a smile. **16. crack hardy** or **hearty.** Austral. & N.Z. inf. to disguise one's discomfort, etc.; put on a bold front. ~n. **17.** a sudden sharp noise. **18.** a break or fracture without complete separation of the two parts. **19.** a narrow opening or fissure. **20.** Inf. a resounding blow. **21.** a physical or mental defect; flaw. **22.** a moment or specific instant: the crack of day. **23.** a broken or cracked tone of voice, as a boy's during puberty. **24.** (often foll. by *at*) *Inf.* an attempt; opportunity to try. **25.** *Sl.* a gibe; wisecrack; joke. **26.** *Sl.* a person that excels. **27.** *Scot. & N English dialect.* a talk; chat. **28.** *Sl.* a concentrated highly addictive form of cocaine made into pellets or powder and smoked. **29. a fair crack of the whip.** *Inf.* a fair chance or opportunity. **30. crack of doom.** doomsday; the end of the world; the Day of Judgment. ~*adj.* **31.** (*prenominal*) *Sl.* first-class; excellent: *a crack shot.* ~See also **crack down, crack up.** [OE *cracian*]

crackbrained ('kræk,breɪnd) *adj.* insane, idiotic, or crazy.

crack down *vb.* (*intr., adv.; often foll. by on*) **1.** to take severe measures (against); become stricter (with). ~*n.* **crackdown.** **2.** severe or repressive measures.

cracked (krækt) *adj.* **1.** damaged by cracking. **2.** *Inf.* crazy.

cracker ('krækə) *n.* **1.** a decorated cardboard tube that emits a bang when pulled apart, releasing a toy, a joke, or a paper hat. **2.** short for **firecracker.** **3.** a thin crisp biscuit, usually unsweetened. **4.** a person or thing that cracks. **5.** *Brit. sl.* a thing or person of notable qualities or abilities. **6.** See **catalytic cracker.**

crackerjack ('krækə,dʒæk) *Inf.* ~*adj.* **1.** excellent. ~*n.* **2.** a person or thing of exceptional quality or ability. [C20: changed from CRACK (first-class) + JACK (man)]

crackers ('krækəz) *adj.* (*postpositive*) *Brit.* a slang word for **insane.**

cracking ('krækɪŋ) *adj.* **1.** (*prenominal*) *Inf.* fast; vigorous (esp. in **a cracking pace**). **2. get cracking.** *Inf.* to start doing something quickly or with increased speed. ~*adv., adj.* **3.** *Brit. inf.* first-class; excellent. ~*n.* **4.** the process in which molecules are cracked, esp. the oil-refining process in which heavy oils are broken down into hydrocarbons of lower molecular weight by heat or catalysis.

crackjaw ('kræk,dʒɔ:) *Inf.* ~*adj.* **1.** difficult to pronounce. ~*n.* **2.** a word or phrase that is difficult to pronounce.

crackle ('kræk°l) *vb.* **1.** to make or cause to make a series of slight sharp noises, as of paper being crushed. **2.** (*tr.*) to decorate (porcelain or pottery) by causing fine cracks to appear in the glaze. **3.** (*intr.*) to abound in vivacity or energy. ~*n.* **4.** the act or sound of crackling. **5.** intentional crazing in the glaze of porcelain or pottery. **6.** Also called: **crackleware.** porcelain or pottery so decorated. —'**crackly** *adj.*

crackling ('kræklɪŋ) *n.* the crisp browned skin of roast pork.

crackpot ('kræk,pɒt) *Inf.* ~*n.* **1.** an eccentric person; crank. ~*adj.* **2.** eccentric; crazy.

crack up *vb.* (*adv.*) **1.** (*intr.*) to break into pieces. **2.** (*intr.*) *Inf.* to undergo a physical or mental breakdown. **3.** (*tr.*) *Inf.* to present or report, esp. in glowing terms: *it's not all it's cracked up to be.* ~*n.* **crackup.** **4.** *Inf.* a physical or mental breakdown.

Cracow ('krækaʊ, -əʊ, -ɒf) *n.* an industrial city in S Poland, on the River Vistula: former capital of the country (1320–1609); university (1364). Pop.: 722 900 (1981 est.). Polish name: **Kraków.** German name: **Krakau.**

-cracy *n. combining form.* indicating a type of government or rule: *plutocracy; mobocracy.* See also **-crat.** [from Gk *-kratia*, from *kratos* power]

cradle ('kreɪd°l) *n.* **1.** a baby's bed, often with rockers. **2.** a place where something originates. **3.** a frame, rest, or trolley made to support a piece of equipment, aircraft, ship, etc. **4.** a platform or trolley in which workmen are suspended on the side of a building or ship. **5.** *Agriculture.* **a.** a framework of several wooden fingers attached to a scythe to gather the grain into bunches as it is cut. **b.** a scythe with such a cradle. **6.** Also called: **rocker.** a boxlike apparatus for washing rocks, sand, etc., containing gold or gemstones. **7. rob the cradle.** *Inf.* to take for a lover, husband, or wife a person much younger than oneself. ~*vb.* (*tr.*) **8.** to rock or place in or as if in a cradle; hold tenderly. **9.** to nurture in or bring up from infancy. **10.** to wash (soil bearing gold, etc.) in a cradle. [OE *cradol*]

cradle snatcher *n. Inf.* another name for **baby snatcher** (sense 2).

cradlesong ('kreɪd°l,sɒŋ) *n.* a lullaby.

craft (krɑ:ft) *n.* **1.** skill or ability. **2.** skill in deception and trickery. **3.** an occupation or trade requiring special skill, esp. manual dexterity. **4. a.** the members of such a trade, regarded collectively. **b.** (*as modifier*): *a craft union.* **5.** a single vessel, aircraft, or spacecraft. **6.** (*functioning as pl.*) ships, boats, aircraft, or spacecraft collectively. ~*vb.* **7.** (*tr.*) to make or fashion with skill, esp. by hand. [OE *cræft* skill, strength]

craftsman ('krɑ:ftsmən) *n., pl.* **-men.** **1.** a member of a skilled trade; someone who practises a craft; artisan. **2.** an artist skilled in an art or craft. —'**craftsman,ship** *n.*

crafty ('krɑ:ftɪ) *adj.* **-tier, -tiest.** **1.** skilled in deception; shrewd; cunning. **2.** *Arch.* skilful. —'**craftily** *adv.* —'**craftiness** *n.*

crag (kræg) *n.* a steep rugged rock or peak. [C13: of Celtic origin]

craggy ('krægɪ) *or U.S.* **cragged** ('krægɪd) *adj.* **-gier, -giest.** **1.** having many crags. **2.** (of the face) rugged; rocklike. —'**cragginess** *n.*

Craig (kreɪg) *n.* **Edward Gordon.** 1872–1966, English theatrical designer, actor, and director. His nonrealistic scenic design greatly influenced theatre in Europe and the U.S.

Craigie ('kreɪgɪ) *n.* Sir **William A(lexander).** 1867–1957, Scottish lexicographer; joint editor of the *Oxford English Dictionary* (1901–33), and of *A Dictionary of American English on Historical Principles* (1938–44).

Craiova (*Romanian* krɑ'jova) *n.* a city in SW Romania, on the Jiul River. Pop.: 275 098 (1985).

crake (kreɪk) *n. Zool.* any of several rails of the Old World, such as the corncrake. [C14: from ON *krāka* crow or *krākr* raven, imit.]

cram (kræm) *vb.* **cramming, crammed.** **1.** (*tr.*) to force more (people, material, etc.) into (a room, container, etc.) than it can hold; stuff. **2.** to eat or cause to eat more than necessary. **3.** *Inf.* to study or cause to study (facts, etc.), esp. for an examination, by hastily memorizing. ~*n.* **4.** the act or condition of cramming. **5.** a crush. [OE *crammian*]

Cram (kræm) *n.* **Steve.** born 1960, English middle-distance runner: European 1500 m champion (1981, 1986); world 1500 m champion (1983); world one mile record holder (1985).

crambo ('kræmbəʊ) *n., pl.* **-boes.** a word game in which one team says a rhyme or rhyming line for a word or line given by the other team. [C17: from earlier *crambe*, prob. from L *crambē repetīta* cabbage repeated, hence an old story]

crammer ('kræmə) *n.* a person or school that prepares pupils for an examination.

cramp¹ (kræmp) *n.* **1.** a painful involuntary contraction of a muscle, typically caused by overexertion, heat, or chill. **2.** temporary partial paralysis of a muscle group: *writer's cramp.* **3.** (*usually pl. in the U.S. and Canada*) severe abdominal pain. ~*vb.* **4.** (*tr.*) to affect with or as if with a cramp. [C14: from OF *crampe*, of Gmc origin]

cramp² (kræmp) *n.* **1.** Also called: **cramp iron.** a strip of metal with its ends bent at right angles, used to bind masonry. **2.** a device for holding pieces of wood while they are glued; clamp. **3.** something that confines or restricts. ~*vb.* (*tr.*) **4.** to hold with a cramp. **5.** to confine or restrict. **6. cramp (someone's) style.** *Inf.* to prevent (a person) from using his abilities or acting freely and confidently. [C15: from MDu. *crampe* cramp, hook, of Gmc origin]

cramped (kræmpt) *adj.* **1.** closed in; restricted. **2.** (esp. of handwriting) small and irregular.

crampon ('kræmpən) *or* **crampoon** (kræm'puːn) *n.* **1.** one of a pair of pivoted steel levers used to lift heavy objects; grappling iron. **2.** (*often pl.*) one of a pair of frames each with 10 or 12 metal spikes, strapped to boots for climbing or walking on ice or snow. [C15: from F, from MDu. *crampe* hook; see CRAMP²]

cran (kræn) *n.* a unit of capacity used for fresh herring, equal to 37.5 gallons. [C18: from ?]

Cranach (*German* 'krɑːnax) *n.* **Lucas** ('luːkas). 1472–1553, German painter, etcher, and designer of woodcuts.

cranberry ('krænbərɪ, -brɪ) *n., pl.* **-ries.** **1.** any of several trailing shrubs that bear sour edible red berries. **2.** the berry of this plant. [C17: from Low G *kraanbere*, from *kraan* CRANE + *bere* BERRY]

crane (kreɪn) *n.* **1.** a large long-necked long-legged wading bird inhabiting marshes and plains in most parts of the world. **2.** (not in ornithological use) any similar bird, such as a heron. **3.** a device for lifting and moving heavy objects, typically consisting of a pivoted boom rotating about a vertical axis with lifting gear suspended from the end of the boom. ~*vb.* **4.** (*tr.*) to lift or move (an object) by or as if by a crane. **5.** to stretch out (esp. the neck), as to see over other people's heads. [OE *cran*]

Crane (kreɪn) *n.* **1.** (**Harold**) **Hart.** 1899–1932, U.S. poet; author of *The Bridge* (1930). **2. Stephen.** 1871–1900, U.S. novelist and short-story writer, noted particularly for his novel *The Red Badge of Courage* (1895).

crane fly *n.* a dipterous fly having long legs, slender wings, and a narrow body. Also called (Brit.): **daddy-longlegs.**

cranesbill ('kreɪnz,bɪl) *n.* any of various plants of the genus *Geranium*, having pink or purple flowers and long slender beaked fruits.

cranial ('kreɪnɪəl) *adj.* of or relating to the skull. —'**cranially** *adv.*

cranial index *n.* the ratio of the greatest length to the greatest width of the cranium, multiplied by 100.

cranial nerve *n.* any of the 12 paired nerves that have their origin in the brain.

craniate ('kreɪnɪɪt, -,eɪt) *adj.* **1.** having a skull or cranium. ~*adj.*, *n.* **2.** another word for **vertebrate.**

cranio- *or before a vowel* **crani-** *combining form.* indicating the cranium or cranial.

craniology (,kreɪnɪ'ɒlədʒɪ) *n.* the branch of science concerned with the shape and size of the human skull. —**craniological** (,kreɪnɪə'lɒdʒɪkəl) *adj.* —,**cranio'logically** *adv.* —,**crani'ologist** *n.*

craniometry (,kreɪnɪ'ɒmɪtrɪ) *n.* the study and measurement of skulls. —**craniometric** (,kreɪnɪə'metrɪk) *or* ,**cranio'metrical** *adj.* —,**cranio'metrically** *adv.* —,**crani'ometrist** *n.*

craniotomy (,kreɪnɪ'ɒtəmɪ) *n.*, *pl.* **-mies. 1.** surgical incision into the skull. **2.** surgical crushing of a fetal skull to extract a dead fetus.

cranium ('kreɪnɪəm) *n.*, *pl.* **-niums** *or* **-nia** (-nɪə). **1.** the skull of a vertebrate. **2.** the part of the skull that encloses the brain. [C16: from Med. L *crānium* skull, from Gk *kranion*]

crank (kræŋk) *n.* **1.** a device for communicating or converting motion, consisting of an arm projecting from a shaft, often with a second member attached to it parallel to the shaft. **2.** Also called: **crank handle, starting handle.** a handle incorporating a crank, used to start an engine or motor. **3.** *Inf.* **a.** an eccentric or odd person. **b.** *U.S. & Canad.* a bad-tempered person. ~*vb.* (*tr.*) **4.** to rotate (a shaft) by means of a crank. **5.** to start (an engine, motor, etc.) by means of a crank handle. [OE *cranc*]

crankcase ('kræŋk,keɪs) *n.* the metal housing that encloses the crankshaft, connecting rods, etc., in an internal-combustion engine.

Cranko ('kræŋkəʊ) *n.* **John.** 1927–73, British choreographer, born in South Africa: director of the Stuttgart Ballet (1961–73).

crankpin ('kræŋk,pɪn) *n.* a short cylindrical surface fitted between two arms of a crank parallel to the main shaft of the crankshaft.

crankshaft ('kræŋk,ʃɑːft) *n.* a shaft having one or more cranks, to which the connecting rods are attached.

crank up *vb.* (*tr.*, *adv.*) **1.** to start (an engine, motor, etc.) with a crank handle. **2.** *Sl.* to speed up.

cranky ('kræŋkɪ) *adj.* **crankier, crankiest. 1.** *Inf.* eccentric. **2.** *U.S., Canad., & Irish inf.* fussy and bad-tempered. **3.** shaky; out of order. —'**crankily** *adv.* —'**crankiness** *n.*

Cranmer ('krænmə) *n.* **Thomas.** 1489–1556, the first Protestant archbishop of Canterbury (1533–56) and principal author of the Book of Common Prayer. He was burnt as a heretic by Mary I.

crannog ('krænəg) *n.* an ancient Celtic lake or bog dwelling. [C19: from Irish Gaelic *crannóg*, from OIrish *crann* tree]

cranny ('krænɪ) *n.*, *pl.* **-nies.** a narrow opening, as in a wall or rock face; chink; crevice (esp. in **every nook and cranny**). [C15: from OF *cran* notch, fissure; cf. CRENEL] —'**crannied** *adj.*

Cranwell ('krænwəl) *n.* a village in E England, in Lincolnshire: Royal Air Force College (1920).

crap[1] (kræp) *n.* **1.** a losing throw in the game of craps. **2.** another name for **craps.** [C20: back formation from CRAPS]

crap[2] (kræp) *Sl.* ~*n.* **1.** nonsense. **2.** rubbish **3.** a taboo word for **faeces.** ~*vb.* **crapping, crapped. 4.** (*intr.*) a taboo word for **defecate.** [C15 *crappe* chaff, from MDu., prob. from *crappen* to break off]

crape (kreɪp) *n.* **1.** a variant spelling of **crepe. 2.** crepe, esp. when used for mourning clothes. **3.** a band of black crepe worn in mourning.

crap out *vb.* (*intr.*, *adv.*) *Sl.* **1.** *U.S.* to make a losing throw in craps. **2.** *U.S.* to fail; withdraw. **3.** to fail to attempt something through fear.

craps (kræps) *n.* (*usually functioning as sing.*) **1.** a gambling game using two dice. **2. shoot craps.** to play this game. [C19: prob. from *crabs* lowest throw at dice, pl. of CRAB[1]] —'**crap,shooter** *n.*

crapulent ('kræpjʊlənt) *or* **crapulous** ('kræpjʊləs) *adj.* **1.** given to or resulting from intemperance. **2.** suffering from intemperance; drunken. [C18: from LL *crāpulentus* drunk, from L *crāpula*, from Gk *kraipalē* drunkenness, headache resulting therefrom] —'**crapulence** *n.*

crash[1] (kræʃ) *vb.* **1.** to make or cause to make a loud noise as of solid objects smashing or clattering. **2.** to fall or cause to fall with force, breaking in pieces with a loud noise. **3.** (*intr.*) to break or smash in pieces with a loud noise. **4.** (*intr.*) to collapse or fail suddenly. **5.** to cause (an aircraft) to land violently resulting in severe damage or (of an aircraft) to land in this way. **6.** to cause (a car, etc.) to collide with another car or other object or (of two or more cars) to be involved in a collision. **7.** to move or cause to move violently or noisily. **8.** (*intr.*) (of a computer system or program) to fail suddenly because of a malfunction. **9.** *Brit. inf.* short for **gate-crash.** ~*n.* **10.** an act or instance of breaking and falling to pieces. **11.** a sudden loud noise. **12.** a collision, as between vehicles. **13.** a sudden descent of an aircraft as a result of which it hits land or water. **14.** the sudden collapse of a business, stock exchange, etc. **15.** (*modifier*) requiring or using intensive effort and all possible resources in order to accomplish something quickly: *a crash course*. [C14: prob. from *crasen* to smash, shatter + *dasshen* to strike violently, DASH[1]; see CRAZE]

crash[2] (kræʃ) *n.* a coarse cotton or linen cloth. [C19: from Russian *krashenina* coloured linen]

Crashaw ('kræʃɔː) *n.* **Richard.** 1613–49, English religious poet, noted esp. for the *Steps to the Temple* (1646).

crash barrier *n.* a barrier erected along the centre of a motorway, around a racetrack, etc., for safety purposes.

crash dive *n.* **1.** a sudden steep dive from the surface by a submarine. ~*vb.* **crash-dive. 2.** (*intr.*) (usually of an aircraft) to descend steeply and rapidly, before hitting the ground. **3.** to perform or cause to perform a crash dive.

crash helmet *n.* a padded helmet worn for motorcycling, flying, etc., to protect the head.

crashing ('kræʃɪŋ) *adj.* (*prenominal*) *Inf.* (intensifier) (esp. in **a crashing bore**).

crash-land *vb.* to land (an aircraft) causing some damage to it or (of an aircraft) to land in this way. —'**crash-,landing** *n.*

crass (kræs) *adj.* **1.** stupid; gross. **2.** *Rare.* thick or coarse. [C16: from L *crassus* thick, dense, gross] —'**crassly** *adv.* —'**crassness** *or* '**crassi,tude** *n.*

Crassus ('kræsəs) *n.* **Marcus Licinius** ('mɑːkəs lɪ'sɪnɪəs). ?115–53 B.C., Roman general; member of the first triumvirate with Caesar and Pompey.

-crat *n. combining form.* indicating a person who takes part in or is a member of a form of government or class. [from Gk *-kratēs*, from *-kratia* -CRACY] —**-cratic** *or* **-cratical** *adj. combining form.*

crate (kreɪt) *n.* **1.** a fairly large container, usually made of wooden slats or wickerwork, used for packing, storing, or transporting goods. **2.** *Sl.* an old car, aeroplane, etc. ~*vb.* **3.** (*tr.*) to pack or place in a crate. [C16: from L *crātis* wickerwork, hurdle] —'**crater** *n.* —'**crateful** *n.*

crater ('kreɪtə) *n.* **1.** the bowl-shaped opening in a volcano or a geyser. **2.** a similar depression formed by the impact of a meteorite or exploding bomb. **3.** any of the roughly circular or polygonal walled formations on the moon and some other planets. **4.** a large open bowl with two handles, used for mixing wines, esp. in ancient Greece. ~*vb.* **5.** to make or form craters in (a surface, such as the ground). [C17: from L: mixing bowl, crater, from Gk *kratēr*, from *kerannunai* to mix] —'**crater-,like** *adj.* —'**craterous** *adj.*

cravat (krə'væt) n. a scarf worn round the neck instead of a tie, esp. by men. [C17: from F *cravate*, from Serbo-Croatian *Hrvat* Croat; so called because worn by Croats in the French army during the Thirty Years' War]

crave (kreɪv) vb. **1.** (when *intr.*, foll. by *for* or *after*) to desire intensely; long (for). **2.** (*tr.*) to need greatly or urgently. **3.** (*tr.*) to beg or plead for. [OE *crafian*] —'**craver** n. —'**craving** n.

craven ('kreɪvᵊn) adj. **1.** cowardly. ~n. **2.** a coward. [C13 *cravant*, prob. from OF *crevant* bursting, from *crever* to burst, die, from L *crepāre* to burst, crack] —'**cravenly** adv. —'**cravenness** n.

craw (krɔː) n. **1.** a less common word for **crop** (sense 6). **2.** the stomach of an animal. **3. stick in one's craw.** *Inf.* to be difficult, or against one's conscience, for one to accept, utter, etc. [C14: rel. to MHG *krage*, MDu. *crāghe* neck, Icelandic *kragi* collar]

crawfish ('krɔːˌfɪʃ) n., pl. **-fish** or **-fishes.** a variant of **crayfish** (esp. sense 2).

crawl¹ (krɔːl) vb. (*intr.*) **1.** to move slowly, either by dragging the body along the ground or on the hands and knees. **2.** to proceed very slowly or laboriously. **3.** to act in a servile manner; fawn. **4.** to be or feel as if overrun by crawling creatures: *the pile of refuse crawled with insects.* **5.** (of insects, worms, snakes, etc.) to move with the body close to the ground. **6.** to swim the crawl. ~n. **7.** a slow creeping pace or motion. **8.** *Swimming.* a stroke in which the feet are kicked like paddles while the arms reach forward and pull back through the water. [C14: prob. from ON *krafla* to creep] —'**crawler** n. —'**crawlingly** adv.

crawl² (krɔːl) n. an enclosure in shallow, coastal water for fish, lobsters, etc. [C17: from Du. KRAAL]

crawler lane n. a lane on an uphill section of a motorway reserved for slow vehicles.

Crawley ('krɔːlɪ) n. a town in S England, in NE West Sussex: designated a new town in 1956. Pop.: 73 081 (1981).

crawly ('krɔːlɪ) adj. **crawlier, crawliest.** *Inf.* feeling or causing a sensation like creatures crawling on one's skin.

Craxi ('kræksɪ) n. **Bettino** (be'tiːno). born 1934, Italian socialist statesman; prime minister (1983–87).

crayfish ('kreɪˌfɪʃ) or esp. U.S. **crawfish** n., pl. **-fish** or **-fishes.** **1.** a freshwater decapod crustacean resembling a small lobster. **2.** any of various similar crustaceans, esp. the spiny lobster. [C14: *cray*, by folk etymology, from OF *crevice* crab, from OHG *krebiz* + fish]

crayon ('kreɪən, -ɒn) n. **1.** a small stick or pencil of charcoal, wax, clay, or chalk mixed with coloured pigment. **2.** a drawing made with crayons. ~vb. **3.** to draw or colour with crayons. [C17: from F, from *craie*, from L *crēta* chalk] —'**crayonist** n.

craze (kreɪz) n. **1.** a short-lived fashion. **2.** a wild or exaggerated enthusiasm. ~vb. **3.** to make or become mad. **4.** *Ceramics, metallurgy.* to develop or cause to develop fine cracks. [C14 (in the sense: to break, shatter): prob. from ON]

crazy ('kreɪzɪ) adj. **-zier, -ziest. 1.** *Inf.* insane. **2.** fantastic; strange; ridiculous. **3.** (*postpositive;* foll. by *about* or *over*) *Inf.* extremely fond (of). —'**crazily** adv. —'**craziness** n.

crazy paving n. *Brit.* a form of paving, as for a path, made of irregular slabs of stone.

creak (kriːk) vb. **1.** to make or cause to make a harsh squeaking sound. **2.** (*intr.*) to make such sounds while moving: *the old car creaked along.* ~n. **3.** a harsh squeaking sound. [C14: var. of CROAK, imit.] —'**creaky** adj. —'**creakily** adv. —'**creakiness** n. —'**creakingly** adv.

cream (kriːm) n. **1. a.** the fatty part of milk, which rises to the top. **b.** (*as modifier*): *cream buns.* **2.** anything resembling cream in consistency. **3.** the best one or most essential part of something; pick. **4.** a soup containing cream or milk: *cream of chicken soup.* **5.** any of various foods resembling or containing cream. **6. a.** a yellowish-white colour. **b.** (*as adj.*): *cream wallpaper.* ~vb. (*tr.*) **7.** to skim or otherwise separate the cream from (milk). **8.** to beat (foodstuffs) to a light creamy consistency. **9.** to add or apply cream or any creamlike substance to. **10.** (sometimes foll. by *off*) to take away the best part of. **11.** to prepare or cook (vegetables, chicken, etc.) with cream or milk. [C14: from OF *cresme*, from LL *crāmum* cream, of Celtic origin; infl. by Church L *chrisma* unction, CHRISM] —'**cream,like** adj.

cream cheese n. a smooth soft white cheese made from soured cream or milk.

cream cracker n. *Brit.* a crisp unsweetened biscuit, often eaten with cheese.

creamer ('kriːmə) n. **1.** a vessel or device for separating cream from milk. **2.** a powdered substitute for cream, used in coffee. **3.** *Now chiefly U.S. & Canad.* a small jug or pitcher for serving cream.

creamery ('kriːmərɪ) n., pl. **-eries. 1.** an establishment where milk and cream are made into butter and cheese. **2.** a place where dairy products are into.

cream of tartar n. potassium hydrogen tartrate, esp. when used in baking powders.

cream puff n. a shell of light pastry with a custard or cream filling.

cream soda n. a soft drink flavoured with vanilla.

cream tea n. afternoon tea including bread or scones served with clotted cream and jam.

creamy ('kriːmɪ) adj. **creamier, creamiest. 1.** resembling cream in colour, taste, or consistency. **2.** containing cream. —'**creaminess** n.

crease (kriːs) n. **1.** a line or mark produced by folding, pressing, or wrinkling. **2.** a wrinkle or furrow, esp. on the face. **3.** *Cricket.* any three lines near each wicket marking positions for the bowler or batsman. ~vb. **4.** to make or become wrinkled or furrowed. **5.** (*tr.*) to graze with a bullet. [C15: from earlier *crēst;* prob. rel. to OF *cresté* wrinkled] —'**creaser** n. —'**creasy** adj.

create (kriː'eɪt) vb. **1.** (*tr.*) to cause to come into existence. **2.** (*tr.*) to invest with a new honour, office, or title; appoint. **3.** (*tr.*) to be the cause of. **4.** (*tr.*) to act (a role) in the first production of a play. **5.** (*intr.*) *Brit. sl.* to make a fuss or uproar. [C14 *creat* created, from L *creātus,* from *creāre* to produce, make]

creatine ('kriːəˌtiːn, -tɪn) n. an important compound involved in many biochemical reactions and present in many types of living cells. [C19: from Gk *kreas* flesh + -INE²]

creation (kriː'eɪʃən) n. **1.** the act or process of creating. **2.** the fact of being created or produced. **3.** something brought into existence or created. **4.** the whole universe.

Creation (kriː'eɪʃən) n. *Christianity.* **1.** (often preceded by *the*) God's act of bringing the universe into being. **2.** the universe as thus brought into being by God.

creative (kriː'eɪtɪv) adj. **1.** having the ability to create. **2.** characterized by originality of thought; having or showing imagination. **3.** designed to or tending to stimulate the imagination. —**cre'atively** adv. —**cre'ativeness** n. —,**crea'tivity** n.

creator (kriː'eɪtə) n. a person or thing that creates; originator. —**cre'ator,ship** n.

Creator (kriː'eɪtə) n. (usually preceded by *the*) an epithet of God.

creature ('kriːtʃə) n. **1.** a living being, esp. an animal. **2.** something that has been created, whether animate or inanimate. **3.** a human being; person: used as a term of scorn, pity, or endearment. **4.** a person who is dependent upon another; tool. [C13: from Church L *crēatūra,* from L *crēare* to create] —'**creatural** or '**creaturely** adj.

crèche (krɛʃ, kreɪʃ) n. **1.** *Chiefly Brit.* a day nursery for very young children. **2.** a tableau of Christ's Nativity. [C19: from OF: manger, crib, ult. of Gmc origin]

Crécy ('kresɪ; *French* kresi) n. a village in N France: scene of the first decisive battle of the Hundred Years' War when the English defeated the French (1346). Official name: **Crécy-en-Ponthieu** (-ãpɔ̃tjø). English name: **Cressy.**

credence ('kriːdᵊns) n. **1.** acceptance or belief, esp. with regard to the evidence of others. **2.** something supporting a claim to belief; credential (esp. in **letters of credence**). **3.** short for **credence table.** [C14: from Med. L *crēdentia* trust, credit, from L *crēdere* to believe]

credence table n. *Christianity.* a small table on which the Eucharistic bread and wine are placed.

credential (krɪ'dɛnʃəl) n. **1.** something that entitles a person to confidence, authority, etc. **2.** (*pl.*) a letter or certificate giving evidence of the bearer's identity or competence. [C16: from Med. L *crēdentia* credit, trust; see CREDENCE]

credenza (krɪ'dɛnzə) n. another name for **credence table.** [It.: see CREDENCE]

credibility gap *n.* a disparity between claims or statements made and the evident facts of the situation or circumstances to which they relate.

credible ('krɛdɪbªl) *adj.* **1.** capable of being believed. **2.** trustworthy. [C14: from L *crēdibilis*, from L *crēdere* to believe] —'**credibleness** *or* ,credi'**bility** *n.* —'**credibly** *adv.*

credit ('krɛdɪt) *n.* **1.** commendation or approval, as for an act or quality. **2.** a person or thing serving as a source of good influence, repute, etc. **3.** influence or reputation coming from the good opinion of others. **4.** belief in the truth, reliability, quality, etc., of someone or something. **5.** a sum of money or equivalent purchasing power, available for a person's use. **6. a.** the positive balance in a person's bank account. **b.** the sum of money that a bank makes available to a client in excess of any deposit. **7. a.** the practice of permitting a buyer to receive goods or services before payment. **b.** the time permitted for paying for such goods or services. **8.** reputation for solvency and probity, inducing confidence among creditors. **9.** *Accounting.* **a.** acknowledgment of an income, liability, or capital item by entry on the right-hand side of an account. **b.** the right-hand side of an account. **c.** an entry on this side. **d.** the total of such entries. **e.** (*as modifier*): *credit entries*. **10.** *Education.* **a.** a distinction awarded to an examination candidate obtaining good marks. **b.** a section of an examination syllabus satisfactorily completed. **11. on credit.** with payment to be made at a future date. ~*vb.* (*tr.*) **12.** (foll. by *with*) to ascribe (to); give credit (for). **13.** to accept as true; believe. **14.** to do credit to. **15.** *Accounting.* **a.** to enter (an item) as a credit in an account. **b.** to acknowledge (a payer) by making such an entry. ~See also **credits.** [C16: from OF *crédit*, from It. *credito*, from L *crēditum* loan, from *crēdere* to believe]

creditable ('krɛdɪtəbªl) *adj.* deserving credit, honour, etc.; praiseworthy. —'**creditableness** *or* ,credita'**bility** *n.* —'**creditably** *adv.*

credit account *n. Brit.* a credit system by means of which customers may obtain goods and services before payment.

credit card *n.* a card issued by banks, businesses, etc., enabling the holder to obtain goods and services on credit.

Creditiste (,krɛdɪ'ti:st) *Canad.* ~*adj.* **1.** of, supporting, or relating to the Social Credit Rally of Quebec. ~*n.* **2.** a supporter or member of this organization.

creditor ('krɛdɪtə) *n.* a person or commercial enterprise to whom money is owed.

credit rating *n.* an evaluation of the creditworthiness of an individual or business.

credits ('krɛdɪts) *pl. n.* a list of those responsible for the production of a film or a television programme.

creditworthy ('krɛdɪt,wɜːðɪ) *adj.* (of an individual or business) adjudged as meriting credit on the basis of earning power, previous record of debt repayment, etc. —'**credit,worthiness** *n.*

credo ('kri:dəʊ, 'kreɪ-) *n., pl.* **-dos.** any formal statement of beliefs, principles, or opinions.

Credo ('kri:dəʊ, 'kreɪ-) *n., pl.* **-dos.** **1.** the Apostles' or Nicene Creed. **2.** a musical setting of the Creed. [C12: from L, lit.: I believe; first word of the Apostles' and Nicene Creeds]

credulity (krɪ'dju:lɪtɪ) *n.* disposition to believe something on little evidence; gullibility.

credulous ('krɛdjʊləs) *adj.* **1.** tending to believe something on little evidence. **2.** arising from or characterized by credulity: *credulous beliefs*. [C16: from L *crēdulus*, from *crēdere* to believe] —'**credulously** *adv.* —'**credulousness** *n.*

Cree (kri:) *n.* **1.** (*pl.* **Cree** *or* **Crees**) a member of a N American Indian people living in Ontario, Saskatchewan, and Manitoba. **2.** the language of this people.

creed (kri:d) *n.* **1.** a concise, formal statement of the essential articles of Christian belief, such as the Apostles' Creed or the Nicene Creed. **2.** any statement or system of beliefs or principles. [OE *crēda*, from L *crēdo* I believe] —'**creedal** *or* '**credal** *adj.*

Creed (kri:d) *n.* Frederick. 1871–1957, Canadian inventor, resident in Scotland from 1897, noted for his invention of the teleprinter, first used in 1912.

creek (kri:k) *n.* **1.** *Chiefly Brit.* a narrow inlet or bay, esp. of the sea. **2.** *U.S., Canad., Austral., & N.Z.* a small stream or tributary. **3. up the creek.** *Sl.* in trouble; in a difficult position. [C13: from ON *kriki* nook; rel. to MDu. *krēke* creek, inlet]

Creek (kri:k) *n.* **1.** (*pl.* **Creek** *or* **Creeks**) a member of a confederacy of N American Indian tribes formerly living in Georgia and Alabama. **2.** any of their languages.

creel (kri:l) *n.* **1.** a wickerwork basket, esp. one used to hold fish. **2.** a wickerwork trap for catching lobsters, etc. [C15: from Scot., from ?]

creep (kri:p) *vb.* **creeping, crept.** (*intr.*) **1.** to crawl with the body near to or touching the ground. **2.** to move slowly, quietly, or cautiously. **3.** to act in a servile way; fawn; cringe. **4.** to move or slip out of place, as from pressure or wear. **5.** (of plants) to grow along the ground or over rocks. **6.** to develop gradually: *creeping unrest.* **7.** to have the sensation of something crawling over the skin. ~*n.* **8.** the act of creeping or a creeping movement. **9.** *Sl.* a person considered to be obnoxious or servile. **10.** *Geol.* the gradual downward movement of loose rock material, soil, etc., on a slope. [OE *crēopan*]

creeper ('kri:pə) *n.* **1.** a person or animal that creeps. **2.** a plant, such as the ivy, that grows by creeping. **3.** the U.S. and Canad. name for the **tree creeper.** **4.** a hooked instrument for dragging deep water. **5.** *Inf.* a shoe with a soft sole.

creeps (kri:ps) *pl. n.* (preceded by *the*) *Inf.* a feeling of fear, repulsion, disgust, etc.

creepy ('kri:pɪ) *adj.* **-ier, -iest. 1.** *Inf.* having or causing a sensation of repulsion or fear, as of creatures crawling on the skin. **2.** creeping; slow-moving. —'**creepily** *adv.* —'**creepiness** *n.*

creepy-crawly *Brit. inf.* ~*n., pl.* **-crawlies. 1.** a small crawling creature. ~*adj.* **2.** feeling or causing a sensation as of creatures crawling on one's skin.

cremate (krɪ'meɪt) *vb.* (*tr.*) to burn up (something, esp. a corpse) and reduce to ash. [C19: from L *cremāre*] —**cre'mation** *n.* —**cre'mator** *n.* —**crematory** ('krɛmətərɪ, -trɪ) *adj.*

crematorium (,krɛmə'tɔːrɪəm) *n., pl.* **-riums** *or* **-ria** (-rɪə). *Brit.* a building in which corpses are cremated. Also called (esp. U.S.): **crematory.**

crème (krɛm, kri:m, kreɪm; *French* krɛm) *n.* **1.** cream. **2.** any of various sweet liqueurs: *crème de moka.* ~*adj.* **3.** (of a liqueur) rich and sweet.

crème de la crème *French.* (krɛm də la krɛm) *n.* the very best. [lit.: cream of the cream]

crème de menthe ('krɛm də 'mɛnθ, 'mɪnt; 'kri:m, 'kreɪm) *n.* a liqueur flavoured with peppermint. [F, lit.: cream of mint]

Cremona (*Italian* kre'mo:na) *n.* a city in N Italy, in Lombardy on the River Po: noted for the manufacture of fine violins in the 16th–18th centuries. Pop.: 80 929 (1981).

crenate ('kri:neɪt) *or* **crenated** *adj.* having a scalloped margin, as certain leaves. [C18: from NL *crēnātus*, from Med. L, prob. from LL *crēna* a notch] —'**crenately** *adv.* —**crenation** (krɪ'neɪʃən) *n.*

crenel ('krɛnªl) *or* **crenelle** (krɪ'nɛl) *n.* any of a set of openings formed in the top of a wall or parapet and having slanting sides, as in a battlement. [C15: from OF, lit.: a little notch, from *cren* notch, from LL *crēna*]

crenellate *or U.S.* **crenelate** ('krɛnɪ,leɪt) *vb.* (*tr.*) to supply with battlements. [C19: from OF *creneler*, from CRENEL] —'**crenel,lated** *or U.S.* '**crenel,ated** *adj.* —,**crenel'lation** *or U.S.* ,**crenel'ation** *n.*

creole ('kri:əʊl) *n.* **1.** a language that has its origin in extended contact between two language communities, one of which is European. ~*adj.* **2.** of or relating to creole. **3.** (of a sauce or dish) containing or cooked with tomatoes, green peppers, onions, etc. [C17: via F & Sp., prob. from Port. *crioulo* slave born in one's household, prob. from *criar* to bring up, from L *creāre* to CREATE]

Creole ('kri:əʊl) *n.* **1.** (*sometimes not cap.*) (in the West Indies and Latin America) **a.** a native-born person of European ancestry. **b.** a native-born person of mixed European and Negro ancestry who speaks a creole. **2.** (in Louisiana and other Gulf States of the U.S.) a native-born person of French ancestry. **3.** the French Creole spoken in Louisiana. ~*adj.* **4.** of or relating to any of these peoples.

Creon ('kri:ɒn) *n. Greek myth.* the successor to Oedipus as king of Thebes; the brother of Jocasta. See also **Antigone.**

creosol ('kri:ə,sɒl) *n.* a colourless or pale yellow insoluble oily liquid with a smoky odour and a burning taste. [C19: from CREOS(OTE) + -OL¹]

creosote ('krɪə,səʊt) *n.* **1. a** colourless or pale yellow liquid with a burning taste and penetrating odour distilled from wood tar. It is used as an antiseptic. **2.** a thick dark liquid mixture prepared from coal tar: used as a preservative for wood. ~*vb.* **3.** to treat (wood) with creosote. [C19: from Gk *kreas* flesh + *sōtēr* preserver, from *sōzein* to keep safe] —**creosotic** (,krɪə'sɒtɪk) *adj.*

crepe *or* **crape** (kreɪp) *n.* **1. a.** a light cotton, silk, or other fabric with a fine ridged or crinkled surface. **b.** (*as modifier*): *a crepe dress.* **2.** a black armband originally made of this, worn as a sign of mourning. **3.** a very thin pancake, often folded around a filling. **4.** short for **crepe paper** *or* **crepe rubber**. [C19: from F *crêpe*, from L *crispus* curled, uneven, wrinkled]

crepe de Chine (kreɪp də ʃiːn) *n.* a very thin crepe of silk or a similar light fabric. [C19: from F: Chinese crepe]

crepe paper *n.* thin crinkled coloured paper, resembling crepe and used for decorations.

creperie ('krepərɪ, 'kreɪp-) *n.* an eating establishment that specializes in pancakes.

crepe rubber *n.* a type of rubber in the form of colourless or pale yellow crinkled sheets: used for the soles of shoes.

crêpe suzette (kreɪp suːˈzɛt) *n.*, *pl.* **crêpes suzettes.** (*sometimes pl.*) an orange-flavoured pancake flambéed in a liqueur or brandy.

crepitate ('krepɪ,teɪt) *vb.* (*intr.*) to make a rattling or crackling sound. [C17: from L *crepitāre*] —**crepitant** *adj.* —,**crepi'tation** *n.*

crepitus ('krepɪtəs) *n.* **1.** a crackling chest sound heard in pneumonia, etc. **2.** the grating sound of two ends of a broken bone rubbing together. [C19: from L, from *crepāre* to crack, creak]

crept (krept) *vb.* the past tense and past participle of **creep.**

crepuscular (krɪˈpʌskjʊlə) *adj.* **1.** of or like twilight; dim. **2.** (of certain creatures) active at twilight or just before dawn. [C17: from L *crepusculum* dusk, from *creper* dark]

crepy *or* **crepey** ('kreɪpɪ) *adj.* **crepier, crepiest.** (esp. of the skin) having a dry wrinkled appearance.

Cres. *abbrev. for* Crescent.

crescendo (krɪˈʃendəʊ) *n.*, *pl.* **-dos** *or* **-di** (-dɪ). **1.** *Music.* **a.** a gradual increase in loudness or the musical direction or symbol indicating this. Abbrev.: **cresc.** Symbol: < **b.** (*as modifier*): *a crescendo passage.* **2.** any similar gradual increase in loudness. ~*vb.* **-doing, -doed. 3.** (*intr.*) to increase in loudness or force. ~*adv.* **4.** with a crescendo. [C18: from It., lit.: increasing, from *crescere* to grow, from L]

crescent ('kresᵊnt, -zᵊnt) *n.* **1.** the biconcave shape of the moon in its first or last quarter. **2.** any shape or object resembling this. **3.** *Chiefly Brit.* a crescent-shaped street. **4.** (*often cap.* and preceded by *the*) **a.** the emblem of Islam or Turkey. **b.** Islamic or Turkish power. ~*adj.* **5.** *Arch. or poetic.* increasing or growing. [C14: from L *crescēns* increasing, from *crescere* to grow]

cresol ('kri:sɒl) *n.* an aromatic compound found in coal tar and creosote and used in making synthetic resins and as an antiseptic and disinfectant. Formula: $C_6H_4(CH_3)OH$.

cress (kres) *n.* any of various plants having pungent-tasting leaves often used in salads and as a garnish. [OE *cressa*]

cresset ('kresɪt) *n. History.* a metal basket mounted on a pole in which oil or pitch was burned for illumination. [C14: from OF *craisset*, from *craisse* GREASE]

Cressida ('kresɪdə), **Criseyde,** *or* **Cressid** *n.* (in medieval adaptations of the story of Troy) a lady who deserts her Trojan lover Troilus for the Greek Diomedes.

Cressy ('kresɪ) *n. Rare.* the English name for **Crécy.**

crest (krest) *n.* **1.** a tuft or growth of feathers, fur, or skin along the top of the heads of some birds, reptiles, and other animals. **2.** something resembling or suggesting this. **3.** the top, highest point, or highest stage of something. **4.** an ornamental piece, such as a plume, on top of a helmet. **5.** *Heraldry.* a symbol of a family or office, borne in addition to a coat of arms and used in medieval times to decorate the helmet. ~*vb.* **6.** (*intr.*) to come or rise to a high point. **7.** (*tr.*) to lie at the top of; cap. **8.** (*tr.*) to reach the top of (a hill, wave, etc.). [C14: from OF *creste*, from L *crista*] —**crested** *adj.* —**crestless** *adj.*

crestfallen ('krest,fɔːlən) *adj.* dejected or disheartened. —**crest,fallenly** *adv.*

cretaceous (krɪˈteɪʃəs) *adj.* consisting of or resembling chalk. [C17: from L *crētāceus*, from *crēta*, lit.: Cretan earth, that is, chalk]

Cretaceous (krɪˈteɪʃəs) *adj.* **1.** of, denoting, or formed in the last period of the Mesozoic era, during which chalk deposits were formed. ~*n.* **2. the.** the Cretaceous period or rock system.

Crete (kriːt) *n.* a mountainous island in the E Mediterranean, the largest island of Greece: of archaeological importance for the ruins of Minoan civilization. Capital: Canea (Khaniá). Pop.: 502 165 (1981). Area: 8331 sq. km (3216 sq. miles). Modern Greek name: **Kríti.** —**'Cretan** *adj., n.*

cretin ('kretɪn) *n.* **1.** a person afflicted with cretinism. **2.** a person considered to be extremely stupid. [C18: from F *crétin*, from Swiss F *crestin*, from L *Christiānus* Christian, alluding to the humanity of such people, despite their handicaps] —**'cretinous** *adj.*

cretinism ('kretɪ,nɪzəm) *n.* a condition arising from a deficiency of thyroid hormone, present from birth, characterized by dwarfism and mental retardation. See also **myxoedema.**

cretonne (kreˈtɒn, 'kretɒn) *n.* a heavy cotton or linen fabric with a printed design, used for furnishing. [C19: from F, from *Creton* Norman village where it originated]

Creuse (*French* krøz) *n.* a department of central France, in Limousin region. Capital: Guéret. Pop.: 139 968 (1982). Area: 5606 sq. km (2186 sq. miles).

crevasse (krɪˈvæs) *n.* **1.** a deep crack or fissure, esp. in the ice of a glacier. **2.** *U.S.* a break in a river embankment. ~*vb.* **3.** (*tr.*) *U.S.* to make a break or fissure in (a dyke, wall, etc.). [C19: from F: CREVICE]

crevice ('krevɪs) *n.* a narrow fissure or crack; split; cleft. [C14: from OF *crevace*, from *crever* to burst, from L *crepāre* to crack]

crew¹ (kruː) *n.* (*sometimes functioning as pl.*) **1.** the men who man a ship, boat, aircraft, etc. **2.** *Naut.* a group of people assigned to a particular job or type of work. **3.** *Inf.* a gang, company, or crowd. ~*vb.* **4.** to serve on (a ship) as a member of the crew. [C15 *crue* (military) reinforcement, from OF *creue* augmentation, from OF *creistre* to increase, from L *crescere*]

crew² (kruː) *vb. Arch.* a past tense of **crow¹.**

crew cut *n.* a closely cropped haircut for men. [C20: from the style of haircut worn by the boat crews at Harvard and Yale Universities]

Crewe (kruː) *n.* a town in NW England, in Cheshire: major railway junction. Pop.: 47 759 (1981).

crewel ('kruːɪl) *n.* a loosely twisted worsted yarn, used in fancy work and embroidery. [C15: from ?] —**'crewelist** *n.* —**'crewel,work** *n.*

crew neck *n.* a plain round neckline in sweaters. —**'crew-,neck** *or* **'crew-,necked** *adj.*

crib (krɪb) *n.* **1.** a child's bed with slatted wooden sides; cot. **2.** a cattle stall or pen. **3.** a fodder rack or manger. **4.** a small crude cottage or room. **5.** *N.Z.* a weekend cottage: term is South Island usage only. **6.** any small confined space. **7.** a representation of the manger in which the infant Jesus was laid at birth. **8.** *Inf.* a theft, esp. of another's writing or thoughts. **9.** *Inf.*, *chiefly Brit.* a translation of a foreign text or a list of answers used by students, often illicitly, as an aid in lessons, examinations, etc. **10.** short for **cribbage. 11.** *Cribbage.* the discard pile. **12.** Also called: **cribwork.** a framework of heavy timbers used in the construction of foundations, mines, etc. ~*vb.* **cribbing, cribbed. 13.** (*tr.*) to put or enclose in or as if in a crib; furnish with a crib. **14.** (*tr.*) *Inf.* to steal (another's writings or thoughts). **15.** (*intr.*) *Inf.* to copy either from a crib or from someone else during a lesson or examination. **16.** (*intr.*) *Inf.* to grumble. [OE *cribb*] —**'cribber** *n.*

cribbage ('krɪbɪdʒ) *n.* a game of cards for two to four, in which players try to win a set number of points before their opponents. [C17: from ?]

cribbage board *n.* a board, with pegs and holes, used for scoring at cribbage.

crib-biting *n.* a harmful habit of horses in which the animal leans on the manger or seizes it with the teeth and swallows a gulp of air.

Crichton ('kraɪtᵊn) n. **James.** 1560–82, Scottish scholar and poet, called *the Admirable Crichton* because of his talents.

crick (krɪk) *Inf.* ~n. **1.** a painful muscle spasm or cramp, esp. in the neck or back. ~vb. **2.** (*tr.*) to cause a crick in. [C15: from ?]

Crick (krɪk) n. **Francis Harry Compton.** born 1916, English molecular biologist: helped to discover the helical structure of DNA; Nobel prize for physiology or medicine shared with James Watson and Maurice Wilkins 1962.

cricket¹ ('krɪkɪt) n. an insect having long antennae and, in the males, the ability to produce a chirping sound by rubbing together the leathery forewings. [C14: from OF *criquet*, from *criquer* to creak, imit.]

cricket² ('krɪkɪt) n. **1. a.** a game played by two teams of eleven players on a field with a wicket at either end of a 22-yard pitch, the object being for one side to score runs by hitting a hard leather-covered ball with a bat while the other side tries to dismiss them by bowling, catching, running them out, etc. **b.** (*as modifier*): *a cricket bat.* **2. not cricket.** *Inf.* not fair play. ~vb. (*intr.*) **3.** to play cricket. [C16: from OF *criquet* goal post, wicket, from ?] —'**cricketer** n.

cricket³ ('krɪkɪt) n. a small low stool. [C17: from ?]

cricoid ('kraɪkɔɪd) *adj.* **1.** of or relating to the ring-shaped lowermost cartilage of the larynx. ~n. **2.** this cartilage. [C18: from NL *cricoïdes*, from Gk *krikoeidēs* ring-shaped, from *krikos* ring]

cri de coeur (kri: də kɜ:) n., *pl.* **cris de coeur.** (kri: dəkɜ:) a heartfelt or impassioned appeal. [C20: altered from F *cri du coeur*]

crier ('kraɪə) n. **1.** a person or animal that cries. **2.** (formerly) an official who made public announcements, esp. in a town or court.

crime (kraɪm) n. **1.** an act or omission prohibited and punished by law. **2.** unlawful acts in general. **3.** an evil act. **4.** *Inf.* something to be regretted. [C14: from OF, from L *crīmen* verdict, accusation, crime]

Crimea (kraɪ'mɪə) n. a peninsula of the SW Soviet Union, in the S Ukrainian SSR between the Black Sea and the Sea of Azov: a former autonomous republic of the Soviet Union (until 1946). Russian name: **Krym.** —**Cri'mean** *adj.*, n.

criminal ('krɪmɪnᵊl) n. **1.** a person charged with and convicted of crime. **2.** a person who commits crimes for a living. ~adj. **3.** of, involving, or guilty of crime. **4.** (*prenominal*) of or relating to crime or its punishment. **5.** *Inf.* senseless or deplorable. [C15: from LL *criminālis*; see CRIME, -AL¹] —'**criminally** *adv.* —,**crimi'nality** n.

criminal conversation n. another term for **adultery.**

criminal law n. the body of law dealing with offences and offenders.

criminate ('krɪmɪˌneɪt) vb. (*tr.*) *Rare.* **1.** to charge with a crime; accuse. **2.** short for **incriminate.** [C17: from L *crīmināri* to accuse] —,**crimi'nation** n. —'**criminative** or **criminatory** ('krɪmɪnətərɪ, -trɪ) *adj.* —'**crimi,nator** n.

criminology (ˌkrɪmɪ'nɒlədʒɪ) n. the scientific study of crime. [C19: from L *crimin-* CRIME, + -LOGY] —**criminological** (ˌkrɪmɪnə'lɒdʒɪkᵊl) or ,**crimino'logic** *adj.* —,**crimino'logically** *adv.* —,**crimi'nologist** n.

crimp (krɪmp) vb. (*tr.*) **1.** to fold or press into ridges. **2.** to fold and pinch together (something, such as two pieces of metal). **3.** to curl or wave (the hair) tightly, esp. with curling tongs. **4.** *U.S. inf.* to hinder. ~n. **5.** the act or result of folding or pressing together or into ridges. **6.** a tight wave or curl in the hair. [OE *crympan*; rel. to *crump* bent; see CRAMP] —'**crimper** n. —'**crimpy** *adj.*

Crimplene ('krɪmpliːn) n. *Trademark.* a synthetic material similar to Terylene, characterized by its crease-resistance.

crimson ('krɪmzən) n. **1. a.** a deep or vivid red colour. **b.** (*as adj.*): *a crimson rose.* ~vb. **2.** to make or become crimson. **3.** (*intr.*) to blush. [C14: from OSp. *cremesin*, from Ar. *qirmizi* red of the kermes, from *qirmiz* KERMES] —'**crimsonness** n.

cringe (krɪndʒ) vb. (*intr.*) **1.** to shrink or flinch, esp. in fear or servility. **2.** to behave in a servile or timid way. **3.** *Inf.* to experience a sudden feeling of embarrassment or distaste. ~n. **4.** the act of cringing. [OE *cringan* to yield in battle] —'**cringer** n.

cringle ('krɪŋgᵊl) n. an eyelet at the edge of a sail. [C17: from Low G *Kringel* small ring]

crinkle ('krɪŋkᵊl) vb. **1.** to form or cause to form wrinkles, twists, or folds. **2.** to make or cause to make a rustling noise. ~n. **3.** a wrinkle, twist, or fold. **4.** a rustling noise. [OE *crincan* to bend, give way] —'**crinkly** *adj.*

crinoid ('kraɪnɔɪd, 'krɪn-) n. **1.** a primitive echinoderm having delicate feathery arms radiating from a central disc. ~adj. **2.** of, relating to, or belonging to the *Crinoidea.* **3.** shaped like a lily. [C19: from Gk *krinoeidēs* lily-like] —**cri'noidal** *adj.*

crinoline ('krɪnᵊlɪn) n. **1.** a stiff fabric, originally of horsehair and linen used in lining garments. **2.** a petticoat stiffened with this, worn to distend skirts, esp. in the mid-19th century. **3.** a framework of steel hoops worn for the same purpose. [C19: from F, from It. *crinolino*, from *crino* horsehair, from L *crinis* hair + *lino* flax, from L *līnum*]

Crippen ('krɪpᵊn) n. **Hawley Harvey**, known as *Doctor Crippen.* 1862–1910, U.S. doctor living in England: executed for poisoning his wife; the first criminal to be apprehended by the use of radiotelegraphy.

cripple ('krɪpᵊl) n. **1.** a person who is lame. **2.** a person who is or seems disabled or deficient in some way: *a mental cripple.* ~vb. **3.** (*tr.*) to make a cripple of; disable. [OE *crypel*; rel. to *crēopan* to creep] —'**crippler** n.

Cripple Creek n. a village in central Colorado: gold-mining centre since 1891, once the richest in the world.

Cripps (krɪps) n. **Sir Stafford.** 1889–1952, British Labour statesman; Chancellor of the Exchequer (1947–50).

Criseyde (krɪ'seɪd) n. a variant of **Cressida.**

crisis ('kraɪsɪs) n., *pl.* **-ses** (-siːz). **1.** a crucial stage or turning point, esp. in a sequence of events or a disease. **2.** an unstable period, esp. one of extreme trouble or danger. **3.** *Pathol.* a sudden change in the course of a disease. [C15: from L: decision, from Gk *krisis*, from *krinein* to decide]

crisp (krɪsp) *adj.* **1.** dry and brittle. **2.** fresh and firm. **3.** invigorating or bracing: *a crisp breeze.* **4.** clear; sharp: *crisp reasoning.* **5.** lively or stimulating. **6.** clean and orderly. **7.** concise and pithy. **8.** wrinkled or curly: *crisp hair.* ~vb. **9.** to make or become crisp. ~n. **10.** *Brit.* a very thin slice of potato fried and eaten cold as a snack. **11.** something that is crisp. [OE, from L *crispus* curled, uneven, wrinkled] —'**crisply** *adv.* —'**crispness** n.

crispbread ('krɪsp,brɛd) n. a thin dry biscuit made of wheat or rye.

crisper ('krɪspə) n. a compartment in a refrigerator for storing salads, vegetables, etc., in order to keep them fresh.

Crispi (*Italian* 'krispi) n. **Francesco** (fran'tʃesko). 1819–1901, Italian statesman; premier (1887–91; 1893–96).

Crispin ('krɪspɪn) n. **Saint,** 3rd century A.D., legendary Roman Christian martyr, with his brother **Crispinian** (krɪ'spɪnɪən): they are the patron saints of shoemakers. Feast day: Oct. 25.

crispy ('krɪspɪ) *adj.* **crispier, crispiest. 1.** crisp. **2.** having waves or curls. —'**crispiness** n.

crisscross ('krɪs,krɒs) vb. **1.** to move or cause to move in a crosswise pattern. **2.** to mark with or consist of a pattern of crossing lines. ~adj. **3.** (esp. of lines) crossing one another in different directions. ~n. **4.** a pattern made of crossing lines. ~adv. **5.** in a crosswise manner or pattern.

crit. *abbrev. for:* **1.** *Med.* critical. **2.** criticism.

criterion (kraɪ'tɪərɪən) n., *pl.* **-ria** (-rɪə) *or* **-rions** a standard by which something can be judged or decided. [C17: from Gk *kritērion*, from *kritēs* judge, from *krinein* to decide]
▷ *Usage. Criteria*, the plural of *criterion*, is not acceptable as a singular noun in careful English.

critic ('krɪtɪk) n. **1.** a person who judges something. **2.** a professional judge of art, music, literature, etc. **3.** a person who often finds fault and criticizes. [C16: from L *criticus*, from Gk *kritikos* capable of judging, from *kritēs* judge; see CRITERION]

critical ('krɪtɪkᵊl) *adj.* **1.** containing or making severe or negative judgments. **2.** containing analytical evaluations. **3.** of a critic or criticism. **4.** of or forming a crisis; crucial. **5.** urgently needed. **6.** *Physics.* of, denoting, or concerned with a state in which the properties of a system undergo an abrupt change. **7. go critical.** (of a nuclear power station or reactor) to reach a state in which a nuclear-fission chain reaction becomes self-sustaining. —,**criti'cality** n. —'**critically** *adv.* —'**criticalness** n.

critical mass n. the minimum mass of fissionable material that can sustain a nuclear chain reaction.

critical path analysis n. a technique for planning projects with reference to the critical path, which is the sequence of stages requiring the longest time.

critical temperature n. the temperature of a substance in its critical state. A gas can only be liquefied at temperatures below this.

criticism ('krɪtɪˌsɪzəm) n. 1. the act or an instance of making an unfavourable or severe judgment, comment, etc. 2. the analysis or evaluation of a work of art, literature, etc. 3. the occupation of a critic. 4. a work that sets out to evaluate or analyse.

criticize or **-ise** ('krɪtɪˌsaɪz) vb. 1. to judge (something) with disapproval; censure. 2. to evaluate or analyse (something). —'**criti,cizable** or -,**cisable** adj. —'**crit-i,cizer** or -,**ciser** n.

critique (krɪ'tiːk) n. 1. a critical essay or commentary. 2. the act or art of criticizing. [C17: from F, from Gk kritikē, from kritikos able to discern]

croak (krəʊk) vb. 1. (intr.) (of frogs, crows, etc.) to make a low, hoarse cry. 2. to utter (something) in this manner. 3. (intr.) to grumble or be pessimistic. 4. Sl. a. (intr.) to die. b. (tr.) to kill. ~n. 5. a low hoarse utterance or sound. [OE crācettan] —'**croaky** adj. —'**croakiness** n.

croaker ('krəʊkə) n. 1. an animal, bird, etc., that croaks. 2. a grumbling person.

Croat ('krəʊæt) n. 1. a. a native or inhabitant of Croatia. b. a speaker of Croatian. ~n., adj. 2. another word for **Croatian**.

Croatia (krəʊ'eɪʃə) n. a constituent republic of NW Yugoslavia: settled by Croats in the 7th century; belonged successively to Hungary, Turkey, and Austria, until the formation of Yugoslavia (1918). Capital: Zagreb. Pop.: 4 665 000 (1986 est.). Area: 56 538 sq. km (21 825 sq. miles). Serbo-Croatian name: **Hrvatska**.

Croatian (krəʊ'eɪʃən) adj. 1. of or relating to Croatia, its people, or their dialect of Serbo-Croatian. ~n. 2. the dialect of Croatia. 3. a. a native or inhabitant of Croatia. b. a speaker of Croatian.

Croce (Italian 'krotʃe) n. **Benedetto** (bene'detto). 1866–1952, Italian philosopher, critic, and statesman: an opponent of Fascism, he helped re-establish liberalism in postwar Italy.

crochet ('krəʊʃeɪ, -ʃɪ) vb. -**cheting** (-ʃeɪɪŋ, -ʃɪɪŋ), -**cheted** (-ʃeɪd, -ʃɪd). 1. to make (a piece of needlework, a garment, etc.) by looping and intertwining thread with a hooked needle (**crochet hook**). ~n. 2. work made by crocheting. [C19: from F crochet, dim. of croc hook, prob. of Scand. origin] —'**crocheter** n.

crock[1] (krɒk) n. 1. an earthen pot, jar, etc. 2. a piece of broken earthenware. [OE crocc pot]

crock[2] (krɒk) n. Sl., chiefly Brit. a person or thing that is old or decrepit (esp. in **old crock**). [C15: orig. Scot.; rel. to Norwegian krake unhealthy animal, Du. kraak decrepit person or animal]

crockery ('krɒkərɪ) n. china dishes, earthen vessels, etc., collectively.

crocket ('krɒkɪt) n. a carved ornament in the form of a curled leaf or cusp, used in Gothic architecture. [C17: from Anglo-F croket a little hook, from croc hook, of Scand. origin]

Crockett ('krɒkɪt) n. **David**, known as Davy Crockett. 1786–1836, U.S. frontiersman, politician, and soldier.

crocodile ('krɒkəˌdaɪl) n. 1. a large tropical reptile having a broad head, tapering snout, massive jaws, and a thick outer covering of bony plates. 2. a. leather made from the skin of any of these animals. b. (as modifier): crocodile shoes. 3. Brit. inf. a line of schoolchildren walking two by two. [C13: via OF, from L crocodīlus, from Gk krokodeilos lizard, ult. from krokē pebble + drilos worm; referring to its basking on shingle]

crocodile clip n. a clasp with serrated interlocking edges used for making electrical connections, etc.

Crocodile River n. another name for the **Limpopo**.

crocodile tears pl. n. an insincere show of grief; false tears. [from the belief that crocodiles wept over their prey to allure further victims]

crocodilian (ˌkrɒkə'dɪlɪən) n. 1. any large predatory reptile of the order Crocodilia, which includes the crocodiles, alligators, and caymans. ~adj. 2. of, relating to, or resembling the Crocodilia. 3. of, relating to, or resem-

crocus ('krəʊkəs) n., pl. -**cuses**. any plant of the iridaceous genus Crocus, having white, yellow, or purple flowers. [C17: from NL, from L crocus, from Gk krokos saffron]

Croesus ('kriːsəs) n. 1. died ?546 B.C., the last king of Lydia (560–546), noted for his great wealth. 2. any very rich man.

croft (krɒft) n. Brit. a small enclosed plot of land, adjoining a house, worked by the occupier and his family, esp. in Scotland. [OE croft] —'**crofter** n. —'**crofting** adj., n.

croissant ('krwɑːsɒŋ) n. a flaky crescent-shaped bread roll. [F, lit.: crescent]

Croix de Guerre French. (krwa də gɛr) n. a French military decoration awarded for gallantry in battle: established 1915. [lit.: cross of war]

Cro-Magnon man ('krəʊ'mænjɒn, -'mægnɒn) n. an early type of modern man, Homo sapiens, who lived in Europe during late Palaeolithic times. [C19: after the cave (Cro-Magnon), Dordogne, France, where the remains were first found]

Crome (krəʊm) n. **John**, known as Old Crome. 1768–1821, English landscape painter and etcher.

cromlech ('krɒmlɛk) n. 1. a circle of prehistoric standing stones. 2. (no longer in technical usage) a megalithic chamber tomb or dolmen. [C17: from Welsh, from crom, fem. of crwm bent, arched + llech flat stone]

Crompton ('krɒmptən) n. **Samuel**. 1753–1827, English inventor of the spinning mule (1779).

Cromwell ('krɒmwəl, -wɛl) n. 1. **Oliver**. 1599–1658, English general and statesman. A convinced Puritan, he was an effective leader of the parliamentary army in the Civil War. After the execution of Charles I he quelled the Royalists in Scotland and Ireland, and became Lord Protector of the Commonwealth (1653–58). 2. his son, **Richard**. 1626–1712, Lord Protector of the Commonwealth (1658–59). 3. **Thomas**, Earl of Essex. ?1485–1540, English statesman. He was secretary to Cardinal Wolsey (1514), after whose fall he became chief adviser to Henry VIII. He drafted most of the Reformation legislation, securing its passage through parliament, the power of which he thereby greatly enhanced. He was executed after losing Henry's favour. —**Cromwellian** (krɒm'wɛlɪən) adj., n.

crone (krəʊn) n. a witchlike old woman. [C14: from OF carogne carrion, ult. from L caro flesh]

Cronin ('krəʊnɪn) n. **A(rchibald) J(oseph)**. 1896–1981, British novelist and physician. His works include Hatter's Castle (1931), The Judas Tree (1961), and Dr Finlay's Casebook, a TV series based on his medical experiences.

cronk (krɒŋk) adj. Austral. sl. 1. unfit; unsound. 2. dishonest. [C19: from G krank ill]

Cronus ('krəʊnəs), **Cronos**, or **Kronos** ('krəʊnɒs) n. Greek myth. a Titan, son of Uranus (sky) and Gaea (earth), who ruled the world until his son Zeus dethroned him. Roman counterpart: **Saturn**.

crony ('krəʊnɪ) n., pl. -**nies**. a friend or companion. [C17: student sl. (Cambridge), from Gk khronios of long duration, from khronos time]

crook (krʊk) n. 1. a curved or hooked thing. 2. a staff with a hooked end, such as a bishop's crosier or shepherd's staff. 3. a turn or curve; bend. 4. Inf. a dishonest person, esp. a swindler or thief. ~vb. 5. to bend or curve or cause to bend or curve. ~adj. 6. Austral. & N.Z. sl. a. ill. b. of poor quality. c. unpleasant; bad. 7. **go (off) crook**. Austral. & N.Z. sl. to lose one's temper. 8. **go crook at** or **on**. Austral. & N.Z. sl. to rebuke or upbraid. [C12: from ON krokr hook]

crooked ('krʊkɪd) adj. 1. bent, angled or winding. 2. set at an angle; not straight. 3. deformed or contorted. 4. Inf. dishonest or illegal. 5. **crooked on**. (also krʊkt) Austral. inf. hostile or averse to. —'**crookedly** adv. —'**crookedness** n.

Crookes (krʊks) n. Sir **William**. 1832–1919, English chemist and physicist: he investigated the properties of cathode rays and invented a type of radiometer and the lens named after him.

croon (kruːn) vb. 1. to sing or speak in a soft low tone. ~n. 2. a soft low singing or humming. [C14: via MDu. crōnen to groan] —'**crooner** n.

crop (krɒp) n. 1. the produce of cultivated plants, esp. cereals, vegetables, and fruit. 2. a. the amount of such produce in any particular season. b. the yield of some other farm produce: the lamb crop. 3. a group of products, thoughts, people, etc., appearing at one time or in one season. **4.** the stock of a thonged whip. **5.** short for **riding crop. 6.** a pouchlike part of the oesophagus of birds, in which food is stored or partially digested before passing on to the gizzard. **7.** a short cropped hairstyle. **8.** a notch in or a piece cut out of the ear of an animal. **9.** the act of cropping. ~*vb.* **cropping, cropped.** (*mainly tr.*) **10.** to cut (hair, grass, etc.) very short. **11.** to cut and collect (mature produce) from the land or plant on which it has been grown. **12.** to clip part of (the ear or ears) of (an animal), esp. as a means of identification. **13.** (of herbivorous animals) to graze on (grass or similar vegetation). ~See also **crop out, crop up.** [OE *cropp*]

crop-dusting *n.* the spreading of fungicide, etc., on crops in the form of dust, often from an aircraft.

crop-eared *adj.* having the ears or hair cut short.

crop out *vb.* (*intr., adv.*) (of a formation of rock strata) to appear or be exposed at the surface.

cropper ('krɒpə) *n.* **1.** a person who cultivates or harvests a crop. **2. come a cropper.** *Inf.* **a.** to fall heavily. **b.** to fail completely.

crop rotation *n.* the system of growing a sequence of different crops on the same ground so as to maintain or increase its fertility.

crop up *vb.* (*intr., adv.*) *Inf.* to occur or appear unexpectedly.

croquet ('krəʊkeɪ, -kɪ) *n.* a game for two to four players who hit a wooden ball through iron hoops with mallets in order to hit a peg. [C19: ?from F dialect, var. of CROCHET (little hook)]

croquette (krəʊ'kɛt, krɒ-) *n.* a savoury cake of minced meat, fish, etc., fried in breadcrumbs. [C18: from F, from *croquer* to crunch, imit.]

Crosby[1] ('krɒzbɪ) *n.* a town in NW England, in Merseyside. Pop.: 53 660 (1981).

Crosby[2] ('krɒzbɪ) *n.* **Bing,** real name *Harry Lillis Crosby.* 1904–77, U.S. singer and film actor; famous for his style of crooning: best known for the song "White Christmas" from the film *Holiday Inn* (1942).

crosier *or* **crozier** ('krəʊʒə) *n.* a staff surmounted by a crook or cross, carried by bishops as a symbol of pastoral office. [C14: from OF *crossier* staff bearer, from *crosse* pastoral staff]

cross (krɒs) *n.* **1.** a structure or symbol consisting of two intersecting lines or pieces at right angles to one another. **2.** a wooden structure used as a means of execution, consisting of an upright post with a transverse piece to which people were nailed or tied. **3.** a representation of the Cross used as an emblem of Christianity or as a reminder of Christ's death. **4.** any mark or shape consisting of two intersecting lines, esp. such a symbol (✕) used as a signature, error mark, etc. **5.** a sign representing the Cross made either by tracing a figure in the air or by touching the forehead, breast, and either shoulder in turn. **6.** any variation of the Christian symbol, such as a Maltese or Greek cross. **7.** a cruciform emblem awarded to indicate membership of an order or as a decoration for distinguished service. **8.** (*sometimes cap.*) Christianity or Christendom, esp. as contrasted with non-Christian religions. **9.** the place in a town or village where a cross has been set up. **10.** *Biol.* **a.** the process of crossing; hybridization. **b.** an individual produced as a result of this process. **11.** a mixture of two qualities or types. **12.** an opposition, hindrance, or misfortune; affliction (esp. in **bear one's cross**). **13.** *Boxing.* a straight punch delivered from the side, esp. with the right hand. **14.** *Football.* the act or an instance of passing the ball from a wing to the middle of the field. ~*vb.* **15.** (sometimes foll. by *over*) to move or go across (something); traverse or intersect. **16. a.** to meet and pass. **b.** (of each of two letters in the post) to be dispatched before receipt of the other. **17.** (*tr.; usually foll. by out, off, or through*) to cancel with a cross or with lines; delete. **18.** (*tr.*) to place or put in a form resembling a cross: *to cross one's legs.* **19.** (*tr.*) to mark with a cross or crosses. **20.** (*tr.*) *Brit.* to draw two parallel lines across the face of (a cheque) and so make it payable only into a bank account. **21.** (*tr.*) **a.** to trace the form of the Cross upon (someone or something) in token of blessing. **b.** to make the sign of the Cross upon (oneself). **22.** (*intr.*) (of telephone lines) to interfere with each other so that several callers are connected together at one time. **23.** to cause fertilization between (plants or animals of different breeds, races, varieties, etc.). **24.**

(*tr.*) to oppose the wishes or plans of; thwart. **25.** *Football.* to pass the (ball) from a wing to the middle of the field. **26. cross one's fingers.** to fold one finger across another in the hope of bringing good luck. **27. cross one's heart.** to promise or pledge, esp. by making the sign of a cross over one's heart. **28. cross one's mind.** to occur to one briefly or suddenly. **29. cross the path (of).** to meet or thwart (someone). **30. cross swords.** to argue or fight. ~*adj.* **31.** angry; ill-humoured; vexed. **32.** lying or placed across; transverse: *a cross timber.* **33.** involving interchange; reciprocal. **34.** contrary or unfavourable. **35.** another word for **crossbred.** [OE *cros,* from OIrish *cross* (unattested), from L *crux;* see CRUX] —'**crossly** *adv.* —'**crossness** *n.*

Cross (krɒs) *n.* **the. 1.** the cross on which Jesus Christ was crucified. **2.** the Crucifixion of Jesus.

cross- *combining form.* **1.** indicating action from one individual, group, etc., to another: *cross-cultural; cross-fertilize; cross-refer.* **2.** indicating movement, position, etc., across something: *crosscurrent; crosstalk.* **3.** indicating a crosslike figure or intersection: *crossbones.* [from CROSS (in various senses)]

crossbar ('krɒs,bɑː) *n.* **1.** a horizontal bar, line, stripe, etc. **2.** a horizontal beam across a pair of goal posts. **3.** the horizontal bar on a man's bicycle.

crossbeam ('krɒs,biːm) *n.* a beam that spans from one support to another.

cross-bench *n.* (*usually pl.*) *Brit.* a seat in Parliament occupied by a neutral or independent member. —'**cross-,bencher** *n.*

crossbill ('krɒs,bɪl) *n.* any of various widely distributed finches that occur in coniferous woods and have a bill with crossed tips.

crossbones ('krɒs,bəʊnz) *pl. n.* See **skull and crossbones.**

crossbow ('krɒs,bəʊ) *n.* a type of medieval bow fixed transversely on a stock grooved to direct a square-headed arrow. —'**cross,bowman** *n.*

crossbred ('krɒs,brɛd) *adj.* **1.** (of plants or animals) produced as a result of crossbreeding. ~*n.* **2.** a crossbred plant or animal.

crossbreed ('krɒs,briːd) *vb.* **-breeding, -bred. 1.** Also: **interbreed.** to breed (animals or plants) using parents of different races, varieties, breeds, etc. ~*n.* **2.** the offspring produced by such a breeding.

crosscheck (,krɒs'tʃɛk) *vb.* **1.** to verify (a fact, report, etc.) by considering conflicting opinions or consulting other sources. ~*n.* **2.** the act or an instance of crosschecking.

cross-country *adj., adv.* **1.** by way of fields, etc., as opposed to roads. **2.** across a country. ~*n.* **3.** a long race held over open ground.

crosscurrent ('krɒs,kʌrənt) *n.* **1.** a current flowing across another current. **2.** a conflicting tendency moving counter to the usual trend.

crosscut ('krɒs,kʌt) *adj.* **1.** cut at right angles or obliquely to the major axis. ~*n.* **2.** a transverse cut or course. **3.** *Mining.* a tunnel through a vein of ore or from the shaft to a vein. ~*vb.* **-cutting, -cut. 4.** to cut across.

crosscut saw *n.* a saw for cutting timber across the grain.

crosse (krɒs) *n.* a light staff with a triangular frame to which a network is attached, used in playing lacrosse. [F, from *croce* CROSIER]

cross-examine *vb.* (*tr.*) **1.** *Law.* to examine (a witness for the opposing side), as in attempting to discredit his testimony. **2.** to examine closely or relentlessly. —'**cross-ex,ami'nation** *n.* —,**cross-ex'aminer** *n.*

cross-eye *n.* a turning inwards towards the nose of one or both eyes, caused by abnormal alignment. —'**cross-,eyed** *adj.*

cross-fertilize *vb.* **1.** to fertilize by fusion of male and female gametes from different individuals of the same species. **2.** a non-technical term for **cross-pollinate.** —'**cross-,fertili'zation** *n.*

crossfire ('krɒs,faɪə) *n.* **1.** *Mil.* etc. converging fire from one or more positions. **2.** a lively exchange of ideas, opinions, etc.

cross-grained *adj.* **1.** (of timber) having the fibres arranged irregularly or across the axis of the piece. **2.** perverse, cantankerous, or stubborn.

cross hairs *pl. n.* two fine mutually perpendicular lines or wires that cross in the focal plane of a theodolite, gunsight, or other optical instrument and are used to define the line of sight. Also called: **cross wires.**

crosshatch ('krɒs,hætʃ) *vb. Drawing.* to shade or hatch with two or more sets of parallel lines that cross one another.

crossing ('krɒsɪŋ) *n.* **1.** the place where one thing crosses another. **2.** a place where a street, railway, etc., may be crossed. **3.** the act or an instance of travelling across something, esp. the sea. **4.** the act or process of crossbreeding.

crossing over *n. Biol.* the interchange of sections between pairing chromosomes during meiosis that produces variations in inherited characteristics by rearranging genes.

cross-legged ('krɒs'lɛgɪd, -'lɛgd) *adj.* standing or sitting with one leg crossed over the other.

cross-match *vb. Immunol.* to test the compatibility of (a donor's and recipient's blood) by checking that the red cells of each do not agglutinate in the other's serum.

crossover network *n. Electronics.* an arrangement in a loudspeaker system that separates the signal into two or more frequency bands for feeding into different speakers.

crosspatch ('krɒs,pætʃ) *n. Inf.* a bad-tempered person. [C18: from CROSS + obs. *patch* fool]

crosspiece ('krɒs,piːs) *n.* a transverse beam, joist, etc.

cross-ply *adj.* (of a motor tyre) having the fabric cords in the outer casing running diagonally to stiffen the sidewalls.

cross-pollinate *vb.* to transfer pollen from the anthers of one flower to the stigma of another. —,**cross-polli'nation** *n.*

cross-purpose *n.* **1.** a contrary aim or purpose. **2. at cross-purposes.** conflicting; opposed; disagreeing.

cross-question *vb.* **1.** to cross-examine. ~*n.* **2.** a question asked in cross-examination.

cross-refer *vb.* to refer from one part of something, esp. a book, to another.

cross-reference *n.* **1.** a reference within a text to another part of the text. ~*vb.* **2.** to cross-refer.

Cross River *n.* a state of SE Nigeria, on the Gulf of Guinea. Capital: Calabar. Pop.: 4 626 317 (1976 est.). Area: 35 149 sq. km (13 568 sq. miles). Former name (until 1976): **South-Eastern State.**

crossroad ('krɒs,rəud) *n. U.S. & Canad.* **1.** a road that crosses another road. **2.** Also called: **crossway.** a road that crosses from one main road to another.

crossroads ('krɒs,rəudz) *n. (functioning as sing.)* **1.** the point at which two or more roads cross each other. **2.** the point at which an important choice has to be made (esp. in **at the crossroads**).

crossruff ('krɒs,rʌf) *Bridge, whist.* ~*n.* **1.** the alternate trumping of each other's leads by two partners, or by declarer and dummy. ~*vb.* **2.** (*intr.*) to trump alternately in this way.

cross section *n.* **1.** *Maths.* a plane surface formed by cutting across a solid, esp. perpendicular to its longest axis. **2.** a section cut off in this way. **3.** the act of cutting anything in this way. **4.** a random sample, esp. one regarded as representative. —,**cross-'sectional** *adj.*

cross-stitch *n.* **1.** an embroidery stitch made by two stitches forming a cross. **2.** embroidery worked with this stitch. ~*vb.* **3.** to embroider (a piece of needlework) with cross-stitch.

crosstalk ('krɒs,tɔːk) *n.* **1.** unwanted signals in one channel of a communications system as a result of a transfer of energy from other channels. **2.** *Brit.* rapid or witty talk.

crosstree ('krɒs,triː) *n. Naut.* either of a pair of wooden or metal braces on the head of a lower mast to support the topmast, etc.

crosswise ('krɒs,waɪz) or **crossways** ('krɒs,weɪz) *adj., adv.* **1.** across; transversely. **2.** in the shape of a cross.

crossword puzzle ('krɒs,wɜːd) *n.* a puzzle in which the solver guesses words suggested by numbered clues and writes them into a grid to form a vertical and horizontal pattern.

crotch (krɒtʃ) *n.* **1.** Also called (Brit.): **crutch. a.** the angle formed by the legs where they join the human trunk. **b.** the human genital area. **c.** the corresponding part of a pair of trousers, pants, etc. **2.** a forked region formed by

the junction of two members. **3.** a forked pole or stick. [C16: prob. var. of CRUTCH] —**crotched** *adj.*

crotchet ('krɒtʃɪt) *n.* **1.** *Music.* a note having the time value of a quarter of a semibreve. **2.** a perverse notion. [C14: from OF *crochet*, lit.: little hook, from *croche* hook; see CROCKET]

crotchety ('krɒtʃɪtɪ) *adj.* **1.** *Inf.* irritable; contrary. **2.** full of crotchets. —'**crotchetiness** *n.*

croton ('krəʊtⁿn) *n.* **1.** any shrub or tree of the chiefly tropical genus *Croton*, esp. *C. tiglium*, the seeds of which yield croton oil, formerly used as a purgative. **2.** any of various tropical plants of the related genus *Codiaeum*. [C18: from NL, from Gk *krotōn* tick, castor-oil plant (whose berries resemble ticks)]

Crotone (*Italian* kro'toːne) *n.* a town in S Italy, on the coast of Calabria: founded in about 700 B.C. by the Achaeans; chemical works and zinc-smelting. Pop.: 58 281 (1981 est.).

crouch (krautʃ) *vb.* (*intr.*) **1.** to bend low with the limbs pulled up close together, esp. (of an animal) in readiness to pounce. **2.** to cringe, as in humility or fear. ~*n.* **3.** the act of stooping or bending. [C14: ?from OF *crochir* to become bent like a hook, from *croche* hook]

croup[1] (kruːp) *n.* a throat condition, occurring usually in children, characterized by a hoarse cough and laboured breathing, resulting from inflammation of the larynx. [C18: *croup* to cry hoarsely, prob. imit.] —'**croupous** or '**croupy** *adj.*

croup[2] (kruːp) *n.* the hindquarters, esp. of a horse. [C13: from OF *croupe*; rel. to G *Kruppe*]

croupier ('kruːpɪə) *n.* a person who deals cards, collects bets, etc., at a gaming table. [C18: lit.: one who rides behind another, from *croupe* CROUP[2]]

crouton ('kruːtɒn) *n.* a small piece of fried or toasted bread, usually served in soup. [F: dim. of *croûte* CRUST]

crow[1] (krəʊ) *n.* **1.** any large gregarious songbird of the genus *Corvus* of Europe and Asia, such as the raven, rook, and jackdaw. All have a heavy bill, glossy black plumage, and rounded wings. **2.** any of various similar birds. **3.** *Sl.* an old or ugly woman. **4. as the crow flies.** as directly as possible. **5. eat crow.** *U.S. & Canad. inf.* to be forced to do something humiliating. **6. stone the crows.** (*interj.*) *Brit. & Austral. sl.* an expression of surprise, dismay, etc. [OE *crāwa*]

crow[2] (krəʊ) *vb.* (*intr.*) **1.** (p.t. **crowed** or **crew**) to utter a shrill squawking sound, as a cock. **2.** (often foll. by *over*) to boast one's superiority. **3.** (esp. of babies) to utter cries of pleasure. ~*n.* **4.** an act or instance of crowing. [OE *crāwan*; rel. to OHG *krāen*, Du. *kraaien*] —'**crowingly** *adv.*

crowbar ('krəʊ,bɑː) *n.* a heavy iron lever with one end forged into a wedge shape.

crowd[1] (kraʊd) *n.* **1.** a large number of things or people gathered or considered together. **2.** a particular group of people, esp. considered as a set: *the crowd from the office.* **3.** (preceded by *the*) the common people; the masses. ~*vb.* **4.** (*intr.*) to gather together in large numbers; throng. **5.** (*tr.*) to press together into a confined space. **6.** (*tr.*) to fill to excess; fill by pushing into. **7.** (*tr.*) *Inf.* to urge or harass by urging. [OE *crūdan*] —'**crowded** *adj.* —'**crowdedness** *n.*

crowd[2] (kraʊd) *n. Music.* an ancient bowed stringed instrument. [C13: from Welsh *crwth*]

crowfoot ('krəʊ,fʊt) *n., pl.* **-foots.** any of several plants that have yellow or white flowers and divided leaves resembling the foot of a crow.

crown (kraʊn) *n.* **1.** an ornamental headdress denoting sovereignty, usually made of gold embedded with precious stones. **2.** a wreath or garland for the head, awarded as a sign of victory, success, honour, etc. **3.** (*sometimes cap.*) monarchy or kingship. **4.** an award, distinction, or title, given as an honour to reward merit, victory, etc. **5.** anything resembling or symbolizing a crown. **6. a.** a coin worth 25 pence (five shillings). **b.** any of several continental coins, such as the krona or krone, with a name meaning *crown.* **7.** the top or summit of something: *crown of a hill.* **8.** the centre part of a road, esp. when it is cambered. **9.** the outstanding quality, achievement, state, etc.: *the crown of his achievements.* **10. a.** the enamel-covered part of a tooth above the gum. **b. artificial crown.** a substitute crown, usually of gold, porcelain, or acrylic resin, fitted over a decayed or broken tooth. **11.** the part of an anchor where the arms are joined to the shank. ~*vb.* (*tr.*) **12.** to put a crown on the head of, symbolically vesting with royal title, powers, etc. **13.** to place a crown, wreath, garland, etc., on the head of. **14.** to place something on or over the head or top of. **15.** to confer a title, dignity, or reward upon. **16.** to form the summit or topmost part of. **17.** to cap or put the finishing touch to (a series of events): *to crown it all it rained, too.* **18.** *Draughts.* to promote (a draught) to a king by placing another draught on top of it. **19.** to attach a crown to (a tooth). **20.** *Sl.* to hit over the head. [C12: from OF *corone*, from L *corōna* wreath, crown, from Gk *korōnē* crown, something curved]

Crown (kraʊn) *n.* (*sometimes not cap.;* usually preceded by *the*) **1.** the sovereignty or realm of a monarch. **2. a.** the government of a monarchy. **b.** (*as modifier*): *Crown property.*

crown colony *n.* a British colony whose administration is controlled by the Crown.

crown court *n. English law.* a court of criminal jurisdiction holding sessions in towns throughout England and Wales.

Crown Derby *n.* **1.** a type of porcelain manufactured at Derby from 1784–1848. **2.** *Trademark.* shortened form of Royal Crown Derby.

crown glass *n.* **1.** another name for **optical crown. 2.** an old form of window glass made by blowing a globe and spinning it until it forms a flat disc.

crown green *n.* a type of bowling green in which the sides are lower than the middle.

crown jewels *pl. n.* the jewellery, including the regalia, used by a sovereign on a state occasion.

Crown Office *n.* (in Britain) an administrative office of the Queen's Bench Division of the High Court, where actions are entered for trial.

crown prince *n.* the male heir to a sovereign throne.

crown princess *n.* **1.** the wife of a crown prince. **2.** the female heir to a sovereign throne.

crown wheel *n.* **1.** *Horology.* a wheel that has one set of teeth at right angles to another. **2.** the larger of two wheels in a bevel gear.

crow's-foot *n., pl.* **-feet.** (*often pl.*) a wrinkle at the outer corner of the eye.

crow's-nest *n.* a lookout platform high up on a ship's mast.

crow step *n.* another term for **corbie-step.**

Croydon ('krɔɪdᵊn) *n.* a Greater London borough (since 1965): formerly important for its airport (1915–59). Pop.: 319 300 (1986 est.).

crozier ('krəʊʒə) *n.* a variant spelling of **crosier.**

CRT *abbrev. for:* **1.** cathode-ray tube. **2.** (in Britain) composite rate tax: a system of paying interest to savers by which a rate of tax for a period is determined in advance and interest is paid net of tax which is deducted at source.

crucial ('kru:ʃəl) *adj.* **1.** involving a final or supremely important decision or event; decisive; critical. **2.** *Inf.* very important. **3.** *Sl.* very good. [C18: from F, from L *crux* CROSS] —**'crucially** *adv.*

crucible ('kru:sɪbᵊl) *n.* **1.** a vessel in which substances are heated to high temperatures. **2.** the hearth at the bottom of a metallurgical furnace in which the metal collects. **3.** a severe trial or test. [C15 *corusible*, from Med. L *crūcibulum* night lamp, crucible, from ?]

crucifix ('kru:sɪfɪks) *n.* a cross or image of a cross with a figure of Christ upon it. [C13: from Church L *crucifixus* the crucified Christ, from *crucifigere* to CRUCIFY]

crucifixion (ˌkru:sɪ'fɪkʃən) *n.* a method of putting to death by nailing or binding to a cross, normally by the hands and feet.

Crucifixion (ˌkru:sɪ'fɪkʃən) *n.* **1.** (usually preceded by *the*) the crucifying of Christ. **2.** a picture or representation of this.

cruciform ('kru:sɪˌfɔ:m) *adj.* shaped like a cross. [C17: from L *crux* cross + -FORM] —**'cruci,formly** *adv.*

crucify ('kru:sɪˌfaɪ) *vb.* **-fying, -fied.** (*tr.*) **1.** to put to death by crucifixion. **2.** *Sl.* to defeat, ridicule, etc., totally. **3.** to treat very cruelly; torment. [C13: from OF *crucifier*, from LL *crucifigere* to crucify, to fasten to a cross, from L *crux* cross + *figere* to fasten] —**'cruci,fier** *n.*

crud (krʌd) *n.* **1.** *Sl.* **a.** a sticky substance, esp. when dirty and encrusted. **b.** a despicable person. **2.** an undesirable residue, esp. one inside a nuclear reactor. [C14: earlier form of CURD] —**'cruddy** *adj.*

crude (kru:d) *adj.* **1.** lacking taste, tact, or refinement; vulgar. **2.** in a natural or unrefined state. **3.** lacking care, knowledge, or skill. **4.** (*prenominal*) stark; blunt. ~*n.* **5.** short for **crude oil.** [C14: from L *crūdus* bloody, raw; rel. to L *cruor* blood] —**'crudely** *adv.* —**'crudity** *or* **'crudeness** *n.*

Cruden ('kru:dᵊn) *n.* **Alexander.** 1701–70, Scottish bookseller and compiler of a well-known biblical concordance (1737).

crude oil *n.* unrefined petroleum.

cruel ('krʊəl) *adj.* **1.** causing or inflicting pain without pity. **2.** causing pain or suffering. ~*vb.* **3. cruel someone's pitch.** *Austral. sl.* to ruin someone's chances. [C13: from OF, from L *crūdēlis*, from *crūdus* raw, bloody] —**'cruelly** *adv.* —**'cruelness** *n.*

cruelty ('krʊəltɪ) *n., pl.* **-ties. 1.** deliberate infliction of pain or suffering. **2.** the quality or characteristic of being cruel. **3.** a cruel action. **4.** *Law.* conduct that causes danger to life or limb or a threat to bodily or mental health.

cruet ('kru:ɪt) *n.* **1.** a small container for holding pepper, salt, vinegar, oil, etc., at table. **2.** a set of such containers, esp. on a stand. [C13: from Anglo-F, dim. of OF *crue* flask, of Gmc origin]

Cruikshank ('krʊk,ʃæŋk) *n.* **George.** 1792–1878, English illustrator and caricaturist.

cruise (kru:z) *vb.* **1.** (*intr.*) to make a trip by sea for pleasure, usually calling at a number of ports. **2.** to sail or travel over (a body of water) for pleasure. **3.** (*intr.*) to search for enemy vessels in a warship. **4.** (*intr.*) (of a vehicle, aircraft, or vessel) to travel at a moderate and efficient speed. ~*n.* **5.** an act or instance of cruising, esp. a trip by sea. [C17: from Du. *kruisen* to cross, from *cruis* CROSS]

cruise missile *n.* a low-flying subsonic missile that is guided throughout its flight.

cruiser ('kru:zə) *n.* **1.** a high-speed, long-range warship armed with medium-calibre weapons. **2.** Also called: **cabin cruiser.** a pleasure boat, esp. one that is power-driven and has a cabin. **3.** any person or thing that cruises.

cruiserweight ('kru:zə,weɪt) *n. Boxing.* another term (esp. Brit.) for **light heavyweight.**

crumb (krʌm) *n.* **1.** a small fragment of bread, cake, or other baked foods. **2.** a small piece or bit. **3.** the soft inner part of bread. **4.** *Sl.* a contemptible person. ~*vb.* **5.** (*tr.*) to prepare or cover (food) with breadcrumbs. **6.** to break into small fragments. [OE *cruma*]

crumble ('krʌmbᵊl) *vb.* **1.** to break or be broken into crumbs or fragments. **2.** (*intr.*) to fall apart or away. ~*n.* **3.** *Brit.* a baked pudding consisting of a crumbly mixture of flour, fat, and sugar over stewed fruit: *apple crumble.* [C16: var. of *crimble*, of Gmc origin]

crumbly ('krʌmblɪ) *adj.* **-blier, -bliest.** easily crumbled or crumbling. —**'crumbliness** *n.*

crumby ('krʌmɪ) *adj.* **crumbier, crumbiest. 1.** full of or littered with crumbs. **2.** soft, like the inside of bread. **3.** a variant spelling of **crummy.**

Crummock Water ('krʌmək) *n.* a lake in NW England, in Cumbria in the Lake District. Length: 4 km (2.5 miles).

crummy ('krʌmɪ) *adj.* **-mier, -miest.** *Sl.* **1.** of little value; contemptible. **2.** unwell or depressed: *to feel crummy.* [C19: var. spelling of CRUMBY]

crumpet ('krʌmpɪt) *n. Chiefly Brit.* **1.** a light soft yeast cake, eaten toasted and buttered. **2.** *Sl.* women collectively. [C17: from ?]

crumple ('krʌmpᵊl) *vb.* **1.** (when *intr.*, often foll. by *up*) to collapse or cause to collapse. **2.** (when *tr.*, often foll. by *up*) to crush or cause to be crushed so as to form wrinkles or creases. ~*n.* **3.** a loose crease or wrinkle. [C16: from obs. *crump* to bend] —**'crumply** *adj.*

crunch (krʌntʃ) *vb.* **1.** to bite or chew with a crushing or crackling sound. **2.** to make or cause to make a crisp or brittle sound. ~*n.* **3.** the sound or act of crunching. **4.** **the crunch.** *Inf.* the critical moment or situation. ~*adj.* **5.** *Inf.* critical; decisive: *crunch time.* [C19: changed (through infl. of MUNCH) from earlier *craunch*, imit.] —**'crunchy** *adj.* —**'crunchily** *adv.* —**'crunchiness** *n.*

crupper ('krʌpə) *n.* **1.** a strap from the back of a saddle that passes under a horse's tail. **2.** the horse's rump. [C13: from OF *crupiere*, from *crupe* CROUP²]

crusade (kruː'seɪd) n. **1.** (often cap.) any of the military expeditions undertaken in the 11th, 12th, and 13th centuries by the Christian powers of Europe to recapture the Holy Land from the Muslims. **2.** (formerly) any holy war. **3.** a vigorous and dedicated action or movement in favour of a cause. ~vb. (intr.) **4.** to campaign vigorously for something. **5.** to go on a crusade. [C16: from earlier croisade, from OF crois cross, from L crux; infl. also by Sp. cruzada, from cruzar to take up the cross] —cru'sader n.

cruse (kruːz) n. a small earthenware container used, esp. formerly, for liquids. [OE crūse]

crush (krʌʃ) vb. (mainly tr.) **1.** to press, mash, or squeeze so as to injure, break, crease, etc. **2.** to break or grind into small particles. **3.** to put down or subdue, esp. by force. **4.** to extract (juice, water, etc.) by pressing. **5.** to oppress harshly. **6.** to hug or clasp tightly. **7.** to defeat or humiliate utterly, as in argument or by a cruel remark. **8.** (intr.) to crowd; throng. **9.** (intr.) to become injured, broken, or distorted by pressure. ~n. **10.** a dense crowd, esp. at a social occasion. **11.** the act of crushing; pressure. **12.** a drink or pulp prepared by or as if by crushing fruit: orange crush. **13.** Inf. **a.** an infatuation: she had a crush on him. **b.** the person with whom one is infatuated. [C14: from OF croissir, of Gmc origin] —'crushable adj. —'crusher n.

crush barrier n. a barrier erected to separate sections of large crowds.

Crusoe ('kruːsəʊ, -zəʊ) n. Robinson. See Robinson Crusoe.

crust (krʌst) n. **1. a.** the hard outer part of bread. **b.** a piece of bread consisting mainly of this. **2.** the baked shell of a pie, tart, etc. **3.** any hard or stiff outer covering or surface: a crust of ice. **4.** the solid outer shell of the earth. **5.** the dry covering of a skin sore or lesion; scab. **6.** Sl. impertinence. **7.** Brit., Austral., & N.Z. sl. a living (esp. in earn a crust). ~vb. **8.** to cover with or acquire a crust. **9.** to form or be formed into a crust. [C14: from L crūsta hard surface, rind, shell]

crustacean (krʌ'steɪʃən) n. **1.** any arthropod of the mainly aquatic class Crustacea, typically having a carapace and including the lobsters, crabs, woodlice, and water fleas. ~adj. also **crustaceous**. **2.** of, relating to, or belonging to the Crustacea. [C19: from NL crūstāceus hard-shelled, from L crūsta shell]

crustal ('krʌstəl) adj. of or relating to the earth's crust.

crusty ('krʌstɪ) adj. **crustier, crustiest**. **1.** having or characterized by a crust. **2.** having a rude or harsh character or exterior. —'crustily adv. —'crustiness n.

crutch (krʌtʃ) n. **1.** a long staff having a rest for the armpit, for supporting the weight of the body. **2.** something that supports, helps, or sustains. **3.** Brit. another word for **crotch** (sense 1). ~vb. **4.** (tr.) to support or sustain (a person or thing) as with a crutch. **5.** Austral. & N.Z. to clip (wool) from the hindquarters of a sheep. [OE crycc]

crutchings ('krʌtʃɪŋz) pl. n. Austral. & N.Z. wool clipped from a sheep's hindquarters.

crux (krʌks) n., pl. **cruxes** or **cruces** ('kruːsiːz). **1.** a vital or decisive stage, point, etc. (often in **the crux of the matter**). **2.** a baffling problem or difficulty. [C18: from L: cross]

Cruyff (krɔɪf; Dutch krœjf) n. Johan (jɔː'hɑn). born 1947, Dutch footballer: one of the world's leading strikers; played for Ajax of Amsterdam (1965–73) and Barcelona (1973–78); captained the Dutch team in the 1974 World Cup.

cruzado (kruː'zeɪdəʊ) n., pl. **-does** or **-dos** (-dəʊz). the standard monetary unit of Brazil. [C16: lit., marked with a cross, from cruzar to bear a cross; see CRUSADE]

cruzeiro (kruː'zɛərəʊ) n., pl. **-ros** (-rəʊz). the former standard monetary unit of Brazil. [Port.: from cruz CROSS]

cry (kraɪ) vb. **crying, cried**. **1.** (intr.) to utter inarticulate sounds, esp. when weeping; sob. **2.** (intr.) to shed tears; weep. **3.** (intr.; usually foll. by out) to scream or shout in pain, terror, etc. **4.** (tr.; often foll. by out) to utter or shout (words of appeal, exclamation, fear, etc.). **5.** (intr.; often foll. by out) (of animals, birds, etc.) to utter loud characteristic sounds. **6.** (tr.) to hawk or sell by public announcement: to cry newspapers. **7.** to announce (something) publicly or in the streets. **8.** (intr.; foll. by for) to clamour or beg. **9. cry for the moon.** to desire the unattainable. **10. cry one's eyes** or **heart out.** to weep bitterly. ~n., pl. **cries. 11.** the act or sound of crying; a

shout, scream, or wail. **12.** the characteristic utterance of an animal or bird. **13.** a fit of weeping. **14.** Hunting. the baying of a pack of hounds hunting their quarry by scent. **15. a far cry. a.** a long way. **b.** something very different. **16. in full cry.** (esp. of a pack of hounds) in hot pursuit of a quarry. ~See also **cry down, cry off**, etc. [C13: from OF crier, from L quirītāre to call for help]

crybaby ('kraɪ,beɪbɪ) n., pl. **-bies.** a person, esp. a child, given to frequent crying or complaint.

cry down vb. (tr., adv.) to belittle; disparage.

crying ('kraɪɪŋ) adj. (prenominal) notorious; lamentable (esp. in **crying shame**).

cryo- combining form. cold or freezing: cryogenics. [from Gk kruos icy cold, frost]

cryobiology (,kraɪəʊbaɪ'ɒlədʒɪ) n. the biology of the effects of very low temperatures on organisms. —,cryobi'ologist n.

cry off vb. (intr.) Inf. to withdraw from or cancel (an agreement or arrangement).

cryogen ('kraɪədʒən) n. a substance used to produce low temperatures; a freezing mixture.

cryogenics (,kraɪə'dʒɛnɪks) n. (functioning as sing.) the branch of physics concerned with very low temperatures and the phenomena occurring at these temperatures. —,cryo'genic adj.

cryolite ('kraɪə,laɪt) n. a white or colourless fluoride of sodium and aluminium: used in the production of aluminium, glass, and enamel. Formula: Na_3AlF_6.

cryonics (kraɪ'ɒnɪks) n. (functioning as sing.) the practice of freezing a human corpse in the hope of restoring it to life later.

cryostat ('kraɪə,stæt) n. an apparatus for maintaining a constant low temperature.

cryosurgery (,kraɪəʊ'sɜːdʒərɪ) n. surgery involving quick freezing for therapeutic benefit.

cry out vb. (intr., adv.) **1.** to scream or shout aloud, esp. in pain, terror, etc. **2.** (often foll. by for) Inf. to demand in an obvious manner.

crypt (krɪpt) n. a vault or underground chamber, esp. beneath a church, often used as a chapel, burial place, etc. [C18: from L crypta, from Gk kruptē vault, secret place, ult. from kruptein to hide]

cryptanalysis (,krɪptə'nælɪsɪs) n. the study of codes and ciphers; cryptography. [C20: from CRYPTO- + ANALYSIS] —**cryptanalytic** (,krɪptænə'lɪtɪk) adj. —**crypt'analyst** n.

cryptic ('krɪptɪk) adj. **1.** hidden; secret. **2.** esoteric or obscure in meaning. **3.** (of coloration) effecting camouflage or concealment. [C17: from LL crypticus, from Gk kruptikos, from kruptos concealed; see CRYPT] —'cryptically adv.

crypto- or before a vowel **crypt-** combining form. secret, hidden, or concealed. [NL, from Gk kruptos hidden, from kruptein to hide]

cryptocrystalline (,krɪptəʊ'krɪstəlaɪn) adj. (of rocks) composed of crystals visible only under a polarizing microscope.

cryptogam ('krɪptəʊ,gæm) n. (in former classification schemes) any plant that does not produce seeds, including algae, fungi, mosses, and ferns. [C19: from NL Cryptogamia, from CRYPTO-+ Gk gamos marriage] —,crypto'gamic or **cryptogamous** (krɪp'tɒgəməs) adj.

cryptograph ('krɪptəʊ,grɑːf) n. **1.** something written in code or cipher. **2.** a code using secret symbols (**cryptograms**).

cryptography (krɪp'tɒgrəfɪ) n. the science or study of analysing and deciphering codes, ciphers, etc. Also called: **cryptanalysis.** —**cryp'tographer** or **cryp'tographist** n. —**cryptographic** (,krɪptə'græfɪk) or ,**crypto'graphical** adj. —,**crypto'graphically** adv.

crystal ('krɪstəl) n. **1.** a solid, such as quartz, with a regular shape in which plane faces intersect at definite angles. **2.** a single grain of a crystalline substance. **3.** anything resembling a crystal, such as a piece of cut glass. **4. a.** a highly transparent and brilliant type of glass. **b.** (as modifier): a crystal chandelier. **5.** something made of or resembling crystal. **6.** crystal glass articles collectively. **7.** Electronics. **a.** a crystalline element used in certain electronic devices as a detector, oscillator, etc. **b.** (as modifier): crystal pick-up. **8.** a transparent cover for the face of a watch. **9.** (modifier) of or relating to a crystal or the regular atomic arrangement of crystals: crystal structure. ~adj. **10.** resembling crystal; transparent: crystal water.

[OE *cristalla*, from L *crystallum*, from Gk *krustallos* ice, crystal, from *krustainein* to freeze]

crystal ball *n.* the glass globe used in crystal gazing.

crystal class *n. Crystallography.* any of 32 possible types of crystals, classified according to their rotational symmetry about axes through a point. Also called: **point group.**

crystal detector *n. Electronics.* a demodulator, used esp. in early radio receivers, incorporating a semiconductor crystal.

crystal gazing *n.* **1.** the act of staring into a crystal ball supposedly in order to arouse visual perceptions of the future, etc. **2.** the act of trying to foresee or predict. —**crystal gazer** *n.*

crystal lattice *n.* the regular array of points about which the atoms, ions, or molecules composing a crystal are centred.

crystalline ('krɪstə‚laɪn) *adj.* **1.** having the characteristics or structure of crystals. **2.** consisting of or containing crystals. **3.** made of or like crystal; transparent; clear.

crystalline lens *n.* a biconvex transparent elastic lens in the eye.

crystallize *or* **-ise** ('krɪstə‚laɪz) *vb.* **1.** to form or cause to form crystals; assume or cause to assume a crystalline form or structure. **2.** to coat or become coated with sugar. **3.** to give a definite form or expression to (an idea, argument, etc.) or (of an idea, argument, etc.) to assume a definite form. —'**crystal‚lizable** *or* **-isable** *adj.* —‚**crystalli'zation** *or* **-i'sation** *n.*

crystallo- *or before a vowel* **crystall-** *combining form.* crystal: *crystallography.*

crystallography (‚krɪstə'lɒɡrəfɪ) *n.* the science of crystal structure. —‚**crystal'lographer** *n.* —**crystallographic** (‚krɪstələʊ'ɡræfɪk) *adj.*

crystalloid ('krɪstə‚lɔɪd) *adj.* **1.** resembling or having the properties of a crystal. ~*n.* **2.** a substance that in solution can pass through a semipermeable membrane.

Crystal Palace *n.* a building of glass and iron designed by Joseph Paxton to house the Great Exhibition of 1851. Erected in Hyde Park, London, it was moved to Sydenham (1852–53): destroyed by fire in 1936.

crystal pick-up *n.* a gramophone pick-up incorporating a piezoelectric crystal.

crystal set *n.* an early form of radio receiver having a crystal detector.

cry up *vb.* (*tr., adv.*) to praise highly; extol.

Cs *the chemical symbol for* caesium.

CS *abbrev. for:* **1.** Also: **cs.** capital stock. **2.** chartered surveyor. **3.** Christian Science. **4.** Civil Service. **5.** Also: **cs.** Court of Session.

csc *abbrev. for* cosecant.

CSC *abbrev. for* Civil Service Commission.

CSE (in Britain) *abbrev. for* Certificate of Secondary Education; an examination the first grade pass of which is an equivalent to a GCE O level.

CSEU *abbrev. for* Confederation of Shipbuilding and Engineering Unions.

CS gas *n.* a gas causing tears, salivation, and painful breathing, used in civil disturbances. [C20: from the surname initials of its U.S. inventors, Ben Carson and Roger Staughton]

CSIRO (in Australia) *abbrev. for* Commonwealth Scientific and Industrial Research Organization.

CSM (in Britain) *abbrev. for* Company Sergeant-Major.

CST (in the U.S. and Canada) *abbrev. for* Central Standard Time.

CSU *abbrev. for* Civil Service Union.

ct *abbrev. for:* **1.** carat. **2.** cent. **3.** court.

CTC (in Britain) *abbrev. for* city technology college.

ctenophore ('tɛnə‚fɔ:, 'ti:nə-) *n.* any marine invertebrate of the phylum *Ctenophora*, whose body bears eight rows of fused cilia, for locomotion. [C19: from NL *ctenophorus*, from Gk *kteno-, kteis* comb + -PHORE]

Ctesiphon ('tɛsɪ‚fɒn) *n.* an ancient city on the River Tigris about 100 km (60 miles) above Babylon. First mentioned in 221 B.C., it was destroyed in the 7th and 8th centuries A.D.

ctn *abbrev. for* cotangent.

CT scanner *n.* an x-ray machine that can produce stereographic images. Former name: **CAT scanner** [C20: from Computerized Tomography]

CTT *abbrev. for* Capital Transfer Tax.

CTV *abbrev. for* Canadian Television (Network Limited).

Cu *the chemical symbol for* copper. [from LL *cuprum*]

cu. *abbrev. for* cubic.

cub (kʌb) *n.* **1.** the young of certain animals, such as the lion, bear, etc. **2.** a young or inexperienced person. ~*vb.* **cubbing, cubbed.** **3.** to give birth to (cubs). [C16: ?from ON *kubbi* young seal] —'**cubbish** *adj.*

Cub (kʌb) *n.* short for **Cub Scout.**

Cuba ('kju:bə) *n.* a republic and the largest island in the West Indies, at the entrance to the Gulf of Mexico: became a Spanish colony after its discovery by Columbus in 1492; gained independence after the Spanish-American War of 1898 but remained subject to U.S. influence until declared a people's republic under Castro in 1960; subject of an international crisis in 1962, when the U.S. blockaded the island in order to compel the Soviet Union to dismantle its nuclear missile base. Sugar comprises about 80 per cent of total exports. Language: Spanish. Currency: peso. Capital: Havana. Pop.: 10 462 000 (1988 est.). Area: 110 922 sq. km (42 827 sq. miles). —'**Cuban** *adj., n.*

cubby ('kʌbɪ) *n., pl.* **-bies.** *Austral.* a small room or enclosed area, esp. one used as a child's play area. Also: **cubbyhole, cubby-house.**

cubbyhole ('kʌbɪ‚həʊl) *n.* a small enclosed space or room. [C19: from dialect *cub* cattle pen]

cube (kju:b) *n.* **1.** a solid having six plane square faces in which the angle between two adjacent sides is a right angle. **2.** the product of three equal factors. **3.** something in the form of a cube. ~*vb.* **4.** to raise (a number or quantity) to the third power. **5.** (*tr.*) to make, shape, or cut (something) into cubes. [C16: from L *cubus* die, cube, from Gk *kubos*] —'**cuber** *n.*

cubeb ('kju:bɛb) *n.* **1.** a SE Asian treelike climbing plant. **2.** its spicy fruit, dried and used as a stimulant and diuretic and sometimes smoked in cigarettes. [C14: from OF *cubebe*, from Med. L *cubēba*, from Ar. *kubābah*]

cube root *n.* the number or quantity whose cube is a given number or quantity: 2 is the cube root of 8 (usually written $^3\sqrt{8}$ or $8^{1/3}$).

cubic ('kju:bɪk) *adj.* **1.** having the shape of a cube. **2. a.** having three dimensions. **b.** denoting or relating to a linear measure that is raised to the third power: *a cubic metre.* **3.** *Maths.* of, relating to, or containing a variable to the third power or a term in which the sum of the exponents of the variables is three. —'**cubical** *adj.*

cubicle ('kju:bɪk³l) *n.* a partially or totally enclosed section of a room, as in a dormitory. [C15: from L *cubiculum*, from *cubāre* to lie down]

cubic measure *n.* a system of units for the measurement of volumes.

cubiform ('kju:bɪ‚fɔ:m) *adj.* having the shape of a cube.

cubism ('kju:bɪzəm) *n.* (*often cap.*) a French school of art, initiated in 1907 by Picasso and Braque, which amalgamated viewpoints of natural forms into a multifaceted surface of geometrical planes. —'**cubist** *adj., n.* —**cu'bistic** *adj.*

cubit ('kju:bɪt) *n.* an ancient measure of length based on the length of the forearm. [C14: from L *cubitum* elbow, cubit]

cuboid ('kju:bɔɪd) *adj. also* **cuboidal** (kju:'bɔɪd³l). **1.** shaped like a cube; cubic. **2.** of or denoting the cuboid bone. ~*n.* **3.** the cubelike bone of the foot. **4.** *Maths.* a geometric solid whose six faces are rectangles.

Cub Scout *or* **Cub** *n.* a member of the junior branch of the Scout Association.

Cuchulain, Cuchulainn, *or* **Cuchullain** (ku:'kʌlɪn, kʊ-'xʊlɪn) *n. Celtic myth.* a legendary hero of Ulster.

cucking stool ('kʌkɪŋ) *n. History.* a stool to which suspected witches, scolds, etc., were tied and pelted or ducked into water. [C13 *cucking stol*, lit.: defecating chair, from *cukken* to defecate]

cuckold ('kʌkəld) *n.* **1.** a man whose wife has committed adultery. ~*vb.* **2.** (*tr.*) to make a cuckold of. [C13 *cukeweld*, from OF *cucuault*, from *cucu* CUCKOO; ? an allusion to cuckoos that lay eggs in the nests of other birds] —'**cuckoldry** *n.*

cuckoo ('kʊku:) *n., pl.* **-oos.** **1.** any bird of the family Cuculidae, having pointed wings and a long tail. Many species, including the **European cuckoo**, lay their eggs in the nests of other birds and have a two-note call. **2.** *Inf.* an insane or foolish person. ~*adj.* **3.** *Inf.* insane or foolish. ~*interj.* **4.** an imitation or representation of the call of a cuckoo. ~*vb.* **-ooing, -ooed. 5.** (*intr.*) to make the sound imitated by the word *cuckoo.* [C13: from OF *cucu,* imit.]

cuckoo clock *n.* a clock in which a mechanical cuckoo pops out with a sound like a cuckoo's call when the clock strikes.

cuckoopint ('kʊkuː,paɪnt) *n.* a European plant with arrow-shaped leaves, a spathe marked with purple, a pale purple spadix, and scarlet berries. Also called: **lords-and-ladies.**

cuckoo spit *n.* a white frothy mass on the stems and leaves of many plants, produced by froghopper larvae.

cucullate ('kjuːkə,leɪt, -lɪt) *adj.* shaped like a hood or having a hoodlike part: *cucullate sepals.* [C18: from LL *cucullātus,* from L *cucullus* hood, cap]

cucumber ('kjuː,kʌmbə) *n.* **1.** a creeping plant cultivated in many forms for its edible fruit. **2.** the cylindrical fruit of this plant, which has hard thin green rind and white crisp flesh. [C14: from L *cucumis,* from ?]

cucurbit (kjuː'kɜːbɪt) *n.* any of a family of creeping flowering plants that includes the pumpkin, cucumber, and gourds. [C14: from OF, from L *cucurbita* gourd, cup] — **cu,curbi'taceous** *adj.*

Cúcuta (*Spanish* 'kukuta) *n.* a city in E Colombia: commercial centre of a coffee-producing region. Pop.: 407 236 (1985). Official name: **San José de Cúcuta** (san xo'se ðe).

cud (kʌd) *n.* **1.** partially digested food regurgitated from the first stomach of ruminants to the mouth for a second chewing. **2. chew the cud.** to reflect or think over something. [OE *cudu,* from *cwidu* what has been chewed]

cuddle ('kʌdəl) *vb.* **1.** to hold close or (of two people, etc.) to hold each other close, as for affection or warmth; hug. **2.** (*intr.*; foll. by *up*) to curl or snuggle up into a comfortable or warm position. ~*n.* **3.** a close embrace, esp. when prolonged. [C18: from ?] — **'cuddlesome** *adj.* — **'cuddly** *adj.*

cuddy ('kʌdɪ) *n.*, *pl.* **-dies.** a small cabin in a boat. [C17: ?from Du. *kajute*]

cudgel ('kʌdʒəl) *n.* **1.** a short stout stick used as a weapon. **2. take up the cudgels.** (often foll. by *for* or *on behalf of*) to join in a dispute, esp. to defend oneself or another. ~*vb.* **-elling, -elled** or *U.S.* **-eling, -eled. 3.** (*tr.*) to strike with a cudgel. **4. cudgel one's brains.** to think hard. [OE *cycgel*]

cudgerie ('kʌdʒərɪ) *n. Austral.* any of various large rainforest trees, such as the pink poplar or blush cudgerie, with pink wood. [from Abor.]

cudweed ('kʌd,wiːd) *n.* any of various temperate woolly plants having clusters of whitish or yellow button-like flowers.

cue[1] (kjuː) *n.* **1. a.** (in the theatre, films, music, etc.) anything that serves as a signal to an actor, musician, etc., to follow with specific lines or action. **b. on cue.** at the right moment. **2.** a signal or reminder to do something. ~*vb.* **cueing, cued. 3.** (*tr.*) to give a cue or cues to (an actor). **4.** (usually foll. by *in* or *into*) to signal (to something or somebody) at a specific moment in a musical or dramatic performance. [C16: prob. from name of the letter *q,* used in an actor's script to represent L *quando* when]

cue[2] (kjuː) *n.* **1.** *Billiards, etc.* a long tapered shaft used to drive the balls. **2.** hair caught at the back forming a tail or braid. ~*vb.* **cueing, cued. 3.** to drive (a ball) with a cue. [C18: var. of QUEUE]

cue ball *n. Billiards, etc.* the ball struck by the cue, as distinguished from the object balls.

Cuenca (*Spanish* 'kweŋka) *n.* **1.** a city in SW Ecuador: university (1868). Pop.: 272 397 (1982). **2.** a town in central Spain: prosperous in the Middle Ages for its silver and textile industries. Pop.: 39 860 (1982 est.).

Cuernavaca (*Spanish* kwɛrna'βaka) *n.* a city in S central Mexico, capital of Morelos state: resort with nearby Cacahuamilpa Caverns. Pop.: 232 355 (1980).

cuesta ('kwɛstə) *n.* a long low ridge with a steep scarp slope and a gentle back slope. [Sp.: shoulder, from L *costa* side, rib]

cuff[1] (kʌf) *n.* **1.** the end of a sleeve, sometimes turned back. **2.** the part of a glove that extends past the wrist. **3.** the U.S., Canad., and Austral. name for **turn-up** (sense 5). **4. off the cuff.** *Inf.* improvised; extemporary. [C14 *cuffe* glove, from ?]

cuff[2] (kʌf) *vb.* **1.** (*tr.*) to strike with an open hand. ~*n.* **2.** a blow of this kind. [C16: from ?]

cuff link *n.* one of a pair of linked buttons, used to join the buttonholes on the cuffs of a shirt.

Cuiabá or **Cuyabá** (*Portuguese* kuia'ba) *n.* **1.** a port in W Brazil, capital of Mato Grosso state, on the Cuiabá River. Pop.: 158 700 (1980 est.). **2.** a river in SW Brazil, rising on the Mato Grosso plateau and flowing southwest into the São Lourenço River. Length: 483 km (300 miles).

cui bono *Latin.* (kwi: 'bəʊnəʊ) for whose benefit? for what purpose?

cuirass (kwɪ'ræs) *n.* **1.** a piece of armour covering the chest and back. ~*vb.* **2.** (*tr.*) to equip with a cuirass. [C15: from F *cuirasse,* from LL *coriacea,* from *coriaceus* made of leather]

cuirassier (,kwɪərə'sɪə) *n.* a mounted soldier, esp. of the 16th century, who wore a cuirass.

Cuisenaire rod (,kwɪzə'nɛə) *n. Trademark.* one of a set of rods of various colours and lengths representing different numbers, used to teach arithmetic to young children. [C20: after Emil-Georges *Cuisenaire* (?1891–1976), Belgian educationalist]

cuisine (kwɪ'ziːn) *n.* **1.** a style or manner of cooking: *French cuisine.* **2.** the food prepared by a restaurant, household, etc. [C18: from F, lit.: kitchen, from LL *coquīna,* from L *coquere* to cook]

cuisse (kwɪs) or **cuish** (kwɪʃ) *n.* a piece of armour for the thigh. [C15: back formation from *cuisses* (pl.), from OF *cuisseaux,* from *cuisse* thigh]

Culbertson ('kʌlbətsən) *n. Ely* ('iːlaɪ). 1891–1955, U.S. authority on contract bridge.

cul-de-sac ('kʌldə,sæk, 'kʊl-) *n.*, *pl.* **culs-de-sac** or **cul-de-sacs. 1.** a road with one end blocked off; dead end. **2.** an inescapable position. [C18: from F, lit.: bottom of the bag]

-cule *suffix forming nouns.* indicating smallness. [from L *-culus,* dim. suffix]

Culebra Cut (kuː'lɛbrə) *n.* the former name of the **Gaillard Cut.**

culex ('kjuːlɛks) *n.*, *pl.* **-lices** (-lɪ,siːz). any mosquito of the genus *Culex,* such as *C. pipiens,* the common mosquito. [C15: from L: midge, gnat]

Culiacán (*Spanish* kulja'kan) *n.* a city in NW Mexico, capital of Sinaloa state. Pop.: 560 011 (1980).

culinary ('kʌlɪnərɪ) *adj.* of, relating to, or used in the kitchen or in cookery. [C17: from L *culīnārius,* from *culīna* kitchen] — **'culinarily** *adv.*

cull (kʌl) *vb.* (*tr.*) **1.** to choose or gather the best or required examples of. **2.** to seek out (an animal, esp. an inferior one) from a herd. **3.** to reduce the size of (a herd, etc.) by killing a proportion of its members. **4.** to gather (flowers, fruit, etc.). ~*n.* **5.** the act or product of culling. **6.** an inferior animal taken from a herd. [C15: from OF *coillir* to pick, from L *colligere;* see COLLECT[1]] — **'culler** *n.*

Culloden (kə'lɒdən) *n.* a moor near Inverness in N Scotland: site of a battle in 1746 in which government troops under the Duke of Cumberland defeated the Jacobites under Prince Charles Edward Stuart.

culm[1] (kʌlm) *n. Mining.* **1.** coal-mine waste. **2.** inferior anthracite. [C14: prob. rel. to COAL]

culm[2] (kʌlm) *n.* the hollow jointed stem of a grass or sedge. [C17: from L *culmus* stalk; see HAULM]

culminate ('kʌlmɪ,neɪt) *vb.* **1.** (when *intr.,* usually foll. by *in*) to reach or bring to a final or climactic stage. **2.** (*intr.*) (of a celestial body) to cross the meridian. [C17: from LL *culmināre* to reach the highest point, from L *culmen* top] — **'culminant** *adj.*

culmination (,kʌlmɪ'neɪʃən) *n.* **1.** the final or highest point. **2.** the act of culminating.

culottes (kjuː'lɒts) *pl. n.* women's flared trousers cut to look like a skirt. [C20: from F, lit.: breeches, from *cul* bottom]

culpable ('kʌlpəbəl) *adj.* deserving censure; blameworthy. [C14: from OF *coupable,* from L *culpābilis,* from *culpāre* to blame, from *culpa* fault] — **,culpa'bility** *n.* — **'culpably** *adv.*

culpable homicide *n. Scots Law.* manslaughter.

culprit ('kʌlprɪt) *n.* **1.** *Law.* a person awaiting trial. **2.** the person responsible for a particular offence, misdeed, etc. [C17: from Anglo-F *cul-,* short for *culpable* guilty + *prit* ready, indicating that the prosecution was ready to prove the guilt of the one charged]

cult (kʌlt) *n.* **1.** a specific system of religious worship. **2.** a sect devoted to the beliefs of a cult. **3.** intense interest in and devotion to a person, idea, or activity. **4.** the person, idea, etc., arousing such devotion. **5.** any popular fashion; craze. **6.** (*modifier*) of, relating to, or characteristic of a cult or cults: *a cult figure*. [C17: from L *cultus* cultivation, refinement, from *colere* to till] —'**cultic** *adj.* —'**cultism** *n.* —'**cultist** *n.*

cultivable ('kʌltɪvəb²l) *or* **cultivatable** ('kʌltɪ,veɪtəb²l) *adj.* (of land) capable of being cultivated. [C17: from F, from OF *cultiver* to CULTIVATE] —,**cultiva'bility** *n.*

cultivar ('kʌltɪ,vɑː) *n.* a variety of a plant produced from a natural species and maintained by cultivation. [C20: from CULTI(VATED) + VAR(IETY)]

cultivate ('kʌltɪ,veɪt) *vb.* (*tr.*) **1.** to prepare (land or soil) for the growth of crops. **2.** to plant, tend, harvest, or improve (plants). **3.** to break up (land or soil) with a cultivator or hoe. **4.** to improve (the mind, body, etc.) as by study, education, or labour. **5.** to give special attention to: *to cultivate a friendship*. [C17: from Med. L *cultivāre* to till, from *cultivus* cultivable, from L *cultus* cultivated, from *colere* to till, toil over] —'**culti,vated** *adj.*

cultivation (,kʌltɪ'veɪʃən) *n.* **1.** *Agriculture*. **a.** the cultivating of crops or plants. **b.** the preparation of ground to promote their growth. **2.** development, esp. through education, training, etc. **3.** culture or sophistication.

cultivator ('kʌltɪ,veɪtə) *n.* **1.** a farm implement used to break up soil and remove weeds. **2.** a person or thing that cultivates.

cultural ('kʌltʃərəl) *adj.* **1.** of or relating to artistic or social pursuits or events considered valuable or enlightened. **2.** of or relating to a culture. **3.** obtained by specialized breeding.

culture ('kʌltʃə) *n.* **1.** the total of the inherited ideas, beliefs, values, and knowledge, which constitute the shared bases of social action. **2.** the total range of activities and ideas of a people. **3.** a particular civilization at a particular period. **4.** the artistic and social pursuits, expression, and tastes valued by a society or class. **5.** the enlightenment or refinement resulting from these pursuits. **6.** the cultivation of plants to improve stock or to produce new ones. **7.** the rearing and breeding of animals, esp. with a view to improving the strain. **8.** the act or practice of tilling or cultivating the soil. **9.** *Biol.* **a.** the experimental growth of microorganisms in a nutrient substance. **b.** a group of microorganisms grown in this way. ~*vb.* (*tr.*) **10.** to cultivate (plants or animals). **11.** to grow (microorganisms) in a culture medium. [C15: from OF, from L *cultūra* a cultivating, from *colere* to till; see CULT] —'**culturist** *n.*

cultured ('kʌltʃəd) *adj.* **1.** showing or having good taste, manners, and education. **2.** artificially grown or synthesized: *cultured pearls*. **3.** treated by a culture of microorganisms.

cultured pearl *n.* a pearl induced to grow in the shell of an oyster or clam, by the insertion of a small object.

culture shock *n.* *Sociol.* the feelings of isolation, rejection, etc., experienced when one culture is brought into sudden contact with another.

culture vulture *n.* *Inf.* a person considered to be excessively eager to acquire culture.

cultus ('kʌltəs) *n.*, *pl.* -**tuses** *or* -**ti** (-taɪ). another word for **cult** (sense 1). [C17: from L: a toiling over something, refinement, CULT]

culverin ('kʌlvərɪn) *n.* **1.** a medium-to-heavy cannon used during the 15th, 16th, and 17th centuries. **2.** a medieval musket. [C15: from OF *coulevrine*, from *couleuvre*, from L *coluber* serpent]

culvert ('kʌlvət) *n.* **1.** a drain or covered channel that crosses under a road, railway, etc. **2.** a channel for an electric cable. [C18: from ?]

cum (kʌm) *prep.* used between nouns to designate a combined nature: *a kitchen-cum-dining room*. [L: with, together with]

Cumae ('kjuːmiː) *n.* the oldest Greek colony in Italy, founded about 750 B.C. near Naples. —**Cu'maean** *adj.*

Cumaná (*Spanish* kuma'na) *n.* a city in NE Venezuela: founded in 1523; the oldest European settlement in South America. Pop.: 173 000 (1981 est.).

cumber ('kʌmbə) *vb.* (*tr.*) **1.** to obstruct or hinder. **2.** *Obs.* to inconvenience. [C13: prob. from OF *combrer* to impede, from *combre* barrier; see ENCUMBER]

Cumberland[1] ('kʌmbələnd) *n.* (until 1974) a county of NW England, now part of Cumbria.

Cumberland[2] ('kʌmbələnd) *n.* **William Augustus,** Duke of Cumberland, known as *Butcher Cumberland*. 1721–65, English soldier, younger son of George II, noted for his defeat of Charles Edward Stuart at Culloden (1746) and his subsequent ruthless destruction of Jacobite rebels.

Cumbernauld (,kʌmbə'nɔːld) *n.* a town in central Scotland, in E central Strathclyde region, northeast of Glasgow: developed as a new town since 1956. Pop.: 49 500 (1985 est.).

cumbersome ('kʌmbəsəm) *or* **cumbrous** ('kʌmbrəs) *adj.* **1.** awkward because of size, weight, or shape. **2.** difficult because of extent or complexity: *cumbersome accounts*. [C14: *cumber*, short for ENCUMBER + -SOME[1]] —'**cumbersomeness** *or* '**cumbrousness** *n.*

cumbrance ('kʌmbrəns) *n.* **1.** a burden, obstacle, or hindrance. **2.** trouble or bother.

Cumbria ('kʌmbrɪə) *n.* (since 1974) a county of NW England comprising the former counties of Westmorland and Cumberland together with N Lancashire: includes the Lake District mountain area and surrounding coastal lowlands with the Pennine uplands in the extreme east. Administrative centre: Carlisle. Pop.: 486 600 (1986 est.). Area: 6810 sq. km (2629 sq. miles). —'**Cumbrian** *adj., n.*

Cumbrian Mountains ('kʌmbrɪən) *pl. n.* a mountain range in NW England, in Cumbria. Highest peak: Scafell Pike, 978 m (3210 ft.).

cumin *or* **cummin** ('kʌmɪn) *n.* **1.** an umbelliferous Mediterranean plant with small white or pink flowers. **2.** the aromatic seeds (collectively) of this plant, used as a condiment and a flavouring. [C12: from OF, from L *cumīnum*, from Gk *kuminon*, of Semitic origin]

cummerbund ('kʌmə,bʌnd) *n.* a wide sash, worn with a dinner jacket. [C17: from Hindi *kamarband*, from Persian, from *kamar* loins, waist + *band* band]

Cummings ('kʌmɪŋz) *n.* **Edward Estlin** ('ɛstlɪn), (preferred typographical representation of name *e. e. cummings*). 1894–1962, U.S. poet and artist.

cumquat ('kʌmkwɒt) *n.* a variant spelling of **kumquat.**

cumulate *vb.* ('kjuːmjʊ,leɪt). **1.** to accumulate. **2.** (*tr.*) to combine (two or more sequences) into one. ~*adj.* ('kjuːmjʊlɪt). **3.** heaped up. [C16: from L *cumulāre* from *cumulus* heap] —,**cumu'lation** *n.*

cumulative ('kjuːmjʊlətɪv) *adj.* **1.** growing in quantity, strength, or effect by successive additions. **2.** (of dividends or interest) intended to be accumulated. **3.** *Statistics*. **a.** (of a frequency) including all values of a variable either below or above a specified value. **b.** (of error) tending to increase as the sample size is increased. —'**cumulatively** *adv.* —'**cumulativeness** *n.*

cumulonimbus (,kjuːmjʊləʊ'nɪmbəs) *n., pl.* -**bi** (-baɪ) *or* -**buses**. *Meteorol.* a cumulus cloud of great vertical extent, the bottom being dark-coloured, indicating rain or hail.

cumulus ('kjuːmjʊləs) *n., pl.* -**li** (-,laɪ). a bulbous or billowing white or dark grey cloud. [C17: from L: mass] —'**cumulous** *adj.*

Cunaxa (kjuː'næksə) *n.* the site near the lower Euphrates where Artaxerxes II defeated Cyrus the Younger in 401 B.C.

cuneate ('kjuːnɪɪt, -,eɪt) *adj.* wedge-shaped. [C19: from L *cuneāre* to make wedge-shaped, from *cuneus* a wedge] —'**cuneately** *adv.* —'**cuneal** *adj.*

cuneiform ('kjuːnɪ,fɔːm) *adj.* **1.** Also: **cuneal.** wedge-shaped. **2.** of, relating to, or denoting the wedge-shaped characters in several ancient languages of Mesopotamia and Persia. **3.** of or relating to a tablet in which this script is employed. ~*n.* **4.** cuneiform characters. [C17: prob. from OF *cunéiforme*, from L *cuneus* wedge]

Cuneo (*Italian* 'kuːneo) *n.* a city in NW Italy, in Piedmont. Pop.: 55 875 (1981).

cunjevoi ('kʌndʒɪ,vɔɪ) *n. Austral.* **1.** an arum of tropical Asia and Australia, cultivated for its edible rhizome. **2.** a sea squirt. Often shortened to **cunjie, cunjy.** [C19: from Abor.]

cunnilingus (,kʌnɪ'lɪŋgəs) *or* **cunnilinctus** (,kʌnɪ-'lɪŋktəs) *n.* a sexual activity in which the female genitalia are stimulated by the partner's lips and tongue. Cf. **fellatio.** [C19: from NL, from L *cunnus* vulva + *lingere* to lick]

cunning ('kʌnɪŋ) *adj.* **1.** crafty and shrewd, esp. in deception. **2.** made with or showing skill; ingenious. ~*n.* **3.** craftiness, esp. in deceiving. **4.** skill or ingenuity. [OE *cunnende;* rel. to *cunnan* to know (see CAN¹)] —'**cunningly** *adv.* —'**cunningness** *n.*

Cunningham ('kʌnɪŋəm) *n.* **Merce** (mɜːs). born 1919, U.S. dancer and choreographer. His experimental ballets include *Suit for Five* (1956) and *Travelogue* (1977).

cunt (kʌnt) *n. Taboo.* **1.** the female genitals. **2.** *Offens. sl.* a woman considered sexually. **3.** *Offens. sl.* a mean or obnoxious person. [C13: of Gmc origin; rel. to ON *kunta,* MLow G *kunte*]

cup (kʌp) *n.* **1.** a small open container, usually having one handle, used for drinking from. **2.** the contents of such a container. **3.** Also called: **teacup, cupful.** a unit of capacity used in cooking. **4.** something resembling a cup. **5.** either of two cup-shaped parts of a brassiere. **6.** a cup-shaped trophy awarded as a prize. **7.** *Brit.* **a.** a sporting contest in which a cup is awarded to the winner. **b.** (*as modifier*): *a cup competition.* **8.** a mixed drink with one ingredient as a base: *claret cup.* **9.** *Golf.* the hole or metal container in the hole on a green. **10.** the chalice or the consecrated wine used in the Eucharist. **11.** one's lot in life. **12. in one's cups.** drunk. **13. one's cup of tea.** *Inf.* one's chosen or preferred thing, task, company, etc. ~*vb.* **cupping, cupped.** (*tr.*) **14.** to form (something, such as the hands) into the shape of a cup. **15.** to put into or as if into a cup. **16.** to draw blood to the surface of the body of (a person) by cupping. [OE *cuppe,* from LL *cuppa* cup, alteration of L *cūpa* cask]

cupbearer ('kʌp,beərə) *n.* an attendant who fills and serves wine cups, as in a royal household.

cupboard ('kʌbəd) *n.* a piece of furniture or a recessed area of a room, with a door concealing storage space.

cupboard love *n.* a show of love inspired only by some selfish or greedy motive.

cupcake ('kʌp,keɪk) *n.* a small cake baked in a cup-shaped foil or paper case.

cupel ('kjuːp³l, kjʊ'pɛl) *n.* **1.** a refractory pot in which gold or silver is refined. **2.** a small bowl in which gold and silver are recovered during assaying. ~*vb.* **-pelling, -pelled** *or U.S.* **-peling, -peled.** **3.** (*tr.*) to refine (gold or silver) using a cupel. [C17: from F *coupelle,* dim. of *coupe* CUP] —,**cupel'lation** *n.*

Cup Final *n.* **1.** (*often preceded by the*) the annual final of the FA or Scottish Cup soccer competition. **2.** (*often not cap.*) the final of any cup competition.

Cupid ('kjuːpɪd) *n.* **1.** the Roman god of love, represented as a winged boy with a bow and arrow. Greek counterpart: **Eros.** **2.** (*not cap.*) any similar figure. [C14: from L *Cupīdō,* from *cupīdō* desire, from *cupidus* desirous; see CUPIDITY]

cupidity (kjuː'pɪdɪtɪ) *n.* strong desire, esp. for wealth; greed. [C15: from L *cupiditās,* from *cupidus* eagerly desiring, from *cupere* to long for]

cupola ('kjuːpələ) *n.* **1.** a roof or ceiling in the form of a dome. **2.** a small structure, usually domed, on the top of a roof or dome. **3.** a protective dome for a gun on a warship. **4.** a furnace in which metals are remelted. [C16: from It., from LL *cūpula* a small cask, from L *cūpa* tub] —'**cupo,lated** *adj.*

cuppa *or* **cupper** ('kʌpə) *n. Brit. inf.* a cup of tea.

cupping ('kʌpɪŋ) *n. Med.* formerly, the use of an evacuated glass cup to draw blood to the surface of the skin for blood-letting.

cupreous ('kjuːprɪəs) *adj.* **1.** of, containing, or resembling copper. **2.** of the colour of copper. [C17: from LL *cupreus,* from *cuprum* COPPER¹]

cupressus (kə'prɛsəs) *n.* any evergreen tree of the genus *Cupressus.*

cupric ('kjuːprɪk) *adj.* of or containing copper in the divalent state. [C18: from LL *cuprum* copper]

cupriferous (kjuː'prɪfərəs) *adj.* (of a substance such as an ore) containing or yielding copper.

cupro-, cupri-, *or before a vowel* **cupr-** *combining form.* indicating copper. [from L *cuprum*]

cupronickel (,kjuːprəʊ'nɪk³l) *n.* any copper alloy containing up to 40 per cent nickel.

cuprous ('kjuːprəs) *adj.* of or containing copper in the monovalent state.

cup tie *n. Sport.* an eliminating match or round between two teams in a cup competition.

cupule ('kjuːpjuːl) *n. Biol.* a cup-shaped part or structure. [C19: from LL *cūpula;* see CUPOLA]

cur (kɜː) *n.* **1.** any vicious dog, esp. a mongrel. **2.** a despicable or cowardly person. [C13: from *kurdogge;* prob. rel. to ON *kurra* to growl]

curable ('kjʊərəb³l) *adj.* capable of being cured. —,**cur-a'bility** *or* '**curableness** *n.*

Curaçao (,kjʊərə'səʊ) *n.* **1.** an island in the Caribbean, the largest in the Netherlands Antilles. Capital: Willemstad. Pop.: 165 011 (1983). Area: 444 sq. km (171 sq. miles). **2.** an orange-flavoured liqueur originally made there.

curacy ('kjʊərəsɪ) *n., pl.* **-cies.** the office or position of a curate.

curare *or* **curari** (kjʊ'rɑːrɪ) *n.* **1.** black resin obtained from certain tropical South American trees, which causes muscular paralysis: used medicinally as a muscle relaxant and by South American Indians as an arrow poison. **2.** any of various trees from which this resin is obtained. [C18: from Port. & Sp., from Carib *kurari*]

curassow ('kjʊərə,səʊ) *n.* any of various ground-nesting birds of S North, Central, and South America, having long legs and tail and a crest of curled feathers. [C17: anglicized from CURAÇAO (island)]

curate ('kjʊərɪt) *n.* a clergyman appointed to assist a parish priest. [C14: from Med. L *cūrātus,* from *cūra* spiritual oversight, CURE]

curate's egg *n.* something that is bad but may be euphemistically described as being only partly so. [C20: simile from a cartoon in *Punch* (Nov., 1895) in which a timid curate, who has been served a bad egg while dining with his bishop, says that parts of the egg are excellent]

curative ('kjʊərətɪv) *adj.* **1.** able or tending to cure. ~*n.* **2.** anything able to heal or cure. —'**curatively** *adv.* —'**curativeness** *n.*

curator (kjʊə'reɪtə) *n.* the administrative head of a museum, art gallery, etc. [C14: from L: one who cares, from *cūrāre* to care for, from *cūra* care] —**curatorial** (,kjʊərə'tɔːrɪəl) *adj.* —**cu'rator,ship** *n.*

curb (kɜːb) *n.* **1.** something that restrains or holds back. **2.** any enclosing framework, such as a wall around the top of a well. **3.** Also called: **curb bit.** a horse's bit with an attached chain or strap, which checks the horse. ~*vb.* (*tr.*) **4.** to control with or as if with a curb; restrain. ~See also **kerb.** [C15: from OF *courbe* curved piece of wood or metal, from L *curvus* curved]

curcuma ('kɜːkjʊmə) *n.* any tropical Asian tuberous plant of the genus *Curcuma,* such as *C. longa,* which is the source of turmeric. [C17: from NL, from Ar. *kurkum* turmeric]

curd (kɜːd) *n.* **1.** (*often pl.*) a substance formed by the coagulation of milk, used in making cheese or eaten as a food. **2.** something similar in consistency. ~*vb.* **3.** to turn into or become curd. [C15: from earlier *crud,* from ?] —'**curdy** *adj.*

curdle ('kɜːd³l) *vb.* **1.** to turn or cause to turn into curd. **2. curdle someone's blood.** to fill someone with fear. [C16 (*crudled,* p.p.): from CURD]

cure (kjʊə) *vb.* **1.** (*tr.*) to get rid of (an ailment or problem); heal. **2.** (*tr.*) to restore to health or good condition. **3.** (*intr.*) to bring about a cure. **4.** (*tr.*) to preserve (meat, fish, etc.) by salting, smoking, etc. **5.** (*tr.*) **a.** to treat or finish (a substance) by chemical or physical means. **b.** to vulcanize (rubber). **6.** (*tr.*) to assist the hardening of (concrete, mortar, etc.) by keeping it moist. ~*n.* **7.** a return to health. **8.** any course of medical therapy, esp. one proved effective. **9.** a means of restoring health or improving a situation, etc. **10.** the spiritual and pastoral charge of a parish. **11.** a process or method of preserving meat, fish, etc. [(n.) C13: from OF, from L *cūra* care; in ecclesiastical sense, from Med. L *cūra* spiritual charge; (vb.) C14: from OF *curer,* from L *cūrāre* to attend to, heal, from *cūra* care] —'**cureless** *adj.* —'**curer** *n.*

curé ('kjʊəreɪ) *n.* a parish priest in France. [F, from Med. L *cūrātus;* see CURATE]

cure-all *n.* something reputed to cure all ailments.

curet *or* **curette** (kjʊə'rɛt) *n.* **1.** a surgical instrument for removing dead tissue, growths, etc., from the walls of body cavities. ~*vb.* **-retting, -retted.** **2.** (*tr.*) to scrape or clean with such an instrument. [C18: from F *curette,* from *curer* to heal, make clean; see CURE]

curettage (,kjʊərɪ'tɑːʒ, kjʊə'rɛtɪdʒ) *or* **curettement** (kjʊə'rɛtmənt) *n.* the process of using a curet. See also **D** and **C.**

curfew ('kɜːfjuː) *n.* **1.** an official regulation setting restrictions on movement, esp. after a specific time at night.

2. the time set as a deadline by such a regulation. **3.** (in medieval Europe) **a.** the ringing of a bell to prompt people to extinguish fires and lights. **b.** the time at which the curfew bell was rung. **c.** the bell itself. [C13: from OF *cuevrefeu*, lit.: cover the fire]

curia ('kjʊərɪə) *n.*, *pl.* **-riae** (-rɪˌiː). **1.** (*sometimes cap.*) the papal court and government of the Roman Catholic Church. **2.** (in the Middle Ages) a court held in the king's name. [C16: from L, from OL *coviria* (unattested), from co- + *vir* man] —**'curial** *adj.*

curie ('kjʊərɪ, -riː) *n.* a unit of radioactivity equal to 3.7 × 10¹⁰ disintegrations per second. [C20: after Pierre CURIE]

Curie ('kjʊərɪ, -riː; *French* kyri) *n.* **1. Marie** (mari). 1867–1934, French physicist and chemist, born in Poland: discovered with her husband Pierre the radioactivity of thorium, and discovered and isolated radium and polonium. She shared a Nobel prize for physics (1903) with her husband and Henri Becquerel, and was awarded a Nobel prize for chemistry (1911). **2.** her husband, **Pierre** (pjɛr). 1859–1906, French physicist and chemist.

curio ('kjʊərɪˌəʊ) *n.*, *pl.* **-rios.** a small article valued as a collector's item, esp. something unusual. [C19: shortened from CURIOSITY]

curiosity (ˌkjʊərɪ'ɒsɪtɪ) *n.*, *pl.* **-ties. 1.** an eager desire to know; inquisitiveness. **2.** the quality of being curious; strangeness. **3.** something strange or fascinating.

curious ('kjʊərɪəs) *adj.* **1.** eager to learn; inquisitive. **2.** overinquisitive; prying. **3.** interesting because of oddness or novelty. [C14: from L *cūriōsus* taking pains over something, from *cūra* care] —**'curiously** *adv.* —**'curiousness** *n.*

Curitiba (ˌkʊərɪ'tiːbə) *n.* a city in SE Brazil, capital of Paraná state: seat of the University of Paraná (1946). Pop.: 1 285 027 (1985).

curium ('kjʊərɪəm) *n.* a silvery-white metallic transuranic element artificially produced from plutonium. Symbol: Cm; at. no.: 96; half-life of most stable isotope, ²⁴⁷Cm: 1.6 × 10⁷ years. [C20: NL, after Pierre & Marie CURIE]

curl (kɜːl) *vb.* **1.** (*intr.*) (esp. of hair) to grow into curves or ringlets. **2.** (*tr.*; sometimes foll. by *up*) to twist or roll (esp. hair) into coils or ringlets. **3.** (often foll. by *up*) to become or cause to become spiral-shaped or curved. **4.** (*intr.*) to move in a curving or twisting manner. **5.** (*intr.*) to play the game of curling. **6. curl one's lip.** to show contempt, as by raising a corner of the lip. ~*n.* **7.** a curve or coil of hair. **8.** a curved or spiral shape or mark. **9.** the act of curling or state of being curled. ~See also **curl up.** [C14: prob. from MDu. *crullen* to curl]

curler ('kɜːlə) *n.* **1.** any of various pins, clasps, or rollers used to curl or wave hair. **2.** a person or thing that curls. **3.** a person who plays curling.

curlew ('kɜːljuː) *n.* any of certain large shore birds of Europe and Asia. They have a long downward-curving bill and occur in northern and arctic regions. [C14: from OF *corlieu*, ? imit.]

curlicue ('kɜːlɪˌkjuː) *n.* an intricate ornamental curl or twist. [C19: from CURLY + CUE²]

curling ('kɜːlɪŋ) *n.* a game played on ice, esp. in Scotland, in which heavy stones with handles (**curling stones**) are slid towards a target (**tee**).

curling tongs *pl. n.* a metal scissor-like device that is heated, so that strands of hair may be twined around it in order to form curls. Also called: **curling iron, curling irons, curling pins.**

curl up *vb.* (*adv.*) **1.** (*intr.*) to adopt a reclining position with the legs close to the body and the back rounded. **2.** to become or cause to become spiral-shaped or curved. **3.** (*intr.*) to retire to a quiet cosy setting: *to curl up with a good novel.* **4.** *Brit. inf.* to be or cause to be disgusted.

curly ('kɜːlɪ) *adj.* **curlier, curliest. 1.** tending to curl; curling. **2.** having curls. **3.** (of timber) having waves in the grain. —**'curliness** *n.*

curmudgeon (kɜː'mʌdʒən) *n.* a surly or miserly person. [C16: from ?] —**cur'mudgeonly** *adj.*

Curnow (kɜːnaʊ) *n.* **T.A.M.** born 1911, New Zealand poet and anthologist.

currach *or* **curragh** *Gaelic.* ('kʌrəx, 'kʌrə) *n.* a Scottish or Irish name for **coracle.** [C15: from Irish Gaelic *currach;* Cf. CORACLE]

currajong ('kʌrəˌdʒɒŋ) *n.* a variant spelling of **kurrajong.**

currant ('kʌrənt) *n.* **1.** a small dried seedless grape of the Mediterranean region. **2.** any of several mainly N temperate shrubs, esp. redcurrant and blackcurrant. **3.** the small acid fruit of any of these plants. [C16: shortened from *rayson of Corannte* raisin of Corinth]

currawong ('kʌrəˌwɒŋ) *n.* any Australian crowlike songbird of the genus *Strepera*, having black, grey, and white plumage. Also called: **bell-magpie.** [from Abor.]

currency ('kʌrənsɪ) *n.*, *pl.* **-cies. 1.** a metal or paper medium of exchange in current use in a particular country. **2.** general acceptance or circulation; prevalence. **3.** the period of time during which something is valid, accepted, or in force. ~*adj.* **4.** *Austral. inf.* native-born as distinct from immigrant: *a currency lad.* [C17: from Med. L *currentia*, lit.: a flowing, from L *currere* to run, flow]

current ('kʌrənt) *adj.* **1.** of the immediate present; in progress. **2.** most recent; up-to-date. **3.** commonly known, practised, or accepted. **4.** circulating and valid at present: *current coins.* ~*n.* **5.** (esp. of water or air) a steady, usually natural, flow. **6.** a mass of air, body of water, etc., that has a steady flow in a particular direction. **7.** the rate of flow of such a mass. **8.** *Physics.* **a.** a flow of electric charge through a conductor. **b.** the rate of flow of this charge. **9.** a general trend or drift: *currents of opinion.* [C13: from OF *corant*, lit.: running, from *corre* to run, from L *currere*] —**'currently** *adv.* —**'currentness** *n.*

current account *n.* a bank account that usually carries no interest and against which cheques may be drawn at any time.

curricle ('kʌrɪkəl) *n.* a two-wheeled open carriage drawn by two horses side by side. [C18: from L *curriculum* from *currus* chariot, from *currere* to run]

curriculum (kə'rɪkjʊləm) *n.*, *pl.* **-la** (-lə) *or* **-lums. 1.** a course of study in one subject at a school or college. **2.** a list of all the courses of study offered by a school or college. **3.** any programme or plan of activities. [C19: from L: course, from *currere* to run] —**cur'ricular** *adj.*

curriculum vitae (kə'rɪkjʊləm 'viːtaɪ, 'vaɪtiː) *n.*, *pl.* **curricula vitae** (kə'rɪkjʊlə). an outline of a person's educational and professional history, usually prepared for job applications. [L, lit.: the course of one's life]

currish ('kɜːrɪʃ) *adj.* of or like a cur; rude or bad-tempered. —**'currishly** *adv.* —**'currishness** *n.*

curry¹ ('kʌrɪ) *n.*, *pl.* **-ries. 1.** a spicy dish of oriental, esp. Indian, origin that usually consists of meat or fish prepared in a hot piquant sauce. **2.** curry seasoning or sauce. **3. give someone curry.** *Austral. sl.* to assault (a person) verbally or physically. ~*vb.* **-rying, -ried. 4.** (*tr.*) to prepare (food) with curry powder or sauce. [C16: from Tamil *kari* sauce, relish]

curry² ('kʌrɪ) *vb.* **-rying, -ried. 1.** to beat vigorously, as in order to clean. **2.** to dress and finish (leather) after it has been tanned. **3.** to groom (a horse). **4. curry favour.** to ingratiate oneself, esp. with superiors. [C13: from OF *correer* to make ready]

Curry ('kʌrɪ) *n.* **John.** born 1949, English ice skater: won the figure-skating gold medal in the 1976 Olympic Games.

currycomb ('kʌrɪˌkəʊm) *n.* a square comb used for grooming horses.

curry powder *n.* a mixture of finely ground pungent spices, such as turmeric, cumin, coriander, ginger, etc., used in making curries.

curse (kɜːs) *n.* **1.** a profane or obscene expression of anger, disgust, surprise, etc.; oath. **2.** an appeal to a supernatural power for harm to come to a specific person, group, etc. **3.** harm resulting from an appeal to a supernatural power. **4.** something that brings or causes great trouble or harm. **5.** (preceded by *the*) *Inf.* menstruation or a menstrual period. ~*vb.* **cursing, cursed** *or* (*Arch.*) **curst. 6.** (*intr.*) to utter obscenities or oaths. **7.** (*tr.*) to abuse (someone) with obscenities or oaths. **8.** (*tr.*) to invoke supernatural powers to bring harm to (someone or something). **9.** (*tr.*) to bring harm upon. [OE *cursian* to curse, from *curs* a curse] —**'curser** *n.*

cursed ('kɜːsɪd, kɜːst) *or* **curst** *adj.* **1.** under a curse. **2.** deserving to be cursed; detestable; hateful. —**'cursedly** *adv.* —**'cursedness** *n.*

cursive ('kɜːsɪv) *adj.* **1.** of or relating to handwriting in which letters are joined in a flowing style. **2.** *Printing.* of or relating to typefaces that resemble handwriting. ~*n.*

3. a cursive letter or printing type. [C18: from Med. L *cursivus* running, ult. from L *currere* to run] —**'cursively** *adv.*

cursor ('kɜ:sə) *n.* **1.** the sliding part of a measuring instrument, esp. on a slide rule. **2.** a movable point of light, etc., that identifies a specific position on a visual display unit.

cursorial (kɜː'sɔːrɪəl) *adj. Zool.* adapted for running: *a cursorial skeleton; cursorial birds.*

cursory ('kɜːsərɪ) *adj.* hasty and usually superficial; quick. [C17: from LL *cursōrius* of running, from L *cursus* a course, from *currere* to run] —**'cursorily** *adv.* —**'cursoriness** *n.*

curst (kɜːst) *vb.* **1.** *Arch.* a past tense and past participle of **curse.** ~*adj.* **2.** a variant of **cursed.**

curt (kɜːt) *adj.* **1.** rudely blunt and brief. **2.** short or concise. [C17: from L *curtus* cut short, mutilated] —**'curtly** *adv.* —**'curtness** *n.*

curtail (kɜː'teɪl) *vb.* (*tr.*) to cut short; abridge. [C16: changed (through infl. of TAIL[1]) from obs. *curtal* to dock] —**cur'tailer** *n.* —**cur'tailment** *n.*

curtain ('kɜːt³n) *n.* **1.** a piece of material that can be drawn across an opening or window, to shut out light or to provide privacy. **2.** a barrier to vision, access, or communication. **3.** a hanging cloth or similar barrier for concealing all or part of a theatre stage from the audience. **4.** (often preceded by *the*) the end of a scene of a play, opera, etc., marked by the fall or closing of the curtain. **5.** the rise or opening of the curtain at the start of a performance. ~*vb.* **6.** (*tr.*; sometimes foll. by *off*) to shut off or conceal as with a curtain. **7.** (*tr.*) to provide (a window, etc.) with curtains. [C13: from OF *courtine*, from LL *cortina* enclosed place, curtain, prob. from L *cohors* courtyard]

curtain call *n.* the appearance of performers at the end of a theatrical performance to acknowledge applause.

curtain lecture *n.* a scolding or rebuke given in private, esp. by a wife to her husband. [alluding to the curtained beds where such rebukes were once given]

curtain-raiser *n.* **1.** *Theatre.* a short dramatic piece presented before the main play. **2.** any preliminary event.

curtains ('kɜːt³nz) *pl. n. Inf.* death or ruin: the end.

curtain wall *n.* a non-load-bearing external wall attached to a framed structure.

Curtin ('kɜːtɪn) *n.* **John Joseph.** 1885–1945, Australian statesman; prime minister of Australia (1941–45).

curtsy *or* **curtsey** ('kɜːtsɪ) *n.*, *pl.* **-sies** *or* **-seys. 1.** a formal gesture of greeting and respect made by women, in which the knees are bent and the head slightly bowed. ~*vb.* **-sying, -sied** *or* **-seying, -seyed. 2.** (*intr.*) to make a curtsy. [C16: var. of COURTESY]

curvaceous (kɜː'veɪʃəs) *adj. Inf.* (of a woman) having a well-rounded body.

curvature ('kɜːvətʃə) *n.* **1.** something curved or a curved part of a thing. **2.** any curving of a bodily part. **3.** the act of curving or the state or degree of being curved or bent.

curve (kɜːv) *n.* **1.** a continuously bending line that has no straight parts. **2.** something that curves or is curved. **3.** the act or extent of curving; curvature. **4.** *Maths.* a system of points whose coordinates satisfy a given equation. **5.** a line representing data on a graph. ~*vb.* **6.** to take or cause to take the shape or path of a curve; bend. [C15: from L *curvāre* to bend, from *curvus* crooked] —**'curvedness** *n.* —**'curvy** *adj.*

curvet (kɜː'vɛt) *n.* **1.** *Dressage.* a low leap with all four feet off the ground. ~*vb.* **-vetting, -vetted** *or* **-veting, -veted. 2.** *Dressage.* to make or cause to make such a leap. **3.** (*intr.*) to prance or frisk about. [C16: from OIt. *corvetta*, from OF *courbette*, from *courber* to bend, from L *curvāre*]

curvilinear (ˌkɜːvɪ'lɪnɪə) *or* **curvilineal** *adj.* consisting of, bounded by, or characterized by a curved line.

Curzon ('kɜːz³n) *n.* **1.** Sir **Clifford.** 1907–82, English pianist. **2. George Nathaniel,** 1st Marquis Curzon of Kedleston. 1859–1925, British Conservative statesman; viceroy of India (1898–1905).

Cusco (*Spanish* 'kusko) *n.* a variant of **Cuzco.**

cuscus ('kʌskʌs) *n.*, *pl.* **-cuses.** any of several large nocturnal phalangers of N Australia, New Guinea, and adjacent islands, having dense fur, prehensile tails, large eyes, and a yellow nose. [C17: NL, prob. from a native name in New Guinea]

cusec ('kjuːsɛk) *n.* a unit of flow equal to 1 cubic foot per second. [C20: from *cu(bic foot per) sec(ond)*]

Cush *or* **Kush** (kʌʃ, kʊʃ) *n. Old Testament.* **1.** the son of Ham and brother of Canaan (Genesis 10:6). **2.** the country of the supposed descendants of Cush (ancient Ethiopia), comprising approximately Nubia and the modern Sudan, and the territory of southern (or Upper) Egypt.

cushat ('kʌʃət) *n.* another name for **wood pigeon.** [OE *cūscote*; ? rel. to *sceōtan* to shoot]

Cushing ('kʊʃɪŋ) *n.* **Harvey Williams.** 1869–1939, U.S. neurosurgeon: identified **Cushing's disease,** a hormonal disorder.

cushion ('kʊʃən) *n.* **1.** a bag filled with a yielding substance, used for sitting on, leaning against, etc. **2.** something resembling a cushion in function or appearance, esp. one to support or pad or to absorb shock. **3.** the resilient felt-covered rim of a billiard table. ~*vb.* (*tr.*) **4.** to place on or as on a cushion. **5.** to provide with cushions. **6.** to protect. **7.** to lessen or suppress the effects of. **8.** to provide with a means of absorbing shock. [C14: from OF *coussin*, from Vulgar L *coxīnus* (unattested) hip-pillow, from L *coxa* hip] —**'cushiony** *adj.*

Cushitic (kʊ'ʃɪtɪk) *n.* **1.** a group of languages of Somalia, Ethiopia, and adjacent regions. ~*adj.* **2.** of or relating to this group of languages.

cushy ('kʊʃɪ) *adj.* **cushier, cushiest.** *Inf.* easy; comfortable. [C20: from Hindi *khush* pleasant, from Persian *khōsh*]

CUSO ('kjuːsəʊ) *n. acronym for* Canadian University Services Overseas; an organization that sends students to work as volunteers in developing countries.

cusp (kʌsp) *n.* **1.** any of the small elevations on the grinding or chewing surface of a tooth. **2.** any of the triangular flaps of a heart valve. **3.** a point or pointed end. **4.** *Geom.* a point at which two arcs of a curve intersect and at which the two tangents are coincident. **5.** *Archit.* a carving at the meeting place of two arcs. **6.** *Astron.* either of the points of a crescent moon. **7.** *Astrol.* any division between houses or signs of the zodiac. [C16: from L *cuspis* point, pointed end] —**'cuspate** *adj.*

cuspid ('kʌspɪd) *n.* a tooth having one point; canine tooth.

cuspidate ('kʌspɪˌdeɪt), **cuspidated,** *or* **cuspidal** ('kʌspɪd³l) *adj.* **1.** having a cusp or cusps. **2.** (esp. of leaves) narrowing to a point. [C17: from L *cuspidāre* to make pointed, from *cuspis* a point]

cuspidor ('kʌspɪˌdɔː) *n.* another name (esp. U.S.) for **spittoon.** [C18: from Port., from *cuspir* to spit, from L *conspuere*, from *spuere* to spit]

cuss (kʌs) *Inf.* ~*n.* **1.** a curse; an oath. **2.** a person or animal, esp. an annoying one. ~*vb.* **3.** another word for **curse** (senses 6, 7).

cussed ('kʌsɪd) *adj. Inf.* **1.** another word for **cursed. 2.** obstinate. **3.** annoying: *a cussed nuisance.* —**'cussedly** *adv.* —**'cussedness** *n.*

custard ('kʌstəd) *n.* **1.** a baked sweetened mixture of eggs and milk. **2.** a sauce made of milk and sugar thickened with cornflour. [C15: alteration of ME *crustade* kind of pie]

custard apple *n.* **1.** a West Indian tree. **2.** its large heart-shaped fruit, which has a fleshy edible pulp.

custard pie *n.* **a.** a flat, open pie filled with real or artificial custard, as thrown in slapstick comedy. **b.** (*as modifier*): *custard-pie humour.*

Custer ('kʌstə) *n.* **George Armstrong.** 1839–76, U.S. cavalry general: Civil War hero, killed fighting the Sioux Indians at Little Bighorn, Montana.

custodian (kʌ'stəʊdɪən) *n.* **1.** a person who has custody, as of a prisoner, ward, etc. **2.** a keeper of an art collection, etc. —**cus'todian,ship** *n.*

custody ('kʌstədɪ) *n.*, *pl.* **-dies. 1.** the act of keeping safe or guarding. **2.** the state of being held by the police; arrest. [C15: from L *custōdia*, from *custōs* guard, defender] —**custodial** (kʌ'stəʊdɪəl) *adj.*

custom ('kʌstəm) *n.* **1.** a usual or habitual practice; typical mode of behaviour. **2.** the long-established habits or traditions of a society collectively; convention. **3. a.** a practice which by long-established usage has come to have the force of law. **b.** such practices collectively (esp. in **custom and practice**). **4.** habitual patronage, esp. of a shop or business. **5.** the customers of a shop or business collectively. ~*adj.* **6.** made to the specifications of an individual customer. ~See also **customs.** [C12: from

OF *costume*, from L *consuētūdō*, from *consuēscere* to grow accustomed to]

customary ('kʌstəməri, -təmri) *adj.* **1.** in accordance with custom or habitual practice; usual. **2.** *Law.* **a.** founded upon long-continued practices and usage. **b.** (of land) held by custom. ~*n., pl.* **-aries. 3.** a statement in writing of customary laws and practices. —'**customarily** *adv.* —'**customariness** *n.*

custom-built *adj.* (of cars, houses, etc.) made according to the specifications of an individual buyer.

customer ('kʌstəmə) *n.* **1.** a person who buys. **2.** *Inf.* a person with whom one has dealings.

custom house *n.* a government office, esp. at a port, where customs are collected and ships cleared for entry.

customize *or* **-ise** ('kʌstə,maɪz) *vb.* (*tr.*) to make (something) according to a customer's individual requirements.

custom-made *adj.* (of suits, dresses, etc.) made according to the specifications of an individual buyer.

customs ('kʌstəmz) *n.* (*functioning as sing. or pl.*) **1.** duty on imports or exports. **2.** the government department responsible for the collection of these duties. **3.** the part of a port, airport, etc., where baggage and freight are examined for dutiable goods and contraband.

cut (kʌt) *vb.* **cutting, cut. 1.** to open up or incise (a person or thing) with a sharp edge or instrument. **2.** (of a sharp instrument) to penetrate or incise (a person or thing). **3.** to divide or be divided with or as if with a sharp instrument. **4.** (*intr.*) to use an instrument that cuts. **5.** (*tr.*) to trim or prune by or as if by clipping. **6.** (*tr.*) to reap or mow (a crop, grass, etc.). **7.** (*tr.*; sometimes foll. by *out*) to make, form, or shape by cutting. **8.** (*tr.*) to hollow or dig out; excavate. **9.** to strike (an object) sharply. **10.** *Cricket.* to hit (the ball) to the off side with a roughly horizontal bat. **11.** to hurt the feelings of (a person). **12.** (*tr.*) *Inf.* to refuse to recognize; snub. **13.** (*tr.*) *Inf.* to absent oneself from, esp. without permission or in haste: *to cut a class.* **14.** (*tr.*) to abridge or shorten. **15.** (*tr.*; often foll. by *down*) to lower, reduce, or curtail. **16.** (*tr.*) to dilute or weaken: *to cut whisky with water.* **17.** (*tr.*) to dissolve or break up: *to cut fat.* **18.** (when *intr.*, foll. by *across* or *through*) to cross or traverse. **19.** (*intr.*) to make a sharp or sudden change in direction; veer. **20.** to grow (teeth) through the gums or (of teeth) to appear through the gums. **21.** (*intr.*) *Films.* **a.** to call a halt to a shooting sequence. **b.** (foll. by *to*) to move quickly to another scene. **22.** *Films.* to edit (film). **23.** to switch off (a light, car engine, etc.). **24.** (*tr.*) to make (a record or tape of a song, performance, etc.). **25.** *Cards.* **a.** to divide (the pack) at random into two parts after shuffling. **b.** (*intr.*) to pick cards from a spread pack to decide dealer, partners, etc. **26.** (*tr.*) (of a tool) to bite into (an object). **27. cut a dash.** to make a stylish impression. **28. cut (a person) dead.** *Inf.* to ignore (a person) completely. **29. cut a (good, poor, etc.) figure.** to appear or behave in a specified manner. **30. cut and run.** *Inf.* to make a rapid escape. **31. cut both ways. a.** to have both good and bad effects. **b.** to affect both sides, as two parties in an argument, etc. **32. cut it fine.** *Inf.* to allow little margin of time, space etc. **33. cut loose.** to free or become freed from restraint, custody, anchorage, etc. **34. cut no ice.** *Inf.* to fail to make an impression. **35. cut one's teeth on.** *Inf.* **a.** to use at an early age or stage. **b.** to practise on. ~*adj.* **36.** detached, divided, or separated by cutting. **37.** made, shaped, or fashioned by cutting. **38.** reduced or diminished as by cutting: *cut prices.* **39.** weakened or diluted. **40.** *Brit.* a slang word for **drunk**: *half cut.* **41. cut and dried.** *Inf.* settled or arranged in advance. ~*n.* **42.** the act of cutting. **43.** a stroke or incision made by cutting; gash. **44.** a piece or part cut off: *a cut of meat.* **45.** the edge of anything cut or sliced. **46.** a passage, channel, path, etc., cut or hollowed out. **47.** an omission or deletion, esp. in a text, film, or play. **48.** a reduction in price, salary, etc. **49.** a decrease in government finance in a particular department or area. **50.** *Inf.* a portion or share. **51.** *Inf.* a straw, slip of paper, etc., used in drawing lots. **52.** the manner or style in which a thing, esp. a garment, is cut. **53.** a direct route; short cut. **54.** the U.S. name for **block** (sense 13). **55.** *Cricket.* a stroke made with the bat in a roughly horizontal position. **56.** *Films.* an immediate transition from one shot to the next. **57.** words or an action that hurt another person's feelings. **58.** a refusal to recognize an acquaintance; snub. **59.** *Brit.* a stretch of water, esp. a canal. **60. a cut**

above. *Inf.* superior to; better than. ~See also **cut across, cutback**, etc. [C13: prob. from ON]

cut across *vb.* (*intr., prep.*) **1.** to be contrary to ordinary procedure or limitations. **2.** to cross or traverse, making a shorter route.

cutaneous (kju:'teɪnɪəs) *adj.* of or relating to the skin. [C16: from NL *cutāneus*, from L *cutis* skin]

cutaway ('kʌtə,weɪ) *n.* **1.** a man's coat cut diagonally from the front waist to the back of the knees. **2. a.** a drawing or model of a machine, engine, etc., in which part of the casing is omitted to reveal the workings. **b.** (*as modifier*): *a cutaway drawing.* **3.** *Films, television.* a shot separate from the main action of a scene.

cutback ('kʌt,bæk) *n.* **1.** a decrease or reduction. ~*vb.* **cut back** (*adv.*) **2.** (*tr.*) to shorten by cutting off the end; prune. **3.** (when *intr.*, foll. by *on*) to reduce or make a reduction (in).

Cutch (kʌtʃ) *n.* a variant spelling of **Kutch.**

cut down *vb.* (*adv.*) **1.** (*tr.*) to fell. **2.** (when *intr.*, often foll. by *on*) to make or make a reduction (in). **3.** (*tr.*) to remake (an old garment) in order to make a smaller one. **4.** (*tr.*) to kill. **5. cut (a person) down to size.** to reduce in importance or decrease the conceit of (a person).

cute (kju:t) *adj.* **1.** appealing or attractive, esp. in a pretty way. **2.** *Inf., chiefly U.S. & Canad.* affecting cleverness or prettiness. **3.** clever; shrewd. [C18 (in the sense: clever): shortened from ACUTE] —'**cutely** *adv.* —'**cuteness** *n.*

cut glass *n.* **1. a.** glass, esp. bowls, vases, etc., decorated by facet-cutting or grinding. **b.** (*as modifier*): *a cut-glass vase.* **2.** (*modifier*) (of an accent) upper-class; refined.

Cuthbert ('kʌθbət) *n.* **Saint.** ?635–87A.D., English monk; bishop of Lindisfarne. Feast day: March 20.

cuticle ('kju:tɪkəl) *n.* **1.** dead skin, esp. round the base of a fingernail or toenail. **2.** another name for **epidermis. 3.** the protective layer that covers the epidermis of higher plants. **4.** the protective layer covering the epidermis of many invertebrates. [C17: from L *cutícula* dim. of *cutis* skin] —**cuticular** (kju:'tɪkjʊlə) *adj.*

cut in *vb.* (*adv.*) **1.** (*intr.*; often foll. by *on*) Also: **cut into.** to break in or interrupt. **2.** (*intr.*) to interrupt a dancing couple to dance with one of them. **3.** (*intr.*) (of a driver, motor vehicle, etc.) to draw in front of another vehicle leaving too little space. **4.** (*tr.*) *Inf.* to allow to have a share. **5.** (*intr.*) to take the place of a person in a card game.

cutis ('kju:tɪs) *n., pl.* **-tes** (-ti:z) *or* **-tises.** *Anat.* a technical name for the **skin.** [C17: from L: skin]

cutlass ('kʌtləs) *n.* a curved, one-edged sword formerly used by sailors. [C16: from F *coutelas*, from *coutel* knife, ult. from L *culter* knife]

cutler ('kʌtlə) *n.* a person who makes or sells cutlery. [C14: from F *coutelier*, ult. from L *culter* knife]

cutlery ('kʌtlərɪ) *n.* **1.** implements used for eating, such as knives, forks, and spoons. **2.** instruments used for cutting. **3.** the art or business of a cutler.

cutlet ('kʌtlɪt) *n.* **1.** a piece of meat taken esp. from the best end of neck of lamb, pork, etc. **2.** a flat croquette of minced chicken, lobster, etc. [C18: from OF *costelette*, lit.: a little rib, from *coste* rib, from L *costa*]

cut off *vb.* (*tr., adv.*) **1.** to remove by cutting. **2.** to intercept or interrupt something, esp. a telephone conversation. **3.** to discontinue the supply of. **4.** to bring to an end. **5.** to deprive of rights; disinherit: *cut off without a penny.* **6.** to sever or separate. **7.** to occupy a position so as to prevent or obstruct (a retreat or escape). ~*n.* **cutoff. 8. a.** the act of cutting off; limit or termination. **b.** (*as modifier*): *the cutoff point.* **9.** *Chiefly U.S.* a short cut. **10.** a device to terminate the flow of a fluid in a pipe or duct.

cut out *vb.* (*adv.*) **1.** (*tr.*) to delete or remove. **2.** (*tr.*) to shape or form by cutting. **3.** (*tr.*; *usually passive*) to suit or equip for: *you're not cut out for this job.* **4.** (*intr.*) (of an engine, etc.) to cease to operate suddenly. **5.** (*tr.*) (of an electrical device) to switch off, usually automatically. **6.** (*tr.*) *Inf.* to oust and supplant (a rival). **7.** (*intr.*) (of a person) to be excluded from a card game. **8.** (*tr.*) *Inf.* to cease doing something, esp. something undesirable (esp. in **cut it out**). **9.** (*tr.*) *Soccer.* to intercept (a pass). **10.** (*tr.*) to separate (cattle) from a herd. **11.** (*intr.*) *Austral.* to end or finish: *the road cuts out at the creek.* **12. have one's work cut out.** to have as much work as one can manage. ~*n.* **cutout. 13.** something that has been or is intended to be cut out from something else. **14.** a device that switches off or interrupts an electric circuit, esp. as a safety device. **15.** *Austral. sl.* the end of shearing.

cut-price *or esp. U.S.* **cut-rate** *adj.* **1.** available at prices or rates below the standard price or rate. **2.** (*prenominal*) offering goods or services at prices below the standard price.

cutpurse ('kʌt,pɜːs) *n.* an archaic word for **pickpocket.**

Cuttack (kʌ'tæk) *n.* a city in NE India, in E Orissa near the mouth of the Mahanadi River: former state capital until 1948. Pop.: 327 412 (1981).

cutter ('kʌtə) *n.* **1.** a person or thing that cuts, esp. a person who cuts cloth for clothing. **2.** a sailing boat with its mast stepped further aft than that of a sloop. **3.** a ship's boat, powered by oars or sail, for carrying passengers or light cargo. **4.** a small lightly armed boat, as used in the enforcement of customs regulations.

cutthroat ('kʌt,θrəut) *n.* **1.** a person who cuts throats; murderer. **2.** Also called: **cutthroat razor.** *Brit.* a razor with a long blade that usually folds into the handle. ~*adj.* **3.** bloodthirsty or murderous; cruel. **4.** fierce or relentless in competition: *cutthroat prices.* **5.** (of some games) played by three people: *cutthroat poker.*

cutting ('kʌtɪŋ) *n.* **1.** a piece cut off from something. **2.** *Horticulture.* **a.** a method of propagation in which a part of a plant is induced to form its own roots. **b.** a part separated for this purpose. **3.** Also called (esp. U.S. and Canad.): **clipping.** an article, photograph, etc., cut from a publication. **4.** the editing process of a film. **5.** an excavation in a piece of high land for a road, railway, etc. **6.** (*modifier*) designed for or adapted to cutting; sharp: *a cutting tool.* ~*adj.* **7.** keen; piercing. **8.** tending to hurt the feelings: *a cutting remark.* —'**cuttingly** *adv.*

cuttlebone ('kʌt³l,bəun) *n.* the internal calcareous shell of the cuttlefish, used as a mineral supplement to the diet of cagebirds and as a polishing agent. [C16: OE *cudele* + BONE]

cuttlefish ('kʌt³l,fɪʃ) *n.*, *pl.* -**fish** *or* -**fishes.** a cephalopod mollusc which occurs near the bottom of inshore waters and has a broad flattened body. Sometimes shortened to **cuttle.**

cut up *vb.* (*tr.*, *adv.*) **1.** to cut into pieces. **2.** to inflict injuries on. **3.** (*usually passive*) *Inf.* to affect the feelings of deeply. **4.** *Inf.* to subject to severe criticism. **5. cut up rough.** *Brit. inf.* to become angry or bad-tempered.

cutwater ('kʌt,wɔːtə) *n.* the forward part of the stem of a vessel, which cuts through the water.

cutworm ('kʌt,wɜːm) *n.* the caterpillar of various noctuid moths, which is a pest of young crop plants in North America.

cuvée (kuː'veɪ) *n.* an individual batch or blend of wine. [C19: from F, lit.: put in a cask, from *cuve* cask]

Cuvier ('kjuːvɪeɪ; *French* kyvje) *n.* **Georges** (**Jean-Leopold-Nicolas-Frédéric**) (ʒɔrʒ), Baron. 1769–1832, French zoologist and statesman; founder of the sciences of comparative anatomy and palaeontology.

Cuxhaven ('kʊks,hɑːvᵊn; *German* kʊks'haːfən) *n.* a port in N West Germany, at the mouth of the River Elbe. Pop.: 57 200 (1984 est.).

Cuyabá (*Portuguese* kuja'ba) *n.* a variant spelling of **Cuiabá.**

Cuyp *or* **Kuyp** (kaɪp; *Dutch* kœip) *n.* **Aelbert** ('aːlbert). 1620–91, Dutch painter of landscapes and animals.

Cuzco (*Spanish* 'kuθko) *or* **Cusco** *n.* a city in S central Peru: former capital of the Inca Empire, with extensive Inca remains; university (1692). Pop.: 181 604 (1981).

CV *abbrev. for* curriculum vitae.

CVS *abbrev. for* chorionic villus sampling.

Cwlth *abbrev. for* Commonwealth.

cwm (kuːm) *n.* **1.** (in Wales) a valley. **2.** *Geol.* another name for **cirque.**

Cwmbran (,kuːm'brɑːn) *n.* a new town in SE Wales, in central Gwent, developed in the 1950s. Pop.: 44 876 (1981).

c.w.o. *or* **CWO** *abbrev. for* cash with order.

CWS *abbrev. for* Cooperative Wholesale Society.

cwt *abbrev. for* hundredweight. [*c*, from the L numeral *C* one hundred (*centum*)]

-cy *suffix.* **1.** indicating state, quality, or condition: *plutocracy; lunacy.* **2.** rank or office: *captaincy.* [via OF from L *-cia, -cia* & Gk *-kia, -tia,* abstract noun suffixes]

cyan ('saɪæn, 'saɪən) *n.* **1.** a green-blue colour. ~*adj.* **2.** of this colour. [C19: from Gk *kuanos* dark blue]

cyanate ('saɪə,neɪt) *n.* any salt or ester of cyanic acid.

cyanic (saɪ'ænɪk) *adj.* **1.** of or containing cyanogen. **2.** blue.

cyanic acid *n.* a colourless poisonous volatile liquid acid. Formula: HOCN.

cyanide ('saɪə,naɪd) *or* **cyanid** ('saɪənɪd) *n.* any salt of hydrocyanic acid. Cyanides are extremely poisonous. —,**cyani'dation** *n.*

cyanite ('saɪə,naɪt) *n.* a grey, green, or blue mineral consisting of aluminium silicate in crystalline form. —**cyanitic** (,saɪə'nɪtɪk) *adj.*

cyano- *or before a vowel* **cyan-** *combining form.* **1.** blue or dark blue. **2.** indicating cyanogen. **3.** indicating cyanide. [from Gk *kuanos* (adj.) dark blue, (n.) dark blue enamel, lapis lazuli]

cyanocobalamin (,saɪənəʊkəʊ'bæləmɪn) *n.* vitamin B$_{12}$, a complex crystalline compound of cobalt and cyanide, lack of which leads to pernicious anaemia. [C20: from CY-ANO- + COBAL(T) + (VIT)AMIN]

cyanogen (saɪ'ænədʒɪn) *n.* an extremely poisonous colourless flammable gas. Formula: (CN)$_2$. [C19: from F *cyanogène*; see CYANO-, -GEN; so named because it is one of the constituents of Prussian blue]

cyanosis (,saɪə'nəʊsɪs) *n.* *Pathol.* a bluish-purple discoloration of skin and mucous membranes usually resulting from a deficiency of oxygen in the blood. —**cyanotic** (,saɪə'nɒtɪk) *adj.*

Cybele ('sɪbɪlɪ) *n.* *Classical myth.* the Phrygian goddess of nature, mother of all living things and consort of Attis; identified with the Greek Rhea or Demeter.

cybernate ('saɪbə,neɪt) *vb.* to control with a servomechanism or to be controlled by a servomechanism. [C20: from CYBER(NETICS) + -ATE¹] —,**cyber'nation** *n.*

cybernetics (,saɪbə'nɛtɪks) *n.* (*functioning as sing.*) the branch of science concerned with control systems and comparisons between man-made and biological systems. [C20: from Gk *kubernētēs* steersman, from *kubernan* to steer] —,**cyber'netic** *adj.* —,**cyber'neticist** *n.*

cycad ('saɪkæd) *n.* a tropical or subtropical plant, having an unbranched stem with fernlike leaves crowded at the top. [C19: from NL *Cycas* name of genus, from Gk *kukas,* scribe's error for *koikas,* from *koïx* a kind of palm] —,**cyca'daceous** *adj.*

Cyclades ('sɪklə,diːz) *pl. n.* a group of over 200 islands in the S Aegean Sea, forming a department of Greece. Capital: Hermoupolis (Siros). Pop.: 88 458 (1981). Area: 2572 sq. km (993 sq. miles). Modern Greek name: **Kikládhes.** —**Cycladic** (sɪ'klædɪk) *adj.*

cyclamate ('saɪklə,meɪt, 'sɪkləmeɪt) *n.* any of certain compounds formerly used as food additives and sugar substitutes. [C20: cycl(ohexyl-sulph)amate]

cyclamen ('sɪkləmən, -,mɛn) *n.* **1.** any Old World plant of the genus *Cyclamen,* having white, pink, or red flowers, with reflexed petals. ~*adj.* **2.** of a dark reddish-purple colour. [C16: from Med. L, from L *cyclamīnos,* from Gk *kuklaminos,* prob. from *kuklos* circle, referring to the bulblike roots]

cycle ('saɪkᵊl) *n.* **1.** a recurring period of time in which certain events or phenomena occur and reach completion. **2.** a completed series of events that follows or is followed by another series of similar events occurring in the same sequence. **3.** the time taken or needed for one such series. **4.** a vast period of time; age; aeon. **5.** a group of poems or prose narratives about a central figure or event: *the Arthurian cycle.* **6.** short for **bicycle, motorcycle,** etc. **7.** a recurrent series of events or processes in plants and animals: *a life cycle.* **8.** one of a series of repeated changes in the magnitude of a periodically varying quantity, such as current or voltage. ~*vb.* **9.** (*tr.*) to process through a cycle or system. **10.** (*intr.*) to move in or pass through cycles. **11.** to travel by or ride a bicycle or tricycle. [C14: from LL *cyclus,* from Gk *kuklos* cycle, circle, ring, wheel]

cyclic ('saɪklɪk, 'sɪklɪk) *or* **cyclical** *adj.* **1.** recurring or revolving in cycles. **2.** (of an organic compound) containing a closed saturated or unsaturated ring of atoms. **3.** *Bot.* **a.** arranged in whorls: *cyclic petals.* **b.** having parts arranged in this way: *cyclic flowers.* —'**cyclically** *adv.*

cyclist ('saɪklɪst) *or U.S.* **cycler** *n.* a person who rides or travels by bicycle, motorcycle, etc.

cyclo- *or before a vowel* **cycl-** *combining form.* **1.** indicating a circle or ring: *cyclotron.* **2.** denoting a cyclic compound: *cyclopropane.* [from Gk *kuklos* CYCLE]

cycloid ('saɪklɔɪd) *adj.* **1.** resembling a circle. ~*n.* **2.** *Geom.* the curve described by a point on the circumference of a circle as the circle rolls along a straight line. —**cy'cloidal** *adj.*

cyclometer (saɪ'klɒmɪtə) *n.* a device that records the number of revolutions made by a wheel and hence the distance travelled.

cyclone ('saɪkləʊn) *n.* **1.** another name for **depression** (sense 6). **2.** a violent tropical storm; hurricane. ~*adj.* **3.** *Austral. & N.Z.* (of fencing) made of interlaced wire and metal. [C19: from Gk *kuklōn* a turning around, from *kuklos* wheel] —**cyclonic** (saɪ'klɒnɪk) *adj.* —**cy'clonically** *adv.*

Cyclopean (ˌsaɪkləʊ'piːən, saɪ'kləʊpɪən) *adj.* **1.** of, relating to, or resembling the Cyclops. **2.** denoting or having the kind of masonry used in preclassical Greek architecture, characterized by large undressed blocks of stone.

cyclopedia *or* **cyclopaedia** (ˌsaɪkləʊ'piːdɪə) *n.* a less common word for **encyclopedia**.

cyclopropane (ˌsaɪkləʊ'prəʊpeɪn) *n.* a colourless gaseous hydrocarbon, used as an anaesthetic. Formula: C_3H_6.

Cyclops ('saɪklɒps) *n., pl.* **Cyclopes** (saɪ'kləʊpiːz) *or* **Cyclopses.** *Classical myth.* one of a race of giants having a single eye in the middle of the forehead. [C15: from L *Cyclōps*, from Gk *Kuklōps*, lit.: round eye, from *kuklos* circle + *ōps* eye]

cyclorama (ˌsaɪkləʊ'rɑːmə) *n.* **1.** a large picture on the interior wall of a cylindrical room, designed to appear in natural perspective to a spectator. **2.** *Theatre.* a curtain or wall curving along the back of a stage, usually painted to represent the sky. [C19: CYCLO- + Gk *horama* view, sight, on the model of *panorama*] —**cycloramic** (ˌsaɪkləʊ'ræmɪk) *adj.*

cyclosporin-A (ˌsaɪkləʊ'spɔːrɪn-) *n.* a drug extracted from a fungus and used in transplant surgery to suppress the body's immune mechanisms, and so prevent rejection of an organ.

cyclostome ('saɪkləˌstəʊm, 'sɪk-) *n.* any primitive aquatic jawless vertebrate, such as the lamprey, having a round sucking mouth. —**cyclostomate** (saɪ'klɒstəmɪt, -ˌmeɪt) *or* **cyclostomatous** (ˌsaɪkləʊ'stɒmətəs, -'stəʊmə-, ˌsɪk-) *adj.*

cyclostyle ('saɪkləˌstaɪl) *n.* **1.** a kind of pen with a small toothed wheel, used for cutting holes in a specially prepared stencil. **2.** an office duplicator using such a stencil. ~*vb.* **3.** (*tr.*) to print using such a stencil. —**'cyclo,styled** *adj.*

cyclothymia (ˌsaɪkləʊ'θaɪmɪə) *n. Psychiatry.* a condition characterized by alternating periods of excitement and depression. [from CYCLO- + Gk *thumos*, cast of mind + -IA] —**,cyclo'thymic** *adj.*

cyclotron ('saɪkləˌtrɒn) *n.* a type of particle accelerator in which the particles spiral under the effect of a strong vertical magnetic field.

cyder ('saɪdə) *n.* a variant spelling of **cider.**

Cydnus ('sɪdnəs) *n.* the ancient name for the (River) **Tarsus.**

cygnet ('sɪgnɪt) *n.* a young swan. [C15 *sygnett*, from OF *cygne* swan, from L *cygnus*, from Gk *kuknos*]

cylinder ('sɪlɪndə) *n.* **1.** a solid consisting of two parallel planes bounded by identical closed curves, usually circles, that are interconnected at every point by a set of parallel lines, usually perpendicular to the planes. **2.** a surface formed by a line moving round a closed plane curve at a fixed angle to it. **3.** any object shaped like a cylinder. **4.** the chamber in a reciprocating internal-combustion engine, pump, or compressor within which the piston moves. The cylinders are housed in the metal **cylinder block,** which is topped by the **cylinder head. 5.** the rotating mechanism of a revolver, containing cartridge chambers. **6.** *Printing.* any of the rotating drums on a printing press. **7.** Also called: **cylinder seal.** an ancient cylindrical seal found in the Middle East and Balkans. [C16: from L *cylindrus*, from Gk *kulindros* a roller, from *kulindein* to roll] —**'cylinder-,like** *adj.*

cylindrical (sɪ'lɪndrɪkᵊl) *or* **cylindric** *adj.* of, shaped like, or characteristic of a cylinder. —**cy,lindri'cality** *n.* —**cy'lindrically** *adv.*

cymbal ('sɪmbᵊl) *n.* a percussion instrument consisting of a thin circular piece of brass, which vibrates when clashed together with another cymbal or struck with a stick. [OE *cymbala*, from L *cymbalum*, from Gk

kumbalon, from *kumbē* something hollow] —**'cymbalist** *n.*

cyme (saɪm) *n.* an inflorescence in which the first flower is the terminal bud of the main stem and subsequent flowers develop as terminal buds of lateral stems. [C18: from L *cyma* cabbage sprout, from Gk *kuma* anything swollen] —**cymiferous** (saɪ'mɪfərəs) *adj.* —**cymose** ('saɪməʊs, -məʊz, saɪ'məʊs) *adj.*

Cymric *or* **Kymric** ('kɪmrɪk) *n.* **1.** the Welsh language. **2.** the Brythonic group of Celtic languages. ~*adj.* **3.** of or relating to the Cymry, any of their languages, Wales, or the Welsh.

Cymru (*Welsh* kum'ri) *n.* the Welsh name for **Wales.**

Cymry *or* **Kymry** ('kɪmrɪ) *n.* **the.** (*functioning as pl.*) **1.** the Brythonic Celts, comprising the present-day Welsh, Cornish, and Bretons. **2.** the Welsh people. [Welsh: the Welsh]

Cynewulf, Kynewulf ('kɪnɪˌwʊlf), *or* **Cynwulf** ('kɪn,wʊlf) *n.* ?8th century A.D., Anglo-Saxon poet; author of *Juliana, The Ascension, Elene,* and *The Fates of the Apostles.*

cynic ('sɪnɪk) *n.* **1.** a person who believes the worst about people or the outcome of events. ~*adj.* **2.** a less common word for **cynical.** [C16: via L from Gk *Kunikos,* from *kuōn* dog]

Cynic ('sɪnɪk) *n.* a member of an ancient Greek sect that scorned worldly things.

cynical ('sɪnɪkᵊl) *adj.* **1.** believing the worst of others, esp. that all acts are selfish. **2.** sarcastic; mocking. **3.** showing contempt for accepted standards, esp. of honesty or morality. —**'cynically** *adv.* —**'cynicalness** *n.*

cynicism ('sɪnɪˌsɪzəm) *n.* **1.** the attitude or beliefs of a cynic. **2.** a cynical action, idea, etc.

Cynicism ('sɪnɪˌsɪzəm) *n.* the doctrines of the Cynics.

cynosure ('sɪnəˌzjʊə, -ʃʊə) *n.* **1.** a person or thing that attracts notice. **2.** something that serves as a guide. [C16: from L *Cynosūra* the constellation of Ursa Minor, from Gk *Kunosoura,* from *kuōn* dog + *oura* tail]

Cynthia ('sɪnθɪə) *n.* another name for **Artemis** (Diana).

cypher ('saɪfə) *n., vb.* a variant spelling of **cipher.**

cypress ('saɪprəs) *n.* **1.** any coniferous tree of a N temperate genus having dark green scalelike leaves and rounded cones. **2.** any of several similar and related trees. **3.** the wood of any of these trees. **4.** cypress branches used as a symbol of mourning. [OE *cypresse,* from L *cyparissus,* from Gk *kuparissos;* rel. to L *cupressus*]

cypress pine *n.* any coniferous tree of an Australian genus yielding valuable timber.

Cyprian ('sɪprɪən) *n.* **Saint.** ?200–258 A.D., bishop of Carthage and martyr. Feast day: Sept. 16.

cyprinid (sɪ'praɪnɪd, 'sɪprɪnɪd) *n.* **1.** any teleost fish of the mainly freshwater family Cyprinidae, typically having toothless jaws and including the carp, tench, and dace. ~*adj.* **2.** of, relating to, or belonging to the Cyprinidae. **3.** resembling a carp; cyprinoid. [C19: from NL *Cyprīnidae,* from L *cyprīnus* carp, from Gk *kuprinos*]

cyprinoid ('sɪprɪˌnɔɪd, sɪ'praɪnɔɪd) *adj.* **1.** of or relating to the Cyprinoidea, a large suborder of teleost fishes including the cyprinids, electric eels, and loaches. **2.** of, relating to, or resembling the carp. ~*n.* **3.** any fish belonging to the Cyprinoidea. [C19: from L *cyprīnus* carp]

Cypriot ('sɪprɪət) *or* **Cypriote** ('sɪprɪ,əʊt) *n.* **1.** a native or inhabitant of Cyprus. **2.** the dialect of Greek spoken in Cyprus. ~*adj.* **3.** denoting or relating to Cyprus, its inhabitants, or dialects.

cypripedium (ˌsɪprɪ'piːdɪəm) *n.* any orchid of a genus having large flowers with an inflated pouchlike lip. See also **lady's-slipper.** [C18: from NL, from L *Cypria* the Cyprian, that is, Venus + *pēs* foot (that is, Venus' slipper)]

Cyprus ('saɪprəs) *n.* an island in the E Mediterranean: ceded to Britain by Turkey in 1878 and made a colony in 1925; became an independent republic in 1960; invaded by Turkey in 1974 following a Greek-supported military coup, leading to the virtual partition of the island. In 1983 the Turkish-controlled northern sector declared itself to be an independent state as the Turkish Republic of Northern Cyprus but failed to receive international recognition. Languages: Greek and Turkish. Religions: Greek Orthodox and Muslim. Currency: pound. Capital: Nicosia. Pop.: 689 000 (1988 est.). Area: 9251 sq. km (3571 sq. miles).

Cyrano de Bergerac (*French* sirano də bɛrʒərak) *n.* **Savinien** (savinjɛ̃). 1619–55, French writer and soldier, famous as a duellist and for his large nose.

Cyrenaic (ˌsaɪrəˈneɪɪk, ˌsɪrə-) *adj.* **1.** of or relating to the ancient Greek city of Cyrene. **2.** of or relating to the philosophical school founded by Aristippus in Cyrene that held pleasure to be the highest good. ~*n.* **3.** a follower of the Cyrenaic school of philosophy.

Cyrenaica *or* **Cirenaica** (ˌsaɪrəˈneɪɪkə, ˌsɪrə-) *n.* a region and former province (1951–63) of E Libya: largely desert; settled by the Greeks in about 630 B.C.; ruled successively by the Egyptians, Romans, Arabs, Turks, and Italians. Area: 855 370 sq. km (330 258 sq. miles).

Cyrene (saɪˈriːnɪ) *n.* an ancient Greek city of N Africa, near the coast of Cyrenaica: famous for its medical school.

Cyril (ˈsɪrəl) *n.* **Saint.** ?827–869 A.D., Greek Christian theologian, missionary to the Moravians and inventor of the Cyrillic alphabet; he and his brother Saint Methodius were called *the Apostles of the Slavs.* Feast day: July 7.

Cyrillic (sɪˈrɪlɪk) *adj.* **1.** denoting or relating to the alphabet devised supposedly by Saint Cyril, for Slavonic languages: now used primarily for Russian and Bulgarian. ~*n.* **2.** this alphabet.

Cyrus (ˈsaɪrəs) *n.* **1.** known as *Cyrus the Great* or *Cyrus the Elder.* died ?529 B.C., king of Persia and founder of the Persian empire. **2.** called *the Younger.* died 401 B.C., Persian satrap of Lydia: revolted against his brother Artaxerxes II, but was killed at the battle of Cunaxa. See also **anabasis, katabasis.**

cyst (sɪst) *n.* **1.** *Pathol.* any abnormal membranous sac or blister-like pouch containing fluid or semisolid material. **2.** *Anat.* any normal sac in the body. **3.** a protective membrane enclosing a cell, larva, or organism. [C18: from NL *cystis,* from Gk *kustis* pouch, bag, bladder]

-cyst *n. combining form.* indicating a bladder or sac: *otocyst.* [from Gk *kustis* bladder]

cystectomy (sɪˈstɛktəmɪ) *n., pl.* **-mies.** **1.** surgical removal of the gall bladder or part of the urinary bladder. **2.** surgical removal of a cyst.

cystic (ˈsɪstɪk) *adj.* **1.** of, relating to, or resembling a cyst. **2.** having or enclosed within a cyst; encysted. **3.** relating to the gall bladder or urinary bladder.

cysticercus (ˌsɪstɪˈsɜːkəs) *n., pl.* **-ci** (-saɪ). an encysted larval form of many tapeworms, consisting of a head inverted in a fluid-filled bladder. [C19: from NL, from Gk *kustis* pouch, bladder + *kerkos* tail]

cystic fibrosis *n.* a congenital disease of the exocrine glands, usually affecting young children, characterized by chronic infection of the respiratory tract and by pancreatic insufficiency.

cystitis (sɪˈstaɪtɪs) *n.* inflammation of the urinary bladder.

cysto- *or before a vowel* **cyst-** *combining form.* indicating a cyst or bladder: *cystoscope.*

cystoid (ˈsɪstɔɪd) *adj.* **1.** resembling a cyst or bladder. ~*n.* **2.** a tissue mass that resembles a cyst but lacks an outer membrane.

cystoscope (ˈsɪstəˌskəʊp) *n.* a slender tubular medical instrument for examining the interior of the urethra and urinary bladder. —**cystoscopic** (ˌsɪstəˈskɒpɪk) *adj.* —**cystoscopy** (sɪsˈtɒskəpɪ) *n.*

-cyte *n. combining form.* indicating a cell. [from NL *-cyta,* from Gk *kutos* vessel]

Cythera (sɪˈθɪərə) *n.* **1.** a Greek island off the SE coast of the Peloponnese: in ancient times a centre of the worship of Aphrodite. Pop.: 4102 (1970). Area: about 285 sq. km (110 sq. miles). **2.** the chief town of this island, on the S coast. Pop.: 682 (1970). ~Modern Greek name: **Kíthira.**

Cytherea (ˌsɪθəˈrɪːə) *n.* another name for **Aphrodite** (Venus). —ˌCytherˈean *adj.*

cyto- *combining form.* indicating a cell: *cytoplasm.* [from Gk *kutos* vessel]

cytogenetics (ˌsaɪtəʊdʒɪˈnɛtɪks) *n.* (*functioning as sing.*) the branch of genetics that correlates the structure of chromosomes with heredity and variation. —ˌcytogeˈnetic *adj.*

cytology (saɪˈtɒlədʒɪ) *n.* the study of plant and animal cells. —**cytological** (ˌsaɪtəˈlɒdʒɪkəl) *adj.* —ˌcytoˈlogically *adv.* —cyˈtologist *n.*

cytoplasm (ˈsaɪtəʊˌplæzəm) *n.* the protoplasm of a cell excluding the nucleus. —ˌcytoˈplasmic *adj.*

cytosine (ˈsaɪtəsɪn) *n.* a white crystalline base occurring in nucleic acids. [C19: from CYTO- + -OSE^2 + -INE^2]

cytotoxic (ˌsaɪtəʊˈtɒksɪk) *adj.* destructive to cells, esp. to cancer cells: *cytotoxic drugs.* —**cytotoxicity** (ˌsaɪtəʊtɒkˈsɪsɪtɪ) *n.*

cytotoxin (ˌsaɪtəʊˈtɒksɪn) *n.* any substance that is poisonous to living cells.

Cyzicus (ˈsɪzɪkəs) *n.* an ancient Greek colony in NW Asia Minor on the S shore of the Sea of Marmara: site of Alcibiades' naval victory over the Peloponnesians (410 B.C.).

czar (zɑː) *n.* a variant spelling (esp. U.S.) of **tsar.** —ˈczardom *n.* —ˈCzarevitch, czaˈrevna, czaˈrina, ˈczarism, ˈczarist: see **ts-** spellings.

czardas (ˈtʃɑːdæʃ) *n.* **1.** a Hungarian national dance of alternating slow and fast sections. **2.** music for this dance. [from Hungarian *csárdás*]

Czech (tʃɛk) *adj.* **1. a.** of, relating to, or characteristic of Bohemia and Moravia, their people, or their language. **b.** (loosely) of, relating to, or characteristic of Czechoslovakia or its people. ~*n.* **2.** one of the two official languages of Czechoslovakia, belonging to the West Slavonic branch of the Indo-European family. Czech and Slovak are closely related and mutually intelligible. **3. a.** a native or inhabitant of Bohemia or Moravia. **b.** (loosely) a native, inhabitant, or citizen of Czechoslovakia. [C19: from Polish, from Czech *Cech*]

Czech. *abbrev. for:* **1.** Czechoslovak. **2.** Czechoslovakian. **3.** Czechoslovakia.

Czechoslovak (ˌtʃɛkəʊˈsləʊvæk) *or* **Czechoslovakian** (ˌtʃɛkəʊsləʊˈvækɪən) *adj.* **1.** of or relating to Czechoslovakia, its peoples, or languages. ~*n.* **2.** (loosely) either of the two languages of Czechoslovakia: Czech or Slovak.

Czechoslovakia (ˌtʃɛkəʊsləʊˈvækɪə) *n.* a republic in central Europe: formed after the defeat of Austro-Hungary (1918) as a nation of Czechs in Bohemia and Moravia and Slovaks in Slovakia; occupied by Germany from 1939 until its liberation by the Soviet Union in 1945; became a people's republic under the Communists in 1948; invaded by Warsaw Pact troops in 1968, ending Dubček's attempt to liberalize communism. It now consists of two federal republics, the **Czech Socialist Republic** and the **Slovak Socialist Republic.** It is mostly wooded and mountainous, with the Carpathians in the east rising over 2400 m (8000 ft.). Languages: Czech and Slovak. Currency: crown. Capital: Prague. Pop.: 15 723 000 (1988 est.). Area: 127 870 sq. km (49 360 sq. miles). Czech name: **Československo.** —ˌCzechosloˈvakian *adj., n.*

Czernowitz (ˈtʃɛrnovɪts) *n.* the German name for **Chernovtsy.**

Czerny (*German* ˈtʃɛrni) *n.* **Karl** (karl). 1791–1857, Austrian pianist, composer, and teacher, noted for his studies.

Częstochowa (*Polish* tʃɛ̃stɔˈxɔva) *n.* an industrial city in S Poland, on the River Warta: pilgrimage centre. Pop.: 247 000 (1985).

D

d *or* **D** (diː) *n., pl.* **d's, D's,** *or* **Ds. 1.** the fourth letter of the modern English alphabet. **2.** a speech sound represented by this letter.

d *symbol for Physics.* density.

D *symbol for:* **1.** *Music.* **a.** the second note of the scale of C major. **b.** the major or minor key having this note as its tonic. **2.** *Chem.* deuterium. ~ **3.** *the Roman numeral for* 500.

d. *abbrev. for:* **1.** date. **2.** daughter. **3.** degree. **4.** delete. **5.** *Brit.* currency before decimalization. penny *or* pennies. [L *denarius* or *denarii*] **6.** depart(s). **7.** diameter. **8.** died.

D. *abbrev. for:* **1.** *U.S.* Democrat(ic). **2.** Department. **3.** Deus. [L: God] **4.** *Optics.* diopter. **5.** Director. **6.** Dominus. [L: Lord] **7.** Dutch.

'd *contraction for* would *or* had: *I'd; you'd.*

DA (in the U.S.) *abbrev. for* District Attorney.

dab[1] (dæb) *vb.* **dabbing, dabbed. 1.** to touch or pat lightly and quickly. **2.** (*tr.*) to daub with short tapping strokes: *to dab the wall with paint.* **3.** (*tr.*) to apply (paint, cream, etc.) with short tapping strokes. ~*n.* **4.** a small amount, esp. of something soft or moist. **5.** a light stroke or tap, as with the hand. **6.** (*often pl.*) *Chiefly Brit.* a slang word for **fingerprint.** [C14: imit.] —**'dabber** *n.*

dab[2] (dæb) *n.* **1.** a small common European flatfish covered with rough toothed scales. **2.** any of various other small flatfish. [C15: from Anglo-F *dabbe*, from ?]

dabble ('dæb³l) *vb.* **1.** to dip, move, or splash (the fingers, feet, etc.) in a liquid. **2.** (*intr.*; usually foll. by *in, with,* or *at*) to deal (with) or work (at) frivolously or superficially. **3.** (*tr.*) to splash or smear. [C16: prob. from Du. *dabbelen*] —**'dabbler** *n.*

dabchick ('dæb,tʃɪk) *n.* any of several small grebes. [C16: prob. from OE *dop* to dive + CHICK]

dab hand *n. Brit. inf.* a person who is particularly skilled at something: *a dab hand at chess.* [?from DAB¹]

da capo (daː 'kɑːpəʊ) *adj., adv. Music.* to be repeated from the beginning. [C18: from It., lit.: from the head]

Dacca ('dækə) *n.* the former name (until 1982) of **Dhaka.**

dace (deɪs) *n., pl.* **dace** *or* **daces. 1.** a European freshwater fish of the carp family. **2.** any of various similar fishes. [C15: from OF *dars* DART]

dacha *or* **datcha** ('dætʃə) *n.* a country house or cottage in Russia. [from Russian: a giving, gift]

Dachau (*German* 'daxau) *n.* a Nazi concentration camp near Munich.

dachshund ('dæks,hʊnd) *n.* a long-bodied short-legged breed of dog. [C19: from G, from *Dachs* badger + *Hund* dog]

Dacia ('deɪsɪə) *n.* an ancient region bounded by the Carpathians, the Tisza, and the Danube, roughly corresponding to modern Romania. United under kings from about 60 B.C., it later contained the Roman province of the same name (about 105 to 270 A.D.). —**'Dacian** *adj., n.*

dacoit (də'kɔɪt) *n.* (in India and Burma) a member of a gang of armed robbers. [C19: from Hindi *dakait*, from *dākā* robbery]

Dacron ('deɪkrɒn, 'dæk-) *n.* the U.S. name (trademark) for **Terylene.**

dactyl ('dæktɪl) *n. Prosody.* a metrical foot of three syllables, one long followed by two short (¯ ˘ ˘). [C14: via L from Gk *daktulos* finger, comparing the finger's three joints to the three syllables]

dactylic (dæk'tɪlɪk) *adj.* **1.** of, relating to, or having a dactyl: *dactylic verse.* ~*n.* **2.** a variant of **dactyl.** —**dac'tyli-cally** *adv.*

dad (dæd) *n.* an informal word for **father.** [C16: childish word]

Dada ('dɑːdɑː) *or* **Dadaism** ('dɑːdɑː,ɪzəm) *n.* a nihilistic artistic movement of the early 20th century, founded on principles of irrationality, incongruity, and irreverence towards accepted aesthetic criteria. [C20: from F, from children's word for hobbyhorse] —**'Dadaist** *n., adj.* —,**Dada'istic** *adj.*

daddy ('dædɪ) *n., pl.* **-dies. 1.** an informal word for **father. 2. the daddy.** *Sl., chiefly U.S., Canad., & Austral.* the supreme or finest example.

daddy-longlegs *n.* **1.** *Brit.* an informal name for **crane fly. 2.** *U.S. & Canad.* an informal name for **harvestman** (sense 2).

dado ('deɪdəʊ) *n., pl.* **-does** *or* **-dos. 1.** the lower part of an interior wall that is decorated differently from the upper part. **2.** *Archit.* the part of a pedestal between the base and the cornice. ~*vb.* **3.** (*tr.*) to provide with a dado. [C17: from It.: die, die-shaped pedestal]

Dadra and Nagar Haveli (də'drɑː; 'nʌgə ə'vɛlɪ) *n.* a union territory of W India, on the Gulf of Cambay: until 1961 administratively part of Portuguese Damão. Capital: Silvassa. Pop.: 103 677 (1981). Area: 489 sq. km (191 sq. miles).

Daedalus ('diːdələs) *n. Greek myth.* an Athenian architect and inventor who built the labyrinth for Minos on Crete and fashioned wings for himself and his son Icarus to flee their imprisonment on the island. —**Daedalian, Daedalean** (dɪ'deɪlɪən) *or* **Daedalic** (dɪ'dælɪk) *adj.*

daemon ('diːmən) *or* **daimon** *n.* **1.** a demigod. **2.** the guardian spirit of a place or person. **3.** a variant spelling of **demon** (sense 3). —**daemonic** (diː'mɒnɪk) *adj.*

daff (dæf) *n. Inf.* short for **daffodil.**

daffodil ('dæfədɪl) *n.* **1.** Also called: **Lent lily.** a widely cultivated Eurasian plant, *Narcissus pseudonarcissus,* having spring-blooming yellow nodding flowers. **2.** any other plant of the genus *Narcissus.* **3. a.** a brilliant yellow colour. **b.** (*as adj.*): *daffodil paint.* **4.** a daffodil as a national emblem of Wales. [C14: from Med. L *affodillus,* var. of L *asphodelus* ASPHODEL]

daffy ('dæfɪ) *adj.* **daffier, daffiest.** *Inf.* another word for **daft** (senses 1, 2). [C19: from obs. *daff* fool]

daft (dɑːft) *adj. Chiefly Brit.* **1.** *Inf.* foolish, simple, or stupid. **2.** a slang word for **insane. 3.** (*postpositive; foll. by about*) *Inf.* extremely fond (of). **4.** *Sl.* frivolous; giddy. [OE *gedæfte* gentle, foolish] —**'daftness** *n.*

daftie ('dɑːftɪ) *n. Inf.* a daft person.

dag[1] (dæg) *n.* **1.** short for **daglock.** ~*vb.* **dagging, dagged. 2.** to cut the daglock away from (a sheep). [C18: from ?] —**'dagger** *n.*

dag[2] (dæg) *n. Inf.* **1.** *Austral.* a character; eccentric. **2.** *Austral.* a person who is untidily dressed. **3.** *Austral.* a conventional person. **4.** *N.Z.* a person with a good sense of humour. [back formation from DAGGY]

Da Gama (də 'gɑːmə) *n.* See (Vasco da) **Gama.**

Dagan ('dɑːgən) *n.* an earth god of the Babylonians and Assyrians.

Dagenham ('dægənəm) *n.* part of the Greater London borough of Barking and Dagenham: motor-vehicle manufacturing.

Dagestan Autonomous Soviet Socialist Republic (,dɑːgɪ'stɑːn) *n.* an administrative division of the S Soviet Union, on the Caspian Sea: annexed from Persia in 1813; rich mineral resources. Capital: Makhachkala. Pop.: 1 697 000 (1982 est.). Area: 50 278 sq. km (19 416 sq. miles). Also called: **Dagestan** *or* **Daghestan.**

dagga ('daxə, 'dɑːgə) *n.* hemp smoked as a narcotic. [C19: from Afrik., from Hottentot *dagab*]

dagger ('dægə) *n.* **1.** a short stabbing weapon with a pointed blade. **2.** Also called: **obelisk.** a character (†) used in printing to indicate a cross reference. **3. at daggers drawn.** in a state of open hostility. **4. look daggers.** to glare with hostility; scowl. [C14: from ?]

daggy ('dægɪ) *adj.* **-gier, -giest.** *Austral. & N.Z. inf.* untidy; dishevelled. [from DAG¹]

daglock ('dæg,lɒk) *n.* a dung-caked lock of wool around the hindquarters of a sheep. [C17: see DAG¹, LOCK²]

dago ('deɪgəʊ) *n., pl.* **-gos** *or* **-goes.** *Derog.* a foreigner, esp. a Spaniard or Portuguese. [C19: from *Diego,* a common Sp. name]

Dagon ('deɪgɒn) *n. Bible.* a god worshipped by the Philistines, represented as half man and half fish. [C14: via L and Gk from Heb. *Dāgōn,* lit.: little fish]

Daguerre (*French* dagɛr) *n.* **Louis Jacques Mandé** (lwi ʒak mɑ̃de). 1789–1851, French inventor, who devised one of the first practical photographic processes (1838).

daguerreotype (dəˈgɛrəʊˌtaɪp) *n.* **1.** one of the earliest photographic processes, in which the image was produced on iodine-sensitized silver and developed in mercury vapour. **2.** a photograph formed by this process. —da'guerreo,typy *n.*

Dahl (dɑːl) *n.* **Roald** (ˈrəʊəld). born 1916, British writer with Norwegian parents. His short stories include *Kiss Kiss* (1954) and *Switch Bitch* (1974). His children's books include *Charlie and the Chocolate Factory* (1964).

dahlia (ˈdeɪljə) *n.* **1.** any herbaceous perennial plant of the Mexican genus *Dahlia*, having showy flowers and tuberous roots. **2.** the flower or root of any of these plants. [C19: after Anders *Dahl*, 18th-cent. Swedish botanist]

Dahna (ˈdɑːxnɑː) *n.* another name for **Rub' al Khali.**

Dahomey (dəˈhəʊmɪ) *n.* the former name (until 1975) of **Benin.**

Dáil Éireann (ˈdaːl ˈɛːrɪn) *or* **Dáil** *n.* (in the Republic of Ireland) the lower chamber of parliament. [from Irish *dáil* assembly + *Eireann* of Eire]

daily (ˈdeɪlɪ) *adj.* **1.** of or occurring every day or every weekday. *~n., pl.* **-lies. 2.** a daily newspaper. **3.** *Brit.* a charwoman. *~adv.* **4.** every day. **5.** constantly; often. [OE *dæglic*]

daimon (ˈdaɪmɒn) *n.* a variant spelling of **daemon** or **demon** (sense 3). —**dai'monic** *adj.*

daimyo *or* **daimio** (ˈdaɪmjəʊ) *n., pl.* **-myo, -myos** *or* **-mio, -mios.** (in Japan) one of the territorial magnates who formerly dominated much of the country. [from Japanese, from Ancient Chinese *d'âi miâng* great name]

dainty (ˈdeɪntɪ) *adj.* **-tier, -tiest. 1.** delicate or elegant. **2.** choice; delicious: *a dainty morsel.* **3.** excessively genteel; fastidious. *~n., pl.* **-ties. 4.** a choice piece of food; delicacy. [C13: from OF *deintié*, from L *dignitās* DIGNITY] —**'daintily** *adv.*

daiquiri (ˈdaɪkɪrɪ, ˈdæk-) *n., pl.* **-ris.** an iced drink containing rum, lime juice, and sugar. [C20: after *Daiquiri*, town in Cuba]

Dairen (daɪˈrɛn) *n.* a former name of **Lüda.**

dairy (ˈdɛərɪ) *n., pl.* **dairies. 1.** a company that supplies milk and milk products. **2.** a room or building where milk and cream are stored or made into butter and cheese. **3. a.** (*modifier*) of milk and milk products. **b.** (*in combination*): *a dairymaid.* **4.** a general shop, selling provisions, esp. milk and milk products. [C13 *daierie*, from OE *dæge* servant girl, one who kneads bread]

dairying (ˈdɛərɪɪŋ) *n.* the business of producing, processing, and selling dairy products.

dairyman (ˈdɛərɪmən) *n., pl.* **-men.** a man who works in a dairy.

dais (ˈdeɪɪs, deɪs) *n.* a raised platform, usually at one end of a hall, used by speakers, etc. [C13: from OF *deis*, from L *discus* DISCUS]

daisy (ˈdeɪzɪ) *n., pl.* **-sies. 1.** a small low-growing European plant having flower heads with a yellow centre and pinkish-white outer rays. **2.** any of various other composite plants having conspicuous ray flowers. **3.** *Sl.* an excellent person or thing. **4. pushing up the daisies.** dead and buried. [OE *dægesége* day's eye] —**'daisied** *adj.*

daisy chain *n.* a garland made, esp. by children, by threading daisies together.

daisycutter (ˈdeɪzɪˌkʌtə) *n. Cricket.* a ball bowled so that it rolls along the ground.

daisywheel (ˈdeɪzɪˌwiːl) *n. Computers.* a component of a computer printer shaped like a wheel with many spokes that prints using a disk with characters around the circumference. Also called: **printwheel.**

Dakar (ˈdækə) *n.* the capital and chief port of Senegal, on the SE side of Cape Verde peninsula. Pop.: 671 000 (1984).

Dakota (dəˈkəʊtə) *n.* a former territory of the U.S.: divided into the states of North Dakota and South Dakota in 1889. —**Da'kotan** *adj., n.*

daks (dæks) *pl. n. Austral. inf.* trousers. [C20: from trade name *Daks*]

dal (dɑːl) *n.* **1.** split grain, a common foodstuff in India; pulse. **2.** a variant spelling of **dhal.**

Daladier (*French* daladje) *n.* **Édouard** (edwar). 1884–1970, French radical socialist statesman; premier of France (1933; 1934; 1938–40) and signatory of the Munich Pact (1938).

Dalai Lama (ˈdælaɪ ˈlɑːmə) *n.* **1.** (until 1959) the chief lama and ruler of Tibet. **2.** the 14th holder of this office (1940), who fled to India (1959). [from Mongolian *dalai* ocean; see LAMA]

dale (deɪl) *n.* an open valley. [OE *dæl*]

Dale (deɪl) *n.* Sir **Henry Hallet.** 1875–1968, English physiologist: shared a Nobel prize for physiology or medicine in 1936 with Otto Loewi for their work on the chemical transmission of nerve impulses.

Dalek (ˈdɑːlɛk) *n.* a fictional robot-like creation that is aggressive, mobile, and produces rasping staccato speech. [C20: from a children's television series, *Dr Who*]

Dales (deɪlz) *pl. n.* (*sometimes not cap.*) **the.** short for the **Yorkshire Dales.**

dalesman (ˈdeɪlzmən) *n., pl.* **-men.** a person living in a dale, esp. in the dales of N England.

Dalglish (dælˈgliːʃ, dəl-) *n.* **Kenny,** born 1951, Scottish footballer: a striker, he played for Glasgow Celtic (1968–77) and for Liverpool from 1977: player-manager of Liverpool from 1985: Scotland's most-capped footballer.

Dalhousie (dælˈhaʊzɪ) *n.* **1. 9th Earl of,** title of *George Ramsay.* 1770–1838, British general; governor of the British colonies in Canada (1819–28). **2.** his son, **1st Marquis and 10th Earl of,** title of *James Andrew Broun Ramsay.* 1812–60, British statesman: governor general of India (1848–56).

Dali (ˈdɑːlɪ) *n.* **Salvador** (ˈsælvədɔː). 1904–89, Spanish surrealist painter.

Dallapiccola (*Italian* dallaˈpikkola) *n.* **Luigi** (luˈiːdʒi). 1904–75, Italian composer of twelve-tone music. His works include the opera *Il Prigioniero* (1944–48) and the ballet *Marsia* (1948).

Dallas (ˈdæləs) *n.* a city in NE Texas, on the Trinity River: scene of the assassination of President John F. Kennedy (1963). Pop.: 1 003 520 (1986).

dalliance (ˈdælɪəns) *n.* waste of time in frivolous action or in dawdling.

dally (ˈdælɪ) *vb.* **-lying, -lied.** (*intr.*) **1.** to waste time idly; dawdle. **2.** (usually foll. by *with*) to deal frivolously; trifle: *to dally with someone's affections.* [C14: from Anglo-F *dalier* to gossip, from ?]

Dalmatia (dælˈmeɪʃə) *n.* a region of W Yugoslavia, in Croatia along the Adriatic: mountainous, with many offshore islands.

Dalmatian (dælˈmeɪʃən) *n.* **1.** a large breed of dog having a short smooth white coat with black or brown spots. **2.** a native or inhabitant of Dalmatia. *~adj.* **3.** of Dalmatia or its inhabitants.

dalmatic (dælˈmætɪk) *n.* a wide-sleeved tunic-like vestment open at the sides, worn by deacons and bishops, and by a king at his coronation. [C15: from LL *dalmatica* (*vestis*) Dalmatian (robe) (orig. made of Dalmatian wool)]

dal segno (ˈdæl ˈsɛnjəʊ) *adj., adv. Music.* to be repeated from the point marked with a sign to the word *fine.* [It., lit.: from the sign]

dalton (ˈdɔːltən) *n.* another name for **atomic mass unit.** [C20: after J. DALTON]

Dalton (ˈdɔːltən) *n.* **John.** 1766–1844, English chemist and physicist, who formulated the modern form of the atomic theory and the law of partial pressures for gases. He also gave the first accurate description of colour blindness, from which he suffered.

daltonism (ˈdɔːltəˌnɪzəm) *n.* colour blindness, esp. the confusion of red and green. [C19: from F *daltonisme*, after J. DALTON]

dam[1] (dæm) *n.* **1.** a barrier of concrete, earth, etc., built across a river to create a body of water. **2.** a reservoir of water created by such a barrier. **3.** something that resembles or functions as a dam. *~vb.* **damming, dammed. 4.** (*tr.*; often foll. by *up*) to restrict by a dam. [C12: prob. from MLow G]

dam[2] (dæm) *n.* the female parent of an animal, esp. of domestic livestock. [C13: var. of DAME]

Dam (*Danish* dam) *n.* (**Carl Peter**) **Henrik** (ˈhɛnrəg). 1895–1976, Danish biochemist who discovered vitamin K (1934): Nobel prize for physiology or medicine 1943.

damage (ˈdæmɪdʒ) *n.* **1.** injury or harm impairing the function or condition of a person or thing. **2.** loss of something desirable. **3.** *Inf.* cost; expense. *~vb.* **4.** (*tr.*) to cause damage to. **5.** (*intr.*) to suffer damage. [C14: from OF, from L *damnum* injury, loss] —**'damaging** *adj.*

damages (ˈdæmɪdʒɪz) *pl. n. Law.* money to be paid as compensation for injury, loss, etc.

Daman and Diu (dɑː'mɑːn; 'diːuː) *n.* **1.** a Union Territory in W India: formerly a district of Portuguese India (1559–1961) then part of the Union Territory of Goa, Daman, and Diu (1961–87). Area: 72 sq. km (28 sq. miles). **2.** the chief town of this region, on the coast. Pop.: 21 003 (1981). ~Portuguese name: **Damão.**

Damanhûr (ˌdɑːmən'huə) *n.* a city in NE Egypt, in the Nile delta. Pop.: 221 500 (1985).

Damão (də'mau) *n.* the Portuguese name for **Daman.**

Damaraland (də'mɑːrəˌlænd) *n.* a plateau region of central Namibia. Pop.: 64 973 (1970).

damascene ('dæməˌsiːn) *vb.* **1.** (*tr.*) to ornament (metal, esp. steel) by etching or by inlaying other metals, usually gold or silver. ~*n.* **2.** a design or article produced by this process. ~*adj.* **3.** of or relating to this process. [C14: from L *damascênus* of Damascus]

Damascene ('dæməˌsiːn) *adj.* **1.** of Damascus. ~*n.* **2.** a native or inhabitant of Damascus.

Damascus (də'mɑːskəs, -'mæs-) *n.* the capital of Syria, in the southwest: reputedly the oldest city in the world, having been inhabited continuously since before 1000 B.C. Pop.: 1 292 000 (1987). Arabic names: **Dimashq, Esh Sham** (ɛʃ ʃæm).

Damascus steel *or* **damask steel** *n. History.* a hard flexible steel with wavy markings, used for sword blades.

damask ('dæməsk) *n.* **1. a.** a reversible fabric, usually silk or linen, with a pattern woven into it. It is used for table linen, curtains, etc. **b.** table linen made from this. **c.** (*as modifier*): *a damask tablecloth.* **2.** short for **Damascus steel. 3.** the wavy markings on such steel. **4. a.** the greyish-pink colour of the damask rose. **b.** (*as adj.*): *damask wallpaper.* ~*vb.* **5.** (*tr.*) another word for **damascene.** [C14: from Med. L *damascus*, from Damascus, where fabric orig. made]

damask rose *n.* a rose with fragrant flowers, which are used to make the perfume attar. [C16: from Med. L *rosa damascêna* rose of Damascus]

dame (deɪm) *n.* **1.** (formerly) a woman of rank or dignity; lady. **2.** *Arch.*, *chiefly Brit.* an elderly woman. **3.** *Sl.*, *chiefly U.S. & Canad.* a woman. **4.** *Brit.* the role of a comic old woman in a pantomime, usually played by a man. [C13: from OF, from L *domina* lady, mistress of household]

Dame (deɪm) *n.* (in Britain) **1.** the title of a woman who has been awarded the Order of the British Empire or any of certain other orders of chivalry. **2.** the title of the wife of a knight or baronet.

dame school *n.* (formerly) a small school, offering basic education, usually run by an elderly woman in her own home.

Damien (*French* damjɛ̃) *n.* **Joseph** (ʒozɛf), known as *Father Damien.* 1840–89, Belgian Roman Catholic missionary to the leper colony at Molokai, Hawaii.

Damietta (ˌdæmɪ'ɛtə) *n.* a town in NE Egypt, in the Nile delta: important medieval commercial centre. Pop.: 111 900 (1983 est.). Arabic name: **Dumyat.**

damn (dæm) *interj.* **1.** *Sl.* an exclamation of annoyance. **2.** *Inf.* an exclamation of surprise or pleasure. ~*adj.* **3.** (*prenominal*) *Sl.* deserving damnation. ~*adv.*, *adj.* (*prenominal*) **4.** *Sl.* (intensifier): *a damn good pianist.* ~*adv.* **5. damn all.** *Sl.* absolutely nothing. ~*vb.* (*mainly tr.*) **6.** to condemn as bad, worthless, etc. **7.** to curse. **8.** to condemn to eternal damnation. **9.** (*often passive*) to doom to ruin. **10.** (*also intr.*) to prove (someone) guilty: *damning evidence.* **11. damn with faint praise.** to praise so unenthusiastically that the effect is condemnation. ~*n.* **12.** *Sl.* something of negligible value (esp. in **not worth a damn**). **13. not give a damn.** *Inf.* not care. [C13: from OF *dampner*, from L *damnāre*, from *damnum* loss, injury]

damnable ('dæmnəbəl) *adj.* **1.** execrable; detestable. **2.** liable to or deserving damnation. —'**damnableness** *or* ˌdamna'bility *n.*

damnation (dæm'neɪʃən) *n.* **1.** the act of damning or state of being damned. ~*interj.* **2.** an exclamation of anger, disappointment, etc.

damnatory ('dæmnətərɪ) *adj.* threatening or occasioning condemnation.

damned (dæmd) *adj.* **1. a.** condemned to hell. **b.** (*as collective n.; preceded by the*): *the damned.* ~*adv.*, *adj. Sl.* **2.** (intensifier): *a damned good try.* **3.** used to indicate amazement, disavowal, or refusal (as in **damned if I care**).

damnify ('dæmnɪˌfaɪ) *vb.* **-fying, -fied.** (*tr.*) *Law.* to cause loss or damage to (a person); injure. [C16: from OF *damnifier*, ult. from L *damnum* harm, + *facere* to make] —ˌdamnifi'cation *n.*

Damocles ('dæməˌkliːz) *n. Classical legend.* a sycophant forced by Dionysius, tyrant of Syracuse, to sit under a sword suspended by a hair to demonstrate that being a king was not the happy state Damocles had said it was. See also **Sword of Damocles.** —ˌDamo'clean *adj.*

Damodar ('dæməˌdɑː) *n.* a river in NE India, rising in Bihar and flowing east through West Bengal to the Hooghly River: the **Damodar Valley** is an important centre of heavy industry.

damoiselle, damosel, *or* **damozel** (ˌdæmə'zɛl) *n.* archaic variants of **damsel.**

Damon and Pythias ('deɪmən) *n. Classical legend.* two friends noted for their mutual loyalty. Damon offered himself as a hostage for Pythias, who was to be executed for treason by Dionysius of Syracuse. When Pythias returned to save his friend's life, he was pardoned.

damp (dæmp) *adj.* **1.** slightly wet. ~*n.* **2.** slight wetness; moisture. **3.** rank air or poisonous gas, esp. in a mine. **4.** a discouragement; damper. ~*vb.* (*tr.*) **5.** to make slightly wet. **6.** (often foll. by *down*) to stifle or deaden: *to damp one's ardour.* **7.** (often foll. by *down*) to reduce the flow of air to (a fire) to make it burn more slowly. **8.** *Physics.* to reduce the amplitude of (an oscillation or wave). **9.** *Music.* to muffle (the sound of an instrument). [C14: from MLow G *damp* steam] —'**dampness** *n.*

dampcourse ('dæmpˌkɔːs) *n.* a layer of impervious material in a wall, to stop moisture rising. Also called: **damp-proof course.**

dampen ('dæmpən) *vb.* **1.** to make or become damp. **2.** (*tr.*) to stifle; deaden. —'**dampener** *n.*

damper ('dæmpə) *n.* **1.** a person, event, or circumstance that depresses or discourages. **2. put a damper on.** to produce a depressing or stultifying effect on. **3.** a movable plate to regulate the draught in a stove or furnace flue. **4.** a device to reduce electronic, mechanical, acoustic, or aerodynamic oscillations in a system. **5.** the pad in a piano or harpsichord that deadens the vibration of each string as its key is released. **6.** *Chiefly Austral. & N.Z.* any of various unleavened loaves and scones, typically cooked on an open fire.

Dampier ('dæmpɪə) *n.* **William.** 1652–1715, English navigator, pirate, and writer: sailed around the world twice.

damping off *n.* any of various diseases of plants caused by fungi in conditions of excessive moisture.

damsel ('dæmzəl) *n. Arch. or poetic.* a young unmarried woman; maiden. [C13: from OF *damoisele*, from Vulgar L *domnicella* (unattested) young lady, from L *domina* mistress]

damselfly ('dæmzəlˌflaɪ) *n., pl.* **-flies.** any of various insects similar to dragonflies but usually resting with the wings closed over the back.

damson ('dæmzən) *n.* **1.** a small tree cultivated for its blue-black edible plumlike fruit. **2.** the fruit of this tree. [C14: from L *prūnum damascênum* Damascus plum]

dan (dæn) *n. Judo, karate.* **1.** any one of the 10 black-belt grades of proficiency. **2.** a competitor entitled to dan grading. [Japanese]

Dan (dæn) *n. Old Testament.* **1. a.** the fourth son of Jacob (Genesis 30:1–6). **b.** the tribe descended from him. **2.** a city in the northern territory of Canaan.

Dan. *abbrev. for:* **1.** *Bible.* Daniel. **2.** Danish.

Dana ('deɪnə) *n.* **James Dwight** (dwaɪt). 1813–95, American geologist; noted for his work *The System of Mineralogy* (1837).

Danaë ('dæneɪˌiː) *n. Greek myth.* the mother of Perseus by Zeus, who came to her in prison as a shower of gold.

Danaides (də'neɪɪˌdiːz) *pl. n., sing.* **Danaid.** *Greek myth.* the fifty daughters of Danaüs. All but Hypermnestra murdered their bridegrooms and were punished in Hades by having to pour water perpetually into a jar with a hole in the bottom. —**Danaidean** (ˌdænɪ'ɪdɪən, ˌdænɪə'diːən) *adj.*

Da Nang (dɑː næŋ) *n.* a port in central Vietnam, on the South China Sea. Pop.: 318 655 (1979). Former name: **Tourane.**

Danaüs ('dænɪəs) *n. Greek myth.* a king of Argos who told his fifty daughters, the Danaides, to kill their bridegrooms on their wedding night.

dance (dɑːns) *vb.* **1.** (*intr.*) to move the feet and body rhythmically, esp. in time to music. **2.** (*tr.*) to perform (a particular dance). **3.** (*intr.*) to skip or leap. **4.** to move or cause to move in a rhythmical way. **5. dance attendance on** (**someone**). to attend (someone) solicitously or obsequiously. ~*n.* **6.** a series of rhythmical steps and movements, usually in time to music. **7.** an act of dancing. **8. a.** a social meeting arranged for dancing. **b.** (*as modifier*): *a dance hall.* **9.** a piece of music in the rhythm of a particular dance form. **10.** dancelike movements. **11. lead** (**someone**) **a dance.** *Brit. inf.* to cause (someone) continued worry and exasperation. [C13: from OF *dancier*] —'**danceable** *adj.* —'**dancer** *n.* —'**dancing** *n.*, *adj.*

dance floor *n.* **a.** an area of floor in a disco, nightclub, etc., where patrons may dance. **b.** (*as modifier*): *dancefloor music.*

dance of death *n.* a medieval representation of a dance in which people are led off to their graves, by a personification of death. Also called (French): **danse macabre.**

dancing girl *n.* a professional female dancer.

D and C *n. Med.* dilation (of the cervix) and curettage (of the uterus).

dandelion ('dændı,laɪən) *n.* **1.** a plant native to Europe and Asia and naturalized as a weed in North America, having yellow rayed flowers and deeply notched leaves. **2.** any of several similar plants. [C15: from OF *dent de lion*, lit.: tooth of a lion, referring to its leaves]

dander ('dændə) *n.* **1.** small particles of hair or feathers. **2. get one's** (*or* **someone's**) **dander up.** *Inf.* to become (*or* cause to become) annoyed or angry. [C19: from DAN-DRUFF]

dandify ('dændı,faɪ) *vb.* -**fying**, -**fied.** (*tr.*) to dress like or cause to resemble a dandy.

dandle ('dændºl) *vb.* (*tr.*) **1.** to move (a young child) up and down (on the knee or in the arms). **2.** to pet; fondle. [C16: from ?] —'**dandler** *n.*

dandruff ('dændrəf) *n.* loose scales of dry dead skin shed from the scalp. [C16: *dand*- from ? + -*ruff*, prob. from ME *roufe* scab, from ON *hrúfa*]

dandy ('dændı) *n.*, *pl.* -**dies.** **1.** a man greatly concerned with smartness of dress. ~*adj.* -**dier**, -**diest.** **2.** *Inf.* very good or fine. [C18: ? short for *jack-a-dandy*] —'**dandyish** *adj.*

dandy-brush *n.* a stiff brush used for grooming a horse.

dandy roll *or* **roller** *n.* a roller used in the manufacture of paper to produce watermarks.

Dane (deɪn) *n.* **1.** a native, citizen, or inhabitant of Denmark. **2.** any of the Vikings who invaded England from the late 8th to the 11th century A.D.

Danegeld ('deɪn,gɛld) *or* **Danegelt** ('deɪn,gɛlt) *n.* the tax levied in Anglo-Saxon England to provide protection money for or to finance forces to oppose Viking invaders. [C11: from *Dan* Dane + *geld* tribute; see YIELD]

Danelaw ('deɪn,lɔː) *n.* the parts of Anglo-Saxon England in which Danish law and custom were observed. [OE *Dena lagu* Danes' law]

danger ('deɪndʒə) *n.* **1.** the state of being vulnerable to injury, loss, or evil; risk. **2.** a person or thing that may cause injury, pain, etc. **3. in danger of.** liable to. **4. on the danger list.** critically ill in hospital. [C13 *daunger* power, hence power to inflict injury, from OF *dongier* from L *dominium* ownership] —'**dangerless** *adj.*

danger money *n.* extra money paid to compensate for the risks involved in certain dangerous jobs.

dangerous ('deɪndʒərəs) *adj.* causing danger; perilous. —'**dangerously** *adv.*

dangle ('dæŋgºl) *vb.* **1.** to hang or cause to hang freely: *his legs dangled over the wall.* **2.** (*tr.*) to display as an enticement. [C16: ?from Danish *dangle*, prob. imit.] —'**dangler** *n.*

Daniel ('dænjəl) *n.* **1.** *Old Testament.* **a.** a youth who was taken into the household of Nebuchadnezzar, received guidance and apocalyptic visions from God, and was given divine protection when thrown into the lions' den. **b.** the book that recounts these experiences and visions, (in full **The Book of the Prophet Daniel**). **2.** (often preceded by *a*) a wise upright person. [sense 2: referring to Daniel in the Apocryphal *Book of Susanna*]

Danish ('deɪnɪʃ) *adj.* **1.** of Denmark, its people, or their language. ~*n.* **2.** the official language of Denmark.

Danish blue *n.* a strong-tasting white cheese with blue veins.

Danish pastry *n.* a rich puff pastry filled with apple, almond paste, icing, etc.

Danish West Indies *pl. n.* the former possession of Denmark in the W Lesser Antilles, sold to the U.S. in 1917 and since then named the **Virgin Islands of the United States.**

dank (dæŋk) *adj.* (esp. of cellars, caves, etc.) unpleasantly damp and chilly. [C14: prob. from ON] —'**dankly** *adv.* —'**dankness** *n.*

Dankworth ('dæŋkwɛːθ) *n.* **John.** born 1927, British jazz composer and saxophonist. His works include *String Quartet* (1971) and various film scores.

Danmark ('danmark) *n.* the Danish name for **Denmark.**

danseur French. (dɑ̃sœr) *or* (*fem.*) *danseuse* (dɑ̃søz) *n.* a ballet dancer.

Dante ('dæntı, 'dɑːnteɪ; *Italian* 'dante) *n.* full name **Dante Alighieri** (*Italian* ali'gjɛːri). 1265–1321, Italian poet famous for *La Divina Commedia* (?1309–?1320), an allegorical account of his journey through Hell, Purgatory, and Paradise, guided by Virgil and his idealized love Beatrice. His other works include *La Vita Nuova* (?1292), in which he celebrates his love for Beatrice. —**Dantean** ('dæntɪən, dæn'tiːən) *or* **Dantesque** (dæn'tɛsk) *adj.*

Danton ('dæntən; *French* dɑ̃tɔ̃) *n.* **Georges Jacques** (ʒɔrʒ ʒɑk). 1759–94, French revolutionary leader: a founder member of the Committee of Public Safety (1793) and minister of justice (1792–94). He was overthrown by Robespierre and guillotined.

Danube ('dænjuːb) *n.* a river in central and SE Europe, rising in the Black Forest in West Germany and flowing to the Black Sea. Length: 2859 km (1776 miles). German name: **Donau.** Czech name: **Dunaj.** Hungarian name: **Duna.** Serbo-Croat name: **Dunav** (dunaf). Romanian name: **Dunărea.** —**Danubian** (dæn'juːbɪən) *adj.*

Danzig ('dænsıg; *German* 'dantsıç) *n.* the German name for **Gdańsk.**

dap (dæp) *vb.* **dapping, dapped.** **1.** *Angling.* to fly-fish so that the fly bobs on and off the water. **2.** (*intr.*) to dip lightly into water. **3.** to bounce or cause to bounce. [C17: imit.]

daphne ('dæfnı) *n.* any of various Eurasian ornamental shrubs with shiny evergreen leaves and clusters of small bell-shaped flowers. [via L from Gk: laurel]

Daphne ('dæfnı) *n. Greek myth.* a nymph who was saved from the amorous attentions of Apollo by being changed into a laurel tree.

daphnia ('dæfnɪə) *n.* any of several waterfleas having a rounded body enclosed in a transparent shell. [C19: prob. from DAPHNE]

Daphnis ('dæfnıs) *n. Greek myth.* a Sicilian shepherd, the son of Hermes and a nymph, who was regarded as the inventor of pastoral poetry.

dapper ('dæpə) *adj.* **1.** neat in dress and bearing. **2.** small and nimble. [C15: from MDu.: active, nimble] —'**dapperly** *adv.* —'**dapperness** *n.*

dapple ('dæpºl) *vb.* **1.** to mark or become marked with spots of a different colour; mottle. ~*n.* **2.** mottled or spotted markings. **3.** a dappled horse, etc. ~*adj.* **4.** marked with dapples or spots. [C14: from ?]

dapple-grey *n.* a horse with a grey coat having spots of darker colour.

Dapsang (dʌp'sʌŋ) *n.* another name for **K2.**

darbies ('dɑːbız) *pl. n. Brit.* a slang term for **handcuffs.** [C16: ?from *Father Derby's* (or *Darby's*) *bonds*, a rigid agreement between a usurer and his client]

d'Arblay ('dɑːbleɪ) *n.* **Madame.** married name of (Fanny) **Burney.**

Darby and Joan ('dɑːbı; dʒəʊn) *n.* **1.** an ideal elderly married couple living in domestic harmony. **2. Darby and Joan Club.** a club for elderly people. [C18: couple in 18th-cent. English ballad]

Darcy ('dɑːsı) *n.* (**James**) **Les**(lie). 1895–1917, Australian boxer and folk hero, who lost only five professional fights and was never knocked out, considered a martyr after his death from septicaemia during a tour of the United States.

Dardanelles (,dɑːdə'nɛlz) *n.* the strait between the Aegean and the Sea of Marmara, separating European from Asian Turkey. Ancient name: **Hellespont.**

Dardanus ('dɑːdənəs) *n. Classical myth.* the son of Zeus and Electra who founded the royal house of Troy.

dare (dɛə) *vb.* **1.** (*tr.*) to challenge (a person to do something) as proof of courage. **2.** (can take an infinitive with or without *to*) to be courageous enough to try (to do something). **3.** (*tr.*) *Rare.* to oppose without fear; defy. **4. I dare say. a.** (it is) quite possible (that). **b.** probably. ~*n.* **5.** a challenge to do something as proof of courage. **6.** something done in response to such a challenge. [OE *durran*] — '**darer** *n.*

▷ **Usage.** When used negatively or interrogatively and not followed by an infinitive with *to*, *dare* does not add -*s: he dare not; dare she come?*

daredevil ('dɛə,dɛvªl) *n.* **1.** a recklessly bold person. ~*adj.* **2.** reckless; daring; bold. — '**dare,devilry** *or* '**dare,deviltry** *n.*

Dar es Salaam ('dɑːr ɛs səˈlɑːm) *n.* the chief port of Tanzania, on the Indian Ocean: capital of German East Africa (1891–1916); capital of Tanzania until 1983 when it was replaced by Dodoma; university (1963). Pop.: 1 394 000 (1985).

Darfur (dɑːˈfʊə) *n.* a province of the W Sudan since 1916; an independent kingdom until conquered by Egypt in 1874. Capital: El Fasher. Pop.: 1 838 707 (1973). Area: 496 373 sq. km (191 650 sq. miles).

Darien ('dɛərɪən, 'dæ-) *n.* **1.** the E part of the Isthmus of Panama, between the **Gulf of Darien** on the Caribbean coast and the Gulf of San Miguel on the Pacific coast; chiefly within the republic of Panama but extending also into Colombia: site of a disastrous attempt to establish a Scottish colony in 1698. **2. Isthmus of.** the former name of the Isthmus of **Panama.** ~Spanish name: **Darién** (daˈrjen).

daring ('dɛərɪŋ) *adj.* **1.** bold or adventurous. ~*n.* **2.** courage in taking risks; boldness.

Dario (*Spanish* da'rio) *n.* **Rubén** (ruˈβen), real name *Félix Rubén García Sarmiento.* 1867–1916, Nicaraguan poet whose poetry includes *Prosas Profanas* (1896).

Darius I (dəˈraɪəs) *n.* known as *Darius the Great*, surname *Hystaspis.* ?550–486 B.C., king of Persia (521–486), who extended the Persian empire and crushed the revolt of the Ionian city states (500). He led two expeditions against Greece but was defeated at Marathon (490).

Darius III *n.* died 330 B.C., last Achaemenid king of Persia (336–330), who was defeated by Alexander the Great.

Darjeeling (dɑːˈdʒiːlɪŋ) *n.* **1.** a town in NE India, in West Bengal in the Himalayas, at an altitude of about 2250 m (7500 ft.). Pop.: 57 603 (1981). **2.** a high-quality black tea grown in the mountains around Darjeeling.

dark (dɑːk) *adj.* **1.** having little or no light. **2.** (of a colour) reflecting or transmitting little light: *dark brown.* **3.** (of complexion, hair colour, etc.) not fair; swarthy; brunette. **4.** gloomy or dismal. **5.** sinister; evil: *a dark purpose.* **6.** sullen or angry. **7.** ignorant or unenlightened: *a dark period in our history.* **8.** secret or mysterious. ~*n.* **9.** absence of light; darkness. **10.** night or nightfall. **11.** a dark place. **12.** a state of ignorance (esp. in **the dark**). [OE *deorc*] — '**darkish** *adj.* — '**darkly** *adv.* — '**darkness** *n.*

Dark Ages *pl. n. European history.* the period from about the late 5th century A.D. to about 1000 A.D., once considered an unenlightened period.

Dark Continent *n.* **the.** a term for Africa when it was relatively unexplored by Europeans.

darken ('dɑːkən) *vb.* **1.** to make or become dark or darker. **2.** to make or become gloomy, angry, or sad. **3. darken (someone's) door.** (*usually used with a negative*) to visit someone: *never darken my door again!* — '**darkener** *n.*

dark horse *n.* **1.** a competitor in a race or contest about whom little is known. **2.** a person who reveals little about himself, esp. one who reveals unexpected talents. **3.** *U.S. politics.* a candidate who is unexpectedly nominated or elected.

dark lantern *n.* a lantern having a sliding shutter or panel to dim or hide the light.

darkling ('dɑːklɪŋ) *adv., adj. Poetic.* in the dark or night. [C15: from DARK + -LING²]

dark matter *n. Astron.* matter, as in galaxies, that is assumed to exist, but which is invisible at any wavelength of the electromagnetic spectrum.

darkroom ('dɑːk,ruːm, -,rʊm) *n.* a room in which photographs are processed in darkness or safe light.

darksome ('dɑːksəm) *adj. Literary.* dark or darkish.

dark star *n.* an invisible star known to exist only from observation of its radio, infrared, or other spectrum or of its gravitational effect.

Darlan (*French* darlɑ̃) *n.* **Jean Louis Xavier François** (ʒɑ̃ lwi gzavje frɑ̃swa). 1881–1942, French admiral and member of the Vichy government. He cooperated with the Allies after their invasion of North Africa; assassinated.

darling ('dɑːlɪŋ) *n.* **1.** a person very much loved. **2.** a favourite. ~*adj.* (*prenominal*) **3.** beloved. **4.** much admired; pleasing: *a darling hat.* [OE *dēorling*; see DEAR, -LING¹]

Darling ('dɑːlɪŋ) *n.* **Grace.** 1815–42, English national heroine, famous for her rescue (1838) of some shipwrecked sailors with her father, a lighthouse keeper.

Darling Downs *pl. n.* a plateau in NE Australia, in SE Queensland: a vast agricultural and stock-raising area.

Darling Range *n.* a ridge in SW Western Australia, parallel to the coast. Highest point: about 582 m (1669 ft.).

Darling River *n.* a river in SE Australia, rising in the Eastern Highlands and flowing southwest to the Murray River. Length: 2740 km (1702 miles).

Darlington ('dɑːlɪŋtən) *n.* an industrial town in NE England in S Durham: developed mainly with the opening of the Stockton-Darlington railway (1825). Pop.: 96 000 (1985).

Darmstadt ('dɑːmstæt; *German* 'darmʃtat) *n.* an industrial city in central West Germany, in Hesse: former capital of the grand duchy of Hesse-Darmstadt (1567–1945). Pop.: 133 600 (1987).

darn¹ (dɑːn) *vb.* **1.** to mend (a hole or a garment) with a series of crossing or interwoven stitches. ~*n.* **2.** a patch of darned work on a garment. [C16: prob. from F (dialect) *darner*] — '**darner** *n.*

darn² (dɑːn) *interj., adj., adv., n.* a euphemistic word for **damn** (senses 1–4).

darnel ('dɑːnªl) *n.* any of several grasses that grow as weeds in grain fields in Europe and Asia. [C14: prob. rel. to F (dialect) *darnelle*, from ?]

darning ('dɑːnɪŋ) *n.* **1.** the act of mending a hole using interwoven stitches. **2.** garments needing to be darned.

darning needle *n.* **1.** a long needle with a large eye used for darning. **2.** *U.S. & Canad.* a dialect name for a **dragonfly.**

Darnley ('dɑːnlɪ) *n.* **Lord.** title of *Henry Stuart* (or *Stewart*). 1545–67, Scottish nobleman; second husband of Mary Queen of Scots and father of James I of England. After murdering his wife's secretary, Rizzio (1566), he was himself assassinated (1567).

dart (dɑːt) *n.* **1.** a small narrow pointed missile that is thrown or shot, as in the game of darts. **2.** a sudden quick movement. **3.** *Zool.* a slender pointed structure, as in snails for aiding copulation. **4.** a tapered tuck made in dressmaking. ~*vb.* **5.** to move or throw swiftly and suddenly; shoot. [C14: from OF, of Gmc origin] — '**darting** *adj.*

dartboard ('dɑːt,bɔːd) *n.* a circular piece of wood, cork, etc., used as the target in the game of darts.

darter ('dɑːtə) *n.* Also called: **anhinga, snakebird.** any of various aquatic birds of tropical and subtropical inland waters, having a long slender neck and bill. **2.** any of various small brightly coloured North American freshwater fish.

Dartford ('dɑːtfəd) *n.* a town in SE England, in NW Kent. Pop.: 77 315 (1983 est.).

Dartmoor ('dɑːt,mʊə) *n.* **1.** a moorland plateau in SW England, in SW Devon: a national park since 1951. Area: 945 sq. km (365 sq. miles). **2.** a prison in SW England, on Dartmoor: England's main prison for long-term convicts.

Dartmouth ('dɑːtməθ) *n.* **1.** a port in SW England, in S Devon: Royal Naval College (1905). Pop.: 6298 (1981). **2.** a city in SE Canada, in S Nova Scotia, on Halifax Harbour: oil refineries and shipyards. Pop.: 65 243 (1986).

darts (dɑːts) *n.* (*functioning as sing.*) any of various competitive games in which darts are thrown at a dartboard.

Darwin¹ ('dɑːwɪn) *n.* a port in N Australia, capital of the Northern Territory: destroyed by a cyclone in 1974 but rebuilt on the same site. Pop.: 66 131 (1986). Former name (1869–1911): **Palmerston.**

Darwin² ('dɑːwɪn) *n.* **1. Charles (Robert).** 1809–82, English naturalist who formulated the theory of evolution by natural selection, expounded in *On the Origin of Species* (1859) and applied to man in *The Descent of Man* (1871). **2.** his grandfather, **Erasmus.** 1731–1802, English physician and poet; author of *Zoonomia, or the Laws of Organic Life* (1794–96), anticipating Lamarck's views on evolution. **3.** Sir **George Howard,** son of Charles Darwin. 1845–1912, English astronomer and mathematician noted for his work on tidal friction.

Darwinian (dɑːˈwɪnɪən) *adj.* **1.** of or relating to Charles Darwin or his theory of evolution. ~*n.* **2.** a person who accepts, supports, or uses this theory.

Darwinism (ˈdɑːwɪˌnɪzəm) *or* **Darwinian theory** *n.* the theory of the origin of animal and plant species by evolution through a process of natural selection. —**'Darwinist** *n., adj.*

dash[1] (dæʃ) *vb.* (*mainly tr.*) **1.** to hurl; crash: *he dashed the cup to the floor.* **2.** to mix: *white paint dashed with blue.* **3.** (*intr.*) to move hastily or recklessly; rush. **4.** (usually foll. by *off* or *down*) to write (down) or finish (off) hastily. **5.** to frustrate: *his hopes were dashed.* **6.** to daunt (someone); discourage. ~*n.* **7.** a sudden quick movement. **8.** a small admixture: *coffee with a dash of cream.* **9.** a violent stroke or blow. **10.** the sound of splashing or smashing. **11.** panache; style: *he rides with dash.* **12.** the punctuation mark —, used to indicate a sudden change of subject or to enclose a parenthetical remark. **13.** the symbol (–) used, in combination with the symbol *dot* (.), in the written representation of Morse and other telegraphic codes. **14.** *Athletics.* another word (esp. U.S. and Canad.) for **sprint.** [ME *daschen, dassen,* ?from ON]

dash[2] (dæʃ) *interj., adj., adv., vb. Inf.* a euphemistic word for **damn** (senses 1, 3, 4).

dashboard (ˈdæʃˌbɔːd) *n.* **1.** Also called (Brit.): **fascia.** the instrument panel in a car, boat, or aircraft. **2.** *Obs.* a board at the side of a carriage or boat to protect against splashing.

dasher (ˈdæʃə) *n.* **1.** one that dashes. **2.** *Canad.* the ledge along the top of the boards of an ice hockey rink.

dashiki (dɑːˈʃiːkɪ) *n.* a large loose-fitting upper garment worn esp. by Negroes in the U.S., Africa, and the Caribbean. [C20: of W African origin]

dashing (ˈdæʃɪŋ) *adj.* **1.** spirited; lively: *a dashing young man.* **2.** stylish; showy.

dashlight (ˈdæʃˌlaɪt) *n.* a light that illuminates the dashboard of a car, esp. at night.

Dasht-i-Kavir *or* **Dasht-e-Kavir** (ˌdæʃtiːkæˈvɪə) *n.* a salt waste on the central plateau of Iran: a treacherous marsh beneath a salt crust. Also called: **Kavir Desert.**

Dasht-i-Lut *or* **Dasht-e-Lut** (ˌdæʃtiːˈlʊt) *n.* a desert plateau in central and E central Iran.

dassie (ˈdæsɪ) *n.* another name for a **hyrax,** esp. the rock hyrax. [C19: from Afrik.]

dastard (ˈdæstəd) *n. Arch.* a contemptible sneaking coward. [C15 (in the sense: dullard): prob. from ON *dæstr* exhausted, out of breath]

dastardly (ˈdæstədlɪ) *adj.* mean and cowardly. —**'dastardliness** *n.*

dasyure (ˈdæsɪˌjʊə) *n.* **1.** any of several small carnivorous marsupials of Australia, New Guinea, and adjacent islands. **2.** the ursine dasyure. See **Tasmanian devil.** [C19: from NL, from Gk *dasus* shaggy + *oura* tail]

dat. *abbrev. for* dative.

DAT *abbrev. for* digital audio tape.

data (ˈdeɪtə, ˈdɑːtə) *n.* **1.** a series of observations, measurements, or facts; information. **2.** Also called: **information.** *Computers.* the information operated on by a computer program. [C17: from L, lit.: (things) given, from *dare* to give]

▷ **Usage.** Although now generally used as a singular noun, *data* is properly a plural.

data base *or* **data bank** *n.* a store of a large amount of information, esp. in a form that can be handled by a computer.

data capture *n.* any process for converting information into a form that can be handled by a computer.

data pen *n.* a device for reading or scanning magnetically coded data on labels, packets, etc.

data processing *n.* **a.** a sequence of operations performed on data, esp. by a computer, in order to extract information, reorder files, etc. **b.** (*as modifier*): *a data-processing centre.*

data set *n. Computers.* another name for **file**[1] (sense 6).

date[1] (deɪt) *n.* **1.** a specified day of the month. **2.** the particular day or year of an event. **3.** an inscription on a coin, letter, etc., stating when it was made or written. **4. a.** an appointment for a particular time, esp. with a person

of the opposite sex. **b.** the person with whom the appointment is made. **5.** the present moment; now (esp. in **to date, up to date**). ~*vb.* **6.** (*tr.*) to mark (a letter, coin, etc.) with the day, month, or year. **7.** (*tr.*) to assign a date of occurrence or creation to. **8.** (*intr.*; foll. by *from* or *back to*) to have originated (at a specified time). **9.** (*tr.*) to reveal the age of: *that dress dates her.* **10.** to make or become old-fashioned: *some good films hardly date at all.* **11.** *Inf., chiefly U.S. & Canad.* **a.** to be a boyfriend or girlfriend of (someone of the opposite sex). **b.** to accompany (a member of the opposite sex) on a date. [C14: from OF, from L *dare* to give, as in *epistula data Romae* letter handed over at Rome] —**'datable** *or* **'dateable** *adj.*

▷ **Usage.** See at **year.**

date[2] (deɪt) *n.* **1.** the fruit of the date palm, having sweet edible flesh and a single large woody seed. **2.** short for **date palm.** [C13: from OF, from L, from Gk *daktulos* finger]

dated (ˈdeɪtɪd) *adj.* unfashionable; outmoded.

dateless (ˈdeɪtlɪs) *adj.* likely to remain fashionable, good, or interesting regardless of age.

dateline (ˈdeɪtˌlaɪn) *n. Journalism.* the date and location of a story, placed at the top of an article.

date line *n.* (*often caps.*) short for **International Date Line.**

date palm *n.* a tall feather palm grown in tropical regions for its sweet edible fruit.

date stamp *n.* **1.** an adjustable rubber stamp for recording the date. **2.** an inked impression made by this.

dating (ˈdeɪtɪŋ) *n.* any of several techniques, such as radioactive dating, dendrochronology, or varve dating, for establishing the age of rocks, palaeontological or archaeological specimens, etc.

dative (ˈdeɪtɪv) *Grammar.* ~*adj.* **1.** denoting a case of nouns, pronouns, and adjectives used to express the indirect object, to identify the recipients, and for other purposes. ~*n.* **2. a.** the dative case. **b.** a word or speech element in this case. [C15: from L *datīvus,* from *dare* to give] —**datival** (deɪˈtaɪvəl) *adj.* —**'datively** *adv.*

datum (ˈdeɪtəm, ˈdɑːtəm) *n., pl.* **-ta.** **1.** a single piece of information; fact. **2.** a proposition taken as unquestionable, often in order to construct some theoretical framework upon it. See also **sense datum.** [C17: from L: something given; see DATA]

datura (dəˈtjʊərə) *n.* any of various chiefly Indian plants and shrubs with large trumpet-shaped flowers. [C16: from NL, from Hindi]

daub (dɔːb) *vb.* **1.** (*tr.*) to smear or spread (paint, mud, etc.), esp. carelessly. **2.** (*tr.*) to cover or coat (with paint, plaster, etc.) carelessly. **3.** to paint (a picture) clumsily or badly. ~*n.* **4.** an unskilful or crude painting. **5.** something daubed on, esp. as a wall covering. **6.** a smear (of paint, mud, etc.) [C14: from OF *dauber* to paint, whitewash, from L *dealbāre,* from *albāre* to whiten] —**'dauber** *n.*

Daubigny (*French* dobiɲi) *n.* **Charles François** (ʃarl frɑ̃swa). 1817–78, French landscape painter associated with the Barbizon School.

Daudet (*French* dodɛ) *n.* **Alphonse** (alfɔ̃s). 1840–97, French novelist, short-story writer, and dramatist: noted particularly for his humorous sketches of Provençal life, as in *Lettres de mon moulin* (1866).

Daugava (ˈdaʊɡəˌva) *n.* the Latvian name for the Western **Dvina.**

Daugavpils (*Latvian* ˈdaʊɡafˌpils) *n.* a city in the W Soviet Union, in the SE Latvian SSR on the Western Dvina River: founded in 1274 by Teutonic Knights; ruled by Poland (1559–1772) and Russia (1772–1915); retaken by the Russians in 1940. Pop.: 122 000 (1983 est.). German name (until 1893): **Dünaburg.** Former Russian name (1893–1920): **Dvinsk.**

daughter (ˈdɔːtə) *n.* **1.** a female offspring; a girl or woman in relation to her parents. **2.** a female descendant. **3.** a female from a certain country, etc., or one closely connected with a certain environment, etc.: *a daughter of the church.* ~(*modifier*) **4.** *Biol.* denoting a cell or unicellular organism produced by the division of one of its own kind. **5.** *Physics.* (of a nuclide) formed from another nuclide by radioactive decay. [OE *dohtor*] —**'daughterhood** *n.* —**'daughterless** *adj.* —**'daughterly** *adj.*

daughter-in-law *n., pl.* **daughters-in-law.** the wife of one's son.

Daumier (*French* domje) *n.* **Honoré** (ɔnɔre). 1808–79, French painter and lithographer, noted particularly for his political and social caricatures.

daunt (dɔ:nt) *vb.* (*tr.; often passive*) **1.** to intimidate. **2.** to dishearten. [C13: from OF *danter*, changed from *donter* to conquer, from L *domitāre* to tame] — **'daunting** *adj.* — **'dauntingly** *adv.*

dauntless ('dɔ:ntlɪs) *adj.* bold; fearless; intrepid. — **'dauntlessly** *adv.* — **'dauntlessness** *n.*

dauphin ('dɔ:fɪn; *French* dofɛ̃) *n.* (from 1349–1830) the title of the eldest son of the king of France. [C15: from OF: orig. a family name]

dauphine ('dɔ:fiːn; *French* dofin) *or* **dauphiness** ('dɔ:fɪnɪs) *n. French history.* the wife of a dauphin.

Dauphiné (*French* dofine) *n.* a former province of SE France; its rulers, the Counts of Vienne, assumed the title of *dauphin;* annexed to France in 1457.

Davao (da'vaːo) *n.* a port in the S Philippines, in SE Mindanao. Pop.: 610 375 (1980).

davenport ('dævən,pɔːt) *n.* **1.** *Chiefly Brit.* a tall narrow writing desk with drawers. **2.** *U.S. & Canad.* a large sofa, esp. one convertible into a bed. [C19: sense 1 supposedly after Captain *Davenport,* who commissioned the first ones]

David ('deɪvɪd) *n.* **1.** the second king of the Hebrews (about 1000–962 B.C.), who united Israel as a kingdom with Jerusalem as its capital. **2. Elizabeth.** born 1914, British cookery writer. Her books include *Mediterranean Food* (1950) and *French Country Cooking* (1951). **3.** (*French* david). **Jacques Louis** (ʒɑk lwi). 1748–1825, French neoclassical painter of such works as the *Oath of the Horatii* (1784), *Death of Socrates* (1787), and *The Intervention of the Sabine Women* (1799). He actively supported the French Revolution and became court painter to Napoleon Bonaparte in 1804; banished at the Bourbon restoration. **4. Saint.** 6th century A.D., Welsh bishop; patron saint of Wales. Feast day: March 1.

David I *n.* 1084–1153, king of Scotland (1124–53) who supported his niece Matilda's claim to the English throne and unsuccessfully invaded England on her behalf.

David II *n.* 1324–71, king of Scotland (1329–71): he was forced into exile in France (1334–41) by Edward de Baliol; captured following the battle of Neville's Cross (1346), and imprisoned by the English (1346–57).

Davies ('deɪvɪs) *n.* **1.** Sir **Peter Maxwell.** born 1934, English composer. His style owes a considerable debt to medieval music; works include the opera *Taverner* (1970). **2. William Henry.** 1871–1940, Welsh poet, noted also for his *Autobiography of a Super-tramp* (1908).

Davis ('deɪvɪs) *n.* **1. Bette** ('bɛtɪ), real name *Ruth Elizabeth Davis* born 1908, U.S. film actress, whose films include *Of Human Bondage* (1934), *Jezebel* (1938) for which she won an Oscar, *Now Voyager* (1942), *Whatever Happened to Baby Jane?* (1962), *The Nanny* (1965), and *Death on the Nile* (1978). **2.** Sir **Colin.** born 1927, English conductor, noted for his interpretation of the music of Berlioz. **3. Jefferson.** 1808–89, president of the Confederate States of America during the Civil War (1861–65). **4. Joe.** 1901–78, English billiards and snooker player: world champion from 1927 to 1946. **5. John.** Also called: **John Davys.** ?1550–1605, English navigator: discovered the Falkland Islands (1592); searched for a Northwest Passage. **6. Miles.** born 1926, U.S. jazz trumpeter and composer. **7. Steve.** born 1957, English snooker player: world champion 1981, 1983, 1984, 1987, and 1988.

Davis Strait *n.* a strait between Baffin Island, in Canada, and Greenland. [after John **Davis**]

davit ('dævɪt, 'deɪ-) *n.* a cranelike device, usually one of a pair, fitted with a tackle for suspending or lowering equipment, esp. a lifeboat. [C14: from Anglo-F *daviot,* dim. of *Davi* David]

Davy ('deɪvɪ) *n.* Sir **Humphry.** 1778–1829, English chemist who isolated sodium, magnesium, chlorine, and other elements and suggested the electrical nature of chemical combination. He invented the **Davy lamp.**

Davy Jones *n.* **1.** Also called: **Davy Jones's locker.** the ocean's bottom, esp. when regarded as the grave of those lost or buried at sea. **2.** the spirit of the sea. [C18: from ?]

Davy lamp *n.* See **safety lamp.** [C19: after Sir H. Davy, who invented it]

daw (dɔː) *n.* an archaic, dialect, or poetic name for a **jackdaw.** [C15: rel. to OHG *taha*]

dawdle ('dɔ:dəl) *vb.* **1.** (*intr.*) to be slow or lag behind. **2.** (when *tr.,* often foll. by *away*) to waste (time); trifle. [C17: from ?] — **'dawdler** *n.*

Dawes (dɔ:z) *n.* **Charles Gates.** 1865–1951, U.S. financier, diplomat, and statesman, who devised the Dawes Plan for German reparations payments after World War I; vice president of the U.S. (1925–29); Nobel peace prize 1925.

dawn (dɔːn) *n.* **1.** daybreak. Related adj.: **auroral. 2.** the sky when light first appears in the morning. **3.** the beginning of something. ~*vb.* (*intr.*) **4.** to begin to grow light after the night. **5.** to begin to develop or appear. **6.** (usually foll. by *on* or *upon*) to begin to become apparent (to). [OE *dagian* to dawn] — **'dawn,like** *adj.*

dawn chorus *n.* the singing of large numbers of birds at dawn.

Dawson ('dɔ:sⁿn) *n.* a town in NW Canada, in the Yukon on the Yukon River: a boom town during the Klondike gold rush (at its height in 1899). Pop.: 1000 (1985 est.).

Dawson Creek *n.* a town in W Canada, in NE British Columbia: SE terminus of the Alaska Highway. Pop.: 12 000 (1985 est.).

day (deɪ) *n.* **1.** Also called: **civil day.** the period of time, the **calendar day,** of 24 hours duration reckoned from one midnight to the next. **2. a.** the period of time between sunrise and sunset. **b.** (*as modifier*): *the day shift.* **3.** the part of a day occupied with regular activity, esp. work. **4.** (*sometimes pl.*) a period or point in time: *in days gone by; any day now.* **5.** the period of time, **sidereal day,** during which the earth makes one complete revolution on its axis relative to a particular star. **6.** the period of time, the **solar day,** during which the earth makes one complete revolution on its axis relative to the sun. **7.** the period of time taken by a specified planet to make one complete rotation on its axis: *the Martian day.* **8.** (*often cap.*) a day designated for a special observance: *Christmas Day.* **9.** a time of success, recognition, etc.: *his day will come.* **10.** a struggle or issue at hand: *the day is lost.* **11. all in a day's work.** part of one's normal activity. **12. at the end of the day.** in the final reckoning. **13. call it a day.** to stop work or other activity. **14. day after day.** without respite; relentlessly. **15. day by day.** gradually or progressively. **16. day in, day out.** every day and all day long. **17. day of rest.** the Sabbath; Sunday. **18. every dog has his day.** one's luck will come. **19. in this day and age.** nowadays. **20. that will be the day. a.** that is most unlikely to happen. **b.** I look forward to that. ~Related adj.: **diurnal.** ~See also **days.** [OE *dæg*]

▷ *Usage.* Numerals are used for the day of the month: in formal written English, either cardinal or ordinal numbers may be used either preceding or following the month. In this dictionary the date is given in this manner: *May 15, 1974.*

Dayak ('daɪæk) *n., pl.* **-aks** *or* **-ak.** a variant spelling of **Dyak.**

Dayan (daɪ'jɑːn) *n.* **Moshe** ('mɒʃɛ). 1915–81, Israeli soldier and statesman; minister of defence (1967; 1969–74) and foreign minister (1977–79).

day bed *n.* a narrow bed intended for use as a seat and as a bed.

daybook ('deɪ,bʊk) *n. Book-keeping.* a book in which the transactions of each day are recorded as they occur.

dayboy ('deɪ,bɔɪ) *n. Brit.* a boy who attends a boarding school daily, but returns home each evening. — **'day,girl** *n.*

daybreak ('deɪ,breɪk) *n.* the time in the morning when light first appears; dawn; sunrise.

daycare ('deɪ,kɛə) *n. Brit. social welfare.* **1.** occupation, treatment, or supervision during the working day for people who might be at risk if left on their own. **2.** welfare services provided by a local authority, health service, etc., during the day.

daycentre ('deɪ,sɛntə) *or* **day centre** *n. Social welfare.* (in Britain) **1.** a building used for daycare or other welfare services. **2.** the enterprise itself, including staff, users, and organization.

daydream ('deɪ,driːm) *n.* **1.** a pleasant dreamlike fantasy indulged in while awake. **2.** a pleasant scheme or wish that is unlikely to be fulfilled. ~*vb.* **3.** (*intr.*) to indulge in idle fantasy. — **'day,dreamer** *n.* — **'day,dreamy** *adj.*

Day-Glo n. Trademark. **a.** a brand of fluorescent colouring materials, as of paint. **b.** (as modifier): Day-Glo colours.

day labourer n. an unskilled worker hired and paid by the day.

Day-Lewis ('deɪ'luːɪs) or **Day Lewis** n. **C(ecil).** 1904–72, English poet, critic, and (under the pen name Nicholas Blake) author of detective stories; poet laureate (1968–72).

daylight ('deɪˌlaɪt) n. **1.** light from the sun. **2.** daytime. **3.** daybreak. **4. see daylight. a.** to understand something previously obscure. **b.** to realize that the end of a difficult task is approaching.

daylight robbery n. Inf. blatant overcharging.

daylights ('deɪˌlaɪts) pl. n. consciousness or wits (esp. in **scare, knock,** or **beat the (living) daylights out of** someone).

daylight-saving time n. time set usually one hour ahead of the local standard time, widely adopted in the summer to provide extra daylight in the evening.

daylong ('deɪˌlɒŋ) adj., adv. lasting the entire day; all day.

day release n. Brit. a system whereby workers are released for part-time education without loss of pay.

day return n. a reduced fare for a journey (by train, etc.) travelling both ways in one day.

day room n. a communal living room in a residential institution such as a hospital.

days (deɪz) adv. Inf. during the day, esp. regularly: he works days.

day school n. **1.** a private school taking day students only. **2.** a school giving instruction during the daytime.

daytime ('deɪˌtaɪm) n. the time between dawn and dusk.

day-to-day adj. routine; everyday.

Dayton ('deɪtᵊn) n. an industrial city in SW Ohio: aviation research centre. Pop.: 193 444 (1980).

Daytona Beach (deɪ'təʊnə) n. a city in NE Florida, on the Atlantic: a resort with a beach of hard white sand, used since 1903 for motor speed trials. Pop.: 54 176 (1980).

day trip n. a journey made to and from a place within one day. —'**day-ˌtripper** n.

Da Yunhe ('dæ 'juːnhə) n. Pinyin transliteration of the Chinese name for the **Grand Canal** (sense 1).

daze (deɪz) vb. (tr.) **1.** to stun, esp. by a blow or shock. **2.** to bewilder or amaze. ~n. **3.** a state of stunned confusion or shock (esp. in **in a daze**). [C14: from ON dasa-, as in dasast to grow weary]

dazzle ('dæzᵊl) vb. **1.** (usually tr.) to blind or be blinded partially and temporarily by sudden excessive light. **2.** (tr.) to amaze, as with brilliance. ~n. **3.** bright light that dazzles. **4.** bewilderment caused by glamour, brilliance, etc.: the dazzle of fame. [C15: from DAZE] —'**dazzler** n. —'**dazzling** adj. —'**dazzlingly** adv.

dB or **db** symbol for decibel or decibels.

DBE abbrev. for Dame Commander of the Order of the British Empire (a Brit. title).

DBS abbrev. for direct broadcasting by satellite.

DC abbrev. for: **1.** Music. da capo. **2.** direct current. Cf. **AC. 3.** Also: **D.C.** District of Columbia.

DCB abbrev. for Dame Commander of the Order of the Bath (a Brit. title).

DCM Brit. mil. abbrev. for Distinguished Conduct Medal.

DD abbrev. for: **1.** Doctor of Divinity. **2.** direct debit.

D-day n. the day selected for the start of some operation, esp. of the Allied invasion of Europe on June 6, 1944. [C20: from D(ay)-day]

DDR abbrev. for Deutsche Demokratische Republik (East Germany; GDR).

DDS or **DDSc** abbrev. for Doctor of Dental Surgery or Science.

DDT n. dichlorodiphenyltrichloroethane; a colourless odourless substance used as an insecticide. It is now banned in the UK.

de- prefix forming verbs and verbal derivatives. **1.** removal of or from something: deforest; dethrone. **2.** reversal of something: decode; desegregate. **3.** departure from: decamp. [from L, from dē (prep.) from, away from, out of, etc. In compound words of Latin origin, de- also means away, away from (decease); down (degrade); reversal (detect); removal (defoliate); and is used intensively (devote) and pejoratively (detest)]

deacon ('diːkən) n. Christianity. **1.** (in the Roman Catholic and other episcopal churches) an ordained minister ranking immediately below a priest. **2.** (in Protestant churches) a lay official who assists the minister, esp. in secular affairs. [OE, ult. from Gk diakonos servant] —'**deaconate** n. —'**deaconˌship** n.

deaconess ('diːkənɪs) n. Christianity. (in the early church and in some modern Churches) a female member of the laity with duties similar to those of a deacon.

deactivate (diː'æktɪˌveɪt) vb. **1.** (tr.) to make (a bomb, etc.) harmless or inoperative. **2.** (intr.) to become less radioactive. —de'actiˌvator n.

dead (dɛd) adj. **1. a.** no longer alive. **b.** (as collective n; preceded by the): the dead. **2.** not endowed with life; inanimate. **3.** no longer in use, effective, or relevant: a dead issue; a dead language. **4.** unresponsive or unaware. **5.** lacking in freshness or vitality. **6.** devoid of physical sensation; numb. **7.** resembling death: a dead sleep. **8.** no longer burning or hot: dead coals. **9.** (of flowers or foliage) withered; faded. **10.** (prenominal) (intensifier): a dead stop. **11.** Inf. very tired. **12.** Electronics. **a.** drained of electric charge. **b.** not connected to a source of potential difference or electric charge. **13.** lacking acoustic reverberation: a dead sound. **14.** Sport. (of a ball, etc.) out of play. **15.** accurate; precise (esp. in **a dead shot**). **16.** lacking resilience or bounce: a dead ball. **17.** not yielding a return: dead capital. **18.** (of colours) not glossy or bright. **19.** stagnant: dead air. **20.** Mil. shielded from view, as by a geographic feature. **21. dead from the neck up.** Inf. stupid. **22. dead to the world.** Inf. unaware of one's surroundings, esp. asleep or drunk. ~n. **23.** a period during which coldness, darkness, etc. is at its most intense: the dead of winter. ~adv. **24.** (intensifier): dead easy; stop dead. **25. dead on.** exactly right. [OE dēad] —'**deadness** n.

dead-and-alive adj. Brit. (of a place, activity, or person) dull; uninteresting.

dead-ball line n. Rugby. a line behind the goal line beyond which the ball is out of play.

deadbeat ('dɛdˌbiːt) n. **1.** Inf., chiefly U.S. & Canad. a lazy or socially undesirable person. **2.** a high grade escapement used in pendulum clocks. **3.** (modifier) without recoil.

dead beat adj. Inf. very tired; exhausted.

dead centre n. **1.** the exact top or bottom of the piston stroke in a reciprocating engine or pump. **2.** a rod mounted in the tailstock or headstock of a lathe to support a workpiece. ~Also called: **dead point.**

dead duck n. Sl. a person or thing doomed to death, failure, etc., esp. because of a mistake.

deaden ('dɛdᵊn) vb. **1.** to make or become less sensitive, intense, lively, etc. **2.** (tr.) to make acoustically less resonant. —'**deadening** adj.

dead end n. **1.** a cul-de-sac. **2.** a situation in which further progress is impossible.

deadeye ('dɛdˌaɪ) n. **1.** Naut. either of a pair of disclike wooden blocks, supported by straps in grooves around them, between which a line is rove so as to draw them together to tighten a shroud. **2.** Inf., chiefly U.S. an expert marksman.

deadfall ('dɛdˌfɔːl) n. a trap in which a heavy weight falls to crush the prey.

dead finish n. Austral. **1.** Inf. the last straw; the extreme of tolerance. **2.** any of various trees or shrubs of Australia that form impenetrable thickets.

deadhead ('dɛdˌhɛd) n. U.S. & Canad. **1.** Inf. a person who uses a free ticket, as for the theatre, etc. **2.** Inf. a train, etc., travelling empty. **3.** Sl. a dull person. **4.** a log sticking out of the water as a snag to navigation. ~vb. **5.** Inf. (intr.) to drive an empty bus, train, etc. **6.** (tr.) to remove dead flower heads.

Dead Heart n. (usually preceded by the) Austral. the remote interior of Australia. [C20: from The Dead Heart of Australia (1906) by J. W. Gregory]

dead heat n. **a.** a race or contest in which two or more participants tie for first place. **b.** a tie between two or more contestants in any position.

dead letter n. **1.** a law or ordinance that is no longer enforced. **2.** a letter that cannot be delivered or returned because it lacks adequate directions.

deadlight ('dɛdˌlaɪt) n. **1.** Naut. **a.** a bull's-eye to admit light to a cabin. **b.** a shutter for sealing off a porthole or cabin window. **2.** a skylight designed not to be opened.

deadline ('dɛdˌlaɪn) n. a time limit for any activity.

deadlock ('dɛdˌlɒk) n. **1.** a state of affairs in which further action between two opposing forces is impossible.

2. a tie between opponents. **3.** a lock having a bolt that can be opened only with a key. ~*vb.* **4.** to bring or come to a deadlock.

dead loss *n.* **1.** a complete loss for which no compensation is paid. **2.** *Inf.* a useless person or thing.

deadly ('dɛdlɪ) *adj.* **-lier, -liest. 1.** likely to cause death. **2.** *Inf.* extremely boring. ~*adv., adj.* **3.** like death in appearance or certainty.

deadly nightshade *n.* a poisonous Eurasian plant having purple bell-shaped flowers and black berries. Also called: **belladonna, dwale.**

deadly sins *pl. n.* the sins of pride, covetousness, lust, envy, gluttony, anger, and sloth.

dead man's handle *or* **pedal** *n.* a safety switch on a piece of machinery that allows operation only while depressed by the operator.

dead march *n.* a piece of solemn funeral music played to accompany a procession.

dead marine *n. Austral. & N.Z. inf.* an empty beer bottle.

dead-nettle *n.* any of several Eurasian plants having leaves resembling nettles but lacking stinging hairs.

deadpan ('dɛd,pæn) *adj., adv.* with a deliberately emotionless face or manner.

dead reckoning *n.* a method of establishing one's position using the distance and direction travelled rather than astronomical observations.

Dead Sea *n.* a lake between Israel and Jordan, 397 m (1302 ft.) below sea level: the lowest lake in the world, with no outlet and very high salinity. Area: 1020 sq. km (394 sq. miles).

dead set *adv.* **1.** absolutely: *he is dead set against going to Spain.* ~*n.* **2.** the motionless position of a dog when pointing towards game. ~*adj.* **3.** (of a hunting dog) in this position.

dead time *n. Electronics.* the time immediately following a stimulus, during which an electrical device, component, etc. is insensitive to a further stimulus.

dead weight *n.* **1.** a heavy weight or load. **2.** an oppressive burden. **3.** the difference between the loaded and the unloaded weights of a ship. **4.** the intrinsic invariable weight of a structure, such as a bridge.

dead wood *n.* **1.** dead trees or branches. **2.** *Inf.* a useless person; encumbrance.

deaf (dɛf) *adj.* **1. a.** partially or totally unable to hear. **b.** (*as collective n.;* preceded by *the*): *the deaf.* **2.** refusing to heed. [OE *dēaf*] — '**deafness** *n.*

deaf-and-dumb *Offens.* ~*adj.* **1.** unable to hear or speak. ~*n.* **2.** a deaf-mute person.

deafen ('dɛfᵊn) *vb.* (*tr.*) to make deaf, esp. momentarily, as by a loud noise. — '**deafeningly** *adv.*

deaf-mute *n.* **1.** a person who is unable to hear or speak. See also **mute** (sense 7). ~*adj.* **2.** unable to hear or speak. [C19: translation of F *sourd-muet*]

Deakin ('diːkɪn) *n.* **Alfred.** 1856–1919, Australian statesman. He was a leader of the movement for Australian federation; prime minister of Australia (1903–04; 1905–08; 1909–10).

deal[1] (diːl) *vb.* **dealing, dealt. 1.** (*intr.*) foll. by *in*) to engage in commercially: *to deal in upholstery.* **2.** (often foll. by *out*) to apportion or distribute. **3.** (*tr.*) to give (a blow, etc.) to (someone); inflict. **4.** (*intr.*) *Sl.* to sell any illegal drug. ~*n.* **5.** *Inf.* a bargain, transaction, or agreement. **6.** a particular type of treatment received, esp. as the result of an agreement: *a fair deal.* **7.** an indefinite amount (esp. in **good** *or* **great deal**). **8.** *Cards.* **a.** the process of distributing the cards. **b.** a player's turn to do this. **c.** a single round in a card game. **9. big deal.** *Sl.* an important person, event, or matter: often used sarcastically. ~See also **deal with.** [OE *dǣlan,* from *dǣl* a part; cf. OHG *teil* a part, ON *deild* a share]

deal[2] (diːl) *n.* **1.** a plank of softwood timber, such as fir or pine, or such planks collectively. **2.** the sawn wood of various coniferous trees. ~*adj.* **3.** of fir or pine. [C14: from MLow G *dele* plank]

dealer ('diːlə) *n.* **1.** a person or firm engaged in commercial purchase and sale; trader: *a car dealer.* **2.** *Cards.* the person who distributes the cards. **3.** *Sl.* a person who sells illegal drugs.

dealings ('diːlɪŋz) *pl. n.* (*sometimes sing.*) transactions or business relations.

dealt (dɛlt) *vb.* the past tense and past participle of **deal**[1].

deal with *vb.* (*tr., adv.*) **1.** to take action on: *to deal with each problem in turn.* **2.** to punish: *the headmaster will*

deal with the culprit. **3.** to treat or be concerned with: *the book deals with architecture.* **4.** to conduct onself (towards others), esp. with regard to fairness. **5.** to do business with.

dean (diːn) *n.* **1.** the chief administrative official of a college or university faculty. **2.** (at Oxford and Cambridge universities) a college fellow with responsibility for undergraduate discipline. **3.** *Chiefly Church of England.* the head of a chapter of canons and administrator of a cathedral or collegiate church. **4.** *R.C. Church.* the cardinal bishop senior by consecration and head of the college of cardinals. Related adj.: **decanal.** See also **rural dean.** [C14: from OF *deien,* from LL *decānus* one set over ten persons, from L *decem* ten]

Dean (diːn) *n.* **1. Christopher.** See **Torvill and Dean. 2. James (Byron).** 1931–55, U.S. film actor, who became a cult figure; his films include *East of Eden* and *Rebel Without a Cause* (both 1955). He died in a car crash.

deanery ('diːnərɪ) *n., pl.* **-eries. 1.** the office or residence of dean. **2.** the group of parishes presided over by a rural dean.

dear (dɪə) *adj.* **1.** beloved; precious. **2.** used in conventional forms of address, as in *Dear Sir.* **3.** (*postpositive;* foll. by *to*) important; close. **4. a.** highly priced. **b.** charging high prices. **5.** appealing. **6. for dear life.** with extreme vigour or desperation. ~*interj.* **7.** used in exclamations of surprise or dismay, such as *Oh dear!* ~*n.* **8.** Also: **dearest.** (*often used in direct address*) someone regarded with affection and tenderness. ~*adv.* **9.** dearly. [OE *dēore*] — '**dearness** *n.*

Dearborn ('dɪəbən, -,bɔːn) *n.* a city in SE Michigan, near Detroit: automobile industry. Pop.: 90 660 (1980).

dearly ('dɪəlɪ) *adv.* **1.** very much. **2.** affectionately. **3.** at a great cost.

dearth (dɜːθ) *n.* an inadequate amount, esp. of food; scarcity. [C13 *derthe,* from *dēr* DEAR]

deary *or* **dearie** ('dɪərɪ) *n.* **1.** (*pl.* **dearies**) *Inf.* a term of affection: now often sarcastic or facetious. **2. deary** *or* **dearie me!** an exclamation of surprise or dismay.

death (dɛθ) *n.* **1.** the permanent end of all functions of life in an organism. **2.** an instance of this: *his death ended an era.* **3.** a murder or killing. **4.** termination or destruction. **5.** a state of affairs or an experience considered as terrible as death. **6.** a cause or source of death. **7.** (*usually cap.*) a personification of death, usually a skeleton or an old man holding a scythe. **8. at death's door.** likely to die soon. **9. catch one's death (of cold).** *Inf.* to contract a severe cold. **10. do to death. a.** to kill. **b.** to overuse. **11. in at the death. a.** present when a hunted animal is killed. **b.** present at the finish or climax. **12. like death warmed up.** *Inf.* very ill. **13. like grim death.** as if afraid of one's life. **14. put to death.** to kill deliberately or execute. **15. to death.** until dead. **b.** very much. ~Related adjs.: **fatal, lethal, mortal.** [OE *dēath*]

death adder *n.* a venomous thick-bodied Australian snake.

deathbed ('dɛθ,bɛd) *n.* the bed in which a person is about to die.

deathblow ('dɛθ,bləʊ) *n.* a thing or event that destroys life or hope, esp. suddenly.

death cap *or* **angel** *n.* a poisonous woodland fungus with white gills and a cuplike structure at the base of the stalk.

death certificate *n.* a legal document issued by a qualified medical practitioner certifying the death of a person and stating the cause if known.

death duty *n.* a tax on property inheritances, in Britain replaced by capital transfer tax since 1975. Also called: **estate duty.**

death knell *or* **bell** *n.* **1.** something that heralds death or destruction. **2.** a bell rung to announce a death.

deathless ('dɛθlɪs) *adj.* immortal, esp. because of greatness; everlasting. — '**deathlessness** *n.*

deathly ('dɛθlɪ) *adj.* **1.** deadly. **2.** resembling death: *a deathly quiet.*

death mask *n.* a cast of a dead person's face.

death rate *n.* the ratio of deaths in a specified area, group, etc., to the population of that area, group, etc. Also called: **mortality rate.**

death rattle *n.* a low-pitched gurgling sound sometimes made by a dying person.

death's-head *n.* a human skull or a representation of one.

death's-head moth *n.* a European hawk moth having markings resembling a human skull on its upper thorax.

deathtrap ('dɛθˌtræp) *n.* a building, vehicle, etc., that is considered very unsafe.

Death Valley *n.* a desert valley in E California and W Nevada: the lowest, hottest, and driest area of the U.S. Lowest point: 86 m (282 ft.) below sea level. Area: about 3885 sq. km (1500 sq. miles).

death warrant *n.* **1.** the official authorization for carrying out a sentence of death. **2. sign one's (own) death warrant.** to cause one's own destruction.

deathwatch ('dɛθˌwɒtʃ) *n.* **1.** a vigil held beside a dying or dead person. **2. deathwatch beetle.** a beetle whose woodboring larvae are a serious pest. The adult produces a tapping sound that was once supposed to presage death.

death wish *n.* (in Freudian psychology) the desire for self-annihilation.

Deauville ('dəʊviːl; *French* dovil) *n.* a town and resort in NW France: casino. Pop.: 4769 (1982 est.).

deb (dɛb) *n. Inf.* short for **debutante.**

debacle (deɪ'bɑːkəl, dɪ-) *n.* **1.** a sudden disastrous collapse or defeat; rout. **2.** the breaking up of ice in a river, often causing flooding. **3.** a violent rush of water carrying along debris. [C19: from F, from OF *desbacler* to unbolt]

debag (diː'bæg) *vb.* **-bagging, -bagged.** (*tr.*) *Brit. sl.* to remove the trousers from (someone) by force.

debar (dɪ'bɑː) *vb.* **-barring, -barred.** (*tr.*; usually foll. by *from*) to exclude from a place, a right, etc.; bar. **—de'barment** *n.*

debark[1] (dɪ'bɑːk) *vb.* another word for **disembark.** [C17: from F *débarquer,* from *dé-* DIS-[1] + *barque* BARQUE] **—debarkation** (ˌdiːbɑː'keɪʃən) *n.*

debark[2] (diː'bɑːk) *vb.* (*tr.*) to remove the bark from (a tree). [C18: from DE-+ BARK[2]]

debase (dɪ'beɪs) *vb.* (*tr.*) to lower in quality, character, or value; adulterate. [C16: see DE-, BASE[2]] **—de'basement** *n.* **—de'baser** *n.*

debate (dɪ'beɪt) *n.* **1.** a formal discussion, as in a legislative body, in which opposing arguments are put forward. **2.** discussion or dispute. **3.** the formal presentation and opposition of a specific motion, followed by a vote. ~*vb.* **4.** to discuss (a motion, etc.), esp. in a formal assembly. **5.** to deliberate upon (something). [C13: from OF *debatre* to discuss, argue, from L *battuere*] **—de'batable** *adj.* **—de'bater** *n.*

debauch (dɪ'bɔːtʃ) *vb.* **1.** (when *tr.,* usually passive) to lead into a life of depraved self-indulgence. **2.** (*tr.*) to seduce (a woman). ~*n.* **3.** an instance or period of extreme dissipation. [C16: from OF *desbaucher* to corrupt, lit.: to shape (timber) roughly, from *bauch* beam, of Gmc origin] **—de'baucher** *n.* **—de'bauchery** *n.*

debauchee (ˌdɛbɔː'tʃiː) *n.* a man who leads a life of promiscuity and self-indulgence.

debenture (dɪ'bɛntʃə) *n.* **1.** a long-term bond, bearing fixed interest and usually unsecured, issued by a company or governmental agency. **2.** a certificate acknowledging a debt. **3.** a customs certificate providing for a refund of excise or import duty. [C15: from L *debentur mihi* there are owed to me, from *debere*] **—de'bentured** *adj.*

debenture stock *n.* shares issued by a company, which guarantee a fixed return at regular intervals.

debilitate (dɪ'bɪlɪˌteɪt) *vb.* (*tr.*) to make feeble; weaken. [C16: from L, from *debilis* weak] **—deˌbili'tation** *n.* **—de'bilitative** *adj.*

debility (dɪ'bɪlɪtɪ) *n., pl.* **-ties.** weakness or infirmity.

debit ('dɛbɪt) *n.* **1. a.** acknowledgment of a sum owing by entry on the left side of an account. **b.** the left side of an account. **c.** an entry on this side. **d.** the total of such entries. **e.** (*as modifier*): *a debit balance.* ~*vb.* **2.** (*tr.*) **a.** to record (an item) as a debit in an account. **b.** to charge (a person or his account) with a debt. [C15: from L *debitum* DEBT]

debit card *n.* (in cashless shopping developments) a card that would enable customers to pay for goods and services by immediate debit from their current account without using a cheque or card.

debonair *or* **debonnaire** (ˌdɛbə'nɛə) *adj.* **1.** suave and refined. **2.** carefree; gay. **3.** courteous and cheerful. [C13: from OF, from *de bon aire* having a good disposition] **—ˌdebo'nairly** *adv.* **—ˌdebo'nairness** *n.*

Deborah ('dɛbərə, -brə) *n. Old Testament.* **1.** a prophetess and judge of Israel who fought the Canaanites (Judges 4, 5). **2.** Rebekah's nurse (Genesis 35:8).

debouch (dɪ'baʊtʃ) *vb.* (*intr.*) **1.** (esp. of troops) to move into a more open space. **2.** (of a river, glacier, etc.) to

flow into a larger area or body. [C18: from F *déboucher,* from *dé-* DIS-[1] + *bouche* mouth] **—de'bouchment** *n.*

Debrecen ('dɛbrɛtsɛn) *n.* a city in E Hungary: seat of the revolutionary government of 1849. Pop.: 211 823 (1986).

Debrett (də'brɛt) *n.* a list, considered exclusive, of the British aristocracy. In full: **Debrett's Peerage.** [C19: after J. *Debrett* (c 1750-1822), London publisher who first issued it]

debrief (diː'briːf) *vb.* (of a soldier, diplomat, etc.) to make or (of his superiors) to elicit a report after a mission or event. **—de'briefing** *n.*

debris *or* **débris** ('deɪbriː, 'dɛbriː) *n.* **1.** fragments of something destroyed or broken; rubble. **2.** a collection of loose material derived from rocks, or an accumulation of animal or vegetable matter. [C18: from F, from obs. *débrisier* to break into pieces, of Celtic origin]

de Broglie (*French* də brɔj) *n.* See (Louis Victor de) Broglie.

Debs (dɛbz) *n.* **Eugene Victor.** 1855–1926, U.S. labour leader; five times Socialist presidential candidate (1900–20).

debt (dɛt) *n.* **1.** something owed, such as money, goods, or services. **2. bad debt.** a debt that has little prospect of being paid. **3.** an obligation to pay or perform something. **4.** the state of owing something, or of being under an obligation (esp. in **in debt,** or **in (someone's) debt**). [C13: from OF *dette,* from L *debitum,* from *debere* to owe, from DE- + *habere* to have]

debt collector *n.* a person employed to collect debts for creditors.

debt of honour *n.* a debt that is morally but not legally binding.

debtor ('dɛtə) *n.* a person or commercial enterprise that owes a financial obligation.

debug (diː'bʌg) *vb.* **-bugging, -bugged.** (*tr.*) *Inf.* **1.** to locate and remove concealed microphones from (a room, etc.). **2.** to locate and remove defects in (a device, system, plan, etc.). **3.** to remove insects from. [C20: from DE- + BUG]

debunk (diː'bʌŋk) *vb.* (*tr.*) *Inf.* to expose the pretensions or falseness of, esp. by ridicule. [C20: from DE-+ BUNK[2]] **—de'bunker** *n.*

debus (diː'bʌs) *vb.* **debusing, debused** *or* **debussing, debussed.** to unload (goods, etc.) or (esp. of troops) to alight from a bus.

Debussy (də'bjuːsɪ, 'deɪbjuːsɪ; *French* dəbysi) *n.* (**Achille**) **Claude** (klod). 1862–1918, French composer and critic, the creator of impressionism in music and a profound influence on contemporary composition. His works include *Prélude à l'après-midi d'un faune* (1894) and *La Mer* (1905) for orchestra, the opera *Pelléas et Mélisande* (1902), and many piano pieces and song settings.

debut ('deɪbjuː, 'dɛbjuː) *n.* **1. a.** the first public appearance of an actor, musician, etc. **b.** (*as modifier*): *debut album.* **2.** the presentation of a debutante. [C18: from F, from OF *desbuter* to play first, from *des-* DE- + *but* goal, target]

debutante ('dɛbjuˌtɑːnt, -ˌtænt) *n.* **1.** a young upper-class woman who is formally presented to society. **2.** a young woman regarded as being upper-class, wealthy, and frivolous. [C19: from F, from *débuter* to lead off in a game, make one's first appearance; see DEBUT]

dec. *abbrev. for:* **1.** deceased. **2.** decimal. **3.** decimetre. **4.** declaration. **5.** declension. **6.** declination. **7.** decrease. **8.** *Music.* decrescendo.

Dec. *abbrev. for* December.

deca-, deka- *or before a vowel* **dec-, dek-** *prefix.* denoting ten: *decagon.* In conjunction with scientific units the symbol **da** is used. [from Gk *deka*]

decade ('dɛkeɪd, dɪ'keɪd) *n.* **1.** a period of ten years. **2.** a group of ten items. [C15: from OF, from LL, from Gk, from *deka* ten] **—de'cadal** *adj.*

▷ **Usage.** Specific decades are referred to as follows: *the 1660s: the 1970s.* Where ambiguity does not arise contractions are allowable though it is preferable to write out the contracted forms in words rather than numerals: *the sixties* rather than *the 60s* or *the '60s.*

decadence ('dɛkədəns) *or* **decadency** *n.* **1.** deterioration, esp. of morality or culture. **2.** the state reached through such a process. [C16: from F, from Med. L *decadentia,* lit.: a falling away; see DECAY]

decadent ('dɛkədənt) *adj.* **1.** characterized by decline, as in being self-indulgent or morally corrupt. **2.** belonging to a period of decline in artistic standards. ~*n.* **3.** a decadent person.

decaffeinate (diˈkæfɪˌneɪt) *vb.* (*tr.*) to remove all or part of the caffeine from (coffee, etc.).

decagon (ˈdɛkəˌgɒn) *n.* a polygon having ten sides. —**decagonal** (dɪˈkægənˀl) *adj.*

decahedron (ˌdɛkəˈhiːdrən) *n.* a solid figure having ten plane faces. —ˌdeca'**hedral** *adj.*

decal (dɪˈkæl, ˈdiːkæl) *n.* **1.** short for **decalcomania**. ~*vb.* **2.** to transfer (a design, etc.) by decalcomania.

decalcify (diːˈkælsɪˌfaɪ) *vb.* **-fying, -fied.** (*tr.*) to remove calcium or lime from (bones, etc.). —de'**calci,fier** *n.*

decalcomania (dɪˌkælkəˈmeɪnɪə) *n.* **1.** the process of transferring a design from prepared paper onto another surface, such as glass or paper. **2.** a design so transferred. [C19: from F, from *décalquer*, from *de-* DE- + *calquer* to trace + *-manie* -MANIA]

decalitre *or U.S.* **decaliter** (ˈdɛkəˌliːtə) *n.* a metric measure of volume equivalent to 10 litres.

Decalogue (ˈdɛkəˌlɒg) *n.* another name for the **Ten Commandments**. [C14: from Church L *decalogus*, from Gk, from *deka* ten + *logos* word]

decametre *or U.S.* **decameter** (ˈdɛkəˌmiːtə) *n.* a metric measure of length equivalent to 10 metres.

decamp (dɪˈkæmp) *vb.* (*intr.*) **1.** to leave a camp; break camp. **2.** to depart secretly or suddenly; abscond. —de'**campment** *n.*

decanal (dɪˈkeɪnˀl) *adj.* **1.** of a dean or deanery. **2.** on the same side of a cathedral, etc., as the dean; on the S side of the choir. [C18: from Med. L *decānālis*, *decānus* DEAN]

decani (dɪˈkeɪnaɪ) *adj., adv. Music.* to be sung by the decanal side of a choir. Cf. *cantoris.* [L: genitive of *decānus*]

decant (dɪˈkænt) *vb.* **1.** to pour (a liquid, such as wine) from one container to another, esp. without disturbing any sediment. **2.** (*tr.*) to rehouse (people) while their homes are being rebuilt or refurbished. [C17: from Med. L *dēcanthāre*, from *canthus* spout, rim]

decanter (dɪˈkæntə) *n.* a stoppered bottle, into which a drink is poured for serving.

decapitate (dɪˈkæpɪˌteɪt) *vb.* (*tr.*) to behead. [C17: from LL *dēcapitāre*, from *de-* + *caput* head] —de,capi'**tation** *n.* —de'**capi,tator** *n.*

decapod (ˈdɛkəˌpɒd) *n.* **1.** any crustacean having five pairs of walking limbs, as a crab, lobster, shrimp, etc. **2.** any cephalopod mollusc having eight short tentacles and two longer ones, as a squid or cuttlefish. —**decapodal** (dɪˈkæpədˀl), *or* de'**capodous** *adj.*

Decapolis (dɪˈkæpəlɪs) *n.* a league of ten cities, including Damascus, in the northeast of ancient Palestine: established in 63 B.C. by Pompey and governed by Rome.

decarbonate (diːˈkɑːbəˌneɪt) *vb.* (*tr.*) to remove carbon dioxide from. —de,carbon'**ation** *n.* —de'**carbon,ator** *n.*

decarbonize *or* **-ise** (diːˈkɑːbəˌnaɪz) *vb.* (*tr.*) to remove carbon from (an internal-combustion engine, etc.). Also: **decoke, decarburize.** —de,carboni'**zation** *or* **-i'sation** *n.* —de'**carbon,izer** *or* **-,iser** *n.*

decastyle (ˈdɛkəˌstaɪl) *n. Archit.* a portico consisting of ten columns.

decasyllable (ˈdɛkəˌsɪləbˀl) *n.* a word or line of verse consisting of ten syllables. —**decasyllabic** (ˌdɛkəsɪˈlæbɪk) *adj.*

decathlon (dɪˈkæθlɒn) *n.* an athletic contest in which each athlete competes in ten different events. [C20: from DECA-+ Gk *athlon* contest, prize; see ATHLETE] —de'**cathlete** *n.*

decay (dɪˈkeɪ) *vb.* **1.** to decline or cause to decline gradually in health, prosperity, excellence, etc.; deteriorate. **2.** to rot or cause to rot; decompose. **3.** (*intr.*) Also: **disintegrate.** *Physics.* **a.** (of an atomic nucleus) to undergo radioactive disintegration. **b.** (of an elementary particle) to transform into two or more different elementary particles. **4.** (*intr.*) *Physics.* (of a stored charge, magnetic flux, etc.) to decrease gradually when the source of energy has been removed. ~*n.* **5.** the process of decline, as in health, mentality, etc. **6.** the state brought about by this process. **7.** decomposition. **8.** rotten or decayed matter. **9.** *Physics.* **a.** See **radioactive decay. b.** a spontaneous transformation of an elementary particle into two or more different particles. **10.** *Physics.* a gradual decrease of a stored charge, current, etc., when the source of energy has been removed. [C15: from OF *decaïr*, from

LL *dēcadere*, lit.: to fall away, from L *cadere* to fall] —de'**cayable** *adj.*

Deccan (ˈdɛkən) *n.* **the. 1.** a plateau in S India, between the Eastern Ghats, the Western Ghats, and the Narmada River. **2.** the whole Indian peninsula south of the Narmada River.

decease (dɪˈsiːs) *n.* **1.** a more formal word for **death**. ~*vb.* **2.** (*intr.*) a more formal word for **die**[1]. [C14 (n.): from OF, from L *dēcēdere* to depart]

deceased (dɪˈsiːst) *adj.* **a.** a more formal word for **dead** (sense 1). **b.** (*as n.*; preceded by *the*): *the deceased.*

deceit (dɪˈsiːt) *n.* **1.** the act or practice of deceiving. **2.** a statement, act, or device intended to mislead; fraud; trick. **3.** a tendency to deceive. [C13: from OF, from *deceivre* to DECEIVE]

deceitful (dɪˈsiːtfʊl) *adj.* full of deceit.

deceive (dɪˈsiːv) *vb.* (*tr.*) **1.** to mislead by deliberate misrepresentation or lies. **2.** to delude (oneself). **3.** to be unfaithful to (one's sexual partner). **4.** *Arch.* to disappoint. [C13: from OF *deceivre*, from L *dēcipere* to ensnare, cheat, from *capere* to take] —de'**ceivable** *adj.* —de'**ceiver** *n.*

decelerate (diːˈsɛləˌreɪt) *vb.* to slow down or cause to slow down. [C19: from DE- + (AC)CELERATE] —de,cel**er'ation** *n.* —de'**celer,ator** *n.*

December (dɪˈsɛmbə) *n.* the twelfth month of the year, consisting of 31 days. [C13: from OF, from L: the tenth month (the Roman year began with March), from *decem* ten]

decemvir (dɪˈsɛmvə) *n., pl.* **-virs** *or* **-viri** (-vɪˌriː). (in ancient Rome) a member of a board of ten magistrates. [C17: from L, from *decem* ten + *virī* men] —de'**cemviral** *adj.* —de'**cemvirate** *n.*

decencies (ˈdiːsˀnsɪz) *pl. n.* **1. the.** those things that are considered necessary for a decent life. **2.** another word for **proprieties.**

decency (ˈdiːsˀnsɪ) *n., pl.* **-cies. 1.** conformity to the prevailing standards of propriety, morality, modesty, etc. **2.** the quality of being decent.

decennial (dɪˈsɛnɪəl) *adj.* **1.** lasting for ten years. **2.** occurring every ten years. ~*n.* **3.** a tenth anniversary. —de'**cennially** *adv.*

decent (ˈdiːsˀnt) *adj.* **1.** polite or respectable. **2.** proper and suitable; fitting. **3.** conforming to conventions of sexual behaviour; not indecent. **4.** free of oaths, blasphemy, etc. **5.** good or adequate: *a decent wage.* **6.** *Inf.* kind; generous. **7.** *Inf.* sufficiently clothed to be seen by other people: *are you decent?* [C16: from L *decēns* suitable, from *decēre* to be fitting] —**decently** *adv.*

decentralize *or* **-ise** (diːˈsɛntrəˌlaɪz) *vb.* **1.** to reorganize into smaller more autonomous units. **2.** to disperse (a concentration, as of industry or population). —de'**centralist** *n., adj.* —de,centrali'**zation** *or* **-i'sation** *n.*

deception (dɪˈsɛpʃən) *n.* **1.** the act of deceiving or the state of being deceived. **2.** something that deceives; trick.

deceptive (dɪˈsɛptɪv) *adj.* likely or designed to deceive; misleading. —de'**ceptively** *adv.* —de'**ceptiveness** *n.*

deci- *prefix.* denoting one tenth: *decimetre.* Symbol: **d** [from F *déci-*, from L *decimus* tenth]

decibel (ˈdɛsɪˌbɛl) *n.* **1.** a unit for comparing two currents, voltages, or power levels, equal to one tenth of a bel. **2.** a similar unit for measuring the intensity of a sound. Abbrev.: **dB.**

decide (dɪˈsaɪd) *vb.* **1.** (*may take a clause or an infinitive as object*; when *intr.*, sometimes foll. by *on* or *about*) to reach a decision: *decide what you want; he decided to go.* **2.** (*tr.*) to cause to reach a decision. **3.** (*tr.*) to determine or settle (a contest or question). **4.** (*tr.*) to influence decisively the outcome of (a contest or question). **5.** (*intr.*; foll. by *for* or *against*) to pronounce a formal verdict. [C14: from OF, from L *dēcīdere*, lit.: to cut off, from *caedere* to cut] —de'**cidable** *adj.* —de'**cider** *n.*

decided (dɪˈsaɪdɪd) *adj.* (*prenominal*) **1.** unmistakable. **2.** determined; resolute: *a girl of decided character.* —de'**cidedly** *adv.*

deciduous (dɪˈsɪdjʊəs) *adj.* **1.** (of trees and shrubs) shedding all leaves annually at the end of the growing season. Cf. **evergreen. 2.** (of antlers, teeth, etc.) being shed at the end of a period of growth. [C17: from L: falling off, from *dēcidere* to fall down, from *cadere* to fall] —de'**ciduousness** *n.*

decilitre *or U.S.* **deciliter** (ˈdɛsɪˌliːtə) *n.* a metric measure of volume equivalent to one-tenth of a litre.

decillion (dɪ'sɪljən) n. 1. (in Britain, France, and Germany) the number represented as one followed by 60 zeros (10⁶⁰). 2. (in the U.S. and Canada) the number represented as one followed by 33 zeros (10³³). [C19: from L *decem* ten + *-illion* as in *million*] —de'cillionth *adj*.

decimal ('dɛsɪməl) n. 1. Also called: **decimal fraction.** a fraction that has an unwritten denominator of a power of ten. It is indicated by a decimal point to the left of the numerator: *.2* = 2/10. 2. any number used in the decimal system. ~adj. 3. a. relating to or using powers of ten. b. of the base ten. 4. (*prenominal*) expressed as a decimal. [C17: from Med. L *decimālis* of tithes, from L *decima* a tenth] —'decimally *adv*.

decimal classification n. another term for **Dewey Decimal System.**

decimal currency n. a system of currency in which the monetary units are parts or powers of ten.

decimalize or **-ise** ('dɛsɪmə,laɪz) vb. to change (a system, number, etc.) to the decimal system. —,decimali'zation or **-i'sation** n.

decimal place n. 1. the position of a digit after the decimal point. 2. the number of digits to the right of the decimal point.

decimal point n. a full stop or a raised full stop placed between the integral and fractional parts of a number in the decimal system.

▷ **Usage.** Conventions relating to the use of the decimal point are confused. The IX General Conference on Weights and Measures resolved in 1948 that the decimal point should be a point on the line or a comma, but not a centre dot. It also resolved that figures could be grouped in threes about the decimal point, but that no point or comma should be used for this purpose. These conventions are adopted in this dictionary. However, the Decimal Currency Board recommended that for sums of money the centre dot should be used as the decimal point and that the comma should be used as the thousand marker. Moreover, in some countries the position is reversed, the comma being used as the decimal point and the dot as the thousand marker.

decimal system n. 1. the number system in general use, having a base of ten, in which numbers are expressed by combinations of the ten digits 0 to 9. 2. a system of measurement in which the multiple and submultiple units are related to a basic unit by powers of ten.

decimate ('dɛsɪ,meɪt) vb. (*tr.*) 1. to destroy or kill a large proportion of. 2. (esp. in the ancient Roman army) to kill every tenth man of (a mutinous section). [C17: from L *decimāre*, from *decem* ten] —,deci'mation n. —'deci,mator n.

▷ **Usage.** The use of *decimate* as in definition 1 was formerly regarded as unacceptable by many careful users of English, but is now by far the more common sense of the word, as in *myxomatosis decimated the rabbit population*.

decimetre or U.S. **decimeter** ('dɛsɪ,miːtə) n. one tenth of a metre. Symbol: **dm.**

decipher (dɪ'saɪfə) vb. (*tr.*) 1. to determine the meaning of (something obscure or illegible). 2. to convert from code into plain text; decode. —de'cipherable *adj*. —de'cipherment n.

decision (dɪ'sɪʒən) n. 1. a judgment, conclusion, or resolution reached or given; verdict. 2. the act of making up one's mind. 3. firmness of purpose or character; determination. [C15: from OF, from L *dēcīsiō*, lit.: a cutting off; see DECIDE]

decisive (dɪ'saɪsɪv) adj. 1. influential; conclusive. 2. characterized by the ability to make decisions, esp. quickly; resolute. —de'cisively *adv*. —de'cisiveness n.

deck (dɛk) n. 1. *Naut.* any of various platforms built into a vessel. 2. a similar platform, as in a bus. 3. a. the horizontal platform that supports the turntable and pick-up of a record player. b. See **tape deck.** 4. *Chiefly U.S.* a pack of playing cards. 5. *Computers.* a collection of punched cards relevant to a particular program. 6. **clear the decks.** *Inf.* to prepare for action, as by removing obstacles. 7. **hit the deck.** *Inf.* a. to fall to the ground, esp. to avoid injury. b. to prepare for action. c. to get out of bed. ~vb. (*tr.*) 8. (often foll. by *out*) to dress or decorate. 9. to build a deck on (a vessel). [C15: from MDu. *dec* a covering]

deck-access adj. (of a block of flats) having a continuous balcony at each level onto which the front door of each flat opens.

deck chair n. a folding chair consisting of a wooden frame suspending a length of canvas.

Decker ('dɛkə) n. a variant spelling of (Thomas) **Dekker.**

-decker adj. (*in combination*): having a certain specified number of levels or layers: *a double-decker bus.*

deck hand n. 1. a seaman assigned duties on the deck of a ship. 2. (in Britain) a seaman who has seen sea duty for at least one year. 3. a helper aboard a yacht.

deckle or **deckel** ('dɛkəl) n. 1. a frame used to contain pulp on the mould in the making of handmade paper. 2. a strap on a paper-making machine that fixes the width of the paper. [C19: from G *Deckel* lid, from *decken* to cover]

deckle edge n. 1. the rough edge of paper made using a deckle, often left as ornamentation. 2. an imitation of this. —'deckle-'edged *adj*.

declaim (dɪ'kleɪm) vb. 1. to make (a speech, etc.) loudly and in a rhetorical manner. 2. to speak lines from (a play, poem, etc.) with studied eloquence. 3. (*intr.*; foll. by *against*) to protest (against) loudly and publicly. [C14: from L *dēclāmāre*, from *clāmāre* to call out] —de'claimer n. —declamatory (dɪ'klæmətərɪ) *adj*.

declamation (,dɛklə'meɪʃən) n. 1. a rhetorical or emotional speech, made esp. in order to protest; tirade. 2. a speech, verse, etc., that is or can be spoken. 3. the act or art of declaiming.

declaration (,dɛklə'reɪʃən) n. 1. an explicit or emphatic statement. 2. a formal statement or announcement. 3. the act of declaring. 4. the ruling of a judge or court on a question of law. 5. *Law.* an unsworn statement of a witness admissible in evidence under certain conditions. 6. *Cricket.* the voluntary closure of an innings before all ten wickets have fallen. 7. *Contract bridge.* the final contract. 8. a statement or inventory of goods, etc., submitted for tax assessment. —de'clarer n.

declarative (dɪ'klærətɪv) adj. making or having the nature of a declaration. —de'claratively *adv*.

declare (dɪ'klɛə) vb. (*mainly tr.*) 1. (*may take a clause as object*) to make clearly known or announce officially: *war was declared.* 2. to state officially that (a person, fact, etc.) is as specified: *he declared him fit.* 3. (*may take a clause as object*) to state emphatically; assert. 4. to show, reveal, or manifest. 5. (*intr.*; often foll. by *for* or *against*) to make known one's choice or opinion. 6. to make a statement of (dutiable goods, etc.). 7. (*also intr.*) *Cards.* a. to display (cards) on the table so as to add to one's score. b. to decide (the trump suit) by making the winning bid. 8. (*intr.*) *Cricket.* to close an innings voluntarily before all ten wickets have fallen. 9. to authorize payment of (a dividend). [C14: from L *dēclārāre* to make clear, from *clārus* clear] —de'clarable *adj*.

declassify (diː'klæsɪ,faɪ) vb. **-fying, -fied.** (*tr.*) to release (a document or information) from the security list. —de,classifi'cation n.

declension (dɪ'klɛnʃən) n. 1. *Grammar.* a. inflection of nouns, pronouns, or adjectives for case, number, and gender. b. the complete set of the inflections of such a word. 2. a decline or deviation. 3. a downward slope. [C15: from L *dēclīnātiō*, lit.: a bending aside, hence variation; see DECLINE] —de'clensional *adj*.

declination (,dɛklɪ'neɪʃən) n. 1. *Astron.* the angular distance of a star, planet, etc., north or south from the celestial equator. Symbol: δ. 2. the angle made by a compass needle with the direction of the geographical north pole. 3. a refusal, esp. a courteous or formal one. —,decli'national *adj*.

decline (dɪ'klaɪn) vb. 1. to refuse to do or accept (something), esp. politely. 2. (*intr.*) to grow smaller; diminish. 3. to slope or cause to slope downwards. 4. (*intr.*) to deteriorate gradually. 5. *Grammar.* to list the inflections of (a noun, adjective, or pronoun), or (of a noun, adjective, or pronoun) to be inflected for number, case, or gender. ~n. 6. gradual deterioration or loss. 7. a movement downward; diminution. 8. a downward slope. 9. *Arch.* any slowly progressive disease, such as tuberculosis. [C14: from OF *decliner*, from L *dēclīnāre* to bend away, inflect grammatically] —de'clinable *adj*. —de'cliner n.

declivity (dɪ'klɪvɪtɪ) n., *pl.* **-ties.** a downward slope, esp. of the ground. [C17: from L *dēclīvitās*, from DE- + *clīvus* a slope, hill] —de'clivitous *adj*.

declutch (diːˈklʌtʃ) *vb.* (*intr.*) to disengage the clutch of a motor vehicle.

decoct (dɪˈkɒkt) *vb.* to extract (the essence or active principle) from (a medicinal or similar substance) by boiling. [C15: see DECOCTION]

decoction (dɪˈkɒkʃən) *n.* **1.** *Pharmacol.* the extraction of the water-soluble substances of a drug or medicinal plants by boiling. **2.** the liquor resulting from this. [C14: from OF, from LL, from *décoquere* to boil down, from *coquere* to cook]

decode (diːˈkəʊd) *vb.* to convert from code into ordinary language. —**de'coder** *n.*

decoke (diːˈkəʊk) *vb.* (*tr.*) another word for **decarbonize.**

décolletage (ˌdeɪkɒlˈtɑːʒ) *n.* a low-cut dress or neckline. [C19: from F; see DÉCOLLETÉ]

décolleté (deɪˈkɒlteɪ) *adj.* **1.** (of a woman's garment) low-cut. **2.** wearing a low-cut garment. [C19: from *décolleter* to cut out the neck (of a dress), from *collet* collar]

decolonize *or* -**ise** (diːˈkɒləˌnaɪz) *vb.* (*tr.*) to grant independence to (a colony). —**de,coloni'zation** *or* -**i'sation** *n.*

decolour, *U.S.* **decolor** (diːˈkʌlə) *or* **decolorize,** -**ise** *vb.* (*tr.*) to deprive of colour. —**de,colori'zation** *or* -**i'sation** *n.*

decommission (ˌdiːkəˈmɪʃən) *vb.* (*tr.*) to dismantle (an industrial plant or nuclear reactor which is no longer required for use), to an extent such that it can be safely abandoned.

decompose (ˌdiːkəmˈpəʊz) *vb.* **1.** to break down or be broken down into constituent elements by bacterial or fungal action; rot. **2.** *Chem.* to break down or cause to break down into simpler chemical compounds. **3.** to break up or separate into constituent parts. —**decomposition** (ˌdiːkɒmpəˈzɪʃən) *n.*

decomposer (ˌdiːkəmˈpəʊzə) *n.* a person or thing that causes decomposition, esp. any of the organisms, such as bacteria, that do so in an ecosystem.

decompress (ˌdiːkəmˈprɛs) *vb.* **1.** to relieve or be relieved of pressure. **2.** to return (a diver, etc.) to a condition of normal atmospheric pressure or to be returned to such a condition. —**decom'pression** *n.*

decompression chamber *n.* a chamber in which the pressure of air can be varied slowly for returning people safely from abnormal pressures to atmospheric pressure.

decompression sickness *or* **illness** *n.* a disorder characterized by severe pain, cramp, and difficulty in breathing, caused by a sudden and substantial change in atmospheric pressure.

decongestant (ˌdiːkənˈdʒɛstənt) *adj.* **1.** relieving congestion, esp. nasal congestion. ~*n.* **2.** a decongestant drug.

deconsecrate (diːˈkɒnsɪˌkreɪt) *vb.* (*tr.*) to transfer (a church, etc.) to secular use. —**de,conse'cration** *n.*

deconstruct (ˌdiːkənˈstrʌkt) *vb.* (*tr.*) **1.** to apply the theories of deconstruction to (a text, film, etc.). **2.** to expose or dismantle the existing structure in (a system, organization, etc.).

deconstruction (ˌdiːkənˈstrʌkʃən) *n.* a development in the theory of criticism (esp. literary and film criticism) that seeks to expose the latent contradictions in a work of art arising from the rhetorical elements embedded in the very structure of language itself.

decontaminate (ˌdiːkənˈtæmɪˌneɪt) *vb.* (*tr.*) to render harmless by the removal or neutralization of poisons, radioactivity, etc. —**decon,tami'nation** *n.*

decontrol (ˌdiːkənˈtrəʊl) *vb.* -**trolling,** -**trolled.** (*tr.*) to free of restraints or controls, esp. government controls: *to decontrol prices.*

décor *or* **decor** (ˈdeɪkɔː) *n.* **1.** a style or scheme of interior decoration, furnishings, etc. in a room or house. **2.** stage decoration; scenery. [C19: from F, from *décorer* to DECORATE]

decorate (ˈdɛkəˌreɪt) *vb.* **1.** (*tr.*) to ornament; adorn. **2.** to paint or wallpaper. **3.** (*tr.*) to confer a mark of distinction, esp. a medal, upon. [C16: from L *decorāre*, from *decus* adornment] —**'decorative** *adj.*

Decorated style *n.* a 14th-century style of English architecture characterized by geometrical tracery and floral decoration.

decoration (ˌdɛkəˈreɪʃən) *n.* **1.** an addition that renders something more attractive or ornate. **2.** the act or art of decorating. **3.** a medal, etc., conferred as a mark of honour.

decorator (ˈdɛkəˌreɪtə) *n.* **1.** *Brit.* a person whose profession is the painting and wallpapering of buildings or their interiors. **2.** a person who decorates.

decorous (ˈdɛkərəs) *adj.* characterized by propriety in manners, conduct, etc. [C17: from L, from *decor* elegance] —**'decorously** *adv.* —**'decorousness** *n.*

decorum (dɪˈkɔːrəm) *n.* **1.** propriety, esp. in behaviour or conduct. **2.** a requirement of correct behaviour in polite society. [C16: from L: propriety]

decoupage (ˌdeɪkuːˈpɑːʒ) *n.* the decoration of a surface with cutout shapes or illustrations. [C20: from F, from *découper*, from DE- + *couper* to cut]

decoy *n.* (ˈdiːkɔɪ, dɪˈkɔɪ). **1.** a person or thing used to lure someone into danger. **2.** *Mil.* something designed to deceive an enemy. **3.** a bird or animal, or an image of one, used to lure game into a trap or within shooting range. **4.** a place into which game can be lured for capture. ~*vb.* (dɪˈkɔɪ). **5.** to lure or be lured by or as if by means of a decoy. **6.** (*tr.*) *Canad.* another word for **deke.** [C17: prob. from Du. *de kooi*, lit.: the cage, from L *cavea* CAGE]

decrease *vb.* (dɪˈkriːs). **1.** to diminish or cause to diminish in size, strength, etc. ~*n.* (ˈdiːkriːs, dɪˈkriːs). **2.** a diminution; reduction. **3.** the amount by which something has been diminished. [C14: from OF, from L *dēcrescere* to grow less, from DE- + *crescere* to grow] —**de'creasingly** *adv.*

decree (dɪˈkriː) *n.* **1.** an edict, law, etc., made by someone in authority. **2.** an order or judgment of a court. ~*vb.* **decreeing, decreed.** **3.** to order, adjudge, or ordain by decree. [C14: from OF, from L *dēcrētum* ordinance, from *dēcrētus* decided, p.p. of *dēcernere*]

decree absolute *n.* the final decree in divorce proceedings, which leaves the parties free to remarry. Cf. **decree nisi.**

decree nisi (ˈnaɪsaɪ) *n.* a provisional decree, esp. in divorce proceedings, which will later be made absolute unless cause is shown why it should not. Cf. **decree absolute.**

decrement (ˈdɛkrɪmənt) *n.* **1.** the act of decreasing; diminution. **2.** *Maths.* a negative increment. **3.** *Physics.* a measure of the damping of an oscillator, expressed by the ratio of amplitudes in successive cycles. [C17: from L *dēcrēmentum*, from *dēcrescere* to DECREASE]

decrepit (dɪˈkrɛpɪt) *adj.* **1.** enfeebled by old age; infirm. **2.** broken down or worn out by hard or long use; dilapidated. [C15: from L *dēcrepitus*, from *crepāre* to creak] —**de'crepi,tude** *n.*

decrescendo (ˌdiːkrɪˈʃɛndəʊ) *n., adj.* another word for **diminuendo.** [It., from *decrescere* to DECREASE]

decrescent (dɪˈkrɛsənt) *adj.* (esp. of the moon) decreasing; waning. [C17: from L *dēcrescēns* growing less; see DECREASE] —**de'crescence** *n.*

decretal (dɪˈkriːtᵊl) *n.* **1.** *R.C. Church.* a papal decree; edict on doctrine or church law. ~*adj.* **2.** of or relating to a decree. [C15: from OF, from LL *dēcrētālis;* see DECREE]

decriminalize *or* -**ise** (diːˈkrɪmɪnᵊˌlaɪz) *vb.* (*tr.*) to remove (an action) from the legal category of criminal offence: *to decriminalize the possession of marijuana.*

decry (dɪˈkraɪ) *vb.* -**crying,** -**cried.** (*tr.*) **1.** to express open disapproval of; disparage. **2.** to depreciate by proclamation: *to decry obsolete coinage.* [C17: from OF *descrier*, from *des-* DIS-¹ + *crier* to CRY]

decumbent (dɪˈkʌmbənt) *adj.* **1.** lying down. **2.** *Bot.* (of stems) lying flat with the tip growing upwards. [C17: from L, present participle of *dēcumbere* to lie down] —**de'cumbency** *n.*

Dedéagach, Dedeagatch, *or* **Dedeağaç** (ˈdɛdeɪɑːˈgɑːtʃ) *n.* a former name (until the end of World War I) of **Alexandroúpolis.**

dedicate (ˈdɛdɪˌkeɪt) *vb.* (*tr.*) **1.** (often foll. by *to*) to devote (oneself, one's time, etc.) wholly to a special purpose or cause. **2.** (foll. by *to*) to address a book, performance, etc. to a person, cause, etc. as a token of affection or respect. **3.** (foll. by *to*) to request or play (a record) on radio for another person as a greeting. **4.** to assign or allocate to a particular project, function, etc. **5.** to set apart for a deity or for sacred uses. [C15: from L *dēdicāre* to announce, from *dicāre* to make known] —**'dedi,cator** *n.* —**dedicatory** (ˈdɛdɪˌkeɪtərɪ, ˈdɛdɪkətərɪ) *or* **'dedi,cative** *adj.*

dedicated ('dɛdɪˌkeɪtɪd) *adj.* **1.** devoted to a particular purpose or cause. **2.** assigned or allocated to a particular project, function, etc.: *a dedicated transmission line.* **3.** *Computers.* designed to fulfil one function.

dedication (ˌdɛdɪ'keɪʃən) *n.* **1.** the act of dedicating or being dedicated. **2.** an inscription prefixed to a book, etc., dedicating it to a person or thing. **3.** wholehearted devotion, esp. to a career, ideal, etc. —ˌdedi'cational *adj.*

deduce (dɪ'djuːs) *vb.* (*tr.*) **1.** (*may take a clause as object*) to reach (a conclusion) by reasoning; conclude (that); infer. **2.** *Arch.* to trace the origin or derivation of. [C15: from L *dēdūcere* to lead away, derive, from DE-+ *dūcere* to lead] —de'ducible *adj.*

deduct (dɪ'dʌkt) *vb.* (*tr.*) to take away or subtract (a number, quantity, part, etc.). [C15: from L *dēductus*, p.p. of *dēdūcere* to DEDUCE]

deductible (dɪ'dʌktɪbªl) *adj.* **1.** capable of being deducted. **2.** *U.S.* short for **tax-deductible.** ~*n.* **3.** *Insurance.* the U.S. name for **excess** (sense 5).

deduction (dɪ'dʌkʃən) *n.* **1.** the act or process of deducting or subtracting. **2.** something that is or may be deducted. **3.** *Logic.* **a.** a process of reasoning by which a specific conclusion necessarily follows from a set of general premises. **b.** a logical conclusion reached by this process. —de'ductive *adj.*

Dee (diː) *n.* **1.** a river in N Wales and NW England, rising in S Gwynedd and flowing east and north to the Irish Sea. Length: about 112 km (70 miles). **2.** a river in NE Scotland, rising in the Cairngorms and flowing east to the North Sea. Length: about 140 km (87 miles). **3.** a river in S Scotland, flowing south to the Solway Firth. Length: about 80 km (50 miles).

deed (diːd) *n.* **1.** something that is done or performed; act. **2.** a notable achievement. **3.** action as opposed to words. **4.** *Law.* a legal document signed, sealed, and delivered to effect a conveyance or transfer of property or to create a legal contract. ~*vb.* **5.** (*tr.*) *U.S.* to convey or transfer (property) by deed. [OE *dēd*]

deed box *n.* a strong box in which deeds and other documents are kept.

deed poll *n. Law.* a deed made by one party only, esp. one by which a person changes his name.

deejay ('diːˌdʒeɪ) *n.* an informal name for **disc jockey.** [C20: from the initials DJ (disc jockey)]

deem (diːm) *vb.* (*tr.*) to judge or consider. [OE *dēman*]

de-emphasize *or* **-ise** (diːˈɛmfəˌsaɪz) *vb.* (*tr.*) to remove emphasis from.

deemster ('diːmstə) *n.* the title of one of the two justices in the Isle of Man. Also called: **dempster.**

deep (diːp) *adj.* **1.** extending or situated far down from a surface: *a deep pool.* **2.** extending or situated far inwards, backwards, or sideways. **3.** *Cricket.* far from the pitch: *the deep field.* **4.** (*postpositive*) of a specified dimension downwards, inwards, or backwards: *six feet deep.* **5.** coming from or penetrating to a great depth. **6.** difficult to understand; abstruse. **7.** intellectually demanding: *a deep discussion.* **8.** of great intensity: *deep trouble.* **9.** (*postpositive;* foll. by *in*) absorbed (by); immersed (in): *deep in study.* **10.** very cunning; devious. **11.** mysterious: *a deep secret.* **12.** (of a colour) having an intense or dark hue. **13.** low in pitch: *a deep voice.* **14. go off the deep end.** *Inf.* **a.** to lose one's temper; react angrily. **b.** *Chiefly U.S.* to act rashly. **15. in deep water.** *Inf.* in a tricky position or in trouble. ~*n.* **16.** any deep place on land or under water. **17. the deep. a.** a poetic term for the ocean. **b.** *Cricket.* the area of the field relatively far from the pitch. **18.** the most profound, intense, or central part: *the deep of winter.* **19.** a vast extent, as of space or time. ~*adv.* **20.** far on in time; late: *they worked deep into the night.* **21.** profoundly or intensely. **22. deep down.** *Inf.* in reality, esp. as opposed to appearance. [OE *dēop*] —'deeply *adv.* —'deepness *n.*

deepen ('diːpªn) *vb.* to make or become deep, deeper, or more intense. —'deepener *n.*

deepfreeze (ˌdiːp'friːz) *n.* **1.** a refrigerator in which food, etc., is stored for long periods at temperatures below freezing. **2.** storage in a deepfreeze. **3.** *Inf.* a state of suspended activity. ~*vb.* **deep-freeze**, **-froze** *or* **-freezed**, **-frozen** *or* **-freezed.** **4.** (*tr.*) to freeze or keep in a deepfreeze.

deep-fry *vb.* **-frying**, **-fried.** to cook (fish, etc.) in sufficient hot fat to cover the food.

deep-laid *adj.* (of a plot or plan) carefully worked out and kept secret.

deep-rooted *or* **deep-seated** *adj.* (of ideas, beliefs, etc.) firmly fixed or held; ingrained.

deep-sea *n.* (*modifier*) of, found in, or characteristic of the deep parts of the sea.

deep-set *adj.* (esp. of eyes) deeply set.

Deep South *n.* the SE part of the U.S., esp. South Carolina, Georgia, Alabama, Mississippi, and Louisiana.

deep space *n.* any region of outer space beyond the system of the earth and moon.

deep structure *n. Generative grammar.* a representation of a sentence at a level where logical or grammatical relations are made explicit. Cf. **surface structure.**

deer (dɪə) *n., pl.* **deer** *or* **deers.** any of a family of hoofed, ruminant mammals including reindeer, elk, and roe deer, typically having antlers in the male. Related adj.: **cervine.** [OE *dēor* beast]

deer lick *n.* a naturally or artificially salty area of ground where deer come to lick the salt.

deerskin ('dɪəˌskɪn) *n.* **a.** the hide of a deer. **b.** (*as modifier*): *a deerskin jacket.*

deerstalker ('dɪəˌstɔːkə) *n.* **1.** a person who stalks deer, esp. in order to shoot them. **2.** a hat, peaked in front and behind, with earflaps usually tied together on the top. —'deerˌstalking *adj., n.*

de-escalate (diːˈɛskəˌleɪt) *vb.* to reduce the level or intensity of. —de-ˌesca'lation *n.*

def (dɛf) *adj. Sl.* (esp. of hip-hop) very good. [C20: ?from *definitive*]

def. *abbrev. for:* **1.** defective. **2.** defence. **3.** defendant. **4.** deferred. **5.** definite. **6.** definition.

deface (dɪ'feɪs) *vb.* (*tr.*) to spoil or mar the surface or appearance of; disfigure. —de'faceable *adj.* —de'facement *n.* —de'facer *n.*

de facto (deɪ 'fæktəʊ) *adv.* **1.** in fact. ~*adj.* **2.** existing in fact, whether legally recognized or not: *a de facto regime.* Cf. **de jure.** ~*n., pl.* **-tos.** **3.** *Austral. & N.Z.* a de facto wife or husband. [C17: L]

defalcate ('diːfælˌkeɪt) *vb.* (*intr.*) *Law.* to misuse or misappropriate property or funds entrusted to one. [C15: from Med. L *dēfalcāre* to cut off, from L DE- + *falx* sickle] —'defalˌcator *n.*

defame (dɪ'feɪm) *vb.* (*tr.*) to attack the good name or reputation of; slander; libel. [C14: from OF, from L, from *diffāmāre* to spread by unfavourable report, from *fāma* FAME] —**defamation** (ˌdɛfə'meɪʃən) *n.* —**defamatory** (dɪ'fæmətərɪ) *adj.*

default (dɪ'fɔːlt) *n.* **1.** a failure to act, esp. a failure to meet a financial obligation or to appear in a court of law at a time specified. **2.** absence. **3. in default of.** through or in the lack or absence of. **4. judgment by default.** *Law.* a judgment in the plaintiff's favour when the defendant fails to plead or to appear. **5.** lack, want, or need. ~*vb.* **6.** (*intr.;* often foll. by *on* or *in*) to fail to make payment when due. **7.** (*intr.*) to fail to fulfil an obligation. **8.** *Law.* to lose (a case) by failure to appear in court. [C13: from OF *defaute*, from *defaillir* to fail, from Vulgar L *dēfallīre* (unattested) to be lacking]

defaulter (dɪ'fɔːltə) *n.* **1.** a person who defaults. **2.** *Chiefly Brit.* a person, esp. a soldier, who has broken the disciplinary code of his service.

defeat (dɪ'fiːt) *vb.* (*tr.*) **1.** to overcome; win a victory over. **2.** to thwart or frustrate. **3.** *Law.* to render null and void. ~*n.* **4.** a defeating or being defeated. [C14: from OF, from *desfaire* to undo, ruin, from *des-* DIS-[1] + *faire* to do, from L *facere*]

defeatism (dɪ'fiːtɪzəm) *n.* a ready acceptance or expectation of defeat. —de'featist *n., adj.*

defecate ('dɛfɪˌkeɪt) *vb.* **1.** (*intr.*) to discharge waste from the body through the anus. **2.** (*tr.*) to remove impurities from. [C16: from L *dēfaecāre* to cleanse from dregs, from DE- + *faex* dregs] —ˌdefe'cation *n.* —'defeˌcator *n.*

defect *n.* (dɪ'fɛkt, 'diːfɛkt) **1.** a lack of something necessary for completeness; deficiency. **2.** an imperfection or blemish. ~*vb.* (dɪ'fɛkt) **3.** (*intr.*) to desert one's country, cause, etc., esp. in order to join the opposing forces. [C15: from L, from *dēficere* to forsake, fail] —de'fector *n.*

defection (dɪ'fɛkʃən) *n.* **1.** abandonment of duty, allegiance, principles, etc. **2.** a shortcoming.

defective (dɪ'fɛktɪv) *adj.* **1.** having a defect or flaw; imperfect. **2.** (of a person) below the usual standard or level, esp. in intelligence. **3.** *Grammar.* lacking the full range of inflections characteristic of its form class. **—de'fectiveness** *n.*

defence *or U.S.* **defense** (dɪ'fɛns) *n.* **1.** resistance against danger or attack. **2.** a person or thing that provides such resistance. **3.** a plea, essay, etc., in support of something. **4.** a country's military measures or resources. **5.** *Law.* a defendant's denial of the truth of the allegations or charge against him. **6.** *Law.* the defendant and his legal advisers collectively. **7.** *Sport.* **a.** the action of protecting oneself or part of the playing area against an opponent's attacks. **b.** (usually preceded by *the*) the players in a team whose function is to do this. **8.** (*pl.*) fortifications. [C13: from OF, from LL *dēfensum*, p.p. of *dēfendere* to DEFEND] **—de'fenceless** *or U.S.* **de'fenseless** *adj.*

defence mechanism *n.* **1.** *Psychoanalysis.* an unconscious mental process designed to reduce anxiety or shame. **2.** *Physiol.* the protective response of the body against disease.

defend (dɪ'fɛnd) *vb.* **1.** to protect from harm or danger. **2.** (*tr.*) to support in the face of criticism, esp. by argument. **3.** to represent (a defendant) in court. **4.** *Sport.* to guard (one's goal, etc.) against attack. **5.** (*tr.*) to protect (a title, etc.) against a challenge. [C13: from OF, from L *dēfendere* to ward off, from DE- + *-fendere* to strike] **—de'fender** *n.*

defendant (dɪ'fɛndənt) *n.* **1.** a person against whom an action or claim is brought in a court of law. Cf. **plaintiff.** ~*adj.* **2.** defending.

defenestration (diː,fɛnɪ'streɪʃən) *n.* the act of throwing someone out of a window. [C17: from NL *dēfenestrātiō*, from L DE- + *fenestra* window]

defensible (dɪ'fɛnsɪbəl) *adj.* capable of being defended, as in war, an argument, etc. **—de,fensi'bility** *or* **de'fensibleness** *n.*

defensive (dɪ'fɛnsɪv) *adj.* **1.** intended for defence. **2.** rejecting criticisms of oneself. ~*n.* **3.** a position of defence. **4. on the defensive.** in a position of defence, as in being ready to reject criticism. **—de'fensively** *adv.*

defer[1] (dɪ'fɜː) *vb.* **-ferring, -ferred.** (*tr.*) to delay until a future time; postpone. [C14: from OF *differer* to be different, postpone; see DIFFER] **—de'ferment** *or* **de'ferral** *n.* **—de'ferrer** *n.*

defer[2] (dɪ'fɜː) *vb.* **-ferring, -ferred.** (*intr.; foll. by to*) to yield (to) or comply (with) the wishes or judgments of another. [C15: from L *dēferre*, lit.: to bear down, from DE- + *ferre* to bear]

deference ('dɛfərəns) *n.* **1.** compliance with the wishes of another. **2.** courteous regard; respect. [C17: from F *déférence*; see DEFER[2]]

deferent[1] ('dɛfərənt) *adj.* another word for **deferential.**

deferent[2] ('dɛfərənt) *adj.* (esp. of a nerve or duct) conveying an impulse, fluid, etc., down or away; efferent. [C17: from L *dēferre*; see DEFER[2]]

deferential (,dɛfə'rɛnʃəl) *adj.* showing deference; respectful. **—,defer'entially** *adv.*

defiance (dɪ'faɪəns) *n.* **1.** open or bold resistance to authority, opposition, or power. **2.** a challenge. **—de'fiant** *adj.*

defibrillation (dɪ,faɪbrɪ'leɪʃən) *n.* *Med.* the application of an electric current to the heart to restore normal contractions after a heart attack caused by fibrillation.

defibrillator (dɪ'faɪbrɪ,leɪtə) *n.* *Med.* an apparatus for stopping fibrillation of the heart by application of an electric current.

deficiency (dɪ'fɪʃənsɪ) *n., pl.* **-cies.** **1.** the state or quality of being deficient. **2.** a lack or insufficiency; shortage. **3.** a deficit.

deficiency disease *n.* any condition, such as pellagra, beriberi, or scurvy, produced by a lack of vitamins or other essential substances.

deficient (dɪ'fɪʃənt) *adj.* **1.** lacking some essential; incomplete; defective. **2.** inadequate in quantity or supply; insufficient. [C16: from L *dēficiēns* lacking, from *dēficere* to fall short] **—de'ficiently** *adv.*

deficit ('dɛfɪsɪt, dɪ'fɪsɪt) *n.* **1.** the amount by which an actual sum is lower than that expected or required. **2. a.** an excess of liabilities over assets. **b.** an excess of expenditures over revenues. [C18: from L, lit.: there is lacking, from *dēficere*]

deficit financing *n.* government spending in excess of revenues so that a budget deficit is incurred, which is financed by borrowing: recommended by some economists as a remedy for economic depression and unemployment.

defile[1] (dɪ'faɪl) *vb.* (*tr.*) **1.** to make foul or dirty; pollute. **2.** to taint; corrupt. **3.** to damage or sully (someone's reputation, etc.). **4.** to make unfit for ceremonial use. **5.** to violate the chastity of. [C14: from earlier *defoilen*, from OF *defouler* to trample underfoot, abuse, from DE- + *fouler* to tread upon; see FULL[2]] **—de'filement** *n.*

defile[2] ('diːfaɪl, dɪ'faɪl) *n.* **1.** a narrow pass or gorge. **2.** a single file of soldiers, etc. ~*vb.* **3.** to march in single file. [C17: from F, from *défiler* to file off, from *filer* to march in a column, from OF, from L *fīlum* thread]

define (dɪ'faɪn) *vb.* (*tr.*) **1.** to state precisely the meaning of. **2.** to describe the nature of. **3.** to determine the boundary or extent of. **4.** (*often passive*) to delineate the form or outline of. **5.** to fix with precision; specify. [C14: from OF: to determine, from L *dēfīnīre* to set bounds to, from *fīnīre* to FINISH] **—de'finable** *adj.* **—de'finer** *n.*

definite ('dɛfɪnɪt) *adj.* **1.** clearly defined; exact. **2.** having precise limits or boundaries. **3.** known for certain. [C15: from L *dēfīnītus* limited, distinct; see DEFINE] **—'definiteness** *n.*

▷ **Usage.** *Definite* and *definitive* should be carefully distinguished. *Definite* indicates precision and firmness, as in a *definite decision. Definitive* includes these senses but also indicates conclusiveness. A *definite answer* indicates a clear and firm answer to a particular question; a *definitive answer* implies an authoritative resolution of a complex question.

definite article *n. Grammar.* a determiner that expresses specificity of reference, such as *the* in English. Cf. **indefinite article.**

definite integral *n.* See **integral.**

definitely ('dɛfɪnɪtlɪ) *adv.* **1.** in a definite manner. **2.** (*sentence modifier*) certainly: *he said he was coming, definitely.* ~*sentence substitute.* **3.** unquestionably.

definition (,dɛfɪ'nɪʃən) *n.* **1.** a formal and concise statement of the meaning of a word, phrase, etc. **2.** the act of defining. **3.** specification of the essential properties of something. **4.** the act of making clear or definite. **5.** the state of being clearly defined. **6.** a measure of the clarity of an optical, photographic, or television image as characterized by its sharpness and contrast.

definitive (dɪ'fɪnɪtɪv) *adj.* **1.** serving to decide or settle finally. **2.** most reliable or authoritative. **3.** serving to define or outline. **4.** *Zool.* fully developed. **5.** (of postage stamps) permanently on sale. ~*n.* **6.** *Grammar.* a word indicating specificity of reference. **—de'finitively** *adv.*

▷ **Usage.** See at **definite.**

deflagrate ('dɛflə,greɪt, 'diː-) *vb.* to burn with great heat and light. [C18: from L *dēflagrāre*, from DE-+ *flagrāre* to burn] **—,defla'gration** *n.*

deflate (diː'fleɪt) *vb.* **1.** to collapse through the release of gas. **2.** (*tr.*) to take away the self-esteem or conceit from. **3.** *Econ.* to cause deflation of (an economy, the money supply, etc.). [C19: from DE- + (IN)FLATE] **—de'flator** *n.*

deflation (diː'fleɪʃən) *n.* **1.** a deflating or being deflated. **2.** *Econ.* a reduction in spending and economic activity resulting in lower levels of output, employment, investment, trade, profits, and prices. **3.** the removal of loose rock material, etc., by wind. **—de'flationary** *adj.* **—de'flationist** *n., adj.*

deflect (dɪ'flɛkt) *vb.* to turn or cause to turn aside from a course; swerve. [C17: from L *dēflectere*, from *flectere* to bend] **—de'flector** *n.*

deflection *or* **deflexion** (dɪ'flɛkʃən) *n.* **1.** a deflecting or being deflected. **2.** the amount of deviation. **3.** the change in direction of a light beam as it crosses a boundary between two media with different refractive indexes. **4.** a deviation of the indicator of a measuring instrument from its zero position. **—de'flective** *adj.*

deflocculate (diː'flɒkyʊ,leɪt) *vb.* (*tr.*) to cause (an aggregate) to separate into particles. **—de,floccu'lation** *n.*

deflower (diː'flaʊə) *vb.* (*tr.*) **1.** to deprive (esp. a woman) of virginity. **2.** to despoil of beauty, innocence, etc. **3.** to rob or despoil of flowers. **—,deflo'ration** *n.*

Defoe (dɪ'fəʊ) *n.* **Daniel.** ?1660–1731, English novelist, journalist, spymaster, and pamphleteer, noted particularly for his novel *Robinson Crusoe* (1719). His other novels include *Moll Flanders* (1722) and *A Journal of the Plague Year* (1722).

defoliant (diːˈfəʊliənt) n. a chemical sprayed or dusted onto trees to cause their leaves to fall, esp. to remove cover from an enemy in warfare.

defoliate (diːˈfəʊlɪˌeɪt) vb. to deprive (a plant) of its leaves. [C18: from Med. L dēfoliāre, from L DE- + folium leaf] —de,foliˈation n.

deforest (diːˈfɒrɪst) vb. (tr.) to clear of trees. Also: **disforest**. —de,foresˈtation n.

De Forest (də ˈfɒrɪst) n. **Lee**. 1873–1961, U.S. inventor of telegraphic, telephonic, and radio equipment: patented the first triode valve (1907).

deform (dɪˈfɔːm) vb. 1. to make or become misshapen or distorted. 2. (tr.) to mar the beauty of; disfigure. 3. (tr.) to subject or be subjected to a stress that causes a change of dimensions. [C15: from L dēformāre, from DE- + forma shape, beauty] —deˈformable adj. —deforˈmation n.

deformed (dɪˈfɔːmd) adj. 1. disfigured or misshapen. 2. morally perverted; warped.

deformity (dɪˈfɔːmɪtɪ) n., pl. **-ties**. 1. a deformed condition. 2. Pathol. a distortion of an organ or part. 3. a deformed person or thing. 4. a defect, esp. of the mind or morals; depravity.

defraud (dɪˈfrɔːd) vb. (tr.) to take away or withhold money, rights, property, etc., from (a person) by fraud; swindle. —deˈfrauder n.

defray (dɪˈfreɪ) vb. (tr.) to provide money for (costs, expenses, etc.); pay. [C16: from OF deffroier to pay expenses, from de- DIS-¹ + frai expenditure] —deˈfrayable adj. —deˈfrayal or deˈfrayment n.

defrock (diːˈfrɒk) vb. (tr.) to deprive (a person in holy orders) of ecclesiastical status; unfrock.

defrost (diːˈfrɒst) vb. 1. to make or become free of frost or ice. 2. to thaw, esp. through removal from a deep-freeze.

defroster (diːˈfrɒstə) n. a device by which a de-icing process, as of a refrigerator, is accelerated.

deft (dɛft) adj. quick and neat in movement; nimble; dexterous. [C13 (in the sense: gentle): see DAFT] —ˈdeftly adv. —ˈdeftness n.

defunct (dɪˈfʌŋkt) adj. 1. no longer living; dead or extinct. 2. no longer operative or valid. [C16: from L dēfungī to discharge (one's obligations), die; see DE-, FUNCTION] —deˈfunctness n.

defuse or U.S. (sometimes) **defuze** (diːˈfjuːz) vb. (tr.) 1. to remove the triggering device of (a bomb, etc.). 2. to remove the cause of tension from (a crisis, etc.).

defy (dɪˈfaɪ) vb. **-fying, -fied**. (tr.) 1. to resist openly and boldly. 2. to elude, esp. in a baffling way. 3. Formal. to challenge (someone to do something); dare. 4. Arch. to invite to do battle or combat. [C14: from OF desfier, from des- DE- + fier to trust, from L fīdere] —deˈfier n.

deg. abbrev. for degree.

Degas (ˈdeɪɡɑː; French dəɡɑ) n. **Hilaire Germain Edgar** (ilɛr ʒɛrmɛ̃ ɛdɡar). 1834–1917, French impressionist painter and sculptor, noted for his brilliant draughtsmanship and ability to convey movement, esp. in his studies of horse racing and ballet dancers.

degauss (diːˈɡaʊs) vb. (tr.) to neutralize by producing an opposing magnetic field. —deˈgausser n.

degeneracy (dɪˈdʒɛnərəsɪ) n., pl. **-cies**. 1. the act or state of being degenerate. 2. the process of becoming degenerate.

degenerate vb. (dɪˈdʒɛnəˌreɪt). (intr.) 1. to become degenerate. 2. Biol. (of organisms or their parts) to become less specialized or functionally useless. ~adj. (dɪˈdʒɛnərɪt). 3. having declined or deteriorated to a lower mental, moral, or physical level; degraded; corrupt. ~n. (dɪˈdʒɛnərɪt). 4. a degenerate person. [C15: from L, from dēgener departing from its kind, ignoble, from DE- + genus race] —deˈgenerately adv. —deˈgenerateness n. —deˈgenerative adj.

degenerate matter n. Astrophysics. the highly compressed state of a star's matter when its atoms virtually touch in the final stage of its evolution into a white dwarf.

degeneration (dɪ,dʒɛnəˈreɪʃən) n. 1. the process of degenerating. 2. the state of being degenerate. 3. Biol. the loss of specialization, function, or structure by organisms and their parts. 4. impairment or loss of the function and structure of cells or tissues, as by disease or injury. 5. Electronics. negative feedback of a signal.

degradable (dɪˈɡreɪdəb³l) adj. 1. capable of being decomposed chemically or biologically. 2. capable of being degraded.

degradation (,dɛɡrəˈdeɪʃən) n. 1. a degrading or being degraded. 2. a state of degeneration or squalor. 3. some act, constraint, etc., that is degrading. 4. the wearing down of the surface of rocks, cliffs, etc., by erosion. 5. Chem. a breakdown of a molecule into atoms or smaller molecules. 6. Physics. an irreversible process in which the energy available to do work is decreased. 7. R.C. Church. the permanent unfrocking of a priest.

degrade (dɪˈɡreɪd) vb. 1. (tr.) to reduce in worth, character, etc.; disgrace. 2. (diːˈɡreɪd) (tr.) to reduce in rank or status; demote. 3. (tr.) to reduce in strength, quality, etc. 4. to reduce or be reduced by erosion or down-cutting, as a land surface or bed of a river. 5. Chem. to decompose into atoms or smaller molecules. [C14: from LL dēgradāre, from L DE- + gradus rank, degree] —deˈgrader n.

degrading (dɪˈɡreɪdɪŋ) adj. causing humiliation; debasing. —deˈgradingly adv.

degree (dɪˈɡriː) n. 1. a stage in a scale of relative amount or intensity: a high degree of competence. 2. an academic award conferred by a university or college on successful completion of a course or as an honorary distinction (**honorary degree**). 3. any of three categories of seriousness of a burn. 4. (in the U.S.) any of the categories into which a crime is divided according to its seriousness. 5. Genealogy. a step in a line of descent. 6. Grammar. any of the forms of an adjective used to indicate relative amount or intensity: in English they are positive, comparative, and superlative. 7. Music. any note of a diatonic scale relative to the other notes in that scale. 8. a unit of temperature on a specified scale. Symbol: °. See also **Celsius scale, Fahrenheit scale**. 9. a measure of angle equal to one three-hundred-and-sixtieth of the angle traced by one complete revolution of a line about one of its ends. Symbol: °. 10. a unit of latitude or longitude used to define points on the earth's surface. Symbol: °. 11. a unit on any of several scales of measurement, as for specific gravity. Symbol: °. 12. Maths. **a**. the highest power or the sum of the powers of any term in a polynomial or by itself: $x^4 + x + 3$ and xyz^2 are of the fourth degree. **b**. the greatest power of the highest order derivative in a differential equation. 13. Obs. a step; rung. 14. Arch. a stage in social status or rank. 15. **by degrees**. little by little; gradually. 16. **one degree under**. Inf. off colour; ill. 17. **to a degree**. somewhat; rather. [C13: from OF degre, from L DE- + gradus step]

degree of freedom n. 1. Chem. the least number of independently variable properties needed to determine the state of a system. See also **phase rule**. 2. one of the independent components of motion (translation, vibration, and rotation) of an atom or molecule.

De Havilland (də ˈhævɪlənd) n. Sir **Geoffrey**. 1882–1965, British aircraft designer. He produced many military aircraft and the first jet airliners.

dehisce (dɪˈhɪs) vb. (intr.) (of fruits, anthers, etc.) to burst open spontaneously, releasing seeds, pollen, etc. [C17: from L dēhiscere to split open, from DE- + hiscere to yawn, gape] —deˈhiscent adj.

dehorn (diːˈhɔːn) vb. (tr.) to remove the horns of (cattle, sheep, or goats).

Dehra Dun (ˈdɛərə ˈduːn) n. a city in N India, in NW Uttar Pradesh: Indian military academy (1932). Pop.: 294 000 (1981).

dehumanize or **-ise** (diːˈhjuːməˌnaɪz) vb. (tr.) 1. to deprive of human qualities. 2. to render mechanical, artificial, or routine. —de,humaniˈzation or -iˈsation n.

dehumidify (,diːhjuːˈmɪdɪˌfaɪ) vb. **-fying, -fied**. (tr.) to remove water from (the air, etc.) —,dehu,midifiˈcation n. —,dehuˈmidiˌfier n.

dehydrate (diːˈhaɪdreɪt, ,diːhaɪˈdreɪt) vb. 1. to lose or cause to lose water. 2. to lose or deprive of water, as the body or tissues. —deˈhydration n. —deˈhydrator n.

dehydrogenate (diːˈhaɪdrədʒəˌneɪt), **dehydrogenize**, or **-ise** (diːˈhaɪdrədʒəˌnaɪz) vb. (tr.) to remove hydrogen from. —de,hydrogeˈnation, de,hydrogeniˈzation, or -iˈsation n.

Deianira (,diːəˈnaɪərə, ,deɪə-) n. Greek myth. a sister of Meleager and wife of Hercules. She unintentionally killed Hercules by dipping his tunic in the poisonous blood of the Centaur Nessus, thinking it to be a love charm.

de-ice (diːˈaɪs) vb. to free or be freed of ice.

de-icer (diːˈaɪsə) n. **1.** a mechanical or thermal device designed to melt or stop the formation of ice on an aircraft. **2.** a substance used for this purpose, esp. an aerosol that can be sprayed on car windscreens to remove ice or frost.

deictic (ˈdaɪktɪk) adj. **1.** Logic. proving by direct argument. Cf. **elenctic** (see **elenchus**). **2.** Grammar. **a.** denoting a word whose reference is determined by the context of its utterance. **b.** (as n.): the word "here" is a deictic. [C17: from Gk deiktikos concerning proof, from deiknunai to show]

deify (ˈdiːɪˌfaɪ, ˈdeɪɪ-) vb. **-fying, -fied.** (tr.) **1.** to exalt to the position of a god or personify as a god. **2.** to accord divine honour or worship to. [C14: from OF, from LL deificāre, from L deus god + facere to make] —ˌdeifiˈcation n. —ˈdeiˌfier n.

Deighton (ˈdeɪtʲn) n. Len. born 1929, British thriller writer. His books include The Ipcress File (1962), Bomber (1970), and the trilogy Berlin Game, Mexico Set, and London Match (1983–85).

deign (deɪn) vb. **1.** (intr.) to think it fit or worthy of oneself (to do something); condescend. **2.** (tr.) Arch. to vouchsafe. [C13: from OF, from L dignārī to consider worthy, from dignus]

de-industrialization or **-isation** (diːɪndʌstrɪəlaɪˈzeɪʃən) n. a decline in importance of a country's manufacturing industry.

Deirdre (ˈdɪədrɪ) n. Irish myth. a beautiful girl who was raised by Conchobar to be his wife but eloped with Naoise. When Conchobar treacherously killed Naoise she took her own life: often used to symbolize Ireland. See also **Naoise**.

deism (ˈdiːɪzəm, ˈdeɪ-) n. belief in the existence of God based solely on natural reason, without reference to revelation. Cf. **theism**. [C17: from F déisme, from L deus god] —ˈdeist n., adj. —deˈistic or deˈistical adj. —deˈistically adv.

deity (ˈdiːɪtɪ, ˈdeɪ-) n., pl. **-ties. 1.** a god or goddess. **2.** the state of being divine; godhead. **3.** the rank of a god. **4.** the nature or character of God. [C14: from OF, from LL deitās, from L deus god]

Deity (ˈdiːɪtɪ, ˈdeɪ-) n. **the.** God.

déjà vu (ˈdeɪʒæ ˈvuː) n. the experience of perceiving a new situation as if it had occurred before. [from F, lit.: already seen]

deject (dɪˈdʒɛkt) vb. (tr.) to have a depressing effect on; dispirit; dishearten. [C15: from L dēicere to cast down, from DE- + iacere to throw]

dejected (dɪˈdʒɛktɪd) adj. miserable; despondent; downhearted. —deˈjectedly adv.

dejection (dɪˈdʒɛkʃən) n. **1.** lowness of spirits; depression. **2. a.** faecal matter. **b.** defecation.

de jure (deɪ ˈdʒʊəreɪ) adv. according to law; by right; legally. Cf. **de facto**. [L]

deka- or **dek-** combining form. variants of **deca-**.

deke (diːk) Canad. sl. ~vb. **1.** (tr.) (in ice hockey or box lacrosse) to draw a defending player out of position by faking a shot or movement. ~n. **2.** such a shot or movement.

Dekker or **Decker** (ˈdɛkə) n. Thomas. ?1572–?1632, English dramatist and pamphleteer, noted particularly for his comedy The Shoemaker's Holiday (1600) and his satirical pamphlet The Gull's Hornbook (1609).

dekko (ˈdɛkəʊ) n., pl. **-kos.** Brit. sl. a look; glance (esp. in **take a dekko (at)**). [C19: from Hindi dekho! look! from dekhnā to see]

de Kooning (də ˈkuːnɪŋ) n. Willem. See (Willem de) **Kooning.**

del. abbrev. for delegate.

Del. abbrev. for Delaware.

De la Beche (biːtʃ) n. Henry. 1796–1855, English geologist. His work led to the founding of the Geological Survey (1835).

Delacroix (French dəlakrwa) n. (Ferdinand Victor) Eugène (øʒɛn). 1798–1863, French romantic painter whose use of colour and free composition influenced impressionism. His paintings of historical and contemporary scenes include The Massacre at Chios (1824).

Delagoa Bay (ˌdɛləˈɡəʊə) n. an inlet of the Indian Ocean, in S Mozambique. Official name: **Baía de Lourenço Marques.**

de la Mare (də lɑː: mɛə) n. Walter (John). 1873–1956, English poet and novelist, noted esp. for his evocative verse for children. His works include the volumes of poetry The Listeners and Other Poems (1912) and Peacock Pie (1913) and the novel Memoirs of a Midget (1921).

Delaunay (French dəlonɛ) n. Robert (rɔbɛr). 1885–1941, French painter, whose abstract use of colour characterized Orphism, an attempt to introduce more colour into austere forms of Cubism.

Delaware[1] (ˈdɛləˌwɛə) n. **1.** (pl. **-wares** or **-ware**) a member of a North American Indian people formerly living near the Delaware River **2.** the language of this people.

Delaware[2] (ˈdɛləˌwɛə) n. **1.** a state of the northeastern U.S., on the Delmarva Peninsula: mostly flat and low-lying, with hills in the extreme north and cypress swamps in the extreme south. Capital: Dover. Pop.: 633 000 (1986 est.). Area: 5004 sq. km. (1932 sq. miles). Abbrevs.: **Del.** or (with zip code) **DE 2.** a river in the northeastern U.S., rising in the Catskill Mountains and flowing south into **Delaware Bay**, an inlet of the Atlantic. Length 660 km (410 miles). —ˌDelaˈwarean adj.

De La Warr (ˈdɛləˌwɛə) n. Baron, title of Thomas West, known as Lord Delaware. 1577–1618, English administrator in America; first governor of Virginia (1610).

delay (dɪˈleɪ) vb. **1.** (tr.) to put off to a later time; defer. **2.** (tr.) to slow up or cause to be late. **3.** (intr.) to be irresolute or put off doing something. **4.** (intr.) to linger; dawdle. ~n. **5.** a delaying or being delayed. **6.** the interval between one event and another. [C13: from OF, from des- off + laier to leave, from L laxāre to loosen] —deˈlayer n.

delayed action or **delay action** n. a device for operating a mechanism, such as a camera shutter, a short time after setting.

delayed drop n. a parachute descent in which the opening of the parachute is delayed for a predetermined time.

dele (ˈdiːlɪ) n., pl. **deles. 1.** a sign ( ) indicating that typeset matter is to be deleted. ~vb. **deleing, deled. 2.** (tr.) to mark (matter to be deleted) with a dele. [C18: from L: delete (imperative), from dēlēre to destroy, obliterate]

delectable (dɪˈlɛktəbʲl) adj. highly enjoyable, esp. pleasing to the taste; delightful. [C14: from L dēlectābilis, from dēlectāre to DELIGHT] —deˈlectableness or deˌlectaˈbility n.

delectation (ˌdiːlɛkˈteɪʃən) n. pleasure; enjoyment.

Deledda (Italian deˈledda) n. Grazia (ˈɡrattsja). 1875–1936, Italian novelist, noted for works, such as La Madre (1920), on peasant life in Sardinia: Nobel prize for literature 1926.

delegate n. (ˈdɛlɪˌɡeɪt, -ɡɪt). **1.** a person chosen to act for another or others, esp. at a conference or meeting. ~vb. (ˈdɛlɪˌɡeɪt). **2.** to give (duties, powers, etc.) to another as representative; depute. **3.** (tr.) to authorize (a person) as representative. [C14: from L dēlēgāre to send on a mission, from lēgāre to send, depute] —**delegable** (ˈdɛlɪɡəbʲl) adj.

delegation (ˌdɛlɪˈɡeɪʃən) n. **1.** a person or group chosen to represent another or others. **2.** a delegating or being delegated.

delete (dɪˈliːt) vb. (tr.) to remove (something printed or written); erase; strike out. [C17: from L dēlēre to destroy, obliterate] —deˈletion n.

deleterious (ˌdɛlɪˈtɪərɪəs) adj. harmful; injurious; hurtful. [C17: from NL, from Gk dēlētērios, from dēleisthai to hurt] —ˌdeleˈteriousness n.

Delft (dɛlft) n. **1.** a town in the SW Netherlands, in South Holland province. Pop.: 87 736 (1987). **2.** Also called: **'delftware.** tin-glazed earthenware made in Delft since the 17th century, typically having blue decoration on a white ground. **3.** a similar earthenware made in England.

Delgado (dɛlˈɡɑːdəʊ) n. Cape. a headland on the extreme NE coast of Mozambique.

Delhi (ˈdɛlɪ) n. **1.** the capital of India, in the N central part, on the Jumna river: consists of **Old Delhi** (a walled city reconstructed in 1639 on the site of former cities of Delhi, which date from the 15th century B.C.) and **New Delhi** to the south, chosen as the capital in 1911, replacing Calcutta; university (1922). Pop.: (total) 5 714 000 (1981). **2.** a Union Territory of N India. Capital: Delhi. Area: 1418 sq. km (553 sq. miles). Pop.: 6 196 414 (1981).

deli (ˈdɛlɪ) n., pl. **delis.** an informal word for **delicatessen.**

deliberate adj. (dɪ'lɪbərɪt). **1.** carefully thought out in advance; intentional. **2.** careful or unhurried: a deliberate pace. ~vb. (dɪ'lɪbəˌreɪt). **3.** to consider (something) deeply; think over. [C15: from L dēlīberāre, from lībrāre to weigh, from lībra scales] —de'liberately adv. —de'liberateness n. —de'liberˌator n.

deliberation (dɪˌlɪbə'reɪʃən) n. **1.** careful consideration. **2.** (often pl.) formal discussion, as of a committee. **3.** care or absence of hurry.

deliberative (dɪ'lɪbərətɪv) adj. **1.** of or for deliberating: a deliberative assembly. **2.** characterized by deliberation. —de'liberatively adv. —de'liberativeness n.

Delibes (French dəlib) n. (Clément Philibert) Léo (leo). 1836–91, French composer, noted particularly for his ballets Coppélia (1870) and Sylvia (1876), and the opera Lakmé (1883).

delicacy ('dɛlɪkəsɪ) n., pl. -cies. **1.** fine or subtle quality, character, construction, etc. **2.** fragile or graceful beauty. **3.** something that is considered choice to eat, such as caviar. **4.** fragile construction or constitution. **5.** refinement of feeling, manner, or appreciation. **6.** fussy or squeamish refinement, esp. in matters of taste, propriety, etc. **7.** need for tactful or sensitive handling. **8.** sensitivity of response, as of an instrument.

delicate ('dɛlɪkɪt) adj. **1.** fine or subtle in quality, character, construction, etc. **2.** having a soft or fragile beauty. **3.** (of colour, tone, taste, etc.) pleasantly subtle. **4.** easily damaged or injured; fragile. **5.** precise or sensitive in action: a delicate mechanism. **6.** requiring tact. **7.** showing regard for the feelings of others. **8.** excessively refined; squeamish. [C14: from L dēlicātus affording pleasure, from dēliciae (pl.) delight, pleasure] —'delicately adv. —'delicateness n.

delicatessen (ˌdɛlɪkə'tɛsən) n. **1.** various foods, esp. unusual or imported foods, already cooked or prepared. **2.** a shop selling these foods. [C19: from G Delikatessen, lit.: delicacies, from F délicatesse]

delicious (dɪ'lɪʃəs) adj. **1.** very appealing, esp. to taste or smell. **2.** extremely enjoyable. [C13: from OF, from LL dēliciōsus, from L dēliciae delights, from dēlicere to entice; see DELIGHT] —de'liciously adv. —de'liciousness n.

delight (dɪ'laɪt) vb. **1.** (tr.) to please greatly. **2.** (intr.; foll. by in) to take great pleasure (in). ~n. **3.** extreme pleasure. **4.** something that causes this. [C13: from OF, from deleitier to please, from L dēlectāre, from dēlicere to allure, from DE- + lacere to entice] —de'lighted adj. —de'lightedly adv.

delightful (dɪ'laɪtfʊl) adj. giving great delight; very pleasing, beautiful, charming, etc. —de'lightfully adv. —de'lightfulness n.

Delilah (dɪ'laɪlə) n. **1.** Samson's Philistine mistress, who betrayed him (Judges 16). **2.** a voluptuous and treacherous woman; temptress.

delimit (diː'lɪmɪt) or **delimitate** vb. (tr.) to mark or prescribe the limits or boundaries of. —deˌlimi'tation n. —de'limitative adj.

delineate (dɪ'lɪnɪˌeɪt) vb. (tr.) **1.** to trace the outline of. **2.** to represent pictorially; depict. **3.** to portray in words; describe. [C16: from L dēlineāre to sketch out, from linea LINE¹] —deˌline'ation n. —de'lineative adj.

delinquency (dɪ'lɪŋkwənsɪ) n., pl. -cies. **1.** an offence or misdeed, esp. one committed by a young person. See **juvenile delinquency. 2.** failure or negligence in duty or obligation. **3.** a delinquent nature or delinquent behaviour. [C17: from LL dēlinquentia fault, offence, from L dēlinquere to transgress, from DE- + linquere to forsake]

delinquent (dɪ'lɪŋkwənt) n. **1.** someone, esp. a young person, guilty of delinquency. ~adj. **2.** guilty of an offence or misdeed. **3.** failing in or neglectful of duty or obligation. [C17: from L dēlinquēns offending; see DELINQUENCY]

deliquesce (ˌdɛlɪ'kwɛs) vb. (intr.) (esp. of certain salts) to dissolve gradually in water absorbed from the air. [C18: from L dēliquēscere, from DE- + liquēscere to melt, from liquēre to be liquid] —ˌdeli'quescence n. —ˌdeli'quescent adj.

delirious (dɪ'lɪrɪəs) adj. **1.** affected with delirium. **2.** wildly excited, esp. with joy or enthusiasm. —de'liriously adv.

delirium (dɪ'lɪrɪəm) n., pl. -liriums or -liria (-'lɪrɪə). **1.** a state of excitement and mental confusion, often accompanied by hallucinations, caused by high fever, poisoning,

brain injury, etc. **2.** violent excitement or emotion; frenzy. [C16: from L: madness, from dēlīrāre, lit.: to swerve from a furrow, hence to be crazy, from DE- + līra furrow]

delirium tremens ('trɛmɛnz, 'triː-) n. a severe psychotic condition occurring in some persons with chronic alcoholism, characterized by delirium, tremor, anxiety, and vivid hallucinations. Abbrevs.: **DT's** (informal), **dt.** [C19: NL, lit.: trembling delirium]

Delius ('diːlɪəs) n. **Frederick.** 1862–1934, English composer, who drew inspiration from folk tunes and the sounds of nature. His works include the opera A Village Romeo and Juliet (1901), A Mass of Life (1905), and the orchestral variations Brigg Fair (1907).

deliver (dɪ'lɪvə) vb. (mainly tr.) **1.** to carry to a destination, esp. to distribute (goods, mail, etc.) to several places. **2.** (often foll. by over or up) to hand over or transfer. **3.** (often foll. by from) to release or rescue (from captivity, harm, etc.). **a.** to aid in the birth of (offspring). **b.** to give birth to (offspring). **c.** (usually foll. by of) to aid (a female) in the birth (of offspring). **d.** (passive; foll. by of) to give birth (to offspring). **5.** to present (a speech, idea, etc.). **6.** to utter: to deliver a cry of exultation. **7.** to discharge or release (something, such as a blow or shot) suddenly. **8.** (intr.) Inf. Also: **deliver the goods.** to produce something promised or expected. **9.** Chiefly U.S. to cause (voters, etc.) to support a given candidate, cause, etc. **10. deliver oneself of.** to speak with deliberation or at length. [C13: from OF, from LL dēlīberāre to set free, from L DE- + līberāre to free] —de'liverable adj. —de'liverer n.

deliverance (dɪ'lɪvərəns) n. **1.** a formal expression of opinion. **2.** rescue from moral corruption or evil; salvation.

delivery (dɪ'lɪvərɪ) n., pl. -eries. **1. a.** the act of delivering or distributing goods, mail, etc. **b.** something that is delivered. **2.** the act of giving birth to a child. **3.** manner or style of utterance, esp. in public speaking: the chairman had a clear delivery. **4.** the act of giving or transferring or the state of being given or transferred. **5.** a rescuing or being rescued; liberation. **6.** Sport. the act or manner of bowling or throwing a ball. **7.** the handing over of property, a deed, etc.

dell (dɛl) n. a small, esp. wooded hollow. [OE]

Delmarva Peninsula (dɛl'mɑːvə) n. a peninsula of the northeast U.S., between Chesapeake Bay and the Atlantic.

Delorme (French dəlɔrm) or **de l'Orme** n. **Philibert** (filibɛr). ?1510–70, French Renaissance architect of the Tuileries, Paris.

Delos ('diːlɒs) n. a Greek island in the SW Aegean Sea, in the Cyclades: a commercial centre in ancient times; the legendary birthplace of Apollo and Artemis. Area: about 5 sq. km (2 sq. miles). Modern Greek name: **Dhílos.**

delouse (diː'laʊs, -'laʊz) vb. (tr.) to rid (a person or animal) of lice as a sanitary measure.

Delphi ('dɛlfɪ) n. an ancient Greek city on the S slopes of Mount Parnassus: site of the most famous oracle of Apollo.

Delphic ('dɛlfɪk) or **Delphian** adj. **1.** of or relating to the ancient Greek city of Delphi or its oracle or temple. **2.** obscure or ambiguous.

delphinium (dɛl'fɪnɪəm) n., pl. -iums or -ia (-ɪə). a plant with spikes of blue, pink, or white spurred flowers. See also **larkspur.** [C17: NL, from Gk delphinion larkspur, from delphis dolphin, referring to the shape of the nectary]

delta ('dɛltə) n. **1.** the fourth letter in the Greek alphabet (Δ or δ). **2.** (cap. when part of name) the flat alluvial area at the mouth of some rivers where the mainstream splits up into several distributaries. **3.** Maths. a finite increment in a variable. [C16: via L from Gk, of Semitic origin] —**deltaic** (dɛl'teɪɪk) or **'deltic** adj.

delta connection n. a connection used in a three-phase electrical system in which three elements in series form a triangle, the supply being input and output at the three junctions.

delta ray n. a particle, esp. an electron, ejected from matter by ionizing radiation.

delta rhythm or **wave** n. Physiol. the normal electrical activity of the cerebral cortex during deep sleep. See also **brain wave.**

delta wing *n.* a triangular swept-back aircraft wing.

deltiology (ˌdɛltɪˈɒlədʒɪ) *n.* the collection and study of postcards. [C20: from Gk *deltion*, dim. of *deltos* a writing tablet + -LOGY] —ˌdelti'ologist *n.*

deltoid ('dɛltɔɪd) *n.* a thick muscle of the shoulder that acts to raise the arm. [C18: from Gk *deltoeidēs* triangular, from DELTA]

delude (dɪ'luːd) *vb.* (*tr.*) to deceive; mislead; beguile. [C15: from L *dēlūdere* to mock, play false, from DE- + *lūdere* to play] —de'ludable *adj.* —de'luder *n.*

deluge ('dɛljuːdʒ) *n.* **1.** a great flood of water. **2.** torrential rain. **3.** an overwhelming rush or number. ~*vb.* (*tr.*) **4.** to flood. **5.** to overwhelm; inundate. [C14: from OF, from L *dīluvium*, from *dīluere* to wash away, drench, from *di-* DIS-¹ + -*luere*, from *lavere* to wash]

Deluge ('dɛljuːdʒ) *n.* **the.** another name for the **Flood**.

delusion (dɪ'luːʒən) *n.* **1.** a mistaken idea, belief, etc. **2.** *Psychiatry.* a belief held in the face of evidence to the contrary, that is resistant to all reason. **3.** a deluding or being deluded. —de'lusional *adj.* —de'lusive *adj.* —delusory (dɪ'luːsərɪ) *adj.*

de luxe (də 'lʌks, 'luks) *adj.* **1.** rich or sumptuous; superior in quality: *the de luxe model of a car.* ~*adv.* **2.** *Chiefly U.S.* in a luxurious manner. [C19: from F, lit.: of luxury]

delve (dɛlv) *vb.* (*mainly intr.; often foll. by in or into*) **1.** to research deeply or intensively (for information, etc.). **2.** to search or rummage. **3.** to dig or burrow deeply. **4.** (*also tr.*) *Arch. or Brit. dialect.* to dig. [OE *delfan*] —'delver *n.*

Dem. (in the U.S.) *abbrev. for* Democrat(ic).

demagnetize *or* -**ise** (diː'mægnəˌtaɪz) *vb.* to remove or lose magnetic properties. Also: **degauss.** —deˌmagnet·i'zation *or* -i'sation *n.* —de'magnetˌizer *or* -ˌiser *n.*

demagogue *or U.S.* (*sometimes*) **demagog** ('dɛməˌgɒg) *n.* **1.** a political agitator who appeals with crude oratory to the prejudice and passions of the mob. **2.** (esp. in the ancient world) any popular political leader or orator. [C17: from Gk *dēmagōgos* people's leader, from *dēmos* people + *agein* to lead] —ˌdema'gogic *adj.* —ˌdema'goguery *n.*

demagogy ('dɛməˌgɒgɪ) *n., pl.* -**gogies.** **1.** demagoguery. **2.** rule by a demagogue or by demagogues. **3.** a group of demagogues.

demand (dɪ'mɑːnd) *vb.* (*tr.; may take a clause as object or an infinitive*) **1.** to request peremptorily or urgently. **2.** to require as just, urgent, etc.: *the situation demands attention.* **3.** to claim as a right; exact. **4.** *Law.* to make a formal legal claim to (property). ~*n.* **5.** an urgent or peremptory requirement or request. **6.** something that requires special effort or sacrifice. **7.** the act of demanding something or the thing demanded. **8.** an insistent question. **9.** *Econ.* **a.** willingness and ability to purchase goods and services. **b.** the amount of a commodity that consumers are willing and able to purchase at a specified price. Cf. **supply**¹. **10.** *Law.* a formal legal claim, esp. to real property. **11. in demand.** sought after. **12. on demand.** as soon as requested. [C13: from Anglo-F, from Med. L *dēmandāre*, from L: to commit to, from DE- + *mandāre* to command, entrust] —de'mandable *adj.* —de'mander *n.*

demanding (dɪ'mɑːndɪŋ) *adj.* requiring great patience, skill, etc.: *a demanding job.*

demarcate ('diːmɑːˌkeɪt) *vb.* (*tr.*) **1.** to mark the boundaries, limits, etc., of. **2.** to separate; distinguish. —'demarˌcator *n.*

demarcation *or* **demarkation** (ˌdiːmɑː'keɪʃən) *n.* **1.** the act of establishing limits or boundaries. **2.** a limit or boundary. **3. a.** a strict separation of the kinds of work performed by members of different trade unions. **b.** (*as modifier*): *demarcation dispute.* **4.** separation or distinction (as in **line of demarcation**). [C18: from Sp. *demarcar* to appoint the boundaries of, from *marcar* to mark, from It., of Gmc origin]

démarche *French.* (demarʃ) *n.* a move, step, or manoeuvre, esp. in diplomatic affairs. [C17: lit.: walk, gait, from OF *demarcher* to tread, trample]

dematerialize *or* -**ise** (diːmə'tɪərɪəˌlaɪz) *vb.* (*intr.*) **1.** to cease to have material existence, as in science fiction or spiritualism. **2.** to vanish. —demaˌteriali'zation *or* -i'sation *n.*

Demavend ('dɛməvɛnd) *n.* **Mount.** a volcanic peak in N Iran, in the Elburz Mountains. Height: 5601 m (18 376 ft.).

deme (diːm) *n.* **1.** (in ancient Attica) a geographical unit of local government. **2.** *Biol.* a group of individuals within a species that possess particular characteristics of cytology, genetics, etc. [C19: from Gk *dēmos* district in local government, the populace]

demean¹ (dɪ'miːn) *vb.* (*tr.*) to lower (oneself) in dignity, status, or character; humble; debase. [C17: see DE-, MEAN²]

demean² (dɪ'miːn) *vb.* (*tr.*) *Rare.* to behave or conduct (oneself). [C13: from OF, from DE- + *mener* to lead, from L *mināre* to drive (animals), from *mināri* to use threats]

demeanour *or U.S.* **demeanor** (dɪ'miːnə) *n.* **1.** the way a person behaves towards others. **2.** bearing or mien. [C15: see DEMEAN²]

dement (dɪ'mɛnt) *vb.* **1.** (*intr.*) to deteriorate mentally, esp. because of old age. **2.** (*tr.*) *Rare.* to drive mad; make insane. [C16: from LL *dēmentāre* to drive mad, from L DE- + *mēns* mind]

demented (dɪ'mɛntɪd) *adj.* mad; insane. —de'mentedly *adv.* —de'mentedness *n.*

dementia (dɪ'mɛnʃə, -ʃɪə) *n.* a state of serious mental deterioration, of organic or functional origin. [C19: from L: madness; see DEMENT]

dementia praecox ('priːkɒks) *n.* a former name for **schizophrenia.** [C19: NL, lit.: premature dementia]

demerara (ˌdɛmə'rɛərə, -'rɑːrə) *n.* brown crystallized cane sugar from the West Indies. [C19: after *Demerara*, a region of Guyana]

Demerara (ˌdɛmə'rɛərə, -'rɑːrə) *n.* **the.** a river in Guyana, rising in the central forest area and flowing north to the Atlantic at Georgetown. Length: 346 km (215 miles).

demerit (diː'mɛrɪt) *n.* **1.** something that deserves censure. **2.** *U.S. & Canad.* a mark given against a student, etc., for failure or misconduct. **3.** a fault. [C14 (orig.: worth, desert, ult.: something worthy of blame): from L *dēmerērī* to deserve] —de'meri'torious *adj.*

demersal (dɪ'mɜːs³l) *adj.* living or occurring in deep water or on the bottom of a sea or lake. [C19: from L *dēmersus* submerged (from *mergere* to dip) + -AL¹]

demesne (dɪ'meɪn, -'miːn) *n.* **1.** land surrounding a house or manor. **2.** *Property law.* the possession and use of one's own property or land. **3.** realm; domain. **4.** a region or district. [C14: from OF *demeine*; see DOMAIN]

Demeter (dɪ'miːtə) *n.* *Greek myth.* the goddess of agricultural fertility and protector of marriage and women. Roman counterpart: **Ceres.**

demi- *prefix.* **1.** half: *demirelief.* **2.** of less than full size, status, or rank: *demigod.* [via F from Med. L, from L *dīmīdius* half, from *dis-* apart + *medius* middle]

demigod ('dɛmɪˌgɒd) *n.* **1. a.** a being who is part mortal, part god. **b.** a lesser deity. **2.** a person with godlike attributes. [C16: translation of L *sēmideus*] —'demiˌgoddess *fem. n.*

demijohn ('dɛmɪˌdʒɒn) *n.* a large bottle with a short narrow neck, often encased in wickerwork. [C18: prob. from F *dame-jeanne*, from *dame* lady + *Jeanne* Jane]

demilitarize *or* -**ise** (diː'mɪlɪtəˌraɪz) *vb.* (*tr.*) **1.** to remove and prohibit any military presence or function in (an area): *demilitarized zone.* **2.** to free of military character, purpose, etc. —deˌmilitari'zation *or* -i'sation *n.*

De Mille (də 'mɪl) *n.* **Cecil B(lount).** 1881–1959, U.S. film producer and director.

demimondaine (ˌdɛmɪ'mɒndeɪn) *n.* a woman of the demimonde. [C19: from F]

demimonde (ˌdɛmɪ'mɒnd) *n.* **1.** (esp. in the 19th century) those women considered to be outside respectable society, esp. on account of sexual promiscuity. **2.** any group considered to be not wholly respectable. [C19: from F, lit.: half-world]

Demirel (*Turkish* dɛmɪ'rɛl) *n.* **Süleyman** (sylɛi'man). born 1924, Turkish statesman; prime minister of Turkey (1965–71; 1975–77; 1977; 1979–80).

demise (dɪ'maɪz) *n.* **1.** failure or termination. **2.** a euphemistic or formal word for **death.** **3.** *Property law.* a transfer of an estate by lease or on the death of the owner. **4.** the transfer of sovereignty to a successor upon the death, abdication, etc., of a ruler (esp. in **demise of the crown**). ~*vb.* **5.** to transfer or be transferred by inheritance, will, or succession. **6.** (*tr.*) *Property law.* to transfer for a limited period; lease. **7.** (*tr.*) to transfer (sovereignty, a title, etc.). [C16: from OF, fem. of *demis* dismissed, from *demettre* to send away, from L *dīmittere*] —de'misable *adj.*

demisemiquaver ('dɛmɪ,sɛmɪ,kweɪvə) n. Music. a note having the time value of one thirty-second of a semibreve. Usual U.S. and Canad. name: **thirty-second note.**

demist (di:'mɪst) vb. to free or become free of condensation. —**de'mister** n.

demitasse ('dɛmɪ,tæs) n. 1. a small cup for serving black coffee, as after dinner. 2. the coffee itself. [C19: F, lit.: half-cup]

demiurge ('dɛmɪ,ɜ:dʒ) n. 1. (in the philosophy of Plato) the creator of the universe. 2. (in Gnostic philosophy) the creator of the universe, supernatural but subordinate to the Supreme Being. [C17: from Church L, from Gk *dēmiourgos* skilled workman, lit.: one who works for the people, from *dēmos* people + *ergon* work] —,demi'ur- gic or ,demi'urgical adj.

demo ('dɛməʊ) n., pl. -os. Inf. 1. short for **demonstra- tion** (sense 5). 2. a demonstration record or tape.

demo- or before a vowel **dem-** combining form. indicat- ing people or population: *demography*. [from Gk *dēmos*]

demob (di:'mɒb) Brit. inf. ~vb. -mobbing, -mobbed. 1. to demobilize. ~n. 2. demobilization.

demobilize or **-ise** (di:'məʊbɪ,laɪz) vb. to disband, as troops, etc. —**de,mobili'zation** or **-i'sation** n.

democracy (dɪ'mɒkrəsɪ) n., pl. **-cies.** 1. government by the people or their elected representatives. 2. a political or social unit governed ultimately by all its members. 3. the practice or spirit of social equality. 4. a social condi- tion of classlessness and equality. [C16: from F, from LL, from Gk *dēmokratia* government by the people]

democrat ('dɛmə,kræt) n. 1. an advocate of democracy. 2. a member or supporter of a democratic party or move- ment.

Democrat ('dɛmə,kræt) n. Politics. 1. Brit. a member or supporter of the Social and Liberal Democratic Party. 2. U.S. a member or supporter of the Democratic Party. —,Demo'cratic adj.

democratic (,dɛmə'krætɪk) adj. 1. of or relating to the principles of democracy. 2. upholding democracy or the interests of the common people. 3. popular with or for the benefit of all. —,demo'cratically adv.

democratize or **-ise** (dɪ'mɒkrə,taɪz) vb. (tr.) to make democratic. —**de,mocrati'zation** or **-i'sation** n.

Democritus (dɪ'mɒkrɪtəs) n. ?460–?370 B.C., Greek phi- losopher who developed the atomist theory of matter of his teacher, Leucippus. See also **atomism.**

démodé French. (demɔde) adj. outmoded. [F, from dé- out of + mode fashion]

demodulate (di:'mɒdjʊ,leɪt) vb. to carry out demodula- tion on. —**de'modu,lator** n.

demodulation (,di:mɒdjʊ'leɪʃən) n. Electronics. the act or process by which an output wave or signal is obtained having the characteristics of the original modulating wave or signal; the reverse of modulation.

Demogorgon (,di:məʊ'gɔ:gən) n. a mysterious and awe- some god in ancient mythology, often represented as rul- ing in the underworld. [C16: via LL from Gk]

demography (dɪ'mɒgrəfɪ) n. the scientific study of human populations, esp. with references to their size, dis- tribution, etc. [C19: from F, from Gk *dēmos* the populace; see -GRAPHY] —**de'mographer** n. —**demographic** (,di:mə'græfɪk, ,dɛmə-) adj.

demoiselle (dəmwɑ:'zɛl) n. 1. a small crane of central Asia, N Africa, and SE Europe, having a grey plumage with black breast feathers and white ear tufts. 2. a less com- mon name for a **damselfly.** 3. a literary word for **dam- sel.** [C16: from F: young woman; see DAMSEL]

demolish (dɪ'mɒlɪʃ) vb. (tr.) 1. to tear down or break up (buildings, etc.). 2. to put an end to (an argument, etc.). 3. Facetious. to eat up. [C16: from F, from L *dēmōlīrī* to throw down, from DE- + *mōlīrī* to construct, from *mōles* mass] —**de'molisher** n.

demolition (,dɛmə'lɪʃən, ,di:-) n. 1. a demolishing or be- ing demolished. 2. Chiefly mil. destruction by explo- sives. —,demo'litionist n., adj.

demon ('di:mən) n. 1. an evil spirit or devil. 2. a person, obsession, etc., thought of as evil or cruel. 3. Also called: **daemon, daimon.** an attendant or ministering spirit; ge- nius: *the demon of inspiration*. 4. a. a person extremely skilful in or devoted to a given activity, esp. a sport: *a de- mon at cycling*. b. (as modifier): *a demon cyclist*. 5. a variant spelling of **daemon** (sense 1). 6. Austral. & N.Z. sl. a detective or policeman, esp. one in plain clothes.

[C15: from L *daemōn* (evil) spirit, from Gk *daimōn* spirit, deity, fate] —**demonic** (dɪ'mɒnɪk) adj.

demonetize or **-ise** (di:'mʌnɪ,taɪz) vb. (tr.) 1. to deprive (a metal) of its capacity as a monetary standard. 2. to withdraw from use as currency. —**de,moneti'zation** or -i'sation n.

demoniac (dɪ'məʊnɪ,æk) adj. also **demoniacal** (,di:mə'naɪəkᵊl). 1. of or like a demon. 2. suggesting in- ner possession or inspiration: *the demoniac fire of ge- nius*. 3. frantic; frenzied. ~n. 4. a person possessed by a demon. —,demo'niacally adv.

demonism ('di:mə,nɪzəm) n. belief in the existence and power of demons. —'demonist n.

demonolatry (,di:mə'nɒlətrɪ) n. the worship of demons. [C17: see DEMON, -LATRY]

demonology (,di:mə'nɒlədʒɪ) n. the study of demons or demonic beliefs. Also called: **demonism.** —,demon'olo- gist n.

demonstrable ('dɛmənstrəbᵊl, dɪ'mɒn-) adj. able to be demonstrated or proved. —,demonstra'bility n. —'de- monstrably adv.

demonstrate ('dɛmən,streɪt) vb. 1. (tr.) to show or prove, esp. by reasoning, evidence, etc. 2. (tr.) to evince; reveal the existence of. 3. (tr.) to explain by experiment, example, etc. 4. (tr.) to display and explain the workings of (a machine, product, etc.). 5. (intr.) to manifest sup- port, protest, etc., by public parades or rallies. 6. (intr.) to be employed as a demonstrator of machinery, etc. 7. (intr.) Mil. to make a show of force. [C16: from L *dēmon- strāre* to point out, from *monstrāre* to show]

demonstration (,dɛmən'streɪʃən) n. 1. the act of dem- onstrating. 2. proof or evidence leading to proof. 3. an explanation, illustration, or experiment showing how something works. 4. a manifestation of support or pro- test by public rallies, parades, etc. 5. a manifestation of emotion. 6. a show of military force. —,demon- 'strational adj. —,demon'strationist n.

demonstration model n. a nearly new product, such as a car or washing machine, that has been used only to demonstrate its performance by a dealer and is offered for sale at a discount.

demonstrative (dɪ'mɒnstrətɪv) adj. 1. tending to ex- press one's feelings easily or unreservedly. 2. (postposi- tive; foll. by of) serving as proof; indicative. 3. involving or characterized by demonstration. 4. conclusive. 5. Grammar. denoting or belonging to a class of determin- ers used to point out the individual referent or referents intended, such as *this* and *those*. Cf. **interrogative, rela- tive.** ~n. 6. Grammar. a demonstrative word. —de'monstratively adv. —de'monstrativeness n.

demonstrator ('dɛmən,streɪtə) n. 1. a person who dem- onstrates equipment, machines, products, etc. 2. a per- son who takes part in a public demonstration.

demoralize or **-ise** (dɪ'mɒrə,laɪz) vb. (tr.) 1. to under- mine the morale of; dishearten. 2. to corrupt. 3. to throw into confusion. —**de,morali'zation** or -i'sation n.

Demosthenes (dɪ'mɒsθə,ni:z) n. 384–322 B.C., Athenian statesman, orator, and lifelong opponent of the power of Macedonia over Greece.

demote (dɪ'məʊt) vb. (tr.) to lower in rank or position; relegate. [C19: from DE- + (PRO)MOTE] —**de'motion** n.

demotic (dɪ'mɒtɪk) adj. 1. of or relating to the common people; popular. 2. of or relating to a simplified form of hieroglyphics used in ancient Egypt. Cf. **hieratic.** ~n. 3. the demotic script of ancient Egypt. [C19: from Gk *dēmo- tikos* of the people, from *dēmotēs* a man of the people, commoner] —**de'motist** n.

Dempsey ('dɛmpsɪ) n. Jack. real name *William Harri- son Dempsey*. 1895–1983, U.S. boxer; world heavyweight champion (1919–26).

dempster ('dɛmpstə) n. a variant spelling of **deemster.**

demulcent (dɪ'mʌlsᵊnt) adj. 1. soothing. ~n. 2. a drug or agent that soothes irritation. [C18: from L *dēmulcēre*, from DE- + *mulcēre* to stroke]

demur (dɪ'mɜ:) vb. -murring, -murred. (intr.) 1. to show reluctance; object. 2. Law. to raise an objection by entering a demurrer. ~n. also **demurral** (dɪ'mʌrəl). 3. the act of demurring. 4. an objection raised. [C13: from OF, from L *dēmorārī*, from *morārī* to delay] —**de'mur- rable** adj.

demure (dɪ'mjʊə) adj. 1. sedate; decorous; reserved. 2. affectedly modest or prim; coy. [C14: ?from OF *demorer*

to delay, linger; ? infl. by *meur* ripe, MATURE] —**de'murely**
adv. —**de'mureness** *n.*

demurrage (dɪ'mʌrɪdʒ) *n.* **1.** the delaying of a ship, etc.,
caused by the charterer's failure to load, unload, etc.,
before the time of scheduled departure. **2.** the extra
charge required for such delay. [C14: from OF *demorage,*
demourage; see DEMUR]

demurrer (dɪ'mʌrə) *n.* **1.** *Law.* a pleading that admits an
opponent's point but denies that it is relevant or valid. **2.**
any objection raised.

demy (dɪ'maɪ) *n., pl.* **-mies. 1.** a size of printing paper,
17½ by 22½ inches (444.5 × 571.5 mm). **2.** a size of writing paper, 15½ by 20 inches (Brit.) (393.7 × 508 mm) or 16
by 21 inches (U.S.) (406.4 × 533.4 mm). [C16: see DEMI-]

demystify (diː'mɪstɪ,faɪ) *vb.* **-fying, -fied.** (*tr.*) to remove
the mystery from; make clear. —**de,mystifi'cation** *n.*

demythologize *or* **-ise** (,diːmɪ'θɒlə,dʒaɪz) *vb.* (*tr.*) **1.** to
eliminate mythical elements from (a piece of writing, esp.
the Bible). **2.** to restate (a religious message) in rational
terms.

den (dɛn) *n.* **1.** the habitat or retreat of a wild animal; lair.
2. a small or secluded room in a home, often used for carrying on a hobby. **3.** a squalid room or retreat. **4.** a site
or haunt: *a den of vice.* **5.** *Scot.* a small wooded valley.
~*vb.* **denning, denned. 6.** (*intr.*) to live in or as if in a
den. [OE *denn*]

Den. *abbrev. for* Denmark.

denarius (dɪ'nɛərɪəs) *n., pl.* **-narii** (-'nɛərɪ,aɪ). **1.** a silver
coin of ancient Rome, often called a penny in translation.
2. a gold coin worth 25 silver denarii. [C16: from L: coin
orig. equal to ten asses, from *dēnārius* (adj.) containing
ten, from *decem* ten]

denary ('diːnərɪ) *adj.* **1.** calculated by tens; decimal. **2.**
containing ten parts; tenfold. [C16: from L *dēnārius;* see
DENARIUS]

denationalize *or* **-ise** (diː'næʃən³,laɪz) *vb.* **1.** to transfer
(an industry, etc.) from public to private ownership. **2.** to
deprive of national character or nationality. —**de,nation-
ali'zation** *or* **-i'sation** *n.*

denaturalize *or* **-ise** (diː'nætʃrə,laɪz) *vb.* (*tr.*) **1.** to deprive of nationality. **2.** to make unnatural. —**de,natural-
i'zation** *or* **-i'sation** *n.*

denature (diː'neɪtʃə) *or* **denaturize, -ise** (diː-
'neɪtʃə,raɪz) *vb.* (*tr.*) **1.** to change the nature of. **2.** to
change the properties of (a protein), as by the action of
acid or heat. **3.** to render (something, such as alcohol)
unfit for consumption by adding nauseous substances. **4.**
to render (fissile material) unfit for use in nuclear weapons by addition of an isotope. —**de'naturant** *n.* —**de,na-
tur'ation** *n.*

Denbighshire ('dɛnbɪ,ʃɪə, -ʃə) *n.* (until 1974) a county of
N Wales, now part of Clwyd and Gwynedd.

Den Bosch (dən bɔs) *n.* another name for **'s
Hertogenbosch.**

Dench (dɛntʃ) *n.* Dame **Judi (Olivia).** born 1934, British
actress.

dendrite ('dɛndraɪt) *n.* **1.** any of the branched extensions
of a nerve cell, which conduct impulses towards the cell
body. **2.** a branching mosslike crystalline structure in
some rocks and minerals. **3.** a crystal that has branched
during growth. [C18: from Gk *dendritēs* relating to a tree]
—**dendritic** (dɛn'drɪtɪk) *adj.*

dendro-, dendri-, *or before a vowel* **dendr-** *combining
form.* tree: *dendrochronology.* [NL, from Gk, from *dendron* tree]

dendrochronology (,dɛndrəʊkrə'nɒlədʒɪ) *n.* the study
of the annual rings of trees, used esp. to date past events.

dendrology (dɛn'drɒlədʒɪ) *n.* the branch of botany that is
concerned with the natural history of trees. —**dendro-
logical** (,dɛndrə'lɒdʒɪk³l) *or* ,**dendro'logic** *adj.*
—**den'drologist** *n.*

dene[1] *or* **dean** (diːn) *n. Brit.* a narrow wooded valley. [OE
denu valley]

dene[2] *or* **dean** (diːn) *n. Dialect, chiefly southern English.*
a sandy stretch of land or dune near the sea. [C13: prob.
rel. to OE *dūn* hill]

dengue ('dɛŋgɪ) *or* **dandy** ('dændɪ) *n.* an acute viral disease transmitted by mosquitoes, characterized by headache, fever, pains in the joints, and skin rash. [C19: from
Sp., prob. of African origin]

Deng Xiaoping ('dəŋ 'sjaʊpɪŋ) *or* **Teng Hsiao-ping** *n.*
born 1904, Chinese Communist statesman; deputy prime

minister of China (1973–76; 1977–80), having been rehabilitated following his dismissal for the second time in
1976. A moderate and a pragmatist, he was first removed
from office in 1967, during the Cultural Revolution, and
was temporarily rehabilitated in 1973.

Den Haag (dɛn 'haːx) *n.* the Dutch name for (The)
Hague.

Den Helder (*Dutch* dɛn 'hɛldər) *n.* a port in the W Netherlands, in North Holland province: fortified by Napoleon in
1811; naval station. Pop.: 62 943 (1987).

deniable (dɪ'naɪəb³l) *adj.* able to be denied; questionable.
—**de'niably** *adv.*

denial (dɪ'naɪəl) *n.* **1.** a refusal to agree or comply with a
statement. **2.** the rejection of the truth of a proposition,
doctrine, etc. **3.** a rejection of a request. **4.** a refusal to
acknowledge; disavowal. **5.** abstinence; self-denial.

denier[1] *n.* **1.** ('dɛnɪ,eɪ, 'dɛnjə). a unit of weight used to
measure the fineness of silk and man-made fibres, esp.
when woven into women's tights, etc. **2.** (də'njeɪ, -'nɪə).
any of several former European coins of various denominations. [C15: from OF: coin, from L *dēnārius* DENARIUS]

denier[2] (dɪ'naɪə) *n.* a person who denies.

denigrate ('dɛnɪ,greɪt) *vb.* (*tr.*) to belittle or disparage the
character of; defame. [C16: from L *dēnigrāre* to make very
black, from *nigrāre,* from *niger* black] —,**deni'gration**
n. —'**deni,grator** *n.*

denim ('dɛnɪm) *n.* **1.** a hard-wearing twill-weave cotton
fabric used for trousers, work clothes, etc. **2.** a similar
lighter fabric used in upholstery. [C17: from F (*serge*) *de
Nîmes* (serge) of Nîmes, in S France]

denims ('dɛnɪmz) *pl. n.* jeans or overalls made of denim.

De Niro (də'nɪərəʊ) *n.* **Robert.** born 1943, U.S. film actor.
His films include *The Deer Hunter* (1978) and *Raging Bull*
(1980).

Denis ('dɛnɪs; *French* dəni) *n.* **1. Maurice** (mɔris). 1870–
1943, French painter and writer on art. One of the leading
Nabis, he defined a picture as "essentially a flat surface
covered with colours assembled in a certain order." **2.
Saint.** Also: **Denys.** 3rd century A.D., first bishop of Paris;
patron saint of France. Feast day: Oct. 9.

denizen ('dɛnɪzən) *n.* **1.** an inhabitant; resident. **2.** *Brit.*
an individual permanently resident in a foreign country
where he enjoys certain rights of citizenship. **3.** a plant or
animal established in a place to which it is not native. **4.**
a naturalized foreign word. [C15: from Anglo-F *denisein,*
from OF *denzein,* from *denz* within, from L *de intus* from
within]

Denmark ('dɛnmɑːk) *n.* a kingdom in N Europe, between
the Baltic and the North Sea: consists of the mainland of
Jutland and about 100 inhabited islands (chiefly Zealand,
Lolland, Funen, Falster, Langeland, and Bornholm); ex-
tended its territory throughout the Middle Ages, ruling
Sweden until 1523 and Norway until 1814, and incorporat-
ing Greenland as a province in 1953; joined the Common
Market in 1973; an important exporter of dairy produce.
Language: Danish. Religion: chiefly Lutheran. Currency:
krone. Capital: Copenhagen. Pop.: 5 082 000 (1988 est.).
Area: 43 031 sq. km (16 614 sq. miles). Danish name:
Danmark.

Denmark Strait *n.* a channel between SE Greenland and
Iceland, linking the Arctic Ocean with the Atlantic.

Denning ('dɛnɪŋ) *n.* Baron **Alfred Thompson.** born 1899,
English judge; Master of the Rolls 1962–82.

Dennis ('dɛnɪs) *n.* **C(larence) J(ames).** 1876–1938, the
poet of the Australian larrikin, esp. in *The Songs of a Sentimental Bloke* (1915) and *The Moods of Ginger Mick*
(1916).

denominate *vb.* (dɪ'nɒmɪ,neɪt). **1.** (*tr.*) to give a specific
name to; designate. ~*adj.* (dɪ'nɒmɪnɪt, -,neɪt). **2.** *Maths.*
(of a number) representing a multiple of a unit of measurement: *4 is the denominate number in 4 miles.* [C16:
from L *denōminare* from DE- (intensive) + *nōminare* to
name]

denomination (dɪ,nɒmɪ'neɪʃən) *n.* **1.** a group having a
distinctive interpretation of a religious faith and usually
its own organization. **2.** a grade or unit in a series of designations of value, weight, measure, etc. **3.** a name given
to a class or group; classification. **4.** the act of giving a
name. **5.** a name; designation. —**de,nomi'national** *adj.*

denominative (dɪ'nɒmɪnətɪv) *adj.* **1.** giving or constituting a name. **2.** *Grammar.* **a.** formed from or having the
same form as a noun. **b.** (*as n.*): *the verb "to mushroom"
is a denominative.*

denominator (dɪ'nɒmɪ,neɪtə) n. the divisor of a fraction, as 8 in ⅞. Cf. **numerator**.

denotation (,di:nəʊ'teɪʃən) n. 1. a denoting; indication. 2. a particular meaning given by a sign or symbol. 3. specific meaning as distinguished from suggestive meaning and associations. 4. *Logic.* another word for **extension** (sense 10).

denote (dɪ'nəʊt) vb. (tr.; may take a clause as object) 1. to be a sign of; designate. 2. (of words, phrases, etc.) to have as a literal or obvious meaning. [C16: from L *dēnotāre* to mark, from *notāre* to mark, NOTE] —**de'notative** adj.

denouement (deɪ'nu:mɒn) or **dénouement** (French denumɑ̃) n. 1. the clarification or resolution of a plot in a play or other work. 2. final outcome; solution. [C18: from F, lit.: an untying, from OF *desnoer*, from *des-* DE- + *noer* to tie, from L *nōdus* a knot]

denounce (dɪ'naʊns) vb. (tr.) 1. to condemn openly or vehemently. 2. to give information against; accuse. 3. to announce formally the termination of (a treaty, etc.). [C13: from OF *denoncier*, from L *dēnuntiāre* to make an official proclamation, threaten, from DE- + *nuntiāre* to announce] —**de'nouncement** n. —**de'nouncer** n.

de novo Latin. (di: 'nəʊvəʊ) adv. from the beginning; anew.

dense (dɛns) adj. 1. thickly crowded or closely set. 2. thick; impenetrable. 3. *Physics.* having a high density. 4. stupid; dull. 5. (of a photographic negative) having many dark or exposed areas. [C15: from L *densus* thick] —**'densely** adv. —**'denseness** n.

densimeter (dɛn'sɪmɪtə) n. *Physics.* any instrument for measuring density. —**densimetric** (,dɛnsɪ'mɛtrɪk) adj. —**den'simetry** n.

density ('dɛnsɪtɪ) n., pl. **-ties.** 1. the degree to which something is filled or occupied: *high density of building in towns.* 2. stupidity. 3. a measure of the compactness of a substance, expressed as its mass per unit volume. Symbol: ρ. See also **relative density.** 4. a measure of a physical quantity per unit of length, area, or volume. 5. *Physics, photog.* a measure of the extent to which a substance or surface transmits or reflects light.

dent (dɛnt) n. 1. a hollow in a surface, as one made by pressure or a blow. 2. an appreciable effect, esp. of lessening: *a dent in our resources.* ~vb. to make a dent in. [C13 (in the sense: a stroke, blow): var. of DINT]

dental ('dɛntəl) adj. 1. of or relating to the teeth or dentistry. 2. *Phonetics.* pronounced with the tip of the tongue touching the backs of the upper teeth, as for *t* in French *tout.* ~n. 3. *Phonetics.* a dental consonant. [C16: from Med. L *dentālis*, from L *dēns* tooth]

dental floss n. a waxed thread used to remove food particles from between the teeth.

dental plaque n. a filmy deposit on the surface of a tooth consisting of a mixture of mucus, bacteria, food, etc.

dental surgeon n. another name for **dentist.**

dentate ('dɛnteɪt) adj. 1. having teeth or toothlike processes. 2. (of leaves) having a toothed margin. [C19: from L *dentātus*] —**'dentately** adv.

denti- or before a vowel **dent-** combining form. indicating a tooth: *dentine.* [from L *dēns, dent-*]

denticulate (dɛn'tɪkjʊlɪt, -,leɪt) adj. 1. *Biol.* very finely toothed: *denticulate leaves.* 2. *Arch.* having dentils. [C17: from L *denticulātus* having small teeth]

dentifrice ('dɛntɪfrɪs) n. any substance, esp. paste or powder, for use in cleaning the teeth. [C16: from L *dentifricium*, from *dent-, dens* tooth + *fricāre* to rub]

dentil ('dɛntɪl) n. one of a set of small square or rectangular blocks evenly spaced to form an ornamental row. [C17: from F, from obs. *dentille* a little tooth, from *dent* tooth]

dentine ('dɛnti:n) or **dentin** ('dɛntɪn) n. the calcified tissue comprising the bulk of a tooth. [C19: from DENTI- + -IN] —**'dentinal** adj.

dentist ('dɛntɪst) n. a person qualified to practise dentistry. [C18: from F *dentiste*, from *dent* tooth]

dentistry ('dɛntɪstrɪ) n. the branch of medical science concerned with the diagnosis and treatment of disorders of the teeth and gums.

dentition (dɛn'tɪʃən) n. 1. the arrangement, type, and number of the teeth in a particular species. 2. the time or process of teething. [C17: from L *dentītiō* a teething]

Denton ('dɛntən) n. a town in NW England, in Greater Manchester. Pop.: 37 729 (1981).

denture ('dɛntʃə) n. (usually pl.) 1. a partial or full set of artificial teeth. 2. *Rare.* a set of natural teeth. [C19: from F, from *dent* tooth + -URE]

denuclearize or **-ise** (dɪ'nju:klɪə,raɪz) vb. (tr.) to deprive (a state, etc.) of nuclear weapons. —**de,nucleari'zation** or **-i'sation** n.

denudate ('dɛnjʊ,deɪt, dɪ'nju:deɪt) vb. 1. a less common word for **denude.** ~adj. 2. denuded.

denude (dɪ'nju:d) vb. (tr.) 1. to make bare; strip. 2. to expose (rock) by the erosion of the layers above. —**denudation** (,dɛnjʊ'deɪʃən) n.

denumerable (dɪ'nju:mərəbəl) adj. *Maths.* capable of being put into a one-to-one correspondence with the positive integers; countable. —**de'numerably** adv.

denunciate (dɪ'nʌnsɪ,eɪt) vb. (tr.) to condemn; denounce. [C16: from L *dēnuntiāre*; see DENOUNCE] —**de'nunci,ator** n. —**de'nunciatory** adj.

denunciation (dɪ,nʌnsɪ'eɪʃən) n. 1. open condemnation; denouncing. 2. *Law, obsolete.* a charge or accusation of crime made before a public prosecutor or tribunal. 3. a formal announcement of the termination of a treaty.

Denver ('dɛnvə) n. a city in central Colorado: the state capital. Pop.: 492 365 (1980).

deny (dɪ'naɪ) vb. **-nying, -nied.** (tr.) 1. to declare (a statement, etc.) to be untrue. 2. to reject as false. 3. to withhold. 4. to refuse to fulfil the expectations of: *it is hard to deny a child.* 5. to refuse to acknowledge; disown. 6. to refuse (oneself) things desired. [C13: from OF *denier*, from L *dēnegāre*, from *negāre*]

Denys ('dɛnvə; French dəni) n. **Saint.** a variant spelling of (Saint) **Denis.**

deodar ('di:əʊ,dɑ:) n. 1. a Himalayan cedar with drooping branches. 2. the durable fragrant highly valued wood of this tree. [C19: from Hindi, from Sansk. *devadāru*, lit.: wood of the gods]

deodorant (di:'əʊdərənt) n. 1. a substance applied to the body to suppress or mask the odour of perspiration. 2. any substance for destroying or masking odours.

deodorize or **-ise** (di:'əʊdə,raɪz) vb. (tr.) to remove, disguise, or absorb the odour of, esp. when unpleasant. —**de,odori'zation** or **-i'sation** n. —**de'odor,izer** or **-,iser** n.

deontic (di:'ɒntɪk) adj. *Logic.* **a.** of such ethical concepts as obligation and permissibility. **b.** designating the branch of logic that deals with the formalization of these concepts. [C19: from Gk *deon* duty, from impersonal *dei* it behoves, it is binding] —**,deon'tology** n.

deoxidize or **-ise** (di:'ɒksɪ,daɪz) vb. 1. (tr.) to remove oxygen atoms from (a compound, molecule, etc.). 2. another word for **reduce** (sense 11). —**de,oxidi'zation** or **-i'sation** n. —**de'oxi,dizer** or **-iser** n.

deoxycorticosterone (di:,ɒksɪ,kɔ:tɪkəʊ'stɪərəʊn) or **deoxycortone** (di:,ɒksɪ'kɔ:təʊn) n. a corticosteroid hormone important in maintaining sodium and water balance in the body.

deoxygenate (di:'ɒksɪdʒɪ,neɪt) or **deoxygenize, -ise** (di:'ɒksɪdʒɪ,naɪz) vb. (tr.) to remove oxygen from. —**de,oxygen'ation** n.

deoxyribonucleic acid (di:,ɒksɪ,raɪbəʊnju:'kleɪɪk) or **desoxyribonucleic acid** n. the full name for **DNA.**

dep. abbrev. for: 1. department. 2. departure. 3. deposed. 4. deposit. 5. depot. 6. deputy.

depart (dɪ'pɑ:t) vb. (mainly intr.) 1. to leave. 2. to set forth. 3. (usually foll. by from) to differ; vary: *to depart from normal procedure.* 4. (tr.) to quit (arch., except in **depart this life**). [C13: from OF *departir*, from DE- + *partir* to go away, divide, from L *partīrī* to divide, distribute, from *pars* a part]

departed (dɪ'pɑ:tɪd) adj. *Euphemistic.* **a.** dead. **b.** (as sing. or collective n.; preceded by the): *the departed.*

department (dɪ'pɑ:tmənt) n. 1. a specialized division of a large concern, such as a business, store, or university. 2. a major subdivision of the administration of a government. 3. a branch of learning. 4. an administrative division in several countries, such as France. 5. *Inf.* a specialized sphere of skill or activity: *wine-making is my wife's department.* [C18: from F *département*, from *départir* to divide; see DEPART] —**departmental** (,di:pɑ:t'mɛntəl) adj.

departmentalize or **-ise** (,di:pɑ:t'mɛntə,laɪz) vb. (tr.) to organize into departments, esp. excessively. —**,department,mentali'zation** or **-i'sation** n.

department store *n.* a large shop divided into departments selling a great many kinds of goods.

departure (dɪ'pɑːtʃə) *n.* **1.** the act or an instance of departing. **2.** a variation from previous custom. **3.** a course of action, venture, etc.: *selling is a new departure for him.* **4.** *Naut.* the net distance travelled due east or west by a vessel. **5.** a euphemistic word for **death.**

depend (dɪ'pɛnd) *vb.* (*intr.*) **1.** (foll. by *on* or *upon*) to put trust (in); rely (on). **2.** (usually foll. by *on* or *upon*) to be influenced or determined (by); *it all depends on you.* **3.** (foll. by *on* or *upon*) to rely (on) for income, support, etc. **4.** (foll. by *from*) *Rare.* to hang down. **5.** to be undecided. [C15: from OF, from L *dēpendēre* to hang from, from DE- + *pendēre*]

dependable (dɪ'pɛndəbəl) *adj.* able to be depended on; reliable. —**de,penda'bility** *or* **de'pendableness** *n.* —**de'pendably** *adv.*

dependant (dɪ'pɛndənt) *n.* a person who depends on another person, organization, etc., for support, aid, or sustenance, esp. financial support.

dependence *or U.S.* (*sometimes*) **dependance** (dɪ'pɛndəns) *n.* **1.** the state or fact of being dependent, esp. for support or help. **2.** reliance; trust; confidence.

dependency *or U.S.* (*sometimes*) **dependancy** (dɪ'pɛndənsɪ) *n., pl.* **-cies.** **1.** a territory subject to a state on which it does not border. **2.** a dependent or subordinate person or thing. **3.** *Psychol.* overreliance on another person or on a drug, etc. **4.** another word for **dependence.**

dependent *or U.S.* (*sometimes*) **dependant** (dɪ'pɛndənt) *adj.* **1.** depending on a person or thing for aid, support, etc. **2.** (*postpositive*; foll. by *on* or *upon*) influenced or conditioned (by). **3.** subordinate; subject. **4.** *Obs.* hanging down. ~*n.* **5.** a variant spelling (esp. U.S.) of **dependant.** —**de'pendently** *adv.*

dependent clause *n. Grammar.* another term for **subordinate clause.**

dependent variable *n.* a variable in a mathematical equation or statement whose value depends on that taken on by the independent variable.

depersonalize *or* **-ise** (diː'pɜːsnə,laɪz) *vb.* (*tr.*) **1.** to deprive (a person, organization, etc.) of individual or personal qualities. **2.** to cause (someone) to lose his sense of identity. —**de,personali'zation** *or* **-i'sation** *n.*

depict (dɪ'pɪkt) *vb.* (*tr.*) **1.** to represent by drawing, sculpture, painting, etc. **2.** to represent in words; describe. [C17: from L *dēpingere*, from *pingere* to paint] —**de'picter** *or* **de'pictor** *n.* —**de'piction** *n.* —**de'pictive** *adj.*

depilate ('dɛpɪ,leɪt) *vb.* (*tr.*) to remove the hair from. [C16: from L *dēpilāre*, from *pilāre* to make bald, from *pilus* hair] —,**depi'lation** *n.* —'**depi,lator** *n.*

depilatory (dɪ'pɪlətərɪ, -trɪ) *adj.* **1.** able or serving to remove hair. ~*n., pl.* **-ries.** **2.** a chemical used to remove hair from the body.

deplane (diː'pleɪn) *vb.* (*intr.*) *Chiefly U.S. & Canad.* to disembark from an aeroplane. [C20: from DE- + PLANE[1]]

deplete (dɪ'pliːt) *vb.* (*tr.*) **1.** to use up (supplies, money, etc.); exhaust. **2.** to empty entirely or partially. [C19: from L *dēplēre* to empty out, from DE- + *plēre* to fill] —**de'pletion** *n.*

depletion layer *n.* a region at the interface between dissimilar zones of conductivity in a semiconductor, in which there are few charge carriers.

deplorable (dɪ'plɔːrəbəl) *adj.* **1.** lamentable. **2.** worthy of censure or reproach; very bad. —**de'plorably** *adv.*

deplore (dɪ'plɔː) *vb.* (*tr.*) **1.** to express or feel sorrow about. **2.** to express or feel strong disapproval of; censure. [C16: from OF, from L *dēplōrāre* to weep bitterly, from *plōrāre* to weep] —**de'ploringly** *adv.*

deploy (dɪ'plɔɪ) *vb. Chiefly mil.* **1.** to adopt or cause to adopt a battle formation. **2.** (*tr.*) to redistribute (forces) to or within a given area. [C18: from F, from L *displicāre* to unfold; see DISPLAY] —**de'ployment** *n.*

depolarize *or* **-ise** (diː'pəʊlə,raɪz) *vb.* to undergo or cause to undergo a loss of polarity or polarization. —**de,polari'zation** *or* **-i'sation** *n.*

deponent (dɪ'pəʊnənt) *adj.* **1.** *Grammar.* (of a verb, esp. in Latin) having the inflectional endings of a passive verb but the meaning of an active verb. ~*n.* **2.** *Grammar.* a deponent verb. **3.** *Law.* a person who makes an affidavit or a deposition. [C16: from L *dēpōnēns* putting aside, putting down, from *dēpōnere*]

depopulate (dɪ'pɒpjʊ,leɪt) *vb.* to be or cause to be reduced in population. —**de,popu'lation** *n.*

deport (dɪ'pɔːt) *vb.* (*tr.*) **1.** to remove forcibly from a country; expel. **2.** to conduct, hold, or behave (oneself) in a specified manner. [C15: from F, from L *dēportāre* to carry away, banish, from DE- + *portāre* to carry] —**de'portable** *adj.*

deportation (,diːpɔː'teɪʃən) *n.* the act of expelling someone from a country.

deportee (,diːpɔː'tiː) *n.* a person deported or awaiting deportation.

deportment (dɪ'pɔːtmənt) *n.* the manner in which a person behaves, esp. in physical bearing: *military deportment.* [C17: from F, from OF *deporter* to conduct (oneself); see DEPORT]

depose (dɪ'pəʊz) *vb.* **1.** (*tr.*) to remove from an office or position of power. **2.** *Law.* to testify or give (evidence, etc.) on oath. [C13: from OF: to put away, put down, from LL *dēpōnere* to depose from office, from L: to put aside]

deposit (dɪ'pɒzɪt) *vb.* (*tr.*) **1.** to put or set down, esp. carefully; place. **2.** to entrust for safekeeping. **3.** to place (money) in a bank or similar institution to earn interest or for safekeeping. **4.** to give (money) in part payment or as security. **5.** to lay down naturally: *the river deposits silt.* ~*n.* **6. a.** an instance of entrusting money or valuables to a bank or similar institution. **b.** the money or valuables so entrusted. **7.** money given in part payment or as security. **8.** an accumulation of sediments, minerals, coal, etc. **9.** any deposited material, such as a sediment. **10.** a depository or storehouse. **11. on deposit.** payable as the first instalment, as when buying on hire-purchase. [C17: from Med. L *dēpositāre*, from L *dēpositus* put down]

deposit account *n. Brit.* a bank account that earns interest and usually requires notice of withdrawal.

depositary (dɪ'pɒzɪtərɪ, -trɪ) *n., pl.* **-taries.** **1.** a person or group to whom something is entrusted for safety. **2.** a variant spelling of **depository.**

deposition (,dɛpə'zɪʃən) *n.* **1.** *Law.* **a.** the giving of testimony on oath. **b.** the testimony given. **c.** the sworn statement of a witness used in court in his absence. **2.** the act or instance of deposing. **3.** the act or an instance of depositing. **4.** something deposited. [C14: from LL *dēpositiō* a laying down, disposal, burying, testimony]

depositor (dɪ'pɒzɪtə) *n.* a person who places or has money on deposit, esp. in a bank.

depository (dɪ'pɒzɪtərɪ, -trɪ) *n., pl.* **-ries.** **1.** a store for furniture, valuables, etc.; repository. **2.** a variant spelling of **depositary.** [C17 (in the sense: place of a deposit): from Med. L *dēpositōrium;* C18 (in the sense: depositary): see DEPOSIT, -ORY[1]]

depot ('dɛpəʊ) *n.* **1.** a storehouse or warehouse. **2.** *Mil.* **a.** a store for supplies. **b.** a training and holding centre for recruits and replacements. **3.** *Chiefly Brit.* a building used for the storage and servicing of buses or railway engines. **4.** *U.S. & Canad.* a bus or railway station. [C18: from F *dépôt*, from L *dēpositum* a deposit, trust]

deprave (dɪ'preɪv) *vb.* (*tr.*) to make morally bad; corrupt. [C14: from L *dēprāvāre* to distort, corrupt, from DE- + *prāvus* crooked] —**depravation** (,dɛprə'veɪʃən) *n.* —**de'praved** *adj.*

depravity (dɪ'prævɪtɪ) *n., pl.* **-ties.** the state or instance of moral corruption.

deprecate ('dɛprɪ,keɪt) *vb.* (*tr.*) **1.** to express disapproval of; protest against. **2.** to deprecate; belittle. [C17: from L *dēprecārī* to avert, ward off by entreaty, from DE- + *precārī* to PRAY] —'**depre,cating** *adj.* —'**depre,catingly** *adv.* —,**depre'cation** *n.* —'**deprecative** *adj.* —'**depre,cator** *n.*

deprecatory ('dɛprɪkətərɪ) *adj.* **1.** expressing disapproval; protesting. **2.** expressing apology; apologetic. —'**deprecatorily** *adv.*

depreciate (dɪ'priːʃɪ,eɪt) *vb.* **1.** to reduce or decline in value or price. **2.** (*tr.*) to lessen the value by derision, criticism, etc. [C15: from LL *dēpretiāre* to lower the price of, from L DE- + *pretium* PRICE] —**de'preci,atingly** *adv.* —**depreciatory** (dɪ'priːʃɪətərɪ) *or* **de'preciative** *adj.*

depreciation (dɪ,priːʃɪ'eɪʃən) *n.* **1.** *Accounting.* **a.** the reduction in value of a fixed asset due to use, obsolescence, etc. **b.** the amount deducted from gross profit to allow for this. **2.** the act or an instance of depreciating or belittling. **3.** a decrease in the exchange value of a currency brought about by excess supply of that currency under conditions of fluctuating exchange rates.

depredation (ˌdɛprɪ'deɪʃən) n. the act or an instance of plundering; robbery; pillage.

depress (dɪ'prɛs) vb. (tr.) **1.** to lower in spirits; make gloomy. **2.** to weaken the force, or energy of. **3.** to lower prices of. **4.** to press or push down. [C14: from OF *depresser*, from L *dēprimere* from DE- + *premere* to PRESS[1]] —**de'pressing** adj. —**de'pressingly** adv.

depressant (dɪ'prɛs°nt) adj. **1.** Med. able to reduce nervous or functional activity. **2.** causing gloom; depressing. ~n. **3.** a depressant drug.

depressed (dɪ'prɛst) adj. **1.** low in spirits; downcast. **2.** lower than the surrounding surface. **3.** pressed down or flattened. **4.** Also: **distressed.** characterized by economic hardship, such as unemployment: *a depressed area.* **5.** lowered in force, intensity, or amount. **6.** *Bot., zool.* flattened.

depression (dɪ'prɛʃən) n. **1.** a depressing or being depressed. **2.** a depressed or sunken place. **3.** a mental disorder characterized by feelings of gloom and inadequacy. **4.** *Pathol.* an abnormal lowering of the rate of any physiological activity or function. **5.** an economic condition characterized by substantial unemployment, low output and investment, etc.; slump. **6.** Also called: **cyclone, low.** *Meteorol.* a body of moving air below normal atmospheric pressure, which often brings rain. **7.** (esp. in surveying and astronomy) the angular distance of an object below the horizontal plane.

Depression (dɪ'prɛʃən) n. (usually preceded by *the*) the worldwide economic depression of the early 1930s, when there was mass unemployment.

depressive (dɪ'prɛsɪv) adj. **1.** tending to depress. **2.** *Psychol.* tending to be subject to periods of depression. —**de'pressively** adv.

depressor (dɪ'prɛsə) n. **1.** a person or thing that depresses. **2.** any muscle that draws down a part. **3.** any medical instrument used to press down or aside an organ or part.

depressurize or **-ise** (dɪ'prɛʃəˌraɪz) vb. (tr.) to reduce the pressure of a gas inside (a container or enclosed space), as in an aircraft cabin. —**de,pressuri'zation** or **-i'sation** n.

deprive (dɪ'praɪv) vb. (tr.) **1.** (foll. by *of*) to prevent from possessing or enjoying; dispossess (of). **2.** *Arch.* to depose; demote. [C14: from OF, from Med. L *dēprīvāre*, from L DE- + *prīvāre* to deprive of] —**de'prival** n. —**deprivation** (ˌdɛprɪ'veɪʃən) n.

deprived (dɪ'praɪvd) adj. lacking adequate food, shelter, education, etc.: *deprived inner-city areas.*

dept *abbrev. for* department.

depth (dɛpθ) n. **1.** the distance downwards, backwards, or inwards. **2.** the quality of being deep; deepness. **3.** intensity of emotion. **4.** profundity of moral character; sagacity; integrity. **5.** complexity or abstruseness, as of thought. **6.** intensity, as of silence, colour, etc. **7.** lowness of pitch. **8.** (*often pl.*) a deep, inner, or remote part, such as an inaccessible region of a country. **9.** (*often pl.*) the most intense or severe part: *the depths of winter.* **10.** (*usually pl.*) a low moral state. **11.** (*often pl.*) a vast space or abyss. **12.** **beyond** or **out of one's depth. a.** in water deeper than one is tall. **b.** beyond the range of one's competence or understanding. [C14: from *dep* DEEP + -TH[1]]

depth charge or **bomb** n. a bomb used to attack submarines that explodes at a preset depth of water.

depth of field n. the range of distance in front of and behind an object focused by an optical instrument, such as a camera or microscope, within which other objects will also appear clear and sharply defined in the resulting image.

depth psychology n. *Psychol.* the study of unconscious motives and attitudes.

depuration (ˌdɛpjʊ'reɪʃən) n. the act or process of eliminating impurities; self-purification. [C17: from F or Med. L, ult. from L *pūrus* pure]

deputation (ˌdɛpjʊ'teɪʃən) n. **1.** the act of appointing a person or body of people to represent others. **2.** a person or body of people so appointed; delegation.

depute vb. (dɪ'pjuːt). (tr.) **1.** to appoint as an agent. **2.** to assign (authority, duties, etc.) to a deputy. ~n. ('dɛpjuːt). **3.** *Scot.* **a.** a deputy. **b.** (*as modifier, usually postpositive*): *a sheriff-depute.* [C15: from OF, from LL *dēputāre* to assign, allot, from L DE-+ *putāre* to think, consider]

deputize or **-ise** ('dɛpjuːˌtaɪz) vb. to appoint or act as deputy.

deputy ('dɛpjʊtɪ) n., pl. **-ties. 1. a.** a person appointed to act on behalf of or represent another. **b.** (*as modifier*): *the deputy chairman.* **2.** a member of a legislative assembly in various countries, such as France. [C16: from OF, from *deputer* to appoint; see DEPUTE]

De Quincey (də 'kwɪnsɪ) n. **Thomas.** 1785–1859, English critic and essayist, noted particularly for his *Confessions of an English Opium Eater* (1821).

der. *abbrev. for:* **1.** derivation. **2.** derivative.

deracinate (dɪ'ræsɪˌneɪt) vb. (tr.) to pull up by or as if by the roots; uproot. [C16: from OF *desraciner*, from *des-* DIS[1] + *racine* root, from LL, from L *rādīx* a root] —**de,raci'nation** n.

derail (dɪ'reɪl) vb. to go or cause to go off the rails, as a train, tram, etc. —**de'railment** n.

Derain (*French* dərɛ̃) n. **André** (ɑ̃dre). 1880–1954, French painter, noted for his Fauvist pictures (1905–08).

derange (dɪ'reɪndʒ) vb. (tr.) **1.** to throw into disorder; disarrange. **2.** to disturb the action of. **3.** to make insane. [C18: from OF *desrengier*, from des- DIS[1] + *reng* row, order] —**de'rangement** n.

Derbent (*Russian* dɪr'bjɛnt) n. a port in the S Soviet Union, in the Dagestan ASSR on the Caspian Sea: founded by the Persians in the 6th century. Pop.: 76 000 (1983 est.).

derby ('dɜːrbɪ) n., pl. **-bies.** the U.S. and Canad. name for **bowler[2].**

Derby[1] ('dɑːbɪ; *U.S.* 'dɜːrbɪ) n., pl. **-bies. 1. the.** an annual horse race run at Epsom Downs, Surrey, since 1780. **2.** any of various other horse races. **3. local Derby.** a football match between two teams from the same area. [C18: after the twelfth Earl of *Derby* (died 1834), who founded the race in 1780]

Derby[2] ('dɑːbɪ) n. **1.** a city in central England, in Derbyshire: engineering industries (esp. aircraft engines and railway rolling stock). Pop.: 215 000 (1985 est.). **2.** a firm-textured pale-coloured type of cheese. **3. sage Derby.** a green-and-white Derby cheese flavoured with sage.

Derby[3] ('dɑːbɪ) n. **Earl of.** title of *Edward George Geoffrey Smith Stanley.* 1799–1869, British statesman; Conservative prime minister (1852; 1858–59; 1866–68).

Derbyshire ('dɑːbɪˌʃɪə, -ʃə) n. a county of N central England: contains the Peak District and several resorts with mineral springs. Administrative centre: Matlock. Pop.: 916 800 (1986 est.). Area: 2631 sq. km (1016 sq. miles).

deregulate (diː'rɛgjʊˌleɪt) vb. (tr.) to remove regulations or controls from. —**de,regu'lation** n.

derelict ('dɛrɪlɪkt) adj. **1.** deserted or abandoned, as by an owner, occupant, etc. **2.** falling into ruins. **3.** neglectful of duty; remiss. ~n. **4.** a social outcast or vagrant. **5.** property deserted or abandoned by an owner, occupant, etc. **6.** a vessel abandoned at sea. **7.** a person who is neglectful of duty. [C17: from L, from *dērelinquere* to abandon, from DE- + *relinquere* to leave]

dereliction (ˌdɛrɪ'lɪkʃən) n. **1.** conscious or wilful neglect (esp. in **dereliction of duty**). **2.** an abandoning or being abandoned. **3.** *Law.* accretion of dry land gained by the gradual receding of the sea.

derestrict (ˌdiːrɪ'strɪkt) vb. (tr.) to render or leave free from restriction, esp. a road from speed limits. —**de-re'striction** n.

deride (dɪ'raɪd) vb. (tr.) to speak of or treat with contempt or ridicule; scoff at. [C16: from L *dērīdēre* to laugh to scorn, from DE- + *rīdēre* to laugh, smile] —**de'rider** n. —**de'ridingly** adv.

de rigueur *French.* (də rigœr) adj. required by etiquette or fashion. [lit.: of strictness]

derision (dɪ'rɪʒən) n. the act of deriding; mockery; scorn. [C15: from LL *dērīsiō*, from L *dērīsus*; see DERIDE] —**de'risible** adj.

derisive (dɪ'raɪsɪv) adj. characterized by derision; mocking; scornful. —**de'risively** adv. —**de'risiveness** n.

derisory (dɪ'raɪsərɪ) adj. **1.** subject to or worthy of derision. **2.** another word for **derisive.**

deriv. *abbrev. for:* **1.** derivation. **2.** derivative. **3.** derived.

derivation (ˌdɛrɪ'veɪʃən) n. **1.** a deriving or being derived. **2.** the origin or descent of something, such as a word. **3.** something derived; a derivative. **4. a.** the process of deducing a mathematical theorem, formula, etc., as a necessary consequence of a set of accepted statements. **b.** this sequence of statements. —,deri'vational *adj.*

derivative (dɪ'rɪvətɪv) *adj.* **1.** derived. **2.** based on other sources; not original. ~*n.* **3.** a term, idea, etc., that is based on or derived from another in the same class. **4.** a word derived from another word. **5.** *Chem.* a compound that is formed from, or can be regarded as formed from, a structurally related compound. **6.** *Maths.* **a.** Also called: **differential coefficient, first derivative.** the change of a function, $f(x)$, with respect to an infinitesimally small change in the independent variable, x. **b.** the rate of change of one quantity with respect to another. —**de'rivatively** *adv.*

derive (dɪ'raɪv) *vb.* **1.** (usually foll. by *from*) to draw or be drawn (from) in source or origin. **2.** (*tr.*) to obtain by reasoning; deduce; infer. **3.** (*tr.*) to trace the source or development of. **4.** (usually foll. by *from*) to produce or be produced (from) by a chemical reaction. [C14: from OF: to spring from, from L *dērīvāre* to draw off, from DE- + *rivus* a stream] —**de'rivable** *adj.* —**de'river** *n.*

derived unit *n.* a unit of measurement obtained by multiplication or division of the base units of a system without the introduction of numerical factors.

-derm *n. combining form.* indicating skin: *endoderm.* [via F from Gk *derma* skin]

derma ('dɜːmə) *n.* another name for **corium.** Also: **derm.** [C18: NL, from Gk: skin]

dermal ('dɜːməl) *adj.* of or relating to the skin.

dermatitis (,dɜːmə'taɪtɪs) *n.* inflammation of the skin.

dermato-, derma- *or before a vowel* **dermat-, derm-** *combining form.* indicating skin: *dermatitis.* [from Gk *derma* skin]

dermatology (,dɜːmə'tɒlədʒɪ) *n.* the branch of medicine concerned with the skin and its diseases. —**dermatological** (,dɜːmətə'lɒdʒɪkəl) *adj.* —,**derma'tologist** *n.*

dermis ('dɜːmɪs) *n.* another name for **corium.** [C19: NL, from EPIDERMIS] —'**dermic** *adj.*

dernier cri *French.* (dɛrnje kri) *n.* **le** (lə). the latest fashion; the last word. [lit.: last cry]

derogate ('dɛrə,geɪt) *vb.* **1.** (*intr.;* foll. by *from*) to cause to seem inferior; detract. **2.** (*intr.;* foll. by *from*) to deviate in standard or quality. **3.** (*tr.*) to cause to seem inferior, etc.; disparage. **4.** (*tr.*) to curtail the application of (a law or regulation). [C15: from L *dērogāre* to repeal some part of a law, modify it, from DE- + *rogāre* to ask, propose a law] —,**dero'gation** *n.* —**derogative** (dɪ'rɒgətɪv) *adj.*

derogatory (dɪ'rɒgətərɪ) *adj.* tending or intended to detract, disparage, or belittle; intentionally offensive. —**de'rogatorily** *adv.*

derrick ('dɛrɪk) *n.* **1.** a simple crane having lifting tackle slung from a boom. **2.** the framework erected over an oil well to enable drill tubes to be raised and lowered. [C17 (in the sense: gallows): from *Derrick,* celebrated hangman at Tyburn, London]

derrière (,dɛrɪ'ɛə) *n.* a euphemistic word for **buttocks.** [C18: lit.: behind (prep.), from OF *deriere,* from L *dē retrō* from the back]

derring-do ('dɛrɪŋ'duː) *n. Arch. or literary.* boldness or bold action. [C16: from ME *durring don* daring to do, from *durren* to dare + *don* to do]

derringer *or* **deringer** ('dɛrɪndʒə) *n.* a short-barrelled pocket pistol of large calibre. [C19: after Henry *Deringer,* U.S. gunsmith, who invented it]

derris ('dɛrɪs) *n.* **1.** an East Indian woody climbing plant. **2.** an insecticide made from its powdered roots. [C19: NL, from Gk: covering, leather, from *deros* skin, hide, from *derein* to skin]

Derry ('dɛrɪ) *n.* another name for **Londonderry.**

derv (dɜːv) *n.* a Brit. name for **diesel oil** when used for road transport. [C20: from *d(iesel) e(ngine) r(oad) v(ehicle)*]

dervish ('dɜːvɪʃ) *n.* a member of any of various Muslim orders of ascetics, some of which (**whirling dervishes**) are noted for a frenzied, ecstatic, whirling dance. [C16: from Turkish: beggar, from Persian *darvīsh* mendicant monk]

Derwent ('dɜːwənt) *n.* **1.** a river in S Australia, in S Tasmania, flowing southeast to the Tasman Sea. Length: 172 km (107 miles). **2.** a river in N central England, in N Derbyshire, flowing southeast to the River Trent. Length: 96 km (60 miles). **3.** a river in N England, in Yorkshire, rising on the North York Moors and flowing south to the River

Ouse. Length: 92 km (57 miles). **4.** a river in NW England, in Cumbria, rising on the Borrowdale Fells and flowing north and west to the Irish Sea. Length: 54 km (34 miles).

Derwentwater ('dɜːwənt,wɔːtə) *n.* a lake in NW England, in Cumbria in the Lake District. Area: about 8 sq. km (3 sq. miles).

DES (in Britain) *abbrev. for* Department of Education and Science.

Desai (dɛ'saɪ) *n.* **Morarji (Ranchhodji)** (mə'rɑːdʒɪ). born 1896, Indian statesman, noted for his asceticism. He founded the Janata party in opposition to Indira Gandhi, whom he defeated in the 1977 election; prime minister of India (1977–79).

desalination (diː,sælɪ'neɪʃən) *or* **desalinization, -isation** *n.* the process of removing salt, esp. from sea water.

descant ('dɛskænt) *n.* **1.** Also called: **discant.** a decorative counterpoint added above a basic melody. **2.** a comment or discourse. ~*adj.* **3.** Also: **discant.** of the highest member in common use in a family of musical instruments: *a descant recorder.* ~*vb.* (*intr.*) **4.** Also: **discant.** (often foll. by *on* or *upon*) to perform a descant. **5.** (often foll. by *on* or *upon*) to discourse or make comments. **6.** *Arch.* to sing sweetly. [C14: from OF, from Med. L *discanthus,* from L DIS-¹ + *cantus* song] —**des'canter** *n.*

Descartes ('deɪ,kɑːt; *French* dekart) *n.* **René** (rəne). 1596–1650, French philosopher and mathematician. He provided a mechanistic basis for the philosophical theory of dualism and is regarded as the founder of modern philosophy. He also founded analytic geometry and contributed greatly to the science of optics. His works include *Discours de la méthode* (1637), *Meditationes de Prima Philosophia* (1641), and *Principia Philosophiae* (1644). Related adj.: **Cartesian.**

descend (dɪ'sɛnd) *vb.* (*mainly intr.*) **1.** (*also tr.*) to move down (a slope, staircase, etc.) **2.** to lead or extend down; slope. **3.** to move to a lower level, pitch, etc.; fall. **4.** (often foll. by *from*) to be connected by a blood relationship (to a dead or extinct individual, species, etc.). **5.** to be inherited. **6.** to sink or come down in morals or behaviour. **7.** (often foll. by *on* or *upon*) to arrive or attack in a sudden or overwhelming way. **8.** (of the sun, moon, etc.) to move towards the horizon. [C13: from OF, from L *dēscendere,* from DE- + *scandere* to climb] —**de'scendable** *or* **des'cendible** *adj.*

descendant (dɪ'sɛndənt) *n.* **1.** a person, animal, or plant when described as descended from an individual, race, species, etc. **2.** something that derives from an earlier form. ~*adj.* **3.** a variant spelling of **descendent.**

descendent (dɪ'sɛndənt) *adj.* descending.

descender (dɪ'sɛndə) *n.* **1.** a person or thing that descends. **2.** *Printing.* the portion of a letter, such as j, p, or y, below the level of the line.

descent (dɪ'sɛnt) *n.* **1.** the act of descending. **2.** a downward slope. **3.** a path or way leading downwards. **4.** derivation from an ancestor; lineage. **5.** a generation in a particular lineage. **6.** a decline or degeneration. **7.** a movement or passage in degree or state from higher to lower. **8.** (often foll. by *on*) a sudden and overwhelming arrival or attack. **9.** *Property law.* (formerly) the transmission of real property to the heir.

Deschamps (*French* deʃɑ̃) *n.* **Eustache** (østaʃ). ?1346–?1406, French poet, noted for his *Miroir de mariage,* a satirical attack on women.

deschool (,diː'skuːl) *vb.* (*tr.*) to separate education from the institution of school and operate through the pupil's life experience as opposed to a set curriculum.

describe (dɪ'skraɪb) *vb.* (*tr.*) **1.** to give an account or representation of in words. **2.** to pronounce or label. **3.** to draw a line or figure, such as a circle. [C15: from L *dēscrībere* to copy off, write out, from DE- + *scribere* to write] —**de'scribable** *adj.* —**de'scriber** *n.*

description (dɪ'skrɪpʃən) *n.* **1.** a statement or account that describes. **2.** the act, process, or technique of describing. **3.** sort or variety: *reptiles of every description.*

descriptive (dɪ'skrɪptɪv) *adj.* **1.** characterized by or containing description. **2.** *Grammar.* (of an adjective) serving to describe the referent of the noun modified, as for example the adjective *brown* as contrasted with *my.* **3.** relating to description or classification rather than explanation or prescription. —**de'scriptively** *adv.* —**de'scriptiveness** *n.*

descry (dɪ'skraɪ) *vb.* **-scrying, -scried.** (*tr.*) **1.** to catch sight of. **2.** to discover by looking carefully. [C14: from OF *descrier* to proclaim, DECRY]

desecrate ('dɛsɪ,kreɪt) *vb.* (*tr.*) **1.** to violate the sacred character of (an object or place) by destructive, blasphemous, or sacrilegious action. **2.** to deconsecrate. [C17: from DE-+ CONSECRATE] —'dese,crator *or* 'dese,crater *n.* —,dese'cration *n.*

desegregate (diː'sɛgrɪ,geɪt) *vb.* to end racial segregation in (a school or other public institution). —,desegre'gation *n.*

deselect (,diːsɪ'lɛkt) *vb.* (*tr.*) *Brit. politics.* (of a constituency organization) to refuse to select (an existing MP) for re-election. —,dese'lection *n.*

desensitize *or* **-tise** (diː'sɛnsɪ,taɪz) *vb.* (*tr.*) to render less sensitive or insensitive: *the patient was desensitized to the allergen.* —de,sensiti'zation *or* **-ti'sation** *n.* —de'sensi,tizer *or* -,tiser *n.*

desert[1] ('dɛzət) *n.* **1.** a region that is devoid or almost devoid of vegetation, esp. because of low rainfall. **2.** an uncultivated uninhabited region. **3.** a place which lacks some desirable feature or quality: *a cultural desert.* **4.** (*modifier*) of, relating to, or like a desert. [C13: from OF, from Church L *dēsertum*, from L *dēserere* to abandon, lit.: to sever one's links with, from DE- + *serere* to bind together]

desert[2] (dɪ'zɜːt) *vb.* **1.** (*tr.*) to abandon (a person, place, etc.) without intending to return, esp. in violation of a promise or obligation. **2.** *Mil.* to abscond from (a post or duty) with no intention of returning. **3.** (*tr.*) to fail (someone) in time of need. [C15: from F *déserter*, from LL *dēsertāre*, from L *dēserere* to forsake; see DESERT[1]] —de'serter *n.*

desert[3] (dɪ'zɜːt) *n.* **1.** (*often pl.*) just reward or punishment. **2.** the state of deserving a reward or punishment. [C13: from OF *deserte*, from *deservir* to DESERVE]

desert boots *pl. n.* ankle-high boots, often of suede, with laces and soft soles.

desertification (dɪ,zɜːtɪfɪ'keɪʃən) *n.* the transformation of fertile land into an arid or semiarid region as a result of intensive farming, soil erosion, etc.

desertion (dɪ'zɜːʃən) *n.* **1.** a deserting or being deserted. **2.** *Law.* wilful abandonment, esp. of one's spouse or children.

desert island *n.* a small remote tropical island.

desert pea *n.* an Australian trailing leguminous plant with scarlet flowers.

desert rat *n.* **1.** a jerboa inhabiting the deserts of N Africa. **2.** *Brit. inf.* a soldier who served in North Africa with the British 7th Armoured Division in 1941–42.

deserve (dɪ'zɜːv) *vb.* **1.** (*tr.*) to be entitled to or worthy of; merit. **2.** (*intr.*; foll. by *of*) *Obs.* to be worthy. [C13: from OF *deservir*, from L *dēservīre* to serve devotedly, from DE- + *servīre* to SERVE]

deserved (dɪ'zɜːvd) *adj.* rightfully earned; justified; warranted. —deservedly (dɪ'zɜːvɪdlɪ) *adv.* —deservedness (dɪ'zɜːvɪdnɪs) *n.*

deserving (dɪ'zɜːvɪŋ) *adj.* (often *postpositive* and foll. by *of*) worthy, esp. of praise or reward. —de'servingly *adv.* —de'servingness *n.*

deshabille (,deɪzæ'biːl) *n.* a variant of **dishabille.**

desiccant ('dɛsɪkənt) *adj.* **1.** drying. ~*n.* **2.** a substance that absorbs water and is used to remove moisture. [C17: from L *dēsiccāns* drying up; see DESICCATE]

desiccate ('dɛsɪ,keɪt) *vb.* **1.** (*tr.*) to remove most of the water from; dehydrate. **2.** (*tr.*) to preserve (food) by removing moisture; dry. **3.** (*intr.*) to become dried up. [C16: from L *dēsiccāre* to dry up, from DE- + *siccāre*, from *siccus* dry] —'desic,cated *adj.* —,desic'cation *n.*

desiderate (dɪ'zɪdə,reɪt) *vb.* (*tr.*) to feel the lack of or need for; miss. [C17: from L *dēsīderāre*, from DE- + *sīdus* star; see DESIRE] —de,sider'ation *n.*

desideratum (dɪ,zɪdə'rɑːtəm) *n.*, *pl.* **-ta** (-tə). something lacked and wanted. [C17: from L; see DESIDERATE]

design (dɪ'zaɪn) *vb.* **1.** to work out the structure or form of (something), as by making a sketch or plans. **2.** to plan and make (something) artistically or skilfully. **3.** (*tr.*) to invent. **4.** (*tr.*) to intend, as for a specific purpose; plan. ~*n.* **5.** a plan or preliminary drawing. **6.** the arrangement, elements, or features of an artistic or decorative work: *the design of the desk is Chippendale.* **7.** a finished artistic or decorative creation. **8.** the art of designing. **9.** a plan or project. **10.** an intention; purpose. **11.** (*often*

pl.; often foll. by *on* or *against*) a plot, often to gain possession of (something) by illegitimate means. [C16: from L *dēsignāre* to mark out, describe, from DE- + *signāre*, from *signum* a mark] —de'signable *adj.*

designate *vb.* ('dɛzɪg,neɪt). (*tr.*) **1.** to indicate or specify. **2.** to give a name to; style; entitle. **3.** to select or name for an office or duty; appoint. ~*adj.* ('dɛzɪgnɪt, -,neɪt). **4.** (*immediately postpositive*) appointed, but not yet in office: *a minister designate.* [C15: from L *dēsignātus* marked out, defined; see DESIGN] —'desig,nator *n.*

designation (,dɛzɪg'neɪʃən) *n.* **1.** something that designates, such as a name. **2.** the act of designating or the fact of being designated.

designedly (dɪ'zaɪnɪdlɪ) *adv.* by intention or design; on purpose.

designer (dɪ'zaɪnə) *n.* **1.** a person who devises and executes designs, as for clothes, machines, etc. **2.** (*modifier*) designed by and bearing the label of a well-known fashion designer: *designer jeans.* **3.** (*modifier*) (of things, ideas, etc.) having an appearance of fashionable trendiness: *designer pop songs; designer diplomacy.* **4.** a person who devises plots; intriguer.

designer drug *n.* **1.** *Med.* a synthetic antibiotic designed to be effective against a particular bacterium. **2.** any of various narcotic or hallucinogenic substances manufactured illegally from a range of chemicals.

designing (dɪ'zaɪnɪŋ) *adj.* artful and scheming.

desirable (dɪ'zaɪərəb³l) *adj.* **1.** worthy of desire: *a desirable residence.* **2.** arousing desire, esp. sexual desire; attractive. —de,sira'bility *or* de'sirableness *n.* —de'sirably *adv.*

desire (dɪ'zaɪə) *vb.* (*tr.*) **1.** to wish or long for; crave. **2.** to request; ask for. ~*n.* **3.** a wish or longing. **4.** an expressed wish; request. **5.** sexual appetite. **6.** a person or thing that is desired. [C13: from OF, from L *dēsīderāre* to desire earnestly; see DESIDERATE] —de'sirer *n.*

desirous (dɪ'zaɪərəs) *adj.* (usually *postpositive* and foll. by *of*) having or expressing desire (for).

desist (dɪ'zɪst) *vb.* (*intr.;* often foll. by *from*) to cease, as from an action; stop or abstain. [C15: from OF, from L *dēsistere* to leave off, stand apart, from DE- + *sistere* to stand, halt]

desk (dɛsk) *n.* **1.** a piece of furniture with a writing surface and usually drawers or other compartments. **2.** a service counter or table in a public building, such as a hotel. **3.** a support for the book from which services are read in a church. **4.** the editorial section of a newspaper, etc., responsible for a particular subject: *the news desk.* **5.** a music stand shared by two orchestral players. [C14: from Med. L *desca* table, from L *discus* disc, dish]

desk-bound *adj.* obliged by one's occupation to work sitting at a desk.

desk editor *n.* (in a publishing house) an editor responsible for the preparation and checking of manuscripts for printing.

desktop ('dɛsk,tɒp) *n.* (*modifier*) denoting a computer system, esp. for word processing, that is small enough to use at a desk but sophisticated enough to produce print-quality documents: *desktop publishing.*

desman ('dɛsmən) *n.*, *pl.* **-mans.** either of two molelike amphibious mammals, the Russian desman or the Pyrenean desman, with dense fur and webbed feet. [C18: from Swedish *desmansråtta*, from *desman* musk + *råtta* rat]

Des Moines (də 'mɔɪn, 'mɔɪnz) *n.* **1.** a city in S central Iowa: state capital. Pop.: 191 003 (1980). **2.** a river in the N central U.S., rising in SW Minnesota and flowing southeast to join the Mississippi. Length: 861 km (535 miles).

Desmoulins (*French* dɛmulɛ̃) *n.* (**Lucie Simplice**) **Camille** (**Benoit**) (kamij). 1760–94, French revolutionary leader, pamphleteer, and orator.

desolate *adj.* ('dɛsəlɪt). **1.** uninhabited; deserted. **2.** made uninhabitable; laid waste; devastated. **3.** without friends, hope, or encouragement. **4.** dismal; depressing. ~*vb.* ('dɛsə,leɪt). (*tr.*) **5.** to deprive of inhabitants; depopulate. **6.** to lay waste; devastate. **7.** to make wretched or forlorn. **8.** to forsake or abandon. [C14: from L *dēsōlāre* to leave alone, from DE- + *sōlāre* to make lonely, lay waste, from *sōlus* alone] —'deso,later *or* 'deso,lator *n.* —'desolately *adv.* —'desolateness *n.*

desolation (,dɛsə'leɪʃən) *n.* **1.** a desolating or being desolated; ruin or devastation. **2.** solitary misery; wretchedness. **3.** a desolate region.

De Soto (də 'səutəu; *Spanish* de 'soto) *n.* **Hernando** (ɛr'nando). ?1500–42, Spanish explorer, who discovered the Mississippi River (1541). Also called: **Fernando De Soto** (fɛr'nando).

despair (dɪ'spɛə) *vb.* **1.** (*intr.; often foll. by of*) to lose or give up hope: *I despair of his coming.* ~*n.* **2.** total loss of hope. **3.** a person or thing that causes hopelessness or for which there is no hope. [C14: from OF *despoir* hopelessness, from *desperer* to despair, from L *dēspērāre*, from DE- + *spērāre* to hope]

despairing (dɪ'spɛərɪŋ) *adj.* hopeless, despondent; feeling or showing despair. —**de'spairingly** *adv.*

despatch (dɪ'spætʃ) *vb.* (*tr.*) a less common spelling of **dispatch.** —**des'patcher** *n.*

Despenser (dɪs'pɛnsə) *n.* **Hugh le,** Earl of Winchester. 1262–1326, English statesman, a favourite of Edward II. Together with his son **Hugh,** *the Younger* (?1290–1326), he was executed by the king's enemies.

desperado (,dɛspə'rɑːdəu) *n., pl.* **-does** *or* **-dos.** a reckless or desperate person, esp. one ready to commit any violent illegal act. [C17: prob. pseudo-Spanish var. of obs. *desperate* (n.)]

desperate ('dɛspərɪt, -prɪt) *adj.* **1.** careless of danger, as from despair. **2.** (of an act) reckless; risky. **3.** used or undertaken as a last resort. **4.** critical; very grave: *in desperate need.* **5.** (often *postpositive* and foll. by *for*) in distress and having a great need or desire. **6.** moved by or showing despair. [C15: from L *dēspērāre* to have no hope; see DESPAIR] —**'desperately** *adv.* —**'desperateness** *n.*

desperation (,dɛspə'reɪʃən) *n.* **1.** desperate recklessness. **2.** the state of being desperate.

despicable ('dɛspɪkəbəl, dɪ'spɪk-) *adj.* worthy of being despised; contemptible; mean. [C16: from LL *dēspicābilis,* from *dēspicārī* to disdain; cf. DESPISE] —**'despicably** *adv.*

despise (dɪ'spaɪz) *vb.* (*tr.*) to look down on with contempt; scorn: *he despises flattery.* [C13: from OF *despire,* from L *dēspicere* to look down, from DE- + *specere* to look] —**de'spiser** *n.*

despite (dɪ'spaɪt) *prep.* **1.** in spite of; undeterred by. ~*n.* **2.** *Arch.* contempt; insult. **3. in despite of.** (*prep.*) *Rare.* in spite of. [C13: from OF *despit,* from L *dēspectus* contempt; see DESPISE]

despoil (dɪ'spɔɪl) *vb.* (*tr.*) to deprive by force; plunder; loot. [C13: from OF, from L *dēspoliāre,* from DE- + *spoliāre* to rob (esp. of clothing)] —**de'spoiler** *n.* —**de'spoilment** *n.*

despoliation (dɪ,spəulɪ'eɪʃən) *n.* **1.** plunder or pillage. **2.** the state of being despoiled.

despond *vb.* (dɪ'spɒnd) (*intr.*) **1.** to become disheartened; despair. ~*n.* ('dɛspɒnd, dɪ'spɒnd). **2.** *Arch.* despondency. [C17: from L *dēspondēre* to promise, make over to, yield, lose heart, from DE- + *spondēre* to promise] —**de'spondingly** *adv.*

despondent (dɪ'spɒndənt) *adj.* downcast or disheartened; dejected. —**de'spondence** *or* **de'spondency** *n.* —**de'spondently** *adv.*

despot ('dɛspɒt) *n.* **1.** an absolute or tyrannical ruler. **2.** any person in power who acts tyrannically. [C16: from Med. L *despota,* from Gk *despotēs* lord, master] —**despotic** (dɛs'pɒtɪk) *or* **des'potical** *adj.* —**des'potically** *adv.*

despotism ('dɛspə,tɪzəm) *n.* **1.** the rule of a despot; absolute or tyrannical government. **2.** arbitrary or tyrannical authority or behaviour.

des res (dɛz rɛz) *n.* (in estate agents' jargon) a desirable residence.

Dessalines (*French* desalin) *n.* **Jean Jacques** (ʒɑ̃ ʒak). ?1758–1806, emperor of Haiti (1804–06) after driving out the French; assassinated.

Dessau (*German* 'dɛsau) *n.* an industrial city in central East Germany: capital of Anhalt state from 1340 to 1918. Pop.: 103 738 (1982 est.).

dessert (dɪ'zɜːt) *n.* **1.** the sweet, usually last course of a meal. **2.** *Chiefly Brit.* (esp. formerly) fruit, dates, nuts, etc., served at the end of a meal. [C17: from F, from *desservir* to clear a table, from *des-* DIS-[1] + *servir* to SERVE]

dessertspoon (dɪ'zɜːt,spuːn) *n.* a spoon intermediate in size between a tablespoon and a teaspoon.

destination (,dɛstɪ'neɪʃən) *n.* **1.** the predetermined end of a journey. **2.** the end or purpose for which something is created or a person is destined.

destine ('dɛstɪn) *vb.* (*tr.*) to set apart (for a certain purpose or person); intend; design. [C14: from OF, from L *dēstināre* to appoint, from DE- + *-stināre,* from *stāre* to stand]

destined ('dɛstɪnd) *adj.* (*postpositive*) **1.** foreordained; meant. **2.** (usually foll. by *for*) heading (towards a specific destination).

destiny ('dɛstɪnɪ) *n., pl.* **-nies. 1.** the future destined for a person or thing. **2.** the predetermined or inevitable course of events. **3.** the power that predetermines the course of events. [C14: from OF, from *destiner* to DESTINE]

destitute ('dɛstɪ,tjuːt) *adj.* **1.** lacking the means of subsistence; totally impoverished. **2.** (*postpositive; foll. by of*) completely lacking: *destitute of words.* [C14: from L, from *dēstituere* to leave alone, from *statuere* to place]

destitution (,dɛstɪ'tjuːʃən) *n.* the state of being destitute; utter poverty.

destrier ('dɛstrɪə) *n. Arch.* a warhorse. [C13: from OF, from *destre* right hand, from L *dextra;* from the fact that a squire led a knight's horse with his right hand]

destroy (dɪ'strɔɪ) *vb.* (*mainly tr.*) **1.** to ruin; spoil. **2.** to tear down or demolish. **3.** to put an end to. **4.** to kill or annihilate. **5.** to crush or defeat. **6.** (*intr.*) to be destructive or cause destruction. [C13: from OF, from L *dēstruere* to pull down, from DE- + *struere* to pile up, build]

destroyer (dɪ'strɔɪə) *n.* **1.** a small fast lightly armoured but heavily armed warship. **2.** a person or thing that destroys.

destruct (dɪ'strʌkt) *vb.* **1.** to destroy (one's own missile, etc.) for safety. **2.** (*intr.*) (of a missile, etc.) to be destroyed, for safety, by those controlling it. ~*n.* **3.** the act of destructing. ~*adj.* **4.** designed to be capable of destroying itself or the object containing it: *destruct mechanism.*

destructible (dɪ'strʌktɪbəl) *adj.* capable of being or liable to be destroyed.

destruction (dɪ'strʌkʃən) *n.* **1.** the act of destroying or state of being destroyed; demolition. **2.** a cause of ruin or means of destroying. [C14: from L *dēstructiō* a pulling down; see DESTROY]

destructive (dɪ'strʌktɪv) *adj.* **1.** (often *postpositive* and foll. by *of* or *to*) causing or tending to cause the destruction (of). **2.** intended to discredit, esp. without positive suggestions or help; negative: *destructive criticism.* —**de'structively** *adv.* —**de'structiveness** *n.*

destructive distillation *n.* the decomposition of a complex substance, such as wood or coal, by heating it in the absence of air and collecting the volatile products.

destructor (dɪ'strʌktə) *n.* **1.** a furnace or incinerator for the disposal of refuse. **2.** a device used to blow up a defective missile.

desuetude (dɪ'sjuːɪ,tjuːd, ,dɛswɪtjuːd) *n.* the condition of not being in use or practice; disuse. [C15: from L, from *dēsuescere* to lay aside a habit, from DE- + *suescere* to grow accustomed]

desulphurize *or* **-ise** (diː'sʌlfjʊ,raɪz) *vb.* to free or become free from sulphur.

desultory ('dɛsəltərɪ, -trɪ) *adj.* **1.** passing from one thing to another, esp. in a fitful way; unmethodical; disconnected. **2.** random or incidental: *a desultory thought.* [C16: from L: relating to one who vaults or jumps, hence superficial, from *dēsilīre* to jump down, from DE- + *salīre*] —**'desultorily** *adv.* —**'desultoriness** *n.*

Det. *abbrev. for* Detective.

detach (dɪ'tætʃ) *vb.* (*tr.*) **1.** to disengage and separate or remove; unfasten; disconnect. **2.** *Mil.* to separate (a small unit) from a larger, esp. for a special assignment. [C17: from OF *destachier,* from *des-* DIS-[1] + *atachier* to AT-TACH] —**de'tachable** *adj.* —**de,tacha'bility** *n.*

detached (dɪ'tætʃt) *adj.* **1.** disconnected or standing apart; not attached: *a detached house.* **2.** showing no bias or emotional involvement.

detachment (dɪ'tætʃmənt) *n.* **1.** indifference; aloofness. **2.** freedom from self-interest or bias; disinterest. **3.** the act of detaching something. **4.** the condition of being detached; disconnection. **5.** *Mil.* **a.** the separation of a small unit from its main body. **b.** the unit so detached.

detail ('diːteɪl) *n.* **1.** an item that is considered separately; particular. **2.** an item that is unimportant: *passengers' comfort was regarded as a detail.* **3.** treatment of particulars: *this essay includes too much detail.* **4.** items collectively; particulars. **5.** a small section or element in a painting, building, statue, etc., esp. when considered in isolation. **6.** *Mil.* **a.** the act of assigning personnel for a specific duty. **b.** the personnel selected. **c.** the duty. **7. in detail.** including all or most particulars or items thoroughly. ~*vb.* (*tr.*) **8.** to list or relate fully. **9.** *Mil.* to select (personnel) for a specific duty. [C17: from F, from OF *detailler* to cut in pieces, from *de-* DIS-¹ + *tailler* to cut]

detailed ('di:teɪld) *adj.* having many details or giving careful attention to details.

detain (dɪ'teɪn) *vb.* (*tr.*) **1.** to delay; hold back. **2.** to confine or hold in custody. [C15: from OF, from L *dētinēre* to hold off, keep back, from DE- + *tenēre* to hold] —**de'tainable** *adj.* —**detainee** (,di:teɪ'ni:) *n.* —**de'tainment** *n.*

detect (dɪ'tɛkt) *vb.* (*tr.*) **1.** to perceive or notice. **2.** to discover the existence or presence of (esp. something likely to elude observation). **3.** *Obs.* to discover, or reveal (a crime, criminal, etc.). **4.** to extract information from (an electromagnetic wave). [C15: from L *dētectus*, from *dētegere* to uncover, from DE- + *tegere* to cover] —**de'tectable** *or* **de'tectible** *adj.*

detection (dɪ'tɛkʃən) *n.* **1.** the act of discovering or the fact of being discovered. **2.** the act or process of extracting information, esp. at audio or video frequencies, from an electromagnetic wave; demodulation.

detective (dɪ'tɛktɪv) *n.* **1. a.** a police officer who investigates crimes. **b.** See **private detective. c.** (*as modifier*): *a detective story.* ~*adj.* **2.** of or for detection.

detector (dɪ'tɛktə) *n.* **1.** a person or thing that detects. **2.** any mechanical sensing device. **3.** *Electronics.* a device used in the detection of radio signals.

detent (dɪ'tɛnt) *n.* the locking piece of a mechanism, often spring-loaded to check the movement of a wheel in only one direction. [C17: from OF *destente* a loosening, trigger; see DÉTENTE]

détente (deɪ'tɑ:nt; *French* detɑ̃t) *n.* the relaxing or easing of tension, esp. between nations. [F, lit.: a loosening, from OF *destendre* to release, from *tendre* to stretch]

detention (dɪ'tɛnʃən) *n.* **1.** a detaining or being detained. **2. a.** custody or confinement, esp. of a suspect awaiting trial. **b.** (*as modifier*): *a detention order.* **3.** a form of punishment in which a pupil is detained after school. [C16: from L *dētentiō* a keeping back; see DETAIN]

detention centre *n.* a place where young persons may be detained for short periods by order of a court.

deter (dɪ'tɜ:) *vb.* **-terring, -terred.** (*tr.*) to discourage (from acting) or prevent (from occurring), usually by instilling fear, doubt, or anxiety. [C16: from L *dēterrēre*, from DE- + *terrēre* to frighten] —**de'terment** *n.*

deterge (dɪ'tɜ:dʒ) *vb.* (*tr.*) to cleanse: *to deterge a wound.* [C17: from L *dētergēre* to wipe away, from DE- + *tergēre* to wipe]

detergent (dɪ'tɜ:dʒənt) *n.* **1.** a cleansing agent, esp. a chemical such as an alkyl sulphonate, widely used in industry, laundering, etc. ~*adj.* **2.** having cleansing power. [C17: from L *dētergēns* wiping off; see DETERGE]

deteriorate (dɪ'tɪərɪə,reɪt) *vb.* **1.** to make or become worse; depreciate. **2.** (*intr.*) to wear away or disintegrate. [C16: from LL *dēteriōrāre*, from L *dēterior* worse] —**de,terio'ration** *n.* —**de'teriorative** *adj.*

determinacy (dɪ'tɜ:mɪnəsɪ) *n.* **1.** the quality of being defined or fixed. **2.** the condition of being predicted or deduced.

determinant (dɪ'tɜ:mɪnənt) *adj.* **1.** serving to determine. ~*n.* **2.** a factor that influences or determines. **3.** *Maths.* a square array of elements that represents the sum of certain products of these elements, used to solve simultaneous equations, in vector studies, etc.

determinate (dɪ'tɜ:mɪnɪt) *adj.* **1.** definitely limited, defined, or fixed. **2.** determined. **3.** able to be predicted or deduced. **4.** *Bot.* having the main and branch stems ending in flowers. —**de'terminateness** *n.*

determination (dɪ,tɜ:mɪ'neɪʃən) *n.* **1.** the act of making a decision. **2.** the condition of being determined; resoluteness. **3.** an ending of an argument by the decision of an authority. **4.** the act of fixing the quality, limit, position, etc., of something. **5.** a decision or opinion reached. **6.** a resolute movement towards some object or end. **7.** *Law.* the termination of an estate or interest. **8.** *Law.* the decision reached by a court of justice on a disputed matter.

determinative (dɪ'tɜ:mɪnətɪv) *adj.* **1.** serving to settle or determine; deciding. ~*n.* **2.** a factor, circumstance, etc.,

that settles or determines. —**de'terminatively** *adv.* —**de'terminativeness** *n.*

determine (dɪ'tɜ:mɪn) *vb.* **1.** to settle or decide (an argument, question, etc.) conclusively. **2.** (*tr.*) to conclude, esp. after observation or consideration. **3.** (*tr.*) to influence; give direction to. **4.** (*tr.*) to fix in scope, variety, etc.: *the river determined the edge of the property.* **5.** to make or cause to make a decision. **6.** (*tr.*) *Logic.* to define or limit (a notion) by adding or requiring certain features or characteristics. **7.** (*tr.*) *Geom.* to fix or specify the position or form of. **8.** *Chiefly law.* to come or bring to an end, as an estate. [C14: from OF, from L *dētermināre* to set boundaries to, from DE- + *termināre* to limit] —**de'terminable** *adj.*

determined (dɪ'tɜ:mɪnd) *adj.* of unwavering mind; resolute; firm. —**de'terminedly** *adv.*

determiner (dɪ'tɜ:mɪnə) *n.* **1.** a word, such as a number, an article, or *all*, that determines the referent or referents of a noun phrase. **2.** a person or thing that determines.

determinism (dɪ'tɜ:mɪ,nɪzəm) *n.* the philosophical doctrine that all events, including human actions, are fully determined by preceding events, and so freedom of choice is illusory. Cf. **free will.** —**de'terminist** *n., adj.* —**de,termin'istic** *adj.*

deterrent (dɪ'tɛrənt) *n.* **1.** something that deters. **2.** a weapon, esp. nuclear, held by one state, etc., to deter attack by another. ~*adj.* **3.** tending or used to deter. [C19: from L *dēterrēns* hindering; see DETER] —**de'terrence** *n.*

detest (dɪ'tɛst) *vb.* (*tr.*) to dislike intensely; loathe. [C16: from L *dētestārī* to curse (while invoking a god as witness), from DE- + *testārī*, from *testis* a witness] —**de'tester** *n.*

detestable (dɪ'tɛstəb³l) *adj.* being or deserving to be abhorred or detested. —**de,testa'bility** *or* **de'testableness** *n.* —**de'testably** *adv.*

detestation (,di:tɛs'teɪʃən) *n.* **1.** intense hatred; abhorrence. **2.** a person or thing that is detested.

dethrone (dɪ'θrəʊn) *vb.* (*tr.*) to remove from a throne or deprive of any high position or title. —**de'thronement** *n.* —**de'throner** *n.*

Detmold ('dɛtməʊld; *German* 'dɛtmɔlt) *n.* a city in NW West Germany, in North Rhine-Westphalia. Pop.: 67 850 (1984 est.).

detonate ('dɛtə,neɪt) *vb.* to cause (a bomb, mine, etc.) to explode or (of a bomb, mine, etc.) to explode. [C18: from L *dētonāre* to thunder down, from DE- + *tonāre* to THUNDER] —,**deto'nation** *n.*

detonator ('dɛtə,neɪtə) *n.* **1.** a small amount of explosive, as in a percussion cap, used to initiate a larger explosion. **2.** a device, such as an electrical generator, used to set off an explosion from a distance. **3.** an explosive.

detour ('di:tʊə) *n.* **1.** a deviation from a direct route or course of action. ~*vb.* **2.** to deviate or cause to deviate from a direct route or course of action. [C18: from F, from OF *destorner* to divert, turn away, from *des-* DE- + *torner* to TURN]

detoxify (di:'tɒksɪ,faɪ) *vb.* **-fying, -fied.** (*tr.*) to remove poison from. —**de,toxifi'cation** *n.*

detoxification centre *n.* a place that specializes in the treatment of alcoholism or drug addiction.

detract (dɪ'trækt) *vb.* **1.** (when *intr.*, usually foll. by *from*) to take away a part (of); diminish: *her anger detracts from her beauty.* **2.** (*tr.*) to distract or divert. **3.** (*tr.*) *Obs.* to belittle or disparage. [C15: from L *dētractus*, from *dētrahere* to pull away, disparage, from DE- + *trahere* to drag] —**de'tractive** *adj.* —**de'tractor** *n.* —**de'traction** *n.*

detrain (di:'treɪn) *vb.* to leave or cause to leave a railway train. —**de'trainment** *n.*

detriment ('dɛtrɪmənt) *n.* **1.** disadvantage or damage. **2.** a cause of disadvantage or damage. [C15: from L *dētrīmentum*, a rubbing off, hence damage, from *dēterere*, from DE- + *terere* to rub]

detrimental (,dɛtrɪ'mɛnt³l) *adj.* (when *postpositive*, foll. by *to*) harmful; injurious.

detritus (dɪ'traɪtəs) *n.* **1.** a loose mass of stones, silt, etc., worn away from rocks. **2.** debris. [C18: from F, from L: a rubbing away; see DETRIMENT] —**de'trital** *adj.*

Detroit (dɪ'trɔɪt) *n.* **1.** a city in SE Michigan, on the Detroit River: a major Great Lakes port; largest car-manufacturing centre in the world. Pop.: 1 086 220 (1986). **2.** a river in central North America, flowing along the U.S.-Canadian border from Lake St Clair to Lake Erie.

de trop *French.* (də troʊ) *adj.* (*postpositive*) not wanted; in the way. [lit.: of too much]

detumescence (ˌdiːtjʊˈmɛsəns) *n.* the subsidence of a swelling. [C17: from L *dētumēscere* to cease swelling, from DE- + *tumescere*, from *tumēre* to swell]

Deucalion (djuːˈkeɪlɪən) *n.* the son of Prometheus and, with his wife Pyrrha, the only survivor on earth of a flood sent by Zeus (**Deucalion's flood**). Together, they were allowed to repopulate the world by throwing stones over their shoulders, which became men and women.

deuce[1] (djuːs) *n.* **1. a.** a playing card or dice with two spots. **b.** a throw of two in dice. **2.** *Tennis, etc.* a tied score that requires one player to gain two successive points to win the game. [C15: from OF *deus* two, from L *duos*, from *duo* two]

deuce[2] (djuːs) *Inf.* ~*interj.* **1.** an expression of annoyance or frustration. ~*n.* **2. the deuce.** (intensifier) used in such phrases as **what the deuce, where the deuce,** etc. [C17: prob. special use of DEUCE[1] (in the sense: lowest throw at dice)]

deuced (ˈdjuːsɪd, djuːst) *Brit. inf.* ~*adj.* **1.** (intensifier) confounded: *he's a deuced idiot.* ~*adv.* **2.** (intensifier): *deuced good luck.*

Deurne (*Flemish* ˈdøːrnə) *n.* a town in N Belgium, a suburb of E Antwerp: site of Antwerp airport. Pop.: 76 744 (1982 est.).

Deus *Latin.* (ˈdeɪʊs) *n.* God. [rel. to Gk *Zeus*]

deus ex machina *Latin.* (ˈdeɪʊs ɛks ˈmækɪnə) *n.* **1.** (in ancient Greek and Roman drama) a god introduced into a play to resolve the plot. **2.** any unlikely device serving this purpose. [lit.: god out of a machine]

Deut. *Bible. abbrev. for* Deuteronomy.

deuteride (ˈdjuːtəˌraɪd) *n.* a compound of deuterium and another element.

deuterium (djuːˈtɪərɪəm) *n.* a stable isotope of hydrogen, occurring in natural hydrogen and in heavy water. Symbol: D or ^{2}H; atomic no.: 1; atomic wt.: 2.014. [C20: NL; see DEUTERO-, -IUM; from the fact that it is the second heaviest hydrogen isotope]

deuterium oxide *n.* the compound D_2O; water in which the normal hydrogen atoms are replaced by deuterium atoms. See also **heavy water.**

deutero-, deuto- *or before a vowel* **deuter-, deut-** *combining form.* second or secondary: *deuterium.* [from Gk *deuteros* second]

deuteron (ˈdjuːtəˌrɒn) *n.* the nucleus of a deuterium atom.

Deutsch (dɔɪtʃ; *German* dɔytʃ) *n.* **Otto Erich** (ˈɔto ˈeːrɪç). 1883–1967, Austrian music historian and art critic, noted for his catalogue of Schubert's works (1951).

Deutschland (ˈdɔytʃlant) *n.* the German name for **Germany.**

Deutschmark (ˈdɔɪtʃˌmɑːk) *or* **Deutsche Mark** (ˈdɔɪtʃə) *n.* the standard monetary unit of West Germany.

deutzia (ˈdjuːtsɪəˌdɔɪtsɪə) *n.* any of various shrubs with white, pink, or purplish flowers in early summer. [C19: NL, after J. *Deutz,* 18th-cent. Du. patron of botany]

Deux-Sèvres (*French* døsɛvrə) *n.* a department of W France, in Poitou-Charentes region. Capital: Niort. Pop.: 342 812 (1982). Area: 6054 sq. km (2337 sq. miles).

devalue (diːˈvæljuː) *or* **devaluate** (diːˈvæljuːˌeɪt) *vb.* **-valuing, -valued** *or* **-valuating, -valuated. 1.** to reduce (a currency) or (of a currency) to be reduced in exchange value. **2.** (*tr.*) to reduce the value of. —**deˌvaluˈation** *n.*

Devanagari (ˌdeɪvəˈnɑːɡərɪ) *n.* a syllabic script in which Sanskrit, Hindi, and other modern languages of India are written. [C18: from Sansk.: alphabet of the gods]

devastate (ˈdɛvəˌsteɪt) *vb.* (*tr.*) **1.** to lay waste or make desolate; ravage; destroy. **2.** to confound or overwhelm. [C17: from L *dēvastāre*, from DE- + *vastāre* to ravage; rel. to *vastus* waste, empty] —ˌdevasˈtation *n.* —ˈdevasˌtator *n.*

develop (dɪˈvɛləp) *vb.* **1.** to come or bring to a later or more advanced or expanded stage; grow or cause to grow gradually. **2.** (*tr.*) to work out in detail. **3.** to disclose or unfold (thoughts, a plot, etc.) gradually or (of thoughts, etc.) to be gradually disclosed or unfolded. **4.** to come or bring into existence: *he developed a new faith in God.* **5.** (*intr.*) to follow as a result of; ensue; *a row developed after her remarks.* **6.** (*tr.*) to contract (a disease or illness). **7.** (*tr.*) to improve the value or change the use of (land). **8.** to exploit or make available the natural resources of (a country or region). **9.** (*tr.*) *Photog.* to treat (exposed film, plate, or paper) with chemical solutions in order to produce a visible image. **10.** *Biol.* to progress or cause to progress from simple to complex stages in the growth of an individual or the evolution of a species. **11.** (*tr.*) to elaborate upon (a musical theme) by varying the melody, key, etc. **12.** (*tr.*) *Maths.* to expand (a function or expression) in the form of a series. **13.** (*tr.*) *Geom.* to project or roll out (a surface) onto a plane without stretching or shrinking any element. **14.** *Chess.* to bring (a piece) into play from its initial position on the back rank. [C19: from OF *desveloper* to unwrap, from *des-* DIS-[1] + *veloper* to wrap; see ENVELOP] —**deˈvelopable** *adj.*

developer (dɪˈvɛləpə) *n.* **1.** a person or thing that develops something, esp. a person who develops property. **2.** *Photog.* a chemical used to convert the latent image recorded in the emulsion of a film or paper into a visible image.

developing country *n.* a poor or non-industrial country that is seeking to develop its resources by industrialization.

development (dɪˈvɛləpmənt) *n.* **1.** the act or process of growing or developing. **2.** the product of developing. **3.** a fact or event, esp. one that changes a situation. **4.** an area of land that has been developed. **5.** the section of a movement, usually in sonata form, in which the basic musical themes are developed. **6.** *Chess.* the process of developing pieces. —**deˌvelopˈmental** *adj.*

development area *n.* (in Britain) an area which has experienced economic depression because of the decline of its main industry or industries, and which is given government assistance to establish new industry.

Deventer (ˈdeɪvəntə; *Dutch* ˈdeːvəntər) *n.* an industrial city in the E Netherlands, in Overijssel province, on the River IJssel: medieval intellectual centre; early centre of Dutch printing. Pop.: 65 423 (1987).

Devereux (ˈdɛvərə) *n.* **Robert.** See (2nd Earl of) **Essex.**

Devi (ˈdeɪviː) *n.* a Hindu goddess and embodiment of the female energy of Siva. [Sansk.: goddess; see DEVA]

deviant (ˈdiːvɪənt) *adj.* **1.** deviating, as from what is considered acceptable behaviour. ~*n.* **2.** a person whose behaviour, esp. sexual behaviour, deviates from what is considered to be acceptable. —ˈdeviance *or* ˈdeviancy *n.*

deviate *vb.* (ˈdiːvɪˌeɪt). **1.** (*usually intr.*) to differ or cause to differ, as in belief or thought. **2.** (*usually intr.*) to turn aside or cause to turn aside. **3.** (*intr.*) *Psychol.* to depart from an accepted standard. ~*n., adj.* (ˈdiːvɪɪt). **4.** another word for **deviant.** [C17: from LL *dēviāre* to turn aside from the direct road, from DE- + *via* road] —ˈdeviˌator *n.* —ˈdeviatory *adj.*

deviation (ˌdiːvɪˈeɪʃən) *n.* **1.** an act or result of deviating. **2.** *Statistics.* the difference between an observed value in a series of such values and their arithmetic mean. **3.** the error of a compass due to local magnetic disturbances.

device (dɪˈvaɪs) *n.* **1.** a machine or tool used for a specific task. **2.** *Euphemistic.* a bomb. **3.** a plan, esp. a clever or evil one; trick. **4.** any ornamental pattern or picture, as in embroidery. **5.** computer hardware designed for a specific function. **6.** a design or figure, used as a heraldic sign, emblem, etc. **7.** a particular pattern of words, figures of speech, etc., used in literature to produce an effect on the reader. **8. leave (someone) to his own devices.** to leave (someone) alone to do as he wishes. [C13: from OF *devis* purpose, contrivance & *devise* difference, intention, from *deviser* to divide, control; see DEVISE]

devil (ˈdɛvəl) *n.* **1.** *Theol.* (*often cap.*) the chief spirit of evil and enemy of God, often depicted as a human figure with horns, cloven hoofs, and tail. **2.** any subordinate evil spirit. **3.** a person or animal regarded as wicked or ill-natured. **4.** a person or animal regarded as unfortunate or wretched. **5.** a person or animal regarded as daring, mischievous, or energetic. **6.** *Inf.* something difficult or annoying. **7.** *Christian Science.* an error, lie, or false belief. **8.** (in Malaysia) a ghost. **9.** a portable furnace or brazier. **10.** any of various mechanical devices, such as a machine for making wooden screws or a rag-tearing machine. **11.** See **printer's devil. 12.** *Law.* (in England) a junior barrister who does work for another in order to gain experience, usually for a half fee. **13. between the devil and the deep blue sea.** between equally undesirable alternatives. **14. devil of a.** *Inf.* (intensifier): *a devil* *of a fine horse.* **15. give the devil his due.** to acknowledge the talent or success of an unpleasant person. **16. go to the devil. a.** to fail or become dissipated. **b.** (*interj.*) used to express annoyance with the person causing it. **17.** (**let**) **the devil take the hindmost.** look after oneself and leave others to their fate. **18. talk** (*or* **speak**) **of the devil!** (*interj.*) used when an absent person who has been the subject of conversation appears. **19. the devil!** (intensifier): **a.** used in **what the devil, where the devil,** etc. **b.** an exclamation of anger, surprise, disgust, etc. **20. the devil to pay.** trouble to be faced as a consequence of an action. ~*vb.* **-illing, -illed** *or U.S.* **-iling, -iled. 21.** (*tr.*) to prepare (food) by coating with a highly flavoured spiced paste or mixture of condiments before cooking. **22.** (*tr.*) to tear (rags) with a devil. **23.** (*intr.*) to serve as a printer's devil. **24.** (*intr.*) *Chiefly Brit.* to do hackwork, esp. for a lawyer or author. **25.** (*tr.*) *U.S. inf.* to harass, vex, etc. [OE *dēofol*, from L *diabolus*, from Gk *diabolos* enemy, accuser, slanderer]

devilfish ('dɛvl,fɪʃ) *n., pl.* **-fish** *or* **-fishes. 1.** Also called: **devil ray.** another name for **manta** (the fish). **2.** another name for **octopus.**

devilish ('dɛvəlɪʃ) *adj.* **1.** of, resembling, or befitting a devil; diabolic; fiendish. ~*adv., adj.* **2.** *Inf.* (intensifier): *devilish good food.* —**'devilishly** *adv.* —**'devilishness** *n.*

devil-may-care *adj.* careless or reckless; happy-go-lucky: *a devil-may-care attitude.*

devilment ('dɛvəlmənt) *n.* devilish or mischievous conduct.

devilry ('dɛvlrɪ) *or* **deviltry** *n., pl.* **-ries** *or* **-tries. 1.** reckless or malicious fun or mischief. **2.** wickedness. **3.** black magic or other forms of diabolism. [C18: from F *diablerie*, from *diable* DEVIL]

devil's advocate *n.* **1.** a person who advocates an opposing or unpopular view, often for the sake of argument. **2.** *R.C. Church.* the official appointed to put the case against the beatification or canonization of a candidate. [translation of NL *advocātus diaboli*]

devil's coach-horse *n.* a large black beetle with large jaws and ferocious habits.

devil's food cake *n. Chiefly U.S. & Canad.* a rich chocolate cake.

Devil's Island *n.* one of the three Safety Islands, off the coast of French Guiana: formerly a leper colony, then a French penal colony from 1895 until 1938. Area: less than 2 sq. km (1 sq. mile). French name: **Île du Diable.**

devious ('di:vɪəs) *adj.* **1.** not sincere or candid; deceitful. **2.** (of a route or course of action) rambling; indirect. **3.** going astray; erring. [C16: from L *dēvius* lying to one side of the road, from DE- + *via* road] —**'deviously** *adv.* —**'deviousness** *n.*

devise (dɪ'vaɪz) *vb.* **1.** to work out or plan (something) in one's mind. **2.** (*tr.*) *Law.* to dispose of (real property) by will. ~*n. Law.* **3.** a disposition of property by will. **4.** a will or clause in a will disposing of real property. [C15: from OF *deviser* to divide, apportion, intend, from L *dīvidere* to DIVIDE] —**de'viser** *n.*

devitalize *or* **-ise** (di:'vaɪtə,laɪz) *vb.* (*tr.*) to lower or destroy the vitality of; make weak or lifeless. —**de,vitali'zation** *or* **-i'sation** *n.*

devoid (dɪ'vɔɪd) *adj.* (*postpositive*; foll. by *of*) destitute or void (of); free (from). [C15: orig. p.p. of *devoid* (*vb.*) to remove, from OF *devoider* from DE- + *voider* to void]

devoirs (də'vwɑː) *pl. n.* (*sometimes sing.*) compliments or respects. [C13: from OF: duty, from *devoir* to be obliged to, owe, from L *dēbēre*]

devolution (,di:və'lu:ʃən) *n.* **1.** a devolving. **2.** a passing onwards or downwards from one stage to another. **3.** a transfer of authority from a central government to regional governments. [C16: from Med. L *dēvolūtiō* a rolling down, from L *dēvolvere*; see DEVOLVE] —**,devo'lutionary** *adj.* —**,devo'lutionist** *n., adj.*

devolve (dɪ'vɒlv) *vb.* **1.** (foll. by *on, upon, to,* etc.) to pass or cause to pass to a successor or substitute, as duties, power, etc. **2.** (*intr.* foll. by *on* or *upon*) *Law.* (of an estate, etc.) to pass to another by operation of law. [C15: from L *dēvolvere* to roll down, fall into, from DE- + *volvere* to roll] —**de'volvement** *n.*

Devon ('dɛvⁿn) *n.* **1.** Also called: **Devonshire.** a county of SW England, between the Bristol Channel and the English Channel, including the island of Lundy: hilly, rising to the uplands of Exmoor and Dartmoor, with wooded river valleys and a rugged coastline. Administrative centre: Exeter. Pop.: 999 000 (1986 est.). Area: 6711 sq. km (2591 sq. miles). **2.** a breed of large red cattle originally from Devon.

Devonian (də'vəʊnɪən) *adj.* **1.** of, denoting, or formed in the fourth period of the Palaeozoic era, between the Silurian and Carboniferous periods. **2.** of or relating to Devon. ~*n.* **3. the.** the Devonian period or rock system.

Devonshire split ('dɛvⁿn,ʃə) *n.* a kind of yeast bun split open and served with cream or jam.

devote (dɪ'vəʊt) *vb.* (*tr.*) to apply or dedicate (oneself, money, etc.) to some pursuit, cause, etc. [C16: from L *dēvōtus* devoted, solemnly promised, from *dēvovēre* to vow; see DE-, VOW]

devoted (dɪ'vəʊtɪd) *adj.* **1.** feeling or demonstrating loyalty or devotion; devout. **2.** (*postpositive*; foll. by *to*) dedicated or consecrated. —**de'votedly** *adv.* —**de'votedness** *n.*

devotee (,dɛvə'ti:) *n.* **1.** a person ardently enthusiastic about something, such as a sport or pastime. **2.** a zealous follower of a religion.

devotion (dɪ'vəʊʃən) *n.* **1.** (often foll. by *to*) strong attachment (to) or affection (for a cause, person, etc.) marked by dedicated loyalty. **2.** religious zeal; piety. **3.** (*often pl.*) religious observance or prayers. —**de'votional** *adj.*

devour (dɪ'vaʊə) *vb.* (*tr.*) **1.** to eat up greedily or voraciously. **2.** to waste or destroy; consume. **3.** to consume greedily or avidly with the senses or mind. **4.** to engulf or absorb. [C14: from OF, from L *dēvorāre* to gulp down, from DE- + *vorāre*; see VORACIOUS] —**de'vourer** *n.* —**de'vouring** *adj.*

devout (dɪ'vaʊt) *adj.* **1.** deeply religious; reverent. **2.** sincere; earnest; heartfelt. [C13: from OF *devot*, from LL *dēvōtus*, from L: faithful; see DEVOTE] —**de'voutly** *adv.* —**de'voutness** *n.*

De Vries (*Dutch* də vri:s) *n.* **Hugo** ('hy:xo:). 1848–1935, Dutch botanist, who rediscovered Mendel's laws and developed the mutation theory of evolution.

dew (dju:) *n.* **1.** drops of water condensed on a cool surface, esp. at night, from vapour in the air. **2.** something like this, esp. in freshness: *the dew of youth.* **3.** small drops of moisture, such as tears. ~*vb.* **4.** (*tr.*) to moisten with or as with dew. [OE *dēaw*]

Dewar ('dju:ə) *n.* **Sir James.** 1842–1923, Scottish chemist and physicist. He worked on the liquefaction of gases and the properties of matter at low temperature, invented the vacuum flask, and (with Sir Frederick Abel) was the first to prepare cordite.

dewberry ('dju:bərɪ, -brɪ) *n., pl.* **-ries. 1.** any trailing bramble having blue-black fruits. **2.** the fruit of any such plant.

dewclaw ('dju:,klɔ:) *n.* **1.** a nonfunctional claw in dogs. **2.** an analogous rudimentary hoof in deer, goats, etc. —**'dew,clawed** *adj.*

dewdrop ('dju:,drɒp) *n.* a drop of dew.

Dewey ('dju:ɪ) *n.* **John.** 1859–1952, U.S. pragmatist philosopher and educator: an exponent of progressivism in education, he formulated an instrumentalist theory of learning through experience. His works include *The School and Society* (1899), *Democracy and Education* (1916), and *Logic: the Theory of Inquiry* (1938).

Dewey Decimal System ('dju:ɪ) *n.* a system of library book classification with ten main subject classes. Also called: **decimal classification.** [C19: after Melvil *Dewey* (1851–1931), U.S. educator]

de Wint (də 'wɪnt) *n.* **Peter.** 1784–1849, English landscape painter.

dewlap ('dju:,læp) *n.* **1.** a loose fold of skin hanging from beneath the throat in cattle, dogs, etc. **2.** loose skin on an elderly person's throat. [C14 *dewlappe*, from DEW (prob. from an earlier form of different meaning) + LAP¹ (from OE *læppa* hanging flap), ?from ON]

DEW line (dju:) *n. acronym for* distant early warning line, a network of radar stations situated mainly in Arctic regions of North America.

dew point *n.* the temperature at which dew begins to form.

dew pond *n.* a shallow pond, formerly thought to be kept full by dew and mist.

Dewsbury ('dju:zbərɪ, -brɪ) *n.* a town in N England, in West Yorkshire: woollen industry. Pop.: 48 339 (1981).

dewy ('djuːɪ) *adj.* **dewier, dewiest. 1.** moist with or as with dew. **2.** of or resembling dew. **3.** *Poetic.* suggesting, falling, or refreshing like dew: *dewy sleep.* —'**dewily** *adv.* —'**dewiness** *n.*

dexter ('dɛkstə) *adj.* **1.** *Arch.* of or located on the right side. **2.** (*usually postpositive*) *Heraldry.* of, on, or starting from the right side of a shield from the bearer's point of view and therefore on the spectator's left. ~Cf. **sinister.** [C16: from L; cf. Gk *dexios* on the right hand]

dexterity (dɛk'stɛrɪtɪ) *n.* **1.** physical, esp. manual, skill or nimbleness. **2.** mental skill or adroitness. [C16: from L *dexteritās* aptness, readiness; see DEXTER]

dexterous ('dɛkstrəs) *adj.* possessing or done with dexterity. —'**dexterously** *adv.* —'**dexterousness** *n.*

dextral ('dɛkstrəl) *adj.* **1.** of or located on the right side, esp. of the body. **2.** of a person who prefers to use his right foot, hand, or eye; right-handed. **3.** (of shells) coiling in an anticlockwise direction from the apex. —**dextrality** (dɛk'strælɪtɪ) *n.* —'**dextrally** *adv.*

dextran ('dɛkstrən) *n. Biochem.* a chainlike polymer of glucose produced by the action of bacteria on sucrose: used as a substitute for plasma in blood transfusions. [C19: from DEXTRO- + -AN]

dextrin ('dɛkstrɪn) *or* **dextrine** ('dɛkstrɪn, -triːn) *n.* any of a group of sticky substances obtained from starch: used as thickening agents in foods and as gums. [C19: from F *dextrine*; see DEXTRO-, -IN]

dextro- *or before a vowel* **dextr-** *combining form.* on or towards the right: *dextrorotation.* [from L, from *dexter* on the right side]

dextrorotation (,dɛkstrəʊrəʊ'teɪʃən) *n.* a rotation to the right; clockwise rotation. esp. of the plane of polarization of plane-polarized light. Cf. **laevorotation.** —**dextrorotatory** (,dɛkstrəʊ'rəʊtətərɪ, -trɪ) *or* ,**dextro'rotary** *adj.*

dextrorse ('dɛkstrɔːs) *or* **dextrorsal** (dɛk'strɔːsəl) *adj.* (of some climbing plants) growing upwards in a spiral from left to right or anticlockwise. [C19: from L *dextrorsum* towards the right, from DEXTRO- + *versus*, var. of *versus*, from *vertere* to turn] —'**dextrorsely** *adv.*

dextrose ('dɛkstrəʊz, -trəʊs) *n.* a glucose occurring widely in fruit, honey, and in the blood and tissue of animals. Formula: $C_6H_{12}O_6$. Also called: **grape sugar, dextroglucose.**

dextrous ('dɛkstrəs) *adj.* a variant spelling of **dexterous.** —'**dextrously** *adv.* —'**dextrousness** *n.*

Dezhnev (*Russian* dɪʒ'njɔf) *n.* **Cape.** a cape in the NE Soviet Union at the E end of Chukotski Peninsula: the northeasternmost point of Asia. Former name: **East Cape.**

DF *abbrev. for* Defender of the Faith.

D/F *or* **DF** *Telecomm. abbrev. for:* **1.** direction finder. **2.** direction finding.

DFC *abbrev. for* Distinguished Flying Cross.

DFM *abbrev. for* Distinguished Flying Medal.

dg *symbol for* decigram.

Dhahran (dɑː'rɑːn) *n.* a town in E Saudi Arabia: site of the original discovery of oil in the country (1938).

Dhaka *or* **Dacca** ('dækə) *n.* the capital of Bangladesh, in the E central part: capital of Bengal (1608–39; 1660–1704) and of East Pakistan (1949–71); jute and cotton mills; university (1921). Pop.: 3 600 000 (1984 est.).

dhal, dal, *or* **dholl** (dɑːl) *n.* **1.** a tropical African and Asian shrub cultivated for its nutritious pealike seeds. **2.** the seed of this shrub. [C17: from Hindi, from Sansk. *dal* to split]

dharma ('dɑːmə) *n.* **1.** *Hinduism.* social custom regarded as a religious and moral duty. **2.** *Hinduism.* **a.** the essential principle of the cosmos; natural law. **b.** conduct that conforms with this. **3.** *Buddhism.* ideal truth. [Sansk.: habit, usage, law]

Dhaulagiri (,daʊlə'gɪərɪ) *n.* a mountain in W central Nepal, in the Himalayas. Height: 8172 m (26 810 ft.).

Dhílos ('ðilɒs) *n.* transliteration of the Modern Greek name for **Delos.**

dhobi ('dəʊbɪ) *n., pl.* **-bis.** (in India, E Africa, etc.) a washerman. [C19: from Hindi, from *dhōb* washing]

Dhodhekánisos (ðɔðɛ'kanisɔs) *n.* a translation of the modern Greek name for the **Dodecanese.**

dhoti ('dəʊtɪ), **dhooti, dhootie,** *or* **dhuti** ('duːtɪ) *n., pl.* **-tis.** a long loincloth worn by men in India. [C17: from Hindi]

dhow (daʊ) *n.* a lateen-rigged coastal Arab sailing vessel. [C19: from Ar.]

DHSS (in Britain) *abbrev. for* Department of Health and Social Security.

di. *or* **dia.** *abbrev. for* diameter.

di-[1] *prefix.* **1.** twice; two; double: *dicotyledon.* **2. a.** containing two specified atoms or groups of atoms: *carbon dioxide.* **b.** a nontechnical equivalent of **bi-** (sense 5). [via L from Gk, from *dis* twice, double, rel. to *duo* two. Cf. BI-]

di-[2] *combining form.* a variant of **dia-** before a vowel: *diopter.*

dia- *or* **di-** *prefix.* **1.** through or during: *diachronic.* **2.** across: *diactinic.* **3.** apart: *diacritic.* [from Gk *dia* through, between, across, by]

diabetes (,daɪə'biːtɪs, -tiːz) *n.* any of various disorders, esp. diabetes mellitus, characterized by excretion of an abnormally large amount of urine. [C16: from L: siphon, from Gk, lit.: a passing through]

diabetes mellitus (məˈlaɪtəs) *n.* a disorder of carbohydrate metabolism characterized by excessive thirst and excretion of abnormally large quantities of urine containing an excess of sugar, caused by a deficiency of insulin. [C18: NL, lit.: honey-sweet diabetes]

diabetic (,daɪə'bɛtɪk) *adj.* **1.** of, relating to, or having diabetes. **2.** for the use of diabetics. ~*n.* **3.** a person who has diabetes.

diablerie (dɪ'ɑːblərɪ) *n.* **1.** magic or witchcraft connected with devils. **2.** esoteric knowledge of devils. **3.** devilry; mischief. [C18: from OF, from *diable* devil, from L *diabolus;* see DEVIL]

diabolic (,daɪə'bɒlɪk) *adj.* **1.** of the devil; satanic. **2.** extremely cruel or wicked; fiendish. **3.** very difficult or unpleasant. [C14: from LL, from Gk *diabolikos,* from *diabolos* DEVIL] —,**dia'bolically** *adv.* —,**dia'bolicalness** *n.*

diabolical (,daɪə'bɒlɪkəl) *adj. Inf.* **1.** excruciatingly bad. **2.** (intensifier): *a diabolical liberty.* —,**dia'bolically** *adv.* —,**dia'bolicalness** *n.*

diabolism (daɪ'æbə,lɪzəm) *n.* **1. a.** witchcraft or sorcery. **b.** worship of devils or beliefs concerning them. **2.** character or conduct that is devilish. —**di'abolist** *n.*

diabolo (dɪ'æbə,ləʊ) *n., pl.* **-los. 1.** a game in which one throws and catches a top on a cord fastened to two sticks. **2.** the top used in this. [C20: from It., lit.: devil]

diachronic (,daɪə'krɒnɪk) *adj.* of the study of the development of a phenomenon through time; historical. Cf. **synchronic.** [C19: from DIA- + Gk *khronos* time]

diacidic (,daɪə'sɪdɪk) *adj.* (of a base) capable of neutralizing two protons with one of its molecules. Also: **diacid.**

diaconal (daɪ'ækən[ə]l) *adj.* of or associated with a deacon or the diaconate. [C17: from LL *diāconālis,* from *diāconus* DEACON]

diaconate (daɪ'ækənɪt, -,neɪt) *n.* the office, sacramental status, or period of office of a deacon. [C17: from LL *diāconātus;* see DEACON]

diacritic (,daɪə'krɪtɪk) *n.* **1.** a sign placed above or below a character or letter to indicate that it has a different phonetic value, is stressed, or for some other reason. ~*adj.* **2.** another word for **diacritical.** [C17: from Gk *diakritikos* serving to distinguish, from *diakrinein,* from DIA- + *krinein* to separate]

diacritical (,daɪə'krɪtɪk[ə]l) *adj.* **1.** of or relating to a diacritic. **2.** showing up a distinction.

diadem ('daɪə,dɛm) *n.* **1.** a royal crown, esp. a light jewelled circlet. **2.** royal dignity or power. [C13: from L, from Gk: fillet, royal headdress, from *diadein,* from DIA-+ *dein* to bind]

diaeresis *or esp. U.S.* **dieresis** (daɪ'ɛrɪsɪs) *n., pl.* **-ses** (-,siːz). **1.** the mark ¨ placed over the second of two adjacent vowels to indicate that it is to be pronounced separately, as in some spellings of *coöperate, naïve,* etc. **2.** this mark used for any other purpose, such as to indicate a special pronunciation for a particular vowel. **3.** a pause in a line of verse when the end of a foot coincides with the end of a word. [C17: from L, from Gk: a division, from *diairein,* from DIA- + *hairein* to take; cf. HERESY] —**di'aeretic** *or esp. U.S.* **dieretic** (,daɪə'rɛtɪk) *adj.*

diag. *abbrev. for* diagram.

Diaghilev (*Russian* 'djagilif) *n.* **Sergei Pavlovich** (sɪr'gjej 'pavləvitʃ). 1872–1929, Russian ballet impresario. He founded (1909) and directed (1909–29) the *Ballet Russe* in Paris, introducing Russian ballet to the West.

diagnose ('daɪəg,nəʊz) *vb.* **1.** to determine by diagnosis. **2.** (*tr.*) to examine (a person or thing), as for a disease. —,**diag'nosable** *adj.*

diagnosis (,daɪəg'nəʊsɪs) *n.*, *pl.* **-ses** (-siːz). **1. a.** the identification of diseases from the examination of symptoms. **b.** an opinion so reached. **2. a.** thorough analysis of facts or problems in order to gain understanding. **b.** an opinion reached through such analysis. [C17: NL, from Gk: a distinguishing, from *diagignōskein*, from *gignōskein* to perceive, KNOW] —**diagnostic** (,daɪəg'nɒstɪk) *adj.*

diagonal (daɪ'ægən³l) *adj.* **1.** *Maths.* connecting any two vertices that in a polygon are not adjacent and in a polyhedron are not in the same face. **2.** slanting; oblique. **3.** marked with slanting lines or patterns. ~*n.* **4.** a diagonal line, plane, or pattern. **5.** something put, set, or drawn obliquely. [C16: from L, from Gk *diagōnios*, from DIA- + *gōnia* angle] —**di'agonally** *adv.*

diagram ('daɪə,græm) *n.* **1.** a sketch or plan demonstrating the form or workings of something. **2.** *Maths.* a pictorial representation of a quantity or of a relationship. ~*vb.* **-gramming, -grammed** *or U.S.* **-graming, -gramed.** **3.** to show in or as if in a diagram. [C17: from L, from Gk, from *diagraphein*, from *graphein* to write] —**diagrammatic** (,daɪəgrə'mætɪk) *adj.*

dial ('daɪəl) *n.* **1.** the face of a watch, clock, etc., marked with divisions representing units of time. **2.** the graduated disc of various measuring instruments. **3. a.** the control on a radio or television set used to change the station or channel. **b.** the panel on a radio on which the frequency, wavelength, or station is indicated. **4.** a numbered disc on a telephone that is rotated a set distance for each digit of a number being called. **5.** *Brit.* a slang word for **face.** ~*vb.* **dialling, dialled** *or U.S.* **dialing, dialed.** **6.** to try to establish a telephone connection with (a subscriber) by operating the dial or buttons on a telephone. **7.** (*tr.*) to indicate, measure, or operate with a dial. [C14: from Med. L *diālis* daily, from L *diēs* day] —**'dialler** *n.*

dial. *abbrev. for* dialect(al).

dialect ('daɪə,lɛkt) *n.* **a.** a form of a language spoken in a particular geographical area or by members of a particular social class or occupational group, distinguished by its vocabulary, grammar, and pronunciation. **b.** a form of a language that is considered inferior. [C16: from L, from Gk *dialektos* speech, dialect, discourse, from *dialegesthai* to converse, from *legein* to talk, speak] —**dia'lectal** *adj.*

dialectic (,daɪə'lɛktɪk) *n.* **1.** disputation or debate, esp. when intended to resolve differences between two views. **2.** logical argumentation. **3.** a variant of **dialectics** (sense 1). **4.** *Philosophy.* an interpretive method used by Hegel in which contradictions are resolved at a higher level of truth (synthesis). ~*adj.* **5.** of or relating to logical disputation. [C17: from L, from Gk *dialektikē* (*tekhnē*) (the art) of argument; see DIALECT] —,**dialec'tician** *n.*

dialectical (,daɪə'lɛktɪk³l) *adj.* of or relating to dialectic or dialectics. —,**dia'lectically** *adv.*

dialectical materialism *n.* the economic, political, and philosophical system of Marx and Engels that combines traditional materialism and Hegelian dialectic.

dialectics (,daɪə'lɛktɪks) *n.* (*functioning as pl. or* (*sometimes*) *sing.*) **1.** the study of reasoning. **2.** a particular methodology or system. **3.** the application of the Hegelian dialectic or the rationale of dialectical materialism.

dialling code *n.* a sequence of numbers which is dialled for connection with another exchange before an individual subscriber's telephone number is dialled.

dialling tone *or U.S. & Canad.* **dial tone** *n.* a continuous sound, either purring or high-pitched, heard over a telephone indicating that a number can be dialled.

dialogue *or U.S.* (*often*) **dialog** ('daɪə,lɒg) *n.* **1.** conversation between two or more people. **2.** an exchange of opinions; discussion. **3.** the lines spoken by characters in drama or fiction. **4.** a passage of conversation in a literary or dramatic work. **5.** a literary composition in the form of a dialogue. **6.** a political discussion between representatives of two nations or groups. [C13: from OF, from L, from Gk, from *dialegesthai*; see DIALECT]

dialyse *or U.S.* **-lyze** ('daɪə,laɪz) *vb.* (*tr.*) to separate by dialysis. —,**dialy'sation** *or U.S.* **-ly'zation** *n.*

dialyser *or U.S.* **dialyzer** ('daɪə,laɪzə) *n.* a machine that performs dialysis, esp. one that removes impurities from the blood of patients with malfunctioning kidneys; kidney machine.

dialysis (daɪ'ælɪsɪs) *n.*, *pl.* **-ses** (-,siːz). **1.** the separation of the crystalloids from a solution containing crystalloids and colloids by osmosis of the crystalloids. **2.** *Med.* the filtering of blood through a semipermeable membrane to remove waste products. [C16: from LL: a separation, from Gk *dialusis*, from *dialuein* to tear apart, dissolve, from *luein* to loosen] —**dialytic** (,daɪə'lɪtɪk) *adj.*

diam. *abbrev. for* diameter.

diamagnetic (,daɪəmæg'nɛtɪk) *adj.* of, exhibiting, or concerned with diamagnetism.

diamagnetism (,daɪə'mægnɪ,tɪzəm) *n.* the phenomenon exhibited by substances that are repelled by both poles of a magnet and thus lie across the magnet's line of influence.

diamanté (,daɪə'mæntɪ) *adj.* **1.** decorated with glittering ornaments, such as sequins. ~*n.* **2.** a fabric so covered. [C20: from F, from *diamanter* to adorn with diamonds]

diameter (daɪ'æmɪtə) *n.* **1. a.** a straight line connecting the centre of a circle, sphere, etc. with two points on the perimeter or surface. **b.** the length of such a line. **2.** the thickness of something, esp. with circular cross section. [C14: from Med. L, from Gk: diameter, diagonal, from DIA- + *metron* measure]

diametric (,daɪə'mɛtrɪk) *or* **diametrical** *adj.* **1.** Also: **diametral.** of, related to, or along a diameter. **2.** completely opposed.

diametrically (,daɪə'mɛtrɪkəlɪ) *adv.* completely; utterly (esp. in **diametrically opposed**).

diamond ('daɪəmənd) *n.* **1. a.** a usually colourless exceptionally hard form of carbon in cubic crystalline form. It is used as a precious stone and for industrial cutting or abrading. **b.** (*as modifier*): *a diamond ring.* **2.** *Geom.* a figure having four sides of equal length forming two acute angles and two obtuse angles; rhombus. **3. a.** a red lozenge-shaped symbol on a playing card. **b.** a card with one or more of these symbols *or* (*when pl.*) the suit of cards so marked. **4.** *Baseball.* **a.** the whole playing field. **b.** the square formed by the four bases. ~*vb.* **5.** (*tr.*) to decorate with or as with diamonds. [C13: from OF *diamant*, from Med. L *diamas*, from L *adamas* the hardest iron or steel, diamond; see ADAMANT] —**diamantine** (,daɪə'mæntaɪn) *adj.*

diamond anniversary *n.* a 60th, or occasionally 75th, anniversary.

diamondback ('daɪəmənd,bæk) *n.* **1.** Also called: **diamondback terrapin** *or* **turtle.** any edible North American terrapin having diamond-shaped markings on the shell. **2.** a large North American rattlesnake having diamond-shaped markings.

diamond wedding *n.* the 60th, or occasionally the 75th, anniversary of a marriage.

Diana (daɪ'ænə) *n.* **1.** the virginal Roman goddess of the hunt and the moon. Greek counterpart: **Artemis. 2.** title *Princess of Wales*, original name *Lady Diana Frances Spencer.* born 1961, she married Charles, Prince of Wales, in 1981.

dianthus (daɪ'ænθəs) *n.*, *pl.* **-thuses.** any Eurasian plant of the widely cultivated genus *Dianthus*, such as the carnation, pink, and sweet william. [C19: NL, from Gk DI-[1] + *anthos* flower]

diapason (,daɪə'peɪz³n) *n. Music.* **1.** either of two stops (**open** and **stopped diapason**) found throughout the compass of a pipe organ that give it its characteristic tone colour. **2.** the compass of an instrument or voice. **3. a.** a standard pitch used for tuning. **b.** a tuning fork or pitch pipe. **4.** (in classical Greece) an octave. [C14: from L: the whole octave, from Gk: (*hē*) *dia pasōn* (*khordōn sumphōnia*) (concord) through all (the notes)]

diapause ('daɪə,pɔːz) *n.* a period of suspended development and growth accompanied by decreased metabolism in insects and some other animals. [C19: from Gk *diapausis* pause, from *diapauein* to pause, bring to an end, from DIA- + *pauein* to stop]

diaper ('daɪəpə) *n.* **1.** the U.S. and Canad. word for **nappy**[1]. **2. a.** a fabric having a pattern of a small repeating design, esp. diamonds. **b.** such a pattern, used as decoration. ~*vb.* **3.** (*tr.*) to decorate with such a pattern. [C14: from OF *diaspre*, from Med. L *diasprus* made of diaper, from Med. Gk *diaspros* pure white, from DIA- + *aspros* white, shining]

diaphanous (daɪ'æfənəs) *adj.* (usually of fabrics) fine and translucent. [C17: from Med. L, from Gk *diaphanēs* transparent, from DIA- + *phainein* to show] —**di'apha-nously** *adv.*

diaphoresis (ˌdaɪəfə'riːsɪs) *n.* perspiration, esp. when perceptible and excessive. [C17: via LL from Gk, from *diaphorein* to disperse by perspiration, from DIA- + *phorein* to carry]

diaphoretic (ˌdaɪəfə'rɛtɪk) *adj.* **1.** relating to or causing perspiration. ~*n.* **2.** a diaphoretic drug.

diaphragm ('daɪəˌfræm) *n.* **1.** *Anat.* any separating membrane, esp. the muscular partition that separates the abdominal and thoracic cavities in mammals. **2.** another name for **cap** (sense 11). **3.** any thin dividing membrane. **4.** Also called: **stop.** a device to control the amount of light entering an optical instrument, such as a camera. **5.** a thin vibrating disc used to convert sound signals to electrical signals or vice versa in telephones, etc. [C17: from LL, from Gk, from DIA- + *phragma* fence] —**diaphragmatic** (ˌdaɪəfræg'mætɪk) *adj.*

diapositive (ˌdaɪə'pɒzɪtɪv) *n.* a positive transparency; slide.

diarist ('daɪərɪst) *n.* a person who writes a diary, esp. one that is subsequently published.

diarrhoea or esp. U.S. **diarrhea** (ˌdaɪə'rɪə) *n.* frequent and copious discharge of abnormally liquid faeces. [C16: from LL, from Gk, from *diarrhein*, from DIA- + *rhein* to flow] —**diar'rhoeal**, **diar'rhoeic** or esp. U.S. **diar'rheal**, **diar'rheic** *adj.*

diary ('daɪərɪ) *n.*, pl. **-ries. 1.** a personal record of daily events, appointments, observations, etc. **2.** a book for this. [C16: from L *diārium* daily allocation of food or money, journal, from *diēs* day]

Dias or **Diaz** ('diːəs; Portuguese 'diəʃ) *n.* **Bartholomeu** (ˌbərtuluˈmeu). ?1450–1500, Portuguese navigator who discovered the sea route from Europe to the East via the Cape of Good Hope (1488).

Diaspora (daɪ'æspərə) *n.* **1. a.** the dispersion of the Jews after the Babylonian and Roman conquests of Palestine. **b.** the Jewish people and communities outside Israel. **2.** (*often not cap.*) a dispersion, as of people originally belonging to one nation. [C19: from Gk: a scattering, from *diaspeirein*, from DIA- + *speirein* to scatter, sow]

diastalsis (ˌdaɪə'stælsɪs) *n.*, pl. **-ses** (-siːz). *Physiol.* a downward wave of contraction occurring in the intestine during digestion. [C20: NL, from DIA- + (PERI)STALSIS] —**dia'staltic** *adj.*

diastase (ˈdaɪəˌsteɪs, -ˌsteɪz) *n.* any of a group of enzymes that hydrolyse starch to maltose. They are present in germinated barley and in the pancreas. [C19: from F, from Gk *diastasis* a separation] —**dia'stasic** *adj.*

diastole (daɪ'æstəlɪ) *n.* the dilation of the chambers of the heart that follows each contraction, during which they refill with blood. Cf. **systole.** [C16: via LL from Gk, from *diastellein* to expand, from DIA- + *stellein* to place, bring together, make ready] —**diastolic** (ˌdaɪə'stɒlɪk) *adj.*

diastrophism (daɪ'æstrəˌfɪzəm) *n.* the process of movement of the earth's crust that gives rise to mountains, continents, and other large-scale features. [C19: from Gk *diastrophē* a twisting; see DIA-, STROPHE] —**diastrophic** (ˌdaɪə'strɒfɪk) *adj.*

diathermancy (ˌdaɪə'θɜːmənsɪ) *n.*, pl. **-cies.** the property of transmitting infrared radiation. [C19: from F, from DIA- + Gk *thermansis* heating, from *thermos* hot] —**dia'thermanous** *adj.*

diathermy ('daɪəˌθɜːmɪ) or **diathermia** (ˌdaɪə'θɜːmɪə) *n.* local heating of the body tissues with an electric current for medical purposes. [C20: from NL, from DIA- + Gk *thermē* heat]

diatom ('daɪətəm) *n.* a microscopic unicellular alga having a cell wall impregnated with silica. [C19: from NL, from Gk *diatomos* cut in two, from DIA- + *temnein* to cut]

diatomaceous (ˌdaɪətə'meɪʃəs) *adj.* of or containing diatoms or their fossil remains.

diatomic (ˌdaɪə'tɒmɪk) *adj.* (of a compound or molecule) **a.** containing two atoms. **b.** containing two characteristic groups or atoms.

diatomite (daɪ'ætəˌmaɪt) *n.* a soft whitish rock consisting of the siliceous remains of diatoms.

diatonic (ˌdaɪə'tɒnɪk) *adj.* **1.** of, relating to, or based upon any scale of five tones and two semitones produced by playing the white keys of a keyboard instrument. **2.** not involving the sharpening or flattening of the notes of the major or minor scale nor the use of such notes as

modified by accidentals. [C16: from LL, from Gk, from *diatonos* extending, from DIA- + *teinein* to stretch]

diatonic scale *n.* *Music.* the major and minor scales, made up of both tones and semitones.

diatribe ('daɪəˌtraɪb) *n.* a bitter or violent criticism or attack. [C16: from L *diatriba* learned debate, from Gk *diatribē* discourse, pastime, from *diatribein* to while away, from DIA- + *tribein* to rub]

Diaz *n.* **1.** ('diːəs; Portuguese 'diəʃ), **Bartholomeu** (ˌbərtuluˈmeu). a variant spelling of (Bartholomeu) **Dias. 2.** ('diːəs; Spanish 'diaθ), **(José de la Cruz) Porfirio** (pɔr'firjo). 1830–1915, Mexican general and statesman; president of Mexico (1877–80; 1884–1911).

Díaz de Bivar (*Spanish* 'diaθ dɛ bi'βar) *n.* **Rodrigo** (rɔ'ðriγo). the original name of (El) **Cid.**

diazepam (daɪ'eɪzəˌpæm) *n.* a chemical compound used as a tranquillizer and muscle relaxant. [C20: from DI-[1] + *azo*- + *ep(oxide)* + -*am*]

diazo (daɪ'eɪzəʊ) *adj.* **1.** of, consisting of, or containing the divalent group, =N:N, or the divalent group, -N:N-. **2.** of the reproduction of documents using the bleaching action of ultraviolet radiation on diazonium salts. ~*n.*, pl. **-os** or **-oes. 3.** a document produced by this method.

diazonium (ˌdaɪə'zəʊnɪəm) *n.* (modifier) of, consisting of, or containing the group ArN:N–, where Ar is an aryl group: *a diazonium salt.*

dibasic (daɪ'beɪsɪk) *adj.* **1.** (of an acid) containing two acidic hydrogen atoms. **2.** (of a salt) derived by replacing two acidic hydrogen atoms. —**dibasicity** (ˌdaɪbeɪ'sɪsɪtɪ) *n.*

dibble ('dɪbəl) *n.* **1.** Also: **dibber.** a small hand tool used to make holes in the ground for bulbs, seeds, or roots. ~*vb.* **2.** to make a hole in (the ground) with a dibble. **3.** to plant (seeds, etc.) with a dibble. [C15: from ?]

dibs (dɪbz) *pl. n.* **1.** another word for **jacks. 2.** *Sl.* money. **3.** (foll. by *on*) *Inf.* rights (to) or claims (on): used mainly by children. [C18: from *dibstones* game played with knucklebones or pebbles, prob. from *dib* to tap]

dice (daɪs) *pl. n.* **1.** cubes of wood, plastic, etc., each of whose sides has a different number of spots (1 to 6), used in games of chance. **2.** (*functioning as sing.*) Also called: **die.** one of these cubes. **3.** small cubes as of vegetables, meat, etc. **4. no dice.** *Sl.*, *chiefly U.S. & Canad.* an expression of refusal. ~*vb.* **5.** to cut (food, etc.) into small cubes. **6.** (intr.) to gamble or play with dice. **7.** (intr.) to take a chance or risk (esp. in **dice with death**). **8.** (tr.) Austral. inf. to abandon or reject. [C14: pl. of DIE[2]] —**'dicer** *n.*

dicey ('daɪsɪ) *adj.* **dicier, diciest.** *Inf.*, chiefly Brit. difficult or dangerous; risky; tricky.

dichloride (daɪ'klɔːraɪd) *n.* a compound in which two atoms of chlorine are combined with another atom or group. Also called: **bichloride.**

dichlorodiphenyltrichloroethane (daɪˌklɔːrəʊdaɪˌfiːnaɪltraɪˌklɔːrəʊ'iːθeɪn) *n.* the full name for **DDT.**

dichotomy (daɪ'kɒtəmɪ) *n.*, pl. **-mies. 1.** division into two parts or classifications, esp. when they are sharply distinguished or opposed. **2.** *Bot.* a simple method of branching by repeated division into two equal parts. —**di'chotomous** *adj.*

dichroism ('daɪkrəʊˌɪzəm) *n.* a property of a uniaxial crystal of showing a difference in colour when viewed along two different axes (in transmitted white light). Also called: **dichromaticism.** See also **pleochroism.** —**di'chroic** *adj.*

dichromate (daɪ'krəʊmeɪt) *n.* any salt or ester of dichromic acid. Also called: **bichromate.**

dichromatic (ˌdaɪkrəʊ'mætɪk) *adj.* **1.** Also: **dichroic.** having two colours. **2.** (of animal species) having two different colour varieties. **3.** able to perceive only two colours (and mixes of them). —**dichromatism** (daɪ'krəʊməˌtɪzəm) *n.*

dichromic (daɪ'krəʊmɪk) *adj.* of or involving only two colours; dichromatic.

dick (dɪk) *n.* *Sl.* **1.** *Brit.* a fellow or person. **2. clever dick.** *Brit.* an opinionated person; know-all. **3.** a taboo word for **penis.** [C16 (meaning: fellow): from *Dick*, familiar form of *Richard*, applied to any fellow, lad, etc.; hence, C19: penis]

dickens ('dɪkɪnz) *n.* *Inf.* a euphemistic word for **devil** (used as intensifier in **what the dickens**). [C16: from the name *Dickens*]

Dickens ('dɪkɪnz) *n.* **Charles (John Huffam)**, pen name *Boz.* 1812–70, English novelist, famous for the humour and sympathy of his characterization and his criticism of social injustice. His major works include *The Pickwick Papers* (1837), *Oliver Twist* (1839), *Nicholas Nickleby* (1839), *Old Curiosity Shop* (1840–41), *Martin Chuzzlewit* (1844), *David Copperfield* (1850), *Bleak House* (1853), *Little Dorrit* (1857), and *Great Expectations* (1861).

Dickensian (dɪ'kɛnzɪən) *adj.* **1.** of Charles Dickens or his novels. **2. a.** denoting poverty, distress, and exploitation as depicted in the novels of Dickens. **b.** grotesquely comic, as some of the characters of Dickens.

dicker ('dɪkə) *vb.* **1.** to trade (goods) by bargaining; barter. ~*n.* **2.** a petty bargain or barter. [C12: ult. from L *decuria* company of ten, from *decem* ten]

Dickinson ('dɪkɪnsᵊn) *n.* **Emily.** 1830–86, U.S. poet, noted for her short mostly unrhymed mystical lyrics.

dicky[1] *or* **dickey** ('dɪkɪ) *n., pl.* **dickies** *or* **dickeys. 1.** a false blouse or shirt front. **2.** Also called: **dicky bow.** *Brit.* a bow tie. **3.** Also called: **dicky-bird, dickeybird.** a child's word for a bird. **4.** a folding outside seat at the rear of some early cars. [C18 (in the sense: shirt front): from *Dickey*, dim. of *Dick* (name)]

dicky[2] *or* **dickey** ('dɪkɪ) *adj.* **dickier, dickiest.** *Brit. inf.* shaky, unsteady, or unreliable: *I feel a bit dicky today.* [C18: ?from as *queer as Dick's hatband* feeling ill]

diclinous ('daɪklɪnəs) *adj.* (of flowering plants) unisexual. Cf. **monoclinous** — '**diclinism** *n.*

dicotyledon (,daɪkɒtɪ'liːdᵊn) *n.* a flowering plant having two embryonic seed leaves. — ,**dicoty'ledonous** *adj.*

dict. *abbrev. for:* **1.** dictation. **2.** dictator. **3.** dictionary.

dicta ('dɪktə) *n.* a plural of **dictum.**

Dictaphone ('dɪktə,fəʊn) *n. Trademark.* a tape recorder designed esp. for recording dictation for subsequent typing.

dictate *vb.* (dɪk'teɪt). **1.** to say (letters, speeches, etc.) aloud for mechanical recording or verbatim transcription by another person. **2.** (*tr.*) to prescribe (commands, etc.) authoritatively. **3.** (*intr.*) to seek to impose one's will on others. ~*n.* ('dɪkteɪt). **4.** an authoritative command. **5.** a guiding principle: *the dictates of reason.* [C17: from L *dictāre* to say repeatedly, order, from *dīcere* to say]

dictation (dɪk'teɪʃən) *n.* **1.** the act of dictating material to be recorded or taken down in writing. **2.** the material dictated. **3.** authoritative commands or the act of giving them.

dictator (dɪk'teɪtə) *n.* **1. a.** a ruler who is not effectively restricted by a constitution, laws, etc. **b.** an absolute, esp. tyrannical, ruler. **2.** (in ancient Rome) a person appointed during a crisis to exercise supreme authority. **3.** a person who makes pronouncements, which are regarded as authoritative. **4.** a person who behaves in an authoritarian or tyrannical manner.

dictatorial (,dɪktə'tɔːrɪəl) *adj.* **1.** of or characteristic of a dictator. **2.** tending to dictate; tyrannical; overbearing. — ,**dicta'torially** *adv.*

dictatorship (dɪk'teɪtə,ʃɪp) *n.* **1.** the rank, office, or period of rule of a dictator. **2.** government by a dictator. **3.** a country ruled by a dictator. **4.** absolute power or authority.

diction ('dɪkʃən) *n.* **1.** the choice of words in writing or speech. **2.** the manner of enunciating words and sounds. [C15: from L *dictiō* a saying, mode of expression, from *dīcere* to speak, say]

dictionary ('dɪkʃənərɪ) *n., pl.* **-aries. 1. a.** a book that consists of an alphabetical list of words with their meanings, parts of speech, pronunciations, etymologies, etc. **b.** a similar book giving equivalent words in two or more languages. **2.** a reference book listing words or terms and giving information about a particular subject or activity. **3.** a collection of information or examples with the entries alphabetically arranged: *a dictionary of quotations.* [C16: from Med. L *dictiōnārium* collection of words, from LL *dictiō* word; see DICTION]

dictum ('dɪktəm) *n., pl.* **-tums** *or* **-ta. 1.** a formal or authoritative statement; pronouncement. **2.** a popular saying or maxim. **3.** *Law.* See **obiter dictum.** [C16: from L, from *dīcere* to say]

did (dɪd) *vb.* the past tense of **do**[1].

didactic (dɪ'dæktɪk) *adj.* **1.** intended to instruct, esp. excessively. **2.** morally instructive. **3.** (of works of art or literature) containing a political or moral message to

which aesthetic considerations are subordinated. [C17: from Gk *didaktikos* skilled in teaching, from *didaskein*] — **di'dactically** *adv.* — **di'dacticism** *n.*

didactics (dɪ'dæktɪks) *n.* (*functioning as sing.*) the art or science of teaching.

diddle ('dɪdᵊl) *vb.* (*tr.*) *Inf.* to cheat or swindle. [C19: back formation from Jeremy *Diddler*, a scrounger in J. Kenney's farce *Raising the Wind* (1803)] — '**diddler** *n.*

Diderot ('diːdərəʊ; *French* didro) *n.* **Denis** (dəni). 1713–84, French philosopher, noted particularly for his direction (1745–72) of the great French *Encyclopédie*.

didgeridoo (,dɪdʒərɪ'duː) *n. Music.* a native deep-toned Australian wind instrument. [C20: imit.]

didn't ('dɪdᵊnt) *contraction of* did not.

dido ('daɪdəʊ) *n., pl.* **-dos** *or* **-does.** (*usually pl.*) *Inf.* an antic; prank; trick. [C19: from ?]

Dido ('daɪdəʊ) *n. Classical myth.* a princess of Tyre who founded Carthage and became its queen. Virgil tells of her suicide when abandoned by her lover Aeneas.

didst (dɪdst) *vb. Arch.* (used with *thou*) a form of the past tense of **do**[1].

didymium (daɪ'dɪmɪəm) *n.* a mixture of the metallic rare earths neodymium and praseodymium, once thought to be an element. [C19: from NL, from Gk *didumos* twin + -IUM]

die[1] (daɪ) *vb.* **dying, died.** (*mainly intr.*) **1.** (of an organism, organs, etc.) to cease all biological activity permanently. **2.** (of something inanimate) to cease to exist. **3.** (often foll. by *away, down,* or *out*) to lose strength, power, or energy, esp. by degrees. **4.** (often foll. by *away* or *down*) to become calm; subside. **5.** to stop functioning: *the engine died.* **6.** to languish, as with love, longing, etc. **7.** (usually foll. by *of*) *Inf.* to be nearly overcome (with laughter, boredom, etc.). **8.** *Christianity.* to lack spiritual life within the soul. **9.** (*tr.*) to suffer (a death of a specified kind): *he died a saintly death.* **10. be dying.** (foll. by *for* or an infinitive) to be eager or desperate (for something or to do something). **11. die hard.** to cease to exist after a struggle: *old habits die hard.* **12. die in harness.** to die while still working or active. **13. never say die.** *Inf.* never give up. ~See also **die down, die out.** [OE *dīegan*, prob. of Scand. origin]

die[2] (daɪ) *n.* **1. a.** a shaped block used to cut or form metal in a drop forge, press, etc. **b.** a tool with a conical hole through which wires, etc. are drawn to reduce their diameter. **2.** an internally-threaded tool for cutting external threads. **3.** a casting mould. **4.** *Archit.* the dado of a pedestal, usually cubic. **5.** another name for **dice** (sense 2). **6. the die is cast.** the irrevocable decision has been taken. [C13 *dee*, from OF *de*, ?from Vulgar L *datum* (unattested) a piece in games, from L *dare* to give, play]

die-cast *vb.* **-casting, -cast.** (*tr.*) to shape or form (an object) by introducing molten metal or plastic into a reusable mould, esp. under pressure. — '**die-,casting** *n.*

die down *vb.* (*intr., adv.*) **1.** (of plants) to wither above ground, leaving only the root alive during the winter. **2.** to lose strength or power, esp. by degrees. **3.** to become calm.

Diefenbaker ('diːfᵊn,beɪkə) *n.* **John George.** 1895–1979, Canadian Conservative statesman; prime minister of Canada (1957–63).

Diégo-Suarez (*French* djegosɥarɛs) *n.* the former name of **Antseranana.**

die-hard *n.* **1.** a person who resists change or who holds onto an untenable position. **2.** (*modifier*) obstinately resistant to change.

dieldrin ('diːldrɪn) *n.* a crystalline substance, consisting of a chlorinated derivative of naphthalene: a contact insecticide. [C20: from *Diel(s-Al)d(e)r* (*reaction*) + -IN; Diels & Alder were G chemists]

dielectric (,daɪɪ'lɛktrɪk) *n.* **1.** a substance that can sustain an electric field. **2.** a substance of very low electrical conductivity; insulator. ~*adj.* **3.** concerned with or having the properties of a dielectric. — ,**die'lectrically** *adv.*

Dien Bien Phu (djɛn bjɛn fuː) *n.* a village in NE Vietnam: French military post during the Indochina War; scene of a major defeat of French forces by the Vietminh (1954).

-diene *n. combining form.* denoting an organic compound containing two double bonds between carbon atoms: *butadiene.* [from DI-[1] + -ENE]

die out *or* **off** *vb.* (*intr., adv.*) **1.** to die one after another until few or none are left. **2.** to become extinct, esp. after a period of gradual decline.

Dieppe (dɪ'ɛp; French djɛp) n. a port and resort in N France, on the English Channel. Pop.: 39 394 (1983 est.).

dieresis (daɪ'ɛrɪsɪs) n., pl. **-ses** (-ˌsiːz). a variant spelling (esp. U.S.) of **diaeresis**.

diesel ('diːzəl) n. **1.** See **diesel engine**. **2.** a ship, locomotive, lorry, etc., driven by a diesel engine. **3.** Inf. short for **diesel oil** (or **fuel**).

Diesel ('diːzəl) n. **Rudolf** ('ruːdɔlf). 1858–1913, German engineer, who invented the diesel engine (1892).

diesel-electric n. **1.** a locomotive fitted with a diesel engine driving an electric generator that feeds electric traction motors. ~adj. **2.** of or relating to such a locomotive or system.

diesel engine or **motor** n. a type of internal-combustion engine in which atomized fuel oil is ignited by compression alone.

diesel oil or **fuel** n. a fuel obtained from petroleum distillation that is used in diesel engines. Also called (Brit.): **derv**.

Dies Irae Latin. ('diːeɪz 'ɪəraɪ) n. **1.** a Latin hymn of the 13th century, describing the Last Judgment. It is used in the Mass for the dead. **2.** a musical setting of this. [lit.: day of wrath]

diesis ('daɪɪsɪs) n., pl. **-ses** (-ˌsiːz). Printing. another name for **double dagger**. [C16: via L from Gk: a quarter tone, lit.: a sending through, from *diienai*; the double dagger was orig. used in musical notation]

diestock ('daɪˌstɒk) n. the device holding the dies used to cut an external screw thread.

diet¹ ('daɪət) n. **1.** a specific allowance or selection of food, esp. prescribed to control weight or for health reasons: *a salt-free diet*. **2.** the food and drink that a person or animal regularly consumes. **3.** regular activities or occupations. ~vb. **4.** (usually intr.) to follow or cause to follow a dietary regimen. [C13: from OF *diete*, from L *diaeta*, from Gk *diaita* mode of living, from *diaitan* to direct one's own life] —**dieter** n.

diet² ('daɪət) n. **1.** (sometimes cap.) a legislative assembly in various countries. **2.** (sometimes cap.) the assembly of the estates of the Holy Roman Empire. **3.** Scots Law. a single session of a court. [C15: from Med. L *dièta* public meeting, prob. from L *diaeta* DIET¹ but associated with L *diès* day]

dietary ('daɪətərɪ, -trɪ) adj. **1.** of or relating to a diet. ~n., pl. **-taries**. **2.** a regulated diet. **3.** a system of dieting.

dietary fibre n. fibrous substances in fruits and vegetables, such as the structural polymers of cell walls, which aid digestion. Also called: **roughage**.

dietetic (ˌdaɪɪ'tɛtɪk) or **dietetical** adj. **1.** denoting or relating to diet. **2.** prepared for special dietary requirements. —**die'tetically** adv.

dietetics (ˌdaɪɪ'tɛtɪks) n. (functioning as sing.) the scientific study and regulation of food intake and preparation.

diethylene glycol n. a colourless soluble liquid used as an antifreeze and solvent.

dietitian or **dietician** (ˌdaɪɪ'tɪʃən) n. a person who specializes in dietetics.

Dietrich (German 'diːtrɪç) n. **Marlene** (mar'leɪnə), real name *Maria Magdalene von Losch*. born 1901, U.S. film actress and cabaret singer, born in Germany.

differ ('dɪfə) vb. (intr.) **1.** (often foll. by *from*) to be dissimilar in quality, nature, or degree (to); vary (from). **2.** (often foll. by *from* or *with*) to disagree (with). **3.** Dialect. to quarrel or dispute. [C14: from L *differre* to scatter, put off, be different, from *dis-* apart + *ferre* to bear]

difference ('dɪfərəns) n. **1.** the state or quality of being unlike. **2.** a specific instance of being unlike. **3.** a distinguishing mark or feature. **4.** a significant change. **5.** a disagreement or argument. **6.** a degree of distinctness, as between two people or things. **7.** the result of the subtraction of one number, quantity, etc., from another. **8.** Maths. (of two sets) the set of members of the first that are not members of the second. **9.** Heraldry. an addition to the arms of a family to represent a younger branch. **10. make a difference. a.** to have an effect. **b.** to treat differently. **11. split the difference. a.** to compromise. **b.** to divide a remainder equally. **12. with a difference.** with some distinguishing quality, good or bad.

different ('dɪfərənt) adj. **1.** partly or completely unlike. **2.** not identical or the same; other. **3.** unusual. —**differently** adv. —**differentness** n.

▷ **Usage.** The constructions *different from*, *different to*, and *different than* are all found in the works of writers of English during the past. Nowadays, however, the most widely acceptable preposition to use after *different* is *from*.

differentia (ˌdɪfə'rɛnʃɪə) n., pl. **-tiae** (-ʃɪˌiː). Logic. a feature by which two subclasses of the same class of named objects can be distinguished. [C19: from L: diversity]

differential (ˌdɪfə'rɛnʃəl) adj. **1.** of, relating to, or using a difference. **2.** constituting a difference; distinguishing. **3.** Maths. involving one or more derivatives or differentials. **4.** Physics, engineering. relating to, operating on, or based on the difference between two opposing effects, motions, forces, etc. ~n. **5.** a factor that differentiates between two comparable things. **6.** Maths. **a.** an increment in a given function, expressed as the product of the derivative of that function and the corresponding increment in the independent variable. **b.** an increment in a given function of two or more variables, $f(x_1, x_2, \ldots x_n)$, expressed as the sum of the products of each partial derivative and the increment in the corresponding variable. **7.** See **differential gear**. **8.** Chiefly Brit. the difference between rates of pay for different types of labour, esp. when forming a pay structure within an industry. **9.** (in commerce) a difference in rates, esp. between comparable services. —**differentially** adv.

differential calculus n. the branch of calculus concerned with the study, evaluation, and use of derivatives and differentials.

differential equation n. an equation containing differentials or derivatives of a function of one independent variable.

differential gear n. the epicyclic gear mounted in the driving axle of a road vehicle that permits one driving wheel to rotate faster than the other, as when cornering.

differential operator n. a mathematical operator, ∇, used in vector analysis.

differentiate (ˌdɪfə'rɛnʃɪˌeɪt) vb. **1.** (tr.) to serve to distinguish between. **2.** (when intr., often foll. by *between*) to perceive, show, or make a difference (in or between); discriminate. **3.** (intr.) to become dissimilar or distinct. **4.** Maths. to perform a differentiation on (a quantity, expression, etc.). **5.** (intr.) (of unspecialized cells, etc.) to change during development to more specialized forms. —ˌdiffer'enti,ator n.

differentiation (ˌdɪfəˌrɛnʃɪ'eɪʃən) n. **1.** the act, process, or result of differentiating. **2.** Maths. an operation used in calculus in which the derivative of a function or variable is determined.

difficult ('dɪfɪkəlt) adj. **1.** not easy to do; requiring effort. **2.** not easy to understand or solve. **3.** troublesome: *a difficult child*. **4.** not easily convinced, pleased, or satisfied. **5.** full of hardships or trials. [C14: back formation from DIFFICULTY] —'**difficultly** adv.

difficulty ('dɪfɪkəltɪ) n., pl. **-ties. 1.** the state or quality of being difficult. **2.** a task, problem, etc., that is hard to deal with. **3.** (often pl.) a troublesome or embarrassing situation, esp. a financial one. **4.** a disagreement. **5.** (often pl.) an objection or obstacle. **6.** a trouble or source of trouble; worry. **7.** lack of ease; awkwardness. [C14: from L *difficultās*, from *difficilis*, from *dis-* not + *facilis* easy]

diffident ('dɪfɪdənt) adj. lacking self-confidence; shy. [C15: from L *diffīdere*, from *dis-* not + *fīdere* to trust] —'**diffidence** n. —'**diffidently** adv.

diffract (dɪ'frækt) vb. to undergo or cause to undergo diffraction. —**dif'fractive** adj. —**dif'fractively** adv. —**dif'fractiveness** n.

diffraction (dɪ'frækʃən) n. **1.** Physics. a deviation in the direction of a wave at the edge of an obstacle in its path. **2.** any phenomenon caused by diffraction, such as the formation of light and dark fringes by the passage of light through a small aperture. [C17: from NL *diffractiō* a breaking to pieces, from L *diffringere* to shatter, from *dis-* apart + *frangere* to break]

diffraction grating n. a glass plate or a mirror marked with lines or grooves. It causes diffraction of light, ultraviolet radiation, or x-rays.

diffuse vb. (dɪ'fjuːz). **1.** to spread in all directions. **2.** to undergo or cause to undergo diffusion. **3.** to scatter; disperse. ~adj. (dɪ'fjuːs). **4.** spread out over a wide area. **5.** lacking conciseness. **6.** characterized by diffusion. [C15: from L *diffūsus* spread abroad, from *diffundere* to pour forth, from *dis-* away + *fundere* to pour] —**diffusely** (dɪ'fjuːslɪ) adv. —**dif'fuseness** n. —**diffusible** (dɪ'fjuːzɪbᵊl) adj.

diffuser *or* **diffusor** (dɪˈfjuːzə) *n.* **1.** a person or thing that diffuses. **2.** a part of a lighting fixture, as a translucent covering, used to scatter the light and prevent glare. **3.** a cone, wedge, or baffle placed in front of the diaphragm of a loudspeaker to diffuse the sound waves. **4.** a duct, esp. in a wind tunnel or jet engine, that reduces the speed and increases the pressure of the air or fluid. **5.** *Photog.* a light-scattering medium, such as a screen of fine fabric, used to reduce the sharpness of shadows and thus soften the lighting.

diffusion (dɪˈfjuːʒən) *n.* **1.** a diffusing or being diffused; dispersion. **2.** verbosity. **3.** *Physics.* **a.** the random thermal motion of atoms, molecules, etc., in gases, liquids, and some solids. **b.** the transfer of atoms or molecules by their random motion from one part of a medium to another. **4.** *Physics.* the transmission or reflection of electromagnetic radiation, esp. light, in which the radiation is scattered in many directions. **5.** *Anthropol.* the transmission of social institutions, skills, and myths from one culture to another.

diffusive (dɪˈfjuːsɪv) *adj.* characterized by diffusion. —**dif'fusively** *adv.* —**dif'fusiveness** *n.*

dig (dɪg) *vb.* **digging, dug. 1.** (when *tr.,* often foll. by *up*) to cut into, break up, and turn over or remove (earth, etc.), esp. with a spade. **2.** to excavate (a hole, tunnel, etc.) by digging, usually with an implement or (of animals) with claws, etc. **3.** (often foll. by *through*) to make or force (one's way): *he dug his way through the crowd.* **4.** (*tr.;* often foll. by *out* or *up*) to obtain by digging. **5.** (*tr.;* often foll. by *out* or *up*) to find by effort or searching: *to dig out facts.* **6.** (*tr.;* foll. by *in* or *into*) to thrust or jab. **7.** (*tr.;* foll. by *in* or *into*) to mix (compost, etc.) with soil by digging. **8.** (*intr.;* foll. by *in* or *into*) *Inf.* to begin vigorously to do something. **9.** (*tr.*) *Inf.* to like, understand, or appreciate. **10.** (*intr.*) *U.S. sl.* to work hard, esp. for an examination. ~*n.* **11.** the act of digging. **12.** a thrust or poke. **13.** a cutting remark. **14.** *Inf.* an archaeological excavation. **15.** *Austral. & N.Z. inf.* short for **digger** (sense 4). ~See also **dig in.** [C13 *diggen,* from ?]

digest *vb.* (dɪˈdʒɛst, daɪ-). **1.** to subject (food) to a process of digestion. **2.** (*tr.*) to assimilate mentally. **3.** *Chem.* to soften or disintegrate by the action of heat, moisture, or chemicals. **4.** (*tr.*) to arrange in a methodical order; classify. **5.** (*tr.*) to reduce to a summary. ~*n.* ('daɪdʒɛst). **6.** a comprehensive and systematic compilation of information or material, often condensed. **7.** a magazine, periodical, etc., that summarizes news. **8.** a compilation of rules of law. [C14: from LL *digesta* writings grouped under various heads, from L *digerere* to divide, from *di-* apart + *gerere* to bear]

Digest ('daɪdʒɛst) *n. Roman law.* the books of law compiled by order of Justinian in the sixth century A.D.

digestible (dɪˈdʒɛstɪbəl, daɪ-) *adj.* capable of being digested. —**di,gesti'bility** *n.*

digestion (dɪˈdʒɛstʃən, daɪ-) *n.* **1.** the act or process in living organisms of breaking down food into easily absorbed substances by the action of enzymes, etc. **2.** mental assimilation, esp. of ideas. **3.** the decomposition of sewage by bacteria. **4.** *Chem.* the treatment of material with heat, solvents, etc., to cause decomposition. [C14: from OF, from L *digestiō* a dissolving, digestion] —**di'gestional** *adj.*

digestive (dɪˈdʒɛstɪv, daɪ-) *or* **digestant** (daɪˈdʒɛstənt) *adj.* **1.** relating to, aiding, or subjecting to digestion. ~*n.* **2.** any substance that aids digestion. —**di'gestively** *adv.*

digestive biscuit *n.* a round semisweet biscuit made from wholemeal flour.

digger ('dɪgə) *n.* **1.** a person, animal, or machine that digs. **2.** a miner. **3.** a tool or machine used for excavation. **4.** (*sometimes cap.*) *Austral. & N.Z. inf.* an Australian or New Zealander, esp. a soldier: often used as a friendly term of address.

digger wasp *n.* a wasp that digs nest holes in the ground, rotten wood, etc. and stocks them with live insects for the larvae.

diggings ('dɪgɪŋz) *pl. n.* **1.** (*functioning as pl.*) material that has been dug out. **2.** (*functioning as sing. or pl.*) a place where mining has taken place. **3.** (*functioning as pl.*) *Brit. inf.* a less common name for **digs.**

dight (daɪt) *vb.* **dighting, dight** *or* **dighted.** (*tr.*) *Arch.* to adorn or equip, as for battle. [OE *dihtan* to compose, from L *dictāre* to DICTATE]

dig in *vb.* (*adv.*) **1.** *Mil.* to dig foxholes, trenches, etc. **2.** *Inf.* to entrench (oneself). **3.** (*intr.*) *Inf.* to defend a position firmly, as in an argument. **4.** (*intr.*) *Inf.* to begin to eat vigorously: *don't wait, just dig in.* **5. dig one's heels in.** *Inf.* to refuse to move or be persuaded.

digit ('dɪdʒɪt) *n.* **1.** a finger or toe. **2.** any of the ten Arabic numerals from 0 to 9. [C15: from L *digitus* toe, finger]

digital ('dɪdʒɪtəl) *adj.* **1.** of, resembling, or possessing a digit or digits. **2.** performed with the fingers. **3.** representing data as a series of numerical values. **4.** displaying information as numbers rather than by a pointer moving over a dial. ~*n.* **5.** *Music.* a key on a piano, harpsichord, etc. —**'digitally** *adv.*

digital audio tape *n.* magnetic tape on which sound is recorded digitally, giving high-fidelity reproduction. Abbrev.: **DAT.**

digital clock *or* **watch** *n.* a clock or watch in which the time is indicated by digits rather than by hands on a dial.

digital computer *n.* an electronic computer in which the input is discrete, consisting of numbers, letters, etc. that are represented internally in binary notation.

digitalin (,dɪdʒɪˈteɪlɪn) *n.* a poisonous glycoside extracted from digitalis and used in treating heart disease. [C19: from DIGITAL(IS) + -IN]

digitalis (,dɪdʒɪˈteɪlɪs) *n.* **1.** any of a genus of Eurasian plants such as the foxglove, having long spikes of bell-shaped flowers. **2.** a drug prepared from the dried leaves of the foxglove: used medicinally as a heart stimulant. [C17: from NL, from L: relating to a finger; based on G *Fingerhut* foxglove, lit.: finger-hat]

digitalize *or* **-ise** ('dɪdʒɪtə,laɪz) *vb.* (*tr.*) another word for **digitize.**

digital mapping *n.* a method of preparing maps in which the data is stored in a computer for ease of access and updating. —**digital map** *n.*

digital recording *n.* a sound recording process that converts audio or analogue signals into a series of pulses that correspond to the voltage level.

digitate ('dɪdʒɪ,teɪt) *or* **digitated** *adj.* **1.** (of leaves) having the leaflets in the form of a spread hand. **2.** (of animals) having digits. —**'digi,tately** *adv.* —**,digi'tation** *n.*

digitigrade ('dɪdʒɪtɪ,greɪd) *adj.* **1.** (of dogs, cats, horses, etc.) walking so that only the toes touch the ground. ~*n.* **2.** a digitigrade animal.

digitize *or* **-ise** ('dɪdʒɪ,taɪz) *vb.* (*tr.*) to transcribe (data) into a digital form for processing by a computer. —**,digiti'zation** *or* **-i'sation** *n.* —**'digi,tizer** *or* **-iser** *n.*

dignified ('dɪgnɪ,faɪd) *adj.* characterized by dignity of manner or appearance; stately; noble. —**'digni,fiedly** *adv.* —**'digni,fiedness** *n.*

dignify ('dɪgnɪ,faɪ) *vb.* **-fying, -fied.** (*tr.*) **1.** to invest with honour or dignity. **2.** to add distinction to. **3.** to add a semblance of dignity to, esp. by the use of a pretentious name or title. [C15: from OF *dignifier,* from LL *dignificāre,* from L *dignus* worthy + *facere* to make]

dignitary ('dɪgnɪtərɪ) *n., pl.* **-taries.** a person of high official position or rank.

dignity ('dɪgnɪtɪ) *n., pl.* **-ties. 1.** a formal, stately, or grave bearing. **2.** the state or quality of being worthy of honour. **3.** relative importance; rank. **4.** sense of self-importance (often in **stand** (*or* **be**) **on one's dignity, beneath one's dignity**). **5.** high rank, esp. in government or the church. [C13: from OF *dignite,* from L *dignitās* merit, from *dignus* worthy]

digraph ('daɪgrɑːf) *n.* a combination of two letters used to represent a single sound such as *gh* in *tough.* —**digraphic** (daɪˈgræfɪk) *adj.*

digress (daɪˈgrɛs) *vb.* (*intr.*) **1.** to depart from the main subject in speech or writing. **2.** to wander from one's path. [C16: from L *digressus* turned aside, from *digredī,* from *dis-* apart + *gradī* to go] —**di'gresser** *n.* —**di'gression** *n.*

digressive (daɪˈgrɛsɪv) *adj.* characterized by digression or tending to digress. —**di'gressively** *adv.* —**di'gressiveness** *n.*

digs (dɪgz) *pl. n. Brit. inf.* lodgings. [C19: from DIGGINGS, ? referring to where one *digs* or works, but see also DIG IN]

dihedral (daɪˈhiːdrəl) *adj.* **1.** having or formed by two intersecting planes. ~*n.* **2.** Also called: **dihedron, dihedral angle.** the figure formed by two intersecting planes. **3.** the upward inclination of an aircraft wing in relation to the lateral axis.

Dijon (*French* diʒɔ̃) *n.* a city in E France: capital of the former duchy of Burgundy. Pop.: 150 300 (1983 est.).

dik-dik ('dɪk,dɪk) *n.* any of several small antelopes inhabiting semiarid regions of Africa. [C19: E African, prob. imit.]

dike (daɪk) *n.* **1.** *Inf., chiefly Austral.* a lavatory. ~*n.,vb.* **2.** a variant spelling of **dyke.**

diktat ('dɪktɑːt) *n.* **1.** a decree or settlement imposed, esp. by a ruler or a victorious nation. **2.** a dogmatic statement. [from G: dictation, from L *dictātum,* from *dictāre* to DICTATE]

dilapidate (dɪ'læpɪ,deɪt) *vb.* to fall or cause to fall into ruin. [C16: from L *dīlapidāre* to waste, from *dis-*apart + *lapidāre* to stone, from *lapis* stone] —**di,lapi'dation** *n.*

dilapidated (dɪ'læpɪ,deɪtɪd) *adj.* falling to pieces or in a state of disrepair; shabby.

dilate (daɪ'leɪt, dɪ-) *vb.* **1.** to make or become wider or larger. **2.** (*intr.;* often foll. by *on* or *upon*) to speak or write at length. [C14: from L *dīlātāre* to spread out, from *dis-* apart + *lātus* wide] —**di'latable** *adj.* —**di,lata'bility** *n.* —**di'lation** *or* **dilatation** (,daɪlə'teɪʃən) *n.* —**dilative** (daɪ'leɪtɪv) *adj.*

dilatory ('dɪlətərɪ, -trɪ) *adj.* **1.** tending to delay or waste time. **2.** intended to waste time or defer action. [C15: from LL *dīlātōrius* inclined to delay, from *differre* to postpone; see DIFFER] —**'dilatorily** *adv.* —**'dilatoriness** *n.*

dildo *or* **dildoe** ('dɪldəʊ) *n., pl.* **-dos** *or* **-does.** an object used as a substitute for an erect penis. [C17: from ?]

dilemma (dɪ'lɛmə, daɪ-) *n.* **1.** a situation necessitating a choice between two equally undesirable alternatives. **2.** a problem that seems incapable of a solution. **3.** *Logic.* a type of argument which forces the maintainer of a proposition to accept one of two conclusions each of which contradicts the original assertion. **4. on the horns of a dilemma. a.** faced with the choice between two equally unpalatable alternatives. **b.** in an awkward situation. [C16: via L from Gk, from DI-¹ + *lēmma* proposition, from *lambanein* to grasp] —**dilemmatic** (,dɪlɪ'mætɪk) *adj.*

dilettante (,dɪlɪ'tɑːntɪ) *n., pl.* **-tantes** *or* **-tanti** (-'tɑːntɪ). **1.** a person whose interest in a subject is superficial rather than professional. **2.** a person who loves the arts. ~*adj.* **3.** of or characteristic of a dilettante. [C18: from It., from *dilettare* to delight, from L *dēlectāre*] —,**dilet'tantish** *or* ,**dilet'tanteish** *adj.* —,**dilet'tantism** *or* ,**dilet'tanteism** *n.*

Díli *or* **Dilli** ('diːliː) *n.* a port in Indonesia, in N Timor: the former capital (until 1976) of Portuguese Timor. Pop.: 60 150 (1980).

diligence¹ ('dɪlɪdʒəns) *n.* **1.** steady and careful application. **2.** proper attention or care. [C14: from L *dīligentia* care]

diligence² ('dɪlɪdʒəns) *n. History.* a stagecoach. [C18: from F, shortened from *carosse de diligence,* lit.: coach of speed]

diligent ('dɪlɪdʒənt) *adj.* **1.** careful and persevering in carrying out tasks or duties. **2.** carried out with care and perseverance: *diligent work.* [C14: from OF, from L *dīligere* to value, from *dis-* apart + *legere* to read] —**'diligently** *adv.*

dill¹ (dɪl) *n.* **1.** an aromatic Eurasian plant with umbrella-shaped clusters of yellow flowers. **2.** the leaves or fruits of this plant, used for flavouring and in medicine. [OE *dile*]

dill² (dɪl) *n. Austral. & N.Z. sl.* a fool. [C20: from DILLY²]

dill pickle *n.* a pickled cucumber flavoured with dill.

dilly¹ ('dɪlɪ) *n., pl.* **-lies.** *Sl., chiefly U.S. & Canad.* a person or thing that is remarkable. [C20: ?from girl's name *Dilly*]

dilly² ('dɪlɪ) *adj.* **-lier, -liest.** *Austral. sl.* silly. [C20: from E dialect, ?from SILLY]

dilly bag *n. Austral.* a small bag, esp., formerly, one made of plaited grass, etc., often used for carrying food. [from Abor. *dilly* small bag or basket]

dilly-dally (,dɪlɪ'dælɪ) *vb.* **-lying, -lied.** (*intr.*) *Inf.* to loiter or vacillate. [C17: by reduplication from DALLY]

dilute (daɪ'luːt) *vb.* **1.** to make or become less concentrated, esp. by adding water or a thinner. **2.** to make or become weaker in force, effect, etc. ~*adj.* **3.** *Chem.* **a.** (of a solution, etc.) having a low concentration. **b.** (of a substance) present in solution, esp. a weak solution in water: *dilute acetic acid.* [C16: from L *dīluere,* from *dis-* apart + *-luere,* from *lavāre* to wash] —**di'luter** *n.*

dilution (daɪ'luːʃən) *n.* **1.** the act of diluting or state of being diluted. **2.** a diluted solution.

diluvial (daɪ'luːvɪəl, dɪ-) *or* **diluvian** *adj.* of or connected with a deluge, esp. with the great Flood described in Genesis. [C17: from LL *dīluviālis,* from L *dīluere* to wash away; see DILUTE]

dim (dɪm) *adj.* **dimmer, dimmest.** **1.** badly illuminated. **2.** not clearly seen; faint. **3.** having weak or indistinct vision. **4.** mentally dull. **5.** not clear in the mind; obscure: *a dim memory.* **6.** lacking in brightness or lustre. **7.** unfavourable, gloomy or disapproving (esp. in **take a dim view**). ~*vb.* **dimming, dimmed.** **8.** to become or cause to become dim. **9.** (*tr.*) to cause to seem less bright. **10.** the U.S. and Canad. word for **dip** (sense 5). [OE *dimm*] —**'dimly** *adv.* —**'dimness** *n.*

dim. *abbrev. for:* **1.** dimension. **2.** Also: **dimin.** *Music.* diminuendo. **3.** Also: **dimin.** diminutive.

Dimashq (diː'mæʃk) *n.* an Arabic name for **Damascus.**

dime (daɪm) *n.* **1.** a coin of the U.S. and Canada, worth one tenth of a dollar or ten cents. **2. a dime a dozen.** very cheap or common. [C14: from OF *disme,* from L *decimus* tenth, from *decem* ten]

dimenhydrinate (,daɪmɛn'haɪdrɪ,neɪt) *n.* a crystalline substance, used as an antihistamine and for the prevention of nausea, esp. in travel sickness. [from DI-¹ + ME(THYL) + (AMI)N(E) + (*diphen*)*hydr*(*am*)*in*(*e*) -ATE¹]

dime novel *n. U.S.* (formerly) a cheap melodramatic novel, usually in paperback.

dimension (dɪ'mɛnʃən) *n.* **1.** (*often pl.*) a measurement of the size of something in a particular direction, such as the length, width, height, or diameter. **2.** (*often pl.*) scope; size; extent. **3.** aspect: *a new dimension to politics.* **4.** *Maths.* the number of coordinates required to locate a point in space. ~*vb.* **5.** (*tr.*) *Chiefly U.S.* to cut to or mark with specified dimensions. [C14: from OF, from L *dīmensiō* an extent, from *dīmētīrī* to measure out, from *mētīrī*] —**di'mensional** *adj.* —**di'mensionless** *adj.*

dimer ('daɪmə) *n. Chem.* a compound the molecule of which is formed by the linking of two identical molecules. [C20: from DI-¹ + -MER] —**dimeric** (daɪ'mɛrɪk) *adj.*

dimerize *or* **-ise** ('daɪmə,raɪz) *vb.* to react or cause to react to form a dimer. —**dimeri'zation** *or* **-i'sation** *n.*

dimeter ('dɪmɪtə) *n. Prosody.* a line of verse consisting of two metrical feet or a verse written in this metre.

dimethylsulphoxide (daɪ,miːθaɪlsʌl'fɒksaɪd) *n.* a liquid used as a solvent and in medicine to improve the penetration of drugs applied to the skin. Abbrev.: **DMSO.**

diminish (dɪ'mɪnɪʃ) *vb.* **1.** to make or become smaller, fewer, or less. **2.** (*tr.*) *Archit.* to cause to taper. **3.** (*tr.*) *Music.* to decrease (a minor or perfect interval) by a semitone. **4.** to reduce in authority, status, etc. [C15: blend of *diminuen* to lessen (from L *dēminuere,* from *minuere*) + archaic *minish* to lessen] —**di'minishable** *adj.*

diminished (dɪ'mɪnɪʃt) *adj.* **1.** reduced or lessened; made smaller. **2.** *Music.* denoting any minor or perfect interval reduced by a semitone.

diminished responsibility *n. Law.* a plea under which mental derangement is submitted as demonstrating lack of criminal responsibility.

diminishing returns *pl. n. Econ.* progressively smaller increases in output resulting from equal increases in production.

diminuendo (dɪ,mɪnjʊ'ɛndəʊ) *Music.* ~*n., pl.* **-dos. 1. a.** a gradual decrease in loudness. Symbol:⇒. **b.** a musical passage affected by a diminuendo. ~*adj.* **2.** gradually decreasing in loudness. **3.** with a diminuendo. [C18: from It., from *diminuire* to DIMINISH]

diminution (,dɪmɪ'njuːʃən) *n.* **1.** reduction; decrease. **2.** *Music.* the presentation of the subject of a fugue, etc., in which the note values are reduced in length. [C14: from L *dēminūtiō;* see DIMINISH]

diminutive (dɪ'mɪnjʊtɪv) *adj.* **1.** very small; tiny. **2.** *Grammar.* **a.** denoting an affix added to a word to convey the meaning *small* or *unimportant* or to express affection. **b.** denoting a word formed by the addition of a diminutive affix. ~*n.* **3.** *Grammar.* a diminutive word or affix. **4.** a tiny person or thing. —**di'minutively** *adv.* —**di'minutiveness** *n.*

dimissory (dɪ'mɪsərɪ) *adj.* **1.** granting permission to be ordained: *a bishop's dimissory letter.* **2.** granting permission to depart.

Dimitrovo (di'mitrovo) *n.* the former name (1949–62) of **Pernik**.

dimity ('dɪmɪtɪ) *n., pl.* **-ties.** a light strong cotton fabric with woven stripes or squares. [C15: from Med. L *dimitum*, from Gk *dimiton*, from DI-[1] + *mitos* thread of the warp]

dimmer ('dɪmə) *n.* **1.** a device for dimming an electric light. **2.** (*often pl.*) *U.S.* **a.** a dipped headlight on a road vehicle. **b.** a parking light on a car.

dimorphism (daɪ'mɔːfɪzəm) *n.* **1.** the occurrence within a plant of two distinct forms of any part. **2.** the occurrence in an animal species of two distinct types of individual. **3.** a property of certain substances that enables them to exist in two distinct crystalline forms. —**di'morphic** *or* **di'morphous** *adj.*

dimple ('dɪmpəl) *n.* **1.** a small natural dent, esp. on the cheeks or chin. **2.** any slight depression in a surface. ~*vb.* **3.** to make or become dimpled. **4.** (*intr.*) to produce dimples by smiling. [C13 *dympull*] —**'dimply** *adj.*

dim sum (dɪm sʌm) *n.* a Chinese appetizer of steamed dumplings containing various fillings. [Cantonese]

dimwit ('dɪm,wɪt) *n. Inf.* a stupid or silly person. —**,dim-'witted** *adj.* —**,dim-'wittedness** *n.*

din (dɪn) *n.* **1.** a loud discordant confused noise. ~*vb.* **dinning, dinned. 2.** (*tr.*; usually foll. by *into*) to instil by constant repetition. **3.** (*tr.*) to subject to a din. **4.** (*intr.*) to make a din. [OE *dynn*]

DIN *n.* **1.** a logarithmic expression of the speed of a photographic film, plate, etc.; high-speed films have high numbers. **2.** a system of standard plugs, sockets, etc. used for interconnecting domestic audio and video equipment. [C20: from G *D(eutsche) I(ndustrie) N(orm)* German Industry Standard]

Dinah ('daɪnə) *n.* the daughter of Jacob and Leah (Genesis 30:21; 34).

dinar ('diːnɑː) *n.* **1.** the standard monetary unit of Algeria, Iraq, Jordan, Kuwait, Libya, South Yemen, Tunisia, and Yugoslavia. **2.** an Iranian monetary unit. [C17: from Ar., from LGk *dēnarion*, from L *dēnārius* DENARIUS]

Dinaric Alps (dɪ'nærɪk, daɪ-) *pl. n.* a mountain range in W Yugoslavia: connected with the main Alpine system by the Julian Alps. Highest peak: Troglav, 1913 m (6277 ft.).

Dincs *or* **DINKS** (dɪŋks) *pl. n. acronym for* double income no children (*or* kids): used of couples.

dine (daɪn) *vb.* **1.** (*intr.*) to eat dinner. **2.** (*intr.*; often foll. by *on, off,* or *upon*) to make one's meal (of): *the guests dined upon roast beef.* **3.** (*tr.*) *Inf.* to entertain to dinner; (esp. in **wine and dine someone**). [C13: from OF *disner*, from Vulgar L *disjējūnāre* (unattested), from *dis-* not + LL *jējūnāre* to fast]

dine out *vb.* (*intr., adv.*) **1.** to dine away from home. **2.** (foll. by *on*) to have dinner at the expense of someone else mainly for the sake of one's conversation about (a subject or story).

diner ('daɪnə) *n.* **1.** a person eating a meal, esp. in a restaurant. **2.** *Chiefly U.S. & Canad.* a small cheap restaurant. **3.** short for **dining car.**

Dinesen ('dɪnɪsən) *n.* **Isak** ('aɪzək), pen name of *Baroness Karen Blixen.* 1885–1962, Danish author of short stories in Danish and English, including *Seven Gothic Tales* (1934) and *Winter's Tales* (1942). Her life story was told in the film *Out of Africa* (1986).

dinette (daɪ'nɛt) *n.* an alcove or small area for use as a dining room.

ding (dɪŋ) *vb.* **1.** to ring, esp. with tedious repetition. **2.** (*tr.*) another word for **din** (sense 2). ~*n.* **3.** an imitation of the sound of a bell. [C13: prob. imit., but infl. by DIN + RING[2]]

Dingaan ('dɪŋgɑːn) *n.* died 1840, Zulu chief (1828–40), who fought the Boer colonists in Natal.

dingbat ('dɪŋ,bæt) *n. Austral. sl.* a crazy or stupid person.

dingbats ('dɪŋ,bæts) *pl. n. Austral. & N.Z. sl.* an attack of nervousness, irritation, or loathing: *he gives me the dingbats.*

ding-dong *n.* **1.** the sound of a bell or bells. **2.** an imitation of the sound of a bell. **3. a.** a violent exchange of blows or words. **b.** (*as modifier*): *a ding-dong battle.* ~*adj.* **4.** sounding or ringing repeatedly. [C16: imit.; see DING]

dinges ('dɪŋəs) *n. S. African inf.* a jocular word for something whose name is unknown or forgotten; thingumabob. [from Afrik., from Du. *dinges* thing]

dinghy ('dɪŋɪ) *n., pl.* **-ghies.** any small boat, powered by sail, oars, or outboard motor. Also (esp. formerly): **dingy, dingey.** [C19: from Hindi or Bengali *dingi*]

dingle ('dɪŋgəl) *n.* a small wooded dell. [C13: from ?]

dingo ('dɪŋgəʊ) *n., pl.* **-goes.** a wild dog of Australia, having a yellowish-brown coat and resembling a wolf. [C18: from Abor.]

dingy ('dɪndʒɪ) *adj.* **-gier, -giest. 1.** lacking light or brightness; drab. **2.** dirty; discoloured. [C18: perhaps from an earlier dialect word rel. to OE *dynge* dung] —**'dingily** *adv.* —**'dinginess** *n.*

dining car *n.* a railway coach in which meals are served at tables. Also called: **restaurant car.**

dining room *n.* a room where meals are eaten.

dinitrogen oxide (daɪ'naɪtrədʒən) *n.* the systematic name for **nitrous oxide.**

DINKS (dɪŋks) *pl. n.* a variant of **Dincs.**

dinkum ('dɪŋkəm) *adj. Austral. & N.Z. inf.* **1.** genuine or right: *a fair dinkum offer.* **2. dinkum oil.** the truth. [C19: from E dialect: work, from ?]

dinky ('dɪŋkɪ) *adj.* **dinkier, dinkiest.** *Inf.* **1.** *Brit.* small and neat; dainty. **2.** *U.S.* inconsequential; insignificant. [C18: from Scot. & N English dialect *dink* neat, neatly dressed]

dinky-di ('dɪŋkɪ'daɪ) *adj. Austral. inf.* typical: *dinky-di Pom idleness.* [C20: var. of DINKUM]

dinner ('dɪnə) *n.* **1.** a meal taken in the evening. **2.** a meal taken at midday, esp. when it is the main meal of the day; lunch. **3.** a formal meal or banquet in honour of someone or something. **4.** (*as modifier*): *dinner table; dinner hour.* [C13: from OF *disner*; see DINE]

dinner dance *n.* a formal dinner followed by dancing.

dinner jacket *n.* a man's semiformal evening jacket without tails, usually black. U.S. and Canad. name: **tuxedo.**

dinner service *n.* a set of matching plates, dishes, etc., suitable for serving a meal.

dinosaur ('daɪnə,sɔː) *n.* **1.** any of a large order of extinct reptiles many of which were of gigantic size and abundant in the Mesozoic era. **2.** a person or thing that is considered to be out of date. [C19: from NL *dinosaurus*, from Gk *deinos* fearful + *sauros* lizard] —**,dino'saurian** *adj.*

dint (dɪnt) *n.* **1. by dint of.** by means or use of: *by dint of hard work.* **2.** *Arch.* a blow or a mark made by a blow. ~*vb.* **3.** (*tr.*) to mark with dints. [OE *dynt*]

dioc. *abbrev. for:* **1.** diocesan. **2.** diocese.

Dio Cassius ('daɪəʊ 'kæsɪəs) *n.* ?155–?230 A.D., Roman historian. His *History of Rome* covers the period of Rome's transition from Republic to Empire.

diocesan (daɪ'ɒsɪsən) *adj.* **1.** of or relating to a diocese. ~*n.* **2.** the bishop of a diocese.

diocese ('daɪəsɪs) *n.* the district under the jurisdiction of a bishop. [C14: from OF, from LL *diocēsis*, from Gk *dioikēsis* administration, from *dioikein* to manage a household, from *oikos* house]

Diocletian (,daɪə'kliːʃən) *n.* full name *Gaius Aurelius Valerius Diocletianus.* 245–313 A.D., Roman emperor (284–305), who divided the empire into four administrative units (293) and instigated the last severe persecution of the Christians (303).

diode ('daɪəʊd) *n.* **1.** a semiconductor device used in circuits for converting alternating current to direct current. **2.** the earliest type of electronic valve having two electrodes between which a current can flow only in one direction. [C20: from DI-[1] + -ODE[2]]

Diodorus Siculus (,daɪə'dɔːrəs 'sɪkjʊləs) *n.* 1st century B.C., Greek historian, noted for his history of the world in 40 books, of which 15 are extant.

dioecious (daɪ'iːʃəs) *adj.* (of plants) having the male and female reproductive organs on separate plants. [C18: from NL *Dioecia* name of class, from DI-[1] + Gk *oikia* house]

Diogenes (daɪ'ɒdʒɪ,niːz) *n.* ?412–?323 B.C., Greek Cynic philosopher, who rejected social conventions and advocated self-sufficiency and simplicity of life.

Diomede Islands ('daɪə,miːd) *pl. n.* two small islands in the Bering Strait, separated by the international date line and by the boundary line between the U.S. and the Soviet Union.

Diomedes (,daɪə'miːdiːz), **Diomede,** *or* **Diomed** ('daɪə,mɛd) *n. Greek myth.* **1.** a king of Argos, and suitor of Helen, who fought with the Greeks at Troy. **2.** a king of the Bistones in Thrace whose savage horses ate strangers.

Dione (daɪ'əʊnɪ) *n. Greek myth.* a Titaness; the earliest consort of Zeus and mother of Aphrodite.

Dionysian (ˌdaɪəˈnɪzɪən) *adj.* **1.** of or relating to Diony-sus. **2.** (*often not cap.*) wild or orgiastic.

Dionysius (ˌdaɪəˈnɪsɪəs) *n.* called *the Elder.* ?430–367 B.C., tyrant of Syracuse (405–367), noted for his success-ful campaigns against Carthage and S Italy.

Dionysius Exiguus (ɛgˈzɪgjʊəs) *n.* died ?556 A.D., Scyth-ian monk and scholar, who is believed to have introduced the current method of reckoning dates on the basis of the Christian era.

Dionysius of Halicarnassus *n.* died ?7 B.C., Greek his-torian and rhetorician; author of a history of Rome.

Dionysus *or* **Dionysos** (ˌdaɪəˈnaɪsəs) *n.* the Greek god of wine, fruitfulness, and vegetation, worshipped in orgi-astic rites. He was also known as the bestower of ecstasy and god of the drama, and identified with Bacchus.

Diophantine equation (ˌdaɪəʊˈfæntaɪn) *n.* (in number theory) an equation in more than one variable, for which integral solutions are sought.

Diophantus (ˌdaɪəʊˈfæntəs) *n.* 3rd century A.D., Greek mathematician, noted for his treatise on the theory of numbers, *Arithmetica*.

dioptre *or U.S.* **diopter** (daɪˈɒptə) *n.* a unit for measuring the refractive power of a lens: the reciprocal of the focal length of the lens expressed in metres. [C16: from L *diop-tra* optical instrument, from Gk, from *dia-* through + *op-sesthai* to see] —**di'optral** *adj.*

dioptrics (daɪˈɒptrɪks) *n.* (*functioning as sing.*) the branch of geometrical optics concerned with the forma-tion of images by lenses. [C20: from DIOPTRE + -ICS]

Dior (diːˈɔː; *French* djɔr) *n.* **Christian** (ˈkrɪstʃən; *French* kristjᾱ). 1905–57, French couturier, noted for his New Look of narrow waist with a long full skirt (1947); he also created the waistless sack dress.

diorama (ˌdaɪəˈrɑːmə) *n.* **1.** a miniature three-dimen-sional scene, in which models of figures are seen against a background. **2.** a picture made up of illuminated translu-cent curtains, viewed through an aperture. **3.** a museum display, as of an animal, of a specimen in its natural set-ting. [C19: from F, from Gk *dia-* through + *horama* view, from *horan* to see] —**dioramic** (ˌdaɪəˈræmɪk) *adj.*

Dioscuri (ˌdaɪɒsˈkjuːrɪ) *pl. n.* the Greek name for **Castor and Pollux**, when considered together.

dioxide (daɪˈɒksaɪd) *n.* any oxide containing two oxygen atoms per molecule, both of which are bonded to an atom of another element.

dioxin (daɪˈɒksɪn) *n.* any of various chemical by-products of the manufacture of certain herbicides and bactericides, esp. the extremely toxic tetrachlorodibenzoparadioxin (TCDD).

dip (dɪp) *vb.* **dipping, dipped. 1.** to plunge or be plunged quickly or briefly into a liquid, esp. to wet or coat. **2.** (*intr.*) to undergo a slight decline, esp. temporarily: *sales dipped in November.* **3.** (*intr.*) to slope downwards. **4.** (*intr.*) to sink quickly. **5.** (*tr.*) to switch (car headlights) from the main to the lower beam. U.S. and Canad. word: **dim. 6.** (*tr.*) **a.** to immerse (sheep, etc.) briefly in a chem-ical to rid them of or prevent infestation by insects, etc. **b.** to immerse (grain, vegetables, or wood) in a preserva-tive liquid. **7.** (*tr.*) to dye by immersing in a liquid. **8.** (*tr.*) to baptize (someone) by immersion. **9.** (*tr.*) to plate or galvanize (a metal, etc.) by immersion in an electrolyte or electrolytic cell. **10.** (*tr.*) to scoop up a liquid or some-thing from a liquid in the hands or in a container. **11.** to lower or be lowered briefly. **12.** (*tr.*) to make (a candle) by plunging the wick into melted wax. **13.** (*intr.*) to plunge a container, the hands, etc., into something, esp. to obtain an object. **14.** (*intr.*) (of an aircraft) to drop sud-denly and then regain height. ~*n.* **15.** the act of dipping or state of being dipped. **16.** a brief swim in water. **17. a.** any liquid chemical in which sheep, etc. are dipped. **b.** any liquid preservative into which objects are dipped. **18.** a dye into which fabric is immersed. **19.** a depression, esp. in a landscape. **20.** something taken up by dipping. **21.** a container used for dipping; dipper. **22.** a momen-tary sinking down. **23.** the angle of slope of rock strata, etc., from the horizontal plane. **24.** the angle between the direction of the earth's magnetic field and the plane of the horizon; the angle that a magnetic needle free to swing in a vertical plane makes with the horizontal. **25.** a creamy savoury mixture into which pieces of food are dipped before being eaten. **26.** *Surveying.* the angular distance of the horizon below the plane of observation. **27.** a can-dle made by plunging a wick into wax. **28.** a momentary

loss of altitude when flying. ~See also **dip into.** [OE *dyp-pan*]

dip. *or* **Dip.** *abbrev. for* diploma.

DipAD *abbrev. for* Diploma in Art and Design.

DipEd (in Britain) *abbrev. for* Diploma in Education.

diphtheria (dɪpˈθɪərɪə) *n.* an acute contagious disease caused by a bacillus, producing fever, severe prostration, and difficulty in breathing and swallowing as the result of swelling of the throat and formation of a false membrane. [C19: NL, from F *diphthérie*, from Gk *diphthera* leather; from the nature of the membrane] —**diph'therial, diph-theritic** (ˌdɪpθəˈrɪtɪk), *or* **diphtheric** (dɪpˈθɛrɪk) *adj.*

diphthong (ˈdɪfθɒŋ) *n.* **1.** a vowel sound, occupying a single syllable, during the articulation of which the tongue moves continuously from one position to another, as in the pronunciation of *a* in *late.* **2.** a digraph or ligature representing a composite vowel such as this, as *ae* in *Cae-sar.* [C15: from LL *diphthongus*, from Gk *diphthongos*, from DI-¹ + *phthongos* sound] —**diph'thongal** *adj.*

diphthongize *or* **-ise** (ˈdɪfθɒŋˌaɪz) *vb.* (*often passive*) to make (a simple vowel) into a diphthong. —ˌ**diphthong-i'zation** *or* **-i'sation** *n.*

dip into *vb.* (*intr., prep.*) **1.** to draw upon: *he dipped into his savings.* **2.** to dabble (in); play at. **3.** to read passages at random from (a book, newspaper, etc.).

diplodocus (ˌdɪpləʊˈdəʊkəs, dɪˈplɒdəkəs) *n., pl.* **-cuses.** a herbivorous dinosaur characterized by a very long neck and tail and a total body length of 27 metres. [C19: from NL, from Gk *diplo-*, (from *diploos*, from DI-¹ + *-ploos* -fold) + *dokos* beam]

diploid (ˈdɪplɔɪd) *adj.* **1.** *Biol.* (of cells or organisms) having paired homologous chromosomes so that twice the haploid number is present. **2.** double or twofold. ~*n.* **3.** a diploid cell or organism. —**dip'loidic** *adj.*

diploma (dɪˈpləʊmə) *n.* **1.** a document conferring a quali-fication, recording success in examinations or successful completion of a course of study. **2.** an official document that confers an honour or privilege. [C17: from L: official letter or document, lit.: letter folded double, from Gk]

diplomacy (dɪˈpləʊməsɪ) *n., pl.* **-cies. 1.** the conduct of the relations of one state with another by peaceful means. **2.** skill in the management of international relations. **3.** tact, skill, or cunning in dealing with people. [C18: from F *diplomatie*, from *diplomatique* DIPLOMATIC]

diplomat (ˈdɪpləˌmæt) *n.* **1.** an official such as an ambas-sador, engaged in diplomacy. **2.** a person who deals with people tactfully or skilfully. ~Also called: **diplomatist** (dɪˈpləʊmətɪst)

diplomatic (ˌdɪpləˈmætɪk) *adj.* **1.** of or relating to diplo-macy or diplomats. **2.** skilled in negotiating, esp. between states or people. **3.** tactful in dealing with people. [C18: from F *diplomatique* concerning the documents of diplo-macy, from NL *diplomaticus;* see DIPLOMA] —ˌ**diplo'mat-ically** *adv.*

diplomatic bag *n.* a container or bag in which official mail is sent, free from customs inspection, to and from an embassy or consulate.

diplomatic corps *or* **body** *n.* the entire body of diplo-mats accredited to a given state.

diplomatic immunity *n.* the immunity from local juris-diction and exemption from taxation in the country to which they are accredited afforded to diplomats.

Diplomatic Service *n.* **1.** (in Britain) the division of the Civil Service which provides diplomats to represent the UK abroad. **2.** (*not caps.*) the equivalent institution of any other country.

dipole (ˈdaɪpəʊl) *n.* **1.** two equal but opposite electric charges or magnetic poles separated by a small distance. **2.** a molecule in which the centre of positive charge does not coincide with the centre of negative charge. **3.** a di-rectional aerial consisting of two metal rods with a con-necting wire fixed between them in the form of a T. —**di'polar** *adj.*

dipper (ˈdɪpə) *n.* **1.** a ladle used for dipping. **2.** Also called: **water ouzel.** any of a genus of aquatic songbirds that inhabit fast-flowing streams. **3.** a person or thing that dips. **4.** *Arch.* an Anabaptist. ~See also **big dipper.**

dippy (ˈdɪpɪ) *adj.* **-pier, -piest.** *Sl.* odd, eccentric, or crazy. [C20: from ?]

dipsomania (ˌdɪpsəʊˈmeɪnɪə) *n.* a compulsive desire to drink alcoholic beverages. [C19: NL, from Gk *dipsa* thirst + -MANIA] —ˌ**dipso'maniac** *n., adj.*

dipstick ('dɪp,stɪk) n. a graduated rod or strip dipped into a container to indicate the fluid level.

dip switch n. a device for dipping car headlights.

dipteran ('dɪptərən) or **dipteron** ('dɪptə,rɒn) n. **1.** any dipterous insect. ~adj. **2.** another word for **dipterous** (sense 1).

dipterous ('dɪptərəs) adj. **1.** Also: **dipteran.** of a large order of insects having a single pair of wings and sucking or piercing mouthparts. The group includes flies, mosquitoes, and midges. **2.** Bot. having two winglike parts. [C18: from Gk dipteros two-winged]

diptych ('dɪptɪk) n. **1.** a pair of hinged wooden tablets with waxed surfaces for writing. **2.** a painting or carving on two hinged panels.

Dirac ('dɪræk) n. **Paul Adrien Maurice.** 1902–84, English physicist, noted for his work on the application of relativity to quantum mechanics and his prediction of electron spin and the positron: shared the Nobel prize for physics 1933.

dire ('daɪə) adj. (usually prenominal) **1.** Also: **direful.** disastrous; fearful. **2.** desperate; urgent: a dire need. **3.** foreboding disaster; ominous. [C16: from L dīrus ominous] —'**direly** adv. —'**direness** n.

direct (dɪ'rɛkt, daɪ-) vb. (mainly tr.) **1.** to conduct or control the affairs of. **2.** (also intr.) to give commands or orders with authority to (a person or group). **3.** to tell or show (someone) the way to a place. **4.** to aim, point, or cause to move towards a goal. **5.** to address (a letter, etc.). **6.** to address (remarks, etc.). **7.** (also intr.) to provide guidance to (actors, cameramen, etc.) in a play or film. **8.** (also intr.) to conduct (a piece of music or musicians), usually while performing oneself. ~adj. **9.** without delay or evasion; straightforward. **10.** without turning aside; shortest; straight: a direct route. **11.** without intervening persons or agencies: a direct link. **12.** honest; frank. **13.** (usually prenominal) precise; exact: a direct quotation. **14.** diametrical: the direct opposite. **15.** in an unbroken line of descent: a direct descendant. **16.** (of government, decisions, etc.) by or from the electorate rather than through representatives. **17.** Logic, maths. (of a proof) progressing from the premises to the conclusion, rather than eliminating the possibility of the falsehood of the conclusion. Cf. **indirect proof. 18.** Astron. moving from west to east. Cf. **retrograde. 19.** of or relating to direct current. **20.** Music. (of an interval or chord) in root position; not inverted. ~adv. **21.** directly; straight. [C14: from L dīrectus, from dīrigere to guide, from dis- apart + regere to rule] —di'**rectness** n.

direct access n. a method of reading data from a computer file without reading through the file from the beginning.

direct action n. action such as strikes or civil disobedience employed to obtain demands from an employer, government, etc.

direct current n. a continuous electric current that flows in one direction only.

direct-grant school n. (in Britain, formerly) a school financed by endowment, fees, and a state grant conditional upon admittance of a percentage of nonpaying pupils.

direction (dɪ'rɛkʃən, daɪ-) n. **1.** the act of directing or the state of being directed. **2.** management, control, or guidance. **3.** the work of a stage or film director. **4.** the course or line along which a person or thing moves, points, or lies. **5.** the place towards which a person or thing is directed. **6.** a line of action; course. **7.** the name and address on a letter, parcel, etc. **8.** Music. the process of conducting an orchestra, choir, etc. **9.** Music. an instruction to indicate tempo, dynamics, mood, etc.

directional (dɪ'rɛkʃənᵊl, daɪ-) adj. **1.** of or relating to a spatial direction. **2.** Electronics. **a.** having or relating to an increased sensitivity to radio waves, nuclear particles, etc., coming from a particular direction. **b.** (of an aerial) transmitting or receiving radio waves more effectively in some directions than in others. **3.** Physics, electronics. concentrated in, following, or producing motion in a particular direction. —di,**rection'ality** n.

directional drilling n. a method of drilling for oil in which the well is not drilled vertically, as when a number of wells are to be drilled from a single platform. Also called: **deviated drilling.**

direction finder n. a device to determine the direction of incoming radio signals, used esp. as a navigation aid.

directions (dɪ'rɛkʃənz, daɪ-) pl. n. (sometimes sing.) instructions for doing something or for reaching a place.

directive (dɪ'rɛktɪv, daɪ-) n. **1.** an instruction; order. ~adj. **2.** tending to direct; directing. **3.** indicating direction.

directly (dɪ'rɛktlɪ, daɪ-) adv. **1.** in a direct manner. **2.** at once; without delay. **3.** (foll. by before or after) immediately; just. ~conj. **4.** (subordinating) as soon as.

direct object n. Grammar. a noun, pronoun, or noun phrase whose referent receives the direct action of a verb. For example, a book in They bought Anne a book.

directoire (dɪ'rɛktwɑː) adj. (of ladies' knickers) knee-length, with elastic at waist and knees. [C19: after fashions of the period of the French Directoire Directorate (1795–99)]

director (dɪ'rɛktə, daɪ-) n. **1.** a person or thing that directs, controls, or regulates. **2.** a member of the governing board of a business concern. **3.** a person who directs the affairs of an institution, trust, etc. **4.** the person responsible for the artistic and technical aspects of the making of a film or television programme. Compare **producer** (sense 3). **5.** Music. another word (esp. U.S.) for **conductor.** —,direc'**torial** adj. —,di'**rector,ship** n. —di'**rectress** fem. n.

directorate (dɪ'rɛktərɪt, daɪ-) n. **1.** a board of directors. **2.** Also: **directorship.** the position of director.

director-general n., pl. **directors-general.** the head of a large organization such as the CBI or BBC.

directory (dɪ'rɛktərɪ, -trɪ; daɪ-) n., pl. **-ries. 1.** a book listing names, addresses, telephone numbers, etc., of individuals or firms. **2.** a book giving directions. **3.** a book containing the rules to be observed in the forms of worship used in churches. **4.** a directorate. ~adj. **5.** directing.

Directory (dɪ'rɛktərɪ, daɪ-) n. **the.** History. the body of five directors in power in France from 1795 until their overthrow by Napoleon in 1799. Also called: **French Directory.**

direct primary n. U.S. government. a primary in which voters directly select the candidates who will run for office.

direct selling n. the selling of goods by the producer to the consumer, by mail shot, newspaper advertising, door-to-door selling, etc., without intermediaries.

direct speech or esp. U.S. **direct discourse** n. the reporting of what someone has said or written by quoting his exact words.

direct tax n. a tax paid by the person or organization on which it is levied.

dirge (dɜːdʒ) n. **1.** a chant of lamentation for the dead. **2.** the funeral service in its solemn or sung forms. **3.** any mourning song or melody. [C13: from L dīrige direct (imperative), opening word of antiphon used in the office of the dead] —'**dirgeful** adj.

dirham ('dɪəræm) n. **1.** the standard monetary unit of Morocco. **2.** a monetary unit of Kuwait, Tunisia, and Qatar. **3.** any of various N African coins. [C18: from Ar., from L: DRACHMA]

Dirichlet (German diri'kle:) n. **Peter Gustav Lejeune** ('pe:tər 'gustaf lə'ʒœn). 1805–59, German mathematician, noted for his work on number theory and calculus.

dirigible ('dɪrɪdʒɪbᵊl) adj. **1.** able to be steered or directed. ~n. **2.** another name for **airship.** [C16: from L dīrigere to DIRECT] —,dirigi'**bility** n.

dirigisme (diːriː'ʒiːzəm) n. control by the state of economic and social matters. [C20: from F] —diri'**giste** adj.

dirk (dɜːk) n. **1.** a dagger, esp. as formerly worn by Scottish Highlanders. ~vb. **2.** (tr.) to stab with a dirk. [C16: from Scot. durk, ?from G Dolch dagger]

dirndl ('dɜːndᵊl) n. **1.** a woman's dress with a full gathered skirt and fitted bodice; originating from Tyrolean peasant wear. **2.** a gathered skirt of this kind. [G (Bavarian and Austrian): from Dirndlkleid, from Dirndl little girl + Kleid dress]

dirt (dɜːt) n. **1.** any unclean substance, such as mud, etc.; filth. **2.** loose earth; soil. **3. a.** packed earth, gravel, cinders, etc., used to make a racetrack. **b.** (as modifier): a dirt track. **4.** Mining. the gravel or soil from which minerals are extracted. **5.** a person or thing regarded as worthless. **6.** obscene or indecent speech or writing. **7.** moral corruption. **8. do (someone) dirt.** Sl. to do something vicious to (someone). **9. eat dirt.** Sl. to accept insult without complaining. [C13: from ON drit excrement]

dirt-cheap *adj., adv. Inf.* at an extremely low price.

dirty ('dɜ:tɪ) *adj.* **dirtier, dirtiest. 1.** covered or marked with dirt; filthy. **2. a.** obscene: *dirty books.* **b.** sexually clandestine: *a dirty weekend.* **3.** causing one to become grimy: *a dirty job.* **4.** (of a colour) not clear and bright. **5.** unfair; dishonest. **6.** mean; nasty: *a dirty cheat.* **7.** scandalous; unkind. **8.** revealing dislike or anger. **9.** (of weather) rainy or squally; stormy. **10.** (of a nuclear weapon) producing a large quantity of radioactive fallout. **11. dirty linen.** *Inf.* intimate secrets, esp. those that might give rise to gossip. **12. dirty work.** unpleasant or illicit activity. ~*n.* **13. do the dirty on.** *Inf.* to behave meanly towards. ~*vb.* **dirtying, dirtied. 14.** to make or become dirty; stain; soil. —'**dirtily** *adv.* —'**dirtiness** *n.*

Dis (dɪs) *n.* **1.** Also called: **Orcus, Pluto.** the Roman god of the underworld. **2.** the abode of the dead; underworld. ~Greek equivalent: **Hades.**

dis-¹ *prefix.* **1.** indicating reversal: *disconnect.* **2.** indicating negation, lack, or deprivation: *dissimilar; disgrace.* **3.** indicating removal or release: *disembowel.* **4.** expressing intensive force: *dissever.* [from L *dis-* apart; in some cases, via OF *des-*. In compound words of L origin, *dis-* becomes *dif-* before *f*, and *di-* before some consonants]

dis-² *combining form.* a variant of **di-¹** before *s: dissyllable.*

disability (ˌdɪsə'bɪlɪtɪ) *n., pl.* **-ties. 1.** the condition of being physically or mentally impaired. **2.** something that disables; handicap. **3.** lack of necessary intelligence, strength, etc. **4.** an incapacity in the eyes of the law to enter into certain transactions.

disable (dɪs'eɪbᵊl) *vb.* (*tr.*) **1.** to make ineffective, unfit, or incapable, as by crippling. **2.** to make or pronounce legally incapable. —**dis'ablement** *n.*

disabled (dɪ'seɪbᵊld) *adj.* **a.** lacking one or more physical powers, such as the ability to walk or to coordinate one's movements. **b.** (*as collective n.; preceded by the*): *the disabled.*

disabuse (ˌdɪsə'bju:z) *vb.* (*tr.; usually foll. by of*) to rid of a mistaken idea; set right.

disadvantage (ˌdɪsəd'vɑ:ntɪdʒ) *n.* **1.** an unfavourable circumstance, thing, person, etc. **2.** injury, loss, or detriment. **3.** an unfavourable situation (esp. in **at a disadvantage**). ~*vb.* **4.** (*tr.*) to put at a disadvantage; handicap.

disadvantaged (ˌdɪsəd'vɑ:ntɪdʒd) *adj.* socially or economically deprived or discriminated against.

disadvantageous (dɪsˌædvɑ:n'teɪdʒəs, ˌdɪsæd-) *adj.* unfavourable; detrimental. —**dis,advan'tageously** *adv.* —**dis,advan'tageousness** *n.*

disaffect (ˌdɪsə'fɛkt) *vb.* (*tr.; often passive*) to cause to lose loyalty or affection; alienate. —**disaf'fectedly** *adv.* —**disaf'fection** *n.*

disaffiliate (ˌdɪsə'fɪlɪˌeɪt) *vb.* to sever an affiliation (with). —**disaf,fili'ation** *n.*

disafforest (ˌdɪsə'fɒrɪst) *vb.* (*tr.*) *Law.* to reduce (land) from the status of a forest to the state of ordinary ground. —**disaf,fores'tation** *n.*

disagree (ˌdɪsə'gri:) *vb.* **-greeing, -greed.** (*intr.; often foll. by with*) **1.** to dissent in opinion or dispute (about an idea, fact, etc.). **2.** to fail to correspond; conflict. **3.** to be unacceptable (to) or unfavourable (for): *curry disagrees with me.* **4.** to be opposed (to).

disagreeable (ˌdɪsə'grɪəbᵊl) *adj.* **1.** not likable; bad-tempered, esp. disobliging, etc. **2.** not to one's liking; unpleasant. —**disa'greeableness** *n.* —**disa'greeably** *adv.*

disagreement (ˌdɪsə'gri:mənt) *n.* **1.** refusal or failure to agree. **2.** a failure to correspond. **3.** an argument or dispute.

disallow (ˌdɪsə'laʊ) *vb.* (*tr.*) **1.** to reject as untrue or invalid. **2.** to cancel. —**disal'lowable** *adj.* —**disal'lowance** *n.*

disappear (ˌdɪsə'pɪə) *vb.* (*intr.*) **1.** to cease to be visible; vanish. **2.** to go away or become lost, esp. without explanation. **3.** to cease to exist; become extinct or lost. —**disap'pearance** *n.*

disappoint (ˌdɪsə'pɔɪnt) *vb.* (*tr.*) **1.** to fail to meet the expectations, hopes, etc. of; let down. **2.** to prevent the fulfilment of (a plan, etc.); frustrate. [C15 (orig. meaning: to remove from office): from OF *desapointier*; see DIS-¹, APPOINT] —**disap'pointed** *adj.* —**disap'pointing** *adj.* —**disap'pointingly** *adv.*

disappointment (ˌdɪsə'pɔɪntmənt) *n.* **1.** a disappointing or being disappointed. **2.** a person or thing that disappoints.

disapprobation (ˌdɪsæprəʊ'beɪʃən) *n.* moral or social disapproval.

disapproval (ˌdɪsə'pru:vᵊl) *n.* the act or a state or feeling of disapproving; censure.

disapprove (ˌdɪsə'pru:v) *vb.* **1.** (*intr.; often foll. by of*) to consider wrong, bad, etc. **2.** (*tr.*) to withhold approval from. —**disap'proving** *adj.* —**disap'provingly** *adv.*

disarm (dɪs'ɑ:m) *vb.* **1.** (*tr.*) to remove defensive or offensive capability from (a country, army, etc.). **2.** (*tr.*) to deprive of weapons. **3.** (*tr.*) to win the confidence or affection of. **4.** (*intr.*) (of a nation, etc.) to decrease the size and capability of one's armed forces. **5.** (*intr.*) to lay down weapons. —**dis'armer** *n.*

disarmament (dɪs'ɑ:məmənt) *n.* **1.** the reduction of fighting capability, as by a nation. **2.** a disarming or being disarmed.

disarming (dɪs'ɑ:mɪŋ) *adj.* tending to neutralize hostility, suspicion, etc. —**dis'armingly** *adv.*

disarrange (ˌdɪsə'reɪndʒ) *vb.* (*tr.*) to throw into disorder. —**disar'rangement** *n.*

disarray (ˌdɪsə'reɪ) *n.* **1.** confusion, dismay, and lack of discipline. **2.** (esp. of clothing) disorderliness; untidiness. ~*vb.* (*tr.*) **3.** to throw into confusion. **4.** *Arch.* to undress.

disassemble (ˌdɪsə'sɛmbᵊl) *vb.* (*tr.*) to take apart (a piece of machinery, etc.); dismantle.

disassociate (ˌdɪsə'səʊʃɪˌeɪt, -sɪ-) *vb.* a less common word for **dissociate.** —**disas,soci'ation** *n.*

▷ **Usage.** While *disassociate* is sometimes encountered in both written and spoken English, the word *dissociate* is generally regarded as being the only acceptable term.

disaster (dɪ'zɑ:stə) *n.* **1.** an occurrence that causes great distress or destruction. **2.** a thing, project, etc., that fails or has been ruined. [C16 (orig. in the sense: malevolent astral influence): from It. *disastro*, from *dis-* (pejorative) + *astro* star, ult. from Gk *astron*] —**dis'astrous** *adj.*

disavow (ˌdɪsə'vaʊ) *vb.* (*tr.*) to deny knowledge of, connection with, or responsibility for. —**disa'vowal** *n.* —**disavowedly** (ˌdɪsə'vaʊɪdlɪ) *adv.*

disband (dɪs'bænd) *vb.* to cease to function or cause to stop functioning, as a unit, group, etc. —**dis'bandment** *n.*

disbar (dɪs'bɑ:) *vb.* **-barring, -barred.** (*tr.*) *Law.* to deprive of the status of barrister; expel from the Bar. —**dis'barment** *n.*

disbelief (ˌdɪsbɪ'li:f) *n.* refusal or reluctance to believe.

disbelieve (ˌdɪsbɪ'li:v) *vb.* **1.** (*tr.*) to reject as false or lying. **2.** (*intr.; usually foll. by in*) to have no faith (in). —**disbe'liever** *n.* —**disbe'lieving** *adj.*

disbud (dɪs'bʌd) *vb.* **-budding, -budded.** to remove superfluous buds from (a plant).

disburden (dɪs'bɜ:dᵊn) *vb.* **1.** to remove a load from. **2.** (*tr.*) to relieve (one's mind, etc.) of a distressing worry.

disburse (dɪs'bɜ:s) *vb.* (*tr.*) to pay out. [C16: from OF *desborser*, from *des-* DIS-¹ + *borser* to obtain money, from *borse* bag, from LL *bursa*] —**dis'bursable** *adj.* —**dis'bursement** *n.* —**dis'burser** *n.*

disc (dɪsk) *n.* **1.** a flat circular plate. **2.** something resembling this. **3.** a gramophone record. **4.** *Anat.* any approximately circular flat structure in the body, esp. an intervertebral disc. **5.** the flat receptacle of composite flowers, such as the daisy. **6. a.** Also called: **parking disc.** a marker or device for display in a parked vehicle showing the time of arrival or the latest permitted time of departure or both. **b.** (*as modifier*): *disc parking.* **7.** *Computers.* a variant spelling of **disk.** [C18: from L *discus* DISCUS]

disc. *abbrev. for:* **1.** discount. **2.** discovered.

discard *vb.* (dɪs'kɑ:d). **1.** (*tr.*) to get rid of as useless or undesirable. **2.** *Cards.* to throw out (a card or cards) from one's hand. **3.** *Cards.* to play (a card not of the suit led nor a trump) when unable to follow suit. ~*n.* ('dɪskɑ:d). **4.** a person or thing that has been cast aside. **5.** *Cards.* a discarded card. **6.** the act of discarding.

disc brake *n.* a type of brake in which two pads rub against a flat disc attached to the wheel hub when the brake is applied.

disc camera *n.* a type of small compact camera in which the film is on a disc (**disc film**) instead of a spool.

discern (dɪ'sɜ:n) *vb.* **1.** (*tr.*) to recognize or perceive clearly. **2.** to recognize or perceive (differences). [C14:

from OF *discerner*, from L *discernere* to divide, from DIS-[1] apart + *cernere* to separate] —**dis'cernible** *adj.* —**dis'cernibly** *adv.*

discerning (dɪ'sɜ:nɪŋ) *adj.* having or showing good taste or judgment; discriminating.

discernment (dɪ'sɜ:nmənt) *n.* keen perception or judgment.

disc flower *or* **floret** *n.* any of the small tubular flowers at the centre of the flower head of certain composite plants, such as the daisy.

discharge *vb.* (dɪs'tʃɑːdʒ). **1.** (*tr.*) to release or allow to go. **2.** (*tr.*) to dismiss from or relieve of duty, employment, etc. **3.** to fire or be fired, as a gun. **4.** to pour forth or cause to pour forth: *the boil discharges pus.* **5.** (*tr.*) to remove (the cargo) from (a boat, etc.); unload. **6.** (*tr.*) to perform the duties of or meet the demands of (an office, obligation, etc.). **7.** (*tr.*) to relieve (oneself) of (a responsibility, debt, etc.). **8.** (*intr.*) *Physics.* **a.** to lose or remove electric charge. **b.** to form an arc, spark, or corona in a gas. **c.** to take or supply electrical current from a cell or battery. **9.** (*tr.*) *Law.* to release (a prisoner from custody, etc.). ~*n.* ('dɪstʃɑːdʒ, dɪs'tʃɑːdʒ). **10.** a person or thing that is discharged. **11. a.** dismissal or release from an office, job, institution, etc. **b.** the document certifying such release. **12.** the fulfilment of an obligation or release from a responsibility or liability. **13.** the act of removing a load, as of cargo. **14.** a pouring forth of a fluid; emission. **15. a.** the act of firing a projectile. **b.** the volley, bullet, etc., fired. **16.** *Law.* **a.** a release, as of a person held under legal restraint. **b.** an annulment, as of a court order. **17.** *Physics.* **a.** the act or process of removing or losing charge. **b.** a conduction of electricity through a gas by the formation and movement of electrons and ions in an applied electric field. —**dis'chargeable** *adj.* —**dis'charger** *n.*

disc harrow *n.* a harrow with sharp-edged discs used to cut clods on the surface of the soil or to cover seed after planting.

disciple (dɪ'saɪpəl) *n.* **1.** a follower of the doctrines of a teacher or a school of thought. **2.** one of the personal followers of Christ (including his 12 apostles) during his earthly life. [OE *discipul*, from L *discipulus* pupil, from *discere* to learn] —**dis'ciple,ship** *n.* —**discipular** (dɪ'sɪpjʊlə) *adj.*

disciplinarian (,dɪsɪplɪ'nɛərɪən) *n.* a person who imposes or advocates strict discipline.

disciplinary ('dɪsɪ,plɪnərɪ) *adj.* **1.** of, promoting, or used for discipline; corrective. **2.** relating to a branch of learning.

discipline ('dɪsɪplɪn) *n.* **1.** training or conditions imposed for the improvement of physical powers, self-control, etc. **2.** systematic training in obedience. **3.** the state of improved behaviour, etc., resulting from such training. **4.** punishment or chastisement. **5.** a system of rules for behaviour, etc. **6.** a branch of learning or instruction. **7.** the laws governing members of a Church. ~*vb.* (*tr.*) **8.** to improve or attempt to improve the behaviour, orderliness, etc., of by training, conditions, or rules. **9.** to punish or correct. [C13: from L *disciplīna* teaching, from *discipulus* DISCIPLE] —**'disci,plinable** *adj.* —**disciplinal** (,dɪsɪ'plaɪnəl) *adj.* —**'disci,pliner** *n.*

disc jockey *n.* a person who announces and plays recorded music, esp. pop music, on a radio programme, etc.

disclaim (dɪs'kleɪm) *vb.* **1.** (*tr.*) to deny or renounce (any claim, connection, etc.). **2.** (*tr.*) to deny the validity or authority of. **3.** *Law.* to renounce or repudiate (a legal claim or right).

disclaimer (dɪs'kleɪmə) *n.* a repudiation or denial.

disclose (dɪs'kləʊz) *vb.* (*tr.*) **1.** to make known. **2.** to allow to be seen. —**dis'closer** *n.*

disclosure (dɪs'kləʊʒə) *n.* **1.** something that is disclosed. **2.** the act of disclosing; revelation.

disco ('dɪskəʊ) *n.*, *pl.* **-cos.** **1. a.** an occasion at which people dance to pop records. **b.** (*as modifier*): *disco music.* **2.** a nightclub or other public place where such dances are held. **3.** mobile equipment for providing music for a disco.

discobolus (dɪs'kɒbələs) *n.*, *pl.* **-li** (-,laɪ). a discus thrower. [C18: from L, from Gk, from *diskos* DISCUS + *-bolos*, from *ballein* to throw]

discography (dɪs'kɒɡrəfɪ) *n.* a classified list of gramophone records. —**dis'cographer** *n.*

discoid ('dɪskɔɪd) *adj. also* **discoidal.** **1.** like a disc. ~*n.* **2.** a disclike object.

discolour *or U.S.* **discolor** (dɪs'kʌlə) *vb.* to change in colour; fade or stain. —**dis,color'ation** *or* **dis,colour'ation** *n.*

discombobulate (,dɪskəm'bɒbjʊ,leɪt) *vb.* (*tr.*) *Inf., chiefly U.S. & Canad.* to throw into confusion. [C20: prob. a whimsical alteration of DISCOMPOSE or DISCOMFIT]

discomfit (dɪs'kʌmfɪt) *vb.* (*tr.*) **1.** to make uneasy or confused. **2.** to frustrate the plans or purpose of. **3.** *Arch.* to defeat. [C14: from OF *desconfire* to destroy, from *des-* (indicating reversal) + *confire* to make, from L *conficere* to produce] —**dis'comfiture** *n.*

discomfort (dɪs'kʌmfət) *n.* **1.** an inconvenience, distress, or mild pain. **2.** something that disturbs or deprives of ease. ~*vb.* **3.** (*tr.*) to make uncomfortable or uneasy.

discommode (,dɪskə'məʊd) *vb.* (*tr.*) to cause inconvenience to; disturb. —**,discom'modious** *adj.*

discompose (,dɪskəm'pəʊz) *vb.* (*tr.*) **1.** to disturb the composure of; disconcert. **2.** *Now rare.* to disarrange. —**,discom'posure** *n.*

disconcert (,dɪskən'sɜːt) *vb.* (*tr.*) **1.** to disturb the composure of. **2.** to frustrate or upset. —**,discon'certed** *adj.* —**,discon'certing** *adj.* —**,discon'certion** *n.*

disconformity (,dɪskən'fɔːmɪtɪ) *n.*, *pl.* **-ties.** **1.** lack of conformity; discrepancy. **2.** the junction between two parallel series of stratified rocks.

disconnect (,dɪskə'nɛkt) *vb.* (*tr.*) to undo or break the connection of or between (something, as a plug and a socket). —**,discon'nection** *n.*

disconnected (,dɪskə'nɛktɪd) *adj.* **1.** not rationally connected; confused or incoherent. **2.** not connected or joined.

disconsolate (dɪs'kɒnsəlɪt) *adj.* **1.** sad beyond comfort; inconsolable. **2.** disappointed; dejected. [C14: from Med. L *disconsōlātus*, from DIS-[1] + *consōlātus* comforted] —**dis'consolately** *adv.* —**dis'consolateness** *or* **dis,conso'lation** *n.*

discontent (,dɪskən'tɛnt) *n.* **1.** Also called: **discontentment.** lack of contentment, as with one's condition or lot in life. ~*vb.* **2.** (*tr.*) to make dissatisfied. —**,discon'tented** *adj.* —**,discon'tentedness** *n.*

discontinue (,dɪskən'tɪnjuː) *vb.* **-uing, -ued. 1.** to come or bring to an end; interrupt or be interrupted; stop. **2.** (*tr.*) *Law.* to terminate or abandon (an action, suit, etc.). —**,discon'tinuance** *n.* —**,discon,tinu'ation** *n.*

discontinuity (dɪs,kɒntɪ'njuːɪtɪ) *n.*, *pl.* **-ties. 1.** lack of rational connection or cohesion. **2.** a break or interruption.

discontinuous (,dɪskən'tɪnjʊəs) *adj.* characterized by interruptions or breaks; intermittent. —**,discon'tinuously** *adv.* —**,discon'tinuousness** *n.*

discord *n.* ('dɪskɔːd). **1.** lack of agreement or harmony. **2.** harsh confused mingling of sounds. **3.** a combination of musical notes, esp. one containing one or more dissonant intervals. ~*vb.* (dɪs'kɔːd). **4.** (*intr.*) to disagree; clash. [C13: from OF *descort*, from *descorder* to disagree, from L *discordāre*, from *discors* at variance, from DIS-[1] + *cor* heart]

discordant (dɪs'kɔːdənt) *adj.* **1.** at variance; disagreeing. **2.** harsh in sound; inharmonious. —**dis'cordance** *n.* —**dis'cordantly** *adv.*

discotheque ('dɪskə,tɛk) *n.* the full term for **disco.** [C20: from F *discothèque*, from Gk *diskos* disc + *-o-* + Gk *thēkē* case]

discount *vb.* (dɪs'kaʊnt, 'dɪskaʊnt). (*mainly tr.*) **1.** to leave out of account as being unreliable, prejudiced, or irrelevant. **2.** to anticipate and make allowance for. **3. a.** to deduct (an amount or percentage) from the price, cost, etc. **b.** to reduce (the regular price, etc.) by a percentage or amount. **4.** to sell or offer for sale at a reduced price. **5.** to buy or sell (a bill of exchange, etc.) before maturity, with a deduction for interest. **6.** (*also intr.*) to loan money on (a negotiable instrument) with a deduction for interest. ~*n.* ('dɪskaʊnt). **7.** a deduction from the full amount of a price or debt. See also **cash discount, trade discount. 8.** Also called: **discount rate. a.** the amount of interest deducted in the purchase or sale of or the loan of money on unmatured negotiable instruments. **b.** the rate of interest deducted. **9.** (in the issue of shares) a percentage deducted from the par value to give a reduced amount payable by subscribers. **10.** a discounting. **11. at a discount. a.** below the regular price. **b.** held in low regard. **12.** (*modifier*) offering or selling at reduced prices: *a discount shop.* —**dis'countable** *adj.* —'**discounter** *n.*

discounted cash flow *n.* the cash flow of an organization taking into account the future values of benefits and assets in addition to their present values.

discountenance (dɪsˈkaʊntɪnəns) *vb.* (*tr.*) **1.** to make ashamed or confused. **2.** to disapprove of. ~*n.* **3.** disapproval.

discount house *n.* **1.** *Chiefly Brit.* a financial organization engaged in discounting bills of exchange, etc., on a large scale. **2.** Also called: **discount store.** *Chiefly U.S.* a shop offering for sale most of its merchandise at prices below the recommended prices.

discourage (dɪsˈkʌrɪdʒ) *vb.* (*tr.*) **1.** to deprive of the will to persist in something. **2.** to inhibit; prevent: *this solution discourages rust.* **3.** to oppose by expressing disapproval. —*vb.* —**dis'couragement** *n.* —**dis'couragingly** *adv.*

discourse *n.* (ˈdɪskɔːs, dɪsˈkɔːs). **1.** verbal communication; talk; conversation. **2.** a formal treatment of a subject in speech or writing. **3.** a unit of text used by linguists for the analysis of linguistic phenomena that range over more than one sentence. **4.** *Arch.* the ability to reason. ~*vb.* (dɪsˈkɔːs). **5.** (*intr.*; often foll. by *on* or *upon*) to speak or write (about) formally. **6.** (*intr.*) to hold a discussion. **7.** (*tr.*) *Arch.* to give forth (music). [C14: from Med. L *discursus* argument, from L: a running to and fro, from *discurrere*, from DIS-¹ + *currere* to run]

discourteous (dɪsˈkɜːtɪəs) *adj.* showing bad manners; impolite; rude. —**dis'courteously** *adv.* —**dis'courteousness** *n.*

discourtesy (dɪsˈkɜːtɪsɪ) *n.*, *pl.* **-sies. 1.** bad manners; rudeness. **2.** a rude remark or act.

discover (dɪsˈkʌvə) *vb.* (*tr.*; *may take a clause as object*) **1.** to be the first to find or find out about. **2.** to learn about for the first time; realize. **3.** to find after study or search. **4.** to reveal or make known. —**dis'coverable** *adj.* —**dis'coverer** *n.*

discovery (dɪsˈkʌvərɪ) *n.*, *pl.* **-eries. 1.** the act, process, or an instance of discovering. **2.** a person, place, or thing that has been discovered. **3.** *Law.* the compulsory disclosure by a party to an action of relevant documents in his possession.

Discovery Bay *n.* an inlet of the Indian Ocean in SE Australia.

discredit (dɪsˈkrɛdɪt) *vb.* (*tr.*) **1.** to damage the reputation of. **2.** to cause to be disbelieved or distrusted. **3.** to reject as untrue. ~*n.* **4.** something that causes disgrace. **5.** damage to a reputation. **6.** lack of belief or confidence.

discreditable (dɪsˈkrɛdɪtəbᵊl) *adj.* tending to bring discredit; shameful or unworthy.

discreet (dɪsˈkriːt) *adj.* **1.** careful to avoid embarrassment, esp. by keeping confidences secret; tactful. **2.** unobtrusive. [C14: from OF *discret*, from Med. L *discrētus*, from L *discernere* to DISCERN] —**dis'creetly** *adv.* —**dis'creetness** *n.*

discrepancy (dɪsˈkrɛpənsɪ) *n.*, *pl.* **-cies.** a conflict or variation, as between facts, figures, or claims. [C15: from L *discrepāns*, from *discrepāre* to differ in sound, from DIS-¹ + *crepāre* to be noisy] —**dis'crepant** *adj.*

discrete (dɪsˈkriːt) *adj.* **1.** separate or distinct. **2.** consisting of distinct or separate parts. [C14: from L *discrētus* separated; see DISCREET] —**dis'cretely** *adv.* —**dis'creteness** *n.*

discretion (dɪsˈkrɛʃən) *n.* **1.** the quality of behaving so as to avoid social embarrassment or distress. **2.** freedom or authority to make judgments and to act as one sees fit (esp. in **at one's own discretion, at the discretion of**). **3.** *age or* **years of discretion.** the age at which a person is thought able to manage his own affairs.

discretionary (dɪsˈkrɛʃənərɪ, -ʃnrɪ) *or* **discretional** *adj.* having or using the ability to decide at one's own discretion: *discretionary powers.*

discriminate *vb.* (dɪsˈkrɪmɪˌneɪt). **1.** (*intr.*; usu. foll. by *in favour of* or *against*) to single out a particular person, group, etc., for special favour or, esp., disfavour. **2.** (when *intr.*, foll. by *between* or *among*) to recognize or understand the difference (between); distinguish. **3.** (*intr.*) to constitute or mark a difference. **4.** (*intr.*) to be discerning in matters of taste. ~*adj.* (dɪsˈkrɪmɪnɪt). **5.** showing or marked by discrimination. [C17: from L *discrimināre* to divide, from *discrīmen* a separation, from *discernere* to DISCERN] —**dis'criminately** *adv.*

discriminating (dɪsˈkrɪmɪˌneɪtɪŋ) *adj.* **1.** able to see fine distinctions and differences. **2.** discerning in matters of taste. **3.** (of a tariff, import duty, etc.) levied at differential rates.

discrimination (dɪˌskrɪmɪˈneɪʃən) *n.* **1.** unfair treatment of a person, racial group, minority, etc.; action based on prejudice. **2.** subtle appreciation in matters of taste. **3.** the ability to see fine distinctions and differences.

discriminatory (dɪˈskrɪmɪnətərɪ, -trɪ) *or* **discriminative** (dɪˈskrɪmɪnətɪv) *adj.* **1.** based on or showing prejudice; biased. **2.** capable of making fine distinctions.

discursive (dɪsˈkɜːsɪv) *adj.* **1.** passing from one topic to another; digressive. **2.** *Philosophy.* of or relating to knowledge obtained by reason and argument rather than intuition. [C16: from Med. L *discursivus*, from LL *discursus* DISCOURSE] —**dis'cursively** *adv.* —**dis'cursiveness** *n.*

discus (ˈdɪskəs) *n.*, *pl.* **discuses** *or* **disci** (ˈdɪskaɪ). **1.** (originally) a circular stone or plate used in throwing competitions by the ancient Greeks. **2.** *Field sports.* a similar disc-shaped object with a heavy middle, thrown by athletes. **3.** (preceded by *the*) the event or sport of throwing the discus. [C17: from L, from Gk *diskos*, from *dikein* to throw]

discuss (dɪsˈkʌs) *vb.* (*tr.*) **1.** to have a conversation about; consider by talking over. **2.** to treat (a subject) in speech or writing. [C14: from LL *discussus* examined, from *discutere*, from L: to dash to pieces, from DIS-¹ + *quatere* to shake] —**dis'cussant** *or* **dis'cusser** *n.* —**dis'cussible** *or* **dis'cussable** *adj.*

discussion (dɪsˈkʌʃən) *n.* the examination or consideration of a matter in speech or writing.

disdain (dɪsˈdeɪn) *n.* **1.** a feeling or show of superiority and dislike; contempt; scorn. ~*vb.* **2.** (*tr.*; *may take an infinitive*) to refuse or reject with disdain. [C13 *dedeyne*, from OF *desdeign*, from *desdeigner* to reject as unworthy, from L *dēdignārī*; see DIS-¹, DEIGN] —**dis'dainful** *adj.*

disease (dɪˈziːz) *n.* **1.** any impairment of normal physiological function affecting an organism, esp. a change caused by infection, stress, etc., producing characteristic symptoms; illness or sickness in general. **2.** a corresponding condition in plants. **3.** any condition likened to this. [C14: from OF *desaise*; see DIS-¹, EASE] —**dis'eased** *adj.*

diseconomy (ˌdɪsɪˈkɒnəmɪ) *n.* *Econ.* disadvantage, such as lower efficiency or higher costs, resulting from the scale on which an enterprise operates.

disembark (ˌdɪsɪmˈbɑːk) *vb.* to land or cause to land from a ship, aircraft, etc. —**disembarkation** (dɪsˌɛmbɑːˈkeɪʃən) *n.*

disembarrass (ˌdɪsɪmˈbærəs) *vb.* (*tr.*) **1.** to free from embarrassment, entanglement, etc. **2.** to relieve or rid of something burdensome.

disembodied (ˌdɪsɪmˈbɒdɪd) *adj.* **1.** lacking a body or freed from the body. **2.** lacking in substance or any firm relation to reality.

disembody (ˌdɪsɪmˈbɒdɪ) *vb.* **-bodying, -bodied.** (*tr.*) to free from the body or from physical form. —ˌ**disem'bodiment** *n.*

disembogue (ˌdɪsɪmˈbəʊg) *vb.* **-boguing, -bogued. 1.** (of a river, stream, etc.) to discharge (water) at the mouth. **2.** (*intr.*) to flow out. [C16: from Sp. *desembocar*, from *des*-DIS-¹ + *embocar* to put into the mouth] —ˌ**disem'boguement** *n.*

disembowel (ˌdɪsɪmˈbaʊəl) *vb.* **-elling, -elled** *or U.S.* **-eling, -eled.** (*tr.*) to remove the entrails of. —ˌ**disem'bowelment** *n.*

disenchant (ˌdɪsɪnˈtʃɑːnt) *vb.* (*tr.*) to free from or as if from an enchantment; disillusion. —ˌ**disen'chantingly** *adv.* —ˌ**disen'chantment** *n.*

disencumber (ˌdɪsɪnˈkʌmbə) *vb.* (*tr.*) to free from encumbrances. —ˌ**disen'cumberment** *n.*

disenfranchise (ˌdɪsɪnˈfræntʃaɪz) *vb.* another word for **disfranchise.** —**disenfranchisement** (ˌdɪsɪnˈfræntʃɪzmənt) *n.*

disengage (ˌdɪsɪnˈgeɪdʒ) *vb.* **1.** to release or become released from a connection, obligation, etc. **2.** *Mil.* to withdraw (forces) from close action. **3.** *Fencing.* to move (one's blade) from one side of an opponent's blade to another in a circular motion. —ˌ**disen'gaged** *adj.* —ˌ**disen'gagement** *n.*

disentangle (ˌdɪsɪn'tæŋgəl) *vb.* **1.** to release or become free from entanglement or confusion. **2.** (*tr.*) to unravel or work out. —ˌdisen'tanglement *n.*

disequilibrium (ˌdɪsiːkwɪ'lɪbrɪəm) *n.* a loss or absence of equilibrium, esp. in an economy.

disestablish (ˌdɪsɪ'stæblɪʃ) *vb.* (*tr.*) to deprive (a church, custom, institution, etc.) of established status. —ˌdises'tablishment *n.*

disesteem (ˌdɪsɪ'stiːm) *vb.* **1.** (*tr.*) to think little of. ~*n.* **2.** lack of esteem.

disfavour *or U.S.* **disfavor** (dɪs'feɪvə) *n.* **1.** disapproval or dislike. **2.** the state of being disapproved of or disliked. **3.** an unkind act. ~*vb.* **4.** (*tr.*) to treat with disapproval or dislike.

disfigure (dɪs'fɪgə) *vb.* (*tr.*) **1.** to spoil the appearance or shape of; deface. **2.** to mar the effect or quality of. —dis'figurement *n.*

disforest (dɪs'fɒrɪst) *vb.* (*tr.*) **1.** another word for **deforest**. **2.** *English law.* a less common word for **disafforest**. —disˌfores'tation *n.*

disfranchise (dɪs'fræntʃaɪz) *or* **disenfranchise** *vb.* (*tr.*) **1.** to deprive (a person) of the right to vote or other rights of citizenship. **2.** to deprive (a place) of the right to send representatives to an elected body. **3.** to deprive (a person, place, etc.) of any franchise or right. —disfranchisement (dɪs'fræntʃɪzmənt) *or* ˌdisen'franchisement *n.*

disgorge (dɪs'gɔːdʒ) *vb.* **1.** to throw out (food, etc.) from the throat or stomach; vomit. **2.** to discharge or empty of (contents). **3.** (*tr.*) to yield up unwillingly. —dis'gorgement *n.*

disgrace (dɪs'greɪs) *n.* **1.** a condition of shame, loss of reputation, or dishonour. **2.** a shameful person or thing. **3.** exclusion from confidence or trust: *he is in disgrace with his father.* ~*vb.* (*tr.*) **4.** to bring shame upon. **5.** to treat or cause to be treated with disfavour.

disgraceful (dɪs'greɪsful) *adj.* shameful; scandalous. —dis'gracefully *adv.*

disgruntle (dɪs'grʌntəl) *vb.* (*tr.*) to make sulky or discontented. [C17: DIS-¹ + obs. *gruntle* to complain] —dis'gruntlement *n.*

disguise (dɪs'gaɪz) *vb.* **1.** to modify the appearance or manner in order to conceal the identity of (someone or something). **2.** (*tr.*) to misrepresent in order to obscure the actual nature or meaning. ~*n.* **3.** a mask, costume, or manner that disguises. **4.** a disguising or being disguised. [C14: from OF *desguiser*, from *des*- DIS-¹ + *guise* manner] —dis'guised *adj.*

disgust (dɪs'gʌst) *vb.* (*tr.*) **1.** to sicken or fill with loathing. **2.** to offend the moral sense of. ~*n.* **3.** a great loathing or distaste. **4. in disgust.** as a result of disgust. [C16: from OF *desgouster*, from *des*- DIS-¹ + *gouster* to taste, from L *gustus* taste] —dis'gustedly *adv.* —dis'gustedness *n.*

dish (dɪʃ) *n.* **1.** a container used for holding or serving food, esp. an open shallow container. **2.** the food in a dish. **3.** a particular kind of food. **4.** Also called: **dishful.** the amount contained in a dish. **5.** something resembling a dish. **6.** a concavity. **7.** short for **dish aerial. 8.** *Inf.* an attractive person. ~*vb.* (*tr.*) **9.** to put into a dish. **10.** to make concave. **11.** *Brit. inf.* to ruin or spoil. ~See also **dish out, dish up.** [OE *disc*, from L *discus* quoit] —'dishˌlike *adj.*

dishabille (ˌdɪsæ'biːl) *or* **deshabille** *n.* the state of being partly or carelessly dressed. [C17: from F *déshabillé*, from *dés*- DIS-¹ + *habiller* to dress]

dish aerial *n.* a microwave aerial, used esp. in radar, radio telescopes, and satellite broadcasting, consisting of a parabolic reflector.

disharmony (dɪs'hɑːmənɪ) *n.*, *pl.* **-nies. 1.** lack of accord or harmony. **2.** a situation, circumstance, etc., that is inharmonious. —**disharmonious** (ˌdɪshɑː'məʊnɪəs) *adj.*

dishcloth ('dɪʃˌklɒθ) *n.* a cloth or rag for washing or drying dishes.

dishearten (dɪs'hɑːt²n) *vb.* (*tr.*) to weaken or destroy the hope, courage, enthusiasm, etc., of. —dis'hearteningly *adv.* —dis'heartenment *n.*

dished (dɪʃt) *adj.* **1.** shaped like a dish. **2.** (of wheels) closer to one another at the bottom than at the top. **3.** *Inf.* exhausted or defeated.

dishevel (dɪ'ʃɛvəl) *vb.* **-elling, -elled** *or U.S.* **-eling, -eled.** to disarrange (the hair or clothes) of (someone).

[C15: back formation from DISHEVELLED] —di'shevelment *n.*

dishevelled *or U.S.* **-eled** (dɪ'ʃɛvᵊld) *adj.* **1.** (esp. of hair) hanging loosely. **2.** unkempt; untidy. [C15 *dischevelee*, from OF *deschevelé*, from *des*- DIS-¹ + *chevel* hair, from L *capillus*]

dishonest (dɪs'ɒnɪst) *adj.* not honest or fair; deceiving or fraudulent. —dis'honestly *adv.*

dishonesty (dɪs'ɒnɪstɪ) *n.*, *pl.* **-ties. 1.** lack of honesty. **2.** a deceiving act or statement.

dishonour *or U.S.* **dishonor** (dɪs'ɒnə) *vb.* (*tr.*) **1.** to treat with disrespect. **2.** to fail or refuse to pay (a cheque, etc.). **3.** to cause the disgrace of (a woman) by seduction or rape. ~*n.* **4.** a lack of honour or respect. **5.** a state of shame or disgrace. **6.** a person or thing that causes a loss of honour. **7.** an insult; affront. **8.** refusal or failure to accept or pay a commercial paper.

dishonourable *or U.S.* **dishonorable** (dɪs'ɒnərəbᵊl) *adj.* **1.** characterized by or causing dishonour or discredit. **2.** having little or no integrity; unprincipled. —dis'honourableness *or U.S.* dis'honorableness *n.* —dis'honourably *or U.S.* dis'honorably *adv.*

dish out *vb.* **1.** (*tr., adv.*) *Inf.* to distribute. **2. dish it out.** to inflict punishment.

dishtowel ('dɪʃˌtaʊəl) *n.* another name (esp. U.S. and Canad.) for a **tea towel**.

dish up *vb.* (*adv.*) **1.** to serve (a meal, food, etc.). **2.** (*tr.*) *Inf.* to prepare or present, esp. in an attractive manner.

dishwasher ('dɪʃˌwɒʃə) *n.* **1.** a machine for washing dishes, etc. **2.** a person who washes dishes, etc.

dishwater ('dɪʃˌwɔːtə) *n.* **1.** water in which dishes have been washed. **2.** something resembling this.

dishy ('dɪʃɪ) *adj.* **dishier, dishiest.** *Inf., chiefly Brit.* good-looking or attractive.

disillusion (ˌdɪsɪ'luːʒən) *vb.* **1.** (*tr.*) to destroy the ideals, illusions, or false ideas of. ~*n.* also **disillusionment. 2.** the act of disillusioning or the state of being disillusioned.

disincentive (ˌdɪsɪn'sɛntɪv) *n.* **1.** something that acts as a deterrent. ~*adj.* **2.** acting as a deterrent: *a disincentive effect on productivity.*

disincline (ˌdɪsɪn'klaɪn) *vb.* to make or be unwilling, reluctant, or averse. —**disinclination** (ˌdɪsɪnklɪ'neɪʃən) *n.*

disinfect (ˌdɪsɪn'fɛkt) *vb.* (*tr.*) to rid of microorganisms potentially harmful to man, esp. by chemical means. —ˌdisin'fection *n.*

disinfectant (ˌdɪsɪn'fɛktənt) *n.* an agent that destroys or inhibits the activity of microorganisms that cause disease.

disinfest (ˌdɪsɪn'fɛst) *vb.* (*tr.*) to rid of vermin. —ˌdisinfes'tation *n.*

disinflation (ˌdɪsɪn'fleɪʃən) *n. Econ.* a reduction or stabilization of the general price level intended to improve the balance of payments without incurring reductions in output, employment, etc.

disinformation (ˌdɪsɪnfə'meɪʃən) *n.* false information intended to deceive or mislead.

disingenuous (ˌdɪsɪn'dʒɛnjʊəs) *adj.* not sincere; lacking candour. —ˌdisin'genuously *adv.* —ˌdisin'genuousness *n.*

disinherit (ˌdɪsɪn'hɛrɪt) *vb.* (*tr.*) **1.** *Law.* to deprive (an heir or next of kin) of inheritance or right to inherit. **2.** to deprive of a right or heritage. —ˌdisin'heritance *n.*

disintegrate (dɪs'ɪntɪˌgreɪt) *vb.* **1.** to break or be broken into fragments or parts; shatter. **2.** to lose or cause to lose cohesion. **3.** (*intr.*) to lose judgment or control. **4.** *Physics.* **a.** to induce or undergo nuclear fission. **b.** another word for **decay** (sense 3). —disˌinte'gration *n.* —dis'inteˌgrator *n.*

disinter (ˌdɪsɪn'tɜː) *vb.* **-terring, -terred.** (*tr.*) **1.** to remove or dig up; exhume. **2.** to bring to light; expose. —ˌdisin'terment *n.*

disinterest (dɪs'ɪntrɪst, -tərɪst) *n.* **1.** freedom from bias or involvement. **2.** lack of interest.

disinterested (dɪs'ɪntrɪstɪd, -tərɪs-) *adj.* free from bias or partiality; objective. —dis'interestedly *adv.* —dis'interestedness *n.*

▷ **Usage.** In spoken and sometimes written English, *disinterested* (impartial) is used where *uninterested* (showing or feeling lack of interest) is meant. Careful writers and speakers avoid this confusion: *a disinterested judge; he was uninterested in public reaction.*

disinvest (dɪsɪn'vɛst) vb. Econ. **1.** (usually foll. by in) to remove investment (from). **2.** (intr.) to reduce the capital stock of an economy or enterprise, as by not replacing obsolete machinery. — ,disin'vestment n.

disjoin (dɪs'dʒɔɪn) vb. to disconnect or become disconnected; separate. — dis'joinable adj.

disjoint (dɪs'dʒɔɪnt) vb. **1.** to take apart or come apart at the joints. **2.** (tr.) to disunite or disjoin. **3.** to dislocate or become dislocated. **4.** (tr.; usually passive) to end the unity, sequence, or coherence of.

disjointed (dɪs'dʒɔɪntɪd) adj. **1.** having no coherence; disconnected. **2.** separated at the joint. **3.** dislocated. — dis'jointedly adv.

disjunct ('dɪsdʒʌŋkt) n. Logic. one of the propositions in a disjunction.

disjunction (dɪs'dʒʌŋkʃən) n. **1.** Also called: **disjuncture.** a disconnecting or being disconnected; separation. **2.** Logic. **a.** the operator that forms a compound sentence from two given sentences and corresponds to the English or. **b.** the relation between such sentences.

disjunctive (dɪs'dʒʌŋktɪv) adj. **1.** serving to disconnect or separate. **2.** Grammar. denoting a word, esp. a conjunction, that serves to express opposition or contrast: but in She was poor but she was honest. **3.** Logic. relating to, characterized by, or containing disjunction. ~n. **4.** Grammar. a disjunctive word, esp. a conjunction. **5.** Logic. a disjunctive proposition. — dis'junctively adv.

disk (dɪsk) n. **1.** a variant spelling (esp. U.S. and Canad.) of **disc.** **2.** Also called: **disk pack, magnetic disk.** Computers. a direct-access storage device consisting of a stack of plates coated with a magnetic layer, the whole assembly rotating rapidly as a single unit.

disk drive n. Computers. the unit that controls the mechanism for handling a floppy disk.

Disko ('dɪskəʊ) n. an island in Davis Strait, off the W coast of Greenland: extensive coal deposits.

disk pack n. Computers. another name for **disk** (sense 2).

dislike (dɪs'laɪk) vb. **1.** (tr.) to consider unpleasant or disagreeable. ~n. **2.** a feeling of aversion or antipathy. — dis'likable or dis'likeable adj.

dislocate ('dɪslə,keɪt) vb. (tr.) **1.** to disrupt or shift out of place. **2.** to displace from its normal position, esp. a bone from its joint.

dislocation (,dɪslə'keɪʃən) n. **1.** a displacing or being displaced. **2.** the state or condition of being dislocated.

dislodge (dɪs'lɒdʒ) vb. to remove from or leave a lodging place, hiding place, or previously fixed position. — dis'lodgment or dis'lodgement n.

disloyal (dɪs'lɔɪəl) adj. not loyal or faithful; deserting one's allegiance. — dis'loyally adv.

disloyalty (dɪs'lɔɪəltɪ) n., pl. **-ties.** the condition or an instance of being unfaithful or disloyal.

dismal ('dɪzməl) adj. **1.** causing gloom or depression. **2.** causing dismay or terror. [C13: from dismal (n.) list of 24 unlucky days in the year, from Med. L diēs malī, from L diēs day + malus bad] — dismally adv. — dismalness n.

Dismal Swamp or **Great Dismal Swamp** n. a coastal marshland in SE Virginia and NE North Carolina: partly reclaimed. Area: about 1940 sq. km (750 sq. miles). Area before reclamation: 5200 sq. km (2000 sq. miles).

dismantle (dɪs'mænt⁹l) vb. (tr.) **1.** to take apart. **2.** to demolish or raze. **3.** to strip of covering. [C17: from OF desmanteler to remove a cloak from] — dis'mantlement n.

dismast (dɪs'mɑːst) vb. (tr.) to break off the mast or masts of (a sailing vessel).

dismay (dɪs'meɪ) vb. (tr.) **1.** to fill with apprehension or alarm. **2.** to fill with depression or discouragement. ~n. **3.** consternation or agitation. [C13: from OF desmaiier (unattested), from des- DIS-¹ + esmayer to frighten, ult. of Gmc origin] — dis'maying adj.

dismember (dɪs'mɛmbə) vb. (tr.) **1.** to remove the limbs or members of. **2.** to cut to pieces. **3.** to divide or partition (something, such as an empire). — dis'memberment n.

dismiss (dɪs'mɪs) vb. (tr.) **1.** to remove or discharge from employment or service. **2.** to send away or allow to go. **3.** to dispel from one's mind; discard. **4.** to cease to consider (a subject). **5.** to decline further hearing to (a claim or action). **6.** Cricket. to bowl out a side for a particular number of runs. [C15: from Med. L dismissus sent

away, from dīmittere, from dī- DIS-¹ + mittere to send] — dis'missal n. — dis'missible adj. — dis'missive adj.

dismount (dɪs'maʊnt) vb. **1.** to get off a horse, bicycle, etc. **2.** (tr.) to disassemble or remove from a mounting. ~n. **3.** the act of dismounting.

Disney ('dɪznɪ) n. **Walt(er Elias).** 1901–66, U.S. film producer, who pioneered animated cartoons: noted esp. for his creations Mickey Mouse and Donald Duck and films such as Fantasia (1940). — ,Disney'esque adj.

disobedience (,dɪsə'biːdɪəns) n. lack of obedience.

disobedient (,dɪsə'biːdɪənt) adj. not obedient; neglecting or refusing to obey. — ,diso'bediently adv.

disobey (,dɪsə'beɪ) vb. to neglect or refuse to obey (someone, an order, etc.). — ,diso'beyer n.

disoblige (,dɪsə'blaɪdʒ) vb. (tr.) **1.** to disregard the desires of. **2.** to slight; insult. **3.** Inf. to cause trouble or inconvenience to. — ,diso'bliging adj.

disorder (dɪs'ɔːdə) n. **1.** a lack of order; confusion. **2.** a disturbance of public order. **3.** an upset of health; ailment. **4.** a deviation from the normal system or order. ~vb. (tr.) **5.** to upset the order of. **6.** to disturb the health or mind of.

disorderly (dɪs'ɔːdəlɪ) adj. **1.** untidy; irregular. **2.** uncontrolled; unruly. **3.** Law. violating public peace or order. — dis'orderliness n.

disorderly house n. Law. an establishment in which unruly behaviour habitually occurs, esp. a brothel or a gaming house.

disorganize or **-ise** (dɪs'ɔːgə,naɪz) vb. (tr.) to disrupt the arrangement, system, or unity of. — dis,organi'zation or -i'sation n.

disorientate (dɪs'ɔːrɪɛn,teɪt) or **disorient** vb. (tr.) **1.** to cause (someone) to lose his bearings. **2.** to perplex; confuse. — dis,orien'tation n.

disown (dɪs'əʊn) vb. (tr.) to deny any connection with; refuse to acknowledge. — dis'owner n.

disparage (dɪ'spærɪdʒ) vb. (tr.) **1.** to speak contemptuously of; belittle. **2.** to damage the reputation of. [C14: from OF desparagier, from des- DIS-¹ + parage equality, from L par equal] — dis'parragement n. — dis'paraging adj.

disparate ('dɪspərɪt) adj. **1.** utterly different or distinct in kind. ~n. **2.** (pl.) unlike things or people. [C16: from L disparāre to divide, from DIS-¹ + parāre to prepare; also infl. by L dispar unequal] — 'disparately adv. — 'dispa-rateness n.

disparity (dɪ'spærɪtɪ) n., pl. **-ties. 1.** inequality or difference, as in age, rank, wages, etc. **2.** dissimilarity.

dispassionate (dɪs'pæʃənɪt) adj. devoid of or uninfluenced by emotion or prejudice; objective; impartial. — dis'passionately adv.

dispatch or **despatch** (dɪ'spætʃ) vb. (tr.) **1.** to send off promptly, as to a destination or to perform a task. **2.** to discharge or complete (a duty, etc.) promptly. **3.** Inf. to eat up quickly. **4.** to murder or execute. ~n. **5.** the act of sending off a letter, messenger, etc. **6.** prompt action or speed (often in **with dispatch**). **7.** an official communication or report, sent in haste. **8.** a report sent to a newspaper, etc., by a correspondent. **9.** murder or execution. [C16: from It. dispacciare, from Provençal despachar, from OF despeechier to set free, from des- DIS-¹ + -peechier, ult. from L pedica a fetter] — dis'patcher n.

dispatch case n. a case used for carrying papers, documents, books, etc.

dispatch rider n. a horseman or motorcyclist who carries dispatches.

dispel (dɪ'spɛl) vb. **-pelling, -pelled.** (tr.) to disperse or drive away. [C17: from L dispellere, from DIS-¹ + pellere to drive] — dis'peller n.

dispensable (dɪ'spɛnsəb⁹l) adj. **1.** not essential; expendable. **2.** (of a law, vow, etc.) able to be relaxed. — dis,pensa'bility n.

dispensary (dɪ'spɛnsərɪ) n., pl. **-ries.** a place where medicine, etc., is dispensed.

dispensation (,dɪspɛn'seɪʃən) n. **1.** the act of distributing or dispensing. **2.** something distributed or dispensed. **3.** a system or plan of administering or dispensing. **4.** Chiefly R.C. Church. permission to dispense with an obligation of church law. **5.** any exemption from an obligation. **6. a.** the ordering of life and events by God. **b.** a religious system or code of prescriptions for life and conduct regarded as of divine origin. — ,dispen'sational adj.

dispensatory (dɪ'spɛnsətərɪ, -trɪ) n., pl. -ries. a book listing the composition, preparation, and application of various drugs.

dispense (dɪ'spɛns) vb. 1. (tr.) to give out or distribute in portions. 2. (tr.) to prepare and distribute (medicine), esp. on prescription. 3. (tr.) to administer (the law, etc.). 4. (intr.; foll. by with) to do away (with) or manage (without). 5. to grant a dispensation to. 6. to exempt or excuse from a rule or obligation. [C14: from Med. L dispensāre to pardon, from L dispendere to weigh out, from DIS-¹ + pendere]

dispenser (dɪ'spɛnsə) n. 1. a device that automatically dispenses a single item or a measured quantity. 2. a person or thing that dispenses.

dispensing optician n. See **optician**.

dispersal (dɪ'spɜːsəl) n. 1. another word for **dispersion** (sense 1). 2. the spread of animals, plants, or seeds to new areas.

dispersant (dɪs'pɜːsənt) n. a liquid or gas used to disperse small particles or droplets, as in an aerosol.

disperse (dɪ'spɜːs) vb. 1. to scatter; distribute over a wide area. 2. to dissipate. 3. to leave or cause to leave a gathering. 4. to separate or be separated by dispersion. 5. (tr.) to spread (news, etc.). 6. to separate (particles) throughout a solid, liquid, or gas. ~adj. 7. of or consisting of the particles in a colloid or suspension: disperse phase. [C14: from L dispersus, from dispergere to scatter widely, from DI-² + spargere to strew] —**dis'perser** n.

dispersion (dɪ'spɜːʃən) n. 1. a dispersing or being dispersed. 2. Physics. **a.** the separation of electromagnetic radiation into constituents of different wavelengths. **b.** a measure of the ability of a substance to separate by refraction. 3. Statistics. the degree to which values of a frequency distribution are scattered around some central point, usually the arithmetic mean or median. 4. Chem. a system containing particles dispersed in a solid, liquid, or gas.

dispirit (dɪ'spɪrɪt) vb. (tr.) to lower the spirit of; make downhearted; discourage. —**dis'pirited** adj. —**dis'piritedness** n. —**dis'piriting** adj.

displace (dɪs'pleɪs) vb. (tr.) 1. to move from the usual or correct location. 2. to remove from office or employment. 3. to occupy the place of; replace; supplant.

displaced person n. a person forced from his or her home or country, esp. by war or revolution.

displacement (dɪs'pleɪsmənt) n. 1. a displacing or being displaced. 2. the weight or volume displaced by a body in a fluid. 3. Psychoanal. the transferring of emotional feelings from their original object to one that disguises their real nature.

displacement activity n. Psychol. behaviour that occurs typically when there is a conflict of motives and that has no relevance to either motive: e.g. head scratching.

display (dɪ'spleɪ) vb. 1. (tr.) to show or make visible. 2. (tr.) to put out to be seen; exhibit. 3. (tr.) to disclose; reveal. 4. (tr.) to flaunt in an ostentatious way. 5. (tr.) to spread out; unfold. 6. (tr.) to give prominence to. 7. (intr.) Zool. to engage in a display. ~n. 8. an exhibiting or displaying; show. 9. something exhibited or displayed. 10. an ostentatious exhibition. 11. an arrangement of certain typefaces to give prominence to headings, etc. 12. Electronics. **a.** a device capable of representing information visually, as on a cathode-ray tube screen. **b.** the information so presented. 13. Zool. a pattern of behaviour by which the animal attracts attention while it is courting the female, defending its territory, etc. 14. (modifier) designating typefaces that give prominence to the words they are used to set. [C14: from Anglo-F despleier to unfold, from LL displicāre to scatter, from DIS-¹ + plicāre to fold] —**dis'player** n.

displease (dɪs'pliːz) vb. to annoy, offend, or cause displeasure to (someone). —**dis'pleasing** adj. —**dis'pleasingly** adv.

displeasure (dɪs'plɛʒə) n. 1. the condition of being displeased. 2. Arch. **a.** pain. **b.** an act or cause of offence.

disport (dɪ'spɔːt) vb. 1. (tr.) to indulge (oneself) in pleasure. 2. (intr.) to frolic or gambol. ~n. 3. Arch. amusement. [C14: from Anglo-F desporter, from des-DIS-¹ + porter to carry]

disposable (dɪ'spəʊzəbəl) adj. 1. designed for disposal after use: disposable cups. 2. available for use if needed: disposable assets. ~n. 3. something, such as a baby's nappy, that is designed for disposal. —**dis,posa'bility** n.

disposal (dɪ'spəʊzəl) n. 1. the act or means of getting rid of something. 2. arrangement in a particular order. 3. a specific method of tending to matters, as in business. 4. the act or process of transferring something to or providing something for another. 5. the power or opportunity to make use of someone or something (esp. in **at one's disposal**).

dispose (dɪ'spəʊz) vb. 1. (intr.; foll. by of) **a.** to deal with or settle. **b.** to give, sell, or transfer to another. **c.** to throw out or away. **d.** to consume, esp. hurriedly. **e.** to kill. 2. to arrange or settle (matters). 3. (tr.) to make willing or receptive. 4. (tr.) to place in a certain order. 5. (tr.; often foll. by to) to accustom or condition. [C14: from OF disposer, from L dispōnere to set in different places, from DIS-¹ + pōnere to place] —**dis'poser** n.

disposed (dɪ'spəʊzd) adj. **a.** having an inclination as specified (towards something). **b.** (in combination): well-disposed.

disposition (,dɪspə'zɪʃən) n. 1. a person's usual temperament or frame of mind. 2. a tendency, inclination, or habit. 3. another word for **disposal** (senses 2–5). 4. Arch. manner of placing or arranging.

dispossess (,dɪspə'zɛs) vb. (tr.) to take away possession of something, esp. property; expel. —**,dispos'session** n. —**,dispos'sessor** n.

dispraise (dɪs'preɪz) vb. 1. (tr.) to express disapproval or condemnation of. ~n. 2. the disapproval, etc., expressed. —**dis'praiser** n.

disproof (dɪs'pruːf) n. 1. facts that disprove something. 2. the act of disproving.

disproportion (,dɪsprə'pɔːʃən) n. 1. lack of proportion or equality. 2. an instance of disparity or inequality. ~vb. 3. (tr.) to cause to become exaggerated or unequal. —**,dispro'portional** adj.

disproportionate (,dɪsprə'pɔːʃənɪt) adj. out of proportion; unequal. —**,dispro'portionately** adv. —**,dispro'portionateness** n.

disprove (dɪs'pruːv) vb. (tr.) to show (an assertion, claim, etc.) to be incorrect. —**dis'provable** adj. —**dis'proval** n.

disputable (dɪ'spjuːtəbəl, 'dɪspjʊtə-) adj. capable of being argued; debatable. —**dis,puta'bility** or **dis'putableness** n. —**dis'putably** adv.

disputant (dɪ'spjuːtənt, 'dɪspjʊtənt) n. 1. a person who argues; contestant. ~adj. 2. engaged in argument.

disputation (,dɪspjuː'teɪʃən) n. 1. the act or an instance of arguing. 2. a formal academic debate on a thesis. 3. an obsolete word for **conversation**.

disputatious (,dɪspjuː'teɪʃəs) or **disputative** (dɪ'spjuːtətɪv) adj. inclined to argument. —**,dispu'tatiousness** or **dis'putativeness** n.

dispute vb. (dɪ'spjuːt). 1. to argue, debate, or quarrel about (something). 2. (tr.; may take a clause as object) to doubt the validity, etc., of. 3. (tr.) to seek to win; contest for. 4. (tr.) to struggle against; resist. ~n. (dɪ'spjuːt, 'dɪspjuːt). 5. an argument or quarrel. 6. Rare. a fight. [C13: from LL disputāre to contend verbally, from L: to discuss, from DIS-¹ + putāre to think] —**dis'puter** n.

disqualify (dɪs'kwɒlɪ,faɪ) vb. -fying, -fied. (tr.) 1. to make unfit or unqualified. 2. to make ineligible, as for entry to an examination. 3. to debar from a contest. 4. to deprive of rights, powers, or privileges. —**dis,qualifi'cation** n.

disquiet (dɪs'kwaɪət) n. 1. a feeling or condition of anxiety or uneasiness. ~vb. 2. (tr.) to make anxious or upset. —**dis'quieting** adj.

disquietude (dɪs'kwaɪɪ,tjuːd) n. a feeling or state of anxiety or uneasiness.

disquisition (,dɪskwɪ'zɪʃən) n. a formal examination of a subject. [C17: from L disquisitiō, from disquīrere to make an investigation, from DIS-¹ + quaerere to seek] —**,disqui'sitional** adj.

Disraeli (dɪz'reɪlɪ) n. **Benjamin,** 1st Earl of Beaconsfield. 1804–81, British Tory statesman and novelist; prime minister (1868; 1874–80). He gave coherence to the Tory principles of protectionism and imperialism, was responsible for the Reform Bill (1867) and, as prime minister, bought a controlling interest in the Suez Canal. His novels include Coningsby (1844) and Sybil (1845).

disregard (,dɪsrɪ'gɑːd) vb. 1. to give little or no attention to; ignore. 2. to treat as unworthy of consideration or respect. ~n. 3. lack of attention or respect. —**,disre'gardful** adj.

disremember (ˌdɪsrɪˈmɛmbə) *vb. Inf., chiefly U.S.* to fail to recall.

disrepair (ˌdɪsrɪˈpɛə) *n.* the condition of being worn out or in poor working order; a condition requiring repairs.

disreputable (dɪsˈrɛpjʊtəbəl) *adj.* **1.** having or causing a lack of repute. **2.** disordered in appearance. —**disˈreputably** *adv.*

disrepute (ˌdɪsrɪˈpjuːt) *n.* a loss or lack of credit or repute.

disrespect (ˌdɪsrɪˈspɛkt) *n.* contempt; rudeness; lack of respect. —**disreˈspectful** *adj.*

disrobe (dɪsˈrəʊb) *vb.* **1.** to undress. **2.** (*tr.*) to divest of authority, etc. —**disˈrobement** *n.*

disrupt (dɪsˈrʌpt) *vb.* **1.** (*tr.*) to throw into turmoil or disorder. **2.** (*tr.*) to interrupt the progress of. **3.** to break or split apart. [C17: from L *disruptus* burst asunder, from *dirumpere* to dash to pieces, from DIS-[1] + *rumpere* to burst] —**disˈrupter** *or* **disˈruptor** *n.* —**disˈruption** *n.*

disruptive (dɪsˈrʌptɪv) *adj.* involving, causing, or tending to cause disruption.

dissatisfy (dɪsˈsætɪsˌfaɪ) *vb.* **-fying, -fied.** (*tr.*) to fail to satisfy; disappoint. —**ˌdissatisˈfaction** *n.* —**ˌdissatisˈfactory** *adj.*

dissect (dɪˈsɛkt, daɪ-) *vb.* **1.** to cut open and examine the structure of (a dead animal or plant). **2.** (*tr.*) to examine critically and minutely. [C17: from L *dissecāre*, from DIS-[1] + *secāre* to cut] —**disˈsection** *n.* —**disˈsector** *n.*

dissected (dɪˈsɛktɪd, daɪ-) *adj.* **1.** *Bot.* in the form of narrow lobes or segments. **2.** *Geol.* cut by erosion into hills and valleys.

disselboom (ˈdɪsəlˌbuːm) *n. S. African.* the single shaft of a wagon, esp. an ox wagon. [from Du. *dissel* shaft + *boom* beam]

dissemble (dɪˈsɛmbəl) *vb.* **1.** to conceal (one's real motives, emotions, etc.) by pretence. **2.** (*tr.*) to pretend; simulate. [C15: from earlier *dissimulen*, from L *dissimulāre*; prob. infl. by obs. *semble* to resemble] —**disˈsemblance** *n.* —**disˈsembler** *n.*

disseminate (dɪˈsɛmɪˌneɪt) *vb.* (*tr.*) to distribute or scatter about; diffuse. [C17: from L *dissēmināre*, from DIS-[1] + *sēmināre* to sow, from *sēmen* seed] —**disˌsemiˈnation** *n.* —**disˈsemiˌnator** *n.*

disseminated sclerosis *n.* another name for **multiple sclerosis.**

dissension (dɪˈsɛnʃən) *n.* disagreement, esp. when leading to a quarrel. [C13: from L *dissēnsiō*, from *dissentīre* to DISSENT]

dissent (dɪˈsɛnt) *vb.* (*intr.*) **1.** to have a disagreement or withhold assent. **2.** *Christianity.* to reject the doctrines, beliefs, or practices of an established church, and to adhere to a different system of beliefs. ~*n.* **3.** a difference of opinion. **4.** *Christianity.* separation from an established church; Nonconformism. **5.** the voicing of a minority opinion in the decision on a case at law. [C16: from L *dissentīre* to disagree, from DIS-[1] + *sentīre* to feel] —**disˈsenter** *n.* —**disˈsenting** *adj.*

Dissenter (dɪˈsɛntə) *n. Christianity, chiefly Brit.* a Nonconformist or a person who refuses to conform to the established church.

dissentient (dɪˈsɛnʃənt) *adj.* **1.** dissenting, esp. from the opinion of the majority. ~*n.* **2.** a dissenter. —**disˈsentience** *or* **disˈsentiency** *n.*

dissertation (ˌdɪsəˈteɪʃən) *n.* **1.** a written thesis, often based on original research, usually required for a higher degree. **2.** a formal discourse. [C17: from L *dissertāre* to debate, from *disserere* to examine, from DIS-[1] + *serere* to arrange] —**ˌdisserˈtational** *adj.*

disserve (dɪsˈsɜːv) *vb.* (*tr.*) *Arch.* to do a disservice to.

disservice (dɪsˈsɜːvɪs) *n.* an ill turn; wrong; injury, esp. when trying to help.

dissever (dɪˈsɛvə) *vb.* **1.** to break off or become broken off. **2.** (*tr.*) to divide up into parts. [C13: from OF *dessevrer*, from LL DIS-[1] + *sēparāre* to SEPARATE] —**disˈseverance** *or* **disˈseverment** *n.*

dissident (ˈdɪsɪdənt) *adj.* **1.** disagreeing; dissenting. ~*n.* **2.** a person who disagrees, esp. one who disagrees with the government. [C16: from L *dissidēre* to be remote from, from DIS-[1] + *sedēre* to sit] —**ˈdissidence** *n.* —**ˈdissidently** *adv.*

dissimilar (dɪˈsɪmɪlə) *adj.* not alike; not similar; different. —**disˈsimilarly** *adv.* —**ˌdissimiˈlarity** *n.*

dissimilate (dɪˈsɪmɪˌleɪt) *vb.* **1.** to make or become dissimilar. **2.** (usually foll. by *to*) *Phonetics.* to change or displace (a consonant) or (of a consonant) to be changed to or displaced by (another consonant) so that its manner of articulation becomes less similar to a speech sound in the same word. Thus (r) in the final syllable of French *marbre* is dissimilated to (l) in its English form *marble.* [C19: from DIS-[1] + ASSIMILATE]

dissimilation (ˌdɪsɪmɪˈleɪʃən) *n.* **1.** the act or an instance of making dissimilar. **2.** *Phonetics.* the alteration or omission of a consonant as a result of being dissimilated.

dissimilitude (ˌdɪsɪˈmɪlɪˌtjuːd) *n.* **1.** dissimilarity; difference. **2.** a point of difference.

dissimulate (dɪˈsɪmjʊˌleɪt) *vb.* to conceal (one's real feelings) by pretence. —**disˌsimuˈlation** *n.* —**disˈsimuˌlator** *n.*

dissipate (ˈdɪsɪˌpeɪt) *vb.* **1.** to exhaust or be exhausted by dispersion. **2.** (*tr.*) to scatter or break up. **3.** (*intr.*) to indulge in the pursuit of pleasure. [C15: from L *dissipāre* to disperse, from DIS-[1] + *supāre* to throw] —**ˈdissiˌpater** *or* **ˈdissiˌpator** *n.* —**ˈdissiˌpative** *adj.*

dissipated (ˈdɪsɪˌpeɪtɪd) *adj.* **1.** indulging without restraint in the pursuit of pleasure; debauched. **2.** wasted, scattered, or exhausted.

dissipation (ˌdɪsɪˈpeɪʃən) *n.* **1.** a dissipating or being dissipated. **2.** unrestrained indulgence in physical pleasures. **3.** excessive expenditure; wastefulness.

dissociate (dɪˈsəʊʃɪˌeɪt, -sɪ-) *vb.* **1.** to break or cause to break the association between (people, organizations, etc.). **2.** (*tr.*) to regard or treat as separate or unconnected. **3.** to undergo or subject to dissociation. —**disˈsociative** *adj.*

▷ **Usage.** See at **disassociate.**

dissociation (dɪˌsəʊsɪˈeɪʃən, -ʃɪ-) *n.* **1.** a dissociating or being dissociated. **2.** *Chem.* the decomposition of the molecules of a single compound into two or more other compounds, atoms, ions, or radicals. **3.** *Psychiatry.* the separation of a group of mental processes or ideas from the rest of the personality, so that they lead an independent existence, as in cases of multiple personality.

dissoluble (dɪˈsɒljʊbəl) *adj.* a less common word for **soluble.** [C16: from L *dissolūbilis*, from *dissolvere* to DISSOLVE] —**disˌsoluˈbility** *n.*

dissolute (ˈdɪsəˌluːt) *adj.* given to dissipation; debauched. [C14: from L *dissolūtus* loose, from *dissolvere* to DISSOLVE] —**ˈdissoˌlutely** *adv.* —**ˈdissoˌluteness** *n.*

dissolution (ˌdɪsəˈluːʃən) *n.* **1.** separation into component parts; disintegration. **2.** destruction by breaking up and dispersing. **3.** the termination of a meeting or assembly, such as Parliament. **4.** the termination of a formal or legal relationship, such as a business, marriage, etc. **5.** the act or process of dissolving.

dissolve (dɪˈzɒlv) *vb.* **1.** to go or cause to go into solution. **2.** to become or cause to become liquid; melt. **3.** to disintegrate or disperse. **4.** to come or bring to an end. **5.** to dismiss (a meeting, Parliament, etc.) or (of a meeting, etc.) to be dismissed. **6.** to collapse or cause to collapse emotionally: *to dissolve into tears.* **7.** to lose or cause to lose distinctness. **8.** (*tr.*) to terminate legally, as a marriage, etc. **9.** (*intr.*) *Films, television.* to fade out one scene and replace with another to make two scenes merge imperceptibly or slowly overlap. ~*n.* **10.** *Films, television.* a scene filmed or televised by dissolving. [C14: from L *dissolvere* to make loose, from DIS-[1] + *solvere* to release] —**disˈsolvable** *adj.*

dissonance (ˈdɪsənəns) *or* **dissonancy** *n.* **1.** a discordant combination of sounds. **2.** lack of agreement or consistency. **3.** *Music.* **a.** a sensation of harshness and incompleteness associated with certain intervals and chords. **b.** an interval or chord of this kind.

dissonant (ˈdɪsənənt) *adj.* **1.** discordant. **2.** incongruous or discrepant. **3.** *Music.* characterized by dissonance. [C15: from L *dissonāre* to be discordant, from DIS-[1] + *sonāre* to sound]

dissuade (dɪˈsweɪd) *vb.* (*tr.*) **1.** (often foll. by *from*) to deter (someone) by persuasion from a course of action, policy, etc. **2.** to advise against (an action, etc.). [C15: from L *dissuādēre*, from DIS-[1] + *suādēre* to persuade] —**disˈsuader** *n.* —**disˈsuasion** *n.* —**disˈsuasive** *adj.*

dissyllable (dɪˈsɪləbəl) *or* **disyllable** *n.* a word of two syllables. —**dissyllabic** (ˌdɪsɪˈlæbɪk) *or* **disyllabic** (ˌdaɪsɪˈlæbɪk) *adj.*

dissymmetry (dɪˈsɪmɪtrɪ, dɪsˈsɪm-) *n., pl.* **-tries. 1.** lack of symmetry. **2.** the relationship between two objects when one is the mirror image of the other. —**dissymmetric** (ˌdɪsɪˈmɛtrɪk, ˌdɪssɪ-) *or* ˌdissym'metrical *adj.*

dist. *abbrev. for:* **1.** distant. **2.** distinguish(ed). **3.** district.

distaff ('dɪstɑːf) *n.* **1.** the rod on which wool, flax, etc., is wound preparatory to spinning. **2.** *Figurative.* women's work. [OE *distæf*, from *dis-* bunch of flax + *stæf* STAFF[1]]

distaff side *n.* the female side of a family.

distal ('dɪstəl) *adj. Anat.* situated farthest from the centre or point of attachment or origin. [C19: from DISTANT + -AL[1]] —'**distally** *adv.*

distance ('dɪstəns) *n.* **1.** the space between two points. **2.** the length of this gap. **3.** the state of being apart in space; remoteness. **4.** an interval between two points in time. **5.** the extent of progress. **6.** a distant place or time. **7.** a separation or remoteness in relationship. **8.** (preceded by *the*) the most distant or a faraway part of the visible scene. **9.** *Horse racing.* **a.** *Brit.* a point on a racecourse 240 yards from the winning post. **b.** *U.S.* the part of a racecourse that a horse must reach before the winner passes the finishing line in order to qualify for later heats. **10. go the distance. a.** *Boxing.* to complete a bout without being knocked out **b.** to be able to complete an assigned task or responsibility. **11. keep one's distance.** to maintain a reserve in respect of another person. **12. middle distance.** halfway between the foreground or the observer and the horizon. ~*vb.* (*tr.*) **13.** to hold or place at a distance. **14.** to separate (oneself) mentally from something. **15.** to outdo; outstrip.

distance learning *n.* a teaching system consisting of video, audio, and written material designed for a person to use in studying a subject at home.

distant ('dɪstənt) *adj.* **1.** far apart in space or time. **2.** (*postpositive*) separated in space or time by a specified distance. **3.** apart in relationship: *a distant cousin.* **4.** coming from or going to a faraway place. **5.** remote in manner; aloof. **6.** abstracted; absent: *a distant look.* [C14: from L *distāre* to be distant, from DIS-[1] + *stāre* to stand] —'**distantly** *adv.* —'**distantness** *n.*

distaste (dɪsˈteɪst) *n.* (often foll. by *for*) a dislike (of); aversion (to).

distasteful (dɪsˈteɪstful) *adj.* unpleasant or offensive. —dis'**tastefulness** *n.*

distemper[1] (dɪsˈtɛmpə) *n.* **1.** any of various infectious diseases of animals, esp. **canine distemper,** a highly contagious viral disease of dogs. **2.** *Arch.* **a.** a disorder. **b.** disturbance. **c.** discontent. [C14: from LL *distemperāre* to derange the health of, from L DIS-[1] + *temperāre* to mix in correct proportions]

distemper[2] (dɪsˈtɛmpə) *n.* **1.** a technique of painting in which the pigments are mixed with water, glue, size, etc.: used for poster, mural, and scene painting. **2.** the paint used in this technique or any of various water-based paints. ~*vb.* **3.** to paint (something) with distemper. [C14: from Med. L *distemperāre* to soak, from L DIS-[1] + *temperāre* to mingle]

distend (dɪsˈtɛnd) *vb.* **1.** to expand by or as if by pressure from within; swell; inflate. **2.** (*tr.*) to stretch out or extend. [C14: from L *distendere,* from DIS-[1] + *tendere* to stretch] —dis'**tensible** *adj.* —dis'**tension** *or* dis'**tention** *n.*

distich ('dɪstɪk) *n. Prosody.* a unit of two verse lines, usually a couplet. [C16: from Gk *distikhos* having two lines, from DI-[1] + *stikhos* row, line]

distil *or U.S.* **distill** (dɪsˈtɪl) *vb.* -**tilling,** -**tilled.** **1.** to subject to or undergo distillation. **2.** (sometimes foll. by *out* or *off*) to purify, separate, or concentrate, or be purified, separated, or concentrated by distillation. **3.** to obtain or be obtained by distillation. **4.** to exude or give off (a substance) in drops. **5.** (*tr.*) to extract the essence of. [C14: from L *dēstillāre* to distil, from DE- + *stillāre* to drip]

distillate ('dɪstɪlɪt) *n.* **1.** the product of distillation. **2.** a concentrated essence.

distillation (ˌdɪstɪˈleɪʃən) *n.* **1.** a distilling. **2.** the process of evaporating or boiling a liquid and condensing its vapour. **3.** purification or separation of mixtures by using different evaporation rates or boiling points of their components. **4.** the process of obtaining the essence or an extract of a substance, usually by heating it in a solvent. **5.** a distillate. **6.** a concentrated essence. —dis'**tillatory** *adj.*

distiller (dɪsˈtɪlə) *n.* a person or organization that distils, esp. a company that makes spirits.

distillery (dɪsˈtɪlərɪ) *n., pl.* -**eries.** a place where alcoholic drinks, etc., are made by distillation.

distinct (dɪsˈtɪŋkt) *adj.* **1.** easily sensed or understood; clear. **2.** (when postpositive, foll. by *from*) not the same (as); separate (from). **3.** not alike; different. **4.** sharp; clear. **5.** recognizable; definite. **6.** explicit; unequivocal. [C14: from L *distinctus,* from *distinguere* to DISTINGUISH] —dis'**tinctly** *adv.* —dis'**tinctness** *n.*

distinction (dɪsˈtɪŋkʃən) *n.* **1.** the act or an instance of distinguishing or differentiating. **2.** a distinguishing feature. **3.** the state of being different or distinguishable. **4.** special honour, recognition, or fame. **5.** excellence of character; distinctive qualities. **6.** distinguished appearance. **7.** a symbol of honour or rank.

distinctive (dɪsˈtɪŋktɪv) *adj.* serving or tending to distinguish; characteristic. —dis'**tinctively** *adv.* —dis'**tinctiveness** *n.*

distingué *French.* (dɪstɛ̃ge) *adj.* distinguished or noble.

distinguish (dɪsˈtɪŋgwɪʃ) *vb.* (*mainly tr.*) **1.** (when *intr.,* foll. by *between* or *among*) to make, show, or recognize a difference (between or among); differentiate (between). **2.** to be a distinctive feature of; characterize. **3.** to make out; perceive. **4.** to mark for a special honour. **5.** to make (oneself) noteworthy. **6.** to classify. [C16: from L *distinguere* to separate] —dis'**tinguishable** *adj.* —dis'**tinguishing** *adj.*

distinguished (dɪsˈtɪŋgwɪʃt) *adj.* **1.** noble or dignified in appearance or behaviour. **2.** eminent; famous; celebrated.

distort (dɪsˈtɔːt) *vb.* (*tr.*) **1.** (*often passive*) to twist or pull out of shape; contort; deform. **2.** to alter or misrepresent (facts, etc.). **3.** *Electronics.* to reproduce or amplify (a signal) inaccurately. [C16: from L *distortus,* from *distorquēre* to turn different ways, from DIS-[1] + *torquēre* to twist] —dis'**torted** *adj.*

distortion (dɪsˈtɔːʃən) *n.* **1.** a distorting or being distorted. **2.** something that is distorted. **3.** *Electronics.* an undesired change in the shape of an electrical wave or signal resulting in a loss of clarity in radio reception or sound reproduction. —dis'**tortional** *adj.*

distr. *abbrev. for:* **1.** distribution. **2.** distributor.

distract (dɪsˈtrækt) *vb.* (*tr.*) **1.** (*often passive*) to draw the attention of (a person) away from something. **2.** to divide or confuse the attention of (a person). **3.** to amuse or entertain. **4.** to trouble greatly. **5.** to make mad. [C14: from L *distractus* perplexed, from *distrahere* to pull in different directions, from DIS-[1] + *trahere* to drag]

distracted (dɪsˈtræktɪd) *adj.* **1.** bewildered; confused. **2.** mad. —dis'**tractedly** *adv.*

distraction (dɪsˈtrækʃən) *n.* **1.** a distracting or being distracted. **2.** something that serves as a diversion or entertainment. **3.** an interruption; obstacle to concentration. **4.** mental turmoil or madness.

distrain (dɪsˈtreɪn) *vb. Law.* to seize (personal property) as security or indemnity for a debt. [C13: from OF *destreindre,* from L *distringere* to impede, from DIS-[1] + *stringere* to draw tight] —dis'**trainment** *n.* —dis'**trainor** *or* dis'**trainer** *n.*

distraint (dɪsˈtreɪnt) *n. Law.* the act or process of distraining; distress.

distrait (dɪsˈtreɪ; *French* distrɛ) *adj.* absent-minded; abstracted. [C18: from F, from *distraire* to DISTRACT]

distraught (dɪsˈtrɔːt) *adj.* **1.** distracted or agitated. **2.** *Rare.* mad. [C14: changed from obs. *distract* through influence of obs. *straught,* p.p. of STRETCH]

distress (dɪsˈtrɛs) *vb.* (*tr.*) **1.** to cause mental pain to; upset badly. **2.** (*usually passive*) to subject to financial or other trouble. **3.** to treat (something, esp. furniture) in order to make it appear older than it is. **4.** *Law.* a less common word for **distrain.** ~*n.* **5.** mental pain; anguish. **6.** a distressing or being distressed. **7.** physical or financial trouble. **8. in distress.** (of a ship, etc.) in dire need of help. **9.** *Law.* **a.** the seizure of property as security for or in satisfaction of debt, claim, etc.; distraint. **b.** the property thus seized. **c.** (*as modifier*) *U.S.: distress merchandise.* [C13: from OF *destresse,* via Vulgar L, from L *districtus* divided [in mind] —dis'**tressful** *adj.* —dis'**tressing** *adj.* —dis'**tressingly** *adv.*

distressed (dɪsˈtrɛst) *adj.* **1.** much troubled; upset; afflicted. **2.** in financial straits; poor. **3.** (of furniture, fabric, etc.) having signs of ageing artificially applied. **4.** *Econ.* another word for **depressed.**

distress signal *n.* a signal by radio, Very light, etc., from a ship in need of immediate assistance.

distribute (dɪ'strɪbjuːt) *vb.* (*tr.*) **1.** to give out in shares; dispense. **2.** to hand out or deliver. **3.** (*often passive*) to spread throughout an area. **4.** (*often passive*) to divide into classes or categories. **5.** *Printing.* to return (used type) to the correct positions in the typecase. **6.** *Logic.* to incorporate in a distributed term of a categorical proposition. [C15: from L *distribuere*, from DIS-¹ + *tribuere* to give] —**dis'tributable** *adj.*

distributed term *n. Logic.* a term referring to every member of the class it designates, as *men* in *all men are mortal*.

distribution (,dɪstrɪ'bjuːʃən) *n.* **1.** the act of distributing or the state or manner of being distributed. **2.** a thing or portion distributed. **3.** arrangement or location. **4.** the process of physically satisfying the demand for goods and services. **5.** *Econ.* the division of the total income of a community among its members. **6.** *Statistics.* the set of possible values of a random variable, considered in terms of theoretical or observed frequency. **7.** *Law.* the apportioning of the estate of a deceased intestate. —,distri'butional *adj.*

distributive (dɪ'strɪbjʊtɪv) *adj.* **1.** characterized by or relating to distribution. **2.** *Grammar.* referring separately to the individual people or items in a group, as the words *each* and *every.* **3.** *Maths, logic.* obeying the distributive law for a specified pair of operators, enabling one to be validly distributed over the other. See **distribute** (sense 6). —*n.* **4.** *Grammar.* a distributive word. —**dis'tributively** *adv.* —**dis'tributiveness** *n.*

distributor (dɪ'strɪbjʊtə) *n.* **1.** a person or thing that distributes. **2.** a wholesaler or middleman engaged in the distribution of a category of goods, esp. to retailers in a specific area. **3.** the device in a petrol engine that distributes the high-tension voltage to the sparking plugs.

district ('dɪstrɪkt) *n.* **1. a.** an area of land marked off for administrative or other purposes. **b.** (*as modifier*): *district nurse.* **2.** a locality separated by geographical attributes; region. **3.** any subdivision of a territory, region, etc. **4.** a political subdivision of a county, region, etc., that elects a council responsible for certain local services. ~*vb.* **5.** (*tr.*) to divide into districts. [C17: from Med. L *districtus* area of jurisdiction, from L *distringere* to stretch out]

district attorney *n.* (in the U.S.) the state prosecuting officer in a specified judicial district.

District Court *n.* **1.** (in Scotland) a court of summary jurisdiction which deals with minor criminal offences. **2.** (in the U.S.) **a.** a Federal trial court in each U.S. district. **b.** in some states, a court of general jurisdiction. **3.** (in New Zealand) a court lower than a High Court. Formerly called: **magistrates' court.**

district high school *n.* (in New Zealand) a school in a rural area providing both primary and secondary education.

district nurse *n.* (in Britain) a nurse appointed to attend patients within a particular district, usually in the patients' homes.

District of Columbia *n.* a federal district of the eastern U.S., coextensive with the federal capital, Washington. Pop.: 637 651 (1980). Area: 178 sq. km (69 sq. miles). Abbrevs.: **D.C.** or (with zip code) **DC**

Distrito Federal (*Portuguese* dis'tritu fede'ral) *n.* a district in S central Brazil, containing Brasilia: detached from Goiás state in 1960. Pop.: 1 177 393 (1980). Area: 5815 sq. km (2245 sq. miles).

distrust (dɪs'trʌst) *vb.* **1.** to regard as untrustworthy or dishonest. ~*n.* **2.** suspicion; doubt. —**dis'truster** *n.* —**dis'trustful** *adj.*

disturb (dɪ'stɜːb) *vb.* (*tr.*) **1.** to intrude on; interrupt. **2.** to destroy the quietness or peace of. **3.** to disarrange; muddle. **4.** (*often passive*) to upset; trouble. **5.** to inconvenience; put out. [C13: from L *disturbāre*, from DIS-¹ + *turbāre* to confuse] —**dis'turber** *n.* —**dis'turbing** *adj.* —**dis'turbingly** *adv.*

disturbance (dɪ'stɜːbəns) *n.* **1.** a disturbing or being disturbed. **2.** an interruption or intrusion. **3.** an unruly outburst or tumult. **4.** *Law.* an interference with another's rights. **5.** *Geol.* a minor movement of the earth causing a small earthquake. **6.** *Meteorol.* a small depression. **7.** *Psychiatry.* a mental or emotional disorder.

disturbed (dɪ'stɜːbd) *adj. Psychiatry.* emotionally upset, troubled, or maladjusted.

disulphide (daɪ'sʌlfaɪd) *n.* any chemical compound containing two sulphur atoms per molecule.

disunite (,dɪsjʊ'naɪt) *vb.* **1.** to separate; disrupt. **2.** (*tr.*) to set at variance; estrange. —**dis'union** *n.* —**dis'unity** *n.*

disuse (dɪs'juːs) *n.* the condition of being unused; neglect (often in **in** *or* **into disuse**).

disyllable ('daɪ,sɪləbəl) *n.* a variant of **dissyllable.**

ditch (dɪtʃ) *n.* **1.** a narrow channel dug in the earth, usually used for drainage, irrigation, or as a boundary marker. ~*vb.* **2.** to make a ditch in. **3.** (*intr.*) to edge with a ditch. **4.** *Sl.* to crash, esp. deliberately, as to avoid more unpleasant circumstances: *he had to ditch the car.* **5.** (*tr.*) *Sl.* to abandon. **6.** *Sl.* to land (an aircraft) on water in an emergency. **7.** (*tr.*) *U.S. sl.* to evade. [OE *dīc*] —**'ditcher** *n.*

ditchwater ('dɪtʃ,wɔːtə) *n.* **1.** stagnant water, esp. found in ditches. **2. as dull as ditchwater.** very dull; very uninteresting.

dither ('dɪðə) *vb.* (*intr.*) **1.** *Chiefly Brit.* to be uncertain or indecisive. **2.** *Chiefly Brit.* to be in an agitated state. **3.** to tremble, as with cold. ~*n.* **4.** *Chiefly Brit.* a state of indecision. **5.** a state of agitation. [C17: var. of C14 (N English dialect) *didder*, from ?] —**'ditherer** *n.* —**'dithery** *adj.*

dithyramb ('dɪθɪ,ræm, -,ræmb) *n.* **1.** (in ancient Greece) a passionate choral hymn in honour of Dionysus. **2.** any utterance or a piece of writing that resembles this. [C17: from L *dithyrambus*, from Gk *dithurambos*] —,dith'y'rambic *adj.*

dittany ('dɪtənɪ) *n., pl.* **-nies. 1.** an aromatic Cretan plant with pink flowers: formerly credited with medicinal properties. **2.** a North American plant with purplish flowers. [C14: from OF *ditan*, from L *dictamnus*, from Gk *diktamnon*, ?from *Diktē*, mountain in Crete]

ditto ('dɪtəʊ) *n., pl.* **-tos. 1.** the aforementioned; the above; the same. Used in accounts, lists, etc., to avoid repetition, and symbolized by two small marks (,,) known as **ditto marks,** placed under the thing repeated. **2.** *Inf.* a duplicate. ~*adv.* **3.** in the same way. ~*sentence substitute.* **4.** *Inf.* used to avoid repeating or to confirm agreement with an immediately preceding sentence. ~*vb.* **-toing, -toed. 5.** (*tr.*) to copy; repeat. [C17: from It. (dialect): var. of *detto* said, from *dicere* to say, from L]

ditty ('dɪtɪ) *n., pl.* **-ties.** a short simple song or poem. [C13: from OF *ditie* poem, from *ditier* to compose, from L *dictāre* to DICTATE]

ditty bag *or* **box** *n.* a sailor's bag or box for personal belongings or tools. [C19: ?from obs. *dutty* calico, from Hindi *dhōtī* loincloth]

Diu ('diːuː) *n.* a small island off the NW coast of India: together with a mainland area, it formed a district of Portuguese India (1535–1961); formerly part of the Indian Union Territory of Goa, Daman, and Diu (1962–87).

diuretic (,daɪjʊ'rɛtɪk) *adj.* **1.** acting to increase the flow of urine. ~*n.* **2.** a drug or agent that increases the flow of urine. [ME, from LL, from Gk, from *dia-* through + *ourein* to urinate] —**diuresis** (,daɪjʊ'riːsɪs) *n.*

diurnal (daɪ'ɜːnəl) *adj.* **1.** happening during the day or daily. **2.** (of flowers) open during the day and closed at night. **3.** (of animals) active during the day. ~Cf. **nocturnal.** [C15: from LL *diurnālis*, from L *diurnus*, from *diēs* day] —**di'urnally** *adv.*

div. *abbrev. for:* **1.** divide(d). **2.** dividend. **3.** division. **4.** divorce(d).

diva ('diːvə) *n., pl.* **-vas** *or* **-ve** (-vɪ). a highly distinguished female singer; prima donna. [C19: via It. from L: a goddess, from *dīvus* DIVINE]

divagate ('daɪvə,geɪt) *vb.* (*intr.*) *Rare.* to digress or wander. [C16: from L DI-² + *vagārī* to wander] —,di'va'gation *n.*

divalent (daɪ'veɪlənt, 'daɪ,veɪ-) *adj. Chem.* **1.** having a valency of two. **2.** having two valencies. ~Also: **bivalent.** —**di'valency** *n.*

divan (dɪ'væn) *n.* **1. a.** a backless sofa or couch. **b.** a bed resembling such a couch. **2.** (esp. formerly) a smoking room. **3. a.** a Muslim law court, council chamber, or counting house. **b.** a Muslim council of state. [C16: from Turkish *dīvān*, from Persian *dīwān*]

dive (daɪv) *vb.* **diving, dived** *or* *U.S.* **dove** (dəʊv), **dived.** (*mainly intr.*) **1.** to plunge headfirst into water. **2.** (of a submarine, etc.) to submerge under water. **3.** (*also tr.*) to fly in a steep nose-down descending path. **4.** to rush, go, or reach quickly, as in a headlong plunge: *he dived for the ball.* **5.** (*also tr.; foll. by in or into*) to dip or put (one's hand) quickly or forcefully (into). **6.** (usually foll. by *in or into*) to involve oneself (in something), as in eating food. ~*n.* **7.** a headlong plunge into water. **8.** an act or instance of diving. **9.** a steep nose-down descent of an aircraft. **10.** *Sl.* a disreputable bar or club. **11.** *Boxing sl.* the act of a boxer pretending to be knocked down or out. [OE *dūfan*]

dive bomber *n.* a military aircraft designed to release its bombs on a target during a steep dive. — **'dive-bomb** *vb.* (*tr.*)

diver ('daɪvə) *n.* **1.** a person or thing that dives. **2.** a person who works or explores underwater. **3.** any of various aquatic birds of northern oceans: noted for skill in diving. U.S. and Canad. name: **loon.** **4.** any of various other diving birds.

diverge (daɪ'vɜːdʒ) *vb.* **1.** to separate or cause to separate and go in different directions from a point. **2.** (*intr.*) to be at variance; differ. **3.** (*intr.*) to deviate from a prescribed course. **4.** (*intr.*) *Maths.* (of a series) to have no limit. [C17: from Med. L *dīvergere*, from L DI-² + *vergere* to turn]

divergence (daɪ'vɜːdʒəns) *or* **divergency** *n.* **1.** the act or result of diverging or the amount by which something diverges. **2.** the condition of being divergent.

divergent (daɪ'vɜːdʒənt) *adj.* **1.** diverging or causing divergence. **2.** *Maths.* (of a series) having no limit. — **di'vergently** *adv.*

divergent thinking *n.* *Psychol.* thinking in an unusual and unstereotyped way, for instance to generate several possible solutions to a problem.

divers ('daɪvəz) *determiner. Arch. or literary.* various; sundry; some. [C13: from OF, from L *dīversus* turned in different directions]

▷ **Usage.** In spite of the frequency with which *divers* (several) and *diverse* (disparate, set apart by marked differences) are treated as synonyms, and although they were originally the same word, careful writers and speakers always distinguish between these two words: *there were divers persons in the room; the personalities of those present were extremely diverse.*

diverse (daɪ'vɜːs, 'daɪvɜːs) *adj.* **1.** having variety; assorted. **2.** distinct in kind. [C13: from L *dīversus*; see DIVERS] — **di'versely** *adv.*

diversify (daɪ'vɜːsɪ͵faɪ) *vb.* **-fying, -fied.** **1.** (*tr.*) to create different forms of; variegate; vary. **2.** (of an enterprise) to vary (products, operations, etc.) in order to spread risk, expand, etc. **3.** to distribute (investments) among several securities in order to spread risk. [C15: from OF *diversifier*, from Med. L *dīversificāre*, from L *dīversus* DIVERSE + *facere* to make] — **di͵versifi'cation** *n.*

diversion (daɪ'vɜːʃən) *n.* **1.** the act of diverting from a specified course. **2.** *Chiefly Brit.* an official detour used by traffic when a main route is closed. **3.** something that distracts from business, etc.; amusement. **4.** *Mil.* a feint attack designed to draw an enemy away from the main attack. — **di'versional** *or* **di'versionary** *adj.*

diversity (daɪ'vɜːsɪtɪ) *n.* **1.** the state or quality of being different or varied. **2.** a point of difference.

divert (daɪ'vɜːt) *vb.* **1.** to turn aside; deflect. **2.** (*tr.*) to entertain; amuse. **3.** (*tr.*) to distract the attention of. [C15: from F *divertir*, from L *dīvertere* to turn aside, from DI-² + *vertere* to turn] — **di'verting** *adj.* — **di'vertingly** *adv.*

diverticulitis (͵daɪvə͵tɪkjʊ'laɪtɪs) *n.* inflammation of one or more diverticula, esp. of the colon.

diverticulum (͵daɪvə'tɪkjʊləm) *n., pl.* **-la** (-lə). any sac or pouch formed by herniation of the wall of a tubular organ or part, esp. the intestines. [C16: from NL, from L *dēverticulum* by-path, from *dēvertere* to turn aside, from *vertere* to turn]

divertimento (dɪ͵vɜːtɪ'mɛntəʊ) *n., pl.* **-ti** (-tɪ). **1.** a piece of entertaining music, often scored for a mixed ensemble and having no fixed form. **2.** an episode in a fugue. [C18: from It.]

divertissement (dɪ'vɜːtɪsmənt) *n.* a brief entertainment or diversion, usually between the acts of a play. [C18: from F: entertainment]

Dives ('daɪviːz) *n.* **1.** a rich man in the parable in Luke 16:19–31. **2.** a very rich man.

divest (daɪ'vɛst) *vb.* (*tr.; usually foll. by of*) **1.** to strip (of clothes). **2.** to deprive or dispossess. [C17: changed from earlier *devest*] — **divestiture** (daɪ'vɛstɪtʃə), **divesture** (daɪ'vɛstʃə), *or* **di'vestment** *n.*

divi ('dɪvɪ) *n.* an alternative spelling of **divvy.**

divide (dɪ'vaɪd) *vb.* **1.** to separate into parts; split up. **2.** to share or be shared out in parts; distribute. **3.** to diverge or cause to diverge in opinion or aim. **4.** (*tr.*) to keep apart or be a boundary between. **5.** (*intr.*) to vote by separating into two groups. **6.** to categorize; classify. **7.** to calculate the quotient of (one number or quantity) and (another number or quantity) by division. **8.** (*intr.*) to diverge: *the roads divide.* **9.** (*tr.*) to mark increments of (length, angle, etc.). ~*n.* **10.** *Chiefly U.S. & Canad.* an area of relatively high ground separating drainage basins; watershed. **11.** a division; split. [C14: from L *dīvidere* to force apart, from DI-² + *vid-* separate, from the source of *viduus* bereaved]

divided (dɪ'vaɪdɪd) *adj.* **1.** *Bot.* another word for **dissected** (sense 1). **2.** split; not united.

dividend ('dɪvɪ͵dɛnd) *n.* **1. a.** a distribution from the net profits of a company to its shareholders. **b.** a portion of this distribution received by a shareholder. **2.** the share of a cooperative society's surplus allocated to members. **3.** *Insurance.* a sum of money distributed from a company's net profits to the holders of certain policies. **4.** something extra; a bonus. **5.** a number or quantity to be divided by another number or quantity. **6.** *Law.* the proportion of an insolvent estate payable to the creditors. [C15: from L *dīvidendum* what is to be divided]

divider (dɪ'vaɪdə) *n.* **1.** Also called: **room divider.** a screen or piece of furniture placed so as to divide a room into separate areas. **2.** a person or thing that divides.

dividers (dɪ'vaɪdəz) *pl. n.* a type of compass with two pointed arms, used for measuring lines or dividing them.

divination (͵dɪvɪ'neɪʃən) *n.* **1.** the art or practice of discovering future events or unknown things, as though by supernatural powers. **2.** a prophecy. **3.** a guess. — **divinatory** (dɪ'vɪnətərɪ, -trɪ) *adj.*

divine (dɪ'vaɪn) *adj.* **1.** of God or a deity. **2.** godlike. **3.** of or associated with religion or worship. **4.** of supreme excellence or worth. **5.** *Inf.* splendid; perfect. ~*n.* **6.** (*often cap.; preceded by the*) another term for **God.** **7.** a priest, esp. one learned in theology. ~*vb.* **8.** to perceive (something) by intuition. **9.** to conjecture (something); guess. **10.** to discern (a hidden or future reality) as though by supernatural power. **11.** (*tr.*) to search for (water, metal, etc.) using a divining rod. [C14: from L *dīvīnus*, from *dīvus* a god] — **di'vinely** *adv.* — **di'viner** *n.*

divine office *n.* (*sometimes cap.*) the canonical prayers recited daily by priests, etc. Also called: **Liturgy of the Hours.**

divine right of kings *n.* *History.* the concept that the right to rule derives from God and that kings are answerable for their actions to God alone.

diving bell *n.* an early diving submersible having an open bottom and being supplied with compressed air.

diving board *n.* a platform or springboard from which swimmers may dive.

diving suit *or* **dress** *n.* a waterproof suit used by divers, having a heavy detachable helmet and an air supply.

divining rod *n.* a forked twig said to move when held over ground in which water, metal, etc., is to be found. Also called: **dowsing rod.**

divinity (dɪ'vɪnɪtɪ) *n., pl.* **-ties.** **1.** the nature of a deity or the state of being divine. **2.** a god. **3.** (*often cap.; preceded by the*) another term for **God.** **4.** another word for **theology.**

divisible (dɪ'vɪzəbəl) *adj.* capable of being divided, usually with no remainder. — **di͵visi'bility** *or* **di'visibleness** *n.* — **di'visibly** *adv.*

division (dɪ'vɪʒən) *n.* **1.** a dividing or being divided. **2.** the act of sharing out; distribution. **3.** something that divides; boundary. **4.** one of the parts, groups, etc., into which something is divided. **5.** a part of a government, business, etc., that has been made into a unit for administrative or other reasons. **6.** a formal vote in Parliament or a similar legislative body. **7.** a difference of opinion. **8.** (in sports) a section or class organized according to age, weight, skill, etc. **9.** a mathematical operation in which the quotient of two numbers or quantities is calculated.

Usually written: $a \div b$, a/b, $\frac{a}{b}$ **10.** *Army.* a major formation, larger than a brigade but smaller than a corps, containing the necessary arms to sustain independent combat. **11.** *Biol.* a major taxonomic division that corresponds to a phylum. [C14: from L *dīvīsiō*, from *dīvidere* to DIVIDE] —**di'visional** *or* **di'visionary** *adj.* —**di'visionally** *adv.*

division sign *n.* the symbol ÷, placed between the dividend and the divisor to indicate division, as in $12 \div 6 = 2$.

divisive (dɪ'vaɪsɪv) *adj.* tending to cause disagreement or dissension. —**di'visively** *adv.* —**di'visiveness** *n.*

divisor (dɪ'vaɪzə) *n.* **1.** a number or quantity to be divided into another number or quantity (the dividend). **2.** a number that is a factor of another number.

divorce (dɪ'vɔːs) *n.* **1.** the legal dissolution of a marriage. **2.** a judicial decree declaring a marriage to be dissolved. **3.** a separation, esp. one that is total or complete. ~*vb.* **4.** to separate or be separated by divorce; give or obtain a divorce. **5.** (*tr.*) to remove or separate, esp. completely. [C14: from OF, from L *dīvortium*, from *dīvertere* to separate] —**di'vorceable** *adj.*

divorcée (dɪvɔː'siː) *or* (*masc.*) **divorcé** (dɪ'vɔːseɪ) *n.* a person who has been divorced.

divot ('dɪvət) *n.* a piece of turf dug out of a grass surface, esp. by a golf club or by horses' hooves. [C16: from Scot., from ?]

divulge (daɪ'vʌldʒ) *vb.* (*tr.; may take a clause as object*) to make known; disclose. [C15: from L *dīvulgāre*, from DI-² + *vulgāre* to spread among the people, from *vulgus* the common people] —**di'vulgence** *or* **di'vulgement** *n.* —**di'vulger** *n.*

divvy ('dɪvɪ) *Inf.* ~*n.*, *pl.* -**vies. 1.** *Brit.* short for **dividend**, esp. (formerly) one paid by a cooperative society. **2.** *U.S. & Canad.* a share; portion. ~*vb.* -**vying, -vied. 3.** (*tr.; usually foll. by up*) to divide and share.

dixie ('dɪksɪ) *n.* **1.** *Chiefly mil.* a large metal pot for cooking, brewing tea, etc. **2.** a mess tin. [C19: from Hindi *degcī*, dim. of *degcā* pot]

Dixie ('dɪksɪ) *n.* **1.** Also called: **Dixieland.** the southern states of the U.S. ~*adj.* **2.** of the southern states of the U.S. [C19: ?from the nickname of New Orleans, from *dixie* a ten-dollar bill printed there, from F *dix* ten]

Dixieland ('dɪksɪˌlænd) *n.* **1.** a kind of jazz derived from the New Orleans tradition of playing, but with more emphasis on melody, regular rhythms, etc. **2.** See **Dixie.**

DIY *or* **d.i.y.** (in Britain) *abbrev. for* do-it-yourself.

Diyarbakir *or* **Diyarbekir** (diː'jɑːbɛkɪə) *n.* a city in SE Turkey, on the River Tigris: ancient black basalt walls. Pop.: 305 259 (1985). Ancient name: **Amida** (ə'miːdə).

dizzy ('dɪzɪ) *adj.* -**zier, -ziest. 1.** affected with a whirling or reeling sensation; giddy. **2.** mentally confused or bewildered. **3.** causing or tending to cause vertigo or bewilderment. **4.** *Inf.* foolish or flighty. ~*vb.* -**zying, -zied. 5.** (*tr.*) to make dizzy. [OE *dysig* silly] —**'dizzily** *adv.* —**'dizziness** *n.*

DJ *or* **dj** ('diːˌdʒeɪ) *n.* **1.** a variant of **deejay. 2.** an informal term for **dinner jacket.**

Djailolo *or* **Jilolo** (dʒaɪ'ləʊləʊ) *n.* the Dutch name for **Halmahera.**

Djaja ('dʒɑːdʒə) *n.* a variant spelling of (Mount) **Jaya.**

Djajapura (ˌdʒɑːdʒɑː'pʊərə) *n.* a variant spelling of **Jayapura.**

Djakarta *n.* a variant spelling of **Jakarta.**

Djambi *n.* a variant spelling of **Jambi.**

Djerba *or* **Jerba** ('dʒɜːbə) *n.* an island off the SE coast of Tunisia, in the Gulf of Gabès: traditionally Homer's land of the lotus-eaters. Pop.: 92 269 (1984). Area: 510 sq. km (197 sq. miles). Ancient name: **Meninx** ('mɛnɪŋks).

Djibouti *or* **Jibouti** (dʒɪ'buːtɪ) *n.* **1.** a republic in E Africa, on the Gulf of Aden: a French overseas territory (1946–77); became independent in 1977; mainly desert. Official language: Arabic. Currency: Djibouti franc. Capital: Djibouti. Pop.: 470 000 (1987). Area: 23 000 sq. km (8500 sq. miles). Former name (until 1977): (Territory of the) **Afars and the Issas. 2.** the capital of Djibouti, a port on the Gulf of Aden: an outlet for Ethiopian merchandise. Pop.: 62 000 (1970 est.).

djinni *or* **djinny** (dʒɪ'niː, 'dʒɪnɪ) *n.*, *pl.* **djinn** (dʒɪn). variant spellings of **jinni.**

dl *symbol for* decilitre.

D/L *abbrev. for* demand loan.

DLitt *or* **DLit** *abbrev. for:* **1.** Doctor of Letters. **2.** Doctor of Literature. [L *Doctor Litterarum*]

dm *symbol for* decimetre.

DM *abbrev. for* Deutsche Mark.

DMA *Computers. abbrev. for* direct memory access.

DMus *abbrev. for* Doctor of Music.

DMZ *abbrev. for* demilitarized zone.

DNA *n.* deoxyribonucleic acid, the main constituent of the chromosomes of all organisms in the form of a double helix. DNA is self-replicating and is responsible for the transmission of hereditary characteristics.

Dneprodzerzhinsk (*Russian* dnɪprədzɪr'ʒɪnsk) *n.* an industrial city in the SW Soviet Union, in the E central Ukrainian SSR on the Dnieper River. Pop.: 279 000 (1987).

Dnepropetrovsk (*Russian* dnɪprəpɪ'trɔfsk) *n.* a city in the SW Soviet Union, in the E central Ukrainian SSR on the Dnieper River: a major centre of the metallurgical industry. Pop.: 1 182 000 (1987). Former name (1787–1796, 1802–1926): **Yekaterinoslav.**

Dnieper ('dniːpə) *n.* a river in the W Soviet Union, rising in the Valdai Hills NE of Smolensk and flowing south to the Black Sea: the third longest river in Europe; a major navigable waterway. Length: 2200 km (1370 miles). Russian name: **Dnepr** ('dnjɛpə).

Dniester ('dniːstə) *n.* a river in the SW Soviet Union, rising in the Carpathian Mountains and flowing generally southeast to the Black Sea. Length: 1411 km (877 miles). Russian name: **Dnestr** ('dnjɛstə).

D-notice *n. Brit.* an official notice sent to newspapers prohibiting the publication of certain security information. [C20: from their administrative classification letter]

do¹ (duː; *unstressed* dʊ, də) *vb.* **does, doing, did, done. 1.** to perform or complete (a deed or action): *to do a portrait.* **2.** (often *intr.*; foll. by *for*) to serve the needs of; be suitable for; suffice. **3.** (*tr.*) to arrange or fix. **4.** (*tr.*) to prepare or provide; serve: *this restaurant doesn't do lunch on Sundays.* **5.** (*tr.*) to make tidy, elegant, ready, etc.: *to do one's hair.* **6.** (*tr.*) to improve (esp. in **do something to** or **for**). **7.** (*tr.*) to find an answer to (a problem or puzzle). **8.** (*tr.*) to translate or adapt the form or language of: *the book was done into a play.* **9.** (*intr.*) to conduct oneself: *do as you please.* **10.** (*intr.*) to fare or manage. **11.** (*tr.*) to cause or produce: *complaints do nothing to help.* **12.** (*tr.*) to give or render: *do me a favour.* **13.** (*tr.*) to work at, esp. as a course of study or a profession. **14.** (*tr.*) to perform (a play, etc.); act. **15.** (*tr.*) to travel at a specified speed, esp. as a maximum. **16.** (*tr.*) to travel or traverse (a distance). **17.** (takes an infinitive without *to*) used as an auxiliary **a.** before the subject of an interrogative sentence as a way of forming a question: *do you agree?* **b.** to intensify positive statements and commands: *I do like your new house; do hurry!* **c.** before a negative adverb to form negative statements or commands: *do not leave me here alone!* **d.** in inverted constructions: *little did he realize that.* **18.** used as an auxiliary to replace an earlier verb or verb phrase: *he likes you as much as I do.* **19.** (*tr.*) *Inf.* to visit as a sightseer or tourist. **20.** (*tr.*) to wear out; exhaust. **21.** (*intr.*) to happen (esp. in **nothing doing**). **22.** (*tr.*) *Sl.* to serve (a period of time) as a prison sentence. **23.** (*tr.*) *Inf.* to cheat or swindle. **24.** (*tr.*) *Sl.* to rob. **25.** (*tr.*) *Sl.* **a.** to arrest. **b.** to convict of a crime. **26.** (*tr.*) *Austral. sl.* to spend (money). **27.** (*tr.*) *Sl., chiefly Brit.* to treat violently; assault. **28.** *U.S. sl.* to take or use (a drug). **29.** (*tr.*) *Taboo sl.* (of a male) to have sexual intercourse with. **30. do or die.** to make a final or supreme effort. **31. make do.** to manage with whatever is available. ~*n., pl.* **dos** *or* **do's. 32.** *Sl.* an act or instance of cheating or swindling. **33.** *Inf., chiefly Brit. & N.Z.* a formal or festive gathering; party. **34. do's and don'ts.** *Inf.* rules. ~See also **do away with, do by,** etc. [OE *dōn*]

do² (dəʊ) *n., pl.* **dos.** a variant spelling of **doh.**

do. *abbrev. for* ditto.

DOA *abbrev. for* dead on arrival.

doable ('duːəbəl) *adj.* capable of being done.

do away with *vb.* (*intr., adv. prep.*) **1.** to kill or destroy. **2.** to discard or abolish.

dobbin ('dɒbɪn) *n.* a name for a horse, esp. a workhorse. [C16: from *Robin*, pet form of *Robert*]

Dobell (dəʊ'bɛl) *n.* Sir **William.** 1899–1970, Australian portrait and landscape painter. Awarded the Archibald prize (1943) for his famous painting of *Joshua Smith* which resulted in a heated clash between the conservatives and the moderns and led to a lawsuit. His other works include *The Cypriot* (1940), *The Billy Boy* (1943), and *Portrait of a strapper* (1941).

Doberman pinscher ('dəʊbəmən 'pɪnʃə) *or* **Doberman** *n.* a breed of large dog with a glossy black-and-tan coat. [C19: after L *Dobermann* (19th-cent. G dog breeder) who bred it + *Pinscher*, ? after *Pinzgau*, district in Austria]

dob in *vb.* **dobbing, dobbed.** (*adv.*) *Austral. sl.* **1.** (*tr.*) to inform against, esp. to the police. **2.** to contribute to a fund.

Dobruja (*Bulgarian* 'dɔbrudʒa) *n.* a region of E Europe, between the River Danube and the Black Sea: the north passed to Romania and the south to Bulgaria after the Berlin Congress (1878). Romanian name: **Dobrogea** (do'brodʒea).

do by *vb.* (*intr., prep.*) to treat in the manner specified.

doc (dɒk) *n. Inf.* short for **doctor.**

DOCG *abbrev. for* Denominazione di Origine Controllata Garantita: used of wines. [It., lit: name of origin guaranteed controlled]

docile ('dəʊsaɪl) *adj.* **1.** easy to manage or discipline; submissive. **2.** *Rare.* easy to teach. [C15: from L *docilis* easily taught, from *docēre* to teach] —**'docilely** *adv.* —**docility** (dəʊ'sɪlɪtɪ) *n.*

dock[1] (dɒk) *n.* **1.** a wharf or pier. **2.** a space between two wharves or piers for the mooring of ships. **3.** an area of water that can accommodate a ship and can be closed off to allow regulation of the water level. **4.** short for **dry dock.** **5. in** *or* **into dock.** *Brit. inf.* **a.** (of people) in hospital. **b.** (of cars, etc.) in a repair shop. **6.** *Chiefly U.S. & Canad.* a platform from which lorries, goods trains, etc., are loaded and unloaded. ~*vb.* **7.** to moor or be moored at a dock. **8.** to put (a vessel) into, or (of a vessel) to come into a dry dock. **9.** (of two spacecraft) to link together in space or link together (two spacecraft) in space. [C14: from MDu. *docke*; ? rel. to L *ducere* to lead]

dock[2] (dɒk) *n.* **1.** the bony part of the tail of an animal. **2.** the part of an animal's tail left after the major part of it has been cut off. ~*vb.* (*tr.*) **3.** to remove (the tail or part of the tail) of (an animal) by cutting through the bone. **4.** to deduct (an amount) from (a person's wages, pension, etc.). [C14: *dok* from ?]

dock[3] (dɒk) *n.* an enclosed space in a court of law where the accused sits or stands during his trial. [C16: from Flemish *dok* sty]

dock[4] (dɒk) *n.* any of various weedy plants having greenish or reddish flowers and broad leaves. [OE *docce*]

dockage ('dɒkɪdʒ) *n.* **1.** a charge levied upon a vessel for using a dock. **2.** facilities for docking vessels. **3.** the practice of docking vessels.

docker ('dɒkə) *n. Brit.* a man employed in the loading or unloading of ships. U.S. and Canad. equivalent: **longshoreman.** See also **stevedore.**

docket ('dɒkɪt) *n.* **1.** *Chiefly Brit.* a piece of paper accompanying or referring to a package or other delivery, stating contents, delivery instructions, etc., sometimes serving as a receipt. **2.** *Law.* **a.** a summary of the proceedings in a court. **b.** a register containing this. **3.** *Brit.* **a.** a customs certificate declaring that duty has been paid. **b.** a certificate giving particulars of a shipment. **4.** a summary of contents, as in a document. **5.** *U.S.* a list of things to be done. **6.** *U.S. law.* a list of cases awaiting trial. ~*vb.* (*tr.*) **7.** to fix a docket to (a package, etc.). **8.** *Law.* **a.** to make a summary of (a judgment, etc.). **b.** to abstract and enter in a register. **9.** to endorse (a document, etc.) with a summary. [C15: from ?]

dockland ('dɒk,lænd) *n.* the area around the docks.

dockside ('dɒk,saɪd) *n.* an area beside a dock.

dockyard ('dɒk,jɑːd) *n.* a naval establishment with docks, workshops, etc., for the building, fitting out, and repair of vessels.

Doc Martens (dɒk 'mɑːtənz) *pl. n. Trademark.* a brand of lace-up boots with thick lightweight resistant soles. In full: **Doctor Martens.**

doctor ('dɒktə) *n.* **1.** a person licensed to practise medicine. **2.** a person who has been awarded a higher academic degree in any field of knowledge. **3.** *Chiefly U.S. & Canad.* a person licensed to practise dentistry or veterinary medicine. **4.** (*often cap.*) Also called: **Doctor of the Church.** a title given to any of several of the early Fathers of the Christian Church. **5.** *Angling.* any of various artificial flies. **6.** *Inf.* a person who mends or repairs things. **7.** *Sl.* a cook on a ship or at a camp. **8.** *Arch.* a man, esp. a teacher, of learning. **9. go for the doctor.** *Austral. sl.* to

make a great effort or move very fast. **10. what the doctor ordered.** something needed or desired. ~*vb.* **11.** (*tr.*) to give medical treatment to. **12.** (*intr.*) *Inf.* to practise medicine. **13.** (*tr.*) to repair or mend. **14.** (*tr.*) to make different in order to deceive. **15.** (*tr.*) to adapt. **16.** (*tr.*) *Inf.* to castrate (a cat, dog, etc.). [C14: from L: teacher, from *docēre* to teach] —**'doctoral** *or* **doctorial** (dɒk'tɔːrɪəl) *adj.*

doctorate ('dɒktərɪt, -trɪt) *n.* the highest academic degree in any field of knowledge.

Doctor of Philosophy *n.* a doctorate awarded for original research in any subject except law, medicine, or theology.

doctrinaire (,dɒktrɪ'nɛə) *adj.* **1.** stubbornly insistent on the observation of the niceties of a theory, esp. without regard to practicality, suitability, etc. **2.** theoretical; impractical. ~*n.* **3.** a person who stubbornly attempts to apply a theory without regard to practical difficulties. —,**doctri'nairism** *n.* —,**doctri'narian** *n.*

doctrine ('dɒktrɪn) *n.* **1.** a creed or body of teachings of a religious, political, or philosophical group presented for acceptance or belief; dogma. **2.** a principle or body of principles that is taught or advocated. [C14: from OF, from L *doctrīna* teaching, from *doctor*; see DOCTOR] —**doctrinal** (dɒk'traɪnəl) *adj.* —**doc'trinally** *adv.*

docudrama ('dɒkjʊ,drɑːmə) *n.* a film or television programme based on true events, presented in a dramatized form.

document *n.* ('dɒkjʊmənt). **1.** a piece of paper, booklet, etc., providing information, esp. of an official nature. **2.** *Arch.* proof. ~*vb.* ('dɒkjʊ,ment). (*tr.*) **3.** to record or report in detail, as in the press, on television, etc. **4.** to support (statements in a book) with references, etc. **5.** to support (a claim, etc.) with evidence. **6.** to furnish (a vessel) with documents specifying its registration, dimensions, etc. [C15: from L *documentum* a lesson, from *docēre* to teach]

documentary (,dɒkjʊ'mɛntərɪ) *adj.* **1.** Also: **documental.** consisting of or relating to documents. **2.** presenting factual material with few or no fictional additions. ~*n.*, *pl.* **-ries. 3.** a factual film or television programme about an event, person, etc., presenting the facts with little or no fiction. —,**docu'mentarily** *adv.*

documentation (,dɒkjʊmən'teɪʃən) *n.* **1.** the act of supplying with or using documents or references. **2.** the documents or references supplied.

dodder[1] ('dɒdə) *vb.* (*intr.*) **1.** to move unsteadily; totter. **2.** to shake or tremble, as from age. [C17: var. of earlier *dadder*] —**'dodderer** *n.* —**'doddery** *adj.*

dodder[2] ('dɒdə) *n.* any of a genus of rootless parasitic plants lacking chlorophyll and having suckers for drawing nourishment from the host plant. [C13: of Gmc origin]

doddle ('dɒd³l) *n. Brit. inf.* something easily accomplished. [C20: ?from *doddle* (*vb.*) to totter]

dodeca- *combining form.* indicating twelve: *dodecaphonic.* [from Gk *dōdeka* twelve]

dodecagon (dəʊ'dɛkə,gɒn) *n.* a polygon having twelve sides.

dodecahedron (,dəʊdɛkə'hiːdrən) *n.* a solid figure having twelve plane faces. —,**dodeca'hedral** *adj.*

Dodecanese (,dəʊdɪkə'niːz) *pl. n.* a group of islands in the SE Aegean Sea, forming a department of Greece: part of the Southern Sporades. Capital: Rhodes. Pop.: 145 071 (1981). Area: 2663 sq. km (1028 sq. miles). Modern Greek name: **Dhodhekánisos.**

dodecaphonic (,dəʊdɛkə'fɒnɪk) *adj.* of or relating to the twelve-tone system of serial music.

dodge (dɒdʒ) *vb.* **1.** to avoid or attempt to avoid (a blow, discovery, etc.), as by moving suddenly. **2.** to evade by cleverness or trickery. **3.** (*intr.*) *Change-ringing.* to make a bell change places with its neighbour when sounding in successive changes. **4.** (*tr.*) *Photog.* to lighten or darken (selected areas on a print). ~*n.* **5.** a plan contrived to deceive. **6.** a sudden evasive movement. **7.** a clever contrivance. **8.** *Change-ringing.* the act of dodging. [C16: from ?]

Dodge City *n.* a city in SW Kansas, on the Arkansas River: famous as a frontier town on the Santa Fe Trail. Pop.: 18 001 (1980).

Dodgem ('dɒdʒəm) *n. Trademark.* an electrically propelled vehicle driven and bumped against similar cars in a rink at a funfair.

dodger ('dɒdʒə) n. 1. a person who evades or shirks. 2. a shifty dishonest person. 3. a canvas shelter on a ship's bridge, etc., to protect the helmsman from bad weather. 4. *Dialect & Austral.* food, esp. bread.

Dodgson ('dɒdʒsən) n. **Charles Lutwidge** ('lʌtwɪdʒ). the real name of (Lewis) **Carroll.**

dodgy ('dɒdʒɪ) adj. **dodgier, dodgiest.** *Brit., Austral. & N.Z. inf.* 1. risky, difficult, or dangerous. 2. uncertain or unreliable; tricky.

dodo ('dəʊdəʊ) n., pl. **dodos** or **dodoes.** 1. any of a now extinct family of flightless birds formerly found on Mauritius. They had a hooked bill and short stout legs. 2. *Inf.* an intensely conservative person who is unaware of changing fashions, ideas, etc. 3. (**as**) **dead as a dodo.** irretrievably defunct or out of date. [C17: from Port. *doudo*, from *duodo* stupid]

Dodoma ('dəʊdəmə) n. a town in central Tanzania, the new capital of the country. Pop.: 45 703 (1978).

Dodona (dəʊ'dəʊnə) n. an ancient Greek town in Epirus: seat of an ancient sanctuary and oracle of Zeus and later the religious centre of Pyrrhus' kingdom. —**Dodonaean** or **Dodonean** (,dəʊdəʊ'niːən) adj.

do down vb. (tr., adv.) 1. to belittle or humiliate. 2. to deceive or cheat.

doe (dəʊ) n., pl. **does** or **doe.** the female of the deer, hare, rabbit, and certain other animals. [OE *dā*]

Doe (dəʊ) n. *Law.* (formerly) the name of the fictitious plaintiff in an action of ejectment.

DOE (in Britain) abbrev. for Department of the Environment.

doek (dʊk) n. *S. African inf.* a square of cloth worn mainly by African women to cover the head. [C18: from Afrik.: cloth]

Doenitz (German 'dø:nɪts) n. a variant spelling of (Karl) **Dönitz.**

doer ('duːə) n. 1. a person or thing that does something. 2. an active or energetic person. 3. *N.Z.* a thriving farm animal.

does (dʌz) vb. (used with a singular noun or the pronouns *he, she,* or *it*) a form of the present tense (indicative mood) of **do**[1].

doeskin ('dəʊ,skɪn) n. 1. the skin of a deer, lamb, or sheep. 2. a very supple leather made from this. 3. a heavy smooth cloth.

doff (dɒf) vb. (tr.) 1. to take off or lift (one's hat) in salutation. 2. to remove (clothing). [OE *dōn of;* see DO[1], OFF; cf. DON[1]] —'**doffer** n.

do for vb. (prep.) *Inf.* 1. (tr.) to convict of a crime or offence. 2. (intr.) to cause the ruin, death, or defeat of. 3. (intr.) to do housework for. 4. **do well for oneself.** to thrive or succeed.

dog (dɒg) n. 1. a domesticated canine mammal occurring in many breeds that show a great variety in size and form. 2. any other carnivore of the dog family, such as the dingo and coyote. 3. the male of animals of the dog family. 4. (*modifier*) spurious, inferior, or useless. 5. a mechanical device for gripping or holding. 6. *Inf.* a fellow; chap. 7. *Inf.* a man or boy regarded as unpleasant or wretched. 8. *U.S. sl.* an unattractive girl or woman. 9. *U.S. & Canad. inf.* something unsatisfactory or inferior. 10. short for **firedog.** 11. **a dog's chance.** no chance at all. 12. **a dog's dinner** or **breakfast.** *Inf.* something messy or bungled. 13. **a dog's life.** a wretched existence. 14. **dog eat dog.** ruthless competition. 15. **like a dog's dinner.** dressed smartly or ostentatiously. 16. **put on the dog.** *U.S. & Canad. inf.* to behave pretentiously. ~vb. **dogging, dogged.** (tr.) 17. to pursue or follow after like a dog. 18. to trouble; plague. 19. to chase with a dog. 20. to grip or secure by a mechanical device. ~adv. 21. (*usually in combination*) thoroughly; utterly: *dog-tired.* ~See also **dogs.** [OE *docga*, from ?]

dog biscuit n. a hard biscuit for dogs.

dog box n. *N.Z. inf.* disgrace; disfavour: *in the dog box.*

dogcart ('dɒg,kɑːt) n. a light horse-drawn two-wheeled vehicle.

dog-catcher n. *Now chiefly U.S. & Canad.* a local official whose job is to impound and dispose of stray dogs.

dog collar n. 1. a collar for a dog. 2. *Inf.* a clerical collar. 3. *Inf.* a tight-fitting necklace.

dog days pl. n. the hot period of the summer reckoned in ancient times from the heliacal rising of Sirius (the Dog Star). [C16: translation of LL *diēs caniculārēs*, translation of Gk *hēmerai kunades*]

doge (dəʊdʒ) n. (formerly) the chief magistrate in the republics of Venice and Genoa. [C16: via F from It. (Venetian dialect), from L *dux* leader]

dog-ear vb. 1. (tr.) to fold down the corner of (a page). ~n. also **dog's-ear.** 2. a folded-down corner of a page.

dog-eared adj. 1. having dog-ears. 2. shabby or worn.

dog-end n. *Inf.* a cigarette end.

dogfight ('dɒg,faɪt) n. 1. close-quarters combat between fighter aircraft. 2. any rough fight.

dogfish ('dɒg,fɪʃ) n., pl. **-fish** or **-fishes.** 1. any of several small sharks. 2. a less common name for the **bowfin.**

dogged ('dɒgɪd) adj. obstinately determined; wilful or tenacious. —'**doggedly** adv. —'**doggedness** n.

Dogger ('dɒgə) n. *Geology.* a formation of mid-Jurassic rocks in N England.

Dogger Bank ('dɒgə) n. an extensive submerged sandbank in the North Sea between N England and Denmark: fishing ground.

doggerel ('dɒgərəl) or **dogrel** ('dɒgrəl) n. 1. a. comic verse, usually irregular in measure. b. (as modifier): *a doggerel rhythm.* 2. nonsense. [C14 *dogerel* worthless, ?from *dogge* DOG]

doggish ('dɒgɪʃ) adj. 1. of or like a dog. 2. surly; snappish.

doggo ('dɒgəʊ) adv. *Brit. inf.* in hiding and keeping quiet (esp. in **lie doggo**). [C19: prob. from DOG]

doggone ('dɒgɒn) *U.S. & Canad.* ~interj. 1. an exclamation of annoyance, etc. ~adj. (prenominal), adv. 2. Also: **doggoned.** another word for **damn.** [C19: euphemism for *God damn*]

doggy or **doggie** ('dɒgɪ) n., pl. **-gies.** 1. a child's word for a **dog.** ~adj. **-gier, -giest.** 1. of, like, or relating to a dog. 3. fond of dogs.

doggy bag n. a bag in which leftovers from a meal may be taken away for the diner's dog.

doghouse ('dɒg,haʊs) n. 1. the U.S. and Canad. name for **kennel.** 2. *Inf.* disfavour (in **in the doghouse**).

dogie, dogy, or **dogey** ('dəʊgɪ) n., pl. **-gies** or **-geys.** *U.S. & Canad.* a motherless calf. [C19: from *dough-guts,* because they were fed on flour-and-water paste]

dog in the manger n. a person who prevents others from using something he has no use for.

dog Latin n. spurious or incorrect Latin.

dogleg ('dɒg,leg) n. 1. a sharp bend or angle. ~vb. **-legging, -legged.** 2. (intr.) to go off at an angle. ~adj. 3. of or with the shape of a dogleg. —**doglegged** (,dɒg'legɪd, 'dɒg,legd) adj.

dogma ('dɒgmə) n., pl. **-mas** or **-mata** (-mətə). 1. a religious doctrine or system of doctrines proclaimed by ecclesiastical authority as true. 2. a belief, principle, or doctrine or a code of beliefs, principles, or doctrines. [C17: via L from Gk: opinion, from *dokein* to seem good]

dogman ('dɒgmən) n., pl. **-men.** *Austral.* a person who directs the operation of a crane whilst riding on an object being lifted by it.

dogmatic (dɒg'mætɪk) or **dogmatical** adj. 1. a. (of a statement, opinion, etc.) forcibly asserted as if authoritative and unchallengeable. b. (of a person) prone to making such statements. 2. of or constituting dogma. 3. based on assumption rather than observation. —dog'matically adv.

dogmatics (dɒg'mætɪks) n. (functioning as sing.) the study of religious dogmas and doctrines. Also called: **dogmatic** (or **doctrinal**) **theology.**

dogmatize or **-ise** ('dɒgmə,taɪz) vb. to say or state (something) in a dogmatic manner. —'**dogmatism** n. —'**dogmatist** n.

do-gooder n. *Inf.* a well-intentioned person, esp. a naive or impractical one. —,do-'**gooding** n., adj.

dog paddle n. 1. a swimming stroke in which the swimmer paddles his hands in imitation of a swimming dog. ~vb. **dog-paddle.** 2. (intr.) to swim using the dog paddle.

dog rose n. a prickly wild European rose that has pink or white scentless flowers. [from belief that its root was effective against the bite of a mad dog]

dogs (dɒgz) pl. n. 1. *Sl.* the feet. 2. **go to the dogs.** *Inf.* to go to ruin physically or morally. 3. **let sleeping dogs lie.** to leave things undisturbed. 4. **the dogs.** *Brit. inf.* greyhound racing.

Dogs (dɒgz) n. **Isle of.** a district in the East End of London, bounded on three sides by the River Thames.

dogsbody ('dɒgz,bɒdɪ) *Inf.* ~*n.*, *pl.* **-bodies. 1.** a person who carries out menial tasks for others. ~*vb.* (*intr.*) **-bodying, -bodied. 2.** to act as a dogsbody.

dog's disease *n. Austral. inf.* influenza.

dogsled ('dɒg,slɛd) *n. Chiefly U.S. & Canad.* a sleigh drawn by dogs. Also called (Brit.): **dog sledge.**

Dog Star *n.* **the.** another name for **Sirius.**

dog-tired *adj.* (*usually postpositive*) *Inf.* exhausted.

dogtooth ('dɒg,tuːθ) *n.*, *pl.* **-teeth.** *Archit.* a carved ornament in the form of a series of four-cornered pyramids set diagonally and often decorated with leaf shapes along each edge, used in England in the 13th century.

dogtooth violet *n.* any of a genus of plants, esp. a North American plant with yellow flowers, or a European plant with purple flowers.

dogtrot ('dɒg,trɒt) *n.* a gently paced trot.

dog violet *n.* any of three wild violets found in Britain and northern Europe.

dogwatch ('dɒg,wɒtʃ) *n.* either of two two-hour watches aboard ship, from four to six p.m. or from six to eight p.m.

dogwood ('dɒg,wud) *n.* any of various trees or shrubs, esp. a European shrub with small white flowers and black berries.

dogy ('dəʊgɪ) *n.*, *pl.* **-gies.** a variant of **dogie.**

doh (dəʊ) *n. Music.* (in tonic sol-fa) the first degree of any major scale. [C18: from It.; see GAMUT]

Doha ('dəʊhɑː, 'dəʊə) *n.* the capital and chief port of Qatar, on the E coast of the peninsula. Pop.: 190 000 (1983 est.). Former name: **Bida, El Beda.**

Dohnányi (*Hungarian* 'dohnaːnji) *n.* **Ernö** ('ɛrnøː) *or* **Ernst von** (ɛrnst fɔn). 1877–1960, Hungarian pianist and composer whose works include *Variations on a Nursery Theme* (1913) for piano and orchestra.

doily *or* **doyley** ('dɔɪlɪ) *n.*, *pl.* **-lies** *or* **-leys.** a decorative mat of lace or lacelike paper, etc., laid on plates. [C18: after *Doily*, a London draper]

do in *vb.* (*tr.*, *adv.*) *Sl.* **1.** to kill. **2.** to exhaust.

doing ('duːɪŋ) *n.* **1.** an action or the performance of an action: *whose doing is this?* **2.** *Inf.* a beating or castigation.

doings ('duːɪŋz) *n.* **1.** (*functioning as pl.*) deeds, actions, or events. **2.** (*functioning as sing.*) *Inf.* anything of which the name is not known, or euphemistically left unsaid, etc.

do-it-yourself *n.* **a.** the hobby or process of constructing and repairing things oneself. **b.** (*as modifier*): *a do-it-yourself kit.*

dol. *abbrev. for:* **1.** *Music.* dolce. **2.** (*pl.* **dols.**) dollar.

Dolby ('dɒlbɪ) *n. Trademark.* any of various specialized electronic circuits, esp. those used in tape recorders for noise reduction in high-frequency signals. [after R. *Dolby* (born 1933), U.S. inventor]

dolce ('dɒltʃɪ) *adj.*, *adv. Music.* (to be performed) gently and sweetly. [It.]

dolce vita ('dɒltʃɪ 'viːtə) *n.* a life of luxury. [It., lit.: sweet life]

doldrums ('dɒldrəmz) *n.* **the.** **1.** a depressed or bored state of mind. **2.** a state of inactivity or stagnation. **3.** a belt of light winds or calms along the equator. [C19: prob. from OE *dol* DULL, infl. by TANTRUM]

dole¹ (dəʊl) *n.* **1.** (*usually preceded by the*) *Brit. inf.* money received from the state while out of work. **2. on the dole.** *Brit. inf.* receiving such money. **3.** a small portion of money or food given to a poor person. **4.** the act of distributing such portions. **5.** *Arch.* fate. ~*vb.* **6.** (*tr.*; usually foll. by *out*) to distribute, esp. in small portions. [OE *dāl* share]

dole² (dəʊl) *n. Arch.* grief or mourning. [C13: from OF, from LL *dolus*, from L *dolēre* to lament]

dole-bludger *n. Austral. sl.* a person who draws unemployment benefit without making any attempt to get work.

doleful ('dəʊlfʊl) *adj.* dreary; mournful. —**'dolefully** *adv.* —**'dolefulness** *n.*

dolerite ('dɒlə,raɪt) *n.* **1.** a dark basic igneous rock; a coarse-grained basalt. **2.** any dark igneous rock whose composition cannot be determined with the naked eye. [C19: from F *dolérite*, from Gk *doleros* deceitful; from the difficulty in determining its composition]

dolichocephalic (,dɒlɪkəʊsɪ'fælɪk) *or* **dolichocephalous** (,dɒlɪkəʊ'sɛfələs) *adj.* having a head much longer than it is broad. [C19: from Gk *dolichos* long + -CEPHALIC]

doll (dɒl) *n.* **1.** a small model or dummy of a human being, used as a toy. **2.** *Sl.* a pretty girl or woman of little intelligence. [C16: prob. from *Doll*, pet name for *Dorothy*]

dollar ('dɒlə) *n.* **1.** the standard monetary unit of the U.S., divided into 100 cents. **2.** the standard monetary unit, comprising 100 cents, of various other countries including: Australia, the Bahamas, Canada, Hong Kong, Jamaica, Malaysia, Singapore, Taiwan, New Zealand, and Zimbabwe. [C16: from Low G *daler*, from G *Taler*, *Thaler*, short for *Joachimsthaler*, coin made from metal mined in *Joachimsthal* Jachymov, town in Czechoslovakia]

dollarbird ('dɒlə,bɜːd) *n.* a bird of S and SE Asia and Australia with a round white spot on each wing.

dollar diplomacy *n. Chiefly U.S.* **1.** a foreign policy that encourages and protects commercial and financial involvement abroad. **2.** use of financial power as a diplomatic weapon.

Dollfuss (*German* 'dɔlfuːs) *n.* **Engelbert** ('ɛŋəlbɛrt). 1892–1934, Austrian statesman, chancellor (1932–34), who was assassinated by Austrian Nazis.

dollop ('dɒləp) *Inf.* ~*n.* **1.** a semisolid lump. **2.** a measure or serving. ~*vb.* **3.** (*tr.*; foll. by *out*) to serve out (food). [C16: from ?]

doll up *vb.* (*tr.*, *adv.*) *Sl.* to dress in a stylish or showy manner.

dolly ('dɒlɪ) *n.*, *pl.* **-lies. 1.** a child's word for a **doll. 2.** *Films, etc.* a wheeled support on which a camera may be mounted. **3.** a cup-shaped anvil used to hold a rivet. **4.** *Cricket.* **a.** a simple catch. **b.** a full toss bowled in a slow high arc. **5.** Also called: **dolly bird.** *Sl.*, *chiefly Brit.* an attractive and fashionable girl. ~*vb.* **-lying, -lied. 6.** *Films, etc.* to wheel (a camera) backwards or forwards on a dolly.

dolly mixture *n.* **1.** a mixture of tiny coloured sweets. **2.** one such sweet.

dolman sleeve ('dɒlmən) *n.* a sleeve that is very wide at the armhole and tapers to a tight wrist. [C19: from *dolman*, a type of Turkish robe, ult. from Turkish *dolamak* to wind]

dolmen ('dɒlmɛn) *n.* a Neolithic stone formation, consisting of a horizontal stone supported by several vertical stones, and thought to be a tomb. [C19: from F, prob. from OBreton *tol* table, from L *tabula* board + Breton *mēn* stone, of Celtic origin]

Dolmetsch ('dɒlmɛtʃ) *n.* **Arnold.** 1858–1940, British musician, born in France. He contributed greatly to the revival of interest in early music and instruments.

dolomite ('dɒlə,maɪt) *n.* **1.** a mineral consisting of calcium magnesium carbonate. **2.** a rock resembling limestone but consisting principally of the mineral dolomite. [C18: after Déodat de *Dolomieu* (1750–1801), F mineralogist] —**dolomitic** (,dɒlə'mɪtɪk) *adj.*

Dolomites ('dɒlə,maɪts) *pl. n.* a mountain range in NE Italy: part of the Alps; formed of dolomitic limestone. Highest peak: Marmolada, 3342 m (10 965 ft.).

doloroso (,dɒlə'rəʊsəʊ) *adj.*, *adv. Music.* (to be performed) in a sorrowful manner. [It.]

dolorous ('dɒlərəs) *adj.* causing or involving pain or sorrow. —**'dolorously** *adv.*

dolos ('dɒlɒs) *n.*, *pl.* **dolosse.** *S. African.* a knucklebone of a sheep, buck, etc., used esp. by diviners. [from ?]

dolour *or U.S.* **dolor** ('dɒlə) *n. Poetic.* grief or sorrow. [C14: from L, from *dolēre* to grieve]

dolphin ('dɒlfɪn) *n.* **1.** any of various marine mammals that are typically smaller than whales and larger than porpoises and have a beaklike snout. **2. river dolphin.** any of various freshwater mammals inhabiting rivers of North and South America and S Asia. **3.** Also called **dorado.** either of two large marine fishes that have an iridescent coloration. **4.** *Naut.* a post or buoy for mooring a vessel. [C13: from OF *dauphin*, via L, from Gk *delphin-*, *delphis*]

dolphinarium (,dɒlfɪ'nɛərɪəm) *n.*, *pl.* **-iums** *or* **-ia** (-ɪə). a pool or aquarium for dolphins, esp. one in which they give public displays.

dolt (dəʊlt) *n.* a slow-witted or stupid person. [C16: prob. rel. to OE *dol* stupid] —**'doltish** *adj.* —**'doltishness** *n.*

dom. *abbrev. for:* **1.** domain. **2.** domestic.

-dom *suffix forming nouns.* **1.** state or condition: *freedom.* **2.** rank, office, or domain of: *earldom.* **3.** a collection of persons: *officialdom.* [OE -*dōm*]

domain (də'meɪn) *n.* **1.** land governed by a ruler or government. **2.** land owned by one person or family. **3.** a field or scope of knowledge or activity. **4.** a region having specific characteristics. **5.** *Austral. & N.Z.* a park or recreation reserve maintained by a public authority, often the government. **6.** *Law.* the absolute ownership and right to dispose of land. **7.** *Maths.* the set of values of the independent variable of a function for which the functional value exists. **8.** *Logic.* another term for **universe of discourse. 9.** *Philosophy.* range of significance. **10.** *Physics.* one of the regions in a ferromagnetic solid in which all the atoms have their magnetic moments aligned in the same direction. [C17: from F *domaine*, from L *dominium* property, from *dominus* lord]

dome (dəʊm) *n.* **1.** a hemispherical roof or vault. **2.** something shaped like this. **3.** a slang word for the **head.** ~*vb.* (*tr.*) **4.** to cover with or as if with a dome. **5.** to shape like a dome. [C16: from F, from It. *duomo* cathedral, from L *domus* house] —'**dome,like** *adj.* —**domical** ('dəʊmɪk³l, 'dɒm-) *adj.*

Domenico Veneziano (*Italian* do'me:niko venet'tsia:no) *n.* died 1461, Italian painter, noted for the St Lucy Altarpiece.

Domesday Book *or* **Doomsday Book** ('du:mz,deɪ) *n.* *History.* the record of a survey of the land of England carried out by the commissioners of William I in 1086.

domestic (də'mɛstɪk) *adj.* **1.** of the home or family. **2.** enjoying or accustomed to home or family life. **3.** (of an animal) bred or kept by man as a pet or for purposes such as the supply of food. **4.** of one's own country or a specific country: *domestic and foreign affairs.* ~*n.* **5.** a household servant. [C16: from OF *domestique*, from L *domesticus* belonging to the house, from *domus* house] —**do'mestically** *adv.*

domesticate (də'mɛstɪ,keɪt) *or* U.S. (*sometimes*) **domesticize** (də'mɛstɪ,saɪz) *vb.* (*tr.*) **1.** to bring or keep (wild animals or plants) under control or cultivation. **2.** to accustom to home life. **3.** to adapt to an environment. —**do'mesticable** *adj.* —**do,mesti'cation** *n.*

domesticity (,dəʊmɛ'stɪsɪtɪ) *n., pl.* **-ties. 1.** home life. **2.** devotion to or familiarity with home life. **3.** (*usually pl.*) a domestic duty or matter.

domestic science *n.* the study of cooking, needlework, and other subjects concerned with household skills.

Domett ('dɒmɪt) *n.* **Alfred.** 1811–87, New Zealand poet, colonial administrator, and statesman, born in England: prime minister of New Zealand (1862–63).

domicile ('dɒmɪ,saɪl) *or* **domicil** ('dɒmɪsɪl) *n.* **1.** a dwelling place. **2.** a permanent legal residence. **3.** *Commerce.* the place where a bill of exchange is to be paid. ~*vb. also* **domiciliate** (,dɒmɪ'sɪlɪ,eɪt). **4.** to establish or be established in a dwelling place. [C15: from L *domicilium*, from *domus* house] —**domiciliary** (,dɒmɪ'sɪlɪərɪ) *adj.*

dominance ('dɒmɪnəns) *n.* control; ascendancy.

dominant ('dɒmɪnənt) *adj.* **1.** having primary authority or influence; governing; ruling. **2.** predominant or primary: *the dominant topic of the day.* **3.** occupying a commanding position. **4.** *Genetics.* (of a gene) producing the same phenotype in the organism whether its allele is identical or dissimilar. Cf. **recessive. 5.** *Music.* of or relating to the fifth degree of a scale. **6.** *Ecology.* (of a plant or animal species) more prevalent than any other species and determining the appearance and composition of the community. ~*n.* **7.** *Genetics.* a dominant gene. **8.** *Music.* **a.** the fifth degree of a scale. **b.** a key or chord based on this. **9.** *Ecology.* a dominant plant or animal in a community. —'**dominantly** *adv.*

dominant seventh chord *n.* *Music.* a chord consisting of the dominant and the major third, perfect fifth, and minor seventh above it.

dominate ('dɒmɪ,neɪt) *vb.* **1.** to control, rule, or govern. **2.** to tower above (surroundings, etc.). **3.** (*tr.; usually passive*) to predominate in. [C17: from L *dominārī* to be lord over, from *dominus* lord] —'**domi,nating** *adj.* —,**domi'nation** *n.*

dominee ('du:mɪnɪ, 'dʊə-) *n.* (in South Africa) a minister in any of the Afrikaner Churches. [from Afrik., from Du.; cf. DOMINIE]

domineer (,dɒmɪ'nɪə) *vb.* (*intr.; often foll. by over*) to act with arrogance or tyranny; behave imperiously. [C16: from Du. *domineren*, from F *dominer* to DOMINATE] —,**domi'neering** *adj.*

Domingo (do'mɪŋgo) *n.* **Placido** ('plaθiðo). born 1941, Spanish operatic tenor.

Dominic ('dɒmɪnɪk) *n.* **Saint.** original name *Domingo de Guzman.* ?1170–1221, Spanish priest; founder of the Dominican order. Feast day: Aug. 4.

Dominica (,dɒmɪ'ni:kə, də'mɪnɪkə) *n.* a republic in the E West Indies, comprising a volcanic island in the Windward Islands group; a former British colony; became independent in 1978. Official language: English. Religion: mostly Roman Catholic. Currency: Dominican dollar. Capital: Roseau. Pop.: 94 191 (1987). Area: 751 sq. km (290 sq. miles). Official name: **Commonwealth of Dominica.**

dominical (də'mɪnɪk³l) *adj.* **1.** of Jesus Christ as Lord. **2.** of Sunday as the Lord's Day. [C15: from LL *dominicālis*, from L *dominus* lord]

Dominican[1] (də'mɪnɪkən) *n.* **1. a.** a member of an order of preaching friars founded by Saint Dominic in 1215; a Blackfriar. **b.** a nun of one of the orders founded under his patronage. ~*adj.* **2.** of Saint Dominic or the Dominican order.

Dominican[2] (də'mɪnɪkən) *adj.* **1.** of or relating to the Dominican Republic or Dominica. ~*n.* **2.** a native or inhabitant of the Dominican Republic or Dominica.

Dominican Republic *n.* a republic in the West Indies, occupying the eastern half of the island of Hispaniola: colonized by the Spanish after its discovery by Columbus in 1492; gained independence from Spain in 1821. It is generally mountainous, dominated by the Cordillera Central, which rises over 3000 m (10 000 ft.), with fertile lowlands. Language: Spanish. Religion: mostly Roman Catholic. Currency: peso. Capital: Santo Domingo. Pop.: 6 708 000 (1987). Area: 48 441 sq. km (18 703 sq. miles). Former name (until 1844): **Santo Domingo.**

dominie ('dɒmɪnɪ) *n.* **1.** a Scots word for **schoolmaster. 2.** a minister or clergyman. [C17: from L *dominē*, vocative case of *dominus* lord]

dominion (də'mɪnjən) *n.* **1.** rule; authority. **2.** the land governed by one ruler or government. **3.** sphere of influence; area of control. **4.** a name formerly applied to self-governing divisions of the British Empire. **5. the Dominion.** New Zealand. [C15: from OF, from L *dominium* ownership, from *dominus* master]

Dominion Day *n.* the former name for **Canada Day.**

domino[1] ('dɒmɪ,nəʊ) *n., pl.* **-noes.** a small rectangular block marked with dots, used in dominoes. [C19: from F, from It., ?from *domino!* master!, said by the winner]

domino[2] ('dɒmɪ,nəʊ) *n., pl.* **-noes** *or* **-nos. 1.** a large hooded cloak worn with an eye mask at a masquerade. **2.** the eye mask worn with such a cloak. [C18: from F or It., prob. from L *dominus* lord, master]

Domino ('dɒmɪnəʊ) *n.* **Fats.** real name *Antoine Domino.* born 1928, U.S. jazz and rock-and-roll pianist, singer, and songwriter. His singles include "Ain't that a Shame" (1955) and "Blueberry Hill" (1956).

domino effect *n.* a series of similar or related events occurring as a direct and inevitable result of one initial event. [C20: alluding to a row of dominoes, each standing on end, all of which fall when one is pushed]

dominoes ('dɒmɪ,nəʊz) *n.* (*functioning as sing.*) any of several games in which dominoes with matching halves are laid together.

Domitian (də'mɪʃən) *n.* full name *Titus Flavius Domitianus.* 51–96 A.D., Roman emperor (81–96): instigated a reign of terror (93); assassinated.

domkop ('dɒm,kɒp) *n.* S. African sl. an idiot; thickhead. [Afrik.]

Domrémy-la-Pucelle (*French* dɔremilapysɛl) *or* **Domrémy** *n.* a village in NE France, in the Vosges: birthplace of Joan of Arc.

don[1] (dɒn) *vb.* **donning, donned.** (*tr.*) to put on (clothing). [C14: from DO[1] + ON; cf. DOFF]

don[2] (dɒn) *n.* **1.** *Brit.* a member of the teaching staff at a university or college, esp. at Oxford or Cambridge. **2.** the head of a student dormitory at certain Canadian universities and colleges. **3.** a Spanish gentleman or nobleman. **4.** *Arch.* a person of rank. **5.** *Austral. & N.Z. inf.* an expert. [C17: ult. from L *dominus* lord]

Don (dɒn) *n.* a Spanish title equivalent to *Mr.* [C16: via Sp., from L *dominus* lord]

Don (dɒn) *n.* **1.** a river in the SE Soviet Union, rising southeast of Tula and flowing generally south to the Sea of Azov: linked by canal to the River Volga. Length: 1870 km (1162 miles). **2.** a river in NE Scotland, rising in the Cairngorm Mountains and flowing east to the North Sea. Length: 100 km (62 miles). **3.** a river in N central England, rising in S Yorkshire and flowing northeast to the Humber. Length: about 96 km (60 miles).

Doña ('dɒnjə) n. a Spanish title of address equivalent to *Mrs* or *Madam*. [C17: via Sp., from L *domina*]

Donald ('dɒnᵊld) n. ?1031–1100, king of Scotland (1093–94; 1094–97).

Donar ('dəʊnɑː; *German* 'doːnar) n. the Germanic god of thunder, corresponding to Thor in Norse mythology.

donate (dəʊ'neɪt) vb. to give (money, time, etc.), esp. to a charity. —**do'nator** n.

Donatello (*Italian* donaˈtɛllo) n. real name *Donato di Betto Bardi*. 1386–1466, Florentine sculptor, regarded as the greatest sculptor of the quattrocento, who was greatly influenced by classical sculpture and contemporary humanist theories. His marble relief of *St George Killing the Dragon* (1416–17) shows his innovative use of perspective. Other outstanding works are the classic bronze *David*, and the bronze equestrian monument to Gattamalata, which became the model of subsequent equestrian sculpture.

donation (dəʊ'neɪʃən) n. **1.** the act of donating. **2.** a contribution. [C15: from L *dōnātiō* a presenting, from *dōnāre* to give, from *dōnum* gift]

donative ('dəʊnətɪv) n. **1.** a gift or donation. **2.** a benefice capable of being conferred as a gift. ~adj. **3.** of or like a donation. **4.** being or relating to a benefice. [C15: from L *dōnātīvum* a donation made to soldiers by a Roman emperor, from *dōnāre* to present]

Donatus (dəʊ'nɑːtəs) n. **1. Aelius** ('iːlɪəs). 4th century A.D., Latin grammarian, who taught Saint Jerome; his textbook *Ars Grammatica* was used throughout the Middle Ages. **2.** 4th century A.D., bishop of Carthage; leader of the Donatists, a heretical Christian sect originating in N Africa in 311 A.D.

Donau ('doːnaʊ) n. the German name for the **Danube**.

Donbass *or* **Donbas** (dɒn'bɑːs) n. an industrial region of the SW Soviet Union, in the E Ukrainian SSR in the plain of the Rivers Donets and lower Dnieper: the largest coalfield in the Soviet Union. Also called: **Donets Basin**.

Doncaster ('dɒŋkəstə) n. an industrial town in South Yorkshire, on the River Don. Pop.: 81 610 (1981).

donder ('dɒndə) *S. African sl.* ~vb. **1.** (tr.) to beat someone up. ~n. **2.** a wretch; swine. [from Afrik., from Du. *donderen* to swear, bully]

done (dʌn) vb. **1.** the past participle of **do**[1]. **2. be** *or* **have done with.** to end relations with. **3. have done.** to be completely finished: *have you done?* ~interj. **4.** an expression of agreement, as on the settlement of a bargain. ~adj. **5.** completed. **6.** cooked enough. **7.** used up. **8.** socially acceptable. **9.** *Inf.* cheated; tricked. **10. done for.** *Inf.* **a.** dead or almost dead. **b.** in serious difficulty. **11. done in** *or* **up.** *Inf.* exhausted.

donee (dəʊ'niː) n. a person who receives a gift. [C16: from DON(OR) + -EE]

Donegal ('dɒnɪˌgɔːl, ˌdɒnɪ'gɔːl) n. a county in NW Ireland, on the Atlantic: mountainous, with a rugged coastline and many offshore islands. County town: Lifford. Pop.: 129 428 (1986). Area: 4830 sq. km (1865 sq. miles).

Donets (*Russian* da'njɛts) n. a river in the SW Soviet Union, rising in the Kursk steppe and flowing southeast to the Don River. Length: about 1078 km (670 miles).

Donets Basin (də'nɛts) n. another name for the **Donbass**.

Donetsk (*Russian* da'njɛtsk) n. a city in the SW Soviet Union, in the E Ukrainian SSR: the chief industrial centre of the Donbass; first ironworks founded by a Welshman, John Hughes (1872), after whom the town was named **Yuzovka** (Hughesovka). Pop.: 1 090 000 (1987). Former names (from after the Revolution until 1961): **Stalin** or **Stalino.**

dong (dɒŋ) n. **1.** an imitation of the sound of a bell. **2.** *Austral. & N.Z. inf.* a heavy blow. ~vb. **3.** (intr.) to make such a sound. **4.** *Austral. & N.Z. inf.* to strike or punch. [C19: imit.]

donga ('dɒŋgə) n. *S. African, Austral. & N.Z.* a steepsided gully created by soil erosion. [C19: from Afrik., from Zulu]

Dongola ('dɒŋgələ) n. a small town in the N Sudan, on the Nile: built on the site of Old Dongola, the capital of the Christian Kingdom of Nubia (6th to 14th centuries). Pop.: 5937 (1973).

Dongting ('dʊŋ'tɪŋ), **Tungting,** *or* **Tung-t'ing** n. a lake in S China, in NE Hunan province: main outlet flows to the

Yangtze; rice-growing in winter. Area: (in winter) 3900 sq. km (1500 sq. miles).

Dönitz *or* **Doenitz** (*German* 'døːnɪts) n. **Karl** (karl). 1891–1980, German admiral; commander in chief of the German navy (1943–45); as head of state after Hitler's death he surrendered to the Allies (May 7, 1945).

Donizetti (ˌdɒnɪ'zɛtɪ; *Italian* donid'dzetti) n. **Gaetano** (gae'taːno). 1797–1848, Italian operatic composer: his works include *Lucia di Lammermoor* (1835), *La Fille du régiment* (1840), and *Don Pasquale* (1843).

donjon ('dʌndʒən, 'dɒn-) n. the heavily fortified central tower or keep of a medieval castle. Also: **dungeon.** [C14: arch. var. of *dungeon*]

Don Juan ('dɒn 'dʒuːən) n. **1.** a legendary Spanish nobleman and philanderer: hero of many poems, plays, and operas. **2.** a successful seducer of women.

donkey ('dɒŋkɪ) n. **1.** a long-eared member of the horse family. **2.** a person who is considered to be stupid or stubborn. **3.** (modifier) auxiliary: *a donkey engine.* **4. talk the hind leg(s) off a donkey.** to talk endlessly. [C18: ?from *dun* dark + -*key*, as in *monkey*]

donkey jacket n. a thick hip-length jacket, usually navy blue, with a waterproof panel across the shoulders.

donkey's years pl., n. *Inf.* a long time.

donkey vote n. *Austral.* a vote in which the voter's order of preference follows the order in which the candidates are listed.

donkey-work n. **1.** groundwork. **2.** drudgery.

Donleavy (dɒn'lɪvɪ) n. **J(ames) P(atrick).** born 1926, Irish-American novelist. His books include *The Ginger Man* (1956), *The Onion Eaters* (1971), and *Are You Listening Rabbi Löw?* (1987).

Donna ('dɒnə) n. an Italian title of address equivalent to *Madam.* [C17: from It., from L *domina* lady]

Donne (dʌn) n. **John.** 1573–1631, English metaphysical poet and preacher. He wrote love and religious poems, sermons, epigrams, and elegies. His *Divine Sonnets* are among his best-known works.

donnish ('dɒnɪʃ) adj. of or resembling a university don, esp. denoting pedantry or fussiness. —'**donnishness** n.

donnybrook ('dɒnɪˌbrʊk) n. a rowdy brawl. [C19: after *Donnybrook Fair*, an annual event until 1855 near Dublin]

donor ('dəʊnə) n. **1.** a person who makes a donation. **2.** *Med.* any person who gives blood, organs, etc., for use in the treatment of another person. **3.** the atom supplying both electrons in a coordinate bond. [C15: from OF *doneur*, from L *dōnātor*, from *dōnāre* to give]

donor card n. a card carried to show that the bodily organs specified on it may be used for transplants after the carrier's death.

Don Quixote ('dɒn kiː'həʊtiː, 'kwɪksət) n. an impractical idealist. [after the hero of Cervantes' *Don Quixote de la Mancha* (1605)]

don't (dəʊnt) *contraction of* do not.

▷ **Usage.** The use of *don't* for *doesn't* (*he don't care*) is not generally acceptable in either written or spoken English.

don't know n. a person who has no definite opinion, esp. as a response to a questionnaire.

doodah ('duːdɑː) *or U.S. & Canad.* **doodad** ('duːdæd) n. *Inf.* an unnamed thing, esp. an object the name of which is unknown or forgotten. [C20: from ?]

doodle ('duːdᵊl) *Inf.* ~vb. **1.** to scribble or draw aimlessly. **2.** to play or improvise idly. **3.** (intr.; often foll. by *away*) *U.S.* to dawdle or waste time. ~n. **4.** a shape, picture, etc., drawn aimlessly. [C20: ?from C17: a foolish person, but infl. in meaning by DAWDLE] —'**doodler** n.

doodlebug ('duːdᵊlˌbʌg) n. **1.** another name for the **V-1.** **2.** a diviner's rod. **3.** a U.S. name for an **antlion** (the larva). [C20: prob. from DOODLE + BUG]

Doolittle ('duːˌlɪtᵊl) n. **Hilda.** known as *H.D.* 1886–1961, U.S. imagist poet and novelist, lived in Europe.

doom (duːm) n. **1.** death or a terrible fate. **2.** a judgment. **3.** (sometimes cap.) another term for the **Last Judgment.** ~vb. **4.** (tr.) to destine or condemn to death or a terrible fate. [OE *dōm*]

doomsday *or* **domesday** ('duːmzˌdeɪ) n. **1.** (sometimes cap.) the day on which the Last Judgment will occur. **2.** any day of reckoning. **3.** (modifier) characterized by predictions of disaster: *doomsday scenario* [OE *dōmes dæg* Judgment Day]

doona ('duːnə) n. the Austral. name for **continental quilt.** [from a trademark]

door (dɔ:) *n.* **1.** a hinged or sliding panel for closing the entrance to a room, cupboard, etc. **2.** a doorway or entrance. **3.** a means of access or escape: *a door to success.* **4. lay at someone's door.** to lay (the blame or responsibility) on someone. **5. out of doors.** in or into the open air. **6. show someone the door.** to order someone to leave. [OE *duru*]

do-or-die *adj.* (*prenominal*) of a determined and sometimes reckless effort to succeed.

doorjamb ('dɔ:,dʒæm) *n.* one of the two vertical members forming the sides of a doorframe. Also called: **doorpost.**

doorkeeper ('dɔ:,ki:pə) *n.* a person attending or guarding a door or gateway.

doorman ('dɔ:,mæn, -mən) *n., pl.* **-men.** a man employed to attend the doors of certain buildings.

doormat ('dɔ:,mæt) *n.* **1.** a mat, placed at an entrance, for wiping dirt from shoes. **2.** *Inf.* a person who offers little resistance to ill-treatment.

Doorn (*Dutch* do:rn) *n.* a town in the central Netherlands, in Utrecht province: residence of Kaiser William II of Germany from his abdication (1919) until his death (1941).

doornail ('dɔ:,neɪl) *n.* (**as**) **dead as a doornail.** dead beyond any doubt.

Doornik ('do:rnɪk) *n.* the Flemish name for **Tournai.**

Doors (dɔ:z) *pl. n.* **the.** U.S. rock group (1965–73), originally comprising Jim Morrison, Ray Manzarek, Robby Krieger, and John Densmore. See also (Jim) **Morrison.**

doorsill ('dɔ:,sɪl) *n.* a horizontal member of wood, stone, etc., forming the bottom of a doorframe.

doorstep ('dɔ:,stɛp) *n.* **1.** a step in front of a door. **2.** *Inf.* a thick slice of bread. ~*vb.* **-stepping, -stepped.** (*tr.*) **3.** to canvass or interview by or in the course of door-to-door visiting.

doorstop ('dɔ:,stɒp) *n.* **1.** any device which prevents an open door from moving. **2.** a piece of rubber, etc., fixed to the floor to stop a door striking a wall.

door to door *adj.* (**door-to-door** *when prenominal*), *adv.* **1.** (of selling, etc.) from one house to the next. **2.** (of journeys, etc.) direct.

doorway ('dɔ:,weɪ) *n.* **1.** an opening into a building, room, etc., esp. one that has a door. **2.** a means of access or escape: *a doorway to freedom.*

do over *vb.* (*tr., adv.*) **1.** *Inf.* to redecorate. **2.** *Brit., Austral. & N.Z. sl.* to beat up; thrash.

doo-wop ('du:,wɒp) *n.* vocalizing based on rhythm-and-blues harmony. [C20: imit.]

dop (dɒp) *n. S. African sl.* **1.** Cape brandy. **2.** a tot of this. [from Afrik., from ?]

dope (dəʊp) *n.* **1.** any of a number of preparations applied to fabric in order to improve strength, tautness, etc. **2.** an additive, such as an antiknock compound added to petrol. **3.** a thick liquid, such as a lubricant, applied to a surface. **4.** a combustible absorbent material used to hold the nitroglycerin in dynamite. **5.** *Sl.* an illegal drug, usually cannabis. **6.** a drug administered to a racehorse or greyhound to affect its performance. **7.** *Inf.* a stupid or slow-witted person. **8.** *Inf.* news or facts, esp. confidential information. ~*vb.* (*tr.*) **9.** *Electronics.* to add impurities to (a semiconductor) in order to produce or modify its properties. **10.** to apply or add dope to. **11.** to administer a drug to (oneself or another). [C19: from Du. *doop* sauce, from *doopen* to dip]

dopey or **dopy** ('dəʊpɪ) *adj.* **dopier, dopiest. 1.** *Sl.* silly. **2.** *Inf.* half-asleep or semiconscious, as when under the influence of a drug.

doppelgänger ('dɒpəl,gɛŋə) *n. Legend.* a ghostly duplicate of a living person. [from G *Doppelgänger*, lit.: double-goer]

Doppler effect ('dɒplə) *n.* a change in the apparent frequency of a sound or light wave, etc., as a result of relative motion between the observer and the source. Also called: **Doppler shift.** [C19: after C. J. *Doppler* (1803–53), Austrian physicist]

Dorcas ('dɔ:kəs) *n.* a charitable woman of Joppa (Acts 9:36–42).

Dorchester ('dɔ:tʃɪstə) *n.* a town in S England, administrative centre of Dorset: associated with Thomas Hardy, esp. as the Casterbridge of his novels. Pop.: 14 000 (1985). Latin name: **Durnovaria** (,djʊərnəʊ'veɪrɪə).

Dordogne (*French* dɔrdɔɲ) *n.* **1.** a river in SW France, rising in the Auvergne Mountains and flowing southwest and west to join the Garonne river and form the Gironde

estuary. Length: 472 km (293 miles). **2.** a department of SW France, in Aquitaine region. Capital: Périgueux. Pop.: 377 356 (1982). Area: 9224 sq. km (3597 sq. miles).

Dordrecht (*Dutch* 'dɔrdrɛxt) *n.* a port in the SW Netherlands, in South Holland province: chief port of the Netherlands until the 17th century. Pop.: 106 987 (1987). Also called: **Dort.**

Doré (*French* dɔre) *n.* (**Paul**) **Gustave** (gystav). 1832–83, French illustrator, whose style tended towards the grotesque. He illustrated the Bible, Dante's *Inferno,* Cervantes' *Don Quixote,* and works by Rabelais.

Doric ('dɒrɪk) *adj.* **1.** of the inhabitants of Doris in ancient Greece or their dialect. **2.** of or denoting one of the five classical orders of architecture: characterized by a heavy fluted column and a simple capital. **3.** (*sometimes not cap.*) rustic. ~*n.* **4.** one of four chief dialects of Ancient Greek. **5.** any rural dialect of English, esp. a Scots one.

Doris[1] ('dɒrɪs) *n.* (in ancient Greece) **1.** a small landlocked area north of the Gulf of Corinth. Traditionally regarded as the home of the Dorians, it was perhaps settled by some of them during their southward migration. **2.** the coastal area of Caria in SW Asia Minor, settled by Dorians.

Doris[2] ('dɒrɪs) *n. Greek myth.* a sea nymph.

dorm (dɔ:m) *n. Inf.* short for **dormitory.**

dormant ('dɔ:mənt) *adj.* **1.** quiet and inactive, as during sleep. **2.** latent or inoperative. **3.** (of a volcano) neither extinct nor erupting. **4.** *Biol.* alive but in a resting condition with reduced metabolism. **5.** (*usually postpositive*) *Heraldry.* (of a beast) in a sleeping position. [C14: from OF *dormant,* from *dormir* to sleep, from L *dormīre*] —'**dormancy** *n.*

dormer ('dɔ:mə) *n.* a construction with a gable roof and a window that projects from a sloping roof. Also called: **dormer window.** [C16: from OF *dormoir,* from L *dormītōrium* DORMITORY]

dormie or **dormy** ('dɔ:mɪ) *adj. Golf.* as many holes ahead of an opponent as there are still to play: *dormie three.* [C19: from ?]

dormitory ('dɔ:mɪtərɪ, -trɪ) *n., pl.* **-ries. 1.** a large room, esp. at a school, containing several beds. **2.** *U.S.* a building, esp. at a college or camp, providing living and sleeping accommodation. **3.** (*modifier*) *Brit.* denoting or relating to an area from which most of the residents commute to work (esp. in **dormitory suburb**). [C15: from L *dormītōrium,* from *dormīre* to sleep]

Dormobile ('dɔ:məʊ,bi:l) *n. Trademark.* a vanlike vehicle specially equipped for living in while travelling.

dormouse ('dɔ:,maʊs) *n., pl.* **-mice.** a small Eurasian rodent resembling a mouse with a furry tail. [C15: from OF, ?from OF *dormir* to sleep, (from L *dormīre*) + MOUSE]

Dornbirn (*German* 'dɔrnbɪrn) *n.* a city in W Austria, in Vorarlberg. Pop.: 38 641 (1981).

doronicum (də'rɒnɪkəm) *n.* any of a genus of plants, such as leopard's-bane, with yellow daisy-like flowers. [C17: NL, from Ar.]

dorp (dɔ:p) *n. S. African.* a small town or village. [C16: from Du.]

Dorpat ('dɔ:pæt) *n.* the German name for **Tartu.**

dorsal ('dɔ:s³l) *adj. Anat., zool.* relating to the back or spinal part of the body. [C15: from Med. L *dorsālis,* from L *dorsum* back] —'**dorsally** *adv.*

dorsal fin *n.* an unpaired fin on the back of a fish that maintains balance during locomotion.

Dorset ('dɔ:sɪt) *n.* a county in SW England, on the English Channel: mainly hilly but low-lying in the east. Administrative centre: Dorchester. Pop.: 638 200 (1986 est.). Area: 2654 sq. km (1024 sq. miles).

Dort (*Dutch* dɔrt) *n.* another name for **Dordrecht.**

Dortmund ('dɔ:tmənd; *German* 'dɔrtmʊnt) *n.* an industrial city in W West Germany, in North Rhine-Westphalia at the head of the **Dortmund–Ems Canal.** Pop.: 569 800 (1986).

dory[1] ('dɔ:rɪ) *n., pl.* **-ries.** any of various spiny-finned food fishes, esp. the John Dory. [C14: from F *dorée* gilded, from LL *deaurāre* to gild, ult. from L *aurum* gold]

dory[2] ('dɔ:rɪ) *n., pl.* **-ries.** *U.S. & Canad.* a flat-bottomed boat with a high bow and stern. [C18: from Amerind *dóri* dugout]

dosage ('dəʊsɪdʒ) *n.* **1.** the administration of a drug or agent in prescribed amounts. **2.** the optimum therapeutic dose and interval between doses. **3.** another name for **dose** (senses 3, 4).

dose (dəʊs) n. **1.** Med. a specific quantity of a therapeutic drug or agent taken at any one time or at specified intervals. **2.** Inf. something unpleasant to experience: a dose of influenza. **3.** Also called: **dosage**. the total energy of ionizing radiation absorbed by unit mass of material, esp. of living tissue; usually measured in grays (SI unit) or rads. **4.** Also called: **dosage**. a small amount of syrup added to wine during bottling. **5.** Sl. a venereal infection. ~vb. (tr.) **6.** to administer a dose to (someone). **7.** Med. to prescribe (a drug) in appropriate quantities. **8.** to add syrup to (wine) during bottling. [C15: from F, from LL dosis, from Gk: a giving, from didonai to give]

dosimeter (dəʊ'sɪmɪtə) n. an instrument for measuring the dose of radiation absorbed by matter or the intensity of a source of radiation. —**dosimetric** (,dəʊsɪ'mɛtrɪk) adj.

dosing strip n. (in New Zealand) an area set aside for treating dogs suspected of having hydatid disease.

Dos Passos (dɒs 'pæsɒs) n. **John** (Roderigo). 1896–1970, U.S. novelist of the Lost Generation; author of Three Soldiers (1921), Manhattan Transfer (1925), and the trilogy U.S.A. (1930–36).

doss (dɒs) Brit. sl. ~vb. **1.** (intr.; often foll. by down) to sleep, esp. in a dosshouse. ~n. **2.** a bed, esp. in a dosshouse. **3.** another word for **sleep**. **4.** short for **dosshouse**. [C18: from ?]

dosser ('dɒsə) n. **1.** Brit. sl. a person who sleeps in dosshouses. **2.** Brit. sl. another word for **dosshouse**. **3.** Dublin dialect. a lazy person.

dosshouse ('dɒs,haʊs) n. Brit. sl. a cheap lodging house, esp. one used by tramps. U.S. name: **flophouse**.

dossier ('dɒsɪ,eɪ) n. a collection of papers about a subject or person. [C19: from F: a file with a label on the back, from dos back, from L dorsum]

dost (dʌst) vb. Arch. or dialect. (used with thou) a singular form of the present tense (indicative mood) of **do**[1].

Dostoevsky, Dostoyevsky, Dostoevski, or **Dostoyevski** (,dɒstɔɪ'ɛfski; Russian dəstɑ'jɛfskij) n. **Fyodor Mikhailovich** ('fjɔdər mɪ'xajləvɪtʃ). 1821–81, Russian novelist, the psychological perception of whose works has greatly influenced the subsequent development of the novel. His best-known works are Crime and Punishment (1866), The Idiot (1868), The Possessed (1871), and The Brothers Karamazov (1879–80).

dot[1] (dɒt) n. **1.** a small round mark; spot; point. **2.** anything resembling a dot; a small amount. **3.** the mark (˙) above the letters i, j. **4.** Music. **a.** the symbol (·) placed after a note or rest to increase its time value by half. **b.** this symbol written above or below a note indicating staccato. **5.** Maths, logic. **a.** the symbol (.) indicating multiplication or logical conjunction. **b.** a decimal point. **6.** the symbol (·) used, in combination with the symbol for dash (—), in Morse and other codes. **7. on the dot.** at exactly the arranged time. ~vb. **dotting, dotted. 8.** (tr.) to mark or form with a dot. **9.** (tr.) to scatter or intersperse (as with dots): bushes dotting the plain. **10.** (intr.) to make a dot or dots. **11. dot one's i's and cross one's t's.** Inf. to pay meticulous attention to detail. [OE dott head of a boil] —'**dotter** n.

dot[2] (dɒt) n. a woman's dowry. [C19: from F from L dōs; rel. to dōtāre to endow, dāre to give]

dotage ('dəʊtɪdʒ) n. **1.** feebleness of mind, esp. as a result of old age. **2.** foolish infatuation. [C14: from DOTE + -AGE]

dotard ('dəʊtəd) n. a person who is weak-minded, esp. through senility. [C14: from DOTE + -ARD] —'**dotardly** adj.

dote (dəʊt) vb. (intr.) **1.** (foll. by on or upon) to love to an excessive or foolish degree. **2.** to be foolish or weak-minded, esp. as a result of old age. [C13: rel. to MDu. doten to be silly] —'**doter** n.

doth (dʌθ) vb. Arch. or dialect. (used with he, she, or it) a singular form of the present tense of **do**[1].

dot matrix printer n. Computers. a printer in which each character is produced by a subset of an array of needles.

dotterel or **dottrel** ('dɒtrəl) n. **1.** a rare Eurasian plover with white bands around the head and neck. **2.** Dialect. a person who is foolish or easily duped. [C15 dotrelle; see DOTE]

dottle ('dɒtᵊl) n. the plug of tobacco left in a pipe after smoking. [C15: dim. of dot lump]

dotty ('dɒtɪ) adj. **-tier, -tiest. 1.** Sl., chiefly Brit. feeble-minded; slightly crazy. **2.** Brit. sl. (foll. by about) extremely fond (of). **3.** marked with dots. [C19: from DOT[1]] —'**dottily** adv. —'**dottiness** n.

Dou, Dow, or **Douw** (daʊ; Dutch dɔu) n. **Gerard** ('xeːrɑrt). 1613–75, Dutch portrait and genre painter.

Douai ('duːeɪ; French dwɛ) n. an industrial city in N France: the political and religious centre of exiled English Roman Catholics in the 16th and 17th centuries. Pop.: 44 738 (1983 est.).

Douala or **Duala** (dʊ'ɑːlə) n. the chief port and largest city in W Cameroon, on the Bight of Bonny: capital of the German colony of Kamerun (1901–16). Pop.: 852 700 (1985).

Douay Bible or **Version** ('duːeɪ) n. an English translation of the Bible from the Latin Vulgate text completed by Roman Catholic scholars at Douai, N France in 1610.

double ('dʌbᵊl) adj. (usually prenominal) **1.** as much again in size, strength, number, etc.: a double portion. **2.** composed of two equal or similar parts. **3.** designed for two users: a double room. **4.** folded in two; composed of two layers. **5.** stooping; bent over. **6.** having two aspects; ambiguous: a double meaning. **7.** false, deceitful, or hypocritical: a double life. **8.** (of flowers) having more than the normal number of petals. **9.** Music. **a.** (of an instrument) sounding an octave lower: a double bass. **b.** (of time) duple. ~adv. **10.** twice over; twofold. **11.** two together; two at a time (esp. in **see double**). ~n. **12.** twice the number, amount, size, etc. **13.** a double measure of spirits. **14.** a duplicate or counterpart, esp. a person who closely resembles another; understudy. **15.** a ghostly apparition of a living person; doppelgänger. **16.** a sharp turn, esp. a return on one's own tracks. **17.** Bridge. a call that increases certain scoring points if the last preceding bid becomes the contract. **18.** Billiards, etc. a strike in which the object ball is struck so as to make it rebound against the cushion to an opposite pocket. **19.** a bet on two horses in different races in which any winnings from the first race are placed on the horse in the later race. **20. a.** the narrow outermost ring on a dartboard. **b.** a hit on this ring. **21. at** or **on the double. a.** at twice normal marching speed. **b.** quickly or immediately. ~vb. **22.** to make or become twice as much. **23.** to bend or fold (material, etc.). **24.** (tr.; sometimes foll. by up) to clench (a fist). **25.** (tr.; often foll. by together or up) to join or couple. **26.** (tr.) to repeat exactly; copy. **27.** (intr.) to play two parts or serve two roles. **28.** (intr.) to turn sharply; follow a winding course. **29.** Naut. to sail around (a headland or other point). **30.** Music. **a.** to duplicate (a part) either in unison or at the octave above or below it. **b.** (intr.; usually foll. by on) to be capable of performing (upon an additional instrument). **31.** Bridge. to make a call that will double certain scoring points if the preceding bid becomes the contract. **32.** Billiards, etc. to cause (a ball) to rebound or (of a ball) to rebound from a cushion. **33.** (intr.; foll. by for) to act as substitute. **34.** (intr.) to go or march at twice the normal speed. ~See also **double back, doubles, double up**. [C13: from OF, from L duplus twofold, from duo two + -plus -FOLD] —'**doubler** n.

double agent n. a spy employed by two mutually antagonistic countries, companies, etc.

double back vb. (intr., adv.) to go back in the opposite direction (esp. in **double back on one's tracks**).

double-bank vb. Austral. & N.Z. inf. to carry (a second person) on (a horse, bicycle, etc.). Also: **dub**.

double bar n. Music. a symbol, consisting of two ordinary bar lines or a single heavy one, that marks the end of a composition or section.

double-barrelled or U.S. **-barreled** adj. **1.** (of a gun) having two barrels. **2.** extremely forceful. **3.** Brit. (of surnames) having hyphenated parts. **4.** serving two purposes; ambiguous: a double-barrelled remark.

double bass (beɪs) n. Also called (U.S.): **bass viol**. a stringed instrument, the largest and lowest member of the violin family with a range of almost three octaves. Inf. name: **bass fiddle**. ~adj. **double-bass**. **1.** of an instrument whose pitch lies below the bass; contrabass.

double bassoon n. Music. the lowest and largest instrument in the oboe class; contrabassoon.

double-blind adj. of or denoting an experimental study of a new drug in which neither the experimenters nor the patients know which are the test subjects and which are the controls.

double boiler *n.* the U.S. and Canad. name for **double saucepan.**

double-breasted *adj.* (of a garment) having overlapping fronts.

double-check *vb.* **1.** to check again; verify. ~*n.* **double check. 2.** a second examination or verification. **3.** *Chess.* a simultaneous check from two pieces.

double chin *n.* a fold of fat under the chin. —,**double-'chinned** *adj.*

double concerto *n.* a concerto for two solo instruments.

double cream *n.* thick cream with a high fat content.

double-cross *vb.* **1.** (*tr.*) to cheat or betray. ~*n.* **2.** the act or an instance of double-crossing; betrayal. —,**double-'crosser** *n.*

double dagger *n.* a character (‡) used in printing to indicate a cross-reference.

double-dealing *n.* **a.** action characterized by treachery or deceit. **b.** (*as modifier*): *double-dealing treachery.* —,**double-'dealer** *n.*

double-decker *n.* **1.** *Chiefly Brit.* a bus with two passenger decks. **2.** *Inf.* **a.** a thing or structure having two decks, layers, etc. **b.** (*as modifier*): *a double-decker sandwich.*

double-declutch *vb.* (*intr.*) *Brit.* to change to a lower gear in a motor vehicle by first placing the gear lever into neutral before engaging the desired gear. U.S. term: **double-clutch.**

double Dutch *n. Brit. inf.* incomprehensible talk; gibberish.

double-edged *adj.* **1.** acting in two ways. **2.** (of a remark, etc.) having two possible interpretations, esp. applicable both for and against, or being malicious though apparently innocuous. **3.** (of a knife, etc.) having a cutting edge on either side of the blade.

double entendre (ɑːn'tɑːndrə) *n.* **1.** a word, phrase, etc., that can be interpreted in two ways, esp. one having one meaning that is indelicate. **2.** the type of humour that depends upon this. [C17: from obs. F: double meaning]

double entry *n.* **a.** a book-keeping system in which any commercial transaction is entered as a debit in one account and as a credit in another. **b.** (*as modifier*): *double-entry book-keeping.*

double exposure *n.* **1.** the act or process of recording two superimposed images on a photographic medium. **2.** the photograph resulting from such an act.

double-faced *adj.* **1.** (of textiles) having a finished nap on each side; reversible. **2.** insincere or deceitful.

double feature *n.* a programme showing two full-length films. Inf. name (U.S.): **twin bill.**

double first *n. Brit.* a first-class honours degree in two subjects.

double glazing *n.* **1.** two panes of glass in a window, fitted to reduce heat loss, etc. **2.** the fitting of glass in such a manner.

double-header *n.* **1.** a train drawn by two locomotives coupled together. **2.** Also called: **twin bill.** *Sport, U.S. & Canad.* two games played consecutively. **3.** *Austral. & N.Z. inf.* a coin with the impression of a head on each side. **4.** *Austral. inf.* a double ice-cream cone.

double helix *n.* the form of the molecular structure of DNA, consisting of two helical chains coiled around the same axis.

double-jointed *adj.* having unusually flexible joints permitting an abnormal degree of motion.

double knitting *n.* a widely used medium thickness of knitting wool.

double negative *n.* a construction, often considered ungrammatical, in which two negatives are used where one is needed, as in *I wouldn't never have believed it.*

▷ **Usage.** There are two contexts where double negatives are found. An adjective with negative force is often used with a negative in order to express a nuance of meaning somewhere between the positive and the negative: *it is not an uncommon sight.* Two negatives are also found together where they reinforce each other rather than conflict: *he never went back, not even to collect his belongings.* These two uses of a double negative are acceptable. A third case, illustrated by *I shouldn't wonder if it didn't rain today,* has the force of a weak positive statement (*I expect it to rain today*) and is common in informal English.

double-park *vb.* to park (a vehicle) alongside or opposite another already parked by the roadside, thereby causing an obstruction.

double pneumonia *n.* pneumonia affecting both lungs.

double-quick *adj.* **1.** very quick; rapid. ~*adv.* **2.** in a very quick or rapid manner.

double-reed *adj.* relating to or denoting a wind instrument having two reeds that vibrate against each other.

double refraction *n.* the splitting of a ray of unpolarized light into two unequally refracted rays polarized in mutually perpendicular planes. Also called: **birefringence.**

doubles ('dʌbəlz) *n.* (*functioning as pl.*) **a.** a game between two pairs of players. **b.** (*as modifier*): *a doubles match.*

double saucepan *n. Brit.* a cooking utensil consisting of two saucepans: the lower pan is used to boil water to heat food in the upper pan. U.S. and Canad. name: **double boiler.**

double-space *vb.* to type (copy) with a full space between lines.

double standard *n.* a set of principles that allows greater freedom to one person or group than to another.

double-stop *vb.* **-stopping, -stopped.** to play (two notes or parts) simultaneously on a violin or related instrument.

doublet ('dʌblɪt) *n.* **1.** (formerly) a man's close-fitting jacket, with or without sleeves (esp. in **doublet and hose**). **2. a.** a pair of similar things, esp. two words deriving ultimately from the same source. **b.** one of such a pair. **3.** *Jewellery.* a false gem made by welding or fusing stones together. **4.** *Physics.* a closely spaced pair of related spectral lines. **5.** (*pl.*) two dice each showing the same number of spots on one throw. [C14: from OF, from DOUBLE]

double take *n.* (esp. in comedy) a delayed reaction by a person to a remark, situation, etc.

double talk *n.* **1.** rapid speech with a mixture of nonsense syllables and real words; gibberish. **2.** empty, deceptive, or ambiguous talk.

doublethink ('dʌbəl,θɪŋk) *n.* deliberate, perverse, or unconscious acceptance or promulgation of conflicting facts, principles, etc.

double time *n.* **1.** a doubled wage rate, paid for working on public holidays, etc. **2.** *Music.* two beats per bar. **3.** *U.S. Army.* **a.** a fast march. **b.** a slow running pace, keeping in step.

doubletree ('dʌbəl,triː) *n.* a horizontal pivoted bar on a vehicle to the ends of which swingletrees are attached for harnessing two horses.

double up *vb.* (*adv.*) **1.** to bend or cause to bend in two. **2.** (*intr.*) to share a room or bed designed for one person, family, etc. **3.** (*intr.*) *Brit.* to use the winnings from one bet as the stake for another. U.S. and Canad. term: **parlay.**

doubloon (dʌ'bluːn) *n.* **1.** a former Spanish gold coin. **2.** (*pl.*) *Sl.* money. [C17: from Sp. *doblón*, from *dobla*, from L *dupla*, fem. of *duplus* twofold]

doubly ('dʌblɪ) *adv.* **1.** to or in a double degree, quantity, or measure. **2.** in two ways.

Doubs (*French* du) *n.* **1.** a department of E France, in Franche-Comté region. Capital: Besançon. Pop.: 477 163 (1982). Area: 5258 sq. km (2030 sq. miles). **2.** a river in E France, rising in the Jura Mountains, becoming part of the border between France and Switzerland and flowing generally southwest to the Saône River. Length: 430 km (267 miles).

doubt (daʊt) *n.* **1.** uncertainty about the truth, fact, or existence of something (esp. in **in doubt, without doubt,** etc.). **2.** (*often pl.*) lack of belief in or conviction about something. **3.** an unresolved difficulty, point, etc. **4.** *Obs.* fear. **5. give (someone) the benefit of the doubt.** to presume (someone suspected of guilt) innocent. **6. no doubt.** almost certainly. ~*vb.* **7.** (*tr.; may take a clause as object*) to be inclined to disbelieve. **8.** (*tr.*) to distrust or be suspicious of. **9.** (*intr.*) to feel uncertainty or be undecided. **10.** (*tr.*) *Arch.* to fear. [C13: from OF *douter,* from L *dubitāre*] —'**doubtable** *adj.* —'**doubter** *n.* —'**doubtingly** *adv.*

▷ **Usage.** Where a clause follows *doubt* in a positive statement, the conjunction may be *whether, that,* or *if. Whether* (*I doubt whether he is there*) is universally accepted; *that* (*I doubt that he is there*) is less widely accepted and *if* (*I doubt if he is there*) is usually restricted to informal contexts. In negative statements, *doubt* is followed by *that: I do not doubt that he is telling the truth.*

In such sentences, but (*I do not doubt but that he is telling the truth*) is redundant.

doubtful ('dautful) *adj.* **1.** unlikely; improbable. **2.** uncertain: *a doubtful answer.* **3.** unsettled; unresolved. **4.** of questionable reputation or morality. **5.** having reservations or misgivings. —'**doubtfully** *adv.* —'**doubtfulness** *n.*

doubting Thomas *n.* a person who insists on proof before he will believe anything. [after THOMAS (the apostle), who did not believe that Jesus had been resurrected until he had proof]

doubtless ('dautlıs) *adv. also* **doubtlessly** (*sentence modifier*), *sentence substitute.* **1.** certainly. **2.** probably. ~*adj.* **3.** certain; assured. —'**doubtlessness** *n.*

douche (du:ʃ) *n.* **1.** a stream of water directed onto or into the body for cleansing or medical purposes. **2.** the application of such a stream of water. **3.** an instrument for applying a douche. ~*vb.* **4.** to cleanse or treat or be cleansed or treated by means of a douche. [C18: from F, from It. *doccia* pipe]

dough (dəu) *n.* **1.** a thick mixture of flour or meal and water or milk, used for making bread, pastry, etc. **2.** any similar pasty mass. **3.** a slang word for **money.** [OE *dāg*]

doughboy ('dəu,bɔı) *n.* **1.** *U.S. inf.* an infantryman, esp. in World War I. **2.** dough that is boiled or steamed as a dumpling.

doughnut ('dəunʌt) *n.* **1.** a small cake of sweetened dough, often ring-shaped, cooked in hot fat. **2.** anything shaped like a ring, such as the reaction vessel of a thermonuclear reactor.

doughty ('dautı) *adj.* **-tier, -tiest.** hardy; resolute. [OE *dohtig*] —'**doughtily** *adv.* —'**doughtiness** *n.*

Doughty ('dautı) *n.* **Charles Montagu.** 1843–1926, English writer and traveller; author of *Travels in Arabia Deserta* (1888).

doughy ('dəuı) *adj.* **doughier, doughiest.** resembling dough; soft, pallid, or flabby.

Douglas[1] ('dʌgləs) *n.* a town and resort on the Isle of Man, capital of the island, on the E coast. Pop.: 19 944 (1981).

Douglas[2] ('dʌgləs) *n.* **1. Clifford Hugh.** 1879–1952, English economist, who originated the theory of social credit. **2. Gavin.** ?1474–1522, Scottish poet, the first British translator of the *Aeneid.* **3. (George) Norman.** 1868–1952, English writer, esp. of books on southern Italy such as *South Wind* (1917).

Douglas fir, spruce, *or* **hemlock** *n.* a North American pyramidal coniferous tree, widely planted for ornament and for timber. [C19: after David *Douglas* (1798–1834), Scot. botanist]

Douglas-Home (,dʌgləs'hju:m) *n.* Sir **Alexander.** See (Baron Alexander) **Home.**

Doukhobor *or* **Dukhobor** ('du:kəu,bɔ:) *n.* a member of a Russian sect of Christians that originated in the 18th century. In the late 19th century a large number emigrated to W Canada, where most Doukhobors now live. [C19: from Russian *dukhoborets* spirit wrestlers]

do up *vb.* (*adv.; mainly tr.*) **1.** to wrap and make into a bundle: *to do up a parcel.* **2.** to beautify or adorn. **3.** (*also intr.*) to fasten or be fastened. **4.** *Inf.* to renovate or redecorate. **5.** *Sl.* to assault. **6.** (*Inf.*) to cause the downfall of (a person).

dour (duə) *adj.* **1.** sullen. **2.** hard or obstinate. [C14: prob. from L *dūrus* hard] —'**dourly** *adv.* —'**dourness** *n.*

Douro ('duərəu; *Portuguese* 'doru) *n.* a river in SW Europe, rising in N central Spain and flowing west to NE Portugal, then south as part of the border between the two countries and finally west to the Atlantic. Length: 895 km (556 miles). Spanish name: **Duero.**

douroucouli (,du:ru:'ku:lı) *n.* a nocturnal New World monkey of Central and South America with thick fur and large eyes. [from Amerind]

douse *or* **dowse** (daus) *vb.* **1.** to plunge or be plunged into liquid; duck. **2.** (*tr.*) to drench with water. **3.** (*tr.*) to put out (a light, candle, etc.). ~*n.* **4.** an immersion. [C16: ? rel. to obs. *douse* to strike, from ?]

dove (dʌv) *n.* **1.** any of a family of birds having a heavy body, small head, short legs, and long pointed wings. **2.** *Politics.* a person opposed to war. **3.** a gentle or innocent person: used as a term of endearment. **4. a.** a greyish-brown colour. **b.** (*as adj.*): *dove walls.* [OE *dūfe* (untested except as a fem. proper name)] —'**dove,like** *adj.*

Dove (dʌv) *n.* **the.** *Christianity.* a manifestation of the Holy Spirit (John 1:32).

dovecote ('dʌv,kəut) *or* **dovecot** ('dʌv,kɒt) *n.* a structure for housing pigeons.

Dover ('dəuvə) *n.* **1.** a port in SE England, in E Kent on the Strait of Dover: the only one of the Cinque Ports that is still important; a stronghold since ancient times and Caesar's first point of attack in the invasion of Britain (55 B.C.). Pop.: 32 843 (1981). **2. Strait of.** a strait between SE England and N France, linking the English Channel with the North Sea. Width: about 32 km (20 miles). French name: **Pas de Calais.**

dovetail ('dʌv,teıl) *n.* **1.** a wedge-shaped tenon. **2.** Also called: **dovetail joint.** a joint containing such tenons. ~*vb.* **3.** (*tr.*) to join by means of dovetails. **4.** to fit or cause to fit together closely or neatly.

Dow (dau; *Dutch* dɔu) *n.* See (Gerard) **Dou.**

dowager ('dauədʒə) *n.* **1. a.** a widow possessing property or a title obtained from her husband. **b.** (*as modifier*): *the dowager duchess.* **2.** a wealthy or dignified elderly woman. [C16: from OF *douagiere*, from *douage* DOWER]

Dowding ('daudıŋ) *n.* Baron **Hugh Caswall Tremenheere,** nicknamed *Stuffy.* 1882–1970, British air chief marshal. As commander in chief of Fighter Command (1936–40), he contributed greatly to the British victory in the Battle of Britain (1940).

dowdy ('daudı) *adj.* **-dier, -diest. 1.** (esp. of a woman or a woman's dress) shabby or old-fashioned. ~*n., pl.* **-dies. 2.** a dowdy woman. [C14: *dowd* slut, from ?] —'**dowdily** *adv.* —'**dowdiness** *n.* —'**dowdyish** *adj.*

dowel ('dauəl) *n.* a wooden or metal peg that fits into two corresponding holes to join two adjacent parts. [C14: from MLow G *dövel* plug, from OHG *tubili*]

Dowell ('dauəl) *n.* **Anthony.** born 1943, British ballet dancer. He became director of the Royal Ballet in 1986.

dower ('dauə) *n.* **1.** the life interest in a part of her husband's estate allotted to a widow by law. **2.** an archaic word for **dowry** (sense 1). **3.** a natural gift. ~*vb.* **4.** (*tr.*) to endow. [C14: from OF *douaire*, from Med. L *dōtārium*, from L *dōs* gift]

dower house *n.* a house for the use of a widow, often on her deceased husband's estate.

dowitcher ('dauıtʃə) *n.* either of two snipelike shore birds of arctic and subarctic North America. [C19: from Amerind]

do with *vb.* **1. could** *or* **can do with.** to find useful; benefit from. **2. have to do with.** to be involved in or connected with. **3. to do with.** concerning; related to. **4. what . . . do with. a.** to put or place: *what did you do with my coat?* **b.** to handle or treat. **c.** to fill one's time usefully: *she didn't know what to do with herself when the project was finished.*

do without *vb.* (*intr.*) **1.** to forgo; manage without. **2.** (*prep.*) not to require (uncalled-for comments): *we can do without your criticisms.*

Dow-Jones average ('dau'dʒəunz) *n. U.S.* a daily index of stock-exchange prices based on the average price of a selected number of securities. [C20: after Charles H. *Dow* (died 1902) & Edward D. *Jones* (died 1920), American financial statisticians]

Dowland ('daulənd) *n.* **John.** ?1563–1626, English lutenist and composer of songs and lute music.

down[1] (daun) *prep.* **1.** used to indicate movement from a higher to a lower position. **2.** at a lower or further level or position on, in, or along: *he ran down the street.* ~*adv.* **3.** downwards; at or to a lower level or position. **4.** (*particle*) used with many verbs when the result of the verb's action is to lower or destroy its object: *knock down.* **5.** (*particle*) used with several verbs to indicate intensity or completion: *calm down.* **6.** immediately: *cash down.* **7.** on paper: *write this down.* **8.** arranged; scheduled. **9.** in a helpless position. **10. a.** away from a more important place. **b.** away from a more northerly place. **c.** (of a member of some British universities) away from the university. **d.** in a particular part of a country: *down south.* **11.** *Naut.* (of a helm) having the rudder to windward. **12.** reduced to a state of lack or want: *down to the last pound.* **13.** lacking a specified amount. **14.** lower in price. **15.** including all intermediate grades. **16.** from an earlier to a later time. **17.** to a finer or more concentrated state: *to grind down.* **18.** *Sport.* being a specified number of points, goals, etc., behind another competitor, team, etc.

19. (of a person) being inactive, owing to illness: *down with flu.* **20.** (*functioning as imperative*) (to dogs): *down, Rover!* **21.** (*functioning as imperative*) **down with.** wanting the end of somebody or something: *down with the king!* ~*adj.* **22.** (*postpositive*) depressed. **23.** (*prenominal*) of or relating to a train or trains from a more important place or one regarded as higher: *the down line.* **24.** made in cash: *a down payment.* ~*vb.* (*tr.*) **25.** to knock, push, or pull down. **26.** to cause to go or come down. **27.** *Inf.* to drink, esp. quickly. **28.** to bring (someone) down, esp. by tackling. ~*n.* **29.** a descent; downward movement. **30.** a lowering or a poor period (esp. in **ups and downs**). **31.** (in Canadian football) any of a series of three attempts to advance the ball ten yards. **32. have a down on.** *Inf.* to bear ill will towards. [OE *dūne*, short for *adūne*, var. of *of dūne*, lit.: from the hill]

down² (daʊn) *n.* **1.** soft fine feathers. **2.** another name for **eiderdown** (sense 1). **3.** *Bot.* a fine coating of soft hairs, as on certain leaves, fruits, and seeds. **4.** any growth or coating of soft fine hair. [C14: from ON]

down³ (daʊn) *n.* *Arch.* a hill, esp. a sand dune. See also **downs.** [OE *dūn*]

Down (daʊn) *n.* a district (former county) of SE Northern Ireland, on the Irish Sea: generally hilly, rising to the Mountains of Mourne. Pop.: 55 800 (1986 est.). Area: 639 sq. km (247 sq. miles).

down-and-out *adj.* **1.** without any means of livelihood; poor and, often, socially outcast. ~*n.* **2.** a person who is destitute and, often, homeless.

downbeat (ˈdaʊnˌbiːt) *n.* **1.** *Music.* the first beat of a bar or the downward gesture of a conductor's baton indicating this. ~*adj.* *Inf.* **2.** depressed; gloomy. **3.** relaxed.

downcast (ˈdaʊnˌkɑːst) *adj.* **1.** dejected. **2.** (esp. of the eyes) directed downwards. ~*n.* **3.** *Mining.* a ventilation shaft.

downer (ˈdaʊnə) *n.* *Sl.* **1.** a barbiturate, tranquillizer, or narcotic. **2.** a depressing experience. **3.** a state of depression.

downfall (ˈdaʊnˌfɔːl) *n.* **1.** a sudden loss of position, health, or reputation. **2.** a fall of rain, snow, etc., esp. a sudden heavy one.

downgrade (ˈdaʊnˌɡreɪd) *vb.* (*tr.*) **1.** to reduce in importance or value, esp. to demote (a person) to a poorer job. **2.** to speak of disparagingly. ~*n.* **3.** *Chiefly U.S. & Canad.* a downward slope. **4. on the downgrade.** waning in importance, health, etc.

downhearted (ˌdaʊnˈhɑːtɪd) *adj.* discouraged; dejected. —ˌdown'heartedly *adv.*

downhill (ˈdaʊnˈhɪl) *adj.* **1.** going or sloping down. ~*adv.* **2.** towards the bottom of a hill; downwards. **3. go downhill.** *Inf.* to decline; deteriorate. ~*n.* **4.** the downward slope of a hill; a descent. **5.** a skiing race downhill.

downhole (ˈdaʊnˌhəʊl) *adj.* (in the oil industry) denoting any piece of equipment which is used in the well itself.

Downing Street (ˈdaʊnɪŋ) *n.* **1.** a street in W central London: official residences of the prime minister of Great Britain and the chancellor of the exchequer. **2.** *Inf.* the prime minister or the British Government. [after Sir George *Downing* (1623–84), E statesman]

download (ˈdaʊnˌləʊd) *vb.* (*tr.*) to copy or transfer (data or a program) from one computer's memory to that of another, esp. in a network of computers.

down-market *adj.* relating to commercial products, services, etc., that are cheap, have little prestige, or are poor in quality.

Downpatrick (ˌdaʊnˈpætrɪk) *n.* a market town in Northern Ireland: associated with Saint Patrick who is said to have been buried here. Pop.: 8245 (1981).

down payment *n.* the deposit paid on an item purchased on hire-purchase, mortgage, etc.

downpipe (ˈdaʊnˌpaɪp) *n.* *Brit. and N.Z.* a pipe for carrying rainwater from a roof gutter to ground level. Usual U.S. & Canad. name: **downspout.**

downpour (ˈdaʊnˌpɔː) *n.* a heavy continuous fall of rain.

downrange (ˈdaʊnˈreɪndʒ) *adj., adv.* in the direction of the intended flight path of a rocket or missile.

downright (ˈdaʊnˌraɪt) *adj.* **1.** frank or straightforward; blunt. ~*adv., adj.* (*prenominal*) **2.** (intensifier): *downright rude.* —ˈdownˌrightly *adv.* —ˈdownˌrightness *n.*

downs (daʊnz) *pl. n.* **1.** rolling upland, esp. in the chalk areas of S Britain, characterized by lack of trees and used mainly as pasture. **2.** *Austral. & N.Z.* a flat grassy area, not necessarily of uplands.

Downs (daʊnz) *n.* **the.** **1.** any of various ranges of low chalk hills in S England, esp. the **South Downs** in Sussex. **2.** a roadstead off the SE coast of Kent, protected by the Goodwin Sands.

downside (ˈdaʊnˌsaɪd) *n.* the disadvantageous aspect of a situation: *the downside of twentieth-century living.*

Down's syndrome (daʊnz) *n.* **a.** *Pathol.* a chromosomal abnormality resulting in a flat face and nose, a vertical fold of skin at the inner edge of the eye, and mental retardation. Former name: **mongolism.** **b.** (*as modifier*): *a Down's syndrome baby.* [C19: after John *Langdon-Down* (1828–96), E physician]

downstage (ˈdaʊnˈsteɪdʒ) *Theatre.* ~*adv.* **1.** at or towards the front of the stage. ~*adj.* **2.** of or relating to the front of the stage.

downstairs (ˈdaʊnˈstɛəz) *adv.* **1.** down the stairs; to or on a lower floor. ~*n.* **2. a.** a lower or ground floor. **b.** (*as modifier*): *a downstairs room.* **3.** *Brit. inf.* the servants of a household collectively.

downstream (ˈdaʊnˈstriːm) *adv., adj.* in or towards the lower part of a stream; with the current.

downswing (ˈdaʊnˌswɪŋ) *n.* a statistical downward trend in business activity, the death rate, etc.

downtime (ˈdaʊnˌtaɪm) *n.* *Commerce.* time during which a computer or machine is not working, as when under repair.

down-to-earth *adj.* sensible; practical; realistic.

downtown (ˈdaʊnˈtaʊn) *Chiefly U.S., Canad., & N.Z.* ~*n.* **1.** the central or lower part of a city, esp. the main commercial area. ~*adv.* **2.** towards, to, or into this area. ~*adj.* **3.** of, relating to, or situated in the downtown area: *a downtown cinema.*

downtrodden (ˈdaʊnˌtrɒdᵊn) *adj.* **1.** subjugated; oppressed. **2.** trodden down.

downturn (ˈdaʊnˌtɜːn) *n.* another term for **downswing.**

down under *Inf.* ~*n.* **1.** Australia or New Zealand. ~*adv.* **2.** in or to Australia or New Zealand.

downward (ˈdaʊnwəd) *adj.* **1.** descending from a higher to a lower level, condition, position, etc. **2.** descending from a beginning. ~*adv.* **3.** a variant of **downwards.** —ˈdownwardly *adv.*

downwards (ˈdaʊnwədz) or **downward** *adv.* **1.** from a higher to a lower place, level, etc. **2.** from an earlier time or source to a later.

downwind (ˈdaʊnˈwɪnd) *adv., adj.* in the same direction towards which the wind is blowing; with the wind from behind.

downy (ˈdaʊnɪ) *adj.* **downier, downiest.** **1.** covered with soft fine hair or feathers. **2.** light, soft, and fluffy. **3.** made from or filled with down. **4.** *Brit. sl.* sharp-witted. —ˈdowniness *n.*

dowry (ˈdaʊərɪ) *n., pl.* **-ries.** **1.** the property brought by a woman to her husband at marriage. **2.** a natural talent or gift. [C14: from Anglo-F *douarie*, from Med. L *dōtārium*; see DOWER]

dowse (daʊz) *vb.* (*intr.*) to search for underground water, minerals, etc., using a divining rod; divine. [C17: from ?] —ˈdowser *n.*

Dowson (ˈdaʊsᵊn) *n.* **Ernest (Christopher).** 1867–1900, English Decadent poet noted for his lyric *Cynara.*

doxology (dɒkˈsɒlədʒɪ) *n., pl.* **-gies.** a hymn, verse, or form of words in Christian liturgy glorifying God. [C17: from Med. L *doxologia,* from Gk, from *doxologos* uttering praise, from *doxa* praise; see -LOGY] —**doxological** (ˌdɒksəˈlɒdʒɪkᵊl) *adj.*

doxy (ˈdɒksɪ) *n., pl.* **doxies.** *Arch. sl.* a prostitute or mistress. [C16: prob. from MFlemish *docke* doll]

doyen (ˈdɔɪən) *n.* the senior member of a group, profession, or society. [C17: from F, from LL *decānus* leader of a group of ten] —**doyenne** (dɔɪˈɛn) *fem. n.*

Doyle (dɔɪl) *n.* See (Sir Arthur) **Conan Doyle.**

doyley (ˈdɔɪlɪ) *n.* a variant spelling of **doily.**

doz. *abbrev. for* dozen.

doze (dəʊz) *vb.* (*intr.*) **1.** to sleep lightly or intermittently. **2.** (often foll. by *off*) to fall into a light sleep. ~*n.* **3.** a short sleep. [C17: prob. from ON *dūs* lull] —ˈdozer *n.*

dozen (ˈdʌzᵊn) *determiner.* **1.** (preceded by *a* or a numeral) twelve or a group of twelve: *two dozen oranges.* ~*n., pl.* **dozens** or **dozen.** **2. by the dozen.** in large quantities. **3. daily dozen.** *Brit.* regular physical exercises. **4. talk nineteen to the dozen.** to talk without stopping. [C13: from OF *douzaine,* from *douze* twelve, from L *duodecim*, from *duo* two + *decem* ten] —'**doz-enth** *adj*.

dozy ('dəʊzɪ) *adj*. **dozier, doziest. 1.** drowsy. **2.** *Brit. inf*. stupid. —'**dozily** *adv*. —'**doziness** *n*.

DP *abbrev. for*: **1.** data processing. **2.** displaced person.

DPhil *or* **DPh** *abbrev. for* Doctor of Philosophy. Also: **PhD.**

DPP (in Britain) *abbrev. for* Director of Public Prosecutions.

dpt *abbrev. for*: **1.** department. **2.** depot.

dr *abbrev. for*: **1.** Also: **dr.** dram. **2.** debtor.

Dr *abbrev. for*: **1.** Doctor. **2.** Drive.

DR *abbrev. for* dry riser.

dr. *abbrev. for*: **1.** debit. **2.** drachma.

drab[1] (dræb) *adj*. **drabber, drabbest. 1.** dull; dingy. **2.** cheerless; dreary. **3.** of the colour drab. ~*n*. **4.** a light olive-brown colour. [C16: from OF *drap* cloth, from LL *drappus*, ? of Celtic origin] —'**drably** *adv*. —'**drabness** *n*.

drab[2] (dræb) *Arch*. ~*n*. **1.** a slatternly woman. **2.** a whore. ~*vb*. **drabbing, drabbed. 3.** (*intr*.) to consort with prostitutes. [C16: of Celtic origin]

Drabble ('dræb°l) *n*. **Margaret.** born 1939, British novelist and editor. Her novels include *The Needle's Eye* (1972) and *The Radiant Way* (1987). She edited the 1985 edition of the *Oxford Companion to Literature*.

drachm (dræm) *n*. **1.** Also called: **fluid dram.** *Brit*. one eighth of a fluid ounce. **2.** *U.S.* another name for **dram** (sense 2). **3.** another name for **drachma.** [C14: learned var. of DRAM]

drachma ('drækmə) *n., pl*. **-mas** *or* **-mae** (-miː). **1.** the standard monetary unit of Greece. **2.** *U.S.* another name for **dram** (sense 2). **3.** a silver coin of ancient Greece. [C16: from L, from Gk *drakhmē* a handful, from *drassesthai* to seize]

drack *or* **drac** (dræk) *adj. Austral. sl*. (of a woman) unattractive. [C20: ?from *Dracula's* daughter]

Draco ('dreɪkəʊ) *n*. 7th century B.C., Athenian statesman and lawmaker, whose code of laws (621) prescribed death for almost every offence.

Draconian (dreɪ'kəʊnɪən) *or* **Draconic** (dreɪ'kɒnɪk) *adj*. (*sometimes not cap*.) **1.** of or relating to Draco or his code of laws. **2.** harsh. —**Dra'conianism** *n*. —**Dra'conically** *adv*.

draff (dræf) *n*. the residue of husks after fermentation of the grain in brewing, used as cattle fodder. [C13: from ON *draf*]

draft (drɑːft) *n*. **1.** a plan, sketch, or drawing of something. **2.** a preliminary outline of a book, speech, etc. **3.** another word for **bill of exchange. 4.** a demand or drain on something. **5.** *U.S. & Austral.* selection for compulsory military service. **6.** detachment of military personnel from one unit to another. **7.** *Austral. & N.Z.* a group of livestock separated from the rest of the herd or flock. ~*vb*. (*tr*.) **8.** to draw up an outline or sketch for. **9.** to prepare a plan or design of. **10.** to detach (military personnel) from one unit to another. **11.** *U.S.* to select for compulsory military service. **12.** *Austral. & N.Z.* **a.** to select (cattle or sheep) from a herd or flock. **b.** to select (farm stock) for sale. ~*n., vb*. **13.** the usual U.S. spelling of **draught.** [C16: var. of DRAUGHT] —'**drafter** *n*.

draftee (drɑːf'tiː) *n. U.S.* a conscript.

drafty ('drɑːftɪ) *adj*. **draftier, draftiest.** the usual U.S. spelling of **draughty.**

drag (dræg) *vb*. **dragging, dragged. 1.** to pull or be pulled with force, esp. along the ground. **2.** (*tr.; often foll. by* *away* *or* *from*) to persuade to come away. **3.** to trail or cause to trail on the ground. **4.** (*tr*.) to move with effort or difficulty. **5.** to linger behind. **6.** (often foll. by *on* or *out*) to prolong or be prolonged unnecessarily or tediously: *his talk dragged on for hours.* **7.** (when *intr*., usually foll. by *for*) to search (the bed of a river, etc.) with a dragnet or hook. **8.** (*tr.; foll. by* *out* *or* *from*) to crush (clods) or level (a soil surface) by use of a drag. **9.** (of hounds) to follow (a fox or its trail). **10.** (*intr*.) *Sl*. to draw (on a cigarette, etc.). **11. drag anchor.** (of a vessel) to move away from its mooring because the anchor has failed to hold. **12. drag one's feet** *or* **heels.** *Inf*. to act with deliberate slowness. ~*n*. **13.** the act of dragging or the state of being dragged. **14.** an implement, such as a dragnet, dredge, etc., used for dragging. **15.** a type of harrow used to crush clods, level soil, etc. **16.** a coach with seats inside and out, usually drawn by four horses. **17.** a

braking device. **18.** a person or thing that slows up progress. **19.** slow progress or movement. **20.** *Aeronautics*. the resistance to the motion of a body passing through a fluid, esp. through air. **21.** the trail of scent left by a fox, etc. **22.** an artificial trail of scent drawn over the ground for hounds to follow. **23.** See **drag hunt. 24.** *Inf*. a person or thing that is very tedious. **25.** *Sl*. a car. **26.** short for **drag race. 27.** *Sl*. **a.** women's clothes worn by a man (esp. in **in drag**). **b.** (*as modifier*): *a drag show.* **c.** clothes collectively. **28.** *Inf*. a draw on a cigarette, etc. **29.** *U.S. sl*. influence. **30.** *Chiefly U.S. sl*. a street (esp. in **main drag**). ~See also **drag out of, drag up.** [OE *dragan* to DRAW]

dragée (dræ'ʒeɪ) *n*. **1.** a sweet coated with a hard sugar icing. **2.** a tiny beadlike sweet used for decorating cakes, etc. **3.** a medicinal pill coated with sugar. [C19: from F; see DREDGE[2]]

draggle ('dræg°l) *vb*. **1.** to make or become wet or dirty by trailing on the ground; bedraggle. **2.** (*intr*.) to lag; dawdle. [ME, prob. frequentative of DRAG]

drag hunt *n*. **1.** a hunt in which hounds follow an artificial trail of scent. **2.** a club that organizes such hunts. —'**drag-,hunt** *vb*.

dragnet ('dræg,nɛt) *n*. **1.** a net used to scour the bottom of a pond, river, etc., as when searching for something. **2.** any system of coordinated efforts to track down wanted persons.

dragoman ('dræɡəʊmən) *n., pl*. **-mans** *or* **-men.** (in some Middle Eastern countries, esp. formerly) a professional interpreter or guide. [C14: from F, from It., from Med. Gk *dragoumanos*, from Ar. *targumān*, ult. from Akkadian]

dragon ('dræɡən) *n*. **1.** a mythical monster usually represented as breathing fire and having a scaly reptilian body, wings, claws, and a long tail. **2.** *Inf*. a fierce person, esp. a woman. **3.** any of various very large lizards, esp. the Komodo dragon. **4. chase the dragon.** *Sl*. to smoke opium or heroin. [C13: from OF, from L *dracō*, from Gk *drakōn*]

dragonet ('dræɡənɪt) *n*. a small fish with spiny fins, a flat head, and a tapering brighty coloured body. [C14 (meaning: small dragon): from F; applied to fish C18]

dragonfly ('dræɡən,flaɪ) *n., pl*. **-flies.** a predatory insect having a long slender body and two pairs of iridescent wings that are outspread at rest.

dragonnade (,dræɡə'neɪd) *n*. **1.** *History*. the persecution of French Huguenots during the reign of Louis XIV by dragoons quartered in their villages and homes. **2.** subjection by military force. ~*vb*. **3.** (*tr*.) to subject to persecution by military troops. [C18: from F, from *dragon* DRAGOON]

dragoon (drə'ɡuːn) *n*. **1.** (originally) a mounted infantryman armed with a carbine. **2.** (*sometimes cap*.) a domestic fancy pigeon. **3. a.** a type of cavalryman. **b.** (*pl.; cap. when part of a name*): *the Royal Dragoons*. ~*vb*. (*tr*.) **4.** to coerce; force. **5.** to persecute by military force. [C17: from F *dragon* (special use of DRAGON), soldier armed with a carbine]

drag out of *vb*. (*tr., adv. prep*.) to obtain or extract (a confession, statement, etc.), esp. by force. Also: **drag from.**

drag race *n*. a type of motor race in which specially built or modified cars or motorcycles are timed over a measured course. —**drag racing** *n*.

dragster ('dræɡstə) *n*. a car specially built or modified for drag racing.

drag up *vb*. (*tr., adv*.) *Inf*. **1.** to rear (a child) poorly and in an undisciplined manner. **2.** to introduce or revive (an unpleasant fact or story).

drain (dreɪn) *n*. **1.** a pipe or channel that carries off water, sewage, etc. **2.** an instance or cause of continuous diminution in resources or energy; depletion. **3.** *Surgery*. a device, such as a tube, to drain off pus, etc. **4. down the drain.** wasted. ~*vb*. **5.** (*tr.; often foll. by* *off*) to draw off or remove (liquid) from. **6.** (*intr.; often foll. by* *away*) to flow (away) or filter (off). **7.** (*intr*.) to dry or be emptied as a result of liquid running off or flowing away. **8.** (*tr*.) to drink the entire contents of (a glass, etc.). **9.** (*tr*.) to consume or make constant demands on (resources, energy, etc.); exhaust. **10.** (*intr*.) to disappear or leave, esp. gradually. **11.** (*tr*.) (of a river, etc.) to carry off the surface water from an area. **12.** (*intr*.) (of an area) to discharge its surface water into rivers, streams, etc. [OE *drēahnian*] —'**drainer** *n*.

drainage ('dreinidʒ) *n.* **1.** the process or a method of draining. **2.** a system of watercourses or drains. **3.** liquid, sewage, etc., that is drained away.

drainage basin *or* **area** *n.* another name for **catchment area.**

draining board *n.* a sloping grooved surface at the side of a sink, used for draining washed dishes, etc. Also called: **drainer.**

drainpipe ('drein,paip) *n.* a pipe for carrying off rainwater, sewage, etc.; downpipe.

drake (dreik) *n.* the male of any duck. [C13: ?from Low G]

Drake (dreik) *n.* Sir **Francis.** ?1540–96, English navigator and buccaneer, the first Englishman to sail around the world (1577–80). He commanded a fleet against the Spanish Armada (1588) and contributed greatly to its defeat.

Drakensberg ('drɑːkənz,bɜːg) *n.* a mountain range in southern Africa, extending through Lesotho, E South Africa, and Swaziland. Highest peak: Thabana Ntlenyana, 3482 m (11 425 ft.). Sotho name: **Quathlamba.**

Drake Passage *n.* a strait between S South America and the South Shetland Islands, connecting the Atlantic and Pacific Oceans.

Dralon ('dreilon) *n. Trademark.* an acrylic fibre fabric used esp. for upholstery.

dram (dræm) *n.* **1.** one sixteenth of an ounce (avoirdupois). 1 dram is equivalent to 0.0018 kilogram. **2.** *U.S.* one eighth of an apothecaries' ounce; 60 grains. 1 dram is equivalent to 0.0039 kilogram. **3.** a small amount of an alcoholic drink, esp. a spirit; tot. [C15: from OF *dragme*, from LL *dragma*, from Gk *drakhmē*; see DRACHMA]

drama ('drɑːmə) *n.* **1.** a work to be performed by actors; play. **2.** the genre of literature represented by works intended for the stage. **3.** the art of the writing and production of plays. **4.** a situation that is highly emotional, tragic, or turbulent. [C17: from LL: a play, from Gk: something performed, from *drān* to do]

Dramamine ('dræmə,miːn) *n.* a trademark for **dimenhydrinate.**

dramatic (drə'mætɪk) *adj.* **1.** of drama. **2.** like a drama in suddenness, emotional impact, etc. **3.** striking; effective. **4.** acting or performed in a flamboyant way. —**dra'matically** *adv.*

dramatic irony *n. Theatre.* the irony occurring when the implications of a situation, speech, etc., are understood by the audience but not by the characters in the play.

dramatics (drə'mætɪks) *n.* **1.** (*functioning as sing. or pl.*) **a.** the art of acting or producing plays. **b.** dramatic productions. **2.** (*usually functioning as pl.*) histrionic behaviour.

dramatis personae ('drɑːmətɪs pɜ'səʊnaɪ) *pl. n.* (*often functioning as sing.*) the characters in a play. [C18: from NL]

dramatist ('dræmətɪst) *n.* a playwright.

dramatize *or* **-tise** ('dræmə,taɪz) *vb.* **1.** (*tr.*) to put into dramatic form. **2.** to express (something) in a dramatic or exaggerated way. —,**dramati'zation** *or* **-ti'sation** *n.*

dramaturge ('dræmə,tɜːdʒ) *n.* **1.** Also called: **dramaturgist.** a dramatist. **2.** Also called: **dramaturg.** a literary adviser on the staff of a theatre, film company, etc. [C19: prob. from F, from Gk *dramatourgos* playwright, from DRAMA + *ergon* work]

dramaturgy ('dræmə,tɜːdʒɪ) *n.* the art and technique of the theatre; dramatics. —,**drama'turgic** *or* ,**drama'turgical** *adj.*

Drammen (*Norwegian* 'drɑmən) *n.* a port in S Norway. Pop.: 51 481 (1987).

Drancy (*French* drɑ̃si) *n.* a residential suburb of NE Paris. Pop.: 64 363 (1983 est.).

drank (dræŋk) *vb.* the past tense of **drink.**

drape (dreip) *vb.* **1.** (*tr.*) to hang or cover with material or fabric, usually in folds. **2.** to hang or arrange or be hung or arranged, esp. in folds. **3.** (*tr.*) to place casually and loosely. —*n.* **4.** (*often pl.*) a cloth or hanging that covers something in folds. **5.** the way in which fabric hangs. [C15: from OF *draper*, from *drap* piece of cloth; see DRAB¹]

draper ('dreipə) *n.* **1.** *Brit.* a dealer in fabrics and sewing materials. **2.** *Arch.* a maker of cloth.

Draper ('dreipə) *n.* **1. Henry.** 1837–82, U.S. astronomer, who contributed to stellar classification and spectroscopy. **2.** his father, **John William.** 1811–82, U.S. chemist and historian, born in England, made the first photograph of the moon.

drapery ('dreipəri) *n., pl.* **-peries. 1.** fabric or clothing arranged and draped. **2.** (*often pl.*) curtains or hangings that drape. **3.** *Brit.* the occupation or shop of a draper. **4.** fabrics and cloth collectively. —'**draperied** *adj.*

drapes (dreips) *or* **draperies** ('dreipəriz) *pl. n. Chiefly U.S. & Canad.* curtains, esp. ones of heavy fabric.

drastic ('dræstɪk) *adj.* extreme or forceful; severe. [C17: from Gk *drastikos*, from *drān* to do, act] —'**drastically** *adv.*

drat (dræt) *interj. Sl.* an exclamation of annoyance. [C19: prob. alteration of *God rot*]

draught *or U.S.* **draft** (drɑːft) *n.* **1.** a current of air, esp. in an enclosed space. **2. a.** the act of pulling a load, as by a vehicle or animal. **b.** (*as modifier*): *a draught horse.* **3.** the load or quantity drawn. **4.** a portion of liquid to be drunk, esp. a dose of medicine. **5.** the act or an instance of drinking; a gulp or swallow. **6.** the act or process of drawing air, etc., into the lungs. **7.** the amount of air, etc., inhaled. **8. a.** beer, wine, etc., stored in bulk, esp. in a cask. **b.** (*as modifier*): *draught beer.* **c. on draught.** drawn from a cask or keg. **9.** any one of the flat discs used in the game of draughts. *U.S. and Canad.* equivalent: **checker. 10.** the depth of a loaded vessel in the water. **11. feel the draught.** to be short of money. [C14: prob. from ON *drahtr*, of Gmc origin]

draughtboard ('drɑːft,bɔːd) *n.* a square board divided into 64 squares of alternating colours, used for playing draughts or chess.

draughts (drɑːfts) *n.* (*functioning as sing.*) a game for two players using a draughtboard and 12 draughtsmen each. *U.S. and Canad.* name: **checkers.** [C14: pl. of DRAUGHT (in obs. sense: a chess move)]

draughtsman *or U.S.* **draftsman** ('drɑːftsmən) *n., pl.* **-men. 1.** a person employed to prepare detailed scale drawings of machinery, buildings, etc. **2.** a person skilled in drawing. **3.** *Brit.* any of the flat discs used in the game of draughts. *U.S. and Canad.* equivalent: **checker.** —'**draughtsman,ship** *or U.S.* '**draftsman,ship** *n.*

draughty *or U.S.* **drafty** ('drɑːftɪ) *adj.* **draughtier, draughtiest** *or U.S.* **draftier, draftiest.** characterized by or exposed to draughts of air. —'**draughtily** *or U.S.* '**draftily** *adv.* —'**draughtiness** *or U.S.* '**draftiness** *n.*

Drava *or* **Drave** ('drɑːvə) *n.* a river in S central Europe, rising in N Italy and flowing east through Austria, then southeast as part of the border between Yugoslavia and Hungary to join the River Danube. Length: 725 km (450 miles). German name: **Drau** (drau).

Dravidian (drə'vɪdɪən) *n.* **1.** a family of languages spoken in S and central India and Sri Lanka, including Tamil, Malayalam, etc. **2.** a member of one of the aboriginal races of India, pushed south by the Indo-Europeans and now mixed with them. ~*adj.* **3.** of or denoting this family of languages or these peoples.

draw (drɔː) *vb.* **drawing, drew, drawn. 1.** to cause (a person or thing) to move towards or away by pulling. **2.** to bring, take, or pull (something) out, as from a drawer, holster, etc. **3.** (*tr.*) to extract or pull or take out: *to draw teeth.* **4.** (*tr.*; often foll. by *off*) to take (liquid) out of a cask, etc., by means of a tap. **5.** (*intr.*) to move, esp. in a specified direction: *to draw alongside.* **6.** (*tr.*) to attract: *to draw attention.* **7.** (*tr.*) to cause to flow: *to draw blood.* **8.** to depict or sketch (a figure, picture, etc.) in lines, as with a pencil or pen. **9.** (*tr.*) to make, formulate, or derive: *to draw conclusions.* **10.** (*tr.*) to write (a legal document) in proper form. **11.** (*tr.*; sometimes foll. by *in*) to suck or take in (air, etc.). **12.** (*intr.*) to induce or allow a draught to carry off air, smoke, etc. **13.** (*tr.*) to take or receive from a source: *to draw money from the bank.* **14.** (*tr.*) to earn: *draw interest.* **15.** (*tr.*) to write out (a bill of exchange, etc.): *to draw a cheque.* **16.** (*tr.*) to choose at random. **17.** (*tr.*) to reduce the diameter of (a wire) by pulling it through a die. **18.** (*tr.*) to shape (metal or glass) by rolling, by pulling through a die, or by stretching. **19.** *Archery.* to bend (a bow) by pulling the string. **20.** to steep (tea) or (of tea) to steep in boiling water. **21.** (*tr.*) to disembowel. **22.** (*tr.*) to cause (pus, etc.) to discharge from an abscess or wound. **23.** (*intr.*) (of two teams, etc.) to finish a game with an equal number of points, goals, etc.; tie. **24.** (*tr.*) *Bridge, whist.* to keep leading a suit in order to force out (all outstanding cards). **25. draw trumps.** *Bridge, whist.* to play the trump suit until the opponents have none left. **26.** (*tr.*) *Billiards.* to cause (the cue ball) to spin back after a direct impact with another ball. **27.** (*tr.*) to search (a place) in order to find wild animals, etc., for hunting. **28.** *Golf.* to drive (the ball) too far to the left. **29.** (*tr.*) *Naut.* (of a vessel) to require (a certain depth) in which to float. **30. draw and quarter.** to disembowel and dismember (a person) after hanging. **31. draw stumps.** *Cricket.* to close play. **32. draw the shot.** *Bowls.* to deliver the bowl in such a way that it approaches the jack. ~*n.* **33.** the act of drawing. **34.** *U.S.* a sum of money advanced to finance anticipated expenses. **35.** *Inf.* an event, act, etc., that attracts a large audience. **36.** a raffle or lottery. **37.** something taken at random, as a ticket in a lottery. **38.** a contest or game ending in a tie. **39.** *U.S. & Canad.* a small natural drainage way or gully. ~See also **drawback, draw in,** etc. [OE *dragan*]

drawback ('drɔː,bæk) *n.* **1.** a disadvantage or hindrance. **2.** a refund of customs or excise paid on goods that are being exported or used in making goods for export. ~*vb.* **draw back.** (*intr., adv.; often foll. by from*) **3.** to retreat; move backwards. **4.** to turn aside from an undertaking.

drawbridge ('drɔː,brɪdʒ) *n.* a bridge that may be raised to prevent access or to enable vessels to pass.

drawee (drɔː'iː) *n.* the person or organization on which an order for payment is drawn.

drawer ('drɔːə) *n.* **1.** a person or thing that draws, esp. a draughtsman. **2.** a person who draws a cheque. **3.** a person who draws up a commercial paper. **4.** *Arch.* a person who draws beer, etc., in a bar. **5.** (drɔː). a boxlike container in a chest, table, etc., made for sliding in and out.

drawers (drɔːz) *pl. n.* a legged undergarment for either sex, worn below the waist.

draw in *vb.* (*intr., adv.*) **1.** (of hours of daylight) to become shorter. **2.** (of a train) to arrive at a station.

drawing ('drɔːɪŋ) *n.* **1.** a picture or plan made by means of lines on a surface, esp. one made with a pencil or pen. **2.** a sketch or outline. **3.** the art of making drawings; draughtsmanship.

drawing pin *n. Brit.* a short tack with a broad smooth head for fastening papers to a drawing board, etc. U.S. and Canad. names: **thumbtack, pushpin.**

drawing room *n.* **1.** a room where visitors are received and entertained; living room; sitting room. **2.** *Arch.* a formal reception.

drawknife ('drɔː,naɪf) *or* **drawshave** *n., pl.* **-knives** *or* **-shaves.** a tool with two handles, used to shave wood. U.S. name: **spokeshave.**

drawl (drɔːl) *vb.* **1.** to speak or utter (words) slowly, esp. prolonging the vowel sounds. ~*n.* **2.** the way of speech of someone who drawls. [C16: prob. frequentative of DRAW] —'**drawling** *adj.*

drawn (drɔːn) *adj.* haggard, tired, or tense in appearance.

drawn work *n.* ornamental needlework done by drawing threads out of the fabric and using the remaining threads to form lacelike patterns. Also called: **drawn-thread work.**

draw off *vb.* (*adv.*) **1.** (*tr.*) to cause (a liquid) to flow from something. **2.** to withdraw (troops).

draw on *vb.* **1.** (*intr., prep.*) to use or exploit (a source, fund, etc.). **2.** (*intr., adv.*) to come near. **3.** (*tr., prep.*) to withdraw (money) from (an account). **4.** (*tr., adv.*) to put on (clothes). **5.** (*tr., adv.*) to lead further; entice.

draw out *vb.* (*adv.*) **1.** to extend. **2.** (*tr.*) to cause (a person) to talk freely. **3.** (*tr.; foll. by of*) Also: **draw from.** to elicit (information) (from). **4.** (*tr.*) to withdraw (money) as from a bank account. **5.** (*intr.*) (of hours of daylight) to become longer. **6.** (*intr.*) (of a train) to leave a station. **7.** (*tr.*) to extend (troops) in line. **8.** (*intr.*) (of troops) to proceed from camp.

drawstring ('drɔː,strɪŋ) *n.* a cord, etc., run through a hem around an opening, so that when it is pulled tighter, the opening closes.

draw up *vb.* (*adv.*) **1.** to come or cause to come to a halt. **2.** (*tr.*) **a.** to prepare a draft of (a document, etc.). **b.** to formulate and write out: *to draw up a contract.* **3.** (*used reflexively*) to straighten oneself. **4.** to form or arrange (a body of soldiers, etc.) in order or formation.

dray[1] (dreɪ) *n.* **a.** a low cart used for carrying heavy loads. **b.** (*in combination*): *a drayman.* [OE *drǣge* dragnet]

dray[2] (dreɪ) *n.* a variant spelling of **drey.**

Drayton ('dreɪt³n) *n.* **Michael.** 1563–1631, English poet. His work includes odes and pastorals, and *Poly-Olbion* (1613–22), on the topography of England.

dread (drɛd) *vb.* (*tr.*) **1.** to anticipate with apprehension or terror. **2.** to fear greatly. **3.** *Arch.* to be in awe of. ~*n.* **4.** great fear. **5.** an object of terror. **6.** *Sl.* a Rastafarian. **7.** *Arch.* deep reverence. [OE *ondrǣdan*]

dreadful ('drɛdfʊl) *adj.* **1.** extremely disagreeable, shocking, or bad. **2.** (intensifier): *a dreadful waste of time.* **3.** causing dread; terrifying. **4.** *Arch.* inspiring awe.

dreadfully ('drɛdfʊlɪ) *adv.* **1.** in a shocking or disagreeable manner. **2.** (intensifier): *you're dreadfully kind.*

dreadlocks ('drɛd,lɒks) *pl. n. Inf.* hair worn in the Rastafarian style of long tightly-curled strands.

dreadnought ('drɛd,nɔːt) *n.* **1.** a battleship armed with heavy guns of uniform calibre. **2.** an overcoat made of heavy cloth.

dream (driːm) *n.* **1. a.** mental activity, usually an imagined series of events, occurring during sleep. **b.** (*as modifier*): *a dream sequence.* **c.** (*in combination*): *dreamland.* **2. a.** a sequence of imaginative thoughts indulged in while awake; daydream; fantasy. **b.** (*as modifier*): *a dream world.* **3.** a person or thing seen or occurring in a dream. **4.** a cherished hope; aspiration. **5.** a vain hope. **6.** a person or thing that is as pleasant or seemingly unreal as a dream. **7. go like a dream.** to move, develop, or work very well. ~*vb.* **dreaming, dreamt** *or* **dreamed.** **8.** (*may take a clause as object*) to undergo or experience (a dream or dreams). **9.** (*intr.*) to indulge in daydreams. **10.** (*intr.*) to suffer delusions; be unrealistic. **11.** (when *intr.,* foll. by *of* or *about*) to have an image (of) or fantasy (about) in or as if in a dream. **12.** (*intr.; foll. by of*) to consider the possibility (of). ~*adj.* **13.** too good to be true; ideal: *dream kitchen.* [OE *drēam* song] —'**dreamer** *n.*

dreamboat ('driːm,bəʊt) *n. Sl.* an ideal or desirable person, esp. one of the opposite sex.

dreamt (drɛmt) *vb.* a past tense and past participle of **dream.**

dream time *n.* **1.** another name for **alcheringa.** **2.** *Austral. inf.* any remote period, out of touch with the realities of the present.

dream up *vb.* (*tr., adv.*) to invent by ingenuity and imagination: *to dream up an excuse.*

dreamy ('driːmɪ) *adj.* **dreamier, dreamiest.** **1.** vague or impractical. **2.** resembling a dream. **3.** relaxing; gentle: *dreamy music.* **4.** *Inf.* wonderful. **5.** having dreams, esp. daydreams. —'**dreamily** *adv.* —'**dreaminess** *n.*

dreary ('drɪərɪ) *adj.* **drearier, dreariest.** **1.** sad or dull; dismal. **2.** wearying; boring. ~Also (literary): **drear.** [OE *drēorig* gory] —'**drearily** *adv.* —'**dreariness** *n.*

dredge[1] (drɛdʒ) *n.* **1.** a machine used to scoop or suck up material from a riverbed, channel, etc. **2.** another name for **dredger.** ~*vb.* **3.** to remove (material) from a riverbed, etc., by means of a dredge. **4.** (*tr.*) to search for (a submerged object) with or as if with a dredge; drag. [C16: ? ult. from OE *dragan* to DRAW]

dredge[2] (drɛdʒ) *vb.* to sprinkle or coat (food) with flour, etc. [C16: from OF *dragie,* ?from L *tragēmata* spices, from Gk] —'**dredging** *n.*

dredger ('drɛdʒə) *n.* **1.** a vessel used for dredging. **2.** another name for **dredge**[1].

dredge up *vb.* (*tr., adv.*) **1.** *Inf.* to bring to notice, esp. with effort and from an obscure source. **2.** to raise, as with a dredge.

dree (driː) *Scot., literary.* ~*vb.* **dreeing, dreed.** **1.** (*tr.*) to endure. ~*adj.* **2.** dreary. [OE *drēogan*]

D region *or* **layer** *n.* the lowest region of the ionosphere, extending from a height of about 60 kilometres to about 90 kilometres.

dregs (drɛgz) *pl. n.* **1.** solid particles that settle at the bottom of some liquids. **2.** residue or remains. **3.** *Brit. sl.* a despicable person. [C14 *dreg,* from ON *dregg*]

dreich *or* **dreigh** (driːx) *adj. Scot. dialect.* dreary. [ME *dreig, drih* enduring, from OE *drēog* (unattested)]

Dreiser ('draɪsə, -zə) *n.* **Theodore (Herman Albert).** 1871–1945, U.S. novelist; his works include *Sister Carrie* (1900) and *An American Tragedy* (1925).

drench (drɛntʃ) *vb.* (*tr.*) **1.** to make completely wet; soak. **2.** to give liquid medicine to (an animal). ~*n.* **3.** a drenching. **4.** a dose of liquid medicine given to an animal. [OE *drencan* to cause to drink] —'**drenching** *n., adj.*

Drenthe (*Dutch* 'drɛntə) *n*. a province of the NE Netherlands: a low plateau, with many raised bogs, partially reclaimed; agricultural, with oil deposits. Capital: Assen. Pop.: 427 336 (1984 est.). Area: 2647 sq. km (1032 sq. miles).

Dresden ('drɛzdⁿn) *n*. **1.** an industrial city in SE East Germany, on the River Elbe: capital of Saxony from the 16th century until 1952; it was severely damaged in the Seven Years' War (1760); the baroque city was almost totally destroyed in World War II by Allied bombing (1945). Pop.: 519 737 (1986). ~*adj*. **2.** relating to, designating, or made of Dresden china.

Dresden china *n*. porcelain ware, esp. delicate and elegantly decorative objects and figures of high quality, made at Meissen, near Dresden, since 1710.

dress (drɛs) *vb*. **1.** to put clothes on; attire. **2.** (*intr*.) to put on more formal attire. **3.** (*tr*.) to provide (someone) with clothing; clothe. **4.** (*tr*.) to arrange merchandise in (a shop window). **5.** (*tr*.) to arrange (the hair). **6.** (*tr*.) to apply protective or therapeutic covering to (a wound, sore, etc.). **7.** (*tr*.) to prepare (food, esp. fowl and fish) by cleaning, gutting, etc. **8.** (*tr*.) to put a finish on (stone, metal, etc.). **9.** (*tr*.) to cultivate (land), esp. by applying fertilizer. **10.** (*tr*.) to trim (trees, etc.). **11.** (*tr*.) to groom (a horse). **12.** (*tr*.) to convert (tanned hides) into leather. **13.** *Mil*. to bring (troops) into line or (of troops) to come into line (esp. in **dress ranks**). **14. dress ship.** *Naut*. to decorate a vessel by displaying signal flags on lines. ~*n*. **15.** a one-piece garment for a woman, consisting of a skirt and bodice. **16.** complete style of clothing; costume: *military dress*. **17.** (*modifier*) suitable for a formal occasion: *a dress shirt*. **18.** outer covering or appearance. ~See also **dress down, dress up**. [C14: from OF *drecier*, ult. from L *dīrigere* to DIRECT]

dressage ('drɛsɑːʒ) *n*. **a.** the training of a horse to perform manoeuvres in response to the rider's body signals. **b.** the manoeuvres performed. [F: preparation, from OF *dresser* to prepare; see DRESS]

dress circle *n*. a tier of seats in a theatre or other auditorium, usually the first gallery.

dress down *vb*. (*tr., adv.*) *Inf*. to reprimand severely or scold (a person).

dresser¹ ('drɛsə) *n*. **1.** a set of shelves, usually also with cupboards, for storing or displaying dishes, etc. **2.** *U.S.* a chest of drawers for storing clothing, often having a mirror on top. [C14 *dressour*, from OF *dreceore*, from *drecier* to arrange; see DRESS]

dresser² ('drɛsə) *n*. **1.** a person who dresses in a specified way: *a fashionable dresser*. **2.** *Theatre*. a person employed to assist actors with their costumes. **3.** a tool used for dressing stone, etc. **4.** *Brit*. a person who assists a surgeon during operations. **5.** *Brit*. See **windowdresser**.

dressing ('drɛsɪŋ) *n*. **1.** a sauce for food, esp. for salad. **2.** the U.S. and Canad. name for **stuffing** (sense 2). **3.** a covering for a wound, etc. **4.** fertilizer spread on land. **5.** size used for stiffening textiles. **6.** the processes in the conversion of hides into leather.

dressing-down *n*. *Inf*. a severe scolding.

dressing gown *n*. a full robe worn before dressing or for lounging.

dressing room *n*. **1.** *Theatre*. a room backstage for an actor to change clothing and to make up. **2.** any room used for changing clothes.

dressing station *n*. *Mil*. a first-aid post close to a combat area.

dressing table *n*. a piece of bedroom furniture with a mirror and a set of drawers for clothes, cosmetics, etc.

dressmaker ('drɛsˌmeɪkə) *n*. a person whose occupation is making clothes, esp. for women. — **'dressˌmaking** *n*.

dress parade *n*. *Mil*. a formal parade in dress uniform.

dress rehearsal *n*. **1.** the last rehearsal of a play, etc., using costumes, lighting, etc., as for the first night. **2.** any full-scale practice.

dress shirt *n*. a man's evening shirt, worn as part of formal evening dress.

dress suit *n*. a man's evening suit, esp. tails.

dress uniform *n*. *Mil*. formal ceremonial uniform.

dress up *vb*. (*adv.*) **1.** to attire (oneself or another) in one's best clothes. **2.** to put fancy dress, etc., on. **3.** (*tr.*) to improve the appearance or impression of: *to dress up the facts*.

dressy ('drɛsɪ) *adj*. **dressier, dressiest.** **1.** (of clothes) elegant. **2.** (of persons) dressing stylishly. **3.** overelegant. — **'dressiness** *n*.

drew (druː) *vb*. the past tense of **draw**.

drey *or* **dray** (dreɪ) *n*. a squirrel's nest. [C17: from ?]

Dreyfus ('dreɪfəs; *French* drɛfys) *n*. **Alfred** (alfrɛd). 1859 – 1935, French army officer, a Jew whose false imprisonment for treason (1894) raised issues of anti-semitism and militarism that dominated French politics until his release (1906).

dribble ('drɪbⁿl) *vb*. **1.** (*usually intr.*) to flow or allow to flow in a thin stream or drops; trickle. **2.** (*intr.*) to allow saliva to trickle from the mouth. **3.** (in soccer, basketball, hockey, etc.) to propel (the ball) by repeatedly tapping it with the hand, foot, or a stick. ~*n*. **4.** a small quantity of liquid falling in drops or flowing in a thin stream. **5.** a small quantity or supply. **6.** an act or instance of dribbling. [C16: frequentative of *drib*, var. of DRIP] — **'dribbler** *n*. — **'dribbly** *adj*.

driblet *or* **dribblet** ('drɪblɪt) *n*. a small amount. [C17: from obs. *drib* to fall bit by bit + -LET]

dribs and drabs (drɪbz) *pl. n*. *Inf*. small sporadic amounts.

dried (draɪd) *vb*. the past tense and past participle of **dry**.

drier¹ ('draɪə) *adj*. a comparative of **dry**.

drier² ('draɪə) *n*. a variant spelling of **dryer**¹.

driest ('draɪɪst) *adj*. a superlative of **dry**.

drift (drɪft) *vb*. (*mainly intr.*) **1.** (*also tr.*) to be carried along as by currents of air or water or (of a current) to carry (a vessel, etc.) along. **2.** to move aimlessly from one place or activity to another. **3.** to wander away from a fixed course or point; stray. **4.** (*also tr.*) (of snow, etc.) to accumulate in heaps or to drive (snow, etc.) into heaps. ~*n*. **5.** something piled up by the wind or current, as a snowdrift. **6.** tendency or meaning: *the drift of the argument*. **7.** a state of indecision or inaction. **8.** the extent to which a vessel, aircraft, etc., is driven off course by winds, etc. **9.** a general tendency of surface ocean water to flow in the direction of the prevailing winds. **10.** a driving movement, force, or influence; impulse. **11.** a controlled four-wheel skid used to take bends at high speed. **12.** a deposit of sand, gravel, etc., esp. one transported and deposited by a glacier. **13.** a horizontal passage in a mine that follows the mineral vein. **14.** something, esp. a group of animals, driven along. **15.** a steel tool driven into holes to enlarge or align them. **16.** an uncontrolled slow change in some operating characteristic of a piece of equipment. **17.** *S. African*. a ford. [C13: from ON: snowdrift]

driftage ('drɪftɪdʒ) *n*. **1.** the act of drifting. **2.** matter carried along by drifting. **3.** the amount by which an aircraft or vessel has drifted.

drifter ('drɪftə) *n*. **1.** a person or thing that drifts. **2.** a person who moves aimlessly from place to place. **3.** a boat used for drift-net fishing.

drift ice *n*. masses of ice floating in the sea.

drift net *n*. a large fishing net that is allowed to drift with the tide or current.

driftwood ('drɪftˌwʊd) *n*. wood floating on or washed ashore by the sea or other body of water.

drill¹ (drɪl) *n*. **1.** a machine or tool for boring holes. **2.** *Mil*. **a.** training in procedures or movements, as for parades or the use of weapons. **b.** (*as modifier*): *drill hall*. **3.** strict and often repetitious training or exercises used in teaching. **4.** *Inf*. correct procedure. **5.** a marine mollusc that preys on oysters. ~*vb*. **6.** to pierce, bore, or cut (a hole) in (material) with or as if with a drill. **7.** to instruct or be instructed in military procedures or movements. **8.** (*tr.*) to teach by rigorous exercises or training. **9.** (*tr.*) *Inf*. to riddle with bullets. [C17: from MDu. *drillen*] — **'driller** *n*.

drill² (drɪl) *n*. **1.** a machine for planting seeds in rows. **2.** a furrow in which seeds are sown. **3.** a row of seeds planted by means of a drill. ~*vb*. **4.** to plant (seeds) by means of a drill. [C18: from ?; cf. G *Rille* furrow] — **'driller** *n*.

drill³ (drɪl) *n*. a hard-wearing twill-weave cotton cloth, used for uniforms, etc. [C18: var. of G *Drillich*, from L *trilix*, from TRI- + *licium* thread]

drill⁴ (drɪl) *n*. an Old World monkey of W Africa, related to the mandrill. [C17: from a West African word]

drilling fluid *n.* a fluid, usually consisting of a suspension of clay in water, pumped down when an oil well is being drilled. Also called: **mud**.

drilling platform *n.* a structure, either fixed to the sea bed or mobile, which supports the machinery and equipment (**drilling rig**), together with the stores, etc., required for drilling an offshore oil well.

drilling rig *n.* **1.** the complete machinery, equipment, and structures needed to drill an oil well. **2.** a mobile drilling platform used for exploratory offshore drilling.

drillmaster ('drɪl,mɑːstə) *n.* **1.** Also called: **drill sergeant.** a military drill instructor. **2.** a person who instructs in a strict manner.

drill press *n.* a machine tool for boring holes.

drily ('draɪlɪ) *adv.* a variant spelling of **dryly**.

Drin (drɪn) *n.* a river in S Europe, rising on the border between Albania and Yugoslavia and flowing north and west into the Adriatic Sea. Length: about 270 km (170 miles).

drink (drɪŋk) *vb.* **drinking, drank, drunk. 1.** to swallow (a liquid). **2.** (*tr.*) to soak up (liquid); absorb. **3.** (*tr.; usually foll. by *in*) to pay close attention to. **4.** (*tr.*) to bring (oneself) into a certain condition by consuming alcohol. **5.** (*tr.; often foll. by *away*) to dispose of or ruin by excessive expenditure on alcohol. **6.** (*intr.*) to consume alcohol, esp. to excess. **7.** (when *intr.*, foll. by *to*) to drink (a toast). **8. drink the health of.** to salute or celebrate with a toast. **9. drink with the flies.** *Austral. inf.* to drink alone. ~*n.* **10.** liquid suitable for drinking. **11.** alcohol or its habitual or excessive consumption. **12.** a portion of liquid for drinking; draught. **13. the drink.** *Inf.* the sea. [OE *drincan*] —**'drinkable** *adj.* —**'drinker** *n.*

drink-driving *n.* (*modifier*) of or relating to driving a car after drinking alcohol: *drink-driving offences; drink-driving campaign.*

drinking fountain *n.* a device for providing a flow or jet of drinking water, esp. in public places.

drinking-up time *n.* (in Britain) a short time allowed for finishing drinks before closing time in a public house.

drinking water *n.* water reserved or suitable for drinking.

Drinkwater ('drɪŋk,wɔːtə) *n.* **John.** 1882–1937, English dramatist, poet, and critic; author of chronicle plays such as *Abraham Lincoln* (1918) and *Mary Stuart* (1921).

drip (drɪp) *vb.* **dripping, dripped. 1.** to fall or let fall in drops. ~*n.* **2.** the formation and falling of drops of liquid. **3.** the sound made by falling drops. **4.** a projection at the edge of a sill or cornice designed to throw water clear of the wall. **5.** *Inf.* an inane, insipid person. **6.** *Med.* the usually intravenous drop-by-drop administration of a solution. [OE *dryppan*, from *dropa* DROP]

drip-dry *adj.* **1.** designating clothing or a fabric that will dry relatively free of creases if hung up when wet. ~*vb.* -**drying, -dried. 2.** to dry or become dry thus.

drip feed *vb.* (*tr.*) **1.** to feed someone a liquid drop by drop, esp. intravenously. ~*n.* **drip-feed. 2.** another term for **drip** (sense 6).

dripping ('drɪpɪŋ) *n.* **1.** the fat that exudes from meat while it is being roasted or fried. **2.** (*often pl.*) liquid that falls in drops. ~*adv.* **3.** (intensifier): *dripping wet.*

drippy ('drɪpɪ) *adj.* -**pier, -piest. 1.** *Inf.* mawkish, insipid, or inane. **2.** tending to drip.

drive (draɪv) *vb.* **driving, drove, driven. 1.** to push, propel, or be pushed or propelled. **2.** to guide the movement of (a vehicle, animal, etc.). **3.** (*tr.*) to compel or urge to work or act, esp. excessively. **4.** (*tr.*) to goad into a specified attitude or state: *work drove him to despair.* **5.** (*tr.*) to cause (an object) to make (a hole, crack, etc.). **6.** to move rapidly by striking or throwing with force. **7.** *Sport.* to hit (a ball) very hard and straight. **8.** *Golf.* to strike (the ball) with a driver. **9.** (*tr.*) to chase (game) from cover. **10.** to transport or be transported in a vehicle. **11.** (*intr.*) to rush or dash violently, esp. against an obstacle. **12.** (*tr.*) to transact with vigour (esp. in **drive a hard bargain**). **13.** (*tr.*) to force (a component) into or out of its location by means of blows or a press. **14.** (*tr.*) *Mining.* to excavate horizontally. **15. drive home. a.** to cause to penetrate to the fullest extent. **b.** to make clear by special emphasis. ~*n.* **16.** the act of driving. **17.** a journey in a driven vehicle. **18.** a road for vehicles, esp. a private road leading to a house. **19.** vigorous pressure, as in business. **20.** a united effort, esp. towards a common goal. **21.** *Brit.* a large gathering of persons to play cards, etc. **22.** energy, ambition, or initiative. **23.** *Psychol.* a motive or interest, such as sex, hunger, or ambition. **24.** a

sustained and powerful military offensive. **25. a.** the means by which force, motion, etc., is transmitted in a mechanism: *fluid drive.* **b.** (*as modifier*): *a drive shaft.* **26.** *Sport.* a hard straight shot or stroke. **27.** a search for and chasing of game towards waiting guns. [OE *drīfan*] —**'drivable** *or* **'driveable** *adj.*

drive at *vb.* (*intr.*, *prep.*) *Inf.* to intend or mean: *what are you driving at?*

drive-in *adj.* **1.** denoting a public facility or service designed to be used by patrons seated in their cars: *a drive-in bank.* ~*n.* **2.** *Chiefly U.S. & Canad.* a cinema designed to be used in such a manner.

drivel ('drɪvəl) *vb.* -**elling, -elled** *or U.S.* -**eling, -eled. 1.** to allow (saliva) to flow from the mouth; dribble. **2.** (*intr.*) to speak foolishly. ~*n.* **3.** foolish or senseless talk. **4.** saliva flowing from the mouth; slaver. [OE *dreflian* to slaver] —**'driveller** *n.*

driven ('drɪvən) *vb.* the past participle of **drive**.

driver ('draɪvə) *n.* **1.** a person who drives a vehicle. **2. in the driver' seat.** in a position of control. **3.** a person who drives animals. **4.** a mechanical component that exerts a force on another to produce motion. **5.** *Golf.* a club, a No. 1 wood, used for tee shots. **6.** *Electronics.* a circuit whose output provides the input of another circuit. —**'driverless** *adj.*

driveway ('draɪv,weɪ) *n.* a path for vehicles, often connecting a house with a public road.

driving licence *n.* an official document authorizing a person to drive a motor vehicle.

drizzle ('drɪzəl) *n.* **1.** very light rain. ~*vb.* **2.** (*intr.*) to rain lightly. [OE *drēosan* to fall] —**'drizzly** *adj.*

Drobny ('drɔbnɪ; *Czech* 'drɔbniː) *n.* **Jaroslav** ('jærəʊˌslɑːv; *Czech* 'jarɔslaf). born 1921, British tennis and ice-hockey player, born in Czechoslovakia: Wimbledon champion 1954: a member of the Czech ice-hockey team in the 1948 Olympic Games.

Drogheda ('drɔɪɪdə) *n.* a port in NE Ireland, in Co. Louth near the mouth of the River Boyne: captured by Cromwell in 1649 and its inhabitants massacred. Pop.: 23 247 (1981).

drogue (drəʊg) *n.* **1.** any funnel-like device used as a sea anchor. **2. a.** a small parachute released behind an aircraft to reduce its landing speed. **b.** a small parachute released during the landing of a spacecraft. **3.** a device towed behind an aircraft as a target for firing practice. **4.** a device on the end of the hose of a tanker aircraft, to assist location of the probe of the receiving aircraft. **5.** a windsock. [C18: prob. based ult. on OE *dragan* to DRAW]

droll (drəʊl) *adj.* amusing in a quaint or odd manner; comical. [C17: from F *drôle* scamp, from MDu.: imp] —**'drollness** *n.* —**'drolly** *adv.*

drollery ('drəʊlərɪ) *n.*, *pl.* -**eries. 1.** humour; comedy. **2.** *Rare.* a droll act, story, or remark.

Drôme (*French* drom) *n.* a department of SE France, in Rhône-Alpes region. Capital: Valence. Pop.: 389 781 (1982). Area: 6561 sq. km (2559 sq. miles).

-drome *n. combining form.* **1.** a course or race-course: *hippodrome.* **2.** a large place for a special purpose: *aerodrome.* [via L from Gk *dromos* race, course]

dromedary ('drʌmədərɪ) *n.*, *pl.* -**daries.** a type of Arabian camel bred for racing and riding, having a single hump. [C14: from LL *dromedārius* (*camēlus*), from Gk *dromas* running]

-dromous *adj. combining form.* moving or running: *anadromous; catadromous.* [via NL from Gk *-dromos*, from *dromos* a running]

drone[1] (drəʊn) *n.* **1.** a male honeybee whose sole function is to mate with the queen. **2.** a person who lives off the work of others. **3.** a pilotless radio-controlled aircraft. [OE *drān*; see DRONE[2]]

drone[2] (drəʊn) *vb.* **1.** (*intr.*) to make a monotonous low dull sound. **2.** (when *intr.*, often foll. by *on*) to utter (words) in a monotonous tone, esp. to talk without stopping. ~*n.* **3.** a monotonous low dull sound. **4.** *Music.* a sustained bass note or chord. **5.** one of the single-reed pipes in a set of bagpipes. **6.** a person who speaks in a low monotonous tone. [C16: rel. to DRONE[1] & MDu. *drōnen*, G *dröhnen*] —**'droning** *adj.*

drongo ('drɒŋgəʊ) *n.*, *pl.* -**gos. 1.** any of various songbirds of the Old World tropics, having a glossy black plumage. **2.** *Austral. & N.Z. sl.* a slow-witted person. [C19: from Malagasy]

drool (druːl) *vb.* **1.** (*intr.; often foll. by *over*) to show excessive enthusiasm (for) or pleasure (in); gloat (over).

~*vb.*, *n.* **2.** another word for **drivel** (senses 1, 2, 4). [C19: prob. alteration of DRIVEL]

droop (dru:p) *vb.* **1.** to sag or allow to sag, as from weakness. **2.** (*intr.*) to be overcome by weariness. **3.** (*intr.*) to lose courage. ~*n.* **4.** the act or state of drooping. [C13: from ON *drúpa*] —'**drooping** *adj.* —'**droopy** *adj.*

drop (drɒp) *n.* **1.** a small quantity of liquid that forms or falls in a spherical mass. **2.** a very small quantity of liquid. **3.** a very small quantity of anything. **4.** something resembling a drop in shape or size.: **5.** the act or an instance of falling; descent. **6.** a decrease in amount or value. **7.** the vertical distance that anything may fall. **8.** a steep incline or slope. **9.** the act of unloading troops, etc., by parachute. **10.** *Theatre.* See **drop curtain. 11.** another word for **trap door** or **gallows. 12.** *Chiefly U.S. & Canad.* a slot through which an object can be dropped into a receptacle. **13.** *Austral. cricket sl.* a fall of the wicket. **14.** See **drop shot. 15. at the drop of a hat.** without hesitation or delay. **16. have the drop on (someone).** *U.S. & N.Z.* to have the advantage over (someone). ~*vb.* **dropping, dropped. 17.** (of liquids) to fall or allow to fall in globules. **18.** to fall or allow to fall vertically. **19.** (*tr.*) to allow to fall by letting go of. **20.** to sink or fall or cause to sink to the ground, as from a blow, weariness, etc. **21.** (*intr.*; foll. by *back, behind,* etc.) to move in a specified manner, direction, etc. **22.** (*intr.*; foll. by *in, by,* etc.) *Inf.* to pay a casual visit (to). **23.** to decrease in amount or value. **24.** to sink or cause to sink to a lower position. **25.** to make or become less in strength, volume, etc. **26.** (*intr.*) to decline in health or condition. **27.** (*intr.*; sometimes foll. by *into*) to pass easily into a condition: *to drop into a habit.* **28.** (*intr.*) to move gently as with a current of air. **29.** (*tr.*) to mention casually: *to drop a hint.* **30.** (*tr.*) to leave out (a word or letter). **31.** (*tr.*) to set down (passengers or goods). **32.** (*tr.*) to send or post: *drop me a line.* **33.** (*tr.*) to discontinue: *let's drop the matter.* **34.** (*tr.*) to cease to associate with. **35.** (*tr.*) *Sl., chiefly U.S.* to cease to employ. **36.** (*tr.*; sometimes foll. by *in, off,* etc.) *Inf.* to leave or deposit. **37.** (of animals) to give birth to (offspring). **38.** *Sl., chiefly U.S. & Canad.* to lose (money). **39.** (*tr.*) to lengthen (a hem, etc.). **40.** (*tr.*) to unload (troops, etc.) by parachute. **41.** (*tr.*) *Naut.* to sail out of sight of. **42.** (*tr.*) *Sport.* to omit (a player) from a team. **43.** (*tr.*) to lose (a game, etc.). **44.** (*tr.*) *Golf, basketball, etc.* to hit or throw (a ball) into a goal. **45.** (*tr.*) to hit (a ball) with a drop shot. ~*n., vb.* **46.** *Rugby.* short for **drop kick** or **drop-kick.** ~See also **drop off, dropout, drops.** [OE *dropian*]

drop curtain *n. Theatre.* a curtain that can be raised and lowered onto the stage.

drop forge *n.* a device for forging metal between two dies, one of which is fixed, the other acting by gravity or by pressure. —'**drop-forge** *vb.* (*tr.*)

drop goal *n. Rugby.* a goal scored with a drop kick during the run of play.

drop hammer *n.* another name for **drop forge.**

drop-in *n.* (*modifier*) denoting a social service or meeting place provided where people may attend if and when they please.

drop kick *n.* **1.** a kick in which the ball is dropped and kicked as it bounces from the ground. **2.** a wrestling attack in which a wrestler leaps in the air and kicks his opponent. ~*vb.* **drop-kick. 3.** to kick (a ball, a wrestling opponent, etc.) by the use of a drop kick.

drop leaf *n.* **a.** a hinged flap on a table that can be raised to extend the surface. **b.** (*as modifier*): *a drop-leaf table.*

droplet ('drɒplɪt) *n.* a tiny drop.

drop off *vb.* (*adv.*) **1.** (*intr.*) to grow smaller or less. **2.** (*tr.*) to set down. **3.** (*intr.*) *Inf.* to fall asleep. ~*n.* **dropoff. 4.** a steep descent. **5.** a sharp decrease.

dropout ('drɒp,aut) *n.* **1.** a student who fails to complete a course. **2.** a person who rejects conventional society. **3.** *Rugby.* a drop kick taken to restart play. ~*vb.* **drop out.** (*intr., adv.*; often foll. by *of*) **4.** to abandon or withdraw from (a school, job, etc.).

dropper ('drɒpə) *n.* **1.** a small tube having a rubber bulb at one end for dispensing drops of liquid. **2.** a person or thing that drops.

droppings ('drɒpɪŋz) *pl. n.* the dung of certain animals, such as rabbits, sheep, and birds.

drops (drɒps) *pl. n.* any liquid medication applied by means of a dropper.

drop scone *n.* a flat spongy cake made by dropping a spoonful of batter on a hot griddle.

drop shot *n. Tennis, etc.* a softly played return that drops abruptly after clearing the net.

dropsy ('drɒpsɪ) *n.* **1.** *Pathol.* a condition characterized by an accumulation of watery fluid in the tissues or in a body cavity. **2.** *Sl.* a tip or bribe. [C13: from *ydropesie,* from L *hydrōpisis,* from Gk *hudrōps,* from *hudōr* water] —**dropsical** ('drɒpsɪkᵊl) *adj.*

droshky ('drɒʃkɪ) *or* **drosky** ('drɒskɪ) *n., pl.* **-kies.** an open four-wheeled carriage, formerly used in Russia. [C19: from Russian, dim. of *drogi* wagon]

drosophila (drɒ'sɒfɪlə) *n., pl.* **-las** *or* **-lae** (-ˌliː). any of a genus of small flies that are widely used in laboratory genetics studies. Also called: **fruit fly.** [C19: NL, from Gk *drosos* dew + *-phila* -PHILE]

dross (drɒs) *n.* **1.** the scum formed on the surfaces of molten metals. **2.** worthless matter; waste. [OE *drōs* dregs] —'**drossy** *adj.* —'**drossiness** *n.*

drought (draut) *n.* **1.** a prolonged period of scanty rainfall. **2.** a prolonged shortage. [OE *drūgoth*] —'**droughty** *adj.*

drove[1] (drəuv) *vb.* the past tense of **drive.**

drove[2] (drəuv) *n.* **1.** a herd of livestock being driven together. **2.** (*often pl.*) a moving crowd of people. ~*vb.* (*tr.*) **3.** to drive (livestock), usually for a considerable distance. [OE *drāf* herd]

drover ('drəuvə) *n.* a person who drives sheep or cattle, esp. to and from market.

drown (draun) *vb.* **1.** to die or kill by immersion in liquid. **2.** (*tr.*) to get rid of: *he drowned his sorrows in drink.* **3.** (*tr.*) to drench thoroughly. **4.** (*tr.*; sometimes foll. by *out*) to render (a sound) inaudible by making a loud noise. [C13: prob. from OE *druncnian*]

drowse (drauz) *vb.* **1.** to be or cause to be sleepy, dull, or sluggish. ~*n.* **2.** the state of being drowsy. [C16: prob. from OE *drūsian* to sink]

drowsy ('drauzɪ) *adj.* **drowsier, drowsiest. 1.** heavy with sleepiness; sleepy. **2.** inducing sleep; soporific. **3.** sluggish or lethargic; dull. —'**drowsily** *adv.* —'**drowsiness** *n.*

drub (drʌb) *vb.* **drubbing, drubbed.** (*tr.*) **1.** to beat as with a stick. **2.** to defeat utterly, as in a contest. **3.** to drum or stamp (the feet). **4.** to instil with force or repetition. ~*n.* **5.** a blow, as from a stick. [C17: prob. from Ar. *dáraba* to beat]

drudge (drʌdʒ) *n.* **1.** a person who works hard at wearisome menial tasks. ~*vb.* **2.** (*intr.*) to toil at **such tasks.** [C16: ?from *druggen* to toil] —'**drudger** *n.* —'**drudgingly** *adv.*

drudgery ('drʌdʒərɪ) *n., pl.* **-eries.** hard, menial, and monotonous work.

drug (drʌg) *n.* **1.** any substance used in the treatment, prevention, or diagnosis of disease. Related adj.: **pharmaceutical. 2.** a chemical substance, esp. a narcotic, taken for the effects it produces. **3. drug on the market.** a commodity available in excess of demand. ~*vb.* **drugging, drugged.** (*tr.*) **4.** to mix a drug with (food, etc.). **5.** to administer a drug to. **6.** to stupefy or poison with or as if with a drug. [C14: from OF *drogue,* prob. of Gmc origin]

drug addict *n.* any person who is abnormally dependent on narcotic drugs.

drugget ('drʌgɪt) *n.* a coarse fabric used as a protective floor covering, etc. [C16: from F *droguet* useless fabric, from *drogue* trash]

druggist ('drʌgɪst) *n.* a U.S. and Canad. term for **pharmacist.**

drugstore ('drʌg,stɔː) *n. U.S. & Canad.* a shop where medical prescriptions are made up and a wide variety of goods and usually light meals are sold.

druid ('dru:ɪd) *n.* (*sometimes cap.*) **1.** a member of an ancient order of priests in Gaul, Britain, and Ireland in the pre-Christian era. **2.** a member of any of several modern movements attempting to revive druidism. [C16: from L *druides* of Gaulish origin] —**druidess** ('dru:ɪdɪs) *fem. n.* —**dru'idic** *or* **dru'idical** *adj.* —'**druid,ism** *n.*

drum (drʌm) *n.* **1.** a percussion instrument sounded by striking a membrane stretched across the opening of a hollow cylinder or hemisphere. **2.** the sound produced by a drum or any similar sound. **3.** an object that resembles a drum in shape, such as a large spool or a cylindrical container. **4.** *Archit.* a cylindrical block of stone used to construct the shaft of a column. **5.** short for **eardrum.**

6. any of various North American fishes that utter a drumming sound. **7.** a type of hollow rotor for steam turbines or axial compressors. **8.** *Arch.* a drummer. **9.** *Austral. sl.* a brothel. **10. beat the drum for.** *Inf.* to attempt to arouse interest in. **11. the drum.** *Austral. inf.* the necessary information (esp. in **give (someone) the drum**). ~*vb.* **drumming, drummed. 12.** to play (music) on or as if on a drum. **13.** to tap rhythmically or regularly. **14.** (*tr.*; sometimes foll. by *up*) to summon or call by drumming. **15.** (*tr.*) to instil by constant repetition. ~See also **drum up.** [C16: prob. from MDu. *tromme*, imit.]

drumbeat ('drʌm,biːt) *n.* the sound made by beating a drum.

drum brake *n.* a type of brake used on the wheels of vehicles, consisting of two shoes that rub against the brake drum when the brake is applied.

drumfish ('drʌm,fɪʃ) *n.*, *pl.* **-fish** or **-fishes.** another name for **drum** (sense 6).

drumhead ('drʌm,hɛd) *n.* **1.** the part of a drum that is actually struck. **2.** the head of a capstan. **3.** another name for **eardrum.**

drumlin ('drʌmlɪn) *n.* a streamlined mound of glacial drift. [C19: from Irish Gaelic *druim* ridge + *-lin* -LING[1]]

drum machine *n.* a synthesizer specially programmed to reproduce the sound of drums and other percussion instruments in variable rhythms and combinations selected by the musician; the resulting beat is produced continually until stopped or changed.

drum major *n.* the noncommissioned officer, usually of warrant officer's rank, who commands the corps of drums of a military band and who is in command of both the drums and the band when paraded together.

drum majorette *n.* a girl who marches at the head of a procession, twirling a baton.

drummer ('drʌmə) *n.* **1.** a drum player. **2.** *Chiefly U.S.* a travelling salesman.

drumstick ('drʌm,stɪk) *n.* **1.** a stick used for playing a drum. **2.** the lower joint of the leg of a cooked fowl.

drum up *vb.* (*tr.*, *adv.*) to obtain (support, business, etc.) by solicitation or canvassing.

drunk (drʌŋk) *adj.* **1.** intoxicated with alcohol to the extent of losing control over normal functions. **2.** overwhelmed by strong influence or emotion. ~*n.* **3.** a person who is drunk. **4.** *Inf.* a drinking bout.

drunkard ('drʌŋkəd) *n.* a person who is frequently or habitually drunk.

drunken ('drʌŋkən) *adj.* **1.** intoxicated. **2.** habitually drunk. **3.** (*prenominal*) caused by or relating to alcoholic intoxication: *a drunken brawl.* —**'drunkenly** *adv.* —**'drunkenness** *n.*

drupe (druːp) *n.* any fruit that has a fleshy or fibrous part around a stone that encloses a seed, as the peach, plum, and cherry. [C18: from L *druppa* wrinkled overripe olive, from Gk: olive] —**drupaceous** (druːˈpeɪʃəs) *adj.*

drupelet ('druːplɪt) or **drupel** ('druːpᵊl) *n.* a small drupe, usually one of a number forming a compound fruit.

Drury Lane ('drʊərɪ) *n.* a street in the West End of London, formerly famous for its theatres.

dry (draɪ) *adj.* **drier, driest** or **dryer, dryest. 1.** lacking moisture; not damp or wet. **2.** having little or no rainfall. **3.** not in or under water. **4.** having the water drained away or evaporated: *a dry river.* **5.** not providing milk: *a dry cow.* **6.** (of the eyes) free from tears. **7. a.** *Inf.* thirsty. **b.** causing thirst. **8.** eaten without butter, jam, etc.: *dry toast.* **9.** (of wine, etc.) not sweet. **10.** not producing a mucous or watery discharge: *a dry cough.* **11.** consisting of solid as opposed to liquid substances. **12.** without adornment; plain: *dry facts.* **13.** lacking interest: *a dry book.* **14.** lacking warmth: *a dry greeting.* **15.** (of humour) shrewd and keen in an impersonal, sarcastic, or laconic way. **16.** *Inf.* opposed to or prohibiting the sale of alcoholic liquor: *a dry country.* ~*vb.* **drying, dried. 17.** (when *intr.*, often foll. by *off*) to make or become dry. **18.** (*tr.*) to preserve (fruit, etc.) by removing the moisture. ~*n.*, *pl.* **drys** or **dries. 19.** *Brit. inf.* a Conservative politician who is a hardliner. **20. the dry.** (*sometimes cap.*) *Austral. inf.* the dry season. ~See also **dry out, dry up.** [OE *drẏge*] —**'dryness** *n.*

dryad ('draɪəd, -æd) *n.*, *pl.* **-ads** or **-ades** (-ə,diːz). *Greek myth.* a nymph or divinity of the woods. [C14: from L *Dryas*, from Gk *Druas*, from *drus* tree]

dry battery *n.* an electric battery consisting of two or more dry cells.

dry cell *n.* a primary cell in which the electrolyte is in the form of a paste or is treated in some way to prevent it from spilling.

dry-clean *vb.* (*tr.*) to clean (fabrics, etc.) with a solvent other than water. —**dry-'cleaner** *n.* —**dry-'cleaning** *n.*

Dryden ('draɪdᵊn) *n.* **John.** 1631–1700, English poet, dramatist, and critic of the Augustan period, commonly regarded as the chief exponent of heroic tragedy. His major works include the tragedy *All for Love* (1677), the verse satire *Absalom and Achitophel* (1681), and the *Essay of Dramatick Poesie* (1668).

dry dock *n.* a dock that can be pumped dry for work on a ship's bottom.

dryer[1] ('draɪə) *n.* **1.** a person or thing that dries. **2.** an apparatus for removing moisture by forced draught, heating, or centrifuging. **3.** any of certain chemicals added to oils to accelerate their drying when used in paints, etc.

dryer[2] ('draɪə) *adj.* a variant spelling of **drier**[1].

dry farming *n.* a system of growing crops in semiarid regions without irrigation, by reducing evaporation, etc. —**dry farmer** *n.*

dry fly *n. Angling.* **a.** an artificial fly designed to be floated on the surface of the water. **b.** (*as modifier*): *dry-fly fishing.*

dry hole *n.* (in the oil industry) a well which proves unsuccessful.

dry ice *n.* solid carbon dioxide used as a refrigerant. Also called: **carbon dioxide snow.**

drying ('draɪɪŋ) *n.* the processing of timber until it has a moisture content suitable for the purposes for which it is to be used.

dryly or **drily** ('draɪlɪ) *adv.* in a dry manner.

dry measure *n.* a unit or system of units for measuring dry goods, such as fruit, grains, etc.

dry out *vb.* (*adv.*) **1.** to make or become dry. **2.** to undergo or cause to undergo treatment for alcoholism or drug addiction.

dry point *n.* **1.** a technique of intaglio engraving with a hard steel needle, without acid, on a copper plate. **2.** the sharp steel needle used. **3.** the engraving or print produced.

dry riser *n.* a vertical pipe, not containing water, having connections on different floors of a building for a fireman's hose to be attached. A fire tender can be connected at the lowest level to make water rise under pressure within the pipe. Abbrev.: **DR.**

dry rot *n.* **1.** crumbling and drying of timber, bulbs, potatoes, or fruit, caused by certain fungi. **2.** any fungus causing this decay. **3.** moral degeneration or corrupt practices.

dry run *n.* **1.** *Mil.* practice in firing without live ammunition. **2.** *Inf.* a rehearsal.

drysalter ('draɪ,sɔːltə) *n. Obs.* a dealer in dyestuffs and gums, and in dried, tinned, or salted foods and edible oils.

Drysdale ('draɪzdeɪl) *n.* **Sir George Russell.** 1912–81, Australian painter, esp. of landscapes.

dry-stone *adj.* (of a wall) made without mortar.

Dry Tortugas (tɔːˈtuːgəz) *n.* a group of eight coral islands at the entrance to the Gulf of Mexico: part of Florida.

dry up *vb.* (*adv.*) **1.** (*intr.*) to become barren or unproductive; fail. **2.** to dry (dishes, cutlery, etc.) with a tea towel after they have been washed. **3.** (*intr.*) *Inf.* to stop talking or speaking.

DS or **ds** *Music. abbrev. for* dal segno.

DSc *abbrev. for* Doctor of Science.

DSC *Mil. abbrev. for* Distinguished Service Cross.

DSM *Mil. abbrev. for* Distinguished Service Medal.

DSO *Brit. mil. abbrev. for* Distinguished Service Order.

DST *abbrev. for* Daylight Saving Time.

DSW (in New Zealand) *abbrev. for* Department of Social Welfare.

DTI (in Britain) *abbrev. for* Department of Trade and Industry.

DT's *Inf. abbrev. for* delirium tremens.

Du. *abbrev. for* Dutch.

dual ('djuːəl) *adj.* **1.** relating to or denoting two. **2.** twofold; double. **3.** (in the grammar of some languages) denoting a form of a word indicating that exactly two referents are being referred to. **4.** *Maths, logic.* (of a pair of operators) convertible into one another by the distribution of negation over either. ~*n.* **5.** *Grammar.* **a.** the dual number. **b.** a dual form of a word. [C17: from L *duālis* concerning two, from *duo* two] —'**dually** *adv.* —**duality** (djuː'ælɪtɪ) *n.*

dual carriageway *n. Brit.* a road on which traffic travelling in opposite directions is separated by a central strip of turf, etc. U.S. and Canad. name: **divided highway.**

dualism ('djuːə,lɪzəm) *n.* **1.** the state of being twofold or double. **2.** *Philosophy.* the doctrine that reality consists of two basic types of substance, usually taken to be mind and matter or mental and physical entities. **3. a.** the theory that the universe has been ruled from its origins by two conflicting powers, one good and one evil. **b.** the theory that there are two personalities, one human and one divine, in Christ. —'**dualist** *n.* —**dual'istic** *adj.*

dub¹ (dʌb) *vb.* **dubbing, dubbed. 1.** (*tr.*) to invest (a person) with knighthood by tapping on the shoulder with a sword. **2.** (*tr.*) to invest with a title, name, or nickname. **3.** (*tr.*) to dress (leather) by rubbing. **4.** *Angling.* to dress (a fly). [OE *dubbian*]

dub² (dʌb) *vb.* **dubbing, dubbed. 1.** to alter the soundtrack of (a film, etc.). **2.** (*tr.*) to provide (a film) with a new soundtrack, esp. in a different language. **3.** (*tr.*) to provide (a film or tape) with a soundtrack. ~*n.* **4.** the new sounds added. **5.** *Music.* a style of record production associated with reggae, involving exaggeration of instrumental parts, the use of echo, etc. [C20: shortened from DOUBLE]

dub³ (dʌb) *vb.* **dubbing, dubbed.** *Austral. & N.Z. inf.* short for **double-bank.**

Dubai (duː'baɪ) *n.* a sheikdom in the NE United Arab Emirates, consisting principally of the port of Dubai, on the Persian Gulf: oilfields. Pop.: 419 104 (1985).

dubbin ('dʌbɪn) *n. Brit.* a greasy preparation applied to leather to soften it and make it waterproof. [C18: from *dub* to dress leather]

dubbing¹ ('dʌbɪŋ) *n. Films.* **1.** the replacement of a soundtrack, esp. by one in another language. **2.** the combination of several soundtracks. **3.** the addition of a soundtrack to a film, etc.

dubbing² ('dʌbɪŋ) *n.* **1.** *Angling.* fibrous material used for the body of an artificial fly. **2.** a variant of **dubbin.**

Dubček (*Czech* 'duptʃɛk) *n.* **Alexander** ('aleksand²r). born 1921, Czechoslovak statesman. His reforms as first secretary of the Czechoslovak Communist Party (1968–69) prompted the Russian occupation (1968) and his enforced resignation.

dubiety (djuː'baɪɪtɪ) *n., pl.* **-ties. 1.** the state of being doubtful. **2.** a doubtful matter. [C18: from LL *dubietās*, from L *dubius* DUBIOUS]

dub in *or* **up** *vb.* (*adv.*) *Sl.* to contribute to the cost of something: *we'll all dub in a fiver for the trip.*

dubious ('djuːbɪəs) *adj.* **1.** marked by or causing doubt. **2.** uncertain; doubtful. **3.** of doubtful quality; untrustworthy. **4.** not certain in outcome. [C16: from L *dubius* wavering] —'**dubiously** *adv.* —'**dubiousness** *n.*

Dublin ('dʌblɪn) *n.* **1.** the capital of the Republic of Ireland, on **Dublin Bay:** under English rule from 1171 until 1922; commercial and cultural centre; contains one of the world's largest breweries and exports whiskey, stout, and agricultural produce. Pop.: 502 337 (1986). Gaelic name: **Baile Átha Cliath. 2.** a county in E Ireland, in Leinster on the Irish Sea: mountainous in the south but low-lying in the north and centre. County seat: Dublin. Pop.: 1 020 796 (1986). Area: 922 sq. km (356 sq. miles). —'**Dubliner** *n.*

Dublin Bay prawn ('dʌblɪn) *n.* a large prawn usually used in a dish of scampi.

Dubrovnik (dʊ'brɒvnɪk) *n.* a port in S Yugoslavia, in Croatia on the Dalmatian coast: an important commercial centre in the Middle Ages; tourist centre. Pop.: 35 000 (1985). Former Italian name (until 1918): **Ragusa.**

Dubuffet (*French* dybyfɛ) *n.* **Jean** (ʒã). 1901–85, French painter, inspired by graffiti and the untrained art of children and psychotics.

ducal ('djuːk²l) *adj.* of a duke or duchy. [C16: from F, from LL *ducālis* of a leader, from L *dux* leader]

ducat ('dʌkət) *n.* **1.** any of various former European gold or silver coins. **2.** (*often pl.*) money. [C14: from OF, from OIt. *ducato* coin stamped with the doge's image]

Duccio di Buoninsegna (*Italian* 'duttʃo di buonin'seɲɲa) *n.* ?1255–?1318, Italian painter; founder of the Sienese school.

duce ('duːtʃɪ) *n.* leader. [C20: from It., from L *dux*]

Duce (*Italian* 'duːtʃe) *n.* **Il** (il). the title assumed by Mussolini as leader of Fascist Italy (1922–43).

Duchamp (*French* dyʃã) *n.* **Marcel** (marsɛl). 1887–1968, U.S. painter and sculptor, born in France; noted as a leading exponent of Dada. His best-known work is *Nude Descending a Staircase* (1912).

duchess ('dʌtʃɪs) *n.* **1.** the wife or widow of a duke. **2.** a woman who holds the rank of duke in her own right. ~*vb.* **3.** (*tr.*) *Austral. inf.* to overwhelm with flattering attention. [C14: from OF *duchesse*]

duchy ('dʌtʃɪ) *n., pl.* **duchies.** the territory of a duke or duchess; dukedom. [C14: from OF *duche*, from *duc* DUKE]

duck¹ (dʌk) *n., pl.* **ducks** *or* **duck. 1.** any of a family of aquatic birds, esp. those having short legs, webbed feet, and a broad blunt bill. **2.** the flesh of this bird, used as food. **3.** the female of such a bird, as opposed to the male (drake). **4.** Also: **ducks.** *Brit. inf.* dear or darling: used as a term of address. See also **ducky. 5.** *Cricket.* a score of nothing by a batsman. **6. like water off a duck's back.** *Inf.* without effect. [OE *dūce* duck, diver; rel. to DUCK²]

duck² (dʌk) *vb.* **1.** to move (the head or body) quickly downwards or away, esp. to escape observation or evade a blow. **2.** to plunge suddenly under water. **3.** (when *intr.*, often foll. by *out*) *Inf.* to dodge or escape (a person, duty, etc.). **4.** (*intr.*) *Bridge.* to play a low card rather than try to win a trick. ~*n.* **5.** the act or an instance of ducking. [C14: rel. to OHG *tūhhan* to dive, MDu. *dūken*] —'**ducker** *n.*

duck³ (dʌk) *n.* a heavy cotton fabric of plain weave, used for clothing, tents, etc. [C17: from MDu. *doek*]

duck⁴ (dʌk) *n.* an amphibious vehicle used in World War II. [C20: from code name DUKW]

duck-billed platypus *n.* an amphibious egg-laying mammal of E Australia having dense fur, a broad bill and tail, and webbed feet.

duckboard ('dʌk,bɔːd) *n.* a board or boards laid so as to form a path over wet or muddy ground.

ducking stool *n. History.* a chair used for punishing offenders by plunging them into water.

duckling ('dʌklɪŋ) *n.* a young duck.

ducks and drakes *n.* (*functioning as sing.*) **1.** a game in which a flat stone is bounced across the surface of water. **2. make ducks and drakes** of *or* **play (at) ducks and drakes with.** *Inf.* to use recklessly; squander.

duck soup *n. U.S. sl.* something that is easy to do.

duckweed ('dʌk,wiːd) *n.* any of various small stemless aquatic plants that occur floating on still water in temperate regions.

ducky *or* **duckie** ('dʌkɪ) *Inf.* ~*n., pl.* **duckies. 1.** *Brit.* darling or dear: a term of endearment. ~*adj.* **duckier, duckiest. 2.** delightful; fine.

duct (dʌkt) *n.* **1.** a tube, pipe, or canal by means of which a substance, esp. a fluid or gas, is conveyed. **2.** any bodily passage, esp. one conveying secretions or excretions. **3.** a narrow tubular cavity in plants. **4.** a channel or pipe carrying electric wires. **5.** a passage through which air can flow, as in air conditioning. [C17: from L *ductus* a leading (in Med. L: aqueduct), from *dūcere* to lead] —'**ductless** *adj.*

ductile ('dʌktaɪl) *adj.* **1.** (of a metal) able to sustain large deformations without fracture and able to be hammered into sheets or drawn out into wires. **2.** able to be moulded. **3.** easily led or influenced. [C14: from OF, from L *ductilis*, from *dūcere* to lead] —**ductility** (dʌk'tɪlɪtɪ) *n.*

ductless gland *n. Anat.* See **endocrine gland.**

dud (dʌd) *Inf.* ~*n.* **1.** a person or thing that proves ineffectual. **2.** a shell, etc., that fails to explode. **3.** (*pl.*) *Old-fashioned.* clothes or other belongings. ~*adj.* **4.** failing in its purpose or function. [C15 (in the sense: an article of clothing, a thing, used disparagingly): from ?]

dude (djuːd) *n. Inf.* **1.** *Western U.S.* a city dweller, esp. one holidaying on a ranch. **2.** *U.S. & Canad.* a dandy. **3.** *U.S. & Canad.* any person. [C19: from ?] —'**dudish** *adj.* —'**dudishly** *adv.*

dude ranch *n. U.S. & Canad.* a ranch used as a holiday resort.

dudgeon ('dʌdʒən) *n.* anger or resentment (arch., except in **in high dudgeon**). [C16: from ?]

Dudley¹ ('dʌdlɪ) *n.* a town in W central England, in the West Midlands: wrought-iron industry. Pop.: 187 228 (1981).

Dudley[2] ('dʌdlɪ) *n.* **Robert.** See (Earl of) **Leicester.**

due (djuː) *adj.* **1.** (*postpositive*) immediately payable. **2.** (*postpositive*) owed as a debt. **3.** fitting; proper. **4.** (*prenominal*) adequate or sufficient. **5.** (*postpositive*) expected or appointed to be present or arrive. **6. due to.** attributable to or caused by. ~*n.* **7.** something that is owed, required, or due. **8. give (a person) his due.** to give or allow what is deserved or right. ~*adv.* **9.** directly or exactly. [C13: from OF *deu*, from *devoir* to owe, from L *debēre*]

▷ **Usage.** There is considerable controversy over the use of *due* to as a compound preposition equivalent to *because of.* Careful users of English prefer *because of* or *owing to.* There is no dispute about the postpositive adjectival use of *due to* to mean *caused by* (*the error was due to carelessness*), but *owing to* is not ordinarily used in this way.

duel ('djuːəl) *n.* **1.** a formal prearranged combat with deadly weapons between two people in the presence of seconds, usually to settle a quarrel. **2.** a contest or conflict between two persons or parties. ~*vb.* **duelling, duelled** *or U.S.* **dueling, dueled.** (*intr.*) **3.** to fight in a duel. **4.** to contest closely. [C15: from Med. L *duellum,* from L, poetical var. of *bellum* war; associated with L *duo* two] — **'dueller** *or* **'duellist** *n.*

duenna (djuː'ɛnə) *n.* (in Spain and Portugal, etc.) an elderly woman retained by a family to act as governess and chaperon to girls. [C17: from Sp. *dueña,* from L *domina* lady]

due process of law *n.* the administration of justice in accordance with established rules and principles.

Duero ('duero) *n.* the Spanish name for the **Douro.**

dues (djuːz) *pl. n.* (*sometimes sing.*) charges, as for membership of a club or organization; fees.

duet (djuː'ɛt) *n.* **1.** a musical composition for two performers or voices. **2.** a pair of closely connected individuals; duo. [C18: from It. *duetto* a little duet, from *duo* duet, from L: two] — **du'ettist** *n.*

duff[1] (dʌf) *n.* **1.** a thick flour pudding boiled in a cloth bag. **2. up the duff.** *Sl.,* *chiefly Austral.* pregnant. [C19: N English var. of DOUGH]

duff[2] (dʌf) *vb.* (*tr.*) **1.** *Sl.* to give a false appearance to (old or stolen goods); fake. **2.** (foll. by *up*) *Brit. sl.* to beat (a person) severely. **3.** *Austral. sl.* to steal (cattle), altering the brand. **4.** *Golf. inf.* to bungle a shot by hitting the ground behind the ball. ~*adj.* **5.** *Brit. inf.* bad or useless: *a duff engine.* [C19: prob. back formation from DUFFER]

duffel *or* **duffle** ('dʌf[ə]l) *n.* **1.** a heavy woollen cloth. **2.** *Chiefly U.S. & Canad.* equipment or supplies. [C17: after *Duffel,* Belgian town]

duffel coat *n.* a usually knee-length wool coat, usually with a hood and fastened with toggles.

duffer ('dʌfə) *n.* **1.** *Inf.* a dull or incompetent person. **2.** *Sl.* something worthless. **3.** *Austral. sl.* **a.** a mine that proves unproductive. **b.** a person who steals cattle. [C19: from ?]

Dufy (*French* dyfi) *n.* **Raoul** (raul). 1877–1953, French painter and designer whose style is characterized by swift calligraphic draughtsmanship and bright colouring.

dug[1] (dʌg) *vb.* the past tense and past participle of **dig.**

dug[2] (dʌg) *n.* a nipple, teat, udder, or breast. [C16: of Scand. origin]

dugong ('duːgɒŋ) *n.* a whalelike mammal occurring in shallow tropical waters from E Africa to Australia. [C19: from Malay *duyong*]

dugout ('dʌg,aʊt) *n.* **1.** a canoe made by hollowing out a log. **2.** *Mil.* a covered excavation dug to provide shelter. **3.** (at a sports ground) the covered bench where managers, substitutes, etc. sit. **4.** (in the Canadian prairies) a reservoir dug on a farm in which water from rain and snow is collected for use in irrigation, watering livestock, etc.

Du Guesclin (*French* dy geklɛ̃) *n.* **Bertrand** (bɛrtrɑ̃). ?1320–80, French military leader; as constable of France (1370–80), he helped to drive the English from France.

Duhamel (*French* dyamɛl) *n.* **Georges** (ʒɔrʒ). 1884–1966, French novelist, poet, and dramatist; author of *La Chronique des Pasquier* (1933–45).

duiker *or* **duyker** ('daɪkə) *n., pl.* **-kers** *or* **-ker. 1.** *Also:* **duikerbok.** any of various small African antelopes. **2.** *S. African.* any of several cormorants, esp. the long-tailed shag. [C18: via Afrik., from Du. *duiker* diver, from *duiken* to dive]

Duisburg (*German* 'dyːsbʊrk) *n.* an industrial city in NW West Germany, in North Rhine-Westphalia at the confluence of the Rivers Rhine and Ruhr: one of the world's largest and busiest inland ports. Pop.: 516 600 (1986).

Dukas (*French* dykɑs) *n.* **Paul** (pɔl). 1865–1935, French composer best known for the orchestral scherzo *The Sorcerer's Apprentice* (1897).

duke (djuːk) *n.* **1.** a nobleman of high rank: in the British Isles standing above the other grades of the nobility. **2.** the prince or ruler of a small principality or duchy. [C12: from OF *duc,* from L *dux* leader] — **'dukedom** *n.*

dukes (djuːks) *pl. n. Sl.* the fists. [C19: from *Duke of Yorks* rhyming sl. for *forks* (fingers)]

dulcet ('dʌlsɪt) *adj.* (of a sound) soothing or pleasant; sweet. [C14: from L *dulcis* sweet]

dulcimer ('dʌlsɪmə) *n.* **1.** a tuned percussion instrument consisting of a set of strings stretched over a sounding board and struck with hammers. **2.** an instrument used in U.S. folk music, with an elliptical body and usually three strings plucked with a goose quill. [C15: from OF *doulcemer,* from OIt. *dolcimelo,* from *dolce* (from L *dulcis* sweet) + *-melo,* ?from Gk *melos* song]

dull (dʌl) *adj.* **1.** slow to think or understand; stupid. **2.** lacking in interest. **3.** lacking in perception; insensitive. **4.** lacking sharpness. **5.** not acute, intense, or piercing. **6.** (of weather) not bright or clear. **7.** not active, busy, or brisk. **8.** lacking in spirit; listless. **9.** (of colour) lacking brilliance; sombre. **10.** not loud or clear; muffled. ~*vb.* **11.** to make or become dull. [OE *dol*] — **'dullish** *adj.* — **'dullness** *or* **'dulness** *n.* — **'dully** *adv.*

dullard ('dʌləd) *n.* a dull or stupid person.

Dulles ('dʌlɪs) *n.* **John Foster.** 1888–1959, U.S. statesman and lawyer; secretary of state (1953–59).

dulse (dʌls) *n.* any of several seaweeds that occur on rocks and have large red edible fronds. [C17: from OIrish *duilesc* seaweed]

Duluth (də'luːθ) *n.* a port in E Minnesota, at the W end of Lake Superior. Pop.: 92 811 (1980).

duly ('djuːlɪ) *adv.* **1.** in a proper manner. **2.** at the proper time. [C14: see DUE, -LY[2]]

duma *Russian* ('duːmə) *n. Russian history.* **1.** (*usually cap.*) the elective legislative assembly established by Tsar Nicholas II in 1905: overthrown in 1917. **2.** (before 1917) any official assembly or council. [C20: from *duma* thought, of Gmc origin]

Dumas (*French* dyma) *n.* **1. Alexandre** (alɛksɑ̃drə), known as *Dumas père.* 1802–70, French novelist and dramatist, noted for his historical romances *The Count of Monte Cristo* (1844) and *The Three Musketeers* (1844). **2.** his son, **Alexandre,** known as *Dumas fils.* 1824–95, French novelist and dramatist, noted esp. for the play he adapted from an earlier novel, *La Dame aux camélias* (1852). **3. Jean-Baptiste André** (ʒɑ̃batist ɑ̃dre). 1800–84, French chemist, noted for his research on vapour density and atomic weight.

Du Maurier (djuː 'mɒrɪ,eɪ) *n.* **1.** Dame **Daphne.** born 1907, English novelist; author of *Rebecca* (1938) and *My Cousin Rachel* (1951). **2.** her grandfather, **George Louis Palmella Busson** ('pælmɛlə 'bjuːs[ə]n). 1834–96, English novelist, caricaturist, and illustrator; author of *Peter Ibbetson* (1891) and *Trilby* (1894).

dumb (dʌm) *adj.* **1.** lacking the power to speak; mute. **2.** lacking the power of human speech: *dumb animals.* **3.** temporarily bereft of the power to speak: *struck dumb.* **4.** refraining from speech; uncommunicative. **5.** producing no sound: *a dumb piano.* **6.** made, done, or performed without speech. **7.** *Inf.* **a.** dim-witted. **b.** foolish. [OE] — **'dumbly** *adv.* — **'dumbness** *n.*

Dumbarton (dʌm'bɑːt[ə]n) *n.* a town in W Scotland, in Strathclyde region near the confluence of the Rivers Leven and Clyde: centred around the **Rock of Dumbarton,** an important stronghold since ancient times; engineering and distilling. Pop.: 23 204 (1981).

Dumbarton Oaks ('dʌm,bɑːt[ə]n) *n.* an estate in the District of Columbia in the U.S: scene of conferences in 1944 concerned with creating the United Nations.

dumbbell ('dʌm,bɛl) *n.* **1.** an exercising weight consisting of a single bar with a heavy ball or disc at either end. **2.** *Sl.,* *chiefly U.S. & Canad.* a fool.

dumbfound *or* **dumfound** (dʌm'faʊnd) *vb.* (*tr.*) to strike dumb with astonishment; amaze. [C17: from DUMB + (CON)FOUND]

dumb show *n.* **1.** formerly, a part of a play acted in pantomime. **2.** meaningful gestures.

dumbstruck ('dʌm,strʌk) *adj.* temporarily deprived of speech through shock or surprise.

dumbwaiter ('dʌm,weɪtə) *n.* **1.** *Brit.* **a.** a stand placed near a dining table to hold food. **b.** a revolving circular tray placed on a table to hold food. U.S. and Canad. name: **lazy Susan. 2.** a lift for carrying food, rubbish, etc., between floors.

dumdum ('dʌm,dʌm) *n.* a soft-nosed bullet that expands on impact and inflicts extensive laceration. [C19: after *Dum-Dum*, town near Calcutta where orig. made]

Dumfries (dʌm'friːs) *n.* a town in S Scotland on the River Nith, administrative centre of Dumfries and Galloway Region. Pop.: 32 084 (1981).

Dumfries and Galloway Region *n.* a local government region in SW Scotland. Administrative centre: Dumfries. Pop.: 146 770 (1986 est.). Area: 6475 sq. km (2500 sq. miles).

Dumfriesshire (dʌm'friːs,ʃɪə, -ʃə) *n.* (until 1975) a county in S Scotland, on the Solway Firth, now part of Dumfries and Galloway region.

dummy ('dʌmɪ) *n., pl.* **-mies. 1.** a figure representing the human form, used for displaying clothes, as a target, etc. **2. a.** a copy of an object, often lacking some essential feature of the original. **b.** (*as modifier*): *a dummy drawer.* **3.** *Sl.* a stupid person. **4.** *Derog., sl.* a person without the power of speech. **5.** *Inf.* a person who says or does nothing. **6. a.** a person who appears to act for himself while acting on behalf of another. **b.** (*as modifier*): *a dummy buyer.* **7.** *Mil.* a weighted round without explosives. **8.** *Bridge.* **a.** the hand exposed on the table by the declarer's partner and played by the declarer. **b.** the declarer's partner. **9. a.** a prototype of a book, indicating the appearance of the finished product. **b.** a designer's layout of a page. **10.** *Sport.* a feigned pass or move. **11.** *Brit.* a rubber teat for babies to suck or bite on. U.S. and Canad. equivalent: **pacifier. 12.** (*modifier*) counterfeit; sham. **13.** (*modifier*) (of a card game) played with one hand exposed or unplayed. **14. sell (someone) a dummy.** *Sport.* to trick (an opponent) with a dummy pass. [C16: see DUMB, -Y³]

dummy run *n.* an experimental run; practice; rehearsal.

dump (dʌmp) *vb.* **1.** to drop, fall, or let fall heavily or in a mass. **2.** (*tr.*) to empty (objects or material) out of a container. **3.** to unload or empty (a container), as by overturning. **4.** (*tr.*) **a.** *Inf.* to dispose of without subtlety or proper care. **b.** to dispose of (nuclear waste). **5.** *Commerce.* to market (goods) in bulk and at low prices, esp. abroad, in order to maintain a high price in the home market and obtain a share of the foreign markets. **6.** (*tr.*) to store (supplies, etc.) temporarily. **7.** (*tr.*) *Surfing.* (of a wave) to hurl a swimmer or surfer down. **8.** (*tr.*) *Austral. & N.Z.* to compact (bales of wool) by hydraulic pressure. **9.** (*tr.*) *Computers.* to record (the contents of the memory) on a storage device at a series of points during a computer run. ~*n.* **10.** a place or area where waste materials are dumped. **11.** a pile or accumulation of rubbish. **12.** the act of dumping. **13.** *Inf.* a dirty or unkempt place. **14.** *Mil.* a place where weapons, supplies, etc., are stored. [C14: prob. from ON]

dumper ('dʌmpə) *n.* **1.** a person or thing that dumps. **2.** *Surfing.* a wave that hurls a swimmer or surfer down.

dumpling ('dʌmplɪŋ) *n.* **1.** a small ball of dough cooked and served with stew. **2.** a pudding consisting of a round pastry case filled with fruit: *apple dumpling.* **3.** *Inf.* a short plump person. [C16: *dump-*, ? var. of LUMP¹ + -LING¹]

dumps (dʌmps) *pl. n. Inf.* a state of melancholy or depression (esp. in **down in the dumps**). [C16: prob. from MDu. *domp* haze]

dump truck *or* **dumper-truck** *n.* a small truck used on building sites, having a load-bearing container at the front that can be tipped up to dump the contents.

dumpy ('dʌmpɪ) *adj.* **dumpier, dumpiest.** short and plump; squat. [C18: ? rel. to DUMPLING] —**'dumpily** *adv.* —**'dumpiness** *n.*

Dumyat (dʊm'jæt) *n.* the Arabic name for **Damietta.**

dun¹ (dʌn) *vb.* **dunning, dunned. 1.** (*tr.*) to press (a debtor) for payment. ~*n.* **2.** a person, esp. a hired agent, who importunes another for the payment of a debt. **3.** a demand for payment. [C17: from ?]

dun² (dʌn) *n.* **1.** a brownish-grey colour. **2.** a horse of this colour. **3.** *Angling. a.* an immature mayfly. **b.** an artificial fly resembling this. ~*adj.* **dunner, dunnest. 4.** of a dun colour. **5.** dark and gloomy. [OE *dunn*]

Duna ('dunɔ) *n.* the Hungarian name for the **Danube.**

Dünaburg ('dyːnabʊrk) *n.* the German name (until 1893) for **Daugavpils.**

Dunaj ('dunaj) *n.* the Czech name for the **Danube.**

Dunant (*French* dynɑ̃) *n.* **Jean Henri** (ʒɑ̃ ɑ̃ri). 1828–1910, Swiss humanitarian, founder of the International Red Cross (1864): shared the Nobel peace prize 1901.

Dunărea ('dunərjɑ) *n.* the Romanian name for the **Danube.**

Dunbar¹ (dʌn'bɑː) *n.* a port and resort in SE Scotland, in Lothian region: scene of Cromwell's defeat of the Scots (1650). Pop.: 6015 (1981).

Dunbar² (dʌn'bɑː) *n.* **William.** ?1460–?1520, Scottish poet, noted for his satirical and humorous verse.

Dunbartonshire (dʌn'bɑːtᵊnʃɪə, -ʃə) *n.* (until 1975) a county of W Scotland, now part of Strathclyde region.

Duncan ('dʌŋkən) *n.* **Isadora** (,ɪzə'dɔːrə). 1878–1927, U.S. dancer and choreographer, who influenced modern ballet by introducing greater freedom of movement.

Duncan I ('dʌŋkən) *n.* died 1040, king of Scotland (1034–40); killed by Macbeth.

dunce (dʌns) *n.* a person who is stupid or slow to learn. [C16: from *Dunses* or *Dunsmen*, term of ridicule applied to the followers of John *Duns Scotus* (?1265–1308), Scot. scholastic theologian, esp. by 16th-cent. humanists]

dunce cap *or* **dunce's cap** *n.* a conical paper hat, formerly placed on the head of a dull child at school.

Dundalk (dʌn'dɔːk) *n.* a town in NE Ireland, on **Dundalk Bay:** county town of Co. Louth. Pop.: 25 610 (1981).

Dundee (dʌn'diː) *n.* a port in E Scotland on the Firth of Tay, administrative centre of Tayside region: centre of the British jute industry. Pop.: 177 674 (1985 est.).

Dundee cake (dʌn'diː) *n. Chiefly Brit.* a fairly rich fruit cake decorated with almonds.

dunderhead ('dʌndə,hɛd) *n.* a slow-witted person. [C17: prob. from Du. *donder* thunder + HEAD] —**'dunder,headed** *adj.*

dune (djuːn) *n.* a mound or ridge of drifted sand. [C18: via OF from MDu. *düne*]

Dunedin (dʌn'iːdɪn) *n.* a port in New Zealand, on SE South Island: founded (1848) by Scottish settlers. Pop. (urban area): 113 300 (1981).

Dunfermline (dʌn'fɜːmlɪn) *n.* a city in E Scotland, in SW Fife: ruined palace, a former residence of Scottish kings. Pop.: 52 057 (1981).

dung (dʌŋ) *n.* **1.** excrement, esp. of animals; manure. **2.** something filthy. ~*vb.* **3.** (*tr.*) to cover with manure. [OE: prison; rel. to OHG *tunc* cellar roofed with dung, ON *dyngja* manure heap]

dungaree (,dʌŋɡə'riː) *n.* **1.** a coarse cotton fabric used chiefly for work clothes, etc. **2.** (*pl.*) **a.** a suit of workman's overalls made of this material, consisting of trousers with a bib attached. **b.** a casual garment resembling this, usually worn by women or children. **3.** *U.S.* trousers. [C17: from Hindi, after *Dungrī*, district of Bombay, where this fabric originated]

Dungeness (,dʌndʒə'nɛs) *n.* a low shingle headland on the S coast of England, in Kent: two nuclear power stations: automatic lighthouse.

dungeon ('dʌndʒən) *n.* **1.** a prison cell, often underground. **2.** a variant spelling of **donjon.** [C14: from OF *donjon*]

dunghill ('dʌŋ,hɪl) *n.* **1.** a heap of dung. **2.** a foul place, condition, or person.

dunk (dʌŋk) *vb.* **1.** to dip (bread, etc.) in tea, soup, etc., before eating. **2.** to submerge or be submerged. [C20: from Pennsylvania Du., from MHG *dunken*, from OHG *dunkōn*] —**'dunker** *n.*

Dunkerque (*French* dœ̃kɛrk) *n.* a port in N France, on the Strait of Dover: scene of the evacuation of British and other Allied troops after the fall of France in 1940; industrial centre with an oil refinery and naval shipbuilding yards. Pop.: 83 296 (1983 est.). English name: **Dunkirk** (dʌn'kɜːk).

Dún Laoghaire (duːn 'lɛərə) *n.* a port in E Ireland, on Dublin Bay. Pop.: 53 171 (1971). Former names: **Dunleary** (until 1821), **Kingstown** (1821–1921).

dunlin ('dʌnlɪn) n. a small sandpiper of northern and arctic regions, having a brown back and black breast in summer. [C16: DUN² + -LING¹]

Dunlop ('dʌnlɒp) n. **John Boyd.** 1840–1921, Scottish veterinary surgeon, who devised the first successful pneumatic tyre, which was manufactured by the company named after him.

dunnage ('dʌnɪdʒ) n. loose material used for packing cargo. [C14: from ?]

dunno (dʌ'nəʊ, dʊ-, də-) Sl. contraction of (I) do not know.

dunnock ('dʌnək) n. another name for a **hedge sparrow.** [C15: from DUN² + -OCK]

dunny ('dʌnɪ) n., pl. **-nies. 1.** Scot. dialect. a cellar or basement. **2.** Austral. & N.Z. inf. a lavatory, esp. one which is outside. [C20: from ?]

Dunois (French dynwa) n. **Jean** (ʒɑ̃), Comte de Dunois, known as the Bastard of Orléans. ?1403–68, French military commander, who defended Orléans against the English until the siege was raised by Joan of Arc (1429).

Dunoon (də'nuːn) n. a town and resort in W Scotland, in central Strathclyde region on the Firth of Clyde. Pop.: 9372 (1981).

Dunsany (dʌn'seɪnɪ) n. **18th Baron,** title of Edward John Moreton Drax Plunkett. 1878–1957, Irish dramatist and short-story writer.

Dunsinane ('dʌnsɪˌneɪn) n. a hill in central Scotland, in the Sidlaw Hills: the ruined fort at its summit is regarded as Macbeth's castle. Height: 308 m (1012 ft.).

Duns Scotus ('dʌnz 'skɒtəs) n. **John.** ?1265–1308, Scottish scholastic theologian and Franciscan priest: opposed the theology of St. Thomas Aquinas.

Dunstable¹ ('dʌnstəbᵊl) n. an industrial town in SE central England, in central Bedfordshire. Pop.: 35 716 (1984).

Dunstable² ('dʌnstəbᵊl) n. **John.** died 1453, English composer, esp. of motets and mass settings, noted for his innovations in harmony and rhythm.

Dunstan ('dʌnstən) n. **Saint.** ?909–988 A.D., English prelate and statesman; archbishop of Canterbury (959–988). He revived monasticism in England on Benedictine lines and promoted education. Feast day: May 19.

Duntroon (dʌn'truːn) n. a suburb of Canberra: seat of the Royal Military College of Australia.

duo ('djuːəʊ) n., pl. **duos** or **dui** ('djuːiː). **1.** Music. **a.** a pair of performers. **b.** a duet. **2.** a pair of actors, etc. **3.** Inf. a pair of closely connected individuals. [C16: via It. from L: two]

duo- combining form. indicating two. [from L]

duodecimal (ˌdjuːəʊ'dɛsɪməl) adj. **1.** relating to twelve or twelfths. ~n. **2.** a twelfth. **3.** one of the numbers used in a duodecimal number system. —ˌduo'decimally adv.

duodecimo (ˌdjuːəʊ'dɛsɪˌməʊ) n., pl. **-mos. 1.** Also called: **twelvemo.** a book size resulting from folding a sheet of paper into twelve leaves. **2.** a book of this size. [C17: from L in duodecimō in twelfth]

duodenum (ˌdjuːəʊ'diːnəm) n., pl. **-na** (-nə) or **-nums.** the first part of the small intestine, between the stomach and the jejunum. [C14: from Med. L, from intestinum duodenum digitorum intestine of twelve fingers' length] —ˌduo'denal adj.

duologue or U.S. (sometimes) **duolog** ('djuːəˌlɒg) n. **1.** a part or all of a play in which the speaking roles are limited to two actors. **2.** a less common word for **dialogue.**

dup. abbrev. for duplicate.

Duparc (French dypark) n. **Henri** (ɑ̃ri), full name Marie Eugène Henri Fouques Duparc. 1848–1933, French composer of songs noted for their sad brooding quality.

dupe (djuːp) n. **1.** a person who is easily deceived. ~vb. **2.** (tr.) to deceive; cheat; fool. [C17: from F, from OF duppe, contraction of de huppe of (a) hoopoe; from the bird's reputation for extreme stupidity] —'dupable adj. —'duper n. —'dupery n.

duple ('djuːpᵊl) adj. **1.** a less common word for **double. 2.** Music. (of time or music) having two beats in a bar. [C16: from L duplus twofold, double]

Dupleix (French dyplɛks) n. Marquis **Joseph François** (ʒozɛf frɑ̃swa). 1697–1763, French governor general in India (1742–54). His plan to establish a French empire in India was frustrated by Clive.

Duplessis-Mornay (French dyplɛsimɔrnɛ) n. a variant of (Philippe de) **Mornay.**

duplex ('djuːplɛks) n. **1.** U.S. & Canad. a duplex apartment or house. ~adj. **2.** having two parts. **3.** having pairs of components of independent but identical function. **4.** permitting the transmission of simultaneous signals in both directions. [C19: from L: twofold, from duo two + -plex -FOLD] —du'plexity n.

duplex apartment n. U.S. & Canad. an apartment on two floors.

duplex house n. U.S. & Canad. a semidetached house.

duplicate adj. ('djuːplɪkɪt). **1.** copied exactly from an original. **2.** identical. **3.** existing as a pair or in pairs. ~n. ('djuːplɪkɪt). **4.** an exact copy. **5.** something additional of the same kind. **6.** two exact copies (esp. in **in duplicate).** ~vb. ('djuːplɪˌkeɪt). (tr.) **7.** to make a replica of. **8.** to do or make again. **9.** to make in a pair; make double. [C15: from L duplicāre to double, from duo two + plicāre to fold] —'duplicable adj. —ˌdupli'cation n.

duplicator ('djuːplɪˌkeɪtə) n. an apparatus for making replicas of an original, such as a machine using a stencil wrapped on an ink-loaded drum.

duplicity (djuː'plɪsɪtɪ) n., pl. **-ties.** deception; double-dealing. [C15: from OF duplicite, from LL duplicitās a being double, from L DUPLEX]

du Pré (duː preɪ) n. **Jacqueline.** 1945–87, English cellist. Multiple sclerosis ended her performing career (1973) after which she became a cello teacher. She was married to the pianist and conductor Daniel Barenboim.

Dupré (French dypre) n. **Marcel** (marsɛl). 1886–1971, French organist and composer, noted as an improviser.

Duque de Caxias (Portuguese 'duːke 'dɛ: kə'ʃiaʃ) n. a city in SE Brazil, near Rio de Janeiro. Pop.: 306 057 (1980).

durable ('djʊərəbᵊl) adj. long-lasting; enduring. [C14: from OF, from L dūrābilis, from dūrāre to last] —ˌdura'bility n. —'durably adv.

durable goods pl. n. goods that require infrequent replacement. Also called: **durables.**

Duralumin (djʊ'ræljʊmɪn) n. Trademark. a light strong aluminium alloy containing copper, silicon, magnesium, and manganese.

dura mater ('djʊərə 'meɪtə) n. the outermost and toughest of the three membranes covering the brain and spinal cord. Often shortened to **dura.** [C15: from Med. L: hard mother]

duramen (djʊ'reɪmɛn) n. another name for **heartwood.** [C19: from L: hardness, from dūrāre to harden]

durance ('djʊərəns) n. Arch. or literary. **1.** imprisonment. **2.** duration. [C15: from OF, from durer to last, from L dūrāre]

Durance (French dyrɑ̃s) n. a river in S France, rising in the Alps and flowing generally southwest into the Rhône. Length: 304 km (189 miles).

Durango (djʊ'ræŋgəʊ; Spanish du'raŋgo) n. **1.** a state in N central Mexico: high plateau, with the Sierra Madre Occidental in the west; irrigated agriculture (esp. cotton) and rich mineral resources. Capital: Durango. Pop.: 1 160 196 (1980). Area: 119 648 sq. km (46 662 sq. miles). **2.** a city in NW central Mexico, capital of Durango state: mining centre. Pop.: 321 148 (1980). Official name: **Victoria de Durango.**

Duras (French dyra) n. **Marguerite.** born 1914, French novelist born in Indochina. Her works include The Sea Wall (1950) and the script for the film Hiroshima mon amour (1960).

duration (djʊ'reɪʃən) n. the length of time that something lasts or continues. [C14: from Med. L dūrātiō, from L dūrāre to last] —du'rational adj.

durative ('djʊərətɪv) Grammar. ~adj. **1.** denoting an aspect of verbs that includes the imperfective and the progressive. ~n. **2. a.** the durative aspect of a verb. **b.** a verb in this aspect.

Durazzo (du'rattso) n. the Italian name for **Durrës.**

Durban ('dɜːbᵊn) n. a port in E South Africa, in E Natal on the Indian Ocean: University of Natal (1909); resort and industrial centre, with oil refineries, shipbuilding yards, etc. Pop.: 982 075 (1985).

durbar ('dɜːbɑː, ˌdɜː'bɑː) n. **a.** (formerly) the court of a native ruler or a governor in India. **b.** a levee at such a court. [C17: from Hindi darbār, from Persian, from dar door + bār entry, audience]

Düren (German 'dyːrən) n. a city in W West Germany, in North Rhine-Westphalia. Pop.: 85 867 (1983 est.).

Dürer (*German* 'dy:rər) *n.* **Albrecht** ('albrɛçt). 1471– 1528, German painter and engraver, regarded as the greatest artist of the German Renaissance and noted particularly as a draughtsman and for his copper engravings and woodcuts.

duress (dju'rɛs, djuə-) *n.* **1.** compulsion by use of force or threat; coercion (often in **under duress**). **2.** imprisonment. [C14: from OF *duresse*, from L *dūritia* hardness, from *dūrus* hard]

Durham ('dʌrəm) *n.* **1.** a county of NE England, on the North Sea: rises to the N Pennines in the west, with a coalfield to the east. Administrative centre: Durham. Pop.: 599 600 (1986 est.). Area: 2436 sq. km (940 sq. miles). Abbrev.: **Dur.** **2.** a city in NE England, administrative centre of Co. Durham, on the River Wear: Norman cathedral; 11th-century castle (founded by William the Conqueror), now occupied by the University of Durham (1832). Pop.: 39 600 (1986).

during ('djʊərɪŋ) *prep.* **1.** concurrently with (some other activity). **2.** within the limit of (a period of time). [C14: from *duren* to last, ult. from L *dūrare* to last]

Durkheim ('dɜ:khaɪm; *French* dyrkɛm) *n.* **Émile** (eml). 1858–1917, French sociologist, whose pioneering works include *De la Division du travail social* (1893).

durmast *or* **durmast oak** ('dɜ:,mɑ:st) *n.* a large Eurasian oak tree with lobed leaves and sessile acorns. Also called: **sessile oak**. [C18: prob. from DUN² MAST²]

durra ('dʌrə) *n.* an Old World variety of sorghum, cultivated for grain and fodder. [C18: from Ar. *dhurah* grain]

Durrell ('dʌrəl) *n.* **Lawrence** (**George**). born 1912, English poet and novelist; author of *The Alexandria Quartet* of novels, consisting of *Justine* (1957), *Balthazar* (1958), *Mountolive* (1958), and *Clea* (1960). Later works include the novels *Tunc* (1968) and *Nunquam* (1970).

Dürrenmatt ('dyrənmat) *n.* **Friedrich** ('fri:drɪç). born 1921, Swiss dramatist and writer of detective stories, noted for his grotesque and paradoxical treatment of the modern world: author of *The Visit* (1956) and *The Physicists* (1962).

Durrës ('durrəs) *n.* a port in W Albania, on the Adriatic. Pop.: 72 000 (1983). Ancient names: **Epidamnus** (epɪ'dæmnəs), **Dyrrachium** (də'reɪkɪəm). Italian name: **Durazzo**.

durry ('dʌrɪ) *n.*, *pl.* **-ries.** *Austral. sl.* a cigarette. [from *durrie* a type of Indian carpet]

durst (dɜ:st) *vb.* an archaic past tense of **dare**.

durum *or* **durum wheat** ('djʊərəm) *n.* a variety of wheat with a high gluten content, used chiefly to make pastas. [C20: from NL *triticum dūrum*, lit.: hard wheat]

Duse ('du:zɪ) *n.* **Eleonora** (,ɛlɪə'nɔ:rə). 1858–1924, Italian actress, noted as a tragedienne.

Dushanbe (du:'ʃɑ:nbɪ) *n.* an industrial city in the SW Soviet Union, capital of the Tadzhik SSR. Pop.: 582 000 (1987). Former name (1929–61): **Stalinabad**.

dusk (dʌsk) *n.* **1.** the darker part of twilight. **2.** *Poetic.* gloom; shade. ~*adj.* **3.** *Poetic.* shady; gloomy. ~*vb.* **4.** *Poetic.* to make or become dark. [OE *dox*]

dusky ('dʌskɪ) *adj.* **duskier, duskiest. 1.** dark in colour; swarthy or dark-skinned. **2.** dim. —**'duskily** *adv.* —**'duskiness** *n.*

Düsseldorf ('dʊsəl,dɔ:f; *German* 'dysəldɔrf) *n.* an industrial city in W West Germany, capital of North Rhine-Westphalia, on the Rhine: commercial centre of the Rhine-Ruhr industrial area. Pop.: 561 200 (1986).

dust (dʌst) *n.* **1.** dry fine powdery material, such as particles of dirt, earth, or pollen. **2.** a cloud of such fine particles. **3. a.** the mortal body of man. **b.** the corpse of a dead person. **4.** the earth; ground. **5.** *Inf.* a disturbance; fuss (esp. in **kick up a dust, raise a dust**). **6.** something of little worth. **7.** short for **gold dust**. **8.** ashes or household refuse. **9. dust and ashes.** something that is very disappointing. **10. shake the dust off** (*or* **from**) **one's feet.** to depart angrily or contemptuously. **11. throw dust in the eyes of.** to confuse or mislead. ~*vb.* **12.** (*tr.*) to sprinkle or cover (something) with (dust or some other powdery substance). **13.** to remove dust (from) by wiping, sweeping, or brushing. **14.** *Arch.* to make or become dirty with dust. ~See also **dust down, dust-up**. [OE *dūst*] —**'dustless** *adj.*

dustbin ('dʌst,bɪn) *n.* a large, usually cylindrical container for rubbish, esp. one used by a household. U.S. and Canad. names: **garbage can, trash can**.

dust bowl *n.* a semiarid area in which the surface soil is exposed to wind erosion.

Dust Bowl *n.* **the.** the area of the south central U.S. that became denuded of topsoil by wind erosion during the droughts of the mid-1930s.

dustcart ('dʌst,kɑ:t) *n.* a road vehicle for collecting refuse. U.S. and Canad. name: **garbage truck**.

dust cover *n.* **1.** another name for **dustsheet**. **2.** another name for **dust jacket**. **3.** a perspex cover for the turntable of a record player.

dust devil *n.* a strong miniature whirlwind that whips up dust, litter, leaves, etc., into the air.

dust down *vb.* (*tr., adv.*). **1.** to remove dust from by brushing or wiping. **2.** to reprimand severely. —**dusting down** *n.*

duster ('dʌstə) *n.* **1.** a cloth used for dusting. U.S. name: **dust cloth**. **2.** a machine for blowing out dust. **3.** a person or thing that dusts.

dusting-powder *n.* fine powder (such as talcum powder) used to absorb moisture, etc.

dust jacket *or* **cover** *n.* a removable paper cover used to protect a bound book.

dustman ('dʌstmən) *n.*, *pl.* **-men.** *Brit.* a man whose job is to collect domestic refuse.

dustpan ('dʌst,pæn) *n.* a short-handled hooded shovel into which dust is swept from floors, etc.

dustsheet ('dʌst,ʃi:t) *n.* *Brit.* a large cloth used to protect furniture from dust.

dust storm *n.* a windstorm that whips up clouds of dust.

dust-up *Inf.* ~*n.* **1.** a fight or argument. ~*vb.* **dust up. 2.** (*tr., adv.*) to attack (someone).

dusty ('dʌstɪ) *adj.* **dustier, dustiest. 1.** covered with or involving dust. **2.** like dust. **3.** (of a colour) tinged with grey; pale. **4. give** (*or* **get**) **a dusty answer.** to give (*or* get) an unhelpful or bad-tempered reply. —**'dustily** *adv.* —**'dustiness** *n.*

Dutch (dʌtʃ) *n.* **1.** the language of the Netherlands. **2. the Dutch.** (*functioning as pl.*) the natives, citizens, or inhabitants of the Netherlands. **3.** See **double Dutch**. **4. in Dutch.** *Sl.* in trouble. ~*adj.* **5.** of the Netherlands, its inhabitants, or their language. ~*adv.* **6. go Dutch.** *Inf.* to share expenses equally.

Dutch auction *n.* an auction in which the price is lowered by stages until a buyer is found.

Dutch barn *n.* *Brit.* a farm building consisting of a steel frame and a curved roof.

Dutch courage *n.* **1.** false courage gained from drinking alcohol. **2.** alcoholic drink.

Dutch door *n.* the U.S. and Canad. name for **stable door**.

Dutch East Indies *n.* **the.** a former name (1798–1945) of **Indonesia**. Also called: **Netherlands East Indies**.

Dutch elm disease *n.* a fungal disease of elm trees characterized by withering of the foliage and stems and eventual death of the tree.

Dutch Guiana *or* **Netherlands Guiana** *n.* the former name of **Surinam**.

Dutchman ('dʌtʃmən) *n.*, *pl.* **-men. 1.** a native, citizen, or inhabitant of the Netherlands. **2.** *S. African derog.* an Afrikaner.

Dutch medicine *n.* *S. African.* patent medicine, esp. made of herbs.

Dutch New Guinea *n.* a former name (until 1963) of **Irian Jaya**.

Dutch oven *n.* **1.** an iron or earthenware container with a cover, used for stews, etc. **2.** a metal box, open in front, for cooking in front of an open fire.

Dutch treat *n.* *Inf.* an entertainment, meal, etc., where each person pays for himself.

Dutch uncle *n.* *Inf.* a person who criticizes or reproves frankly and severely.

Dutch West Indies *pl. n.* **the.** a former name of the **Netherlands Antilles**.

duteous ('dju:tɪəs) *adj.* *Formal or arch.* dutiful; obedient. —**'duteously** *adv.*

dutiable ('dju:tɪəb³l) *adj.* (of goods) liable to duty. —**,dutia'bility** *n.*

dutiful ('dju:tɪful) *adj.* **1.** exhibiting or having a sense of duty. **2.** characterized by or resulting from a sense of duty: *a dutiful answer*.

Dutton ('dʌt³n) *n.* **Clarence Edward.** 1841–1912, American geologist who first developed the theory of isostasy.

duty ('dju:tɪ) *n.*, *pl.* **-ties. 1.** a task or action that a person is bound to perform for moral or legal reasons. **2.** respect or obedience due to a superior, older persons, etc. **3.** the force that binds one morally or legally to one's obligations. **4.** a government tax, esp. on imports. **5.** *Brit.* **a.** the quantity of work for which a machine is designed. **b.** a measure of the efficiency of a machine. **6. a.** a job or service allocated. **b.** (*as modifier*): *duty rota.* **7. do duty for.** to act as a substitute for. **8. on** (*or* **off**) **duty.** at (*or* not at) work. [C13: from Anglo-F *dueté*, from OF *deu* DUE]

duty-bound *adj.* morally obliged.

duty-free *adj., adv.* with exemption from customs or excise duties.

duty-free shop *n.* a shop, esp. one at a port or on board a ship, that sells perfume, tobacco, etc., at duty-free prices.

duumvir (djuː'ʌmvə) *n., pl.* **-virs** *or* **-viri** (-vɪˌriː). **1.** *Roman history.* one of two coequal magistrates. **2.** either of two men who exercise a joint authority. [C16: from L, from *duo* two + *vir* man] —**duumvirate** (djuː'ʌmvɪrɪt) *n.*

Duvalier (*French* dyvalje) *n.* **1. François** (frɑ̃swa), known as *Papa Doc.* 1907–71, president of Haiti (1957–71). **2.** his son, **Jean-Claude** (ʒɑ̃klod), known as *Baby Doc.* born 1951, Haitian statesman; president of Haiti 1971–86; deposed and exiled.

duvet ('duːveɪ) *n.* **1.** another name for **continental quilt.** **2.** Also called: **duvet jacket.** a down-filled jacket. [C18: from F, from earlier *dumet*, from OF *dum* DOWN[2]]

dux (dʌks) *n.* (esp. in Scottish schools) the top pupil in a class or school. [L: leader]

DV *abbrev. for:* **1.** Deo volente. [L: God willing] **2.** Douay Version (of the Bible).

Dvina (*Russian* dvi'na) *n.* **1. Northern.** a river in the NW Soviet Union, formed by the confluence of the Sukhona and Yug Rivers and flowing northwest to *Dvina Bay* in the White Sea. Length: 750 km (466 miles). Russian name: **Severnaya Dvina. 2. Western.** a river in the W Soviet Union, rising in the Valdai Hills and flowing south and southwest then northwest to the Gulf of Riga. Length: 1021 km (634 miles). Russian name: **Zapadnaya Dvina** ('zapədnəjə). Latvian name: **Daugava.**

Dvina Bay *or* **Dvina Gulf** *n.* an inlet of the White Sea, off the coast of the NW Soviet Union.

Dvinsk (dvinsk) *n.* transliteration of the former Russian name for **Daugavpils.**

Dvořák (ˈdvɔːʒæk; *Czech* ˈdvɔrʒaːk) *n.* **Antonín** (ˈantɔnjiːn), known as *Anton Dvořák.* 1841–1904, Czech composer, much of whose work reflects the influence of folk music. His best-known work is the *Symphony No. 9 From the New World* (1893).

dwaal (dwaːl) *n. S. African.* a state of befuddlement; daze. [from Afrik. *dwaal* wander]

dwale (dweɪl) *n.* another name for **deadly nightshade.** [C14: ?from ON]

dwarf (dwɔːf) *n., pl.* **dwarfs** *or* **dwarves** (dwɔːvz). **1.** an abnormally undersized person. **2. a.** an animal or plant much below the average height for the species. **b.** (*as modifier*): *a dwarf tree.* **3.** (in folklore) a small ugly manlike creature, often possessing magical powers. **4.** *Astron.* short for **dwarf star.** ~*vb.* **5.** to become or cause to become small in size, importance, etc. **6.** (*tr.*) to stunt the growth of. [OE *dweorg*] —**dwarfish** *adj.*

dwarf star *n.* any of a class of faint stars having a very high density and small diameter compared to the much brighter **giant stars.**

dwell (dwɛl) *vb.* **dwelling, dwelt** *or* **dwelled.** (*intr.*) **1.** *Formal, literary.* to live as a permanent resident. **2.** to live (in a specified state): *to dwell in poverty.* ~*n.* **3.** a regular pause in the operation of a machine. [OE *dwellan* to seduce, get lost] —**'dweller** *n.*

dwelling ('dwɛlɪŋ) *n. Formal, literary.* a place of residence.

dwell on *or* **upon** *vb.* (*intr., prep.*) to think, speak, or write at length.

dwelt (dwɛlt) *vb.* a past tense and past participle of **dwell.**

dwindle ('dwɪndl) *vb.* to grow or cause to grow less in size, intensity, or number. [C16: from OE *dwīnan* to waste away]

Dy *the chemical symbol for* dysprosium.

dyad ('daɪæd) *n.* **1.** *Maths.* an operator that is the unspecified product of two vectors. **2.** an atom or group that has a valency of two. **3.** a group of two; couple. [C17: from LL *dyas*, from Gk *duas* two] —**dy'adic** *adj.*

Dyak *or* **Dayak** ('daɪæk) *n., pl.* **-aks** *or* **-ak.** a member of a Malaysian people of Borneo. [from Malay: upcountry, from *darat* land]

dybbuk ('dɪbək) *n., pl.* **-buks** *or* **-bukkim.** *Judaism.* (in folklore) the soul of a dead sinner that has transmigrated into the body of a living person. [from Yiddish: devil, from Heb.]

dye (daɪ) *n.* **1.** a staining or colouring substance. **2.** a liquid that contains a colouring material and can be used to stain fabrics, skins, etc. **3.** the colour produced by dyeing. ~*vb.* **dyeing, dyed. 4.** (*tr.*) to impart a colour or stain to (fabric, hair, etc.) by or as if by the application of a dye. [OE *dēagian*, from *dēag* a dye] —**'dyable** *or* **'dyeable** *adj.* —**'dyer** *n.*

dyed-in-the-wool *adj.* **1.** uncompromising or unchanging in attitude, opinion, etc. **2.** (of a fabric) made of dyed yarn.

dyeing ('daɪɪŋ) *n.* the process or industry of colouring yarns, fabrics, etc.

dyestuff ('daɪˌstʌf) *n.* a substance that can be used as a dye or which yields a dye.

Dyfed ('dʌvɛd) *n.* a county in SW Wales, formed in 1974 from Cardiganshire, Pembrokeshire, and Carmarthenshire: coastal lowlands rising to a high plateau in the north and mountains in the south. Administrative centre: Carmarthen. Pop.: 339 000 (1986 est.). Area: 5768 sq. km (2227 sq. miles).

dying ('daɪɪŋ) *vb.* **1.** the present participle of **die**[1]. ~*adj.* **2.** relating to or occurring at the moment of death: *a dying wish.*

dyke[1] *or esp. U.S.* **dike** (daɪk) *n.* **1.** an embankment constructed to prevent flooding or keep out the sea. **2.** a ditch or watercourse. **3.** a bank made of earth alongside a ditch. **4.** *Scot.* a wall, esp. a dry-stone wall. **5.** a barrier or obstruction. **6.** a wall-like mass of igneous rock in older sedimentary rock. **7.** *Austral. inf.* a lavatory. ~*vb.* **8.** (*tr.*) to protect, enclose, or drain (land) with a dyke. [C13: from OE *dīc* ditch]

dyke[2] *or* **dike** (daɪk) *n. Sl.* a lesbian. [C20: from ?]

Dylan ('dɪlən) *n.* **Bob.** real name *Robert Allen Zimmerman.* born 1941, U.S. rock singer and songwriter, also noted for his acoustic protest songs in the early 1960s. His albums include *The Freewheelin' Bob Dylan* (1963), *Highway 61 Revisited* (1965), *Blonde on Blonde* (1966), *John Wesley Harding* (1968), *Blood on the Tracks* (1974), and *Infidels* (1983).

dynamic (daɪ'næmɪk) *adj.* **1.** of or concerned with energy or forces that produce motion, as opposed to *static.* **2.** of or concerned with dynamics. **3.** Also: **dynamical.** characterized by force of personality, ambition, energy, etc. **4.** *Computers.* (of a memory) needing its contents refreshed periodically. [C19: from F *dynamique*, from Gk *dunamikos* powerful, from *dunamis* power, from *dunasthai* to be able] —**dy'namically** *adv.*

dynamics (daɪ'næmɪks) *n.* **1.** (*functioning as sing.*) the branch of mechanics concerned with the forces that change or produce the motions of bodies. **2.** (*functioning as sing.*) the branch of mechanics that includes statics and kinetics. **3.** (*functioning as sing.*) the branch of any science concerned with forces. **4.** (*functioning as pl.*) those forces that produce change in any field or system. **5.** (*functioning as pl.*) *Music.* **a.** the various degrees of loudness called for in performance. **b.** directions and symbols used to indicate degrees of loudness.

dynamism ('daɪnəˌmɪzəm) *n.* **1.** *Philosophy.* any of several theories that attempt to explain phenomena in terms of an immanent force or energy. **2.** the forcefulness of an energetic personality. —**'dynamist** *n.* —ˌdyna'mistic *adj.*

dynamite ('daɪnəˌmaɪt) *n.* **1.** an explosive consisting of nitroglycerin mixed with an absorbent. **2.** *Inf.* a spectacular or potentially dangerous person or thing. ~*vb.* **3.** (*tr.*) to mine or blow up with dynamite. [C19 (coined by Alfred Nobel): from DYNAMO- + -ITE[1]] —**'dynaˌmiter** *n.*

dynamo ('daɪnəˌmoʊ) *n., pl.* **-mos. 1.** a device for converting mechanical energy into electrical energy. **2.** *Inf.* an energetic hard-working person. [C19: short for *dynamoelectric machine*]

dynamo- *or sometimes before a vowel* **dynam-** *combining form.* indicating power: *dynamite.* [from Gk, from *dunamis* power]

dynamoelectric (ˌdaɪnəməʊɪˈlɛktrɪk) *or* **dynamoelectrical** *adj.* of or concerned with the interconversion of mechanical and electrical energy.

dynamometer (ˌdaɪnəˈmɒmɪtə) *n.* an instrument for measuring power or force.

dynamotor (ˈdaɪnəˌməʊtə) *n.* an electrical machine having two independent armature windings of which one acts as a motor and the other a generator: used to convert direct current into alternating current.

dynast (ˈdɪnəst, -æst) *n.* a ruler, esp. a hereditary one. [C17: from L *dynastēs*, from Gk, from *dunasthai* to be powerful]

dynasty (ˈdɪnəstɪ) *n.*, *pl.* **-ties.** **1.** a sequence of hereditary rulers. **2.** any sequence of powerful leaders of the same family. [C15: via LL from Gk, from *dunastēs* DYNAST] —**dynastic** (dɪˈnæstɪk) *adj.*

dyne (daɪn) *n.* the cgs unit of force; the force that imparts an acceleration of 1 centimetre per second per second to a mass of 1 gram. 1 dyne is equivalent to 10^{-5} newton or 7.233×10^{-5} poundal. [C19: from F, from Gk *dunamis* power, force]

dys- *prefix.* **1.** diseased, abnormal, or faulty. **2.** difficult or painful. **3.** unfavourable or bad. [via L from Gk *dus-*]

dysentery (ˈdɪsᵊntrɪ) *n.* infection of the intestine marked by severe diarrhoea with the passage of mucus and blood. [C14: via L from Gk, from *dusentera*, lit.: bad bowels, from DYS-+ *enteron* intestine] —**dysenteric** (ˌdɪsᵊnˈtɛrɪk) *adj.*

dysfunction (dɪsˈfʌŋkʃən) *n. Med.* any disturbance or abnormality in the function of an organ or part. —ˌdys'**functional** *adj.*

dyslexia (dɪsˈlɛksɪə) *n.* impaired ability to read, not caused by low intelligence. [C19: NL, from DYS- + *-lexia*, from *legein* to speak] —**dyslectic** (dɪsˈlɛktɪk) *adj., n.* —dys'**lexic** *adj.*

dysmenorrhoea *or esp. U.S.* **dysmenorrhea** (ˌdɪsmɛnəˈrɪə) *n.* abnormally difficult or painful menstruation. [C19: from DYS- + Gk *mēn* month + *rhoiā* a flowing]

dyspepsia (dɪsˈpɛpsɪə) *n.* indigestion or upset stomach. [C18: from L, from Gk *duspepsia*, from DYS- + *pepsis* digestion]

dyspeptic (dɪsˈpɛptɪk) *adj.* **1.** relating to or suffering from dyspepsia. **2.** irritable. ~*n.* **3.** a person suffering from dyspepsia.

dysphasia (dɪsˈfeɪzɪə) *n.* impaired coordination of speech. —**dys'phasic** *adj., n.*

dysphoria (dɪsˈfɔːrɪə) *n.* a feeling of being ill at ease. [C20: NL, from Gk DYS- + *-phoria*, from *pherein* to bear]

dyspnoea *or U.S.* **dyspnea** (dɪspˈniːə) *n.* difficulty in breathing or in catching the breath. [C17: via L from Gk *duspnoia*, from DYS- + *pnoē* breath, from *pnein* to breathe] —**dysp'noeal, dysp'noeic** *or U.S.* **dysp'neal, dysp'neic** *adj.*

dysprosium (dɪsˈprəʊsɪəm) *n.* a metallic element of the lanthanide series: used in laser materials and as a neutron absorber in nuclear control rods. Symbol: Dy; atomic no.: 66; atomic wt.: 162.50. [C20: NL, from Gk *dusprositos* difficult to get near + -IUM]

dysthymia (dɪsˈθaɪmɪə) *n. Psychiatry.* the characteristics of the neurotic and introverted, including anxiety, depression, and compulsive behaviour. [C19: NL, from Gk *dusthumia*, from DYS-+ *thumos* mind] —**dys'thymic** *adj.*

dystrophy (ˈdɪstrəfɪ) *n.* any of various bodily disorders, characterized by wasting of tissues. See also **muscular dystrophy.** [C19: NL *dystrophia*, from DYS- + Gk *trophē* food] —**dystrophic** (dɪsˈtrɒfɪk) *adj.*

Dzaudzhikau (dzəʊdʒiˈkau) *n.* the former name (1944–54) of **Ordzhonikidze.**

Dzerzhinsk (*Russian* dzɪrˈʒinsk) *n.* an industrial city in the central Soviet Union, in the RSFSR. Pop.: 281 000 (1987).

Dzhambul (*Russian* dʒamˈbul) *n.* a city in the S central Soviet Union, in the Kazakh SSR: chemical manufacturing. Pop.: 292 000 (1983 est.). Former name (until 1938): **Auliye-Ata** (ˈaʊlijəaˈta).

dzo (zəʊ) *n., pl.* **dzos** *or* **dzo.** a variant spelling of **zo.**

Dzungaria (dzʊŋˈgɛərɪə, zʊŋ-) *n.* a variant transliteration of the Chinese name for **Junggar Pendi.**

E

e *or* **E** (iː) *n., pl.* **e's, E's,** *or* **Es. 1.** the fifth letter and second vowel of the English alphabet. **2.** any of several speech sounds represented by this letter, as in *he, bet,* or *below.*

e *symbol for:* **1.** *Maths.* a transcendental number used as the base of natural logarithms. Approximate value: 2.718 282 … **2.** electron.

E *symbol for:* **1.** *Music.* **a.** the third note of the scale of C major. **b.** the major or minor key having this note as its tonic. **2.** earth. **3.** East. **4.** English. **5.** Egypt(ian). **6.** *Physics.* **a.** energy. **b.** electromotive force. **7.** exa-.

e. *abbrev. for* engineer(ing).

E. *abbrev. for* Earl.

E- *prefix.* used with numbers indicating a standardized system within the European Economic Community, as of food additives. See also **E number.**

ea. *abbrev. for* each.

each (iːtʃ) *determiner.* **1. a.** every (one) of two or more considered individually: *each day; each person.* **b.** *(as pron.):* *each gave according to his ability.* ~*adv.* **2.** for, to, or from each one; apiece: *four apples each.* [OE *ǣlc*]

eager (ˈiːgə) *adj.* **1.** *(postpositive; often foll. by to or for)* impatiently desirous (of); anxious or avid (for). **2.** characterized by or feeling expectancy or great desire: *an eager look.* **3.** *Arch.* biting; sharp. [C13: from OF *egre,* from L *acer* sharp, keen] — ˈeagerly *adv.* — ˈeagerness *n.*

eager beaver *n. Inf.* a person who displays conspicuous diligence.

eagle (ˈiːgəl) *n.* **1.** any of various birds of prey having large broad wings and strong soaring flight. Related adj.: **aquiline. 2.** a representation of an eagle used as an emblem, etc., esp. representing power: *the Roman eagle.* **3.** a standard, seal, etc., bearing the figure of an eagle. **4.** *Golf.* a score of two strokes under par for a hole. **5.** a former U.S. gold coin worth ten dollars. [C14: from OF *aigle,* from OProvençal *aigla,* from L *aquila*]

eagle-eyed *adj.* having keen or piercing eyesight.

eagle-hawk *n.* a large brown Australian eagle. Also called: **wedge-tailed eagle.**

eagle owl *n.* a large Eurasian owl with brownish speckled plumage and large ear tufts.

eaglet (ˈiːglɪt) *n.* a young eagle.

ealdorman (ˈɔːldəmən) *n., pl.* **-men.** an official of Anglo-Saxon England, appointed by the king, and responsible for law and order in his shire and for leading local militia. [OE *ealdor* lord + MAN]

Ealing (ˈiːlɪŋ) *n.* a borough of W Greater London, formed in 1965 from Acton, Ealing, and Southall. Pop.: 295 500 (1986 est.).

-ean *suffix forming adjectives and nouns.* a variant of **-an:** *Caesarean.*

Eanes (*Portuguese* eˈanəʃ) *n.* **António (dos Santos Ramalho)** (ənˈtɔniu). born 1935, Portuguese statesman and general; president of Portugal 1976–86.

ear¹ (ɪə) *n.* **1.** the organ of hearing and balance in higher vertebrates (see **middle ear**). Related adj.: **aural. 2.** the outermost cartilaginous part of the ear in mammals, esp. man. **3.** the sense of hearing. **4.** sensitivity to musical sounds, poetic diction, etc.: *he has an ear for music.* **5.** attention; consideration (esp. in **give ear to, lend an ear**). **6.** an object resembling the external ear. **7. all ears.** very attentive; listening carefully. **8. a thick ear.** *Inf.* a blow on the ear. **9. fall on deaf ears.** to be ignored or pass unnoticed. **10. in one ear and out the other.** heard but unheeded. **11. keep** (*or* **have**) **one's ear to the ground.** to be or try to be well informed about current trends and opinions. **12. out on one's ear.** *Inf.* dismissed unceremoniously. **13. play by ear. a.** *Inf.* to act according to the demands of a situation; improvise. **b.** to perform a musical piece on an instrument without written music. **14. turn a deaf ear.** to be deliberately unresponsive. **15. up to one's ears.** *Inf.* deeply involved, as in work or debt. [OE *ēare*] — **eared** *adj.* — ˈearless *adj.*

ear² (ɪə) *n.* **1.** the part of a cereal plant, such as wheat or barley, that contains the seeds, grains, or kernels. ~*vb.* **2.** *(intr.)* (of cereal plants) to develop such parts. [OE *ēar*]

earache (ˈɪərˌeɪk) *n.* pain in the ear.

eardrum (ˈɪəˌdrʌm) *n.* the nontechnical name for **tympanic membrane.**

earful (ˈɪəfʊl) *n. Inf.* **1.** something heard or overheard. **2.** a rebuke or scolding.

Earhart (ˈɛəˌhɑːt) *n.* **Amelia.** 1898–1937, U.S. aviator: the first woman to fly the Atlantic (1928). She disappeared on a Pacific flight (1937).

earl (ɜːl) *n.* (in Britain) a nobleman ranking below a marquess and above a viscount. Female equivalent: **countess.** [OE *eorl*] — ˈearldom *n.*

Earl Marshal *n.* an officer of the English peerage who presides over the College of Heralds and organizes royal processions and other important ceremonies.

early (ˈɜːlɪ) *adj., adv.* **-lier, -liest. 1.** before the expected or usual time. **2.** occurring in or characteristic of the first part of a period or sequence. **3.** occurring in or characteristic of a period far back in time. **4.** occurring in the near future. **5. in the early days. a.** during the first years of any enterprise, such as marriage. **b.** *Austral. & N.Z.* during the 19th-century pioneering period in Australia and New Zealand. [OE *ǣrlice,* from *ǣr* ERE + *-lice* -LY²] — ˈearliness *n.*

early closing *n. Brit.* the shutting of shops in a town one afternoon each week.

Early English *n.* a style of architecture used in England in the 12th and 13th centuries, characterized by lancet arches and plate tracery.

early warning *n.* advance notice of some impending event.

earmark (ˈɪəˌmɑːk) *vb.* *(tr.)* **1.** to set aside or mark out for a specific purpose. **2.** to make an identification mark on the ear of (a domestic animal). ~*n.* **3.** such a mark of identification. **4.** any distinguishing mark or characteristic.

earmuff (ˈɪəˌmʌf) *n.* one of a joined pair of pads of fur or cloth for keeping the ears warm.

earn (ɜːn) *vb.* **1.** to gain or be paid (money or other payment) in return for work or service. **2.** *(tr.)* to acquire or deserve through behaviour or action. **3.** *(tr.)* (of securities, investments, etc.) to gain (interest, profit, etc.). [OE *earnian*] — **earner** *n.*

earned income *n.* income derived from paid employment.

earnest¹ (ˈɜːnɪst) *adj.* **1.** serious in mind or intention. **2.** characterized by sincerity of intention. **3.** demanding or receiving serious attention. ~*n.* **4. in earnest.** with serious or sincere intentions. [OE *eornost*] — ˈearnestly *adv.* — ˈearnestness *n.*

earnest² (ˈɜːnɪst) *n.* **1.** a part of something given in advance as a guarantee or the remainder. **2.** Also called: **earnest money.** *Contract law.* something given, usually a nominal sum of money, to confirm a contract. **3.** any token of something to follow. [C13: from OF *erres* pledges, pl. of *erre* earnest money, from L *arrha,* from *arrabō* pledge, from Gk *arrabon,* from Heb. *'ērābhōn* pledge]

earnings (ˈɜːnɪŋz) *pl. n.* **1.** money or other payment earned. **2. a.** the profits of an enterprise. **b.** an individual's investment income.

EAROM (ˈɪərɒm) *n. Computers. acronym for* electrically alterable read only memory.

earphone (ˈɪəˌfəʊn) *n.* a device for converting electric currents into sound waves, held close to or inserted into the ear.

ear piercing *n.* **1.** the making of a hole in the lobe of an ear, using a sterilized needle, so that earrings may be worn fastened in the hole. ~*adj.* **ear-piercing. 2.** so loud or shrill as to hurt the ears.

earplug (ˈɪəˌplʌg) *n.* a piece of soft material placed in the ear to keep out noise or water.

earring (ˈɪəˌrɪŋ) *n.* an ornament for the ear, usually clipped onto the lobe or fastened through a hole pierced in the lobe.

earshot (ˈɪəˌʃɒt) *n.* the range or distance within which sound may be heard (esp. in **out of earshot,** etc.)

ear-splitting *adj.* so loud or shrill as to hurt the ears.
earth (ɜːθ) *n.* **1.** (*sometimes cap.*) the third planet from the sun, the only planet on which life is known to exist. Related adjs.: **terrestrial, telluric.** **2.** the inhabitants of this planet: *the whole earth rejoiced.* **3.** the dry surface of this planet; land; ground. **4.** the loose soft material on the surface of the ground that consists of disintegrated rock particles, mould, clay, etc.; soil. **5.** worldly or temporal matters as opposed to the concerns of the spirit. **6.** the hole in which a burrowing animal, esp. a fox, lives. **7.** *Chem.* See **rare earth, alkaline earth.** **8. a.** a connection between an electric circuit or device and the earth, which is at zero potential. **b.** a terminal to which this connection is made. **9.** (*modifier*) *Astrol.* of or relating to a group of three signs of the zodiac: Taurus, Virgo, and Capricorn. **10. come back** *or* **down to earth.** to return to reality from a fantasy or daydream. **11. on earth.** used as an intensifier in **what on earth, who on earth,** etc. **12. run to earth. a.** to hunt (an animal, esp. a fox) to its earth and trap it there. **b.** to find (someone) after hunting. ~*vb.* **13.** (*tr.*) to connect (a circuit, device, etc.) to earth. ~See also **earth up.** [OE *eorthe*]
earthbound ('ɜːθ,baʊnd) *adj.* **1.** confined to the earth. **2.** heading towards the earth.
earth closet *n.* a type of lavatory in which earth is used to cover excreta.
earthen ('ɜːθən) *adj.* (*prenominal*) **1.** made of baked clay: *an earthen pot.* **2.** made of earth.
earthenware ('ɜːθən,wɛə) *n.* **a.** vessels, etc., made of baked clay. **b.** (*as adj.*): *an earthenware pot.*
earthly ('ɜːθlɪ) *adj.* **-lier, -liest.** **1.** of or characteristic of the earth as opposed to heaven; materialistic; worldly. **2.** (*usually with a negative*) *Inf.* conceivable or possible (in **not an earthly (chance),** etc.). — '**earthliness** *n.*
earthman ('ɜːθ,mæn) *n., pl.* **-men.** (esp. in science fiction) an inhabitant or native of the earth. Also called: **earthling.**
earthnut ('ɜːθ,nʌt) *n.* **1.** a perennial umbelliferous plant of Europe and Asia, having edible dark brown tubers. **2.** any of various plants having an edible root, tuber, or underground pod, such as the peanut or truffle.
earthquake ('ɜːθ,kweɪk) *n.* a series of vibrations at the earth's surface caused by movement along a fault plane, volcanic activity, etc. Related adj.: **seismic.**
earth science *n.* any of various sciences, such as geology and geography, that are concerned with the structure, age, etc., of the earth.
Earthshaker ('ɜːθ,ʃeɪkə) *n.* **the.** *Classical myth.* Poseidon (or Neptune) in his capacity as the bringer of earthquakes.
earth up *vb.* (*tr., adv.*) to cover (part of a plant) with soil to protect from frost, light, etc.
earthward ('ɜːθwəd) *adj.* **1.** directed towards the earth. ~*adv.* **2.** a variant of **earthwards.**
earthwards ('ɜːθwədz) *or* **earthward** *adv.* towards the earth.
earthwork ('ɜːθ,wɜːk) *n.* **1.** excavation of earth, as in engineering construction. **2.** a fortification made of earth.
earthworm ('ɜːθ,wɜːm) *n.* any of numerous worms which burrow in the soil and help aerate and break up the ground.
earthy ('ɜːθɪ) *adj.* **earthier, earthiest.** **1.** of, composed of, or characteristic of earth. **2.** unrefined, coarse, or crude. — '**earthily** *adv.* — '**earthiness** *n.*
ear trumpet *n.* a trumpet-shaped instrument held to the ear: an old form of hearing aid.
earwax ('ɪə,wæks) *n.* the nontechnical name for **cerumen.**
earwig ('ɪə,wɪg) *n.* **1.** any of various insects that typically have an elongated body with small leathery forewings, semicircular membranous hindwings, and curved forceps at the tip of the abdomen. ~*vb.* **-wigging, -wigged.** **2.** (*tr.*) *Arch.* to attempt to influence (a person) by private insinuation. [OE *ēarwicga,* from *ēare* ear + *wicga* beetle, insect; prob. from superstition that the insect crept into human ears]
ease (iːz) *n.* **1.** freedom from discomfort, worry, or anxiety. **2.** lack of difficulty, labour, or awkwardness. **3.** rest, leisure, or relaxation. **4.** freedom from poverty; affluence: *a life of ease.* **5.** lack of restraint, embarrassment, or stiffness: *ease of manner.* **6. at ease. a.** *Mil.* (of a standing soldier, etc.) in a relaxed position with the feet apart, rather than at attention. **b.** a command to adopt

such a position. **c.** in a relaxed attitude or frame of mind. ~*vb.* **7.** to make or become less burdensome. **8.** (*tr.*) to relieve (a person) of worry or care; comfort. **9.** (*tr.*) to make comfortable or give rest to. **10.** (*tr.*) to make less difficult; facilitate. **11.** to move or cause to move into, out of, etc., with careful manipulation. **12.** (when *intr.,* often foll. by *off* or *up*) to lessen or cause to lessen in severity, pressure, tension, or strain. **13. ease oneself** *or* **ease nature.** *Arch., euphemistic.* to urinate or defecate. [C13: from OF *aise* ease, opportunity, from L *adjacēns* neighbouring (area); see ADJACENT] — '**easer** *n.* — '**easeful** *adj.*
easel ('iːzªl) *n.* a frame, usually an upright tripod, for supporting or displaying an artist's canvas, a blackboard, etc. [C17: from Du. *ezel;* ult. from L *asinus* ass]
easement ('iːzmənt) *n.* **1.** *Property law.* the right enjoyed by a landowner of making limited use of his neighbour's land, as by crossing it to reach his own property. **2.** the act of easing or something that brings ease.
easily ('iːzɪlɪ) *adv.* **1.** with ease; without difficulty or exertion. **2.** by far; undoubtedly: *easily the best.* **3.** probably; almost certainly.
▷ **Usage.** See at **easy.**
easiness ('iːzɪnɪs) *n.* **1.** the quality or condition of being easy to accomplish, do, obtain, etc. **2.** ease or relaxation of manner; nonchalance.
east (iːst) *n.* **1.** the direction along a parallel towards the sunrise, at 90° to north; the direction of the earth's rotation. **2. the east.** (*often cap.*) any area lying in or towards the east. Related adj.: **oriental.** **3.** (*usually cap.*) *Cards.* the player or position at the table corresponding to east on the compass. ~*adj.* **4.** situated in, moving towards, or facing the east. **5.** (esp. of the wind) from the east. ~*adv.* **6.** in, to, or towards the east. **7. back East.** *Canad.* in or to E Canada, esp. east of Quebec. [OE *ēast*]
East (iːst) *n.* **the. 1.** the continent of Asia regarded as culturally distinct from Europe and the West; the Orient. **2.** the countries under Communist rule, lying mainly in the E hemisphere. ~*adj.* **3.** of or denoting the eastern part of a specified country, area, etc.
East Africa *n.* a region of Africa comprising Kenya, Uganda, and Tanzania. —**East African** *adj., n.*
East Anglia ('æŋglɪə) *n.* **1.** a region of E England south of the Wash: consists of Norfolk and Suffolk, and parts of Essex and Cambridgeshire. **2.** an Anglo-Saxon kingdom that consisted of Norfolk and Suffolk in the 6th century A.D.; became a dependency of Mercia in the 8th century. —**East Anglian** *adj., n.*
East Bengal *n.* the part of the former Indian province of Bengal assigned to Pakistan in 1947 (now Bangladesh). —**East Bengali** *adj., n.*
East Berlin *n.* the part of Berlin under East German control. —**East Berliner** *n.*
eastbound ('iːst,baʊnd) *adj.* going or leading towards the east.
Eastbourne ('iːst,bɔːn) *n.* a resort in SE England, in East Sussex on the English Channel. Pop.: 77 608 (1981).
east by north *n.* one point on the compass north of east.
east by south *n.* one point on the compass south of east.
East Cape *n.* **1.** the easternmost point of New Guinea, on Milne Bay. **2.** the easternmost point of New Zealand, on North Island. **3.** the former name for Cape **Dezhnev.**
East China Sea *n.* part of the N Pacific, between the E coast of China and the Ryukyu Islands.
East End *n.* **the.** a densely populated part of E London containing former industrial and dock areas. —**East Ender** *n.*
Easter ('iːstə) *n.* **1.** a festival of the Christian Church commemorating the Resurrection of Christ: falls on the Sunday following the first full moon after the vernal equinox. **2.** Also called: **Easter Sunday, Easter Day.** the day on which this festival is celebrated. **3.** the period between Good Friday and Easter Monday. Related adj.: **Paschal.** [OE *ēastre*]
Easter egg *n.* an egg given to children at Easter, usually a chocolate egg or a hen's egg with its shell painted.
Easter Island *n.* an isolated volcanic island in the Pacific, 3700 km (2300 miles) west of Chile, of which it is a dependency: discovered on Easter Sunday, 1722; annexed by Chile in 1888; noted for the remains of an aboriginal culture, which includes gigantic stone figures. Pop.: 1931 (1982). Area: 166 sq. km (64 sq. miles). Also called: **Rapa Nui.** —**Easter Islander** *n.*

easterly ('iːstəlɪ) *adj.* **1.** of or in the east. ~*adv.*, *adj.* **2.** towards the east. **3.** from the east: *an easterly wind.* ~*n.*, *pl.* **-lies. 4.** a wind from the east.
eastern ('iːstən) *adj.* **1.** situated in or towards the east. **2.** facing or moving towards the east.
Eastern Church *n.* **1.** any of the Christian Churches of the former Byzantine Empire. **2.** any Church owing allegiance to the Orthodox Church. **3.** any Church having Eastern forms of liturgy and institutions.
Easterner ('iːstənə) *n.* (*sometimes not cap.*) a native or inhabitant of the east of any specified region.
Eastern Ghats *pl. n.* a mountain range in S India, parallel to the Bay of Bengal: united with the Western Ghats by the Nilgiri Hills; forms the E margin of the Deccan plateau.
eastern hemisphere *n.* (*often caps.*) **1.** that half of the globe containing Europe, Asia, Africa, and Australia, lying east of the Greenwich meridian. **2.** the lands in this, esp. Asia.
Eastern Orthodox Church *n.* another name for the **Orthodox Church.**
Eastern Townships *n.* an area of central Canada, in S Quebec: consists of 11 townships south of the St Lawrence.
Eastertide ('iːstə,taɪd) *n.* the Easter season.
East Flanders *n.* a province of W Belgium: low-lying, with reclaimed land in the northwest: textile industries. Capital: Ghent. Pop.: 1 332 547 (1981 est.). Area: 2979 sq. km (1150 sq. miles).
East Germany *n.* a republic in N central Europe, on the Baltic: established in 1949 and declared a sovereign state by the Soviet Union in 1954; low-lying in the north, with many lakes; mountainous and forested in the south. Language: German. Currency: East German mark. Capital: East Berlin. Pop.: 16 724 000 (1983 est.). Area: 108 178 sq. km (42 189 sq. miles). Official name: **German Democratic Republic.** Abbrevs.: **DDR, GDR.** See also **Germany.** —**East German** *adj.*, *n.*
East Indies *pl. n.* **the. 1.** the Malay Archipelago, including or excluding the Philippines. **2.** SE Asia in general.
easting ('iːstɪŋ) *n.* **1.** *Naut.* the net distance eastwards made by a vessel moving towards the east. **2.** *Cartography.* the distance eastwards of a point from a given meridian indicated by the first half of a map grid reference.
East Kilbride (kɪl'braɪd) *n.* a town in W Scotland, in Strathclyde region near Glasgow: designated a new town in 1947. Pop.: 72 000 (1985).
Eastleigh ('iːst,liː) *n.* a town in S England, in S Hampshire: railway engineering industry. Pop.: 53 113 (1981).
East London *n.* a port in S South Africa, in SE Cape Province. Pop.: 160 582 (1980 est.).
East Lothian *n.* (until 1975) a county of E central Scotland, now part of Lothian region.
Eastman ('iːstmən) *n.* **George.** 1854–1932, U.S. manufacturer of photographic equipment: noted for the introduction of roll film and developments in colour photography.
east-northeast *n.* **1.** the point on the compass or the direction midway between northeast and east. ~*adj.*, *adv.* **2.** in, from, or towards this direction.
East Pakistan *n.* the former name (until 1971) of **Bangladesh.** —**East Pakistani** *adj.*, *n.*
East Prussia *n.* a former province of NE Germany on the Baltic Sea: separated in 1919 from the rest of Germany by the Polish Corridor and Danzig: in 1945 Poland received the south part, the Soviet Union the north. German name: **Ostpreussen** (ost'prɔysən). —**East Prussian** *adj.*, *n.*
East Riding *n.* (until 1974) an administrative division of Yorkshire, now mostly in Humberside.
east-southeast *n.* **1.** the point on the compass or the direction midway between east and southeast. ~*adj.*, *adv.* **2.** in, from, or towards this direction.
East Sussex *n.* a county of SE England comprising part of the former county of Sussex: mainly undulating agricultural land, with the South Downs and seaside resorts in the south. Administrative centre: Lewes. Pop.: 652 568 (1981). Area: 1795 sq. km (693 sq. miles). Abbrev.: **E. Sussex.**
eastward ('iːstwəd) *adj.* **1.** situated or directed towards the east. ~*adv.* **2.** a variant of **eastwards.** ~*n.* **3.** the eastward part, direction, etc. —'**eastwardly** *adv.*, *adj.*
eastwards ('iːstwədz) *or* **eastward** *adv.* towards the east.

Eastwood ('iːstwʊd) *n.* **Clint.** born 1930, U.S. film actor and director. His films include *The Good The Bad and The Ugly* (1966), *Dirty Harry* (1971), and *Bird* (1988; as director).
easy ('iːzɪ) *adj.* **easier, easiest. 1.** not requiring much labour or effort; not difficult. **2.** free from pain, care, or anxiety. **3.** not restricting; lenient: *easy laws.* **4.** tolerant and undemanding; easy-going: *an easy disposition.* **5.** readily influenced; pliant: *an easy victim.* **6.** not constricting; loose: *an easy fit.* **7.** not strained or extreme; moderate: *an easy pace.* **8.** *Inf.* ready to fall in with any suggestion made; not predisposed: *he is easy about what to do.* **9.** *Sl.* sexually available. ~*adv.* **10.** *Inf.* in an easy or relaxed manner. **11. easy does it.** *Inf.* go slowly and carefully; be careful. **12. go easy.** (*usually imperative*; often foll. by *on*) to exercise moderation. **13. stand easy.** *Mil.* a command to soldiers standing at ease that they may relax further. **14. take it easy. a.** to avoid stress or undue hurry. **b.** to remain calm. [C12: from OF *aisié*, p.p. of *aisier* to relieve, EASE]
▷ **Usage.** *Easy* is not used as an adverb by careful speakers and writers except in certain set phrases: *to take it easy; easy does it.* Where a fixed expression is not involved, the usual adverbial form of *easy* is preferred: *this polish goes on more easily* (not *easier*) *than the other.*
easy-care *adj.* (esp. of a fabric or garment) hard-wearing and requiring no special treatment during washing, etc.
easy chair *n.* a comfortable upholstered armchair.
easy-going ('iːzɪ'gəʊɪŋ) *adj.* **1.** relaxed in manner or attitude; excessively tolerant. **2.** moving at a comfortable pace: *an easy-going horse.*
easy meat *n.* *Inf.* **1.** someone easily seduced or deceived. **2.** something easy.
easy money *n.* **1.** money made with little effort, sometimes dishonestly. **2.** *Commerce.* money that can be borrowed at a low interest rate.
Easy Street *n.* (*sometimes not caps.*) *Inf.* a state of financial security.
eat (iːt) *vb.* **eating, ate, eaten. 1.** to take into the mouth and swallow (food, etc.), esp. after biting and chewing. **2.** (*tr.*; often foll. by *away* or *up*) to destroy as if by eating: *the damp had eaten away the woodwork.* **3.** (often foll. by *into*) to use up or waste: *taxes ate into his inheritance.* **4.** (often foll. by *into* or *through*) to make (a hole, passage, etc.) by eating or gnawing: *rats ate through the floor.* **5.** to take or have (a meal or meals): *we eat at six.* **6.** (*tr.*) to include as part of one's diet: *he doesn't eat fish.* **7.** (*tr.*) *Inf.* to cause to worry; make anxious: *what's eating you?* ~See also **eat out, eats, eat up.** [OE *etan*] —'**eater** *n.*
eatable ('iːtəbªl) *adj.* fit or suitable for eating; edible.
eatables ('iːtəblz) *pl. n.* (*sometimes sing.*) food.
eating ('iːtɪŋ) *n.* **1.** food, esp. in relation to quality or taste: *this fruit makes excellent eating.* ~*adj.* **2.** suitable for eating uncooked: *eating apples.* **3.** relating to or for eating: *an eating house.*
eat out *vb.* (*intr.*, *adv.*) to eat away from home, esp. in a restaurant.
eats (iːts) *pl. n.* *Inf.* articles of food; provisions.
eat up *vb.* (*adv.*, *mainly tr.*) **1.** (*also intr.*) to eat or consume entirely. **2.** *Inf.* to listen to with enthusiasm or appreciation: *the audience ate up his every word.* **3.** (often passive) *Inf.* to affect grossly: *she was eaten up by jealousy.* **4.** *Inf.* to travel (a distance) quickly: *we just ate up the miles.*
eau de Cologne (əʊ də kə'ləʊn) *n.* See **cologne.** [F, lit.: water of Cologne]
eau de nil (əʊ də niːl) *n.*, *adj.* (of) a pale yellowish-green colour. [F, lit.: water of (the) Nile]
eau de vie (əʊ də viː) *n.* brandy or other spirits. [F, lit.: water of life]
eaves (iːvz) *pl. n.* the edge of a roof that projects beyond the wall. [OE *efes*]
eavesdrop ('iːvz,drɒp) *vb.* **-dropping, -dropped.** (*intr.*) to listen secretly to the private conversation of others. [C17: back formation from *evesdropper*, from OE *yfesdrype* water dripping from the eaves] —'**eaves,dropper** *n.*
ebb (εb) *vb.* (*intr.*) **1.** (of tide water) to flow back or recede. Cf. **flow** (sense 8). **2.** to fall away or decline. ~*n.* **3. a.** the flowing back of the tide from high to low water or the period in which this takes place. **b.** (*as modifier*):

the ebb tide. Cf. **flood** (sense 3). **4. at a low ebb.** in a state of weakness or decline. [OE *ebba*]

Ebbinghaus ('ɛbɪŋhaʊs) *n.* **Hermann** ('hɛrman). 1850–1909, German experimental psychologist who undertook the first systematic and large-scale studies of memory and devised tests using nonsense syllables.

Ebbw Vale ('ɛbuː veɪl) *n.* a town in S Wales, in W Gwent: coal mines. Pop.: 24 422 (1981).

EBCDIC ('ɛpsɪˌdɪk) *n. acronym for* extended binary-coded decimal-interchange code: a computer code for representing alphanumeric characters.

Ebert (*German* 'eːbərt) *n.* **Friedrich** ('friːdrɪç). 1871–1925, German Social Democratic statesman; first president of the German Republic (1919–25).

ebon ('ɛbᵊn) *adj., n.* a poetic word for **ebony.** [C14: from L *hebenus;* see EBONY]

ebonite ('ɛbəˌnaɪt) *n.* another name for **vulcanite.**

ebonize *or* **-ise** ('ɛbəˌnaɪz) *vb.* (*tr.*) to stain or otherwise finish in imitation of ebony.

ebony ('ɛbənɪ) *n., pl.* **-onies. 1.** any of various tropical and subtropical trees that have hard dark wood. **2.** the wood of such a tree. **3. a.** a black colour. **b.** (*as adj.*): *an ebony skin.* [C16 *hebeny,* from LL, from Gk, from *ebenos* ebony, from Egyptian]

Eboracum (iːˈbɒrəkəm, ˌiːbɔːˈrɑːkəm) *n.* the Roman name for **York¹** (sense 1).

Ebro ('iːbrəʊ; *Spanish* 'eβro) *n.* the second largest river in Spain, rising in the Cantabrian Mountains and flowing southeast to the Mediterranean. Length: 910 km (565 miles).

ebullient (ɪˈbʌljənt, ɪˈbʊl-) *adj.* **1.** overflowing with enthusiasm or excitement. **2.** boiling. [C16: from L *ēbullīre* to bubble forth, be boisterous, from *bullīre* to BOIL¹] —e'**bullience** *or* e'**bulliency** *n.*

ebullition (ˌɛbəˈlɪʃən) *n.* **1.** the process of boiling. **2.** a sudden outburst, as of intense emotion. [C16: from LL *ēbullītiō;* see EBULLIENT]

EC *abbrev. for:* **1.** East Central. **2.** European Community.

ec- *combining form.* out from; away from: *eccentric; ecdysis.* [from Gk *ek* (before a vowel *ex*) out of, away from; see EX-¹]

Ecbatana (ɛkˈbætənə) *n.* an ancient city in Iran, on the site of modern Hamadān; capital of Media and royal residence of the Persians and Parthians.

eccentric (ɪkˈsɛntrɪk) *adj.* **1.** deviating or departing from convention; irregular or odd. **2.** situated away from the centre or the axis. **3.** not having a common centre: *eccentric circles.* **4.** not precisely circular. ~*n.* **5.** a person who deviates from normal forms of behaviour. **6.** a device for converting rotary motion to reciprocating motion. [C16: from Med. L *eccentricus,* from Gk *ekkentros,* from *ek-* EX-¹ + *kentron* centre] —ec'**centrically** *adv.*

eccentricity (ˌɛksɛnˈtrɪsɪtɪ) *n., pl.* **-ties. 1.** unconventional or irregular behaviour. **2.** the state of being eccentric. **3.** deviation from a circular path or orbit. **4.** *Geom.* a number that expresses the shape of a conic section. **5.** the degree of displacement of the geometric centre of a part from the true centre, esp. of the axis of rotation of a wheel.

eccl. *or* **eccles.** *abbrev. for* ecclesiastic(al).

Eccles ('ɛkᵊlz) *n.* a town in NW England, in Greater Manchester. Pop.: 37 166 (1981).

Eccles. *or* **Eccl.** *Bible. abbrev. for* Ecclesiastes.

ecclesiastic (ɪˌkliːzɪˈæstɪk) *n.* **1.** a clergyman or other person in holy orders. ~*adj.* **2.** of or associated with the Christian Church or clergy.

ecclesiastical (ɪˌkliːzɪˈæstɪkᵊl) *adj.* of or relating to the Christian Church. —ec,clesi'**astically** *adv.*

ecclesiasticism (ɪˌkliːzɪˈæstɪˌsɪzəm) *n.* exaggerated attachment to the practices or principles of the Christian Church.

ecclesiology (ɪˌkliːzɪˈɒlədʒɪ) *n.* **1.** the study of the Christian Church. **2.** the study of Church architecture and decoration. —ecclesiological (ɪˌkliːzɪəˈlɒdʒɪkᵊl) *adj.*

eccrine ('ɛkrɪn) *adj.* of or denoting glands that secrete externally, esp. the sweat glands. Cf. **apocrine.** [from Gk *ek-krinein,* from *ek-* EC- + *krinein* to separate] —**eccrinology** (ˌɛkrɪˈnɒlədʒɪ) *n.*

ecdysis ('ɛkdɪsɪs) *n., pl.* **-ses** (-ˌsiːz). the periodic shedding of the cuticle in insects and other arthropods or the outer epidermal layer in reptiles. [C19: NL, from Gk *ekdusis,* from *ekduein* to strip, from *ek-* EX-¹ + *duein* to put on]

Ecevit ('ɛtʃəvɪt) *n.* **Bülent** ('buːlənt). born 1925, Turkish statesman; prime minister (1974; 1978–79).

ECG *abbrev. for:* **1.** electrocardiogram. **2.** electrocardiograph.

echelon ('ɛʃəˌlɒn) *n.* **1.** a level of command, responsibility, etc. (esp. in **the upper echelons**). **2.** *Mil.* **a.** a formation in which units follow one another but are offset sufficiently to allow each unit a line of fire ahead. **b.** a group formed in this way. ~*vb.* **3.** to assemble in echelon. [C18: from F *échelon,* lit.: rung of a ladder, from OF *eschiele* ladder, from L *scāla*]

echidna (ɪˈkɪdnə) *n., pl.* **-nas** *or* **-nae** (-niː). a spine-covered monotreme mammal of Australia and New Guinea, having a long snout and claws. Also called: **spiny anteater.** [C19: from NL, from L: viper, from Gk *ekhidna*]

echinoderm (ɪˈkaɪnəʊˌdɜːm) *n.* any of various marine invertebrates characterized by tube feet, a calcite body-covering, and a five-part symmetrical body. The group includes the starfish, sea urchins, and sea cucumbers.

echinus (ɪˈkaɪnəs) *n., pl.* **-ni** (-naɪ). **1.** *Archit.* a moulding between the shaft and the abacus of a Doric column. **2.** any sea urchin of the genus *Echinus,* such as the Mediterranean edible sea urchin. [C14: from L, from Gk *ekhinos*]

echo ('ɛkəʊ) *n., pl.* **-oes. 1. a.** the reflection of sound or other radiation by a reflecting medium, esp. a solid object. **b.** the sound so reflected. **2.** a repetition or imitation, esp. an unoriginal reproduction of another's opinions. **3.** something that evokes memories. **4.** (*sometimes pl.*) an effect that continues after the original cause has disappeared: *echoes of the French Revolution.* **5.** a person who copies another, esp. one who obsequiously agrees with another's opinions. **6. a.** the signal reflected by a radar target. **b.** the trace produced by such a signal on a radar screen. ~*vb.* **-oing, -oed. 7.** to resound or cause to resound with an echo. **8.** (*intr.*) (of sounds) to repeat or resound by echoes; reverberate. **9.** (*tr.*) (of persons) to repeat (words, opinions, etc.) in imitation, agreement, or flattery. **10.** (*tr.*) (of things) to resemble or imitate (another style, an earlier model, etc.). [C14: via L from Gk *ēkhō;* rel. to Gk *ēkhē* sound] —'**echoing** *adj.* —'**echoless** *adj.* —'**echo-ˌlike** *adj.*

Echo ('ɛkəʊ) *n. Greek myth.* a nymph who, spurned by Narcissus, pined away until only her voice remained.

echo chamber *n.* a room with walls that reflect sound. It is used to make acoustic measurements and as a recording studio when echo effects are required. Also called: **reverberation chamber.**

echoic (ɛˈkəʊɪk) *adj.* **1.** characteristic of or resembling an echo. **2.** onomatopoeic; imitative.

echolalia (ˌɛkəʊˈleɪlɪə) *n. Psychiatry.* the tendency to repeat mechanically words just spoken by another person. [C19: from NL, from ECHO + Gk *lalia* talk, chatter]

echolocation (ˌɛkəʊləʊˈkeɪʃən) *n.* determination of the position of an object by measuring the time taken for an echo to return from it and its direction.

echo sounder *n.* a navigation device that determines depth by measuring the time taken for a pulse of sound to reach the sea bed or a submerged object and for the echo to return. —**echo sounding** *n.*

echovirus *or* **ECHO virus** ('ɛkəʊˌvaɪrəs) *n.* any of a group of viruses that can cause symptoms of mild meningitis, the common cold, or infections of the intestinal and respiratory tracts. [C20: from initials of *Enteric Cytopathic Human Orphan* ("orphan" because orig. believed to be unrelated to any disease) + VIRUS]

Eck (ɛk) *n.* **Johann** (joˈhan), original name *Johann Mayer.* 1486–1543, German Roman Catholic theologian; opponent of Luther and the Reformation.

Eckhart (*German* 'ɛkhart) *n.* **Johannes** (joˈhanəs), called *Meister Eckhart.* ?1260–?1327, German Dominican theologian, mystic, and preacher.

éclair (eɪˈklɛə, ɪˈklɛə) *n.* a finger-shaped cake of choux pastry, usually filled with cream and covered with chocolate. [C19: from F, lit.: lightning (prob. because it does not last long)]

eclampsia (ɪˈklæmpsɪə) *n. Pathol.* a toxic condition that sometimes develops in the last three months of pregnancy, characterized by high blood pressure, weight gain, and convulsions. [C19: from NL, from Gk *eklampsis* a shining forth]

éclat (eɪ'klɑ:) n. **1.** brilliant or conspicuous success, effect, etc. **2.** showy display; ostentation. **3.** social distinction. **4.** approval; acclaim; applause. [C17: from F, from *éclater* to burst]

eclectic (ɪ'klɛktɪk, ɛ'klɛk-) adj. **1.** selecting from various styles, ideas, methods, etc. **2.** composed of elements drawn from a variety of sources, styles, etc. ~n. **3.** a person who favours an eclectic approach. [C17: from Gk *eklektikos*, from *eklegein* to select, from *legein* to gather] —e'**clectically** adv. —e'**clecticism** n.

eclipse (ɪ'klɪps) n. **1.** the total or partial obscuring of one celestial body by another (**total eclipse** or **partial eclipse**). A **solar eclipse** occurs when the moon passes between the sun and the earth; a **lunar eclipse** when the earth passes between the sun and the moon. **2.** the period of time during which such a phenomenon occurs. **3.** any dimming or obstruction of light. **4.** a loss of importance, power, fame, etc., esp. through overshadowing by another. ~vb. (tr.) **5.** to cause an eclipse of. **6.** to cast a shadow upon; obscure. **7.** to overshadow or surpass. [C13: back formation from OE *eclypsis*, from Gk *ekleipsis* a forsaking, from *ekleipein* to abandon] —e'**clipser** n.

eclipsing binary n. a binary star whose orbital plane lies in or near the line of sight so that one component is regularly eclipsed by its companion.

ecliptic (ɪ'klɪptɪk) n. **1.** *Astron.* **a.** the great circle on the celestial sphere representing the apparent annual path of the sun relative to the stars. **b.** (as modifier): *the ecliptic plane.* **2.** an equivalent great circle on the terrestrial globe. ~adj. **3.** of or relating to an eclipse. —e'**cliptically** adv.

eclogue ('ɛklɒg) n. a pastoral or idyllic poem, usually in the form of a conversation. [C15: from L *ecloga* short poem, collection of extracts, from Gk *eklogē* selection, from *eklegein* to select]

eclosion (ɪ'kləʊʒən) n. the emergence of an insect larva from the egg or an adult from the pupal case. [C19: from F, from *éclore* to hatch, ult. from L *exclūdere* to shut out]

Eco ('ɛkəʊ) n. Umberto. born 1932, Italian semiologist and writer. He is noted for his novel *The Name of the Rose* (1981).

eco- combining form. denoting ecology or ecological: *ecocide; ecosphere.*

ecol. abbrev. for: **1.** ecological. **2.** ecology.

ecology (ɪ'kɒlədʒɪ) n. **1.** the study of the relationships between living organisms and their environment. **2.** the set of relationships of a particular organism with its environment. [C19: from G *Ökologie*, from Gk *oikos* house (hence, environment)] —**ecological** (,i:kə'lɒdʒɪk°l) adj. —e'**cologist** n.

econ. abbrev. for: **1.** economical. **2.** economics. **3.** economy.

econometrics (ɪ,kɒnə'mɛtrɪks) n. (functioning as sing.) the application of mathematical and statistical techniques to economic theories. —**e,cono'metric** or **e,cono'metrical** adj. —**econometrician** (ɪ,kɒnəmə'trɪʃən) or **e,cono'metrist** n.

economic (,i:kə'nɒmɪk, ,ɛkə-) adj. **1.** of or relating to an economy, economics, or finance. **2.** *Brit.* capable of being produced, operated, etc., for profit; profitable. **3.** concerning or affecting material resources or welfare: *economic pests.* **4.** concerned with or relating to the necessities of life; utilitarian. **5.** a variant of **economical**. **6.** *Inf.* inexpensive; cheap.

economical (,i:kə'nɒmɪk°l, ,ɛkə-) adj. **1.** using the minimum required; not wasteful. **2.** frugal; thrifty. **3.** a variant of **economic** (senses 1–4). —,**eco'nomically** adv.

economics (,i:kə'nɒmɪks, ,ɛkə-) n. **1.** (functioning as sing.) the social science concerned with the production and consumption of goods and services and the analysis of the commercial activities of a society. **2.** (functioning as pl.) financial aspects.

economist (ɪ'kɒnəmɪst) n. a specialist in economics.

economize or **-ise** (ɪ'kɒnə,maɪz) vb. (often foll. by *on*) to limit or reduce (expense, waste, etc.). —**e,conomi'zation** or **-i'sation** n.

economy (ɪ'kɒnəmɪ) n., pl. **-mies**. **1.** careful management of resources to avoid unnecessary expenditure or waste; thrift. **2.** a means or instance of this; saving. **3.** sparing, restrained, or efficient use. **4. a.** the complex of activities concerned with the production, distribution, and consumption of goods and services. **b.** a particular type or branch of this: *a socialist economy.* **5.** the management of the resources, finances, income, and expenditure of a community, business enterprise, etc. **6. a.** a class of travel in aircraft, cheaper and less luxurious than first class. **b.** (as modifier): *economy class.* **7.** (modifier) purporting to offer a larger quantity for a lower price: *economy pack.* **8.** the orderly interplay between the parts of a system or structure. [C16: via L from Gk *oikonomia* domestic management, from *oikos* house + *-nomia*, from *nemein* to manage]

ecosphere ('i:kəʊ,sfɪə, 'ɛkəʊ-) n. the parts of the universe, esp. on earth, where life can exist.

écossaise (,eɪkɒ'seɪz) n. **1.** a lively dance in two-four time. **2.** the tune for such a dance. [C19: F, lit.: Scottish (dance)]

ecosystem ('i:kəʊ,sɪstəm, 'ɛkəʊ-) n. *Ecology.* a system involving the interactions between a community and its non-living environment. [C20: from ECO(LOGY) + SYSTEM]

ecru ('ɛkru:, 'eɪkru:) n., adj. (of) a greyish-yellow to a light greyish colour. [C19: from F, from *é-* (intensive) + *cru* raw, from L *crūdus*; see CRUDE]

ecstasy ('ɛkstəsɪ) n., pl. **-sies**. **1.** (often pl.) a state of exalted delight, joy, etc.; rapture. **2.** intense emotion of any kind: *an ecstasy of rage.* **3.** *Psychol.* overpowering emotion sometimes involving temporary loss of consciousness: often associated with mysticism. **4.** *Sl.* 3,4-methylenedioxymethamphetamine: a powerful drug that acts as a stimulant and can produce hallucinations. [C14: from OF via Med. L from Gk *ekstasis* displacement, trance, from *ex-* out + *histanai* to cause to stand]

ecstatic (ɛk'stætɪk) adj. **1.** in a trancelike state of rapture or delight. **2.** showing or feeling great enthusiasm. ~n. **3.** a person who has periods of intense trancelike joy. —**ec'statically** adv.

ECT abbrev. for electroconvulsive therapy.

ecto- combining form. indicating outer, outside. [from Gk *ektos* outside, from *ek, ex* out]

ectoblast ('ɛktəʊ,blæst) n. another name for **ectoderm**. —,**ecto'blastic** adj.

ectoderm ('ɛktəʊ,dɜ:m) or **exoderm** n. the outer germ layer of an animal embryo, which gives rise to epidermis and nervous tissue. —,**ecto'dermal** or ,**ecto'dermic** adj.

ectomorph ('ɛktəʊ,mɔ:f) n. a type of person having a body build characterized by thinness, weakness, and a lack of weight. —,**ecto'morphic** adj. — 'ecto,**morphy** n.

-ectomy n. combining form. indicating surgical excision of a part: *appendectomy.* [from NL *-ectomia*, from Gk *ek-* out + -TOMY]

ectopic pregnancy (ɛk'tɒpɪk) n. *Pathol.* the abnormal development of a fertilized egg outside the uterus, usually within a Fallopian tube.

ectoplasm ('ɛktəʊ,plæzəm) n. **1.** *Cytology.* the outer layer of cytoplasm. **2.** *Spiritualism.* the substance supposedly emanating from the body of a medium during trances. —,**ecto'plasmic** adj.

ECU (also 'eɪku:, 'ɛkju:) abbrev. for European Currency Unit.

Ecuador ('ɛkwə,dɔ:) n. a republic in South America, on the Pacific: under the Incas when Spanish colonization began in 1532; gained independence in 1822; declared a republic in 1830. It consists chiefly of a coastal plain in the west, separated from the densely forested upper Amazon basin (Oriente) by ranges and plateaus of the Andes. Official language: Spanish; Quechua is also widely spoken. Religion: Roman Catholic. Currency: sucre. Capital: Quito. Pop.: 9 640 000 (1986). Area: 283 560 sq. km (109 483 sq. miles). —,**Ecua'dorian** or ,**Ecua'doran** adj., n.

ecumenical, oecumenical (,i:kju'mɛnɪk°l, ,ɛk-) or **ecumenic, oecumenic** adj. **1.** of or relating to the Christian Church throughout the world, esp. with regard to its unity. **2.** tending to promote unity among Churches. [C16: via LL from Gk *oikoumenikos*, from *oikein* to inhabit, from *oikos* house] —,**ecu'menically** or ,**oecu'menically** adv.

ecumenicalism (,i:kju'mɛnɪkə,lɪzəm, ,ɛk-), **ecumenicism** or **ecumenism** n. the aim of unity among all Christian churches throughout the world.

eczema ('ɛksɪmə) n. *Pathol.* a skin inflammation with lesions that scale, crust, or ooze a serous fluid, often accompanied by intense itching. [C18: from NL, from Gk *ekzema*, from *ek-* out + *zein* to boil] —**eczematous** (ɛk'sɛmətəs) adj.

ed. *abbrev. for:* **1.** edited. **2.** (*pl.* **eds.**) edition. **3.** (*pl.* **eds.**) editor. **4.** education.

-ed[1] *suffix.* forming the past tense of most English verbs. [OE *-de, -ede, -ode, -ade*]

-ed[2] *suffix.* forming the past participle of most English verbs. [OE *-ed, -od, -ad*]

-ed[3] *suffix forming adjectives from nouns.* possessing or having the characteristics of: *salaried; red-blooded.* [OE *-ede*]

Edam ('iːdæm) *n.* a round yellow cheese with a red outside covering. [after *Edam,* in Holland]

Edberg ('ɛdbɜːg) *n.* **Stefan.** born 1966, Swedish tennis player: Wimbledon champion 1988.

Edda ('ɛdə) *n.* **1.** Also called: **Elder Edda, Poetic Edda.** a 12th-century collection of mythological Old Norse poems. **2.** Also called: **Younger Edda, Prose Edda.** a treatise on versification together with a collection of Scandinavian myths, legends, and poems (?1222). [C18: ON] — **Eddaic** (ɛ'deɪɪk) *adj.*

Eddington ('ɛdɪŋtən) *n.* Sir **Arthur Stanley.** 1882–1944, English astronomer and physicist, noted for his research on the motion, internal constitution, and luminosity of stars and for his elucidation of the theory of relativity.

eddy ('ɛdɪ) *n., pl.* **-dies. 1.** a movement in air, water, or other fluid in which the current doubles back on itself causing a miniature whirlwind or whirlpool. **2.** a deviation from or disturbance in the main trend of thought, life, etc. ~*vb.* **-dying, -died. 3.** to move or cause to move against the main current. [C15: prob. from ON]

Eddy ('ɛdɪ) *n.* **Mary Baker.** 1821–1910, U.S. religious leader; founder of the Christian Science movement (1866).

eddy current *n.* an electric current induced in a massive conductor by an alternating magnetic field.

Eddystone Rocks ('ɛdɪstən) *n.* a dangerous group of rocks at the W end of the English Channel, southwest of Plymouth: lighthouse.

Ede ('eɪdə) *n.* a city in the central Netherlands, in Gelderland province. Pop.: 85 025 (1982 est.).

edelweiss ('eɪd°l,vaɪs) *n.* a small alpine flowering plant having white woolly oblong leaves and a tuft of floral leaves surrounding the flowers. [C19: G, lit.: noble white]

edema (ɪ'diːmə) *n., pl.* **-mata** (-mətə). the usual U.S. spelling of **oedema.**

Eden[1] ('iːd°n) *n.* **1.** Also called: **Garden of Eden.** *Bible.* the garden in which Adam and Eve were placed at the Creation. **2.** a place or state of great delight or contentment. [C14: from LL, from Heb. *'ēdhen* place of pleasure] — **Edenic** (iː'dɛnɪk) *adj.*

Eden[2] ('iːd°n) *n.* Sir (**Robert**) **Anthony,** Earl of Avon. 1897–1977, British Conservative statesman; foreign secretary (1935–38; 1940–45; 1951–55) and prime minister (1955–57). He resigned after the controversy caused by the occupation of the Suez Canal zone by British and French forces (1956).

edentate (iː'dɛnteɪt) *n.* **1.** any mammal of the order *Edentata,* of tropical Central and South America, which have few or no teeth. The order includes anteaters, sloths, and armadillos. ~*adj.* **2.** of or relating to the order *Edentata.* [C19: from L *ēdentātus* lacking teeth, from *ēdentāre* to render toothless, from *e-* out + *dēns* tooth]

Edessa (ɪ'dɛsə) *n.* **1.** an ancient city on the N edge of the Syrian plateau, founded as a Macedonian colony by Seleucus I: a centre of early Christianity. Modern name: **Urfa. 2.** a market town in Greece: ancient capital of Macedonia. Pop.: 15 980 (1981). Ancient name: **Aegae** ('iːgiː). Modern Greek name: **Édhessa.**

Edgar ('ɛdgə) *n.* **1.** 944–975 A.D., king of Mercia and Northumbria (957–975) and of England (959–975). **2.** ?1074–1107, king of Scotland (1097–1107), fourth son of Malcolm III. He overthrew his uncle Donald to gain the throne.

Edgar Atheling ('æθɪlɪŋ) *n.* ?1050–?1125, grandson of Edmund II; Anglo-Saxon pretender to the English throne in 1066.

edge (ɛdʒ) *n.* **1.** a border, brim, or margin. **2.** a brink or verge. **3.** a line along which two faces or surfaces of a solid meet. **4.** the sharp cutting side of a blade. **5.** keenness, sharpness, or urgency. **6.** force, effectiveness, or incisiveness: *the performance lacked edge.* **7.** a ridge. **8. have the edge on** *or* **over.** to have a slight advantage or superiority over. **9. on edge. a.** nervously irritable; tense. **b.** nervously excited or eager. **10. set (someone's)**

teeth on edge. to make (someone) acutely irritated or uncomfortable. ~*vb.* **11.** (*tr.*) to provide an edge or border for. **12.** (*tr.*) to shape or trim the edge or border of (something). **13.** to push (one's way, someone, something, etc.) gradually, esp. edgeways. **14.** (*tr.*) *Cricket.* to hit (a bowled ball) with the edge of the bat. **15.** (*tr.*) to sharpen (a knife, etc.). [OE *ecg*] — **edger** *n.*

edgeways ('ɛdʒ,weɪz) *or esp. U.S. & Canad.* **edgewise** ('ɛdʒ,waɪz) *adv.* **1.** with the edge forwards or uppermost. **2.** on, by, with, or towards the edge. **3. get a word in edgeways.** (*usually with a negative*) to interrupt a conversation in which someone else is talking incessantly.

Edgeworth ('ɛdʒwɜːθ) *n.* **Maria.** 1767–1849, English novelist: her works include *Castle Rackrent* (1800) and *The Absentee* (1812).

edging ('ɛdʒɪŋ) *n.* **1.** anything placed along an edge to finish it, esp. as an ornament. **2.** the act of making an edge. ~*adj.* **3.** relating to or used for making an edge: *edging shears.*

edgy ('ɛdʒɪ) *adj.* **edgier, edgiest.** (*usually postpositive*) nervous, irritable, tense, or anxious. — '**edgily** *adv.* — '**edginess** *n.*

edh (ɛð) *or* **eth** (ɛθ, ɛð) *n.* a character of the runic alphabet (ð) used to represent the voiced dental fricative as in *then, mother, bathe.*

Édhessa (*Greek* 'ɔðɛsa) *n.* transliteration of the Modern Greek name for **Edessa.**

edible ('ɛdɪb°l) *adj.* fit to be eaten; eatable. [C17: from LL *edibilis,* from L *edere* to eat] — ,**edi'bility** *or* '**edibleness** *n.*

edibles ('ɛdɪb°lz) *pl. n.* articles fit to eat; food.

edict ('iːdɪkt) *n.* **1.** a decree or order issued by any authority. **2.** any formal or authoritative command, proclamation, etc. [C15: from L *ēdictum,* from *ēdīcere* to declare] — **e'dictal** *adj.*

edifice ('ɛdɪfɪs) *n.* **1.** a building, esp. a large or imposing one. **2.** a complex or elaborate institution or organization. [C14: from OF, from L *aedificium,* from *aedificāre* to build; see EDIFY]

edify ('ɛdɪ,faɪ) *vb.* **-fying, -fied.** (*tr.*) to improve the morality, intellect, etc., of, esp. by instruction. [C14: from OF, from L *aedificāre* to construct, from *aedēs* a dwelling, temple + *facere* to make] — ,**edifi'cation** *n.* — '**edi,fier** *n.* — '**edi,fying** *adj.*

Edinburgh[1] ('ɛdɪnbərə, -brə) *n.* the capital of Scotland, in Lothian region on the S side of the Firth of Forth: became the capital in the 15th century; university (1583); commercial and cultural centre, noted for its annual festival. Pop.: 439 672 (1985 est.).

Edinburgh[2] ('ɛdɪnbərə, -brə) *n.* **Duke of,** title of Prince *Philip Mountbatten.* born 1921, husband of Elizabeth II of Great Britain and Northern Ireland.

Edirne (ɛ'dirnɛ) *n.* a city in NW Turkey: a Thracian town, rebuilt and renamed by the Roman emperor Hadrian. Pop.: 71 914 (1980). Former name: **Adrianople.**

Edison ('ɛdɪs°n) *n.* **Thomas Alva.** 1847–1931, U.S. inventor. He patented more than a thousand inventions, including the phonograph, the incandescent electric lamp, the microphone, and the kinetoscope.

edit ('ɛdɪt) *vb.* (*tr.*) **1.** to prepare (text) for publication by checking and improving its accuracy, clarity, etc. **2.** to be in charge of (a publication, esp. a periodical). **3.** to prepare (a film, tape, etc.) by rearrangement or selection of material. **4.** (often foll. by *out*) to remove, as from a manuscript or film. [C18: back formation from EDITOR]

edit. *abbrev. for:* **1.** edited. **2.** edition. **3.** editor.

edition (ɪ'dɪʃən) *n.* **1.** *Printing.* **a.** the entire number of copies of a book or other publication printed at one time. **b.** a copy from this number: *a first edition.* **2.** one of a number of printings of a book or other publication, issued at separate times with alterations, amendments, etc. **3. a.** an issue of a work identified by its format: *a leather-bound edition.* **b.** an issue of a work identified by its editor or publisher: *the Oxford edition.* [C16: from L *ēditiō* a bringing forth, publishing, from *ēdere* to give out; see EDITOR]

editor ('ɛdɪtə) *n.* **1.** a person who edits written material for publication. **2.** a person in overall charge of a newspaper or periodical. **3.** a person in charge of one section of a newspaper or periodical: *the sports editor.* **4.** *Films.* a person who makes a selection and arrangement of shots. **5.** a person in overall control of a television or radio programme that consists of various items. [C17: from

LL: producer, exhibitor, from *ēdere* to give out, publish, from *ē-* out + *dāre* to give] —'**editor,ship** *n.*

editorial (,ɛdɪ'tɔːrɪəl) *adj.* **1.** of or relating to editing or editors. **2.** of, relating to, or expressed in an editorial. **3.** of or relating to the content of a publication. ~*n.* **4.** an article in a newspaper, etc., expressing the opinion of the editor or the publishers. —,**edi'torially** *adv.*

editorialize *or* **-ise** (,ɛdɪ'tɔːrɪə,laɪz) *vb.* (*intr.*) to express an opinion as in an editorial. —,**edi,toriali'zation** *or* **-i'sation** *n.* —,**edi'torial,izer** *or* **-iser** *n.*

Edmonton ('ɛdməntən) *n.* a city in W Canada, capital of Alberta: oil industry. Pop.: 785 465 (1986).

Edmund I ('ɛdmənd) *n.* ?922–946 A.D., king of England (940–946).

Edmund II *n.* called *Edmund Ironside.* ?980–1016, king of England in 1016. His succession was contested by Canute and they divided the kingdom between them.

EDP *abbrev. for* electronic data processing.

EDT (in the U.S. and Canada) *abbrev. for* Eastern Daylight Time.

educate ('ɛdjʊ,keɪt) *vb.* (*mainly tr.*) **1.** (*also intr.*) to impart knowledge by formal instruction to (a pupil); teach. **2.** to provide schooling for. **3.** to improve or develop (a person, taste, skills, etc.). **4.** to train for some particular purpose or occupation. [C15: from L *ēducāre* to rear, educate, from *dūcere* to lead] —'**educable** *or* '**edu,catable** *adj.* —,**educa'bility** *or* ,**edu,cata'bility** *n.* —'**educative** *adj.*

educated ('ɛdjʊ,keɪtɪd) *adj.* **1.** having an education, esp. a good one. **2.** displaying culture, taste, and knowledge; cultivated. **3.** (*prenominal*) based on experience or information (esp. in an **educated guess**).

education (,ɛdjʊ'keɪʃən) *n.* **1.** the act or process of acquiring knowledge. **2.** the knowledge or training acquired by this process. **3.** the act or process of imparting knowledge, esp. at a school, college, or university. **4.** the theory of teaching and learning. **5.** a particular kind of instruction or training: *a university education.* —,**edu'cational** *adj.* —,**edu'cationalist** *or* ,**edu'cationist** *n.*

educator ('ɛdjʊ,keɪtə) *n.* **1.** a person who educates; teacher. **2.** a specialist in education.

educe (ɪ'djuːs) *vb.* (*tr.*) *Rare.* **1.** to evolve or develop. **2.** to draw out or elicit (information, solutions, etc.). [C15: from L *ēdūcere*, from *ē-* out + *dūcere* to lead] —**e'ducible** *adj.* —**eductive** (ɪ'dʌktɪv) *adj.*

Edward¹ ('ɛdwəd) *n.* **Lake.** a lake in central Africa, between Uganda and Zaïre in the Great Rift Valley: empties through the Semliki River into Lake Albert. Area: about 2150 sq. km (830 sq. miles). Former official name: **Lake Amin.**

Edward² ('ɛdwəd) *n.* **1.** known as *the Black Prince.* 1330–76, Prince of Wales, the son of Edward III of England. He won victories over the French at Crécy (1346) and Poitiers (1356) in the Hundred Years' War. **2. Prince.** born 1964, third son of Elizabeth II of Great Britain and Northern Ireland.

Edward I *n.* 1239–1307, king of England (1272–1307); son of Henry III. He conquered Wales (1284) but failed to subdue Scotland.

Edward II *n.* 1284–1327, king of England (1307–27); son of Edward I. He invaded Scotland but was defeated by Robert Bruce at Bannockburn (1314). He was deposed by his wife Isabella and Roger Mortimer; died in prison.

Edward III *n.* 1312–77, king of England (1327–77); son of Edward II. His claim to the French throne in right of his mother Isabella provoked the Hundred Years' War (1337).

Edward IV *n.* 1442–83, king of England (1461–70; 1471–83); son of Richard, duke of York. He defeated Henry VI in the Wars of the Roses and became king (1461). In 1470 Henry was restored to the throne, but Edward recovered the crown by his victory at Tewkesbury.

Edward V *n.* 1470–?83, king of England in 1483; son of Edward IV. He was deposed by his uncle, Richard, Duke of Gloucester (Richard III), and is thought to have been murdered with his brother in the Tower of London.

Edward VI *n.* 1537–53, king of England (1547–53), son of Henry VIII and Jane Seymour. His uncle the Duke of Somerset was regent until 1552, when he was executed. Edward then came under the control of Dudley, Duke of Northumberland.

Edward VII *n.* 1841–1910, king of Great Britain and Ireland (1901–10); son of Queen Victoria.

Edward VIII *n.* 1894–1972, king of Great Britain and Ireland in 1936; son of George V and brother of George VI. He abdicated in order to marry an American divorcée, Mrs Wallis Simpson; created Duke of Windsor (1937).

Edwardian (ɛd'wɔːdɪən) *adj.* of or characteristic of the reign of Edward VII. —**Ed'wardianism** *n.*

Edwards ('ɛdwədz) *n.* **1. Gareth (Owen).** born 1947, Welsh Rugby Union footballer: halfback for Wales (1967–78) and the British Lions (1968–74). **2. Jonathan.** 1703–58, American Calvinist theologian and metaphysician; author of *The Freedom of the Will* (1754).

Edward the Confessor *n.* **Saint.** ?1002–66, king of England (1042–66); son of Ethelred II; founder of Westminster Abbey. Feast day: Oct. 13.

Edwin ('ɛdwɪn) *n.* ?585–633 A.D., king of Northumbria (617–633) and overlord of all England except Kent.

-ee *suffix forming nouns.* **1.** indicating a recipient of an action (as opposed, esp. in legal terminology, to the agent): *assignee; lessee.* **2.** indicating a person in a specified state or condition: *absentee.* **3.** indicating a diminutive form of something: *bootee.* [via OF *-é*, *-ée*, p.p. endings, from L *-ātus*, *-āta* -ATE¹]

EEC *abbrev. for* European Economic Community (the Common Market).

EEG *abbrev. for:* **1.** electroencephalogram. **2.** electroencephalograph.

eel (iːl) *n.* **1.** any teleost fish such as the European freshwater eel, having a long snakelike body, a smooth slimy skin, and reduced fins. **2.** any of various similar animals, such as the mud eel and the electric eel. **3.** an evasive or untrustworthy person. [OE *ǣl*] —'**eel-,like** *adj.* —'**eely** *adj.*

eelgrass ('iːl,grɑːs) *n.* any of several perennial submerged marine plants having grasslike leaves.

eelpout ('iːl,paʊt) *n.* **1.** a marine eel-like fish. **2.** another name for **burbot.** [OE *ǣlepūte*]

eelworm ('iːl,wɜːm) *n.* any of various nematode worms, esp. the wheatworm and the vinegar eel.

e'en (iːn) *adv., n. Poetic or arch.* contraction of **even²** or **evening.**

e'er (ɛə) *adv. Poetic or arch.* contraction of **ever.**

-eer *or* **-ier** *suffix.* **1.** (*forming nouns*) indicating a person who is concerned with or who does something specified: *auctioneer; engineer; profiteer; mutineer.* **2.** (*forming verbs*) to be concerned with something specified: *electioneer.* [from OF *-ier*, from L *-arius* -ARY]

eerie ('ɪərɪ) *adj.* **eerier, eeriest.** uncannily frightening or disturbing; weird. [C13: orig. Scot. & N English, prob. from OE *earg* cowardly] —'**eerily** *adv.* —'**eeriness** *n.*

EETPU (in Britain) *abbrev. for* Electrical, Electronic, Telecommunications, and Plumbing Union.

eff (ɛf) *vb.* **1.** euphemism for **fuck** (esp. in **eff off**). **2. eff and blind.** *Sl.* to use obscene language. —'**effing** *n., adj., adv.*

efface (ɪ'feɪs) *vb.* (*tr.*) **1.** to obliterate or make dim. **2.** to make (oneself) inconspicuous or humble. **3.** to rub out; erase. [C15: from F *effacer*, lit.: to obliterate the face; see FACE] —**ef'faceable** *adj.* —**ef'facement** *n.* —**ef'facer** *n.*

effect (ɪ'fɛkt) *n.* **1.** something produced by a cause or agent; result. **2.** power to influence or produce a result. **3.** the condition of being operative (esp. in **in** or **into effect**). **4. take effect.** to become operative or begin to produce results. **5.** basic meaning or purpose (esp. in **to that effect**). **6.** an impression, usually contrived (esp. in **for effect**). **7.** a scientific phenomenon: *the Doppler effect.* **8. in effect. a.** in fact; actually. **b.** for all practical purposes. **9.** the overall impression or result. ~*vb.* **10.** (*tr.*) to cause to occur; accomplish. [C14: from L *effectus* a performing, tendency, from *efficere* to accomplish, from *facere* to do] —**ef'fecter** *n.* —**ef'fectible** *adj.*

effective (ɪ'fɛktɪv) *adj.* **1.** productive of or capable of producing a result. **2.** in effect; operative. **3.** impressive: *an effective entrance.* **4.** (*prenominal*) actual rather than theoretical. **5.** (of a military force, etc.) equipped and prepared for action. ~*n.* **6.** a serviceman equipped and prepared for action. —**ef'fectively** *adv.* —**ef'fectiveness** *n.*

effects (ɪ'fɛkts) *pl. n.* **1.** Also called: **personal effects.** personal belongings. **2.** lighting, sounds, etc., to accompany a stage, film, or broadcast production.

effectual (ɪˈfɛktjʊəl) *adj.* **1.** capable of or successful in producing an intended result; effective. **2.** (of documents, etc.) having legal force. —**efˌfectuˈality** *or* **efˈfectualness** *n.*

effectually (ɪˈfɛktjʊəlɪ) *adv.* **1.** with the intended effect. **2.** in effect.

effectuate (ɪˈfɛktjʊˌeɪt) *vb.* (*tr.*) to cause to happen; effect; accomplish. —**efˌfectuˈation** *n.*

effeminate (ɪˈfɛmɪnɪt) *adj.* (of a man or boy) displaying characteristics regarded as typical of a woman; not manly. [C14: from L *effēmināre* to make into a woman, from *fēmina* woman] —**efˈfeminacy** *or* **efˈfeminateness** *n.*

effendi (ɛˈfɛndɪ) *n.,* pl. **-dis.** **1.** (in the Ottoman Empire) a title of respect. **2.** (in Turkey since 1934) the oral title of address equivalent to *Mr.* [C17: from Turkish *efendi* master, from Mod. Gk *aphéntēs*, from Gk *authéntēs* lord, doer]

efferent (ˈɛfərənt) *adj. Physiol.* carrying or conducting outwards, esp. from the brain or spinal cord. Cf. **afferent.** [C19: from L *efferre* to bear off, from *ferre* to bear] —**ˈefference** *n.*

effervesce (ˌɛfəˈvɛs) *vb.* (*intr.*) **1.** (of a liquid) to give off bubbles of gas. **2.** (of a gas) to issue in bubbles from a liquid. **3.** to exhibit great excitement, vivacity, etc. [C18: from L *effervescere* to foam up, ult. from *fervēre* to boil, ferment] —ˌ**efferˈvescingly** *adv.*

effervescent (ˌɛfəˈvɛsᵊnt) *adj.* **1.** (of a liquid) giving off bubbles of gas. **2.** high-spirited; vivacious. —ˌ**efferˈvescence** *n.*

effete (ɪˈfiːt) *adj.* **1.** weak or decadent. **2.** exhausted; spent. **3.** (of animals or plants) no longer capable of reproduction. [C17: from L *effētus* exhausted by bearing, from *fētus* having brought forth; see FETUS] —**efˈfeteness** *n.*

efficacious (ˌɛfɪˈkeɪʃəs) *adj.* capable of or successful in producing an intended result; effective. [C16: from L *efficāx* powerful, efficient, from *efficere* to achieve] —**efficacy** (ˈɛfɪkəsɪ) *or* ˌ**effiˈcaciousness** *n.*

efficiency (ɪˈfɪʃənsɪ) *n.,* pl. **-cies.** **1.** the quality or state of being efficient. **2.** the ratio of the useful work done by a machine, etc., to the energy input, often expressed as a percentage.

efficient (ɪˈfɪʃənt) *adj.* **1.** functioning or producing effectively and with the least waste of effort; competent. **2.** *Philosophy.* producing a direct effect. [C14: from L *efficiēns* effecting]

effigy (ˈɛfɪdʒɪ) *n.,* pl. **-gies.** **1.** a portrait, esp. as a monument. **2.** a crude representation of someone, used as a focus for contempt or ridicule (often in **burn** *or* **hang in effigy**). [C18: from L *effigiēs*, from *effingere* to form, portray, from *fingere* to shape]

effloresce (ˌɛflɔːˈrɛs) *vb.* (*intr.*) **1.** to burst forth as into flower; bloom. **2.** to become powdery by loss of water crystallization. **3.** to become encrusted with powder or crystals as a result of chemical change or evaporation. [C18: from L *efflorēscere* to blossom, from *florēscere*, from *flōs* flower]

efflorescence (ˌɛflɔːˈrɛsᵊns) *n.* **1.** a bursting forth or flowering. **2.** *Chem., geol.* **a.** the process of efflorescing. **b.** the powdery substance formed as a result of this process. **3.** any skin rash or eruption. —ˌ**effloˈrescent** *adj.*

effluence (ˈɛflʊəns) *or* **efflux** (ˈɛflʌks) *n.* **1.** the act or process of flowing out. **2.** something that flows out.

effluent (ˈɛflʊənt) *n.* **1.** liquid discharged as waste, as from an industrial plant or sewage works. **2.** radioactive waste released from a nuclear power station. **3.** a stream that flows out of another body of water. **4.** something that flows out or forth. ~*adj.* **5.** flowing out or forth. [C18: from L *effluere* to run forth, from *fluere* to flow]

effluvium (ɛˈfluːvɪəm) *n.,* pl. **-via** (-vɪə) *or* **-viums.** an unpleasant smell or exhalation, as of gaseous waste or decaying matter. [C17: from L: a flowing out; see EFFLUENT] —**efˈfluvial** *adj.*

effort (ˈɛfət) *n.* **1.** physical or mental exertion. **2.** a determined attempt. **3.** achievement; creation. [C15: from OF *esfort*, from *esforcier* to force, ult. from L *fortis* strong] —ˈ**effortful** *adj.* —ˈ**effortless** *adj.*

effrontery (ɪˈfrʌntərɪ) *n.,* pl. **-eries.** shameless or insolent boldness. [C18: from F, from OF *esfront* barefaced, shameless, from LL *effrons,* lit.: putting forth one's forehead]

effulgent (ɪˈfʌldʒənt) *adj.* radiant; brilliant. [C18: from L *effulgēre* to shine forth, from *fulgēre* to shine] —**efˈfulgence** *n.* —**efˈfulgently** *adv.*

effuse *vb.* (ɪˈfjuːz). **1.** to pour or flow out. **2.** to spread out; diffuse. ~*adj.* (ɪˈfjuːs). **3.** *Bot.* (esp. of an inflorescence) spreading out loosely. [C16: from L *effūsus* poured out, from *effundere* to shed]

effusion (ɪˈfjuːʒən) *n.* **1.** an unrestrained outpouring in speech or words. **2.** the act or process of being poured out. **3.** something that is poured out.

effusive (ɪˈfjuːsɪv) *adj.* **1.** extravagantly demonstrative of emotion; gushing. **2.** (of rock) formed by the solidification of magma. —**efˈfusively** *adv.* —**efˈfusiveness** *n.*

EFL *abbrev. for* English as a Foreign Language.

eft (ɛft) *n.* a dialect or archaic name for a **newt.** [OE *efeta*]

EFTA (ˈɛftə) *n. acronym for* European Free Trade Association; established in 1960 to eliminate trade tariffs on industrial products; originally comprised Britain, Denmark, Norway, Sweden, Switzerland, Austria, and Portugal.

Eftpos *or* **EFTPOS** (ˈɛftpɒs) *n. acronym for* electronic funds transfer at point of sale.

EFTS *abbrev. for* electronic funds transfer system.

eftsoons (ɛftˈsuːnz) *adv. Arch.* **1.** soon afterwards. **2.** repeatedly. [OE *eft sōna*]

Eg. *abbrev. for:* **1.** Egypt(ian). **2.** Egyptology.

e.g., eg, *or* **eg.** *abbrev. for* exempli gratia. [L: for example]

egad (ɪˈgæd, iːˈgæd) *interj. Arch.* a mild oath. [C17: prob. var. of *Ah God!*]

egalitarian (ɪˌgælɪˈtɛərɪən) *adj.* **1.** of or upholding the doctrine of the equality of mankind. ~*n.* **2.** an adherent of egalitarian principles. [C19: alteration of *equalitarian,* through infl. of F *égal* equal] —**eˌgaliˈtarianˌism** *n.*

Egbert (ˈɛgbɜːt) *n.* ?775–839 A.D., king of Wessex (802–839); first overlord of all England (829–830).

Eger *n.* **1.** (*Hungarian* ˈɛgɛr). a city in N central Hungary. Pop.: 66 000 (1985). **2.** (ˈeːgər). the German name for **Cheb.**

egg[1] (ɛg) *n.* **1.** the oval or round reproductive body laid by the females of birds, reptiles, fishes, insects, and some other animals, consisting of a developing embryo, its food store, and sometimes jelly or albumen, all surrounded by an outer shell or membrane. **2.** Also called: **egg cell.** any female gamete; ovum. **3.** the egg of the domestic hen used as food. **4.** something resembling an egg, esp. in shape. **5. good** (*or* **bad**) **egg.** *Old-fashioned inf.* a good (or bad) person. **6. put** *or* **have all one's eggs in one basket.** to stake everything on a single venture. **7. teach one's grandmother to suck eggs.** *Inf.* to presume to teach someone something that he knows already. **8. with egg on one's face.** *Inf.* made to look ridiculous. [C14: from ON *egg*; rel. to OE *æg*]

egg[2] (ɛg) *vb.* (*tr.;* usually foll. by *on*) to urge or incite, esp. to daring or foolish acts. [OE *eggian*]

egg-and-spoon race *n.* a race in which runners carry an egg balanced in a spoon.

eggbeater (ˈɛgˌbiːtə) *n.* **1.** Also called: **eggwhisk.** a utensil for beating eggs; whisk. **2.** *Chiefly U.S. & Canad.* an informal name for **helicopter.**

egger *or* **eggar** (ˈɛgə) *n.* any of various European moths having brown bodies and wings. [C18: from EGG[1], from the egg-shaped cocoon]

egghead (ˈɛgˌhɛd) *n. Inf.* an intellectual.

eggnog (ˌɛgˈnɒg) *n.* a drink made of eggs, milk, sugar, spice, and brandy, rum, or other spirit. Also called: **egg flip.** [C19: from EGG[1] + NOG]

eggplant (ˈɛgˌplɑːnt) *n.* another name (esp. U.S. and Canad.) for **aubergine.**

eggshell (ˈɛgˌʃɛl) *n.* **1.** the hard porous outer layer of a bird's egg. **2.** (*modifier*) (of paint) having a very slight sheen.

eggshell porcelain *or* **china** *n.* a very thin translucent porcelain originally from China.

egg tooth *n.* (in embryo reptiles) a temporary tooth or (in birds) projection of the beak used for piercing the egg-shell.

Egham (ˈɛgəm) *n.* a town in S England, in N Surrey on the River Thames. Pop.: 27 817 (1981).

eglantine (ˈɛglənˌtaɪn) *n.* another name for **sweetbrier.** [C14: from OF *aiglent,* ult. from L *acus* needle, from *acer* sharp, keen]

Egmont[1] (ˈɛgmɒnt) *n.* an extinct volcano in New Zealand, in W central North Island in the **Egmont National Park:** an almost perfect cone. Height: 2518 m (8261 ft.).

Egmont[2] ('ɛgmɒnt) n. **Lamoral** (lamo'ral), Count of Egmont, Prince of Gavre. 1522–68, Flemish statesman and soldier. He attempted to secure limited reforms and religious tolerance in the Spanish government of the Netherlands, refused to join William the Silent's rebellion, but was nevertheless executed for treason by the Duke of Alva.

ego ('iːgəʊ, 'ɛgəʊ) n., pl. **egos. 1.** the self of an individual person; the conscious subject. **2.** *Psychoanalysis.* the conscious mind, based on perception of the environment: responsible for modifying the antisocial instincts of the id and itself modified by the conscience (superego). **3.** one's image of oneself; morale. **4.** egotism; conceit. [C19: from L: I]

egocentric (ˌiːgəʊ'sɛntrɪk, ˌɛg-) adj. **1.** regarding everything only in relation to oneself; self-centred. ~n. **2.** a self-centred person; egotist. —ˌegocen'tricity n. —ˌego'centrism n.

egoism ('iːgəʊˌɪzəm, 'ɛg-) n. **1.** concern for one's own interests and welfare. **2.** *Ethics.* the theory that the pursuit of one's own welfare is the highest good. **3.** self-centredness; egotism. —'egoist n.

egomania (ˌiːgəʊ'meɪnɪə, ˌɛg-) n. *Psychiatry.* obsessive love for oneself. —ˌego'maniˌac n. —egomaniacal (ˌiːgəʊmə'naɪkəl, ˌɛg-) adj.

egotism ('iːgəˌtɪzəm, 'ɛgə-) n. **1.** an inflated sense of self-importance or superiority; self-centredness. **2.** excessive reference to oneself. [C18: from L *ego* I + -ISM] —'egotist n.

ego trip n. *Inf.* something undertaken to boost or draw attention to a person's own image or appraisal of himself.

egregious (ɪ'griːdʒəs, -dʒɪəs) adj. **1.** outstandingly bad; flagrant. **2.** *Arch.* distinguished; eminent. [C16: from L *ēgregius* outstanding (lit.: standing out from the herd), from *ē-* out + *grex* flock, herd] —e'gregiousness n.

egress ('iːgrɛs) n. **1.** Also: **egression.** the act of going or coming out; emergence. **2.** a way out; exit. **3.** the right to go out or depart. [C16: from L *ēgredī* to come forth, depart, from *gradī* to move, step]

egret ('iːgrɪt) n. any of various wading birds similar to herons but usually having white plumage and, in the breeding season, long feathery plumes. [C15: from OF *aigrette*, from OProvençal *aigreta*, from *aigron* heron, of Gmc origin]

Egypt ('iːdʒɪpt) n. a republic in NE Africa, on the Mediterranean and Red Sea: its history dates back about 5000 years. Occupied by the British from 1882, it became an independent kingdom in 1922 and a republic in 1953. Over 96 per cent of the total area is desert, with the chief areas of habitation and cultivation in the Nile delta and valley. Cotton is the main export. Language: Arabic. Religion: chiefly Sunni Muslim. Currency: pound. Capital: Cairo. Pop.: 50 000 000 (1986 est.). Area: 1 002 000 sq. km (386 900 sq. miles). Official name: **Arab Republic of Egypt.** Former official name (1958–71): **United Arab Republic.**

Egyptian (ɪ'dʒɪpʃən) adj. **1.** of or relating to Egypt, its inhabitants, or their dialect of Arabic. **2.** of or characteristic of the ancient Egyptians, their language, or culture. ~n. **3.** a native or inhabitant of Egypt. **4.** a member of a people who established an advanced civilization in Egypt that flourished from the late fourth millennium B.C. **5.** the extinct language of the ancient Egyptians.

Egyptology (ˌiːdʒɪp'tɒlədʒɪ) n. the study of the archaeology and language of ancient Egypt. —ˌEgyp'tologist n.

eh (eɪ) interj. an exclamation used to express questioning surprise or to seek the repetition or confirmation of a statement or question.

EHF abbrev. for extremely high frequency.

Ehrenburg or **Erenburg** ('ɛrənbɜːg; *Russian* erɪn'burk) n. **Ilya Grigorievich** (ilj'ja gri'gɔrjɪvitʃ). 1891–1967, Soviet novelist and journalist. His novel *The Thaw* (1954) was the first published in the Soviet Union to deal with repression under Stalin.

Ehrlich (*German* 'eːrlɪç) n. **Paul** (paul). 1854–1915, German bacteriologist, noted for his pioneering work in immunology and chemotherapy and for his discovery of a remedy for syphilis: Nobel prize for physiology or medicine 1908.

Eichendorff (*German* 'aiçəndɔrf) n. **Joseph** ('joːzɛf), Freiherr von Eichendorff. 1788–1857, German poet and novelist, regarded as one of the greatest German romantic lyricists.

Eichmann (*German* 'aiçman) n. (**Karl**) **Adolf** ('aːdɔlf). 1902–62, Austrian Nazi official. He escaped to Argentina after World War II, but was captured and executed in Israel as a war criminal.

eider or **eider duck** ('aidə) n. any of several sea ducks of the N hemisphere. See **eiderdown.** [C18: from ON *æthr*]

eiderdown ('aidəˌdaʊn) n. **1.** the breast down of the female eider duck, used for stuffing pillows, quilts, etc. **2.** a thick, warm cover for a bed, enclosing a soft filling.

eidetic (ai'dɛtɪk) adj. *Psychol.* **1.** (of visual, or sometimes auditory, images) very vivid and allowing detailed recall of something previously perceived: thought to be common in children. **2.** relating to or subject to such imagery. [C20: from Gk *eidētikos*, from *eidos* shape, form] —ei'detically adv.

Eiffel ('aifl; *French* ɛfɛl) n. **Alexandre Gustave** (alɛksɔ̃drə gystav). 1832–1923, French engineer.

Eiffel Tower ('aifl) n. a tower in Paris: designed by A. G. Eiffel; erected for the 1889 Paris Exposition. Height: 300 m (984 ft.), raised in 1959 to 321 m (1052 ft.).

Eiger (*German* 'aigər) n. a mountain in central Switzerland, in the Bernese Alps. Height: 3970 m (13 025 ft.).

eight (eit) n. **1.** the cardinal number that is the sum of one and seven and the product of two and four. **2.** a numeral, 8, VIII, etc., representing this number. **3.** the amount or quantity that is one greater than seven. **4.** something representing, represented by, or consisting of eight units. **5.** *Rowing.* **a.** a racing shell propelled by eight oarsmen. **b.** the crew of such a shell. **6.** Also called: **eight o'clock.** eight hours after noon or midnight. **7. have one over the eight.** *Sl.* to be drunk. ~determiner. **8. a.** amounting to eight. **b.** (as pron.): *I could only find eight.* [OE *eahta*]

eighteen ('ei'tiːn) n. **1.** the cardinal number that is the sum of ten and eight and the product of two and nine. **2.** a numeral, 18, XVIII, etc., representing this number. **3.** the amount or quantity that is eight more than ten. **4.** something represented by, representing, or consisting of 18 units. ~determiner. **5. a.** amounting to eighteen: *eighteen weeks.* **b.** (as pron.): *eighteen of them knew.* [OE *eahtatēne*] —'eigh'teenth adj., n.

eightfold ('eit,fəʊld) adj. **1.** equal to or having eight times as many or as much. **2.** composed of eight parts. ~adv. **3.** by eight times as much.

eighth (eitθ) adj. **1.** (usually prenominal) **a.** coming after the seventh and before the ninth in numbering, position, etc.; being the ordinal number of *eight*: often written 8th. **b.** (as n.): *the eighth in line.* ~n. **2. a.** one of eight equal parts of something. **b.** (as modifier): *an eighth part.* **3.** the fraction one divided by eight (1/8). **4.** another word for **octave.** ~adv. **5.** Also: **eighthly.** after the seventh person, position, event, etc.

eighth note n. *Music.* the usual U.S. and Canad. name for **quaver.**

eightsome reel ('eitsəm) n. a Scottish dance for eight people.

eighty ('eiti) n., pl. **eighties. 1.** the cardinal number that is the product of ten and eight. **2.** a numeral, 80, LXXX, etc., representing this number. **3.** (pl.) the numbers 80–89, esp. the 80th to the 89th year of a person's life or of a century. **4.** the amount or quantity that is eight times ten. **5.** something represented by, representing, or consisting of 80 units. ~determiner. **6. a.** amounting to eighty: *eighty pages of nonsense.* **b.** (as pron.): *eighty are expected.* [OE *eahtatig*] —'eightieth adj., n.

Eijkman (*Dutch* 'eikman) n. **Christiaan** ('kriːstiˌaːn). 1858–1930, Dutch physician, who discovered that beriberi is caused by nutritional deficiency: Nobel prize for physiology or medicine 1929.

Eilat, Elat, or **Elath** (ei'laːt) n. a port in S Israel, on the Gulf of Aqaba: Israel's only outlet to the Red Sea. Pop.: 19 500 (1982 est.).

Eindhoven ('aint,həʊvᵊn, *Dutch* 'ɛinthoːvə) n. a city in the SE Netherlands, in North Brabant province: radio and electrical industry. Pop.: 190 962 (1987).

Einstein ('ainstain) n. **Albert.** 1879–1955, U.S. physicist and mathematician, born in Germany. He formulated the special theory of relativity (1905) and the general theory of relativity (1916), and made major contributions to the quantum theory, for which he was awarded the Nobel prize for physics in 1921. He was noted also for his work for world peace. —Ein'steinian adj.

einsteinium (aɪn'staɪnɪəm) *n.* a radioactive metallic transuranic element artificially produced from plutonium. Symbol: Es; atomic no.: 99; half-life of most stable isotope, ²⁵⁴Es: 276 days. [C20: NL, after Albert EINSTEIN]

Eire ('ɛərə) *n.* **1.** the Irish Gaelic name for **Ireland**¹: often used to mean the **Republic of Ireland**. **2.** a former name for the **Republic of Ireland** (1937–49).

EIS *abbrev. for* Educational Institute of Scotland.

Eisenach (*German* 'aizənax) *n.* a city in SW East Germany, in Erfurt district. Pop.: 50 796 (1983 est.).

Eisenhower ('aɪzənhauə) *n.* **Dwight David,** known as *Ike.* 1890–1969, U.S. general and Republican statesman; Supreme Commander of the Allied Expeditionary Force (1943–45) and 34th president of the U.S. (1953–61). He commanded Allied forces in Europe and North Africa (1942), directed the invasion of Italy (1943), and was Supreme Commander of the combined land forces of NATO (1950–52).

Eisenstadt (*German* 'aizənʃtat) *n.* a town in E Austria, capital of Burgenland province: Hungarian until 1921. Pop.: 10 150 (1981).

Eisenstein ('aɪzᵊn,staɪn; *Russian* ejzɪn'ʃtjejn) *n.* **Sergei Mikhailovich** (sɪr'gjej mi'xaɪləvitʃ). 1898–1948, Soviet film director. His films include *Battleship Potemkin* (1925), *Alexander Nevsky* (1938), and *Ivan the Terrible* (1944).

Eisk *or* **Eysk** (*Russian* jejsk) *n.* variant transliterations of the Russian name for **Yeisk.**

eisteddfod (aɪ'stɛdfəd) *n., pl.* **-fods** *or* **eisteddfodau** (*Welsh* aɪ,stɛð'vɒdaɪ). any of a number of annual festivals in Wales in which competitions are held in music, poetry, drama, and the fine arts. [C19: from Welsh, lit.: session, from *eistedd* to sit + *-fod*, from *bod* to be] —,**eisteddfodic** *adj.*

either ('aɪðə, 'iːðə) *determiner.* **1. a.** one or the other (of two). **b.** (*as pron.*): *either is acceptable.* **2.** both one and the other: *at either end of the table. ~conj.* **3.** (*coordinating*) used preceding two or more possibilities joined by "*or*". *~adv.* (*sentence modifier*) **4.** (*with a negative*) used to indicate that the clause immediately preceding is a partial reiteration of a previous clause: *John isn't a liar, but he isn't exactly honest either.* [OE *ǣgther,* short for *ǣghwæther* each of two; see WHETHER]
▷ *Usage. Either* is followed by a singular verb in good usage: *either of these books is useful.* Careful writers and speakers are cautious in using *either* to mean *both* or *each* because of possible ambiguity, as in: *a ship could be moored on either side of the channel.* Agreement between verb and subject in *either... or...* constructions follows the pattern for *neither... nor...* See at **neither.**

ejaculate *vb.* (ɪ'dʒækjʊ,leɪt). **1.** to eject or discharge (semen) in orgasm. **2.** (*tr.*) to utter abruptly; blurt out. *~n.* (ɪ'dʒækjʊlɪt). **3.** another word for **semen.** [C16: from L *ējaculārī* to hurl out, from *jaculum* javelin, from *jacere* to throw] —**e,jacu'lation** *n.* —**e'jaculatory** *or* **e'jaculative** *adj.* —**e'jacu,lator** *n.*

eject (ɪ'dʒɛkt) *vb.* **1.** (*tr.*) to force out; expel or emit. **2.** (*tr.*) to compel (a person) to leave; evict. **3.** (*tr.*) to dismiss, as from office. **4.** (*intr.*) to leave an aircraft rapidly, using an ejection seat or capsule. [C15: from L *ejicere,* from *jacere* to throw] —**e'jection** *n.* —**e'jective** *adj.* —**e'jector** *n.*

ejection seat *or* **ejector seat** *n.* a seat, esp. in military aircraft, fired by a cartridge or rocket to eject the occupant in an emergency.

Ekaterinburg (*Russian* jɪkətɪrim'burk) *n.* the former name (until 1924) of **Sverdlovsk.**

Ekaterinodar (*Russian* jɪkətrina'dar) *n.* the former name (until 1920) of **Krasnodar.**

Ekaterinoslav (*Russian* jɪkətrina'slaf) *n.* the former name (1787–96, 1802–1926) of **Dnepropetrovsk.**

eke (iːk) *sentence connector. Arch.* also; moreover. [OE *eac*]

eke out (iːk) *vb.* (*tr., adv.*) **1.** to make (a supply) last, esp. by frugal use. **2.** to support (existence) with difficulty and effort. **3.** to add to (something insufficient), esp. with effort. [from obs. *eke* to enlarge]

El Aaiún (ɛl aɪ'juːn) *n.* a city in Morocco: the former capital of Spanish Sahara; port facilities begun in 1967 at **Playa de El Aaiún,** 20 km (12 miles) away, following the discovery of rich phosphate deposits. Pop.: 50 000 (1982 est.).

elaborate *adj.* (ɪ'læbərɪt). **1.** planned with care and exactness. **2.** marked by complexity or detail. *~vb.* (ɪ'læbə,reɪt). **3.** (*intr.*; usually foll. by *on* or *upon*) to add detail (to an account); expand (upon). **4.** (*tr.*) to work out in detail; develop. **5.** (*tr.*) to produce by careful labour. **6.** (*tr.*) *Physiol.* to change (food or simple substances) into more complex substances for use in the body. [C16: from L *ēlabōrāre* to take pains, from *labōrāre* to toil] —**e'laborateness** *n.* —**e,labo'ration** :*n.* —**elaborative** (ɪ'læbərətɪv) *adj.* —**e'labo,rator** *n.*

Elagabalus (,ɛlə'gæbələs, ,iːlə-) *n.* a variant of **Heliogabalus.**

Elaine (ɪ'leɪn) *n. Arthurian legend.* **1.** the half sister of Arthur and mother by him of Modred. **2.** the mother of Sir Galahad.

El Alamein *or* **Alamein** (ɛl 'ælə,meɪn) *n.* a village on the N coast of Egypt, about 112 km (70 miles) west of Alexandria: scene of a decisive Allied victory over the Germans (1942).

Elam ('iːləm) *n.* an ancient kingdom east of the River Tigris: established before 4000 B.C.; probably inhabited by a non-Semitic people.

élan (eɪ'lɑːn) *n.* a combination of style and vigour. [C19: from F, from *élancer* to throw forth, ult. from L *lancea* LANCE]

eland ('iːlənd) *n.* **1.** a large spiral-horned antelope inhabiting bushland in eastern and southern Africa. **2. giant eland.** a similar but larger animal of central and W Africa. [C18: via Afrik., from Du. *eland* elk]

elapse (ɪ'læps) *vb.* (*intr.*) (of time) to pass by. [C17: from L *ēlābī* to slip away, from *lābī* to slip, glide]

elasmobranch (ɪ'læsmə,bræŋk) *n.* **1.** any cartilaginous fish of the subclass Elasmobranchii, which includes sharks, rays, and skates. *~adj.* **2.** of or relating to the Elasmobranchii. [C19: from NL *elasmobranchii,* from Gk *elasmos* metal plate + *brankhia* gills]

elastic (ɪ'læstɪk) *adj.* **1.** (of a body or material) capable of returning to its original shape after compression, stretching, or other deformation. **2.** capable of adapting to change. **3.** quick to recover from fatigue, dejection, etc. **4.** springy or resilient. **5.** made of elastic. *~n.* **6.** tape, cord, or fabric containing flexible rubber or similar substance allowing it to stretch and return to its original shape. [C17: from NL *elasticus* impulsive, from Gk *elastikos,* from *elaunein* to beat, drive] —**e'lastically** *adv.* —**elas'ticity** *n.*

elasticate (ɪ'læstɪ,keɪt) *vb.* (*tr.*) to insert elastic into (a fabric or garment). —**e,lasti'cation** *n.*

elastic band *n.* another name for **rubber band.**

elasticize *or* **-ise** (ɪ'læstɪ,saɪz) *vb.* **1.** to make elastic. **2.** another word for **elasticate.**

elastomer (ɪ'læstəmə) *n.* any material, such as rubber, able to resume its original shape when a deforming force is removed. [C20: from ELASTIC + -MER] —**elastomeric** (ɪ,læstə'mɛrɪk) *adj.*

Elastoplast (ɪ'læstə,plɑːst) *n. Trademark.* a gauze surgical dressing backed by adhesive tape.

Elat *or* **Elath** (eɪ'lɑːt) *n.* variant spellings of **Eilat.**

elate (ɪ'leɪt) *vb.* (*tr.*) to fill with high spirits, exhilaration, pride, or optimism. [C16: from p.p. of L *efferre* to bear away, from *ferre* to carry] —**e'lated** *adj.* —**e'latedly** *adv.* —**e'latedness** *n.*

elation (ɪ'leɪʃən) *n.* joyfulness or exaltation of spirit, as from success, pleasure, or relief.

E layer *n.* another name for **E region.**

Elba ('ɛlbə) *n.* a mountainous island off the W coast of Italy, in the Mediterranean: Napoleon Bonaparte's first place of exile (1814–15). Pop.: 27 309 (1981 est.). Area: 223 sq. km (86 sq. miles).

Elbe (ɛlb; *German* 'ɛlbə) *n.* a river in central Europe, rising in N Czechoslovakia and flowing generally northwest through East and West Germany to the North Sea at Hamburg. Length: 1165 km (724 miles). Czech name: **Labe.**

Elbert ('ɛlbət) *n.* **Mount.** a mountain in central Colorado, in the Sawatch range. Height: 4399 m (14 431 ft.).

Elblag (*Polish* 'ɛlblɔŋk) *n.* a port in N Poland: metallurgical industries. Pop.: 112 100 (1981 est.). German name: **Elbing** ('ɛlbɪŋ).

elbow ('ɛlbəʊ) *n.* **1.** the joint between the upper arm and the forearm. **2.** the corresponding joint of birds or mammals. **3.** the part of a garment that covers the elbow. **4.** something resembling an elbow, such as a sharp bend in a road. **5. at one's elbow.** within easy reach. **6. out at elbow(s).** ragged or impoverished. ~*vb.* **7.** to make (one's way) by shoving, jostling, etc. **8.** (*tr.*) to knock or shove as with the elbow. **9.** (*tr.*) to reject; dismiss (esp. in **give** or **get the elbow**). [OE *elnboga*]

elbow grease *n. Facetious.* vigorous physical labour, esp. hard rubbing.

elbowroom ('ɛlbəʊˌruːm, -ˌrʊm) *n.* sufficient scope to move or function.

Elbrus (ɪl'bruːs) *n.* a mountain in the S Soviet Union, in the Caucasus Mountains, with two extinct volcanic peaks: the highest mountain in Europe. Height: 5642 m (18 510 ft.).

Elburz Mountains (ɛl'bʊəz) *pl. n.* a mountain range in N Iran, parallel to the SW and S shores of the Caspian Sea. Highest peak: Mount Demavend, 5601 m (18 376 ft.).

El Capitan (ɛl ˌkæpɪ'tæn) *n.* a mountain in E central California, in the Sierra Nevada: a monolith with a precipice rising over 1100 m (3600 ft.) above the floor of the Yosemite Valley. Height: 2306 m (7564 ft.).

El Cid Campeador (*Spanish* kampeaˈðɔr) *n.* See (**El**) **Cid.**

elder[1] ('ɛldə) *adj.* **1.** born earlier; senior. Cf. **older. 2.** (in certain card games) denoting or relating to the nondealer (the **elder hand**), who has certain advantages in the play. **3.** *Arch.* **a.** prior in rank or office. **b.** of a previous time. ~*n.* **4.** an older person; one's senior. **5.** *Anthropol.* a senior member of a tribe who has authority. **6.** (in certain Protestant Churches) a lay office. **7.** another word for **presbyter.** [OE *eldra,* comp. of *eald* OLD] —'**elderˌship** *n.*

elder[2] ('ɛldə) *n.* any of various shrubs or small trees having clusters of small white flowers and red, purple, or black berry-like fruits. Also called: **elderberry.** [OE *ellern*]

elderberry ('ɛldəˌbɛrɪ) *n., pl.* -**ries. 1.** the fruit of the elder. **2.** another name for **elder**[2].

elder brother *n.* one of the senior members of Trinity House.

elderly ('ɛldəlɪ) *adj.* (of people) quite old; past middle age. —'**elderliness** *n.*

eldest ('ɛldɪst) *adj.* being the oldest, esp. the oldest surviving child of the same parents. [OE *eldesta,* sup. of *eald* OLD]

El Dorado (ɛl dɒ'rɑːdəʊ) *n.* **1.** a fabled city in South America, rich in treasure. **2.** Also: **eldorado.** any place of great riches or fabulous opportunity. [C16: from Sp., lit.: the gilded (place)]

eldritch *or* **eldrich** ('ɛldrɪtʃ) *adj. Poetic, Scot.* unearthly; weird. [C16: ?from OE *ælf* elf + *rice* realm]

Elea ('iːlɪə) *n.* (in ancient Italy) a Greek colony on the Tyrrhenian coast of Lucania.

Eleanor of Aquitaine ('ɛlɪnə, -ˌnɔː) *n.* ?1122–1204, queen of France (1137–52) by her marriage to Louis VII and queen of England (1154–89) by her marriage to Henry II; mother of the English kings Richard I and John.

elect (ɪ'lɛkt) *vb.* **1.** (*tr.*) to choose (someone) to be (a representative or official) by voting. **2.** to select; choose. **3.** (*tr.*) (of God) to predestine for the grace of salvation. ~*adj.* **4.** (*immediately postpositive*) voted into office but not yet installed: *president elect.* **5. a.** chosen; elite. **b.** (*as collective n.; preceded by the*): *the elect.* **6.** *Christian theol.* **a.** predestined by God to receive salvation. **b.** (*as collective n.; preceded by the*): *the elect.* [C15: from L *ēligere* to select, from *legere* to choose] —**e'lectable** *adj.*

elect. *or* **elec.** *abbrev. for:* **1.** electric(al). **2.** electricity.

election (ɪ'lɛkʃən) *n.* **1.** the selection by vote of a person or persons for a position, esp. a political office. **2.** a public vote. **3.** the act or an instance of choosing. **4.** *Christian theol.* **a.** the doctrine that God chooses individuals for salvation without reference to faith or works. **b.** the doctrine that God chooses for salvation those who, by grace, persevere in faith and works.

electioneer (ɪˌlɛkʃə'nɪə) *vb.* (*intr.*) **1.** to be active in a political election or campaign. ~*n.* **2.** a person who engages in this activity. —**e,lection'eering** *n., adj.*

elective (ɪ'lɛktɪv) *adj.* **1.** of or based on selection by vote. **2.** selected by vote. **3.** having the power to elect. **4.** open to choice; optional. —**electivity** (ˌiːlɛk'tɪvɪtɪ) *or* **e'lectiveness** *n.*

elector (ɪ'lɛktə) *n.* **1.** someone who is eligible to vote in the election of a government. **2.** (*often cap.*) a member of

the U.S. electoral college. **3.** (*often cap.*) (in the Holy Roman Empire) any of the German princes entitled to take part in the election of a new emperor. —**e'lectoral** *adj.* —**e'lectorˌship** *n.* —**e'lectress** *fem. n.*

electoral college *n.* (*often cap.*) **1.** *U.S.* a body of electors chosen by the voters who formally elect the president and vice president. **2.** any body of electors.

electorate (ɪ'lɛktərɪt) *n.* **1.** the body of all qualified voters. **2.** the rank, position, or territory of an elector in the Holy Roman Empire. **3.** *Austral. & N.Z.* the area represented by a Member of Parliament. **4.** *Austral. & N.Z.* the voters in a constituency.

Electra (ɪ'lɛktrə) *n. Greek myth.* the daughter of Agamemnon and Clytemnestra. She persuaded her brother Orestes to avenge their father by killing his murderess Clytemnestra and her lover Aegisthus.

electret (ɪ'lɛktrət) *n.* a permanently polarized dielectric material; its field is similar to that of a permanent magnet. [C20: from *electr(icity)* + *magn)et*]

electric (ɪ'lɛktrɪk) *adj.* **1.** of, derived from, produced by, producing, transmitting, or powered by electricity. **2.** (of a musical instrument) amplified electronically. **3.** very tense or exciting; emotionally charged. ~*n.* **4.** *Inf.* an electric train, car, etc. **5.** (*pl.*) an electric circuit or electric appliances. [C17: from NL *electricus* amber-like (because friction causes amber to become charged), from L *ēlectrum* amber, from Gk *ēlektron*, from ?]
▷ **Usage.** See at **electronic.**

electrical (ɪ'lɛktrɪkˀl) *adj.* of, relating to, or concerned with electricity. —**e'lectrically** *adv.*
▷ **Usage.** See at **electronic.**

electrical engineering *n.* the branch of engineering concerned with practical applications of electricity. —**electrical engineer** *n.*

electric blanket *n.* a blanket that contains an electric heating element, used to warm a bed.

electric chair *n.* (in the U.S.) **a.** an electrified chair for executing criminals. **b.** (usually preceded by *the*) execution by this method.

electric constant *n.* the permittivity of free space, which has the value 8.854 185 × 10^{-12} farad per metre.

electric eel *n.* an eel-like freshwater fish of N South America, having electric organs in the body.

electric eye *n.* another name for **photocell.**

electric field *n.* a field of force surrounding a charged particle within which another charged particle experiences a force.

electric guitar *n.* an electrically amplified guitar, used mainly in pop music.

electrician (ɪlɛk'trɪʃən, ˌiːlɛk-) *n.* a person whose occupation is the installation, maintenance, and repair of electrical devices.

electricity (ɪlɛk'trɪsɪtɪ, ˌiːlɛk-) *n.* **1.** any phenomenon associated with stationary or moving electrons, ions, or other charged particles. **2.** the science of electricity. **3.** an electric current or charge. **4.** emotional tension or excitement.

electric organ *n.* **1.** *Music.* **a.** a pipe organ operated by electrical means. **b.** another name for **electronic organ. 2.** a group of cells on certain fishes, such as the electric eel, that gives an electric shock to any animal touching them.

electric potential *n.* **a.** the work required to transfer a unit positive electric charge from an infinite distance to a given point. **b.** the potential difference between the point and some other point. Sometimes shortened to **potential.**

electric ray *n.* any ray of tropical and temperate seas, having a flat rounded body with an electric organ in each fin.

electrify (ɪ'lɛktrɪˌfaɪ) *vb.* -**fying, -fied.** (*tr.*) **1.** to adapt or equip (a system, device, etc.) for operation by electrical power. **2.** to charge with or subject to electricity. **3.** to startle or excite intensely. —**e'lectriˌfiable** *adj.* —**e,lectrifi'cation** *n.* —**e'lectriˌfier** *n.*

electro (ɪ'lɛktrəʊ) *n., pl.* -**tros.** short for **electroplate** or **electrotype.**

electro- *or sometimes before a vowel* **electr-** *combining form.* **1.** electric or electrically: *electrodynamic.* **2.** electrolytic: *electrodialysis.* [from NL, from L *ēlectrum* amber, from Gk *ēlektron*]

electrocardiograph (ɪˌlɛktrəʊ'kɑːdɪəʊˌgrɑːf) *n.* an instrument for making tracings (**electrocardiograms**) recording the electrical activity of the heart.

—e,lectro,cardio'graphic *or* e,lectro,cardio'graphical *adj.* —**electrocardiography** (ɪ,lɛktrəʊ,kɑːdɪ'ɒgrəfɪ) *n.*

electrochemistry (ɪ,lɛktrəʊ'kɛmɪstrɪ) *n.* the branch of chemistry concerned with electric cells and electrolysis. —**electrochemical** (ɪ,lɛktrəʊ'kɛmɪkəl) *adj.* —e,lectro'chemist *n.*

electroconvulsive therapy (ɪ,lɛktrəʊkən'vʌlsɪv) *n. Med.* the treatment of certain psychotic conditions by passing an electric current through the brain to induce coma or convulsions. See also **shock therapy.**

electrocute (ɪ'lɛktrə,kjuːt) *vb.* (*tr.*) **1.** to kill as a result of an electric shock. **2.** *U.S.* to execute in the electric chair. [C19: from ELECTRO- + (EXE)CUTE] —e,lectro'cution *n.*

electrode (ɪ'lɛktrəʊd) *n.* **1.** a conductor through which an electric current enters or leaves an electrolyte, an electric arc, or an electronic valve or tube. **2.** an element in a semiconducting device that emits, collects, or controls the movement of electrons or holes.

electrodeposit (ɪ,lɛktrəʊdɪ'pɒzɪt) *vb.* **1.** (*tr.*) to deposit (a metal) by electrolysis. ~*n.* **2.** the deposit so formed. —**electrodeposition** (ɪ,lɛktrəʊ,dɛpə'zɪʃən) *n.*

electrodynamics (ɪ,lɛktrəʊdaɪ'næmɪks) *n.* (*functioning as sing.*) the branch of physics concerned with the interactions between electrical and mechanical forces.

electroencephalograph (ɪ,lɛktrəʊɛn'sɛfələ,grɑːf) *n.* an instrument for making tracings (**electroencephalograms**) recording the electrical activity of the brain, usually by means of electrodes placed on the scalp. See also **brain wave.** —e,lectroen,cephalo'graphic *adj.* —**electroencephalography** (ɪ,lɛktrəʊɛn,sɛfə'lɒgrəfɪ) *n.*

electrolyse *or U.S.* **-lyze** (ɪ'lɛktrəʊ,laɪz) *vb.* (*tr.*) **1.** to decompose (a chemical compound) by electrolysis. **2.** to destroy (living tissue, such as hair roots) by electrolysis. —e,lectroly'sation *or U.S.* -ly'zation *n.* —e'lectro,lyser *or U.S.* -,lyzer *n.*

electrolysis (ɪlɛk'trɒlɪsɪs) *n.* **1.** the conduction of electricity by an electrolyte, esp. the use of this process to induce chemical changes. **2.** the destruction of living tissue, such as hair roots, by an electric current, usually for cosmetic reasons.

electrolyte (ɪ'lɛktrəʊ,laɪt) *n.* a solution or molten substance that conducts electricity.

electrolytic (ɪ,lɛktrəʊ'lɪtɪk) *adj.* **1.** *Physics.* **a.** of, concerned with, or produced by electrolysis or electrodeposition. **b.** of, relating to, or containing an electrolyte. ~*n.* **2.** *Electronics.* Also called: **electrolytic capacitor.** a small capacitor consisting of two electrodes separated by an electrolyte. —e,lectro'lytically *adv.*

electromagnet (ɪ,lɛktrəʊ'mægnɪt) *n.* a magnet consisting of an iron or steel core wound with a coil of wire, through which a current is passed.

electromagnetic (ɪ,lɛktrəʊmæg'nɛtɪk) *adj.* **1.** of, containing, or operated by an electromagnet. **2.** of, relating to, or consisting of electromagnetism. **3.** of or relating to electromagnetic radiation. —e,lectromag'netically *adv.*

electromagnetic radiation *n.* radiation consisting of an electric and magnetic field at right angles to each other and to the direction of propagation.

electromagnetic spectrum *n.* the complete range of electromagnetic radiation from the longest radio waves to the shortest gamma radiation.

electromagnetic unit *n.* any unit of a system of electrical cgs units in which the magnetic constant is given the value of unity.

electromagnetic wave *n.* a wave of energy propagated in an electromagnetic field.

electromagnetism (ɪ,lɛktrəʊ'mægnɪ,tɪzəm) *n.* **1.** magnetism produced by electric current. **2.** the branch of physics concerned with this magnetism and with the interaction of electric and magnetic fields.

electrometer (ɪlɛk'trɒmɪtə, ,iːlɛk-) *n.* an instrument for detecting or measuring a potential difference or charge by the electrostatic forces between charged bodies. —**electrometric** (ɪ,lɛktrəʊ'mɛtrɪk) *or* e,lectro'metrical *adj.* —elec'trometry *n.*

electromotive (ɪ,lɛktrəʊ'məʊtɪv) *adj.* of, concerned with, or producing an electric current.

electromotive force *n. Physics.* **a.** a source of energy that can cause current to flow in an electrical circuit. **b.** the rate at which energy is drawn from this source when unit current flows through the circuit, measured in volts.

electron (ɪ'lɛktrɒn) *n.* an elementary particle in all atoms, orbiting the nucleus in numbers equal to the atomic number of the element. [C19: from ELECTRO- + -ON]

electronegative (ɪ,lɛktrəʊ'nɛgətɪv) *adj.* **1.** having a negative electric charge. **2.** (of an atom, molecule, etc.) tending to attract electrons and form negative ions or polarized bonds.

electron gun *n.* a heated cathode for producing and focusing a beam of electrons, used esp. in cathode-ray tubes.

electronic (ɪlɛk'trɒnɪk, ,iːlɛk-) *adj.* **1.** of, concerned with, using, or operated by devices, such as transistors, in which electrons are conducted through a semiconductor, free space, or gas. **2.** of or concerned with electronics. **3.** of or concerned with electrons. **4.** making use of electronic systems, such as computerized banking transactions: *electronic shopping.* —elec'tronically *adv.*

▷**Usage.** *Electronic* is used to refer to equipment, such as television sets, computers, etc., in which current is controlled by transistors, valves, etc., and also to these components themselves. *Electrical* is used in a more general sense, often to refer to the use of electricity as opposed to other forms of energy: *an electrical appliance. Electric*, in many cases used interchangeably with *electrical*, is often restricted to the description of devices or to concepts relating to the flow of current: *electric fire.*

electronic data processing *n.* data processing largely performed by electronic equipment, such as computers.

electronic flash *n. Photog.* an electronic device for producing a very bright flash of light by means of an electric discharge in a gas-filled tube.

electronic funds transfer system *n.* a system of conducting financial transactions by a network of computers, without using cheques or cash: debits and credits are recorded when a card is inserted in an electronic machine as, for instance, when a person buys something in a shop.

electronic keyboard *n.* a typewriter keyboard used to operate an electronic device such as a computer.

electronic mail *n.* the transmission of information, facsimiles, etc., from one computer terminal to another.

electronic music *n.* music consisting of sounds produced by electric currents either controlled from an instrument panel or keyboard or prerecorded on magnetic tape.

electronic organ *n. Music.* an instrument played by means of a keyboard, in which sounds are produced by electronic or electrical means.

electronics (ɪlɛk'trɒnɪks, ,iːlɛk-) *n.* **1.** (*functioning as sing.*) the science and technology concerned with the development, behaviour, and applications of electronic devices and circuits. **2.** (*functioning as pl.*) the circuits and devices of a piece of electronic equipment.

electronic publishing *n.* the publication of information on magnetic tape, discs, etc., so that it can be accessed by a computer.

electronic surveillance *n.* **1.** the use of such electronic devices as television monitors, video cameras, etc., to prevent burglary, shop lifting, break-ins, etc. **2.** monitoring events, conversations, etc. at a distance by electronic means, esp. by such covert means as wire tapping or bugging.

electronic tagging *n.* a method of monitoring the whereabouts of a convicted person given a noncustodial sentence, in which the person wears an electronic wristlet linked to a central computer through the telephone system.

electron lens *n.* a system, such as an arrangement of electrodes or magnets, that produces a field for focusing a beam of electrons.

electron microscope *n.* a powerful microscope that uses electrons, rather than light, and electron lenses to produce a magnified image.

electron tube *n.* an electrical device, such as a valve, in which a flow of electrons between electrodes takes place.

electronvolt (ɪ,lɛktrɒn'vəʊlt) *n.* a unit of energy equal to the work done on an electron accelerated through a potential difference of 1 volt.

electrophoresis (ɪ,lɛktrəʊfə'riːsɪs) *n.* the motion of charged particles in a colloid under the influence of an applied electric field. —**electrophoretic** (ɪ,lɛktrəʊfə-'rɛtɪk) *adj.*

electrophorus (ɪlɛk'trɒfərəs, ˌiːlɛk-) *n.* an apparatus for generating static electricity by induction. [C18: from ELECTRO- + *-phorus*, from Gk, from *pherein* to bear]

electroplate (ɪ'lɛktrəʊˌpleɪt) *vb.* **1.** (*tr.*) to plate (an object) by electrolysis. ~*n.* **2.** electroplated articles collectively, esp. when plated with silver. — **e'lectro,plater** *n.*

electropositive (ɪˌlɛktrəʊ'pɒzɪtɪv) *adj.* **1.** having a positive electric charge. **2.** (of an atom, molecule, etc.) tending to release electrons and form positive ions or polarized bonds.

electroscope (ɪ'lɛktrəʊˌskəʊp) *n.* an apparatus for detecting an electric charge, typically consisting of a rod holding two gold foils that separate when a charge is applied. — **electroscopic** (ɪˌlɛktrəʊ'skɒpɪk) *adj.*

electroshock therapy (ɪ'lɛktrəʊˌʃɒk) *n.* another name for **electroconvulsive therapy.**

electrostatics (ɪˌlɛktrəʊ'stætɪks) *n.* (*functioning as sing.*) the branch of physics concerned with static electricity. — **e,lectro'static** *adj.*

electrostatic unit *n.* any unit of a system of electrical cgs units in which the electric constant is given the value of unity.

electrotherapeutics (ɪˌlɛktrəʊˌθɛrə'pjuːtɪks) *n.* (*functioning as sing.*) the branch of medical science concerned with the use of electricity (**electrotherapy**) in treating disease. — **e,lectro,thera'peutic** *or* **e,lectro,thera'peutical** *adj.* — **e,lectro'therapist** *n.*

electrotype (ɪ'lɛktrəʊˌtaɪp) *n.* **1.** a duplicate printing plate made by electrolytically depositing a layer of copper or nickel onto a mould of the original. ~*vb.* **2.** (*tr.*) to make an electrotype of (printed matter, etc.). — **e'lectro,typer** *n.*

electrovalent bond (ɪˌlɛktrəʊ'veɪlənt) *n.* a type of chemical bond in which one atom loses an electron to form a positive ion and the other atom gains the electron to form a negative ion. The resulting ions are held together by electrostatic attraction. — **e,lectro'valency** *n.*

electrum (ɪ'lɛktrəm) *n.* an alloy of gold and silver. [C14: from L, from Gk *ēlektron* amber]

electuary (ɪ'lɛktjʊərɪ) *n., pl.* **-aries.** *Med.* a paste taken orally, containing a drug mixed with syrup or honey. [C14: from LL *ēlēctuārium*, prob. from Gk *ēkleikton*, from *leikhein* to lick]

eleemosynary (ˌɛliːiː'mɒsɪnərɪ) *adj.* **1.** of or dependent on charity. **2.** given as an act of charity. [C17: from Church L *eleēmosyna* ALMS]

elegance ('ɛlɪgəns) *or* **elegancy** *n., pl.* **-gances** *or* **-gancies. 1.** dignified grace. **2.** good taste in design, style, arrangement, etc. **3.** something elegant; a refinement.

elegant ('ɛlɪgənt) *adj.* **1.** tasteful in dress, style, or design. **2.** dignified and graceful. **3.** cleverly simple; ingenious: *an elegant solution.* [C16: from L *ēlegāns* tasteful; see ELECT]

elegiac (ˌɛlɪ'dʒaɪək) *adj.* **1.** resembling, characteristic of, relating to, or appropriate to an elegy. **2.** lamenting; mournful. **3.** denoting or written in elegiac couplets (which consist of a dactylic hexameter followed by a dactylic pentameter) or elegiac stanzas (which consist of a quatrain in iambic pentameters with alternate lines rhyming). ~*n.* **4.** (*often pl.*) an elegiac couplet or stanza. — **,ele'giacally** *adv.*

elegize *or* **-gise** ('ɛlɪˌdʒaɪz) *vb.* **1.** to compose an elegy (in memory of). **2.** (*intr.*) to write elegiacally. — **'elegist** *n.*

elegy ('ɛlɪdʒɪ) *n., pl.* **-gies. 1.** a mournful poem or song, esp. a lament for the dead. **2.** poetry written in elegiac couplets or stanzas. [C16: via F & L from Gk, from *elegos* lament sung to flute accompaniment]

Eleia ('iːlɪə) *n.* a variant spelling of **Elia[1].**

elem. *abbrev. for:* **1.** element(s). **2.** elementary.

element ('ɛlɪmənt) *n.* **1.** any of the 105 known substances that consist of atoms with the same number of protons in their nuclei. **2.** one of the fundamental or irreducible components making up a whole. **3.** any group that is part of a larger unit, such as a military formation. **4.** a small amount; hint. **5.** a distinguishable section of a social group. **6.** the most favourable environment for an animal or plant. **7.** the situation in which a person is happiest or most effective (esp. in **in** *or* **out of one's element**). **8.** the resistance wire that constitutes the electrical heater in a cooker, heater, etc. **9.** one of the

four substances thought in ancient and medieval cosmology to constitute the universe (earth, air, water, or fire). **10.** (*pl.*) atmospheric conditions, esp. wind, rain, and cold. **11.** (*pl.*) the basic principles. **12.** *Christianity.* the bread or wine consecrated in the Eucharist. [C13: from L *elementum* a first principle, element]

elemental (ˌɛlɪ'mɛntəl) *adj.* **1.** fundamental; basic. **2.** motivated by or symbolic of primitive powerful natural forces or passions. **3.** of or relating to earth, air, water, and fire considered as elements. **4.** of or relating to atmospheric forces, esp. wind, rain, and cold. **5.** of or relating to a chemical element. ~*n.* **6.** *Rare.* a disembodied spirit. — **,ele'mental,ism** *n.*

elementary (ˌɛlɪ'mɛntərɪ) *adj.* **1.** not difficult; rudimentary. **2.** of or concerned with the first principles of a subject; introductory or fundamental. **3.** *Chem.* another word for **elemental** (sense 5). — **,ele'mentariness** *n.*

elementary particle *n.* any of several entities, such as electrons, neutrons, or protons, that are less complex than atoms.

elementary school *n.* **1.** *Brit.* a former name for **primary school. 2.** *U.S. & Canad.* a state school for the first six to eight years of a child's education.

elenchus (ɪ'lɛŋkəs) *n., pl.* **-chi** (-kaɪ). *Logic.* refutation of an argument by proving the contrary of its conclusion, esp. syllogistically. [C17: from L, from Gk, from *elenkhein* to refute] — **e'lenctic** *adj.*

elephant ('ɛlɪfənt) *n., pl.* **-phants** *or* **-phant.** either of two proboscidean mammals. The **African elephant** is the larger species, with large flapping ears and a less humped back than the **Indian elephant,** of S and SE Asia. [C13: from L, from Gk *elephas* elephant, ivory] — **'elephan,toid** *adj.*

elephantiasis (ˌɛlɪfən'taɪəsɪs) *n. Pathol.* a complication of chronic filariasis, in which nematode worms block the lymphatic vessels, usually in the legs or scrotum, causing extreme enlargement of the affected area. [C16: via L from Gk, from *elephas* ELEPHANT + -IASIS]

elephantine (ˌɛlɪ'fæntaɪn) *adj.* **1.** denoting, relating to, or characteristic of an elephant or elephants. **2.** huge, clumsy, or ponderous.

elephant seal *n.* either of two large earless seals, of southern oceans or of the N Atlantic, the males of which have a trunklike snout.

Eleusinian mysteries (ˌɛljʊ'sɪnɪən) *pl. n.* a mystical religious festival, held at Eleusis in SE Greece in classical times, to celebrate the gods Persephone, Demeter, and Dionysus.

Eleusis (ɪ'luːsɪs) *n.* a town in Greece, in Attica about 23 km (14 miles) west of Athens, of which it is now an industrial suburb. Modern Greek name: **Elevsís. — Eleusinian** (ˌɛljʊ'sɪnɪən) *n., adj.*

elev. *or* **el.** *abbrev. for* elevation.

elevate (ˈɛlɪˌveɪt) *vb.* (*tr.*) **1.** to move to a higher place. **2.** to raise in rank or status. **3.** to put in a cheerful mood; elate. **4.** to put on a higher cultural plane; uplift. **5.** to raise the axis of (a gun). **6.** to raise the intensity or pitch of (the voice). [C15: from L *ēlevāre*, from *levāre* to raise, from *levis* (adj.) light] — **'ele,vatory** *adj.*

elevated ('ɛlɪˌveɪtɪd) *adj.* **1.** raised to or being at a higher level. **2.** inflated or lofty; exalted. **3.** in a cheerful mood. **4.** *Inf.* slightly drunk.

elevation (ˌɛlɪ'veɪʃən) *n.* **1.** the act of elevating or the state of being elevated. **2.** the height of something above a given place, esp. above sea level. **3.** a raised area; height. **4.** nobleness or grandeur. **5.** a drawing to scale of the external face of a building or structure. **6.** a ballet dancer's ability to leap high. **7.** *Astron.* another name for **altitude** (sense 3). **8.** the angle formed between the muzzle of a gun and the horizontal. — **,ele'vational** *adj.*

elevator ('ɛlɪˌveɪtə) *n.* **1.** a person or thing that elevates. **2.** a mechanical hoist, often consisting of a chain of scoops linked together on a conveyor belt. **3.** the U.S. and Canad. name for **lift** (sense 14a). **4.** *Chiefly U.S. & Canad.* a granary equipped with an elevator and, usually, facilities for cleaning and grading the grain. **5.** a control surface on the tailplane of an aircraft, for making it climb or descend. **6.** any muscle that raises a part of the body.

eleven (ɪ'lɛvən) *n.* **1.** the cardinal number that is the sum of ten and one. **2.** a numeral, 11, XI, etc., representing this number. **3.** something representing, represented by, or consisting of 11 units. **4.** (*functioning as sing. or pl.*) a team of 11 players in football, cricket, etc. **5.** Also called:

eleven o'clock. eleven hours after noon or midnight. ~*determiner.* **6. a.** amounting to eleven. **b.** (*as pron.*): *another eleven.* [OE *endleofan*] —**e'leventh** *adj., n.*

eleven-plus *n.* (in Britain, esp. formerly) an examination taken by children aged 11 or 12 that determines the type of secondary education a child will be given.

elevenses (ɪ'lɛvᵊnzɪz) *pl. n.* (*sometimes functioning as sing.*) *Brit. inf.* a light snack, usually with tea or coffee, taken in mid-morning.

eleventh hour *n.* the latest possible time; last minute.

Elevsís (ˌɛlɛf'sis) *n.* transliteration of the Modern Greek name for **Eleusis.**

elf (ɛlf) *n., pl.* **elves. 1.** (in folklore) one of a kind of legendary beings, usually characterized as small, manlike, and mischievous. **2.** a mischievous or whimsical child or girl. [OE *ælf*] —**'elfish** *or* **'elvish** *adj.*

El Faiyûm (ɛl faɪ'juːm) *or* **Al Faiyûm** (æl faɪ'juːm) *n.* a city in N Egypt: a site of towns going back at least to the 12th dynasty. Pop.: 206 100 (1983 est.).

El Ferrol (*Spanish* ɛl fɛ'rrɔl) *n.* a port in NW Spain, on the Atlantic: fortified naval base, with a deep natural harbour. Pop.: 91 764 (1981). Official name (since 1939): **El Ferrol del Caudillo** (dɛl kau'ðiʎo).

elfin ('ɛlfɪn) *adj.* **1.** of or like an elf or elves. **2.** small, delicate, and charming.

elflock ('ɛlfˌlɒk) *n.* a lock of hair, fancifully regarded as having been tangled by the elves.

Elgar ('ɛlgɑː) *n.* Sir **Edward** (**William**). 1857–1934, English composer, whose works include the *Enigma Variations* (1899), the oratorio *The Dream of Gerontius* (1900), two symphonies, a cello concerto, and a violin concerto.

El Giza (ɛl 'giːzə) *n.* a city in NE Egypt, on the W bank of the Nile opposite Cairo: nearby are the Great Pyramid of Cheops (Khufu) and the Sphinx. Pop.: 1 509 600 (1983 est.).

Elgon ('ɛlgɒn) *n.* **Mount.** an extinct volcano in E Africa, on the Kenya-Uganda border. Height: 4321 m (14 178 ft.).

El Greco (ɛl 'grɛkəʊ) *n.* real name *Domenikos Theotocopoulos.* 1541–1614, Spanish painter, born in Crete; noted for his elongated human forms and dramatic use of colour.

Eli ('iːlaɪ) *n. Old Testament.* the highest priest at Shiloh and teacher of Samuel (I Samuel 1–3).

Elia¹ *or* **Eleia** ('iːlɪə) *n.* a department of SW Greece, in the W Peloponnese: in ancient times most of the region formed the state of Elis. Pop.: 160 305 (1981). Area: 2681 sq. km (1035 sq. miles). Modern Greek name: **Ilia.**

Elia² ('iːlɪə) *n.* the pen name of (Charles) **Lamb.**

Elias (ɪ'laɪəs) *n. Bible.* the Douay spelling of **Elijah.**

elicit (ɪ'lɪsɪt) *vb.* (*tr.*) **1.** to give rise to; evoke. **2.** to bring to light. [C17: from L *ēlicere*, from *licere* to entice] —**e'licitable** *adj.* —**e,lici'tation** *n.* —**e'licitor** *n.*

elide (ɪ'laɪd) *vb.* to undergo or cause to undergo elision. [C16: from L *ēlīdere* to knock, from *laedere* to hit, wound] —**e'lidible** *adj.*

eligible ('ɛlɪdʒəbᵊl) *adj.* **1.** fit, worthy, or qualified, as for office. **2.** desirable, esp. as a spouse. [C15: from LL *ēligere* to ELECT] —**,eligi'bility** *n.* —**'eligibly** *adv.*

Elijah (ɪ'laɪdʒə) *n. Old Testament.* a Hebrew prophet of the 9th century B.C., who was persecuted for denouncing Ahab and Jezebel. (I Kings 17–21: 21; II Kings 1–2:18).

Elikón (ɛli'kɒn) *n.* transliteration of the Modern Greek name for **Helicon.**

eliminate (ɪ'lɪmɪˌneɪt) *vb.* (*tr.*) **1.** to remove or take out. **2.** to reject; omit from consideration. **3.** to remove (a competitor, team, etc.) from a contest, usually by defeat. **4.** *Sl.* to murder in cold blood. **5.** *Physiol.* to expel (waste) from the body. **6.** *Maths.* to eliminate (an unknown variable) from simultaneous equations. [C16: from L *ēlīmināre* to turn out of the house, from *e-* out + *līmen* threshold] —**e'liminable** *adj.* —**e,limi'nation** *n.* —**e'liminative** *adj.* —**e'limi,nator** *n.*

Eliot ('ɛlɪət) *n.* **1. George,** real name *Mary Ann Evans.* 1819–80, English novelist, noted for her analysis of provincial Victorian society. Her best-known novels include *Adam Bede* (1859), *The Mill on the Floss* (1860), *Silas Marner* (1861), and *Middlemarch* (1872). **2.** Sir **John.** 1592–1632, English statesman, a leader of parliamentary opposition to Charles I. **3. T(homas) S(tearns).** 1888–1965, British poet, dramatist, and critic, born in the U.S. His poetry includes *Prufrock and Other Observations* (1917), *The Waste Land* (1922), *Ash Wednesday* (1930), and *Four Quartets* (1943). Among his verse plays are

Murder in the Cathedral (1935), *The Family Reunion* (1939), *The Cocktail Party* (1950), and *The Confidential Clerk* (1954): Nobel prize for literature 1948.

Elis ('iːlɪs) *n.* an ancient city-state of SW Greece, in the NW Peloponnese: site of the ancient Olympic games.

Elisabeth (ɪ'lɪzəbəθ) *n.* a variant spelling of **Elizabeth²** (sense 1).

Elisabethville (ɪ'lɪzəbəθˌvɪl) *n.* the former name (until 1966) of **Lubumbashi.**

Elisavetgrad (*Russian* jɪliza'vjɛtgrət) *n.* a former name (until 1924) of **Kirovograd.**

Elisavetpol (*Russian* jɪliza'vjɛtpəlj) *n.* a former name (until 1920) of **Kirovabad.**

Elisha (ɪ'laɪʃə) *n. Old Testament.* a Hebrew prophet of the 9th century B.C.: successor of Elijah (II Kings 3–9).

elision (ɪ'lɪʒən) *n.* **1.** omission of a syllable or vowel at the beginning or end of a word. **2.** omission of parts of a book, etc. [C16: from L *ēlīdere* to ELIDE]

elite *or* **élite** (ɪ'liːt, eɪ-) *n.* (*sometimes functioning as pl.*) the most powerful, rich, or gifted members of a group, community, etc. **2.** a typewriter type size having 12 characters to the inch. ~*adj.* **3.** of or suitable for an elite. [C18: from F, from OF *eslit* chosen, from L *ēligere* to ELECT]

elitism (ɪ'liːtɪzəm, eɪ-) *n.* **1. a.** the belief that society should be governed by an elite. **b.** such government. **2.** pride in or awareness of being one of an elite group. —**e'litist** *n.*

elixir (ɪ'lɪksə) *n.* **1.** an alchemical preparation supposed to be capable of prolonging life (**elixir of life**) or of transmuting base metals into gold. **2.** anything that purports to be a sovereign remedy. **3.** a quintessence. **4.** a liquid containing a medicine with syrup, glycerin, or alcohol added to mask its unpleasant taste. [C14: from Med. L, from Ar., prob. from Gk *xērion* powder used for drying wounds]

Eliz. *abbrev. for* Elizabethan.

Elizabeth¹ (ɪ'lɪzəbəθ) *n.* **1.** a city in NE New Jersey, on Newark Bay. Pop.: 106 201 (1980). **2.** a town in SE South Australia, near Adelaide. Pop.: 33 310 (1981 est.).

Elizabeth² (ɪ'lɪzəbəθ) *n.* **1.** Also: **Elisabeth.** *New Testament.* the wife of Zacharias, mother of John the Baptist, and kinswoman of the Virgin Mary. **2.** pen name *Carmen Sylva.* 1843–1916, queen of Romania (1881–1914) and author. **3.** Russian name *Yelizaveta Petrovna.* 1709–62, empress of Russia (1741–62); daughter of Peter the Great. **4. Saint.** 1207–31, Hungarian princess who devoted herself to charity and asceticism. Feast day: Nov. 19. **5.** title *the Queen Mother;* original name Lady *Elizabeth Bowes-Lyon.* born 1900, queen of Great Britain and Northern Ireland (1936–52) as the wife of George VI; mother of Elizabeth II.

Elizabeth I *n.* 1533–1603, queen of England (1558–1603); daughter of Henry VIII and Anne Boleyn. She established the Church of England (1559) and put an end to Catholic plots, notably by executing Mary Queen of Scots (1587) and defeating the Spanish Armada (1588). Her reign was notable for commercial growth, maritime expansion, and the flourishing of literature, music, and architecture.

Elizabeth II *n.* born 1926, queen of Great Britain and Northern Ireland from 1952; daughter of George VI.

Elizabethan (ɪˌlɪzə'biːθən) *adj.* **1.** of, characteristic of, or relating to the reigns of Elizabeth I or Elizabeth II. **2.** of, relating to, or designating a style of architecture used in England during the reign of Elizabeth I. ~*n.* **3.** a person who lived in England during the reign of Elizabeth I.

Elizabethan sonnet *n.* another term for **Shakespearean sonnet.**

elk (ɛlk) *n., pl.* **elks** *or* **elk. 1.** a large deer of N Europe and Asia: also occurs in N America, where it is called a moose. **2. American elk.** another name for **wapiti.** [OE *eolh*]

El Khalil (æl xɒ'liːl) *n.* transliteration of the Arabic name for **Hebron.**

ell (ɛl) *n.* an obsolete unit of length, approximately 45 inches. [OE *eln* forearm (the measure orig. being from elbow to fingertips)]

Ellás (ɛ'las) *n.* transliteration of the Modern Greek name for **Greece.**

Ellesmere Island ('ɛlzmɪə) *n.* a Canadian island in the Arctic Ocean: part of the Northwest Territories; mountainous, with many glaciers. Area: 212 688 sq. km (82 119 sq. miles).

Ellesmere Port n. a port in NW England, in NW Cheshire on the Manchester Ship Canal. Pop.: 63 134 (1981).

Ellice Islands ('ɛlɪs) pl. n. the former name (until 1975) of **Tuvalu**.

Ellington ('ɛlɪŋtən) n. **Duke**, nickname of *Edward Kennedy Ellington*. 1899–1974, U.S. jazz composer, pianist, and conductor, famous for such works as "Mood Indigo" and "Creole Love Call".

ellipse (ɪ'lɪps) n. a closed conic section shaped like a flattened circle and formed by an inclined plane that does not cut the base of the cone. [C18: back formation from ELLIPSIS]

ellipsis (ɪ'lɪpsɪs) n., pl. **-ses** (-siːz). **1.** omission of parts of a word or sentence. **2.** *Printing.* a sequence of three dots (. . .) indicating an omission in text. [C16: from L, from Gk, from *en* in + *leipein* to leave]

ellipsoid (ɪ'lɪpsɔɪd) n. **a.** a geometric surface, symmetrical about the three coordinate axes, whose plane sections are ellipses or circles. **b.** a solid having this shape. —**ellipsoidal** (ɪlɪp'sɔɪdᵊl, ˌɛl-) adj.

ellipsoid of revolution n. a geometric surface produced by rotating an ellipse about one of its two axes and having circular plane sections perpendicular to the axis of revolution.

elliptical (ɪ'lɪptɪkᵊl) adj. **1.** relating to or having the shape of an ellipse. **2.** relating to or resulting from ellipsis. **3.** (of speech, literary style, etc.) **a.** very concise, often so as to be obscure or ambiguous. **b.** circumlocutory. ~Also (for senses 1 and 2): **elliptic**. —**el'lipticalness** n.

▷**Usage.** The use of *elliptical* to mean *circumlocutory* is avoided by many careful speakers and writers.

Ellis ('ɛlɪs) n. **1. Alexander John.** 1814–90, English philologist: made the first systematic survey of the phonology of British dialects. **2. (Henry) Havelock** ('hævlɒk). 1859–1939, English essayist: author of works on the psychology of sex.

elm (ɛlm) n. **1.** any tree of the genus *Ulmus*, occurring in the N hemisphere, having serrated leaves and winged fruits (samaras). **2.** the hard heavy wood of this tree. [OE *elm*]

El Mansûra (ɛl mæn'suərə) or **Al Mansûrah** n. a city in NE Egypt: scene of a battle (1250) in which the Crusaders were defeated by the Mamelukes and Louis IX of France was captured; cotton-manufacturing centre. Pop.: 310 900 (1983 est.).

El Minya (ɛl 'mɪnjə) n. a river port in central Egypt on the Nile. Pop.: 197 000 (1983 est.).

El Misti (ɛl 'miːstiː) n. a volcano in S Peru, in the Andes. Height: 5852 m (19 199 ft.).

El Obeid (ɛl əʊ'beɪd) n. a city in the central Sudan, in Kordofan province: scene of the defeat of a British and Egyptian army by the Mahdi (1883). Pop.: 140 025 (1984).

elocution (ˌɛlə'kjuːʃən) n. the art of public speaking. [C15: from L *ēloquī*, from *loquī* to speak] —ˌelo'cutionary adj. —ˌelo'cutionist n.

Elohist (ɛ'ləʊhɪst) n. *Bible.* the supposed author or authors of the Pentateuch, identified chiefly by the use of the word *Elohim* for God.

elongate ('iːlɒŋgeɪt) vb. **1.** to make or become longer; stretch. ~adj. **2.** long and narrow. **3.** lengthened or tapered. [C16: from LL *ēlongāre* to keep at a distance, from *ē-* away + L *longē* (adv.) far] —ˌelon'gation n.

elope (ɪ'ləʊp) vb. (intr.) to run away secretly with a lover, esp. in order to marry. [C16: from Anglo-F *aloper*, ?from MDu. *lōpen* to run; see LOPE] —**e'lopement** n. —**e'loper** n.

eloquence ('ɛləkwəns) n. **1.** ease in using language. **2.** powerful and effective language. **3.** the quality of being persuasive or moving.

eloquent ('ɛləkwənt) adj. **1.** (of speech, writing, etc.) fluent and persuasive. **2.** visibly or vividly expressive: *an eloquent yawn*. [C14: from L *ēloquēns*, from *loquī* to speak] —**'eloquentness** n.

El Paso (ɛl 'pæsəʊ) n. a city in W Texas, on the Rio Grande opposite Ciudad Juárez, Mexico. Pop.: 425 259 (1980).

El Salvador (ɛl 'sælvəˌdɔː) n. a republic in Central America, on the Pacific: colonized by the Spanish from 1524; declared independence in 1841, becoming a republic in 1856. It consists of coastal lowlands rising to a central plateau. Coffee constitutes about half of the total exports. Language: Spanish. Religion: Roman Catholic. Currency: colón. Capital: San Salvador. Pop.: 5 480 000 (1985 est.).

Area: 21 330 sq. km (8236 sq. miles). —ˌSalva'doran, ˌSalva'dorean, or ˌSalva'dorian adj., n.

Elsan ('ɛlsæn) n. *Trademark.* a type of portable chemical lavatory. [C20: from initials of *E. L.* Jackson, manufacturer + SAN(ITATION)]

Elsass ('ɛlzas) n. the German name for **Alsace**.

Elsass-Lothringen ('ɛlzas'loːtrɪŋən) n. the German name for **Alsace-Lorraine**.

else (ɛls) determiner. (postpositive; used after an indefinite pronoun or an interrogative) **1.** in addition; more: *there is nobody else here.* **2.** other; different: *where else could he be?* ~adv. **3. or else. a.** if not, then: *go away or else I won't finish my work today.* **b.** or something terrible will result: used as a threat: *sit down, or else!* [OE *elles,* genitive of *el-* strange, foreign]

▷**Usage.** The possessive of the expressions *anybody else, everybody else,* etc., is formed by adding 's to *else: somebody else's letter. Who else* is an exception in that *whose else* is an acceptable alternative to *who else's: whose else can it be?* or *who else's can it be?*

elsewhere (ˌɛls'wɛə) adv. in or to another place; somewhere else. [OE *elles hwǣr;* see ELSE, WHERE]

Elsinore ('ɛlsɪˌnɔː, ˌɛlsɪ'nɔː) n. the English name for **Helsingør**.

ELT abbrev. for English Language Teaching.

Éluard (French elɥar) n. **Paul** (pɔl). 1895–1952, French surrealist poet, noted for his political and love poems.

eluate ('ɛljuˌeɪt) n. a solution of adsorbed material in the eluant obtained during the process of elution.

elucidate (ɪ'luːsɪˌdeɪt) vb. to make clear (something obscure or difficult); clarify. [C16: from LL *ēlūcidāre* to enlighten; see LUCID] —**e,luci'dation** n. —**e'luci,dative** or **e'luci,datory** adj. —**e'luci,dator** n.

elude (ɪ'luːd) vb. (tr.) **1.** to escape from or avoid, esp. by cunning. **2.** to avoid fulfilment of (a responsibility, obligation, etc.); evade. **3.** to escape discovery or understanding by; baffle. [C16: from L *ēlūdere* to deceive, from *lūdere* to play] —**e'luder** n. —**elusion** (ɪ'luːʒən) n.

eluent or **eluant** ('ɛljuːənt) n. a solvent used for eluting.

elusive (ɪ'luːsɪv) adj. **1.** difficult to catch. **2.** preferring or living in solitude and anonymity. **3.** difficult to remember. —**e'lusiveness** n.

elute (iː'luːt, ɪ'luːt) vb. (tr.) to wash out (a substance) by the action of a solvent, as in chromatography. [C18: from L *ēlūtus* rinsed out, from *luere* to wash, LAVE] —**e'lution** n.

elutriate (ɪ'luːtrɪˌeɪt) vb. (tr.) to purify or separate (a substance or mixture) by washing and straining or decanting. [C18: from L *ēluere,* from *ē-* out + *lavere* to wash] —**e,lutri'ation** n.

elver ('ɛlvə) n. a young eel, esp. one migrating up a river. [C17: var. of *eelfare,* lit.: eel-journey; see EEL, FARE]

elves (ɛlvz) n. the plural of **elf**.

elvish ('ɛlvɪʃ) adj. a variant of **elfish**: see **elf**.

Ely ('iːlɪ) n. **1.** a cathedral city in E England, in E Cambridgeshire on the River Ouse. Pop.: 11 030 (1983 est.). **2. Isle of.** a former county of E England, part of Cambridgeshire since 1965.

Elyot ('ɛlɪət) n. Sir **Thomas**. ?1490–1546, English scholar and diplomat; author of *The Boke named the Governour* (1531), a treatise in English on education.

Élysée (eɪ'liːzeɪ) n. a palace in Paris, in the Champs Elysées: official residence of the president of France.

Elysium (ɪ'lɪzɪəm) n. **1.** Also called: **Elysian fields.** *Greek myth.* the dwelling place of the blessed after death. **2.** a state or place of perfect bliss. [C16: from L, from Gk *Ēlusion pedion* Elysian (that is, blessed) fields]

elytron ('ɛlɪˌtrɒn) or **elytrum** ('ɛlɪtrəm) n., pl. **-tra** (-trə). either of the horny front wings of beetles and some other insects. [C18: from Gk *elutron* sheath]

em (ɛm) n. *Printing.* **1.** the square of a body of any size of type, used as a unit of measurement. **2.** Also called: **pica em, pica.** a unit of measurement in printing, equal to twelve points or one sixth of an inch. [C19: from the name of the letter *M*]

em- prefix. a variant of **en-**¹ and **en-**² before *b, m,* and *p*.

'em (əm) pron. an informal variant of **them**.

emaciate (ɪ'meɪsɪˌeɪt) vb. (usually tr.) to become or cause to become abnormally thin. [C17: from L, from *macer* thin] —**e'maci,ated** adj. —**e,maci'ation** n.

emanate ('ɛməˌneɪt) vb. **1.** (intr.; often foll. by *from*) to issue or proceed from or as from a source. **2.** (tr.) to send forth; emit. [C18: from L *ēmānāre* to flow out, from

mānāre to flow] —**emanative** ('ɛmənətɪv) *adj.*
—'**ema,nator** *n.* —'**ema,natory** *adj.*
emanation (,ɛmə'neɪʃən) *n.* **1.** an act or instance of emanating. **2.** something that emanates or is produced. **3.** a gaseous product of radioactive decay. —,**ema'national** *adj.*

emancipate (ɪ'mænsɪ,peɪt) *vb.* (*tr.*) **1.** to free from restriction or restraint, esp. social or legal restraint. **2.** (*often passive*) to free from the inhibitions of conventional morality. **3.** to liberate (a slave) from bondage. [C17: from L *ēmancipāre* to give independence (to a son), from *mancipāre* to transfer property; see MANCIPLE] —e'**manci,pated** *adj.* —e,**manci'pation** *n.* —e'**manci,pator** *n.* —**emancipatory** (ɪ'mænsɪpətərɪ, -trɪ) *adj.*

emasculate *vb.* (ɪ'mæskjʊ,leɪt). (*tr.*) **1.** to remove the testicles of; castrate; geld. **2.** to deprive of vigour, effectiveness, etc. ~*adj.* (ɪ'mæskjʊlɪt, -,leɪt). **3.** castrated; gelded. **4.** Also: **emasculated.** deprived of strength, effectiveness, etc. [C17: from L *ēmasculāre*, from *masculus* male; see MASCULINE] —e,**mascu'lation** *n.* —e'**mascu,lator** *n.* —e'**masculatory** *adj.*

embalm (ɪm'bɑːm) *vb.* (*tr.*) **1.** to treat (a dead body) with preservatives to retard putrefaction. **2.** to preserve or cherish the memory of. **3.** *Poetic.* to give a sweet fragrance to. [C13: from OF *embaumer;* see BALM] —**em'balmer** *n.* —**em'balmment** *n.*

embank (ɪm'bæŋk) *vb.* (*tr.*) to protect, enclose, or confine with an embankment.

embankment (ɪm'bæŋkmənt) *n.* a man-made ridge of earth or stone that carries a road or railway or confines a waterway.

embargo (ɛm'bɑːgəʊ) *n., pl.* -**goes.** **1.** a government order prohibiting the departure or arrival of merchant ships in its ports. **2.** any legal stoppage of commerce. **3.** a restraint or prohibition. ~*vb.* -**going, -goed.** (*tr.*) **4.** to lay an embargo upon. **5.** to seize for use by the state. [C16: from Sp., from *embargar*, from L IM- + *barra* BAR[1]]

embark (ɛm'bɑːk) *vb.* **1.** to board (a ship or aircraft). **2.** (*intr.;* usually foll. by *on* or *upon*) to commence or engage (in) a new project, venture, etc. [C16: via F from OF, from EM- + *barca* boat, BARQUE] —,**embar'kation** *n.* —**em'barkment** *n.*

embarrass (ɪm'bærəs) *vb.* (*mainly tr.*) **1.** to cause to feel confusion or self-consciousness; disconcert. **2.** (*usually passive*) to involve in financial difficulties. **3.** *Arch.* to complicate. **4.** *Arch.* to impede or hamper. [C17 (in the sense: to impede): via F & Sp. from It., from *imbarrare* to confine within bars] —**em'barrassed** *adj.* —**em'barrassing** *adj.* —**em'barrassment** *n.*

embassy ('ɛmbəsɪ) *n., pl.* -**sies.** **1.** the residence or place of business of an ambassador. **2.** an ambassador and his entourage collectively. **3.** the position, business, or mission of an ambassador. **4.** any important or official mission. [C16: from OF *ambaisada;* see AMBASSADOR]

embattle (ɪm'bæt²l) *vb.* (*tr.*) **1.** to deploy (troops) for battle. **2.** to fortify (a position, town, etc.). **3.** to provide with battlements. [C14: from OF *embataillier;* see EN-[1] BATTLE]

embay (ɪm'beɪ) *vb.* (*tr.*) (*usually passive*) **1.** to form into a bay. **2.** to enclose in or as if in a bay.

embed (ɪm'bɛd) *vb.* -**bedding, -bedded. 1.** (usually foll. by *in*) to fix or become fixed firmly and deeply in a surrounding solid mass. **2.** (*tr.*) to surround closely. **3.** (*tr.*) to fix or retain (a thought, idea, etc.) in the mind. ~Also: **imbed.** —**em'bedment** *n.*

embellish (ɪm'bɛlɪʃ) *vb.* (*tr.*) **1.** to beautify; adorn. **2.** to make (a story, etc.) more interesting by adding detail. [C14: from OF *embelir*, from *bel* beautiful, from L *bellus*] —**em'bellisher** *n.* —**em'bellishment** *n.*

ember ('ɛmbə) *n.* **1.** a glowing or smouldering piece of coal or wood, as in a dying fire. **2.** the remains of a past emotion. [OE *ǣmyrge*]

Ember days *pl. n. R.C. & Anglican Church.* any of four groups in the year of three days (always Wednesday, Friday, and Saturday) of prayer and fasting. [OE *ymbrendæg*, from *ymb* around + *ryne* a course + *dæg* day]

embezzle (ɪm'bɛz²l) *vb.* to convert (money or property entrusted to one) fraudulently to one's own use. [C15: from Anglo-F *embeseiller* to destroy, from OF *beseiller* to make away with, from ?] —**em'bezzlement** *n.* —**em'bezzler** *n.*

embitter (ɪm'bɪtə) *vb.* (*tr.*) **1.** to make (a person) bitter. **2.** to aggravate (a hostile feeling, difficult situation, etc.). —**em'bittered** *adj.* —**em'bitterment** *n.*

emblazon (ɪm'bleɪz²n) *vb.* (*tr.*) **1.** to portray heraldic arms on (a shield, one's notepaper, etc.). **2.** to make bright or splendid, as with colours, flowers, etc. **3.** to glorify, praise, or extol. —**em'blazonment** *n.*

emblem ('ɛmbləm) *n.* a visible object or representation that symbolizes a quality, type, group, etc. [C15: from L *emblēma*, from Gk, from *emballein* to insert, from *en* in + *ballein* to throw] —,**emblem'atic** *or* ,**emblem'atical** *adj.* —,**emblem'atically** *adv.*

embody (ɪm'bɒdɪ) *vb.* -**bodying, -bodied.** (*tr.*) **1.** to give a tangible, bodily, or concrete form to (an abstract concept). **2.** to be an example of or express (an idea, principle, etc.). **3.** (often foll. by *in*) to collect or unite in a comprehensive whole. **4.** to invest (a spiritual entity) with bodily form. —**em'bodiment** *n.*

embolden (ɪm'bəʊld²n) *vb.* (*tr.*) to encourage; make bold.

embolism ('ɛmbə,lɪzəm) *n.* the occlusion of a blood vessel by an embolus. [C14: from Med. L, from Gk *embolismos;* see EMBOLUS] —**embolic** (ɛm'bɒlɪk) *adj.*

embolus ('ɛmbələs) *n., pl.* -**li** (-,laɪ). material, such as part of a blood clot or an air bubble, that becomes lodged within a small blood vessel and impedes the circulation. [C17: via L from Gk *embolos* stopper; see EMBLEM]

embonpoint *French.* (ɑ̃bɔ̃pwɛ̃) *n.* **1.** plumpness or stoutness. ~*adj.* **2.** plump; stout. [C18: from *en bon point* in good condition]

embosom (ɪm'bʊzəm) *vb.* (*tr.*) *Arch.* **1.** to enclose or envelop, esp. protectively. **2.** to clasp to the bosom; hug. **3.** to cherish.

emboss (ɪm'bɒs) *vb.* **1.** to mould or carve (a decoration) on (a surface) so that it is raised above the surface in low relief. **2.** to cause to bulge; make protrude. [C14: from OF *embocer*, from EM- + *boce* BOSS[2]] —**em'bossed** *adj.* —**em'bosser** *n.* —**em'bossment** *n.*

embouchure (,ɒmbʊ'ʃʊə) *n.* **1.** the mouth of a river or valley. **2.** *Music.* **a.** the correct application of the lips and tongue in playing a wind instrument. **b.** the mouthpiece of a wind instrument. [C18: from F, from OF *bouche* mouth, from L *bucca* cheek]

embower (ɪm'baʊə) *vb.* (*tr.*) *Arch.* to enclose in or as in a bower.

embrace (ɪm'breɪs) *vb.* (*mainly tr.*) **1.** (*also intr.*) (of a person) to take or clasp (another person) in the arms, or (of two people) to clasp each other, as in affection, greeting, etc.; hug. **2.** to accept willingly or eagerly. **3.** to take up (a new idea, faith, etc.); adopt. **4.** to comprise or include as an integral part. **5.** to encircle or enclose. **6.** *Rare.* to perceive or understand. ~*n.* **7.** the act of embracing. [C14: from OF, from EM- + *brace* a pair of arms, from L *bracchia* arms] —**em'braceable** *adj.* —**em'bracement** *n.* —**em'bracer** *n.*

embrasure (ɪm'breɪʒə) *n.* **1.** *Fortifications.* an opening or indentation, as in a battlement, for shooting through. **2.** a door or window having splayed sides that increase the width of the opening in the interior. [C18: from F, from obs. *embraser* to widen] —**em'brasured** *adj.*

embrocate ('ɛmbrəʊ,keɪt) *vb.* (*tr.*) to apply a liniment or lotion to (a part of the body). [C17: from Med. L *embrocha* poultice, from Gk, from *brokhē* a moistening]

embrocation (,ɛmbrəʊ'keɪʃən) *n.* a drug or agent for rubbing into the skin; liniment.

embroider (ɪm'brɔɪdə) *vb.* **1.** to do decorative needlework (upon). **2.** to add fictitious or exaggerated detail to (a story, account, etc.). [C15: from OF *embroder*] —**em'broiderer** *n.*

embroidery (ɪm'brɔɪdərɪ) *n., pl.* -**deries. 1.** decorative needlework done usually on loosely woven cloth or canvas, often being a picture or pattern. **2.** elaboration or exaggeration, esp. in writing or reporting; embellishment.

embroil (ɪm'brɔɪl) *vb.* (*tr.*) **1.** to involve (a person, oneself, etc.) in trouble, conflict, or argument. **2.** to throw (affairs, etc.) into a state of confusion or disorder; complicate; entangle. [C17: from F *embrouiller*, from *brouiller* to mingle, confuse] —**em'broiler** *n.* —**em'broilment** *n.*

embryo ('ɛmbrɪ,əʊ) *n., pl.* -**bryos. 1.** an animal in the early stages of development up to birth or hatching. **2.** the human product of conception up to approximately the end of the second month of pregnancy. Cf. **fetus.** **3.** a plant in the early stages of development. **4.** an undeveloped or rudimentary state (esp. in **in embryo**). **5.** something in an early stage of development. [C16: from LL, from Gk *embruon*, from *bruein* to swell]

embryology (ˌɛmbrɪˈɒlədʒɪ) *n.* **1.** the scientific study of embryos. **2.** the structure and development of the embryo of a particular organism. —**embryological** (ˌɛmbrɪəˈlɒdʒɪkᵊl) *or* ˌembryoˈlogic *adj.* —ˌembryˈologist *n.*

embryonic (ˌɛmbrɪˈɒnɪk) *or* **embryonal** (ˈɛmbrɪənᵊl) *adj.* **1.** of or relating to an embryo. **2.** in an early stage; rudimentary; undeveloped. —ˌembryˈonically *adv.*

emcee (ˌɛmˈsiː) *Inf.* ~*n.* **1.** a master of ceremonies. ~*vb.* **-ceeing, -ceed.** **2.** to act as master of ceremonies (for or at). [C20: from MC]

Emden (*German* ˈɛmdən) *n.* a port in NW West Germany, in Lower Saxony at the mouth of the River Ems. Pop.: 50 500 (1984).

-eme *suffix forming nouns. Linguistics.* indicating a minimal distinctive unit of a specified type in a language: *morpheme; phoneme*. [C20: via F, abstracted from PHONEME]

emend (ɪˈmɛnd) *vb.* (*tr.*) to make corrections or improvements in (a text) by critical editing. [C15: from L, from *ē*out + *mendum* a mistake] —eˈmendable *adj.*
▷ **Usage.** See at **amend.**

emendation (ˌiːmɛnˈdeɪʃən) *n.* **1.** a correction or improvement in a text. **2.** the act or process of emending. —ˈemenˌdator *n.* —**emendatory** (ɪˈmɛndətərɪ, -trɪ) *adj.*

emerald (ˈɛmərəld, ˈɛmrəld) *n.* **1.** a green transparent variety of beryl: highly valued as a gem. **2. a.** its clear green colour. **b.** (*as adj.*): *an emerald carpet.* [C13: from OF *esmeraude*, from L *smaragdus*, from Gk *smaragdos*]

Emerald Isle *n.* a poetic name for **Ireland**[1].

emerge (ɪˈmɜːdʒ) *vb.* (*intr.; often foll. by from*) **1.** to come up to the surface of or rise from water or other liquid. **2.** to come into view, as from concealment or obscurity. **3.** (foll. by *from*) to come out (of) or live (through (a difficult experience, etc.)). **4.** to become apparent. [C17: from L *ēmergere* to rise up from, from *mergere* to dip] —eˈmergence *n.* —eˈmerging *adj.*

emergency (ɪˈmɜːdʒənsɪ) *n.*, *pl.* **-cies.** **1. a.** an unforeseen or sudden occurrence, esp. of danger demanding immediate action. **b.** (*as modifier*): *an emergency exit.* **2. a.** a patient requiring urgent treatment. **b.** (*as modifier*): *an emergency ward.* **3.** *N.Z.* a player selected to stand by to replace an injured member of a team; reserve. **4. state of emergency.** a condition, declared by a government, in which martial law applies, usually because of civil unrest or natural disaster.

emergent (ɪˈmɜːdʒənt) *adj.* **1.** coming into being or notice. **2.** (of a nation) recently independent. —eˈmergently *adv.*

emeritus (ɪˈmɛrɪtəs) *adj.* (*usually postpositive*) retired or honourably discharged from full-time work, but retaining one's title on an honorary basis: *a professor emeritus.* [C19: from L, from *merēre* to deserve; see MERIT]

emersion (ɪˈmɜːʃən) *n.* **1.** the act or an instance of emerging. **2.** *Astron.* the reappearance of a celestial body after an eclipse or occultation. [C17: from L *ēmersus*; see EMERGE]

Emerson (ˈɛməsᵊn) *n.* **Ralph Waldo.** (rælf ˈwɔːldəʊ). 1803–82, U.S. poet, essayist, and transcendentalist.

emery (ˈɛmərɪ) *n.* **a.** a hard greyish-black mineral consisting of corundum with either magnetite or haematite: used as an abrasive and polishing agent. **b.** (*as modifier*): *emery paper.* [C15: from OF *esmeril*, ult. from Gk *smuris* powder for rubbing]

emery board *n.* a strip of cardboard or wood with a rough surface of crushed emery, for filing one's nails.

emetic (ɪˈmɛtɪk) *adj.* **1.** causing vomiting. ~*n.* **2.** an emetic agent or drug. [C17: from LL, from Gk *emetikos*, from *emein* to vomit]

emf *or* **EMF** *abbrev. for* electromotive force.

-emia *n. combining form.* a U.S. variant of **-aemia.**

emigrant (ˈɛmɪɡrənt) *n.* **a.** a person who leaves one place, esp. his native country, to settle in another. **b.** (*as modifier*): *an emigrant worker.*

emigrate (ˈɛmɪˌɡreɪt) *vb.* (*intr.*) to leave one place, esp. one's native country, to settle in another. [C18: from L *ēmigrāre*, from *migrāre* to depart, MIGRATE] —ˌemiˈgration *n.* —ˈemiˌgratory *adj.*

émigré (ˈɛmɪˌɡreɪ) *n.* an emigrant, esp. one forced to leave his native country for political reasons. [C18: from F, from *émigrer* to EMIGRATE]

Emilia-Romagna (ɪˈmiːliərəʊˈmɑːnjə; *Italian* eˈmiːliaroˈmaɲɲa) *n.* a region of N central Italy, on the Adriatic: rises from the plains of the Po valley in the north to the Apennines in the south. Capital: Bologna. Pop.: 3 931 014 (1985 est.). Area: 22 123 sq. km (8628 sq. miles).

eminence (ˈɛmɪnəns) *n.* **1.** a position of superiority or fame. **2.** a high or raised piece of ground. ~*Also:* **eminency.** [C17: from F, from L *ēminentia* a standing out; see EMINENT]

Eminence (ˈɛmɪnəns) *or* **Eminency** *n.*, *pl.* **-nences** *or* **-nencies.** (preceded by *Your* or *His*) a title used to address or refer to a cardinal.

éminence grise *French.* (eminɑ̃s ɡriz) *n.*, *pl.* **éminences grises** (eminɑ̃s ɡriz). a person who wields power and influence unofficially or behind the scenes. [lit.: grey eminence, orig. applied to Père Joseph, F monk, secretary of Cardinal RICHELIEU]

eminent (ˈɛmɪnənt) *adj.* **1.** above others in rank, merit, or reputation; distinguished. **2.** (*prenominal*) noteworthy or outstanding. **3.** projecting or protruding; prominent. [C15: from L *ēminēre* to project, stand out, from *minēre* to stand]

eminent domain *n. Law.* the right of a state to confiscate private property for public use, payment usually being made in compensation.

emir (ɛˈmɪə) *n.* (in the Islamic world) **1.** an independent ruler or chieftain. **2.** a military commander or governor. **3.** a descendant of Mohammed. [C17: via F from Sp., from Ar. *'amīr* commander] —eˈmirate *n.*

emissary (ˈɛmɪsərɪ, -ɪsrɪ) *n.*, *pl.* **-saries.** **1. a.** an agent sent on a mission, esp. one who represents a government or head of state. **b.** (*as modifier*): *an emissary delegation.* **2.** an agent sent on a secret mission, as a spy. [C17: from L *ēmissārius*, from *ēmittere* to send out; see EMIT]

emission (ɪˈmɪʃən) *n.* **1.** the act of emitting or sending forth. **2.** energy, in the form of heat, light, radio waves, etc., emitted from a source. **3.** a substance, fluid, etc., that is emitted; discharge. **4.** *Physiol.* any bodily discharge, esp. of semen. [C17: from L *ēmissiō*, from *ēmittere* to send forth, EMIT] —eˈmissive *adj.*

emission spectrum *n.* the spectrum or pattern of bright lines or bands seen when the electromagnetic radiation emitted by a substance is passed into a spectrometer.

emit (ɪˈmɪt) *vb.* **emitting, emitted.** (*tr.*) **1.** to give or send forth; discharge. **2.** to give voice to; utter. **3.** *Physics.* to give off (radiation or particles). [C17: from L *ēmittere* to send out, from *mittere* to send]

emitter (ɪˈmɪtə) *n.* **1.** a person or thing that emits. **2.** a substance that emits radiation. **3.** the region in a transistor in which the charge-carrying holes or electrons originate.

Emmanuel (ɪˈmænjʊəl) *n.* a variant spelling of **Immanuel.**

Emmen (ˈɛmən; *Dutch* ˈɛmə) *n.* a city in the NE Netherlands, in Drenthe province: a new town developed since World War II. Pop.: 91 968 (1987).

Emmenthal, Emmental (ˈɛmənˌtɑːl), *or* **Emmenthaler** *n.* a hard Swiss cheese with holes in it. [C20: after *Emmenthal*, valley in Switzerland]

Emmy (ˈɛmɪ) *n.*, *pl.* **-mys** *or* **-mies.** (in the U.S.) one of the statuettes awarded annually for outstanding television performances and productions. [C20: from *Immy*, short for *image orthicon tube*]

emollient (ɪˈmɒljənt) *adj.* **1.** softening or soothing, esp. to the skin. ~*n.* **2.** any preparation or substance that has this effect. [C17: from L *ēmollīre* to soften, from *mollis* soft] —eˈmollience *n.*

emolument (ɪˈmɒljʊmənt) *n.* the profit arising from an office or employment; fees or wages. [C15: from L *ēmolumentum* benefit; orig., fee paid to a miller, from *molere* to grind]

emote (ɪˈməʊt) *vb.* (*intr.*) to display exaggerated emotion, as in acting. [C20: back formation from EMOTION] —eˈmoter *n.*

emotion (ɪˈməʊʃən) *n.* any strong feeling, as of joy, sorrow, or fear. [C16: from F, from OF, from L *ēmovēre* to disturb, from *movēre* to MOVE]

emotional (ɪˈməʊʃənᵊl) *adj.* **1.** of, characteristic of, or expressive of emotion. **2.** readily or excessively affected by emotion. **3.** appealing to or arousing emotion. **4.**

caused or determined by emotion rather than reason: *an emotional argument.* —**e,motion'ality** *n.*

emotionalism (ɪ'məʊʃənə,lɪzəm) *n.* **1.** emotional nature or quality. **2.** a tendency to yield readily to the emotions. **3.** an appeal to the emotions, esp. as to an audience. —**e'motionalist** *n.* —**e,motional'istic** *adj.*

emotionalize *or* **-ise** (ɪ'məʊʃənə,laɪz) *vb.* (*tr.*) to make emotional; subject to emotional treatment. —**e,motionali'zation** *or* **-i'sation** *n.*

emotive (ɪ'məʊtɪv) *adj.* **1.** tending or designed to arouse emotion. **2.** of or characterized by emotion. —**e'motiveness** *or* ,emo'tivity *n.*

Emp. *abbrev. for:* **1.** Emperor. **2.** Empire. **3.** Empress.

empanel *or* **impanel** (ɪm'pænᵊl) *vb.* **-elling, -elled** *or* *U.S.* **-eling, -eled.** (*tr.*) *Law.* **1.** to enter on a list (names of persons to be summoned for jury service). **2.** to select (a jury) from such a list. —**em'panelment** *or* **im'panelment** *n.*

empathize *or* **-ise** ('ɛmpə,θaɪz) *vb.* (*intr.*) to engage in or feel empathy.

empathy ('ɛmpəθɪ) *n.* **1.** the power of understanding and imaginatively entering into another person's feelings. **2.** the attribution to an object, such as a work of art, of one's own feelings about it. [C20: from Gk *empatheia* affection, passion] —**em'pathic** *or* ,empa'thetic *adj.* — 'em**pathist** *n.*

Empedocles (ɛm'pɛdə,kliːz) *n.* ?490–430 B.C., Greek philosopher and scientist, who held that the world is composed of four elements, air, fire, earth, and water, which are governed by the opposing forces of love and discord.

emperor ('ɛmpərə) *n.* a monarch who rules or reigns over an empire. [C13: from OF, from L *imperāre* to command, from IM- + *parāre* to make ready] —'**emperor,ship** *n.*

emperor penguin *n.* an Antarctic penguin with orange-yellow patches on the neck: the largest penguin, reaching a height of 1.3 m (4 ft.).

emphasis ('ɛmfəsɪs) *n., pl.* **-ses** (-siːz). **1.** special importance or significance. **2.** an object, idea, etc., that is given special importance or significance. **3.** stress on a particular syllable, word, or phrase in speaking. **4.** force or intensity of expression. **5.** sharpness or clarity of form or outline. [C16: via L from Gk: meaning, (in rhetoric) significant stress; see EMPHATIC]

emphasize *or* **-ise** ('ɛmfə,saɪz) *vb.* (*tr.*) to give emphasis or prominence to; stress.

emphatic (ɪm'fætɪk) *adj.* **1.** expressed, spoken, or done with emphasis. **2.** forceful and positive; definite; direct. **3.** sharp or clear in form, contour, or outline. **4.** important or significant; stressed. [C18: from Gk, from *emphainein* to display, from *phainein* to show] —**em'phatically** *adv.*

emphysema (,ɛmfɪ'siːmə) *n. Pathol.* **1.** a condition in which the air sacs of the lungs are grossly enlarged, causing breathlessness and wheezing. **2.** the abnormal presence of air in a tissue or part. [C17: from NL, from Gk *emphusēma* a swelling up, from *phusan* to blow]

empire ('ɛmpaɪə) *n.* **1.** an aggregate of peoples and territories under the rule of a single person, oligarchy, or sovereign state. **2.** any monarchy that has an emperor as head of state. **3.** the period during which a particular empire exists. **4.** supreme power; sovereignty. **5.** a large industrial organization with many ramifications. [C13: from OF, from L, from *imperāre* to command, from *parāre* to prepare]

Empire ('ɛmpaɪə) *n.* **the. 1.** See **British Empire. 2.** *French history.* **a.** the period of imperial rule in France from 1804 to 1815 under Napoleon Bonaparte. **b.** Also called: **Second Empire.** the period from 1852 to 1870 when Napoleon III ruled as emperor. ~*adj.* **3.** denoting, characteristic of, or relating to the British Empire. **4.** denoting, characteristic of, or relating to either French Empire, esp. the first.

empire-builder *n. Inf.* a person who seeks extra power, esp. by increasing the number of his staff. —'**empire-,building** *n., adj.*

Empire Day *n.* the former name of **Commonwealth Day.**

empiric (ɛm'pɪrɪk) *n.* **1.** a person who relies on empirical methods. **2.** a medical quack. ~*adj.* **3.** a variant of **empirical.** [C16: from L, from Gk *empeirikos* practised, from *peiran* to attempt]

empirical (ɛm'pɪrɪkᵊl) *adj.* **1.** derived from or relating to experiment and observation rather than theory. **2.** (of medical treatment) based on practical experience rather

than scientific proof. **3.** *Philosophy.* (of knowledge) derived from experience rather than by logic from first principles. **4.** of or relating to medical quackery. —**em'piricalness** *n.*

empiricism (ɛm'pɪrɪ,sɪzəm) *n.* **1.** *Philosophy.* the doctrine that all knowledge derives from experience. **2.** the use of empirical methods. **3.** medical quackery. —**em'piricist** *n., adj.*

emplace (ɪm'pleɪs) *vb.* (*tr.*) to put in position.

emplacement (ɪm'pleɪsmənt) *n.* **1.** a prepared position for a gun or other weapon. **2.** the act of putting or state of being put in place. [C19: from F, from obs. *emplacer* to put in position, from PLACE]

emplane (ɪm'pleɪn) *vb.* to board or put on board an aeroplane.

employ (ɪm'plɔɪ) *vb.* (*tr.*) **1.** to engage or make use of the services of (a person) in return for money; hire. **2.** to provide work or occupation for; keep busy. **3.** to use as a means. ~*n.* **4.** the state of being employed (esp. in **in someone's employ**). [C15: from OF *employer*, from L *implicāre* to entangle, engage, from *plicāre* to fold] —**em'ployable** *adj.* —**em,ploya'bility** *n.*

employee *or U.S.* **employe** (ɛm'plɔɪiː, ,ɛmplɔɪ'iː) *n.* a person who is hired to work for another or for a business, firm, etc., in return for payment.

employer (ɪm'plɔɪə) *n.* **1.** a person, firm, etc., that employs workers. **2.** a person who employs.

employment (ɪm'plɔɪmənt) *n.* **1.** the act of employing or state of being employed. **2.** a person's work or occupation.

employment exchange *n. Brit.* a former name for **employment office.**

employment office *n. Brit.* any government office established to collect and supply to the unemployed information about job vacancies and to employers information about availability of prospective workers. See also **Jobcentre.**

emporium (ɛm'pɔːriəm) *n., pl.* **-riums** *or* **-ria** (-rɪə). a large retail shop offering for sale a wide variety of merchandise. [C16: from L, from Gk, from *emporos* merchant, from *poros* a journey]

empower (ɪm'paʊə) *vb.* (*tr.*) **1.** to give power or authority to; authorize. **2.** to give ability to; enable or permit. —**em'powerment** *n.*

empress ('ɛmprɪs) *n.* **1.** the wife or widow of an emperor. **2.** a woman who holds the rank of emperor in her own right. [C12: from OF *empereriz*, from L *imperātrix*; see EMPEROR]

Empson ('ɛmpsᵊn) *n.* Sir **William.** 1906–84, English poet and critic; author of *Seven Types of Ambiguity* (1930).

empty ('ɛmptɪ) *adj.* **-tier, -tiest. 1.** containing nothing. **2.** without inhabitants; vacant or unoccupied. **3.** carrying no load, passengers, etc. **4.** without purpose, substance, or value: *an empty life.* **5.** insincere or trivial: *empty words.* **6.** not expressive or vital; vacant: *an empty look.* **7.** *Inf.* hungry. **8.** (*postpositive;* foll. by *of*) devoid; destitute. **9.** *Inf.* drained of energy or emotion. **10.** *Maths, logic.* (of a set or class) containing no members. ~*vb.* **-tying, -tied. 11.** to make or become empty. **12.** (when *intr.,* foll. by *into*) to discharge (contents). **13.** (*tr.;* often foll. by *of*) to unburden or rid (oneself). ~*n., pl.* **-ties. 14.** an empty container, esp. a bottle. [OE *æmtig*] —'**emptiable** *adj.* —'**emptier** *n.* —'**emptily** *adv.* —'**emptiness** *n.*

empty-handed *adj.* **1.** carrying nothing in the hands. **2.** having gained nothing.

empty-headed *adj.* lacking sense; frivolous.

Empty Quarter *n.* another name for **Rub' al Khali.**

empyema (,ɛmpaɪ'iːmə) *n., pl.* **-emata** (-'iːmətə) *or* **-emas.** a collection of pus in a body cavity, esp. in the chest. [C17: from Med. L, from Gk *empuēma* abscess, from *empuein* to suppurate, from *puon* pus] —,empy'emic *adj.*

empyrean (,ɛmpaɪ'riːən) *n.* **1.** *Arch.* the highest part of the heavens, thought in ancient times to contain the pure element of fire and by early Christians to be the abode of God. **2.** *Poetic.* the heavens or sky. ~*adj. also* **empyreal. 3.** of or relating to the sky. **4.** heavenly or sublime. [C17: from Gk, from *empurios* fiery]

empyreuma (,ɛmpɪ'ruːmə) *n., pl.* **-mata** (-mətə). the smell and taste associated with burning vegetable and animal matter. [C17: from Gk, from *empureuein* to set on fire]

Ems (ɛmz) n. **1.** a town in W West Germany, in the Rhineland-Palatinate: famous for the **Ems Telegram** (1870), Bismarck's dispatch that led to the outbreak of the Franco-Prussian War. Pop.: 10 241 (1983 est.). **2.** a river in West Germany, rising in the Teutoburger Wald and flowing generally north to the North Sea. Length: about 370 km (230 miles).

EMS abbrev. for European Monetary System.

emu ('iːmjuː) n. a large Australian flightless bird, similar to the ostrich. [C17: changed from Port. ema ostrich]

e.m.u. or **EMU** abbrev. for electromagnetic unit.

emu-bob Austral. inf. ~vb. **-bobbing, -bobbed. 1.** (intr.) to bend over to collect litter or small pieces of wood. ~n. **2.** Also called: **emu parade.** a parade of soldiers or schoolchildren for litter collection. —'emu-,bobbing n.

emulate ('ɛmjuˌleɪt) vb. (tr.) **1.** to attempt to equal or surpass, esp. by imitation. **2.** to rival or compete with. [C16: from L aemulus competing with] —'emulative adj. —ˌemu'lation n. —'emuˌlator n.

emulous ('ɛmjuləs) adj. **1.** desiring or aiming to equal or surpass another. **2.** characterized by or arising from emulation. [C14: from L; see EMULATE] —'emulousness n.

emulsifier (ɪ'mʌlsɪˌfaɪə) n. an agent that forms an emulsion, esp. a food additive that prevents separation of processed foods.

emulsify (ɪ'mʌlsɪˌfaɪ) vb. **-fying, -fied.** to make or form into an emulsion. —eˌmulsi'fiable or e'mulsible adj. —eˌmulsifi'cation n.

emulsion (ɪ'mʌlʃən) n. **1.** Photog. a light-sensitive coating on a base, such as paper or film, consisting of silver bromide suspended in gelatin. **2.** Chem. a colloid in which both phases are liquids. **3.** a type of paint in which the pigment is suspended in a vehicle that is dispersed in water as an emulsion. **4.** Pharmacol. a mixture in which an oily medicine is dispersed in another liquid. **5.** any liquid resembling milk. [C17: from NL ēmulsiō, from L, from ēmulgēre to milk out, from mulgēre to milk] —e'mulsive adj.

emu-wren n. an Australian wren having long plumy tail feathers.

en (ɛn) n. Printing. a unit of measurement, half the width of an em.

en-¹ or **em-** prefix forming verbs. **1.** (from nouns) **a.** put in or on: entomb; enthrone. **b.** go on or into: enplane. **c.** surround or cover with: enmesh. **d.** furnish with: empower. **2.** (from adjectives and nouns) cause to be in a certain condition: enable; enslave. [via OF from L in- IN-¹]

en-² or **em-** prefix forming nouns and adjectives. in; into; inside: endemic. [from Gk (often via L); cf. IN-¹, IN-²]

-en¹ suffix forming verbs from adjectives and nouns. cause to be; become; cause to have: blacken; heighten. [OE -n-, as in fæst-n-ian to fasten, of Gmc origin]

-en² suffix forming adjectives from nouns. of; made of; resembling: ashen; wooden. [OE -en]

enable (ɪn'eɪbᵊl) vb. (tr.) **1.** to provide (someone) with adequate power, means, opportunity, or authority (to do something). **2.** to make possible or easy. —en'abler n.

enabling act n. a legislative act conferring certain specified powers on a person or organization.

enact (ɪn'ækt) vb. (tr.) **1.** to make into an act or statute. **2.** to establish by law; decree. **3.** to represent or perform as in a play. —en'actable adj. —en'active or en'actory adj. —en'actment or en'action n. —en'actor n.

enamel (ɪ'næməl) n. **1.** a coloured glassy substance, translucent or opaque, fused to the surface of articles made of metal, glass, etc., for ornament or protection. **2.** an article or articles ornamented with enamel. **3.** an enamel-like paint or varnish. **4.** any coating resembling enamel. **5.** the hard white substance that covers the crown of each tooth. **6.** (modifier) decorated or covered with enamel. ~vb. **-elling, -elled** or U.S. **-eling, -eled.** (tr.) **7.** to decorate with enamel. **8.** to ornament with glossy variegated colours, as if with enamel. **9.** to portray in enamel. [C15: from OF esmail, of Gmc origin] —e'nameller, e'namellist or U.S. e'nameler, e'namelist n. —e'namel,work n.

enamour or U.S. **enamor** (ɪn'æmə) vb. (tr.; usually passive and foll. by of) to inspire with love; captivate. [C14: from OF, from amour love, from L amor] —en'amoured or U.S. en'amored adj.

en bloc French. (ã blɔk) adv. in a lump or block; as a body or whole; all together.

en brosse French. (ã brɔs) adj., adv. (of the hair) cut very short so that the hair stands up stiffly. [lit.: in the style of a brush]

enc. abbrev. for: **1.** enclosed. **2.** enclosure.

encamp (ɪn'kæmp) vb. to lodge or cause to lodge in a camp.

encampment (ɪn'kæmpmənt) n. **1.** the act of setting up a camp. **2.** the place where a camp, esp. a military camp, is set up.

encapsulate or **incapsulate** (ɪn'kæpsjuˌleɪt) vb. **1.** to enclose or be enclosed as in a capsule. **2.** (tr.) to put in a short or concise form. —enˌcapsu'lation or inˌcapsu'lation n.

encase or **incase** (ɪn'keɪs) vb. (tr.) to place or enclose as in a case. —en'casement or in'casement n.

encash (ɪn'kæʃ) vb. (tr.) Brit., formal. to exchange (a cheque) for cash. —en'cashable adj. —en'cashment n.

encaustic (ɪn'kɒstɪk) Ceramics, etc. ~adj. **1.** decorated by any process involving burning in colours, esp. by inlaying coloured clays and baking or by fusing wax colours to the surface. ~n. **2.** the process of burning in colours. **3.** a product of such a process. [C17: from L encausticus, from Gk, from enkaiein to burn in, from kaiein to burn] —en'caustically adv.

-ence or **-ency** suffix forming nouns. indicating an action, state, condition, or quality: benevolence; residence; patience. [via OF from L -entia, from -ēns, present participial ending]

enceinte (ɒn'sænt) adj. another word for **pregnant.** [C17: from F, from L inciēns pregnant]

Enceladus (ɛn'sɛlədəs) n. Greek myth. a giant who was punished for his rebellion against the gods by a fatal blow from a stone cast by Athena. He was believed to be buried under Mount Etna in Sicily.

encephalic (ˌɛnsɪ'fælɪk) adj. of or relating to the brain.

encephalin (ɛn'sɛfəlɪn) n. a variant of **enkephalin.**

encephalitis (ˌɛnsɛfə'laɪtɪs) n. inflammation of the brain. —encephalitic (ˌɛnsɛfə'lɪtɪk) adj.

encephalitis lethargica (lɪ'θɑːdʒɪkə) n. a technical name for **sleeping sickness** (sense 2).

encephalo- or before a vowel **encephal-** combining form. indicating the brain: encephalogram; encephalitis. [from NL, from Gk enkephalos, from en- in + kephalē head]

encephalogram (ɛn'sɛfələˌgræm) n. **1.** an x-ray photograph of the brain, esp. one (a **pneumoencephalogram**) taken after replacing some of the cerebrospinal fluid with air or oxygen. **2.** short for **electroencephalogram;** see **electroencephalograph.**

encephalon (ɛn'sɛfəˌlɒn) n., pl. **-la** (-lə). a technical name for **brain.** [C18: from NL, from Gk enkephalos brain, from EN-² + kephalē head] —en'cephalous adj.

enchain (ɪn'tʃeɪn) vb. (tr.) **1.** to bind with chains. **2.** to hold fast or captivate (the attention, etc.). —en'chainment n.

enchant (ɪn'tʃɑːnt) vb. (tr.) **1.** to cast a spell on; bewitch. **2.** to delight or captivate utterly. [C14: from OF, from L incantāre, from cantāre to chant, from canere to sing] —en'chanted adj. —en'chanter n. —en'chantress fem. n.

enchanting (ɪn'tʃɑːntɪŋ) adj. pleasant; delightful. —en'chantingly adv.

enchantment (ɪn'tʃɑːntmənt) n. **1.** the act of enchanting or state of being enchanted. **2.** a magic spell. **3.** great charm or fascination.

enchase (ɪn'tʃeɪs) vb. (tr.) a less common word for **chase³.** [C15: from OF enchasser to enclose, set, from EN-¹ + casse CASE²] —en'chaser n.

enchilada (ˌɛntʃɪ'lɑːdə) n. a Mexican dish of a tortilla filled with meat, served with a chilli sauce. [American Sp., from enchilado, from enchilar to spice with chilli, from chile CHILLI]

-enchyma n. combining form. denoting cellular tissue. [C20: abstracted from PARENCHYMA]

encipher (ɪn'saɪfə) vb. (tr.) to convert (a message, etc.) into code or cipher. —en'cipherer n. —en'cipherment n.

encircle (ɪn'sɜːkᵊl) vb. (tr.) **1.** to form a circle around; enclose within a circle; surround. —en'circlement n. —en'circling adj.

enclave ('ɛnkleɪv) n. a part of a country entirely surrounded by foreign territory: viewed from the position of the surrounding territories. [C19: from F, from OF *enclaver* to enclose, from Vulgar L *inclāvāre* (unattested) to lock up, from L IN-² + *clavis* key]

enclitic (ɪn'klɪtɪk) *adj.* **1.** denoting or relating to a monosyllabic word or form that is treated as a suffix of the preceding word. ~*n.* **2.** an enclitic word or form. [C17: from LL, from Gk, from *enklinein* to cause to lean, from EN-² + *klinein* to lean] —**en'clitically** *adv.*

enclose *or* **inclose** (ɪn'kləʊz) *vb.* (*tr.*) **1.** to close; hem in; surround. **2.** to surround (land) with or as if with a fence. **3.** to put in an envelope or wrapper, esp. together with a letter. **4.** to contain or hold. —**en'closable** *or* **in'closable** *adj.* —**en'closer** *or* **in'closer** *n.*

enclosed order *n.* a Christian religious order that does not permit its members to go into the outside world.

enclosure *or* **inclosure** (ɪn'kləʊʒə) *n.* **1.** the act of enclosing or state of being enclosed. **2.** an area enclosed as by a fence. **3.** the act of appropriating land by setting up a fence, hedge, etc., around it. **4.** a fence, wall, etc., that encloses. **5.** something enclosed within an envelope or wrapper, esp. together with a letter. **6.** *Brit.* a section of a sports ground, racecourse, etc., allotted to certain spectators.

encode (ɪn'kəʊd) *vb.* (*tr.*) to convert (a message) into code. —**en'codement** *n.* —**en'coder** *n.*

encomiast (ɛn'kəʊmɪˌæst) *n.* a person who speaks or writes an encomium. [C17: from Gk, from *enkōmiazein* to utter an ENCOMIUM] —**en,comi'astic** *or* **en,comi'astical** *adj.*

encomium (ɛn'kəʊmɪəm) *n.,* *pl.* **-miums** *or* **-mia** (-mɪə). a formal expression of praise; eulogy. [C16: from L, from Gk, from EN-² + *kōmos* festivity]

encompass (ɪn'kʌmpəs) *vb.* (*tr.*) **1.** to enclose within a circle; surround. **2.** to bring about: *he encompassed the enemy's ruin.* **3.** to include entirely or comprehensively. —**en'compassment** *n.*

encore ('ɒŋkɔː) *sentence substitute.* **1.** again: used by an audience to demand an extra or repeated performance. ~*n.* **2.** an extra or repeated performance given in response to enthusiastic demand. ~*vb.* **3.** (*tr.*) to demand an extra or repeated performance of (a work, piece of music, etc.) by (a performer). [C18: from F: still, again, ?from L *in hanc hōram* until this hour]

encounter (ɪn'kaʊntə) *vb.* **1.** to come upon or meet casually or unexpectedly. **2.** to meet (an enemy, army, etc.) in battle or contest. **3.** (*tr.*) to be faced with; contend with. ~*n.* **4.** a casual or unexpected meeting. **5.** a hostile meeting; contest. [C13: from OF, from Vulgar L *incontrāre* (unattested), from L IN-² + *contrā* against, opposite] —**en'counterer** *n.*

encounter group *n.* a group of people who meet in order to develop self-awareness and mutual understanding by openly expressing their feelings, by confrontation, etc.

encourage (ɪn'kʌrɪdʒ) *vb.* (*tr.*) **1.** to inspire (someone) with the courage or confidence (to do something). **2.** to stimulate (something or someone) by approval or help. —**en'couragement** *n.* —**en'courager** *n.* —**en'couraging** *adj.* —**en'couragingly** *adv.*

encroach (ɪn'krəʊtʃ) *vb.* (*intr.*) **1.** (often foll. by *on* or *upon*) to intrude gradually or stealthily upon the rights, property, etc., of another. **2.** to advance beyond certain limits. [C14: from OF *encrochier* to seize, lit.: fasten upon with hooks, of Gmc origin] —**en'croacher** *n.* —**en'croachment** *n.*

encrust *or* **incrust** (ɪn'krʌst) *vb.* **1.** (*tr.*) to cover or overlay with or as with a crust or hard coating. **2.** to form or cause to form a crust or hard coating. **3.** (*tr.*) to decorate lavishly, as with jewels. —**,encrus'tation** *or* **,incrus'tation** *n.*

encumber *or* **incumber** (ɪn'kʌmbə) *vb.* (*tr.*) **1.** to hinder or impede; hamper. **2.** to fill with superfluous or useless matter. **3.** to burden with debts, obligations, etc. [C14: from OF, from EN-¹ + *combre* a barrier, from LL *combrus*, from ?]

encumbrance *or* **incumbrance** (ɪn'kʌmbrəns) *n.* **1.** a thing that impedes or is burdensome; hindrance. **2.** *Law.* a burden or charge upon property, such as a mortgage or lien.

ency., encyc., *or* **encycl.** *abbrev. for* encyclopedia.

-ency *suffix forming nouns.* a variant of **-ence:** *fluency; permanency.*

encyclical (ɛn'sɪklɪk²l) *n.* **1.** a letter sent by the pope to all Roman Catholic bishops. ~*adj. also* **encyclic. 2.** (of

letters) intended for general circulation. [C17: from LL, from Gk, from *kuklos* circle]

encyclopedia *or* **encyclopaedia** (ɛn,saɪkləʊ'piːdɪə) *n.* a book, often in many volumes, containing articles, often arranged in alphabetical order, dealing either with the whole range of human knowledge or with one particular subject. [C16: from NL, erroneously for Gk *enkuklios paideia* general education, from *enkuklios* general + *paideia* education] —**en,cyclo'pedic** *or* **en,cyclo'paedic** *adj.*

encyclopedist *or* **encyclopaedist** (ɛn,saɪkləʊ'piːdɪst) *n.* a person who compiles or contributes to an encyclopedia. —**en,cyclo'pedism** *or* **en,cyclo'paedism** *n.*

encyst (ɛn'sɪst) *vb. Biol.* to enclose or become enclosed by a cyst, thick membrane, or shell. —**en'cystment** *or* **,encys'tation** *n.*

end (ɛnd) *n.* **1.** the extremity of the length of something, such as a road, line, etc. **2.** the surface at either extremity of an object. **3.** the extreme extent, limit, or degree of something. **4.** the most distant place or time that can be imagined: *the ends of the earth.* **5.** the time at which something is concluded. **6.** the last section or part. **7.** a share or part. **8.** (*often pl.*) a remnant or fragment (esp. in **odds and ends**). **9.** a final state, esp. death; destruction. **10.** the purpose of an action or existence. **11.** *Sport.* either of the two defended areas of a playing field, rink, etc. **12.** *Bowls.* a section of play from one side of the green to the other. **13. at an end.** exhausted or completed. **14. come to an end.** to become completed or exhausted. **15. have one's end away.** *sl.* to have sexual intercourse. **16. in the end.** finally. **17. make (both) ends meet.** to spend no more than the money one has. **18. no end (of).** *Inf.* (intensifier): *I had no end of work.* **19. on end.** *Inf.* without pause or interruption. **20. the end.** *Sl.* the worst, esp. something that goes beyond the limits of endurance. ~*vb.* **21.** to bring or come to a finish; conclude. **22.** to die or cause to die. **23.** (*tr.*) to surpass or outdo: *a novel to end all novels.* **24. end it all.** *Inf.* to commit suicide. ~See also **end up.** [OE *ende*] —**'ender** *n.*

end- *combining form.* a variant of **endo-** before a vowel.

-end *suffix forming nouns.* See **-and.**

endamoeba *or* U.S. **endameba** (,ɛndə'miːbə) *n.* variant spellings of **entamoeba.**

endanger (ɪn'deɪndʒə) *vb.* (*tr.*) to put in danger or peril; imperil. —**en'dangerment** *n.*

endangered (ɪn'deɪndʒəd) *adj.* in danger, esp. of extinction: *an endangered species.*

endear (ɪn'dɪə) *vb.* (*tr.*) to cause to be beloved or esteemed. —**en'dearing** *adj.*

endearment (ɪn'dɪəmənt) *n.* something that endears, such as an affectionate utterance.

endeavour *or* U.S. **endeavor** (ɪn'dɛvə) *vb.* **1.** to try (to do something). ~*n.* **2.** an effort to do or attain something. [C14 *endeveren*, from EN-¹ + *-deveren* from *dever* duty, from OF *deveir; see* DEVOIRS] —**en'deavourer** *or* U.S. **en'deavorer** *n.*

endemic (ɛn'dɛmɪk) *adj. also* **endemial** (ɛn'dɛmɪəl) *or* **endemical. 1.** present within a localized area or peculiar to persons in such an area. ~*n.* **2.** an endemic disease or plant. [C18: from NL *endēmicus,* from Gk *endēmos* native, from EN-² + *dēmos* the people] —**en'demically** *adv.* —**'endemism** *or* **,ende'micity** *n.*

Enderby Land ('ɛndəbɪ) *n.* part of the coastal region of Antarctica, between Kempland and Queen Maud Land: the westernmost part of the Australian Antarctic Territory; discovered in 1831.

endermic (ɛn'dɜːmɪk) *adj.* (of a medicine, etc.) acting by absorption through the skin. [C19: from EN-² + Gk *derma* skin]

endgame ('ɛnd,geɪm) *n.* the closing stage of any of certain games, esp. chess, when there are only a few pieces left in play.

ending ('ɛndɪŋ) *n.* **1.** the act of bringing to or reaching an end. **2.** the last part of something. **3.** the final part of a word, esp. a suffix.

endive ('ɛndaɪv) *n.* a plant cultivated for its crisp curly leaves, which are used in salads. Cf. **chicory.** [C15: from OF, from Med. L, from var. of L *intubus, entubus*]

endless ('ɛndlɪs) *adj.* **1.** having or seeming to have no end; eternal or infinite. **2.** continuing too long or continually recurring. **3.** formed with the ends joined. —**'endlessness** *n.*

endmost ('ɛnd,məʊst) *adj.* nearest the end; most distant.

endo- *or before a vowel* **end-** *combining form.* inside; within: *endocrine.* [from Gk, from *endon* within]

endoblast ('ɛndəʊ,blæst) *n.* **1.** *Embryol.* a less common name for **endoderm. 2.** another name for **hypoblast.** —,endo'blastic *adj.*

endocarditis (,ɛndəʊkɑː'daɪtɪs) *n.* inflammation of the lining of the heart. [C19: from NL, from ENDO- + Gk *kardia* heart + -ITIS] —**endocarditic** (,ɛndəʊkɑː'dɪtɪk) *adj.*

endocarp ('ɛndə,kɑːp) *n.* the inner layer of the pericarp of a fruit, such as the stone of a peach. —,endo'carpal *or* ,endo'carpic *adj.*

endocrine ('ɛndəʊ,kraɪn) *adj. also* **endocrinal** (,ɛndəʊ'kraɪnᵊl), **endocrinic** (,ɛndəʊ'krɪnɪk). **1.** of or denoting endocrine glands or their secretions. ~*n.* **2.** an endocrine gland. [C20: from ENDO- + -*crine*, from Gk *krinein* to separate]

endocrine gland *n.* any of the glands that secrete hormones directly into the bloodstream, e.g. the pituitary, pineal, and thyroid.

endocrinology (,ɛndəʊkraɪ'nɒlədʒɪ, -krɪ-) *n.* the branch of medical science concerned with the endocrine glands and their secretions. —,endocri'nologist *n.*

endoderm ('ɛndəʊ,dɜːm) *or* **entoderm** *n.* the inner germ layer of an animal embryo, which gives rise to the lining of the digestive and respiratory tracts. —,endo'dermal, ,endo'dermic *or* ,ento'dermal, ,ento'dermic *adj.*

end of steel *n. Canad.* **1.** a point up to which railway tracks have been laid. **2.** a town located at such a point.

endogamy (ɛn'dɒgəmɪ) *n.* **1.** *Anthropol.* marriage within one's own tribe or similar unit. **2.** pollination between two flowers on the same plant. —**en'dogamous** *or* **endogamic** (,ɛndəʊ'gæmɪk) *adj.*

endogenous (ɛn'dɒdʒɪnəs) *adj.* **1.** *Biol.* developing or originating within an organism or part of an organism. **2.** having no apparent external cause: *endogenous depression.* —**en'dogeny** *n.*

endomorph ('ɛndəʊ,mɔːf) *n.* **1.** a type of person having a body build characterized by fatness and heaviness. **2.** a mineral that naturally occurs enclosed within another mineral. —,endo'morphic *adj.* —'endo,morphy *n.*

endomorphism (,ɛndəʊ'mɔː,fɪzəm) *n. Geol.* metamorphism in which changes are induced in cooling molten rock by contact with older rocks.

endophyte ('ɛndəʊ,faɪt) *n.* any plant that lives within another plant. —**endophytic** (,ɛndəʊ'fɪtɪk) *adj.*

endoplasm ('ɛndəʊ,plæzəm) *n. Cytology.* the inner cytoplasm of a cell. —,endo'plasmic *adj.*

end organ *n. Anat.* the expanded end of a peripheral motor or sensory nerve.

endorphin (ɛn'dɔːfɪn) *n.* any of a class of chemicals occurring in the brain, including enkephalin, which have a similar effect to morphine.

endorsation (,ɛndɔː'seɪʃən) *n. Canad.* approval or support.

endorse *or* **indorse** (ɪn'dɔːs) *vb. (tr.)* **1.** to give approval or sanction to. **2.** to sign (one's name) on the back of (a cheque, etc.) to specify oneself as payee. **3.** *Commerce.* **a.** to sign the back of (a document) to transfer ownership of the rights to a specified payee. **b.** to specify (a sum) as transferable to another as payee. **4.** to write (a qualifying comment, etc.) on the back of a document. **5.** to sign a document, as when confirming receipt of payment. **6.** *Chiefly Brit.* to record a conviction on (a driving licence). [C16: from OF *endosser* to put on the back, from EN-¹ + *dos* back] —**en'dorsable** *or* **in'dorsable** *adj.* —**en'dorser, en'dorsor** *or* **in'dorser, in'dorsor** *n.* —**en,dor'see** *or* **in,dor'see** *n.*

endorsement *or* **indorsement** (ɪn'dɔːsmənt) *n.* **1.** the act or an instance of endorsing. **2.** something that endorses, such as a signature. **3.** approval or support. **4.** a record of a motoring offence on a driving licence.

endoscope ('ɛndəʊ,skəʊp) *n.* a medical instrument for examining the interior of hollow organs such as the stomach or bowel. —**endoscopic** (,ɛndəʊ'skɒpɪk) *adj.*

endoskeleton (,ɛndəʊ'skɛlɪtᵊn) *n.* an internal skeleton, esp. the bony or cartilaginous skeleton of vertebrates. —,endo'skeletal *adj.*

endosperm ('ɛndəʊ,spɜːm) *n.* the tissue within the seed of a flowering plant that surrounds and nourishes the embryo. —,endo'spermic *adj.*

endothermic (,ɛndəʊ'θɜːmɪk) *or* **endothermal** *adj.* (of a chemical reaction or compound) occurring or formed with the absorption of heat. —,endo'thermically *adv.* —,endo'thermism *n.*

endow (ɪn'daʊ) *vb. (tr.)* **1.** to provide with or bequeath a source of permanent income. **2.** (usually foll. by *with*) to provide (with qualities, characteristics, etc.). [C14: from OF, from EN-¹ + *douer* from L *dōtāre*, from *dōs* dowry] —**en'dower** *n.*

endowment (ɪn'daʊmənt) *n.* **1.** the income with which an institution, etc., is endowed. **2.** the act or process of endowing. **3.** (*usually pl.*) natural talents or qualities. **4.** *Austral.* Also: **child endowment.** a social-security payment for dependent children.

endowment assurance *or* **insurance** *n.* a form of life insurance that provides for the payment of a specified sum directly to the policyholder at a designated date or to his beneficiary should he die before this date.

endpaper ('ɛnd,peɪpə) *n.* either of two leaves at the front and back of a book pasted to the inside of the board covers and the first leaf of the book.

end point *n.* **1.** *Chem.* the point at which a titration is complete. **2.** the point at which anything is complete.

end product *n.* the final result of a process, series, etc., esp. in manufacturing.

endue *or* **indue** (ɪn'djuː) *vb.* **-duing, -dued.** *(tr.)* (usually foll. by *with*) to invest or provide, as with some quality or trait. [C15: from OF, from L *indūcere*, from *dūcere* to lead]

end up *vb. (adv.)* **1.** *(copula)* to become eventually; turn out to be. **2.** *(intr.)* to arrive, esp. by a circuitous or lengthy route or process.

endurance (ɪn'djʊərəns) *n.* **1.** the capacity, state, or an instance of enduring. **2.** something endured; a hardship, strain, or privation.

endure (ɪn'djʊə) *vb.* **1.** to undergo (hardship, strain, etc.) without yielding; bear. **2.** *(tr.)* to permit or tolerate. **3.** *(intr.)* to last or continue to exist. [C14: from OF, from L *indūrāre* to harden, from *dūrus* hard] —**en'durable** *adj.* —**en,dura'bility** *or* **en'durableness** *n.*

enduring (ɪn'djʊərɪŋ) *adj.* **1.** permanent; lasting. **2.** having forbearance; long-suffering. —**en'duringly** *adv.* —**en'duringness** *n.*

end user *n.* **1.** (in international trading) the person, organization, or nation that will be the ultimate recipient of goods such as arms. **2.** *Computers.* the ultimate destination of information that is being transferred within a system.

endways ('ɛnd,weɪz) *or esp. U.S. & Canad.* **endwise** ('ɛnd,waɪz) *adv.* **1.** having the end forwards or upwards. ~*adj.* **2.** vertical or upright. **3.** lengthways. **4.** standing or lying end to end.

Endymion (ɛn'dɪmɪən) *n. Greek myth.* a handsome youth who was visited every night by the moon goddess Selene, who loved him.

ENE *symbol for* east-northeast.

-ene *n. combining form.* (in chemistry) indicating an unsaturated compound containing double bonds: *benzene; ethylene.* [from Gk -*ēnē*, fem. patronymic suffix]

enema ('ɛnɪmə) *n., pl.* **-mas** *or* **-mata** (-mətə). *Med.* **1.** the introduction of liquid into the rectum to evacuate the bowels, medicate, or nourish. **2.** the liquid so introduced. [C15: from NL, from Gk: injection, from *enienai* to send in, from *hienai* to send]

enemy ('ɛnəmɪ) *n., pl.* **-mies. 1.** a person hostile or opposed to a policy, cause, person, or group. **2. a.** an armed adversary; opposing military force. **b.** (*as modifier*): *enemy aircraft.* **3. a.** a hostile nation or people. **b.** (*as modifier*): *an enemy alien.* **4.** something that harms or opposes. ~Related adj.: **inimical.** [C13: from OF, from L *inimicus* hostile, from EN-¹ + *amīcus* friend]

energetic (,ɛnə'dʒɛtɪk) *adj.* having or showing energy; vigorous. —,ener'getically *adv.*

energize *or* **-ise** ('ɛnə,dʒaɪz) *vb.* **1.** to have or cause to have energy; invigorate. **2.** *(tr.)* to apply electric current or electromotive force to (a circuit, etc.). —'ener,gizer *or* **-iser** *n.*

energy ('ɛnədʒɪ) *n., pl.* **-gies. 1.** intensity or vitality of action or expression; forcefulness. **2.** capacity or tendency for intense activity; vigour. **3.** *Physics.* **a.** the capacity of a body or system to do work. **b.** a measure of this capacity, measured in joules (SI units). [C16: from LL, from Gk *energeia* activity, from EN-² + *ergon* work]

energy band n. Physics. a range of energies associated with the quantum states of electrons in a crystalline solid.
enervate vb. ('ɛnə,veɪt). **1.** (tr.) to deprive of strength or vitality. ~adj. (ɪ'nɜːvɪt). **2.** deprived of strength or vitality. [C17: from L ēnervāre to remove the nerves from, from nervus nerve] —'ener,vating adj. —,ener'vation n.
Enesco (ɛ'nɛskəʊ) n. **Georges** (ʒɔrʒ), original name George Enescu. 1881–1955, Romanian violinist and composer.
en famille French. (ɑ̃ famij) adv. **1.** with one's family; at home. **2.** in a casual way; informally.
enfant terrible French. (ɑ̃fɑ̃ tɛriblə) n., pl. **enfants terribles** (ɑ̃fɑ̃ tɛriblə). a person given to unconventional conduct or indiscreet remarks. [C19: lit.: terrible child]
enfeeble (ɪn'fiːbªl) vb. (tr.) to make weak. —en'feeblement n. —en'feebler n.
en fête French. (ɑ̃ fɛt) adv. dressed for or engaged in a festivity. [C19: lit.: in festival]
Enfield ('ɛnfiːld) n. a borough of Greater London: a N residential suburb. Pop.: 265 400 (1986 est.).
enfilade (,ɛnfɪ'leɪd) Mil. ~n. **1.** gunfire directed along the length of a position or formation. **2.** a position or formation subject to such fire. ~vb. (tr.) **3.** to attack (a position or formation) with enfilade. [C18: from F: suite, from enfiler to thread on string, from fil thread]
enfold or **infold** (ɪn'fəʊld) vb. (tr.) **1.** to cover by enclosing. **2.** to embrace. —en'folder or in'folder n. —en'foldment or in'foldment n.
enforce (ɪn'fɔːs) vb. (tr.) **1.** to ensure obedience to (a law, decision, etc.). **2.** to impose (obedience, etc.) as by force. **3.** to emphasize or reinforce (an argument, etc.). —en'forceable adj. —en,forcea'bility n. —enforcedly (ɪn'fɔːsɪdlɪ) adv. —en'forcement n. —en-'forcer n.
enfranchise (ɪn'fræntʃaɪz) vb. (tr.) **1.** to grant the power of voting to. **2.** to liberate, as from servitude. **3.** (in England) to invest (a town, city, etc.) with the right to be represented in Parliament. —en'franchisement n. —en'franchiser n.
Eng. abbrev. for: **1.** England. **2.** English.
Engadine ('ɛŋgə,diːn) n. the upper part of the valley of the River Inn in Switzerland, in Graubünden canton: tourist and winter sports centre.
engage (ɪn'geɪdʒ) vb. (mainly tr.) **1.** to secure the services of. **2.** to secure for use; reserve. **3.** to involve (a person or his attention) intensely. **4.** to attract the affection) of (a person). **5.** to draw (somebody) into conversation. **6.** (intr.) to take part; participate. **7.** to promise (to do something). **8.** (also intr.) Mil. to begin an action with (an enemy). **9.** to bring (a mechanism) into operation. **10.** (also intr.) to undergo or cause to undergo interlocking, as of the components of a driving mechanism. **11.** Machinery. to locate (a locking device) in its operative position or to advance (a tool) into a workpiece to commence cutting. [C15: from OF, from EN-¹ + gage a pledge; see GAGE¹] —en'gager n.
engagé or (fem.) **engagée** French. (ɑ̃gaʒe) adj. (of an artist) committed to some ideology.
engaged (ɪn'geɪdʒd) adj. **1.** pledged to be married; betrothed. **2.** occupied or busy. **3.** Archit. built against or attached to a wall or similar structure. **4.** (of a telephone line) in use.
engaged tone n. Brit. a repeated single note heard on a telephone when the number called is already in use.
engagement (ɪn'geɪdʒmənt) n. **1.** a pledge of marriage; betrothal. **2.** an appointment or arrangement, esp. for business or social purposes. **3.** the act of engaging or condition of being engaged. **4.** a promise, obligation, or other condition that binds. **5.** a period of employment, esp. a limited period. **6.** an action; battle.
engagement ring n. a ring given by a man to a woman as a token of their betrothal.
engaging (ɪn'geɪdʒɪŋ) adj. pleasing, charming, or winning. —en'gagingness n.
en garde French. (ɑ̃ gard) sentence substitute. **1.** on guard; a call to a fencer to adopt a defensive stance in readiness for an attack or bout. ~adj. **2.** (of a fencer) in such a stance.
Engels (German 'ɛŋªls) n. **Friedrich** ('friːdrɪç). 1820–95, German socialist leader and political philosopher, in England from 1849. He collaborated with Marx on The Communist Manifesto (1848) and his own works include

Condition of the Working Classes in England (1844) and The Origin of the Family, Private Property and the State (1884).
engender (ɪn'dʒɛndə) vb. (tr.) to bring about or give rise to; cause to be born. [C14: from OF, from L ingenerāre, from generāre to beget]
engin. abbrev. for engineering.
engine ('ɛndʒɪn) n. **1.** any machine designed to convert energy into mechanical work. **2.** a railway locomotive. **3.** Mil. any piece of equipment formerly used in warfare, such as a battering ram. **4.** any instrument or device. [C13: from OF, from L ingenium nature, talent, ingenious contrivance, from IN-² + -genium, rel. to gignere to beget, produce]
engine driver n. Chiefly Brit. a man who drives a railway locomotive; train driver.
engineer (,ɛndʒɪ'nɪə) n. **1.** a person trained in any branch of engineering. **2.** the originator or manager of a situation, system, etc. **3.** U.S. & Canad. the driver of a railway locomotive. **4.** an officer responsible for a ship's engines. **5.** a member of the armed forces trained in engineering and construction work. ~vb. (tr.) **6.** to originate, cause, or plan in a clever or devious manner. **7.** to design, plan, or construct as a professional engineer. [C14 enginer, from OF, from enginier to contrive, ult. from L ingenium skill, talent; see ENGINE]
engineering (,ɛndʒɪ'nɪərɪŋ) n. the profession of applying scientific principles to the design, construction, and maintenance of engines, cars, machines, etc. (**mechanical engineering**), buildings, bridges, roads, etc. (**civil engineering**), electrical machines and communication systems (**electrical engineering**), chemical plant and machinery (**chemical engineering**), or aircraft (**aeronautical engineering**).
England ('ɪŋglənd) n. the largest division of Great Britain, bordering on Scotland and Wales: unified in the mid-tenth century and conquered by the Normans in 1066; united with Wales in 1536 and Scotland in 1707; monarchy overthrown in 1649 but restored in 1660. Capital: London. Pop.: 47 254 500 (1986 est.). Area: 130 439 sq. km (50 352 sq. miles). See **United Kingdom, Great Britain**.
English ('ɪŋglɪʃ) n. **1.** the official language of Britain, the U.S., most of the Commonwealth, and certain other countries. **2. the English.** (functioning as pl.) the natives or inhabitants of England collectively. **3.** (often not cap.) the usual U.S. & Canad. term for **side** (in billiards). ~adj. **4.** of or relating to the English language. **5.** relating to or characteristic of England or the English. ~vb. (tr.) **6.** Arch. to translate or adapt into English. —'**Englishness** n.
▷ **Usage.** The United Kingdom consists of England, Scotland, Wales, and Northern Ireland. Careful writers and speakers avoid the use of England to mean Britain or English to mean British as these usages are considered offensive by Scottish, Welsh, and Irish people.
English Channel n. an arm of the Atlantic Ocean between S England and N France, linked with the North Sea by the Strait of Dover. Length: about 560 km (350 miles). Width: between 32 km (20 miles) and 161 km (100 miles).
English horn n. Music. another name for **cor anglais**.
Englishman ('ɪŋglɪʃmən) or (fem.) **Englishwoman** n., pl. **-men** or **-women**. a native or inhabitant of England.
engorge (ɪn'gɔːdʒ) vb. (tr.) **1.** Pathol. to congest with blood. **2.** to eat (food) greedily. **3.** to gorge (oneself); glut. —en'gorgement n.
engr abbrev. for: **1.** engineer. **2.** engraver.
engr. abbrev. for: engraved.
engraft or **ingraft** (ɪn'grɑːft) vb. (tr.) **1.** to graft (a shoot, bud, etc.) onto a stock. **2.** to incorporate in a firm or permanent way; implant. —,engraf'tation, ,ingraf'tation or en'graftment, in'graftment n.
engrain (ɪn'greɪn) vb. a variant spelling of **ingrain**.
engrave (ɪn'greɪv) vb. (tr.) **1.** to inscribe (a design, writing, etc.) onto (a block, plate, or other printing surface) by carving, etching, or other process. **2.** to print (designs or characters) from a plate so made. **3.** to fix deeply or permanently in the mind. [C16: from EN-¹ + GRAVE³, on the model of F engraver] —en'graver n.
engraving (ɪn'greɪvɪŋ) n. **1.** the art of a person who engraves. **2.** a printing surface that has been engraved. **3.** a print made from this.
engross (ɪn'grəʊs) vb. (tr.) **1.** to occupy one's attention completely; absorb. **2.** to write or copy (manuscript) in

large legible handwriting. **3.** *Law.* to write or type out formally (a document) preparatory to execution. [C14 (in the sense: to buy up wholesale); C15 (in the sense: to write in large letters): from L *grossus* thick, GROSS] —**en'grossed** *adj.* —**engrossedly** (ın'grəʊsıdlı) *adv.* —**en'grossing** *adj.* —**en'grossment** *n.*

engulf *or* **ingulf** (ın'gʌlf) *vb.* (*tr.*) **1.** to immerse, plunge, bury, or swallow up. **2.** (*often passive*) to overwhelm. —**en'gulfment** *n.*

enhance (ın'hɑːns) *vb.* (*tr.*) to intensify or increase in quality, value, power, etc.; improve; augment. [C14: from OF, from EN-¹ + *haucier* to raise, from Vulgar L *altiāre* (unattested), from L *altus* high] —**en'hancement** *n.* —**en'hancer** *n.*

enharmonic (ˌɛnhɑː'mɒnık) *adj. Music.* **1.** denoting or relating to a small difference in pitch between two notes such as A flat and G sharp: not present in instruments of equal temperament such as the piano, but significant in the intonation of stringed and wind instruments. **2.** denoting or relating to enharmonic modulation. [C17: from L, from Gk, from EN-² + *harmonia*; see HARMONY] —ˌen**har'monically** *adv.*

Enid ('iːnıd) *n.* (in Arthurian legend) the faithful wife of Geraint.

enigma (ı'nıgmə) *n.* a person, thing, or situation that is mysterious, puzzling, or ambiguous. [C16: from L, from Gk, from *ainissesthai* to speak in riddles, from *ainos* fable, story] —**enigmatic** (ˌɛnıg'mætık) *or* ˌenig**matical** *adj.* —**enig'matically** *adv.*

Eniwetok (ˌɛnə'wiːtɒk, əˈniːwıˌtɔːk) *n.* an atoll in the W Pacific Ocean, in the NW Marshall Islands: taken by the U.S. from Japan in 1944; became a naval base and later a testing ground for atomic weapons.

enjambment *or* **enjambement** (ın'dʒæmmənt) *n. Prosody.* the running over of a sentence from one line of verse into the next. [C19: from F, lit.: a straddling, from EN-¹ + *jambe* leg; see JAMB] —**en'jambed** *adj.*

enjoin (ın'dʒɔın) *vb.* (*tr.*) **1.** to order (someone) to do something. **2.** to impose or prescribe (a mode of behaviour, etc.). **3.** *Law.* to require (a person) to do or refrain from some act, esp. by an injunction. [C13: from OF *enjoindre*, from L *injungere* to fasten to, from IN-² + *jungere* to JOIN] —**en'joiner** *n.* —**en'joinment** *n.*

enjoy (ın'dʒɔı) *vb.* (*tr.*) **1.** to receive pleasure from; take joy in. **2.** to have the benefit of; use. **3.** to have as a condition; experience. **4. enjoy oneself.** to have a good time. [C14: from OF, from EN-¹ + *joir* to find pleasure in, from L *gaudēre* to rejoice] —**en'joyable** *adj.* —**en'joyableness** *n.* —**en'joyably** *adv.* —**en'joyer** *n.*

enjoyment (ın'dʒɔımənt) *n.* **1.** the act or condition of receiving pleasure from something. **2.** the use or possession of something that is satisfying. **3.** something that provides joy or satisfaction.

enkephalin (ɛn'kɛfəlın) *or* **encephalin** (ɛn'sɛfəlın) *n.* a chemical occurring in the brain, having effects similar to those of morphine.

enkindle (ın'kındᵊl) *vb.* (*tr.*) **1.** to set on fire; kindle. **2.** to excite to activity or ardour; arouse.

enlace (ın'leıs) *vb.* (*tr.*) **1.** to bind or encircle with or as with laces. **2.** to entangle; intertwine. —**en'lacement** *n.*

enlarge (ın'lɑːdʒ) *vb.* **1.** to make or grow larger; increase or expand. **2.** (*tr.*) to make (a photographic print) of a larger size than the negative. **3.** (*intr.*; foll. by *on* or *upon*) to speak or write (about) in greater detail. —**en'largeable** *adj.* —**en'largement** *n.* —**en'larger** *n.*

enlighten (ın'laıtᵊn) *vb.* (*tr.*) **1.** to give information or understanding to; instruct. **2.** to free from prejudice, superstition, etc. **3.** to give spiritual or religious revelation to. **4.** *Poetic.* to shed light on. —**en'lightener** *n.* —**en'lightening** *adj.*

enlightened (ın'laıtᵊnd) *adj.* **1.** well-informed, tolerant, and guided by rational thought: *an enlightened administration.* **2.** privy to or claiming a spiritual revelation of truth.

enlightenment (ın'laıtᵊnmənt) *n.* the act or means of enlightening or the state of being enlightened.

Enlightenment (ın'laıtᵊnmənt) *n.* **the.** an 18th-century philosophical movement stressing the importance of reason.

enlist (ın'lıst) *vb.* **1.** to enter or persuade to enter the armed forces. **2.** (*tr.*) to engage or secure (a person or his support) for a venture, cause, etc. **3.** (*intr.*; foll. by *in*) to

enter into or join an enterprise, cause, etc. —**en'lister** *n.* —**en'listment** *n.*

enlisted man *n. U.S.* a serviceman who holds neither a commission nor a warrant.

enliven (ın'laıvᵊn) *vb.* (*tr.*) **1.** to make active, vivacious, or spirited. **2.** to make cheerful or bright; gladden. —**en'livening** *adj.* —**en'livenment** *n.*

en masse (*French* ɑ̃ mas) *adv.* in a group or mass; as a whole; all together. [C19: from F]

enmesh, inmesh (ın'mɛʃ), *or* **immesh** *vb.* (*tr.*) to catch or involve in or as if in a net or snare; entangle. —**en'meshment** *n.*

enmity ('ɛnmıtı) *n.*, *pl.* **-ties.** a feeling of hostility or ill will, as between enemies. [C13: from OF; see ENEMY]

Ennerdale Water ('ɛnəˌdeıl) *n.* a lake in NW England, in Cumbria in the Lake District. Length: 4 km (2.5 miles).

Ennis ('ɛnıs) *n.* a town in W Republic of Ireland, county town of Co. Clare. Pop.: 6223 (1981).

Enniskillen (ˌɛnıs'kılın) *or* (*formerly*) **Inniskilling** *n.* a town in SW Northern Ireland, in Fermanagh, on an island in the River Erne: scene of the defeat of James II's forces in 1689. Pop.: 10 429 (1981).

Ennius ('ɛnıəs) *n.* **Quintus** ('kwıntəs). 239–169 B.C., Roman epic poet and dramatist.

ennoble (ı'nəʊbᵊl) *vb.* (*tr.*) **1.** to make noble, honourable, or excellent; dignify; exalt. **2.** to raise to a noble rank. —**en'noblement** *n.* —**en'nobler** *n.* —**en'nobling** *adj.*

ennui ('ɒnwiː) *n.* a feeling of listlessness and general dissatisfaction resulting from lack of activity or excitement. [C18: from F: apathy, from OF *enui* annoyance, vexation; see ANNOY]

Enoch ('iːnɒk) *n. Old Testament.* **1.** the eldest son of Cain after whom the first city was named (Genesis 4:17). **2.** the father of Methuselah: said to have walked with God and to have been taken by God at the end of his earthly life (Genesis 5:24).

enology (iː'nɒlədʒı) *n.* the usual U.S. spelling of **oenology.**

enormity (ı'nɔːmıtı) *n.*, *pl.* **-ties.** **1.** the quality or character of extreme wickedness. **2.** an act of great wickedness; atrocity. **3.** *Inf.* vastness of size or extent. [C15: from OF, from LL *ēnormitās* hugeness; see ENORMOUS]

▷ **Usage.** In careful usage, the noun *enormity* is not employed to convey the idea of great size.

enormous (ı'nɔːməs) *adj.* **1.** unusually large in size, extent, or degree; immense; vast. **2.** *Arch.* extremely wicked; heinous. [C16: from L, from *ē-* out of, away from + *norma* rule, pattern] —**e'normously** *adv.* —**e'normousness** *n.*

Enos ('iːnɒs) *n. Old Testament.* a son of Seth (Genesis 4:26; 5:6).

enosis ('ɛnəʊsıs) *n.* the union of Greece and Cyprus: the aim of a group of Greek Cypriots. [C20: Mod. Gk: from Gk *henoun* to unite, from *heis* one]

enough (ı'nʌf) *determiner.* **1. a.** sufficient to answer a need, demand or supposition. **b.** (*as pron.*): *enough is now known.* **2. that's enough!** that will do: used to put an end to an action, speech, performance, etc. ~*adv.* **3.** so as to be sufficient; as much as necessary. **4.** (*not used with a negative*) very or quite; rather. **5.** (intensifier): *oddly enough.* **6.** just adequately; tolerably. [OE *genōh*]

enow (ı'naʊ) *adj., adv.* an archaic word for **enough.**

en passant (ɒn pæ'sɑːnt) *adv.* in passing: in chess, said of capturing a pawn that has made an initial move of two squares. The capture is made as if the captured pawn moved one square instead of two. [C17: from F]

enquire (ın'kwaıə) *vb.* a variant of **inquire.** —**en'quirer** *n.* —**en'quiry** *n.*

enrage (ın'reıdʒ) *vb.* (*tr.*) to provoke to fury; put into a rage. —**en'raged** *adj.* —**en'ragement** *n.*

en rapport *French.* (ɑ̃ rapɔr) *adj.* (*postpositive*), *adv.* in sympathy, harmony, or accord.

enrapture (ın'ræptʃə) *vb.* (*tr.*) to fill with delight; enchant.

enrich (ın'rıtʃ) *vb.* (*tr.*) **1.** to increase the wealth of. **2.** to endow with fine or desirable qualities. **3.** to make more beautiful; adorn; decorate. **4.** to improve in quality, colour, flavour, etc. **5.** to increase the food value of by adding nutrients. **6.** to fertilize (soil). **7.** *Physics.* to increase the concentration or abundance of one component or isotope in (a solution or mixture). —**en'riched** *adj.* —**en'richment** *n.*

enrol *or U.S.* **enroll** (ɪnˈrəʊl) *vb.* **-rolling, -rolled.** (*mainly tr.*) **1.** to record or note in a roll or list. **2.** (*also intr.*) to become or cause to become a member; enlist; register. **3.** tо put on record. —,enrolˈlee *n.* —enˈroller *n.*

enrolment *or U.S.* **enrollment** (ɪnˈrəʊlmənt) *n.* **1.** the act of enrolling or state of being enrolled. **2.** a list of people enrolled. **3.** the total number of people enrolled.

en route (ɒn ˈruːt) *adv.* on or along the way. [C18: from F]

Ens. *abbrev. for* Ensign.

ENSA (ˈɛnsə) *n. acronym for* Entertainments National Service Association.

Enschede (*Dutch* ˈɛnsxədeː) *n.* a city in the E Netherlands, in Overijssel province: a major centre of the Dutch cotton industry. Pop.: 144 227 (1987).

ensconce (ɪnˈskɒns) *vb.* (*tr.; often passive*) **1.** to establish or settle firmly or comfortably. **2.** to place in safety; hide. [C16: see EN-¹, SCONCE²]

ensemble (ɒnˈsɒmbəl) *n.* **1.** all the parts of something considered together. **2.** a person's complete costume; outfit. **3.** the cast of a play other than the principals. **4.** *Music.* a group of soloists singing or playing together. **5.** *Music.* the degree of precision and unity exhibited by a group of instrumentalists or singers performing together. **6.** the general effect of something made up of individual parts. ~*adv.* **7.** all together or at once. [C15: from F: together, from L, from IN-² + *simul* at the same time]

enshrine *or* **inshrine** (ɪnˈʃraɪn) *vb.* (*tr.*) **1.** to place or enclose as in a shrine. **2.** to hold as sacred; cherish; treasure. —enˈshrinement *n.*

enshroud (ɪnˈʃraʊd) *vb.* (*tr.*) to cover or hide as with a shroud.

ensign (ˈɛnsaɪn) *n.* **1.** (*also* ˈɛnsən). a flag flown by a ship, branch of the armed forces, etc., to indicate nationality, allegiance, etc. See also **Red Ensign, White Ensign. 2.** any flag, standard, or banner. **3.** a standard-bearer. **4.** a symbol, token, or emblem; sign. **5.** (in the U.S. Navy) a commissioned officer of the lowest rank. **6.** (in the British infantry) a colours bearer. **7.** (formerly in the British infantry) a commissioned officer of the lowest rank. [C14: from OF *enseigne,* from L INSIGNIA] —ˈensign,ship *or* ˈensigncy *n.*

ensilage (ˈɛnsɪlɪdʒ) *n.* **1.** the process of ensiling green fodder. **2.** a less common name for **silage.**

ensile (ɛnˈsaɪl, ˈɛnsaɪl) *vb.* (*tr.*) **1.** to store and preserve (green fodder) in a silo. **2.** to turn (green fodder) into silage by causing it to ferment in a silo. [C19: from F, from Sp., from EN-¹ + *silo* SILO]

enslave (ɪnˈsleɪv) *vb.* (*tr.*) to make a slave of; subjugate. —enˈslavement *n.* —enˈslaver *n.*

ensnare *or* **insnare** (ɪnˈsnɛə) *vb.* (*tr.*) to catch or trap as in a snare. —enˈsnarement *n.* —enˈsnarer *n.*

Ensor (ˈɛnsɔː) *n.* **James.** 1860–1949, Belgian expressionist painter, noted for his macabre subjects.

ensue (ɪnˈsjuː) *vb.* **-suing, -sued. 1.** (*intr.*) to come next or afterwards. **2.** (*intr.*) to occur as a consequence; result. **3.** (*tr.*) *Obs.* to pursue. [C14: from Anglo-F, from OF, from EN-¹ + *suivre* to follow, from L *sequī*] —enˈsuing *adj.*

en suite *French.* (ã sɥit) *adv.* forming a unit: *a room with bathroom en suite.* [lit.: in sequence]

ensure (ɛnˈʃʊə, -ˈʃɔː) *or esp. U.S.* **insure** *vb.* (*tr.*) **1.** (*may take a clause as object*) to make certain or sure; guarantee. **2.** to make safe or secure; protect. —enˈsurer *n.*

ENT *Med. abbrev. for* ear, nose, and throat.

-ent *suffix forming adjectives and nouns.* causing or performing an action or existing in a certain condition; the agent that performs an action: *astringent; dependent.* [from L *-ent-, -ens,* present participial ending]

entablature (ɛnˈtæblətʃə) *n. Archit.* **1.** the part of a classical temple above the columns, having an architrave, a frieze, and a cornice. **2.** any similar construction. [C17: from F, from It. *intavolatura* something put on a table, hence, something laid flat, from *tavola* table, from L *tabula* TABLE]

entablement (ɪnˈteɪbəlmənt) *n.* the platform of a pedestal, above the dado, that supports a statue. [C17: from OF]

entail (ɪnˈteɪl) *vb.* (*tr.*) **1.** to bring about or impose inevitably: *this task entails careful thought.* **2.** *Property law.* to restrict the descent of an estate) to designated heirs. **3.** *Logic.* to have as a necessary consequence. ~*n.* **4.** *Property law.* **a.** such a limitation. **b.** an entailed estate.

[C14 *entaillen,* from EN-¹ + *taille* limitation, TAIL²] —enˈtailer *n.* —enˈtailment *n.*

entamoeba (,ɛntəˈmiːbə), **endamoeba** *or U.S.* **entameba, endameba** *n., pl.* **-bae** (-biː) *or* **-bas.** any parasitic amoeba of the genus *Entamoeba* (or *Endamoeba*) which lives in the intestines of man and causes amoebic dysentery.

entangle (ɪnˈtæŋgəl) *vb.* (*tr.*) **1.** to catch or involve in or as if in a tangle; ensnare or enmesh. **2.** to make tangled or twisted; snarl. **3.** to make complicated; confuse. **4.** to involve in difficulties. —enˈtanglement *n.* —enˈtangler *n.*

entasis (ˈɛntəsɪs) *n., pl.* **-ses** (-siːz). a slightly convex curve given to the shaft of a column, or similar structure, to correct the illusion of concavity produced by a straight shaft. [C18: from Gk, from *enteinein* to stretch tight, from *teinein* to stretch]

Entebbe (ɛnˈtɛb) *n.* a town in S Uganda, on Lake Victoria: British administrative centre of Uganda (1893–1958); international airport. Pop.: 20 472 (1980).

entellus (ɛnˈtɛləs) *n.* an Old World monkey of S Asia. [C19: NL, apparently after a character in Virgil's *Aeneid*]

entente (*French* ãtãt) *n.* **1.** short for **entente cordiale. 2.** the parties to an entente cordiale collectively. [C19: F: understanding]

entente cordiale (*French* ãtãt kɔrdjal) *n.* **1.** a friendly understanding between political powers. **2.** (*often caps.*) the understanding reached by France and Britain in April 1904, over colonial disputes. [C19: F: cordial understanding]

enter (ˈɛntə) *vb.* **1.** to come or go into (a place, house, etc.). **2.** to penetrate or pierce. **3.** (*tr.*) to introduce or insert. **4.** to join (a party, organization, etc.). **5.** (when *intr.*, foll. by *into*) to become involved or take part (in). **6.** (*tr.*) to record (an item) in a journal, account, etc. **7.** (*tr.*) to record (a name, etc.) on a list. **8.** (*tr.*) to present or submit: *to enter a proposal.* **9.** (*intr.*) *Theatre.* to come on stage: used as a stage direction: *enter Juliet.* **10.** (when *intr.,* often foll. by *into, on,* or *upon*) to begin; start: *to enter upon a new career.* **11.** (*intr.;* often foll. by *upon*) to come into possession (of). **12.** (*tr.*) to place (evidence, etc.) before a court of law. [C13: from OF, from L *intrāre,* from *intrā* within] —ˈenterable *adj.* —ˈenterer *n.*

enteric (ɛnˈtɛrɪk) *or* **enteral** (ˈɛntərəl) *adj.* intestinal. [C19: from Gk, from *enteron* intestine]

enter into *vb.* (*intr., prep.*) **1.** to be considered as a necessary part of (one's plans, calculations, etc.). **2.** to be in sympathy with.

enteritis (,ɛntəˈraɪtɪs) *n.* inflammation of the intestine.

entero- *or before a vowel* **enter-** *combining form.* indicating an intestine: *enterovirus; enteritis.* [from NL, from Gk *enteron* intestine]

enterprise (ˈɛntə,praɪz) *n.* **1.** a project or undertaking, esp. one that requires boldness or effort. **2.** participation in such projects. **3.** readiness to embark on new ventures; boldness and energy. **4.** a company or firm. [C15: from OF *entreprise* (n.), from *entreprendre* from *entre-* between (from L: INTER-) + *prendre* to take, from L *prehendere* to grasp] —ˈenter,priser *n.*

enterprise zone *n.* one of several areas in the UK in which industrial development is encouraged by tax and other concessions.

enterprising (ˈɛntə,praɪzɪŋ) *adj.* ready to embark on new ventures; full of boldness and initiative. —ˈenter,prisingly *adv.*

entertain (,ɛntəˈteɪn) *vb.* **1.** to provide amusement for (a person or audience). **2.** to show hospitality to (guests). **3.** (*tr.*) to hold in the mind. [C15: from OF, from *entremutually* + *tenir* to hold]

entertainer (,ɛntəˈteɪnə) *n.* **1.** a professional performer in public entertainments. **2.** any person who entertains.

entertaining (,ɛntəˈteɪnɪŋ) *adj.* serving to entertain or give pleasure; diverting; amusing.

entertainment (,ɛntəˈteɪnmənt) *n.* **1.** the act or art of entertaining or state of being entertained. **2.** an act, production, etc., that entertains; diversion; amusement.

enthral *or U.S.* **enthrall** (ɪnˈθrɔːl) *vb.* **-thralling, -thralled.** (*tr.*) **1.** to hold spellbound; enchant; captivate. **2.** *Obs.* to hold as thrall; enslave. —enˈthraller *n.* —enˈthralling *adj.* —enˈthralment *or U.S.* enˈthrallment *n.*

enthrone (ɛn'θrəʊn) vb. (tr.) **1.** to place on a throne. **2.** to honour or exalt. **3.** to assign authority to. —**en'thronement** n.

enthuse (ɪn'θjuːz) vb. to feel or show or cause to feel or show enthusiasm.

enthusiasm (ɪn'θjuːzɪˌæzəm) n. **1.** ardent and lively interest or eagerness. **2.** an object of keen interest. **3.** Arch. extravagant religious fervour. [C17: from LL, from Gk, from enthousiazein to be possessed by a god, from EN-² + theos god]

enthusiast (ɪn'θjuːzɪˌæst) n. **1.** a person motivated by enthusiasm; fanatic. **2.** Arch. one whose zeal for religion is extravagant. —**en,thusi'astic** adj. —**en,thusi'astically** adv.

enthymeme ('ɛnθɪˌmiːm) n. Logic. a syllogism in which one or more premises are unexpressed. [C16: via L from Gk enthumeisthai to infer, from EN-² + thumos mind]

entice (ɪn'taɪs) vb. (tr.) to attract by exciting hope or desire; tempt; allure. [C13: from OF, from Vulgar L intitiāre (unattested) to incite] —**en'ticement** n. —**en'ticer** n. —**en'ticing** adj. —**en'ticingly** adv.

entire (ɪn'taɪə) adj. **1.** (prenominal) whole; complete. **2.** (prenominal) without reservation or exception. **3.** not broken or damaged. **4.** undivided; continuous. **5.** (of leaves, petals, etc.) having a smooth margin not broken up into teeth or lobes. **6.** not castrated: an entire horse. **7.** Obs. unmixed; pure. ~n. **8.** an uncastrated horse. [C14: from OF, from L integer whole, from IN-¹ + tangere to touch] —**en'tireness** n.

entirely (ɪn'taɪəlɪ) adv. **1.** wholly; completely. **2.** solely or exclusively.

entirety (ɪn'taɪərɪtɪ) n., pl. -**ties. 1.** the state of being entire or whole; completeness. **2.** a thing, sum, amount, etc., that is entire; whole; total.

entitle (ɪn'taɪtəl) vb. (tr.) **1.** to give (a person) the right to do or have something; qualify; allow. **2.** to give a name or title to. **3.** to confer a title of rank or honour upon. [C14: from OF entituler, from LL, from L titulus TITLE] —**en'titlement** n.

entity ('ɛntɪtɪ) n., pl. -**ties. 1.** something having real or distinct existence. **2.** existence or being. [C16: from Med. L, from ēns being, from L esse to be] —**entitative** ('ɛntɪtətɪv) adj.

ento- combining form. inside; within: entoderm. [NL, from Gk entos within]

entomb (ɪn'tuːm) vb. (tr.) **1.** to place in or as if in a tomb; bury; inter. **2.** to serve as a tomb for. —**en'tombment** n.

entomo- combining form. indicating an insect: entomology. [from Gk entomon insect]

entomol. or **entom.** abbrev. for entomology.

entomology (ˌɛntəˈmɒlədʒɪ) n. the branch of science concerned with the study of insects. —**entomological** (ˌɛntəməˈlɒdʒɪkəl) or **entomoˈlogic** adj. —**entoˈmologist** n.

entophyte ('ɛntəʊˌfaɪt) n. Bot. a variant spelling of **endophyte.** —**entophytic** (ˌɛntəʊˈfɪtɪk) adj.

entourage (ˌɒntʊˈrɑːʒ) n. **1.** a group of attendants or retainers; retinue. **2.** surroundings. [C19: from F, from entourer to surround, from tour circuit; see TOUR, TURN]

entr'acte (ɒn'trækt) n. **1.** an interval between two acts of a play or opera. **2.** (esp. formerly) an entertainment during such an interval. [C19: F, lit.: between-act]

entrails ('ɛntreɪlz) pl. n. **1.** the internal organs of a person or animal; intestines; guts. **2.** the innermost parts of anything. [C13: from OF, from Med. L intrālia, changed from L interānea intestines]

entrain (ɪn'treɪn) vb. to board or put aboard a train. —**en'trainment** n.

entrance¹ ('ɛntrəns) n. **1.** the act or an instance of entering; entry. **2.** a place for entering, such as a door. **3. a.** the power, liberty, or right of entering. **b.** (as modifier): an entrance fee. **4.** the coming of an actor or other performer onto a stage. [C16: from F, from entrer to ENTER]

entrance² (ɪn'trɑːns) vb. (tr.) **1.** to fill with wonder and delight; enchant. **2.** to put into a trance; hypnotize. —**en'trancement** n. —**en'trancing** adj.

entrant ('ɛntrənt) n. a person who enters. [C17: from F, lit.: entering, from entrer to ENTER]

entrap (ɪn'træp) vb. -**trapping, -trapped.** (tr.) **1.** to catch or snare as in a trap. **2.** to trick into danger, difficulty, or embarrassment. —**en'trapment** n. —**en'trapper** n.

entreat or **intreat** (ɪn'triːt) vb. **1.** to ask (a person) earnestly; beg or plead with; implore. **2.** to make an earnest request or petition for (something). **3.** an archaic word for **treat** (sense 4). [C15: from OF, from EN-¹ traiter to TREAT] —**en'treatment** or **in'treatment** n.

entreaty (ɪn'triːtɪ) n., pl. -**treaties.** an earnest request or petition; supplication; plea.

entrechat (French ātrəʃa) n. a leap in ballet during which the dancer repeatedly crosses his feet or beats them together. [C18: from F entrechase, changed by folk etymology from It. (capriola) intrecciata, lit.: entwined (caper)]

entrecôte (French ātrəkot) n. a beefsteak cut from between the ribs. [F, from entre- INTER- + côte rib, from L costa]

entrée ('ɒntreɪ) n. **1.** a dish served before a main course. **2.** Chiefly U.S. the main course of a meal. **3.** the power or right of entry. [C18: from F, from entrer to ENTER; in cookery, so called because formerly the course was served after an intermediate course called the relevé (remove)]

entremets (French ātrəmɛ) n., pl. -**mets** (French -mɛ). **1.** a dessert. **2.** a light dish formerly served between the main course and the dessert. [C18: from F, from OF, from entre- between + mes dish]

entrench or **intrench** (ɪn'trɛntʃ) vb. **1.** (tr.) to construct a defensive position by digging trenches around it. **2.** (tr.) to fix or establish firmly. **3.** (intr.; foll. by on or upon) to trespass or encroach. —**en'trenched** or **in'trenched** adj. —**en'trenchment** or **in'trenchment** n.

entrepôt (French ātrəpo) n. **1.** a warehouse for commercial goods. **2. a.** a trading centre or port at which goods are imported and re-exported without incurring duty. **b.** (as modifier): an entrepôt trade. [C18: F, from entreposer, from entre between + poser to place; formed on the model of DEPOT]

entrepreneur (ˌɒntrəprə'nɜː) n. **1.** the owner or manager of a business enterprise who, by risk and initiative, attempts to make profits. **2.** a middleman or commercial intermediary. [C19: from F, from entreprendre to undertake; see ENTERPRISE] —**,entrepre'neurial** adj. —**,entrepre'neurship** n.

entropy ('ɛntrəpɪ) n., pl. -**pies. 1.** a thermodynamic quantity that changes in a reversible process by an amount equal to the heat absorbed or emitted divided by the thermodynamic temperature. It is measured in joules per kelvin. **2.** lack of pattern or organization; disorder. [C19: from EN-² + -TROPE]

entrust or **intrust** (ɪn'trʌst) vb. (tr.) **1.** (usually foll. by with) to invest or charge (with a duty, responsibility, etc.). **2.** (often foll. by to) to put into the care or protection of someone. —**en'trustment** or **in'trustment** n.

entry ('ɛntrɪ) n., pl. -**tries. 1.** the act or an instance of entering; entrance. **2.** a point or place for entering, such as a door, etc. **3. a.** the right or liberty of entering. **b.** (as modifier): an entry permit. **4.** the act of recording an item in a journal, account, etc. **5.** an item recorded, as in a diary, dictionary, or account. **6.** a person, horse, car, etc., entering a competition or contest. **7.** the competitors entering a contest considered collectively. **8.** the action of an actor in going on stage. **9.** Property law. the act of going upon land with the intention of asserting the right to possession. **10.** any point in a piece of music at which a performer commences or resumes singing or playing. **11.** Bridge, etc. a card that enables one to transfer the lead from one's own hand to that of one's partner or to the dummy hand. **12.** Dialect. a passage between the backs of two rows of houses. [C13: from OF entree, p.p. of entrer to ENTER]

entryism ('ɛntriːˌɪzəm) n. the policy or practice of joining an existing political party with the intention of changing it instead of forming a new party. —**'entryist** n., adj.

entwine or **intwine** (ɪn'twaɪn) vb. (of two or more things) to twine together or (of one or more things) to twine around (something else). —**en'twinement** or **in'twinement** n.

Enugu (ɛ'nuːguː) n. a city in S Nigeria, capital of Anambra state: capital of the former Eastern region and of the breakaway state of Biafra during the Civil War (1967–70): coal-mining. Pop.: 228 400 (1983 est.).

E number n. any of a series of numbers with the prefix E indicating a specific food additive recognized by the European Economic Community.

enumerate (ɪ'njuːməˌreɪt) vb. (tr.) **1.** to name one by one; list. **2.** to determine the number of; count. [C17: from L, from numerāre to count, reckon; see NUMBER] —e'**numerable** adj. —eˌnumer'**ation** n. —e'**numerative** adj.

enumerator (ɪ'njuːməˌreɪtə) n. **1.** a person or thing that enumerates. **2.** Brit. a person who issues and retrieves census forms.

enunciable (ɪ'nʌnsɪəb²l) adj. capable of being enunciated.

enunciate (ɪ'nʌnsɪˌeɪt) vb. **1.** to articulate or pronounce (words), esp. clearly and distinctly. **2.** (tr.) to state precisely or formally. [C17: from L ēnuntiāre to declare, from nuntiāre to announce] —e'**nunci'ation** n. —e'**nunciative** or e'**nunciatory** adj. —e'**nunci'ator** n.

enuresis (ˌɛnjuˈriːsɪs) n. involuntary discharge of urine, esp. during sleep. [C19: from NL, from Gk EN-² + ouron urine] —**enuretic** (ˌɛnjuˈrɛtɪk) adj.

envelop (ɪn'vɛləp) vb. (tr.) **1.** to wrap or enclose as in a covering. **2.** to conceal or obscure. **3.** to surround (an enemy force). [C14: from OF envoluper, from EN-¹ + voluper, voloper, from ?] —en'**velopment** n.

envelope ('ɛnvəˌləʊp, 'ɒn-) n. **1.** a flat covering of paper, usually rectangular and with a flap that can be sealed, used to enclose a letter, etc. **2.** any covering or wrapper. **3.** Biol. any enclosing structure, such as a membrane, shell, or skin. **4.** the bag enclosing gas in a balloon. **5.** Maths. a curve or surface that is tangential to each one of a group of curves or surfaces. [C18: from F, from enveloper to wrap around; see ENVELOP]

envenom (ɪn'vɛnəm) vb. (tr.) **1.** to fill or impregnate with venom; make poisonous. **2.** to fill with bitterness or malice.

Enver Pasha ('ɛnvə 'pɑːʃə) n. 1881–1922, Turkish soldier and leader of the Young Turks.

enviable ('ɛnvɪəb²l) adj. exciting envy; fortunate or privileged. —'**enviableness** n.

envious ('ɛnvɪəs) adj. feeling, showing, or resulting from envy. [C13: from Anglo-Norman, ult. from L invidiōsus full of envy, INVIDIOUS; see ENVY] —'**enviously** adv. —'**enviousness** n.

environ (ɪn'vaɪrən) vb. (tr.) to encircle or surround. [C14: from OF environner to surround, from EN-¹ + viron a circle, from virer to turn, VEER]

environment (ɪn'vaɪrənmənt) n. **1.** external conditions or surroundings. **2.** Ecology. the external surroundings in which a plant or animal lives, which influence its development and behaviour. **3.** the state of being environed. —enˌviron'**mental** adj.

environmentalist (ɪnˌvaɪrən'mɛntəlɪst) n. **1.** a specialist in the maintenance of ecological balance and the conservation of the environment. **2.** a person concerned with issues that affect the environment, such as pollution.

environs (ɪn'vaɪrənz) pl. n. a surrounding area or region, esp. the suburbs or outskirts of a city.

envisage (ɪn'vɪzɪdʒ) vb. (tr.) **1.** to form a mental image of; visualize. **2.** to conceive of as a possibility in the future. **3.** Arch. to look in the face of. [C19: from F, from EN-¹ + visage face, VISAGE] —en'**visagement** n.

▷ Usage. In careful English, envisage is usually used with a direct object rather than a clause to refer to conceptions of future possibilities: he envisaged great success for his project.

envision (ɪn'vɪʒən) vb. (tr.) to conceive of as a possibility, esp. in the future; foresee.

envoy¹ ('ɛnvɔɪ) n. **1.** a diplomat ranking between an ambassador and a minister resident. **2.** an accredited agent or representative. [C17: from F, from envoyer to send, from Vulgar L inviāre (unattested) to send on a journey, from IN-² + via road] —'**envoyship** n.

envoy² or **envoi** ('ɛnvɔɪ) n. **1.** a brief concluding stanza, notably in ballades. **2.** a postscript in other forms of verse or prose. [C14: from OF, from envoyer to send; see ENVOY¹]

envy ('ɛnvɪ) n., pl. -**vies**. **1.** a feeling of grudging or somewhat admiring discontent aroused by the possessions, achievements, or qualities of another. **2.** the desire to have something possessed by another; covetousness. **3.** an object of envy. ~vb. -**vying**, -**vied**. **4.** to be envious of (a person or thing). [C13: via OF from L invidia, from invidēre to eye maliciously, from IN-² + vidēre to see] —'**envier** n. —'**envyingly** adv.

enwrap or **inwrap** (ɪn'ræp) vb. -**wrapping**, -**wrapped**. (tr.) **1.** to wrap or cover up; envelop. **2.** (usually passive) to engross or absorb.

enwreath (ɪn'riːð) vb. (tr.) to surround or encircle with or as with a wreath or wreaths.

enzootic (ˌɛnzəʊ'ɒtɪk) adj. **1.** (of diseases) affecting animals within a limited region. ~n. **2.** an enzootic disease. [C19: from EN-² + Gk zōion animal + -OTIC] —ˌenzo'**otically** adv.

enzyme ('ɛnzaɪm) n. any of a group of complex proteins produced by living cells, that act as catalysts in specific biochemical reactions. [C19: from Med. Gk enzumos leavened, from Gk EN-²+ zumē leaven] —**enzymatic** (ˌɛnzaɪ'mætɪk, -zɪ-) or **enzymic** (ɛn'zaɪmɪk, -'zɪm-) adj.

eo- combining form. early or primeval: Eocene; eohippus. [from Gk, from ēōs dawn]

EOC abbrev. for Equal Opportunities Commission.

Eocene ('iːəʊˌsiːn) adj. **1.** of or denoting the second epoch of the Tertiary period, during which hooved mammals appeared. ~n. **2.** the. the Eocene epoch or rock series. [C19: from EO- + -CENE]

eohippus (ˌiːəʊ'hɪpəs) n., pl. -**puses**. the earliest horse: an extinct Eocene dog-sized animal. [C19: NL, from EO-+ Gk hippos horse]

Eolithic (ˌiːəʊ'lɪθɪk) adj. denoting or relating to the early part of the Stone Age, characterized by the use of crude stone tools (**eoliths**).

eon ('iːən, 'iːɒn) n. the usual U.S. spelling of **aeon**.

Eos ('iːɒs) n. Greek myth. the winged goddess of the dawn, the daughter of Hyperion. Roman counterpart: **Aurora**.

eosin ('iːəʊsɪn) or **eosine** ('iːəʊsɪn, -ˌsiːn) n. **1.** a red fluorescent crystalline water-insoluble compound. Its soluble salts are used as dyes. **2.** any of several similar dyes. [C19: from Gk ēōs dawn + -IN; referring to colour it gives to silk] —ˌeo'**sinic** adj.

Eötvös ('ɜːtvɒs) n. Baron **Roland von**. 1848–1919, Hungarian physicist noted for his studies of gravity and surface tension.

-eous suffix forming adjectives. relating to or having the nature of: gaseous. [from L -eus]

EP n. **1.** Also called: **maxisingle**. an extended-play gramophone record, usually 7 inches (18 cm) in diameter: a longer recording than a single. ~adj. **2.** denoting such a record.

epact ('iːpækt) n. **1.** the difference in time, about 11 days, between the solar year and the lunar year. **2.** the number of days between the beginning of the calendar year and the new moon immediately preceding this. [C16: via LL from Gk epaktē, from epagein to bring in, intercalate]

Epaminondas (ɛˌpæmɪ'nɒndæs) n. ?418–362 B.C., Greek Theban statesman and general: defeated the Spartans at Leuctra (371) and Mantinea (362) and restored power in Greece to Thebes.

eparch ('ɛpɑːk) n. **1.** a bishop or metropolitan in the Orthodox Church. **2.** a governor of a subdivision of a province of modern Greece. [C17: from Gk eparkhos, from epi- over, on + -ARCH] —'**eparchy** n.

epaulette or U.S. **epaulet** ('ɛpəˌlɛt, -lɪt) n. a piece of ornamental material on the shoulder of a garment, esp. a military uniform. [C18: from F, from épaule shoulder, from L spatula shoulder blade]

épée ('ɛpeɪ) n. a sword similar to the foil but with a heavier blade. [C19: from F: sword, from L spatha, from Gk spathē blade; see SPADE¹] —'**épéeist** n.

epeirogeny (ˌɛpaɪ'rɒdʒɪnɪ) or **epeirogenesis** (ɪˌpaɪrəʊ'dʒɛnɪsɪs) n. the formation of continents by relatively slow displacements of the earth's crust. [C19: from Gk ēpeiros continent + -GENY] —**epeirogenic** (ɪˌpaɪrəʊ'dʒɛnɪk) or **epeirogenetic** (ɪˌpaɪrəʊdʒɪ'nɛtɪk) adj.

epergne (ɪ'pɜːn) n. an ornamental centrepiece for a table, holding fruit, flowers, etc. [C18: prob. from F épergne a saving, from épargner to economize, of Gmc origin]

epexegesis (ɛˌpɛksɪ'dʒiːsɪs) n., pl. -**ses** (-ˌsiːz). Rhetoric. **1.** the addition of a phrase, clause, or sentence to a text to provide further explanation. **2.** the phrase, clause, or sentence added for this purpose. [C17: from Gk; see EPI-, EXEGESIS] —**epexegetic** (ɛˌpɛksɪ'dʒɛtɪk) or **epˌexe'getical** adj.

Eph. *or* **Ephes.** *Bible. abbrev. for* Ephesians.

ephah *or* **epha** ('iːfə) *n.* a Hebrew unit of measure equal to approximately one bushel or about 33 litres. [C16: from Heb., from Egyptian]

ephedrine *or* **ephedrin** (ɪ'fɛdrɪn, 'ɛfɪˌdriːn, -drɪn) *n.* a white crystalline alkaloid used for the treatment of asthma and hay fever. [C19: from NL from L from Gk, from EPI- + *hedra* seat + -INE²]

ephemera (ɪ'fɛmərə) *n., pl.* **-eras** *or* **-erae** (-əˌriː). **1.** a mayfly, esp. one of the genus *Ephemera*. **2.** something transitory or short-lived. **3.** *(functioning as pl.)* collectable items not originally intended to be long-lasting, such as tickets, posters, etc. **4.** a plural of **ephemeron**. [C16: see EPHEMERAL]

ephemeral (ɪ'fɛmərəl) *adj.* **1.** transitory; short-lived: *ephemeral pleasure.* ~*n.* **2.** a short-lived organism, such as the mayfly. [C16: from Gk *ephēmeros* lasting only a day, from *hēmera* day] —**e‚phemer'ality** *or* **e'phemeralness** *n.*

ephemerid (ɪ'fɛmərɪd) *n.* any insect of the order *Ephemeroptera* (or *Ephemerida*), which comprises the mayflies. Also: **ephemeropteran.** [C19: from NL, from Gk *ephēmeros* short-lived + -ID¹]

ephemeris (ɪ'fɛmərɪs) *n., pl.* **ephemerides** (‚ɛfɪ'mɛrɪˌdiːz). a table giving the future positions of a planet, comet, or satellite during a specified period. [C16: from L, from Gk: diary, journal; see EPHEMERAL]

ephemeron (ɪ'fɛməˌrɒn) *n., pl.* **-era** (-ərə) *or* **-erons.** *(usually pl.).* something transitory or short-lived. [C16: see EPHEMERAL]

Ephesus ('ɛfɪsəs) *n.* (in ancient Greece) a major trading city on the W coast of Asia Minor: famous for its temple of Artemis (Diana); sacked by the Goths (262 A.D.).

ephod ('iːfɒd) *n. Bible.* an embroidered vestment worn by priests in ancient Israel. [C14: from Heb.]

ephor ('ɛfɔː) *n., pl.* **-ors** *or* **-ori** (-əˌraɪ) (in ancient Greece) a senior magistrate, esp. one of the five Spartan ephors, who wielded effective power. [C16: from Gk, from *ephoran* to supervise, from EPI- + *horan* to look] —**'ephoral** *adj.* —**'ephorate** *n.*

Ephraim ('iːfreɪɪm) *n. Old Testament.* **1. a.** the younger son of Joseph, who received the principal blessing of his grandfather Jacob (Genesis 48:8–22). **b.** the tribe descended from him. **c.** the territory of this tribe, west of the River Jordan. **2.** the northern kingdom of Israel after the kingdom of Solomon had been divided into two.

epi-, eph-, *or before a vowel* **ep-** *prefix.* **1.** upon; above; over: *epidermis; epicentre.* **2.** in addition to: *epiphenomenon.* **3.** after: *epilogue.* **4.** near; close to: *epicalyx.* [from Gk, from *epi* (prep.)]

epic ('ɛpɪk) *n.* **1.** a long narrative poem recounting in elevated style the deeds of a legendary hero. **2.** the genre of epic poetry. **3.** any work of literature, film, etc., having qualities associated with the epic. **4.** an episode in the lives of men in which heroic deeds are performed. ~*adj.* **5.** denoting, relating to, or characteristic of an epic or epics. **6.** of heroic or impressive proportions. [C16: from L, from Gk *epikos*, from *epos* speech, word, song]

epicalyx (‚ɛpɪ'keɪlɪks, -'kæl-) *n., pl.* **-lyxes** *or* **-lyces** (-lɪˌsiːz). *Bot.* a series of small sepal-like bracts forming an outer calyx beneath the true calyx in some flowers.

epicanthus (‚ɛpɪ'kænθəs) *n., pl.* **-thi** (-θaɪ). a fold of skin extending vertically over the inner angle of the eye: characteristic of Mongolian peoples. [C19: NL, from EPI- + L *canthus* corner of the eye, from Gk *kanthos*] —**‚epi'canthic** *adj.*

epicardium (‚ɛpɪ'kɑːdɪəm) *n., pl.* **-dia** (-dɪə). *Anat.* the innermost layer of the pericardium. [C19: NL, from EPI- + Gk *kardia* heart] —**‚epi'cardiac** *or* **‚epi'cardial** *adj.*

epicarp ('ɛpɪˌkɑːp) *n.* **exocarp** *n.* the outermost layer of the pericarp of fruits. [C19: from F, from EPI- + Gk *karpos* fruit]

epicene ('ɛpɪˌsiːn) *adj.* **1.** having the characteristics of both sexes. **2.** of neither sex; sexless. **3.** effeminate. **4.** *Grammar.* **a.** denoting a noun that may refer to a male or a female. **b.** (in Latin, Greek, etc.) denoting a noun that retains the same gender regardless of the sex of the referent. [C15: from L *epicoenus* of both genders, from Gk *epikoinos* common to many, from *koinos* common] —**‚epi'cenism** *n.*

epicentre *or U.S.* **epicenter** ('ɛpɪˌsɛntə) *n.* the point on the earth's surface immediately above the origin of an earthquake. [C19: from NL, from Gk *epikentros* over the centre, from EPI- + CENTRE] —**‚epi'central** *adj.*

Epictetus (‚ɛpɪk'tiːtəs) *n.* ?50–?120 A.D., Greek Stoic philosopher, who stressed self-renunciation and the brotherhood of man.

epicure ('ɛpɪˌkjʊə) *n.* **1.** a person who cultivates a discriminating palate for good food and drink. **2.** a person devoted to sensual pleasures. [C16: from Med. L *epicūrus*, after EPICURUS] —**'epicur‚ism** *n.*

epicurean (‚ɛpɪkjʊ'riːən) *adj.* **1.** devoted to sensual pleasures, esp. food and drink. **2.** suitable for an epicure. ~*n.* **3.** an epicure; gourmet. —**‚epicu'reanism** *n.*

Epicurean (‚ɛpɪkjʊ'riːən) *adj.* **1.** of or relating to the philosophy of Epicurus. ~*n.* **2.** a follower of the philosophy of Epicurus. —**‚Epicu'reanism** *n.*

Epicurus (‚ɛpɪ'kjʊərəs) *n.* 341–270 B.C., Greek philosopher, who held that the highest good is pleasure and that the world is a series of fortuitous combinations of atoms.

epicycle ('ɛpɪˌsaɪkʰl) *n.* a circle that rolls around the inside or outside of another circle. [C14: from LL, from Gk; see EPI-, CYCLE] —**epicyclic** (‚ɛpɪ'saɪklɪk, -'sɪklɪk) *or* **‚epi'cyclical** *adj.*

epicyclic train *n.* a cluster of gears consisting of a central gearwheel, a coaxial gearwheel of greater diameter, and one or more planetary gears engaging with both of them.

epicycloid (‚ɛpɪ'saɪklɔɪd) *n.* the curve described by a point on the circumference of a circle as this circle rolls around the outside of another fixed circle. —**‚epicy'cloidal** *adj.*

Epidaurus (‚ɛpɪ'dɔːrəs) *n.* an ancient port in Greece, in the NE Peloponnese, in Argolis on the Saronic Gulf.

epideictic (‚ɛpɪ'daɪktɪk) *adj.* designed to display something, esp. the skill of the speaker in rhetoric. Also: **epidictic** (‚ɛpɪ'dɪktɪk). [C18: from Gk, from *epideiknunai* to display, from *deiknunai* to show]

epidemic (‚ɛpɪ'dɛmɪk) *adj.* **1.** (esp. of a disease) attacking or affecting many persons simultaneously in a community or area. ~*n.* **2.** a widespread occurrence of a disease. **3.** a rapid development, spread, or growth of something. [C17: from F, via LL from Gk *epidēmia*, lit.: among the people, from EPI- + *dēmos* people] —**‚epi'demically** *adv.*

epidemiology (‚ɛpɪˌdiːmɪ'ɒlədʒɪ) *n.* the branch of medical science concerned with the occurrence, distribution, and control of diseases in populations. —**epidemiological** (‚ɛpɪˌdiːmɪə'lɒdʒɪkʰl) *adj.* —**‚epiˌdemi'ologist** *n.*

epidermis (‚ɛpɪ'dɜːmɪs) *n.* **1.** the thin protective outer layer of the skin. **2.** the outer layer of cells of an invertebrate. **3.** the outer protective layer of cells of a plant. [C17: via LL from Gk, from EPI- + *derma* skin] —**‚epi'dermal, ‚epi'dermic,** *or* **‚epi'dermoid** *adj.*

epidiascope (‚ɛpɪ'daɪəˌskəʊp) *n.* an optical device for projecting a magnified image onto a screen.

epididymis (‚ɛpɪ'dɪdɪmɪs) *n., pl.* **-didymides** (-dɪ'dɪmɪˌdiːz). *Anat.* a convoluted tube behind each testis, in which spermatozoa are stored and conveyed to the vas deferens. [C17: from Gk *epididumis*, from EPI- + *didumos* twin, testicle]

epidural (‚ɛpɪ'djʊərəl) *adj.* **1.** upon or outside the dura mater. ~*n.* **2.** Also: **epidural anaesthesia. a.** injection of anaesthetic into the space outside the dura mater enveloping the spinal cord. **b.** anaesthesia induced by this method. [C19: from EPI- + DUR(A MATER) + -AL¹]

epigeal (‚ɛpɪ'dʒiːəl), **epigean,** *or* **epigeous** *adj.* **1.** of or relating to seed germination in which the cotyledons appear above the ground. **2.** living or growing on or close to the surface of the ground. [C19: from Gk *epigeios* of the earth, from EPI- + *gē* earth]

epiglottis (‚ɛpɪ'glɒtɪs) *n., pl.* **-tises** *or* **-tides** (-tɪˌdiːz). a thin cartilaginous flap that covers the entrance to the larynx during swallowing, preventing food from entering the trachea. —**‚epi'glottal** *or* **‚epi'glottic** *adj.*

Epigoni (ɪ'pɪgəˌnaɪ) *pl. n., sing.* **-onus** (-ənəs). *Greek myth.* the descendants of the Seven against Thebes, who undertook a second expedition against the city and eventually captured and destroyed it. [C20: from Gk *epigonoi* those born after]

epigram ('ɛpɪˌgræm) *n.* **1.** a witty, often paradoxical remark, concisely expressed. **2.** a short poem, esp. one having a witty and ingenious ending. [C15: from L *epigramma*, from Gk: inscription, from *graphein* to write] —**‚epigram'matic** *adj.* —**‚epigram'matically** *adv.*

epigrammatize *or* **-ise** (,ɛpɪ'græmə,taɪz) *vb.* to make an epigram (about). —,**epi'grammatism** *n.* —,**epi'grammatist** *n.*

epigraph ('ɛpɪ,grɑːf) *n.* **1.** a quotation at the beginning of a book, chapter, etc. **2.** an inscription on a monument or building. [C17: from Gk; see EPIGRAM] —**epigraphic** (,ɛpɪ'græfɪk) *or* ,**epi'graphical** *adj.*

epigraphy (ɪ'pɪgrəfɪ) *n.* **1.** the study of ancient inscriptions. **2.** epigraphs collectively. — e'**pigraphist** *or* e'**pigrapher** *n.*

epilepsy ('ɛpɪ,lɛpsɪ) *n.* a disorder of the central nervous system characterized by periodic loss of consciousness with or without convulsions. [C16: from LL *epilēpsia*, from Gk, from *epilambanein* to attack, seize, from *lambanein* to take]

epileptic (,ɛpɪ'lɛptɪk) *adj.* **1.** of, relating to, or having epilepsy. ~*n.* **2.** a person who has epilepsy. —,**epi'leptically** *adv.*

epilogue ('ɛpɪ,lɒg) *n.* **1. a.** a speech addressed to the audience by an actor at the end of a play. **b.** the actor speaking this. **2.** a short postscript to any literary work. **3.** *Brit.* the concluding programme of the day on a radio or television station. [C15: from Gk *epilogos*, from *logos* word, speech] —**epilogist** (ɪ'pɪlədʒɪst) *n.*

epinephrine (,ɛpɪ'nɛfrɪn, -riːn) *or* **epinephrin** *n.* a U.S. name for **adrenaline**. [C19: from EPI- + *nephro-* + -INE²]

epiphany (ɪ'pɪfənɪ) *n.*, *pl.* **-nies. 1.** the manifestation of a supernatural or divine reality. **2.** any moment of great or sudden revelation. —**epiphanic** (,ɛpɪ'fænɪk) *adj.*

Epiphany (ɪ'pɪfənɪ) *n.*, *pl.* **-nies.** a Christian festival held on Jan. 6, commemorating, in the Western Church, the manifestation of Christ to the Magi. [C17: via Church L from Gk *epiphaneia* an appearing, from EPI- + *phainein* to show]

epiphenomenon (,ɛpɪfɪ'nɒmɪnən) *n.*, *pl.* **-na** (-nə). **1.** a secondary or additional phenomenon. **2.** *Philosophy.* mind or consciousness regarded as a by-product of the biological activity of the human brain. **3.** *Pathol.* an unexpected symptom or occurrence during the course of a disease. — ,**epiphe'nomenal** *adj.*

epiphyte ('ɛpɪ,faɪt) *n.* a plant that grows on another plant but is not parasitic on it. [C19: via NL from Gk, from EPI- + *phusis* growth] —**epiphytic** (,ɛpɪ'fɪtɪk) , **epi'phytal**, *or* ,**epi'phytical** *adj.*

Epirus (ɪ'paɪərəs) *n.* **1.** a region of NW Greece, part of ancient Epirus ceded to Greece after independence in 1830. **2.** (in ancient Greece) a region between the Pindus mountains and the Ionian Sea, straddling the modern border with Albania.

Epis. *abbrev. for:* **1.** Also: **Episc.** Episcopal *or* Episcopalian. **2.** *Bible.* Also: **Epist.** Epistle.

episcopacy (ɪ'pɪskəpəsɪ) *n.*, *pl.* **-cies. 1.** government of a Church by bishops. **2.** another word for **episcopate**.

episcopal (ɪ'pɪskəpᵊl) *adj.* of, denoting, governed by, or relating to a bishop or bishops. [C15: from Church L, from *episcopus* BISHOP]

Episcopal (ɪ'pɪskəpᵊl) *adj.* of or denoting the Episcopal Church, the autonomous church of Scotland and the U.S. which is in full communion with the Church of England.

episcopalian (ɪ,pɪskə'peɪlɪən) *adj.* also **episcopal. 1.** practising or advocating the principle of Church government by bishops. ~*n.* **2.** an advocate of such Church government. —e,**pisco'palianism** *n.*

Episcopalian (ɪ,pɪskə'peɪlɪən) *adj.* **1.** belonging to or denoting the Episcopal Church. ~*n.* **2.** a member or adherent of this Church.

episcopate (ɪ'pɪskəpɪt, -,peɪt) *n.* **1.** the office, status, or term of office of a bishop. **2.** bishops collectively.

episiotomy (ə,piːzɪ'ɒtəmɪ) *n.*, *pl.* **-mies.** surgical incision into the perineum during labour to prevent its laceration during childbirth. [C20: from Gk *epision* pubic region + -TOMY]

episode ('ɛpɪ,səʊd) *n.* **1.** an event or series of events. **2.** any of the sections into which a serialized novel or radio or television programme is divided. **3.** an incident or sequence that forms part of a narrative but may be a digression from the main story. **4.** (in ancient Greek tragedy) a section between two choric songs. **5.** *Music.* a contrasting section between statements of the subject, as in a fugue. [C17: from Gk *epeisodion* something added, from *epi-* (in addition) + *eisodios* coming in, from *eis-* in + *hodos* road]

episodic (,ɛpɪ'sɒdɪk) *or* **episodical** *adj.* **1.** resembling or relating to an episode. **2.** divided into episodes. **3.** irregular or sporadic. —,**epi'sodically** *adv.*

epistaxis (,ɛpɪ'stæksɪs) *n.* the technical name for **nosebleed**. [C18: from Gk: a dropping, from *epistazein* to drop on, from *stazein* to drip]

epistemology (ɪ,pɪstɪ'mɒlədʒɪ) *n.* the theory of knowledge, esp. the critical study of its validity, methods, and scope. [C19: from Gk *epistēmē* knowledge] —**epistemological** (ɪ,pɪstɪmə'lɒdʒɪkᵊl) *adj.* —e,**piste'mologist** *n.*

epistle (ɪ'pɪsᵊl) *n.* **1.** a letter, esp. one that is long, formal, or didactic. **2.** a literary work in letter form, esp. a verse letter. [OE *epistol*, via L from Gk *epistolē*]

Epistle (ɪ'pɪsᵊl) *n.* **1.** *Bible.* any of the letters of the apostles. **2.** a reading from one of the Epistles, part of the Eucharistic service in many Christian Churches.

epistolary (ɪ'pɪstələrɪ) *or* (*arch.*) **epistolatory** *adj.* **1.** relating to, denoting, conducted by, or contained in letters. **2.** (of a novel, etc.) in the form of a series of letters.

epistyle ('ɛpɪ,staɪl) *n.* another name for **architrave** (sense 1). [C17: via L from Gk, from EPI- + *stulos* column, STYLE]

epitaph ('ɛpɪ,tɑːf) *n.* **1.** a commemorative inscription on a tombstone or monument. **2.** a commemorative speech or written passage. **3.** a final judgment on a person or thing. [C14: via L from Gk, from EPI- + *taphos* tomb] —**epitaphic** (,ɛpɪ'tæfɪk) *adj.* — 'epi,**taphist** *n.*

epitaxy ('ɛpɪ,tæksɪ) *n.* the growth of a layer of one substance on the surface of a crystal so that the layer has the same structure as the underlying crystal. —**epitaxial** (,ɛpɪ'tæksɪəl) *adj.*

epithalamium (,ɛpɪθə'leɪmɪəm) *or* **epithalamion** *n.*, *pl.* **-mia** (-mɪə). a poem or song written to celebrate a marriage. [C17: from L, from Gk *epithalamion* marriage song, from *thalamos* bridal chamber] —**epithalamic** (,ɛpɪθə'læmɪk) *adj.*

epithelium (,ɛpɪ'θiːlɪəm) *n.*, *pl.* **-liums** *or* **-lia** (-lɪə). an animal cellular tissue covering the external and internal surfaces of the body. [C18: NL, from EPI- + Gk *thēlē* nipple] —,**epi'thelial** *adj.*

epithet ('ɛpɪ,θɛt) *n.* a descriptive word or phrase added to or substituted for a person's name. [C16: from L, from Gk, from *epitithenai* to add, from *tithenai* to put] —,**epi'thetic** *or* ,**epi'thetical** *adj.*

epitome (ɪ'pɪtəmɪ) *n.* **1.** a typical example of a characteristic or class; embodiment; personification. **2.** a summary of a written work; abstract. [C16: via L from Gk, from *epitemnein* to abridge, from EPI- + *temnein* to cut] —**epitomical** (,ɛpɪ'tɒmɪkᵊl) *or* ,**epi'tomic** *adj.*

epitomize *or* **-ise** (ɪ'pɪtə,maɪz) *vb.* (*tr.*) **1.** to be a personification of; typify. **2.** to make an epitome of. —e'**pitomist** *n.* —e,**pitomi'zation** *or* **-i'sation** *n.* —e'**pito,mizer** *or* **-iser** *n.*

epizootic (,ɛpɪzəʊ'ɒtɪk) *adj.* **1.** (of a disease) suddenly and temporarily affecting a large number of animals. ~*n.* **2.** an epizootic disease.

EPNS *abbrev. for* electroplated nickel silver.

epoch ('iːpɒk) *n.* **1.** a point in time beginning a new or distinctive period. **2.** a long period of time marked by some predominant characteristic; era. **3.** *Astron.* a precise date to which information relating to a celestial body is referred. **4.** a unit of geological time within a period during which a series of rocks is formed. [C17: from NL, from Gk *epokhē* cessation] —**epochal** ('ɛp,ɒkᵊl) *adj.*

epode ('ɛpəʊd) *n. Greek prosody.* **1.** the part of a lyric ode that follows the strophe and the antistrophe. **2.** a type of lyric poem composed of couplets in which a long line is followed by a shorter one. [C16: via L from Gk, from *epaidein* to sing after, from *aidein* to sing]

eponym ('ɛpənɪm) *n.* **1.** a name, esp. a place name, derived from the name of a real or mythical person. **2.** the name of the person from which such a name is derived. [C19: from Gk *epōnumos* giving a significant name] —**eponymous** (ɪ'pɒnɪməs) *adj.* —e'**ponymously** *adv.* —e'**ponymy** *n.*

EPOS *abbrev. for* electronic point of sale.

epoxidize *or* **-ise** *vb.* (*tr.*) to convert into or treat with an epoxy resin.

epoxy (ɪ'pɒksɪ) *adj. Chem.* **1.** of, consisting of, or containing an oxygen atom joined to two different groups that are themselves joined to other groups: *epoxy group.* **2.** of, relating to, or consisting of an epoxy resin. ~*n.*, *pl.* **epoxies. 3.** short for **epoxy resin.** [C20: from EPI- OXY-²]

epoxy or **epoxide resin** (ɪ'pɒksaɪd) n. any of various tough resistant thermosetting synthetic resins containing epoxy groups: used in surface coatings, laminates, and adhesives.

Epping Forest ('ɛpɪŋ) n. a forest in E England, northeast of London: formerly a royal hunting ground.

epsilon ('ɛpsɪ,lɒn) n. the fifth letter of the Greek alphabet (E, ε). [Gk e psilon, lit.: simple e]

Epsom ('ɛpsəm) n. a town in SE England, in Surrey: famous for its mineral springs and for horse racing. Pop. (with Ewell): 69 200 (1985 est.).

Epsom salts n. (functioning as sing. or pl.) a medicinal preparation of hydrated magnesium sulphate, used as a purgative, etc. [C18: after EPSOM, where they occur in the water]

Epstein ('ɛpstaɪn) n. Sir **Jacob**. 1880–1959, British sculptor, born in the U.S. of Russo-Polish parents.

equable ('ɛkwəb²l) adj. 1. even-tempered; placid. 2. unvarying; uniform: an equable climate. [C17: from L aequābilis, from aequāre to make equal] —,**equa'bility** or **'equableness** n.

equal ('iːkwəl) adj. 1. (often foll. by to or with) identical in size, quantity, degree, intensity, etc. 2. having identical privileges, rights, status, etc. 3. having uniform effect or application: equal opportunities. 4. evenly balanced or proportioned. 5. (usually foll. by to) having the necessary or adequate strength, ability, means, etc. (for). ~n. 6. a person or thing equal to another, esp. in merit, ability, etc. ~vb. **equalling, equalled** or U.S. **equaling, equaled.** 7. (tr.) to be equal to; match. 8. (intr.; usually foll. by out) to become equal. 9. (tr.) to make or do something equal to. [C14: from L aequālis, from aequus level] — '**equally** adv.

▷ Usage. Equally should not be followed by as: the two were equally important not the two were equally as important.

equalitarian (ɪ,kwɒlɪ'tɛərɪən) adj., n. a less common word for **egalitarian.** —**e,quali'tarianism** n.

equality (ɪ'kwɒlɪtɪ) n., pl. **-ties.** the state of being equal.

equalize or **-ise** ('iːkwə,laɪz) vb. 1. (tr.) to make equal or uniform. 2. (intr.) (in sports) to reach the same score as one's opponent or opponents. —,**equali'zation** or **-i'sation** n.

equal opportunity n. **a.** the offering of employment, pay, or promotion without discrimination as to sex, race, etc. **b.** (as modifier): an equal-opportunities employer.

equal sign or **equals sign** n. the symbol =, used to indicate a mathematical equality.

equanimity (,iːkwə'nɪmɪtɪ, ,ɛkwə-) n. calmness of mind or temper; composure. [C17: from L, from aequus even, EQUAL + animus mind, spirit] —**equanimous** (ɪ'kwænɪməs) adj.

equate (ɪ'kweɪt) vb. (mainly tr.) 1. to make or regard as equivalent or similar. 2. Maths. to indicate the equality of; form an equation from. 3. (intr.) to be equal. [C15: from L aequāre to make EQUAL] —**e'quatable** adj. —**e,quata'bility** n.

equation (ɪ'kweɪʒən, -ʃən) n. 1. a mathematical statement that two expressions are equal. 2. the act of equating. 3. the state of being equal, equivalent, or equally balanced. 4. a representation of a chemical reaction using symbols of the elements. —**e'quational** adj. —**e'quationally** adv.

equator (ɪ'kweɪtə) n. 1. the great circle of the earth, equidistant from the poles, dividing the N and S hemispheres. 2. a circle dividing a sphere into two equal parts. 3. Astron. See **celestial equator.** [C14: from Med. L (circulus) aequātor (diei et noctis) (circle) that equalizes (the day and night), from L aequāre to make EQUAL]

equatorial (,ɛkwə'tɔːrɪəl) adj. 1. of, like, or existing at or near the equator. 2. (of a telescope) mounted on perpendicular axes, one of which is parallel to the earth's axis. ~n. 3. an equatorial telescope or its mounting.

Equatorial Guinea n. a republic of W Africa, consisting of Rio Muni on the mainland and the island of Bioko in the Gulf of Guinea, with four smaller islands: ceded by Portugal to Spain in 1778; gained independence in 1968. Official language: Spanish. Currency: ekpwele. Capital: Malabo. Pop.: 384 000 (1987 est.). Area: 28 049 sq. km (10 830 sq. miles). Former name (until 1964): **Spanish Guinea.**

equerry ('ɛkwərɪ; at the British court ɪ'kwɛrɪ) n., pl. **-ries.** 1. an officer attendant upon the British sovereign.

2. (formerly) an officer in a royal household responsible for the horses. [C16: alteration (through infl. of L equus horse) of earlier escuirie, from OF: stable]

equestrian (ɪ'kwɛstrɪən) adj. 1. of or relating to horses and riding. 2. on horseback; mounted. 3. of, relating to, or composed of knights. ~n. 4. a person skilled in riding and horsemanship. [C17: from L equestris, from equus horse] —**e'questrian,ism** n.

equi- combining form. equal or equally: equidistant; equilateral.

equiangular (,iːkwɪ'æŋgjʊlə) adj. having all angles equal.

equidistant (,iːkwɪ'dɪstənt) adj. equally distant. —,**equi'distance** n. —,**equi'distantly** adv.

equilateral (,iːkwɪ'lætərəl) adj. 1. having all sides of equal length. ~n. 2. a geometric figure having all sides of equal length. 3. a side that is equal in length to other sides.

equilibrant (ɪ'kwɪlɪbrənt) n. a force capable of balancing another force.

equilibrate (,iːkwɪ'laɪbreɪt, ɪ'kwɪlɪ,breɪt) vb. to bring to or be in equilibrium; balance. [C17: from LL, from aequilibris in balance; see EQUILIBRIUM] —**equilibration** (,iːkwɪlaɪ'breɪʃən, ɪ,kwɪlɪ-) n. —**equilibrator** (ɪ'kwɪlɪ,breɪtə) n.

equilibrist (ɪ'kwɪlɪbrɪst) n. a person who performs balancing feats, esp. on a high wire. —**e,quili'bristic** adj.

equilibrium (,iːkwɪ'lɪbrɪəm) n., pl. **-riums** or **-ria** (-rɪə). 1. a stable condition in which forces cancel one another. 2. any unchanging state of a body, system, etc., resulting from the balance of the influences to which it is subjected. 3. Physiol. a state of bodily balance, maintained primarily by receptors in the inner ear. [C17: from L, from aequi- EQUI- + libra pound, balance]

equine ('ɛkwaɪn) adj. of, relating to, or resembling a horse. [C18: from L, from equus horse]

equinoctial (,iːkwɪ'nɒkʃəl) adj. 1. relating to or occurring at either or both equinoxes. 2. Astron. of or relating to the celestial equator. ~n. 3. a storm or gale at or near an equinox. 4. another name for **celestial equator.** [C14: from L: see EQUINOX]

equinoctial circle or **line** n. another name for **celestial equator.**

equinoctial point n. either of two points at which the celestial equator intersects the ecliptic.

equinoctial year n. another name for **solar year.** See **year** (sense 4).

equinox ('iːkwɪ,nɒks) n. 1. either of the two occasions, six months apart, when day and night are of equal length. In the N hemisphere the **vernal equinox** occurs around March 21 (Sept. 23 in the S hemisphere). The **autumnal equinox** occurs around Sept. 23 in the N hemisphere (March 21 in the S hemisphere). 2. another name for **equinoctial point.** [C14: from Med. L equinoxium, changed from L aequinoctium, from aequi- EQUI- + nox night]

equip (ɪ'kwɪp) vb. **equipping, equipped.** (tr.) 1. to furnish (with necessary supplies, etc.). 2. (usually passive) to provide with abilities, understanding, etc. 3. to dress out; attire. [C16: from OF eschiper to embark, fit out (a ship), of Gmc origin] —**e'quipper** n.

equipage ('ɛkwɪpɪdʒ) n. 1. a horse-drawn carriage, esp. one attended by liveried footmen. 2. the stores and equipment of a military unit. 3. Arch. a set of useful articles.

equipment (ɪ'kwɪpmənt) n. 1. an act or instance of equipping. 2. the items provided. 3. a set of tools, kit, etc., assembled for a specific purpose.

equipoise ('ɛkwɪ,pɔɪz) n. 1. even balance of weight; equilibrium. 2. a counterbalance; counterpoise. ~vb. 3. (tr.) to offset or balance.

equipollent (,iːkwɪ'pɒlənt) adj. 1. equal or equivalent in significance, power, or effect. ~n. 2. something that is equipollent. [C15: from L aequipollēns of equal importance, from EQUI- + pollēre to be able, be strong] —,**equi'pollence** or ,**equi'pollency** n.

equisetum (,ɛkwɪ'siːtəm) n., pl. **-tums** or **-ta** (-tə). any plant of the horsetail genus. [C19: NL, from L, from equus horse + saeta bristle]

equitable ('ɛkwɪtəb²l) adj. 1. fair; just. 2. Law. relating to or valid in equity, as distinct from common law or statute law. [C17: from F, from équité EQUITY] —'**equitableness** n.

equitation (ˌɛkwɪˈteɪʃən) n. the study and practice of riding and horsemanship. [C16: from L equitātiō, from equitāre to ride, from equus horse]

equities (ˈɛkwɪtɪz) pl. n. another name for **ordinary shares.**

equity (ˈɛkwɪtɪ) n., pl. **-ties. 1.** the quality of being impartial; fairness. **2.** an impartial or fair act, decision, etc. **3.** Law. a system of jurisprudence founded on principles of natural justice and fair conduct. It supplements common law, as by providing a remedy where none exists at law. **4.** Law. an equitable right or claim. **5.** the interest of ordinary shareholders in a company. **6.** the value of a debtor's property in excess of debts to which it is liable. [C14: from OF, from L aequitās, from aequus level, EQUAL]

Equity (ˈɛkwɪtɪ) n. Brit. the actors' trade union.

equiv. abbrev. for equivalent.

equivalence (ɪˈkwɪvələns) or **equivalency** n. **1.** the state of being equivalent. **2.** Logic, maths. another term for **biconditional.**

equivalent (ɪˈkwɪvələnt) adj. **1.** equal in value, quantity, significance, etc. **2.** having the same or a similar effect or meaning. **3.** Logic, maths. (of two propositions) having a biconditional between them. ~n. **4.** something that is equivalent. **5.** Also called: **equivalent weight.** the weight of a substance that will combine with or displace 8 grams of oxygen or 1.007 97 grams of hydrogen. [C15: from LL, from L aequi- EQUI- + valēre to be worth] —e'quivalently adv.

equivocal (ɪˈkwɪvəkəl) adj. **1.** capable of varying interpretations; ambiguous. **2.** deliberately misleading or vague. **3.** of doubtful character or sincerity. [C17: from LL, from L EQUI- + vōx voice] —e,quivo'cality or —e'quivocalness n.

equivocate (ɪˈkwɪvəˌkeɪt) vb. (intr.) to use equivocal language, esp. to avoid speaking directly or honestly. [C15: from Med. L, from LL aequivocus ambiguous, EQUIVOCAL] —e'quivo,catingly adv. —e,quivo'cation n. —e'quivo,cator n. —e'quivocatory adj.

er (ə, ɜː) interj. a sound made when hesitating in speech.

Er the chemical symbol for erbium.

ER abbrev. for: **1.** Elizabeth Regina. [L: Queen Elizabeth] **2.** Eduardus Rex. [L: King Edward]

-er[1] suffix forming nouns. **1.** a person or thing that performs a specified action: reader; lighter. **2.** a person engaged in a profession, occupation, etc.: writer; baker. **3.** a native or inhabitant of: Londoner; villager. **4.** a person or thing having a certain characteristic: newcomer; fiver. [OE -ere]

-er[2] suffix. forming the comparative degree of adjectives (deeper, freer, etc.) and adverbs (faster, slower, etc.). [OE -rd, -re (adj.), -or (adv.)]

era (ˈɪərə) n. **1.** a period of time considered as being of a distinctive character; epoch. **2.** an extended period of time the years of which are numbered from a fixed point: the Christian era. **3.** a point in time beginning a new or distinctive period. **4.** a major division of geological time, divided into periods. [C17: from L aera counters, pl. of aes brass, pieces of brass money]

eradicate (ɪˈrædɪˌkeɪt) vb. (tr.) **1.** to obliterate. **2.** to pull up by the roots. [C16: from L ērādicāre to uproot, from EX-[1] + rādix root] —e'radicable adj. —e,radi'cation n. —e'radicative adj. —e'radi,cator n.

erase (ɪˈreɪz) vb. **1.** to obliterate or rub out (something written, typed, etc.). **2.** (tr.) to destroy all traces of. **3.** to remove (a recording) from (magnetic tape). [C17: from L, from EX-[1] + rādere to scratch, scrape] —e'rasable adj.

eraser (ɪˈreɪzə) n. an object, such as a piece of rubber, for erasing something written, typed, etc.

Erasmus (ɪˈræzməs) n. **Desiderius** (ˌdɛzɪˈdɪərɪəs), real name Gerhard Gerhards. ?1466–1536, Dutch humanist, the leading scholar of the Renaissance in northern Europe. He published the first Greek edition of the New Testament in 1516; his other works include the satirical Encomium Moriae (1509); Colloquia (1519), a series of dialogues; and an attack on the theology of Luther, De Libero Arbitrio (1524).

erasure (ɪˈreɪʒə) n. **1.** the act or an instance of erasing. **2.** the place or mark, as on a piece of paper, where something has been erased.

Erato (ˈɛrəˌtəʊ) n. Greek myth. the Muse of love poetry.

Eratosthenes (ˌɛrəˈtɒsθɪˌniːz) n. ?276–?194 B.C., Greek mathematician and astronomer, who calculated the circumference of the earth by observing the angle of the sun's rays at different places.

Erbil, Irbil (ˈɜːbɪl), or **Arbil** n. a city in N Iraq: important in Assyrian times. Pop.: 368 000 (1980 est.). Ancient name: **Arbela.**

erbium (ˈɜːbɪəm) n. a soft malleable silvery-white element of the lanthanide series of metals. Symbol: Er; atomic no.: 68; atomic wt.: 167.26. [C19: from NL, from (Ytt)erb(y), Sweden, where it was first found + -IUM]

Erciyas Daği (Turkish ˈɛrdʒijas daˈi) n. an extinct volcano in central Turkey. Height 3916 m (12 848 ft.).

ere (εə) conj., prep. a poetic word for **before.** [OE ǣr]

Erebus[1] (ˈɛrɪbəs) n. Greek myth. **1.** the god of darkness, son of Chaos and brother of Night. **2.** the darkness below the earth, thought to be the abode of the dead or the region they pass through on their way to Hades.

Erebus[2] (ˈɛrɪbəs) n. **Mount.** a volcano in Antarctica, on Ross Island: discovered by Sir James Ross in 1841 and named after his ship. Height: 3794 m (12 448 ft.).

Erechtheum (ɪˈrɛkθɪəm, ˌɛrəkˈθiːəm) or **Erechtheion** (ɪˈrɛkθɪən, ˌɛrəkˈθiːən) n. a temple on the Acropolis at Athens, which has a porch of caryatids.

Erechtheus (εˈrɛkθjuːs, -θɪəs) n. Greek myth. a king of Athens who sacrificed one of his daughters because the oracle at Delphi said this was the only way to win the war against the Eleusinians.

erect (ɪˈrɛkt) adj. **1.** upright in posture or position. **2.** Physiol. (of the penis, clitoris, or nipples) firm or rigid after swelling with blood, esp. as a result of sexual excitement. **3.** (of plant parts) growing vertically or at right angles to the parts from which they arise. ~vb. (mainly tr.) **4.** to put up; build. **5.** to raise to an upright position. **6.** to found or form; set up. **7.** (also intr.) Physiol. to become or cause to become firm or rigid by filling with blood. **8.** to exalt. **9.** to draw or construct (a line, figure, etc.) on a given line or figure. [C14: from L ērigere to set up, from regere to control, govern] —e'rectable adj. —e'recter or e'rector n. —e'rectness n.

erectile (ɪˈrɛktaɪl) adj. **1.** Physiol. (of tissues or organs, such as the penis or clitoris) capable of becoming erect. **2.** capable of being erected. —**erectility** (ɪrɛkˈtɪlɪtɪ, ˌiːrɛk-) n.

erection (ɪˈrɛkʃən) n. **1.** the act of erecting or the state of being erected. **2.** a building or construction. **3.** Physiol. the enlarged state of erectile tissues or organs, esp. the penis, when filled with blood. **4.** an erect penis.

E region or **layer** n. a region of the ionosphere, extending from a height of 90 to about 150 kilometres. It reflects radio waves of medium wavelength.

erelong (εəˈlɒŋ) adv. Arch. or poetic. before long; soon.

eremite (ˈɛrɪˌmaɪt) n. a Christian hermit or recluse. [C13: see HERMIT] —**eremitic** (ˌɛrɪˈmɪtɪk) or ,ere'mitical adj. —'eremit,ism n.

Erenburg (ˈɛrənbɜːg; Russian erɪnˈburk) n. a variant spelling of (Ilya Grigorievich) **Ehrenburg.**

erepsin (ɪˈrɛpsɪn) n. a mixture of proteolytic enzymes secreted by the small intestine. [C20: er-, from L ēripere to snatch + (P)EPSIN]

erethism (ˈɛrɪˌθɪzəm) n. **1.** Physiol. an abnormal irritability or sensitivity in any part of the body. **2.** Psychiatry. an abnormal tendency to become aroused quickly, esp. sexually, as the result of a verbal or psychic stimulus. [C18: from F, from Gk, from erethizein to excite, irritate]

Eretria (ɪˈrɛtrɪə) n. an ancient city in Greece, on the S coast of Euboea: founded as an Ionian colony; destroyed by the Persians in 490 B.C. following which it never regained its former significance.

Erevan (Russian jɪrɪˈvan) n. a variant spelling of **Yerevan.**

erf (ɜːf) n., pl. **erven** (ˈɜːvən). S. African. a plot of land, usually urban. [from Afrik., from Du.: inheritance, piece of land]

Erfurt (German ˈɛrfurt) n. an industrial city in SW East Germany: university (1392). Pop.: 216 646 (1986).

erg[1] (ɜːg) n. the cgs unit of work or energy. [C19: from Gk ergon work]

erg[2] (ɜːg) n., pl. **ergs** or **areg** (əˈrɛg). an area of shifting sand dunes, esp. in the Sahara Desert in N Africa. [C19: from Ar. 'irj]

ergo ('ɜːgəʊ) *sentence connector.* therefore; hence. [C14: from L: therefore]

ergonomics (ˌɜːgəˈnɒmɪks) *n.* (*functioning as sing.*) the study of the relationship between workers and their environment. [C20: from Gk *ergon* work + (ECO)NOMICS] —ˌergoˈnomic *adj.* —**ergonomist** (ɜːˈgɒnəmɪst) *n.*

ergosterol (ɜːˈgɒstəˌrɒl) *n.* a plant sterol that is converted into vitamin D by the action of ultraviolet radiation.

ergot ('ɜːgət, -gɒt) *n.* **1.** a disease of cereals and other grasses caused by fungi of the genus *Claviceps.* **2.** any fungus causing this disease. **3.** the dried fungus, used as the source of certain alkaloids used in medicine. [C17: from F: spur (of a cock), from ?]

ergotism ('ɜːgəˌtɪzəm) *n.* ergot poisoning, producing either burning pains and eventually gangrene or itching skin and convulsions.

Erhard (*German* 'eːrhart) *n.* **Ludwig** ('luːtvɪç). 1897–1977, German statesman: chief architect of the *Wirtschaftswunder* ("economic miracle") of West Germany's recovery after World War II; chancellor (1963–66).

erica ('ɛrɪkə) *n.* any shrub of the ericaceous genus *Erica,* including the heaths and some heathers. [C19: via L from Gk *erikē* heath]

ericaceous (ˌɛrɪˈkeɪʃəs) *adj.* of or relating to the Ericaceae, a family of trees and shrubs with typically bell-shaped flowers: includes heather, rhododendron, azalea, and arbutus. [C19: from NL, from L *erīca* heath, from Gk *ereikē*]

Ericson *or* **Ericsson** ('ɛrɪksᵊn) *n.* **Leif** (liːf). 10th–11th centuries A.D., Norse navigator, who discovered Vinland (?1000), variously identified as the coast of New England, Labrador, or Newfoundland; son of Eric the Red.

Eric the Red ('ɛrɪk) *n.* ?940–?1010 A.D., Norse navigator: discovered and colonized Greenland; father of Leif Ericson.

Erie ('ɪərɪ) *n.* **1. Lake.** a lake between the U.S. and Canada: the southernmost and the shallowest of the Great Lakes; empties by the Niagara River into Lake Ontario. Area: 25 718 sq. km (9930 sq. miles). **2.** a port in NW Pennsylvania, on Lake Erie. Pop.: 119 123 (1981).

Erie Canal *n.* a canal in New York State between Albany and Buffalo, linking the Hudson River with Lake Erie. Length: 579 km (360 miles).

erigeron (ɪˈrɪdʒərən, -ˈrɪg-) *n.* any plant of the genus *Erigeron,* whose flowers resemble asters. [C17: via L from Gk, from *ēri* early + *gerōn* old man; from the white down of some species]

Erin ('ɪərɪn, 'ɛərɪn) *n.* an archaic or poetic name for **Ireland**[1]. [from Irish Gaelic *Éirinn,* dative of Ireland]

Erinyes (ɪˈrɪnɪˌiːz) *pl. n.,* *sing.* **Erinys** (ɪˈrɪnɪs, ɪˈraɪ-). *Myth.* another name for the **Furies.** [Gk]

Eris ('ɛrɪs) *n. Greek myth.* the goddess of discord, sister of Ares.

Eritrea (ˌɛrɪˈtreɪə) *n.* a province of N Ethiopia, on the Red Sea: became an Italian colony in 1890; federated with Ethiopia in 1952; an independence movement has been engaged in war with the government since 1961; consists of hot and arid coastal lowlands, rising to the foothills of the Ethiopian highlands. Capital: Asmara. Pop.: 2 426 200 (1980 est.). Area: 117 600 sq. km (45 396 sq. miles). —ˌEriˈtrean *n.*

Erivan (*Russian* jɪrɪˈvan) *n.* a variant spelling of **Yerevan.**

erk (ɜːk) *n. Brit. sl.* an aircraftman or naval rating. [C20: ? a corruption of *AC* (aircraftman)]

Erlangen (*German* 'ɛrlaŋən) *n.* a town in SW West Germany, in Bavaria: university (1743). Pop.: 102 400 (1983 est.).

Erlanger ('ɜːlæŋə) *n.* **Joseph.** 1874–1965, U.S. physiologist. He shared a Nobel prize for physiology or medicine (1944) with Gasser for their work on the electrical signs of nervous activity.

Ermanaric (əˈmænərɪk) *n.* died ?375 A.D., king of the Ostrogoths: ruled an extensive empire in eastern Europe, which was overrun by the Huns in the 370s.

ermine ('ɜːmɪn) *n., pl.* **-mines** *or* **-mine. 1.** the stoat in northern regions, where it has a white winter coat with a black-tipped tail. **2.** the fur of this animal. **3.** the dignity or office of a judge, noble, etc., whose state robes are trimmed with ermine. [C12: from OF, from Med. L *Armenius* (*mūs*) Armenian (mouse)]

erne *or* **ern** (ɜːn) *n.* a fish-eating sea eagle. [OE *earn*]

Erne (ɜːn) *n.* a river in N central Ireland, rising in County Cavan and flowing north across the border, through **Upper Lough Erne** and **Lower Lough Erne,** and then west to Donegal Bay. Length: about 96 km (60 miles).

Ernie ('ɜːnɪ) *n.* (in Britain) a computer that randomly selects winning numbers of Premium Bonds. [C20: acronym of *E*lectronic *R*andom *N*umber *I*ndicator *E*quipment]

Ernst (*German* ɛrnst) *n.* **Max** (maks). 1891–1976, German painter, resident in France and the U.S., a prominent exponent of Dada and surrealism: developed the technique of collage.

erode (ɪˈrəʊd) *vb.* **1.** to grind or wear down or away or become ground or worn down or away. **2.** to deteriorate or cause to deteriorate. [C17: from L, from EX-[1] + *rōdere* to gnaw] —eˈrodent *adj., n.* —eˈrodible *adj.*

erogenous (ɪˈrɒdʒɪnəs) *or* **erogenic** (ˌɛrəˈdʒɛnɪk) *adj.* **1.** sensitive to sexual stimulation. **2.** arousing sexual desire or giving sexual pleasure. [C19: from Gk *erōs* love, desire + -GENOUS] —**erogeneity** (ˌɛrədʒɪˈniːɪtɪ) *n.*

Eros ('ɪərɒs, 'ɛrɒs) *n. Greek myth.* the god of love, son of Aphrodite. Roman counterpart: **Cupid.**

erosion (ɪˈrəʊʒən) *n.* **1.** the wearing away of rocks, soil, etc., by the action of water, ice, wind, etc. **2.** the act or process of eroding or the state of being eroded. —eˈrosive *or* eˈrosional *adj.*

erotic (ɪˈrɒtɪk) *adj.* **1.** of, concerning, or arousing sexual desire or giving sexual pleasure. **2.** marked by strong sexual desire or being especially sensitive to sexual stimulation. Also: **erotical.** [C17: from Gk *erōtikos,* from *erōs* love] —eˈrotically *adv.*

erotica (ɪˈrɒtɪkə) *pl. n.* explicitly sexual literature or art. [C19: from Gk: see EROTIC]

eroticism (ɪˈrɒtɪˌsɪzəm) *or* **erotism** ('ɛrəˌtɪzəm) *n.* **1.** erotic quality or nature. **2.** the use of sexually arousing or pleasing symbolism in literature or art. **3.** sexual excitement or desire.

erotogenic (ɪˌrɒtəˈdʒɛnɪk) *adj.* originating from or causing sexual stimulation; erogenous.

err (ɜː) *vb.* (*intr.*) **1.** to make a mistake; be incorrect. **2.** to deviate from a moral standard. **3.** to act with bias, esp. favourable bias: *to err on the right side.* [C14 *erren* to wander, stray, from OF, from L *errāre*] —ˈerrancy *n.*

errand ('ɛrənd) *n.* **1.** a short trip undertaken to perform a task or commission (esp. in **run errands**). **2.** the purpose or object of such a trip. [OE *ærende*]

errant ('ɛrənt) *adj.* (*often postpositive*) **1.** *Arch. or literary.* wandering in search of adventure. **2.** erring or straying from the right course or accepted standards. [C14: from OF: journeying, from Vulgar L *iterāre* (unattested), from L *iter* journey; infl. by L *errāre* to err] —ˈerrantry *n.*

erratic (ɪˈrætɪk) *adj.* **1.** irregular in performance, behaviour, or attitude; unpredictable. **2.** having no fixed or regular course. ~*n.* **3.** a piece of rock that has been transported from its place of origin, esp. by glacial action. [C14: from L, from *errāre* to wander, err] —erˈratically *adv.*

erratum (ɪˈrɑːtəm) *n., pl.* **-ta** (-tə). **1.** an error in writing or printing. **2.** another name for **corrigendum.** [C16: from L: mistake, from *errāre* to err]

Er Rif (ɛə rɪf) *n.* a mountainous region of N Morocco, near the Mediterranean coast.

erroneous (ɪˈrəʊnɪəs) *adj.* based on or containing error; incorrect. [C14 (in the sense: deviating from what is right), from L, from *errāre* to wander] —erˈroneousness *n.*

error ('ɛrə) *n.* **1.** a mistake or inaccuracy. **2.** an incorrect belief or wrong judgment. **3.** the condition of deviating from accuracy or correctness. **4.** deviation from a moral standard; wrongdoing. **5.** *Maths, statistics.* a measure of the difference between some quantity and an approximation of it, often expressed as a percentage. [C13: from L, from *errāre* to err] —ˈerror-ˌfree *adj.*

ersatz ('ɛəzæts, 'ɜː-) *adj.* **1.** made in imitation; artificial. ~*n.* **2.** an ersatz substance or article. [C20: G, from *ersetzen* to substitute]

Erse (ɜːs) *n.* **1.** another name for **Gaelic.** ~*adj.* **2.** of or relating to the Gaelic language. [C14: from Lowland Scots *Erisch* Irish]

Ershad ('ɜːʃæd) *n.* **Hussain Mohammed.** born 1930, Bangladeshi soldier and statesman. He seized power in a coup in 1982, becoming president in 1983.

Erskine ('ɜːskɪn) *n.* **Thomas,** 1st Baron Erskine. 1750–1823, Scottish lawyer: noted as a defence advocate, esp. in cases involving civil liberties.

erst (ɜːst) *adv. Arch.* **1.** long ago; formerly. **2.** at first. [OE ǣrest earliest, sup. of ǣr early]

erstwhile ('ɜːst,waɪl) *adj.* **1.** former; one-time. ~*adv.* **2.** *Arch.* long ago; formerly.

Erté (ɛrte) *n.* real name *Romain de Tirtoff.* born 1892, French fashion illustrator and designer, born in Russia, noted for his extravagant costumes and tableaux for the Folies-Bergère in Paris.

eruct (ɪ'rʌkt) *or* **eructate** *vb.* **1.** to belch. **2.** (of a volcano) to pour out (fumes or volcanic matter). [C17: from L, from *ructāre* to belch] —**eructation** (,ɪrʌk'teɪʃən, ,iːrʌk-) *n.*

erudite ('ɛrʊ,daɪt) *adj.* having or showing extensive scholarship; learned. [C15: from L, from *ērudīre* to polish] —**erudition** (,ɛrʊ'dɪʃən) *or* **'eru,diteness** *n.*

erupt (ɪ'rʌpt) *vb.* **1.** to eject (steam, water, and volcanic material) violently or (of volcanic material, etc.) to be so ejected. **2.** (*intr.*) (of a blemish) to appear on the skin. **3.** (*intr.*) (of a tooth) to emerge through the gum during normal tooth development. **4.** (*intr.*) to burst forth suddenly and violently. [C17: from L *ēruptus* having burst forth, from *ērumpere*, from *rumpere* to burst] —**e'ruptive** *adj.* —**e'ruption** *n.*

-ery *or* **-ry** *suffix forming nouns.* **1.** indicating a place of business or activity: *bakery; refinery.* **2.** indicating a class or collection of things: *cutlery.* **3.** indicating qualities or actions: *snobbery; trickery.* **4.** indicating a practice or occupation: *husbandry.* **5.** indicating a state or condition: *slavery.* [from OF -*erie*; see -ER¹, -Y³]

Erymanthus (,ɛrɪ'mænθəs) *n.* **Mount.** a mountain in SW Greece, in the NW Peloponnese. Height: 2224 m (7297 ft.). Modern Greek name: **Erimanthos** (e'rimanθɔs).

erysipelas (,ɛrɪ'sɪpɪləs) *n.* an acute streptococcal infectious disease of the skin, characterized by fever and purplish lesions. [C16: from L, from Gk, from *erusi-* red + *-pelas* skin]

erythro- *or before a vowel* **erythr-** *combining form.* red: *erythrocyte.* [from Gk *eruthros* red]

erythrocyte (ɪ'rɪθrəʊ,saɪt) *n.* a blood cell of vertebrates that transports oxygen and carbon dioxide, combined with haemoglobin. —**erythrocytic** (ɪ,rɪθrəʊ'sɪtɪk) *adj.*

erythromycin (ɪ,rɪθrəʊ'maɪsɪn) *n.* an antibiotic used in treating certain bacterial infections. [C20: from ERYTHRO- + Gk *mukēs* fungus + -IN]

Erzgebirge (*German* 'eːrtsgəbɪrgə) *pl. n.* a mountain range on the border between East Germany and Czechoslovakia: formerly rich in mineral resources. Highest peak: Mount Klínovec (Keilberg), 1244 m (4081 ft.). Czech name: **Krušné Hory.** Also called: **Ore Mountains.**

Erzurum ('ɛəzʊrʊm) *n.* a city in E Turkey: a strategic centre; scene of two major battles against Russian forces (1877 and 1916); important military base and a closed city to unofficial visitors. Pop.: 252 648 (1985).

Es *the chemical symbol for* einsteinium.

-es *suffix.* **1.** a variant of -s¹ for nouns ending in *ch, s, sh, z,* postconsonantal *y,* for some nouns ending in a vowel, and nouns in *f* with *v* in the plural: *ashes; heroes; calves.* **2.** a variant of -s² for verbs ending in *ch, s, sh, z,* postconsonantal *y,* or a vowel: *preaches; steadies; echoes.*

Esau ('iːsɔː) *n. Bible.* son of Isaac and Rebecca and twin brother of Jacob, to whom he sold his birthright (Genesis 25).

Esbjerg (*Danish* 'ɛsbjɛr) *n.* a port in SW Denmark, in Jutland on the North Sea: Denmark's chief fishing port. Pop.: 80 825 (1987).

escadrille (,ɛskə'drɪl) *n.* a French squadron of aircraft, esp. in World War I. [from F: flotilla, from Sp., from *escuadra* SQUADRON]

escalade (,ɛskə'leɪd) *n.* **1.** an assault using ladders, esp. on a fortification. ~*vb.* **2.** to gain access to (a place) by ladders. [C16: from F, from It., from *scalare* to mount, SCALE³]

escalate ('ɛskə,leɪt) *vb.* to increase or be increased in extent, intensity, or magnitude. [C20: back formation from ESCALATOR] —**esca'lation** *n.*

▷ **Usage.** *Escalate* is very commonly used in journalistic contexts in the sense of gradually increasing the intensity or scope of a war, etc. This word is, however, not yet completely accepted as appropriate in formal English.

escalator ('ɛskə,leɪtə) *n.* **1.** a moving staircase consisting of stair treads fixed to a conveyor belt. **2.** short for **escalator clause.** [C20: orig. a trademark]

escalator clause *n.* a clause in a contract stipulating an adjustment in wages, prices, etc., in the event of specified changes in conditions, such as a large rise in the cost of living.

escallop (ɛ'skɒləp, ɛ'skæl-) *n., vb.* another word for **scallop.**

escalope ('ɛskə,lɒp) *n.* a thin slice of meat, usually veal. [C19: from OF: shell]

escapade ('ɛskə,peɪd, ,ɛskə'peɪd) *n.* **1.** an adventure, esp. one that is mischievous or unlawful. **2.** a prank; romp. [C17: from F, from OIt., from Vulgar L *excappāre* (unattested) to ESCAPE]

escape (ɪ'skeɪp) *vb.* **1.** to get away or break free from (confinements, etc.). **2.** to manage to avoid (danger, etc.). **3.** (*intr.*; usually foll. by *from*) (of gases, liquids, etc.) to issue gradually, as from a crack; seep; leak. **4.** (*tr.*) to elude; be forgotten by: *the figure escapes me.* **5.** (*tr.*) to be articulated inadvertently or involuntarily from: *a roar escaped his lips.* ~*n.* **6.** the act of escaping or state of having escaped. **7.** avoidance of injury, harm, etc. **8. a.** a means or way of escape. **b.** (*as modifier*): *an escape route.* **9.** a means of distraction or relief. **10.** a gradual outflow; leakage; seepage. **11.** Also called: **escape valve, escape cock.** a valve that releases air, steam, etc., above a certain pressure. **12.** a plant originally cultivated but now growing wild. [C14: from OF, from Vulgar L *excappāre* (unattested) to escape (lit.: to slip out of one's cloak, hence free oneself), from EX-¹ + LL *cappa* cloak] —**es'capable** *adj.* —**es'caper** *n.*

escapee (ɪ,skeɪ'piː) *n.* a person who has escaped, esp. an escaped prisoner.

escapement (ɪ'skeɪpmənt) *n.* **1.** a mechanism consisting of a toothed wheel (**escape wheel**) and anchor, used in timepieces to provide periodic impulses to the pendulum or balance. **2.** any similar mechanism that regulates movement. **3.** in pianos, the mechanism which allows the hammer to clear the string after striking, so the string can vibrate. **4.** *Rare.* an act or means of escaping.

escape road *n.* a road provided on a hill for a driver to drive into if his brakes fail or on a bend if he loses control of the turn.

escape velocity *n.* the minimum velocity necessary for a body to escape from the gravitational field of the earth or other celestial body.

escapism (ɪ'skeɪpɪzəm) *n.* an inclination to retreat from unpleasant reality, as through diversion or fantasy. —**es'capist** *n., adj.*

escapologist (,ɛskə'pɒlədʒɪst) *n.* an entertainer who specializes in freeing himself from confinement. —,**esca'pology** *n.*

escargot *French.* (ɛskargo) *n.* a variety of edible snail.

escarpment (ɪ'skɑːpmənt) *n.* **1.** the long continuous steep face of a ridge or plateau formed by erosion or faulting; scarp. **2.** a steep artificial slope made immediately in front of a fortified place. [C19: from F *escarpe*; see SCARP]

Escaut (ɛsko) *n.* the French name for the **Scheldt.**

-escent *suffix forming adjectives.* beginning to be, do, show, etc.: *convalescent; luminescent.* [via OF from L -*ēscent-,* stem of present participial suffix of -*ēscere,* ending of inceptive verbs] —**-escence** *suffix forming nouns.*

eschatology (,ɛskə'tɒlədʒɪ) *n.* the branch of theology concerned with the end of the world. [C19: from Gk *eskhatos* last] —**eschatological** (,ɛskətə'lɒdʒɪk²l) *adj.* —,**escha'tologist** *n.*

escheat (ɪs'tʃiːt) *Law.* ~*n.* **1.** (in England before 1926) the reversion of property to the Crown in the absence of legal heirs. **2.** *Feudalism.* the reversion of property to the feudal lord in the absence of legal heirs. **3.** the property so reverting. ~*vb.* **4.** to take (land) by escheat or (of land) to revert by escheat. [C14: from OF, from *escheoir* to fall to the lot of, from LL *excadere* (unattested), from L *cadere* to fall] —**es'cheatable** *adj.* —**es'cheatage** *n.*

Escherichia (,ɛʃə'rɪkɪə) *n.* a genus of bacteria that form acid and gas on many carbohydrates and are found in the intestines of man and many animals. [C19: after Theodor *Escherich* (1857-1911), G paediatrician]

eschew (ɪs'tʃuː) *vb.* (*tr.*) to keep clear of or abstain from (something disliked, injurious, etc.); shun; avoid. [C14: from OF *eschiver,* of Gmc origin; see SHY¹, SKEW] —**es'chewal** *n.* —**es'chewer** *n.*

eschscholzia (ɪsˌkɒlʃə) *n.* any of a genus of N American herbs having showy flowers. [C19: after J. F. von *Eschscholz* (1793–1831), G botanist]

Escoffier (*French* ɛskɔfje) *n.* **Auguste** (ogyst). 1846–1935, French chef at the Savoy Hotel, London (1890–99).

Escorial (ˌɛskɒrɪˈɑːl, ɛˈskɔːrɪəl) *or* **Escurial** *n.* a village in central Spain, northwest of Madrid: site of an architectural complex containing a monastery, palace, and college, built by Philip II between 1563 and 1584.

escort *n.* (ˈɛskɔːt). **1.** one or more persons, soldiers, vehicles, etc., accompanying another or others for protection, as a mark of honour, etc. **2.** a man or youth who accompanies a woman or girl on a social occasion. ~*vb.* (ɪsˈkɔːt). **3.** (*tr.*) to accompany or attend as an escort. [C16: from F, from It., from *scorgere* to guide, from L *corrigere* to straighten; see CORRECT]

escritoire (ˌɛskrɪˈtwɑː) *n.* a writing desk with compartments and drawers. [C18: from F, from Med. L *scriptōrium* writing room in a monastery, from L *scribere* to write]

escrow (ˈɛskrəʊ, ɛˈskrəʊ) *Law.* ~*n.* **1.** money, goods, or a written document, held by a third party pending fulfilment of some condition. **2.** the state or condition of being an escrow (esp. in **in escrow**). ~*vb.* (*tr.*) **3.** to place (money, a document, etc.) in escrow. [C16: from OF *escroe*, of Gmc origin; see SCREED, SHRED, SCROLL]

escudo (ɛˈskrəʊdəʊ) *n., pl.* **-dos. 1.** the standard monetary unit of Portugal. **2.** the standard monetary unit of Chile. **3.** an old Spanish silver coin. [C19: Sp., lit.: shield, from L *scūtum*]

esculent (ˈɛskjʊlənt) *n.* **1.** any edible substance. ~*adj.* **2.** edible. [C17: from L *ēsculentus* good to eat, from *ēsca* food, from *edere* to eat]

Escurial (ɛˌskjʊərɪˈɑːl, ɛˈskjʊərɪəl) *n.* a variant of **Escorial.**

escutcheon (ɪˈskʌtʃən) *n.* **1.** a shield, esp. a heraldic one that displays a coat of arms. **2.** a plate or shield around a keyhole, door handle, etc. **3.** the place on the stern of a vessel where the name is shown. **4. blot on one's escutcheon**, a stain on one's honour. [C15: from OF *escuchon*, ult. from L *scūtum* shield] —**es'cutcheoned** *adj.*

Esdraelon (ˌɛsdreɪˈiːlɒn) *n.* a plain in N Israel, east of Mount Carmel. Also called: (Plain of) **Jezreel.**

ESE *symbol for* east-southeast.

-ese *suffix forming adjectives and nouns.* indicating place of origin, language, or style: *Cantonese; Japanese; journalese.*

Eşfahān (ˌɛʃfəˈhɑːn) *n.* a variant of **Isfahan.**

Esher (ˈiːʃə) *n.* a town in SE England, in NE Surrey near London: racecourse. Pop.: 61 446 (1981).

esker (ˈɛskə) *or* **eskar** (ˈɛskɑː, -kə) *n.* a long winding ridge of gravel, sand, etc., originally deposited by a meltwater stream running under a glacier. [C19: from Olrish *escir* ridge]

Eskilstuna (*Swedish* ˈɛskilstuːna) *n.* an industrial city in SE Sweden. Pop.: 90 104 (1981 est.).

Eskimo (ˈɛskɪˌməʊ) *n.* **1.** (*pl.* **-mos** *or* **-mo**) a member of a group of peoples inhabiting N Canada, Greenland, Alaska, and E Siberia. The Eskimos are more properly referred to as the **Inuit. 2.** the language of these peoples. ~*adj.* **3.** of or relating to the Eskimos. [C18 *Esquimawes*: rel. to *esquimantsic* (from a native language) eaters of raw flesh]

Eskimo dog *n.* a large powerful breed of dog with a long thick coat and curled tail, developed for hauling sledges.

Eskişehir (*Turkish* ɛsˈkiʃɛˌhir) *n.* an industrial city in NW Turkey: founded around hot springs in Byzantine times. Pop.: 367 328 (1985).

Esky (ˈɛskɪ) *n., pl.* **-kies.** (*sometimes not cap.*) *Austral. trademark.* a portable insulated container for keeping food and drink cool. [C20: from ESKIMO, alluding to the Eskimos' cold habitat]

ESN *abbrev. for* educationally subnormal.

esophagus (iːˈsɒfəgəs) *n.* the U.S. spelling of **oesophagus.**

esoteric (ˌɛsəʊˈtɛrɪk) *adj.* **1.** restricted to or intended for an enlightened or initiated minority. **2.** difficult to understand; abstruse. **3.** not openly admitted; private. [C17: from Gk, from *esōterō* inner] —**eso'terically** *adv.* —**eso'teri,cism** *n.*

ESP *abbrev. for* extrasensory perception.

esp. *abbrev. for* especially.

espadrille (ˌɛspəˈdrɪl) *n.* a light shoe with a canvas upper, esp. with a braided cord sole. [C19: from F, from Provençal *espardilho*, dim. of *espart* ESPARTO; from use of esparto for the soles]

espalier (ɪˈspæljə) *n.* **1.** an ornamental shrub or fruit tree trained to grow flat, as against a wall. **2.** the trellis or framework on which such plants are trained. ~*vb.* **3.** (*tr.*) to train (a plant) on an espalier. [C17: from F: trellis, from OIt.: shoulder supports, from *spalla* shoulder, from LL SPATULA]

España (esˈpaɲa) *n.* the Spanish name for **Spain.**

esparto *or* **esparto grass** (ɛˈspaːtəʊ) *n., pl.* **-tos.** any of various grasses of S Europe and N Africa, used to make ropes, mats, etc. [C18: from Sp., via L from Gk *spartos* a kind of rush]

especial (ɪˈspɛʃəl) *adj.* (*prenominal*) **1.** unusual; notable. **2.** applying to one person or thing in particular; specific; peculiar: *he had an especial dislike of relatives.* [C14: from OF, from L *speciālis* individual; see SPECIAL] —**es'pecially** *adv.*

▷ **Usage.** *Special* is always used in preference to *especial* when the sense is one of being out of the ordinary: *a special lesson. Special* is also used when something is referred to as being for a particular purpose: *the word was specially underlined for you.* Where an idea of pre-eminence or individuality is involved, either *especial* or *special* may be used: *he is my especial* (or *special*) *friend; he is especially* (or *specially*) *good at his job.* In informal English, however, *special* is usually preferred in all contexts.

Esperanto (ˌɛspəˈræntəʊ) *n.* an international artificial language based on words common to the chief European languages. [C19: lit.: the one who hopes, pseudonym of Dr L. L. Zamenhof (1859–1917), its Polish inventor] —**Espe'rantist** *n.*, *adj.*

espial (ɪˈspaɪəl) *n. Arch.* **1.** the act or fact of being seen or discovered. **2.** the act of noticing. **3.** the act of spying upon; secret observation.

espionage (ˈɛspɪəˌnɑːʒ) *n.* **1.** the use of spies to obtain secret information, esp. by governments. **2.** the act of spying. [C18: from F, from *espion* spy, from OIt. *spione*, of Gmc origin]

Espírito Santo (*Portuguese* ɪʃˈpiritu ˈsəntu) *n.* a state of E Brazil, on the Atlantic: swampy coastal plain with mountains in the west: heavily forested. Capital: Vitória. Pop.: 2 019 877 (1980). Area: 45 597 sq. km (17 601 sq. miles).

Espíritu Santo (esˈpɪrɪtu: ˈsæntəʊ) *n.* an island in the SW Pacific: the largest and westernmost of the Vanuatu islands. Area: 4856 sq. km (1875 sq. miles).

esplanade (ˌɛspləˈneɪd) *n.* **1.** a long open level stretch of ground for walking along, esp. beside the seashore. Cf. **promenade** (sense 1). **2.** an open area in front of a fortified place. [C17: from F, from OIt. *spianata*, from *spianare* to make level, from L *explānāre*; see EXPLAIN]

Espoo (*Finnish* ˈɛspoː) *n.* a city in S Finland. Pop.: 160 406 (1986).

espousal (ɪˈspaʊzᵊl) *n.* **1.** adoption or support: *an espousal of new beliefs.* **2.** (*sometimes pl.*) *Arch.* a marriage or betrothal ceremony.

espouse (ɪˈspaʊz) *vb.* (*tr.*) **1.** to adopt or give support to (a cause, ideal, etc.): *to espouse socialism.* **2.** *Arch.* (esp. of a man) to take as spouse; marry. [C15: from OF *espouser*, from L *spōnsāre* to affiance, espouse] —**es'pouser** *n.*

espressivo (ɛsprɛˈsiːvəʊ) *adv. Music.* in an expressive manner. [It.]

espresso (ɛˈsprɛsəʊ) *n., pl.* **-sos. 1.** coffee made by forcing steam or boiling water through ground coffee beans. **2.** an apparatus for making coffee in this way. [C20: It., lit.: pressed]

esprit (ɛˈspriː) *n.* spirit and liveliness, esp. in wit. [C16: from F, from L *spīritus* a breathing, SPIRIT¹]

esprit de corps (ɛˈspriː də ˈkɔː) *n.* consciousness of and pride in belonging to a particular group; the sense of shared purpose and fellowship.

espy (ɪˈspaɪ) *vb.* **espying, espied.** (*tr.*) to catch sight of or perceive; detect. [C14: from OF *espier* to SPY, of Gmc origin] —**es'pier** *n.*

Esq. *abbrev. for* esquire.

-esque *suffix forming adjectives.* indicating a specified character, manner, style, or resemblance: *picturesque; Romanesque; statuesque.* [via F from It. *-esco*, of Gmc origin]

Esquiline ('ɛskwə,laɪn) *n.* one of the seven hills on which ancient Rome was built.

Esquimau ('ɛskɪ,məʊ) *n., pl.* **-maus** *or* **-mau,** *adj.* a former spelling of **Eskimo.**

esquire (ɪ'skwaɪə) *n.* **1.** *Chiefly Brit.* a title of respect, usually abbreviated *Esq.*, placed after a man's name. **2.** (in medieval times) the attendant of a knight, subsequently often knighted himself. [C15: from OF *escuier*, from LL *scūtārius* shield bearer, from L *scūtum* shield]

ESRC (in Britain) *abbrev. for* Economic and Social Research Council.

ESRO ('ɛzrəʊ) *n.* acronym for European Space Research Organization.

-ess *suffix forming nouns.* indicating a female: *waitress; lioness.* [via OF from LL *-issa*, from Gk]

▷ **Usage.** The suffix *-ess* in such words as *poetess, authoress* is now often regarded as disparaging; a sexually neutral term *poet, author* is preferred.

Essaouira (,ɛsə'wɪərə) *n.* a port in SW Morocco on the Atlantic. Pop.: 30 061 (1971). Former name (until 1956): **Mogador.**

essay *n.* ('ɛseɪ; *senses 2, 3 also* ɛ'seɪ). **1.** a short literary composition. **2.** an attempt; effort. **3.** a test or trial. ~*vb.* (ɛ'seɪ). (*tr.*) **4.** to attempt or try. **5.** to test or try out. [C15: from OF *essai* an attempt, from LL *exagium* a weighing, from L *agere* to do, infl. by *exigere* to investigate]

essayist ('ɛseɪɪst) *n.* a person who writes essays.

Essen (*German* 'ɛsən) *n.* a city in W West Germany, in North Rhine-Westphalia: the leading industrial centre of the Ruhr, with extensive iron and steel factories. Pop.: 617 700 (1986).

essence ('ɛs³ns) *n.* **1.** the characteristic or intrinsic feature of a thing, which determines its identity; fundamental nature. **2.** a perfect or complete form of something. **3.** *Philosophy.* the unchanging and unchangeable inward nature of something. **4. a.** the constituent of a plant, usually an oil, alkaloid, or glycoside, that determines its chemical properties. **b.** an alcoholic solution of such a substance. **5.** a rare word for **perfume. 6. in essence.** essentially; fundamentally. **7. of the essence.** indispensable; vitally important. [C14: from Med. L *essentia*, from L: the being (of something), from *esse* to be]

Essene ('ɛsiːn, ɛ'siːn) *n. Judaism.* a member of an ascetic sect that flourished in Palestine from the second century B.C. to the second century A.D. —**Essenian** (ɛ'siːnɪən) *or* **Essenic** (ɛ'sɛnɪk) *adj.*

essential (ɪ'sɛnʃəl) *adj.* **1.** vitally important; absolutely necessary. **2.** basic; fundamental. **3.** absolute; perfect. **4.** derived from or relating to an extract of a plant, drug, etc.: *an essential oil.* ~*n.* **5.** something fundamental or indispensable. —**essentiality** (ɪ,sɛnʃɪ'ælɪtɪ) *or* **es'sentialness** *n.* —**es'sentially** *adv.*

essentialism (ɪ'sɛnʃə,lɪzəm) *n. Philosophy.* any doctrine that material objects have an essence distinguishable from their attributes and existence. —**es'sentialist** *n.*

essential oil *n.* any of various volatile oils in plants, having the odour or flavour of the plant from which they are extracted.

Essequibo (,ɛsɪ'kwiːbəʊ) *n.* a river in Guyana, rising near the Brazilian border and flowing north to the Atlantic: drains over half of Guyana. Length: 1014 km (630 miles).

Essex¹ ('ɛsɪks) *n.* **1.** a county of SE England, on the North Sea and the Thames estuary. Administrative centre: Chelmsford. Pop.: 1 512 100 (1986 est.). Area: 3672 sq. km (1417 sq. miles). **2.** an Anglo-Saxon kingdom that in the early 7th century A.D. comprised the modern county of Essex and much of Hertfordshire and Surrey. By the late 8th century, Essex had become a dependency of the kingdom of Mercia.

Essex² ('ɛsɪks) *n.* **2nd Earl of,** title of *Robert Devereux.* ?1566–1601, English soldier and favourite of Queen Elizabeth I; executed for treason.

Essonne (*French* ɛsɔn) *n.* a department of N France, south of Paris in Île-de-France region: formed in 1964. Capital: Évry. Pop.: 988 000 (1982). Area: 1811 sq. km (706 sq. miles).

EST *abbrev. for:* **1.** (in the U.S. and Canada) Eastern Standard Time. **2.** electric-shock treatment.

est. *abbrev. for:* **1.** established. **2.** estimate(d).

-est¹ *suffix.* forming the superlative degree of adjectives and adverbs: *fastest.* [OE *-est, -ost*]

-est² *or* **-st** *suffix.* forming the archaic second person singular present and past indicative tense of verbs: *thou goest; thou hadst.* [OE *-est, -ast*]

establish (ɪ'stæblɪʃ) *vb.* (*tr.*) **1.** to make secure or permanent in a certain place, condition, job, etc. **2.** to create or set up (an organization, etc.) as on a permanent basis. **3.** to prove correct; validate: *establish a fact.* **4.** to cause (a principle, theory, etc.) to be accepted: *establish a precedent.* **5.** to give (a Church) the status of a national institution. **6.** to cause (a person) to become recognized and accepted. **7.** (in works of imagination) to cause (a character, place, etc.) to be credible and recognized. [C14: from OF, from L *stabilis* STABLE²] —**es'tablisher** *n.*

Established Church *n.* a Church that is officially recognized as a national institution, esp. the Church of England.

establishment (ɪ'stæblɪʃmənt) *n.* **1.** the act of establishing or state of being established. **2. a.** a business organization or other large institution. **b.** a place of business. **3.** the staff and equipment of an organization. **4.** any large organization or system. **5.** a household; residence. **6.** a body of employees or servants. **7.** (*modifier*) belonging to or characteristic of the Establishment.

Establishment (ɪ'stæblɪʃmənt) *n.* **the.** a group or class having institutional authority within a society: usually seen as conservative.

estate (ɪ'steɪt) *n.* **1.** a large piece of landed property, esp. in the country. **2.** *Chiefly Brit.* a large area of property development, esp. of new houses or (**trading estate**) of factories. **3.** *Law.* **a.** property or possessions. **b.** the nature of interest that a person has in land or other property. **c.** the total extent of the property of a deceased person or bankrupt. **4.** Also called: **estate of the realm.** an order or class in a political community, regarded as a part of the body politic: the lords spiritual (**first estate**), lords temporal or peers (**second estate**), and commons (**third estate**). See also **fourth estate. 5.** state, period, or position in life: *youth's estate; a poor man's estate.* [C13: from OF *estat*, from L *status* condition, STATE]

estate agent *n.* **1.** *Brit.* an agent concerned with the valuation, management, lease, and sale of property. **2.** the administrator of a large landed property; estate manager.

estate car *n. Brit.* a car containing a large carrying space, reached through a rear door: usually the back seats fold forward to increase the carrying space.

estate duty *n.* another name for **death duty.**

Este ('ɛste) *n.* a noble family of Italy founded by Alberto Azzo II (996–1097), who was invested with the town of Este in NE Italy as a fief of the Holy Roman Empire. The family governed Ferrara (13th–16th centuries), Modena, and Reggio (13th–18th centuries).

esteem (ɪ'stiːm) *vb.* (*tr.*) **1.** to have great respect or high regard for. **2.** *Formal.* to judge or consider; deem. ~*n.* **3.** high regard or respect; good opinion. **4.** *Arch.* judgment; opinion. [C15: from OF *estimer*, from L *aestimāre* ESTIMATE] —**es'teemed** *adj.*

ester ('ɛstə) *n. Chem.* any of a class of compounds produced by reaction between acids and alcohols with the elimination of water. [C19: from G, prob. a contraction of *Essigäther* acetic ether, from *Essig* vinegar (ult. from L *acētum*) + *Äther* ETHER]

Esth. *Bible. abbrev. for* Esther.

Esther ('ɛstə) *n. Old Testament.* **1.** a beautiful Jewess who became queen of Persia and saved her people from massacre. **2.** the book in which this episode is recounted.

esthesia (iːs'θiːzɪə) *n.* a U.S. spelling of **aesthesia.**

esthete ('iːsθiːt) *n.* a U.S. spelling of **aesthete.**

Esthonia (ɛ'stəʊnɪə, ɛ'stθəʊ-) *n.* See **Estonian Soviet Socialist Republic.**

Estienne *or* **Étienne** (*French* etjɛn) *n.* a family of French printers, scholars, and dealers in books, including **Henri** (āri), ?1460–1520, who founded the printing business in Paris, his son **Robert** (rɔbɛr), 1503–59, and his grandson **Henri,** 1528–98.

estimable ('ɛstɪməb³l) *adj.* worthy of respect; deserving of admiration. —**'estimableness** *n.* —**'estimably** *adv.*

estimate *vb.* ('ɛstɪ,meɪt). **1.** to form an approximate idea of (size, cost, etc.); calculate roughly. **2.** (*tr.; may take a clause as object*) to form an opinion about; judge. **3.** to submit (an approximate price) for (a job) to a prospective client. ~*n.* (ˈɛstɪmɪt). **4.** an approximate calculation. **5.** a statement of the likely charge for certain work. **6.** a judgment; appraisal. [C16: from L *aestimāre* to assess the worth of, from ?] — **ˈestiˌmator** *n.* — **ˈestimative** *adj.*

estimation (ˌɛstɪˈmeɪʃən) *n.* **1.** a considered opinion; judgment. **2.** esteem; respect. **3.** the act of estimating.

estival (iːˈstaɪvəl, ˈɛstɪ-) *adj.* the usual U.S. spelling of **aestival.**

estivate (ˈiːstɪˌveɪt, ˈɛs-) *vb.* (*intr.*) the usual U.S. spelling of **aestivate.**

Estonian *or* **Esthonian** (ɛˈstəʊnɪən, ɛˈsθəʊ-) *adj.* **1.** of, relating to, or characteristic of the Estonian SSR, its people, or their language. ~*n.* **2.** an official language of the Estonian SSR. **3.** a native or inhabitant of Estonia.

Estonian Soviet Socialist Republic *n.* a constituent republic of the W Soviet Union, on the Gulf of Finland and the Baltic: low-lying with many lakes and forests. As **Estonia** or **Esthonia** it was under Scandinavian and Teutonic rule from the 13th century to 1721, when it passed to Russia: it was an independent republic from 1920 to 1940, when it was annexed by the Soviet Union. Capital: Tallinn. Pop.: 1 556 000 (1987). Area: 45 100 sq. km (17 410 sq. miles).

estop (ɪˈstɒp) *vb.* **-topping, -topped.** (*tr.*) **1.** *Law.* to preclude by estoppel. **2.** *Arch.* to stop. [C15: from OF *estoper* to plug, ult. from L *stuppa* tow; see STOP] — **esˈtoppage** *n.*

estoppel (ɪˈstɒpəl) *n.* *Law.* a rule of evidence whereby a person is precluded from denying the truth of a statement he has previously asserted. [C16: from OF *estoupail* plug; see ESTOP]

estovers (ɛˈstəʊvəz) *pl. n.* *Law.* necessaries allowed to tenant of land, esp. wood for fuel and repairs. [C15: from Anglo-F., pl. of *estover*, from OF *estovoir* to be necessary, from L *est opus* there is need]

estradiol (ˌɛstrəˈdaɪɒl, ˌiːstrə-) *n.* the usual U.S. spelling of **oestradiol.**

estrange (ɪˈstreɪndʒ) *vb.* (*tr.*) to antagonize or lose the affection of (someone previously friendly); alienate. [C15: from OF *estranger*, from LL *extrāneāre* to treat as a stranger, from L *extrāneus* foreign; see STRANGE] — **esˈtranged** *adj.* — **esˈtrangement** *n.*

Estremadura (*Portuguese* ɪʃtrəməˈðʊrə) *n.* **1.** a region of W Spain: arid and sparsely populated except in the valleys of the Tagus and Guadiana Rivers. Area: 41 593 sq. km (16 059 sq. miles). Spanish name: **Extremadura.** **2.** a province in Portugal around Lisbon. Pop.: 1 600 000 (1970 est.). Area: 5348 sq. km (2065 sq. miles).

estrogen (ˈɛstrədʒən, ˈiːstrə-) *n.* the usual U.S. spelling of **oestrogen.**

estrus (ˈɛstrəs, ˈiːstrəs) *n.* the usual U.S. spelling of **oestrus.**

estuary (ˈɛstjʊərɪ) *n.*, *pl.* **-aries.** the widening channel of a river where it nears the sea. [C16: from L *aestuārium* marsh, channel, from *aestus* tide] — **estuarial** (ˌɛstjʊˈɛərɪəl) *adj.* — **ˈestuarine** *adj.*

e.s.u. *or* **ESU** *abbrev. for* electrostatic unit.

-et *suffix of nouns.* small or lesser: *islet; baronet.* [from OF *-et, -ete*]

eta (ˈiːtə) *n.* the seventh letter in the Greek alphabet (H, η). [Gk, from Phoenician]

ETA *abbrev. for* estimated time of arrival.

et al. *abbrev. for:* **1.** et alibi. [L: and elsewhere] **2.** et alii. [L: and others]

etalon (ˈɛtəˌlɒn) *n.* *Physics.* a device used in spectroscopy to measure wavelengths by interference effects produced by multiple reflections between parallel half-silvered glass plates. [C20: F *étalon* a standard of weights & measures]

etc. *abbrev. for* et cetera.

et cetera *or* **etcetera** (ɪt ˈsɛtrə) *n. and vb. substitute.* **1.** and the rest; and others; and so forth. **2.** or the like; or something similar. [from L *et* and + *cetera* the other (things)]

▷ **Usage.** Since *et cetera* (or *etc.*) means *and other things,* careful writers do not use the expression *and etc.* The repetition of *etc.,* as in *notebooks, etc., etc.,* is avoided in formal contexts.

etceteras (ɪtˈsɛtrəz) *pl. n.* miscellaneous extra things or persons.

etch (ɛtʃ) *vb.* **1.** (*tr.*) to wear away the surface of (a metal, glass, etc.) by the action of an acid. **2.** to cut or corrode (a design, etc.) on (a metal or other printing plate) by the

action of acid on parts not covered by an acid-resistant coating. **3.** (*tr.*) to cut as with a sharp implement. **4.** (*tr.; usually passive*) to imprint vividly. [C17: from Du. *etsen,* from OHG *azzen* to feed, bite] — **ˈetcher** *n.*

etching (ˈɛtʃɪŋ) *n.* **1.** the art, act, or process of preparing etched surfaces or of printing designs from them. **2.** an etched plate. **3.** an impression made from an etched plate.

ETD *abbrev. for* estimated time of departure.

Eteocles (ɪˈtiːəˌkliːz, ˈɛtɪə-) *n. Greek myth.* a son of Oedipus and Jocasta. He expelled his brother Polynices from Thebes; they killed each other in single combat when Polynices returned as leader of the Seven against Thebes.

eternal (ɪˈtɜːnˀl) *adj.* **1. a.** without beginning or end; lasting for ever. **b.** (*as n.*): *the eternal.* **2.** (*often cap.*) a name applied to God. **3.** unchanged by time; immutable: *eternal truths.* **4.** seemingly unceasing. [C14: from LL, from L *aeternus*; rel. to L *aevum* age] — **ˌeterˈnality** *or* **eˈternalness** *n.*

eternalize (ɪˈtɜːnəˌlaɪz) *or* **eternize** (ɪˈtɜːnaɪz), **-ise** *vb.* (*tr.*) **1.** to make eternal. **2.** to make famous for ever; immortalize. — **eˌternaliˈzation** *or* **eˌterniˈzation, -iˈsation** *n.*

eternal triangle *n.* an emotional relationship in which there are conflicts involving a man and two women or a woman and two men.

eternity (ɪˈtɜːnɪtɪ) *n.*, *pl.* **-ties. 1.** endless or infinite time. **2.** the quality, state, or condition of being eternal. **3.** (*usually pl.*) any aspect of life and thought considered timeless. **4.** the timeless existence, believed by some to characterize the afterlife. **5.** a seemingly endless period of time.

eternity ring *n.* a ring given as a token of lasting affection, esp. one set all around with stones to symbolize continuity.

etesian (ɪˈtiːʒɪən) *adj.* (of NW winds) recurring annually in the summer in the E Mediterranean. [C17: from L *etēsius* yearly, from Gk *etos* year]

Eth. *abbrev. for:* **1.** Ethiopia(n). **2.** Ethiopic.

-eth[1] *suffix.* forming the archaic third person singular present indicative tense of verbs: *goeth; taketh.* [OE *-eth, -th*]

-eth[2] *suffix forming ordinal numbers.* a variant of **-th**[2]: *twentieth.*

ethane (ˈiːθeɪn, ˈɛθ-) *n.* a colourless odourless flammable gaseous alkane obtained from natural gas and petroleum: used as a fuel. Formula: C_2H_6. [C19: from ETH(YL) + -ANE]

ethanediol (ˈiːθeɪnˌdaɪɒl, ˈɛθ-) *n.* a colourless soluble liquid used as an antifreeze and solvent. Formula: $C_2H_4(OH)_2$. [C20: from ETHANE + DI-[1] + -OL[1]]

ethanoic acid (ˌɛθəˈnəʊɪk, ˌiːθə-) *n.* the systematic name for **acetic acid.**

ethanal (ˈɛθəˌnæl) *n.* the systematic name for **acetaldehyde.**

ethanol (ˈɛθəˌnɒl, ˈiːθə-) *n.* the systematic name for **alcohol** (sense 1).

Ethelbert (ˈɛθəlˌbɜːt) *or* **Æthelbert** (ˈæθəlˌbɜːt) *n.* ?552–616 A.D., king of Kent (560–616): converted to Christianity by St. Augustine; issued the earliest known code of English laws.

Ethelred I (ˈɛθəlˌrɛd) *or* **Æthelred** (ˈæθəlˌrɛd) *n.* died 871, king of Wessex (866–71). He led resistance to the Danish invasion of England; died following his victory at Ashdown.

Ethelred II *or* **Æthelred** *n.* known as *Ethelred the Unready.* ?968–1016 A.D., king of England (978–1016). He was temporarily deposed by the Danish king Sweyn (1013) but was recalled on Sweyn's death (1014).

ethene (ˈɛθiːn) *n.* the systematic name for **ethylene.**

ether (ˈiːθə) *n.* **1.** Also called: **diethyl ether, ethyl ether, ethoxyethane.** a colourless volatile highly flammable liquid: used as a solvent and anaesthetic. Formula: $C_2H_5OC_2H_5$. **2.** any of a class of organic compounds with the general formula ROR′, as in methyl ethyl ether, $CH_3OC_2H_5$. **3.** the medium formerly believed to fill all space and to support the propagation of electromagnetic waves. **4.** *Greek myth.* the upper regions of the atmosphere; clear sky or heaven. ~Also (for senses 3 and 4): **aether.** [C17: from L, from Gk *aithein* to burn] — **etheric** (iːˈθɛrɪk) *adj.*

ethereal (ɪˈθɪərɪəl) *adj.* **1.** extremely delicate or refined. **2.** almost as light as air; airy. **3.** celestial or spiritual. **4.** of, containing, or dissolved in an ether, esp. diethyl ether.

5. of or relating to the ether. [C16: from L, from Gk *aithēr* ETHER] —**e,there'ality** or **e'therealness** n.

etherealize or **-ise** (ɪ'θɪərɪə,laɪz) vb. (tr.) **1.** to make or regard as being ethereal. **2.** to add ether to or make into ether. —**e,thereali'zation** or **-i'sation** n.

Etherege ('εθərɪdʒ) n. Sir George. ?1635–?92, English Restoration dramatist; author of the comedies *The Comical Revenge* (1664), *She would if she could* (1668), and *The Man of Mode* (1676).

etherize or **-ise** ('i:θə,raɪz) vb. (tr.) Obs. to subject (a person) to the anaesthetic influence of ether fumes; anaesthetize. —**,etheri'zation** or **-i'sation** n. —**'ether,izer** or **-,iser** n.

ethic ('εθɪk) n. **1.** a moral principle or set of moral values held by an individual or group. ~adj. **2.** another word for **ethical**. [C15: from L, from Gk *ēthos* custom]

ethical ('εθɪkəl) adj. **1.** in accordance with principles of conduct that are considered correct, esp. those of a given profession or group. **2.** of or relating to ethics. **3.** (of a medicinal agent) available legally only with a doctor's prescription. —**'ethicalness** or **,ethi'cality** n.

ethics ('εθɪks) n. **1.** (functioning as sing.) the philosophical study of the moral value of human conduct and of the rules and principles that ought to govern it. **2.** (functioning as pl.) a code of behaviour considered correct, esp. that of a particular group, profession, or individual. **3.** (functioning as pl.) the moral fitness of a decision, course of action, etc. —**ethicist** ('εθɪsɪst) n.

Ethiopia (,i:θɪ'əupɪə) n. a state in NE Africa, on the Red Sea: consolidated as an empire under Menelik II (1889–1913); federated with Eritrea in 1952; Emperor Haile Selassie was deposed by the military in 1974 and the monarchy was abolished in 1975; an independence movement in Eritrea, has been engaged in war with the government since 1961. It lies along the Great Rift Valley and consists of deserts in the southeast and northeast and a high central plateau with many rivers (including the Blue Nile) and mountains rising over 4500 m (15 000 ft.); the main export is coffee. Official language: Amharic. Currency: birr. Capital: Addis Ababa. Pop.: 46 000 000 (1986 est.). Area: 1 221 894 sq. km (471 776 sq. miles). Former name: **Abyssinia**.

Ethiopian (,i:θɪ'əupɪən) adj. **1.** of or relating to Ethiopia, its people, or any of their languages. ~n. **2.** a native or inhabitant of Ethiopia. **3.** any of the languages of Ethiopia, esp. Amharic. ~n., adj. **4.** an archaic word for **Negro**.

Ethiopic (,i:θɪ'ɒpɪk, -'əupɪk) n. **1.** the ancient Semitic language of Ethiopia: a Christian liturgical language. **2.** the group of languages developed from this language, including Amharic. ~adj. **3.** denoting or relating to this language or group of languages. **4.** a less common word for **Ethiopian**.

ethnic ('εθnɪk) or **ethnical** adj. **1.** of or relating to a human group having racial, religious, linguistic, and other traits in common. **2.** relating to the classification of mankind into groups, esp. on the basis of racial characteristics. **3.** denoting or deriving from the cultural traditions of a group of people. **4.** characteristic of another culture, esp. a peasant one. ~n. **5.** Chiefly U.S. a member of an ethnic group, esp. a minority one. [C14 (in the senses: heathen, Gentile): from LL *ethnicus*, from Gk *ethnos* race] —**ethnicity** (εθ'nɪsɪtɪ) n.

ethno- combining form. indicating race, people, or culture. [via F from Gk *ethnos* race]

ethnocentrism (,εθnəʊ'sεn,trɪzəm) n. belief in the intrinsic superiority of the nation, culture, or group to which one belongs. —**,ethno'centric** adj. —**,ethno'centrically** adv. —**,ethnocen'tricity** n.

ethnography (εθ'nɒɡrəfɪ) n. the branch of anthropology that deals with the scientific description of individual human societies. —**eth'nographer** n. —**ethnographic** (,εθnəʊ'ɡræfɪk) or **,ethno'graphical** adj.

ethnology (εθ'nɒlədʒɪ) n. the branch of anthropology that deals with races and peoples, their origins, characteristics, etc. —**ethnologic** (,εθnə'lɒdʒɪk) or **,ethno'logical** adj. —**eth'nologist** n.

ethnomusicology (,εθnəʊ,mju:zɪ'kɒlədʒɪ) n. the study of the origins of music, esp. from non-European cultures.

ethology (ɪ'θɒlədʒɪ) n. the study of the behaviour of animals in their normal environment. [C17 (in the obs. sense: mimicry): via L from Gk *ēthos* character; current sense, C19] —**ethological** (,εθə'lɒdʒɪkəl) adj. —**e'thologist** n.

ethos ('i:θɒs) n. the distinctive character, spirit, and attitudes of a people, culture, era, etc.: *the revolutionary ethos*. [C19: from LL: habit, from Gk]

ethyl ('i:θaɪl, 'εθɪl) n. (modifier) of, consisting of, or containing the monovalent group C_2H_5-. [C19: from ETH(ER) + -YL] —**ethylic** (ɪ'θɪlɪk) adj.

ethyl acetate n. a colourless volatile flammable liquid ester: used in perfumes and flavourings and as a solvent. Formula: $CH_3COOC_2H_5$.

ethyl alcohol n. another name for **alcohol** (sense 1).

ethylene ('εθɪ,li:n) or **ethene** ('εθi:n) n. a colourless flammable gaseous alkene used in the manufacture of polythene and other chemicals. Formula: $CH_2:CH_2$. —**ethylenic** (,εθɪ'li:nɪk) adj.

ethylene glycol n. another name for **ethanediol**.

ethylene group or **radical** n. Chem. the divalent group, $-CH_2CH_2-$, derived from ethylene.

ethylene series n. Chem. another name for **alkene series**.

ethyne ('εθaɪn) n. Chem. the systematic name for **acetylene**.

ethyne series n. Chem. another name for **acetylene series**.

Étienne (French etjεn) n. a variant spelling of **Estienne**.

etiolate ('i:tɪəʊ,leɪt) vb. **1.** Bot. to whiten (a green plant) through lack of sunlight. **2.** to become or cause to become pale and weak. [C18: from F *étioler* to make pale, prob. from OF *estuble* straw, from L *stipula*] —**,etio'lation** n.

etiology or **aetiology** (,i:tɪ'ɒlədʒɪ) n., pl. **-gies**. **1.** the philosophy or study of causation. **2.** the study of the causes of diseases. **3.** the cause of a disease. [C16: from LL *aetiologia*, from Gk *aitiologia* from *aitia* cause] —**etiological** or **aetiological** (,i:tɪə'lɒdʒɪkəl) adj. —**,eti'ologist** or **,aeti'ologist** n.

etiquette ('εtɪ,kεt, ,εtɪ'kεt) n. **1.** the customs or rules governing behaviour regarded as correct in social life. **2.** a conventional code of practice followed in certain professions or groups. [C18: from F, from OF *estiquette* label, from *estiquier* to attach; see STICK[2]]

Etna ('εtnə) n. Mount. an active volcano in E Sicily: the highest volcano in Europe and the highest peak in Italy south of the Alps. Height: 3323 m (10 902 ft.).

Eton ('i:t[2]n) n. **1.** a town in S England, in Berkshire near the River Thames: site of **Eton College**, a public school for boys founded in 1440. Pop.: 3473 (1983). **2.** this college. —**Etonian** (i:'təʊnɪən) adj., n.

Eton collar n. a broad stiff white collar worn outside a Eton jacket.

Eton crop n. a very short mannish hairstyle worn by women in the 1920s.

Eton jacket n. a waist-length jacket with a V-shaped back, open in front, formerly worn by pupils of Eton College.

Etruria (ɪ'trʊərɪə) n. **1.** an ancient country of central Italy, between the Rivers Arno and Tiber, roughly corresponding to present-day Tuscany and part of Umbria. **2.** a factory established in Staffordshire by Josiah Wedgwood in 1769.

Etruscan (ɪ'trʌskən) or **Etrurian** (ɪ'trʊərɪən) n. **1.** a member of an ancient people of Etruria whose civilization greatly influenced the Romans. **2.** the language of the ancient Etruscans. ~adj. **3.** of or relating to Etruria, the Etruscans, their culture, or their language.

et seq. abbrev. for: **1.** et sequens [L: and the following] **2.** Also: **et seqq.** et sequentia [L: and those that follow]

-ette suffix of nouns. **1.** small: *cigarette*. **2.** female: *majorette*. **3.** (esp. in trade names) imitation: *Leatherette*. [from F, fem. of -ET]

étude ('eɪtju:d) n. a short musical composition for a solo instrument, esp. one designed as an exercise or exploiting virtuosity. [C19: from F: STUDY]

ety., etym., or **etymol.** abbrev. for: **1.** etymological. **2.** etymology.

etymology (,εtɪ'mɒlədʒɪ) n., pl. **-gies**. **1.** the study of the sources and development of words. **2.** an account of the source and development of a word. [C14: via L from Gk; see ETYMON, -LOGY] —**etymological** (,εtɪmə'lɒdʒɪkəl) adj. —**,ety'mologize** or **-gise** vb.

etymon ('εtɪ,mɒn) n., pl. **-mons** or **-ma** (-mə). a form of a word, usually the earliest recorded form or a reconstructed form, from which another word is derived. [C16: via L from Gk *etumon* basic meaning, from *etumos* true, actual]

Etzel ('ɛtsəl) *n. German legend.* a great king who, according to the *Nibelungenlied*, was the second husband of Kriemhild after the death of Siegfried: identified with Attila the Hun. Compare **Atli.**

Eu *the chemical symbol for* europium.

eu- *prefix.* well, pleasant, or good: *eupeptic; euphony.* [via L from Gk, from *eus* good]

Euboea (ju:'bɪə) *n.* an island in the W Aegean Sea: the largest island after Crete of the Greek archipelago; linked with the mainland by a bridge across the Euripus channel. Capital: Chalcis. Pop.: 188 410 (1981). Area: 3908 sq. km (1509 sq. miles). Modern Greek name: **Évvoia.** Former English name: **Eu'boean** *adj., n.*

eucalyptus (ˌjuːkə'lɪptəs) *or* **eucalypt** ('juːkə,lɪpt) *n., pl.* **-lyptuses, -lypti** (-'lɪptaɪ), *or* **-lypts.** any tree of the mostly Australian genus *Eucalyptus,* widely cultivated for timber and gum, as ornament, and for the medicinal oil in their leaves (**eucalyptus oil**). [C19: NL, from EU- + Gk *kaluptos* covered, from *kaluptein* to cover, hide]

Eucharist ('juːkərɪst) *n.* **1.** the Christian sacrament in which Christ's Last Supper is commemorated by the consecration of bread and wine. **2.** the consecrated elements of bread and wine offered in the sacrament. [C14: via Church L from Gk *eukharistos* thankful, from EU- + *kharis* favour] —,**Eucha'ristic** *or* ,**Eucha'ristical** *adj.*

euchre ('juːkə) *n.* **1.** a U.S. and Canad. card game for two, three, or four players, using a poker pack. **2.** an instance of euchring another player. ~*vb.* (*tr.*) **3.** to prevent (a player) from making his contracted tricks. **4.** (usually foll. by *out*) *U.S., Canad., Austral., & N.Z. inf.* to outwit or cheat. [C19: from ?]

Eucken (*German* 'ɔykən) *n.* **Rudolph Christoph** ('ruːdɔlf 'krɪstɔf). 1846–1926, German idealist philosopher: Nobel prize for literature 1908.

Euclid ('juːklɪd) *n.* **1.** 3rd century B.C., Greek mathematician of Alexandria; author of *Elements,* which sets out the principles of geometry and remained a text until the 19th century at least. **2.** the works of Euclid, esp. his system of geometry. —**Euclidean** *or* **Euclidian** (ju:'klɪdɪən) *adj.*

eucryphia (ju:'krɪfɪə) *n.* any of various mostly evergreen trees and shrubs of S America and Australia. [NL, from EU- + Gk *kryphios* covered]

eudiometer (ˌjuːdɪ'ɒmɪtə) *n.* a graduated glass tube used in the study and volumetric analysis of gas reactions. [C18: from Gk *eudios,* lit.: clear-skied + -METER]

Eudoxus of Cnidus (ju:'dɒksəs; 'naɪdəs) *n.* ?406–?355 B.C., Greek astronomer and mathematician; believed to have calculated the length of the solar year.

Eugène (*French* øʒɛn) *n.* **Prince,** title of *François Eugène de Savoie-Carignan.* 1663–1736, Austrian general, born in France: with Marlborough defeated the French at Blenheim (1704), Oudenaarde (1708), and Malplaquet (1709).

eugenics (ju:'dʒɛnɪks) *n.* (*functioning as sing.*) the study of methods of improving the quality of the human race, esp. by selective breeding. [C19: from Gk *eugenēs* well-born, from EU- + *-genēs* born; see -GEN] —**eu'genic** *adj.* —**eu'genically** *adv.* —**eu'genicist** *n.* —**eugenist** ('juːdʒənɪst) *n., adj.*

Eugénie (*French* øʒeni) *n.* original name *Eugénia Maria de Montijo de Guzman, Comtesse de Téba.* 1826–1920, Empress of France (1853–71) as wife of Napoleon III.

eukaryote *or* **eucaryote** (ju:'kærɪɒt) *n.* an organism having cells each with a nucleus in which the genetic material is carried on chromosomes. Cf. **prokaryote.** [from EU- from KARYO- + -ote as in zygote]

Euler (*German* 'ɔylər) *n.* **Leonhard** ('leːɔnhart). 1707–83, Swiss mathematician, noted esp. for his work on the calculus of variation: considered the founder of modern mathematical analysis.

eulogize *or* **-gise** ('juːlə,dʒaɪz) *vb.* to praise (a person or thing) highly in speech or writing. —**'eulogist, 'eulo,gizer,** *or* **-giser** *n.* —,**eulo'gistic** *or* ,**eulo'gistical** *adj.*

eulogy ('juːlədʒɪ) *n., pl.* **-gies. 1.** a speech or piece of writing praising a person or thing, esp. a person who has recently died. **2.** high praise or commendation. ~Also called (*archaic*): **eulogium** (ju:'ləʊdʒɪəm). [C16: from LL, from Gk: praise, from EU- + -LOGY]

Eumenides (ju:'mɛnɪ,diːz) *pl. n.* another name for the **Furies,** used by the Greeks as a euphemism. [from Gk, lit: the benevolent ones, from *eumenēs* benevolent, from EU- + *menos* spirit]

eunuch ('juːnək) *n.* **1.** a man who has been castrated, esp. (formerly) for some office such as a guard in a harem. **2.** *Inf.* an ineffective man. [C15: via L from Gk *eunoukhos* bedchamber attendant, from *eunē* bed + *ekhein* to have, keep]

euonymus (ju:'ɒnɪməs) *or* **evonymus** (ɛ'vɒnɪməs) *n.* any tree or shrub of the N temperate genus *Euonymus,* such as the spindle tree. [C18: from L: spindle tree, from Gk *euōnumos* fortunately named, from EU- + *onoma* NAME]

Eupen and Malmédy (*French* øpɛn; malmedi) *n.* a region of Belgium in Liège province: ceded by Germany in 1919. Pop.: 18 540 (1983 est.).

eupepsia (ju:'pɛpsɪə) *or* **eupepsy** (ju:'pɛpsɪ) *n. Physiol.* good digestion. [C18: from NL, from Gk, from EU- + *pepsis* digestion] —**eupeptic** (ju:'pɛptɪk) *adj.*

euphemism ('juːfɪ,mɪzəm) *n.* **1.** an inoffensive word or phrase substituted for one considered offensive or hurtful. **2.** the use of such inoffensive words or phrases. [C17: from Gk, from EU- + *phēmē* speech] —,**euphe'mistic** *adj.* —,**euphe'mistically** *adv.*

euphemize *or* **-mise** ('juːfɪ,maɪz) *vb.* to speak in euphemisms or refer to by means of a euphemism. —'**euphe,mizer** *or* -,**miser** *n.*

euphonic (ju:'fɒnɪk) *or* **euphonious** (ju:'fəʊnɪəs) *adj.* **1.** denoting or relating to euphony; pleasing to the ear. **2.** (of speech sounds) altered for ease of pronunciation. —**eu'phonically** *or* **eu'phoniously** *adv.* —**eu'phoniousness** *n.*

euphonium (ju:'fəʊnɪəm) *n.* a brass musical instrument with four valves. [C19: NL, from EUPH(ONY + HARM)O-NIUM]

euphonize *or* **-nise** ('juːfə,naɪz) *vb.* **1.** to make pleasant to hear. **2.** to change (speech sounds) so as to facilitate pronunciation.

euphony ('juːfənɪ) *n., pl.* **-nies. 1.** the alteration of speech sounds, esp. by assimilation, so as to make them easier to pronounce. **2.** a pleasing sound, esp. in speech. [C17: from LL, from Gk, from EU- + *phōnē* voice]

euphorbia (ju:'fɔːbɪə) *n.* any plant of the genus *Euphorbia,* such as the spurges. [C14 *euforbia,* from L *euphorbea* African plant, after *Euphorbus,* first-cent. A.D. Gk physician]

euphoria (ju:'fɔːrɪə) *n.* a feeling of great elation, esp. when exaggerated. [C19: from Gk: good ability to endure, from EU- + *pherein* to bear] —**euphoric** (ju:'fɒrɪk) *adj.*

euphoriant (ju:'fɔːrɪənt) *adj.* **1.** able to produce euphoria. ~*n.* **2.** a euphoriant drug or agent.

euphotic (ju:'fəʊtɪk, -'fɒt-) *adj.* denoting or relating to the uppermost part of a sea or lake, which receives enough light for photosynthesis to take place. [C20: from EU- + PHOTIC]

euphrasy ('juːfrəsɪ) *n., pl.* **-sies.** another name for **eyebright.** [C15: *eufrasie,* from Med. L, from Gk *euphrasia* gladness, from EU- + *phrēn* mind]

Euphrates (ju:'freɪtiːz) *n.* a river in SW Asia, rising in E Turkey and flowing south across Syria and Iraq to join the Tigris, forming the Shatt-al-Arab, which flows to the head of the Persian Gulf: important in ancient times for the extensive irrigation of its valley (in Mesopotamia). Length: 3598 km (2235 miles).

Euphrosyne (ju:'frɒzɪ,niː) *n. Greek myth.* one of the three Graces. [from Gk: mirth, merriment]

euphuism ('juːfjuː,ɪzəm) *n.* **1.** an artificial prose style of the Elizabethan period, marked by extreme use of antithesis, alliteration, and extended similes and allusions. **2.** any stylish affectation in speech or writing. [C16: after *Euphues,* prose romance by John LYLY] —'**euphuist** *n.* —,**euphu'istic** *or* ,**euphu'istical** *adj.* —,**euphu'istically** *adv.*

Eur. *abbrev. for* Europe(an).

Eur- *combining form.* a variant of **Euro-** before a vowel.

Eurasia (jʊə'reɪʃə, -ʒə) *n.* the continents of Europe and Asia considered as a whole.

Eurasian (jʊə'reɪʃən, -ʒən) *adj.* **1.** of or relating to Eurasia. **2.** of mixed European and Asian descent. ~*n.* **3.** a person of mixed European and Asian descent.

Euratom (jʊə'rætəm) *n.* short for **European Atomic Energy Community;** an authority established by the Common Market to develop peaceful uses of nuclear energy.

Eure (*French* œr) *n.* a department of N France, in Haute-Normandie region. Capital: Évreux. Pop.: 462 323 (1982). Area: 6037 sq. km (2354 sq. miles).

Eure-et-Loir (*French* œrelwar) *n.* a department of N central France, in Centre region. Capital: Chartres. Pop.: 362 813 (1982). Area: 5940 sq. km (2317 sq. miles).

eureka (ju'ri:kə) *interj.* an exclamation of triumph on discovering or solving something. [C17: from Gk *heurēka* I have found (it), from *heuriskein* to find; traditionally the exclamation of Archimedes when he realized, during bathing, that the volume of an irregular solid could be calculated by measuring the water displaced when it was immersed]

eurhythmic (ju:'rıðmık), **eurhythmical**, *or esp. U.S.* **eurythmic, eurythmical** *adj.* **1.** having a pleasing and harmonious rhythm, order, or structure. **2.** of or relating to eurhythmics. [C19: from L, from Gk, from EU- + *rhuthmos* proportion, RHYTHM]

eurhythmics *or esp. U.S.* **eurythmics** (ju:'rıðmıks) *n.* (*functioning as sing.*) **1.** a system of training through physical movement to music. **2.** dancing of this style. [C20: from EURHYTHMIC] —**eu'rhythmy** *or* **eu'rythmy** *n.*

Euripides (ju'rıpı,di:z) *n.* ?480–406 B.C., Greek tragic dramatist. His plays, 18 of which are extant, include *Alcestis, Medea, Hippolytus, Hecuba, Trojan Women, Electra, Iphigeneia in Tauris, Iphigeneia in Aulis*, and *Bacchae.*

Euro- ('juərəʊ) *or before a vowel* **Eur-** *combining form.* Europe *or* European.

Eurobond ('juərəʊ,bɒnd) *n.* a bond sold in countries other than the country in the currency of which it is issued.

Eurocommunism (,juərəʊ'kɒmju,nızəm) *n.* the policies, doctrines, and practices of Communist Parties in Western Europe, esp. insofar as these favour nonalignment with Russia or China. —,**Euro'communist** *n., adj.*

Eurocrat ('juərə,kræt) *n.* a member of the administration of the Common Market.

Eurocurrency ('juːrəʊ,kʌrənsı) *n.* the currency of any country held on deposit in Europe outside its home market: used as a source of short- or medium-term finance because of easy convertibility.

Europa (ju'rəʊpə) *n. Greek myth.* a Phoenician princess who had three children by Zeus in Crete, where he had taken her after assuming the guise of a white bull. Their offspring were Rhadamanthys, Minos, and Sarpedon.

Europe ('juərəp) *n.* **1.** the second smallest continent, forming the W extension of Eurasia: the border with Asia runs from the Urals to the Caspian and the Black Sea. The coastline is generally extremely indented and there are several peninsulas (notably Scandinavia, Italy, and Iberia) and offshore islands (including the British Isles and Iceland). It contains a series of great mountain systems in the south (Pyrenees, Alps, Apennines, Carpathians, Caucasus), a large central plain, and a N region of lakes and mountains in Scandinavia. Pop.: 492 000 000 (1985). Area: about 10 400 000 sq. km (4 000 000 sq. miles). **2.** *Brit.* the continent of Europe except for the British Isles: *we're going to Europe for our holiday.* **3.** *Brit.* the Common Market: *when did Britain go into Europe?*

European (,juərə'pıən) *adj.* **1.** of or relating to Europe or its inhabitants. **2.** native to or derived from Europe. ~*n.* **3.** a native or inhabitant of Europe. **4.** a person of European descent. **5.** *S. African.* any White person. —,**Euro'pean,ism** *n.*

European Community *or* **European Economic Community** *n.* the official name for the **Common Market.** Abbrev.: **EEC.**

European Currency Unit *n.* a unit of account used as a reserve asset within the European Monetary System. Abbrev.: **ECU**

Europeanize *or* **-ise** (,juərə'pıə,naız) *vb.* (*tr.*) **1.** to make European. **2.** to integrate (a country, economy, etc.) into the Common Market. —,**Euro,peani'zation** *or* **-i'sation** *n.*

European Monetary System *n.* the system enabling members of the EEC to coordinate their exchange rates by linking them to the ECU. Abbrev.: **EMS**

European Parliament *n.* the assembly of the European Economic Community in Strasbourg.

europium (ju'rəʊpıəm) *n.* a silvery-white element of the lanthanide series of metals. Symbol: Eu; atomic no.: 63; atomic wt.: 151.96. [C20: after EUROPE + -IUM]

Europoort (*Dutch* 'ø:ro:po:rt) *n.* a port in the Netherlands near Rotterdam: developed in the 1960s; handles chiefly oil.

Eurus ('juərəs) *n. Greek myth.* the east or southeast wind personified. [L, from Gk *euros*]

Euryale (ju'raıəlı) *n. Greek myth.* one of the three Gorgons.

Eurydice (ju'rıdısı) *n. Greek myth.* a dryad married to Orpheus, who sought her in Hades after she died. She would have been able to leave Hades with him had he not broken his pact and looked back at her.

Eurystheus (ju'rısθju:s, -θıəs) *n. Greek myth.* a grandson of Perseus, who, through the favour of Hera, inherited the kingship of Mycenae, which Zeus had intended for Hercules.

eurythmics (ju:'rıðmıks) *n.* a variant spelling (esp. U.S.) of **eurhythmics.**

Eusebius (ju:'si:bıəs) *n.* ?265–?340 A.D., bishop of Caesarea: author of a history of the Christian Church to 324 A.D.

Eustachian tube (ju:'steıʃən) *n.* a tube that connects the middle ear with the pharynx and equalizes the pressure between the two sides of the eardrum. [C18: after Bartolomeo *Eustachio*, 16th-cent. It. anatomist]

eustatic (ju:'stætık) *adj.* denoting or relating to worldwide changes in sea level, caused by the melting of ice sheets, sedimentation, etc. [C20: from Gk, from EU- + STATIC] —**eustasy** ('ju:stəsı) *n.*

eutectic (ju:'tɛktık) *adj.* **1.** (of a mixture of substances) having the lowest freezing point of all possible mixtures of the substances. **2.** concerned with or suitable for the formation of eutectic mixtures. ~*n.* **3.** a eutectic mixture. **4.** the temperature at which a eutectic mixture forms. [C19: from Gk *eutēktos* melting readily, from EU- + *tēkein* to melt]

Euterpe (ju:'tɜːpı) *n. Greek myth.* the Muse of lyric poetry and music. —**Eu'terpean** *adj.*

euthanasia (,ju:θə'neızıə) *n.* the act of killing someone painlessly, esp. to relieve suffering from an incurable illness. [C17: via NL from Gk: easy death, from EU- + *thanatos* death]

euthenics (ju:'θɛnıks) *n.* (*functioning as sing.*) the study of the control of the environment, esp. with a view to improving the health and living standards of the human race. [C20: from Gk *euthēnein* to thrive] —**eu'thenist** *n.*

eutrophic (ju:'trɒfık, -'trəʊ-) *adj.* (of lakes, etc.) rich in organic and mineral nutrients and supporting an abundant plant life. [C18: prob. from *eutrophy*, from Gk, from *eutrophos* well-fed, from EU- + *trephein* to nourish] —'**eutrophy** *n.*

Euxine Sea ('ju:ksaın) *n.* another name for the **Black Sea.**

eV *abbrev. for* electronvolt.

EVA *Astronautics. abbrev. for* extravehicular activity.

evacuate (ı'vækju,eıt) *vb.* (*mainly tr.*) **1.** (*also intr.*) to withdraw or cause to withdraw (from a place of danger) to a place of safety. **2.** to make empty. **3.** (*also intr.*) *Physiol.* **a.** to eliminate or excrete (faeces). **b.** to discharge (any waste) from (the body). **4.** (*tr.*) to create a vacuum in (a bulb, flask, etc.). [C16: from L *ēvacuāre* to void, from *vacuus* empty] —**e,vacu'ation** *n.* —**e'vacuative** *adj.* —**e'vacu,ator** *n.* —**e,vacu'ee** *n.*

evade (ı'veıd) *vb.* (*mainly tr.*) **1.** to get away from or avoid (imprisonment, captors, etc.). **2.** to get around, shirk, or dodge (the law, a duty, etc.). **3.** (*also intr.*) to avoid answering (a question). [C16: from F, from L *ēvādere* to go forth] —**e'vadable** *adj.* —**e'vader** *n.* —**e'vadingly** *adv.*

evaginate (ı'vædʒı,neıt) *vb.* (*tr.*) *Med.* to turn (an organ or part) inside out. [C17: from LL *ēvāginare* to unsheathe, from L *vāgina* sheath]

evaluate (ı'vælju,eıt) *vb.* (*tr.*) **1.** to ascertain or set the amount or value of. **2.** to judge or assess the worth of. [C19: back formation from *evaluation*, from F, from *évaluer*; see VALUE] —**e,valu'ation** *n.* —**e'valuative** *adj.* —**e'valu,ator** *n.*

evanesce (,ɛvə'nɛs) *vb.* (*intr.*) (of smoke, mist, etc.) to fade gradually from sight; vanish. [C19: from L *ēvānēscere* to disappear; see VANISH]

evanescent (,ɛvə'nɛs²nt) *adj.* **1.** passing out of sight; fading away; vanishing. **2.** ephemeral or transitory. —,**eva'nescence** *n.*

evangel (ı'vændʒəl) *n.* **1.** *Arch.* the gospel of Christianity. **2.** (*often cap.*) any of the four Gospels of the New Testament. **3.** any body of teachings regarded as basic. [C14: from Church L, from Gk *evangelion* good news, from EU- + *angelos* messenger; see ANGEL]

evangelical (ˌiːvænˈdʒɛlɪkəl) *Christianity.* ~*adj.* **1.** of or following from the Gospels. **2.** denoting or relating to any of certain Protestant sects, which emphasize personal conversion and faith in atonement through the death of Christ as a means of salvation. **3.** denoting or relating to an evangelical. ~*n.* **4.** a member of an evangelical sect. —ˌevanˈgelicalism *n.*

evangelism (ɪˈvændʒɪˌlɪzəm) *n.* **1.** the practice of spreading the Christian gospel. **2.** ardent or missionary zeal for a cause.

evangelist (ɪˈvændʒɪlɪst) *n.* **1.** an occasional preacher, sometimes itinerant. **2.** a preacher of the Christian gospel. —eˌvangeˈlistic *adj.*

Evangelist (ɪˈvændʒɪlɪst) *n.* any of the writers of the New Testament Gospels: Matthew, Mark, Luke, or John.

evangelize *or* **-lise** (ɪˈvændʒɪˌlaɪz) *vb.* **1.** to preach the Christian gospel (to). **2.** (*intr.*) to advocate a cause with the object of making converts. —eˌvangeliˈzation *or* -liˈsation *n.* —eˈvangeˌlizer *or* -ˌliser *n.*

Evans (ˈɛvənz) *n.* **1.** Sir **Arthur John.** 1851–1941, English archaeologist, whose excavations of the palace of Knossos in Crete provided evidence for the existence of the Minoan civilization. **2.** (**Arthur**) **Mostyn,** known as *Moss Evans.* born 1925, British trade-union leader; general secretary of the Transport and General Workers' Union from 1978. **3.** Dame **Edith.** 1888–1976, English actress. **4.** Sir **Geraint** (**Llewellyn**). born 1922, Welsh operatic baritone. **5.** **Herbert McLean.** 1882–1971, U.S. anatomist and embryologist; discoverer of vitamin E (1922). **6.** **Mary Ann.** real name of (George) **Eliot.**

Evanston (ˈɛvənstən) *n.* a city in NE Illinois, on Lake Michigan north of Chicago: Northwestern University (1851). Pop.: 73 706 (1980).

Evansville (ˈɛvənzˌvɪl) *n.* a city in SW Indiana, on the Ohio River. Pop.: 129 480 (1986 est.).

evaporate (ɪˈvæpəˌreɪt) *vb.* **1.** to change or cause to change from a liquid or solid state to a vapour. **2.** to lose or cause to lose liquid by vaporization leaving a more concentrated residue. **3.** to disappear or cause to disappear. [C16: from LL, from L *vapor* steam; see VAPOUR] —eˈvaporable *adj.* —eˌvapoˈration *n.* —eˈvaporative *adj.* —eˈvapoˌrator *n.*

evaporated milk *n.* thick unsweetened tinned milk from which some of the water has been evaporated.

evasion (ɪˈveɪʒən) *n.* **1.** the act of evading, esp. a distasteful duty, responsibility, etc., by cunning or by illegal means: *tax evasion.* **2.** cunning or deception used to dodge a question, duty, etc.; means of evading. [C15: from LL *ēvāsio;* see EVADE]

evasive (ɪˈveɪsɪv) *adj.* **1.** tending or seeking to evade; not straightforward. **2.** avoiding or seeking to avoid trouble or difficulties. **3.** hard to catch or obtain; elusive. —eˈvasively *adv.* —eˈvasiveness *n.*

Evatt (ˈɛvæt) *n.* **Herbert Vere.** 1894–1965, Australian jurist and Labor political leader, president of the General Assembly of the United Nations 1948–49.

eve (iːv) *n.* **1.** the evening or day before some special event. **2.** the period immediately before an event: *the eve of war.* **3.** an archaic word for **evening.** [C13: var. of EVEN²]

Eve (iːv) *n. Old Testament.* the first woman; mother of the human race, fashioned by God from the rib of Adam (Genesis 2:18-25).

Evelyn (ˈiːvlɪn, ˈɛv-) *n.* **John.** 1620–1706, English author, noted chiefly for his diary (1640–1706).

even¹ (ˈiːvən) *adj.* **1.** level and regular; flat. **2.** (*postpositive;* foll. by *with*) on the same level or in the same plane (as). **3.** without variation or fluctuation; regular; constant. **4.** not readily moved or excited; calm: *an even temper.* **5.** equally balanced between two sides: *an even game.* **6.** equal or identical in number, quantity, etc. **7. a.** (of a number) divisible by two. **b.** characterized or indicated by such a number: *the even pages.* **8.** relating to or denoting two or either of two alternatives, events, etc., that have an equal probability: *an even chance of missing or catching a train.* **9.** having no balance of debt; neither owing nor being owed. **10.** just and impartial; fair. **11.** exact in number, amount, or extent: *an even pound.* **12.** equal, as in score; level. **13.** *even money.* **a.** a bet that wins an identical sum if it succeeds. **b.** (*as modifier*): *the even-money favourite.* **14. get even** (**with**). *Inf.* to exact

revenge (on); settle accounts (with). ~*adv.* **15.** (intensifier; used to suggest that the content of a statement is unexpected or paradoxical): *even an idiot can do that.* **16.** (intensifier; used with comparative forms): *even better.* **17.** notwithstanding; in spite of. **18.** used to introduce a more precise version of a word, phrase, or statement: *he is base, even depraved.* **19.** used preceding a clause or supposition or hypothesis to emphasize that whether or not the condition in it is fulfilled, the statement in the main clause remains valid: *even if she died he wouldn't care.* **20.** *Arch.* all the way; fully: *I love thee even unto death.* **21. even as.** (*conj.*) at the very same moment or in the very same way that. **22. even so.** in spite of any assertion to the contrary: nevertheless. ~See also **even out, evens, even up.** [OE *efen*] —ˈevener *n.* —ˈevenly *adv.* —ˈevenness *n.*

even² (ˈiːvən) *n.* an archaic word for **eve** or **evening.** [OE *æfen*]

even-handed *adj.* fair; impartial. —ˌevenˈhandedly *adv.* —ˌevenˈhandedness *n.*

evening (ˈiːvnɪŋ) *n.* **1.** the latter part of the day, esp. from late afternoon until nightfall. **2.** the latter or concluding period: *the evening of one's life.* **3.** the early part of the night spent in a specified way: *an evening at the theatre.* **4.** (*modifier*) of, used in, or occurring in the evening: *the evening papers.* [OE *æfnung*]

evening dress *n.* attire for a formal occasion during the evening.

evening primrose *n.* any plant of the genus *Oenothera,* typically having yellow flowers that open in the evening.

evenings (ˈiːvnɪŋz) *adv. Inf.* in the evening, esp. regularly.

evening star *n.* a planet, usually Venus, seen shining brightly in the west just after sunset.

even out *vb.* (*adv.*) to make or become even, as by the removal of bumps, inequalities, etc.

evens (ˈiːvənz) *adj., adv.* **1.** (of a bet) winning an identical sum if successful. **2.** (of a runner) offered at such odds.

evensong (ˈiːvənˌsɒŋ) *n.* **1.** Also called: **Evening Prayer, vespers.** *Church of England.* the daily evening service. **2.** *R.C. Church, arch.* another name for **vespers.**

event (ɪˈvɛnt) *n.* **1.** anything that takes place, esp. something important; an incident. **2.** the actual or final outcome (esp. in **in the event, after the event**). **3.** any one contest in a programme of sporting or other contests. **4. at all events** *or* **in any event.** regardless of circumstances; in any case. **5. in the event of.** in case of; if (such a thing) happens. **6. in the event that.** if it should happen that. [C16: from L *ēvenīre* to come forth, happen, from *venīre* to come]

even-tempered *adj.* not easily angered or excited; calm.

eventful (ɪˈvɛntfʊl) *adj.* full of events. —eˈventfully *adv.* —eˈventfulness *n.*

event horizon *n. Astron.* the spherical boundary of a black hole: objects passing through it would disappear completely and for ever, as no information can escape across the event horizon from the interior.

eventide (ˈiːvənˌtaɪd) *n. Arch. or poetic.* another word for **evening.**

eventide home *n. Euphemistic.* an old people's home.

eventing (ɪˈvɛntɪŋ) *n. Chiefly Brit.* the sport of taking part in equestrian competitions (esp. **three-day events**), usually involving cross-country riding, jumping, and dressage.

eventual (ɪˈvɛntʃʊəl) *adj.* **1.** (*prenominal*) happening in due course of time; ultimate. **2.** *Arch.* contingent or possible.

eventuality (ɪˌvɛntʃʊˈælɪtɪ) *n., pl.* **-ties.** a possible event, occurrence, or result; contingency.

eventually (ɪˈvɛntʃʊəlɪ) *adv.* **1.** at the very end; finally. **2.** (*sentence modifier*) after a long time or long delay: *eventually, he arrived.*

eventuate (ɪˈvɛntʃʊˌeɪt) *vb.* (*intr.*) **1.** (often foll. by *in*) to result ultimately (in). **2.** to come about as a result. —eˌventuˈation *n.*

even up *vb.* (*adv.*) to make or become equal, esp. in respect of claims or debts.

ever (ˈɛvə) *adv.* **1.** at any time. **2.** by any chance; in any case: *how did you ever find out?* **3.** at all times; always. **4.** in any possible way or manner: *come as fast as ever you can.* **5.** *Inf., chiefly Brit.* (intensifier, in **ever so, ever such,** and **ever such a**). **6. is he** *or* **she ever!** *U.S.*

& *Canad. sl.* he *or* she displays the quality concerned in abundance. ~See also **for ever.** [OE *æfre*, from ?]

Everest ('ɛvərɪst) *n.* **1. Mount.** a mountain in S Asia on the border between Nepal and Tibet, in the Himalayas: the highest mountain in the world; first climbed by a British expedition (1953). Height: 8848 m (29 028 ft.). **2.** any high point of ambition or achievement. [C19: after Sir G. *Everest* (1790–1866), Surveyor-General of India]

Everglades ('ɛvə,gleɪdz) *pl. n.* **the.** a subtropical marshy region of Florida, south of Lake Okeechobee: contains the **Everglades National Park,** established to preserve the flora and fauna of the swamps. Area: over 13 000 sq. km (5000 sq. miles).

evergreen ('ɛvə,griːn) *adj.* **1.** (of certain trees and shrubs) bearing foliage throughout the year. Cf. **deciduous. 2.** remaining fresh and vital. ~*n.* **3.** an evergreen tree or shrub.

everlasting (,ɛvə'lɑːstɪŋ) *adj.* **1.** never coming to an end; eternal. **2.** lasting for an indefinitely long period. **3.** lasting so long or occurring so often as to become tedious. ~*n.* **4.** eternity. **5.** Also called: **everlasting flower.** another name for **immortelle.** —,ever'lastingly *adv.*

Everly Brothers ('ɛvəlɪ) *pl. n.* **the.** U.S. pop singing duo comprising Don Everly (born 1937) and Phil Everly (born 1939), noted for their close harmonies.

evermore (,ɛvə'mɔː) *adv.* (often preceded by *for*) all time to come.

evert (ɪ'vɜːt) *vb.* (*tr.*) to turn (an eyelid or other bodily part) outwards or inside out. [C16: from L *ēvertere* to overthrow, from *vertere* to turn] —e'versible *adj.* —e'version *n.*

Evert ('ɛvət) *n.* **Chris(tine).** born 1954, U.S. tennis player: Wimbledon champion 1974, 1976, and 1981; U.S. champion 1975–78, 1980, and 1982.

every ('ɛvrɪ) *determiner.* **1.** each one (of the class specified), without exception. **2.** (*not used with a negative*) the greatest or best possible: *every hope.* **3.** each: used before a noun phrase to indicate the recurrent, intermittent, or serial nature of a thing: *every third day.* **4. every bit.** (used in comparisons with *as*) quite; just; equally. **5. every other.** each alternate; every second. **6. every which way.** *U.S. & Canad.* **a.** in all directions; everywhere. **b.** from all sides. [C15 *everich,* from OE *æfre ælc,* from *æfre* EVER + *ælc* EACH]

everybody ('ɛvrɪ,bɒdɪ) *pron.* every person; everyone.
▷ **Usage.** See at **everyone.**

everyday ('ɛvrɪ,deɪ) *adj.* **1.** happening each day. **2.** commonplace or usual. **3.** suitable for or used on ordinary days.

Everyman ('ɛvrɪ,mæn) *n.* **1.** a medieval English morality play in which the central figure represents mankind. **2.** (*often not cap.*) the ordinary person; common man.

everyone ('ɛvrɪ,wʌn, -wən) *pron.* every person; everybody.
▷ **Usage.** Anybody, anyone, everybody, everyone, none, noone, nobody, somebody, someone, and *each* function as singular in careful English: *everyone nodded his head* (not *their heads*). The use of *their* in such constructions is, however, common in informal English.

every one *pron.* each person or thing in a group, without exception.

everything ('ɛvrɪ,θɪŋ) *pron.* **1.** the entirety of a specified or implied class. **2.** a great deal, esp. of something very important.

everywhere ('ɛvrɪ,wɛə) *adv.* to or in all parts or places.

Evesham ('iːvʃəm) *n.* a town in W central England, in E Hereford and Worcester, on the River Avon: scene of the Battle of Evesham in 1265 (Lord Edward's defeat of Simon de Montfort and the barons); centre of the **Vale of Evesham,** famous for market gardens and orchards. Pop.: 15 300 (1985 est.).

evict (ɪ'vɪkt) *vb.* (*tr.*) **1.** to expel (a tenant) from property by process of law; turn out. **2.** to recover (property or the title to property) by judicial process or by virtue of a superior title. [C15: from LL *ēvincere,* from L: to vanquish utterly, from *vincere* to conquer] —e'viction *n.* —e'victor *n.*

evidence ('ɛvɪdəns) *n.* **1.** ground for belief or disbelief; data on which to base proof or to establish truth or falsehood. **2.** a mark or sign that makes evident. **3.** *Law.* matter produced before a court of law in an attempt to prove or disprove a point in issue. **4. in evidence.** on display;

apparent. ~*vb.* (*tr.*) **5.** to make evident; show clearly. **6.** to give proof of or evidence for.

evident ('ɛvɪdənt) *adj.* easy to see or understand; apparent. [C14: from L *ēvidēns,* from *vidēre* to see]

evidential (,ɛvɪ'dɛnʃəl) *adj.* relating to, serving as, or based on evidence. —,evi'dentially *adv.*

evidently ('ɛvɪdəntlɪ) *adv.* **1.** without question; clearly. **2.** to all appearances; apparently.

evil ('iːvəl) *adj.* **1.** morally wrong or bad; wicked. **2.** causing harm or injury. **3.** marked or accompanied by misfortune: *an evil fate.* **4.** (of temper, disposition, etc.) characterized by anger or spite. **5.** infamous: *an evil reputation.* **6.** offensive or unpleasant: *an evil smell.* ~*n.* **7.** the quality or an instance of being morally wrong; wickedness. **8.** (*sometimes cap.*) a force or power that brings about wickedness or harm. ~*adv.* **9.** (*now usually in combination*) in an evil manner; badly: *evil-smelling.* [OE *yfel*] —'evilly *adv.* —'evilness *n.*

evildoer ('iːvəl,duːə) *n.* a person who does evil. —'evil,doing *n.*

evil eye *n.* **the.** **1.** a look or glance superstitiously supposed to have the power of inflicting harm or injury. **2.** the power to inflict harm, etc., by such a look. —,evil-'eyed *adj.*

evil-minded *adj.* inclined to evil thoughts; malicious or spiteful. —,evil-'mindedly *adv.* —,evil-'mindedness *n.*

evince (ɪ'vɪns) *vb.* (*tr.*) to make evident; show (something) clearly. [C17: from L *ēvincere* to overcome; see EVICT] —e'vincible *adj.* —e'vincive *adj.*

eviscerate (ɪ'vɪsə,reɪt) *vb.* (*tr.*) **1.** to remove the internal organs of; disembowel. **2.** to deprive of meaning or significance. [C17: from L *ēviscerāre,* from *viscera* entrails] —e,viscer'ation *n.* —e'viscer,ator *n.*

evocation (,ɛvə'keɪʃən) *n.* the act or an instance of evoking. [C17: from L: see EVOKE] —**evocative** (ɪ'vɒkətɪv) *adj.*

evoke (ɪ'vəʊk) *vb.* (*tr.*) **1.** to call or summon up (a memory, feeling, etc.), esp. from the past. **2.** to provoke; elicit. **3.** to cause (spirits) to appear; conjure up. [C17: from L *ēvocāre* to call forth, from *vocāre* to call] —**evocable** ('ɛvəkəbəl) *adj.* —e'voker *n.*

evolute ('ɛvə,luːt) *n.* a geometric curve that describes the locus of the centres of curvature of another curve (the **involute**). [C19: from L *ēvolūtus* unrolled, from *ēvolvere* to roll out, EVOLVE]

evolution (,iːvə'luːʃən) *n.* **1.** *Biol.* a gradual change in the characteristics of a population of animals or plants over successive generations. **2.** a gradual development, esp. to a more complex form: *the evolution of modern art.* **3.** the act of throwing off, as heat, gas, vapour, etc. **4.** a pattern formed by a series of movements or something similar. **5.** an algebraic operation in which the root of a number, expression, etc., is extracted. **6.** *Mil.* an exercise carried out in accordance with a set procedure or plan. [C17: from L *ēvolūtiō* an unrolling, from *ēvolvere* to EVOLVE] —,evo'lutionary *or* ,evo'lutional *adj.*

evolutionist (,iːvə'luːʃənɪst) *n.* **1.** a person who believes in a theory of evolution. ~*adj.* **2.** of or relating to a theory of evolution. —,evo'lutionism *n.* —,evolution'istic *adj.*

evolve (ɪ'vɒlv) *vb.* **1.** to develop or cause to develop gradually. **2.** (of animal or plant species) to undergo evolution (of organs or parts). **3.** (*tr.*) to yield, emit, or give off (heat, gas, vapour, etc.). [C17: from L *ēvolvere* to unfold, from *volvere* to roll] —e'volvable *adj.* —e'volvement *n.*

Évora (*Portuguese* 'ɛvura) *n.* a city in S central Portugal: ancient Roman settlement; occupied by the Moors from 712 to 1166; residence of the Portuguese court in 15th and 16th centuries. Pop.: 34 072 (1981). Ancient name: **Ebora** ('iːbərə).

Évreux (*French* evrø) *n.* an industrial town in NW France: severely damaged in World War II; cathedral (12th–16th centuries). Pop.: 46 288 (1983 est.).

Évros ('ɛvrɒs) *n.* transliteration of the Modern Greek name for the **Maritsa.**

Évvoia ('ɛvia) *n.* transliteration of the Modern Greek name for **Euboea.**

evzone ('ɛvzəʊn) *n.* a soldier in an elite Greek infantry regiment. [C19: from Mod. Gk, from Gk *euzōnos,* lit.: well-girt, from EU- + *zōnē* girdle]

ewe (juː) *n.* **a.** a female sheep. **b.** (*as modifier*): *a ewe lamb.* [OE *ēowu*]

ewer ('ju:ə) *n.* a large jug or pitcher with a wide mouth. [C14: from OF *evier*, from L *aquārius* water carrier, from *aqua* water]

ex[1] (ɛks) *prep.* **1.** *Finance.* excluding; without: *ex dividend.* **2.** *Commerce.* without charge to the buyer until removed from: *ex warehouse.* [C19: from L: out of, from]

ex[2] (ɛks) *n. Inf.* (a person's) former wife, husband, etc.

Ex. *Bible. abbrev. for* Exodus.

ex-[1] *prefix.* **1.** out of; outside of; from: *exclosure; exurbia.* **2.** former: *ex-wife.* [from L, from *ex* (prep.), identical with Gk *ex, ek*; see EC-]

ex-[2] *combining form.* a variant of **exo-** before a vowel: *exergonic.*

exa- *prefix.* denoting 10^{18}: *exametres.* Symbol: E

exacerbate (ɪg'zæsə,beɪt, ɪk'sæs-) *vb.* (*tr.*) **1.** to make (pain, disease, etc.) more intense; aggravate. **2.** to irritate (a person). [C17: from L *exacerbāre* to irritate, from *acerbus* bitter] —**ex,acer'bation** *n.*

exact (ɪg'zækt) *adj.* **1.** correct in every detail; strictly accurate. **2.** precise, as opposed to approximate. **3.** (*prenominal*) specific; particular. **4.** operating with very great precision. **5.** allowing no deviation from a standard; rigorous; strict. **6.** based on measurement and the formulation of laws, as opposed to description and classification: *an exact science.* ~*vb.* (*tr.*) **7.** to force or compel (payment, etc.); extort: *to exact tribute.* **8.** to demand as a right; insist upon. **9.** to call for or require. [C16: from L *exactus* driven out, from *exigere* to drive forth, from *agere* to drive] —**ex'actable** *adj.* —**ex'actness** *n.* —**ex'actor** *or* **ex'acter** *n.*

exacting (ɪg'zæktɪŋ) *adj.* making rigorous or excessive demands. —**ex'actingness** *n.*

exaction (ɪg'zækʃən) *n.* **1.** the act or an instance of exacting. **2.** an excessive or harsh demand, esp. for money. **3.** a sum or payment exacted.

exactitude (ɪg'zæktɪ,tju:d) *n.* the quality of being exact; precision; accuracy.

exactly (ɪg'zæktlɪ) *adv.* **1.** in an exact manner; accurately or precisely. **2.** in every respect; just. ~*sentence substitute.* **3.** just so!, precisely! **4. not exactly.** *Ironical.* not at all; by no means.

exacum ('ɛksəkəm) *n.* any of various Asian flowering herbs. [NL, from EX-[1] + Gk *ago* to arrive]

exaggerate (ɪg'zædʒə,reɪt) *vb.* **1.** to regard or represent as larger or greater, more important or more successful, etc., than is true. **2.** (*tr.*) to make greater, more noticeable, etc. [C16: from L *exaggerāre* to magnify, from *aggerāre* to heap, from *agger* heap] —**ex'agger,ated** *adj.* —**ex'agger,atingly** *adv.* —**ex,agger'ation** *n.* —**ex'aggerative** *or* **ex'aggeratory** *adj.* —**ex'agger,ator** *n.*

exalt (ɪg'zɔ:lt) *vb.* (*tr.*) **1.** to elevate in rank, dignity, etc. **2.** to praise highly; extol. **3.** to stimulate; excite. **4.** to fill with joy or delight; elate. [C15: from L *exaltāre* to raise, from *altus* high] —**ex'alted** *adj.* —**ex'alter** *n.*

exaltation (,ɛgzɔ:l'teɪʃən) *n.* **1.** the act of exalting or state of being exalted. **2.** exhilaration; elation; rapture.

exam (ɪg'zæm) *n.* short for **examination.**

examination (ɪg,zæmɪ'neɪʃən) *n.* **1.** the act of examining or state of being examined. **2.** *Education.* **a.** written exercises, oral questions, etc., set to test a candidate's knowledge and skill. **b.** (*as modifier*): *an examination paper.* **3.** *Med.* **a.** physical inspection of a patient. **b.** laboratory study of secretory or excretory products, tissue samples, etc. **4.** *Law.* the formal interrogation of a person on oath. —**ex,ami'national** *adj.*

examine (ɪg'zæmɪn) *vb.* (*tr.*) **1.** to inspect or scrutinize carefully or in detail; investigate. **2.** *Education.* to test the knowledge or skill of (a candidate) in (a subject or activity) by written or oral questions, etc. **3.** *Law.* to interrogate (a person) formally on oath. **4.** *Med.* to investigate the state of health of (a patient). [C14: from OF, from L *exāmināre* to weigh, from *exāmen* means of weighing] —**ex'aminable** *adj.* —**ex,ami'nee** *n.* —**ex'aminer** *n.* —**ex'amining** *adj.*

example (ɪg'zɑ:mp[ə]l) *n.* **1.** a specimen or instance that is typical of its group or set; sample. **2.** a person, action, thing, etc., that is worthy of imitation; pattern. **3.** a precedent, illustration of a principle, or model. **4.** a punishment or the recipient of a punishment intended to serve as a warning. **5. for example.** as an illustration; for instance. ~*vb.* **6.** (*tr.; now usually passive*) to present an example of; exemplify. [C14: from OF, from L *exemplum* pattern, from *eximere* to take out]

exanthema (,ɛksæn'θi:mə) *n.*, *pl.* **-themata** (-'θi:mətə) *or* **-themas.** a skin rash occurring in a disease such as measles. [C17: via LL from Gk, from *exanthein* to burst forth, from *anthein* to blossom]

exasperate (ɪg'zɑ:spə,reɪt) *vb.* (*tr.*) **1.** to cause great irritation or anger to. **2.** to cause (something unpleasant) to worsen; aggravate. [C16: from L *exasperāre* to make rough, from *asper* rough] —**ex'asper,atedly** *adv.* —**ex'asper,ater** *n.* —**ex'asper,atingly** *adv.* —**ex,asper'ation** *n.*

ex cathedra (ɛks kə'θi:drə) *adj., adv.* **1.** with authority. **2.** *R.C. Church.* (of doctrines of faith or morals) defined by the pope as infallibly true, to be accepted by all Catholics. [L, lit.: from the chair]

excavate ('ɛkskə,veɪt) *vb.* **1.** to remove (soil, earth, etc.) by digging; dig out. **2.** to make (a hole or tunnel) in (solid matter) by hollowing. **3.** to unearth (buried objects) methodically to discover information about the past. [C16: from L *cavāre* to make hollow, from *cavus* hollow] —,**exca'vation** *n.* —**'exca,vator** *n.*

exceed (ɪk'si:d) *vb.* **1.** to be superior (to); excel. **2.** (*tr.*) to go beyond the limit or bounds of. **3.** (*tr.*) to be greater in degree or quantity than. [C14: from L *excēdere* to go beyond, from *cēdere* to go] —**ex'ceedable** *adj.* —**ex'ceeder** *n.*

exceeding (ɪk'si:dɪŋ) *adj.* **1.** very great; exceptional or excessive. ~*adv.* **2.** *Arch.* to a great or unusual degree. —**ex'ceedingly** *adv.*

excel (ɪk'sɛl) *vb.* **-celling, -celled. 1.** to be superior to (another or others); surpass. **2.** (*intr.*; foll. by *in* or *at*) to be outstandingly good or proficient. [C15: from L *excellere* to rise up]

excellence ('ɛksələns) *n.* **1.** the state or quality of excelling or being exceptionally good; extreme merit. **2.** an action, feature, etc., in which a person excels. —'**excellent** *adj.* —'**excellently** *adv.*

Excellency ('ɛksələnsɪ) *or* **Excellence** *n.*, *pl.* **-lencies** *or* **-lences. 1.** (usually preceded by *Your, His,* or *Her*) a title used to address or refer to a high-ranking official, such as an ambassador. **2.** *R.C. Church.* a title of bishops and archbishops in many non-English-speaking countries.

excelsior (ɪk'sɛlsɪ,ɔ:) *interj., n.* **1.** excellent: used as a motto and as a trademark for various products. **2.** upward. [C19: from L: higher]

except (ɪk'sɛpt) *prep.* **1.** Also: **except for.** other than; apart from. **2. except that.** (*conj.*) but for the fact that; were it not true that. ~*conj.* **3.** an archaic word for **unless.** **4.** *Inf.* (*not standard in the U.S.*) except that; but for the fact that. ~*vb.* **5.** (*tr.*) to leave out; omit; exclude. **6.** (*intr.*; often foll. by *to*) *Rare.* to take exception; object. [C14: from OF *excepter* to leave out, from L *excipere* to take out, from *capere* to take]

excepting (ɪk'sɛptɪŋ) *prep.* **1.** except; except for (esp. in **not excepting**). ~*conj.* **2.** an archaic word for **unless.**

exception (ɪk'sɛpʃən) *n.* **1.** the act of excepting or fact of being excepted; omission. **2.** anything excluded from or not in conformance with a general rule, principle, class, etc. **3.** criticism, esp. adverse; objection. **4.** *Law.* (formerly) a formal objection in legal proceedings. **5. take exception. a.** (usually foll. by *to*) to make objections (to); demur (at). **b.** (often foll. by *at*) to be offended (by); be resentful (at).

exceptionable (ɪk'sɛpʃənəb[ə]l) *adj.* open to or subject to objection; objectionable. —**ex'ceptionableness** *n.* —**ex'ceptionably** *adv.*

exceptional (ɪk'sɛpʃən[ə]l) *adj.* **1.** forming an exception; not ordinary. **2.** having much more than average intelligence, ability, or skill.

excerpt *n.* ('ɛksɜ:pt). **1.** a part or passage taken from a book, speech, etc.; extract. ~*vb.* (ɛk'sɜ:pt). **2.** (*tr.*) to take (a part or passage) from a book, speech, etc. [C17: from L *excerptum*, lit.: (something) picked out, from *excerpere* to select, from *carpere* to pluck] —**ex'cerptible** *adj.* —**ex'cerption** *n.* —**ex'cerptor** *n.*

excess *n.* (ɪk'sɛs, 'ɛksɛs). **1.** the state or act of going beyond normal, sufficient, or permitted limits. **2.** an immoderate or abnormal amount. **3.** the amount, number, etc., by which one thing exceeds another. **4.** overindulgence or intemperance. **5.** *Insurance, chiefly Brit.* a specified contribution towards the cost of a claim, payable by the policyholder. **6. in excess of.** of more than; over. **7. to excess.** to an inordinate extent; immoderately. ~*adj.*

('ɛksɛs, ɪk'sɛs). (*usually prenominal*) **8.** more than normal, necessary, or permitted; surplus: *excess weight.* **9.** payable as a result of previous underpayment: *excess postage.* [C14: from L *excēdere* to go beyond; see EXCEED]
excessive (ɪk'sɛsɪv) *adj.* exceeding the normal or permitted limits; immoderate; inordinate. —**ex'cessively** *adv.* —**ex'cessiveness** *n.*
excess luggage *or* **baggage** *n.* luggage that is more in weight or number of pieces than an airline, etc., will carry free.
exchange (ɪks'tʃeɪndʒ) *vb.* **1.** (*tr.*) to give up or transfer (one thing) for an equivalent. **2.** (*tr.*) to give and receive (information, ideas, etc.); interchange. **3.** (*tr.*) to replace (one thing) with another, esp. to replace unsatisfactory goods. **4.** to hand over (goods) in return for the equivalent value in kind; barter; trade. ~*n.* **5.** the act or process of exchanging. **6. a.** anything given or received as an equivalent or substitute for something else. **b.** (*as modifier*): *an exchange student.* **7.** an argument or quarrel. **8.** Also called: **telephone exchange.** a switching centre in which telephone lines are interconnected. **9.** a place where securities or commodities are sold, bought, or traded, esp. by brokers or merchants. **10. a.** the system by which commercial debts are settled by commercial documents, esp. bills of exchange, instead of by direct payment of money. **b.** the percentage or fee charged for accepting payment in this manner. **11.** a transfer or interchange of sums of money of equivalent value, as between different currencies. **12. win** (*or* **lose**) **the exchange.** *Chess.* to win (*or* lose) a rook in return for a bishop or knight. ~See also **bill of exchange, exchange rate, labour exchange.** [C14: from Anglo-French *eschaungier,* from Vulgar L *excambiāre* (unattested), from L *cambīre* to barter] —**ex'changeable** *adj.* —**ex,changea'bility** *n.* —**ex'changeably** *adv.* —**ex'changer** *n.*
exchange rate *n.* the rate at which the currency unit of one country may be exchanged for that of another.
exchequer (ɪks'tʃɛkə) *n.* **1.** (*often cap.*) *Government.* (in Britain and certain other countries) the accounting department of the Treasury. **2.** *Inf.* personal funds; finances. [C13 (in the sense: chessboard, counting table): from OF *eschequier,* from *eschec* CHECK]
excisable (ɪk'saɪzəb'l) *adj.* **1.** liable to an excise tax. **2.** suitable for deletion.
excise[1] *n.* ('ɛksaɪz, ɛk'saɪz). **1.** Also called: **excise tax.** a tax on goods, such as spirits, produced for the home market. **2.** a tax paid for a licence to carry out various trades, sports, etc. **3.** *Brit.* that section of the government service responsible for the collection of excise, now the Board of Customs and Excise. ~*vb.* (ɪk'saɪz). **4.** (*tr.*) *Rare.* to compel (a person) to pay excise. [C15: prob. from MDu. *excijs,* prob. from OF *assise* a sitting, assessment, from L *assidēre* to sit beside, assist in judging] —**ex'cisable** *adj.*
excise[2] (ɪk'saɪz) *vb.* (*tr.*) **1.** to delete (a passage, sentence, etc.). **2.** to remove (an organ or part) surgically. [C16: from L *excīdere* to cut down] —**excision** (ɪk'sɪʒən) *n.*
exciseman ('ɛksaɪz,mæn) *n., pl.* -**men.** *Brit.* (formerly) a government agent whose function was to collect excise and prevent smuggling.
excitable (ɪk'saɪtəb'l) *adj.* **1.** easily excited; volatile. **2.** (esp. of a nerve) ready to respond to a stimulus. —**ex,cit-a'bility** *or* **ex'citableness** *n.*
excitation (,ɛksɪ'teɪʃən) *n.* **1.** the act or process of exciting or state of being excited. **2.** a means of exciting or cause of excitement. **3.** the current in a field coil of a generator, motor, etc., or the magnetizing current in a transformer. **4.** the action of a stimulus on an animal or plant organ, inducing it to respond.
excite (ɪk'saɪt) *vb.* (*tr.*) **1.** to arouse (a person), esp. to pleasurable anticipation or nervous agitation. **2.** to arouse or elicit (an emotion, response, etc.); evoke. **3.** to cause or bring about; stir up. **4.** to arouse sexually. **5.** *Physiol.* to cause a response in or increase the activity of (an organ, tissue, or part); stimulate. **6.** to raise (an atom, molecule, etc.) from the ground state to a higher energy level. **7.** to supply electricity to (the coils of a generator or motor) in order to create a magnetic field. [C14: from L *excīēre* to stimulate, from *ciēre* to set in motion, rouse] —**ex'citant** *n.* —**ex'citative** *or* **ex'citatory** *adj.* —**ex'citer** *or* **ex'citor** *n.*

excited (ɪk'saɪtɪd) *adj.* **1.** emotionally aroused, esp. to pleasure or agitation. **2.** characterized by excitement. **3.** sexually aroused. **4.** (of an ːɔlecule, etc.) having an energy level above the gɪound state. —**ex'citedness** *n.*
excitement (ɪk'saɪtmənt) *n.* **1.** the state of being excited. **2.** a person or thing that excites.
exciting (ɪk'saɪtɪŋ) *adj.* causing excitement; stirring; stimulating. —**ex'citingly** *adv.*
exclaim (ɪk'skleɪm) *vb.* to cry out or speak suddenly or excitedly, as from surprise, delight, horror, etc. [C16: from L *exclāmāre,* from *clāmāre* to shout] —**ex'claimer** *n.*
exclamation (,ɛksklə'meɪʃən) *n.* **1.** an abrupt or excited cry or utterance; ejaculation. **2.** the act of exclaiming. —,**excla'mational** *adj.* —**ex'clamatory** *adj.*
exclamation mark *or* *U.S.* **point** *n.* **1.** the punctuation mark ! used after exclamations and vehement commands. **2.** this mark used for any other purpose, as to draw attention to an obvious mistake, in road warning signs, etc.
exclave ('ɛkskleɪv) *n.* a part of a country entirely surrounded by foreign territory: viewed from the position of the home country. [C20: from EX-[1] + -*clave,* on the model of ENCLAVE]
exclosure (ɪk'skləʊʒə) *n.* an area of land fenced round to keep out unwanted animals.
exclude (ɪk'skluːd) *vb.* (*tr.*) **1.** to keep out; prevent from entering. **2.** to reject or not consider; leave out. **3.** to expel forcibly; eject. [C14: from L *exclūdere,* from *claudere* to shut] —**ex'cludable** *or* **ex'cludible** *adj.* —**ex'cluder** *n.*
exclusion (ɪk'skluːʒən) *n.* the act or an instance of excluding or the state of being excluded. —**ex'clusionary** *adj.*
exclusion principle *n.* See **Pauli exclusion principle.**
exclusive (ɪk'skluːsɪv) *adj.* **1.** excluding all else; rejecting other considerations, events, etc. **2.** belonging to a particular individual or group and to no other; not shared. **3.** belonging to or catering for a privileged minority, esp. a fashionable clique. **4.** (*postpositive;* foll. by *to*) limited (to); found only in (in). **5.** single; unique; only. **6.** separate and incompatible. **7.** (*immediately postpositive*) not including the numbers, dates, letters, etc., mentioned. **8.** (*postpositive;* foll. by *of*) except (for); not taking account (of). **9.** *Logic.* (of a disjunction) true if only one rather than both of its component propositions is true. ~*n.* **10.** an exclusive story; a story reported in only one newspaper. —**ex'clusiveness** *or* **exclusivity** (,ɛkskluː'sɪvɪtɪ) *n.*
exclusive OR circuit *or* **gate** *n.* *Electronics.* a computer logic circuit having two or more input wires and one output wire and giving a high-voltage output signal if a low-voltage signal is fed to one or more, but not all, of the input wires. Cf. **OR circuit.**
excommunicate *R.C. Church.* ~*vb.* (,ɛkskə'mjuːnɪ,keɪt). **1.** (*tr.*) to sentence (a member of the Church) to exclusion from the communion of believers and from the privileges and public prayers of the Church. ~*adj.* (,ɛkskə'mjuːnɪkɪt, -,keɪt). **2.** having incurred such a sentence. ~*n.* (,ɛkskə'mjuːnɪkɪt, -,keɪt). **3.** an excommunicated person. [C15: from LL *excommūnicāre,* lit.: to exclude from the community, from L *commūnis* COMMON] —,**excom,muni'cation** *n.* —,**excom'municative** *or* ,**excom'municatory** *adj.* —,**excom'muni,cator** *n.* —,**ex- com'municable** *adj.*
excoriate (ɪk'skɔːrɪ,eɪt) *vb.* (*tr.*) **1.** to strip the skin from (a person or animal). **2.** to denounce vehemently. [C15: from LL *excoriāre* to strip, flay, from L *corium* skin, hide] —**ex,cori'ation** *n.*
excrement ('ɛkskrɪmənt) *n.* waste matter discharged from the body, esp. faeces; excreta. [C16: from L *excernere* to sift, EXCRETE] —**excremental** (,ɛkskrɪ'mɛnt'l) *or* **excrementitious** (,ɛkskrɪmɛn'tɪʃəs) *adj.*
excrescence (ɪk'skrɛs'ns) *n.* a projection or protuberance, esp. an outgrowth from an organ or part of the body. —**ex'crescent** *adj.* —**excrescential** (,ɛkskrɪ'sɛnʃəl) *adj.*
excrescency (ɪk'skrɛsənsɪ) *n., pl.* -**cies. 1.** the state or condition of being excrescent. **2.** another word for **excrescence.**
excreta (ɪk'skriːtə) *pl. n.* waste matter, such as urine, faeces, or sweat, discharged from the body. [C19: NL, from L: see EXCRETE] —**ex'cretal** *adj.*

excrete (ɪk'skriːt) *vb.* **1.** to discharge (waste matter, such as urine, sweat, or faeces) from the body. **2.** (of plants) to eliminate (waste matter) through the leaves, roots, etc. [C17: from L *excernere* to separate, discharge, from *cernere* to sift] —**ex'creter** *n.* —**ex'cretion** *n.* —**ex'cretive** *or* **ex'cretory** *adj.*

excruciate (ɪk'skruːʃɪˌeɪt) *vb.* (*tr.*) to inflict mental suffering on; torment. [C16: from L *excruciāre*, from *cruciāre* to crucify, from *crux* cross] —**ex,cruci'ation** *n.*

excruciating (ɪk'skruːʃɪˌeɪtɪŋ) *adj.* **1.** unbearably painful; agonizing. **2.** intense; extreme. **3.** *Inf.* irritating; trying. **4.** *Humorous.* very bad: *an excruciating pun.*

exculpate ('ɛkskʌlˌpeɪt, ɪk'skʌlpeɪt) *vb.* (*tr.*) to free from blame or guilt; vindicate or exonerate. [C17: from Med. L, from L EX-[1] + *culpa* fault, blame] —**exculpable** (ɪk'skʌlpəbᵊl) *adj.* —,**excul'pation** *n.* —**ex'culpatory** *adj.*

excursion (ɪk'skɜːʃən, -ʒən) *n.* **1.** a short outward and return journey, esp. for sightseeing, etc.; outing. **2.** a group going on such a journey. **3.** (*modifier*) of or relating to reduced rates offered on certain journeys by rail: *an excursion ticket.* **4.** a digression or deviation; diversion. **5.** (formerly) a raid or attack. [C16: from L *excursiō* attack, from *excurrere* to run out, from *currere* to run] —**ex'cursionist** *n.*

excursive (ɪk'skɜːsɪv) *adj.* **1.** tending to digress. **2.** involving detours; rambling. [C17: from L *excursus*, from *excurrere* to run forth] —**ex'cursively** *adv.* —**ex'cursiveness** *n.*

excuse *vb.* (ɪk'skjuːz). (*tr.*) **1.** to pardon or forgive. **2.** to seek pardon or exemption for (a person, esp. oneself). **3.** to make allowances for: *to excuse someone's ignorance.* **4.** to serve as an apology or explanation for; justify: *her age excuses her.* **5.** to exempt from a task, obligation, etc. **6.** to dismiss or allow to leave. **7.** to seek permission for (someone, esp. oneself) to leave. **8. be excused.** *Euphemistic.* to go to the lavatory. **9. excuse me!** an expression used to catch someone's attention or to apologize for an interruption, disagreement, etc. ~*n.* (ɪk'skjuːs). **10.** an explanation offered in defence of some fault or as a reason for not fulfilling an obligation, etc. **11.** *Inf.* an inferior example of something; makeshift substitute: *she is a poor excuse for a hostess.* **12.** the act of excusing. [C13: from L, from EX-[1] + *causa* cause, accusation] —**ex'cusable** *adj.* —**ex'cusableness** *n.* —**ex'cusably** *adv.*

excuse-me *n.* a dance in which a person may take another's partner.

ex-directory *adj. Chiefly Brit.* not listed in a telephone directory, by request, and not disclosed to inquirers.

ex dividend *adj., adv.* without the right to the current dividend: *to quote shares ex dividend.*

exeat ('ɛksɪət) *n. Brit.* **1.** leave of absence from school or some other institution. **2.** a bishop's permission for a priest to leave his diocese in order to take up an appointment elsewhere. [C18: L, lit.: he may go out, from *exīre*]

exec. *abbrev. for:* **1.** executive. **2.** executor.

execrable ('ɛksɪkrəbᵊl) *adj.* **1.** deserving to be execrated; abhorrent. **2.** of very poor quality. [C14: from L: see EXECRATE] —'**execrableness** *n.* —'**execrably** *adv.*

execrate ('ɛksɪˌkreɪt) *vb.* **1.** (*tr.*) to loathe; detest; abhor. **2.** (*tr.*) to denounce; deplore. **3.** to curse (a person or thing); damn. [C16: from L *exsecrārī* to curse, from EX-[1] + -*secrārī* from *sacer* SACRED] —,**exe'cration** *n.* —'**exe,crative** *or* '**exe,cratory** *adj.* —'**exe,cratively** *adv.*

execute ('ɛksɪˌkjuːt) *vb.* (*tr.*) **1.** to put (a condemned person) to death; inflict capital punishment upon. **2.** to carry out; complete. **3.** to perform; accomplish; effect. **4.** to make or produce: *to execute a drawing.* **5.** to carry into effect (a judicial sentence, the law, etc.). **6.** *Law.* to render (a deed, etc.) effective, as by signing, sealing, and delivering. **7.** to carry out the terms of (a contract, will, etc.). [C14: from OF *executer*, back formation from *exécuteur* EXECUTOR] —'**exe,cutable** *adj.* —**executant** (ɪg'zɛkjʊtənt) *n.* —'**exe,cuter** *n.*

execution (,ɛksɪ'kjuːʃən) *n.* **1.** the act or process of executing. **2.** the carrying out or undergoing of a sentence of death. **3.** the style or manner in which something is accomplished or performed; technique. **4. a.** the enforcement of the judgment of a court of law. **b.** the writ ordering such enforcement.

executioner (,ɛksɪ'kjuːʃənə) *n.* an official charged with carrying out the death sentence passed upon a condemned person.

executive (ɪg'zɛkjʊtɪv) *n.* **1.** a person or group responsible for the administration of a project, activity, or business. **2. a.** the branch of government responsible for carrying out laws, decrees, etc. **b.** any administration. ~*adj.* **3.** having the function of carrying plans, orders, laws, etc., into effect. **4.** of or relating to an executive. **5.** *Inf.* very expensive or exclusive: *executive housing.* —**ex'ecutively** *adv.*

Executive Council *n.* (in Australia and New Zealand) a body of ministers of the Crown presided over by the governor or governor-general that formally approves cabinet decisions, etc.

executive officer *n.* the second-in-command of any of certain military units.

executor (ɪg'zɛkjʊtə) *n.* **1.** *Law.* a person appointed by a testator to carry out his will. **2.** a person who executes. [C14: from Anglo-F *executour*, from L *execūtor*] —**ex,ecu'torial** *adj.* —**ex'ecutory** *adj.* —**ex'ecutor,ship** *n.*

executrix (ɪg'zɛkjʊtrɪks) *n., pl.* **executrices** (ɪg,zɛkjʊ'traɪsiːz) *or* **executrixes.** *Law.* a female executor.

exegesis (,ɛksɪ'dʒiːsɪs) *n., pl.* -**ses** (-siːz). explanation or critical interpretation of a text, esp. of the Bible. [C17: from Gk, from *exēgeisthai* to interpret, from EX-[1] + *hēgeisthai* to guide] —**exegetic** (,ɛksɪ'dʒɛtɪk) *adj.* —,**exe'getics** *n.* (*functioning as sing.*)

exegete ('ɛksɪ,dʒiːt) *or* **exegetist** (,ɛksɪ'dʒiːtɪst, -'dʒɛt-) *n.* a person who practises exegesis. [C18: from Gk: see EXEGESIS]

exemplar (ɪg'zɛmplə, -plɑː) *n.* **1.** a person or thing to be copied or imitated; model. **2.** a typical specimen or instance; example. [C14: from L, from *exemplum* EXAMPLE]

exemplary (ɪg'zɛmplərɪ) *adj.* **1.** fit for imitation; model. **2.** serving as a warning; admonitory. **3.** representative; typical. —**ex'emplarily** *adv.* —**ex'emplariness** *n.*

exemplary damages *pl. n. Law.* damages awarded to a plaintiff above the value of actual loss sustained so that they serve also as a punishment to the defendant.

exemplify (ɪg'zɛmplɪˌfaɪ) *vb.* -**fying**, -**fied.** (*tr.*) **1.** to show by example. **2.** to serve as an example of. **3.** *Law.* to make an official copy of (a document) under seal. [C15: via OF from Med. L *exemplificāre*, from L *exemplum* EXAMPLE + *facere* to make] —**ex'empli,fiable** *adj.* —**ex,emplifi'cation** *n.* —**ex'emplifi,cative** *adj.* —**ex'empli,fier** *n.*

exempt (ɪg'zɛmpt) *vb.* **1.** (*tr.*) to release from an obligation, tax, etc.; excuse. ~*adj.* (*postpositive*) **2.** freed from or not subject to an obligation, tax, etc.; excused. ~*n.* **3.** a person who is exempt. [C14: from L *exemptus* removed, from *eximere* to take out, from *emere* to buy, obtain] —**ex'emption** *n.*

exequies ('ɛksɪkwɪz) *pl. n., sing.* -**quy.** the rites and ceremonies used at funerals. [C14: from L *exequiae* (pl.) funeral procession, rites, from *exequī* to follow to the end, from *sequī* to follow]

exercise ('ɛksəˌsaɪz) *vb.* (*mainly tr.*) **1.** to put into use; employ. **2.** (*intr.*) to take exercise or perform exercises. **3.** to practise using in order to develop or train. **4.** to perform or make use of: *to exercise one's rights.* **5.** to bring to bear: *to exercise one's influence.* **6.** (*often passive*) to occupy the attentions of, esp. so as to worry or vex: *to be exercised about a decision.* **7.** *Mil.* to carry out or cause to carry out simulated combat, manoeuvres, etc. ~*n.* **8.** physical exertion, esp. for development, training, or keeping fit. **9.** mental or other activity or practice, esp. to develop a skill. **10.** a set of movements, tasks, etc., designed to train, improve, or test one's ability: *piano exercises.* **11.** a performance or work of art done as practice or to demonstrate a technique. **12.** the performance of a function: *the exercise of one's rights.* **13.** (*usually pl.*) *Mil.* a manoeuvre or simulated combat operation. **14.** *Gymnastics.* a particular event, such as the horizontal bar. [C14: from OF, from L, from *exercēre* to drill, from EX-[1] + *arcēre* to ward off] —'**exer,cisable** *adj.* —'**exer,ciser** *n.*

exercise bike *or* **cycle** *n.* a stationary exercise machine that is pedalled like a bicycle as a method of increasing cardiovascular fitness.

exert (ɪg'zɜːt) *vb.* (*tr.*) to apply (oneself) diligently; make a strenuous effort. [C17 (in the sense: push forth, emit): from L *exserere* to thrust out, from EX-[1] + *serere* to bind together, entwine] —**ex'ertion** *n.* —**ex'ertive** *adj.*

Exeter ('ɛksɪtə) *n.* a city in SW England, administrative centre of Devon; university (1955). Pop.: 101 800 (1983 est.).

exeunt ('ɛksɪ,ʌnt) *Latin.* they go out: used as a stage direction.

exeunt omnes ('ɒmneɪz) *Latin.* they all go out: used as a stage direction.

exfoliate (ɛks'fəʊlɪˌeɪt) *vb.* (of bark, skin, minerals, etc.) to peel off in layers, flakes, or scales. [C17: from LL *exfoliāre* to strip off leaves, from L *folium* leaf] —**ex**ˌ**foli'ation** *n.* —**ex'foliative** *adj.*

ex gratia ('greɪʃə) *adj.* given as a favour or gratuitously where no legal obligation exists: *an ex gratia payment.* [NL, lit.: out of kindness]

exhale (ɛks'heɪl, ɪg'zeɪl) *vb.* **1.** to expel (breath, smoke, etc.) from the lungs; breathe out. **2.** to give off (air, fumes, etc.) or (of air, etc.) to be given off. [C14: from L *exhālāre*, from *hālāre* to breathe] —**ex'halable** *adj.* —ˌ**exha'lation** *n.*

exhaust (ɪg'zɔːst) *vb.* (*mainly tr.*) **1.** to drain the energy of; tire out. **2.** to deprive of resources, etc. **3.** to deplete totally; consume. **4.** to empty (a container) by drawing off or pumping out (the contents). **5.** to develop or discuss thoroughly so that no further interest remains. **6.** to remove gas from (a vessel, etc.) in order to reduce pressure or create a vacuum. **7.** (*intr.*) (of steam or other gases) to be emitted or to escape from an engine after being expanded. ~*n.* **8.** gases ejected from an engine as waste products. **9.** the expulsion of expanded gas or steam from an engine. **10. a.** the parts of an engine through which exhausted gases or steam pass. **b.** (*as modifier*): *exhaust pipe.* [C16: from L *exhaustus* made empty, from *exhaurīre* to draw out, from *haurīre* to draw, drain] —**ex'hausted** *adj.* —**ex'haustible** *adj.* —**ex'hausting** *adj.*

exhaustion (ɪg'zɔːstʃən) *n.* **1.** extreme tiredness. **2.** the condition of being used up. **3.** the act of exhausting or the state of being exhausted.

exhaustive (ɪg'zɔːstɪv) *adj.* **1.** comprehensive; thorough. **2.** tending to exhaust. —**ex'haustively** *adv.* —**ex'haustiveness** *n.*

exhibit (ɪg'zɪbɪt) *vb.* (*mainly tr.*) **1.** (*also intr.*) to display (something) to the public. **2.** to manifest; display; show. **3.** *Law.* to produce (a document or object) in court as evidence. ~*n.* **4.** an object or collection exhibited to the public. **5.** *Law.* a document or object produced in court as evidence. [C15: from L *exhibēre* to hold forth, from *habēre* to have] —**ex'hibitor** *n.* —**ex'hibitory** *adj.*

exhibition (ˌɛksɪ'bɪʃən) *n.* **1.** a public display of art, skills, etc. **2.** the act of exhibiting or the state of being exhibited. **3. make an exhibition of oneself.** to behave so foolishly that one excites notice or ridicule. **4.** *Brit.* an allowance or scholarship awarded to a student at a university or school.

exhibitioner (ˌɛksɪ'bɪʃənə) *n. Brit.* a student who has been awarded an exhibition.

exhibitionism (ˌɛksɪ'bɪʃəˌnɪzəm) *n.* **1.** a compulsive desire to attract attention to oneself, esp. by exaggerated behaviour. **2.** a compulsive desire to expose one's genital organs publicly. —ˌ**exhi'bitionist** *n.* —ˌ**exhiˌbition'istic** *adj.*

exhibitive (ɪg'zɪbɪtɪv) *adj.* (*usually postpositive* and foll. by *of*) illustrative or demonstrative.

exhilarate (ɪg'zɪləˌreɪt) *vb.* (*tr.*) to make lively and cheerful; elate. [C16: from L *exhilarāre*, from *hilarāre* to cheer] —**ex'hilaˌrating** *adj.* —**ex**ˌ**hila'ration** *n.* —**ex'hilaˌrative** *adj.*

exhort (ɪg'zɔːt) *vb.* to urge or persuade (someone) earnestly; advise strongly. [C14: from L *exhortārī*, from *hortārī* to urge] —**ex'hortative** *or* **ex'hortatory** *adj.* —ˌ**exhor'tation** *n.* —**ex'horter** *n.*

exhume (ɛks'hjuːm) *vb.* (*tr.*) **1.** to dig up (something buried, esp. a corpse); disinter. **2.** to reveal; disclose. [C18: from Med. L, from L EX-[1] + *humus* to bury, from *humus* the ground] —**exhumation** (ˌɛkshjʊ'meɪʃən) *n.* —**ex'humer** *n.*

ex hypothesi (ɛks haɪ'pɒθəsɪ) *adv.* in accordance with the hypothesis stated. [C17: NL]

exigency ('ɛksɪdʒənsɪ, ɪg'zɪdʒənsɪ) *or* **exigence** ('ɛksɪdʒəns) *n.*, *pl.* **-gencies** *or* **-gences**. **1.** urgency. **2.** (*often pl.*) an urgent demand; pressing requirement. **3.** an emergency.

exigent ('ɛksɪdʒənt) *adj.* **1.** urgent; pressing. **2.** exacting; demanding. [C15: from L *exigere* to drive out, weigh out, from *agere* to drive, compel]

exiguous (ɪg'zɪgjʊəs, ɛk'sɪg-) *adj.* scanty or slender; meagre. [C17: from L *exiguus* from *exigere* to weigh out; see EXIGENT] —**exiguity** (ˌɛksɪ'gjuːɪtɪ) *or* **ex'iguousness** *n.*

exile ('ɛgzaɪl, 'ɛksaɪl) *n.* **1.** a prolonged, usually enforced absence from one's home or country. **2.** the official expulsion of a person from his native land. **3.** a person banished or living away from his home or country; expatriate. ~*vb.* **4.** (*tr.*) to expel from home or country, esp. by official decree; banish. [C13: from L *exsilium* banishment, from *exsul* banished person] —**exilic** (ɛg'zɪlɪk, ɛk'sɪlɪk) *or* **ex'ilian** *adj.*

exist (ɪg'zɪst) *vb.* (*intr.*) **1.** to have being or reality; be. **2.** to eke out a living; stay alive. **3.** to be living; live. **4.** to be present under specified conditions or in a specified place. [C17: from L *exsistere* to step forth, from EX-[1] + *sistere* to stand] —**ex'istent** *adj.* —**ex'isting** *adj.*

existence (ɪg'zɪstəns) *n.* **1.** the fact or state of existing; being. **2.** the continuance or maintenance of life; living, esp. in adverse circumstances. **3.** something that exists; a being or entity. **4.** everything that exists.

existential (ˌɛgzɪ'stɛnʃəl) *adj.* **1.** of or relating to existence, esp. human existence. **2.** *Philosophy.* known by experience rather than reason. **3.** of a formula or proposition asserting the existence of at least one object fulfilling a given condition. **4.** of or relating to existentialism.

existentialism (ˌɛgzɪ'stɛnʃəˌlɪzəm) *n.* a modern philosophical movement stressing personal experience and responsibility and their demands on the individual, who is seen as a free agent in a deterministic and seemingly meaningless universe. —ˌ**exis'tentialist** *adj.*, *n.*

exit ('ɛgzɪt, 'ɛksɪt) *n.* **1.** a way out. **2.** the act or an instance of going out. **3. a.** the act of leaving or right to leave a particular place. **b.** (*as modifier*): *an exit visa.* **4.** departure from life; death. **5.** *Theatre.* the act of going offstage. **6.** *Brit.* a point at which vehicles may leave or join a motorway. **7.** *Computers.* (in processing) an instruction to leave a routine. ~*vb.* (*intr.*) **8.** to go away or out; depart. **9.** *Theatre.* to go offstage: used as a stage direction: *exit Hamlet.* **10.** to leave; withdraw (from). [C17: from L *exitus* a departure, from *exīre* to go out, from EX-[1] + *īre* to go]

exitance ('ɛksɪtəns) *n.* a measure of the ability of a surface to emit radiation. [C20: from EXIT + -ANCE]

exit poll *n.* a poll taken by an organization by asking people how they voted in an election as they leave a polling station.

ex libris (ɛks 'liːbrɪs) *prep.* **1.** from the collection or library of. ~*n.* **ex-libris**, *pl.* **ex-libris.** **2.** a bookplate bearing the owner's name, coat of arms, etc. [C19: from L, lit.: from the books (of)]

Exmoor ('ɛksˌmʊə, -ˌmɔː) *n.* a high moorland in SW England, in NW Somerset and Devon: largely forested until the 19th century, now chiefly grazing ground for Exmoor ponies, sheep, and red deer.

exo- *combining form.* external, outside, or beyond: *exothermal.* [from Gk *exō* outside]

exobiology (ˌɛksəʊbaɪ'ɒlədʒɪ) *n.* another name for **astrobiology.** —ˌ**exobi'ologist** *n.*

exocarp ('ɛksəʊˌkɑːp) *n.* another name for **epicarp.**

exocrine ('ɛksəʊˌkraɪn) *adj.* **1.** of or relating to exocrine glands or their secretions. ~*n.* **2.** an exocrine gland. [C20: EXO- + -*crine* from Gk *krinein* to separate]

exocrine gland *n.* any gland, such as a salivary or sweat gland, that secretes its products through a duct onto an epithelial surface.

Exod. *Bible. abbrev. for* Exodus.

exodus ('ɛksədəs) *n.* the act or an instance of going out. [C17: via L from Gk *exodos*, from EX-[1] + *hodos* way]

Exodus ('ɛksədəs) *n.* **1.** the departure of the Israelites from Egypt. **2.** the second book of the Old Testament, recounting the events connected with this.

ex officio ('ɛks ə'fɪʃɪəʊ, ə'fɪsɪəʊ) *adv.*, *adj.* by right of position or office. [L]

exogamy (ɛk'sɒgəmɪ) *n. Anthropol., sociol.* marriage outside one's own tribe or similar unit. —**ex'ogamous** *or* **exogamic** (ˌɛksəʊ'gæmɪk) *adj.*

exogenous (ɛk'sɒdʒɪnəs) *adj.* **1.** having an external origin. **2.** *Biol.* **a.** originating outside an organism. **b.** of or relating to external factors, such as light, that influence an organism.

exon ('ɛksɒn) *n. Brit.* one of the four officers who command the Yeomen of the Guard. [C17: a pronunciation spelling of F *exempt* EXEMPT]

exonerate (ɪg'zɒnəˌreɪt) *vb.* (*tr.*) **1.** to absolve from blame or a criminal charge. **2.** to relieve from an obligation. [C16: from L *exonerāre* to free from a burden, from *onus* a burden] —**ex,oner'ation** *n.* —**ex'onerative** *adj.* —**ex'oner,ator** *n.*

exophthalmos (,ɛksɒf'θælmɒs), **exophthalmus** (,ɛksɒf'θælməs), *or* **exophthalmia** (,ɛksɒf'θælmɪə) *n.* abnormal protrusion of the eyeball, as caused by hyperthyroidism. [C19: via NL from Gk, from EX-[1] + *ophthalmos* eye] —**exoph'thalmic** *adj.*

exorbitant (ɪg'zɔːbɪt⁰nt) *adj.* (of prices, demands, etc.) excessive; extravagant; immoderate. [C15: from LL *exorbitāre* to deviate, from L *orbita* track] —**ex'orbitance** *n.* —**ex'orbitantly** *adv.*

exorcise *or* **-cize** ('ɛksɔː,saɪz) *vb.* (*tr.*) to expel (evil spirits) from (a person or place), by adjurations and religious rites. [C15: from LL, from Gk, from EX-[1] + *horkizein* to adjure] —**exor,ciser** *or* **-,cizer** *n.* —**'exorcism** *n.* —**'exorcist** *n.*

exordium (ɛk'sɔːdɪəm) *n., pl.* **-diums** *or* **-dia** (-dɪə). an introductory part or beginning, esp. of an oration or discourse. [C16: from L, from *exōrdīrī* to begin, from *ōrdīrī* to begin] —**ex'ordial** *adj.*

exoskeleton (,ɛksəʊ'skɛlɪt⁰n) *n.* the protective or supporting structure covering the outside of the body of many animals, such as the thick cuticle of arthropods. —**,exo'skeletal** *adj.*

exosphere ('ɛksəʊ,sfɪə) *n.* the outermost layer of the earth's atmosphere. It extends from about 400 kilometres above the earth's surface.

exothermic (,ɛksəʊ'θɜːmɪk) *or* **exothermal** *adj.* (of a chemical reaction or compound) occurring or formed with the evolution of heat. —**,exo'thermically** *or* **,exo'thermally** *adv.*

exotic (ɪg'zɒtɪk) *adj.* **1.** originating in a foreign country, esp. one in the tropics; not native: *an exotic plant.* **2.** having a strange or bizarre allure, beauty, or quality. ~*n.* **3.** an exotic person or thing. [C16: from L, from Gk *exōtikos* foreign, from *exō* outside] —**ex'otically** *adv.* —**ex'oti,cism** *n.* —**ex'oticness** *n.*

exotica (ɪg'zɒtɪkə) *pl. n.* exotic objects, esp. when forming a collection. [C19: L, neuter pl. of *exōticus*; see EXOTIC]

exotic dancer *n.* a striptease or belly dancer.

expand (ɪk'spænd) *vb.* **1.** to make or become greater in extent, volume, size, or scope. **2.** to spread out; unfold; stretch out. **3.** (*intr.; often foll. by on*) to enlarge or expatiate (on a story, topic, etc.). **4.** (*intr.*) to become increasingly relaxed, friendly, or talkative. **5.** *Maths.* to express (a function or expression) as the sum or product of terms. [C15: from L *expandere* to spread out] —**ex'pandable** *adj.* —**ex'pander** *n.*

expanded (ɪk'spændɪd) *adj.* (of a plastic) having been foamed during manufacture by a gas to make a light packaging material or heat insulator: *expanded polystyrene.*

expanded metal *n.* an open mesh of metal used for reinforcing brittle or friable materials and in fencing.

expander (ɪk'spændə) *n.* **1.** a device for exercising and developing the muscles of the body. **2.** an electronic device for increasing the variations in signal amplitude in a transmission system according to a specified law.

expanse (ɪk'spæns) *n.* **1.** an uninterrupted surface of something that extends, esp. over a wide area; stretch. **2.** expansion or extension. [C17: from NL *expansum*, from L *expansus* spread out, from *expandere* to expand]

expansible (ɪk'spænsəb⁰l) *adj.* able to expand or be expanded. —**ex,pansi'bility** *n.*

expansion (ɪk'spænʃən) *n.* **1.** the act of expanding or the state of being expanded. **2.** something expanded. **3.** the degree or amount by which something expands. **4.** an increase or development, esp. in the activities of a company. **5.** the increase in the dimensions of a body or substance when subjected to an increase in temperature, internal pressure, etc. —**ex'pansionary** *adj.*

expansionism (ɪk'spænʃə,nɪzəm) *n.* the doctrine or practice of expanding the economy or territory of a country. —**ex'pansionist** *n., adj.* —**ex,pansion'istic** *adj.*

expansive (ɪk'spænsɪv) *adj.* **1.** able or tending to expand or characterized by expansion. **2.** wide; extensive. **3.** friendly, open, or talkative. **4.** grand or extravagant. —**ex'pansiveness** *n.*

expansivity (,ɛkspæn'sɪvɪtɪ) *n.* the fractional increase in length or volume of a substance or body on being heated through a one degree rise in temperature; coefficient of expansion.

ex parte (ɛks 'pɑːtɪ) *adj. Law.* (of an application in a judicial proceeding) on behalf of one side or party only: *an ex parte injunction.*

expat (,ɛks'pæt) *n., adj. Inf.* short for **expatriate.**

expatiate (ɪk'speɪʃɪ,eɪt) *vb.* (*intr.*) **1.** (foll. by *on* or *upon*) to enlarge (on a theme, topic, etc.); elaborate (on). **2.** *Rare.* to wander about. [C16: from L *exspatiārī* to digress, from *spatiārī* to walk about] —**ex,pati'ation** *n.* —**ex'pati,ator** *n.*

expatriate *adj.* (ɛks'pætrɪt, -,eɪt). **1.** resident outside one's native country. **2.** exiled or banished from one's native country. ~*n.* (ɛks'pætrɪt, -,eɪt). **3.** a person living outside his native country **4.** an exile; expatriate person. ~*vb.* (ɛks'pætrɪ,eɪt). (*tr.*) **5.** to exile (oneself) from one's native country or cause (another) to go into exile. [C18: from Med. L, from L EX-[1] + *patria* native land] —**ex-,patri'ation** *n.*

expect (ɪk'spɛkt) *vb.* (*tr.; may take a clause as object or an infinitive*) **1.** to regard as likely; anticipate. **2.** to look forward to or be waiting for. **3.** to decide that (something) is necessary; require: *the teacher expects us to work late.* ~See also **expecting.** [C16: from L *exspectāre* to watch for, from *spectāre* to look at] —**ex'pectable** *adj.*

expectancy (ɪk'spɛktənsɪ) *or* **expectance** *n.* **1.** something expected, esp. on the basis of a norm or average: *his life expectancy was 30 years.* **2.** anticipation; expectation. **3.** the prospect of a future interest or possession.

expectant (ɪk'spɛktənt) *adj.* **1.** expecting, anticipating, or hopeful. **2.** having expectations, esp. of possession of something. **3.** pregnant. ~*n.* **4.** a person who expects something.

expectation (,ɛkspɛk'teɪʃən) *n.* **1.** the act or state of expecting or the state of being expected. **2.** (*usually pl.*) something looked forward to, whether feared or hoped for. **3.** an attitude of expectancy or hope. **4.** *Statistics.* **a.** the numerical probability that an event will occur. **b.** another term for **expected value.** —**expectative** (ɪk'spɛktətɪv) *adj.*

expected frequency *n. Statistics.* the number of occasions on which an event may be presumed to occur on average in a given number of trials.

expected value *n. Statistics.* the sum or integral of all possible values of a random variable, or any given function of it, multiplied by the respective probabilities of the values of the variable.

expecting (ɪk'spɛktɪŋ) *adj. Inf.* pregnant.

expectorant (ɪk'spɛktərənt) *Med.* ~*adj.* **1.** promoting the secretion, liquefaction, or expulsion of sputum from the respiratory passages. ~*n.* **2.** an expectorant drug or agent.

expectorate (ɪk'spɛktə,reɪt) *vb.* to cough up and spit out (sputum from the respiratory passages). [C17: from L *expectorāre*, lit.: to drive from the breast, expel, from *pectus* breast] —**ex,pecto'ration** *n.* —**ex'pecto,rator** *n.*

expediency (ɪk'spiːdɪənsɪ) *or* **expedience** *n., pl.* **-encies** *or* **-ences.** **1.** appropriateness; suitability. **2.** the use of or inclination towards methods that are advantageous rather than fair or just. **3.** another word for **expedient** (sense 3).

expedient (ɪk'spiːdɪənt) *adj.* **1.** suitable to the circumstances; appropriate. **2.** inclined towards methods that are advantageous rather than fair or just. ~*n.* also **expediency.** **3.** something suitable or appropriate, esp. during an urgent situation. [C14: from L *expediēns* setting free; see EXPEDITE]

expedite ('ɛkspɪ,daɪt) *vb.* (*tr.*) **1.** to facilitate the progress of; hasten or assist. **2.** to do or process with speed and efficiency. [C17: from L *expedīre*, lit.: to free the feet (as from a snare), hence, liberate, from EX-[1] + *pēs* foot] —**'expe,diter** *or* **'expe,ditor** *n.*

expedition (,ɛkspɪ'dɪʃən) *n.* **1.** an organized journey or voyage, esp. for exploration or for a scientific or military purpose. **2.** the people and equipment comprising an expedition. **3.** promptness; dispatch. [C15: from L *expedīre* to prepare, EXPEDITE] —**,expe'ditionary** *adj.*

expeditious (,ɛkspɪ'dɪʃəs) *adj.* characterized by or done with speed and efficiency; prompt; quick. —**,expe'ditiously** *adv.* —**,expe'ditiousness** *n.*

expel (ɪk'spɛl) *vb.* **-pelling, -pelled.** (*tr.*) **1.** to eject or drive out with force. **2.** to deprive of participation in or membership of a school, club, etc. [C14: from L *expellere* to drive out, from *pellere* to thrust, drive] —**ex'pellable** *adj.* —**expellee** (ˌɛkspɛ'liː) *n.* —**ex'peller** *n.*

expellant *or* **expellent** (ɪk'spɛlənt) *adj.* **1.** forcing out or able to force out. ~*n.* **2.** a medicine used to expel undesirable substances or organisms from the body.

expend (ɪk'spɛnd) *vb.* (*tr.*) **1.** to spend; disburse. **2.** to consume or use up. [C15: from L *expendere*, from *pendere* to weigh] —**ex'pender** *n.*

expendable (ɪk'spɛndəbᵊl) *adj.* **1.** that may be expended or used up. **2.** able to be sacrificed to achieve an objective, esp. a military one. ~*n.* **3.** something expendable. —**ex,penda'bility** *n.*

expenditure (ɪk'spɛndɪtʃə) *n.* **1.** something expended, esp. money. **2.** the act of expending.

expense (ɪk'spɛns) *n.* **1.** a particular payment of money; expenditure. **2.** money needed for individual purchases; cost; charge. **3.** (*pl.*) money spent in the performance of a job, etc., usually reimbursed by an employer or allowable against tax. **4.** something requiring money for its purchase or upkeep. **5. at the expense of.** to the detriment of. [C14: from LL, from L *expēnsus* weighed out; see EXPEND]

expense account *n.* **1.** an arrangement by which an employee's expenses are refunded by his employer or deducted from his income for tax purposes. **2.** a record of such expenses.

expensive (ɪk'spɛnsɪv) *adj.* high-priced; costly; dear. —**ex'pensiveness** *n.*

experience (ɪk'spɪərɪəns) *n.* **1.** direct personal participation or observation. **2.** a particular incident, feeling, etc., that a person has undergone. **3.** accumulated knowledge, esp. of practical matters. ~*vb.* (*tr.*) **4.** to participate in or undergo. **5.** to be moved by; feel. [C14: from L *experīrī* to prove; rel. to L *perīculum* PERIL] —**ex'perienceable** *adj.*

experienced (ɪk'spɪərɪənst) *adj.* having become skilful or knowledgeable from extensive participation or observation.

experiential (ɪkˌspɪərɪ'ɛnʃəl) *adj. Philosophy.* relating to or derived from experience; empirical.

experiment *n.* (ɪk'spɛrɪmənt) **1.** a test or investigation, esp. one planned to provide evidence for or against a hypothesis. **2.** the act of conducting such an investigation or test; research. **3.** an attempt at something new or original. ~*vb.* (ɪk'spɛrɪˌmɛnt) **4.** (*intr.*) to make an experiment or experiments. [C14: from L *experīmentum* proof, trial, from *experīrī* to test; see EXPERIENCE] —**ex'peri,menter** *n.*

experimental (ɪkˌspɛrɪ'mɛntᵊl) *adj.* **1.** relating to, based on, or having the nature of experiment. **2.** based on or derived from experience; empirical. **3.** tending to experiment. **4.** tentative or provisional. —**ex,peri'mentalism** *n.*

experimentation (ɪkˌspɛrɪmɛn'teɪʃən) *n.* the act, process, or practice of experimenting.

expert ('ɛkspɜːt) *n.* **1.** a person who has extensive skill or knowledge in a particular field. ~*adj.* **2.** skilful or knowledgeable. **3.** of, involving, or done by an expert: *an expert job.* [C14: from L *expertus* known by experience; see EXPERIENCE] —**'expertly** *adv.* —**'expertness** *n.*

expertise (ˌɛkspɜː'tiːz) *n.* special skill, knowledge, or judgment; expertness. [C19: from F: expert skill, from EXPERT]

expiate ('ɛkspɪˌeɪt) *vb.* (*tr.*) to atone for (sin or wrongdoing); make amends for. [C16: from L *expiāre*, from *pius* dutiful; see PIOUS] —**'expiable** *adj.* —**,expi'ation** *n.* —**'expi,ator** *n.*

expiatory ('ɛkspɪətərɪ, -trɪ) *adj.* **1.** capable of making expiation. **2.** offered in expiation.

expiration (ˌɛkspɪ'reɪʃən) *n.* **1.** the finish of something; expiry. **2.** the act, process, or sound of breathing out. —**expiratory** (ɪk'spaɪərətərɪ, -trɪ) *adj.*

expire (ɪk'spaɪə) *vb.* **1.** (*intr.*) to finish or run out; come to an end. **2.** to breathe out (air). **3.** (*intr.*) to die. [C15: from OF, from L *exspīrāre* to breathe out, from *spīrāre* to breathe] —**ex'pirer** *n.*

expiry (ɪk'spaɪərɪ) *n., pl.* **-ries. 1. a.** a coming to an end, esp. of a contract period; termination. **b.** (*as modifier*): *the expiry date.* **2.** death.

explain (ɪk'spleɪn) *vb.* **1.** (when *tr., may take a clause as object*) to make (something) comprehensible, esp. by giving a clear and detailed account of it. **2.** (*tr.*) to justify or attempt to justify (oneself) by reasons for one's actions.

[C15: from L *explānāre* to flatten, from *plānus* level] —**ex'plainable** *adj.* —**ex'plainer** *n.*

explain away *vb.* (*tr., adv.*) to offer excuses or reasons for (bad conduct, mistakes, etc.).

explanation (ˌɛksplə'neɪʃən) *n.* **1.** the act or process of explaining. **2.** something that explains. **3.** a clarification of disputed points.

explanatory (ɪk'splænətərɪ, -trɪ) *or* **explanative** *adj.* serving or intended to serve as an explanation. —**ex'planatorily** *adv.*

expletive (ɪk'spliːtɪv) *n.* **1.** an exclamation or swearword; an oath or sound expressing emotion rather than meaning. **2.** any syllable, word, or phrase conveying no independent meaning, esp. one inserted in verse for the sake of metre. ~*adj. also* **expletory** (ɪk'spliːtərɪ, -trɪ). **3.** without particular meaning, esp. when filling out a line of verse. [C17: from LL *explētīvus* for filling out, from *explēre*, from *plēre* to fill]

explicable ('ɛksplɪkəbᵊl, ɪk'splɪk-) *adj.* capable of being explained.

explicate ('ɛksplɪˌkeɪt) *vb.* (*tr.*) *Formal.* **1.** to make clear or explicit; explain. **2.** to formulate or develop (a theory, hypothesis, etc.). [C16: from L *explicāre* to unfold, from *plicāre* to fold] —**,expli'cation** *n.* —**explicative** (ɪk'splɪkətɪv) *or* **explicatory** (ɪk'splɪkətərɪ, -trɪ) *adj.* —**'expli,cator** *n.*

explicit (ɪk'splɪsɪt) *adj.* **1.** precisely and clearly expressed, leaving nothing to implication; fully stated. **2.** leaving little to the imagination; graphically detailed. **3.** openly expressed without reservations; unreserved. [C17: from L *explicitus* unfolded; see EXPLICATE] —**ex'plicitly** *adv.* —**ex'plicitness** *n.*

explode (ɪk'spləʊd) *vb.* **1.** to burst or cause to burst with great violence, esp. through detonation of an explosive; blow up. **2.** to destroy or be destroyed in this manner. **3.** (of a gas) to undergo or cause (a gas) to undergo a sudden violent expansion, as a result of a fast exothermic chemical or nuclear reaction. **4.** (*intr.*) to react suddenly or violently with emotion, etc. **5.** (*intr.*) (esp. of a population) to increase rapidly. **6.** (*tr.*) to show (a theory, etc.) to be baseless. [C16: from L *explōdere* to drive off by clapping, from EX-[1] + *plaudere* to clap] —**ex'ploder** *n.*

exploded view *n.* a drawing or photograph of a mechanism that shows its parts separately, usually indicating their relative positions.

exploit *n.* ('ɛksplɔɪt). **1.** a notable deed or feat, esp. one that is heroic. ~*vb.* (ɪk'splɔɪt). (*tr.*) **2.** to take advantage of (a person, situation, etc.) for one's own ends. **3.** to make the best use of. [C14: from OF: accomplishment, from L *explicitum* (something) unfolded, from *explicāre* to EXPLICATE] —**ex'ploitable** *adj.* —**,exploi'tation** *n.* —**ex'ploitive** *or* **ex'ploitative** *adj.*

exploration (ˌɛksplə'reɪʃən) *n.* **1.** the act or process of exploring. **2.** an organized trip into unfamiliar regions, esp. for scientific purposes. —**exploratory** (ɪk-'splɒrətərɪ, -trɪ) *or* **ex'plorative** *adj.*

explore (ɪk'splɔː) *vb.* **1.** (*tr.*) to examine or investigate, esp. systematically. **2.** to travel into (unfamiliar regions), esp. for scientific purposes. **3.** (*tr.*) *Med.* to examine (an organ or part) for diagnostic purposes. [C16: from L, from EX-[1] + *plōrāre* to cry aloud; prob. from the shouts of hunters sighting prey] —**ex'plorer** *n.*

explosion (ɪk'spləʊʒən) *n.* **1.** the act or an instance of exploding. **2.** a violent release of energy resulting from a rapid chemical or nuclear reaction. **3.** a sudden or violent outburst of activity, noise, emotion, etc. **4.** a rapid increase, esp. in a population. [C17: from L *explōsiō*, from *explōdere* to EXPLODE]

explosive (ɪk'spləʊsɪv) *adj.* **1.** of, involving, or characterized by explosion. **2.** capable of exploding or tending to explode. **3.** potentially violent or hazardous: *an explosive situation.* ~*n.* **4.** a substance capable of exploding or tending to explode. —**ex'plosiveness** *n.*

expo ('ɛkspəʊ) *n., pl.* **-pos.** short for **exposition** (sense 3).

exponent (ɪk'spəʊnənt) *n.* **1.** (usually foll. by *of*) a person or thing that acts as an advocate (of an idea, cause, etc.). **2.** a person or thing that explains or interprets. **3.** a performer or artist. **4.** Also called: **power, index.** *Maths.* a number or variable placed as a superscript to another number or quantity indicating the number of times the number or quantity is to be multiplied by itself. ~*adj.* **5.**

offering a declaration, explanation, or interpretation. [C16: from L *exponere* to set out, expound]

exponential (,ɛkspəʊ'nɛnʃəl) *adj.* **1.** *Maths.* (of a function, curve, etc.) of or involving numbers or quantities raised to an exponent, esp. e^x. **2.** *Maths.* raised to the power of e, the base of natural logarithms. **3.** of or involving an exponent or exponents. **4.** *Inf.* very rapid. ~*n.* **5.** *Maths.* an exponential function, etc.

exponential distribution *n. Statistics.* a continuous single-parameter distribution used esp. when making statements about the length of life of materials or times between random events.

export *n.* ('ɛkspɔːt). **1.** (*often pl.*) **a.** goods (**visible exports**) or services (**invisible exports**) sold to a foreign country or countries. **b.** (*as modifier*): *an export licence.* ~*vb.* (ɪk'spɔːt, 'ɛkspɔːt). **2.** to sell (goods or services) or ship (goods) to a foreign country. **3.** (*tr.*) to transmit or spread (an idea, institution, etc.) abroad. [C15: from L *exportāre* to carry away] —**ex'portable** *adj.* —ex,port-a'bility *n.* —**ex'porter** *n.*

export reject *n.* an article that fails to meet a standard of quality required for export and that is sold on the home market.

expose (ɪk'spəʊz) *vb.* (*tr.*) **1.** to display for viewing; exhibit. **2.** to bring to public notice; disclose. **3.** to divulge the identity of; unmask. **4.** (foll. by *to*) to make subject or susceptible (to attack, criticism, etc.). **5.** to abandon (a child, etc.) in the open to die. **6.** (foll. by *to*) to introduce (to) or acquaint (with). **7.** *Photog.* to subject (a film or plate) to light, x-rays, etc. **8. expose oneself.** to display one's sexual organs in public. [C15: from OF *exposer*, from L *expōnere* to set out] —**ex'posable** *adj.* —**ex'posal** *n.* —**ex'poser** *n.*

exposé (ɛks'pəʊzeɪ) *n.* the act or an instance of bringing a scandal, crime, etc., to public notice.

exposed (ɪk'spəʊzd) *adj.* **1.** not concealed; displayed for viewing. **2.** without shelter from the elements. **3.** susceptible to attack or criticism; vulnerable. —**exposedness** (ɪk'spəʊzɪdnɪs) *n.*

exposition (,ɛkspə'zɪʃən) *n.* **1.** a systematic, usually written statement about or explanation of a subject. **2.** the act of expounding or setting forth information or a viewpoint. **3.** a large public exhibition, esp. of industrial products or arts and crafts. **4.** the act of exposing or the state of being exposed. **5.** *Music.* the first statement of the subjects or themes of a movement in sonata form or a fugue. **6.** *R.C. Church.* the exhibiting of the consecrated Eucharistic Host or a relic for public veneration. [C14: from L *expositiō* a setting forth, from *expōnere* to display] —,expo'sitional *adj.*

expositor (ɪk'spɒzɪtə) *n.* a person who expounds.

expository (ɪk'spɒzɪtərɪ, -trɪ) *or* **expositive** *adj.* of or involving exposition; explanatory. —**ex'positorily** *or* **ex'positively** *adv.*

ex post facto (ɛks pəʊst 'fæktəʊ) *adj.* having retrospective effect. [C17: from L *ex* from + *post* afterwards + *factus* done, from *facere* to do]

expostulate (ɪk'spɒstjʊ,leɪt) *vb.* (*intr.;* usually foll. by *with*) to argue or reason (with), esp. in order to dissuade. [C16: from L *expostulāre* to require, from *postulāre* to demand; see POSTULATE] —**ex,postu'lation** *n.* —**ex'postu,lator** *n.* —**ex'postulatory** *or* **ex'postulative** *adj.*

exposure (ɪk'spəʊʒə) *n.* **1.** the act of exposing or the condition of being exposed. **2.** the position or outlook of a house, building, etc.: *a southern exposure.* **3.** lack of shelter from the weather, esp. the cold. **4.** a surface that is exposed. **5.** *Photog.* **a.** the act of exposing a film or plate to light, x-rays, etc. **b.** an area on a film or plate that has been exposed. **6.** *Photog.* **a.** the intensity of light falling on a film or plate multiplied by the time for which it is exposed. **b.** a combination of lens aperture and shutter speed used in taking a photograph. **7.** appearance before the public, as in a theatre, on television, etc.

exposure meter *n. Photog.* an instrument for measuring the intensity of light so that suitable camera settings can be determined. Also called: **light meter.**

expound (ɪk'spaʊnd) *vb.* (when *intr.,* foll. by *on* or *about*) to explain or set forth (an argument, theory, etc.) in detail. [C13: from OF, from L *expōnere* to set forth, from *pōnere* to put] —**ex'pounder** *n.*

express (ɪk'sprɛs) *vb.* (*tr.*) **1.** to transform (ideas) into words; utter; verbalize. **2.** to show or reveal. **3.** to communicate (emotion, etc.) without words, as through music, painting, etc. **4.** to indicate through a symbol, formula, etc. **5.** to squeeze out: *to express the juice from an orange.* **6. express oneself.** to communicate one's thoughts or ideas. ~*adj.* (*prenominal*) **7.** clearly indicated; explicitly stated. **8.** done or planned for a definite reason; particular. **9.** of or designed for rapid transportation of people, mail, etc.: *express delivery.* ~*n.* **10. a.** a system for sending mail, money, etc., rapidly. **b.** mail, etc., conveyed by such a system. **c.** *Chiefly U.S. & Canad.* an enterprise operating such a system. **11.** Also: **express train.** a fast train stopping at no or only a few stations between its termini. ~*adv.* **12.** by means of express delivery. [C14: from L *expressus,* lit.: squeezed out, hence, prominent, from *exprimere* to force out, from EX-[1] + *premere* to press] —**ex'presser** *n.* —**ex'pressible** *adj.*

expressage (ɪk'sprɛsɪdʒ) *n.* **1.** the conveyance of merchandise by express. **2.** the fee for this.

expression (ɪk'sprɛʃən) *n.* **1.** the act or an instance of transforming ideas into words. **2.** a manifestation of an emotion, feeling, etc., without words. **3.** communication of emotion through music, painting, etc. **4.** a look on the face that indicates mood or emotion. **5.** the choice of words, intonation, etc., in communicating. **6.** a particular phrase used conventionally to express something. **7.** the act or process of squeezing out a liquid. **8.** *Maths.* a variable, function, or some combination of these. —**ex'pressional** *adj.* —**ex'pressionless** *adj.*

expressionism (ɪk'sprɛʃə,nɪzəm) *n.* (*sometimes cap.*) an artistic and literary movement originating in the early 20th century, which sought to express emotions rather than to represent external reality: characterized by symbolism and distortion. —**ex'pressionist** *n.,* *adj.* —**ex,pression'istic** *adj.*

expression mark *n.* one of a set of musical directions, usually in Italian, indicating how a piece or passage is to be performed.

expressive (ɪk'sprɛsɪv) *adj.* **1.** of, involving, or full of expression. **2.** (*postpositive;* foll. by *of*) indicative or suggestive (of). **3.** having a particular meaning or force; significant. —**ex'pressiveness** *n.*

expressly (ɪk'sprɛslɪ) *adv.* **1.** for an express purpose. **2.** plainly, exactly, or unmistakably.

expresso (ɪk'sprɛsəʊ) *n., pl.* **-sos.** a variant of **espresso.**

expressway (ɪk'sprɛs,weɪ) *n.* a motorway.

expropriate (ɛks'prəʊprɪ,eɪt) *vb.* (*tr.*) to deprive (an owner) of (property), esp. by taking it for public use. [C17: from Med. L *expropriāre* to deprive of possessions, from *proprius* own] —**ex,propri'ation** *n.* —**ex'propri,ator** *n.*

expulsion (ɪk'spʌlʃən) *n.* the act of expelling or the fact or condition of being expelled. [C14: from L *expulsiō* a driving out, from *expellere* to EXPEL] —**ex'pulsive** *adj.*

expunge (ɪk'spʌndʒ) *vb.* (*tr.*) to delete or erase; blot out; obliterate. [C17: from L *expungere* to blot out, from *pungere* to prick] —**expunction** (ɪk'spʌŋkʃən) *n.* —**ex'punger** *n.*

expurgate ('ɛkspə,geɪt) *vb.* (*tr.*) to amend (a book, text, etc.) by removing (offensive sections). [C17: from L *expurgāre* to clean out, from *purgāre* to purify; see PURGE] —,expur'gation *n.* —'expur,gator *n.* —expurgatory (ɛks'pɜːgətərɪ) *or* **expurgatorial** (ɛk,spɜːgə'tɔːrɪəl) *adj.*

exquisite (ɪk'skwɪzɪt, 'ɛkskwɪzɪt) *adj.* **1.** possessing qualities of unusual delicacy and craftsmanship. **2.** extremely beautiful. **3.** outstanding or excellent. **4.** sensitive; discriminating. **5.** fastidious and refined. **6.** intense or sharp in feeling. ~*n.* **7.** *Obs.* a dandy. [C15: from L *exquīsītus* excellent, from *exquīrere* to search out, from *quaerere* to seek] —**ex'quisiteness** *n.*

ex-serviceman *or* (*fem.*) **ex-servicewoman** *n., pl.* **-men** *or* **-women.** a person who has served in the armed forces.

extant (ɛk'stænt, 'ɛkstənt) *adj.* still in existence; surviving. [C16: from L *exstāns* standing out, from *exstāre,* from *stāre* to stand]
▷ **Usage.** Careful writers distinguish between *extant* and *existent.* Both are used of that which exists at the present time, but *extant* has a further connotation of survival.

extemporaneous (ɪk,stɛmpə'reɪnɪəs) *or* **extemporary** (ɪk'stɛmpərərɪ) *adj.* **1.** spoken, performed, etc., without preparation; extempore. **2.** done in a temporary manner; improvised. —**ex,tempo'raneously** *or* **ex'temporarily** *adv.* —**ex,tempo'raneousness** *or* **ex'temporariness** *n.*

extempore (ɪkˈstɛmpərɪ) *adv., adj.* without planning or preparation. [C16: from L *ex tempore* instantaneously, from EX-[1] out of + *tempus* time]

extemporize *or* -**rise** (ɪkˈstɛmpəˌraɪz) *vb.* **1.** to perform, speak, or compose (an act, speech, music, etc.) without preparation. **2.** to use a temporary solution; improvise. —**ex,tempori'zation** *or* -**ri'sation** *n.* —**ex'tempo,rizer** *or* -,**riser** *n.*

extend (ɪkˈstɛnd) *vb.* **1.** to draw out or be drawn out; stretch. **2.** to last or cause to last for a certain time. **3.** (*intr.*) to reach a certain point in time or distance. **4.** (*intr.*) to exist or occur. **5.** (*tr.*) to increase (a building, etc.) in size; add to or enlarge. **6.** (*tr.*) to broaden the meaning or scope of: *the law was extended.* **7.** (*tr.*) to present or offer. **8.** to stretch forth (an arm, etc.). **9.** (*tr.*) to lay out (a body) at full length. **10.** (*tr.*) to strain or exert (a person or animal) to the maximum. **11.** (*tr.*) to prolong (the time) for payment of (a debt or loan), completion of (a task), etc. [C14: from L *extendere* to stretch out, from *tendere* to stretch] —**ex'tendible** *or* **ex'tendable** *adj.* —**ex,tendi'bility** *or* **ex,tenda'bility** *n.*

extended family *n. Sociol., anthropol.* the nuclear family together with blood relatives, often spanning three or more generations.

extended-play *adj.* denoting an EP record.

extender (ɪkˈstɛndə) *n.* **1.** a person or thing that extends. **2.** a substance added to paints to give body and decrease their rate of settlement. **3.** a substance added to glues and resins to dilute them or to modify their viscosity.

extensible (ɪkˈstɛnsɪbəl) *or* **extensile** (ɪkˈstɛnsaɪl) *adj.* capable of being extended. —**ex,tensi'bility** *or* **ex'tensibleness** *n.*

extension (ɪkˈstɛnʃən) *n.* **1.** the act of extending or the condition of being extended. **2.** something that can be extended or that extends another object. **3.** the length, range, etc., over which something is extended. **4.** an additional telephone set connected to the same telephone line as another set. **5.** a room or rooms added to an existing building. **6.** a delay in the date originally set for payment of a debt or completion of a contract. **7.** the property of matter by which it occupies space. **8. a.** the act of straightening or extending an arm or leg. **b.** its position after being straightened or extended. **9. a.** a service by which the facilities of an educational establishment, library, etc., are offered to outsiders. **b.** (*as modifier*): *a university extension course.* **10.** *Logic.* the class of entities to which a given word correctly applies. [C14: from LL *extensiō* a stretching out; see EXTEND] —**ex'tensional** *adj.* —**ex,tension'ality** *or* **ex'tensional,ism** *n.*

extensive (ɪkˈstɛnsɪv) *adj.* **1.** having a large extent, area, degree, etc. **2.** widespread. **3.** *Agriculture.* involving or farmed with minimum expenditure of capital or labour, esp. depending on a large extent of land. Cf. **intensive** (sense 3). **4.** of or relating to logical extension. —**ex'tensiveness** *n.*

extensor (ɪkˈstɛnsə, -sɔː) *n.* any muscle that stretches or extends an arm, leg, or other bodily part. Cf. **flexor.** [C18: from NL, from L *extensus* stretched out]

extent (ɪkˈstɛnt) *n.* **1.** the range over which something extends; scope. **2.** an area or volume. [C14: from OF, from L *extentus* extensive, from *extendere* to EXTEND]

extenuate (ɪkˈstɛnjʊˌeɪt) *vb.* (*tr.*) **1.** to represent (an offence, fault, etc.) as being less serious than it appears, as by showing mitigating circumstances. **2.** to cause to be or appear less serious; mitigate. **3.** *Arch.* **a.** to emaciate or weaken. **b.** to dilute or thin out. [C16: from L *extenuāre* to make thin, from *tenuis* thin, frail] —**ex'ten,u,ating** *adj.* —**ex,tenu'ation** *n.* —**ex'tenu,ator** *n.* —**ex'tenuatory** *adj.*

exterior (ɪkˈstɪərɪə) *n.* **1.** a part, surface, or region that is on the outside. **2.** the outward behaviour or appearance of a person. **3.** a film or scene shot outside a studio. ~*adj.* **4.** of, situated on, or suitable for the outside. **5.** coming or acting from without. [C16: from L, comp. of *exterus* on the outside, from *ex* out of] —**ex'teriorly** *adv.*

exterior angle *n.* **1.** an angle of a polygon contained between one side extended and the adjacent side. **2.** any of the four angles made by a transversal that are outside the region between the two intersected lines.

exteriorize *or* -**ise** (ɪkˈstɪərɪəˌraɪz) *vb.* (*tr.*) **1.** *Surgery.* to expose (an attached organ or part) outside the body. **2.** another word for **externalize.** —**ex,teriori'zation** *or* -**i'sation** *n.*

exterminate (ɪkˈstɜːmɪˌneɪt) *vb.* (*tr.*) to destroy (living things, esp. pests or vermin) completely; annihilate; eliminate. [C16: from L *extermināre* to drive away, from *terminus* boundary] —**ex'terminable** *adj.* —**ex,termi'nation** *n.* —**ex'terminative** *or* **ex'terminatory** *adj.* —**ex'termi,nator** *n.*

external (ɪkˈstɜːnəl) *adj.* **1.** of, situated on, or suitable for the outside; outer. **2.** coming or acting from without. **3.** of or involving foreign nations. **4.** of, relating to, or designating a medicine that is applied to the outside of the body. **5.** *Anat.* situated on or near the outside of the body. **6.** *Austral. & N.Z.* (of a student) studying a university subject extramurally. **7.** *Philosophy.* (of objects, etc.) taken to exist independently of a perceiving mind. ~*n.* **8.** (*often pl.*) an external circumstance or aspect, esp. one that is superficial. **9.** *Austral. & N.Z.* an extramural student. [C15: from L *externus* outward, from *exterus* on the outside, from *ex* out of] —,**exter'nality** *n.*

externalize *or* -**ise** (ɪkˈstɜːnəˌlaɪz) *vb.* (*tr.*) **1.** to make external; give outward shape to. **2.** *Psychol.* to project (one's feelings) to one's surroundings. —**ex,ternali'zation** *or* -**i'sation** *n.*

extinct (ɪkˈstɪŋkt) *adj.* **1.** (of an animal or plant species) having died out. **2.** quenched or extinguished. **3.** (of a volcano) no longer liable to erupt; inactive. [C15: from L *exstinctus* quenched, from *exstinguere* to EXTINGUISH]

extinction (ɪkˈstɪŋkʃən) *n.* **1.** the act of making extinct or the state of being extinct. **2.** the act of extinguishing or the state of being extinguished. **3.** complete destruction; annihilation. **4.** *Physics.* reduction of the intensity of radiation as a result of absorption or scattering by matter.

extinguish (ɪkˈstɪŋgwɪʃ) *vb.* (*tr.*) **1.** to put out or quench (a light, flames, etc.). **2.** to remove or destroy entirely; annihilate. **3.** *Arch.* to eclipse or obscure. [C16: from L *exstinguere*, from *stinguere* to quench] —**ex'tinguishable** *adj.* —**ex'tinguisher** *n.* —**ex'tinguishment** *n.*

extirpate (ˈɛkstəˌpeɪt) *vb.* (*tr.*) **1.** to remove or destroy completely. **2.** to pull up or root; uproot. [C16: from L *exstirpāre* to root out, from *stirps* root, stock] —,**extir'pation** *n.* —**'extir,pative** *adj.* —**'extir,pator** *n.*

extol *or U.S.* **extoll** (ɪkˈstəʊl) *vb.* -**tolling, -tolled.** (*tr.*) to praise lavishly; exalt. [C15: from L *extollere* to elevate, from *tollere* to raise] —**ex'toller** *n.* —**ex'tolment** *n.*

extort (ɪkˈstɔːt) *vb.* (*tr.*) **1.** to secure (money, favours, etc.) by intimidation, violence, or the misuse of authority. **2.** to obtain by importunate demands. [C16: from L *extortus* wrenched out, from *extorquēre* to wrest away, from *torquēre* to twist, wrench] —**ex'tortion** *n.* —**ex'tortioner, ex'tortionist,** *or* **ex'torter** *n.* —**ex'tortive** *adj.*

extortionate (ɪkˈstɔːʃənɪt) *adj.* **1.** (of prices, etc.) excessive; exorbitant. **2.** (of persons) using extortion. —**ex'tortionately** *adv.*

extra (ˈɛkstrə) *adj.* **1.** being more than what is usual or expected; additional. ~*n.* **2.** a person or thing that is additional. **3.** something for which an additional charge is made. **4.** an additional edition of a newspaper, esp. to report a new development. **5.** *Films.* a person temporarily engaged, usually for crowd scenes. **6.** *Cricket.* a run not scored from the bat, such as a wide, no-ball, or bye. ~*adv.* **7.** unusually; exceptionally: *an extra fast car.* [C18: ? shortened from EXTRAORDINARY]

extra- *prefix.* outside or beyond an area or scope: *extrasensory; extraterritorial.* [from L *extrā* outside, beyond, from *extera,* from *exterus* outward]

extra cover *n. Cricket.* a fielding position between cover and mid-off.

extract *vb.* (ɪkˈstrækt). (*tr.*) **1.** to pull out or uproot by force. **2.** to remove or separate. **3.** to derive (pleasure, information, etc.) from some source. **4.** to deduce or develop (a doctrine, policy, etc.). **5.** *Inf.* to extort (money, etc.). **6.** to obtain (a substance) from a mixture or material by a process, such as digestion, distillation, mechanical separation, etc. **7.** to cut out or copy out (an article, passage, etc.) from a publication. **8.** to determine the value of (the root of a number). ~*n.* (ˈɛkstrækt). **9.** something extracted, such as a passage from a book, etc. **10.** a preparation containing the active principle or concentrated essence of a material. [C15: from L *extractus* drawn forth, from *extrahere,* from *trahere* to drag]

—**ex'tractable** *adj.* —**ex,tracta'bility** *n.* —**ex'trac-tive** *adj.* —**ex'tractor** *n.*

extraction (ɪk'strækʃən) *n.* **1.** the act of extracting or the condition of being extracted. **2.** something extracted. **3.** the act or an instance of extracting a tooth. **4.** origin or ancestry.

extracurricular (,ɛkstrəkə'rɪkjʊlə) *adj.* **1.** taking place outside the normal school timetable. **2.** beyond the regular duties, schedule, etc.

extradite ('ɛkstrə,daɪt) *vb.* (*tr.*) **1.** to surrender (an alleged offender) for trial to a foreign state. **2.** to procure the extradition of. [C19: back formation from EXTRADITION] —'**extra,ditable** *adj.*

extradition (,ɛkstrə'dɪʃən) *n.* the surrender of an alleged offender to the state where the alleged offence was committed. [C19: from F, from L *trāditiō* a handing over; see TRADITION]

extrados (ɛk'streɪdɒs) *n.*, *pl.* -**dos** (-dəʊz) *or* -**doses**. *Archit.* the outer curve of an arch or vault. [C18: from F, from EXTRA- + *dos* back]

extragalactic (,ɛkstrəgə'læktɪk) *adj.* occurring or existing beyond the Galaxy.

extramarital (,ɛkstrə'mærɪt³l) *adj.* (esp. of sexual relations) occurring outside marriage.

extramural (,ɛkstrə'mjʊərəl) *adj.* **1.** connected with but outside the normal courses of a university, college, etc. **2.** beyond the boundaries or walls of a city, castle, etc.

extraneous (ɪk'streɪnɪəs) *adj.* **1.** not essential. **2.** not pertinent; irrelevant. **3.** coming from without. **4.** not belonging. [C17: from L *extrāneus* external, from *extrā* outside] —**ex'traneousness** *n.*

extraordinary (ɪk'strɔːd³nrɪ) *adj.* **1.** very unusual or surprising. **2.** not in an established manner or order. **3.** employed for particular purposes. **4.** (*usually postpositive*) (of an official, etc.) additional or subordinate. [C15: from L *extraordinārius* beyond what is usual; see ORDINARY] —**ex'traordinarily** *adv.* —**ex'traordinariness** *n.*

extrapolate (ɪk'stræpə,leɪt) *vb.* **1.** *Maths.* to estimate (a value of a function etc.) beyond the known values, by the extension of a curve. Cf. **interpolate** (sense 4). **2.** to infer (something) by using but not strictly deducing from known facts. [C19: EXTRA- + -*polate*, as in INTERPOLATE] —**ex,trapo'lation** *n.* —**ex'trapolative** *or* **ex'trapo-latory** *adj.* —**ex'trapo,lator** *n.*

extrasensory (,ɛkstrə'sɛnsərɪ) *adj.* of or relating to extrasensory perception.

extrasensory perception *n.* the supposed ability of certain individuals to obtain information about the environment without the use of normal sensory channels.

extraterritorial (,ɛkstrə,tɛrɪ'tɔːrɪəl) *or* **exterritorial** *adj.* **1.** beyond the limits of a country's territory. **2.** of, relating to, or possessing extraterritoriality.

extraterritoriality (,ɛkstrə,tɛrɪ,tɔːrɪ'ælɪtɪ) *n.* **1.** the privilege granted to some aliens, esp. diplomats, of being exempt from the jurisdiction of the state in which they reside. **2.** the right of a state to exercise authority in certain circumstances beyond the limits of its territory.

extra time *n. Sport.* an additional period played at the end of a match, to compensate for time lost through injury or (in certain circumstances) to allow the teams to achieve a conclusive result.

extravagance (ɪk'strævɪgəns) *n.* **1.** excessive outlay of money; wasteful spending. **2.** immoderate or absurd speech or behaviour.

extravagant (ɪk'strævɪgənt) *adj.* **1.** spending money excessively or immoderately. **2.** going beyond usual bounds; unrestrained. **3.** ostentatious; showy. **4.** exorbitant in price; overpriced. [C14: from Med. L *extravagāns*, from L EXTRA- + *vagārī* to wander]

extravaganza (ɪk,strævə'gænzə) *n.* **1.** an elaborately staged light entertainment. **2.** any lavish or fanciful display, literary composition, etc. [C18: from It.: extravagance]

extravasate (ɪk'strævə,seɪt) *vb. Pathol.* to cause (blood or lymph) to escape or (of blood or lymph) to escape into the surrounding tissues from their proper vessels. [C17: from L EXTRA-+ *vās* vessel] —**ex,trava'sation** *n.*

extravehicular (,ɛkstrəvɪ'hɪkjʊlə) *adj.* occurring or used outside a spacecraft, either in space or on the surface of a planet.

extraversion (,ɛkstrə'vɜːʃən) *n.* a variant spelling of extroversion. —'**extra,vert** *n.*, *adj.*

Extremadura (estrema'ðura) *n.* the Spanish name for **Estremadura**.

extreme (ɪk'striːm) *adj.* **1.** being of a high or of the highest degree or intensity. **2.** exceeding what is usual or reasonable; immoderate. **3.** very strict or severe; drastic. **4.** (*prenominal*) farthest or outermost. ~*n.* **5.** the highest or furthest degree (often in **in the extreme, go to extremes**). **6.** (*often pl.*) either of the two limits or ends of a scale or range. **7.** *Maths.* the first or last term of a series or a proportion. [C15: from L *extrēmus* outermost, from *exterus* on the outside; see EXTERIOR] —**ex'tremely** *adv.* —**ex'tremeness** *n.*

extreme unction *n. R.C. Church.* the former name of the sacrament of the anointing of the sick.

extremist (ɪk'striːmɪst) *n.* **1.** a person who favours immoderate or fanatical methods, esp. in being politically radical. ~*adj.* **2.** of or characterized by immoderate or excessive actions, opinions, etc. —**ex'tremism** *n.*

extremity (ɪk'strɛmɪtɪ) *n.*, *pl.* -**ties**. **1.** the farthest or outermost point or section. **2.** the greatest degree. **3.** an extreme condition or state, as of adversity. **4.** a limb, such as a leg or wing, or the end of such a limb. **5.** (*usually pl.*) *Arch.* a drastic or severe measure.

extricate ('ɛkstrɪ,keɪt) *vb.* (*tr.*) **1.** to remove or free from complication, hindrance, or difficulty; disentangle. [C17: from L *extricāre* to disentangle, from EX-¹ + *tricae* vexations] —'**extricable** *adj.* —**ex'trication** *n.*

extrinsic (ɛk'strɪnsɪk) *adj.* **1.** not contained or included within; extraneous. **2.** originating or acting from outside. [C16: from LL *extrinsecus* (adj.) outward, from L (adv.), ult. from *exter* outward + *secus* alongside] —**ex'trinsically** *adv.*

extroversion *or* **extraversion** (,ɛkstrə'vɜːʃən) *n. Psychol.* the directing of one's interest outwards, esp. towards social contacts. [C17: from *extro-* (var. of EXTRA-), contrasting with *intro-*) + -*version*, from L *vertere* to turn] —,**extro'versive** *or* ,**extra'versive** *adj.*

extrovert *or* **extravert** ('ɛkstrə,vɜːt) *Psychol.* ~*n.* **1.** a person concerned more with external reality than inner feelings. ~*adj.* **2.** of or characterized by extroversion. [C20: from *extro-* (var. of EXTRA-, contrasting with *intro-*) + -*vert*, from L *vertere* to turn] —'**extro,verted** *or* '**extra,verted** *adj.*

extrude (ɪk'struːd) *vb.* (*tr.*) **1.** to squeeze or force out. **2.** to produce (moulded sections of plastic, metal, etc.) by ejection from a shaped nozzle or die. **3.** to chop up or pulverize (an item of food) and re-form it to look like a whole. [C16: from L *extrūdere* to thrust out, from *trūdere* to push, thrust] —**ex'truded** *adj.*

extrusion (ɪk'struːʒən) *n.* **1.** the act or process of extruding. **2. a.** the movement of magma through volcano craters and cracks in the earth's crust, forming igneous rock. **b.** any igneous rock formed in this way. **3.** anything formed by the process of extruding. [C16: from Med. L *extrūsiō*, from *extrūdere* to EXTRUDE] —**ex'trusive** *adj.*

exuberant (ɪg'zjuːbərənt) *adj.* **1.** abounding in vigour and high spirits. **2.** lavish or effusive; excessively elaborate. **3.** growing luxuriantly or in profusion. [C15: from L *exūberāns*, from *ūberāre* to be fruitful] —**ex'uberance** *n.*

exuberate (ɪg'zjuːbə,reɪt) *vb.* (*intr.*) *Rare.* **1.** to be exuberant. **2.** to abound. [C15: from L *exūberāre* to be abundant; see EXUBERANT]

exude (ɪg'zjuːd) *vb.* **1.** to release or be released through pores, incisions, etc., as sweat or sap. **2.** (*tr.*) to make apparent by mood or behaviour. [C16: from L *exsūdāre*, from *sūdāre* to sweat] —**exudation** (,ɛksjʊ'deɪʃən) *n.*

exult (ɪg'zʌlt) *vb.* (*intr.*) **1.** to be joyful or jubilant, esp. because of triumph or success. **2.** (*often foll. by over*) to triumph (over). [C16: from L *exsultāre* to jump or leap for joy, from *saltāre* to leap] —**exultation** (,ɛgzʌl'teɪʃən) *n.* —**ex'ultingly** *adv.*

exultant (ɪg'zʌltənt) *adj.* elated or jubilant, esp. because of triumph or success. —**ex'ultantly** *adv.*

exurbia (ɛks'ɜːbɪə) *n. Chiefly U.S.* the region outside the suburbs of a city, consisting of residential areas (**exurbs**) occupied predominantly by rich commuters (**exurbanites**). [C20: from EX-¹ + L *urbs* city] —**ex'urban** *adj.*

exuviate (ɪg'zjuːvɪ,eɪt) *vb.* to shed (a skin or similar outer covering). —**ex,uvi'ation** *n.*

-ey *suffix.* a variant of **-y**^{1} and **-y**^{2}.

eyas ('aɪəs) *n.* a nestling hawk or falcon, esp. one reared for falconry. [C15: mistaken division of earlier *a nyas*, from OF *niais* nestling, from L *nīdus* nest]

eye^1 (aɪ) *n.* **1.** the organ of sight of animals. Related adjs.: **ocular, ophthalmic. 2.** (*often pl.*) the ability to see; sense of vision. **3.** the external part of an eye, often including the area around it. **4.** a look, glance, expression, or gaze. **5.** a sexually inviting or provocative look (esp. in **give (someone) the (glad) eye, make eyes at**). **6.** attention or observation (often in **catch someone's eye, keep an eye on, cast an eye over**). **7.** ability to recognize, judge, or appreciate. **8.** (*often pl.*) opinion, judgment, point of view, or authority: *in the eyes of the law*. **9.** a structure or marking resembling an eye, such as the bud on a potato tuber or a spot on a butterfly wing. **10.** a small loop or hole, as at one end of a needle. **11.** a small area of low pressure and calm in the centre of a tornado. **12. electric eye.** another name for **photocell. 13. all eyes.** *Inf.* acutely vigilant or observant. **14. (all) my eye.** *Inf.* nonsense. **15. an eye for an eye.** retributive or vengeful justice; retaliation. **16. get one's eye in.** *Chiefly sport.* to become accustomed to the conditions, light, etc., with a consequent improvement in one's performance. **17. go eyes out.** *Austral. & N.Z.* to make every possible effort. **18. half an eye.** a modicum of perceptiveness. **19. have eyes for.** to be interested in. **20. in one's mind's eye.** pictured within the mind; imagined or remembered vividly. **21. in the public eye.** exposed to public curiosity or publicity. **22. keep an eye open** *or* **out (for).** to watch with special attention (for). **23. keep one's eyes skinned** (*or* **peeled**). to watch vigilantly (for). **24. lay, clap,** *or* **set eyes on.** (*usually with a negative*) to see. **25. look (someone) in the eye.** to look openly and without shame or embarrassment at (someone). **26. make sheep's eyes (at).** *Old-fashioned.* to ogle amorously. **27. more than meets the eye.** hidden motives, meaning, or facts. **28. see eye to eye (with).** to agree (with). **29. shut one's eyes (to)** *or* **turn a blind eye (to).** to pretend not to notice or to ignore deliberately. **30. up to one's eyes (in).** extremely busy (with). **31. with** *or* **having an eye to.** (*prep.*) **a.** regarding; with reference to. **b.** with the intention or purpose of. **32. with one's eyes open.** in the full knowledge of all relevant facts. **33. with one's eyes shut. a.** with great ease, esp. as a result of thorough familiarity. **b.** without being aware of all the facts. ~*vb.* **eyeing** *or* **eying, eyed.** (*tr.*) **34.** to look at carefully or warily. **35.** Also: **eye up.** to look at in a manner indicating sexual interest; ogle. [OE *ēage*] — **'eyeless** *adj.* — **'eye,like** *adj.*

eye^2 (aɪ) *n.* another word for **nye.**

eyeball ('aɪ,bɔːl) *n.* **1.** the entire ball-shaped part of the eye. **2. eyeball to eyeball.** in close confrontation. ~*vb.* **3.** (*tr.*) *Sl., chiefly U.S.* to stare at.

eyebank ('aɪ,bæŋk) *n.* a place in which corneas are stored for use in corneal grafts.

eyebath ('aɪ,bɑːθ) *n.* a small vessel for applying medicated or cleansing solutions to the eye. Also called (U.S. and Canad.) **eyecup.**

eyeblack ('aɪ,blæk) *n.* another name for **mascara.**

eyebright ('aɪ,braɪt) *n.* an annual plant having small white-and-purple flowers: formerly used in the treatment of eye disorders.

eyebrow ('aɪ,braʊ) *n.* **1.** the transverse bony ridge over each eye. **2.** the arch of hair that covers this ridge. **3. raise an eyebrow.** to give rise to doubt or disapproval.

eyebrow pencil *n.* a cosmetic in pencil form for applying colour and shape to the eyebrows.

eye-catching *adj.* tending to attract attention; striking. — **'eye-,catcher** *n.*

eye contact *n.* a direct look between two people; meeting of eyes.

eyed (aɪd) *adj.* **a.** having an eye or eyes (as specified). **b.** (*in combination*): *brown-eyed*.

eye dog *n.* *N.Z.* a dog trained to control sheep by staring fixedly at them. Also called: **strong-eye dog.**

eyeful ('aɪ,fʊl) *n.* *Inf.* **1.** a view, glance, or gaze. **2.** a beautiful or attractive sight, esp. a woman.

eyeglass ('aɪ,glɑːs) *n.* **1.** a lens for aiding or correcting defective vision, esp. a monocle. **2.** another word for **eyepiece** or **eyebath.**

eyeglasses ('aɪ,glɑːsɪz) *pl. n.* *Now chiefly U.S.* another word for **spectacles.**

eyehole ('aɪ,həʊl) *n.* **1.** a hole through which a rope, hook, etc., is passed. **2.** the cavity that contains the eyeball. **3.** another word for **peephole.**

eyelash ('aɪ,læʃ) *n.* **1.** any one of the short curved hairs that grow from the edge of the eyelids. **2.** a row or fringe of these hairs.

eyelet ('aɪlɪt) *n.* **1.** a small hole for a lace, cord, or hook to be passed through. **2.** a small metal ring or tube reinforcing an eyehole in fabric. **3.** a small opening, such as a peephole. **4.** *Embroidery.* a small hole with finely stitched edges. **5.** a small eye or eyelike marking. ~*vb.* **6.** (*tr.*) to supply with an eyelet or eyelets. [C14: from OF *oillet*, lit.: a little eye, from *oill* eye, from L *oculus* eye]

eyelevel ('aɪ,lɛvˀl) *adj.* level with a person's eyes when looking straight ahead: *an eyelevel grill*.

eyelid ('aɪ,lɪd) *n.* either of the two muscular folds of skin that can be moved to cover the exposed portion of the eyeball.

eyeliner ('aɪ,laɪnə) *n.* a cosmetic used to outline the eyes.

eye-opener *n.* *Inf.* **1.** something startling or revealing. **2.** *U.S. & Canad.* an alcoholic drink taken early in the morning.

eyepiece ('aɪ,piːs) *n.* the lens or lenses in an optical instrument nearest the eye of the observer.

eye rhyme *n.* a rhyme involving words that are similar in spelling but not in sound, such as *stone* and *none*.

eye shadow *n.* a coloured cosmetic put around the eyes.

eyeshot ('aɪ,ʃɒt) *n.* range of vision; view.

eyesight ('aɪ,saɪt) *n.* the ability to see; faculty of sight.

eyesore ('aɪ,sɔː) *n.* something very ugly.

eyespot ('aɪ,spɒt) *n.* **1.** a small area of light-sensitive pigment in some simple organisms. **2.** an eyelike marking, as on a butterfly wing.

eyestrain ('aɪ,streɪn) *n.* fatigue or irritation of the eyes, resulting from excessive use or uncorrected defects of vision.

Eyetie ('aɪtaɪ) *n., adj. Brit. sl., offensive.* Italian. [C20: from jocular mispronunciation of *Italian*]

eyetooth (,aɪ'tuːθ) *n., pl.* **-teeth.** **1.** either of the two canine teeth in the upper jaw. **2. give one's eyeteeth for.** to go to any lengths to achieve or obtain (something).

eyewash ('aɪ,wɒʃ) *n.* **1.** a lotion for the eyes. **2.** *Inf.* nonsense; rubbish.

eyewitness ('aɪ,wɪtnɪs) *n.* a person present at an event who can describe what happened.

Eyre (ɛə) *n.* **Lake.** a shallow salt lake in NE central South Australia, about 11 m (35 ft.) below sea level. Area: 9600 sq. km (3700 sq. miles). [C19: after E. J. *Eyre* (1815–1901), E explorer, who discovered it]

Eyre Peninsula *n.* a peninsula of South Australia, between the Great Australian Bight and Spencer Gulf.

eyrie ('ɪərɪ, 'ɛərɪ, 'aɪərɪ) *or* **aerie** *n.* **1.** the nest of an eagle or other bird of prey, built in a high inaccessible place. **2.** any high isolated position or place. [C16: from Med. L *airea*, from L *ārea* open field, hence, nest]

eyrir ('eɪrɪə) *n., pl.* **aurar** ('ɔɪraː). an Icelandic monetary unit worth one hundredth of a krona. [ON: ounce (of silver), money; rel. to L *aureus* golden]

Eysenck ('aɪzɛŋk) *n.* **Hans Jürgen** (hænz 'jɜːgən). born 1916, British psychologist, born in Germany, who developed a dimensional theory of personality that stressed the influence of heredity.

Ez. *or* **Ezr.** *Bible. abbrev. for* Ezra.

Ezek. *Bible. abbrev. for* Ezekiel.

Ezekiel (ɪ'ziːkɪəl) *n. Old Testament.* **1.** a Hebrew prophet of the 6th century B.C., exiled to Babylon in 597 B.C. **2.** the book containing his oracles, which describe the downfall of Judah and Jerusalem and their subsequent restoration. Douay spelling: **Ezechiel.**

Ezra ('ɛzrə) *n. Old Testament.* **1.** a Jewish priest of the 5th century B.C., who was sent from Babylon by the Persian king Artaxerxes I to reconstitute observance of the Jewish law and worship in Jerusalem after the captivity. **2.** the book recounting his efforts to perform this task.

F

f *or* **F** (ɛf) *n., pl.* **f's, F's,** *or* **Fs.** **1.** the sixth letter of the English alphabet. **2.** a speech sound represented by this letter, as in *fat.*

f *symbol for:* **1.** *Music.* forte: an instruction to play loudly. **2.** *Physics.* frequency. **3.** *Maths.* function (of). **4.** *Physics.* femto-.

f, f/, *or* **f:** *symbol for* f- number.

F *symbol for:* **1.** *Music.* **a.** the fourth note of the scale of C major. **b.** the major or minor key having this note as its tonic. **2.** Fahrenheit. **3.** farad(s). **4.** *Chem.* fluorine. **5.** *Physics.* force. **6.** franc(s). **7.** *Genetics.* a generation of filial offspring, F_1 being the first generation of offspring.

f. *or* **F.** *abbrev. for:* **1.** fathom(s). **2.** female. **3.** *Grammar.* feminine. **4.** *(pl.* **ff.** *or* **FF.)** folio. **5.** *(pl.* **ff.)** following (page).

F- (of U.S. military aircraft) *abbrev. for* fighter.

fa (fɑː) *n. Music.* a variant spelling of **fah.**

FA (in Britain) *abbrev. for* Football Association.

f.a. *or* **FA** *abbrev. for* fanny adams.

Fabergé ('fæbə,ʒeɪ) *n.* **Peter Carl.** 1846–1920, Russian goldsmith and jeweller, known for the golden Easter eggs and other ornate and fanciful objects that he created for the Russian and other royal families.

Fabian ('feɪbɪən) *adj.* **1.** of or resembling the delaying tactics of Q. Fabius Maximus; cautious. ~*n.* **2.** a member of or sympathizer with the Fabian Society. [C19: from L *Fabiānus* of Fabius] —'**Fabia,nism** *n.*

Fabian Society *n.* an association of British socialists advocating the establishment of socialism by gradual reforms.

Fabius Maximus ('feɪbɪəs 'mæksɪməs) *n.* full name *Quintus Fabius Maximus Verrucosus,* called *Cunctator* (the delayer). died 203 B.C., Roman general and statesman. As commander of the Roman army during the Second Punic War, he withstood Hannibal by his strategy of harassing the Carthaginians while avoiding a pitched battle.

fable ('feɪbʰl) *n.* **1.** a short moral story, esp. one with animals as characters. **2.** a false, fictitious, or improbable account. **3.** a story or legend about supernatural or mythical characters or events. **4.** legends or myths collectively. ~*vb.* **5.** to relate or tell (fables). **6.** *(intr.)* to tell lies. **7.** *(tr.)* to talk about or describe in the manner of a fable. [C13: from L *fābula* story, narrative, from *fārī* to speak, say] —'**fabler** *n.*

fabled ('feɪbʰld) *adj.* **1.** made famous in fable. **2.** fictitious.

fabliau ('fæblɪ,əʊ) *n., pl.* **fabliaux** ('fæblɪ,əʊz). a comic usually ribald verse tale, popular in France in the 12th and 13th centuries. [C19: from F: a little tale, from *fable* tale]

Fablon ('fæblən, -lɒn) *n. Trademark.* a brand of adhesive-backed plastic material used to cover and decorate shelves, worktops, etc.

Fabre (*French* fabrə) *n.* **Jean Henri** (ʒɑ̃ ɑ̃ri). 1823–1915, French entomologist; author of many works on insect life, remarkable for their vivid and minute observation, esp. *Souvenirs Entomologiques* (1879–1907). Nobel prize for literature 1910.

fabric ('fæbrɪk) *n.* **1.** any cloth made from yarn or fibres by weaving, knitting, felting, etc. **2.** the texture of a cloth. **3.** a structure or framework: *the fabric of society.* **4.** a style or method of construction. **5.** *Rare.* a building. [C15: from L *fabrica* workshop, from *faber* craftsman]

fabricate ('fæbrɪ,keɪt) *vb. (tr.)* **1.** to make, build, or construct. **2.** to devise or concoct (a story, etc.). **3.** to fake or forge. [C15: from L, from *fabrica* workshop; see FABRIC] —,**fabri'cation** *n.* —'**fabri,cator** *n.*

fabulist ('fæbjʊlɪst) *n.* **1.** a person who invents or recounts fables. **2.** a person who lies.

fabulous ('fæbjʊləs) *adj.* **1.** almost unbelievable; astounding; legendary: *fabulous wealth.* **2.** *Inf.* extremely good: *a fabulous time at the party.* **3.** of, relating to, or based upon fable: *a fabulous beast.* [C15: from L *fābulōsus* celebrated in fable, from *fābula* FABLE] —'**fabulously** *adv.* —'**fabulousness** *n.*

Fac. *abbrev. for* Faculty.

façade *or* **facade** (fə'sɑːd, fæ-) *n.* **1.** the face of a building, esp. the main front. **2.** a front or outer appearance, esp. a deceptive one. [C17: from F, from It., from *faccia* FACE]

face (feɪs) *n.* **1. a.** the front of the head from the forehead to the lower jaw. **b.** *(as modifier):* *face flannel.* **2. a.** the expression of the countenance: *a sad face.* **b.** a distorted expression, esp. to indicate disgust. **3.** *Inf.* make-up (esp. in **put one's face on**). **4.** outward appearance: *the face of the countryside is changing.* **5.** appearance or pretence (esp. in **put a bold, good, bad,** etc., **face on**). **6.** dignity (esp. in **lose** *or* **save face**). **7.** *Inf.* impudence or effrontery. **8.** the main side of an object, building, etc., or the front: *a cliff face.* **9.** the marked surface of an instrument, esp. the dial of a timepiece. **10.** the functional or working side of an object, as of a tool or playing card. **11. a.** the exposed area of a mine from which coal, ore, etc., may be mined. **b.** *(as modifier):* *face worker.* **12.** the uppermost part or surface: *the face of the earth.* **13.** Also called: **side.** any one of the plane surfaces of a crystal or other solid figure. **14.** Also called: **typeface.** *Printing.* **a.** the printing surface of any type character. **b.** the style or design of the character on the type. **15.** *N.Z.* the exposed slope of a hill. **16. in (the) face of.** despite. **17. on the face of it.** to all appearances. **18. set one's face against.** to oppose with determination. **19. show one's face.** to make an appearance. **20. to someone's face.** in someone's presence: *I told him the truth to his face.* ~*vb.* **21.** (when *intr.,* often foll. by *to, towards,* or *on*) to look or be situated or placed (in a specified direction): *the house faces onto the square.* **22.** to be opposite: *facing page 9.* **23.** *(tr.)* to be confronted by: *he faces many problems.* **24.** *(tr.)* to provide with a surface of a different material. **25.** to dress the surface of (stone or other material). **26.** *(tr.)* to expose (a card) with the face uppermost. **27.** *Mil.* to order (a formation) to turn in a certain direction or (of a formation) to turn as required: *right face!* ~See also **face up to.** [C13: from OF, from Vulgar L *facia* (unattested), from L *faciēs* form]

face card *n.* the usual U.S. and Canad. term for **court card.**

face cloth *or* **face flannel** *n. Brit.* a small piece of cloth used to wash the face and hands. U.S. equivalent: **washcloth.**

faceless ('feɪslɪs) *adj.* **1.** without a face. **2.** without identity; anonymous. —'**facelessness** *n.*

face-lift *n.* **1.** cosmetic surgery for tightening sagging skin and smoothing wrinkles on the face. **2.** any improvement or renovation. ~*vb. (tr.)* **3.** to improve the appearance of, as by a face-lift.

face-off *Ice hockey, etc.* ~*n.* **1.** the method of starting a game, in which the referee drops the puck, etc. between two opposing players. ~*vb.* **face off.** *(adv.)* **2.** to start play by (a face-off).

face powder *n.* a cosmetic powder worn to make the face look less shiny, softer, etc.

facer ('feɪsə) *n.* **1.** a person or thing that faces. **2.** *Brit. inf.* a difficulty or problem.

face-saving *adj.* maintaining dignity or prestige. —'**face,saver** *n.*

facet ('fæsɪt) *n.* **1.** any of the surfaces of a cut gemstone. **2.** an aspect or phase, as of a subject or personality. ~*vb.* **-eting, -eted** *or* **-etting, -etted.** **3.** *(tr.)* to cut facets in (a gemstone). [C17: from F *facette* a little FACE]

facetiae (fə'siːʃɪ,iː) *pl. n.* **1.** humorous or witty sayings. **2.** obscene or coarsely witty books. [C17: from L: jests, pl. of *facētia* witticism, from *facētus* elegant]

facetious (fə'siːʃəs) *adj.* **1.** characterized by love of joking. **2.** jocular or amusing, esp. at inappropriate times: *facetious remarks.* [C16: from OF *facetieux,* from *facetie* witticism; see FACETIAE] —**fa'cetiously** *adv.* —**fa'cetiousness** *n.*

face to face *adv., adj.* **(face-to-face** *as adj.)* **1.** opposite one another. **2.** in confrontation.

face up to vb. (intr., adv. + prep.) to accept (an unpleasant fact, reality, etc.).

face value n. **1.** the value written or stamped on the face of a commercial paper or coin. **2.** apparent worth or value.

facia ('feɪʃɪə) n. a variant spelling of **fascia**.

facial ('feɪʃəl) adj. **1.** of or relating to the face. ~n. **2.** a beauty treatment for the face involving massage and cosmetic packs. — **'facially** adv.

facial eczema n. a disease of sheep and cattle characterized by impairment of liver function, itching, scab formation, and swelling of the skin, esp. on the face.

-facient suffix forming adjectives and nouns. indicating a state or quality: absorbefacient. [from L facient-, faciēns, present participle of facere to do]

facies ('feɪʃɪ,iːz) n., pl. **-cies**. **1.** the general form and appearance of an individual or a group. **2.** the characteristics of a rock or rocks reflecting their appearance and conditions of formation. **3.** Med. the general facial expression of a patient. [C17: from L: appearance, FACE]

facile ('fæsaɪl) adj. **1.** easy to perform or achieve. **2.** working or moving easily or smoothly. **3.** superficial: a facile solution. [C15: from L facilis easy, from facere to do] — **'facilely** adv. — **'facileness** n.

facilitate (fə'sɪlɪ,teɪt) vb. (tr.) to assist the progress of. — **fa,cili'tation** n.

facility (fə'sɪlɪtɪ) n., pl. **-ties**. **1.** ease of action or performance. **2.** ready skill or ease deriving from practice or familiarity. **3.** (often pl.) the means or equipment facilitating the performance of an action. **4.** Rare. easy-going disposition. **5.** (usually pl.) a euphemistic word for **lavatory**. [C15: from L facilitās, from facilis easy; see FACILE]

facing ('feɪsɪŋ) n. **1.** a piece of material used esp. to conceal the seam of a garment and prevent fraying. **2.** (usually pl.) the collar, cuffs, etc., of the jacket of a military uniform. **3.** an outer layer or coat of material applied to the surface of a wall.

facsimile (fæk'sɪmɪlɪ) n. **1.** an exact copy or reproduction. **2.** a telegraphic system in which a written or pictorial document is scanned photoelectrically, the resulting signals being transmitted and reproduced photographically. Often shortened to **fax**. ~vb. **-leing, -led**. **3.** (tr.) to make an exact copy of. [C17: from L fac simile! make something like it!, from facere to make + similis similar, like]

fact (fækt) n. **1.** an event or thing known to have happened or existed. **2.** a truth verifiable from experience or observation. **3.** a piece of information: get me all the facts of this case. **4.** (often pl.) Law. an actual event, happening, etc., as distinguished from its legal consequences. **5. after** (or **before**) **the fact**. Criminal law. after (or before) the commission of the offence. **6. as a matter of fact, in fact, in point of fact**. in reality or actuality. **7. fact of life**. an inescapable truth, esp. an unpleasant one. See also **facts of life**. [C16: from L factum something done, from factus made, from facere to do, make]

faction[1] ('fækʃən) n. **1.** a group of people forming a minority within a larger body, esp. a dissentious group. **2.** strife or dissension within a group. [C16: from L factiō a making, from facere to do, make] — **'factional** adj.

faction[2] ('fækʃən) n. a television programme, film, or literary work comprising a dramatized presentation of actual events. [C20: a blend of FACT & FICTION]

faction fight n. conflict between different groups within a larger body, esp. in S Africa in a fight between Blacks of different tribes.

factious ('fækʃəs) adj. given to, producing, or characterized by faction. — **'factiously** adv.

factitious (fæk'tɪʃəs) adj. **1.** artificial rather than natural. **2.** not genuine; sham: factitious enthusiasm. [C17: from L factīcius, from facere to do, make] — **fac'titiously** adv. — **fac'titiousness** n.

factitive ('fæktɪtɪv) adj. Grammar. denoting a verb taking a direct object as well as a noun in apposition, as for example elect in They elected John president, where John is the direct object and president is the complement. [C19: from NL, from L factitāre to do frequently, from facere to do, make]

factoid ('fæktɔɪd) n. a piece of unreliable information believed to be true because of the way it is presented or repeated in print. [C20: coined by Norman MAILER, from FACT + -OID]

factor ('fæktə) n. **1.** an element or cause that contributes to a result. **2.** Maths. one of two or more integers or polynomials whose product is a given integer or polynomial: 2 and 3 are factors of 6. **3.** a person who acts on another's behalf, esp. one who transacts business for another. **4.** former name for a **gene**. **5.** Commercial law. a person to whom goods are consigned for sale and who is paid a commission. **6.** (in Scotland) the manager of an estate. ~vb. **7.** (intr.) to engage in the business of a factor. [C15: from L: one who acts, from facere to do, make] — **'factorable** adj. — **'factorship** n.

factor 8 n. a protein that participates in the clotting of blood. It is extracted from donated serum and used in the treatment of haemophilia.

factorial (fæk'tɔːrɪəl) Maths. ~n. **1.** the product of all the positive integers from one up to and including a given integer: factorial four is 1 × 2 × 3 × 4. ~adj. **2.** of or involving factorials or factors. — **fac'torially** adv.

factorize or **-rise** ('fæktə,raɪz) vb. (tr.) Maths. to resolve (an integer or polynomial) into factors. — ,factori'zation or -ri'sation n.

factory ('fæktərɪ) n., pl. **-ries. a.** a building or group of buildings containing a plant assembly for the manufacture of goods. **b.** (as modifier): a factory worker. [C16: from LL factorium; see FACTOR] — **'factory-,like** adj.

factory farm n. a farm in which animals are intensively reared using modern industrial methods. — **factory farming** n.

factory ship n. a vessel that processes fish supplied by a fleet.

factotum (fæk'təʊtəm) n. a person employed to do all kinds of work. [C16: from Med. L, from L fac! do! + tōtum, from tōtus (adj.) all]

facts and figures pl. n. details.

facts of life pl. n. **the.** the details of sexual behaviour and reproduction.

factual ('fæktʃʊəl) adj. **1.** of, relating to, or characterized by facts. **2.** real; actual. — **'factually** adv. — **'factualness** or ,factu'ality n.

facula ('fækjʊlə) n., pl. **-lae** (-,liː). any of the bright areas on the sun's surface, usually appearing just before a sunspot. [C18: from L: little torch, from fax torch] — **'facular** adj.

facultative ('fækəltətɪv) adj. **1.** empowering but not compelling the doing of an act. **2.** that may or may not occur. **3.** Biol. able to exist under more than one set of environmental conditions. **4.** of or relating to a faculty. — **'facultatively** adv.

faculty ('fækəltɪ) n., pl. **-ties. 1.** one of the inherent powers of the mind or body, such as memory, sight, or hearing. **2.** any ability or power, whether acquired or inherent. **3.** a conferred power or right. **4. a.** a department within a university or college devoted to a particular branch of knowledge. **b.** the staff of such a department. **c.** Chiefly U.S. & Canad. all administrative and teaching staff at a university, school, etc. **5.** all members of a learned profession. [C14 (in the sense: department of learning): from L facultās capability; rel. to L facilis easy]

FA Cup n. Soccer. (in England and Wales) **1.** an annual knockout competition among member teams of the Football Association. **2.** the trophy itself.

fad (fæd) n. Inf. **1.** an intense but short-lived fashion. **2.** a personal idiosyncrasy. [C19: from ?] — **'faddish** or **'faddy** adj.

Fadden ('fædⁿ) n. Sir **Arthur William**. 1895–1973, Australian statesman; prime minister of Australia (1941).

fade (feɪd) vb. **1.** to lose or cause to lose brightness, colour, or clarity. **2.** (intr.) to lose vigour or youth. **3.** (intr.; usually foll. by away or out) to vanish slowly. **4. a.** to decrease the brightness or volume of (a television or radio programme) or (of a television programme, etc.) to decrease in this way. **b.** to decrease the volume of (a sound) in a recording system or (of a sound) to be so reduced in volume. **5.** (intr.) (of the brakes of a vehicle) to lose power. **6.** to cause (a golf ball) to veer from a straight line or (of a golf ball) to veer from a straight flight. ~n. **7.** the act or an instance of fading. [C14: from fade (adj.) dull, from OF, from Vulgar L fatidus (unattested), prob. blend of L vapidus VAPID + L fatuus FATUOUS] — **'fadeless** adj. — **'fadedness** n. — **'fader** n.

fade-in n. **1.** Films. an optical effect in which a shot appears gradually out of darkness. ~vb. **fade in.** (adv.) **2.**

to increase or cause to increase gradually, as vision or sound in a film or broadcast.

fade-out n. **1.** *Films.* an optical effect in which a shot slowly disappears into darkness. **2.** a gradual and temporary loss of a radio or television signal. **3.** a slow or gradual disappearance. ~vb. **fade out.** (adv.) **4.** to decrease or cause to decrease gradually, as vision or sound in a film or broadcast.

faeces or esp. U.S. **feces** ('fiːsiːz) pl. n. bodily waste matter discharged through the anus. [C15: from L *faecēs*, pl. of *faex* sediment, dregs] —**faecal** or esp. U.S. **fecal** ('fiːk°l) adj.

Faenza (*Italian* fa'ɛntsa) n. a city in N Italy, in Emilia-Romagna: famous in the 15th and 16th centuries for its majolica earthenware, esp. faience. Pop.: 54 904 (1981 est.).

faerie or **faery** ('feɪərɪ, 'fɛərɪ) n., pl. **-ries.** Arch. or poetic. **1.** the land of fairies. ~adj., n. **2.** a variant spelling of **fairy.**

Faeroes or **Faroes** ('fɛərəʊz) pl. n. a group of 21 basalt islands in the North Atlantic between Iceland and the Shetland Islands: a self-governing community within the kingdom of Denmark; fishing. Capital: Thorshavn. Pop.: 46 000 (1988 est.). Area: 1400 sq. km (540 sq. miles). Also called: **Faeroe Islands** or **Faroe Islands.**

Faeroese or **Faroese** (,fɛərəʊ'iːz) adj. **1.** of or characteristic of the Faeroes, their inhabitants, or their language. ~n. **2.** the language of the Faeroes, closely related to Icelandic. **3.** (pl. **-ese**) a native or inhabitant of the Faeroes.

faff (fæf) vb. (intr.; often foll. by about) Brit. inf. to dither or fuss.

Fafnir ('fæfnɪə, 'fæv-) n. Norse myth. the son of Hreidmar, whom he killed to gain the cursed treasure of Andvari. He became a dragon and was slain by Sigurd while guarding the treasure.

fag[1] (fæg) n. **1.** Inf. a boring or wearisome task. **2.** Brit. (esp. formerly) a young public school boy who performs menial chores for an older boy or prefect. ~vb. **fagging, fagged. 3.** (when tr., often foll. by out) Inf. to become or cause to become exhausted by hard work **4.** (usually intr.) Brit. to do or cause to do menial chores in a public school. [C18: from ?]

fag[2] (fæg) n. Brit. sl. a cigarette. [C16 (in the sense: something hanging loose, flap): from ?]

fag[3] (fæg) n. Sl., chiefly U.S. & Canad. short for **faggot**[2].

fag end n. **1.** the last and worst part. **2.** Brit. inf. the stub of a cigarette. [C17: see FAG[2]]

faggot[1] or esp. U.S. **fagot** ('fægət) n. **1.** a bundle of sticks or twigs, esp. when used as fuel. **2.** a bundle of iron bars, esp. to be forged into wrought iron. **3.** a ball of chopped meat bound with herbs and bread and eaten fried. ~vb. (tr.) **4.** to collect into a bundle or bundles. **5.** Needlework. to do faggoting on (a garment, etc.). [C14: from OF, ?from Gk *phakelos* bundle]

faggot[2] ('fægət) n. Sl., chiefly U.S. & Canad. a male homosexual. [C20: special use of FAGGOT[1]]

faggoting or esp. U.S. **fagoting** ('fægətɪŋ) n. **1.** decorative needlework done by tying vertical threads together in bundles. **2.** a decorative way of joining two hems by crisscross stitches.

fah or **fa** (faː) n. Music. **1.** (in the fixed system of solmization) the note F. **2.** (in tonic sol-fa) the fourth degree of any major scale. [C14: see GAMUT]

Fah. or **Fahr.** abbrev. for Fahrenheit.

Fahd ibn Abdul Aziz (faːd 'ɪbᵊn 'æbdʊl ə'ziːz) n. born 1923, king of Saudi Arabia from 1982.

Fahrenheit[1] ('færən,haɪt) adj. of or measured according to the Fahrenheit scale of temperature. Symbol: F

Fahrenheit[2] (German 'faːrənhait) n. **Gabriel Daniel** ('gaːbrieːl 'daːnieːl). 1686–1736, German physicist, who invented the mercury thermometer and devised the temperature scale that bears his name.

Fahrenheit scale n. a scale of temperatures in which 32° represents the melting point of ice and 212° represents the boiling point of pure water under standard atmospheric pressure. Cf. **Celsius scale.**

Faial or **Fayal** (Portuguese fə'ial) n. an island in the central Azores archipelago. Chief town: Horta. Area: 171 sq. km (66 sq. miles).

faïence (faɪ'ɑːns, feɪ-) n. tin-glazed earthenware, usually that of French, German, Italian, or Scandinavian origin. [C18: from F, strictly: pottery from FAENZA]

fail (feɪl) vb. **1.** to be unsuccessful in an attempt (at something or to do something). **2.** (intr.) to stop operating or working properly: *the steering failed suddenly.* **3.** to judge or be judged as being below the officially accepted standard required in (a course, examination, etc.). **4.** (tr.) to prove disappointing or useless to (someone). **5.** (tr.) to neglect or be unable (to do something). **6.** (intr.) to prove insufficient in quantity or extent. **7.** (intr.) to weaken. **8.** (intr.) to go bankrupt. ~n. **9.** a failure to attain the required standard. **10. without fail.** definitely. [C13: from OF *faillir*, ult. from L *fallere* to disappoint]
▷ **Usage.** *Fail* is often used to emphasize the fact that something did not occur: *the expected number of visitors failed to materialize; the car failed to stop at the lights.* Careful users of English, however, at least in formal contexts, restrict the use of the word to the sense of something that has been tried but did not succeed: *the England team failed to win a place in the finals; she failed in her attempt to swim to France.*

failing ('feɪlɪŋ) n. **1.** a weak point. ~prep. **2.** (used to express a condition) in default of: *failing a solution, the problem will have to wait until Monday.*

fail-safe adj. **1.** designed to return to a safe condition in the event of a failure or malfunction. **2.** safe from failure; foolproof.

failure ('feɪljə) n. **1.** the act or an instance of failing. **2.** a person or thing that is unsuccessful or disappointing. **3.** nonperformance of something required or expected: *failure to attend will be punished.* **4.** cessation of normal operation: *a power failure.* **5.** an insufficiency: *a crop failure.* **6.** a decline or loss, as in health. **7.** the fact of not reaching the required standard in an examination, test, etc. **8.** bankruptcy.

fain (feɪn) adv. **1.** (usually with would) Arch. gladly: *she would fain be dead.* ~adj. **2.** Obs. **a.** willing. **b.** compelled. [OE *fægen*; see FAWN[2]]

faint (feɪnt) adj. **1.** lacking clarity, brightness, volume, etc. **2.** lacking conviction or force: *faint praise.* **3.** feeling dizzy or weak as if about to lose consciousness. **4.** timid (esp. in **faint-hearted**). **5. not the faintest** (idea or **notion**). no idea whatsoever: *I haven't the faintest.* ~vb. (intr.) **6.** to lose consciousness, as through weakness. **7.** Arch. or poetic. to become weak, esp. in courage. ~n. **8.** a sudden spontaneous loss of consciousness caused by an insufficient supply of blood to the brain. [C13: from OF, from *faindre* to be idle] —**faintish** adj. —**faintly** adv. —**faintness** n.

fair[1] (fɛə) adj. **1.** free from discrimination, dishonesty, etc. **2.** in conformity with rules or standards: *a fair fight.* **3.** (of the hair or complexion) light in colour. **4.** beautiful to look at. **5.** quite good: *a fair piece of work.* **6.** unblemished; untainted. **7.** (of the tide or wind) favourable to the passage of a vessel. **8.** fine or cloudless. **9.** pleasant or courteous. **10.** apparently good or valuable: *fair words.* **11. fair and square.** in a correct or just way. ~adv. **12.** in a fair way: *act fair, now!* **13.** absolutely or squarely; quite. ~vb. **14.** (intr.) Dialect. (of the weather) to become fine. ~n. **15.** Arch. a person or thing that is beautiful or valuable. [OE *fæger*] —**fairish** adj. —**fairness** n.

fair[2] (fɛə) n. **1.** a travelling entertainment with sideshows, rides, etc. **2.** a gathering of producers of and dealers in a given class of products to facilitate business: *a world fair.* **3.** a regular assembly at a specific place for the sale of goods, esp. livestock. [C13: from OF *feire*, from LL *fēria* holiday, from L *fēriae* days of rest]

Fairbanks[1] ('fɛə,bæŋks) n. a city in central Alaska, at the terminus of the Alaska Highway. Pop.: 64 800 (1983 est.).

Fairbanks[2] ('fɛə,bæŋks) n. **1. Douglas (Elton)**, real name *Julius Ullman.* 1883–1939, U.S. film actor. **2.** his son, **Douglas, Jnr.** born 1909, U.S. film actor.

Fairfax ('fɛəfæks) n. **Thomas**, 3rd Baron Fairfax. 1612–71, English general and statesman: commanded the Parliamentary army (1645–50), defeating Charles I at Naseby (1645). He was instrumental in restoring Charles II to the throne (1660).

fair game n. a legitimate object for ridicule or attack.

fairground ('fɛə,graʊnd) n. an open space used for a fair or exhibition.

fairing[1] ('fɛərɪŋ) n. an external metal structure fitted around parts of an aircraft, car, etc., to reduce drag. [C20: from *fair* to streamline + -ING[1]]

fairing[2] ('fɛərɪŋ) n. Arch. a present, esp. from a fair.
Fair Isle n. an intricate multicoloured pattern knitted with Shetland wool into various garments, such as sweaters. [C19: after one of the Shetland Islands where this type of pattern originated]
fairly ('fɛəlɪ) adv. **1.** (not used with a negative) moderately. **2.** as deserved; justly. **3.** (not used with a negative) positively: the hall fairly rang with applause.
fair-minded adj. just or impartial. —ˌfair'mindedness n.
fair play n. **1.** an established standard of decency, etc. **2.** abidance by this standard.
fair sex n. **the.** women collectively.
fair-spoken adj. civil, courteous, or elegant in speech. —ˌfair'spokenness n.
fairway ('fɛəˌweɪ) n. **1.** (on a golf course) the avenue approaching a green bordered by rough. **2.** Naut. the navigable part of a river, harbour, etc.
fair-weather adj. **1.** suitable for use in fair weather only. **2.** not reliable in situations of difficulty: fair-weather friend.
Fairweather ('fɛəˌwɛðə) n. Mount. a mountain in W North America, on the border between Alaska and British Columbia. Height: 4663 m (15 300 ft.).
fairy ('fɛərɪ) n., pl. **fairies. 1.** an imaginary supernatural being, usually represented in diminutive human form and characterized as having magical powers. **2.** Sl. a male homosexual. ~adj. (prenominal) **3.** of a fairy or fairies. **4.** resembling a fairy or fairies. [C14: from OF faerie fairyland, from feie fairy, from L Fāta the Fates; see FATE, FAY] —ˈfairy-ˌlike adj.
fairy cycle n. a child's bicycle.
fairyfloss ('fɛərɪˌflɒs) n. the Australian word for **candyfloss.**
fairy godmother n. a benefactress, esp. an unknown one.
fairyland ('fɛərɪˌlænd) n. **1.** the imaginary domain of the fairies. **2.** a fantasy world, esp. one resulting from a person's wild imaginings.
fairy lights pl. n. small coloured electric bulbs strung together and used as decoration, esp. on a Christmas tree.
fairy penguin n. a small penguin with a bluish head and back, found on the Australian coast. Also called: **little** or **blue penguin.**
fairy ring n. a ring of dark luxuriant vegetation in grassy ground corresponding to the outer edge of an underground fungal mycelium.
fairy tale or **story** n. **1.** a story about fairies or other mythical or magical beings. **2.** a highly improbable account.
fairy-tale adj. **1.** of or relating to a fairy tale. **2.** resembling a fairy tale, esp. in being extremely happy or fortunate: a fairy-tale ending. **3.** highly improbable: a fairy-tale account.
Faisal I or **Feisal I** ('faɪsəl) n. 1885–1933, king of Syria (1920) and first king of Iraq (1921–33).
Faisal II or **Feisal II** n. 1935–58, last king of Iraq (1939–58).
Faisalabad (faɪˈʒɑːlə,bɑːd) n. a city in NE Pakistan: commercial and manufacturing centre of a cotton- and wheat-growing region; university (1961). Pop.: 1 092 000 (1981). Former name (until 1979): **Lyallpur.**
fait accompli French. (fɛt akɔ̃pli) n., pl. *faits accomplis* (fɛz akɔ̃pli). something already done and beyond alteration. [lit.: accomplished fact]
faith (feɪθ) n. **1.** strong or unshakeable belief in something, esp. without proof. **2.** a specific system of religious beliefs: the Jewish faith. **3.** Christianity. trust in God and in his actions and promises. **4.** a conviction of the truth of certain doctrines of religion. **5.** complete confidence or trust in a person, remedy, etc. **6.** loyalty, as to a person or cause (esp. in **keep faith, break faith**). **7.** bad faith. dishonesty. **8.** good faith. honesty. **9.** (modifier) using or relating to the supposed ability to cure bodily ailments by means of religious faith: a faith healer. ~interj. **10.** Arch. indeed. [C12: from Anglo-F feid, from L fidēs trust, confidence]
faithful ('feɪθfʊl) adj. **1.** remaining true or loyal. **2.** maintaining sexual loyalty to one's lover or spouse. **3.** consistently reliable: a faithful worker. **4.** reliable or truthful. **5.** accurate in detail: a faithful translation. ~n. **6. the faithful. a.** the believers in a religious faith, esp. Christianity. **b.** any group of loyal and steadfast followers. —ˈfaithfully adv. —ˈfaithfulness n.

faithless ('feɪθlɪs) adj. **1.** unreliable or treacherous. **2.** dishonest or disloyal. **3.** lacking religious faith. —ˈfaithlessness n.
Faiyûm or **Fayum** (faɪˈjuːm) n. See **El Faiyûm.**
fake (feɪk) vb. **1.** (tr.) to cause (something inferior or not genuine) to appear more valuable or real by fraud or pretence. **2.** to pretend to have (an illness, emotion, etc.). ~n. **3.** an object, person, or act that is not genuine; sham. ~adj. **4.** not genuine. [C18: prob. ult. from It. facciare to make or do] —ˈfaker n. —ˈfakery n.
fakir ('feɪkɪə, fəˈkɪə) n. **1.** a member of any religious order of Islam. **2.** a Hindu ascetic mendicant. [C17: from Ar. faqīr poor]
Falange ('fælændʒ) n. the Fascist movement founded in Spain in 1933. [Sp.: PHALANX] —**Faˈlangist** n., adj.
falcate ('fælkeɪt) or **falciform** ('fælsɪˌfɔːm) adj. Biol. shaped like a sickle. [C19: from L falcātus, from falx sickle]
falchion ('fɔːltʃən, 'fɔːlʃən) n. **1.** a short and slightly curved medieval sword. **2.** an archaic word for **sword.** [C14: from It., from falce, from L falx sickle]
falcon ('fɔːlkən, 'fɔːkən) n. **1.** a diurnal bird of prey such as the gyrfalcon, peregrine falcon, etc., having pointed wings and a long tail. **2. a.** any of these or related birds, trained to hunt small game. **b.** the female of such a bird (cf. **tercel**). [C13: from OF, from LL falcō hawk, prob. of Gmc origin; ? rel. to L falx sickle]
falconet ('fɔːlkə,nɛt, 'fɔːkə-) n. **1.** any of various small falcons. **2.** a small light cannon used from the 15th to 17th centuries.
falconry ('fɔːlkənrɪ, 'fɔːkən-) n. the art of keeping falcons and training them to return from flight to a lure or to hunt quarry. —ˈfalconer n.
falderal ('fældə,ræl) or **folderol** ('fɒldə,rɒl) n. **1.** a showy but worthless trifle. **2.** foolish nonsense. **3.** a nonsensical refrain in old songs.
Faldo ('fældəʊ) n. Nick. born 1957, British golfer: won the British Open Championship (1987).
faldstool ('fɔːld,stuːl) n. a backless seat, sometimes capable of being folded, used by bishops and certain other prelates. [C11 fyldestol, prob. a translation of Med. L faldistolium folding stool, of Gmc origin; cf. OHG faldstuol]
Falerii (fəˈlɪərɪ,aɪ) n. an ancient city in S Italy, in Latium: important in pre-Roman times.
Falkirk ('fɔːlkɜːk) n. a town in Scotland, in the Central region: scene of Edward I's defeat of Wallace (1298) and Prince Charles Edward's defeat of General Hawley (1746); iron works. Pop.: 36 875 (1981).
Falkland Islands ('fɔːlkland) pl. n. a group of over 100 islands in the S Atlantic: a British crown colony; invaded by Argentina, who had long laid claim to the islands, on 2 April 1982; recaptured by a British expeditionary force on 14 June 1982. Chief town: Stanley. Pop.: 1916 (1986). Area: about 12 200 sq. km (4700 sq. miles). Spanish name: **Islas Malvinas.**
Falkland Islands Dependencies pl. n. a group of almost uninhabited islands south of the Falkland Islands: consisting of the South Sandwich Islands and South Georgia. Area: 4090 sq. km (1580 sq. miles).
Falkner ('fɔːknə) n. a variant spelling of (William) **Faulkner.**
fall (fɔːl) vb. **falling, fell, fallen.** (mainly intr.) **1.** to descend by the force of gravity from a higher to a lower place. **2.** to drop suddenly from an erect position. **3.** to collapse to the ground, esp. in pieces. **4.** to become less or lower in number, quality, etc.: prices fell. **5.** to become lower in pitch. **6.** to extend downwards: her hair fell to her waist. **7.** to be badly wounded or killed. **8.** to slope in a downward direction. **9.** to yield to temptation or sin. **10.** to diminish in status, estimation, etc. **11.** to yield to attack: the city fell under the assault. **12.** to lose power: the government fell after the riots. **13.** to pass into or take on a specified condition: to fall asleep. **14.** to adopt a despondent expression: her face fell. **15.** to be averted: her gaze fell. **16.** to come by chance or presumption: suspicion fell on the butler. **17.** to occur; take place: night fell. **18.** (foll. by back, behind, etc.) to move in a specified direction. **19.** to occur at a specified place: the accent falls on the last syllable. **20.** (foll. by to) to be inherited (by): the estate falls to the eldest son. **21.** (often foll. by into, under, etc.) to be classified: the subject falls into two main areas. **22.** to issue forth: a curse fell from her

lips. **23.** *Cricket.* (of a batsman's wicket) to be taken by the bowling side: *the sixth wicket fell for 96.* **24. fall short. a.** to prove inadequate. **b.** (often foll. by *of*) to fail to reach or measure up to (a standard). ~*n.* **25.** an act or instance of falling. **26.** something that falls: *a fall of snow.* **27.** *Chiefly U.S. & Canad.* autumn. **28.** the distance that something falls: *a hundred-foot fall.* **29.** a sudden drop from an upright position. **30.** (*often pl.*) **a.** a waterfall or cataract. **b.** (*cap. when part of a name*): *Niagara Falls.* **31.** a downward slope or decline. **32.** a decrease in value, number, etc. **33.** a decline in status or importance. **34.** a capture or overthrow: *the fall of the city.* **35.** *Machinery, naut.* the end of a tackle to which power is applied to hoist it. **36.** Also called: **pinfall.** *Wrestling.* a scoring move, pinning both shoulders of one's opponent to the floor for a specified period. **37. a.** the birth of an animal. **b.** the animals produced at a single birth. ~See also **fall about, fall away,** etc. [OE *feallan:* cf. FELL[2]]

Fall (fɔːl) *n.* **the.** *Theol.* Adam's sin of disobedience and the state of innate sinfulness ensuing from this for himself and all mankind.

Falla (*Spanish* 'faʎa) *n.* **Manuel de** (ma'nuɛl de). 1876–1946, Spanish composer and pianist, composer of the opera *La Vida Breve* (1905), the ballet *The Three-Cornered Hat* (1919), guitar and piano music, and songs.

fall about *vb.* (*intr., adv.*) to laugh in an uncontrolled manner: *we fell about at the sight.*

fallacious (fə'leɪʃəs) *adj.* **1.** containing or involving a fallacy. **2.** tending to mislead. **3.** delusive or disappointing. —**fal'laciously** *adv.*

fallacy ('fæləsɪ) *n., pl.* **-cies. 1.** an incorrect or misleading notion or opinion based on inaccurate facts or invalid reasoning. **2.** unsound reasoning. **3.** the tendency to mislead. **4.** *Logic.* an error in reasoning that renders an argument logically invalid. [C15: from L, from *fallax* deceitful, from *fallere* to deceive]

fall away *vb.* (*intr., adv.*) **1.** (of friendship, etc.) to be withdrawn. **2.** to slope down.

fall back *vb.* (*intr., adv.*) **1.** to recede or retreat. **2.** (foll. by *on* or *upon*) to have recourse (to). ~*n.* **fall-back.** **3.** a retreat. **4.** a reserve, esp. money, that can be called upon in need. **5. a.** anything to which one can have recourse as a second choice. **b.** (*as modifier*): *a fall-back position.*

fall behind *vb.* (*intr., adv.*) **1.** to drop back; fail to keep up. **2.** to be in arrears, as with a payment.

fall down *vb.* (*intr., adv.*) **1.** to drop suddenly or collapse. **2.** (often foll. by *on*) *Inf.* to fail.

fallen ('fɔːlən) *vb.* **1.** the past participle of **fall.** ~*adj.* **2.** having sunk in reputation or honour: *a fallen woman.* **3.** killed in battle with glory.

fallen arch *n.* collapse of the arch formed by the instep of the foot, resulting in flat feet.

fall for *vb.* (*intr., prep.*) **1.** to become infatuated with (a person). **2.** to allow oneself to be deceived by (a lie, trick, etc.).

fall guy *n. Inf.* **1.** a person who is the victim of a confidence trick. **2.** a scapegoat.

fallible ('fælɪbəl) *adj.* **1.** capable of being mistaken. **2.** liable to mislead. [C15: from Med. L *fallibilis,* from L *fallere* to deceive] —**falli'bility** *n.*

fall in *vb.* (*intr., adv.*) **1.** to collapse. **2.** to adopt a military formation, esp. as a soldier taking his place in a line. **3.** (of a lease) to expire. **4.** (often foll. by *with*) **a.** to meet and join. **b.** to agree with or support a person, suggestion, etc.

falling sickness *or* **evil** *n.* a former name (nontechnical) for **epilepsy.**

falling star *n.* an informal name for **meteor.**

Fall Line *n.* a natural junction, running parallel to the E coast of the U.S., between the hard rocks of the Appalachians and the softer coastal plain, along which rivers form falls and rapids.

fall off *vb.* (*intr.*) **1.** to drop unintentionally to the ground from (a high object, bicycle, etc.), esp. after losing one's balance. **2.** (*adv.*) to diminish in size, intensity, etc. ~*n.* **fall-off. 3.** a decline or drop.

fall on *vb.* (*intr., prep.*) **1.** Also: **fall upon.** to attack or snatch (an army, booty, etc.). **2. fall on one's feet.** to emerge unexpectedly well from a difficult situation.

Fallopian tube (fə'ləʊpɪən) *n.* either of a pair of slender tubes through which ova pass from the ovaries to the

uterus in female mammals. [C18: after Gabriello *Fallopio* (1523–62), It. anatomist who first described the tubes]

fallout ('fɔːl,aʊt) *n.* **1.** the descent of radioactive material following a nuclear explosion. **2.** any particles that so descend. **3.** secondary consequences. ~*vb.* **fall out.** (*intr., adv.*) **4.** *Inf.* to disagree. **5.** (*intr.*) to occur. **6.** *Mil.* to leave a disciplinary formation.

fallow[1] ('fæləʊ) *adj.* **1.** (of land) left unseeded after being ploughed to regain fertility for a crop. **2.** (of an idea, etc.) undeveloped, but potentially useful. ~*n.* **3.** land treated in this way. ~*vb.* **4.** (*tr.*) to leave (land) unseeded after ploughing it. [OE *fealga*] —**'fallowness** *n.*

fallow[2] ('fæləʊ) *n., adj.* (of) a light yellowish-brown colour. [OE *fealu*]

fallow deer *n.* either of two species of deer, one of which is native to the Mediterranean region and the other to Persia. The summer coat is reddish with white spots.

fall through *vb.* (*intr., adv.*) to fail.

fall to *vb.* (*intr.*) **1.** (*adv.*) to begin some activity, as eating, working, or fighting. **2.** (*prep.*) to devolve on (a person): *the task fell to me.*

Falmouth ('fælməθ) *n.* a port and resort in SW England, in S Cornwall. Pop.: 18 525 (1981).

false (fɔːls) *adj.* **1.** not in accordance with the truth or facts. **2.** irregular or invalid: *a false start.* **3.** untruthful or lying: *a false account.* **4.** artificial; fake: *false teeth.* **5.** being or intended to be misleading or deceptive: *a false rumour.* **6.** treacherous: *a false friend.* **7.** based on mistaken or irrelevant ideas or facts: *a false argument.* **8.** (*prenominal*) (esp. of plants) superficially resembling the species specified: *false hellebore.* **9.** serving to supplement or replace, often temporarily: *a false keel.* **10.** *Music.* (of a note, interval, etc.) out of tune. ~*adv.* **11.** in a false or dishonest manner (esp. in **play** (**someone**) **false**). [OE *fals*] —**'falsely** *adv.* —**'falseness** *n.*

False Bay *n.* a bay in SW South Africa, near the Cape of Good Hope.

false dawn *n.* light appearing just before sunrise.

falsehood ('fɔːls,hʊd) *n.* **1.** the quality of being untrue. **2.** an untrue statement; lie. **3.** the act of deceiving or lying.

false imprisonment *n. Law.* the restraint of a person's liberty without lawful authority.

false pretences *pl. n.* a misrepresentation used to obtain anything, such as trust or affection (esp. in **under false pretences**).

false ribs *pl. n.* any of the lower five pairs of ribs in man, not attached directly to the breastbone.

false step *n.* **1.** an unwise action. **2.** a stumble; slip.

falsetto (fɔːl'sɛtəʊ) *n., pl.* **-tos.** a form of vocal production used by male singers to extend their range upwards by limiting the vibration of the vocal cords. [C18: from It., from *falso* false]

falsies ('fɔːlsɪz) *pl. n. Inf.* pads of soft material, such as foam rubber, worn to exaggerate the size of a woman's breasts.

falsify ('fɔːlsɪ,faɪ) *vb.* **-fying, -fied.** (*tr.*) **1.** to make (a report, evidence, etc.) false or inaccurate by alteration, esp. in order to deceive. **2.** to prove false. [C15: from OF, from LL, from L *falsus* FALSE + *facere* to do, make] —**'falsi,fiable** *adj.* —**falsification** (,fɔːlsɪfɪ'keɪʃən) *n.*

falsity ('fɔːlsɪtɪ) *n., pl.* **-ties. 1.** the state of being false or untrue. **2.** a lie or deception.

Falstaffian (fɔːl'stɑːfɪən) *adj.* jovial, plump, and dissolute. [C19: after Sir John *Falstaff,* a character in Shakespeare's play *Henry IV*]

Falster ('fɑːlstə) *n.* an island in the Baltic Sea, part of SE Denmark. Chief town: Nykøbing. Pop.: 49 556 (1981 est.). Area: 513 sq. km (198 sq. miles).

falter ('fɔːltə) *vb.* **1.** (*intr.*) to be hesitant, weak, or unsure. **2.** (*intr.*) to move unsteadily or hesitantly. **3.** to utter haltingly or hesitantly. ~*n.* **4.** hesitancy in speech or action. **5.** a quavering sound. [C14: prob. from ON] —**'falterer** *n.* —**'falteringly** *adv.*

Falun (,fɑː'luːn) *n.* a city in central Sweden: iron and pyrites mines. Pop.: 51 900 (1986).

Famagusta (,fæmə'gʊstə) *n.* a port in E Cyprus, on **Famagusta Bay:** became one of the richest cities in Christendom in the 14th century. Pop.: 19 428 (1985).

fame (feɪm) *n.* **1.** the state of being widely known or recognized. **2.** *Arch.* rumour or public report. ~*vb.* **3.** (*tr.; now usually passive*) to make famous: *he was famed for* *his ruthlessness.* [C13: from L *fāma* report; rel. to *fārī* to say]

familial (fə'mɪlɪəl) *adj.* **1.** of or relating to the family. **2.** occurring in the members of a family: *a familial disease.*

familiar (fə'mɪlɪə) *adj.* **1.** well-known: *a familiar figure.* **2.** frequent or customary: *a familiar excuse.* **3.** (*postpositive*; foll. by *with*) acquainted. **4.** friendly; informal. **5.** close; intimate. **6.** more intimate than is acceptable; presumptuous. *~n.* **7.** Also called: **familiar spirit.** a supernatural spirit supposed to attend and aid a witch, wizard, etc. **8.** a person attached to the household of the pope or a bishop, who renders service in return for support. **9.** a friend. [C14: from L *familiāris* domestic, from *familia* FAMILY] —**fa'miliarly** *adv.* —**fa'miliarness** *n.*

familiarity (fə,mɪlɪ'ærɪtɪ) *n., pl.* **-ties. 1.** knowledge, as of a subject or place. **2.** close acquaintanceship. **3.** undue intimacy. **4.** (*sometimes pl.*) an instance of unwarranted intimacy.

familiarize *or* **-rise** (fə'mɪljə,raɪz) *vb.* (*tr.*) **1.** to make (oneself or someone else) familiar, as with a particular subject. **2.** to make (something) generally known. —**fa,miliari'zation** *or* **-ri'sation** *n.*

famille *French.* (famij) *n.* a type of Chinese porcelain characterized either by a design on a background of yellow (***famille jaune***) or black (***famille noire***) or by a design in which the predominant colour is pink (***famille rose***) or green (***famille verte***). [C19: lit.: family]

family ('fæmɪlɪ, 'fæmlɪ) *n., pl.* **-lies. 1. a.** a primary social group consisting of parents and their offspring. **b.** (*as modifier*): *a family unit.* **2.** one's wife or husband and one's children. **3.** one's children, as distinguished from one's husband or wife. **4.** a group descended from a common ancestor. **5.** all the persons living together in one household. **6.** any group of related things or beings, esp. when scientifically categorized. **7.** *Biol.* any of the taxonomic groups into which an order is divided and which contains one or more genera. **8.** a group of historically related languages assumed to derive from one original language. **9.** *Maths.* a group of curves or surfaces whose equations differ from a given equation only in the values assigned to one or more constants. **10. in the family way.** *Inf.* pregnant. [C15: from L *familia* a household, servants of the house, from *famulus* servant]

Family Allowance *n.* **1.** (in Britain) a former name for **child benefit. 2.** (in Canada) an allowance paid by the Federal Government to the parents of dependent children.

family benefit *n. N.Z.* a child allowance paid to the mothers of children under 18 years of age. Also called: **child benefit.**

family Bible *n.* a large Bible in which births, marriages, and deaths of the members of a family are recorded.

Family Compact *n. Canad.* **1. the.** the ruling oligarchy in Upper Canada in the early 19th century. **2.** (*often not cap.*) any influential clique.

family credit *n.* (in Britain) an allowance paid to families whose earnings from full-time work are low. It replaces Family Income Supplement.

Family Income Supplement *n.* (in Britain) formerly a means-tested benefit for families whose earnings from full-time work are low. Abbrev.: **FIS.**

family man *n.* a man who is married and has children, esp. one who is devoted to his family.

family name *n.* a surname, esp. when regarded as representing the family honour.

family planning *n.* the control of the number of children in a family and of the intervals between them, esp. by the use of contraceptives.

family tree *n.* a chart showing the genealogical relationships and lines of descent of a family. Also called: **genealogical tree.**

famine ('fæmɪn) *n.* **1.** a severe shortage of food, as through crop failure or overpopulation. **2.** acute shortage of anything. **3.** violent hunger. [C14: from OF, via Vulgar L, from L *famēs* hunger]

famish ('fæmɪʃ) *vb.* (*now usually passive*) to be or make very hungry or weak. [C14: from OF, from L *famēs* FAMINE]

famous ('feɪməs) *adj.* **1.** known to or recognized by many people. **2.** *Inf.* excellent; splendid. [C14: from L *fāmōsus*; see FAME] —**'famously** *adv.* —**'famousness** *n.*

fan[1] (fæn) *n.* **1.** any device for creating a current of air by movement of a surface or number of surfaces, esp. a rotating device consisting of a number of blades attached to a central hub. **2.** any of various hand-agitated devices for cooling oneself, esp. a collapsible semicircular series of flat segments of paper, ivory, etc. **3.** something shaped like such a fan, such as the tail of certain birds. **4.** *Agriculture.* a kind of basket formerly used for winnowing grain. *~vb.* **fanning, fanned.** (*mainly tr.*) **5.** to cause a current of air to blow upon, as by means of a fan: *to fan one's face.* **6.** to agitate or move (air, etc.) with or as if with a fan. **7.** to make fiercer, more ardent, etc.: *fan one's passion.* **8.** (*also intr.*; often foll. by *out*) to spread out or cause to spread out in the shape of a fan. **9.** to winnow (grain) by blowing the chaff away from it. [OE *fann*, from L *vannus*] —**'fanlike** *adj.* —**'fanner** *n.*

fan[2] (fæn) *n.* **1.** an ardent admirer of a pop star, football team, etc. **2.** a devotee of a sport, hobby, etc. [C17, reformed C19: from FAN(ATIC)]

Fanagalo ('fænəgələʊ) *or* **Fanakalo** *n.* (in South Africa) a Zulu-based pidgin with English and Afrikaans components. [C20: from Fanagalo *fana ga lo,* lit.: be like this]

fanatic (fə'nætɪk) *n.* **1.** a person whose enthusiasm or zeal for something is extreme or beyond normal limits. **2.** *Inf.* a person devoted to a particular hobby or pastime. *~adj.* **3.** a variant of **fanatical.** [C16: from L *fānāticus* belonging to a temple, hence, inspired by a god, frenzied, from *fānum* temple]

fanatical (fə'nætɪkᵊl) *adj.* surpassing what is normal or accepted in enthusiasm for or belief in something. —**fa'natically** *adv.*

fanaticism (fə'nætɪ,sɪzəm) *n.* wildly excessive or irrational devotion, dedication, or enthusiasm.

fan belt *n.* the belt that drives a cooling fan in a car engine.

fancied ('fænsɪd) *adj.* **1.** imaginary; unreal. **2.** thought likely to win or succeed: *a fancied runner.*

fancier ('fænsɪə) *n.* **1.** a person with a special interest in something. **2.** a person who breeds special varieties of plants or animals: *a pigeon fancier.*

fanciful ('fænsɪfʊl) *adj.* **1.** not based on fact: *fanciful notions.* **2.** made or designed in a curious, intricate, or imaginative way. **3.** indulging in or influenced by fancy. —**'fancifully** *adv.* —**'fancifulness** *n.*

fancy ('fænsɪ) *adj.* **-cier, -ciest. 1.** ornamented or decorative: *fancy clothes.* **2.** requiring skill to perform: *a fancy dance routine.* **3.** capricious or illusory. **4.** (often used ironically) superior in quality. **5.** higher than expected: *fancy prices.* **6.** (of a domestic animal) bred for particular qualities. *~n., pl.* **-cies. 7.** a sudden capricious idea. **8.** a sudden or irrational liking for a person or thing. **9.** the power to conceive and represent decorative and novel imagery, esp. in poetry. **10.** an idea or thing produced by this. **11.** a mental image. **12.** *Music.* a composition for solo lute, keyboard, etc., current during the 16th and 17th centuries. **13. the fancy.** *Arch.* those who follow a particular sport, esp. prize fighting. *~vb.* **-cying, -cied.** (*tr.*) **14.** to picture in the imagination. **15.** to imagine: *I fancy it will rain.* **16.** (*often used with a negative*) to like: *I don't fancy your chances!* **17.** (*reflexive*) to have a high or ill-founded opinion of oneself. **18.** *Inf.* to have a wish for: *she fancied some chocolate.* **19.** *Brit. inf.* to be physically attracted to (another person). **20.** to breed (animals) for particular characteristics. *~interj.* **21.** Also: **fancy that!** an exclamation of surprise. [C15 *fantsy,* shortened from *fantasie*; see FANTASY] —**'fancily** *adv.* —**'fanciness** *n.*

fancy dress *n.* **a.** a costume worn at masquerades, etc., representing an historical figure, etc. **b.** (*as modifier*): *a fancy-dress ball.*

fancy-free *adj.* having no commitments.

fancy goods *pl. n.* small decorative gifts.

fancy man *n. Sl.* **1.** a woman's lover. **2.** a pimp.

fancy woman *n. Sl.* a mistress or prostitute.

fancywork ('fænsɪ,wɜːk) *n.* any ornamental needlework, such as embroidery or crochet.

fan dance *n.* a dance in which large fans are manipulated in front of the body, partially revealing or suggesting nakedness.

fandangle (fæn'dæŋgᵊl) *n. Inf.* **1.** elaborate ornament. **2.** nonsense. [C19: ?from FANDANGO]

fandango (fæn'dæŋgəʊ) *n.*, *pl.* **-gos. 1.** an old Spanish courtship dance in triple time. **2.** a piece of music composed for or in the rhythm of this dance. [C18: from Sp., from ?]

fane (feɪn) *n. Arch. or poetic.* a temple or shrine. [C14: from L *fānum*]

fanfare ('fænfɛə) *n.* **1.** a flourish or short tune played on brass instruments. **2.** an ostentatious flourish or display. [C17: from F, back formation from *fanfarer*, from Sp, from *fanfarron* boaster, from Ar. *farfār* garrulous]

fang (fæŋ) *n.* **1.** the long pointed hollow or grooved tooth of a venomous snake through which venom is injected. **2.** any large pointed tooth, esp. the canine tooth of a carnivorous mammal. **3.** the root of a tooth. **4.** (*usually pl.*) *Brit. inf.* a tooth. [OE *fang* what is caught, prey] —**fanged** *adj.* —'**fangless** *adj.*

Fangio (*Spanish* 'faŋxjo) *n.* **Juan Manuel** (xwan ma'nwɛl). born 1911, Argentinian racing driver who won the World Championship five times between 1951 and 1957.

fan heater *n.* a space heater consisting of an electrically heated element with an electrically driven fan to disperse the heat.

fanjet ('fæn,dʒɛt) *n.* another name for **turbofan.**

fanlight ('fæn,laɪt) *n.* **1.** a semicircular window over a door or window, often having sash bars like the ribs of a fan. **2.** a small rectangular window over a door. U.S. name: **transom.**

fan mail *n.* mail sent to a famous person, such as a pop musician or film star, by admirers.

fanny ('fænɪ) *n.*, *pl.* **-nies.** *Sl.* **1.** *Taboo, Brit.* the female pudendum. **2.** *Chiefly U.S. & Canad.* the buttocks. [C20: ?from *Fanny*, pet name from *Frances*]

fanny adams *n. Brit. sl.* **1.** (usually preceded by *sweet*) absolutely nothing at all. **2.** *Chiefly naut.* (formerly) tinned meat. [C19: from the name of a young murder victim whose body was cut up into small pieces. For sense 1: a euphemism for *fuck all*]

fantail ('fæn,teɪl) *n.* **1.** a breed of domestic pigeon having a large tail that can be opened like a fan. **2.** an Old World flycatcher of Australia, New Zealand, and SE Asia, having a broad fan-shaped tail. **3.** a tail shaped like an outspread fan. **4.** an auxiliary sail on the upper portion of a windmill. **5.** *U.S.* a part of the deck projecting aft of the sternpost of a ship. —'**fan-,tailed** *adj.*

fan-tan *n.* **1.** a Chinese gambling game. **2.** a card game played in sequence, the winner being the first to use up all his cards. [C19: from Chinese (Cantonese) *fan t'an* repeated divisions, from *fan* times + *t'an* division]

fantasia (fæn'teɪzɪə) *n.* **1.** any musical composition of a free or improvisatory nature. **2.** a potpourri of popular tunes woven loosely together. [C18: from It.: fancy; see FANTASY]

fantasize *or* **-sise** ('fæntə,saɪz) *vb.* **1.** (when *tr.*, takes a clause as object) to conceive extravagant or whimsical ideas, images, etc. **2.** (*intr.*) to conceive pleasant mental images.

fantastic (fæn'tæstɪk) *adj. also* **fantastical. 1.** strange or fanciful in appearance, conception, etc. **2.** created in the mind; illusory. **3.** unrealistic: *fantastic plans.* **4.** incredible or preposterous: *a fantastic verdict.* **5.** *Inf.* very large or extreme: *a fantastic fortune.* **6.** *Inf.* very good; excellent. **7.** of or characterized by fantasy. **8.** capricious; fitful. [C14 *fantastik* imaginary, via L from Gk *phantastikos* capable of imagining, from *phantazein* to make visible] —**fan,tasti'cality** *or* **fan'tasticalness** *n.* —**fan'tastically** *adv.*

fantasy *or* **phantasy** ('fæntəsɪ) *n.*, *pl.* **-sies. 1. a.** imagination unrestricted by reality. **b.** (*as modifier*): *a fantasy world.* **2.** a creation of the imagination, esp. a weird or bizarre one. **3.** *Psychol.* a series of pleasing mental images, usually serving to fulfil a need not gratified in reality. **4.** a whimsical or far-fetched notion. **5.** an illusion or phantom. **6.** a highly elaborate imaginative design or creation. **7.** *Music.* another word for **fantasia. 8.** literature, etc., having a large fantasy content. ~*vb.* **-sying, -sied. 9.** a less common word for **fantasize.** [C14 *fantasie*, from L, from Gk *phantazein* to make visible]

Fantin-Latour (*French* fãtēlatur) *n.* (**Ignace**) **Henri** (**Joseph Théodore**) (ãri). 1836–1904, French painter, noted for his still lifes and portrait groups.

fan vaulting *n. Archit.* vaulting having ribs that radiate like those of a fan and spring from the top of a capital. Also called: **palm vaulting.**

fanzine ('fæn,ziːn) *n.* a magazine produced by amateurs for fans of a specific interest, pop group, etc. [C20: from FAN[2] + (MAGA)ZINE]

FAO *abbrev. for* Food and Agriculture Organization (of the United Nations).

far (fɑː) *adv.*, *adj.* **farther** *or* **further, farthest** *or* **furthest.** *adv.* **1.** at, to, or from a great distance. **2.** at or to a remote time: *far in the future.* **3.** to a considerable degree: *a far better plan.* **4. as far as. a.** to the degree or extent that. **b.** to the distance or place of. **c.** *Inf.* with reference to; as for. **5. by far.** by a considerable margin. **6. far and away.** by a very great margin. **7. far and wide.** everywhere. **8. far be it from me.** on no account: *far be it from me to tell you what to do.* **9. go far. a.** to be successful: *your son will go far.* **b.** to be sufficient or last long: *the wine didn't go far.* **10. go too far.** to exceed reasonable limits. **11. so far. a.** up to the present moment. **b.** up to a certain point, extent, degree, etc. ~*adj.* (*prenominal*) **12.** remote in space or time: *in the far past.* **13.** extending a great distance. **14.** more distant: *the far end of the room.* **15. far from.** in a degree, state, etc. remote from: *he is far from happy.* [OE *feorr*] —'**farness** *n.*

farad ('færəd) *n. Physics.* the derived SI unit of electric capacitance; the capacitance of a capacitor between the plates of which a potential of 1 volt is created by a charge of 1 coulomb. Symbol: F [C19: see FARADAY]

faraday ('færə,deɪ) *n.* a quantity of electricity, used in electrochemical calculations, equivalent to unit amount of substance of electrons. Symbol: *F* [C20: after Michael FARADAY]

Faraday ('færə,deɪ) *n.* **Michael.** 1791–1867, English physicist and chemist who discovered electromagnetic induction, leading to the invention of the dynamo. He also carried out research into the principles of electrolysis.

faradic (fə'rædɪk) *adj.* of or concerned with an intermittent alternating current such as that induced in the secondary winding of an induction coil. [C19: from F *faradique*; from Michael FARADAY]

farandole ('færən,dəʊl) *n.* **1.** a lively dance from Provence. **2.** a piece of music composed for or in the rhythm of this dance. [C19: from F, from Provençal *farandoulo*, from ?]

faraway ('fɑːrə,weɪ) *adj.* (**far away** *when postpositive*). **1.** very distant. **2.** absent-minded.

farce (fɑːs) *n.* **1.** a broadly humorous play based on the exploitation of improbable situations. **2.** the genre of comedy represented by works of this kind. **3.** a ludicrous situation or action. **4.** another name for **forcemeat.** [C14 (in the sense: stuffing): from OF, from L *farcīre* to stuff, interpolate passages (in the mass, in religious plays, etc.)]

farcical ('fɑːsɪk[ə]l) *adj.* **1.** absurd. **2.** of or relating to farce. —,**farci'cality** *n.* —'**farcically** *adv.*

fardel ('fɑːd[ə]l) *n. Arch.* a bundle or burden. [C13: from OF *farde*, ult. from Ar. *fardah*]

fare (fɛə) *n.* **1.** the sum charged or paid for conveyance in a bus, train, etc. **2.** a paying passenger, esp. when carried by taxi. **3.** a range of food and drink. ~*vb.* (*intr.*) **4.** to get on (as specified): *he fared well.* **5.** (with *it* as a subject) to happen as specified: *it fared badly with him.* **6.** *Arch.* to eat: *we fared sumptuously.* **7.** (often foll. by *forth*) *Arch.* to travel. [OE *faran*] —'**farer** *n.*

Far East *n.* **the.** the countries of E Asia, including China, Japan, North and South Korea, E Siberia, Indonesia, Malaysia, and the Philippines: sometimes extended to include all territories east of Afghanistan. —**Far Eastern** *adj.*

Fareham ('fɛərəm) *n.* a market town in S England, in S Hampshire. Pop.: 90 875 (1983 est.).

fare stage *n.* **1.** a section of a bus journey for which a set charge is made. **2.** the bus stop marking the end of such a section.

farewell (,fɛə'wɛl) *sentence substitute.* **1.** goodbye; adieu. ~*n.* **2.** a parting salutation. **3.** an act of departure. **4.** (*modifier*) expressing leave-taking: *a farewell speech.*

far-fetched *adj.* unlikely.

far-flung *adj.* **1.** widely distributed. **2.** far distant; remote.

farina (fə'ri:nə) n. 1. flour or meal made from any kind of cereal grain. 2. *Chiefly Brit.* starch. [C18: from L *far* spelt, coarse meal]

farinaceous (,færɪ'neɪʃəs) adj. 1. consisting or made of starch. 2. having a mealy texture or appearance. 3. containing starch: *farinaceous seeds*.

farm (fa:m) n. 1. a. a tract of land, usually with house and buildings, cultivated as a unit or used to rear livestock. b. (*as modifier*): *farm produce*. c. (*in combination*): *farmland*. 2. a unit of land or water devoted to the growing or rearing of some particular type of vegetable, fruit, animal, or fish: *a fish farm*. 3. an installation for storage or disposal: *a sewage farm*. ~vb. 4. (*tr.*) a. to cultivate (land). b. to rear (stock, etc.) on a farm. 5. (*intr.*) to engage in agricultural work, esp. as a way of life. 6. (*tr.*) to look after a child for a fixed sum. 7. to collect the moneys due and retain the profits from (a tax district, business, etc.) for a specified period. ~See also **farm out**. [C13: from OF *ferme* rented land, ult. from L *firmāre* to settle] —'**farmable** adj.

farmer ('fa:mə) n. 1. a person who operates or manages a farm. 2. a person who obtains the right to collect and retain a tax, rent, etc., on payment of a fee. 3. a person who looks after a child for a fixed sum.

Farmer ('fa:mə) n. **John.** ?1565–1605, English madrigal composer and organist.

farm hand n. a person who is hired to work on a farm.

farmhouse ('fa:m,haʊs) n. a house attached to a farm, esp. the dwelling from which the farm is managed.

farming ('fa:mɪŋ) n. a. the business or skill of agriculture. b. (*as modifier*): *farming methods*.

farm out vb. (*tr., adv.*) 1. to send (work) to be done by another person, firm, etc. 2. to put (a child, etc.) into the care of a private individual. 3. to lease to another for a fee the right to collect (taxes).

farmstead ('fa:m,stɛd) n. a farm or the part of a farm comprising its main buildings together with adjacent grounds.

farmyard ('fa:m,ja:d) n. an area surrounded by or adjacent to farm buildings.

Farnborough ('fa:nbərə, -brə) n. a town in S England, in NE Hampshire: military base, with an aeronautical research centre. Pop.: 42 496 (1982 est.).

Farnese (*Italian* far'ne:se) n. 1. **Alessandro** (ales'sandro). original name of (Pope) **Paul III.** 2. **Alessandro,** duke of Parma and Piacenza. 1545–92, Italian general, statesman, and diplomat in the service of Philip II of Spain. As governor of the Netherlands (1578–92), he successfully suppressed revolts against Spanish rule.

Farnham ('fa:nəm) n. a town in S England, in NW Surrey. Pop.: 35 289 (1981).

Far North n. **the.** the Arctic and sub-Arctic regions of the world.

faro ('fɛərəʊ) n. a gambling game in which players bet against the dealer on what cards he will turn up. [C18: prob. spelling var. of *Pharoah*]

Faroes ('fɛərəʊz) n. a variant spelling of **Faeroes.** —**Faroese** (,fɛərəʊ'i:z) adj., n.

far-off adj. (**far off** *when postpositive*). remote in space or time; distant.

farouche *French.* (faruʃ) adj. sullen or shy. [C18: from F, from OF, from LL *forasticus* from without, from L *foras* out of doors]

Farouk I *or* **Faruk I** (fə'ru:k) n. 1920–65, last king of Egypt (1936–52). He was forced to abdicate (1952).

far-out *Sl.* ~adj. (**far out** *when postpositive*) 1. bizarre or avant-garde. 2. wonderful. ~interj. **far out.** 3. an expression of amazement or delight.

Farquhar ('fa:kwə, -kə) n. **George.** 1678–1707, Irish-born dramatist; author of comedies such as *The Recruiting Officer* (1706) and *The Beaux' Stratagem* (1707).

Farquhar Islands *pl. n.* an island group in the Indian Ocean: administratively part of the Seychelles.

farrago (fə'ra:gəʊ) n., *pl.* **-gos** *or* **-goes.** a hotchpotch. [C17: from L: mash for cattle (hence, a mixture), from *far* spelt] —**farraginous** (fə'rædʒɪnəs) adj.

far-reaching adj. extensive in influence, effect, or range.

farrier ('færɪə) n. *Chiefly Brit.* 1. a person who shoes horses. 2. another name for **veterinary surgeon.** [C16: from OF, from L *ferrārius* smith, from *ferrum* iron] —'**farriery** n.

farrow ('færəʊ) n. 1. a litter of piglets. ~vb. 2. (of a sow) to give birth to (a litter). [OE *fearh*]

far-seeing adj. having shrewd judgment.

Farsi ('fa:sɪ) n. a language spoken in Iran.

far-sighted adj. 1. possessing prudence and foresight. 2. another word for **long-sighted.** — ,far-'sightedly adv. — ,far-'sightedness n.

fart (fa:t) *Taboo.* ~n. 1. an emission of intestinal gas from the anus. 2. *Sl.* a contemptible person. ~vb. (*intr.*) 3. to break wind. 4. **fart about** *or* **around.** *Sl.* **a.** to behave foolishly. **b.** to waste time. [ME *farten*]

farther ('fa:ðə) adv. 1. to or at a greater distance in space or time. 2. in addition. ~adj. 3. more distant or remote in space or time. 4. additional. [C13: see FAR, FURTHER]

▷ **Usage.** In careful usage, *farther* and *farthest* are preferred when referring to literal distance: *the farthest planet. Further* and *furthest* are regarded as more correct for figurative senses: *nothing could be further from the truth.*

farthermost ('fa:ðə,məʊst) adj. most distant or remote.

farthest ('fa:ðɪst) adv. 1. to or at the greatest distance in space or time. ~adj. 2. most distant in space or time. 3. most extended. [C14 *ferthest,* from *ferther* FURTHER]

farthing ('fa:ðɪŋ) n. 1. a former British bronze coin worth a quarter of an old penny: withdrawn in 1961. 2. something of negligible value; jot. [OE *fēorthing* from *fēortha* FOURTH + -ING[1]]

farthingale ('fa:ðɪŋ,geɪl) n. a hoop or framework worn under skirts, esp. in the Elizabethan period, to shape and spread them. [C16: from F *verdugale,* from OSp. *verdugado,* from *verdugo* rod]

Faruk I (fə'ru:k) n. a variant spelling of **Farouk I.**

fasces ('fæsi:z) pl. n., *sing.* **-cis** (-sɪs). 1. (in ancient Rome) one or more bundles of rods containing an axe with its blade protruding; a symbol of a magistrate's power. 2. (in modern Italy) such an object used as the symbol of Fascism. [C16: from L, pl. of *fascis* bundle]

fascia *or* **facia** ('feɪʃɪə) n., *pl.* **-ciae** (-ʃɪ,i:). 1. the flat surface above a shop window. 2. *Archit.* a flat band or surface, esp. a part of an architrave. 3. ('fæʃɪə). fibrous connective tissue occurring in sheets between muscles. 4. *Biol.* a distinctive band of colour, as on an insect or plant. 5. *Brit.* the outer panel which covers the dashboard of a motor vehicle. [C16: from L: band; rel. to *fascis* bundle] —'**fascial** *or* '**facial** adj.

fasciate ('fæʃɪ,eɪt) *or* **fasciated** adj. 1. *Bot.* (of stems and branches) abnormally flattened due to coalescence. 2. (of birds, insects, etc.) marked by bands of colour. [C17: prob. from NL *fasciātus* (unattested) having bands; see FASCIA]

fascicle ('fæsɪkəl) n. 1. a bundle of branches, leaves, etc. 2. Also called: **fasciculus.** *Anat.* a small bundle of fibres, esp. nerve fibres. [C15: from L *fasciculus* a small bundle, from *fascis* a bundle] —'**fascicled** adj. —**fascicular** (fə'sɪkjʊlə) *or* **fasciculate** (fə'sɪkjʊ,leɪt) adj. —**fas,cic·u'lation** n.

fascicule ('fæsɪ,kju:l) n. one part of a printed work that is published in instalments. Also called: **fascicle, fasciculus.**

fascinate ('fæsɪ,neɪt) vb. (*mainly tr.*) 1. to attract and delight by arousing interest: *his stories fascinated me for hours.* 2. to render motionless, as by arousing terror or awe. 3. *Arch.* to put under a spell. [C16: from L, from *fascinum* a bewitching] —,**fasci'nation** n.

fascinating ('fæsɪ,neɪtɪŋ) adj. 1. arousing great interest. 2. enchanting or alluring.

fascinator ('fæsɪ,neɪtə) n. *Rare.* a lace or crocheted head covering for women.

Fascism ('fæʃɪzəm) n. the political movement, doctrine, system, or regime of Benito Mussolini in Italy. Fascism encouraged militarism and nationalism, organizing the country along hierarchical authoritarian lines. [C20: from It. *fascismo,* from *fascio* political group, from L *fascis* bundle; see FASCES]

Fascist ('fæʃɪst) n. 1. a supporter or member of a Fascist movement. 2. (*sometimes not cap.*) any person regarded as having right-wing authoritarian views. ~adj. 3. characteristic of or relating to Fascism.

fashion ('fæʃən) n. 1. a. style in clothes, behaviour, etc., esp. the latest style. b. (*as modifier*): *a fashion magazine.* 2. (modifier) designed to be in the current fashion. 3. a. manner of performance: *in a striking fashion.* b. (*in combination*): *crab-fashion.* 4. a way of life that revolves around the activities, dress, interests, etc., that are most fashionable. 5. shape or form. 6. sort; kind. 7. **after** *or* **in a fashion.** in some manner, but not very well: *I* *mended it, after a fashion.* **8. of fashion.** of high social standing. ~*vb.* (*tr.*) **9.** to give a particular form to. **10.** to make suitable or fitting. **11.** *Obs.* to contrive. [C13 *facioun* form, manner, from OF *faceon*, from L, from *facere* to make] — **'fashioner** *n.*

fashionable ('fæʃənəbªl) *adj.* **1.** conforming to fashion; in vogue. **2.** of or patronized by people of fashion: *a fashionable café.* **3.** (usually foll. by *with*) patronized (by). — **'fashionableness** *n.* — **'fashionably** *adv.*

fashion plate *n.* **1.** an illustration of the latest fashion in dress. **2.** a fashionably dressed person.

Fashoda (fə'ʃəʊdə) *n.* a small town in SE Sudan: scene of a diplomatic incident (1898) in which French occupation of the fort at Fashoda caused a crisis between France and Great Britain. Modern name: **Kodok.**

Fassbinder (*German* 'fasbındər) *n.* **Rainer Werner** ('raɪnər 'vɛrnər). 1946–82, West German film director. His films include *The Bitter Tears of Petra von Kant* (1972), *Fear Eats the Soul* (1974), and *The Marriage of Maria Braun* (1978).

fast[1] (fɑːst) *adj.* **1.** acting or moving or capable of acting or moving quickly. **2.** accomplished in or lasting a short time: *a fast visit.* **3.** (*prenominal*) adapted to or facilitating rapid movement: *the fast lane of a motorway.* **4.** (of a clock, etc.) indicating a time in advance of the correct time. **5.** given to an active dissipated life. **6.** of or characteristic of such activity: *a fast life.* **7.** not easily moved; firmly fixed; secure. **8.** firmly fastened or shut. **9.** steadfast; constant (esp. in **fast friends**). **10.** *Sport.* (of a playing surface, running track, etc.) conducive to rapid speed, as of a ball used on it or of competitors racing on it. **11.** that will not fade or change colour readily. **12.** proof against fading. **13.** *Photog.* **a.** requiring a relatively short time of exposure to produce a given density: *a fast film.* **b.** permitting a short exposure time: *a fast shutter.* **14. a fast one.** *Inf.* a deceptive or unscrupulous trick (esp. in **pull a fast one**). **15. fast worker.** a person who achieves results quickly, esp. in seductions. ~*adv.* **16.** quickly; rapidly. **17.** soundly; deeply: *fast asleep.* **18.** firmly; tightly. **19.** in quick succession. **20.** in advance of the correct time: *my watch is running fast.* **21.** in a reckless or dissipated way. **22. fast by** *or* **beside.** *Arch.* close by. **23. play fast and loose.** *Inf.* to behave in an insincere or unreliable manner. [OE *fæst* strong, tight]

fast[2] (fɑːst) *vb.* **1.** (*intr.*) to abstain from eating all or certain foods or meals, esp. as a religious observance. ~*n.* **2. a.** an act or period of fasting. **b.** (*as modifier*): *a fast day.* [OE *fæstan*] — **'faster** *n.*

fastback ('fɑːst,bæk) *n.* a car having a back that forms one continuous slope from roof to rear.

fast-breeder reactor *n.* a nuclear reactor that uses little or no moderator and produces more fissionable material than it consumes.

fasten ('fɑːsªn) *vb.* **1.** to make or become fast or secure. **2.** to make or become attached or joined. **3.** to close or become closed by fixing firmly in place, locking, etc. **4.** (*tr.*; foll. by *in* or *up*) to enclose or imprison. **5.** (*tr.*; usually foll. by *on*) to cause (blame, a nickname, etc.) to be attached (to). **6.** (usually foll. by *on* or *upon*) to direct or be directed in a concentrated way. **7.** (*intr.*; usually foll. by *on*) to take a firm hold (of). [OE *fæstnian*; see FAST[1]] — **'fastener** *n.*

fastening ('fɑːsªnɪŋ) *n.* something that fastens, such as a clasp or lock.

fast food *n.* **a.** food, esp. hamburgers, fried chicken, etc., that is prepared and served very quickly. **b.** (*as modifier*): *a fast-food restaurant.*

fast-forward *vb.* (*intr.*) to move on rapidly. [C20: from the fast-forward wind control on a tape deck]

fastidious (fæ'stɪdɪəs) *adj.* **1.** hard to please. **2.** excessively particular about details. **3.** exceedingly delicate. [C15: from L *fastīdiōsus* scornful, from *fastīdium* loathing, from *fastus* pride, + *taedium* weariness] — **fas'tidiously** *adv.* — **fas'tidiousness** *n.*

fastigiate (fæ'stɪdʒɪɪt) *or* **fastigiated** *adj.* *Biol.* (of parts or organs) united in a tapering group. [C17: from Med. L *fastigiātus* lofty, from L *fastīgium* height]

fast lane *n.* **1.** the outside lane on a motorway for vehicles overtaking or travelling at high speed. **2.** *Inf.* the quickest but most competitive route to success.

fastness ('fɑːstnɪs) *n.* **1.** a stronghold; fortress. **2.** the state or quality of being firm or secure. [OE *fæstnes*; see FAST[1]]

fast-track *adj.* taking the quickest but most competitive route to success or personal advancement: *fast-track executives.*

fat (fæt) *n.* **1.** any of a class of naturally occurring soft greasy solids that are present in some plants and animals, and are used in making soap and paint and in the food industry. **2.** vegetable or animal tissue containing fat. **3.** corpulence, obesity, or plumpness. **4.** the best or richest part of something. **5. the fat is in the fire.** an irrevocable action has been taken from which dire consequences are expected. **6. the fat of the land.** the best that is obtainable. ~*adj.* **fatter, fattest. 7.** having much or too much flesh or fat. **8.** consisting of or containing fat; greasy. **9.** profitable; lucrative. **10.** affording great opportunities: *a fat part in the play.* **11.** fertile or productive: *a fat land.* **12.** thick, broad, or extended: *a fat log of wood.* **13.** *Sl.* very little or none (in **a fat chance, a fat lot of good,** etc.). ~*vb.* **fatting, fatted. 14.** to make or become fat; fatten. [OE *fætt*, p.p. of *fǣtan* to cram] — **'fatless** *adj.* — **'fatly** *adv.* — **'fatness** *n.* — **'fattish** *adj.*

fatal ('feɪtªl) *adj.* **1.** resulting in death: *a fatal accident.* **2.** bringing ruin. **3.** decisively important. **4.** inevitable. [C14: from OF or L from L *fātum;* see FATE] — **'fatally** *adv.*

fatalism ('feɪtə,lɪzəm) *n.* **1.** the philosophical doctrine that all events are predetermined so that man is powerless to alter his destiny. **2.** the acceptance of and submission to this doctrine. — **'fatalist** *n.* — ,**fatal'istic** *adj.*

fatality (fə'tælɪtɪ) *n., pl.* -**ties. 1.** an accident or disaster resulting in death. **2.** a person killed in an accident or disaster. **3.** the power of causing death or disaster. **4.** the quality or condition of being fated. **5.** something caused by fate.

fate (feɪt) *n.* **1.** the ultimate agency that predetermines the course of events. **2.** the inevitable fortune that befalls a person or thing. **3.** the end or final result. **4.** death, destruction, or downfall. ~*vb.* **5.** (*tr.; usually passive*) to predetermine: *he was fated to lose.* [C14: from L *fātum* oracular utterance, from *fārī* to speak]

fated ('feɪtɪd) *adj.* **1.** destined. **2.** doomed to death or destruction.

fateful ('feɪtful) *adj.* **1.** having important consequences. **2.** bringing death or disaster. **3.** controlled by or as if by fate. **4.** prophetic. — **'fatefully** *adv.* — **'fatefulness** *n.*

Fates (feɪts) *pl. n.* **1.** *Greek myth.* the three goddesses who control the destinies of the lives of man, which are likened to skeins of thread that they spin, measure out, and at last cut. See **Atropos, Clotho, Lachesis. 2.** *Norse myth.* another name for the **Norns.**

fathead ('fæt,hɛd) *n. Inf.* a stupid person; fool. — **'fat,headed** *adj.*

father ('fɑːðə) *n.* **1.** a male parent. **2.** a person who founds a line or family; forefather. **3.** any male acting in a paternal capacity. **4.** (*often cap.*) a respectful term of address for an old man. **5.** a male who originates something: *the father of modern psychology.* **6.** a leader of an association, council, etc.: *a city father.* **7.** *Brit.* the eldest or most senior member in a union, profession, etc. **8.** (*often pl.*) a senator in ancient Rome. ~*vb.* (*tr.*) **9.** to procreate or generate (offspring). **10.** to create, found, etc. **11.** to act as a father to. **12.** to acknowledge oneself as father or originator of. **13.** (foll. by *on* or *upon*) to impose or foist upon. [OE *fæder*] — **'fatherhood** *n.* — **'fatherless** *adj.* — **'father-,like** *adj.*

Father ('fɑːðə) *n.* **1.** God, esp. when considered as the first person of the Christian Trinity. **2.** any of the early writers on Christian doctrine. **3.** a title used for Christian priests.

father confessor *n.* **1.** *Christianity.* a priest who hears confessions. **2.** any person to whom one tells private matters.

father-in-law *n., pl.* **fathers-in-law.** the father of one's wife or husband.

fatherland ('fɑːðə,lænd) *n.* **1.** a person's native country. **2.** the country of a person's ancestors.

fatherly ('fɑːðəlɪ) *adj.* of, resembling, or suitable to a father, esp. in kindliness, encouragement, etc. — **'fatherliness** *n.*

Father's Day *n.* the third Sunday in June, observed as a day in honour of fathers.

fathom ('fæðəm) *n.* **1.** a unit of length equal to six feet, used to measure depths of water. ~*vb.* (*tr.*) **2.** to measure the depth of, esp. with a sounding line. **3.** to penetrate (a mystery, problem, etc.). [OE *fæthm*] —'**fathomable** *adj.*

Fathometer (fə'ðɒmɪtə) *n. Trademark.* a type of echo sounder used for measuring the depth of water.

fathomless ('fæðəmlɪs) *adj.* another word for **unfathomable.** —'**fathomlessness** *n.*

fatigue (fə'tiːg) *n.* **1.** physical or mental exhaustion due to exertion. **2.** a tiring activity or effort. **3.** *Physiol.* the temporary inability of an organ or part to respond to a stimulus because of overactivity. **4.** the weakening of a material subjected to alternating stresses, esp. vibrations. **5.** any of the mainly domestic duties performed by military personnel, esp. as a punishment. **6.** (*pl.*) special clothing worn by military personnel to carry out such duties. ~*vb.* **-tiguing, -tigued. 7.** to make or become weary or exhausted. [C17: from F, from *fatiguer* to tire, from L *fatigāre*] —**fatigable** *or* **fatiguable** ('fætɪgəbᵊl) *adj.*

Fatima ('fætɪmə) *n.* ?606–632 A.D., daughter of Mohammed; wife of Ali.

Fátima (*Portuguese* 'fatimə) *n.* a village in central Portugal: Roman Catholic shrine and pilgrimage centre.

Fatshan ('faːt'ʃaːn) *n.* a variant transliteration of the Chinese name for **Foshan.**

fatshedera (fæts'hɛdərə) *n.* a hybrid plant with five-lobed leaves. [from NL, from *Fatsia japonica* + *Hedera hibernica*]

fatsia ('fætsɪə) *n.* an evergreen hardy shrub. Also known as the **false castor-oil plant.** [from NL]

fatso ('fætsəʊ) *n. Sl.* a fat person.

fat-soluble *adj.* soluble in substances, such as ether, chloroform, and oils. Fat-soluble compounds are often insoluble in water.

fat stock *n.* livestock fattened and ready for market.

fatten ('fætᵊn) *vb.* **1.** to grow or cause to grow fat or fatter. **2.** (*tr.*) to cause (an animal or fowl) to become fat by feeding it. **3.** (*tr.*) to make fuller or richer. **4.** (*tr.*) to enrich (soil). —'**fattening** *adj.*

fatty ('fætɪ) *adj.* **-tier, -tiest. 1.** containing or derived from fat. **2.** greasy; oily. **3.** (esp. of tissues, organs, etc.) characterized by the excessive accumulation of fat. ~*n., pl.* **-ties. 4.** *Inf.* a fat person. —'**fattily** *adv.* —'**fattiness** *n.*

fatty acid *n.* an aliphatic carboxylic acid, esp. one found in lipids, such as palmitic acid, stearic acid, and oleic acid.

fatty degeneration *n. Pathol.* the abnormal formation of tiny globules of fat within the cytoplasm of a cell.

fatuity (fə'tjuːɪtɪ) *n., pl.* **-ties. 1.** inanity. **2.** a fatuous remark, act, sentiment, etc. —**fa'tuitous** *adj.*

fatuous ('fætjʊəs) *adj.* complacently or inanely foolish. [C17: from L *fatuus*; rel. to *fatiscere* to gape] —'**fatuously** *adv.* —'**fatuousness** *n.*

fauces ('fɔːsiːz) *n., pl.* **-ces.** *Anat.* the area between the cavity of the mouth and the pharynx. [C16: from L: throat] —**faucal** ('fɔːkᵊl) *or* **faucial** ('fɔːʃəl) *adj.*

faucet ('fɔːsɪt) *n.* **1.** a tap fitted to a barrel **2.** the U.S. and Canad. name for **tap².** [C14: from OF from Provençal *falsar* to bore]

Faulkner *or* **Falkner** ('fɔːknə) *n.* **William.** 1897–1962, U.S. novelist and short-story writer. Most of his works portray the problems of the southern U.S., esp. the novels set in the imaginary county of Yoknapatawpha in Mississippi. Other novels include *The Sound and the Fury* (1929) and *Light in August* (1932): Nobel prize for literature 1949.

fault (fɔːlt) *n.* **1.** a failing or defect; flaw. **2.** a mistake or error. **3.** a misdeed. **4.** responsibility for a mistake or misdeed. **5.** *Electronics.* a defect in a circuit, component, or line, such as a short circuit. **6.** *Geol.* a fracture in the earth's crust resulting in the relative displacement of the rocks on either side of it. **7.** *Tennis, squash, etc.* an invalid serve. **8.** (in showjumping) a penalty mark given for failing to clear, or refusing, a fence, etc. **9. at fault.** guilty of error; culpable. **10. find fault (with).** to seek out minor imperfections or errors (in). **11. to a fault.** excessively. ~*vb.* **12.** *Geol.* to undergo or cause to undergo a fault. **13.** (*tr.*) to criticize or blame. **14.** (*intr.*) to commit a fault. [C13: from OF *faute*, ult. from L *fallere* to fail]

fault-finding *n.* **1.** continual criticism. ~*adj.* **2.** given to finding fault. —'**fault-,finder** *n.*

faultless ('fɔːltlɪs) *adj.* perfect or blameless. —'**faultlessly** *adv.* —'**faultlessness** *n.*

faulty ('fɔːltɪ) *adj.* **faultier, faultiest.** defective or imperfect. —'**faultily** *adv.* —'**faultiness** *n.*

faun (fɔːn) *n.* (in Roman legend) a rural deity represented as a man with a goat's ears, horns, tail, and hind legs. [C14: back formation from *Faunes* (pl.), from L *Faunus* deity of forests] —'**faun,like** *adj.*

fauna ('fɔːnə) *n., pl.* **-nas** *or* **-nae** (-niː). **1.** all the animal life of a given place or time. **2.** a descriptive list of such animals. [C18: from NL, from LL *Fauna* a goddess of living things] —'**faunal** *adj.*

Faunus ('fɔːnəs) *n.* an ancient Italian deity of pastures and forests, later identified with the Greek Pan.

Fauré ('fɔːreɪ; *French* fore) *n.* **Gabriel (Urbain)** (gabriɛl). 1845–1924, French composer and teacher, noted particularly for his song settings of French poems, esp. those of Verlaine, his piano music, and his *Messe de Requiem* (1887).

Faust (faʊst) *or* **Faustus** ('faʊstəs) *n. German legend.* a magician and alchemist who sells his soul to the devil in exchange for knowledge and power. —'**Faustian** *adj.*

Fauvism ('fəʊvɪzəm) *n.* a form of expressionist painting characterized by the use of bright colours and simplified forms. [C20: from F, from *fauve* wild beast] —**Fauve** *n., adj.* —'**Fauvist** *n., adj.*

faux pas (fəʊ pɑː) *n., pl.* **faux pas** (fəʊ pɑːz). a social blunder. [C17: from F: false step]

favour *or U.S.* **favor** ('feɪvə) *n.* **1.** an approving attitude; good will. **2.** an act performed out of good will or mercy. **3.** prejudice and partiality. **4.** a condition of being regarded with approval (esp. in **in favour, out of favour**). **5.** a token of love, goodwill, etc. **6.** a small gift or toy given to a guest at a party. **7.** *History.* a badge or ribbon worn or given to indicate loyalty. **8. find favour with.** to be approved of by someone. **9. in favour of. a.** approving. **b.** to the benefit of. **c.** (of a cheque, etc.) made out to. **d.** in order to show preference for. ~*vb.* (*tr.*) **10.** to regard with especial kindness. **11.** to treat with partiality. **12.** to support; advocate. **13.** to oblige. **14.** to help; facilitate. **15.** *Inf.* to resemble: *he favours his father.* **16.** to wear habitually: *she favours red.* **17.** to treat gingerly: *a footballer favouring an injured leg.* [C14: from L, from *favēre* to protect] —'**favourer** *or U.S.* '**favorer** *n.*

favourable *or U.S.* **favorable** ('feɪvərəbᵊl) *adj.* **1.** advantageous, encouraging or promising. **2.** giving consent. —'**favourably** *or U.S.* '**favorably** *adv.*

-favoured *adj.* (*in combination*) having an appearance (as specified): *ill-favoured.*

favourite *or U.S.* **favorite** ('feɪvərɪt) *adj.* **1.** (*prenominal*) most liked. ~*n.* **2.** a person or thing regarded with especial preference or liking. **3.** *Sport.* a competitor thought likely to win. [C16: from It., from *favorire* to favour, from L *favēre*]

favouritism *or U.S.* **favoritism** ('feɪvərɪ,tɪzəm) *n.* the practice of giving special treatment to a person or group.

Fawkes (fɔːks) *n.* **Guy.** 1570–1606, English conspirator, executed for his part in the Gunpowder Plot to blow up King James I and the Houses of Parliament (1605). Effigies of him (guys) are burnt in Britain on Guy Fawkes Day (Nov. 5).

fawn¹ (fɔːn) *n.* **1.** a young deer of either sex aged under one year. **2. a.** a light greyish-brown colour. **b.** (*as adj.*): *a fawn raincoat.* ~*vb.* **3.** (of deer) to bear (young). [C14: from OF, from L *fētus* offspring; see FETUS] —'**fawn,like** *adj.*

fawn² (fɔːn) *vb.* (*intr.;* often foll. by *on* or *upon*) **1.** to seek attention and admiration (from) by cringing and flattering. **2.** (of animals, esp. dogs) to try to please by a show of extreme friendliness. [OE *fægnian* to be glad, from *fægen* glad; see FAIN] —'**fawner** *n.* —'**fawning** *adj.*

fax (fæks) *n.* **1.** short for **facsimile** (sense 2). **2.** a message or document sent by facsimile. ~*vb.* **3.** (*tr.*) to send (a document) by a telegraphic facsimile system.

fay (feɪ) *n.* a fairy or sprite. [C14: from OF *feie*, ult. from L *fātum* FATE]

Fayal (*Portuguese* fə'ial) *n.* a variant spelling of **Faial.**

Fayum (faɪ'juːm) *n.* See **El Faiyûm.**

faze (feɪz) *vb.* (*tr.*) *Inf., chiefly U.S. & Canad.* to disconcert; worry; disturb. [C19: var. of arch. *feeze* to beat off]

FBA *abbrev. for* Fellow of the British Academy.
FBI (in the U.S.) *abbrev. for* Federal Bureau of Investigation; an agency responsible for investigating violations of Federal laws.
FC (in Britain) *abbrev. for:* **1.** Football Club. **2.** Free Church.
fcap *abbrev. for* foolscap.
F clef *n.* another name for **bass clef.**
FD *abbrev. for* Fidei Defensor. [L: Defender of the Faith]
Fe *the chemical symbol for* iron. [from NL *ferrum*]
fealty ('fi:əltɪ) *n., pl.* **-ties.** (in feudal society) the loyalty sworn to one's lord on becoming his vassal. [C14: from OF, from L *fidēlitās* FIDELITY]
fear (fɪə) *n.* **1.** a feeling of distress, apprehension, or alarm caused by impending danger, pain, etc. **2.** a cause of this feeling. **3.** awe; reverence: *fear of God.* **4.** concern; anxiety. **5.** possibility; chance. **6. for fear of, that** *or* **lest.** to forestall or avoid. **7. no fear.** certainly not. *~vb.* **8.** to be afraid (of doing something) or of (a person or thing). **9.** (*tr.*) to revere; respect. **10.** (*tr.; takes a clause as object*) to be sorry: *I fear that you have not won.* **11.** (*intr.;* foll. by *for*) to feel anxiety about something. [OE *fǣr*] —**'fearless** *adj.* —**'fearlessly** *adv.* —**'fearlessness** *n.*
fearful ('fɪəful) *adj.* **1.** afraid. **2.** causing fear. **3.** *Inf.* very unpleasant: *a fearful cold.* —**'fearfully** *adv.* —**'fearfulness** *n.*
fearsome ('fɪəsəm) *adj.* **1.** frightening. **2.** timorous; afraid. —**'fearsomely** *adv.*
feasibility study *n.* a study designed to determine the practicability of a system or plan.
feasible ('fi:zəb³l) *adj.* **1.** able to be done or put into effect; possible. **2.** likely; probable. [C15: from Anglo-F *faisable,* from *faire* to do, from L *facere*] —**,feasi'bility** *n.* —**'feasibly** *adv.*
feast (fi:st) *n.* **1.** a large and sumptuous meal. **2.** a periodic religious celebration. **3.** something extremely pleasing: *a feast for the eyes.* **4. moveable feast.** a festival of variable date. *~vb.* **5.** (*intr.*) **a.** to eat a feast. **b.** (usually foll. by *on*) to enjoy the eating (of): *to feast on cakes.* **6.** (*tr.*) to give a feast to. **7.** (*intr.;* foll. by *on*) to take great delight (in): *to feast on beautiful paintings.* **8.** (*tr.*) to regale or delight: *to feast one's eyes.* [C13: from OF, from L *festa,* neuter pl. (later assumed to be fem. sing.) of *festus* joyful; rel. to L *fānum* temple, *fēriae* festivals] —**'feaster** *n.*
feat (fi:t) *n.* a remarkable, skilful, or daring action. [C14: from Anglo-F *fait,* from L *factum* deed; see FACT]
feather ('fɛðə) *n.* **1.** any of the flat light waterproof structures forming the plumage of birds, each consisting of a hollow shaft having a vane of barbs on either side. **2.** something resembling a feather, such as a tuft of hair or grass. **3.** *Archery.* **a.** a bird's feather or artificial substitute fitted to an arrow to direct its flight. **b.** the feathered end of an arrow. **4.** *Rowing.* the position of an oar turned parallel to the water between strokes. **5.** condition of spirits; fettle: *in fine feather.* **6.** something of negligible value: *I don't care a feather.* **7. feather in one's cap.** a cause for pleasure at one's achievements. *~vb.* **8.** (*tr.*) to fit, cover, or supply with feathers. **9.** *Rowing.* to turn (an oar) parallel to the water during recovery between strokes, in order to lessen wind resistance. **10.** to change the pitch of (an aircraft propeller) so that the chord lines of the blades are in line with the airflow. **11.** (*intr.*) (of a bird) to grow feathers. **12. feather one's nest.** to provide oneself with comforts. [OE *fether*] —**'feathering** *n.* —**'feather-,like** *adj.* —**'feathery** *adj.*
feather bed *n.* **1.** a mattress filled with feathers or down. *~vb.* **featherbed, -bedding, -bedded. 2.** (*tr.*) to pamper; spoil.
featherbedding ('fɛðə,bɛdɪŋ) *n.* the practice of limiting production or of overmanning in order to prevent redundancies or create jobs.
featherbrain ('fɛðə,breɪn) *or* **featherhead** *n.* a frivolous or forgetful person. —**'feather,brained** *or* **'feather-,headed** *adj.*
featheredge ('fɛðər,ɛdʒ) *n.* a board or plank that tapers to a thin edge at one side.
featherstitch ('fɛðə,stɪtʃ) *n.* **1.** a zigzag embroidery stitch. *~vb.* **2.** to decorate (cloth) with featherstitch.
featherweight ('fɛðə,weɪt) *n.* **1. a.** something very light or of little importance. **b.** (*as modifier*): *featherweight considerations.* **2. a.** a professional boxer weighing 118–

126 pounds (53.5–57 kg). **b.** an amateur boxer weighing 54–57 kg (119–126 pounds). **3.** an amateur wrestler weighing usually 127–137 pounds (58–62 kg).
feature ('fi:tʃə) *n.* **1.** any one of the parts of the face, such as the nose, chin, or mouth. **2.** a prominent or distinctive part, as of a landscape, book, etc. **3.** the principal film in a programme at a cinema. **4.** an item or article appearing at intervals in a newspaper, magazine, etc.: *a gardening feature.* **5.** Also called: **feature story.** a prominent story in a newspaper, etc.: *a feature on prison reform.* **6.** a programme given special prominence on radio or television. **7.** *Arch.* general form. *~vb.* **8.** (*tr.*) to have as a feature or make a feature of. **9.** to give prominence to (an actor, famous event, etc.) in a film or (of an actor, etc.) to have prominence in a film. **10.** (*tr.*) to draw the main features or parts of. [C14: from Anglo-F *feture,* from L *factūra* a making, from *facere* to make] —**'featureless** *adj.*
-featured *adj.* (*in combination*) having features as specified: *heavy-featured.*
Feb. *abbrev. for* February.
febri- *combining form.* indicating fever: *febrifuge.* [from L *febris* fever]
febrifuge ('fɛbrɪ,fju:dʒ) *n.* **1.** any drug or agent for reducing fever. *~adj.* **2.** serving to reduce fever. [C17: from Med. L *febrifugia* feverfew; see FEBRI-, -FUGE] —**febrifugal** (fɪ'brɪfjʊg³l) *adj.*
febrile ('fi:braɪl) *adj.* of or relating to fever; feverish. [C17: from Medical L *febrīlis,* from L *febris* fever] —**febrility** (fɪ'brɪlɪtɪ) *n.*
February ('fɛbruərɪ) *n., pl.* **-aries.** the second month of the year, consisting of 28 or (in a leap year) 29 days. [C13: from L *Februārius mēnsis* month of expiation, from *februa* Roman festival of purification held on February 15, from pl. of *februum* a purgation]
feces ('fi:si:z) *pl. n.* the usual U.S. spelling of **faeces.** —**fecal** ('fi:k³l) *adj.*
Fechner (*German* 'fɛçnər) *n.* **Gustav Theodor** ('gʊstaf 'te:odo:ər). 1801–87, German physicist, philosopher, and psychologist, noted particularly for his work on psychophysics, *Elemente der Psychophysik* (1860).
feckless ('fɛklɪs) *adj.* feeble; weak; ineffectual. [C16: from obs. *feck* value, effect + -LESS] —**'fecklessly** *adv.* —**'fecklessness** *n.*
feculent ('fɛkjʊlənt) *adj.* **1.** filthy or foul. **2.** of or containing waste matter. [C15: from L *faeculentus;* see FAECES] —**'feculence** *n.*
fecund ('fi:kənd, 'fɛk-) *adj.* **1.** fertile. **2.** intellectually productive. [C14: from L *fēcundus*] —**fecundity** (fɪ'kʌndɪtɪ) *n.*
fecundate ('fi:kən,deɪt, 'fɛk-) *vb.* (*tr.*) **1.** to make fruitful. **2.** to fertilize. [C17: from L *fēcundāre* to fertilize] —**,fe-cun'dation** *n.*
fed (fɛd) *vb.* **1.** the past tense and past participle of **feed. 2. fed to death** *or* **fed (up) to the (back) teeth.** *Inf.* bored or annoyed.
Fed. *or* **fed.** *abbrev. for:* **1.** Federal. **2.** Federation. **3.** Federated.
fedayee (fə'dɑ:ji:) *n., pl.* **-yeen** (-ji:n). **a.** (*sometimes cap.*) (in Arab states) a commando, esp. one fighting against Israel. **b.** (esp. in Iran and Afghanistan) a member of a guerrilla organization. [from Ar. *fidā'ī* one who risks his life in a cause, from *fidā'* redemption]
federal ('fɛdərəl) *adj.* **1.** of or relating to a form of government or a country in which power is divided between one central and several regional governments. **2.** of or relating to the central government of a federation. [C17: from L *foedus* league] —**'federa,lism** *n.* —**'federalist** *n., adj.* —**'federally** *adv.*
Federal ('fɛdərəl) *adj.* characteristic of or supporting the Union government during the American Civil War. *~n.* **2.** a supporter of the Union government during the American Civil War.
Federal Government *n.* the national government of a federated state, such as the Canadian national government located in Ottawa.
federalize *or* **-lise** ('fɛdərə,laɪz) *vb.* (*tr.*) **1.** to unite in a federal union. **2.** to subject to federal control. —**,feder-ali'zation** *or* **-li'sation** *n.*
Federal Republic of Germany *n.* the official name of **West Germany.**
Federal Reserve System *n.* (in the U.S.) a banking system consisting of twelve **Federal Reserve Banks** and

their member banks. It performs functions similar to those of the Bank of England.

federate vb. ('fɛdə,reɪt). **1.** to unite or cause to unite in a federal union. ~adj. ('fɛdərɪt). **2.** federal; federated. — **'federative** adj.

Federated Malay States pl. n. See **Malay States.**

federation (,fɛdə'reɪʃən) n. **1.** the act of federating. **2.** the union of several provinces, states, etc., to form a federal union. **3.** a political unit formed in such a way. **4.** any league, alliance, or confederacy.

Federation of Rhodesia and Nyasaland n. a federation (1953–63) of Northern Rhodesia, Southern Rhodesia, and Nyasaland.

fedora (fɪ'dɔːrə) n. a soft felt brimmed hat, usually with a band. [C19: allegedly after *Fédora* (1882), play by Victorien Sardou (1831–1908)]

fed up adj. (usually postpositive) Inf. annoyed or bored: I'm fed up with your conduct.

fee (fiː) n. **1.** a payment asked by professional people or public servants for their services: school fees. **2.** a charge made for a privilege: an entrance fee. **3.** Property law. an interest in land capable of being inherited. The interest can be with unrestricted rights of disposal (**fee simple**) or with restricted rights to one class of heirs (**fee tail**). **4.** (in feudal Europe) the land granted by a lord to his vassal. **5. in fee.** Law. (of land) in absolute ownership. ~vb. **feeing, feed. 6.** Rare. to give a fee to. **7.** Chiefly Scot. to hire for a fee. [C14: from OF fie, of Gmc origin; see FIEF]

feeble ('fiːbªl) adj. **1.** lacking in physical or mental strength. **2.** unconvincing: feeble excuses. **3.** easily influenced. [C12: from OF feble, fleible, from L flēbilis to be lamented, from flēre to weep] — **'feebleness** n. — **'feebly** adv.

feeble-minded adj. **1.** lacking in intelligence. **2.** mentally defective.

feed (fiːd) vb. **feeding, fed.** (mainly tr.) **1.** to give food to: to feed the cat. **2.** to give as food: to feed meat to the cat. **3.** (intr.) to eat food: the horses feed at noon. **4.** to provide food for. **5.** to gratify; satisfy. **6.** (also intr.) to supply (a machine, furnace, etc.) with (the necessary materials or fuel) for its operation, or (of such materials) to flow or move forwards into a machine, etc. **7.** Theatre, inf. to cue (an actor, esp. a comedian) with lines. **8.** Sport. to pass a ball to (a team-mate). **9.** (also intr.; foll. by on or upon) to eat or cause to eat. ~n. **10.** the act or an instance of feeding. **11.** food, esp. that of animals or babies. **12.** the process of supplying a machine or furnace with a material or fuel. **13.** the quantity of material or fuel so supplied. **14.** Theatre, inf. a performer, esp. a straight man, who provides cues. **15.** Inf. a meal. [OE fēdan] — **'feedable** adj.

feedback ('fiːd,bæk) n. **1. a.** the return of part of the output of an electronic circuit, device, or mechanical system to its input. In **negative feedback** a rise in output energy reduces the input energy; in **positive feedback** an increase in output energy reinforces the input energy. **b.** that part of the output signal fed back into the input. **2.** the return of part of the sound output of a loudspeaker to the microphone or pick-up, so that a high-pitched whistle is produced. **3.** the whistling noise so produced. **4.** the effect of a product or action in a cyclic biological reaction on another stage in the same reaction. **5.** information in response to an inquiry, experiment, etc.

feeder ('fiːdə) n. **1.** a person or thing that feeds or is fed. **2.** a child's feeding bottle or bib. **3.** a person or device that feeds the working material into a system or machine. **4.** a tributary channel. **5.** a road, service, etc., that links secondary areas to the main traffic network. **6.** a power line for transmitting electrical power from a generating station to a distribution network.

feeding bottle n. a bottle fitted with a rubber teat from which infants suck liquids.

feel (fiːl) vb. **feeling, felt. 1.** to perceive (something) by touching. **2.** to have a physical or emotional sensation of (something): to feel anger. **3.** (tr.) to examine (something) by touch. **4.** (tr.) to find (one's way) by testing or cautious exploration. **5.** (copula) to seem in respect of the sensation given: it feels warm. **6.** to sense (esp. in **feel (it) in one's bones**). **7.** to consider; believe; think. **8.** (intr.; foll. by for) to show sympathy or compassion (towards): I feel for you in your sorrow. **9.** (tr.; often foll. by up) Sl. to pass one's hands over the sexual organs

of. **10. feel like.** to have an inclination (for something or doing something): I don't feel like going to the pictures. **11. feel up to.** (usually used with a negative or in a question) to be fit enough for (something or doing something): I don't feel up to going out. ~n. **12.** the act or an instance of feeling. **13.** the quality of or an impression from something perceived through feeling: a homely feel. **14.** the sense of touch. **15.** an instinctive aptitude; knack: she's got a feel for this sort of work. [OE fēlan]
▷ **Usage.** The verbs feel, look, and smell can be followed by an adverb or an adjective according to the sense in which they are used. Where a quality of the subject is involved, an adjective is used: I feel sick; he looks strong. For other senses an adverb would be used: she feels strongly about that; I must look closely at his record.

feeler ('fiːlə) n. **1.** a person or thing that feels. **2.** an organ in certain animals, such as an antenna, that is sensitive to touch. **3.** a remark designed to probe the reactions or intentions of others.

feeler gauge n. a thin metal strip of known thickness used to measure a narrow gap or to set a gap between two parts.

feeling ('fiːlɪŋ) n. **1.** the sense of touch. **2. a.** the ability to experience physical sensations, such as heat, etc. **b.** the sensation so experienced. **3.** a state of mind. **4.** a physical or mental impression: a feeling of warmth. **5.** fondness; sympathy: to have a great deal of feeling for someone. **6.** a sentiment: a feeling that the project is feasible. **7.** an emotional disturbance, esp. anger or dislike: a lot of bad feeling. **8.** intuitive appreciation and understanding: a feeling for words. **9.** sensibility in the performance or intentions of something. **10.** (pl.) emotional or moral sensitivity (esp. in **hurt** or **injure the feelings of**). ~adj. **11.** sentient; sensitive. **12.** expressing or containing emotion. — **'feelingly** adv.

feet (fiːt) n. **1.** the plural of **foot. 2. at (someone's) feet.** as someone's disciple. **3. be run** or **rushed off one's feet.** to be very busy. **4. carry** or **sweep off one's feet.** to fill with enthusiasm. **5. feet of clay.** a weakness that is not widely known. **6. have (** or **keep) one's feet on the ground.** to be practical and reliable. **7. on one's** or **its feet. a.** standing up. **b.** in good health. **8. stand on one's own feet.** to be independent.

feign (feɪn) vb. **1.** to pretend: to feign innocence. **2.** (tr.) to invent: to feign an excuse. **3.** (tr.) to copy; imitate. [C13: from OF, from L fingere to form, shape, invent] — **'feigningly** adv.

Feininger ('faɪnɪŋə) n. **Lyonel.** 1871–1956, U.S. artist, who worked at the Bauhaus, noted for his use of superimposed translucent planes of colour.

feint[1] (feɪnt) n. **1.** a mock attack or movement designed to distract an adversary, as in boxing, fencing, etc. **2.** a misleading action or appearance. ~vb. **3.** (intr.) to make a feint. [C17: from F, from OF feindre to FEIGN]

feint[2] (feɪnt) n. Printing. a narrow rule used in the production of ruled paper. [C19: var. of FAINT]

Feisal ('faɪsªl) n. a variant spelling of **Faisal.**

feldspar ('fɛld,spɑː, 'fɛl,spɑː) or **felspar** n. any of a group of hard rock-forming minerals consisting of aluminium silicates of potassium, sodium, calcium, or barium: the principal constituents of igneous rocks. [C18: from G, from Feld field + Spat(h) SPAR[3]] — **feldspathic** (fɛld'spæθɪk, fɛl'spæθ-) or **fel'spathic** adj.

felicitate (fɪ'lɪsɪ,teɪt) vb. to congratulate. — **fe,lici'tation** n. — **fe'lici,tator** n.

felicitous (fɪ'lɪsɪtəs) adj. **1.** well-chosen; apt. **2.** possessing an agreeable style. **3.** marked by happiness. — **fe'licitously** adv.

felicity (fɪ'lɪsɪtɪ) n., pl. **-ties. 1.** happiness. **2.** a cause of happiness. **3.** an appropriate expression or style. **4.** the display of such expressions or style. [C14: from L fēlīcitās happiness, from fēlix happy]

feline ('fiːlaɪn) adj. **1.** of, relating to, or belonging to a family of predatory mammals, including cats, lions, leopards, and cheetahs, having a round head and retractile claws. **2.** resembling or suggestive of a cat, esp. in stealth or grace. ~n. **3.** any member of the cat family; a cat. [C17: from L, from fēlēs cat] — **'felinely** adv. — **felinity** (fɪ'lɪnɪtɪ) n.

fell[1] (fɛl) vb. the past tense of **fall.**

fell[2] (fɛl) vb. (tr.) **1.** to cut or knock down: to fell a tree. **2.** Needlework. to fold under and sew flat (the edges of a seam). ~*n.* **3.** *U.S. & Canad.* the timber felled in one season. **4.** a seam finished by felling. [OE *fellan;* cf. FALL] —'**feller** *n.*

fell[3] (fɛl) *adj.* **1.** *Arch.* cruel or fierce. **2.** *Arch.* destructive or deadly. **3. one fell swoop.** a single hasty action or occurrence. [C13 *fel,* from OF: cruel, from Med. L *fellō* villain; see FELON[1]]

fell[4] (fɛl) *n.* an animal skin or hide. [OE]

fell[5] (fɛl) *n.* (*often pl.*) *Scot. & N English.* **a.** a mountain, hill, or moor. **b.** (*in combination*): *fell-walking.* [C13: from ON *fjall;* rel. to OHG *felis* rock]

fellah ('fɛlə) *n., pl.* **fellahs, fellahin,** *or* **fellaheen** (ˌfɛlə'hiːn). a peasant in Arab countries. [C18: from Ar., dialect var. of *fallāh,* from *falaha* to cultivate]

fellatio (fɪ'leɪʃɪəʊ) *n.* a sexual activity in which the penis is stimulated by the mouth. [C19: NL, from L *fellāre* to suck]

Felling ('fɛlɪŋ) *n.* a coal-mining town in N England, in Tyneside. Pop.: 36 431 (1981).

Fellini (fə'liːnɪ) *n.* **Federico** (fedeˈriko). born 1920, Italian film director. His films include *La Dolce Vita* (1959), *8½* (1963), *Satyricon* (1969), and *Intervista* (1987).

felloe ('fɛləʊ) *or* **felly** ('fɛlɪ) *n., pl.* **-loes** *or* **-lies.** a segment or the whole rim of a wooden wheel to which the spokes are attached. [OE *felge*]

fellow ('fɛləʊ) *n.* **1.** a man or boy. **2.** an informal word for **boyfriend. 3.** *Inf.* one or oneself: *a fellow has to eat.* **4.** a person considered to be of little worth. **5. a.** (*often pl.*) a companion; associate. **b.** (*as modifier*): *fellow travellers.* **6.** a member of the governing body at any of various universities or colleges. **7.** a postgraduate student employed, esp. for a fixed period, to undertake research. **8. a.** a person in the same group, class, or condition: *the surgeon asked his fellows.* **b.** (*as modifier*): *a fellow sufferer.* **9.** one of a pair; counterpart; mate. [OE *fēolaga*]

Fellow ('fɛləʊ) *n.* a member of any of various learned societies: *Fellow of the British Academy.*

fellow feeling *n.* **1.** mutual sympathy or friendship. **2.** an opinion held in common.

fellowship ('fɛləʊˌʃɪp) *n.* **1.** the state of sharing mutual interests, activities, etc. **2.** a society of people sharing mutual interests, activities, etc. **3.** companionship; friendship. **4.** the state or relationship of being a fellow. **5.** *Education.* **a.** a financed research post providing study facilities, privileges, etc., often in return for teaching services. **b.** an honorary title carrying certain privileges awarded to a postgraduate student.

fellow traveller *n.* **1.** a companion on a journey. **2.** a non-Communist who sympathizes with Communism.

felon[1] ('fɛlən) *n.* **1.** *Criminal law.* (formerly) a person who has committed a felony. ~*adj.* **2.** *Arch.* evil. [C13: from OF: villain, from Med. L *fellō,* from ?]

felon[2] ('fɛlən) *n.* a purulent inflammation of the end joint of a finger. [C12: from Med. L *fellō,* ?from L *fel* poison]

felonious (fɪ'ləʊnɪəs) *adj.* **1.** *Criminal law.* of, involving, or constituting a felony. **2.** *Obs.* wicked. —**fe'loniously** *adv.* —**fe'loniousness** *n.*

felony ('fɛlənɪ) *n., pl.* **-nies.** *Criminal law.* (formerly) a serious crime, such as murder or arson.

felspar ('fɛlˌspaː) *n.* a variant spelling (esp. Brit.) of **feldspar.** —**felspathic** (fɛl'spæθɪk) *adj.*

felt[1] (fɛlt) *vb.* the past tense and past participle of **feel.**

felt[2] (fɛlt) *n.* **1.** a matted fabric of wool, hair, etc., made by working the fibres together under pressure or by heat or chemical action. **2.** any material, such as asbestos, made by a similar process of matting. ~*vb.* **3.** (*tr.*) to make into or cover with felt. **4.** (*intr.*) to become matted. [OE]

felt-tip pen *n.* a pen whose writing point is made from pressed fibres. Also called: **fibre-tip pen.**

felucca (fɛ'lʌkə) *n.* a narrow lateen-rigged vessel of the Mediterranean. [C17: from It., prob. from obs. Sp. *faluca,* prob. from Ar. *fulūk* ships, from Gk, from *ephelkein* to tow]

fem. *abbrev. for:* **1.** female. **2.** feminine.

female ('fiːmeɪl) *adj.* **1.** of, relating to, or designating the sex producing gametes (ova) that can be fertilized by male gametes (spermatozoa). **2.** of or characteristic of a woman. **3.** for or composed of women or girls: *a female choir.* **4.** (of reproductive organs such as the ovary and carpel) capable of producing female gametes. **5.** (of flowers) lacking or having nonfunctional, stamens. **6.** having

an internal cavity into which a projecting male counterpart can be fitted: *a female thread.* ~*n.* **7.** a female animal or plant. [C14: from earlier *femelle* (infl. by *male*), from L *fēmella* a young woman, from *fēmina* a woman] —'**femaleness** *n.*

female impersonator *n.* a male theatrical performer who acts as a woman.

feminine ('fɛmɪnɪn) *adj.* **1.** suitable to or characteristic of a woman. **2.** possessing qualities or characteristics considered typical of or appropriate to a woman. **3.** effeminate; womanish. **4.** *Grammar.* **a.** denoting or belonging to a gender of nouns that includes all kinds of referents as well as some female animate referents. **b.** (*as n.*): *German Zeit "time" and Ehe "marriage" are feminines.* [C14: from L, from *fēmina* woman] —'**femininely** *adv.* —'**feminineness** *n.*

feminism ('fɛmɪˌnɪzəm) *n.* a doctrine or movement that advocates equal rights for women. —'**feminist** *n., adj.*

feminize *or* **-ise** ('fɛmɪˌnaɪz) *vb.* **1.** to make or become feminine. **2.** to cause (a male animal) to develop female characteristics. —ˌ**femini'zation** *or* **-i'sation** *n.*

femme fatale *French.* (fam fatal) *n., pl.* **femmes fatales** (fam fatal). an alluring or seductive woman, esp. one who causes men to love her to their own distress. [fatal woman]

femto- *prefix.* denoting 10⁻¹⁵: *femtometer.* Symbol: f [from Danish or Norwegian *femten* fifteen]

femur ('fiːmə) *n., pl.* **femurs** *or* **femora** ('fɛmərə). **1.** the longest thickest bone of the human skeleton, with the pelvis above and the knee below. Nontechnical name: **thighbone. 2.** the corresponding bone in other vertebrates or the corresponding segment of an insect's leg. [C18: from L: thigh] —'**femoral** *adj.*

fen (fɛn) *n.* low-lying flat land that is marshy or artificially drained. [OE *fenn*] —'**fenny** *adj.*

fence (fɛns) *n.* **1.** a structure that serves to enclose an area such as a garden or field, usually made of posts of timber, concrete, or metal connected by wire netting, rails, or boards. **2.** *Sl.* a dealer in stolen property. **3.** an obstacle for a horse to jump in steeplechasing or showjumping. **4.** *Machinery.* a guard or guide, esp. in a circular saw or plane. **5.** (**sit**) **on the fence.** (to be) unable or unwilling to commit oneself. ~*vb.* **6.** (*tr.*) to construct a fence on or around (a piece of land, etc.). **7.** (*tr.;* foll. by *in* or *off*) to close (in) or separate (off) with or as if with a fence: *he fenced in the livestock.* **8.** (*tr.*) to fight using swords or foils. **9.** (*intr.*) to evade a question or argument. **10.** (*intr.*) *Sl.* to receive stolen property. [C14 *fens,* shortened from *defens* DEFENCE] —'**fenceless** *adj.* —'**fencer** *n.*

fencible ('fɛnsəbʰl) *n.* (formerly) a person who undertook military service in immediate defence of his homeland only.

fencing ('fɛnsɪŋ) *n.* **1.** the practice, art, or sport of fighting with foils, épées, sabres, etc. **2. a.** wire, stakes, etc., used as fences. **b.** fences collectively.

fend (fɛnd) *vb.* **1.** (*intr.;* foll. by *for*) to give support (to someone, esp. oneself). **2.** (*tr.;* usually foll. by *off*) to ward off or turn aside (blows, questions, etc.). ~*n.* **3.** *Scot. & N English dialect.* a shift or effort. [C13 *fenden,* shortened from *defenden* to DEFEND]

fender ('fɛndə) *n.* **1.** a low metal frame which confines falling coals to the hearth. **2.** *Chiefly U.S.* a metal frame fitted to the front of locomotives to absorb shock, etc. **3.** a cushion-like device, such as a car tyre hung over the side of a vessel to reduce damage resulting from collision. **4.** the U.S. and Canad. name for the wing of a car.

Fénelon (*French* fenlɔ̃) *n.* **François de Salignac de La Mothe** (frãswa də saliɲak də la mɔt). 1651–1715, French theologian and writer; author of *Maximes des saints* (1697), a defence of quietism, and *Les aventures de Télémaque* (1699), which was construed as criticizing the government of Louis XIV.

fenestra (fɪ'nɛstrə) *n., pl.* **-trae** (-triː). **1.** *Biol.* a small opening, esp. either of two openings between the middle and inner ears. **2.** *Zool.* a transparent marking or spot, as on the wings of moths. [C19: via NL from L: wall opening, window]

fenestrated (fɪ'nɛstreɪtɪd, 'fɛnɪˌstreɪtɪd) *or* **fenestrate** *adj.* **1.** *Archit.* having windows. **2.** *Biol.* perforated or having fenestrae.

fenestration (ˌfɛnɪ'streɪʃən) *n.* **1.** the arrangement of windows in a building. **2.** an operation to restore hearing by making an artificial opening into the labyrinth of the ear.

Fenian ('fi:nɪən, 'fi:njən) n. **1.** (formerly) a member of an Irish revolutionary organization founded in the U.S. in the 19th century to fight for an independent Ireland. ~adj. **2.** of or relating to the Fenians. [C19: from Irish Gaelic féinne, after Fiann Irish folk hero] — 'Fenianism n.

fennec ('fɛnɛk) n. a very small nocturnal fox inhabiting deserts of N Africa and Arabia, having enormous ears. [C18: from Ar. fenek fox]

fennel ('fɛnᵊl) n. a strong-smelling yellow-flowered umbelliferous plant whose seeds, feathery leaves, and bulbous aniseed-flavoured root are used in cookery. [OE fenol]

Fenrir ('fɛnrɪə), **Fenris** ('fɛnrɪs), or **Fenriswolf** ('fɛnrɪs-‚wʊlf) n. Norse myth. an enormous wolf, fathered by Loki, which killed Odin.

Fens (fɛnz) pl. n. **the.** a flat low-lying area of E England, west and south of the Wash: consisted of marshes until reclaimed in the 17th to 19th centuries.

fenugreek ('fɛnjʊ‚gri:k) n. an annual heavily scented Mediterranean leguminous plant with hairy stems and white flowers. [OE fēnogrēcum]

feoff (fi:f) History. ~n. **1.** a variant spelling of **fief.** ~vb. **2.** (tr.) to invest with a benefice or fief. [C13: from Anglo-F a FIEF] — 'feoffee n. — 'feoffment n. — 'feoffor or 'feoffer n.

-fer n. combining form. indicating a person or thing that bears something specified: crucifer; conifer. [from L, from ferre to bear]

feral ('fɪərəl) adj. **1.** (of animals and plants) existing in a wild or uncultivated state. **2.** savage; brutal. [C17: from Med. L, from L, from ferus savage]

fer-de-lance (‚fɛədə'lɑ:ns) n. a large highly venomous tropical American snake with a greyish-brown mottled coloration. [C19: from F, lit.: iron (head) of a lance]

Ferdinand ('fɛ:dɪ‚nænd; German 'fɛrdinant) n. See **Franz Ferdinand.**

Ferdinand I ('fɛ:dɪ‚nænd) n. **1.** known as Ferdinand the Great. ?1016–65, king of Castile (1035–65) and León (1037–65): achieved control of the Moorish kings of Saragossa, Seville, and Toledo. **2.** 1503–64, king of Hungary and Bohemia (1526–64); Holy Roman Emperor (1558–64), bringing years of religious warfare to an end. **3.** 1751–1825, king of the Two Sicilies (1816–25); king of Naples (1759–1806; 1815–25), as Ferdinand IV, being dispossessed by Napoleon (1806–15). **4.** 1793–1875, king of Hungary (1830–48) and emperor of Austria (1835–48); abdicated after the Revolution of 1848 in favour of his nephew, Franz Josef I. **5.** 1861–1948, ruling prince of Bulgaria (1887–1908) and tsar from 1908 until his abdication in 1918. **6.** 1865–1927, king of Romania (1914–27); sided with the Allies in World War I.

Ferdinand II n. **1.** 1578–1637, Holy Roman Emperor (1619–37); king of Bohemia (1617–19; 1620–37) and of Hungary (1617–37). His anti-Protestant policies led to the Thirty Years' War. **2.** title as king of Aragon and Sicily of **Ferdinand V.**

Ferdinand III n. **1.** 1608–57, Holy Roman Emperor (1637–57) and king of Hungary (1625–57); son of Ferdinand II. **2.** title as king of Naples of **Ferdinand V.**

Ferdinand V n. known as Ferdinand the Catholic. 1452–1516, king of Castile (1474–1504); as Ferdinand II, king of Aragon (1479–1516) and Sicily (1468–1516); as Ferdinand III, king of Naples (1504–16). His marriage to Isabella I of Castile (1469) led to the union of Aragon and Castile and his reconquest of Granada from the Moors (1492) completed the unification of Spain. He introduced the Inquisition (1478), expelled the Jews from Spain (1492), and financed Columbus' voyage to the New World.

feretory ('fɛrɪtərɪ, -trɪ) n., pl. -ries. Chiefly R.C. Church. **1.** a shrine, usually portable, for a saint's relics. **2.** the chapel in which a shrine is kept. [C14: from MF fiertre, from L feretrum a bier, from Gk, from pherein to bear]

Fergana or **Ferghana** (fə'gɑ:nə) n. **1.** a region of W central Asia, surrounded by high mountains and accessible only from the west; mainly in the Uzbek SSR and partly in the Tadzhik and Kirgiz SSRs. **2.** the chief city of this region, in the E Uzbek SSR. Pop.: 195 000 (1985 est.).

Fergus ('fɛ:gəs) n. (in Irish legend) a warrior king of Ulster, who was supplanted by Conchobar.

feria ('fɪərɪə) n., pl. -rias or -riae (-rɪ‚i:). R.C. Church. a weekday, other than Saturday, on which no feast occurs.

[C19: from LL: day of the week (as in prīma fēria Sunday), sing. of L fēriae festivals] — 'ferial adj.

Fermanagh (fə'mænə) n. a district (former county) of SW Northern Ireland: contains the Upper and Lower Lough Erne. Pop.: 51 000 (1986). Area (excluding water): 1700 sq. km (656 sq. miles).

Fermat (fɛ:'mæt; French fɛrma) n. **Pierre de** (pjɛr də). 1601–65, French mathematician, regarded as the founder of the modern theory of numbers. He studied the properties of whole numbers and, with Pascal, investigated the theory of probability.

fermata (fə'mɑ:tə) n., pl. -tas or -te (-tɪ). Music. another word for **pause** (sense 5). [from It., from fermare to stop, from L firmāre to establish]

ferment n. ('fɛ:mɛnt). **1.** any agent or substance, such as a bacterium, mould, yeast, or enzyme, that causes fermentation. **2.** another word for **fermentation. 3.** commotion; unrest. ~vb. (fə'mɛnt). **4.** to undergo or cause to undergo fermentation. **5.** to stir up or seethe with excitement. [C15: from L fermentum yeast, from fervēre to seethe] — 'fer'mentable adj.

fermentation (‚fɛ:mɛn'teɪʃən) n. a chemical reaction in which an organic molecule splits into simpler substances, esp. the conversion of sugar to ethyl alcohol by yeast. — 'fer'mentative adj.

fermentation lock n. a valve placed on the top of bottles of fermenting wine to allow bubbles to escape.

fermi ('fɛ:mɪ) n. a unit of length used in nuclear physics equal to 10^{-15} metre. [C20: after Enrico FERMI]

Fermi ('fɛ:mɪ; Italian 'fermi) n. **Enrico** (en'ri:ko). 1901–54, Italian nuclear physicist, in the U.S. from 1939. He was awarded a Nobel prize for physics in 1938 for his work on radioactive substances and neutron bombardment and headed the group that produced the first controlled nuclear reaction (1942).

fermion ('fɛ:mɪ‚ɒn) n. any of a group of elementary particles, such as a nucleon, that has half-integral spin and obeys the Pauli exclusion principle. Cf. **boson.** [C20: after Enrico FERMI; see -ON]

fermium ('fɛ:mɪəm) n. a transuranic element artificially produced by neutron bombardment of plutonium. Symbol: Fm; atomic no.: 100; half-life of most stable isotope, ^{257}Fm: 80 days (approx.). [C20: after Enrico FERMI]

fern (fɛ:n) n. **1.** a plant having roots, stems, and fronds and reproducing by spores formed in structures (sori) on the fronds. **2.** any of certain similar but unrelated plants, such as the sweet fern. [OE fearn] — 'ferny adj.

Fernandel (French fɛrnɑ̃dɛl) n. real name Fernand Joseph Désiré Contandin. 1903–71, French comic film actor.

Fernando de Noronha (Portuguese fer'nəndu di no'roɲa) n. a volcanic island in the S Atlantic northeast of Cape São Roque: constitutes a federal territory of Brazil; a penal colony since the 18th century. Pop.: 1323 (1980). Area: 26 sq. km (10 sq. miles).

Fernando Po (fə'nændəʊ pəʊ) n. a former name (until 1973) of **Bioko.**

fernbird ('fɛ:n‚bɜ:d) n. a New Zealand swamp bird with a fern-like tail.

ferocious (fə'rəʊʃəs) adj. savagely fierce or cruel: a ferocious tiger. [C17: from L ferox fierce, warlike] — **ferocity** (fə'rɒsɪtɪ) n.

-ferous adj. combining form. bearing or producing: coniferous. [from -FER + -OUS]

Ferrara (fə'rɑ:rə; Italian fer'rara) n. a city in N Italy, in Emilia–Romagna: a centre of the Renaissance under the House of Este; university (1391). Pop.: 143 950 (1986).

Ferrari (Italian fer'rari) n. **Enzo** ('ɛntso). 1898–1988, Italian designer and manufacturer of racing cars.

ferrate ('fɛreɪt) n. a salt containing the divalent ion, FeO_4^{2-}. [C19: from L ferrum iron]

ferret ('fɛrɪt) n. **1.** a domesticated albino variety of the polecat bred for hunting rats, rabbits, etc. **2.** an assiduous searcher. ~vb. **3.** to hunt (rabbits, rats, etc.) with ferrets. **4.** (tr.; usually foll. by out) to drive from hiding: to ferret out snipers. **5.** (tr.; usually foll. by out) to find by persistent investigation. **6.** (intr.) to search around. [C14: from OF furet, from L fur thief] — 'ferreter n. — 'ferrety adj.

ferri- combining form. indicating the presence of iron, esp. in the trivalent state: ferricyanide; ferriferous. Cf. **ferro-.** [from L ferrum iron]

ferriage ('fɛrɪɪdʒ) *n.* **1.** transportation by ferry. **2.** the fee charged for passage on a ferry.

ferric ('fɛrɪk) *adj.* of or containing iron in the trivalent state; designating an iron(III) compound. [C18: from L *ferrum* iron]

ferric oxide *n.* a red crystalline insoluble oxide of iron that occurs as haematite and rust, used as a pigment and metal polish (**jeweller's rouge**), and as a sensitive coating on magnetic tape. Formula: Fe$_2$O$_3$. Systematic name: **iron(III) oxide**.

Ferrier ('fɛrɪə) *n.* **Kathleen**. 1912–53, English contralto; her early death from cancer ended a brilliant career.

ferrimagnetism (ˌfɛrɪ'mæɡnɪˌtɪzəm) *n.* a phenomenon exhibited by certain substances, such as ferrites, in which the magnetic moments of neighbouring ions are nonparallel and unequal in magnitude. —**ferrimagnetic** (ˌfɛrɪmæɡ'nɛtɪk) *adj.*

Ferris wheel ('fɛrɪs) *n.* a fairground wheel having seats freely suspended from its rim. [C19: after G.W.G. *Ferris* (1859–96), American engineer]

ferrite ('fɛraɪt) *n.* any of a class of nonconducting magnetic mixed-oxide ceramics.

ferrite-rod aerial *n.* a type of aerial, normally used in radio reception, consisting of a small coil of wire mounted on a ferromagnetic ceramic core, the coil serving as a tuning inductance.

ferro- *combining form.* **1.** indicating a property of iron or the presence of iron: *ferromagnetism.* **2.** indicating the presence of iron in the divalent state: *ferrocyanide.* Cf. **ferri-**. [from L *ferrum* iron]

ferroconcrete (ˌfɛrəʊ'kɒnkriːt) *n.* another name for **reinforced concrete**.

Ferrol (*Spanish* fɛ'rrɔl) *n.* See **El Ferrol**.

ferromagnetism (ˌfɛrəʊ'mæɡnɪˌtɪzəm) *n.* the phenomenon exhibited by substances, such as iron, that have relative permeabilities much greater than unity and increasing magnetization with applied magnetizing field. Certain of these substances retain their magnetization in the absence of the applied field. —**ferromagnetic** (ˌfɛrəʊmæɡ'nɛtɪk) *adj.*

ferromanganese (ˌfɛrəʊ'mæŋɡəˌniːz) *n.* an alloy of iron and manganese, used in making additions of manganese to cast iron and steel.

ferrous ('fɛrəs) *adj.* of or containing iron in the divalent state; designating an iron(II) compound. [C19: from FERRI- + -OUS]

ferrous sulphate *n.* an iron salt usually obtained as greenish crystals: used in inks, tanning, etc. Formula: FeSO$_4$. Systematic name: **iron(II) sulphate**. Also called: **copperas**.

ferruginous (fɛ'ruːdʒɪnəs) *adj.* **1.** (of minerals, rocks, etc.) containing iron: *a ferruginous clay.* **2.** rust-coloured. [C17: from L *ferrūgineus* of a rusty colour, from *ferrum* iron]

ferrule ('fɛruːl) *n.* **1.** a metal ring, tube, or cap placed over the end of a stick or post for added strength or to increase wear. **2.** a small length of tube, etc., esp. one used for making a joint. [C17: from ME *virole*, from OF, from L, from *viria* bracelet; infl. by L *ferrum* iron]

ferry ('fɛrɪ) *n., pl.* **-ries**. **1.** Also called: **ferryboat**. a vessel for transporting passengers and usually vehicles across a body of water, esp. as a regular service. **2. a.** such a service. **b.** (*in combination*): *a ferryman.* **3.** the delivering of aircraft by flying them to their destination. ~*vb.* **-rying**, **-ried**. **4.** to transport or go by ferry. **5.** to deliver (an aircraft) by flying it to its destination. **6.** (*tr.*) to convey (passengers, goods, etc.). [OE *ferian* to carry, bring]

fertile ('fɜːtaɪl) *adj.* **1.** capable of producing offspring. **2. a.** (of land) capable of sustaining an abundant growth of plants. **b.** (of farm animals) capable of breeding stock. **3.** *Biol.* capable of undergoing growth and development: *fertile seeds; fertile eggs.* **4.** producing many offspring; prolific. **5.** highly productive: *a fertile brain.* **6.** *Physics.* (of a substance) able to be transformed into fissile or fissionable material. [C15: from L *fertilis*, from *ferre* to bear] —**'fertilely** *adv.* —**'fertileness** *n.*

Fertile Crescent *n.* an area of fertile land in the Middle East, extending around the Rivers Tigris and Euphrates in a semicircle from Israel to the Persian Gulf.

fertility (fɜː'tɪlɪtɪ) *n.* **1.** the ability to produce offspring. **2.** the state or quality of being fertile.

fertility drug *n.* any of a group of preparations used to stimulate ovulation in women hitherto infertile.

fertilize *or* **-lise** ('fɜːtɪˌlaɪz) *vb.* (*tr.*) **1.** to provide (an animal, plant, etc.) with sperm or pollen to bring about fertilization. **2.** to supply (soil or water) with nutrients to aid the growth of plants. **3.** to make fertile. —**ˌfertili'zation** *or* **-li'sation** *n.*

fertilizer *or* **-liser** ('fɜːtɪˌlaɪzə) *n.* **1.** any substance, such as manure, added to soil or water to increase its productivity. **2.** an object or organism that fertilizes an animal or plant.

ferula ('fɛrʊlə) *n., pl.* **-las** *or* **-lae** (-ˌliː). a large umbelliferous plant having thick stems and dissected leaves. [C14: from L: giant fennel]

ferule ('fɛruːl) *n.* **1.** a flat piece of wood, such as a ruler, used in some schools to cane children on the hand. ~*vb.* **2.** (*tr.*) to punish with a ferule. [C16: from L *ferula* giant fennel]

fervent ('fɜːvənt) *or* **fervid** ('fɜːvɪd) *adj.* **1.** intensely passionate; ardent. **2.** *Arch. or poetic.* burning or glowing. [C14: from L *fervēre* to boil, glow] —**'fervency** *n.* —**'fervently** *or* **'fervidly** *adv.*

fervour *or U.S.* **fervor** ('fɜːvə) *n.* **1.** great intensity of feeling or belief. **2.** *Rare.* intense heat. [C14: from L: heat, from *fervēre* to glow, boil]

Fès (fɛs) *or* **Fez** *n.* a city in N central Morocco, traditional capital of the north: became an independent kingdom in the 11th century, at its height in the 14th century; religious centre; university (850). Pop.: 448 823 (1982).

fescue ('fɛskjuː) *or* **fescue grass** *n.* a widely cultivated pasture and lawn grass, having stiff narrow leaves. [C14: from OF *festu*, ult. from L *festūca* stem, straw]

fesse *or* **fess** (fɛs) *n.* *Heraldry.* an ordinary consisting of a horizontal band across a shield. [C15: from Anglo-F, from L *fascia* band, fillet]

festal ('fɛstəl) *adj.* another word for **festive**. [C15: from L *festum* holiday] —**'festally** *adv.*

fester ('fɛstə) *vb.* **1.** to form or cause to form pus. **2.** (*intr.*) to become rotten; decay. **3.** to become or cause to become bitter, irritated, etc., esp. over a long period of time. ~*n.* **4.** a small ulcer or sore containing pus. [C13: from OF *festre* suppurating sore, from L: FISTULA]

festival ('fɛstɪvəl) *n.* **1.** a day or period set aside for celebration or feasting, esp. one of religious significance. **2.** any occasion for celebration. **3.** an organized series of special events and performances: *a festival of drama.* **4.** *Arch.* a time of revelry. **5.** (*modifier*) relating to or characteristic of a festival. [C14: from Church L *festīvālis* of a feast, from L *festīvus* FESTIVE]

Festival Hall *n.* a concert hall in London, on the South Bank of the Thames: constructed for the 1951 Festival of Britain; completed 1964–65. Official name: **Royal Festival Hall**.

festive ('fɛstɪv) *adj.* appropriate to or characteristic of a holiday, etc. [C17: from L *festīvus* joyful, from *festus* of a FEAST] —**'festively** *adv.*

festivity (fɛs'tɪvɪtɪ) *n., pl.* **-ties**. **1.** merriment characteristic of a festival, etc. **2.** any festival or other celebration. **3.** (*pl.*) celebrations.

festoon (fɛ'stuːn) *n.* **1.** a decorative chain of flowers, ribbons, etc., suspended in loops. **2.** a carved or painted representation of this, as in architecture, furniture, or pottery. ~*vb.* (*tr.*) **3.** to decorate or join together with festoons. **4.** to form into festoons. [C17: from F, from It. *festone* ornament for a feast, from *festa* FEAST]

festoon blind *n.* a window blind consisting of vertical rows of horizontally gathered fabric that may be drawn up to form a series of ruches.

feta ('fɛtə) *n.* a white sheep or goat cheese popular in Greece. [Mod. Gk, from the phrase *turi pheta*, from *turi* cheese + *pheta*, from It. *fetta* a slice]

fetch[1] (fɛtʃ) *vb.* (*mainly tr.*) **1.** to go after and bring back: *to fetch help.* **2.** to cause to come; bring or draw forth. **3.** (*also intr.*) to cost or sell for (a certain price): *the table fetched six hundred pounds.* **4.** to utter (a sigh, groan, etc.). **5.** *Inf.* to deal (a blow, slap, etc.). **6.** (used esp. as a command to dogs) to retrieve (an object thrown, etc.). **7. fetch and carry.** to perform menial tasks or run errands. ~*n.* **8.** the reach, stretch, etc., of a mechanism. **9.** a trick or stratagem. [OE *feccan*] —**'fetcher** *n.*

fetch[2] (fɛtʃ) *n.* the ghost or apparition of a living person. [C18: from ?]

fetching ('fɛtʃɪŋ) *adj. Inf.* **1.** attractively befitting. **2.** charming.

fetch up *vb. (adv.)* **1.** *(intr.;* usually foll. by *at* or *in*) *Inf.* to arrive (at) or end up (in): *to fetch up in New York.* **2.** *Sl.* to vomit (food, etc.).

fête *or* **fete** (feɪt) *n.* **1.** a gala, bazaar, or similar entertainment, esp. one held outdoors in aid of charity. **2.** a feast day or holiday, esp. one of religious significance. ~*vb.* **3.** *(tr.)* to honour or entertain with or as if with a fête: *the author was fêted.* [C18: from F: FEAST]

fetid *or* **foetid** ('fɛtɪd, 'fiː-) *adj.* having a stale nauseating smell, as of decay. [C16: from L, from *fētēre* to stink; rel. to *fūmus* smoke] —'**fetidly** *or* '**foetidly** *adv.* —'**fetidness** *or* '**foetidness** *n.*

fetish ('fɛtɪʃ, 'fiːtɪʃ) *n.* **1.** something, esp. an inanimate object, that is believed to have magical powers. **2. a.** a form of behaviour involving fetishism. **b.** any object that is involved in fetishism. **3.** any object, activity, etc., to which one is excessively devoted. [C17: from F, from Port. *feitiço* (n.) sorcery, from adj.: artificial, from L *facticius* made by art, FACTITIOUS]

fetishism ('fɛtɪˌʃɪzəm, 'fiː-) *n.* **1.** a condition in which the handling of an inanimate object or a part of the body other than the sexual organs is a source of sexual satisfaction. **2.** belief in or recourse to a fetish for magical purposes. —'**fetishist** *n.* —ˌfetish'**istic** *adj.*

fetlock ('fɛtˌlɒk) *n.* **1.** a projection behind and above a horse's hoof. **2.** Also called: **fetlock joint.** the joint at this part of the leg. **3.** the tuft of hair growing from this part. [C14 *fetlak*]

fetor *or* **foetor** ('fiːtə) *n.* an offensive stale or putrid odour. [C15: from L, from *fētēre* to stink]

fetter ('fɛtə) *n.* **1.** *(often pl.)* a chain or bond fastened round the ankle. **2.** *(usually pl.)* a check or restraint: *in fetters.* ~*vb. (tr.)* **3.** to restrict or confine. **4.** to bind in fetters. [OE *fetor*]

fettle ('fɛtªl) *vb. (tr.)* **1.** to line or repair (the walls of a furnace). **2.** *Brit. dialect.* **a.** to prepare or arrange (a thing, oneself, etc.). **b.** to repair or mend (something). ~*n.* **3.** state of health, spirits, etc. (esp. in **in fine fettle**). [C14 (in the sense: to put in order): back formation from *fetled* girded up, from OE *fetel* belt]

fettler ('fɛtlə) *n. Austral.* a person employed to maintain railway tracks.

fetus *or* **foetus** ('fiːtəs) *n., pl.* **-tuses.** the embryo of a mammal in the later stages of development, esp. a human embryo from the end of the second month of pregnancy until birth. [C14: from L offspring] —'**fetal** *adj.*

feu (fjuː) *n.* **1.** *Scot. legal history.* **a.** a feudal tenure of land for which rent was paid in money or grain instead of by the performance of military service. **b.** the land so held. **2.** *Scots Law.* a right to the use of land in return for a fixed annual payment (**feu duty**). [C15: from OF; see FEE]

Feuchtwanger (German 'fɔʏçtvaŋər) *n.* **Lion** ('liːɔn). 1884–1958, German novelist and dramatist, lived in the U.S. (1940–58): noted for his historical novels, including *Die hässliche Herzogin* (1923) and *Jud Süss* (1925).

feud[1] (fjuːd) *n.* **1.** long and bitter hostility between two families, clans, or individuals. **2.** a quarrel or dispute. ~*vb.* **3.** *(intr.)* to take part in or carry on a feud. [C13 *fede,* from OF, from OHG *fēhida;* rel. to OE *fæhth* hostility; see FOE] —'**feudal** *adj.* —'**feudist** *n.*

feud[2] *or* **feod** (fjuːd) *n. Feudal law.* land held in return for service. [C17: from Med. L *feodum,* of Gmc origin; see FEE]

feudal ('fjuːdªl) *adj.* **1.** of or characteristic of feudalism or its institutions. **2.** of or relating to a fief. **3.** *Disparaging.* old-fashioned. [C17: from Med. L, from *feudum* FEUD[2]]

feudalism ('fjuːdəˌlɪzəm) *n.* the legal and social system that evolved in W Europe in the 8th and 9th centuries, in which vassals were protected and maintained by their lords, usually through the granting of fiefs, and were required to serve under them in war. Also called: **feudal system.** —'**feudalist** *n.* —ˌfeudal'**istic** *adj.*

feudality (fjuː'dælɪtɪ) *n., pl.* **-ties.** **1.** the state or quality of being feudal. **2.** a fief or fee.

feudalize *or* **-lise** ('fjuːdəˌlaɪz) *vb. (tr.)* to create feudal institutions in (a society, etc.). —ˌfeudali'**zation** *or* **-li'sation** *n.*

feudatory ('fjuːdətərɪ) (in feudal Europe) ~*n.* **1.** a person holding a fief; vassal. ~*adj.* **2.** relating to or characteristic of the relationship between lord and vassal. [C16: from Med. L *feudātor*]

Feuerbach (German 'fɔʏərbax) *n.* **Ludwig Andreas** ('luːtvɪç an'dreːas). 1804–72, German materialist philosopher: in *The Essence of Christianity* (1841), translated into English by George Eliot (1853), he maintained that God is merely an outward projection of man's inner self.

feuilleton (French fœjtɔ̃) *n.* **1.** the part of a European newspaper carrying reviews, serialized fiction, etc. **2.** such a review or article. [C19: from F, from *feuillet* sheet of paper, dim. of *feuille* leaf, from L *folium*]

fever ('fiːvə) *n.* **1.** an abnormally high body temperature, accompanied by a fast pulse rate, dry skin, etc. Related adj.: **febrile. 2.** any of various diseases, such as yellow fever or scarlet fever, characterized by a high temperature. **3.** intense nervous excitement. ~*vb.* **4.** *(tr.)* to affect with or as if with fever. [OE *fēfor,* from L *febris*] —'**fevered** *adj.*

feverfew ('fiːvəˌfjuː) *n.* a bushy European strong-scented perennial plant with white flower heads, formerly used medicinally. [OE *feferfuge,* from LL, from L *febris* fever + *fugāre* to put to flight]

feverish ('fiːvərɪʃ) *or* **feverous** *adj.* **1.** suffering from fever. **2.** in a state of restless excitement. **3.** of, caused by, or causing fever. —'**feverishly** *or* '**feverously** *adv.*

fever pitch *n.* a state of intense excitement.

fever therapy *n.* a former method of treating disease by raising the body temperature.

few (fjuː) *determiner.* **1. a.** hardly any: *few men are so cruel.* **b.** *(as pronoun; functioning as pl.):* *many are called but few are chosen.* **2.** (preceded by *a*) **a.** a small number of: *a few drinks.* **b.** *(as pronoun; functioning as pl.):* *a few of you.* **3. a good few.** *Inf.* several. **4. few and far between. a.** widely spaced. **b.** scarce. **5. not** *or* **quite a few.** *Inf.* several. ~*n.* **6. the few.** a small number of people considered as a class: *the few who fell at Thermopylae.* [OE *fēawa*] —'**fewness** *n.*
▷ **Usage.** See at **less.**

fey (feɪ) *adj.* **1.** interested in or believing in the supernatural. **2.** clairvoyant; visionary. **3.** *Chiefly Scot.* fated to die; doomed. **4.** *Chiefly Scot.* in a state of high spirits. [OE *fæge* marked out for death] —'**feyness** *n.*

Feydeau (French fɛdo) *n.* **Georges** (ʒɔrʒ). 1862–1921, French dramatist, noted for his farces, esp. *La Dame de chez Maxim* (1899) and *Occupe-toi d'Amélie* (1908).

Feynman ('faɪnmən) *n.* **Richard.** 1918–88, U.S. physicist, noted for his research on quantum electrodynamics; shared the Nobel prize for physics in 1965.

fez (fɛz) *n., pl.* **fezzes.** an originally Turkish brimless felt or wool cap, shaped like a truncated cone. [C19: via F from Turkish, from FÈS]

Fez (fɛz) *n.* a variant of **Fès.**

Fezzan (fɛ'zɑːn) *n.* a region of SW Libya, in the Sahara: a former province (until 1963).

ff *Music. symbol for* fortissimo.

ff. 1. *abbrev. for* folios. **2.** *symbol for* and the following (pages, lines, etc.).

fiacre (fɪ'ɑːkrə) *n.* a small four-wheeled horse-drawn carriage. [C17: after the Hotel de St *Fiacre,* Paris, where these vehicles were first hired out]

fiancé *or (fem.)* **fiancée** (fɪ'ɒnseɪ) *n.* a person who is engaged to be married. [C19: from F, from OF *fiancier* to promise, betroth, from *fiance* a vow, from *fier* to trust, from L *fidere*]

fiasco (fɪ'æskəʊ) *n., pl.* **-cos** *or* **-coes.** a complete failure, esp. one that is ignominious or humiliating. [C19: from It., lit.: FLASK; sense development obscure]

fiat ('faɪət) *n.* **1.** official sanction. **2.** an arbitrary order or decree. [C17: from L, lit.: let it be done]

fib (fɪb) *n.* **1.** a trivial and harmless lie. ~*vb.* **fibbing, fibbed. 2.** *(intr.)* to tell such a lie. [C17: ?from *fibble-fable* an unlikely story; see FABLE] —'**fibber** *n.*

Fibonacci sequence *or* **series** (ˌfiːbəʊ'nɑːtʃɪ) *n.* the infinite sequence of numbers, 0, 1, 1, 2, 3, 5, 8, etc., in which each member (**Fibonacci number**) is the sum of the previous two. [after Leonardo *Fibonacci* (?1170–?1250), Florentine mathematician]

fibre *or U.S.* **fiber** ('faɪbə) *n.* **1.** a natural or synthetic filament that may be spun into yarn, such as cotton or nylon. **2.** cloth or other material made from such yarn. **3.** a long fine continuous thread or filament. **4.** the texture of any material or substance. **5.** essential substance or nature. **6.** strength of character (esp. in **moral fibre**). **7.** *Bot.* **a.** a narrow elongated thick-walled cell. **b.** a very small root or twig. **8.** a fibrous substance, such as bran, as part of someone's diet: *dietary fibre.* [C14: from L *fibra* filament, entrails] — **'fibred** *or U.S.* **'fibered** *adj.*

fibreboard *or U.S.* **fiberboard** ('faɪbə,bɔːd) *n.* a building material made of compressed wood or other plant fibres.

fibreglass ('faɪbə,glɑːs) *n.* **1.** material consisting of matted fine glass fibres, used as insulation in buildings, etc. **2.** a light strong material made by bonding fibreglass with a synthetic resin; used for car bodies, etc.

fibre optics *n.* (*functioning as sing.*) the transmission of information modulated on light down very thin flexible fibres of glass. See also **optical fibres.** — **fibre optic** *adj.*

fibrescope *or U.S.* **fiberscope** ('faɪbə,skəʊp) *n.* a medical instrument using fibre optics used to examine internal organs, such as the stomach.

fibril ('faɪbrɪl) *or* **fibrilla** (faɪ'brɪlə) *n., pl.* **-brils** *or* **-brillae** (-'brɪliː). **1.** a small fibre or part of a fibre. **2.** *Biol.* a root hair. [C17: from NL *fibrilla* a little FIBRE] — **fi'brillar** *or* **fi'brillose** *adj.*

fibrillation (,faɪbrɪ'leɪʃən, ,fɪb-) *n.* **1.** a local and uncontrollable twitching of muscle fibres. **2.** irregular twitchings of the muscular wall of the heart.

fibrin ('faɪbrɪn) *n.* a white insoluble elastic protein formed from fibrinogen when blood clots: forms a network that traps red cells and platelets.

fibrinogen (faɪ'brɪnədʒən) *n.* a soluble protein in blood plasma, converted to fibrin by the action of the enzyme thrombin when blood clots.

fibro ('faɪbrəʊ) *n. Austral. inf.* **a.** short for **fibrocement.** **b.** (*as modifier*): *a fibro shack.*

fibro- *combining form.* **1.** indicating fibrous tissue: *fibrosis.* **2.** indicating fibre: *fibrocement.* [from L *fibra* FIBRE]

fibrocement (,faɪbrəʊsɪ'mɛnt) *n.* cement combined with asbestos fibre, used esp. in sheets for building.

fibroid ('faɪbrɔɪd) *adj.* **1.** *Anat.* (of structures or tissues) containing or resembling fibres. ~*n.* **2.** another word for **fibroma.**

fibroin ('faɪbrəʊɪn) *n.* a tough elastic protein that is the principal component of spiders' webs and raw silk.

fibroma (faɪ'brəʊmə) *n., pl.* **-mata** (-mətə) *or* **-mas.** a benign tumour derived from fibrous connective tissue.

fibrosis (faɪ'brəʊsɪs) *n.* the formation of an abnormal amount of fibrous tissue in an organ or part.

fibrositis (,faɪbrə'saɪtɪs) *n.* inflammation of white fibrous tissue, esp. that of muscle sheaths.

fibrous ('faɪbrəs) *adj.* consisting of or resembling fibres: *fibrous tissue.* — **'fibrously** *adv.*

fibula ('fɪbjʊlə) *n., pl.* **-lae** (-,liː) *or* **-las.** **1.** the outer and thinner of the two bones between the knee and ankle of the human leg. Cf. **tibia. 2.** the corresponding bone in other vertebrates. **3.** a metal brooch resembling a safety pin. [C17: from L: clasp, prob. from *fīgere* to fasten] — **'fibular** *adj.*

-fic *suffix forming adjectives.* making or producing: *honorific.* [from L *-ficus,* from *facere* to do, make]

fiche (fiːʃ) *n.* See **microfiche, ultrafiche.**

Fichte (*German* 'fɪçtə) *n.* **Johann Gottlieb** (jo'han 'gɔtliːp). 1762–1814, German philosopher: expounded ethical idealism.

fichu ('fiːʃuː) *n.* a woman's shawl worn esp. in the 18th century. [C19: from F: small shawl, from *ficher* to fix with a pin, from L *fīgere* to fasten, FIX]

Ficino (*Italian* fi'tʃiːno) *n.* **Marsilio** (mar'siːlio). 1433–99, Italian Neoplatonist philosopher: attempted to integrate Platonism with Christianity.

fickle ('fɪkəl) *adj.* changeable in purpose, affections, etc. [OE *ficol* deceitful] — **'fickleness** *n.*

fictile ('fɪktaɪl) *adj.* **1.** moulded or capable of being moulded from clay. **2.** made of clay by a potter. [C17: from L *fictilis* that can be moulded, from *fingere* to shape]

fiction ('fɪkʃən) *n.* **1.** literary works invented by the imagination, such as novels or short stories. **2.** an invented story or explanation. **3.** the act of inventing a story. **4.** *Law.* something assumed to be true for the sake of convenience, though probably false. [C14: from L *fictiō* a fashioning, hence something imaginary, from *fingere* to shape] — **'fictional** *adj.* — **'fictionally** *adv.* — **'fictive** *adj.*

fictionalize *or* **-lise** ('fɪkʃənə,laɪz) *vb.* (*tr.*) to make into fiction. — **,fictionali'zation** *or* **-li'sation** *n.*

fictitious (fɪk'tɪʃəs) *adj.* **1.** not genuine or authentic: *to give a fictitious address.* **2.** of, related to, or characteristic of fiction. — **fic'titiously** *adv.* — **fic'titiousness** *n.*

fid (fɪd) *n. Naut.* **1.** a spike for separating strands of rope in splicing. **2.** a wooden or metal bar for supporting the topmast. [C17: from ?]

-fid *adj. combining form.* divided into parts or lobes: *bifid.* [from L *-fidus,* from *findere* to split]

fiddle ('fɪdəl) *n.* **1.** *Inf. or disparaging.* the violin. **2.** a violin played as a folk instrument. **3.** *Naut.* a small railing around the top of a table to prevent objects from falling off it. **4.** *Brit. inf.* an illegal transaction or arrangement. **5.** *Brit. inf.* a manually delicate or tricky operation. **6. at** *or* **on the fiddle.** *Inf.* engaged in an illegal or fradulent undertaking. **7. fit as a fiddle.** *Inf.* in very good health. **8. play second fiddle.** *Inf.* to play a minor part. ~*vb.* **9.** to play (a tune) on the fiddle. **10.** (*intr.; often foll. by with*) to make aimless movements with the hands. **11.** (when *intr.,* often foll. by *about* or *around*) *Inf.* to waste (time). **12.** (often foll. by *with*) *Inf.* to interfere (with). **13.** *Inf.* to contrive to do (something) by illicit means or deception. **14.** (*tr.*) *Inf.* to falsify (accounts, etc.). [OE *fithele;* see VIOLA[1]]

fiddle-faddle ('fɪdəl,fædəl) *n., interj.* **1.** trivial matter. ~*vb.* **2.** (*intr.*) to fuss or waste time. [C16: reduplication of FIDDLE] — **'fiddle-,faddler** *n.*

fiddler ('fɪdlə) *n.* **1.** a person who plays the fiddle. **2.** See **fiddler crab. 3.** *Inf.* a petty rogue.

fiddler crab *n.* any of various burrowing crabs of American coastal regions, the males of which have one of their pincer-like claws enlarged. [C19: referring to the rapid fiddling movement of the enlarged anterior claw of the males, used to attract females]

fiddlestick ('fɪdəl,stɪk) *n.* **1.** *Inf.* a violin bow. **2.** any trifle. **3. fiddlesticks!** an expression of annoyance or disagreement.

fiddling ('fɪdlɪŋ) *adj.* **1.** trifling or insignificant. **2.** another word for **fiddly.**

fiddly ('fɪdlɪ) *adj.* **-dlier, -dliest.** small and awkward to do or handle.

Fidei Defensor *Latin.* ('faɪdiː,aɪ dɪ'fɛnsɔː) *n.* defender of the faith; a title given to Henry VIII by Pope Leo X, and appearing on British coins as FID DEF (before decimalization) or FD (after decimalization).

fidelity (fɪ'dɛlɪtɪ) *n., pl.* **-ties. 1.** devotion to duties, obligations, etc. **2.** loyalty or devotion, as to a person or cause. **3.** faithfulness to one's spouse, lover, etc. **4.** accuracy in reporting detail. **5.** *Electronics.* the degree to which an amplifier or radio accurately reproduces the characteristics of the input signal. [C15: from L, from *fidēs* faith, loyalty]

fidget ('fɪdʒɪt) *vb.* **1.** (*intr.*) to move about restlessly. **2.** (*intr.; often foll. by with*) to make restless or uneasy movements (with something). **3.** (*tr.*) to cause to fidget. ~*n.* **4.** (*often pl.*) a state of restlessness or unease: *he's got the fidgets.* **5.** a person who fidgets. [C17: from earlier *fidge,* prob. from ON *fikjast* to desire eagerly] — **'fidgety** *adj.*

fiducial (fɪ'djuːʃɪəl) *adj.* **1.** *Physics, etc.* used as a standard of reference or measurement: *a fiducial point.* **2.** of or based on trust or faith. [C17: from LL *fidūciālis,* from L *fidūcia* confidence, from *fidere* to trust]

fiduciary (fɪ'djuːʃɪərɪ) *Law.* ~*n.* **1.** a person bound to act for another's benefit, as a trustee. ~*adj.* **2. a.** having the nature of a trust. **b.** of or relating to a trust or trustee. [C17: from L *fidūciārius* relating to something held in trust, from *fidūcia* trust]

fiduciary issue *n.* an issue of bank notes not backed by gold.

fie (faɪ) *interj. Obs. or facetious.* an exclamation of distaste or mock dismay. [C13: from OF *fi,* from L *fī,* exclamation of disgust]

fief *or* **feoff** (fiːf) *n.* (in feudal Europe) the property or fee granted to a vassal for his maintenance by his lord in return for service. [C17: from OF *fie,* of Gmc origin; cf. OE *fēo* cattle, money, L *pecus* cattle, *pecūnia* money, Gk *pokos* fleece]

field (fiːld) *n.* **1.** an open tract of uncultivated grassland; meadow. **2.** a piece of land cleared of trees and undergrowth used for pasture or growing crops: *a field of barley.* **3.** a limited or marked off area on which any of various sports, athletic competitions, etc., are held: *a soccer field.* **4.** an area that is rich in minerals or other natural resources: *a coalfield.* **5.** short for **battlefield** or **airfield.** **6.** the mounted followers that hunt with a pack of hounds. **7. a.** all the runners in a race or competitors in a competition. **b.** the runners in a race or competitors in a competition excluding the favourite. **8.** *Cricket.* the fielders collectively, esp. with regard to their positions. **9.** a wide or open expanse: *a field of snow.* **10. a.** an area of human activity: *the field of human knowledge.* **b.** a sphere or division of knowledge, etc.: *his field is physics.* **11.** a place away from the laboratory, office, library, etc., where practical work is done. **12.** the surface or background, as of a flag, coin, or heraldic shield, on which a design is displayed. **13.** Also called: **field of view.** the area within which an object may be observed with a telescope, etc. **14.** *Physics.* See **field of force.** **15.** *Maths.* a set of entities, such as numbers, subject to two binary operations, addition and multiplication, such that the set is a commutative group under addition and the set, minus the zero, is a commutative group under multiplication. **16.** *Computers.* a set of one or more characters comprising a unit of information. **17. play the field.** *Inf.* to disperse one's interests or attentions among a number of activities, people, or objects. **18. take the field.** to begin or carry on activity, esp. in sport or military operations. **19.** *(modifier) Mil.* of or relating to equipment, personnel, etc., specifically trained for operations in the field: *a field gun.* ~*vb.* **20.** *(tr.) Sport.* to stop, catch, or return (the ball) as a fielder. **21.** *(tr.) Sport.* to send (a player or team) onto the field to play. **22.** *(intr.) Sport.* (of a player or team) to act or take turn as a fielder or fielders. **23.** *(tr.)* to enter (a person) in a competition: *each party fielded a candidate.* **24.** *(tr.) Inf.* to deal with or handle: *to field a question.* [OE *feld*]

Field (fi:ld) *n.* **John.** 1782–1837, Irish composer and pianist, lived in Russia from 1803: invented the nocturne.

field artillery *n.* artillery capable of deployment in support of front-line troops, due mainly to its mobility.

field day *n.* **1.** a day spent in some special outdoor activity, such as nature study. **2.** *Mil.* a day devoted to manoeuvres or exercises, esp. before an audience. **3.** *Inf.* a day or time of exciting activity: *the children had a field day with their new toys.*

field effect transistor *n.* a unipolar transistor in which the transverse application of an electric field produces amplification.

fielder ('fi:ldə) *n. Cricket, etc.* **a.** a player in the field. **b.** a member of the fielding side.

field event *n.* a competition, such as the discus, etc., that takes place on a field or similar area as opposed to those on the running track.

fieldfare ('fi:ld,fɛə) *n.* a large Old World thrush having a pale grey head, brown wings and back, and a blackish tail. [OE *feldefare*; see FIELD, FARE]

field glasses *pl. n.* another name for **binoculars.**

field hockey *n. U.S. & Canad.* hockey played on a field, as distinguished from ice hockey.

field hospital *n.* a temporary hospital set up near a battlefield for emergency treatment.

Fielding ('fi:ldɪŋ) *n.* **Henry.** 1707–54, English novelist and dramatist, noted particularly for his picaresque novel *Tom Jones* (1749) and for *Joseph Andrews* (1742), which starts as a parody of Richardson's *Pamela:* also noted as an enlightened magistrate and a founder of the Bow Street runners (1749).

field magnet *n.* a permanent magnet or an electromagnet that produces the magnetic field in a generator, electric motor, or similar device.

field marshal *n.* an officer holding the highest rank in certain armies.

fieldmouse ('fi:ld,maʊs) *n., pl.* **-mice.** a nocturnal mouse inhabiting woods, fields, and gardens of the Old World that has yellowish-brown fur.

field officer *n.* an officer holding the rank of major, lieutenant colonel, or colonel.

field of force *n.* the region of space surrounding a body, such as a charged particle or a magnet, within which it can exert a force on another similar body not in contact with it.

Fields (fi:ldz) *n.* **1.** Dame **Gracie.** real name *Grace Stansfield.* 1898–1979, English popular singer and comedienne. **2. W. C.** real name *William Claude Dukenfield.*

1880–1946, U.S. film actor, noted for his portrayal of comic roles.

fieldsman ('fi:ldzmən) *n., pl.* **-men.** *Cricket.* another name for **fielder.**

field sports *pl. n.* sports carried on in the countryside, such as hunting or fishing.

field tile *n. Brit. & N.Z.* an earthenware drain used in farm drainage.

field trial *n. (often pl.)* a test to display performance, efficiency, or durability, as of a vehicle or invention.

field trip *n.* an expedition, as by a group of students, to study something at first hand.

field winding ('waɪndɪŋ) *n.* the current-carrying coils on a field magnet that produce the magnetic field intensity required to set up the electrical excitation in a generator or motor.

fieldwork ('fi:ld,wɜ:k) *n. Mil.* a temporary structure used in fortifying a place or position.

field work *n.* an investigation or search for material, data, etc., made in the field as opposed to the classroom or laboratory. —**field worker** *n.*

fiend (fi:nd) *n.* **1.** an evil spirit. **2.** a cruel, brutal, or spiteful person. **3.** *Inf.* **a.** a person who is intensely interested in or fond of something: *a fresh-air fiend.* **b.** an addict: *a drug fiend.* [OE *fēond*]

Fiend (fi:nd) *n.* **the.** the devil; Satan.

fiendish ('fi:ndɪʃ) *adj.* **1.** of or like a fiend. **2.** diabolically wicked or cruel. **3.** *Inf.* extremely difficult or unpleasant: *a fiendish problem.*

fierce (fɪəs) *adj.* **1.** having a violent and unrestrained nature: *a fierce dog.* **2.** wild or turbulent in force, action, or intensity: *a fierce storm.* **3.** intense or strong: *fierce competition.* **4.** *Inf.* very unpleasant. [C13: from OF *fiers,* from L *ferus*] —**fiercely** *adv.* —**fierceness** *n.*

fiery ('faɪərɪ) *adj.* **fierier, fieriest.** **1.** of, containing, or composed of fire. **2.** resembling fire in heat, colour, ardour, etc.: *a fiery speaker.* **3.** easily angered or aroused: *a fiery temper.* **4.** (of food) producing a burning sensation: *a fiery curry.* **5.** (of the skin or a sore) inflamed. **6.** flammable. —**'fierily** *adv.* —**'fieriness** *n.*

Fiesole[1] (*Italian* 'fiɛːzole) *n.* a town in central Italy, in Tuscany near Florence: Etruscan and Roman remains. Pop.: 14 486 (1981 est.). Ancient name: **Faesulae** ('fi:sʊli:).

Fiesole[2] (*Italian* 'fiɛːzole) *n.* **Giovanni da** (dʒo'vanni da). the monastic name of (Fra) **Angelico.**

fiesta (fɪ'ɛstə) *n.* (esp. in Spain and Latin America) **1.** a religious festival or celebration. **2.** a holiday or carnival. [Sp., from L *festa;* see FEAST]

FIFA ('fi:fə) *n. acronym for* Fédération Internationale de Football Association. [from F]

fife (faɪf) *n.* **1.** a small high-pitched flute similar to the piccolo, used esp. in military bands. ~*vb.* **2.** to play (music) on a fife. [C16: from OHG *pfifa;* see PIPE[1]] —**'fifer** *n.*

Fife (faɪf) *n.* **1.** a local government region of E central Scotland, bordering on the North Sea between the Firths of Tay and Forth: coastal lowlands in the north and east, with several ranges of hills; mainly agricultural. Administrative centre: Glenrothes. Pop.: 348 825 (1986 est.). Area: 1305 sq. km (504 sq. miles). **2.** (until 1975) a county of E central Scotland, coextensive with Fife region.

fifteen ('fɪf'ti:n) *n.* **1.** the cardinal number that is the sum of ten and five. **2.** a numeral, 15, XV, etc., representing this number. **3.** something represented by, representing, or consisting of 15 units. **4.** a rugby football team. ~*determiner.* **5. a.** amounting to fifteen: *fifteen jokes.* **b.** (as *pronoun*): *fifteen of us danced.* [OE *fiftēne*] —**'fif'teenth** *adj., n.*

fifth (fɪfθ) *adj.* (*usually prenominal*) **1. a.** coming after the fourth in order, position, etc. Often written 5th. **b.** (as *n.*): *he came on the fifth.* ~*n.* **2. a.** one of five equal parts of an object, quantity, etc. **b.** (as *modifier*): *a fifth part.* **3.** the fraction equal to one divided by five (1/5). **4.** *Music.* **a.** the interval between one note and another five notes away from it in a diatonic scale. **b.** one of two notes constituting such an interval in relation to the other. ~*adv.* **5.** Also: **fifthly.** after the fourth person, position, event, etc. ~*sentence connector.* **6.** Also: **fifthly.** as the fifth point. [OE *fifta*]

fifth column *n.* **1.** (originally) a group of Falangist sympathizers in Madrid during the Spanish Civil War who were prepared to join the insurgents marching on the city. **2.** any group of hostile infiltrators. —**fifth columnist** *n.*

fifth wheel *n.* **1.** a spare wheel for a four-wheeled vehicle. **2.** a superfluous or unnecessary person or thing.

fifty ('fıftı) *n., pl.* **-ties. 1.** the cardinal number that is the product of ten and five. **2.** a numeral, 50, L, etc., representing this number. **3.** something represented by, representing, or consisting of 50 units. ~*determiner.* **4. a.** amounting to fifty: *fifty people.* **b.** (*as pronoun*): *fifty should be sufficient.* [OE *fīftig*] —'**fiftieth** *adj., n.*

fifty-fifty *adj., adv. Inf.* in equal parts.

fig (fıg) *n.* **1.** a tree or shrub that produces a closed pearshaped receptacle which becomes fleshy and edible when mature. **2.** the receptacle of any of these trees, having sweet flesh containing numerous seedlike fruits. **3.** (*used with a negative*) something of negligible value: *I don't care a fig for your opinion.* [C13: from OF, from *figa*, from L *ficus* fig tree]

fig. *abbrev. for:* **1.** figurative(ly). **2.** figure.

fight (faıt) *vb.* **fighting, fought. 1.** to oppose or struggle against (an enemy) in battle. **2.** to oppose or struggle against (a person, cause, etc.) in any manner. **3.** (*tr.*) to engage in or carry on (a battle, contest, etc.). **4.** (when *intr.*, often foll. by *for*) to uphold or maintain (a cause, etc.) by fighting or struggling: *to fight for freedom.* **5.** (*tr.*) to make or achieve (a way) by fighting. **6.** to engage (another or others) in combat. **7. fight it out.** to contend until a decisive result is obtained. **8. fight shy.** to keep aloof from. ~*n.* **9.** a battle, struggle, or physical combat. **10.** a quarrel, dispute, or contest. **11.** resistance (esp. in **to put up a fight**). **12.** a boxing match. ~See also **fight off.** [OE *feohtan*]

fighter ('faıtə) *n.* **1.** a person who fights, esp. a professional boxer. **2.** a person who has determination. **3.** *Mil.* an armed aircraft designed for destroying other aircraft.

fighter-bomber *n.* an aircraft that combines the roles of fighter and bomber.

fighting chance *n.* a slight chance of success dependent on a struggle.

fighting cock *n.* **1.** a gamecock. **2.** a pugnacious person.

fighting fish *n.* any of various tropical fishes of the genus *Betta*, esp. the Siamese fighting fish.

fight off *vb.* (*tr., adv.*) **1.** to repulse; repel. **2.** to struggle to avoid or repress: *to fight off a cold.*

fight-or-flight *n.* (*modifier*) involving or relating to an involuntary response to stress in which the hormone adrenaline is secreted into the blood in readiness for physical action, such as fighting or running away.

fig leaf *n.* **1.** a leaf from a fig tree. **2.** a representation of a fig leaf used in sculpture, etc. to cover the genitals of nude figures. **3.** a device to conceal something regarded as shameful.

figment ('fıgmənt) *n.* a fantastic notion or fabrication: *a figment of the imagination.* [C15: from LL *figmentum* a fiction, from L *fingere* to shape]

figurant ('fıgjʊrənt) *n.* a ballet dancer who does group work but no solo roles. [C18: from F, from *figurer* to represent, appear, FIGURE] —**figurante** (,fıgjʊ'rɒnt) *fem. n.*

figuration (,fıgə'reıʃən) *n.* **1.** *Music.* **a.** the employment of characteristic patterns of notes, esp. in variations on a theme. **b.** florid ornamentation. **2.** an instance of representing figuratively, as by means of allegory. **3.** a figurative representation. **4.** the act of decorating with a design.

figurative ('fıgərətıv) *adj.* **1.** involving a figure of speech; not literal; metaphorical. **2.** using or filled with figures of speech. **3.** representing by means of an emblem, likeness, etc. — 'figuratively *adv.* — 'figurativeness *n.*

figure ('fıgə) *n.* **1.** any written symbol other than a letter, esp. a whole number. **2.** another name for **digit** (sense 2). **3.** an amount expressed numerically: *a figure of £1800 was suggested.* **4.** (*pl.*) calculations with numbers: *he's good at figures.* **5.** visible shape or form; outline. **6.** the human form: *a girl with a slender figure.* **7.** a slim bodily shape (esp. in **keep** *or* **lose one's figure**). **8.** a character or personage: *a figure in politics.* **9.** the impression created by a person through behaviour (esp. in **to cut a fine, bold,** etc., **figure**). **10. a.** a person as impressed on the mind. **b.** (*in combination*): *father-figure.* **11.** a representation in painting or sculpture, esp. of the human form. **12.** an illustration or diagram in a text. **13.** a representative object or symbol. **14.** a pattern or design, as in wood. **15.** a predetermined set of movements in dancing or skating. **16.** *Geom.* any combination

of points, lines, curves, or planes. **17.** *Logic.* one of four possible arrangements of the terms in the major and minor premises of a syllogism that give the same conclusion. **18.** *Music.* **a.** a numeral written above or below a note in a part. **b.** a characteristic short pattern of notes. ~*vb.* **19.** (when *tr.*, often foll. by *up*) to calculate or compute (sums, amounts, etc.). **20.** (*tr.; usually takes a clause as object*) *Inf., U.S., Canad., & N.Z.* to consider. **21.** (*tr.*) to represent by a diagram or illustration. **22.** (*tr.*) to pattern or mark with a design. **23.** (*tr.*) to depict or portray in a painting, etc. **24.** (*tr.*) to imagine. **25.** (*tr.*) *Music.* to decorate (a melody line or part) with ornamentation. **26.** (*intr.; usually foll. by in*) to be included: *his name figures in the article.* **27.** (*intr.*) *Inf.* to accord with expectation: *it figures that he wouldn't come.* ~See also **figure out.** [C13: from L *figūra* a shape, from *fingere* to mould] —'**figurer** *n.*

figured ('fıgəd) *adj.* **1.** depicted as a figure in painting or sculpture. **2.** decorated with a design. **3.** having a form. **4.** *Music.* **a.** ornamental. **b.** (of a bass part) provided with numerals indicating accompanying harmonies.

figured bass (beıs) *n.* a shorthand method of indicating a thorough-bass part in which each bass note is accompanied by figures indicating the intervals to be played in the chord above it.

figurehead ('fıgə,hɛd) *n.* **1.** a person nominally having a prominent position, but no real authority. **2.** a carved bust on the bow of some sailing vessels.

figure of speech *n.* an expression of language, such as metaphor, by which the literal meaning of a word is not employed.

figure out *vb.* (*tr., adv.; may take a clause as object*) *Inf.* **1.** to calculate. **2.** to understand.

figure skating *n.* **1.** ice skating in which the skater traces outlines of selected patterns. **2.** the whole art of skating, as distinct from skating at speed. —**figure skater** *n.*

figurine (,fıgə'riːn) *n.* a small carved or moulded figure; statuette. [C19: from F, from It. *figurina* a little FIGURE]

figwort ('fıg,wɜːt) *n.* a plant related to the foxglove having square stems and small greenish flowers.

Fiji ('fiːdʒiː, fiː'dʒiː) *n.* **1.** an independent republic (formerly within the British Commonwealth), consisting of 844 islands (chiefly Viti Levu and Vanua Levu) in the SW Pacific: a British colony (1874-1970); the large islands are of volcanic origin, surrounded by coral reefs; smaller ones are of coral. Official language: English. Religion: Christian and Hindu. Currency: dollar. Capital: Suva. Pop.: 726 000 (1987). Area: 18 272 sq. km (7055 sq. miles). ~*n., adj.* **2.** another word for **Fijian.**

Fijian (fiː'dʒiːən) *n.* **1.** a member of the indigenous people inhabiting Fiji. **2.** the language of this people, belonging to the Malayo-Polynesian family. ~*adj.* **3.** of or characteristic of Fiji or its inhabitants. ~Also: **Fiji.**

filagree ('fılə,griː) *n., adj.* a less common spelling of **filigree.**

filament ('fıləmənt) *n.* **1.** the thin wire, usually tungsten, inside a light bulb that emits light when heated to incandescence by an electric current. **2.** *Electronics.* a high-resistance wire forming the cathode in some valves. **3.** a single strand of a natural or synthetic fibre. **4.** *Bot.* the stalk of a stamen. **5.** any slender structure or part. [C16: from NL, from Med. L *fīlāre* to spin, from L *fīlum* thread] —**filamentary** (,fılə'mɛntərı) *or* ,fila'mentous *adj.*

filaria (fı'lɛərıə) *n., pl.* **-iae** (-ı,iː). a parasitic nematode worm that lives in the blood of vertebrates and is transmitted by insects: the cause of filariasis. [C19: NL (former name of genus), from L *fīlum* thread] —**fi'larial** *adj.*

filariasis (,fılə'raıəsıs, fı,lɛərı'eısıs) *n.* a disease common in tropical and subtropical countries resulting from infestation of the lymphatic system with nematode worms transmitted by mosquitoes: characterized by inflammation. See also **elephantiasis.** [C19: from NL; see FILARIA]

filbert ('fılbət) *n.* **1.** any of several N temperate shrubs that have edible rounded brown nuts. **2.** Also called: **hazelnut, cobnut.** the nut of any of these shrubs. [C14: after St *Philbert*, 7th-century Frankish abbot, because the nuts are ripe around his feast day, Aug. 22]

filch (fıltʃ) *vb.* (*tr.*) to steal or take in small amounts. [C16 *filchen* to steal, attack, ?from OE *gefylce* band of men] —'**filcher** *n.*

file¹ (faıl) *n.* **1.** a folder, box, etc., used to keep documents or other items in order. **2.** the documents, etc., kept in this way. **3.** documents or information about a specific subject, person, etc. **4.** a line of people in marching formation, one behind another. **5.** any of the eight vertical rows of squares on a chessboard. **6.** Also called: **data set.** *Computers.* an organized collection of related records, accessible from a storage device via an assigned address. **7. on file.** recorded or catalogued for reference, as in a file. ~*vb.* **8.** to place (a document, etc.) in a file. **9.** (*tr.*) to place (a legal document) on official or public record. **10.** (*tr.*) to bring (a suit, esp. a divorce suit) in a court of law. **11.** (*tr.*) to submit (copy) to a newspaper. **12.** (*intr.*) to march or walk in a file or files: *the ants filed down the hill.* [C16 (in the sense: string on which documents are hung): from OF, from Med. L *filāre;* see FILAMENT] —'**filer** *n.*

file² (faɪl) *n.* **1.** a hand tool consisting of a steel blade with small cutting teeth on some or all of its faces. It is used for shaping or smoothing. ~*vb.* **2.** (*tr.*) to shape or smooth (a surface) with a file. [OE *fīl*] —'**filer** *n.*

filefish ('faɪl,fɪʃ) *n., pl.* **-fish** *or* **-fishes.** any tropical triggerfish having a narrow compressed body and a very long dorsal spine. [C18: referring to its file-like scales]

filet ('fɪlɪt, 'fɪleɪ) *n.* a variant spelling of **fillet** (senses 1-3). [C20: from F: net, from OF, from *fil* thread, from L *fīlum*]

filet mignon ('fɪleɪ 'miːnjɒn) *n.* a small tender boneless cut of beef. [from F, lit.: dainty fillet]

filial ('fɪlɪəl) *adj.* **1.** of, resembling, or suitable to a son or daughter: *filial affection.* **2.** *Genetics.* designating any of the generations following the parental generation. [C15: from LL *fīliālis,* from L *fīlius* son] —'**filially** *adv.*

filibeg *or* **philibeg** ('fɪlɪ,bɛɡ) *n.* the kilt worn by Scottish Highlanders. [C18: from Scot. Gaelic *fèileadhbeag,* from *fèileadh* kilt + *beag* small]

filibuster ('fɪlɪ,bʌstə) *n.* **1.** the process of obstructing legislation by means of delaying tactics. **2.** Also called: **filibusterer.** a legislator who engages in such obstruction. **3.** a freebooter or military adventurer, esp. in a foreign country. ~*vb.* **4.** to obstruct (legislation) with delaying tactics. **5.** (*intr.*) to engage in unlawful military action. [C16: from Sp., from F *flibustier,* prob. from Du. *vrijbuiter* pirate, lit.: one plundering freely; see FREEBOOTER] —'**fili,busterer** *n.*

filigree ('fɪlɪ,ɡriː) *or* **filagree** *n.* **1.** delicate ornamental work of twisted gold, silver, or other wire. **2.** any fanciful delicate ornamentation. ~*adj.* **3.** made of or as if with filigree. [C17: from earlier *filigreen,* from F *filigrane,* from L *fīlum* thread + *grānum* GRAIN] —'**fili,greed** *adj.*

filings ('faɪlɪŋz) *pl. n.* shavings or particles removed by a file: *iron filings.*

Filipino (,fɪlɪ'piːnəʊ) *n., pl.* **-nos. 1.** a native or inhabitant of the Philippines. **2.** another name for **Tagalog.** ~*adj.* **3.** of or relating to the Philippines or their inhabitants.

fill (fɪl) *vb. (mainly tr.; often foll. by up)* **1.** (*also intr.*) to make or become full: *to fill up a bottle.* **2.** to occupy the whole of: *the party filled the house.* **3.** to plug (a gap, crevice, etc.). **4.** to meet (a requirement or need) satisfactorily. **5.** to cover (a page or blank space) with writing, drawing, etc. **6.** to hold and perform the duties of (an office or position). **7.** to appoint or elect an occupant to (an office or position). **8.** (*also intr.*) to swell or cause to swell with wind, as in manoeuvring the sails of a sailing vessel. **9.** *Chiefly U.S. & Canad.* to put together the necessary materials for (a prescription or order). **10. fill the bill.** *Inf.* to serve or perform adequately. ~*n.* **11.** material such as gravel, stones, etc., used to bring an area of ground up to a required level. **12. one's fill.** the quantity needed to satisfy one. ~See also **fill in, fill out,** etc. [OE *fyllan*]

filler ('fɪlə) *n.* **1.** a person or thing that fills. **2.** an object or substance used to add weight or size to something or to fill in a gap. **3.** a paste, used for filling in cracks, holes, etc., in a surface before painting. **4.** the inner portion of a cigar. **5.** *Journalism.* articles, photographs, etc., to fill space between more important articles in a newspaper or magazine.

fillet ('fɪlɪt) *n.* **1. a.** Also called: **fillet steak.** a strip of boneless meat. **b.** the boned side of a fish. **2.** a narrow strip of any material. **3.** a thin strip of ribbon, lace, etc., worn in the hair or around the neck. **4.** a narrow flat moulding, esp. one between other mouldings. **5.** a narrow band between flutings on the shaft of a column. **6.** *Heraldry.* a horizontal division of a shield. **7.** a narrow decorative line, impressed on the cover of a book. ~*vb.*

(*tr.*) **8.** to cut or prepare (meat or fish) as a fillet. **9.** to cut fillets from (meat or fish). **10.** to bind or decorate with or as if with a fillet. ~Also (for senses 1-3): **filet.** [C14: from OF *filet,* from *fil* thread, from L *fīlum*]

fill in *vb. (adv.)* **1.** (*tr.*) to complete (a form, drawing, etc.). **2.** (*intr.*) to act as a substitute. **3.** (*tr.*) to put material into (a hole or cavity), esp. so as to make it level with a surface. **4.** (*tr.*) *Inf.* to inform with facts or news. ~*n.* **fill-in. 5.** a substitute.

filling ('fɪlɪŋ) *n.* **1.** the substance or thing used to fill a space or container: *pie filling.* **2.** *Dentistry.* any of various substances (metal, plastic, etc.) for inserting into the prepared cavity of a tooth. **3.** *Chiefly U.S.* the weft in weaving. ~*adj.* **4.** (of food or a meal) substantial and satisfying.

filling station *n.* a place where petrol and other supplies for motorists are sold.

fillip ('fɪlɪp) *n.* **1.** something that adds stimulation or enjoyment. **2.** the action of holding a finger towards the palm with the thumb and suddenly releasing it outwards to produce a snapping sound. **3.** a quick blow or tap made by this. ~*vb.* **4.** (*tr.*) to stimulate or excite. **5.** (*tr.*) to strike or project sharply with a fillip. **6.** (*intr.*) to make a fillip. [C15 *philippe,* imit.]

Fillmore ('fɪlmɔː) *n.* **Millard.** 1800–74, 13th president of the U.S. (1850-53); a leader of the Whig Party.

fill out *vb. (adv.)* **1.** to make or become fuller, thicker, or rounder. **2.** to make more substantial. **3.** (*tr.*) *Chiefly U.S. & Canad.* to fill in (a form, etc.).

fill up *vb. (adv.)* **1.** (*tr.*) to complete (a form, application, etc.). **2.** to make or become full. ~*n.* **fill-up. 3.** the act of filling something completely, esp. the petrol tank of a car.

filly ('fɪlɪ) *n., pl.* **-lies.** a female horse or pony under the age of four. [C15: from ON *fylja;* see FOAL]

film (fɪlm) *n.* **1. a.** a sequence of images of moving objects photographed by a camera and providing the optical illusion of continuous movement when projected onto a screen. **b.** a form of entertainment, etc., composed of such a sequence of images. **c.** (*as modifier*): *film techniques.* **2.** a thin flexible strip of cellulose coated with a photographic emulsion, used to make negatives and transparencies. **3.** a thin coating or layer. **4.** a thin sheet of any material, as of plastic for packaging. **5.** a fine haze, mist, or blur. **6.** a gauzy web of filaments or fine threads. ~*vb.* **7. a.** to photograph with a cine camera. **b.** to make a film of (a screenplay, event, etc.). **8.** (*often foll. by over*) to cover or become covered or coated with a film. [OE *filmen* membrane] —'**filmic** *adj.*

film noir (nwɑː) *n.* a gangster thriller, made esp. in the 1940s in Hollywood, characterized by contrasty lighting and often somewhat impenetrable plots. [C20: F, lit.: black film]

filmography (fɪl'mɒɡrəfɪ) *n.* **1.** a list of the films made by a particular director, actor, etc. **2.** any writing that deals with films or the cinema.

filmset ('fɪlm,sɛt) *vb.* **-setting, -set.** (*tr.*) *Brit.* to set (type matter) by filmsetting. —'**film,setter** *n.*

filmsetting ('fɪlm,sɛtɪŋ) *n. Brit., printing.* typesetting by exposing type characters onto photographic film from which printing plates are made.

film strip *n.* a strip of film composed of different images projected separately as slides.

filmy ('fɪlmɪ) *adj.* **filmier, filmiest. 1.** transparent or gauzy. **2.** hazy; blurred. —'**filmily** *adv.* —'**filminess** *n.*

filo ('fiːləʊ) *n.* a type of Greek flaky pastry in very thin sheets. [C20: Mod. Gk *phullon* leaf]

Filofax ('faɪləʊ,fæks) *n. Trademark.* a type of loose-leaf ring binder with sets of different-coloured paper, used as a portable personal filing system, including appointments, addresses, etc.

filter ('fɪltə) *n.* **1.** a porous substance, such as paper or sand, that allows fluid to pass but retains suspended solid particles. **2.** any device containing such a porous substance for separating suspensions from fluids. **3.** any of various porous substances built into the mouth end of a cigarette or cigar for absorbing impurities such as tar. **4.** any electronic, optical, or acoustic device that blocks signals or radiations of certain frequencies while allowing others to pass. **5.** any transparent disc of gelatin or glass used to eliminate or reduce the intensity of given frequencies from the light leaving a lamp, entering a camera, etc. **6.** *Brit.* a traffic signal at a road junction which permits vehicles to turn either left or right when the main signals are red. ~*vb.* **7.** (often foll. by *out*) to remove or separate (suspended particles, etc.) from (a liquid, gas, etc.) by the action of a filter. **8.** (*tr.*) to obtain by filtering. **9.** (*intr.;* foll. by *through*) to pass (through a filter or something like a filter). **10.** (*intr.*) to flow slowly; trickle. [C16 *filtre,* from Med. L *filtrum* piece of felt used as a filter, of Gmc origin]

filterable ('fɪltərəbəl) *or* **filtrable** ('fɪltrəbəl) *adj.* **1.** capable of being filtered. **2.** (of most viruses and certain bacteria) capable of passing through the pores of a fine filter.

filter bed *n.* a layer of sand or gravel in a tank or reservoir through which a liquid is passed so as to purify it.

filter out *or* **through** *vb.* (*intr., adv.*) to become known gradually; leak.

filter paper *n.* a porous paper used for filtering liquids.

filter tip *n.* **1.** an attachment to the mouth end of a cigarette for trapping impurities such as tar during smoking. **2.** a cigarette having such an attachment. —**'filter-,tipped** *adj.*

filth (fɪlθ) *n.* **1.** foul or disgusting dirt; refuse. **2.** extreme physical or moral uncleanliness. **3.** vulgarity or obscenity. **4. the filth.** *Sl.* the police. [OE *fylth*]

filthy ('fɪlθɪ) *adj.* **filthier, filthiest. 1.** very dirty or obscene. **2.** offensive or vicious: *that was a filthy trick to play.* **3.** *Inf., chiefly Brit.* extremely unpleasant: *filthy weather.* ~*adv.* **4.** extremely; disgustingly (esp. in **filthy rich**). — **'filthily** *adv.* — **'filthiness** *n.*

filtrate ('fɪltreɪt) *n.* **1.** a liquid or gas that has been filtered. ~*vb.* **2.** to filter. [C17: from Med. L *filtrāre* to FILTER] —**fil'tration** *n.*

fin (fɪn) *n.* **1.** any of the firm appendages that are the organs of locomotion and balance in fishes and some other aquatic animals. **2.** a part or appendage that resembles a fin. **3. a.** *Brit.* a vertical surface to which the rudder is attached at the rear of an aeroplane. **b.** a tail surface fixed to a rocket or missile to give stability. **4.** *Naut.* a fixed or adjustable blade projecting under water from the hull of a vessel to give it stability or control. **5.** a projecting rib to dissipate heat from the surface of an engine cylinder or radiator. ~*vb.* **6.** (*tr.*) to provide with fins. [OE *finn*] — **'finless** *adj.* —**finned** *adj.*

fin. *abbrev. for:* **1.** finance. **2.** financial.

Fin. *abbrev. for:* **1.** Finland. **2.** Finnish.

finable *or* **fineable** ('faɪnəbəl) *adj.* liable to a fine. — **'finableness** *or* **'fineableness** *n.*

finagle (fɪ'neɪɡəl) *vb. Inf.* **1.** (*tr.*) to get or achieve by craftiness or persuasion. **2.** to use trickery on (a person). [C20: ?from dialect *fainaigue* cheat] — **fi'nagler** *n.*

final ('faɪnəl) *adj.* **1.** of or occurring at the end; last. **2.** having no possibility of further discussion, action, or change: *a final decree of judgment.* **3.** relating to or constituting an end or purpose: *a final clause may be introduced by "in order to".* **4.** *Music.* another word for **perfect** (sense 9b.). ~*n.* **5.** a last thing; end. **6.** a deciding contest between the winners of previous rounds in a competition. ~See also **finals.** [C14: from L *fīnālis,* from *fīnis* limit, boundary]

finale (fɪ'nɑːlɪ) *n.* **1.** the concluding part of any performance or presentation. **2.** the closing section or movement of a musical composition. [C18: from It., n. use of adj. *finale,* from L *fīnālis* FINAL]

finalist ('faɪnəlɪst) *n.* a contestant who has reached the last stage of a competition.

finality (faɪ'nælɪtɪ) *n., pl.* **-ties. 1.** the condition or quality of being final or settled: *the finality of death.* **2.** a final or conclusive act.

finalize *or* **-lise** ('faɪnə,laɪz) *vb.* **1.** (*tr.*) to put into final form; settle: *to finalize plans for the merger.* **2.** to reach agreement on a transaction. — **,finali'zation** *or* **-li'sation** *n.*

▷ **Usage.** Although *finalize* has been in widespread use for some time, it carries strong associations of bureaucratic or commercial jargon for many careful speakers and writers, who usually prefer *complete, conclude,* or *make final,* esp. in formal contexts.

finally ('faɪnəlɪ) *adv.* **1.** at last; eventually. **2.** at the end or final point; lastly. **3.** completely; conclusively. ~*sentence connector.* **4.** in the end; lastly: *finally, he put his tie on.* **5.** as the last or final point.

finals ('faɪnəlz) *pl. n.* **1.** the deciding part of a competition. **2.** *Education.* the last examinations in an academic or professional course.

finance (fɪ'næns, 'faɪnæns) *n.* **1.** the system of money, credit, etc., esp. with respect to government revenues and expenditures. **2.** funds or the provision of funds. **3.** (*pl.*) financial condition. ~*vb.* **4.** (*tr.*) to provide or obtain funds or credit for. [C14: from OF, from *finer* to end, settle by payment]

finance company *or* **house** *n.* an enterprise engaged in the loan of money against collateral, esp. one specializing in the financing of hire-purchase contracts.

financial (fɪ'nænʃəl, faɪ-) *adj.* **1.** of or relating to finance or finances. **2.** of or relating to persons who manage money, capital, or credit. **3.** *Austral. & N.Z. inf.* having money; in funds. **4.** *Austral. & N.Z.* (of a club member) fully paid-up. —**fi'nancially** *adv.*

financial year *n. Brit.* **1.** any annual period at the end of which a firm's accounts are made up. **2.** the annual period ending April 5, over which Budget estimates are made by the British Government. ~U.S. and Canad. equivalent: **fiscal year.**

financier (fɪ'nænsɪə, faɪ-) *n.* a person who is engaged in large-scale financial operations.

finback ('fɪn,bæk) *n.* another name for **rorqual.**

finch (fɪntʃ) *n.* any of various songbirds having a short stout bill for feeding on seeds, such as the bullfinch, chaffinch, siskin, and canary. [OE *finc*]

Finchley ('fɪntʃlɪ) *n.* a residential district of N London, part of the Greater London borough of Barnet from 1965.

find (faɪnd) *vb.* **finding, found.** (*mainly tr.*) **1.** to meet with or discover by chance. **2.** to discover or obtain, esp. by search or effort: *to find happiness.* **3.** (*may take a clause as object*) to realize: *he found that nobody knew.* **4.** (*may take a clause as object*) to consider: *I find this wine a little sour.* **5.** to look for and point out (something to be criticized). **6.** (*also intr.*) *Law.* to determine an issue and pronounce a verdict (upon): *the court found the accused guilty.* **7.** to regain (something lost or not functioning): *to find one's tongue.* **8.** to reach (a target): *the bullet found its mark.* **9.** to provide, esp. with difficulty: *we'll find room for you too.* **10.** to be able to pay: *I can't find that amount of money.* **11. find oneself.** to realize and accept one's true character; discover one's vocation. **12. find one's feet.** to become capable or confident. ~*n.* **13.** a person, thing, etc., that is found, esp. a valuable discovery. [OE *findan*]

finder ('faɪndə) *n.* **1.** a person or thing that finds. **2.** *Physics.* a small telescope fitted to a more powerful larger telescope. **3.** *Photog.* short for **viewfinder. 4. finders keepers.** *Inf.* whoever finds something has the right to keep it.

fin de siècle French. (fɛ̃ də sjɛklə) *n.* **1.** the end of the 19th century. ~*adj.* **fin-de-siècle. 2.** of or relating to the close of the 19th century. **3.** decadent, esp. in artistic tastes.

finding ('faɪndɪŋ) *n.* **1.** a thing that is found or discovered. **2.** *Law.* the conclusion reached after a judicial inquiry; verdict.

find out *vb.* (*adv.*) **1.** to gain knowledge of (something); learn. **2.** to detect the crime, deception, etc., of (someone).

fine[1] (faɪn) *adj.* **1.** very good of its kind: *a fine speech.* **2.** superior in skill or accomplishment: *a fine violinist.* **3.** (of weather) clear and dry. **4.** enjoyable or satisfying: *a fine time.* **5.** (*postpositive*) *Inf.* quite well: *I feel fine.* **6.** satisfactory; acceptable: *that's fine by me.* **7.** of delicate composition or careful workmanship: *fine crystal.* **8.** (of precious metals) pure or having a high degree of purity: *fine silver.* **9.** discriminating: *a fine eye for antique brasses.* **10.** abstruse or subtle: *a fine point.* **11.** very thin or slender: *fine hair.* **12.** very small: *fine print.* **13.** (of edges, blades, etc.) sharp; keen. **14.** ornate, showy, or smart. **15.** good-looking: *a fine young woman.* **16.** polished, elegant, or refined: *a fine gentleman.* **17.** *Cricket.* (of a fielding position) oblique to and behind the wicket: *fine leg.* **18.** (*prenominal*) *Inf.* disappointing or terrible: *a fine mess.* ~*adv.* **19.** *Inf.* all right: *that suits me fine.* **20.** finely. ~*vb.* **21.** to make or become finer; refine. **22.** (often foll. by *down* or *away*) to make or become smaller. [C13: from OF *fin,* from L *fīnis* end, boundary, as in *fīnis honōrum* the highest degree of honour] — **'finely** *adv.* — **'fineness** *n.*

fine[2] (faɪn) *n.* **1.** a certain amount of money exacted as a penalty: *a parking fine.* **2.** a payment made by a tenant at the start of his tenancy to reduce his subsequent rent; premium. **3. in fine. a.** in short. **b.** in conclusion. ~*vb.* **4.** (*tr.*) to impose a fine on. [C12 (in the sense: conclusion, settlement): from OF *fin;* see FINE[1]]

fine[3] ('fi:neɪ) *n. Music.* the point at which a piece is to end. [It., from L *finis* end]

fine art *n.* **1.** art produced chiefly for its aesthetic value. **2.** (*often pl.*) any of the fields in which such art is produced, such as painting, sculpture, and engraving.

fine-draw *vb.* **-drawing, -drew, -drawn.** (*tr.*) to sew together so finely that the join is scarcely noticeable.

fine-drawn *adj.* **1.** (of arguments, distinctions, etc.) precise or subtle. **2.** (of wire, etc.) drawn out until very fine.

fine-grained *adj.* (of wood, leather, etc.) having a fine smooth even grain.

finery[1] ('faɪnərɪ) *n.* elaborate or showy decoration, esp. clothing and jewellery.

finery[2] ('faɪnərɪ) *n., pl.* **-eries.** a hearth for converting cast iron into wrought iron. [C17: from OF *finerie,* from *finer* to refine; see FINE[1]]

fines herbes (*French* finz ɛrb) *pl. n.* a mixture of finely chopped herbs, used to flavour omelettes, salads, etc.

finespun ('faɪn'spʌn) *adj.* **1.** spun or drawn out to a fine thread. **2.** excessively subtle or refined.

finesse (fɪ'nɛs) *n.* **1.** elegant skill in style or performance. **2.** subtlety and tact in handling difficult situations. **3.** *Bridge, whist.* an attempt to win a trick when opponents hold a high card in the suit led by playing a lower card. **4.** a trick, artifice, or strategy. ~*vb.* **5.** to bring about with finesse. **6.** to play (a card) as a finesse. [C15: from OF, from *fin* fine, delicate; see FINE[1]]

fine-tooth comb *or* **fine-toothed comb** *n.* **1.** a comb with fine teeth set closely together. **2. go over** (*or* **through**) **with a fine-tooth(ed) comb.** to examine very thoroughly.

fine-tune *vb.* (*tr.*) to make fine adjustments to (something) in order to obtain optimum performance.

Fingal's Cave ('fɪŋg°lz) *n.* a cave in W Scotland, on Staffa Island in the Inner Hebrides: basaltic pillars. Length: 69 m (227 ft.). Height: 36 m (117 ft.).

finger ('fɪŋgə) *n.* **1. a.** any of the digits of the hand, often excluding the thumb. **b.** (*as modifier*): *a finger bowl.* **c.** (*in combination*): *a fingernail.* Related adj.: **digital. 2.** the part of a glove made to cover a finger. **3.** something that resembles a finger in shape or function: *a finger of land.* **4.** the length or width of a finger used as a unit of measurement. **5.** a quantity of liquid in a glass, etc., as deep as a finger is wide. **6. get** *or* **pull one's finger out.** *Brit. inf.* to begin or speed up activity, esp. after initial delay. **7. have a** (*or* **one's**) **finger in the pie. a.** to have an interest in or take part in some activity. **b.** to meddle or interfere. **8. lay** *or* **put one's finger on.** to indicate or locate accurately. **9. not lift** (*or* **raise**) **a finger.** (*foll. by an infinitive*) not to make any effort (to do something). **10. twist** *or* **wrap around one's little finger.** to have easy and complete control or influence over. **11. put the finger on.** *Inf., U.S. & N.Z.* to inform on or identify, esp. for the police. ~*vb.* **12.** (*tr.*) to touch or manipulate with the fingers; handle. **13.** to use one's fingers in playing (an instrument, such as a piano or clarinet). **14.** to indicate on (a composition or part) the fingering required by a pianist, etc. [OE] —**'fingerless** *adj.*

fingerboard ('fɪŋgə,bɔ:d) *n.* the long strip of hard wood on a violin, guitar, etc. upon which the strings are stopped by the fingers.

finger bowl *n.* a small bowl filled with water for rinsing the fingers at the table after a meal.

finger buffet ('bʊfeɪ) *n.* a buffet meal at which food that may be picked up in the fingers (**finger food**), such as canapés or vol-au-vents, is served.

fingered ('fɪŋgəd) *adj.* **1.** marked or dirtied by handling. **2. a.** having a finger or fingers. **b.** (*in combination*): *redfingered.* **3.** (of a musical part) having numerals indicating the fingering.

fingering ('fɪŋgərɪŋ) *n.* **1.** the technique or art of using one's fingers in playing a musical instrument, esp. the piano. **2.** the numerals in a musical part indicating this.

fingerling ('fɪŋgəlɪŋ) *n.* a very young fish, esp. the parr of salmon or trout.

fingermark ('fɪŋgə,mɑ:k) *n.* a mark left by dirty or greasy fingers on paintwork, walls, etc.

fingernail ('fɪŋgə,neɪl) *n.* a thin horny translucent plate covering part of the dorsal surface of the end joint of each finger.

finger painting *n.* the process or art of painting with **finger paints** of starch, glycerin, and pigments, using the fingers, hand, or arm.

finger post *n.* a signpost showing a pointing finger or hand.

fingerprint ('fɪŋgə,prɪnt) *n.* **1.** an impression of the pattern of ridges on the surface of the end joint of each finger and thumb. **2.** any unique identifying characteristic. ~*vb.* (*tr.*) **3.** to take an inked impression of the fingerprints of (a person). **4.** to take a sample of (a person's) DNA.

fingerstall ('fɪŋgə,stɔːl) *n.* a protective covering for a finger. Also called: **cot.**

fingertip ('fɪŋgə,tɪp) *n.* **1.** the end joint or tip of a finger. **2. at one's fingertips.** readily available.

finial ('faɪnɪəl) *n.* **1.** an ornament on top of a spire, etc., esp. in the form of a fleur-de-lis. **2.** an ornament at the top of a piece of furniture, etc. [C14: from *finial* (adj.), var. of FINAL]

finicky ('fɪnɪkɪ) *or* **finicking** *adj.* **1.** excessively particular; fussy. **2.** overelaborate. [C19: from *finical,* from FINE[1]]

finis ('fɪnɪs) *n.* the end; finish: used at the end of books, films, etc. [C15: from L]

finish ('fɪnɪʃ) *vb.* (*mainly tr.*) **1.** to bring to an end; conclude or stop. **2.** (*intr.;* sometimes foll. by *up*) to be at or come to the end; use up. **3.** to bring to a desired or complete condition. **4.** to put a particular surface texture on (wood, cloth, etc.). **5.** (often foll. by *off*) to destroy or defeat completely. **6.** to train (a person) in social graces and talents. **7.** (*intr.;* foll. by *with*) to end a relationship or association. ~*n.* **8.** the final or last stage or part; end. **9.** the death or absolute defeat of a person or one side in a conflict: *a fight to the finish.* **10.** the surface texture or appearance of wood, cloth, etc.: *a rough finish.* **11.** a thing, event, etc., that completes. **12.** completeness and high quality of workmanship. **13.** *Sport.* ability to sprint at the end of a race. [C14: from OF, from L *finire;* see FINE[1]] —**'finished** *adj.* —**'finisher** *n.*

finishing school *n.* a private school for girls that teaches social graces.

Finistère (,fɪnɪ'stɛə; *French* finistɛr) *n.* a department of NW France, at the tip of the Breton peninsula. Capital: Quimper. Pop.: 828 364 (1982). Area: 7029 sq. km (2741 sq. miles).

Finisterre (,fɪnɪ'stɛə) *n.* **1. Cape.** a headland in NW Spain: the westernmost point of the Spanish mainland. **2.** an English name for **Finistère.**

finite ('faɪnaɪt) *adj.* **1.** bounded in magnitude or spatial or temporal extent. **2.** *Maths, logic.* having a countable number of elements. **3.** limited or restricted in nature: *human existence is finite.* **4.** denoting any form of a verb inflected for grammatical features such as person, number, and tense. [C15: from L *finitus* limited, from *finire* to limit, end] —**'finitely** *adv.* —**'finiteness** *or* **finitude** ('faɪnɪ,tjuːd) *n.*

fink (fɪŋk) *n. Sl., chiefly U.S. & Canad.* **1.** a strikebreaker. **2.** an unpleasant or contemptible person. [C20: from ?]

Finland ('fɪnlənd) *n.* **1.** a republic in N Europe, on the Baltic Sea: ceded to Russia by Sweden in 1809; gained independence in 1917; Soviet invasion successfully withstood in 1939–40, with the loss of Karelia. It is generally low-lying, with about 50 000 lakes, extensive forests, and peat bogs. Official languages: Finnish and Swedish. Religion: chiefly Lutheran. Currency: markka. Capital: Helsinki. Pop.: 4 942 000 (1987). Area: 337 000 sq. km (130 120 sq. miles). Finnish name: **Suomi. 2. Gulf of.** an arm of the Baltic Sea between Finland and the Soviet Union.

Finn (fɪn) *n.* a native, inhabitant, or citizen of Finland. [OE *Finnas* (pl.)]

finnan haddock ('fɪnən) *or* **haddie** ('hædɪ) *n.* smoked haddock. [C18: *finnan* after *Findon,* a village in NE Scotland]

Finney ('fɪnɪ) *n.* **Albert.** born 1936, English stage and film actor.

Finnic ('fɪnɪk) *n.* **1.** one of the two branches of the Finno-Ugric family of languages, including Finnish and several languages of the N Soviet Union in Europe. ~*adj.* **2.** of or relating to this group of languages or to the Finns.

Finnish ('fɪnɪʃ) *adj.* **1.** of or characteristic of Finland, the Finns, or their language. ~*n.* **2.** the official language of Finland, belonging to the Finno-Ugric family.

Finnmark ('fɪn,mɑːk) *n.* a county of N Norway: the largest, northernmost, and least populated county; mostly a barren plateau. Capital: Vadsø. Pop.: 78 356 (1980). Area: 48 649 sq. km (18 779 sq. miles).

Finno-Ugric ('fɪnəʊ'uːgrɪk, -'juː-) *or* **Finno-Ugrian** *n.* **1.** a family of languages spoken in Scandinavia, Hungary, and the Soviet Union, including Finnish, Estonian, and Hungarian. ~*adj.* **2.** of, relating to, or belonging to this family of languages.

finny ('fɪnɪ) *adj.* **-nier, -niest. 1.** *Poetic.* relating to or containing many fishes. **2.** having or resembling a fin or fins.

fino ('fiːnəʊ) *n.* a very dry sherry. [Sp.: FINE¹]

Finsen (*Danish* 'fensən) *n.* **Niels Ryberg** (neːls 'ryber). 1860–1904, Danish physician; founder of phototherapy: Nobel prize for physiology or medicine 1903.

Finsteraarhorn (*German* ˌfɪnstər'aːrhɔrn) *n.* a mountain in S central Switzerland: highest peak in the Bernese Alps. Height: 4274 m (14 022 ft.).

fiord (fjɔːd) *n.* a variant spelling of **fjord.**

fioritura (ˌfjɔːrɪ'tʊərɛɪ) *pl. n. Music.* flourishes; embellishments. [C19: It, from *fiorire* to flower]

fipple ('fɪp³l) *n.* a wooden plug forming a flue in the end of a pipe, as the mouthpiece of a recorder. [C17: from ?]

fipple flute *n.* an end-blown flute provided with a fipple, such as the recorder or flageolet.

fir (fɜː) *n.* **1.** any of a genus of pyramidal coniferous trees having single needle-like leaves and erect cones. **2.** any of various other related trees, such as the Douglas fir. **3.** the wood of any of these trees. [OE *furh*]

Firbank ('fɜːbæŋk) *n.* (**Arthur Annesley**) **Ronald.** 1886–1926, English novelist, whose works include *Valmouth* (1919), *The Flower beneath the Foot* (1923), and *Concerning the Eccentricities of Cardinal Pirelli* (1926).

Firdausi (fɪə'daʊsɪ) *or* **Firdusi** (fɪə'duːsɪ) *n.* pen name of *Abul Qasim Mansur.* ?935–1020 A.D., Persian epic poet; author of *Shah Nama* (*The Book of Kings*), a chronicle of the legends and history of Persia.

fire ('faɪə) *n.* **1.** the state of combustion in which inflammable material burns, producing heat, flames, and often smoke. **2. a.** a mass of burning coal, wood, etc., used esp. in a hearth to heat a room. **b.** (*in combination*): *firelighter.* **3.** a destructive conflagration, as of a forest, building, etc. **4.** a device for heating a room, etc. **5.** something resembling a fire in light or brilliance: *a diamond's fire.* **6.** the act of discharging weapons, artillery, etc. **7.** a burst or rapid volley: *a fire of questions.* **8.** intense passion; ardour. **9.** liveliness, as of imagination, etc. **10.** fever and inflammation. **11.** a severe trial or torment (esp. in **go through fire and water**). **12. between two fires.** under attack from two sides. **13. catch fire.** to ignite. **14. on fire. a.** in a state of ignition. **b.** ardent or eager. **15. open fire.** to start firing a gun, artillery, etc. **16. play with fire.** to be involved in something risky. **17. set fire to** *or* **set on fire. a.** to ignite. **b.** to arouse or excite. **18. under fire.** being attacked, as by weapons or by harsh criticism. **19.** (*modifier*) *Astrol.* of or relating to a group of three signs of the zodiac, Aries, Leo, and Sagittarius. ~*vb.* **20.** to discharge (a firearm or projectile), or (of a firearm, etc.) to be discharged. **21.** to detonate (an explosive charge or device), or (of such a charge or device) to be detonated. **22.** (*tr.*) *Inf.* to dismiss from employment. **23.** (*tr.*) *Ceramics.* to bake in a kiln to harden the clay, etc. **24.** to kindle or be kindled. **25.** (*tr.*) to provide with fuel: *oil fires the heating system.* **26.** (*tr.*) to subject to heat. **27.** (*tr.*) to heat slowly so as to dry. **28.** (*tr.*) to arouse to strong emotion. **29.** to glow or cause to glow. ~*sentence substitute.* **30.** a cry to warn others of a fire. **31.** the order to begin firing a gun, artillery, etc. [OE *fȳr*] —'**firer** *n.*

fire alarm *n.* a device to give warning of fire, esp. a bell, siren, or hooter.

firearm ('faɪəˌrɑːm) *n.* a weapon from which a projectile can be discharged by an explosion caused by igniting gunpowder, etc.

fireback ('faɪəˌbæk) *n.* an ornamental iron slab against the back wall of a hearth.

fireball ('faɪəˌbɔːl) *n.* **1.** a ball-shaped discharge of lightning. **2.** the region of hot ionized gas at the centre of a

nuclear explosion. **3.** *Astron.* a large bright meteor. **4.** *Sl.* an energetic person.

fire blight *n.* a disease of apples, pears, and similar fruit trees, caused by a bacterium and characterized by blackening of the blossoms and leaves.

fireboat ('faɪəˌbəʊt) *n.* a motor vessel equipped with fire-fighting apparatus.

firebomb ('faɪəˌbɒm) *n.* another name for **incendiary** (sense 6).

firebox ('faɪəˌbɒks) *n.* the furnace chamber of a boiler in a steam locomotive.

firebrand ('faɪəˌbrænd) *n.* **1.** a piece of burning wood. **2.** a person who causes unrest.

firebreak ('faɪəˌbreɪk) *n.* a strip of open land in forest or prairie, serving to arrest the advance of a fire.

firebrick ('faɪəˌbrɪk) *n.* a refractory brick made of fire clay, used for lining furnaces, flues, etc.

fire brigade *n. Chiefly Brit.* an organized body of firemen.

firebug ('faɪəˌbʌg) *n. Inf.* a person who deliberately sets fire to property.

fire clay *n.* a heat-resistant clay used in the making of firebricks, furnace linings, etc.

fire company *n.* **1.** an insurance company selling policies relating to fire risk. **2.** *U.S.* an organized body of firemen.

fire control *n. Mil.* the procedures by which weapons are brought to engage a target.

firecracker ('faɪəˌkrækə) *n.* a small cardboard container filled with explosive powder.

firecrest ('faɪəˌkrɛst) *n.* a small European warbler having a crown striped with yellow, black, and white.

firedamp ('faɪəˌdæmp) *n.* an explosive of hydrocarbons, chiefly methane, formed in coal mines. See also **afterdamp.**

firedog ('faɪəˌdɒg) *n.* either of a pair of metal stands used to support logs in an open fire.

fire door *n.* **1.** a door made of noncombustible material that prevents a fire spreading within a building. **2.** a similar door leading to the outside of a building that can be easily opened from inside; emergency exit.

fire-eater *n.* **1.** a performer who simulates the swallowing of fire. **2.** a belligerent person.

fire engine *n.* a vehicle that carries firemen and fire-fighting equipment to a fire.

fire escape *n.* a means of evacuating persons from a building in the event of fire.

fire-extinguisher *n.* a portable device for extinguishing fires, usually consisting of a canister with a directional nozzle used to direct a spray of water, etc., onto the fire.

firefly ('faɪəˌflaɪ) *n., pl.* **-flies.** a nocturnal beetle common in warm and tropical regions, having luminescent abdominal organs.

fireguard ('faɪəˌgɑːd) *n.* a meshed frame put before an open fire to protect against falling logs, sparks, etc.

fire hall *n. Canad.* a fire station.

fire hydrant *n.* a hydrant for use as an emergency supply for fighting fires.

fire insurance *n.* insurance covering damage or loss caused by fire or lightning.

fire irons *pl. n.* metal fireside implements, such as poker, shovel, and tongs.

firelock ('faɪəˌlɒk) *n.* **1.** an obsolete type of gunlock with a priming mechanism ignited by sparks. **2.** a gun or musket having such a lock.

fireman ('faɪəmən) *n., pl.* **-men. 1.** a person who fights fires, usually a trained volunteer or public employee. **2. a.** (on steam locomotives) the man who stokes the fire. **b.** (on diesel and electric locomotives) the driver's assistant. **3.** a man who tends furnaces; stoker.

Firenze (fi'rɛntse) *n.* the Italian name for **Florence.**

fire opal *n.* an orange-red translucent variety of opal, valued as a gemstone.

fireplace ('faɪəˌpleɪs) *n.* an open recess at the base of a chimney, etc., for a fire; hearth.

fireplug ('faɪəˌplʌg) *n.* another name (esp. U.S. and N.Z.) for **fire hydrant.**

fire power *n. Mil.* **1.** the amount of fire that can be delivered by a unit or weapon. **2.** the capability of delivering fire.

fireproof ('faɪəˌpruːf) *adj.* **1.** capable of resisting damage by fire. ~*vb.* **2.** (*tr.*) to make resistant to fire.

fire raiser *n.* a person who deliberately sets fire to property, etc. —**fire raising** *n.*

fire screen *n.* **1.** a decorative screen placed in the hearth when there is no fire. **2.** a screen placed before a fire to protect the face.

fire ship *n.* a vessel loaded with explosives and used, esp. formerly, as a bomb by igniting it and directing it to drift among an enemy's warships.

fireside ('faɪə,saɪd) *n.* **1.** the hearth. **2.** family life; the home.

fire station *n.* a building where fire-fighting vehicles and equipment are stationed. Also called (U.S.): **firehouse, station house.**

firestorm ('faɪə,stɔ:m) *n.* an uncontrollable blaze sustained by violent winds that are drawn into the column of rising hot air over the burning area: often the result of heavy bombing.

firetrap ('faɪə,træp) *n.* a building that would burn easily or one without fire escapes.

firewater ('faɪə,wɔ:tə) *n.* any strong spirit, esp. whisky.

fireweed ('faɪə,wi:d) *n.* any of various plants that appear as first vegetation in burnt-over areas.

firework ('faɪə,wɜ:k) *n.* a device, such as a Catherine wheel or rocket, in which combustible materials are ignited and produce coloured flames, sparks, and smoke.

fireworks ('faɪə,wɜ:ks) *pl. n.* **1.** a show in which large numbers of fireworks are let off. **2.** *Inf.* an exciting exhibition, as of musical virtuosity or wit. **3.** *Inf.* a burst of temper.

firing ('faɪərɪŋ) *n.* **1.** the process of baking ceramics, etc., in a kiln. **2.** the act of stoking a fire or furnace. **3.** a discharge of a firearm. **4.** something used as fuel, such as coal or wood.

firing line *n.* **1.** *Mil.* the positions from which fire is delivered. **2.** the leading or most advanced position in an activity.

firkin ('fɜ:kɪn) *n.* **1.** a small wooden barrel. **2.** *Brit.* a unit of capacity equal to nine gallons. [C14 *fir,* from MDu. *vierde* FOURTH + -KIN]

firm¹ (fɜ:m) *adj.* **1.** not soft or yielding to a touch or pressure. **2.** securely in position; stable or stationary. **3.** decided; settled. **4.** enduring or steady. **5.** having determination or strength. **6.** (of prices, markets, etc.) tending to rise. ~*adv.* **7.** in a secure or unyielding manner: *he stood firm.* ~*vb.* **8.** (sometimes foll. by *up*) to make or become firm. [C14: from L *firmus*] —'**firmly** *adv.* —'**firmness** *n.*

firm² (fɜ:m) *n.* **1.** a business partnership. **2.** any commercial enterprise. **3.** a team of doctors and their assistants. [C16 (in the sense: signature): from Sp. *firma* signature, from *firmar* to sign, from L *firmāre* to confirm, from *firmus* firm]

firmament ('fɜ:məmənt) *n.* the expanse of the sky; heavens. [C13: from LL *firmāmentum* sky (considered as fixed above the earth), from L: prop, support, from *firmāre* to make FIRM¹]

first (fɜ:st) *adj.* (*usually prenominal*) **1. a.** coming before all others. **b.** (*as n.*): *I was the first to arrive.* **2.** preceding all others in numbering or counting order; the ordinal number of *one.* Often written: 1st. **3.** rated, graded, or ranked above all other levels. **4.** denoting the lowest forward ratio of a gearbox in a motor vehicle. **5.** *Music.* **a.** denoting the highest part assigned to one of the voice parts in a chorus or one of the sections of an orchestra: *the first violins.* **b.** denoting the principal player in a specific orchestral section: *he plays first horn.* **6.** first thing. as the first action of the day: *I'll see you first thing tomorrow.* ~*n.* **7.** the beginning; outset: *I couldn't see at first because of the mist.* **8.** *Education, chiefly Brit.* an honours degree of the highest class. Full term: **first-class honours degree. 9.** the lowest forward ratio of a gearbox in a motor vehicle. ~*adv.* **10.** Also: **firstly.** before anything else in order, time, importance, etc.: *do this first.* **11.** **first and last.** on the whole. **12.** **from first to last.** throughout. **13.** for the first time: *I've loved you since I first saw you.* **14.** (*sentence modifier*) in the first place or beginning of a series of actions. [OE *fyrest*]

first aid *n.* **a.** immediate medical assistance given in an emergency. **b.** (*as modifier*): *first-aid box.*

first-born *adj.* **1.** eldest of the children in a family. ~*n.* **2.** the eldest child in a family.

first class *n.* **1.** the class or grade of the best or highest value, quality, etc. ~*adj.* (**first-class** when prenominal).

2. of the best or highest class or grade: *a first-class citizen.* **3.** excellent. **4.** of or denoting the most comfortable class of accommodation in a hotel, aircraft, train, etc. **5.** (in Britain) of letters that are handled faster than second-class letters. ~*adv.* **first-class. 6.** by first-class mail, means of transportation, etc.

first-day cover *n.* *Philately.* an envelope postmarked on the first day of the issue of its stamps.

first-degree burn *n.* *Pathol.* the least severe type of burn, in which the skin surface is red and painful.

first-foot *Chiefly Scot.* ~*n.* also **first-footer. 1.** the first person to enter a household in the New Year. ~*vb.* **2.** to enter (a house) as first-foot. —'**first-'footing** *n.*

first fruits *pl. n.* **1.** the first results or profits of an undertaking. **2.** fruit that ripens first.

first-hand *adj., adv.* **1.** from the original source: *he got the news first-hand.* **2. at first hand.** directly.

first lady *n.* (*often caps.*) (in the U.S.) the wife or official hostess of a state governor or a president.

firstling ('fɜ:stlɪŋ) *n.* the first, esp. the first offspring.

firstly ('fɜ:stlɪ) *adv.* another word for **first.**

first mate *n.* an officer second in command to the captain of a merchant ship.

first mortgage *n.* a mortgage that has priority over other mortgages on the same property.

first name *n.* another term for **Christian name.**

first night *n.* **a.** the first public performance of a play, etc. **b.** (*as modifier*): *first-night nerves.*

first offender *n.* a person convicted of a criminal offence for the first time.

first officer *n.* **1.** another name for **first mate. 2.** the member of an aircraft crew who is second in command to the captain.

first-past-the-post *n.* (*modifier*) of a voting system in which a candidate may be elected by a simple majority.

first person *n.* a grammatical category of pronouns and verbs used by the speaker to refer to or talk about himself.

first-rate *adj.* **1.** of the best or highest rated class or quality. **2.** *Inf.* very good; excellent.

first reading *n.* the introduction of a bill into a legislative assembly.

first refusal *n.* the right to buy something before it is offered to others.

first-strike *adj.* (of a nuclear missile) intended for use in an opening attack calculated to destroy the enemy's nuclear weapons.

first water *n.* **1.** the finest quality of diamond or other precious stone. **2.** the highest grade or best quality.

firth (fɜ:θ) *or* **frith** *n.* a narrow inlet of the sea, esp. in Scotland. [C15: from ON *fjörthr* FJORD]

fiscal ('fɪskəl) *adj.* **1.** of or relating to government finances, esp. tax revenues. **2.** of or involving financial matters. ~*n.* **3. a.** (in some countries) a public prosecutor. **b.** *Scot.* short for **procurator fiscal.** [C16: from L *fiscālis* concerning the state treasury, from *fiscus* public money] —'**fiscally** *adv.*

fiscal year *n.* the U.S. and Canad. term for **financial year.**

Fischer ('fɪʃər) *n.* **1. Emil Hermann** ('e:mi:l 'hɛrman). 1852–1919, German chemist, noted particularly for his work on synthetic sugars and the purine group: Nobel prize for chemistry 1902. **2. Hans** (hans). 1881–1945, German chemist, noted particularly for his work on chlorophyll, haemin, and the porphyrins: Nobel prize for chemistry 1930. **3. Robert James,** known as *Bobby.* born 1943, U.S. chess player; world champion 1972–75.

Fischer-Dieskau (*German* -'di:skau) *n.* **Dietrich** ('di:trɪç). born 1925, German baritone, noted particularly for his interpretation of Schubert's song cycles.

fish (fɪʃ) *n., pl.* **fish** *or* **fishes. 1. a.** any of a large group of cold-blooded aquatic vertebrates having jaws, gills, and usually fins and a skin covered in scales: includes the sharks, rays, teleosts, lungfish, etc. **b.** (*in combination*): *fishpond.* Related adj.: **piscine. 2.** any of various similar but jawless vertebrates, such as the hagfish and lamprey. **3.** (*not in technical use*) any of various aquatic invertebrates, such as the cuttlefish and crayfish. **4.** the flesh of fish used as food. **5.** *Inf.* a person of little emotion or intelligence: *a poor fish.* **6. drink like a fish.** to drink to excess. **7. have other fish to fry.** to have other activities to do, esp. more important ones. **8. like a fish out of water.** out of one's usual place. **9. neither fish,**

flesh, nor fowl. neither this nor that. ~*vb.* **10.** (*intr.*) to attempt to catch fish, as with a line and hook or with nets, traps, etc. **11.** (*tr.*) to fish in (a particular area of water). **12.** to search (a body of water) for something or to search for something, esp. in a body of water. **13.** (*intr.*; foll. by *for*) to seek something indirectly: *to fish for compliments*. ~See also **fish out.** [OE *fisc*] —'**fish,like** *adj.*

fish and chips *n.* fish fillets coated with batter and deep-fried, eaten with potato chips.

fish cake *n.* a fried flattened ball of flaked fish mixed with mashed potatoes.

fisher ('fıʃə) *n.* **1.** a fisherman. **2.** Also called: **pekan. a.** a large North American marten having dark brown fur. **b.** the fur of this animal.

Fisher ('fıʃə) *n.* **1. Andrew.** 1862–1928, Australian statesman, born in Scotland: prime minister of Australia (1908–09; 1910–13; 1914–15). **2. Saint John.** ?1469–1535, English prelate and scholar: executed for refusing to acknowledge Henry VIII as supreme head of the church. Feast day: June 20. **3. John Arbuthnot,** 1st Baron Fisher of Kilverstone. 1841–1920, British admiral; First Sea Lord (1904–10; 1914–15); introduced the dreadnought.

fisherman ('fıʃəmən) *n.*, *pl.* **-men. 1.** a person who fishes as a profession or for sport. **2.** a vessel used for fishing.

fishery ('fıʃərı) *n.*, *pl.* **-eries. 1. a.** the industry of catching, processing, and selling fish. **b.** a place where this is carried on. **2.** a place where fish are reared. **3.** a fishing ground.

Fishes ('fıʃız) *n.* **the.** the constellation Pisces, the twelfth sign of the zodiac.

fish-eye lens *n. Photog.* a lens of small focal length, having a highly curved protruding front element that covers almost 180°.

fishfinger ('fıʃ'fıŋgə) *or U.S. & Canad.* **fish stick** *n.* an oblong piece of filleted or minced fish coated in breadcrumbs.

fish hawk *n.* another name for the **osprey.**

fish-hook *n.* a sharp hook used in angling, esp. one with a barb.

fishing ('fıʃıŋ) *n.* **a.** the occupation of catching fish. **b.** (*as modifier*): *a fishing match.*

fishing rod *n.* a long tapered flexible pole for use with a fishing line and, usually, a reel.

fish joint *n.* a connection formed by fishplates at the meeting point of two rails, beams, etc.

fish meal *n.* ground dried fish used as feed for farm animals, as a fertilizer, etc.

fishmonger ('fıʃ,mʌŋgə) *n. Chiefly Brit.* a retailer of fish.

fishnet ('fıʃ,nɛt) *n.* **a.** an open mesh fabric resembling netting. **b.** (*as modifier*): *fishnet tights.*

fish out *vb.* (*tr.*, *adv.*) to find or extract (something): *to fish keys out of a pocket.*

fishplate ('fıʃ,pleıt) *n.* a flat piece of metal joining one rail or beam to the next, esp. on railway tracks.

fishtail ('fıʃ,teıl) *n.* **1.** an aeroplane manoeuvre in which the tail is moved from side to side to reduce speed. **2.** a nozzle having a long narrow slot at the top, placed over a Bunsen burner to produce a thin fanlike flame.

fishwife ('fıʃ,waıf) *n.*, *pl.* **-wives. 1.** a woman who sells fish. **2.** a coarse scolding woman.

fishy ('fıʃı) *adj.* **fishier, fishiest. 1.** of, involving, or suggestive of fish. **2.** abounding in fish. **3.** *Inf.* suspicious, doubtful, or questionable. **4.** dull and lifeless: *a fishy look.* —'**fishily** *adv.*

fissile ('fısaıl) *adj.* **1.** *Brit.* capable of undergoing nuclear fission. **2.** fissionable. **3.** tending to split or capable of being split. [C17: from L, from *fissus* split]

fission ('fıʃən) *n.* **1.** the act or process of splitting or breaking into parts. **2.** *Biol.* a form of asexual reproduction involving a division into two or more equal parts. **3.** short for **nuclear fission.** [C19: from L *fissiō* a cleaving] —'**fissionable** *adj.*

fission-track dating *n.* the dating of samples of minerals by comparing the tracks in them made by fission fragments of the uranium nuclei they contain, before and after irradiation by neutrons.

fissiparous (fı'sıpərəs) *adj. Biol.* reproducing by fission. —fis'**siparously** *adv.*

fissure ('fıʃə) *n.* **1.** any long narrow cleft or crack, esp. in a rock. **2.** a weakness or flaw. **3.** *Anat.* a narrow split or groove that divides an organ such as the brain, lung, or liver into lobes. ~*vb.* **4.** to crack or split apart. [C14: from Medical L *fissūra,* from L *fissus* split]

fist (fıst) *n.* **1.** a hand with the fingers clenched into the palm, as for hitting. **2.** Also called: **fistful.** the quantity that can be held in a fist or hand. **3.** *Inf.* handwriting. **4.** an informal word for **index** (sense 9). ~*vb.* **5.** (*tr.*) to hit with the fist. [OE *fýst*]

fisticuffs ('fıstı,kʌfs) *pl. n.* combat with the fists. [C17: prob. from *fisty* with the fist + CUFF²]

fistula ('fıstjʊlə) *n.*, *pl.* **-las** *or* **-lae** (-,liː). *Pathol.* an abnormal opening between one hollow organ and another or between a hollow organ and the surface of the skin, caused by ulceration, malformation, etc. [C14: from L: pipe, tube, hollow reed, ulcer] —'**fistulous** *or* '**fistular** *adj.*

fit¹ (fıt) *vb.* **fitting, fitted. 1.** to be appropriate or suitable for (a situation, etc.). **2.** to be of the correct size or shape for (a container, etc.). **3.** (*tr.*) to adjust in order to render appropriate. **4.** (*tr.*) to supply with that which is needed. **5.** (*tr.*) to try clothes on (someone) in order to make adjustments if necessary. **6.** (*tr.*) to make competent or ready. **7.** (*tr.*) to locate with care. **8.** (*intr.*) to correspond with the facts or circumstances. ~*adj.* **fitter, fittest. 9.** appropriate. **10.** having the right qualifications; qualifying. **11.** in good health. **12.** worthy or deserving. **13.** (*foll. by an infinitive*) *Inf.* ready (to); strongly disposed (to): *she was fit to scream.* ~*n.* **14.** the manner in which something fits. **15.** the act or process of fitting. **16.** *Statistics.* the correspondence between observed and predicted characteristics of a distribution or model. ~See also **fit in, fit out.** [C14: prob. from MDu. *vitten*; rel. to ON *fitja* to knit] —'**fitly** *adv.* —'**fitness** *n.* —'**fittable** *adj.*

fit² (fıt) *n.* **1.** *Pathol.* a sudden attack or convulsion, such as an epileptic seizure. **2.** a sudden spell of emotion: *a fit of anger.* **3.** an impulsive period of activity or lack of activity. **4. by** *or* **in fits (and starts).** in spasmodic spells. **5. have** *or* **throw a fit.** *Inf.* to become very angry. [OE *fitt* conflict]

fitch (fıtʃ) *n.* **1.** a polecat. **2.** the fur of the polecat. [C16: prob. from *ficheux,* from OF, from ?]

fitful ('fıtfʊl) *adj.* characterized by or occurring in irregular spells. —'**fitfully** *adv.*

fit in *vb.* **1.** (*tr.*) to give a place or time to. **2.** (*intr.*, *adv.*) to belong or conform, esp. after adjustment: *he didn't fit in with their plans.*

fitment ('fıtmənt) *n.* **1.** *Machinery.* an accessory attached to an assembly of parts. **2.** *Chiefly Brit.* a detachable part of the furnishings of a room.

fit out *vb.* (*tr.*, *adv.*) to equip.

fitted ('fıtıd) *adj.* **1.** designed for excellent fit: *a fitted suit.* **2.** (of a carpet) cut or sewn to cover a floor completely. **3. a.** (of furniture) built to fit a particular space: *a fitted cupboard.* **b.** (of a room) equipped with fitted furniture: *a fitted kitchen.* **4.** (of sheets) having ends that are elasticated and shaped to fit tightly over a mattress.

fitter ('fıtə) *n.* **1.** a person who fits a garment, esp. when it is made for a particular person. **2.** a person who is skilled in the assembly and adjustment of machinery, esp. of a specified sort.

fitting ('fıtıŋ) *adj.* **1.** appropriate or proper. ~*n.* **2.** an accessory or part: *an electrical fitting.* **3.** (*pl.*) furnishings or accessories in a building. **4.** work carried out by a fitter. **5.** the act of trying on clothes so that they can be adjusted to fit. —'**fittingly** *adv.*

Fittipaldi (,fıtı'pældı) *n.* **Emerson.** born 1946, Brazilian motor-racing driver: world champion in 1972 and 1974.

Fitzgerald (fıts'dʒɛrəld) *n.* **1. Edward.** 1809–83, English poet, noted particularly for his free translation of the *Rubáiyát of Omar Khayyám* (1859). **2. Ella.** born 1918, U.S. jazz singer, noted for her vocal range, clarity, and rhythm. **3. F(rancis) Scott (Key).** 1896–1940, U.S. novelist and short-story writer, noted particularly for his portrayal of the 1920s in *The Great Gatsby* (1925) and *Tender is the Night* (1934).

FitzGerald (fıts'dʒɛrəld) *n.* **Garret.** born 1926, Irish politician; leader of Fine Gael Party (1977–87); prime minister of the Republic of Ireland (1981–82; 1986–87).

Fitzgerald-Lorentz contraction (fıts'dʒɛrəldlɔː'rɛnts) *n. Physics.* the contraction that a moving body exhibits when its velocity approaches that of light. [C19: after G. F. *Fitzgerald* (1851–1901), Irish physicist and H. A. LORENTZ]

Fitzsimmons (ˌfɪtˈsɪmənz) n. **Bob.** 1862–1917, New Zealand boxer, born in England: world middleweight (1891–97), heavyweight (1897–99), and light-heavyweight (1903–05) champion.

Fiume (ˈfiːme) n. the Italian name for **Rijeka.**

five (faɪv) n. **1.** the cardinal number that is the sum of four and one. **2.** a numeral, 5, V, etc., representing this number. **3.** the amount or quantity that is one greater than four. **4.** something representing, represented by, or consisting of five units, such as a playing card with five symbols on it. **5. five o'clock.** five hours after noon or midnight. ~*determiner.* **6. a.** amounting to five: *five nights.* **b.** (*as pronoun*): *choose any five you like.* ~See also **fives.** [OE *fīf*]

five-a-side n. a version of soccer with five players on each side.

five-eighth n. *Austral. & N.Z.* a rugby player positioned between the half-backs and three-quarters.

five-finger n. any of various plants having five-petalled flowers or five lobed leaves, such as cinquefoil and Virginia creeper.

fivefold (ˈfaɪvˌfəʊld) adj. **1.** equal to or having five times as many or as much. **2.** composed of five parts. ~*adv.* **3.** by or up to five times as many or as much.

five-o'clock shadow n. beard growth visible late in the day on a man's shaven face.

fivepins (ˈfaɪvˌpɪnz) n. (*functioning as sing.*) a bowling game using five pins, played esp. in Canada. — **'five,pin** *adj.*

fiver (ˈfaɪvə) n. *Brit. inf.* a five-pound note.

fives (faɪvz) n. (*functioning as sing.*) a ball game similar to squash but played with bats or the hands.

Five-Year Plan n. (in socialist economies) a government plan for economic development over a period of five years.

fix (fɪks) vb. (*mainly tr.*) **1.** (*also intr.*) to make or become firm, stable, or secure. **2.** to attach or place permanently. **3.** (often foll. by *up*) to settle definitely; decide. **4.** to hold or direct (eyes, etc.) steadily: *he fixed his gaze on the woman.* **5.** to call to attention or rivet. **6.** to make rigid: *to fix one's jaw.* **7.** to place or ascribe: *to fix the blame.* **8.** to mend or repair. **9.** *Inf.* to provide or be provided with: *how are you fixed for supplies?* **10.** *Inf.* to influence (a person, etc.) unfairly, as by bribery. **11.** *Sl.* to take revenge on. **12.** *Inf.* to give (someone) his just deserts: *that'll fix him.* **13.** *Inf., chiefly U.S. & Canad.* to prepare: *to fix a meal.* **14.** *Dialect or inf.* to spay or castrate (an animal). **15.** *Photog.* to treat (a film, plate, or paper) with fixer to make permanent the image rendered visible by developer. **16.** to convert (atmospheric nitrogen) into nitrogen compounds, as in the manufacture of fertilizers or the action of bacteria in the soil. **17.** to reduce (a substance) to a solid state or a less volatile state. **18.** (*intr.*) *Sl.* to inject a narcotic drug. ~n. **19.** *Inf.* a predicament; dilemma. **20.** the ascertaining of the navigational position, as of a ship, by radar, etc. **21.** *Sl.* an intravenous injection of a narcotic such as heroin. ~See also **fix up.** [C15: from Med. L *fixāre*, from L *fixus* fixed, from L *fīgere*] — **'fixable** *adj.*

fixate (ˈfɪkseɪt) vb. **1.** to become or cause to become fixed. **2.** *Psychol.* to engage in fixation. **3.** (*tr.; usually passive*) *Inf.* to obsess. [C19: from L *fixus* fixed + -ATE[1]]

fixation (fɪkˈseɪʃən) n. **1.** the act of fixing or the state of being fixed. **2.** a preoccupation or obsession. **3.** *Psychol.* **a.** the situation of being set in a certain way of thinking or acting. **b.** a strong attachment of a person to another person or an object in early life. **4.** *Chem.* the conversion of nitrogen in the air into a compound, esp. a fertilizer. **5.** the reduction of a substance to a nonvolatile or solid form.

fixative (ˈfɪksətɪv) adj. **1.** serving or tending to fix. ~n. **2.** a fluid sprayed over drawings to prevent smudging or one that fixes tissues and cells for microscopic study. **3.** a substance added to a liquid, such as a perfume, to make it less volatile.

fixed (fɪkst) adj. **1.** attached or placed so as to be immovable. **2.** stable: *fixed prices.* **3.** steadily directed: *a fixed expression.* **4.** established as to relative position: *a fixed point.* **5.** always at the same time: *a fixed holiday.* **6.** (of ideas, etc.) firmly maintained. **7.** (of an element) held in chemical combination: *fixed nitrogen.* **8.** (of a substance) nonvolatile. **9.** arranged. **10.** *Inf.* equipped or provided for, as with money, possessions, etc. **11.** *Inf.*

illegally arranged: *a fixed trial.* — **fixedly** (ˈfɪksɪdlɪ) adv. — **'fixedness** n.

fixed assets pl. n. nontrading business assets of a relatively permanent nature, such as plant, fixtures, or goodwill. Also called: **capital assets.**

fixed oil n. a natural animal or vegetable oil that is not volatile: a mixture of esters of fatty acids.

fixed-point representation n. *Computers.* the representation of numbers by a single set of digits such that the radix point has a predetermined location. Cf. **floating-point representation.**

fixed satellite n. a satellite revolving in a stationary orbit so that it appears to remain over a fixed point on the earth's surface.

fixed star n. an extremely distant star whose position appears to be almost stationary over a long period of time.

fixer (ˈfɪksə) n. **1.** *Photog.* a solution used to dissolve unexposed silver halides after developing. **2.** *Sl.* a person who makes arrangements, esp. by underhand or illegal means.

fixity (ˈfɪksɪtɪ) n., pl. **-ties. 1.** the state or quality of being fixed. **2.** a fixture.

fixture (ˈfɪkstʃə) n. **1.** an object firmly fixed in place, esp. a household appliance. **2.** a person or thing regarded as fixed in a particular place or position. **3.** *Property law.* an article attached to land and regarded as part of it. **4.** *Chiefly Brit.* **a.** a sports match or social occasion. **b.** the date of such an event. [C17: from LL *fīxūra* a fastening (with *-t-* by analogy with *mixture*)]

fix up vb. (*tr., adv.*) **1.** to arrange: *let's fix up a date.* **2.** (often foll. by *with*) to provide: *I'm sure we can fix you up with a room.*

fizgig (ˈfɪzˌgɪg) n. **1.** a frivolous or flirtatious girl. **2.** a firework that fizzes as it moves. [C16: prob. from obs. *fise* a breaking of wind + *gig* girl]

fizz (fɪz) vb. (*intr.*) **1.** to make a hissing or bubbling sound. **2.** (of a drink) to produce bubbles of carbon dioxide. ~n. **3.** a hissing or bubbling sound. **4.** the bubbly quality of a drink; effervescence. **5.** any effervescent drink. [C17: imit.] — **'fizzy** adj. — **'fizziness** n.

fizzle (ˈfɪzəl) vb. (*intr.*) **1.** to make a hissing or bubbling sound. **2.** (often foll. by *out*) *Inf.* to fail or die out, esp. after a promising start. ~n. **3.** a hissing or bubbling sound. **4.** *Inf.* a failure. [C16: prob. from obs. *fist* to break wind]

fjord or **fiord** (fjɔːd) n. a long narrow inlet of the sea between high steep cliffs, common in Norway. [C17: from Norwegian, from ON *fjörthr*; see FIRTH, FORD]

FL abbrev. for Flight Lieutenant.

fl. abbrev. for: **1.** floor. **2.** floruit. **3.** fluid.

Fl. abbrev. for: **1.** Flanders. **2.** Flemish.

flab (flæb) n. unsightly or unwanted fat on the body. [C20: back formation from FLABBY]

flabbergast (ˈflæbəˌɡɑːst) vb. (*tr.; usually passive*) *Inf.* to amaze utterly; astound. [C18: from ?]

flabby (ˈflæbɪ) adj. **-bier, -biest. 1.** loose or yielding: *flabby muscles.* **2.** having flabby flesh, esp. through being overweight. **3.** lacking vitality; weak. [C17: alteration of *flappy* from FLAP + -Y[1]; cf. Du. *flabbe* drooping lip] — **'flabbiness** n.

flaccid (ˈflæksɪd) adj. lacking firmness; soft and limp. [C17: from L *flaccidus*, from *flaccus*] — **flac'cidity** n.

flacon (French flakɔ̃) n. a small stoppered bottle, esp. used for perfume. [C19: from F; see FLAGON]

flag[1] (flæg) n. **1.** a piece of cloth, esp. bunting, often attached to a pole or staff, decorated with a design and used as an emblem, symbol, or standard or as a means of signalling. **2.** a small piece of paper, etc., sold on flag days. **3.** the conspicuously marked or shaped tail of a deer or of certain dogs. **4.** anything used like a flag to attract attention, esp. a code inserted into a computer file to distinguish certain information. **5.** *Brit., Austral., & N.Z.* the part of a taximeter that is raised when a taxi is for hire. **6. show the flag. a.** to assert a claim by military presence. **b.** *Inf.* to make an appearance. ~vb. **flagging, flagged.** (*tr.*) **7.** to decorate or mark with a flag or flags. **8.** (often foll. by *down*) to warn or signal (a vehicle) to stop. **9.** to send or communicate (messages, information, etc.) by flag. [C16: from ?] — **'flagger** n.

flag[2] (flæg) n. **1.** any of various plants that have long swordlike leaves, esp. an iris (**yellow flag**). **2.** the leaf of any such plant. [C14: prob. from ON]

flag[3] (flæg) *vb.* **flagging, flagged.** (*intr.*) **1.** to hang down; droop. **2.** to become weak or tired. [C16: from ?]

flag[4] (flæg) *n.* **1.** short for **flagstone.** ~*vb.* **flagging, flagged. 2.** (*tr.*) to furnish (a floor, etc.) with flagstones.

flag day *n.* a day on which money is collected by a charity and small flags or emblems are given to contributors.

flagellant (ˈflædʒɪlənt, fləˈdʒɛlənt) *or* **flagellator** (ˈflædʒɪˌleɪtə) *n.* a person who whips himself or others either as part of a religious penance or for sexual gratification. [C16: from L *flagellāre* to whip, from FLAGELLUM]

flagellate *vb.* (ˈflædʒɪˌleɪt) **1.** (*tr.*) to whip; flog. ~*adj.* (ˈflædʒɪlɪt), *also* **flagellated. 2.** possessing one or more flagella. **3.** whiplike. ~*n.* (ˈflædʒɪlɪt). **4.** a flagellate organism. — ˌflagelˈlation *n.*

flagellum (fləˈdʒɛləm) *n., pl.* **-la** (-lə) *or* **-lums. 1.** *Biol.* a long whiplike outgrowth from a cell that acts as an organ of locomotion: occurs in some protozoans, gametes, etc. **2.** *Bot.* a long thin shoot or runner. [C19: from L: a little whip, from *flagrum* a whip, lash] — flaˈgellar *adj.*

flageolet[1] (ˌflædʒəˈlɛt) *n.* a high-pitched musical instrument of the recorder family. [C17: from F, modification of OF *flajolet* a little flute, from Vulgar L *flabeolum* (unattested), from L *flāre* to blow]

flageolet[2] (ˌflædʒəˈlɛt) *n.* a type of kidney bean. [C19: from F, corruption of *fageolet*, dim. of *fageol*, from L *faseolus*]

flag fall *n. Austral.* the minimum charge for hiring a taxi.

flag of convenience *n.* a national flag flown by a ship registered in that country to gain financial or legal advantage.

flag of truce *n.* a white flag indicating an invitation to an enemy to negotiate.

flagon (ˈflægən) *n.* **1.** a large bottle of wine, cider, etc. **2.** a vessel having a handle, spout, and narrow neck. [C15: from OF *flascon*, from LL *flascō*, prob. of Gmc origin; see FLASK]

flagpole (ˈflægˌpəʊl) *or* **flagstaff** (ˈflægˌstɑːf) *n., pl.* **-poles, -staffs,** *or* **-staves** (-ˌsteɪvz). a pole or staff on which a flag is hoisted and displayed.

flagrant (ˈfleɪɡrənt) *adj.* blatant; outrageous. [C15: from L *flagrāre* to blaze, burn] — ˈflagrancy *n.* — ˈflagrantly *adv.*

flagrante delicto (fləˈɡræntɪ dɪˈlɪktəʊ) *adv.* See **in flagrante delicto.**

flagship (ˈflægˌʃɪp) *n.* **1.** a ship, esp. in a fleet, aboard which the commander of the fleet is quartered. **2.** the most important ship belonging to a shipping company. **3.** the item in a group considered most important esp. in establishing a public image: *costume drama is the flagship of the BBC.*

Flagstad (ˈflægstæd; *Norwegian* ˈflaksta) *n.* **Kirsten** (ˈçɪrstən). 1895–1962, Norwegian operatic soprano, noted particularly for her interpretations of Wagner.

flagstone (ˈflægˌstəʊn) *n.* **1.** a hard fine-textured rock that can be split up into slabs for paving. **2.** a slab of such a rock. [C15 *flag* (in the sense: sod, turf), from ON *flaga* slab; cf. OE *flǣcg* plaster, poultice]

flag-waving *n. Inf.* an emotional appeal intended to arouse patriotic feeling. — ˈflagˌwaver *n.*

flail (fleɪl) *n.* **1.** an implement used for threshing grain, consisting of a wooden handle with a free-swinging metal or wooden bar attached to it. ~*vb.* **2.** (*tr.*) to beat with or as if with a flail. **3.** to thresh about: *with arms flailing.* [C12 *fleil*, ult. from LL *flagellum* flail, from L: whip]

flair (flɛə) *n.* **1.** natural ability; talent. **2.** perceptiveness. **3.** *Inf.* stylishness or elegance: *to dress with flair.* [C19: from F, lit.: sense of smell, from OF: scent, ult. from L *frāgrāre* to smell sweet; see FRAGRANT]

flak (flæk) *n.* **1.** anti-aircraft fire or artillery. **2.** *Inf.* adverse criticism. [C20: from G *Fl(ieger)a(bwehr)k(anone)*, lit.: aircraft defence gun]

flake[1] (fleɪk) *n.* **1.** a small thin piece or layer chipped off or detached from an object or substance. **2.** a small piece or particle: *a flake of snow.* **3.** *Archaeol.* a fragment removed by chipping from a larger stone used as a tool or weapon. ~*vb.* **4.** to peel or cause to peel off in flakes. **5.** to cover or become covered with or as with flakes. **6.** (*tr.*) to form into flakes. [C14: from ON]

flake[2] (fleɪk) *n.* a rack or platform for drying fish. [C14: from ON *flaki*; rel. to Du. *vlaak* hurdle]

flake out *vb.* (*intr., adv.*) *Inf.* to collapse or fall asleep as through extreme exhaustion.

flake white *n.* a pigment made from flakes of white lead.

flak jacket *n.* a reinforced jacket for protection against gunfire or shrapnel worn by soldiers, policemen, etc.

flaky (ˈfleɪkɪ) *adj.* **flakier, flakiest. 1.** like or made of flakes. **2.** tending to break easily into flakes. **3.** Also spelt: **flakey.** *U.S. sl.* eccentric; crazy. — ˈflakily *adv.* — ˈflakiness *n.*

flambé (ˈflɑːmbeɪ) *adj.* (of food, such as steak or pancakes) served in flaming brandy, etc. [F, p.p. of *flamber* to FLAME]

flambeau (ˈflæmbəʊ) *n., pl.* **-beaux** (-bəʊ, -bəʊz) *or* **-beaus.** a burning torch, as used in night processions, etc. [C17: from OF: torch, lit.: a little flame, from *flambe* FLAME]

Flamborough Head (ˈflæmbərə, -brə) *n.* a chalk promontory in NE England, on the coast of Humberside.

flamboyant (flæmˈbɔɪənt) *adj.* **1.** elaborate or extravagant; showy. **2.** rich or brilliant in colour. **3.** exuberant or ostentatious. **4.** of the French Gothic style of architecture characterized by flamelike tracery and elaborate carving. [C19: from F: flaming, from *flamboyer* to FLAME] — flamˈboyance *or* flamˈboyancy *n.* — flamˈboyantly *adv.*

flame (fleɪm) *n.* **1.** a hot usually luminous body of burning gas emanating in flickering streams from burning material or produced by a jet of ignited gas. **2.** (*often pl.*) the state or condition of burning with flames: *to burst into flames.* **3.** a brilliant light. **4. a.** a strong reddish-orange colour. **b.** (*as adj.*): *a flame carpet.* **5.** intense passion or ardour. **6.** *Inf.* a lover or sweetheart (esp. in **an old flame**). ~*vb.* **7.** to burn or cause to burn brightly. **8.** (*intr.*) to become red or fiery: *his face flamed with anger.* **9.** (*intr.*) to become angry or excited. **10.** (*tr.*) to apply a flame to (something). [C14: from Anglo-F, from OF *flambe*, from L *flammula* a little flame, from *flamma* flame] — ˈflameˌlike *adj.* — ˈflamy *adj.*

flame gun *n.* a type of flame-thrower for destroying garden weeds, etc.

flamen (ˈfleɪmɛn) *n., pl.* **flamens** *or* **flamines** (ˈflæmɪˌniːz). (in ancient Rome) any of 15 priests who each served a particular deity. [C14: from L; prob. rel. to OE *blōtan* to sacrifice, Gothic *blotan* to worship]

flamenco (fləˈmɛŋkəʊ) *n., pl.* **-cos. 1.** a type of dance music for vocal soloist and guitar, characterized by sad mood. **2.** the dance performed to such music. [from Sp.: like a Gipsy, lit.: Fleming, from MDu. *Vlaminc* Fleming]

flameout (ˈfleɪmˌaʊt) *n.* the failure of an aircraft jet engine in flight due to extinction of the flame.

flame-thrower *n.* a weapon that ejects a stream or spray of burning fluid.

flame tree *n.* any of various tropical trees with red or orange flowers.

flaming (ˈfleɪmɪŋ) *adj.* **1.** burning with or emitting flames. **2.** glowing brightly. **3.** intense or ardent: *a flaming temper.* **4.** *Inf.* (intensifier): *you flaming idiot.*

flamingo (fləˈmɪŋɡəʊ) *n., pl.* **-gos** *or* **-goes.** a large wading bird having a pink-and-red plumage and downward-bent bill and inhabiting brackish lakes. [C16: from Port., from Provençal, from L *flamma* flame + Gmc suffix *-ing* denoting descent from; cf. -ING[3]]

Flaminian Way (fləˈmɪnɪən) *n.* an ancient road in Italy, extending north from Rome to Rimini: constructed in 220 B.C. by Gaius Flaminius. Length: over 322 km (200 miles). Latin name: **Via Flaminia.**

Flamininus (ˌflæmɪˈnaɪnəs) *n.* **Titus Quinctius** (ˈtaɪtəs ˈkwɪŋktɪəs). ?230–?174 B.C., Roman general and statesman: defeated Macedonia (197) and proclaimed the independence of the Greek states (196).

Flaminius (fləˈmɪnɪəs) *n.* **Gaius** (ˈɡaɪəs). died 217 B.C., Roman statesman and general: built the Flaminian Way; defeated by Hannibal at Trasimene (217).

flammable (ˈflæməbəl) *adj.* readily combustible; inflammable. — ˌflammaˈbility *n.*

▷ **Usage.** *Flammable* and *inflammable* are interchangeable when used of the properties of materials. *Flammable* is, however, often preferred for warning labels as there is less likelihood of misunderstanding (*inflammable* being sometimes taken to mean *not flammable*). The word that does mean *not flammable* is *nonflammable.*

Flamsteed (ˈflæmˌstiːd) *n.* **John.** 1646–1719, English astronomer: the first Astronomer Royal and first director of the Royal Observatory, Greenwich (1675). He increased the accuracy of existing stellar catalogues, greatly aiding navigation.

flan (flæn) *n.* **1.** an open pastry or sponge tart filled with fruit or a savoury mixture. **2.** a piece of metal ready to receive the die or stamp in the production of coins. [C19: from F, from OF *flaon*, from LL *flādō* flat cake, of Gmc origin]

Flanders ('flɑːndəz) *n.* a powerful medieval principality in the SW part of the Low Countries, now in the Belgian provinces of East and West Flanders, the Netherlands province of Zeeland, and the French department of the Nord; scene of battles in many wars.

flange (flændʒ) *n.* **1.** a radially projecting collar or rim on an object for strengthening it or for attaching it to another object. **2.** a flat outer face of a rolled-steel joist. ~*vb.* **3.** (*tr.*) to provide (a component) with a flange. [C17: prob. changed from earlier *flaunche* curved segment at side of a heraldic field, from F *flanc* FLANK] —**flanged** *adj.* — **'flangeless** *adj.*

flank (flæŋk) *n.* **1.** the side of a man or animal between the ribs and the hip. **2.** a cut of beef from the flank. **3.** the side of anything, such as a mountain or building. **4.** the side of a naval or military formation. ~*vb.* **5.** (when *intr.*, often foll. by *on* or *upon*) to be located at the side of (an object, etc.). **6.** *Mil.* to position or guard on or beside the flank of (a formation, etc.). [C12: from OF *flanc*, of Gmc origin]

flanker ('flæŋkə) *n.* **1.** one of a detachment of soldiers detailed to guard the flanks. **2.** a fortification used to protect a flank. **3.** Also called: **flank forward.** *Rugby.* another name for **winger.**

flannel ('flænəl) *n.* **1.** a soft light woollen fabric with a slight nap, used for clothing, etc. **2.** (*pl.*) trousers or other garments made of flannel. **3.** *Brit.* a small piece of cloth used to wash the face and hands; face flannel. U.S. and Canad. equivalent: **washcloth. 4.** *Brit. inf.* indirect or evasive talk. ~*vb.* **-nelling, -nelled** or *U.S.* **-neling, -neled.** (*tr.*) **5.** to cover or wrap with flannel. **6.** to rub or polish with flannel. **7.** *Brit. inf.* to flatter. [C14: prob. var. of *flanen* sackcloth, from Welsh, from *gwlân* wool] — **'flannelly** *adj.*

flannelette (ˌflænə'let) *n.* a cotton imitation of flannel.

flap (flæp) *vb.* **flapping, flapped. 1.** to move (wings or arms) up and down, esp. in or as if in flying, or (of wings or arms) to move in this way. **2.** to move or cause to move noisily back and forth or up and down: *the curtains flapped in the breeze.* **3.** (*intr.*) *Inf.* to become agitated or flustered. **4.** to deal (a person or thing) a blow with a broad flexible object. ~*n.* **5.** the action, motion, or noise made by flapping: *with one flap of its wings the bird was off.* **6.** a piece of material, attached at one edge and usually used to cover an opening, as on a tent, envelope, or pocket. **7.** a blow dealt with a flat object. **8.** a movable surface fixed to an aircraft wing that increases lift during takeoff and drag during landing. **9.** *Inf.* a state of panic or agitation. [C14: prob. imit.]

flapdoodle ('flæpˌduːdəl) *n. Sl.* foolish talk; nonsense. [C19: from ?]

flapjack ('flæpˌdʒæk) *n.* **1.** a chewy biscuit made with rolled oats. **2.** *Chiefly U.S. & Canad.* another word for **pancake.**

flapper ('flæpə) *n.* (in the 1920s) a young woman, esp. one flaunting her unconventional behaviour.

flare (flɛə) *vb.* **1.** to burn or cause to burn with an unsteady or sudden bright flame. **2.** to burn off excess gas or oil. **3.** to spread or cause to spread outwards from a narrow to a wider shape. ~*n.* **4.** an unsteady flame. **5.** a sudden burst of flame. **6. a.** a blaze of light or fire used to illuminate, signal distress, alert, etc. **b.** the device producing such a blaze. **7.** a spreading shape or anything with a spreading shape: *a skirt with a flare.* **8.** an open flame used to burn off unwanted gas at an oil well. **9.** *Astron.* short for **solar flare.** [C16 (to spread out): from ?]

flare-up *n.* **1.** a sudden burst of fire or light. **2.** *Inf.* a sudden burst of emotion or violence. ~*vb.* **flare up.** (*intr., adv.*) **3.** to burst suddenly into fire or light. **4.** *Inf.* to burst into anger.

flash (flæʃ) *n.* **1.** a sudden short blaze of intense light or flame: *a flash of sunlight.* **2.** a sudden occurrence or display, esp. one suggestive of brilliance: *a flash of understanding.* **3.** a very brief space of time: *over in a flash.* **4.** Also called: **news flash.** a short news announcement concerning a new event. **5.** Also called: **patch.** *Chiefly Brit.* an insignia or emblem worn on a uniform, vehicle,

etc., to identify its military formation. **6.** a sudden rush of water down a river or watercourse. **7.** *Photog., inf.* short for **flashlight** (sense 2). **8.** (*modifier*) involving, using, or produced by a flash of heat, light, etc.: *flash distillation.* **9. flash in the pan.** a project, person, etc., that enjoys only short-lived success. ~*adj.* **10.** *Inf.* ostentatious or vulgar. **11.** sham or counterfeit. **12.** *Inf.* relating to or characteristic of the criminal underworld. **13.** brief and rapid: *flash freezing.* ~*vb.* **14.** to burst or cause to burst suddenly or intermittently into flame. **15.** to emit or reflect or cause to emit or reflect light suddenly or intermittently. **16.** (*intr.*) to move very fast: *he flashed by on his bicycle.* **17.** (*intr.*) to come rapidly (into the mind or vision). **18.** (*intr.*; foll. by *out* or *up*) to appear like a sudden light. **19. a.** to signal or communicate very fast: *to flash a message.* **b.** to signal by use of a light, such as car headlights. **20.** (*tr.*) *Inf.* to display ostentatiously: *to flash money around.* **21.** (*tr.*) *Inf.* to show suddenly and briefly. **22.** (*intr.*) *Brit. sl.* to expose oneself indecently. **23.** to send a sudden rush of water down (a river, etc.), or to carry (a vessel) down by this method. [C14 (in the sense: to rush, as of water): from ?] — **'flasher** *n.*

flashback ('flæʃˌbæk) *n.* a transition in a novel, film, etc., to an earlier scene or event.

flashboard ('flæʃˌbɔːd) *n.* a board or boarding that is placed along the top of a dam to increase its height and capacity.

flashbulb ('flæʃˌbʌlb) *n. Photog.* a small expendable glass light bulb that is triggered, usually electrically, to produce a bright flash of light.

flash burn *n. Pathol.* a burn caused by momentary exposure to intense radiant heat.

flash card *n.* a card on which are written or printed words for children to look at briefly, used as an aid to learning.

flashcube ('flæʃˌkjuːb) *n.* a boxlike camera attachment, holding four flashbulbs, that turns so that each flashbulb can be used.

flash flood *n.* a sudden short-lived torrent, usually caused by a heavy storm, esp. in desert regions.

flash gun *n.* a device, sometimes incorporated in a camera, for holding and electrically firing a flashbulb as the shutter opens.

flashing ('flæʃɪŋ) *n.* a weatherproof material, esp. thin sheet metal, used to cover the valleys between the slopes of a roof, the junction between a chimney and a roof, etc.

flashlight ('flæʃˌlaɪt) *n.* **1.** another word (esp. *U.S.* and Canad.) for **torch. 2.** *Photog.* the brief bright light emitted by a flashbulb or electronic flash. Often shortened to **flash.**

flash point *n.* **1.** the lowest temperature at which the vapour above a liquid can be ignited in air. **2.** a critical time or place beyond which a situation will inevitably erupt into violence.

flashy ('flæʃɪ) *adj.* **flashier, flashiest. 1.** brilliant and dazzling, esp. for a short time or in a superficial way. **2.** cheap and ostentatious. — **'flashily** *adv.* — **'flashiness** *n.*

flask (flɑːsk) *n.* **1.** a bottle with a narrow neck, esp. used in a laboratory or for wine, oil, etc. **2.** Also called: **hip flask.** a small flattened container of glass or metal designed to be carried in a pocket, esp. for liquor. **3.** See **vacuum flask.** [C14: from OF, from Med. L *flasca, flasco,* ? of Gmc origin; cf. OE *flasce, flaxe*]

flat¹ (flæt) *adj.* **flatter, flattest. 1.** horizontal; level: *a flat roof.* **2.** even or smooth, without projections or depressions: *a flat surface.* **3.** lying stretched out at full length: *he lay flat on the ground.* **4.** having little depth or thickness: *a flat dish.* **5.** (*postpositive*; often foll. by *against*) having a surface or side in complete contact with another surface: *flat against the wall.* **6.** (of a tyre) deflated. **7.** (of shoes) having an unraised heel. **8.** *Chiefly Brit.* **a.** (of races, racetracks, or racecourses) not having obstacles to be jumped. **b.** of, relating to, or connected with flat racing as opposed to steeplechasing and hurdling. **9.** without qualification; total: *a flat denial.* **10.** fixed: *a flat rate.* **11.** (*prenominal* or *immediately postpositive*) neither more nor less; exact: *he did the journey in thirty minutes flat.* **12.** unexciting: *a flat joke.* **13.** without variation or resonance; monotonous: *a flat voice.* **14.** (of beer, sparkling wines, etc.) having lost effervescence, as by exposure to air. **15.** (of trade, business, etc.) commercially inactive. **16.** (of a battery) fully discharged. **17.** (of a print, photograph, or painting) lacking contrast. **18.** (of paint) without gloss or lustre. **19.** *Music.* **a.** (*immediately postpositive*) denoting a note of a given letter name (or the sound it represents) that has been lowered in pitch by one chromatic semitone: *B flat.* **b.** (of an instrument, voice, etc.) out of tune by being too low in pitch. Cf. **sharp** (sense 12). **20.** *Phonetics.* **flat a.** the vowel sound of *a* as in the usual U.S. or S Brit. pronunciation of *hand, cat.* ~*adv.* **21.** in or into a prostrate, level, or flat state or position: *he held his hand out flat.* **22.** completely or utterly; absolutely. **23.** exactly; precisely: *in three minutes flat.* **24.** *Music.* **a.** lower than a standard pitch. **b.** too low in pitch: *she sings flat.* Cf. **sharp** (sense 17). **25. fall flat** (**on one's face**). to fail to achieve a desired effect. **26. flat out.** *Inf.* **a.** with the maximum speed or effort. **b.** totally exhausted. ~*n.* **27.** a flat object, surface, or part. **28.** (*often pl.*) a low-lying tract of land, esp. a marsh or swamp. **29.** (*often pl.*) a mud bank exposed at low tide. **30.** *Music.* **a.** an accidental that lowers the pitch of a note by one chromatic semitone. Usual symbol: ♭ **b.** a note affected by this accidental. Cf. **sharp** (sense 18). **31.** *Theatre.* a wooden frame covered with painted canvas, etc., used to form part of a stage setting. **32.** a punctured car tyre. **33.** (*often cap.; preceded by the*) *Chiefly Brit.* **a.** flat racing, esp. as opposed to steeplechasing and hurdling. **b.** the season of flat racing. ~*vb.* **flatting, flatted.** **34.** to make or become flat. [C14: from ON *flatr*] — **'flatly** *adv.* — **'flatness** *n.* — **'flattish** *adj.*

flat² (flæt) *n.* a set of rooms comprising a residence entirely on one floor of a building. Usual U.S. and Canad. name: **apartment.** [OE *flett* floor, hall, house]

flatbed lorry ('flæt,bɛd) *n.* a lorry with a flat platform for its body.

flatboat ('flæt,bəʊt) *n.* any boat with a flat bottom, usually for transporting goods on a canal.

flatette (,flæt'ɛt) *n.* *Austral.* a flat having only a few rooms.

flatfish ('flæt,fɪʃ) *n., pl.* -**fish** *or* -**fishes.** any of an order of marine spiny-finned fish including the halibut, plaice, turbot, and sole, all of which have a flat body which has both eyes on the uppermost side.

flatfoot ('flæt,fʊt) *n.* **1.** Also called: **splayfoot.** a condition in which the instep arch of the foot is flattened. **2.** (*pl.* -**foots** *or* -**feet**) a slang word (usually derogatory) for a **policeman.**

flat-footed (,flæt'fʊtɪd) *adj.* **1.** having flatfoot. **2.** *Inf.* **a.** awkward. **b.** downright. **3.** *Inf.* off guard (often in **catch flat-footed**). — ,**flat-'footedly** *adv.* — ,**flat-'footedness** *n.*

flathead ('flæt,hɛd) *n., pl.* -**head** *or* -**heads.** a Pacific food fish which resembles the gurnard.

flatiron ('flæt,aɪən) *n.* (formerly) an iron for pressing clothes that was heated by being placed on a stove, etc.

flatlet ('flætlɪt) *n.* a flat having only a few rooms.

flatmate ('flæt,meɪt) *n.* a person with whom one shares a flat.

flat racing *n.* **a.** the racing of horses on racecourses without jumps. **b.** (*as modifier*): *the flat-racing season.*

flat spin *n.* **1.** an aircraft spin in which the longitudinal axis is more nearly horizontal than vertical. **2.** *Inf.* a state of confusion; dither.

flatten ('flæt²n) *vb.* **1.** (sometimes foll. by *out*) to make or become flat or flatter. **2.** (*tr.*) *Inf.* **a.** to knock down or injure. **b.** to crush or subdue. **3.** (*tr.*) *Music.* to lower the pitch of (a note) by one chromatic semitone. — **'flattener** *n.*

flatter ('flætə) *vb.* **1.** to praise insincerely, esp. in order to win favour or reward. **2.** to show to advantage: *that dress flatters her.* **3.** (*tr.*) to make to appear more attractive, etc., than in reality. **4.** to gratify the vanity of (a person). **5.** (*tr.*) to encourage, esp. falsely. **6.** (*tr.*) to deceive (oneself): *I flatter myself that I am the best.* [C13: prob. from OF *flater* to lick, fawn upon, of Frankish origin] — **'flatterable** *adj.* — **'flatterer** *n.*

flattery ('flætərɪ) *n., pl.* -**teries.** **1.** the act of flattering. **2.** excessive or insincere praise.

flattie ('flætɪ) *n.* *N.Z. inf.* a flounder or other flatfish.

flatties ('flætɪz) *pl. n.* shoes with flat heels or no heels.

flat top *n.* a style of haircut in which the hair is cut shortest on the top of the head so that it stands up from the scalp and appears flat from the crown to the forehead.

flatulent ('flætjʊlənt) *adj.* **1.** suffering from or caused by an excessive amount of gas in the alimentary canal. **2.** generating excessive gas in the alimentary canal. **3.** pretentious. [C16: from NL *flātulentus*, from L *flatus*, from *flāre* to breathe, blow] — **'flatulence** *or* **'flatulency** *n.* — **'flatulently** *adv.*

flatus ('fleɪtəs) *n., pl.* -**tuses.** gas generated in the alimentary canal. [C17: from L: a blowing, from *flāre* to breathe, blow]

flatworm ('flæt,wɜːm) *n.* any parasitic or free-living invertebrate of the phylum *Platyhelminthes,* including flukes and tapeworms, having a flattened body.

Flaubert ('fləʊbɛə; *French* flobɛr) *n.* **Gustave** (gystav). 1821–80, French novelist and short-story writer, regarded as a leader of the 19th-century naturalist school. His most famous novel, *Madame Bovary* (1857), for which he was prosecuted (and acquitted) on charges of immorality, and *L'Éducation sentimentale* (1869) deal with the conflict of romantic attitudes and bourgeois society. His other major works include *Salammbô* (1862), *La Tentation de Saint Antoine* (1874), and *Trois contes* (1877).

flaunt (flɔːnt) *vb.* **1.** to display (possessions, oneself, etc.) ostentatiously. **2.** to wave or cause to wave freely. ~*n.* **3.** the act of flaunting. [C16: ? of Scand. origin]
▷ **Usage.** See at **flout.**

flautist ('flɔːtɪst) *or U.S.* **flutist** ('fluːtɪst) *n.* a player of the flute. [C19: from It. *flautista,* from *flauto* FLUTE]

flavescent (flə'vɛsənt) *adj.* turning yellow; yellowish. [C19: from L *flāvēscere* to become yellow, from *flāvus* yellow]

flavin *or* **flavine** ('fleɪvɪn) *n.* **1.** a heterocyclic ketone that forms the nucleus of certain natural yellow pigments, such as riboflavin. **2.** any yellow pigment based on flavin. [C19: from L *flāvus* yellow]

flavine ('fleɪvɪn) *n.* another name for **acriflavine hydrochloride.**

flavone ('fleɪvəʊn) *n.* **1.** a crystalline compound occurring in plants. **2.** any of a class of plant pigments derived from flavone. [C19: from G, from L *flāvus* yellow + -ONE]

flavoprotein (,fleɪvəʊ'prəʊtiːn) *n.* any of a group of enzymes that contain a derivative of riboflavin linked to a protein and catalyse oxidation in cells.

flavour *or U.S.* **flavor** ('fleɪvə) *n.* **1.** taste perceived in food or liquid in the mouth. **2.** a substance added to food, etc., to impart a specific taste. **3.** a distinctive quality or atmosphere. **4.** *Physics.* a hypothetical property of particles that distinguishes one from another. ~*vb.* **5.** (*tr.*) to impart a flavour or quality to. [C14: from OF *flaour,* from LL *flātor* (unattested) bad smell, breath, from L *flāre* to blow] — **'flavourless** *or U.S.* **'flavorless** *adj.* — **'flavourful** *or U.S.* **'flavorful** *adj.*

flavour enhancer *n.* another term for **monosodium glutamate.**

flavouring *or U.S.* **flavoring** ('fleɪvərɪŋ) *n.* a substance used to impart a particular flavour to food: *rum flavouring.*

flaw¹ (flɔː) *n.* **1.** an imperfection or blemish. **2.** a crack or rift. **3.** *Law.* an invalidating defect in a document or proceeding. ~*vb.* **4.** to make or become blemished or imperfect. [C14: prob. from ON *flaga* stone slab] — **'flawless** *adj.*

flaw² (flɔː) *n.* a sudden short gust of wind; squall. [C16: of Scand. origin]

flax (flæks) *n.* **1.** a herbaceous plant or shrub that has blue flowers and is cultivated for its seeds (flaxseed) and for the fibres of its stems. **2.** the fibre of this plant, made into thread and woven into linen fabrics. **3.** any of various similar plants. **4.** *N.Z.* a swamp plant producing a fibre that is used by Maoris for decorative work, baskets, etc. [OE *fleax*]

flaxen ('flæksən) *adj.* **1.** of or resembling flax. **2.** of a soft yellow colour: *flaxen hair.*

Flaxman ('flæksmən) *n.* **John.** 1755–1826, English neoclassical sculptor and draughtsman, noted particularly for his monuments and his engraved illustrations for the *Iliad,* the *Odyssey,* and works by Dante and Aeschylus.

flaxseed ('flæks,siːd) *n.* the seed of the flax plant, which yields linseed oil. Also called: **linseed.**

flay (fleɪ) *vb.* (*tr.*) **1.** to strip off the skin or outer covering of, esp. by whipping. **2.** to attack with savage criticism. [OE *flēan*] — **'flayer** *n.*

flea (fliː) *n.* **1.** a small wingless parasitic blood-sucking jumping insect living on the skin of mammals and birds. **2. flea in one's ear.** *Inf.* a sharp rebuke. [OE *flēah*]

fleabane ('fliː,beɪn) *n.* any of several plants, including one having purplish tubular flower heads with orange centres and one having yellow daisy-like flower heads, that are reputed to ward off fleas.

fleabite ('fliː,baɪt) *n.* **1.** the bite of a flea. **2.** a slight or trifling annoyance or discomfort.

flea-bitten *adj.* **1.** bitten by or infested with fleas. **2.** *Inf.* shabby or decrepit.

flea market *n.* an open-air market selling cheap and often second-hand goods.

fleapit ('fliː,pɪt) *n. Inf.* a shabby cinema or theatre.

fleawort ('fliː,wɜːt) *n.* **1.** any of various plants with yellow daisy-like flowers and rosettes of downy leaves. **2.** a Eurasian plantain whose seeds were formerly used as a flea repellent.

flèche (fleɪʃ, fleʃ) *n.* a slender spire, esp. over the intersection of the nave and transept ridges of a church roof. Also called: **spirelet.** [C18: from F: spire (lit.: arrow), prob. of Gmc origin]

fleck (flɛk) *n.* **1.** a small marking or streak. **2.** a speck: *a fleck of dust.* ~*vb.* **3.** (*tr.*) Also: **flecker.** to speckle. [C16: prob. from ON *flekkr* stain, spot]

Flecker ('flɛkə) *n.* **James Elroy.** 1884–1915, English poet and dramatist; author of *Hassan* (1922).

fled (flɛd) *vb.* the past tense and past participle of **flee.**

fledge (flɛdʒ) *vb.* (*tr.*) **1.** to feed and care for (a young bird) until it is able to fly. **2.** Also called: **fletch.** to fit (something, esp. an arrow) with a feather or feathers. **3.** to cover or adorn with or as if with feathers. [OE *-flycge*, as in *unflycge* unfledged; see FLY[1]]

fledgling *or* **fledgeling** ('flɛdʒlɪŋ) *n.* **1.** a young bird that has grown feathers. **2.** a young and inexperienced person.

flee (fliː) *vb.* **fleeing, fled. 1.** to run away from (a place, danger, etc.). **2.** (*intr.*) to run or move quickly. [OE *flēon*] —'**fleer** *n.*

fleece (fliːs) *n.* **1.** the coat of wool that covers the body of a sheep or similar animal. **2.** the wool removed from a single sheep. **3.** something resembling a fleece. **4.** sheepskin or a fabric with soft pile, used as a lining for coats, etc. ~*vb.* (*tr.*) **5.** to defraud or charge exorbitantly. **6.** another term for **shear** (sense 1). [OE *flēos*]

fleecie ('fliːsɪ) *n. N.Z.* a person who collects fleeces after shearing and prepares them for baling. Also called: **fleece-oh.**

fleecy ('fliːsɪ) *adj.* **fleecier, fleeciest.** of or resembling fleece. —'**fleecily** *adv.*

fleer (flɪə) *Arch.* ~*vb.* **1.** to scoff; sneer. ~*n.* **2.** a derisory glance. [C14: from ON; cf. Norwegian *flire* to snigger]

fleet[1] (fliːt) *n.* **1.** a number of warships organized as a tactical unit. **2.** all the warships of a nation. **3.** a number of aircraft, ships, buses, etc., operating together or under the same ownership. [OE *flēot*]

fleet[2] (fliːt) *adj.* **1.** rapid in movement; swift. **2.** *Poetic.* fleeting. ~*vb.* **3.** (*intr.*) to move rapidly. **4.** (*tr.*) *Obs.* to cause (time) to pass rapidly. [prob. OE *flēotan* to float, glide rapidly] —'**fleetly** *adv.* —'**fleetness** *n.*

Fleet (fliːt) *n.* **the.** a stream that formerly ran into the Thames between Ludgate Hill and Fleet Street and is now a covered sewer.

Fleet Air Arm *n.* the aviation branch of the Royal Navy.

fleet chief petty officer *n.* a noncommissioned officer in the Royal Navy comparable in rank to a warrant officer in the army or the Royal Air Force.

fleeting ('fliːtɪŋ) *adj.* rapid and transient: *a fleeting glimpse of the sea.* —'**fleetingly** *adv.*

fleet rate *or* **rating** *n.* a reduced rate quoted by an insurance company to underwrite the risks to a fleet of vehicles, aircraft, etc.

Fleet Street *n.* **1.** a street in central London in which many newspaper offices are situated. **2.** British journalism or journalists collectively.

Fleetwood ('fliːt,wʊd) *n.* a fishing port in NW England, in Lancashire. Pop.: 28 467 (1981).

Fleming[1] ('flɛmɪŋ) *n.* a native or inhabitant of Flanders or of Flemish-speaking Belgium.

Fleming[2] ('flɛmɪŋ) *n.* **1. Sir Alexander.** 1881–1955, Scottish bacteriologist: discovered lysozyme (1922) and penicillin (1928): shared the Nobel prize for physiology or medicine in 1945. **2. Ian (Lancaster).** 1908–64, English

author of spy novels; creator of the secret agent James Bond. **3. Sir John Ambrose.** 1849–1945, English electrical engineer: invented the thermionic valve (1904).

Flemish ('flɛmɪʃ) *n.* **1.** one of the two official languages of Belgium. **2. the Flemish.** (*functioning as pl.*) the Flemings collectively. ~*adj.* **3.** of or characteristic of Flanders, the Flemings, or their language.

Flensburg (*German* 'flɛnsbʊrk) *n.* a port in N West Germany, in Schleswig-Holstein: taken from Denmark by Prussia in 1864; voted to remain German in 1920. Pop.: 86 700 (1984 est.).

flense (flɛns), **flench** (flɛntʃ), *or* **flinch** (flɪntʃ) *vb.* (*tr.*) to strip (a whale, seal, etc.) of (its blubber or skin). [C19: from Danish *flense*; rel. to Du. *flensen*]

flesh (flɛʃ) *n.* **1.** the soft part of the body of an animal or human, esp. muscular tissue, as distinct from bone and viscera. **2.** *Inf.* excess weight; fat. **3.** *Arch.* the edible tissue of animals as opposed to that of fish or, sometimes, fowl. **4.** the thick soft part of a fruit or vegetable. **5.** the human body and its physical or sensual nature as opposed to the soul or spirit. Related adj.: **carnal. 6.** mankind in general. **7.** animate creatures in general. **8.** one's own family; kin (esp. in **one's own flesh and blood**). **9. a.** a yellowish-pink colour. **b.** (*as adj.*): *flesh tights.* **10. in the flesh.** in person; actually present. ~*vb.* **11.** (*tr.*) *Hunting.* to stimulate the hunting instinct of (hounds or falcons) by giving them small quantities of raw flesh. **12.** *Arch. or poetic.* to accustom or incite to bloodshed or battle by initial experience. **13.** to fatten; fill out. [OE *flǣsc*]

fleshings ('flɛʃɪŋz) *pl. n.* flesh-coloured tights.

fleshly ('flɛʃlɪ) *adj.* **-lier, -liest. 1.** relating to the body; carnal: *fleshly desire.* **2.** worldly as opposed to spiritual. **3.** fat. —'**fleshliness** *n.*

flesh out *vb.* (*adv.*) **1.** (*tr.*) to give substance to (an argument, description, etc.). **2.** (*intr.*) to expand or become more substantial.

fleshpots ('flɛʃ,pɒts) *pl. n. Often facetious.* **1.** luxurious living. **2.** places where bodily desires are gratified. [C16: from the Biblical use as applied to Egypt (Exodus 16:3)]

flesh wound (wuːnd) *n.* a wound affecting superficial tissues.

fleshy ('flɛʃɪ) *adj.* **fleshier, fleshiest. 1.** plump. **2.** related to or resembling flesh. **3.** *Bot.* (of some fruits, etc.) thick and pulpy. —'**fleshiness** *n.*

fletcher ('flɛtʃə) *n.* a person who makes arrows. [C14: from OF *flechier*, from *fleche* arrow; see FLÈCHE]

Fletcher ('flɛtʃə) *n.* **John.** 1579–1625, English Jacobean dramatist, noted for his romantic tragicomedies written in collaboration with Francis Beaumont, esp. *Philaster* (1610) and *The Maid's Tragedy* (1611).

fleur-de-lis *or* **fleur-de-lys** (,flɜːdə'liː) *n., pl.* **fleurs-de-lis** *or* **fleurs-de-lys** (,flɜːdə'liːz). **1.** *Heraldry.* a charge representing a lily with three distinct petals. **2.** another name for **iris** (sense 2). [C19: from OF *flor de lis*, lit.: lily flower]

fleurette *or* **fleuret** (flʊə'rɛt) *n.* an ornament or motif resembling a flower. [C19: F, lit.: a small flower, from *fleur* flower]

Fleury (*French* flœri) *n.* **André Hercule de** (ɑ̃dre ɛrkyl də). 1653–1743, French cardinal and statesman: Louis XV's chief adviser and virtual ruler of France (1726–43).

flew (fluː) *vb.* the past tense of **fly**[1].

flews (fluːz) *pl. n.* the fleshy hanging upper lip of a bloodhound or similar dog. [C16: from ?]

flex (flɛks) *n.* **1.** *Brit.* a flexible insulated electric cable, used esp. to connect appliances to mains. U.S. and Canad. name: **cord.** ~*vb.* **2.** to bend or be bent: *he flexed his arm.* **3.** to contract (a muscle) or (of a muscle) to contract. **4.** (*intr.*) to work flexitime. [C16: from L *flexus* bent, winding, from *flectere* to bend, bow]

flexible ('flɛksɪb°l) *adj.* **1.** Also **flexile** ('flɛksaɪl). able to be bent easily without breaking. **2.** adaptable or variable: *flexible working hours.* **3.** able to be persuaded easily. —,**flexi'bility** *n.* —'**flexibly** *adv.*

flexion ('flɛkʃən) *or* **flection** *n.* **1.** the act of bending a joint or limb. **2.** the condition of the joint or limb so bent. —'**flexional** *adj.*

flexitime ('flɛksɪ,taɪm) *n.* a system permitting flexibility of working hours at the beginning or end of the day, provided an agreed period (**core time**) is spent at work. Also called: **flextime.**

flexor ('flɛksə) *n.* any muscle whose contraction serves to bend a joint or limb. Cf. **extensor.** [C17: NL; see FLEX]

flexuous ('flɛksjʊəs) *adj.* full of bends or curves; winding. [C17: from L *flexuōsus* full of bends, tortuous, from *flexus* a bending; see FLEX] — **'flexuously** *adv.*

flexure ('flɛkʃə) *n.* **1.** the act of flexing or the state of being flexed. **2.** a bend, turn, or fold.

flibbertigibbet ('flɪbətɪ,dʒɪbɪt) *n.* an irresponsible, silly, or gossipy person. [C15: from ?]

flick[1] (flɪk) *vb.* **1.** (*tr.*) to touch with or as if with the finger or hand in a quick jerky movement. **2.** (*tr.*) to propel or remove by a quick jerky movement, usually of the fingers or hand. **3.** to move or cause to move quickly or jerkily. **4.** (*intr.*; foll. by *through*) to read or look at (a book, etc.) quickly or idly. ~*n.* **5.** a tap or quick stroke with the fingers, a whip, etc. **6.** the sound made by such a stroke. **7.** a fleck or particle. [C15: imit.; cf. F *flicflac*]

flick[2] (flɪk) *n. Sl.* **1.** a cinema film. **2. the flicks.** the cinema: *what's on at the flicks tonight?*

flicker[1] ('flɪkə) *vb.* **1.** (*intr.*) to shine with an unsteady or intermittent light. **2.** (*intr.*) to move quickly to and fro. **3.** (*tr.*) to cause to flicker. ~*n.* **4.** an unsteady or brief light or flame. **5.** a swift quivering or fluttering movement. [OE *flicorian*]

flicker[2] ('flɪkə) *n.* a North American woodpecker which has a yellow undersurface to the wings and tail. [C19: ? imit. of the bird's call]

flick knife *n.* a knife with a retractable blade that springs out when a button is pressed.

flier *or* **flyer** ('flaɪə) *n.* **1.** a person or thing that flies or moves very fast. **2.** an aviator or pilot. **3.** *Inf.* a long flying leap. **4.** a rectangular step in a straight flight of stairs. Cf. **winder** (sense 5). **5.** *Athletics. inf.* a flying start. **6.** *Chiefly U.S.* a speculative business transaction.

flight[1] (flaɪt) *n.* **1.** the act, skill, or manner of flying. **2.** a journey made by a flying animal or object. **3.** a group of flying birds or aircraft: *a flight of swallows.* **4.** the basic tactical unit of a military air force. **5.** a journey through space, esp. of a spacecraft. **6.** an aircraft flying on a scheduled journey. **7.** a soaring mental journey above or beyond the normal everyday world: *a flight of fancy.* **8.** a single line of hurdles across a track in a race. **9.** a feather or plastic attachment fitted to an arrow or dart to give it stability in flight. **10.** a set of steps or stairs between one landing or floor and the next. ~*vb.* (*tr.*) **11.** *Sport.* to cause (a ball, dart, etc.) to float slowly towards its target. **12.** to shoot (a bird) in flight. **13.** to fledge (an arrow or dart). [OE *flyht*]

flight[2] (flaɪt) *n.* **1.** the act of fleeing or running away, as from danger. **2. put to flight.** to cause to run away. **3. take (to) flight.** to run away; flee. [OE *flyht* (unattested)]

flight deck *n.* **1.** the crew compartment in an airliner. **2.** the upper deck of an aircraft carrier from which aircraft take off.

flightless ('flaɪtlɪs) *adj.* (of certain birds and insects) unable to fly. See also **ratite.**

flight lieutenant *n.* an officer holding a commissioned rank senior to a flying officer and junior to a squadron leader in the Royal Air Force.

flight path *n.* the course through the air of an aircraft, rocket, or projectile.

flight recorder *n.* an electronic device fitted to an aircraft for collecting and storing information concerning its performance in flight. It is often used to determine the cause of a crash. Also called: **black box.**

flight sergeant *n.* a noncommissioned officer in the Royal Air Force, junior in rank to that of master aircrew.

flight simulator *n.* a ground-training device that reproduces exactly the conditions experienced on the flight deck of an aircraft.

flighty ('flaɪtɪ) *adj.* **flightier, flightiest. 1.** frivolous and irresponsible. **2.** mentally erratic or wandering. — **'flightiness** *n.*

flimflam ('flɪm,flæm) *Inf.* ~*n.* **1. a.** nonsense; rubbish; foolishness. **b.** (*as modifier*): *flimflam arguments.* **2.** a deception; trick; swindle. ~*vb.* **-flamming, -flammed. 3.** (*tr.*) to deceive; trick; swindle; cheat. [C16: prob. of Scand. origin] — **'flim,flammer** *n.*

flimsy ('flɪmzɪ) *adj.* **-sier, -siest. 1.** not strong or substantial: *a flimsy building.* **2.** light and thin: *a flimsy dress.* **3.** unconvincing; weak: *a flimsy excuse.* ~*n.* **4.** thin paper used for making carbon copies of a letter, etc. **5.** a copy made on this paper. [C17: from ?] — **'flimsiness** *n.*

flinch (flɪntʃ) *vb.* (*intr.*) **1.** to draw back suddenly, as from pain, shock, etc.; wince. **2.** (often foll. by *from*) to avoid contact (with): *he never flinched from his duty.* [C16: from OF *flenchir*; rel. to MHG *lenken* to bend, direct] — **'flinchingly** *adv.*

flinders ('flɪndəz) *pl. n. Rare.* small fragments or splinters (esp. in **fly into flinders**). [C15: prob. from ON; cf. Norwegian *flindra* thin piece of stone]

Flinders Island *n.* an island off the coast of NE Tasmania: the largest of the Furneaux Islands. Pop.: 1039 (1981). Area: 2077 sq. km (802 sq. miles).

Flinders Range *n.* a mountain range in E South Australia, between Lake Torrens and Lake Frome. Highest peak: 1188 m (3898 ft.).

fling (flɪŋ) *vb.* **flinging, flung.** (*mainly tr.*) **1.** to throw, esp. with force or abandon. **2.** to put or send without warning or preparation: *to fling someone into jail.* **3.** (*also intr.*) to move (oneself or a part of the body) with abandon or speed. **4.** (usually foll. by *into*) to apply (oneself) diligently and with vigour (to). **5.** to cast aside: *she flung away her scruples.* ~*n.* **6.** the act or an instance of flinging. **7.** a period or occasion of unrestrained or extravagant behaviour. **8.** any of various vigorous Scottish reels full of leaps and turns, such as the Highland fling. **9.** a trial; try: *to have a fling at something different.* [C13: from ON] — **'flinger** *n.*

flint (flɪnt) *n.* **1.** an impure greyish-black form of quartz that occurs in chalk. It produces sparks when struck with steel and is used in the manufacture of pottery and road-construction materials. Formula: SiO_2. **2.** any piece of flint, esp. one used as a primitive tool or for striking fire. **3.** a small cylindrical piece of an iron alloy, used in cigarette lighters. **4.** Also called: **flint glass.** colourless glass other than plate glass. [OE]

Flint (flɪnt) *n.* **1.** a town in NE Wales, in Clwyd, on the Dee estuary. Pop.: 16 454 (1981). **2.** a city in SE Michigan: car production. Pop.: 159 611 (1980).

flintlock ('flɪnt,lɒk) *n.* **1.** an obsolete gunlock in which the charge is ignited by a spark produced by a flint in the hammer. **2.** a firearm having such a lock.

Flintshire ('flɪnt,ʃɪə, -ʃə) *n.* (until 1974) a county of NE Wales, now part of Clwyd.

flinty ('flɪntɪ) *adj.* **flintier, flintiest. 1.** of or resembling flint. **2.** hard or cruel; unyielding. — **'flintily** *adv.* — **'flintiness** *n.*

flip (flɪp) *vb.* **flipping, flipped. 1.** to throw (something light or small) carelessly or briskly. **2.** to throw or flick (an object such as a coin) so that it turns or spins in the air. **3.** to flick: *to flip a crumb across the room.* **4.** (foll. by *through*) to read or look at (a book, etc.) quickly, idly, or incompletely. **5.** (*intr.*) to make a snapping movement or noise with the finger and thumb. **6.** (*intr.*) *Sl.* to fly into a rage or an emotional outburst (also in **flip one's lid, flip one's top**). ~*n.* **7.** a snap or tap, usually with the fingers. **8.** a rapid jerk. **9.** any alcoholic drink containing beaten egg. ~*adj.* **10.** *Inf.* flippant or pert. [C16: prob. imit.; see FILLIP]

flip-flop *n.* **1.** a backward handspring. **2.** an electronic device or circuit that can assume either of two states by the application of a suitable pulse. **3.** a complete change of opinion, policy, etc. **4.** a repeated flapping noise. **5.** Also called (esp. U.S., Austral., N.Z., and Canad.): **thong.** a rubber-soled sandal attached to the foot by a thong between the big toe and the next toe. ~*vb.* **-flopping, -flopped. 6.** (*intr.*) to move with repeated flaps. [C16: reduplication of FLIP]

flippant ('flɪpənt) *adj.* **1.** marked by inappropriate levity; frivolous. **2.** impertinent; saucy. [C17: ?from FLIP] — **'flippancy** *n.* — **'flippantly** *adv.*

flipper ('flɪpə) *n.* **1.** the flat broad limb of seals, whales, etc., specialized for swimming. **2.** (*often pl.*) either of a pair of rubber paddle-like devices worn on the feet as an aid in swimming.

flip side *n.* **1.** another term for **B-side. 2.** another, less familiar, aspect of a person or thing.

flirt (flɜːt) *vb.* **1.** (*intr.*) to behave or act amorously without emotional commitment. **2.** (*intr.*; usually foll. by *with*) to deal playfully or carelessly (with something dangerous or serious): *the motorcyclist flirted with death.* **3.** (*intr.*; usually foll. by *with*) to toy (with): *to flirt with the idea of leaving.* **4.** (*intr.*) to dart; flit. **5.** (*tr.*) to flick or toss. ~*n.* **6.** a person who acts flirtatiously. [C16: from ?] — **'flirter** *n.*

flirtation (flɜː'teɪʃən) *n.* **1.** behaviour intended to arouse sexual feelings or advances without emotional commitment. **2.** any casual involvement.

flirtatious (flɜː'teɪʃəs) *adj.* **1.** given to flirtation. **2.** expressive of playful sexual invitation: *a flirtatious glance.* — **flir'tatiously** *adv.*

flirty ('flɜːtɪ) *adj.* **flirtier, flirtiest. 1.** flirtatious. **2.** (of a skirt) full, frilly, and often short.

flit (flɪt) *vb.* **flitting, flitted.** (*intr.*) **1.** to move along rapidly and lightly. **2.** to fly rapidly and lightly. **3.** to pass quickly: *a memory flitted into his mind.* **4.** *Scot. & N English dialect.* to move house. **5.** *Brit. inf.* to depart hurriedly and stealthily in order to avoid obligations. ~*n.* **6.** the act or an instance of flitting. **7.** *Brit. inf.* a hurried and stealthy departure in order to avoid obligations. [C12: from ON *flytja* to carry] — **'flitter** *n.*

flitch (flɪtʃ) *n.* **1.** a side of pork salted and cured. **2.** a piece of timber cut lengthways from a tree trunk. [OE *flicce*; cf. FLESH]

flitter ('flɪtə) *vb.* a less common word for **flutter.**

flittermouse ('flɪtə,maʊs) *n., pl.* **-mice.** a dialect name for **bat**². [C16: translation of G *Fledermaus*]

float (fləʊt) *vb.* **1.** to rest or cause to rest on the surface of a fluid or in a fluid or space without sinking: *oil floats on water.* **2.** to move or cause to move buoyantly, lightly, or freely across a surface or through air, water, etc. **3.** to move about aimlessly, esp. in the mind: *thoughts floated before him.* **4.** (*tr.*) **a.** to launch or establish (a commercial enterprise, etc.). **b.** to offer for sale (stock or bond issues, etc.) on the stock market. **5.** (*tr.*) *Finance.* to allow (a currency) to fluctuate against other currencies in accordance with market forces. **6.** (*tr.*) to flood, inundate, or irrigate (land). ~*n.* **7.** something that floats. **8.** *Angling.* an indicator attached to a baited line that sits on the water and moves when a fish bites. **9.** a small hand tool with a rectangular blade used for smoothing plaster, etc. **10.** Also called: **paddle.** a blade of a paddle wheel. **11.** *Brit.* a buoyant garment or device to aid a person in staying afloat. **12.** a structure fitted to the underside of an aircraft to allow it to land on water. **13.** a motor vehicle used to carry a tableau or exhibit in a parade, esp. a civic parade. **14.** a small delivery vehicle, esp. one powered by batteries: *a milk float.* **15.** *Austral. & N.Z.* a vehicle for transporting horses. **16.** a sum of money used by shopkeepers to provide change at the start of the day's business. **17.** the hollow floating ball of a ballcock. [OE *flotian;* see FLEET²] — **'floatable** *adj.* — ,**floata'bility** *n.* — '**floaty** *adj.*

floatage ('fləʊtɪdʒ) *n.* a variant spelling of **flotage.**

floatation (fləʊ'teɪʃən) *n.* a variant spelling of **flotation.**

floatel (fləʊ'tɛl) *n.* a variant spelling of **flotel.**

floater ('fləʊtə) *n.* **1.** a person or thing that floats. **2.** a dark spot that appears in one's vision as a result of dead cells or cell fragments in the eye. **3.** *U.S. & Canad.* a person of no fixed political opinion. **4.** *U.S. inf.* a person who often changes employment, residence, etc.

float glass *n.* polished glass made by floating molten glass on liquid metal in a reservoir.

floating ('fləʊtɪŋ) *adj.* **1.** having little or no attachment. **2.** (of an organ or part) displaced from the normal position or abnormally movable: *a floating kidney.* **3.** uncommitted or unfixed: *floating voters.* **4.** *Finance.* **a.** (of capital) available for current use. **b.** (of debt) short-term and unfunded, usually raised to meet current expenses. **c.** (of a currency) free to fluctuate against other currencies in accordance with market forces. — '**floatingly** *adv.*

floating-point representation *n. Computers.* the representation of numbers by two sets of digits (*a, b*), the set *a* indicating the significant digits, the set *b* giving the position of the radix point. Also called: **floating decimal point representation.** Cf. **fixed-point representation.**

floating rib *n.* any rib of the lower two pairs of ribs in man, which are not attached to the breastbone.

floats (fləʊts) *pl. n. Theatre.* another word for **footlights.**

flocculate ('flɒkjʊ,leɪt) *vb.* to form or be formed into an aggregated flocculent mass. — ,**floccu'lation** *n.*

flocculent ('flɒkjʊlənt) *adj.* **1.** like wool; fleecy. **2.** *Chem.* aggregated in woolly cloudlike masses: *a flocculent precipitate.* **3.** *Biol.* covered with tufts or flakes. [C19: from L *floccus* FLOCK² + -ULENT] — '**flocculence** *n.*

flocculus ('flɒkjʊləs) *n., pl.* **-li** (-,laɪ). **1.** a cloudy marking on the sun's surface. It consists of calcium when lighter than the surroundings and of hydrogen when

darker. **2.** *Anat.* a tiny prominence on each side of the cerebellum.

flock¹ (flɒk) *n.* (*sometimes functioning as pl.*) **1.** a group of animals of one kind, esp. sheep or birds. **2.** a large number of people. **3.** a body of Christians regarded as the pastoral charge of a priest, bishop, etc. ~*vb.* (*intr.*) **4.** to gather together or move in a flock. **5.** to go in large numbers: *people flocked to the church.* [OE *flocc*]

flock² (flɒk) *n.* **1.** a tuft, as of wool, hair, cotton, etc. **2.** waste from fabrics such as cotton or wool used for stuffing mattresses, etc. **3.** Also called: **flocking.** very small tufts of wool applied to fabrics, wallpaper, etc., to give a raised pattern. [C13: from OF *floc,* from L *floccus*] — '**flocky** *adj.*

Flodden ('flɒdʰn) *n.* a hill in Northumberland where invading Scots were defeated by the English in 1513 and James IV of Scotland was killed. Also called: **Flodden Field.**

floe (fləʊ) *n.* See **ice floe.** [C19: prob. from Norwegian *flo* slab, layer, from ON; see FLAW¹]

flog (flɒg) *vb.* **flogging, flogged. 1.** (*tr.*) to beat harshly, esp. with a whip, strap, etc. **2.** *Brit. sl.* to sell. **3.** (*intr.*) to make progress by painful work. **4. flog a dead horse.** *Chiefly Brit.* **a.** to harp on some long discarded subject. **b.** to pursue the solution of a problem long realized to be insoluble. [C17: prob. from L *flagellāre;* see FLAGELLANT] — '**flogger** *n.*

flong (flɒŋ) *n. Printing.* a material used for making moulds in stereotyping. [C20: var. of FLAN]

flood (flʌd) *n.* **1. a.** the inundation of land that is normally dry through the overflowing of a body of water, esp. a river. **b.** the state of a river that is at an abnormally high level. Related adj.: **diluvial. 2.** a great outpouring or flow: *a flood of words.* **3. a.** the rising of the tide from low to high water. **b.** (*as modifier*): *the flood tide.* Cf. **ebb** (sense 3). **4.** *Theatre.* short for **floodlight.** ~*vb.* **5.** (of water) to inundate or submerge (land) or (of land) to be inundated or submerged. **6.** to fill or be filled to overflowing, as with a flood. **7.** (*intr.*) to flow; surge: *relief flooded through him.* **8.** to supply an excessive quantity of petrol to (a carburettor or petrol engine) or (of a carburettor, etc.) to be supplied with such an excess. **9.** (*intr.*) to overflow. **10.** (*intr.*) to bleed profusely from the uterus, as following childbirth. [OE *flōd;* see FLOW, FLOAT]

Flood (flʌd) *n. Old Testament.* **the.** the flood from which Noah and his family and livestock were saved in the ark (Genesis 7–8).

floodgate ('flʌd,geɪt) *n.* **1.** Also called: **head gate, water gate.** a gate in a sluice that is used to control the flow of water. **2.** (*often pl.*) a control or barrier against an outpouring or flow.

floodlight ('flʌd,laɪt) *n.* **1.** a broad intense beam of artificial light, esp. as used in the theatre or to illuminate the exterior of buildings. **2.** the lamp producing such light. ~*vb.* **-lighting, -lit. 3.** (*tr.*) to illuminate as by floodlight.

flood plain *n.* the flat area bordering a river, composed of sediment deposited during flooding.

floor (flɔː) *n.* **1.** Also called: **flooring.** the inner lower surface of a room. **2.** a storey of a building: *the second floor.* **3.** a flat bottom surface in or on any structure: *a dance floor.* **4.** the bottom surface of a tunnel, cave, sea, etc. **5.** that part of a legislative hall in which debate and other business is conducted. **6.** the right to speak in a legislative body (esp. in **get, have,** *or* **be given the floor**). **7.** the room in a stock exchange where trading takes place. **8.** the earth; ground. **9.** a minimum price charged or paid. **10. take the floor.** to begin dancing on a dance floor. ~*vb.* **11.** to cover with or construct a floor. **12.** (*tr.*) to knock to the floor or ground. **13.** (*tr.*) *Inf.* to disconcert, confound, or defeat. [OE *flōr*]

floorboard ('flɔː,bɔːd) *n.* one of the boards forming a floor.

flooring ('flɔːrɪŋ) *n.* **1.** the material used in making a floor. **2.** another word for **floor** (sense 1).

floor manager *n.* **1.** the stage manager of a television programme. **2.** a person in overall charge of one floor of a large shop.

floor plan *n.* a drawing to scale of the arrangement of rooms on one floor of a building.

floor show *n.* a series of entertainments, such as singing and dancing, performed in a nightclub.

floozy, floozie, or **floosie** ('flu:zı) n., pl. **-zies** or **-sies.** Sl. a disreputable woman. [C20: from ?]

flop (flɒp) vb. **flopping, flopped. 1.** (intr.) to bend, fall, or collapse loosely or carelessly: his head flopped backwards. **2.** (when intr., often foll. by into, onto, etc.) to fall, cause to fall, or move with a sudden noise. **3.** (intr.) Inf. to fail: the scheme flopped. **4.** (intr.) to fall flat onto the surface of water. **5.** (intr.; often foll. by out) Sl. to go to sleep. ~n. **6.** the act of flopping. **7.** Inf. a complete failure. [C17: var. of FLAP]

floppy ('flɒpı) adj. **-pier, -piest. 1.** limp or hanging loosely. ~n. **2.** short for **floppy disk.** —'**floppily** adv. —'**floppiness** n.

floppy disk n. a flexible magnetic disk that stores information and can be used to store data in the memory of a digital computer.

flora ('flɔːrə) n., pl. **-ras** or **-rae** (-riː). **1.** all the plant life of a given place or time. **2.** a descriptive list of such plants, often including a key for identification. [C18: from NL, FLORA, from flōs FLOWER]

Flora ('flɔːrə) n. the Roman goddess of flowers. [C16: from L, from flōs flower]

floral ('flɔːrəl) adj. **1.** decorated with or consisting of flowers or patterns of flowers. **2.** of or associated with flowers. —'**florally** adv.

Florence ('flɒrəns) n. a city in central Italy, on the River Arno in Tuscany: became an independent republic in the 14th century; under Austrian and other rule intermittently from 1737 to 1859; capital of Italy 1865–70. It was the major cultural and artistic centre of the Renaissance and is still one of the world's chief art centres. Pop.: 425 835 (1986). Ancient name: **Florentia** (flɒ'rɛntsɪə, -rɛntɪə). Italian name: **Firenze.**

Florentine ('flɒrən,taın) adj. **1.** of or relating to Florence, in Italy. ~n. **2.** a native or inhabitant of Florence.

Flores ('flɔːrɛs) n. **1.** an island in Indonesia, one of the Lesser Sunda Islands, between the Flores Sea and the Savu Sea: mountainous, with active volcanoes and unexplored forests. Chief town: Ende. Area: 17 150 sq. km (6622 sq. miles). **2.** (also Portuguese **Florı**ʃ). an island in the Atlantic, the westernmost of the Azores. Chief town: Santa Cruz. Area: 142 sq. km (55 sq. miles).

florescence (flɔː'rɛsəns) n. the process, state, or period of flowering. [C18: from NL, from L flōrēscere to come into flower]

Flores Sea n. a part of the Pacific Ocean in Indonesia between Celebes and the Lesser Sunda Islands.

floret ('flɔːrɪt) n. a small flower, esp. one of many making up the head of a composite flower. [C17: from OF, from flor FLOWER]

Florey ('flɔːrı) n. **Howard Walter,** Baron Florey. 1898–1968, British pathologist: shared the Nobel prize for physiology or medicine (1945) with E. B. Chain and Alexander Fleming for their work on penicillin.

Florianópolis (Portuguese floriə'nɔpulis) n. a port in S Brazil, capital of Santa Caterina state, on the W coast of Santa Caterina Island. Pop.: 154 000 (1984 est.).

floriated or **floreated** ('flɔːrı,eıtıd) adj. Archit. having ornamentation based on flowers and leaves. [C19: from L flōs FLOWER]

floribunda (,flɔːrı'bʌndə) n. any of several varieties of cultivated hybrid roses whose flowers grow in large sprays. [C19: from NL, fem. of flōribundus flowering freely]

floriculture ('flɔːrı,kʌltʃə) n. the cultivation of flowering plants. —,**flori'cultural** adj. —,**flori'culturist** n.

florid ('flɒrıd) adj. **1.** having a red or flushed complexion. **2.** excessively ornate; flowery: florid architecture. [C17: from L flōridus blooming] —**flo'ridity** n. —'**floridly** adv.

Florida ('flɒrıdə) n. **1.** a state of the southeastern U.S., between the Atlantic and the Gulf of Mexico: consists mostly of a low-lying peninsula ending in the **Florida Keys,** a chain of small islands off the coast of S Florida, extending southwest for over 160 km (100 miles). Capital: Tallahassee. Pop.: 11 675 000 (1986 est.). Area: 143 900 sq. km (55 560 sq. miles). Abbrevs.: **Fla.** or (with zip code) **FL 2. Straits of.** a sea passage between the Florida Keys and Cuba, linking the Atlantic with the Gulf of Mexico. —**Flo'ridian** adj.

floriferous (flɔː'rıfərəs) adj. bearing or capable of bearing many flowers.

florin ('flɒrın) n. **1.** a former British coin, originally silver, equivalent to ten (new) pence. **2.** (formerly) another name for **guilder** (sense 1). [C14: from F, from OIt. fiorino Florentine coin, from fiore flower, from L flōs]

Florio ('flɔːrı,əʊ) n. **John.** ?1553–?1625, English lexicographer, noted for his translation of Montaigne's Essays (1603).

florist ('flɒrıst) n. a person who grows or deals in flowers.

floristic (flɒ'rıstık) adj. of or relating to flowers or a flora. —**flo'ristically** adv.

-florous adj. combining form. indicating number or type of flowers: tubuliflorous.

floruit Latin. ('flɒruːıt) vb. (he or she) flourished: used to indicate the period when a figure, whose birth and death dates are unknown, was most active.

floss (flɒs) n. **1.** the mass of fine silky fibres obtained from cotton and similar plants. **2.** any similar fine silky material. **3.** untwisted silk thread used in embroidery, etc. **4.** See **dental floss.** [C18: ?from OF flosche down]

flossy ('flɒsı) adj. **flossier, flossiest.** consisting of or resembling floss.

flotage or **floatage** ('fləʊtıdʒ) n. **1.** the act or state of floating. **2.** power or ability to float. **3.** flotsam.

flotation or **floatation** (fləʊ'teıʃən) n. **1. a.** the launching or financing of a commercial enterprise by bond or share issues. **b.** the raising of a loan or new capital by bond or share issues. **2.** power or ability to float. **3.** Also called: **froth flotation.** a process to concentrate the valuable ore in low-grade ores by using induced differences in surface tension to carry the valuable fraction to the surface.

flotel or **floatel** (fləʊ'tɛl) n. a rig used for accommodation of workers in off-shore oil fields. [C20: FLO(ATING) + (HO)TEL]

flotilla (flə'tılə) n. a small fleet or a fleet of small vessels. [C18: from Sp., from F flotte, ult. from ON floti]

Flotow (German 'flo:to) n. **Friedrich von** ('friːdrıç fɔn). 1812–83, German composer of operas, esp. Martha (1847).

flotsam ('flɒtsəm) n. **1.** wreckage from a ship found floating. Cf. **jetsam. 2.** odds and ends (esp. in **flotsam and jetsam**). **3.** vagrants. [C16: from Anglo-F floteson, from floter to FLOAT]

flounce[1] (flaʊns) vb. **1.** (intr.; often foll. by about, away, out, etc.) to move or go with emphatic movements. ~n. **2.** the act of flouncing. [C16: of Scand. origin]

flounce[2] (flaʊns) n. an ornamental gathered ruffle sewn to a garment by its top edge. [C18: from OF, from froncir to wrinkle, of Gmc origin]

flounder[1] ('flaʊndə) vb. (intr.) **1.** to move with difficulty, as in mud. **2.** to make mistakes. ~n. **3.** the act of floundering. [C16: prob. a blend of FOUNDER[2] + BLUNDER; ? infl. by FLOUNDER[2]]

flounder[2] ('flaʊndə) n., pl. **-der** or **-ders.** a European flatfish having a greyish-brown body covered with prickly scales: an important food fish. [C14: from ON]

flour ('flaʊə) n. **1.** a powder, which may be either fine or coarse, prepared by grinding the meal of a grass, esp. wheat. **2.** any finely powdered substance. ~vb. (tr.) **3.** to make (grain, etc.) into flour. **4.** to dredge or sprinkle (food or utensils) with flour. [C13 flur finer portion of meal, FLOWER] —'**floury** adj.

flourish ('flʌrıʃ) vb. **1.** (intr.) to thrive; prosper. **2.** (intr.) to be at the peak of condition. **3.** (intr.) to be healthy: plants flourish in the light. **4.** to wave or cause to wave in the air with sweeping strokes. **5.** to display or make a display. **6.** to play (a fanfare, etc.) on a musical intrument. ~n. **7.** the act of waving or brandishing. **8.** a showy gesture: he entered with a flourish. **9.** an ornamental embellishment in writing. **10.** a display of ornamental language or speech. **11.** a grandiose passage of music. [C13: from OF, ult. from L flōrēre to flower, from flōs a flower] —'**flourisher** n.

flout (flaʊt) vb. (when intr., usually foll. by at) to show contempt (for). [C16: ?from ME flouten to play the flute, from OF flauter] —'**floutingly** adv.

▷ **Usage.** Confusion sometimes arises between flout and flaunt although the meanings of the words are quite different. Flout, to defy or disregard, is typically used in relation to law or authority: both the law and the party rules were flouted by this disregard of precedent; be prepared to flout convention — serve red wine with your fish *course. Flaunt* implies a deliberate and ostentatious displaying of possessions, abilities, etc.: *she flaunted her large engagement ring; flaunting his indifference to the danger.*

flow (fləʊ) *vb.* (*mainly intr.*) **1.** (of liquids) to move or be conveyed as in a stream. **2.** (of blood) to circulate around the body. **3.** to move or progress freely as if in a stream: *the crowd flowed into the building.* **4.** to be produced continuously and effortlessly: *ideas flowed from her pen.* **5.** to be marked by smooth or easy movement. **6.** to hang freely or loosely: *her hair flowed down her back.* **7.** to be present in abundance: *wine flows at their parties.* **8.** (of tide water) to advance or rise. Cf. **ebb** (sense 1). **9.** (of rocks such as slate) to yield to pressure so that the structure and arrangement of the constituent minerals are altered. ~*n.* **10.** the act, rate, or manner of flowing: *a fast flow.* **11.** a continuous stream or discharge. **12.** continuous progression. **13.** the advancing of the tide. **14.** *Scot.* **a.** a marsh or swamp. **b.** an inlet or basin of the sea. **c.** (*cap. when part of a name*): *Scapa Flow.* [OE *flōwan*]

flow chart *or* **sheet** *n.* a diagrammatic representation of the sequence of operations in an industrial process, computer program, etc.

flower ('flaʊə) *n.* **1. a.** a bloom or blossom on a plant. **b.** a plant that bears blooms or blossoms. **2.** the reproductive structure of angiosperm plants, consisting of stamens and carpels surrounded by petals and sepals. In some plants it is brightly coloured and attracts insects for pollination. Related adj.: **floral**. **3.** any similar reproductive structure in other plants. **4.** the prime; peak: *in the flower of his youth.* **5.** the choice or finest product, part, or representative. **6.** a decoration or embellishment. **7.** (*pl.*) fine powder, usually produced by sublimation: *flowers of sulphur.* ~*vb.* **8.** (*intr.*) to produce flowers; bloom. **9.** (*intr.*) to reach full growth or maturity. **10.** (*tr.*) to deck or decorate with flowers or floral designs. [C13: from OF *flor*, from L *flōs*] — **'flowerless** *adj.* — **'flower-,like** *adj.*

flowered ('flaʊəd) *adj.* **1.** having flowers. **2.** decorated with flowers or a floral design.

floweret ('flaʊərɪt) *n.* another name for **floret**.

flower girl *n.* a girl or woman who sells flowers in the street.

flowering ('flaʊərɪŋ) *adj.* (of certain species of plants) capable of producing conspicuous flowers.

flowerpot ('flaʊə,pɒt) *n.* a pot in which plants are grown.

flower power *n. Inf.* a youth cult of the late 1960s advocating peace and love; associated with drug-taking. Its adherents were known as **flower children** or **flower people.**

flowery ('flaʊərɪ) *adj.* **1.** abounding in flowers. **2.** decorated with flowers or floral patterns. **3.** like or suggestive of flowers. **4.** (of language or style) elaborate. — **'flow-eriness** *n.*

flown (fləʊn) *vb.* the past participle of **fly**¹.

flow-on *n. Austral. & N.Z.* **a.** a wage or salary increase granted to one group of workers as a consequence of a similar increase granted to another group. **b.** (*as modifier*): *a flow-on effect.*

fl. oz. *abbrev. for* fluid ounce.

flu (fluː) *n. Inf.* **1.** (often preceded by *the*) short for **influenza**. **2.** any of various viral infections, esp. a respiratory or intestinal infection.

fluctuate ('flʌktjʊ,eɪt) *vb.* **1.** to change or cause to change position constantly. **2.** (*intr.*) to rise and fall like a wave. [C17: from L, from *fluctus* a wave, from *fluere* to flow] — **'fluctuant** *adj.* — **,fluctu'ation** *n.*

flue (fluː) *n.* a shaft, tube, or pipe, esp. as used in a chimney, to carry off smoke, gas, etc. [C16: from ?]

fluent ('fluːənt) *adj.* **1.** able to speak or write a specified foreign language with facility. **2.** spoken or written with facility. **3.** graceful in motion or shape. **4.** flowing or able to flow freely. [C16: from L: flowing, from *fluere* to flow] — **'fluency** *n.* — **'fluently** *adv.*

flue pipe *or* **flue** *n.* an organ pipe whose sound is produced by the passage of air across a fissure in the side, as distinguished from a **reed pipe.**

fluff (flʌf) *n.* **1.** soft light particles, such as the down or nap of cotton or wool. **2.** any light showy substance. **3.** *Inf.* a mistake, esp. in speaking or reading lines or performing music. **4.** *Inf.* a young woman (esp. in **a bit of fluff**). ~*vb.* **5.** to make or become soft and puffy. **6.** *Inf.* to make a mistake in performing (an action, music, etc.). [C18: ?from *flue* downy matter]

fluffy ('flʌfɪ) *adj.* **fluffier, fluffiest. 1.** of, resembling, or covered with fluff. **2.** soft and light. — **'fluffily** *adv.* — **'fluffiness** *n.*

flugelhorn ('fluːgl,hɔːn) *n.* a type of valved brass instrument consisting of a tube of conical bore with a cup-shaped mouthpiece, used esp. in brass bands. [G, from *Flügel* wing + *Horn* HORN]

fluid ('fluːɪd) *n.* **1.** a substance, such as a liquid or gas, that can flow, has no fixed shape, and offers little resistance to an external stress. ~*adj.* **2.** capable of flowing and easily changing shape. **3.** of or using a fluid or fluids. **4.** constantly changing or apt to change. **5.** flowing. [C15: from L, from *fluere* to flow] — **'fluidal** *adj.* — **flu'idity** *or* **'fluidness** *n.*

fluidics (fluː'ɪdɪks) *n.* (*functioning as sing.*) the study and use of systems in which the flow of fluids in tubes simulates the flow of electricity in conductors. — **flu'idic** *adj.*

fluidize *or* **-dise** ('fluːɪ,daɪz) *vb.* (*tr.*) to make fluid, esp. to make (solids) fluid by pulverizing them so that they can be transported in gas as if they were liquids. — **,fluidi'zation** *or* **-di'sation** *n.*

fluid mechanics *n.* (*functioning as sing.*) the study of the mechanical and flow properties of fluids, esp. as they apply to practical engineering. Also called: **hydraulics.**

fluid ounce *n.* **1.** *Brit.* a unit of capacity equal to one twentieth of an Imperial pint. **2.** *U.S.* a unit of capacity equal to one sixteenth of a U.S. pint.

fluke¹ (fluːk) *n.* **1.** a flat bladelike projection at the end of the arm of an anchor. **2.** either of the two lobes of the tail of a whale. **3.** the barb of a harpoon, arrow, etc. [C16: ? a special use of FLUKE³ (in the sense: a flounder)]

fluke² (fluːk) *n.* **1.** an accidental stroke of luck. **2.** any chance happening. ~*vb.* **3.** (*tr.*) to gain, make, or hit by a fluke. [C19: from ?]

fluke³ (fluːk) *n.* any parasitic flatworm, such as the blood fluke and liver fluke. [OE *flōc*; rel. to ON *flóki* flounder]

fluky *or* **flukey** ('fluːkɪ) *adj.* **flukier, flukiest.** *Inf.* **1.** done or gained by an accident, esp. a lucky one. **2.** variable; uncertain. — **'flukiness** *n.*

flume (fluːm) *n.* **1.** a ravine through which a stream flows. **2.** a narrow artificial channel made for providing water for power, floating logs, etc. ~*vb.* **3.** (*tr.*) to transport (logs) in a flume. [C12: from OF, ult. from L *flūmen* stream, from *fluere* to flow]

flummery ('flʌmərɪ) *n.*, *pl.* **-meries. 1.** *Inf.* meaningless flattery. **2.** *Chiefly Brit.* a cold pudding of oatmeal, etc. [C17: from Welsh *llymru*]

flummox ('flʌməks) *vb.* (*tr.*) to perplex or bewilder. [C19: from ?]

flung (flʌŋ) *vb.* the past tense and past participle of **fling.**

flunk (flʌŋk) *Inf.*, *U.S.*, *Canad.*, & *N.Z.* ~*vb.* **1.** to fail or cause to fail to reach the required standard in (an examination, course, etc.). **2.** (*intr.*; foll. by *out*) to be dismissed from a school. [C19: ?from FLINCH + FUNK¹]

flunky *or* **flunkey** ('flʌŋkɪ) *n.*, *pl.* **flunkies** *or* **flunkeys. 1.** a servile person. **2.** a person who performs menial tasks. **3.** *Usually derog.* a manservant in livery. [C18: ?]

fluor ('fluːɔː) *n.* another name for **fluorspar.** [C17: from L: a flowing; so called from its use as a metallurgical flux]

fluor- *combining form.* a variant of **fluoro-** before a vowel: *fluorine.*

fluoresce (,fluə'rɛs) *vb.* (*intr.*) to exhibit fluorescence. [C19: back formation from FLUORESCENCE]

fluorescence (,fluə'rɛsəns) *n.* **1.** *Physics.* **a.** the emission of light or other radiation from atoms or molecules that are bombarded by particles, such as electrons, or by radiation from a separate source. **b.** an emission of photons that ceases as soon as the bombarding radiation is discontinued. **2.** the radiation emitted as a result of fluorescence. Cf. **phosphorescence.** [C19: FLUOR + -*escence* (as in *opalescence*)] — **,fluo'rescent** *adj.*

fluorescent lamp *n.* a type of lamp in which ultraviolet radiation from an electrical gas discharge causes a thin layer of phosphor on a tube's inside surface to fluoresce.

fluoridate ('fluərɪ,deɪt) *vb.* to subject (water) to fluoridation.

fluoridation (,fluərɪ'deɪʃən) *n.* the addition of fluorides to the public water supply as a protection against tooth decay.

fluoride ('fluə,raɪd) n. **1.** any salt of hydrofluoric acid, containing the fluoride ion, F⁻. **2.** any compound containing fluorine, such as methyl fluoride.

fluorinate ('fluərɪ,neɪt) vb. to treat or combine with fluorine. —,fluori'nation n.

fluorine ('fluəri:n) n. a toxic pungent pale yellow gas of the halogen group that is the most electronegative and reactive of all the elements: used in the production of uranium, fluorocarbons, and other chemicals. Symbol: F; atomic no.: 9; atomic wt.: 18.998.

fluorite ('fluəraɪt) n. the U.S. and Canad. name for **fluorspar.**

fluoro- or before a vowel **fluor-** combining form. **1.** indicating the presence of fluorine: fluorocarbon. **2.** indicating fluorescence: fluoroscope.

fluorocarbon (,fluərəʊ'ka:bʰn) n. any compound derived by replacing all or some of the hydrogen atoms in hydrocarbons by fluorine atoms. Many of them are used as lubricants, solvents, coatings, and aerosol propellants. See also **Freon.**

fluorometer (,fluə'rɒmɪtə) or **fluorimeter** (,fluə'rɪmɪtə) n. a device for detecting and measuring ultraviolet radiation by determining the amount of fluorescence that it produces from a phosphor.

fluoroscope ('fluərə,skəʊp) n. a device consisting of a fluorescent screen and an x-ray source that enables an x-ray image of an object, person, or part to be observed directly.

fluoroscopy (fluə'rɒskəpɪ) n. examination of a person or object by means of a fluoroscope.

fluorosis (fluə'rəʊsɪs) n. fluoride poisoning, due to ingestion of too much fluoride.

fluorspar ('fluə,spa:), **fluor,** or U.S. & Canad. **fluorite** n. a white or colourless soft mineral, sometimes fluorescent or tinted by impurities, consisting of calcium fluoride (CaF) in crystalline form: the chief ore of fluorine.

flurry ('flʌrɪ) n., pl. **-ries. 1.** a sudden commotion. **2.** a light gust of wind or rain or fall of snow. ~vb. **-rying, -ried. 3.** to confuse or bewilder or be confused or bewildered. [C17: from obs. flurr to scatter, ? formed on analogy with HURRY]

flush¹ (flʌʃ) vb. **1.** to blush or cause to blush. **2.** to flow or flood or cause to flow or flood with or as if with water. **3.** to glow or shine or cause to glow or shine with a rosy colour. **4.** to send a volume of water quickly through (a pipe, etc.) or into (a toilet) for the purpose of cleansing, etc. **5.** (tr.; usually passive) to excite or elate. ~n. **6.** a rosy colour, esp. in the cheeks. **7.** a sudden flow or gush, as of water. **8.** a feeling of excitement or elation: the flush of success. **9.** freshness: the flush of youth. **10.** redness of the skin, as from the effects of a fever, alcohol, etc. [C16: (in the sense: to gush forth): ?from FLUSH³] —'flusher n.

flush² (flʌʃ) adj. (usually postpositive) **1.** level or even with another surface. **2.** directly adjacent; continuous. **3.** Inf. having plenty of money. **4.** Inf. abundant or plentiful, as money. **5.** full to the brim. ~adv. **6.** so as to be level or even. **7.** directly or squarely. ~vb. (tr.) **8.** to cause (surfaces) to be on the same level or in the same plane. ~n. **9.** a period of fresh growth of leaves, shoots, etc. [C16: prob. from FLUSH¹ (in the sense: spring out)] —'flushness n.

flush³ (flʌʃ) vb. (tr.) to rouse (game, etc.) and put to flight. [C13 flusshen, ? imit.]

flush⁴ (flʌʃ) n. (in poker and similar games) a hand containing only one suit. [C16: from OF, from L fluxus FLUX]

Flushing ('flʌʃɪŋ) n. a port in the SW Netherlands, in Zeeland province, on Walcheren Island, at the mouth of the West Scheldt river: the first Dutch city to throw off Spanish rule (1572). Pop.: 45 742 (1984 est.). Dutch name: **Vlissingen.**

fluster ('flʌstə) vb. **1.** to make or become nervous or upset. ~n. **2.** a state of confusion or agitation. [C15: from ON]

flute (flu:t) n. **1.** a wind instrument consisting of an open cylindrical tube of wood or metal having holes in the side stopped either by the fingers or by pads controlled by keys. The breath is directed across a mouth hole cut in the side. **2.** Archit. a rounded shallow concave groove on the shaft of a column, pilaster, etc. ~vb. **3.** to produce or utter (sounds) in the manner or tone of a flute. **4.** (tr.) to make grooves or furrows in. [C14: from OF flahute, from

Vulgar L flabeolum (unattested); ? also infl. by OF laut lute] —'flute,like adj. —'fluty adj.

fluting ('flu:tɪŋ) n. a design or decoration of flutes on a column, pilaster, etc.

flutist ('flu:tɪst) n. Now chiefly U.S. a variant spelling of **flautist.**

flutter ('flʌtə) vb. **1.** to wave or cause to wave rapidly. **2.** (intr.) (of birds, butterflies, etc.) to flap the wings. **3.** (intr.) to move, esp. downwards, with an irregular motion. **4.** (intr.) Pathol. (of the heart) to beat abnormally rapidly, esp. in a regular rhythm. **5.** to be or make nervous or restless. **6.** (intr.) to move about restlessly. ~n. **7.** a quick flapping or vibrating motion. **8.** a state of nervous excitement or confusion. **9.** excited interest; stir. **10.** Brit. inf. a modest bet or wager. **11.** Pathol. an abnormally rapid beating of the heart, esp. in a regular rhythm. **12.** Electronics. a slow variation in pitch in a sound-reproducing system, similar to wow but occurring at higher frequencies. **13.** a potentially dangerous oscillation of an aircraft, or part of an aircraft. **14.** Also called: **flutter tonguing.** Music. a method of sounding a wind instrument, esp. the flute, with a rolling movement of the tongue. [OE floterian to float to and fro] —'flutterer n. —'fluttery adj.

fluvial ('flu:vɪəl) adj. of or occurring in a river: fluvial deposits. [C14: from L, from fluvius river, from fluere to flow]

flux (flʌks) n. **1.** a flow or discharge. **2.** continuous change; instability. **3.** a substance, such as borax or salt, that gives a low melting-point mixture with a metal oxide to assist in fusion. **4.** Metallurgy. a chemical used to increase the fluidity of refining slags. **5.** Physics. **a.** the rate of flow of particles, energy, or a fluid, such as that of neutrons (**neutron flux**) or of light energy (**luminous flux**). **b.** the strength of a field in a given area: magnetic flux. **6.** Pathol. an excessive discharge of fluid from the body, such as watery faeces in diarrhoea. ~vb. **7.** to make or become fluid. **8.** (tr.) to apply flux to (a metal, soldered joint, etc.). [C14: from L fluxus a flow, from fluere to flow]

flux density n. Physics. the amount of flux per unit of cross-sectional area.

fluxion ('flʌkʃən) n. Maths., obs. the rate of change of a function; derivative. [C16: from LL fluxiō a flowing]

fly¹ (flaɪ) vb. **flying, flew, flown. 1.** (intr.) (of birds, aircraft, etc.) to move through the air in a controlled manner using aerodynamic forces. **2.** to travel over (an area of land or sea) in an aircraft. **3.** to operate (an aircraft or spacecraft). **4.** to float, flutter, or be displayed in the air or cause to float, etc., in this way: they flew the flag. **5.** to transport or be transported by or through the air by aircraft, wind, etc. **6.** (intr.) to move or be moved very quickly, or suddenly: the door flew open. **7.** (intr.) to pass swiftly: time flies. **8.** to escape from (an enemy, place, etc.); flee. **9.** (intr.; may be foll. by at or upon) to attack a person. **10. fly a kite. a.** to procure money by an accommodation bill. **b.** to release information or take a step in order to test public opinion. **11. fly high.** Inf. **a.** to have a high aim. **b.** to prosper or flourish. **12. let fly.** Inf. **a.** to lose one's temper (with a person): she really let fly at him. **b.** to shoot or throw (an object). ~n., pl. **flies. 13.** (often pl.) Also called: **fly front.** a closure that conceals a zip, buttons, or other fastening, by having one side overlapping, as on trousers. **14. a.** a flap forming the entrance to a tent. **b.** a piece of canvas drawn over the ridgepole of a tent to form an outer roof. **15.** short for **flywheel. 16. a.** the outer edge of a flag. **b.** the distance from the outer edge of a flag to the staff. **17.** Brit. a light one-horse covered carriage formerly let out on hire. **18.** (pl.) Theatre. the space above the stage out of view of the audience, used for storing scenery, etc. **19.** Rare. the act of flying. [OE flēogan] —'flyable adj.

fly² (flaɪ) n., pl. **flies. 1.** any dipterous insect, esp. the housefly, characterized by active flight. **2.** any of various similar but unrelated insects, such as the caddis fly, firefly, and dragonfly. **3.** Angling. a lure made from a fishhook dressed with feathers, tinsel, etc., to resemble any of various flies or nymphs: used in fly-fishing. **4. fly in the ointment.** Inf. a slight flaw that detracts from value or enjoyment. **5. fly on the wall. a.** a person who watches others, while not being noticed himself. **b.** (as modifier): a fly-on-the-wall documentary. **6. there are no flies on him, her,** etc. Inf. he, she, etc., is no fool. [OE flēoge] —'flyless adj.

fly³ (flaɪ) *adj. Sl., chiefly Brit.* knowing and sharp; smart. [C19: from ?]

fly agaric *n.* a woodland fungus having a scarlet cap with white warts and white gills: poisonous but rarely fatal. [so named from its use as a poison on flypaper]

fly ash *n.* fine solid particles of ash carried into the air during combustion.

flyaway ('flaɪə,weɪ) *adj.* **1.** (of hair or clothing) loose and fluttering. **2.** frivolous or flighty; giddy.

flyblow ('flaɪ,bləʊ) *vb.* **-blowing, -blew, -blown. 1.** (*tr.*) to contaminate, esp. with the eggs or larvae of the blowfly; taint. ~*n.* **2.** (*usually pl.*) the eggs or young larva of a blowfly.

flyblown ('flaɪ,bləʊn) *adj.* **1.** covered with flyblows. **2.** contaminated; tainted.

flybook ('flaɪ,bʊk) *n.* a small case or wallet used by anglers for storing artificial flies.

flyby ('flaɪ,baɪ) *n., pl.* **-bys.** a flight past a particular position or target, esp. the close approach of a spacecraft to a planet or satellite.

fly-by-night *Inf.* ~*adj.* **1.** unreliable or untrustworthy, esp. in finance. ~*n.* **2.** an untrustworthy person, esp. one who departs secretly or by night to avoid paying debts.

flycatcher ('flaɪ,kætʃə) *n.* **1.** a small insectivorous songbird of the Old World having a small slender bill fringed with bristles. **2.** an American passerine bird.

flyer ('flaɪə) *n.* a variant spelling of **flier.**

fly-fish *vb.* (*intr.*) *Angling.* to fish using artificial flies as lures. — 'fly-,fishing *n.*

fly half *n. Rugby.* another name for **stand-off half.**

flying ('flaɪɪŋ) *adj.* **1.** (*prenominal*) hurried; fleeting: *a flying visit.* **2.** (*prenominal*) designed for fast action. **3.** (*prenominal*) moving or passing quickly on or as if on wings: *flying hours.* **4.** hanging, waving, or floating freely: *flying hair.* ~*n.* **5.** the act of piloting, navigating, or travelling in an aircraft. **6.** (*modifier*) relating to, accustomed to, or adapted for flight: *a flying machine.*

flying boat *n.* a seaplane in which the fuselage consists of a hull that provides buoyancy.

flying bridge *n.* an auxiliary bridge of a vessel.

flying buttress *n.* a buttress supporting a wall or other structure by an arch that transmits the thrust outwards and downwards.

flying colours *pl. n.* conspicuous success; triumph: *he passed his test with flying colours.*

flying doctor *n.* (in areas of sparse or scattered population) a doctor who visits patients by aircraft.

flying fish *n.* a fish common in warm and tropical seas, having enlarged winglike pectoral fins used for gliding above the surface of the water.

flying fox *n.* **1.** any large fruit bat of tropical Africa and Asia. **2.** *Austral. & N.Z.* a cable mechanism used for transportation across a river, gorge, etc.

flying gurnard *n.* a marine spiny-finned gurnard-like fish having enlarged fan-shaped pectoral fins used to glide above the surface of the sea.

flying jib *n.* the jib set furthest forward or outboard on a vessel with two or more jibs.

flying lemur *n.* either of the two arboreal mammals of S and SE Asia that resemble lemurs but have a fold of skin between the limbs enabling movement by gliding leaps.

flying officer *n.* an officer holding commissioned rank senior to a pilot officer but junior to a flight lieutenant in the British and certain other air forces.

flying phalanger *n.* a nocturnal arboreal phalanger of E Australia and New Guinea, moving with gliding leaps using folds of skin between the hind limbs and forelimbs.

flying picket *n.* (in industrial disputes) a member of a group of pickets organized to be able to move quickly from place to place.

flying saucer *n.* any unidentified disc-shaped flying object alleged to come from outer space.

flying squad *n.* a small group of police, soldiers, etc., ready to move into action quickly.

flying squirrel *n.* a nocturnal rodent of Asia and North America, related to the squirrel. Furry folds of skin between the forelegs and hind legs enable these animals to move by gliding leaps.

flying start *n.* **1.** (in sprinting) a start by a competitor anticipating the starting signal. **2.** a start to a race in which the competitor is already travelling at speed as he passes the starting line. **3.** any promising beginning. **4.** an initial advantage.

flying wing *n.* **1.** an aircraft consisting mainly of one large wing or tailplane and no fuselage. **2.** (in Canadian football) the twelfth player, who has a variable position behind the scrimmage line.

flyleaf ('flaɪ,li:f) *n., pl.* **-leaves.** the inner leaf of the endpaper of a book, pasted to the first leaf.

Flynn (flɪn) *n.* **1. Errol.** 1909–59, Australian actor, who was noted for his swashbuckling roles; his films included *Captain Blood* (1935), *The Adventures of Robin Hood* (1938), and *Too Much Too Soon* (1958). **2.** Rev. **John.** 1880–1951, founder of the Australian flying doctor service.

flyover ('flaɪ,əʊvə) *n.* **1.** *Brit.* an intersection of two roads at which one is carried over the other by a bridge. **2.** the U.S. name for **fly-past.**

flypaper ('flaɪ,peɪpə) *n.* paper with a sticky and poisonous coating, usually hung from the ceiling to trap flies.

fly-past *n.* a ceremonial flight of aircraft over a given area.

flyposting ('flaɪ,pəʊstɪŋ) *n.* the posting of advertising or political posters, etc., in unauthorized places.

Fly River *n.* a river in W Papua New Guinea, flowing southeast to the Gulf of Papua. Length: about 1300 km (800 miles).

flyscreen ('flaɪ,skri:n) *n.* a wire-mesh screen over a window to prevent flies entering a room.

fly sheet *n.* **1.** another term for **fly**¹ (sense 14). **2.** a short handbill.

flyspeck ('flaɪ,spɛk) *n.* **1.** the small speck of the excrement of a fly. **2.** a small spot or speck. ~*vb.* **3.** (*tr.*) to mark with flyspecks.

fly spray *n.* a liquid used to destroy flies and other insects, sprayed from an aerosol.

fly-tipping *n.* the deliberate dumping of rubbish in an unauthorized place.

flytrap ('flaɪ,træp) *n.* **1.** any of various insectivorous plants. **2.** a device for catching flies.

fly way *n.* the usual route used by birds when migrating.

flyweight ('flaɪ,weɪt) *n.* **1. a.** a professional boxer weighing not more than 112 pounds (51 kg). **b.** an amateur boxer weighing 48–51 kg (106–112 pounds). **2.** an amateur wrestler weighing 107–115 pounds (49–52 kg).

flywheel ('flaɪ,wi:l) *n.* a heavy wheel that stores kinetic energy and smoothes the operation of a reciprocating engine by maintaining a constant speed of rotation over the whole cycle.

fm *abbrev. for:* **1.** fathom. **2.** from.

Fm *the chemical symbol for* fermium.

FM *abbrev. for:* **1.** frequency modulation. **2.** Field Marshal.

f-number *or* **f number** *n. Photog.* the numerical value of the relative aperture. If the relative aperture is f8, 8 is the f-number.

Fo (fəʊ) *n.* **Dario** ('dærɪəʊ). born 1926, Italian playwright and actor. His plays include *The Accidental Death of an Anarchist* (1970) and *Trumpets and Raspberries* (1984).

FO *abbrev. for:* **1.** *Army.* Field Officer. **2.** *Air Force.* Flying Officer. **3.** Foreign Office.

fo. *abbrev. for* folio.

foal (fəʊl) *n.* **1.** the young of a horse or related animal. ~*vb.* **2.** to give birth to (a foal). [OE *fola*]

foam (fəʊm) *n.* **1.** a mass of small bubbles of gas formed on the surface of a liquid, such as the froth produced by a solution of soap or detergent in water. **2.** frothy saliva sometimes formed in and expelled from the mouth, as in rabies. **3.** the frothy sweat of a horse or similar animal. **4. a.** any of a number of light cellular solids made by creating bubbles of gas in the liquid material: used as insulation and packaging. **b.** (*as modifier*): *foam rubber; foam plastic.* ~*vb.* **5.** to produce or cause to produce foam; froth. **6.** (*intr.*) to be very angry (esp. in **foam at the mouth**). [OE *fām*] —'**foamless** *adj.*

foamy ('fəʊmɪ) *adj.* **foamier, foamiest.** of, resembling, consisting of, or covered with foam.

fob¹ (fɒb) *n.* **1.** a chain or ribbon by which a pocket watch is attached to a waistcoat. **2.** any ornament hung on such a chain. **3.** a small pocket in a man's waistcoat, etc., for holding a watch. [C17: prob. of Gmc origin]

fob² (fɒb) *vb.* **fobbing, fobbed.** (*tr.*) *Arch.* to cheat. [C15: prob. from G *foppen* to trick]

f.o.b. *or* **FOB** *Commerce. abbrev. for* free on board.

fob off *vb.* (*tr., adv.*) **1.** to trick (a person) with lies or excuses. **2.** to dispose of (goods) by trickery.

focal ('fəʊkªl) *adj.* **1.** of or relating to a focus. **2.** situated at or measured from the focus.

focalize *or* **-lise** ('fəʊkə,laɪz) *vb.* a less common word for **focus.** —,**focali'zation** *or* **-li'sation** *n.*

focal length *or* **distance** *n.* the distance from the focal point of a lens or mirror to the reflecting surface of the mirror or the centre point of the lens.

focal plane *n.* the plane that is perpendicular to the axis of a lens or mirror and passes through the focal point.

focal point *n.* the point on the axis of a lens or mirror to which parallel rays of light converge or from which they appear to diverge after refraction or reflection. Also called: **focus.**

Foch (*French* fɔʃ) *n.* **Ferdinand** (fɛrdinã). 1851–1929, marshal of France; commander in chief of Allied armies on the Western front in World War I (1918).

fo'c's'le *or* **fo'c'sle** ('fəʊksªl) *n.* a variant spelling of **forecastle.**

focus ('fəʊkəs) *n., pl.* **-cuses** *or* **-ci** (-saɪ). **1.** a point of convergence of light or sound waves, etc., or a point from which they appear to diverge. **2.** another name for **focal point** or **focal length. 3.** *Optics.* the state of an optical image when it is distinct and clearly defined or the state of an instrument producing this image: *the telescope is out of focus.* **4.** a point upon which attention, activity, etc., is concentrated. **5.** *Geom.* a fixed reference point on the concave side of a conic section, used when defining its eccentricity. **6.** the point beneath the earth's surface at which an earthquake originates. **7.** *Pathol.* the main site of an infection. ~*vb.* **-cusing, -cused** *or* **-cussing, -cussed. 8.** to bring or come to a focus or into focus. **9.** (*tr.;* often foll. by *on*) to concentrate. [C17: via NL from L: hearth, fireplace] —**'focuser** *n.*

fodder ('fɒdə) *n.* **1.** bulk feed for livestock, esp. hay, straw, etc. ~*vb.* **2.** (*tr.*) to supply (livestock) with fodder. [OE *fódor*]

foe (fəʊ) *n. Formal or literary.* another word for **enemy.** [OE *fāh* hostile]

FoE *or* **FOE** *abbrev. for* Friends of the Earth.

foehn (fɜːn; *German* føːn) *n. Meteorol.* a variant spelling of **föhn.**

foeman ('fəʊmən) *n., pl.* **-men.** *Arch. & poetic.* an enemy in war; foe.

foetid ('fɛtɪd, 'fiː-) *adj.* a variant spelling of **fetid.** —**'foetidly** *adv.* —**'foetidness** *n.*

foetus ('fiːtəs) *n., pl.* **-tuses.** a variant spelling of **fetus.** —**'foetal** *adj.*

fog¹ (fɒg) *n.* **1.** a mass of droplets of condensed water vapour suspended in the air, often greatly reducing visibility. **2.** a cloud of any substance in the atmosphere reducing visibility. **3.** a state of mental uncertainty. **4.** *Photog.* a blurred area on a developed negative, print, or transparency. ~*vb.* **fogging, fogged. 5.** to envelop or become enveloped with or as if with fog. **6.** to confuse or become confused. **7.** *Photog.* to produce fog on (a negative, print, or transparency) or (of a negative, print, or transparency) to be affected by fog. [C16: ? back formation from *foggy* damp, boggy, from FOG²]

fog² (fɒg) *n.* a second growth of grass after the first mowing. [C14: prob. from ON]

fog bank *n.* a distinct mass of fog, esp. at sea.

fogbound ('fɒg,baʊnd) *adj.* prevented from operation by fog: *the airport was fogbound.*

fogbow ('fɒg,bəʊ) *n.* a faint arc of light sometimes seen in a fog bank.

Foggia (*Italian* 'fɔddʒa) *n.* a city in SE Italy, in Apulia; seat of Emperor Frederick II; centre for Carbonari revolutionary societies in the revolts of 1820, 1848, and 1860. Pop.: 159 051 (1986).

foggy ('fɒgɪ) *adj.* **-gier, -giest. 1.** thick with fog. **2.** obscure or confused. **3. not the foggiest** (**idea** *or* **notion**). no idea whatsoever: *I haven't the foggiest.* —**'fogginess** *n.*

foghorn ('fɒg,hɔːn) *n.* **1.** a mechanical instrument sounded at intervals to serve as a warning to vessels in fog. **2.** *Inf.* a loud deep resounding voice.

fog signal *n.* a signal used to warn railway engine drivers in fog, consisting of a detonator placed on the line.

fogy *or* **fogey** ('fəʊgɪ) *n., pl.* **-gies** *or* **-geys.** an extremely fussy or conservative person (esp. in **old fogy**). [C18: from ?] —**'fogyish** *or* **'fogeyish** *adj.*

föhn *or* **foehn** (fɜːn; *German* føːn) *n.* a warm dry wind blowing down the northern slopes of the Alps. [G, from OHG, from L *favōnius*; rel. to *fovēre* to warm]

foible ('fɔɪbªl) *n.* **1.** a slight peculiarity or minor weakness; idiosyncrasy. **2.** the most vulnerable part of a sword's blade, from the middle to the tip. [C17: from obs. F, from obs. adj.: FEEBLE]

foie gras (*French* fwa grɑ) *n.* See **pâté de foie gras.**

foil¹ (fɔɪl) *vb.* (*tr.*). **1.** to baffle or frustrate (a person, attempt, etc.). **2.** *Hunting.* (of hounds, hunters, etc.) to obliterate the scent left by a hunted animal or (of a hunted animal) to run back over its own trail. ~*n.* **3.** *Arch.* a setback or defeat. [C13 *foilen* to trample, from OF, *fuler* tread down] —**'foilable** *adj.*

foil² (fɔɪl) *n.* **1.** metal in the form of very thin sheets: *tin foil.* **2.** the thin metallic sheet forming the backing of a mirror. **3.** a thin leaf of shiny metal set under a gemstone to add brightness or colour. **4.** a person or thing that gives contrast to another. **5.** *Archit.* a small arc between cusps. **6.** short for **hydrofoil.** ~*vb.* (*tr.*) **7.** Also: **foliate.** *Archit.* to ornament (windows, etc.) with foils. [C14: from OF, from L *folia* leaves]

foil³ (fɔɪl) *n.* a light slender flexible sword tipped by a button. [C16: from ?]

foist (fɔɪst) *vb.* (*tr.*). **1.** (often foll. by *off* or *on*) to sell or pass off (something, esp. an inferior article) as genuine, valuable, etc. **2.** (usually foll. by *in* or *into*) to insert surreptitiously or wrongfully. [C16: prob. from obs. Du. *vuisten* to enclose in one's hand, from MDu. *vuist* fist]

Fokine (*Russian* 'fɔkin; *French* fɔkin) *n.* **Michel** (miʃɛl). 1880–1942, U.S. choreographer, born in Russia, regarded as the creator of modern ballet. He worked with Diaghilev as director of the Ballet Russe (1909–15), producing works such as *Les Sylphides* and *Petrushka.*

Fokker ('fɔkə; *Dutch* 'fɔkər) *n.* **Anthony Herman Gerard** (an'toːni; 'hɛrman 'xeːrɑrt). 1890–1939, U.S. designer and builder of aircraft, born in Java.

FOL (in New Zealand) *abbrev. for* Federation of Labour.

fol. *abbrev. for:* **1.** folio. **2.** following.

fold¹ (fəʊld) *vb.* **1.** to bend or be bent double so that one part covers another. **2.** (*tr.*) to bring together and intertwine (the arms, legs, etc.). **3.** (*tr.*) (of birds, insects, etc.) to close (the wings) together from an extended position. **4.** (*tr.;* often foll. by *up* or *in*) to enclose in or as if in a surrounding material. **5.** (*tr.;* foll. by *in*) to clasp (a person) in the arms. **6.** (*tr.;* usually foll. by *round, about,* etc.) to wind (around); entwine. **7.** Also: **fold in.** (*tr.*) to mix (a whisked mixture) with other ingredients by gently turning one part over the other with a spoon. **8.** (*intr.;* often foll. by *up*) *Inf.* to collapse; fail: *the business folded.* ~*n.* **9.** a piece or section that has been folded: *a fold of cloth.* **10.** a mark, crease, or hollow made by folding. **11.** a hollow in undulating terrain. **12.** a bend in stratified rocks that results from movements within the earth's crust. **13.** a coil, as in a rope, etc. [OE *fealdan*] —**'foldable** *adj.*

fold² (fəʊld) *n.* **1. a.** a small enclosure or pen for sheep or other livestock, where they can be gathered. **b.** a flock of sheep. **2.** a church or the members of it. ~*vb.* **3.** (*tr.*) to gather or confine (sheep, etc.) in a fold. [OE *falod*]

-fold *suffix forming adjectives and adverbs.* having so many parts or being so many times as much or as many: *three-hundredfold.* [OE *-fald, -feald*]

foldaway ('fəʊldə,weɪ) *adj.* (*prenominal*) (of a bed, etc.) able to be folded away when not in use.

folded dipole *n.* a type of aerial consisting of two parallel dipoles connected together at their outer ends and fed at the centre of one of them. The length is usually half the operating wavelength.

folder ('fəʊldə) *n.* **1.** a binder or file for holding loose papers, etc. **2.** a folded circular. **3.** a person or thing that folds.

folderol ('fɒldə,rɒl) *n.* a variant spelling of **falderal.**

folding door *n.* a door in the form of one or more vertical hinged leaves that can be folded one against another.

foliaceous (,fəʊlɪ'eɪʃəs) *adj.* **1.** having the appearance of the leaf of a plant. **2.** bearing leaves or leaflike structures. **3.** *Geol.* consisting of thin layers. [C17: from L *foliāceus*]

foliage ('fəʊlɪɪdʒ) *n.* **1.** the green leaves of a plant. **2.** sprays of leaves used for decoration. **3.** an ornamental leaflike design. [C15: from OF *fuellage*, from *fuelle* leaf; infl. in form by L *folium*]

foliar ('fəuliə) *adj.* of or relating to a leaf or leaves. [C19: from F, from L *folium* leaf]

foliate *adj.* ('fəuliɪt, -ˌeɪt). **1. a.** relating to, possessing, or resembling leaves. **b.** (*in combination*): *trifoliate.* ~*vb.* ('fəuliˌeɪt). **2.** (*tr.*) to ornament with foliage or with leaf forms such as foils. **3.** to hammer or cut (metal) into thin plates or foil. **4.** (*tr.*) to number the leaves of (a book, etc.). Cf. **paginate. 5.** (*intr.*) (of plants) to grow leaves. [C17: from L *foliātus* leaved, leafy]

foliation (ˌfəuliˈeɪʃən) *n.* **1.** *Bot.* **a.** the process of producing leaves. **b.** the state of being in leaf. **c.** the arrangement of leaves in a leaf bud. **2.** *Archit.* ornamentation consisting of cusps and foils. **3.** the consecutive numbering of the leaves of a book. **4.** *Geol.* the arrangement of the constituents of a rock in leaflike layers, as in schists.

folic acid ('fəulɪk) *n.* any of a group of vitamins of the B complex, used in the treatment of anaemia. Also called: **folacin.** [C20: from L *folium* leaf; so called because it may be obtained from green leaves]

folio ('fəuliəu) *n.*, *pl.* **-lios. 1.** a sheet of paper folded in half to make two leaves for a book. **2.** a book of the largest common size made up of such sheets. **3. a.** a leaf of paper numbered on the front side only. **b.** the page number of a book. **4.** *Law.* a unit of measurement of the length of legal documents, determined by the number of words, generally 72 or 90 in Britain and 100 in the U.S. ~*adj.* **5.** relating to or having the format of a folio: *a folio edition.* [C16: from L phrase *in foliō* in a leaf, from *folium* leaf]

folk (fəuk) *n.*, *pl.* **folk** *or* **folks. 1.** (*functioning as pl.; often pl. in form*) people in general, esp. those of a particular group or class: *country folk.* **2.** (*functioning as pl.; usually pl. in form*) *Inf.* members of a family. **3.** (*functioning as sing.*) *Inf.* short for **folk music. 4.** a people or tribe. **5.** (*modifier*) originating from or traditional to the common people of a country: *a folk song.* [OE *folc*] —'**folkish** *adj.*

folk dance *n.* **1.** any of various traditional rustic dances. **2.** a piece of music composed for or in the rhythm of this dance. —**folk dancing** *n.*

Folkestone ('fəukstən) *n.* a port and resort in SE England, in E Kent. Pop.: 44 200 (1983 est.).

folk etymology *n.* the gradual change in the form of a word through the influence of a more familiar word or phrase with which it becomes associated, as for example *sparrow-grass* for *asparagus.*

folkie *or* **folky** ('fəukɪ) *n.*, *pl.* **folkies.** *Inf.* a devotee of folk music.

folklore ('fəukˌlɔː) *n.* **1.** the unwritten literature of a people as expressed in folk tales, songs, etc. **2.** the body of stories and legends attacked to a particular place, group, etc.: *rugby folklore.* **3.** study of folkloric materials. —'**folkˌloric** *adj.* —'**folkˌlorist** *n.*, *adj.*

folk medicine *n.* medicine as practised among rustic communities and primitive peoples, consisting typically of the use of herbal remedies.

folk music *n.* **1.** music that is passed on from generation to generation. **2.** any music composed in this idiom.

folk-rock *n.* a combination of folk-oriented lyrics with a pop accompaniment.

folk song *n.* **1.** a song which has been handed down among the common people. **2.** a modern song which reflects the folk idiom.

folksy ('fəuksɪ) *adj.* **-sier, -siest.** *Inf.*, *chiefly U.S. & Canad.* **1.** of or like ordinary people. **2.** friendly; affable.

folk tale *or* **story** *n.* a tale or legend originating among a people and becoming part of an oral tradition.

folk weave *n.* a type of fabric with a loose weave.

follicle ('fɒlɪkªl) *n.* **1.** any small sac or cavity in the body having an excretory, secretory, or protective function: *a hair follicle.* **2.** *Bot.* a dry fruit that splits along one side only to release its seeds. [C17: from L *folliculus* small bag, from *follis* pair of bellows, leather money-bag] —**follicular** (fɒˈlɪkjʊlə), **folliculate** (fɒˈlɪkjʊˌleɪt), *or* **fol'licuˌlated** *adj.*

follow ('fɒləu) *vb.* **1.** to go or come after in the same direction. **2.** (*tr.*) to accompany: *she followed her sister everywhere.* **3.** (*tr.*) to come after as a logical or natural consequence. **4.** (*tr.*) to keep to the course or track of: *she followed the towpath.* **5.** (*tr.*) to act in accordance with: *to follow instructions.* **6.** (*tr.*) to accept the ideas or beliefs of (a previous authority, etc.): *he followed*

Donne in most of his teachings. **7.** to understand (an explanation, etc.): *the lesson was difficult to follow.* **8.** to watch closely or continuously: *she followed his progress.* **9.** (*tr.*) to have a keen interest in: *to follow athletics.* **10.** (*tr.*) to help in the cause of: *the men who followed Napoleon.* [OE *folgian*]

follower ('fɒləuə) *n.* **1.** a person who accepts the teachings of another: *a follower of Marx.* **2.** an attendant. **3.** a supporter, as of a sport or team. **4.** (*esp. formerly*) a male admirer.

following ('fɒləuɪŋ) *adj.* **1. a.** (*prenominal*) about to be mentioned, specified, etc.: *the following items.* **b.** (*as n.*): *will the following please raise their hands?* **2.** (of winds, currents, etc.) moving in the same direction as a vessel. ~*n.* **3.** a group of supporters or enthusiasts: *he attracted a large following.*

follow-on *Cricket.* ~*n.* **1.** an immediate second innings forced on a team scoring a prescribed number of runs fewer than its opponents in the first innings. ~*vb.* **follow on. 2.** (*intr.*, *adv.*) (of a team) to play a follow-on.

follow out *vb.* (*tr.*, *adv.*) to implement (an idea or action) to a conclusion.

follow through *vb.* (*adv.*) **1.** *Sport.* to complete (a stroke or shot) by continuing the movement to the end of its arc. **2.** (*tr.*) to pursue (an aim) to a conclusion. ~*n.* **follow-through. 3.** the act of following through.

follow up *vb.* (*tr.*, *adv.*) **1.** to pursue or investigate (a person, etc.) closely. **2.** to continue (action) after a beginning, esp. to increase its effect. ~*n.* **follow-up. 3. a.** something done to reinforce an initial action. **b.** (*as modifier*): *a follow-up letter.* **4.** *Med.* an examination of a patient at intervals after treatment.

folly ('fɒlɪ) *n.*, *pl.* **-lies. 1.** the state or quality of being foolish. **2.** a foolish action, idea, etc. **3.** a building in the form of a castle, temple, etc., built to satisfy a fancy or conceit. **4.** (*pl.*) *Theatre.* an elaborately costumed review. [C13: from OF *folie* madness, from *fou* mad; see FOOL¹]

foment (fəˈmɛnt) *vb.* (*tr.*) **1.** to encourage or instigate (trouble, discord, etc.). **2.** *Med.* to apply heat and moisture to (a part of the body) to relieve pain. [C15: from LL, from L *fōmentum* a poultice, ult. from *fovēre* to foster] —**fomentation** (ˌfəumɛnˈteɪʃən) *n.* —**fo'menter** *n.*

fond (fɒnd) *adj.* **1.** (*postpositive;* foll. by *of*) having a liking (for). **2.** loving; tender. **3.** indulgent: *a fond mother.* **4.** (of hopes, wishes, etc.) cherished but unlikely to be realized: *he had fond hopes of starting his own firm.* **5.** *Arch.* or *dialect.* **a.** foolish. **b.** credulous. [C14 *fonned,* from *fonne* a fool] —'**fondly** *adv.* —'**fondness** *n.*

Fonda ('fɒndə) *n.* **1. Henry.** 1905–82, U.S. film actor. His many films include *Young Mr Lincoln* (1939), *The Grapes of Wrath* (1940), *Twelve Angry Men* (1957), and *On Golden Pond* (1981) for which he won an Oscar. **2.** his daughter **Jane.** born 1937, U.S. film actress. Her films include *Klute* (1971) for which she won an Oscar, *Julia* (1977), *The China Syndrome* (1979), and *On Golden Pond* (1981). **3.** her brother, **Peter.** born 1939, U.S. film actor, who made his name in *Easy Rider* (1969).

fondant ('fɒndənt) *n.* **1.** a thick flavoured paste of sugar and water, used in sweets and icings. **2.** a sweet made of this mixture. ~*adj.* **3.** (of a colour) soft, pastel. [C19: from F, lit.: melting, from *fondre* to melt, from L *fundere*; see FOUND³]

fondle ('fɒndªl) *vb.* (*tr.*) to touch or stroke tenderly. [C17: from (obs.) vb. *fond* to fondle; see FOND] —'**fondler** *n.*

fondue ('fɒndjuː; *French* fɔ̃dy) *n.* a Swiss dish, consisting of melted cheese into which small pieces of bread are dipped. [C19: from F, fem. of *fondu* melted; see FONDANT]

Fonseca (*Spanish* fɒnˈseka) *n.* **Gulf of.** an inlet of the Pacific Ocean in W Central America.

font¹ (fɒnt) *n.* **1. a.** a large bowl for baptismal water. **b.** a receptacle for holy water. **2.** the reservoir for oil in an oil lamp. **3.** *Arch.* or *poetic.* a fountain or well. [OE, from Church L *fons* from L: fountain]

font² (fɒnt) *n. Printing.* another name (esp. U.S. and Canad.) for **fount**².

Fontainebleau ('fɒntɪnˌbləu; *French* fɔ̃tɛnblo) *n.* a town in N France, in the **Forest of Fontainebleau:** famous for its palace (now a museum), one of the largest royal residences in France, built largely by Francis I (16th century). Pop.: 18 753 (1982).

fontanelle *or chiefly U.S.* **fontanel** (ˌfɒntəˈnɛl) *n. Anat.* any of the soft membranous gaps between the bones of the skull in a fetus or infant. [C16 (in the sense: hollow between muscles): from OF *fontanele*, lit.: a little spring, from *fontaine* FOUNTAIN]

Fonteyn (fɒn'teɪn) n. Dame **Margot**. real name *Margaret Hookham*. born 1919, English classical ballerina.

Foochow ('fuː'tʃaʊ) n. a variant transliteration of the Chinese name for **Fuzhou**.

food (fuːd) n. **1.** any substance that can be ingested by a living organism and metabolized into energy and body tissue. Related adj.: **alimentary**. **2.** nourishment in more or less solid form: *food and drink*. **3.** anything that provides mental nourishment or stimulus. [OE *fōda*]

food additive n. any of various natural or synthetic substances, such as salt or citric acid, used in the commercial processing of food as preservatives, antioxidants, emulsifiers, etc.

food chain n. *Ecology*. a series of organisms in a community, each member of which feeds on another in the chain and is in turn eaten.

foodie or **foody** ('fuːdɪ) n., pl. **foodies**. a person having an enthusiastic interest in the preparation and consumption of good food.

food poisoning n. an acute illness caused by food that is either naturally poisonous or contaminated by bacteria.

food processor n. *Cookery*. an electric domestic appliance for automatic chopping, grating, blending, etc.

foodstuff ('fuːd,stʌf) n. any material, substance, etc., that can be used as food.

food value n. the relative degree of nourishment obtained from different foods.

fool[1] (fuːl) n. **1.** a person who lacks sense or judgement. **2.** a person who is made to appear ridiculous. **3.** (formerly) a professional jester living in a royal or noble household. **4.** *Obs.* an idiot or imbecile: *the village fool*. **5.** act or **play the fool**. to deliberately act foolishly. ~vb. **6.** (tr.) to deceive (someone), esp. in order to make him look ridiculous. **7.** (intr.; foll. by *with, around with*, or *about with*) *Inf.* to act or play (with) irresponsibly or aimlessly. **8.** (intr.) to speak or act in a playful or jesting manner. **9.** (tr.; foll. by *away*) to squander; fritter. ~adj. **10.** *U.S. inf.* short for **foolish**. [C13: from OF *fol* mad person, from LL *follis* empty-headed fellow, from L: bellows]

fool[2] (fuːl) n. *Chiefly Brit.* a dessert made from a purée of fruit with cream. [C16: ?from FOOL[1]]

foolery ('fuːlərɪ) n., pl. **-eries**. **1.** foolish behaviour. **2.** an instance of this.

foolhardy ('fuːl,hɑːdɪ) adj. **-hardier**, **-hardiest**. heedlessly rash or adventurous. [C13: from OF, from *fol* foolish + *hardi* bold] — 'fool,hardily adv. — 'fool,hardiness n.

foolish ('fuːlɪʃ) adj. **1.** unwise; silly. **2.** resulting from folly or stupidity. **3.** ridiculous or absurd. **4.** weakminded; simple. — 'foolishly adv. — 'foolishness n.

foolproof ('fuːl,pruːf) adj. *Inf.* **1.** proof against failure. **2.** (esp. of machines, etc.) proof against human misuse, error, etc.

foolscap ('fuːlz,kæp) n. *Chiefly Brit.* a size of writing or printing paper, 13½ by 17 inches. [C17: see FOOL[1], CAP; so called from the watermark formerly used on this kind of paper]

fool's cap n. **1.** a hood or cap with bells or tassels, worn by court jesters. **2.** a dunce's cap.

fool's errand n. a fruitless undertaking.

fool's gold n. any of various yellow minerals, esp. pyrite, that can be mistaken for gold.

fool's paradise n. illusory happiness.

fool's-parsley n. an evil-smelling Eurasian umbelliferous plant with small white flowers.

foot (fʊt) n., pl. **feet**. **1.** the part of the vertebrate leg below the ankle joint that is in contact with the ground during standing and walking. Related adj.: **pedal**. **2.** the part of a garment covering a foot. **3.** any of various organs of locomotion or attachment in invertebrates, including molluscs. **4.** *Bot.* the lower part of some plants or plant structures. **5.** a unit of length equal to one third of a yard or 12 inches. 1 foot is equivalent to 0.3048 metre. **6.** any part resembling a foot in form or function: *the foot of a chair*. **7.** the lower part of something; bottom: *the foot of a hill*. **8.** the end of a series or group: *the foot of the list*. **9.** manner of walking or moving: *a heavy foot*. **10. a.** infantry, esp. in the British army. **b.** (as modifier): *a foot soldier*. **11.** any of various attachments on a sewing machine that hold the fabric in position. **12.** *Prosody*. a group of two or more syllables in which one syllable has the major

stress, forming the basic unit of poetic rhythm. **13. my foot!** an expression of disbelief, often of the speaker's own preceding statement. **14. of foot**. *Arch.* in manner of movement: *fleet of foot*. **15. one foot in the grave**. *Inf.* near to death. **16. on foot**. **a.** walking or running. **b.** astir; afoot. **17. put a foot wrong**. to make a mistake. **18. put one's best foot forward**. **a.** to try to do one's best. **b.** to hurry. **19. put one's foot down**. *Inf.* to act firmly. **20. put one's foot in it**. *Inf.* to blunder. **21. under foot**. on the ground; beneath one's feet. ~vb. **22.** to dance to music (esp. in **foot it**). **23.** (tr.) to walk over or set foot on (esp. in **foot it**). **24.** (tr.) to pay the entire cost of (esp. in **foot the bill**). [OE *fōt*] ~See also **feet**. — 'footless adj.

Foot (fʊt) n. **Michael**. born 1913, British Labour politician, and a leader of the left-wing Tribune Group; secretary of state for employment (1974–76); leader of the House of Commons (1976–79); leader of the Labour Party (1980–83).

footage ('fʊtɪdʒ) n. **1.** a length or distance measured in feet. **2.** the extent of film material shot and exposed.

foot-and-mouth disease n. an acute highly infectious viral disease of cattle, pigs, sheep, and goats, characterized by the formation of vesicular eruptions in the mouth and on the feet.

football ('fʊt,bɔːl) n. **1. a.** any of various games played with a round or oval ball and usually based on two teams competing to kick, head, carry, or otherwise propel the ball into each other's goal, territory, etc. **b.** (as modifier): *a football supporter*. **2.** the ball used in any of these games or their variants. **3.** a problem, issue, etc., that is continually passed from one group or person to another as a pretext for argument. — 'foot,baller n.

footboard ('fʊt,bɔːd) n. **1.** a board for a person to stand or rest his feet on. **2.** a treadle or foot-operated lever on a machine. **3.** a vertical board at the foot of a bed.

footbridge ('fʊt,brɪdʒ) n. a narrow bridge for the use of pedestrians.

-footed adj. **1.** having a foot or feet as specified: *four-footed*. **2.** having a tread as specified: *heavy-footed*.

footer[1] ('fʊtə) n. (in combination) a person or thing of a specified length or height in feet: *a six-footer*.

footer[2] ('fʊtə) n. *Brit. inf.* short for **football** (the game).

footfall ('fʊt,fɔːl) n. the sound of a footstep.

foot fault n. *Tennis*. a fault that occurs when the server fails to keep both feet behind the baseline until he has served.

foothill ('fʊt,hɪl) n. (often pl.) a relatively low hill at the foot of a mountain.

foothold ('fʊt,həʊld) n. **1.** a ledge or other place affording a secure grip, as during climbing. **2.** a secure position from which further progress may be made.

footing ('fʊtɪŋ) n. **1.** the basis or foundation on which something is established: *the business was on a secure footing*. **2.** the relationship or status existing between two persons, groups, etc. **3.** a secure grip by or for the feet. **4.** the lower part of a foundation of a column, wall, building, etc.

footle ('fuːtᵊl) vb. (intr.; often foll. by *around* or *about*) *Inf.* to loiter aimlessly. [C19: prob. from F *foutre* to copulate with, from L *futuere*] — 'footling adj.

footlights ('fʊt,laɪts) pl. n. *Theatre*. lights set in a row along the front of the stage floor.

footloose ('fʊt,luːs) adj. **1.** free to go or do as one wishes. **2.** restless: *to feel footloose*.

footman ('fʊtmən) n., pl. **-men**. **1.** a male servant, esp. one in livery. **2.** (formerly) a foot soldier.

footnote ('fʊt,nəʊt) n. **1.** a note printed at the bottom of a page, to which attention is drawn by means of a mark in the text. ~vb. **2.** (tr.) to supply (a page, etc.) with footnotes.

footpad ('fʊt,pæd) n. *Arch.* a robber or highwayman, on foot rather than horseback.

footpath ('fʊt,pɑːθ) n. a narrow path for walkers only.

footplate ('fʊt,pleɪt) n. *Chiefly Brit.* a platform in the cab of a locomotive on which the crew stand to operate the controls.

foot-pound-second n. See **fps units**.

footprint ('fʊt,prɪnt) n. an indentation or outline of the foot of a person or animal on a surface.

footrest ('fʊt,rest) n. something that provides a support for the feet, such as a low stool, rail, etc.

foot rot *n. Vet. science.* See **rot** (sense 10).

footsie ('fʊtsɪ) *n. Inf.* flirtation involving the touching together of feet, etc.

Footsie ('fʊtsɪ) *n. Brit. sl.* the Financial Times Stock Exchange 100 index (of companies' shares).

foot soldier *n.* an infantryman.

footsore ('fʊt,sɔː) *adj.* having sore or tired feet, esp. from much walking. —'**foot,soreness** *n.*

footstep ('fʊt,stɛp) *n.* **1.** the action of taking a step in walking. **2.** the sound made by walking. **3.** the distance covered with a step. **4.** a footmark. **5.** a single stair. **6. follow in someone's footsteps.** to continue the example of another.

footstool ('fʊt,stuːl) *n.* a low stool used for supporting or resting the feet of a seated person.

footwear ('fʊt,wɛə) *n.* anything worn to cover the feet.

footwork ('fʊt,wɜːk) *n.* skilful use of the feet, as in sports, dancing, etc.

fop (fɒp) *n.* a man who is excessively concerned with fashion and elegance. [C15: rel. to G *foppen* to trick] —'**foppery** *n.* —'**foppish** *adj.*

for (fɔː; *unstressed* fə) *prep.* **1.** directed or belonging to: *there's a phone call for you.* **2.** to the advantage of: *I only did it for you.* **3.** in the direction of: *heading for the border.* **4.** over a span of (time or distance): *working for six days.* **5.** in favour of: *vote for me.* **6.** in order to get or achieve: *I do it for money.* **7.** designed to meet the needs of: *these kennels are for puppies.* **8.** at a cost of: *I got it for hardly any money.* **9.** such as explains or results in: *his reason for changing his job was not given.* **10.** in place of: *a substitute for the injured player.* **11.** because of: *she wept for pure relief.* **12.** with regard or consideration to the usual characteristics of: *it's cool for this time of year.* **13.** concerning: *desire for money.* **14.** as being: *I know that for a fact.* **15.** at a specified time: *a date for the next evening.* **16.** to do or partake of: *an appointment for supper.* **17.** in the duty or task of: *that's for him to say.* **18.** to allow of: *too big a job for us to handle.* **19.** despite: *she's a good wife, for all her nagging.* **20.** in order to preserve, retain, etc.: *to fight for survival.* **21.** as a direct equivalent to: *word for word.* **22.** in order to become or enter: *to train for the priesthood.* **23.** in recompense for: *I paid for it last week.* **24. for it.** *Brit. inf.* liable for punishment or blame: *you'll be for it if she catches you.* ~*conj.* **25.** (*coordinating*) because; seeing that: *I couldn't stay, for the area was violent.* [OE]

for- *prefix.* **1.** indicating rejection or prohibition: *forbid.* **2.** indicating falsity: *forswear.* **3.** used to give intensive force: *forlorn.* [OE *for-*]

▷ **Usage.** The difference in meaning between the prefixes *for-* and *fore-* helps to distinguish between pairs of similar words like *forbear, forebear* and *forgo, forego. For-* implies negation or prohibition, so that *forbear* means "not to do something" and *forgo* means "to deny oneself something". *Fore-* has the sense "before, earlier", hence *forebear* means "one who has gone before, i.e., an ancestor", and *forego* means "to go or have happened before", as in *a foregone conclusion.* In practice, the above words are used interchangeably with or without the *e*, but careful writers of English may prefer to maintain the distinction between them.

forage ('fɒrɪdʒ) *n.* **1.** food for horses or cattle, esp. hay or straw. **2.** the act of searching for food or provisions. ~*vb.* **3.** to search (the countryside or a town) for food, etc. **4.** (*intr.*) *Mil.* to carry out a raid. **5.** (*tr.*) to obtain by searching about. **6.** (*tr.*) to give food or other provisions to. **7.** (*tr.*) to feed (cattle or horses) with such food. [C14: from OF *fourrage,* prob. of Gmc origin] —'**forager** *n.*

forage cap *n.* a soldier's undress cap.

foramen (fɒ'reɪmɛn) *n., pl.* **-ramina** (-'ræmɪnə) *or* **-ramens.** a natural hole, esp. one in a bone. [C17: from L, from *forāre* to bore, pierce]

foraminifer (,fɒrə'mɪnɪfə) *n.* a protozoan of the order *Foraminifera,* having a shell with numerous openings through which the pseudopodia protrude. [C19: from NL, from FORAMEN + -FER]

forasmuch as (fərəz'mʌtʃ) *conj.* (*subordinating*) *Arch. or legal.* seeing that.

foray ('fɒreɪ) *n.* **1.** a short raid or incursion. ~*vb.* **2.** to raid or ravage (a town, district, etc.). [C14: from *forrayen* to pillage, from OF, from *fuerre* fodder]

forbade (fə'bæd, -'beɪd) *or* **forbad** (fə'bæd) *vb.* the past tense of **forbid.**

forbear[1] (fɔː'bɛə) *vb.* **-bearing, -bore, -borne. 1.** (when *intr.,* often foll. by *from* or an infinitive) to cease or refrain (from doing something). **2.** *Arch.* to tolerate (misbehaviour, etc.). [OE *forberan*]

▷ **Usage.** See at **for-.**

forbear[2] ('fɔː,bɛə) *n.* a variant spelling of **forebear.**

forbearance (fɔː'bɛərəns) *n.* **1.** the act of forbearing. **2.** self-control; patience.

Forbes (fɔːbz) *n.* **George William.** 1869–1947, New Zealand statesman; prime minister of New Zealand (1930–35).

forbid (fə'bɪd) *vb.* **-bidding, -bade** *or* **-bad, -bidden** *or* **-bid.** (*tr.*) **1.** to prohibit (a person) in a forceful or authoritative manner (from doing or having something). **2.** to make impossible. **3.** to shut out or exclude. [OE *forbēodan;* see FOR-, BID] —**for'bidder** *n.*

forbidden (fə'bɪd²n) *adj.* **1.** not permitted by order or law. **2.** *Physics.* involving a change in quantum numbers that is not permitted by certain rules derived from quantum mechanics.

Forbidden City *n.* **the. 1.** Lhasa, Tibet: once famed for its inaccessibility and hostility to strangers. **2.** a walled section of Peking, China, enclosing the Imperial Palace and associated buildings of the former Chinese Empire.

forbidden fruit *n.* any pleasure or enjoyment regarded as illicit, esp. sexual indulgence.

forbidding (fə'bɪdɪŋ) *adj.* **1.** hostile or unfriendly. **2.** dangerous or ominous.

forbore (fɔː'bɔː) *vb.* the past tense of **forbear**[1].

forborne (fɔː'bɔːn) *vb.* the past participle of **forbear**[1].

force[1] (fɔːs) *n.* **1.** strength or energy; power: *the force of the blow.* **2.** exertion or the use of exertion against a person or thing that resists. **3.** *Physics.* **a.** a dynamic influence that changes a body from a state of rest to one of motion or changes its rate of motion. **b.** a static influence that produces a strain in a body or system. Symbol: *F* **4. a.** intellectual, political, or moral influence or strength: *the force of his argument.* **b.** a person or thing with such influence: *he was a force in the land.* **5.** vehemence or intensity: *she spoke with great force.* **6.** a group of persons organized for military or police functions: *armed forces.* **7.** (*sometimes cap.;* preceded by *the*) *Inf.* the police force. **8.** a group of persons organized for particular duties or tasks: *a workforce.* **9.** *Criminal law.* violence unlawfully committed or threatened. **10. in force. a.** (of a law) having legal validity. **b.** in great strength or numbers. ~*vb.* (*tr.*) **11.** to compel or cause (a person, group, etc.) to do something through effort, superior strength, etc. **12.** to acquire or produce through effort, superior strength, etc.: *to force a confession.* **13.** to propel or drive despite resistance. **14.** to break down or open (a lock, door, etc.). **15.** to impose or inflict: *he forced his views on them.* **16.** to cause (plants or farm animals) to grow or fatten artificially at an increased rate. **17.** to strain to the utmost: *to force the voice.* **18.** to rape. **19.** *Cards.* **a.** to compel a player by the lead of a particular suit to play (a certain card). **b.** (in bridge) to induce (a bid) from one's partner. [C13: from OF, from Vulgar L *fortia* (unattested), from L *fortis* strong] —'**forceable** *adj.* —'**forceless** *adj.* —'**forcer** *n.*

force[2] (fɔːs) *n.* (in N England) a waterfall. [C17: from ON *fors*]

forced (fɔːst) *adj.* **1.** done because of force: *forced labour.* **2.** false or unnatural: *a forced smile.* **3.** due to an emergency or necessity: *a forced landing.*

force-feed *vb.* **-feeding, -fed.** (*tr.*) to force (a person or animal) to eat or swallow food.

forceful ('fɔːsful) *adj.* **1.** powerful. **2.** persuasive or effective. —'**forcefully** *adv.* —'**forcefulness** *n.*

forcemeat ('fɔːs,miːt) *n.* a mixture of chopped ingredients used for stuffing. Also called: **farce.** [C17: from *force* (see FARCE) + MEAT]

forceps ('fɔːsɪps) *n., pl.* **-ceps. 1. a.** a surgical instrument in the form of a pair of pincers, used esp. in the delivery of babies. **b.** (*as modifier*): *a forceps baby.* **2.** any part of an organism shaped like a forceps. [C17: from L, from *formus* hot + *capere* to seize]

force pump *n.* a pump that ejects fluid under pressure. Cf. **lift pump.**

Forces ('fɔːsɪz) *pl. n.* (usually preceded by *the*) the armed services of a nation.

forcible ('fɔːsəbᵊl) *adj.* **1.** done by, involving, or having force. **2.** convincing or effective: *a forcible argument.* —'**forcibly** *adv.*

ford (fɔːd) *n.* **1.** a shallow area in a river that can be crossed by car, on horseback, etc. ~*vb.* **2.** (*tr.*) to cross (a river, brook, etc.) over a shallow area. [OE] —'**fordable** *adj.*

Ford (fɔːd) *n.* **1. Ford Madox** ('mædəks), real name *Ford Madox Hueffer.* 1873–1939, English novelist, editor, and critic; works include *The Good Soldier* (1915) and the war tetralogy *Parade's End* (1924–28). **2. Gerald.** born 1913, U.S. politician; 38th president of the U.S. (1974–77). **3. Henry.** 1863–1947, U.S. car manufacturer, who pioneered mass production. **4. John.** 1586–?1639, English dramatist; author of revenge tragedies such as *'Tis Pity She's a Whore* (1633). **5. John,** real name *Sean O'Feeney.* 1895–1973, U.S. film director, esp. of Westerns such as *Stagecoach* (1939) and *She Wore a Yellow Ribbon* (1949).

fore[1] (fɔː) *adj.* **1.** (*usually in combination*) located at, in, or towards the front: *the forelegs of a horse.* ~*n.* **2.** the front part. **3.** something located at, or towards the front. **4. fore and aft.** located at both ends of a vessel: *a fore-and-aft rig.* **5. to the fore.** to the front or conspicuous position. ~*adv.* **6.** at or towards a ship's bow. **7.** *Obs.* before. ~*prep., conj.* **8.** a less common word for **before.** [OE]

fore[2] (fɔː) *sentence substitute.* (in golf) a warning shout made by a player about to make a shot. [C19: prob. short for BEFORE]

fore- *prefix.* **1.** before in time or rank: *forefather.* **2.** at or near the front: *forecourt.* [OE, from *fore* (adv.)]
▷ **Usage. See at for-.**

fore-and-after *n. Naut.* **1.** any vessel with a fore-and-aft rig. **2.** a double-ended vessel.

forearm[1] ('fɔːrˌɑːm) *n.* the part of the arm from the elbow to the wrist. [C18: from FORE- + ARM[1]]

forearm[2] (fɔːrˈɑːm) *vb.* (*tr.*) to prepare or arm (someone) in advance. [C16: from FORE- + ARM[2]]

forebear *or* **forbear** ('fɔːˌbɛə) *n.* an ancestor.
▷ **Usage. See at for-.**

forebode (fɔːˈbəʊd) *vb.* **1.** to warn of or indicate (an event, result, etc.) in advance. **2.** to have a premonition of (an event).

foreboding (fɔːˈbəʊdɪŋ) *n.* **1.** a feeling of impending evil, disaster, etc. **2.** an omen or portent. ~*adj.* **3.** presaging something.

forebrain ('fɔːˌbreɪn) *n.* the nontechnical name for **prosencephalon.**

forecast ('fɔːˌkɑːst) *vb.* **-casting, -cast** *or* **-casted. 1.** to predict or calculate (weather, events, etc.) in advance. **2.** (*tr.*) to serve as an early indication of. ~*n.* **3.** a statement of probable future weather calculated from meteorological data. **4.** a prediction. **5.** the practice or power of forecasting. — '**fore**, **caster** *n.*

forecastle, fo'c's'le, *or* **fo'c'sle** ('fəʊksᵊl) *n.* the part of a vessel at the bow where the crew is quartered.

foreclose (fɔːˈkləʊz) *vb.* **1.** *Law.* to deprive (a mortgagor, etc.) of the right to redeem (a mortgage or pledge). **2.** (*tr.*) to shut out; bar. **3.** (*tr.*) to prevent or hinder. [C15: from OF, from *for-* out + *clore* to close, from L *claudere*] —**fore'closable** *adj.* —**foreclosure** (fɔːˈkləʊʒə) *n.*

forecourt ('fɔːˌkɔːt) *n.* **1.** a courtyard in front of a building, as one in a filling station. **2.** the section of the court in tennis, badminton, etc., between the service line and the net.

foredoom (fɔːˈduːm) *vb.* (*tr.*) to doom or condemn beforehand.

forefather ('fɔːˌfɑːðə) *n.* an ancestor, esp. a male. — '**fore**, **fatherly** *adj.*

forefinger ('fɔːˌfɪŋɡə) *n.* the finger next to the thumb. Also called: **index finger.**

forefoot ('fɔːˌfʊt) *n., pl.* **-feet.** either of the front feet of a quadruped.

forefront ('fɔːˌfrʌnt) *n.* **1.** the extreme front. **2.** the position of most prominence or action.

foregather (fɔːˈɡæðə) *vb.* a variant spelling of **forgather.**

forego[1] (fɔːˈɡəʊ) *vb.* **-going, -went, -gone.** to precede in time, place, etc. [OE *foregān*]
▷ **Usage. See at for-.**

forego[2] (fɔːˈɡəʊ) *vb.* **-going, -went, -gone.** (*tr.*) a variant spelling of **forgo.**

foregoing (fɔːˈɡəʊɪŋ) *adj.* (*prenominal*) (esp. of writing or speech) going before; preceding.

foregone (fɔːˈɡɒn, 'fɔːˌɡɒn) *adj.* gone or completed; past. —**fore'goneness** *n.*

foregone conclusion *n.* an inevitable result or conclusion.

foreground ('fɔːˌɡraʊnd) *n.* **1.** the part of a scene situated towards the front or nearest to the viewer. **2.** a conspicuous position.

forehand ('fɔːˌhænd) *adj.* (*prenominal*) **1.** *Tennis, squash, etc.* (of a stroke) made with the palm of the hand facing the direction of the stroke. ~*n.* **2.** *Tennis, squash, etc.* **a.** a forehand stroke. **b.** the side on which such strokes are made. **3.** the part of a horse in front of the saddle.

forehead ('fɒrɪd, 'fɔːˌhɛd) *n.* the part of the face between the natural hairline and the eyes. Related adj.: **frontal.** [OE *forhēafod*]

foreign ('fɒrɪn) *adj.* **1.** of, located in, or coming from another country, area, people, etc.: *a foreign resident.* **2.** dealing or concerned with another country, area, people, etc.: *a foreign office.* **3.** not pertinent or related: *a matter foreign to the discussion.* **4.** not familiar; strange. **5.** in an abnormal place or position: *foreign matter.* [C13: from OF, from Vulgar L *forānus* (unattested) on the outside, from L *foris* outside] —'**foreignness** *n.*

foreign affairs *pl. n.* matters abroad that involve the homeland, such as relations with another country.

foreigner ('fɒrɪnə) *n.* **1.** a person from a foreign country. **2.** an outsider. **3.** something from a foreign country, such as a ship or product.

foreign minister *or* **secretary** *n.* (*often caps.*) a cabinet minister who is responsible for a country's dealings with other countries. U.S. equivalent: **secretary of state.**

foreign office *n.* the ministry of a country or state that is concerned with dealings with other states. U.S. equivalent: **State Department.**

foreknowledge (fɔːˈnɒlɪdʒ) *n.* knowledge of a thing before it exists or occurs; prescience. —**fore'know** *vb.* —**fore'knowable** *adj.*

foreland ('fɔːlənd) *n.* **1.** a headland, cape, or promontory. **2.** land lying in front of something, such as water.

Foreland ('fɔːlənd) *n.* either of two headlands (**North Foreland** and **South Foreland**) in SE England, on the coast of Kent.

foreleg ('fɔːˌlɛɡ) *n.* either of the front legs of a horse, sheep, or other quadruped.

forelimb ('fɔːˌlɪm) *n.* either of the front or anterior limbs of a four-limbed vertebrate.

forelock ('fɔːˌlɒk) *n.* a lock of hair growing or falling over the forehead.

foreman ('fɔːmən) *n., pl.* **-men. 1.** a person, often experienced, who supervises other workmen. **2.** *Law.* the principal juror, who presides at the deliberations of a jury.

foremast ('fɔːˌmɑːst; *Naut.* 'fɔːməst) *n.* the mast nearest the bow on vessels with two or more masts.

foremost ('fɔːˌməʊst) *adj., adv.* first in time, place, rank, etc. [OE, from *forma* first]

forename ('fɔːˌneɪm) *n.* another term for **Christian name.**

forenamed ('fɔːˌneɪmd) *adj.* (*prenominal*) named or mentioned previously; aforesaid.

forenoon ('fɔːˌnuːn) *n.* the daylight hours before or just before noon.

forensic (fəˈrɛnsɪk) *adj.* used in, or connected with a court of law: *forensic science.* [C17: from L *forēnsis* public, from *forum*] —**fo'rensically** *adv.*

forensic medicine *n.* the use of medical knowledge, esp. pathology, to the purposes of the law, as in determining the cause of death. Also called: **medical jurisprudence.**

foreordain (ˌfɔːrɔːˈdeɪn) *vb.* (*tr.; may take a clause as object*) to determine (events, etc.) in the future. —**foreordination** (ˌfɔːrɔːdɪˈneɪʃən) *n.*

forepaw ('fɔːˌpɔː) *n.* either of the front feet of most land mammals that do not have hoofs.

foreplay ('fɔːˌpleɪ) *n.* mutual sexual stimulation preceding sexual intercourse.

forequarter ('fɔːˌkwɔːtə) *n.* the front portion, including the leg, of half of a carcass, as of beef.

forequarters ('fɔːˌkwɔːtəz) *pl. n.* the part of the body of a horse, etc. that consists of the forelegs, shoulders, and adjoining parts.

forerun (fɔːˈrʌn) *vb.* **-running, -ran, -run.** (*tr.*) **1.** to serve as a herald for. **2.** to precede. **3.** to forestall.

forerunner ('fɔːˌrʌnə) *n.* **1.** a person or thing that precedes another. **2.** a person or thing coming in advance to herald the arrival of someone or something. **3.** an omen; portent.

foresail ('fɔːˌseɪl; *Naut.* 'fɔːsˀl) *n. Naut.* **1.** the aftermost headsail of a fore-and-aft rigged vessel. **2.** the lowest sail set on the foremast of a square-rigged vessel.

foresee (fɔː'siː) *vb.* **-seeing, -saw, -seen.** (*tr.; may take a clause as object*) to see or know beforehand: *he did not foresee that.* **—fore'seeable** *adj.* **—fore'seer** *n.*

foreshadow (fɔː'ʃædəʊ) *vb.* (*tr.*) to show, indicate, or suggest in advance; presage.

foreshank ('fɔːˌʃæŋk) *n.* **1.** the top of the front leg of an animal. **2.** a cut of meat from this part.

foresheet ('fɔːˌʃiːt) *n.* **1.** the sheet of a foresail. **2.** (*pl.*) the part forward of the foremost thwart of a boat.

foreshock ('fɔːˌʃɒk) *n. Chiefly U.S.* a relatively small earthquake heralding the arrival of a much larger one.

foreshore ('fɔːˌʃɔː) *n.* **1.** the part of the shore that lies between the limits for high and low tides. **2.** the part of the shore that lies just above the high-water mark.

foreshorten (fɔː'ʃɔːtˀn) *vb.* (*tr.*) to represent (a line, form, object, etc.) as shorter than actual length in order to give an illusion of recession or projection.

foreshow (fɔː'ʃəʊ) *vb.* **-showing, -showed, -shown.** (*tr.*) *Arch.* to indicate in advance.

foresight ('fɔːˌsaɪt) *n.* **1.** provision for or insight into future problems, needs, etc. **2.** the act or ability of foreseeing. **3.** the act of looking forward. **4.** *Surveying.* a reading taken looking forwards. **5.** the front sight on a firearm. **—ˌfore'sighted** *adj.* **—ˌfore'sightedly** *adv.* **—ˌfore'sightedness** *n.*

foreskin ('fɔːˌskɪn) *n. Anat.* the nontechnical name for **prepuce.**

forest ('fɒrɪst) *n.* **1.** a large wooded area having a thick growth of trees and plants. **2.** the trees of such an area. **3.** *N.Z.* an area planted with pines or similar trees, not native trees. Cf. **bush** (sense 4). **4.** something resembling a large wooded area, esp. in density: *a forest of telegraph poles.* **5.** *Law.* (formerly) an area of woodland, esp. one owned by the sovereign and set apart as a hunting ground. **6.** (*modifier*) of, involving, or living in a forest or forests: *a forest glade.* ~*vb.* **7.** (*tr.*) to create a forest. [C13: from OF, from Med. L *forestis* unfenced woodland, from L *foris* outside] **—'forested** *adj.*

forestall (fɔː'stɔːl) *vb.* (*tr.*) **1.** to delay, stop, or guard against beforehand. **2.** to anticipate. **3.** to buy up merchandise for profitable resale. [C14 *forestallen* to waylay, from OE, from *fore-* in front of + *steall* place] **—fore'staller** *n.* **—fore'stalment** *n.*

forestation (ˌfɒrɪ'steɪʃən) *n.* the planting of trees over a wide area.

forestay ('fɔːˌsteɪ) *n. Naut.* an adjustable stay leading from the truck of the foremast to the deck, for controlling the bending of the mast.

forester ('fɒrɪstə) *n.* **1.** a person skilled in forestry or in charge of a forest. **2.** a person or animal that lives in a forest. **3.** (*cap.*) a member of the Ancient Order of Foresters, a friendly society.

Forester ('fɒrɪstə) *n.* **C(ecil) S(cott).** 1899–1966, English novelist; creator of Captain Horatio Hornblower in a series of novels on the Napoleonic Wars.

forest park *n. N.Z.* a recreational reserve which may include bush and exotic trees.

forestry ('fɒrɪstrɪ) *n.* **1.** the science of planting and caring for trees. **2.** the planting and management of forests. **3.** *Rare.* forest land.

foretaste ('fɔːˌteɪst) *n.* an early but limited experience of something to come.

foretell (fɔː'tɛl) *vb.* **-telling, -told.** (*tr.; may take a clause as object*) to tell or indicate (an event, a result, etc.) beforehand.

forethought ('fɔːˌθɔːt) *n.* **1.** advance consideration or deliberation. **2.** thoughtful anticipation of future events.

foretoken *n.* ('fɔːˌtəʊkən). **1.** a sign of a future event. ~*vb.* (fɔː'təʊkən). **2.** (*tr.*) to foreshadow.

foretop ('fɔːˌtɒp; *Naut.* 'fɔːtəp) *n. Naut.* a platform at the top of the foremast.

fore-topgallant (ˌfɔːtɒp'gælənt; *Naut.* ˌfɔːtə'gælənt) *adj. Naut.* of, relating to, or being the topmost portion of a foremast.

fore-topmast (fɔː'tɒpˌmɑːst; *Naut.* fɔː'tɒpməst) *n. Naut.* a mast stepped above a foremast.

fore-topsail (fɔː'tɒpˌseɪl; *Naut.* fɔː'tɒpsˀl) *n. Naut.* a sail set on a fore-topmast.

for ever *or* **forever** (fɔː'rɛvə, fə-) *adv.* **1.** without end; everlastingly. **2.** at all times. **3.** *Inf.* for a very long time: *he went on speaking for ever.* ~*n.* **forever. 4.** (*as object*) *Inf.* a very long time: *it took him forever to reply.*

for evermore *or* **forevermore** (fɔːˌrɛvə'mɔː, fə-) *adv.* a more emphatic or emotive term for **for ever.**

forewarn (fɔː'wɔːn) *vb.* (*tr.*) to warn beforehand. **—fore'warner** *n.*

forewent (fɔː'wɛnt) *vb.* the past tense of **forego.**

forewing ('fɔːˌwɪŋ) *n.* either wing of the anterior pair of an insect's two pairs of wings.

foreword ('fɔːˌwɜːd) *n.* an introductory statement to a book. [C19: literal translation of G *Vorwort*]

Forfar ('fɔːfər, -fɑː) *n.* a market town in E Scotland, in Tayside region: site of a castle, residence of Scottish kings between the 11th and 14th centuries. Pop.: 12 742 (1981).

forfeit ('fɔːfɪt) *n.* **1.** something lost or given up as a penalty for a fault, mistake, etc. **2.** the act of losing or surrendering something in this manner. **3.** *Law.* something confiscated as a penalty for an offence, etc. **4.** (*sometimes pl.*) **a.** a game in which a player has to give up an object, perform a specified action, etc., if he commits a fault. **b.** an object so given up. ~*vb.* (*tr.*) **5.** to lose or be liable to lose in consequence of a mistake, fault, etc. **6.** *Law.* to confiscate as punishment. ~*adj.* **7.** surrendered or liable to be surrendered as a penalty. [C13: from OF *forfet* offence, from *forfaire* to commit a crime, from Med. L, from L *foris* outside + *facere* to do] **—'forfeiter** *n.*

forfeiture ('fɔːfɪtʃə) *n.* **1.** something forfeited. **2.** the act of forfeiting or paying a penalty.

forfend *or* **forefend** (fɔː'fɛnd) *vb.* (*tr.*) **1.** *U.S.* to protect or secure. **2.** *Obs.* to prevent.

forgather *or* **foregather** (fɔː'gæðə) *vb.* (*intr.*) **1.** to gather together. **2.** (foll. by *with*) to socialize.

forgave (fə'geɪv) *vb.* the past tense of **forgive.**

forge[1] (fɔːdʒ) *n.* **1.** a place in which metal is worked by heating and hammering; smithy. **2.** a hearth or furnace used for heating metal. ~*vb.* **3.** (*tr.*) to shape (metal) by heating and hammering. **4.** (*tr.*) to form, make, or fashion (objects, etc.). **5.** (*tr.*) to invent or devise (an agreement, etc.). **6.** to make a fraudulent imitation of (a signature, etc.) or to commit forgery. [C14: from OF *forgier* to construct, from L *fabricāre*, from *faber* craftsman] **—'forger** *n.*

forge[2] (fɔːdʒ) *vb.* (*intr.*) **1.** to move at a steady pace. **2. forge ahead.** to increase speed. [C17: from ?]

forgery ('fɔːdʒərɪ) *n., pl.* **-geries. 1.** the act of reproducing something for a fraudulent purpose. **2.** something forged, such as an antique. **3.** *Criminal law.* **a.** the false making or altering of a document, such as a cheque, etc., or any tape or disc storing information, with intent to defraud. **b.** something forged.

forget (fə'gɛt) *vb.* **-getting, -got, -gotten** *or* (*Arch. or dialect*) **-got. 1.** (when *tr., may take a clause as object or an infinitive*) to fail to recall (someone or something once known). **2.** (*tr.; may take a clause as object or an infinitive*) to neglect, either as the result of an unintentional error or intentionally. **3.** (*tr.*) to leave behind by mistake. **4. forget oneself. a.** to act in an improper manner. **b.** to be unselfish. **c.** to be deep in thought. [OE *forgietan*] **—for'gettable** *adj.* **—for'getter** *n.*

forgetful (fə'gɛtfʊl) *adj.* **1.** tending to forget. **2.** (*often postpositive; foll. by of*) inattentive (to) or neglectful (of). **—for'getfully** *adv.*

forget-me-not *n.* a temperate low-growing plant having clusters of small blue flowers.

forgive (fə'gɪv) *vb.* **-giving, -gave, -given. 1.** to cease to blame (someone or something). **2.** to grant pardon for (a mistake, etc.). **3.** (*tr.*) to free (someone) from penalty. **4.** (*tr.*) to free from the obligation of (a debt, etc.). [OE *forgiefan*] **—for'givable** *adj.* **—for'giver** *n.*

forgiveness (fə'gɪvnɪs) *n.* **1.** the act of forgiving or the state of being forgiven. **2.** willingness to forgive.

forgiving (fə'gɪvɪŋ) *adj.* willing to forgive.

forgo *or* **forego** (fɔː'gəʊ) *vb.* **-going, -went, -gone.** (*tr.*) to give up or do without. [OE *forgān*]
▷ **Usage.** See at **for-.**

forgot (fə'gɒt) *vb.* **1.** the past tense of **forget. 2.** *Arch. or dialect.* a past participle of **forget.**

forgotten (fə'gɒtᵊn) vb. a past participle of **forget.**
forint (*Hungarian* 'forint) n. the standard monetary unit of Hungary. [from Hungarian, from It. *fiorino* FLORIN]
fork (fɔːk) n. 1. a small usually metal implement consisting of two, three, or four long thin prongs on the end of a handle, used for lifting food to the mouth, etc. 2. a similar-shaped agricultural tool, used for lifting, digging, etc. 3. a pronged part of any machine, device, etc. 4. (of a road, river, etc.) a. a division into two or more branches. b. the point where the division begins. c. such a branch. ~vb. 5. (tr.) to pick up, dig, etc., with a fork. 6. (tr.) *Chess.* to place (two enemy pieces) under attack with one of one's own pieces. 7. (intr.) to be divided into two or more branches. 8. to take one or other branch at a fork in a road, etc. [OE *forca*, from L *furca*]
forked (fɔːkt) adj. 1. a. having a fork or forklike parts. b. (in combination): two-forked. 2. zigzag: forked lightning. —**forkedly** ('fɔːkɪdlɪ) adv.
fork-lift truck n. a vehicle having two power-operated horizontal prongs that can be raised and lowered for transporting and unloading goods. Sometimes shortened to **fork-lift.**
fork out, over, or **up** vb. (adv.) Sl. to pay (money, goods, etc.), esp. with reluctance.
Forlì (Italian for'li) n. a city in N Italy, in Emilia-Romagna. Pop.: 110 482 (1986). Ancient name: **Forum Livii** ('lɪvɪaɪ).
forlorn (fə'lɔːn) adj. 1. miserable or cheerless. 2. forsaken. 3. (postpositive; foll. by of) bereft: forlorn of hope. 4. desperate: the last forlorn attempt. [OE *forloren* lost, from *forlēosan* to lose] —**for'lornness** n.
forlorn hope n. 1. a hopeless enterprise. 2. a faint hope. 3. Obs. a group of soldiers assigned to an extremely dangerous duty. [C16 (in the obs. sense): changed (by folk etymology) from Du. *verloren hoop* lost troop, from *verloren*, p.p. of *verliezen* to lose + *hoop* troop (lit.: heap)]
form (fɔːm) n. 1. the shape or configuration of something as distinct from its colour, texture, etc. 2. the particular mode, appearance, etc., in which a thing or person manifests itself: water in the form of ice. 3. a type or kind: imprisonment is a form of punishment. 4. a printed document, esp. one with spaces in which to insert facts or answers: an application form. 5. physical or mental condition, esp. good condition, with reference to ability to perform: off form. 6. the previous record of a horse, athlete, etc., esp. with regard to fitness. 7. Brit. sl. a criminal record. 8. a fixed mode of artistic expression or representation in literary, musical, or other artistic works: sonata form. 9. a mould, frame, etc., that gives shape to something. 10. Education, chiefly Brit. a group of children who are taught together. 11. behaviour or procedure, esp. as governed by custom or etiquette: good form. 12. formality or ceremony. 13. a prescribed set or order of words, terms, etc., as in a religious ceremony or legal document. 14. Philosophy. a. the structure of anything as opposed to its content. b. essence as opposed to matter. 15. See **logical form.** 16. Brit. a bench, esp. one that is long, low, and backless. 17. a hare's nest. 18. any of the various ways in which a word may be spelt or inflected. ~vb. 19. to give shape or form to or to take shape or form, esp. a particular shape. 20. to come or bring into existence: a scum formed. 21. to make or construct or be made or constructed. 22. to construct or develop in the mind: to form an opinion. 23. (tr.) to train or mould by instruction or example. 24. (tr.) to acquire or develop: to form a habit. 25. (tr.) to be an element of or constitute: this plank will form a bridge. 26. (tr.) to organize: to form a club. [C13: from OF, from L *forma* shape, model]
-form adj. combining form. having the shape or form of or resembling: cruciform; vermiform. [from NL -formis, from L, from *fōrma* FORM]
formal ('fɔːməl) adj. 1. of or following established forms, conventions, etc.: a formal document. 2. characterized by observation of conventional forms of ceremony, behaviour, etc.: a formal dinner. 3. methodical or stiff. 4. suitable for occasions organized according to conventional ceremony: formal dress. 5. denoting idiom, vocabulary, etc., used by educated speakers and writers of a language. 6. acquired by study in academic institutions. 7. symmetrical in form: a formal garden. 8. of or relating to the appearance, form, etc., of something as distinguished from its substance. 9. logically deductive: formal

proof. 10. denoting a second-person pronoun in some languages: in French the pronoun "vous" is formal, while "tu" is informal. [C14: from L formālis] —**'formally** adv. —**'formalness** n.
formaldehyde (fɔː'mældɪ,haɪd) n. a colourless poisonous irritating gas with a pungent characteristic odour, used as formalin and in the manufacture of synthetic resins. Formula: HCH₃. Systematic name: **methanal.** [C19: FORM(IC) ALDEHYDE; on the model of G *Formaldehyd*]
formalin ('fɔːməlɪn) n. a solution of formaldehyde in water, used as a disinfectant, preservative for biological specimens, etc.
formalism ('fɔːmə,lɪzəm) n. 1. scrupulous or excessive adherence to outward form at the expense of content. 2. the mathematical or logical structure of a scientific argument as distinguished from its subject matter. 3. Theatre. a stylized mode of production. 4. (in Marxist criticism, etc.) excessive concern with artistic technique at the expense of social values, etc. —**'formalist** n. —**,formal'istic** adj.
formality (fɔː'mælɪtɪ) n., pl. -ties. 1. a requirement of custom, etiquette, etc. 2. the quality of being formal or conventional. 3. strict or excessive observance of ceremony, etc.
formalize or **-lise** ('fɔːmə,laɪz) vb. 1. to be or make formal. 2. (tr.) to make official or valid. 3. (tr.) to give a definite shape or form to. —**,formali'zation** or **-li'sation** n.
formal language n. any of various languages designed for use in fields such as mathematics, logic, or computer programming, the symbols and formulas of which stand in precisely specified syntactic and semantic relations to one another.
formal logic n. the study of systems of deductive argument in which symbols are used to represent precisely defined categories of expressions.
Forman ('fɔːmən) n. **Miloš** ('mi:ləʊʃ). born 1932, Czech film director working in the U.S.A. since 1968. His films include Taking Off (1970) and One Flew over the Cuckoo's Nest (1976).
formant ('fɔːmənt) n. Acoustics, phonetics. any of the constituents of a sound, esp. a vowel sound, that impart to the sound its own special quality, tone colour, or timbre.
format ('fɔːmæt) n. 1. the general appearance of a publication, including type style, paper, binding, etc. 2. style, plan, or arrangement, as of a television programme. 3. Computers. the arrangement of data on magnetic tape, etc., to comply with a computer's input device. ~vb. -matting, -matted. (tr.) 4. to arrange (a book, page, etc.) into a specified format. [C19: via F from G, from L *liber formātus* volume formed]
formation (fɔː'meɪʃən) n. 1. the act of giving or taking form or existence. 2. something that is formed. 3. the manner in which something is arranged. 4. a. a formal arrangement of a number of persons or things acting as a unit, such as a troop of soldiers or a football team. b. (as modifier): formation dancing. 5. a series of rocks with certain characteristics in common.
formative ('fɔːmətɪv) adj. 1. of or relating to formation, development, or growth: formative years. 2. shaping; moulding: a formative experience. 3. functioning in the formation of derived, inflected, or compound words. ~n. 4. an inflectional or derivational affix. —**'formatively** adv. —**'formativeness** n.
Formby ('fɔːmbɪ) n. **George.** Real name George Booth. 1904–61, British comedian. He made many musical films in the 1930s, accompanying his songs on the ukulele.
form class n. 1. another term for **part of speech.** 2. a group of words distinguished by common inflections, such as the weak verbs of English.
forme or U.S. **form** (fɔːm) n. Printing. type matter, blocks, etc., assembled in a chase and ready for printing. [C15: from F: FORM]
former¹ ('fɔːmə) adj. (prenominal) 1. belonging to or occurring in an earlier time: former glory. 2. having been at a previous time: a former colleague. 3. denoting the first or first mentioned of two. ~n. 4. **the former.** the first or first mentioned of two: distinguished from latter.
former² ('fɔːmə) n. 1. a person or thing that forms or shapes. 2. Electrical engineering. a tool for giving a coil or winding the required shape.

formerly ('fɔːməlɪ) *adv.* at or in a former time; in the past.

formic ('fɔːmɪk) *adj.* **1.** of, relating to, or derived from ants. **2.** of, containing, or derived from formic acid. [C18: from L *formica* ant; the acid occurs naturally in ants]

Formica (fɔː'maɪkə) *n. Trademark.* any of various laminated plastic sheets used esp. for heat-resistant surfaces.

formic acid *n.* a colourless corrosive liquid carboxylic acid found in some insects, esp. ants, and many plants: used in the manufacture of insecticides. Formula: HCOOH. Systematic name: **methanoic acid.**

formidable ('fɔːmɪdəbᵊl) *adj.* **1.** arousing or likely to inspire fear or dread. **2.** extremely difficult to defeat, overcome, manage, etc. **3.** tending to inspire awe or admiration because of great size, excellence, etc. [C15: from L, from *formīdāre* to dread, from *formīdō* fear] — **'formidably** *adv.*

formless ('fɔːmlɪs) *adj.* without a definite shape or form; amorphous. — **'formlessly** *adv.*

form letter *n.* a single copy of a letter that has been mechanically reproduced in large numbers for circulation.

Formosa (fɔː'məʊsə) *n.* the former name of **Taiwan.**

Formosa Strait *n.* an arm of the Pacific between Taiwan and mainland China, linking the East and South China Seas. Also called: **Taiwan Strait.**

formula ('fɔːmjʊlə) *n., pl.* **-las** *or* **-lae** (-,liː). **1.** an established form or set of words, as used in religious ceremonies, legal proceedings, etc. **2.** *Maths., physics.* a general relationship, principle, or rule stated, often as an equation, in the form of symbols. **3.** *Chem.* a representation of molecules, radicals, ions, etc., expressed in the symbols of the atoms of their constituent elements. **4. a.** a method, pattern, or rule for doing or producing something, often one proved to be successful. **b.** (*as modifier*): *formula fiction.* **5.** *U.S. & Canad.* a prescription for making up a medicine, baby's food, etc. **6.** *Motor racing.* the category in which a type of car competes, judged according to engine size, weight, and fuel capacity. [C17: from L: dim. of *forma* FORM] — **formulaic** (,fɔːmjʊ'leɪɪk) *adj.*

formularize *or* **-ise** ('fɔːmjʊlə,raɪz) *vb.* a less common word for **formulate** (sense 1).

formulary ('fɔːmjʊlərɪ) *n., pl.* **-laries. 1.** a book of prescribed formulas, esp. relating to religious procedure or doctrine. **2.** a formula. **3.** *Pharmacol.* a book containing a list of pharmaceutical products with their formulas. ~*adj.* **4.** of or relating to a formula.

formulate ('fɔːmjʊ,leɪt) *vb.* (*tr.*) **1.** to put into or express in systematic terms; express in or as if in a formula. **2.** to devise. — **,formu'lation** *n.*

formwork ('fɔːm,wɜːk) *n.* an arrangement of wooden boards, etc., used to shape concrete while it is setting.

fornicate ('fɔːnɪ,keɪt) *vb.* (*intr.*) to commit fornication. [C16: from LL *fornicārī*, from L *fornix* vault, brothel situated therein] — **'forni,cator** *n.*

fornication (,fɔːnɪ'keɪʃən) *n.* **1.** voluntary sexual intercourse outside marriage. **2.** *Bible.* sexual immorality in general, esp. adultery.

Forrest ('fɒrɪst) *n.* **John,** 1st Baron Forrest. 1847–1918, Australian statesman and explorer; first premier of Western Australia (1890–1901).

forsake (fə'seɪk) *vb.* **-saking, -sook, -saken.** (*tr.*) **1.** to abandon. **2.** to give up (something valued or enjoyed). [OE *forsacan*] — **for'saker** *n.*

forsaken (fə'seɪkən) *vb.* **1.** the past participle of **forsake.** ~*adj.* **2.** completely deserted or helpless. — **for'sakenly** *adv.* — **for'sakenness** *n.*

forsook (fə'sʊk) *vb.* the past tense of **forsake.**

forsooth (fə'suːθ) *adv. Arch.* in truth; indeed. [OE *forsóth*]

Forster ('fɔːstə) *n.* **E(dward) M(organ).** 1879–1970, English novelist, short-story writer, and essayist. His best-known novels are *A Room with a View* (1908), *Howard's End* (1910), and *A Passage to India* (1924), in all of which he stresses the need for sincerity and sensitivity in human relationships and criticizes English middle-class values.

forswear (fɔː'swɛə) *vb.* **-swearing, -swore, -sworn. 1.** (*tr.*) to reject or renounce with determination or as upon oath. **2.** (*tr.*) to deny or disavow absolutely or upon oath. **3.** to perjure (oneself). [OE *forswearian*] — **for'swearer** *n.*

forsworn (fɔː'swɔːn) *vb.* the past participle of **forswear.** — **for'swornness** *n.*

Forsyth ('fɔːsaɪθ) *n.* **1. Bill.** born 1947, Scottish writer and director. His films include *Gregory's Girl* (1981) and

Local Hero (1983). **2. Frederick.** born 1938, British thriller writer. His books include *The Day of the Jackal* (1970), *The Odessa File* (1972), and *The Fourth Protocol* (1984).

forsythia (fɔː'saɪθɪə) *n.* a shrub native to China, Japan, and SE Europe but widely cultivated for its showy yellow bell-shaped flowers, which appear in spring before the foliage. [C19: NL, after William *Forsyth* (1737–1804), E botanist]

fort (fɔːt) *n.* **1.** a fortified enclosure, building, or position able to be defended against an enemy. **2. hold the fort.** *Inf.* to guard something temporarily. [C15: from OF, from *fort* (adj.) strong, from L *fortis*]

fort. *abbrev. for:* **1.** fortification. **2.** fortified.

Fortaleza (*Portuguese* fortə'leza) *n.* a port in NE Brazil, capital of Ceará state. Pop.: 648 815 (1980). Also called: **Ceará.**

Fort-de-France (*French* fɔrdəfrɑ̃s) *n.* the capital of Martinique, a port on the W coast: commercial centre of the French Antilles. Pop.: 99 844 (1982).

forte¹ (fɔːt, 'fɔːteɪ) *n.* **1.** something at which a person excels: *cooking is my forte.* **2.** *Fencing.* the stronger section of a sword, between the hilt and the middle. [C17: from F, from *fort* (adj.) strong, from L *fortis*]

forte² ('fɔːtɪ) *Music.* ~*adj., adv.* **1.** loud or loudly. Symbol: f ~*n.* **2.** a loud passage in music. [C18: from It., from L *fortis* strong]

forte-piano (,fɔːtɪ'pjɑːnəʊ) *Music.* ~*adj., adv.* **1.** loud and then immediately soft. Symbol: fp ~*n.* **2.** a note played in this way.

forth (fɔːθ) *adv.* **1.** forward in place, time, order, or degree. **2.** out, as from concealment or inaction. **3.** away, as from a place or country. **4. and so forth.** and so on. ~*prep.* **5.** *Arch.* out of. [OE]

Forth (fɔːθ) *n.* **1. Firth of.** an inlet of the North Sea in SE Scotland: spanned by a cantilever railway bridge 1600 m (almost exactly 1 mile) long (1889), and by a road bridge (1964). **2.** a river in S Scotland, flowing generally east to the Firth of Forth. Length: about 104 km (65 miles).

forthcoming (,fɔːθ'kʌmɪŋ) *adj.* **1.** approaching in time: *the forthcoming debate.* **2.** about to appear: *his forthcoming book.* **3.** available or ready. **4.** open or sociable.

forthright *adj.* ('fɔːθ,raɪt). **1.** direct and outspoken. ~*adv.* (,fɔːθ'raɪt, 'fɔːθ,raɪt), *also* **forthrightly. 2.** in a direct manner; frankly. **3.** at once. — **'forth,rightness** *n.*

forthwith (,fɔːθ'wɪθ) *adv.* at once.

fortification (,fɔːtɪfɪ'keɪʃən) *n.* **1.** the act, art, or science of fortifying or strengthening. **2. a.** a wall, mound, etc., used to fortify a place. **b.** such works collectively.

fortify ('fɔːtɪ,faɪ) *vb.* **-fying, -fied.** (*mainly tr.*) **1.** (*also intr.*) to make (a place) defensible, as by building walls, etc. **2.** to strengthen physically, mentally, or morally. **3.** to add alcohol to (wine), in order to produce sherry, port, etc. **4.** to increase the nutritious value of (a food), as by adding vitamins. **5.** to confirm: *to fortify an argument.* [C15: from OF, from LL, from L *fortis* strong + *facere* to make] — **'forti,fiable** *adj.* — **'forti,fier** *n.*

fortissimo (fɔː'tɪsɪ,məʊ) *Music.* ~*adj., adv.* **1.** very loud. Symbol: ff ~*n.* **2.** a very loud passage in music. [C18: from It., from L, from *fortis* strong]

fortitude ('fɔːtɪ,tjuːd) *n.* strength and firmness of mind. [C15: from L *fortitūdō* courage]

Fort Knox (nɒks) *n.* a military reservation in N Kentucky: site of the U.S. Gold Bullion Depository. Pop.: 31 055 (1980).

Fort Lamy ('fɔːt 'lɑːmɪ; *French* fɔr lami) *n.* the former name (until 1973) of **Ndjamena.**

Fort Lauderdale ('lɔːdə,deɪl) *n.* a city in SE Florida, on the Atlantic. Pop.: 151 048 (1986 est.).

fortnight ('fɔːt,naɪt) *n.* a period of 14 consecutive days; two weeks. [OE *fēowertiene niht* fourteen nights]

fortnightly ('fɔːt,naɪtlɪ) *Chiefly Brit.* ~*adj.* **1.** occurring or appearing once each fortnight. ~*adv.* **2.** once a fortnight. ~*n., pl.* **-lies. 3.** a publication issued at intervals of two weeks.

Fortran ('fɔːtræn) *n.* a high-level computer programming language for mathematical and scientific purposes. [C20: from *for(mula) tran(slation)*]

fortress ('fɔːtrɪs) *n.* **1.** a large fort or fortified town. **2.** a place or source of refuge or support. ~*vb.* **3.** (*tr.*) to protect. [C13: from OF, from Med. L *fortalitia*, from L *fortis* strong]

fortuitous (fɔː'tjuːɪtəs) *adj.* happening by chance, esp. by a lucky chance. [C17: from L *fortuitus* happening by chance, from *fors* chance, luck] —**for'tuitously** *adv.*

fortuity (fɔː'tjuːɪtɪ) *n., pl.* **-ties.** **1.** a chance or accidental occurrence. **2.** chance or accident.

Fortuna (fɔː'tjuːnə) *n.* the Roman goddess of fortune and good luck. Greek counterpart: **Tyche.**

fortunate ('fɔːtʃənɪt) *adj.* **1.** having good luck. **2.** occurring by or bringing good fortune or luck. —**'fortunately** *adv.*

fortune ('fɔːtʃən) *n.* **1.** an amount of wealth or material prosperity, esp. a great amount. **2. small fortune.** a large sum of money. **3.** a power or force, often personalized, regarded as being responsible for human affairs. **4.** luck, esp. when favourable. **5.** (*often pl.*) a person's destiny. ~*vb.* **6.** (*intr.*) *Arch.* to happen by chance. [C13: from OF, from L, from *fors* chance]

fortune-hunter *n.* a person who seeks to secure a fortune, esp. through marriage.

fortune-teller *n.* a person who makes predictions about the future as by looking into a crystal ball, etc. —**'fortune-,telling** *adj., n.*

Fort Wayne (weɪn) *n.* a city in NE Indiana. Pop: 172 900 (1986 est.).

Fort William *n.* a town in W Scotland, in the Highland region at the head of Loch Linnhe: tourist centre; the fort itself, built in 1655 and renamed after William III in 1690, was demolished in 1866. Pop.: 4400 (1985 est.).

Fort Worth (wɜːθ) *n.* a city in N Texas, at the junction of the Clear and West forks of the Trinity River. Pop.: 385 164 (1980).

forty ('fɔːtɪ) *n., pl.* **-ties.** **1.** the cardinal number that is the product of ten and four. **2.** a numeral, 40, XL, etc., representing this number. **3.** something representing, represented by, or consisting of 40 units. ~*determiner.* **4. a.** amounting to forty: *forty thieves.* **b.** (*as pronoun*): *there were forty in the herd.* [OE *fēowertig*] —**'fortieth** *adj., n.*

forty-five *n.* a gramophone record played at 45 revolutions per minute.

Forty-Five *n.* **the.** *British history.* another name for the **Jacobite Rebellion.** See **Young Pretender.**

forty-niner *n.* (*sometimes cap.*) *U.S. history.* a prospector who took part in the California gold rush of 1849.

forty winks *n.* (*functioning as sing. or pl.*) *Inf.* a short light sleep; nap.

forum ('fɔːrəm) *n., pl.* **-rums** *or* **-ra** (-rə). **1.** a meeting for the open discussion of subjects of public interest. **2.** a medium for open discussion, such as a magazine. **3.** a public meeting place for open discussion. **4.** a court; tribunal. **5.** (in ancient Italy) an open space serving as a city's marketplace and centre of public business. [C15: from L: public place]

Forum *or* **Forum Romanum** (rəʊ'mɑːnəm) *n.* **the.** the main forum of ancient Rome.

forward ('fɔːwəd) *adj.* **1.** directed or moving ahead. **2.** lying or situated in or near the front part of something. **3.** presumptuous, pert, or impudent. **4.** well developed or advanced, esp. in physical or intellectual development. **5. a.** of or relating to the future or favouring change. **b.** (*in combination*): *forward-looking.* **6.** (*often postpositive*) *Arch.* ready, eager, or willing. **7.** *Commerce.* relating to fulfilment at a future date. ~*n.* **8.** an attacking player in any of various sports, such as soccer. ~*adv.* **9.** a variant of **forwards.** **10.** ('fɔːwəd; *Naut.* 'fɒrəd). towards the front or bow of an aircraft or ship. **11.** into a position of being subject to public scrutiny: *the witness came forward.* ~*vb.* (*tr.*) **12.** to send forward or pass on to an ultimate destination: *the letter was forwarded.* **13.** to advance or promote: *to forward one's career.* [OE *foreweard*] —**'forwarder** *n.* —**'forwardly** *adv.* —**'forwardness** *n.*

forwards ('fɔːwədz) *or* **forward** *adv.* **1.** towards or at a place ahead or in advance, esp. in space but also in time. **2.** towards the front.

forwent (fɔː'wɛnt) *vb.* the past tense of **forgo.**

forza ('fɔːtsə) *n. Music.* force. [C19: It., lit.: force]

Foshan (fɔː'ʃɑːn) *or* **Fatshan** *n.* a city in SE China, in W Guangdong province. Pop.: 122 500 (1953). Also called: **Namhoi.**

fossa ('fɒsə) *n., pl.* **-sae** (-siː). an anatomical depression or hollow area. [C19: from L: ditch, from *fossus* dug up, from *fodere* to dig up]

fosse *or* **foss** (fɒs) *n.* a ditch or moat, esp. one dug as a fortification. [C14: from OF, from L *fossa*; see FOSSA]

Fosse Way (fɒs) *n.* a Roman road in Britain between Lincoln and Exeter, with a fosse on each side.

fossick ('fɒsɪk) *vb. Austral. & N.Z.* **1.** (*intr.*) to search for gold or precious stones in abandoned workings, rivers, etc. **2.** to rummage or search for (something): *to fossick around for.* [C19: Austral., prob. from E dialect *fussock* to bustle about, from FUSS] —**'fossicker** *n.*

fossil ('fɒsəl) *n.* **1. a.** a relic or representation of a plant or animal that existed in a past geological age, occurring in the form of mineralized bones, shells, etc. **b.** (*as modifier*): *fossil insects.* **2.** *Inf., derog.* a person, idea, thing, etc., that is outdated or incapable of change. **3.** *Linguistics.* a form once current but now appearing only in one or two special contexts. [C17: from L *fossilis* dug up, from *fodere* to dig]

fossil fuel *n.* any naturally occurring fuel, such as coal, and natural gas, formed by the decomposition of prehistoric organisms.

fossiliferous (,fɒsɪ'lɪfərəs) *adj.* (of sedimentary rocks) containing fossils.

fossilize *or* **-lise** ('fɒsɪ,laɪz) *vb.* **1.** to convert or be converted into a fossil. **2.** to become or cause to become antiquated or inflexible. —**,fossili'zation** *or* **-li'sation** *n.*

fossorial (fɒ'sɔːrɪəl) *adj.* (of the forelimbs and skeleton of burrowing animals) adapted for digging. [C19: from Med. L, from L *fossor* digger, from *fodere* to dig]

foster ('fɒstə) *vb.* (*tr.*) **1.** to promote the growth or development of. **2.** to bring up (a child, etc.). **3.** to cherish (a plan, hope, etc.) in one's mind. **4.** *Chiefly Brit.* **a.** to place (a child) in the care of foster parents. **b.** to bring up under fosterage. ~*adj.* **5.** (*in combination*) of or involved in the rearing of a child by persons other than his natural parents: *foster home.* [OE *fōstrian* to feed, from *fōstor* FOOD] —**'fosterer** *n.* —**'fostering** *n.*

Foster ('fɒstə) *n.* **1. Norman.** born 1935, British architect. His works include the Willis Faber building (1978) in Ipswich and the Sainsbury Centre for Visual Art (1974). **2. Stephen Collins.** 1826–64, U.S. composer of songs such as *The Old Folks at Home* and *Oh Susanna.*

fosterage ('fɒstərɪdʒ) *n.* **1.** the act of caring for a foster child. **2.** the state of being a foster child. **3.** the act of encouraging.

Fotheringhay ('fɒðərɪŋ,geɪ) *n.* a village in E England, in NE Northamptonshire: ruined castle, scene of the imprisonment and execution of Mary Queen of Scots (1587).

Foucault (*French* fuko) *n.* **Jean Bernard Léon** (ʒɑ̃ bɛrnar leɔ̃). 1819–68, French physicist. He determined the velocity of light and proved that light travels more slowly in water than in air (1850). He demonstrated by means of the pendulum named after him the rotation of the earth on its axis (1851) and invented the gyroscope (1852).

Foucquet (*French* fukɛ) *n.* a variant spelling of (Nicolas) **Fouquet.**

fought (fɔːt) *vb.* the past tense and past participle of **fight.**

foul (faʊl) *adj.* **1.** offensive to the senses; revolting. **2.** stinking. **3.** charged with or full of dirt or offensive matter. **4.** (of food) putrid; rotten. **5.** morally or spiritually offensive. **6.** obscene; vulgar: *foul language.* **7.** unfair: *to resort to foul means.* **8.** (esp. of weather) unpleasant or adverse. **9.** blocked or obstructed with dirt or foreign matter: *a foul drain.* **10.** (of the bottom of a vessel) covered with barnacles that slow forward motion. **11.** *Inf.* unsatisfactory; bad: *a foul book.* ~*n.* **12.** *Sport.* **a.** a violation of the rules. **b.** (*as modifier*): *a foul blow.* **13.** an entanglement or collision, esp. in sailing or fishing. ~*vb.* **14.** to make or become polluted. **15.** to become or cause to become entangled. **16.** (*tr.*) to disgrace. **17.** to become or cause to become clogged. **18.** (*tr.*) *Naut.* (of underwater growth) to cling to (the bottom of a vessel) so as to slow its motion. **19.** (*tr.*) *Sport.* to commit a foul against (an opponent). **20.** (*intr.*) *Sport.* to infringe the rules. **21.** to collide (with a boat, etc.). ~*adv.* **22.** in a foul manner. **23. fall foul of. a.** come into conflict with. **b.** *Naut.* to come into collision with. [OE *fūl*] —**'foully** *adv.* —**'foulness** *n.*

foulard (fuː'lɑːd) *n.* a soft light fabric of plain-weave or twill-weave silk or rayon, usually with a printed design. [C19: from F, from ?]

Foulds (fəʊldz) *n.* **Neal.** born 1963, British snooker player.

Foulness (faʊl'nɛs) n. a flat marshy island in SE England, in Essex north of the Thames estuary.

foul play n. **1.** unfair conduct esp. with violence. **2.** a violation of the rules in a game or sport.

foul up vb. (adv.) **1.** (tr.) to bungle. **2.** (tr.) to contaminate. **3.** to be or cause to be blocked, choked, or entangled.

found[1] (faʊnd) vb. **1.** the past tense and past participle of **find.** ~adj. **2.** furnished or fitted out. **3.** Brit. with meals, heating, etc., provided without extra charge.

found[2] (faʊnd) vb. **1.** (tr.) to bring into being or establish (something, such as an institution, etc.). **2.** (tr.) to build or establish the foundation of. **3.** (also intr.; foll. by on or upon) to have a basis (in). [C13: from OF, from L, from fundus bottom]

found[3] (faʊnd) vb. (tr.) **1.** to cast (a material, such as metal or glass) by melting and pouring into a mould. **2.** to make (articles) in this way. [C14: from OF, from L fundere to melt]

foundation (faʊn'deɪʃən) n. **1.** that on which something is founded. **2.** (often pl.) a construction below the ground that distributes the load of a building, wall, etc. **3.** the base on which something stands. **4.** the act of founding or establishing or the state of being founded or established. **5.** an endowment for the support of an institution such as a school. **6.** an institution supported by an endowment, often one that provides funds for charities, research, etc. **7.** a cosmetic used as a base for make-up. —**foun'dational** adj.

foundation garment n. a woman's undergarment worn to shape and support the figure. Also called: **foundation.**

foundation stone n. a stone laid at a ceremony to mark the foundation of a new building.

founder[1] ('faʊndə) n. a person who establishes an institution, society, etc. [C14: see FOUND[2]]

founder[2] ('faʊndə) vb. (intr.) **1.** (of a ship, etc.) to sink. **2.** to break down or fail: the project foundered. **3.** to sink into or become stuck in soft ground. **4.** to collapse. **5.** (of a horse) to stumble or go lame. [C13: from OF fondrer to submerge, from L fundus bottom]

founder[3] ('faʊndə) n. **a.** a person who makes metal castings. **b.** (in combination): an iron founder. [C15: see FOUND[3]]

foundling ('faʊndlɪŋ) n. an abandoned infant whose parents are not known. [C13 foundeling; see FIND]

foundry ('faʊndrɪ) n., pl. -ries. a place in which metal castings are produced. [C17: from OF, from fondre; see FOUND[3]]

fount[1] (faʊnt) n. **1.** Poetic. a spring or fountain. **2.** source. [C16: back formation from FOUNTAIN]

fount[2] (faʊnt, font) n. Printing. a complete set of type of one style and size. Also called (esp. U.S. and Canad.): **font.** [C16: from OF fonte a founding, casting, from Vulgar L funditus (unattested) a casting, from L fundere to melt]

fountain ('faʊntɪn) n. **1.** a jet or spray of water or some other liquid. **2.** a structure from which such a jet or a number of such jets spurt. **3.** a natural spring of water, esp. the source of a stream. **4.** a stream, jet, or cascade of sparks, lava, etc. **5.** a principal source. **6.** a reservoir, as for oil in a lamp. [C15: from OF, from LL, from L fons spring, source] —**'fountained** adj.

fountainhead ('faʊntɪn,hɛd) n. **1.** a spring that is the source of a stream. **2.** a principal or original source.

fountain pen n. a pen the nib of which is supplied with ink from a cartridge or a reservoir in its barrel.

Fouqué (German fu'ke:) n. **Friedrich Heinrich Karl** ('fri:drɪç 'haɪnrɪç karl), Baron de la Motte. 1777–1843, German romantic writer; author of Undine (1811).

Fouquet (French fukɛ) n. **1. Jean** (ʒɑ̃). ?1420–?80, French painter and miniaturist. **2.** Also: **Foucquet. Nicolas** (nikɔla), Marquis de Belle-Isle. 1615–80, French statesman; superintendent of finance (1653–61) under Louis XIV. He was imprisoned for embezzlement, having been denounced by Colbert.

Fouquier-Tinville (French fukjetɛ̃vil) n. **Antoine Quentin** (ɑ̃twan kɑ̃tɛ̃). 1746–95, French revolutionary; as public prosecutor (1793–94) during the Reign of Terror, he sanctioned the guillotining of Desmoulins, Danton, and Robespierre.

four (fɔː) n. **1.** the cardinal number that is the sum of three and one. **2.** a numeral, 4, IV, etc., representing this number. **3.** something representing, represented by, or consisting of four units, such as a playing card with four symbols on it. **4.** Also called: **four o'clock.** four hours after noon or midnight. **5.** Cricket. **a.** a shot that crosses the boundary after hitting the ground. **b.** the four runs scored for such a shot. **6.** Rowing. **a.** a racing shell propelled by four oarsmen. **b.** the crew of such a shell. ~determiner. **7. a.** amounting to four: four times. **b.** (as pronoun): four are ready. [OE fēower]

four flush n. a useless poker hand, containing four of a suit and one odd card.

fourfold ('fɔː,fəʊld) adj. **1.** equal to or having four times as many or as much. **2.** composed of four parts. ~adv. **3.** by or up to four times as many or as much.

Fourier ('fʊərɪ,eɪ; French furje) n. **1. (François Marie) Charles** (ʃarl). 1772–1837, French social reformer: propounded a system of cooperatives known as Fourierism, esp. in his work Le Nouveau monde industriel (1829–30). **2. Jean Baptiste Joseph** (ʒɑ̃ batist ʒɔzɛf). 1768–1830, French mathematician, Egyptologist, and administrator, noted particularly for his research on the theory of heat and the method of analysis named after him.

four-in-hand n. **1.** a road vehicle drawn by four horses and driven by one driver. **2.** a four-horse team. **3.** U.S. a long narrow tie tied in a flat slipknot with the ends dangling.

four-leaf clover or **four-leaved clover** n. a clover with four leaves rather than three, supposed to bring good luck.

four-letter word n. any of several short English words referring to sex or excrement: regarded generally as offensive or obscene.

Fournier (French furnje) n. See **Alain-Fournier.**

four-o'-clock n. a tropical American plant, cultivated for its tubular yellow, red, or white flowers that open in late afternoon. Also called: **marvel-of-Peru.**

four-poster n. a bed with posts at each corner supporting a canopy and curtains.

fourscore (,fɔː'skɔː) determiner. an archaic word for **eighty.**

foursome ('fɔːsəm) n. **1.** a set or company of four. **2.** Also called: **four-ball.** Golf. a game between two pairs of players.

foursquare (,fɔː'skwɛə) adv. **1.** squarely; firmly. ~adj. **2.** solid and strong. **3.** forthright. **4.** a rare word for **square.**

four-stroke adj. designating an internal-combustion engine in which the piston makes four strokes for every explosion.

fourteen ('fɔː'tiːn) n. **1.** the cardinal number that is the sum of ten and four. **2.** a numeral, 14, XIV, etc., representing this number. **3.** something represented by or consisting of 14 units. ~determiner. **4. a.** amounting to fourteen: fourteen cats. **b.** (as pronoun): the fourteen who remained. [OE fēowertiene] —**'four'teenth** adj., n.

fourth (fɔːθ) adj. (usually prenominal) **1. a.** coming after the third in order, position, time, etc. Often written: 4th. **b.** (as n.): the fourth in succession. **2.** denoting the highest forward ratio of a gearbox in most motor vehicles. ~n. **3.** Music. **a.** the interval between one note and another four notes away from it in a diatonic scale. **b.** one of two notes constituting such an interval in relation to the other. **4.** the fourth forward ratio of a gearbox in a motor vehicle, usually the highest gear in cars. **5.** a less common word for **quarter** (sense 2). ~adv. also: **fourthly. 6.** after the third person, position, event, etc. ~sentence connector. also: **fourthly. 7.** as the fourth point.

fourth dimension n. **1.** the dimension of time, which in addition to three spatial dimensions specifies the position of a point or particle. **2.** the concept in science fiction of a dimension in addition to three spatial dimensions. —**,fourth-di'mensional** adj.

fourth estate n. (sometimes caps.) journalists or their profession; the press.

fovea ('fəʊvɪə) n., pl. -veae (-vɪ,iː). Anat. any small pit or depression in the surface of a bodily organ or part. [C19: from L: a small pit]

Fowey (fɔɪ) n. a resort and fishing village in SW England, in Cornwall, linked administratively with St Austell in 1968. Pop. (with St Austell): 36 639 (1981).

fowl (faʊl) n. **1.** Also called: **domestic fowl.** a domesticated gallinaceous bird occurring in many varieties. **2.** any other bird that is used as food or hunted as game. **3.** the flesh or meat of fowl, esp. of chicken. **4.** an archaic word for any **bird**. ~*vb*. **5**. (*intr.*) to hunt or snare wildfowl. [OE *fugol*] — **'fowler** *n*. — **'fowling** *n*., *adj*.

Fowler ('faʊlə) *n*. **Henry Watson**. 1858–1933, English lexicographer and grammarian; compiler of *Modern English Usage* (1926).

Fowles (faʊlz) *n*. **John**. born 1926, English novelist, noted for his psychological novels, often playing on the complexities of existential possibilities. They include *The Collector* (1963), *The French Lieutenant's Woman* (1969), and *A Maggot* (1985).

Fowliang or **Fou-liang** ('fuː'ljæŋ) *n*. a variant transliteration of the Chinese name for **Jingdezhen**.

fowl pest *n*. an acute and usually fatal viral disease of domestic fowl, characterized by discoloration of the comb and wattles.

fox (fɒks) *n*., *pl*. **foxes** or **fox**. **1**. any canine mammal of the genus *Vulpes* and related genera. They are mostly predators and have a pointed muzzle and a bushy tail. **2**. the fur of any of these animals, usually reddish-brown or grey in colour. **3**. a person who is cunning and sly. ~*vb*. **4**. (*tr.*) *Inf*. to perplex: *to fox a person with a problem*. **5**. to cause (paper, wood, etc.) to become discoloured with spots, or (of paper, etc.) to become discoloured. **6**. (*tr.*) to trick; deceive. **7**. (*intr.*) to act deceitfully or craftily. [OE] — **'fox,like** *adj*.

Fox (fɒks) *n*. **1. Charles James**. 1749–1806, British Whig statesman and orator. He opposed North over taxation of the American colonies and Pitt over British intervention against the French Revolution. He advocated parliamentary reform and the abolition of the slave trade. **2. George**. 1624–91, English religious leader; founder (1647) of the Society of Friends (Quakers). **3. Sir William**. 1812–93, New Zealand statesman, born in England: prime minister of New Zealand (1856; 1861–62; 1869–72; 1873).

Foxe (fɒks) *n*. **John**. 1516–87, English Protestant clergyman; author of *History of the Acts and Monuments of the Church* (1563), popularly known as the *Book of Martyrs*.

Foxe Basin *n*. an arm of the Atlantic in NE Canada, between Melville Peninsula and Baffin Island.

foxfire ('fɒks,faɪə) *n*. a luminescent glow emitted by certain fungi on rotting wood.

foxglove ('fɒks,glʌv) *n*. a plant having spikes of purple or white thimble-like flowers. The soft wrinkled leaves are a source of digitalis. [OE]

foxhole ('fɒks,həʊl) *n*. *Mil*. a small pit dug to provide shelter against hostile fire.

foxhound ('fɒks,haʊnd) *n*. a breed of short-haired hound, usually kept for hunting foxes.

fox hunt *n*. **1. a.** the hunting of foxes with hounds. **b.** an instance of this. **2.** an organization for fox hunting within a particular area. — **'fox-,hunter** *n*. — **'fox-,hunting** *n*.

foxtail ('fɒks,teɪl) *n*. any grass of Europe, Asia, and South America, having soft cylindrical spikes of flowers: cultivated as a pasture grass.

Fox Talbot ('tɔːlbət) *n*. **William Henry**. 1800–77, English physicist; a pioneer of photography.

fox terrier *n*. either of two breeds of small tan-black-and-white terrier, the wire-haired and the smooth.

foxtrot ('fɒks,trɒt) *n*. **1**. a ballroom dance in quadruple time, combining short and long steps in various sequences. ~*vb*. **-trotting**, **-trotted**. **2**. (*intr.*) to perform this dance.

foxy ('fɒksɪ) *adj*. **foxier**, **foxiest**. **1**. of or resembling a fox, esp. in craftiness. **2**. of a reddish-brown colour. **3**. (of paper, etc.) spotted, esp. by mildew. — **'foxily** *adv*. — **'foxiness** *n*.

foyer ('fɔɪeɪ, 'fɔɪə) *n*. a hall, lobby, or anteroom, as in a hotel, theatre, cinema, etc. [C19: from F: fireplace, from Med. L, from L *focus* fire]

fp *Music. abbrev. for* forte-piano.

FP *abbrev. for:* **1**. fire plug. **2**. former pupil. **3**. Also: **fp**. freezing point.

FPA *abbrev. for* Family Planning Association.

fps *abbrev. for:* **1**. feet per second. **2**. foot-pound-second. **3**. *Photog.* frames per second.

fps units *pl.*, *n*. an Imperial system of units based on the foot, pound, and second as the units of length, mass, and time.

Fr *abbrev. for:* **1**. *Christianity:* **a.** Father. **b.** Frater. [L: brother] **2**. *the chemical symbol for* francium.

fr. *abbrev. for:* **1**. fragment. **2**. franc. **3**. from.

Fr. *abbrev. for:* **1**. France. **2**. French.

Fra (fraː) *n*. a title given to an Italian monk or friar. [It., short for *frate* brother, from L *frāter* BROTHER]

fracas ('frækaː) *n*. a noisy quarrel; brawl. [C18: from F, from *fracasser* to shatter, from L *frangere* to break, infl. by *quassāre* to shatter]

fractal ('fræktəl) *n*. any of various irregular and fragmented shapes or surfaces that are not normally represented in geometry. [C20: from L *frāctus*, p.p. of *frangere* to break]

fraction ('frækʃən) *n*. **1**. *Maths*. a ratio of two expressions or numbers other than zero. **2**. any part or subdivision. **3**. a small piece; fragment. **4**. *Chem*. a component of a mixture separated by fractional distillation. **5**. *Christianity*. the formal breaking of the bread in Communion. [C14: from LL, from L *fractus* broken, from *frangere* to break] — **'fractional** *adj*. — **'fraction,ize** or **-,ise** *vb*.

fractional distillation *n*. the process of separating the constituents of a liquid mixture by heating it and condensing separately the components according to their different boiling points. Sometimes shortened to **distillation**.

fractionate ('frækʃə,neɪt) *vb*. **1**. to separate or cause to separate into constituents. **2**. (*tr.*) *Chem*. to obtain (a constituent of a mixture) by a fractional process. — **,fraction'ation** *n*.

fractious ('frækʃəs) *adj*. **1**. irritable. **2**. unruly. [C18: from (obs.) *fraction* discord + -OUS] — **'fractiously** *adv*. — **'fractiousness** *n*.

fracture ('fræktʃə) *n*. **1**. the act of breaking or the state of being broken. **2. a.** the breaking or cracking of a bone or the tearing of a cartilage. **b.** the resulting condition. **3**. a division, split, or breach. **4**. *Mineralogy*. **a.** the characteristic appearance of the surface of a freshly broken mineral or rock. **b.** the way in which a mineral or rock naturally breaks. ~*vb*. **5**. to break or cause to break. **6**. to break or crack (a bone) or (of a bone) to become broken or cracked. [C15: from OF, from L, from *frangere* to break] — **'fractural** *adj*.

fraenum or **frenum** ('friːnəm) *n*., *pl*. **-na** (-nə). a fold of membrane or skin, such as the fold beneath the tongue. [C18: from L: bridle]

fragile ('frædʒaɪl) *adj*. **1**. able to be broken easily. **2**. in a weakened physical state. **3**. delicate; light: *a fragile touch*. **4**. slight; tenuous. [C17: from L *fragilis*, from *frangere* to break] — **'fragilely** *adv*. — **fragility** (frə'dʒɪlɪtɪ) *n*.

fragment *n*. ('frægmənt). **1**. a piece broken off or detached. **2**. an incomplete piece: *fragments of a novel*. **3**. a scrap; bit. ~*vb*. (fræg'ment). **4**. to break or cause to break into fragments. [C15: from L *fragmentum*, from *frangere* to break] — **,fragmen'tation** *n*.

fragmentary ('frægməntərɪ) *adj*. made up of fragments; disconnected. Also: **fragmental**.

Fragonard (*French* fragɔnar) *n*. **Jean Honoré** (ʒɑ̃ ɔnɔre). 1732–1806, French artist, noted for richly coloured paintings typifying the frivolity of 18th-century French court life.

fragrance ('freɪɡrəns) or **fragrancy** *n*., *pl*. **-grances** or **-grancies**. **1**. a pleasant or sweet odour. **2**. the state of being fragrant.

fragrant ('freɪɡrənt) *adj*. having a pleasant or sweet smell. [C15: from L, from *frāgrāre* to emit a smell] — **'fragrantly** *adv*.

frail[1] (freɪl) *adj*. **1**. physically weak and delicate. **2**. fragile: *a frail craft*. **3**. easily corrupted or tempted. [C13: from OF *frele*, from L *fragilis*, FRAGILE]

frail[2] (freɪl) *n*. **1**. a rush basket for figs or raisins. **2**. a quantity of raisins or figs equal to between 50 and 75 pounds. [C13: from OF *fraiel*, from ?]

frailty ('freɪltɪ) *n*., *pl*. **-ties**. **1**. physical or moral weakness. **2**. (*often pl.*) a fault symptomatic of moral weakness.

framboesia or *U.S.* **frambesia** (fræm'biːzɪə) *n*. *Pathol*. another name for **yaws**. [C19: from NL, from F *framboise* raspberry; from its raspberry-like excrescences]

frame (freɪm) *n*. **1**. an open structure that gives shape and support to something, such as the ribs of a ship's hull or an aircraft's fuselage or the beams of a building. **2**. an enclosing case or border into which something is fitted: *the frame of a picture*. **3**. the system around which something is built up: *the frame of government*. **4**. the structure of the human body. **5.** a condition; state (esp. in **frame of mind**). **6. a.** one of a series of exposures on film used in making motion pictures. **b.** an exposure on a film used in still photography. **7.** a television picture scanned by one or more electron beams at a particular frequency. **8.** *Snooker, etc.* **a.** the wooden triangle used to set up the balls. **b.** the balls when set up. **c.** a single game finished when all the balls have been potted. **9.** short for **cold frame**. **10.** one of the sections of which a beehive is composed, esp. one designed to hold a honeycomb. **11.** *Statistics.* an enumeration of a population for the purposes of sampling. **12.** *Sl.* another word for **frame-up**. **13.** *Obs.* shape; form. ~*vb.* (*mainly tr.*) **14.** to construct by fitting parts together. **15.** to draw up the plans or basic details for: *to frame a policy.* **16.** to compose or conceive: *to frame a reply.* **17.** to provide, support, or enclose with a frame: *to frame a picture.* **18.** to form (words) with the lips, esp. silently. **19.** *Sl.* to conspire to incriminate (someone) on a false charge. [OE *framiae* to avail] — **'frameless** *adj.* — **'framer** *n.*

Frame (freɪm) *n.* **Janet.** born 1924, New Zealand novelist. Her works include *Owls Do Cry* (1957), *Faces in the Water* (1961), and *The Pocket Mirror* (1967).

frame house *n.* a house that has a timber framework and cladding.

frame of reference *n.* **1.** *Sociol.* a set of standards that determines and sanctions behaviour. **2.** any set of planes or curves, such as the three coordinate axes, used to locate a point in space.

frame-up *n.* *Sl.* **1.** a conspiracy to incriminate someone on a false charge. **2.** a plot to bring about a dishonest result, as in a contest.

framework ('freɪm,wɜːk) *n.* **1.** a structural plan or basis of a project. **2.** a structure or frame supporting or containing something.

franc (fræŋk; *French* frɑ̃) *n.* **1.** the standard monetary unit of France, French dependencies, and Monaco, divided into 100 centimes. **2.** the standard monetary and currency unit, comprising 100 centimes, of various countries including Belgium, the Central African Republic, Gabon, Guinea, Liechtenstein, Luxembourg, Mauritania, Niger, the Republic of Congo, Senegal, Switzerland, Togo, etc. **3.** a Moroccan monetary unit worth one hundredth of a dirham. [C14: from OF; from L *Rex Francōrum* King of the Franks, inscribed on 14th-century francs]

France[1] (frɑːns) *n.* a republic in W Europe, between the English Channel, the Mediterranean, and the Atlantic: the largest country wholly in Europe; became a republic in 1793 after the French Revolution and an empire in 1804 under Napoleon; reverted to a monarchy (1815–48), followed by the Second Republic (1848–52), the Second Empire (1852–70), the Third Republic (1870–1940), and the Fourth and Fifth Republics (1946 and 1958); a member of the Common Market. It is generally flat or undulating in the north and west and mountainous in the south and east. Language: French. Religion: mostly Roman Catholic. Currency: franc. Capital: Paris. Pop.: 55 623 000 (1987). Area: (including Corsica) 551 600 sq. km (212 973 sq. miles). Related adj.: **Gallic.**

France[2] (*French* frɑ̃s) *n.* **Anatole** (anatɔl), real name *Anatole François Thibault.* 1844–1924, French novelist, short-story writer, and critic. His works include *Le Crime de Sylvestre Bonnard* (1881), *I'lle des Pingouins* (1908), and *La Révolte des anges* (1914): Nobel prize for literature 1921.

Francesca (*Italian* fran'tʃeska) *n.* See **Piero Della Francesca.**

Franche-Comté (*French* frɑ̃ʃkõte) *n.* a region of E France, covering the Jura and the low country east of the Saône: part of the Kingdom of Burgundy (6th cent. A.D.– 1137); autonomous as the Free County of Burgundy (1137–1384); under Burgundian rule again (1384–1477) and Hapsburg rule (1493–1674); annexed by France (1678).

franchise ('fræntʃaɪz) *n.* **1.** (usually preceded by *the*) the right to vote, esp. for representatives in a legislative body. **2.** any exemption, privilege, or right granted to an individual or group by a public authority. **3.** *Commerce.* authorization granted by a manufacturing enterprise to a distributor to market the manufacturer's products. **4.** the full rights of citizenship. ~*vb.* **5.** (*tr.*) *Commerce, chiefly U.S. & Canad.* to grant (a person, firm, etc.) a franchise.

[C13: from OF, from *franchir* to set free, from *franc* free] — **franchisement** ('fræntʃɪzmənt) *n.*

Francis I ('frɑːnsɪs) *n.* **1.** 1494–1547, king of France (1515–47). His reign was dominated by his rivalry with Emperor Charles V for the control of Italy. He was a noted patron of the arts and learning. **2.** title as emperor of Austria of **Francis II.**

Francis II *n.* 1768–1835, last Holy Roman Emperor (1792–1806) and, as Francis I, first emperor of Austria (1804–35). The Holy Roman Empire was dissolved (1806) following his defeat by Napoleon at Austerlitz.

Franciscan (fræn'sɪskən) *n.* **a.** a member of a Christian religious order of friars or nuns tracing their origins back to Saint Francis of Assisi. **b.** (*as modifier*): *a Franciscan friary.*

Francis of Assisi *n.* **Saint.** original name *Giovanni di Bernardone.* ?1181–1226, Italian monk; founder of the Franciscan order of friars. He is remembered for his humility and love for all creation and, according to legend, he received the stigmata (1224). Feast day: Oct. 4.

Francis of Sales (seɪlz; *French* sal) *n.* **Saint.** 1567–1622, French ecclesiastic and theologian; bishop of Geneva (1602–22) and an opponent of Calvinism; author of *Introduction to a Devout Life* (1609) and founder of the Order of the Visitation (1610). Feast day: Jan. 29.

Francis Xavier ('zeɪvɪə) *n.* **Saint.** See (Saint Francis) **Xavier.**

francium ('frænsɪəm) *n.* an unstable radioactive element of the alkali-metal group, occurring in minute amounts in uranium ores. Symbol: Fr; atomic no.: 87; half-life of most stable isotope, ^{223}Fr: 22 minutes. [C20: from NL, from FRANCE + -IUM; because first found in France]

Franck *n.* **1.** (*French* frɑ̃k). **César (Auguste)** (sezar). 1822–90, French composer, organist, and teacher, born in Belgium. His works, some of which make use of cyclic form, include a violin sonata, a string quartet, the *Symphony in D Minor* (1888), and much organ music. **2.** (fræŋk). **James.** 1882–1964, U.S. physicist, born in Germany: shared a Nobel prize for physics with Gustav Hertz (1925) for work on the quantum theory, particularly the effects of bombarding atoms with electrons.

Franco ('fræŋkəʊ; *Spanish* 'fraŋko) *n.* **Francisco** (fran'θisko), called *el Caudillo.* 1892–1975, Spanish general and statesman; head of state (1939–1975). He was commander-in-chief of the Falangists in the Spanish Civil War (1936–39), defeating the republican government and establishing a dictatorship (1939). He kept Spain neutral in World War II.

Franco- ('fræŋkəʊ-) *combining form.* indicating France or French: *Franco-Prussian.* [from Med. L *Francus,* from LL: FRANK]

francolin ('fræŋkəʊlɪn) *n.* an African or Asian partridge. [C17: from F, from OIt. *francolino,* from ?]

Francome ('fræŋkəm) *n.* **John.** born 1953, British jockey and trainer. He retired as a jockey in 1985.

Franconia (fræŋ'kəʊnɪə) *n.* a medieval duchy of Germany, inhabited by the Franks from the 7th century, now chiefly in Bavaria, Hesse, and Baden-Württemberg.

Francophone ('fræŋkəʊ,fəʊn) (*often not cap.*) ~*n.* **1.** a person who speaks French, esp. a native speaker. ~*adj.* **2.** speaking French as a native language. **3.** using French as a lingua franca.

frangible ('frændʒɪbəl) *adj.* breakable or fragile. [C15: from OF, ult. from L *frangere* to break] — ,**frangi'bility** *or* **'frangibleness** *n.*

frangipane ('frændʒɪ,peɪn) *n.* **1.** a pastry filled with cream and flavoured with almonds. **2.** a variant of **frangipani** (the perfume).

frangipani (,frændʒɪ'pɑːnɪ) *n., pl.* -**panis** *or* -**pani.** **1.** a tropical American shrub cultivated for its waxy white or pink flowers, which have a sweet overpowering scent. **2.** a perfume prepared from the flowers or resembling the odour of its flowers. **3.** **native frangipani.** *Austral.* an Australian evergreen tree with large fragrant yellow flowers. [C17: via F from It.: perfume for scenting gloves, after the Marquis Muzio *Frangipani,* 16th-century Roman nobleman who invented it]

Franglais (*French* frɑ̃glɛ) *n.* informal French containing a high proportion of English. [C20: from F *français* French + *anglais* English]

frank (fræŋk) *adj.* **1.** honest and straightforward in speech or attitude: *a frank person.* **2.** outspoken or blunt. **3.** open and avowed: *frank interest.* ~*vb.* (*tr.*) **4.**

Chiefly Brit. to put a mark on (a letter, etc.), either cancelling the postage stamp or in place of a stamp, ensuring free carriage. **5.** to mark (a letter, etc.) with an official mark or signature, indicating the right of free delivery. **6.** to facilitate or assist (a person) to enter easily. **7.** to obtain immunity for (a person). ~*n.* **8.** an official mark or signature affixed to a letter, etc., ensuring free delivery or delivery without stamps. [C13: from OF, from Med. L *francus* free; identical with FRANK (in Frankish Gaul only members of this people enjoyed full freedom)] —'**frankable** *adj.* —'**franker** *n.* —'**frankness** *n.*

Frank[1] (fræŋk) *n.* a member of a group of West Germanic peoples who spread from the east in the late 4th century A.D., gradually conquering most of Gaul and Germany. [OE *Franca;* ?from the name of a Frankish weapon (cf. OE *franca* javelin)]

Frank[2] (*Dutch* fraŋk) *n.* **Anne.** 1929–45, Dutch Jewess, whose *Diary* (1947) recorded the experiences of her family while in hiding from the Nazis in Amsterdam (1942–44). They were betrayed and she died in a concentration camp.

Frankenstein ('fræŋkɪn‚staɪn) *n.* **1.** a person who creates something that brings about his ruin. **2.** Also called: **Frankenstein's monster.** a thing that destroys its creator. [C19: after Baron *Frankenstein,* who created a destructive monster from parts of corpses in the novel by Mary Shelley (1818)] —‚**Franken'steinian** *adj.*

Frankfort ('fræŋkfət) *n.* **1.** a city in N Kentucky: the state capital. Pop.: 25 973 (1980). **2.** *Now rare.* an English spelling of **Frankfurt.**

Frankfurt (am Main) (*German* 'fraŋkfʊrt (am 'maɪn)) *n.* a city in central West Germany, in Hesse on the Main River: a Roman settlement in the 1st century; a free imperial city (1372–1806); seat of the federal assembly (1815–66); university (1914); trade fairs since the 13th century. Pop.: 593 400 (1986).

Frankfurt (an der Oder) (*German* 'fraŋkfʊrt (an der 'oːdər)) *n.* a city in E East Germany on the Polish border: member of the Hanseatic League (1368–1450). Pop.: 707 600 (1986).

frankfurter ('fræŋk‚fɜːtə) *n.* a smoked sausage, made of finely minced pork or beef. [C20: short for G *Frankfurter Wurst* sausage from FRANKFURT AM MAIN]

Frankfurter ('fræŋk‚fɜːtə) *n.* an inhabitant or native of Frankfurt.

frankincense ('fræŋkɪn‚sɛns) *n.* an aromatic gum resin obtained from trees of the genus *Boswellia,* which occur in Asia and Africa. [C14: from OF *franc* free, pure + *encens* INCENSE; see FRANK]

Frankish ('fræŋkɪʃ) *n.* **1.** the ancient West Germanic language of the Franks. ~*adj.* **2.** of or relating to the Franks or their language.

franklin ('fræŋklɪn) *n.* (in 14th- and 15th-century England) a substantial landholder of free but not noble birth. [C13: from Anglo-F, from OF *franc* free, on the model of CHAMBERLAIN]

Franklin ('fræŋklɪn) *n.* **1. Benjamin.** 1706–90, American statesman, scientist, and author. He helped draw up the Declaration of Independence (1776) and, as ambassador to France (1776–85), he negotiated an alliance with France and a peace settlement with Britain. As a scientist, he is noted particularly for his researches in electricity, esp. his invention of the lightning conductor. **2. Sir John.** 1786–1847, English explorer of the Arctic: lieutenant-governor of Van Diemen's Land (now Tasmania) (1836–43): died while on a voyage to discover the Northwest Passage. **3. Rosalind.** 1920–58, British X-ray crystallographer. She contributed to the discovery of the structure of DNA, before her premature death from cancer.

frankly ('fræŋklɪ) *adv.* **1.** (*sentence modifier*) to be honest. **2.** in a frank manner.

frantic ('fræntɪk) *adj.* **1.** distracted with fear, pain, joy, etc. **2.** marked by or showing frenzy: *frantic efforts.* [C14: from OF, from L *phrenēticus* mad] —'**frantically** *or* '**franticly** *adv.*

Franz Ferdinand (*German* frants 'fɛrdinant) *n.* English name *Francis Ferdinand.* 1863–1914, archduke of Austria; heir apparent of Franz Josef I. His assassination contributed to the outbreak of World War I.

Franz Josef I (*German* frants 'joːzɛf) *n.* English name *Francis Joseph I.* 1830–1916, emperor of Austria (1848–1916) and king of Hungary (1867–1916).

Franz Josef Land *n.* an archipelago of over 100 islands in the Arctic Ocean, administratively part of the Soviet Union. Area: about 21 000 sq. km (8000 sq. miles). Russian name: **Zemlya Frantsa Iosifa** (zji'mlja 'frantsə 'jɔsifə).

frappé ('fræpeɪ) *n.* **1.** a drink consisting of a liqueur, etc., poured over crushed ice. ~*adj.* **2.** (*postpositive*) (esp. of drinks) chilled. [C19: from F, from *frapper* to strike, hence, chill]

Fraser[1] ('freɪzə) *n.* a river in SW Canada, in S central British Columbia, flowing northwest, south, and west through spectacular canyons in the Coast Mountains to the Strait of Georgia. Length: 1370 km (850 miles).

Fraser[2] ('freɪzə) *n.* **1. (John) Malcolm.** born 1930, Australian statesman; prime minister of Australia (1975–83). **2. Peter.** 1884–1950, New Zealand statesman, born in Scotland; prime minister (1940–49).

frater ('freɪtə) *n. Arch.* a refectory. [C13: from OF *fraiteur,* from *refreitor,* from LL *rēfectōrium* REFECTORY]

fraternal (frə'tɜːn²l) *adj.* **1.** of or suitable to a brother; brotherly. **2.** of a fraternity. **3.** designating twins of the same or opposite sex that developed from two separate fertilized ova. Cf. **identical** (sense 3). [C15: from L, from *frāter* brother] —**fra'ternalism** *n.*

fraternity (frə'tɜːnɪtɪ) *n., pl.* -ties. **1.** a body of people united in interests, aims, etc.: *the teaching fraternity.* **2.** brotherhood. **3.** *U.S. & Canad.* a secret society joined by male students, functioning as a social club.

fraternize *or* **-nise** ('frætə‚naɪz) *vb.* (*intr.;* often foll. by *with*) to associate on friendly terms. —‚**frater'nization** *or* -‚**ni'sation** *n.* —'**frater‚nizer** *or* -‚**niser** *n.*

fratricide ('frætrɪ‚saɪd, 'freɪ-) *n.* **1.** the act of killing one's brother. **2.** a person who kills his brother. [C15: from L, from *frāter* brother + -CIDE] —‚**fratri'cidal** *adj.*

Frau (frau) *n., pl.* **Frauen** ('frauən) *or* **Fraus.** a married German woman: usually used as a title equivalent to *Mrs.* [from OHG *frouwa*]

fraud (frɔːd) *n.* **1.** deliberate deception, trickery, or cheating intended to gain an advantage. **2.** an act or instance of such deception. **3.** *Inf.* a person who acts in a false or deceitful way. [C14: from OF, from L *fraus* deception] —'**fraudster** *n.*

fraudulent ('frɔːdjʊlənt) *adj.* **1.** acting with or having the intent to deceive. **2.** relating to or proceeding from fraud. [C15: from L *fraudulentus* deceitful] —'**fraudulence** *n.* —'**fraudulently** *adv.*

Frauenfeld (*German* 'frauənfɛlt) *n.* a town in NE Switzerland, capital of Thurgau canton. Pop.: 18 607 (1980).

fraught (frɔːt) *adj.* **1.** (*usually postpositive* and foll. by *with*) filled or charged with: *a venture fraught with peril.* **2.** *Inf.* showing or producing tension or anxiety. [C14: from MDu. *vrachten,* from *vracht* FREIGHT]

Fräulein (*German* 'frɔylaɪn) *n., pl.* -lein *or English* -leins. an unmarried German woman: often used as a title equivalent to *Miss.* [from MHG *vrouwelīn,* dim. of *vrouwe* lady]

Fraunhofer (*German* 'fraunhoːfər) *n.* **Joseph von** ('jɔːzɛf fɔn). 1787–1826, German physicist and optician, who investigated spectra of the sun, planets, and fixed stars, and improved telescopes and other optical instruments.

Fraunhofer lines *pl. n.* a set of dark lines appearing in the continuous emission spectrum of the sun.

fraxinella (‚fræksɪ'nɛlə) *n.* another name for **gas plant.** [C17: from NL: a little ash tree, from L *frāxinus* ash]

fray[1] (freɪ) *n.* **1.** a noisy quarrel. **2.** a fight or brawl. [C14: short for AFFRAY]

fray[2] (freɪ) *vb.* **1.** to wear or cause to wear away into loose threads, esp. at an edge or end. **2.** to make or become strained or irritated. **3.** to rub or chafe (another object). [C14: from F *frayer* to rub, from L *fricāre* to rub]

Frazer ('freɪzə) *n.* Sir **James George.** 1854–1941, Scottish anthropologist; author of many works on primitive religion, and magic, esp. *The Golden Bough* (1890).

Frazier ('freɪzjə) *n.* **Joe.** born 1944, U.S. boxer: won the world heavyweight title in 1970 and was the first to beat Muhammad Ali professionally (1971).

frazil ('freɪzɪl) *n.* small pieces of ice that form in water moving turbulently enough to prevent the formation of a sheet of ice. [C19: from Canad. F, from F *fraisil* cinders, ult. from L *fax* torch]

frazzle ('fræz²l) *Inf.* ~*vb.* **1.** to make or become exhausted or weary. ~*n.* **2.** the state of being frazzled or exhausted. **3. to a frazzle.** completely (esp. in **burnt to**

a frazzle). [C19: prob. from ME *faselen* to fray, from *fasel* fringe; infl. by FRAY[2]]

freak (friːk) *n.* **1.** a person, animal, or plant that is abnormal or deformed. **2. a.** an object, event, etc., that is abnormal. **b.** (*as modifier*): *a freak storm*. **3.** a personal whim or caprice. **4.** *Inf.* a person who acts or dresses in a markedly unconventional way. **5.** *Inf.* a person who is ardently fond of something specified: *a jazz freak*. ~*vb.* **6.** See **freak out**. [C16: from ?] —'**freakish** *adj.* —'**freaky** *adj.*

freak out *vb.* (*adv.*) *Inf.* to be or cause to be in a heightened emotional state.

freckle ('frɛkəl) *n.* **1.** a small brownish spot on the skin developed by exposure to sunlight. Technical name: **lentigo.** **2.** any small area of discoloration. ~*vb.* **3.** to mark or become marked with freckles or spots. [C14: from ON *freknur*] —'**freckled** *or* '**freckly** *adj.*

Fredericia (*Danish* freðə'redsja) *n.* a port in Denmark, in E Jutland at the N end of the Little Belt. Pop.: 46 085 (1982).

Frederick I ('frɛdrɪk) *n.* **1.** See **Frederick Barbarossa.** **2.** 1657–1713, first king of Prussia (1701–13); son of Frederick William.

Frederick II *n.* **1.** 1194–1250, Holy Roman Emperor (1220–50), king of Germany (1212–50), and king of Sicily (1198–1250). **2.** See **Frederick the Great.**

Frederick III *n.* called *the Wise.* 1463–1525, elector of Saxony (1486–1525). He protected Martin Luther in Wartburg Castle after the Diet of Worms (1521).

Frederick IX *n.* 1899–1972, king of Denmark (1947–72).

Frederick Barbarossa (ˌbɑːbə'rɒsə) *n.* official title *Frederick I.* ?1123–90, Holy Roman Emperor (1155–90), king of Germany (1152–90). His attempt to assert imperial rights in Italy ended in his defeat at Legnano (1176) and the independence of the Lombard cities (1183).

Frederick the Great *n.* official title *Frederick II.* 1712–86, king of Prussia (1740–86); son of Frederick William I. He gained Silesia during the War of Austrian Succession (1740–48) and his military genius during the Seven Years' War (1756–63) established Prussia as a European power. He was also a noted patron of the arts.

Frederick William *n.* called *the Great Elector.* 1620–88, elector of Brandenburg (1640–88).

Frederick William I *n.* 1688–1740, king of Prussia (1713–40); son of Frederick I: reformed the Prussian army.

Frederick William III *n.* 1770–1840, king of Prussia (1797–1840).

Frederick William IV *n.* 1795–1861, king of Prussia (1840–61). He submitted to the 1848 Revolution but refused the imperial crown offered by the Frankfurt Parliament (1849). In 1857 he became insane and his brother, William I, became regent (1858–61).

Fredericton ('frɛdrɪktən) *n.* a city in SE Canada, capital of New Brunswick, on the St John River. Pop.: 44 352 (1986).

Frederiksberg (*Danish* frɛðregs'bɛr) *n.* a city in E Denmark, within the area of greater Copenhagen: founded in 1651 by King Frederick III. Pop.: 88 047 (1982 est.).

Fredrikstad (*Norwegian* 'freːdrikstad) *n.* a port in SE Norway at the entrance to Oslo Fjord. Pop.: 26 650 (1987).

free (friː) *adj.* **freer, freest.** **1.** able to act at will; not under compulsion or restraint. **2. a.** not enslaved or confined. **b.** (*as n.*): *land of the free.* **3.** (*often postpositive* and foll. by *from*) not subject (to) or restricted (by some regulation, constraint, etc.): *free from pain.* **4.** (of a country, etc.) autonomous or independent. **5.** exempt from external direction: *free will.* **6.** not subject to conventional constraints: *free verse.* **7.** not exact or literal: *a free translation.* **8.** provided without charge: *free entertainment.* **9.** *Law.* (of property) **a.** not subject to payment of rent or performance of services; freehold. **b.** not subject to any burden or charge; unencumbered. **10.** (*postpositive*; often foll. by *of* or *with*) ready or generous in using or giving: *free with advice.* **11.** not occupied or in use; available: *a free cubicle.* **12.** (of a person) not busy. **13.** open or available to all. **14.** without charge to the subscriber or user: *freepost; freephone.* **15.** not fixed or joined; loose: *the free end of a chain.* **16.** without obstruction or impediment: *free passage.* **17.** *Chem.* chemically uncombined: *free nitrogen.* **18.** *Logic.* denoting an occurrence of a variable not bound by a quantifier. Cf.

bound[1] (sense 8). **19.** (of routines in figure skating competitions) chosen by the competitor. **20. for free.** *Nonstandard.* without charge or cost. **21. free and easy.** casual or tolerant; easy-going. **22. make free with.** to behave too familiarly towards. ~*adv.* **23.** in a free manner; freely. **24.** without charge or cost. **25.** *Naut.* with the wind blowing from the quarter. ~*vb.* **freeing, freed.** (*tr.*) **26.** to set at liberty; release. **27.** to remove obstructions or impediments from. **28.** (often foll. by *of* or *from*) to relieve or rid (of obstacles, pain, etc.). [OE *frēo*] —'**freely** *adv.* —'**freeness** *n.*

-free *adj. combining form.* free from: *trouble-free; lead-free petrol.*

free alongside ship *adj.* (of a shipment of goods) delivered to the dock without charge to the buyer, but excluding the cost of loading onto the vessel. Cf. **free on board.**

free association *n. Psychoanal.* a method of exploring a person's unconscious by eliciting words and thoughts that are associated with key words provided by a psychoanalyst.

freebase ('friːˌbeɪs) *vb. Sl.* to refine (cocaine) for smoking.

freebie ('friːbɪ) *n. Sl.* something provided without charge.

freeboard ('friːˌbɔːd) *n.* the space or distance between the deck of a vessel and the waterline.

freebooter ('friːˌbuːtə) *n.* a person, such as a pirate, living from plunder. [C16: from Du., from *vrijbuit* booty; see FILIBUSTER] —'**freeboot** *vb.* (*intr.*)

freeborn ('friːˌbɔːn) *adj.* **1.** not born in slavery. **2.** of or suitable for people not born in slavery.

Free Church *n. Chiefly Brit.* any Protestant Church, esp. the Presbyterian, other than the Established Church.

free city *n.* a sovereign or autonomous city.

freedman ('friːdˌmæn) *n., pl.* **-men.** a man who has been freed from slavery.

freedom ('friːdəm) *n.* **1.** personal liberty, as from slavery, serfdom, etc. **2.** liberation, as from confinement or bondage. **3.** the quality or state of being free, esp. to enjoy political and civil liberties. **4.** (usually foll. by *from*) exemption or immunity: *freedom from taxation.* **5.** the right or privilege of unrestricted use or access: *the freedom of a city.* **6.** autonomy, self-government, or independence. **7.** the power or liberty to order one's own actions. **8.** *Philosophy.* the quality, esp. of the will or the individual, of not being totally constrained. **9.** ease or frankness of manner: *she talked with complete freedom.* **10.** excessive familiarity of manner. **11.** ease and grace, as of movement. [OE *frēodōm*]

freedom fighter *n.* a militant revolutionary.

free energy *n.* a thermodynamic property that expresses the capacity of a system to perform work under certain conditions.

free enterprise *n.* an economic system in which commercial organizations compete for profit with little state control.

free fall *n.* **1.** free descent of a body in which the gravitational force is the only force acting on it. **2.** the part of a parachute descent before the parachute opens.

free flight *n.* the flight of a rocket, missile, etc., when its engine has ceased to produce thrust.

free-for-all *n. Inf.* a disorganized brawl or argument, usually involving all those present.

free-form *adj. Arts.* freely flowing, spontaneous.

free hand *n.* **1.** unrestricted freedom to act (esp. in **give** (**someone**) **a free hand**). ~*adj., adv.* **freehand.** **2.** (done) by hand without the use of guiding instruments: *a freehand drawing.*

free-handed *adj.* generous or liberal; unstinting. —,**free-'handedly** *adv.*

freehold ('friːˌhəʊld) *Property law.* ~*n.* **1. a.** tenure by which land is held in fee simple, fee tail, or for life. **b.** an estate held by such tenure. ~*adj.* **2.** relating to or having the nature of freehold. —'**freeholder** *n.*

free house *n. Brit.* a public house not bound to sell only one brewer's products.

free kick *n. Soccer.* a place kick awarded for a foul or infringement.

freelance ('friːˌlɑːns) *n.* **1. a.** Also called: **freelancer.** a self-employed person, esp. a writer or artist, who is hired to do specific assignments. **b.** (*as modifier*): *a freelance journalist.* **2.** (in medieval Europe) a mercenary soldier or adventurer. ~*vb.* **3.** to work as a freelance on (an assignment, etc.). ~*adv.* **4.** as a freelance. [C19 (in sense 3): later applied to politicians, writers, etc.]

free-living *adj.* **1.** given to ready indulgence of the appetites. **2.** (of animals and plants) not parasitic. — ,**free-'liver** *n.*

freeloader ('fri:,ləʊdə) *n. Sl.* a person who habitually depends on others for food, shelter, etc.

free love *n.* the practice of sexual relationships without fidelity to a single partner.

freeman ('fri:mən) *n., pl.* -**men.** **1.** a person who is not a slave. **2.** a person who enjoys political and civil liberties. **3.** a person who enjoys a privilege, such as the freedom of a city.

free market economy *n.* an economic system which allows supply and demand to regulate prices, wages, etc. rather than government policy.

freemartin ('fri:,mɑːtɪn) *n.* the female of a pair of twin calves of unlike sex that is imperfectly developed and sterile. [C17: from ?]

Freemason ('fri:,meɪsᵊn) *n.* a member of the widespread secret order, constituted in London in 1717, of **Free and Accepted Masons,** pledged to brotherliness and mutual aid. Sometimes shortened to **Mason.**

freemasonry ('fri:,meɪsᵊnrɪ) *n.* natural or tacit sympathy and understanding.

Freemasonry ('fri:,meɪsᵊnrɪ) *n.* **1.** the institutions, rites, practices, etc., of Freemasons. **2.** Freemasons collectively.

free on board *adj.* (of a shipment of goods) delivered on board ship or other carrier without charge to the buyer. Cf. **free alongside ship.**

free port *n.* **1.** a port open to all commercial vessels on equal terms. **2.** a port that permits the duty-free entry of foreign goods intended for re-export.

free radical *n.* an atom or group of atoms containing at least one unpaired electron and existing for a brief period of time before reacting to produce a stable molecule.

free-range *adj. Chiefly Brit.* kept or produced in natural conditions: *free-range eggs.*

free-select *vb.* (*tr.*) *Austral. history.* to select (areas of crown land) and acquire the freehold by a series of annual payments. — '**free-se'lection** *n.* — '**free-se'lector** *n.*

freesia ('fri:zɪə) *n.* a plant of Southern Africa, cultivated for its white, yellow, or pink tubular fragrant flowers. [C19: NL, after F. H. T. *Freese* (died 1876), G physician]

free skating *n.* either of two parts in a figure-skating competition in which the skater chooses the sequence of figures and the music and which are judged on technique and artistic presentation. The short programme consists of specified movements and the long programme is entirely the skater's own choice.

free space *n.* a region that has no gravitational and electromagnetic fields. It is used as an absolute standard and was formerly referred to as a vacuum.

free-spoken *adj.* speaking frankly or without restraint. — ,**free-'spokenly** *adv.*

freestanding (,fri:'stændɪŋ) *adj.* not attached to or supported by another object.

freestone ('fri:,stəʊn) *n.* **1.** any fine-grained stone, esp. sandstone or limestone, that can be worked in any direction without breaking. **2.** *Bot.* a fruit, such as a peach, in which the flesh separates readily from the stone.

freestyle ('fri:,staɪl) *n.* **1.** a competition or race, as in swimming, in which each participant may use a style of his or her choice instead of a specified style. **2. a. International freestyle.** an amateur style of wrestling with an agreed set of rules. **b.** Also called: **all-in wrestling.** a style of professional wrestling with no internationally agreed set of rules.

freethinker (,fri:'θɪŋkə) *n.* a person who forms his ideas and opinions independently of authority or accepted views, esp. in matters of religion. —**free thought** *n.*

Freetown ('fri:,taʊn) *n.* the capital and chief port of Sierra Leone: founded in 1787 for slaves freed and destitute in England. Pop.: 469 776 (1985).

free trade *n.* **1.** international trade that is free of such government interference as protective tariffs. **2.** *Arch.* smuggling.

free verse *n.* unrhymed verse without a metrical pattern.

freeway ('fri:,weɪ) *n. U.S.* **1.** an expressway. **2.** a major road that can be used without paying a toll.

freewheel (,fri:'wi:l) *n.* **1.** a ratchet device in the rear hub of a bicycle wheel that permits the wheel to rotate freely while the pedals are stationary. ~*vb.* **2.** (*intr.*) to coast on a bicycle using the freewheel.

free will *n.* **1. a.** the apparent human ability to make choices that are not externally determined. **b.** the doctrine that such human freedom of choice is not illusory. Cf. **determinism. 2.** the ability to make a choice without outside coercion: *he left of his own free will.*

Free World *n.* **the.** the non-Communist countries collectively.

freeze (fri:z) *vb.* **freezing, froze, frozen. 1.** to change (a liquid) into a solid as a result of a reduction in temperature, or (of a liquid) to solidify in this way. **2.** (when *intr.,* sometimes foll. by *over* or *up*) to cover, clog, or harden with ice, or become so covered, clogged, or hardened. **3.** to fix fast or become fixed (to something) because of the action of frost. **4.** (*tr.*) to preserve (food) by subjection to extreme cold, as in a freezer. **5.** to feel or cause to feel the sensation or effects of extreme cold. **6.** to die or cause to die of extreme cold. **7.** to become or cause to become paralysed, fixed, or motionless, esp. through fear, shock, etc. **8.** (*tr.*) to cause (moving film) to stop at a particular frame. **9.** to make or become formal, haughty, etc., in manner. **10.** (*tr.*) to fix (prices, incomes, etc.) at a particular level. **11.** (*tr.*) to forbid by law the exchange, liquidation, or collection of (loans, assets, etc.). **12.** (*tr.*) to stop (a process) at a particular stage of development. **13.** (*intr.;* foll. by *onto*) *Inf., chiefly U.S.* to cling. ~*n.* **14.** the act of freezing or state of being frozen. **15.** *Meteorol.* a spell of temperatures below freezing point, usually over a wide area. **16.** the fixing of incomes, prices, etc., by legislation. ~*sentence substitute.* **17.** *Chiefly U.S.* a command to stop instantly or risk being shot. [OE *frēosan*] —'**freezable** *adj.*

freeze-dry *vb.* -**drying,** -**dried.** (*tr.*) to preserve (a substance) by rapid freezing and subsequently drying in a vacuum.

freeze-frame *n.* **1.** *Films, television.* a single frame of a film repeated to give an effect like a still photograph. **2.** *Video.* a single frame of a video recording viewed as a still by stopping the tape.

freeze out *vb.* (*tr., adv.*) *Inf.* to exclude, as by unfriendly behaviour, etc.

freezer ('fri:zə) *n.* an insulated cold-storage cabinet for long-term storage of perishable foodstuffs. Also called: **deepfreeze.**

freezing point *n.* the temperature below which a liquid turns into a solid.

freezing works *n. Austral. & N.Z.* a slaughterhouse at which animal carcasses are frozen for export.

Frege (*German* 'freːgə) *n.* **Gottlob.** 1848–1925, German logician and philosopher, who laid the foundations of modern formal logic and semantics in his *Begriffsschrift* (1879).

Freiburg (*German* 'fraɪbʊrk) *n.* **1.** a city in West Germany, in SW Baden-Württemberg: under Austrian rule (1368–1805); university (1457). Pop.: 184 800 (1986). Official name: **Freiburg im Breisgau** (ɪm 'braɪsɡaʊ). **2.** the German name for **Fribourg.**

freight (freɪt) *n.* **1. a.** commercial transport that is slower and cheaper than express. **b.** the price charged for such transport. **c.** goods transported by this means. **d.** (*as modifier*): *freight transport.* **2.** *Chiefly Brit.* a ship's cargo or part of it. ~*vb.* (*tr.*) **3.** to load with goods for transport. [C16: from MDu *vrecht,* var. of *vracht*]

freightage ('freɪtɪdʒ) *n.* **1.** the commercial conveyance of goods. **2.** the goods so transported. **3.** the price charged for such conveyance.

freighter ('freɪtə) *n.* **1.** a ship or aircraft designed for transporting cargo. **2.** a person concerned with the loading of a ship.

freightliner ('freɪt,laɪnə) *n.* a type of goods train carrying containers that can be transferred onto lorries or ships.

Fremantle ('fri:,mæntᵊl) *n.* a port in SW Western Australia, on the Indian Ocean. Pop.: 24 010 (1986).

French[1] (frɛntʃ) *n.* **1.** the official language of France: also an official language of Switzerland, Belgium, Canada, and certain other countries. Historically, French is an Indo-European language belonging to the Romance group. **2. the French.** (*functioning as pl.*) the natives, citizens, or inhabitants of France collectively. ~*adj.* **3.** relating to, denoting, or characteristic of France, the French, or their language. **4.** (in Canada) of French Canadians. [OE *Frencisc* French, Frankish] —'**Frenchness** *n.*

French² (frɛntʃ) *n.* Sir **John Denton Pinkstone,** 1st Earl of Ypres. 1852–1925, British field marshal in World War I: commanded the British Expeditionary Force in France and Belgium (1914–15); Lord Lieutenant of Ireland (1918–21).

French bread *n.* white bread in a long slender loaf that has a crisp brown crust.

French Cameroons *pl. n.* the part of Cameroon formerly administered by France (1919–60).

French Canada *n.* the areas of Canada, esp. in the province of Quebec, where French Canadians predominate.

French Canadian *n.* **1.** a Canadian citizen whose native language is French. ~*adj.* **French-Canadian. 2.** of or relating to French Canadians or their language.

French chalk *n.* a variety of talc used to mark cloth, remove grease stains, or as a dry lubricant.

French doors *pl. n.* the U.S. and Canad. name for **French windows.**

French dressing *n.* a salad dressing made from oil and vinegar with seasonings; vinaigrette.

French Equatorial Africa *n.* the former French overseas territories of Chad, Gabon, Middle Congo, and Ubangi-Shari (1910–58).

French fried potatoes *pl. n.* a more formal name for **chips.** Also called (U.S. and Canad.): **French fries.**

French Guiana *n.* a French overseas region in NE South America, on the Atlantic: colonized by the French in about 1637; tropical forests. Capital: Cayenne. Pop.: 88 800 (1987). Area: about 91 000 sq. km (23 000 sq. miles). —**French Guianese** or **Guianan** *adj., n.*

French Guinea *n.* a former French territory of French West Africa: became independent as Guinea in 1958.

French horn *n. Music.* a valved brass instrument with a funnel-shaped mouthpiece and a tube of conical bore coiled into a spiral.

Frenchify ('frɛntʃɪˌfaɪ) *vb.* -**fying,** -**fied.** *Inf.* to make or become French in appearance, etc.

French India *n.* a former French overseas territory in India, including Chandernagore and Pondicherry: restored to India between 1949 and 1954.

French Indochina *n.* the territories of SE Asia that were colonized by France and held mostly until 1954: included Cochin China, Annam, and Tonkin (now largely Vietnam), Cambodia (now Kampuchea), Laos, and Kuang-Chou Wan (returned to China in 1945, now Zhanjiang).

French kiss *n.* a kiss involving insertion of the tongue into the partner's mouth.

French knickers *pl. n.* women's wide-legged underpants.

French leave *n.* an unauthorized or unannounced absence or departure. [C18: alluding to a custom in France of leaving without saying goodbye to one's host or hostess]

French letter *n. Brit.* a slang term for **condom.**

Frenchman ('frɛntʃmən) *n., pl.* -**men.** a native, citizen, or inhabitant of France. —'**French,woman** *fem. n.*

French Morocco *n.* a former French protectorate in NW Africa, united in 1956 with Spanish Morocco and Tangier to form the kingdom of Morocco.

French mustard *n.* a mild mustard paste made with vinegar rather than water.

French North Africa *n.* the former French possessions of Algeria, French Morocco, and Tunisia.

French Oceania *n.* a former name (until 1958) of **French Polynesia.**

French polish *n.* **1.** a varnish for wood consisting of shellac dissolved in alcohol. **2.** the gloss finish produced by this polish.

French-polish *vb.* to treat with French polish or give a French polish (to).

French Polynesia *n.* a French Overseas Territory in the S Pacific Ocean, including the Society Islands, the Tuamotu group, the Gambier group, the Tubuai Islands, and the Marquesas Islands. Capital: Papeete, on Tahiti. Pop.: 183 000 (1987). Area: about 4000 sq. km (1500 sq. miles). Former name (until 1958): **French Oceania.**

French seam *n.* a seam in which the edges are not visible.

French Somaliland *n.* a former name (until 1967) of **Djibouti.**

French Southern and Antarctic Territories *pl. n.* a French overseas territory, comprising Adélie Land in Antarctica and the islands of Amsterdam and St Paul and the Kerguelen and Crozet archipelagos in the S Indian Ocean.

French Sudan *n.* a former name (1898–1959) of **Mali.**

French toast *n.* **1.** *Brit.* toast cooked on one side only. **2.** bread dipped in beaten egg and lightly fried.

French Togoland *n.* a former United Nations Trust Territory in W Africa, administered by France (1946–60), now the independent republic of Togo.

French West Africa *n.* a former group (1895–1958) of French Overseas Territories: consisted of Senegal, Mauritania, French Sudan, Burkina-Faso, Niger, French Guinea, the Ivory Coast, and Dahomey.

French West Indies *pl. n.* **the.** a group of islands in the Lesser Antilles, administered by France. Pop.: 632 754 (1967). Area: 2792 sq. km (1077 sq. miles).

French windows *pl. n.* (*sometimes sing.*) *Brit.* a pair of casement windows extending to floor level and opening onto a balcony, garden, etc.

frenetic (frɪ'nɛtɪk) *adj.* distracted or frantic. [C14: via OF, from L, from Gk, from *phrenitis* insanity, from *phrēn* mind] —**fre'netically** *adv.*

frenum ('friːnəm) *n., pl.* -**na** (-nə). a variant spelling (esp. U.S.) of **fraenum.**

frenzy ('frɛnzɪ) *n., pl.* -**zies. 1.** violent mental derangement. **2.** wild excitement or agitation. **3.** a bout of wild or agitated activity: *a frenzy of preparations.* ~*vb.* -**zying,** -**zied. 4.** (*tr.*) to drive into a frenzy. [C14: from OF, from LL *phrēnēsis* madness, from LGk, ult. from Gk *phrēn* mind] —'**frenzied** *adj.*

Freon ('friːˌɒn) *n. Trademark.* any of a group of chemically unreactive gaseous or liquid derivatives of methane in which hydrogen atoms have been replaced by chlorine and fluorine atoms: used as aerosol propellants, refrigerants, and solvents.

freq. *abbrev. for:* **1.** frequent(ly). **2.** frequentative.

frequency ('friːkwənsɪ) *n., pl.* -**cies. 1.** the state of being frequent. **2.** the number of times that an event occurs within a given period. **3.** *Physics.* the number of times that a periodic function or vibration repeats itself in a specified time, often 1 second. It is usually measured in hertz. **4.** *Statistics.* **a.** the number of individuals in a class (**absolute frequency**). **b.** the ratio of this number to the total number of individuals under survey (**relative frequency**). [C16: from L, from *frequēns* crowded]

frequency distribution *n. Statistics.* the function of the distribution of a sample corresponding to the probability density function of the underlying population and tending to it as the sample size increases.

frequency modulation *n.* a method of transmitting information using a radio-frequency carrier wave. The frequency of the carrier wave is varied in accordance with the amplitude of the input signal, the amplitude of the carrier remaining unchanged. Cf. **amplitude modulation.**

frequent *adj.* ('friːkwənt). **1.** recurring at short intervals. **2.** habitual. ~*vb.* (frɪ'kwɛnt). **3.** (*tr.*) to visit repeatedly or habitually. [C16: from L *frequēns* numerous] —,**frequen'tation** *n.* —**fre'quenter** *n.* —'**frequently** *adv.*

frequentative (frɪ'kwɛntətɪv) *Grammar.* ~*adj.* **1.** denoting an aspect of verbs in some languages used to express repeated or habitual action. **2.** (in English) denoting a verb or an affix meaning repeated action, such as the verb *wrestle,* from *wrest.* ~*n.* **3.** a frequentative verb or affix.

fresco ('frɛskəʊ) *n., pl.* -**coes** or -**cos. 1.** a very durable method of wall-painting using watercolours on wet plaster. **2.** a painting done in this way. [C16: from It.: fresh plaster, from *fresco* (adj.) fresh, cool, of Gmc origin]

Frescobaldi (*Italian* fresko'baldi) *n.* **Girolamo** (dʒiˈrɔːlamo). 1583–1643, Italian organist and composer, noted esp. for his organ and harpsichord music.

fresh (frɛʃ) *adj.* **1.** newly made, harvested, etc.: *fresh bread; fresh strawberries.* **2.** newly acquired, found, etc.: *fresh publications.* **3.** novel; original: *a fresh outlook.* **4.** most recent: *fresh developments.* **5.** further; additional: *fresh supplies.* **6.** not canned, frozen, or otherwise preserved: *fresh fruit.* **7.** (of water) not salt. **8.** bright or clear: *a fresh morning.* **9.** chilly or invigorating: *a fresh breeze.* **10.** not tired; alert. **11.** not worn or faded: *fresh colours.* **12.** having a healthy or ruddy appearance. **13.**

newly or just arrived: *fresh from the presses*. **14.** youthful or inexperienced. **15.** *Inf.* presumptuous or disrespectful; forward. ~*n.* **16.** the fresh part or time of something. **17.** another name for **freshet**. ~*adv.* **18.** in a fresh manner. [OE *fersc* fresh, unsalted] — '**freshly** *adv.* — '**freshness** *n.*

fresh breeze *n.* a wind of force 5 on the Beaufort scale, blowing at speeds between 19 and 24 mph.

freshen ('frɛʃən) *vb.* **1.** to make or become fresh or fresher. **2.** (often foll. by *up*) to refresh (oneself), esp. by washing. **3.** (*intr.*) (of the wind) to increase.

fresher ('frɛʃə) *or* **freshman** ('frɛʃmən) *n., pl.* **-ers** *or* **-men.** a first-year student at college or university.

freshet ('frɛʃɪt) *n.* **1.** the sudden overflowing of a river caused by heavy rain or melting snow. **2.** a stream of fresh water emptying into the sea.

freshwater ('frɛʃ,wɔːtə) *n.* (*modifier*) **1.** of or living in fresh water. **2.** (esp. of a sailor who has not sailed on the sea) inexperienced. **3.** *U.S.* little known: *a freshwater school.*

fresnel ('freɪnɛl) *n.* a unit of frequency equivalent to 10¹² hertz. [C20: after A. J. FRESNEL]

Fresnel (*French* frɛnɛl) *n.* **Augustin Jean** (ogystɛ̃ ʒɑ̃). 1788–1827, French physicist: worked on the interference of light, contributing to the wave theory of light.

Fresno ('frɛznəʊ) *n.* a city in central California, in the San Joaquin Valley. Pop.: 218 202 (1980).

fret¹ (frɛt) *vb.* **fretting, fretted. 1.** to distress or be distressed. **2.** to rub or wear away. **3.** to feel or give annoyance or vexation. **4.** to eat away or be eaten away, as by chemical action. **5.** (*tr.*) to make by wearing away; erode. ~*n.* **6.** a state of irritation or anxiety. [OE *fretan* to eat]

fret² (frɛt) *n.* **1.** a repetitive geometrical figure, esp. one used as an ornamental border. **2.** such a pattern made in relief; fretwork. ~*vb.* **fretting, fretted. 3.** (*tr.*) to ornament with fret or fretwork. [C14: from OF *frete* interlaced design used on a shield, prob. of Gmc origin] — '**fretless** *adj.*

fret³ (frɛt) *n.* any of several small metal bars set across the fingerboard of a musical instrument of the lute, guitar, or viol family at various points along its length so as to produce the desired notes. [C16: from ?] — '**fretless** *adj.*

fretful ('frɛtfʊl) *adj.* peevish, irritable, or upset. — '**fretfully** *adv.* — '**fretfulness** *n.*

fret saw *n.* a fine-toothed saw with a long thin narrow blade, used for cutting designs in thin wood or metal.

fretwork ('frɛt,wɜːk) *n.* decorative geometrical carving or openwork.

Freud (frɔɪd) *n.* **1. Lucian.** born 1922, British painter, esp. of nudes and portraits. **2.** his grandfather, **Sigmund** ('ziːkmʊnt). 1856–1939, Austrian psychiatrist; originator of psychoanalysis, based on free association of ideas and analysis of dreams. He stressed the importance of infantile sexuality in later development, evolving the concept of the Oedipus complex. His works include *The Interpretation of Dreams* (1900) and *The Ego and the Id* (1923).

Freudian ('frɔɪdɪən) *adj.* **1.** of or relating to Sigmund Freud or his ideas. ~*n.* **2.** a person who follows or believes in the basic ideas of Sigmund Freud. — '**Freudian,ism** *n.*

Freudian slip *n.* any action, such as a slip of the tongue, that may reveal an unconscious thought.

Frey (freɪ) *or* **Freyr** (freɪə) *n. Norse myth.* the god of earth's fertility and dispenser of prosperity.

Freya *or* **Freyja** ('freɪə) *n. Norse myth.* the goddess of love and fecundity, sister of Frey.

Freytag (*German* 'fraɪtaːk) *n.* **Gustav** ('gʊstaf). 1816–95, German novelist and dramatist; author of the comedy *Die Journalisten* (1853) and *Soll und Haben* (1855), a novel about German commercial life.

Fri. *abbrev. for* Friday.

friable ('fraɪəbəl) *adj.* easily broken up; crumbly. [C16: from L, from *friāre* to crumble] — ,**fria'bility** *or* '**friableness** *n.*

friar ('fraɪə) *n.* a member of any of various chiefly mendicant religious orders of the Roman Catholic Church. [C13 *frere*, from OF: brother, from L *frāter* BROTHER]

friar's balsam *n.* a compound produced benzoin, mixed with hot water and used as an inhalant to relieve colds and sore throats.

friary ('fraɪərɪ) *n., pl.* **-aries.** *Christianity.* a convent or house of friars.

Fribourg (*French* fribur) *n.* **1.** a canton in W Switzerland. Capital: Fribourg. Pop.: 185 246 (1980). Area: 1676 sq. km (645 sq. miles). **2.** a town in W Switzerland, capital of Fribourg canton: university (1889). Pop.: 37 100 (1983 est.). ~German name: **Freiburg.**

fricandeau ('frɪkən,dəʊ) *n., pl.* **-deaus** *or* **-deaux** (-,dəʊz). a larded and braised veal fillet. [C18: from OF, prob. based on FRICASSEE]

fricassee (,frɪkə'siː, 'frɪkəsɪ) *n.* **1.** stewed meat, esp. chicken or veal, served in a thick white sauce. ~*vb.* **-seeing, -seed. 2.** (*tr.*) to prepare (meat, etc.) as a fricassee. [C16: from OF, from *fricasser* to fricassee]

fricative ('frɪkətɪv) *n.* **1.** a consonant produced by partial occlusion of the airstream, such as (f) or (z). ~*adj.* **2.** relating to or denoting a fricative. [C19: from NL, from L *fricāre* to rub]

friction ('frɪkʃən) *n.* **1.** a resistance encountered when one body moves relative to another body with which it is in contact. **2.** the act, effect, or an instance of rubbing one object against another. **3.** disagreement or conflict. [C16: from F, from L *frictiō* a rubbing, from *fricāre* to rub] — '**frictional** *adj.* — '**frictionless** *adj.*

Friday ('fraɪdɪ) *n.* **1.** the sixth day of the week; fifth day of the working week. **2.** See **man Friday.** [OE *Frīgedæg*]

fridge (frɪdʒ) *n.* short for **refrigerator.**

fried (fraɪd) *vb.* the past tense and past participle of **fry¹.**

Friedman ('friːdmən) *n.* **Milton.** born 1912. U.S. economist, particularly associated with monetarism; a forceful advocate of free market capitalism. — '**Friedman,ite** *n., adj.*

Friedrich (*German* 'friːdrɪç) *n.* **Caspar David** ('kaspar 'daːfɪt). 1774–1840, German romantic landscape painter, noted for his skill in rendering changing effects of light.

friend (frɛnd) *n.* **1.** a person known well to another and regarded with liking, affection, and loyalty. **2.** an acquaintance or associate. **3.** an ally in a fight or cause. **4.** a fellow member of a party, society, etc. **5.** a patron or supporter. **6. be friends** (**with**). to be friendly (with). **7. make friends** (**with**). to become friendly (with). ~*vb.* **8.** (*tr.*) an archaic word for **befriend.** [OE *frēond*] — '**friendless** *adj.* — '**friendship** *n.*

Friend (frɛnd) *n.* a member of the Society of Friends; Quaker.

friend at court *n.* an influential acquaintance who can promote one's interests.

friendly ('frɛndlɪ) *adj.* **-lier, -liest. 1.** showing or expressing liking, goodwill, or trust. **2.** on the same side; not hostile. **3.** tending or disposed to help or support: *a friendly breeze helped them escape.* ~*n., pl.* **-lies. 4.** Also: **friendly match.** *Sport.* a match played for its own sake. — '**friendlily** *adv.* — '**friendliness** *n.*

-friendly *adj. combining form.* helpful, easy, or good for the person or thing specified: *ozone-friendly.*

Friendly Islands *pl. n.* another name for **Tonga².**

friendly society *n. Brit.* an association of people who pay regular dues or other sums in return for old-age pensions, sickness benefits, etc.

Friends of the Earth *n.* an organization of environmentalists and conservationists.

frier ('fraɪə) *n.* a variant spelling of **fryer.** See **fry¹.**

Friese-Greene (,friːz'griːn) *n.* **William.** 1855–1921, British photographer. He invented (with Mortimer Evans) the first practicable motion-picture camera.

Friesian ('friːʒən) *n.* **1.** *Brit.* any of several breeds of black-and-white dairy cattle having a high milk yield. **2.** see **Frisian.**

Friesland ('friːzlənd; *Dutch* 'friːslɑnt) *n.* a province of the N Netherlands, on the IJsselmeer and the North Sea: includes four of the West Frisian Islands; flat, with sand dunes and fens (under reclamation), canals, and lakes. Capital: Leeuwarden. Pop.: 598 068 (1986 est.). Area: 3319 sq. km (1294 sq. miles).

frieze¹ (friːz) *n.* **1.** *Archit.* **a.** the horizontal band between the architrave and cornice of a classical entablature. **b.** the upper part of the wall of a room, below the cornice. **2.** any ornamental band on a wall. [C16: from F *frise*, ?from Med. L *frisium*, changed from L *Phrygium* Phrygian (work), from Phrygia, famous for embroidery in gold]

frieze² (friːz) *n.* a heavy woollen fabric used for coats, etc. [C15: from OF, from MDu. ?from *Vriese* Frisian]

frigate ('frɪgɪt) *n.* **1.** a medium-sized square-rigged warship of the 18th and 19th centuries. **2. a.** *Brit.* a warship smaller than a destroyer. **b.** *U.S.* (formerly) a warship larger than a destroyer. **c.** *U.S.* a small escort vessel. [C16: from F *frégate*, from It. *fregata*, from ?]

frigate bird *n.* a bird of tropical and subtropical seas, having a long bill, a wide wingspan, and a forked tail.

Frigg (frɪg) *or* **Frigga** ('frɪgə) *n. Norse myth.* the wife of Odin; goddess of the heavens and married love.

fright (fraɪt) *n.* **1.** sudden fear or alarm. **2.** a sudden alarming shock. **3.** *Inf.* a horrifying or ludicrous person or thing: *she looks a fright.* **4. take fright.** to become frightened. ~*vb.* **5.** a poetic word for **frighten.** [OE *fryhto*]

frighten ('fraɪt³n) *vb.* (*tr.*) **1.** to terrify; scare. **2.** to drive or force to go (away, off, out, in, etc.) by making afraid. — **'frightener** *n.* — **'frighteningly** *adv.*

frightful ('fraɪtfʊl) *adj.* **1.** very alarming or horrifying. **2.** unpleasant, annoying, or extreme: *a frightful hurry.* — **'frightfully** *adv.* — **'frightfulness** *n.*

frigid ('frɪdʒɪd) *adj.* **1.** formal or stiff in behaviour or temperament. **2.** (esp. of women) lacking sexual responsiveness. **3.** characterized by physical coldness: *a frigid zone.* [C15: from L *frigidus* cold, from *frigēre* to be cold] — **fri'gidity** *or* **'frigidness** *n.* — **'frigidly** *adv.*

Frigid Zone *n.* the cold region inside the Arctic or Antarctic Circle where the sun's rays are very oblique.

frijol (*Spanish* fri'xol) *n.*, *pl.* **-joles** (*Spanish* -'xoles). a variety of bean extensively cultivated for food in Mexico. [C16: from Sp., ult. from L *phaseolus*, from Gk *phasēlos* bean with edible pod]

frill (frɪl) *n.* **1.** a gathered, ruched, or pleated strip of cloth sewn on at one edge only, as on garments, as ornament, or to give extra body. **2.** a ruff of hair or feathers around the neck of a dog or bird or a fold of skin around the neck of a reptile or amphibian. **3.** (*often pl.*) *Inf.* a superfluous or pretentious thing or manner; affectation: *he made a plain speech with no frills.* ~*vb.* **4.** (*tr.*) to adorn or fit with a frill or frills. **5.** to form into a frill or frills. [C14: ? of Flemish origin] — **'frilliness** *n.* — **'frilly** *adj.*

frilled lizard *n.* a large arboreal insectivorous Australian lizard having an erectile fold of skin around the neck.

fringe (frɪndʒ) *n.* **1.** an edging consisting of hanging threads, tassels, etc. **2. a.** an outer edge; periphery. **b.** (*as modifier*): *a fringe area.* **3.** (*modifier*) unofficial; not conventional in form: *fringe theatre.* **4.** *Chiefly Brit.* a section of the front hair cut short over the forehead. **5.** an ornamental border. **6.** *Physics.* any of the light and dark bands produced by diffraction or interference of light. ~*vb.* (*tr.*) **7.** to adorn with a fringe or fringes. **8.** to be a fringe for. [C14: from OF *frenge*, ult. from L *fimbria* fringe, border] — **'fringeless** *adj.*

fringe benefit *n.* an additional advantage, esp. a benefit provided by an employer to supplement an employee's regular pay.

fringing reef *n.* a coral reef close to the shore to which it is attached, having a steep seaward edge.

Frink (frɪŋk) *n.* Dame **Elizabeth.** born 1930, British sculptress.

frippery ('frɪpərɪ) *n.*, *pl.* **-peries. 1.** ornate or showy clothing or adornment. **2.** ostentation. **3.** trifles; trivia. [C16: from OF, from *frepe* frill, rag, from Med. L *faluppa* a straw, splinter, from ?]

Frisbee ('frɪzbiː) *n. Trademark.* a light plastic disc thrown with a spinning motion for recreation or in competition.

Frisch (frɪʃ) *n.* **1. Max** (maks). born 1911, Swiss dramatist and novelist. His works are predominantly satirical and include the plays *Biedermann und die Brandstifter* (1953) and *Andorra* (1961), and the novel *Stiller* (1954). **2. Otto.** 1904–79, British nuclear physicist, born in Austria.

Frisches Haff ('frɪʃəs haf) *n.* the German name for **Vistula** (sense 2).

Frisian ('frɪʒən) *or* **Friesian** *n.* **1.** a language spoken in the NW Netherlands and adjacent islands. **2.** a speaker of this language. ~*adj.* **3.** of or relating to this language or its speakers. [C16: from L *Frīsiī* people of northern Germany]

Frisian Islands *pl. n.* a chain of islands in the North Sea along the coasts of the Netherlands, West Germany, and Denmark: separated from the mainland by shallows.

frisk (frɪsk) *vb.* **1.** (*intr.*) to leap, move about, or act in a playful manner. **2.** (*tr.*) (esp. of animals) to whisk or wave briskly: *the dog frisked its tail.* **3.** (*tr.*) *Inf.* to search (someone) by feeling for concealed weapons, etc.

~*n.* **4.** a playful antic or movement. **5.** *Inf.* an instance of frisking a person. [C16: from OF *frisque*, of Gmc origin] — **'frisker** *n.*

frisky ('frɪskɪ) *adj.* **friskier, friskiest.** lively, high-spirited, or playful. — **'friskily** *adv.*

frisson *French.* (frisɔ̃) *n.* a shiver; thrill. [C18 (but in common use only from C20): lit.: shiver]

frit (frɪt) *n.* **1. a.** the basic materials, partially or wholly fused, for making glass, glazes for pottery, enamel, etc. **b.** a glassy substance used in some soft-paste porcelain. ~*vb.* **fritting, fritted. 2.** (*tr.*) to fuse (materials) in making frit. [C17: from It. *fritta*, lit.: fried, from *friggere* to fry, from L *frigere*]

fritillary (frɪ'tɪlərɪ) *n.*, *pl.* **-laries. 1.** a liliaceous plant having purple or white drooping bell-shaped flowers, typically marked in a chequered pattern. **2.** any of various butterflies having brownish wings chequered with black and silver. [C17: from NL *fritillāria*, from L *fritillus* dice box; prob. with reference to the markings]

fritter¹ ('frɪtə) *vb.* (*tr.*) **1.** (usually foll. by *away*) to waste: *to fritter away time.* **2.** to break into small pieces. [C18: prob. from obs. *fitter* to break into small pieces, ult. from OE *fitt* a piece]

fritter² ('frɪtə) *n.* a piece of food, such as apple, that is dipped in batter and fried in deep fat. [C14: from OF, from L *frictus* fried, from *frigere* to fry]

Friuli (*Italian* fri'uːli) *n.* a historic region of SW Europe, between the Carnic Alps and the Gulf of Venice: the W part (**Venetian Friuli**) was ceded by Austria to Italy in 1866 and **Eastern Friuli** in 1919; in 1947 Eastern Friuli (except Gorizia) was ceded to Yugoslavia. — **Friulian** (frɪ'uːlɪən) *adj.*, *n.*

Friuli-Venezia Giulia (*Italian* 'dʒuːlja) *n.* a region of NE Italy, formed in 1947 from **Venetian Friuli** and part of **Eastern Friuli.** Capital: Trieste. Pop.: 1 214 557 (1985 est.). Area: 7851 sq. km (3031 sq. miles).

frivolous ('frɪvələs) *adj.* **1.** not serious or sensible in content, attitude, or behaviour. **2.** unworthy of serious or sensible treatment: *frivolous details.* [C15: from L *frivolus*] — **'frivolously** *adv.* — **'frivolousness** *or* **frivolity** (frɪ'vɒlɪtɪ) *n.*

frizz (frɪz) *vb.* **1.** (of the hair, nap, etc.) to form or cause (the hair, etc.) to form tight curls or crisp tufts. ~*n.* **2.** hair that has been frizzed. **3.** the state of being frizzed. [C19: from F *friser* to curl]

frizzle¹ ('frɪz²l) *vb.* **1.** to form (the hair) into tight crisp curls. ~*n.* **2.** a tight curl. [C16: prob. rel. to OE *frīs* curly]

frizzle² ('frɪz²l) *vb.* **1.** to scorch or be scorched, esp. with a sizzling noise. **2.** (*tr.*) to fry (bacon, etc.) until crisp. [C16: prob. blend of FRY¹ + SIZZLE]

frizzy ('frɪzɪ) *or* **frizzly** ('frɪzlɪ) *adj.* **-zier, -ziest** *or* **-zlier, -zliest.** (of the hair) in tight crisp wiry curls. — **'frizziness** *or* **'frizzliness** *n.*

fro (frəʊ) *adv.* back or from. [C12: from ON *frā*]

Frobisher ('frəʊbɪʃə) *n.* Sir **Martin.** ?1535–94, English navigator and explorer: made three unsuccessful voyages in search of the Northwest Passage (1576; 1577; 1578), visiting Labrador and Baffin Island.

Frobisher Bay *n.* **1.** an inlet of the Atlantic in NE Canada, in the SE coast of Baffin Island. **2.** a town in N Canada in the Northwest Territories of Baffin Island.

frock (frɒk) *n.* **1.** a girl's or woman's dress. **2.** a loose garment of several types, such as a peasant's smock. **3.** a wide-sleeved outer garment worn by members of some religious orders. ~*vb.* **4.** (*tr.*) to invest (a person) with the office of a cleric. [C14: from OF *froc*]

frock coat *n.* a man's single- or double-breasted skirted coat, as worn in the 19th century.

Froebel *or* **Fröbel** (*German* 'frøːbəl) *n.* **1. Friedrich** (**Wilhelm August**) ('friːdrɪç). 1782–1852, German educator: founded the first kindergarten (1840). ~*adj.* **2.** of, denoting, or relating to a system of kindergarten education developed by him or to the training and qualification of teachers to use this system.

frog¹ (frɒg) *n.* **1.** an insectivorous amphibian, having a short squat tailless body with a moist smooth skin and very long hind legs specialized for hopping. **2.** any of various similar amphibians, such as the tree frog. **3.** any spiked object used to support plant stems in a flower arrangement. **4. a frog in one's throat.** phlegm on the vocal cords that affects one's speech. [OE *frogga*] — **'froggy** *adj.*

frog² (frɒg) *n.* **1.** (*often pl.*) a decorative fastening of looped braid or cord, as on a military uniform. **2.** an attachment on a belt to hold the scabbard of a sword, etc. [C18: ? ult. from L *floccus* tuft of hair] —**frogged** *adj.* —**'frogging** *n.*

frog³ (frɒg) *n.* a tough elastic horny material in the centre of the sole of a horse's foot. [C17: from ?]

frog⁴ (frɒg) *n.* a plate of iron or steel to guide train wheels over an intersection of railway lines. [C19: from ?; ? a special use of FROG¹]

Frog (frɒg) *or* **Froggy** ('frɒgɪ) *n., pl.* **Frogs** *or* **Froggies.** *Brit. sl.* a derogatory word for a French person.

froghopper ('frɒg,hɒpə) *n.* any small leaping insect whose larvae secrete a protective spittle-like substance around themselves.

frogman ('frɒgmən) *n., pl.* **-men.** a swimmer equipped with a rubber suit, flippers, and breathing equipment for working underwater.

frogmarch ('frɒg,mɑːtʃ) *Chiefly Brit.* ~*n.* **1.** a method of carrying a resisting person in which each limb is held and the victim is carried horizontally and face downwards. **2.** any method of making a person move against his will. ~*vb.* **3.** (*tr.*) to carry in a frogmarch or cause to move forward unwillingly.

frogmouth ('frɒg,maʊθ) *n.* a nocturnal insectivorous bird of SE Asia and Australia, similar to the nightjars.

frogspawn ('frɒg,spɔːn) *n.* a mass of fertilized frogs' eggs surrounded by a protective nutrient jelly.

frog spit *or* **spittle** *n.* **1.** another name for **cuckoo spit.** **2.** a foamy mass of threadlike green algae floating on ponds.

Froissart (*French* frwasar) *n.* **Jean** (ʒã). ?1333–?1400, French chronicler and poet, noted for his *Chronique*, a vivid history of Europe from 1325 to 1400.

frolic ('frɒlɪk) *n.* **1.** a light-hearted entertainment or occasion. **2.** light-hearted activity; gaiety. ~*vb.* **-icking, -icked. 3.** (*intr.*) to caper about. ~*adj.* **4.** *Arch.* full of fun; gay. [C16: from Du. *vrolijk*, from MDu. *vro* happy] —**'frolicker** *n.*

frolicsome ('frɒlɪksəm) *adj.* merry and playful. — **'frolicsomely** *adv.*

from (frɒm; *unstressed* frəm) *prep.* **1.** used to indicate the original location, situation, etc.: *from behind the bushes.* **2.** in a period of time starting at: *he lived from 1910 to 1970.* **3.** used to indicate the distance between two things or places: *a hundred miles from here.* **4.** used to indicate a lower amount: *from five to fifty pounds.* **5.** showing the model of: *painted from life.* **6.** used with the gerund to mark prohibition, etc.: *nothing prevents him from leaving.* **7.** because of: *exhausted from his walk.* [OE *fram*]
▷ **Usage.** See at **off.**

Frome (fraʊm) *n.* **Lake.** a shallow salt lake in NE South Australia: intermittently filled with water. Length: 100 km (60 miles). Width: 48 km (30 miles).

frond (frɒnd) *n.* **1.** the compound leaf of a fern. **2.** the leaf of a palm. [C18: from *frōns*]

front (frʌnt) *n.* **1.** that part or side that is forward, or most often seen or used. **2.** a position or place directly before or ahead: *a fountain stood at the front of the building.* **3.** the beginning, opening, or first part. **4.** the position of leadership: *in the front of scientific knowledge.* **5.** land bordering a lake, street, etc. **6.** land along a seashore or large lake, esp. a promenade. **7.** *Mil.* **a.** the total area in which opposing armies face each other. **b.** the space in which a military unit is operating: *to advance on a broad front.* **8.** *Meteorol.* the dividing line or plane between two air masses of different origins. **9.** outward aspect or bearing, as when dealing with a situation: *a bold front.* **10.** *Inf.* a business or other activity serving as a respectable cover for another, usually criminal, organization. **11.** Also called: **front man.** a nominal leader of an organization etc.; figurehead. **12.** *Inf.* outward appearance of rank or wealth. **13.** a particular field of activity: *on the wages front.* **14.** a group of people with a common goal: *a national liberation front.* **15.** a false shirt front; a dicky. **16.** *Arch.* the forehead or the face. ~*adj.* (*prenominal*) **17.** of, at, or in the front: *a front seat.* **18.** *Phonetics.* of or denoting a vowel articulated with the tongue brought forward, as for the sound of *ee* in English *see* or *a* in English *hat.* ~*vb.* **19.** (when *intr.*, foll. by *on* or *onto*) to face (onto): *this house fronts the river.* **20.** (*tr.*) to be a front of or for. **21.** (*tr.*) to appear as a presenter in a

television show. **22.** (*tr.*) to be the lead singer or player in (a band). **23.** (*tr.*) to confront. **24.** to supply a front for. **25.** (*intr.*; often foll. by *up*) *Austral. inf.* to appear (at): *to front up at the police station.* [C13 (in the sense: forehead, face): from L *frōns* forehead, foremost part] —**'frontless** *adj.*

frontage ('frʌntɪdʒ) *n.* **1.** the façade of a building or the front of a plot of ground. **2.** the extent of the front of a shop, plot of land, etc. **3.** the direction in which a building faces.

frontal ('frʌntᵊl) *adj.* **1.** of, at, or in the front. **2.** of or relating to the forehead: *frontal artery.* ~*n.* **3.** a decorative hanging for the front of an altar. [C14 (in the sense: adornment for forehead, altarcloth): via OF *frontel*, from L *frōns* forehead] —**'frontally** *adv.*

frontal lobe *n. Anat.* the anterior portion of each cerebral hemisphere.

front bench *n.* **1.** *Brit.* **a.** the foremost bench of either the Government or Opposition in the House of Commons. **b.** the leadership (**frontbenchers**) of either group, who occupy this bench. **2.** the leadership of the government or opposition in various legislative assemblies.

Frontenac (**et Palluau**) (*French* frõtnak (e palyo)) *n.* **Comte de** (kɔ̃t də). title of *Louis de Buade.* 1620–98, governor of New France (1672–82; 1689–98).

front-end *adj.* (of money, costs, etc.) required or incurred in advance of a project in order to get it under way.

frontier ('frʌntɪə, frʌn'tɪə) *n.* **1. a.** the region of a country bordering on another or a line, barrier, etc., marking such a boundary. **b.** (*as modifier*): *a frontier post.* **2.** *U.S.* the edge of the settled area of a country. **3.** (*often pl.*) the limit of knowledge in a particular field: *the frontiers of physics have been pushed back.* [C14: from OF, from *front* (in the sense: part which is opposite)]

frontiersman ('frʌntɪəzmən, frʌn'tɪəz-) *n., pl.* **-men.** (formerly) a man living on a frontier, esp. in a newly pioneered territory of the U.S.

frontispiece ('frʌntɪs,piːs) *n.* **1.** an illustration facing the title page of a book. **2.** the principal façade of a building. **3.** a pediment over a door, window, etc. [C16 *frontispice*, from F, from LL *frontispicium* façade, from L *frōns* forehead + *specere* to look at; infl. by PIECE]

frontlet ('frʌntlɪt) *n. Judaism.* a phylactery attached to the forehead. [C15: from OF *frontelet* a little FRONTAL]

front line *n.* **1.** *Military.* **a.** the most advanced military units in a battle. **b.** (*modifier*): of, relating to, or suitable for the military front line: *frontline troops.* **2.** (*modifier*) close to a hostile country or scene of armed conflict: *the frontline states.*

front loader *n.* a washing machine with a door at the front which opens one side of the drum into which washing is placed.

front-page *n.* (*modifier*) important enough to be put on the front page of a newspaper.

frontrunner ('frʌnt,rʌnə) *n. Inf.* the leader or a favoured contestant in a race, election, etc.

frost (frɒst) *n.* **1.** a white deposit of ice particles, esp. one formed on objects out of doors at night. **2.** an atmospheric temperature of below freezing point, characterized by the production of this deposit. **3. degrees of frost.** degrees below freezing point. **4.** *Inf.* something given a cold reception; failure. **5.** *Inf.* coolness of manner. **6.** the act of freezing. ~*vb.* **7.** to cover or be covered with frost. **8.** (*tr.*) to give a frostlike appearance to (glass, etc.), as by means of a fine-grained surface. **9.** (*tr.*) *Chiefly U.S. & Canad.* to decorate (cakes, etc.) with icing or frosting. **10.** (*tr.*) to kill or damage (crops, etc.) with frost. [OE *frost*]

Frost (frɒst) *n.* **Robert** (**Lee**). 1874–1963, U.S. poet, noted for his lyrical verse on country life in New England. His books include *A Boy's Will* (1913), *North of Boston* (1914), and *New Hampshire* (1923).

frostbite ('frɒst,baɪt) *n.* destruction of tissues, esp. those of the fingers, ears, toes, and nose, by freezing. —**'frost,bitten** *adj.*

frosted ('frɒstɪd) *adj.* **1.** covered or injured by frost. **2.** covered with icing, as a cake. **3.** (of glass, etc.) having a surface roughened to prevent clear vision through it.

frosting ('frɒstɪŋ) *n.* **1.** another word (esp. U.S. and Canad.) for **icing. 2.** a rough or matt finish on glass, silver, etc.

frosty ('frɒstɪ) *adj.* **frostier, frostiest. 1.** characterized by frost: *a frosty night.* **2.** covered by or decorated with frost. **3.** lacking warmth or enthusiasm: *the new plan had a frosty reception.* —'**frostily** *adv.* —'**frostiness** *n.*

froth (froθ) *n.* **1.** a mass of small bubbles of air or a gas in a liquid, produced by fermentation, etc. **2.** a mixture of saliva and air bubbles formed at the lips in certain diseases, such as rabies. **3.** trivial ideas or entertainment. ~*vb.* **4.** to produce or cause to produce froth. **5.** (*tr.*) to give out in the form of froth. [C14: from ON *frotha* or *frauth*] —'**frothy** *adj.* —'**frothily** *adv.*

Froude (fru:d) *n.* **1. James Anthony.** 1818–94, English historian; author of a controversial biography (1882–84) of Carlyle. **2.** his brother **William.** 1810–79, English civil engineer.

froufrou ('fru:,fru:) *n.* a swishing sound, as made by a long silk dress. [C19: from F, imit.]

froward ('frəuəd) *adj. Arch.* obstinate; contrary. [C14: see FRO, -WARD] —'**frowardly** *adv.* —'**frowardness** *n.*

frown (fraun) *vb.* **1.** (*intr.*) to draw the brows together and wrinkle the forehead, esp. in worry, anger, or concentration. **2.** (*intr.*; foll. by *on* or *upon*) to look disapprovingly (upon). **3.** (*tr.*) to express (worry, etc.) by frowning. ~*n.* **4.** the act of frowning. **5.** a show of dislike or displeasure. [C14: from OF *froigner*, of Celtic origin] —'**frowner** *n.* —'**frowningly** *adv.*

frowst (fraust) *n. Brit. inf.* a hot and stale atmosphere; fug. [C19: back formation from *frowsty* musty, stuffy, var. of FROWZY]

frowsty ('frausti) *adj.* ill-smelling; stale; musty. —'**frowstiness** *n.*

frowzy *or* **frowsy** ('frauzi) *adj.* **frowzier, frowziest,** *or* **frowsier, frowsiest.** **1.** untidy or unkempt in appearance. **2.** ill-smelling; frowsty. [C17: from ?] —'**frowziness** *or* '**frowsiness** *n.*

froze (frəuz) *vb.* the past tense of **freeze.**

frozen ('frəuz³n) *vb.* **1.** the past participle of **freeze.** ~*adj.* **2.** turned into or covered with ice. **3.** killed or stiffened by extreme cold. **4.** (of a region or climate) icy or snowy. **5.** (of food) preserved by a freezing process. **6. a.** (of prices, wages, etc.) arbitrarily pegged at a certain level. **b.** (of business assets) not convertible into cash. **7.** frigid or disdainful in manner. **8.** motionless or unyielding: *he was frozen with horror.* —'**frozenly** *adv.*

frozen shoulder *n. Pathol.* painful stiffness in a shoulder joint.

FRS (in Britain) *abbrev. for* Fellow of the Royal Society.

FRSNZ *abbrev. for* Fellow of the Royal Society of New Zealand.

fructify ('frʌktɪ,faɪ) *vb.* **-fying, -fied. 1.** to bear or cause to bear fruit. **2.** to make or become fruitful. [C14: from OF, from LL *frūctificāre*, from L *frūctus* fruit + *facere* to produce] —,**fructifi'cation** *n.* —**fruc'tiferous** *adj.* —'**fructi,fier** *n.*

fructose ('frʌktəus) *n.* a white crystalline sugar occurring in many fruits. Formula: $C_6H_{12}O_6$. [C19: from L *frūctus* fruit + -OSE²]

frugal ('fru:g³l) *adj.* **1.** practising economy; thrifty. **2.** not costly; meagre. [C16: from L, from *frūgi* useful, temperate, from *frux* fruit] —**fru'gality** *n.* —'**frugally** *adv.*

frugivorous (fru:'dʒɪvərəs) *adj.* fruit-eating. [C18: from *frugi-* (as in FRUGAL) + -VOROUS]

fruit (fru:t) *n.* **1.** *Bot.* the ripened ovary of a flowering plant, containing one or more seeds. It may be dry, as in the poppy, or fleshy, as in the peach. **2.** any fleshy part of a plant that supports the seeds and is edible, such as the strawberry. **3.** any plant product useful to man, including grain, vegetables, etc. **4.** (*often pl.*) the result or consequence of an action or effort. **5.** *Arch.* offspring of man or animals. ~*vb.* **6.** to bear or cause to bear fruit. [C12: from OF, from L *frūctus* enjoyment, fruit, from *fruī* to enjoy] —'**fruit,like** *adj.*

fruit bat *n.* a large Old World bat occurring in tropical and subtropical regions and feeding on fruit.

fruitcake ('fru:t,keɪk) *n.* a rich cake containing mixed dried fruit, lemon peel, etc.

fruiterer ('fru:tərə) *n. Chiefly Brit.* a fruit dealer or seller.

fruit fly *n.* **1.** a small dipterous fly which feeds on and lays its eggs in plant tissues. **2.** any dipterous fly of the genus *Drosophila.* See **drosophila.**

fruitful ('fru:tful) *adj.* **1.** bearing fruit in abundance. **2.** productive or prolific. **3.** producing results or profits: *a fruitful discussion.* —'**fruitfully** *adv.* —'**fruitfulness** *n.*

fruition (fru:'ɪʃən) *n.* **1.** the attainment of something worked for or desired. **2.** enjoyment of this. **3.** the act or condition of bearing fruit. [C15: from LL, from L *fruī* to enjoy]

fruitless ('fru:tlɪs) *adj.* **1.** yielding nothing or nothing of value; unproductive. **2.** without fruit. —'**fruitlessly** *adv.* —'**fruitlessness** *n.*

fruit machine *n. Brit.* a gambling machine that pays out when certain combinations of diagrams, usually of fruit, appear on a dial.

fruit salad *n.* a dessert consisting of sweet fruits cut up and served in a syrup.

fruit sugar *n.* another name for **fructose.**

fruit tree *n.* any tree that bears edible fruit.

fruity ('fru:tɪ) *adj.* **fruitier, fruitiest. 1.** of or resembling fruit. **2.** (of a voice) mellow or rich. **3.** *Inf., chiefly Brit.* erotically stimulating; salacious. —'**fruitiness** *n.*

frumenty ('fru:məntɪ) *or* **furmenty** *n. Brit.* a kind of porridge made from hulled wheat boiled with milk, sweetened, and spiced. [C14: from OF, from *frument* grain, from L *frūmentum*]

frump (frʌmp) *n.* a woman who is dowdy, drab, or unattractive. [C16 (in the sense: to be sullen; C19: dowdy woman): from MDu. *verrompelen* to wrinkle] —'**frumpish** *or* '**frumpy** *adj.*

Frunze (*Russian* 'frunzɪ) *n.* a city in the SW Soviet Union, capital of the Kirghiz SSR. Pop.: 604 000 (1985 est.). Former name (until 1926): **Pishpek.**

frustrate (frʌ'streɪt) *vb.* (*tr.*) **1.** to hinder or prevent (the efforts, plans, or desires) of. **2.** to upset, agitate, or tire. ~*adj.* **3.** *Arch.* frustrated or thwarted. [C15: from L *frustrāre* to cheat, from *frustrā* in error] —**frus'tration** *n.*

frustrated (frʌ'streɪtɪd) *adj.* having feelings of dissatisfaction or lack of fulfilment.

frustum ('frʌstəm) *n., pl.* **-tums** *or* **-ta** (-tə). *Geom.* **a.** the part of a solid, such as a cone or pyramid, contained between the base and a plane parallel to the base that intersects the solid. **b.** the part of such a solid contained between two parallel planes intersecting the solid. [C17: from L: piece]

fry¹ (fraɪ) *vb.* **frying, fried. 1.** (when *tr.*, sometimes foll. by *up*) to cook or be cooked in fat, oil, etc., usually over direct heat. **2.** *Sl., chiefly U.S.* to kill or be killed by electrocution. ~*n., pl.* **fries. 3.** a dish of something fried, esp. the offal of a specified animal: *pig's fry.* **4. fry-up.** *Brit. inf.* the act of preparing a mixed fried dish or the dish itself. [C13: from OF *frire*, from L *frīgere* to fry] —'**fryer** *or* '**frier** *n.*

fry² (fraɪ) *pl. n.* **1.** the young of various species of fish. **2.** the young of certain other animals, such as frogs. [C14 (in the sense: young, offspring): from OF *freier* to spawn, from L *fricāre* to rub]

Fry (fraɪ) *n.* **1. Christopher.** born 1907, English dramatist; author of the verse dramas *A Phoenix Too Frequent* (1946), *The Lady's Not For Burning* (1948), and *Venus Observed* (1950). **2. Elizabeth.** 1780–1845, English prison reformer and Quaker. **3. Roger Eliot.** 1866–1934, English art critic and painter who helped to introduce the postimpressionists to Britain. His books include *Vision and Design* (1920) and *Cézanne* (1927).

frying pan *n.* **1.** a long-handled shallow pan used for frying. **2. out of the frying pan into the fire.** from a bad situation to a worse one.

f-stop ('ɛf,stɒp) *n.* any of the settings for the f-number of a camera.

ft. *abbrev. for* foot or feet.

fth. *or* **fthm.** *abbrev. for* fathom.

FT Index *abbrev. for* Financial Times Industrial Ordinary Share Index. A listing designed to show the general trend in share prices, produced daily by the Financial Times newspaper.

Fuad I (fu:'a:d) *n.* original name *Ahmed Fuad Pasha.* 1868–1936, sultan of Egypt (1917–22) and king (1922–36).

Fu-chou ('fu:'tʃau) *n.* a variant transliteration of the Chinese name for **Fuzhou.**

Fuchs (fuks, fu:ks) *n.* **1. Klaus Emil** (klaus 'e:mi:l). 1911–88, East German physicist. He was born in Germany, became a British citizen (1942), and was imprisoned (1950–59) for giving secret atomic research information to the Soviet Union. **2. Sir Vivian Ernest.** born 1908, English explorer and geologist: led the Commonwealth Trans-Antarctic Expedition (1955–58).

fuchsia ('fju:ʃə) n. **1.** a shrub widely cultivated for its showy drooping purple, red, or white flowers. **2. a.** a reddish-purple to purplish-pink colour. **b.** (as adj.): a fuchsia dress. [C18: from NL, after Leonhard Fuchs (1501–66), G botanist]

fuchsin ('fu:ksɪn) or **fuchsine** ('fu:ksi:n, -sɪn) n. an aniline dye forming a red solution in water: used as a textile dye and a biological stain. [C19: from FUCHS(IA) + -IN; from its similarity in colour to the flower]

fuck (fʌk) Taboo. ~vb. **1.** to have sexual intercourse with (someone). ~n. **2.** an act of sexual intercourse. **3.** Sl. a partner in sexual intercourse. **4. not care** or **give a fuck.** not to care at all. ~interj. **5.** Offens. an expression of strong disgust or anger. [C16: of Gmc origin]

fucus ('fju:kəs) n., pl. **-ci** (-saɪ) or **-cuses.** a seaweed of the genus Fucus, having greenish-brown slimy fronds. [C16: from L: rock lichen, from Gk phukos seaweed, of Semitic origin]

fuddle ('fʌdəl) vb. **1.** (tr.; often passive) to cause to be confused or intoxicated. ~n. **2.** a muddled or confused state. [C16: from ?]

fuddy-duddy ('fʌdɪˌdʌdɪ) n., pl. **-dies.** Inf. a person, esp. an elderly one, who is extremely conservative or dull. [C20: from ?]

fudge[1] (fʌdʒ) n. a soft variously flavoured sweet made from sugar, butter, etc. [C19: from ?]

fudge[2] (fʌdʒ) n. **1.** foolishness; nonsense. ~interj. **2.** a mild exclamation of annoyance. [C18: from ?]

fudge[3] (fʌdʒ) n. **1.** a small section of type matter in a box in a newspaper allowing late news to be included without the whole page having to be remade. **2.** the late news so inserted. ~vb. **3.** (tr.) to make or adjust in a false or clumsy way. **4.** (tr.) to misrepresent; falsify. **5.** to evade (a problem, issue, etc.). [C19: ? rel. to arch. fadge to agree, succeed]

fuel (fjʊəl) n. **1.** any substance burned as a source of heat or power, such as coal or petrol. **2.** the material, containing a fissile substance such as uranium-235, that produces energy in a nuclear reactor. **3.** something that nourishes or builds up emotion, action, etc. ~vb. **fuelling, fuelled** or U.S. **fueling, fueled. 4.** to supply with or receive fuel. [C14: from OF, from feu fire, ult. from L focus hearth]

fuel cell n. a cell in which chemical energy is converted directly into electrical energy.

fuel injection n. a system for introducing fuel directly into the combustion chambers of an internal-combustion engine without the use of a carburettor.

fuel oil n. a liquid petroleum product used as a substitute for coal in industrial furnaces, ships, and locomotives.

fug (fʌg) n. Chiefly Brit. a hot, stale, or suffocating atmosphere. [C19: ? var. of FOG[1]] — **'fuggy** adj.

fugacity (fju:'gæsɪtɪ) n. Thermodynamics. a property of a gas that expresses its tendency to escape or expand.

Fugard ('fu:gɑ:d) n. Athol ('æθəl). born 1932, South African dramatist and theatre director. His plays include Blood-Knot (1961), The Island (1973), Statements after an Arrest under the Immorality Act (1974), and Dimetos (1976).

-fuge n. combining form. indicating an agent or substance that expels or drives away: vermifuge. [from L fugāre to expel]

Fugger (German 'fʊgər) n. a German family of merchants and bankers, prominent in 15th- and 16th-century Europe.

fugitive ('fju:dʒɪtɪv) n. **1.** a person who flees. **2.** a thing that is elusive or fleeting. ~adj. **3.** fleeing, esp. from arrest or pursuit. **4.** not permanent; fleeting. [C14: from L, from fugere to take flight] — **'fugitively** adv.

fugleman ('fju:gəlmən) n., pl. **-men. 1.** (formerly) a soldier used as an example for those learning drill. **2.** a leader or spokesman. [C19: from G Flügelmann, from Flügel wing + Mann MAN]

fugue (fju:g) n. **1.** a musical form consisting of a theme repeated a fifth above or a fourth below the continuing first statement. **2.** Psychiatry. a dreamlike altered state of consciousness, during which a person may lose his memory and wander away. [C16: from F, from It. fuga, from L: a running away] — **'fugal** adj.

Führer or **Fuehrer** German. ('fy:rər) n. a leader: applied esp. to Adolf Hitler while he was Chancellor. [G, from führen to lead]

Fuji ('fu:dʒɪ) n. Mount. an extinct volcano in central Japan, in S central Honshu: the highest mountain in Japan, famous for its symmetrical snow-capped cone. Height: 3776 m (12 388 ft.). Also called: **Fujiyama, Fuji-san.**

Fujian or **Fukien** ('fu:'kjen) n. **1.** a province of SE China: mountainous and forested, drained chiefly by the Min River; noted for the production of flower-scented teas. Capital: Fuzhou. Pop.: 27 130 000 (1986 est.). Area: 123 000 sq. km (47 970 sq. miles). **2.** any of the Chinese dialects of this province. See also **Min.**

Fukuoka (ˌfu:ku:'əʊkə) n. an industrial city and port in SW Japan, in N Kyushu: an important port in ancient times; site of Kyushu university. Pop.: 1 182 000 (1987).

-ful suffix. **1.** (forming adjectives) full of or characterized by: painful; restful. **2.** (forming adjectives) able or tending to: useful. **3.** (forming nouns) indicating as much as will fill the thing specified: mouthful. [OE -ful, -full, from FULL[1]]

▷ **Usage.** Where the amount held by a spoon, etc., is used as a rough unit of measurement, the correct form is spoonful, etc.: take a spoonful of this medicine every day. The plural of a word like spoonful is spoonfuls and not spoonsful.

fulcrum ('fʊlkrəm, 'fʌl-) n., pl. **-crums** or **-cra** (-krə). **1.** the pivot about which a lever turns. **2.** something that supports or sustains; prop. [C17: from L: foot of a couch, from fulcire to prop up]

fulfil or U.S. **fulfill** (fʊl'fɪl) vb. **-filling, -filled.** (tr.) **1.** to bring about the completion or achievement of (a desire, promise, etc.). **2.** to carry out or execute (a request, etc.). **3.** to conform with or satisfy (regulations, etc.). **4.** to finish or reach the end of. **5. fulfil oneself.** to achieve one's potentials or desires. [OE fulfyllan] — **ful'filment** or U.S. **ful'fillment** n.

fulgent ('fʌldʒənt) adj. Poetic. shining brilliantly; gleaming. [C15: from L fulgēre to shine]

fulgurate ('fʌlgjʊˌreɪt) vb. (intr.) Rare. to flash like lightning. [C17: from L, from fulgur lightning]

fulgurite ('fʌlgjʊˌraɪt) n. glassy mineral matter found in sand and rock, formed by the action of lightning. [C19: from L fulgur lightning]

Fulham ('fʊləm) n. a district of the Greater London borough of Hammersmith and Fulham (since 1965): contains **Fulham Palace** (16th century), residence of the Bishop of London.

fuliginous (fju:'lɪdʒɪnəs) adj. **1.** sooty or smoky. **2.** of the colour of soot. [C16: from LL fūliginōsus full of soot, from L fūligō soot]

full[1] (fʊl) adj. **1.** holding or containing as much as possible. **2.** abundant in supply, quantity, number, etc.: full of energy. **3.** having consumed enough food or drink. **4.** (esp. of the face or figure) rounded or plump. **5.** (prenominal) complete: a full dozen. **6.** (prenominal) with all privileges, rights, etc.: a full member. **7.** (prenominal) having the same parents: a full brother. **8.** filled with emotion or sentiment: a full heart. **9.** (postpositive; foll. by of) occupied or engrossed (with): full of his own projects. **10.** Music. **a.** powerful or rich in volume and sound. **b.** completing a piece or section; concluding: a full close. **11.** (of a garment, esp. a skirt) containing a large amount of fabric. **12.** (of sails, etc.) distended by wind. **13.** (of wine, such as a burgundy) having a heavy body. **14.** (of a colour) rich; saturated. **15.** Inf. drunk. **16. full of oneself.** full of pride or conceit. **17. full up.** filled to capacity. **18. in full swing.** at the height of activity: the party was in full swing. ~adv. **19. a.** completely; entirely. **b.** (in combination): full-fledged. **20.** directly; right: he hit him full in the stomach. **21.** very; extremely (esp. in **full well**). ~n. **22.** the greatest degree, extent, etc. **23. in full.** without omitting or shortening: we paid in full for our mistake. **24. to the full.** thoroughly; fully. ~vb. **25.** (tr.) Needlework. to gather or tuck. **26.** (intr.) (of the moon) to be fully illuminated. [OE] — **'fullness** or esp. U.S. **'fulness** n.

full[2] (fʊl) vb. (of cloth, yarn, etc.) to become or to make (cloth, yarn, etc.) more compact during manufacture through shrinking and pressing. [C14: from OF fouler, ult. from L fullō a FULLER]

fullback ('fʊlˌbæk) n. Soccer, hockey, rugby. **a.** a defensive player. **b.** the position held by this player.

full-blooded adj. **1.** (esp. of horses) of unmixed ancestry. **2.** having great vigour or health; hearty. — **full-'bloodedness** n.

full-blown adj. **1.** characterized by the fullest, strongest, or best development. **2.** in full bloom.

full-bodied *adj.* having a full rich flavour or quality.

full dress *n.* **a.** a formal style of dress, such as white tie and tails for a man. **b.** (*as modifier*): *full-dress uniform.*

fuller ('fʊlə) *n.* a person who fulls cloth for his living. [OE *fullere*]

Fuller ('fʊlə) *n.* **1. (Richard) Buckminster.** 1895–1983, U.S. architect and engineer: developed the geodesic dome. **2. Roy.** born 1912, English poet, whose collections of poetry include *The Middle of a War* (1942) and *A Lost Season* (1944), both of which are concerned with World War II, and *Epitaphs and Occasions* (1949), *Brutus's Orchard* (1957), and *New Poems* (1968). **3. Thomas.** 1608–61, English clergyman and antiquarian; author of *The Worthies of England* (1662).

fuller's earth *n.* a natural absorbent clay used, after heating, for clarifying oils and fats, fulling cloth, etc.

full face *adj.* facing towards the viewer, with the entire face visible.

full-fledged *adj.* See **fully fledged.**

full-frontal *adj. Inf.* **1.** (of a nude person or a photograph of a nude person) exposing the genitals to full view. **2.** all-out; unrestrained.

full house *n.* **1.** *Poker.* a hand with three cards of the same value and another pair. **2.** a theatre, etc., filled to capacity. **3.** (in bingo, etc.) the set of numbers needed to win.

full-length *n.* (*modifier*) **1.** showing the complete length. **2.** not abridged.

full moon *n.* one of the four phases of the moon when the moon is visible as a fully illuminated disc.

full nelson *n.* a wrestling hold in which a wrestler places both arms under his opponent's arms from behind and exerts pressure on the back of the neck.

full pitch *or* **full toss** *n.* *Cricket.* a bowled ball that reaches the batsman without bouncing.

full sail *adv.* **1.** at top speed. ~*adj.* (*postpositive*), *adv.* **2.** with all sails set.

full-scale *n.* (*modifier*) **1.** (of a plan, etc.) of actual size. **2.** using all resources; all-out.

full stop *or* **full point** *n.* the punctuation mark (.) used at the end of a sentence that is not a question or exclamation, after abbreviations, etc. Also called (esp. U.S. and Canad.): **period.**

full time *n.* the end of a football or other match.

full-time *adj.* **1.** for the entire time appropriate to an activity: *a full-time job.* ~*adv.* **full time. 2.** on a full-time basis: *he works full time.* ~Cf. **part-time. —,full'timer** *n.*

fully ('fʊlɪ) *adv.* **1.** to the greatest degree or extent. **2.** amply; adequately: *they were fully fed.* **3.** at least: *it was fully an hour before she came.*

fully fashioned *adj.* (of stockings, knitwear, etc.) shaped and seamed so as to fit closely.

fully fledged *or* **full-fledged** *adj.* **1.** (of a young bird) having acquired its adult feathers and thus able to fly. **2.** developed or matured to the fullest degree. **3.** of full rank or status.

fulmar ('fʊlmə) *n.* a heavily built short-tailed oceanic bird of polar regions. [C17: of Scand. origin]

fulminate ('fʌlmɪˌneɪt) *vb.* **1.** (*intr.; often foll. against*) to make severe criticisms or denunciations; rail. **2.** to explode with noise and violence. ~*n.* **3.** any salt or ester of **fulminic acid,** an isomer of cyanic acid, which is used as a detonator. [C15: from Med. L, from L *fulmen* lightning that strikes] — **'fulminant** *adj.* — ˌ**fulmi'nation** *n.* — **'fulmiˌnatory** *adj.*

fulsome ('fʊlsəm) *adj.* excessive or insincere, esp. in an offensive or distasteful way: *fulsome compliments.* — **'fulsomely** *adv.* — **'fulsomeness** *n.*

Fulton ('fʊlt³n) *n.* **Robert.** 1765–1815, U.S. engineer and inventor: designed the first commercially successful steamboat (1807) and the first steam warship (1814).

fulvous ('fʌlvəs) *adj.* of a dull brownish-yellow colour. [C17: from L *fulvus* reddish yellow]

fumarole ('fju:məˌrəʊl) *n.* a vent in or near a volcano from which hot gases, esp. steam, are emitted. [C19: from F, from LL *fūmāriolum* smoke hole, from L *fūmus* smoke]

fumble ('fʌmb³l) *vb.* **1.** (*intr.;* often foll. by *for* or *with*) to grope about clumsily or blindly, esp. in searching. **2.** (*intr.;* foll. by *at* or *with*) to finger or play with, esp. in an absent-minded way. **3.** to say or do awkwardly: *he fumbled the introduction badly.* **4.** to fail to catch or grasp (a ball, etc.) cleanly. ~*n.* **5.** the act of fumbling. [C16: prob. of Scand. origin] — **'fumbler** *n.* — **'fumblingly** *adv.*

fume (fju:m) *vb.* **1.** (*intr.*) to be overcome with anger or fury. **2.** to give off (fumes) or (of fumes) to be given off, esp. during a chemical reaction. **3.** (*tr.*) to fumigate. ~*n.* **4.** (*often pl.*) a pungent or toxic vapour, gas, or smoke. **5.** a sharp or pungent odour. [C14: from OF *fum*, from L *fūmus* smoke, vapour] — **'fumeless** *adj.* — **'fumingly** *adv.* — **'fumy** *adj.*

fumed (fju:md) *adj.* (of wood, esp. oak) having a dark colour and distinctive grain from exposure to ammonia fumes.

fumigant ('fju:mɪgənt) *n.* a substance used for fumigating.

fumigate ('fju:mɪˌgeɪt) *vb.* to treat (something contaminated or infected) with fumes or smoke. [C16: from L, from *fūmus* smoke + *agere* to drive] — ˌ**fumi'gation** *n.* — **'fumiˌgator** *n.*

fuming sulphuric acid *n.* a mixture of acids, made by dissolving sulphur trioxide in concentrated sulphuric acid. Also called: **oleum.**

fumitory ('fju:mɪtərɪ) *n., pl.* **-ries.** any plant of the genus *Fumaria* having spurred flowers and formerly used medicinally. [C14: from OF, from Med. L *fūmus terrae*, lit.: smoke of the earth]

fun (fʌn) *n.* **1.** a source of enjoyment, amusement, diversion, etc. **2.** pleasure, gaiety, or merriment. **3.** jest or sport (esp. in **in** *or* **for fun**). **4. fun and games.** *Ironic or facetious.* frivolous or hetic activity. **5. make fun of** *or* **poke fun at.** to ridicule or deride. **6.** (*modifier*) full of amusement, diversion, gaiety, etc.: *a fun sport.* [C17: ?from obs. *fon* to make a fool of; see FOND]

funambulist (fju:'næmbjʊlɪst) *n.* a tightrope walker. [C18: from L, from *fūnis* rope + *ambulāre* to walk] — **fu'nambulism** *n.*

Funchal (*Portuguese* fū'ʃal) *n.* the capital and chief port of the Madeira Islands, on the S coast of Madeira. Pop.: 44 111 (1984).

function ('fʌŋkʃən) *n.* **1.** the natural action of a person or thing: *the function of the kidneys is to filter waste products from the blood.* **2.** the intended purpose of a person or thing in a specific role: *the function of a hammer is to hit nails into wood.* **3.** an official or formal social gathering or ceremony. **4.** a factor dependent upon another or other factors. **5.** *Maths, logic.* a relation between two sets that associates a unique element (the value) of the second (the range) with each element (the argument) of the first (the domain). Symbol: $f(x)$. The value of $f(x)$ for $x = 2$ is $f(2)$. Also called: **map, mapping.** ~*vb.* (*intr.*) **6.** to operate or perform as specified. **7.** (foll. by *as*) to perform the action or role (of something or someone else): *a coin may function as a screwdriver.* [C16: from L *functio*, from *fungi* to perform]

functional ('fʌŋkʃən³l) *adj.* **1.** of, involving, or containing a function or functions. **2.** practical rather than decorative; utilitarian. **3.** capable of functioning; working. **4.** *Med.* affecting a function of an organ without structural change. — **'functionally** *adv.*

functionalism ('fʌŋkʃənəˌlɪzəm) *n.* **1.** the theory of design that the form of a thing should be determined by its use. **2.** any doctrine that stresses purpose. — **'functionalist** *n., adj.*

functionary ('fʌŋkʃənərɪ) *n., pl.* **-aries.** a person acting in an official capacity, as for a government; an official.

fund (fʌnd) *n.* **1.** a reserve of money, etc., set aside for a certain purpose. **2.** a supply or store of something; stock: *it exhausted his fund of wisdom.* ~*vb.* (*tr.*) **3.** to furnish money to in the form of a fund. **4.** to place or store up in a fund. **5.** to convert (short-term floating debt) into long-term debt bearing fixed interest and represented by bonds. **6.** to accumulate a fund for the discharge of (a recurrent liability): *to fund a pension plan.* ~See also **funds.** [C17: from L *fundus* the bottom, piece of land]

fundament ('fʌndəmənt) *n. Euphemistic or facetious.* the buttocks. [C13: from *fundāre* to FOUND²]

fundamental (ˌfʌndə'mɛnt³l) *adj.* **1.** of, involving, or comprising a foundation; basic. **2.** of, involving, or comprising a source; primary. **3.** *Music.* denoting or relating to the principal or lowest note of a harmonic series. ~*n.* **4.** a principle, law, etc., that serves as the basis of an idea or system. **5. a.** the principal or lowest note of a harmonic series. **b.** the bass note of a chord in root position. — ˌ**fundamen'tality** *n.* — ˌ**funda'mentally** *adv.*

fundamental interaction *n.* any of the four basic interactions that occur in nature: the gravitational, electromagnetic, strong, and weak interactions.

fundamentalism (ˌfʌndəˈmɛntəˌlɪzəm) *n.* **1.** *Christianity.* the view that the Bible is divinely inspired and is therefore literally true. **2.** *Islam.* a movement favouring strict observance of the teachings of the Koran and Islamic law. — ˌfunda'mentalist *n., adj.*

fundamental particle *n.* another name for **elementary particle.**

fundamental unit *n.* one of a set of unrelated units that form the basis of a system of units. For example, the metre, kilogram, and second are fundamental units of the SI system.

funded debt *n.* that part of the British national debt which the government is not obliged to repay by a fixed date.

funds (fʌndz) *pl. n.* **1.** money that is readily available. **2.** British government securities representing national debt.

fundus (ˈfʌndəs) *n., pl.* **-di** (-daɪ). *Anat.* the base of an organ or the part farthest away from its opening. [C18: from L, lit.: the bottom]

Fundy (ˈfʌndɪ) *n.* **Bay of.** an inlet of the Atlantic in SE Canada, between S New Brunswick and W Nova Scotia: remarkable for its swift tides of up to 21 m (70 ft.).

Fünen (ˈfyːnən) *n.* the German name for **Fyn.**

funeral (ˈfjuːnərəl) *n.* **1. a.** a ceremony at which a dead person is buried or cremated. **b.** (*as modifier*): *a funeral service.* **2.** a procession of people escorting a corpse to burial. **3.** *Inf.* concern; affair: *that's your funeral.* [C14: from Med. L, from LL, from L *fūnus* funeral] — ˈfunerary *adj.*

funeral director *n.* an undertaker.

funeral parlour *n.* a place where the dead are prepared for burial or cremation. Usual U.S. name: **funeral home.**

funereal (fjuːˈnɪərɪəl) *adj.* suggestive of a funeral; gloomy or mournful. Also: **funebrial.** [C18: from L *fūnereus*] — fu'nereally *adv.*

funfair (ˈfʌnˌfɛə) *n. Brit.* an amusement park or fairground.

fungible (ˈfʌndʒɪbəl) *n. Law.* (*often pl.*) moveable perishable goods of a sort that may be estimated by number or weight, such as grain, wine, etc. [C18: from Med. L *fungibilis*, from L *fungī* to perform] — ˌfungiˈbility *n.*

fungicide (ˈfʌndʒɪˌsaɪd) *n.* a substance or agent that destroys or is capable of destroying fungi. — ˌfungiˈcidal *adj.* — ˌfungiˈcidally *adv.*

fungoid (ˈfʌngɔɪd) *adj.* resembling a fungus or fungi: *a fungoid growth.*

fungous (ˈfʌngəs) *adj.* appearing suddenly and spreading quickly like a fungus.

fungus (ˈfʌngəs) *n., pl.* **fungi** (ˈfʌngaɪ, ˈfʌndʒaɪ, ˈfʌndʒɪ) *or* **funguses.** **1.** any plant of the division *Fungi*, lacking chlorophyll, leaves, true stems, and roots, and reproducing by spores. The group includes moulds, yeasts, and mushrooms. **2.** something resembling a fungus, esp. in suddenly growing. **3.** *Pathol.* any soft tumorous growth. [C16: from L: mushroom, fungus] — ˈfungal *adj.*

funicular (fjuːˈnɪkjʊlə) *n.* **1.** Also called: **funicular railway.** a railway up the side of a mountain, consisting of two cars at either end of a cable passing round a driving wheel at the summit. ~*adj.* **2.** relating to or operated by a rope, etc. [C17: from L, from *fūnis* rope]

funk¹ (fʌnk) *Inf., chiefly Brit.* ~*n.* **1.** Also called: **blue funk.** a state of nervousness, fear, or depression. **2.** a coward. ~*vb.* **3.** to flinch from (responsibility, etc.) through fear. **4.** (*tr.; usually passive*) to make afraid. [C18: university sl., ? rel. to *funk* to smoke]

funk² (fʌnk) *n. Inf.* a type of polyrhythmic Black dance music with heavy syncopation. [C20: back formation from FUNKY]

Funk (fʌnk) *n.* **Casimir** (ˈkæzɪˌmɪə). 1884–1967, U.S. biochemist, born in Poland: studied and named vitamins.

funky (ˈfʌnkɪ) *adj.* **funkier, funkiest.** *Inf.* (of jazz, pop, etc.) passionate; soulful. [C20: from *funk* to smoke (tobacco), ? alluding to music that was smelly, that is, earthy]

funnel (ˈfʌnəl) *n.* **1.** a hollow utensil with a wide mouth tapering to a small hole, used for pouring liquids, etc., into a narrow-necked vessel. **2.** something resembling this in shape or function. **3.** a smokestack for smoke and exhaust gases, as on a steam locomotive. ~*vb.* **-nelling, -nelled** *or U.S.* **-neling, -neled. 4.** to move or cause to move or pour through or as if through a funnel. [C15: from OProvençal *fonilh*, ult. from L *infundibulum*, from *infundere* to pour in] — ˈfunnel-,like *adj.*

funnel-web *n. Austral.* a large poisonous black spider that constructs funnel-shaped webs.

funny (ˈfʌnɪ) *adj.* **-nier, -niest. 1.** causing amusement or laughter; humorous. **2.** peculiar; odd. **3.** suspicious or dubious (esp. in **funny business**). **4.** *Inf.* faint or ill. ~*n., pl.* **-nies. 5.** *Inf.* a joke or witticism. — ˈfunnily *adv.* — ˈfunniness *n.*

funny bone *n.* the area near the elbow where the ulnar nerve is close to the surface of the skin: when it is struck, a sharp tingling sensation is experienced.

fun run *n.* a long run or part-marathon run for exercise and pleasure, often by large numbers of people.

fuoco (fuˈɔːkəʊ) *Music.* ~*n.* **1.** fire. ~*adv., adj.* **2. con fuoco.** in a fiery manner. [C19: It., lit.: fire]

fur (fɜː) *n.* **1.** the dense coat of fine silky hairs on such mammals as the cat and mink. **2. a.** the dressed skin of certain fur-bearing animals, with the hair left on. **b.** (*as modifier*): *a fur coat.* **3.** a garment made of fur, such as a stole. **4.** a pile fabric made in imitation of animal fur. **5.** *Heraldry.* any of various stylized representations of animal pelts used in coats of arms. **6. make the fur fly.** to cause a scene or disturbance. **7.** *Inf.* a whitish coating on the tongue, caused by excessive smoking, an upset stomach, etc. **8.** *Brit.* a whitish-grey deposit precipitated from hard water onto the insides of pipes, kettles, etc. ~*vb.* **furring, furred. 9.** (*tr.*) to line or trim a garment, etc., with fur. **10.** (often foll. by *up*) to cover or become covered with a furlike lining or deposit. [C14: from OF *forrer* to line a garment, from *fuerre* sheath, of Gmc origin] — ˈfurless *adj.*

fur. *abbrev. for* furlong.

furbelow (ˈfɜːbɪˌləʊ) *n.* **1.** a flounce, ruffle, or other ornamental trim. **2.** (*often pl.*) showy ornamentation. ~*vb.* **3.** (*tr.*) to put a furbelow on (a garment, etc.). [C18: by folk etymology from F dialect *farbella* a frill]

furbish (ˈfɜːbɪʃ) *vb.* (*tr.*) **1.** to make bright by polishing. **2.** (often foll. by *up*) to renovate; restore. [C14: from OF *fourbir* to polish, of Gmc origin] — ˈfurbisher *n.*

furcate (ˈfɜːkeɪt) *vb.* **1.** to divide into two parts. ~*adj.* **2.** forked: *furcate branches.* [C19: from LL, from L *furca* a fork] — ˈfur'cation *n.*

furfuraceous (ˌfɜːfjʊˈreɪʃəs) *adj.* **1.** relating to or resembling bran. **2.** *Med.* resembling dandruff. [C17: from L *furfur* bran, scurf + -ACEOUS]

Furies (ˈfjʊərɪz) *pl. n., sing.* **Fury.** *Classical myth.* the snake-haired goddesses of vengeance, usually three in number, who pursued unpunished criminals. Also called: **Erinyes, Eumenides.**

furioso (ˌfjʊərɪˈəʊsəʊ) *Music.* ~*adj., adv.* **1.** in a frantically rushing manner. ~*n.* **2.** a passage or piece to be performed in this way. [C19: It., lit.: furious]

furious (ˈfjʊərɪəs) *adj.* **1.** extremely angry or annoyed. **2.** violent or unrestrained, as in speed, energy, etc. — ˈfuriously *adv.* — ˈfuriousness *n.*

furl (fɜːl) *vb.* **1.** to roll up (an umbrella, flag, etc.) neatly and securely or (of an umbrella, flag, etc.) to be rolled up in this way. ~*n.* **2.** the act or an instance of furling. **3.** a single rolled-up section. [C16: from OF, from *ferm* tight (from L *firmus* FIRM¹) + *lier* to bind, from L *ligāre*] — ˈfurlable *adj.*

furlong (ˈfɜːlɒŋ) *n.* a unit of length equal to 220 yards (201.168 metres). [OE *furlang*, from *furh* furrow + *lang* long]

furlough (ˈfɜːləʊ) *n.* **1.** leave of absence from military duty. ~*vb.* (*tr.*) **2.** to grant a furlough to. [C17: from Du. *verlof*, from *ver-* FOR- + *lof* leave, permission]

furnace (ˈfɜːnɪs) *n.* **1.** an enclosed chamber in which heat is produced to destroy refuse, smelt or refine ores, etc. **2.** a very hot place. [C13: from OF, from L *fornax* oven, furnace]

Furness (ˈfɜːnɪs) *n.* a region in NW England in Cumbria, forming a peninsula between the Irish Sea and Morecambe Bay.

furnish (ˈfɜːnɪʃ) *vb.* (*tr.*) **1.** to provide (a house, room, etc.) with furniture, etc. **2.** to equip with what is necessary. **3.** to supply: *the records furnished the information.* [C15: from OF *fournir*, of Gmc origin] — ˈfurnisher *n.*

furnishings (ˈfɜːnɪʃɪŋz) *pl. n.* furniture, carpets, etc., with which a room or house is furnished.

furniture ('fɜːnɪtʃə) n. **1.** the movable articles that equip a room, house, etc. **2.** the equipment necessary for a ship, factory, etc. **3.** *Printing.* lengths of wood, plastic, or metal, used in assembling formes to surround the type. **4.** Also called: **door furniture.** locks, handles, etc., designed for use on doors. [C16: from F, from *fournir* to equip]

Furnivall ('fɜːnɪvˀl) n. **Frederick James.** 1825–1910, English philologist: founder of the Early English Text Society and one of the founders of the *Oxford English Dictionary.*

furore (fjʊ'rɔːrɪ) *or esp. U.S.* **furor** ('fjʊərɔː) n. **1.** a public outburst; uproar. **2.** a sudden widespread enthusiasm; craze. **3.** frenzy; rage. [C15: from L: frenzy, from *furere* to rave]

furphy ('fɜːfɪ) n., pl. **-phies.** *Austral. sl.* a rumour or fictitious story. [C20: from *Furphy* carts (used for water or sewage in World War I), made at a foundry established by the Furphy family]

Furphy ('fɜːfɪ) n. **Joseph,** pen name *Tom Collins.* 1843–1912, Australian author. His works include the classic Australian novel *Such is Life* (1903) and *The Buln-Buln and the Brolga* (1948).

furred (fɜːd) adj. **1.** made of, lined with, or covered in fur. **2.** wearing fur. **3.** (of animals) having fur. **4.** another word for **furry** (sense 3). **5.** provided with furring strips. **6.** (of a pipe, kettle, etc.) lined with hard lime.

furrier ('fʌrɪə) n. a person whose occupation is selling, making, or repairing fur garments. [C14: *furour,* from OF *fourrer* to trim with FUR] —'**furriery** n.

furring ('fɜːrɪŋ) n. **1.** short for **furring strip. 2.** the formation of fur on the tongue. **3.** trimming of animal fur, as on a coat.

furring strip n. a strip of wood or metal fixed to a wall, floor, or ceiling to provide a surface for the fixing of plasterboard, floorboards, etc.

furrow ('fʌrəʊ) n. **1.** a long narrow trench made in the ground by a plough. **2.** any long deep groove, esp. a deep wrinkle on the forehead. ~vb. **3.** to develop or cause to develop furrows or wrinkles. **4.** to make a furrow or furrows in (land). [OE *furh*] —'**furrower** n. —'**furrowless** adj. —'**furrowy** adj.

furry ('fɜːrɪ) adj. **-rier, -riest. 1.** covered with fur or something furlike. **2.** of, relating to, or resembling fur. **3.** Also: **furred.** (of the tongue) coated with whitish cellular debris. —'**furrily** adv. —'**furriness** n.

Fur Seal Islands pl. n. another name for the **Pribilof Islands.**

Fürth (*German* fyːrt) n. a city in S West Germany, in Bavaria northwest of Nuremberg. Pop.: 98 500 (1984 est.).

further ('fɜːðə) adv. **1.** in addition; furthermore. **2.** to a greater degree or extent. **3.** to or at a more advanced point. **4.** to or at a greater distance in time or space. ~adj. **5.** additional; more. **6.** more distant or remote in time or space. ~vb. **7.** (tr.) to assist the progress of. ~See also **far, furthest.** [OE *furthor*]
▷ **Usage.** See at **farther.**

furtherance ('fɜːðərəns) n. **1.** the act of furthering. **2.** something that furthers.

further education n. (in Britain) formal education beyond school other than at a university or polytechnic.

furthermore ('fɜːðə,mɔː) adv. in addition; moreover.

furthermost ('fɜːðə,məʊst) adj. most distant; furthest.

furthest ('fɜːðɪst) adv. **1.** to the greatest degree or extent. **2.** to or at the greatest distance in time or space; farthest. ~adj. **3.** most distant or remote in time or space; farthest.

furtive ('fɜːtɪv) adj. characterized by stealth; sly and secretive. [C15: from L *furtīvus* stolen, from *furtum* a theft, from *fūr* a thief] —'**furtively** adv. —'**furtiveness** n.

Furtwängler (*German* 'fʊrtvɛŋlər) n. **Wilhelm** ('vɪlhɛlm). 1886–1954, German conductor, noted for his interpretations of Wagner.

furuncle ('fjʊərʌŋkˀl) n. *Pathol.* the technical name for **boil**[2]. [C17: from L *fūrunculus* pilferer, sore, from *fūr* thief] —**furuncular** (fjʊ'rʌŋkjʊlə) *or* **fu'runculous** adj.

furunculosis (fjʊ,rʌŋkjʊ'ləʊsɪs) n. **1.** a skin condition characterized by the presence of multiple boils. **2.** a disease of salmon and trout caused by a bacterium.

fury ('fjʊərɪ) n., pl. **-ries. 1.** violent or uncontrolled anger. **2.** an outburst of such anger. **3.** uncontrolled violence: *the fury of the storm.* **4.** a person, esp. a woman, with a violent temper. **5.** See **Furies. 6. like fury.** *Inf.* violently; furiously. [C14: from L, from *furere* to be furious]

furze (fɜːz) n. another name for **gorse.** [OE *fyrs*] —'**furzy** adj.

fuscous ('fʌskəs) adj. of a brownish-grey colour. [C17: from L *fuscus* dark, swarthy, tawny]

fuse[1] *or U.S.* **fuze** (fjuːz) n. **1.** a lead of combustible black powder (**safety fuse**), or a lead containing an explosive (**detonating fuse**), used to fire an explosive charge. **2.** any device by which an explosive charge is ignited. ~vb. **3.** (tr.) to equip with such a fuse. [C17: from It. *fuso* spindle, from L *fūsus*] —'**fuseless** adj.

fuse[2] (fjuːz) vb. **1.** to unite or become united by melting, esp. by the action of heat. **2.** to become or cause to become liquid, esp. by the action of heat. **3.** to join or become combined. **4.** (tr.) to equip (a plug, etc.) with a fuse. **5.** *Brit.* to fail or cause to fail as a result of the blowing of a fuse: *the lights fused.* ~n. **6.** a protective device for safeguarding electric circuits, etc., containing a wire that melts and breaks the circuit when the current exceeds a certain value. [C17: from L *fūsus* melted, cast, from *fundere* to pour out; sense 5 infl. by FUSE[1]]

fusee *or* **fuzee** (fjuː'ziː) n. **1.** (in early clocks and watches) a spirally grooved spindle, functioning as an equalizing force on the unwinding of the mainspring. **2.** a friction match with a large head. [C16: from F *fusée* spindleful of thread, from OF *fus* spindle, from L *fūsus*]

fuselage ('fjuːzɪ,lɑːʒ) n. the main body of an aircraft. [C20: from F, from *fuseler* to shape like a spindle, from OF *fusel* spindle]

fusel oil *or* **fusel** ('fjuːzˀl) n. a poisonous by-product formed in the distillation of fermented liquors and used as a source of amyl alcohols. [C19: from G *Fusel* bad spirits]

Fushih *or* **Fu-shih** ('fuː'ʃiː) n. another name for **Yanan.**

Fushun ('fuː'ʃʌn) n. a city in NE China, in central Liaoning province near Shenyang: situated on one of the richest coalfields in the world; site of the largest thermal power plant in NE Asia. Pop.: 1 240 000 (1986).

fusible ('fjuːzəbˀl) adj. capable of being fused or melted. —,**fusi'bility** n. —'**fusibly** adv.

fusiform ('fjuːzɪ,fɔːm) adj. elongated and tapering at both ends. [C18: from L *fūsus* spindle]

fusil ('fjuːzɪl) n. a light flintlock musket. [C16 (in the sense: steel for a tinderbox): from OF, from Vulgar L *focīlis* (unattested), from L *focus* fire]

fusilier (,fjuːzɪ'lɪə) n. **1.** (formerly) an infantryman armed with a light musket. **2.** Also: **fusileer. a.** a soldier, esp. a private, serving in any of certain British or other infantry regiments. **b.** (pl.; cap. when part of a name): *the Royal Welsh Fusiliers.* [C17: from F; see FUSIL]

fusillade (,fjuːzɪ'leɪd) n. **1.** a rapid continual discharge of firearms. **2.** a sudden outburst, as of criticism. ~vb. **3.** (tr.) to attack with a fusillade. [C19: from F, from *fusiller* to shoot; see FUSIL]

fusion ('fjuːʒən) n. **1.** the act or process of fusing or melting together. **2.** the state of being fused. **3.** something produced by fusing. **4.** a kind of popular music that is a blend of two or more styles, such as jazz and funk. **5.** See **nuclear fusion. 6.** a coalition of political parties. [C16: from L *fūsiō* a pouring out, melting, from *fundere* to pour out, FOUND[3]]

fusion bomb n. a type of bomb in which most of the energy is provided by nuclear fusion. Also called: **thermonuclear bomb, fission-fusion bomb.**

fuss (fʌs) n. **1.** nervous activity or agitation, esp. when unnecessary. **2.** complaint or objection: *he made a fuss over the bill.* **3.** an exhibition of affection or admiration: *they made a great fuss over the new baby.* **4.** a quarrel. ~vb. **5.** (intr.) to worry unnecessarily. **6.** (intr.) to be excessively concerned over trifles. **7.** (when intr., usually foll. by *over*) to show great or excessive concern, affection, etc. (for). **8.** (tr.) to bother (a person). [C18: from ?] —'**fusser** n.

fusspot ('fʌs,pɒt) n. *Brit. inf.* a person who fusses unnecessarily.

fussy ('fʌsɪ) adj. **fussier, fussiest. 1.** inclined to fuss over minor points. **2.** very particular about detail. **3.** characterized by overelaborate detail. —'**fussily** adv. —'**fussiness** n.

fustanella (,fʌstə'nɛlə) n. a white knee-length pleated skirt worn by men in Greece and Albania. [C19: from It., from Mod. Gk *phoustani,* prob. from It. *fustagno* FUSTIAN]

fustian ('fʌstɪən) n. **1. a.** a hard-wearing fabric of cotton mixed with flax or wool. **b.** (as modifier): *a fustian jacket.* **2.** pompous talk or writing. ~adj. **3.** cheap;

worthless. **4.** bombastic. [C12: from OF, from Med. L *fustāneum*, from L *fustis* cudgel]

fustic ('fʌstɪk) *n.* **1.** Also called: **old fustic.** a large tropical American tree. **2.** the yellow dye obtained from the wood of this tree. **3.** any of various trees or shrubs that yield a similar dye, esp. a European sumach (**young fustic**). [C15: from F *fustoc*, from Sp., from Ar. *fustuq*, from Gk *pistake* pistachio tree]

fusty ('fʌstɪ) *adj.* **-tier, -tiest. 1.** smelling of damp or mould. **2.** old-fashioned in attitude. [C14: from *fust* wine cask, from OF: cask, from L *fustis* cudgel] —**'fustily** *adv.* —**'fustiness** *n.*

fut. *abbrev. for* future.

futhark ('fu:θɑːk) *or* **futhorc, futhork** ('fu:θɔːk) *n.* a phonetic alphabet consisting of runes. [C19: from the first six letters: *f, u, th, a, r, k*]

futile ('fju:taɪl) *adj.* **1.** having no effective result; unsuccessful. **2.** pointless; trifling. **3.** inane or foolish. [C16: from L *futtilis* pouring out easily, from *fundere* to pour out] —**'futilely** *adv.* —**futility** (fju:'tɪlɪtɪ) *n.*

futon ('fu:,tɒn) *n.* a Japanese padded quilt, laid on the floor as a bed. [C19: from Japanese]

futtock ('fʌtək) *n. Naut.* one of the ribs in the frame of a wooden vessel. [C13: ? var. of *foothook*]

future ('fju:tʃə) *n.* **1.** the time yet to come. **2.** undetermined events that will occur in that time. **3.** the condition of a person or thing at a later date: *the future of the school is undecided.* **4.** likelihood of later improvement: *he has a future as a singer.* **5.** *Grammar.* **a.** a tense of verbs used when the action or event described is to occur after the time of utterance. **b.** a verb in this tense. **6. in future.** from now on. ~*adj.* **7.** that is yet to come or be. **8.** of or expressing time yet to come. **9.** (*prenominal*) destined to become. **10.** *Grammar.* in or denoting the future as a tense of verbs. ~*See also* **futures.** [C14: from L *futūrus* about to be, from *esse* to be] —**'futureless** *adj.*

future perfect *Grammar.* ~*adj.* **1.** denoting a tense of verbs describing an action that will have been performed by a certain time. ~*n.* **2. a.** the future perfect tense. **b.** a verb in this tense.

futures ('fju:tʃəz) *pl. n.* commodities bought or sold at an agreed price for delivery at a specified future date.

futurism ('fju:tʃə,rɪzəm) *n.* an artistic movement that arose in Italy in 1909 to replace traditional aesthetic values with the characteristics of the machine age. —**'futurist** *n., adj.*

futuristic (,fju:tʃə'rɪstɪk) *adj.* **1.** denoting or relating to design, etc., that is thought likely to be fashionable at some future time. **2.** of or relating to futurism. —**,futur'istically** *adv.*

futurity (fju:'tjʊərɪtɪ) *n., pl.* **-ties. 1.** a less common word for **future. 2.** the quality of being in the future. **3.** a future event.

futurology (,fju:tʃə'rɒlədʒɪ) *n.* the study or prediction of the future of mankind. —**,futur'ologist** *n.*

fuze (fju:z) *n. U.S.* a variant spelling of **fuse**[1].

fuzee (fju:'zi:) *n.* a variant spelling of **fusee.**

Fuzhou ('fu:'dʒəʊ), **Foochow,** *or* **Fuchou** *n.* a port in SE China, capital of Fujian province on the Min Jiang: one of the original five treaty ports (1842). Pop.: 1 190 000 (1986).

fuzz[1] (fʌz) *n.* **1.** a mass or covering of fine or curly hairs, fibres, etc. **2.** a blur. ~*vb.* **3.** to make or become fuzzy. **4.** to make or become indistinct. [C17: ?from Low G *fussig* loose]

fuzz[2] (fʌz) *n.* a slang word for **police** or **policeman.** [C20: from ?]

fuzzy ('fʌzɪ) *adj.* **fuzzier, fuzziest. 1.** of, resembling, or covered with fuzz. **2.** unclear or distorted. **3.** (of the hair) tightly curled or very wavy. —**'fuzzily** *adv.* —**'fuzziness** *n.*

fwd *abbrev. for* forward.

-fy *suffix forming verbs.* to make or become: *beautify.* [from OF *-fier,* from L *-ficāre,* from *-ficus* -FIC]

Fylde (faɪld) *n.* a region in NW England in Lancashire between the Wyre and Ribble estuaries.

fylfot ('faɪlfɒt) *n.* a rare word for **swastika.** [C16 (apparently meaning: a sign or device for the lower part or foot of a painted window): from *fillen* to fill + *fot* foot]

Fyn (*Danish* fy:n) *n.* the second largest island of Denmark, between the Jutland peninsula and the island of Sjælland. Pop.: 453 483 (1987). Area: 3481 sq. km (1344 sq. miles). German name: **Fünen.**

G

g *or* **G** (dʒiː) *n.*, *pl.* **g's, G's,** *or* **Gs. 1.** the seventh letter of the English alphabet. **2.** a speech sound represented by this letter, usually either as in *grass*, or as in *page*.

g *symbol for:* **1.** gallon(s). **2.** gram(s). **3.** grav. **4.** acceleration of free fall (due to gravity).

G *symbol for:* **1.** *Music.* **a.** the fifth note of the scale of C major. **b.** the major or minor key having this note as its tonic. **2.** gauss. **3.** gravitational constant. **4.** *Physics.* conductance. **5.** German. **6.** giga. **7.** good. **8.** *Sl.*, *chiefly U.S.* grand (a thousand dollars or pounds).

G. *or* **g.** *abbrev. for:* **1.** gauges. **2.** gelding. **3.** guilder(s). **4.** guinea(s). **5.** Gulf.

Ga *the chemical symbol for* gallium.

gab (gæb) *Inf.* ~*vb.* **gabbing, gabbed. 1.** (*intr.*) to talk excessively or idly; gossip; chatter. ~*n.* **2.** idle or trivial talk. **3. gift of the gab.** ability to speak glibly or persuasively. [C18: prob. from Irish Gaelic *gob* mouth] —'**gabber** *n.*

gabble ('gæbᵊl) *vb.* **1.** to utter (words, etc.) rapidly and indistinctly; jabber. **2.** (*intr.*) (of geese, etc.) to utter rapid cackling noises. ~*n.* **3.** rapid and indistinct speech or noises. [C17: from MDu. *gabbelen*, imit.] —'**gabbler** *n.*

gabbro ('gæbrəʊ) *n.*, *pl.* **-bros.** a dark coarse-grained igneous rock consisting of feldspar, pyroxene, and often olivine. [C19: from It., prob. from L *glaber* smooth, bald]

gabby ('gæbɪ) *adj.* **-bier, -biest.** *Inf.* inclined to chatter; talkative.

gaberdine ('gæbə,diːn, ,gæbə'diːn) *n.* **1.** a twill-weave worsted, cotton, or spun-rayon fabric. **2.** Also called: **gabardine.** an ankle-length loose coat or frock worn by men, esp. by Jews, in the Middle Ages. **3.** any of various other garments made of gaberdine, esp. a child's raincoat. [C16: from OF *gauvardine* pilgrim's garment, from MHG *wallewart* pilgrimage]

Gaberones (,gæbə'rəʊnɛs) *n.* the former name for **Gaborone.**

Gabès ('gɑːbɛs; *French* gabɛs) *n.* **1.** a port in E Tunisia. Pop.: 92 259 (1984). **2. Gulf of.** an inlet of the Mediterranean on the E coast of Tunisia. Ancient name: **Syrtis Minor.**

gabfest ('gæb,fɛst) *n. Inf., chiefly U.S. & Canad.* **1.** prolonged gossiping or conversation. **2.** an informal gathering for conversation. [C19: from GAB + G *Fest* festival]

gabion ('geɪbɪən) *n.* **1.** a cylindrical metal container filled with stones, used in the construction of underwater foundations. **2.** a wickerwork basket filled with stones or earth, used (esp. formerly) as part of a fortification. [C16: from F: basket, from It., from *gabbia* cage, from L *cavea*; see CAGE]

gable ('geɪbᵊl) *n.* **1.** the triangular upper part of a wall between the sloping ends of a pitched roof (**gable roof**). **2.** a triangular ornamental feature, esp. as used over a door or window. [C14: OF, prob. from ON *gafl*] —'**gabled** *adj.*

Gable ('geɪbᵊl) *n.* (**William**) **Clark.** 1901–60, U.S. film actor. His films include *It Happened One Night* (1934), *San Francisco* (1936), *Gone with the Wind* (1939), *Mogambo* (1953), and *The Misfits* (1960).

gable end *n.* the end wall of a building on the side which is topped by a gable.

Gabo ('gɑːbəʊ, -bə) *n.* **Naum** (naʊm). 1890–1977, U.S. sculptor, born in Russia: a leading constructivist.

Gabon (gə'bɒn; *French* gabɔ̃) *n.* a republic in W central Africa, on the Atlantic: settled by the French in 1839; made part of the French Congo in 1888; became independent in 1960; almost wholly forested. Official language: French. Religion: Christian and animist. Currency: franc. Capital: Libreville. Pop.: 1 224 000 (1987). Area: 267 675 sq. km (103 350 sq. miles). —**Gabonese** (,gæbə'niːz) *adj.*, *n.*

Gabor (gə'bɔː) *n.* **Dennis.** 1900–79, British electrical engineer, born in Hungary. He invented holography: Nobel prize for physics 1971.

Gaborone (,gæbə'rəʊnɪ) *n.* the capital of Botswana (since 1964), in the extreme southeast. Pop.: 96 000 (1986). Former name: **Gaberones.**

Gabriel[1] ('geɪbrɪəl) *n. Bible.* one of the archangels, the messenger of good news (Daniel 8:16–26; Luke 1:11–20, 26–38).

Gabriel[2] (*French* gabrɛl) *n.* **Jacques-Ange** (ʒakɑ̃ʒ). 1698–1782, French architect: designed the Petit Trianon at Versailles.

Gabrieli (*Italian* ga'brjɛːli) *or* **Gabrielli** (*Italian* ga'brjɛlli) *n.* **1. Andrea** (an'drɛːa). 1520–86, Italian organist and composer; chief organist of St Mark's, Venice. **2.** his nephew, **Giovanni** (dʒo'vanni). 1558–1612, Italian organist and composer.

gaby ('geɪbɪ) *n.*, *pl.* **-bies.** *Arch.* or *dialect.* a simpleton. [C18: from ?]

gad (gæd) *vb.* **gadding, gadded. 1.** (*intr.*; often foll. by *about* or *around*) to go out in search of pleasure; gallivant. ~*n.* **2.** carefree adventure (esp. in **on the gad**). [C15: back formation from obs. *gadling* companion, from OE, from *gæd* fellowship] —'**gadder** *n.*

Gad (gæd) *n. Old Testament.* **1. a.** Jacob's sixth son, whose mother was Zilpah, Leah's maid. **b.** the Israelite tribe descended from him. **c.** the territory of this tribe, lying to the east of the Jordan and extending southwards from the Sea of Galilee. **2.** a prophet and admonisher of David (I Samuel 22; II Samuel 24).

gadabout ('gædə,baʊt) *n. Inf.* a person who restlessly seeks amusement, etc.

Gadarene ('gædə,riːn) *adj.* relating to or engaged in a headlong rush. [C19: via LL from Gk *Gadarēnos*, of Gadara (Palestine), alluding to the Gadarene swine (Matthew 8:28ff.)]

Gaddafi *or* **Qaddafi** (gə'dɑːfɪ) *n.* **Moamar al** ('məʊə,mɑː æl). born 1942, Libyan army officer and statesman; head of state from 1969.

gadfly ('gæd,flaɪ) *n.*, *pl.* **-flies. 1.** any of various large dipterous flies, esp. the horsefly, that annoy livestock by sucking their blood. **2.** a constantly irritating person. [C16: from *gad* sting + FLY[2]]

gadget ('gædʒɪt) *n.* **1.** a small mechanical device or appliance. **2.** any object that is interesting for its ingenuity. [C19: from ?]

gadgetry ('gædʒɪtrɪ) *n.* **1.** gadgets collectively. **2.** use of or preoccupation with gadgets.

gadoid ('geɪdɔɪd) *adj.* **1.** of or belonging to an order of marine soft-finned fishes typically having the pectoral and pelvic fins close together and small cycloid scales. The group includes cod and hake. ~*n.* **2.** any gadoid fish. [C19: from NL *Gadidae*, from *gadus* cod; see -OID]

gadolinium (,gædə'lɪnɪəm) *n.* a ductile malleable silvery-white ferromagnetic element of the lanthanide series of metals. Symbol: Gd; atomic no.: 64; atomic wt.: 157.25. [C19: NL, after Johan *Gadolin* (1760–1852), Finnish mineralogist]

gadroon *or* **godroon** (gə'druːn) *n.* a decorative moulding composed of a series of convex flutes and curves, used esp. as an edge to silver articles. [C18: from F *godron*, ?from OF *godet* cup, goblet]

Gadsden Purchase ('gædzdən) *n.* an area of about 77 000 sq. km (30 000 sq. miles) in present-day Arizona and New Mexico, bought by the U.S. from Mexico for 10 million dollars in 1853. The purchase was negotiated by James Gadsden (1788–1858), U.S. diplomat.

gadwall ('gæd,wɔːl) *n.*, *pl.* **-walls** *or* **-wall.** a duck related to the mallard. The male has a grey body and black tail. [C17: from ?]

gadzooks (gæd'zuːks) *interj. Arch.* a mild oath. [C17: ?from *God's hooks* (the nails of the cross) from *Gad* arch. euphemism for God]

Gaea ('dʒiːə), **Gaia,** *or* **Ge** *n. Greek myth.* the goddess of the earth, who bore Uranus and by him Oceanus, Cronus and the Titans. [from Gk *gaia* earth]

Gael (geɪl) *n.* a person who speaks a Gaelic language, esp. a Highland Scot or an Irishman. [C19: from Gaelic *Gaidheal*] —'**Gaeldom** *n.*

Gaelic ('geɪlɪk, 'gæ-) *n.* **1.** any of the closely related languages of the Celts in Ireland, Scotland, or the Isle of Man. ~*adj.* **2.** of, denoting, or relating to the Celtic people of

Ireland, Scotland, or the Isle of Man or their language or customs.

Gaelic coffee *n.* another name for **Irish coffee.**

Gaeltacht ('ge:ltəxt) *n.* any of the regions in Ireland in which Irish Gaelic is the vernacular speech. [C20: from Irish Gaelic]

gaff[1] (gæf) *n.* **1.** *Angling.* a stiff pole with a stout prong or hook attached for landing large fish. **2.** *Naut.* a boom hoisted aft of a mast to support a fore-and-aft sail. **3.** a metal spur fixed to the leg of a gamecock. ~*vb.* **4.** (*tr.*) *Angling.* to hook or land (a fish) with a gaff. [C13: from F *gaffe*, from Provençal *gaf* boat hook]

gaff[2] (gæf) *n.* **1.** *Sl.* nonsense. **2. blow the gaff.** *Brit. sl.* to divulge a secret. [C19: from ?]

gaffe (gæf) *n.* a social blunder, esp. a tactless remark. [C19: from F]

gaffer ('gæfə) *n.* **1.** an old man: often used affectionately or patronizingly. **2.** *Inf., chiefly Brit.* a boss, foreman, or owner of a factory, etc. **3.** *Inf.* the senior electrician on a television or film set. [C16: from GODFATHER]

gag[1] (gæg) *vb.* **gagging, gagged. 1.** (*tr.*) to stop up (a person's mouth), esp. with a piece of cloth, etc., to prevent him from speaking or crying out. **2.** (*tr.*) to suppress or censor (free expression, information, etc.). **3.** to retch or cause to retch. **4.** (*intr.*) to struggle for breath; choke. ~*n.* **5.** a piece of cloth, rope, etc., stuffed into or tied across the mouth. **6.** any restraint on or suppression of information, free speech, etc. **7.** *Parliamentary procedure.* another word for **closure** (sense 4). [C15 *gaggen*; ? imit. of a gasping sound]

gag[2] (gæg) *Inf.* ~*n.* **1.** a joke or humorous story, esp. one told by a professional comedian. **2.** a hoax, practical joke, etc. ~*vb.* **gagging, gagged. 3.** (*intr.*) to tell jokes or funny stories, as comedians in nightclubs, etc. [C19: ? special use of GAG[1]]

gaga ('gɑ:gɑ:) *adj. Inf.* **1.** senile; doting. **2.** slightly crazy. [C20: from F, imit.]

Gagarin (*Russian* ga'garin) *n.* **Yuri** ('juri). 1934–68, Soviet cosmonaut: made the first manned space flight (1961).

gage[1] (geidʒ) *n.* **1.** something deposited as security against the fulfilment of an obligation; pledge. **2.** (formerly) a glove or other object thrown down to indicate a challenge to combat. ~*vb.* **3.** (*tr.*) *Arch.* to stake, pledge, or wager. [C14: from OF, of Gmc origin]

gage[2] (geidʒ) *n.* short for **greengage.**

gage[3] (geidʒ) *n., vb. U.S.* a variant spelling (esp. in technical senses) of **gauge.**

Gage (geidʒ) *n.* **Thomas.** 1721–87, British general and governor in America; commander in chief of British forces at Bunker Hill (1775).

gaggle ('gægəl) *vb.* **1.** (*intr.*) (of geese) to cackle. ~*n.* **2.** a flock of geese. **3.** *Inf.* a disorderly group of people. [C14: of Gmc origin; imit.]

Gaia ('geiə) *n.* a variant of **Gaea.**

gaiety ('geiəti) *n., pl.* **-ties. 1.** the state or condition of being gay. **2.** festivity; merrymaking. **3.** colourful bright appearance.

Gaillard Cut (gil'jɑ:d, 'geilɑ:d) *n.* the SE section of the Panama Canal, cut through Culebra Mountain. Length: about 13 km (8 miles). Former name: **Culebra Cut.** [C19: after David Du Bose *Gaillard* (1859–1913), U.S. army engineer in charge of the work]

gaillardia (gei'lɑ:diə) *n.* a plant of the composite family having ornamental flower heads with yellow or red rays and purple discs. [C19: from NL, after *Gaillard* de Marentonneau, 18th-cent. F amateur botanist]

gaily ('geili) *adv.* **1.** in a gay manner; merrily. **2.** with bright colours; showily.

gain (gein) *vb.* **1.** (*tr.*) to acquire (something desirable); obtain. **2.** (*tr.*) to win in competition: *to gain the victory.* **3.** to increase, improve, or advance: *the car gained speed.* **4.** (*tr.*) to earn (a wage, living, etc.). **5.** (*intr.; usually foll. by *on* or *upon*)* **a.** to get nearer (to) or catch up (on). **b.** to get farther away (from). **6.** (*tr.*) (esp. of ships) to get to; reach: *the steamer gained port.* **7.** (of a timepiece) to operate too fast, so as to indicate a time ahead of the true time. ~*n.* **8.** something won, acquired, earned, etc.; profit; advantage. **9.** an increase in size, amount, etc. **10.** the act of gaining; attainment; acquisition. **11.** Also called: **amplification.** *Electronics.* the ratio of the output signal of an amplifier to the input signal, usually measured in decibels. [C15: from OF *gaaignier*, of Gmc origin]

gainer ('geinə) *n.* **1.** a person or thing that gains. **2.** a type of dive in which the diver leaves the board facing forward and completes a full backward somersault to enter the water feet first with his back to the diving board.

gainful ('geinful) *adj.* profitable; lucrative. —**'gainfully** *adv.* —**'gainfulness** *n.*

gainsay (gein'sei) *vb.* **-saying, -said.** (*tr.*) *Arch. or literary.* to deny (an allegation, statement, etc.); contradict. [C13 *gainsaien*, from *gain-* AGAINST + *saien* to SAY] —**gain'sayer** *n.*

Gainsborough ('geinzbərə, -brə) *n.* **Thomas.** 1727–88, English painter, noted particularly for his informal portraits and for his naturalistic landscapes.

'gainst *or* **gainst** (genst, geinst) *prep. Poetic.* short for **against.**

Gaiseric ('gaizərik) *n.* a variant of **Genseric.**

gait (geit) *n.* **1.** manner of walking or running. **2.** (used esp. of horses and dogs) the pattern of footsteps at a particular speed, as the walk, canter, etc. ~*vb.* **3.** (*tr.*) to teach (a horse) a particular gait. [C16: var. of GATE]

gaiter ('geitə) *n.* (*often pl.*) **1.** a cloth or leather covering for the leg or ankle. **2.** Also called: **spat.** a similar covering extending from the ankle to the instep. [C18: from F *guêtre*, prob. of Gmc origin]

Gaitskell ('geitskil) *n.* **Hugh (Todd Naylor).** 1906–63, British politician; leader of the Labour Party (1955–63).

Gaius ('gaiəs) *or* **Caius** *n.* **1.** ?110–?180 A.D., Roman jurist. His *Institutes* were later used as the basis for those of Justinian. **2. Gaius Caesar.** See **Caligula.**

gal (gæl) *n. Sl.* a girl.

gal. *or* **gall.** *abbrev. for* gallon.

Gal. *Bible. abbrev. for* Galatians.

gala ('gɑ:lə, 'geilə) *n.* **1. a.** a celebration; festive occasion. **b.** (*as modifier*): *a gala occasion.* **2.** *Chiefly Brit.* a sporting occasion involving competitions in several events: *a swimming gala.* [C17: from F or It., from OF *gale*, from *galer* to make merry, prob. of Gmc origin]

galactic (gə'læktik) *adj.* **1.** *Astron.* of or relating to a galaxy, esp. the Galaxy. **2. galactic plane.** the plane passing through the spiral arms of the Galaxy, contained by the great circle of the celestial sphere (**galactic equator**) and perpendicular to an imaginary line joining opposite points (**galactic poles**) on the celestial sphere. **3.** *Med.* of or relating to milk. [C19: from Gk *galaktikos*; see GALAXY]

galago (gə'lɑ:gəʊ) *n., pl.* **-gos.** another name for **bushbaby.** [C19: from NL, ?from Wolof *golokh* monkey]

galah (gə'lɑ:) *n.* **1.** an Australian cockatoo, having grey wings, back, and crest, and a pink body. **2.** *Austral. sl.* a fool or simpleton. [C19: from Abor.]

Galahad ('gælə,hæd) *n.* **1. Sir.** (in Arthurian legend) the most virtuous knight of the Round Table. **2.** a pure or noble man.

galantine ('gælən,ti:n) *n.* a cold dish of meat or poultry, which is boned, cooked, then pressed and glazed. [C14: from OF, from Med. L *galatina*, prob. from L *gelātus* frozen, set]

Galápagos Islands (gə'læpəgəs; *Spanish* ga'lapaɣɔs) *pl. n.* a group of 15 islands in the Pacific west of Ecuador, of which they form a province: discovered (1535) by the Spanish; main settlement on San Cristóbal. Pop.: 8000 (1986 est.). Area: 7844 sq. km (3028 sq. miles). Official Spanish name: **Archipiélago de Colón.**

Galashiels (,gælə'ʃiːlz) *n.* a town in SE Scotland, in the central Borders region. Pop.: 12 294 (1981).

Galata ('gælətə) *n.* a port in NW Turkey, a suburb and the chief business section of Istanbul.

Galatea (,gælə'tiə) *n. Greek myth.* a statue of a maiden brought to life by Aphrodite in response to the prayers of the sculptor Pygmalion, who had fallen in love with his creation.

Galaţi (*Romanian* ga'latsj) *n.* an inland port in SE Romania, on the River Danube. Pop.: 292 805 (1985).

Galatia (gə'leiʃə, -ʃiə) *n.* an ancient region in central Asia Minor, conquered by Gauls 278–277 B.C.: later a Roman province. —**Ga'latian** *adj., n.*

galaxy ('gæləksi) *n., pl.* **-axies. 1.** any of a vast number of star systems held together by gravitational attraction. **2.** a splendid gathering, esp. one of famous or distinguished people. [C14 (in the sense: the Milky Way): from Med. L *galaxia*, from L, from Gk, from *gala* milk]

Galaxy ('gæləksɪ) *n.* **the.** the spiral galaxy that contains the solar system about three fifths of the distance from its centre. Also called: the **Milky Way System.**

Galba ('gælbə) *n.* **Servius Sulpicius** ('sɜːvɪəs sʌl'pɪʃəs). ?3 B.C.–69 A.D., Roman emperor (68–69) after the assassination of Nero.

galbanum ('gælbənəm) *n.* a bitter aromatic gum resin extracted from any of several Asian umbelliferous plants. [C14: from L, from Gk, from Heb. *helbenāh*]

Galbraith (gæl'breɪθ) *n.* **John Kenneth.** born 1908, U.S. economist and diplomat born in Canada; author of *The Affluent Society* (1958) and *The New Industrial State* (1967). —**Gal'braithian** *adj.*

gale (geɪl) *n.* **1.** a strong wind, specifically one of force 8 on the Beaufort scale or from 39-46 mph. **2.** (*often pl.*) a loud outburst, esp. of laughter. **3.** *Arch. & poetic.* a gentle breeze. [C16: from ?]

galea ('geɪlɪə) *n., pl.* **-leae** (-lɪ,iː). a part shaped like a helmet, such as the petals of certain flowers. [C18: from L: helmet] — '**gale,ate** *or* '**gale,ated** *adj.*

Galen ('geɪlən) *n.* Latin name *Claudius Galenus.* ?130–?200 A.D., Greek physician, anatomist, and physiologist. He codified existing medical knowledge and his authority continued until the Renaissance.

galena (gə'liːnə) *or* **galenite** (gə'liːnaɪt) *n.* a soft heavy bluish-grey or black mineral consisting of lead sulphide: the chief source of lead. Formula: PbS. [C17: from L: lead ore]

Galenic (geɪ'lɛnɪk, gə-) *adj.* of or relating to Galen or his teachings or methods.

Galicia *n.* **1.** (gə'lɪʃɪə, -'lɪʃə). a region of E central Europe on the N side of the Carpathians, now in SE Poland and the SW Soviet Union. **2.** (*Spanish* ga'liθja). an autonomous region and former kingdom of NW Spain, on the Bay of Biscay and the Atlantic. —**Galician** (gə'lɪʃɪən, -ʃən) *adj., n.*

Galilean[1] (,gælɪ'liːən) *n.* **1.** a native or inhabitant of Galilee. **2. the.** an epithet of Jesus Christ. ~*adj.* **3.** of Galilee.

Galilean[2] (,gælɪ'leɪən) *adj.* of or relating to Galileo.

Galilee ('gælɪ,liː) *n.* **1. Sea of.** Also called: Lake **Tiberias.** a lake in NE Israel, 209 m (686 ft.) below sea level, through which the River Jordan flows. Area: 165 sq. km (64 sq. miles). **2.** a northern region of Israel: scene of Christ's early ministry.

Galileo (,gælɪ'leɪəʊ) *n.* full name *Galileo Galilei.* 1564–1642, Italian mathematician, astronomer, and physicist. He discovered the isochronism of the pendulum and demonstrated that falling bodies of different weights descend at the same rate. He perfected the refracting telescope, which led to his discovery of Jupiter's satellites, sunspots, and craters on the moon. He was forced by the Inquisition to recant his support of the Copernican system.

galingale ('gælɪŋ,geɪl) *or* **galangal** (gə'læŋgəl) *n.* a European plant with rough-edged leaves, reddish spikelets of flowers, and aromatic roots. [C13: from OF, from Ar., from Chinese]

galiot *or* **galliot** ('gælɪət) *n.* **1.** a small swift galley formerly sailed on the Mediterranean. **2.** a ketch formerly used along the coasts of Germany and the Netherlands. [C14: from OF, from It., from Med. L *galea* GALLEY]

galipot ('gælɪ,pɒt) *n.* a resin obtained from several species of pine. [C18: from F, from ?]

gall[1] (gɔːl) *n.* **1.** *Inf.* impudence. **2.** bitterness; rancour. **3.** something bitter or disagreeable. **4.** *Physiol.* an obsolete term for **bile.** See also **gall bladder.** [from ON, replacing OE *gealla*]

gall[2] (gɔːl) *n.* **1.** a sore on the skin caused by chafing. **2.** something that causes vexation or annoyance. **3.** irritation; exasperation. ~*vb.* **4.** to abrade (the skin, etc.) as by rubbing. **5.** (*tr.*) to irritate or annoy; vex. [C14: of Gmc origin; rel. to OE *gealla* sore on a horse, & ? to GALL[1]]

gall[3] (gɔːl) *n.* an abnormal outgrowth in plant tissue caused by certain parasitic insects, fungi, or bacteria. [C14: from OF, from L *galla*]

gall. *or* **gal.** *abbrev. for* gallon.

gallant *adj.* ('gælənt). **1.** brave and high-spirited; courageous and honourable: *a gallant warrior.* **2.** (gə'lænt, 'gælənt). (of a man) attentive to women; chivalrous. **3.** imposing; dignified; stately: *a gallant ship.* **4.** *Arch.* showy in dress. ~*n.* ('gælənt, gə'lænt). **5.** a woman's lover or suitor. **6.** a dashing or fashionable young man,

esp. one who pursues women. **7.** a brave, high-spirited, or adventurous man. ~*vb.* (gə'lænt, 'gælənt). *Rare.* **8.** (when *intr.*, usually foll. by *with*) to court or flirt (with). [C15: from OF, from *galer* to make merry, from *gale* enjoyment, of Gmc origin] — '**gallantly** *adv.*

gallantry ('gæləntrɪ) *n., pl.* **-ries. 1.** conspicuous courage, esp. in war. **2.** polite attentiveness to women. **3.** a gallant action, speech, etc.

gall bladder *n.* a muscular sac, attached to the right lobe of the liver, that stores bile.

Galle ('gɑːlə) *n.* a port in SW Sri Lanka. Pop.: 77 183 (1981). Former name: **Point de Galle.**

galleass ('gælɪ,æs) *n.* a three-masted galley used as a warship in the Mediterranean from the 15th to the 18th centuries. [C16: from F, from It., from Med. L *galea* GALLEY]

galleon ('gælɪən) *n.* a large sailing ship having three or more masts, used as a warship or trader from the 15th to the 18th centuries. [C16: from Sp. *galeón*, from F, from OF *galie* GALLEY]

gallery ('gælərɪ) *n., pl.* **-leries. 1.** a covered passageway open on one side or on both sides. **2.** a balcony running along or around the inside wall of a church, hall, etc. **3.** *Theatre.* **a.** an upper floor that projects from the rear and contains the cheapest seats. **b.** the seats there. **c.** the audience seated there. **4.** a glass-fronted soundproof room overlooking a television studio, used for lighting, etc. **5.** a long narrow room, esp. one used for a specific purpose: *a shooting gallery.* **6.** a room or building for exhibiting works of art. **7.** an underground passage, as in a mine, etc. **8.** a small ornamental railing, esp. one surrounding the top of a desk, table, etc. **9.** any group of spectators, as at a golf match. **10. play to the gallery.** to try to gain popular favour, esp. by crude appeals. [C15: from OF, from Med. L, prob. from *galilea* galilee, porch or chapel at entrance to medieval church] — '**galleried** *adj.*

galley ('gælɪ) *n.* **1.** any of various kinds of ship propelled by oars or sails used in ancient or medieval times. **2.** the kitchen of a ship, boat, or aircraft. **3.** any of various long rowing boats. **4.** *Printing.* **a.** a tray for holding composed type. **b.** short for **galley proof.** [C13: from OF *galie*, from Med. L *galea*, from Gk *galaia*, from ?]

galley proof *n.* a printer's proof, esp. one taken from type in a galley, used to make corrections before the matter has been split into pages. Often shortened to **galley.**

galley slave *n.* **1.** a criminal or slave condemned to row in a galley. **2.** *Inf.* a drudge.

gallfly ('gɔːl,flaɪ) *n., pl.* **-flies.** any of several small insects that produce galls in plant tissues.

galliard ('gæljəd) *n.* **1.** a spirited dance in triple time for two persons, popular in the 16th and 17th centuries. **2.** a piece of music composed for or in the rhythm of this dance. [C14: from OF *gaillard* valiant, ? of Celtic origin]

Gallic ('gælɪk) *adj.* **1.** of or relating to France. **2.** of or relating to ancient Gaul or the Gauls.

gallic acid *n.* a colourless crystalline compound obtained from tannin: used as a tanning agent and in making inks and paper. [C18: from F *gallique*; see GALL[3]]

Gallicism ('gælɪ,sɪzəm) *n.* a word or idiom borrowed from French.

Gallicize *or* **-cise** ('gælɪ,saɪz) *vb.* to make or become French in attitude, language, etc.

galligaskins (,gælɪ'gæskɪnz) *pl. n.* **1.** loose wide breeches or hose, esp. as worn by men in the 17th century. **2.** leather leggings, as worn in the 19th century. [C16: from obs. F, from It. *grechesco* Greek, from L *Graecus*]

gallimaufry (,gælɪ'mɔːfrɪ) *n., pl.* **-fries.** a jumble; hotchpotch. [C16: from F *galimafrée* ragout, hash, from ?]

gallinacean (,gælɪ'neɪʃən) *n.* any gallinaceous bird.

gallinaceous (,gælɪ'neɪʃəs) *adj.* of, relating to, or belonging to an order of birds, including domestic fowl, pheasants, grouse, etc., having a heavy rounded body, short bill, and strong legs. [C18: from L, from *gallīna* hen]

Gallinas Point (gɑː'jiːnəs) *n.* a cape in NE Colombia: the northernmost point of South America. Spanish name: **Punta Gallinas** ('punta ga'ʎinas).

galling ('gɔːlɪŋ) *adj.* irritating, exasperating, or bitterly humiliating. — '**gallingly** *adv.*

gallinule ('gælɪ,njuːl) *n.* any of various aquatic birds, typically having a dark plumage, red bill, and a red shield above the bill. [C18: from NL *Gallīnula*, from LL, from L *gallīna* hen]

galliot ('gælɪət) n. a variant spelling of **galiot**.

Gallipoli (gə'lɪpəlɪ) n. **1.** a peninsula in NW Turkey, between the Dardanelles and the Gulf of Saros: scene of a costly but unsuccessful Allied campaign in 1915. **2.** a port in NW Turkey, at the entrance to the Sea of Marmara: historically important for its strategic position. Pop.: 14 721 (1980). Turkish name: **Gelibolu**.

gallipot ('gælɪ,pɒt) n. a small earthenware pot used by pharmacists as a container for ointments, etc. [C16: prob. from GALLEY + POT¹; because imported in galleys]

gallium ('gælɪəm) n. a silvery metallic element that is liquid for a wide temperature range. It is used in high-temperature thermometers, semiconductors, and low-melting alloys. Symbol: Ga; atomic no.: 31; atomic wt.: 69.72. [C19: from NL, from L *gallus* cock, translation of F *coq* in the name of its discoverer, *Lecoq* de Boisbaudran, 19th-cent. F chemist]

gallivant ('gælɪ,vænt) vb. (intr.) to go about in search of pleasure, etc.; gad about. [C19: ? whimsical from GALLANT]

Gällivare (Swedish 'jɛliva:rə) n. a town in N Sweden, within the Arctic Circle: iron mines. Pop.: 25 276 (1976).

galliwasp ('gælɪ,wɒsp) n. a lizard of the West Indies. [C18: from ?]

gallnut ('gɔːl,nʌt) or **gall-apple** n. a type of plant gall that resembles a nut.

Gallo- ('gæləʊ) combining form. denoting Gaul or France: *Gallo-Roman*. [from L *Gallus* a Gaul]

gallon ('gælən) n. **1.** Also called: **imperial gallon**. Brit. a unit of capacity equal to 277.42 cubic inches. 1 Brit. gallon is equivalent to 1.20 U.S. gallons or 4.55 litres. **2.** U.S. a unit of capacity equal to 231 cubic inches. 1 U.S. gallon is equivalent to 0.83 imperial gallon or 3.79 litres. **3.** (pl.) Inf. great quantities. [C13: from ONorthern F *galon* (OF *jalon*), ? of Celtic origin]

gallonage ('gælənɪdʒ) n. a capacity measured in gallons.

galloon (gə'luːn) n. a narrow band of cord, embroidery, silver or gold braid, etc., used on clothes and furniture. [C17: from F, from OF *galonner* to trim with braid, from ?]

gallop ('gæləp) vb. **1.** (intr.) (of a horse or other quadruped) to run fast with a two-beat stride in which all four legs are off the ground at once. **2.** to ride (a horse, etc.) at a gallop. **3.** (intr.) to move, read, progress, etc., rapidly. ~n. **4.** the fast two-beat gait of horses. **5.** an instance of galloping. [C16: from OF *galoper*, from ?] — **'galloper** n.

Galloway ('gæləˌweɪ) n. **1.** an area of SW Scotland, on the Solway Firth: consists of the former counties of Kirkcudbright and Wigtown, now part of Dumfries and Galloway region; in the west is a large peninsula, the **Rhinns of Galloway**, with the **Mull of Galloway**, a promontory, at the south end of it (the southernmost point of Scotland). Related adj.: **Galwegian**. **2.** a breed of hardy black cattle originally bred in Galloway.

gallows ('gæləʊz) n., pl. **-lowses** or **-lows**. **1.** a wooden structure usually consisting of two upright posts with a crossbeam, used for hanging criminals. **2.** any timber structure resembling this. **3. the gallows**. execution by hanging. [C13: from ON *galgi*, replacing OE *gealga*]

gallows bird n. Inf. a person considered deserving of hanging.

gallows humour n. sinister and ironic humour.

gallows tree or **gallow tree** n. another name for **gallows** (sense 1).

gallstone ('gɔːl,stəʊn) n. a small hard concretion formed in the gall bladder or its ducts.

Gallup ('gæləp) n. **George Horace**. 1901–84, U.S. statistician: devised the Gallup Poll; founded the American Institute of Public Opinion (1935) and its British counterpart (1936).

Gallup Poll n. a sampling of the views of a representative cross section of the population, used esp. as a means of forecasting voting.

galluses ('gæləsɪz) pl. n. Dialect. braces for trousers. [C18: var. of *gallowses*, from GALLOWS (in the obs. sense: braces)]

gall wasp n. any small solitary wasp that produces galls in plant tissue.

galoot or **galloot** (gə'luːt) n. Sl., chiefly U.S. a clumsy or uncouth person. [C19: from ?]

galop ('gæləp) n. **1.** a 19th-century dance in quick duple time. **2.** a piece of music for this dance. [C19: from F; see GALLOP]

galore (gə'lɔː) determiner. (immediately postpositive) in great numbers or quantity: *there were daffodils galore in the park*. [C17: from Irish Gaelic *go leór* to sufficiency]

galoshes or **goloshes** (gə'lɒʃɪz) pl. n. (sometimes sing.) a pair of waterproof overshoes. [C14 (in the sense: wooden shoe): from OF, from LL *gallicula* Gallic shoe]

Galsworthy ('gɔːlz,wɜːðɪ) n. **John**. 1867–1933, English novelist and dramatist, noted for *The Forsyte Saga* (1906–28): Nobel prize for literature 1932.

Galt (gɔːlt) n. **John**. 1779–1839, Scottish novelist, noted for his ironic humour, esp. in *Annals of the Parish* (1821), *The Provost* (1822), and *The Entail* (1823).

Galton ('gɔːltən) n. Sir **Francis**. 1822–1911, English explorer and scientist, a cousin of Charles Darwin, noted for his researches in heredity, meteorology, and statistics. He founded the study of eugenics and the theory of anticyclones.

galumph (gə'lʌmpf, -'lʌmf) vb. (intr.) Inf. to leap or move about clumsily or joyfully. [C19 (coined by Lewis Carroll): prob. a blend of GALLOP + TRIUMPH]

Galvani (Italian gal'va:ni) n. **Luigi** (lu'iːdʒi). 1737–98, Italian physiologist: observed that muscles contracted on contact with dissimilar metals. This led to the galvanic cell and the electrical theory of muscle control by nerves.

galvanic (gæl'vænɪk) adj. **1.** of, producing, or concerned with an electric current, esp. a direct current produced chemically. **2.** Inf. resembling the effect of an electric shock; convulsive, startling, or energetic. — **gal'vanically** adv.

galvanism ('gælvə,nɪzəm) n. **1.** Obs. electricity, esp. when produced by chemical means as in a cell or battery. **2.** Med. treatment involving the application of electric currents to tissues. [C18: via F from It. *galvanismo*, after GALVANI]

galvanize or **-ise** ('gælvə,naɪz) vb. (tr.) **1.** to stimulate to action; excite; startle. **2.** to cover (iron, steel, etc.) with a protective zinc coating. **3.** to stimulate by application of an electric current. — **galvani'zation** or **-i'sation** n.

galvano- combining form. indicating a galvanic current: *galvanometer*.

galvanometer (,gælvə'nɒmɪtə) n. any sensitive instrument for detecting or measuring small electric currents. — **galvanometric** (,gælvənəʊ'mɛtrɪk, gæl,vænəʊ-) adj. — **,galva'nometry** n.

Galway¹ ('gɔːlweɪ) n. **1.** a county of W Ireland, in S Connacht, on **Galway Bay** and the Atlantic: it has a deeply indented coastline and many offshore islands, including the Aran Islands. County town: Galway. Pop.: 178 180 (1986). Area: 5939 sq. km (2293 sq. miles). **2.** a port in W Ireland, county town of Co. Galway, on Galway Bay: important fisheries (esp. for salmon). Pop.: 47 008 (1986).

Galway² ('gɔːlweɪ) n. **James**. born 1939, Irish flautist.

gam (gæm) n. Sl. a leg. [C18: from F *jambe* leg]

Gama ('gɑːmə) n. **Vasco da** ('væskəʊ də). ?1469–1524, Portuguese navigator, who discovered the sea route from Portugal to India around the Cape of Good Hope (1498).

Gambetta (gæm'bɛtə; French gɑ̃bɛta) n. **Léon** (leɔ̃). 1838–82, French statesman; prime minister (1881–82). He organized resistance during the Franco-Prussian War (1870–71) and was a founder of the Third Republic (1871).

Gambia ('gæmbɪə) n. **The.** a republic in W Africa, entirely surrounded by Senegal except for an outlet to the Atlantic: sold to English merchants by the Portuguese in 1588; became a British colony in 1843; gained independence within the Commonwealth in 1965; joined with Senegal in 1982 to form the Confederation of Senegambia; consists of a strip of land about 16 km (10 miles) wide, on both banks of the **Gambia River**, extending inland for about 480 km (300 miles). Official language: English. Religion: Muslim majority. Currency: dalasi. Capital: Banjul. Pop.: 698 817 (1986 est.). Area: 11 295 sq. km (4361 sq. miles). — **'Gambian** adj., n.

gambier or **gambir** ('gæmbɪə) n. an astringent resinous substance obtained from a tropical Asian plant: used as an astringent and tonic and in tanning. [C19: from Malay]

Gambier Islands ('gæmbɪə) pl. n. a group of islands in the S Pacific Ocean, in French Polynesia. Chief settlement: Rikitéa. Pop.: 556 (1977). Area: 30 sq. km (11 sq. miles).

gambit ('gæmbɪt) n. **1.** *Chess.* an opening move in which a chessman, usually a pawn, is sacrificed to secure an advantageous position. **2.** an opening comment, manoeuvre, etc., intended to secure an advantage. [C17: from F, from It. *gambetto* a tripping up, from *gamba* leg]

gamble ('gæmbªl) vb. **1.** (*intr.*) to play games of chance to win money, etc. **2.** to risk or bet (money, etc.) on the outcome of an event, sport, etc. **3.** (*intr.*; often foll. by *on*) to act with the expectation of: *to gamble on its being a sunny day.* **4.** (often foll. by *away*) to lose by or as if by betting; squander. ~*n.* **5.** a risky act or venture. **6.** a bet or wager. [C18: prob. var. of GAME[1]] —'**gambler** *n.* —'**gambling** *n.*

gamboge (gæm'bəʊdʒ, -'buːʒ) n. **1. a.** a gum resin used as the source of a yellow pigment and as a purgative. **b.** the pigment made from this resin. **2. gamboge tree.** any of several tropical Asian trees that yield this resin. [C18: from NL *gambaugium*, from CAMBODIA (now Kampuchea), where first found]

gambol ('gæmbªl) vb. **-bolling**, **-bolled** or U.S. **-boling**, **-boled**. **1.** (*intr.*) to skip or jump about in a playful manner; frolic. ~*n.* **2.** a playful antic; frolic. [C16: from F *gambade*; see JAMB]

gambrel ('gæmbrəl) n. **1.** the hock of a horse or similar animal. **2.** short for **gambrel roof.** [C16: from OF, from *gambe* leg]

gambrel roof n. **1.** *Chiefly Brit.* a hipped roof having a small gable at both ends. **2.** *Chiefly U.S. & Canad.* a roof having two slopes on both sides, the lower slopes being steeper than the upper.

game[1] (geɪm) n. **1.** an amusement or pastime; diversion. **2.** a contest with rules, the result being determined by skill, strength, or chance. **3.** a single period of play in such a contest, sport, etc. **4.** the score needed to win a contest. **5.** a single contest in a series; match. **6.** (*pl.; often cap.*) an event consisting of various sporting contests, esp. in athletics: *Olympic Games.* **7.** equipment needed for playing certain games. **8.** style or ability in playing a game. **9.** a scheme, proceeding, etc., practised like a game: *the game of politics.* **10.** an activity undertaken in a spirit of levity; joke: *marriage is just a game to him.* **11. a.** wild animals, including birds and fish, hunted for sport, food, or profit. **b.** (*as modifier*): *game laws.* **12.** the flesh of such animals, used as food. **13.** an object of pursuit; quarry; prey (esp. in **fair game**). **14.** *Inf.* work or occupation. **15.** *Inf.* a trick, strategy, or device: *I can see through your little game.* **16.** *Sl., chiefly Brit.* prostitution (esp. in **on the game**). **17. give the game away.** to reveal one's intentions or a secret. **18. make (a) game of.** to make fun of; ridicule; mock. **19. play the game.** to behave fairly or in accordance with the rules. **20. the game is up.** there is no longer a chance of success. ~*adj.* **21.** *Inf.* full of fighting spirit; plucky; brave. **22.** (usually foll. by *for*) *Inf.* prepared or ready; willing: *I'm game for a try.* ~*vb.* **23.** (*intr.*) to play games of chance for money, stakes, etc.; gamble. [OE *gamen*] —'**gamely** *adv.* —'**gameness** *n.*

game[2] (geɪm) adj. a less common word for **lame** (esp. in **game leg**). [C18: prob. from Irish *cam* crooked]

gamecock ('geɪm,kɒk) n. a cock bred and trained for fighting. Also called: **fighting cock.**

game fish n. any fish providing sport for the angler.

gamekeeper ('geɪm,kiːpə) n. a person employed to take care of game, as on an estate.

gamelan ('gæmɪ,læn) n. a type of percussion orchestra common in the East Indies. [from Javanese]

game laws pl. n. laws governing the hunting and preservation of game.

game point n. *Tennis, etc.* a stage at which winning one further point would enable one player or side to win a game.

gamesmanship ('geɪmzmən,ʃɪp) n. *Inf.* the art of winning games or defeating opponents by cunning practices without actually cheating.

gamesome ('geɪmsəm) adj. full of merriment; sportive. —'**gamesomeness** *n.*

gamester ('geɪmstə) n. a person who habitually plays games for money; gambler.

gametangium (,gæmɪ'tændʒɪəm) n., pl. **-gia** (-dʒɪə). *Bot.* an organ or cell in which gametes are produced, esp. in algae and fungi. [C19: NL, from GAMETO- + Gk *angeion* vessel]

gamete ('gæmiːt, gə'miːt) n. a haploid germ cell that fuses with another during fertilization. [C19: from NL, from Gk *gametē* wife, from *gamos* marriage] —**gametic** (gə'mɛtɪk) adj.

game theory n. mathematical theory concerned with the optimum choice of strategy in situations involving a conflict of interest.

gameto- or sometimes before a vowel **gamet-** combining form. gamete: *gametophyte.*

gametophyte (gə'miːtəʊ,faɪt) n. the plant body, in species showing alternation of generations, that produces the gametes. —**gametophytic** (,gæmɪtəʊ'fɪtɪk) adj.

gamin ('gæmɪn) n. a street urchin. [from F]

gamine ('gæmiːn) n. a slim and boyish girl or young woman; an elfish tomboy. [from F]

gaming ('geɪmɪŋ) n. **a.** gambling on games of chance. **b.** (*as modifier*): *gaming house.*

gamma ('gæmə) n. **1.** the third letter in the Greek alphabet (Γ, γ). **2.** the third in a group or series. [C14: from Gk]

gamma distribution n. *Statistics.* a continuous two-parameter distribution from which the chi-square and exponential distributions are derived.

gamma globulin n. any of a group of proteins in blood plasma that includes most known antibodies.

gamma radiation n. electromagnetic radiation of shorter wavelength and higher energy than x-rays.

gamma rays pl. n. streams of gamma radiation.

gammer ('gæmə) n. *Rare, chiefly Brit.* a dialect word for an old woman: now chiefly humorous or contemptuous. [C16: prob. from GODMOTHER or GRANDMOTHER]

gammon[1] ('gæmən) n. **1.** a cured or smoked ham. **2.** the hindquarter of a side of bacon, cooked either whole or in rashers. [C15: from OF *gambon*, from *gambe* leg]

gammon[2] ('gæmən) n. **1.** a double victory in backgammon in which one player throws off all his pieces before his opponent throws any. ~*vb.* **2.1**(*tr.*) to score such a victory over. [C18: prob. special use of ME *gamen* GAME[1]]

gammon[3] ('gæmən) *Brit. inf.* ~*n.* **1.** deceitful nonsense; humbug. ~*vb.* **2.** to deceive (a person). [C18: ? special use of GAMMON[1]]

gammy ('gæmɪ) adj. **-mier**, **-miest**. *Brit. sl.* (esp. of the leg) malfunctioning, injured, or lame; game. [C19: dialect var. of GAME[2]]

gamo- or before a vowel **gam-** combining form. **1.** indicating sexual union or reproduction: *gamogenesis.* **2.** united or fused: *gamopetalous.* [from Gk *gamos* marriage]

gamopetalous (,gæməʊ'pɛtələs) adj. (of flowers) having petals that are united or partly united, as the primrose.

gamp (gæmp) n. *Brit. inf.* an umbrella. [C19: after Mrs Sarah *Gamp*, a nurse in Dickens' *Martin Chuzzlewit*, who carried a faded cotton umbrella]

gamut ('gæmʌt) n. **1.** entire range or scale, as of emotions. **2.** *Music.* **a.** a scale, or scale. (in medieval theory) one starting on the G on the bottom line of the bass staff. **b.** the whole range of notes. [C15: from Med. L, from *gamma*, the lowest note of the hexachord as established by Guido d'Arezzo + *ut* (now, *doh*), the first of the notes of the scale *ut, re, mi, fa, sol, la, si*]

gamy or **gamey** ('geɪmɪ) adj. **gamier**, **gamiest**. **1.** having the smell or flavour of game, esp. high game. **2.** *Inf.* spirited; plucky; brave. —'**gamily** adv. —'**gaminess** n.

-gamy n. combining form. denoting marriage or sexual union: *bigamy.* [from Gk, from *gamos* marriage] —'**-gamous** adj. combining form.

Gance (French gɑ̃s) n. **Abel** (abɛl). 1889–1981, French film director, whose works include *J'accuse* (1919, 1937) and *Napoléon* (1927), which introduced the split-screen technique.

Gand (gɑ̃) n. the French name for **Ghent.**

gander ('gændə) n. **1.** a male goose. **2.** *Inf.* a quick look (esp. in **take** (or **have**) **a gander**). **3.** *Inf.* a simpleton. [OE *gandra, ganra*]

Gandhi ('gændɪ) n. **1.** Mrs **Indira (Priyadarshini)** (ɪn'dɪərə, 'ɪndərə), daughter of Jawaharlal Nehru. 1917–84, Indian stateswoman; prime minister of India (1966–77; 1980–84); assassinated. **2. Mohandas Karamchand** (,məʊhən'dʌs ,kʌrəm'tʃʌnd), known as *Mahatma Gandhi.* 1869–1948, Indian political and spiritual leader and social reformer. He played a major part in India's struggle for home rule and was frequently imprisoned by the British for organizing acts of civil disobedience. He advocated passive resistance and hunger strikes as means of achieving reform, campaigned for the untouchables, and attempted to unite Muslims and Hindus. He was assassinated by a Hindu extremist. **3. Rajiv** (ræ'dʒiːv), son of Indira Gandhi. born 1944, Indian statesman; prime minister of India from 1984. —**Gandhian** ('gændɪən) adj.

Gandzha (Russian gan'dʒa) n. a former name (until 1813 and 1920–35) of **Kirovabad.**

Ganesa (gə'niːsə) n. the Hindu god of prophecy, represented as having an elephant's head.

gang¹ (gæŋ) n. **1.** a group of people who associate together or act as an organized body, esp. for criminal or illegal purposes. **2.** an organized group of workmen. **3.** a series of similar tools arranged to work simultaneously in parallel. ~vb. **4.** to form into, become part of, or act as a gang. ~See also **gang up.** [OE: journey]

gang² (gæŋ) n. a variant spelling of **gangue.**

gang³ (gæŋ) vb. (intr.) Scot. to go or walk. [OE gangan]

gangbang ('gæŋ,bæŋ) n. Sl. an instance of sexual intercourse between one woman and several men one after the other, esp. against her will.

ganger ('gæŋə) n. Chiefly Brit. the foreman of a gang of labourers.

Ganges ('gændʒiːz) n. the great river of N India and central Bangladesh: rises in two headstreams in the Himalayas and flows southeast to Allahabad, where it is joined by the Jumna; continues southeast into Bangladesh, where it enters the Bay of Bengal in a great delta; the most sacred river to Hindus, with many places of pilgrimage, esp. Varanasi. Length: 2507 km (1557 miles). Hindi name: **Ganga** ('gʌŋgə, 'gɑːŋ-). —**Gangetic** (gæn'dʒɛtɪk) adj.

gangland ('gæŋ,lænd, -lənd) n. the criminal underworld.

gangling ('gæŋglɪŋ) or **gangly** adj. tall, lanky, and awkward in movement. [see GANG³]

ganglion ('gæŋglɪən) n., pl. **-glia** (-glɪə) or **-glions. 1.** an encapsulated collection of nerve-cell bodies, usually located outside the brain and spinal cord. **2.** any concentration or centre of energy, activity, or strength. **3.** a cystic tumour on a tendon sheath. [C17: from LL: swelling, from Gk: cystic tumour] —**'gangliar** adj. —**,gangli'onic** or **'gangli,ated** adj.

gangplank ('gæŋ,plæŋk) or **gangway** n. Naut. a portable bridge for boarding and leaving a vessel at dockside.

gangrene ('gæŋgriːn) n. **1.** death and decay of tissue as the result of interrupted blood supply, disease, or injury. ~vb. **2.** to become or cause to become affected with gangrene. [C16: from L, from Gk gangraina an eating sore] —**gangrenous** ('gæŋgrɪnəs) adj.

gang-saw n. a multiple saw used in a timber mill to cut planks from logs.

gangster ('gæŋstə) n. a member of an organized gang of criminals.

Gangtok ('gʌŋtɒk) n. a city in NE India: capital of Sikkim state. Pop.: 36 768 (1981).

gangue or **gang** (gæŋ) n. valueless and undesirable material in an ore. [C19: from F, from G Gang vein of metal, course]

gang up vb. (intr., adv.; often foll. by on or against) Inf. to combine in a group (against).

gangway ('gæŋ,weɪ) n. **1.** another word for **gangplank. 2.** an opening in a ship's side to take a gangplank. **3.** Brit. an aisle between rows of seats. **4.** temporary planks over mud or earth, as on a building site. ~sentence substitute. **5.** clear a path!

ganister or **gannister** ('gænɪstə) n. a refractory siliceous sedimentary rock occurring beneath coal seams: used for lining furnaces.

gannet ('gænɪt) n. **1.** any of several heavily built marine birds having a long stout bill and typically white plumage with dark markings. **2.** Sl. a greedy person. [OE ganot]

ganoid ('gænɔɪd) adj. **1.** (of the scales of certain fishes) consisting of an inner bony layer and an outer layer of an enamel-like substance (**ganoin**). **2.** denoting fishes, including the sturgeon and bowfin, having such scales. ~n. **3.** a ganoid fish. [C19: from F, from Gk ganos brightness + -OID]

Gansu ('gæn'suː) or **Kansu** n. a province of NW China, between Tibet and Inner Mongolia: mountainous, with desert regions; forms a corridor, the Old Silk Road, much used in early and medieval times for trade with Turkestan, India, and Persia. Capital: Lanzhou. Pop.: 20 160 000 (1985). Area: 366 500 sq. km (141 500 sq. miles).

gantry ('gæntrɪ) n., pl. **-tries. 1.** a bridgelike framework used to support a travelling crane, signals over a railway track, etc. **2.** Also called: **gantry scaffold.** the framework tower used to attend to a large rocket on its launching pad. **3.** a supporting framework for a barrel. **4. a.** the area behind a bar where bottles, esp. spirit bottles mounted in optics, are kept. **b.** the range or quality of the spirits on display there. [C16 (in the sense: wooden platform for barrels): from OF chantier, from Med. L, from L canthērius supporting frame, pack ass]

Ganymede ('gænɪ,miːd) n. Classical myth. a beautiful Trojan youth who was abducted by Zeus to Olympus and made the cupbearer of the gods.

Gao ('gɑːəʊ, gaʊ) n. a town in E Mali, on the River Niger: a small river port. Pop.: 30 714 (1976).

gaol (dʒeɪl) n., vb. Brit. a variant spelling of **jail.** —**'gaoler** n.

gap (gæp) n. **1.** a break or opening in a wall, fence, etc. **2.** a break in continuity; interruption; hiatus. **3.** a break in a line of hills or mountains affording a route through. **4.** Chiefly U.S. a gorge or ravine. **5.** a divergence or difference; disparity: the generation gap. **6.** Electronics. **a.** a break in a magnetic circuit that increases the inductance and saturation point of the circuit. **b.** See **spark gap. 7. bridge, close, fill,** or **stop a gap.** to remedy a deficiency. ~vb. **gapping, gapped. 8.** (tr.) to make a breach or opening in. [C14: from ON gap chasm] —**'gappy** adj.

gape (geɪp) vb. (intr.) **1.** to stare in wonder, esp. with the mouth open. **2.** to open the mouth wide, esp. involuntarily, as in yawning. **3.** to be or become wide open: the crater gaped under his feet. ~n. **4.** the act of gaping. **5.** a wide opening. **6.** the width of the widely opened mouth of a vertebrate. **7.** a stare of astonishment. [C13: from ON gapa] —**'gaper** n. —**'gaping** adj.

gapes (geɪps) n. (functioning as sing.) **1.** a disease of young domestic fowl, characterized by gaping and caused by parasitic worms (**gapeworms**). **2.** Inf. a fit of yawning.

gar (gɑː) n., pl. **gar** or **gars.** short for **garpike.**

garage ('gærɑːʒ, -rɪdʒ) n. **1.** a building used to house a motor vehicle. **2.** a commercial establishment in which motor vehicles are repaired, serviced, bought, and sold, and which usually also sells motor fuels. ~vb. **3.** (tr.) to put into or keep in a garage. [C20: from F, from OF: to protect, from OHG warōn]

garage band n. a rough-and-ready amateurish rock group. [?from the practice of such bands rehearsing in a garage]

garage sale n. a sale of personal belongings or household effects held at a person's home, usually in the garage.

garb (gɑːb) n. **1.** clothes, esp. the distinctive attire of an occupation: clerical garb. **2.** style of dress; fashion. **3.** external appearance, covering, or attire. ~vb. **4.** (tr.) to clothe; attire. [C16: from OF: graceful contour, from OIt. garbo grace, prob. of Gmc origin]

garbage ('gɑːbɪdʒ) n. **1.** worthless, useless, or unwanted matter. **2.** another word (esp. U.S. and Canad.) for **rubbish. 3.** Computers. invalid data. [C15: prob. from Anglo-F garbelage removal of discarded matter, from ?]

garble ('gɑːbəl) vb. (tr.) **1.** to jumble (a story, quotation, etc.), esp. unintentionally. **2.** to distort the meaning of (an account, text, etc.), as by making misleading omissions; corrupt. ~n. **3. a.** the act of garbling. **b.** garbled matter. [C15: from OIt. garbellare to strain, sift, from Ar., from LL cribellum small sieve] —**'garbler** n.

Garbo ('gɑːbəʊ) n. **Greta** ('greɪə), real name Greta Lovisa Gustafson. born 1905, U.S. film actress, born in Sweden. Her films include Grand Hotel (1932), Queen Christina (1933), Anna Karenina (1935), Camille (1936), and Ninotchka (1939).

garboard ('gɑː,bɔːd) n. Naut. the bottommost plank of a vessel's hull. Also called: **garboard strake.** [C17: from Du. gaarboord, prob. from MDu. gaderen to GATHER + boord BOARD]

García Lorca (Spanish gar'θia 'lɔrka) n. See (Federico García) **Lorca.**

garçon (French gars5) n. a waiter or male servant, esp. if French. [C19: from OF gars lad, prob. of Gmc origin]

Gard (French gar) n. a department of S France, in Languedoc-Roussillon region. Capital: Nîmes. Pop.: 530 478 (1982). Area: 5881 sq. km (2294 sq. miles).

garda ('gɑːrdə) *n.*, *pl.* **gardaí** ('gɑːrdɪ). a member of the **Garda Síochána**, the police force of the Republic of Ireland.

Garda ('gɑːdə) *n.* **Lake.** a lake in N Italy: the largest lake in the country. Area: 370 sq. km (143 sq. miles).

garden ('gɑːdᵊn) *n.* **1.** *Brit.* **a.** an area of land, usually planted with grass, trees, flowerbeds, etc., adjoining a house. U.S. and Canad. word: **yard. b.** (*as modifier*): *a garden chair.* **2. a.** an area of land used for the cultivation of ornamental plants, herbs, fruit, vegetables, trees, etc. **b.** (*as modifier*): *garden tools.* Related adj.: **horticultural. 3.** (*often pl.*) such an area of land that is open to the public, sometimes part of a park: *botanical gardens.* **4.** a fertile and beautiful region. **5. lead** (**a person**) **up the garden path.** *Inf.* to mislead or deceive. ~*vb.* **6.** to work in, cultivate, or take care of (a garden, plot of land, etc.). [C14: from OF *gardin*, of Gmc origin] —'**gardener** *n.* —'**gardening** *n.*

garden centre *n.* a place where gardening tools and equipment, plants, seeds, etc., are sold.

garden city *n. Brit.* a planned town of limited size surrounded by a rural belt.

gardenia (gɑːˈdiːnɪə) *n.* **1.** any evergreen shrub or tree of the Old World tropical genus *Gardenia,* cultivated for their large fragrant waxlike typically white flowers. **2.** the flower of any of these shrubs. [C18: NL, after Dr Alexander *Garden* (1730–91), American botanist]

Garden of Eden *n.* the full name for **Eden.**

garderobe ('gɑːdˌrəʊb) *n. Arch.* **1.** a wardrobe or its contents. **2.** a private room. **3.** a privy. [C14: from F, from *garder* to keep + *robe* dress, clothing; see WARDROBE]

Gardiner ('gɑːdnə) *n.* **Stephen.** ?1483–1555, English bishop and statesman; lord chancellor (1553–55). He opposed Protestantism, supporting the anti-Reformation policies of Mary I.

Garfield ('gɑːˌfiːld) *n.* **James Abram.** 1831–81, 20th president of the U.S. (1881); assassinated in office.

garfish ('gɑːˌfɪʃ) *n.*, *pl.* **-fish** *or* **-fishes.** **1.** another name for **garpike** (sense 1). **2.** an elongated marine teleost fish with long toothed jaws: related to the flying fishes. [OE *gār* spear + FISH]

garganey ('gɑːgənɪ) *n.* a small Eurasian duck closely related to the mallard. The male has a white stripe over each eye. [C17: from It. dialect *garganei,* imit.]

gargantuan (gɑːˈgæntjʊən) *adj.* (*sometimes cap.*) huge; enormous. [after *Gargantua,* a giant in Rabelais' satire *Gargantua and Pantagruel* (1534)]

gargle ('gɑːgᵊl) *vb.* **1.** to rinse the mouth and throat with (a liquid, esp. a medicinal fluid) by slowly breathing through the liquid. ~*n.* **2.** the liquid used for gargling. **3.** the sound produced by gargling. [C16: from OF, from *gargouille* throat, ? imit.]

gargoyle ('gɑːgɔɪl) *n.* **1.** a waterspout carved in the form of a grotesque face or creature and projecting from a roof gutter. **2.** a person with a grotesque appearance. [C15: from OF *gargouille* gargoyle; throat; see GARGLE]

garibaldi (ˌgærɪˈbɔːldɪ) *n. Brit.* a type of biscuit having a layer of currants in the centre.

Garibaldi (ˌgærɪˈbɔːldɪ) *n.* **Giuseppe** (dʒuˈzɛppe). 1807–82, Italian patriot; a leader of the Risorgimento. He fought against the Austrians and French in Italy (1848–49; 1859) and, with 1000 volunteers, conquered Sicily and Naples for the emerging kingdom of Italy (1860).

garish ('gɛərɪʃ) *adj.* gay or colourful in a crude manner; gaudy. [C16: from earlier *gaure* to stare + -ISH] —'**garishly** *adv.* —'**garishness** *n.*

garland ('gɑːlənd) *n.* **1.** a wreath of flowers, leaves, etc., worn round the head or neck or hung up. **2.** a collection of short literary pieces, such as poems; anthology. ~*vb.* **3.** (*tr.*) to adorn with a garland or garlands. [C14: from OF *garlande,* ? of Gmc origin]

Garland ('gɑːlənd) *n.* **Judy,** real name *Frances Gumm.* 1922–69, U.S. singer and film actress. Already a child star, she achieved international fame with *The Wizard of Oz* (1939). Later films included *Meet Me in St Louis* (1944) and *A Star is Born* (1954).

garlic ('gɑːlɪk) *n.* **1.** a hardy widely cultivated Asian alliaceous plant having whitish flowers. **2.** the bulb of this plant, made up of small segments (cloves) that have a strong odour and pungent taste and are used in cooking. [OE *gārlēac,* from *gār* spear + *lēac* LEEK] —'**garlicky** *adj.*

garment ('gɑːmənt) *n.* **1.** (*often pl.*) an article of clothing. **2.** outer covering. ~*vb.* **3.** (*tr.; usually passive*) to cover or clothe. [C14: from OF *garniment,* from *garnir* to equip; see GARNISH]

garner ('gɑːnə) *vb.* (*tr.*) **1.** to gather or store as in a granary. ~*n.* **2.** an archaic word for **granary. 3.** a place for storage. [C12: from OF: granary, from L *grānārium,* from *grānum* grain]

Garner ('gɑːnə) *n.* **Erroll.** 1921–77, U.S. jazz pianist and songwriter.

garnet ('gɑːnɪt) *n.* any of a group of hard glassy red, yellow, or green minerals consisting of silicates in cubic crystalline form: used as a gemstone and abrasive. [C13: from OF, from *grenat* (adj.) red, from *pome grenate* POMEGRANATE]

Garnett ('gɑːnɪt) *n.* **Constance.** 1862–1946, English translator of Russian novels.

garnish ('gɑːnɪʃ) *vb.* (*tr.*) **1.** to decorate; trim. **2.** to add something to (food) in order to improve its appearance or flavour. **3.** *Law.* **a.** to serve with notice of proceedings; warn. **b.** to attach (a debt). ~*n.* **4.** a decoration; trimming. **5.** something, such as parsley, added to a dish for its flavour or decorative effect. [C14: from OF *garnir* to adorn, equip, of Gmc origin] —'**garnisher** *n.*

garnishee (ˌgɑːnɪˈʃiː) *Law.* ~*n.* **1.** a person upon whom a garnishment has been served. ~*vb.* **-nisheeing, -nisheed.** (*tr.*) **2.** to attach (a debt or other property) by garnishment. **3.** to serve (a person) with a garnishment.

garnishment ('gɑːnɪʃmənt) *n.* **1.** decoration or embellishment. **2.** *Law.* **a.** a notice or warning. **b.** *Obs.* a summons to court proceedings already in progress. **c.** a notice warning a person holding money or property belonging to a debtor whose debt has been attached to hold such property until directed by the court to apply it.

garniture ('gɑːnɪtʃə) *n.* decoration or embellishment. [C16: from F, from *garnir* to GARNISH]

Garonne (*French* garɔn) *n.* a river in SW France, rising in the central Pyrenees in Spain and flowing northeast then northwest into the Gironde estuary. Length: 580 km (360 miles).

garpike ('gɑːˌpaɪk) *n.* **1.** Also called: **garfish, gar.** any primitive freshwater elongated bony fish of North and Central America, having very long toothed jaws and a body covering of thick scales. **2.** another name for **garfish** (sense 2).

garret ('gærɪt) *n.* another word for **attic** (sense 1). [C14: from OF: watchtower, from *garir* to protect, of Gmc origin]

Garrick ('gærɪk) *n.* **David.** 1717–79, English actor and theatre manager.

garrison ('gærɪsᵊn) *n.* **1.** the troops who maintain and guard a base or fortified place. **2.** the place itself. ~*vb.* **3.** (*tr.*) to station (troops) in (a fort, etc.). [C13: from OF, from *garir* to defend, of Gmc origin]

garrotte *or* **garotte** (gəˈrɒt) *n.* **1.** a Spanish method of execution by strangulation. **2.** the device, usually an iron collar, used in such executions. **3.** *Obs.* strangulation of one's victim while committing robbery. ~*vb.* (*tr.*) **4.** to execute by means of the garrotte. **5.** to strangle, esp. in order to commit robbery. [C17: from Sp. *garrote,* ?from OF *garrot* cudgel; from ?] —ga'**rotter** *or* ga'**rotter** *n.*

garrulous ('gærʊləs) *adj.* **1.** given to constant chatter; talkative. **2.** wordy or diffuse. [C17: from L *garrīre* to chatter] —'**garrulously** *adv.* —'**garrulousness** *or* **garrulity** (gæˈruːlɪtɪ) *n.*

garryowen (ˌgærɪˈəʊɪn) *n.* (in rugby union) another term for **up-and-under.** [from *Garryowen* RFC, Ireland]

garter ('gɑːtə) *n.* **1.** a band, usually of elastic, worn round the leg to hold up a sock or stocking. **2.** the U.S. and Canad. word for **suspender.** ~*vb.* **3.** (*tr.*) to fasten or secure as with a garter. [C14: from OF *gartier,* from *garet* bend of the knee, prob. of Celtic origin]

Garter ('gɑːtə) *n.* **the. 1. Order of the Garter.** the highest order of British knighthood, open to women since 1987. **2.** (*sometimes not cap.*) **a.** the badge of this Order. **b.** membership of this Order.

garter snake *n.* a nonvenomous North American snake, typically marked with longitudinal stripes.

garter stitch *n.* knitting in which all the rows are knitted in plain stitch.

garth (gɑːθ) *n.* **1.** a courtyard surrounded by a cloister. **2.** *Arch.* a yard or garden. [C14: from ON *garthr*]

Gary ('gærɪ) *n.* a port in NW Indiana, on Lake Michigan: a major world steel producer. Pop.: 136 790 (1986 est.).

gas (gæs) *n., pl.* **gases** *or* **gasses. 1.** a substance in a physical state in which it does not resist change of shape and will expand indefinitely to fill any container. **2.** any substance that is gaseous at room temperature and atmospheric pressure. **3.** any gaseous substance that is above its critical temperature and therefore not liquefiable by pressure alone. Cf. **vapour** (sense 2). **4. a.** a fossil fuel in the form of a gas, used as a source of domestic and industrial heat. **b.** (*as modifier*): *a gas cooker; gas fire.* **5.** a gaseous anaesthetic, such as nitrous oxide. **6.** *Mining.* firedamp or the explosive mixture of firedamp and air. **7.** the usual U.S., Canad., Austral., and N.Z. word for **petrol. 8. step on the gas.** *Inf.* **a.** to accelerate a motor vehicle. **b.** to hurry. **9.** a toxic, etc., substance in suspension in air used against an enemy, etc. **10.** *Inf.* idle talk or boasting. **11.** *Sl.* a delightful or successful person or thing: *his latest record is a gas.* ~*vb.* **gases** *or* **gasses, gassing, gassed. 12.** (*tr.*) to provide or fill with gas. **13.** (*tr.*) to subject to gas fumes, esp. so as to asphyxiate or render unconscious. **14.** (*intr.; foll. by to*) *Inf.* to talk in an idle or boastful way (to a person). [C17 (coined by J. B. van Helmont (1577–1644), Flemish chemist): from Gk *khaos* atmosphere]

gasbag ('gæs,bæg) *n.* *Inf.* a person who talks in a vapid or empty way.

gas chamber *or* **oven** *n.* an airtight room into which poison gas is introduced to kill people or animals.

gas chromatography *n.* a technique for analysing a mixture of volatile substances in which the mixture is carried by an inert gas through a column packed with a selective adsorbent and a detector records on a moving strip the conductivity of the gas leaving the tube.

Gascon ('gæskən) *n.* **1.** a native or inhabitant of Gascony. **2.** the dialect of French spoken in Gascony. ~*adj.* **3.** of or relating to Gascony, its inhabitants, or their dialect of French.

gasconade (,gæskə'neɪd) *Rare.* ~*n.* **1.** boastful talk or bluster. ~*vb.* **2.** (*intr.*) to boast, brag, or bluster. [C18: from F, from *gasconner* to chatter, boast like a GASCON]

gas constant *n.* the constant in the gas equation, having the value 8.3143 joules per kelvin per mole. Symbol *R* Also called: **universal gas constant.**

Gascony ('gæskənɪ) *n.* a former province of SW France. French name: **Gascogne** (gaskɔ̃).

gas-cooled reactor *n.* a nuclear reactor using a gas as the coolant.

gaseous ('gæsɪəs, -ʃəs, -ʃɪəs, 'geɪ-) *adj.* of, concerned with, or having the characteristics of a gas. —'**gaseousness** *n.*

gas equation *n.* an equation relating the product of the pressure and the volume of an ideal gas to the product of its thermodynamic temperature and the gas constant.

gas gangrene *n.* gangrene resulting from infection of a wound by anaerobic bacteria that cause gas bubbles in the surrounding tissues.

gash (gæʃ) *vb.* **1.** (*tr.*) to make a long deep cut in; slash. ~*n.* **2.** a long deep cut. [C16: from OF *garser* to scratch, wound, from Vulgar L, from Gk *kharassein*]

gasholder ('gæs,həʊldə) *n.* **1.** Also called: **gasometer.** a large tank for storing coal gas or natural gas prior to distribution to users. **2.** any vessel for storing or measuring a gas.

gasify ('gæsɪ,faɪ) *vb.* **-fying, -fied.** to make into or become a gas. —,**gasifi'cation** *n.*

Gaskell ('gæskəl) *n.* **Mrs.** married name of *Elizabeth Cleghorn Stevenson.* 1810–65, English novelist. Her novels include *Mary Barton* (1848), an account of industrial life in Manchester, and *Cranford* (1853), a social study of a country village.

gasket ('gæskɪt) *n.* **1.** a compressible packing piece of paper, rubber, asbestos, etc., sandwiched between the faces of a metal joint to provide a seal. **2.** *Naut.* a piece of line used as a sail stop. [C17 (in the sense: rope lashing a furled sail): prob. from F *garcette* rope's end, lit.: little girl, from OF]

gaslight ('gæs,laɪt) *n.* **1.** a type of lamp in which the illumination is produced by an incandescent mantle heated by a jet of gas. **2.** the light produced by such a lamp.

gasman ('gæs,mæn) *n., pl.* **-men.** a man employed to read household gas meters, supervise gas fittings, etc.

gas mantle *n.* a mantle for use in a gaslight. See **mantle** (sense 3).

gas mask *n.* a mask fitted with a chemical filter to enable the wearer to breathe air free of poisonous or corrosive gases.

gas meter *n.* an apparatus for measuring and recording the amount of gas passed through it.

gasoline *or* **gasolene** ('gæsə,liːn) *n.* a U.S. and Canad. name for **petrol.**

gasometer (gæs'ɒmɪtə) *n.* a nontechnical name for **gasholder.**

gasp (gɑːsp) *vb.* **1.** (*intr.*) to draw in the breath sharply or with effort, esp. in expressing awe, horror, etc. **2.** (*intr.; foll. by after or for*) to crave. **3.** (*tr.; often foll. by out*) to utter breathlessly. ~*n.* **4.** a short convulsive intake of breath. **5. at the last gasp. a.** at the point of death. **b.** at the last moment. [C14: from ON *geispa* to yawn]

Gaspar ('gæspə, 'gæspɑː) *n.* a variant of **Caspar.**

Gaspé Peninsula (gæ'speɪ; *French* gaspe) *n.* a peninsula in E Canada, in SE Quebec between the St Lawrence River and New Brunswick: mountainous and wooded with many lakes and rivers. Area: about 29 500 sq. km (11 400 sq. miles). Also called: **the Gaspé.**

gasper ('gɑːspə) *n.* **1.** a person who gasps. **2.** *Brit. sl.* a cheap cigarette.

gas plant *n.* an aromatic white-flowered Eurasian plant that emits vapour capable of being ignited. Also called: **burning bush, dittany, fraxinella.**

gas ring *n.* a circular assembly of gas jets, used esp. for cooking.

Gasser ('gæsə) *n.* **Herbert Spencer.** 1888–1963, U.S. physiologist: shared a Nobel prize for physiology or medicine (1944) with Erlanger for work on electrical signs of nervous activity.

gassy ('gæsɪ) *adj.* **-sier, -siest. 1.** filled with, containing, or resembling gas. **2.** *Inf.* full of idle or vapid talk. —'**gassiness** *n.*

gasteropod ('gæstərə,pɒd) *n., adj.* a variant spelling of **gastropod.**

gas thermometer *n.* a device for measuring temperature by observing the pressure of a gas at a constant volume or the volume of a gas kept at a constant pressure.

gastric ('gæstrɪk) *adj.* of, relating to, near, or involving the stomach.

gastric juice *n.* a digestive fluid secreted by the stomach, containing hydrochloric acid, pepsin, rennin, etc.

gastric ulcer *n.* an ulcer of the mucous membrane lining the stomach.

gastritis (gæs'traɪtɪs) *n.* inflammation of the stomach.

gastro- *or often before a vowel* **gastr-** *combining form.* stomach: *gastroenteritis; gastritis.* [from Gk *gastēr*]

gastroenteritis (,gæstrəʊ,ɛntə'raɪtɪs) *n.* inflammation of the stomach and intestines.

gastrointestinal (,gæstrəʊm'tɛstɪnəl) *adj.* of or relating to the stomach and intestinal tract.

gastronome ('gæstrə,nəʊm), **gastronomer** (gæs-'trɒnəmə), *or* **gastronomist** *n.* less common words for **gourmet.**

gastronomy (gæs'trɒnəmɪ) *n.* the art of good eating. [C19: from F, from Gk, from *gastēr* stomach; see -NOMY] —**gastronomic** (,gæstrə'nɒmɪk) *or* ,**gastro'nomical** *adj.* —,**gastro'nomically** *adv.*

gastropod ('gæstrə,pɒd) *or* **gasteropod** *n.* any of a class of molluscs typically having a flattened muscular foot for locomotion and a head that bears stalked eyes. The class includes the snails, whelks and slugs. —**gastropodous** (gæs'trɒpədəs) *adj.*

gastroscope ('gæstrə,skəʊp) *n.* a medical instrument for examining the interior of the stomach.

gastrula ('gæstrʊlə) *n., pl.* **-las** *or* **-lae** (-,liː). a saclike animal embryo consisting of three layers of cells surrounding a central cavity with a small opening to the exterior. [C19: NL: little stomach, from Gk *gastēr* belly]

gas turbine *n.* an internal-combustion engine in which the expanding gases emerging from one or more combustion chambers drive a turbine.

gasworks ('gæs,wɜːks) *n.* (*functioning as sing.*) a plant in which gas, esp. coal gas, is made.

gat (gæt) *vb. Arch.* a past tense of **get.**

gate (geɪt) *n.* **1.** a movable barrier, usually hinged, for closing an opening in a wall, fence, etc. **2.** an opening to allow passage into or out of an enclosed place. **3.** any means of entrance or access. **4.** a mountain pass or gap, esp. one providing entry into another country or region. **5. a.** the number of people admitted to a sporting event or entertainment. **b.** the total entrance money received from them. **6.** *Electronics.* a logic circuit having one or more input terminals and one output terminal, the output being switched between two voltage levels determined by the combination of input signals. **7.** a component in a motion-picture camera or projector that holds each frame flat and momentarily stationary behind the lens. **8.** a slotted metal frame that controls the positions of the gear lever in a motor vehicle. ~*vb.* **9.** (*tr.*) *Brit.* to restrict (a student) to the school or college grounds as a punishment. [OE *geat*]

gâteau ('gætəu) *n., pl.* **-teaux** (-təuz). a rich cake usually layered with cream and elaborately decorated. [F: cake]

gate-crash *vb. Inf.* to gain entry to (a party, concert, etc.) without invitation or payment. — **'gate-,crasher** *n.*

gatefold ('geɪt,fəuld) *n.* an oversize page in a book or magazine that is folded in. Also called: **foldout.**

gatehouse ('geɪt,haus) *n.* **1.** a building at or above a gateway, used by a porter or guard, or, formerly, as a fortification. **2.** a small house at the entrance to the grounds of a country mansion.

gatekeeper ('geɪt,ki:pə) *n.* **1.** a person who has charge of a gate and controls who may pass through it. **2.** any of several Eurasian butterflies having brown-bordered orange wings.

gate-leg table *or* **gate-legged table** *n.* a table with one or two leaves supported by a hinged leg swung out from the frame.

gatepost ('geɪt,pəust) *n.* **1. a.** the post on which a gate is hung. **b.** the post to which a gate is fastened when closed. **2. between you, me, and the gatepost.** confidentially.

Gates (geɪts) *n.* **Horatio.** ?1728 – 1806, American Revolutionary general: defeated the British at Saratoga (1777).

Gateshead ('geɪts,hɛd) *n.* a port in NE England, in Tyne and Wear: engineering works. Pop.: 81 367 (1981).

gateway ('geɪt,weɪ) *n.* **1.** an entrance that may be closed by or as by a gate. **2.** a means of entry or access: *Bombay, gateway to India.*

Gath (gæθ) *n. Old Testament.* one of the five cities of the Philistines, from which Goliath came (I Samuel 17:4) and near which Saul fell in battle (II Samuel 1:20). Douay spelling: **Geth** (geθ).

gather ('gæðə) *vb.* **1.** to assemble or cause to assemble. **2.** to collect or be collected gradually; muster. **3.** (*tr.*) to learn from information given; conclude or assume. **4.** (*tr.*) to pick or harvest (flowers, fruit, etc.). **5.** (*tr.*) to bring close (to). **6.** to increase or cause to increase gradually, as in force, speed, intensity, etc. **7.** to contract (the brow) or (of the brow) to become contracted into wrinkles; knit. **8.** (*tr.*) to assemble (sections of a book) in the correct sequence for binding. **9.** (*tr.*) to prepare or make ready: *to gather one's wits.* **10.** to draw (material) into a series of small tucks or folds. **11.** (*intr.*) (of a boil or other sore) to come to a head; form pus. ~*n.* **12. a.** the act of gathering. **b.** the amount gathered. **13.** a small fold in material, as made by a tightly pulled stitch; tuck. [OE *gadrian*] — **'gatherer** *n.*

gathering ('gæðərɪŋ) *n.* **1.** a group of people, things, etc., that are gathered together; assembly. **2.** *Sewing.* a series of gathers in material. **3.** *Inf.* **a.** the formation of pus in a boil. **b.** the pus so formed. **4.** *Printing.* an informal name for **section** (sense 16).

Gatling gun ('gætlɪŋ) *n.* a machine gun equipped with a rotating cluster of barrels that are fired in succession. [C19: after R. J. *Gatling* (1818 – 1903), its U.S. inventor]

GATT (gæt) *n. acronym for* General Agreement on Tariffs and Trade: a multilateral international treaty signed in 1947 to promote trade.

Gatún Lake (*Spanish* ga'tun) *n.* a lake in Panama, part of the Panama Canal: formed in 1912 on the completion of the **Gatún Dam** across the Chagres River. Area: 424 sq. km (164 sq. miles).

gauche (gəuʃ) *adj.* lacking ease of manner; tactless. [C18: F: awkward, left, from OF *gauchir* to swerve, ult. of Gmc origin] — **'gauchely** *adv.* — **'gaucheness** *n.*

gaucherie (,gəuʃə'ri:, 'gəuʃərɪ) *n.* **1.** the quality of being gauche. **2.** a gauche act.

gaucho ('gautʃəu) *n., pl.* **-chos.** a cowboy of the South American pampas, usually one of mixed Spanish and Indian descent. [C19: from American Sp., prob. from Quechuan *wáhcha* orphan, vagabond]

gaud (gɔ:d) *n.* an article of cheap finery. [C14: prob. from OF *gaudir* to be joyful, from L *gaudēre*]

Gaudí ('gaudɪ; *Spanish* gau'ði) *n.* **Antonio** (an'tonjo). 1852 – 1926, Spanish architect, regarded as one of the most original exponents of Art Nouveau in Europe and noted esp. for the church of the Sagrada familia, Barcelona.

Gaudier-Brzeska (*French* godjebʒɛska) *n.* **Henri** (ɑ̃ri). 1891 – 1915, French vorticist sculptor.

gaudy[1] ('gɔ:dɪ) *adj.* **gaudier, gaudiest.** bright or colourful in a crude or vulgar manner. [C16: from GAUD] — **'gaudily** *adv.* — **'gaudiness** *n.*

gaudy[2] ('gɔ:dɪ) *n., pl.* **gaudies.** *Brit.* a celebratory feast held at some schools and colleges. [C16: from L *gaudium* joy, from *gaudēre* to rejoice]

gauge *or* **gage** (geɪdʒ) *vb.* (*tr.*) **1.** to measure or determine the amount, quantity, size, condition, etc., of. **2.** to estimate or appraise; judge. **3.** to check for conformity or bring into conformity with a standard measurement, etc. ~*n.* **4.** a standard measurement, dimension, capacity, or quantity. **5.** any of various instruments for measuring a quantity: *a pressure gauge.* **6.** any of various devices used to check for conformity with a standard measurement. **7.** a standard or means for assessing; test; criterion. **8.** scope, capacity, or extent. **9.** the diameter of the barrel of a gun, esp. a shotgun. **10.** the thickness of sheet metal or the diameter of wire. **11.** the distance between the rails of a railway track. **12.** the distance between two wheels on the same axle of a vehicle, truck, etc. **13.** *Naut.* the position of a vessel in relation to the wind and another vessel. **14.** a measure of the fineness of woven or knitted fabric. ~*adj.* **15.** (of a pressure measurement) measured on a pressure gauge that registers zero at atmospheric pressure. [C15: from OF, prob. of Gmc origin] — **'gaugeable** *or* **'gageable** *adj.*

Gauguin (*French* gogɛ̃) *n.* **Paul** (pɔl). 1848 – 1903, French postimpressionist painter, who worked in the South Pacific from 1891. Inspired by primitive art, his work is characterized by flat contrasting areas of pure colours.

Gauhati (gau'ha:tɪ) *n.* a city in NE India, in Assam on the River Brahmaputra: centre of British administration in Assam (1826 – 74). Pop.: 123 784 (1971).

Gaul (gɔ:l) *n.* **1.** an ancient region of W Europe corresponding to N Italy, France, Belgium, part of Germany, and the S Netherlands: divided into Cisalpine Gaul, which became a Roman province before 100 B.C., and Transalpine Gaul, which was conquered by Julius Caesar (58 – 51 B.C.). Latin name: **Gallia.** **2.** a native of ancient Gaul. **3.** a Frenchman.

Gauleiter ('gau,laɪtə) *n.* **1.** a provincial governor in Germany under Hitler. **2.** (*sometimes not cap.*) a person in a position of petty authority who behaves in an overbearing manner. [G, from *Gau* district + *Leiter* leader]

Gaulish ('gɔ:lɪʃ) *n.* **1.** the extinct Celtic language of the pre-Roman Gauls. ~*adj.* **2.** of ancient Gaul, the Gauls, or their language.

Gaulle (gəul, gɔ:l; *French* gol) *n.* **Charles de.** See (Charles) **de Gaulle.**

gaunt (gɔ:nt) *adj.* **1.** bony and emaciated in appearance. **2.** (of places) bleak or desolate. [C15: ?from ON] — **'gauntly** *adv.* — **'gauntness** *n.*

gauntlet[1] ('gɔ:ntlɪt) *n.* **1.** a medieval armoured leather glove. **2.** a heavy glove with a long cuff. **3. take up** (*or* **throw down) the gauntlet.** to accept (*or* offer) a challenge. [C15: from OF *gantelet*, dim. of *gant* glove, of Gmc origin]

gauntlet[2] ('gɔ:ntlɪt) *n.* **1.** a punishment in which the victim is forced to run between two rows of men who strike at him as he passes: formerly a military punishment. **2. run the gauntlet. a.** to suffer this punishment. **b.** to endure an onslaught, as of criticism. **3.** a testing ordeal. [C15: changed (through infl. of GAUNTLET[1]) from earlier *gantlope*, from Swedish *gatlopp* passageway]

gaur ('gauə) *n.* a large wild ox of mountainous regions of S Asia. [C19: from Hindi, from Sansk. *gāura*]

gauss (gaus) *n., pl.* **gauss.** the cgs unit of magnetic flux density. 1 gauss is equivalent to 10^{-4} tesla. [after K. F. GAUSS]

Gauss (*German* gaus) *n.* **Karl Friedrich** (karl 'friːdrɪç). 1777–1855, German mathematician: developed the theory of numbers and applied mathematics to astronomy, electricity and magnetism, and geodesy. —**Gaussian** ('gausɪən) *adj.*

Gaussian distribution *n.* another name for **normal distribution.**

Gautier (*French* gotje) *n.* **Théophile** (teɔfil). 1811–72, French poet, novelist, and critic. His early extravagant romanticism gave way to a preoccupation with poetic form and expression that anticipated the Parnassians.

gauze (gɔːz) *n.* **1.** a transparent cloth of loose weave. **2.** a surgical dressing of muslin or similar material. **3.** any thin openwork material, such as wire. **4.** a fine mist or haze. [C16: from F *gaze*, ?from GAZA, where it was believed to originate]

gauzy ('gɔːzɪ) *adj.* **gauzier, gauziest.** resembling gauze; thin and transparent. —'**gauzily** *adv.* —'**gauziness** *n.*

Gavaskar (gæ'væskaː) *n.* **Sunil Manohar** ('sʊnɪl 'mænəʊhaː). born 1949, Indian cricketer. He captained India 1978–83 and 1984–85.

gave (geɪv) *vb.* the past tense of **give.**

gavel ('gævᵊl) *n.* a small hammer used by a chairman, auctioneer, etc., to call for order or attention. [C19: from ?]

gavial ('geɪvɪəl), **gharial,** *or* **garial** ('gærɪəl) *n.* a large fish-eating crocodile with a very long slender snout. [C19: from F, from Hindi]

Gävle (*Swedish* 'jɛːvlə) *n.* a port in E Sweden, on an inlet of the Gulf of Bothnia. Pop.: 87 431 (1986).

gavotte *or* **gavot** (gə'vɒt) *n.* **1.** an old formal dance in quadruple time. **2.** a piece of music composed for or in the rhythm of this dance. [C17: from F, from Provençal, from *gavot* mountaineer, dweller in the Alps (where the dance originated)]

gawk (gɔːk) *n.* **1.** a clumsy stupid person; lout. ~*vb.* **2.** (*intr.*) to stare in a stupid way; gape. [C18: from ODanish *gaukr*; prob. rel. to GAPE]

gawky ('gɔːkɪ) *adj.* **gawkier, gawkiest.** clumsy or ungainly; awkward. Also: **gawkish.** —'**gawkily** *adv.* —'**gawkiness** *n.*

gawp *or* **gaup** (gɔːp) *vb.* (*intr.; often foll. by at*) *Brit. sl.* to stare stupidly; gape. [C14 *galpen;* prob. rel. to OE *gielpan* to boast, YELP]

gay (geɪ) *adj.* **1. a.** homosexual. **b.** (*as n.*): *a group of gays* **2.** carefree and merry: *a gay temperament.* **3.** brightly coloured; brilliant: *a gay hat.* **4.** given to pleasure, esp. in social entertainment: *a gay life.* [C13: from OF *gai,* from OProvençal, of Gmc origin] —'**gayness** *n.*

Gay (geɪ) *n.* **John.** 1685–1732, English poet and dramatist; author of *The Beggar's Opera* (1728).

Gaya ('gɑːjə, 'gaɪə) *n.* a city in NE India, in central Bihar: Hindu place of pilgrimage and one of the holiest sites of Buddhism. Pop.: 344 941 (1981).

Gay-Lussac ('geɪ'luːsæk; *French* gɛlysak) *n.* **Joseph Louis** (ʒozɛf lwi). 1778–1850, French physicist and chemist: discovered the law named after him (1808). He also investigated the effects of terrestrial magnetism, isolated boron and cyanogen, and discovered new methods of manufacturing sulphuric and oxalic acids.

Gaza ('gɑːzə) *n.* a city in the Gaza Strip: a Philistine city in biblical times. It was under Egyptian administration from 1949 until occupied by Israel (1967). Pop.: 120 000 (1979). Arabic name: **Ghazzah.**

gazania (gæ'zeɪnɪə) *n.* any of a genus of S. African plants of the composite family having large showy flowers. [? after Theodore of *Gaza* (1398–1478), who translated the botanical works of Theophrastus into Latin]

Gazankulu (,gazaŋ'kuːluː) *n.* a Bantustan in South Africa: consists of four exclaves, three in N Transvaal and one in E Transvaal. Capital: Giyani.

Gaza Strip *n.* a coastal region on the SE corner of the Mediterranean: administered by Egypt from 1949; occupied by Israel in 1967. Pop. (with North Sinai): 635 000 (1988).

gaze (geɪz) *vb.* **1.** (*intr.*) to look long and fixedly, esp. in wonder. ~*n.* **2.** a fixed look. [C14: from Swedish dialect *gasa* to gape at] —'**gazer** *n.*

gazebo (gə'ziːbəʊ) *n., pl.* **-bos** *or* **-boes.** a summerhouse, garden pavilion, or belvedere, sited to command a view. [C18: ? a pseudo-Latin coinage based on GAZE]

gazelle (gə'zɛl) *n., pl.* **-zelles** *or* **-zelle.** any small graceful usually fawn-coloured antelope of Africa and Asia. [C17: from OF, from Ar. *ghazāl*]

gazette (gə'zɛt) *n.* **1.** a newspaper or official journal. **2.** *Brit.* an official document containing public notices, appointments, etc. ~*vb.* **3.** (*tr.*) *Brit.* to announce or report (facts or an event) in a gazette. [C17: from F, from It., from Venetian dialect *gazeta* news-sheet costing one *gazet,* small copper coin]

gazetteer (,gæzɪ'tɪə) *n.* **1.** a book or section of a book that lists and describes places. **2.** *Arch.* a writer for a gazette.

Gaziantep (,gɑːziːɑːn'tɛp) *n.* a city in S Turkey: base for Ibrahim Pasha's campaign against the Turks (1839) and centre of Turkish resistance to French forces (1921). Pop.: 466 302 (1985). Former name (until 1921): **Aintab.**

gazpacho (gəz'pɑːtʃəʊ, gæs-) *n.* a Spanish soup made from tomatoes, peppers, etc., and served cold. [from Sp.]

gazump (gə'zʌmp) *Brit.* ~*vb.* **1.** to raise the price of something, esp. a house, after agreeing a price verbally with (an intending buyer). **2.** (*tr.*) to swindle or overcharge. ~*n.* **3.** an instance of gazumping. [C20: from ?] —**ga'zumper** *n.*

GB *abbrev. for* Great Britain.

GBE *abbrev. for* (Knight or Dame) Grand Cross of the British Empire (a Brit. title).

GBH *abbrev. for* grievous bodily harm.

GC *abbrev. for* George Cross (a Brit. award for bravery).

GCB *abbrev. for* (Knight) Grand Cross of the Bath (a Brit. title).

gcd *or* **GCD** *abbrev. for* greatest common divisor.

GCE (in Britain) **1.** *abbrev. for* General Certificate of Education: either of two public examinations in specified subjects taken as school-leaving qualifications or as qualifying examinations for entry into a university, college, etc. See also **O level, A level.** ~*n.* **2.** *Inf.* any subject taken for one of these examinations.

GCHQ (in Britain) *abbrev. for* Government Communications Headquarters.

G clef *n.* another name for **treble clef.**

GCMG *abbrev. for* (Knight or Dame) Grand Cross of the Order of St Michael and St George (a Brit. title).

GCSE (in Britain) *abbrev. for* General Certificate of Secondary Education: a public examination in specified subjects for 16-year-old schoolchildren. It replaces the GCE O-level and CSE.

GCVO *abbrev. for* (Knight or Dame) Grand Cross of the Royal Victorian Order (a Brit. title).

Gd *the chemical symbol for* gadolinium.

Gdańsk (*Polish* gdaisk) *n.* **1.** the chief port of Poland, on the Baltic: a member of the Hanseatic league; under Prussian rule (1793–1807 and 1814–1919); a free city under the League of Nations from 1919 until annexed by Germany in 1939; returned to Poland in 1945. Pop.: 467 000 (1985). German name: **Danzig. 2. Bay of.** a wide inlet of the Baltic Sea on the N coast of Poland.

Gdns *abbrev. for* Gardens.

Gdynia (*Polish* 'gdinja) *n.* a port in N Poland, near Gdańsk: developed 1924–39 as the outlet for trade through the Polish Corridor; naval base. Pop.: 243 000 (1985).

Ge[1] (dʒiː) *n.* another name for **Gaea.**

Ge[2] *the chemical symbol for* germanium.

gean (giːn) *n.* a white-flowered tree of the rose family of Europe, W Asia, and N Africa; the ancestor of the cultivated sweet cherries.

gear (gɪə) *n.* **1.** a toothed wheel that engages with another toothed wheel or with a rack in order to change the speed or direction of transmitted motion. **2.** a mechanism for transmitting motion by gears. **3.** the engagement or specific ratio of a system of gears: *in gear; high gear.* **4.** personal belongings. **5.** equipment and supplies for a particular operation, sport, etc. **6.** *Naut.* all equipment or appurtenances belonging to a certain vessel, sailor, etc. **7.** short for **landing gear. 8.** *Inf.* up-to-date clothes and accessories. **9.** *Sl.* drugs of any type. **10.** a less common word for **harness** (sense 1). **11. out of gear.** out of order; not functioning properly. ~*vb.* **12.** (*tr.*) to adjust or adapt (one thing) so as to fit in or work with another: *to gear our output to current demand.* **13.** (*tr.*) to equip with or connect by gears. **14.** (*intr.*) to be in or come into gear. **15.** (*tr.*) to equip with a harness. [C13: from ON *gervi*]

gearbox ('gɪə,bɒks) *n.* **1.** the metal casing within which a train of gears is sealed. **2.** this metal casing and its contents, esp. in a motor vehicle.

gearing ('gɪərɪŋ) *n.* **1.** an assembly of gears designed to transmit motion. **2.** the act or technique of providing gears to transmit motion. **3.** *Accounting, Brit.* the ratio of a company's debt capital to its equity capital.

gear lever *or U.S. & Canad.* **gearshift** ('gɪə,ʃɪft) *n.* a lever used to move gearwheels relative to each other, esp. in a motor vehicle.

gearwheel ('gɪə,wiːl) *n.* another name for **gear** (sense 1).

Geber ('dʒiːbə) *n.* Latinized form of Jabir, assumed in honour of **Jabir ibn Hayyan** by a 14th-century alchemist, probably Spanish: he described the preparation of nitric and sulphuric acids.

gecko ('gekəʊ) *n., pl.* **geckos** *or* **geckoes.** a small insectivorous terrestrial lizard of warm regions. [C18: from Malay *ge'kok,* imit.]

gee¹ (dʒiː) *interj.* **1.** Also: **gee up!** an exclamation, as to a horse or draught animal, to encourage it to turn to the right, go on, or go faster. ~*vb.* **geeing, geed. 2.** (usually foll. by *up*) to move (an animal, esp. a horse) ahead; urge on. [C17: from ?]

gee² (dʒiː) *interj. U.S. & Canad. inf.* a mild exclamation. Also: **gee whiz.** [C20: euphemism for JESUS]

Gee (dʒiː) *n.* **Maurice.** born 1931, New Zealand novelist.

geebung ('dʒiːbʌŋ) *n.* **1.** any of several Australian trees or shrubs with edible but tasteless fruit. **2.** the fruit of these trees. [from Abor.]

geek (giːk) *n. Sl.* a degenerate.

geelbek ('xiːl,bɛk) *n. S. African.* an edible marine fish with yellow jaws. Also called: **Cape salmon.** [from Afrik. *geel* yellow + *bek* mouth]

Geelong (dʒə'lɒŋ) *n.* a port in SE Australia, in S Victoria on Port Phillip Bay. Pop.: 139 792 (1986).

geese (giːs) *n.* the plural of **goose¹.**

geezer ('giːzə) *n. Inf.* a man, esp. an old one regarded as eccentric. [C19: prob. from dialect pronunciation of GUISER]

Gehenna (gɪ'hɛnə) *n.* **1.** *Old Testament.* the valley below Jerusalem, where children were sacrificed and, later, unclean things were burnt. **2.** *New Testament, Judaism.* a place where the wicked are punished after death. **3.** a place or state of pain and torment. [C16: from LL, from Gk, from Heb. *Gê' Hinnōm,* lit.: valley of Hinnom, symbolic of hell]

Geiger ('gaɪgə) *n.* **Hans.** 1882–1945, German physicist: developed the Geiger counter.

Geiger counter *or* **Geiger-Müller counter** ('gaɪgə 'mʊlə) *n.* an instrument for detecting and measuring the intensity of ionizing radiation. [C20: after Hans GEIGER and W. *Müller,* 20th-cent. G physicist]

Geikie (giːkɪ) *n.* **Sir Archibald.** 1835–1924, Scottish geologist noted for his study of British volcanic rocks.

geisha ('geɪʃə) *n., pl.* **-sha** *or* **-shas.** a professional female companion for men in Japan, trained in music, dancing, and the art of conversation. [C19: from Japanese, from Ancient Chinese]

Geissler tube ('gaɪslə) *n.* a glass or quartz vessel for maintaining an electric discharge in a low-pressure gas as a source of visible or ultraviolet light for spectroscopy, etc. [C19: after Heinrich *Geissler* (1814–79), G mechanic]

gel (dʒel) *n.* **1.** a semirigid jelly-like colloid in which a liquid is dispersed in a solid: *nondrip paint is a gel.* **2.** a jelly-like substance applied to the hair before styling in order to retain the style. ~*vb.* **gelling, gelled. 3.** to become or cause to become a gel. **4.** a variant spelling of **jell.** [C19: from GELATIN]

gelatin ('dʒelətɪn) *or* **gelatine** ('dʒelə,tiːn) *n.* **1.** a colourless or yellowish water-soluble protein prepared by boiling animal hides and bones: used in foods, glue, photographic emulsions, etc. **2.** an edible jelly made of this substance. [C19: from F *gélatine,* from Med. L, from L *gelāre* to freeze]

gelatinize *or* **-ise** (dʒɪ'lætɪ,naɪz) *vb.* **1.** to make or become gelatinous. **2.** (*tr.*) *Photog.* to coat (glass, paper, etc.) with gelatin. —**ge,lati'zation** *or* **-i'sation** *n.*

gelatinous (dʒɪ'lætɪnəs) *adj.* **1.** consisting of or resembling jelly; viscous. **2.** of, containing, or resembling gelatin. —**ge'latinously** *adv.* —**ge'latinousness** *n.*

gelation¹ (dʒɪ'leɪʃən) *n.* the act or process of freezing a liquid. [C19: from L *gelātiō* a freezing; see GELATIN]

gelation² (dʒɪ'leɪʃən) *n.* the act or process of forming into a gel. [C20: from GEL]

geld (gɛld) *vb.* **gelding, gelded** *or* **gelt** (gɛlt). (*tr.*) **1.** to castrate (a horse or other animal). **2.** to deprive of virility

or vitality; emasculate; weaken. [C13: from ON, from *geldr* barren]

Gelderland *or* **Guelderland** ('gɛldə,lænd; *Dutch* 'xɛldər,lɑnt) *n.* a province of the E Netherlands: formerly a duchy, belonging successively to several different European powers. Capital: Arnhem. Pop.: 1 771 972 (1986). Area: 5014 sq. km (1955 sq. miles). Also called: **Guelders.**

gelding ('gɛldɪŋ) *n.* a castrated male horse. [C14: from ON *geldingr;* see GELD, -ING¹]

Geldof ('gɛldɒf) *n.* **Sir Bob.** Full name *Robert Frederick Zenon Geldof.* born 1952, Irish rock singer and philanthropist: formerly lead vocalist with the Boomtown Rats (1977–86). Now a solo singer, he organized the Band Aid charity for famine relief in Africa.

Gelée (*French* ʒəle) *n.* **Claude** (klod). the original name of **Claude Lorrain.**

Gelibolu (gɛ'libəlu) *n.* the Turkish name for **Gallipoli.**

gelid ('dʒelɪd) *adj.* very cold, icy, or frosty. [C17: from L *gelidus,* from *gelu* frost] —**ge'lidity** *n.*

gelignite ('dʒelɪg,naɪt) *n.* a type of dynamite in which the nitrogelatin is absorbed in a base of wood pulp and potassium or sodium nitrate. Also called (*informal*): **gelly.** [C19: from GEL(ATIN) + L *ignis* fire + -ITE¹]

Gelligaer (*Welsh* ,gɛhliː'gaɪr) *n.* a town in S Wales, in Mid Glamorgan. Pop.: 34 118 (1981).

Gell-Mann ('gɛl,mæn) *n.* **Murray.** born 1929, U.S. physicist, noted for his research on the interaction and classification of elementary particles: Nobel prize for physics in 1969.

Gelsenkirchen (*German* gɛlzən'kɪrçən) *n.* an industrial city in W West Germany, in North Rhine-Westphalia. Pop.: 284 400 (1986).

gem (dʒem) *n.* **1.** a precious or semiprecious stone used in jewellery as a decoration; jewel. **2.** a person or thing held to be a perfect example; treasure. ~*vb.* **gemming, gemmed. 3.** (*tr.*) to set or ornament with gems. [C14: from OF, from L *gemma* bud, precious stone] —**'gem,like** *adj.* —**'gemmy** *adj.*

Gemara (gɛ'mɑːrə; *Hebrew* gema'ra) *n. Judaism.* the later main part of the Talmud, being a commentary on the Mishnah: the primary source of Jewish religious law. [C17: from Aramaic *gemārā* completion]

geminate *adj.* ('dʒemɪnɪt, -,neɪt) *also* **geminated. 1.** combined in pairs; doubled: *a geminate leaf.* ~*vb.* ('dʒemɪ,neɪt). **2.** to arrange or be arranged in pairs: *the "t"s in Italian "gatto" are geminated.* [C17: from L *gemināre* to double, from *geminus* twin] —**'geminately** *adv.* —**,gemi'nation** *n.*

Gemini ('dʒemɪ,naɪ, -,niː) *n.* **1.** *Astron.* a zodiacal constellation in the N hemisphere containing the stars Castor and Pollux. **2.** *Classical myth.* another name for **Castor and Pollux. 3.** *Astrol.* Also called: the **Twins.** the third sign of the zodiac. The sun is in this sign between about May 21 and June 20.

gemma ('dʒemə) *n., pl.* **-mae** (-miː). **1.** a small asexual reproductive structure in mosses, etc., that becomes detached from the parent and develops into a new individual. **2.** *Zool.* another name for **gemmule.** [C18: from L: bud, GEM]

gemmate ('dʒemeɪt) *adj.* **1.** (of some plants and animals) having or reproducing by gemmae. ~*vb.* **2.** (*intr.*) to produce or reproduce by gemmae. —**gem'mation** *n.*

gemmiparous (dʒe'mɪpərəs) *adj.* (of plants and animals) reproducing by gemmae or buds.

gemmule ('dʒemjuːl) *n.* **1.** *Zool.* a cell or mass of cells produced asexually by sponges and developing into a new individual; bud. **2.** *Bot.* a small gemma. [C19: from F, from L *gemmula* a little bud; see GEM]

gemology *or* **gemmology** (dʒe'mɒlədʒɪ) *n.* the branch of mineralogy concerned with gems and gemstones. —**gem'ologist** *or* **gem'mologist** *n.*

gemsbok *or* **gemsbuck** ('gemz,bʌk) *n., pl.* **-bok, -boks** *or* **-buck, -bucks.** an oryx of southern Africa, marked with a broad black band along its flanks. [C18: from Afrik., from G *Gemsbock,* from *Gemse* chamois + *Bock* BUCK¹]

gemstone ('dʒem,stəʊn) *n.* a precious or semiprecious stone, esp. one cut and polished.

gen (dʒen) *n. Brit. inf.* information: *give me the gen on your latest project.* See also **gen up.** [C20: from *gen(eral information)*]

gen. *abbrev. for:* **1.** gender. **2.** general(ly). **3.** generic. **4.** genitive. **5.** genus.

Gen. *abbrev. for:* **1.** General. **2.** *Bible.* Genesis.

-gen *suffix forming nouns.* **1.** producing or that which produces: *hydrogen.* **2.** something produced: *carcinogen.* [via F *-gène,* from Gk *-genēs* born]

Genck *(Flemish* xɛŋk) *n.* a variant spelling of **Genk.**

gendarme ('ʒɒndɑːm) *n.* **1.** a member of the police force in France or in countries influenced or controlled by France. **2.** a sharp pinnacle of rock on a mountain ridge. [C16: from F, from *gens d'armes* people of arms]

gendarmerie *or* **gendarmery** (ʒɒn'dɑːmərɪ) *n.* **1.** the whole corps of gendarmes. **2.** the headquarters of a body of gendarmes.

gender ('dʒɛndə) *n.* **1.** a set of two or more grammatical categories into which the nouns of certain languages are divided. **2.** any of the categories, such as masculine, feminine, neuter, or common, within such a set. **3.** *Inf.* the state of being male, female, or neuter. **4.** *Inf.* all the members of one sex: *the female gender.* [C14: from OF, from L *genus* kind]

gender-bender *n. Inf.* a person who adopts an androgynous style of dress, hair, etc.

gene (dʒiːn) *n.* a unit of heredity composed of DNA occupying a fixed position on a chromosome and transmitted from parent to offspring during reproduction. [C20: from G *Gen,* shortened from *Pangen;* see PAN-, -GEN]

-gene *suffix forming nouns.* a variant of **-gen.**

genealogy (,dʒiːnɪ'ælədʒɪ) *n., pl.* **-gies. 1.** the direct descent of an individual or group from an ancestor. **2.** the study of the evolutionary development of animals and plants from earlier forms. **3.** a chart showing the relationships and descent of an individual, group, etc. [C13: from OF, from LL, from Gk, from *genea* race] —**genealogical** (,dʒiːnɪə'lɒdʒɪkᵊl) *adj.* —,genea'logically *adv.* —,gene'alogist *n.*

gene pool *n.* the total of all the genes and their alleles in a population of a plant or animal species.

genera ('dʒɛnərə) *n.* a plural of **genus.**

general ('dʒɛnərəl, 'dʒɛnrəl) *adj.* **1.** common; widespread. **2.** of, applying to, or participated in by all or most of the members of a group, category, or community. **3.** relating to various branches of an activity, profession, etc.; not specialized: *general office work.* **4.** including various or miscellaneous items: *general knowledge; a general store.* **5.** not specific as to detail; overall: *a general description.* **6.** not definite; vague: *the general idea.* **7.** applicable or true in most cases; usual. **8.** *(prenominal or immediately postpositive)* having superior or extended authority or rank: *general manager; consul general.* ~*n.* **9.** an officer of a rank senior to lieutenant general, esp. one who commands a large military formation. **10.** any person acting as a leader and applying strategy or tactics. **11.** a general condition or principle: opposed to *particular.* **12.** a title for the head of a religious order, congregation, etc. **13.** *Arch.* the people; public. **14. in general.** generally; mostly or usually. [C13: from L *generālis* of a particular kind, from *genus* kind] —'**generalness** *n.*

general anaesthetic *n.* See **anaesthesia.**

General Assembly *n.* **1.** the deliberative assembly of the United Nations. Abbrev.: **GA. 2.** *N.Z.* an older name for **parliament. 3.** the supreme governing body of certain religious denominations, esp. of the Presbyterian Church.

General Certificate of Education *n.* See **GCE.**

General Certificate of Secondary Education *n.* See **GCSE.**

general election *n.* **1.** an election in which representatives are chosen in all constituencies of a state. **2.** *U.S.* a final election from which successful candidates are sent to a legislative body. **3.** *U.S. & Canad.* a national, state, or provincial election.

generalissimo (,dʒɛnərə'lɪsɪ,məʊ, ,dʒɛnrə-) *n., pl.* **-mos.** a supreme commander of combined military, naval, and air forces. [C17: from It., sup. of *generale* GENERAL]

generality (,dʒɛnə'rælɪtɪ) *n., pl.* **-ties. 1.** a principle or observation having general application. **2.** the state or quality of being general. **3.** *Arch.* the majority.

generalization *or* **-isation** (,dʒɛnrəlaɪ'zeɪʃən) *n.* **1.** a principle, theory, etc., with general application. **2.** the act or an instance of generalizing. **3.** *Logic.* **a.** the derivation of a universal statement from a particular one by replacing its subject term with a bound variable and prefixing

the universal quantifier. **b.** the analogous derivation of any general statement from a particular one.

generalize *or* **-ise** ('dʒɛnrə,laɪz) *vb.* **1.** to form (general principles or conclusions) from (detailed facts, experience, etc.); infer. **2.** *(intr.)* to think or speak in generalities, esp. in a prejudiced way. **3.** *(tr.; usually passive)* to cause to become widely used or known.

generally ('dʒɛnrəlɪ) *adv.* **1.** usually; as a rule. **2.** commonly or widely. **3.** without reference to specific details or facts; broadly.

general practitioner *n.* a physician who does not specialize but has a medical practice (**general practice**) in which he treats all illnesses. Informal name: **family doctor.** Abbrev.: **GP.**

general-purpose *adj.* having a range of uses; not restricted to one function.

generalship ('dʒɛnrəl,ʃɪp) *n.* **1.** the art or duties of exercising command of a major military formation or formations. **2.** tactical or administrative skill.

general staff *n.* officers assigned to advise commanders in the planning and execution of military operations.

general strike *n.* a strike by all or most of the workers of a country, province, city, etc.

generate ('dʒɛnə,reɪt) *vb.* *(mainly tr.)* **1.** to produce or bring into being; create. **2.** *(also intr.)* to produce (electricity). **3.** to produce (a substance) by a chemical process. **4.** *Maths, linguistics.* to provide a precise criterion for membership in (a set): *these rules will generate all the noun phrases in English.* **5.** *Geom.* to trace or form by moving a point, line, or plane in a specific way: *circular motion of a line generates a cylinder.* [C16: from L *generāre* to beget, from *genus* kind] —**generable** ('dʒɛnərəbᵊl) *adj.*

generation (,dʒɛnə'reɪʃən) *n.* **1.** the act or process of bringing into being; production or reproduction, esp. of offspring. **2.** a successive stage in natural descent of people or animals or the individuals produced at each stage. **3.** the average time between two such generations of a species: about 35 years for humans. **4.** all the people of approximately the same age, esp. when considered as sharing certain attitudes, etc. **5.** production of electricity, heat, etc. **6.** *(modifier, in combination)* **a.** belonging to a generation specified as having been born in or as having parents, grandparents, etc., born in a given country: *a third-generation American.* **b.** belonging to a specified stage of development in manufacture: *a second-generation computer.*

generation gap *n.* the years separating one generation from the next, esp. when regarded as representing the difference in outlook and the lack of understanding between them.

generative ('dʒɛnərətɪv) *adj.* **1.** of or relating to the production of offspring, parts, etc. **2.** capable of producing or originating.

generative grammar *n.* a description of a language in terms of explicit rules that ideally generate all and only the grammatical sentences of the language.

generator ('dʒɛnə,reɪtə) *n.* **1.** *Physics.* **a.** any device for converting mechanical energy into electrical energy. **b.** a device for producing a voltage electrostatically. **2.** an apparatus for producing a gas. **3.** a person or thing that generates.

generatrix ('dʒɛnə,reɪtrɪks) *n., pl.* **generatrices** ('dʒɛnə-,reɪtrɪ,siːz). a point, line, or plane moved in a specific way to produce a geometric figure.

generic (dʒɪ'nɛrɪk) *adj.* **1.** applicable or referring to a whole class or group; general. **2.** *Biol.* of, relating to, or belonging to a genus: *the generic name.* **3.** (of a drug, food product, etc.) not having a trademark. [C17: from F; see GENUS] —**ge'nerically** *adv.*

generosity (,dʒɛnə'rɒsɪtɪ) *n., pl.* **-ties. 1.** willingness and liberality in giving away one's money, time, etc.; magnanimity. **2.** freedom from pettiness in character and mind. **3.** a generous act. **4.** abundance; plenty.

generous ('dʒɛnərəs, 'dʒɛnrəs) *adj.* **1.** willing and liberal in giving away one's money, time, etc.; munificent. **2.** free from pettiness in character and mind. **3.** full or plentiful: *a generous portion.* **4.** (of wine) rich in alcohol. [C16: via OF from L *generōsus* nobly born, from *genus* race] —'**generously** *adv.* —'**generousness** *n.*

genesis ('dʒɛnɪsɪs) *n., pl.* **-ses** (-,siːz). a beginning or origin of anything. [OE: via L from Gk; rel. to Gk *gignesthai* to be born]

Genesis ('dʒɛnɪsɪs) *n.* the first book of the Old Testament recounting the Creation of the world.

-genesis *n. combining form.* indicating genesis, development, or generation: *biogenesis; parthenogenesis.* [NL, from L: GENESIS] —**genetic** *or* **-genic** *adj. combining form.*

genet[1] ('dʒɛnɪt) *or* **genette** (dʒɪ'nɛt) *n.* 1. an agile cat-like mammal of Africa and S Europe, having thick spotted fur and a very long tail. 2. the fur of such an animal. [C15: from OF, from Ar. *jarnayt*]

genet[2] ('dʒɛnɪt) *n.* an obsolete spelling of **jennet.**

Genet (*French* ʒɔnɛ) *n.* **Jean** (ʒɑ̃). 1910–86, French dramatist and novelist; his novels include *Notre-Dame des Fleurs* (1944) and his plays *Les Bonnes* (1947) and *Le Balcon* (1956).

genetic (dʒɪ'nɛtɪk) *or* **genetical** *adj.* of or relating to genetics, genes, or the origin of something. [C19: from GENESIS] —**ge'netically** *adv.*

genetic code *n. Biochem.* the order in which the four nitrogenous bases of DNA are arranged in the molecule, which determines the type and amount of protein synthesized in the cell.

genetic engineering *n.* alteration of the DNA of a cell as a means of manufacturing animal proteins, making improvements to plants and animals bred by man, etc.

genetic fingerprinting *n.* the pattern of DNA unique to each individual which can be analysed in a sample of blood, saliva, or tissue: used as a means of identification.

genetics (dʒɪ'nɛtɪks) *n.* 1. (*functioning as sing.*) the study of heredity and variation in organisms. 2. (*functioning as pl.*) the genetic features and constitution of a single organism, species, or group. —**ge'neticist** *n.*

Geneva (dʒɪ'niːvə) *n.* 1. a city in SW Switzerland, in the Rhône valley on Lake Geneva: centre of Calvinism; headquarters of the International Red Cross (1864), the International Labour Office (1925), the League of Nations (1929–46), the World Health Organization, and the European office of the United Nations; banking centre. Pop.: 159 900 (1985). 2. a canton in SW Switzerland. Capital: Geneva. Pop.: 349 040 (1980). Area: 282 sq. km (109 sq. miles). 3. **Lake.** a lake between SW Switzerland and E France: fed and drained by the River Rhône, it is the largest of the Alpine lakes; the surface is subject to considerable changes of level. Area: 580 sq. km (224 sq. miles). French name: **Lac Léman.** German name: **Genfersee.** ~(for senses 1 and 2) French name: **Genève;** German name: **Genf.**

Geneva bands *pl. n.* a pair of white lawn or linen strips hanging from the front of the neck or collar of some ecclesiastical and academic robes. [C19: after GENEVA, where orig. worn by Swiss Calvinist clergy]

Geneva Convention *n.* the international agreement, first formulated in 1864 at Geneva, establishing a code for wartime treatment of the sick or wounded: revised and extended to cover maritime warfare and prisoners of war.

Geneva gown *n.* a long loose black gown with very wide sleeves worn by Protestant clerics. [C19: after GENEVA; see GENEVA BANDS]

Genevan (dʒɪ'niːvən) *or* **Genevese** (,dʒɛnɪ'viːz) *adj.* 1. of, relating to, or characteristic of Geneva. 2. of, adhering to, or relating to the teachings of Calvin or the Calvinists. ~*n., pl.* **-vans** *or* **-vese.** 3. a native or inhabitant of Geneva. 4. a less common name for a **Calvinist.**

Genève (ʒɔnɛv) *n.* the French name for **Geneva.**

Geneviève ('dʒɛnɪ,viːv; *French* ʒɔnvjɛv) *n.* **Saint.** ?422–?512 A.D., French nun; patron saint of Paris. Feast day: Jan. 3.

Genf (gɛnf) *n.* the German name for **Geneva** (senses 1, 2).

Genfersee ('gɛnfərzeː) *n.* the German name for (Lake) **Geneva.**

Genghis Khan ('dʒɛŋgɪs kɑːn) *n.* original name *Temuchin* or *Temujin.* ?1162–1227, Mongol ruler, whose empire stretched from the Black Sea to the Pacific. Also called: **Jinghis Khan, Jenghis Khan.**

genial[1] ('dʒiːnjəl, -nɪəl) *adj.* 1. cheerful, easy-going, and warm in manner. 2. pleasantly warm, so as to give life, growth, or health. [C16: from L *geniālis* relating to birth or marriage, from *genius* tutelary deity; see GENIUS] —**geniality** (,dʒiːnɪ'ælɪtɪ) *n.* —'**genially** *adv.*

genial[2] (dʒɪ'niːəl) *adj. Anat.* of or relating to the chin. [C19: from Gk, from *genus* jaw]

genic ('dʒɛnɪk) *adj.* of or relating to a gene or genes.

-genic *adj. combining form.* 1. relating to production or generation: *carcinogenic.* 2. suited to or suitable for: *photogenic.* [from -GEN + -IC]

genie ('dʒiːnɪ) *n., pl.* **-nies** *or* **-nii** (-nɪ,aɪ). 1. (in fairy tales and stories) a servant who appears by magic and fulfils a person's wishes. 2. another word for **jinni.** [C18: from F, from Ar. *jinni* demon, infl. by L *genius* attendant spirit; see GENIUS]

genista (dʒɪ'nɪstə) *n.* any of a genus of leguminous deciduous shrubs, usually having yellow, often fragrant, flowers; broom. [C17: from L]

genital ('dʒɛnɪtᵊl) *adj.* 1. of or relating to the sexual organs or to reproduction. 2. *Psychoanal.* relating to the mature stage of psychosexual development. [C14: from L *genitālis* concerning birth, from *gignere* to beget]

genital herpes *n.* a sexually transmitted disease caused by a variety of the herpes simplex virus, in which painful blisters occur in the genital region.

genitals ('dʒɛnɪtᵊlz) *or* **genitalia** (,dʒɛnɪ'teɪlɪə, -'teɪljə) *pl. n.* the external sexual organs.

genitive ('dʒɛnɪtɪv) *Grammar.* ~*adj.* 1. denoting a case of nouns, pronouns, and adjectives in inflected languages used to indicate a relation of ownership or association. ~*n.* 2. a. the genitive case. b. a word or speech element in this case. [C14: from L *genetīvus* relating to birth, from *gignere* to produce] —**genitival** (,dʒɛnɪ'taɪvᵊl) *adj.* —,**geni'tivally** *adv.*

genitourinary (,dʒɛnɪtəʊ'jʊərɪnərɪ) *adj.* another name for **urogenital.**

genius ('dʒiːnɪəs, -njəs) *n., pl.* **-uses** *or* (*for senses 5, 6*) **genii** ('dʒiːnɪ,aɪ). 1. a person with exceptional ability, esp. of a highly original kind. 2. such ability. 3. the distinctive spirit of a nation, era, language, etc. 4. a person considered as exerting influence of a certain sort: *an evil genius.* 5. *Roman myth.* a. the guiding spirit who attends a person from birth to death. b. the guardian spirit of a place. 6. (*usually pl.*) *Arabic myth.* a demon; jinn. [C16: from L, from *gignere* to beget]

genizah (gɛ'niːzə) *n. Judaism.* a repository for sacred objects which can no longer be used but which may not be destroyed. [C19: from Heb., lit.: a hiding place]

Genk *or* **Genck** (*Flemish* xɛŋk) *n.* a town in NE Belgium, in Limburg province: coal-mining. Pop.: 61 391 (1987).

genoa ('dʒɛnəʊə) *n. Yachting.* a large jib sail.

Genoa ('dʒɛnəʊə) *n.* a port in NW Italy, capital of Liguria, on the **Gulf of Genoa:** Italy's main port; an independent commercial city with many colonies in the Middle Ages; university (1243); heavy industries. Pop.: 727 427 (1986). Italian name: **Genova.**

genocide ('dʒɛnəʊ,saɪd) *n.* the policy of deliberately killing a nationality or ethnic group. [C20: from Gk *genos* race + -CIDE] —,**geno'cidal** *adj.*

Genoese (,dʒɛnəʊ'iːz) *or* **Genovese** (,dʒɛnə'viːz) *n., pl.* **-ese** *or* **-vese.** 1. a native or inhabitant of Genoa. ~*adj.* 2. of or relating to Genoa or its inhabitants.

genome ('dʒiːnəʊm) *n.* the complete set of heploid chromosomes that an organism passes on to its offspring in its reproductive cells. [C20: from GEN(E) + (CHROMOS)OME]

genotype ('dʒɛnəʊ,taɪp) *n.* 1. the genetic constitution of an organism. 2. a group of organisms with the same genetic constitution. —**genotypic** (,dʒɛnəʊ'tɪpɪk) *adj.*

-genous *adj. combining form.* 1. yielding or generating: *erogenous.* 2. generated by or issuing from: *endogenous.* [from -GEN + -OUS]

Genova ('dʒɛːnova) *n.* the Italian name for **Genoa.**

genre ('ʒɑːnrə) *n.* 1. kind, category, or sort, esp. of literary or artistic work. 2. a. a category of painting in which incidents from everyday life are depicted. b. (*as modifier*): *genre painting.* [C19: from F, from OF *gendre;* see GENDER]

gens (dʒɛnz) *n., pl.* **gentes** ('dʒɛntiːz). 1. (in ancient Rome) any of a group of families, having a common name and claiming descent from a common ancestor in the male line. 2. *Anthropol.* a group based on descent in the male line. [C19: from L: race]

Genseric ('gɛnsərɪk, 'dʒɛn-) *or* **Gaiseric** *n.* ?390–477 A.D., king of the Vandals (428–77). He seized Roman lands, esp. extensive parts of N Africa, and sacked Rome (455).

gent (dʒɛnt) *n. Inf.* short for **gentleman**.

Gent (xɛnt) *n.* the Flemish name for **Ghent**.

genteel (dʒɛn'tiːl) *adj.* **1.** affectedly proper or refined; excessively polite. **2.** respectable, polite, and well-bred. **3.** appropriate to polite or fashionable society. [C16: from F *gentil* well-born; see GENTLE] —**gen'teelly** *adv.* —**gen'teelness** *n.*

gentian ('dʒɛnʃən) *n.* **1.** any plant of the genus *Gentiana*, having blue, yellow, white, or red showy flowers. **2.** the bitter-tasting roots of the yellow gentian, which can be used as a tonic. [C14: from L *gentiāna*; ? after *Gentius*, a second-century B.C. Illyrian king, reputedly the first to use it medicinally]

gentian violet *n.* a greenish crystalline substance that forms a violet solution in water, used as an indicator, antiseptic, and in the treatment of burns.

Gentile[1] ('dʒɛntaɪl) *n.* **1.** a person, esp. a Christian, who is not a Jew. **2.** a Christian, as contrasted with a Jew. **3.** a person who is not a member of one's own church: used esp. by Mormons. **4.** a heathen or pagan. ~*adj.* **5.** of or relating to a race or religion that is not Jewish. **6.** Christian, as contrasted with Jewish. **7.** not being a member of one's own church: used esp. by Mormons. **8.** pagan or heathen. [C15 *gentil*, from LL *gentīlis*, from L: one belonging to the same tribe]

Gentile[2] (*Italian* dʒen'tiːle) *n.* **Giovanni** (dʒo'vanni). 1875–1944, Italian Idealist philosopher and Fascist politician: minister of education (1922–24).

gentility (dʒɛn'tɪlɪtɪ) *n., pl.* -**ties. 1.** respectability and polite good breeding. **2.** affected politeness. **3.** noble birth or ancestry. **4.** people of noble birth. [C14: from OF, from L *gentīlitās* relationship of those belonging to the same tribe or family; see GENS]

gentle ('dʒɛntəl) *adj.* **1.** having a mild or kindly nature or character. **2.** soft or temperate; mild; moderate. **3.** gradual: *a gentle slope*. **4.** easily controlled; tame. **5.** *Arch.* of good breeding; noble: *gentle blood*. **6.** *Arch.* gallant; chivalrous. ~*vb. (tr.)* **7.** to tame or subdue (a horse, etc.). **8.** to appease or mollify. ~*n.* **9.** a maggot, esp. when used as bait in fishing. [C13: from OF *gentil* noble, from L *gentīlis* belonging to the same family; see GENS] —**'gentleness** *n.* —**'gently** *adv.*

gentle breeze *n.* a wind of force 3 on the Beaufort scale, blowing at 8-12 mph.

gentlefolk ('dʒɛntəl,fəʊk) *or* **gentlefolks** *pl. n.* persons regarded as being of good breeding.

gentleman ('dʒɛntəlmən) *n., pl.* -**men. 1.** a man regarded as having qualities of refinement associated with a good family. **2.** a man who is cultured, courteous, and well-educated. **3.** a polite name for a man. **4.** the personal servant of a gentleman (esp. in **gentleman's gentleman**). —**'gentlemanly** *adj.* —**'gentlemanliness** *n.*

gentleman-farmer *n., pl.* **gentlemen-farmers. 1.** a person who engages in farming but does not depend on it for his living. **2.** a person who owns farmland but does not farm it personally.

gentlemen's agreement *or* **gentleman's agreement** *n.* an understanding or arrangement based on honour and not legally binding.

gentlewoman ('dʒɛntəl,wʊmən) *n., pl.* -**women. 1.** *Arch.* a woman regarded as being of good family or breeding; lady. **2.** (formerly) a woman in personal attendance on a high-ranking lady.

gentrification (,dʒɛntrɪfɪ'keɪʃən) *n. Brit.* a process by which middle-class people take up residence in a traditionally working-class area, changing its character. —**'gentri,fy** *vb. (tr.)*

gentry ('dʒɛntrɪ) *n.* **1.** *Brit.* persons just below the nobility in social rank. **2.** people of a particular class, esp. one considered to be inferior. [C14: from OF *genterie*, from *gentil* GENTLE]

gents (dʒɛnts) *n. (functioning as sing.) Brit. inf.* a men's public lavatory.

genuflect ('dʒɛnjʊ,flɛkt) *vb. (intr.)* **1.** to act in a servile or deferential manner. **2.** *R.C. Church.* to bend one or both knees as a sign of reverence. [C17: from Med. L, from L *genu* knee + *flectere* to bend] —**,genu'flection** *or (esp. Brit.)* **,genu'flexion** *n.* —**'genu,flector** *n.*

genuine ('dʒɛnjʊɪn) *adj.* **1.** not fake or counterfeit; original; real; authentic. **2.** not pretending; frank; sincere. **3.** being of authentic or original stock. [C16: from L *genuīnus* inborn, hence (in LL) authentic] —**'genuinely** *adv.* —**'genuineness** *n.*

gen up *vb.* **genning, genned.** *(adv.; often passive;* when *intr.,* usually foll. by *on*) *Brit. inf.* to make or become fully conversant (with).

genus ('dʒiːnəs) *n., pl.* **genera** *or* **genuses. 1.** *Biol.* any of the taxonomic groups into which a family is divided and which contains one or more species. **2.** *Logic.* a class of objects or individuals that can be divided into two or more groups or species. **3.** a class, group, etc., with common characteristics. [C16: from L: race]

-geny *n. combining form.* origin or manner of development: *phylogeny*. [from Gk, from *-genēs* born] —**-genic** *adj. combining form.*

geo- *combining form.* indicating earth: *geomorphology*. [from Gk, from *gē* earth]

geocentric (,dʒiːəʊ'sɛntrɪk) *adj.* **1.** having the earth at its centre. **2.** measured as from the centre of the earth. —,**geo'centrically** *adv.*

geochronology (,dʒiːəʊkrə'nɒlədʒɪ) *n.* the branch of geology concerned with ordering and dating events in the earth's history. —**geochronological** (,dʒiːəʊ,krɒnə'lɒdʒɪkəl) *adj.*

geode ('dʒiːəʊd) *n.* a cavity, usually lined with crystals, within a rock mass or nodule. [C17: from L *geōdēs* a precious stone, from Gk: earthlike; see GEO-, -ODE[1]] —**geodic** (dʒɪ'ɒdɪk) *adj.*

geodesic (,dʒiːəʊ'dɛsɪk, -'diː-) *adj.* **1.** Also: **geodetic.** relating to the geometry of curved surfaces. ~*n.* **2.** Also called: **geodesic line.** the shortest line between two points on a curved surface.

geodesic dome *n.* a light structural framework arranged as a set of polygons in the form of a shell.

geodesy (dʒɪ'ɒdɪsɪ) *n.* the branch of science concerned with determining the exact position of geographical points and the shape and size of the earth. [C16: from F, from Gk *geōdaisia*, from GEO- + *daiein* to divide] —**ge'odesist** *n.*

geodetic (,dʒiːəʊ'dɛtɪk) *adj.* **1.** of or relating to geodesy. **2.** another word for **geodesic.** —,**geo'detically** *adv.*

Geoffrey of Monmouth ('dʒɛfrɪ) *n.* ?1100–54, Welsh bishop and chronicler; author of *Historia Regum Britanniae,* the chief source of Arthurian legends.

geog. *abbrev. for:* **1.** geographer. **2.** geographic(al). **3.** geography.

geographical mile *n.* another name for **nautical mile.**

geography (dʒɪ'ɒgrəfɪ) *n., pl.* -**phies. 1.** the study of the natural features of the earth's surface, including topography, climate, soil, vegetation, etc., and man's response to them. **2.** the natural features of a region. —**ge'ographer** *n.* —**geographical** (,dʒɪə'græfɪkəl) *or* ,**geo'graphic** *adj.* —,**geo'graphically** *adv.*

geoid ('dʒiːɔɪd) *n.* **1.** a hypothetical surface that corresponds to mean sea level and extends under the continents. **2.** the shape of the earth.

geol. *abbrev. for:* **1.** geologic(al). **2.** geologist. **3.** geology.

geology (dʒɪ'ɒlədʒɪ) *n.* **1.** the scientific study of the origin, structure, and composition of the earth. **2.** the geological features of a district or country. —**geological** (,dʒɪə'lɒdʒɪkəl) *or* ,**geo'logic** *adj.* —,**geo'logically** *adv.* —**ge'ologist** *n.*

geom. *abbrev. for:* **1.** geometric(al). **2.** geometry.

geomagnetism (,dʒiːəʊ'mægnɪ,tɪzəm) *n.* **1.** the magnetic field of the earth. **2.** the branch of physics concerned with this. —**geomagnetic** (,dʒiːəʊmæg'nɛtɪk) *adj.*

geometric (,dʒɪə'mɛtrɪk) *or* **geometrical** *adj.* **1.** of, relating to, or following the methods and principles of geometry. **2.** consisting of, formed by, or characterized by points, lines, curves, or surfaces. **3.** (of design or ornamentation) composed predominantly of simple geometric forms, such as circles, triangles, etc. —,**geo'metrically** *adv.*

geometric mean *n.* the average value of a set of *n* integers, terms, or quantities, expressed as the *n*th root of their product.

geometric progression *n.* **1.** a sequence of numbers, each of which differs from the succeeding one by a constant ratio, as 1, 2, 4, 8, ... Cf. **arithmetic progression. 2.** geometric series. such numbers written as a sum.

geometrid (dʒɪ'ɒmɪtrɪd) *n.* any of a family of moths, the larvae of which are called measuring worms, inchworms, or loopers. [C19: from NL, from L, from Gk *geometrēs* land measurer, from the looping gait of the larvae]

geometry (dʒɪ'ɒmɪtrɪ) *n.* **1.** the branch of mathematics concerned with the properties, relationships, and measurement of points, lines, curves, and surfaces. **2.** a shape, configuration, or arrangement. [C14: from L, from Gk, from *geōmetrein* to measure the land] —**ge₁ome'trician** *n.*

geomorphology (₁dʒiːəʊmɔː'fɒlədʒɪ) *n.* the branch of geology that is concerned with the structure, origin, and development of the topographical features of the earth's crust. —**geomorphological** (₁dʒiːəʊ₁mɔːfə'lɒdʒɪkᵊl) *or* ₁**geo₁morpho'logic** *adj.*

geophysics (₁dʒiːəʊ'fɪzɪks) *n.* (*functioning as sing.*) the study of the earth's physical properties and of the physical processes acting upon, above, and within the earth. It includes seismology, meteorology, and oceanography. —₁**geo'physical** *adj.* —₁**geo'physicist** *n.*

geopolitics (₁dʒiːəʊ'pɒlɪtɪks) *n.* **1.** (*functioning as sing.*) the study of the effect of geographical factors on politics. **2.** (*functioning as pl.*) the combination of geographical and political factors affecting a country or area. **3.** (*functioning as pl.*) politics as they affect the whole world; global politics. —**geopolitical** (₁dʒiːəʊpə'lɪtɪkᵊl) *adj.* —₁**geo₁poli'tician** *n.*

George (dʒɔːdʒ) *n.* **1.** David Lloyd. See **Lloyd George**. **2. Henry.** 1839–97, U.S. economist: advocated a single tax on land values, esp. in *Progress and Poverty* (1879). **3. Saint.** died ?303 A.D., Christian martyr, the patron saint of England; the hero of a legend in which he slew a dragon. Feast day: April 23. **4.** (*German* ge'ɔrgə). **Stefan** (**Anton**) ('ʃtɛfan). 1868–1933, German poet and aesthete. Influenced by the French Symbolists, esp. Mallarmé and later by Nietzsche, he sought for an idealized purity of form in his verse. Refused Nazi honours and went into exile in 1933.

George I *n.* 1660–1727, first Hanoverian king of Great Britain and Ireland (1714–27) and elector of Hanover (1698–1727). His dependence in domestic affairs on his ministers led to the emergence of Walpole as the first prime minister.

George II *n.* **1.** 1683–1760, king of Great Britain and Ireland and elector of Hanover (1727–60); son of George I. His victory over the French at Dettingen (1743) in the War of the Austrian Succession was the last appearance on a battlefield by a British king. **2.** 1890–1947, king of Greece (1922–24; 1935–47). He was overthrown by the republicans (1924) and exiled during the German occupation of Greece (1941–45).

George III *n.* 1738–1820, king of Great Britain and Ireland (1760–1820) and of Hanover (1815–20). During his reign the American colonies were lost. He became insane in 1811, and his son acted as regent for the rest of the reign.

George IV *n.* 1762–1830, king of Great Britain and Ireland (1820–30); regent (1811–20). He was on bad terms with his father (George III) because of his profligate ways, which undermined the prestige of the crown, and his association with the Whig opposition.

George V *n.* 1865–1936, king of Great Britain and Northern Ireland and emperor of India (1910–36).

George VI *n.* 1895–1952, king of Great Britain and Northern Ireland (1936–52) and emperor of India (1936–47). The second son of George V, he succeeded to the throne after the abdication of his brother, Edward VIII.

George Cross (dʒɔːdʒ) *n.* a British award for bravery, esp. of civilians. Abbrev.: **GC.**

Georgetown ('dʒɔːdʒ₁taʊn) *n.* **1.** the capital and chief port of Guyana, at the mouth of the Demerara River: became capital of the Dutch colonies of Essequibo and Demerara in 1784; seat of the University of Guyana. Pop.: 200 000 (1985 est.). Former name (until 1812): **Stabroek. 2.** the capital of the Cayman Islands: a port on Grand Cayman Island. Pop.: 7617 (1979).

George Town *n.* a port in NW Malaysia, capital of Penang state, in NE Penang Island: the first chartered city of the Malayan federation. Pop.: 250 578 (1980). Also called: **Penang.**

georgette *or* **georgette crepe** (dʒɔː'dʒɛt) *n.* a thin silk or cotton crepe fabric. [C20: from Mme *Georgette*, a F modiste]

Georgia ('dʒɔːdʒə) *n.* **1.** a state of the southeastern U.S., on the Atlantic: consists of coastal plains with forests and swamps, rising to the Cumberland Plateau and the Appalachians in the northwest. Capital: Atlanta. Pop.: 6 104 000 (1986 est.). Area: 152 489 sq. km (58 876 sq.

miles). Abbrevs.: **Ga.** or (with zip code) **GA 2.** short for the **Georgian Soviet Socialist Republic.**

Georgian ('dʒɔːdʒən) *adj.* **1.** of or relating to any or all of the four kings who ruled Great Britain from 1714 to 1830, or to their reigns: *Georgian architecture.* **2.** of or relating to George V of Great Britain or his reign (1910–36): *the Georgian poets.* **3.** of or relating to the Georgian SSR, its people, or their language. **4.** of or relating to the American State of Georgia or its inhabitants. **5.** (of furniture, furnishings, etc.) in or imitative of the style prevalent in England during the 18th century. ~*n.* **6.** the official language of the Georgian SSR, belonging to the South Caucasian family. **7.** a native or inhabitant of the Georgian SSR. **8.** a native or inhabitant of the American State of Georgia.

Georgian Bay *n.* a bay in S central Canada, in Ontario, containing many small islands: the NE part of Lake Huron. Area: 15 000 sq. km (5800 sq. miles).

Georgian Soviet Socialist Republic *or* **Georgia** *n.* an administrative division of the SW Soviet Union, on the Black Sea: an independent kingdom for over 2000 years, at its height in the 12th and 13th centuries; joined the Soviet Union in 1921; a major source of manganese, coal, and oil. Capital: Tbilisi. Pop.: 5 300 000 (1982 est.). Area: 69 700 sq. km (26 900 sq. miles).

geostatics (₁dʒiːəʊ'stætɪks) *n.* (*functioning as sing.*) the branch of physics concerned with the statics of rigid bodies, esp. the balance of forces within the earth.

geostationary (₁dʒiːəʊ'steɪʃənərɪ) *adj.* (of a satellite, etc.) orbiting at such speed that it appears to remain stationary with respect to the earth's surface. Also: **geosynchronous** (₁dʒiːəʊ'sɪŋkrənəs).

geostrophic (₁dʒiːəʊ'strɒfɪk) *adj.* of, relating to, or caused by the force produced by the rotation of the earth: *geostrophic wind.*

geosyncline (₁dʒiːəʊ'sɪŋklaɪn) *n.* a broad elongated depression in the earth's crust.

geothermal (₁dʒiːəʊ'θɜːməl) *or* **geothermic** *adj.* of or relating to the heat in the interior of the earth.

geotropism (dʒɪ'ɒtrə₁pɪzəm) *n.* the response of a plant part to the stimulus of gravity. Plant stems, which grow upwards irrespective of the position in which they are placed, show **negative geotropism.** —**geotropic** (₁dʒiːəʊ'trɒpɪk) *adj.*

ger. *abbrev. for:* **1.** gerund. **2.** gerundive.

Ger. *abbrev. for:* **1.** German. **2.** Germany.

Gera (*German* 'geːra) *n.* an industrial city in S East Germany. Pop.: 132 303 (1986).

geranium (dʒɪ'reɪnɪəm) *n.* **1.** a cultivated plant of the genus *Pelargonium* having scarlet, pink, or white showy flowers. See also **pelargonium. 2.** any plant such as cranesbill and herb Robert, having divided leaves and pink or purplish flowers. [C16: from L: cranesbill, from Gk, from *geranos* CRANE]

gerbera ('dʒɜːbərə) *n.* a genus of African or Asian plants belonging to the composite family, esp. the Transvaal daisy. [C19: from NL, after T. *Gerber* (died 1743), G naturalist]

gerbil *or* **gerbille** ('dʒɜːbɪl) *n.* a burrowing rodent inhabiting hot dry regions of Asia and Africa. [C19: from F, from NL *gerbillus* a little JERBOA]

gerfalcon ('dʒɜː₁fɔːlkən, -₁fɔːkən) *n.* a variant spelling of **gyrfalcon.**

geriatric (₁dʒɛrɪ'ætrɪk) *adj.* **1.** of or relating to geriatrics or to elderly people. **2.** *Inf.* old, decrepit, or useless. ~*n.* **3.** an elderly person. [C20: from Gk *gēras* old age + -IATRIC]

geriatrics (₁dʒɛrɪ'ætrɪks) *n.* (*functioning as sing.*) the branch of medical science concerned with the diagnosis and treatment of diseases affecting elderly people. —₁**geria'trician** *n.*

Géricault (*French* ʒeriko) *n.* (**Jean Louis André**) **Théodore** (teɔdɔr). 1791–1824, French romantic painter, noted for his skill in capturing movement, esp. of horses.

Gerlachovka (*Czech* 'ɡɛrlaxɔfka) *n.* a mountain in E Czechoslovakia, in the Tatra Mountains: the highest peak of the Carpathian Mountains. Height: 2663 m (8737 ft.).

germ (dʒɜːm) *n.* **1.** a microorganism, esp. one that produces disease. **2.** (*often pl.*) the rudimentary or initial form of something: *the germs of revolution.* **3.** a simple structure that is capable of developing into a complete organism. [C17: from F, from L *germen* sprout, seed]

german ('dʒɜːmən) *adj.* **1.** (used in combination) **a.** having the same parents as oneself: *a brother-german*. **b.** having a parent that is a brother or sister of either of one's own parents: *cousin-german*. **2.** a less common word for **germane**. [C14: via OF, from L *germānus* of the same race, from *germen* sprout, offshoot]

German ('dʒɜːmən) *n.* **1.** the official language of East and West Germany and Austria and one of the official languages of Switzerland. **2.** a native, inhabitant, or citizen of East or West Germany. **3.** a person whose native language is German. ~*adj.* **4.** denoting, relating to, or using the German language. **5.** relating to, denoting, or characteristic of any German state or its people.

German Democratic Republic *n.* the official name of **East Germany**. Abbrevs.: **GDR, DDR**.

germander (dʒɜː'mændə) *n.* any of several plants of Europe, having two-lipped flowers with a very small upper lip. [C15: from Med. L, ult. from Gk *khamai*: on the ground + *drus* oak tree]

germane (dʒɜː'meɪn) *adj.* (*postpositive;* usually foll. by *to*) related (to the topic being considered); akin; relevant. [var. of GERMAN] —**ger'manely** *adv.* —**ger'maneness** *n.*

German East Africa *n.* a former German territory in E Africa, consisting of Tanganyika and Ruanda-Urundi: divided in 1919 between Great Britain and Belgium; now in Tanzania, Rwanda, and Burundi.

Germanic (dʒɜː'mænɪk) *n.* **1.** a branch of the Indo-European family of languages that includes English, Dutch, German, the Scandinavian languages, and Gothic. Abbrev.: **Gmc. 2.** Also called: **Proto-Germanic.** the unrecorded language from which all of these languages developed. ~*adj.* **3.** of, denoting, or relating to this group of languages. **4.** of, relating to, or characteristic of the German language or any people that speaks a Germanic language. **5.** (formerly) of the German people.

Germanicus Caesar (dʒɜː'mænɪkəs) *n.* 15 B.C.–19 A.D., Roman general; nephew of the emperor Tiberius; waged decisive campaigns against the Germans (14–16).

germanium (dʒɜː'meɪnɪəm) *n.* a brittle crystalline grey element that is a semiconducting metalloid: used in transistors, and to strengthen alloys. Symbol: Ge; atomic no.: 32; atomic wt.: 72.59. [C19: NL, after GERMANY]

German measles *n.* (*functioning as sing.*) a nontechnical name for **rubella**.

German Ocean *n.* a former name for the **North Sea**.

German shepherd dog *n.* another name for **Alsatian**.

German silver *n.* another name for **nickel silver**.

Germany ('dʒɜːmənɪ) *n.* **1.** a country in central Europe: in the Middle Ages the centre of the Holy Roman Empire; dissolved into numerous principalities; united under the leadership of Prussia in 1871 after the Franco-Prussian War; became a republic with reduced size in 1919 after being defeated in World War I; under the dictatorship of Hitler from 1933 to 1945; defeated in World War II and divided by the Allied Powers into four zones, which became established as East and West Germany in the late 1940s. German name: **Deutschland**. See also **East Germany, West Germany**. Related adj.: **Teutonic. 2. Federal Republic of.** the official name of **West Germany**.

germ cell *n.* a sexual reproductive cell.

germicide ('dʒɜːmɪˌsaɪd) *n.* any substance that kills germs. —ˌgermi'cidal *adj.*

germinal ('dʒɜːmɪnəl) *adj.* **1.** of, relating to, or like germs or a germ cell. **2.** of or in the earliest stage of development. [C19: from NL, from L *germen* bud; see GERM] —'germinally *adv.*

germinate ('dʒɜːmɪˌneɪt) *vb.* **1.** to cause (seeds or spores) to sprout or (of seeds or spores) to sprout. **2.** to grow or cause to grow; develop. **3.** to come or bring into existence; originate: *the idea germinated with me.* [C17: from L *germināre* to sprout; see GERM] —**germinative** *adj.* —ˌgermi'nation *n.* —'germiˌnator *n.*

Germiston ('dʒɜːmɪstən) *n.* a city in South Africa, in the S Transvaal, southeast of Johannesburg: industrial centre, with the world's largest gold refinery, serving the Witwatersrand mines. Pop.: 155 435 (1980 est.).

germ plasm *n.* **a.** the part of a germ cell that contains hereditary material. **b.** the germ cells collectively.

germ warfare *n.* the military use of disease-spreading bacteria against an enemy.

Gerona (*Spanish* xe'rona) *n.* a city in NE Spain: city walls and 14th-century cathedral; often besieged, in particular

by the French (1809). Pop.: 86 624 (1981). Ancient name: **Gerunda** (dʒə'ruːndə).

Geronimo (dʒə'rɒnɪˌməʊ) *n.* 1829–1909, Apache Indian chieftain: led a campaign against the White settlers until his final capture in 1886.

gerontology (ˌdʒɛrɒn'tɒlədʒɪ) *n.* the scientific study of ageing and the problems associated with elderly people. —**gerontological** (ˌdʒɛrɒntə'lɒdʒɪk[ə]l) *adj.* —ˌger-on'tologist *n.*

-gerous *adj. combining form.* bearing or producing: *armigerous.* [from L *-ger* bearing + -OUS]

gerrymander ('dʒɛrɪˌmændə) *vb.* **1.** to divide the constituencies of (a voting area) so as to give one party an unfair advantage. **2.** to manipulate or adapt to one's advantage. ~*n.* **3.** an act or result of gerrymandering. [C19: from Elbridge *Gerry*, U.S. politician + (SALA)MANDER; from the salamander-like outline of an electoral district reshaped (1812) for political purposes while Gerry was governor of Massachusetts]

Gers (*French* ʒɛr) *n.* a department of SW France, in Midi-Pyrénées region. Capital: Auch. Pop.: 174 154 (1982). Area: 6291 sq. km (2453 sq. miles).

Gershwin ('gɜːʃwɪn) *n.* **George.** 1898–1937, U.S. composer: incorporated jazz into works such as *Rhapsody in Blue* (1924) for piano and jazz band and the opera *Porgy and Bess* (1935).

gerund ('dʒɛrənd) *n.* a noun formed from a verb, ending in *-ing*, denoting an action or state: *the living is easy.* [C16: from LL, from L *gerundum* something to be carried on, from *gerere* to wage] —**gerundial** (dʒɪ'rʌndɪəl) *adj.*

gerundive (dʒɪ'rʌndɪv) *n.* **1.** (in Latin grammar) an adjective formed from a verb, expressing the desirability, etc., of the activity denoted by the verb. ~*adj.* **2.** of or relating to the gerund or gerundive. [C17: from LL, from *gerundium* GERUND] —**gerundival** (ˌdʒɛrən'daɪv[ə]l) *adj.*

Geryon ('gɛrɪən) *n. Greek myth.* a winged monster with three bodies joined at the waist, killed by Hercules, who stole the monster's cattle as his tenth labour.

gesso ('dʒɛsəʊ) *n.* **1.** a white ground of plaster and size, used to prepare panels or canvas for painting or gilding. **2.** any white substance, esp. plaster of Paris, that forms a ground when mixed with water. [C16: from It.: chalk, GYPSUM]

gest *or* **geste** (dʒɛst) *n. Arch.* **1.** a notable deed or exploit. **2.** a tale of adventure or romance, esp. in verse. [C14: from OF, from L *gesta* deeds, from *gerere* to carry out]

Gestalt psychology (gə'ʃtælt) *n.* a system of thought that regards all mental phenomena as being arranged in patterns or structures (**gestalts**) perceived as a whole and not merely as the sum of their parts. [C20: from G *Gestalt* form]

Gestapo (gɛ'stɑːpəʊ) *n.* the secret state police in Nazi Germany. [from G *Ge(heime) Sta(ats)po(lizei)* lit.: secret state police]

gestate ('dʒɛsteɪt) *vb.* **1.** (*tr.*) to carry (developing young) in the uterus during pregnancy. **2.** (*tr.*) to develop (a plan or idea) in the mind. **3.** (*intr.*) to be in the process of gestating. [C19: from L p.p. of *gestare*, from *gerere* to bear] —**ges'tation** *n.*

gesticulate (dʒɛ'stɪkjʊˌleɪt) *vb.* to express by or make gestures. [C17: from L, from *gesticulus* (unattested except in LL) gesture, from *gerere* to bear, conduct] —**ge**ˌsticu'lation *n.* —**ge'sticulative** *adj.* —**ges'ticuˌlator** *n.* —**ges'ticulatory** *adj.*

gesture ('dʒɛstʃə) *n.* **1.** a motion of the hands, head, or body to express or emphasize an idea or emotion. **2.** something said or done as a formality or as an indication of intention. ~*vb.* **3.** to express by or make gestures; gesticulate. [C15: from Med. L *gestūra* bearing, from L *gestus*, p.p. of *gerere* to bear] —**'gestural** *adj.* —**'gesturer** *n.*

Gesualdo (*Italian* dʒezu'aldo) *n.* **Carlo** ('karlo), Prince of Venosa. ?1560–1613, Italian composer, esp. of madrigals.

get (gɛt) *vb.* **getting, got.** (*mainly tr.*) **1.** to come into possession of; receive or earn. **2.** to bring or fetch. **3.** to contract or be affected by: *he got a chill.* **4.** to capture or seize: *the police got him.* **5.** (*also intr.*) to become or cause to become or act as specified: *to get one's hair cut; get wet.* **6.** (*intr.;* foll. by a preposition or adverbial particle) to succeed in going, coming, leaving, etc.: *get off the bus.* **7.** (*takes an infinitive*) to manage or contrive: *how did you get to be captain?* **8.** to make ready or prepare:

to get a meal. **9.** to hear, notice, or understand: *I didn't get your meaning.* **10.** to learn or master by study. **11.** (*intr.; often foll. by to*) to come (to) or arrive (at): *we got home safely; to get to London.* **12.** to catch or enter: *to get a train.* **13.** to induce or persuade: *get him to leave.* **14.** to reach by calculation: *add 2 and 2 and you will get 4.* **15.** to receive (a broadcast signal). **16.** to communicate with (a person or place), as by telephone. **17.** (*also intr.; foll. by to*) *Inf.* to have an emotional effect (on): *that music really gets me.* **18.** *Inf.* to annoy or irritate: *her voice gets me.* **19.** *Inf.* to bring a person into a difficult position from which he cannot escape. **20.** *Inf.* to puzzle; baffle. **21.** *Inf.* to hit: *the blow got him in the back.* **22.** *Inf.* to be revenged on, esp. by killing. **23.** *Inf.* to have the better of: *your extravagant habits will get you in the end.* **24.** (*intr.; foll. by present participle*) *Inf.* to begin: *get moving.* **25.** (used as a command) *Inf.* go! leave now! **26.** *Arch.* to beget or conceive. **27. get with child.** *Arch.* to make pregnant. ~*n.* **28.** *Rare.* the act of begetting. **29.** *Rare.* something begotten; offspring. **30.** *Brit. sl.* a variant of **git.** ~See also **get about, get across,** etc. [OE *gietan*] —'**getable** *or* 'gettable *adj.* —'getter *n.*

get about *or* **around** *vb.* (*intr., adv.*) **1.** to move around, as when recovering from an illness. **2.** to be socially active. **3.** (of news, rumour, etc.) to become known; spread.

get across *vb.* **1.** to cross or cause to cross. **2.** (*adv.*) to be or cause to be understood.

get at *vb.* (*intr., prep.*) **1.** to gain access to. **2.** to mean or intend: *what are you getting at?* **3.** to irritate or annoy persistently; criticize: *she is always getting at him.* **4.** to influence or seek to influence, esp. illegally by bribery, intimidation, etc.: *someone had got at the witness before the trial.*

get away *vb.* (*adv., mainly intr.*) **1.** to make an escape; leave. **2.** to make a start. **3. get away with. a.** to steal and escape with (money, goods, etc.). **b.** to do (something wrong, illegal, etc.) without being discovered or punished. ~*interj.* **4.** an exclamation indicating mild disbelief. ~*n.* **getaway.** **5.** the act of escaping, esp. by criminals. **6.** a start or acceleration. **7.** (*modifier*) used for escaping: *a getaway car.*

get back *vb.* (*adv.*) **1.** (*tr.*) to recover or retrieve. **2.** (*intr.; often foll. by to*) to return, esp. to a former position or activity. **3.** (*intr.; foll. by at*) to retaliate (against); wreak vengeance (on). **4. get one's own back.** *Inf.* to obtain one's revenge.

get by *vb.* **1.** to pass; go past or overtake. **2.** (*intr., adv.*) *Inf.* to manage, esp. in spite of difficulties. **3.** (*intr.*) to be accepted or permitted: *that book will never get by the authorities.*

Gethsemane (geθ'sɛmənɪ) *n. New Testament.* the garden in Jerusalem where Christ was betrayed on the night before his Crucifixion (Matthew 26:36–56).

get in *vb.* (*mainly adv.*) **1.** (*intr.*) to enter a car, train, etc. **2.** (*intr.*) to arrive, esp. at one's home or place of work. **3.** (*tr.*) to bring in or inside: *get the milk in.* **4.** (*tr.*) to insert or slip in: *he got his suggestion in before anyone else.* **5.** (*tr.*) to gather or collect (crops, debts, etc.). **6.** to be elected or cause to be elected. **7.** (*intr.*) to obtain a place at university, college, etc. **8.** (foll. by *on*) to join or cause to join (an activity or organization).

get off *vb.* **1.** (*intr., adv.*) to escape the consequences of an action: *he got off very lightly.* **2.** (*adv.*) to be or cause to be acquitted: *a good lawyer got him off.* **3.** (*adv.*) to depart or cause to depart: *to get the children off to school.* **4.** (*intr.*) to descend (from a bus, train, etc.); dismount: *she got off at the terminus.* **5.** to move or cause to move to a distance (from): *get off the field.* **6.** (*tr., adv.*) to remove; take off: *get your coat off.* **7.** (*adv.*) to go or send to sleep. **8.** (*adv.*) to send (letters) or (of letters) to be sent. **9. get off with.** *Brit. inf.* to establish an amorous or sexual relationship (with).

get on *vb.* (*mainly adv.*) **1.** Also (*when prep.*): **get onto.** to board or cause or help to board (a bus, train, etc.). **2.** (*tr.*) to dress in (clothes as specified). **3.** (*intr.*) to grow late or (of time) to elapse: *it's getting on and I must go.* **4.** (*intr.*) (of a person) to grow old. **5.** (*intr.; foll. by for*) to approach (a time, age, amount, etc.): *she is getting on for seventy.* **6.** (*intr.*) to make progress, manage, or fare: *how did you get on in your exam?* **7.** (*intr.; often foll. by with*) to establish a friendly relationship: *he gets on well with other people.* **8.** (*intr.; foll. by with*) to continue to do: *get on with your homework!*

get out *vb.* (*adv.*) **1.** to leave or escape or cause to leave or escape: used in the imperative when dismissing a person. **2.** to make or become known; publish or be published. **3.** (*tr.*) to express with difficulty. **4.** (*tr.; often foll. by of*) to extract (information or money) (from a person): *to get a confession out of a criminal.* **5.** (*tr.*) to gain or receive something, esp. something of significance or value. **6.** (foll. by *of*) to avoid or cause to avoid: *she always gets out of swimming.* **7.** *Cricket.* to dismiss or be dismissed.

get over *vb.* **1.** to cross or surmount (something). **2.** (*intr., prep.*) to recover from (an illness, shock, etc.). **3.** (*intr., prep.*) to overcome or master (a problem). **4.** (*intr., prep.*) to appreciate fully: *I can't get over seeing you again.* **5.** (*tr., adv.*) to communicate effectively. **6.** (*tr., adv.; sometimes foll. by with*) to bring (something necessary but unpleasant) to an end: *let's get this job over with quickly.*

get round *or* **around** *vb.* (*intr.*) **1.** (*prep.*) to circumvent or overcome. **2.** (*prep.*) *Inf.* to have one's way with; cajole: *that girl can get round anyone.* **3.** (*prep.*) to evade (a law or rules). **4.** (*adv.; foll. by to*) to reach or come to at length: *I'll get round to that job in an hour.*

get through *vb.* **1.** to succeed or cause or help to succeed in an examination, test, etc. **2.** to bring or come to a destination, esp. after overcoming problems: *we got through the blizzards to the survivors.* **3.** (*intr., adv.*) to contact, as by telephone. **4.** (*intr., prep.*) to use, spend, or consume (money, supplies, etc.). **5.** to complete or cause to complete (a task, process, etc.): *to get a bill through Parliament.* **6.** (*adv.; foll. by to*) to reach the awareness and understanding (of a person): *I just can't get the message through to him.*

get-together *n.* **1.** *Inf.* a small informal meeting or social gathering. ~*vb.* **get together.** (*adv.*) **2.** (*tr.*) to gather or collect. **3.** (*intr.*) (of people) to meet socially. **4.** (*intr.*) to discuss, esp. in order to reach an agreement.

Getty ('gɛtɪ) *n.* **J(ean) Paul.** 1892–1976, U.S. oil executive, millionaire, and art collector.

Gettysburg ('gɛtɪz,bɜːg) *n.* a small town in S Pennsylvania, southwest of Harrisburg: scene of a crucial battle (1863) during the American Civil War, in which Meade's Union forces defeated Lee's Confederate army; site of the national cemetery dedicated by President Lincoln. Pop.: 7194 (1980).

get up *vb.* (*mainly adv.*) **1.** to wake and rise from one's bed or cause to wake and rise from bed. **2.** (*intr.*) to rise to one's feet; stand up. **3.** (*also prep.*) to ascend or cause to ascend. **4.** to increase or cause to increase in strength: *the wind got up at noon.* **5.** (*tr.*) *Inf.* to dress (oneself) in a particular way, esp. elaborately. **6.** (*tr.*) *Inf.* to devise or create: *to get up an entertainment for Christmas.* **7.** (*tr.*) *Inf.* to study or improve one's knowledge of: *I must get up my history.* **8.** (*intr.; foll. by to*) *Inf.* to be involved in: *he's always getting up to mischief.* ~*n.* **get-up.** *Inf.* **9.** a costume or outfit. **10.** the arrangement or production of a book, etc.

get-up-and-go *n. Inf.* energy or drive.

geum ('dʒiːəm) *n.* any herbaceous plant of the rose type, having compound leaves and red, orange, yellow, or white flowers. [C19: NL, from L: herb bennet, avens]

gewgaw ('gjuːgɔː, 'guː-) *n.* a showy but valueless trinket. [C15: from ?]

geyser ('giːzə; *U.S.* 'gaɪzər) *n.* **1.** a spring that discharges steam and hot water. **2.** *Brit.* a domestic gas water heater. [C18: from Icelandic *Geysir*, from ON *geysa* to gush]

Gezira (dʒə'zɪərə) *n.* a region of the E central Sudan between the Blue and White Niles: site of a large-scale irrigation system.

G-force *n.* the force of gravity.

Ghana ('gɑːnə) *n.* a republic in W Africa, on the Gulf of Guinea: a powerful empire from the 4th to the 13th centuries; a major source of gold and slaves for Europeans after 1471; British colony of the Gold Coast established in 1874; united with British Togoland in 1957 and became a republic within the Commonwealth in 1960. Official language: English. Religions: Christian and animist. Currency: new cedi. Capital: Accra. Pop.: 13 004 000 (1985). Area: 238 539 sq. km (92 100 sq. miles). —**Ghanaian** (gɑː'neɪən) *or* 'Ghanian *adj., n.*

gharry *or* **gharri** ('gærɪ) *n., pl.* **-ries.** a horse-drawn vehicle used in India. [C19: from Hindi *gārī*]

ghastly ('gɑːstlı) *adj.* **-lier, -liest. 1.** *Inf.* very bad or unpleasant. **2.** deathly pale; wan. **3.** *Inf.* extremely unwell; ill. **4.** terrifying; horrible. ~*adv.* **5.** unhealthily; sickly: *ghastly pale.* [OE *gǣstlīc* spiritual] — '**ghastliness** *n.*

ghat (gɔːt) *n.* (in India) **1.** stairs or a passage leading down to a river. **2.** a mountain pass. [C17: from Hindi, from Sansk.]

Ghats (gɔːts) *pl. n.* See **Eastern Ghats** and **Western Ghats.**

ghazi ('gɑːzı) *n., pl.* **-zis. 1.** a Muslim fighter against infidels. **2.** (*often cap.*) a Turkish warrior of high rank. [C18: from Ar., from *ghazā* he made war]

Ghazzah ('gɑːzə, 'gʌzə) *n.* transliteration of the Arabic name for **Gaza.**

ghee (giː) *n.* a clarified butter used in Indian cookery. [C17: from Hindi *ghī*, from Sansk. *ghri* sprinkle]

Ghent (gɛnt) *n.* an industrial city and port in NW Belgium, capital of East Flanders province, at the confluence of the Rivers Lys and Scheldt: formerly famous for its cloth industry; university (1816). Pop.: 233 856 (1982 est.). Flemish name: **Gent.** French name: **Gand.**

gherkin ('gɜːkın) *n.* **1.** the small immature fruit of any of various cucumbers, used for pickling. **2. a.** a tropical American climbing plant. **b.** its small spiny edible fruit. [C17: from Du., dim. of *gurk*, ult. from Gk *angourion*]

ghetto ('gɛtəʊ) *n., pl.* **-tos** *or* **-toes. 1.** a densely populated slum area of a city inhabited by a socially and economically deprived minority. **2.** an area or community that is segregated or isolated. **3.** an area in a European city in which Jews were formerly required to live. [C17: from It., ?from *borghetto*, dim. of *borgo* settlement outside a walled city, or from *gheto* foundry, because one occupied the site of the later Venetian ghetto]

ghetto blaster *n. Inf.* a portable cassette recorder with built-in speakers.

Ghiberti (*Italian* gi'bɛrti) *n.* **Lorenzo** (lo'rɛntso). 1378–1455, Italian sculptor, painter, and goldsmith of the quattrocento: noted esp. for the bronze doors of the baptistry of Florence Cathedral.

ghillie ('gılı) *n.* a variant spelling of **gillie.**

Ghirlandaio *or* **Ghirlandajo** (*Italian* girlan'daːjo) *n.* **Domenico** (do'meːniko). original name *Domenico Bigordi.* 1449–94, Italian painter of frescoes.

ghost (gəʊst) *n.* **1.** the disembodied spirit of a dead person, supposed to haunt the living as a pale or shadowy vision; phantom. Related adj.: **spectral. 2.** a haunting memory: *the ghost of his former life rose up before him.* **3.** a faint trace or possibility of something; glimmer: *a ghost of a smile.* **4.** the spirit; soul (archaic, except in **the Holy Ghost**). **5.** *Physics.* **a.** a faint secondary image produced by an optical system. **b.** a similar image on a television screen. **6. give up the ghost.** to die. ~*vb.* **7.** See **ghostwrite. 8.** (*tr.*) to haunt. [OE *gāst*] — '**ghost,like** *adj.* — '**ghostly** *adj.*

ghost town *n.* a deserted town, esp. one in the western U.S. that was formerly a boom town.

ghost word *n.* a word that has entered the language through the perpetuation, in dictionaries, etc., of an error.

ghostwrite ('gəʊst,raɪt) *vb.* **-writing, -wrote, -written.** to write (an article, etc.) on behalf of a person who is then credited as author. Often shortened to **ghost.** — '**ghost,writer** *n.*

ghoul (guːl) *n.* **1.** a malevolent spirit or ghost. **2.** a person interested in morbid or disgusting things. **3.** a person who robs graves. **4.** (in Muslim legend) an evil demon thought to eat corpses. [C18: from Ar. *ghūl*, from *ghāla* he seized] — '**ghoulish** *adj.* — '**ghoulishly** *adv.* — '**ghoulishness** *n.*

GHQ *Mil. abbrev. for* General Headquarters.

ghyll (gıl) *n.* a variant spelling of **gill**[3].

GI *n., U.S. inf.* **1.** (*pl.* **GIs** *or* **GI's**) a soldier in the U.S. Army, esp. an enlisted man. ~*adj.* **2.** conforming to U.S. Army regulations. [C20: abbrev. of *government issue*]

gi. *abbrev. for* gill (unit of measure).

Giacometti (*Italian* dʒako'metti) *n.* **Alberto** (al'bɛrto). 1901–66, Swiss sculptor and painter, noted particularly for his long skeletal statues of isolated figures.

giant ('dʒaɪənt) *n.* **1.** Also (fem.): **giantess** ('dʒaɪəntıs). a mythical figure of superhuman size and strength, esp. in folklore or fairy tales. **2.** a person or thing of exceptional size, reputation, etc. ~*adj.* **3.** remarkably or supernaturally large. [C13: from OF *geant*, from L *gigant-, gigās*, from Gk]

giant hogweed *n.* a species of cow parsley that grows up to 3½ metres (10 ft.) and whose irritant hairs and sap can cause a severe reaction.

giantism ('dʒaɪən,tɪzəm) *n.* another term for **gigantism** (sense 1).

giant panda *n.* See **panda.**

Giant's Causeway *n.* a promontory of columnar basalt on the N coast of Northern Ireland, in Antrim: consists of several thousand pillars, mostly hexagonal, that were formed by the rapid cooling of lava and the inward contraction of the lava flow.

giant star *n.* any of a class of very bright stars having a diameter up to 100 times that of the sun.

giaour ('dʒaʊə) *n.* a derogatory term for a non-Muslim, esp. a Christian. [C16: from Turkish: unbeliever, from Persian *gaur*]

gib (gıb) *n.* **1.** a metal wedge, pad, or thrust bearing, esp. a brass plate let into a steam engine crosshead. ~*vb.* **gibbing, gibbed. 2.** (*tr.*) to fasten or supply with a gib. [C18: from ?]

Gib (dʒıb) *n.* an informal name for **Gibraltar.**

gibber[1] ('dʒıbə) *vb.* **1.** to utter rapidly and unintelligibly; prattle. **2.** (*intr.*) (of monkeys and related animals) to make characteristic chattering sounds. [C17: imit.]

gibber[2] ('dʒıbə) *n. Austral.* **1.** a stone or boulder. **2.** (*modifier*) of or relating to a dry flat area of land covered with wind-polished stones: *gibber plains.* [C19: from Abor.]

Gibberd ('gıbəd) *n.* Sir **Frederick.** 1908–84, British architect and town planner. His buildings include the Liverpool Roman Catholic cathedral (1960–67) and the Regent's Park Mosque in London (1977). Harlow in the U.K. and Santa Teresa in Venezuela were built to his plans.

gibberellin (,dʒıbə'rɛlın) *n.* any of several plant hormones whose main action is to cause elongation of the stem. [C20: from NL *Gibberella*, lit.: a little hump, from L *gibber* hump + -IN]

gibberish ('dʒıbərɪʃ) *n.* **1.** rapid chatter. **2.** incomprehensible talk; nonsense.

gibbet ('dʒıbıt) *n.* **1. a.** a wooden structure resembling a gallows, from which the bodies of executed criminals were formerly hung to public view. **b.** a gallows. ~*vb.* (*tr.*) **2.** to put to death by hanging on a gibbet. **3.** to hang (a corpse) on a gibbet. **4.** to expose to public ridicule. [C13: from OF: gallows, lit.: little cudgel, from *gibe* cudgel; from ?]

gibbon ('gıbⁿn) *n.* a small agile arboreal anthropoid ape inhabiting forests in S Asia. [C18: from F, prob. from an Indian dialect word]

Gibbon ('gıbⁿn) *n.* **Edward.** 1737–94, English historian; author of *The History of the Decline and Fall of the Roman Empire* (1776–88), controversial in its historical criticism of Christianity.

Gibbons ('gıbⁿnz) *n.* **1. Grinling.** 1648–1721, English sculptor and woodcarver, noted for his delicate carvings of fruit, flowers, birds, etc. **2. Orlando.** 1583–1625, English organist and composer, esp. of anthems, motets, and madrigals.

gibbous ('gıbəs) *or* **gibbose** ('gıbəʊs) *adj.* **1.** (of the moon or a planet) more than half but less than fully illuminated. **2.** hunchbacked. **3.** bulging. [C17: from LL *gibbōsus* humpbacked, from L *gibba* hump] — '**gibbously** *adv.* — '**gibbousness** *or* **gibbosity** (gı'bɒsıtı) *n.*

gibe[1] *or* **jibe** (dʒaɪb) *vb.* **1.** to make jeering or scoffing remarks (at); taunt. ~*n.* **2.** a derisive or provoking remark. [C16: ?from OF *giber* to treat roughly, from ?] — '**giber** *or* '**jiber** *n.*

gibe[2] (dʒaɪb) *vb., n. Naut.* a variant spelling of **gybe.**

Gibeon ('gıbıən) *n.* an ancient town of Palestine probably about 9 kilometres (6 miles) northwest of Jerusalem.

giblets ('dʒıblıts) *pl. n.* (*sometimes sing.*) the gizzard, liver, heart, and neck of a fowl. [C14: from OF *gibelet* stew of game birds, prob. from *gibier* game, of Gmc origin]

Gibraltar (dʒı'brɔːltə) *n.* **1. City of.** a city on the **Rock of Gibraltar,** a limestone promontory at the tip of S Spain: settled by Moors in 711 and taken by Spain in 1462; ceded to Britain in 1713; a British crown colony (1830–1969), still politically associated with Britain; a naval and air base of strategic importance. Pop.: 29 000 (1987 est.). Area: 6.5 sq. km (2.5 sq. miles). Ancient name: **Calpe. 2. Strait of.** a narrow strait between the S tip of Spain and the NW tip of Africa, linking the Mediterranean with the Atlantic. —**Gibraltarian** (ˌdʒɪbrɔːˈlɛ əriən) *adj.*, *n.*

Gibran (dʒɪ'brɑːn) *n.* **Kahlil** ('kɑːliːl). 1883–1931, Syro-Lebanese poet, mystic, and painter, resident in the U.S. after 1910; author of *The Prophet* (1923).

Gibson Desert ('gɪbsən) *n.* a desert in W central Australia, between the Great Sandy Desert and the Victoria Desert: salt marshes, salt lakes, and scrub. Area: about 220 000 sq. km (85 000 sq. miles).

gidday (gə'daɪ) *sentence substitute.* an Austral. and N.Z. informal variant of **good day.**

giddy ('gɪdɪ) *adj.* **-dier, -diest. 1.** affected with a reeling sensation and feeling as if about to fall; dizzy. **2.** causing or tending to cause vertigo. **3.** impulsive; scatterbrained. ~*vb.* **giddying, giddied. 4.** to make or become giddy. [OE *gydig* mad, frenzied, possessed by God; rel. to GOD] —'**giddily** *adv.* —'**giddiness** *n.*

Gide (*French* ʒid) *n.* **André** (ɑ̃dre). 1869–1951, French novelist, dramatist, critic, diarist, and translator, noted particularly for his exploration of the conflict between self-fulfilment and conventional morality. His novels include *L'Immoraliste* (1902), *La Porte étroite* (1909), and *Les Faux-Monnayeurs* (1926): Nobel prize for literature 1947.

Gideon ('gɪdɪən) *n. Old Testament.* a Hebrew judge who led the Israelites to victory over their Midianite oppressors (Judges 6:11–8:35).

gidgee *or* **gidjee** ('gɪdʒiː) *n. Austral.* **1.** a small acacia tree yielding useful timber. **2.** a spear made of this. [C19: from Abor.]

gie (giː) *vb.* a Scot. word for **give.**

Gielgud ('giːlɡud) *n.* Sir **John.** born 1904, English stage, film, and television actor and director.

Giessen (*German* 'giːsən) *n.* a city in W central West Germany, in Hesse: university (1607). Pop.: 71 800 (1984).

gift (ɡɪft) *n.* **1.** something given; a present. **2.** a special aptitude, ability, or power; talent. **3.** the power or right to give or bestow (esp. in **in the gift of, in (someone's) gift**). **4.** the act or process of giving. **5. look a gift-horse in the mouth.** (*usually negative*) to find fault with a free gift or chance benefit. ~*vb.* (*tr.*) **6.** to present (something) as a gift to (a person). [OE *gift* payment for a wife, dowry; see GIVE]

GIFT (ɡɪft) *n. acronym for* Gamete In (*or* Intra-) Fallopian Transfer: a technique, similar to IVF, that enables some people with unexplained infertility or subfertility to have children.

gifted ('ɡɪftɪd) *adj.* having or showing natural talent or aptitude: *a gifted musician.* —'**giftedly** *adv.* —'**giftedness** *n.*

gift of tongues *n.* an utterance, partly or wholly unintelligible, produced under the influence of ecstatic religious emotion. Also called: **glossolalia.**

giftwrap ('ɡɪft,ræp) *vb.* **-wrapping, -wrapped.** to wrap (a gift) attractively.

Gifu ('ɡiːfuː) *n.* a city in Japan, on central Honshu: hot springs. Pop.: 412 000 (1985).

gig[1] (ɡɪɡ) *n.* **1.** a light two-wheeled one-horse carriage without a hood. **2.** *Naut.* a light tender for a vessel. **3.** a long light rowing boat, used esp. for racing. ~*vb.* **gigging, gigged. 4.** (*intr.*) to travel in a gig. [C13 (in the sense: flighty girl, spinning top): ?from ON]

gig[2] (ɡɪɡ) *n.* **1.** a cluster of barbless hooks drawn through a shoal of fish to try to impale them. ~*vb.* **gigging, gigged. 2.** to catch (fish) with a gig. [C18: ? shortened from obs. *fishgig* or *fizgig* kind of harpoon]

gig[3] (ɡɪɡ) *n.* **1.** a job, esp. a single booking for jazz or pop musicians. **2.** the performance itself. ~*vb.* **gigging, gigged. 3.** (*intr.*) to perform a gig. [C20: from ?]

giga- ('ɡɪɡə-, 'ɡaɪɡə) *combining form.* **1.** denoting 10[9]: *gigavolt.* **2.** *Computers.* denoting 2[30]: *gigabyte.* Symbol: G [from Gk *gigas* GIANT]

gigahertz ('ɡaɪɡə,hɜːts, 'dʒɪɡ-) *n., pl.* **-hertz.** a unit of frequency equal to 10[9] hertz. Symbol: GHz

gigantic (dʒaɪ'ɡæntɪk) *adj.* **1.** very large; enormous. **2.** Also: **gigantesque** (ˌdʒaɪɡæn'tɛsk). of or suitable for giants. [C17: from Gk *gigantikos*, from *gigas* GIANT] —**gi'gantically** *adv.*

gigantism ('dʒaɪɡæn,tɪzəm, dʒaɪ'ɡæntɪzəm) *n.* **1.** Also called: **giantism.** excessive growth of the entire body, caused by overproduction of growth hormone by the pituitary gland. **2.** the state or quality of being gigantic.

giggle ('ɡɪɡ²l) *vb.* **1.** (*intr.*) to laugh nervously or foolishly. ~*n.* **2.** such a laugh. **3.** *Inf.* something or someone that causes amusement. [C16: imit.] —'**giggler** *n.* —'**gig-gling** *adj., n.* —'**giggly** *adj.*

Gigli (*Italian* 'dʒiʎʎi) *n.* **Beniamino** (benja'miːno). 1890–1957, Italian operatic tenor.

gigolo ('ʒɪɡə,ləʊ) *n., pl.* **-los. 1.** a man who is kept by a woman, esp. an older woman. **2.** a man who is paid to dance with or escort women. [C20: from F, back formation from *gigolette* girl for hire as a dancing partner, prostitute, ult. from *gigue* a fiddle]

gigot ('dʒɪɡət) *n.* **1.** a leg of lamb or mutton. **2.** a leg-of-mutton sleeve. [C16: from OF: leg, a small fiddle, from *gigue* a fiddle, of Gmc origin]

gigue (ʒiːɡ) *n.* a piece of music, usually in six-eight time, incorporated into the classical suite. [C17: from F, from It. *giga*, of Gmc origin; see GIGOT]

Gijón (giː'hɔːn; *Spanish* xi'xon) *n.* a port in NW Spain, on the Bay of Biscay: capital of the kingdom of Asturias until 791. Pop.: 255 969 (1981). Ancient name: **Gigia.**

Gila monster ('hiːlə) *n.* a large venomous brightly coloured lizard inhabiting deserts of the southwestern U.S. and Mexico.

gilbert ('ɡɪlbət) *n.* the cgs unit of magnetomotive force. Symbol: Gb, Gi [C19: after William GILBERT, E scientist]

Gilbert ('ɡɪlbət) *n.* **1. Grove Karl.** 1843–1918, U.S. geologist who pioneered the study of river development and valley erosion. **2.** Sir **Humphrey.** ?1539–83, English navigator: founded the colony at St John's, Newfoundland (1583). **3. William.** 1540–1603, English physician and physicist, noted for his study of terrestrial magnetism in *De Magnete* (1600). **4.** Sir **W(illiam) S(chwenck).** 1836–1911, English dramatist, humorist, and librettist. He collaborated (1871–96) with Arthur Sullivan on the famous series of comic operettas, including *The Pirates of Penzance* (1879), *Iolanthe* (1882), and *The Mikado* (1885).

Gilbert Islands *pl. n.* a group of islands in the W Pacific: with Banaba, the Phoenix Islands, and three of the Line Islands they constitute the independent state of Kiribati; until 1975 they formed part of the British colony of **Gilbert and Ellice Islands;** achieved full independence in 1979. Pop.: 66 250 (1987 est.). Area: 295 sq. km (114 sq. miles).

gild[1] (ɡɪld) *vb.* **gilding, gilded** *or* **gilt.** (*tr.*) **1.** to cover with or as if with gold. **2. gild the lily. a.** to adorn unnecessarily something already beautiful. **b.** to praise someone inordinately. **3.** to give a falsely attractive or valuable appearance to. [OE *gyldan*, from *gold* GOLD] —'**gilder** *n.*

gild[2] (ɡɪld) *n.* a variant spelling of **guild.**

gilding ('ɡɪldɪŋ) *n.* **1.** the act or art of applying gilt to a surface. **2.** the surface so produced. **3.** another word for **gilt**[1] (sense 2).

Gilead[1] ('ɡɪlɪ,æd) *n.* a historic mountainous region east of the River Jordan, rising over 1200 m (4000 ft.).

Gilead[2] ('ɡɪlɪ,æd) *n. Old Testament.* a grandson of Manasseh; ancestor of the Coileadites (Numbers 26: 29–30).

Giles (dʒaɪlz) *n.* **1. Saint.** 7th century A.D., Greek hermit in France; patron saint of cripples, beggars, and lepers. Feast day: Sept. 1. **2. William Ernest Powell.** 1835–97, Australian explorer, born in England. He was noted esp. for his exploration of the western desert (1875–76).

gilet (dʒi'leɪ) *n.* a garment resembling a waistcoat. [C20: F, lit.: waistcoat]

gill[1] (ɡɪl) *n.* **1.** the respiratory organ in many aquatic animals. **2.** any of the radiating leaflike spore-producing structures on the undersurface of the cap of a mushroom. [C14: from ON] —**gilled** *adj.*

gill[2] (dʒɪl) *n.* a unit of liquid measure equal to one quarter of a pint. [C14: from OF *gille* vat, tub, from LL *gillō*, from ?]

gill[3] *or* **ghyll** (ɡɪl) *n. Dialect.* **1.** a narrow stream; rivulet. **2.** a wooded ravine. [C11: from ON *gil* steep-sided valley]

Gillespie (ɡɪ'lɛspɪ) *n.* **Dizzy,** nickname of *John Birks Gillespie.* born 1917, U.S. jazz trumpeter.

gillie, ghillie, *or* **gilly** ('ɡɪlɪ) *n., pl.* **-lies.** *Scot.* **1.** an attendant or guide for hunting or fishing. **2.** (formerly) a Highland chieftain's male attendant. [C17: from Scot. Gaelic *gille* boy, servant]

Gillingham ('dʒɪlɪŋəm) *n.* a town in SE England, in N Kent on the Medway estuary: former dockyards. Pop.: 93 741 (1981).

Gillray ('ɡɪlreɪ) *n.* **James.** 1757–1815, English caricaturist.

gills (gɪlz) *pl. n.* **1.** (*sometimes sing.*) the wattle of birds such as domestic fowl. **2.** the cheeks and jowls of a person. **3. green about the gills.** *Inf.* looking or feeling nauseated.

gillyflower *or* **gilliflower** ('dʒɪlɪ,flaʊə) *n.* **1.** any of several plants having fragrant flowers, such as the stock and wallflower. **2.** an archaic name for **carnation.** [C14: from *gilofre*, from OF *girofle*, from Med. L, from Gk: clove tree, from *karuon* nut + *phullon* leaf]

Gilolo (dʒaɪ'ləʊləʊ, dʒɪ-) *n.* See **Halmahera.**

gilt[1] (gɪlt) *vb.* **1.** a past tense and past participle of **gild**[1]. ~*n.* **2.** gold or a substance simulating it, applied in gilding. **3.** another word for **gilding** (senses 1, 2). **4.** superficial or false appearance of excellence. **5.** a gilt-edged security. **6. take the gilt off the gingerbread.** to destroy the part of something that gives it its appeal. ~*adj.* **7.** covered with or as if with gold or gilt; gilded.

gilt[2] (gɪlt) *n.* a young female pig, esp. one that has not had a litter. [C15: from ON *gyltr*]

gilt-edged *adj.* **1.** denoting government securities on which interest payments will certainly be met and that will certainly be repaid at par on the due date. **2.** (of books, papers, etc.) having gilded edges.

gimbals ('dʒɪmbᵊlz, 'gɪm-) *pl. n.* a device, consisting of two or three pivoted rings at right angles to each other, that provides free suspension in all planes for a compass, chronometer, etc. Also called: **gimbal ring.** [C16: var. of earlier *gimmal*, from OF *gemel* double finger ring, from L *gemellus*, dim. of *geminus* twin]

gimcrack ('dʒɪm,kræk) *adj.* **1.** cheap; shoddy. ~*n.* **2.** a cheap showy trifle or gadget. [C18: from C14 *gibecrake* little ornament, from ?] — '**gim,crackery** *n.*

gimlet ('gɪmlɪt) *n.* **1.** a small hand tool consisting of a pointed spiral tip attached at right angles to a handle, used for boring small holes in wood. **2.** *U.S.* a cocktail consisting of half gin or vodka and half lime juice. ~*vb.* **3.** (*tr.*) to make holes in (wood) using a gimlet. ~*adj.* **4.** penetrating; piercing (esp. in **gimlet-eyed**). [C15: from OF *guimbelet*, of Gmc origin, see WIMBLE]

gimmick ('gɪmɪk) *n. Inf.* **1.** something designed to attract extra attention, interest, or publicity. **2.** any clever device, gadget, or stratagem, esp. one used to deceive. [C20: orig. U.S. sl., from ?] — '**gimmickry** *n.* — '**gimmicky** *adj.*

gimp *or* **guimpe** (gɪmp) *n.* a tapelike trimming. [C17: prob. from Du. *gimp*, from ?]

gin[1] (dʒɪn) *n.* an alcoholic drink obtained by distillation of the grain of malted barley, rye, or maize, flavoured with juniper berries. [C18: from Du. *genever*, via OF from L *jūniperus* JUNIPER]

gin[2] (dʒɪn) *n.* **1.** a primitive engine in which a vertical shaft is turned by horses driving a horizontal beam in a circle. **2.** Also called: **cotton gin.** a machine of this type used for separating seeds from raw cotton. **3.** a trap for catching small mammals, consisting of a noose of thin strong wire. ~*vb.* **ginning, ginned.** (*tr.*) **4.** to free (cotton) of seeds with a gin. **5.** to trap or snare (game) with a gin. [C13 *gyn*, from ENGINE]

gin[3] (gɪn) *vb.* **ginning, gan** (gæn), **gun** (gʌn). an archaic word for **begin.**

gin[4] (dʒɪn) *n. Austral. derog. sl.* an Aboriginal woman. [C19: from Abor.]

ginger ('dʒɪndʒə) *n.* **1.** any of several plants of the East Indies, cultivated throughout the tropics for their spicy hot-tasting underground stems. **2.** the underground stem of this plant, which is used fresh or powdered as a flavouring or crystallized as a sweetmeat. **3. a.** a reddish-brown or yellowish-brown colour. **b.** (*as adj.*): *ginger hair.* **4.** *Inf.* liveliness; vigour. [C13: from OF *gingivre*, ult. from Sansk. *śṛṅgaveram*, from *śṛṅga-* horn + *vera-* body, referring to its shape] — '**gingery** *adj.*

ginger ale *n.* a sweetened effervescent nonalcoholic drink flavoured with ginger extract.

ginger beer *n.* a slightly alcoholic drink made by fermenting a mixture of syrup and root ginger.

gingerbread ('dʒɪndʒə,brɛd) *n.* **1.** a moist brown cake, flavoured with ginger and treacle. **2. a.** a biscuit, similarly flavoured, cut into various shapes. **b.** (*as modifier*): *gingerbread man.* **3.** an elaborate but unsubstantial ornamentation.

ginger group *n. Chiefly Brit.* a group within a party, association, etc., that enlivens or radicalizes its parent body.

gingerly ('dʒɪndʒəlɪ) *adv.* **1.** in a cautious, reluctant, or timid manner. ~*adj.* **2.** cautious, reluctant, or timid. [C16: ?from OF *gensor* dainty, from *gent* of noble birth; see GENTLE]

ginger snap *or* **nut** *n.* a crisp biscuit flavoured with ginger.

gingham ('gɪŋəm) *n.* a cotton fabric, usually woven of two coloured yarns in a checked or striped design. [C17: from F, from Malay *ginggang* striped cloth]

gingili ('dʒɪndʒɪlɪ) *n.* **1.** the oil obtained from sesame seeds. **2.** another name for **sesame.** [C18: from Hindi *jin-gali*]

gingiva ('dʒɪndʒɪvə, dʒɪn'dʒaɪvə) *n., pl.* **-givae** (-dʒɪ,viː, -'dʒaɪviː). *Anat.* the technical name for the **gum**[2]. [from L] — '**gingival** *adj.*

gingivitis (,dʒɪndʒɪ'vaɪtɪs) *n.* inflammation of the gums.

ginglymus ('dʒɪŋglɪməs, 'gɪŋ-) *n., pl.* **-mi** (-,maɪ). *Anat.* a hinge joint. [C17: NL, from Gk *ginglumos* hinge]

gink (gɪŋk) *n. Sl.* a man or boy, esp. one considered to be odd. [C20: from ?]

ginkgo ('gɪŋkgəʊ) *or* **gingko** ('gɪŋkəʊ) *n., pl.* **-goes** *or* **-koes.** a widely planted ornamental Chinese tree with fan-shaped deciduous leaves and fleshy yellow fruit. Also called: **maidenhair tree.** [C18: from Japanese, from Ancient Chinese: silver + apricot]

ginormous (dʒaɪ'nɔːməs) *adj. Inf.* very large. [C20: blend of *giant* or *gigantic* & *enormous*]

gin palace (dʒɪn) *n.* (formerly) a gaudy drinking house.

gin rummy (dʒɪn) *n.* a version of rummy in which a player may go out if the odd cards outside his sequences total less than ten points. [C20: from GIN[1] + RUMMY]

Ginsberg ('gɪnzbɜːg) *n.* **Allen.** born 1926, U.S. poet of the Beat Generation. His poetry includes *Howl* (1956).

ginseng ('dʒɪnsɛŋ) *n.* **1.** either of two plants of China or of North America, whose forked aromatic roots are used medicinally in China. **2.** the root of either of these plants or a substance obtained from the roots, believed to possess tonic and energy-giving properties. [C17: from Mandarin Chinese *jen shen*]

Gioconda (*Italian* dʒo'konda) *n.* **1. La.** Also called: **Mona Lisa.** the portrait by Leonardo da Vinci of a young woman with an enigmatic smile. ~*adj.* **2.** mysterious or enigmatic. [It.: the smiling (lady)]

giocoso (dʒɒ'kəʊzəʊ) *adj. Music.* jocose. [It.]

Giorgione (*Italian* dʒor'dʒoːne) *n.* **Il.** original name *Giorgio Barbarelli.* ?1478–1511, Italian painter of the Venetian school, who introduced a new unity between figures and landscape.

Giotto (*Italian* 'dʒɔtto) *n.* also known as *Giotto di Bondone.* ?1267–1337, Florentine painter, who broke away from the stiff linear design of the Byzantine tradition and developed the more dramatic and naturalistic style characteristic of the Renaissance: his work includes cycles of frescoes in Assisi, the Arena Chapel in Padua, and the Church of Santa Croce, Florence.

gip (dʒɪp) *vb.* **gipping, gipped. 1.** a variant spelling of **gyp**[1]. ~*n.* **2.** a variant spelling of **gyp**[2].

Gippsland ('gɪps,lænd) *n.* a fertile region of SE Australia, in SE Victoria, extending east along the coast from Melbourne to the New South Wales border. Area: 35 200 sq. km (13 600 sq. miles).

Gipsy ('dʒɪpsɪ) *n., pl.* **-sies.** (*sometimes not cap.*) a variant spelling of **Gypsy.**

gipsy moth *n.* a variant spelling of **gypsy moth.**

giraffe (dʒɪ'rɑːf, -'ræf) *n., pl.* **-raffes** *or* **-raffe.** a large ruminant mammal inhabiting savannas of tropical Africa: the tallest mammal, with very long legs and neck. [C17: from It. *giraffa*, from Ar. *zarāfah*, prob. of African origin]

Giraldus Cambrensis (dʒɪ'rældəs kæm'brɛnsɪs) *n.* literary name of *Gerald de Barri.* ?1146–?1223, Welsh chronicler and churchman, noted for his accounts of his travels in Ireland and Wales.

girandole ('dʒɪrən,dəʊl) *n.* **1.** a branched wall candleholder. **2.** an earring or pendant having a central gem surrounded by smaller ones. **3.** a revolving firework. **4.** *Artillery.* a group of connected mines. [C17: from F, from It. *girandola*, from L *gȳrāre* to GYRATE]

girasol *or* **girasole** ('dʒɪrə,sɒl, -,səʊl) *n.* a type of opal that has a red or pink glow; fire opal. [C16: from It., from *girare* to revolve (see GYRATE) + *sole* the sun]

Giraud (*French* ʒiro) *n.* **Henri Honoré** (ãri ɔnɔre). 1879–1949, French general, who commanded French forces in North Africa (1942–43).

Giraudoux (*French* ʒirodu) *n.* **Jean** (ʒã). 1882–1944, French dramatist. His works, noted for their use of paradox and imagery, include the novel *Suzanne et le Pacifique* (1921) and the plays *Amphitryon 38* (1929) and *La Guerre de Troie n'aura pas lieu* (1935).

gird[1] (gɜːd) *vb.* **girding, girded** *or* **girt.** (*tr.*) **1.** to put a belt, girdle, etc., around (the waist or hips). **2.** to bind or secure with or as if with a belt: *to gird on one's armour.* **3.** to surround; encircle. **4.** to prepare (oneself) for action (esp. in **gird (up) one's loins**). [OE *gyrdan*, of Gmc origin]

gird[2] (gɜːd) *N English dialect.* ~*vb.* **1.** (when *intr.*, foll. by *at*) to jeer (at someone); mock. ~*n.* **2.** a taunt; gibe. [C13 *girden* to strike, cut, from ?]

girder ('gɜːdə) *n.* a large beam, esp. one made of steel, used in the construction of bridges, buildings, etc.

girdle[1] ('gɜːd°l) *n.* **1.** a woman's elastic corset covering the waist to the thigh. **2.** anything that surrounds or encircles. **3.** a belt or sash. **4.** *Jewellery.* the outer edge of a gem. **5.** *Anat.* any encircling structure or part. **6.** the mark left on a tree trunk after the removal of a ring of bark. ~*vb.* (*tr.*) **7.** to put a girdle on or around. **8.** to surround or encircle. **9.** to remove a ring of bark from (a tree). [OE *gyrdel*, of Gmc origin; see GIRD[1]] —'**girdle-like** *adj.*

girdle[2] ('gɜːd°l) *n. Scot. & N English dialect.* another word for **griddle**.

Girgenti (*Italian* dʒir'dʒɛnti) *n.* a former name (until 1927) of **Agrigento**.

girl (gɜːl) *n.* **1.** a female child from birth to young womanhood. **2.** a young unmarried woman; lass; maid. **3.** *Inf.* a sweetheart or girlfriend. **4.** *Inf.* a woman of any age. **5.** a female employee, esp. a female 'servant. **6.** *S. African derog.* a Black female servant. [C13: from ?; ? rel. to Low G *Göre* boy, girl] —'**girlish** *adj.*

girlfriend ('gɜːl,frɛnd) *n.* **1.** a female friend with whom a person is romantically or sexually involved. **2.** any female friend.

Girl Guide *n.* See **Guide**.

girlhood ('gɜːl,hʊd) *n.* the state or time of being a girl.

girlie ('gɜːlɪ) *n.* (*modifier*) *Inf.* featuring nude or scantily dressed women: *a girlie magazine.*

giro ('dʒaɪrəʊ) *n., pl.* **-ros.** **1.** a system of transferring money within a financial organization, such as a bank or post office, directly from the account of one person into that of another. **2.** *Brit. inf.* an unemployment or supplementary benefit payment by giro cheque. [C20: ult. from Gk *guros* circuit]

Gironde (*French* ʒirɔ̃d) *n.* **1.** a department of SW France, in Aquitaine region. Capital: Bordeaux. Pop.: 1 127 546 (1982). Area: 10 726 sq. km (4183 sq. miles). **2.** an estuary in SW France, formed by the confluence of the Rivers Garonne and Dordogne. Length: 72 km (45 miles).

girt[1] (gɜːt) *vb.* a past tense and past participle of **gird**[1].

girt[2] (gɜːt) *vb.* **1.** (*tr.*) to bind or encircle; gird. **2.** to measure the girth of (something).

girth (gɜːθ) *n.* **1.** the distance around something; circumference. **2.** a band around a horse's belly to keep the saddle in position. ~*vb.* **3.** (usually foll. by *up*) to fasten a girth on (a horse). **4.** (*tr.*) to encircle or surround. [C14: from ON *gjörth* belt; see GIRD[1]]

Gisborne ('gɪzbən) *n.* a port in N New Zealand, on E North Island on Poverty Bay. Pop.: 32 000 (1987).

Giscard d'Estaing (*French* ʒiskardɛstɛ̃) *n.* **Valéry** (valeri). born 1926, French politician; minister of finance and economic affairs (1962–66; 1969–74); president (1974–81).

Gish (gɪʃ) *n.* **1. Dorothy**, original name *Dorothy de Guiche.* 1898–1968, U.S. film actress, chiefly in silent films. **2.** her sister, **Lillian**, original name *Lillian Diana de Guiche.* born 1899, U.S. film and stage actress, noted esp. for her roles in such silent films as *Birth of a Nation* (1914) and *Intolerance* (1916).

gismo *or* **gizmo** ('gɪzməʊ) *n., pl.* **-mos.** *Sl., chiefly U.S. & Canad.* a device; gadget [C20: from ?]

Gissing ('gɪsɪŋ) *n.* **George (Robert).** 1857–1903, English novelist, noted for his depiction of middle-class poverty. His works include *Demos* (1886) and *New Grub Street* (1891).

gist (dʒɪst) *n.* the point or substance of an argument, speech, etc. [C18: from Anglo-F, as in *cest action gist en* this action consists in, lit.: lies in, from OF *gésir*, from L *jacēre*]

git (gɪt) *n. Brit. sl.* **1.** a contemptible person, often a fool. **2.** a bastard. [C20: from GET (in the sense: *to beget*, hence a bastard, fool)]

gîte (ʒiːt) *n.* a self-catering holiday cottage for let in France. [C20: F]

gittern ('gɪtɜːn) *n.* an obsolete medieval stringed instrument resembling the guitar. [C14: from OF, ult. from OSp. *guitarra* GUITAR; see CITTERN]

Giulini (*Italian* dʒu'liːni) *n.* **Carlo Maria** ('karlo ma'riːa). born 1914, Italian orchestral conductor, esp. of opera.

Giulio Romano (*Italian* 'dʒuːljo ro'maːno) *n.* ?1499–1546, Italian architect and painter; a founder of mannerism.

giusto ('dʒuːstəʊ) *adj. Music.* (of tempo) exact; strict. [It.]

give (gɪv) *vb.* **giving, gave, given.** (*mainly tr.*) **1.** (*also intr.*) to present or deliver voluntarily (something that is one's own) to another. **2.** (often foll. by *for*) to transfer (something that is one's own, esp. money) to the possession of another as part of an exchange: *to give fifty pounds for a painting.* **3.** to place in the temporary possession of another: *I gave him my watch while I went swimming.* **4.** (when *intr.*, foll. by *of*) to grant, provide, or bestow: *give me some advice.* **5.** to administer: *to give a reprimand.* **6.** to award or attribute: *to give blame, praise,* etc. **7.** to be a source of: *he gives no trouble.* **8.** to impart or communicate: *to give news.* **9.** to utter or emit: *to give a shout.* **10.** to perform, make, or do: *the car gave a jolt.* **11.** to sacrifice or devote: *he gave his life for his country.* **12.** to surrender: *to give place to others.* **13.** to concede or yield: *I will give you this game.* **14.** (*intr.*) *Inf.* to happen: *what gives?* **15.** (often foll. by *to*) to cause; lead: *she gave me to believe that she would come.* **16.** to perform or present as an entertainment: *to give a play.* **17.** to act as a host of (a party, etc.). **18.** (*intr.*) to yield or break under force or pressure: *this surface will give if you sit on it.* **19. give as good as one gets.** to respond to verbal or bodily blows to at least an equal extent as those received. **20. give or take.** plus or minus: *three thousand people came, give or take a few hundred.* ~*n.* **21.** tendency to yield under pressure; resilience. ~See also **give away, give in,** etc. [OE *giefan*] —'**givable** *or* '**giveable** *adj.* —'**giver** *n.*

give-and-take *n.* **1.** mutual concessions, shared benefits, and cooperation. **2.** a smoothly flowing exchange of ideas and talk. ~*vb.* **give and take.** (*intr.*) **3.** to make mutual concessions.

give away *vb.* (*tr., adv.*) **1.** to donate or bestow as a gift, prize, etc. **2.** to sell very cheaply. **3.** to reveal or betray. **4.** to fail to use (an opportunity) through folly or neglect. **5.** to present (a bride) formally to her husband in a marriage ceremony. ~*n.* **giveaway.** **6.** a betrayal or disclosure esp. when unintentional. **7.** (*modifier*) **a.** very cheap (esp. in **giveaway prices**). **b.** free of charge: *a giveaway property magazine.*

give in *vb.* (*adv.*) **1.** (*intr.*) to yield; admit defeat. **2.** (*tr.*) to submit or deliver (a document).

given ('gɪv°n) *vb.* **1.** the past participle of **give.** ~*adj.* **2.** (*postpositive*; foll. by *to*) tending (to); inclined or addicted (to). **3.** specific or previously stated. **4.** assumed as a premise. **5.** *Maths.* known or determined independently: *a given volume.* **6.** (on official documents) issued or executed, as on a stated date.

given name *n.* another term (esp. U.S.) for **Christian name.**

give off *vb.* (*tr., adv.*) to emit or discharge: *the mothballs gave off an acrid odour.*

give out *vb.* (*adv.*) **1.** (*tr.*) to emit or discharge. **2.** (*tr.*) to publish or make known: *the chairman gave out that he would resign.* **3.** (*tr.*) to hand out or distribute: *they gave out free chewing gum.* **4.** (*intr.*) to become exhausted; fail: *the supply of candles gave out.*

give over *vb.* (*adv.*) **1.** (*tr.*) to transfer, esp. to the care or custody of another. **2.** (*tr.*) to assign or resign to a specific purpose or function: *the day was given over to pleasure.* **3.** *Inf.* to cease (an activity): *give over fighting, will you!*

give up *vb.* (*adv.*) **1.** to abandon hope (for). **2.** (*tr.*) to renounce (an activity, belief, etc.): *I have given up smoking.* **3.** (*tr.*) to relinquish or resign from: *he gave up the presidency.* **4.** (*tr.; usually reflexive*) to surrender: *the escaped convict gave himself up.* **5.** (*intr.*) to admit one's defeat or inability to do something. **6.** (*tr.; often* *passive or reflexive*) to devote completely (to): *she gave herself up to caring for the sick.*

Gîza ('gi:zə) *n*. See **El Gîza.**

gizzard ('gizəd) *n*. **1.** the thick-walled part of a bird's stomach, in which hard food is broken up. **2.** *Inf*. the stomach and entrails generally. [C14: from OF *guisier* fowl's liver, from L *gigēria* entrails of poultry when cooked, from ?]

Gk *abbrev. for* Greek.

glabella (glə'bɛlə) *n*., *pl*. **-lae** (-li:). *Anat*. a smooth elevation of the frontal bone just above the bridge of the nose. [C19: NL, from L, from *glaber* bald, smooth] —**gla'bellar** *adj*.

glabrous ('gleɪbrəs) *adj*. *Biol*. without hair or a similar growth; smooth. [C17 *glabrous*, from L *glaber*] —**'glabrousness** *n*.

glacé ('glæsɪ) *adj*. **1.** crystallized or candied: *glacé cherries*. **2.** covered in icing. **3.** (of leather, silk, etc.) having a glossy finish. ~*vb*. **-céing, -céed. 4.** (*tr*.) to ice or candy (cakes, fruits, etc.). [C19: from F *glacé*, lit.: iced, from *glacer* to freeze, from L *glaciēs* ice]

glacial ('gleɪsɪəl, -ʃəl) *adj*. **1.** characterized by the presence of masses of ice. **2.** relating to, caused by, or deposited by a glacier. **3.** extremely cold; icy. **4.** cold or hostile in manner. **5.** (of a chemical compound) of or tending to form crystals that resemble ice. **6.** very slow in progress: *a glacial pace*. —**'glacially** *adv*.

glacial acetic acid *n*. pure acetic acid.

glacial period *n*. **1.** any period of time during which a large part of the earth's surface was covered with ice, due to the advance of glaciers. **2.** (*often caps*.) the Pleistocene epoch. ~Also called: **glacial epoch, ice age.**

glaciate ('gleɪsɪ,eɪt) *vb*. **1.** to cover or become covered with glaciers or masses of ice. **2.** (*tr*.) to subject to the effects of glaciers, such as denudation and erosion. —**,glaci'ation** *n*.

glacier ('glæsɪə, 'gleɪs-) *n*. a slowly moving mass of ice originating from an accumulation of snow. [C18: from F (dialect), from OF *glace* ice, from LL, from L *glaciēs* ice]

glaciology (,glæsɪ'ɒlədʒɪ, ,gleɪ-) *n*. the study of the distribution, character, and effects of glaciers. —**glaciological** (,glæsɪə'lɒdʒɪkəl, ,gleɪ-) *adj*. —**glaci'ologist** *n*.

glacis ('glæsɪs, 'glæsɪ, 'gleɪ-) *n*., *pl*. **-ises** *or* **-is** (-i:z, -ɪz). **1.** a slight incline; slope. **2.** an open slope in front of a fortified place. [C17: from F, from OF *glacier* to freeze, slip, from L, from *glaciēs* ice]

glad¹ (glæd) *adj*. **gladder, gladdest. 1.** happy and pleased; contented. **2.** causing happiness or contentment. **3.** (*postpositive; foll. by to*) very willing: *he was glad to help.* ~*vb*. **gladding, gladded. 4.** (*tr*.) an archaic word for **gladden.** [OE *glæd*] —**'gladly** *adv*. —**'gladness** *n*.

glad² (glæd) *n*. *Inf*. short for **gladiolus.**

Gladbeck (*German* 'glatbɛk) *n*. a city in N West Germany, in North Rhine-Westphalia. Pop.: 78 727 (1983 est.).

gladden ('glædⁿn) *vb*. to make or become glad and joyful. —**'gladdener** *n*.

glade (gleɪd) *n*. an open place in a forest; clearing. [C16: from ?; ? rel. to GLAD¹ (in obs. sense: bright); see GLEAM]

glad eye *n*. *Inf*. an inviting or seductive glance (esp. in **give (someone) the glad eye**).

gladiator ('glædɪ,eɪtə) *n*. **1.** (in ancient Rome) a man trained to fight in arenas to provide entertainment. **2.** a person who supports and fights publicly for a cause. [C16: from L: swordsman, from *gladius* sword] —**gladiatorial** (,glædɪə'tɔ:rɪəl) *adj*.

gladiolus (,glædɪ'əʊləs) *n*., *pl*. **-lus, -li** (-laɪ), *or* **-luses.** any plant of a widely cultivated genus having swordshaped leaves and spikes of funnel-shaped brightly coloured flowers. Also called: **gladiola.** [C16: from L: a small sword, sword lily, from *gladius* a sword]

glad rags *pl. n*. *Inf*. best clothes or clothes used on special occasions.

gladsome ('glædsəm) *adj*. an archaic word for **glad¹.** —**'gladsomely** *adv*. —**'gladsomeness** *n*.

Gladstone ('glædstən) *n*. **William Ewart.** 1809–98, British statesman. He became leader of the Liberal Party in 1867 and was four times prime minister (1868–74; 1880–85; 1886; 1892–94). In his first ministry he disestablished the Irish Church (1869) and introduced educational reform (1870) and the secret ballot (1872). He succeeded in carrying the Reform Act of 1884 but failed to gain support

for a Home Rule Bill for Ireland, to which he devoted much of the latter part of his career.

Gladstone bag *n*. a piece of hand luggage consisting of two equal-sized hinged compartments. [C19: after W. E. GLADSTONE]

Glagolitic (,glægə'lɪtɪk) *adj*. of, relating to, or denoting a Slavic alphabet whose invention is attributed to Saint Cyril. [C19: from NL, from Serbo-Croatian *glagolica* the Glagolitic alphabet]

glair (glɛə) *n*. **1.** white of egg, esp. when used as a size, glaze, or adhesive. **2.** any substance resembling this. ~*vb*. **3.** (*tr*.) to apply glair to (something). [C14: from OF *glaire*, from Vulgar L *clāria* (unattested) CLEAR, from L *clārus*] —**'glairy** *or* **'glaireous** *adj*.

Glamorgan (glə'mɔ:gən) *or* **Glamorganshire** (glə'mɔ:gən,ʃɪə, -ʃə) *n*. (until 1974) a county of SE Wales, now divided into West Glamorgan, Mid Glamorgan, and South Glamorgan.

glamorize, -ise, *or U.S.* (*sometimes*) **glamourize** ('glæmə,raɪz) *vb*. **1.** to cause to be or seem glamorous; romanticize or beautify. —**,glamori'zation** *or* **-i'sation** *n*.

glamorous ('glæmərəs) *adj*. **1.** possessing glamour; alluring and fascinating. **2.** beautiful and smart, esp. in a showy way: *a glamorous woman.* —**'glamorously** *adv*.

glamour *or U.S.* (*sometimes*) **glamor** ('glæmə) *n*. **1.** charm and allure; fascination. **2. a.** fascinating or voluptuous beauty. **b.** (*as modifier*): *a glamour girl.* **3.** *Arch*. a magic spell; charm. [C18: Scot. var. of GRAMMAR (hence a magic spell, because occult practices were popularly associated with learning)]

glance¹ (glɑ:ns) *vb*. **1.** (*intr*.) to look hastily or briefly. **2.** (*intr.;* foll. by *over, through,* etc.) to look over briefly: *to glance through a report.* **3.** (*intr*.) to reflect, glint, or gleam: *the sun glanced on the water.* **4.** (*intr.;* usually foll. by *off*) to depart (from an object struck) at an oblique angle: *the arrow glanced off the tree.* ~*n*. **5.** a hasty or brief look; peep. **6.** a flash or glint of light; gleam. **7.** the act or an instance of an object glancing off another. **8.** a brief allusion. [C15: from *glacen* to strike obliquely, from OF *glacier* to slide (see GLACIS)] —**'glancingly** *adv*.

glance² (glɑ:ns) *n*. any mineral having a metallic lustre. [C19: from G *Glanz* brightness, lustre]

gland¹ (glænd) *n*. **1.** a cell or organ in man and other animals that synthesizes chemical substances and secretes them for the body to use or eliminate, either through a duct (exocrine gland) or directly into the bloodstream (endocrine gland). **2.** a structure, such as a lymph node, that resembles a gland in form. **3.** a cell or organ in plants that synthesizes and secretes a particular substance. [C17: from L *glāns* acorn]

gland² (glænd) *n*. a device that prevents leakage of fluid along a rotating shaft or reciprocating rod passing between areas of high and low pressure. It often consists of a flanged metal sleeve bedding into a stuffing box. [C19: from ?]

glanders ('glændəz) *n*. (*functioning as sing.*) a highly infectious bacterial disease of horses, sometimes communicated to man, characterized by inflammation and ulceration of the mucous membranes of the air passages, skin and lymph glands. [C16: from OF *glandres*, from L *glandulae*, lit.: little acorns, from *glāns* acorn; see GLAND¹]

glandular ('glændjʊlə) *or* **glandulous** ('glændjʊləs) *adj*. of, relating to, containing, functioning as, or affecting a gland. [C18: from L *glandula*, lit.: a little acorn; see GLANDERS] —**'glandularly** *or* **'glandulously** *adv*.

glandular fever *n*. another name for **infectious mononucleosis.**

glandule ('glændju:l) *n*. a small gland.

glans (glænz) *n*., *pl*. **glandes** ('glændi:z). *Anat*. any small rounded body or glandlike mass, such as the head of the penis (**glans penis**). [C17: from L: acorn; see GLAND¹]

glare (glɛə) *vb*. **1.** (*intr*.) to stare angrily; glower. **2.** (*tr*.) to express by glowering. **3.** (*intr*.) (of light, colour, etc.) to be very bright and intense. **4.** (*intr*.) to be dazzlingly ornamented or garish. ~*n*. **5.** an angry stare. **6.** a dazzling light or brilliance. **7.** garish ornamentation or appearance. [C13: prob. from MLow G, MDu. *glaren* to gleam]

glaring ('glɛərɪŋ) *adj*. **1.** conspicuous: *a glaring omission.* **2.** dazzling or garish. —**'glaringly** *adv*. —**'glaringness** *n*.

Glarus (*German* 'gla:rʊs) *n.* **1.** an Alpine canton of E central Switzerland. Capital: Glarus. Pop.: 36 718 (1980). Area 684 sq. km (264 sq. miles). **2.** a town in E central Switzerland, the capital of Glarus canton. Pop.: 5800 (1980). ~French name: **Glaris** (glari).

Glaser ('gleɪzə) *n.* **Donald Arthur.** born 1926, U.S. physicist: invented the bubble chamber; Nobel prize for physics 1960.

Glasgow ('gla:zgəʊ, 'glæz-) *n.* a port in W central Scotland, administrative centre of Strathclyde region on the River Clyde: the largest city in Scotland; centre of a major industrial region, chiefly brewing and engineering; university (1451). Pop.: 733 794 (1985 est.). Related adj.: **Glaswegian.**

glasnost ('glæs,nɒst) *n.* the policy of public frankness and accountability developed in Russia under the leadership of Mikhail Gorbachov. [C20: Russian, lit.: openness]

glass (gla:s) *n.* **1. a.** a hard brittle transparent or translucent noncrystalline solid, consisting of metal silicates or similar compounds. It is made from a fused mixture of oxides, such as lime, silicon dioxide, phosphorus pentoxide, etc. **b.** (*as modifier): a glass bottle.* Related adj.: **vitreous. 2.** something made of glass, esp. a drinking vessel, a barometer, or a mirror. **3.** Also called: **glassful.** the amount or volume contained in a drinking glass: *he drank a glass of wine.* **4.** glassware collectively. **5.** See **fibreglass.** ~*vb.* **6.** (*tr.*) to cover with, enclose in, or fit with glass. [OE *glæs*] —**'glassless** *adj.* —**'glass,like** *adj.*

Glass (gla:s) *n.* **Philip.** born 1937, U.S. avant-garde composer, whose works include *Music in Fifths* (1970), *Music for Voices* (1972), and *North Star* (1975).

glass-blowing *n.* the process of shaping a mass of molten glass by blowing air into it through a tube. —**'glass,blower** *n.*

glasses ('gla:sɪz) *pl. n.* a pair of lenses for correcting faulty vision, in a frame that rests on the bridge of the nose and hooks behind the ears. Also called: **spectacles, eyeglasses.**

glass harmonica *n.* a musical instrument of the 18th century consisting of a set of glass bowls of graduated pitches, played by rubbing the fingers over the moistened rims or by a keyboard mechanism. Sometimes shortened to **harmonica.** Also called: **musical glasses.**

glasshouse ('gla:s,haʊs) *n.* **1.** *Brit.* a glass building, esp. a greenhouse, used for growing plants in protected or controlled conditions. **2.** *Inf., chiefly Brit.* a military detention centre.

glassine (glæ'si:n) *n.* a glazed translucent paper.

glass snake *n.* any snakelike lizard of Europe, Asia, or North America, with vestigial hind limbs and a tail that breaks off easily.

glassware ('gla:s,wɛə) *n.* articles made of glass, esp. drinking glasses.

glass wool *n.* fine spun glass massed into a wool-like bulk, used in insulation, filtering, etc.

glasswort ('gla:s,wɜ:t) *n.* **1.** any plant of salt marshes having fleshy stems and scalelike leaves: formerly used as a source of soda for glass-making. **2.** another name for **saltwort.**

glassy ('gla:sɪ) *adj.* **glassier, glassiest. 1.** resembling glass, esp. in smoothness or transparency. **2.** void of expression, life, or warmth: *a glassy stare.* —**'glassily** *adv.* —**'glassiness** *n.*

Glastonbury ('glæstənbərɪ, -brɪ) *n.* a town in SW England, in Somerset: remains of prehistoric lake villages; the reputed burial place of King Arthur; site of a ruined Benedictine abbey, probably the oldest in England. Pop.: 6773 (1981).

Glaswegian (glæz'wi:dʒən) *adj.* **1.** of or relating to Glasgow or its inhabitants. ~*n.* **2.** a native or inhabitant of Glasgow. [C19: infl. by NORWEGIAN]

Glauber's salt ('glaʊbəz) *or* **Glauber salt** *n.* the crystalline decahydrate of sodium sulphate: used in making glass, detergents and pulp. [C18: after J. R. *Glauber* (1604–68), G chemist]

Glauce ('glɔ:sɪ) *n. Greek myth.* **1.** the second bride of Jason, murdered on her wedding day by Medea, whom Jason had deserted. **2.** a sea nymph, one of the Nereids.

glaucoma (glɔ:'kəʊmə) *n.* a disease of the eye in which increased pressure within the eyeball causes impaired vision, sometimes progressing to blindness. [C17: from L, from Gk, from *glaukos*; see GLAUCOUS] —**glau'comatous** *adj.*

glaucous ('glɔ:kəs) *adj.* **1.** *Bot.* covered with a waxy or powdery bloom. **2.** bluish-green. [C17: from L *glaucus* silvery, bluish-green, from Gk *glaukos*]

glaze (gleɪz) *vb.* **1.** (*tr.*) to fit or cover with glass. **2.** (*tr.*) *Ceramics.* to cover with a vitreous solution, rendering impervious to liquid. **3.** (*tr.*) to cover (foods) with a shiny coating by applying beaten egg, sugar, etc. **4.** (*tr.*) to make glossy or shiny. **5.** (when *intr.*, often foll. by *over*) to become or cause to become glassy: *his eyes were glazing over.* ~*n.* **6.** *Ceramics.* **a.** a vitreous coating. **b.** the substance used to produce such a coating. **7.** a smooth lustrous finish on a fabric produced by applying various chemicals. **8.** something used to give a glossy surface to foods: *a syrup glaze.* [C14 *glasen*, from *glas* GLASS] —**glazed** *adj.* —**'glazer** *n.*

glaze ice *n. Brit.* a thin clear layer of ice caused by the freezing of rain in the air or by refreezing after a thaw.

glazier ('gleɪzɪə) *n.* a person who fits windows, doors, etc., with glass. —**'glaziery** *n.*

glazing ('gleɪzɪŋ) *n.* **1.** the surface of a glazed object. **2.** glass fitted, or to be fitted, in a door, frame, etc.

Glazunov ('glæzʊnɒf; *Russian* gləzu'nɔf) *n.* **Aleksandr Konstantinovich** (alık'sandr kənstan'tinəvitʃ). 1865–1936, Russian composer, in France from 1928. A pupil of Rimsky-Korsakov, he wrote eight symphonies and concertos for piano and for violin among other works.

GLC *abbrev. for* Greater London Council; abolished 1986.

gleam (gli:m) *n.* **1.** a small beam or glow of light, esp. reflected light. **2.** a brief or dim indication: *a gleam of hope.* ~*vb.* (*intr.*) **3.** to send forth or reflect a beam of light. **4.** to appear, esp. briefly. [OE *glǣm*] —**'gleaming** *adj.* —**'gleamingly** *adv.* —**'gleamy** *adj.*

glean (gli:n) *vb.* **1.** to gather (something) slowly and carefully in small pieces: *to glean information.* **2.** to gather (the useful remnants of a crop) from the field after harvesting. [C14: from OF *glener*, from LL *glennāre*, prob. of Celtic origin] —**'gleaner** *n.*

gleanings ('gli:nɪŋz) *pl. n.* the useful remnants of a crop that can be gathered from the field after harvesting.

glebe (gli:b) *n.* **1.** *Brit.* land granted to a clergyman as part of his benefice. **2.** *Poetic.* land, esp. for growing things. [C14: from L *glaeba*]

glee (gli:) *n.* **1.** great merriment; joy. **2.** a type of song originating in 18th-century England, sung by three or more unaccompanied voices. [OE *glēo*]

glee club *n.* Now *chiefly U.S. & Canad.* a society organized for the singing of choral music.

gleeful ('gli:fʊl) *adj.* full of glee; merry. —**'gleefully** *adv.* —**'gleefulness** *n.*

gleeman ('gli:mən) *n., pl.* -**men.** *Obs.* a minstrel.

Gleiwitz ('glaɪvɪts) *n.* the German name for **Gliwice.**

glen (glɛn) *n.* a narrow and deep mountain valley, esp. in Scotland or Ireland. [C15: from Scot. Gaelic *gleann*, from OIrish *glend*]

Glen Albyn ('ælbɪn, 'ɔ:l-) *n.* another name for the **Great Glen.**

Glencoe (glɛn'kəʊ) *n.* a glen in W Scotland, in S Highland region: site of a massacre of Macdonalds by Campbells and English troops (1692).

Glendower (glɛn'daʊə) *n.* **Owen,** Welsh name *Owain Glyndŵr.* ?1350–?1416, Welsh chieftain, who led a revolt against Henry IV's rule in Wales (1400–15).

glengarry (glɛn'gærɪ) *n., pl.* -**ries.** a brimless Scottish cap with a crease down the crown, often with ribbons at the back. Also called: **glengarry bonnet.** [C19: after *Glengarry*, Scotland]

Glen More (mɔ:) *n.* another name for the **Great Glen.**

Glenn (glɛn) *n.* **John.** born 1921, U.S. astronaut and politician. The first American to orbit the earth (Feb., 1962), he later became a senator.

Glenrothes (glɛn'rɒθɪs) *n.* a new town in E central Scotland, the administrative centre of Fife region: founded in 1948. Pop.: 37 400 (1985 est.).

glib (glɪb) *adj.* **glibber, glibbest.** fluent and easy, often in an insincere or deceptive way. [C16: prob. from MLow G *glibberich* slippery] —**'glibly** *adv.* —**'glibness** *n.*

glide (glaɪd) *vb.* **1.** to move or cause to move easily without jerks or hesitations. **2.** (*intr.*) to pass slowly or without perceptible change: *to glide into sleep.* **3.** to cause (an aircraft) to come into land without engine power, or (of an aircraft) to land in this way. **4.** (*intr.*) to fly a glider. **5.** (*intr.*) *Music.* to execute a portamento from one note to another. **6.** (*intr.*) *Phonetics.* to produce a glide. ~n. **7.** a smooth easy movement. **8. a.** any of various dances featuring gliding steps. **b.** a step in such a dance. **9.** a manoeuvre in which an aircraft makes a gentle descent without engine power. **10.** the act or process of gliding. **11.** *Music.* a portamento or slur. **12.** *Phonetics.* a transitional sound as the speech organs pass from the articulatory position of one speech sound to that of the next. [OE *glidan*] — **'glidingly** *adv.*

glide path *n.* the path of an aircraft as it descends to land.

glider ('glaɪdə) *n.* **1.** an aircraft capable of gliding and soaring in air currents without the use of an engine. **2.** a person or thing that glides.

glide time *n.* the N.Z. term for **flexitime.**

glimmer ('glɪmə) *vb.* (*intr.*) **1.** (of a light) to glow faintly or flickeringly. **2.** to be indicated faintly: *hope glimmered in his face.* ~n. **3.** a glow or twinkle of light. **4.** a faint indication. [C14: cf. MHG *glimmern*] — **'glimmeringly** *adv.*

glimpse (glɪmps) *n.* **1.** a brief or incomplete view: *to catch a glimpse of the sea.* **2.** a vague indication. **3.** *Arch.* a glimmer of light. ~vb. **4.** (*tr.*) to catch sight of momentarily. [C14: of Gmc origin; cf. MHG *glimsen* to glimmer] — **'glimpser** *n.*

Glinka (*Russian* 'glinkə) *n.* **Mikhail Ivanovich** (mixa'il i'vanəvitʃ). 1803–57, Russian composer who pioneered the Russian national school of music. His works include the operas *A Life for the Tsar* (1836) and *Russlan and Ludmilla* (1842).

glint (glɪnt) *vb.* **1.** to gleam or cause to gleam brightly. ~n. **2.** a bright gleam or flash. **3.** brightness or gloss. **4.** a brief indication. [C15: prob. from ON]

glioma (glaɪ'əʊmə) *n., pl.* **-mata** (-mətə) *or* **-mas.** a tumour of the brain and spinal cord, composed of neuroglia cells and fibres. [C19: from NL, from Gk *glia* glue + -OMA]

glissade (glɪ'sɑːd, -'seɪd) *n.* **1.** a gliding step in ballet. **2.** a controlled slide down a snow slope. ~vb. **3.** (*intr.*) to perform a glissade. [C19: from F, from *glisser* to slip, from OF *glicier*, of Frankish origin]

glissando (glɪ'sændəʊ) *n., pl.* **-di** (-diː) *or* **-dos.** a rapidly executed series of notes, each of which is discretely audible. [C19: prob. It. var. of GLISSADE]

glisten ('glɪs²n) *vb.* (*intr.*) **1.** (of a wet or glossy surface) to gleam by reflecting light. **2.** (of light) to reflect with brightness: *the sunlight glistens on wet leaves.* ~n. **3.** *Rare.* a gleam or gloss. [OE *glisnian*]

glister ('glɪstə) *vb., n.* an archaic word for **glitter.** [C14: prob. from MDu. *glisteren*]

glitch (glɪtʃ) *n.* **1.** a sudden instance of malfunctioning in an electronic system. **2.** a change in the rotation rate of a pulsar. [C20: from ?]

glitter ('glɪtə) *vb.* (*intr.*) **1.** (of a hard, wet, or polished surface) to reflect light in bright flashes. **2.** (of light) to be reflected in bright flashes. **3.** (usually foll. by *with*) to be decorated or enhanced by the glamour (of): *the show glitters with famous actors.* ~n. **4.** sparkle or brilliance. **5.** show and glamour. **6.** tiny pieces of shiny decorative material. **7.** *Canad.* Also called: **silver thaw.** ice formed from freezing rain. [C14: from ON *glitra*] — **'glitteringly** *adv.* — **'glittery** *adj.*

glitterati (ˌglɪtə'rɑːtiː) *pl. n. Inf.* the leaders of society, esp. the rich and beautiful. [C20: from GLITTER + -*ati* as in LITERATI]

glitzy ('glɪtsɪ) *adj.* **glitzier, glitziest.** *Sl.* showily attractive; flashy or glittery. [C20: prob. via Yiddish from G *glitzern* to glitter]

Gliwice (*Polish* gli'vitsɛ) *n.* an industrial city in S Poland. Pop.: 213 000 (1985 est.). German name: **Gleiwitz.**

gloaming ('gləʊmɪŋ) *n. Scot. or poetic.* twilight or dusk. [OE *glōmung*, from *glōm*]

gloat (gləʊt) *vb.* **1.** (*intr.; often foll. by *over*) to dwell (on) with malevolent smugness or exultation. ~n. **2.** the act of gloating. [C16: prob. of Scand. origin; cf. ON *glotta* to grin, MHG *glotzen* to stare] — **'gloater** *n.*

glob (glɒb) *n. Inf.* a rounded mass of some thick fluid substance. [C20: prob. from GLOBE, infl. by BLOB]

global ('gləʊb²l) *adj.* **1.** covering or relating to the whole world. **2.** comprehensive; total — **'globally** *adv.*

globe (gləʊb) *n.* **1.** a sphere on which a map of the world is drawn. **2. the globe.** the world; the earth. **3.** a planet or some other astronomical body. **4.** an object shaped like a sphere, such as a glass lampshade or fishbowl. **5.** an orb, usually of gold, symbolic of sovereignty. ~vb. **6.**

to form or cause to form into a globe. [C16: from OF, from L *globus*] — **'globe,like** *adj.*

globefish ('gləʊb,fɪʃ) *n., pl.* **-fish** *or* **-fishes.** another name for **puffer.**

globeflower ('gləʊb,flaʊə) *n.* a plant having pale yellow, white, or orange globe-shaped flowers.

globetrotter ('gləʊb,trɒtə) *n.* a habitual worldwide traveller, esp. a tourist. — **'globe,trotting** *n., adj.*

globigerina (gləʊ,bɪdʒə'raɪnə) *n., pl.* **-nas** *or* **-nae** (-niː). **1.** a marine protozoan having a rounded shell with spiny processes. **2. globigerina ooze.** a deposit on the ocean floor consisting of the shells of these protozoans. [C19: from NL, from L *globus* GLOBE + *gerere* to bear]

globoid ('gləʊbɔɪd) *adj.* **1.** shaped like a globe. ~n. **2.** a globoid body.

globose ('gləʊbəʊs, gləʊ'bəʊs) *or* **globous** ('gləʊbəs) *adj.* spherical or approximately spherical. [C15: from L *globōsus*; see GLOBE] — **'globosely** *adv.*

globular ('glɒbjʊlə) *or* **globulous** ('glɒbjʊləs) *adj.* **1.** shaped like a globe or globule. **2.** having or consisting of globules. — **'globularly** *adv.*

globule ('glɒbjuːl) *n.* a small globe, esp. a drop of liquid. [C17: from L *globulus*, dim. of *globus* GLOBE]

globulin ('glɒbjʊlɪn) *n.* any of a group of simple proteins that are generally insoluble in water but soluble in salt solutions.

glockenspiel ('glɒkən,spiːl, -,ʃpiːl) *n.* a percussion instrument consisting of a set of tuned metal plates played with a pair of small hammers. [C19: G, from *Glocken* bells + *Spiel* play]

glomerate ('glɒmərɪt) *adj.* **1.** gathered into a compact rounded mass. **2.** *Anat.* (esp. of glands) conglomerate in structure. [C18: from L *glomerāre*, from *glomus* ball] — **,glome'ration** *n.*

glomerule ('glɒmə,ruːl) *n. Bot.* an inflorescence in the form of a ball-like cluster of flowers. [C18: from NL *glomerulus*]

Glomma (*Norwegian* 'glɒmə) *n.* a river in SE Norway, rising near the border with Sweden and flowing generally south to the Skagerrak: the largest river in Scandinavia; important for hydroelectric power and floating timber. Length: 588 km (365 miles).

gloom (gluːm) *n.* **1.** partial or total darkness. **2.** a state of depression or melancholy. **3.** an appearance or expression of despondency or melancholy. **4.** *Poetic.* a dim or dark place. ~vb. **5.** (*intr.*) to look sullen or depressed. **6.** to make or become dark or gloomy. [C14 *gloumben* to look sullen]

gloomy ('gluːmɪ) *adj.* **gloomier, gloomiest. 1.** dark or dismal. **2.** causing depression, dejection, or gloom: *gloomy news.* **3.** despairing; sad. — **'gloomily** *adv.* — **'gloominess** *n.*

gloria ('glɔːrɪə) *n.* a halo or nimbus, esp. as represented in art. [C16: from L GLORY]

Gloria ('glɔːrɪə, -ɑː) *n.* **1.** any of several doxologies beginning with the word *Gloria.* **2.** a musical setting of one of these.

glorify ('glɔːrɪ,faɪ) *vb.* **-fying, -fied.** (*tr.*) **1.** to make glorious. **2.** to make more splendid; adorn. **3.** to worship, exalt, or adore. **4.** to extol. **5.** to cause to seem more splendid or imposing than reality. — **,glorifi'cation** *n.* — **'glori,fier** *n.*

gloriole ('glɔːrɪ,əʊl) *n.* another name for a **halo.** [C19: from L *glōriola*, lit.: a small GLORY]

glorious ('glɔːrɪəs) *adj.* **1.** having or full of glory; illustrious. **2.** conferring glory or renown: *a glorious victory.* **3.** brilliantly beautiful. **4.** delightful or enjoyable. — **'gloriously** *adv.* — **'gloriousness** *n.*

glory ('glɔːrɪ) *n., pl.* **-ries. 1.** exaltation, praise, or honour. **2.** something that brings or is worthy of praise (esp. in **crowning glory**). **3.** thanksgiving, adoration, or worship: *glory be to God.* **4.** pomp; splendour: *the glory of the king's reign.* **5.** radiant beauty; resplendence: *the glory of the sunset.* **6.** the beauty and bliss of heaven. **7.** a state of extreme happiness or prosperity. **8.** another word for **halo** or **nimbus.** ~vb. **-rying, -ried. 9.** (*intr.; often foll. by *in*) to triumph or exult. ~*interj.* **10.** *Inf.* a mild interjection to express pleasure or surprise (often **glory be!**). [C13: from OF *glorie*, from L *glōria*, from ?]

glory box *n. Austral. & N.Z.* (esp. formerly) a box in which a young woman stores clothes, etc., in preparation for marriage.

glory hole *n.* **1.** a cupboard or storeroom, esp. one which is very untidy. **2.** *Naut.* another term for **lazaretto** (sense 1).

Glos *abbrev. for* Gloucestershire.

gloss[1] (glɒs) *n.* **1. a.** lustre or sheen, as of a smooth surface. **b.** (*as modifier*): *gloss paint.* **2.** a superficially attractive appearance. **3.** a cosmetic used to give a sheen. ~*vb.* **4.** to give a gloss to or obtain a gloss. **5.** (*tr.*; often foll. by *over*) to hide under a deceptively attractive surface or appearance. [C16: prob. of Scand. origin] — **'glosser** *n.*

gloss[2] (glɒs) *n.* **1.** a short or expanded explanation or interpretation of a word, expression, or foreign phrase in the margin or text of a manuscript, etc. **2.** an intentionally misleading explanation. **3.** short for **glossary.** ~*vb.* (*tr.*) **4.** to add glosses to. **5.** (often foll. by *over*) to give a false or misleading interpretation of. [C16: from L *glōssa* unusual word requiring explanatory note, from Ionic Gk] — **'glosser** *n.*

glossary ('glɒsərɪ) *n., pl.* **-ries.** an alphabetical list of terms peculiar to a field of knowledge with explanations. [C14: from LL *glossārium;* see GLOSS[2]] —**glossarial** (glɒ'sɛərɪəl) *adj.* — **'glossarist** *n.*

glosseme ('glɒsi:m) *n.* the smallest meaningful unit of a language, such as stress, form, etc. [C20: from Gk; see GLOSS[2], -EME]

glossitis (glɒ'saɪtɪs) *n.* inflammation of the tongue. — **glossitic** (glɒ'sɪtɪk) *adj.*

glosso- *or before a vowel* **gloss-** *combining form.* indicating a tongue or language: *glossolaryngeal.* [from Gk *glossa* tongue]

glossolalia (ˌglɒsə'leɪlɪə) *n.* another term for **gift of tongues.** [C19: NL, from GLOSSO- + Gk *lalein* to babble]

glossy ('glɒsɪ) *adj.* **glossier, glossiest. 1.** smooth and shiny; lustrous. **2.** superficially attractive; plausible. **3.** (of a magazine) lavishly produced on shiny paper. ~*n., pl.* **glossies. 4.** Also called (U.S.): **slick.** an expensively produced magazine, printed on shiny paper and containing high-quality colour photography. **5.** a photograph printed on paper that has a smooth shiny surface. — **'glossily** *adv.* — **'glossiness** *n.*

glottal ('glɒt³l) *adj.* **1.** of or relating to the glottis. **2.** *Phonetics.* articulated or pronounced at or with the glottis.

glottal stop *n.* a plosive speech sound produced by tightly closing the glottis and allowing the air pressure to build up before opening the glottis, causing the air to escape with force.

glottis ('glɒtɪs) *n., pl.* **-tises** *or* **-tides** (-tɪˌdi:z). the vocal apparatus of the larynx, consisting of the two true vocal cords and the opening between them. [C16: from NL, from Gk, from Attic form of Ionic *glōssa* tongue; see GLOSS[2]]

Gloucester[1] ('glɒstə) *n.* a city in SW England, administrative centre of Gloucestershire, on the River Severn; cathedral (founded 1100). Pop.: 92 200 (1983 est.). Latin name: **Glevum** ('gli:vʊm).

Gloucester[2] ('glɒstə) *n.* **1. Humphrey,** Duke of. 1391–1447, English soldier and statesman; son of Henry IV. He acted as protector during Henry VI's minority (1422–29) and was noted for his patronage of humanists. **2. Duke of.** See **Richard III. 3. Duke of.** See **Thomas of Woodstock.**

Gloucestershire ('glɒstəˌʃɪə, -ʃə) *n.* a county of SW England, situated around the lower Severn valley: includes the Forest of Dean and the main part of the Cotswold Hills. Administrative centre: Gloucester. Pop.: 506 100 (1983 est.). Area: 2643 sq. km (1020 sq. miles). Abbrev.: **Glos.**

glove (glʌv) *n.* **1.** (*often pl.*) a shaped covering for the hand with individual sheaths for the fingers and thumb, made of leather, fabric, etc. **2.** any of various large protective hand covers worn in sports, such as a boxing glove. ~*vb.* **3.** (*tr.*) to cover or provide with or as if with gloves. [OE *glōfe*]

glove box *n.* a closed box in which toxic or radioactive substances can be handled by an operator who places his hands through protective gloves sealed to the box.

glove compartment *n.* a small compartment in a car dashboard for the storage of miscellaneous articles.

glover ('glʌvə) *n.* a person who makes or sells gloves.

glow (gləʊ) *n.* **1.** light emitted by a substance or object at a high temperature. **2.** a steady even light without flames. **3.** brilliance of colour. **4.** brightness of complexion. **5.** a

feeling of well-being or satisfaction. **6.** intensity of emotion. ~*vb.* (*intr.*) **7.** to emit a steady even light without flames. **8.** to shine intensely, as if from great heat. **9.** to be exuberant, as from excellent health or intense emotion. **10.** to experience a feeling of wellbeing or satisfaction: *to glow with pride.* **11.** (esp. of the complexion) to show a strong bright colour, esp. red. **12.** to be very hot. [OE *glōwan*]

glow discharge *n.* a silent luminous discharge of electricity through a low-pressure gas.

glower ('glaʊə) *vb.* **1.** (*intr.*) to stare hard and angrily. ~*n.* **2.** a sullen or angry stare. [C16: prob. of Scand. origin] — **'gloweringly** *adv.*

glowing ('gləʊɪŋ) *adj.* **1.** emitting light without flames: *glowing embers.* **2.** warm and rich in colour: *glowing shades of gold and orange.* **3.** flushed and rosy: *glowing cheeks.* **4.** displaying or indicative of extreme pride or emotion: *a glowing account of his son's achievements.*

glow-worm *n.* a European beetle, the females and larvae of which bear luminescent organs producing a soft greenish light.

gloxinia (glɒk'sɪnɪə) *n.* any of several tropical plants cultivated for their large white, red, or purple bell-shaped flowers. [C19: after Benjamin P. *Gloxin,* 18th-cent. G physician & botanist]

gloze (gləʊz) *vb. Arch.* **1.** (*tr.*; often foll. by *over*) to explain away; minimize the effect or importance of. **2.** to make explanatory notes or glosses on (a text). **3.** to use flattery (on). [C13: from OF *gloser* to comment; see GLOSS[2]]

Gluck (*German* glʊk) *n.* **Christoph Willibald von** ('krɪstɔf 'vɪlɪbalt fɔn). 1714–87, German composer, esp. of operas, including *Orfeo ed Euridice* (1762) and *Alceste* (1767).

glucose ('glu:kəʊz, -kəʊs) *n.* **1.** a white crystalline sugar, the most abundant form being dextrose. Formula: $C_6H_{12}O_6$. **2.** a yellowish syrup obtained by incomplete hydrolysis of starch: used in confectionery, fermentation, etc. [C19: from F, from Gk *gleukos* sweet wine; rel. to Gk *glukus* sweet]

glucoside ('glu:kəʊˌsaɪd) *n. Biochem.* any of a large group of glycosides that yield glucose on hydrolysis. — **glucosidic** (ˌglu:kəʊ'sɪdɪk) *adj.*

glue (glu:) *n.* **1.** any natural or synthetic adhesive, esp. a sticky gelatinous substance prepared by boiling animal products such as bones, skin, and horns. **2.** any other sticky or adhesive substance. ~*vb.* **gluing** *or* **glueing, glued. 3.** (*tr.*) to join or stick together as with glue. [C14: from OF *glu,* from LL *glūs*] — **'glue,like** *adj.* — **'gluer** *n.* — **'gluey** *adj.*

glue-sniffing *n.* the practice of inhaling the fumes of certain types of glue to produce intoxicating or hallucinatory effects. — **'glue-,sniffer** *n.*

gluhwein ('glu:,vaɪn) *n.* mulled wine. [G]

glum (glʌm) *adj.* **glummer, glummest.** silent or sullen, as from gloom. [C16: var. of GLOOM] — **'glumly** *adv.* — **'glumness** *n.*

glume (glu:m) *n. Bot.* one of a pair of dry membranous bracts at the base of the spikelet of grasses. [C18: from L *glūma* husk of corn] — **glu'maceous** *adj.*

gluon ('glu:ɒn) *n.* a hypothetical particle believed to be exchanged between quarks in order to bind them together to form particles. [C20: coined from GLUE + -ON]

glut (glʌt) *n.* **1.** an excessive amount, as in the production of a crop. **2.** the act of glutting or state of being glutted. ~*vb.* **glutting, glutted.** (*tr.*) **3.** to feed or supply beyond capacity. **4.** to supply (a market, etc.) with a commodity in excess of the demand for it. [C14: prob. from OF *gloutir,* from L *gluttīre;* see GLUTTON[1]]

glutamic acid (glu:'tæmɪk) *n.* an amino acid, occurring in proteins.

gluten ('glu:t³n) *n.* a protein present in cereal grains, esp. wheat. [C16: from L: GLUE] — **'glutenous** *adj.*

gluteus (glu'ti:əs) *n., pl.* **-tei** (-'ti:aɪ). any one of the three large muscles that form the human buttock. [C17: from NL, from Gk *gloutos* buttock, rump] — **glu'teal** *adj.*

glutinous ('glu:tɪnəs) *adj.* resembling glue in texture; sticky. — **'glutinously** *adv.*

glutton[1] ('glʌt³n) *n.* **1.** a person devoted to eating and drinking to excess; greedy person. **2.** a person who has or appears to have a voracious appetite for something: *a glutton for punishment.* [C13: from OF *glouton,* from L from *gluttire* to swallow] —'**gluttonous** *adj.* —'**gluttonously** *adv.*

glutton[2] ('glʌt³n) *n.* another name for **wolverine**. [C17: from GLUTTON[1], apparently translating G *Vielfass* great eater]

gluttony ('glʌtənɪ) *n.*, *pl.* **-tonies.** the act or practice of eating to excess.

glyceride ('glɪsə,raɪd) *n.* any fatty-acid ester of glycerol.

glycerin ('glɪsərɪn) *or* **glycerine** ('glɪsəri:n, ,glɪsə'ri:n) *n.* another name (not in technical usage) for **glycerol**. [C19: from F, from Gk *glukeros* sweet + *-ine* -IN; rel. to Gk *glukus* sweet]

glycerol ('glɪsə,rɒl) *n.* a colourless odourless syrupy liquid: a by-product of soap manufacture, used as a solvent, antifreeze, plasticizer, and sweetener (**E422**). Formula: $CH_2OHCHOHCH_2OH$. [C19: from GLYCER(IN) + -OL[1]]

glycine ('glaɪsi:n, glaɪ'si:n) *n.* a white sweet crystalline amino acid occurring in most proteins. [C19: GLYCO- + -INE[2]]

glyco- *or before a vowel* **glyc-** *combining form.* sugar: *glycogen.* [from Gk *glukus* sweet]

glycogen ('glaɪkəʊdʒən) *n.* a polysaccharide consisting of glucose units: the form in which carbohydrate is stored in animals. —**glycogenic** (,glaɪkəʊ'dʒɛnɪk) *adj.* —,**glyco'genesis** *n.*

glycol ('glaɪkɒl) *n.* another name (not in technical usage) for **ethanediol.**

glycolic acid (glaɪ'kɒlɪk) *n.* a colourless crystalline compound found in sugar cane and sugar beet: used in the manufacture of pharmaceuticals, pesticides, and plasticizers.

glycolysis (glaɪ'kɒlɪsɪs) *n.* *Biochem.* the breakdown of glucose by enzymes with the liberation of energy.

glycoside ('glaɪkəʊ,saɪd) *n.* any of a group of substances derived from simple sugars by replacing the hydroxyl group by another group. —**glycosidic** (,glaɪkəʊ'sɪdɪk) *adj.*

glycosuria (,glaɪkəʊ'sjʊərɪə) *n.* the presence of excess sugar in the urine, as in diabetes. [C19: from NL, from F *glycose* GLUCOSE + -URIA]

Glyndebourne ('glaɪnd,bɔːn) *n.* an estate in SE England, in East Sussex: site of a famous annual festival of opera founded in 1934 by John Christie.

glyph (glɪf) *n.* **1.** a carved channel or groove, esp. a vertical one. **2.** *Now rare.* another word for **hieroglyphic.** [C18: from F, from Gk, from *gluphein* to carve] —'**glyphic** *adj.*

glyptic ('glɪptɪk) *adj.* of or relating to engraving or carving, esp. on precious stones. [C19: from F, from Gk, from *gluphein* to carve]

glyptodont ('glɪptə,dɒnt) *n.* an extinct mammal of South America that resembled the giant armadillo. [C19: from Gk *gluptos* carved + -ODONT]

GM *abbrev. for:* **1.** general manager. **2.** (in Britain) George Medal. **3.** Grand Master.

G-man *n.*, *pl.* **G-men. 1.** *U.S. sl.* an FBI agent. **2.** *Irish.* a political detective.

Gmc *abbrev. for* Germanic.

GMT *abbrev. for* Greenwich Mean Time.

GMWU (in Britain) *abbrev. for* National Union of General and Municipal Workers.

gnarl (nɑːl) *n.* **1.** any knotty swelling on a tree. ~*vb.* **2.** (*tr.*) to knot or cause to knot. [C19: back formation from *gnarled*]

gnarled (nɑːld) *or* **gnarly** *adj.* **1.** having gnarls: *the gnarled trunk of the old tree.* **2.** (esp. of hands) rough, twisted, and weather-beaten.

gnash (næʃ) *vb.* **1.** to grind (the teeth) together, as in pain or anger. **2.** (*tr.*) to bite or chew as by grinding the teeth. ~*n.* **3.** the act of gnashing the teeth. [C15: prob. from ON; cf. *gnastan* gnashing of teeth]

gnat (næt) *n.* any of various small fragile biting two-winged insects. [OE *gnætt*]

gnathic ('næθɪk) *adj.* *Anat.* of or relating to the jaw. [C19: from Gk *gnathos* jaw]

-gnathous *adj.* *combining form.* indicating or having a jaw of a specified kind: *prognathous.* [from NL, from Gk *gnathos* jaw]

gnaw (nɔː) *vb.* **gnawing, gnawed; gnawed** *or* **gnawn. 1.** (when *intr.*, often foll. by *at* or *upon*) to bite (at) or chew (upon) constantly so as to wear away little by little. **2.** (*tr.*) to form by gnawing: *to gnaw a hole.* **3.** to cause erosion of (something). **4.** (when *intr.*, often foll. by *at*) to

cause constant distress or anxiety (to). ~*n.* **5.** the act or an instance of gnawing. [OE *gnagan*]

gnawing ('nɔːɪŋ) *n.* a dull persistent pang or pain, esp. of hunger.

gneiss (naɪs) *n.* any coarse-grained metamorphic rock that is banded or foliated. [C18: from G *Gneis*, prob. from MHG *ganeist* spark] —'**gneissic, 'gneissoid,** *or* '**gneissose** *adj.*

gnocchi ('nɒkɪ) *pl. n.* dumplings made of pieces of semolina pasta, or sometimes potato, served with cheese sauce. [It., pl. of *gnocco* lump, prob. of Gmc origin]

gnome (nəʊm) *n.* **1.** one of a species of legendary creatures, usually resembling small misshapen old men, said to live in the depths of the earth and guard buried treasure. **2.** the statue of a gnome, esp. in a garden. **3.** a very small or ugly person. **4.** *Facetious or derog.* an international banker or financier (esp. in **gnomes of Zürich**). [C18: from F, from NL *gnomus*, coined by Paracelsus (1493-1541), Swiss alchemist, from ?] —'**gnomish** *adj.*

gnomic ('nəʊmɪk, 'nɒm-) *adj.* of or relating to aphorisms; pithy. —'**gnomically** *adv.*

gnomon ('nəʊmɒn) *n.* **1.** the stationary arm that projects the shadow on a sundial. **2.** a geometric figure remaining after a parallelogram has been removed from one corner of a larger parallelogram. [C16: from L, from Gk: interpreter, from *gignōskein* to know] —'**gno'monic** *adj.*

-gnosis *n. combining form.* (esp. in medicine) recognition or knowledge: *diagnosis.* [via L from Gk: knowledge] —**-gnostic** *adj. combining form.*

gnostic ('nɒstɪk) *adj.* of, relating to, or possessing knowledge, esp. spiritual knowledge.

Gnostic ('nɒstɪk) *n.* **1.** an adherent of Gnosticism. ~*adj.* **2.** of or relating to Gnostics or to Gnosticism. [C16: from LL, from Gk *gnōstikos* relating to knowledge]

Gnosticism ('nɒstɪ,sɪzəm) *n.* a religious movement characterized by a belief in intuitive spiritual knowledge: regarded as a heresy by the Christian Church.

gnotobiotic (,nəʊtəʊbaɪ'ɒtɪk) *adj.* of or pertaining to germ-free conditions, esp. in a laboratory in which animals are injected with known strains of organisms. [C20: from Gk *gnōtos*, from *gignōskein* to know + BIOTIC]

GNP *abbrev. for* gross national product.

gnu (nuː) *n.*, *pl.* **gnus** *or* **gnu.** either of two sturdy antelopes inhabiting the savannas of Africa, having an ox-like head and a long tufted tail. Also called: **wildebeest.** [C18: from Xhosa *nqu*]

go (gəʊ) *vb.* **going, went, gone.** (*mainly intr.*) **1.** to move or proceed, esp. to or from a point or in a certain direction: *go home.* **2.** (*tr.*; *takes an infinitive*, often with *to* omitted or replaced by *and*) to proceed towards a particular person or place with some specified purpose: *I must go and get that book.* **3.** to depart: *we'll have to go at eleven.* **4.** to start, as in a race: often used in commands. **5.** to make regular journeys: *this train service goes to the east coast.* **6.** to operate or function effectively: *the radio won't go.* **7.** (*copula*) to become: *his face went red.* **8.** to make a noise as specified: *the gun went bang.* **9.** to enter into a specified state or condition: *to go into hysterics.* **10.** to be or continue to be in a specified state or condition: *to go in rags; to go in poverty.* **11.** to lead, extend, or afford access: *this route goes to the north.* **12.** to proceed towards an activity: *to go to sleep.* **13.** (*tr.*; *takes an infinitive*) to serve or contribute: *this letter goes to prove my point.* **14.** to follow a course as specified: *the lecture went badly.* **15.** to be applied or allotted to a particular purpose or recipient: *his money went on drink.* **16.** to be sold: *the necklace went for three thousand pounds.* **17.** to be ranked; compare: *this meal is good as my meals go.* **18.** to blend or harmonize: *these chairs won't go with the rest of your furniture.* **19.** (foll. by *by* or *under*) to be known (by a name or disguise). **20.** to have a usual or proper place: *those books go on this shelf.* **21.** (of music, poetry, etc.) to be sounded; expressed, etc.: *how does that song go?* **22.** to fail or give way: *my eyesight is going.* **23.** to break down or collapse abruptly: *the ladder went at the critical moment.* **24.** to die: *the old man went at 2 a.m.* **25.** (often foll. by *by*) **a.** (of time, etc.) to elapse: *the hours go by so slowly.* **b.** to travel past: *the train goes by her house.* **c.** to be guided (by). **26.** to occur: *happiness does not always go with riches.* **27.** to be eliminated, abolished, or given up: *this entry must go to save space.* **28.** to be spent or finished: *all his money has gone.* **29.** to attend: *go to school.* **30.**

to join a stated profession: *go on the stage.* **31.** (foll. by *to*) to have recourse (to); turn: *to go to arbitration.* **32.** (foll. by *to*) to subject or put oneself (to): *she goes to great pains to please him.* **33.** to proceed, esp. up to or beyond certain limits: *you will go too far one day and then you will be punished.* **34.** to be acceptable or tolerated: *anything goes.* **35.** to carry the weight of final authority: *what the boss says goes.* **36.** (*tr.*) *Nonstandard.* to say: *Then she goes, "Give it to me!" and she just snatched it.* **37.** (foll. by *into*) to be contained in: *four goes into twelve three times.* **38.** (often foll. by *for*) to endure or last out: *we can't go for much longer without water.* **39.** (*tr.*) *Cards.* to bet or bid: *I go two hearts.* **40. be going.** to intend or be about to start (to do or be doing something): often used as an alternative future construction: *what's going to happen to us?* **41. go and.** *Inf.* to be so foolish or unlucky as to: *then she had to go and lose her hat.* **42. go it.** *Sl.* to do something or move energetically. **43. go it alone.** *Inf.* to act or proceed without allies or help. **44. go one better.** *Inf.* to surpass or outdo (someone). **45. let go. a.** to relax one's hold (on); release. **b.** to discuss or consider no further. **46. let oneself go. a.** to act in an uninhibited manner. **b.** to lose interest in one's appearance, manners, etc. **47. to go. a.** remaining. **b.** *U.S. & Canad. inf.* (of food served by a restaurant) for taking away. ~*n., pl.* **goes.** **48.** the act of going. **49. a.** an attempt or try: *he had a go at the stamp business.* **b.** an attempt at stopping a person suspected of a crime: *the police are not always in favour of the public having a go.* **c.** an attack, esp. verbal: *she had a real go at them.* **50.** a turn: *it's my go next.* **51.** *Inf.* the quality of being active and energetic: *she has much more go than I.* **52.** *Inf.* hard or energetic work: *it's all go.* **53.** *Inf.* a successful venture or achievement: *he made a go of it.* **54.** *Inf.* a bargain or agreement. **55. from the word go.** *Inf.* from the very beginning. **56. no go.** *Inf.* impossible; abortive or futile: *it's no go, I'm afraid.* **57. on the go.** *Inf.* active and energetic. ~*adj.* **58.** (*postpositive*) *Inf.* functioning properly and ready for action: esp. used in astronautics: *all systems are go.* ~See also **go about, go against,** etc. [OE *gān*]

Goa ('gəuə) *n.* a state on the W coast of India: a Portuguese overseas territory from 1510 until annexed by India in 1961. Area: 3496 sq. km (1363 sq. miles).

Goa, Daman, and Diu *n.* a former Union Territory of India consisting of the widely separated districts of Goa and Daman and the island of Diu. Capital: Panaji. Area: 3814 sq. km (1472 sq. miles).

go about *vb.* (*intr.*) **1.** (*prep.*) to busy oneself with: *to go about one's duties.* **2.** (*prep.*) to tackle (a problem or task). **3.** (*prep.*) to circulate (in): *there's a lot of flu going about.* **4.** (*adv.*) (of a sailing ship) to change from one tack to another.

goad (gəud) *n.* **1.** a sharp pointed stick for urging on cattle, etc. **2.** anything that acts as a spur or incitement. ~*vb.* **3.** (*tr.*) to drive as if with a goad; spur; incite. [OE *gād*, of Gmc origin]

go against *vb.* (*intr., prep.*) **1.** to be contrary to (principles or beliefs). **2.** to be unfavourable to (a person): *the case went against him.*

go-ahead *n.* **1.** (usually preceded by *the*) *Inf.* permission to proceed. ~*adj.* **2.** enterprising or ambitious.

goal (gəul) *n.* **1.** the aim or object towards which an endeavour is directed. **2.** the terminal point of a journey or race. **3.** (in various sports) the net, basket, etc., into or over which players try to propel the ball, puck, etc., to score. **4.** *Sport.* **a.** a successful attempt at scoring. **b.** the score so made. **5.** (in soccer, hockey, etc.) the position of goalkeeper. [C16: ? rel. to ME *gol* boundary, OE *gælan* to hinder] —'**goalless** *adj.*

goalie ('gəuli) *n. Inf.* short for **goalkeeper.**

goalkeeper ('gəul,ki:pə) *n. Sport.* a player in the goal whose duty is to prevent the ball, puck, etc., from entering or crossing it.

goal kick *n. Soccer.* a kick taken from the six-yard line by the defending team after the ball has been put out of play by an opposing player.

goal line *n. Sport.* the line marking each end of the pitch, on which the goals stand.

go along *vb.* (*intr., adv.;* often foll. by *with*) to refrain from disagreement; assent.

goal post *n.* **1.** either of two upright posts supporting the crossbar of a goal. **2. move the goal posts.** to change the target required during negotiations, etc.

goanna (gəu'ænə) *n.* any of various Australian monitor lizards. [C19: from IGUANA]

goat (gəut) *n.* **1.** any sure-footed agile ruminant mammal with hollow horns, naturally inhabiting rough stony ground in Europe, Asia, and N Africa. **2.** *Inf.* a lecherous man. **3.** a foolish person. **4. get (someone's) goat.** *Sl.* to cause annoyance to (someone). [OE *gāt*] —'**goatish** *adj.*

go at *vb.* (*intr., prep.*) **1.** to make an energetic attempt at (something). **2.** to attack vehemently.

Goat (gəut) *n.* **the.** the constellation Capricorn, the tenth sign of the zodiac.

goatee (gəu'ti:) *n.* a pointed tuftlike beard on the chin. [C19: from GOAT + *-ee* (see -Y²)]

goatherd ('gəut,hɜ:d) *n.* a person employed to tend or herd goats.

goatsbeard *or* **goat's-beard** ('gəuts,biəd) *n.* **1.** Also called: **Jack-go-to-bed-at-noon.** a Eurasian plant of the composite family, with woolly stems and large heads of yellow rayed flowers. **2.** an American plant with long spikes of small white flowers.

goatskin ('gəut,skin) *n.* **1.** the hide of a goat. **2.** something made from the hide of a goat, such as leather or a container for wine.

goatsucker ('gəut,sʌkə) *n.* the U.S. and Canad. name for **nightjar.**

gob¹ (gob) *n.* **1.** a lump or chunk, esp. of a soft substance. **2.** (*often pl.*) *Inf.* a great quantity or amount. **3.** *Inf.* a globule of spittle or saliva. ~*vb.* **gobbing, gobbed.** **4.** (*intr.*) *Brit. inf.* to spit. [C14: from OF *gobe* lump, from *gober;* see GOBBET]

gob² (gob) *n.* a slang word (esp. Brit.) for the **mouth.** [C16: ?from Gaelic *gob*]

go back *vb.* (*intr., adv.*) **1.** to return. **2.** (often foll. by *to*) to originate (in): *the links with France go back to the Norman Conquest.* **3.** (foll. by *on*) to change one's mind about; repudiate (esp. in **go back on one's word**).

gobbet ('gobit) *n.* a chunk, lump, or fragment, esp. of raw meat. [C14: from OF *gobet*, from *gobe* or gulp down]

Gobbi (*Italian* 'gɔbbi) *n.* **Tito** ('ti:to). 1915–84, Italian operatic baritone.

gobble¹ ('gɒb³l) *vb.* **1.** (when *tr.*, often foll. by *up*) to eat or swallow (food) hastily and in large mouthfuls. **2.** (*tr.*; often foll. by *up*) *Inf.* to snatch. [C17: prob. from GOB¹]

gobble² ('gɒb³l) *n.* **1.** the loud rapid gurgling sound made by male turkeys. ~*vb.* **2.** (*intr.*) (of a turkey) to make this sound. [C17: prob. imit.]

gobbledegook *or* **gobbledygook** ('gɒb³l dɪ,guːk) *n.* pretentious language, esp. as characterized by obscure phraseology. [C20: whimsical formation from GOBBLE²]

gobbler ('gɒblə) *n. Inf.* a male turkey.

Gobelin ('gəubəlin; *French* gɔblɛ̃) *adj.* **1.** of or resembling tapestry made at the Gobelins' factory in Paris, having vivid pictorial scenes. ~*n.* **2.** a tapestry of this kind. [C19: from the *Gobelin* family, who founded the factory]

go-between *n.* a person who acts as agent or intermediary for two people or groups in a transaction or dealing.

Gobi ('gəubi) *n.* a desert in E Asia, mostly in the Mongolian People's Republic and the Inner Mongolian Autonomous Region of China: sometimes considered to include all the arid regions east of the Pamirs and north of the plateau of Tibet and the Great Wall of China: one of the largest deserts in the world. Length: about 1600 km (1000 miles). Width: about 1000 km (625 miles). Average height: 900 m (3000 ft.). Chinese name: **Shamo.** —'**Gobian** *adj.*

goblet ('gɒblit) *n.* **1.** a vessel for drinking, with a base and stem but without handles. **2.** *Arch.* a large drinking cup. [C14: from OF *gobelet* a little cup, from *gobel*, ult. of Celtic origin]

goblin ('gɒblin) *n.* (in folklore) a small grotesque supernatural creature, regarded as malevolent towards human beings. [C14: from OF, from MHG *kobolt;* cf. COBALT]

gobo ('gəubəu) *n., pl.* **-bos** *or* **-boes.** a shield placed round a microphone to exclude unwanted sounds, or round a camera lens, etc., to reduce the incident light. [C20: from ?]

gobsmacked ('gɒb,smækt) *adj. Brit. Sl.* astounded; astonished. [C20: from GOB² + SMACK]

goby ('gəʊbɪ) n., pl. **-by** or **-bies**. a small spiny-finned fish of coastal or brackish waters, having a large head, an elongated tapering body, and the ventral fins modified as a sucker. [C18: from L *gōbius* gudgeon from Gk *kōbios*]

go by vb. (*intr.*) **1.** to pass: *as the years go by*. **2.** (*prep.*) to be guided by: *in the darkness we could only go by the stars*. **3.** (*prep.*) to use as a basis for forming an opinion or judgment: *it's wise not to go only by appearances*.

go-by n. Sl. a deliberate snub or slight (esp. in **give** (a **person**) **the go-by**).

go-cart n. See **kart**.

god (gɒd) n. **1.** a supernatural being, who is worshipped as the controller of some part of the universe or some aspect of life in the world or is the personification of some force. **2.** an image, idol, or symbolic representation of such a deity. **3.** any person or thing to which excessive attention is given: *money was his god*. **4.** a man who has qualities regarded as making him superior to other men. **5.** (*pl.*) the gallery of a theatre. [OE *god*]

God (gɒd) n. **1.** the sole Supreme Being, eternal, spiritual, and transcendent, who is the Creator and ruler of all and is infinite in all attributes; the object of worship in monotheistic religions. ~*interj.* **2.** an oath or exclamation used to indicate surprise, annoyance, etc. (and in such expressions as **My God!** or **God Almighty!**).

Godard (*French* gɔdar) n. **Jean-Luc** (ʒɑ̃lyk). born 1930, French film director and writer. Influenced by surrealism, his early works explored the political and documentary use of film. His works include *A bout de souffle* (1960), *Weekend* (1967), *Pravda* (1969), and *Je vous salue, Marie* (1985).

Godavari (gəʊˈdɑːvərɪ) n. a river in central India, rising in the Western Ghats and flowing southeast to the Bay of Bengal: extensive delta, linked by canal with the Krishna delta; a sacred river to Hindus. Length: about 1500 km (900 miles).

godchild ('gɒd,tʃaɪld) n., pl. **-children**. a person who is sponsored by adults at baptism.

Goddard ('gɒdɑːd) n. **Robert Hutchings**. 1882–1945, U.S. physicist. He made the first workable liquid-fuelled rocket.

goddaughter ('gɒd,dɔːtə) n. a female godchild.

goddess ('gɒdɪs) n. **1.** a female divinity. **2.** a woman who is adored or idealized, esp. by a man.

Godefroy de Bouillon (*French* gɔdfrwa də bujɔ̃) n. ?1060–1100, French leader of the First Crusade (1096–99), becoming first ruler of the Latin kingdom of Jerusalem.

Gödel ('gɜːdəl) n. **Kurt** (kʊrt). 1906–78, U.S. logician and mathematician, born in Austria-Hungary. He showed (**Gödel's proof**) that in a formal axiomatic system, such as logic or mathematics, it is impossible to prove consistency without using methods from outside the system.

Goderich ('gəʊdrɪtʃ) n. **Viscount**, title of *Frederick John Robinson*, 1st Earl of Ripon. 1782–1859, British statesman; prime minister (1827–28).

Godesberg (*German* 'gɔːdəsbɛrk) n. a town and spa in West Germany, in North Rhine-Westphalia on the Rhine: a SE suburb of Bonn. Official name: **Bad Godesberg**.

godetia (gəˈdiːʃə) n. any plant of the American genus *Godetia*, esp. one grown as a showy-flowered annual garden plant. [C19: after C. H. *Godet* (died 1879), Swiss botanist]

godfather ('gɒd,fɑːðə) n. **1.** a male godparent. **2.** the head of a Mafia family or other criminal ring.

God-fearing adj. pious; devout.

godforsaken ('gɒdfə,seɪkən) adj. (*sometimes cap.*) **1.** (*usually prenominal*) desolate; dreary; forlorn. **2.** wicked.

Godhead ('gɒd,hɛd) n. (*sometimes not cap.*) **1.** the essential nature and condition of being God. **2. the Godhead**. God.

godhood ('gɒd,hʊd) n. the state of being divine.

Godiva (gəˈdaɪvə) n. **Lady**. ?1040–1080, wife of Leofric, Earl of Mercia. According to legend, she rode naked through Coventry in order to obtain remission for the townspeople from the heavy taxes imposed by her husband.

godless ('gɒdlɪs) adj. **1.** wicked or unprincipled. **2.** lacking a god. **3.** refusing to acknowledge God. —'**godlessly** adv. —'**godlessness** n.

godlike ('gɒd,laɪk) adj. resembling or befitting a god or God; divine.

godly ('gɒdlɪ) adj. **-lier, -liest**. having a religious character; pious; devout. —'**godliness** n.

godmother ('gɒd,mʌðə) n. a female godparent.

Godolphin (gəˈdɒlfɪn) n. **Sidney**. 1st Earl of Godolphin. 1645–1712, English statesman; as Lord Treasurer, he managed the financing of Marlborough's campaigns in the War of the Spanish Succession.

godown ('gəʊ,daʊn) n. (in the East, esp. in India) a warehouse. [C16: from Malay *godong*]

go down vb. (*intr., mainly adv.*) **1.** (*also prep.*) to move or lead to or as if to a lower place or level; sink, decline, decrease, etc. **2.** to be defeated; lose. **3.** to be remembered or recorded (esp. in **go down in history**). **4.** to be received: *his speech went down well*. **5.** (of food) to be swallowed. **6.** *Brit.* to leave a college or university at the end of a term. **7.** (usually foll. by *with*) to fall ill; be infected. **8.** (of a celestial body) to sink or set.

godparent ('gɒd,pɛərənt) n. a person who stands sponsor to another at baptism.

God's acre n. Literary. a churchyard or burial ground. [C17: translation of G *Gottesacker*]

godsend ('gɒd,sɛnd) n. a person or thing that comes unexpectedly but is particularly welcome. [C19: from C17 *God's send*, alteration of *goddes sand* God's message, from OE *sand*; see SEND]

godson ('gɒd,sʌn) n. a male godchild.

Godspeed ('gɒd'spiːd) *sentence substitute, n.* an expression of good wishes for a person's success and safety. [C15: from *God spede* may God prosper (you)]

Godthaab (*Danish* 'gɒdhɔːb) n. the capital of Greenland, in the southwest on **Godthaab Fiord**: the oldest Danish settlement in Greenland, founded in 1721. Pop.: 11 209 (1986).

Godunov ('gɒdə,nɒf, 'gʊd-; *Russian* gədu'nɔf) n. **Boris Fyodorovich** (ba'ris 'fjɔdərəvɪtʃ). ?1551–1605, Russian regent (1584–98) and tsar (1598–1605).

Godwin ('gɒdwɪn) n. **1.** died 1053, Earl of Wessex. He was chief adviser to Canute and Edward the Confessor. His son succeeded Edward to the throne as Harold II. **2. Mary**, *née* **Wollstonecraft**. 1759–97, English feminist and writer; author of *Vindication of the Rights of Women* (1792). **3.** her husband, **William**. 1756–1836, English political philosopher and novelist. In *An Enquiry concerning Political Justice* (1793), he rejected government and social institutions, including marriage. His views greatly influenced English romantic writers.

Godwin Austen n. another name for **K2**.

godwit ('gɒdwɪt) n. a large shore bird of the sandpiper family having long legs and a long upturned bill. [C16: from ?]

Goebbels (*German* 'gœbəls) n. **Paul Joseph** (paul 'joːzɛf). 1897–1945, German Nazi politician; minister of propaganda (1933–45).

goer ('gəʊə) n. **1. a.** a person who attends something regularly. **b.** (*in combination*): *filmgoer*. **2.** a person or thing that goes. esp. one that goes very fast. **3.** an energetic person. **4.** *Austral. inf.* an acceptable or feasible idea, proposal, etc.

Goering (*German* 'gøːrɪŋ) n. See (Hermann Wilhelm) **Göring**.

Goethe (*German* 'gøːtə) n. **Johann Wolfgang von** (jo'han 'vɔlfgaŋ fɔn). 1749–1832, German poet, novelist, and dramatist, who settled in Weimar in 1775. His early works include the play *Götz von Berlichingen* (1773) and the novel *The Sorrows of Young Werther* (1774). After a journey to Italy (1786–88) his writings, such as the epic play *Iphigenie auf Tauris* (1787) and the epic idyll *Hermann und Dorothea* (1797), showed the influence of classicism. Other works include the *Wilhelm Meister* novels (1796–1829) and his greatest masterpiece *Faust* (1808; 1832).

gofer ('gəʊfə) n. Sl. a person who runs errands. [C20: from GO + FOR]

goffer ('gəʊfə) vb. (tr.) **1.** to press pleats into (a frill). **2.** to decorate (the edges of a book). ~n. **3.** an ornamental frill made by pressing pleats. **4.** the decoration formed by goffering books. **5.** the iron or tool used in making goffers. [C18: from F *gaufrer* to impress a pattern, from *gaufre*, from MLow G *wāfel*; see WAFFLE[1], WAFER]

go for vb. (*intr., prep.*) **1.** to go somewhere in order to have or fetch: *he went for a drink*. **2.** to seek to obtain: *I'd go for that job if I were you*. **3.** to prefer or choose; like: *I really go for that new idea of yours*. **4.** to make a physical or verbal attack on. **5.** to be considered to be of a stated importance or value: *his twenty years went for nothing when he was made redundant.*

Gog and Magog (gɒg; 'meɪgɒg) *n.* **1.** *Old Testament.* a hostile prince and the land from which he comes to attack Israel (Ezekiel 38). **2.** *New Testament.* two kings, who are to attack the Church in a climactic battle, but are then to be destroyed by God (Revelation 20:8–10).

go-getter *n. Inf.* an ambitious enterprising person. —**,go-getting** *adj.*

gogga ('xɒxə) *n. S. African inf.* any small animal that crawls or flies, esp. an insect. [C20: from Hottentot *xoxon* insects collectively]

goggle ('gɒgəl) *vb.* **1.** (*intr.*) to stare fixedly, as in astonishment. **2.** to cause (the eyes) to roll or bulge or (of the eyes) to roll or bulge. ~*n.* **3.** a bulging stare. **4.** (*pl.*) spectacles, often of coloured glass or covered with gauze: used to protect the eyes. [C14: from *gogelen* to look aside, from ?; see AGOG] —**'goggle-,eyed** *adj.*

gogglebox ('gɒgəl,bɒks) *n. Brit. sl.* a television set.

Gogh (gɒx; *Dutch* xɔx) *n.* See (Vincent) **van Gogh.**

Go-Go *n.* a form of soul music originating in Washington, DC, characterized by the use of funk rhythms and a brass section.

go-go dancer *n.* a dancer, usually scantily dressed, who performs rhythmic and often erotic modern dance routines, esp. in a nightclub.

Gogol ('gɒugɒl; *Russian* 'gɔgəlj) *n.* **Nikolai Vasilievich** (nika'laj va'siljivitʃ). 1809–52, Russian novelist, dramatist, and short-story writer. His best-known works are *The Government Inspector* (1836), a comedy satirizing bureaucracy, and the novel *Dead Souls* (1842).

Gogra ('gɒgrə) *n.* a river in N India, rising in Tibet, in the Himalayas, and flowing southeast through Nepal as the Karnali, then through Uttar Pradesh to join the Ganges. Length: about 1000 km (600 miles).

Goiânia (gɔɪ'ɑːnɪə; *Portuguese* go'jənja) *n.* a city in central Brazil, capital of Goiás state: planned in 1933 to replace the old capital, Goiás; two universities. Pop.: 928 046 (1985).

Goiás (*Portuguese* gɔ'jas) *n.* a state of central Brazil, in the Brazilian Highlands: contains Brasília, the capital of Brazil. Capital: Goiânia. Pop.: 3 864 629 (1980). Area: 642 092 sq. km (247 860 sq. miles).

Goidelic (gɔɪ'dɛlɪk) *n.* **1.** the N group of Celtic languages, consisting of Irish Gaelic, Scottish Gaelic, and Manx. ~*adj.* **2.** of, relating to, or characteristic of this group of languages. [C19: from OIrish *Goidel* a Celt, from OWelsh, from *gwydd* savage]

go in *vb.* (*intr., adv.*) **1.** to enter. **2.** (*prep.*) See **go into.** **3.** (of the sun) to become hidden behind a cloud. **4. go in for. a.** to enter as a competitor or contestant. **b.** to adopt as an activity, interest, or guiding principle: *she went in for nursing.*

going ('gɒuɪŋ) *n.* **1.** a departure or farewell. **2.** the condition of a surface such as a road or field with regard to walking, riding, etc.: *muddy going.* **3.** *Inf.* speed, progress, etc.: *we made good going on the trip.* ~*adj.* **4.** thriving (esp. in **a going concern**). **5.** current or accepted: *the going rate.* **6.** (*postpositive*) available: *the best going.*

going-over *n., pl.* **goings-over.** *Inf.* **1.** a check, examination, or investigation. **2.** a castigation or thrashing.

goings-on *pl. n. Inf.* **1.** actions or conduct, esp. when regarded with disapproval. **2.** happenings or events, esp. when mysterious or suspicious.

go into *vb.* (*intr., prep.*) **1.** to enter. **2.** to start a career in: *to go into publishing.* **3.** to investigate or examine. **4.** to discuss: *we won't go into that now.* **5.** to be admitted to, esp. temporarily: *she went into hospital.* **6.** to enter a specified state: *she went into fits of laughter.*

goitre *or U.S.* **goiter** ('gɔɪtə) *n. Pathol.* a swelling of the thyroid gland, in some cases nearly doubling the size of the neck. [C17: from F, from OF *goitron* ult. from L *guttur* throat] —**'goitred** *or U.S.* **'goitered** *adj.* —**'goitrous** *adj.*

go-kart *or* **go-cart** *n.* See **kart.**

Golan Heights ('gɒu,læn) *pl. n.* a range of hills in the Middle East, possession of which is disputed between Israel and Syria: under Syrian control until 1967 when they were stormed by Israeli forces; Jewish settlements have since been established. Highest peak: 2224 m (7297 ft.).

Golconda (gɒl'kɒndə) *n.* **1.** a ruined town and fortress in S central India, in W Andhra Pradesh near Hyderabad city: capital of one of the five Muslim kingdoms of the Deccan from 1512 to 1687, then annexed to the Mogul empire; renowned for its diamonds. **2.** (*sometimes not cap.*) a source of wealth or riches, esp. a mine.

gold (gəuld) *n.* **1. a.** a dense inert bright yellow element that is the most malleable and ductile metal, occurring in rocks and alluvial deposits: used as a monetary standard and in jewellery, dentistry, and plating. Symbol: Au; atomic no.: 79; atomic wt.: 196.97. Related adj.: **auric. b.** (*as modifier*): *a gold mine.* **2.** a coin or coins made of this metal. **3.** money; wealth. **4.** something precious, beautiful, etc., such as a noble nature (esp. in **heart of gold**). **5. a.** a deep yellow colour, sometimes with a brownish tinge. **b.** (*as adj.*): *a gold carpet.* **6.** short for **gold medal.** [OE *gold*]

Gold Coast *n.* **1.** the former name (until 1957) of **Ghana. 2.** a line of resort towns and beaches in E Australia, extending for over 30 km (20 miles) along the S coast of Queensland.

goldcrest ('gəuld,krɛst) *n.* a small Old World warbler having a greenish plumage and a bright yellow-and-black crown.

gold-digger *n.* **1.** a person who prospects or digs for gold. **2.** *Inf.* a woman who uses her sexual attractions to accumulate gifts and wealth.

gold dust *n.* gold in the form of small particles or powder.

golden ('gəuldən) *adj.* **1.** of the yellowish colour of gold: *golden hair.* **2.** made from or largely consisting of gold: *a golden statue.* **3.** happy or prosperous: *golden days.* **4.** (*sometimes cap.*) (of anniversaries) the 50th in a series: *Golden Jubilee; golden wedding.* **5.** *Inf.* very successful or destined for success: *the golden girl of tennis.* **6.** extremely valuable or advantageous: *a golden opportunity.* —**'goldenly** *adv.* —**'goldenness** *n.*

golden age *n.* **1.** *Classical myth.* the first and best age of mankind, when existence was happy, prosperous, and innocent. **2.** the most flourishing and outstanding period, esp. in the history of an art or nation: *the golden age of poetry.*

golden eagle *n.* a large eagle of mountainous regions of the N hemisphere, having a plumage that is golden brown on the back.

goldeneye ('gəuldən,aɪ) *n., pl.* **-eyes** *or* **-eye.** either of two black-and-white diving ducks of northern regions.

Golden Fleece *n. Greek myth.* the fleece of a winged ram stolen by Jason and the Argonauts.

Golden Gate *n.* a strait between the Pacific and San Francisco Bay: crossed by the **Golden Gate Bridge,** with a central span of 1280 m (4200 ft.).

golden goose *n.* a goose in folklore that laid a golden egg every day until its greedy owner killed it in an attempt to get all the gold at once.

golden handcuffs *pl. n.* payments deferred over a number of years that induce a person to stay with a particular company or in a particular job.

golden handshake *n. Inf.* a sum of money given to an employee, either on retirement or as compensation for loss of employment.

golden hello *n.* a payment made to a sought-after recruit on signing a contract of employment with a company.

Golden Horn *n.* an inlet of the Bosporus in NW Turkey, forming the harbour of Istanbul. Turkish name: **Haliç.**

golden mean *n.* **1.** the middle course between extremes. **2.** another term for **golden section.**

golden number *n.* a number between 1 and 19, used to indicate the position of any year in the Metonic cycle: so called from its importance in fixing the date of Easter.

golden retriever *n.* a breed of retriever with a silky wavy coat of a golden colour.

goldenrod (,gəuldən'rɒd) *n.* a plant of the composite family of North America, Europe, and Asia, having spikes of small yellow flowers.

golden rule *n.* **1.** the rule of conduct formulated by Christ: *Whatsoever ye would that men should do to you, do ye even so to them* (Matthew 7:12). **2.** any important principle: *a golden rule of sailing is to wear a life jacket.* **3.** another name for **rule of three.**

golden section *or* **mean** *n.* the proportion of the two divisions of a straight line such that the smaller is to the larger as the larger is to the sum of the two.

golden syrup *n. Brit.* a light golden-coloured treacle produced by the evaporation of cane sugar juice, used to flavour cakes, puddings, etc.

golden wattle *n.* **1.** an Australian yellow-flowered plant that yields a useful gum and bark. **2.** any of several similar and related Australian plants.

goldfinch ('gəʊld,fɪntʃ) *n.* a common European finch, the male of which has a red-and-white face and yellow-and-black wings.

goldfish ('gəʊld,fɪʃ) *n., pl.* **-fish** *or* **-fishes.** a freshwater fish of E Europe and Asia, esp. China, widely introduced as a pond or aquarium fish. It resembles the carp and has a typically golden or orange-red coloration.

gold foil *n.* thin gold sheet that is thicker than gold leaf.

Golding ('gəʊldɪŋ) *n.* **Sir William (Gerald).** born 1911, English novelist noted for his allegories of man's proclivity for evil. His novels include *Lord of the Flies* (1954), *Darkness Visible* (1979), *Rites of Passage* (1980), and *Close Quarters* (1987). Nobel prize for literature 1983.

gold leaf *n.* very thin gold sheet produced by rolling or hammering gold and used for gilding woodwork, etc.

gold medal *n.* a medal of gold, awarded to the winner of a competition or race.

Goldoni (*Italian* gol'dɔːni) *n.* **Carlo** ('karlo). 1707–93, Italian dramatist; author of over 250 plays in Italian or French, including *La Locandiera* (1753). His work introduced realistic Italian comedy, superseding the commedia dell'arte.

gold plate *n.* **1.** a thin coating of gold, usually produced by electroplating. **2.** vessels or utensils made of gold. — ,gold-'plate *vb.* (*tr.*)

gold reserve *n.* the gold reserved by a central bank to support domestic credit expansion, to cover balance of payments deficits, and to protect currency.

gold rush *n.* a large-scale migration of people to a territory where gold has been found.

Goldschmidt ('gəʊld,ʃmɪt) *n.* **Richard Benedikt.** 1878–1958, U.S. geneticist, born in Germany. He advanced the theory that heredity is determined by the chemical configuration of the chromosome molecule rather than by the qualities of the individual genes.

goldsmith ('gəʊld,smɪθ) *n.* **1.** a dealer in articles made of gold. **2.** an artisan who makes such articles.

Goldsmith ('gəʊld,smɪθ) *n.* **Oliver.** ?1730–74, Irish poet, dramatist, and novelist. His works include the novel *The Vicar of Wakefield* (1766), the poem *The Deserted Village* (1770), and the comedy *She Stoops to Conquer* (1773).

gold standard *n.* a monetary system in which the unit of currency is defined with reference to gold.

Goldwyn ('gəʊldwɪn) *n.* **Samuel,** original name *Samuel Goldfish.* 1882–1974, U.S. film producer, born in Poland.

golf (gɒlf) *n.* **1.** a game played on a large open course, the object of which is to hit a ball using clubs, with as few strokes as possible, into each of usually 18 holes. ~*vb.* **2.** (*intr.*) to play golf. [C15: ?from MDu. *colf* CLUB] — 'golfer *n.*

golf ball *n.* **1.** a small resilient white ball of strands of rubber wound at high tension around a core with a cover made of gutta-percha, etc., used in golf. **2.** (in some electric typewriters) a small detachable metal sphere, around the surface of which type characters are arranged.

golf club *n.* **1.** any of various long-shafted clubs with wood or metal heads used to strike a golf ball. **2. a.** an association of golf players, usually having its own course and facilities. **b.** the premises of such an association.

golf course *or* **links** *n.* an area of ground laid out for the playing of golf.

Golgi (*Italian* 'gɔldʒi) *n.* **Camillo** (ka'millo). 1844–1926, Italian neurologist and histologist, noted for his work on the central nervous system and his discovery in animal cells of the bodies known by his name: shared the Nobel prize for physiology or medicine 1906.

Golgotha ('gɒlgəθə) *n.* **1.** another name for **Calvary. 2.** (*sometimes not cap.*) *Now rare.* a place of burial. [C17: from LL, from Gk, from Aramaic, based on Heb. *gulgōleth* skull]

Goliath (gə'laɪəθ) *n. Bible.* a Philistine giant who was killed by David with a stone from his sling (I Samuel 17).

golliwog ('gɒlɪ,wɒg) *n.* a soft doll with a black face, usually made of cloth or rags. [C19: from a doll in a series of American children's books]

gollop ('gɒləp) *vb.* to eat or drink (something) quickly or greedily. [dialect var. of GULP]

golly ('gɒlɪ) *interj.* an exclamation of mild surprise. [C19: orig. a euphemism for GOD]

goloshes (gə'lɒʃɪz) *pl. n.* a less common spelling of **galoshes.**

Gomberg ('gɒmbɜːg) *n.* **Mo-ses.** 1866–1947, U.S. chemist, born in Russia, noted for his work on free radicals.

Gomel (*Russian* 'gɒmɪlj) *n.* an industrial city in the W Soviet Union, in the SE Byelorussian SSR: belonged to Lithuania until 1772. Pop.: 488 000 (1987).

Gomorrah *or* **Gomorrha** (gə'mɒrə) *n.* **1.** *Old Testament.* one of two ancient cities near the Dead Sea, the other being Sodom, that were destroyed by God as a punishment for the wickedness of their inhabitants (Genesis 19:24). **2.** any place notorious for vice and depravity. —Go'morrean *or* Go'morrhean *adj.*

Gompers ('gɒmpəz) *n.* **Samuel.** 1850–1924, U.S. labour leader, born in England; a founder of the American Federation of Labor and its president (1886–94; 1896–1924).

Gomulka (gə'mʊlkə) *n.* **Władysław** (vwa'diswaf). 1905–82, Polish statesman; first secretary of the Polish Communist Party (1956–70).

-gon *n. combining form.* indicating a figure having a specified number of angles: *pentagon.* [from Gk *-gōnon*, from *gōnia* angle]

gonad ('gɒnæd) *n.* an animal organ in which gametes are produced, such as a testis or an ovary. [C19: from NL *gonas*, from Gk *gonos* seed] — 'gonadal *or* gonadial (gə'neɪdɪəl) *adj.*

gonadotrophic (,gɒnədəʊ'trɒfɪk) *adj.* stimulating the gonads.

Gonaïves (*French* gɔnaiv) *n.* a port in W Haiti, on the **Gulf of Gonaïves;** scene of the proclamation of Haiti's independence (1804). Pop.: 37 034 (1987).

Goncourt (*French* gɔ̃kur) *n.* **Edmond Louis Antoine Huot de** (ɛdmɔ̃ lwi ɑ̃twan yo də), 1822–96, and his brother, **Jules Alfred Huot de** (ʒyl alfrɛd), 1830–70, French writers, noted for their collaboration, esp. on their *Journal,* and for the Académie Goncourt founded by Edmond's will.

Gondar ('gɒndɑː) *n.* a city in NW Ethiopia: capital of Ethiopia from the 17th century until 1868. Pop.: 68 958 (1984).

gondola ('gɒndələ) *n.* **1.** a long narrow flat-bottomed boat with a high ornamented stem: traditionally used on the canals of Venice. **2. a.** a car or cabin suspended from an airship or balloon. **b.** a moving cabin suspended from a cable across a valley, etc. **3.** a flat-bottomed barge used on canals and rivers of the U.S. **4.** *U.S. & Canad.* a low open flat-bottomed railway goods wagon. **5.** a set of island shelves in a self-service shop: used for displaying goods. **6.** *Canad.* a broadcasting booth built close to the roof of an ice-hockey stadium. [C16: from It. (dialect), from Med. L, ? ult. from Gk *kondu* drinking vessel]

gondolier (,gɒndə'lɪə) *n.* a man who propels a gondola.

Gondwanaland (gɒnd'wɑːnə,lænd) *n.* one of the two ancient supercontinents comprising chiefly what are now Africa, South America, Australia, Antarctica, and the Indian subcontinent. [C19: from *Gondwana,* region in central north India, where the rock series was orig. found]

gone (gɒn) *vb.* **1.** the past participle of **go.** ~*adj.* (*usually postpositive*) **2.** ended; past. **3.** lost; ruined. **4.** dead. **5.** spent; consumed; used up. **6.** *Inf.* faint or weak. **7.** *Inf.* having been pregnant (for a specified time): *six months gone.* **8.** (usually foll. by *on*) *Sl.* in love (with).

goner ('gɒnə) *n. Sl.* a person or thing beyond help or recovery, esp. a person who is about to die.

gonfalon ('gɒnfələn) *n.* **1.** a banner hanging from a crossbar, used esp. by certain medieval Italian republics. **2.** a battle flag suspended crosswise on a staff, usually having a serrated edge. [C16: from OIt., from OF, of Gmc origin]

gong (gɒŋ) *n.* **1.** a percussion instrument consisting of a metal platelike disc struck with a soft-headed drumstick. **2.** a rimmed metal disc, hollow metal hemisphere, or metal strip, tube, or wire that produces a note when struck. **3.** a fixed saucer-shaped bell, as on an alarm clock, struck by a mechanically operated hammer. **4.** *Brit. sl.* a medal, esp. a military one. ~*vb.* **5.** (*intr.*) to sound a gong. **6.** (*tr.*) (of traffic police) to summon (a driver) to stop by sounding a gong. [C17: from Malay, imit.]

Gongola (gɒŋ'gəʊlə) *n.* a state of E Nigeria, formed in 1976 from part of Northeastern State. Capital: Yola. Pop.: 4 367 600 (1984). Area: 13 664 sq. km (5275 sq. miles).

Góngora y Argote (*Spanish* 'gɔŋgora i ar'ɣote) *n.* **Luis de** (lwis de). 1561–1627, Spanish lyric poet, noted for the exaggerated pedantic style of works such as *Las Soledades.*

goniometer (ˌgəʊnɪ'ɒmɪtə) *n.* **1.** an instrument for measuring the angles between the faces of a crystal. **2.** an instrument used to determine the bearing of a distant radio station. [C18: via F from Gk *gōnia* angle] —**goniometric** (ˌgəʊnɪə'mɛtrɪk) *adj.* — ˌgoni'ometry *n.*

-gonium *n. combining form.* indicating a seed or reproductive cell: *archegonium.* [from NL, from Gk *gonos* seed]

gonococcus (ˌgɒnəʊ'kɒkəs) *n., pl.* **-cocci** (-'kɒksaɪ). a spherical bacterium that causes gonorrhoea.

gonorrhoea *or esp. U.S.* **gonorrhea** (ˌgɒnə'rɪə) *n.* an infectious venereal disease characterized by a discharge of mucus and pus from the urethra or vagina. [C16: from L, from Gk *gonos* semen + *rhoia* flux] — ˌgonor'rhoeal *or esp. U.S.* ˌgonor'rheal *adj.*

-gony *n. combining form.* genesis, origin, or production: *cosmogony.* [from L, from Gk, from *gonos* seed, procreation]

Gonzales (gən'zɑːlɪs) *n.* **Ricardo Alonzo** (rɪ'kɑːdəʊ ə'lɒnzəʊ), known as *Pancho.* born 1928, U.S. tennis player.

González (*Spanish* gɔn'θaleθ) *n.* **Julio** ('xuljo). 1876–1942, Spanish sculptor: one of the first to create abstract geometric forms with soldered iron.

González Márquez (*Spanish* gɔn'θaleθ 'markeθ) *n.* **Felipe** (fe'lipe). born 1942, Spanish statesman; prime minister of Spain from 1982.

goo (guː) *n. Inf.* **1.** a sticky substance. **2.** coy or sentimental language or ideas. [C20: from ?]

good (gʊd) *adj.* **better, best.** **1.** having admirable, pleasing, superior, or positive qualities; not negative, bad, or mediocre: *a good teacher.* **2. a.** morally excellent or admirable; virtuous; righteous: *a good man.* **b.** (*as collective n.; preceded by the*): *the good.* **3.** suitable or efficient for a purpose: *a good winter coat.* **4.** beneficial or advantageous: *vegetables are good for you.* **5.** not ruined or decayed: *the meat is still good.* **6.** kindly or generous: *you are good to him.* **7.** valid or genuine: *I would not do this without good reason.* **8.** honourable or held in high esteem: *a good family.* **9.** financially secure, sound, or safe: *a good investment.* **10.** (of a draft, etc.) drawn for a stated sum. **11.** (of debts) expected to be fully paid. **12.** clever, competent, or talented: *he's good at science.* **13.** obedient or well-behaved: *a good dog.* **14.** reliable, safe, or recommended: *a good make of clothes.* **15.** affording material pleasure: *the good life.* **16.** having a well-proportioned or generally fine appearance: *a good figure.* **17.** complete; full: *I took a good look round the house.* **18.** propitious; opportune: *a good time to ask for a rise.* **19.** satisfying or gratifying: *a good rest.* **20.** comfortable: *did you have a good night?* **21.** newest or of the best quality: *keep the good plates for guests.* **22.** fairly large, extensive, or long: *a good distance away.* **23.** sufficient; ample: *we have a good supply of food.* **24. a good one. a.** an unbelievable assertion. **b.** a very funny joke. **25. as good as.** virtually; practically: *it's as good as finished.* **26. good and.** *Inf.* (intensifier): *good and mad.* ~*interj.* **27.** an exclamation of approval, agreement, pleasure, etc. ~*n.* **28.** moral or material advantage or use; benefit or profit: *for the good of our workers; what is the good of worrying?* **29.** positive moral qualities; goodness; virtue; righteousness; piety. **30.** (*sometimes cap.*) moral qualities seen as an abstract entity: *we must pursue the Good.* **31.** a good thing. **32. for good (and all).** forever; permanently: *I have left them for good.* **33. good for** *or* **on you.** well done, well said, etc.: a term of congratulation. **34. make good. a.** to recompense or repair damage or injury. **b.** to be successful. **c.** to prove the truth of (a statement or accusation). **d.** to secure and retain (a position). **e.** to effect or fulfil (something intended or promised). ~See also **goods.** [OE *gōd*] — 'goodish *adj.*

▷ **Usage.** Careful speakers and writers of English do not use *good* and *bad* as adverbs: *she dances well* (not *good*); *he sings really badly* (not *really bad*).

Good Book *n.* a name for the **Bible.**

goodbye (ˌgʊd'baɪ) *sentence substitute.* **1.** farewell: a conventional expression used at leave-taking or parting with people. ~*n.* **2.** a leave-taking; parting: *they prolonged their goodbyes.* **3.** a farewell: *they said goodbyes to each other.* [C16: from *God be with ye*]

good day *sentence substitute.* a conventional expression of greeting or farewell used during the day.

good-for-nothing *n.* **1.** an irresponsible or worthless person. ~*adj.* **2.** irresponsible; worthless.

Good Friday *n.* the Friday before Easter, observed as a commemoration of the Crucifixion of Jesus.

Good Hope *n.* **Cape of.** See **Cape of Good Hope.**

good-humoured *adj.* being in or expressing a pleasant, tolerant, and kindly state of mind. — ˌgood-'humouredly *adv.*

goodies ('gʊdɪz) *pl. n.* any objects, rewards, etc., considered particularly desirable.

good-looking *adj.* handsome or pretty.

goodly ('gʊdlɪ) *adj.* **-lier, -liest.** **1.** considerable: *a goodly amount of money.* **2.** *Obs.* attractive, pleasing, or fine. — 'goodliness *n.*

goodman ('gʊdmən) *n., pl.* **-men.** *Arch.* **1.** a husband. **2.** a man not of gentle birth: used as a title. **3.** a master of a household.

Goodman ('gʊdmən) *n.* **Benny,** full name *Benjamin David Goodman.* 1909–86, U.S. jazz clarinetist and bandleader, whose treatment of popular songs created the jazz idiom known as swing.

good morning *sentence substitute.* a conventional expression of greeting or farewell used in the morning.

good-natured *adj.* of a tolerant and kindly disposition. — ˌgood-'naturedly *adv.*

goodness ('gʊdnɪs) *n.* **1.** the state or quality of being good. **2.** generosity; kindness. **3.** moral excellence; piety; virtue. **4.** what is good in something; essence. ~*interj.* **5.** a euphemism for **God:** used as an exclamation of surprise.

goodness of fit *n. Statistics.* the extent to which observed sample values of a variable approximate to values derived from a theoretical density.

good night *sentence substitute.* a conventional expression of farewell, used in the evening or at night, esp. when departing to bed.

good-oh *or* **good-o** (ˌgʊd'əʊ) *interj. Brit. & Austral. inf.* an exclamation of pleasure, agreement, etc.

good oil *n.* (usually preceded by *the*) *Austral. sl.* true or reliable facts, information, etc.

goods (gʊdz) *pl. n.* **1.** possessions and personal property. **2.** (*sometimes sing.*) *Econ.* commodities that are tangible, usually movable, and generally not consumed at the same time as they are produced. **3.** articles of commerce; merchandise. **4.** *Chiefly Brit.* **a.** merchandise when transported, esp. by rail; freight. **b.** (*as modifier*): *a goods train.* **5. the goods. a.** *Inf.* that which is expected or promised: *to deliver the goods.* **b.** *Sl.* the real thing. **c.** *U.S. & Canad. sl.* incriminating evidence (esp. in **have the goods on someone**).

Good Samaritan *n.* **1.** *New Testament.* a figure in one of Christ's parables (Luke 10:30–37) who is an example of compassion towards those in distress. **2.** a kindly person who helps another in difficulty or distress.

Good Shepherd *n. New Testament.* a title given to Jesus Christ in John 10:11–12.

good-sized *adj.* quite large.

good-tempered *adj.* of a kindly and generous disposition.

good turn *n.* a helpful and friendly act; favour.

goodwife ('gʊdˌwaɪf) *n., pl.* **-wives.** *Arch.* **1.** the mistress of a household. **2.** a woman not of gentle birth: used as a title.

goodwill (ˌgʊd'wɪl) *n.* **1.** benevolence, approval, and kindly interest. **2.** willingness or acquiescence. **3.** an intangible asset of an enterprise reflecting its commercial reputation, customer connections, etc.

Goodwin Sands ('gʊdwɪn) *pl. n.* a dangerous stretch of shoals at the entrance to the Strait of Dover: separated from the E coast of Kent by the Downs roadstead.

goody[1] ('gʊdɪ) *interj.* **1.** a child's exclamation of pleasure. ~*n., pl.* **goodies. 2.** short for **goody-goody. 3.** *Inf.* the hero in a film, book, etc. **4.** See **goodies.**

goody[2] ('gʊdɪ) *n., pl.* **goodies.** *Arch. or literary.* a married woman of low rank: used as a title: *Goody Two-Shoes.* [C16: from GOODWIFE]

Goodyear ('gʊdˌjɪə) *n.* **Charles.** 1800–60, U.S. inventor of vulcanized rubber.

goody-goody *n., pl.* **-goodies. 1.** *Inf.* a smugly virtuous or sanctimonious person. ~*adj.* **2.** smug and sanctimonious.

gooey ('gu:ɪ) *adj.* **gooier, gooiest.** *Inf.* **1.** sticky, soft, and often sweet. **2.** oversweet and sentimental. —'**gooily** *adv.*

goof (gu:f) *Inf.* ~*n.* **1.** a foolish error. **2.** a stupid person. ~*vb.* **3.** to bungle (something); botch. **4.** (*intr.;* often foll. by *about* or *around*) to fool (around); mess (about). [C20: prob. from (dialect) *goff* simpleton, from OF *goffe* clumsy, from It. *goffo*, from ?]

go off *vb.* (*intr.*) **1.** (*adv.*) (of power, a water supply, etc.) to cease to be available or functioning: *the lights suddenly went off.* **2.** (*adv.*) to explode. **3.** (*adv.*) to occur as specified: *the meeting went off well.* **4.** to leave (a place): *the actors went off stage.* **5.** (*adv.*) (of a sensation) to gradually cease to be felt. **6.** (*adv.*) to fall asleep. **7.** (*adv.*) (of concrete, mortar, etc.) to harden. **8.** (*adv.*) *Brit. inf.* (of food, etc.) to become stale or rotten. **9.** (*prep.*) *Brit. inf.* to cease to like.

goofy ('gu:fɪ) *adj.* **goofier, goofiest.** *Inf.* foolish; silly. —'**goofily** *adv.* —'**goofiness** *n.*

goog (gʊg) *n. Austral. sl.* an egg. [?from Du. *oog*]

googly ('gu:glɪ) *n., pl.* **-lies.** *Cricket.* an off break bowled with a leg break action. [C20: Austral.]

Goole (gu:l) *n.* an inland port in NE England, in Humberside at the confluence of the Ouse and Don Rivers, 75 km (47 miles) from the North Sea. Pop.: 18 630 (1985 est.).

goolie *or* **gooly** ('gu:lɪ) *n., pl.* **goolies. 1.** (*usually pl.*) *Taboo sl.* a testicle. **2.** *Austral. sl.* a stone or pebble. [from Hindi *goli* ball]

goon (gu:n) *n.* **1.** a stupid or deliberately foolish person. **2.** *U.S. inf.* a thug hired to commit acts of violence or intimidation, esp. in an industrial dispute. [C20: partly from dialect *gooney* fool, partly after the character Alice the *Goon*, created by E. C. Segar (1894–1938), American cartoonist]

go on *vb.* (*intr., mostly adv.*) **1.** to continue or proceed. **2.** to happen: *there's something peculiar going on here.* **3.** (*prep.*) to ride on, esp. as a treat: *children love to go on donkeys at the seaside.* **4.** *Theatre.* to make an entrance on stage. **5.** to talk excessively; chatter. **6.** to continue talking, esp. after a short pause. **7.** to criticize or nag: *stop going on at me all the time!* ~*sentence substitute.* **8.** I don't believe what you're saying.

gooney bird ('gu:nɪ) *n.* an informal name for **albatross,** esp. the black-footed albatross. [C19 *gony* (orig. sailors' sl.), prob. from dialect *gooney* fool, from ?]

goop (gu:p) *n. U.S. & Canad. sl.* a rude or ill-mannered person. [C20: coined by G. Burgess (1866–1951), American humorist] —'**goopy** *adj.*

goorie *or* **goory** ('gu:rɪ) *n., pl.* **goories.** *N.Z. inf.* a mongrel dog. [from Maori *kuri*]

goosander (gu:'sændə) *n.* a common merganser (a duck) of Europe and North America, having a dark head and white body in the male. [C17: prob. from GOOSE¹ + ON *önd* (genitive *andar*) duck]

goose¹ (gu:s) *n., pl.* **geese. 1.** any of various web-footed long-necked birds typically larger and less aquatic than ducks. They are gregarious and migratory. **2.** the female of such a bird, as opposed to the male (gander). **3.** *Inf.* a silly person. **4.** (*pl.* **gooses**) a pressing iron with a long curving handle, used esp. by tailors. **5.** the flesh of the goose, used as food. **6. cook someone's goose.** *Inf.* **a.** to spoil someone's chances or plans completely. **b.** to bring about someone's downfall. **7. kill the goose that lays the golden eggs.** See **golden goose.** [OE *gōs*]

goose² (gu:s) *Sl.* ~*vb.* **1.** (*tr.*) to prod (a person) playfully in the bottom. ~*n., pl.* **gooses. 2.** such a prod. [C19: from GOOSE¹, prob. from a comparison with the jabbing of a goose's bill]

gooseberry ('gʊzbərɪ, -brɪ) *n., pl.* **-ries. 1.** a Eurasian shrub having ovoid yellow-green or red-purple berries. **2. a.** the berry of this plant. **b.** (*as modifier*): *gooseberry jam.* **3.** *Brit. inf.* an unwanted single person, esp. a third person with a couple (often in **play gooseberry**).

goose flesh *n.* the bumpy condition of the skin induced by cold, fear, etc., caused by contraction of the muscles at the base of the hair follicles with consequent erection of papillae. Also called: **goose bumps, goose pimples, goose skin.**

goosefoot ('gu:s,fʊt) *n., pl.* **-foots.** any typically weedy plant having small greenish flowers and leaves shaped like a goose's foot.

goosegog ('gʊzgɒg) *n. Brit.* a dialect or informal word for **gooseberry.** [from *goose* in GOOSEBERRY + *gog*, var. of GOB¹]

goosegrass ('gu:s,grɑ:s) *n.* another name for **cleavers.**

gooseneck ('gu:s,nɛk) *n.* something, such as a jointed pipe, in the form of the neck of a goose.

goose step *n.* **1.** a military march step in which the leg is swung rigidly to an exaggerated height. ~*vb.* **goose-step, -stepping, -stepped. 2.** (*intr.*) to march in goose step.

go out *vb.* (*intr., adv.*) **1.** to depart from a room, house, country, etc. **2.** to cease to illuminate, burn, or function: *the fire has gone out.* **3.** to cease to be fashionable or popular: *that style went out ages ago!* **4.** (of a broadcast) to be transmitted. **5.** to go to entertainments, social functions, etc. **6.** (usually foll. by *with* or *together*) to associate (with a person of the opposite sex) regularly. **7.** (of workers) to begin to strike. **8.** *Card games, etc.* to get rid of the last card, token, etc., in one's hand.

go over *vb.* (*intr.*) **1.** to be received in a specified manner: *the concert went over very well.* **2.** (*prep.*) Also: **go through.** to examine and revise as necessary: *he went over the accounts.* **3.** (*prep.*) to check and repair: *can you go over my car, please?* **4.** (*prep.*) Also: **go through.** to rehearse: *I'll go over my lines before the play.*

gopak ('gəʊ,pæk) *n.* a spectacular high-leaping Russian peasant dance for men. [from Russian]

gopher ('gəʊfə) *n.* **1.** Also called: **pocket gopher.** a burrowing rodent of North and Central America, having a thickset body, short legs, and cheek pouches. **2.** another name for **ground squirrel.** **3.** a burrowing tortoise of SE North America. [C19: from earlier *megopher* or *magopher*, from ?]

Gorakhpur ('gɔ:rək,pʊə) *n.* a city in N India, in SE Uttar Pradesh: formerly an important Muslim garrison. Pop.: 306 000 (1981).

goral ('gɔ:rəl) *n.* a small goat antelope inhabiting mountainous regions of S Asia. [C19: from Hindi, prob. from Sansk.]

Gorbachov (gɔrba'tʃɒf) *n.* **Mikhail Sergeevich** (mixa'il-sir'gjejivitʃ). born 1931, Soviet statesman; general secretary of the Soviet Communist Party from 1985: president from 1988.

Gorbals ('gɔ:bᵊlz) *n.* **the.** a district of Glasgow, formerly known for its slums.

Gordian knot ('gɔ:dɪən) *n.* **1.** (in Greek legend) a complicated knot, tied by King Gordius of Phrygia, that Alexander the Great cut with a sword. **2.** a complicated and intricate problem (esp. in **cut the Gordian knot**).

Gordimer ('gɔ:dɪmə) *n.* **Nadine.** born 1923, South African novelist. Her books include *The Lying Days* (1952) and *July's People* (1981), which have been banned in South Africa for their condemnation of apartheid.

Gordon ('gɔ:dᵊn) *n.* **1. Adam Lindsay.** 1833–70, Australian poet and horseman, born in the Azores, who developed the bush ballad as a literary form, esp. in *Bush Ballads and Galloping Rhymes* (1870). **2. Charles George,** known as *Chinese Gordon.* 1833–85, British general and administrator. He helped to crush the Taiping rebellion (1863–64), and was governor of the Sudan (1877–80), returning in 1884 to aid Egyptian forces against the Mahdi. He was killed in the siege of Khartoum. **3. Lord George.** 1751–93, English religious agitator. He led the Protestant opposition to legislation relieving Roman Catholics of certain disabilities, which culminated in the Gordon riots (1780). **4. George Hamilton.** See (4th Earl of) **Aberdeen.**

gore¹ (gɔ:) *n.* **1.** blood shed from a wound, esp. when coagulated. **2.** *Inf.* killing, fighting, etc. [OE *gor* dirt]

gore² (gɔ:) *vb.* (*tr.*) (of an animal, such as a bull) to pierce or stab (a person or another animal) with a horn or tusk. [C16: prob. from OE *gār* spear]

gore³ (gɔ:) *n.* **1.** a tapering or triangular piece of material used in making a shaped skirt, umbrella, etc. ~*vb.* **2.** (*tr.*) to make into or with a gore or gores. [OE *gāra*] —**gored** *adj.*

gorge (gɔ:dʒ) *n.* **1.** a deep ravine, esp. one through which a river runs. **2.** the contents of the stomach. **3.** feelings of disgust or resentment (esp. in **one's gorge rises**). **4.** an obstructing mass: *an ice gorge.* **5.** *Fortifications.* a narrow rear entrance to a work. **6.** *Arch.* the throat or gullet. ~*vb.* **7.** to swallow (food) ravenously. **8.** (*tr.*) to stuff (oneself) with food. [C14: from OF *gorger* to stuff, from *gorge* throat, from LL *gurga*, from L *gurges* whirl-pool]

gorgeous ('gɔːdʒəs) *adj.* **1.** strikingly beautiful or magnificent: *a gorgeous array; a gorgeous girl.* **2.** *Inf.* extremely pleasing, fine, or good: *gorgeous weather.* [C15: from OF *gorgias* elegant, from *gorge*; see GORGE] — **'gorgeously** *adv.* — **'gorgeousness** *n.*

gorget ('gɔːdʒɪt) *n.* **1.** a collar-like piece of armour worn to protect the throat. **2.** a part of a wimple worn by women to cover the throat and chest, esp. in the 14th century. **3.** a band of distinctive colour on the throat of an animal, esp. a bird. [C15: from OF, from *gorge*; see GORGE]

Gorgias ('gɔːdʒɪəs) *n.* ?485–?380 B.C., Greek sophist and rhetorician, subject of a dialogue by Plato.

Gorgio ('gɔːdʒɪəʊ) *n., pl.* **-gios.** the Gypsy name for a non-Gypsy. [C19: from Romany]

Gorgon ('gɔːgən) *n.* **1.** *Greek myth.* any of three winged monstrous sisters who had live snakes for hair, huge teeth, and brazen claws. **2.** (*often not cap.*) *Inf.* a fierce or unpleasant woman. [via L *Gorgō* from Gk, from *gorgos* terrible]

gorgonian (gɔː'gəʊnɪən) *n.* any of various corals having a horny or calcareous branching skeleton, such as the sea fans and red corals.

Gorgonzola (,gɔːgən'zəʊlə) *n.* a semihard blue-veined cheese of sharp flavour, made from pressed milk. [C19: after *Gorgonzola*, It. town where it originated]

Gorica ('gɔːritsə) *n.* the Serbo-Croatian name for **Gorizia.**

gorilla (gə'rɪlə) *n.* **1.** the largest anthropoid ape, inhabiting the forests of central W Africa. It is stocky with a short muzzle and coarse dark hair. **2.** *Inf.* a large, strong, and brutal-looking man. [C19: NL, from Gk *Gorillai*, an African tribe renowned for their hirsute appearance]

Göring *or* **Goering** (*German* 'gøːrɪŋ) *n.* **Hermann Wilhelm** ('hɛrman 'vɪlhɛlm). 1893–1946, German Nazi leader and field marshal. He commanded Hitler's storm troops (1923) and as Prussian prime minister and German commissioner for aviation (1933–45) he founded the Gestapo and mobilized Germany for war. Sentenced to death at Nuremberg, he committed suicide.

Gorizia (*Italian* go'rittsja) *n.* a city in NE Italy, in Friuli-Venezia Giulia, on the Isonzo River: cultural centre under the Hapsburgs. Pop.: 41 557 (1981). German name: **Görz.** Serbo-Croatian name: **Gorica.**

Gorki[1] *or* **Gorky** (*Russian* 'gɔrjkij) *n.* an industrial city and port in the central Soviet Union, at the confluence of the Volga and Oka Rivers: situated on the Volga route from the Baltic to central Asia; birthplace of Maxim Gorki. Pop.: 1 425 000 (1987). Former name (until 1932): **Nizhni Novgorod.**

Gorki[2] *or* **Gorky** (*Russian* 'gɔrjkij) *n.* **Maxim** (mak'sim), pen name of *Aleksey Maximovich Peshkov.* 1868–1936, Russian novelist, dramatist, and short-story writer, noted for his depiction of the outcasts of society. His works include the play *The Lower Depths* (1902), the novel *Mother* (1907), and an autobiographical trilogy (1913–23).

Gorky ('gɔːkɪ) *n.* **Arshile** ('ɑːʃɪl). 1904–48, U.S. abstract expressionist painter. Influenced by Picasso and Miró, his style is characterized by fluid lines and resonant colours.

Görlitz (*German* 'gœrlɪts) *n.* a city in SE East Germany, on the Neisse River: divided in 1945, the area on the E bank of the river becoming the Polish town of **Zgorzelec.** Pop.: 80 492 (1983).

Gorlovka (*Russian* 'gɔrləfkə) *n.* a city in the SW Soviet Union, in the SE Ukrainian SSR in the centre of the Donets Basin: a major coal-mining centre. Pop.: 345 000 (1987).

gormand ('gɔːmənd) *n.* a less common spelling of **gourmand.**

gormandize *or* **-ise** ('gɔːmən,daɪz) *vb.* to eat (food) greedily and voraciously. — **'gormand,izer** *or* **-,iser** *n.*

gormless ('gɔːmlɪs) *adj. Brit. inf.* stupid; dull. [C19: var. of C18 *gaumless*, from dialect *gome*, from OE *gom, gome*, from ON *gaumr* heed]

Gorno-Altai Autonomous Region ('gɔːnəʊæl'taɪ, -'æltaɪ) *n.* an administrative division of the S central Soviet Union: mountainous, rising over 4350 m (14 500 ft.) in the Altai Mountains of the south. Capital: Gorno-Altaisk. Pop.: 179 000 (1986). Area: 92 600 sq. km (35 740 sq. miles).

Gorno-Badakhshan Autonomous Region (-bə-'dækʃɑːn) *n.* an administrative division of the S Soviet Union, in the Tadzhik SSR: generally mountainous and inaccessible. Capital: Khorog. Pop.: 149 000 (1986). Area: 63 700 sq. km (24 590 sq. miles).

go round *vb.* (*intr.*) **1.** (*adv.*) to be sufficient: *are there enough sweets to go round?* **2.** to circulate (in): *measles is going round the school.* **3.** to be long enough to encircle: *will that belt go round you?*

gorse (gɔːs) *n.* an evergreen shrub which has yellow flowers and thick green spines instead of leaves. Also called: **furze, whin.** [OE *gors*] — **'gorsy** *adj.*

Gorton ('gɔːtᵊn) *n.* Sir **John Grey.** born 1911, Australian statesman; prime minister (1968–71).

gory ('gɔːrɪ) *adj.* **gorier, goriest. 1.** horrific or bloodthirsty: *a gory story.* **2.** involving bloodshed and killing: *a gory battle.* **3.** covered in gore. — **'gorily** *adv.* — **'goriness** *n.*

Görz (gœrts) *n.* the German name for **Gorizia.**

gosh (gɒʃ) *interj.* an exclamation of mild surprise or wonder. [C18: euphemistic for GOD]

goshawk ('gɒs,hɔːk) *n.* a large hawk of Europe, Asia, and North America, having a bluish-grey back and wings and paler underparts: used in falconry. [OE *gōshafoc*; see GOOSE[1], HAWK[1]]

Goshen ('gəʊʃən) *n.* **1.** a region of ancient Egypt, east of the Nile delta: granted to Jacob and his descendants by the king of Egypt and inhabited by them until the Exodus (Genesis 45:10). **2.** a place of comfort and plenty.

gosling ('gɒzlɪŋ) *n.* **1.** a young goose. **2.** an inexperienced or youthful person. [C15: from ON *gæslingr*; rel. to Danish *gåsling*; see GOOSE[1], -LING[1]]

go-slow *n.* **1.** *Brit.* a deliberate slackening of the rate of production by organized labour as a tactic in industrial conflict. U.S. and Canad. equivalent: **slowdown.** ~*vb.* **go slow. 2.** (*intr.*) to work deliberately slowly as a tactic in industrial conflict.

gospel ('gɒspᵊl) *n.* **1.** Also called: **gospel truth.** an unquestionable truth: *to take someone's word as gospel.* **2.** a doctrine maintained to be of great importance. **3.** Black religious music originating in the churches of the Southern states of the United States. **4.** the message or doctrine of a religious teacher. **5. a.** the story of Christ's life and teachings as narrated in the Gospels. **b.** the good news of salvation in Jesus Christ. **c.** (*as modifier*): *the gospel story.* [OE *gōdspell*, from *gōd* GOOD + *spell* message; see SPELL[2]]

Gospel ('gɒspᵊl) *n.* **1.** any of the first four books of the New Testament, namely Matthew, Mark, Luke, and John. **2.** a reading from one of these in a religious service.

Gosport ('gɒs,pɔːt) *n.* a town in S England, in Hampshire on Portsmouth harbour: naval base since the 16th century. Pop.: 82 000 (1985 est.).

gossamer ('gɒsəmə) *n.* **1.** a gauze or silk fabric of the very finest texture. **2.** a filmy cobweb often seen on foliage or floating in the air. **3.** anything resembling gossamer in fineness or filminess. [C14 (in sense 2): prob. from *gos* GOOSE[1] + *somer* SUMMER; the phrase refers to *St Martin's summer*, a period in November when goose was traditionally eaten; from the prevalence of the cobweb in the autumn] — **'gossamery** *adj.*

Gosse (gɒs) *n.* Sir **Edmund William.** 1849–1928, English critic and poet, noted particularly for his autobiographical work *Father and Son* (1907).

gossip ('gɒsɪp) *n.* **1.** casual and idle chat. **2.** a conversation involving malicious chatter or rumours about other people. **3.** Also called: **gossipmonger.** a person who habitually talks about others, esp. maliciously. **4.** light easy communication: *to write a letter full of gossip.* **5.** *Arch.* a close woman friend. ~*vb.* **6.** (*intr.*; often foll. by *about*) to talk casually or maliciously (about other people). [OE *godsibb* godparent, from GOD + SIB; came to be applied esp. to a woman's female friends at the birth of a child, hence a woman fond of light talk] — **'gossiper** *n.* — **'gossipy** *adj.*

gossypol ('gɒsɪ,pɒl) *n.* a toxic crystalline pigment that is a constituent of cottonseed oil: discovered to have medical applications and currently the subject of research as a male contraceptive. [C19: from Mod. L *gossypium* cotton plant + -OL[1]]

got (gɒt) *vb.* **1.** the past tense and past participle of **get. 2. have got. a.** to possess. **b.** (*takes an infinitive*) used as an auxiliary to express compulsion: *I've got to get a new coat.*

Göta (*Swedish* 'jø:ta) *n*. a river in S Sweden, draining Lake Vänern and flowing south-southwest to the Kattegat: forms part of the **Göta Canal**, which links Göteborg in the west with Stockholm in the east. Length: 93 km (58 miles).

Göteborg (*Swedish* jœtə'bɔrj) *or* **Gothenburg** *n*. a port in SW Sweden, at the mouth of the Göta River: the largest port and second largest city in the country; developed through the Swedish East India Company and grew through Napoleon's continental blockade and with the opening of the Göta Canal (1832); university (1891). Pop.: 429 339 (1986).

Goth (gɒθ) *n*. **1.** a member of an East Germanic people from Scandinavia who settled south of the Baltic early in the first millennium A.D. They moved on to the Ukrainian steppes and raided and later invaded many parts of the Roman Empire from the 3rd to the 5th century. **2.** a rude or barbaric person.

Gotha ('gəʊθə; *German* 'goːta) *n*. a town in SW East Germany, on the N edge of the Thuringian forest: capital of Saxe-Coburg-Gotha (1826-1918); noted for the *Almanach de Gotha* (a record of the royal and noble houses of Europe, first published in 1764). Pop.: 57 876 (1983).

Gotham *n*. ('gəʊtəm, 'gɒtəm). a village in N central England, in Nottinghamshire near Nottingham: renowned for the legend of its early inhabitants, the Wise Men of Gotham, who feigned stupidity in order to dissuade King John from residing in their neighbourhood.

Gothenburg ('gɒθən,bɜːg) *n*. the English name for **Göteborg**.

Gothic ('gɒθɪk) *adj*. **1.** denoting, relating to, or resembling the style of architecture that was used in W Europe from the 12th to the 16th centuries, characterized by the lancet arch, the ribbed vault, and the flying buttress. **2.** of or relating to the style of sculpture, painting, or other arts as practised in W Europe from the 12th to the 16th centuries. **3.** (*sometimes not cap.*) of or relating to a literary style characterized by gloom, the grotesque, and the supernatural, popular esp. in the late 18th century: when used of modern literature, films, etc., sometimes spelt: **Gothick. 4.** of, relating to, or characteristic of the Goths or their language. **5.** (*sometimes not cap.*) primitive and barbarous in style, behaviour, etc. **6.** of or relating to the Middle Ages. ~*n*. **7.** Gothic architecture or art. **8.** the extinct language of the ancient Goths, known mainly from fragments of a translation of the Bible made in the 4th century by Bishop Wulfila. See also **East Germanic. 9.** Also called (esp. Brit): **black letter.** the family of heavy script typefaces in use from about the 15th to 18th centuries. — '**Gothically** *adv*.

go through *vb*. (*intr*.) **1.** (*adv*.) to be approved or accepted: *the amendment went through*. **2.** (*prep*.) to consume; exhaust: *we went through our supplies in a day*. **3.** (*prep*.) Also: **go over**. to examine: *he went through the figures*. **4.** (*prep*.) to suffer: *she went through tremendous pain*. **5.** (*prep*.) Also: **go over**. to rehearse: *let's just go through the details again*. **6.** (*prep*.) to search: *she went through the cupboards*. **7.** (*adv*.; foll. by *with*) to come or bring to a successful conclusion, often by persistence.

Gotland ('gɒtlənd; *Swedish* 'gɔtlant), **Gothland** ('gɒθlənd) *or* **Gottland** ('gɒtlənd) *n*. an island in the Baltic Sea, off the SE coast of Sweden: important trading centre since the Bronze Age; long disputed between Sweden and Denmark, finally becoming Swedish in 1645; tourism and agriculture now important. Capital: Visby. Pop.: (including associated islands) 56 174 (1986 est.). Area: 3140 sq. km (1212 sq. miles).

go together *vb*. (*intr*., *adv*.) **1.** to be mutually suited; harmonize: *the colours go well together*. **2.** *Inf*. (of two people of opposite sex) to associate frequently with each other: *they had been going together for two years*.

gotten ('gɒtʰn) *vb*. U.S. a past participle of **get**.

Götterdämmerung (,gɒtə'dɛmə,rʊŋ) *n. German myth*. the twilight of the gods; their ultimate destruction in a battle with the forces of evil.

Gottfried von Strassburg (*German* 'gɔtfriːt fɔn 'ʃtraːsbʊrk) *n*. early 13th-century German poet; author of the incomplete epic *Tristan and Isolde*, the version of the legend that served as the basis of Wagner's opera.

Göttingen ('gœtɪŋən) *n*. a city in central West Germany, in Lower Saxony; important member of the Hanseatic League (14th century); university, founded in 1734 by George II of England. Pop.: 133 700 (1987).

Götz von Berlichingen (*German* gœts fɔn 'bɛrlɪçɪŋən). See **Berlichingen**.

gouache (gʊ'ɑː.ʃ) *n*. **1.** Also called: **body colour**. a painting technique using opaque watercolour in which the pigments are bound with glue. **2.** the paint used in this technique. **3.** a painting done by this method. [C19: from F, from It. *guazzo* puddle, from L, from *aqua* water]

Gouda ('gaʊdə; *Dutch* 'xɔuda:) *n*. **1.** a town in the W Netherlands, in South Holland province: important medieval cloth trade; famous for its cheese. Pop.: 61 458 (1987). **2.** a large flat round Dutch cheese, mild and similar in taste to Edam.

gouge (gaʊdʒ) *vb*. (*mainly tr*.) **1.** (usually foll. by *out*) to scoop or force (something) out of its position. **2.** (sometimes foll. by *out*) to cut (a hole or groove) in (something) with a sharp instrument or tool. **3.** *U.S. & Canad. inf*. to extort from. **4.** (*also intr*.) *Austral*. to dig for (opal). ~*n*. **5.** a type of chisel with a blade that has a concavo-convex section. **6.** a mark or groove made as with a gouge. **7.** *U.S. & Canad. inf*. extortion; swindling. [C15: from F, from LL *gulbia* a chisel, of Celtic origin] — '**gouger** *n*.

goulash ('guːlæ.ʃ) *n*. **1.** Also called: **Hungarian goulash**. a rich stew, originating in Hungary, made of beef, lamb, or veal highly seasoned with paprika. **2.** *Bridge*. a method of dealing in threes and fours without first shuffling the cards, to produce freak hands. [C19: from Hungarian *gulyás hus* herdsman's meat]

Gould (guːld) *n*. **Benjamin Apthorp**. 1824–96, U.S. astronomer: the first to use the telegraph to determine longitudes; founded the *Astronomical Journal* (1849).

go under *vb*. (*intr*., *mainly adv*.) **1.** (*also prep*.) to sink below (a surface). **2.** to be overwhelmed: *the firm went under in the economic crisis*.

Gounod ('guːnəʊ; *French* guno) *n*. **Charles François** (ʃarl frɑːswa). 1818–93, French composer of the operas *Faust* (1859) and *Romeo and Juliet* (1867).

go up *vb*. (*intr*., *mainly adv*.) **1.** (*also prep*.) to move or lead as to a higher place or level; rise; increase: *prices are always going up*. **2.** to be destroyed: *the house went up in flames*. **3.** *Brit*. to go or return (to college or university).

gourami ('gʊərəmɪ) *n*., *pl*. **-mi** *or* **-mis**. **1.** a large SE Asian labyrinth fish used for food. **2.** any of various other labyrinth fishes, many of which are brightly coloured and popular aquarium fishes. [from Malay *gurami*]

gourd (gʊəd) *n*. **1.** the fruit of any of various plants of the cucumber family, esp. the bottle gourd and some squashes, whose dried shells are used for ornament, drinking cups, etc. **2.** any plant that bears this fruit. **3.** a bottle or flask made from the dried shell of the bottle gourd. [C14: from OF *gourde*, ult. from L *cucurbita*]

gourmand ('gʊəmənd) *or* **gormand** *n*. a person devoted to eating and drinking, esp. to excess. [C15: from OF *gourmant*, from ?] — '**gourmand,ism** *n*.

gourmet ('gʊəmeɪ) *n*. a person who cultivates a discriminating palate for the enjoyment of good food and drink. [C19: from F, from OF *gromet* serving boy]

Gourmont (*French* gurmɔ̃) *n*. **Remy de** (rəmi də). 1858–1915, French symbolist critic and novelist.

gout (gaʊt) *n*. **1.** a metabolic disease characterized by painful inflammation of certain joints, esp. of the big toe, caused by deposits of sodium urate. **2.** *Arch*. a drop or splash, esp. of blood. [C13: from OF, from L *gutta* a drop] — '**gouty** *adj*. — '**goutily** *adv*. — '**goutiness** *n*.

Gov. *or* **gov.** *abbrev. for*: **1.** government. **2.** governor.

govern ('gʌvʰn) *vb*. (*mainly tr*.) **1.** (*also intr*.) to direct and control the actions, affairs, policies, functions, etc., of (an organization, nation, etc.). **2.** to exercise restraint over; regulate or direct: *to govern one's temper*. **3.** to decide or determine (something): *his injury governed his decision to avoid sports*. **4.** to control the speed of (an engine, machine, etc.) using a governor. **5.** (of a word) to determine the inflection of (another word): *Latin nouns govern adjectives that modify them*. [C13: from OF, from L *gubernāre* to steer, from Gk *kubernan*] — '**governable** *adj*.

governance ('gʌvənəns) *n*. **1.** government, control, or authority. **2.** the action, manner, or system of governing.

governess ('gʌvənɪs) *n*. a woman teacher employed in a private household to teach and train the children.

government ('gʌvənmənt, 'gʌvəmənt) n. **1.** the exercise of political authority over the actions, affairs, etc., of a political unit, people, etc.; the action of governing; political rule and administration. **2.** the system or form by which a community, etc., is ruled: *tyrannical government.* **3. a.** the executive policy-making body of a political unit, community, etc.; ministry or administration. **b.** (*cap. when of a specific country*): *the British Government.* **4. a.** the state and its administration: *blame it on the government.* **b.** (*as modifier*): *a government agency.* **5.** regulation; direction. **6.** *Grammar.* the determination of the form of one word by another word. —**governmental** (ˌgʌvən'mɛnt²l, ˌgʌvə'mɛnt²l) adj. —ˌgovern'mentally adv.

governor ('gʌvənə) n. **1.** a person who governs. **2.** the ruler or chief magistrate of a colony, province, etc. **3.** the representative of the Crown in a British colony. **4.** *Brit.* the senior administrator of a society, prison, etc. **5.** the chief executive of any state in the U.S. **6.** a device that controls the speed of an engine, esp. by regulating the supply of fuel. **7.** *Brit. inf.* a name or title of respect for a father, employer, etc. —'governorˌship n.

governor general n., pl. **governors general** or **governor generals. 1.** the representative of the Crown in a dominion of the Commonwealth or a British colony; vice-gerent. **2.** *Brit.* a governor with jurisdiction or precedence over other governors. —ˌgovernor-'generalˌship n.

Govt or **govt** abbrev. for government.

Gower[1] ('gauə) n. **1. David** (**Ivon**). born 1957, English cricketer: captained England (1984–86). **2. John.** ?1330–1408, English poet, noted particularly for his tales of love, the *Confessio Amantis.*

Gower[2] ('gauə) n. **the.** a peninsula in S Wales, in West Glamorgan in the Bristol Channel: mainly agricultural with several resorts.

go with vb. (*intr., prep.*) **1.** to accompany. **2.** to blend or harmonize: *that new wallpaper goes well with the furniture.* **3.** to be a normal part of: *three acres of land go with the house.* **4.** (*of two people of the opposite sex*) to associate frequently with each other.

go without vb. (*intr.*) *Chiefly Brit.* to be denied or deprived of (something, esp. food): *if you don't like your tea you can go without.*

gowk (gauk) n. *Scot. & N English dialect.* **1.** a fool. **2.** a cuckoo. [from ON *gaukr* cuckoo]

gown (gaun) n. **1.** any of various outer garments, such as a woman's elegant or formal dress, a dressing robe, or a protective garment, esp. one worn by surgeons during operations. **2.** a loose wide garment indicating status, such as worn by academics. **3.** the members of a university as opposed to the other residents of the university town. ~vb. **4.** (*tr.*) to supply with or dress in a gown. [C14: from OF, from LL *gunna* garment made of leather or fur, of Celtic origin]

Gowon ('gauən) n. **Yakubu** ('ja:ku,bu:). born 1934, Nigerian general and statesman; head of state from 1966 until his overthrow in 1975.

goy (gɔɪ) n., pl. **goyim** ('gɔɪɪm) or **goys.** *Sl.* a Jewish word for a **Gentile.** [from Yiddish, from Heb. *goi* people] —'goyish adj.

Goya ('gɔɪə; *Spanish* 'goja) n. **Francisco de** (fran'θisko de), full name *Francisco José de Goya y Lucientes.* 1746–1828, Spanish painter and etcher; well known for his portraits, he became court painter to Charles IV of Spain (1799). He recorded the French invasion of Spain in a series of etchings *The Disasters of War* (1810–14) and two paintings *2 May 1808* and *3 May 1808* (1814).

GP abbrev. for: **1.** Gallup Poll. **2.** *Music.* general pause. **3.** general practitioner. **4.** (in Britain) graduated pension. **5.** Grand Prix.

GPO abbrev. for general post office.

Gr. abbrev. for: **1.** Grecian. **2.** Greece. **3.** Greek.

Graafian follicle ('grɑːfɪən) n. a fluid-filled vesicle in the mammalian ovary containing a developing egg cell. [C17: after R. de *Graaf* (1641–73), Du. anatomist]

grab (græb) vb. **grabbing, grabbed. 1.** to seize hold of (something). **2.** (*tr.*) to seize illegally or unscrupulously. **3.** (*tr.*) to arrest; catch. **4.** (*tr.*) *Inf.* to catch the attention or interest of; impress. ~n. **5.** the act or an instance of grabbing. **6.** a mechanical device for gripping objects,

esp. the hinged jaws of a mechanical excavator. **7.** something that is grabbed. [C16: prob. from MLow G or MDu. *grabben*] —'grabber n.

Gracchus ('grækəs) n. **Tiberius Sempronius** (taɪ-'bɪərɪəs sɛm'prəʊnɪəs). ?163–133 B.C., and his younger brother, **Gaius Sempronius** ('gaɪəs), 153–121 B.C., known as *the Gracchi.* Roman tribunes and reformers. Tiberius attempted to redistribute public land among the poor but was murdered in the ensuing riot. Violence again occurred when the reform was revived by Gaius, and he too was killed.

grace (greɪs) n. **1.** elegance and beauty of movement, form, expression, or proportion. **2.** a pleasing or charming quality. **3.** goodwill or favour. **4.** a delay granted for the completion of a task or payment of a debt. **5.** a sense of propriety and consideration for others. **6.** (*pl.*) a. affectation of manner (esp. in **airs and graces**). **b. in** (**someone's**) **good graces.** regarded favourably and with kindness by (someone). **7.** mercy; clemency. **8.** *Christian theol.* **a.** the free and unmerited favour of God shown towards man. **b.** the divine assistance given to man in spiritual rebirth. **c.** the condition of being favoured or sanctified by God. **d.** an unmerited gift, favour, etc., granted by God. **9.** a short prayer recited before or after a meal to give thanks for it. **10.** *Music.* a melodic ornament or decoration. **11. with (a) bad grace.** unwillingly or grudgingly. **12. with (a) good grace.** willingly or cheerfully. ~vb. **13.** (*tr.*) to add elegance and beauty to: *flowers graced the room.* **14.** (*tr.*) to honour or favour: *to grace a party with one's presence.* **15.** to ornament or decorate (a melody, part, etc.) with nonessential notes. [C12: from OF, from L *grātia*, from *grātus* pleasing]

Grace[1] (greɪs) n. (preceded by *your, his,* or *her*) a title used to address or refer to a duke, duchess, or archbishop.

Grace[2] (greɪs) n. **W(illiam) G(ilbert).** 1848–1915, English cricketer.

grace-and-favour n. (*modifier*) *Brit.* (of a house, flat, etc.) owned by the sovereign and granted free of rent to a person to whom the sovereign wishes to express gratitude.

graceful ('greɪsful) adj. characterized by beauty of movement, style, form, etc. —'gracefully adv. —'gracefulness n.

graceless ('greɪslɪs) adj. **1.** lacking manners. **2.** lacking elegance. —'gracelessly adv. —'gracelessness n.

grace note n. *Music.* a note printed in small type to indicate that it is melodically and harmonically nonessential.

Graces ('greɪsɪz) pl. n. *Greek myth.* three sister goddesses, givers of charm and beauty.

gracious ('greɪʃəs) adj. **1.** characterized by or showing kindness and courtesy. **2.** condescendingly courteous, benevolent, or indulgent. **3.** characterized by or suitable for a life of elegance, ease, and indulgence: *gracious living.* **4.** merciful or compassionate. ~interj. **5.** an expression of mild surprise or wonder. —'graciously adv. —'graciousness n.

grackle ('græk²l) n. **1.** an American songbird of the oriole family, having a dark iridescent plumage. **2.** any of various starlings, such as the Indian grackle or hill myna. [C18: from NL, from L *grāculus* jackdaw]

grad. abbrev. for: **1.** *Maths.* gradient. **2.** *Education.* graduate(d).

gradate (grə'deɪt) vb. **1.** to change or cause to change imperceptibly, as from one colour, tone, or degree to another. **2.** (*tr.*) to arrange in grades or ranks.

gradation (grə'deɪʃən) n. **1.** a series of systematic stages; gradual progression. **2.** (*often pl.*) a stage or degree in such a series or progression. **3.** the act or process of arranging or forming in stages, grades, etc., or of progressing evenly. **4.** (in painting, drawing, or sculpture) transition from one colour, tone, or surface to another through a series of very slight changes. **5.** *Linguistics.* any change in the quality or length of a vowel within a word indicating certain distinctions, such as inflectional or tense differentiations. See also **ablaut.** —gra'dational adj.

grade (greɪd) n. **1.** a position or degree in a scale, as of quality, rank, size, or progression: *high-grade timber.* **2.** a group of people or things of the same category. **3.** *Chiefly U.S.* a military or other rank. **4.** a stage in a course of progression. **5.** a mark or rating indicating achievement or the worth of work done, as at school. **6.** *U.S. & Canad.* a unit of pupils of similar age or ability taught together at school. **7. make the grade.** *Inf.* **a.** to reach the required standard. **b.** to succeed. ~*vb.* **8.** (*tr.*) to arrange according to quality, rank, etc. **9.** (*tr.*) to determine the grade of or assign a grade to. **10.** (*intr.*) to achieve or deserve a grade or rank. **11.** to change or blend (something) gradually; merge. **12.** (*tr.*) to level (ground, a road, etc.) to a suitable gradient. [C16: from F, from L *gradus* step, from *gradī* to step]

-grade *adj. combining form.* indicating a kind or manner of movement or progression: *plantigrade; retrograde.* [via F from L *-gradus*, from *gradus* a step, from *gradī* to walk]

gradely ('greɪdlɪ) *adj.* **-lier, -liest.** *Midland English dialect.* fine; excellent. [C13: from ON *greidhligr*, from *greidhr* ready]

grader ('greɪdə) *n.* **1.** a person or thing that grades. **2.** a machine that levels earth, rubble, etc., as in road construction.

gradient ('greɪdɪənt) *n.* **1.** Also called (esp. U.S.): **grade.** a part of a railway, road, etc., that slopes upwards or downwards; inclination. **2.** Also called (esp. U.S. and Canad.): **grade.** a measure of such a slope, esp. the ratio of the vertical distance between two points on the slope to the horizontal distance between them. **3.** *Physics.* a measure of the change of some physical quantity, such as temperature or electric potential, over a specified distance. **4.** *Maths.* (of a curve) the slope of the tangent at any point on a curve with respect to the horizontal axis. ~*adj.* **5.** sloping uniformly. [C19: from L *gradiēns* stepping, from *gradī* to go]

gradin ('greɪdɪn) *or* **gradine** (grə'diːn) *n.* **1.** a ledge above or behind an altar for candles, etc., to stand on. **2.** one of a set of steps or seats arranged on a slope, as in an amphitheatre. [C19: from F, from It. *gradino*, dim. of *grado* a step]

gradual ('grædjʊəl) *adj.* **1.** occurring, developing, moving, etc., in small stages: *a gradual improvement in health.* **2.** not steep or abrupt: *a gradual slope.* ~*n.* **3.** (*often cap.*) *Christianity.* **a.** an antiphon usually from the Psalms, sung or recited immediately after the epistle at Mass. **b.** a book of plainsong containing the words and music of the parts of the Mass that are sung by the cantors and choir. [C16: from Med. L: relating to steps, from L *gradus* a step] — '**gradually** *adv.* — '**gradualness** *n.*

gradualism ('grædjʊə,lɪzəm) *n.* **1.** the policy of seeking to change something gradually, esp. in politics. **2.** the theory that explains major changes in fossils, rock strata, etc., in terms of gradual evolutionary processes rather than sudden violent catastrophes. — '**gradualist** *n., adj.* — ,gradual'istic *adj.*

graduand ('grædjʊ,ænd) *n. Chiefly Brit.* a person who is about to graduate. [C19: from Med. L gerundive of *graduārī* to GRADUATE]

graduate *n.* ('grædjʊɪt). **1.** a person who has been awarded a first degree from a university or college. **2.** *U.S. & Canad.* a student who has completed a course of studies at a high school and received a diploma. ~*vb.* ('grædjʊ,eɪt). **3.** to receive or cause to receive a degree or diploma. **4.** *Chiefly U.S. & Canad.* to confer a degree, diploma, etc., upon. **5.** (*tr.*) to mark (a thermometer, flask, etc.) with units of measurement; calibrate. **6.** (*tr.*) to arrange or sort into groups according to type, quality, etc. **7.** (*intr.; often foll. by to*) to change by degrees (from something to something else). [C15: from Med. L *graduārī* to take a degree, from L *gradus* a step] — '**gradu,ator** *n.*

graduated pension *n.* (in Britain) a national pension scheme in which employees' contributions are scaled in accordance with their wage rate.

graduation (,grædjʊ'eɪʃən) *n.* **1.** the act of graduating or the state of being graduated. **2.** the ceremony at which school or college degrees and diplomas are conferred. **3.** a mark or division or all the marks or divisions that indicate measure on an instrument or vessel.

Graeae ('griːiː) *or* **Graiae** *pl. n. Greek myth.* three aged sea deities, having only one eye and one tooth among them, guardians of their sisters, the Gorgons.

Graecism *or esp. U.S.* **Grecism** ('griːsɪzəm) *n.* **1.** Greek characteristics or style. **2.** admiration for or imitation of these, as in sculpture or architecture. **3.** a form of words characteristic or imitative of the idiom of the Greek language.

Graeco- *or esp. U.S.* **Greco-** ('griːkəʊ, 'grɛkəʊ) *combining form.* Greek: *Graeco-Roman.*

Graeco-Roman *or esp. U.S.* **Greco-Roman** *adj.* of, characteristic of, or relating to Greek and Roman influences.

Graf (græf) *n.* **Steffi.** born 1969, West German tennis player: Wimbledon champion 1988.

graffiti (græ'fiːtɪ) *pl. n.* (*sometimes functioning as sing.*) drawings, messages, etc., often obscene, scribbled on the walls of public lavatories, advertising premises, etc. [C19: see GRAFFITO]

graffito (græ'fiːtəʊ) *n., pl.* **-ti** (-tɪ). **1.** *Archaeol.* any inscription or drawing scratched onto a surface, esp. rock or pottery. **2.** See **graffiti.** [C19: from It.: a little scratch, from L *graphium* stylus, from Gk *grapheion*; see GRAFT[1]]

graft[1] (grɑːft) *n.* **1.** *Horticulture.* **a.** a small piece of plant tissue (the scion) that is made to unite with an established plant (the stock), which supports and nourishes it. **b.** the plant resulting from the union of scion and stock. **c.** the point of union between the scion and the stock. **2.** *Surgery.* a piece of tissue transplanted from a donor or from the patient's own body to an area of the body in need of the tissue. **3.** the act of joining one thing to another as by grafting. ~*vb.* **4.** *Horticulture.* **a.** to induce (a plant or part of a plant) to unite with another part or (of a plant or part of a plant) to unite in this way. **b.** to produce (fruit, flowers, etc.) by this means or (of fruit, etc.) to grow by this means. **5.** to transplant (tissue) or (of tissue) to be transplanted. **6.** to attach or incorporate or become attached or incorporated: *to graft a happy ending onto a sad tale.* [C15: from OF *graffe*, from Med. L *graphium*, from L: stylus, from Gk *grapheion*, from *graphein* to write] — '**grafter** *n.* — '**grafting** *n.*

graft[2] (grɑːft) *n.* **1.** *Inf.* work (esp. in **hard graft**). **2. a.** the acquisition of money, power, etc., by dishonest or unfair means, esp. by taking advantage of a position of trust. **b.** something gained in this way. **c.** a payment made to a person profiting by such a practice. ~*vb.* **3.** (*intr.*) *Inf.* to work, esp. hard. **4.** to acquire by or practise graft. [C19: from ?] — '**grafter** *n.*

Graham ('greɪəm) *n.* **1. Martha.** born 1893, U.S. dancer and choreographer. **2. William Franklin,** known as *Billy Graham.* born 1918, U.S. evangelist.

Grahame ('greɪəm) *n.* **Kenneth.** 1859–1932, Scottish author, noted for the children's classic *The Wind in the Willows* (1908).

Graham Land *n.* the N part of the Antarctic Peninsula: became part of the British Antarctic Territory in 1962 (formerly part of the Falkland Islands Dependencies).

Graiae ('greɪiː, 'graɪiː) *pl. n.* a variant of **Graeae.**

Graian Alps ('greɪən, 'graɪ-) *pl. n.* the N part of the Western Alps, in France and NW Piedmont, Italy. Highest peak: Gran Paradiso, 4061 m (13 323 ft.).

Grail (greɪl) *n.* See **Holy Grail.**

grain (greɪn) *n.* **1.** the small hard seedlike fruit of a grass, esp. a cereal plant. **2.** a mass of such fruits, esp. when gathered for food. **3.** the plants, collectively, from which such fruits are harvested. **4.** a small hard particle: *a grain of sand.* **5. a.** the general direction or arrangement of the fibres, layers, or particles in wood, leather, stone, etc. **b.** the pattern or texture resulting from such an arrangement. **6.** the relative size of the particles of a substance: *sugar of fine grain.* **7.** the granular texture of a rock, mineral, etc. **8.** the outer layer of a hide or skin from which the hair or wool has been removed. **9.** the smallest unit of weight in the avoirdupois, Troy, and apothecaries' systems: equal to 0.0648 gram. **10.** the threads or direction of threads in a woven fabric. **11.** *Photog.* any of a large number of particles in a photographic emulsion. **12.** cleavage lines in crystalline material. **13.** *Chem.* any of a large number of small crystals forming a solid. **14.** a very small amount: *a grain of truth.* **15.** natural disposition, inclination, or character (esp. in **go against the grain**). **16.** *Astronautics.* a homogenous mass of solid propellant in a form designed to give the required combustion characteristics for a particular rocket. **17.** (not in technical usage) kermes or a red dye made from this insect. ~*vb.* (*mainly tr.*) **18.** (*also intr.*) to form grains or cause to form into grains; granulate; crystallize. **19.** to give a granular or roughened appearance or texture to. **20.** to paint, stain, etc., in imitation of the grain of wood or leather. **21. a.** to remove the hair or wool from (a hide or skin) before tanning. **b.** to raise the grain pattern on (leather). [C13: from OF, from L *grānum*]

grain alcohol *n.* ethanol containing about 10 per cent of water, made by the fermentation of grain.

grain elevator *n.* a machine for raising grain to a higher level, esp. one having an endless belt fitted with scoops.

Grainger ('greɪndʒə) *n.* **Percy Aldridge.** 1882–1961, Australian pianist, composer, and collector of folk music on which many of his works are based.

graining ('greɪnɪŋ) *n.* **1.** the pattern or texture of the grain of wood, leather, etc. **2.** the process of painting, printing, staining, etc., a surface in imitation of a grain. **3.** a surface produced by such a process.

grainy ('greɪnɪ) *adj.* **grainier, grainiest. 1.** resembling, full of, or composed of grain; granular. **2.** resembling the grain of wood, leather, etc. **3.** *Photog.* having poor definition because of large grain size. — **'graininess** *n.*

grallatorial (ˌgrælə'tɔːrɪəl) *adj.* of or relating to long-legged wading birds. [C19: from NL, from L *grallātor* one who walks on stilts, from *grallae* stilts]

gram[1] *or* **gramme** (græm) *n.* a metric unit of mass equal to one thousandth of a kilogram. Symbol: g [C18: from F *gramme*, from LL *gramma*, from Gk: small weight, from *graphein* to write]

gram[2] (græm) *n.* **1.** any of several leguminous plants whose seeds are used as food in India. **2.** the seed of any of these plants. [C18: from Port. *gram* (modern spelling: *grão*), from L *grānum* GRAIN]

gram. *abbrev. for:* **1.** grammar. **2.** grammatical.

-gram *n. combining form.* indicating a drawing or something written or recorded: *hexagram; telegram.* [from L *-gramma*, from Gk, from *gramma* letter & *grammē* line]

gram atom *or* **gram-atomic weight** *n.* an amount of an element equal to its atomic weight expressed in grams: now replaced by the mole.

gramineous (grə'mɪnɪəs) *adj.* **1.** of, relating to, or belonging to the grass family. **2.** resembling a grass; grass-like. ~Also: **graminaceous** (ˌgræmɪ'neɪʃəs). [C17: from L, from *grāmen* grass]

graminivorous (ˌgræmɪ'nɪvərəs) *adj.* (of animals) feeding on grass. [C18: from L *grāmen* grass + -VOROUS]

grammar ('græmə) *n.* **1.** the branch of linguistics that deals with syntax and morphology, sometimes also phonology and semantics. **2.** the abstract system of rules in terms of which a person's mastery of his native language can be explained. **3.** a systematic description of the grammatical facts of a language. **4.** a book containing an account of the grammatical facts of a language or recommendations as to rules for the proper use of a language. **5.** the use of language with regard to its correctness or social propriety, esp. in syntax: *the teacher told him to watch his grammar.* [C14: from OF, from L, from Gk *grammatikē (tekhnē)* the grammatical (art), from *grammatikos* concerning letters, from *gramma* letter]

grammarian (grə'mɛərɪən) *n.* **1.** a person whose occupation is the study of grammar. **2.** the author of a grammar.

grammar school *n.* **1.** *Brit.* (esp. formerly) a state-maintained secondary school providing an education with an academic bias. **2.** *U.S.* another term for **elementary school. 3.** *Austral.* a private school, esp. one controlled by a church. **4.** *N.Z.* a secondary school forming part of the public education system.

grammatical (grə'mætɪkəl) *adj.* **1.** of or relating to grammar. **2.** (of a sentence) well formed; regarded as correct. — **gram'matically** *adv.* — **gram'maticalness** *n.*

gramme (græm) *n.* a variant spelling of **gram**[1].

gram molecule *or* **gram-molecular weight** *n.* an amount of a compound equal to its molecular weight expressed in grams: now replaced by the mole. See **mole**[3].

Grammy ('græmɪ) *n., pl.* **-mys** *or* **-mies.** (in the U.S.) one of the gold-plated discs awarded annually for outstanding achievement in the record industry. [C20: from GRAM(O-PHONE) + -*my* as in EMMY]

gramophone ('græməˌfəʊn) *n.* **1. a.** Also called: **record player.** a device for reproducing the sounds stored on a record: now usually applied to the early type that uses an acoustic horn. U.S. and Canad. word: **phonograph. b.** (*as modifier*): *a gramophone record.* **2.** the technique of recording sound on disc: *the gramophone has made music widely available.* [C19: orig. a trademark, ? based on an inversion of *phonogram*; see PHONO-, -GRAM]

Grampian Mountains ('græmpɪən) *pl. n.* **1.** a mountain system of central Scotland, extending from the southwest to the northeast and separating the Highlands from the Lowlands. Highest peak: Ben Nevis, 1343 m (4406 ft.). **2.**

a mountain range in SE Australia, in W Victoria. ~Also called: **the Grampians.**

Grampian Region *n.* a local government region in NE Scotland, formed in 1975 from Aberdeenshire, Kincardineshire, and most of Banffshire and Morayshire. Administrative centre: Aberdeen. Pop.: 502 850 (1986 est.). Area: 8700 sq. km (3360 sq. miles).

grampus ('græmpəs) *n., pl.* **-puses. 1.** a widely distributed slaty-grey dolphin with a blunt snout. **2.** another name for **killer whale.** [C16: from OF *graspois*, from *gras* fat (from L *crassus*) + *pois* fish (from L *piscis*)]

Gram's method (græmz) *n. Bacteriol.* **1.** a technique used to classify bacteria by staining them with a violet iodine solution. **2. Gram-positive** (*or* **Gram-negative**). *adj.* denoting bacteria that (*or* do not) retain this stain. [C19: after H. C. J. *Gram* (1853–1938), Danish physician]

Granada (grə'nɑːdə) *n.* **1.** a former kingdom of S Spain, in Andalusia: founded in the 13th century and divided in 1833 into the present-day provinces of Granada, Almería, and Málaga. **2.** a city in S Spain, in Andalusia: capital of the Moorish kingdom of Granada from 1238 to 1492 and a great commercial and cultural centre, containing the Alhambra palace (13th and 14th centuries); university (1531). Pop.: 246 642 (1981). **3.** a city in SW Nicaragua, on the NW shore of Lake Nicaragua: the oldest city in the country, founded in 1523 by Córdoba; attacked frequently by pirates in the 17th century. Pop.: 88 636 (1985).

granadilla (ˌgrænə'dɪlə) *n.* **1.** any of various passionflowers that have edible egg-shaped fleshy fruit. **2.** Also called: **passion fruit.** the fruit of such a plant. [C18: from Sp., dim. of *granada* pomegranate, from LL *grānātum*]

Granados (*Spanish* grɑ'naðɔs) *n.* **Enrique** (en'rrike), full name *Enrique Granados y Campina.* 1867–1916, Spanish composer, noted for the *Goyescas* (1911) for piano, which formed the basis for an opera of the same name.

granary ('grænərɪ; *U.S.* 'greɪnərɪ) *n., pl.* **-ries. 1.** a building for storing threshed grain. **2.** a region that produces a large amount of grain. [C16: from L *grānārium*, from *grānum* GRAIN]

Gran Canaria (graŋ ka'narja) *n.* the Spanish name for **Grand Canary.**

Gran Chaco (*Spanish* gran 'tʃako) *n.* a plain of S central South America, between the Andes and the Paraguay River in SE Bolivia, E Paraguay, and N Argentina: huge swamps and scrub forest. Area: about 780 000 sq. km (300 000 sq. miles). Often shortened to: **Chaco.**

grand (grænd) *adj.* **1.** large or impressive in size, extent, or consequence: *grand mountain scenery.* **2.** characterized by or attended with magnificence or display; sumptuous: *a grand feast.* **3.** of great distinction or pretension; dignified or haughty. **4.** designed to impress: *grand gestures.* **5.** very good; wonderful. **6.** comprehensive; complete: *a grand total.* **7.** worthy of respect; fine: *a grand old man.* **8.** large or impressive in conception or execution: *grand ideas.* **9.** most important; chief: *the grand arena.* ~*n.* **10.** See **grand piano. 11.** (*pl.* **grand**) *Sl.* a thousand pounds or dollars. [C16: from OF, from L *grandis*] — **'grandly** *adv.* — **'grandness** *n.*

grand- *prefix.* (in designations of kinship) one generation removed in ascent or descent: *grandson; grandfather.* [from F *grand-*, on the model of L *magnus* in such phrases as *avunculus magnus* great-uncle]

grandam ('grændəm, -dæm) *or* **grandame** ('grændeɪm, -dəm) *n.* an archaic word for **grandmother.** [C13: from Anglo-F *grandame*, from OF GRAND- + *dame* lady, mother]

grandaunt ('grændˌɑːnt) *n.* another name for **great-aunt.**

Grand Bahama *n.* an island in the Atlantic, in the W Bahamas. Pop.: 33 102 (1980). Area: 1114 sq. km (430 sq. miles).

Grand Banks *pl. n.* a part of the continental shelf in the Atlantic, extending for about 560 km (350 miles) off the SE coast of Newfoundland: meeting place of the cold Labrador Current and the warm Gulf Stream, producing frequent fogs and rich fishing grounds.

Grand Canal *n.* **1.** a canal in E China, extending north from Hangzhou to Tianjin: the longest canal in China, now partly silted up; central section, linking the Yangtze and Yellow Rivers, finished in 486 B.C.; north section finished by Kublai Khan between 1282 and 1292. Length: about 1600 km (1000 miles). Chinese name: **Da Yunhe. 2.** a canal in Venice, forming the main water thoroughfare: noted for its bridges, the Rialto, and the fine palaces along its banks.

Grand Canary *n.* an island in the Atlantic, in the Canary Islands: part of the Spanish province of Las Palmas. Capital: Las Palmas. Pop.: 630 937 (1981). Area: 1533 sq. km (592 sq. miles). Spanish name: **Gran Canaria.**

Grand Canyon *n.* a gorge of the Colorado River in N Arizona, extending from its junction with the Little Colorado River to Lake Mead; cut by vertical river erosion through the multicoloured strata of a high plateau; partly contained in the **Grand Canyon National Park,** covering 2610 sq. km (1008 sq. miles). Length: 451 km (280 miles). Width: 6 km (4 miles) to 29 km (18 miles). Greatest depth: over 1.5 km (1 mile).

grandchild ('græn,tʃaɪld) *n., pl.* **-children.** the son or daughter of one's child.

Grand Coulee ('ku:lɪ) *n.* a canyon in central Washington State, over 120 m (400 ft.) deep, at the N end of which is situated the **Grand Coulee Dam,** on the Columbia River. Height of dam: 168 m (550 ft.). Length of dam: 1310 m (4300 ft.).

granddad ('græn,dæd) *or* **granddaddy** *n., pl.* **-dads** *or* **-daddies.** informal words for **grandfather.**

granddaughter ('græn,dɔ:tə) *n.* a daughter of one's son or daughter.

grand duchess *n.* **1.** the wife or widow of a grand duke. **2.** a woman who holds the rank of grand duke in her own right.

grand duchy *n.* the territory, state, or principality of a grand duke or grand duchess.

grand duke *n.* **1.** a prince or nobleman who rules a territory, state, or principality. **2.** a son or a male descendant in the male line of a Russian tsar. **3.** a medieval Russian prince who ruled over other princes.

grande dame *French.* (grãd dam) *n.* a woman regarded as the most experienced, prominent, or venerable member of her profession, etc.

grandee (græn'di:) *n.* **1.** a Spanish or Portuguese prince or nobleman of the highest rank. **2.** a person of high station. [C16: from Sp. *grande*]

Grande-Terre (*French* grãdtɛr) *n.* an island in the French West Indies, in the Lesser Antilles: one of the two main islands which constitute Guadeloupe. Chief town: Pointe-à-Pitre.

grandeur ('grændʒə) *n.* **1.** personal greatness, esp. when based on dignity, character, or accomplishments. **2.** magnificence; splendour. **3.** pretentious or bombastic behaviour.

Grand Falls *pl. n.* the former name (until 1965) of **Churchill Falls.**

grandfather ('græn,fɑ:ðə, 'grænd-) *n.* **1.** the father of one's father or mother. **2.** (*often pl.*) a male ancestor. **3.** (*often cap.*) a familiar term of address for an old man. —'**grand,fatherly** *adj.*

grandfather clock *n.* a long-pendulum clock in a tall standing wooden case.

Grand Guignol *French.* (grã giɲɔl) *n.* **a.** a brief sensational play intended to horrify. **b.** (*modifier*) of or like plays of this kind. [C20: after *Le Grand Guignol,* a small theatre in Montmartre, Paris]

grandiloquent (græn'dɪləkwənt) *adj.* inflated, pompous, or bombastic in style or expression. [C16: from L *grandiloquus,* from *grandis* great + *loquī* to speak] —**gran'diloquence** *n.* —**gran'diloquently** *adv.*

grandiose ('grændɪ,əʊs) *adj.* **1.** pretentiously grand or stately. **2.** imposing in conception or execution. [C19: from F, from It., from *grande* great; see GRAND] —'**grandi,osely** *adv.* —**grandiosity** (,grændɪ'ɒsɪtɪ) *n.*

grand jury *n. Law.* (esp. in the U.S. and, now rarely, in Canada) a jury summoned to inquire into accusations of crime and ascertain whether the evidence is adequate to found an indictment. Abolished in England in 1948.

grand larceny *n.* **1.** (formerly, in England) the theft of property valued at over 12 pence. Abolished in 1827. **2.** (in some states of the U.S.) the theft of property of which the value is above a specified figure.

grandma ('græn,mɑ:), **grandmama,** *or* **grandmamma** ('grænmə,mɑ:) *n.* informal words for **grandmother.**

grand mal (grɒn mæl) *n.* a form of epilepsy characterized by loss of consciousness for up to five minutes and violent convulsions. Cf. **petit mal.** [F: great illness]

Grand Manan (mə'næn) *n.* a Canadian island, off the SW coast of New Brunswick: separated from the coast of

Maine by the **Grand Manan Channel.** Area: 147 sq. km (57 sq. miles).

grandmaster ('grænd,mɑːstə) *n.* **1.** *Chess.* one of the top chess players of a particular country. **2.** a leading exponent of any of various arts.

Grand Master *n.* the title borne by the head of any of various societies, orders, and other organizations, such as the Templars, Freemasons, or the various martial arts.

grandmother ('græn,mʌðə, 'grænd-) *n.* **1.** the mother of one's father or mother. **2.** (*often pl.*) a female ancestor. —'**grand,motherly** *adj.*

Grand National *n.* **the.** an annual steeplechase run at Aintree, Liverpool, since 1839.

grandnephew ('græn,nɛvjuː, -,nɛfjuː, 'grænd-) *n.* another name for **great-nephew.**

grandniece ('græn,niːs, 'grænd-) *n.* another name for **great-niece.**

grand opera *n.* an opera that has a serious plot and is entirely in musical form, with no spoken dialogue.

grandpa ('græn,pɑː) *or* **grandpapa** ('grænpə,pɑː) *n.* informal words for **grandfather.**

grandparent ('græn,pɛərənt, 'grænd-) *n.* the father or mother of either of one's parents.

grand piano *n.* a form of piano in which the strings are arranged horizontally.

Grand Pré (grɒn preɪ; *French* grã pre) *n.* a village in SE Canada, in W Nova Scotia: setting of Longfellow's *Evangeline.*

Grand Prix (*French* grã pri) *n.* **1.** any of a series of formula motor races to determine the annual Driver's World Championship. **2.** a very important competitive event in various other sports, such as athletics, snooker, or powerboating. [F: great prize]

Grand Rapids *n.* (*functioning as sing.*) a city in SW Michigan. Pop.: 181 843 (1980).

grandsire ('græn,saɪə, 'grænd-) *n.* an archaic word for **grandfather.**

grand slam *n.* **1.** *Bridge, etc.* the winning of 13 tricks by one player or side or the contract to do so. **2.** the winning of all major competitions in a season, esp. in tennis and golf.

grandson ('grænsʌn, 'grænd-) *n.* a son of one's son or daughter.

grandstand ('græn,stænd, 'grænd-) *n.* **1.** a terraced block of seats commanding the best view at racecourses, football pitches, etc. **2.** the spectators in a grandstand.

grand tour *n.* **1.** (formerly) an extended tour through the major cities of Europe, esp. one undertaken by a rich or aristocratic Englishman to complete his education. **2.** *Inf.* an extended sightseeing trip, tour of inspection, etc.

granduncle ('grænd,ʌŋkəl) *n.* another name for **great-uncle.**

Grand Union Canal *n.* a canal in S England linking London and the Midlands: opened in 1801.

grange (greɪndʒ) *n.* **1.** *Chiefly Brit.* a farm, esp. a farmhouse or country house with its various outbuildings. **2.** *Arch.* a granary or barn. [C13: from Anglo-F *graunge,* from Med. L *grānica,* from L *grānum* GRAIN]

Grangemouth ('greɪndʒməʊθ, -məθ) *n.* a port in Scotland, in the Central region: now Scotland's second port, with oil refineries, shipyards, and chemical industries. Pop.: 21 666 (1981).

Granicus (grə'naɪkəs) *n.* an ancient river in NW Asia Minor where Alexander the Great won his first major battle against the Persians (334 B.C.).

granite (grænɪt) *n.* **1.** a light-coloured coarse-grained acid plutonic igneous rock consisting of quartz and feldspars: widely used for building. **2.** great hardness, endurance, or resolution. [C17: from It. *granito* grained, from *grano* grain, from L *grānum*] —**granitic** (grə'nɪtɪk) *adj.*

graniteware ('grænɪt,wɛə) *n.* **1.** iron vessels coated with enamel of a granite-like appearance. **2.** a type of pottery with a speckled glaze.

granivorous (græ'nɪvərəs) *adj.* (of animals) feeding on seeds and grain. —**granivore** ('grænɪ,vɔː) *n.*

granny *or* **grannie** ('grænɪ) *n., pl.* **-nies. 1.** informal words for **grandmother.** Often shortened to **gran. 2.** *Inf.* an irritatingly fussy person. **3.** See **granny knot.**

granny bond *n. Brit. inf.* a savings scheme available originally only to people over retirement age.

granny flat *n.* self-contained accommodation within or built onto a house, suitable for an elderly parent.

granny knot or **granny's knot** n. a reef knot with the ends crossed the wrong way, making it liable to slip or jam.

Gran Paradiso (*Italian* gram para'di:zo) n. a mountain in NW Italy, in NW Piedmont: the highest peak of the Graian Alps. Height: 4061 m (13 323 ft.).

grant (grɑ:nt) vb. (tr.) **1.** to consent to perform or fulfil: *to grant a wish.* **2.** (*may take a clause as object*) to permit as a favour, indulgence, etc.: *to grant an interview.* **3.** (*may take a clause as object*) to acknowledge the validity of; concede: *I grant what you say is true.* **4.** to bestow, esp. in a formal manner. **5.** to transfer (property) to another, esp. by deed; convey. **6. take for granted. a.** to accept (something) as true and not requiring verification. **b.** to take advantage of the benefits of (something) without due appreciation. ~n. **7.** a sum of money provided by a government or public fund to finance educational study, overseas aid, etc. **8.** a privilege, right, etc., that has been granted. **9.** the act of granting. **10.** a transfer of property by deed; conveyance. [C13: from OF *graunter*, from Vulgar L *credentāre* (unattested), from L *crēdere* to believe] —'**grantable** adj. —'**granter** or (*Law.*) '**grantor** n.

Grant (grɑ:nt) n. **1. Cary,** real name *Alexander Archibald Leach.* 1904–86, U.S. film actor, born in England. His many films include *Bringing up Baby* (1938), *The Philadelphia Story* (1940), *Arsenic and Old Lace* (1944), and *Mr Blandings Builds his Dream House* (1948). **2. Duncan (James Corrowr).** 1885–1978, British painter and designer. **3. Ulysses S(impson),** real name *Hiram Ulysses Grant.* 1822–85, 18th president of the U.S. (1869–77); commander in chief of Union forces in the American Civil War (1864–65).

Granta ('græntə, 'grɑ:ntə) n. the original name, still in use locally, for the River Cam.

grantee (grɑ:n'ti:) n. *Law.* a person to whom a grant is made.

Granth (grʌnt) n. the sacred scripture of the Sikhs. [from Hindi, from Sansk. *grantha* a book]

grant-in-aid n., pl. **grants-in-aid.** a sum of money granted by one government to a lower level of government for a programme, etc.

gran turismo ('græn tuə'rizməu) n., pl. **gran turismos.** See GT. [C20: from It.]

granular ('grænjulə) adj. **1.** of, like, or containing granules. **2.** having a grainy surface. —**granularity** (,grænju'læriti) n. —'**granularly** adv.

granulate ('grænju,leit) vb. **1.** (tr.) to make into grains: *granulated sugar.* **2.** to make or become roughened in surface texture. —,**granu'lation** n. —'**granulative** adj. —'**granu,lator** or '**granu,later** n.

granule ('grænju:l) n. a small grain. [C17: from LL *grānulum* a small GRAIN]

granulocyte ('grænjulə,sait) n. any of a group of unpigmented blood cells having cytoplasmic granules that take up various dyes.

Granville-Barker ('grænvil'bɑ:kə) n. **Harley.** 1877–1946, English dramatist, theatre director, and critic, noted particularly for his *Prefaces to Shakespeare* (1927–47).

grape (greip) n. **1.** the fruit of the grapevine, which has a purple or green skin and sweet flesh: eaten raw, dried to make raisins, currants, or sultanas, or used for making wine. **2.** See **grapevine** (sense 1). **3. the grape.** *Inf.* wine. **4.** See **grapeshot.** [C13: from OF *grape* bunch of grapes, of Gmc origin; rel. to CRAMP[2], GRAPPLE] —'**grapey** or '**grapy** adj.

grapefruit ('greip,fru:t) n., pl. **-fruit** or **-fruits. 1.** a tropical or subtropical evergreen tree. **2.** the large round edible fruit of this tree, which has yellow rind and juicy slightly bitter pulp.

grape hyacinth n. any of various Eurasian bulbous plants of the lily family with clusters of rounded blue flowers resembling tiny grapes.

grapeshot ('greip,ʃɒt) n. ammunition for cannons consisting of a cluster of iron balls that scatter after firing.

grape sugar n. another name for **dextrose.**

grapevine ('greip,vain) n. **1.** any of several vines of E Asia, widely cultivated for its fruit (grapes). **2.** *Inf.* an unofficial means of relaying information, esp. from person to person.

graph (grɑ:f) n. **1.** Also called: **chart.** a drawing depicting the relation between certain sets of numbers or quantities by means of a series of dots, lines, etc., plotted with reference to a set of axes. **2.** *Maths.* a drawing depicting a functional relation between two or three variables by means of a curve or surface containing only those points whose coordinates satisfy the relation. **3.** *Linguistics.* a symbol in a writing system not further subdivisible into other such symbols. ~vb. **4.** (tr.) to draw or represent in a graph. [C19: short for *graphic formula*]

-graph n. combining form. **1.** an instrument that writes or records: *telegraph.* **2.** a writing, record, or drawing: *autograph; lithograph.* [via L from Gk, from *graphein* to write] —**-graphic** or **-graphical** adj. combining form. —**-graphically** adv. combining form.

grapheme ('græfi:m) n. *Linguistics.* the complete class of letters or combinations of letters that represent one speech sound: for instance, the *f* in *full*, the *gh* in *cough*, and the *ph* in *photo* are members of the same grapheme. [C20: from Gk *graphēma* a letter] —**gra'phemically** adv.

-grapher n. combining form. **1.** indicating a person skilled in a subject: *geographer; photographer.* **2.** indicating a person who writes or draws in a specified way: *stenographer; lithographer.*

graphic ('græfik) or **graphical** adj. **1.** vividly or clearly described: *a graphic account of the disaster.* **2.** of or relating to writing: *graphic symbols.* **3.** *Maths.* using, relating to, or determined by a graph: *a graphic representation of the figures.* **4.** of or relating to the graphic arts. **5.** *Geol.* having or denoting a texture resembling writing: *graphic granite.* [C17: from L *graphicus*, from Gk *graphikos*, from *graphein* to write] —'**graphically** adv. —'**graphicness** n.

graphicacy ('græfikəsi) n. the ability to understand and use maps, symbols, etc. [C20: formed on the model of *literacy*]

graphic arts pl. n. any of the fine or applied visual arts based on drawing or the use of line, esp. illustration and printmaking of all kinds.

graphic equalizer n. an electronic device for cutting or boosting selected frequencies, using small linear faders.

graphics ('græfiks) n. **1.** (functioning as sing.) the process or art of drawing in accordance with mathematical principles. **2.** (functioning as sing.) the study of writing systems. **3.** (functioning as pl.) the drawings, photographs, etc., in a magazine or book, or in a television or film production. **4.** (functioning as pl.) Computers. information displayed in the form of diagrams, graphs, etc.

graphite ('græfait) n. a blackish soft form of carbon used in pencils, electrodes, as a lubricant, as a moderator in nuclear reactors, and, in carbon fibre form, for tough lightweight sports equipment. [from G *Graphit*, from Gk *graphein* to write + -ITE[1]] —**graphitic** (grə'fitik) adj.

graphology (græ'fɒlədʒi) n. **1.** the study of handwriting, esp. to analyse the writer's character. **2.** *Linguistics.* the study of writing systems. —,**grapho'logical** adj. —**gra'phologist** n.

graph paper n. paper printed with intersecting lines for drawing graphs, diagrams, etc.

-graphy n. combining form. **1.** indicating a form of writing, representing, etc.: *calligraphy; photography.* **2.** indicating an art or descriptive science: *choreography; oceanography.* [via L from Gk, from *graphein* to write]

grapnel ('græpn²l) n. **1.** a device with a multiple hook at one end and attached to a rope, which is thrown or hooked over a firm mooring to secure an object attached to the other end of the rope. **2.** a light anchor for small boats. [C14: from OF *grapin*, from *grape* a hook; see GRAPE]

grappa ('græpə) n. a spirit distilled from the fermented remains of grapes after pressing. [It.: grape stalk, of Gmc origin; see GRAPE]

Grappelli or **Grappelly** (grə'pɛli) n. **Stéphane** ('stɛf²n). born 1908, French jazz violinist: with Django Reinhardt, he led the Quintet of the Hot Club of France between 1934 and 1939.

grapple ('græp²l) vb. **1.** to come to grips with (one or more persons), esp. to struggle in hand-to-hand combat. **2.** (intr.; foll. by with) to cope or contend: *to grapple with a financial problem.* **3.** (tr.) to secure with a grapple. ~n. **4.** any form of hook or metal instrument by which something is secured, such as a grapnel. **5. a.** the act of gripping or seizing, as in wrestling. **b.** a grip or hold. [C16: from OF *grappelle* a little hook, from *grape* hook; see GRAPNEL] —'**grappler** n.

grappling iron or **hook** n. a grapnel, esp. one used for securing ships.

graptolite ('græptə,laɪt) *n.* an extinct Palaeozoic colonial animal: a common fossil. [C19: from Gk *graptos* written, from *graphein* to write + -LITE]

Grasmere ('grɑːs,mɪə) *n.* a village in NW England, in Cumbria at the head of **Lake Grasmere**: home of William Wordsworth and of Thomas de Quincey.

grasp (grɑːsp) *vb.* 1. to grip (something) firmly as with the hands. 2. (when *intr.*, often foll. by *at*) to struggle, snatch, or grope (for). 3. (*tr.*) to understand, esp. with effort. ~*n.* 4. the act of grasping. 5. a grip or clasp, as of a hand. 6. total rule or possession. 7. understanding; comprehension. [C14: from Low G *grapsen;* rel. to OE *græppian* to seize] —'**graspable** *adj.* —'**grasper** *n.*

grasping ('grɑːspɪŋ) *adj.* greedy; avaricious. —'**graspingly** *adv.* —'**graspingness** *n.*

grass (grɑːs) *n.* 1. any of a family of plants having jointed stems sheathed by long narrow leaves, flowers in spikes, and seedlike fruits. The family includes cereals, bamboo, etc. 2. such plants collectively, in a lawn, meadow, etc. Related adj.: **verdant.** 3. ground on which such plants grow; a lawn, field, etc. 4. ground on which animals are grazed; pasture. 5. a slang word for **marijuana.** 6. *Brit. sl.* a person who informs, esp. on criminals. 7. **let the grass grow under one's feet.** to squander time or opportunity. ~*vb.* 8. to cover or become covered with grass. 9. to feed or be fed with grass. 10. (*tr.*) to spread (cloth, etc.) out on grass for drying or bleaching in the sun. 11. (*intr.;* usually foll. by *on*) *Brit. sl.* to inform, esp. to the police. [OE *græs*] —'**grass,like** *adj.*

Grass (*German* gras) *n.* **Günter** (**Wilhelm**) ('gyntər) born 1927, German novelist, dramatist, and poet, noted particularly for his novels *The Tin Drum* (1959), *Dog Years* (1963), and *The Meeting at Telgte* (1981).

grass hockey *n.* in W Canada, field hockey, as contrasted with ice hockey.

grasshopper ('grɑːs,hɒpə) *n.* an insect having hind legs adapted for leaping: typically terrestrial, feeding on plants, and producing a ticking sound by rubbing the hind legs against the leathery forewings.

grassland ('grɑːs,lænd) *n.* 1. land, such as a prairie, on which grass predominates. 2. land reserved for natural grass pasture.

grass roots *pl. n.* 1. ordinary people as distinct from the active leadership of a group or organization, esp. a political party. 2. the essentials.

grass snake *n.* 1. a harmless nonvenomous European snake having a brownish-green body with variable markings. 2. any of several similar related European snakes.

grass tree *n.* 1. Also called: **blackboy.** an Australian plant of the lily family, having a woody stem, stiff grass-like leaves, and a spike of small white flowers. 2. any of several similar Australasian plants.

grass widow *or* (*masc.*) **grass widower** *n.* a person whose spouse is regularly away for a short period. [C16: ? an allusion to a grass bed as representing an illicit relationship]

grassy ('grɑːsɪ) *adj.* **grassier, grassiest.** covered with, containing, or resembling grass. —'**grassiness** *n.*

grate[1] (greɪt) *vb.* 1. (*tr.*) to reduce to small shreds by rubbing against a rough or sharp perforated surface: *to grate carrots.* 2. to scrape (an object) against something or (objects) together, producing a harsh rasping sound, or (of objects) to scrape with such a sound. 3. (*intr.;* foll. by *on* or *upon*) to annoy. [C15: from OF *grater* to scrape, of Gmc origin] —'**grater** *n.*

grate[2] (greɪt) *n.* 1. a framework of metal bars for holding fuel in a fireplace, stove, or furnace. 2. a less common word for **fireplace.** 3. another name for **grating**[1](sense 1). ~*vb.* 4. (*tr.*) to provide with a grate or grates. [C14: from OF, from L *crātis* hurdle]

grateful ('greɪtfʊl) *adj.* 1. thankful for gifts, favours, etc.; appreciative. 2. showing gratitude: *a grateful letter.* 3. favourable or pleasant: *a grateful rest.* [C16: from obs. *grate,* from L *grātus* + -FUL] —'**gratefully** *adv.* —'**gratefulness** *n.*

Gratian ('greɪʃɪən) *n.* Latin name *Flavius Gratianus.* 359–383 A.D., Roman emperor (367–383): ruled with his father Valentinian I (367–375); ruled the Western Roman Empire with his brother Valentinian II (375-83); appointed Theodosius I emperor of the Eastern Roman Empire (379).

graticule ('grætɪ,kjuːl) *n.* 1. the grid of intersecting lines of latitude and longitude on which a map is drawn. 2.

another name for **reticle.** [C19: from F, from L *crāticula,* from *crātis* wickerwork]

gratify ('grætɪ,faɪ) *vb.* **-fying, -fied.** (*tr.*) 1. to satisfy or please. 2. to yield to or indulge (a desire, whim, etc.). [C16: from L *grātificārī,* from *grātus* grateful + *facere* to make] —,**gratifi'cation** *n.* —'**grati,fier** *n.* —'**grati,fying** *adj.* —'**grati,fyingly** *adv.*

grating[1] ('greɪtɪŋ) *n.* 1. Also called: **grate.** a framework of metal bars in the form of a grille set into a wall, pavement, etc., serving as a cover or guard but admitting air and sometimes light. 2. short for **diffraction grating.**

grating[2] ('greɪtɪŋ) *adj.* 1. (of sounds) harsh and rasping. 2. annoying; irritating. ~*n.* 3. (*often pl.*) something produced by grating. —'**gratingly** *adv.*

gratis ('greɪtɪs, 'grætɪs, 'grɑːtɪs) *adv., adj.* (*postpositive*) without payment; free of charge. [C15: from L: out of kindness, from *grātiis,* ablative pl. of *grātia* favour]

gratitude ('grætɪ,tjuːd) *n.* a feeling of thankfulness, as for gifts or favours. [C16: from Med. L *grātitūdō,* from L *grātus* GRATEFUL]

Grattan ('græt³n) *n.* **Henry.** 1746–1820, Irish statesman and orator: led the movement that secured legislative independence for Ireland (1782), opposed union with England (1800), and campaigned for Catholic emancipation.

gratuitous (grə'tjuːɪtəs) *adj.* 1. given or received without payment or obligation. 2. without cause; unjustified. [C17: from L *grātuītus* from *grātia* favour] —**gra'tuitously** *adv.* —**gra'tuitousness** *n.*

gratuity (grə'tjuːɪtɪ) *n., pl.* **-ties.** 1. a gift or reward, usually of money, for services rendered; tip. 2. *Mil.* a financial award granted for long or meritorious service.

gratulatory ('grætjʊlətərɪ) *adj.* expressing congratulation. [C16: from L *grātulārī* to congratulate]

Graubünden (*German* grau'byndən) *n.* an Alpine canton of E Switzerland: the largest of the cantons, but sparsely populated. Capital: Chur. Pop.: 164 641 (1980). Area: 7109 sq. km (2773 sq. miles). Italian name: **Grigioni.** Romansch name: **Grishun.** French name: **Grisons.**

grav (græv) *n.* a unit of acceleration equal to the standard acceleration of free fall. 1 grav is equivalent to 9.806 65 metres per second per second. Symbol: g

gravamen (grə'veɪmɛn) *n., pl.* **-vamina** (-'væmɪnə). 1. *Law.* that part of an accusation weighing most heavily against an accused. 2. *Law.* the substance or material grounds of a complaint. 3. a rare word for **grievance.** [C17: from LL: trouble, from L *gravāre* to load, from *gravis* heavy]

grave[1] (greɪv) *n.* 1. a place for the burial of a corpse, esp. beneath the ground and usually marked by a tombstone. Related adj.: **sepulchral.** 2. something resembling a grave or resting place: *the ship went to its grave.* 3. (often preceded by *the*) a poetic term for **death.** 4. **make (someone) turn in his grave.** to do something that would have shocked or distressed a person now dead. [OE *græf*]

grave[2] (greɪv) *adj.* 1. serious and solemn: *a grave look.* 2. full of or suggesting danger: *a grave situation.* 3. important; crucial: *grave matters of state.* 4. (of colours) sober or dull. 5. (grɑːv). *Phonetics.* of or relating to an accent (`) over vowels, denoting a pronunciation with lower or falling musical pitch (as in ancient Greek), with certain special quality (as in French), or in a manner that gives the vowel status as a syllable (as in English *agèd*). ~*n.* 6. (*also* grɑːv). a grave accent. [C16: from OF, from L *gravis*] —'**gravely** *adv.* —'**graveness** *n.*

grave[3] (greɪv) *vb.* **graving, graved; graved** *or* **graven.** (*tr.*) *Arch.* 1. to carve or engrave. 2. to fix firmly in the mind. [OE *grafan*]

grave[4] ('grɑːveɪ) *adj. Music.* solemn. [It.]

grave clothes (greɪv) *pl. n.* the wrappings in which a dead body is interred.

gravel ('græv³l) *n.* 1. a mixture of rock fragments and pebbles that is coarser than sand. 2. *Pathol.* small rough calculi in the kidneys or bladder. ~*vb.* **-elling, -elled** *or U.S.* **-eling, -eled.** (*tr.*) 3. to cover with gravel. 4. to confound or confuse. 5. *U.S. inf.* to annoy or disturb. [C13: from OF *gravele,* dim. of *grave,* ? of Celtic origin]

gravel-blind *adj. Literary.* almost completely blind. [C16: from GRAVEL + BLIND]

gravelly ('græv³lɪ) *adj.* 1. consisting of or abounding in gravel. 2. of or like gravel. 3. (esp. of a voice) harsh and grating.

graven ('greɪvᵊn) vb. **1.** a past participle of **grave**³. ~adj. **2.** strongly fixed.

Gravenhage (xraːvənˈhaːxə) n. **'s.** a Dutch name for (The) **Hague**.

graven image n. Chiefly Bible. a carved image used as an idol.

graver ('greɪvə) n. any of various engraving or sculpting tools, such as a burin.

Graves¹ (graːv) n. (functioning as sing.) **1.** (sometimes not cap.) a white or red wine from the district around Bordeaux, France. **2.** a dry or medium sweet white wine from any country: Spanish Graves.

Graves² (greɪvz) n. **Robert** (**Ranke**). 1895–1985, English poet, novelist, and critic, whose works include his World War I autobiography, Goodbye to All That (1929), and the historical novels I, Claudius (1934) and Claudius the God (1934).

Gravesend (ˌgreɪvˈɛnd) n. a river port in SE England, in NW Kent on the Thames. Pop.: 52 963 (1981).

gravestone ('greɪvˌstəʊn) n. a stone marking a grave.

graveyard ('greɪvˌjɑːd) n. a place for graves; a burial ground, esp. a small one or one in a churchyard.

gravid ('grævɪd) adj. the technical word for **pregnant**. [C16: from L gravidus, from gravis heavy]

gravimeter (grəˈvɪmɪtə) n. **1.** an instrument for measuring the earth's gravitational field at points on its surface. **2.** an instrument for measuring relative density. [C18: from F gravimètre, from L gravis heavy] — **graˈvimetry** n.

gravimetric (ˌgrævɪˈmɛtrɪk) adj. **1.** of, concerned with, or using measurement by weight. **2.** Chem. of analysis of quantities by weight.

graving dock n. another term for **dry dock**.

gravitate ('grævɪˌteɪt) vb. (intr.) **1.** Physics. to move under the influence of gravity. **2.** (usually foll. by to or towards) to be influenced or drawn, as by strong impulses. **3.** to sink or settle. — **'graviˌtater** n. — **'graviˌtative** adj.

gravitation (ˌgrævɪˈteɪʃən) n. **1.** the force of attraction that bodies exert on one another as a result of their mass. **2.** any process or result caused by this interaction. ~Also called: **gravity.** — **ˌgraviˈtational** adj. — **ˌgraviˈtationally** adv.

gravitational constant n. the factor relating force to mass and distance in Newton's law of gravitation. Symbol: G

gravitational field n. the field of force surrounding a body of finite mass in which another body would experience an attractive force that is proportional to the product of the masses and inversely proportional to the square of the distance between them.

gravitational mass n. the mass of a body expressed in terms of the gravitational force between it and the earth. Cf. **inertial mass**.

graviton ('grævɪˌtɒn) n. a postulated quantum of gravitational energy, usually considered to be a particle with zero charge and rest mass and a spin of 2.

gravity ('grævɪtɪ) n., pl. **-ties. 1.** the force of attraction that moves or tends to move bodies towards the centre of a celestial body, such as the earth or moon. **2.** the property of being heavy or having weight. **3.** another name for **gravitation. 4.** seriousness or importance, esp. as a consequence of an action or opinion. **5.** manner or conduct that is solemn or dignified. **6.** lowness in pitch. **7.** (modifier) of or relating to gravity or gravitation or their effects: gravity feed. [C16: from L gravitās weight, from gravis heavy]

gravlax ('grævˌlæks) n. dry-cured salmon, marinated in salt, sugar, and spices, as served in Scandinavia. [C20: from Norwegian, from grav grave (because the salmon is left to ferment) + laks or Swedish lax salmon]

gravure (grəˈvjʊə) n. **1.** a method of intaglio printing using a plate with many small etched recesses. See also **rotogravure. 2.** See **photogravure. 3.** matter printed by this process. [C19: from F, from graver to engrave, of Gmc origin]

gravy ('greɪvɪ) n., pl. **-vies. 1. a.** the juices that exude from meat during cooking. **b.** the sauce made by thickening and flavouring such juices. **2.** Sl. money or gain acquired with little effort, esp. above that needed for ordinary living. [C14: from OF gravé, from ?]

gravy boat n. a small often boat-shaped vessel for serving gravy or other sauces.

Gray (greɪ) n. **Thomas.** 1716–71, English poet, best known for his Elegy written in a Country Churchyard (1751).

gray¹ (greɪ) adj., n., vb. a variant spelling (now esp. U.S.) of **grey**.

gray² (greɪ) n. the derived SI unit of the absorbed dose of ionizing radiation: equal to 1 joule per kilogram. Symbol: Gy [C20: after L. H. Gray, Brit. radiobiologist]

grayling ('greɪlɪŋ) n., pl. **-ling** or **-lings. 1.** a freshwater food fish of the salmon family of the N hemisphere, having a long spiny dorsal fin, a silvery back, and greyish-green sides. **2.** any of various European butterflies having grey or greyish-brown wings.

Graz (German graːts) n. an industrial city in SE Austria, capital of Styria province: the second largest city in the country. Pop.: 243 405 (1981).

graze¹ (greɪz) vb. **1.** to allow (animals) to consume the vegetation on (an area of land), or (of animals) to feed thus. **2.** (tr.) to tend (livestock) while at pasture. [OE grasian, from græs GRASS]

graze² (greɪz) vb. **1.** (when intr., often foll. by against or along) to brush or scrape (against) gently, esp. in passing. **2.** (tr.) to break the skin of (a part of the body) by scraping. ~n. **3.** the act of grazing. **4.** a scrape or abrasion made by grazing. [C17: prob. special use of GRAZE¹]

grazier ('greɪzɪə) n. a rancher or farmer who rears or fattens cattle or sheep on grazing land.

grazing ('greɪzɪŋ) n. **1.** the vegetation on pastures that is available for livestock to feed upon. **2.** the land on which this is growing.

grazioso (ˌgrɑːtsɪˈəʊsəʊ) adj. Music. graceful. [It.]

grease (griːs, griːz) n. **1.** animal fat in a soft or melted condition. **2.** any thick fatty oil, esp. one used as a lubricant for machinery, etc. ~vb. (tr.) **3.** to soil, coat, or lubricate with grease. **4. grease the palm** (or hand) **of.** Sl. to bribe; influence by giving money to. [C13: from OF craisse, from L crassus thick] — **'greaser** n.

grease gun n. a device for forcing grease through nipples into bearings.

grease monkey n. Inf. a mechanic, esp. one who works on cars or aircraft.

greasepaint ('griːsˌpeɪnt) n. **1.** a waxy or greasy substance used as make-up by actors. **2.** theatrical make-up.

greasy ('griːsɪ, -zɪ) adj. **greasier, greasiest. 1.** coated or soiled with or as if with grease. **2.** composed of or full of grease. **3.** resembling grease. **4.** unctuous or oily in manner. — **'greasily** adv. — **'greasiness** n.

greasy wool n. untreated wool still retaining the lanolin; used for waterproof clothing.

great (greɪt) adj. **1.** relatively large in size or extent; big. **2.** relatively large in number; having many parts or members: a great assembly. **3.** of relatively long duration: a great wait. **4.** of larger size or more importance than others of its kind: the great auk. **5.** extreme or more than usual: great worry. **6.** of significant importance or consequence: a great decision. **7. a.** of exceptional talents or achievements; remarkable: a great writer. **b.** (as n.): the great; one of the greats. **8.** doing or exemplifying (something) on a large scale: she's a great reader. **9.** arising from or possessing idealism in thought, action, etc.; heroic: great deeds. **10.** illustrious or eminent: a great history. **11.** impressive or striking: a great show of wealth. **12.** active or enthusiastic: a great walker. **13.** (often foll. by at) skilful or adroit: a great carpenter; you are great at singing. **14.** Inf. excellent; fantastic. ~n. **15.** Also called: **great organ.** the principal manual on an organ. [OE grēat] — **'greatly** adv. — **'greatness** n.

great- prefix. **1.** being the parent of a person's grandparent (in the combinations **great-grandfather, great-grandmother, great-grandparent**). **2.** being the child of a person's grandchild (in the combinations **great-grandson, great-granddaughter, great-grandchild**).

great auk n. a large flightless auk, extinct since the middle of the 19th century.

great-aunt or **grandaunt** n. an aunt of one's father or mother; sister of one's grandfather or grandmother.

Great Australian Bight n. a wide bay of the Indian Ocean, in S Australia, extending from Cape Pasley to the Eyre Peninsula: notorious for storms.

Great Barrier Reef n. a coral reef in the Coral Sea, off the NE coast of Australia, extending for about 2000 km (1250 miles) from the Torres Strait along the coast of Queensland; the largest coral reef in the world.

Great Basin n. a semiarid region of the western U.S., between the Wasatch and the Sierra Nevada Mountains, having no drainage to the ocean: includes Nevada, W Utah, and parts of E California, S Oregon, and Idaho. Area: about 490 000 sq. km (189 000 sq. miles).

Great Bear n. **the.** the English name for **Ursa Major.**

Great Bear Lake n. a lake in NW Canada, in the Northwest Territories: the largest freshwater lake entirely in Canada; drained by the **Great Bear River,** which flows to the Mackenzie River. Area: 31 792 sq. km (12 275 sq. miles).

Great Belt n. a strait in Denmark, between Sjælland and Fyn islands, linking the Kattegat with the Baltic. Danish name: **Store Bælt.**

Great Britain n. England, Wales, and Scotland including those adjacent islands governed from the mainland (i.e. excluding the Isle of Man and the Channel Islands). The United Kingdom of Great Britain was formed by the Act of Union (1707), although the term Great Britain had been in use since 1603, when James VI of Scotland became James I of England (including Wales). Later unions created the United Kingdom of Great Britain and Ireland (1801) and the United Kingdom of Great Britain and Northern Ireland (1922). Pop.: 55 196 400 (1986 est.). Area: 229 523 sq. km (88 619 sq. miles). See also **United Kingdom.**

great circle n. a circular section of a sphere that has a radius equal to that of the sphere.

greatcoat ('greɪt,kəʊt) n. a heavy overcoat.

Great Dane n. one of a very large breed of dog with a short smooth coat.

Great Dividing Range pl. n. a series of mountain ranges and plateaus roughly parallel to the E coast of Australia, in Queensland, New South Wales, and Victoria; the highest range is the Australian Alps, in the south.

Greater Antilles pl. n. **the.** a group of islands in the West Indies, including Cuba, Jamaica, Hispaniola, and Puerto Rico.

Greater London n. See **London**[1] (sense 2).

Greater Manchester n. a metropolitan county of NW England, comprising the districts of Wigan, Bolton, Bury, Rochdale, Salford, Manchester, Oldham, Trafford, Stockport, and Tameside. Administrative centre: Manchester. Pop.: 2 579 500 (1986 est.). Area: 1286 sq. km (496 sq. miles).

Greater Sunda Islands pl. n. a group of islands in the W Malay Archipelago, forming the larger part of the Sunda Islands: consists of Borneo, Sumatra, Java, and Sulawesi.

Great Glen n. **the.** a fault valley across the whole of Scotland, extending southwest from the Moray Firth in the east to Loch Linnhe and containing Loch Ness and Loch Lochy. Also called: **Glen More, Glen Albyn.**

great gross n. a unit of quantity equal to one dozen gross (or 1728.)

great-hearted adj. benevolent or noble; magnanimous. — ˌgreat-'heartedness n.

Great Indian Desert n. another name for the **Thar Desert.**

Great Karoo or **Central Karoo** (kə'ruː) n. an arid plateau of S central South Africa, in Cape Province, separated from the Little Karoo to the southwest by the Swartberg range. Average height: 750 m (2500 ft.).

Great Lakes pl. n. a group of five lakes in central North America with connecting waterways: the largest group of lakes in the world: consists of Lakes Superior, Huron, Erie, and Ontario, which are divided by the border between the U.S. and Canada and Lake Michigan, which is wholly in the U.S.; constitutes the most important system of inland waterways in the world, discharging through the St Lawrence into the Atlantic. Total length: 3767 km (2340 miles). Area: 246 490 sq. km (95 170 sq. miles).

great-nephew or **grandnephew** n. a son of one's nephew or niece; grandson of one's brother or sister. — ˌgreat-'niece or ˈgrand,niece fem. n.

Great Ouse n. See **Ouse** (sense 1).

Great Plains pl. n. a vast region of North America east of the Rocky Mountains, extending from the lowlands of the Mackenzie River (Canada), south to the Big Bend of the Rio Grande.

Great Rift Valley n. the most extensive rift in the earth's surface, extending from the Jordan valley in Syria to Mozambique; marked by a chain of steep-sided lakes, volcanoes, and escarpments.

Great Russian n. **1.** Linguistics. the technical name for **Russian. 2.** a member of the chief East Slavonic people of Russia. ~adj. **3.** of or relating to this people or their language.

Greats (greɪts) pl. n. (at Oxford University) **1.** the Honour School of Literae Humaniores, involving the study of Greek and Roman history and literature and philosophy. **2.** the final examinations at the end of this course.

Great Salt Lake n. a shallow salt lake in NW Utah, in the Great Basin at an altitude of 1260 m (4200 ft.): the area has fluctuated from less than 2500 sq. km (1000 sq. miles) to over 5000 sq. km (2000 sq. miles).

Great Sandy Desert n. **1.** a desert in NW Australia. Area: about 415 000 sq. km (160 000 sq. miles). **2.** the English name for the **Rub' al Khali.**

great seal n. (often caps.) the principal seal of a nation, sovereign, etc., used to authenticate documents of the highest importance.

Great Slave Lake n. a lake in NW Canada, in the Northwest Territories: drained by the Mackenzie River into the Arctic Ocean. Area: 28 440 sq. km (10 980 sq. miles).

Great Slave River n. another name for the **Slave River.**

Great Smoky Mountains or **Great Smokies** pl. n. the W part of the Appalachians, in W North Carolina and E Tennessee. Highest peak: Clingman's Dome, 2024 m (6642 ft.).

Great St Bernard Pass n. a pass over the W Alps, between SW central Switzerland and N Italy: noted for the hospice at the summit, founded in the 11th century. Height: 2469 m (8100 ft.).

great tit n. a Eurasian tit with yellow-and-black underparts and a black-and-white head.

great-uncle or **granduncle** n. an uncle of one's father or mother; brother of one's grandfather or grandmother.

Great Victoria Desert n. a desert in S Australia, in SE Western Australia and W South Australia. Area: 323 750 sq. km (125 000 sq. miles).

Great Wall of China n. a defensive wall in N China, extending from W Gansu to the Gulf of Liaodong: constructed in the 3rd century B.C. as a defence against the Mongols; substantially rebuilt in the 15th century. Length: over 2400 km (1500 miles). Average height: 6 m (20 ft.). Average width: 6 m (20 ft.).

Great War n. another name for **World War I.**

Great Yarmouth ('jɑːməθ) n. a port and resort in E England, in E Norfolk. Pop.: 48 273 (1981).

greave (griːv) n. (often pl.) a piece of armour worn to protect the shin. [C14: from OF greve, ?from graver to part the hair, of Gmc origin]

grebe (griːb) n. an aquatic bird, such as the great crested grebe and little grebe, similar to the divers but with lobate rather than webbed toes and a vestigial tail. [C18: from F grèbe, from ?]

Grecian ('griːʃən) adj. **1.** (esp. of beauty or architecture) conforming to Greek ideals. ~n. **2.** a scholar of Greek. ~adj., n. **3.** another word for **Greek.**

Grecism ('griːˌsɪzəm) n. a variant spelling (esp. U.S.) of **Graecism.**

Greco ('grɛkəʊ) n. **El.** See **El Greco.**

Greco- ('griːkəʊ, 'grɛkəʊ) combining form. a variant (esp. U.S.) of **Graeco-.**

Greece (griːs) n. a republic in SE Europe, occupying the S part of the Balkan Peninsula and many islands in the Ionian and Aegean Seas; site of two of Europe's earliest civilizations (the Minoan and Mycenaean); in the classical eras divided into many small independent city-states, the most important being Athens and Sparta; part of the Roman and Byzantine Empires; passed under Turkish rule in the late Middle Ages; became an independent kingdom in 1827; taken over by a military junta (1967–74); the monarchy was abolished in 1973; became a republic in 1975. Language: Greek. Religion: predominantly Greek Orthodox. Currency: drachma. Capital: Athens. Pop.: 10 018 000 (1988). Area: 131 944 sq. km (50 944 sq. miles). Modern Greek name: **Ellás.** Related adj.: **Hellenic.**

greed (griːd) n. **1.** excessive consumption of or desire for food. **2.** excessive desire, as for wealth or power. [C17: back formation from GREEDY]

greedy ('griːdɪ) adj. **greedier, greediest. 1.** excessively desirous of food or wealth, esp. in large amounts; voracious. **2.** (postpositive; foll. by for) eager (for): a man greedy for success. [OE grǣdig] —'**greedily** adv. —'**greediness** n.

greegree ('gri:gri:) n. a variant spelling of **grigri.**

Greek (gri:k) n. **1.** the official language of Greece, constituting the Hellenic branch of the Indo-European family of languages. **2.** a native or inhabitant of Greece or a descendant of such a native. **3.** a member of the Greek Orthodox Church. **4.** *Inf.* anything incomprehensible (esp. in **it's (all) Greek to me).** ~adj. **5.** denoting, relating to, or characteristic of Greece, the Greeks, or the Greek language; Hellenic. **6.** of, relating to, or designating the Greek Orthodox Church. —'**Greekness** n.

Greek cross n. a cross with each of the four arms of the same length.

Greek fire n. a Byzantine weapon consisting of an unknown mixture that caught fire when wetted.

Greek gift n. a gift given with the intention of tricking and causing harm to the recipient. [C19: in allusion to Virgil's *Aeneid* ii 49; see also TROJAN HORSE]

Greek Orthodox Church n. **1.** Also called: **Greek Church.** the established Church of Greece, governed by the holy synod of Greece, in which the Metropolitan of Athens has primacy of honour. **2.** another name for **Orthodox Church.**

Greeley ('gri:lɪ) n. Horace. 1811–72, U.S. journalist and political leader: founder (1841) and editor of the *New York Tribune*, which championed the abolition of slavery.

green (gri:n) n. **1.** any of a group of colours, such as that of fresh grass, that lie between yellow and blue in the visible spectrum. Related adj.: **verdant. 2.** a dye or pigment of or producing these colours. **3.** something of the colour green. **4.** a small area of grassland, esp. in the centre of a village. **5.** an area of smooth turf kept for a special purpose: *a putting green.* **6.** (*pl.*) **a.** the edible leaves and stems of certain plants, eaten as a vegetable. **b.** freshly cut branches of ornamental trees, shrubs, etc., used as a decoration. **7.** (*sometimes cap.*) a person, esp. a politician, who supports environmentalist issues. ~adj. **8.** of the colour green. **9.** greenish in colour or having parts or marks that are greenish. **10.** vigorous; not faded: *a green old age.* **11.** envious or jealous. **12.** immature, unsophisticated, or gullible. **13.** characterized by foliage or green plants: *a green wood; a green salad.* **14.** denoting a unit of account that is adjusted in accordance with fluctuations between the currencies of the EEC nations and is used to make payments to agricultural producers within the EEC: *green pound.* **15.** (*sometimes cap.*) of or concerned with conservation of natural resources and improvement of the environment: used esp. in a political context. **16.** fresh, raw, or unripe: *green bananas.* **17.** unhealthily pale in appearance: *he was green after his boat trip.* **18.** (of meat) not smoked or cured: *green bacon.* **19.** (of timber) freshly felled; not dried or seasoned. ~vb. **20.** to make or become green. [OE *grēne*] —'**greenish** or '**greeny** adj. —'**greenly** adv. —'**greenness** n.

Green (gri:n) n. **1. John Richard.** 1837–83, English historian; author of *A Short History of the English People* (1874). **2. Thomas Hill.** 1836–82, English idealist philosopher. His chief work, *Prolegomena to Ethics*, was unfinished at his death.

Greenaway ('gri:nə,weɪ) n. Kate. 1846–1901, English painter, noted as an illustrator of children's books.

greenback ('gri:n,bæk) n. U.S. **1.** *Inf.* a legal-tender U.S. currency note. **2.** *Sl.* a dollar bill.

green bean n. any bean plant, such as the French bean, having narrow green edible pods.

green belt n. a zone of farmland, parks, and open country surrounding a town or city.

Green Cross Code n. *Brit.* a code for children giving rules for road safety.

Greene (gri:n) n. **1. Graham.** born 1904, English novelist and dramatist; his works include the novels *Brighton Rock* (1938), *The Power and the Glory* (1940), and *The Captain and the Enemy* (1988), and the film script *The Third Man* (1949). **2. Robert.** ?1558–92, English poet, dramatist, and prose writer, noted for his autobiographical tract *A Groatsworth of Wit bought with a Million of Repentance* (1592), which contains an attack on Shakespeare.

greenery ('gri:nərɪ) n., pl. **-eries.** green foliage, esp. when used for decoration.

green-eyed adj. **1.** jealous or envious. **2. the green-eyed monster.** jealousy or envy.

greenfield ('gri:n,fi:ld) n. (*modifier*). denoting or located in a rural area which has not previously been built on.

greenfinch ('gri:n,fɪntʃ) n. a European finch the male of which has a dull green plumage with yellow patches on the wings and tail.

green fingers pl. n. considerable talent or ability to grow plants.

greenfly ('gri:n,flaɪ) n., pl. **-flies.** a greenish aphid commonly occurring as a pest on garden and crop plants.

greengage ('gri:n,geɪdʒ) n. **1.** a cultivated variety of plum tree with edible green plumlike fruits. **2.** the fruit of this tree. [C18: GREEN + -*gage*, after Sir W. *Gage* (1777–1864), E botanist who brought it from France]

greengrocer ('gri:n,grəʊsə) n. *Chiefly Brit.* a retail trader in fruit and vegetables. —'**green,grocery** n.

greenheart ('gri:n,hɑ:t) n. **1.** Also called: **bebeeru.** a tropical American tree that has dark green durable wood. **2.** any of various similar trees. **3.** the wood of any of these trees.

greenhorn ('gri:n,hɔ:n) n. **1.** an inexperienced person, esp. one who is extremely gullible. **2.** *Chiefly U.S.* a newcomer. [C17: orig. an animal with *green* (that is, young) horns]

greenhouse ('gri:n,haʊs) n. a building with glass walls and roof for the cultivation of plants under controlled conditions.

greenhouse effect n. **1.** an effect occurring in greenhouses, etc., in which radiant heat from the sun passes through the glass warming the contents, the radiant heat from inside being trapped by the glass. **2.** the application of this effect to a planet's atmosphere, esp. the warming up of the earth's surface as man-made carbon dioxide in the atmosphere traps the sun's heat.

greenkeeper ('gri:n,ki:pə) n. a person responsible for maintaining a golf course or bowling green.

Greenland ('gri:nlənd) n. a large island, lying mostly within the Arctic Circle off the NE coast of North America: first settled by Icelanders in 986; resettled by Danes from 1721 onwards; integral part of Denmark (1953–79); granted internal autonomy 1979; mostly covered by an icecap up to 3300 m (11 000 ft.) thick, with ice-free coastal strips and coastal mountains; the population is largely Eskimo, with a European minority; fishing, hunting, and mining. Capital: Godthaab. Pop.: 53 733 (1987). Area: 2 175 600 sq. km (840 000 sq. miles). Danish name: **Grønland.** —'**Greenlander** n. —**Greenlandic** (gri:n-'lændɪk) adj., n.

Greenland Sea n. the S part of the Arctic Ocean, off the NE coast of Greenland.

green leek n. any of several Australian parrots with a green or mostly green plumage.

green light n. **1.** a signal to go, esp. a green traffic light. **2.** permission to proceed with a project, etc.

greenmail ('gri:n,meɪl) n. (esp. in the U.S.) the practice of a company buying sufficient shares in another company to threaten takeover and making a quick profit as a result of the threatened company buying back its shares at a higher price.

Green Mountains pl. n. a mountain range in E North America, extending from Canada through Vermont into W Massachusetts: part of the Appalachian system. Highest peak: Mount Mansfield, 1338 m (4393 ft.).

Greenock ('gri:nək) n. a port in SW Scotland, in Strathclyde region on the Firth of Clyde: shipbuilding and other marine industries. Pop.: 57 324 (1981).

Greenough ('gri:nəʊ) n. George Bellas. 1778–1855, English geologist, founder of the Geological Society of London.

green paper n. (*often caps.*) (in Britain) a government document containing policy proposals to be discussed, esp. by Parliament.

Green Party n. (esp. in West Germany and now in Britain) a political party whose policies are based on concern for the environment.

green pepper n. the green unripe fruit of the sweet pepper, eaten raw or cooked.

green pound n. a unit of account used in calculating Britain's contributions to and payments from the Community Agricultural Fund of the EEC. See also **green** (sense 14).

Green River n. a river in the western U.S., rising in W central Wyoming and flowing south into Utah, east through NW Colorado, re-entering Utah before joining the Colorado River. Length: 1175 km (730 miles).

greenroom ('gri:n,ru:m, -,rʊm) n. (esp. formerly) a backstage room in a theatre where performers may rest or receive visitors. [C18: prob. from its original colour]

greensand ('gri:n,sænd) n. an olive-green sandstone consisting mainly of quartz and glauconite.

Greensboro ('gri:nzbərə, -brə) n. a city in N central North Carolina. Pop.: 155 642 (1980).

greenshank ('gri:n,ʃæŋk) n. a large European sandpiper with greenish legs and a slightly upturned bill.

greensickness ('gri:n,sɪknɪs) n. an informal name for **chlorosis.**

greenstick fracture ('gri:n,stɪk) n. a fracture in children in which the bone is partly bent and splinters only on the convex side of the bend. [C20: alluding to the similar way in which a green stick splinters]

greenstone ('gri:n,stəʊn) n. **1.** any basic dark green igneous rock. **2.** a variety of jade formerly used in New Zealand by Maoris for ornaments and tools, now used for jewellery.

greensward ('gri:n,swɔ:d) n. Arch. or literary. fresh green turf or an area of such turf.

green tea n. a sharp tea made from tea leaves that have been dried quickly without fermenting.

green turtle n. a mainly tropical edible turtle, with greenish flesh.

green-wellie n. (modifier) characterizing or belonging to the upper-class set devoted to hunting, shooting, and fishing: the green-wellie brigade.

Greenwich ('grɪnɪdʒ, -ɪtʃ, 'gren-) n. a Greater London borough on the Thames: site of a Royal Naval College and of the original Royal Observatory designed by Christopher Wren (1675), accepted internationally as the prime meridian of longitude since 1884, and the basis of Greenwich Mean Time. Pop.: 217 800 (1986 est.).

Greenwich Mean Time or **Greenwich Time** n. the local time of the 0° meridian passing through Greenwich, England: a standard time for Britain and formerly a basis for calculating times throughout most of the world. Abbrev.: **GMT.**

Greenwich Village ('grenɪtʃ, 'grɪn-) n. a part of New York City in the lower west side of Manhattan; traditionally the home of many artists and writers.

greenwood ('gri:n,wʊd) n. a forest or wood when the leaves are green.

Greer ('grɪə) n. **Germaine.** born 1939, Australian writer and feminist. Her books include The Female Eunuch (1970) and Sex and Destiny (1984).

greet[1] (gri:t) vb. (tr.) **1.** to meet or receive with expressions of gladness or welcome. **2.** to send a message of friendship to. **3.** to receive in a specified manner: her remarks were greeted by silence. **4.** to become apparent to: the smell of bread greeted him. [OE grētan] —**'greeter** n.

greet[2] (gri:t) Scot. or dialect. ~vb. **1.** (intr.) to weep; lament. ~n. **2.** weeping; lamentation. [from OE grētan, N dialect var. of grǣtan]

greeting ('gri:tɪŋ) n. **1.** the act or an instance of welcoming or saluting on meeting. **2.** (often pl.) **a.** an expression of friendly salutation. **b.** (as modifier): a greetings card.

gregarious (grɪ'geərɪəs) adj. **1.** enjoying the company of others. **2.** (of animals) living together in herds or flocks. **3.** (of plants) growing close together. **4.** of or characteristic of crowds or communities. [C17: from L, from grex flock] —**gre'gariously** adv. —**gre'gariousness** n.

Gregorian calendar (grɪ'gɔ:rɪən) n. the revision of the Julian calendar introduced in 1582 by Pope Gregory XIII and still in force, whereby the ordinary year is made to consist of 365 days.

Gregorian chant n. another name for plainsong.

Gregorian telescope n. a type of reflecting astronomical telescope with a concave secondary mirror and the eyepiece set in the centre of the parabolic primary mirror. [C18: after J. Gregory (died 1675), Scot. mathematician]

Gregory ('gregərɪ) n. Lady (**Isabella**) **Augusta (Persse).** 1852–1932, Irish dramatist; a founder and director of the Abbey Theatre, Dublin.

Gregory I n. **Saint,** known as Gregory the Great. ?540–604 A.D., pope (590–604), who greatly influenced the medieval Church. He strengthened papal authority by centralizing administration, tightened discipline, and revised the liturgy. He appointed Saint Augustine missionary to England. Feast day: Sept. 3.

Gregory VII n. **Saint,** monastic name Hildebrand. ?1020–85, pope (1073–85), who did much to reform abuses in the Church. His assertion of papal supremacy and his prohibition (1075) of lay investiture was opposed by the Holy Roman Emperor Henry IV, whom he excommunicated (1076). He was driven into exile when Henry captured Rome (1084). Feast day: May 25.

Gregory XIII n. 1502–85, pope (1572–85). He promoted the Counter-Reformation and founded seminaries. His reformed (Gregorian) calendar was issued in 1582.

Gregory of Tours n. **Saint.** ?538–?594 A.D., Frankish bishop and historian. His Historia Francorum is the chief source of knowledge of 6th-century Gaul. Feast day: Nov. 17.

gremial ('gri:mɪəl) n. R.C. Church. a cloth spread upon the lap of a bishop when seated during a solemn High Mass. [C17: from L gremium lap]

gremlin ('gremlɪn) n. **1.** an imaginary imp jokingly said to be responsible for mechanical troubles in aircraft, esp. in World War II. **2.** any mischievous troublemaker. [C20: from ?]

Grenada (gre'neɪdə) n. an island state in the West Indies, in the Windward Islands: formerly a British colony; since 1974 an independent state within the British Commonwealth. Capital: St George's. Pop.: 92 000 (1987 est.). Area: 344 sq. km (133 sq. miles). —**Gre'nadian** n., adj.

grenade (grɪ'neɪd) n. **1.** a small container filled with explosive thrown by hand or fired from a rifle. **2.** a sealed glass vessel that is thrown and shatters to release chemicals, such as tear gas. [C16: from F, from Sp.: pomegranate, from LL, from L grānātus seedy; see GRAIN]

grenadier (,grenə'dɪə) n. **1.** Mil. **a.** (in the British Army) a member of the senior regiment of infantry in the Household Brigade. **b.** (formerly) a member of a special formation, usually selected for strength and height. **c.** (formerly) a soldier trained to throw grenades. **2.** any of various deep-sea fish, typically having a large head and a long tapering tail. [C17: from F; see GRENADE]

grenadine[1] (,grenə'di:n) n. a light thin fabric of silk, wool, rayon, or nylon, used for dresses, etc. [C19: from F]

grenadine[2] (,grenə'di:n, 'grenə,di:n) n. a syrup made from pomegranate juice, used as a sweetening and colouring agent in various drinks. [C19: from F: a little pomegranate; see GRENADE]

Grenadines (,grenə'di:nz, 'grenə,di:nz) pl. n. **the.** a chain of about 600 islets in the West Indies, part of the Windward Islands, extending for about 100 km (60 miles) between St Vincent and Grenada and divided administratively between the two states. Largest island: Carriacou.

Grendel ('grend³l) n. (in Old English legend) a man-eating monster defeated by the hero Beowulf.

Grenoble (grə'nəʊb³l; French grənɔblə) n. a city in SE France, on the Isère River: university (1339). Pop.: 165 746 (1982).

Grenville ('grenvɪl) n. **1. George.** 1712–70, British statesman; prime minister (1763–65). His policy of taxing the American colonies precipitated the War of Independence. **2. Sir Richard.** ?1541–91, English naval commander. He was fatally wounded aboard his ship, the Revenge, during a lone battle with a fleet of Spanish treasure ships. **3. William Wyndham,** Baron Grenville, son of George Grenville. 1759–1834, British statesman; prime minister (1806–07) of the coalition government known as the "ministry of all the talents".

Gresham ('greʃəm) n. Sir **Thomas.** ?1519–79, English financier, who founded the Royal Exchange in London (1568).

Gresham's law or **theorem** n. the economic hypothesis that bad money drives good money out of circulation; the superior currency will tend to be hoarded and the inferior will thus dominate the circulation. [C16: after Sir T. GRESHAM]

gressorial (gre'sɔ:rɪəl) or **gressorious** adj. **1.** (of the feet of certain birds) specialized for walking. **2.** (of birds, such as the ostrich) having such feet. [C19: from NL, from gressus having walked, from gradī to step]

Gretna Green ('gretnə) n. a village in S Scotland, in Dumfries and Galloway region on the border with England: famous smithy where eloping couples were married by the blacksmith from 1754 until 1940, when such marriages became illegal. Pop.: 3000 (1981 est.).

Greuze (*French* grøz) *n.* **Jean Baptiste** (ʒã batist). 1725–1805, French genre and portrait painter.

grew (gruː) *vb.* the past tense of **grow**.

grey *or U.S.* **gray** (greɪ) *adj.* **1.** of a neutral tone, intermediate between black and white, that has no hue and reflects and transmits only a little light. **2.** greyish in colour or having greyish marks. **3.** dismal or dark, esp. from lack of light; gloomy. **4.** neutral or dull, esp. in character or opinion. **5.** having grey hair. **6.** of or characteristic of old age; wise. **7.** ancient; venerable. ~*n.* **8.** any of a group of grey tones. **9.** grey cloth or clothing. **10.** an animal, esp. a horse, that is grey or whitish. ~*vb.* **11.** to become or make grey. [OE *grǣg*] —'**greyish** *or U.S.* '**grayish** *adj.* —'**greyly** *or U.S.* '**grayly** *adv.* —'**greyness** *or U.S.* '**grayness** *n.*

Grey (greɪ) *n.* **1. Charles,** 2nd Earl Grey. 1764–1845, British statesman. As Whig prime minister (1830–34), he carried the Reform Bill of 1832 and the bill for the abolition of slavery throughout the British Empire (1833). **2. Sir Edward,** 1st Viscount Grey of Fallodon. 1862–1933, British statesman; foreign secretary (1905–16). **3. Sir George.** 1812–98, British statesman and colonial administrator; prime minister of New Zealand (1877–79). **4. Lady Jane.** 1537–54, queen of England (July 9–19, 1553); great-granddaughter of Henry VII. Her father-in-law, the Duke of Northumberland, persuaded Edward VI to alter the succession in her favour, but after ten days as queen she was imprisoned and later executed. **5. Zane.** 1875–1939, U.S. author of Westerns, including *Riders of the Purple Sage* (1912).

grey area *n.* **1.** an area or part of something existing between two extremes and having mixed characteristics of both. **2.** an area, situation, etc., lacking clearly defined characteristics.

greybeard *or U.S.* **graybeard** ('greɪ‚bɪəd) *n.* **1.** an old man, esp. a sage. **2.** a large stoneware or earthenware jar or jug for spirits.

grey eminence *n.* the English equivalent of *éminence grise.*

Grey Friar *n.* a Franciscan friar.

greyhen ('greɪ‚hɛn) *n.* the female of the black grouse.

greyhound ('greɪ‚haʊnd) *n.* a tall slender fast-moving breed of dog.

greylag *or* **greylag goose** ('greɪ‚læg) *n.* a large grey Eurasian goose: the ancestor of many domestic breeds of goose. U.S. spelling: **graylag.** [C18: from GREY + LAG[1], from its migrating later than other species]

grey matter *n.* **1.** the greyish tissue of the brain and spinal cord, containing nerve cell bodies and fibres. **2.** *Inf.* brains or intellect.

grey squirrel *n.* a grey-furred squirrel, native to E North America but now widely established.

greywacke ('greɪ‚wækə) *n.* any dark sandstone or grit having a matrix of clay minerals. [C19: partial translation of G *Grauwacke*; see WACKE]

grey wolf *n.* another name for **timber wolf.**

grid (grɪd) *n.* **1.** See **gridiron. 2.** a network of horizontal and vertical lines superimposed over a map, building plan, etc., for locating points. **3. the grid.** the national network of transmission lines, pipes, etc., by which electricity, gas, or water is distributed. **4.** Also called: **control grid.** *Electronics.* an electrode usually consisting of a cylindrical mesh of wires, that controls the flow of electrons between the cathode and anode of a valve. **5.** any interconnecting system of links: *the bus service formed a grid across the country.* [C19: back formation from GRIDIRON]

grid bias *n.* the fixed voltage applied between the control grid and cathode of a valve.

griddle ('grɪd²l) *n.* **1.** Also called: **girdle.** *Brit.* a thick round iron plate with a half hoop handle over the top, for making scones, etc. **2.** any flat heated surface, esp. on the top of a stove, for cooking food. ~*vb.* **3.** (*tr.*) to cook (food) on a griddle. [C13: from OF *gridil,* from LL *crātīculum* (unattested) fine wickerwork; see GRILL]

griddlecake ('grɪd²l‚keɪk) *n.* another name for **drop scone.**

gridiron ('grɪd‚aɪən) *n.* **1.** a utensil of parallel metal bars, used to grill meat, fish, etc. **2.** any framework resembling this utensil. **3.** a framework above the stage in a theatre from which suspended scenery, lights, etc., are manipulated. **4.** the field of play in American football. ~Often shortened to **grid.** [C13 *gredire*, ? a var. (through influence of *ire* IRON) of *gredile* GRIDDLE]

grief (griːf) *n.* **1.** deep or intense sorrow, esp. at the death of someone. **2.** something that causes keen distress. **3. come to grief.** *Inf.* to end unsuccessfully or disastrously. [C13: from Anglo-F *gref*, from *grever* to GRIEVE]

Grieg (griːg) *n.* **Edvard (Hagerup)** ('ɛdvard). 1843–1907, Norwegian composer. His works, often inspired by Norwegian folk music, include the incidental music for *Peer Gynt* (1876), a piano concerto, and many songs.

Grierson ('grɪəs²n) *n.* **John.** 1898–1972, Scottish film director. He coined the word *documentary*, of which genre his *Industrial Britain* (1931) and *Song of Ceylon* (1934) are notable examples.

grievance ('griːv²ns) *n.* **1.** a real or imaginary wrong causing resentment and regarded as grounds for complaint. **2.** a feeling of resentment or injustice at having been unfairly treated. [C15 *grevance*, from OF, from *grever* to GRIEVE]

grieve (griːv) *vb.* to feel or cause to feel great sorrow or distress, esp. at the death of someone. [C13: from OF *grever*, from L *gravāre* to burden, from *gravis* heavy] —'**griever** *n.* —'**grieving** *n., adj.*

grievous ('griːvəs) *adj.* **1.** very severe or painful: *a grievous injury.* **2.** very serious; heinous: *a grievous sin.* **3.** showing or marked by grief. **4.** causing great pain or suffering. —'**grievously** *adv.* —'**grievousness** *n.*

grievous bodily harm *n. Criminal law.* serious injury caused by one person to another.

griffin ('grɪfɪn), **griffon,** *or* **gryphon** *n.* a winged monster with an eagle-like head and the body of a lion. [C14: from OF *grifon*, from L *grȳphus*, from Gk *grups*, from *grupos* hooked]

Griffith ('grɪfɪθ) *n.* **D(avid L°welyn) W(ark).** 1875–1948, U.S. film director and producer. He introduced several cinematic techniques, including the flashback and the fade-out, in his masterpiece *The Birth of a Nation* (1915).

Griffiths ('grɪfɪθs) *n.* **Terry.** born 1947, British snooker player.

griffon ('grɪf²n) *n.* **1.** any of various small wire-haired breeds of dog, originally from Belgium. **2.** a large vulture of Africa, S Europe, and SW Asia, having a pale plumage with black wings. [C19: from F: GRIFFIN]

Grigioni (griˈdʒoːni) *n.* the Italian name for **Graubünden.**

grigri, gris-gris, *or* **greegree** ('griːgriː) *n., pl.* **-gris** (-griːz) *or* **-grees.** an African talisman, amulet, or charm. [of African origin]

grill (grɪl) *vb.* **1.** to cook (meat, etc.) by direct heat, as under a grill or over a hot fire, or (of meat, etc.) to be cooked in this way. Usual U.S. and Canad. word: **broil. 2.** (*tr.; usually passive*) to torment with or as if with extreme heat: *the travellers were grilled by the scorching sun.* **3.** (*tr.*) *Inf.* to subject to insistent or prolonged questioning. ~*n.* **4.** a device with parallel bars of thin metal on which meat, etc., may be cooked by a fire; gridiron. **5.** a device on a cooker that radiates heat downwards for grilling meat, etc. **6.** food cooked by grilling. **7.** See **grillroom.** [C17: from F *gril* gridiron, from L *crātīcula* fine wickerwork; see GRILLE] —'**grilled** *adj.* —'**griller** *n.*

grillage ('grɪlɪdʒ) *n.* an arrangement of beams and crossbeams used as a foundation on soft ground. [C18: from F, from *griller* to furnish with a grille]

grille *or* **grill** (grɪl) *n.* **1.** a framework, esp. of metal bars arranged to form an ornamental pattern, used as a screen or partition. **2.** Also called: **radiator grille.** a grating that admits cooling air to the radiator of a motor vehicle. **3.** a metal or wooden openwork grating used as a screen or divider. **4.** a protective screen, usually plastic or metal, in front of the loudspeaker in a radio, record player, etc. [C17: from OF, from L *crātīcula* fine hurdlework, from *crātis* a hurdle]

Grillparzer (*German* 'grɪlpartsər) *n.* **Franz** (frants). 1791–1872, Austrian dramatist and poet, noted for his historical and classical tragedies, which include *Sappho* (1818), the trilogy *The Golden Fleece* (1819–22), and *The Jewess of Toledo* (1872).

grillroom ('grɪl‚ruːm, -‚rʊm) *n.* a restaurant where grilled steaks and other meat are served.

grilse (grɪls) *n., pl.* **grilses** *or* **grilse.** a salmon at the stage when it returns for the first time from the sea to fresh water. [C15 *grilles* (pl.), from ?]

grim (grɪm) *adj.* **grimmer, grimmest. 1.** stern; resolute: *grim determination.* **2.** harsh or formidable in manner or appearance. **3.** harshly ironic or sinister: *grim laughter.* **4.** cruel, severe, or ghastly: *a grim accident.* **5.** *Arch. or poetic.* fierce: *a grim warrior.* **6.** *Inf.* unpleasant; disagreeable. [OE *grimm*] —'**grimly** *adv.* —'**grimness** *n.*

grimace (grɪ'meɪs) *n.* **1.** an ugly or distorted facial expression, as of wry humour, disgust, etc. ~*vb.* **2.** (*intr.*) to contort the face. [C17: from F, of Gmc origin; rel. to Sp. *grimazo* caricature] —**gri'macer** *n.*

Grimaldi (grɪ'mɔːldɪ) *n.* **Joseph.** 1779–1837, English actor, noted as a clown in pantomime.

grimalkin (grɪ'mælkɪn, -'mɔːl-) *n.* **1.** an old cat, esp. an old female cat. **2.** a crotchety or shrewish old woman. [C17: from GREY + *malkin*, dim. of female name *Maud*]

grime (graɪm) *n.* **1.** dirt, soot, or filth, esp. when ingrained. ~*vb.* **2.** (*tr.*) to make dirty or coat with filth. [C15: from MDu. *grime*] —'**grimy** *adj.* —'**griminess** *n.*

Grimm (grɪm) *n.* **Jakob Ludwig Karl** ('jaːkɔp 'luːtvɪç karl), 1785–1863, and his brother, **Wilhelm Karl** ('vɪlhɛlm karl), 1786–1859, German philologists and folklorists, who collaborated on *Grimm's Fairy Tales* (1812–22) and began a German dictionary. Jakob is noted also for his philological work *Deutsche Grammatik* (1819–37), in which he formulated the law named after him.

Grimsby ('grɪmzbɪ) *n.* a former fishing port in E England, in S Humberside. Pop.: 95 000 (1985).

grin (grɪn) *vb.* **grinning, grinned.** **1.** to smile with the lips drawn back revealing the teeth or express (something) by such a smile: *to grin a welcome.* **2.** (*intr.*) to draw back the lips revealing the teeth, as in a snarl or grimace. **3. grin and bear it.** *Inf.* to suffer trouble or hardship without complaint. ~*n.* **4.** a broad smile. **5.** a snarl or grimace. [OE *grennian*] —'**grinning** *adj., n.*

grind (graɪnd) *vb.* **grinding, ground.** **1.** to reduce or be reduced to small particles by pounding or abrading: *to grind corn.* **2.** (*tr.*) to smooth, sharpen, or polish by friction or abrasion: *to grind a knife.* **3.** to scrape or grate together (two things, esp. the teeth) with a harsh rasping sound or (of such objects) to be scraped together. **4.** (*tr.; foll. by out*) to speak or say something in a rough voice. **5.** (*tr.; often foll. by down*) to hold down; oppress; tyrannize. **6.** (*tr.*) to operate (a machine) by turning a handle. **7.** (*tr.; foll. by out*) to produce in a routine or uninspired manner: *he ground out his weekly article for the paper.* **8.** (*intr.*) *Inf.* to study or work laboriously. ~*n.* **9.** *Inf.* laborious or routine work or study. **10.** a specific grade of pulverization, as of coffee beans: *coarse grind.* **11.** the act or sound of grinding. [OE *grindan*] —'**grindingly** *adv.*

Grindelwald (German 'grɪndəlvalt) *n.* a valley and resort in central Switzerland, in the Bernese Oberland: mountaineering centre, with the Wetterhorn and the Eiger nearby.

grinder ('graɪndə) *n.* **1.** a person who grinds, esp. one who grinds cutting tools. **2.** a machine for grinding. **3.** a molar tooth.

grindstone ('graɪnd,stəʊn) *n.* **1. a.** a machine having a circular block of stone rotated for sharpening tools or grinding metal. **b.** the stone used in this machine. **c.** any stone used for sharpening; whetstone. **2. keep** *or* **have one's nose to the grindstone.** to work hard and perseveringly.

gringo ('grɪŋgəʊ) *n., pl.* **-gos.** a person from an English-speaking country: used as a derogatory term by Latin Americans. [C19: from Sp.: foreigner, prob. from *griego* Greek, hence an alien]

grip (grɪp) *n.* **1.** the act or an instance of grasping and holding firmly: *he lost his grip on the slope.* **2.** Also called: **handgrip.** the strength or pressure of such a grasp, as in a handshake. **3.** the style or manner of grasping an object, such as a tennis racket. **4.** understanding, control, or mastery of a subject, problem, etc. **5.** a person who manoeuvres the cameras in a film or television studio. **6. come** *or* **get to grips.** (often foll. by *with*) **a.** to deal with (a problem or subject). **b.** to tackle (an assailant). **7.** Also called: **handgrip.** a part by which an object is grasped; handle. **8.** Also called: **handgrip.** a travelling bag or holdall. **9.** See **hairgrip.** **10.** any device that holds by friction, such as certain types of brake. ~*vb.* **gripping, gripped.** **11.** to take hold of firmly or tightly, as by a clutch. **12.** to hold the interest or attention of: *to grip an audience.* [OE *gripe* grasp] —'**gripper** *n.* —'**gripping** *adj.*

gripe (graɪp) *vb.* **1.** (*intr.*) *Inf.* to complain, esp. in a persistent nagging manner. **2.** to cause sudden intense pain in the intestines of (a person) or (of a person) to experience this pain. **3.** *Arch.* to clutch; grasp. **4.** (*tr.*) *Arch.* to afflict. ~*n.* **5.** (*usually pl.*) a sudden intense pain in the intestines; colic. **6.** *Inf.* a complaint or grievance. **7.** *Now rare.* **a.** the act of gripping. **b.** a firm grip. **c.** a device that grips. [OE *grīpan*] —'**griper** *n.*

Gripe Water *n. Trademark. Brit.* a solution given to infants to relieve colic.

grippe *or* **grip** (grɪp) *n.* a former name for **influenza.** [C18: from F *grippe*, from *gripper* to seize, of Gmc origin; see GRIP]

Grips (grɪps) *n.* (*functioning as sing.*) *Films.* the member of the film crew who carries heavy camera equipment from place to place.

Griqualand East ('griːkwə,lænd, 'grɪk-) *n.* an area of South Africa, in E Cape Province: settled in 1861 by Griquas led by Adam Kok III; annexed to the Cape in 1879; became part of the Transkei in 1903. Chief town: Kokstad. Area: 17 100 sq. km (6602 sq. miles).

Griqualand West *n.* an area of South Africa, in N Cape Province north of the Orange river: settled after 1803 by the Griquas; annexed by the British in 1871 following a dispute with the Orange Free State; became part of the Cape in 1880. Chief town: Kimberley. Area: 39 360 sq. km (15 197 sq. miles).

Gris (*Spanish* gris) *n.* **Juan** (xwan). 1887–1927, Spanish cubist painter, resident in France from 1906.

grisaille (grɪ'zeɪl) *n.* **1.** a technique of monochrome painting in shades of grey, imitating the effect of relief. **2.** a painting, stained-glass window, etc., in this manner. [C19: from F, from *gris* grey]

griseofulvin (,grɪzɪəʊ'fʊlvɪn) *n.* an antibiotic used to treat fungal infections of the skin and hair. [C20: from NL, ult. from Med. L *griseus* grey + L *fulvus* reddish-yellow]

grisette (grɪ'zɛt) *n.* (esp. formerly) a French working girl. [C18: from F, from grey fabric used for dresses, from *gris* grey]

gris-gris ('griːgriː) *n., pl.* **-gris** (-griːz). a variant spelling of **grigri.**

Grishun (griː'ʃʊn) *n.* the Romansch name for **Graubünden.**

grisly ('grɪzlɪ) *adj.* **-lier, -liest.** causing horror or dread; gruesome. [OE *grislic*] —'**grisliness** *n.*

Grisons (griːzɔ̃) *n.* the French name for **Graubünden.**

grist (grɪst) *n.* **1. a.** grain intended to be or that has been ground. **b.** the quantity of such grain processed in one grinding. **2.** *Brewing.* malt grains that have been cleaned and cracked. **3. grist to** (*or* **for**) **the** (*or* **one's**) **mill.** anything that can be turned to profit or advantage. [OE *grist*]

gristle ('grɪsᵊl) *n.* cartilage, esp. when in meat. [OE *gristle*] —'**gristly** *adj.* —'**gristliness** *n.*

grit (grɪt) *n.* **1.** small hard particles of sand, earth, stone, etc. **2.** Also called: **gritstone.** any coarse sandstone that can be used as a grindstone or millstone. **3.** indomitable courage, toughness, or resolution. ~*vb.* **gritting, gritted.** **4.** to clench or grind together (two objects, esp. the teeth). **5.** to cover (a surface, such as icy roads) with grit. [OE *grēot*] —'**gritter** *n.*

Grit (grɪt) *n., adj. Canad.* an informal word for **Liberal.**

grits (grɪts) *pl. n.* **1.** hulled or coarsely ground grain. **2.** *U.S.* See **hominy grits.** [OE *grytt*]

gritty ('grɪtɪ) *adj.* **-tier, -tiest. 1.** courageous; hardy; resolute. **2.** of, like, or containing grit. —'**grittily** *adv.* —'**grittiness** *n.*

grizzle[1] ('grɪzᵊl) *vb.* **1.** to make or become grey. ~*n.* **2.** a grey colour. **3.** grey hair. [C15: from OF *grisel*, from *gris*, of Gmc origin]

grizzle[2] ('grɪzᵊl) *vb.* (*intr.*) *Inf., chiefly Brit.* (esp. of a child) to fret; whine. [C18: of Gmc origin] —'**grizzler** *n.*

grizzled ('grɪzᵊld) *adj.* **1.** streaked or mixed with grey; grizzly. **2.** having grey hair.

grizzly ('grɪzlɪ) *adj.* **-zlier, -zliest. 1.** somewhat grey; grizzled. ~*n., pl.* **-zlies. 2.** See **grizzly bear.**

grizzly bear *n.* a variety of the brown bear, formerly widespread in W North America; its brown fur has cream or white tips on the back, giving a grizzled appearance. Often shortened to **grizzly.**

groan (grəʊn) *n.* **1.** a prolonged stressed dull cry expressive of agony, pain, or disapproval. **2.** a loud harsh creaking sound, as of a tree bending in the wind. **3.** *Inf.* a

grumble or complaint, esp. a persistent one. ~*vb.* **4.** to utter (low inarticulate sounds) expressive of pain, grief, disapproval, etc. **5.** (*intr.*) to make a sound like a groan. **6.** (*intr.; usually foll. by beneath* or *under*) to be weighed down (by) or suffer greatly (under). **7.** (*intr.*) *Inf.* to complain or grumble. [OE *grānian*] —'**groaner** *n.* —'**groaning** *adj., n.* —'**groaningly** *adv.*

groat (grəʊt) *n.* an obsolete English silver coin worth four pennies. [C14: from MDu. *groot*, from MLow G *gros*, from Med. L (*denarius*) *grossus* thick (coin); see GROSCHEN]

groats (grəʊts) *pl. n.* the hulled and crushed grain of oats, wheat, or certain other cereals. [OE *grot* particle]

grocer ('grəʊsə) *n.* a dealer in foodstuffs and other household supplies. [C15: from OF *grossier*, from *gros* large; see GROSS]

groceries ('grəʊsərɪz) *pl. n.* merchandise, esp. foodstuffs, sold by a grocer.

grocery ('grəʊsərɪ) *n., pl.* -ceries. the business or premises of a grocer.

Grodno (*Russian* 'grɔdnə) *n.* a city in the W central Soviet Union, in the Byelorussian SSR on the Neman River: part of Poland (1921–39). Pop.: 263 000 (1987).

grog (grɒg) *n.* **1.** diluted spirit, usually rum, as an alcoholic drink. **2.** *Austral. & N.Z. inf.* alcoholic drink in general, esp. spirits. [C18: from Old *Grog*, nickname of Edward Vernon (1684–1757), Brit. admiral, who in 1740 issued naval rum diluted with water; his nickname arose from his grogram cloak]

groggy ('grɒgɪ) *adj.* -gier, -giest. *Inf.* **1.** dazed or staggering, as from exhaustion, blows, or drunkenness. **2.** faint or weak. —'**groggily** *adv.* —'**grogginess** *n.*

grogram ('grɒgrəm) *n.* a coarse fabric of silk, wool, or silk mixed with wool or mohair, often stiffened with gum, formerly used for clothing. [C16: from F *gros grain* coarse grain; see GROSGRAIN]

groin (grɔɪn) *n.* **1.** the depression or fold where the legs join the abdomen. **2.** *Euphemistic.* the genitals, esp. the testicles. **3.** a variant spelling (esp. U.S.) of **groyne**. **4.** *Archit.* a curved arris formed where two intersecting vaults meet. ~*vb.* **5.** (*tr.*) *Archit.* to provide or construct with groins. [C15: ?from E *grynde* abyss]

grommet ('grɒmɪt) *or* **grummet** *n.* a ring of rubber or plastic or a metal eyelet designed to line a hole to prevent a cable or pipe passed through it from chafing. [C15: from obs. F *gourmette* chain linking the ends of a bit, from *gourmer* bridle, from ?]

Gromyko (*Russian* grɑ'mikə) *n.* **Andrei Andreyevich** (an'drjej an'drjejɪvɪtʃ). born 1909, Soviet statesman and diplomat; foreign minister (1957–85); president (1985–88).

Groningen ('grəʊnɪŋən; *Dutch* 'xro:nɪŋə) *n.* **1.** a province in the NE Netherlands: mainly agricultural. Capital: Groningen. Pop.: 558 378 (1987). Area: 2336 sq. km (902 sq. miles). **2.** a city in the NE Netherlands, capital of Groningen province. Pop.: 168 019 (1987).

Grønland ('grœnlɑn) *n.* the Danish name for **Greenland.**

groom (gru:m, grʊm) *n.* **1.** a person employed to clean and look after horses. **2.** See **bridegroom**. **3.** any of various officers of a royal or noble household. **4.** *Arch.* a male servant. ~*vb.* (*tr.*) **5.** to make or keep (clothes, appearance, etc.) clean and tidy. **6.** to rub down, clean, and smarten (a horse, dog, etc.). **7.** to train or prepare for a particular task, occupation, etc.: *to groom someone for the Presidency.* [C13 *grom* manservant; ? rel. to OE *grōwan* to GROW]

groomsman ('gru:mzmən, 'grʊmz-) *n., pl.* -men. a man who attends the bridegroom at a wedding, usually the best man.

groove (gru:v) *n.* **1.** a long narrow channel or furrow, esp. one cut into wood by a tool. **2.** the spiral channel in a gramophone record. **3.** a settled existence, routine, etc., to which one is suited or accustomed. **4.** *Dated sl.* an experience, event, etc., that is groovy. **5. in the groove. a.** *Jazz.* playing well and apparently effortlessly, with a good beat, etc. **b.** *U.S.* fashionable. ~*vb.* **6.** (*tr.*) to form or cut a groove in. **7.** (*intr.*) *Dated sl.* to enjoy oneself or feel in rapport with one's surroundings. **8.** (*intr.*) *Jazz.* to play well, with a good beat, etc. [C15: from obs. Du. *groeve*, of Gmc origin]

groovy ('gru:vɪ) *adj.* groovier, grooviest. *Dated sl.* attractive, fashionable, or exciting.

grope (grəʊp) *vb.* **1.** (*intr.; usually foll. by for*) to feel or search about uncertainly (for something) with the hands.

2. (*intr.; usually foll. by for* or *after*) to search uncertainly or with difficulty (for a solution, answer, etc.). **3.** (*tr.*) to find (one's way) by groping. **4.** (*tr.*) *Sl.* to fondle the body of (someone) for sexual gratification. ~*n.* **5.** the act of groping. [OE *grāpian*] —'**gropingly** *adv.*

groper ('grəʊpə) *or* **grouper** *n., pl.* -er *or* -ers. a large marine fish of warm and tropical seas. [C17: from Port. *garupa*, prob. from a South American Indian word]

Gropius ('grəʊpɪəs) *n.* **Walter.** 1883–1969, U.S. architect, designer, and teacher, born in Germany. He founded (1919) and directed (1919–28) the Bauhaus in Germany. His influence stemmed from his adaptation of architecture to modern social needs and his pioneering use of industrial materials, such as concrete and steel. His buildings include the Fagus factory at Alfeld (1911) and the Bauhaus at Dessau (1926).

Gros (*French* gro) *n.* Baron **Antoine Jean** (ātwan ʒā). 1771–1835, French painter, noted for his battle scenes.

grosbeak ('grəʊs,bi:k, 'grɒs-) *n.* any of various finches that have a massive powerful bill. [C17: from F *grosbec*, from OF *gros* large, thick + *bec* BEAK]

groschen ('grəʊʃən) *n., pl.* -schen. **1.** an Austrian monetary unit worth one hundredth of a schilling. **2.** a German coin worth ten pfennigs. **3.** a former German silver coin. [C17: from G: alteration of MHG *grosse*, from Med. L (*denarius*) *grossus* thick (penny); see GROSS, GROAT]

grosgrain ('grəʊ,greɪn) *n.* a heavy ribbed silk or rayon fabric or tape for trimming clothes, etc. [C19: from F *gros grain* coarse grain; see GROSS, GRAIN]

gros point (grəʊ) *n.* **1.** a needlepoint stitch covering two horizontal and two vertical threads. **2.** work done in this stitch.

gross (grəʊs) *adj.* **1.** repellently or excessively fat or bulky. **2.** with no deductions for expenses, tax, etc.; total: *gross sales.* Cf. net[2]. **3.** (of personal qualities, tastes, etc.) conspicuously coarse or vulgar. **4.** obviously or exceptionally culpable or wrong; flagrant: *gross inefficiency.* **5.** lacking in perception, sensitivity, or discrimination: *gross judgments.* **6.** (esp. of vegetation) dense; thick; luxuriant. ~*n.* **7.** (*pl.* **gross**). a unit of quantity equal to 12 dozen. **8.** (*pl.* **grosses**). **a.** the entire amount. **b.** the great majority. ~*vb.* (*tr.*) **9.** to earn as total revenue, before deductions for expenses, tax, etc. [C14: from OF *gros* large, from LL *grossus* thick] —'**grossly** *adv.* —'**grossness** *n.*

gross domestic product *n.* the total value of all goods and services produced domestically by a nation during a year. It is equivalent to gross national product minus net investment incomes from foreign nations. Abbrev.: **GDP.**

Grosseteste ('grəʊs,test) *n.* **Robert.** ?1175–1253, English prelate and scholar; bishop of Lincoln (1235–53). He attacked ecclesiastical abuses and wrote commentaries on Aristotle and treatises on theology, philosophy, and science.

gross national product *n.* the total value of all final goods and services produced annually by a nation. Abbrev.: **GNP.**

gross profit *n. Accounting.* the difference between total revenue from sales and the total cost of purchases or materials, with an adjustment for stock.

Grosswardein (gro:svar'dain) *n.* the German name for **Oradea.**

gross weight *n.* total weight of an article inclusive of the weight of the container and packaging.

Grosz (grəʊs) *n.* **George.** 1893–1959, German painter, in the U.S. from 1932, whose works satirized German militarism and bourgeois society.

grot (grɒt) *n. Sl.* rubbish; dirt. [C20: from GROTTY]

Grote (grəʊt) *n.* **George.** 1794–1871, English historian, noted particularly for his *History of Greece* (1846–56).

grotesque (grəʊ'tesk) *adj.* **1.** strangely or fantastically distorted; bizarre. **2.** of or characteristic of the grotesque in art. **3.** absurdly incongruous; in a ludicrous context. ~*n.* **4.** a 16th-century decorative style in which parts of human, animal, and plant forms are distorted and mixed. **5.** a decorative device, as in painting or sculpture, in this style. **6.** *Printing.* the family of 19th-century sans serif display types. **7.** any grotesque person or thing. [C16: from F, from OIt. (*pittura*) *grottesca* cave painting, from *grotta* cave; see GROTTO] —**gro'tesquely** *adv.* —**gro'tesqueness** *n.* —**gro'tesquery** *or* **gro'tesquerie** *n.*

Grotius ('grəʊtɪəs) n. **Hugo,** original name *Huig de Groot.* 1583–1645, Dutch jurist and statesman, whose *De Jure Belli ac Pacis* (1625) is regarded as the foundation of modern international law. —'**Grotian** *adj.* —'**Grotianism** *n.*

grotto ('grɒtəʊ) n., pl. **-toes** or **-tos. 1.** a small cave, esp. one with attractive features. **2.** a construction in the form of a cave, esp. as in landscaped gardens during the 18th century. [C17: from OIt. *grotta,* from LL *crypta* vault; see CRYPT]

grotty ('grɒtɪ) *adj.* **-tier, -tiest.** *Brit. sl.* **1.** nasty or unattractive. **2.** of poor quality or in bad condition. [C20: from GROTESQUE]

grouch (graʊtʃ) *Inf.* ~*vb.* (*intr.*) **1.** to complain; grumble. ~*n.* **2.** a complaint, esp. a persistent one. **3.** a person who is always grumbling. [C20: from obs. *grutch,* from OF *grouchier* to complain; see GRUDGE] —'**grouchy** *adj.* —'**grouchily** *adv.* —'**grouchiness** *n.*

ground[1] (graʊnd) n. **1.** the land surface. **2.** earth or soil. **3.** (*pl.*) the land around a dwelling house or other building. **4.** (*sometimes pl.*) an area of land given over to a purpose: *football ground.* **5.** land having a particular characteristic: *high ground.* **6.** matter for consideration or debate; field of research or inquiry: *the report covered a lot of ground.* **7.** a position or viewpoint, as in an argument or controversy (esp. in **give ground, hold, stand,** or **shift one's ground**). **8.** position or advantage, as in a subject or competition (esp. in **gain ground, lose ground,** etc.). **9.** (*often pl.*) reason; justification: *grounds for complaint.* **10.** *Arts.* **a.** the prepared surface applied to a wall, canvas, etc., to prevent it reacting with or absorbing the paint. **b.** the background of a painting against which the other parts of a work of art appear superimposed. **11. a.** the first coat of paint applied to a surface. **b.** (*as modifier*): *ground colour.* **12.** the bottom of a river or the sea. **13.** (*pl.*) sediment or dregs, esp. from coffee. **14.** *Chiefly Brit.* the floor of a room. **15.** *Cricket.* the area from the popping crease back past the stumps, in which a batsman may legally stand. **16.** *Electrical.* the usual U.S. and Canad. word for **earth** (sense 8). **17. break new ground.** to do something that has not been done before. **18. common ground.** an agreed basis for identifying issues in an argument. **19. cut the ground from under someone's feet.** to anticipate someone's action or argument and thus make it irrelevant or meaningless. **20.** (**down**) **to the ground.** *Brit. inf.* completely; absolutely: *it suited him down to the ground.* **21. home ground.** a familiar area or topic. **22. into the ground.** beyond what is requisite or can be endured; to exhaustion. **23.** (*modifier*) on or concerned with the ground: *ground frost; ground forces.* ~*vb.* **24.** (*tr.*) to put or place on the ground. **25.** (*tr.*) to instruct in fundamentals. **26.** (*tr.*) to provide a basis or foundation for; establish. **27.** (*tr.*) to confine (an aircraft, pilot, etc.) to the ground. **28.** the usual U.S. and Canad. word for **earth** (sense 8). **29.** (*tr.*) *Naut.* to run (a vessel) aground. **30.** (*intr.*) to hit or reach the ground. [OE *grund*]

ground[2] (graʊnd) *vb.* **1.** the past tense and past participle of **grind.** ~*adj.* **2.** having the surface finished, thickness reduced, or an edge sharpened by grinding. **3.** reduced to fine particles by grinding.

groundage ('graʊndɪdʒ) n. *Brit.* a fee levied on a vessel entering a port or anchored off a shore.

groundbait ('graʊnd,beɪt) n. *Angling.* bait, such as bread or maggots, thrown into an area of water to attract fish.

ground bass (beɪs) n. *Music.* a short melodic bass line that is repeated over and over.

ground control n. **1.** the personnel, radar, computers, etc., on the ground that monitor the progress of aircraft or spacecraft. **2.** a system for feeding continuous radio messages to an aircraft pilot to enable him to make a blind landing.

ground cover n. dense low herbaceous plants and shrubs that grow over the surface of the ground.

ground elder n. a widely naturalized Eurasian umbelliferous plant with white flowers and creeping underground stems. Also called: **bishop's weed, goutweed.**

ground floor n. **1.** the floor of a building level or almost level with the ground. **2. get in on the ground floor.** *Inf.* to be in a project, undertaking, etc., from its inception.

ground glass n. **1.** glass that has a rough surface produced by grinding, used for diffusing light. **2.** glass in the form of fine particles produced by grinding, used as an abrasive.

groundhog ('graʊnd,hɒg) n. another name for **woodchuck.**

grounding ('graʊndɪŋ) n. a foundation, esp. the basic general knowledge of a subject.

ground ivy n. a creeping or trailing Eurasian aromatic herbaceous plant with scalloped leaves and purplish-blue flowers.

groundless ('graʊndlɪs) *adj.* without reason or justification: *his suspicions were groundless.* —'**groundlessly** *adv.* —'**groundlessness** *n.*

groundling ('graʊndlɪŋ) n. **1.** any animal or plant that lives close to the ground or at the bottom of a lake, river, etc. **2.** (in Elizabethan theatre) a spectator standing in the yard in front of the stage and paying least. **3.** a person on the ground as distinguished from one in an aircraft.

groundnut ('graʊnd,nʌt) n. **1.** a North American climbing leguminous plant with small edible underground tubers. **2.** the tuber of this plant. **3.** *Brit.* another name for **peanut.**

ground plan n. **1.** a drawing of the ground floor of a building, esp. one to scale. **2.** a preliminary or basic outline.

ground rule n. a procedural or fundamental principle.

groundsel ('graʊnsəl) n. any of certain plants of the composite family, esp. a Eurasian weed with heads of small yellow flowers. [OE *gundeswilge,* from *gund* pus + *swelgan* to swallow; after its use in poultices]

groundsheet ('graʊnd,ʃiːt) n. a waterproof rubber, plastic, or polythene sheet placed on the ground in a tent, etc., to keep out damp.

groundsill ('graʊnd,sɪl) n. a joist forming the lowest member of a timber frame. Also called: **ground plate.**

groundsman ('graʊndzmən) n., pl. **-men.** a person employed to maintain a sports ground, park, etc.

groundspeed ('graʊnd,spiːd) n. the speed of an aircraft relative to the ground.

ground squirrel n. a burrowing rodent resembling a chipmunk and occurring in North America, E Europe, and Asia. Also called: **gopher.**

ground swell n. **1.** a considerable swell of the sea, often caused by a distant storm or earthquake. **2.** a rapidly developing general feeling or opinion.

ground water n. underground water that is held in the soil and in pervious rocks.

groundwork ('graʊnd,wɜːk) n. **1.** preliminary work as a foundation or basis. **2.** the ground or background of a painting, etc.

ground zero n. a point on the ground directly below the centre of a nuclear explosion.

group (gruːp) n. **1.** a number of persons or things considered as a collective unit. **2. a.** a number of persons bound together by common social standards, interests, etc. **b.** (*as modifier*): *group behaviour.* **3.** a small band of players or singers, esp. of pop music. **4.** a number of animals or plants considered as a unit because of common characteristics, habits, etc. **5.** an association of companies under a single ownership and control. **6.** two or more figures or objects forming a design in a painting or sculpture. **7.** a military formation comprising complementary arms and services: *a brigade group.* **8.** an air force organization of higher level than a squadron. **9.** *Also called:* **radical.** *Chem.* two or more atoms that are bound together in a molecule and behave as a single unit: *a methyl group* -CH₃. **10.** a vertical column of elements in the periodic table that all have similar electronic structures, properties, and valencies: *the halogen group.* **11.** *Maths.* a set under an operation involving any two members of the set such that the set is closed, associative, and contains both an identity and the inverse of each member. **12.** See **blood group.** ~*vb.* **13.** to arrange or place (things, people, etc.) in or into a group, or (of things, etc.) to form into a group. [C17: from F *groupe,* of Gmc origin; cf. It. *gruppo;* see CROP]

group captain n. an officer holding commissioned rank senior to a wing commander but junior to an air commodore in the RAF and certain other air forces.

group dynamics n. (*functioning as sing.*) *Psychol.* a field of social psychology concerned with the nature of human groups, their development, and their interactions.

grouper ('gru:pə) n. a variant spelling of **groper**.

groupie ('gru:pɪ) n. Sl. an ardent fan of a celebrity, esp. a girl who follows the members of a pop group on tour in order to have sexual relations with them.

group practice n. a group of doctors who together run a general practice.

group therapy n. Psychol. the simultaneous treatment of a number of individuals who are brought together to share their problems in group discussion.

grouse[1] (graus) n., pl. **grouse** or **grouses**. a game bird occurring mainly in the N hemisphere, having a stocky body and feathered legs and feet. [C16: from ?]

grouse[2] (graus) vb. 1. (intr.) to grumble; complain. ~n. 2. a persistent complaint. [C19: from ?] — **'grouser** n.

grouse[3] (graus) adj. Austral. & N.Z. sl. fine; excellent. [from ?]

grout (graut) n. 1. a thin mortar for filling joints between tiles, masonry, etc. 2. a fine plaster used as a finishing coat. 3. (pl.) sediment or dregs. ~vb. 4. (tr.) to fill (joints) or finish (walls, etc.) with grout. [OE grūt] — **'grouter** n.

grove (grəʊv) n. 1. a small wooded area or plantation. 2. a road lined with houses and often trees, esp. in a suburban area. [OE grāf]

grovel ('grɒvəl) vb. **-elling, -elled** or U.S. **-eling, -eled**. (intr.) 1. to humble or abase oneself, as in making apologies or showing respect. 2. to lie or crawl face downwards, as in fear or humility. 3. (often foll. by in) to indulge or take pleasure (in sensuality or vice). [C16: back formation from obs. groveling (adv.), from ME on grufe on the face, of Scand. origin; see -LING[2]] — **'groveller** n.

Groves (grəʊvz) n. Sir **Charles**. born 1915, English orchestral conductor.

grow (grəʊ) vb. **growing, grew, grown.** 1. (of an organism or part of an organism) to increase in size or develop (hair, leaves, or other structures). 2. (intr.; usually foll. by out of or from) to originate, as from an initial cause or source: the federation grew out of the Empire. 3. (intr.) to increase in size, number, degree, etc.: the population is growing rapidly. 4. (intr.) to change in length or amount in a specified direction: some plants grow downwards. 5. (copula; may take an infinitive) (esp. of emotions, physical states, etc.) to develop or come into existence or being gradually: to grow cold; he grew to like her. 6. (intr.; foll. by together) to be joined gradually by or as by growth: the branches on the tree grew together. 7. (when intr., foll. by with) to become covered with a growth: the path grew with weeds. 8. to produce (plants) by controlling or encouraging their growth, esp. for home consumption or on a commercial basis. ~See also **grow into, grow on,** etc. [OE grōwan] — **'growable** adj. — **'grower** n.

grow bag n. a plastic bag containing a sterile growing medium that enables a plant to be grown to full size in it, usually for one season only. [C20: from Gro-bag, trademark for the first ones marketed]

growing pains pl. n. 1. pains in muscles or joints sometimes experienced by growing children. 2. difficulties besetting a new enterprise in its early stages.

grow into vb. (intr., prep.) to become big or mature enough for: his clothes were always big enough for him to grow into.

growl (graul) vb. 1. (of animals, esp. when hostile) to utter (sounds) in a low inarticulate manner: the dog growled. 2. to utter (words) in a gruff or angry manner. 3. (intr.) to make sounds suggestive of an animal growling: the thunder growled. ~n. 4. the act or sound of growling. [C18: from earlier grolle, from OF grouller to grumble] — **'growler** n. — **'growlingly** adv.

grown (grəʊn) adj. **a.** developed or advanced: fully grown. **b.** (in combination): half-grown.

grown-up adj. 1. having reached maturity; adult. 2. suitable for or characteristic of an adult. ~n. 3. an adult.

grow on vb. (intr., prep.) to become progressively more acceptable or pleasant to.

grow out of vb. (intr., adv. + prep.) to become too big or mature for: she soon grew out of her girlish ways.

growth (grəʊθ) n. 1. the process or act of growing. 2. an increase in size, number, significance, etc. 3. something grown or growing: a new growth of hair. 4. a stage of development: a full growth. 5. any abnormal tissue, such as a tumour. 6. (modifier) of, relating to, causing, or

characterized by growth: a growth industry; growth hormone.

grow up vb. (intr., adv.) 1. to reach maturity; become adult. 2. to come into existence; develop.

groyne or esp. U.S. **groin** (grɔɪn) n. a wall or jetty built out from a riverbank or seashore to control erosion. Also called: **spur, breakwater.** [C16: ?from OF groign snout, promontory]

Grozny (Russian 'grɔznɪj) n. a city in the S Soviet Union, capital of the Checheno-Ingush ASSR: a major oil centre. Pop.: 404 000 (1987).

grub (grʌb) vb. **grubbing, grubbed.** 1. (when tr., often foll. by up or out) to search for and pull up (roots, stumps, etc.) by digging in the ground. 2. to dig up the surface of (ground, soil, etc.), esp. to clear away roots, stumps, etc. 3. (intr.; often foll. by in or among) to search carefully. 4. (intr.) to work unceasingly, esp. at a dull task. ~n. 5. the short legless larva of certain insects, esp. beetles. 6. Sl. food; victuals. 7. a person who works hard, esp. in a dull plodding way. [C13: of Gmc origin; cf. OHG grubilōn to dig] — **'grubber** n.

grubby ('grʌbɪ) adj. **-bier, -biest.** 1. dirty; slovenly. 2. mean; beggarly. 3. infested with grubs. — **'grubbily** adv. — **'grubbiness** n.

grub screw n. a small headless screw used to secure a sliding component in position.

grubstake ('grʌb,steɪk) n. U.S. & Canad. inf. ~ 1. supplies provided for a prospector on the condition that the donor has a stake in any finds. ~vb. (tr.) 2. to furnish with such supplies. 3. Chiefly U.S. & Canad. to supply (a person) with a stake in a gambling game. — **'grub,staker** n.

Grub Street n. 1. a former street in London frequented by literary hacks and needy authors. 2. the world or class of literary hacks, etc. ~adj. also **Grubstreet.** 3. (sometimes not cap.) relating to or characteristic of hack literature.

grudge (grʌdʒ) n. 1. a persistent feeling of resentment, esp. one due to an insult or injury. ~vb. 2. (tr.) to give unwillingly. 3. to feel resentful or envious about (someone else's success, possessions, etc.). [C15: from OF grouchier to grumble, prob. of Gmc origin] — **'grudging** adj. — **'grudgingly** adv.

gruel ('gru:əl) n. a drink or thin porridge made by boiling meal, esp. oatmeal, in water or milk. [C14: from OF, of Gmc origin]

gruelling or U.S. **grueling** ('gru:əlɪŋ) adj. 1. extremely severe or tiring. ~n. 2. Inf. a severe or tiring experience, esp. punishment. [C19: from obs. gruel (vb.) to punish]

gruesome ('gru:səm) adj. inspiring repugnance and horror; ghastly. [C16: orig. Northern E and Scot., of Scand. origin] — **'gruesomely** adv. — **'gruesomeness** n.

gruff (grʌf) adj. 1. rough or surly in manner, speech, etc. 2. (of a voice, bark, etc.) low and throaty. [C16: orig. Scot., from Du. grof, of Gmc origin; rel. to OE hrēof] — **'gruffly** adv. — **'gruffness** n.

grumble ('grʌmbəl) vb. 1. to utter (complaints) in a nagging way. 2. (intr.) to make low dull rumbling sounds. ~n. 3. a complaint; grouse. 4. a low rumbling sound. [C16: from MLow G grommelen, of Gmc origin] — **'grumbler** n. — **'grumblingly** adv. — **'grumbly** adj.

grumbling appendix n. Inf. a condition in which the appendix causes intermittent pain or discomfort but appendicitis has not developed.

grummet ('grʌmɪt) n. a variant of **grommet**.

grump (grʌmp) Inf. ~n. 1. a surly or bad-tempered person. 2. (pl.) a sulky or morose mood (esp. in **have the grumps**). ~vb. 3. (intr.) to complain or grumble. [C18: dialect: surly remark, prob. imit.]

grumpy ('grʌmpɪ) or **grumpish** adj. **grumpier, grumpiest.** peevish; sulky. [C18: from GRUMP + -Y[1]] — **'grumpily** or **'grumpishly** adv. — **'grumpiness** or **'grumpishness** n.

Grundy ('grʌndɪ) n. a narrow-minded person who keeps critical watch on the propriety of others. [C18: after Mrs Grundy, the character in T. Morton's play Speed the Plough (1798)] — **'Grundy,ism** n. — **'Grundyist** or **'Grundyite** n.

Grünewald (German 'gry:nəvalt) n. **Matthias** (ma'ti:as), original name Mathis Gothardt. ?1470–1528, German painter, the greatest exponent of late Gothic art in Germany. The Isenheim Altarpiece is regarded as his masterpiece.

grungy ('grʌndʒɪ) *adj.* **-gier, -giest.** *Sl., chiefly U.S. & Canad.* squalid, seedy, grotty. [from ?]

grunion ('grʌnjən) *n.* a Californian marine fish that spawns on beaches. [C20: prob. from Sp. *gruñón* a grunter]

grunt (grʌnt) *vb.* **1.** (*intr.*) (esp. of pigs and some other animals) to emit a low short gruff noise. **2.** (when *tr., may take a clause as object*) to express something gruffly: *he grunted his answer.* ~*n.* **3.** the characteristic low short gruff noise of pigs, etc., or a similar sound, as of disgust. **4.** any of various mainly tropical marine fishes that utter a grunting sound when caught. [OE *grunnettan*, prob. imit.; cf. OHG *grunnizōn, grunni* moaning] — '**grunter** *n.*

Gruyère *or* **Gruyère cheese** ('gru:jɛə) *n.* a hard flat whole-milk cheese, pale yellow in colour and with holes. [C19: after *Gruyère*, Switzerland, where it originated]

gr. wt. *abbrev. for* gross weight.

gryphon ('grɪfⁿn) *n.* a variant spelling of **griffin.**

grysbok ('graɪs,bɒk) *n.* either of two small antelopes of central and southern Africa, having small straight horns. [C18: Afrik., from Du. *grijs* grey + *bok* BUCK¹]

GS *abbrev. for:* **1.** General Secretary. **2.** General Staff.

G-string *n.* **1.** a piece of cloth worn by striptease artistes covering the pubic area only and attached to a very narrow waistband. **2.** a strip of cloth attached to the front and back of a waistband and covering the loins. **3.** *Music.* a string tuned to G.

G-suit *n.* a close-fitting garment that is worn by the crew of high-speed aircraft and can be pressurized to prevent blackout during certain manoeuvres. [C20: from *g*(*ravity*) *suit*]

GT *abbrev. for* gran turismo: a touring car; usually a fast sports car with a hard fixed roof.

gtd *abbrev. for* guaranteed.

Guadalajara (ˌgwɑːdⁿlə'hɑːrə; *Spanish* gwaðala'xara) *n.* **1.** a city in W Mexico, capital of Jalisco state: the second largest city of Mexico: centre of the Indian slave trade until its abolition, declared here in 1810; two universities (1792 and 1935). Pop.: 2 244 715 (1980). **2.** a city in central Spain, in New Castile. Pop.: 56 922 (1981).

Guadalcanal (ˌgwɑːdⁿlkə'næl; *Spanish* gwaðalka'nal) *n.* a mountainous island in the SW Pacific, the largest of the Solomon Islands: under British protection until 1978; occupied by the Japanese (1942–43). Pop.: 63 335 (1984). Area: 6475 sq. km (2500 sq. miles).

Guadalquivir (ˌgwɑːdⁿlkwɪ'vɪə; *Spanish* gwaðalki'βir) *n.* the chief river of S Spain, rising in the Sierra de Segura and flowing west and southwest to the Gulf of Cádiz: navigable by ocean-going vessels to Seville. Length: 560 km (348 miles).

Guadalupe Hidalgo (ˌgwɑːdⁿ'luːp hɪ'dælgəʊ; *Spanish* gwaða'lupe i'ðalɣo) *n.* a city in central Mexico, northwest of Mexico City: became the foremost pilgrimage centre in the Americas after an Indian convert reported seeing a vision of the Virgin Mary here in 1531. Pop.: 370 524 (1980). Former name (1931–71): **Gustavo A. Madero.**

Guadeloupe (ˌgwɑːdⁿ'luːp) *n.* an overseas region of France in the E Caribbean, in the Leeward Islands, formed by the islands of Basse Terre and Grande Terre and their five dependencies. Capital: Basse-Terre. Pop.: 335 300 (1987 est.). Area: 1702 sq. km (657 sq. miles).

Guadiana (*Spanish* gwa'ðjana; *Portuguese* gwə'ðjənə) *n.* a river in SW Europe, rising in S central Spain and flowing west, then south as part of the border between Spain and Portugal, to the Gulf of Cádiz. Length: 578 km (359 miles).

guaiacum ('gwaɪəkəm) *n.* **1.** any of a family of tropical American evergreen trees such as the lignum vitae. **2.** the hard heavy wood of any of these trees. **3.** a brownish resin obtained from the lignum vitae, used medicinally and in making varnishes. [C16: NL, from Sp. *guayaco*, of Amerind origin]

Guam (gwɑːm) *n.* an island in the N Pacific, the largest and southernmost of the Marianas: belonged to Spain from the 17th century until 1898, when it was ceded to the U.S.: site of naval and air force bases. Capital: Agaña. Pop.: 115 756 (1984 est.). Area: 541 sq. km (209 sq. miles). —**Guamanian** (gwɑː'meɪnɪən) *n., adj.*

Guanabara (*Portuguese* gwənə'bara) *n.* (until 1975) a state of SE Brazil, on the Atlantic and **Guanabara Bay,** now amalgamated with the state of Rio de Janeiro.

guanaco (gwɑː'nɑːkəʊ) *n., pl.* **-cos.** a cud-chewing South American mammal closely related to the domesticated llama. [C17: from Sp., from Quechuan *huanacu*]

Guanajuato (*Spanish* gwana'xwato) *n.* **1.** a state of central Mexico, on the great central plateau: mountainous in the north, with fertile plains in the south; important mineral resources. Capital: Guanajuato. Pop.: 3 044 402 (1980). Area: 30 588 sq. km (11 810 sq. miles). **2.** a city in central Mexico, capital of Guanajuato state: founded in 1554, it became one of the world's richest silver-mining centres. Pop.: 48 000 (1980).

Guangdong ('gwæŋ'dʊŋ) *or* **Kwangtung** *n.* a province of SE China, on the South China Sea: includes the Leizhou Peninsula and Hainan Island, with densely populated river valleys; the only true tropical climate in China, and the only remaining foreign enclaves (Macao and Hong Kong). Capital: Canton. Pop.: 61 660 000 (1985). Area: 231 400 sq. km (90 246 sq. miles).

Guangxi Zhuang Autonomous Region ('gwæŋ'siː 'dʒwæŋ) *or* **Kwangsi-Chuang Autonomous Region** *n.* an administrative division of S China: the least developed of Chinese regions. Capital: Nanning. Pop.: 38 060 000 (1985). Area: 220 400 sq. km (85 100 sq. miles).

Guangzhou ('gwæŋ'dzəʊ) *n.* the Pinyin transliteration of the Chinese name for **Canton.**

guanine ('gwɑːniːn, 'guːə,niːn) *n.* a white almost insoluble compound: one of the purine bases in nucleic acids. [C19: from GUANO + -INE²]

guano ('gwɑːnəʊ) *n., pl.* **-nos.** **1.** the dried excrement of fish-eating sea birds, deposited in rocky coastal regions of South America: used as a fertilizer. **2.** any similar but artificially produced fertilizer. [C17: from Sp., from Quechuan *huano* dung]

Guantánamo (*Spanish* gwan'tanamo) *n.* a city in SE Cuba, on **Guantánamo Bay.** Pop.: 174 400 (1986 est.).

Guaporé (*Portuguese* gwapo're) *n.* **1.** a river in W central South America, rising in SW Brazil and flowing northwest as part of the border between Brazil and Bolivia, to join the Mamoré River. Length: 1750 km (1087 miles). Spanish name: **Iténez.** **2.** the former name (until 1956) of **Rondônia.**

Guarani (ˌgwɑːrə'niː) *n.* **1.** (*pl.* **-ni** *or* **-nis**) a member of a South American Indian people of Paraguay, S Brazil, and Bolivia. **2.** the language of this people.

guarantee (ˌgærən'tiː) *n.* **1.** a formal assurance, esp. in writing, that a product, service, etc., will meet certain standards or specifications. **2.** *Law.* a promise, esp. a collateral agreement, to answer for the debt, default, or miscarriage of another. **3. a.** a person, company, etc., to whom a guarantee is made. **b.** a person, company, etc., who gives a guarantee. **4.** a person who acts as a guarantor. **5.** something that makes a specified condition or outcome certain. **6.** a variant spelling of **guaranty.** ~*vb.* **-teeing, -teed.** (*mainly tr.*) **7.** (*also intr.*) to take responsibility for (someone else's debts, obligations, etc.). **8.** to serve as a guarantee for. **9.** to secure or furnish security for: *a small deposit will guarantee any dress.* **10.** (usually foll. by *from* or *against*) to undertake to protect or keep secure, as against injury, loss, etc. **11.** to ensure: *good planning will guarantee success.* **12.** (*may take a clause as object or an infinitive*) to promise or make certain. [C17: ?from Sp. *garante* or F *garant*, of Gmc origin; cf. WARRANT]

guarantor (ˌgærən'tɔː) *n.* a person who gives or is bound by a guarantee or guaranty; surety.

guaranty ('gærəntɪ) *n., pl.* **-ties. 1.** a pledge of responsibility for fulfilling another person's obligations in case of that person's default. **2.** a thing given or taken as security for a guaranty. **3.** the act of providing security. **4.** a person who acts as a guarantor. ~*vb.* **-tying, -tied. 5.** a variant spelling of **guarantee.** [C16: from OF *garantie*, var. of *warantie*, of Gmc origin; see WARRANTY]

guard (gɑːd) *vb.* **1.** to watch over or shield (a person or thing) from danger or harm; protect. **2.** to keep watch over (a prisoner or other potentially dangerous person or thing), as to prevent escape. **3.** (*tr.*) to control: *to guard one's tongue.* **4.** (*intr.*; usually foll. by *against*) to take precautions. **5.** to control entrance and exit through (a gate, door, etc.). **6.** (*tr.*) to provide (machinery, etc.) with a device to protect the operator. **7.** (*tr.*) **a.** *Chess, cards.* to protect or cover (a chessman or card) with another. **b.** *Curling, bowling.* to protect or cover (a stone or bowl) by placing one's own stone or bowl between it and another player. ~n. **8.** a person or group who keeps a protecting, supervising, or restraining watch or control over people, such as prisoners, things, etc. Related adj.: **custodial. 9.** a person or group of people, such as soldiers, who form a ceremonial escort. **10.** *Brit.* the official in charge of a train. **11. a.** the act or duty of protecting, restraining, or supervising. **b.** (*as modifier*): *guard duty.* **12.** a device, part, or attachment on an object, such as a weapon or machine tool, designed to protect the user against injury. **13.** anything that provides or is intended to provide protection: *a guard against infection.* **14.** *Sport.* an article of light tough material worn to protect any of various parts of the body. **15.** the posture of defence or readiness in fencing, boxing, cricket, etc. **16. mount guard. a.** (of a sentry, etc.) to begin to keep watch. **b.** (with *over*) to take a protective or defensive stance (towards something). **17. off** (one's) **guard.** having one's defences down; unprepared. **18. on** (one's) **guard.** prepared to face danger, difficulties, etc. **19. stand guard.** (of a sentry, etc.) to keep watch. [C15: from OF, from *garder* to protect, of Gmc origin; see WARD] —'**guarder** *n.*

Guardafui (ˌgwɑːdəˈfuːɪ) *n.* **Cape.** a cape at the NE tip of Somalia, extending into the Indian Ocean.

guarded ('gɑːdɪd) *adj.* **1.** protected or kept under surveillance. **2.** prudent, restrained, or noncommittal: *a guarded reply.* —'**guardedly** *adv.* —'**guardedness** *n.*

guard hair *n.* any of the coarse hairs that form the outer fur in certain mammals.

guardhouse ('gɑːd,haʊs) *n. Mil.* a building serving as headquarters for military police and in which military prisoners are detained.

Guardi (*Italian* 'guardi) *n.* **Francesco** (fran'tʃesko). 1712–93, Venetian landscape painter.

guardian ('gɑːdɪən) *n.* **1.** one who looks after, protects, or defends: *the guardian of public morals.* **2.** *Law.* someone legally appointed to manage the affairs of a person incapable of acting for himself, as a minor or person of unsound mind. ~adj. **3.** protecting or safeguarding. —'**guardian,ship** *n.*

Guardian Angels *pl. n.* vigilante volunteers who patrol the New York Underground and elsewhere, wearing red berets, to deter violent crime.

guard ring *n.* **1.** Also called: **keeper ring.** a ring worn to prevent another from slipping off the finger. **2.** an electrode used to counteract distortion of the electric fields at the edges of other electrodes.

Guards (gɑːdz) *pl. n.* (esp. in European armies) any of various regiments responsible for ceremonial duties and, formerly, the protection of the head of state: *the Life Guards.*

guardsman ('gɑːdzmən) *n., pl.* **-men. 1.** (in Britain) a member of a Guards battalion or regiment. **2.** (in the U.S.) a member of the National Guard. **3.** a guard.

guard's van *n. Railways, Brit. & N.Z.* the van in which the guard travels, usually attached to the rear of a train. U.S. and Canad. equivalent: **caboose.**

Guarneri (gwɑːˈnɪərɪ; *Italian* gwar'nɛːri), **Guarnieri** (*Italian* gwar'njɛːri), *or* **Guarnerius** (gwɑːˈnɛərɪəs) *n., pl.* **Guarneris, Guarnieris,** *or* **Guarneriuses.** an Italian family of 17th- and 18th-century violin-makers.

Guatemala (ˌgwɑːtəˈmɑːlə) *n.* a republic in Central America: original Maya Indians conquered by the Spanish in 1523; became the centre of Spanish administration in Central America; gained independence and was annexed to Mexico in 1821, becoming an independent republic in 1839. Official language: Spanish. Religion: Roman Catholic. Currency: quetzal. Capital: Guatemala City. Pop.: 7 714 000 (1983 est.). Area: 108 889 sq. km (42 042 sq. miles). —ˌGuate'**malan** *adj., n.*

Guatemala City *n.* the capital of Guatemala, in the southeast: founded in 1776 to replace the former capital, Antigua; university (1676). Pop.: 1 300 000 (1983 est.).

guava ('gwɑːvə) *n.* **1.** any of various tropical American trees, grown esp. for their edible fruit. **2.** the fruit of such a tree, having yellow skin and pink pulp. [C16: from Sp. *guayaba*, from a South American Indian word]

Guayaquil (*Spanish* gwaja'kil) *n.* a port in W Ecuador: the largest city in the country and its chief port; university (1867). Pop.: 1 572 615 (1987).

guayule (gwəˈjuːlɪ) *n.* **1.** a bushy shrub of the southwestern U.S. **2.** rubber derived from the sap of this plant. [from American Sp., from Nahuatl *cuauhuli*, from *cuahuitl* tree + *uli* gum]

gubbins ('gʌbɪnz) *n.* **1.** (*functioning as sing.*) an object of little value. **2.** (*functioning as sing.*) a small gadget. **3.** (*functioning as pl.*) odds and ends; rubbish. **4.** (*functioning as sing.*) a silly person. [C16 (meaning: fragments): from obs. *gobbon*]

gubernatorial (ˌgjuːbənəˈtɔːrɪəl, ˌguː-) *adj. Chiefly U.S.* of or relating to a governor. [C18: from L *gubernātor* governor]

guddle ('gʌdəl) *Scot.* ~vb. **1.** to catch (fish) by groping with the hands under the banks or stones of a stream. ~n. **2.** a muddle; confusion. [C19: from ?]

gudgeon[1] ('gʌdʒən) *n.* **1.** a small slender European freshwater fish with a barbel on each side of the mouth: used as bait by anglers. **2.** any of various other fishes, such as the goby. **3.** *Sl.* a person who is easy to trick or cheat. ~vb. **4.** (*tr.*) *Sl.* to trick or cheat. [C15: from OF *gougon*, prob. from L *gōbius*; see GOBY]

gudgeon[2] ('gʌdʒən) *n.* **1.** the female or socket portion of a pinned hinge. **2.** *Naut.* one of two or more looplike sockets, fixed to the transom of a boat, into which the pintles of a rudder are fitted. [C14: from OF *goujon*, ?from LL *gulbia* chisel]

gudgeon pin *n. Brit.* the pin through the skirt of a piston in an internal-combustion engine, to which the little end of the connecting rod is attached. U.S. and Canad. name: **wrist pin.**

Gudrun ('gʊdruːn), **Guthrun** ('gʊθruːn), *or* **Kudrun** ('kʊdruːn) *n. Norse myth.* the wife of Sigurd and, after his death, of Atli, whom she slew for his murder of her brother Gunnar. She corresponds to Kriemhild in the *Nibelungenlied.*

guelder-rose ('gɛldə,rəʊz) *n.* a Eurasian shrub with clusters of white flowers and small red fruits. [C16: from Du. *geldersche roos*, from *Gelderland* or *Gelders*, province of Holland]

Guelders ('gɛldəz) *n.* another name for **Gelderland.**

Guelph (gwɛlf) *n.* a city in Canada, in SE Ontario. Pop.: 71 207 (1981).

guenon (gə'nɒn) *n.* a slender agile Old World monkey inhabiting wooded regions of Africa and having long hind limbs and tail and long hair surrounding the face. [C19: from F, from ?]

guerdon ('gɜːdən) *Poetic.* ~n. **1.** a reward or payment. ~vb. **2.** (*tr.*) to give a guerdon to. [C14: from OF *gueredon*, of Gmc origin; final element infl. by L *dōnum* gift]

Guernica (gɜːˈniːkə, 'gɜːnɪkə; *Spanish* gɛr'nika) *n.* a town in N Spain: formerly the seat of a Basque parliament; destroyed in 1937 by German bombers during the Spanish Civil War, an event depicted in one of Picasso's most famous paintings. Pop.: 17 836 (1981).

Guernsey ('gɜːnzɪ) *n.* **1.** an island in the English Channel: the second largest of the Channel Islands, which, with Alderney and Sark, Herm, Jethou, and some islets, forms the bailiwick of Guernsey; market gardening, dairy farming, and tourism. Capital: St Peter Port. Pop.: 55 482 (1986). Area: 63 sq. km (24.5 sq. miles). **2.** a breed of dairy cattle producing rich creamy milk, originating from the island of Guernsey. **3.** (*sometimes not cap.*) a seaman's knitted woollen sweater. **4.** (*not cap.*) *Austral.* a sleeveless woollen shirt or jumper worn by a football player. **5. get a guernsey.** *Austral.* to be selected or gain recognition for something.

Guerrero (*Spanish* gɛ'rrɛro) *n.* a mountainous state of S Mexico, on the Pacific: rich mineral resources. Capital: Chilpancingo. Pop.: 2 174 162 (1980). Area: 63 794 sq. km (24 631 sq. miles).

guerrilla *or* **guerilla** (gə'rɪlə) *n.* **a.** a member of an irregular usually politically motivated armed force that combats stronger regular forces. **b.** (*as modifier*): *guerrilla warfare.* [C19: from Sp., dim. of *guerra* WAR]

guess (gɛs) *vb.* (when *tr.*, *may take a clause as object*) **1.** (when *intr.*, often foll. by *at* or *about*) to form or express an uncertain estimate or conclusion (about something), based on insufficient information: *guess what we're having for dinner.* **2.** to arrive at a correct estimate of (something) by guessing: *he guessed my age.* **3.** *Inf., chiefly U.S. & Canad.* to believe, think, or suppose (something): *I guess I'll go now.* ~n. **4.** an estimate or conclusion arrived at by guessing: *a bad guess.* **5.** the act of guessing. [C13: prob. from ON] —'**guesser** *n.*

guesstimate or **guestimate** *Inf.* ~*n.* ('gɛstɪmɪt). **1.** an estimate calculated mainly or only by guesswork. ~*vb.* ('gɛstɪˌmeɪt). (*tr.*) **2.** to form a guesstimate of.

guesswork ('gɛsˌwɜːk) *n.* **1.** a set of conclusions, estimates, etc., arrived at by guessing. **2.** the process of making guesses.

guest (gɛst) *n.* **1.** a person who is entertained, taken out to eat, etc., and paid for by another. **2. a.** a person who receives hospitality at the home of another. **b.** (*as modifier*): *the guest room.* **3. a.** a person who receives the hospitality of a government, establishment, or organization. **b.** (*as modifier*): *a guest speaker.* **4. a.** an actor, contestant, entertainer, etc., taking part as a visitor in a programme in which there are also regular participants. **b.** (*as modifier*): *a guest appearance.* **5.** a patron of a hotel, boarding house, restaurant, etc. ~*vb.* **6.** (*intr.*) (in theatre and broadcasting) to be a guest: *to guest on a show.* [OE *giest* guest, stranger, enemy]

guesthouse ('gɛstˌhaʊs) *n.* a private home or boarding house offering accommodation.

guest rope *n. Naut.* any line trailed over the side of a vessel as a convenience for boats drawing alongside, as an aid in towing, etc.

Guevara (gəˈvɑːrə; *Spanish* geˈβara) *n.* **Ernesto** (ɛrˈnesto), known as *Che Guevara.* 1928–67, Latin American politician and soldier, born in Argentina. He developed guerrilla warfare as a tool for revolution and was instrumental in Castro's victory in Cuba (1959), where he held government posts until 1965. He was killed while training guerrillas in Bolivia.

guff (gʌf) *n. Sl.* ridiculous or insolent talk. [C19: imit. of empty talk]

guffaw (gʌˈfɔː) *n.* **1.** a crude and boisterous laugh. ~*vb.* **2.** to laugh or express (something) in this way. [C18: imit.]

Guiana (gaɪˈænə, gɪˈɑːnə) or **The Guianas** *n.* a region of NE South America, including Guyana, Surinam, French Guiana, and the **Guiana Highlands** (largely in SE Venezuela and partly in N Brazil). Area: about 1 787 000 sq. km (690 000 sq. miles). —**Guianese** (ˌgaɪəˈniːz, ˌgɪə-) or **Guianan** (gaɪˈænən, gɪˈɑːnən) *adj.,* *n.*

guidance ('gaɪdᵊns) *n.* **1.** leadership, instruction, or direction. **2. a.** counselling or advice on educational, vocational, or psychological matters. **b.** (*as modifier*): *the marriage-guidance counsellor.* **3.** something that guides. **4.** any process by which the flight path of a missile is controlled in flight.

guide (gaɪd) *vb.* **1.** to lead the way for (a person). **2.** to control the movement or course of (an animal, vehicle, etc.) by physical action; steer. **3.** to supervise or instruct (a person). **4.** (*tr.*) to direct the affairs of (a person, company, nation, etc.). **5.** (*tr.*) to advise or influence (a person) in his standards or opinions: *let truth guide you.* ~*n.* **6. a.** a person, animal, or thing that guides. **b.** (*as modifier*): *a guide dog.* **7.** a person, usually paid, who conducts tour expeditions, etc. **8.** a model or criterion, as in moral standards or accuracy. **9.** Also called: **guidebook.** a handbook with information for visitors to a place. **10.** a book that instructs or explains the fundamentals of a subject or skill. **11.** any device that directs the motion of a tool or machine part. **12.** a mark, sign, etc., that points the way. **13. a.** *Naval.* a ship in a formation used as a reference for manoeuvres. **b.** *Mil.* a soldier stationed to one side of a column or line to regulate alignment, show the way, etc. [C14: from (O)F *guider,* of Gmc origin] —'**guidable** *adj.* —'**guider** *n.*

Guide (gaɪd) *n.* (*sometimes not cap.*) a member of the organization for girls equivalent to the Scouts. U.S. equivalent: **Girl Scout.**

guided missile *n.* a missile, esp. one that is rocket-propelled, having a flight path controlled either by radio signals or by internal preset or self-actuating homing devices.

guide dog *n.* a dog that has been specially trained to accompany someone who is blind, enabling the blind person to move about safely.

guideline ('gaɪdˌlaɪn) *n.* a principle put forward to set standards or determine a course of action.

guidepost ('gaɪdˌpəʊst) *n.* **1.** a sign on a post by a road indicating directions. **2.** a principle or guideline.

Guider ('gaɪdə) *n.* (*sometimes not cap.*) a woman leader of a company of Guides or of a pack of Brownie Guides.

Guido d'Arezzo (*Italian* 'gwiːdo daˈrettso) *n.* ?995–?1050 A.D., Italian Benedictine monk and musical theorist: reputed inventor of solmization.

guidon ('gaɪdᵊn) *n.* **1.** a small pennant, used as a marker or standard, esp. by cavalry regiments. **2.** the man or vehicle that carries this. [C16: from F, from OProvençal *guidoo,* from *guida* GUIDE]

Guienne or **Guyenne** (*French* gɥijɛn) *n.* a former province of SW France: formed, with Gascony, the duchy of Aquitaine during the 12th century.

guild or **gild** (gɪld) *n.* **1.** an organization, club, or fellowship. **2.** (esp. in medieval Europe) an association of men sharing the same interests, such as merchants or artisans: formed for mutual aid and protection and to maintain craft standards. [C14: from ON; cf. *gjald* payment, *gildi* guild; rel. to OE *gield* offering, OHG *gelt* money] —'**guildsman,** '**gildsman** or (*fem.*) '**guildswoman,** '**gildswoman** *n.*

guilder ('gɪldə) or **gulden** *n.,* pl. **-ders, -der** or **-dens, -den.** **1.** Also: **gilder.** the standard monetary unit of the Netherlands, divided into 100 cents. **2.** any of various former gold or silver coins of Germany, Austria, or the Netherlands. [C15: from MDu. *gulden,* lit.: GOLDEN]

Guildford ('gɪlfəd) *n.* a city in S England: cathedral (1936–68); seat of the University of Surrey (1966). Pop.: 56 652 (1981).

guildhall ('gɪldˌhɔːl) *n. Brit.* **a.** the hall of a guild or corporation. **b.** a town hall.

guile (gaɪl) *n.* clever or crafty character or behaviour. [C18: from OF *guile,* of Gmc origin; see WILE] —'**guileful** *adj.* —'**guilefully** *adv.* —'**guilefulness** *n.* —'**guileless** *adj.* —'**guilelessly** *adv.* —'**guilelessness** *n.*

Guilin ('gweɪˈlɪn), **Kweilin,** or **Kuei-lin** *n.* a city in S China, in Guangxi Zhuang AR on the Li River: noted for the unusual caves and formations of the surrounding karst scenery; trade and manufacturing centre. Pop.: 347 000 (1980 est.).

Guillaume de Lorris (*French* gijom də lɔris) *n.* 13th century, French poet who wrote the first 4058 lines of the allegorical romance, the *Roman de la rose,* continued by Jean de Meung.

guillemot ('gɪlɪˌmɒt) *n.* a northern oceanic diving bird having a black-and-white plumage and long narrow bill. [C17: from F, dim. of *Guillaume* William]

guilloche (gɪˈləʊʃ) *n.* an ornamental border with a repeating pattern of two or more interwoven wavy lines, as in architecture. [C19: from F: tool used in ornamental work, ?from *Guillaume* William]

guillotine *n.* ('gɪləˌtiːn). **1. a.** a device for beheading persons, consisting of a weighted blade set between two upright posts. **b. the guillotine.** execution by this instrument. **2.** a device for cutting or trimming sheet material, such as paper or sheet metal, consisting of a slightly inclined blade that descends onto the sheet. **3.** a surgical instrument for removing tonsils, growths in the throat, etc. **4.** (in Parliament, etc.) a form of closure under which a bill is divided into compartments, groups of which must be completely dealt with each day. ~*vb.* (ˌgɪləˈtiːn). (*tr.*) **5.** to behead (a person) by guillotine. **6.** (in Parliament, etc.) to limit debate on (a bill, motion, etc.) by the guillotine. [C18: from F, after Joseph Ignace *Guillotin* (1738–1814), F physician, who advocated its use in 1789] —'**guillo'tiner** *n.*

guilt (gɪlt) *n.* **1.** the fact or state of having done wrong or committed an offence. **2.** responsibility for a criminal or moral offence deserving punishment or a penalty. **3.** remorse or self-reproach caused by feeling that one is responsible for a wrong or offence. **4.** *Arch.* sin or crime. [OE *gylt,* from ?]

guiltless ('gɪltlɪs) *adj.* free of all responsibility for wrongdoing or crime; innocent. —'**guiltlessly** *adv.* —'**guiltlessness** *n.*

guilty ('gɪltɪ) *adj.* **guiltier, guiltiest. 1.** responsible for an offence or misdeed. **2.** *Law.* having committed an offence or adjudged to have done so: *the accused was found guilty.* **3.** of, showing, or characterized by guilt. —'**guiltily** *adv.* —'**guiltiness** *n.*

guimpe (gɪmp) *n.* a variant spelling of **gimp.**

guinea ('gɪnɪ) *n.* **1. a.** a British gold coin taken out of circulation in 1813, worth 21 shillings. **b.** the sum of 21 shillings (1.05), still used in quoting professional fees. **2.** See **guinea fowl.** [C16: the coin was orig. made of gold from Guinea]

Guinea ('gɪnɪ) n. **1.** a republic in West Africa, on the Atlantic: established as the colony of French Guinea in 1890 and became an independent republic in 1958. Official language: French. Religion: Muslim majority and animist. Currency: franc. Capital: Conakry. Pop.: 6 339 000 (1981 UN est.). Area: 245 855 sq. km (94 925 sq. miles). **2.** (formerly) the coastal region of West Africa, between Cape Verde and Namibe (formerly Moçâmedes; Angola): divided by a line of volcanic peaks into **Upper Guinea** (between The Gambia and Cameroon) and **Lower Guinea** (between Cameroon and S Angola). **3. Gulf of.** a large inlet of the S Atlantic on the W coast of Africa, extending from Cape Palmas, Liberia, to Cape Lopez, Gabon: contains two large bays, the Bight of Biafra and the Bight of Benin, separated by the Niger delta. —'**Guinean** *adj.*

Guinea-Bissau n. a republic in West Africa, on the Atlantic: first discovered by the Portuguese in 1446 and of subsequent importance in the slave trade; made a colony in 1879; became an independent republic in 1974. Languages: Portuguese and Cape Verde creole. Religion: animist majority and Muslim. Currency: Guinean peso. Capital: Bissau. Pop.: 935 000 (1987 est.). Area: 36 125 sq. km (13 948 sq. miles). Former name (until 1974): **Portuguese Guinea.**

guinea fowl *or* **guinea** n. a domestic fowl of Africa and SW Asia, having a dark plumage mottled with white, a naked head and neck, and a heavy rounded body.

guinea hen n. a guinea fowl, esp. a female.

guinea pig n. **1.** a domesticated cavy, commonly kept as a pet and used in scientific experiments. **2.** a person or thing used for experimentation. [C17: from ?]

Guinevere ('gwɪnɪ,vɪə), **Guenevere** ('gwɛnɪ,vɪə), *or* **Guinever** ('gwɪnɪvə) n. (in Arthurian legend) the wife of King Arthur and paramour of Lancelot.

Guinness ('gɪnɪs) n. Sir **Alec.** born 1914, British stage and film actor. His films include *Kind Hearts and Coronets* (1949) and *The Bridge on the River Kwai* (1957), for which he won an Oscar.

guipure (gɪ'pjʊə) n. **1.** Also called: **guipure lace.** any of many types of heavy lace that have their pattern connected by threads, rather than supported on a net mesh. **2.** a heavy corded trimming; gimp. [C19: from OF, from *guiper* to cover with cloth, of Gmc origin]

Guiscard (*French* giskar) n. **Robert** (rɔbɛr). ?1015–85, Norman conqueror in S Italy.

guise (gaɪz) n. **1.** semblance or pretence: *under the guise of friendship.* **2.** external appearance in general. **3.** *Arch.* manner or style of dress. [C13: from OF *guise*, of Gmc origin]

guising ('gaɪzɪŋ) n. (in Scotland and N England) the practice or custom of disguising oneself in fancy dress, often with mask, and visiting people's houses, esp. at Hallowe'en. — '**guiser** n.

guitar (gɪ'tɑː) n. a plucked stringed instrument originating in Spain, usually having six strings, a flat sounding board with a circular sound hole in the centre, a flat back, and a fretted fingerboard. [C17: from Sp. *guitarra*, from Ar. *qītār*, from Gk: CITHARA] —**gui'tarist** n.

Guitry (*French* gitri) n. **Sacha** (saʃa). 1885–1957, French actor, dramatist, and film director, born in Russia: plays include *Nono* (1905).

Guiyang ('gweɪ'jæŋ), **Kweiyang,** *or* **Kuei-yang** n. a city in S China, capital of Guizhou province: reached by rail in 1959, with subsequent industrial growth. Pop.: 1 380 000 (1986).

Guizhou ('gweɪ'dʒəʊ), **Kweichow,** *or* **Kueichou** n. a province of SW China, between the Yangtze and Xi Rivers: a high plateau. Capital: Guiyang. Pop.: 29 320 000 (1985). Area: 174 000 sq. km (69 278 sq. miles).

Guizot (*French* gizo) n. **François Pierre Guillaume** (frãswa pjɛr gijom). 1787–1874, French statesman and historian. As chief minister (1840–48), his reactionary policies contributed to the outbreak of the revolution of 1848.

Gujarat *or* **Gujerat** (,gʊdʒə'rɑːt) n. **1.** a state of W India: formed in 1960 from the N and W parts of Bombay State; one of India's most industrialized states. Capital: Gandhinagar. Pop.: 34 085 799 (1984). Area: 187 114 sq. km (72 245 sq. miles). **2.** a region of W India, north of the Narmada River: generally includes the areas north of Bombay city where Gujarati is spoken.

Gujranwala (gu:dʒ'rɑːn,wʌlə) n. a city in NE Pakistan: textile manufacturing. Pop.: 597 000 (1981 est.).

Gulag ('gu:læg) n. **1.** the central administrative department of the Soviet security service, responsible for maintaining prisons and labour camps. **2.** (*not cap.*) any system used to silence dissidents. [C20: from Russian *G(lavnoye) U(pravleniye Ispravitelno-Trudovykh) Lag(erei)* Main Administration for Corrective Labour Camps]

Gulbenkian (gʊl'bɛŋkɪən) n. **1. Calouste Sarkis** (kæ'lu:st 'sɑːkɪz). 1869–1955, British industrialist, born in Turkey. He endowed the international Gulbenkian Foundation for the advancement of the arts, science, and education. **2.** his son, **Nubar Sarkis** ('nu:bɑː 'sɑːkɪz). 1896–1972, British industrialist, diplomat, and philanthropist.

gulch (gʌltʃ) n. U.S. & Canad. a narrow ravine cut by a fast stream. [C19: from ?]

gulden ('gʊldən) n., pl. **-dens** or **-den.** a variant spelling of **guilder.**

Gülek Bogaz (gu:'lɛk bəʊ'gɑːz) n. the Turkish name for the **Cilician Gates.**

gules (gju:lz) adj. (*usually postpositive*), n. Heraldry. red. [C14: from OF *gueules* red fur worn around the neck, from *gole* throat, from L *gula* GULLET]

gulf (gʌlf) n. **1.** a large deep bay. **2.** a deep chasm. **3.** something that divides or separates, such as a lack of understanding. **4.** something that engulfs, such as a whirlpool. ~vb. **5.** (*tr.*) to swallow up; engulf. [C14: from OF *golfe*, from It. *golfo*, from Gk *kolpos*]

Gulf (gʌlf) n. **1.** *Austral.* **a. the.** the Gulf of Carpentaria. **b.** (*modifier*) of, relating to, or adjoining the Gulf: *Gulf country.* **2. the.** N.Z. the Hauraki Gulf.

Gulf States pl. n. **the. 1.** the oil-producing states around the Persian Gulf: Iran, Iraq, Kuwait, Saudi Arabia, Bahrain, Qatar, the United Arab Emirates, and Oman. **2.** the states of the U.S. that border on the Gulf of Mexico: Alabama, Florida, Louisiana, Mississippi, and Texas.

Gulf Stream n. a relatively warm ocean current flowing northeastwards from the Gulf of Mexico towards NW Europe. Also called: **North Atlantic Drift.**

gulfweed ('gʌlf,wi:d) n. a brown seaweed having air bladders and forming dense floating masses in tropical Atlantic waters, esp. the Gulf Stream. Also called: **sargasso, sargasso weed.**

gull[1] (gʌl) n. an aquatic bird such as the common gull or mew having long pointed wings, short legs, and a mostly white plumage. [C15: of Celtic origin]

gull[2] (gʌl) Arch. ~n. **1.** a person who is easily fooled or cheated. ~vb. **2.** (*tr.*) to fool, cheat, or hoax. [C16: ?from dialect *gull* unfledged bird, prob. from *gul*, from ON *gulr* yellow]

gullet ('gʌlɪt) n. **1.** a less formal name for the **oesophagus. 2.** the throat or pharynx. [C14: from OF *goulet*, dim. of *goule* throat, from L *gula* throat]

gullible ('gʌlɪb²l) adj. easily taken in or tricked. —,**gulli'bility** n. —'**gullibly** adv.

gully *or* **gulley** ('gʌlɪ) n., pl. **-lies** or **-leys. 1.** a channel or small valley, esp. one cut by heavy rainwater. **2.** N.Z. a bush-clad small valley. **3.** Cricket. **a.** a fielding position between the slips and point. **b.** a fielder in this position. ~vb. **-lying, -lied. 4.** (*tr.*) to make channels in (the ground, sand, etc.). [C16: from F *goulet* neck of a bottle; see GULLET]

gulp (gʌlp) vb. **1.** (*tr.*; often foll. by *down*) to swallow rapidly, esp. in large mouthfuls. **2.** (*tr.*; often foll. by *back*) to stifle or choke: *to gulp back sobs.* **3.** (*intr.*) to swallow air convulsively because of nervousness, surprise, etc. **4.** (*intr.*) to make a noise, as when swallowing too quickly. ~n. **5.** the act of gulping. **6.** the quantity taken in a gulp. [C15: from MDu. *gulpen*, imit.] —'**gulper** n. —'**gulpingly** adv. —'**gulpy** adj.

gum[1] (gʌm) n. **1.** any of various sticky substances that exude from certain plants, hardening on exposure to air and dissolving or forming viscous masses in water. **2.** any of various products, such as adhesives, that are made from such substances. **3.** any sticky substance used as an adhesive; mucilage; glue. **4.** See **chewing gum, bubble gum,** and **gumtree. 5.** N.Z. See **kauri gum. 6.** Chiefly Brit. a gumdrop. ~vb. **gumming, gummed. 7.** to cover or become covered, clogged, or stiffened as with gum. **8.** (*tr.*) to stick together or in place with gum. **9.** (*intr.*) to emit or form gum. ~See also **gum up.** [C14: from OF *gomme*, from L *gummi*, from Gk *kommi*, from Egyptian *kemai*]

gum[2] (gʌm) n. the fleshy tissue that covers the jawbones around the bases of the teeth. Technical name: **gingiva**. Related adj.: **gingival**. [OE *gōma* jaw]

gum ammoniac n. another name for **ammoniac**.

gum arabic n. a gum exuded by certain acacia trees, used in the manufacture of ink, food thickeners, pills, emulsifiers, etc. Also called: **gum acacia**.

gumbo ('gʌmbəu) n., pl. **-bos**. *U.S.* **1.** the mucilaginous pods of okra. **2.** another name for **okra**. **3.** a soup or stew thickened with okra pods. **4.** a fine soil in the W prairies that becomes muddy when wet. [C19: from Louisiana F *gombo*, of Bantu origin]

gumboil ('gʌm,bɔɪl) n. an abscess on the gums.

gumboots ('gʌm,buːts) pl. n. another name for **Wellington boots** (sense 1).

gum-digger n. *N.Z.* a person who digs for fossilized kauri gum in a **gum-field**, an area where it is found buried.

gumdrop ('gʌm,drɒp) n. a small jelly-like sweet containing gum arabic and various colourings and flavourings. Also called (esp. Brit.): **gum**.

gummy[1] ('gʌmɪ) adj. **-mier, -miest. 1.** sticky or tacky. **2.** consisting of, coated with, or clogged by gum or a similar substance. **3.** producing gum. [C14: from GUM[1] + -Y[1]] —'**gumminess** n.

gummy[2] ('gʌmɪ) adj. **-mier, -miest. 1.** toothless. ~n., pl. **-mies. 2.** Also called: **gummy shark**. *Austral.* a small crustacean-eating shark with flat crushing teeth. [C20: from GUM[2] + -Y[1]]

gum nut n. *Austral.* the hardened seed container of the gumtree *Eucalyptus gummifera*.

gumption ('gʌmpʃən) n. *Inf.* **1.** *Brit.* common sense or resourcefulness. **2.** initiative or courage. [C18: orig. Scot., from ?]

gum resin n. a mixture of resin and gum obtained from various plants and trees.

gumtree ('gʌm,triː) n. **1.** any of various trees that yield gum, such as the eucalyptus, sweet gum, and sour gum. Sometimes shortened to: **gum**. **2. up a gumtree.** *Inf.* in a very awkward position; in difficulties.

gum up vb. (tr., adv.) **1.** to cover, dab, or stiffen with gum. **2.** *Inf.* to make a mess of; bungle (often in **gum up the works**).

gun (gʌn) n. **1. a.** a weapon with a metallic tube or barrel from which a missile is discharged, usually by force of an explosion. It may be portable or mounted. **b.** (as modifier): *a gun barrel.* **2.** the firing of a gun as a salute or signal, as in military ceremonial. **3.** a member of or a place in a shooting party or syndicate. **4.** any device used to project something under pressure: *a spray gun.* **5.** *U.S. sl.* an armed criminal; gunman. **6.** *Austral. & N.Z. sl.* **a.** an expert. **b.** (as modifier): *a gun shearer.* **7. give it the gun.** *Sl.* to increase speed, effort, etc., to a considerable or maximum degree. **8. go great guns.** *Sl.* to act or function with great speed, intensity, etc. **9. jump** or **beat the gun. a.** (of a runner, etc.) to set off before the starting signal is given. **b.** *Inf.* to act prematurely. **10. stick to one's guns.** *Inf.* to maintain one's opinions or intentions in spite of opposition. ~vb. **gunning, gunned. 11.** (when tr., often foll. by *down*) to shoot (someone) with a gun. **12.** (tr.) to press hard on the accelerator of (an engine): *to gun the engine of a car.* **13.** (intr.) to hunt with a gun. ~See also **gun for.** [C14: prob. from a female pet name, from the Scand. name *Gunnhildr* (from ON *gunnr* war + *hildr* war)]

gunboat ('gʌn,bəut) n. a small shallow-draft vessel carrying mounted guns and used by coastal patrols, etc.

gunboat diplomacy n. diplomacy conducted by threats of military intervention.

guncotton ('gʌn,kɒtˀn) n. cellulose nitrate containing a relatively large amount of nitrogen: used as an explosive.

gun dog n. **1.** a dog trained to work with a hunter or gamekeeper, esp. in retrieving, pointing at, or flushing game. **2.** a dog belonging to any breed adapted to these activities.

gunfight ('gʌn,faɪt) n. *Chiefly U.S.* a fight between persons using firearms. —'**gun,fighter** n.

gunfire ('gʌn,faɪə) n. **1.** the firing of one or more guns, esp. when done repeatedly. **2.** the use of firearms, as contrasted with other military tactics.

gun for vb. (intr., prep.) **1.** to search for in order to reprimand, punish, or kill. **2.** to try earnestly for: *he was gunning for promotion.*

gunge (gʌndʒ) *Inf.* ~n. **1.** sticky, rubbery, or congealed matter. ~vb. **2.** (tr.; usually passive; foll. by *up*) to block or encrust with gunge; clog. [C20: imit., ? infl. by GOO & SPONGE] —'**gungy** adj.

gunk (gʌŋk) n. *Inf.* slimy, oily, or filthy matter. [C20: ? imit.]

gunlock ('gʌn,lɒk) n. the mechanism in some firearms that causes the charge to be exploded.

gunman ('gʌnmən) n., pl. **-men. 1.** a man who is armed with a gun, esp. unlawfully. **2.** a man who is skilled with a gun.

gunmetal ('gʌn,mɛtˀl) n. **1.** a type of bronze containing copper, tin, and zinc. **2. a.** a dark grey colour. **b.** (as adj.): *gunmetal chiffon.*

Gunn (gʌn) n. **Thom(son William)**. born 1929, British poet resident in the U.S.A. His works include *Fighting Terms* (1954), *My Sad Captains* (1961), and *Jack Straw's Castle* (1976).

Gunnar ('gunɑː) n. *Norse myth.* brother of Gudrun and husband of Brynhild, won for him by Sigurd. He corresponds to Gunther in the *Nibelungenlied*.

gunnel[1] ('gʌnˀl) n. any eel-like fish occurring in coastal regions of northern seas. [C17: from ?]

gunnel[2] ('gʌnˀl) n. a variant spelling of **gunwale**.

gunner ('gʌnə) n. **1.** a serviceman who works with, uses, or specializes in guns. **2.** *Naval.* (formerly) a warrant officer responsible for the training of gun crews, their performance in action, and accounting for ammunition. **3.** (in the British Army) an artilleryman, esp. a private. **4.** a person who hunts with a rifle or shotgun.

gunnery ('gʌnərɪ) n. **1.** the art and science of the efficient design and use of ordnance, esp. artillery. **2.** guns collectively. **3.** the use and firing of guns.

gunny ('gʌnɪ) n., pl. **-nies.** *Chiefly U.S.* **1.** a coarse hard-wearing fabric usually made from jute and used for sacks, etc. **2.** Also called: **gunny sack.** a sack made from this fabric. [C18: from Hindi, from Sansk. *gōnī* sack, prob. of Dravidian origin]

gunplay ('gʌn,pleɪ) n. *Chiefly U.S.* the use of firearms, as by criminals, etc.

gunpoint ('gʌn,pɔɪnt) n. **1.** the muzzle of a gun. **2. at gunpoint.** being under or using the threat of being shot.

gunpowder ('gʌn,paudə) n. an explosive mixture of potassium nitrate, charcoal, and sulphur: used in time fuses and in fireworks.

gun room n. **1.** (esp. in the Royal Navy) the mess allocated to junior officers. **2.** a room where guns are stored.

gunrunning ('gʌn,rʌnɪŋ) n. the smuggling of guns and ammunition or other weapons of war into a country. —'**gun,runner** n.

gunshot ('gʌn,ʃɒt) n. **1. a.** shot fired from a gun. **b.** (as modifier): *gunshot wounds.* **2.** the range of a gun. **3.** the shooting of a gun.

gunslinger ('gʌn,slɪŋə) n. *Sl.* a gunfighter or gunman, esp. in the Old West.

gunsmith ('gʌn,smɪθ) n. a person who makes or repairs firearms, esp. portable guns.

gunstock ('gʌn,stɒk) n. the wooden handle or support to which is attached the barrel of a rifle.

Gunter ('gʌntə) n. **Edmund.** 1581–1626, English mathematician and astronomer, who invented various measuring instruments, including Gunter's chain.

Gunter's chain n. *Surveying.* a measuring chain 22 yards in length, or this length as a unit. [C17: after E. GUNTER]

Gunther ('gontə) n. (in the *Nibelungenlied*) a king of Burgundy, allied with Siegfried, who won for him his wife Brunhild. He corresponds to Gunnar in Norse mythology.

Guntur (gun'tuə) n. a city in E India, in central Andhra Pradesh: founded by the French in the 18th century; ceded to Britain in 1788. Pop.: 367 219 (1981).

gunwale or **gunnel** ('gʌnˀl) n. *Naut.* the top of the side of a boat or ship. [C15: from GUN + WALE from its use to support guns]

gunyah ('gʌnjɑː) n. *Austral.* a bush hut or shelter. [C19: from Abor.]

guppy ('gʌpɪ) n., pl. **-pies.** a small brightly coloured freshwater fish of N South America and the West Indies: a popular aquarium fish. [C20: after R. J. L. *Guppy*, 19th-cent. clergyman of Trinidad who first presented specimens to the British Museum]

gurdwara ('gɜːdwɑːrə) n. a Sikh place of worship. [C20: from Punjabi *gurduārā*, from Sansk. *guru* teacher + *dvārā* door]

gurgle ('gɜ:gᵊl) vb. (intr.) **1.** (of liquids, esp. of streams, etc.) to make low bubbling noises when flowing. **2.** to utter low throaty bubbling noises, esp. as a sign of contentment: *the baby gurgled with delight.* ~n. **3.** the act or sound of gurgling. [C16: ?from Vulgar L *gurgulāre*, from L *gurguliō* gullet]

gurnard ('gɜ:nəd) or **gurnet** ('gɜ:nɪt) n., pl. **-nard, -nards** or **-net, -nets.** a European marine fish having a heavily armoured head and finger-like pectoral fins. [C14: from OF *gornard*, from *grognier* to grunt, from L *grunnīre*]

guru ('gʊru:, 'gu:ru:) n. **1.** a Hindu or Sikh religious teacher or leader, giving personal spiritual guidance to his disciples. **2.** *Often derog.* a leader or chief theoretician of a movement, esp. a spiritual or religious cult. [C17: from Hindi *gurū*, from Sansk. *guruh* weighty]

gush (gʌʃ) vb. **1.** to pour out or cause to pour out suddenly and profusely, usually with a rushing sound. **2.** to act or utter in an overeffusive, affected, or sentimental manner. ~n. **3.** a sudden copious flow or emission, esp. of liquid. **4.** something that flows out or is emitted. **5.** an extravagant and insincere expression of admiration, sentiment, etc. [C14: prob. imit.; cf. ON *gjósa*] —'**gushing** adj. —'**gushingly** adv.

gusher ('gʌʃə) n. **1.** a person who gushes, as in being effusive or sentimental. **2.** something, such as a spurting oil well, that gushes.

gushy ('gʌʃɪ) adj. **gushier, gushiest.** *Inf.* displaying excessive admiration or sentimentality. —'**gushily** adv. —'**gushiness** n.

gusset ('gʌsɪt) n. **1.** an inset piece of material used esp. to strengthen or enlarge a garment. **2.** a triangular metal plate for strengthening a corner joint. ~vb. **3.** (tr.) to put a gusset in (a garment). [C15: from OF *gousset* a piece of mail, dim. of *gousse* pod, from ?] —'**gusseted** adj.

gust (gʌst) n. **1.** a sudden blast of wind. **2.** a sudden rush of smoke, sound, etc. **3.** an outburst of emotion. ~vb. **4.** (intr.) to blow in gusts. [C16: from ON *gustr*; rel. to *gjósa* to GUSH; see GEYSER]

gustation (gʌ'steɪʃən) n. the act of tasting or the faculty of taste. [C16: from L *gustātiō*, from *gustāre* to taste] —**gustatory** ('gʌstətərɪ) adj.

Gustavo A. Madero (Spanish gus'taβo a ma'ðero) n. the former name (1931–71) of **Guadalupe Hidalgo.**

Gustavus I (gʊ'stɑ:vəs) n. called *Gustavus Vasa.* ?1496–1560, king of Sweden (1523–60). He was elected king after driving the Danes from Sweden (1520–23).

Gustavus II n. See **Gustavus Adolphus.**

Gustavus VI n. title of *Gustaf Adolf.* 1882–1973, king of Sweden (1950–73).

Gustavus Adolphus (ə'dɒlfəs) or **Gustavus II** n. 1594–1632, king of Sweden (1611–32). A brilliant general, he waged successful wars with Denmark, Russia, and Poland and in the Thirty Years' War led a Protestant army against the Catholic League and the Holy Roman Empire (1630–32). He defeated Tilly at Leipzig (1631) and Lech (1632) but was killed at the battle of Lützen.

gusto ('gʌstəʊ) n. vigorous enjoyment, zest, or relish: *the aria was sung with great gusto.* [C17: from Sp.: taste, from L *gustus* a tasting]

gusty ('gʌstɪ) adj. **gustier, gustiest. 1.** blowing in gusts or characterized by blustery weather: *a gusty wind.* **2.** given to sudden outbursts, as of emotion. —'**gustily** adv. —'**gustiness** n.

gut (gʌt) n. **1. a.** the lower part of the alimentary canal; intestine. **b.** the entire alimentary canal. Related adj.: **visceral. 2.** (often pl.) the bowels or entrails, esp. of an animal. **3.** *Sl.* the belly; paunch. **4.** See **catgut. 5.** a silky fibrous substance extracted from silkworms, used in the manufacture of fishing tackle. **6.** a narrow channel or passage. **7.** (pl.) *Inf.* courage, willpower, or daring; forcefulness. **8.** (pl.) *Inf.* the essential part: *the guts of a problem.* ~vb. **gutting, gutted.** (tr.) **9.** to remove the entrails from (fish, etc.). **10.** (esp. of fire) to destroy the inside of (a building). **11.** to take out the central points of (an article, etc.), esp. in summary form. ~adj. **12.** *Inf.* arising from or characterized by what is basic, essential, or natural: *a gut problem; a gut reaction.* [OE *gutt*; rel. to *gēotan* to flow]

Gutenberg ('gu:tᵊn,bɜ:g; German 'gu:tənberk) n. **Johann** (jo'han), original name *Johannes Gensfleisch.* ?1398–1468, German printer; inventor of printing by movable type.

Gütersloh (German 'gy:tərslo:) n. a town in NW West Germany, in North Rhine-Westphalia. Pop.: 78 299 (1983 est.).

Guthrie ('gʌθrɪ) n. **1. Samuel.** 1782–1848, U.S. chemist: invented percussion priming powder and a punch lock for exploding it, and discovered chloroform (1831). **2.** Sir **(William) Tyrone.** 1900–71, English theatrical director. **3. Woody,** real name *Woodrow Wilson Guthrie.* 1912–67, U.S. folk singer and songwriter. His songs include "So Long, it's been Good to Know you" (1940) and "This Land is your Land" (1944).

Guthrun ('gʊðru:n) n. a variant of **Gudrun.**

gutless ('gʌtlɪs) adj. *Inf.* lacking courage or determination.

gut reaction n. a reaction to a situation derived from a person's instinct and experience.

gutsy ('gʌtsɪ) adj. **gutsier, gutsiest.** *Sl.* **1.** gluttonous; greedy. **2.** full of courage or boldness. **3.** passionate; lusty.

gutta-percha ('gʌtə'pɜ:tʃə) n. **1.** any of several tropical trees with leathery leaves. **2.** a whitish rubber substance derived from the coagulated milky latex of any of these trees: used in electrical insulation and dentistry. [C19: from Malay *getah* gum + *percha* tree that produces it]

guttate ('gʌteɪt) adj. *Biol.* (esp. of plants) covered with small drops or droplike markings. [C19: from L *guttātus* dappled, from *gutta* a drop]

gutter ('gʌtə) n. **1.** a channel along the eaves or on the roof of a building, used to collect and carry away rainwater. **2.** a channel running along the kerb or the centre of a road to collect and carry away rainwater. **3.** either of the two channels running parallel to a tenpin bowling lane. **4.** *Printing.* the white space between the facing pages of an open book. **5.** *Surfing.* a dangerous deep channel formed by currents and waves. **6. the gutter.** a povertystricken, degraded, or criminal environment. ~vb. **7.** (tr.) to make gutters in. **8.** (intr.) to flow in a stream. **9.** (intr.) (of a candle) to melt away as the wax forms channels and runs down in drops. **10.** (intr.) (of a flame) to flicker and be about to go out. [C13: from Anglo-F *goutiere*, from OF *goute* a drop, from L *gutta*] —'**guttering** n.

gutter press n. the section of the popular press that seeks sensationalism in its coverage.

guttersnipe ('gʌtə,snaɪp) n. a child who spends most of his time in the streets, esp. in a slum area.

guttural ('gʌtərəl) adj. **1.** *Anat.* of or relating to the throat. **2.** *Phonetics.* pronounced in the throat or the back of the mouth. **3.** raucous. ~n. **4.** *Phonetics.* a guttural consonant. [C16: from NL *gutturālis*, from L *guttur* gullet] —'**gutturally** adv.

guy¹ (gaɪ) n. **1.** *Inf.* a man or youth. **2.** *Brit.* a crude effigy of Guy Fawkes, usually made of old clothes stuffed with straw or rags, that is burnt on top of a bonfire on Guy Fawkes Day. **3.** *Brit.* a person in shabby or ludicrously odd clothes. ~vb. **4.** (tr.) to make fun of; ridicule. [C19: short for Guy FAWKES]

guy² (gaɪ) n. **1.** a rope, chain, wire, etc., for anchoring an object in position or for steadying or guiding it. ~vb. **2.** (tr.) to anchor, steady, or guide with a guy or guys. [C14: prob. from Low G; cf. OF *guie* guide, from *guier* to GUIDE]

Guyana (gaɪ'ænə) n. a republic in NE South America, on the Atlantic: colonized chiefly by the Dutch in the 17th and 18th centuries; became a British colony in 1831 and an independent republic within the Commonwealth in 1966. Official language: English. Religions: Christian and Hindu. Currency: dollar. Capital: Georgetown. Pop.: 812 000 (1987). Area: about 215 000 sq. km (83 000 sq. miles). Former name (until 1966): **British Guiana.** —**Guyanese** (,gaɪə'ni:z) or **Guy'anan** adj., n.

Guyenne (French gɥijɛn) n. a variant spelling of **Guienne.**

Guzmán Blanco (Spanish guð'man 'blaŋko) n. **Antonio** (an'tonjo). 1829–99, Venezuelan statesman; president (1873–77; 1879–84; 1886–87). He was virtual dictator of Venezuela from 1870 until his overthrow (1889).

guzzle ('gʌzᵊl) vb. to consume (food or drink) excessively or greedily. [C16: from ?] —'**guzzler** n.

Gwalior ('gwɑ:lɪ,ɔ:) n. **1.** a city in N central India, in Madhya Pradesh: built around the fort, which dates from before 525; industrial and commercial centre. Pop.: 542 924 (1981). **2.** a former princely state of central India, established in the 18th century: merged with Madhya

Bharat in 1948, which in turn merged with Madhya Pradesh in 1956.

Gwent (gwɛnt) *n.* a county in SE Wales, formed in 1974 from most of Monmouthshire, part of Breconshire, and the county borough of Newport: generally hilly. Administrative centre: Cwmbran. Pop.: 441 800 (1986 est.). Area: 1376 sq. km (531 sq. miles).

Gweru ('gweiru:) *n.* a city in central Zimbabwe. Pop.: 79 000 (1982). Former name (until 1982): **Gwelo** ('gwi:ləʊ).

Gwyn (gwɪn) *n.* **Nell,** original name *Eleanor Gwynne.* 1650–87, English actress; mistress of Charles II.

Gwynedd ('gwɪnɛð) *n.* a county of NW Wales, formed in 1974 from Anglesey, Caernarvonshire, part of Denbighshire, and most of Merionethshire: the mainland is generally mountainous with many lakes, much of it lying in the Snowdonia National Park. Administrative centre: Caernarfon. Pop.: 234 600 (1986 est.). Area: 3869 sq. km (1493 sq. miles).

gwyniad ('gwɪnɪˌæd) *n.* a freshwater white fish occurring in Lake Bala in Wales. [Welsh, from *gwyn* white]

gybe *or* **jibe** (dʒaɪb) *Naut.* ~*vb.* **1.** (*intr.*) (of a fore-and-aft sail) to shift suddenly from one side of the vessel to the other when running before the wind. **2.** to cause (a sailing vessel) to gybe or (of a sailing vessel) to undergo gybing. ~*n.* **3.** an instance of gybing. [C17: from obs. Du. *gijben* (now *gijpen*), from ?]

gym (dʒɪm) *n*, *adj.* short for **gymnasium, gymnastics, gymnastic.**

gymkhana (dʒɪmˈkɑːnə) *n.* **1.** *Chiefly Brit.* an event in which horses and riders display skill and aptitude in various races and contests. **2.** (in Anglo-India) a place providing sporting and athletic facilities. [C19: from Hindi *gend-khānā*, lit.: ball house]

gymnasium (dʒɪmˈneɪzɪəm) *n.*, *pl.* **-siums** *or* **-sia** (-zɪə). **1.** a large room or hall equipped with bars, weights, ropes, etc., for physical training. **2.** (in various European countries) a secondary school that prepares pupils for university. [C16: from L: school for gymnastics, from Gk *gumnasion*, from *gumnazein* to exercise naked]

gymnast ('dʒɪmnæst) *n.* a person who is skilled or trained in gymnastics.

gymnastic (dʒɪmˈnæstɪk) *adj.* of, like, or involving gymnastics. —**gym'nastically** *adv.*

gymnastics (dʒɪmˈnæstɪks) *n.* **1.** (*functioning as sing.*) practice or training in exercises that develop physical strength and agility or mental capacity. **2.** (*functioning as pl.*) gymnastic exercises.

gymno- *combining form.* naked, bare, or exposed: *gymnosperm.* [from Gk *gumnos* naked]

gymnosperm ('dʒɪmnəʊˌspɜːm, 'gɪm-) *n.* any seed-bearing plant in which the ovules are borne naked on open scales, which are often arranged in cones; any conifer or related plant. Cf. **angiosperm.** —ˌgymno'spermous *adj.*

gympie ('gɪmpɪ) *n.* a tall Australian tree with stinging hairs on its leaves. Also: **nettle tree.**

gym shoe *n.* another name for **plimsoll.**

gymslip ('dʒɪmˌslɪp) *n.* a tunic or pinafore dress worn by schoolgirls, often part of a school uniform.

gyn- *combining form.* a variant of **gyno-** before a vowel.

gynaeco- *or U.S.* **gyneco-** *combining form.* relating to women; female: *gynaecology.* [from Gk, from *gunē, gunaik-* woman, female]

gynaecology *or U.S.* **gynecology** (ˌgaɪnɪˈkɒlədʒɪ) *n.* the branch of medicine concerned with diseases of women. —**gynaecological** (ˌgaɪnɪkəˈlɒdʒɪk*ə*l), ˌgynaeco'logic *or U.S.* ˌgyneco'logical, ˌgyneco'logic *adj.* —ˌgynae'cologist *or U.S.* ˌgyne'cologist *n.*

gynandromorph (dʒɪˈnændrəʊˌmɔːf, gaɪ-) *n.* an abnormal organism, esp. an insect, that has both male and female physical characteristics.

gynandrous (dʒaɪˈnændrəs, gaɪ-) *adj.* (of flowers such as the orchid) having the stamens and styles united in a column. [C19: from Gk *gunandros* of uncertain sex, from *gunē* woman + *anēr* man]

gyno- *or before a vowel* **gyn-** *combining form.* **1.** relating to women; female: *gynarchy.* **2.** denoting a female reproductive organ: *gynophore.* [from Gk, from *gunē* woman]

gynoecium, gynaeceum, *or esp. U.S.* **gynecium** (dʒaɪˈniːsɪəm, gaɪ-) *n.*, *pl.* **-cia** *or* **-cea** (-sɪə). the carpels of a flowering plant collectively. [C18: NL, from Gk *gunaikeion* women's quarters, from *gunaik-, gunē* woman + *-eion*, suffix indicating place]

gynophore ('dʒaɪnəʊˌfɔː, 'gaɪ-) *n.* a stalk in some plants that bears the gynoecium above the level of the other flower parts.

-gynous *adj. combining form.* **1.** of or relating to women or females: *androgynous; misogynous.* **2.** relating to female organs: *epigynous.* [from NL, from Gk, from *gunē* woman] —**-gyny** *n. combining form.*

Györ (*Hungarian* djoːr) *n.* an industrial town in NW Hungary: medieval Benedictine abbey. Pop.: 130 000 (1985).

gyp[1] *or* **gip** (dʒɪp) *Sl.* ~*vb.* **gypping, gypped** *or* **gipping, gipped. 1.** (*tr.*) to swindle, cheat, or defraud. ~*n.* **2.** an act of cheating. **3.** a person who gyps. [C18: back formation from GYPSY]

gyp[2] *or* **gip** (dʒɪp) *n. Brit. & N.Z. sl.* severe pain; torture: *his arthritis gave him gyp.* [C19: prob. a contraction of *gee up!*; see GEE[1]]

gyp[3] (dʒɪp) *n.* a college servant at the universities of Cambridge or Durham. [C18: ?from obs. *gippo* scullion]

gypsophila (dʒɪpˈsɒfɪlə) *n.* any of a Mediterranean genus of plants, having small white or pink fragrant flowers. [C18: NL, from Gk *gupsos* chalk + *philos* loving]

gypsum ('dʒɪpsəm) *n.* a mineral consisting of hydrated calcium sulphate that occurs in sedimentary rocks and clay and is used principally in making plasters and cements, esp. plaster of Paris. Formula: $CaSO_4.2H_2O$. [C17: from L, from Gk *gupsos* chalk, plaster, cement, of Semitic origin] —**gypseous** ('dʒɪpsɪəs) *adj.*

Gypsy *or* **Gipsy** ('dʒɪpsɪ) *n.*, *pl.* **-sies.** (*sometimes not cap.*) **1. a.** a member of a people scattered throughout Europe and North America, who maintain a nomadic way of life in industrialized societies. They migrated from NW India about the 9th century onwards. **b.** (*as modifier*): *a Gypsy fortune-teller.* **2.** the language of the Gypsies; Romany. **3.** a person who looks or behaves like a Gypsy. [C16: from EGYPTIAN, since they were thought to have come orig. from Egypt] —'**Gypsyish** *or* '**Gipsyish** *adj.*

gypsy moth *or* **gipsy moth** *n.* a European moth whose caterpillars are pests on deciduous trees.

gyrate *vb.* (dʒaɪˈreɪt). **1.** (*intr.*) to rotate or spiral, esp. about a fixed point or axis. ~*adj.* ('dʒaɪrɪt). **2.** *Biol.* curved or coiled into a circle. [C19: from LL *gȳrāre*, from L *gȳrus* circle, from Gk *guros*] —**gy'ration** *n.* —**gy'rator** *n.* —**gyratory** ('dʒaɪrətərɪ) *adj.*

gyre ('dʒaɪə) *Chiefly literary.* ~*n.* **1.** a circular or spiral movement or path. **2.** a ring, circle, or spiral. ~*vb.* **3.** (*intr.*) to whirl. [C16: from L *gȳrus* circle, from Gk *guros*]

gyrfalcon *or* **gerfalcon** ('dʒɜː, fɔːlkən, -, fɔːkən) *n.* a very large rare falcon of northern and arctic regions. [C14: from OF *gerfaucon*, ?from ON *geirfalki*, from *geirr* spear + *falki* falcon]

gyro ('dʒaɪrəʊ) *n.*, *pl.* **-ros. 1.** See **gyrocompass. 2.** See **gyroscope.**

gyro- *or before a vowel* **gyr-** *combining form.* **1.** indicating rotating or gyrating motion: *gyroscope.* **2.** indicating a gyroscope: *gyrocompass.* [via L from Gk, from *guros* circle]

gyrocompass ('dʒaɪrəʊˌkʌmpəs) *n.* a nonmagnetic compass that uses a motor-driven gyroscope to indicate true north.

gyromagnetic (ˌdʒaɪrəʊmæɡˈnɛtɪk) *adj.* of or caused by magnetic properties resulting from the spin of a charged particle, such as an electron.

gyroscope ('dʒaɪrəˌskəʊp) *n.* a device containing a disc rotating on an axis that can turn freely in any direction so that the disc maintains the same orientation irrespective of the movement of the surrounding structure. —**gyroscopic** (ˌdʒaɪrəˈskɒpɪk) *adj.* —ˌgyro'scopically *adv.*

gyrostabilizer *or* **-liser** (ˌdʒaɪrəʊˈsteɪbɪˌlaɪzə) *n.* a gyroscopic device used to stabilize the rolling motion of a ship.

gyve (dʒaɪv) *Arch.* ~*vb.* **1.** (*tr.*) to shackle or fetter. ~*n.* **2.** (*usually pl.*) fetter. [C13: from ?]

H

h *or* **H** (eɪtʃ) *n.*, *pl.* **h's, H's,** *or* **Hs.** **1.** the eighth letter of the English alphabet. **2.** a speech sound represented by this letter. **3. a.** something shaped like an H. **b.** (*in combination*): *an H-beam*.

h *symbol for:* **1.** *Physics.* Planck constant. **2.** hecto-. **3.** hour.

H *symbol for:* **1.** *Chem.* hydrogen. **2.** *Physics.* magnetic field strength. **3.** *Electronics.* henry. **4.** (on Brit. pencils, signifying degree of hardness of lead) hard.

h. *or* **H.** *abbrev. for:* **1.** harbour. **2.** height. **3.** high. **4.** hour. **5.** hundred. **6.** husband.

ha[1] *or* **hah** (hɑː) *interj.* **1.** an exclamation expressing derision, triumph, surprise, etc. **2.** (*reiterated*) a representation of the sound of laughter.

ha[2] *symbol for* hectare.

Haakon VII ('hɑːkɒn) *n.* 1872–1957, king of Norway (1905–57). During the Nazi occupation of Norway (1940–45), he led Norwegian resistance from England.

haar (hɑː) *n. Eastern Brit.* a cold sea mist or fog off the North Sea. [C17: rel. to Du. dialect *harig* damp]

Haarlem (*Dutch* 'hɑːrlɛm) *n.* a city in the W Netherlands, capital of North Holland province. Pop.: 149 099 (1987).

Hab. *Bible. abbrev. for* Habakkuk.

Habakkuk ('hæbəkək) *n. Old Testament.* a Hebrew prophet.

Habana (a'βana) *n.* the Spanish name for **Havana**.

habanera (ˌhæbə'nɛərə) *n.* **1.** a slow Cuban dance in duple time. **2.** a piece of music for this dance. [from Sp. *danza habanera* Havanan dance]

habeas corpus ('heɪbɪəs 'kɔːpəs) *n. Law.* a writ ordering a person to be brought before a court or judge, esp. so that the court may ascertain whether his detention is lawful. [C15: from the opening of the L writ, lit.: you may have the body]

haberdasher ('hæbəˌdæʃə) *n.* **1.** *Brit.* a dealer in small articles for sewing, such as buttons and ribbons. **2.** *U.S.* a men's outfitter. [C14: from Anglo-F *hapertas* small items of merchandise, from ?]

haberdashery ('hæbəˌdæʃərɪ) *n.*, *pl.* **-eries.** the goods or business kept by a haberdasher.

habergeon ('hæbədʒən) *n.* a light sleeveless coat of mail worn in the 14th century under the plated hauberk. [C14: from OF *haubergeon* a little HAUBERK]

habiliment (hə'bɪlɪmənt) *n.* (*often pl.*) dress or attire. [C15: from OF *habillement*, from *habiller* to dress]

habilitate (hə'bɪlɪˌteɪt) *vb.* **1.** (*tr.*) *U.S.* to equip and finance (a mine). **2.** (*intr.*) to qualify for office. [C17: from Med. L *habilitāre* to make fit, from L *habilitās* aptness] —**ha,bili'tation** *n.*

habit ('hæbɪt) *n.* **1.** a tendency or disposition to act in a particular way. **2.** established custom, usual practice, etc. **3.** *Psychol.* a learned behavioural response to a particular situation. **4.** mental disposition or attitude: *a good working habit of mind.* **5. a.** a practice or substance to which a person is addicted: *drink has become a habit with him.* **b.** the state of being dependent on something, esp. a drug. **6.** *Bot., zool.* method of growth, type of existence, or general appearance: *a burrowing habit.* **7.** the customary apparel of a particular occupation, rank, etc., now esp. the costume of a nun or monk. **8.** Also called: **riding habit.** a woman's riding dress. ~*vb.* (*tr.*) **9.** to clothe. **10.** an archaic word for **inhabit.** [C13: from L *habitus* custom, from *habēre* to have]

habitable ('hæbɪtəb⁀l) *adj.* able to be lived in. —ˌhabit-a'bility *or* 'habitableness *n.* —'habitably *adv.*

habitant ('hæbɪ⁀nt) *n.* **1.** a less common word for **inhabitant.** **2. a.** an early French settler in Canada or Louisiana. **b.** a descendant of these settlers, esp. a farmer.

habitat ('hæbɪˌtæt) *n.* **1.** the natural home of an animal or plant. **2.** the place in which a person, group, class, etc., is normally found. [C18: from L: it inhabits, from *habitāre* to dwell, from *habēre* to have]

habitation (ˌhæbɪ'teɪʃən) *n.* **1.** a dwelling place. **2.** occupation of a dwelling place.

habit-forming *adj.* tending to become a habit or addiction.

habitual (hə'bɪtjʊəl) *adj.* **1.** (*usually prenominal*) done or experienced regularly and repeatedly: *the habitual Sunday walk.* **2.** (*usually prenominal*) by habit: *a habitual drinker.* **3.** customary; usual. —**ha'bitually** *adv.* —**ha'bitualness** *n.*

habituate (hə'bɪtjʊˌeɪt) *vb.* **1.** to accustom; make used to. **2.** *U.S. arch. & Canad.* to frequent. —**ha,bitu'ation** *n.*

habitude ('hæbɪˌtjuːd) *n. Rare.* habit; tendency.

habitué (hə'bɪtjʊˌeɪ) *n.* a frequent visitor to a place. [C19: from F, from *habituer* to frequent]

Habsburg ('hɑːpsbʊrk) *n.* the German name for **Hapsburg.**

HAC *abbrev. for* Honourable Artillery Company.

hachure (hæ'ʃjʊə) *n.* shading of short lines drawn on a relief map to indicate gradients. [C19: from F, from *hacher* to chop up]

hacienda (ˌhæsɪ'ɛndə) *n.* (in Spain or Spanish-speaking countries) **1. a.** a ranch or large estate. **b.** any substantial manufacturing establishment in the country. **2.** the main house on such a ranch or establishment. [C18: from Sp., from L *facienda* things to be done, from *facere* to do]

hack[1] (hæk) *vb.* **1.** (when *intr.*, usually foll. by *at* or *away*) to chop (at) roughly or violently. **2.** to cut and clear (a way), as through undergrowth. **3.** (in sport, esp. rugby) to foul (an opposing player) by kicking his shins. **4.** (*intr.*) to cough in short dry bursts. **5.** (*tr.*) to cut (a story, article, etc.) in a damaging way. ~*n.* **6.** a cut or gash. **7.** any tool used for shallow digging, such as a mattock or pick. **8.** a chopping blow. **9.** a dry spasmodic cough. **10.** a kick on the shins, as in rugby. [OE *haccian*]

hack[2] (hæk) *n.* **1.** a horse kept for riding. **2.** an old or overworked horse. **3.** a horse kept for hire. **4.** *Brit.* a country ride on horseback. **5.** a drudge. **6.** a person who produces mediocre literary work. **7.** *U.S. inf.* **a.** a cab driver. **b.** a taxi. ~*vb.* **8.** *Brit.* to ride (a horse) cross-country for pleasure. **9.** (*tr.*) *Inf.* to write (an article, etc.) in the manner of a hack. ~*adj.* **10.** (*prenominal*) banal, mediocre, or unoriginal: *hack writing.* [C17: short for HACKNEY]

hack[3] (hæk) *n.* **1.** a rack used for fodder for livestock. **2.** a board on which meat is placed for a hawk. **3.** a pile or row of unfired bricks stacked to dry. [C16: var. of HATCH[2]]

hackamore ('hækəˌmɔː) *n. U.S. & N.Z.* a rope or rawhide halter used for unbroken foals. [C19: from Sp. *jáquima* headstall, ult. from Ar. *shaqīmah*]

hackberry ('hækˌbɛrɪ) *n.*, *pl.* **-ries.** **1.** an American tree having edible cherry-like fruits. **2.** the fruit. [C18: var. of C16 *hagberry*, of Scand. origin]

hacker ('hækə) *n.* **1.** a person that hacks. **2.** *Sl.* a computer fanatic, esp. one who through a personal computer breaks into the computer system of a company, government, etc.

hackery ('hækərɪ) *n.* **1.** *Ironic.* journalism; hackwork. **2.** *Inf.* the practice of gaining illegal access to a computer system.

hacking ('hækɪŋ) *adj.* (of a cough) harsh, dry, and spasmodic.

hackle ('hæk⁀l) *n.* **1.** any of the long slender feathers on the neck of poultry and other birds. **2.** *Angling.* parts of an artificial fly made from hackle feathers, representing the legs and sometimes the wings of a real fly. **3.** a feathered ornament worn in the headdress of some Highland regiments. **4.** a steel flax comb. ~*vb.* (*tr.*) **5.** to comb (flax) using a hackle. [C15: *hakell* prob. from OE]

hackles ('hæk⁀lz) *pl. n.* **1.** the hairs on the back of the neck and the back of a dog, cat, etc., which rise when the animal is angry or afraid. **2.** anger or resentment: *to make one's hackles rise.*

hackney ('hæknɪ) *n.* **1.** a compact breed of harness horse with a high-stepping trot. **2.** a coach or carriage that is for hire. **3.** a popular term for **hack**[2] (sense 1). ~*vb.* **4.** (*tr.*; *usually passive*) to make commonplace and banal by too frequent use. [C14: prob. after HACKNEY, where horses were formerly raised]

Hackney ('hæknɪ) *n.* a borough of NE Greater London: formed in 1965 from the former boroughs of Shoreditch,

Stoke Newington, and Hackney; nearby are **Hackney Marshes**, the largest recreation ground in London. Pop.: 187 100 (1986 est.).

hackneyed ('hæknɪd) *adj.* used so often as to be trite, dull, and stereotyped.

hacksaw ('hæk,sɔː) *n.* a handsaw for cutting metal, with a blade in a frame under tension.

hackwork ('hæk,wɜːk) *n.* undistinguished literary work produced to order.

had (hæd) *vb.* the past tense and past participle of **have**.

haddock ('hædək) *n., pl.* **-docks** *or* **-dock**. a North Atlantic gadoid food fish similar to but smaller than the cod. [C14: from ?]

hade (heɪd) *Geol.* ~*n.* **1.** the angle made to the vertical by the plane of a fault or vein. ~*vb.* **2.** (*intr.*) to incline from the vertical. [C18: from ?]

hadedah ('hɑːdɪ,dɑː) *n.* a large grey-green S. African ibis. [imit.]

Hades ('heɪdiːz) *n.* **1.** *Greek myth.* **a.** the underworld abode of the souls of the dead. **b.** Pluto, the god of the underworld. **2.** (*often not cap.*) hell.

Hadhramaut *or* **Hadramaut** (,hɑːdrə'mɔːt) *n.* a plateau region of the S Arabian Peninsula, in E Southern Yemen on the Indian Ocean: corresponds roughly to the former East Aden Protectorate. Area: about 151 500 sq. km (58 500 sq. miles).

Hadith ('hædɪθ, hɑː'diːθ) *n.* the body of tradition about Mohammed and his followers. [Ar.]

hadj (hædʒ) *n.* a variant spelling of **hajj**.

hadji ('hædʒɪ) *n., pl.* **hadjis**. a variant spelling of **hajji**.

Hadlee ('hædlɪ) *n.* Richard (**John**). born 1951, New Zealand cricketer.

hadn't ('hædᵊnt) *contraction of* had not.

Hadrian ('heɪdrɪən) *or* **Adrian** *n.* Latin name *Publius Aelius Hadrianus*. 76–138 A.D., Roman emperor (117–138); adopted son and successor of Trajan. He travelled throughout the Roman Empire, strengthening its frontiers and encouraging learning and architecture, and in Rome he reorganized the army and codified Roman law.

Hadrian's Wall *n.* a fortified Roman wall across N England, of which substantial parts remain, extending from the Solway Firth in the west to the mouth of the River Tyne in the east. It was built in 120–123 A.D. on the orders of the emperor Hadrian as a defence against the N British tribes.

hadron ('hædrɒn) *n.* an elementary particle capable of taking part in a strong nuclear interaction. [C20: from Gk *hadros* heavy, from *hadēn* enough + -ON] —**had'ronic** *adj.*

hadst (hædst) *vb. Arch. or dialect.* (used with the pronoun *thou*) a singular form of the past tense (indicative mood) of **have**.

haecceity (hɛk'siːɪtɪ, hiːk-) *n., pl.* **-ties.** *Philosophy.* the property that uniquely identifies an object. [C17: from Med. L *haecceitas*, lit.: thisness, from *haec*, fem. of *hic* this]

Haeckel (German 'hɛkəl) *n.* **Ernst Heinrich** (ɛrnst 'haɪnrɪç). 1834–1919, German biologist and philosopher. He formulated the recapitulation theory of evolution and was an exponent of the philosophy of materialistic monism. —**Haeckelian** (hɛ'kiːlɪən) *adj.*

haem *or U.S.* **heme** (hiːm) *n. Biochem.* a complex red organic pigment containing ferrous iron, present in haemoglobin. [C20: from HAEMATIN]

haem- *combining form.* a variant of **haemo-** before a vowel. Also (U.S.): **hem-**.

haemal *or U.S.* **hemal** ('hiːməl) *adj.* **1.** of the blood. **2.** denoting or relating to the region of the body containing the heart.

haematemesis *or U.S.* **hematemesis** (,hiːmə'tɛmɪsɪs) *n.* vomiting of blood, esp. as the result of a bleeding ulcer. [C19: from HAEMATO- + Gk *emesis* vomiting]

haematic *or U.S.* **hematic** (hiː'mætɪk) *adj.* relating to, acting on, having the colour of, or containing blood. Also: **haemic**.

haematin *or U.S.* **hematin** ('hɛmətɪn, 'hiː-) *n. Biochem.* a dark bluish or brownish pigment obtained by the oxidation of haem.

haematite *or U.S.* **hematite** ('hiːmə,taɪt, 'hɛm-) *n.* a variant spelling of **hematite**.

haemato- *or before a vowel* **haemat-** *combining form.* indicating blood: *haematology*. Also: **haemo-** *or* (U.S.) **hemato-**, **hemat-**. [from Gk *haima, haimat-* blood]

haematocrit *or U.S.* **hematocrit** ('hɛmətəʊkrɪt, 'hiː-) *n.* **1.** a centrifuge for separating blood cells from plasma. **2.** the ratio of the volume occupied by these cells, esp. the red cells, to the total volume of blood, expressed as a percentage. [C20: from HAEMATO- + -*crit*, from Gk *kritēs* judge, from *krinein* to separate]

haematology *or U.S.* **hematology** (,hiːmə'tɒlədʒɪ) *n.* the branch of medical science concerned with diseases of the blood. —**haematologic** (,hiːmətə'lɒdʒɪk), **haemato'logical** *or U.S.* **hemato'logic**, **hemato'logical** *adj.*

haematoma *or U.S.* **hematoma** (,hiːmə'təʊmə) *n., pl.* **-mas** *or* **-mata** (-mətə). *Pathol.* a tumour of clotted blood.

haematuria *or U.S.* **hematuria** (,hiːmə'tjʊərɪə) *n. Pathol.* the presence of blood or red blood cells in the urine.

-haemia *or esp. U.S.* **-hemia** *n. combining form.* variants of **-aemia**.

haemo-, haema-, *or before a vowel* **haem-** *combining form.* denoting blood. Also:(U.S.)**hemo-, hema-**, *or* **hem-**. [from Gk *haima* blood]

haemocyanin *or U.S.* **hemocyanin** (,hiːmə'saɪənɪn) *n.* a blue copper-containing respiratory pigment in crustaceans and molluscs that functions as haemoglobin.

haemocytometer *or U.S.* **hemocytometer** (,hiːməʊsaɪ'tɒmɪtə) *n. Med.* an apparatus for counting the number of cells in a quantity of blood.

haemodialysis *or U.S.* **hemodialysis** (,hiːməʊdaɪ'ælɪsɪs) *n., pl.* **-ses** (-,siːz). *Med.* the filtering of circulating blood through a membrane in an apparatus (**haemodialyser** *or* **artificial kidney**) to remove waste products: performed in cases of kidney failure. [C20: from HAEMO- + DIALYSIS]

haemoglobin *or U.S.* **hemoglobin** (,hiːməʊ'gləʊbɪn) *n.* a protein that gives red blood cells their characteristic colour. It combines reversibly with oxygen and is thus very important in the transportation of oxygen to tissues. [C19: shortened from *haematoglobulin*: see HAEMATIN + GLOBULIN]

haemolysis (hɪ'mɒlɪsɪs), **haematolysis** (,hiːmə'tɒlɪsɪs) *or U.S.* **hemolysis, hematolysis** *n., pl.* **-ses** (-,siːz). the disintegration of red blood cells, with the release of haemoglobin. —**haemolytic** *or U.S.* **hemolytic** (,hiːməʊ'lɪtɪk) *adj.*

haemophilia *or U.S.* **hemophilia** (,hiːməʊ'fɪlɪə) *n.* an inheritable disease, usually affecting only males, characterized by loss or impairment of the normal clotting ability of blood. —**,haemo'philiac** *or U.S.* **,hemo'philiac** *n.* —**,haemo'philic** *or U.S.* **,hemo'philic** *adj.*

haemoptysis *or U.S.* **hemoptysis** (hɪ'mɒptɪsɪs) *n., pl.* **-ses** (-,siːz). spitting or coughing up of blood, as in tuberculosis. [C17: from HAEMO- + -*ptysis*, from Gk *ptyein* to spit]

haemorrhage *or U.S.* **hemorrhage** ('hɛmərɪdʒ) *n.* **1.** profuse bleeding from ruptured blood vessels. ~*vb.* **2.** (*intr.*) to bleed profusely. [C17: from L *haemorrhagia*; see HAEMO-, -RRHAGIA]

haemorrhoids *or U.S.* **hemorrhoids** ('hɛmə,rɔɪdz) *pl. n. Pathol.* swollen and twisted veins in the region of the anus. Nontechnical name: **piles**. [C14: from L *haemorrhoidae* (pl.), from Gk, from *haimorrhoos* discharging blood, from *haimo*-HAEMO- + *rhein* to flow] —**haemor'rhoidal** *or U.S.* **,hemor'rhoidal** *adj.*

haemostasis *or U.S.* **hemostasis** (,hiːməʊ'steɪsɪs) *n.* the stopping of bleeding or of blood circulation, as during a surgical operation. [C18: from NL, from HAEMO- + Gk *stasis* a standing still] —**,haemo'static** *or U.S.* **,hemo'static** *adj.*

haemostat *or U.S.* **hemostat** ('hiːməʊ,stæt) *n.* a surgical instrument or chemical agent that retards or stops bleeding.

haeremai ('haɪrə,maɪ) *N.Z.* ~*sentence substitute.* **1.** an expression of greeting or welcome. ~*n.* **2.** the act of saying "haeremai". [C18: Maori, lit.: come hither]

Ha-erh-pin ('hɑː'ɛə'pɪn) *n.* transliteration of the Chinese name for Harbin.

hafiz ('hɑːfɪz) *n. Islam.* a title for a person who knows the Koran by heart. [from Persian, from Ar., from *hafiza* to guard]

hafnium ('hæfnɪəm) *n.* a bright metallic element found in zirconium ores. Symbol: Hf; atomic no.: 72; atomic wt.: 178.49. [C20: NL, after *Hafnia*, L name of Copenhagen + -IUM]

haft (hɑːft) n. **1.** the handle of an axe, knife, etc. ~vb. **2.** (tr.) to provide with a haft. [OE hæft]

hag[1] (hæg) n. **1.** an unpleasant or ugly old woman. **2.** a witch. **3.** short for **hagfish**. [OE hægtesse witch] — '**haggish** adj.

hag[2] (hæg) n. Scot. & N English dialect. **1.** a firm spot in a bog. **2.** a soft place in a moor. [C13: from ON]

Hag. Bible. abbrev. for Haggai.

Hagar ('heɪgɑː, -gə) n. Old Testament. an Egyptian maid of Sarah, who bore Ishmael to Abraham, Sarah's husband.

Hagen[1] ('hɑːgən) n. (in the Nibelungenlied) Siegfried's killer, who in turn is killed by Siegfried's wife, Kriemhild.

Hagen[2] (German 'haːgən) n. an industrial city in NE West Germany, in North Rhine-Westphalia. Pop.: 206 100 (1986).

Hagen[3] ('heɪgən) n. **Walter.** 1892–1969, U.S. golfer.

hagfish ('hæg,fɪʃ) n., pl. **-fish** or **-fishes**. an eel-like marine vertebrate having a round sucking mouth and feeding on the tissues of other animals and on dead organic material.

Haggadah or **Haggadoth** (hə'gɑːdə) n., pl. **Haggadahs**, **Haggadas** or **Haggadoth** (hægə'dəʊt). Judaism. **a.** a book containing the order of service of the traditional Passover meal. **b.** the narrative of the Exodus from Egypt that constitutes the main part of that service. ~See also **Seder**. [C19: from Heb.: story, from hagged to tell] — **haggadic** (hə'gædɪk, -'gɑː-) adj.

Haggai ('hægeɪ,aɪ) n. Old Testament. **1.** a Hebrew prophet, whose oracles are usually dated between August and December of 520 B.C. **2.** the book in which these oracles are contained, chiefly concerned with the rebuilding of the Temple after the Exile. Douay spelling: **Aggeus** (ə'dʒiːəs).

haggard ('hægəd) adj. **1.** careworn or gaunt, as from anxiety or starvation. **2.** wild or unruly. **3.** (of a hawk) having reached maturity in the wild before being caught. ~n. **4.** Falconry. a haggard hawk. [C16: from OF hagard, ? rel. to HEDGE] — '**haggardly** adv. — '**haggardness** n.

Haggard ('hægəd) n. Sir (**Henry**) **Rider.** 1856–1925, English author of romantic adventure stories, including King Solomon's Mines (1885).

haggis ('hægɪs) n. a Scottish dish made from sheep's or calf's offal, oatmeal, suet, and seasonings boiled in a skin made from the animal's stomach. [C15: ?from haggen to HACK[1]]

haggle ('hæg°l) vb. (intr.; often foll. by over) to bargain or wrangle (over a price, terms of an agreement, etc.); barter. [C16: of Scand. origin] — '**haggler** n.

hagio- or before a vowel **hagi-** combining form. indicating a saint, saints, or holiness: hagiography. [via LL from Gk, from hagios holy]

Hagiographa (,hægɪ'ɒgrəfə) n. the third of the three main parts into which the books of the Old Testament are divided in Jewish tradition (the other two parts being the Law and the Prophets).

hagiographer (,hægɪ'ɒgrəfə) or **hagiographist** n. **1.** a person who writes about the lives of the saints. **2.** one of the writers of the Hagiographa.

hagiography (,hægɪ'ɒgrəfɪ) n., pl. **-phies**. **1.** the writing of the lives of the saints. **2.** a biography that idealizes or idolizes its subject. — **hagiographic** (,hægɪə'græfɪk) or ,**hagio'graphical** adj.

hagiolatry (,hægɪ'ɒlətrɪ) n. worship or veneration of saints.

hagiology (,hægɪ'ɒlədʒɪ) n., pl. **-gies**. literature concerned with the lives and legends of saints. —**hagiological** (,hægɪə'lɒdʒɪk°l) adj. —,**hagi'ologist** n.

hag-ridden adj. tormented or worried, as if by a witch.

Hague (heɪg) n. **The.** the seat of government of the Netherlands and capital of South Holland province, situated about 3 km (2 miles) from the North Sea. Pop.: 445 127 (1987). Dutch names: '**s Gravenhage**, **Den Haag**.

hah (hɑː) interj. a variant spelling of **ha**[1].

ha-ha[1] ('hɑː'hɑː) or **haw-haw** ('hɔː'hɔː) interj. **1.** a representation of the sound of laughter. **2.** an exclamation expressing derision, mockery, etc.

ha-ha[2] ('hɑːhɑː) or **haw-haw** ('hɔːhɔː) n. a sunk fence bordering a garden or park, that allows uninterrupted views from within. [C18: from F haha, prob. based on ha! ejaculation denoting surprise]

Hahn (German haːn) n. **Otto** ('ɔto). 1879–1968, German physicist: discovered the radioactive element protactinium with Meitner (1917); with Strassmann, demonstrated the nuclear fission of uranium, when it is bombarded with neutrons: Nobel prize for chemistry 1944.

Hahnemann (German 'haːnəman) n. (**Christian Friedrich**) **Samuel** ('zaːmueːl). 1755–1843, German physician; founder of homeopathy.

hahnium ('hɑːnɪəm) n. a transuranic element artificially produced from californium. Symbol: Ha; atomic no.: 105; half-life of most stable isotope, ^{262}Ha: 40 seconds. [C20: after Otto HAHN]

Haidar Ali ('haɪdər 'ɑːlɪ) n. a variant spelling of **Hyder Ali.**

Haifa ('haɪfə) n. a port in NW Israel, near Mount Carmel, on the Bay of Acre: Israel's chief port, with an oil refinery and other heavy industry. Pop.: 223 400 (1986).

Haig (heɪg) n. **Douglas,** 1st Earl Haig. 1861–1928, British field marshal; commander in chief of the British forces in France and Flanders (1915–18).

haik or **haick** (haɪk, heɪk) n. an Arab's outer garment for the head and body. [C18: from Ar.]

haiku ('haɪkuː) or **hokku** ('hɒkuː) n., pl. **-ku.** an epigrammatic Japanese verse form in 17 syllables. [from Japanese, from hai amusement + ku verse]

hail[1] (heɪl) n. **1.** small pellets of ice falling from cumulonimbus clouds when there are strong rising air currents. **2.** a storm of such pellets. **3.** words, ideas, missiles, etc., directed with force and in great quantity: a hail of abuse. ~vb. **4.** (intr.; with it as subject) to be the case that hail is falling. **5.** (often with it as subject) to fall or cause to fall as or like hail. [OE hægl]

hail[2] (heɪl) vb. (mainly tr.) **1.** to greet, esp. enthusiastically: the crowd hailed the actress with joy. **2.** to acclaim or acknowledge: they hailed him as their hero. **3.** to attract the attention of by shouting or gesturing: to hail a taxi. **4.** (intr.; foll. by from) to be a native of: she hails from India. ~n. **5.** the act or an instance of hailing. **6.** a distance across which one can attract attention (esp. in **within hail**). ~sentence substitute. **7.** Poetic. an exclamation of greeting. [C12: from ON heill WHOLE]

Haile Selassie ('haɪlɪ sə'læsɪ) n. title of Ras Tafari Makonnen. 1892–1975, emperor of Ethiopia (1930–36; 1941–74). During the Italian occupation of Ethiopia (1936–41), he lived in exile in England. He was a prominent figure in the Pan-African movement: deposed 1974.

hail-fellow-well-met adj. genial and familiar, esp. in an offensive or ingratiating way.

Hail Mary n. R.C. Church. a prayer to the Virgin Mary, based on the salutations of the angel Gabriel (Luke 1:28) and Elizabeth (Luke 1:42) to her. Also called: **Ave Maria.**

Hailsham ('heɪlʃəm) n. **Quintin (McGarel) Hogg** ('kwɪntɪn), Baron. born 1907, British Conservative politician; Lord Chancellor (1970–74; 1979–87). He renounced his viscountcy in 1963 when he made an unsuccessful bid for the Conservative Party leadership; he became a life peer in 1970.

hailstone ('heɪl,stəʊn) n. a pellet of hail.

hailstorm ('heɪl,stɔːm) n. a storm during which hail falls.

Hailwood ('heɪlwʊd) n. **Mike,** full name Stanley Michael Bailey Hailwood. 1940–81, English racing motorcyclist: world champion (250 cc.) 1961 and 1966–67; (350 cc.) 1966–67; and (500 cc.) 1962–67.

Hainan ('haɪ'næn) or **Hainan Tao** (taʊ) n. an island in the South China Sea, separated from the mainland of S China by **Hainan Strait:** administratively part of Guangdong province; China's second largest offshore island. Pop.: 2 700 000 (1956 est.). Area: 33 991 sq. km (13 124 sq. miles).

Hainaut or **Hainault** (French ɛno) n. a province of SW Belgium: stretches from the Flanders Plain in the north to the Ardennes in the south; coal mines. Capital: Mons. Pop.: 1 274 034 (1986). Area: 3797 sq. km (1466 sq. miles).

Haiphong ('haɪ'fɒŋ) n. a port in N Vietnam, on the Red River delta: a major industrial centre. Pop.: 1 305 163 (1980).

hair (hɛə) n. **1.** any of the threadlike structures that grow from follicles beneath the skin of mammals. **2.** a growth of such structures, as on an animal's body, which helps prevent heat loss. **3.** Bot. any threadlike outgrowth, such as a root hair. **4.** a fabric made from the hair of some animals. **5.** another word for **hair's-breadth**: to lose by a *hair.* **6. get in someone's hair.** *Inf.* to annoy someone persistently. **7. hair of the dog (that bit one).** an alcoholic drink taken as an antidote to a hangover. **8. keep your hair on!** *Brit. inf.* keep calm. **9. let one's hair down.** to behave without reserve. **10. not turn a hair.** to show no surprise, anger, fear, etc. **11. split hairs.** to make petty and unnecessary distinctions. [OE *hær*] — '**hairless** *adj.* — '**hair,like** *adj.*

haircloth ('hɛə,klɒθ) *n.* a cloth woven from horsehair, used (esp. formerly) in upholstery, etc.

haircut ('hɛə,kʌt) *n.* **1.** the act of cutting the hair. **2.** the style in which hair has been cut.

hairdo ('hɛə,du:) *n., pl.* **-dos.** the arrangement of a person's hair, esp. after styling and setting.

hairdresser ('hɛə,drɛsə) *n.* **1.** a person whose business is cutting, colouring and arranging hair. **2.** a hairdresser's establishment. ~Related adj.: **tonsorial.** — '**hair,dressing** *n.*

-haired *adj.* having hair as specified: *long-haired.*

hair gel *n.* a preparation used in hair styling.

hairgrip ('hɛə,grɪp) *n. Chiefly Brit.* a small tightly bent metal hair clip. Also called (U.S., Canad., and N.Z.): **bobby pin.**

hairline ('hɛə,laɪn) *n.* **1.** the natural margin formed by hair on the head. **2. a.** a very narrow line. **b.** (*as modifier*): *a hairline crack.*

hairnet ('hɛə,nɛt) *n.* any of several kinds of light netting worn over the hair to keep it in place.

hairpiece ('hɛə,pi:s) *n.* **1.** a wig or toupee. **2.** a section of extra hair attached to a woman's real hair to give it greater bulk or length.

hairpin ('hɛə,pɪn) *n.* **1.** a thin double-pronged pin used to fasten the hair. **2.** (*modifier*) (esp. of a bend in a road) curving very sharply.

hair-raising *adj.* inspiring horror; terrifying.

hair's-breadth *n.* **a.** a very short or imperceptible margin or distance. **b.** (*as modifier*): *a hair's-breadth escape.*

hair shirt *n.* **1.** a shirt made of haircloth worn next to the skin as a penance. **2.** a secret trouble or affliction.

hair slide *n.* a hinged clip with a tortoiseshell, bone, or similar back, used to fasten a girl's hair.

hairsplitting ('hɛə,splɪtɪŋ) *n.* **1.** the making of petty distinctions. ~*adj.* **2.** occupied with or based on petty distinctions. — '**hair,splitter** *n.*

hairspring ('hɛə,sprɪŋ) *n.* a fine spiral spring in some timepieces which, in combination with the balance wheel, controls the timekeeping.

hairstreak ('hɛə,stri:k) *n.* a small butterfly having fringed wings with narrow white streaks.

hairstyle ('hɛə,staɪl) *n.* a particular mode of arranging the hair. — '**hair,stylist** *n.*

hair trigger *n.* **1.** a trigger of a firearm that responds to very slight pressure. **2.** *Inf.* any mechanism, reaction, etc., set in operation by slight provocation.

hairy ('hɛərɪ) *adj.* **hairier, hairiest. 1.** covered with hair. **2.** *Sl.* **a.** difficult or problematic. **b.** dangerous or exciting. — '**hairiness** *n.*

Haiti ('heɪtɪ, hɑː'iːtɪ) *n.* **1.** a republic occupying the W part of the island of Hispaniola in the Caribbean, the E part consisting of the Dominican Republic: ceded by Spain to France in 1697 and became one of the richest colonial possessions in the world, with numerous plantations; slaves rebelled under Toussaint L'Ouverture in 1793 and defeated the French; taken over by the U.S. (1915–41) after long political and economic chaos; under the authoritarian regimes of François Duvalier (1957–71) and his son Jean-Claude Duvalier (1971–86). Official language: French; Haitian creole is the common spoken language. Religions: Roman Catholic and voodoo. Currency: gourde. Capital: Port-au-Prince. Pop.: 6 096 000 (1988 est.). Area: 27 749 sq. km (10 714 sq. miles). **2.** a former name for **Hispaniola.** — **Haitian** ('heɪʃɪən, hɑː'iːʃən) *adj., n.*

Haitink ('haɪ,tɪŋk) *n.* Sir **Bernard.** born 1929, Dutch orchestral conductor.

hajj *or* **hadj** (hædʒ) *n.* the pilgrimage to Mecca that every Muslim is required to make at least once in his life. [from Ar.]

hajji, hadji, *or* **haji** ('hædʒɪ) *n., pl.* **hajjis, hadjis,** *or* **hajis. 1.** a Muslim who has made a pilgrimage to Mecca: also used as a title. **2.** a Christian who has visited Jerusalem.

haka ('hɑːkə) *n. N.Z.* **1.** a Maori war chant accompanied by gestures. **2.** a similar performance by, for instance, a rugby team.

hake (heɪk) *n., pl.* **hake** *or* **hakes. 1.** a gadoid food fish of the N hemisphere, having an elongated body with a large head and two dorsal fins. **2.** a similar North American fish. [C15: ?from ON *haki* hook]

hakea ('hɑːkɪə, 'heɪkɪə) *n.* any shrub or tree of the Australian genus *Hakea*, having a hard woody fruit and often yielding a useful wood. [C19: NL, after C. L. von *Hake* (died 1818), G botanist]

hakim *or* **hakeem** (hɑː'kiːm) *n.* **1.** a Muslim judge, ruler, or administrator. **2.** a Muslim physician. [C17: from Ar., from *hakama* to rule]

Hakluyt ('hæklu:t) *n.* **Richard.** ?1552–1616, English geographer, who compiled *The Principal Navigations, Voyages, and Discoveries of the English Nation* (1589).

Hakodate (,hɑːkəʊ'dɑːteɪ) *n.* a port in N Japan, on S Hokkaido: fishing industry and shipbuilding. Pop.: 19 000 (1985).

Halakah *or* **Halacha** (,hɑːlə'kɑː, hə'lɑːkə) *n.* that part of traditional Jewish literature concerned with the law, as contrasted with Haggadah. [C19: from Heb.: way, from *hālakh* to go] — **Halakic** *or* **Halachic** (hə'lækɪk) *adj.*

halal *or* **hallal** (hɑː'lɑːl) *n.* **1.** meat from animals that have been killed according to Muslim law. ~*adj.* **2.** of or relating to such meat: *a halal butcher.* ~*vb.* **-alling, -alled** (*tr.*) **3.** to kill (animals) in this way. [from Ar.: lawful]

halation (hə'leɪʃən) *n. Photog.* fogging usually seen as a bright ring surrounding a source of light. [C19: from HALO + -ATION]

halberd ('hælbəd) *or* **halbert** ('hælbət) *n.* a weapon consisting of a long shaft with an axe blade and a pick, topped by a spearhead: used in 15th- and 16th-century warfare. [C15: from OF *halebarde*, from MHG *helm* handle + *barde* axe] — ,**halber'dier** *n.*

halcyon ('hælsɪən) *adj.* **1.** peaceful, gentle, and calm. **2. halcyon days. a.** a fortnight of calm weather during the winter solstice. **b.** a period of peace and happiness. ~*n.* **3.** *Greek myth.* a fabulous bird associated with the winter solstice. **4.** a poetic name for the **kingfisher.** [C14: from L *alcyon*, from Gk *alkuōn* kingfisher, from ?]

Halcyone (hæl'saɪənɪ) *n.* a variant of **Alcyone**[1].

Haldane ('hɔːldeɪn) *n.* **1. J(ohn) B(urdon) S(anderson).** 1892–1964, Scottish biochemist, geneticist, and writer on science. **2.** his father, **John Scott.** 1860–1936, Scottish physiologist, noted particularly for his research into industrial diseases. **3.** his brother, **Richard Burdon,** 1st Viscount Haldane of Cloan. 1856–1928, British statesman and jurist. As secretary of state for war (1905–12) he reorganized the army and set up the territorial reserve.

hale[1] (heɪl) *adj.* healthy and robust (esp. in **hale and hearty**). [OE *hæl* WHOLE] — '**haleness** *n.*

hale[2] (heɪl) *vb.* (*tr.*) to pull or drag. [C13: from OF *haler*, of Gmc origin] — '**haler** *n.*

Hale (heɪl) *n.* **1. George Ellery.** 1868–1938, U.S. astronomer: undertook research into sunspots and invented the spectroheliograph. **2.** Sir **Matthew.** 1609–76, English judge and scholar; Lord Chief Justice (1671–76).

Haleakala (,hɑːli:,ɑːkɑː'lɑː) *n.* a volcano in Hawaii, on E Mani Island. Height: 3057 m (10 032 ft.). Area of crater: 49 sq. km (19 sq. miles). Depth of crater: 829 m (2720 ft.).

Halesowen (heɪlz'əʊɪn) *n.* a town in W central England, in the SW West Midlands. Pop.: 57 453 (1981).

Halévy (*French* alevi) *n.* **Ludovic** (lydɔvik). 1834–1908, French dramatist and novelist, who collaborated with Meilhac on opera libretti.

half (hɑːf) *n., pl.* **halves** (hɑːvz). **1. a.** either of two equal or corresponding parts that together comprise a whole. **b.** a quantity equalling such a part: *half a dozen.* **2.** half a pint, esp. of beer. **3.** *Scot.* a small drink of spirits, esp. whisky. **4.** *Football, hockey, etc.* the half of the pitch regarded as belonging to one team. **5.** *Golf.* an equal score with an opponent. **6.** (in various games) either of two periods of play separated by an interval. **7.** a half-price ticket on a bus, etc. **8.** short for **half-hour. 9.** *Sport.* short for **halfback. 10.** *Obs.* a half-year period. **11. by halves.** (*used with a negative*) without being thorough: *we don't do things by halves.* **12. go halves.** (often foll. by *on, in,* etc.) **a.** to share expenses. **b.** to share the whole amount (of something): *to go halves on an orange.* ~*determiner.* **13. a.** being a half or approximately a half: *half the kingdom.* **b.** (*as pron.; functioning as sing. or* *pl.*): *half of them came.* ~*adj.* **14.** not perfect or complete: *he only did a half job on it.* ~*adv.* **15.** to the amount or extent of a half. **16.** to a great amount or extent. **17.** partially; to an extent. **18. by half.** to an excessive degree: *he's too arrogant by half.* **19. half two,** etc. *Inf.* 30 minutes after two o'clock, etc. **20. have half a mind to.** to have a vague intention to. **21. not half.** *Inf.* **a.** not in any way: *he's not half clever enough.* **b.** *Brit.* very: *he isn't half stupid.* **c.** yes, indeed. [OE *healf*]

half- *prefix.* **1.** one of two equal parts: *half-moon.* **2.** related through one parent only: *half-brother.* **3.** not completely, partly: *half-baked.*

half-and-half *n.* **1.** a mixture of half one thing and half another thing. **2.** a drink consisting of equal parts of beer and stout, or equal parts of bitter and mild.

halfback ('hɑːf,bæk) *n.* **1.** *Soccer.* any of three players positioned behind the line of forwards and in front of the fullbacks. **2.** *Rugby.* either the scrum half or the stand-off half. **3.** any of certain similar players in other team sports.

half-baked *adj.* **1.** insufficiently baked. **2.** *Inf.* foolish; stupid. **3.** *Inf.* poorly planned.

halfbeak ('hɑːf,biːk) *n.* a marine and freshwater teleost fish having an elongated body with a short upper jaw and a long protruding lower jaw.

half-binding *n.* a type of bookbinding in which the backs are bound in one material and the sides in another.

half-blood *n.* **1. a.** the relationship between individuals having only one parent in common. **b.** an individual having such a relationship. **2.** a less common name for a **half-breed.** —,half-'blooded *adj.*

half board *n.* the daily provision by a hotel of bed, breakfast, and one main meal. Also called: **demi-pension.**

half-boot *n.* a boot reaching to the midcalf.

half-breed *n.* **1.** a person whose parents are of different races, esp. the offspring of a White person and an American Indian. ~*adj. also* **half-bred.** **2.** of, relating to, or designating offspring of people or animals of different races or breeds.

half-brother *n.* the son of either of one's parents by another partner.

half-butt *n.* a snooker cue that is longer than an ordinary cue.

half-caste *n.* **1.** a person having parents of different races, esp. the offspring of a European and an Indian. ~*adj.* **2.** of, relating to, or designating such a person.

half-cock *n.* **1.** the halfway position of a firearm's hammer when the trigger is cocked by the hammer and the hammer cannot reach the primer to fire the weapon. **2. go off at half-cock** *or* **half-cocked.** to fail as a result of inadequate preparation or premature starting.

half-crown *n.* a former British coin worth two shillings and sixpence (12½p). Also called: **half-a-crown.**

half gainer *n.* a type of dive in which the diver completes a half backward somersault to enter the water headfirst facing the diving board.

half-hardy *adj.* (of a cultivated plant) able to survive out of doors except during severe frost.

half-hearted *adj.* without enthusiasm or determination. —,half-'heartedly *adv.*

half-hitch *n.* a knot made by passing the end of a piece of rope around itself and through the loop thus made.

half-hour *n.* **1.** a period of 30 minutes. **2.** the point of time 30 minutes after the beginning of an hour. —,half-'hourly *adv., adj.*

half-hunter *n.* a watch with a hinged lid in which a small circular opening or crystal allows the approximate time to be read.

half landing *n.* a landing halfway up a flight of stairs.

half-life *n.* the time taken for half of the atoms in a radioactive material to undergo decay.

half-light *n.* a dim light, as at dawn or dusk.

half-mast *n.* the lower than normal position to which a flag is lowered on a mast as a sign of mourning.

half measure *n.* (*often pl.*) an inadequate measure or action; compromise.

half-moon *n.* **1.** the moon at first or last quarter when half its face is illuminated. **2.** the time at which a half-moon occurs. **3.** something shaped like a half-moon.

half-nelson *n.* a wrestling hold in which a wrestler places an arm under one of his opponent's arms from behind and exerts pressure with his palm on the back of his opponent's neck.

half-note *n.* the usual U.S. name for **minim.**

halfpenny *or* **ha'penny** ('heɪpnɪ, *for sense 1* 'hɑːf,penɪ) *n.* **1.** (*pl.* **-pennies**) a small British coin worth half a new penny (withdrawn 1985). **2.** (*pl.* **-pennies**) an old British coin worth half an old penny. **3.** (*pl.* **-pence**) something of negligible value. —**halfpennyworth** *or* **ha'p'orth** ('heɪpəθ) *n.*

half-pie *adj. N.Z. inf.* ill planned; not properly thought out: *a half-pie scheme.* [from Maori *pai* good]

half-pint *n. Sl.* a small or insignificant person.

half-plate *or* **half-print** *n. Photog.* a size of plate measuring 16.5 cm by 10.8 cm.

half seas over *adj. Brit. inf.* drunk.

half-sister *n.* the daughter of either of one's parents by another partner.

half-size *n.* any size, esp. in clothing, that is halfway between two sizes.

half-sole *n.* a sole from the shank of a shoe to the toe.

half term *n. Brit. education.* a short holiday midway through an academic term.

half-timbered *or* **half-timber** *adj.* (of a building) having an exposed timber framework filled with brick, stone, or plastered laths, as in Tudor architecture. —,half-'timbering *n.*

half-time *n. Sport.* **a.** a rest period between the two halves of a game. **b.** (*as modifier*): *the half-time score.*

half-title *n.* **1.** the short title of a book as printed on the right-hand page preceding the title page. **2.** a title on a separate page preceding a section of a book.

halftone ('hɑːf,təʊn) *n.* **1.** a process used to reproduce an illustration by photographing it through a fine screen to break it up into dots. **2.** the print obtained.

half-track *n.* a vehicle with caterpillar tracks on the wheels that supply motive power only.

half-truth *n.* a partially true statement intended to mislead. —,half-'true *adj.*

half volley *n. Sport.* a stroke or shot in which the ball is hit immediately after it bounces.

halfway (,hɑːf'weɪ) *adv., adj.* **1.** at or to half the distance. **2.** in or of an incomplete manner. **3. meet halfway.** to compromise with.

halfway house *n.* **1.** a place to rest midway on a journey. **2.** the halfway point in any progression. **3.** a centre or hostel designed to facilitate the readjustment to private life of released prisoners, mental patients, etc.

,half-a'fraid *adj.*	,half-con'cealed *adj.*	,half-'drunk *adj.*	,half-'mile *n.*
,half-a'live *adj.*	,half-'conscious *adj.*	,half-'eaten *adj.*	,half-'naked *adj.*
,half-a'shamed *adj.*	,half-con'sumed *adj.*	,half-'edu,cated *adj.*	,half-'open *adj.*
,half-a'sleep *adj.*	,half-con'vinced *adj.*	,half-'filled *adj.*	,half-pro'testing *adj.*
,half-a'wake *adj.*	,half-'cooked *adj.*	,half-'finished *adj.*	,half-'raw *adj.*
,half-'barrel *n.*	,half-'covered *adj.*	,half-for'gotten *adj.*	,half-re'luctantly *adv.*
,half-be'gun *adj.*	,half-'crazy *adj.*	,half-'formed *adj.*	,half-re'membered *adj.*
,half-'blind *adj.*	,half-'day *n.*	,half-'frozen *adj.*	,half-'rotten *adj.*
,half-'bottle *n.*	,half-'dazed *adj.*	,half-'full *adj.*	,half-'seriously *adv.*
,half-'buried *adj.*	,half-'deaf *adj.*	,half-'grown *adj.*	,half-'shut *adj.*
,half-'century *n.*	,half-de'veloped *adj.*	,half-'heard *adj.*	,half-'starved *adj.*
,half-'civil,ized *or* -,ised *adj.*	,half-di'gested *adj.*	,half-'human *adj.*	,half-sub'merged *adj.*
	,half-'done *adj.*	,half-in'clined *adj.*	,half-'trained *adj.*
,half-'clad *adj.*	,half-'dozen *n.*	,half-in'formed *adj.*	,half-under'stood *adj.*
,half-'closed *adj.*	,half-'dressed *adj.*	,half-in'stinctive *adj.*	,half-'used *adj.*
,half-'clothed *adj.*	,half-'drowned *adj.*	,half-'joking *adj.*	,half-'wild *adj.*
,half-com'pleted *adj.*			

halfwit ('hɑːf,wɪt) *n.* **1.** a feeble-minded person. **2.** a foolish or inane person. —,**half'witted** *adj.*

halibut ('hælɪbət) *n.*, *pl.* **-buts** *or* **-but.** the largest flatfish: a dark green North Atlantic species that is a very important food fish. [C15: from *hali* HOLY (because it was eaten on holy days) + *butte* flat-fish, from MDu.]

Haliç (ha'liːtʃ) *n.* the Turkish name for the **Golden Horn.**

Halicarnassus (,hælɪkɑː'næsəs) *n.* a Greek colony on the SW coast of Asia Minor: one of the major Hellenistic cities. —,**Halicar'nassian** *adj.*

halide ('hælaɪd) *or* **halid** ('hælɪd) *n.* any binary salt of a halogen acid; a chloride, bromide, iodide, or fluoride.

Halifax[1] ('hælɪ,fæks) *n.* **1.** a port in SE Canada, capital of Nova Scotia, on the Atlantic: founded in 1749 as a British stronghold. Pop.: 113 577 (1986). **2.** a town in N England, in West Yorkshire: textiles. Pop.: 87 488 (1981).

Halifax[2] ('hælɪ,fæks) *n.* **1. Charles Montagu,** Earl of Halifax. 1661–1715, English statesman; founder of the National Debt (1692) and the Bank of England (1694). **2. Edward Frederick Lindley Wood,** Earl of Halifax. 1881–1959, British Conservative statesman. He was viceroy of India (1926–31), foreign secretary (1938–40), and ambassador to the U.S. (1941–46).

halite ('hælaɪt) *n.* a mineral consisting of sodium chloride in cubic crystalline form, occurring in sedimentary beds and dried salt lakes: an important source of table salt. Also called: **rock salt.** [C19: from NL *halites*, from Gk *hals* salt + -ITE[2]]

halitosis (,hælɪ'təʊsɪs) *n.* the state or condition of having bad breath. [C19: NL, from L *hālitus* breath, from *hālāre* to breathe]

hall (hɔːl) *n.* **1.** a room serving as an entry area. **2.** (*sometimes cap.*) a building for public meetings. **3.** (*often cap.*) the great house of an estate; manor. **4.** a large building or room used for assemblies, dances, etc. **5.** a residential building, esp. in a university; hall of residence. **6. a.** a large room, esp. for dining, in a college or university. **b.** a meal eaten in this room. **7.** the large room of a house, castle, etc. **8.** *U.S. & Canad.* a corridor into which rooms open. **9.** (*often pl.*) *Inf.* short for **music hall.** [OE *heall*]

Hall (hɔːl) *n.* **1. Charles Martin.** 1863–1914, U.S. chemist: discovered the electrolytic process for producing aluminium. **2. Sir John.** 1824–1907, New Zealand statesman, born in England: prime minister of New Zealand (1879–82). **3. Sir Peter.** born 1930, English stage director: director of the Royal Shakespeare Company (1960–73) and of the National Theatre (1973–88).

Halle (*German* 'halə) *n.* a city in SW East Germany, on the River Saale: early saltworks; a Hanseatic city in the late Middle Ages; university (1694). Pop.: 234 768 (1986). Official name: **Halle an der Saale** (an der 'zɑːlə).

hallelujah, halleluiah (,hælɪ'luːjə), *or* **alleluia** (,ælɪ'luːjə) *interj.* **1.** an exclamation of praise to God. ~*n.* **2.** an exclamation of "Hallelujah". **3.** a musical composition that uses the word *Hallelujah* as its text. [C16: from Heb. *hellēl* to praise + *yāh* the Lord]

Haller (*German* 'halər) *n.* **Albrecht von** ('albrɛçt fɔn). 1708–77, Swiss biologist: founder of experimental physiology.

Hallett ('hælɪt) *n.* **Michael,** known as *Mike.* born 1959, British snooker player.

Halley ('hælɪ) *n.* **Edmund.** 1656–1742, English astronomer and mathematician. He predicted the return of the comet now known as **Halley's comet,** constructed charts of magnetic declination, and produced the first wind maps.

halliard ('hæljəd) *n.* a variant spelling of **halyard.**

Hall-Jones ('hɔːl'dʒəʊnz) *n.* **Sir William.** 1851–1936, New Zealand statesman, born in England: prime minister of New Zealand (1906).

hallmark ('hɔːl,mɑːk) *n.* **1.** *Brit.* an official series of marks stamped by the London Guild of Goldsmiths on gold, silver, or platinum articles to guarantee purity, date of manufacture, etc. **2.** a mark of authenticity or excellence. **3.** an outstanding feature. ~*vb.* **4.** (*tr.*) to stamp with or as if with a hallmark. [C18: after Goldsmiths' *Hall* in London, where items were graded and stamped]

hallo (ha'ləʊ) *sentence substitute, n.* **1.** a variant spelling of **hello.** ~*sentence substitute, n., vb.* **2.** a variant spelling of **halloo.**

halloo (ha'luː), **hallo,** *or* **halloa** (ha'ləʊ) *sentence substitute.* **1.** a shout to attract attention, esp. to call hounds at a hunt. ~*n.*, *pl.* **-loos, -los,** *or* **-loas.** **2.** a shout of "halloo". ~*vb.* **-looing, -looed; -loing, -loed,** *or* **-loaing, -loaed.** **3.** to shout. **4.** (*tr.*) to urge on (dogs) with shouts. [C16: ? var. of *hallow* to encourage hounds by shouting]

hallow ('hæləʊ) *vb.* (*tr.*) **1.** to consecrate or set apart as being holy. **2.** to venerate as being holy. [OE *hālgian,* from *hālig* HOLY] —'**hallower** *n.*

hallowed ('hæləʊd; *liturgical* 'hæləʊɪd) *adj.* **1.** set apart as sacred. **2.** consecrated or holy.

Hallowe'en *or* **Halloween** (,hæləʊ'iːn) *n.* the eve of All Saints' Day celebrated on Oct. 31; Allhallows Eve. [C18: see ALLHALLOWS, EVEN[2]]

hall stand *or esp. U.S.* **hall tree** *n.* a piece of furniture for hanging coats, hats, etc., on.

Hallstatt ('hælstæt) *adj.* of a late Bronze Age culture extending from central Europe to Britain and lasting from the 9th to the 5th century B.C. [C19: after *Hallstatt,* Austrian village where remains were found]

hallucinate (hə'luːsɪ,neɪt) *vb.* (*intr.*) to experience hallucinations. [C17: from L *ālūcinārī* to wander in mind] —**hal'luci,nator** *n.*

hallucination (hə,luːsɪ'neɪʃən) *n.* the alleged perception of an object when no object is present, occurring under hypnosis, in some mental disorders, etc. —**hal'lucinatory** *adj.*

hallucinogen (hə'luːsɪnə,dʒɛn) *n.* any drug that induces hallucinations. —**hallucinogenic** (hə,luːsɪnə'dʒɛnɪk) *adj.*

hallux ('hæləks) *n.* the first digit on the hind foot of a mammal, bird, reptile, or amphibian; the big toe of man. [C19: NL, from LL *allex* big toe]

hallway ('hɔːl,weɪ) *n.* a hall or corridor.

halm (hɔːm) *n.* a variant spelling of **haulm.**

halma ('hælmə) *n.* a board game in which players attempt to transfer their pieces from their own to their opponents' bases. [C19: from Gk *halma* leap]

Halmahera (,hælmə'hɪərə) *n.* an island in NE Indonesia, the largest of the Moluccas: consists of four peninsulas enclosing three bays; mountainous and forested. Area: 17 780 sq. km (6865 sq. miles). Dutch name: **Djailolo, Gilolo,** or **Jilolo.**

Halmstad (*Swedish* 'halmstɑːd) *n.* a port in SW Sweden, on the Kattegat. Pop.: 76 042 (1980).

halo ('heɪləʊ) *n.*, *pl.* **-loes** *or* **-los.** **1.** a disc or ring of light around the head of an angel, saint, etc., as in painting. **2.** the aura surrounding a famous or admired person, thing, or event. **3.** a circle of light around the sun or moon, caused by the refraction of light by particles of ice. ~*vb.* **-loes** *or* **-los, -loing, -loed.** **4.** to surround with or form a halo. [C16: from Med. L, from L *halos* circular threshing floor, from Gk]

halogen ('hælə,dʒɛn) *n.* any of the chemical elements fluorine, chlorine, bromine, iodine, and astatine. They are all monovalent and readily form negative ions. [C19: from Swedish, from Gk *hals* salt + -GEN] —**halogenous** (hə'lɒdʒɪnəs) *adj.*

halogenate ('hælədʒə,neɪt) *vb. Chem.* to treat or combine with a halogen. —,**halogen'ation** *n.*

haloid ('hæləɪd) *Chem.* ~*adj.* **1.** derived from a halogen: *a haloid salt.* ~*n.* **2.** a compound containing halogen atoms in its molecules.

Hals (*Dutch* hals) *n.* **Frans** (frans). ?1580–1666, Dutch portrait and genre painter: his works include *The Laughing Cavalier* (1624).

Hälsingborg *or* **Helsingborg** (*Swedish* helsiŋ'bɔrj) *n.* a port in SW Sweden, on the Sound opposite Helsingor, Denmark: changed hands several times between Denmark and Sweden, finally becoming Swedish in 1710; shipbuilding. Pop.: 106 275 (1986).

halt[1] (hɔːlt) *n.* **1.** an interruption or end to movement or progress. **2.** *Chiefly Brit.* a minor railway station, without permanent buildings. **3. call a halt** (**to**). to put an end (to); stop. ~*n., sentence substitute.* **4.** a command to halt, esp. as an order when marching. ~*vb.* **5.** to come or bring to a halt. [C17: from *to make halt,* translation of G *halt machen,* from *halten* to stop]

halt[2] (hɔːlt) *vb.* (*intr.*) **1.** (esp. of verse) to falter or be defective. **2.** to be unsure. **3.** *Arch.* to be lame. ~*adj.* **4.**

,**half-'wrong** *adj.*

Arch. **a.** lame. **b.** (*as collective n.*; preceded by *the*): *the halt.* [OE *healt* lame]

halter ('hɔːltə) *n.* **1.** headgear for a horse, usually with a rope for leading. **2.** a style of woman's top fastened behind the neck and waist, leaving the back and arms bare. **3.** a rope having a noose for hanging a person. **4.** death by hanging. ~*vb.* (*tr.*) **5.** to put on a halter. **6.** to hang (someone). [OE *hælfter*]

haltere ('hæltɪə) *n.*, *pl.* **halteres** (hæl'tɪəriːz). one of a pair of short projections in dipterous insects that are modified hind wings, used for maintaining equilibrium during flight. [C18: from Gk *haltēres* (pl.) hand-held weights used as balancers or to give impetus in leaping, from *hallesthai* to leap]

halting ('hɔːltɪŋ) *adj.* **1.** hesitant: *halting speech.* **2.** lame. —'**haltingly** *adv.*

halvah, halva ('hælvɑː), *or* **halavah** ('hæləvɑː) *n.* an Eastern sweetmeat made of honey and containing sesame seeds, nuts, etc. [from Yiddish *halva*, ult. from Ar. *halwā*]

halve (hɑːv) *vb.* (*tr.*) **1.** to divide into two approximately equal parts. **2.** to share equally. **3.** to reduce by half, as by cutting. **4.** *Golf.* to take the same number of strokes on (a hole or round) as one's opponent. [OE *hielfan*]

halyard *or* **halliard** ('hæljəd) *n. Naut.* a line for hoisting or lowering a sail, flag, or spar. [C14 *halier*, infl. by YARD¹; see HALE²]

ham¹ (hæm) *n.* **1.** the part of the hindquarters of a pig between the hock and the hip. **2.** the meat of this part. **3.** *Inf.* the back of the leg above the knee. [OE *hamm*]

ham² (hæm) *n.* **1.** *Theatre, inf.* **a.** an actor who overacts or relies on stock gestures. **b.** overacting or clumsy acting. **c.** (*as modifier*): *a ham actor.* **2.** *Inf.* a licensed amateur radio operator. ~*vb.* **hamming, hammed.** **3.** *Inf.* to overact. [C19: special use of HAM¹; in some senses prob. infl. by AMATEUR]

Hama ('hɑːmɑː) *n.* a city in W Syria, on the Orontes River: an early Hittite settlement; famous for its huge water wheels, used for irrigation since the Middle Ages. Pop.: 214 000 (1987). Biblical name: **Hamath.**

Hamadān *or* **Hamedān** ('hæmə,dæn) *n.* city in W central Iran, at an altitude of over 1830 m (6000 ft.): changed hands several times from the 17th century between Iraq, Persia, and Turkey; trading centre. Pop.: 274 274 (1986).

hamadryad (,hæmə'draɪəd) *n.* **1.** *Classical myth.* a nymph who inhabits a tree and dies with it. **2.** another name for **king cobra.** [C14: from L *Hamādryas*, from Gk *Hamadruas*, from *hama* together with + *drus* tree]

hamadryas (,hæmə'draɪəs) *n.* a baboon of Arabia and NE Africa, having long silvery hair on the head, neck, and chest. [C19: via NL from L; see HAMADRYAD]

Hamamatsu (,hæmə'mætsuː) *n.* a city in central Japan, in S central Honshu: cotton textiles and musical instruments. Pop.: 514 000 (1985).

hamba ('hæmbə) *sentence substitute. S. African, usually offens.* go away; be off. [from a Bantu language, from *ukuttamba* to go]

Hamburg ('hæmbɜːg) *n.* a city-state and port in N West Germany, on the River Elbe: the largest port in Germany; a founder member of the Hanseatic League; became a free imperial city in 1510 and a state of the German empire in 1871; university (1919); extensive shipyards. Pop.: 1 575 700 (1986).

hamburger ('hæm,bɜːgə) *n.* a cake of minced beef, often served in a bread roll. Also called: **beefburger.** [C20: from *Hamburger steak* (steak in the fashion of HAMBURG)]

hame (heɪm) *n.* either of the two curved bars holding the traces of the harness, attached to the collar of a draught animal. [C14: from MDu. *hame*]

Hameln (*German* 'haːməln) *n.* an industrial town in N West Germany, in Lower Saxony on the Weser River: famous for the legend of the Pied Piper (supposedly took place in 1284). Pop.: 56 000 (1984). English name: **Hamelin** ('hæməlɪn, 'hæmlɪn).

Hamersley Range ('hæməzlɪ) *n.* a mountain range in N Western Australia: iron-ore deposits. Highest peak: 1236 m (4056 ft.).

ham-handed *or* **ham-fisted** *adj. Inf.* lacking dexterity or elegance; clumsy.

Hamhung *or* **Hamheung** ('haːm'hʊŋ) *n.* an industrial city in central North Korea: commercial and governmental centre of NE Korea during the Yi dynasty (1392–1910). Pop.: 775 000 (1981).

Hamilcar Barca (hæ'mɪlkɑː 'bɑːkə, 'hæmɪl,kɑː) *n.* died ?228 B.C., Carthaginian general; father of Hannibal. He held command (247–41) during the first Punic War and established Carthaginian influence in Spain (237–?228).

Hamilton¹ ('hæmɪltən) *n.* **1.** a port in central Canada, in S Ontario on Lake Ontario: iron and steel industry. Pop.: 306 728 (1986). **2.** a city in New Zealand, on central North Island. Pop. (urban area): 169 000 (1987). **3.** a town in S Scotland, in Strathclyde region near Glasgow. Pop.: 51 529 (1981). **4.** the capital and chief port of Bermuda. Pop.: 1617 (1980). **5.** the former name of the **Churchill** River in Labrador.

Hamilton² ('hæmɪltən) *n.* **1. Alexander.** ?1757–1804, American statesman. He was a leader of the Federalists and as first secretary of the Treasury (1789–95) established a federal bank. **2. Lady Emma.** ?1765–1815, mistress of Nelson. **3.** Sir **William Rowan.** 1805–65, Irish mathematician: founded Hamiltonian mechanics and formulated the theory of quaternions.

Hamitic (hæ'mɪtɪk, hə-) *n.* **1.** a group of N African languages related to Semitic. ~*adj.* **2.** denoting or belonging to this group of languages. **3.** denoting or characteristic of the Hamites, a group of peoples of N Africa, including the ancient Egyptians, supposedly descended from Noah's son Ham.

hamlet ('hæmlɪt) *n.* a small village, esp. (in Britain) one without its own church. [C14: from OF *hamelet*, dim. of *hamel*, from *ham*, of Gmc origin]

Hamm (*German* ham) *n.* an industrial city in NW West Germany, in North Rhine-Westphalia: a Hanse town from 1417; severely damaged in World War II. Pop.: 166 200 (1986).

Hammarskjöld ('hæmə,ʃʊld; *Swedish* 'hamarʃœld) *n.* **Dag** (**Hjalmar Agne Carl**) (dɑːg). 1905–61, Swedish statesman; secretary-general of the United Nations (1953–61): Nobel peace prize 1961.

hammer ('hæmə) *n.* **1.** a hand tool consisting of a heavy usually steel head held transversely on the end of a handle, used for driving in nails, etc. **2.** any tool or device with a similar function, such as the striking head on a bell. **3.** a power-driven striking tool, esp. one used in forging. **4.** a part of a gunlock that strikes the primer or percussion cap when the trigger is pulled. **5.** *Field sports.* **a.** a heavy metal ball attached to a flexible wire: thrown in competitions. **b.** the sport of throwing the hammer. **6.** an auctioneer's gavel. **7.** a device on a piano that is made to strike a string or group of strings causing them to vibrate. **8.** *Anat.* the nontechnical name for **malleus.** **9. go under the hammer.** to be offered for sale by an auctioneer. **10. hammer and tongs.** with great effort or energy. **11. on someone's hammer.** *Austral. & N.Z. sl.* in hot pursuit of someone. ~*vb.* **12.** to strike or beat with or as if with a hammer. **13.** (*tr.*) to shape with or as if with a hammer. **14.** (*tr.*; foll. by *in* or *into*) to force (facts, ideas, etc.) into (someone) through constant repetition. **15.** (*intr.*) to feel or sound like hammering. **16.** (*intr.*; often foll. by *away*) to work at constantly. **17.** (*tr.*) *Brit.* to criticize severely. **18.** (*tr.*) *Inf.* to defeat. **19.** (*tr.*) *Stock Exchange.* **a.** to announce the default of (a member). **b.** to cause prices of (securities, the market, etc.) to fall by bearish selling. [OE *hamor*] —'**hammer-,like** *adj.*

hammer and sickle *n.* the emblem on the flag of the Soviet Union, representing the industrial workers and the peasants respectively.

hammer beam *n.* either of a pair of short horizontal beams that project from opposite walls to support arched braces and struts.

Hammerfest (*Norwegian* 'hamərfɛst) *n.* a port in N Norway, on the W coast of Kvaløy Island: the northernmost town in the world, with uninterrupted daylight from May 17 to July 19 and no sun between Nov. 21 and Jan. 21; fishing and tourist centre. Pop.: 7500 (1985).

hammerhead ('hæmə,hɛd) *n.* **1.** a ferocious shark having a flattened hammer-shaped head. **2.** a tropical African wading bird having a dark plumage and a long backward-pointing crest. **3.** a large African fruit bat with a hammer-shaped muzzle. —'**hammer,headed** *adj.*

hammerlock ('hæmə,lɒk) *n.* a wrestling hold in which a wrestler twists his opponent's arm upwards behind his back.

hammer out *vb.* (*tr., adv.*) **1.** to shape or remove with or as if with a hammer. **2.** to settle or reconcile (differences, problems, etc.).

Hammersmith and Fulham ('hæmə,smiθ) n. a borough of Greater London on the River Thames: established in 1965 by the amalgamation of Fulham and Hammersmith. Pop.: 150 800 (1986 est.).

Hammerstein II ('hæmə,staɪn) n. **Oscar.** 1895–1960, U.S. librettist and songwriter: collaborated with the composer Richard Rodgers in musicals such as *South Pacific* (1949) and *The Sound of Music* (1959).

hammertoe ('hæmə,təʊ) n. a deformity causing the toe to be bent in a clawlike arch.

hammock ('hæmək) n. a length of canvas, net, etc., suspended at the ends and used as a bed. [C16: from Sp. *hamaca*, from Amerind]

Hammond[1] ('hæmənd) n. a city in NW Indiana, adjacent to Chicago. Pop.: 93 714 (1980).

Hammond[2] ('hæmənd) n. **1. Dame Joan.** born 1912, Australian operatic singer, born in New Zealand. **2. Walter Reginald,** known as *Wally.* 1903–65, English cricketer. An all-rounder, he played for England 85 times between 1928 and 1946.

Hammurabi (,hæmʊ'rɑːbɪ) or **Hammurapi** n. ?18th century B.C., king of Babylonia; promulgator of one of the earliest known codes of law.

hammy ('hæmɪ) adj. **-mier, -miest.** *Inf.* **1.** (of an actor) tending to overact. **2.** (of a play, performance, etc.) overacted or exaggerated.

Hampden ('hæmpdən, 'hæmdən) n. **John.** 1594–1643, English statesman; one of the leaders of the Parliamentary opposition to Charles I.

hamper[1] ('hæmpə) vb. **1.** (tr.) to prevent the progress or free movement of. ~n. **2.** *Naut.* gear aboard a vessel that, though essential, is often in the way. [C14: from ?; ? rel. to OE *hamm* enclosure, *hemm* HEM[1]]

hamper[2] ('hæmpə) n. **1.** a large basket, usually with a cover. **2.** *Brit.* a selection of food and drink packed in a hamper or other container. [C14: var. of earlier *hanaper* a small basket, from OF, of Gmc origin]

Hampshire ('hæmp,ʃɪə, -ʃə) n. a county of S England, on the English Channel: crossed by the **Hampshire Downs** and the South Downs, with the New Forest in the southwest and many prehistoric and Roman remains. Administrative centre: Winchester. Pop.: 1 527 700 (1986 est.). Area: 3777 sq. km (1458 sq. miles). Abbrev.: **Hants.**

Hampstead ('hæmpstɪd) n. a residential district in N London: part of the Greater London borough of Camden since 1965; nearby is **Hampstead Heath,** a popular recreation area.

Hampton[1] ('hæmptən) n. **1.** a city in SE Virginia, on the harbour of **Hampton Roads** on Chesapeake Bay. Pop.: 122 617 (1980). **2.** a district of the Greater London borough of Richmond-upon-Thames, on the River Thames: famous for **Hampton Court Palace** (built in 1515 by Cardinal Wolsey).

Hampton[2] ('hæmptən) n. **Lionel.** born 1913, U.S. jazz-band leader and vibraphone player.

hamster ('hæmstə) n. a Eurasian burrowing rodent having a stocky body, short tail, and cheek pouches: a popular pet. [C17: from G, from OHG *hamustro*, of Slavic origin]

hamstring ('hæm,strɪŋ) n. **1.** one of the tendons at the back of the knee. **2.** the large tendon at the back of the hind leg of a horse, etc. ~vb. **-stringing, -strung.** (tr.) **3.** to cripple by cutting the hamstring of. **4.** to thwart. [C16: HAM[1] + STRING]

Hamsun (*Norwegian* 'hamsun) n. **Knut** (knuːt), pen name of *Knut Pedersen.* 1859–1952, Norwegian novelist, whose works include *The Growth of the Soil* (1917): Nobel prize for literature 1920.

hamulus ('hæmjʊləs) n., pl. **-li** (-,laɪ). *Biol.* a hook or hooklike process, between the fore and hind wings of a bee. [C18: from L: a little hook, from *hāmus* hook]

Han[1] (hæn) n. **1.** the imperial dynasty that ruled China for most of the time from 206 B.C. to 221 A.D., expanding its territory and developing its bureaucracy. **2.** the Chinese people as contrasted with Mongols, Manchus, etc.

Han[2] (hæn) n. a river in E central China, rising in S Shaanxi and flowing southeast through Hubei to the Yangtze River at Wuhan. Length: about 1450 km (900 miles).

Hanau (*German* 'haːnau) n. a city in central West Germany, in Hesse east of Frankfurt am Main: a centre of the jewellery industry. Pop.: 86 261 (1983 est.).

Han Cities pl. n. a group of three cities in E central China, in SE Hubei at the confluence of the Han and Yangtze Rivers: Hanyang, Hankow, and Wuchang; united in 1950 to form the conurbation of Wuhan, the capital of Hubei province.

Hancock ('hænkɒk) n. **1. Anthony John,** known as *Tony.* 1924–68, British comedian, noted for his radio series *Hancock's Half Hour.* **2. John.** 1737–93, American statesman; first signatory of the Declaration of Independence.

hand (hænd) n. **1.** the prehensile part of the body at the end of the arm, consisting of a thumb, four fingers, and a palm. Related adj.: **manual. 2.** the corresponding part in animals. **3.** something resembling this in shape or function. **4. a.** the cards dealt in one round of a card game. **b.** a player holding such cards. **c.** one round of a card game. **5.** agency or influence: *the hand of God.* **6.** a part in something done: *he had a hand in the victory.* **7.** assistance: *to give someone a hand.* **8.** a pointer on a dial, indicator, or gauge, esp. on a clock. **9.** acceptance or pledge of partnership, as in marriage. **10.** a position indicated by its location to the side of an object or the observer: *on the right hand.* **11.** a contrastive aspect, condition, etc.: *on the other hand.* **12.** source or origin: *a story heard at third hand.* **13.** a person, esp. one who creates something: *a good hand at painting.* **14.** a manual worker. **15.** a member of a ship's crew: *all hands on deck.* **16.** a person's handwriting: *the letter was in his own hand.* **17.** a round of applause: *give him a hand.* **18.** a characteristic way of doing something: *the hand of a master.* **19.** a unit of length equalling four inches, used for measuring the height of horses. **20.** a cluster of bananas. **21. a free hand.** freedom to do as desired. **22.** (*modifier*) **a.** of or involving the hand: *a hand grenade.* **b.** carried in or worn on the hand: *hand luggage.* **c.** operated by hand: *a hand drill.* **23.** (*in combination*) made by hand rather than machine: *hand-sewn.* **24. a heavy hand.** tyranny or oppression: *he ruled with a heavy hand.* **25. a high hand.** a dictatorial manner. **26. by hand. a.** by manual rather than mechanical means. **b.** by messenger or personally: *the letter was delivered by hand.* **27. force someone's hand.** to force someone to act. **28. from hand to mouth. a.** in poverty: *living from hand to mouth.* **b.** without preparation or planning. **29. hand and foot.** in all ways possible; completely: *they waited on him hand and foot.* **30. hand in glove.** in close association. **31. hand over fist.** steadily and quickly: *he makes money hand over fist.* **32. hold one's hand.** to stop or postpone a planned action or punishment. **33. hold someone's hand.** to support, help, or guide someone, esp. by giving sympathy. **34. in hand. a.** under control. **b.** receiving attention. **c.** available in reserve. **d.** with deferred payment: *he works a week in hand.* **35. keep one's hand in.** to continue or practise. **36. (near) at hand.** very close, esp. in time. **37. on hand.** close by; present. **38. out of hand. a.** beyond control. **b.** without reservation or deeper examination: *he condemned him out of hand.* **39. show one's hand.** to reveal one's stand, opinion, or plans. **40. take in hand.** to discipline; control. **41. throw one's hand in.** to give up a venture, game, etc. **42. to hand.** accessible. **43. try one's hand.** to attempt to do something. ~vb. (tr.) **44.** to transmit or offer by the hand or hands. **45.** to help or lead with the hand. *Naut.* to furl (a sail). **47. hand it to someone.** to give credit to someone. ~See also **hand down, hand in,** etc., **hands.** [OE *hand*] —**handless** adj.

handbag ('hænd,bæg) n. **1.** Also called: **bag, purse** (U.S. and Canad.), **pocketbook** (chiefly U.S.). a woman's small bag used to contain personal articles. **2.** a small suitcase that can be carried by hand.

handball ('hænd,bɔːl) n. **1.** a game in which two or four people strike a ball against a wall with the hand. **2.** the small hard rubber ball used. ~vb. **3.** *Australian Rules football.* to pass (the ball) with a blow of the fist.

handbarrow ('hænd,bærəʊ) n. a flat tray for transporting loads, usually carried by two men.

handbill ('hænd,bɪl) n. a small printed notice for distribution by hand.

handbook ('hænd,bʊk) n. a reference book listing brief facts on a subject or place or directions for maintenance or repair, as of a car.

handbrake ('hænd,breɪk) n. **1.** a brake operated by a hand lever. **2.** the lever that operates the handbrake.

handbreadth ('hænd,brɛtθ, -,brɛdθ) *or* **hand's-breadth** *n.* the width of a hand used as an indication of length.

h and c *adj. abbrev. for* hot and cold (water).

handcart ('hænd,kɑːt) *n.* a simple cart, usually with one or two wheels, pushed or drawn by hand.

handcraft ('hænd,krɑːft) *n.* **1.** another word for **handicraft.** ~*vb.* **2.** (*tr.*) to make by handicraft. — **'hand,crafted** *adj.*

handcuff ('hænd,kʌf) *vb.* **1.** (*tr.*) to put handcuffs on (a person); manacle. ~*n.* **2.** (*pl.*) a pair of locking metal rings joined by a short bar or chain for securing prisoners, etc.

hand down *vb.* (*tr., adv.*) **1.** to bequeath. **2.** to pass (an outgrown garment) on from one member of a family to a younger one. **3.** U.S. & Canad. law. to announce (a verdict).

-handed *adj.* of, for, or using a hand or hands as specified: *left-handed; a four-handed game of cards.*

Handel ('hændəl) *n.* **George Frederick.** German name *Georg Friedrich Händel.* 1685–1759, German composer, resident in England, noted particularly for his oratorios, including the *Messiah* (1741) and *Samson* (1743). Other works include over 40 operas, 12 concerti grossi, organ concertos, chamber and orchestral music, esp. *Water Music* (1717).

handful ('hændful) *n., pl.* **-fuls. 1.** the amount or number that can be held in the hand. **2.** a small number or quantity. **3.** Inf. a person or thing difficult to manage or control.

handgun ('hænd,gʌn) *n.* U.S. & Canad. a firearm that can be fired with one hand, such as a pistol.

handicap ('hændɪ,kæp) *n.* **1.** something that hampers or hinders. **2. a.** a contest, esp. a race, in which competitors are given advantages or disadvantages of weight, distance, etc., in an attempt to equalize their chances. **b.** the advantage or disadvantage prescribed. **3.** Golf. the number of strokes by which a player's averaged score exceeds par for the course. **4.** any disability or disadvantage resulting from physical, mental, or social impairment or abnormality. ~*vb.* **-capping, -capped.** (*tr.*) **5.** to be a hindrance or disadvantage to. **6.** to assign a handicap to. **7.** to organize (a contest) by handicapping. [C17: prob. from *hand in cap*, a lottery game in which players drew forfeits from a cap or deposited money in it] — **'hand i,capper** *n.*

handicapped ('hændɪ,kæpt) *adj.* **1. a.** physically or mentally disabled. **b.** (*as collective n.*; preceded by *the*): *the handicapped.* **2.** (of a competitor) assigned a handicap.

handicraft ('hændɪ,krɑːft) *n.* **1.** skill in working with the hands. **2.** a particular skill performed with the hands, such as weaving. **3.** the work so produced. ~Also called: **handcraft.** [C15: changed from HANDCRAFT through infl. of HANDIWORK]

hand in *vb.* (*tr., adv.*) to return or submit (something, such as an examination paper).

handiwork ('hændɪ,wɜːk) *n.* **1.** work produced by hand. **2.** the result of the action or endeavours of a person or thing. [OE *handgeweorc*, from HAND + *ge-* (collective prefix) + *weorc* WORK]

handkerchief ('hæŋkətʃɪf, -tʃiːf) *n.* a small square of soft absorbent material carried and used to wipe the nose, etc.

handle ('hændəl) *n.* **1.** the part of a utensil, drawer, etc., designed to be held in order to move, use, or pick up the object. **2.** N.Z. a glass beer mug with a handle. **3.** Sl. a title put before a person's name. **4.** CB radio. a slang name for **call sign. 5.** an excuse for doing something: *his background served as a handle for their mockery.* **6.** the quality, as of textiles, perceived by feeling. **7. fly off the handle.** Inf. to become suddenly extremely angry. ~*vb.* (*mainly tr.*) **8.** to hold, move, or touch with the hands. **9.** to operate using the hands: *the boy handled the reins well.* **10.** to control: *my wife handles my investments.* **11.** to manage successfully: *a secretary must be able to handle clients.* **12.** to discuss (a theme, subject, etc.). **13.** to deal with in a specified way: *I was handled with great tact.* **14.** to trade or deal in (specified merchandise). **15.** (*intr.*) to react in a specified way to operation: *the car handles well on bends.* [OE] — **'handled** *adj.* — **'handling** *n.*

handlebar moustache ('hændəl,bɑː) *n.* a bushy extended moustache with curled ends.

handlebars ('hændəl,bɑːz) *pl. n.* (*sometimes sing.*) a metal bar having its ends curved to form handles, used for steering a bicycle, etc.

handler ('hændlə) *n.* **1.** a person who trains and controls an animal, esp. a police dog. **2.** the trainer or second of a boxer.

handmade (,hænd'meɪd) *adj.* made by hand, not by machine, esp. with care or craftsmanship.

handmaiden ('hænd,meɪdən) *or* **handmaid** *n.* **1.** a person or thing that serves a useful but subordinate purpose. **2.** Arch. a female servant.

hand-me-down *n. Inf.* **1.** something, esp. an outgrown garment, passed down from one person to another. **2.** anything that has already been used by another.

hand-off *Rugby.* ~*n.* **1.** the act of warding off an opposing player with the open hand. ~*vb.* **hand off. 2.** (*tr., adv.*) to ward off thus.

hand on *vb.* (*tr., adv.*) to pass to the next in a succession.

hand organ *n.* another name for **barrel organ.**

hand-out *n.* **1.** clothing, food, or money given to a needy person. **2.** a leaflet, free sample, etc., given out to publicize something. **3.** a statement distributed to the press or an audience to confirm or replace an oral presentation. ~*vb.* **hand out. 4.** (*tr., adv.*) to distribute.

hand over *vb.* **1.** (*tr., adv.*) to surrender possession of; transfer. ~*n.* **handover. 2.** a transfer; surrender.

hand-pick *vb.* (*tr.*) to select with great care, as for a special job. — **,hand-'picked** *adj.*

handrail ('hænd,reɪl) *n.* a rail alongside a stairway, etc., to provide support.

hands (hændz) *pl. n.* **1.** power or keeping: *your welfare is in his hands.* **2.** Also called: **handling.** Soccer. the infringement of touching the ball with the hand or arm. **3. change hands.** to pass from the possession of one person to another. **4. hands down.** without effort; easily. **5. have one's hands full. a.** to be completely occupied. **b.** to be beset with problems. **6. have one's hands tied.** to be unable to act. **7. lay hands on** *or* **upon. a.** to get possession of. **b.** to beat up; assault. **c.** to find. **d.** Christianity. to confirm or ordain by the imposition of hands. **8. off one's hands.** for which one is no longer responsible. **9. on one's hands. a.** for which one is responsible: *I've got too much on my hands to help.* **b.** to spare: *time on my hands.* **10. wash one's hands of.** to have nothing more to do with; refuse to accept responsibility for.

handsaw ('hænd,sɔː) *n.* any saw for use in one hand only.

hand's-breadth *n.* another name for **handbreadth.**

handsel *or* **hansel** ('hænsəl) *Arch. or dialect.* ~*n.* **1.** a gift for good luck at the beginning of a new year, new venture, etc. ~*vb.* **-selling, -selled** *or* U.S. **-seling, -seled.** (*tr.*) **2.** to give a handsel to (a person). **3.** to inaugurate. [OE *handselen* delivery into the hand]

handset ('hænd,sɛt) *n.* a telephone mouthpiece and earpiece mounted as a single unit.

handshake ('hænd,ʃeɪk) *n.* the act of grasping and shaking a person's hand, as when being introduced or agreeing on a deal.

handsome ('hændsəm) *adj.* **1.** (of a man) good-looking. **2.** (of a woman) fine-looking in a dignified way. **3.** well-proportioned; stately: *a handsome room.* **4.** liberal: *a handsome allowance.* **5.** gracious or generous: *a handsome action.* [C15 *handsom* easily handled] — **'handsomely** *adv.* — **'handsomeness** *n.*

hands-on *adj.* involving practical experience of equipment, etc.: *hands-on training in computers.*

handspring ('hænd,sprɪŋ) *n.* a gymnastic feat in which a person starts from a standing position and leaps forwards or backwards into a handstand and then onto his feet.

handstand ('hænd,stænd) *n.* the act of supporting the body on the hands in an upside-down position.

hand-to-hand *adj., adv.* at close quarters.

hand-to-mouth *adj., adv.* with barely enough money or food to satisfy immediate needs.

handwork ('hænd,wɜːk) *n.* work done by hand rather than by machine. — **'hand,worked** *adj.*

handwriting ('hænd,raɪtɪŋ) *n.* **1.** writing by hand rather than by typing or printing. **2.** a person's characteristic writing style: *that is in my handwriting.* — **'hand,written** *adj.*

handy ('hændɪ) *adj.* **handier, handiest. 1.** conveniently within reach. **2.** easy to handle or use. **3.** skilful with one's hands. — **'handily** *adv.* — **'handiness** *n.*

Handy ('hændɪ) n. **W(illiam) C(hristopher).** 1873–1958, U.S. blues musician and songwriter, esp. noted for the song "St Louis Blues".

handyman ('hændɪ,mæn) n., pl. **-men.** a man employed to do or skilled in odd jobs, etc.

hanepoot ('hɑːnə,pɔːt) n. S. African. a kind of grape for eating or wine making. [from Du.]

hang (hæŋ) vb. **hanging, hung. 1.** to fasten or be fastened from above, esp. by a cord, chain, etc. **2.** to place or be placed in position as by a hinge so as to allow free movement: to hang a door. **3.** (intr.; sometimes foll. by over) to be suspended; hover: a pall of smoke hung over the city. **4.** (intr.; sometimes foll. by over) to threaten. **5.** (intr.) to be or remain doubtful (esp. in **hang in the balance**). **6.** (p.t. & p.p. **hanged**) to suspend or be suspended by the neck until dead. **7.** (tr.) to decorate, furnish, or cover with something suspended. **8.** (tr.) to fasten to a wall: to hang wallpaper. **9.** to exhibit or be exhibited in an art gallery, etc. **10.** to droop or allow to droop: to hang one's head. **11.** (of cloth, clothing, etc.) to drape, fall, or flow: her skirt hangs well. **12.** (tr.) to suspend (game such as pheasant) so that it becomes slightly decomposed and therefore more tasty. **13.** (of a jury) to prevent or be prevented from reaching a verdict. **14.** (p.t. & p.p. **hanged**) Sl. to damn or be damned: used in mild curses or interjections. **15.** (intr.) to pass slowly (esp. in **time hangs heavily**). **16. hang fire.** to be delayed or to procrastinate. ~n. **17.** the way in which something hangs. **18.** (usually used with a negative) Sl. a damn: I don't care a hang. **19. get the hang of.** Inf. **a.** to understand the technique of doing something. **b.** to perceive the meaning of. ~See also **hang about, hang back,** etc. [OE hangian]

hang about or **around** vb. (intr.) **1.** to waste time; loiter. **2.** (adv.; foll. by with) to frequent the company of (someone).

hangar ('hæŋə) n. a large building for storing and maintaining aircraft. [C19: from F: shed, ?from Med. L angārium shed used as a smithy, from ?]

hang back vb. (intr., adv.; often foll. by from) to be reluctant to go forward or carry on.

Hangchow n. a variant transliteration of the Chinese name for **Hangzhou.**

hangdog ('hæŋ,dɒg) adj. downcast, furtive, or guilty in appearance or manner.

hanger ('hæŋə) n. **1. a.** any support, such as a peg or loop, on or by which something may be hung. **b.** See **coat hanger. 2. a.** a person who hangs something. **b.** (in combination): paperhanger. **3.** a type of dagger worn on a sword belt. **4.** Brit. a wood on a steep hillside.

hanger-on n., pl. **hangers-on.** a sycophantic follower or dependant.

hang-glider n. an unpowered aircraft consisting of a large cloth wing stretched over a light framework from which the pilot hangs in a harness. —'**hang-,gliding** n.

hangi ('hʌŋi) n. N.Z. **1.** an open-air cooking pit. **2.** the food cooked in it. **3.** the social gathering at the resultant meal. [from Maori]

hang in vb. (intr., prep.) Inf., chiefly U.S. & Canad. to persist: just hang in there for a bit longer.

hanging ('hæŋɪŋ) n. **1. a.** the putting of a person to death by suspending the body by the neck. **b.** (as modifier): a hanging offence. **2.** (often pl.) a decorative drapery hung on a wall or over a window. ~adj. **3.** not supported from below; suspended. **4.** undecided; still under discussion. **5.** projecting downwards; overhanging. **6.** situated on a steep slope. **7.** (prenominal) given to issuing death sentences: a hanging judge.

Hanging Gardens of Babylon n. (in ancient Babylon) gardens, probably planted on terraces of a ziggurat: one of the Seven Wonders of the World.

hanging valley n. Geog. a tributary valley entering a main valley at a much higher level because of overdeepening of the main valley, esp. by glacial erosion.

hangman ('hæŋmən) n., pl. **-men.** an official who carries out a sentence of hanging.

hangnail ('hæŋ,neɪl) n. a piece of skin torn away from, but still attached to, the base or side of a fingernail. [C17: from OE angnægl, from enge tight + nægl nail; infl. by HANG]

hang on vb. (intr.) **1.** (adv.) to continue or persist, esp. with effort or difficulty. **2.** (adv.) to grasp or hold. **3.** (prep.) to depend on: everything hangs on this deal. **4.**

(prep.) Also: **hang onto, hang upon.** to listen attentively to. **5.** (adv.) Inf. to wait: hang on for a few minutes.

hang out vb. (adv.) **1.** to suspend, be suspended, or lean. **2.** (intr.) Inf. to frequent a place. **3. let it all hang out.** Inf., chiefly U.S. **a.** to relax to an unassuming way. **b.** to act or speak freely. ~n. **hang-out. 4.** Inf. a place that one frequents.

hangover ('hæŋ,əʊvə) n. **1.** the delayed aftereffects of drinking too much alcohol. **2.** a person or thing left over from or influenced by a past age.

hang together vb. (intr., adv.) **1.** to be cohesive or united. **2.** to be consistent: your statements don't quite hang together.

Hanguk ('hæn'gʊk) n. the Korean name for **South Korea.**

hang up vb. (adv.) **1.** (tr.) to put on a hook, hanger, etc. **2.** to replace (a telephone receiver) on its cradle at the end of a conversation. **3.** (tr.; usually passive; usually foll. by on) Inf. to cause to have an emotional or psychological preoccupation or problem: he's really hung up on his mother. ~n. **hang-up.** Inf. **4.** an emotional or psychological preoccupation or problem. **5.** a persistent cause of annoyance.

Hangzhou ('hæŋ'dʒəʊ) or **Hangchow** n. a port in E China, capital of Zhejiang province, on **Hangzhou Bay** (an inlet of the East China Sea), at the foot of the Eye of Heaven Mountains: regarded by Marco Polo as the finest city in the world; seat of two universities (1927, 1959). Pop.: 1 250 000 (1986).

hank (hæŋk) n. **1.** a loop, coil, or skein, as of rope. **2.** Naut. a ringlike fitting that can be opened to admit a stay for attaching the luff of a sail. **3.** a unit of measurement of cloth, yarn, etc., such as a length of 840 yards (767 m) of cotton or 560 yards (512 m) of worsted yarn. [C13: from ON]

hanker ('hæŋkə) vb. (foll. by for, after, or an infinitive) to have a yearning. [C17: prob. from Du. dialect hankeren] —'**hankering** n.

Hankow or **Han-k'ou** ('hæn'kaʊ) n. a former city in SE China, in SE Hubei at the confluence of the Han and Yangtze Rivers: one of the Han Cities; merged with Hanyang and Wuchang in 1950 to form the conurbation of Wuhan.

hanky or **hankie** ('hæŋkɪ) n., pl. **hankies.** Inf. short for **handkerchief.**

hanky-panky ('hæŋkɪ'pæŋkɪ) n. Inf. **1.** dubious or foolish behaviour. **2.** illicit sexual relations. [C19: var. of HOCUS-POCUS]

Hannah ('hænə) n. Old Testament. the woman who gave birth to Samuel (I Samuel 1–2).

Hannibal ('hænɪbəl) n. 247–182 B.C., Carthaginian general; son of Hamilcar Barca. He commanded the Carthaginian army in the Second Punic War (218–201). After capturing Sagunto in Spain, he invaded Italy (218), crossing the Alps with an army of about 40 000 men and defeating the Romans at Trasimene (217) and Cannae (216). In 203 he was recalled to defend Carthage and was defeated by Scipio at Zama (202). He was later forced into exile and committed suicide to avoid capture.

Hannover (German ha'noːfər) n. a city in N West Germany, capital of Lower Saxony: capital of the kingdom of Hannover (1815–66); situated on the Mittelland canal. Pop.: 506 400 (1986). English spelling: **Hanover.**

Hanoi (hæ'nɔɪ) n. the capital of Vietnam, on the Red River: became capital of Tonkin in 1802, of French Indochina in 1887, of Vietnam in 1945, and of North Vietnam (1954–75); university (1917); industrial centre. Pop.: 2 674 400 (1983 est.).

Hanover[1] ('hænəʊvə) n. the English spelling of **Hannover.**

Hanover[2] ('hænəʊvə) n. **1.** a princely house of Germany (1692–1815), the head of which succeeded to the British throne as George I in 1714. **2.** the royal house of Britain (1714–1901). —,**Hano'verian** adj.

Hanratty (hæn'rætɪ) n. James. 1936–62, Englishman executed, despite conflicting evidence, for a murder on the A6 road. Subsequent public concern played a major part in the abolition of capital punishment in Britain.

Hansard ('hænsɑːd) n. **1.** the official verbatim report of the proceedings of the British Parliament. **2.** a similar report kept by the Canadian House of Commons and other legislative bodies. [C19: after L. Hansard (1752–1828) and his descendants, who compiled the reports until 1889]

Hanse (hæns) n. **1.** a medieval guild of merchants. **2.** a fee paid by the new members of a medieval trading guild.

3. another name for the **Hanseatic League.** [C12: of Gmc origin] —**Hanseatic** (ˌhænsɪˈætɪk) adj.

Hanseatic League n. a commercial organization of towns in N Germany formed in the mid-14th century to protect and control trade.

hansel ('hænsᵊl) n., vb. a variant spelling of **handsel.**

hansom ('hænsəm) n. (sometimes cap.) a two-wheeled one-horse carriage with a fixed hood. The driver sits on a high outside seat at the rear. Also called: **hansom cab.** [C19: after its designer J. A. Hansom (1803–82)]

Hants (hænts) abbrev. for Hampshire.

Hanukkah ('hɑːnəkə, -nʊˌkɑː) n. a variant of **Chanukah.**

Hanuman (ˌhʌnʊˈmɑːn) n. **1.** (pl. -mans) another word for **entellus** (the monkey). **2.** the monkey chief of Hindu mythology. [from Hindi, from Sansk. hanumant having (conspicuous) jaws, from hanu jaw]

Hanyang or **Han-yang** ('hænˈjæŋ) n. a former city in SE China, in SE Hubei at the confluence of the Han and Yangtze Rivers: one of the Han Cities; merged with Hankow and Wuchang in 1950 to form the conurbation of Wuhan.

hap (hæp) Arch. ~n. **1.** luck; chance. **2.** an occurrence. ~vb. **happing, happed. 3.** (intr.) to happen. [C13: from ON happ good luck]

ha'penny ('heɪpnɪ) n., pl. -nies. Brit. a variant spelling of **halfpenny.**

haphazard (hæpˈhæzəd) adv., adj. **1.** at random. ~adj. **2.** careless; slipshod. —**hapˈhazardly** adv. —**hapˈhazardness** n.

hapless ('hæplɪs) adj. unfortunate; wretched. —**haplessly** adv. —**haplessness** n.

haplography (hæpˈlɒɡrəfɪ) n., pl. -phies. the accidental omission of a letter or syllable which recurs, as in spelling endodontics as endontics. [C19: from Gk, from haplous single + -GRAPHY]

haploid ('hæplɔɪd) Biol. ~adj. **1.** (esp. of gametes) having a single set of unpaired chromosomes. ~n. **2.** a haploid cell or organism. [C20: from Gk haploeidēs, from haplous single]

haplology (hæpˈlɒlədʒɪ) n. omission of a repeated occurrence of a sound or syllable in fluent speech, as for example in the pronunciation of library as ('laɪbrɪ).

haply ('hæplɪ) adv. (sentence modifier) an archaic word for **perhaps.**

happen ('hæpᵊn) vb. **1.** (intr.) to take place; occur. **2.** (intr.; foll. by to) (of some unforeseen event, esp. death) to fall to the lot (of): if anything happens to me it'll be your fault. **3.** (tr.) to chance (to be or do something): I happen to know him. **4.** (tr.; takes a clause as object) to be the case, esp. by chance: it happens that I know him. ~adv., sentence substitute. **5.** N English dialect. another word for **perhaps.** [C14: see HAP, -EN¹]

▷ **Usage.** See at **occur.**

happening ('hæpənɪŋ, 'hæpnɪŋ) n. **1.** an event. **2.** an improvised or spontaneous performance consisting of bizarre events.

happen on or **upon** vb. (intr.; prep.) to find by chance.

happy ('hæpɪ) adj. -pier, -piest. **1.** feeling or expressing joy; pleased. **2.** causing joy or gladness. **3.** fortunate: the happy position of not having to work. **4.** aptly expressed; appropriate: a happy turn of phrase. **5.** (postpositive) Inf. slightly intoxicated. [C14: see HAP, -Y¹] —**happily** adv. —**happiness** n.

happy event n. Inf. the birth of a child.

happy-go-lucky adj. carefree or easy-going.

happy hour n. a time when some pubs or bars sell drinks at reduced prices.

happy hunting ground n. **1.** (in Amerind legend) the paradise to which a person passes after death. **2.** a productive or profitable area to explore: jumble sales can be a happy hunting grounds.

happy medium n. a course or state that avoids extremes.

Hapsburg ('hæps,bɜːɡ) n. a German princely family founded by Albert, count of Hapsburg (1153). From 1440 to 1806, the Hapsburgs wore the imperial crown of the Holy Roman Empire almost uninterruptedly. They also provided rulers for Austria, Spain, Hungary, Bohemia, etc. The line continued as the royal house of **Hapsburg-Lorraine,** ruling in Austria (1806–48) and Austria-Hungary (1848–1918). German name: **Habsburg.**

haptic ('hæptɪk) adj. relating to or based on the sense of touch. [C19: from Gk, from haptein to touch]

hapuka or **hapuku** (hə'puːkə, 'hɑːpʊkə) n. N.Z. another name for **groper.** [from Maori]

hara-kiri (ˌhærəˈkɪrɪ) or **hari-kari** (ˌhærɪˈkɑːrɪ) n. (formerly, in Japan) ritual suicide by disembowelment when disgraced or under sentence of death. [C19: from Japanese taboo sl., from hara belly + kiri cut]

Harald I ('hærəld) n. called Harald Fairhair. ?850–933, first king of Norway: his rule caused emigration to the British Isles.

harangue (həˈræŋ) vb. **1.** to address (a person or crowd) in an angry, vehement, or forcefully persuasive way. ~n. **2.** a loud, forceful, or angry speech. [C15: from OF, from Olt. aringa public speech, prob. of Gmc origin] —**haˈranguer** n.

Harappa (hə'ræpə) n. an ancient city in the Punjab in NW Pakistan: one of the centres of the Indus civilization that flourished from 2500 to 1700 B.C.; probably destroyed by Indo-European invaders. —**Haˈrappan** adj., n.

Harar or **Harrar** ('hɑːrə) n. a city in E Ethiopia: former capital of the Muslim state of Adal. Pop.: 62 160 (1984).

Harare (hə'rɑːrɪ) n. the capital of Zimbabwe, in the northeast: University of Zimbabwe (1957); industrial and commercial centre. Pop.: 681 000 (1983). Former name (until 1982): **Salisbury.**

harass ('hærəs, hə'ræs) vb. (tr.) to trouble, torment, or confuse by continual persistent attacks, questions, etc. [C17: from F harasser, var. of OF harer to set a dog on, of Gmc origin] —**harassed** adj. —**harassment** n.

Harbin (hɑːˈbiːn, -ˈbɪn) n. a city in NE China, capital of Heilongjiang province on the Songhua River: founded by the Russians in 1897; centre of tsarist activities after the October Revolution in Russia (1917). Pop.: 2 630 000 (1986). Also called: **Ha-erh-pin.**

harbinger ('hɑːbɪndʒə) n. **1.** a person or thing that announces or indicates the approach of something; forerunner. ~vb. **2.** (tr.) to announce the approach or arrival of. [C12: from OF herbergere, from herberge lodging, from OSaxon]

harbour or U.S. **harbor** ('hɑːbə) n. **1.** a sheltered port. **2.** a place of refuge or safety. ~vb. **3.** (tr.) to give shelter to: to harbour a criminal. **4.** (tr.) to maintain secretly: to harbour a grudge. **5.** to shelter (a vessel) in a harbour or (of a vessel) to seek shelter. [OE herebeorg, from here army + beorg shelter]

harbourage or U.S. **harborage** ('hɑːbərɪdʒ) n. shelter or refuge, as for a ship.

harbour master n. an official in charge of a harbour.

hard (hɑːd) adj. **1.** firm or rigid. **2.** toughened; not soft or smooth: hard skin. **3.** difficult to do or accomplish: a hard task. **4.** difficult to understand: a hard question. **5.** showing or requiring considerable effort or application: hard work. **6.** demanding: a hard master. **7.** harsh; cruel: a hard fate. **8.** inflicting pain, sorrow, or hardship: hard times. **9.** tough or violent: a hard man. **10.** forceful: a hard knock. **11.** cool or uncompromising: we took a long hard look at our profit factor. **12.** indisputable; real: hard facts. **13.** Chem. (of water) impairing the formation of a lather by soap. **14.** practical, shrewd, or calculating: he is a hard man in business. **15.** harsh: hard light. **16. a.** (of currency) high and stable in exchange value. **b.** (of credit) difficult to obtain; tight. **17.** (of alcoholic drink) being a spirit rather than a wine, beer, etc. **18.** (of a drug) highly addictive. **19.** Physics. (of radiation) having high energy and the ability to penetrate solids. **20.** Chiefly U.S. (of goods) durable. **21.** short for **hard-core. 22.** Phonetics. (not in technical usage) denoting the consonants c and g when they are pronounced as in cat and got. **23. a.** heavily fortified. **b.** (of nuclear missiles) located underground. **24.** politically extreme: the hard left. **25.** Brit. & N.Z. inf. incorrigible or disreputable (esp. in **a hard case**). **26. a hard nut to crack. a.** a person not easily won over. **b.** a thing not easily done or understood. **27. hard by.** close by. **28. hard of hearing.** slightly deaf. **29. hard up.** Inf. **a.** in need of money. **b.** (foll. by for) in great need (of): hard up for suggestions. ~adv. **30.** with great energy, force, or vigour: the team always played hard. **31.** as far as possible: hard left. **32.** earnestly or intently: she thought hard about the formula. **33.** with great intensity: his son's death hit him hard. **34.** (foll. by on, upon, by, or after) close; near: hard on his heels. **35.** (foll. by at) assiduously; devotedly. **36. a.** with effort or difficulty: their victory was hard won. **b.** (in combination): hard-earned. **37.** slowly: prejudice dies hard. **38. go hard with.** to cause pain or difficulty to (someone). **39. hard put (to it).** scarcely having the capacity (to do something). ~*n.* **40.** *Brit.* a roadway across a foreshore. **41.** *Sl.* hard labour. **42.** *Taboo sl.* an erection of the penis (esp. in **get** or **have a hard on**). [OE *heard*] — **'hardness** *n.*

hard and fast *adj.* (**hard-and-fast** *when prenominal*). (of rules, etc.) invariable or strict.

hardback ('hɑːd,bæk) *n.* **1.** a book with covers of cloth, cardboard, or leather. ~*adj.* **2.** Also: **casebound, hardbound, hardcover.** of or denoting a hardback or the publication of hardbacks.

hard-bitten *adj. Inf.* tough and realistic.

hardboard ('hɑːd,bɔːd) *n.* a thin stiff sheet made of compressed sawdust and woodchips bound together under heat and pressure.

hard-boiled *adj.* **1.** (of an egg) boiled until solid. **2.** *Inf.* **a.** tough, realistic. **b.** cynical.

hard cash *n.* money or payment in money, as opposed to payment by cheque, credit, etc.

hard coal *n.* another name for **anthracite.**

hard copy *n.* computer output printed on paper, as contrasted with machine-readable output such as magnetic tape.

hard core *n.* **1.** the members of a group who form an intransigent nucleus resisting change. **2.** material, such as broken stones, used to form a foundation for a road, etc. ~*adj.* **hard-core. 3.** (of pornography) describing or depicting sexual acts in explicit detail. **4.** completely established in a belief, etc.: *hard-core Communists.*

hard disk *n. Computers.* an inflexible disk in a sealed container, usually with a storage capacity of several megabytes.

Hardecanute ('hɑːdɪkə,njuːt) *n.* a variant of **Harthacanute.**

harden ('hɑːd²n) *vb.* **1.** to make or become hard or harder; freeze, stiffen, or set. **2.** to make or become tough or unfeeling. **3.** to make or become stronger or firmer. **4.** (*intr.*) *Commerce.* **a.** (of prices, a market, etc.) to cease to fluctuate. **b.** (of price) to rise higher. — **'hardener** *n.*

Hardenberg (*German* 'hɑːdənbɛrk) *n.* **Friedrich von** ('friːdrɪç fɔn). the original name of **Novalis.**

hardened ('hɑːd²nd) *adj.* **1.** rigidly set, as in a mode of behaviour. **2.** toughened; seasoned.

harden off *vb.* (*tr., adv.*) to cause (plants) to become resistant to cold, frost, etc., by gradually exposing them to such conditions.

hard feeling *n.* (*often pl.; often used with a negative*) resentment; ill will: *no hard feelings?*

hard hat *n.* **1.** a hat made of a hard material for protection, worn esp. by construction workers. **2.** *Inf., chiefly U.S.* a construction worker.

hard-headed *adj.* tough, realistic, or shrewd; not moved by sentiment.

hardhearted (,hɑːd'hɑːtɪd) *adj.* unkind or intolerant. — ,**hard'heartedness** *n.*

Hardicanute ('hɑːdɪkə,njuːt) *n.* a variant of **Harthacanute.**

Hardie ('hɑːdɪ) *n.* (**James**) **Keir** (kɪə). 1856–1915, British Labour leader and politician, born in Scotland; the first parliamentary leader of the Labour Party.

hardihood ('hɑːdɪ,hʊd) *n.* courage or daring.

Harding ('hɑːdɪŋ) *n.* **Warren G(amaliel).** 1865–1923, 29th president of the U.S. (1921–23).

hard labour *n. Criminal law.* (formerly) the penalty of compulsory physical labour imposed in addition to a sentence of imprisonment.

hard landing *n.* a landing by a rocket or spacecraft in which the vehicle is destroyed on impact.

hard line *n.* an uncompromising course or policy. — ,**hard'liner** *n.*

hardly ('hɑːdlɪ) *adv.* **1.** scarcely; barely: *we hardly knew the family.* **2.** only just: *he could hardly hold the cup.* **3.** Often used ironically. not at all: *he will hardly incriminate himself.* **4.** with difficulty. **5.** *Rare.* harshly or cruelly.

▷ **Usage.** Since *hardly, scarcely,* and *barely* already have negative force, it is redundant to use another negative in the same clause: *he had hardly had* (not *he hadn't hardly had*) *time to think.*

hard-nosed *adj. Inf.* tough, shrewd, and practical.

hard pad *n.* (in dogs) an abnormal increase in the thickness of the foot pads: one of the clinical signs of canine distemper. See **distemper**[1].

hard palate *n.* the anterior bony portion of the roof of the mouth.

hardpan ('hɑːd,pæn) *n.* a hard impervious layer of clay below the soil.

hard paste *n.* **a.** porcelain made with kaolin and petuntse, of Chinese origin and made in Europe from the early 18th century. **b.** (*as modifier*): *hard-paste porcelain.*

hard-pressed *adj.* **1.** in difficulties. **2.** subject to severe competition or attack. **3.** closely pursued.

hard rock *n.* rhythmically simple rock music that is very loud.

hard sauce *n.* another name for **brandy butter.**

hard science *n.* one of the natural or physical sciences, such as physics, chemistry, biology, geology, or astronomy. — **hard scientist** *n.*

hard sell *n.* an aggressive insistent technique of selling or advertising.

hard-shell *adj.* also **hard-shelled. 1.** *Zool.* having a shell or carapace that is thick, heavy, or hard. **2.** *U.S.* strictly orthodox.

hardship ('hɑːdʃɪp) *n.* **1.** conditions of life difficult to endure. **2.** something that causes suffering or privation.

hard shoulder *n. Brit.* a surfaced verge running along the edge of a motorway for emergency stops.

hardtack ('hɑːd,tæk) *n.* a kind of hard saltless biscuit, formerly eaten esp. by sailors as a staple aboard ship. Also called: **ship's biscuit, sea biscuit.**

hardtop ('hɑːd,tɒp) *n.* a car with a metal or plastic roof that is sometimes detachable.

hardware ('hɑːd,wɛə) *n.* **1.** metal tools, implements, etc., esp. cutlery or cooking utensils. **2.** *Computers.* the physical equipment used in a computer system, such as the central processing unit, peripheral devices, and memory. Cf. **software. 3.** mechanical equipment, components, etc. **4.** heavy military equipment, such as tanks and missiles. **5.** *Inf.* a gun.

hard-wired *adj.* (of a circuit or instruction) permanently wired into a computer, replacing separate software.

hardwood ('hɑːd,wʊd) *n.* **1.** the wood of any of numerous broad-leaved trees, such as oak, beech, ash, etc., as distinguished from the wood of a conifer. **2.** any tree from which this wood is obtained.

hardy ('hɑːdɪ) *adj.* **-dier, -diest. 1.** having or demanding a tough constitution; robust. **2.** bold; courageous. **3.** foolhardy; rash. **4.** (of plants) able to live out of doors throughout the winter. [C13: from OF *hardi,* p.p. of *hardir* to become bold, of Gmc origin; cf. OE *hierdan* to HARDEN, ON *hertha,* OHG *herten*] — **'hardily** *adv.* — **'hardiness** *n.*

Hardy ('hɑːdɪ) *n.* **Thomas.** 1840–1928, English novelist and poet. Most of his novels are set in his native Dorset (part of his fictional Wessex) and include *Far from the Madding Crowd* (1874), *The Return of the Native* (1878), *The Mayor of Casterbridge* (1886), *Tess of the d'Urbervilles* (1891), and *Jude the Obscure* (1895), after which his work consisted chiefly of verse.

hare (hɛə) *n., pl.* **hares** or **hare. 1.** a solitary mammal which is larger than a rabbit, has longer ears and legs, and lives in a shallow nest (form). **2. run with the hare and hunt with the hounds.** to be on good terms with both sides. **3. start a hare.** to raise a topic for conversation. ~*vb.* **4.** (*intr.;* often foll. by *off, after,* etc.) *Brit. inf.* to run fast or wildly. [OE *hara*] — **'hare,like** *adj.*

hare and hounds *n.* (*functioning as sing.*) a game in which certain players (**hares**) run across country scattering pieces of paper that the other players (**hounds**) follow in an attempt to catch the hares.

harebell ('hɛə,bɛl) *n.* a N temperate plant having slender stems and leaves, and bell-shaped blue flowers.

harebrained *or* **hairbrained** ('hɛə,breɪnd) *adj.* rash, foolish, or badly thought out.

Hare Krishna ('hɑːrɪ 'krɪʃnə) *n.* **1.** a Hindu sect devoted to a form of Hinduism (**Krishna Consciousness**) based on the worship of the god Krishna. **2.** (*pl.* **Hare Krishnas**) a member or follower of this sect. [C20: from Hindi, literally: Lord Krishna (vocative): the opening words of a sacred verse often chanted in public by adherents of the movement]

harelip ('hɛə,lɪp) *n.* a congenital cleft or fissure in the midline of the upper lip, often occurring with cleft palate. — **'hare,lipped** *adj.*

harem ('hɛərəm, hɑː'riːm) *or* **hareem** (hɑː'riːm) *n.* **1.** the part of an Oriental house reserved strictly for wives, concubines, etc. **2.** a Muslim's wives and concubines collectively. **3.** a group of female animals that are the mates of a single male. [C17: from Ar. *harīm* forbidden (place)]

hare's-foot *n.* a plant that grows on sandy soils in Europe and NW Asia and has downy heads of white or pink flowers.

Hargeisa (haˈgeɪsə) *n.* a city in NW Somalia: former capital of British Somaliland (1941–60); trading centre for nomadic herders. Pop.: 400 000 (1987 est.).

Hargreaves (ˈhɑːgriːvz) *n.* **James.** died 1778, English inventor of the spinning jenny.

haricot (ˈhærɪkəʊ) *n.* a variety of French bean with light-coloured edible seeds, which can be dried and stored. [C17: from F, ?from Amerind]

Harijan (ˈhʌrɪdʒən) *n.* a member of certain classes in India, formerly considered inferior and untouchable. [Hindi, lit.: man of God (so called by Mahatma Gandhi)]

hari-kari (ˌhærɪˈkɑːrɪ) *n.* a non-Japanese variant spelling of **hara-kiri.**

Haringey (ˈhærɪŋˌgeɪ) *n.* a borough of N Greater London. Pop.: 196 100 (1986 est.).

hark (hɑːk) *vb.* (*intr., usually imperative*) to listen; pay attention. [OE *heorcnian* to HEARKEN]

hark back *vb.* (*intr., adv.*) to return to an earlier subject in speech or thought.

harken (ˈhɑːkən) *vb.* a variant spelling (esp. U.S.) of **hearken.** — **ˈharkener** *n.*

harl (hɑːl) *n. Angling.* a variant of **herl.**

Harlem (ˈhɑːləm) *n.* a district of New York City, in NE Manhattan: now largely a Black ghetto.

harlequin (ˈhɑːlɪkwɪn) *n.* **1.** (*sometimes cap.*) *Theatre.* a stock comic character originating in the commedia dell'arte; the foppish lover of Columbine in the English harlequinade. He is usually represented in diamond-patterned multicoloured tights, wearing a black mask. **2.** a clown or buffoon. ~*adj.* **3.** varied in colour or decoration. [C16: from OF *Herlequin, Hellequin* leader of band of demon horsemen]

harlequinade (ˌhɑːlɪkwɪˈneɪd) *n.* **1.** (*sometimes cap.*) *Theatre.* a play in which harlequin has a leading role. **2.** buffoonery.

Harley (ˈhɑːlɪ) *n.* **Robert,** 1st Earl of Oxford. 1661–1724, British statesman; head of the government (1710–14), negotiating the treaty of Utrecht (1713).

Harley Street *n.* a street in central London famous for its large number of medical specialists' consulting rooms.

harlot (ˈhɑːlət) *n.* a prostitute. [C13: from OF *herlot* rascal, from ?] — **ˈharlotry** *n.*

Harlow[1] (ˈhɑːləʊ) *n.* a town in SE England, in W Essex: designated a new town in 1947, with a planned population of 80 000. Pop.: 79 276 (1981).

Harlow[2] (ˈhɑːləʊ) *n.* **Jean,** real name *Harlean Carpentier.* 1911–37, U.S. film actress, whose films include *Hell's Angels* (1930), *Red Dust* (1932), and *Bombshell* (1933).

harm (hɑːm) *n.* **1.** physical or mental injury. **2.** moral wrongdoing. ~*vb.* **3.** (*tr.*) to injure physically, morally, or mentally. [OE *hearm*]

harmattan (hɑːˈmætᵊn) *n.* a dry dusty wind from the Sahara blowing towards the W African coast. [C17: from native African language *haramata,* ?from Ar. *harām* forbidden thing; see HAREM]

harmful (ˈhɑːmfʊl) *adj.* causing or tending to cause harm; injurious. — **ˈharmfully** *adv.*

harmless (ˈhɑːmlɪs) *adj.* not causing or tending to cause harm. — **ˈharmlessly** *adv.*

harmonic (hɑːˈmɒnɪk) *adj.* **1.** of, producing, or characterized by harmony; harmonious. **2.** *Music.* of or belonging to harmony. **3.** *Maths.* **a.** capable of expression in the form of sine and cosine functions. **b.** of or relating to numbers whose reciprocals form an arithmetic progression. **4.** *Physics.* of or concerned with a harmonic or harmonics. ~*n.* **5.** *Physics, music.* a component of a periodic quantity, such as a musical tone, with a frequency that is an integral multiple of the fundamental frequency. **6.** *Music.* (not in technical use) overtone. ~*See* also **harmonics.** [C16: from L *harmonicus* relating to HARMONY] — **harˈmonically** *adv.*

harmonica (hɑːˈmɒnɪkə) *n.* **1.** a small wind instrument in which reeds of graduated lengths set into a metal plate enclosed in a narrow oblong box are made to vibrate by blowing and suction. **2.** See **glass harmonica.** [C18: from L *harmonicus* relating to HARMONY]

harmonic analysis *n.* the representation of a periodic function by means of the summation and integration of simple trigonometric functions.

harmonic mean *n.* the reciprocal of the arithmetic mean of the reciprocals of a set of specified numbers: the harmonic mean of 2, 3, and 4 is $3/(\frac{1}{2} + \frac{1}{3} + \frac{1}{4}) = 36/13$.

harmonic minor scale *n. Music.* a minor scale modified from the natural by the sharpening of the seventh degree.

harmonic motion *n.* a periodic motion in which the displacement is symmetrical about a point or a periodic motion that is composed of such motions.

harmonic progression *n.* a sequence of numbers whose reciprocals form an arithmetic progression, as $1, \frac{1}{2}, \frac{3}{4}, \ldots$

harmonics (hɑːˈmɒnɪks) *n.* **1.** (*functioning as sing.*) the science of musical sounds and their acoustic properties. **2.** (*functioning as pl.*) the overtones of a fundamental note, as produced by lightly touching the string of a stringed instrument at one of its node points while playing.

harmonic series *n.* **1.** *Maths.* a series whose terms are in harmonic progression, as in $1 + \frac{1}{2} + \frac{3}{4} + \ldots$. **2.** *Acoustics.* the series of tones with frequencies strictly related to one another and to the fundamental tone, as obtained by touching lightly the node points of a string while playing it.

harmonious (hɑːˈməʊnɪəs) *adj.* **1.** (esp. of colours or sounds) fitting together well. **2.** having agreement. **3.** tuneful or melodious.

harmonist (ˈhɑːmənɪst) *n.* **1.** a person skilled in the art and techniques of harmony. **2.** a person who combines and collates parallel narratives.

harmonium (hɑːˈməʊnɪəm) *n.* a musical keyboard instrument in which air from pedal-operated bellows causes the reeds to vibrate. [C19: from F, from *harmonie* HARMONY]

harmonize *or* **-nise** (ˈhɑːməˌnaɪz) *vb.* **1.** to make or become harmonious. **2.** (*tr.*) *Music.* to provide a harmony for (a tune, etc.). **3.** (*intr.*) to sing in harmony, as with other singers. **4.** to collate parallel narratives. — **ˌharmoniˈzation** *or* **-niˈsation** *n.*

harmony (ˈhɑːmənɪ) *n., pl.* **-nies. 1.** agreement in action, opinion, feeling, etc. **2.** order or congruity of parts to their whole or to one another. **3.** agreeable sounds. **4.** *Music.* **a.** any combination of notes sounded simultaneously. **b.** the vertically represented structure of a piece of music. Cf. **melody** (sense 1b). **c.** the art or science concerned with combinations of chords. **5.** a collation of parallel narratives, esp. of the four Gospels. [C14: from L *harmonia* concord of sounds, from Gk: harmony, from *harmos* a joint]

Harmsworth (ˈhɑːmzwɜːθ) *n.* **1. Alfred Charles William.** See (Viscount) **Northcliffe. 2. Harold Sydney.** See (1st Viscount) **Rothermere.**

harness (ˈhɑːnɪs) *n.* **1.** an arrangement of straps fitted to a draught animal in order that the animal can be attached to and pull a cart. **2.** something resembling this, esp. for attaching something to the body: *a parachute harness.* **3.** *Weaving.* the part of a loom that raises and lowers the warp threads. **4.** *Arch.* armour. **5. in harness.** at one's routine work. ~*vb.* (*tr.*) **6.** to put a harness on (a horse). **7.** (usually foll. by *to*) to attach (a draught animal) to (a cart, etc.). **8.** to control so as to employ the energy or potential power of: *to harness the atom.* **9.** to equip with armour. [C13: from OF *harneis* baggage, prob. from ON *hernest* (unattested), from *herr* army + *nest* provisions] — **ˈharnesser** *n.*

harness race *n. Horse racing.* a trotting or pacing race for horses pulling sulkies.

Harney Peak (ˈhɑːnɪ) *n.* a mountain in SW South Dakota: the highest peak in the Black Hills. Height: 2207 m (7242 ft.).

Harold I (ˈhærəld) *n.* surname *Harefoot.* died 1040, king of England (1037–40); son of Canute.

Harold II *n.* ?1022–66, king of England (1066); son of Earl Godwin and successor of Edward the Confessor. His claim to the throne was disputed by William the Conqueror, who defeated him at the Battle of Hastings (1066).

harp (hɑːp) *n.* **1.** a large triangular plucked stringed instrument consisting of a soundboard connected to an upright pillar by means of a curved crossbar from which the strings extend downwards. ~*vb.* (*intr.*) **2.** to play the harp. **3.** (foll. by *on* or *upon*) to speak or write in a persistent and tedious manner. [OE *hearpe*] — **ˈharper** *or* **ˈharpist** *n.*

harpoon (hɑːˈpuːn) n. **1. a.** a barbed missile attached to a long cord and hurled or fired from a gun when hunting whales, etc. **b.** (as modifier): a harpoon gun. ~vb. **2.** (tr.) to spear with or as if with a harpoon. [C17: prob. from Du. harpoen, from OF harpon clasp, ? of Scand. origin] —**har'pooner** or ,**harpoon'eer** n.

harp seal n. a brownish-grey North Atlantic and Arctic seal, having a dark mark on its back.

harpsichord ('hɑːpsɪˌkɔːd) n. a horizontally strung stringed keyboard instrument, triangular in shape, with strings plucked by plectra mounted on pivoted jacks. [C17: from NL harpichordium, from LL harpa HARP + L chorda CHORD¹] —**'harpsiˌchordist** n.

harpy ('hɑːpɪ) n., pl. -**pies.** a cruel grasping person. [C16: from L Harpyia, from Gk Harpuiai the Harpies, lit.: snatchers, from harpazein to seize]

Harpy ('hɑːpɪ) n., pl. -**pies.** Greek myth. a ravenous creature with a woman's head and trunk and a bird's wings and claws.

harquebus ('hɑːkwɪbəs) n., pl. -**buses.** a variant spelling of **arquebus.**

Harrar ('hɑːrə) n. a variant spelling of **Harar.**

harridan ('hærɪdᵊn) n. a scolding old woman; nag. [C17: from ?; ? rel. to F haridelle, lit.: broken-down horse]

harrier¹ ('hærɪə) n. **1.** a person or thing that harries. **2.** a diurnal bird of prey having broad wings and long legs and tail.

harrier² ('hærɪə) n. **1.** a smallish breed of hound used originally for hare-hunting. **2.** a cross-country runner. [C16: from HARE + -ER¹; infl. by HARRIER¹]

Harriman ('hærɪmən) n. **W(illiam)** Averell. 1891–1986, U.S. diplomat: negotiated the Nuclear Test Ban Treaty with the Soviet Union (1963); governor of New York (1955–58).

Harris¹ ('hærɪs) n. the S part of the island of Lewis with Harris, in the Outer Hebrides. Pop.: (including Lewis) 23 390 (1981). Area: 500 sq. km (193 sq. miles).

Harris² ('hærɪs) n. **1. Arthur** **Travers,** 1st Baron, known as Bomber Harris. 1892–1984, British air marshal. He was commander-in-chief of Bomber Command of the RAF during World War II. **2. Frank.** 1856–1931, British writer and journalist; his books include his autobiography My Life and Loves (1923–27) and Contemporary Portraits (1915–30). **3. Joel Chandler.** 1848–1908, U.S. writer; creator of Uncle Remus. **4. Roy.** 1898–1979, U.S. composer, esp. of orchestral and choral music incorporating American folk tunes.

Harrisburg ('hærɪsˌbɜːɡ) n. a city in S Pennsylvania, on the Susquehanna River: the state capital. Pop.: 53 264 (1980).

Harrison ('hærɪsᵊn) n. **1. Benjamin.** 1833–1901, 23rd president of the U.S. (1889–93). **2. Rex (Carey).** born 1908, British actor. His many films include Major Barbara (1940), Blithe Spirit (1945), and My Fair Lady (1964). **3.** grandfather of Benjamin, **William Henry.** 1773–1841, 9th president of the U.S. (1841).

Harris Tweed n. Trademark. a loose-woven tweed made in the Outer Hebrides.

Harrogate ('hærəˌɡɪt) n. a town in N England, in North Yorkshire: a spa. Pop.: 66 475 (1981).

harrow ('hærəʊ) n. **1.** any of various implements used to level the ground, stir the soil, break up clods, destroy weeds, etc., in soil. ~vb. (tr.) **2.** to draw a harrow over (land). **3.** to distress; vex. [C13: from ON] —**'harrower** n. —**'harrowing** adj.

Harrow ('hærəʊ) n. a borough of NW Greater London; site of an English boys' public school founded in 1571 at **Harrow-on-the-Hill,** a part of this borough. Pop.: 201 900 (1986 est.). —**Harrovian** (həˈrəʊvɪən) adj., n.

harrumph (həˈrʌmf) vb. (intr.) Chiefly U.S. & Canad. to clear or make the noise of clearing the throat.

harry ('hærɪ) vb. -**rying, -ried. 1.** (tr.) to harass; worry. **2.** to ravage (a town, etc.), esp. in war. [OE hergian; rel. to here army, ON herja to lay waste]

harsh (hɑːʃ) adj. **1.** rough or grating to the senses. **2.** stern, severe, or cruel. [C16: prob. of Scand. origin] —**'harshly** adv. —**'harshness** n.

hart (hɑːt) n., pl. **harts** or **hart.** the male of the deer, esp. the red deer aged five years or more. [OE heorot]

Hart (hɑːt) n. **Lorenz.** 1895–1943, U.S. lyricist: collaborated with Richard Rodgers in writing musicals.

hartal (hɑːˈtɑːl) n. (in India) the act of closing shops or suspending work, esp. in political protest. [C20: from

Hindi hartāl, from hāt shop + tālā bolt for a door, from Sansk.]

Harte (hɑːt) n. **(Francis) Bret.** 1836–1902, U.S. poet and short-story writer, noted for his sketches of Californian gold miners, such as The Luck of Roaring Camp (1870).

hartebeest ('hɑːtɪˌbiːst) or **hartbeest** ('hɑːtˌbiːst) n. either of two large African antelopes having an elongated muzzle, lyre-shaped horns, and a fawn-coloured coat. [C18: via Afrik. from Du.; see HART, BEAST]

Hartford ('hɑːtfəd) n. a port in central Connecticut, on the Connecticut River: the state capital. Pop.: 136 392 (1980).

Harthacanute ('hɑːθəkəˌnjuːt), **Hardecanute,** or **Hardicanute** n. ?1019–42, king of Denmark (1035–42) and of England (1040–42); son of Canute.

Hartlepool ('hɑːtlɪˌpuːl) n. a port in NE England, in Cleveland on the North Sea: greatly enlarged in 1967 by its amalgamation with West Hartlepool; shipbuilding and fishing. Pop.: 93 400 (1983 est.).

Hartley ('hɑːtlɪ) n. **1. David.** 1705–57, English philosopher and physician. In Observations of Man (1749) he introduced the theory of psychological associationism. **2. L(esley) P(oles).** 1895–1972, British novelist. His novels include the trilogy The Shrimp and the Anemone (1944), The Sixth Heaven (1940), and Eustace and Hilda (1947) as well as The Go-Between (1953).

Hartnell ('hɑːtnᵊl) n. Sir **Norman.** 1901–79, English couturier.

hartshorn ('hɑːtsˌhɔːn) n. an obsolete name for **sal volatile** [OE heortes horn hart's horn (formerly a chief source of ammonia)]

hart's-tongue n. an evergreen Eurasian fern with narrow undivided fronds.

harum-scarum (ˌhɛərəmˈskɛərəm) adj., adv. **1.** in a reckless way or of a reckless nature. ~n. **2.** a person who is impetuous or rash. [C17: ?from hare (in obs. sense: harass) + scare, var. of STARE]

Harun al-Rashid (hæˈruːn ˈælræˈʃiːd) n. ?763–809 A.D., Abbasid caliph of Islam (786–809), whose court at Baghdad was idealized in the Arabian Nights.

haruspex (həˈrʌspɛks) n., pl. **haruspices** (həˈrʌspɪˌsiːz). (in ancient Rome) a priest who practised divination, esp. by examining the entrails of animals. [C16: from L, prob. from hīra gut + specere to look] —**haruspicy** (həˈrʌspɪsɪ) n.

harvest ('hɑːvɪst) n. **1.** the gathering of a ripened crop. **2.** the crop itself. **3.** the season for gathering crops. **4.** the product of an effort, action, etc.: a harvest of love. ~vb. **5.** to gather (a ripened crop) from (the place where it has been growing). **6.** (tr.) to receive (consequences). [OE hærfest] —**'harvesting** n.

harvester ('hɑːvɪstə) n. **1.** a person who harvests. **2.** a harvesting machine, esp. a combine harvester.

harvest home n. **1.** the bringing in of the harvest. **2.** Chiefly Brit. a harvest supper.

harvestman ('hɑːvɪstmən) n., pl. -**men. 1.** a person engaged in harvesting. **2.** Also called (U.S. and Canad.): **daddy-longlegs.** an arachnid having a small rounded body and very long thin legs.

harvest moon n. the full moon occurring nearest to the autumnal equinox.

harvest mouse n. a very small reddish-brown Eurasian mouse inhabiting cornfields, hedgerows, etc.

Harvey ('hɑːvɪ) n. **William.** 1578–1657, English physician who discovered the mechanism of blood circulation.

Harwich ('hærɪtʃ) n. a port in SE England, in NE Essex on the North Sea. Pop.: 15 076 (1981).

Haryana (hərˈjɑːnə) n. a state of NE India, formed in 1966 from the Hindi-speaking parts of the state of Punjab. Capital: Chandigarh (shared with Punjab). Pop.: 12 850 902 (1981). Area: 44 506 sq. km (17 182 sq. miles).

Harz or **Harz Mountains** (hɑːts) pl. n. a range of wooded hills in central Germany, between the Rivers Weser and Elbe: source of many legends. Highest peak: Brocken, 1142 m (3746 ft.).

has (hæz) vb. (used with he, she, it, or a singular noun) a form of the present tense (indicative mood) of **have.**

Hasa ('hɑːsə) n. See **Al Hasa.**

has-been n. Inf. a person or thing that is no longer popular, successful, effective, etc.

Hasdrubal ('hæzdrʊbᵊl) n. died 207 B.C., Carthaginian general: commanded the Carthaginian army in Spain (218–211); joined his brother Hannibal in Italy and was killed at the Metaurus.

Hašek (*Czech* 'haʃɛk) *n.* **Jaroslav** ('jarɔslaf). 1883–1923, Czech novelist and short-story writer; author of *The Good Soldier Schweik.*

hash[1] (hæʃ) *n.* **1.** a dish of diced cooked meat, vegetables, etc., reheated in a sauce. **2.** a reuse or rework of old material. **3. make a hash of.** *Inf.* to mess up or destroy. **4. settle someone's hash.** *Inf.* to subdue or silence someone. ~*vb.* (*tr.*) **5.** to chop into small pieces. **6.** to mess up. [C17: from OF *hacher* to chop up, from *hache* HATCHET]

hash[2] (hæʃ) *n. Sl.* short for **hashish.**

Hashemite Kingdom of Jordan ('hæʃɪ,maɪt) *n.* the official name of **Jordan.**

hashish ('hæʃiːʃ, -ɪʃ) *or* **hasheesh** *n.* a resinous extract of the dried flower tops of the female hemp plant, used as a hallucinogenic. See also **cannabis.** [C16: from Ar. *hashīsh* hemp]

haslet ('hæzlɪt) *or* **harslet** *n.* a loaf of cooked minced pig's offal, eaten cold. [C14: from OF *hastelet* piece of spit-roasted meat, from *haste* spit, of Gmc origin]

hasn't ('hæzᵊnt) *contraction of* has not.

hasp (hɑːsp) *n.* **1.** a metal fastening consisting of a hinged strap with a slot that fits over a staple and is secured by a pin, bolt, or padlock. ~*vb.* **2.** (*tr.*) to secure (a door, window, etc.) with a hasp. [OE *hæpse*]

Hassan II (hæ'sɑːn, 'hæsᵊn) *n.* born 1929, king of Morocco from 1961.

Hasselt (*Flemish* 'hɑsəlt; *French* asɛlt) *n.* a market town in E Belgium, capital of Limbourg province. Pop.: 65 563 (1987).

Hassid ('hæsɪd) *n.* a variant spelling of **Chassid.**

hassle ('hæsᵊl) *Inf.* ~*n.* **1.** a prolonged argument. **2.** a great deal of trouble. ~*vb.* **3.** (*intr.*) to quarrel or wrangle. **4.** (*tr.*) to cause annoyance or trouble to (someone); harass. [C20: from ?]

hassock ('hæsək) *n.* **1.** a firm upholstered cushion used for kneeling on, esp. in church. **2.** a thick clump of grass. [OE *hassuc* matted grass]

hast (hæst) *vb. Arch. or dialect.* (used with the pronoun *thou*) a singular form of the present tense (indicative mood) of **have.**

hastate ('hæsteɪt) *adj.* (of a leaf) having a pointed tip and two outward-pointing lobes at the base. [C18: from L *hastātus*, from *hasta* spear]

haste (heɪst) *n.* **1.** speed, esp. in an action. **2.** the act of hurrying in a careless manner. **3.** a necessity for hurrying; urgency. **4. make haste.** to hurry; rush. ~*vb.* **5.** a poetic word for **hasten.** [C14: from OF *haste*, of Gmc origin]

hasten ('heɪsᵊn) *vb.* **1.** (*may take an infinitive*) to hurry or cause to hurry; rush. **2.** (*tr.*) to be anxious (to say something). —'**hastener** *n.*

Hastings[1] ('heɪstɪŋz) *n.* **1.** a port in SE England, in East Sussex on the English Channel: near the site of the **Battle of Hastings** (1066), in which William the Conqueror defeated King Harold; chief of the Cinque Ports. Pop.: 74 803 (1981). **2.** a town in New Zealand, on E North Island: centre of a rich agricultural and fruit-growing region. Pop. (urban area): 43 500 (1985).

Hastings[2] ('heɪstɪŋz) *n.* **Warren.** 1732–1818, British administrator in India; first governor general of Bengal (1773–85). He implemented important reforms but was impeached by parliament (1788) on charges of corruption; acquitted in 1795.

hasty ('heɪstɪ) *adj.* **-tier, -tiest. 1.** rapid; swift; quick. **2.** excessively or rashly quick. **3.** short-tempered. **4.** showing irritation or anger: *hasty words.* —'**hastily** *adv.* —'**hastiness** *n.*

hat (hæt) *n.* **1.** a head covering, esp. one with a brim and a shaped crown. **2.** *Inf.* a role or capacity. **3. I'll eat my hat.** *Inf.* I will be greatly surprised if (something that proves me wrong) happens. **4. keep (something) under one's hat.** to keep (something) secret. **5. pass (or send) the hat round.** to collect money, as for a cause. **6. take off one's hat to.** to admire or congratulate. **7. talk through one's hat.** **a.** to talk foolishly. **b.** to deceive or bluff. ~*vb.* **hatting, hatted. 8.** (*tr.*) to supply (a person, etc.) with a hat or put a hat on (someone). [OE *hætt*] —'**hatless** *adj.*

hatband ('hæt,bænd) *n.* a band or ribbon around the base of the crown of a hat.

hatbox ('hæt,bɒks) *n.* a box or case for a hat.

hatch[1] (hætʃ) *vb.* **1.** to cause (the young of various animals, esp. birds) to emerge from the egg or (of young birds, etc.) to emerge from the egg. **2.** to cause (eggs) to break and release the fully developed young or (of eggs) to break and release the young animal within. **3.** (*tr.*) to contrive or devise (a scheme, plot, etc.). ~*n.* **4.** the act or process of hatching. **5.** a group of newly hatched animals. [C13: of OE origin]

hatch[2] (hætʃ) *n.* **1.** a covering for a hatchway. **2. a.** short for **hatchway.** **b.** a door in an aircraft or spacecraft. **3.** Also called: **serving hatch.** an opening in a wall separating a kitchen from a dining area. **4.** the lower half of a divided door. **5.** a sluice in a dam, dyke, or weir. **6. down the hatch.** *Sl.* (used as a toast) drink up! **7. under hatches. a.** below decks. **b.** out of sight. **c.** dead. [OE *hæcc*]

hatch[3] (hætʃ) *vb. Drawing, engraving, etc.* to mark (a figure, etc.) with fine parallel or crossed lines to indicate shading. [C15: from OF *hacher* to chop, from *hache* HATCHET] —'**hatching** *n.*

hatchback ('hætʃ,bæk) *n.* **1.** a sloping rear end of a car having a single door that is lifted to open. **2.** a car having such a rear end.

hatchery ('hætʃərɪ) *n., pl.* **-eries.** a place where eggs are hatched under artificial conditions.

hatchet ('hætʃɪt) *n.* **1.** a short axe used for chopping wood, etc. **2.** a tomahawk. **3.** (*modifier*) of narrow dimensions and sharp features: *a hatchet face.* **4. bury the hatchet.** to cease hostilities and become reconciled. [C14: from OF *hachette*, from *hache* axe, of Gmc origin]

hatchet job *n. Inf.* a malicious or devastating verbal or written attack.

hatchet man *n. Inf.* **1.** a person carrying out unpleasant assignments for an employer or superior. **2.** a severe or malicious critic.

hatchment ('hætʃmənt) *n. Heraldry.* a diamond-shaped tablet displaying the coat of arms of a dead person. [C16: changed from earlier use of *achievement* in this sense]

hatchway ('hætʃ,weɪ) *n.* **1.** an opening in the deck of a vessel to provide access below. **2.** a similar opening in a wall, floor, ceiling, or roof.

hate (heɪt) *vb.* **1.** to dislike (something) intensely; detest. **2.** (*intr.*) to be unwilling (to be or do something). ~*n.* **3.** intense dislike. **4.** *Inf.* a person or thing that is hated (esp. in **pet hate**). [OE *hatian*] —'**hateable** *or* '**hatable** *adj.*

hateful ('heɪtfʊl) *adj.* **1.** causing or deserving hate; loathsome; detestable. **2.** *Arch.* full of hate. —'**hatefully** *adv.* —'**hatefulness** *n.*

Hatfield ('hæt,fiːld) *n.* a market town in S central England, in Hertfordshire, with a new town of the same name built on the outskirts. Pop.: 25 160 (1981).

hath (hæθ) *vb. Arch. or dialect.* (used with the pronouns *he, she,* or *it* or a singular noun) a form of the present tense (indicative mood) of **have.**

Hathaway ('hæθə,weɪ) *n.* **Anne.** ?1557–1623, wife of William Shakespeare.

Hathor ('hæθɔː) *n.* (in ancient Egyptian religion) the mother of Horus and goddess of creation. —**Hathoric** (hæ'θɔːrɪk, -'θɒr-) *adj.*

hatred ('heɪtrɪd) *n.* intense dislike; enmity.

Hatshepsut (hæt'ʃɛpsuːt) *or* **Hatshepset** *n.* queen of Egypt of the 18th dynasty (?1512–1482 B.C.). She built a great mortuary temple at Deir el Bahri near Thebes.

hat stand *or esp. U.S.* **hat tree** *n.* a pole equipped with hooks for hanging up hats, etc.

hatter ('hætə) *n.* **1.** a person who makes and sells hats. **2. mad as a hatter.** eccentric.

Hatteras ('hætərəs) *n.* **Cape.** a promontory off the E coast of North Carolina, on **Hatteras Island,** which is situated between Pamlico Sound and the Atlantic: known as the "Graveyard of the Atlantic" for its danger to shipping.

Hattersley ('hætəzlɪ) *n.* **Roy (Sydney George).** born 1932, British Labour politician; deputy leader of the Labour Party since 1983.

hat trick *n.* **1.** *Cricket.* the achievement of a bowler in taking three wickets with three successive balls. **2.** any achievement of three successive points, victories, etc.

hauberk ('hɔːbɜːk) *n.* a long coat of mail, often sleeveless. [C13: from OF *hauberc*, of Gmc origin; cf. OHG *halsberc*, OE *healsbeorg*, from *heals* neck + *beorg* protection]

Haughey ('hɔːxɪ; *Irish* 'hʌhiː) *n.* **Charles James.** born 1925, Irish politician; leader of the Fianna Fáil party; prime minister of the Republic of Ireland (1979–81; 1982; and from 1987).

haughty ('hɔːtɪ) *adj.* **-tier, -tiest.** having or showing arrogance. [C16: from OF *haut* lofty, from L *altus* high] — **'haughtily** *adv.* — **'haughtiness** *n.*

haul (hɔːl) *vb.* **1.** to drag (something) with effort. **2.** (*tr.*) to transport, as in a lorry. **3.** *Naut.* to alter the course of (a vessel), esp. so as to sail closer to the wind. **4.** (*intr.*) *Naut.* (of the wind) to blow from a direction nearer the bow. ~*n.* **5.** the act of dragging with effort. **6.** (esp. of fish) the amount caught at a single time. **7.** something that is hauled. **8.** a distance of hauling or travelling. [C16: from OF *haler*, of Gmc origin] — **'hauler** *n.*

haulage ('hɔːlɪdʒ) *n.* **1.** the act or labour of hauling. **2.** a rate or charge levied for the transportation of goods, esp. by rail.

haulier ('hɔːljə) *n.* **1.** *Brit.* a person or firm that transports goods by road. **2.** a mine worker who conveys coal from the workings to the foot of the shaft.

haulm *or* **halm** (hɔːm) *n.* **1.** the stalks of beans, peas, potatoes, grasses, etc., collectively. **2.** a single stem of such a plant. [OE *healm*]

haul up *vb.* (*adv.*) **1.** (*tr.*) *Inf.* to call to account or criticize. **2.** *Naut.* to sail (a vessel) closer to the wind.

haunch (hɔːntʃ) *n.* **1.** the human hip or fleshy hindquarter of an animal. **2.** the leg and loin of an animal, used for food. **3.** *Archit.* the part of an arch between the impost and apex. [C13: from OF *hanche*; rel. to Sp., It. *anca*, of Gmc origin]

haunt (hɔːnt) *vb.* **1.** to visit (a person or place) in the form of a ghost. **2.** (*tr.*) to recur to (the memory, thoughts, etc.): *he was haunted by the fear of insanity.* **3.** to visit (a place) frequently. **4.** to associate with (someone) frequently. ~*n.* **5.** (*often pl.*) a place visited frequently. **6.** a place to which animals habitually resort for food, drink, shelter, etc. [C13: from OF *hanter*, of Gmc origin]

haunted ('hɔːntɪd) *adj.* **1.** frequented or visited by ghosts. **2.** (*postpositive*) obsessed or worried.

haunting ('hɔːntɪŋ) *adj.* **1.** (of memories) poignant or persistent. **2.** poignantly sentimental; eerily evocative. — **'hauntingly** *adv.*

Hauptmann (*German* 'hauptman) *n.* **Gerhart** ('geːrhart). 1862–1946, German naturalist, dramatist, novelist, and poet. His works include the historical drama *The Weavers* (1892): Nobel prize for literature 1912.

Hauraki Gulf (hau'rækɪ) *n.* an inlet of the Pacific in New Zealand, on the N coast of North Island.

Hausa ('hausə) *n.* **1.** (*pl.* **-sas** *or* **-sa**) a member of a Negroid people of W Africa, living chiefly in N Nigeria. **2.** the language of this people, widely used as a trading language throughout W Africa.

hausfrau ('haus,frau) *n.* a German housewife. [G, from *Haus* house + *Frau* woman, wife]

hautboy ('əubɔɪ) *n.* **1.** a strawberry with large fruit. **2.** an archaic word for **oboe**. [C16: from F *hautbois*, from *haut* high + *bois* wood, of Gmc origin]

haute couture French. (ot kutyr) *n.* high fashion. [lit.: high dressmaking]

haute cuisine French. (ot kwizin) *n.* high-class cooking. [lit.: high cookery]

haute école French. (ot ekɔl) *n.* the classical art of riding. [lit.: high school]

Haute-Garonne (*French* otgarɔn) *n.* a department of SW France, in Midi-Pyrénées region. Capital: Toulouse. Pop.: 824 501 (1982). Area: 6367 sq. km (2483 sq. miles).

Haute-Loire (*French* otlwar) *n.* a department of S central France, in Auvergne region. Capital: Le Puy. Pop.: 205 895 (1982). Area: 5001 sq. km (1950 sq. miles).

Haute-Marne (*French* otmarn) *n.* a department of NE France, in Champagne-Ardenne region. Capital: Chaumont. Pop.: 210 670 (1982). Area: 6257 sq. km (2440 sq. miles).

Haute-Normandie (*French* otnɔrmãdi) *n.* a region of NW France, on the English Channel: generally fertile and flat.

Hautes-Alpes (*French* otzalp) *n.* a department of SE France in Provence-Alpes-Côte d'Azur region. Capital: Gap. Pop.: 105 070 (1982). Area: 5643 sq. km (2201 sq. miles).

Haute-Saône (*French* otson) *n.* a department of E France, in Franche-Comté region. Capital: Vesoul. Pop.: 231 962 (1982). Area: 5375 sq. km (2096 sq. miles).

Haute-Savoie (*French* otsavwa) *n.* a department of E France, in Rhône-Alpes region. Capital: Annecy. Pop.: 494 505 (1982). Area: 4958 sq. km (1934 sq. miles).

Hautes-Pyrénées (*French* otpirene) *n.* a department of SW France, in Midi-Pyrénées region. Capital: Tarbes. Pop.: 227 922 (1982). Area: 4534 sq. km (1768 sq. miles).

hauteur (əu'tɜː) *n.* pride; haughtiness. [C17: from F, from *haut* high; see HAUGHTY]

Haute-Vienne (*French* otvjɛn) *n.* a department of W central France, in Limousin region. Capital: Limoges. Pop.: 355 737 (1982). Area: 5555 sq. km (2166 sq. miles).

haut monde French. (o mɔ̃d) *n.* high society. [lit.: high world]

Haut-Rhin (*French* orɛ̃) *n.* a department of E France in Alsace region. Capital: Colmar. Pop.: 650 372 (1982). Area: 3566 sq. km (1377 sq. miles).

Hauts-de-Seine (*French* odsɛn) *n.* a department of N central France, in Île-de-France region just west of Paris: formed in 1964. Capital: Nanterre. Pop.: 1 387 039 (1982). Area: 175 km (68 sq. miles).

Havana (hə'vænə) *n.* the capital of Cuba, a port in the northwest on the Gulf of Mexico: the largest city in the West Indies; founded in 1514 as San Cristóbal de la Habana by Diego Velásquez. Pop.: 2 014 800 (1986 est.). Spanish name: **Habana.**

Havana cigar *n.* any of various cigars manufactured in Cuba, known esp. for their high quality. Also: **Havana.**

Havant ('hævənt) *n.* a market town in S England, in SE Hampshire. Pop. (with Waterlooville): 115 600 (1982 est.).

have (hæv) *vb.* **has, having, had.** (*mainly tr.*) **1.** to be in possession of; own: *he has two cars.* **2.** to possess as a quality or attribute: *he has dark hair.* **3.** to receive, take, or obtain: *she had a present; have a look.* **4.** to hold in the mind: *to have an idea.* **5.** to possess a knowledge of: *I have no German.* **6.** to experience: *to have a shock.* **7.** to suffer from: *to have a cold.* **8.** to gain control of or advantage over: *you have me on that point.* **9.** (*usually passive*) *Sl.* to cheat or outwit: *he was had by that dishonest salesman.* **10.** (foll. by *on*) to exhibit (mercy, etc., towards). **11.** to take part in: *to have a conversation.* **12.** to arrange or hold: *to have a party.* **13.** to cause, compel, or require to (be, do, or be done): *have my shoes mended.* **14.** (takes an infinitive with *to*) used as an auxiliary to express compulsion or necessity: *I had to run quickly to escape him.* **15.** to eat, drink, or partake of. **16.** *Taboo sl.* to have sexual intercourse with. **17.** (*used with a negative*) to tolerate or allow: *I won't have all this noise.* **18.** to state or assert: *rumour has it that they will marry.* **19.** to place: *I'll have the sofa in this room.* **20.** to receive as a guest: *to have people to stay.* **21.** to be pregnant with or bear (offspring). **22.** (*takes a past participle*) used as an auxiliary to form compound tenses expressing completed action: *I have gone; I had gone.* **23. had rather** *or* **sooner.** to consider preferable that: *I had rather you left at once.* **24. have had it.** *Inf.* **a.** to be exhausted, defeated, or killed. **b.** to have lost one's last chance. **c.** to become unfashionable. **25. have it away** (*or* **off**). *Taboo, Brit. sl.* to have sexual intercourse. **26. have it so good.** to have so many material benefits. **27. have to do with. a.** to have dealings with. **b.** to be of relevance to. **28. let** (**someone**) **have it.** *Sl.* to launch an attack on (someone). ~*n.* **29.** (*usually pl.*) *Inf.* a person or group in possession of wealth, security, etc.: *the haves and the have-nots.* ~See also **have at, have on,** etc. [OE *habban*]

have at *vb.* (*intr., prep.*) *Arch.* to make an opening attack on, esp. in fencing.

Havel (*German* 'haːfəl) *n.* a river in East Germany, flowing south to Berlin, then west and north to join the River Elbe. Length: about 362 km (225 miles).

havelock ('hævlɒk) *n.* a light-coloured cover for a service cap with a flap extending over the back of the neck to protect the head and neck from the sun. [C19: after Sir H. *Havelock* (1795–1857), E general in India]

haven ('heɪvᵊn) *n.* **1.** a harbour or other sheltered place for shipping. **2.** a place of safety; shelter. ~*vb.* **3.** (*tr.*) to shelter as in a haven. [OE *hæfen* from ON *höfn*]

have-not *n.* (*usually pl.*) a person or group in possession of relatively little material wealth.

haven't ('hævᵊnt) *contraction of* have not.

have on *vb.* (*tr.*) **1.** (*usually adv.*) to wear. **2.** (*usually adv.*) to have a commitment: *what does your boss have on this afternoon?* **3.** (*adv.*) *Inf.* to trick or tease (a person). **4.** (*prep.*) to have available (information, esp. when incriminating) about (a person).

have out *vb.* (*tr., adv.*) **1.** to settle (a matter) or come to (a final decision), esp. by fighting or by frank discussion (often in **have it out**). **2.** to have extracted or removed.

haver ('heivə) *vb.* (*intr.*) **1.** *Scot. & N English dialect.* to babble; talk nonsense. **2.** to dither. ~*n.* **3.** (*usually pl.*) *Scot.* nonsense. [C18: from ?]

Havering ('heivəriŋ) *n.* a borough of NE Greater London, formed in 1965 from Romford and Hornchurch (both previously in Essex). Pop.: 238 100 (1986 est.).

haversack ('hævə,sæk) *n.* a canvas bag for provisions or equipment, carried on the back or shoulder. [C18: from F *havresac*, from G *Habersack* oat bag, from OHG *habaro* oats + *Sack* SACK[1]]

haversine ('hævə,sain) *n.* half the value of the versed sine. [C19: combination of *half* + *versed* + *sine*[1]]

have up *vb.* (*tr., adv.; usually passive*) to cause to appear for trial: *he was had up for breaking and entering.*

havildar ('hævil,dɑ:) *n.* a noncommissioned officer in the Indian army, equivalent in rank to sergeant. [C17: from Hindi, from Persian *hawāldār* one in charge]

havoc ('hævək) *n.* **1.** destruction; devastation; ruin. **2.** *Inf.* confusion; chaos. **3. cry havoc.** *Arch.* to give the signal for pillage and destruction. **4. play havoc.** (often foll. by *with*) to cause a great deal of damage, distress, or confusion (to). [C15: from OF *havot* pillage, prob. of Gmc origin]

Havre ('hɑːvrə; *French* ɑvrə) *n.* See **Le Havre.**

haw[1] (hɔː) *n.* **1.** the fruit of the hawthorn. **2.** another name for **hawthorn.** [OE *haga*, identical with *haga* hedge]

haw[2] (hɔː) *n., interj.* **1.** an inarticulate utterance, as of hesitation, embarrassment, etc.; hem. ~*vb.* **2.** (*intr.*) to make this sound. [C17: imit.]

haw[3] (hɔː) *n.* the nictitating membrane of a horse or other domestic animal. [C15: from ?]

Hawaii (hə'waiı) *n.* a state of the U.S. in the central Pacific, consisting of over 20 volcanic islands and atolls, including Hawaii, Maui, Oahu, Kauai, and Molokai: discovered by Captain Cook in 1778; annexed by the U.S. in 1898; naval base at Pearl Harbor attacked by the Japanese in 1941, a major cause of U.S. entry into World War II; became a state in 1959. Capital: Honolulu. Pop.: 1 062 000 (1986 est.). Area: 16 640 sq. km (6425 sq. miles). Former name: **Sandwich Islands. —Ha'waiian** *adj., n.*

Hawaiki ('hɑ:waiki:) *n. N.Z.* a legendary Pacific island from which the Maoris migrated to New Zealand by canoe. [Maori]

Hawes Water (hɔːz) *n.* a lake in NW England, in the Lake District: provides part of Manchester's water supply; extended by damming from 4 km (2.5 miles) to 6 km (4 miles).

hawfinch ('hɔː,fintʃ) *n.* an uncommon European finch having a very stout bill.

Haw-Haw ('hɔː,hɔː) *n.* **Lord.** See (William) **Joyce.**

Hawick ('hɔːik) *n.* a town in SE Scotland, in the S central Borders region: knitwear industry. Pop.: 16 584 (1984 est.).

hawk[1] (hɔːk) *n.* **1.** any of various diurnal birds of prey of the family Accipitridae, typically having short rounded wings and a long tail. **2.** a person who advocates or supports war or warlike policies. **3.** a ruthless or rapacious person. ~*vb.* **4.** (*intr.*) to hunt with falcons, hawks, etc. **5.** (*intr.*) (of falcons or hawks) to fly in quest of prey. **6.** to pursue or attack on the wing, as a hawk. [OE *hafoc*] — '**hawking** *n.* — '**hawkish** *adj.* — '**hawk,like** *adj.*

hawk[2] (hɔːk) *vb.* **1.** to offer (goods) for sale, as in the street. **2.** (often foll. by *about*) to spread (news, gossip, etc.). [C16: back formation from HAWKER[1]]

hawk[3] (hɔːk) *vb.* **1.** (*intr.*) to clear the throat noisily. **2.** (*tr.*) to force (phlegm, etc.) up from the throat. [C16: imit.]

hawk[4] (hɔːk) *n.* a small square board with a handle underneath, for carrying wet mortar. Also called: **mortarboard.** [from ?]

Hawke (hɔːk) *n.* **Robert (James Lee),** known as *Bob.* born 1929, Australian statesman; prime minister of Australia from 1983.

hawker[1] ('hɔːkə) *n.* a person who travels from place to place selling goods. [C16: prob. from MLow G *hōker*, from *hōken* to peddle; see HUCKSTER]

hawker[2] ('hɔːkə) *n.* a person who hunts with hawks, falcons, etc. [OE *hafecere*]

hawk-eyed *adj.* **1.** having extremely keen sight. **2.** vigilant, watchful, or observant.

Hawking ('hɔːkiŋ) *n.* **Stephen William.** born 1942, British physicist. Stricken with a progressive nervous disease since the 1960s, he has nevertheless been a leader in cosmological theory. His *A Brief History of Time* (1987) is a bestseller.

Hawkins ('hɔːkinz) *n.* **1. Coleman.** 1904–69, U.S. pioneer of the tenor saxophone for jazz. **2.** Sir **John.** 1532–95, English naval commander and slave trader, treasurer of the navy (1577–89); commander of a squadron in the fleet that defeated the Spanish Armada (1588).

hawk moth *n.* any of various moths having long narrow wings and powerful flight, with the ability to hover over flowers when feeding from the nectar.

hawksbill turtle *or* **hawksbill** ('hɔːks,bil) *n.* a small tropical turtle with a hooked beaklike mouth: a source of tortoiseshell.

hawkweed ('hɔːk,wiːd) *n.* a hairy plant with clusters of dandelion-like flowers.

Haworth ('hauəθ) *n.* a village in N England, in West Yorkshire: home of Charlotte, Emily, and Anne Brontë.

hawse (hɔːz) *n. Naut.* **1.** the part of the bows of a vessel where the hawseholes are. **2.** short for **hawsehole** or **hawsepipe. 3.** the distance from the bow of an anchored vessel to the anchor. **4.** the arrangement of port and starboard anchor ropes when a vessel is riding on both anchors. [C14: from earlier *halse*, prob. from ON *háls* neck, ship's bow]

hawsehole ('hɔːz,həul) *n. Naut.* one of the holes in the upper part of the bows of a vessel through which anchor ropes pass.

hawsepipe ('hɔːz,paip) *n. Naut.* a strong metal pipe through which an anchor rope passes.

hawser ('hɔːzə) *n. Naut.* a large heavy rope. [C14: from Anglo-F *hauceour*, from OF *haucier* to hoist, ult. from L *altus* high]

hawthorn ('hɔː,θɔːn) *n.* any of various thorny trees or shrubs of a N temperate genus, having white or pink flowers and reddish fruits (haws). Also called (in Britain): **may, may tree, mayflower.** [OE *haguthorn*, from *haga* hedge + *thorn* thorn]

Hawthorne ('hɔː,θɔːn) *n.* **Nathaniel.** 1804–64, U.S. novelist and short-story writer: his works include the novels *The Scarlet Letter* (1850) and *The House of the Seven Gables* (1851) and the children's stories *Tanglewood Tales* (1853).

hay (hei) *n.* **1. a.** grass, clover, etc., cut and dried as fodder. **b.** (*in combination*): *a hayfield.* **2. hit the hay.** *Sl.* to go to bed. **3. make hay of.** to throw into confusion. **4. make hay while the sun shines.** to take full advantage of an opportunity. **5. roll in the hay.** *Inf.* sexual intercourse or heavy petting. ~*vb.* **6.** to cut, dry, and store (grass, etc.) as fodder. [OE *hieg*]

haybox ('hei,bɒks) *n.* an airtight box full of hay used for cooking preheated food by retained heat.

haycock ('hei,kɒk) *n.* a small cone-shaped pile of hay left in the field until dry.

Haydn ('haidᵊn) *n.* **1.** (**Franz**) **Joseph** ('jɔːzɛf). 1732–1809, Austrian composer, who played a major part in establishing the classical forms of the symphony and the string quartet. His other works include the oratorios *The Creation* (1796–98) and *The Seasons* (1798–1801). **2.** his brother, **Johann Michael** (*German* jo'han 'miçaeːl). 1737–1806, Austrian composer, esp. of Church music.

Hayes (heiz) *n.* **Rutherford B(irchard).** 1822–93, 19th president of the U.S. (1877–81).

hay fever *n.* an allergic reaction to pollen, dust, etc., characterized by sneezing, runny nose, and watery eyes due to inflammation of the mucous membranes of the eyes and nose.

haymaker ('hei,meikə) *n.* **1.** a person who helps to cut, turn, or carry hay. **2.** either of two machines, one designed to crush stems of hay, the other to break and bend them, in order to cause more rapid and even drying. **3.** *Boxing sl.* a wild swinging punch. — '**hay,making** *adj., n.*

haymow ('heɪ,maʊ) n. **1.** a part of a barn where hay is stored. **2.** a quantity of hay stored.

hayseed ('heɪ,siːd) n. **1.** seeds or fragments of grass or straw. **2.** U.S. & Canad. inf., derog. a yokel.

haystack ('heɪ,stæk) or **hayrick** n. a large pile of hay, esp. one built in the open air and covered with thatch.

haywire ('heɪ,waɪə) adj. (postpositive) Inf. **1.** (of things) not functioning properly. **2.** (of people) erratic or crazy. [C20: from the disorderly tangle of wire removed from bales of hay]

hazard ('hæzəd) n. **1.** exposure or vulnerability to injury, loss, etc. **2. at hazard.** at risk; in danger. **3.** a thing likely to cause injury, etc. **4.** Golf. an obstacle such as a bunker, a sand pit, etc. **5.** chance; accident. **6.** a gambling game played with two dice. **7.** Real Tennis. **a.** the receiver's side of the court. **b.** one of the winning openings. **8.** Billiards. a scoring stroke made either when a ball other than the striker's is pocketed (**winning hazard**) or the striker's cue ball itself (**losing hazard**). ~vb. (tr.) **9.** to risk. **10.** to venture (an opinion, guess, etc.). **11.** to expose to danger. [C13: from OF hasard, from Ar. az-zahr the die]

hazardous ('hæzədəs) adj. **1.** involving great risk. **2.** depending on chance. — **'hazardously** adv. — **'hazardousness** n.

hazard warning device n. a mechanism in a motor vehicle which enables both indicators to flash simultaneously: used as a warning signal, as after an accident or breakdown.

haze[1] (heɪz) n. **1.** Meteorol. reduced visibility in the air as a result of condensed water vapour, dust, etc., in the atmosphere. **2.** obscurity of perception, feeling, etc. ~vb. **3.** (when intr., often foll. by over) to make or become hazy. [C18: back formation from HAZY]

haze[2] (heɪz) vb. (tr.) **1.** Chiefly U.S. & Canad. to subject (fellow students) to ridicule or abuse. **2.** Naut. to harass with humiliating tasks. [C17: from ?]

hazel ('heɪz°l) n. **1.** Also called: **cob.** any of several shrubs of a N temperate genus, having edible rounded nuts. **2.** the wood of any of these trees. **3.** short for **hazelnut. 4. a.** a light yellowish-brown colour. **b.** (as adj.): hazel eyes. [OE hæsel]

hazelhen ('heɪz°l,hɛn) n. a European woodland gallinaceous bird with a speckled brown plumage and slightly crested crown.

hazelnut ('heɪz°l,nʌt) n. the nut of a hazel shrub, having a smooth shiny hard shell. Also called: **filbert,** (Brit.) **cobnut, cob.**

Hazlitt ('hæzlɪt) n. **William.** 1778–1830, English critic and essayist: works include Characters of Shakespeare's Plays (1817), Table Talk (1821), and The Plain Speaker (1826).

hazy ('heɪzɪ) adj. **-zier, -ziest.** misty; indistinct; vague. [C17: from ?] — **'hazily** adv. — **'haziness** n.

Hb symbol for haemoglobin.

HB (on Brit. pencils) symbol for hard-black: denoting a medium-hard lead.

HBC abbrev. for Hudson's Bay Company.

HBM (in Britain) abbrev. for His (or Her) Britannic Majesty.

H-bomb n. short for **hydrogen bomb.**

HC abbrev. for: **1.** Holy Communion. **2.** (in Britain) House of Commons.

HCF or **hcf** abbrev. for highest common factor.

hcp abbrev. for handicap.

HD abbrev. for heavy duty.

hdqrs abbrev. for headquarters.

he (hiː; unstressed iː) pron. (subjective) **1.** refers to a male person or animal. **2.** refers to an indefinite antecedent such as whoever or anybody: everybody can do as he likes. **3.** refers to a person or animal of unknown or unspecified sex: a member may vote as he sees fit. ~n. **4. a.** a male person or animal. **b.** (in combination): he-goat. **5.** (in children's play) another name for **tag**[2] (sense 1), **it** (sense 7). [OE hē]

He the chemical symbol for helium.

HE abbrev. for: **1.** high explosive. **2.** His Eminence. **3.** His (or Her) Excellency.

head (hɛd) n. **1.** the upper or front part of the body in vertebrates, including man, that contains and protects the brain, eyes, mouth, nose, and ears. Related adj.: **cephalic. 2.** the corresponding part of an invertebrate animal. **3.** something resembling a head in form or function, such as the top of a tool. **4. a.** the person commanding most authority within a group, organization, etc. **b.** (as modifier): head buyer. **c.** (in combination): headmaster. **5.** the position of leadership or command. **6.** the most forward part of a thing; front: the head of a queue. **7.** the highest part of a thing; upper end: the head of the pass. **8.** the froth on the top of a glass of beer. **9.** aptitude, intelligence, and emotions (esp. in **over one's head, lose one's head,** etc.): she has a good head for figures. **10.** (pl. **head**) a person or animal considered as a unit: the show was two pounds per head; six hundred head of cattle. **11.** the head considered as a measure: he's a head taller than his mother. **12.** Bot. **a.** a dense inflorescence such as that of the daisy. **b.** any other compact terminal part of a plant, such as the leaves of a cabbage. **13.** a culmination or crisis (esp. in **bring** or **come to a head**). **14.** the pus-filled tip or central part of a pimple, boil, etc. **15.** the source of a river or stream. **16.** (cap. when part of a name) a headland or promontory. **17.** the obverse of a coin, usually bearing a portrait of the head of a monarch, etc. **18.** a main point of an argument, discourse, etc. **19.** (often pl.) a headline or heading. **20.** (often pl.) Naut. a lavatory. **21.** the taut membrane of a drum, tambourine, etc. **22. a.** the height of the surface of liquid above a specific point, esp. as a measure of the pressure at that point: a head of four feet. **b.** pressure of water, caused by height or velocity, measured in terms of a vertical column of water. **c.** any pressure: a head of steam in the boiler. **23.** Sl. **a.** a person who regularly takes drugs, esp. LSD or cannabis. **b.** (in combination): an acidhead. **24.** Mining. a road driven into the coalface. **25. a.** the terminal point of a route. **b.** (in combination): railhead. **26.** a device on a turning or boring machine equipped with one or more cutting tools held to the work by this device. **27. cylinder head.** See cylinder (sense 4). **28.** an electromagnet that can read, write, or erase information on a magnetic medium, used in computers, tape recorders, etc. **29.** Inf. short for **headmaster** or **headmistress. 30.** a narrow margin of victory (esp. in (**win**) **by a head**). **31.** Inf. short for **headache. 32. bite** or **snap someone's head off.** to speak sharply to someone. **33. give someone** (or **something**) **his** (or its) **head. a.** to allow a person greater freedom or responsibility. **b.** to allow a horse to gallop by lengthening the reins. **34. go to one's head. a.** to make one dizzy or confused, as might an alcoholic drink. **b.** to make one conceited: his success has gone to his head. **35. head and shoulders above.** greatly superior to. **36. head over heels. a.** turning a complete somersault. **b.** completely; utterly (esp. in **head over heels in love**). **37. hold up one's head.** to be unashamed. **38. keep one's head.** to remain calm. **39. keep one's head above water.** to manage to survive difficulties, esp. financial ones. **40. make head or tail of.** (used with a negative) to attempt to understand (a problem, etc.). **41. off** (or **out of**) **one's head.** Sl. insane or delirious. **42. on one's** (**own**) **head.** at a one's (own) risk or responsibility. **43. over someone's head. a.** without a person in the obvious position being considered: the graduate was promoted over the heads of several of his seniors. **b.** without consulting a person in the obvious position but referring to a higher authority: he went straight to the director, over the head of his immediate boss. **c.** beyond a person's comprehension. **44. put** (**our, their,** etc.) **heads together.** Inf. to consult together. **45. take it into one's head.** to conceive a notion (to do something). **46. turn someone's head.** to make someone vain, conceited, etc. ~vb. **47.** (tr.) to be at the front or top of: to head the field. **48.** (tr.; often foll. by up) to be in the commanding or most important position. **49.** (often foll. by for) to go or cause to go (towards): where are you heading? **50.** to turn or steer (a vessel) as specified: to head into the wind. **51.** Soccer. to propel (the ball) by striking it with the head. **52.** (tr.) to provide with or be a head or heading for. **53.** (tr.) to cut the top branches or shoots off a tree or plant. **54.** (intr.) to form a head, as a plant. **55.** (intr.; often foll. by in) (of streams, rivers, etc.) to originate or rise. ~See also **head off, heads.** [OE hēafod] — **'headless** adj. — **'head,like** adj.

Head (hɛd) n. **Edith.** born 1907, U.S. dress designer: won many Oscars for her Hollywood film costume designs.

headache ('hɛd,eɪk) n. **1.** a continuous pain in the head. **2.** Inf. any cause of worry, difficulty, or annoyance. — **'head,achy** adj.

headband ('hɛd,bænd) n. 1. a ribbon or band worn around the head. 2. a narrow cloth band attached to the top of the spine of a book for protection or decoration.

head-banger n. Sl. 1. a person, esp. a teenager, who shakes his head violently to the beat of loud music. 2. a crazy or stupid person.

headboard ('hɛd,bɔːd) n. a vertical board or terminal at the head of a bed.

headdress ('hɛd,drɛs) n. any head covering, esp. an ornate one or one denoting a rank.

headed ('hɛdɪd) adj. 1. a. having a head or heads. b. (in combination): two-headed; bullet-headed. 2. having a heading: headed notepaper.

header ('hɛdə) n. 1. a machine that trims the heads from castings, forgings, etc., or one that forms heads, as in wire, to make nails. 2. a person who operates such a machine. 3. Also called: **header tank.** a reservoir that maintains a gravity feed or a static fluid pressure in an apparatus. 4. a brick or stone laid across a wall so that its end is flush with the outer surface. 5. the action of striking a ball with the head. 6. Inf. a headlong fall or dive.

headfirst ('hɛd'fɜːst) adj., adv. 1. with the head foremost; headlong. 2. rashly.

headgear ('hɛd,gɪə) n. 1. a hat. 2. any part of a horse's harness that is worn on the head. 3. the hoisting mechanism at the pithead of a mine.

headguard ('hɛd,gɑːd) n. a lightweight helmet-like piece of equipment worn to protect the head in various sports.

head-hunting n. 1. the practice among certain peoples of removing the heads of slain enemies and preserving them as trophies. 2. U.S. sl. the destruction or neutralization of political opponents. 3. (of a company or corporation) the recruitment of, or a drive to recruit, new high-level personnel, esp. in management or in specialist fields. —'**head-,hunter** n.

heading ('hɛdɪŋ) n. 1. a title for a page, chapter, etc. 2. a main division, as of a speech. 3. Mining. **a.** a horizontal tunnel. **b.** the end of such a tunnel. 4. the angle between the direction of an aircraft and a specified meridian, often due north. 5. the compass direction parallel to the keel of a vessel. 6. the act of heading.

headland n. 1. ('hɛdlənd). a narrow area of land jutting out into a sea, lake, etc. 2. ('hɛd,lænd). a strip of land along the edge of an arable field left unploughed to allow space for machines.

headlight ('hɛd,laɪt) or **headlamp** n. a powerful light, equipped with a reflector and attached to the front of a motor vehicle, etc.

headline ('hɛd,laɪn) n. 1. **a.** a phrase at the top of a newspaper or magazine article indicating the subject of the article, usually in larger and heavier type. **b.** a line at the top of a page indicating the title, page number, etc. 2. **hit the headlines.** to become prominent in the news. 3. (usually pl.) the main points of a television or radio news broadcast, read out before the full broadcast. ~vb. 4. (tr.) to furnish (a story or page) with a headline. 5. to have top billing (in).

headlong ('hɛd,lɒŋ) adv., adj. 1. with the head foremost; headfirst. 2. with great haste. ~adj. 3. Arch. (of slopes, etc.) very steep; precipitous.

headman ('hɛdmən) n., pl. -men. 1. Anthropol. a chief or leader. 2. a foreman or overseer.

headmaster (,hɛd'mɑːstə) or (fem.) **headmistress** n. the principal of a school.

headmost ('hɛd,məʊst) adj. foremost.

head off vb. (tr., adv.) 1. to intercept and force to change direction: to head off the stampede. 2. to prevent or forestall.

head-on adv., adj. 1. front foremost: a head-on collision. 2. with directness or without compromise: in his usual head-on fashion.

headphones ('hɛd,fəʊnz) pl. n. an electrical device consisting of two earphones held in position by a flexible metallic strap passing over the head. Informal name: **cans.**

headpiece ('hɛd,piːs) n. 1. Printing. a decorative band at the top of a page, chapter, etc. 2. a helmet. 3. Arch. the intellect.

headpin ('hɛd,pɪn) n. Tenpin bowling. another word for **kingpin** (sense 2).

headquarters (,hɛd'kwɔːtəz) pl. n. (sometimes functioning as sing.) 1. any centre from which operations are directed, as in the police. 2. a military formation comprising the commander and his staff. ~Abbrev.: **HQ, h.q.**

headrace ('hɛd,reɪs) n. a channel that carries water to a water wheel, turbine, etc.

headrest ('hɛd,rɛst) n. a support for the head, as on a dentist's chair or car seat.

head restraint n. an adjustable support for the head, attached to a car seat, to prevent the neck from being jolted backwards sharply in the event of a crash or sudden stop.

headroom ('hɛd,rʊm, -,ruːm) or **headway** n. the height of a bridge, room, etc.; clearance.

heads (hɛdz) interj., adv. with the obverse side of a coin uppermost, esp. if it has a head on it: used as a call before tossing a coin.

headscarf ('hɛd,skɑːf) n., pl. -scarves. a scarf for the head, often worn tied under the chin.

headset ('hɛd,sɛt) n. a pair of headphones, esp. with a microphone attached.

headship ('hɛdʃɪp) n. 1. the position or state of being a leader; command. 2. Brit. the position of headmaster or headmistress of a school.

headshrinker ('hɛd,ʃrɪŋkə) n. 1. a slang name for **psychiatrist.** Often shortened to **shrink.** 2. a head-hunter who shrinks the heads of his victims.

headsman ('hɛdzmən) n., pl. -men. (formerly) an executioner who beheaded condemned persons.

headstall ('hɛd,stɔːl) n. the part of a bridle that fits round a horse's head.

head start n. an initial advantage in a competitive situation.

headstock ('hɛd,stɒk) n. the part of a machine that supports and transmits the drive.

headstone ('hɛd,stəʊn) n. 1. a memorial stone at the head of a grave. 2. Archit. another name for **keystone.**

headstream ('hɛd,striːm) n. a stream that is the source or a source of a river.

headstrong ('hɛd,strɒŋ) adj. 1. self-willed; obstinate. 2. (of an action) heedless; rash.

head-up display n. a projection of readings from instruments onto a windscreen, enabling a pilot or driver to see them without moving his eyes.

head voice or **register** n. the high register of the human voice, in which the vibrations of sung notes are felt in the head.

headwaters ('hɛd,wɔːtəz) pl. n. the tributary streams of a river in the area in which it rises.

headway ('hɛd,weɪ) n. 1. motion forward: the vessel made no headway. 2. progress: he made no headway with the problem. 3. another name for **headroom.** 4. the interval between consecutive trains, buses, etc., on the same route.

headwind ('hɛd,wɪnd) n. a wind blowing directly against the course of an aircraft or ship.

headword ('hɛd,wɜːd) n. a key word placed at the beginning of a line, paragraph, etc., as in a dictionary entry.

headwork ('hɛd,wɜːk) n. 1. mental work. 2. the ornamentation of the keystone of an arch.

heady ('hɛdɪ) adj. **headier, headiest.** 1. (of alcoholic drink) intoxicating. 2. strongly affecting the senses; extremely exciting. 3. rash; impetuous. —'**headily** adv. —'**headiness** n.

heal (hiːl) vb. 1. to restore or be restored to health. 2. (intr.; often foll. by over or up) (of a wound) to repair by natural processes, as by scar formation. 3. (tr.) to cure (a disease or disorder). 4. to restore or be restored to friendly relations, harmony, etc. [OE hǣlan; see HALE[1], WHOLE] —'**healer** n. —'**healing** n., adj.

Healey ('hiːlɪ) n. Denis (Winston). born 1917, British Labour politician; Chancellor of the Exchequer (1974–79); deputy leader of the Labour Party (1980–83).

health (hɛlθ) n. 1. the state of being bodily and mentally vigorous and free from disease. 2. the general condition of body and mind: in poor health. 3. the condition of any unit, society, etc.: the economic health of a nation. 4. a toast to a person. 5. (modifier) of or relating to food or other goods reputed to be beneficial to the health: health food. 6. (modifier) of or relating to health: health service. [OE hǣlth; rel. to hāl HALE[1]]

health centre n. the surgery and offices of a group medical practice.

health farm n. a residential establishment, often in the country, visited by those who wish to improve their health by losing weight, eating health foods, taking exercise, etc.

health food n. vegetarian food organically grown and with no additives, eaten for its benefit to health. **b.** (as modifier): a health-food shop.

healthful ('hɛlθfʊl) adj. a less common word for **healthy** (senses 1–3).

health salts pl. n. magnesium sulphate or similar salts taken as a mild laxative.

health visitor n. (in Britain) a nurse employed to visit esp. mothers of babies, the handicapped, or elderly people in their homes to give help and advice on health and social welfare.

healthy ('hɛlθɪ) adj. **healthier, healthiest. 1.** enjoying good health. **2.** sound: the company's finances are not very healthy. **3.** conducive to health. **4.** indicating soundness of body or mind: a healthy appetite. **5.** Inf. considerable: a healthy sum. — **'healthily** adv. — **'healthiness** n.

heap (hiːp) n. **1.** a collection of articles or mass of material gathered in a pile. **2.** (often pl.; usually foll. by of) Inf. a large number or quantity. **3.** Inf. a thing that is very old, unreliable, etc.: the car was a heap. ~adv. **4. heaps.** (intensifier): he was heaps better. ~vb. **5.** (often foll. by up or together) to collect or be collected into or as if into a pile. **6.** (tr.; often foll. by with, on, or upon) to load (with) abundantly: to heap with riches. [OE héap]

hear (hɪə) vb. **hearing, heard** (hɜːd). **1.** (tr.) to perceive (a sound) with the sense of hearing. **2.** (tr.; may take a clause as object) to listen to: did you hear what I said? **3.** (when intr., sometimes foll. by of or about; when tr., may take a clause as object) to be informed (of); receive information (about). **4.** Law. to give a hearing to (a case). **5.** (when intr., usually foll. by of and used with a negative) to listen (to) with favour, assent, etc.: she wouldn't hear of it. **6.** (intr.; foll. by from) to receive a letter (from). **7. hear! hear!** an exclamation of approval. **8. hear tell (of).** Dialect. to be told (about). [OE hieran] — **'hearer** n.

Heard and McDonald Islands (hɜːd, mək'dɒnəld) pl. n. a group of islands in the S Indian Ocean: an external territory of Australia from 1947. Area: 412 sq. km (159 sq. miles).

hearing ('hɪərɪŋ) n. **1.** the sense by which sound is perceived. **2.** an opportunity to be listened to. **3.** the range within which sound can be heard; earshot. **4.** the investigation of a matter by a court of law, esp. the preliminary inquiry into an indictable crime by magistrates.

hearing aid n. a device for assisting the hearing of partially deaf persons, typically a small battery-powered amplifier worn in or behind the ear.

hearken or U.S. (sometimes) **harken** ('haːkən) vb. Arch. to listen to (something). [OE heorcnian]

hear out vb. (tr., adv.) to listen in regard to every detail and give a proper or full hearing to.

hearsay ('hɪə,seɪ) n. gossip; rumour.

hearsay evidence n. Law. evidence based on what has been reported to a witness by others rather than what he has himself observed.

hearse (hɜːs) n. a vehicle, such as a car or carriage, used to carry a coffin to the grave. [C14: from OF herce, from L hirpex harrow]

Hearst (hɜːst) n. **William Randolph.** 1863–1951, U.S. newspaper publisher, whose newspapers were noted for their sensationalism.

heart (haːt) n. **1.** the hollow muscular organ in vertebrates whose contractions propel the blood through the circulatory system. Related adj.: **cardiac. 2.** the corresponding organ in invertebrates. **3.** this organ considered as the seat of emotions, esp. love. **4.** emotional mood: a change of heart. **5.** tenderness or pity: you have no heart. **6.** courage or spirit. **7.** the most central part: the heart of the city. **8.** the most important part: the heart of the matter. **9.** (of vegetables, such as cabbage) the inner compact part. **10.** the breast: she held him to her heart. **11.** a dearly loved person: dearest heart. **12.** a conventionalized representation of the heart, having two rounded lobes at the top meeting in a point at the bottom. **13. a.** a red heart-shaped symbol on a playing card. **b.** a card with one or more of these symbols or (when pl.) the suit of cards so marked. **14.** a fertile condition in land (esp. in **in good heart**). **15. after one's own heart.** appealing to one's own disposition or taste. **16. break one's** (or **someone's**) **heart.** to grieve (or cause to grieve) very deeply, esp. through love. **17. by heart.** by

committing to memory. **18. eat one's heart out.** to brood or pine with grief or longing. **19. from (the bottom of) one's heart.** very sincerely or deeply. **20. have a change of heart.** to experience a profound change of outlook, attitude, etc. **21. have one's heart in one's mouth** (or throat). to be full of apprehension, excitement, or fear. **22. have one's heart in the right place.** to be kind, thoughtful, or generous. **23. have the heart.** (usually used with a negative) to have the necessary will, callousness, etc. (to do something): I didn't have the heart to tell him. **24. heart of hearts.** the depths of one's conscience or emotions. **25. heart of oak.** a brave person. **26. lose heart.** to become despondent or disillusioned (over something). **27. lose one's heart to.** to fall in love with. **28. set one's heart on.** to have as one's ambition to obtain; covet. **29. take heart.** to become encouraged. **30. take to heart.** to take seriously or be upset about. **31. wear one's heart on one's sleeve.** to show one's feelings openly. **32. with all one's heart.** very willingly. ~vb. (intr.) **33.** (of vegetables) to form a heart. ~See also **hearts.** [OE heorte]

heartache ('haːt,eɪk) n. intense anguish or mental suffering.

heart attack n. any sudden severe instance of abnormal heart functioning, esp. coronary thrombosis.

heartbeat ('haːt,biːt) n. one complete pulsation of the heart.

heart block n. impaired conduction of the impulse that regulates the heartbeat, resulting in a lack of coordination between the beating of the atria and the ventricles.

heartbreak ('haːt,breɪk) n. intense and overwhelming grief, esp. through disappointment in love. — **'heart,breaker** n. — **'heart,breaking** adj.

heartburn ('haːt,bɜːn) n. a burning sensation beneath the breastbone caused by irritation of the oesophagus. Technical names: **cardialgia, pyrosis.**

-hearted adj. having a heart or disposition as specified: cold-hearted; heavy-hearted.

hearten ('haːt°n) vb. to make or become cheerful. — **'heartening** adj.

heart failure n. **1.** a condition in which the heart is unable to pump an adequate amount of blood to the tissues. **2.** sudden cessation of the heartbeat, resulting in death.

heartfelt ('haːt,fɛlt) adj. sincerely and strongly felt.

hearth (haːθ) n. **1. a.** the floor of a fireplace, esp. one that extends outwards into the room. **b.** (as modifier): hearth rug. **2.** this as a symbol of the home, etc. **3.** the bottom part of a metallurgical furnace in which the molten metal is produced or contained. [OE heorth]

hearthstone ('haːθ,stəʊn) n. **1.** a stone that forms a hearth. **2.** soft stone used (esp. formerly) to clean and whiten floors, steps, etc.

heartily ('haːtɪlɪ) adv. **1.** thoroughly or vigorously. **2.** in a sincere manner.

heartland ('haːt,lænd) n. the central or most important region of a country or continent.

heartless ('haːtlɪs) adj. unkind or cruel. — **'heartlessly** adv. — **'heartlessness** n.

heart-lung machine n. a machine used to maintain the circulation and oxygenation of the blood during heart surgery.

heart-rending adj. causing great mental pain and sorrow. — **'heart-,rendingly** adv.

hearts (haːts) n. (functioning as sing.) a card game in which players must avoid winning tricks containing hearts or the queen of spades. Also called: **Black Maria.**

heart-searching n. examination of one's feelings or conscience.

heartsease or **heart's-ease** ('haːts,iːz) n. **1.** another name for the **wild pansy. 2.** peace of mind.

heartsick ('haːt,sɪk) adj. deeply despondent. — **'heart,sickness** n.

heartstrings ('haːt,strɪŋz) pl. n. Often facetious. deep emotions. [C15: orig. referring to the tendons supposed to support the heart]

heart-throb n. **1.** Brit. an object of infatuation. **2.** a heartbeat.

heart-to-heart adj. **1.** (esp. of a conversation) concerned with personal problems or intimate feelings. ~n. **2.** an intimate conversation.

heart-warming adj. **1.** pleasing; gratifying. **2.** emotionally moving.

heartwood ('hɑːt,wud) *n.* the central core of dark hard wood in tree trunks, consisting of nonfunctioning xylem tissue that has become blocked with resins, tannins, and oils.

hearty ('hɑːtɪ) *adj.* **heartier, heartiest. 1.** warm and unreserved in manner. **2.** vigorous and heartfelt: *hearty dislike.* **3.** healthy and strong (esp. in **hale and hearty**). **4.** substantial and nourishing. ~*n., pl.* **hearties.** *Inf.* **5.** a comrade, esp. a sailor. **6.** a vigorous sporting man: *a rugby hearty.* —'**heartily** *adv.* —'**heartiness** *n.*

heat (hiːt) *n.* **1.** the energy transferred as a result of a difference in temperature. Related adjs.: **thermal, calorific. 2.** the sensation caused by heat energy; warmth. **3.** the state of being hot. **4.** hot weather: *the heat of summer.* **5.** intensity of feeling: *the heat of rage.* **6.** the most intense part: *the heat of the battle.* **7.** a period of sexual excitement in female mammals that occurs at oestrus. **8.** *Sport.* **a.** a preliminary eliminating contest in a competition. **b.** a single section of a contest. **9.** *Sl.* police activity after a crime: *the heat is off.* **10.** *Sl., chiefly U.S.* criticism or abuse: *he took a lot of heat for that mistake.* **11. in** *or* **on heat. a.** Also: **in season.** of some female mammals) sexually receptive. **b.** in a state of sexual excitement. **12. in the heat of the moment.** without pausing to think. ~*vb.* **13.** to make or become hot or warm. **14.** to make or become excited or intense. [OE *hǣtu*]

heat barrier *n.* another name for **thermal barrier.**

heat capacity *n.* the heat required to raise the temperature of a substance by unit temperature interval under specified conditions.

heat death *n. Thermodynamics.* the condition of any closed system when its total entropy is a maximum and it has no available energy. If the universe is a closed system it should eventually reach this state.

heated ('hiːtɪd) *adj.* **1.** made hot. **2.** impassioned or highly emotional. —'**heatedly** *adv.*

heat engine *n.* an engine that does work when heat is supplied to it.

heater ('hiːtə) *n.* **1.** any device for supplying heat, such as a convector. **2.** *U.S. sl.* a pistol. **3.** *Electronics.* a conductor carrying a current that indirectly heats the cathode in some types of valve.

heat exchanger *n.* a device for transferring heat from one fluid to another without allowing them to mix.

heat exhaustion *n.* a condition resulting from exposure to intense heat, characterized by dizziness, abdominal cramp, and prostration.

heath (hiːθ) *n.* **1.** *Brit.* a large open area, usually with sandy soil and scrubby vegetation, esp. heather. **2.** Also called: **heather.** a low-growing evergreen shrub having small bell-shaped typically pink or purple flowers. **3.** any of several heathlike plants, such as sea heath. [OE *hǣth*] —'**heath,like** *adj.* —'**heathy** *adj.*

Heath (hiːθ) *n.* **Edward (Richard George).** born 1916, British statesman; leader of the Conservative Party (1965–75); prime minister 1970–74.

heathen ('hiːðən) *n., pl.* **-thens** *or* **-then. 1.** a person who does not acknowledge the God of Christianity, Judaism, or Islam; pagan. **2.** an uncivilized or barbaric person. ~*adj.* **3.** irreligious; pagan. **4.** uncivilized; barbaric. **5.** of or relating to heathen peoples or their customs and beliefs. [OE *hǣthen*] —'**heathendom** *n.* —'**heathenism** *or* '**heathenry** *n.*

heathenize *or* **-nise** ('hiːðə,naɪz) *vb.* to render or become heathen.

heather ('hɛðə) *n.* **1.** Also called: **ling, heath.** a low-growing evergreen Eurasian shrub that grows in dense masses on open ground and has clusters of small bell-shaped typically pinkish-purple flowers. **2.** a purplish-red to pinkish-purple colour. ~*adj.* **3.** of a heather colour. **4.** of or relating to interwoven yarns of mixed colours: *heather mixture.* [C14: orig. Scot. & N English, prob. from HEATH] —'**heathery** *adj.*

Heath Robinson (hiːθ 'rɒbɪnsən) *adj.* (of a mechanical device) absurdly complicated in design and having a simple function. [C20: after William *Heath Robinson* (1872–1944), E cartoonist who drew such contrivances]

heating ('hiːtɪŋ) *n.* **1.** a device or system for supplying heat, esp. central heating, to a building. **2.** the heat supplied.

heat pump *n.* a device for extracting heat from a source and delivering it elsewhere at a much higher temperature.

heat rash *n.* a nontechnical name for **miliaria.**

heat shield *n.* a coating or barrier for shielding from excessive heat, such as that experienced by a spacecraft on re-entry into the earth's atmosphere.

heat sink *n.* **1.** a metal plate designed to conduct and radiate heat from an electrical component. **2.** a layer within the outer skin of high-speed aircraft to absorb heat.

heatstroke ('hiːt,strəuk) *n.* a condition resulting from prolonged exposure to intense heat, characterized by high fever.

heat-treat *vb.* (*tr.*) to apply heat to (a metal or alloy) in one or more temperature cycles to give it desirable properties. —**heat treatment** *n.*

heat wave *n.* **1.** a continuous spell of abnormally hot weather. **2.** an extensive slow-moving air mass at a relatively high temperature.

heave (hiːv) *vb.* **heaving, heaved** *or* **hove. 1.** (*tr.*) to lift or move with a great effort. **2.** (*tr.*) to throw (something heavy) with effort. **3.** to utter (sounds) noisily or unhappily: *to heave a sigh.* **4.** to rise and fall or cause to rise and fall heavily. **5.** (*p.t. & p.p.* **hove**) *Naut.* **a.** to move or cause to move in a specified direction: *to heave in sight.* **b.** (*intr.*) (of a vessel) to pitch or roll. **6.** (*tr.*) to displace (rock strata, etc.) in a horizontal direction. **7.** (*intr.*) to retch. ~*n.* **8.** the act of heaving. **9.** a horizontal displacement of rock strata at a fault. ~See also **heave to, heaves.** [OE *hebban*] —'**heaver** *n.*

heave-ho *interj.* a sailors' cry, as when hoisting anchor.

heaven ('hɛvən) *n.* **1.** (*sometimes cap.*) *Christianity.* **a.** the abode of God and the angels. **b.** a state of communion with God after death. **2.** (*usually pl.*) the firmament surrounding the earth. **3.** (in various mythologies) a place, such as Elysium or Valhalla, to which those who have died in the gods' favour are brought to dwell in happiness. **4.** a place or state of happiness. **5.** (*sing.* or *pl.*; *sometimes cap.*) God or the gods, used in exclamatory phrases: *for heaven's sake.* **6. move heaven and earth.** to do everything possible (to achieve something). [OE *heofon*]

heavenly ('hɛvənlɪ) *adj.* **1.** *Inf.* wonderful. **2.** of or occurring in space: *a heavenly body.* **3.** holy. —'**heavenliness** *n.*

heavenward ('hɛvənwəd) *adj.* **1.** directed towards heaven or the sky. ~*adv.* **2.** Also **heavenwards.** towards heaven or the sky.

heaves (hiːvz) *n.* a chronic respiratory disorder of animals of the horse family, of unknown cause. Also called: **broken wind.**

heave to *vb.* (*adv.*) to stop (a vessel) or (of a vessel) to stop, as by trimming the sails, etc.

Heaviside ('hɛvɪ,saɪd) *n.* **Oliver.** 1850–1925, English physicist. Independently of Kennelly, he predicted (1902) the existence of an ionized gaseous layer in the upper atmosphere (the **Heaviside layer**); he also contributed to telegraphy.

Heaviside layer *n.* another name for **E region** (of the ionosphere). [C20: after O. HEAVISIDE]

heavy ('hɛvɪ) *adj.* **heavier, heaviest. 1.** of comparatively great weight. **2.** having a relatively high density: *lead is a heavy metal.* **3.** great in yield, quality, or quantity: *heavy traffic.* **4.** considerable: *heavy emphasis.* **5.** hard to bear or fulfil: *heavy demands.* **6.** sad or dejected: *heavy at heart.* **7.** coarse or broad: *heavy features.* **8.** (of soil) having a high clay content; cloggy. **9.** solid or fat: *heavy legs.* **10.** (of an industry) engaged in the large-scale complex manufacture of capital goods or extraction of raw materials. **11.** serious; grave. **12.** *Mil.* **a.** equipped with large weapons, armour, etc. **b.** (of guns, etc.) of a large and powerful type. **13.** (of a syllable) having stress or accentuation. **14.** dull and uninteresting: *a heavy style.* **15.** prodigious: *a heavy drinker.* **16.** (of cakes, etc.) insufficiently leavened. **17.** deep and loud: *a heavy thud.* **18.** (of music, literature, etc.) **a.** dramatic and powerful. **b.** not immediately comprehensible or appealing. **19.** *Sl.* (of rock music) having a powerful beat; hard. **20.** burdened: *heavy with child.* **21. heavy on.** *Inf.* using large quantities of: *this car is very heavy on petrol.* **22.** clumsy and slow: *heavy going.* **23.** cloudy or overcast: *heavy skies.* **24.** not easily digestible: *a heavy meal.* **25.** (of an element or compound) being or containing an isotope with greater atomic weight than that of the naturally occurring element: *heavy water.* **26.** (of the going on a racecourse) soft and muddy. **27.** *Sl.* using, or prepared to use, violence or brutality. ~*n.*, *pl.* **heavies. 28. a.** a villainous role. **b.** an actor who plays such a part. **29.** *Mil.* **a.** a large fleet unit, esp. an aircraft carrier or battleship. **b.** a large piece of artillery. **30.** *Inf.* (*usually pl.*; often preceded by *the*) a serious newspaper: *the Sunday heavies.* **31.** *Inf.* a heavyweight boxer, wrestler, etc. **32.** *Sl.* a man hired to threaten violence or deter others by his presence. ~*adv.* **33. a.** in a heavy manner; heavily: *time hangs heavy.* **b.** (*in combination*): *heavy-laden.* [OE *hefig*] — '**heavily** *adv.* — '**heaviness** *n.*

heavy-duty *n.* (*modifier*) made to withstand hard wear, bad weather, etc.

heavy-handed *adj.* **1.** clumsy. **2.** harsh and oppressive. — ,**heavy-'handedly** *adv.*

heavy-hearted *adj.* sad; melancholy.

heavy hydrogen *n.* another name for **deuterium.**

heavy metal *n.* a type of rock music characterized by a strong beat and amplified instrumental effects.

heavy middleweight *n.* a professional wrestler weighing 177–187 pounds (81–85 kg).

heavy spar *n.* another name for **barytes.**

heavy water *n.* water that has been electrolytically decomposed to reduce the amount of normal hydrogen present and enrich it in deuterium in the form D_2O or HDO. See also **deuterium oxide.**

heavyweight ('hɛvɪ,weɪt) *n.* **1.** a person or thing that is heavier than average. **2. a.** a professional boxer weighing more than 175 pounds (79 kg). **b.** an amateur boxer weighing over 81 kg (179 pounds). **3. a.** a professional wrestler weighing over 209 pounds (95 kg). **b.** an amateur wrestler weighing over 220 pounds (100kg). **4.** *Inf.* an important or highly influential person.

Heb. *or* **Hebr.** *abbrev. for:* **1.** Hebrew (language). **2.** *Bible.* Hebrews.

Hebbel (*German* 'hɛbəl) *n.* **Christian Friedrich** ('krɪstian 'friːdrɪç). 1813–63, German dramatist and lyric poet, whose historical works were influenced by Hegel; his major plays are *Maria Magdalena* (1844), *Herodes und Marianne* (1850), and the trilogy *Die Nibelungen* (1862).

hebdomadal (hɛb'dɒmədˀl) *adj.* weekly. [C18: from L, from Gk *hebdomas* seven (days), from *hepta* seven]

Hebe ('hiːbɪ) *n. Greek myth.* the goddess of youth and spring, daughter of Zeus and Hera and wife of Hercules.

Hebei ('hʌ'beɪ), **Hopeh,** *or* **Hopei** *n.* a province of NE China, on the Gulf of Chihli: important for the production of winter wheat, cotton, and coal. Capital: Shijiazhuang. Pop.: 54 870 000 (1985). Area: 202 700 sq. km (79 053 sq. miles).

Hébert (*French* ebɛr) *n.* **Jacques René** (ʒak rəne). 1755–94, French journalist and revolutionary: a leader of the sans-culottes during the French Revolution. He was guillotined under Robespierre.

hebetate ('hɛbɪ,teɪt) *adj.* **1.** (of plant parts) having a blunt or soft point. ~*vb.* **2.** *Rare.* to make or become blunted. [C16: from L *hebetāre* to make blunt, from *hebes* blunt] — ,**hebe'tation** *n.*

Hebraic (hɪ'breɪɪk) *or* **Hebraical** *adj.* of, relating to, or characteristic of the Hebrews or their language or culture. — He'**braically** *adv.*

Hebraism ('hiːbreɪ,ɪzəm) *n.* a linguistic usage, custom, or other feature borrowed from or particular to the Hebrew language, or to the Jewish people or their culture. — 'He**braist** *n.* — 'Hebra,**ize** *or* -,**ise** *vb.*

Hebrew ('hiːbruː) *n.* **1.** the ancient language of the Hebrews, revived as the official language of Israel. **2.** a member of an ancient Semitic people claiming descent from Abraham; an Israelite. **3.** *Arch. or offens.* a Jew. ~*adj.* **4.** of or relating to the Hebrews or their language. **5.** *Arch. or offens.* Jewish. [C13: from OF *Ebreu*, ult. from Heb. '*ibhrī* one from beyond (the river)]

Hebrides ('hɛbrɪ,diːz) *pl. n.* **the.** a group of over 500 islands off the W coast of Scotland: separated by the North Minch, Little Minch, and the Sea of the Hebrides: the chief islands are Skye, Raasay, Rhum, Eigg, Coll, Tiree, Mull, Jura, Colonsay, and Islay (**Inner Hebrides**), and Lewis with Harris, North Uist, Benbecula, South Uist, and Barra (**Outer Hebrides**). Also called: **Western Isles.** — ,Hebri'**dean** *or* **Hebridian** (hɛ'brɪdɪən) *adj.*, *n.*

Hebron ('hɛbrɒn, 'hiː-) *n.* a city on the West Bank of the Jordan: famous for the Haram, which includes the cenotaphs of Abraham and Sarah, Isaac and Rebecca, and Jacob and Leah. Pop.: 75 000 (1984 est.). Arabic name: **El Khalil.**

Hecate *or* **Hekate** ('hɛkətɪ) *n. Greek myth.* a goddess of the underworld.

hecatomb ('hɛkə,təum, -,tuːm) *n.* **1.** (in ancient Greece or Rome) any great public sacrifice and feast, originally one in which 100 oxen were sacrificed. **2.** a great sacrifice. [C16: from L *hecatombē*, from Gk, from *hekaton* hundred + *bous* ox]

heck (hɛk) *interj.* a mild exclamation of surprise, irritation, etc. [C19: euphemistic for *hell*]

heckelphone ('hɛkəl,fəun) *n. Music.* a type of bass oboe. [C20: after W. *Heckel* (1856-1909), G inventor]

heckle ('hɛkˀl) *vb.* **1.** to interrupt (a public speaker, etc.) by comments, questions, or taunts. **2.** (*tr.*) Also: **hackle, hatchel.** to comb (hemp or flax). ~*n.* **3.** an instrument for combing flax or hemp. [C15: N English & East Anglian form of HACKLE] — '**heckler** *n.*

hectare ('hɛktɑː) *n.* one hundred ares (10 000 square metres or 2.471 acres). Symbol: ha [C19: from F; see HECTO-, ARE²]

hectic ('hɛktɪk) *adj.* **1.** characterized by extreme activity or excitement. **2.** associated with or symptomatic of tuberculosis (esp. in **hectic fever, hectic flush**). ~*n.* **3.** a hectic fever or flush. **4.** *Rare.* a person who is consumptive. [C14: from LL *hecticus*, from Gk *hektikos* habitual, from *hexis* state, from *ekhein* to have] — '**hectically** *adv.*

hecto- *or before a vowel* **hect-** *prefix.* denoting 100: *hectogram.* Symbol: h [via F from Gk *hekaton* hundred]

hectog *abbrev. for* hectogram.

hectogram *or* **hectogramme** ('hɛktəu,græm) *n.* one hundred grams (3.527 ounces). Symbol: hg

hectograph ('hɛktəu,grɑːf) *n.* **1.** a process for copying type or manuscript from a glycerin-coated gelatin master to which the original has been transferred. **2.** a machine using this process.

hector ('hɛktə) *vb.* **1.** to bully or torment by teasing. ~*n.* **2.** a blustering bully. [C17: after HECTOR, in the sense: a bully]

Hector ('hɛktə) *n. Classical myth.* a son of King Priam of Troy, who was killed by Achilles.

Hecuba ('hɛkjubə) *n. Classical myth.* the wife of King Priam of Troy, and mother of Hector and Paris.

he'd (hiːd; *unstressed* iːd, hɪd, ɪd) *contraction of* he had *or* he would.

heddle ('hɛdˀl) *n.* one of a set of frames of vertical wires on a loom, each wire having an eye through which a warp thread can be passed. [OE *hefeld* chain]

hedera ('hɛdərə) *n.* the genus name of **ivy** (sense 1). [L]

hedge (hɛdʒ) *n.* **1.** a row of shrubs or bushes forming a boundary. **2.** a barrier or protection against something. **3.** the act or a method of reducing the risk of loss on an investment, etc. **4.** a cautious or evasive statement. **5.** (*as modifier*) low, inferior, or illiterate: *hedge priest.* ~*vb.* **6.** (*tr.*) to enclose or separate with or as if with a hedge. **7.** (*intr.*) to make or maintain a hedge. **8.** (*tr.*) to hinder or restrict. **9.** (*intr.*) to evade decision, esp. by making noncommittal statements. **10.** (*tr.*) to guard against the risk of loss in (a bet, etc.), esp. by laying bets with other bookmakers. **11.** (*intr.*) to protect against loss through future price fluctuations, as by investing in futures. [OE *hecg*] — '**hedger** *n.* — '**hedging** *n.*

hedgehog ('hɛdʒ,hɒg) *n.* a small nocturnal Old World mammal having a protective covering of spines on the back.

hedgehop ('hɛdʒ,hɒp) *vb.* -**hopping, -hopped.** (*intr.*) (of an aircraft) to fly close to the ground, as in crop spraying. — 'hedge,**hopping** *n.*, *adj.*

hedgerow ('hɛdʒ,rəu) *n.* a hedge of shrubs or low trees, esp. one bordering a field.

hedge sparrow *n.* a small brownish European songbird. Also called: **dunnock.**

Hedjaz (hiː'dʒæz) *n.* a variant spelling of **Hejaz.**

hedonics (hiː'dɒnɪks) *n.* (*functioning as sing.*) **1.** the branch of psychology concerned with the study of pleasant and unpleasant sensations. **2.** (in philosophy) the study of pleasure.

hedonism ('hiːdˀ,nɪzəm, 'hɛd-) *n.* **1.** *Ethics.* **a.** the doctrine that moral value can be defined in terms of pleasure. **b.** the doctrine that the pursuit of pleasure is the highest good. **2.** indulgence in sensual pleasures. [C19: from Gk *hēdonē* pleasure] — ,hedon'**istic** *adj.* — '**hedonist** *n.*

-hedron *n. combining form.* indicating a solid having a specified number of surfaces: *tetrahedron.* [from Gk

-edron -sided, from *hedra* seat, base] —*-hedral* adj. combining form.

heebie-jeebies ('hiːbɪ'dʒiːbɪz) pl. n. **the.** Sl. apprehension and nervousness. [C20: coined by W. De Beck (1890–1942), American cartoonist]

heed (hiːd) n. **1.** careful attention; notice: *to take heed.* ∼vb. **2.** to pay close attention to (someone or something). [OE *hēdan*] — **'heedful** adj. — **'heedfully** adv. — **'heedfulness** n.

heedless ('hiːdlɪs) adj. taking no notice; careless or thoughtless. — **'heedlessly** adv. — **'heedlessness** n.

heehaw (ˌhiː'hɔː) interj. an imitation or representation of the braying sound of a donkey.

heel[1] (hiːl) n. **1.** the back part of the human foot. **2.** the corresponding part in other vertebrates. **3.** the part of a stocking, etc., designed to fit the heel. **4.** the outer part of a shoe underneath the heel. **5.** the end or back section of something: *the heel of a loaf.* **6.** *Horticulture.* the small part of the parent plant that remains attached to a young shoot cut for propagation. **7.** the back part of a golf club head where it bends to join the shaft. **8.** Sl. a contemptible person. **9. at** (or **on**) **one's heels.** following closely. **10. cool** (or **kick**) **one's heels.** to wait or be kept waiting. **11. down at heel. a.** shabby or worn. **b.** slovenly. **12. take to one's heels.** to run off. **13. to heel.** under control, as a dog walking by a person's heel. ∼vb. **14.** (tr.) to repair or replace the heel of (a shoe, etc.). **15.** (tr.) Golf. to strike (the ball) with the heel of the club. **16.** to follow at the heels of (a person). [OE *hēla*] — **'heelless** adj.

heel[2] (hiːl) vb. **1.** (of a vessel) to lean over; list. ∼n. **2.** inclined position from the vertical. [OE *hieldan*]

heelball ('hiːlˌbɔːl) n. **a.** a mixture of beeswax and lampblack used by shoemakers to blacken the edges of heels and soles. **b.** a similar substance used to take rubbings, esp. brass rubbings.

heeler ('hiːlə) n. **1.** U.S. See **ward heeler**. **2.** a person or thing that heels. **3.** Austral. & N.Z. a dog that herds cattle, etc., by biting at their heels.

heel in vb. (tr., adv.) to insert (cuttings, shoots, etc.) into the soil before planting to keep them moist.

heeltap ('hiːlˌtæp) n. **1.** a layer of leather, etc., in the heel of a shoe. **2.** a small amount of alcoholic drink left at the bottom of a glass.

Heenan ('hiːnən) n. **John Carmel.** 1905–75, Irish cardinal; archbishop of Westminster (1963–75).

Heerlen ('hɪələn; Dutch 'heːrlə) n. a city in the SE Netherlands, in Limburg province: industrial centre of a coalmining region. Pop.: 91 291 (1982 est.).

Hefei (hʌ'feɪ) or **Hofei** n. a city in SE China, capital of Anhui province: administrative and commercial centre in a rice- and cotton-growing region. Pop.: 815 000 (1983 est.).

heft (hɛft) vb. (tr.) Brit. dialect. & U.S. inf. **1.** to assess the weight of (something) by lifting. **2.** to lift. ∼n. **3.** weight. **4.** U.S. the main part. [C19: prob. from HEAVE, by analogy with *thieve, theft, cleave, cleft*]

hefty ('hɛftɪ) adj. **heftier, heftiest.** Inf. **1.** big and strong. **2.** characterized by vigour or force: *a hefty blow.* **3.** bulky or heavy. **4.** sizable; involving a large amount of money: *a hefty bill.* — **'heftily** adv.

Hegel ('heɪɡəl) n. **Georg Wilhelm Friedrich** (ge'ɔrk 'vɪlhɛlm 'friːdrɪç). 1770–1831, German philosopher, who created a fundamentally influential system of thought. His view of man's mind as the highest expression of the Absolute is expounded in *The Phenomenology of Mind* (1807). He developed his concept of dialectic, in which the contradiction between a proposition (thesis) and its antithesis is resolved at a higher level of truth (synthesis), in *Science of Logic* (1812–16). — **Hegelian** (hɪ'ɡeɪlɪən, heɪ'ɡiː-) adj. — **He'gelian,ism** n.

hegemony (hɪ'ɡɛmənɪ) n., pl. **-nies.** ascendancy or domination of one power or state within a league, confederation, etc. [C16: from Gk *hēgemonia*, from *hēgemōn* leader, from *hēgeisthai* to lead] — **hegemonic** (ˌhɛɡə'mɒnɪk) adj.

Hegira or **Hejira** ('hɛdʒɪrə) n. **1.** the flight of Mohammed from Mecca to Medina in 622 A.D.; the starting point of the Muslim era. **2.** the Muslim era itself. **3.** (often not cap.) an escape or flight. [C16: from Med. L, from Ar. *hijrah* flight]

Heidegger (German 'haidɛɡər) n. **Martin** ('martiːn). 1889–1976, German existentialist philosopher: he expounded his ontological system in *Being and Time* (1927).

Heidelberg ('haɪdˌbɜːɡ; German 'haidəlbɛrk) n. a city in SW West Germany, in NW Baden-Württemberg on the River Neckar: capital of the Palatinate from the 13th century until 1719; famous castle (begun in the 12th century) and university (1386), the oldest in Germany. Pop.: 135 800 (1986).

heifer ('hɛfə) n. a young cow. [OE *heahfore*]

Heifetz ('haɪfɪts) n. **Jascha** ('jæʃə). 1901–87, U.S. violinist, born in Russia.

heigh-ho ('heɪ'həʊ) interj. an exclamation of weariness, surprise, or happiness.

height (haɪt) n. **1.** the vertical distance from the bottom of something to the top. **2.** the vertical distance of a place above sea level. **3.** relatively great altitude. **4.** the topmost point; summit. **5.** Astron. the angular distance of a celestial body above the horizon. **6.** the period of greatest intensity: *the height of the battle.* **7.** an extreme example: *the height of rudeness.* **8.** (often pl.) an area of high ground. [OE *hiehthu*; see HIGH]

heighten ('haɪtᵊn) vb. to make or become higher or more intense. — **'heightened** adj.

height of land n. U.S. & Canad. a watershed.

Heilbronn (German hail'brɔn) n. a city in SW West Germany, in N Baden-Württemberg on the River Neckar. Pop.: 111 400 (1986).

Heilongjiang ('heɪ'tʊŋdʒaɪ'æŋ) or **Heilungkiang** ('heɪ'lʊŋ'kjæŋ, -kaɪ'æŋ) n. a province of NE China, in Manchuria: coal-mining, with placer gold in some rivers. Capital: Harbin. Pop.: 32 950 000 (1985). Area: 464 000 sq. km (179 000 sq. miles).

Heilong Jiang ('heɪ'lʊŋ 'dʒaɪ'æŋ) n. the Pinyin transliteration of the Chinese name for the **Amur.**

Heimdall, Heimdal ('heɪm,daːl), or **Heimdallr** ('heɪm,daːl) n. Norse myth. the god of light and the dawn, and the guardian of the rainbow bridge Bifrost.

Heine (German 'hainə) n. **Heinrich** ('hainrɪç). 1797–1856, German poet and essayist, whose chief poetic work is *Das Buch der Lieder* (1827). Many of his poems have been set to music, notably by Schubert and Schumann.

Heinkel (German 'haɪŋkᵊl) n. **Ernst Heinrich** (ɛrnst 'hainrɪç). 1888–1958, German aircraft designer. His company provided many military aircraft in World Wars I and II, including the first jet-powered plane.

heinous ('heɪnəs, 'hiː-) adj. evil; atrocious. [C14: from OF *haineus*, from *haine* hatred, of Gmc origin] — **'heinously** adv.

heir (ɛə) n. **1.** the person legally succeeding to all property of a deceased person. **2.** any person or thing that carries on some tradition, circumstance, etc., from a forerunner. [C13: from OF, from L *hērēs*] — **'heirdom** or **'heirship** n.

heir apparent n., pl. **heirs apparent.** a person whose right to succeed to certain property cannot be defeated, provided such person survives his ancestor.

heiress ('ɛərɪs) n. **1.** a woman who inherits or expects to inherit great wealth. **2.** a female heir.

heirloom ('ɛəˌluːm) n. **1.** an object that has been in a family for generations. **2.** an item of personal property inherited in accordance with the terms of a will. [C15: from HEIR + *lome* tool; see LOOM[1]]

heir presumptive n. Property law. a person who expects to succeed to an estate but whose right may be defeated by the birth of one nearer in blood to the ancestor.

Heisenberg ('haɪzᵊn,bɜːɡ; German 'haizənbɛrk) n. **Werner Karl** ('vɛrnər karl). 1901–76, German physicist. He contributed to quantum mechanics and formulated the uncertainty principle (1927): Nobel prize for physics 1932.

heist (haɪst) Sl., chiefly U.S. & Canad. ∼n. **1.** a robbery. ∼vb. **2.** (tr.) to steal. [var. of HOIST]

Heitler (German 'haitlər) n. **Walter** ('valtər). 1904–81, German physicist, noted for his work on chemical bonds.

Hejaz, Hedjaz, or **Hijaz** (hiː'dʒæz) n. a provincial area of W Saudi Arabia, along the Red Sea and the Gulf of Aqaba: formerly an independent kingdom; united with Nejd in 1932 to form Saudi Arabia. Capital: Mecca. Pop.: 3 043 189 (1985 est.). Area: about 348 600 sq. km (134 600 sq. miles).

Hejira ('hɛdʒɪrə) *n.* a variant spelling of **Hegira**.
Hekate ('hɛkətɪ) *n.* a variant spelling of **Hecate**.
Hekla ('hɛklə) *n.* a volcano in SW Iceland: several craters, with the last eruption in 1970. Height: 1491 m (4892 ft.).
Hel (hɛl) *or* **Hela** ('hɛlɑː) *n. Norse myth.* **1.** the goddess of the dead. **2.** the underworld realm of the dead.
held (hɛld) *vb.* the past tense and past participle of **hold**[1].
Helen ('hɛlɪn) *n. Greek myth.* the beautiful daughter of Zeus and Leda, whose abduction by Paris from her husband Menelaus caused the Trojan War.
Helena ('hɛlənə) *n.* a city in W Montana: the state capital. Pop.: 24 289 (1982 est.).
helenium (hɛ'liːnɪəm) *n.* a perennial garden plant with yellow, bronze, or crimson flowers. [from Gk *helenion* name of a plant]
Helgoland ('hɛlgolant) *n.* the German name for **Heligoland**.
heliacal rising (hɪ'laɪəkəl) *n.* **1.** the rising of a celestial object at the same time as the sun. **2.** the date at which such a celestial object first becomes visible. [C17: from LL *hēliacus* relating to the sun, from Gk, from *hēlios* sun]
helianthemum (hiːlɪ'ænθəməm) *n.* any of a genus of dwarf shrubs with brightly coloured flowers: often grown in rockeries. [from Gk *helios* sun + *anthemon* flower]
helianthus (hiːlɪ'ænθəs) *n., pl.* -thuses. a plant of the composite family having large yellow daisy-like flowers with yellow, brown, or purple centres. [C18: NL, from Gk *hēlios* sun + *anthos* flower]
helical ('hɛlɪkəl) *adj.* of or like a helix; spiral.
helical gear *n.* a gearwheel having the tooth form generated on a helical path about the axis of the wheel.
helices ('hɛlɪˌsiːz) *n.* a plural of **helix**.
helichrysum (ˌhɛlɪ'kraɪzəm) *n.* any plant of the genus *Helichrysum*, whose flowers retain their shape and colour when dried. [C16: from L, from Gk, from *helix* spiral + *khrusos* gold]
helicoid ('hɛlɪˌkɔɪd) *adj.* **1.** *Biol.* shaped like a spiral: *a helicoid shell.* ~*n.* **2.** *Geom.* any surface resembling that of a screw thread.
helicon ('hɛlɪkən) *n.* a bass tuba made to coil over the shoulder of a band musician. [C19: prob. from HELICON; associated with Gk *helix* spiral]
Helicon ('hɛlɪkən) *n.* a mountain in Greece, in Boeotia: location of the springs of Hippocrene and Aganippe, believed by the Ancient Greeks to be the source of poetic inspiration and the home of the Muses. Height: 1749 m (5738 ft.). Modern Greek name: **Elikón**.
helicopter ('hɛlɪˌkɒptə) *n.* an aircraft capable of hover, vertical flight, and horizontal flight in any direction. Most get all of their lift and propulsion from the rotation of overhead blades. [C19: from F, from Gk *helix* spiral + *pteron* wing]
helicopter gunship *n.* a large heavily armed helicopter used for ground attack.
Heligoland ('hɛlɪgəʊˌlænd) *n.* a small island in the North Sea, one of the North Frisian Islands, separated from the coast of NW West Germany by **Heligoland Bight:** administratively part of the West German state of Schleswig-Holstein: a large island in early medieval times, now eroded to an area of about 150 hectares (380 acres); ceded by Britain to Germany in 1890 in exchange for Zanzibar. German name: **Helgoland**.
helio- *or before a vowel* **heli-** *combining form.* indicating the sun: *heliocentric.* [from Gk, from Gk *hēlios* sun]
heliocentric (ˌhiːlɪəʊ'sɛntrɪk) *adj.* **1.** having the sun at its centre. **2.** measured from or in relation to the sun. —ˌhelio'centrically *adv.*
Heliogabalus (ˌhiːlɪəʊ'gæbələs) *or* **Elagabalus** *n.* original name *Varius Avitus Bassianus.* ?204–222 A.D., Roman emperor (218–222). His reign was notorious for debauchery and extravagance.
heliograph ('hiːlɪəʊˌgrɑːf) *n.* **1.** an instrument with mirrors and a shutter used for sending messages in Morse code by reflecting the sun's rays. **2.** a device used to photograph the sun. —ˌheli'ography *n.*
heliometer (ˌhiːlɪ'ɒmɪtə) *n.* a refracting telescope used to determine angular distances between celestial bodies. —ˌheli'ometry *n.*
Heliopolis (ˌhiːlɪ'ɒpəlɪs) *n.* **1.** (in ancient Egypt) a city near the apex of the Nile delta: a centre of sun worship. Ancient Egyptian name: **On**. **2.** the Ancient Greek name for **Baalbek**.

heliopsis (ˌhɛlɪ'ɒpsɪs) *n.* a perennial plant with yellow daisy-like flowers.
Helios ('hiːlɪˌɒs) *n. Greek myth.* the god of the sun, who drove his chariot daily across the sky. Roman counterpart: **Sol**.
heliostat ('hiːlɪəʊˌstæt) *n.* an astronomical instrument used to reflect the light of the sun in a constant direction. —ˌhelio'static *adj.*
heliotrope ('hiːlɪəˌtrəʊp, 'hɛljə-) *n.* **1.** any plant of the genus *Heliotropium*, esp. the South American variety, cultivated for its small fragrant purple flowers. **2. a.** a bluish-violet to purple colour. **b.** (*as adj.*): *a heliotrope dress.* **3.** another name for **bloodstone**. [C17: from L *hēliotropium*, from Gk, from *hēlios* sun + *trepein* to turn]
heliotropism (ˌhiːlɪ'trəˌpɪzəm) *n.* the growth of a plant in response to the stimulus of sunlight. —**heliotropic** (ˌhiːlɪəʊ'trɒpɪk) *adj.*
heliport ('hɛlɪˌpɔːt) *n.* an airport for helicopters. [C20: from HELI(COPTER) + PORT[1]]
helium ('hiːlɪəm) *n.* a very light nonflammable colourless odourless element that is an inert gas, occurring in certain natural gases. Symbol: He; atomic no.: 2; atomic wt.: 4.0026. [C19: NL, from HELIO- + -IUM; because first detected in the solar spectrum]
helix ('hiːlɪks) *n., pl.* **helices** *or* **helixes**. **1.** a spiral. **2.** the incurving fold that forms the margin of the external ear. **3.** another name for **volute** (sense 2). **4.** any terrestrial mollusc of the genus *Helix*, which includes the garden snail. [C16: from L, from Gk: spiral; prob. rel. to Gk *helissein* to twist]
hell (hɛl) *n.* **1.** (*sometimes cap.*) *Christianity.* **a.** the place or state of eternal punishment of the wicked after death. **b.** forces of evil regarded as residing there. **2.** (*sometimes cap.*) (in various religions and cultures) the abode of the spirits of the dead. **3.** pain, extreme difficulty, etc. **4.** *Inf.* a cause of such suffering: *war is hell.* **5.** *U.S. & Canad.* high spirits or mischievousness. **6.** *Now rare.* a gambling house. **7.** (**come**) **hell or high water.** *Inf.* whatever difficulties may arise. **8. for the hell of it.** *Inf.* for the fun of it. **9. give someone hell.** *Inf.* **a.** to give someone a severe reprimand or punishment. **b.** to be a source of torment to someone. **10. hell for leather.** at great speed. **11. hell to pay.** *Inf.* serious consequences, as of a foolish action. **12. the hell.** *Inf.* **a.** (intensifier): used in such phrases as **what the hell. b.** an expression of strong disagreement: *the hell I will.* **13.** *Inf.* an exclamation of anger, surprise, etc. [OE *hell*]
he'll (hiːl; *unstressed* iːl, hɪl, ɪl) *contraction of* he will *or* he shall.
Helladic (hɛ'lædɪk) *adj.* of or relating to the Bronze Age civilization that flourished about 2900 to 1100 B.C. on the Greek mainland and islands.
Hellas ('hɛləs) *n.* transliteration of the ancient Greek name for **Greece**.
hellbent (ˌhɛl'bɛnt) *adj.* (*postpositive;* foll. by *on*) *Inf.* strongly or rashly intent.
hellcat ('hɛlˌkæt) *n.* a spiteful fierce-tempered woman.
Helle ('hɛlɪ) *n. Greek myth.* a daughter of King Athamas, who was borne away with her brother Phrixus on the golden winged ram. She fell from its back and was drowned in the Hellespont. See also **Phrixus, Golden Fleece**.
hellebore ('hɛlɪˌbɔː) *n.* **1.** any plant of the Eurasian genus *Helleborus*, typically having showy flowers and poisonous parts. See also **Christmas rose**. **2.** any of various plants which yield alkaloids used in the treatment of heart disease. [C14: from Gk *helleboros*, from ?]
Hellen ('hɛlɪn) *n.* (in Greek legend) a Thessalian king and eponymous ancestor of the Hellenes.
Hellene ('hɛliːn) *or* **Hellenian** (hɛ'liːnɪən) *n.* another name for a **Greek**.
Hellenic (hɛ'lɛnɪk, -'liː-) *adj.* **1.** of or relating to the ancient or modern Greeks or their language. **2.** of or relating to ancient Greece or the Greeks of the classical period (776–323 B.C.). Cf. **Hellenistic**. ~*n.* **3.** the Greek language in its various ancient and modern dialects.
Hellenism ('hɛlɪˌnɪzəm) *n.* **1.** the principles, ideals, and pursuits associated with classical Greek civilization. **2.** the spirit or national character of the Greeks. **3.** imitation of or devotion to the culture of ancient Greece. —**Hellenist** *n.*

Hellenistic (ˌhɛlɪˈnɪstɪk) or **Hellenistical** adj. 1. characteristic of or relating to Greek civilization in the Mediterranean world, esp. from the death of Alexander the Great (323 B.C.) to the defeat of Antony and Cleopatra (30 B.C.). 2. of or relating to the Greeks or to Hellenism. —ˌHellen'istically adv.

Hellenize or **-nise** (ˈhɛlɪˌnaɪz) vb. to make or become like the ancient Greeks. —ˌHelleni'zation or **-ni'sation** n.

Heller (ˈhɛlə) n. **Joseph.** born 1923, U.S. novelist. His works include Catch 22 (1961), God Knows (1984), and Picture This (1988).

Helles (ˈhɛlɪs) n. **Cape.** a cape in NW Turkey, at the S end of the Gallipoli Peninsula.

Hellespont (ˈhɛlɪˌspɒnt) n. the ancient name for the **Dardanelles.**

hellfire (ˈhɛlˌfaɪə) n. 1. the torment of hell, envisaged as eternal fire. 2. (modifier) characterizing sermons that emphasize this.

hellion (ˈhɛljən) n. Chiefly U.S. inf. a rowdy person, esp. a child; troublemaker. [C19: prob. from dialect hallion rogue, from ?]

hellish (ˈhɛlɪʃ) adj. 1. of or resembling hell. 2. wicked; cruel. 3. Inf. very unpleasant. ~adv. 4. Brit. inf. (intensifier): a hellish good idea.

hello, hallo, or **hullo** (hɛˈləʊ, hə-; ˈhɛləʊ) sentence substitute. 1. an expression of greeting. 2. a call used to attract attention. 3. an expression of surprise. ~n., pl. **-los.** 4. the act of saying or calling "hello". [C19: see HOLLO]

Hell's Angel n. a member of a motorcycle gang who typically dress in Nazi-style paraphernalia and are noted for their lawless behaviour.

helm[1] (hɛlm) n. 1. Naut. **a.** the wheel or entire apparatus by which a vessel is steered. **b.** the position of the helm: that is, on the side of the keel opposite from that of the rudder. 2. a position of leadership or control (esp. in **at the helm**). ~vb. 3. (tr.) to steer. [OE helma] — **'helmsman** n.

helm[2] (hɛlm) n. an archaic or poetic word for **helmet.** [OE helm]

Helmand (ˈhɛlmənd) n. a river in S Asia, rising in E Afghanistan and flowing generally southwest to a marshy lake, Hamun Helmand, on the border with Iran. Length: 1400 km (870 miles).

helmet (ˈhɛlmɪt) n. 1. a piece of protective or defensive armour for the head worn by soldiers, policemen, firemen, divers, etc. 2. Biol. a part or structure resembling a helmet, esp. the upper part of the calyx of certain flowers. [C15: from OF, dim. of helme, of Gmc origin] — **'helmeted** adj.

Helmholtz (German ˈhɛlmhɒlts) n. Baron **Hermann Ludwig Ferdinand von** (ˈhɛrman ˈluːtvɪç ˈfɛrdinant fɔn). 1821–94, German physiologist, physicist, and mathematician: helped to found the theory of the conservation of energy; invented the ophthalmoscope (1850); and investigated the mechanics of sight and sound.

helminth (ˈhɛlmɪnθ) n. any parasitic worm, esp. a nematode or fluke. [C19: from Gk helmins parasitic worm] — **hel'minthic** or **helminthoid** (ˈhɛlmɪnˌθɔɪd, hɛlˈmɪnθɔɪd) adj.

helminthiasis (ˌhɛlmɪnˈθaɪəsɪs) n. infestation of the body with parasitic worms. [C19: from NL, from Gk helminthian to be infested with worms]

Helmont (Flemish ˈhɛlmɔnt) n. **Jean Baptiste van** (ʒɑ̃ batist vɑn). 1577–1644, Flemish chemist and physician. He was the first to distinguish gases and claimed to have coined the word gas.

Héloïse (ˈɛləʊˌiːz; French elɔiz) n. ?1101–64, pupil, mistress, and wife of Abelard.

helot (ˈhɛlət, ˈhiː-) n. 1. (cap.) (in ancient Sparta) a member of the class of serfs owned by the state. 2. a serf or slave. [C16: from L Hēlōtes, from Gk Heilōtes, alleged to have meant orig.: inhabitants of Helos, who, after its conquest, were serfs of the Spartans] — **'helotism** n. — **'helotry** n.

help (hɛlp) vb. 1. to assist (someone to do something), esp. by sharing the work, cost, or burden of something. 2. to alleviate the burden of (someone else) by giving assistance. 3. (tr.) to assist (a person) to go in a specified direction: help the old lady up. 4. to contribute to: to help the relief operations. 5. to improve (a situation, etc.): crying won't help. 6. (tr.; preceded by can, could, etc.; usually used with a negative) **a.** to refrain from: we can't help wondering who he is. **b.** (usually foll. by it) to be

responsible for: I can't help it if it rains. 7. to alleviate (an illness, etc.). 8. (tr.) to serve (a customer). 9. (tr.; foll. by to) **a.** to serve (someone with food, etc.) (usually in **help oneself**). **b.** to provide (oneself with) without permission. 10. **cannot help but** to be unable to do anything else except: I cannot help but laugh. 11. **so help me. a.** on my honour. **b.** no matter what: so help me, I'll get revenge. ~n. 12. the act of helping or being helped, or a person or thing that helps. 13. **a.** a person hired for a job, esp. a farm worker or domestic servant. **b.** (functioning as sing.) several employees collectively. 14. a remedy: there's no help for it. ~sentence substitute. 15. used to ask for assistance. ~See also **help out.** [OE helpan] — **'helper** n.

helpful (ˈhɛlpfʊl) adj. giving help. — **'helpfully** adv. — **'helpfulness** n.

helping (ˈhɛlpɪŋ) n. a single portion of food.

helping hand n. assistance: many people lent a helping hand in making arrangements.

helpless (ˈhɛlplɪs) adj. 1. unable to manage independently. 2. made weak: they were helpless from giggling. — **'helplessly** adv. — **'helplessness** n.

helpline (ˈhɛlpˌlaɪn) n. a telephone line specially set aside to enable callers to contact an agency or organization for help with a particular problem.

Helpmann (ˈhɛlpmən) n. Sir **Robert.** 1909–86, Australian ballet dancer and choreographer: his ballets include Miracle in the Gorbals (1944), Display (1965), and Yugen (1965).

helpmate (ˈhɛlpˌmeɪt) n. a companion and helper, esp. a wife.

helpmeet (ˈhɛlpˌmiːt) n. a less common word for **helpmate.** [C17: from an helpe meet (suitable) for him Genesis 2:18]

help out vb. (adv.) to assist, esp. by sharing the burden or cost of something with (another person).

Helsingborg (Swedish hɛlsɪŋˈbɔrj) n. a variant spelling of **Hälsingborg.**

Helsingor (Danish hɛlseŋˈoːr) n. a port in NE Denmark, in NE Zealand: site of Kronborg Castle (16th century), famous as the scene of Shakespeare's Hamlet. Pop.: 56 618 (1987). English name: **Elsinore.**

Helsinki (ˈhɛlsɪŋkɪ, hɛlˈsɪŋ-) n. the capital of Finland, a port in the south on the Gulf of Finland: founded by Gustavus I of Sweden in 1550; replaced Turku as capital in 1812, while under Russian rule; university. Pop.: 487 581 (1985). Swedish name: **Helsingfors** (hɛlsɪŋˈfɔrs).

helter-skelter (ˈhɛltəˈskɛltə) adj. 1. haphazard or careless. ~adv. 2. in a helter-skelter manner. ~n. 3. Brit. a high spiral slide, as at a fairground. 4. disorder. [C16: prob. imit.]

helve (hɛlv) n. the handle of a hand tool such as an axe or pick. [OE hielfe]

Helvellyn (hɛlˈvɛlɪn) n. a mountain in NW England, in the Lake District. Height: 950 m (3118 ft.).

Helvetia (hɛlˈviːʃə) n. 1. the Latin name for Switzerland. 2. a Roman province in central Europe (1st century B.C. to the 5th century A.D.), corresponding to part of S Germany and parts of W and N Switzerland.

Helvetian (hɛlˈviːʃən) adj. 1. Swiss. ~n. 2. a native or citizen of Switzerland.

Helvétius (hɛlˈviːʃɪəs; French ɛlvesjys) n. **Claude Adrien** (klod adriɛ̃). 1715–71, French philosopher. In his chief work De l'Esprit (1758), he asserted that the mainspring of human action is self-interest and that differences in human intellects are due only to differences in education.

hem[1] (hɛm) n. 1. an edge to a piece of cloth, made by folding the raw edge under and stitching it down. 2. short for **hemline.** ~vb. **hemming, hemmed.** (tr.) 3. to provide with a hem. 4. (usually foll. by in, around, or about) to enclose or confine. [OE hemm] — **'hemmer** n.

hem[2] (hɛm) n., interj. 1. a representation of the sound of clearing the throat, used to gain attention, etc. ~vb. **hemming, hemmed.** 2. (intr.) to utter this sound. 3. **hem** (or **hum**) **and haw.** to hesitate in speaking.

he-man n., pl. **-men.** Inf. a strongly built muscular man.

hematite or **haematite** (ˈhɛmətaɪt, ˈhiːm-) n. a red, grey, or black mineral, found as massive beds and in veins and igneous rocks. It is the chief source of iron. Composition: iron (ferric) oxide. Crystal structure: hexagonal (rhombohedral). [C16: via L from Gk haimatitēs resembling blood, from haima blood] — **hematitic** or **haematitic** (ˌhɛməˈtɪtɪk, ˌhiː-) adj.

hemato- *or before a vowel* **hemat-** *combining form.* U.S. variants of **haemato-**.

Hemel Hempstead ('hɛməl 'hɛmstɪd) *n.* a town in SE England, in W Hertfordshire: designated a new town in 1947. Pop.: 79 695 (1981).

hemeralopia (,hɛmərə'ləʊpɪə) *n.* inability to see clearly in bright light. Nontechnical name: **day blindness**. [C18: NL, from Gk, from *hēmera* day + *alaos* blind + *ōps* eye]

hemerocallis (hɛmər'ɒkælɪs) *n.* a N temperate plant with large funnel-shaped orange flowers: each single flower lasts for only one day. Also called: **day lily**. [C17: from Gk *hēmera* day + *kallos* beauty]

hemi- *prefix.* half: *hemicycle; hemisphere.* [from L, from Gk *hēmi-*]

-hemia *n. combining form.* a U.S. variant of **-aemia**.

hemidemisemiquaver (,hɛmɪ,dɛmɪ'sɛmɪ,kweɪvə) *n. Music.* a note having the time value of one sixty-fourth of a semibreve. Usual U.S. & Canad. name: **sixty-fourth note**.

Hemingway ('hɛmɪŋ,weɪ) *n.* **Ernest.** 1899–1961, U.S. novelist and short-story writer. His novels include *The Sun Also Rises* (1926), *A Farewell to Arms* (1929), *For Whom the Bell Tolls* (1940), and *The Old Man and the Sea* (1952): Nobel prize for literature 1954.

hemiplegia (,hɛmɪ'pliːdʒɪə) *n.* paralysis of one side of the body. —**hemi'plegic** *adj.*

hemipode ('hɛmɪ,pəʊd) *n.* a small quail-like bird occurring in tropical and subtropical regions of the Old World. Also called: **button quail**.

hemipteran (hɪ'mɪptərən) *n.* any hemipterous insect. [C19: from HEMI- + Gk *pteron* wing]

hemipterous (hɪ'mɪptərəs) *adj.* of or belonging to a large order of insects having sucking or piercing mouthparts.

hemisphere ('hɛmɪ,sfɪə) *n.* **1.** one half of a sphere. **2. a.** half of the terrestrial globe, divided into **northern** and **southern hemispheres** by the equator or into **eastern** and **western hemispheres** by some meridians, usually 0° and 180°. **b.** a map or projection of one of the hemispheres. **3.** *Anat.* short for **cerebral hemisphere**, a half of the cerebrum. —**hemispheric** (,hɛmɪ'sfɛrɪk) *or* ,hem-i'spherical *adj.*

hemistich ('hɛmɪ,stɪk) *n. Prosody.* a half line of verse.

hemline ('hɛm,laɪn) *n.* the level to which the hem of a skirt or dress hangs.

hemlock ('hɛm,lɒk) *n.* **1.** an umbelliferous poisonous Eurasian plant having finely divided leaves, spotted stems, and small white flowers. **2.** a poisonous drug derived from this plant. **3.** Also called: **hemlock spruce**. a coniferous tree of North America and Asia. [OE *hymlic*]

hemo- *combining form.* a U.S. variant of **haemo-**.

hemp (hɛmp) *n.* **1.** Also called: **cannabis, marijuana**. an Asian plant having tough fibres, deeply lobed leaves, and small greenish flowers. See also **Indian hemp**. **2.** the fibre of this plant, used to make canvas, rope, etc. **3.** any of several narcotic drugs obtained from some varieties of this plant, esp. from Indian hemp. [OE *hænep*] —'**hempen** *or* '**hemp,like** *adj.*

hemstitch ('hɛm,stɪtʃ) *n.* **1.** a decorative edging stitch, usually for a hem, in which the cross threads are stitched in groups. ~*vb.* **2.** to decorate (a hem, etc.) with hemstitches.

hen (hɛn) *n.* **1.** the female of any bird, esp. of the domestic fowl. **2.** the female of certain other animals, such as the lobster. **3.** *Scot. dialect.* a term of address used to women. [OE *henn*]

Henan ('hʌ'næn) *or* **Honan** *n.* a province of N central China: the chief centre of early Chinese culture; mainly agricultural (the largest wheat-producing province in China). Capital: Zhengzhou. Pop.: 76 460 000 (1985).

henbane ('hɛn,beɪn) *n.* a poisonous Mediterranean plant with sticky hairy leaves: yields the drug hyoscyamine.

hence (hɛns) *sentence connector.* **1.** for this reason; therefore. ~*adv.* **2.** from this time: *a year hence.* **3.** *Arch.* from here; away. ~*sentence substitute.* **4.** *Arch.* begone! away! [OE *hionane*]

henceforth ('hɛns'fɔːθ), **henceforwards**, *or* **henceforward** *adv.* from now on.

henchman ('hɛntʃmən) *n., pl.* **-men. 1.** a faithful attendant or supporter. **2.** *Arch.* a squire; page. [C14 *hengestman*, from OE *hengest* stallion + MAN]

hendeca- *combining form.* eleven: *hendecagon; hendeca-syllable.* [from Gk *hendeka*, from *hen*, neuter of *heis* one + *deka* ten]

hendecagon (hɛn'dɛkəgən) *n.* a polygon having 11 sides. —**hendecagonal** (,hɛndɪ'kægən³l) *adj.*

hendecasyllable ('hɛndɛkə,sɪləb³l) *n. Prosody.* a verse line of 11 syllables. [C18: from Gk]

hendiadys (hɛn'daɪədɪs) *n.* a rhetorical device by which two nouns joined by a conjunction are used instead of a noun and a modifier, as in *to run with fear and haste* instead of *to run with fearful haste.* [C16: from Med. L, from Gk *hen dia duoin*, lit.: one through two]

Hendrix ('hɛndrɪks) *n.* **Jimi,** full name *James Marshall Hendrix.* 1942–70, U.S. rock guitarist, singer, and songwriter, noted for his innovative guitar technique. His recordings include "Purple Haze" (1967) and *Are you Experienced* (1967).

Hendry ('hɛndrɪ) *n.* **Stephen.** born 1969, British snooker player.

henequen, henequin, *or* **heniquen** ('hɛnɪkɪn) *n.* **1.** an agave plant that is native to Mexico. **2.** the fibre of this plant, used in making rope, twine, and coarse fabrics. [C19: from American Sp. *henequén*, prob. of Amerind origin]

henge (hɛndʒ) *n.* a circular monument, often containing a circle of stones, dating from the Neolithic and Bronze Ages. [back formation from *Stonehenge*, site of important megalithic ruins on Salisbury Plain, S England]

Hengelo (*Dutch* 'hɛŋəlo:) *n.* a city in the E Netherlands, in Overijssel province on the Twente Canal: industrial centre, esp. for textiles. Pop.: 76 399 (1982 est.).

Hengist ('hɛŋgɪst) *n.* died ?488 A.D., a leader, with his brother Horsa, of the first Jutish settlers in Britain; he is thought to have conquered Kent (?455).

Hengyang ('hɛŋ'jæŋ) *n.* a city in SE central China, in Hunan province on the Xiang River. Pop.: 507 000 (1980).

hen harrier *n.* a common harrier that nests in marshes and open land.

henhouse ('hɛn,haʊs) *n.* a coop for hens.

Henie ('hɛnɪ) *n.* **Sonja** ('sɒnjə). 1912–69, Norwegian figure-skater.

Henley-on-Thames ('hɛnlɪ-) *n.* a town in S England, in SE Oxfordshire on the River Thames: a riverside resort with an annual regatta. Pop.: 10 976 (1984 est.). Often shortened to **Henley.**

henna ('hɛnə) *n.* **1.** a shrub or tree of Asia and N Africa. **2.** a reddish dye obtained from the powdered leaves of this plant, used as a cosmetic and industrial dye. **3.** a reddish-brown colour. **b.** (*as adj.*): *henna tresses.* ~*vb.* **4.** (*tr.*) to dye with henna. [C16: from Ar. *hinnā'* ; see ALKANET]

henotheism ('hɛnəʊθiː,ɪzəm) *n.* the worship of one deity (of several) as the special god of one's family, clan, or tribe. [C19: from Gk *heis* one + *theos* god] —,heno-the'istic *adj.*

hen party *n. Inf.* a party at which only women are present.

henpeck ('hɛn,pɛk) *vb.* (*tr.*) (of a woman) to harass or torment (a man, esp. her husband) by persistent nagging. —'**hen,pecked** *adj.*

Henrietta Maria (,hɛnrɪ'ɛtə mə'riːə) *n.* 1609–69, queen of England (1625–49), the wife of Charles I; daughter of Henry IV of France. Her Roman Catholicism contributed to the unpopularity of the crown in the period leading to the Civil War.

henry ('hɛnrɪ) *n., pl.* **-ry, -ries,** *or* **-rys.** the derived SI unit of electric inductance; the inductance of a closed circuit in which an emf of 1 volt is produced when the current varies uniformly at the rate of 1 ampere per second. Symbol: H [C19: after Joseph HENRY]

Henry ('hɛnrɪ) *n.* **1. Joseph.** 1797–1878, U.S. physicist. He discovered the principle of electromagnetic induction independently of Faraday and constructed the first electromagnetic motor (1829). He also discovered self-induction and the oscillatory nature of electric discharges (1842). **2. O.** See **O. Henry.** **3. Patrick.** 1736–99, American statesman and orator, a leading opponent of British rule during the War of American Independence.

Henry I *n.* 1068–1135, king of England (1100–35) and duke of Normandy (1106–35); son of William the Conqueror: crowned in the absence of his elder brother, Robert II, duke of Normandy; conquered Normandy (1106).

Henry II *n.* **1.** 1133–89, first Plantagenet king of England (1154–89): extended his Anglo-French domains and instituted judicial and financial reforms. His attempts to control the church were opposed by Becket. **2.** 1519–59, king of France (1547–59); husband of Catherine de' Medici. He recovered Calais from the English (1558) and suppressed the Huguenots.

Henry III *n.* **1.** 1207–72, king of England (1216–72); son of John. His incompetent rule provoked the Baron's War (1264–65), during which he was captured by Simon de Montfort. **2.** 1551–89, king of France (1574–89). He plotted the massacre of Huguenots on St. Bartholomew's Day (1572) with his mother Catherine de' Medici, thus exacerbating the religious wars in France.

Henry IV *n.* **1.** 1050–1106, Holy Roman Emperor (1084–1105) and king of Germany (1056–1105). He was excommunicated by Pope Gregory VII, whom he deposed (1084). **2.** surnamed *Bolingbroke.* 1367–1413, first Lancastrian king of England (1399–1413); son of John of Gaunt: deposed Richard II (1399) and suppressed rebellions led by Owen Glendower and Sir Henry Percy. **3.** known as *Henry of Navarre.* 1553–1610, first Bourbon king of France (1589–1610). He obtained toleration for the Huguenots with the Edict of Nantes (1598) and restored prosperity to France following the religious wars (1562–98).

Henry V *n.* 1387–1422, king of England (1413–22); son of Henry IV. He defeated the French at the Battle of Agincourt (1415), conquered Normandy (1419), and was recognized as heir to the French throne (1420).

Henry VI *n.* 1421–71, last Lancastrian king of England (1422–61; 1470–71); son of Henry V. He suffered periods of insanity, which led to the loss by 1453 of all his possessions in France except Calais and to the Wars of the Roses (1455–85). He was deposed by Edward IV (1461) but was briefly restored to the throne (1470).

Henry VII *n.* 1457–1509, first Tudor king of England (1485–1509). He came to the throne (1485) after defeating Richard III at the Battle of Bosworth Field, ending the Wars of the Roses. Royal power and the prosperity of the country greatly increased during his reign.

Henry VIII *n.* 1491–1547, king of England (1509–47); second son of Henry VII. The declaration that his marriage to Catherine of Aragon was invalid and his marriage to Anne Boleyn (1533) precipitated the Act of Supremacy, making Henry supreme head of the Church in England. Anne Boleyn was executed (1536) and Henry subsequently married Jane Seymour, Anne of Cleves, Catherine Howard, and Catherine Parr. His reign is also noted for the fame of his succession of advisers, Cardinal Wolsey, Sir Thomas More, and Thomas Cromwell.

Henryson ('hɛnrɪs³n) *n.* **Robert.** ?1430–?1506, Scottish poet. His works include *Testament of Cresseid* (1593), a sequel to Chaucer's *Troilus and Cressida*, the 13 *Moral Fables of Esope the Phrygian*, and the pastoral dialogue *Robene and Makyne.*

Henry the Navigator *n.* 1394–1460, prince of Portugal, noted for his patronage of Portuguese voyages of exploration of the W coast of Africa.

Henslowe ('hɛnzləʊ) *n.* **Philip.** died 1616, English theatre manager, noted also for his diary.

Henze (*German* 'hɛntsə) *n.* **Hans Werner** (hans 'vɛrnər). born 1926, West German composer, whose works, in many styles, include the operas *The Stag King* (1956), *The Bassarids* (1965), and *The Tedious Way to the Place of Natasha Ungeheuer* (1970) and the oratorio *The Raft of the Medusa* (1968).

hep (hɛp) *adj.* **hepper, heppest.** *Sl.* an earlier word for **hip**[4].

heparin ('hɛpərɪn) *n.* a polysaccharide, containing sulphate groups, present in most body tissues: an anticoagulant used in the treatment of thrombosis. [C20: from Gk *hēpar* the liver + -IN]

hepatic (hɪ'pætɪk) *adj.* **1.** of the liver. **2.** having the colour of liver. ~*n.* **3.** any of various drugs for use in treating diseases of the liver. [C15: from L *hēpaticus*, from Gk *hēpar* liver]

hepatica (hɪ'pætɪkə) *n.* a woodland plant of a N temperate genus, having three-lobed leaves and white, mauve, or pink flowers. [C16: from Med. L: liverwort, from L *hēpaticus* of the liver]

hepatitis (ˌhɛpə'taɪtɪs) *n.* inflammation of the liver.

Hepburn ('hɛp,bɜːn) *n.* **Katharine.** born 1909, U.S. film actress, whose films include *The Philadelphia Story* (1940), *Adam's Rib* (1949), *The African Queen* (1951), *The Lion in Winter* (1968) for which she won an Oscar, and *On Golden Pond* (1981).

Hephaestus (hɪ'fiːstəs) *or* **Hephaistos** (hɪ'faɪstɒs) *n.* *Greek myth.* the lame god of fire and metal-working. Roman counterpart: **Vulcan.**

Hepplewhite ('hɛp³l,waɪt) *adj.* of or in a style of ornamental and carved 18th-century English furniture, of which oval or shield-shaped open chairbacks are characteristic. [C18: after George *Hepplewhite* (died 1786), E cabinetmaker]

hepta- *or before a vowel* **hept-** *combining form.* seven: *heptameter.* [from Gk]

heptad ('hɛptæd) *n.* a group or series of seven. [C17: from Gk *heptas* seven]

heptagon ('hɛptəgən) *n.* a polygon having seven sides. —**heptagonal** (hɛp'tægən³l) *adj.*

heptahedron (ˌhɛptə'hiːdrən) *n.* a solid figure having seven plane faces. —ˌhepta'hedral *adj.*

heptameter (hɛp'tæmɪtə) *n.* *Prosody.* a verse line of seven metrical feet. —**heptametrical** (ˌhɛptə'mɛtrɪk³l) *adj.*

heptane ('hɛpteɪn) *n.* an alkane which is found in petroleum and used as an anaesthetic. [C19: from HEPTA- + -ANE, because it has seven carbon atoms]

heptarchy ('hɛptɑːkɪ) *n., pl.* **-chies. 1.** government by seven rulers. **2.** the seven kingdoms into which Anglo-Saxon England is thought to have been divided from about the 7th to the 9th centuries A.D. —'heptarch *n.* —hep'tarchic *or* hep'tarchal *adj.*

heptathlon (hɛp'tæθlɒn) *n.* an athletic contest for women in which each athlete competes in seven different events. [C20: from HEPTA- + Gk *athlon* contest] —hep'tathlete *n.*

heptavalent (hɛp'tævələnt, ˌhɛptə'veɪlənt) *adj.* *Chem.* having a valency of seven.

Hepworth ('hɛpwəθ) *n.* Dame **Barbara.** 1903–75, English sculptress of abstract works.

her (hɜː; *unstressed* hə, ə) *pron.* (*objective*) **1.** refers to a female person or animal: *he loves her.* **2.** refers to things personified as feminine or traditionally to ships and nations. ~*determiner.* **3.** of, belonging to, or associated with her: *her hair.* [OE *hire*, genitive & dative of *hēo* SHE, fem. of *hē* HE]
▷ **Usage.** See at **me.**

Hera *or* **Here** ('hɪərə) *n. Greek myth.* the queen of the Olympian gods and sister and wife of Zeus. Roman counterpart: **Juno.**

Heraclea (ˌhɛrə'kliːə) *n.* any of several ancient Greek colonies. The most famous is the S Italian site where Pyrrhus of Epirus defeated the Romans (280 B.C.).

Heracles *or* **Herakles** ('hɛrə,kliːz) *n.* the usual name (in Greek) for **Hercules.** —,Hera'clean *or* ,Hera'klean *adj.*

Heraclitus (ˌhɛrə'klaɪtəs) *n.* ?535–?475 B.C., Greek philosopher, who held that fire is the primordial substance of the universe and that all things are in perpetual flux.

Herakleion *or* **Heraklion** (*Greek* he'raːklɪɒn) *n.* variants of **Iráklion.**

herald ('hɛrəld) *n.* **1.** a person who announces important news. **2.** *Often literary.* a forerunner; harbinger. **3.** the intermediate rank of heraldic officer, between king-of-arms and pursuivant. **4.** (in the Middle Ages) an official at a tournament. ~*vb.* (*tr.*) **5.** to announce publicly. **6.** to precede or usher in. [C14: from OF *herault*, of Gmc origin]

heraldic (hɛ'rældɪk) *adj.* of or relating to heraldry or heralds. —**he'raldically** *adv.*

heraldry ('hɛrəldrɪ) *n., pl.* **-ries. 1.** the study concerned with the classification of armorial bearings, the tracing of genealogies, etc. **2.** armorial bearings, insignia, etc. **3.** the show and ceremony of heraldry. —'heraldist *n.*

Herat (hɛ'ræt) *n.* a city in NW Afghanistan, on the Hari Rud River: on the site of several ancient cities; at its height as a cultural centre in the 15th century. Pop.: 159 804 (1984).

Hérault (*French* ero) *n.* a department of S France, in Languedoc-Roussillon region. Capital: Montpellier. Pop.: 706 499 (1982). Area: 6224 sq. km (2427 sq. miles).

herb (hɜːb; *U.S.* ɜːrb) *n.* **1.** a plant whose aerial parts do not persist above ground at the end of the growing season; herbaceous plant. **2.** any of various usually aromatic plants, such as parsley and rosemary, that are used in cookery and medicine. [C13: from OF *herbe*, from L *herba* grass, green plants] — 'herb,like adj. — 'herby adj.

herbaceous (hɜːˈbeɪʃəs) adj. **1.** designating or relating to plants that are fleshy as opposed to woody: *a herbaceous plant.* **2.** (of petals and sepals) green and leaflike.

herbaceous border n. a flower bed that contains perennials rather than annuals.

herbage ('hɜːbɪdʒ) n. **1.** herbaceous plants collectively, esp. the edible parts on which cattle, sheep, etc., graze. **2.** the vegetation of pasture land; pasturage.

herbal ('hɜːbªl) adj. **1.** of herbs. ~n. **2.** a book describing the properties of plants.

herbalist ('hɜːbªlɪst) n. **1.** a person who grows or specializes in the use of herbs, esp. medicinal herbs. **2.** (formerly) a descriptive botanist.

herbarium (hɜːˈbɛərɪəm) n., pl. **-iums** or **-ia** (-ɪə). **1.** a collection of dried plants that are mounted and classified systematically. **2.** a room, etc., in which such a collection is kept.

herb bennet ('bɛnɪt) n. a Eurasian and N African plant with yellow flowers. Also called: **wood avens, bennet.** [from OF *herbe benoite*, lit.: blessed herb, from Med. L *herba benedicta*]

Herbert ('hɜːbət) n. **George.** 1593–1633, English Metaphysical poet. His chief work is *The Temple: Sacred Poems and Private Ejaculations* (1633).

herbicide ('hɜːbɪˌsaɪd) n. a chemical that destroys plants, esp. one used to control weeds.

herbivore ('hɜːbɪˌvɔː) n. an animal that feeds on grass and other plants. [C19: from NL *herbivora* grass-eaters] — **herbivorous** (hɜːˈbɪvərəs) adj.

herb Paris ('pærɪs) n., pl. **herbs Paris.** a Eurasian woodland plant with a whorl of four leaves and a solitary yellow flower. [C16: from Med. L *herba paris*, lit.: herb of a pair: because the four leaves on the stalk look like a true lovers' knot]

herb Robert ('rɒbət) n., pl. **herbs Robert.** a low-growing N temperate plant with strongly scented divided leaves and small purplish flowers. [C13: from Med. L *herba Roberti* herb of Robert, prob. after St *Robert*, 11th-cent. F ecclesiastic]

Hercegovina (*Serbo-Croatian* 'hɛrtsɛgɔvina) n. a variant of **Herzegovina.**

Herculaneum (ˌhɜːkjuˈleɪnɪəm) n. an ancient city in SW Italy, of marked Greek character, on the S slope of Vesuvius: buried along with Pompeii by an eruption of the volcano (79 A.D.). Excavation has uncovered well preserved streets, houses, etc.

herculean (ˌhɜːkjuˈliːən) adj. **1.** requiring tremendous effort, strength, etc. **2.** (*sometimes cap.*) resembling Hercules in strength, courage, etc.

Hercules[1] ('hɜːkjuˌliːz), **Heracles,** or **Herakles** n. **1.** Also called: **Alcides.** *Classical myth.* a hero noted for his great strength, courage, and for the performance of twelve immense labours. **2.** a man of outstanding strength or size.

herd[1] (hɜːd) n. **1.** a large group of mammals living and feeding together, esp. cattle. **2.** *Often disparaging.* a large group of people. ~vb. **3.** to collect or be collected into or as if into a herd. [OE *heord*]

herd[2] (hɜːd) n. **1. a.** *Arch.* or *dialect.* a man who tends livestock; herdsman. **b.** (*in combination*): *goatherd.* ~vb. (*tr.*) **2.** to drive forwards in a large group. **3.** to look after (livestock). [OE *hirde*: see HERD[1]]

Herder (*German* 'hɛrdər) n. **Johann Gottfried von** (joˈhan 'gɔtfriːt fɔn). 1744–1803, German philosopher, critic, and poet, the leading figure in the *Sturm und Drang* movement in German literature. His chief work is *Outlines of a Philosophy of the History of Man* (1784–91).

herd instinct n. *Psychol.* the inborn tendency to associate with others and follow the group's behaviour.

herdsman ('hɜːdzmən) n., pl. **-men.** *Chiefly Brit.* a person who breeds or cares for cattle or (rarely) other livestock. U.S. equivalent: **herder.**

here (hɪə) adv. **1.** in, at, or to this place, point, case, or respect: *we come here every summer; here comes Roy.* **2.** **here and there.** at several places in or throughout an area. **3. here's to.** a formula used in proposing a toast to someone or something. **4. neither here nor there.** of no relevance or importance. ~n. **5.** this place or point: *they leave here tonight.* [OE *hēr*]

hereabouts ('hɪərəˌbaʊts) or **hereabout** adv. in this region or neighbourhood.

hereafter (ˌhɪərˈɑːftə) adv. **1.** *Formal or law.* in a subsequent part of this document, matter, case, etc. **2.** a less common word for **henceforth. 3.** at some time in the future. **4.** in a future life after death. ~n. (usually preceded by *the*) **5.** life after death. **6.** the future.

hereat (ˌhɪərˈæt) adv. *Arch.* because of this.

hereby (ˌhɪəˈbaɪ) adv. (used in official statements, etc.) by means of or as a result of this.

hereditable (hɪˈrɛdɪtəbªl) adj. a less common word for **heritable. — he,redita'bility** n.

hereditament (ˌhɛrɪˈdɪtəmənt) n. *Property law.* any kind of property capable of being inherited.

hereditary (hɪˈrɛdɪtərɪ, -trɪ) adj. **1.** of or denoting factors that can be transmitted genetically from one generation to another. **2.** *Law.* **a.** descending to succeeding generations by inheritance. **b.** transmitted according to established rules of descent. **3.** derived from one's ancestors; traditional: *hereditary feuds.* — **he'reditarily** adv. — **he'reditariness** n.

heredity (hɪˈrɛdɪtɪ) n., pl. **-ties. 1.** the transmission from one generation to another of genetic factors that determine individual characteristics. **2.** the sum total of the inherited factors in an organism. [C16: from OF *heredite*, from L *hērēditās* inheritance; see HEIR]

Hereford ('hɛrɪfəd) n. a city in W England, in Hereford and Worcester county on the River Wye: trading centre for agricultural produce; cathedral (begun 1079). Pop.: 47 652 (1981).

Hereford and Worcester n. a county of the W Midlands of England, formed in 1974 from the two former separate counties minus a small area of NW Worcestershire: drained chiefly by the Rivers Wye and Severn: important agriculturally (esp. for fruit and cattle). Administrative centre: Worcester. Pop.: 654 500 (1986 est.). Area: 3926 sq. km (1516 sq. miles).

Herefordshire ('hɛrɪfədˌʃɪə, -ʃə) n. a former county of W England, since 1974 part of Hereford and Worcester.

herein (ˌhɪərˈɪn) adv. **1.** *Formal or law.* in or into this place, thing, document, etc. **2.** *Rare.* in this respect, circumstance, etc.

hereinafter (ˌhɪərɪnˈɑːftə) adv. *Formal or law.* from this point on in this document, etc.

hereinto (ˌhɪərˈɪntuː) adv. *Formal or law.* into this place, circumstance, etc.

hereof (ˌhɪərˈɒv) adv. *Formal or law.* of or concerning this.

hereon (ˌhɪərˈɒn) adv. an archaic word for **hereupon.**

heresiarch (hɪˈriːzɪˌɑːk) n. the leader or originator of a heretical movement or sect.

heresy ('hɛrəsɪ) n., pl. **-sies. 1. a.** an opinion contrary to the orthodox tenets of a religious body. **b.** the act of maintaining such an opinion. **2.** any belief that is or is thought to be contrary to official or established theory. **3.** adherence to unorthodox opinion. [C13: from OF *eresie*, from LL, from L: sect, from Gk, from *hairein* to choose]

heretic ('hɛrətɪk) n. **1.** *Now chiefly R.C. Church.* a person who maintains beliefs contrary to the established teachings of his Church. **2.** a person who holds unorthodox opinions in any field. — **heretical** (hɪˈrɛtɪkªl) adj. — **he'retically** adv.

hereto (ˌhɪəˈtuː) adv. *Formal or law.* to this place, thing, matter, document, etc.

heretofore (ˌhɪətuˈfɔː) adv. *Formal or law.* until now; before this time.

hereunder (ˌhɪərˈʌndə) adv. *Formal or law.* **1.** (in documents, etc.) below this; subsequently; hereafter. **2.** under the terms or authority of this.

hereupon (ˌhɪərəˈpɒn) adv. **1.** following immediately after this; at this stage. **2.** *Formal or law.* upon this thing, point, subject, etc.

Hereward ('hɛrɪwəd) n. called *Hereward the Wake.* 11th-century Anglo-Saxon rebel, who defended the Isle of Ely against William the Conqueror (1070–71): a subject of many legends.

herewith (ˌhɪəˈwɪð, -ˈwɪθ) adv. *Formal.* together with this: *we send you herewith your statement of account.*

Hering ('heriŋ) n. **Ewald** ('ɛvalt). 1834–1918, German physiologist and experimental psychologist who studied

vision and propounded the doctrine of nativism, the policy of favouring the natives of a country over the immigrants.
heriot ('hɛrɪət) n. (in medieval England) a death duty paid by villeins and free tenants to their lord, often consisting of the dead man's best beast or chattel. [OE *heregeatwa*, from *here* army + *geatwa* equipment]
Herisau (*German* 'heːrɪzau) n. a town in NE Switzerland, capital of Appenzell Outer Rhodes demicanton. Pop.: 14 160 (1980).
heritable ('hɛrɪtəbªl) adj. 1. capable of being inherited; inheritable. 2. *Chiefly law.* capable of inheriting. [C14: from OF, from *heriter* to INHERIT] —,herita'bility n. —'heritably adv.
heritage ('hɛrɪtɪdʒ) n. 1. something inherited at birth. 2. anything that has been transmitted from the past or handed down by tradition. 3. the evidence of the past, such as historical sites, and the unspoilt natural environment, considered as the inheritance of present-day society. 4. *Law.* any property, esp. land, that by law has descended or may descend to an heir. [C13: from OF; see HEIR]
herl (hɜːl) or **harl** n. *Angling.* 1. the barb or barbs of a feather, used to dress fishing flies. 2. an artificial fly dressed with such barbs. [C15: from MLow G *herle*, from ?]
Hermann ('hɜːmən; *German* 'hɛrman) n. another name for **Arminius** (sense 1).
Hermannstadt ('hɛrmanʃtat) n. the German name for **Sibiu.**
hermaphrodite (hɜː'mæfrə,daɪt) n. 1. *Biol.* an animal or flower that has both male and female reproductive organs. 2. a person having both male and female sexual characteristics. 3. a person or thing in which two opposite qualities are combined. ~adj. 4. having the characteristics of a hermaphrodite. [C15: from L *her maphroditus*, from Gk, after HERMAPHRODITUS] —her,maphro'ditic or her,maphro'ditical adj. —her'maphrodit,ism n.
hermaphrodite brig n. a sailing vessel with two masts, rigged square on the foremast and fore-and-aft on the aftermast.
Hermaphroditus (hɜː,mæfrə'daɪtəs) n. *Greek myth.* a son of Hermes and Aphrodite who merged with the nymph Salmacis to form one body.
hermeneutic (,hɜːmɪ'njuːtɪk) or **hermeneutical** adj. 1. of or relating to the interpretation of Scripture. 2. interpretive. — ,herme'neutically adv.
hermeneutics (,hɜːmɪ'njuːtɪks) n. (*functioning as sing.*) 1. the science of interpretation, esp. of Scripture. 2. *Philosophy.* the study and interpretation of human behaviour and social institutions. [C18: from Gk *hermēneutikos* expert in interpretation, from *hermēneuein* to interpret, from ?]
Hermes ('hɜːmiːz) n. *Greek myth.* the messenger and herald of the gods; the divinity of commerce, cunning, theft, travellers, and rascals. He was represented as wearing winged sandals. Roman counterpart: **Mercury.**
Hermes Trismegistus (,trɪsmə'dʒɪstəs) n. a Greek name for the Egyptian god Thoth, credited with various works on mysticism and magic. [Gk: Hermes thrice-greatest]
hermetic (hɜː'mɛtɪk) or **hermetical** adj. sealed so as to be airtight. [C17: from Med. L *hermēticus* belonging to HERMES TRISMEGISTUS traditionally the inventor of a magic seal] —her'metically adv.
hermit ('hɜːmɪt) n. 1. one of the early Christian recluses. 2. any person living in solitude. [C13: from OF *hermite*, from LL, from Gk *erēmitēs* living in the desert, from *erēmos* lonely] —her'mitic or her'mitical adj.
hermitage ('hɜːmɪtɪdʒ) n. 1. the abode of a hermit. 2. any retreat.
hermit crab n. a small soft-bodied crustacean living in and carrying about the empty shells of whelks or similar molluscs.
Hermon ('hɜːmən) n. **Mount.** a mountain on the border between Lebanon and SW Syria, in the Anti-Lebanon Range: represented the NE limits of Israeli conquests under Moses and Joshua. Height: 2814 m (9232 ft.).
Hermosillo (*Spanish* ɛrmo'siʎo) n. a city in NW Mexico, capital of Sonora state, on the Sonora River: university (1938); winter resort and commercial centre for an agricultural and mining region. Pop.: 340 779 (1980).

Hermoupolis (hɜː'muːpəlɪs) n. a port in Greece, capital of Cyclades department, on the E coast of Syros Island. Pop.: 14 115 (1981).
Herne (*German* 'hɛrnə) n. an industrial city in W West Germany, in North Rhine-Westphalia, in the Ruhr on the Rhine-Herne Canal. Pop.: 171 500 (1986).
hernia ('hɜːnɪə) n., pl. **-nias** or **-niae** (-nɪ,iː). the projection of an organ or part through the lining of the cavity in which it is normally situated, esp. the intestine through the front wall of the abdominal cavity. Also called: **rupture.** [C14: from L] —'hernial adj. —'herni,ated adj.
hero ('hɪərəʊ) n., pl. **-roes.** 1. a man distinguished by exceptional courage, nobility, etc. 2. a man who is idealized for possessing superior qualities in any field. 3. *Classical myth.* a being of extraordinary strength and courage, often the offspring of a mortal and a god. 4. the principal male character in a novel, play, etc. [C14: from L *hērōs*, from Gk]
Hero[1] ('hɪərəʊ) n. *Greek myth.* a priestess of Aphrodite, who killed herself when her lover Leander drowned while swimming the Hellespont to visit her.
Hero[2] ('hɪərəʊ) or **Heron** n. 1st century A.D., Greek mathematician and inventor.
Herod ('hɛrəd) n. called *the Great.* ?73–4 B.C., king of Judaea (37–4). The latter part of his reign was notable for his cruelty and he ordered the Massacre of the Innocents.
Herod Agrippa I n. 10 B.C.–44 A.D., king of Judaea (41–44), grandson of Herod (the Great). A friend of Caligula and Claudius, he imprisoned Saint Peter and executed Saint James.
Herod Antipas ('æntɪ,pæs) n. died ?40 A.D., tetrarch of Galilee and Peraea (4 B.C.–40 A.D.); son of Herod the Great. At the instigation of his wife Herodias, he ordered the execution of John the Baptist.
Herodias (hɛ'rəʊdɪ,æs) n. ?14 B.C. –?40 A.D., niece and wife of Herod Antipas and mother of Salome, whom she persuaded to ask for the head of John the Baptist. Her ambition led to the banishment of her husband.
Herodotus (hɪ'rɒdətəs) n. called *the Father of History.* ?485–?425 B.C., Greek historian, famous for his *History* dealing with the causes and events of the wars between the Greeks and the Persians (490–479).
heroic (hɪ'rəʊɪk) or **heroical** adj. 1. of, like, or befitting a hero. 2. courageous but desperate. 3. treating of heroes and their deeds. 4. of or resembling the heroes of classical mythology. 5. (of language, manner, etc.) extravagant. 6. *Prosody.* of or resembling heroic verse. 7. (of the arts, esp. sculpture) larger than life-size; smaller than colossal. —he'roically adv.
heroic age n. the period in an ancient culture, when legendary heroes are said to have lived.
heroic couplet n. *Prosody.* a verse form consisting of two rhyming lines in iambic pentameter.
heroics (hɪ'rəʊɪks) pl. n. 1. *Prosody.* short for **heroic verse.** 2. extravagant or melodramatic language, behaviour, etc.
heroic verse n. *Prosody.* a type of verse suitable for epic or heroic subjects, such as the classical hexameter or the French Alexandrine.
heroin ('hɛrəʊɪn) n. a white bitter-tasting crystalline powder derived from morphine: a highly addictive narcotic. [C19: coined in G as a trademark, prob. from HERO, referring to its aggrandizing effect on the personality]
heroine ('hɛrəʊɪn) n. 1. a woman possessing heroic qualities. 2. a woman idealized for possessing superior qualities. 3. the main female character in a novel, play, film, etc.
heroism ('hɛrəʊ,ɪzəm) n. the state or quality of being a hero.
heron ('hɛrən) n. any of various wading birds having a long neck, slim body, and a plumage that is commonly grey or white. [C14: from OF *hairon*, of Gmc origin]
Heron ('hɪərɒn) n. a variant of **Hero**[2].
heronry ('hɛrənrɪ) n., pl. **-ries.** a colony of breeding herons.
Herophilus (hɪə'rɒfɪləs) n. died ?280 B.C., Greek anatomist in Alexandria. He was the first to distinguish sensory from motor nerves.
hero worship n. 1. admiration for heroes or idealized persons. 2. worship by the ancient Greeks and Romans of heroes. ~vb. **hero-worship, -shipping, -shipped** or U.S. **-shiping, -shiped.** 3. (tr.) to feel admiration or adulation for. —'hero-,worshipper n.

herpes ('hɜːpiːz) n. any of several inflammatory diseases of the skin, esp. herpes simplex. [C17: via L from Gk, from *herpein* to creep] —**herpetic** (hɜːˈpɛtɪk) adj., n.

herpes simplex ('sɪmplɛks) n. an acute viral disease characterized by formation of clusters of watery blisters. [NL: simple herpes]

herpes zoster ('zɒstə) n. a technical name for **shingles**. [NL: girdle herpes, from HERPES + Gk *zōstēr* girdle]

herpetology (ˌhɜːpɪˈtɒlədʒɪ) n. the study of reptiles and amphibians. [C19: from Gk *herpeton* creeping animal] —**herpetologic** (ˌhɜːpɪtəˈlɒdʒɪk) or ˌherpeto'logical adj.

Herr (German hɛr) n., pl. **Herren** ('hɛrən). a German man: used before a name as a title equivalent to *Mr*. [G, from OHG *herro* lord]

Herrenvolk German. ('hɛrənfɒlk) n. a race, nation, or group, such as the Germans or Nazis as viewed by Hitler, believed by themselves to be superior to other races. Also called: **master race**. [lit.: master race, from *Herren*, pl. of HERR + *Volk* folk]

Herrick ('hɛrɪk) n. **Robert.** 1591–1674, English poet. His chief work is the *Hesperides* (1648), a collection of short, delicate, sacred, and pastoral lyrics.

herring ('hɛrɪŋ) n., pl. **-rings** or **-ring.** an important food fish of northern seas, having an elongated body covered with large silvery scales. [OE *hæring*]

herringbone ('hɛrɪŋˌbəʊn) n. **1. a.** a pattern consisting of two or more rows of short parallel strokes slanting in alternate directions to form a series of zigzags. **b.** (as modifier): *a herringbone pattern*. **2.** *Skiing*. a method of ascending a slope by walking with the skis pointing outwards and one's weight on the inside edges. ~vb. **3.** to decorate (textiles, brickwork, etc.) with herringbone. **4.** (intr.) *Skiing*. to ascend a slope in herringbone fashion.

herring gull n. a common gull that has a white plumage with black-tipped wings.

Herriot n. **1.** (French ɛrjo) **Édouard** (edwar). 1872–1957, French Radical statesman and writer; premier (1924–25; 1932). **2.** ('hɛrɪət) **James.** real name *James Alfred Wight*. born 1916, British veterinary surgeon and writer. His books based on his experiences in Yorkshire have been adapted for television and films.

hers (hɜːz) pron. **1.** something or someone belonging to her: *hers is the nicest dress; that cat is hers*. **2. of hers.** belonging to her. [C14 *hires*; see HER]

Herschel ('hɜːʃəl) n. **1.** Sir **John Frederick William.** 1792–1871, English astronomer. He discovered and catalogued over 525 nebulae and star clusters. **2.** his father, Sir **William,** original name *Friedrich Wilhelm Herschel*. 1738–1822, British astronomer, born in Germany. He constructed a reflecting telescope, which led to his discovery of the planet Uranus (1781), two of its satellites, and two of the satellites of Saturn. He also discovered the motions of binary stars.

herself (həˈsɛlf) pron. **1. a.** the reflexive form of *she* or *her*. **b.** (intensifier): *the queen herself signed*. **2.** (preceded by a copula) her normal self: *she looks herself again after the operation*.
▷ **Usage.** See at **myself.**

Herstmonceux or **Hurstmonceux** ('hɜːstmənˌsuː, -ˌsəʊ) n. a village in S England, in E Sussex north of Eastbourne: 15th-century castle, site of the Royal Observatory, which was transferred from Greenwich between 1948 and 1958, until 1990.

Hertford ('hɑːtfəd) n. a town in SE England, administrative centre of Hertfordshire. Pop.: 21 412 (1981).

Hertfordshire ('hɑːtfədˌʃɪə, -ʃə) n. a county of S England, bordering on Greater London in the south: mainly lowlying, with the Chiltern Hills in the northwest; largely agricultural; expanding light industries, esp. in the new towns. Administrative centre: Hertford. Pop.: 985 700 (1986 est.). Area: 1634 sq. km (631 sq. miles).

Hertogenbosch (Dutch hɛrtoːxənˈbɔs) n. **'s.** See **'s Hertogenbosch.**

Herts abbrev. for Hertfordshire.

hertz (hɜːts) n., pl. **hertz.** the derived SI unit of frequency; the frequency of a periodic phenomenon that has a periodic time of 1 second; 1 cycle per second. Symbol: Hz [C20: after H. R. HERTZ]

Hertz (hɜːts; German hɛrts) n. **1. Gustav** ('gʊstaf). 1887–1975, German atomic physicist. He provided evidence for the quantum theory by his research with Franck on the effects produced by bombarding atoms with electrons:

they shared the Nobel prize for physics (1925). **2. Heinrich Rudolph** ('hainrɪç 'ruːdɔlf). 1857–94, German physicist. He was the first to produce electromagnetic waves artificially. —'**Hertzian** adj.

Hertzian wave n. an electromagnetic wave with a frequency in the range from about 3×10^{10} hertz to about 1.5×10^5 hertz. [C19: after H. R. HERTZ]

Hertzog ('hɜːtsɒg) n. **James Barry Munnik.** 1866–1942, South African statesman; prime minister (1924–39): founded the Nationalist Party (1913), advocating complete South African independence from Britain; opposed South African participation in World Wars I and II.

Herzegovina (ˌhɜːtsəɡəʊˈviːnə) or **Hercegovina** n. a region of W central Yugoslavia: originally under Austro-Hungarian rule; became part of the province of Bosnia and Herzegovina (1878), which became a constituent republic of Yugoslavia in 1946.

Herzl (German 'hɛrtsəl) n. **Theodor** ('teːodoːr). 1860–1904, Austrian writer, born in Hungary; founder of the Zionist movement. In *The Jewish State* (1896), he advocated resettlement of the Jews in a state of their own.

Herzog (German 'hɛrtsoːk) n. **Werner** ('vɛrnər). born 1942, West German film director. His films include *Signs of Life* (1967), *Fata Morgana* (1970), *Aguirre, Wrath of God* (1973), *Wozzeck* (1979), and *Fitzcarraldo* (1982).

he's (hiːz) contraction of he is or he has.

Hesiod ('hɛsɪˌɒd) n. 8th century B.C., Greek poet and the earliest author of didactic verse. His two complete extant works are the *Works and Days*, dealing with the agricultural seasons, and the *Theogony*, concerning the origin of the world and the genealogies of the gods. —ˌHesi'odic adj.

Hesione (hɪˈsaɪənɪ) n. Greek myth. daughter of King Laomedon, rescued by Hercules from a sea monster.

hesitant ('hɛzɪtᵊnt) adj. wavering, hesitating, or irresolute. —'**hesitantly** adv.

hesitate ('hɛzɪˌteɪt) vb. (intr.) **1.** to be slow in acting; be uncertain. **2.** to be reluctant (to do something). **3.** to stammer or pause in speaking. [C17: from L *haesitāre*, from *haerēre* to cling to] —**hesitancy** ('hɛzɪtᵊnsɪ) or ˌhesi'tation n. —'hesiˌtatingly adv.

Hesperia (hɛˈspɪərɪə) n. a poetic name used by the ancient Greeks for Italy and by the Romans for Spain or beyond. [L, from Gk: land of the west, from *hesperos* western]

Hesperian (hɛˈspɪərɪən) adj. **1.** Poetic. western. **2.** of or relating to the Hesperides or Islands of the Blessed.

Hesperides (hɛˈspɛrɪˌdiːz) pl. n. Greek myth. **1.** the daughters of Hesperus, nymphs who kept watch with a dragon over the garden of the golden apples in the Islands of the Blessed. **2.** (functioning as sing.) the gardens themselves. **3.** another name for the **Islands of the Blessed.** —**Hesperidian** (ˌhɛspəˈrɪdɪən) or ˌHesper'idean adj.

hesperidium (ˌhɛspəˈrɪdɪəm) n. Bot. the fruit of citrus plants, in which the flesh consists of fluid-filled hairs and is protected by a tough rind. [C19: NL; alluding to the fruit in the garden of the HESPERIDES]

Hesperus ('hɛspərəs) n. an evening star, esp. Venus. [from L, from Gk, from *hesperos* western]

Hess (hɛs) n. **1.** Dame **Myra.** 1890–1965, English pianist. **2. (Walther Richard) Rudolf** ('ruːdɔlf). 1894–1987, German Nazi leader. He made a secret flight to Scotland (1941) to negotiate peace with Britain but was held as a prisoner of war; later sentenced to life imprisonment at the Nuremberg trials (1946); committed suicide. **3. Victor Francis.** 1883–1964, U.S. physicist, born in Austria: pioneered the investigation of cosmic rays: shared the Nobel prize for physics (1936).

Hesse[1] (hɛs) n. a state of E central West Germany, formed in 1945 from the former Prussian province of Hesse-Nassau and part of the former state of Hesse. Capital: Wiesbaden. Pop.: 5 531 300 (1986). Area: 21 111 sq. km (8151 sq. miles). German name: **Hessen** (hɛsᵊn).

Hesse[2] (hɛs; German 'hɛsə) n. **Hermann** ('hɛrman). 1877–1962, German novelist, short-story writer, and poet. His novels include *Der Steppenwolf* (1927) and *Das Glasperlenspiel* (1943): Nobel prize for literature 1946.

Hesse-Nassau n. a former province of Prussia, now part of the state of Hesse, West Germany.

hessian ('hɛsɪən) n. a coarse jute fabric similar to sacking. [C18: from HESSIAN]

Hessian ('hɛsɪən) n. **1.** a native or inhabitant of Hesse. **2.** a Hessian soldier in any of the mercenary units of the British Army in the War of American Independence or the Napoleonic Wars. ~adj. **3.** of Hesse or its inhabitants.

Hessian fly n. a small dipterous fly whose larvae damage wheat, barley, and rye. [C18: thought to have been introduced into America by Hessian soldiers]

hest (hɛst) n. an archaic word for **behest**. [OE hǣs]

Hestia ('hɛstɪə) n. Greek myth. the goddess of the hearth. Roman counterpart: **Vesta**.

hetaera (hɪ'tɪərə) or **hetaira** (hɪ'taɪrə) n., pl. **-taerae** (-'tɪəri:) or **-tairai** (-'taɪraɪ). (esp. in ancient Greece) a prostitute, esp. an educated courtesan. [C19: from Gk hetaira concubine]

hetaerism (hɪ'tɪərɪzəm) or **hetairism** (hɪ'taɪrɪzəm) n. **1.** the state of being a concubine. **2.** Sociol., anthropol. a social system attributed to some primitive societies, in which women are communally shared.

hetero- combining form. other, another, or different: heterosexual. [from Gk heteros other]

heteroclite ('hɛtərə,klaɪt) adj. also **heteroclitic** (,hɛtərə'klɪtɪk). **1.** (esp. of the form of a word) irregular or unusual. ~n. **2.** an irregularly formed word. [C16: from LL heteroclitus declining irregularly, from Gk, from HETERO- + klinein to inflect]

heterocyclic (,hɛtərəʊ'saɪklɪk, -'sɪk-) adj. (of an organic compound) containing a closed ring of atoms, at least one of which is not a carbon atom.

heterodox ('hɛtərəʊ,dɒks) adj. **1.** at variance with established or accepted doctrines or beliefs. **2.** holding unorthodox opinions. [C17: from Gk heterodoxos, from HETERO- + doxa opinion] —'hetero,doxy n.

heterodyne ('hɛtərəʊ,daɪn) vb. **1.** Electronics. to combine by modulation (two alternating signals) to produce two signals having frequencies corresponding to the sum and the difference of the original frequencies. ~adj. **2.** produced by, operating by, or involved in heterodyning two signals.

heteroecious (,hɛtə'ri:ʃəs) adj. (of parasites) undergoing different stages of the life cycle on different host species. [from HETERO- + -oecious, from Gk oikia house] —**heteroecism** (,hɛtə'ri:,sɪzəm) n.

heterogamete (,hɛtərəʊgæ'mi:t) n. a gamete that differs in size and form from the one with which it unites in fertilization.

heterogamy (,hɛtə'rɒgəmɪ) n. **1.** a type of sexual reproduction in which the gametes differ in both size and form. **2.** a condition in which different types of reproduction occur in successive generations of an organism. **3.** the presence of both male and female flowers in one inflorescence. —,hetero'gamous adj.

heterogeneous (,hɛtərəʊ'dʒi:nɪəs) adj. **1.** composed of unrelated parts. **2.** not of the same type. [C17: from Med. L heterogeneus, from Gk, from HETERO- + genos sort] —**heterogeneity** (,hɛtərəʊdʒɪ'ni:ɪtɪ) or ,hetero'geneousness n.

heterogony (,hɛtə'rɒgənɪ) n. **1.** Biol. the alternation of parthenogenetic and sexual generations in rotifers and similar animals. **2.** the condition in plants, such as the primrose, of having flowers that differ from each other in the length of their stamens and styles. —,heter'ogonous adj.

heterologous (,hɛtə'rɒləgəs) adj. **1.** Pathol. designating cells or tissues not normally present in a particular part of the body. **2.** differing in structure or origin. —,heter'ology n.

heteromerous (,hɛtə'rɒmərəs) adj. Biol. having parts that differ, esp. in number.

heteromorphic (,hɛtərəʊ'mɔ:fɪk) or **heteromorphous** adj. Biol. **1.** differing from the normal form. **2.** (esp. of insects) having different forms at different stages of the life cycle. —,hetero'morphism n.

heteronomous (,hɛtə'rɒnɪməs) adj. **1.** subject to an external law. **2.** (of parts of an organism), differing in the manner of growth, development, or specialization. —,heter'onomy n.

heteronym ('hɛtərəʊ,nɪm) n. one of two or more words pronounced differently but spelt alike: the two English words spelt "bow" are heteronyms. Cf. **homograph**. [C17: from LGk heteronumos, from Gk HETERO- + onoma name]

heterophyllous (,hɛtərəʊ'fɪləs, ,hɛtə'rɒfɪləs) adj. having more than one type of leaf on the same plant. —'hetero,phylly n.

heteropterous (,hɛtə'rɒptərəs) or **heteropteran** adj. of or belonging to a suborder of hemipterous insects, including bedbugs, water bugs, etc., in which the forewings are membranous but have leathery tips. [C19: from NL Heteroptera, from HETERO- + Gk pteron wing]

heterosexism (,hɛtərəʊ'sɛk,sɪzəm) n. discrimination on the basis of sexual orientation, practised by heterosexuals against homosexuals. —**hetero'sexist** adj., n.

heterosexual (,hɛtərəʊ'sɛksjʊəl) n. **1.** a person who is sexually attracted to the opposite sex. ~adj. **2.** of or relating to heterosexuality. —,hetero,sexu'ality n.

heterotaxis (,hɛtərəʊ'tæksɪs) or **heterotaxy** n. an abnormal or asymmetrical arrangement of parts, as of the organs of the body.

heterotrophic (,hɛtərəʊ'trɒfɪk) adj. (of animals and some plants) using complex organic compounds to manufacture their own organic constituents. [C20: from HETERO- + Gk trophikos concerning food, from trophē nourishment]

heterozygote (,hɛtərəʊ'zaɪgəʊt) n. an animal or plant that is heterozygous; a hybrid.

heterozygous (,hɛtərəʊ'zaɪgəs) adj. Genetics. (of an organism) having dissimilar alleles for any one gene: heterozygous for eye colour.

hetman ('hɛtmən) n., pl. **-mans.** an elected leader of the Cossacks. Also called: **ataman**. [C18: from Polish, from G Hauptmann headman]

het up adj. Inf. angry; excited: don't get het up. [C19: from dialect p.p. of HEAT]

heuchera ('hɔɪkərə) n. a North American shrub with red or pink flowers and ornamental foliage. [after J. H. Heucher (1677–1747), G botanist]

heuristic (hjʊə'rɪstɪk) adj. **1.** helping to learn; guiding in investigation. **2.** (of a method of teaching) allowing pupils to learn things for themselves. **3. a.** Maths, science, philosophy. using or obtained by exploration of possibilities rather than by following set rules. **b.** Computers. denoting a rule of thumb for solving a problem without the exhaustive application of an algorithm. ~n. **4.** (pl.) the science of heuristic procedure. [C19: from NL heuristicus, from Gk heuriskein to discover] —**heu'ristically** adv.

Hevelius (German he'veːlɪʊs) n. **Johannes** (jo'hanəs). 1611–87, German astronomer, who published one of the first detailed maps of the lunar surface.

Hevesy (Hungarian 'hɛvɛʃɪ) n. **Georg von** ('geːɔrg fɔn). 1885–1966, Hungarian chemist. He worked on radioactive tracing and, with D. Coster, discovered the element hafnium (1923): Nobel prize for chemistry 1943.

hew (hju:) vb. **hewing, hewed, hewed** or **hewn. 1.** to strike (something, esp. wood) with cutting blows, as with an axe. **2.** (tr.; often foll. by out) to carve from a substance. **3.** (tr.; often foll. by away, off, etc.) to sever from a larger portion. **4.** (intr.; often foll. by to) U.S. & Canad. to conform. [OE hēawan] —'**hewer** n.

hex[1] (hɛks) n. **a.** short for **hexadecimal** (**notation**). **b.** (as modifier): hex code.

hex[2] (hɛks) U.S. & Canad. inf. ~vb. **1.** (tr.) to bewitch. ~n. **2.** an evil spell. **3.** a witch. [C19: via Pennsylvania Du. from G Hexe witch, from MHG hecse, ?from OHG hagzissa]

hex. abbrev. for: **1.** hexachord. **2.** hexagon(al).

hexa- or before a vowel **hex-** combining form. six: hexachord; hexameter. [from Gk, from hex SIX]

hexachlorophene (,hɛksə'klɔ:rəfi:n) n. an insoluble white bactericidal substance used in antiseptic soaps, deodorants, etc. Formula: $(C_6HCl_3OH)_2CH_2$.

hexachord ('hɛksə,kɔ:d) n. (in medieval music theory) any of three diatonic scales based upon C, F, and G, each consisting of six notes, from which solmization was developed.

hexad ('hɛksæd) n. a group or series of six. [C17: from Gk hexas, from hex six]

hexadecimal notation or **hexadecimal** (,hɛksə'dɛsɪməl) n. a number system having a base 16; the symbols for the numbers 0 – 9 are the same as those used in the decimal system, and the numbers 10 – 15 are usually represented by the letters A – F. The system is used as a convenient way of representing the internal binary code of a computer.

hexagon ('hɛksəgən) *n.* a polygon having six sides. —**hex'agonal** *adj.*

hexagram ('hɛksə,græm) *n.* a star-shaped figure formed by extending the sides of a regular hexagon to meet at six points.

hexahedron (,hɛksə'hi:drən) *n.* a solid figure having six plane faces. —**,hexa'hedral** *adj.*

hexameter (hɛk'sæmɪtə) *n. Prosody.* **1.** a verse line consisting of six metrical feet. **2.** (in Greek and Latin epic poetry) a verse line of six metrical feet, of which the first four are usually dactyls or spondees, the fifth almost always a dactyl, and the sixth a spondee or trochee. —**hexametric** (,hɛksə'mɛtrɪk) *or* **,hexa'metrical** *adj.*

hexane ('hɛkseɪn) *n.* a liquid alkane found in petroleum and used as a solvent. Formula: $CH_3(CH_2)_4CH_3$ (*n-*). [C19: from HEXA- + -ANE]

hexapla ('hɛksəplə) *n.* an edition of the Old Testament compiled by Origen (?185–?254 A.D.), Christian theologian, containing six versions of the text. [C17: from Gk *hexaploos* sixfold] —**'hexaplar** *adj.*

hexapod ('hɛksə,pɒd) *n.* an insect.

hexavalent (hɛk'sævələnt, ,hɛksə'veɪlənt) *adj. Chem.* having a valency of six. Also: **sexivalent.**

hexose ('hɛksəʊs, -əʊz) *n.* a monosaccharide, such as glucose, that contains six carbon atoms per molecule.

hey (heɪ) *interj.* **1.** an expression indicating surprise, dismay, discovery, etc. **2. hey presto.** an exclamation used by conjurers to herald the climax of a trick. [C13: imit.]

heyday ('heɪ,deɪ) *n.* the time of most power, popularity, vigour, etc. [C16: prob. based on HEY]

Heyerdahl (*Norwegian* 'heɪədɑ:l) *n.* **Thor** (tɔː). born 1914, Norwegian anthropologist. In 1947 he demonstrated that the Polynesians could originally have been migrants from South America, by sailing from Peru to the Pacific Islands of Tuamotu in the *Kon-Tiki*, a raft made of balsa wood.

Heysham ('heɪʃəm) *n.* a port in NW England, in NW Lancashire. Pop. (with Morecambe): 41 187 (1981).

Heywood[1] ('heɪ,wʊd) *n.* a town in NW England, in Greater Manchester near Bury. Pop.: 30 672 (1981).

Heywood[2] ('heɪ,wʊd) *n.* **1. John.** ?1497–?1580, English dramatist, noted for his comic interludes. **2. Thomas.** ?1574–1641, English dramatist, noted esp. for his domestic drama *A Woman Killed with Kindness* (1607).

Hezekiah (,hɛzə'kaɪə) *n.* a king of Judah ?715–?687 B.C., noted for his religious reforms (II Kings 18–19). Douay spelling: **Ezechias.** [from Heb. *hizqiyyāhū* God has strengthened]

hf *abbrev. for* half.

Hf *the chemical symbol for* hafnium.

HF *or* **h.f.** *abbrev. for* high frequency.

hg *abbrev. for* hectogram.

Hg *the chemical symbol for* mercury. [from NL *hydrargyrum*]

HG *abbrev. for* His (*or* Her) Grace.

hgt *abbrev. for* height.

HGV (in Britain) *abbrev. for* heavy goods vehicle.

HH *abbrev. for:* **1.** His (*or* Her) Highness. **2.** His Holiness (title of the Pope). ~ **3.** (on British pencils) *symbol for* double hard.

hi (haɪ) *sentence substitute.* an informal word for **hello.** [C20: prob. from *how are you?*]

Hialeah (,haɪə'liːə) *n.* a city in SE Florida, near Miami: racetrack. Pop.: 145 254 (1980).

hiatus (haɪ'eɪtəs) *n., pl.* **-tuses** *or* **-tus. 1.** (esp. in manuscripts) a break or interruption in continuity. **2.** a break between adjacent vowels in the pronunciation of a word. [C16: from L: gap, cleft, from *hiāre* to gape]

hiatus hernia *n.* protrusion of part of the stomach through the diaphragm at the oesophageal opening.

Hiawatha (,haɪə'wɒθə) *n.* a 16th-century Onondaga Indian chief: credited with the organization of the Five Nations.

hibachi (hɪ'bɑːtʃɪ) *n.* a portable brazier for heating and cooking food. [from Japanese, from *hi* fire + *bachi* bowl]

hibernal (haɪ'bɜːnəl) *adj.* of or occurring in winter. [C17: from L *hībernālis*, from *hiems* winter]

hibernate ('haɪbə,neɪt) *vb.* (*intr.*) **1.** (of some animals) to pass the winter in a dormant condition with metabolism greatly slowed down. **2.** to cease from activity. [C19: from L *hībernāre* to spend the winter, from *hībernus* of winter] —**,hiber'nation** *n.* —**'hiber,nator** *n.*

Hibernia (haɪ'bɜːnɪə) *n.* the Roman name for Ireland: used poetically in later times. —**Hi'bernian** *adj., n.*

Hibernicism (haɪ'bɜːnɪ,sɪzəm) *n.* an Irish expression, idiom, trait, custom, etc.

hibiscus (hɪ'bɪskəs) *n., pl.* **-cuses.** any plant of the chiefly tropical and subtropical genus *Hibiscus*, cultivated for its large brightly coloured flowers. [C18: from L, from Gk *hibiskos* marsh mallow]

hiccup ('hɪkʌp) *n.* **1.** a spasm of the diaphragm producing a sudden breathing in of air resulting in a characteristic sharp sound. **2.** the state of having such spasms. **3.** *Inf.* a minor difficulty. ~*vb.* **-cuping, -cuped** *or* **-cupping, -cupped. 4.** (*intr.*) to make a hiccup or hiccups. **5.** (*tr.*) to utter with a hiccup. ~Also: **hiccough** ('hɪkʌp). [C16: imit.]

hic jacet *Latin.* (hɪk 'jækɛt) (on gravestones, etc.) here lies.

hick (hɪk) *n. Inf., chiefly U.S. & Canad.* a country bumpkin. [C16: after *Hick*, familiar form of *Richard*]

Hick (hɪk) *n.* **Graeme (Ashley).** born 1966, British cricketer born in Zimbabwe.

Hickok ('hɪkɒk) *n.* **James Butler,** known as *Wild Bill Hickok.* 1837–76, U.S. frontiersman and marshal.

hickory ('hɪkərɪ) *n., pl.* **-ries. 1.** a tree of a chiefly North American genus having nuts with edible kernels and hard smooth shells. **2.** the hard tough wood of this tree. [C17: ult. from Algonquian *pawcohiccora* food made from ground hickory nuts]

hid (hɪd) *vb.* the past tense and a past participle of **hide**[1].

hidalgo (hɪ'dælgəʊ) *n., pl.* **-gos.** a member of the lower nobility in Spain. [C16: from Sp., from OSp. *fijo dalgo* nobleman, from L *fīlius* son + *dē* of + *aliquid* something]

Hidalgo (hɪ'dælgəʊ; *Spanish* i'ðalɣo) *n.* a state of central Mexico: consists of a high plateau, with the Sierra Madre Oriental in the north and east; ancient remains of Teltec culture (at Tula); rich mineral resources. Capital: Pachuca. Pop.: 1 516 511 (1980). Area: 20 987 sq. km (8103 sq. miles).

hidden ('hɪdən) *vb.* **1.** a past participle of **hide**[1]. ~*adj.* **2.** concealed or obscured: *a hidden cave; a hidden meaning.*

hide[1] (haɪd) *vb.* **hiding, hid, hidden** *or* **hid. 1.** to conceal (oneself or an object) from view or discovery: *to hide a pencil; to hide from the police.* **2.** (*tr.*) to obscure: *clouds hid the sun.* **3.** (*tr.*) to keep secret. **4.** (*tr.*) to turn (one's eyes, etc.) away. ~*n.* **5.** *Brit.* a place of concealment, usually disguised to appear as part of the natural environment, used by hunters, birdwatchers, etc. U.S. and Canad. equivalent: **blind.** [OE *hȳdan*] —**'hider** *n.*

hide[2] (haɪd) *n.* **1.** the skin of an animal, either tanned or raw. **2.** *Inf.* the human skin. ~*vb.* **hiding, hided. 3.** (*tr.*) *Inf.* to flog. [OE *hȳd*]

hide[3] (haɪd) *n.* an obsolete Brit. land measure, varying from about 60 to 120 acres. [OE *hīgid*]

hide-and-seek *or* U.S. & Canad. **hide-and-go-seek** *n.* a game in which one player covers his eyes while the others hide, and he then tries to find them.

hideaway ('haɪdə,weɪ) *n.* a hiding place or secluded spot.

hidebound ('haɪd,baʊnd) *adj.* **1.** restricted by petty rules, a conservative attitude, etc. **2.** (of cattle, etc.) having the skin closely attached to the flesh as a result of poor feeding.

hideous ('hɪdɪəs) *adj.* **1.** extremely ugly; repulsive. **2.** terrifying and horrific. [C13: from OF *hisdos*, from *hisde* fear; from ?] —**'hideously** *adv.* —**'hideousness** *n.*

hide-out *n.* a hiding place, esp. a remote place used by outlaws, etc.; hideaway.

Hideyoshi Toyotomi (,hiːdɛ'jɔːʃɪ ,tɔːjɔː'tɔːmɪ) *n.* 1536–98, Japanese military dictator (1582–98). He unified all Japan under one rule (1590).

hiding[1] ('haɪdɪŋ) *n.* **1.** the state of concealment: *in hiding.* **2. hiding place.** a place of concealment.

hiding[2] ('haɪdɪŋ) *n. Inf.* a flogging; beating.

hidrosis (hɪ'drəʊsɪs) *n.* a technical word for **perspiration** *or* **sweat.** [C18: via NL from Gk, from *hidrōs* sweat] —**hidrotic** (hɪ'drɒtɪk) *adj.*

hidy-hole *or* **hidey-hole** *n. Inf.* a hiding place.

hie (haɪ) *vb.* **hieing** *or* **hying, hied.** *Arch. or poetic.* to hurry; speed. [OE *hīgian* to strive]

hierarch ('haɪə,rɑːk) *n.* **1.** a high priest. **2.** a person at a high level in a hierarchy. —**,hier'archal** *adj.*

hierarchy ('haɪə,rɑːkɪ) *n., pl.* **-chies. 1.** a system of persons or things arranged in a graded order. **2.** a body of persons in holy orders organized into graded ranks. **3.** the collective body of those so organized. **4.** a series of ordered groupings within a system, such as the arrangement of plants into classes, orders, etc. **5.** government by a priesthood. [C14: from Med. L *hierarchia*, from LGk, from *hierarkhēs* high priest; see HIERO-, -ARCHY] —**hier'archical** *or* **,hier'archic** *adj.* — **'hier,archism** *n.*

hieratic (,haɪə'rætɪk) *adj.* **1.** of priests. **2.** of a cursive form of hieroglyphics used by priests in ancient Egypt. **3.** of styles in art that adhere to certain fixed types, as in ancient Egypt. ~*n.* **4.** the hieratic script of ancient Egypt. [C17: from L *hierāticus*, from Gk, from *hiereus* priest] — **,hier'atically** *adv.*

hiero- *or before a vowel* **hier-** *combining form.* holy or divine: *hierarchy.* [from Gk, from *hieros* holy]

hieroglyphic (,haɪərə'glɪfɪk) *adj. also* **hieroglyphical.** **1.** of or relating to a form of writing using picture symbols, esp. as used in ancient Egypt. **2.** difficult to decipher. ~*n. also* **hieroglyph. 3.** a picture or symbol representing an object, concept, or sound. **4.** a symbol that is difficult to decipher. [C16: from LL *hieroglyphicus*, from Gk, from HIERO- + *gluphē*, from *gluphein* to carve] — **,hiero'glyphically** *adv.*

hieroglyphics (,haɪərə'glɪfɪks) *n.* (*functioning as sing. or pl.*) **1.** a form of writing, esp. as used in ancient Egypt, in which pictures or symbols are used to represent objects, concepts, or sounds. **2.** difficult or undecipherable writing.

Hieronymus (,haɪə'rɒnɪməs) *n.* **Eusebius** (ju:'si:bɪəs). the Latin name of (Saint) **Jerome.** —**Hieronymic** (,haɪərə'nɪmɪk) *or* **,Hiero'nymian** *adj.*

hierophant ('haɪərə,fænt) *n.* **1.** (in ancient Greece) a high priest of religious mysteries. **2.** a person who interprets esoteric mysteries. [C17: from LL *hierophanta*, from Gk, from HIERO- + *phainein* to reveal] — **,hiero'phantic** *adj.*

hi-fi ('haɪ,faɪ) *n. Inf.* **1. a.** short for **high fidelity. b.** (*as modifier*): *hi-fi equipment.* **2.** a set of high-quality sound-reproducing equipment.

Higgins ('hɪgɪnz) *n.* **Alex,** known as *Hurricane Higgins.* born 1949, Northern Irish snooker player.

higgledy-piggledy ('hɪgˀldɪ'pɪgˀldɪ) *Inf.* ~*adj., adv.* **1.** in a jumble. ~*n.* **2.** a muddle.

high (haɪ) *adj.* **1.** being a relatively great distance from top to bottom; tall: *a high building.* **2.** situated at a relatively great distance above sea level: *a high plateau.* **3.** (*postpositive*) being a specified distance from top to bottom: *three feet high.* **4.** extending from or performed at an elevation: *a high dive.* **5.** (*in combination*) coming up to a specified level: *knee-high.* **6.** being at its peak: *high noon.* **7.** of greater than average height: *a high collar.* **8.** greater than normal in intensity or amount: *a high wind; high mileage.* **9.** (of sound) acute in pitch. **10.** (of latitudes) relatively far north or south from the equator. **11.** (of meat) slightly decomposed, regarded as enhancing the flavour of game. **12.** very important: *the high priestess.* **13.** exalted in style or character: *high drama.* **14.** expressing contempt or arrogance: *high words.* **15.** elated; cheerful: *high spirits.* **16.** *Inf.* being in a state of altered consciousness induced by alcohol, narcotics, etc. **17.** *Inf.* overexcited: *by Christmas the children are high.* **18.** luxurious or extravagant: *high life.* **19.** advanced in complexity: *high finance.* **20.** (of a gear) providing a relatively great forward speed for a given engine speed. **21.** *Phonetics.* denoting a vowel whose articulation is produced by raising the tongue, such as for the *ee* in *see* or *oo* in *moon.* **22.** (*cap. when part of a name*) formal and elaborate: *High Mass.* **23.** (*usually cap.*) relating to the High Church. **24.** *Cards.* having a relatively great value in a suit. **25. high and dry.** stranded; destitute. **26. high and mighty.** *Inf.* arrogant. **27. high opinion.** a favourable opinion. ~*adv.* **28.** at or to a height: *he jumped high.* **29.** in a high manner. **30.** *Naut.* close to the wind with sails full. ~*n.* **31.** a high place or level. **32.** *Inf.* a state of altered consciousness induced by alcohol, narcotics, etc. **33.** another word for **anticyclone. 34. on high. a.** at a height. **b.** in heaven. [OE *hēah*]

High Arctic *n.* the regions of Canada, esp. the northern islands, within the Arctic Circle.

highball ('haɪ,bɔːl) *n. Chiefly U.S.* a long iced drink consisting of spirits with soda water, etc.

highborn ('haɪ,bɔːn) *adj.* of noble birth.

highboy ('haɪ,bɔɪ) *n. U.S. & Canad.* a tallboy.

highbrow ('haɪ,braʊ) *Often disparaging.* ~*n.* **1.** a person of scholarly and erudite tastes. ~*adj. also* **highbrowed. 2.** appealing to highbrows.

highchair ('haɪ,tʃɛə) *n.* a long-legged chair for a child, esp. one with a table-like tray.

High Church *n.* **1.** the party or movement within the Church of England stressing continuity with Catholic Christendom, the authority of bishops, and the importance of sacraments. ~*adj.* **High-Church. 2.** of or relating to this party or movement. — **'High-'Churchman** *n.*

high-class *adj.* **1.** of very good quality: *a high-class grocer.* **2.** belonging to or exhibiting the characteristics of an upper social class.

high-coloured *adj.* (of the complexion) deep red or purplish; florid.

high comedy *n.* comedy set largely among cultured and articulate people and featuring witty dialogue.

high commissioner *n.* the senior diplomatic representative sent by one Commonwealth country to another instead of an ambassador.

high country *n.* (often preceded by *the*) *N.Z.* sheep pastures in the foothills of the Southern Alps, New Zealand.

High Court *n.* **1.** Also called: **High Court of Justice.** (in England) the supreme court dealing with civil law cases. **2.** (in Australia) the highest court of appeal, deciding esp. constitutional issues. **3.** (in New Zealand) a court of law that is superior to a District Court. Former name: **Supreme Court.**

higher ('haɪə) *adj.* **1.** the comparative of **high.** ~*n.* (*usually cap.*) (in Scotland) **2. a.** the advanced level of the Scottish Certificate of Education. **b.** (*as modifier*): *Higher Latin.* **3.** a pass in a subject at Higher level: *she has four Highers.*

higher education *n.* education and training at colleges, universities, etc.

higher mathematics *n.* (*functioning as sing.*) mathematics that is more abstract than normal arithmetic, algebra, geometry, and trigonometry.

higher-up *n. Inf.* a person of higher rank or in a superior position.

highest common factor *n.* the largest number or quantity that is a factor of each member of a group of numbers or quantities.

high explosive *n.* an extremely powerful chemical explosive, such as TNT or gelignite.

highfalutin (,haɪfə'luːtɪn) *or* **highfaluting** *adj. Inf.* pompous or pretentious. [C19: from HIGH + -*falutin,* ? var. of *fluting,* from FLUTE]

high fidelity *n.* **a.** the reproduction of sound using electronic equipment that gives faithful reproduction with little or no distortion. **b.** (*as modifier*): *a high-fidelity amplifier.* ~Often shortened to **hi-fi.**

high-flier *or* **high-flyer** *n.* **1.** a person who is extreme in aims, ambition, etc. **2.** a person of great ability, esp. in a career. — **'high-,flying** *adj., n.*

high-flown *adj.* extravagant or pretentious in conception or intention: *high-flown ideas.*

high frequency *n.* a radio frequency lying between 30 and 3 megahertz. Abbrev.: **HF.**

High German *n.* the standard German language, historically developed from the form of West Germanic spoken in S Germany.

high-handed *adj.* tactlessly overbearing and inconsiderate. — **,high-'handedness** *n.*

high-hat *adj.* **1.** *Inf.* snobbish and arrogant. ~*vb.* **-hatting, -hatted.** (*tr.*) **2.** *Inf.* chiefly *U.S. & Canad.* to treat in a snobbish or offhand way. ~*n.* **3.** *Inf.* a snobbish person.

high hurdles *n.* (*functioning as sing.*) a race in which competitors leap over hurdles 42 inches (107 cm) high.

Highland fling *n.* a vigorous Scottish solo dance.

highjack ('haɪ,dʒæk) *vb., n.* a less common spelling of **hijack.** — **'high,jacker** *n.*

high jump *n.* **1.** (usually preceded by *the*) an athletic event in which a competitor has to jump over a high bar. **2. the high jump.** *Brit. inf.* a severe reprimand or punishment. — **high jumper** *n.* — **high jumping** *n.*

high-key *adj.* (of a painting, etc.) having a predominance of light tones or colours.

highland ('haɪlənd) *n.* **1.** relatively high ground. **2.** (*modifier*) of or relating to a highland. — **'highlander** *n.*

Highland ('haɪlənd) n. (modifier) of or denoting the Highlands of Scotland. —'**Highlander** n.

Highland cattle n. a breed of cattle with shaggy reddish-brown hair and long horns.

Highland dress n. 1. the historical costume including the plaid and kilt, of Highland clansmen and soldiers. 2. a modern version of this worn for formal occasions.

Highland Region n. a local government region in N Scotland, formed in 1975 from Caithness, Sutherland, Nairnshire, most of Inverness-shire, and Ross and Cromarty except for the Outer Hebrides. Administrative centre: Inverness. Pop.: 200 764 (1986 est.). Area: 25 149 sq. km (9710 sq. miles).

Highlands ('haɪləndz) n. **the.** 1. **a.** the part of Scotland that lies to the northwest of the great fault that runs from Dumbarton to Stonehaven. **b.** a mountainous region of NW Scotland: distinguished by Gaelic culture. 2. (often not cap.) the highland region of any country.

high-level language n. a computer-programming language that is closer to human language or mathematical notation than to machine language.

highlight ('haɪ,laɪt) n. 1. an area of the lightest tone in a painting, photograph, etc. 2. Also called: **high spot.** the most exciting or memorable part or time. 3. (pl.) a lightened or brightened effect produced in the hair by bleaching selected strands. ~vb. (tr.) 4. Painting, photog., etc. to mark with light tone. 5. to bring emphasis to. 6. to produce highlights in (the hair).

highly ('haɪlɪ) adv. 1. (intensifier): highly disappointed. 2. with great approbation: we spoke highly of it. 3. in a high position: placed highly in class. 4. at or for a high cost.

highly strung or U.S. & Canad. **high-strung** adj. tense and easily upset; excitable; nervous.

High Mass n. a solemn and elaborate sung Mass.

high-minded adj. 1. having or characterized by high moral principles. 2. Arch. arrogant; haughty. —,**high-'mindedness** n.

highness ('haɪnɪs) n. the condition of being high.

Highness ('haɪnɪs) n. (preceded by Your, His, or Her) a title used to address or refer to a royal person.

high-octane adj. (of petrol) having a high octane number.

high-pass filter n. Electronics. a filter that transmits all frequencies above a specified value, attenuating frequencies below this value.

high-pitched adj. 1. pitched high in tone. 2. (of a roof) having steeply sloping sides. 3. (of an argument, style, etc.) lofty or intense.

high-powered adj. 1. (of an optical instrument or lens) having a high magnification. 2. dynamic and energetic; highly capable.

high-pressure adj. 1. having, using, or designed to withstand pressure above normal. 2. Inf. (of selling) persuasive in an aggressive and persistent manner.

high priest n. 1. Judaism. the priest of highest rank who alone was permitted to enter the holy of holies of the Temple. 2. Also (fem.): **high priestess.** the head of a cult. —**high priesthood** n.

high-rise adj. (prenominal) of or relating to a building that has many storeys, esp. one used for flats or offices: a high-rise block.

high-risk adj. denoting a group, part, etc., that is particularly subject to a danger.

highroad ('haɪ,rəʊd) n. 1. a main road; highway. 2. (usually preceded by the) the sure way: the highroad to fame.

high school n. 1. Brit. another term for **grammar school.** 2. U.S., Canad., & N.Z. a secondary school.

high seas pl. n. (sometimes sing.) the open seas, outside the jurisdiction of any one nation.

high season n. the most popular time of year at a holiday resort, etc.

Highsmith ('haɪ,smɪθ) n. **Patricia.** born 1921, U.S. author of crime fiction. Her novels include Strangers on a Train (1950) and Ripley's Game (1974).

high-sounding adj. another term for **high-flown.**

high-spirited adj. vivacious, bold, or lively. —,**high-'spiritedness** n.

High Street n. (often not cap.; usually preceded by the) Brit. the main street of a town, usually where the principal shops are situated.

high table n. (sometimes cap.) the table in the dining hall of a school, college, etc., at which the principal teachers, fellows, etc., sit.

hightail ('haɪ,teɪl) vb. (intr.) Inf., chiefly U.S. & Canad. to go or move in a great hurry.

High Tatra n. another name for the **Tatra Mountains.**

high tea n. Brit. a substantial early evening meal consisting of a cooked dish, cakes, etc., and usually accompanied by tea.

high tech (tɛk) n. 1. short for **high technology.** ~adj. **high-tech.** 2. of or relating to a style of interior decoration using features of industrial equipment. Also: **hi-tech.**

high technology n. any type of sophisticated industrial process, esp. electronic.

high-tension n. (modifier) carrying or operating at a relatively high voltage.

high tide n. 1. the tide at its highest level. 2. a culminating point.

high time Inf. ~adv. 1. the latest possible time: it's high time you left. ~n. 2. Also: **high old time.** an enjoyable and exciting time.

high-toned adj. 1. having a superior social, moral, or intellectual quality. 2. affectedly superior. 3. high in tone.

high treason n. an act of treason directly affecting a sovereign or state.

high-up n. Inf. a person who holds an important or influential position.

highveld ('haɪ,fɛlt) n. **the.** the high grassland region of the Transvaal, South Africa.

high water n. 1. another name for **high tide.** 2. the state of any stretch of water at its highest level, as during a flood. ~Abbrev.: **HW.**

high-water mark n. 1. the level reached by sea water at high tide or by other stretches of water in flood. 2. the highest point.

highway ('haɪ,weɪ) n. 1. a public road that all may use. 2. Now chiefly U.S. & Canad. except in legal contexts. a main road, esp. one that connects towns. 3. a direct path or course.

Highway Code n. (in Britain) a booklet compiled by the Department of Transport for the guidance of users of public roads.

highwayman ('haɪweɪmən) n., pl. **-men.** (formerly) a robber, usually on horseback, who held up travellers on public roads.

high wire n. a tightrope stretched high in the air for balancing acts.

High Wycombe ('wɪkəm) n. a town in S central England, in S Buckinghamshire: furniture industry. Pop.: 60 516 (1981).

HIH abbrev. for His (or Her) Imperial Highness.

hijack or **highjack** ('haɪ,dʒæk) vb. 1. (tr.) to seize or divert (a vehicle or the goods it carries) while in transit: to hijack an aircraft. ~n. 2. the act or an instance of hijacking. [C20: from ?] —'**hijacker** or '**highjacker** n.

Hijaz (hɪ'dʒæz) n. a variant spelling of **Hejaz.**

hike (haɪk) vb. 1. (intr.) to walk a long way, usually for pleasure, esp. in the country. 2. (usually foll. by up) to pull or be pulled; hitch. 3. (tr.; usually foll. by up) to raise (prices). ~n. 4. a long walk. 5. a rise in price. [C18: from ?] —'**hiker** n.

hilarious (hɪ'lɛərɪəs) adj. very funny. [C19: from L hilaris glad, from Gk hilaros] —hi'**lariously** adv. —hi'**lariousness** n.

hilarity (hɪ'lærɪtɪ) n. mirth and merriment.

Hilary of Poitiers ('hɪlərɪ) n. **Saint.** ?315–?367 A.D., French bishop, an opponent of Arianism. Feast day: Jan. 13.

Hilary term n. the spring term at Oxford University and some other educational establishments. [C16: after Saint HILARY of Poitiers]

Hilbert ('hɪlbət) n. **David** ('da:fɪt). 1862–1943, German mathematician, who made outstanding contributions to the theories of number fields and invariants and to geometry.

Hildebrand ('hɪldə,brænd) n. the monastic name of **Gregory VII.** —,**Hilde'brandian** adj., n. —'**Hilde,brandine** adj.

Hildesheim (German 'hɪldəshaɪm) n. a city in N West Germany, in Lower Saxony: a member of the Hanseatic League. Pop.: 100 700 (1986).

hill (hɪl) *n.* **1. a.** a natural elevation of the earth's surface, less high or craggy than a mountain. **b.** (*in combination*): *a hillside.* **2. a.** a heap or mound. **b.** (*in combination*): *a dunghill.* **3.** an incline; slope. **4. hill and dale.** (of gramophone records) having vertical groove undulations. **5. over the hill. a.** *Inf.* beyond one's prime. **b.** *Mil. sl.* absent without leave or deserting. ~*vb.* (*tr.*) **6.** to form into a hill. **7.** to cover or surround with a heap of earth. [OE *hyll*] —'**hilly** *adj.*

Hill (hɪl) *n.* **1. Archibald Vivian.** 1886–1977, English biochemist, noted for his research into heat loss in muscle contraction: shared the Nobel prize for physiology or medicine (1922). **2. Octavia.** 1838–1912, English housing reformer; a founder of the National Trust. **3. Sir Rowland.** 1795–1879, English originator of the penny postage.

Hilla ('hɪlə) *n.* a market town in central Iraq, on a branch of the Euphrates: built partly of bricks from the nearby site of Babylon. Pop.: 375 000 (1980 UN est.). Also called: **Al Hillah.**

Hillary ('hɪlərɪ) *n.* Sir **Edmund.** born 1919, New Zealand explorer and mountaineer. He and his Sherpa guide, Tenzing Norgay, were the first to reach the summit of Mount Everest (1953); New Zealand ambassador to India from 1984.

hillbilly ('hɪl,bɪlɪ) *n., pl.* **-lies. 1.** *Usually disparaging.* an unsophisticated person, esp. from the mountainous areas in the southeastern U.S. **2.** another name for **country and western.** [C20: from HILL + *Billy* (the nickname)]

Hillel ('hɪlɛl, -ləl) *n.* ?60 B.C.–?9 A.D., rabbi, born in Babylonia; president of the Sanhedrin. He was the first to formulate principles of biblical interpretation.

Hiller ('hɪlə) *n.* Dame **Wendy.** born 1912, British actress. Her many films include *Pygmalion* (1938) and *Major Barbara* (1940).

Hillery ('hɪlərɪ) *n.* **Patrick John.** born 1923, Irish statesman; president of the Republic of Ireland from 1976.

Hilliard ('hɪlɪəd) *n.* **Nicholas.** 1537–1619, English miniaturist, esp. of portraits.

Hillingdon ('hɪlɪŋdən) *n.* a residential borough of W Greater London. Pop.: 232 000 (1986 est.).

hillock ('hɪlək) *n.* a small hill or mound. [C14 *hilloc*] —'**hillocked** *or* '**hillocky** *adj.*

hills (hɪlz) *pl. n.* **1. as old as the hills.** very old. **2. the.** a hilly and often remote region.

hill station *n.* (in northern India, etc.) a settlement or resort at a high altitude.

hilt (hɪlt) *n.* **1.** the handle or shaft of a sword, dagger, etc. **2. to the hilt.** to the full. [OE]

hilum ('haɪləm) *n., pl.* **-la** (-lə). *Bot.* a scar on a seed marking its point of attachment to the seed stalk. [C17: from L: trifle]

Hilversum ('hɪlvəsəm; *Dutch* 'hɪlvərsym) *n.* a city in the central Netherlands, in North Holland province: Dutch radio and television centre. Pop.: 85 449 (1987).

him (hɪm; *unstressed* ɪm) *pron.* (*objective*) refers to a male person or animal: *they needed him; she baked him a cake; not him again!* [OE *him*, dative of *hē* HE]
▷ *Usage.* See at **me.**

HIM *abbrev. for* His (*or* Her) Imperial Majesty.

Himachal Pradesh (hɪ'mɑːtʃəl prə'dɛʃ) *n.* a state of N India, in the W Himalayas: rises to about 6700 m (22 000 ft.) and is densely forested. Capital: Simla. Pop.: 4 237 569 (1981). Area: 55 658 sq. km (21 707 sq. miles).

Himalayas (,hɪmə'leɪəz, hɪ'mɑːljəz) *pl. n.* **the.** a vast mountain system in S Asia, extending 2400 km (1500 miles) from Kashmir (west) to Assam (east), between the valleys of the Rivers Indus and Brahmaputra: covers most of Nepal, Sikkim, Bhutan, and the S edge of Tibet; the highest range in the world, with several peaks over 7500 m (25 000 ft.). Highest peak: Mount Everest, 8848 m (29 028 ft.). —,**Hima'layan** *adj.*

himation (hɪ'mætɪ,ɒn) *n., pl.* **-ia** (-ɪə). (in ancient Greece) a cloak draped around the body. [C19: from Gk, from *heima* dress, from *hennunai* to clothe]

Himeji ('hiːmɛ,dʒiː) *n.* a city in central Japan, on W Honshu: cotton textile centre. Pop.: 453 636 (1986).

Himmler (*German* 'hɪmlər) *n.* **Heinrich** ('haɪnrɪç). 1900–45, German Nazi leader, head of the SS and the Gestapo (1936–45); committed suicide.

Hims (hɪmz) *n.* a former name of **Homs.**

himself (hɪm'sɛlf; *medially often* ɪm'sɛlf) *pron.* **1. a.** the reflexive form of *he* or *him.* **b.** (intensifier): *the king*

himself waved to me. **2.** (*preceded by a copula*) his normal self: *he seems himself once more.* [OE *him selfum*, dative sing. of *hē self;* see HE, SELF]
▷ *Usage.* See at **myself.**

Hinayana (,hiːnə'jɑːnə) *n.* any of various early forms of Buddhism. [from Sansk., from *hīna* lesser + *yāna* vehicle]

Hinckley ('hɪŋklɪ) *n.* a town in central England, in Leicestershire. Pop.: 29 325 (1983 est.).

hind[1] (haɪnd) *adj.* **hinder, hindmost** *or* **hindermost.** (*prenominal*) (esp. of parts of the body) situated at the back: *a hind leg.* [OE *hindan* at the back, rel. to G *hinten*]

hind[2] (haɪnd) *n., pl.* **hinds** *or* **hind. 1.** the female of the deer, esp. the red deer when aged three years or more. **2.** any of several marine fishes related to the groper. [OE *hind*]

hind[3] (haɪnd) *n.* (formerly) **1.** a simple peasant. **2.** (in Scotland and N England) a skilled farm worker. **3.** a steward. [OE *hīne*, from *hīgna*, genitive pl. of *hīgan* servants]

Hindemith (*German* 'hɪndəmɪt) *n.* **Paul** (paul). 1895–1963, German composer and musical theorist, who opposed the twelve-tone technique. His works include the song cycle *Das Marienleben* (1923) and the opera *Mathis der Maler* (1938).

Hindenburg[1] ('hɪndənbɜːrk) *n.* the German name for **Zabrze.**

Hindenburg[2] ('hɪndən,bɜːɡ; *German* 'hɪndənbʊrk) *n.* **Paul von Beneckendorff und von** (paul fɔn 'bɛnəkəndɔrf ʊnt fɔn). 1847–1934, German field marshal and statesman; president (1925–34). During World War I he directed German strategy together with Ludendorff (1916–18).

hinder[1] ('hɪndə) *vb.* **1.** to be or get in the way of (someone or something); hamper. **2.** (*tr.*) to prevent. [OE *hindrian*]

hinder[2] ('haɪndə) *adj.* (*prenominal*) situated at or further towards the back; posterior. [OE]

Hindi ('hɪndɪ) *n.* **1.** a language or group of dialects of N central India. See also **Hindustani. 2.** a formal literary dialect of this language, the official language of India. **3.** a person whose native language is Hindi. [C18: from Hindi, from *Hind* India, from OPersian *Hindu* the river Indus]

hindmost ('haɪnd,məʊst) *or* **hindermost** ('hɪndə,məʊst) *adj.* furthest back; last.

Hindoo ('hɪnduː, hɪn'duː) *n., pl.* **-doos,** *adj.* an older spelling of **Hindu.** —'**Hindoo,ism** *n.*

hindquarter ('haɪnd,kwɔːtə) *n.* **1.** one of the two back quarters of a carcass of beef, lamb, etc. **2.** (*pl.*) the rear, esp. of a four-legged animal.

hindrance ('hɪndrəns) *n.* **1.** an obstruction or snag; impediment. **2.** the act of hindering.

hindsight ('haɪnd,saɪt) *n.* **1.** the ability to understand, after something has happened, what should have been done. **2.** a firearm's rear sight.

Hindu ('hɪnduː, hɪn'duː) *n., pl.* **-dus. 1.** a person who adheres to Hinduism. **2.** an inhabitant or native of Hindustan or India. ~*adj.* **3.** relating to Hinduism, Hindus, or India. [C17: from Persian *Hindū*, from *Hind* India; see HINDI]

Hinduism ('hɪndʊ,ɪzəm) *n.* the complex of beliefs and customs comprising the dominant religion of India, characterized by the worship of many gods, a caste system, belief in reincarnation, etc.

Hindu Kush (kʊʃ, kuːʃ) *pl. n.* a mountain range in central Asia, extending about 800 km (500 miles) east from the Koh-i-Baba Mountains of central Afghanistan to the Pamirs. Highest peak: Tirich Mir, 7690 m (25 230 ft.).

Hindustan (,hɪndʊ'stɑːn) *n.* **1.** the land of the Hindus, esp. India north of the Deccan and excluding Bengal. **2.** the general area around the Ganges where Hindi is the predominant language. **3.** the areas of India where Hinduism predominates, as contrasted with those areas where Islam predominates.

Hindustani (,hɪndʊ'stɑːnɪ) *n.* **1.** the dialect of Hindi spoken in Delhi: used as a lingua franca throughout India. **2.** all the spoken forms of Hindi and Urdu considered together. ~*adj.* **3.** of or relating to these languages or Hindustan.

Hines (haɪnz) *n.* **Earl,** known as *Earl "Fatha" Hines.* 1905–83, U.S. jazz pianist, conductor, and songwriter.

hinge (hɪndʒ) *n.* **1.** a device for holding together two parts such that one can swing relative to the other. **2.** a natural joint, such as the knee joint, that functions in only one plane. **3.** something on which events, opinions, etc., turn. **4.** Also called: **mount.** *Philately.* a small transparent strip of gummed paper for affixing a stamp to a page. ~*vb.* **5.** (*tr.*) to fit a hinge to (something). **6.** (*intr.; usually foll. by on or upon*) to depend (on). **7.** (*intr.*) to hang or turn on or as if on a hinge. [C13: prob. of Gmc origin] — **hinged** *adj.*

hinny[1] ('hını) *n., pl.* **-nies.** the sterile hybrid offspring of a male horse and a female donkey. [C19: from L *hinnus,* from Gk *hinnos*]

hinny[2] ('hını) *n. Scot. & N English dialect.* a term of endearment, esp. for a woman. [var. of HONEY]

Hinshelwood ('hınʃəl,wod) *n.* Sir **Cyril Norman.** 1897–1967, English chemist, who shared the Nobel prize for chemistry (1956) for the study of reaction kinetics.

hint (hınt) *n.* **1.** a suggestion given in an indirect or subtle manner. **2.** a helpful piece of advice. **3.** a small amount; trace. ~*vb.* **4.** (when *intr.,* often foll. by *at;* when *tr., takes a clause as object*) to suggest indirectly. [C17: from ?]

hinterland ('hıntə,lænd) *n.* **1.** land lying behind something, esp. a coast or the shore of a river. **2.** remote or undeveloped areas. **3.** an area near and dependent on a large city, esp. a port. [C19: from G, from *hinter* behind + *land* LAND]

hip[1] (hıp) *n.* **1.** (*often pl.*) either side of the body below the waist and above the thigh. **2.** another name for **pelvis** (sense 1). **3.** short for **hip joint. 4.** the angle formed where two sloping sides of a roof meet. [OE *hype*] — **hipless** *adj.*

hip[2] (hıp) *n.* the berry-like brightly coloured fruit of a rose plant. Also called: **rosehip.** [OE *héopa*]

hip[3] (hıp) *interj.* an exclamation used to introduce cheers (in **hip, hip, hurrah**). [C18: from ?]

hip[4] (hıp) *adj.* **hipper, hippest.** *Sl.* **1.** aware of or following the latest trends. **2.** (*often postpositive; foll. by to*) informed (about). [var. of earlier *hep*]

hip bath *n.* a portable bath in which the bather sits.

hipbone ('hıp,bəʊn) *n.* the nontechnical name for **innominate bone.**

hip flask *n.* a small metal flask for spirits, etc.

hip-hop ('hıp,hɒp) *n.* a U.S. pop culture movement of the 1980s comprising rap music, graffiti, and break dancing.

hip joint *n.* the ball-and-socket joint that connects each leg to the trunk of the body.

Hipparchus (hı'pɑːkəs) *n.* **1.** 2nd century B.C., Greek astronomer. He discovered the precession of the equinoxes, calculated the length of the solar year, and developed trigonometry. **2.** died 514 B.C., tyrant of Athens (527–514).

hippeastrum (,hıpı'æstrəm) *n.* any plant of a South American genus cultivated for their large funnel-shaped typically red flowers. [C19: NL, from Gk *hippeus* knight + *astron* star]

hipped[1] (hıpt) *adj.* **1. a.** having a hip or hips. **b.** (*in combination*): *broad-hipped.* **2.** (esp. of cows, sheep, etc.) having an injury to the hip, such as a dislocation. **3.** *Archit.* having a hip or hips: *hipped roof.*

hipped[2] (hıpt) *adj.* (*often postpositive; foll. by on*) *U.S. & Canad. dated sl.* very enthusiastic. [C20: from HIP[4]]

hippie *or* **hippy** ('hıpı) *n., pl.* **-pies.** (esp. during the 1960s) a person whose behaviour, dress, use of drugs, etc., implies a rejection of conventional values. [C20: see HIP[4]]

hippo ('hıpəʊ) *n., pl.* **-pos.** *Inf.* short for **hippopotamus.**

hippocampus (,hıpəʊ'kæmpəs) *n., pl.* **-pi** (-paı). **1.** a mythological sea creature with the forelegs of a horse and the tail of a fish. **2.** any of various small sea fishes with a horselike head; sea horse. **3.** a structure in the floor of the brain, which in cross section has the shape of a sea horse. [C16: from L, from Gk *hippos* horse + *kampos* sea monster]

hippocras ('hıpəʊ,kræs) *n.* an old English drink of wine flavoured with spices. [C14 *ypocras,* from OF: HIPPOCRATES, prob. referring to a filter called *Hippocrates' sleeve*]

Hippocrates (hı'pɒkrə,tiːz) *n.* ?460–?377 B.C., Greek physician, commonly regarded as the father of medicine. — ,**Hippo'cratic** *or* ,**Hippo'cratical** *adj.*

Hippocratic oath *n.* an oath taken by a doctor to observe a code of medical ethics derived from that of Hippocrates.

Hippocrene ('hıpəʊ,kriːn, ,hıpəʊ'kriːnı) *n.* a spring on Mount Helicon in Greece, said to engender poetic inspiration. [C17: via L from Gk *hippos* horse + *krēnē* spring] — ,**Hippo'crenian** *adj.*

hippodrome ('hıpə,drəʊm) *n.* **1.** a music hall, variety theatre, or circus. **2.** (in ancient Greece or Rome) an open-air course for horse and chariot races. [C16: from L *hippodromos,* from Gk *hippos* horse + *dromos* race]

hippogriff *or* **hippogryph** ('hıpəʊ,grıf) *n.* a monster with a griffin's head, wings, and claws and a horse's body. [C17: from It. *ippogrifo,* from *ippo-* horse (from Gk) + *grifo* GRIFFIN]

Hippolyta (hı'pɒlıtə) *or* **Hippolyte** (hı'pɒlı,tiː) *n. Greek myth.* a queen of the Amazons, slain by Hercules in battle for her belt, which he obtained as his ninth labour.

Hippolytus (hı'pɒlıtəs) *n. Greek myth.* a son of Theseus, killed after his stepmother Phaedra falsely accused him of raping her. — **Hip'polytan** *adj.*

Hippomenes (hı'pɒmı,niːz) *n. Greek myth.* the husband, in some traditions, of Atalanta.

hippopotamus (,hıpə'pɒtəməs) *n., pl.* **-muses** *or* **-mi** (-,maı). a very large gregarious mammal living in or around the rivers of tropical Africa. [C16: from L, from Gk: river horse, from *hippos* horse + *potamos* river]

Hippo Regius ('hıpəʊ 'riːdʒıəs) *n.* an ancient Numidian city, adjoining present-day Annaba, Algeria. Often shortened to **Hippo.**

hippy[1] ('hıpı) *adj.* **-pier, -piest.** *Inf.* (esp. of a woman) having large hips.

hippy[2] ('hıpı) *n., pl.* **-pies.** a variant spelling of **hippie.**

hip roof *n.* a roof having sloping ends and sides.

hipster ('hıpstə) *n.* **1.** *Sl., now rare.* **a.** an enthusiast of modern jazz. **b.** an outmoded word for **hippie. 2.** (*modifier*) (of trousers) cut so that the top encircles the hips.

hipsters ('hıpstəz) *pl. n. Brit.* trousers cut so that the top encircles the hips. Usual U.S. word: **hip-huggers.**

Hiram ('haıərəm) *n.* 10th century B.C., king of Tyre, who supplied Solomon with materials and craftsmen for the building of the Temple (II Samuel 5:11; I Kings 5:1–18).

hircine ('hɜːsaın, -sın) *adj.* **1.** *Arch.* of or like a goat. **2.** *Literary.* lascivious. [C17: from L *hircīnus,* from *hircus* goat]

hire ('haıə) *vb.* (*tr.*) **1.** to acquire the temporary use of (a thing) or the services of (a person) in exchange for payment. **2.** to employ (a person) for wages. **3.** (often foll. by *out*) to provide (something) or the services of (oneself or others) for payment, usually for an agreed period. **4.** (*tr.; foll. by out*) *Chiefly Brit.* to pay independent contractors for (work to be done). ~*n.* **5. a.** the act of hiring or the state of being hired. **b.** (*as modifier*): *a hire car.* **6.** the price for a person's services or the temporary use of something. **7. for** *or* **on hire.** available for hire. [OE *hȳrian*] — **'hirable** *or* **'hireable** *adj.* — **'hirer** *n.*

hireling ('haıəlıŋ) *n. Derog.* a person who works only for money. [OE *hȳrling*]

hire-purchase *n. Brit.* a system in which a buyer takes possession of merchandise on payment of a deposit and completes the purchase by paying a series of instalments while the seller retains ownership until the final instalment is paid. Abbrev.: **HP, h.p.** U.S. and Canad. equivalents: **installment plan, instalment plan.**

Hirohito (,hıərəʊ'hiːtəʊ) *n.* 1901–89, emperor of Japan 1926–89. In 1946 he became a constitutional monarch.

Hiroshige (,hıərəʊ'ʃiːgeı) *n.* Ando ('ɑːndəʊ). 1797–1858, Japanese artist, esp. of colour wood-block prints.

Hiroshima (,hıro'ʃiːmə, hı'rɒʃımə) *n.* a port in SW Japan, on SW Honshu on the delta of the Ota River: largely destroyed on August 6, 1945, by the first atomic bomb to be used in warfare, dropped by the U.S., which killed over 75 000 of its inhabitants. Pop.: 1 044 000 (1985).

hirsute ('hɜːsjuːt) *adj.* **1.** covered with hair. **2.** (of plants) covered with long but not stiff hairs. **3.** (of a person) having long, thick, or untrimmed hair. [C17: from L *hirsūtus* shaggy] — **'hirsuteness** *n.*

his (hız; *unstressed* ız) *determiner.* **1. a.** of, belonging to, or associated with him: *his knee; I don't like his being out so late.* **b.** (*as pron.*): *his is on the left; that book is his.* **2. his and hers.** for a man and woman respectively. ~*pron.* **3. of his.** belonging to him. [OE *his,* genitive of *hē* HE & of *hit* IT]

Hispania (hı'spænıə) *n.* the Iberian peninsula in the Roman world.

Hispanic (hɪ'spænɪk) *adj.* **1.** of or derived from Spain or the Spanish. ~*n.* **2.** *U.S.* a U.S. citizen of Latin-American descent. —**His'panicism** *n.*

Hispaniola (ˌhɪspən'jəʊlə; *Spanish* ispa'ɲola) *n.* the second largest island in the West Indies, in the Greater Antilles: divided politically into Haiti and the Dominican Republic; discovered in 1492 by Christopher Columbus, who named it La Isla Española. Area: 18 703 sq. km (29 418 sq. miles). Former name: **Santo Domingo.**

hispid ('hɪspɪd) *adj. Biol.* covered with stiff hairs or bristles. [C17: from L *hispidus* bristly]

hiss (hɪs) *n.* **1.** a sound like that of a prolonged *s.* **2.** such a sound as an exclamation of derision, contempt, etc. ~*vb.* **3.** (*intr.*) to produce or utter a hiss. **4.** (*tr.*) to express with a hiss. **5.** (*tr.*) to show derision or anger towards (a speaker, performer, etc.) by hissing. [C14: imit.]

hist (hɪst) *interj.* an exclamation used to attract attention or as a warning to be silent.

histamine ('hɪstəˌmiːn) *n.* an amine released by the body tissues in allergic reactions, causing irritation. [C20: from HIST- + AMINE] —**histaminic** (ˌhɪstə'mɪnɪk) *adj.*

histo- *or before a vowel* **hist-** *combining form.* indicating animal or plant tissue: *histology; histochemistry.* [from Gk, from *histos* web]

histogenesis (ˌhɪstəʊ'dʒɛnɪsɪs) *n.* the formation of tissues and organs from undifferentiated cells. —**histogenetic** (ˌhɪstəʊdʒə'nɛtɪk) *or* ˌhisto'genic *adj.*

histogram ('hɪstəˌgræm) *n.* a figure that represents a frequency distribution, consisting of contiguous rectangles whose width is in proportion to the class interval under consideration and whose area represents relative frequency of the phenomenon in question. [C20: from HISTO(RY) + -GRAM]

histology (hɪ'stɒlədʒɪ) *n.* the study of the tissues of an animal or plant. —**histological** (ˌhɪstə'lɒdʒɪkᵊl) *or* ˌhisto'logic *adj.*

histolysis (hɪ'stɒlɪsɪs) *n.* the disintegration of organic tissues. —**histolytic** (ˌhɪstə'lɪtɪk) *adj.*

historian (hɪ'stɔːrɪən) *n.* a person who writes or studies history, esp. one who is an authority on it.

historic (hɪ'stɒrɪk) *adj.* **1.** famous in history; significant. **2.** *Linguistics.* (of Latin, Greek, or Sanskrit verb tenses) referring to past time.
▷ **Usage.** A distinction is made between *historic* (important, significant) and *historical* (pertaining to history): *a historic decision; a historical perspective.*

historical (hɪ'stɒrɪkᵊl) *adj.* **1.** belonging to or typical of the study of history: *historical methods.* **2.** concerned with events of the past: *historical accounts.* **3.** based on or constituting factual material as distinct from legend or supposition. **4.** based on history: *a historical novel.* **5.** occurring in history. —**his'torically** *adv.*
▷ **Usage.** See at **historic.**

historical linguistics *n.* (*functioning as sing.*) the study of language as it changes in the course of time.

historical present *n.* the present tense used to narrate past events, employed for effect or in informal use, as in *a week ago I see this accident.*

historicism (hɪ'stɒrɪˌsɪzəm) *n.* **1.** the belief that natural laws govern historical events. **2.** the doctrine that each period of history has its own beliefs and values inapplicable to any other. **3.** excessive emphasis on history, past styles, etc. —**his'toricist** *n., adj.*

historicity (ˌhɪstə'rɪsɪtɪ) *n.* historical authenticity.

historiographer (hɪˌstɔːrɪ'ɒgrəfə) *n.* **1.** a historian, esp. one concerned with historical method. **2.** a historian employed to write the history of a group or public institution. —**hiˌstori'ography** *n.*

history ('hɪstərɪ) *n., pl.* **-ries. 1.** a record or account of past events, developments, etc. **2.** all that is preserved of the past, esp. in written form. **3.** the discipline of recording and interpreting past events. **4.** past events, esp. when considered as an aggregate. **5.** an event in the past, esp. one that has been reduced in importance: *their quarrel was just history.* **6.** the past, previous experiences, etc., of a thing or person: *the house had a strange history.* **7.** a play that depicts historical events. **8.** a narrative relating the events of a character's life: *the history of Joseph Andrews.* [C15: from L *historia*, from Gk: inquiry, from *historein* to narrate, from *histōr* judge]

histrionic (ˌhɪstrɪ'ɒnɪk) *adj.* **1.** excessively dramatic or artificial: *histrionic gestures.* **2.** *Now rare.* dramatic. ~*n.* **3.** (*pl.*) melodramatic displays of temperament. **4.** *Rare.*

(*pl.; functioning as sing.*) dramatics. [C17: from LL *histriōnicus*, from L *histriō* actor] —ˌhistri'onically *adv.*

hit (hɪt) *vb.* **hitting, hit.** (*mainly tr.*) **1.** (*also intr.*) to deal (a blow) to (a person or thing); strike. **2.** to come into violent contact with: *the car hit the tree.* **3.** to strike with a missile: *to hit a target.* **4.** to knock or bump: *I hit my arm on the table.* **5.** to propel by striking: *to hit a ball.* **6.** *Cricket.* to score (runs). **7.** to affect (a person, place, or thing), esp. suddenly or adversely: *his illness hit his wife very hard.* **8.** to reach: *unemployment hit a new high.* **9.** to experience: *I've hit a slight snag here.* **10.** *Sl.* to murder (a rival criminal) in fulfilment of an underworld vendetta. **11.** *Inf.* to set out on: *let's hit the road.* **12.** *Inf.* to arrive: *he will hit town tomorrow.* **13.** *Inf., chiefly U.S. & Canad.* to demand or request from: *he hit me for a pound.* **14. hit the bottle.** *Sl.* to drink an excessive amount of alcohol. ~*n.* **15.** an impact or collision. **16.** a shot, blow, etc., that reaches its object. **17.** an apt, witty, or telling remark. **18.** *Inf.* **a.** a person or thing that gains wide appeal: *she's a hit with everyone.* **b.** (*as modifier*): *a hit record.* **19.** *Inf.* a stroke of luck. **20.** *Sl.* **a.** a murder carried out as the result of an underworld vendetta. **b.** (*as modifier*): *a hit squad.* **21. make a hit with.** *Inf.* to make a favourable impression on. ~See also **hit off, hit on, hit out.** [OE *hittan*, from ON *hitta*] —**'hitter** *n.*

hit-and-run *adj.* (*prenominal*) **1.** denoting a motor-vehicle accident in which the driver leaves the scene without stopping to give assistance, inform the police, etc. **2.** (of an attack, raid, etc.) relying on surprise allied to a rapid departure from the scene of operations: *hit-and-run tactics.*

hitch (hɪtʃ) *vb.* **1.** to fasten or become fastened with a knot or tie. **2.** (*tr.*; often foll. by *up*) to pull up (the trousers, etc.) with a quick jerk. **3.** (*intr.*) *Chiefly U.S.* to move in a halting manner. **4.** (*tr.; passive*) *Sl.* to marry (esp. in **get hitched**). **5.** *Inf.* to obtain (a ride) by hitchhiking. ~*n.* **6.** an impediment or obstacle, esp. one that is temporary or minor. **7.** a knot that can be undone by pulling against the direction of the strain that holds it. **8.** a sudden jerk: *he gave it a hitch and it came loose.* **9.** *Inf.* a ride obtained by hitchhiking. [C15: from ?] —'**hitcher** *n.*

Hitchcock ('hɪtʃˌkɒk) *n.* Sir **Alfred (Joseph).** 1899– 1980, English film director, noted for his mastery in creating suspense. His films include *The Thirty-Nine Steps* (1935), *Rebecca* (1940), *Psycho* (1960), and *The Birds* (1963).

hitchhike ('hɪtʃˌhaɪk) *vb.* (*intr.*) to travel by obtaining free lifts in motor vehicles. —'**hitchˌhiker** *n.*

hi-tech (tɛk) *n.* a variant spelling of **high-tech.**

hither ('hɪðə) *adv.* **1.** to or towards this place (esp. in **come hither**). **2. hither and thither.** this way and that, as in confusion. ~*adj.* **3.** *Arch.* or *dialect.* (of a side or part) nearer; closer. [OE *hider*]

hithermost ('hɪðəˌməʊst) *adj. Now rare.* nearest to this place or in this direction.

hitherto (ˌhɪðə'tuː) *adv.* until this time: *hitherto, there have been no problems.*

Hitler ('hɪtlə) *n.* **1. Adolf** ('aːdɔlf). 1889–1945, German dictator, born in Austria. After becoming president of the National Socialist German Workers' Party (Nazi party), he attempted to overthrow the government of Bavaria (1923). While in prison he wrote *Mein Kampf*, expressing his philosophy of the superiority of the Aryan race and the inferiority of the Jews. He was appointed chancellor of Germany (1933), transforming it from a democratic republic into the totalitarian Third Reich, of which he became Führer in 1934. He established concentration camps to exterminate the Jews, rearmed the Rhineland (1936), annexed Austria (1938) and Czechoslovakia, and invaded Poland (1939), which precipitated World War II. He committed suicide. **2.** a person who displays dictatorial characteristics.

Hitlerism ('hɪtləˌrɪzəm) *n.* the policies, principles, and methods of the Nazi party as developed by Adolf Hitler.

hit list *n. Inf.* **1.** a list of people to be murdered: *a terrorist hit list.* **2.** a list of targets to be eliminated in some way: *a hit list of pits to be closed.*

hit man *n.* a hired assassin.

hit off *vb.* **1.** (*tr., adv.*) to represent or mimic accurately. **2. hit it off with.** *Inf.* to have a good relationship with.

hit on *vb.* (*intr., prep.*) to discover unexpectedly or guess correctly. Also: **hit upon.**

hit or miss *adj.* (**hit-or-miss** *when prenominal*) *Inf.* random; haphazard. Also: **hit and miss.**

hit out *vb.* (*intr.*, *adv.*; often foll. by *at*) **1.** to direct blows forcefully and vigorously. **2.** to make a verbal attack (upon someone).

Hittite ('hɪtaɪt) *n.* **1.** a member of an ancient people of Anatolia, who built a great empire in N Syria and Asia Minor in the second millennium B.C. **2.** the extinct language of this people. ~*adj.* **3.** of or relating to this people, their civilization, or their language.

HIV *abbrev. for* human immunodeficiency virus.

hive (haɪv) *n.* **1.** a structure in which social bees live. **2.** a colony of social bees. **3.** a place showing signs of great industry (esp. in **a hive of activity**). **4.** a teeming multitude. ~*vb.* **5.** to cause (bees) to collect or (of bees) to collect inside a hive. **6.** to live or cause to live in or as if in a hive. **7.** (*tr.*; often foll. by *up* or *away*) to store, esp. for future use. [OE *hӯf*]

hive off *vb.* (*adv.*) **1.** to transfer or be transferred from a larger group or unit. **2.** (*usually tr.*) to transfer (profitable activities of a nationalized industry) back to private ownership.

hives (haɪvz) *n.* (*functioning as sing. or pl.*) *Pathol.* a nontechnical name for **urticaria.** [C16: from ?]

hiya ('haɪjə, ˌhaɪ'jɑː) *sentence substitute.* an informal term of greeting. [C20: shortened from *how are you?*]

hl *abbrev. for* hectolitre.

HL (in Britain) *abbrev. for* House of Lords.

hm *symbol for* hectometre.

h'm (*spelling pron.* hmmm) *interj.* used to indicate hesitation, doubt, assent, pleasure, etc.

HM *abbrev. for:* **1.** His (*or* Her) Majesty. **2.** headmaster; headmistress.

HMAS *abbrev. for* His (*or* Her) Majesty's Australian Ship.

HMCS *abbrev. for* His (*or* Her) Majesty's Canadian Ship.

HMI (in Britain) *abbrev. for* Her Majesty's Inspector; a government official who examines and supervises schools.

H.M.S. *or* **HMS** *abbrev. for:* **1.** His (*or* Her) Majesty's Service. **2.** His (*or* Her) Majesty's Ship.

HMSO (in Britain) *abbrev. for* His (*or* Her) Majesty's Stationery Office.

HNC (in Britain) *abbrev. for* Higher National Certificate; a qualification recognized by many national technical and professional institutions.

HND (in Britain) *abbrev. for* Higher National Diploma; a qualification in technical subjects equivalent to an ordinary degree.

ho (həʊ) *interj.* **1.** Also: **ho-ho.** an imitation or representation of a deep laugh. **2.** an exclamation used to attract attention, etc. [C13: imit.]

Ho *the chemical symbol for* holmium.

hoar (hɔː) *n.* **1.** short for **hoarfrost.** ~*adj.* **2.** *Rare.* covered with hoarfrost. **3.** *Arch.* a poetic variant of **hoary.** [OE *hār*]

hoard (hɔːd) *n.* **1.** an accumulated store hidden away for future use. **2.** a cache of ancient coins, treasure, etc. ~*vb.* **3.** to gather or accumulate (a hoard). [OE *hord*] —'**hoarder** *n.*

hoarding ('hɔːdɪŋ) *n.* **1.** Also called (esp. U.S. and Canad.): **billboard.** a large board used for displaying advertising posters, as by a road. **2.** a temporary wooden fence erected round a building or demolition site. [C19: from C15 *hoard* fence, from OF *hourd* palisade, of Gmc origin]

hoarfrost ('hɔːˌfrɒst) *n.* a deposit of needle-like ice crystals formed on the ground by direct condensation at temperatures below freezing point. Also called: **white frost.**

hoarhound ('hɔːˌhaʊnd) *n.* a variant spelling of **horehound.**

hoarse (hɔːs) *adj.* **1.** gratingly harsh in tone. **2.** having a husky voice, as through illness, shouting, etc. [C14: from ON] —'**hoarsely** *adv.* —'**hoarseness** *n.*

hoarsen ('hɔːsᵊn) *vb.* to make or become hoarse.

hoary ('hɔːrɪ) *adj.* **hoarier, hoariest. 1.** having grey or white hair. **2.** white or whitish-grey in colour. **3.** ancient or venerable. —'**hoariness** *n.*

hoatzin (həʊ'ætsɪn) *n.* a unique South American bird with clawed wing digits in the young. [C17: from American Sp., from Nahuatl *uatzin* pheasant]

hoax (həʊks) *n.* **1.** a deception, esp. a practical joke. ~*vb.* **2.** (*tr.*) to deceive or play a joke on (someone). [C18: prob. from HOCUS] —'**hoaxer** *n.*

hob[1] (hɒb) *n.* **1.** the flat top part of a cooking stove, or a separate flat surface, containing hotplates or burners. **2.** a shelf beside an open fire, for keeping kettles, etc., hot. **3.** a steel pattern used in forming a mould or die in cold metal. [C16: var. of obs. *hubbe*; ? rel. to HUB]

hob[2] (hɒb) *n.* **1.** a hobgoblin or elf. **2. raise** *or* **play hob.** *U.S. inf.* to cause mischief. **3.** a male ferret. [C14: var. of *Rob*, short for *Robin* or *Robert*]

Hobart ('həʊbɑːt) *n.* a port in Australia, capital of the island state of Tasmania on the estuary of the Derwent: excellent natural harbour; University of Tasmania (1890). Pop.: 175 082 (1986).

Hobbema ('hɒbɪmə; *Dutch* 'hɔbəmɑː) *n.* **Meindert** ('maɪndərt). 1638–1709, Dutch painter of peaceful landscapes, usually including a watermill.

Hobbes (hɒbz) *n.* **Thomas.** 1588–1679, English political philosopher. His greatest work is the *Leviathan* (1651), which contains his defence of absolute sovereignty. —'**Hobbesian** *n., adj.* —'**Hobbism** *n.* —'**Hobbist** *n.*

hobble ('hɒbᵊl) *vb.* **1.** (*intr.*) to walk with a lame awkward movement. **2.** (*tr.*) to fetter the legs of (a horse) in order to restrict movement. **3.** (*intr.*) to progress with difficulty. ~*n.* **4.** a strap, rope, etc., used to hobble a horse. **5.** a limping gait. ~Also (for senses 2, 4): **hopple.** [C14: prob. from Low G] —'**hobbler** *n.*

hobbledehoy (ˌhɒbᵊldɪ'hɔɪ) *n.* a clumsy or bad-mannered youth. [C16: from earlier *hobbard de hoy,* from ?]

Hobbs (hɒbz) *n.* Sir **John Berry,** known as *Jack Hobbs.* 1882–1963, English cricketer: scored 197 centuries.

hobby[1] ('hɒbɪ) *n., pl.* **-bies. 1.** an activity pursued in spare time for pleasure or relaxation. **2.** *Arch.* a small horse. **3.** short for **hobbyhorse** (sense 1). **4.** an early form of bicycle, without pedals. [C14 *hobyn,* prob. var. of name *Robin*] —'**hobbyist** *n.*

hobby[2] ('hɒbɪ) *n., pl.* **-bies.** any of several small Old World falcons. [C15: from OF *hobet,* from *hobe* falcon]

hobbyhorse ('hɒbɪˌhɔːs) *n.* **1.** a toy consisting of a stick with a figure of a horse's head at one end. **2.** a rocking horse. **3.** a figure of a horse attached to a performer's waist in a morris dance, etc. **4.** a favourite topic (esp. in **on one's hobbyhorse**). [C16: from HOBBY[1], orig. a small horse; then generalized to apply to any pastime]

hobgoblin (ˌhɒb'gɒblɪn) *n.* **1.** a mischievous goblin. **2.** a bogey; bugbear. [C16: from HOB[2] + GOBLIN]

hobnail ('hɒbˌneɪl) *n.* **a.** a short nail with a large head for protecting the soles of heavy footwear. **b.** (*as modifier*): *hobnail boots.* [C16: from HOB[1] (in archaic sense: peg) + NAIL] —'**hob,nailed** *adj.*

hobnob ('hɒbˌnɒb) *vb.* **-nobbing, -nobbed.** (*intr.*; often foll. by *with*) **1.** to socialize or talk informally. **2.** *Obs.* to drink (with). [C18: from *hob* or *nob* to drink to one another in turns, ult. from OE *habban* to HAVE + *nabban* not to have]

hobo ('həʊbəʊ) *n., pl.* **-boes** *or* **-bos.** *Chiefly U.S. & Canad.* **1.** a tramp; vagrant. **2.** a migratory worker. [C19 (U.S.): from ?] —'**hoboism** *n.*

Hoboken ('həʊbəʊkən) *n.* a city in N Belgium, in Antwerp province, on the River Scheldt. Pop.: 34 505 (1982 est.).

Hobson's choice ('hɒbsᵊnz) *n.* the choice of taking what is offered or nothing at all. [C16: after Thomas *Hobson* (1544–1631), E liveryman who gave his customers no choice but had them take the nearest horse]

Hochhuth (*German* 'hɔːxhuːt) *n.* **Rolf** (rɔlf). born 1933, Swiss dramatist. His best-known works are the controversial documentary drama *The Representative* (1963), on the papacy's attitude to the Jews in World War II, *Soldiers* (1967), and *German Love Story* (1980).

Ho Chi Minh ('həʊ 'tʃiː 'mɪn) *n.* original name *Nguyen That Tan.* 1890–1969, Vietnamese statesman; president of North Vietnam (1954–69). He headed the Vietminh (1941), which won independence for Vietnam from the French (1954).

Ho Chi Minh City *n.* a port in S Vietnam, 97 km (60 miles) from the South China Sea, on the Saigon River: captured by the French in 1859; merged with adjoining Cholon in 1932; capital of the former Republic of Vietnam (South Vietnam) from 1954 to 1976; university (1917); U.S. headquarters during the Vietnam War. Pop.: 3 500 000 (1985). Former name (until 1976): **Saigon.**

hock[1] (hɒk) *n.* **1.** the joint at the tarsus of a horse or similar animal, corresponding to the human ankle. ~*vb.* **2.** another word for **hamstring.** [C16: short for *hockshin,* from OE *hōhsinu* heel sinew]

hock[2] (hɒk) *n.* any of several white wines from the German Rhine. [C17: short for obs. *hockamore* from G *Hochheimer*]

hock[3] (hɒk) *Inf., chiefly U.S. & Canad.* ~*vb.* **1.** (*tr.*) to pawn or pledge. ~*n.* **2.** the state of being in pawn. **3. in hock. a.** in prison. **b.** in debt. **c.** in pawn. [C19: from Du. *hok* prison, debt]

hockey (ˈhɒkɪ) *n.* **1.** Also called (esp. U.S. and Canad.): **field hockey.** a game played on a field by two opposing teams of 11 players each, who try to hit a ball into their opponents' goal using long sticks curved at the end. **2.** See **ice hockey.** [C19: from earlier *hawkey*, from ?]

Hockney (ˈhɒknɪ) *n.* **David.** born 1937, English painter, best known for his etchings, such as those to Cavafy's poems (1966), naturalistic portraits such as *Mr and Mrs Clark and Percy* (1971), and for paintings of water, swimmers, and swimming pools.

hocus (ˈhəʊkəs) *vb.* **-cusing, -cused** *or* **-cussing, -cussed.** (*tr.*) *Now rare.* **1.** to trick. **2.** to stupefy, esp. with a drug. **3.** to drug (a drink).

hocus-pocus (ˈhəʊkəsˈpəʊkəs) *n.* **1.** trickery or chicanery. **2.** an incantation used by conjurers or magicians. **3.** conjuring. ~*vb.* **-cusing, -cused** *or* **-cussing, -cussed.** **4.** to deceive or trick (someone). [C17: ? dog Latin invented by jugglers]

hod (hɒd) *n.* **1.** an open wooden box attached to a pole, for carrying bricks, mortar, etc. **2.** a tall narrow coal scuttle. [C14: ?from C13 dialect *hot*, from OF *hotte* pannier, prob. of Gmc origin]

Hodeida (hɒˈdeɪdə) *n.* the chief port of North Yemen, on the Red Sea. Pop.: 155 110 (1986).

hodgepodge (ˈhɒdʒˌpɒdʒ) *n.* a variant spelling (esp. U.S. and Canad.) of **hotchpotch.**

Hodgkin (ˈhɒdʒkɪn) *n.* **1. Alan Lloyd.** born 1914, English physiologist. With A. F. Huxley, he explained the conduction of nervous impulses in terms of the physical and chemical changes involved: shared the Nobel prize for physiology or medicine (1963). **2. Dorothy Crowfoot.** born 1910, English chemist and crystallographer, who determined the three-dimensional structure of insulin: Nobel prize for chemistry (1964).

Hodgkin's disease *n.* a malignant disease characterized by enlargement of the lymph nodes, spleen, and liver. [C19: after Thomas *Hodgkin* (1798–1866), London physician, who first described it]

hodograph (ˈhɒdəˌgrɑːf) *n.* a curve of which the radius vector represents the velocity of a moving particle. [C19: from Gk *hodos* way + -GRAPH]

hodometer (hɒˈdɒmɪtə) *n.* another name for **odometer.** —**ho'dometry** *n.*

hoe (həʊ) *n.* **1.** any of several kinds of long-handled hand implement used to till the soil, weed, etc. ~*vb.* **hoeing, hoed.** **2.** to dig, scrape, weed, or till (surface soil) with or as if with a hoe. [C14: via OF *houe*, of Gmc origin] —**'hoer** *n.*

hoedown (ˈhəʊˌdaʊn) *n. U.S. & Canad.* **1.** a boisterous square dance. **2.** a party at which hoedowns are danced.

Hoek van Holland (ˈhuːk fan ˈhɔlant) *n.* the Dutch name for the **Hook of Holland.**

Hofei (ˈhəʊˈfeɪ) *n.* a variant transliteration of the Chinese name for **Hefei.**

Hoffman (ˈhɒfmən) *n.* **Dustin (Lee).** (ˈdʌstɪn) born 1937, U.S. stage and film actor. His films include *The Graduate* (1967), *Midnight Cowboy* (1969), *All the President's Men* (1976), *Kramer vs Kramer* (1979) for which he won an Oscar, and *Tootsie* (1983).

Hofmannsthal (German ˈhoːfmansˌtaːl) *n.* **Hugo von** (ˈhuːɡo fɔn). 1874–1929, Austrian lyric poet and dramatist, noted as the librettist for Richard Strauss' operas, esp. *Der Rosenkavalier* (1911), *Elektra* (1909), and *Ariadne auf Naxos* (1912).

Hofuf (hɒˈfuːf) *n.* another name for **Al Hufuf.**

hog (hɒg) *n.* **1.** a domesticated pig, esp. a castrated male. **2.** *U.S. & Canad.* any mammal of the family Suidae; pig. **3.** Also: **hogget** (ˈhɒgɪt), **hogg.** *Dialect. Austral. & N.Z.* a young sheep that has yet to be sheared. **4.** *Inf.* a greedy person. **5. go the whole hog.** *Sl.* to do something thoroughly or unreservedly. ~*vb.* **hogging, hogged.** (*tr.*) **6.** *Sl.* to take more than one's share of. **7.** to arch (the back) like a hog. **8.** to cut (the mane) of (a horse) very short. [OE *hogg*, of Celtic origin] —**'hogger** *n.* —**'hog,like** *adj.*

hogan (ˈhəʊɡən) *n.* a wooden dwelling covered with earth, typical of the Navaho Indians of North America. [of Amerind origin]

Hogarth (ˈhəʊɡɑːθ) *n.* **William.** 1697–1764, English engraver and painter. He is noted particularly for his series of engravings satirizing the vices and affectations of his age, such as *A Rake's Progress* (1735) and *Marriage à la Mode* (1745). —**Ho'garthian** *adj.*

hogback (ˈhɒɡˌbæk) *n.* **1.** Also called: **hog's back.** a narrow ridge with steep sides. **2.** *Archaeol.* a tomb with sloping sides.

hogfish (ˈhɒɡˌfɪʃ) *n., pl.* **-fish** *or* **-fishes.** a wrasse that occurs in the Atlantic. The head of the male resembles a pig's snout.

Hogg (hɒg) *n.* **James,** known as *the Ettrick Shepherd.* 1770–1835, Scottish poet and writer. His works include the volume of poems *The Queen's Wake* (1813) and the novel *The Confessions of a Justified Sinner* (1824).

hoggish (ˈhɒɡɪʃ) *adj.* selfish, gluttonous, or dirty.

Hogmanay (ˌhɒɡməˈneɪ) *n.* (*sometimes not cap.*) New Year's Eve in Scotland. [C17: ?from Norman F *hoguinane*, from OF *aguillanneuf* a New Year's Eve gift]

hognose snake (ˈhɒɡˌnəʊz) *n.* a North American nonvenomous snake that has a trowel-shaped snout and inflates its body when alarmed. Also called: **puff adder.**

hogshead (ˈhɒɡzˌhɛd) *n.* **1.** a unit of capacity, used esp. for alcoholic beverages. It has several values. **2.** a large cask. [C14: from ?]

hogtie (ˈhɒɡˌtaɪ) *vb.* **-tying, -tied.** (*tr.*) *Chiefly U.S.* **1.** to tie together the legs or the arms and legs of. **2.** to impede, hamper, or thwart.

hogwash (ˈhɒɡˌwɒʃ) *n.* **1.** nonsense. **2.** pigswill.

hogweed (ˈhɒɡˌwiːd) *n.* any of several coarse weedy plants.

Hohenlohe (ˈhəʊənˌləʊə; German hoːənˈloːə) *n.* **Chlodwig** (ˈkloːtvɪç), Prince of Hohenlohe-Schillingsfürst. 1819–1901, Prussian statesman; chancellor of the German empire (1894–1900).

Hohenstaufen (ˈhəʊənˌʃtaʊfən; German hoːənˈʃtaufən) *n.* a German princely family that provided rulers of Germany (1138–1208, 1215–54), Sicily (1194–1268), and the Holy Roman Empire (1138–1254).

Hohenzollern (ˈhəʊənˌzɒlən; German hoːənˈtsɔlərn) *n.* a German noble family the younger (Franconian) branch of which provided rulers of Brandenburg (1417–1701) and Prussia (1701–1918). The last kings of Prussia (1871–1918) were also emperors of Germany.

Hohhot (hɒˈhɒt), **Huhehot,** *or* **Hu-ho-hao-t'e** *n.* a city in N China, capital of Inner Mongolia Autonomous Region (since 1954) and former capital of Suiyüan province; Inner Mongolia University (1957). Pop.: 747 000 (1983).

hoick (hɔɪk) *vb.* to rise or raise abruptly and sharply. [C20: from ?]

hoi polloi (ˈhɔɪ pəˈlɔɪ) *n.* **the.** *Often derog.* the masses; common people. [Gk, lit.: the many]

hoist (hɔɪst) *vb.* **1.** (*tr.*) to raise or lift up, esp. by mechanical means. ~*n.* **2.** any apparatus or device for hoisting. **3.** the act of hoisting. **4.** *Naut.* a group of signal flags. **5.** the inner edge of a flag next to the staff. [C16: var. of *hoise*, prob. from Low G] —**'hoister** *n.*

hoity-toity (ˌhɔɪtɪˈtɔɪtɪ) *adj. Inf.* arrogant or haughty. [C17: rhyming compound based on C16 *hoit* to romp, from ?]

Hokkaido (hɒˈkaɪdəʊ) *n.* the second largest and northernmost of the four main islands of Japan, separated from Honshu by the Tsugaru Strait and from the island of Sakhalin, Soviet Union, by La Pérouse Strait: constitutes an autonomous administrative division. Capital: Sapporo. Pop.: 5 679 000 (1985). Area: 78 508 sq. km (30 312 sq. miles).

hokonui (ˌhəʊkəˈnuːiː) *n. N.Z.* illicit whisky. [from *Hokonui*, district of Southland Province, N.Z.]

hokum (ˈhəʊkəm) *n. Sl., chiefly U.S. & Canad.* **1.** claptrap; bunk. **2.** obvious or hackneyed material of a sentimental nature in a play, film, etc. [C20: prob. a blend of HOCUS-POCUS & BUNKUM]

Hokusai (ˈhɒkʊˌsaɪ, ˌhɒkʊˈsaɪ) *n.* **Katsushika** (ˌkætsuˈʃiːkə). 1760–1849, Japanese artist, noted for the draughtsmanship of his colour wood-block prints, which influenced the impressionists.

Holarctic (hɒˈlɑːktɪk) *adj.* of or denoting a zoogeographical region consisting of the entire arctic regions. [C19: from HOLO- + ARCTIC]

Holbein (*German* 'hɔlbain) *n.* **1. Hans** (hans), known as *Holbein the Elder.* 1465–1524, German painter. **2.** his son, **Hans,** known as *Holbein the Younger.* 1497–1543, German painter and engraver; court painter to Henry VIII of England (1536–43). He is noted particularly for his portraits, such as those of Erasmus (1524; 1532) and Sir Thomas More (1526).

hold¹ (həʊld) *vb.* **holding, held. 1.** to have or keep (an object) with or within the hands, arms, etc.; clasp. **2.** (*tr.*) to support: *to hold a drowning man's head above water.* **3.** to maintain or be maintained in a specified state: *to hold firm.* **4.** (*tr.*) to set aside or reserve: *they will hold our tickets until tomorrow.* **5.** (when *intr., usually used in commands*) to restrain or be restrained from motion, action, departure, etc.: *hold that man until the police come.* **6.** (*intr.*) to remain fast or unbroken: *that cable won't hold much longer.* **7.** (*intr.*) (of the weather) to remain dry and bright. **8.** (*tr.*) to keep the attention of. **9.** (*tr.*) to engage in or carry on: *to hold a meeting.* **10.** (*tr.*) to have the ownership, possession, etc., of: *he holds a law degree; who's holding the ace?* **11.** (*tr.*) to have the use of or responsibility for: *hold office.* **12.** (*tr.*) to have the capacity for: *the carton will hold eight books.* **13.** (*tr.*) to be able to control the outward effects of drinking beer, spirits, etc. **14.** (often foll. by *to* or *by*) to remain or cause to remain committed (to): *hold him to his promise.* **15.** (*tr.; takes a clause as object*) to claim: *he holds that the theory is incorrect.* **16.** (*intr.*) to remain relevant, valid, or true: *the old philosophies don't hold nowadays.* **17.** (*tr.*) to consider in a specified manner: *I hold him very dear.* **18.** (*tr.*) to defend successfully: *hold the fort against the attack.* **19.** (sometimes foll. by *on*) *Music.* to sustain the sound of (a note) throughout its specified duration. **20.** (*tr.*) *Computers.* to retain (data) in a storage device after copying onto another storage device or location. **21. hold (good) for.** to apply or be relevant to: *the same rules hold for everyone.* **22. there is no holding him.** he is so spirited that he cannot be restrained. ~*n.* **23.** the act or method of holding fast or grasping. **24.** something to hold onto, as for support or control. **25.** an object or device that holds fast or grips something else. **26.** controlling influence: *she has a hold on him.* **27.** a short pause. **28.** a prison or a cell in a prison. **29.** *Wrestling.* a way of seizing one's opponent. **30.** *Music.* a pause or fermata. **31. a.** a tenure, esp. of land. **b.** (*in combination*): *freehold.* **32.** *Arch.* a fortified place. **33. no holds barred.** all limitations removed. ~See also **hold back, hold down,** etc. [OE *healdan*] — '**holdable** *adj.*

hold² (həʊld) *n.* the space in a ship or aircraft for storing cargo. [C16: var. of HOLE]

holdall ('həʊld,ɔːl) *n. Brit.* a large strong bag or basket. Usual U.S. and Canad. name: **carryall.**

hold back *vb.* (*adv.*) **1.** to restrain or be restrained. **2.** (*tr.*) to withhold: *he held back part of the payment.*

hold down *vb.* (*tr., adv.*) **1.** to restrain or control. **2.** *Inf.* to manage to retain or keep possession of: *to hold down two jobs at once.*

holder ('həʊldə) *n.* **1.** a person or thing that holds. **2. a.** a person who has possession or control of something. **b.** (*in combination*): *householder.* **3.** *Law.* a person who has possession of a bill of exchange, cheque, or promissory note that he is legally entitled to enforce.

Hölderlin (*German* 'hœldərliːn) *n.* **Friedrich** ('friːdrɪç). 1770–1843, German lyric poet, whose works include the poems *Menon's Lament for Diotima* and *Bread and Wine* and the novel *Hyperion* (1797–99).

holdfast ('həʊld,faːst) *n.* **1.** the act of gripping strongly. **2.** any device used to secure an object, such as a hook, clamp, etc. **3.** the organ of attachment of a seaweed or related plant.

hold forth *vb.* (*adv.*) **1.** (*intr.*) to speak for a long time or in public. **2.** (*tr.*) to offer (an attraction or enticement).

hold in *vb.* (*tr., adv.*) **1.** to curb, control, or keep in check. **2.** to conceal (feelings).

holding ('həʊldɪŋ) *n.* **1.** land held under a lease. **2.** (*often pl.*) property to which the holder has legal title, such as land, stocks, shares, and other investments. **3.** *Sport.* the obstruction of an opponent with the hands or arms, esp. in boxing.

holding company *n.* a company with controlling shareholdings in one or more other companies.

holding operation *n.* a plan or procedure devised to prolong the existing situation.

holding paddock *n. Austral. & N.Z.* a paddock in which cattle or sheep are kept temporarily, as before shearing, etc.

holding pattern *n.* the oval or circular path of an aircraft flying around an airport awaiting permission to land.

hold off *vb.* (*adv.*) **1.** (*tr.*) to keep apart or at a distance. **2.** (*intr.; often foll. by from*) to refrain (from doing something).

hold on *vb.* (*intr., adv.*) **1.** to maintain a firm grasp. **2.** to continue or persist. **3.** (foll. by *to*) to keep or retain: *hold on to those stamps as they'll soon be valuable.* **4.** *Inf.* to keep a telephone line open. ~*sentence substitute.* **5.** *Inf.* stop! wait!

hold out *vb.* (*adv.*) **1.** (*tr.*) to offer. **2.** (*intr.*) to last or endure. **3.** (*intr.*) to continue to stand firm, as a person refusing to succumb to persuasion. **4.** *Chiefly U.S.* to withhold (something due). **5. hold out for.** to wait patiently for (the fulfilment of one's demands). **6. hold out on.** *Inf.* to keep from telling (a person) some important information.

hold over *vb.* (*tr., mainly adv.*) **1.** to defer or postpone. **2.** (*prep.*) to intimidate (a person) with (a threat).

hold-up *n.* **1.** a robbery, esp. an armed one. **2.** a delay; stoppage. ~*vb.* **hold up.** (*tr., adv.*) **3.** to delay; hinder. **4.** to support. **5.** to waylay in order to rob, esp. using a weapon. **6.** to exhibit or present.

hold with *vb.* (*intr., prep.*) to support; approve of.

hole (həʊl) *n.* **1.** an area hollowed out in a solid. **2.** an opening in or through something. **3.** an animal's burrow. **4.** *Inf.* an unattractive place, such as a town. **5.** a fault (esp. in **pick holes in**). **6.** *Sl.* a difficult and embarrassing situation. **7.** the cavity in various games into which the ball must be thrust. **8.** (on a golf course) **a.** each of the divisions of a course (usually 18) represented by the distance between the tee and a green. **b.** the score made in striking the ball from the tee into the hole. **9.** *Physics.* a vacancy in a nearly full band of quantum states of electrons in a semiconductor or an insulator. Under the action of an electric field holes behave as carriers of positive charge. **10. hole in the wall.** *Inf.* a small dingy place, esp. one difficult to find. **11. in holes.** so worn as to be full of holes. **12. make a hole in.** to consume or use a great amount of (food, drink, money, etc.). ~*vb.* **13.** to make a hole or holes in (something). **14.** (when *intr.*, often foll. by *out*) *Golf.* to hit (the ball) into the hole. [OE *hol*] — '**holey** *adj.*

hole-and-corner *adj.* (*usually prenominal*) *Inf.* furtive or secretive.

hole in one *n. Golf.* a shot from the tee that finishes in the hole. Also (esp. U.S.): **ace.**

hole in the heart *n.* a defect of the heart in which there is an abnormal opening in any of the walls dividing the four heart chambers.

hole up *vb.* (*intr., adv.*) **1.** (of an animal) to hibernate. **2.** *Inf.* to hide or remain secluded.

Holguín (*Spanish* ɔl'ɣin) *n.* a city in NE Cuba, in Oriente province: trading centre. Pop.: 194 700 (1986 est.).

-holic *suffix forming noun* indicating desire for or dependence on; *workaholic; chocoholic.* [C20: abstracted from (*alco*)*holic*]

holiday ('hɒlɪ,deɪ) *n.* **1.** (*often pl.*) *Chiefly Brit.* a period in which a break is taken from work or studies for rest, travel, or recreation. U.S. and Canad. word: **vacation. 2.** a day on which work is suspended by law or custom, such as a religious festival, bank holiday, etc. Related adj.: **ferial.** ~*vb.* **3.** (*intr.*) *Chiefly Brit.* to spend a holiday. [OE *hāligdæg,* lit.: holy day]

Holiday ('hɒlɪ,deɪ) *n.* **Billie.** real name *Eleanora Fagan;* known as *Lady Day.* 1915–59, U.S. jazz singer.

holiday camp *n. Brit.* a place, esp. one at the seaside, providing accommodation, recreational facilities, etc., for holiday-makers.

holiday-maker *n. Brit.* a person who goes on holiday. U.S. and Canad. equivalents: **vacationer, vacationist.**

holily ('həʊlɪlɪ) *adv.* in a holy, devout, or sacred manner.

holiness ('həʊlɪnɪs) *n.* the state or quality of being holy.

Holiness ('həʊlɪnɪs) *n.* (preceded by *His* or *Your*) a title reserved for the pope.

Holinshed ('hɒlɪnʃed) *or* **Holingshed** *n.* **Raphael.** died ?1580, English chronicler. His *Chronicles of England,*

Scotland, and Ireland (1577) provided material for Shakespeare's historical and legendary plays.

holism ('hǝʊlɪzǝm) *n.* **1.** *Philosophy.* the idea that the whole is greater than the sum of its parts. **2.** (in medicine) the consideration of the complete person in the treatment of disease. [C20: from HOLO- + -ISM] —**ho'listic** *adj.*

Holkar State (hɒl'kɑː) *n.* a former state of central India, ruled by the Holkar dynasty of Maratha rulers of Indore (18th century until 1947).

holland ('hɒlǝnd) *n.* a coarse linen cloth. [C15: after HOLLAND, where it was made]

Holland[1] ('hɒlǝnd) *n.* **1.** another name for the **Netherlands.** **2.** a county of the Holy Roman Empire, corresponding to the present-day North and South Holland provinces of the Netherlands. **3. Parts of.** an area in E England constituting a former administrative division of Lincolnshire.

Holland[2] ('hɒlǝnd) *n.* Sir **Sidney George.** 1893–1961, New Zealand statesman; prime minister of New Zealand (1949–57).

hollandaise sauce (,hɒlǝn'deɪz, 'hɒlǝn,deɪz) *n.* a rich sauce of egg yolks, butter, vinegar, etc. [C19: from F *sauce hollandaise* Dutch sauce]

Hollandia (hɒ'lændɪǝ) *n.* a former name of **Jayapura.**

Hollands ('hɒlǝndz) *n.* *(functioning as sing.)* Dutch gin, often sold in stone bottles. [C18: from Du. *hollandsch genever*]

holler ('hɒlǝ) *Inf.* ~*vb.* **1.** to shout or yell (something). ~*n.* **2.** a shout; call. [var. of C16 *hollow*, from *holla*, from F *holà* stop! (lit.: ho there!)]

Holliger (*German* 'hɔlɪgǝ) *n.* **Heinz** (haints). born 1939, Swiss oboist and composer.

hollo ('hɒlǝʊ) *or* **holla** ('hɒlǝ) *n.*, *pl.* **-los** *or* **-las**, *interj.* **1.** a cry for attention, or of encouragement. ~*vb.* **2.** *(intr.)* to shout. [C16: from F *holà* ho there!]

hollow ('hɒlǝʊ) *adj.* **1.** having a hole or space within; not solid. **2.** having a sunken area; concave. **3.** deeply set: *hollow cheeks.* **4.** (of sounds) as if resounding in a hollow place. **5.** without substance or validity. **6.** hungry or empty. **7.** insincere; cynical. ~*adv.* **8. beat (someone) hollow.** *Brit. inf.* to defeat thoroughly. ~*n.* **9.** a cavity, opening, or space in or within something. **10.** a depression in the land. ~*vb.* (often foll. by *out*, usually when *tr.*) **11.** to make or become hollow. **12.** to form (a hole, cavity, etc.) or (of a hole, etc.) to be formed. [C12: from *holu*, inflected form of OE *holh* cave] —**'hollowly** *adv.* —**'hollowness** *n.*

hollow-eyed *adj.* with the eyes appearing to be sunk into the face, as from excessive fatigue.

holly ('hɒlɪ) *n.*, *pl.* **-lies.** **1.** a tree or shrub having bright red berries and shiny evergreen leaves with prickly edges. **2.** its branches, used for Christmas decorations. **3. holly oak.** another name for **holm oak.** [OE *holegn*]

Holly ('hɒlɪ) *n.* **Buddy.** real name *Charles Harden Holley.* 1936–59, U.S. rock-and-roll singer, guitarist, and songwriter. His hits (all 1956–59) include "That'll be the Day", "Maybe Baby", "Peggy Sue", "Oh, Boy", "Think it over", and "It doesn't Matter anymore".

hollyhock ('hɒlɪ,hɒk) *n.* a tall plant with stout hairy stems and spikes of white, yellow, red, or purple flowers. Also called (U.S.): **rose mallow.** [C16: from HOLY + *hock*, from OE *hoc* mallow]

Hollywood ('hɒlɪ,wʊd) *n.* **1.** a NW suburb of Los Angeles, California: centre of the American film industry. **2.** the American film industry.

holm[1] (hǝʊm) *n.* *Dialect, chiefly northwestern English.* **1.** an island in a river or lake. **2.** low flat land near a river. [OE *holm* sea, island]

holm[2] (hǝʊm) *n.* **1.** short for **holm oak.** **2.** *Chiefly Brit.* a dialect word for **holly.** [C14: var. of obs. *holin*, from OE *holegn* holly]

Holmes (hǝʊmz) *n.* **1. Oliver Wendell.** 1809–94, U.S. author, esp. of humorous essays, such as *The Autocrat of the Breakfast Table* (1858) and its sequels. **2.** his son, **Oliver Wendell.** 1841–1935, U.S. jurist, noted for his liberal judgments.

holmium ('hɒlmɪǝm) *n.* a malleable silver-white metallic element of the lanthanide series. Symbol: Ho; atomic no.: 67; atomic wt.: 164.93. [C19: from NL *Holmia* Stockholm]

holm oak *n.* an evergreen Mediterranean oak tree with prickly leaves resembling holly. Also called: **holm, holly oak, ilex.**

holo- *or before a vowel* **hol-** *combining form.* whole or wholly: *holograph.* [from Gk *holos*]

holocaust ('hɒlǝ,kɔːst) *n.* **1.** great destruction or loss of life or the source of such destruction, esp. fire. **2.** *(usually cap.)* **the.** the mass murder of Jews in Nazi Germany. **3.** a rare word for **burnt offering.** [C13: from LL *holocaustum* whole burnt offering, from Gk, from HOLO- + *kaiein* to burn]

Holocene ('hɒlǝ,siːn) *adj.* **1.** of, denoting, or formed in the second and most recent epoch of the Quaternary period, which began 10 000 years ago. ~*n.* **2. the.** the Holocene epoch or rock series. ~Also: **Recent.**

Holofernes (,hɒlǝ'fɜːniːz, hǝ'lɒfǝ,niːz) *n.* the Assyrian general, who was killed by the biblical heroine Judith.

hologram ('hɒlǝ,græm) *n.* a photographic record produced by illuminating the object with coherent light (as from a laser) and, without using lenses, exposing a film to light reflected from this object and to a direct beam of coherent light. When interference patterns on the film are illuminated by the coherent light a three-dimensional image is produced.

holograph ('hɒlǝ,grɑːf) *n.* a book or document handwritten by its author; original manuscript; autograph.

holography (hɒ'lɒgrǝfɪ) *n.* the science or practice of producing holograms. —**holographic** (,hɒlǝ'græfɪk) *adj.* —,**holo'graphically** *adv.*

holohedral (,hɒlǝ'hiːdrǝl) *adj.* (of a crystal) exhibiting all the planes required for the symmetry of the crystal system.

holophytic (,hɒlǝ'fɪtɪk) *adj.* (of plants) capable of synthesizing their food from inorganic molecules, esp. by photosynthesis.

holothurian (,hɒlǝ'θjʊǝrɪǝn) *n.* **1.** an echinoderm of the class *Holothuroidea*, having a leathery elongated body with a ring of tentacles around the mouth. ~*adj.* **2.** of the *Holothuroidea.* [C19: from NL *Holothūria*, name of type genus, from L: water polyp, from Gk, from ?]

hols (hɒlz) *pl. n. Brit. school sl.* holidays.

Holst (hǝʊlst) *n.* **Gustav (Theodore).** 1874–1934, English composer. His works include operas, choral music, and orchestral music such as the suite *The Planets* (1917).

Holstein (*German* 'hɔlʃtain) *n.* a region of N West Germany, in S Schleswig-Holstein: in early times a German duchy of Saxony; became a duchy of Denmark in 1474; finally incorporated into Prussia in 1866.

holster ('hǝʊlstǝ) *n.* a sheathlike leather case for a pistol, attached to a belt or saddle. [C17: via Du., of Gmc origin]

holt[1] (hǝʊlt) *n. Arch. or poetic.* a wood or wooded hill. [OE *holt*]

holt[2] (hǝʊlt) *n.* the lair of an animal, esp. an otter. [C16: from HOLD[1]]

Holt (hǝʊlt) *n.* **Harold Edward.** 1908–67, Australian statesman; prime minister (1966–67); believed drowned.

holy ('hǝʊlɪ) *adj.* **-lier, -liest.** **1.** of or associated with God or a deity; sacred. **2.** endowed or invested with extreme purity. **3.** devout or virtuous. **4. holier-than-thou.** offensively sanctimonious or self-righteous. ~*n.*, *pl.* **-lies.** **5.** a sacred place. [OE *hālig, hælig*]

Holy Communion *n.* **1.** the celebration of the Eucharist. **2.** the consecrated elements.

holy day *n.* a day on which a religious festival is observed.

Holy Father *n. R.C. Church.* the pope.

Holy Ghost *n.* another name for the **Holy Spirit.**

Holy Grail *n.* (in medieval legend) the bowl used by Jesus at the Last Supper. It was brought to Britain by Joseph of Arimathea, where it became the quest of many knights. Also called: **Grail, Sangraal.** [C14: *grail* from OF *graal*, from Med. L *gradālis* bowl, from ?]

Holyhead ('hɒlɪ,hed) *n.* **1.** an island off the NW coast of Anglesey: part of the county of Gwynedd. Area: about 62 sq. km (24 sq. miles). **2.** the chief town of this island, a port on the N coast. Pop.: 10 467 (1981).

Holy Island *n.* an island off the NE coast of Northumberland, linked to the mainland by road but accessible only at low water: site of a monastery founded by St. Aidan in 635. Also called: **Lindisfarne.**

Holy Land *n.* the. another name for Palestine.

Holyoake ('hǝʊlɪ,ǝʊk) *n.* Sir **Keith Jacka** ('dʒækǝ). 1904–83, New Zealand politician; prime minister (1957; 1960–72); governor general (1977–80).

holy of holies *n.* **1.** any place of special sanctity. **2.** *(cap.)* the innermost compartment of the Jewish tabernacle, where the Ark was enshrined.

holy orders *pl. n.* **1.** the sacrament whereby a person is admitted to the Christian ministry. **2.** the grades of the Christian ministry. **3.** the status of an ordained Christian minister.

Holy Roman Empire *n.* the complex of European territories under the rule of the Frankish or German king who bore the title of Roman emperor, beginning with the coronation of Charlemagne in 800 A.D.

Holy Scripture *n.* another term for the **Scriptures**.

Holy See *n. R.C. Church.* **1.** the see of the pope as bishop of Rome. **2.** the Roman curia.

Holy Spirit *n. Christianity.* the third person of the Trinity. Also called: **Holy Ghost**.

holystone ('həʊlɪˌstəʊn) *n.* **1.** a soft sandstone used for scrubbing the decks of a vessel. ~*vb.* **2.** (*tr.*) to scrub (a vessel's decks) with a holystone. [C19: ?from its being used in a kneeling position]

holy synod *n.* the governing body of any of the Orthodox Churches.

holy water *n.* water that has been blessed by a priest for use in symbolic rituals of purification.

Holy Week *n.* the week preceding Easter Sunday.

Holy Willie ('wɪlɪ) *n.* a person who is hypocritically pious. [C18: from Burns' *Holy Willie's Prayer*]

Holy Writ *n.* another term for the **Scriptures**.

homage ('hɒmɪdʒ) *n.* **1.** a public show of respect or honour towards someone or something (esp. in **pay** *or* **do homage to**). **2.** (in feudal society) the act of respect and allegiance made by a vassal to his lord. [C13: from OF, from *home* man, from L *homo*]

homburg ('hɒmbɜːɡ) *n.* a man's hat of soft felt with a dented crown and a stiff upturned brim. [C20: after *Homburg*, in West Germany, where orig. made]

home (həʊm) *n.* **1.** the place where one lives. **2.** a house or other dwelling. **3.** a family or other group living in a house. **4.** a person's country, city, etc., esp. viewed as a birthplace or a place dear to one. **5.** the habitat of an animal. **6.** the place where something is invented, founded, or developed. **7.** a building or organization set up to care for people in a certain category, such as orphans, the aged, etc. **8.** *Sport.* one's own ground: *the match is at home*. **9. a.** the objective towards which a player strives in certain sports. **b.** an area where a player is safe from attack. **10. a home from home.** a place other than one's own home where one can be at ease. **11. at home. a.** in one's own home or country. **b.** at ease. **c.** giving an informal party at one's own home. **12. at home in, on,** *or* **with.** familiar with. **13. home and dry.** *Brit. sl.* definitely safe or successful. Austral. and N.Z. equivalent: **home and hosed. 14. near home.** concerning one deeply. ~*adj.* (*usually prenominal*) **15.** of one's home, country, etc.; domestic. **16.** (of an activity) done in one's house: *home taping.* **17.** *Sport.* relating to one's own ground: *a home game.* **18.** *U.S.* central; principal: *the company's home office.* ~*adv.* **19.** to or at home: *I'll be home tomorrow.* **20.** to or on the point. **21.** to the fullest extent: *hammer the nail home.* **22. bring home to. a.** to make clear to. **b.** to place the blame on. **23. nothing to write home about.** *Inf.* to be of no particular interest: *the film was nothing to write home about.* ~*vb.* **24.** (*intr.*) (of birds and other animals) to return home accurately from a distance. **25.** (often foll. by *in on* or *onto*) to direct or be directed onto a point or target, esp. by automatic navigational aids. **26.** to send or go home. **27.** (*tr.*) to furnish with a home. **28.** (*intr.; often foll. by in* or *in on*) to be directed towards a goal, target, etc. [OE *hām*] —'**homeless** *adj., n.* —'**homelessness** *n.*

Home (hjuːm) *n.* **Alexander,** Baron Home of the Hirsel; title of *Sir Alec Douglas-Home,* formerly 14th Earl of Home. born 1903, British Conservative statesman: he renounced his earldom to become prime minister of Great Britain and Northern Ireland (1963–64); foreign secretary (1970–74).

home banking *n.* a system whereby a person at home or in an office can use a computer with a modem to call up information from a bank or to transfer funds electronically.

home-brew *n.* **1.** a beer or other alcoholic drink brewed at home rather than commercially. **2.** *Canad. inf.* a professional football player who was born in Canada and is not an import. —,**home-'brewed** *adj.*

homecoming ('həʊmˌkʌmɪŋ) *n.* the act of coming home.

Home Counties *pl. n.* the counties surrounding London.

home economics *n.* (*functioning as sing. or pl.*) the study of diet, budgeting, child care, and other subjects concerned with running a home.

home farm *n. Brit.* (esp. formerly) a farm attached to and providing food for a large country house.

Home Guard *n.* a volunteer part-time military force recruited for the defence of the United Kingdom in World War II.

home help *n. Brit.* a woman employed, esp. by a local authority, to do housework in a person's home. N.Z. equivalent: **home aid**.

homeland ('həʊmˌlænd) *n.* **1.** the country in which one lives or was born. **2.** the official name for a **Bantustan**.

homely ('həʊmlɪ) *adj.* **-lier, -liest. 1.** characteristic of or suited to the ordinary home; unpretentious. **2.** (of a person) **a.** *Brit.* warm and domesticated. **b.** *Chiefly U.S. & Canad.* plain. —'**homeliness** *n.*

home-made *adj.* **1.** (esp. of foods) made at home or on the premises, esp. of high-quality ingredients. **2.** crudely fashioned.

homeo-, homoeo-, *or* **homoio-** *combining form.* like or similar: *homeomorphism.* [from L *homoeo-,* from Gk *homoio-,* from *homos* same]

Home Office *n. Brit. government.* the department responsible for the maintenance of law and order, and all other domestic affairs not specifically assigned to another department.

homeopathy *or* **homoeopathy** (ˌhəʊmɪ'ɒpəθɪ) *n.* a method of treating disease by the use of small amounts of a drug that, in healthy persons, produces symptoms similar to those of the disease being treated. —**homeopathic** *or* **homoeopathic** (ˌhəʊmɪə'pæθɪk) *adj.* —**homeopathist, homoeopathist** (ˌhəʊmɪ'ɒpəθɪst) *or* **homeopath, homoeopath** ('həʊmɪəˌpæθ) *n.*

homeostasis *or* **homoeostasis** (ˌhəʊɪəʊ'steɪsɪs) *n.* **1.** the maintenance of metabolic equilibrium within an animal by a tendency to compensate for disrupting changes. **2.** the maintenance of equilibrium within a social group, person, etc.

homer ('həʊmə) *n.* a homing pigeon.

Homer ('həʊmə) *n.* c. 800 B.C., Greek poet to whom are attributed the *Iliad* and the *Odyssey.* Almost nothing is known of him, but it is thought that he was born on the island of Chios and was blind.

Homeric (həʊ'mɛrɪk) *adj.* **1.** of, relating to, or resembling Homer or his poems. **2.** imposing or heroic.

home rule *n.* **1.** self-government, esp. in domestic affairs. **2.** the partial autonomy sometimes granted to a national minority or a colony.

Home Secretary *n. Brit. government.* the head of the Home Office.

homesick ('həʊmˌsɪk) *adj.* depressed or melancholy at being away from home and family. —'**home,sickness** *n.*

homespun ('həʊmˌspʌn) *adj.* **1.** having plain or unsophisticated character. **2.** woven or spun at home. ~*n.* **3.** cloth made at home or made of yarn spun at home.

homestead ('həʊmˌstɛd, -stɪd) *n.* **1.** a house or estate and the adjoining land, buildings, etc., esp. a farm. **2.** (in the U.S.) a house and adjoining land designated by the owner as his fixed residence and exempt under the homestead laws from seizure and forced sale for debts. **3.** (in western Canada) a piece of land granted to a settler by the federal government. **4.** *Austral. & N.Z.* (on a sheep or cattle station) the owner's or manager's residence; in New Zealand, the term includes all outbuildings.

Homestead Act *n.* **1.** an act passed by the U.S. Congress in 1862 making available to settlers 160-acre tracts of public land for cultivation. **2.** (in Canada) a similar act passed by the Canadian Parliament in 1872.

homesteader ('həʊmˌstɛdə) *n. U.S. & Canad.* a person who possesses land under a homestead law.

homestead law *n.* (in the U.S. & Canada) any of various laws conferring privileges on homesteaders.

home straight *n.* **1.** *Horse racing.* the section of a racecourse forming the approach to the finish. **2.** the final stage of an undertaking. ~Also (chiefly U.S.): **home stretch**.

home truth *n.* (often *pl.*) an unpleasant fact told to a person about himself.

home unit n. Austral. & N.Z. a self-contained residence which is part of a series of similar residences. Often shortened to **unit**.

homeward ('həʊmwəd) adj. **1.** going home. **2.** (of a voyage, etc.) returning to the home port. ~adv. also **homewards. 3.** towards home.

homework ('həʊm,wɜːk) n. **1.** school work done at home. **2.** any preparatory study. **3.** work done at home for pay.

homey ('həʊmɪ) adj. **homier, homiest.** a variant spelling (esp. U.S.) of **homy.** —'**homeyness** n.

homicide ('hɒmɪ,saɪd) n. **1.** the killing of a human being by another person. **2.** a person who kills another. [C14: from OF, from L homo man + caedere to slay] —,homi'cidal adj.

homiletics (,hɒmɪ'lɛtɪks) n. (functioning as sing.) the art of preaching or writing sermons. [C17: from Gk homilētikos cordial, from homilein; see HOMILY]

homily ('hɒmɪlɪ) n., pl. **-lies. 1.** a sermon. **2.** moralizing talk or writing. [C14: from Church L homīlia, from Gk: discourse, from homilein to converse with, from homilos crowd, from homou together + ilē crowd] —,homi'letic adj. —'**homilist** n.

homing ('həʊmɪŋ) n. (modifier) **1.** Zool. relating to the ability to return home after travelling great distances. **2.** (of an aircraft, missile, etc.) capable of guiding itself onto a target.

homing pigeon n. any breed of pigeon developed for its homing instinct, used for racing. Also called: **homer.**

hominid ('hɒmɪnɪd) n. **1.** any primate of the family Hominidae, which includes modern man (Homo sapiens) and the extinct precursors of man. ~adj. **2.** of or belonging to the Hominidae. [C19: via NL from L homo man + -ID[1]]

hominoid ('hɒmɪ,nɔɪd) adj. **1.** of or like man; manlike. **2.** of or belonging to the primate family, which includes the anthropoid apes and man. ~n. **3.** a hominoid animal. [C20: from L homin-, homo man + -OID]

hominy ('hɒmɪnɪ) n. Chiefly U.S. coarsely ground maize prepared as a food by boiling in milk or water. [C17: prob. of Algonquian origin]

hominy grits pl. n. U.S. finely ground hominy.

homo ('həʊməʊ) n., pl. **-mos.** Inf. short for **homosexual.**

Homo ('həʊməʊ) n. any primate of the hominid genus Homo, including modern man (see **Homo sapiens**). [L: man]

homo- combining form. same or like: homologous; homosexual. [via L from Gk homos same]

homocyclic (,həʊməʊ'saɪklɪk) adj. (of a chemical compound) containing a closed ring of atoms of the same kind, esp. carbon atoms.

homoeo- combining form. a variant of **homeo-.**

homogamy (hɒ'mɒgəmɪ) n. **1.** a condition in which all the flowers of an inflorescence are either of the same sex or hermaphrodite. **2.** the maturation of the anthers and stigmas at the same time, ensuring self-pollination. —ho'mogamous adj.

homogeneous (,həʊmə'dʒiːnɪəs, ,hɒm-) adj. **1.** composed of similar or identical parts or elements. **2.** of uniform nature. **3.** similar in kind or nature. **4.** Maths. containing terms of the same degree with respect to all the variables, as in $x^2 + 2xy + y^2$. —**homogeneity** (,həʊməʊdʒɪ'niːɪtɪ, ,hɒm-) n. —,homo'geneousness n.

homogenize or **-nise** (hɒ'mɒdʒɪ,naɪz) vb. **1.** (tr.) to break up the fat globules in (milk or cream) so that they are evenly distributed. **2.** to make or become homogeneous. —ho,mogeni'zation or -ni'sation n. —ho'moge,nizer or -,niser n.

homogenous (hə'mɒdʒɪnəs) adj. of, relating to, or exhibiting homogeny.

homogeny (hə'mɒdʒɪnɪ) n. Biol. similarity in structure because of common ancestry. [C19: from Gk homogeneia community of origin, from homogenēs of the same kind]

homograph ('hɒmə,grɑːf) n. one of a group of words spelt in the same way but having different meanings. —,homo'graphic adj.

homoiothermic (həʊ,mɔɪə'θɜːmɪk) or **homothermal** adj. having a constant body temperature, usually higher than the temperature of the surroundings; warm-blooded.

homologize or **-gise** (hɒ'mɒlə,dʒaɪz) vb. to be, show to be, or make homologous.

homologous (hɒ'mɒləgəs, hɒ-), **homological** (,həʊmə'lɒdʒɪk[ə]l, ,hɒm-), or **homologic** adj. **1.** having a related or similar position, structure, etc. **2.** Biol. (of organs and parts) having the same evolutionary origin but different functions: the wing of a bat and the paddle of a whale are homologous. —,homo'logically adv. —'homo,logue or U.S. (sometimes) 'homolog n.

homology (hɒʊ'mɒlədʒɪ) n., pl. **-gies.** the condition of being homologous. [C17: from Gk homologia agreement, from homologos agreeing, from HOMO- + legein to speak]

homolosine projection (hɒ'mɒlə,saɪn) n. a map projection of the world on which the oceans are distorted to allow for greater accuracy in representing the continents. [C20: from Gk homologos agreeing + SINE[1]]

homomorphism (,həʊməʊ'mɔːfɪzəm, ,hɒm-) or **homomorphy** n. Biol. similarity in form. —,homo'morphic or ,homo'morphous adj.

homonym ('hɒmənɪm) n. **1.** one of a group of words pronounced or spelt in the same way but having different meanings. Cf. **homograph, homophone. 2.** Biol. a specific or generic name that has been used for two or more different organisms. [C17: from L homōnymum, from Gk, from homōnumos of the same name; see HOMO-, -ONYM] —,homo'nymic or ho'monymous adj.

homophobia (,həʊməʊ'fəʊbɪə) n. intense hatred or fear of homosexuals or homosexuality. [C20: from HOMO(SEXUAL) + -PHOBIA] —'homo,phobe n.

homophone ('hɒmə,fəʊn) n. **1.** one of a group of words pronounced in the same way but differing in meaning or spelling or both, as bear and bare. **2.** a written letter or combination of letters that represents the same speech sound as another: "ph" is a homophone of "f".

homophonic (,hɒmə'fɒnɪk) adj. of or relating to music in which the parts move together rather than exhibit individual rhythmic independence.

homopterous (həʊ'mɒptərəs) or **homopteran** adj. of or belonging to a suborder of hemipterous insects having wings of a uniform texture held over the back at rest. [C19: from Gk homopteros, from HOMO- + pteron wing]

Homo sapiens ('sæpɪ,ɛnz) n. the specific name of modern man; the only extant species of the genus Homo. This species also includes extinct types of primitive man such as Cro-Magnon man. [NL, from L homo man + sapiens wise]

homosexual (,həʊməʊ'sɛksjʊəl, ,hɒm-) n. **1.** a person who is sexually attracted to members of the same sex. ~adj. **2.** of or relating to homosexuals or homosexuality. **3.** of or relating to the same sex.

homosexuality (,həʊməʊ,sɛksjʊ'ælɪtɪ, ,hɒm-) n. sexual attraction to or sexual relations with members of the same sex.

homozygote (,həʊməʊ'zaɪgəʊt) n. an animal or plant that is homozygous and breeds true to type. —**homozygotic** (,həʊməʊzaɪ'gɒtɪk) adj.

homozygous (,həʊməʊ'zaɪgəs) adj. Genetics. (of an organism) having identical alleles for any one gene: these two fruit flies are homozygous for red eye colour.

Homs (hɒms) or **Hums** (hʊms) n. a city in W Syria, near the Orontes River: important in Roman times as the capital of Phoenicia-Lebanesia. Pop.: 431 000 (1987). Ancient name: **Emesa** ('ɛmɛsə). Former name: **Hims.**

homunculus (hɒ'mʌŋkjʊləs) n., pl. **-li** (-,laɪ). a miniature man; midget. Also called: **homuncule** (həʊ'mʌŋkju:l). [C17: from L, dim. of homo man] —ho'muncular adj.

homy or esp. U.S. **homey** ('həʊmɪ) adj. **homier, homiest.** like a home; cosy. —'hominess or esp. U.S. 'homeyness n.

hon. abbrev. for: **1.** honorary. **2.** honourable.

Hon. abbrev. for Honourable (title).

Honan (hɒʊ'næn) n. a variant transliteration of the Chinese name for **Henan.**

Hondo ('hɒndəʊ) n. another name for **Honshu.**

Honduras (hɒn'djʊərəs) n. **1.** a republic in Central America: an early centre of Mayan civilization; colonized by the Spanish from 1524 onwards; gained independence in 1821. Official language: Spanish; English is also widely spoken. Religion: Roman Catholic. Currency: lempira. Capital: Tegucigalpa. Pop.: 4 300 000 (1986 est.). Area: 112 088 sq. km (43 277 sq. miles). **2. Gulf of.** an inlet of the Caribbean, on the coasts of Honduras, Guatemala, and Belize. —Hon'duran adj., n.

hone (həʊn) n. **1.** a fine whetstone for sharpening. ~vb. **2.** (tr.) to sharpen or polish with or as if with a hone. [OE hān stone]

Honecker (*German* 'hɔːnɛkər) *n.* **Erich** ('eːrɪç). born 1912, East German statesman; head of state of East Germany from 1976.

Honegger ('hɒnɪgə; *French* ɔnɛgɛr) *n.* **Arthur** (artyr). 1892–1955, French composer, one of Les Six. His works include the oratorios *King David* (1921) and *Joan of Arc at the Stake* (1935), and *Pacific 231* (1924) for orchestra.

honest ('ɒnɪst) *adj.* **1.** not given to lying, cheating, stealing, etc.; trustworthy. **2.** not false or misleading; genuine. **3.** just or fair: *honest wages*. **4.** characterized by sincerity: *an honest appraisal*. **5.** without pretensions: *honest farmers*. **6.** *Arch.* (of a woman) respectable. **7. honest broker.** a mediator in disputes, esp. international ones. **8. make an honest woman of.** to marry (a woman, esp. one who is pregnant) to prevent scandal. [C13: from OF *honeste*, from L *honestus* distinguished, from *honōs* HONOUR]

honestly ('ɒnɪstlɪ) *adv.* **1.** in an honest manner. **2.** (intensifier): *I honestly don't believe it.*

honesty ('ɒnɪstɪ) *n., pl.* **-ties. 1.** the condition of being honest. **2.** *Arch.* virtue or respect. **3.** Also called: **moonwort, satinpod.** a purple-flowered European plant cultivated for its flattened silvery pods, which are used for indoor decoration.

honey ('hʌnɪ) *n.* **1.** a sweet viscid substance made by bees from nectar and stored in their nests or hives as food. **2.** anything that is sweet or delightful. **3.** (*often cap.*) *Chiefly U.S. & Canad.* a term of endearment. **4.** *Inf., chiefly U.S. & Canad.* something very good of its kind. ~*vb.* **honeying, honeyed. 5.** (*tr.*) to sweeten with or as if with honey. **6.** (often foll. by *up*) to talk to (someone) in a flattering way. [OE *huneg*] — **'honey-,like** *adj.*

honey badger *n.* another name for **ratel.**

honeybee ('hʌnɪˌbiː) *n.* any of various social bees widely domesticated as a source of honey and beeswax. Also called: **hive bee.**

honey buzzard *n.* a common European bird of prey having broad wings and a typically dull brown plumage with white-streaked underparts.

honeycomb ('hʌnɪˌkəʊm) *n.* **1.** a waxy structure, constructed by bees in a hive, that consists of adjacent hexagonal cells in which honey is stored, eggs are laid, and larvae develop. **2.** something resembling this in structure. **3.** *Zool.* another name for **reticulum** (sense 2). ~*vb.* (*tr.*) **4.** to pierce with holes, cavities, etc. **5.** to permeate: *honeycombed with spies.*

honey creeper *n.* a small tropical American songbird having a slender downward-curving bill and feeding on nectar.

honeydew ('hʌnɪˌdjuː) *n.* **1.** a sugary substance excreted by aphids and similar insects. **2.** a similar substance exuded by certain plants.

honeydew melon *n.* a variety of muskmelon with a smooth greenish-white rind and sweet greenish flesh.

honey-eater ('hʌnɪˌiːtə) *n.* a small Australasian songbird having a downward-curving bill and a brushlike tongue specialized for extracting nectar from flowers.

honeyed *or* **honied** ('hʌnɪd) *adj. Poetic.* **1.** flattering or soothing. **2.** made sweet or agreeable: *honeyed words.* **3.** full of honey.

honey guide *n.* a small bird inhabiting tropical forests of Africa and Asia and feeding on beeswax, honey, and insects.

honeymoon ('hʌnɪˌmuːn) *n.* **1.** a holiday taken by a newly married couple. **2.** a holiday considered to resemble a honeymoon: *a second honeymoon.* **3.** the early, usually calm period of a relationship or enterprise. ~*vb.* **4.** (*intr.*) to take a honeymoon. [C16: traditionally explained as an allusion to the feelings of married couples as changing with the phases of the moon] — **'honey,mooner** *n.*

honeysuckle ('hʌnɪˌsʌkəl) *n.* **1.** a temperate climbing shrub with fragrant white, yellow, or pink tubular flowers. **2.** any of various Australian trees or shrubs of the genus *Banksia*, having flowers in dense spikes. [OE *hunigsūce*, from HONEY + SUCK]

Hong Kong (hɒŋkɒŋ) *n.* **1.** a British Crown Colony on the coast of S China, to be returned to Chinese control in 1997: consists of Hong Kong Island, leased by China to Britain in 1842, Kowloon Peninsula, Stonecutters Island, the New Territories (mainland), leased by China in 1898 for a 99-year period, and over 230 small islands; important entrepôt trade and manufacturing centre, esp. for textiles

and other consumer goods; university (1912). Capital: Victoria. Pop.: 5 431 200 (1986). Area: 1046 sq. km (404 sq. miles). **2.** an island in the British Colony of Hong Kong, south of Kowloon Peninsula: contains the colonial capital, Victoria. Pop.: 996 183 (1971). Area: 75 sq. km (29 sq. miles).

Honiara (ˌhəʊnɪˈɑːrə) *n.* the capital of the Solomon Islands, on NW Guadalcanal Island. Pop.: 18 346 (1979).

honk (hɒŋk) *n.* **1.** a representation of the sound made by a goose. **2.** any sound resembling this, esp. a motor horn. ~*vb.* **3.** to make or cause (something) to make such a sound. **4.** (*intr.*) *Brit. sl.* to vomit.

honky ('hɒŋkɪ) *n., pl.* **honkies.** *Derog. sl., chiefly U.S.* a White man or White men collectively. [C20: from ?]

honky-tonk ('hɒŋkɪˌtɒŋk) *n.* **1.** *U.S. & Canad. sl.* a cheap disreputable nightclub, bar, etc. **2. a.** a style of ragtime piano-playing, esp. on a tinny-sounding piano. **b.** (*as modifier*): *honky-tonk music.* [C19: rhyming compound based on HONK]

Honolulu (ˌhɒnəˈluːluː) *n.* a port in Hawaii, on S Oahu Island: the state capital. Pop.: 372 330 (1986).

honorarium (ˌɒnəˈrɛərɪəm) *n., pl.* **-iums** *or* **-ia** (-ɪə). a fee paid for a nominally free service. [C17: from L: something presented on being admitted to a post of HONOUR]

honorary ('ɒnərərɪ) *adj.* (*usually prenominal*) **1. a.** held or given only as an honour, without the normal privileges or duties: *an honorary degree.* **b.** (of a secretary, treasurer, etc.) unpaid. **2.** having such a position or title. **3.** depending on honour rather than legal agreement.

honorific (ˌɒnəˈrɪfɪk) *adj.* **1.** showing respect. **2. a.** (of a pronoun, verb inflection, etc.) indicating the speaker's respect for the addressee. **b.** (*as n.*): *a Japanese honorific.* — **,honor'ifically** *adv.*

honour *or U.S.* **honor** ('ɒnə) *n.* **1.** personal integrity; allegiance to moral principles. **2. a.** fame or glory. **b.** a person who wins this for his country, school, etc. **3.** (*often pl.*) great respect, esteem, etc., or an outward sign of this. **4.** (*often pl.*) high or noble rank. **5.** a privilege or pleasure: *it is an honour to serve you.* **6.** a woman's chastity. **7. a.** *Bridge, etc.* any of the top five cards in a suit or any of the four aces at no trumps. **b.** *Whist.* any of the top four cards. **8.** *Golf.* the right to tee off first. **9. do the honours.** **a.** to serve as host or hostess. **b.** to perform a social act, such as carving meat, etc. **10. in honour bound.** under a moral obligation. **11. in honour of.** out of respect for. **12. on one's honour.** on the pledge of one's word or good name. ~*vb.* (*tr.*) **13.** to hold in respect. **14.** to show courteous behaviour towards. **15.** to worship. **16.** to confer a distinction upon. **17.** to accept and then pay when due (a cheque, draft, etc.). **18.** to keep (one's promise); fulfil (a previous agreement). **19.** to bow or curtsy to (one's dancing partner). [C12: from OF *onor*, from L *honor* esteem]

Honour ('ɒnə) *n.* (preceded by *Your*, *His*, or *Her*) a title used to or of certain judges.

honourable *or U.S.* **honorable** ('ɒnərəbəl) *adj.* **1.** possessing or characterized by high principles. **2.** worthy of honour or esteem. **3.** consistent with or bestowing honour. — **'honourably** *or U.S.* **'honorably** *adv.*

Honourable *or U.S.* **Honorable** ('ɒnərəbəl) *adj.* (*prenominal*) **the.** a title of respect placed before a name: used of various officials in the English-speaking world, as a courtesy title in Britain for the children of certain peers, and in Parliament by one member speaking of another. Abbrev.: **Hon.**

honours *or U.S.* **honors** ('ɒnəz) *pl. n.* **1.** observances of respect. **2.** (*often cap.*) **a.** (in a university degree course) a rank of the highest academic standard. **b.** (*as modifier*): *an honours degree.* Abbrev.: **Hons.** **3.** a high mark awarded for an examination; distinction. **4. last** (*or funeral*) **honours.** observances of respect at a funeral. **5. military honours.** ceremonies performed by troops in honour of royalty, at the burial of an officer, etc.

honours of war *pl. n. Mil.* the honours granted by the victorious to the defeated, esp. as of marching out with all arms and flags flying.

Honshu ('hɒnʃuː) *n.* the largest of the four main islands of Japan, between the Pacific and the Sea of Japan; regarded as the Japanese mainland; includes a number of offshore islands and contains most of the main cities. Pop.: 96 687 700 (1985). Area: 230 448 sq. km (88 976 sq. miles). Also called: **Hondo.**

hooch or **hootch** (hu:tʃ) n. Inf., chiefly U.S. & Canad. alcoholic drink, esp. illicitly distilled spirits. [C20: of Amerind origin, Hootchinoo, name of a tribe that distilled a type of liquor]

Hooch or **Hoogh** (hu:tʃ; Dutch ho:x) n. **Pieter de** ('pi:tər də). 1629–?1684, Dutch genre painter, noted esp. for his light effects.

hood[1] (hʊd) n. **1.** a loose head covering either attached to a cloak or coat or made as a separate garment. **2.** something resembling this in shape or use. **3.** the U.S. and Canad. name for **bonnet** (of a car). **4.** the folding roof of a convertible car. **5.** a hoodlike garment worn over an academic gown, indicating its wearer's degree and university. **6.** Biol. a hoodlike structure, such as the fold of skin on the head of a cobra ~vb. **7.** (tr.) to cover with or as if with a hood. [OE hōd] —'**hooded** adj. —'**hood,like** adj.

hood[2] (hʊd) n. Sl. short for **hoodlum**.

Hood (hʊd) n. **1.** Robin. See **Robin Hood**. **2.** Thomas. 1799–1845, English poet and humorist: his work includes protest poems, such as The Song of the Shirt (1843) and The Bridge of Sighs (1844).

-hood suffix forming nouns. **1.** indicating state or condition: manhood. **2.** indicating a body of persons: knighthood; priesthood. [OE -hād]

hooded crow n. a crow that has a grey body and black head, wings, and tail. Also called (Scot.): **hoodie** ('hʊdɪ), **hoodie crow**.

hoodlum ('hu:dləm) n. **1.** a petty gangster. **2.** a lawless youth. [C19: ?from Southern G Haderlump ragged good-for-nothing]

hoodman-blind (,hʊdmən'blaɪnd) n. Brit., arch. blind man's buff.

hoodoo ('hu:du:) n., pl. **-doos**. **1.** a variant of **voodoo**. **2.** Inf. a person or thing that brings bad luck. **3.** Inf. bad luck. ~vb. **-dooing, -dooed**. **4.** (tr.) Inf. to bring bad luck to.

hoodwink ('hʊd,wɪŋk) vb. (tr.) **1.** to dupe; trick. **2.** Obs. to cover or hide. [C16: orig., to cover the eyes with a hood, blindfold]

hooey ('hu:ɪ) n., interj. Sl. nonsense. [C20: from ?]

hoof (hu:f) n., pl. **hooves** or **hoofs**. **1. a.** the horny covering of the end of the foot in the horse, deer, and all other ungulate mammals. **b.** (in combination): a hoofbeat. Related adj.: **ungular**. **2.** the foot of an ungulate mammal. **3.** a hoofed animal. **4.** Facetious. a person's foot. **5. on the hoof**. (of livestock) alive. ~vb. **6. hoof it**. Sl. **a.** to walk. **b.** to dance. [OE hōf] —'**hoofed** adj.

Hoogh (Dutch ho:x) n. See (Pieter de) **Hooch**.

Hooghly ('hu:glɪ) n. a river in NE India, in West Bengal: the westernmost and commercially most important channel by which the River Ganges enters the Bay of Bengal. Length: 232 km (144 miles).

hoo-ha ('hu:,ha:) n. a noisy commotion or fuss. [C20: from ?]

hook (hʊk) n. **1.** a curved piece of material, usually metal, used to suspend, hold, or pull something. **2.** short for **fish-hook**. **3.** a trap or snare. **4.** something resembling a hook in design or use. **5. a.** a sharp bend, esp. in a river. **b.** a sharply curved spit of land. **6.** Boxing. a short swinging blow delivered with the elbow bent. **7.** Cricket. a shot in which the ball is hit square on the leg side with the bat held horizontally. **8.** Golf. a shot that causes the ball to go to the player's left. **9.** a hook-shaped stroke used in writing, such as a part of a letter extending above or below the line. **10.** Music. a stroke added to the stem of a note to indicate time values shorter than a crotchet. **11.** a sickle. **12.** Naut. an anchor. **13. by hook or (by) crook**. by any means. **14. hook, line, and sinker**. Inf. completely: he fell for it hook, line, and sinker. **15. off the hook**. Sl. free from obligation or guilt. **16. sling one's hook**. Brit. sl. to leave. ~vb. **17.** (often foll. by up) to fasten or be fastened with or as if with a hook or hooks. **18.** (tr.) to catch (something, such as a fish) on a hook. **19.** to curve like or into the shape of a hook. **20.** (tr.) to make (a rug) by hooking yarn through a stiff fabric backing with a special instrument. **21.** Boxing. to hit (an opponent) with a hook. **22.** Cricket, etc. to play (a ball) with a hook. **23.** Rugby. to obtain and pass (the ball) backwards from a scrum, using the feet. **24.** (tr.) Sl. to steal. [OE hōc] —'**hook,like** adj.

hookah or **hooka** ('hʊkə) n. an oriental pipe for smoking marijuana, tobacco, etc., consisting of one or more long flexible stems connected to a container of water or other liquid through which smoke is drawn and cooled. Also called: **hubble-bubble, water pipe**. [C18: from Ar. huqqah]

Hooke (hʊk) n. Robert. 1635–1703, English physicist, chemist, and inventor. He formulated Hooke's law (1678), built the first Gregorian telescope, and invented a balance spring for watches.

hooked (hʊkt) adj. **1.** bent like a hook. **2.** having a hook or hooks. **3.** caught or trapped. **4.** a slang word for **married**. **5.** Sl. addicted to a drug. **6.** (often foll. by on) obsessed (with).

hooker ('hʊkə) n. **1.** a person or thing that hooks. **2.** U.S. & Canad. sl. a prostitute. **3.** Rugby. the central forward in the front row of a scrum whose main job is to hook the ball.

Hooker ('hʊkə) n. Richard. 1554–1600, English theologian, who influenced Anglican theology with The Laws of Ecclesiastical Polity (1593–97).

Hooke's law n. the principle that the stress imposed on a solid is directly proportional to the strain produced, within the elastic limit. [C18: after R. HOOKE]

Hook of Holland n. the. **1.** a cape on the SW coast of the Netherlands, in South Holland province. **2.** a port on this cape. ~Dutch name: **Hoek van Holland**.

hook-up n. **1.** the contact of an aircraft in flight with the refuelling hose of a tanker aircraft. **2.** an alliance or relationship. **3.** the linking of broadcasting equipment or stations to transmit a special programme. ~vb. **hook up** (adv.). **4.** to connect (two or more people or things).

hookworm ('hʊk,wɜ:m) n. any of various bloodsucking worms which cause disease. They have hooked mouthparts and enter their hosts by boring through the skin. Cf. **ancylostomiasis**.

hooky or **hookey** ('hʊkɪ) n. Inf., chiefly U.S., Canad., & N.Z. truancy, usually from school (esp. in **play hooky**). [C20: ?from hook it to escape?]

hooligan ('hu:lɪgən) n. Sl. a rough lawless young person. [C19: ? var. of Houlihan, Irish surname] —'**hooliganism** n.

hoop[1] (hu:p) n. **1.** a rigid circular band of metal or wood. **2.** something resembling this. **3.** a band of iron that holds the staves of a barrel together. **4.** a child's toy shaped like a hoop and rolled on the ground or whirled around the body. **5.** Croquet. any of the iron arches through which the ball is driven. **6. a.** a light curved frame to spread out a skirt. **b.** (as modifier): a hoop skirt. **7.** Basketball. the round metal frame to which the net is attached to form the basket. **8.** a large ring often with paper stretched over it through which performers or animals jump. **9. go or be put through the hoop**. to be subjected to an ordeal. ~vb. **10.** (tr.) to surround with or as if with a hoop. [OE hōp] —'**hooped** adj.

hoop[2] (hu:p) n., vb. a variant spelling of **whoop**.

hoopla ('hu:pla:) n. **1.** Brit. a fairground game in which a player tries to throw a hoop over an object and so win it. **2.** U.S. & Canad. sl. **a.** noise; bustle. **b.** nonsense; ballyhoo. [C20: see WHOOP, LA²]

hoopoe ('hu:pu:) n. an Old World bird having a pinkish-brown plumage with black-and-white wings and an erectile crest. [C17: from earlier hoopoop, imit.]

hoop pine n. a fast-growing timber tree of Australia having rough bark with hooplike cracks around the trunk and branches.

hooray (hu:'reɪ) or **hoorah** (hu:'ra:) interj., n., vb. **1.** variant spellings of **hurrah**. ~sentence substitute. **2.** Also: **hooroo** (hu:'ru:). Austral. & N.Z. cheerio.

Hooray Henry ('hu:,reɪ 'hɛnrɪ) n., pl. **Hooray Henries** or **-rys**. a young upper-class man, often with affectedly hearty voice and manners. Sometimes shortened to **Hooray**.

hoosegow or **hoosgow** ('hu:sgaʊ) n. U.S. a slang word for jail. [C20: from Mexican Sp. jusgado prison, from Sp. court of justice, ult. from L judex a JUDGE]

hoot[1] (hu:t) n. **1.** the mournful wavering cry of some owls. **2.** a similar sound, such as that of a train whistle. **3.** a jeer of derision. **4.** Inf. an amusing person or thing. ~vb. **5.** (often foll. by at) to jeer or yell (something) contemptuously (at someone). **6.** (tr.) to drive (speakers, actors on stage, etc.) off by hooting. **7.** (intr.) to make a hoot. **8.** (intr.) Brit. to blow a horn. [C13 hoten, imit.]

hoot[2] (hu:t) n. Austral. & N.Z. a slang word for **money**. [from Maori utu price]

hootenanny ('hu:tə,næni) *or* **hootnanny** ('hu:t,næni) *n.*, *pl.* **-nies.** *U.S. & Canad.* an informal performance by folk singers. [C20: from ?]

hooter ('hu:tə) *n. Chiefly Brit.* **1.** a person or thing that hoots, esp. a car horn. **2.** *Sl.* a nose.

Hoover[1] ('hu:və) *n.* **1.** *Trademark.* a type of vacuum cleaner. ~*vb.* **2.** (*usually not cap.*) to vacuum-clean (a carpet, etc.).

Hoover[2] ('hu:və) *n.* **Herbert (Clark).** 1874–1964, U.S. statesman; 31st president of the U.S. (1929–33). He organized relief for Europe during and after World War I, but as president he lost favour after his failure to alleviate the effects of the Depression.

Hoover Dam *n.* a dam in the western U.S., on the Colorado River on the border between Nevada and Arizona; forms Lake Mead. Height: 222 m (727 ft.). Length: 354 m (1180 ft.). Former name (1933–47): **Boulder Dam.**

hooves (hu:vz) *n.* a plural of **hoof.**

hop[1] (hɒp) *vb.* **hopping, hopped. 1.** (*intr.*) to jump forwards or upwards on one foot. **2.** (*intr.*) (esp. of frogs, birds, etc.) to move forwards in short jumps. **3.** (*tr.*) to jump over. **4.** (*intr.*) *Inf.* to move quickly (in, on, out of, etc.): *hop on a bus.* **5.** (*tr.*) *Inf.* to cross (an ocean) in an aircraft. **6.** (*tr.*) *U.S. & Canad. Inf.* to travel by means of: *he hopped a train to Chicago.* **7.** (*intr.*) another word for **limp**[1]. **8. hop it** (*or* **off**). *Brit. sl.* to go away. ~*n.* **9.** the act or an instance of hopping. **10.** *Inf.* an informal dance. **11.** *Inf.* a trip, esp. in an aircraft. **12. on the hop.** *Inf.* **a.** active or busy. **b.** *Brit.* unawares or unprepared. [OE *hoppian*]

hop[2] (hɒp) *n.* **1.** a climbing plant which has green cone-like female flowers and clusters of small male flowers. **2. hop garden.** a field of hops. **3.** *Obs. sl.* opium or any other narcotic drug. ~See also **hops.** [C15: from MDu. *hoppe*] — '**hop-,picker** *n.*

hope (həup) *n.* **1.** (*sometimes pl.*) a feeling of desire for something and confidence in the possibility of its fulfilment: *his hope for peace was justified.* **2.** a reasonable ground for this feeling: *there is still hope.* **3.** a person or thing that gives cause for hope. **4.** a thing, situation, or event that is desired: *my hope is that prices will fall.* **5. not a hope** *or* **some hope.** used ironically to express little confidence that expectations will be fulfilled. ~*vb.* **6.** (*tr.; takes a clause as object or an infinitive*) to desire (something) with some possibility of fulfilment: *I hope to tell you.* **7.** (*intr.; often foll. by for*) to have a wish. **8.** (*tr.; takes a clause as object*) to trust or believe: *we hope that this is satisfactory.* [OE *hopa*]

Hope (həup) *n.* **1. Anthony,** real name *Sir Anthony Hope Hawkins.* 1863–1933, English novelist; author of *The Prisoner of Zenda* (1894). **2. Bob,** real name *Leslie Townes Hope.* born 1903, U.S. comedian and comic actor, born in England. His films include *The Cat and the Canary* (1939), *Road to Morocco* (1942), and *The Paleface* (1947).

hope chest *n.* the U.S., Canad., and N.Z. name for **bottom drawer.**

hopeful ('həupful) *adj.* **1.** having or expressing hope. **2.** inspiring hope; promising. ~*n.* **3.** a person considered to be on the brink of success (esp. in **a young hopeful**). — '**hopefulness** *n.*

hopefully ('həupfuli) *adv.* **1.** in a hopeful manner. **2.** *Inf.* it is hoped: *hopefully they will be married soon.*
▷ **Usage.** The use of *hopefully* to mean 'it is hoped that' is not universally accepted as standard. It does, however, represent a construction well-established in colloquial English, as in the use of *happily* in the *two vehicles crashed, but happily no one was injured.*

Hopeh *or* **Hopei** ('həu'pei) *n.* a variant transliteration of the Chinese name for **Hebei.**

hopeless ('həuplis) *adj.* **1.** having or offering no hope. **2.** impossible to solve. **3.** unable to learn, function, etc. **4.** *Inf.* without skill or ability. — '**hopelessly** *adv.* — '**hopelessness** *n.*

Hopi ('həupi) *n.* **1.** (*pl.* **-pis** *or* **-pi**) a member of a North American Indian people of NE Arizona. **2.** the language of this people. [from Hopi *Hópi* peaceful]

Hopkins ('hɒpkinz) *n.* **1. Sir Frederick Gowland** ('gauland). 1861–1947, English biochemist, who pioneered research into what came to be called vitamins: shared the Nobel prize for physiology or medicine (1929). **2. Gerard Manley.** 1844–89, English poet and Jesuit priest, who experimented with sprung rhythm in his highly original poetry.

hoplite ('hɒplait) *n.* (in ancient Greece) a heavily armed infantryman. [C18: from Gk *hoplitēs*, from *hoplon* weapon, from *hepein* to prepare]

hopper (hɒpə) *n.* **1.** a person or thing that hops. **2.** a funnel-shaped reservoir from which solid materials can be discharged into a receptacle below, esp. for feeding fuel to a furnace, loading a truck, etc. **3.** a machine used for picking hops. **4.** any of various long-legged hopping insects. **5.** an open-topped railway truck for loose minerals, etc., unloaded through doors on the underside. **6.** *S. African.* another name for **cocopan. 7.** *Computers.* a device for holding punched cards and feeding them to a card reader.

hopping ('hɒpiŋ) *adv.* **hopping mad.** in a terrible rage.

hops (hɒps) *pl. n.* the dried flowers of the hop plant, used to give a bitter taste to beer.

hopsack ('hɒp,sæk) *n.* **1.** a roughly woven fabric of wool, cotton, etc., used for clothing. **2.** Also called: **hopsacking.** a coarse fabric used for bags, etc., made generally of hemp or jute.

hopscotch ('hɒp,skɒtʃ) *n.* a children's game in which a player throws a small stone or other object to land in one of a pattern of squares marked on the ground and then hops over to it to pick it up. [C19: HOP[1] + SCOTCH[1]]

Horace ('hɒris) *n.* Latin name *Quintus Horatius Flaccus.* 65–8 B.C., Roman poet and satirist: his verse includes the lyrics in the *Epodes* and the *Odes*, the *Epistles* and *Satires*, and the *Ars Poetica.*

Horae ('hɔ:ri:) *pl. n. Classical myth.* the goddesses of the seasons. Also called: **the Hours.** [L: hours]

horary ('hɔ:rəri) *adj. Arch.* **1.** relating to the hours. **2.** hourly. [C17: from Med. L *hōrārius*, from L *hora*]

Horatian (hə'reiʃən) *adj.* of, relating to, or characteristic of Horace or his poetry.

Horatius Cocles (hɒ'reiʃiəs 'kɒkliːz) *n.* a legendary Roman hero of the 6th century B.C., who defended a bridge over the Tiber against Lars Porsena.

horde (hɔ:d) *n.* **1.** a vast crowd; throng; mob. **2.** a nomadic group of people, esp. an Asiatic group. **3.** a large moving mass of animals, esp. insects. [C16: from Polish *horda*, from Turkish *ordū* camp]

Hordern ('hɔ:dən) *n.* Sir **Michael (Murray).** born 1911, British actor.

Horeb ('hɔ:rɛb) *n. Bible.* a mountain, probably Mount Sinai.

horehound *or* **hoarhound** ('hɔ:,haund) *n.* a downy herbaceous Old World plant with small white flowers that contain a bitter juice formerly used as a cough medicine and flavouring. [OE *hārhūne*, from *hār* grey + *hūne* horehound, from ?]

horizon (hə'raiz°n) *n.* **1.** Also called: **visible horizon, apparent horizon.** the apparent line that divides the earth and the sky. **2.** *Astron.* **a.** Also called: **sensible horizon.** the circular intersection with the celestial sphere of the plane tangential to the earth at the position of the observer. **b.** Also called: **celestial horizon.** the great circle on the celestial sphere, the plane of which passes through the centre of the earth and is parallel to the sensible horizon. **3.** the range or limit of scope, interest, knowledge, etc. **4.** a layer of rock within a stratum that has a particular composition by which the stratum may be dated. [C14: from L, from Gk *horizōn kuklos* limiting circle, from *horizein* to limit]

horizontal (,hɒri'zɒnt°l) *adj.* **1.** parallel to the plane of the horizon; level; flat. **2.** of or relating to the horizon. **3.** in a plane parallel to that of the horizon. **4.** applied uniformly to all members of a group. **5.** *Econ.* relating to identical stages of commercial activity: *horizontal integration.* ~*n.* **6.** a horizontal plane; position, line, etc. — ,**horizon'tality** *n.* — ,**hori'zontally** *adv.*

horizontal bar *n. Gymnastics.* a raised bar on which swinging and vaulting exercises are performed.

hormone ('hɔ:məun) *n.* **1.** a chemical substance produced in an endocrine gland and transported in the blood to a certain tissue, on which it exerts a specific effect. **2.** an organic compound produced by a plant that is essential for growth. **3.** any synthetic substance having the same effects. [C20: from Gk *hormōn*, from *horman* to stir up, from *hormē* impulse] — **hor'monal** *adj.*

Hormuz (hɔ:'mu:z, 'hɔ:mʌz) *or* **Ormuz** *n.* an island off the SE coast of Iran, in the **Strait of Hormuz:** ruins of the ancient city of Hormuz, a major trading centre in the Middle Ages. Area: about 41 sq. km (16 sq. miles).

horn (hɔːn) *n.* **1.** either of a pair of permanent bony outgrowths on the heads of cattle, antelopes, etc. **2.** the outgrowth from the nasal bone of a rhinoceros, consisting of a mass of fused hairs. **3.** any hornlike projection, such as the eyestalk of a snail. **4.** the antler of a deer. **5. a.** the constituent substance, mainly keratin, of horns, hooves, etc. **b.** (*in combination*): *horn-rimmed spectacles.* **6.** a container or device made from this substance or an artificial substitute: *a drinking horn.* **7.** an object resembling a horn in shape, such as a cornucopia. **8.** a primitive musical instrument made from horn. **9.** any musical instrument consisting of a pipe or tube of brass fitted with a mouthpiece. See **French horn, cor anglais. 10.** *Jazz sl.* any wind instrument. **11. a.** a device for producing a warning or signalling noise. **b.** (*in combination*): *a foghorn.* **12.** (*usually pl.*) the imaginary hornlike parts formerly supposed to appear on the forehead of a cuckold. **13. a.** a hollow conical device coupled to a gramophone to control the direction and quality of the sound. **b.** a similar device attached to an electrical loudspeaker, esp. in a public-address system. **14.** a stretch of land or water shaped like a horn. **15.** *Brit. taboo sl.* an erection of the penis. ~*vb.* (*tr.*) **16.** to provide with a horn or horns. **17.** to gore or butt with a horn. **18.** to remove or shorten the horns of (cattle, etc.). ~See also **horn in.** [OE] —**horned** *adj.* —**hornless** *adj.*

Horn (hɔːn) *n.* Cape. See **Cape Horn.**

hornbeam ('hɔːn,biːm) *n.* **1.** a tree of Europe and Asia having smooth grey bark and hard white wood. **2.** its wood. ~Also called: **ironwood.** [C14: from HORN + BEAM, referring to its tough wood]

hornbill ('hɔːn,bɪl) *n.* a bird of tropical Africa and Asia, having a very large bill with a basal bony protuberance.

hornblende ('hɔːn,blɛnd) *n.* a mineral of the amphibole group consisting of the aluminium silicates of calcium, sodium, magnesium, and iron: varies in colour from green to black. [C18: from G *Horn* horn + BLENDE]

hornbook ('hɔːn,bʊk) *n.* a page bearing a religious text or the alphabet, held in a frame with a thin window of horn over it.

horned toad *or* **lizard** *n.* a small insectivorous burrowing lizard inhabiting desert regions of America, having a flattened toadlike body covered with spines.

horned viper *n.* a venomous snake that occurs in desert regions of N Africa and SW Asia and has a small horny spine above each eye.

hornet ('hɔːnɪt) *n.* **1.** any of various large social wasps that can inflict a severe sting. **2. hornet's nest.** a strongly unfavourable reaction (often in **stir up a hornet's nest**). [OE *hyrnetu*]

horn in *vb.* (*intr., adv.*; often foll. by *on*) *Sl.* to interrupt or intrude.

Horn of Africa *n.* a region of NE Africa, comprising Somalia and adjacent territories.

horn of plenty *n.* another term for **cornucopia.**

hornpipe ('hɔːn,paɪp) *n.* **1.** an obsolete reed instrument with a mouthpiece made of horn. **2.** an old British solo dance to a hornpipe accompaniment, traditionally performed by sailors. **3.** a piece of music for such a dance.

hornswoggle ('hɔːn,swɒɡ²l) *vb.* (*tr.*) *Sl.* to cheat or trick; bamboozle. [C19: from ?]

horny ('hɔːnɪ) *adj.* **hornier, horniest. 1.** of, like, or hard as horn. **2.** having a horn or horns. **3.** *Sl.* aroused sexually. — **'horniness** *n.*

horologe ('hɒrə,lɒdʒ) *n.* a rare word for **timepiece.** [C14: from L *hōrologium*, from Gk *hōrologion*, from *hōra* HOUR + *-logos* from *legein* to tell]

horologist (hɒ'rɒlədʒɪst) *or* **horologer** *n.* a person skilled in horology.

horology (hɒ'rɒlədʒɪ) *n.* the art or science of making timepieces or of measuring time. —**horologic** (,hɒrə'lɒdʒɪk) *or* ,**horo'logical** *adj.*

horoscope ('hɒrə,skəʊp) *n.* **1.** the prediction of a person's future based on zodiacal data for the time of birth. **2.** the configuration of the planets, sun, and moon in the sky at a particular moment. **3.** a diagram showing the positions of the planets, sun, moon, etc., at a particular time and place. [C16: from L *horoscopus*, from Gk *hōroskopos*, from *hōra* HOUR + -SCOPE] —**horoscopic** (,hɒrə'skɒpɪk) *adj.* —**horoscopy** (hɒ'rɒskəpɪ) *n.*

Horowitz ('hɒrəvɪts) *n.* **Vladimir.** born 1904, Russian virtuoso pianist, in the U.S. from 1928.

horrendous (hɒ'rɛndəs) *adj.* another word for **horrific.** [C17: from L *horrendus* fearful, from *horrēre* to bristle, shudder, tremble; see HORROR] —**hor'rendously** *adv.*

horrible ('hɒrɪb²l) *adj.* **1.** causing horror; dreadful. **2.** disagreeable. **3.** *Inf.* cruel or unkind. [C14: via OF from L *horribilis*, from *horrēre* to tremble] — **'horribleness** *n.* — **'horribly** *adv.*

horrid ('hɒrɪd) *adj.* **1.** disagreeable; unpleasant: *a horrid meal.* **2.** repulsive or frightening. **3.** *Inf.* unkind. [C16 (in the sense: bristling, shaggy): from L *horridus* prickly, from *horrēre* to bristle] — **'horridly** *adv.* — **'horridness** *n.*

horrific (hɒ'rɪfɪk, hə-) *adj.* provoking horror; horrible. —**hor'rifically** *adv.*

horrify ('hɒrɪ,faɪ) *vb.* **-fying, -fied.** (*tr.*) **1.** to cause feelings of horror in; terrify. **2.** to shock greatly. — ,**horrifi'cation** *n.* — **'horri,fied** *adj.* — **'horri,fying** *adj.* — **'horri,fyingly** *adv.*

horripilation (hɒ,rɪpɪ'leɪʃən) *n. Physiol.* a technical name for **goose flesh.** [C17: from LL *horripilātiō* a bristling, from L *horrēre* to stand on end + *pilus* hair]

horror ('hɒrə) *n.* **1.** extreme fear; terror; dread. **2.** intense hatred. **3.** (*often pl.*) a thing or person causing fear, loathing, etc. **4.** (*modifier*) having a frightening subject: *a horror film.* [C14: from L: a trembling with fear]

horrors ('hɒrəz) *pl. n.* **1.** *Sl.* a fit of depression or anxiety. **2.** *Inf.* See **delirium tremens.** ~*interj.* **3.** an expression of dismay, sometimes facetious.

Horsa ('hɔːsə) *n.* died ?455 A.D., leader, with his brother Hengist, of the first Jutish settlers in Britain. See also **Hengist.**

hors de combat *French.* (ɔr də kɔ̃ba) *adj.* (*postpositive*), *adv.* disabled or injured. [lit.: out of (the) fight]

hors d'oeuvre ('ɔː 'dɜːvr) *n., pl.* **hors d'oeuvre** *or* **hors d'oeuvres** ('dɜːvr). an appetizer, usually served before the main meal. [C18: from F, lit.: outside the work]

horse (hɔːs) *n.* **1.** a solid-hoofed, herbivorous, domesticated mammal used for draught work and riding. Related *adj.:* **equine. 2.** the adult male of this species; stallion. **3. wild horse.** another name for **Przewalski's horse. 4.** (*functioning as pl.*) horsemen, esp. cavalry: *a regiment of horse.* **5.** Also called: **buck.** *Gymnastics.* a padded apparatus on legs, used for vaulting, etc. **6.** a narrow board supported by a pair of legs at each end, used as a frame for sawing or as a trestle, barrier, etc. **7.** a contrivance on which a person may ride and exercise. **8.** a slang word for **heroin. 9.** *Mining.* a mass of rock within a vein of ore. **10.** *Naut.* a rod, rope, or cable, fixed at the ends, along which something may slide; traveller. **11.** *Inf.* short for **horsepower. 12.** (*modifier*) drawn by a horse or horses: *a horse cart.* **13. a horse of another** *or* **a different colour.** a completely different topic, argument, etc. **14. be** (*or* **get**) **on one's high horse.** *Inf.* to act disdainfully aloof. **15. hold one's horses.** to restrain oneself. **16. horses for courses.** a policy, course of action, etc. modified slightly to take account of special circumstances without departing in essentials from the original. **17. the horse's mouth.** the most reliable source. ~*vb.* **18.** (*tr.*) to provide with a horse or horses. **19.** to put or be put on horseback. [OE *hors*] — **'horse,like** *adj.*

horse trading *n.* shrewd bargaining.

horse around *or* **about** *vb.* (*intr., adv.*) *Inf.* to indulge in horseplay.

horseback ('hɔːs,bæk) *n.* **a.** a horse's back (esp. in **on horseback**). **b.** *Chiefly U.S.* (*as modifier*): *horseback riding.*

horsebox ('hɔːs,bɒks) *n. Brit.* a van or trailer used for carrying horses.

horse brass *n.* a decorative brass ornament, originally attached to a horse's harness.

horse chestnut *n.* **1.** a tree having palmate leaves, erect clusters of white, pink, or red flowers, and brown shiny inedible nuts enclosed in a spiky bur. **2.** Also called: **conker.** the nut of this tree. [C16: from its having been used in the treatment of respiratory disease in horses]

horseflesh ('hɔːs,flɛʃ) *n.* **1.** horses collectively. **2.** the flesh of a horse, esp. edible horse meat.

horsefly ('hɔːs,flaɪ) *n., pl.* **-flies.** a large stout-bodied dipterous fly, the female of which sucks the blood of mammals, esp. horses, cattle, and man. Also called: **gadfly, cleg.**

horsehair ('hɔːs,hɛə) n. hair taken chiefly from the tail or mane of a horse, used in upholstery and for fabric, etc.

horsehide ('hɔːs,haɪd) n. **1.** the hide of a horse. **2.** leather made from this hide.

horse latitudes pl. n. Naut. the latitudes near 30°N or 30°S at sea, characterized by baffling winds, calms, and high barometric pressure. [C18: referring either to the high mortality of horses on board ship in these latitudes or to dead horse (nautical slang: advance pay), which sailors expected to work off by this stage of a voyage]

horse laugh n. a coarse or raucous laugh.

horseleech ('hɔːs,liːtʃ) n. **1.** any of several large carnivorous freshwater leeches. **2.** an archaic name for a **veterinary surgeon.**

horse mackerel n. **1.** Also called: **scad.** a mackerel-like fish of European Atlantic waters, with a row of bony scales along the lateral line. Sometimes called (U.S.): **saurel.** **2.** any of various large tunnies or related fishes.

horseman ('hɔːsmən) n., pl. **-men. 1.** a person skilled in riding. **2.** a person who rides a horse. —'**horseman,ship** n. —'**horse,woman** fem. n.

horse mushroom n. a large edible mushroom, with a white cap and greyish gills.

Horsens (Danish 'hɔrsəns) n. a port in Denmark, in E Jutland at the head of **Horsens Fjord.** Pop.: 46 855 (1981 est.).

horse pistol n. a large holstered pistol formerly carried by horsemen.

horseplay ('hɔːs,pleɪ) n. rough or rowdy play.

horsepower ('hɔːs,pauə) n. an fps unit of power, equal to 550 foot-pounds per second (equivalent to 745.7 watts). Abbrev.: **HP, h.p.**

horseradish ('hɔːs,rædɪʃ) n. a coarse Eurasian plant cultivated for its thick white pungent root, which is ground and combined with vinegar, etc., to make a sauce.

horse sense n. another term for **common sense.**

horseshoe ('hɔːs,ʃuː) n. **1.** a piece of iron shaped like a U nailed to the underside of the hoof of a horse to protect the soft part of the foot: commonly thought to be a token of good luck. **2.** an object of similar shape.

horseshoe bat n. any of numerous large-eared Old World bats with a fleshy growth around the nostrils, used in echolocation.

horseshoe crab n. a marine arthropod of North America and Asia, having a rounded heavily armoured body with a long pointed tail. Also called: **king crab.**

horsetail ('hɔːs,teɪl) n. **1.** a plant having jointed stems with whorls of small dark toothlike leaves. **2.** a stylized horse's tail formerly used as the emblem of a pasha.

horsewhip ('hɔːs,wɪp) n. **1.** a whip, usually with a long thong, used for managing horses. ~vb. **-whipping, -whipped. 2.** (tr.) to flog with such a whip. —'**horse-,whipper** n.

horst (hɔːst) n. a ridge of land that has been forced upwards between two faults. [C20: from G Horst thicket]

horsy or **horsey** ('hɔːsɪ) adj. **horsier, horsiest. 1.** of or relating to horses: a horsy smell. **2.** dealing with or devoted to horses. **3.** like a horse: a horsy face. —'**horsily** adv. —'**horsiness** n.

Horta (Portuguese 'ɔrtə) n. a port in the Azores, on the SE coast of Fayal Island.

hortatory ('hɔːtətərɪ) or **hortative** ('hɔːtətɪv) adj. tending to exhort; encouraging. [C16: from LL hortātōrius, from L hortārī to EXHORT] —**hor'tation** n. —'**hortatorily** or '**hortatively** adv.

Hortense (French ɔrtɑ̃s) n. See (Eugénie Hortense de) **Beauharnais.**

Horthy (Hungarian 'horti) n. **Miklós** ('miklo:ʃ), full name Horthy de Nagybánya. 1868–1957, Hungarian admiral: suppressed Kun's Communist republic (1919); regent of Hungary (1920–44).

horticulture ('hɔːtɪ,kʌltʃə) n. the art or science of cultivating gardens. [C17: from L hortus garden + CULTURE; cf. AGRICULTURE] —,**horti'cultural** adj. —,**horti'culturist** n.

Horus ('hɔːrəs) n. a solar god of Egyptian mythology, usually depicted with a falcon's head. [via LL from Gk Hōros, from Egyptian Hur hawk]

Hos. Bible. abbrev. for Hosea.

hosanna (həu'zænə) interj. an exclamation of praise, esp. one to God. [OE osanna, via LL from Gk, from Heb. hōshi 'āh nnā save now, we pray]

hose¹ (həuz) n. **1.** a flexible pipe, for conveying a liquid or gas. ~vb. **2.** (sometimes foll. by down) to wash, water, or sprinkle (a person or thing) with or as if with a hose. [C15: later use of HOSE²]

hose² (həuz) n., pl. **hose** or **hosen. 1.** stockings, socks, and tights collectively. **2.** History. a man's garment covering the legs and reaching up to the waist. **3. half-hose.** socks. [OE hosa]

Hosea (həu'zɪə) n. Old Testament. **1.** a Hebrew prophet of the 8th century B.C. **2.** the book containing his oracles.

hosier ('həuzɪə) n. a person who sells stockings, etc.

hosiery ('həuzɪərɪ) n. stockings, socks, and knitted underclothing collectively.

hospice ('hɒspɪs) n. **1.** a nursing home that specializes in caring for the terminally ill. **2.** Arch. a place of shelter for travellers, esp. one kept by a monastic order. [C19: from F, from L hospitium hospitality, from hospes guest]

hospitable ('hɒspɪtəbəl, hɒ'spɪt-) adj. **1.** welcoming to guests or strangers. **2.** fond of entertaining. [C16: from Med. L hospitāre to receive as a guest, from L hospes guest] —'**hospitableness** n. —'**hospitably** adv.

hospital ('hɒspɪtəl) n. **1.** an institution for the medical or psychiatric care and treatment of patients. **2.** (modifier) having the function of a hospital: a hospital ship. **3.** a repair shop for something specified: a dolls' hospital. **4.** Arch. a charitable home, hospice, or school. [C13: from Med. L hospitāle hospice, from L, from hospes guest]

Hospitalet (Spanish ɔspita'let) n. a city in NE Spain, a SW suburb of Barcelona. Pop.: 294 033 (1981).

hospitality (,hɒspɪ'tælɪtɪ) n., pl. **-ties.** kindness in welcoming strangers or guests.

hospitality suite n. a room or suite, as at a conference, where free drinks are offered.

hospitalize or **-lise** ('hɒspɪtə,laɪz) vb. (tr.) to admit or send (a person) into a hospital. —,**hospitali'zation** or **-li'sation** n.

hospitaller or U.S. **hospitaler** ('hɒspɪtələ) n. a person, esp. a member of certain religious orders, dedicated to hospital work, ambulance services, etc. [C14: from OF hospitalier, from Med. L, from hospitāle hospice; see HOSPITAL]

Hospitaller or U.S. **Hospitaler** ('hɒspɪtələ) n. a member of the order of the Knights Hospitallers.

host¹ (həust) n. **1.** a person who receives or entertains guests, esp. in his own home. **2.** the compere of a show or television programme. **3.** Biol. **a.** an animal or plant that supports a parasite. **b.** an animal into which tissue is experimentally grafted. **4.** the owner or manager of an inn. ~vb. **5.** to be the host of (a party, programme, etc.): to host one's own show. [C13: from F hoste, from L hospes guest]

host² (həust) n. **1.** a great number; multitude. **2.** an archaic word for **army.** [C13: from OF hoste, from L hostis stranger]

Host (həust) n. Christianity. the wafer of unleavened bread consecrated in the Eucharist. [C14: from OF oiste, from L hostia victim]

hosta ('hɒstə) n. a plant cultivated esp. for its ornamental foliage. [C19: NL, after N. T. Host (1761–1834), Austrian physician]

hostage ('hɒstɪdʒ) n. **1.** a person given to or held by another as a security or pledge. **2.** the state of being held as a hostage. **3.** any security or pledge. **4. give hostages to fortune.** to place oneself in a position in which misfortune may strike through the loss of what one values most. [C13: from OF, from hoste guest]

hostel ('hɒstəl) n. **1.** a building providing overnight accommodation, as for homeless people. **2.** See **youth hostel. 3.** Brit. a supervised lodging house for nurses, workers, etc. **4.** Arch. another word for **hostelry.** [C13: from OF, from Med. L hospitāle hospice; see HOSPITAL]

hosteller or U.S. **hosteler** ('hɒstələ) n. **1.** a person who stays at youth hostels. **2.** an archaic word for **innkeeper.**

hostelling or U.S. **hosteling** ('hɒstəlɪŋ) n. the practice of staying at youth hostels when travelling.

hostelry ('hɒstəlrɪ) n., pl. **-ries.** Arch. or facetious. an inn.

hostess ('həustɪs) n. **1.** a woman acting as host. **2.** a woman who receives and entertains patrons of a club, restaurant, etc. **3.** See **air hostess.**

hostile ('hɒstaɪl) adj. **1.** antagonistic; opposed. **2.** of or relating to an enemy. **3.** unfriendly. [C16: from L hostīlis, from hostis enemy] —'**hostilely** adv.

hostility (hɒ'stɪlɪtɪ) n., pl. -ties. 1. enmity. 2. an act expressing enmity. 3. (pl.) fighting; warfare.

hostler ('ɒslə) n. a variant (esp. Brit.) of **ostler**.

hot (hɒt) adj. hotter, hottest. 1. having a relatively high temperature. 2. having a temperature higher than desirable. 3. causing a sensation of bodily heat. 4. causing a burning sensation on the tongue: a hot curry. 5. expressing or feeling intense emotion, such as anger or lust. 6. intense or vehement. 7. recent; new: hot from the press. 8. Ball games. (of a ball) thrown or struck hard, and so difficult to respond to. 9. much favoured: a hot favourite. 10. Inf. having a dangerously high level of radioactivity. 11. Sl. stolen or otherwise illegally obtained. 12. Sl. (of people) being sought by the police. 13. (of a colour) intense; striking: hot pink. 14. following closely: hot on the scent. 15. Inf. at a dangerously high electric potential. 16. Sl. good (esp. in not so hot). 17. Jazz sl. arousing great excitement by inspired improvisation, strong rhythms, etc. 18. Inf. dangerous or unpleasant (esp. in make it hot for someone). 19. (in various games) very near the answer. 20. Metallurgy. (of a process) at a sufficiently high temperature for metal to be in a soft workable state. 21. Austral. & N.Z. inf. (of a price, etc.) excessive. 22. hot on. Inf. a. very severe: the police are hot on drunk drivers. b. particularly knowledgeable about. 23. hot under the collar. Inf. aroused with anger, annoyance, etc. 24. in hot water. Inf. in trouble. ~adv. 25. in a hot manner; hotly. ~See also hot up. [OE hāt] —'hotly adv. —'hotness n. —'hottish adj.

hot air n. Inf. empty and woolly boastful talk.

Hotan ('həʊ'tæn), **Hotien**, or **Ho-t'ien** ('həʊ'tjɛn) n. 1. an oasis in W China, in the Taklimakan Shamo desert of central Xinjiang Uygur Autonomous Region, around the seasonal Hotan River. 2. the chief town of this oasis, situated at the foot of the Kunlun Mountains. Pop.: about 50 000 (1975 est.). Also called: **Khotan**.

hotbed ('hɒt,bɛd) n. 1. a glass-covered bed of soil, usually heated, for propagating plants, forcing early vegetables, etc. 2. a place offering ideal conditions for the growth of an idea, activity, etc., esp. one considered bad.

hot-blooded adj. 1. passionate or excitable. 2. (of a horse) being of thoroughbred stock.

hotchpotch ('hɒtʃ,pɒtʃ) or esp. U.S. & Canad. **hodgepodge** n. 1. a jumbled mixture. 2. a thick soup or stew. [C15: var. of hotchpot from OF, from hocher to shake + POT[1]]

hot cross bun n. a yeast bun marked with a cross and traditionally eaten on Good Friday.

hot dog n. a sausage, esp. a frankfurter, usually served hot in a long roll split lengthways.

hotel (həʊ'tɛl) n. 1. a commercially run establishment providing lodging and usually meals for guests. 2. Austral. & N.Z. a public house. [C17: from F hôtel, from OF hostel; see HOSTEL]

hotelier (hɒ'tɛljeɪ) n. an owner or manager of one or more hotels.

hotel ship n. an accommodation barge anchored near an oil production rig.

hotfoot ('hɒt,fʊt) adv. with all possible speed.

hot-gospeller n. Inf. a revivalist preacher with a highly enthusiastic style of addressing his audience. —'hot-'gospel adj.

hothead ('hɒt,hɛd) n. an excitable person.

hot-headed adj. impetuous, rash, or hot-tempered. —,hot-'headedness n.

hothouse ('hɒt,haʊs) n. 1. a. a greenhouse in which the temperature is maintained at a fixed level. b. (as modifier): a hothouse plant. 2. a. an environment that encourages rapid development. b. (as modifier): a hothouse atmosphere. 3. (modifier) Inf. often disparaging. sensitive or delicate: a hothouse temperament.

Hotien or **Ho-t'ien** ('həʊ'tjɛn) n. a variant transliteration of the Chinese name for **Hotan**.

hot line n. 1. a direct telephone or teletype link between heads of government, etc., for emergency use. 2. any such direct line for urgent use.

hot money n. capital that is transferred from one financial centre to another seeking the best opportunity for short-term gain.

hotplate ('hɒt,pleɪt) n. 1. an electrically heated plate on a cooker or one set into a working surface. 2. a portable device on which food can be kept warm.

hotpot ('hɒt,pɒt) n. Brit. a casserole covered with a layer of potatoes.

hot potato n. Inf. a delicate or awkward matter.

hot-press n. 1. a machine for applying a combination of heat and pressure to give a smooth surface to paper, to express oil from it, etc. ~vb. 2. (tr.) to subject (paper, cloth, etc.) to such a process.

hot rod n. a car with an engine that has been radically modified to produce increased power.

hot seat n. 1. Inf. a difficult or dangerous position. 2. U.S. a slang term for **electric chair**.

hot spot n. 1. an area of potential violence. 2. a lively nightclub. 3. any local area of high temperature in a part of an engine, etc. 4. a small area of exceptionally high radioactivity or of some chemical or mineral considered harmful.

hot spring n. a natural spring of mineral water at 21°C (70°F) or above, found in areas of volcanic activity. Also called: **thermal spring**.

hotspur ('hɒt,spɜː) n. an impetuous or fiery person. [C15: from Hotspur, nickname of Sir Henry Percy (1364-1403), E rebel, killed leading an army against Henry IV]

Hotspur ('hɒt,spɜː) n. **Harry**. nickname of (Sir Henry) **Percy**.

hot stuff n. Inf. 1. a person, object, etc., considered important, attractive, etc. 2. a pornographic or erotic book, play, film, etc.

Hottentot ('hɒtᵊn,tɒt) n. 1. (pl. -tot or -tots) a member of a race of people of southern Africa, who formerly occupied the region near the Cape of Good Hope and are now almost extinct. 2. any of the languages of this people. [C17: from Afrik., from ?]

hot up vb. hotting, hotted. (adv.) Inf. 1. to make or become more exciting, active, or intense. 2. (tr.) another term for **soup up**.

hot-water bottle n. a receptacle now usually made of rubber, designed to be filled with hot water and used for warming a bed.

hot-wire vb. (tr.) Sl. to start the engine of (a motor vehicle) by short-circuiting the ignition.

Houdini (huː'diːnɪ) n. **Harry**, real name Ehrich Weiss. 1874–1926, U.S. magician and escapologist.

Houdon (French udɔ̃) n. **Jean Antoine** (ʒɑ̃ ɑ̃twan). 1741–1828, French neoclassical portrait sculptor.

hough (hɒk) Brit. ~n. 1. a variant of **hock**[1]. ~vb. (tr.) 2. to hamstring (cattle, horses, etc.). [C14: from OE hōh heel]

Houghton-le-Spring ('haʊtᵊnlə'sprɪŋ) n. a town in N England, in E Tyne and Wear: coal-mining. Pop.: 31 036 (1981).

hound (haʊnd) n. 1. a. any of several breeds of dog used for hunting. b. (in combination): a deerhound. 2. a dog, esp. one regarded as annoying. 3. a despicable person. 4. (in hare and hounds) a runner who pursues a hare. 5. Sl., chiefly U.S. & Canad. an enthusiast: an autograph hound. 6. ride to hounds or follow the hounds. to take part in a fox hunt. 7. the hounds. a pack of foxhounds, etc. ~vb. (tr.) 8. to pursue relentlessly. 9. to urge on. [OE hund] —'hounder n.

hound's-tongue n. a plant which has small reddish-purple flowers and spiny fruits. Also called: **dog's-tongue**. [OE hundestunge, translation of L cynoglossos, from Gk, from kuōn dog + glossa tongue; referring to the shape of its leaves]

hound's-tooth check n. a pattern of broken or jagged checks, esp. on cloth. Also called: **dog's-tooth check, dogtooth check**.

Hounslow ('haʊnzləʊ) n. a borough of Greater London, on the River Thames: site of London's first civil airport (1919). Pop.: 199 782 (1981).

Houphouet-Boigny (French ufwɛbwaɲi) n. **Félix** (feliks). born 1905, Côte d'Ivoire statesman; president of the Côte d'Ivoire from 1960.

hour ('aʊə) n. 1. a period of time equal to 3600 seconds; 1/24th of a calendar day. Related adj.: **horary**. 2. any of the points on the face of a timepiece that indicate intervals of 60 minutes. 3. the time. 4. the time allowed for or used for something: the lunch hour. 5. a special moment: our finest hour. 6. the distance covered in an hour: we live an hour from the city. 7. Astron. an angular measurement of right ascension equal to 15° or a 24th part of the celestial equator. 8. **one's last hour**. the time of one's death. 9. **the hour**. an exact number of complete hours: *the bus leaves on the hour.* ~See also **hours.** [C13: from OF *hore*, from L *hōra*, from Gk: season]

hour circle *n.* a great circle on the celestial sphere passing through the celestial poles and a specified point, such as a star.

hourglass ('aʊə,glɑːs) *n.* **1.** a device consisting of two transparent chambers linked by a narrow channel, containing a quantity of sand that takes a specified time to trickle from one chamber to the other. **2.** *(modifier)* well-proportioned with a small waist: *an hourglass figure.*

hour hand *n.* the pointer on a timepiece that indicates the hour.

houri ('hʊərɪ) *n., pl.* **-ris. 1.** (in Muslim belief) any of the nymphs of Paradise. **2.** any alluring woman. [C18: from F, from Persian, from Ar. *hūr*, pl. of *haurā'* woman with dark eyes]

hourly ('aʊəlɪ) *adj.* **1.** of, occurring, or done every hour. **2.** done in or measured by the hour: *an hourly rate.* **3.** continual or frequent. ~*adv.* **4.** every hour. **5.** at any moment.

hours ('aʊəz) *pl. n.* **1.** a period regularly appointed for work, etc. **2.** one's times of rising and going to bed: *he keeps late hours.* **3.** till all hours. until very late. **4.** an indefinite time. **5.** *R.C. Church.* Also called: **canonical hours. a.** the seven times of the day laid down for the recitation of the prayers of the divine office. **b.** the prayers recited at these times.

Hours (aʊəz) *pl. n.* another word for the **Horae.**

house *n.* (haʊs), *pl.* **houses** ('haʊzɪz). **1. a.** a building used as a home; dwelling. **b.** *(as modifier)*: *house dog.* **2.** the people present in a house. **3. a.** a building for some specific purpose. **b.** *(in combination)*: *a schoolhouse.* **4.** *(often cap.)* a family or dynasty: *the House of York.* **5. a.** a commercial company: *a publishing house.* **b.** *(as modifier)*: *a house journal.* **6.** a legislative body. **7.** a quorum in such a body (esp. in **make a house**). **8.** a dwelling for a religious community. **9.** *Astrol.* any of the 12 divisions of the zodiac. **10.** any of several divisions of a large school. **11.** a hotel, restaurant, club, etc., or the management of such an establishment. **12.** the audience in a theatre or cinema. **13.** an informal word for **brothel. 14.** a hall in which a legislative body meets. **15.** See **full house. 16.** *Naut.* any structure or shelter on the weather deck of a vessel. **17. bring the house down.** *Theatre.* to win great applause. **18. like a house on fire.** *Inf.* very well. **19. on the house.** (usually of drinks) paid for by the management of the hotel, bar, etc. **20. put one's house in order.** to settle or organize one's affairs. **21. safe as houses.** *Brit.* very secure. ~*vb.* (haʊz). **22.** *(tr.)* to provide with or serve as accommodation. **23.** to give or receive lodging. **24.** *(tr.)* to contain or cover; protect. **25.** *(tr.)* to fit (a piece of wood) into a mortise, joint, etc. [OE *hūs*] — **'houseless** *adj.*

house agent *n. Brit.* another name for **estate agent.**

house arrest *n.* confinement to one's own home rather than in prison.

houseboat ('haʊs,bəʊt) *n.* a stationary boat or barge used as a home.

housebound ('haʊs,baʊnd) *adj.* unable to leave one's house because of illness, injury, etc.

housebreaking ('haʊs,breɪkɪŋ) *n. Criminal law.* the act of entering a building as a trespasser for an unlawful purpose. Assimilated with burglary (1968). — **'house-ˌbreaker** *n.*

housecoat ('haʊs,kəʊt) *n.* a woman's loose robelike informal garment.

house-craft *n.* skill in domestic management.

housefather ('haʊs,fɑːðə) *n.* a man in charge of the welfare of a particular group of children in an institution. — **'house,mother** *fem. n.*

housefly ('haʊs,flaɪ) *n., pl.* **-flies.** a common dipterous fly that frequents human habitations, spreads disease, and lays its eggs in carrion, decaying vegetables, etc.

household ('haʊs,həʊld) *n.* **1.** the people living together in one house. **2.** *(modifier)* relating to the running of a household: *household management.*

householder ('haʊs,həʊldə) *n.* a person who owns or rents a house. — **'house,holder,ship** *n.*

household name *or* **word** *n.* a person or thing that is very well known.

housekeeper ('haʊs,kiːpə) *n.* a person, esp. a woman, employed to run a household.

housekeeping ('haʊs,kiːpɪŋ) *n.* **1.** the running of a household. **2.** money allotted for this. **3.** general maintenance as of records, data, etc., in an organization.

houseleek ('haʊs,liːk) *n.* an Old World plant which has a rosette of succulent leaves and pinkish flowers: grows on walls.

house lights *pl. n.* the lights in the auditorium of a theatre, cinema, etc.

housemaid ('haʊs,meɪd) *n.* a girl or woman employed to do housework, esp. one who is resident in the household.

housemaid's knee *n.* inflammation and swelling of the bursa in front of the kneecap, caused esp. by constant kneeling on a hard surface. Technical name: **prepatellar bursitis.**

houseman ('haʊsmən) *n., pl.* **-men.** *Med.* a junior doctor who is a member of the medical staff of a hospital. U.S. and Canad. equivalent: **intern.**

house martin *n.* a Eurasian swallow with a slightly forked tail.

house mouse *n.* any of various greyish mice, a common household pest in most parts of the world.

House music *or* **House** *n.* a type of disco music of the late 1980s, based on funk, with fragments of other recordings edited in electronically.

House of Assembly *n.* a legislative assembly or the lower chamber of such an assembly.

house of cards *n.* an unstable situation, etc.

House of Commons *n.* (in Britain, Canada, etc.) the lower chamber of Parliament.

house of correction *n.* (formerly) a place of confinement for persons convicted of minor offences.

house of ill repute *or* **ill fame** *n.* a euphemistic name for **brothel.**

House of Keys *n.* the lower chamber of the legislature of the Isle of Man.

House of Lords *n.* (in Britain) the upper chamber of Parliament, composed of the peers of the realm.

House of Representatives *n.* **1.** (in the U.S.) the lower chamber of Congress, or of many state legislatures. **2.** (in Australia) the lower chamber of Parliament. **3.** the sole chamber of New Zealand's Parliament.

house party *n.* **1.** a party, usually in a country house, at which guests are invited to stay for several days. **2.** the guests who are invited.

house plant *n.* a plant that can be grown indoors.

house-proud *adj.* proud of the appearance, cleanliness, etc., of one's house, sometimes excessively so.

houseroom ('haʊs,rʊm, -,ruːm) *n.* **1.** room for storage or lodging. **2. give (something) houseroom.** (*used with a negative*) to have or keep (something) in one's house.

Houses of Parliament *n.* (in Britain) **1.** the building in which the House of Commons and the House of Lords assemble. **2.** these two chambers considered together.

house sparrow *n.* a small Eurasian bird, now established in North America and Australia. It has a brown plumage with grey underparts. Also called (U.S.): **English sparrow.**

housetop ('haʊs,tɒp) *n.* **1.** the roof of a house. **2. proclaim from the housetops.** to announce (something) publicly.

house-train *vb.* (*tr.*) *Brit.* to train (pets) to urinate and defecate outside the house.

house-warming *n.* a party given after moving into a new home.

housewife *n., pl.* **-wives. 1.** ('haʊs,waɪf). a woman who keeps house. **2.** ('hʌzɪf). Also called: **hussy, huswife.** Chiefly *Brit.* a small sewing kit. — **housewifery** ('haʊs,wɪfərɪ) *n.* — **'housewifely** *adj.*

housework ('haʊs,wɜːk) *n.* the work of running a home, such as cleaning, cooking, etc.

housey-housey ('haʊzɪ'haʊzɪ) *n.* another name for **bingo** or **lotto.** [C20: from the cry of "house!" shouted by the winner, prob. from FULL HOUSE]

housing[1] ('haʊzɪŋ) *n.* **1. a.** houses collectively. **b.** *(as modifier)*: *a housing problem.* **2.** the act of providing with accommodation. **3.** a hole or slot made in one wooden member to receive another. **4.** a part designed to contain or support a component or mechanism: *a wheel housing.*

housing[2] ('haʊzɪŋ) *n.* (*often pl.*) *Arch.* another word for **trappings** (sense 2). [C14: from OF *houce* covering, of Gmc origin]

housing estate *n.* a planned area of housing, often with its own shops and other amenities.

housing scheme *n.* a local-authority housing estate. Often shortened to **scheme.**

Housman ('hausmən) *n.* **A(lfred) E(dward).** 1859–1936, English poet and classical scholar, author of *A Shropshire Lad* (1896) and *Last Poems* (1922).

Houston ('hju:stən) *n.* an inland port in SE Texas, linked by the **Houston Ship Canal** to the Gulf of Mexico and the Gulf Intracoastal Waterway: capital of the Republic of Texas (1837–39; 1842–45); site of the Manned Spacecraft Center (1964). Pop.: 1 728 910 (1986).

hove (həuv) *vb. Chiefly naut.* a past tense and past participle of **heave.**

Hove (həuv) *n.* a town and resort in S England, in East Sussex adjoining Brighton. Pop.: 66 612 (1981).

hovel ('hɒvəl) *n.* **1.** a ramshackle dwelling place. **2.** an open shed for livestock, carts, etc. **3.** the conical building enclosing a kiln. [C15: from ?]

hover ('hɒvə) *vb.* (*intr.*) **1.** to remain suspended in one place. **2.** (of certain birds, esp. hawks) to remain in one place in the air by rapidly beating the wings. **3.** to linger uncertainly. **4.** to be in a state of indecision. ~*n.* **5.** the act of hovering. [C14 *hoveren,* var. of *hoven,* from ?] —'hoverer *n.*

hovercraft ('hɒvə,krɑ:ft) *n.* a vehicle that is able to travel across both land and water on a cushion of air.

hover fly *n.* a dipterous fly with a hovering flight.

hoverport ('hɒvə,pɔ:t) *n.* a port for hovercraft.

hovertrain ('hɒvə,treɪn) *n.* a train that moves over a concrete track and is supported by a cushion of air supplied by powerful fans.

how (hau) *adv.* **1.** in what way? by what means?: *how did it happen?* Also used in indirect questions: *tell me how he did it.* **2.** to what extent?: *how tall is he?* **3.** how good? how well? what . . . like?: *how did she sing? how was the holiday?* **4. and how!** (intensifier) very much so! **5. how about?** used to suggest something: *how about a cup of tea?* **6. how are you?** what is your state of health? **7. how come?** *Inf.* what is the reason (that)?: *how come you told him?* **8. how's that? a.** what is your opinion? **b.** *Cricket.* Also written: **howzat** (hau'zæt). (an appeal to the umpire) is the batsman out? **9. how now?** *or* **how so?** *Arch.* what is the meaning of this? **10.** in whatever way: *do it how you wish.* ~*n.* **11.** the way a thing is done: *the how of it.* [OE *hu*]

Howard ('hauəd) *n.* **1. Catherine.** ?1521–42, fifth wife of Henry VIII of England; beheaded. **2. Charles,** Lord Howard of Effingham and 1st Earl of Nottingham. 1536–1624, Lord High Admiral of England (1585–1618). He commanded the fleet that defeated the Spanish Armada (1588). **3. Sir Ebenezer.** 1850–1928, English town planner, who introduced garden cities. **4. Henry.** See (Earl of) **Surrey. 5. John.** 1726–90, English prison reformer. **6 Leslie.** real name *Leslie Howard Stainer.* 1890–1943, British actor of Hungarian descent. His many films included *The Scarlet Pimpernel* (1938), *Pygmalion* (1938), and *Gone With the Wind* (1939). **7. Trevor.** 1916–88, British actor. His many films include *Brief Encounter* (1946), *The Third Man* (1949), *Ryan's Daughter* (1970), and *White Mischief* (1987).

howbeit (hau'bi:ɪt) *Arch.* ~*sentence connector.* **1.** however. ~*conj.* **2.** (*subordinating*) though; although.

howdah ('haudə) *n.* a seat for riding on an elephant's back, esp. one with a canopy. [C18: from Hindi *haudah,* from Ar. *haudaj* load carried by elephant or camel]

how do you do *sentence substitute.* **1.** a formal greeting said by people who are being introduced to each other. ~*n.* **how-do-you-do. 2.** *Inf.* a difficult situation.

howdy ('haudɪ) *sentence substitute. Chiefly U.S.* an informal word for **hello.** [C16: from *how d'ye do*]

Howe (hau) *n.* **1. Elias.** 1819–67, U.S. inventor of the sewing machine (1846). **2. Sir (Richard Edward) Geoffrey.** born 1926, British Conservative politician; Chancellor of the Exchequer (1979–83); foreign secretary from 1983. **3. Richard,** 4th Viscount Howe. 1726–99, British admiral: served (1776–78) in the War of American Independence and commanded the Channel fleet against France, winning the Battle of the Glorious First of June (1794). **4.** his brother, **William,** 5th Viscount Howe. 1729–1814, British general; commander in chief (1776–78) of British forces in the War of American Independence.

however (hau'ɛvə) *sentence connector.* **1.** still; nevertheless. **2.** on the other hand; yet. ~*adv.* **3.** by whatever means. **4.** (*used with adjectives of quantity or degree*) no matter how: *however long it takes, finish it.* **5.** an emphatic form of **how** (sense 1).

howitzer ('hauɪtsə) *n.* a cannon having a short barrel with a low muzzle velocity and a steep angle of fire. [C16: from Du. *houwitser,* from G, from Czech *houfnice* stone-sling]

howl (haul) *n.* **1.** a long plaintive cry characteristic of a wolf or hound. **2.** a similar cry of pain or sorrow. **3.** a prolonged outburst of laughter. **4.** *Electronics.* an unwanted high-pitched sound produced by a sound-producing system as a result of feedback. ~*vb.* **5.** to express in a howl or utter such cries. **6.** (*intr.*) (of the wind, etc.) to make a wailing noise. **7.** (*intr.*) *Inf.* to shout or laugh. [C14 *houlen*]

Howland Island ('haulənd) *n.* a small island in the central Pacific, near the equator northwest of Phoenix Island: U.S. airfield. Area: 2.6 sq. km (1 sq. mile).

howl down *vb.* (*tr., adv.*) to prevent (a speaker) from being heard by shouting disapprovingly.

howler ('haulə) *n.* **1.** Also called: **howler monkey.** a large New World monkey inhabiting tropical forests in South America and having a loud howling cry. **2.** *Inf.* a glaring mistake. **3.** a person or thing that howls.

howling ('haulɪŋ) *adj.* (*prenominal*) *Inf.* (intensifier) *a howling success; a howling error.*

Howlin' Wolf ('haulɪn) *n.* real name *Chester Burnett.* 1910–76, U.S. blues singer and songwriter.

Howrah ('haurə) *n.* an industrial city in E India, in West Bengal on the Hooghly River opposite Calcutta. Pop.: 742 298 (1981).

howsoever (,hausəu'ɛvə) *sentence connector, adv.* a less common word for **however.**

Hoxha (*Albanian* 'hodʒa) *n.* **Enver** ('emver). 1908–85, Albanian statesman: founded the Albanian Communist Party in 1941 and was its first secretary (1954–85).

hoy[1] (hɔɪ) *n. Naut.* **1.** a freight barge. **2.** a coastal fishing and trading vessel used during the 17th and 18th centuries. [C15: from MDu. *hoei*]

hoy[2] (hɔɪ) *interj.* a cry used to attract attention or drive animals. [C14: var. of HEY]

hoya ('hɔɪə) *n.* any plant of the genus *Hoya,* of E Asia and Australia, esp. the waxplant. [C19: after Thomas *Hoy* (died 1821), E gardener]

hoyden *or* **hoiden** ('hɔɪd³n) *n.* a wild boisterous girl; tomboy. [C16: ?from MDu. *heidijn* heathen] —'hoydenish *or* 'hoidenish *adj.*

Hoylake ('hɔɪ,leɪk) *n.* a town and resort in NW England, in Merseyside on the Irish Sea. Pop.: 32 914 (1981).

Hoyle[1] (hɔɪl) *n.* an authoritative book of rules for card games. [after Sir Edmund *Hoyle,* 18th-cent. E authority on games, its compiler]

Hoyle[2] (hɔɪl) *n.* **Sir Fred.** born 1915, English astronomer and writer: his books include *The Nature of the Universe* (1950) and *Frontiers of Astronomy* (1955), and science-fiction writings.

HP *abbrev. for:* **1.** *Brit.* hire-purchase. **2.** horsepower. **3.** high pressure. **4.** (in Britain) Houses of Parliament. ~Also (for senses 1–3): **h.p.**

HQ *or* **h.q.** *abbrev. for* headquarters.

hr *abbrev. for* hour.

Hradec Králové (*Czech* 'hradɛts 'kra:lɔvɛ:) *n.* a town in NW Czechoslovakia, on the Elbe River. Pop.: 100 000 (1986). German name: **Königgrätz.**

HRH *abbrev. for* His (or Her) Royal Highness.

HRT *abbrev. for* hormone replacement therapy.

Hrvatska ('hrvɑ:tska:) *n.* the Serbo-Croatian name for **Croatia.**

HS (in Britain) *abbrev. for* Home Secretary.

HSH *abbrev. for* His (or Her) Serene Highness.

Hsi (ʃi) *n.* a variant spelling of **Si.**

Hsia-men ('ʃja:'mɛn) *n.* a transliteration of the modern Chinese name for **Amoy.**

Hsian (ʃja:n) *n.* a variant transliteration of the Chinese name for **Xi An.**

Hsiang (ʃja:ŋ) *n.* a variant transliteration of the Chinese name for **Xiang.**

Hsin-hai-lien ('ʃɪn 'haɪ 'ljɛn) *n.* a variant spelling of **Sinhailien.**

Hsining ('ʃi:'nɪŋ) *n.* a variant transliteration of the Chinese name for **Xining.**

Hsinking ('ʃɪn'kɪŋ) *n.* the former name (1932–45) of **Changchun**.

Hsüan T'ung ('ʃwɑːn 'tʊŋ) *n. See* **Xuan-tong**.

Hsü-chou ('ʃuː'tʃaʊ) *n.* a variant transliteration of the Chinese name for **Xuzhou**.

ht *abbrev. for* height.

HT *Physics. abbrev. for* high tension.

HTLV *abbrev. for* human T-cell lymphotrophic virus: any one of a small family of viruses that cause certain rare diseases in the T-cells of human beings.

Hua Guo Feng ('hwɑː gwəʊ 'fɛʃ) *or* **Hua Kuo-feng** ('hwɑː kwəʊ 'fɛŋ) *n.* born c. 1920, Chinese Communist statesman; prime minister of China 1976–80.

Huainan ('hwaɪ'næn) *n.* a city in E China, in Anhui province north of Hefei. Pop.: 1 070 000 (1986 est.).

Huambo (*Portuguese* 'wambu) *n.* a town in central Angola: designated by the Portuguese as the future capital of the country. Pop.: 80 000 (1980 est.). Former name (1928–73): **Nova Lisboa**.

Huang Hai ('hwæŋ 'haɪ) *n.* the Pinyin transliteration of the Chinese name for the **Yellow Sea**.

Huang Ho ('hwæŋ 'həʊ) *n.* the Pinyin transliteration of the Chinese name for the **Yellow River**.

Huang Hua (hwæŋ hwɑː) *n.* born 1913, Chinese Communist statesman; minister for foreign affairs from 1976.

Huáscar (*Spanish* uaskar) *n.* died 1533, Inca ruler (1525–33): murdered by his half brother Atahualpa.

Huascarán (*Spanish* uaska'ran) *or* **Huascán** (*Spanish* uas'kan) *n.* an extinct volcano in W Peru, in the Peruvian Andes: the highest peak in Peru; avalanche in 1962 killed over 3000 people. Height: 6768 m (22 205 ft.).

hub (hʌb) *n.* **1.** the central portion of a wheel, propeller, fan, etc., through which the axle passes. **2.** the focal point. [C17: prob. var. of HOB¹]

Hubble ('hʌbᵊl) *n.* **Edwin Powell.** 1889–1953, U.S. astronomer, noted for his investigations of nebulae and the recession of the galaxies.

hubble-bubble ('hʌbᵊl'bʌbᵊl) *n.* **1.** another name for **hookah. 2.** turmoil. **3.** a gargling sound. [C17: rhyming jingle based on BUBBLE]

hubbub ('hʌbʌb) *n.* **1.** a confused noise of many voices. **2.** tumult; uproar. [C16: prob. from Irish *hooboobbes*]

hubby ('hʌbɪ) *n., pl.* **-bies.** an informal word for **husband.** [C17: by shortening and altering]

hubcap ('hʌb,kæp) *n.* a metal cap fitting over the hub of a wheel.

Hubei ('huː'beɪ), **Hupeh,** *or* **Hupei** *n.* a province of central China: largely low-lying with many lakes. Capital: Wuhan. Pop.: 48 760 000 (1985). Area: 187 500 sq. km (72 394 sq. miles).

Hubli ('huːblɪ) *n.* a city in W India, in NW Mysore: incorporated with Dharwar in 1961; educational and trading centre. Pop. (with Dharwar): 526 493 (1981).

hubris ('hjuːbrɪs) *n.* **1.** pride or arrogance. **2.** (in Greek tragedy) an excess of ambition, pride, etc., ultimately causing the transgressor's ruin. [C19: from Gk] — **hu'bristic** *adj.*

huckaback ('hʌkə,bæk) *n.* a coarse absorbent linen or cotton fabric used for towels, etc. Also: **huck** (hʌk). [C17: from ?]

huckleberry ('hʌkᵊl,bɛrɪ) *n., pl.* **-ries. 1.** an American shrub having edible dark blue berries. **2.** the fruit of this shrub. **3.** a Brit. name for **whortleberry** (sense 1, 2). [C17: prob. var. of *hurtleberry,* from ?]

huckster ('hʌkstə) *n.* **1.** a person who uses aggressive or questionable methods of selling. **2.** *Now rare.* a person who sells small articles or fruit in the street. **3.** *U.S.* a person who writes for radio or television advertisements. ~*vb.* **4.** (*tr.*) to peddle. **5.** (*tr.*) to sell or advertise aggressively or questionably. **6.** to haggle (over). [C12: ?from MDu. *hoekster,* from *hoeken* to carry on the back]

Huddersfield ('hʌdəz,fiːld) *n.* a town in N England, in West Yorkshire on the River Colne: textile industry. Pop.: 123 888 (1981).

huddle ('hʌdᵊl) *n.* **1.** a heaped or crowded mass of people or things. **2.** *Inf.* a private or impromptu conference (esp. in **go into a huddle**). ~*vb.* **3.** to crowd or nestle closely together. **4.** (often foll. by *up*) to hunch (oneself), as through cold. **5.** (*intr.*) *Inf.* to confer privately. **6.** (*tr.*) *Chiefly Brit.* to do (something) in a careless way. **7.** (*tr.*) *Rare.* to put on (clothes) hurriedly. [C16: from ?; cf. ME *hoderen* to wrap up] — **'huddler** *n.*

Huddleston ('hʌdᵊlstən) *n.* **Trevor.** born 1913, English prelate; suffragan bishop of Stepney (1968–78) and bishop of Mauritius (1978–83); president of the Anti-Apartheid Movement from 1981.

Hudson ('hʌdsən) *n.* **1. Henry.** died 1611, English navigator: he explored the Hudson River (1609) and Hudson Bay (1610), where his crew mutinied and cast him adrift to die. **2. W(illiam) H(enry).** 1841–1922, British naturalist and novelist, born in Argentina, noted esp. for his romance *Green Mansions* (1904) and the autobiographical *Far Away and Long Ago* (1918).

Hudson Bay *n.* an inland sea in NE Canada: linked with the Atlantic by **Hudson Strait**; the S extension forms James Bay; discovered in 1610 by Henry Hudson. Area (excluding James Bay): 647 500 sq. km (250 000 sq. miles).

Hudson River *n.* a river in E New York State, flowing generally south into Upper New York Bay: linked to the Great Lakes, the St Lawrence Seaway, and Lake Champlain by the New York State Barge Canal and the canalized Mohawk River. Length: 492 km (306 miles).

hue (hjuː) *n.* **1.** the attribute of colour that enables an observer to classify it as red, blue, etc., and excludes white, black, and grey. **2.** a shade of a colour. **3.** aspect: *a different hue on matters.* [OE *hīw* beauty] — **hued** *adj.*

Hué (*French* ɥe) *n.* a port in central Vietnam, on the delta of the **Hué River** near the South China Sea: former capital of the kingdom of Annam, of French Indochina (1883–1946), and of Central Vietnam (1946–54). Pop.: 165 865 (1979).

hue and cry *n.* **1.** (formerly) the pursuit of a suspected criminal with loud cries in order to raise the alarm. **2.** any loud public outcry. [C16: from Anglo-F *hu et cri,* from OF *hue* outcry, from *hu!* shout of warning + *cri* CRY]

Huelva (*Spanish* 'uɛlβa) *n.* a port in SW Spain, between the estuaries of the Odiel and Tinto Rivers: exports copper and other ores. Pop.: 127 822 (1981).

Huesca (*Spanish* 'ueska) *n.* a city in NE Spain: Roman town, site of Quintus Sertorius' school (76 B.C.); 15th-century cathedral and ancient palace of Aragonese kings. Pop.: 42 554 (1982 est.). Latin name: **Osca** ('ɒskə).

huff (hʌf) *n.* **1.** a passing mood of anger or pique (esp. in **in a huff**). ~*vb.* **2.** to make or become angry or resentful. **3.** (*intr.*) to blow or puff heavily. **4.** Also: **blow.** *Draughts.* to remove (an opponent's draught) from the board for failure to make a capture. **5.** (*tr.*) *Obs.* to bully. **6. huffing and puffing.** empty threats or objections: bluster. [C16: imit.; cf. PUFF] — **'huffish** *or* **'huffy** *adj.* — **'huffily** *or* **'huffishly** *adv.*

Hufuf (huˈfuːf) *n. See* **Al Hufuf.**

hug (hʌg) *vb.* **hugging, hugged.** (*mainly tr.*) **1.** (*also intr.*) to clasp tightly, usually with affection; embrace. **2.** to keep close to a shore, kerb, etc. **3.** to cling to (beliefs, etc.); cherish. **4.** to congratulate (oneself). ~*n.* **5.** a tight or fond embrace. [C16: prob. of Scand. origin] — **'huggable** *adj.*

huge (hjuːdʒ) *adj.* extremely large. [C13: from OF *ahuge,* from ?] — **'hugely** *adv.* — **'hugeness** *n.*

huggermugger ('hʌgə,mʌgə) *n.* **1.** confusion. **2.** *Rare.* secrecy. ~*adj., adv. Arch.* **3.** with secrecy. **4.** in confusion. ~*vb. Obs.* **5.** (*tr.*) to keep secret. **6.** (*intr.*) to act secretly. [C16: from ?]

Hugh Capet ('hjuː 'kæpɪt, 'keɪpɪt) *n. See* **(Hugh) Capet.**

Hughes (hjuːz) *n.* **1. Howard.** 1905–76, U.S. industrialist, aviator, and film producer. He became a total recluse during the last years of his life. **2. Richard (Arthur Warren).** 1900–76, English novelist. He wrote *A High Wind in Jamaica* (1929), *In Hazard* (1938), and *The Fox in the Attic* (1961). **3. Ted.** born 1930, English poet: his works include *The Hawk in the Rain* (1957) and *Crow* (1970). Appointed poet laureate 1984. **4. Thomas.** 1822–96, English novelist; author of *Tom Brown's Schooldays* (1857). **5. William Morris.** 1864–1952, Australian statesman, born in Pimlico to a Welsh-speaking father: prime minister of Australia (1915–23).

Hugo ('hjuːgəʊ; *French* ygo) *n.* **Victor (Marie)** (viktɔr). 1802–85, French poet, novelist, and dramatist; leader of the romantic movement in France. His works include the volumes of verse *Les Feuilles d'automne* (1831) and *Les Contemplations* (1856), the novels *Notre-Dame de Paris* (1831) and *Les Misérables* (1862), and the plays *Hernani* (1830) and *Ruy Blas* (1838).

Huguenot ('hjuːgə,nəʊ, -,nɒt) *n.* **1.** a French Calvinist, esp. of the 16th or 17th centuries. ~*adj.* **2.** designating the French Protestant Church. [C16: from F, from Genevan dialect *eyguenot* one who opposed annexation by Savoy, ult. from Swiss G *Eidgenoss* confederate]

huh (*spelling pron.* hʌ) *interj.* an exclamation of derision, bewilderment, inquiry, etc.

Huhehot (ˌhuːhɪˈhɒt ˌhuːɪ-) *or* **Hu-ho-hao-t'e** (ˌhuːhəʊhəʊˈteɪ) *n.* a variant transliteration of the Chinese name for **Hohhot**.

huhu (ˈhuːhuː) *n.* a New Zealand beetle with a hairy body. [from Maori]

hui (ˈhuːɪ) *n. N.Z.* **1.** a Maori social gathering. **2.** *Inf.* any party. [from Maori]

huia (ˈhuːjə) *n.* an extinct New Zealand bird, prized by early Maoris for its distinctive tail feathers. [from Maori]

hula (ˈhuːlə) *or* **hula-hula** *n.* a Hawaiian dance performed by a woman. [from Hawaiian]

Hula-Hoop *n. Trademark.* a light hoop that is whirled around the body by movements of the waist and hips.

hulk (hʌlk) *n.* **1.** the body of an abandoned vessel. **2.** *Disparaging.* a large or unwieldy vessel. **3.** *Disparaging.* a large ungainly person or thing. **4.** (*often pl.*) the hull of a ship, used as a storehouse, etc., or (esp. in 19th-century Britain) as a prison. [OE *hulc*, from Med. L *hulca*, from Gk *holkas* barge, from *helkein* to tow]

hulking (ˈhʌlkɪŋ) *adj.* big and ungainly.

hull (hʌl) *n.* **1.** the main body of a vessel, tank, etc. **2.** the outer covering of a fruit or seed. **3.** the calyx at the base of a strawberry, raspberry, or similar fruit. **4.** the outer casing of a missile, rocket, etc. ~*vb.* **5.** to remove the hulls from (fruit or seeds). **6.** (*tr.*) to pierce the hull of (a vessel, tank, etc.). [OE *hulu*]

Hull[1] (hʌl) *n.* **1.** a port in NE England: the largest fishing port in Britain; university (1929). Pop.: 268 302 (1981). Official name: **Kingston upon Hull**. **2.** a city in SE Canada, in SW Quebec on the River Ottawa: a centre of the timber trade and associated industries. Pop.: 58 722 (1986).

Hull[2] (hʌl) *n.* **Cordell.** 1871–1955, U.S. statesman; secretary of state (1933–44). He helped to found the U.N.: Nobel peace prize 1945.

hullabaloo *or* **hullaballoo** (ˌhʌləbəˈluː) *n., pl.* **-loos.** loud confused noise; commotion. [C18: ?from HALLO + Scot. *baloo* lullaby]

hullo (hʌˈləʊ) *sentence substitute, n.* a variant spelling of **hello.**

Hulme (hjuːm) *n.* **T(homas) E(rnest).** 1883–1917, English literary critic and poet; a proponent of imagism.

hum (hʌm) *vb.* **humming, hummed.** (*intr.*) **1.** to make a low continuous vibrating sound. **2.** (of a person) to sing with the lips closed. **3.** to utter an indistinct sound, as in hesitation; hem. **4.** *Sl.* to be in a state of feverish activity. **5.** *Sl.* to smell unpleasant. **6. hum and haw.** See **hem**[2](sense 3). ~*n.* **7.** a low continuous murmuring sound. **8.** *Electronics.* an undesired low-frequency noise in the output of an amplifier or receiver. ~*interj., n.* **9.** an indistinct sound of hesitation, embarrassment, etc.; hem. [C14: imit.]

human (ˈhjuːmən) *adj.* **1.** of or relating to mankind: *human nature.* **2.** consisting of people: *a human chain.* **3.** having the attributes of man as opposed to animals, divine beings, or machines: *human failings.* **4. a.** kind or considerate. **b.** natural. ~*n.* **5.** a human being; person. [C14: from L *hūmānus*; rel. to L *homō* man] — **'humanness** *n.*

human being *n.* a member of any of the races of *Homo sapiens*; person; man, woman, or child.

humane (hjuːˈmeɪn) *adj.* **1.** characterized by kindness, sympathy, etc. **2.** inflicting as little pain as possible: *a humane killing.* **3.** civilizing or liberal: *humane studies.* [C16: var. of HUMAN] — **hu'manely** *adv.* — **hu'maneness** *n.*

human interest *n.* (in a newspaper story, etc.) reference to individuals and their emotions, sometimes from exploitative motives.

humanism (ˈhjuːməˌnɪzəm) *n.* **1.** the rejection of religion in favour of a belief in the advancement of humanity by its own efforts. **2.** (*often cap.*) a cultural movement of the Renaissance, based on classical studies. **3.** interest in the welfare of people. — **'humanist** *n.* — **ˌhuman'istic** *adj.*

humanitarian (hjuːˌmænɪˈtɛərɪən) *adj.* **1.** having the interests of mankind at heart. ~*n.* **2.** a philanthropist. — **huˌmani'tarianism** *n.*

humanity (hjuːˈmænɪtɪ) *n., pl.* **-ties. 1.** the human race. **2.** the quality of being human. **3.** kindness or mercy. **4.**

(*pl.;* usually preceded by *the*) the study of literature, philosophy, and the arts, esp. study of Ancient Greece and Rome.

humanize *or* **-nise** (ˈhjuːməˌnaɪz) *vb.* **1.** to make or become human. **2.** to make or become humane. — **ˌhumani'zation** *or* **-ni'sation** *n.*

humankind (ˌhjuːmənˈkaɪnd) *n.* the human race; humanity.

humanly (ˈhjuːmənlɪ) *adv.* **1.** by human powers or means. **2.** in a human or humane manner.

human nature *n.* the qualities common to humanity, esp. with reference to human weakness.

humanoid (ˈhjuːməˌnɔɪd) *adj.* **1.** like a human being in appearance. ~*n.* **2.** a being with human rather than anthropoid characteristics. **3.** (in science fiction) a robot or creature resembling a human being.

human rights *pl. n.* the rights of individuals to liberty, justice, etc.

Humber (ˈhʌmbə) *n.* an estuary in NE England, into which flow the Rivers Ouse and Trent: flows east into the North Sea; navigable for large ocean-going ships as far as Hull; crossed by the **Humber Bridge** (1981), the world's longest single-span suspension bridge with a main span of 1410 m (4626 ft.). Length: 64 km (40 miles).

Humberside (ˈhʌmbəˌsaɪd) *n.* a county of N England around the Humber estuary, formed in 1974 from parts of the East and West Ridings of Yorkshire and N Lincolnshire. Administrative centre: Beverley. Pop.: 848 500 (1986 est.). Area: 3512 sq. km (1356 sq. miles).

humble (ˈhʌmbᵊl) *adj.* **1.** conscious of one's failings. **2.** unpretentious; lowly: *a humble cottage; my humble opinion.* **3.** deferential or servile. ~*vb.* (*tr.*) **4.** to cause to become humble; humiliate. **5.** to lower in status. [C13: from OF, from L *humilis* low, from *humus* the ground] — **'humbleness** *n.* — **'humbly** *adv.*

humblebee (ˈhʌmbᵊlˌbiː) *n.* another name for the **bumblebee.** [C15: rel. to MDu. *hommel* bumblebee, OHG *humbal*]

humble pie *n.* **1.** (formerly) a pie made from the heart, entrails, etc., of a deer. **2. eat humble pie.** to be forced to behave humbly; be humiliated. [C17: earlier *an umble pie*, by mistaken word division from *a numble pie*, from *numbles* offal of a deer, ult. from L *lumbulus* a little loin]

Humboldt (ˈhʌmbəʊlt; German ˈhʊmbɔlt) *n.* **1.** Baron (**Friedrich Heinrich**) **Alexander von** (alɛˈksandər fɔn). 1769–1859, German scientist, who made important scientific explorations in Central and South America (1799–1804). In *Kosmos* (1845–62), he provided a comprehensive description of the physical universe. **2.** his brother, Baron (**Karl**) **Wilhelm von** (ˈvɪlhɛlm fɔn). 1767–1835, German philologist and educational reformer.

humbug (ˈhʌmˌbʌg) *n.* **1.** a person or thing that deceives. **2.** nonsense. **3.** *Brit.* a hard boiled sweet, usually having a striped pattern. ~*vb.* **-bugging, -bugged. 4.** to cheat or deceive (someone). [C18: from ?] — **'humˌbugger** *n.*

humdinger (ˈhʌmˌdɪŋə) *n. Sl.* an excellent person or thing. [C20: from ?]

humdrum (ˈhʌmˌdrʌm) *adj.* **1.** ordinary; dull. ~*n.* **2.** a monotonous routine, task, or person. [C16: rhyming compound, prob. based on HUM]

Hume (hjuːm) *n.* **1.** (**George**) **Basil.** born 1923, English Roman Catholic Benedictine monk and cardinal; archbishop of Westminster from 1976. **2. David.** 1711–76, Scottish empiricist philosopher, economist, and historian, whose sceptic philosophy restricted human knowledge to that which can be perceived by the senses. His works include *A Treatise of Human Nature* (1740), *An Enquiry concerning the Principles of Morals* (1751), *Political Discourses* (1752), and *History of England* (1754–62). — **'Humism** *n.*

humectant (hjuːˈmɛktənt) *adj.* **1.** producing moisture. ~*n.* **2.** a substance added to another to keep it moist. [C17: from L *umectāre* to wet, from *ūmēre* to be moist]

humerus (ˈhjuːmərəs) *n., pl.* **-meri** (-məˌraɪ). **1.** the bone that extends from the shoulder to the elbow in man. **2.** the corresponding bone in other vertebrates. [C17: from L *umerus*; rel. to Gothic *ams* shoulder, Gk *ōmos*] — **'humeral** *adj.*

humid (ˈhjuːmɪd) *adj.* moist; damp. [C16: from L *ūmidus*, from *ūmēre* to be wet] — **'humidly** *adv.* — **'humidness** *n.*

humidex ('hju:mɪ,dɛks) n. Canad. an index of discomfort showing the combined effect of humidity and temperature.

humidify (hju:'mɪdɪ,faɪ) vb. **-fying, -fied.** (tr.) to make (air, etc.) humid or damp. —**hu,midifi'cation** n. —**hu'midi,fier** n.

humidity (hju:'mɪdɪtɪ) n. **1.** dampness. **2.** a measure of the amount of moisture in the air.

humidor ('hju:mɪ,dɔ:) n. a humid place or container for storing cigars, tobacco, etc.

humiliate (hju:'mɪlɪ,eɪt) vb. (tr.) to lower or hurt the dignity or pride of. [C16: from LL humiliāre, from L humilis HUMBLE] —**hu'mili,atingly** adv. —**hu,mili'ation** n. —**hu'mili,ator** n.

humility (hju:'mɪlɪtɪ) n., pl. **-ties.** the state or quality of being humble.

Hummel ('hʊməl) n. **Johann Nepomuk** (jo'han 'neːpomʊk). 1778–1837, German composer and pianist.

hummingbird ('hʌmɪŋ,bɜ:d) n. a very small American bird having a brilliant iridescent plumage, long slender bill, and wings specialized for very powerful vibrating flight.

hummock ('hʌmək) n. **1.** a hillock; knoll. **2.** a ridge or mound of ice in an ice field. **3.** Chiefly southern U.S. a wooded area lying above the level of an adjacent marsh. [C16: from ?; cf. HUMP] —**'hummocky** adj.

hummus or **houmous** ('hʊməs) n. a creamy dip originating in the Middle East, made from puréed chickpeas. [from Turkish humus]

humoral ('hju:mərəl) adj. Obs. of or relating to the four bodily fluids (humours).

humoresque (,hju:mə'rɛsk) n. a short lively piece of music. [C19: from G Humoreske, ult. from E HUMOUR]

humorist ('hju:mərɪst) n. a person who acts, speaks, or writes in a humorous way.

humorous ('hju:mərəs) adj. **1.** funny; comical; amusing. **2.** displaying or creating humour. —**'humorously** adv. —**'humorousness** n.

humour or U.S. **humor** ('hju:mə) n. **1.** the quality of being funny. **2.** Also called: **sense of humour.** the ability to appreciate or express that which is humorous. **4. a.** a state of mind; mood. **b.** (in combination): good humour. **5.** temperament or disposition. **6.** a caprice or whim. **7.** any of various fluids in the body: aqueous humour. **8.** Also called: **cardinal humour.** Arch. any of the four bodily fluids (blood, phlegm, choler or yellow bile, melancholy or black bile) formerly thought to determine emotional and physical disposition. **9. out of humour.** in a bad mood. ~vb. (tr.) **10.** to gratify; indulge: he humoured the boy's whims. **11.** to adapt oneself to: to humour someone's fantasies. [C14: from L: liquid; rel. to L ūmēre to be wet] —**'humourless** or U.S. **'humorless** adj.

hump (hʌmp) n. **1.** a rounded protuberance or projection. **2.** a rounded deformity of the back, consisting of a spinal curvature. **3.** a rounded protuberance on the back of a camel or related animal. **4. the hump.** Brit. inf. a fit of sulking. ~vb. **5.** to form or become a hump; hunch; arch. **6.** (tr.) Sl. to carry or heave. **7.** Taboo sl. to have sexual intercourse with (someone). [C18: prob. from earlier humpbacked] —**'humpy** adj.

humpback ('hʌmp,bæk) n. **1.** another word for **hunchback. 2.** Also called: **humpback whale.** a large whalebone whale with a humped back and long flippers. **3.** a Pacific salmon, the male of which has a humped back. **4.** Also: **humpback bridge.** Brit. a road bridge having a sharp incline and decline and usually a narrow roadway. [C17: alteration of earlier crumpbacked, ? infl. by HUNCHBACK] —**'hump,backed** adj.

Humperdinck (German 'hʊmpərdɪŋk) n. **Engelbert** ('ɛŋəlbɛrt). 1854–1921, German composer, esp. of operas, including Hansel and Gretel (1893).

humph (spelling pron. hʌmf) interj. an exclamation of annoyance, indecision, etc.

Humphrey ('hʌmfrɪ) n. **1. Duke.** See (Humphrey, Duke of) **Gloucester. 2. Hubert Horatio.** 1911–78, U.S. statesman; vice-president of the U.S. under President Johnson (1965–69).

Humphreys Peak ('hʌmfrɪz) n. a mountain in N central Arizona, in the San Francisco Peaks: the highest peak in the state. Height: 3862 m (12 670 ft.).

humpty dumpty ('hʌmptɪ 'dʌmptɪ) n., pl. **dumpties.** Chiefly Brit. **1.** a short fat person. **2.** a person or thing

that once broken cannot be mended. [C18: from the nursery rhyme Humpty Dumpty]

humpy ('hʌmpɪ) n., pl. **humpies.** Austral. a primitive hut. [C19: from Abor.]

Hums (hʊms) n. a variant of **Homs.**

humus ('hju:məs) n. a dark brown or black colloidal mass of partially decomposed organic matter in the soil. It improves the fertility and water retention of the soil. [C18: from L: soil]

Hun (hʌn) n., pl. **Huns** or **Hun. 1.** a member of any of several Asiatic nomadic peoples who dominated much of Asia and E Europe from before 300 B.C., invading the Roman Empire in the 4th and 5th centuries A.D. **2.** Inf. (esp. in World War I) a derogatory name for a **German. 3.** Inf. a vandal. [OE Hūnas, from LL Hūnī, from Turkish Hun-yū] —**'Hunnish** adj. —**'Hun,like** adj.

Hunan ('hu:'næn) n. a province of S China, between the Yangtze River and the Nan Ling Mountains: drained chiefly by the Xiang and Yüan Rivers; valuable mineral resources. Capital: Changsha. Pop.: 55 610 000 (1985). Area: 210 500 sq. km (82 095 sq. miles).

hunch (hʌntʃ) n. **1.** an intuitive guess or feeling. **2.** another word for **hump. 3.** a lump or large piece. ~vb. **4.** to draw (oneself or a part of the body) up or together. **5.** (intr.; usually foll. by up) to sit in a hunched position. [C16: from ?]

hunchback ('hʌntʃ,bæk) n. **1.** a person having an abnormal curvature of the spine. **2.** such a curvature. ~Also called: **humpback.** [C18: from earlier hunchbacked] —**'hunch,backed** adj.

hundred ('hʌndrəd) n., pl. **-dreds** or **-dred. 1.** the cardinal number that is the product of ten and ten; five score. **2.** a numeral, 100, C, etc., representing this number. **3.** (often pl.) a large but unspecified number, amount, or quantity. **4.** (pl.) the 100 years of a specified century: in the sixteen hundreds. **5.** something representing, represented by, or consisting of 100 units. **6.** Maths. the position containing a digit representing that number followed by two zeros: in 4376, 3 is in the hundred's place. **7.** an ancient division of a county. ~determiner. **8.** amounting to or approximately a hundred: a hundred reasons for that. [OE] —**'hundredth** adj., n.

hundreds and thousands pl. n. tiny beads of coloured sugar, used in decorating cakes, etc.

hundredweight ('hʌndrəd,weɪt) n., pl. **-weights** or **-weight. 1.** Also called: **long hundredweight.** Brit. a unit of weight equal to 112 pounds (50.802 kg). **2.** Also called: **short hundredweight.** U.S. & Canad. a unit of weight equal to 100 pounds (45.359 kg). **3.** Also called: **metric hundredweight.** a metric unit of weight equal to 50 kilograms. ~Abbrev. (for senses 1, 2): **cwt.**

hung (hʌŋ) vb. **1.** the past tense and past participle of **hang** (except in the sense of to execute). ~adj. **2.** (of a political party, jury, etc.) not having a majority: a hung parliament. **3. hung over.** Inf. suffering from the effects of a hangover. **4. hung up.** Sl. **a.** impeded by some difficulty or delay. **b.** emotionally disturbed. **5. hung up on.** Sl. obsessively interested in.

Hungarian (hʌŋ'gɛərɪən) n. **1.** the official language of Hungary, also spoken in Romania and elsewhere, belonging to the Finno-Ugric family. **2.** a native, inhabitant, or citizen of Hungary. ~adj. **3.** of or relating to Hungary, its people, or their language. ~Cf. **Magyar.**

Hungary ('hʌŋgərɪ) n. a republic in central Europe: Magyars first unified under Saint Stephen, the first Hungarian king (1001–38); taken by the Hapsburgs from the Turks at the end of the 17th century; gained autonomy with the establishment of the dual monarchy of Austria-Hungary (1867) and became a republic in 1918; passed under Communist control in 1949; a popular rising in 1956 was suppressed by Soviet troops. It consists chiefly of the Middle Danube basin and plains. Language: Hungarian. Currency: forint. Capital: Budapest. Pop.: 10 622 000 (1987). Area: 93 030 sq. km (35 919 sq. miles). Hungarian name: **Magyarország.**

hunger ('hʌŋgə) n. **1.** a feeling of emptiness or weakness induced by lack of food. **2.** desire or craving: hunger for a woman. ~vb. **3.** (intr.; usually foll. by for or after) to have a great appetite or desire (for). [OE]

hunger march n. a procession of protest or demonstration, esp. by the unemployed.

hunger strike n. a voluntary fast undertaken, usually by a prisoner, as a means of protest. —**hunger striker** n.

Hungnam (ˌhʊŋˈnæm) n. a port in E North Korea, on the Sea of Japan southeast of Hamhung. Pop.: 260 000 (1976 est.).

hungry (ˈhʌŋɡrɪ) adj. **-grier, -griest. 1.** desiring food. **2.** (postpositive; foll. by for) having a craving, desire, or need (for). **3.** expressing or appearing to express greed, craving, or desire. **4.** lacking fertility; poor. **5.** Austral. & N.Z. greedy; mean. **6.** N.Z. (of timber) dry and bare. — **ˈhungrily** adv. — **ˈhungriness** n.

hunk (hʌŋk) n. **1.** a large piece. **2.** Sl. a sexually attractive man. [C19: prob. rel. to Flemish hunke]

hunkers (ˈhʌŋkəz) pl. n. haunches. [C18: from ?]

hunky-dory (ˌhʌŋkɪˈdɔːrɪ) adj. Inf. very satisfactory; fine. [C20: from ?]

hunt (hʌnt) vb. **1.** to seek out and kill (animals) for food or sport. **2.** (intr.; often foll. by for) to search (for): to hunt for a book. **3.** (tr.) to use (hounds, horses, etc.) in the pursuit of wild animals, game, etc.: to hunt a pack of hounds. **4.** (tr.) to search (country) to hunt game, etc.: to hunt the parkland. **5.** (tr.; often foll. by down) to track diligently so as to capture: to hunt down a criminal. **6.** (tr.; usually passive) to persecute; hound. **7.** (intr.) (of a gauge indicator, etc.) to oscillate about a mean value or position. **8.** (intr.) (of an aircraft, rocket, etc.) to oscillate about a flight path or its course axis. ~n. **9.** the act or an instance of hunting. **10.** chase or search, esp. of animals. **11.** the area of a hunt. **12.** a party or institution organized for the pursuit of wild animals, esp. for sport. **13.** the members of such a party or institution. [OE huntian]

Hunt (hʌnt) n. **1.** (**William**) **Holman.** 1827–1910, English painter; a founder of the Pre-Raphaelite Brotherhood (1848). **2.** **James.** born 1947, English motor-racing driver: world champion 1976. **3.** (**James Henry**) **Leigh.** 1784–1859, English poet and essayist: a founder of The Examiner (1808) in which he promoted the work of Keats and Shelley.

huntaway (ˈhʌntəˌweɪ) n. N.Z. a dog trained to drive sheep at a long distance from the shepherd.

hunted (ˈhʌntɪd) adj. harassed: a hunted look.

hunter (ˈhʌntə) n. **1.** a person or animal that seeks out and kills or captures game. Fem.: **huntress** (ˈhʌntrɪs). **2. a.** a person who looks diligently for something. **b.** (in combination): a fortune-hunter. **3.** a specially bred horse used in hunting, characterized by strength and stamina. **4.** a watch with a hinged metal lid or case (**hunting case**) to protect the crystal.

hunter-killer adj. denoting a type of submarine designed and equipped to pursue and destroy enemy craft.

hunter's moon n. the full moon following the harvest moon.

hunting (ˈhʌntɪŋ) n. **a.** the pursuit and killing or capture of wild animals, regarded as a sport. **b.** (as modifier): hunting lodge.

Huntingdon[1] (ˈhʌntɪŋdən) n. a town in E central England, in Cambridgeshire: birthplace of Oliver Cromwell. Pop. (with Godmanchester): 17 467 (1981).

Huntingdon[2] (ˈhʌntɪŋdən) n. **Selina,** Countess of Huntingdon. 1707–91, English religious leader, who founded a Calvinistic Methodist sect.

Huntingdonshire (ˈhʌntɪŋdənˌʃɪə, -ʃə) n. (until 1974) a former county of E England, now part of Cambridgeshire.

hunting horn n. a long straight metal tube with a flared end, used in giving signals in hunting.

Huntington's chorea (ˈhʌntɪŋtənz) n. a hereditary form of chorea associated with progressive dementia. [after G. Huntington (1850–1916), U.S. physician]

huntsman (ˈhʌntsmən) n., pl. **-men. 1.** a person who hunts. **2.** a person who trains hounds, beagles, etc., and manages them during a hunt.

Huntsville (ˈhʌntsvɪl) n. a city in NE Alabama: spaceflight and guided-missile research centre. Pop.: 142 513 (1981).

Hunyadi (Hungarian ˈhunjɔdi) n. **János** (ˈjaːnoʃ). ?1387–1456, Hungarian general, who led Hungarian resistance to the Turks, defeating them notably at Belgrade (1456).

Huon pine (ˈhjuːɒn) n. a tree of Australasia, SE Asia, and Chile, with scalelike leaves and cup-shaped berry-like fruits. [after the Huon River, Tasmania]

Hupeh or **Hupei** (ˈxuːˈpeɪ) n. a variant transliteration of the Chinese name for Hubei.

Hurd (hɜːd) n. **Douglas** (**Richard**). born 1930, British Conservative politician; Home Secretary from 1985.

hurdle (ˈhɜːdʳl) n. **1. a.** Athletics. one of a number of light barriers over which runners leap in certain events. **b.** a low barrier used in certain horse races. **2.** an obstacle: the next hurdle in his career. **3.** a light framework of interlaced osiers, etc., used as a temporary fence. **4.** a sledge on which criminals were dragged to their executions. ~vb. **5.** to jump (a hurdle). **6.** (tr.) to surround with hurdles. **7.** (tr.) to overcome. [OE hyrdel] — **ˈhurdler** n.

hurdy-gurdy (ˈhɜːdɪˈɡɜːdɪ) n., pl. **hurdy-gurdies.** any mechanical musical instrument, such as a barrel organ. [C18: rhyming compound, prob. imit.]

hurl (hɜːl) vb. (tr.) **1.** to throw with great force. **2.** to utter with force; yell: to hurl insults. ~n. **3.** the act of hurling. [C13: prob. imit.]

hurling (ˈhɜːlɪŋ) or **hurley** n. a traditional Irish game resembling hockey, played with sticks and a ball between two teams of 15 players.

hurly-burly (ˈhɜːlɪˈbɜːlɪ) n., pl. **hurly-burlies.** confusion or commotion. [C16: from earlier hurling and burling, rhyming phrase based on hurling in obs. sense of uproar]

Huron (ˈhjʊərən) n. **1. Lake.** a lake in North America, between the U.S. and Canada: the second largest of the Great Lakes. Area: 59 570 sq. km (23 000 sq. miles). **2.** (pl. **-rons** or **-ron**) a member of a North American Indian people formerly living in the region east of Lake Huron. **3.** the Iroquoian language of this people.

hurrah (hʊˈrɑː), **hooray** (huːˈreɪ), or **hoorah** (huːˈrɑː) interj., n. **1.** a cheer of joy, victory, etc. ~vb. **2.** to shout "hurrah". [C17: prob. from G hurra; cf. HUZZAH]

hurricane (ˈhʌrɪkˀn) n. **1.** a severe, often destructive storm, esp. a tropical cyclone. **2.** a wind of force 12 on the Beaufort scale, with speeds over 72 mph. [C16: from Sp. huracán, of Amerind origin, from hura wind]

hurricane deck n. a ship's deck that is covered by a light deck as a sunshade.

hurricane lamp n. a paraffin lamp with a glass covering. Also called: **storm lantern.**

hurried (ˈhʌrɪd) adj. performed with great or excessive haste. — **ˈhurriedly** adv. — **ˈhurriedness** n.

hurry (ˈhʌrɪ) vb. **-rying, -ried. 1.** (intr.; often foll. by up) to hasten; rush. **2.** (tr.; often foll. by along) to speed up the completion, progress, etc., of. ~n. **3.** haste. **4.** urgency or eagerness. **5. in a hurry.** Inf. **a.** easily: you won't beat him in a hurry. **b.** willingly: we won't go there again in a hurry. [C16 horyen, prob. imit.]

hurst (hɜːst) n. Arch. **1.** a wood. **2.** a sandbank. [OE hyrst]

Hurstmonceux (ˈhɜːstmənˌsuː, -ˌsəʊ) n. a variant spelling of **Herstmonceux.**

hurt (hɜːt) vb. **hurting, hurt. 1.** (tr.) to cause physical or mental injury to. **2.** (intr.) to produce a painful sensation: the bruise hurts. **3.** (intr.) Inf. to feel pain. ~n. **4.** physical or mental pain or suffering. **5.** a wound, cut, or sore. **6.** damage or injury; harm. ~adj. **7.** injured or pained: a hurt knee; a hurt look. [C12 hurten to hit, from OF hurter to knock against, prob. of Gmc origin]

hurtful (ˈhɜːtfʊl) adj. causing distress or injury: to say hurtful things. — **ˈhurtfully** adv.

hurtle (ˈhɜːtʳl) vb. to project or be projected very quickly, noisily, or violently. [C13 hurtlen, from hurten to strike; see HURT]

Hus (Czech hʊs) n. **Jan** (jan). the Czech name of (John) **Huss.**

Husain (huˈseɪn, -ˈsaɪn) n. **1.** ?629–680 A.D., Islamic caliph, the son of Ali and Fatima and the grandson of Mohammed. **2.** a variant of **Hussein.**

Husák (Czech ˈhusaːk) n. **Gustáv** (ˈɡustaf). born 1913, Czechoslovak statesman; first secretary of the Communist Party (1969–87); president (1975–87).

husband (ˈhʌzbənd) n. **1.** a woman's partner in marriage. **2.** Arch. a manager of an estate. ~vb. **3.** to manage or use (resources, finances, etc.) thriftily. **4.** (tr.) Arch. to find a husband for. **5.** (tr.) Obs. to till (the soil). [OE hūsbonda, from ON hūsbōndi, from hūs house + bōndi one who has a household] — **ˈhusbander** n.

husbandman (ˈhʌzbəndmən) n., pl. **-men.** Arch. a farmer.

husbandry (ˈhʌzbəndrɪ) n. **1.** farming, esp. when regarded as a science, skill, or art. **2.** management of affairs and resources.

Husein ibn-Ali (huˈseɪn ˈɪbᵊnˈɑːlɪ, ˈælɪ, huˈsaɪn) *n.* 1856–1931, first king of Hejaz (1916–24). Advised by T. E. Lawrence, he took part in the Arab revolt against the Turks (1916–18); forced to abdicate by ibn-Saud.

hush (hʌʃ) *vb.* **1.** to make or become silent; quieten; soothe. ~*n.* **2.** stillness; silence. ~*interj.* **3.** a plea or demand for silence. [C16: prob. from earlier *husht* quiet!, the *-t* being thought to indicate a past participle] —**hushed** *adj.*

hushaby (ˈhʌʃəˌbaɪ) *interj.* **1.** used in quietening a baby or child to sleep. ~*n., pl.* **-bies. 2.** a lullaby. [C18: from HUSH + *by*, as in BYE-BYE]

hush-hush *adj. Inf.* (esp. of official work, documents, etc.) secret; confidential.

hush money *n. Sl.* money given to a person to ensure that something is kept secret.

hush up *vb.* (*tr., adv.*) to suppress information or rumours about.

husk (hʌsk) *n.* **1.** the external green or membranous covering of certain fruits and seeds. **2.** any worthless outer covering. ~*vb.* **3.** (*tr.*) to remove the husk from. [C14: prob. based on MDu. *huusken* little house, from *hūs* house]

husky[1] (ˈhʌskɪ) *adj.* **huskier, huskiest. 1.** (of a voice, utterance, etc.) slightly hoarse or rasping. **2.** of or containing husks. **3.** *Inf.* big and strong. [C19: prob. from HUSK, from the toughness of a corn husk] — **'huskily** *adv.* — **'huskiness** *n.*

husky[2] (ˈhʌskɪ) *n., pl.* **huskies. 1.** a breed of Arctic sled dog with a thick dense coat, pricked ears, and a curled tail. **2.** *Canad. sl.* **a.** a member of the Inuit people. **b.** their language. [C19: prob. based on ESKIMO]

Huss (hʌs) *n.* **John,** Czech name *Jan Hus.* ?1372–1415, Bohemian religious reformer. Influenced by Wycliffe, he anticipated the Reformation in denouncing doctrines and abuses of the Church. His death at the stake precipitated the Hussite wars in Bohemia and Moravia.

hussar (huˈzɑː) *n.* **1.** a member of any of various light cavalry regiments, renowned for their elegant dress. **2.** a Hungarian horseman of the 15th century. [C15: from Hungarian *huszár* hussar, formerly freebooter, ult. from Olt. *corsaro* CORSAIR]

Hussein (huˈseɪn) *or* **Husain** *n.* born 1935, king of Jordan from 1952.

Husserl (*German* ˈhʊsərl) *n.* **Edmund** (ˈɛtmʊnt). 1859–1938, German philosopher; founder of phenomenology.

Hussite (ˈhʌsaɪt) *n.* **1.** an adherent of the ideas of John Huss or a member of the movement initiated by him. ~*adj.* **2.** of or relating to John Huss, his teachings, followers, etc. — **'Hussitism** *n.*

hussy (ˈhʌsɪ, -zɪ) *n., pl.* **-sies.** *Contemptuous.* a shameless or promiscuous woman. [C16 (in the sense: housewife): from *hussif* HOUSEWIFE]

hustings (ˈhʌstɪŋz) *n.* (*functioning as pl. or sing.*) **1.** *Brit.* (before 1872) the platform on which candidates were nominated for Parliament and from which they addressed the electors. **2.** the proceedings at a parliamentary election. [C11: from ON *hūsthing*, from *hūs* HOUSE + *thing* assembly]

hustle (ˈhʌsᵊl) *vb.* **1.** to shove or crowd (someone) roughly. **2.** to move hurriedly or furtively: *he hustled her out of sight.* **3.** (*tr.*) to deal with hurriedly: *to hustle legislation through.* **4.** *Sl.* to obtain (something) forcefully. **5.** *U.S. & Canad. sl.* (of procurers and prostitutes) to solicit. ~*n.* **6.** an instance of hustling. [C17: from Du. *husselen* to shake, from MDu. *hutsen*] — **'hustler** *n.*

Huston (ˈhjuːstən) *n.* **John.** 1906–87, U.S. film director. His films include *The Treasure of the Sierra Madre* (1947), for which he won an Oscar, *The African Queen* (1951), *The Man Who Would Be King* (1975), *Prizzi's Honour* (1985), and *The Dead* (1987).

hut (hʌt) *n.* **1.** a small house or shelter. ~*vb.* **hutting, hutted. 2.** to furnish with or live in a hut. [C17: from F *hutte,* of Gmc origin] — **'hut,like** *adj.*

hutch (hʌtʃ) *n.* **1.** a cage, usually of wood and wire mesh, for small animals. **2.** *Inf., derog.* a small house. **3.** a cart for carrying ore. [C14 *hucche,* from OF *huche,* from Med. L *hutica,* from ?]

hutment (ˈhʌtmənt) *n. Chiefly mil.* a number or group of huts.

Hutton (ˈhʌtᵊn) *n.* **James.** 1726–97, Scottish geologist, regarded as the founder of modern geology.

Huxley (ˈhʌkslɪ) *n.* **1. Aldous** (**Leonard**) (ˈɔːldəs). 1894–1963, English novelist and essayist, noted particularly for his novel *Brave New World* (1932), depicting a scientifically controlled civilization of human robots. **2.** his half-brother, Sir **Andrew Fielding,** born 1917, English biologist: noted for his research into nerve cells and the mechanism by which nerve impulses are transmitted; Nobel prize for physiology or medicine shared with Alan Hodgkin and John Eccles 1963; president of the Royal Society from 1980. **3.** his half-brother, Sir **Julian** (**Sorrel**). 1887–1975, English biologist; first director-general of UNESCO (1946–48). His works include *Essays of a Biologist* (1923) and *Evolution: the Modern Synthesis* (1942). **4.** their grandfather, **Thomas Henry.** 1825–95, English biologist, the leading British exponent of Darwin's theory of evolution; his works include *Man's Place in Nature* (1863) and *Evolution and Ethics* (1893).

Hu Yaobang (xu: jaʊˈbɑːŋ) *n.* born 1915, Chinese statesman; leader of the Chinese Communist Party (1981–87).

Huygens (ˈhaɪgənz; *Dutch* ˈhœixəns) *n.* **Christiaan** (ˈkrɪstiːˌaːn). 1629–95, Dutch physicist: first formulated the wave theory of light.

Huysmans (*French* ɥismɑ̃s) *n.* **Joris Karl** (ʒɔrɪs karl). 1848–1907, French novelist of the Decadent school, whose works include *A rebours* (1884).

huzzah (bəˈzɑː) *interj., n., vb.* an archaic word for **hurrah.** [C16: from ?]

HV *or* **h.v.** *abbrev. for* high voltage.

Hwange (ˈhwæŋgeɪ) *n.* a town in W Zimbabwe: coal mines. Pop.: 39 200 (1982 est.). Former name (until 1982): **Wankie.**

Hwang Hai (ˈwæŋ ˈhaɪ) *n.* a variant transliteration of the Chinese name for the **Yellow Sea.**

Hwang Ho (ˈwæŋ ˈhəʊ) *n.* a variant transliteration of the Chinese name for the **Yellow River.**

HWM *abbrev. for* high-water mark.

hwyl (ˈhuːɪl) *n.* emotional fervour, as in the recitation of poetry. [C19: Welsh]

hyacinth (ˈhaɪəsɪnθ) *n.* **1.** any plant of the Mediterranean genus *Hyacinthus,* esp. a cultivated variety having a thick flower stalk bearing bell-shaped fragrant flowers. **2.** the flower or bulb of such a plant. **3.** any similar plant, such as the grape hyacinth. **4.** Also called: **jacinth.** a reddish transparent variety of the mineral zircon, used as a gemstone. **5. a.** a purplish-blue colour. **b.** (*as adj.*): *hyacinth eyes.* [C16: from L *hyacinthus,* from Gk *huakinthos*] — **hyacinthine** (ˌhaɪəˈsɪnθaɪn) *adj.*

Hyacinthus (ˌhaɪəˈsɪnθəs) *n. Greek myth.* a youth beloved of Apollo and inadvertently killed by him. At the spot where the youth died, Apollo caused a flower to grow.

Hyades[1] (ˈhaɪəˌdiːz) *pl. n.* an open cluster of stars in the constellation Taurus, formerly believed to bring rain when they rose with the sun. [C16: via L from Gk *huades,* ?from *huein* to rain]

Hyades[2] (ˈhaɪəˌdiːz) *pl. n. Greek myth.* seven nymphs, daughters of Atlas, whom Zeus placed among the stars after death.

hyaena (haɪˈiːnə) *n.* a variant spelling of **hyena.**

hyaline (ˈhaɪəlɪn) *adj. Biol.* clear and translucent, as a common type of cartilage. [C17: from LL *hyalinus,* from Gk, from *hualos* glass]

hyalite (ˈhaɪəˌlaɪt) *n.* a clear and colourless variety of opal in globular form.

hyaloid (ˈhaɪəˌlɔɪd) *adj. Anat., zool.* clear and transparent; hyaline. [C19: from Gk *hualoeidēs*]

hyaloid membrane *n.* the delicate transparent membrane enclosing the vitreous humour of the eye.

hybrid (ˈhaɪbrɪd) *n.* **1.** an animal or plant resulting from a cross between genetically unlike individuals; usually sterile. **2.** anything of mixed ancestry. **3.** a word, part of which is derived from one language and part from another, such as *monolingual.* ~*adj.* **4.** denoting or being a hybrid; of mixed origin. [C17: from L *hibrida* offspring of a mixed union (human or animal)] — **'hybridism** *n.* — **hy'bridity** *n.*

hybrid computer *n.* a computer that uses both analogue and digital techniques.

hybridize *or* **-ise** (ˈhaɪbrɪˌdaɪz) *vb.* to produce or cause to produce hybrids; crossbreed. — **hybridi'zation** *or* **-i'sation** *n.*

hybridoma (ˌhaɪbrɪˈdəʊmə) *n.* a hybrid cell formed by the fusion of two different types of cell, esp. one capable of producing antibodies fused with an immortal tumour cell. [C20: from HYBRID + -OMA]

hybrid vigour n. Biol. the increased size, strength, etc., of a hybrid as compared to either of its parents. Also called: **heterosis**.

hydatid ('haɪdətɪd) n. **1.** a large bladder containing encysted larvae of the tapeworm Echinococcus: causes serious disease in man. **2.** Also called: **hydatid cyst**. a sterile fluid-filled cyst produced in man and animals during infestation by Echinococcus larval forms. [C17: from Gk hudatis watery vesicle, from hudōr, hudat- water]

Hyde[1] (haɪd) n. a town in NW England, in E Greater Manchester. Pop.: 35 600 (1981).

Hyde[2] (haɪd) n. **1. Douglas**. 1860–1949, Irish scholar and author; first president of Eire (1938–45). **2. Edward**. See (1st Earl of) **Clarendon**.

Hyde Park n. a park in W central London: popular for open-air meetings.

Hyderabad ('haɪdərə,bɑːd, -,bæd, 'haɪdrə-) n. **1.** a city in S central India, capital of Andhra Pradesh state and capital of former Hyderabad state; university (1918). Pop.: 2 142 087 (1981). **2.** a former state of S India: divided in 1956 between the states of Andhra Pradesh, Mysore, and Maharashtra. **3.** a city in SW Pakistan, on the River Indus: seat of the University of Sind (1947). Pop.: 795 000 (1981).

Hyder Ali or **Haidar Ali** ('haɪdər 'ɑːlɪ) n. 1722–82, Indian ruler of Mysore (1766–82), who waged two wars against the British in India (1767–69; 1780–82).

hydr- combining form. a variant of **hydro-** before a vowel.

hydra ('haɪdrə) n., pl. -dras or -drae (-driː). **1.** a freshwater coelenterate in which the body is a slender polyp with tentacles around the mouth. **2.** a persistent trouble or evil. [C16: from L, from Gk hudra water serpent]

Hydra ('haɪdrə) n. Greek myth. a monster with nine heads, each of which, when struck off, was replaced by two new ones.

hydracid (haɪ'dræsɪd) n. an acid, such as hydrochloric acid, that does not contain oxygen.

hydrangea (haɪ'dreɪndʒə) n. a shrub or tree of an Asian and American genus cultivated for their large clusters of white, pink, or blue flowers. [C18: from NL, from Gk hudōr water + angeion vessel: prob. from the cup-shaped fruit]

hydrant ('haɪdrənt) n. an outlet from a water main, usually an upright pipe with a valve attached, from which water can be tapped for fighting fires, etc. [C19: from HYDRO- + -ANT]

hydrate ('haɪdreɪt) n. **1.** a chemical compound containing water that is chemically combined with a substance. **2.** a crystalline chemical compound containing weakly bound water molecules. ~vb. **3.** to undergo or cause to undergo treatment or impregnation with water. —**hy'dration** n. —**'hydrator** n.

hydrated ('haɪdreɪtɪd) adj. (of a compound) chemically bonded to water molecules.

hydraulic (haɪ'drɒlɪk) adj. **1.** operated by pressure transmitted through a pipe by a liquid, such as water or oil. **2.** of or employing liquids in motion. **3.** of hydraulics. **4.** hardening under water: hydraulic cement. [C17: from L hydraulicus, from Gk hudraulikos, from hudraulos water organ, from HYDRO- + aulos pipe] —**hy'draulically** adv.

hydraulic brake n. a type of brake, used in motor vehicles, in which the braking force is transmitted from the brake pedal to the brakes by a liquid under pressure.

hydraulic press n. a press that utilizes liquid pressure to enable a small force applied to a small piston to produce a large force on a larger piston.

hydraulic ram n. **1.** the larger or working piston of a hydraulic press. **2.** a form of water pump utilizing the kinetic energy of running water to provide static pressure to raise water to a reservoir higher than the source.

hydraulics (haɪ'drɒlɪks) n. (functioning as sing.) another name for **fluid mechanics**.

hydraulic suspension n. a system of motor-vehicle suspension using hydraulic members, often with hydraulic compensation between front and rear systems (**hydroelastic suspension**).

hydrazine ('haɪdrə,ziːn, -zɪn) n. a colourless liquid made from sodium hypochlorite and ammonia: used as a rocket fuel. Formula: N_2H_4. [C19: from HYDRO- + AZO + -INE[2]]

hydric ('haɪdrɪk) adj. **1.** of or containing hydrogen. **2.** containing or using moisture.

hydride ('haɪdraɪd) n. any compound of hydrogen with another element.

hydrilla (haɪ'drɪlə) n. a type of underwater aquatic weed that was introduced from Asia into the south U.S., where it has become a serious problem, choking fish and hindering navigation. [C20: NL, prob. from L hydra: see HYDRA]

hydriodic acid (,haɪdrɪ'ɒdɪk) n. a solution of hydrogen iodide in water: a strong acid. [C19: from HYDRO- + IODIC]

hydro[1] ('haɪdrəʊ) n., pl. -dros. Brit. a hotel or resort, often near a spa, offering facilities (esp. formerly) for hydropathic treatment.

hydro[2] ('haɪdrəʊ) adj. **1.** short for **hydroelectric**. ~n. **2.** a Canadian name for **electricity**.

Hydro ('haɪdrəʊ) n. (esp. in Canada) a hydroelectric power company or board.

hydro- or before a vowel **hydr-** combining form. **1.** indicating water or fluid: hydrodynamics. **2.** indicating hydrogen in a chemical compound: hydrochloric acid. **3.** indicating a hydroid: hydrozoan. [from Gk hudōr water]

hydrobromic acid (,haɪdrəʊ'brəʊmɪk) n. a solution of hydrogen bromide in water: a strong acid.

hydrocarbon (,haɪdrəʊ'kɑːbən) n. any organic compound containing only carbon and hydrogen.

hydrocele ('haɪdrəʊ,siːl) n. an abnormal collection of fluid in any saclike space.

hydrocephalus (,haɪdrəʊ'sɛfələs) or **hydrocephaly** (,haɪdrəʊ'sɛfəlɪ) n. accumulation of cerebrospinal fluid within the ventricles of the brain because its normal outlet has been blocked by congenital malformation or disease. Nontechnical name: **water on the brain**. —**hydrocephalic** (,haɪdrəʊsɛ'fælɪk) or ,**hydro'cephalous** adj.

hydrochloric acid (,haɪdrə'klɒrɪk) n. a solution of hydrogen chloride in water: a strong acid used in many industrial and laboratory processes.

hydrochloride (,haɪdrə'klɔːraɪd) n. a quaternary salt formed by the addition of hydrochloric acid to an organic base.

hydrocyanic acid (,haɪdrəʊsaɪ'ænɪk) n. another name for **hydrogen cyanide**.

hydrodynamics (,haɪdrəʊdaɪ'næmɪks, -dɪ-) n. (functioning as sing.) the branch of science concerned with the mechanical properties of fluids, esp. liquids. Also called: **hydromechanics**.

hydroelastic suspension (,haɪdrəʊɪ'læstɪk) n. See **hydraulic suspension**.

hydroelectric (,haɪdrəʊɪ'lɛktrɪk) adj. **1.** generated by the pressure of falling water: hydroelectric power. **2.** of the generation of electricity by water pressure: a hydroelectric scheme. —**hydroelectricity** (,haɪdrəʊɪlɛk'trɪsɪtɪ) n.

hydrofluoric acid (,haɪdrəʊflu'ɒrɪk) n. a solution of hydrogen fluoride in water: a strong acid that attacks glass.

hydrofoil ('haɪdrə,fɔɪl) n. **1.** a fast light vessel the hull of which is raised out of the water on one or more pairs of fixed vanes. **2.** any of these vanes.

hydrogen ('haɪdrɪdʒən) n. **a.** a flammable colourless gas that is the lightest and most abundant element in the universe. It occurs in water and in most organic compounds. Symbol: H; atomic no.: 1; atomic wt.: 1.007 97. **b.** (as modifier): hydrogen bomb. [C18: from F hydrogène, from HYDRO- + -GEN; because its combustion produces water] —**hydrogenous** (haɪ'drɒdʒɪnəs) adj.

hydrogenate ('haɪdrədʒɪ,neɪt, haɪ'drɒdʒɪ,neɪt) vb. to undergo or cause to undergo a reaction with hydrogen: to hydrogenate ethylene. —,**hydrogen'ation** n.

hydrogen bomb n. a type of bomb in which energy is released by fusion of hydrogen nuclei to give helium nuclei. The energy required to initiate the fusion is provided by the detonation of an atom bomb, which is surrounded by a hydrogen-containing substance. Also called: **H-bomb**.

hydrogen bond n. a weak chemical bond between an electronegative atom, such as fluorine, oxygen, or nitrogen, and a hydrogen atom bound to another electronegative atom.

hydrogen bromide n. **1.** a colourless pungent gas used in organic synthesis. Formula: HBr. **2.** an aqueous solution of hydrogen bromide; hydrobromic acid.

hydrogen carbonate n. another name for **bicarbonate**.

hydrogen chloride n. **1.** a colourless pungent corrosive gas obtained by the action of sulphuric acid on sodium chloride: used in making vinyl chloride and other organic chemicals. Formula: HCl. **2.** an aqueous solution of hydrogen chloride; hydrochloric acid.

hydrogen cyanide n. a colourless poisonous liquid with a faint odour of bitter almonds. It forms prussic acid in aqueous solution and is used for making plastics and as a war gas. Formula: HCN. Also called: **hydrocyanic acid.**

hydrogen fluoride n. **1.** a colourless poisonous corrosive gas or liquid made by reaction between calcium fluoride and sulphuric acid: used as a fluorinating agent and catalyst. Formula: HF. **2.** an aqueous solution of hydrogen fluoride; hydrofluoric acid.

hydrogen iodide n. **1.** a colourless poisonous corrosive gas obtained by a catalysed reaction between hydrogen and iodine vapour: used in making iodides. Formula HI. **2.** an aqueous solution of this gas; hydriodic acid.

hydrogen ion n. an ionized hydrogen atom, occurring in aqueous solutions of acids; proton. Formula: H^+.

hydrogenize or **-nise** ('haɪdrədʒɪˌnaɪz, haɪ'drɒdʒɪˌnaɪz) vb. a variant of **hydrogenate.**

hydrogen peroxide n. a colourless oily unstable liquid used as a bleach and as an oxidizer in rocket fuels. Formula: H_2O_2.

hydrogen sulphide n. a colourless poisonous gas with an odour of rotten eggs. Formula: H_2S. Also called: **sulphuretted hydrogen.**

hydrography (haɪ'drɒgrəfɪ) n. the study, surveying, and mapping of the oceans, seas, and rivers. —**hy'drographer** n. —**hydrographic** (ˌhaɪdrə'græfɪk) adj.

hydroid ('haɪdrɔɪd) adj. **1.** of or relating to the Hydroida, an order of hydrozoan coelenterates that have the polyp phase dominant. **2.** having or consisting of hydralike polyps. ~n. **3.** a hydroid colony or individual.

hydrokinetics (ˌhaɪdrəʊkɪ'nɛtɪks, -kaɪ-) n. (functioning as sing.) the branch of science concerned with the behaviour and properties of fluids in motion. Also called: **hydrodynamics.**

hydrology (haɪ'drɒlədʒɪ) n. the study of the distribution, conservation, use, etc., of the water of the earth and its atmosphere. —**hydrological** (ˌhaɪdrə'lɒdʒɪkəl) adj. —**hy'drologist** n.

hydrolyse or U.S. **-lyze** ('haɪdrəˌlaɪz) vb. to subject to or undergo hydrolysis.

hydrolysis (haɪ'drɒlɪsɪs) n. a chemical reaction in which a compound reacts with water to produce other compounds. —**hydrolytic** (ˌhaɪdrə'lɪtɪk) adj.

hydrolyte ('haɪdrəˌlaɪt) n. a substance subjected to hydrolysis.

hydromel ('haɪdrəʊˌmɛl) n. Arch. another word for **mead** (the drink). [C15: from L, from Gk hudromeli, from HYDRO- + meli honey]

hydrometer (haɪ'drɒmɪtə) n. an instrument for measuring the relative density of a liquid. —**hydrometric** (ˌhaɪdrəʊ'mɛtrɪk) or **hydro'metrical** adj.

hydronaut ('haɪdrəʊˌnɔːt) n. U.S. Navy. a person trained to operate deep submergence vessels. [C20: from Gk, from HYDRO- + -naut, as in astronaut]

hydropathy (haɪ'drɒpəθɪ) n. a pseudoscientific method of treating disease by the use of large quantities of water both internally and externally. —**hydropathic** (ˌhaɪdrəʊ'pæθɪk) adj.

hydrophilic (ˌhaɪdrəʊ'fɪlɪk) adj. Chem. tending to dissolve in, mix with, or be wetted by water: a hydrophilic colloid. —**hydrophile** ('haɪdrəʊˌfaɪl) n.

hydrophobia (ˌhaɪdrə'fəʊbɪə) n. **1.** another name for **rabies.** **2.** a fear of drinking fluids, esp. that of a person with rabies, because of painful spasms when trying to swallow. —**hydro'phobic** adj.

hydrophone ('haɪdrəˌfəʊn) n. an electroacoustic transducer that converts sound travelling through water into electrical oscillations.

hydrophyte ('haɪdrəʊˌfaɪt) n. a plant that grows only in water or very moist soil.

hydroplane ('haɪdrəʊˌpleɪn) n. **1.** a motorboat equipped with hydrofoils or with a shaped bottom that raises its hull out of the water at high speeds. **2.** an attachment to an aircraft to enable it to glide along the surface of the water. **3.** another name for a **seaplane.** **4.** a horizontal vane on the hull of a submarine for controlling its vertical motion. ~vb. **5.** (intr.) (of a boat) to rise out of the water in the manner of a hydroplane.

hydroponics (ˌhaɪdrəʊ'pɒnɪks) n. (functioning as sing.) a method of cultivating plants by growing them in gravel, etc., through which water containing dissolved inorganic nutrient salts is pumped. [C20: from HYDRO- + (geo)ponics science of agriculture] —**hydro'ponic** adj. —**hydro'ponically** adv.

hydropower ('haɪdrəʊˌpaʊə) n. hydroelectric power.

hydroquinone (ˌhaɪdrəʊkwɪ'nəʊn) or **hydroquinol** (ˌhaɪdrəʊ'kwɪnɒl) n. a white crystalline soluble phenol used as a photographic developer.

hydrosphere ('haɪdrəˌsfɪə) n. the watery part of the earth's surface, including oceans, lakes, water vapour in the atmosphere, etc.

hydrostatics (ˌhaɪdrəʊ'stætɪks) n. (functioning as sing.) the branch of science concerned with the mechanical properties and behaviour of fluids that are not in motion. —**hydro'static** adj.

hydrotherapeutics (ˌhaɪdrəʊˌθɛrə'pjuːtɪks) n. (functioning as sing.) the branch of medical science concerned with hydrotherapy.

hydrotherapy (ˌhaɪdrəʊ'θɛrəpɪ) n. Med. the treatment of certain diseases by the external application of water, as for mobilizing stiff joints or strengthening weakened muscles.

hydrothermal (ˌhaɪdrəʊ'θɜːməl) adj. of or relating to the action of water under conditions of high temperature, esp. in forming rocks.

hydrotropism (haɪ'drɒtrəˌpɪzəm) n. the directional growth of plants in response to the stimulus of water.

hydrous ('haɪdrəs) adj. containing water.

hydroxide (haɪ'drɒksaɪd) n. **1.** a base or alkali containing the ion OH^-. **2.** any compound containing an -OH group.

hydroxy (haɪ'drɒksɪ) adj. (of a chemical compound) containing one or more hydroxyl groups. [C19: HYDRO- + OXY(GEN)]

hydroxyl (haɪ'drɒksɪl) n. (modifier) of, consisting of, or containing the monovalent group -OH or the ion OH^-: a hydroxyl group or radical.

hydrozoan (ˌhaɪdrəʊ'zəʊən) n. **1.** any coelenterate of the class Hydrozoa, which includes the hydra and the Portuguese man-of-war. ~adj. **2.** of the Hydrozoa.

hyena or **hyaena** (haɪ'iːnə) n. any of several long-legged carnivorous doglike mammals such as the spotted or laughing hyena, of Africa and S Asia. [C16: from Med. L, from L hyaena, from Gk, from hus hog] —**hy'enic** or **hy'aenic** adj.

Hygeia (haɪ'dʒiːə) n. the Greek goddess of health. —**Hy'geian** adj.

hygiene ('haɪdʒiːn) n. **1.** Also called: **hygienics.** the science concerned with the maintenance of health. **2.** clean or healthy practices or thinking: personal hygiene. [C18: from NL hygiēna, from Gk hugieinē, from hugiēs healthy]

hygienic (haɪ'dʒiːnɪk) adj. promoting health or cleanliness; sanitary. —**hy'gienically** adv.

hygienics (haɪ'dʒiːnɪks) n. (functioning as sing.) another word for **hygiene** (sense 1).

hygienist ('haɪdʒiːnɪst) n. a person skilled in the practice of hygiene.

hygro- or before a vowel **hygr-** combining form. indicating moisture: hygrometer. [from Gk hugros wet]

hygrometer (haɪ'grɒmɪtə) n. any of various instruments for measuring humidity. —**hygrometric** (ˌhaɪgrə'mɛtrɪk) adj.

hygroscope ('haɪgrəˌskəʊp) n. any device that indicates the humidity of the air without necessarily measuring it.

hygroscopic (ˌhaɪgrə'skɒpɪk) adj. (of a substance) tending to absorb water from the air. —**hygro'scopically** adv.

hying ('haɪɪŋ) vb. a present participle of **hie.**

hyla ('haɪlə) n. a tree frog of tropical America. [C19: from NL, from Gk hulē forest]

hylomorphism (ˌhaɪlə'mɔːfɪzəm) n. the philosophical doctrine that identifies matter with the first cause of the universe.

hylozoism (ˌhaɪlə'zəʊɪzəm) n. the philosophical doctrine that life is one of the properties of matter. [C17: from Gk hulē wood, matter + zōē life]

hymen ('haɪmɛn) n. Anat. a fold of mucous membrane that partly covers the entrance to the vagina and is usually ruptured when sexual intercourse takes place for the first time. [C17: from Gk: membrane] —**'hymenal** adj.

Hymen ('haɪmɛn) n. the Greek and Roman god of marriage.

hymeneal (ˌhaɪmɛˈniːəl) *adj.* **1.** *Chiefly poetic.* of or relating to marriage. ~*n.* **2.** a wedding song or poem.

hymenopteran (ˌhaɪmɪˈnɒptərən) *or* **hymenopteron** *n.*, *pl.* **-terans, -tera** (-tərə), *or* **-terons.** any hymenopterous insect.

hymenopterous (ˌhaɪmɪˈnɒptərəs) *adj.* of or belonging to an order of insects, including bees, wasps, and ants, having two pairs of membranous wings. [C19: from Gk *humenopteros* membrane wing; see HYMEN, -PTEROUS]

Hymettus (haɪˈmɛtəs) *n.* a mountain in SE Greece, in Attica east of Athens: famous for its marble and for honey. Height: 1026 m (3386 ft.). Modern Greek name: **Imittós.** —**Hy'mettian** *or* **Hy'mettic** *adj.*

hymn (hɪm) *n.* **1.** a Christian song of praise sung to God or a saint. **2.** a similar song praising other gods, a nation, etc. ~*vb.* **3.** to express (praises, thanks, etc.) by singing hymns. [C13: from L *hymnus*, from Gk *humnos*] —**hymnic** (ˈhɪmnɪk) *adj.*

hymnal (ˈhɪmnəl) *n.* **1.** Also: **hymn book.** a book of hymns. ~*adj.* **2.** of, relating to, or characteristic of hymns.

hymnody (ˈhɪmnədɪ) *n.* **1.** the composition or singing of hymns. **2.** hymns collectively. ~Also called: **hymnology.** [C18: from Med. L *hymnōdia*, from Gk, from *humnōidein*, from HYMN + *aeidein* to sing]

hymnology (hɪmˈnɒlədʒɪ) *n.* **1.** the study of hymn composition. **2.** another word for **hymnody.** —**hym'nologist** *n.*

hyoid (ˈhaɪɔɪd) *adj.* of or relating to the **hyoid bone,** the horseshoe-shaped bone that lies at the base of the tongue. [C19: from NL *hyoides*, from Gk *huoeidēs* having the shape of the letter UPSILON, from *hu* upsilon + -OID]

hyoscine (ˈhaɪəˌsiːn) *n.* another name for **scopolamine.** [C19: from *huosc(yamus)* a medicinal plant + -INE²; see HYOSCYAMINE]

hyoscyamine (ˌhaɪəˈsaɪəˌmiːn) *n.* a poisonous alkaloid occurring in henbane and related plants: used in medicine. [C19: from NL, from Gk *huoskuamos* (from *hus* pig + *kuamos* bean) + AMINE]

hyp. *abbrev. for:* **1.** hypotenuse. **2.** hypothesis. **3.** hypothetical.

hypaethral *or U.S.* **hypethral** (hɪˈpiːθrəl, haɪ-) *adj.* (esp. of a classical temple) having no roof. [C18: from L *hypaethrus* uncovered, from Gk, from HYPO- + *aithros* clear sky]

hypallage (haɪˈpæləˌdʒiː) *n. Rhetoric.* a figure of speech in which the natural relations of two words in a statement are interchanged, as in *the fire spread the wind.* [C16: via LL from Gk *hupallagē,* from HYPO- + *allassein* to exchange]

hype[1] (haɪp) *Sl.* ~*n.* **1.** a hypodermic needle or injection. ~*vb.* **2.** (*intr.*; usually foll. by *up*) to inject oneself with a drug. **3.** (*tr.*) to stimulate artificially or excite. [C20: shortened from HYPODERMIC]

hype[2] (haɪp) *Sl.* ~*n.* **1.** a deception or racket. **2.** an intensive or exaggerated publicity or sales promotion. ~*vb.* **3.** (*tr.*) to market or promote (a product) using exaggerated or intensive publicity. [C20: from ?]

hyped up *adj. Sl.* stimulated or excited by or as if by the effect of a stimulating drug.

hyper (ˈhaɪpə) *adj. Inf.* overactive; overexcited. [C20: prob. independent use of HYPER-]

hyper- *prefix.* **1.** above, over, or in excess: *hypercritical.* **2.** denoting an abnormal excess: *hyperacidity.* **3.** indicating that a chemical compound contains a greater than usual amount of an element: *hyperoxide.* [from Gk *huper* over]

hyperacidity (ˌhaɪpərəˈsɪdɪtɪ) *n.* excess acidity of the gastrointestinal tract, esp. the stomach, producing a burning sensation.

hyperactive (ˌhaɪpərˈæktɪv) *adj.* abnormally active.

hyperaemia *or U.S.* **hyperemia** (ˌhaɪpərˈiːmɪə) *n. Pathol.* an excessive amount of blood in an organ or part.

hyperaesthesia *or U.S.* **hyperesthesia** (ˌhaɪpəriːsˈθiːzɪə) *n. Pathol.* increased sensitivity of any of the sense organs. —**hyperaesthetic** *or U.S.* **hyperesthetic** (ˌhaɪpəriːsˈθɛtɪk) *adj.*

hyperbaton (haɪˈpɜːbəˌtɒn) *n. Rhetoric.* a figure of speech in which the normal order of words is reversed, as in *cheese I love.* [C16: via L from Gk, lit.: an overstepping, from HYPER- + *bainein* to step]

hyperbola (haɪˈpɜːbələ) *n.*, *pl.* **-las** *or* **-le** (-ˌliː). a conic section formed by a plane that cuts a cone at a steeper angle to its base than its side. [C17: from Gk *huperbolē,* lit.: excess, extravagance, from HYPER- + *ballein* to throw]

hyperbole (haɪˈpɜːbəlɪ) *n.* a deliberate exaggeration used for effect: *he embraced her a thousand times.* [C16: from Gk, from HYPER- + *bolē,* from *ballein* to throw] —**hy'perbolism** *n.*

hyperbolic (ˌhaɪpəˈbɒlɪk) *or* **hyperbolical** *adj.* **1.** of a hyperbola. **2.** *Rhetoric.* of a hyperbole. —**ˌhyper'bolically** *adv.*

hyperbolic function *n.* any of a group of functions of an angle expressed as a relationship between the distances of a point on a hyperbola to the origin and to the coordinate axes.

hyperbolize *or* **-lise** (haɪˈpɜːbəˌlaɪz) *vb.* to express (something) by means of hyperbole.

hyperboloid (haɪˈpɜːbəˌlɔɪd) *n.* a geometric surface consisting of one sheet, or of two sheets separated by a finite distance, whose sections parallel to the three coordinate planes are hyperbolas or ellipses.

Hyperborean (ˌhaɪpəˈbɔːrɪən) *n.* **1.** *Greek myth.* one of a people believed to have lived beyond the North Wind in a sunny land. **2.** an inhabitant of the extreme north. ~*adj.* **3.** (*sometimes not cap.*) of or relating to the extreme north. [C16: from L *hyperboreus,* from Gk, from HYPER- + *Boreas* the north wind]

hypercharge (ˈhaɪpəˌtʃɑːdʒ) *n.* a property of baryons that is used to account for the absence of certain strong interaction decays.

hypercritical (ˌhaɪpəˈkrɪtɪkəl) *adj.* excessively or severely critical. —**ˌhyper'critically** *adv.*

hyperfocal distance (ˌhaɪpəˈfəʊkəl) *n.* the distance from a camera lens to the point beyond which all objects appear sharp and clearly defined.

hyperglycaemia *or U.S.* **hyperglycemia** (ˌhaɪpəglaɪˈsiːmɪə) *n. Pathol.* an abnormally large amount of sugar in the blood. [C20: from HYPER- + GLYCO- + -AEMIA] —**ˌhypergly'caemic** *or U.S.* **hypergly'cemic** *adj.*

hypergolic (ˌhaɪpəˈgɒlɪk) *adj.* (of a rocket fuel) able to ignite spontaneously on contact with an oxidizer. [C20: from G *Hypergol* (?from HYP(ER-) + ERG¹ + -OL²) + -IC]

hypericum (haɪˈpɛrɪkəm) *n.* any herbaceous plant or shrub of the temperate genus *Hypericum.* See **rose of Sharon, Saint John's wort.** [C16: via L from Gk *hupereikon,* from HYPER- + *ereikē* heath]

hyperinflation (ˌhaɪpəmˈfleɪʃən) *n.* an extremely high level of inflation (with price rises of 50 percent per month), often involving social disorder.

Hyperion (haɪˈpɪərɪən) *n. Greek myth.* a Titan, son of Uranus and Gaea, father of Helios (sun), Selene (moon), and Eos (dawn).

hypermarket (ˈhaɪpəˌmɑːkɪt) *n. Brit.* a huge self-service store, usually built on the outskirts of a town. [C20: translation of F *hypermarché*]

hypermetropia (ˌhaɪpəmɪˈtrəʊpɪə) *or* **hypermetropy** (ˌhaɪpəˈmɛtrəpɪ) *n. Pathol.* a variant of **hyperopia.** [C19: from Gk *hupermetros* beyond measure (from HYPER- + *metron* measure) + -OPIA]

hyperon (ˈhaɪpəˌrɒn) *n. Physics.* any baryon that is not a nucleon. [C20: from HYPER- + -ON]

hyperopia (ˌhaɪpəˈrəʊpɪə) *n.* inability to see near objects clearly because the images received by the eye are focused behind the retina; long-sightedness. —**hyperopic** (ˌhaɪpəˈrɒpɪk) *adj.*

hyperphysical (ˌhaɪpəˈfɪzɪkəl) *adj.* beyond the physical; supernatural or immaterial.

hyperpyrexia (ˌhaɪpəpaɪˈrɛksɪə) *n. Pathol.* an extremely high fever, with a temperature of 41°C (106°F) or above.

hypersensitive (ˌhaɪpəˈsɛnsɪtɪv) *adj.* **1.** having unduly vulnerable feelings. **2.** abnormally sensitive to an allergen, a drug, or other agent. —**ˌhyper'sensitiveness** *or* **ˌhyperˌsensi'tivity** *n.*

ˌhyperac'tivity *n.*
ˌhypera'cute *adj.*
ˌhypercon'formity *n.*
ˌhyper'conscious *adj.*
ˌhypercon'servative *adj.*
ˌhypercor'rect *adj.*
ˌhypere'motional *adj.*
ˌhyper,ener'getic *adj.*
ˌhyperen'thusiasm *n.*
ˌhyper'functional *adj.*
ˌhyper,intel'lectual *adj.*
ˌhyperro'mantic *adj.*
ˌhyper,senti'mental *adj.*

hypersonic (ˌhaɪpəˈsɒnɪk) *adj.* concerned with or having a velocity of at least five times that of sound in the same medium under the same conditions. —ˌhyperˈsonics *n.*

hyperspace (ˌhaɪpəˈspeɪs) *n.* **1.** *Maths.* space having more than three dimensions. **2.** (in science fiction) a theoretical dimension within which conventional space-time relationship does not apply.

hypersthene (ˈhaɪpəˌsθiːn) *n.* a green, brown, or black pyroxene mineral. [C19: from HYPER- + Gk *sthenos* strength]

hypertension (ˌhaɪpəˈtɛnʃən) *n.* *Pathol.* abnormally high blood pressure. —**hypertensive** (ˌhaɪpəˈtɛnsɪv) *adj.*, *n.*

hyperthermia (ˌhaɪpəˈθɜːmɪə) *or* **hyperthermy** (ˌhaɪpəˈθɜːmɪ) *n.* *Pathol.* a variant of **hyperpyrexia.** —ˌhyperˈthermal *adj.*

hyperthyroidism (ˌhaɪpəˈθaɪrɔɪˌdɪzəm) *n.* overproduction of thyroid hormone by the thyroid gland, causing nervousness, insomnia, and sensitivity to heat. —ˌhyperˈthyroid *adj.*, *n.*

hypertonic (ˌhaɪpəˈtɒnɪk) *adj.* **1.** (esp. of muscles) being in a state of abnormally high tension. **2.** (of a solution) having a higher osmotic pressure than that of a specified solution.

hypertrophy (haɪˈpɜːtrəfɪ) *n.*, *pl.* **-phies. 1.** enlargement of an organ or part resulting from an increase in the size of the cells. ~*vb.* **-phying, -phied. 2.** to undergo or cause to undergo this condition.

hyperventilation (ˌhaɪpəˌvɛntɪˈleɪʃən) *n.* an increase in the rate of breathing, sometimes resulting in cramp and dizziness.

hypha (ˈhaɪfə) *n.*, *pl.* **-phae** (-fiː). any of the filaments that constitute the body (mycelium) of a fungus. [C19: from NL, from Gk *huphē* web] —ˈhyphal *adj.*

hyphen (ˈhaɪfⁿn) *n.* **1.** the punctuation mark (-), used to separate parts of compound words, to link the words of a phrase, and between syllables of a word split between two consecutive lines. ~*vb.* **2.** (*tr.*) another word for **hyphenate.** [C17: from LL (meaning: the combining of two words), from Gk *huphen* (adv.) together, from HYPO- + *heis* one]

hyphenate (ˈhaɪfⁿˌneɪt) *vb.* (*tr.*) to separate (words, etc.) with a hyphen. —ˌhyphenˈation *n.*

hyphenated (ˈhaɪfⁿˌneɪtɪd) *adj.* **1.** containing or linked with a hyphen. **2.** *Chiefly U.S.* having a nationality denoted by a hyphenated word: *Irish-American.*

hypno- *or before a vowel* **hypn-** *combining form.* **1.** indicating sleep: *hypnopaedia.* **2.** relating to hypnosis: *hypnotherapy.* [from Gk *hupnos* sleep]

hypnoid (ˈhɪpˌnɔɪd) *or* **hypnoidal** (hɪpˈnɔɪdⁿl) *adj. Psychol.* of or relating to a state resembling sleep or hypnosis.

hypnology (hɪpˈnɒlədʒɪ) *n. Psychol.* the study of sleep and hypnosis. —ˈhypˈnologist *n.*

hypnopaedia (ˌhɪpnəʊˈpiːdɪə) *n.* the learning of lessons heard during sleep. [C20: from HYPNO- + Gk *paideia* education]

hypnopompic (ˌhɪpnəʊˈpɒmpɪk) *adj. Psychol.* relating to the state existing between sleep and full waking, characterized by the persistence of dreamlike imagery. [C20: from HYPNO- + Gk *pompē* a sending forth, escort + -IC]

Hypnos (ˈhɪpnɒs) *n. Greek myth.* the god of sleep. Roman counterpart: **Somnus.** Compare **Morpheus.** [Gk: sleep]

hypnosis (hɪpˈnəʊsɪs) *n.*, *pl.* **-ses** (-siːz). an artificially induced state of relaxation and concentration in which deeper parts of the mind become more accessible.

hypnotherapy (ˌhɪpnəʊˈθɛrəpɪ) *n.* the use of hypnosis in the treatment of emotional and psychogenic problems.

hypnotic (hɪpˈnɒtɪk) *adj.* **1.** of or producing hypnosis or sleep. **2.** (of a person) susceptible to hypnotism. ~*n.* **3.** a drug that induces sleep. **4.** a person susceptible to hypnosis. [C17: from LL *hypnōticus*, from Gk, from *hupnoun* to put to sleep, from *hupnos* sleep] —hypˈnotically *adv.*

hypnotism (ˈhɪpnəˌtɪzəm) *n.* **1.** the scientific study and practice of hypnosis. **2.** the process of inducing hypnosis. —ˈhypnotist *n.*

hypnotize *or* **-tise** (ˈhɪpnəˌtaɪz) *vb.* (*tr.*) **1.** to induce hypnosis in (a person). **2.** to charm or beguile; fascinate. —ˌhypnotiˈzation *or* -tiˈsation *n.* —ˈhypnoˌtizer *or* -ˌtiser *n.*

hypo¹ (ˈhaɪpəʊ) *n.* short for **hyposulphite.** [C19]

hypo² (ˈhaɪpəʊ) *n.*, *pl.* **-pos.** *Inf.* short for **hypodermic syringe.**

hypo- *or before a vowel* **hyp-** *prefix.* **1.** beneath or below: *hypodermic.* **2.** lower: *hypogastrium.* **3.** less than; denoting a deficiency: *hypothyroid.* **4.** indicating that a chemical compound contains an element in a lower oxidation state than usual: *hypochlorous acid.* [from Gk, from *hupo* under]

hypoallergenic (ˌhaɪpəʊˌæləˈdʒɛnɪk) *adj.* (of cosmetics) not likely to cause an allergic reaction.

hypoblast (ˈhaɪpəˌblæst) *n. Embryol.* the inner layer of an embryo at an early stage of development that becomes the endoderm.

hypocaust (ˈhaɪpəˌkɔːst) *n.* an ancient Roman heating system in which hot air circulated under the floor and between double walls. [C17: from L *hypocaustum*, from Gk, from *hupokaiein* to light a fire beneath, from HYPO- + *kaiein* to burn]

hypocentre (ˈhaɪpəʊˌsɛntə) *n.* the point immediately below the centre of explosion of a nuclear bomb. Also called: **ground zero.**

hypochlorite (ˌhaɪpəˈklɔːraɪt) *n.* any salt or ester of hypochlorous acid.

hypochlorous acid (ˌhaɪpəˈklɔːrəs) *n.* an unstable acid known only in solution and in the form of its salts: a strong oxidizing and bleaching agent. Formula: HOCl.

hypochondria (ˌhaɪpəˈkɒndrɪə) *n.* chronic abnormal anxiety concerning the state of one's health. Also called: **hypochondriasis** (ˌhaɪpəkɒnˈdraɪəsɪs). [C18: from LL: abdomen, supposedly the seat of melancholy, from Gk, from *hupokhondrios*, from HYPO- + *khondros* cartilage]

hypochondriac (ˌhaɪpəˈkɒndrɪˌæk) *n.* **1.** a person suffering from hypochondria. ~*adj. also* **hypochondriacal** (ˌhaɪpəkɒnˈdraɪəkⁿl). **2.** relating to or suffering from hypochondria.

hypocorism (haɪˈpɒkəˌrɪzəm) *n.* a pet name, esp. one using a diminutive affix: *"Sally" is a hypocorism for "Sarah".* [C19: from Gk *hupo-korisma*, from *hupokorizesthai* to use pet names, from *hypo-* beneath + *korizesthai*, from *korē* girl, *koros* boy] —**hypocoristic** (ˌhaɪpəkɔːˈrɪstɪk) *adj.*

hypocotyl (ˌhaɪpəˈkɒtɪl) *n.* the part of an embryo plant between the cotyledons and the radicle. [C19: from HYPO- + COTYL(EDON)]

hypocrisy (hɪˈpɒkrəsɪ) *n.*, *pl.* **-sies. 1.** the practice of professing standards, beliefs, etc., contrary to one's real character or actual behaviour. **2.** an act or instance of this.

hypocrite (ˈhɪpəkrɪt) *n.* a person who pretends to be what he is not. [C13: from OF *ipocrite*, via LL from Gk *hupokritēs* one who plays a part, from *hupokrinein* to feign, from *krinein* to judge] —ˌhypoˈcritical *adj.* —ˌhypoˈcritically *adv.*

hypocycloid (ˌhaɪpəˈsaɪklɔɪd) *n.* a curve described by a point on the circumference of a circle as the circle rolls around the inside of a fixed coplanar circle. —ˌhypocyˈcloidal *adj.*

hypodermic (ˌhaɪpəˈdɜːmɪk) *adj.* **1.** of or relating to the region of the skin beneath the epidermis. **2.** injected beneath the skin. ~*n.* **3.** a hypodermic syringe or needle. **4.** a hypodermic injection. —ˌhypoˈdermically *adv.*

hypodermic syringe *n. Med.* a type of syringe consisting of a hollow cylinder, usually of glass or plastic, a tightly fitting piston, and a hollow needle (**hypodermic needle**), used for withdrawing blood samples, etc.

hypodermis (ˌhaɪpəˈdɜːmɪs) *or* **hypoderm** *n.* **1.** *Bot.* a layer of thick-walled supportive or water-storing cells beneath the epidermis in some plants. **2.** *Zool.* the epidermis of arthropods, annelids, etc. [C19: from HYPO- + EPIDERMIS]

hypogastrium (ˌhaɪpəˈgæstrɪəm) *n.*, *pl.* **-tria** (-trɪə). *Anat.* the lower front central region of the abdomen. [C17: from NL, from Gk *hupogastrion*, from HYPO- + *gastrion*, dim. of *gastēr* stomach]

hypogeal (ˌhaɪpəˈdʒiːəl) *or* **hypogeous** *adj.* occurring or living below the surface of the ground. [C19: from L *hypogēus*, from Gk, from HYPO- + *gē* earth]

hypogene (ˈhaɪpəˌdʒiːn) *adj.* formed or originating beneath the surface of the earth.

ˌhyperˈsoˈphistiˌcated *adj.*   ˌhyperˈtechnical *adj.*   ˌhyperˈtoxic *adj.*

hypogeum (ˌhaɪpəˈdʒiːəm) *n., pl.* **-gea** (-ˈdʒiːə). an underground vault, esp. one used for burials. [C18: from L, from Gk *hupogeion;* see HYPOGEAL]

hypoid gear (ˈhaɪpɔɪd) *n.* a gear having a tooth form generated by a hypocycloidal curve. [C20: *hypoid*, shortened from HYPOCYCLOID]

hyponasty (ˈhaɪpəˌnæstɪ) *n.* increased growth of the lower surface of a plant part, resulting in an upward bending of the part. —**hypoˈnastic** *adj.*

hypophosphate (ˌhaɪpəˈfɒsfeɪt) *n.* any salt or ester of hypophosphoric acid.

hypophosphite (ˌhaɪpəˈfɒsfaɪt) *n.* any salt of hypophosphorous acid.

hypophosphoric acid (ˌhaɪpəfɒsˈfɒrɪk) *n.* a tetrabasic acid produced by the slow oxidation of phosphorus in moist air. Formula: $H_4P_2O_6$.

hypophosphorous acid (ˌhaɪpəˈfɒsfərəs) *n.* a monobasic acid and a reducing agent. Formula: H_3PO_2.

hypophysis (haɪˈpɒfɪsɪs) *n., pl.* **-ses** (-ˌsiːz). the technical name for **pituitary gland.** [C18: from Gk: outgrowth, from HYPO- + *phuein* to grow] —**hypophyseal** *or* **hypophysial** (ˌhaɪpəˈfɪzɪəl, haɪˌpɒfɪˈsɪəl) *adj.*

hypostasis (haɪˈpɒstəsɪs) *n., pl.* **-ses** (-ˌsiːz). **1.** *Metaphysics.* the essential nature of a substance. **2.** *Christianity.* **a.** any of the three persons of the Godhead. **b.** the one person of Christ in which the divine and human natures are united. **3.** the accumulation of blood in an organ or part as the result of poor circulation. [C16: from LL: substance, from Gk *hupostasis* foundation, from *huphistasthai*, from HYPO- + *histanai* to cause to stand] —**hypostatic** (ˌhaɪpəˈstætɪk) *or* ˌ**hypoˈstatical** *adj.*

hypostyle (ˈhaɪpəʊˌstaɪl) *adj.* **1.** ⸚having a roof supported by columns. ~*n.* **2.** a building constructed in this way.

hyposulphite (ˌhaɪpəˈsʌlfaɪt) *n.* another name for **sodium thiosulphate,** esp. when used as a photographic fixer. Often shortened to **hypo.**

hyposulphurous acid (ˌhaɪpəˈsʌlfərəs) *n.* an unstable acid known only in solution: a powerful reducing agent. Formula H_2SO_4.

hypotension (ˌhaɪpəʊˈtɛnʃən) *n. Pathol.* abnormally low blood pressure. —**hypotensive** (ˌhaɪpəʊˈtɛnsɪv) *adj.*

hypotenuse (haɪˈpɒtɪˌnjuːz) *n.* the side in a right-angled triangle that is opposite the right angle. Abbrev.: **hyp.** [C16: from L *hypotēnūsa*, from Gk *hupoteinousa grammē* subtending line, from HYPO- + *teinein* to stretch]

hypothalamus (ˌhaɪpəˈθæləməs) *n., pl.* **-mi** (-ˌmaɪ). a neural control centre at the base of the brain, concerned with hunger, thirst, satiety, and other autonomic functions. —**hypothalamic** (ˌhaɪpəθəˈlæmɪk) *adj.*

hypothec (haɪˈpɒθɪk) *n. Roman & Scots. Law.* a charge on property in favour of a creditor. [C16: from LL *hypotheca*, from Gk *hupothēkē* pledge, from *hupotithenai* to deposit as a security, from HYPO- + *tithenai* to place]

hypothecate (haɪˈpɒθɪˌkeɪt) *vb.* (*tr.*) *Law.* to pledge (personal property or a ship) as security for a debt without transferring possession or title. —**hyˌpotheˈcation** *n.* —**hyˈpotheˌcator** *n.*

hypothermia (ˌhaɪpəʊˈθɜːmɪə) *n.* **1.** *Pathol.* an abnormally low body temperature, as induced in the elderly by exposure to cold weather. **2.** *Med.* the intentional reduction of normal body temperature to reduce the patient's metabolic rate.

hypothesis (haɪˈpɒθɪsɪs) *n., pl.* **-ses** (-ˌsiːz). **1.** a suggested explanation for a group of facts or phenomena, either accepted as a basis for further verification (**working hypothesis**) or accepted as likely to be true. **2.** an assumption used in an argument; supposition. [C16: from Gk, from *hupo-tithenai* to propose, lit.: put under; see HYPO-, THESIS] —**hyˈpothesist** *n.*

hypothesize *or* **-ise** (haɪˈpɒθɪˌsaɪz) *vb.* to form or assume as a hypothesis. —**hyˈpotheˌsizer** *or* **-iser** *n.*

hypothetical (ˌhaɪpəˈθɛtɪkəl) *or* **hypothetic** *adj.* **1.** having the nature of a hypothesis. **2.** assumed or thought to exist. **3.** *Logic.* another word for **conditional** (sense 3). —ˌ**hypoˈthetically** *adv.*

hypothyroidism (ˌhaɪpəʊˈθaɪrɔɪˌdɪzəm) *n. Pathol.* **1.** insufficient production of thyroid hormones by the thyroid gland. **2.** any disorder, such as cretinism or myxoedema, resulting from this. —ˌ**hypoˈthyroid** *n., adj.*

hypotonic (ˌhaɪpəˈtɒnɪk) *adj.* **1.** *Pathol.* (of muscles) lacking normal tone or tension. **2.** (of a solution) having a lower osmotic pressure than that of a specified solution.

hypoxia (haɪˈpɒksɪə) *n.* deficiency in the amount of oxygen delivered to the body tissues. [C20: from HYPO- + OXY-[2] + -IA] —**hypoxic** (haɪˈpɒksɪk) *adj.*

Hypsilantis *or* **Hypsilantes** (*Greek* ˌɪpsiˈlandis) *n.* variants of **Ypsilanti.**

hypso- *or before a vowel* **hyps-** *combining form.* indicating height: *hypsometry.* [from Gk *hupsos*]

hypsography (hɪpˈsɒɡrəfɪ) *n.* the scientific study and mapping of the earth's topography above sea level.

hypsometer (hɪpˈsɒmɪtə) *n.* **1.** an instrument for measuring altitudes by determining the boiling point of water at a given altitude. **2.** any instrument used to calculate the heights of trees by triangulation.

hypsometry (hɪpˈsɒmɪtrɪ) *n.* (in mapping) the establishment of height above sea level.

hyrax (ˈhaɪræks) *n., pl.* **hyraxes** *or* **hyraces** (ˈhaɪrəˌsiːz). any of various agile herbivorous mammals of Africa and SW Asia. They resemble rodents but have feet with hooflike toes. Also called: **dassie.** [C19: from NL, from Gk *hurax* shrewmouse]

Hyrcania (hɜːˈkeɪnɪə) *n.* an ancient district of Asia, southeast of the Caspian Sea. —**Hyrˈcanian** *adj.*

hyssop (ˈhɪsəp) *n.* **1.** a widely cultivated Asian plant with spikes of small blue flowers and aromatic leaves, used as a condiment and in perfumery and folk medicine. **2.** a Biblical plant, used for sprinkling in the ritual practices of the Hebrews. [OE *ysope*, from L *hyssōpus*, from Gk *hussōpos*, of Semitic origin]

hysterectomy (ˌhɪstəˈrɛktəmɪ) *n., pl.* **-mies.** surgical removal of the uterus.

hysteresis (ˌhɪstəˈriːsɪs) *n. Physics.* the lag in a variable property of a system with respect to the effect producing it as this effect varies, esp. the phenomenon in which the magnetic induction of a ferromagnetic material lags behind the changing external field. [from Gk *husterēsis*, from *husteros* coming after] —**hysteretic** (ˌhɪstəˈrɛtɪk) *adj.*

hysteresis loop *n.* a closed curve showing the variation of the magnetic induction of a ferromagnetic material with the external magnetic field producing it, when this field is changed through a complete cycle.

hysteria (hɪˈstɪərɪə) *n.* **1.** a mental disorder characterized by emotional outbursts and, often, symptoms such as paralysis. **2.** any frenzied emotional state, esp. of laughter or crying. [C20: from NL, from L *hystericus* HYSTERIC]

hysteric (hɪˈstɛrɪk) *n.* **1.** a hysterical person. ~*adj.* **2.** hysterical. [C17: from L *hystericus*, lit.: of the womb, from Gk, from *hustera* womb; from the belief that hysteria in women originated in disorders of the womb]

hysterical (hɪˈstɛrɪkəl) *adj.* **1.** suggesting hysteria: *hysterical cries.* **2.** suffering from hysteria. **3.** *Inf.* wildly funny. —**hysˈterically** *adv.*

hysterics (hɪˈstɛrɪks) *n.* (*functioning as pl. or sing.*) **1.** an attack of hysteria. **2.** *Inf.* wild uncontrollable bursts of laughter.

hystero- *or before a vowel* **hyster-** *combining form.* the uterus: *hysterectomy.* [from Gk *hustera* womb]

hysteron proteron (ˈhɪstəˌrɒn ˈprɒtəˌrɒn) *n.* **1.** *Logic.* a fallacious argument in which the proposition to be proved is assumed as a premise. **2.** *Rhetoric.* a figure of speech in which the normal order of two sentences, clauses, etc., is reversed: *bred and born* (for *born and bred*). [C16: from LL, from Gk *husteron proteron* the latter (placed as) former]

hystricomorph (hɪˈstraɪkəʊˌmɔːf) *n.* **1.** any rodent of the suborder *Hystricomorpha*, which includes porcupines, cavies, agoutis, and chinchillas. ~*adj.* also: **hystricomorphic** (hɪˌstraɪkəʊˈmɔːfɪk). **2.** of the *Hystricomorpha*. [C19: from L *hystrix* porcupine, from Gk *hustrix*]

Hz *symbol for* hertz.

I

i or **I** (aɪ) n., pl. **i's**, **I's**, or **Is**. 1. the ninth letter and third vowel of the English alphabet. 2. any of several speech sounds represented by this letter. 3. a. something shaped like an I. b. (in combination): an I-beam.

i symbol for the imaginary number √−1.

I¹ (aɪ) pron. (subjective) refers to the speaker or writer. [C12: from OE ic; cf. OSaxon ik, OHG ih, Sansk. ahám]

I² symbol for: 1. Chem. iodine. 2. Physics. current. 3. Physics. isospin. ~ 4. the Roman numeral for one. See **Roman numerals.**

I. abbrev. for: 1. Independence. 2. Independent. 3. Institute. 4. International. 5. Island; Isle.

-ia suffix forming nouns. 1. in place names: Columbia. 2. in names of diseases: pneumonia. 3. in words denoting condition or quality: utopia. 4. in names of botanical genera and zoological classes: Reptilia. 5. in collective nouns borrowed from Latin: regalia. [(for senses 1–4) NL, from L & Gk, suffix of fem. nouns; (for sense 5) from L, neuter pl. suffix]

IAEA abbrev. for International Atomic Energy Agency.

-ial suffix forming adjectives. of or relating to: managerial. [from L -iālis, adj. suffix; cf. -AL¹]

iamb ('aɪæm, 'aɪæmb) or **iambus** (aɪ'æmbəs) n., pl. **iambs, iambi** (aɪ'æmbaɪ), or **iambuses**. Prosody. 1. a metrical foot of two syllables, a short one followed by a long one. 2. a line of verse of such feet. [C19 iamb, from C16 iambus, from L, from Gk iambos]

iambic (aɪ'æmbɪk) Prosody. ~adj. 1. of, relating to, or using an iamb. 2. (in Greek literature) denoting a satirical verse written in iambs. ~n. 3. a metrical foot, line, or stanza consisting of iambs. 4. an ancient Greek satirical verse written in iambs.

-ian suffix. a variant of **-an**: Etonian. [from L -iānus]

-iana suffix forming nouns. a variant of **-ana**.

Iaşi (Romanian 'iaʃj) n. a city in NE Romania: capital of Moldavia (1565–1859); university (1860). Pop.: 314 156 (1985 est.). German name: **Jassy.**

-iasis or **-asis** n. combining form. (in medicine) indicating a diseased condition: psoriasis. Cf. **-osis** (sense 2). [from NL, from Gk, suffix of action]

IATA (aɪ'ɑːtə, iː'ɑːtə) n. acronym for International Air Transport Association.

-iatrics n. combining form. indicating medical care or treatment: paediatrics. [C19: from Gk, from iasthai to heal]

iatrogenic (aɪ,ætrəʊ'dʒɛnɪk) adj. Med. (of an illness) induced in a patient as the result of a physician's action. ──**iatrogenicity** (aɪ,ætrəʊdʒɪ'nɪsɪtɪ) n.

-iatry n. combining form. indicating healing or medical treatment: psychiatry. Cf. **-iatrics.** [from NL -iatria, from Gk iatreia the healing art, from iatros healer, physician] ──**iatric** adj. combining form.

IBA (in Britain) abbrev. for Independent Broadcasting Authority.

Ibadan (ɪ'bædən) n. a city in SW Nigeria, capital of Oyo state: university (1948). Pop.: 1 060 000 (1983 est.).

Ibagué (Spanish iβa'ɣe) n. a city in W central Colombia. Pop.: 306 078 (1985).

Ibáñez (Spanish i'βaɲɛθ) n. See (Vicente) **Blasco Ibáñez.**

Ibarruri (Spanish i'βarruri) n. **Dolores** (do'lores). real name of (La) **Pasionaria.**

Iberia (aɪ'bɪərɪə) n. 1. the Iberian Peninsula. 2. an ancient region south of the Caucasus corresponding approximately to the present-day Georgian SSR.

Iberian (aɪ'bɪərɪən) n. 1. a member of a group of ancient Caucasoid peoples who inhabited the Iberian Peninsula, in classical times. 2. a native or inhabitant of the Iberian Peninsula; a Spaniard or Portuguese. 3. a native or inhabitant of ancient Iberia. ~adj. 4. relating to the pre-Roman peoples of the Iberian Peninsula or of Caucasian Iberia. 5. of or relating to the Iberian Peninsula, its inhabitants, or any of their languages.

Iberian Peninsula n. a peninsula of SW Europe, occupied by Spain and Portugal.

iberis (aɪ'bɪərɪs) n. any of various Mediterranean plants with white, lilac, or purple flowers. Also called: **candytuft.** [from Gk ibēris pepperwort]

Ibert (French ibɛr) n. **Jacques** (**François Antoine**) (ʒak). 1890–1962, French composer; his works include the humorous orchestral Divertissement (1930).

ibex ('aɪbɛks) n., pl. **ibexes, ibices** ('ɪbɪ,siːz, 'aɪ-), or **ibex.** any of three species of wild goat of mountainous regions of Europe, Asia, and North Africa, having large backward-curving horns. [C17: from L: chamois]

ibid. or **ib.** (referring to a book, etc., previously cited) abbrev. for ibidem. [L: in the same place]

ibis ('aɪbɪs) n., pl. **ibises** or **ibis.** any of various wading birds such as the sacred ibis, that occur in warm regions and have a long thin down-curved bill. [C14: via L from Gk, from Egyptian hby]

Ibiza or **Iviza** (Spanish i'βiθa) n. 1. a Spanish island in the W Mediterranean, one of the Balearic Islands: hilly, with a rugged coast; tourism. Pop.: 45 000 (1986). Area: 541 sq. km (209 sq. miles). 2. the capital of Ibiza, a port on the south of the island. Pop.: 15 642 (1970).

-ible suffix forming adjectives. a variant of **-able.** ──**ibly** suffix forming adverbs. ──**ibility** suffix forming nouns.

Ibo or **Igbo** ('iːbəʊ) n. 1. (pl. **-bos** or **-bo**) a member of a Negroid people of W Africa, living in S Nigeria. 2. their language, belonging to the Niger-Congo family.

Ibrahim Pasha (,ɪbrə'hiːm 'pɑːʃə) n. 1789–1848, Albanian general; son of Mehemet Ali, whom he succeeded as viceroy of Egypt (1848).

IBRD abbrev. for International Bank for Reconstruction and Development (the World Bank).

Ibsen ('ɪbsən) n. **Henrik** ('hɛnrɪk). 1828–1906, Norwegian dramatist and poet. After his early verse plays Brand (1866) and Peer Gynt (1867), he began the series of social dramas in prose, including A Doll's House (1879), Ghosts (1881), and The Wild Duck (1886), which have had a profound influence on modern drama. His later plays, such as Hedda Gabler (1890) and The Master Builder (1892), are more symbolic.

ibuprofen (,aɪbju:'prəʊfən) n. a drug that relieves pain and reduces inflammation: used to treat arthritis and muscular strains.

i/c abbrev. for: 1. in charge (of). 2. internal combustion.

-ic suffix forming adjectives. 1. of, relating to, or resembling: periodic. See also **-ical.** 2. (in chemistry) indicating that an element is chemically combined in the higher of two possible valence states: ferric. Cf. **-ous** (sense 2). [from L -icus or Gk -ikos; -ic also occurs in nouns that represent a substantive use of adjectives (magic) and in nouns borrowed directly from L or Gk (critic, music)]

Içá ('iːsɑː; Portuguese i'sa) n. the Brazilian part of the **Putumayo River.**

ICA abbrev. for: 1. (in Britain) Institute of Contemporary Arts. 2. Institute of Chartered Accountants.

-ical suffix forming adjectives. a variant of **-ic,** but having a less literal application than corresponding adjectives ending in -ic: economical. [from L -icālis] ──**-ically** suffix forming adverbs.

ICAO abbrev. for International Civil Aviation Organization.

Icaria (aɪ'kɛərɪə, ɪ-) n. a Greek island in the Aegean Sea, in the Southern Sporades group. Area: 256 sq. km (99 sq. miles). Modern Greek name: **Ikaría.** Also called: **Nikaria.**

Icarian Sea n. the part of the Aegean Sea between the islands of Patmos and Leros and the coast of Asia Minor, where, according to legend, Icarus fell into the sea.

Icarus ('ɪkərəs, 'aɪ-) n. Greek myth. the son of Daedalus, with whom he escaped from Crete, flying with wings made of wax and feathers. Heedless of his father's warning he flew too near the sun, causing the wax to melt, and fell into the Aegean and drowned.

ICBM abbrev. for intercontinental ballistic missile.

ice (aɪs) n. 1. water in the solid state, formed by freezing liquid water. Related adj.: **glacial.** 2. a portion of ice cream. 3. Sl. a diamond or diamonds. 4. **break the ice. a.** to relieve shyness, etc., esp. between strangers. **b.** to be the first of a group to do something. **5. on ice.** in abeyance; pending. **6. on thin ice.** unsafe; vulnerable. ~*vb.* **7.** (often foll. by *up, over,* etc.) to form ice; freeze. **8.** (*tr.*) to mix with ice or chill (a drink, etc.). **9.** (*tr.*) to cover (a cake, etc.) with icing. [OE *īs*] —**iced** *adj.*

ICE (in Britain) *abbrev. for* Institution of Civil Engineers.

Ice. *abbrev. for* Iceland(ic).

ice age *n.* another name for **glacial period.**

ice axe *n.* a light axe used by mountaineers for cutting footholds in ice.

ice bag *n.* a waterproof bag used as an ice pack.

iceberg ('aɪsbɜːg) *n.* **1.** a large mass of ice floating in the sea. **2. tip of the iceberg.** the small visible part of something, esp. a problem, that is much larger. **3.** *Sl., chiefly U.S.* a person considered to have a cold or reserved manner. **4.** *Austral. inf.* a person who swims or surfs in winter. [C18: prob. part translation of MDu. *ijsberg* ice mountain; cf. Norwegian *isberg*]

iceberg lettuce *n.* a type of lettuce with very crisp pale leaves tightly enfolded.

iceblink ('aɪs,blɪŋk) *n.* a reflected glare in the sky over an ice field. Also called: **blink.**

icebound ('aɪs,baʊnd) *adj.* covered or made immobile by ice; frozen in: *an icebound ship.*

icebox ('aɪs,bɒks) *n.* **1.** a compartment in a refrigerator for storing or making ice. **2.** an insulated cabinet packed with ice for storing food. **3.** a U.S. and Canad. name for **refrigerator.**

icebreaker ('aɪs,breɪkə) *n.* **1.** Also called: **iceboat.** a vessel with a reinforced bow for breaking up the ice in bodies of water. **2.** a device for breaking ice into smaller pieces. **3.** something intended to relieve shyness between strangers.

ice bucket *n.* a bucket-shaped container in which ice cubes are kept to be used for serving with drinks or into which a wine bottle is plunged to keep it cool at table.

icecap ('aɪs,kæp) *n.* a thick mass of glacial ice that permanently covers an area, such as the polar regions or the peak of a mountain.

ice cream *n.* a sweetened frozen liquid, made from cream, milk, or a custard base, flavoured in various ways.

ice dance *n.* any of a number of dances, mostly based on ballroom dancing, performed by a couple skating on ice. —**ice dancer** *n.* —**ice dancing** *n.*

icefall ('aɪs,fɔːl) *n.* a steep part of a glacier that resembles a frozen waterfall.

ice field *n.* **1.** a large ice floe. **2.** a large mass of ice permanently covering an extensive area of land.

ice floe *n.* a sheet of ice, of variable size, floating in the sea. See also **ice field** (sense 1).

ice hockey *n.* a game played on ice by two teams wearing skates, who try to propel a flat puck into their opponents' goal with long sticks.

ice house *n.* a building for storing ice.

Içel (iː'tʃɛl) *n.* another name for **Mersin.**

Iceland ('aɪslənd) *n.* an island republic in the N Atlantic, regarded as part of Europe: settled by Norsemen, who established a legislative assembly in 930; under Danish rule (1380–1918); gained independence in 1918 and became a republic in 1944; contains large areas of glaciers, snowfields, and lava beds with many volcanoes and hot springs (the chief source of domestic heat); inhabited chiefly along the SW coast. The economy is based largely on fishing. Language: Icelandic. Religion: mostly Lutheran. Currency: krona. Capital: Reykjavik. Pop.: 244 009 (1986). Area: 102 828 sq. km (39 702 sq. miles).

Icelander ('aɪslændə, 'aɪsləndə) *n.* a native or inhabitant of Iceland.

Icelandic (aɪs'lændɪk) *adj.* **1.** of or relating to Iceland, its people, or their language. ~*n.* **2.** the official language of Iceland.

Iceland poppy *n.* any of various arctic poppies with white or yellow nodding flowers.

Iceland spar *n.* a pure transparent variety of calcite with double-refracting crystals.

ice lolly *n. Brit. inf.* a water ice or an ice cream on a stick. Also called: **lolly.**

ice pack *n.* **1.** a bag or folded cloth containing ice, applied to a part of the body to reduce swelling, etc. **2.** another name for **pack ice. 3.** a sachet containing a gel that retains its temperature for an extended period of time, used esp. in cool bags.

ice pick *n.* a pointed tool used for breaking ice.

ice plant *n.* a low-growing plant of southern Africa, with fleshy leaves covered with icelike hairs and pink or white rayed flowers.

ice point *n.* the temperature at which a mixture of ice and water are in equilibrium at a pressure of one atmosphere. It is 0° on the Celsius scale and 32° on the Fahrenheit scale. Cf. **steam point.**

ice sheet *n.* a thick layer of ice covering a large area of land for a long time, esp. the layer that covered much of the N hemisphere during the last glacial period.

ice shelf *n.* a thick mass of ice that is permanently attached to the land but projects into and floats on the sea.

ice skate *n.* **1.** a boot having a steel blade fitted to the sole to enable the wearer to glide over ice. **2.** the steel blade on such a boot. ~*vb.* **ice-skate. 3.** (*intr.*) to glide over ice on ice skates. —'**ice,skater** *n.*

ice station *n.* a scientific research station in polar regions, where ice movement, weather, and environmental conditions are monitored.

Ichang *or* **I-ch'ang** ('iː'tʃæŋ) *n.* a variant transliteration of the Chinese name of **Yichang.**

IChemE *abbrev. for* Institution of Chemical Engineers.

I Ching ('iː 'tʃɪŋ) *n.* an ancient Chinese book of divination and a source of Confucian and Taoist philosophy.

ichneumon (ɪk'njuːmən) *n.* a mongoose of Africa and S Europe, having greyish-brown speckled fur. [C16: via L from Gk, lit.: tracker, hunter, from *ikhneuein* to track, from *ikhnos* a footprint; so named from the animal's alleged ability to locate the eggs of crocodiles]

ichneumon fly *or* **wasp** *n.* any hymenopterous insect whose larvae are parasitic in caterpillars and other insect larvae.

ichnography (ɪk'nɒgrəfɪ) *n.* **1.** the art of drawing ground plans. **2.** the ground plan of a building. [C16: from L, from Gk, from *ikhnos* trace, track] —**ichnographic** (,ɪknə'græfɪk) *or* ,**ichno'graphical** *adj.*

ichor ('aɪkɔː) *n.* **1.** *Greek myth.* the fluid said to flow in the veins of the gods. **2.** *Pathol.* a foul-smelling watery discharge from a wound or ulcer. [C17: from Gk *ikhōr,* from ?] —'**ichorous** *adj.*

ichthyo- *or before a vowel* **ichthy-** *combining form.* indicating or relating to fishes: *ichthyology.* [from L, from Gk *ikhthus* fish]

ichthyoid ('ɪkθɪ,ɔɪd) *adj. also* **ichthyoidal. 1.** resembling a fish. ~*n.* **2.** a fishlike vertebrate.

ichthyology (,ɪkθɪ'ɒlədʒɪ) *n.* the study of fishes. —**ichthyologic** (,ɪkθɪə'lɒdʒɪk) *or* ,**ichthyo'logical** *adj.* — ,**ichthy'ologist** *n.*

ichthyosaur ('ɪkθɪə,sɔː) *or* **ichthyosaurus** (,ɪkθɪə'sɔːrəs) *n., pl.* **-saurs, -sauruses,** *or* **-sauri** (-'sɔːraɪ). an extinct marine Mesozoic reptile which had a porpoise-like body with dorsal and tail fins and paddlelike limbs. See also **plesiosaur.**

ichthyosis (,ɪkθɪ'əʊsɪs) *n.* a congenital disease in which the skin is coarse, dry, and scaly. —**ichthyotic** (,ɪkθɪ'ɒtɪk) *adj.*

ICI *abbrev. for* Imperial Chemical Industries.

-ician *suffix forming nouns.* indicating a person skilled or involved in a subject or activity: *physician; beautician.* [from F *-icien;* see -IC, -IAN]

icicle ('aɪsɪk²l) *n.* a hanging spike of ice formed by the freezing of dripping water. [C14: from ICE + *ickel,* from OE *gicel* icicle, rel. to ON *jökull* glacier]

icing ('aɪsɪŋ) *n.* **1.** (esp. U.S. and Canad.): **frosting.** a sugar preparation, variously flavoured and coloured, for coating and decorating cakes, etc. **2. icing on the cake** any unexpected extra or bonus. **3.** the formation of ice, as on a ship, due to the freezing of moisture in the atmosphere.

icing sugar *n. Brit.* a very finely ground sugar used for icings, confections, etc. U.S. term: **confectioners' sugar.**

icon *or* **ikon** ('aɪkɒn) *n.* **1.** a representation of Christ or a saint, esp. one painted in oil on a wooden panel in the traditional Byzantine style and venerated in the Eastern Church. **2.** an image, picture, etc. **3.** a symbol resembling or analogous to the thing it represents. [C16: from L, from Gk *eikōn* image, from *eikenai* to be like]

Iconium (aɪ'kəʊnɪəm) *n.* the ancient name for **Konya.**

icono- *or before a vowel* **icon-** *combining form.* indicating an image or likeness: *iconology.*

iconoclast (aɪ'kɒnə,klæst) *n.* **1.** a person who attacks established or traditional concepts, principles, etc. **2. a.** a destroyer of religious images or objects. **b.** an adherent of a heretical iconoclastic movement within the Greek Orthodox Church from 725 to 842 A.D. [C16: from LL, from LGk *eikonoklastes*, from *eikōn* icon + *klastes* breaker] —**i,cono'clastic** *adj.* —**i'cono,clasm** *n.*

iconography (,aɪkɒ'nɒgrəfɪ) *n.*, *pl.* -**phies.** **1. a.** the symbols used in a work of art. **b.** the conventional significance attached to such symbols. **2.** a collection of pictures of a particular subject. **3.** the representation of the subjects of icons or portraits, esp. on coins. —**,ico'nographer** *n.* —**iconographic** (aɪ,kɒnə'græfɪk) *or* **i,cono'graphical** *adj.*

iconolatry (,aɪkɒ'nɒlətrɪ) *n.* the worship of icons as idols. —**,ico'nolater** *n.* —**,ico'nolatrous** *adj.*

iconology (,aɪkɒ'nɒlədʒɪ) *n.* **1.** the study of icons. **2.** icons collectively. **3.** the symbolic representation of icons. —**iconological** (aɪ,kɒnə'lɒdʒɪkəl) *adj.* —**,ico'nologist** *n.*

iconoscope (aɪ'kɒnə,skəʊp) *n.* a television camera tube in which an electron beam scans a surface, converting an optical image into electrical pulses.

iconostasis (,aɪkəʊ'nɒstəsɪs) *or* **iconostas** (aɪ'kɒnə,stæs) *n.*, *pl.* **iconostases** (,aɪkəʊ'nɒstə,siːz). *Eastern Church.* screen with doors and icons set in tiers, which separates the sanctuary from the nave. [C19: Church L, from LGk *eikonostasion* shrine, lit.: area where images are placed, from *icono-* + *histanai* to stand]

icosahedron (,aɪkəsə'hiːdrən) *n.*, *pl.* -**drons** *or* -**dra** (-drə). a solid figure having 20 faces. [C16: from Gk, from *eikosi* twenty + *-edron* -HEDRON] —**,icosa'hedral** *adj.*

-ics *suffix forming nouns; functioning as sing.* **1.** indicating a science, art, or matters relating to a particular subject: *politics.* **2.** indicating certain activities: *acrobatics.* [pl. of *-ic*, representing L *-ica*, from Gk *-ika*]

Ictinus (ɪk'taɪnəs) *n.* 5th century B.C., Greek architect, who designed the Parthenon with Callicrates.

ictus ('ɪktəs) *n.*, *pl.* -**tuses** *or* -**tus.** **1.** *Prosody.* metrical or rhythmical stress in verse feet, as contrasted with the stress accent on words. **2.** *Med.* a sudden attack or stroke. [C18: from L *icere* to strike] —**'ictal** *adj.*

ICU *abbrev. for* intensive care unit.

icy ('aɪsɪ) *adj.* **icier, iciest. 1.** made of, covered with, or containing ice. **2.** resembling ice. **3.** freezing or very cold. **4.** cold or reserved in manner; aloof. —**'icily** *adv.* —**'iciness** *n.*

id (ɪd) *n. Psychoanal.* the primitive instincts and energies in the unconscious mind that, modified by the ego and the superego, underlie all psychic activity. [C20: NL, from L: it; used to render G *Es*]

ID *abbrev. for* **1.** identification. **2.** Also **i.d.** intradermal(ly).

id. *abbrev. for* idem.

I'd (aɪd) *contraction of* I had *or* I would.

-id[1] *suffix forming nouns and adjectives.* indicating members of a zoological family: *cyprinid.* [from NL *-idae* or *-ida*, from Gk *-idēs* suffix indicating offspring]

-id[2] *suffix forming nouns.* a variant of **-ide.**

Ida ('aɪdə) *n. Mount.* **1.** a mountain in central Crete: the highest on the island; in ancient times associated with the worship of Zeus. Height: 2456 m (8057 ft). Modern Greek name: **Idhi. 2.** a mountain in NW Turkey, southeast of the site of ancient Troy. Height: 1767 m (5797 ft.). Turkish name: **Kaz Daği.**

IDA *abbrev. for* International Development Association.

-idae *suffix forming plural proper nouns.* indicating names of zoological families: *Felidae.* [NL, from L, from Gk *-idai*, suffix indicating offspring]

Idaho ('aɪdə,həʊ) *n.* a state of the northwestern U.S.: consists chiefly of ranges of the Rocky Mountains, with the Snake River basin in the south; important for agriculture (**Idaho potatoes**), livestock, and silver-mining. Capital: Boise. Pop.: 1 003 000 (1986 est.). Area: 216 413 sq. km (83 557 sq. miles). Abbrevs.: **Id., Ida.,** or (with zip code) **ID** —**'Ida,hoan** *adj.*, *n.*

-ide *or* **-id** *suffix forming nouns.* **1.** (*added to the combining form of the nonmetallic or electronegative elements*) indicating a binary compound: *sodium chloride.* **2.** indicating an organic compound derived from another: *acetanilide.* **3.** indicating one of a class of compounds or elements: *peptide.* [from G *-id*, from F *oxide* OXIDE, based on the suffix of *acide* ACID]

idea (aɪ'dɪə) *n.* **1.** any product of mental activity; thought. **2.** the thought of something: *the idea appals me.* **3.** a belief; opinion. **4.** a scheme, intention, plan, etc. **5.** a vague notion; inkling: *he had no idea of the truth.* **6.** a person's conception of something: *her idea of honesty is not the same as mine.* **7.** significance or purpose: *the idea of the game is to discover the murderer.* **8.** *Philosophy.* **a.** an immediate object of thought or perception. **b.** (*sometimes cap.*) (in Plato) the universal essence or archetype of any class of things or concepts. **9. get ideas.** to become ambitious, restless, etc. **10. not one's idea of.** not what one regards as (hard work, a holiday, etc.). **11. that's an idea.** that is worth considering. **12. the very idea!** that is preposterous, unreasonable, etc. [C16: via LL from Gk: model, notion, from *idein* to see]

ideal (aɪ'dɪəl) *n.* **1.** a conception of something that is perfect. **2.** a person or thing considered to represent perfection. **3.** something existing only as an idea. **4.** a pattern or model, esp. of ethical behaviour. ~*adj.* **5.** conforming to an ideal. **6.** of, involving, or existing in the form of an idea. **7.** *Philosophy.* **a.** of or relating to a highly desirable and possible state of affairs. **b.** of or relating to idealism. —**i'deally** *adv.* —**i'dealness** *n.*

ideal element *n.* any element added to a mathematical theory in order to eliminate special cases. The ideal element $i = \sqrt{-1}$ allows all algebraic equations to be solved.

ideal gas *n.* a hypothetical gas which obeys Boyle's law exactly at all temperatures and pressures, and which has internal energy that depends only upon the temperature.

idealism (aɪ'dɪə,lɪzəm) *n.* **1.** belief in or pursuance of ideals. **2.** the tendency to represent things in their ideal forms, rather than as they are. **3.** *Philosophy.* the doctrine that material objects and the external world do not exist in reality, but are creations of the mind. Cf. **materialism.** —**i'dealist** *n.* —**i,deal'istic** *adj.* —**i,deal'istically** *adv.*

idealize *or* **-ise** (aɪ'dɪə,laɪz) *vb.* **1.** to consider or represent (something) as ideal. **2.** (*tr.*) to portray as ideal; glorify. **3.** (*intr.*) to form an ideal or ideals. —**i,deali'zation** *or* **-i'sation** *n.* —**i'deal,izer** *or* **-,iser** *n.*

idée fixe *French.* (ide fiks) *n.*, *pl.* **idées fixes** (ide fiks). a fixed idea; obsession.

idem *Latin.* ('aɪdɛm, 'ɪdɛm) *pron.*, *adj.* the same: used to refer to an article, chapter, etc., previously cited.

identic (aɪ'dɛntɪk) *adj. Diplomacy.* (esp. of opinions expressed by two or more governments) having the same wording or intention regarding another power.

identical (aɪ'dɛntɪkəl) *adj.* **1.** being the same: *we got the identical hotel room as last year.* **2.** exactly alike or equal. **3.** designating either or both of a pair of twins of the same sex who developed from a single fertilized ovum that split into two. Cf. **fraternal** (sense 3). [C17: from Med. L *identicus*, from L *idem* the same] —**i'dentically** *adv.*

identification (aɪ,dɛntɪfɪ'keɪʃən) *n.* **1.** the act of identifying or the state of being identified. **2. a.** something that identifies a person or thing. **b.** (*as modifier*): *an identification card.* **3.** *Psychol.* **a.** the process of recognizing specific objects as the result of remembering. **b.** the process by which one incorporates aspects of another person's personality. **c.** the transferring of a response from one situation to another because the two bear similar features.

identification parade *n.* a group of persons, including one suspected of a crime, assembled for the purpose of discovering whether a witness can identify the suspect.

identify (aɪ'dɛntɪ,faɪ) *vb.* -**fying, -fied.** (*mainly tr.*) **1.** to prove or recognize as being a certain person or thing; determine the identity of. **2.** to consider as the same or equivalent. **3.** (*also intr.*; often foll. by *with*) to consider (oneself) as similar to another. **4.** to determine the taxonomic classification of (a plant or animal). **5.** (*intr.*; usually foll. by *with*) *Psychol.* to engage in identification. —**i'denti,fiable** *adj.* —**i'denti,fier** *n.*

Identikit (aɪ'dɛntɪ,kɪt) *n. Trademark.* **a.** a set of transparencies of typical facial characteristics that can be superimposed on one another to build up a picture of a person sought by the police. **b.** (*as modifier*): *an Identikit picture.*

identity (aɪ'dɛntɪtɪ) *n.*, *pl.* -**ties. 1.** the state of having unique identifying characteristics. **2.** the individual characteristics by which a person or thing is recognized. **3.** the state of being the same in nature, quality, etc.: *linked* *by the identity of their tastes.* **4.** the state of being the same as a person or thing described or known: *the identity of the stolen goods was soon established.* **5.** *Maths.* **a.** an equation that is valid for all values of its variables, as in $(x - y)(x + y) = x^2 - y^2$. Often denoted by the symbol ≡. Also called: **identity element.** a member of a set that when operating on another member, *x*, produces that member *x*: the identity for multiplication of numbers is 1 since $x.1 = 1.x = x$. **6.** *Logic.* the relationship between an object and itself. **7.** *Austral. inf.* a well-known local person; figure: *a Barwidgee identity.* **8.** *Austral. & N.Z. inf.* an eccentric; character: *an old identity in the town.* [C16: from LL *identitās*, from L *idem* the same]

identity card *n.* a card that establishes a person's identity, esp. one issued to all members of the population in wartime, to the staff of an organization, or to spectators at a football match as a means of curbing hooliganism.

ideo- *combining form.* of or indicating idea or ideas: *ideology.* [from F *idéo-*, from Gk *idea* IDEA]

ideogram ('ɪdɪəʊ,græm) *or* **ideograph** ('ɪdɪəʊ,grɑ:f) *n.* **1.** a sign or symbol, used in a writing system such as that of China, that directly represents a concept or thing, rather than a word for it. **2.** any graphic sign or symbol, such as % or &.

ideography (,ɪdɪ'ɒgrəfɪ) *n.* the use of ideograms to communicate ideas.

ideology (,aɪdɪ'ɒlədʒɪ) *n., pl.* **-gies. 1.** a body of ideas that reflects the beliefs of a nation, political system, class, etc. **2.** speculation that is imaginary or visionary. **3.** the study of the nature and origin of ideas. —**ideological** (,aɪdɪə'lɒdʒɪkəl) *or* ,**ideo'logic** *adj.* —,**ideo'logically** *adv.*— ,**ide'ologist** *n.*

ides (aɪdz) *n.* (*functioning as sing.*) (in the Roman calendar) the 15th day in March, May, July, and October and the 13th day of each other month. [C15: from OF, from L *īdūs* (pl.), from ?]

id est *Latin.* ('ɪd 'ɛst) the full form of **i.e.**

Idhi ('ɪðɪ) *n.* a transliteration of the Modern Greek name for (Mount) **Ida** (sense 1).

idiocy ('ɪdɪəsɪ) *n., pl.* **-cies. 1.** (*not in technical usage*) severe mental retardation. **2.** foolishness; stupidity. **3.** a foolish act or remark.

idiom ('ɪdɪəm) *n.* **1.** a group of words whose meaning cannot be predicted from the constituent words: (*It was raining*) *cats and dogs.* **2.** linguistic usage that is grammatical and natural to native speakers. **3.** the characteristic vocabulary or usage of a specific human group or subject. **4.** the characteristic artistic style of an individual, school, etc. [C16: from L *idiōma* peculiarity of language, from Gk *idios* private, separate] —**idiomatic** (,ɪdɪə'mætɪk) *adj.* —,**idio'matically** *adv.*

idiosyncrasy (,ɪdɪəʊ'sɪŋkrəsɪ) *n., pl.* **-sies. 1.** a tendency, type of behaviour, etc., of a person; quirk. **2.** the composite physical or psychological make-up of a person. **3.** an abnormal reaction of an individual to specific foods, drugs, etc. [C17: from Gk, from *idios* private, separate + *sunkrasis* mixture, temperament] —**idiosyncratic** (,ɪdɪəʊsɪŋ'krætɪk) *adj.* —,**idiosyn'cratically** *adv.*

idiot ('ɪdɪət) *n.* **1.** a person with severe mental retardation. **2.** a foolish or senseless person. [C13: from L *idiōta* ignorant person, from Gk *idiōtēs* private person, ignoramus]

idiot board *n.* a slang name for **autocue.**

idiot box *n. Sl.* a television set.

idiotic (,ɪdɪ'ɒtɪk) *adj.* of or resembling an idiot; foolish; senseless. —,**idi'otically** *adv.*

idiot savant ('i:djəʊ sæ'vɑ̃, 'ɪdɪət 'sævənt) *n., pl.* **idiots savants** ('i:djəʊ sæ'vɑ̃) *or* **idiot savants.** a person of subnormal intelligence who performs brilliantly at some specialized intellectual task.

idiot tape *n. Computers.* a tape that prints out information in a continuous stream, with no line breaks.

idle ('aɪdəl) *adj.* **1.** unemployed or unoccupied; inactive. **2.** not operating or being used. **3.** (of money) not used to earn interest, etc. **4.** not wanting to work; lazy. **5.** (*usually prenominal*) frivolous or trivial: *idle pleasures.* **6.** ineffective or powerless; vain. **7.** without basis; unfounded. ~*vb.* **8.** (when *tr.*, often foll. by *away*) to waste or pass (time) fruitlessly or inactively. **9.** (*intr.*) (of a shaft, etc.) to turn without doing useful work. **10.** (*intr.*) (of an engine) to run at low speed with the transmission disengaged. [OE *īdel*] —'**idleness** *n.* —'**idly** *adv.*

idle pulley *or* **idler pulley** *n.* a freely rotating pulley used to control the tension or direction of a belt. Also called: **idler.**

idler ('aɪdlə) *n.* **1.** a person who idles. **2.** another name for **idle pulley** or **idle wheel.**

idle wheel *n.* a gearwheel interposed between two others to transmit torque without changing the velocity ratio. Also called: **idler.**

idol ('aɪdəl) *n.* **1.** a material object that is worshipped as a god. **2.** *Christianity, Judaism.* any being (other than the one God) to which divine honour is paid. **3.** a person who is revered, admired, or highly loved. [C13: from LL, from L: image, from Gk, from *eidos* shape, form]

idolatry (aɪ'dɒlətrɪ) *n.* **1.** the worship of idols. **2.** great devotion or reverence. —**i'dolater** *n.* or **i'dolatress** *fem. n.* —**i'dolatrous** *adj.*

idolize *or* **-ise** ('aɪdə,laɪz) *vb.* **1.** (*tr.*) to admire or revere greatly. **2.** (*tr.*) to worship as an idol. **3.** (*intr.*) to worship idols. —,**idoli'zation** *or* **-i'sation** *n.* —'**idol,izer** *or* -,**iser** *n.*

idolum (ɪ'dəʊləm) *n.* **1.** a mental picture; idea. **2.** a false idea; fallacy. [C17: from L: IDOL]

Idomeneus (aɪ'dɒmɪ,nju:s) *n. Greek myth.* a king of Crete who fought on the Greek side in the Trojan War.

IDP *abbrev. for* integrated data processing.

Idun ('i:dʊn) *or* **Ithunn** *n. Norse myth.* the goddess of spring who guarded the apples that kept the gods eternally young; wife of Bragi.

idyll *or U.S.* (*sometimes*) **idyl** ('ɪdɪl) *n.* **1.** a poem or prose work describing an idealized rural life, pastoral scenes, etc. **2.** a charming or picturesque scene or event. **3.** a piece of music with a pastoral character. [C17: from L, from Gk *eidullion*, from *eidos* shape, (literary) form] —**i'dyllic** *adj.* —**i'dyllically** *adv.*

IE *abbrev. for* Indo-European (languages).

i.e. *abbrev. for* id est. [L: that is (to say); in other words]

-ie *suffix forming nouns.* a variant of -y²: *groupie.*

IEE *abbrev. for* Institution of Electrical Engineers.

Ieper ('i:pər) *n.* the Flemish name for **Ypres.**

-ier *suffix forming nouns.* a variant of **-eer**: *brigadier.* [from OE *-ere* -ER¹ or (in some words) from OF *-ier*, from L *-ārius* -ARY]

Ieyasu (,i:jɛ'jɑːsu:) *n.* a variant spelling of (Tokugawa) **Iyeyasu.**

if (ɪf) *conj.* (*subordinating*) **1.** in case that, or on condition that: *if you try hard it might work.* **2.** used to introduce an indirect question. In this sense, *if* approaches the meaning of *whether.* **3.** even though: *an attractive if awkward girl.* **4. a.** used to introduce expressions of desire, with *only*: *if I had only known.* **b.** used to introduce exclamations of surprise, dismay, etc.: *if this doesn't top everything!* ~*n.* **5.** an uncertainty or doubt: *the big if is whether our plan will work.* **6.** a condition or stipulation: *I won't have any ifs or buts.* [OE *gif*]

IF *or* **i.f.** *Electronics. abbrev. for* intermediate frequency.

IFC *abbrev. for* International Finance Corporation.

Ife ('i:fɪ) *n.* a town in W central Nigeria: one of the largest and oldest Yoruba towns; university (1961); centre of the cocoa trade. Pop.: 214 500 (1983 est.).

-iferous *suffix forming adjectives.* containing or yielding: *carboniferous.*

iffy ('ɪfɪ) *adj.* **-fier, -fiest.** *Inf.* uncertain or subject to contingency. [C20: from IF + -Y¹]

Ifni (*Spanish* 'ifni) *n.* a former Spanish province in S Morocco, on the Atlantic: returned to Morocco in 1969.

-ify *suffix forming verbs.* a variant of **-fy**: *intensify.* —**-ification** *suffix forming nouns.*

Igdrasil ('ɪgdrəsɪl) *n.* a variant spelling of **Yggdrasil.**

igloo *or* **iglu** ('ɪglu:) *n., pl.* **-loos** *or* **-lus. 1.** a domeshaped Eskimo house, built of blocks of solid snow. **2.** a hollow made by a seal in the snow over its breathing hole in the ice. [C19: from Eskimo *igdlu* house]

Ignatius (ɪg'neɪʃɪəs) *n.* **Saint,** surnamed *Theophorus.* died ?110 A.D., bishop of Antioch. His seven letters, written on his way to his martyrdom in Rome, give valuable insight into the early Christian Church. Feast day: Feb. 1.

Ignatius Loyola (lɔɪ'əʊlə) *n.* **Saint.** 1491–1556, Spanish ecclesiastic. He founded the Society of Jesus (1534) and was its first general (1541–56). His *Spiritual Exercises* (1548) remains the basic manual for the training of Jesuits. Feast day: July 31.

igneous ('ɪgnɪəs) *adj.* **1.** (of rocks) derived from magma or lava that has solidified on or below the earth's surface.

2. of or relating to fire. [C17: from L *igneus* fiery, from *ignis* fire]

ignis fatuus ('ɪgnɪs 'fætjʊəs) *n.*, *pl.* **ignes fatui** ('ɪgniːz 'fætjʊˌaɪ). another name for **will-o'-the-wisp**. [C16: from Med. L, lit.: foolish fire]

ignite (ɪg'naɪt) *vb.* **1.** to catch fire or set fire to; burn or cause to burn. **2.** (*tr.*) *Chem.* to heat strongly. [C17: from L, from *ignis* fire] —**ig,nitable** *or* **ig'nitible** *adj.* —**ig,nita'bility** *or* **ig,niti'bility** *n.* —**ig'niter** *n.*

ignition (ɪg'nɪʃən) *n.* **1.** the act or process of initiating combustion. **2.** the process of igniting the fuel in an internal-combustion engine. **3.** (preceded by *the*) the devices used to ignite the fuel in an internal-combustion engine.

ignition key *n.* the key used in a motor vehicle to turn the switch that connects the battery to the ignition system.

ignitron (ɪg'naɪtrɒn, 'ɪgnɪˌtrɒn) *n.* a rectifier controlled by a subsidiary electrode, the igniter, partially immersed in a mercury cathode. A current passed between igniter and cathode forms a hot spot sufficient to strike an arc between cathode and anode. [C20: from *igniter* + ELECTRON]

ignoble (ɪg'nəʊbəl) *adj.* **1.** dishonourable; base; despicable. **2.** of low birth or origins; humble; common. **3.** of low quality; inferior. [C16: from L, from IN-² and OL *gnōbilis* NOBLE] —**,igno'bility** *or* **ig'nobleness** *n.* —**ig'nobly** *adv.*

ignominy ('ɪgnəˌmɪnɪ) *n.*, *pl.* **-minies. 1.** disgrace or public shame; dishonour. **2.** a cause of disgrace; a shameful act. [C16: from L *ignōminia* disgrace, from *ig-* (see IN-²) + *nōmen* name, reputation] —**,igno'minious** *adj.* —**,igno'miniously** *adv.* —**,igno'miniousness** *n.*

ignoramus (,ɪgnə'reɪməs) *n.*, *pl.* **-muses.** an ignorant person; fool. [C16: from legal L, lit.: we have no knowledge of, from L *ignōrāre* to be ignorant of; see IGNORE; modern usage originated from use of *Ignoramus* as the name of an unlettered lawyer in a play by G. Ruggle, 17th-century E dramatist]

ignorance ('ɪgnərəns) *n.* lack of knowledge, information, or education; the state of being ignorant.

ignorant ('ɪgnərənt) *adj.* **1.** lacking in knowledge or education; unenlightened. **2.** (*postpositive*; often foll. by *of*) lacking in awareness or knowledge (of): *ignorant of the law.* **3.** resulting from or showing lack of knowledge or awareness: *an ignorant remark.* —**'ignorantly** *adv.*

ignore (ɪg'nɔː) *vb.* (*tr.*) to fail or refuse to notice; disregard. [C17: from L *ignōrāre* not to know, from *ignārus* ignorant of] —**ig'norer** *n.*

Iguaçu *or* **Iguassú** (*Portuguese* igua'su) *n.* a river in SE South America, rising in S Brazil and flowing west to join the Paraná River, forming part of the border between Brazil and Argentina. Length: 1200 km (745 miles).

Iguaçu Falls *n.* a waterfall on the border between Brazil and Argentina, on the Iguaçu River: divided into hundreds of separate falls by forested rocky islands. Width: about 4 km (2.5 miles). Height: 82 m (269 ft.).

iguana (ɪ'gwɑːnə) *n.* either of two large tropical American arboreal herbivorous lizards, esp. the common iguana, having a greyish-green body with a row of spines along the back. [C16: from Sp., from Amerind *iwana*] —**i'guanian** *n.*, *adj.*

iguanodon (ɪ'gwɑːnəˌdɒn) *n.* a massive herbivorous long-tailed bipedal dinosaur common in Europe and N Africa in Jurassic and Cretaceous times. [C19: NL, from IGUANA + Gk *odōn* tooth]

IHC (in New Zealand) *abbrev. for* intellectually handicapped child.

IHS the first three letters of the name Jesus in Greek (IHΣΟΤΣ), often used as a Christian emblem.

Ikaría (ika'ria) *n.* a transliteration of the Modern Greek name for **Icaria**.

ikebana (,iːke'bɑːnə) *n.* the Japanese decorative art of flower arrangement.

Ikeja (ɪ'keɪjə) *n.* a town in SW Nigeria, capital of Lagos state: residential and industrial suburb of Lagos. Pop.: 63 870 (1983 est.).

Ikhnaton (ɪk'nɑːtən) *n.* a variant of **Akhenaten**.

ikon ('aɪkɒn) *n.* a variant spelling of **icon**.

il- *prefix.* a variant of **in-¹** and **in-²** before *l*.

-ile *or* **-il** *suffix forming adjectives and nouns.* indicating capability, liability, or a relationship with something: *agile; juvenile*. [via F from L or directly from L *-ilis*] —**-ility** *suffix forming nouns.*

Île-de-France (*French* ildəfrɑ̃s) *n.* **1.** a region of N France, in the Paris Basin: part of the duchy of France in the 10th century. **2.** a former name (1715–1810) for **Mauritius**.

Île du Diable (il dy djɑblə) *n.* the French name for **Devil's Island**.

ileitis (,ɪlɪ'aɪtɪs) *n.* inflammation of the ileum.

ileostomy (,ɪlɪ'ɒstəmɪ) *n.*, *pl.* **-mies.** the surgical formation of a permanent opening through the abdominal wall into the ileum.

Îles Comores (il kɔmɔr) *n.* the French name for the **Comoros**.

Îles du Salut (il dy saly) *n.* the French name for the **Safety Islands**.

Ilesha (ɪ'leɪʃə) *n.* a town in W Nigeria. Pop.: 273 400 (1983 est.).

Îles Mascareignes (il maskarɛɲ) *n.* the French name for the **Mascarene Islands**.

Îles sous le Vent (il su lə vɑ̃) *n.* the French name for the **Leeward Islands** (sense 3).

ileum ('ɪlɪəm) *n.* the part of the small intestine between the jejunum and the caecum. [C17: NL, from L *ilium*, *īleum* flank, groin, from ?] —**'ile,ac** *adj.*

ilex ('aɪlɛks) *n.* **1.** any of a genus of trees or shrubs such as the holly and inkberry. **2.** another name for the **holm oak**. [C16: from L]

Ilía (i'lɪə) *n.* (in Roman legend) the daughter of Aeneas and Lavinia, who, according to some traditions, was the mother of Romulus and Remus. See also **Rhea Silvia**.

Ilía (i'lɪə) *n.* a transliteration of the Modern Greek name for **Elía¹**.

Iliamna (,ɪlɪ'æmnə) *n.* **1.** a lake in SW Alaska: the largest lake in Alaska. Length: about 130 km (80 miles). Width: 40 km (25 miles). **2.** a volcano in SW Alaska, northwest of Iliamna Lake. Height: 3076 m (10 092 ft.).

Iligan (ɪ'liːgən) *n.* a city in the Philippines, a port on the N coast of Mindanao. Pop.: 167 358 (1980).

Ilion ('ɪlɪən) *n.* a transliteration of the Greek name for ancient **Troy**.

ilium ('ɪlɪəm) *n.*, *pl.* **-ia** (-ɪə). the uppermost and widest of the three sections of the hipbone.

Ilium ('ɪlɪəm) *n.* the Latin name for ancient **Troy**.

ilk (ɪlk) *n.* **1.** a type; class; sort (esp. in **of that, his,** etc., **ilk**): *people of that ilk should not be allowed here.* **2.** of **that ilk.** *Scot.* of the place of the same name: to indicate that the person is laird of the place named: *Moncrieff of that ilk.* [OE *ilca* the same family, same kind]

▷ **Usage.** Although the use of *ilk* in sense 1 is often condemned as being the result of a misunderstanding of the original Scottish expression, it is nevertheless well established and generally acceptable.

Ilkeston ('ɪlkɪstən) *n.* a town in N central England, in SE Derbyshire. Pop.: 33 031 (1981).

Ilkley ('ɪlklɪ) *n.* a town in N England, in West Yorkshire: nearby is **Ilkley Moor** (to the south). Pop.: 24 082 (1981).

ill (ɪl) *adj.* **worse, worst.** **1.** (*usually postpositive*) not in good health; sick. **2.** characterized by or intending harm, etc.; hostile: *ill deeds.* **3.** causing pain, harm, adversity, etc. **4.** ascribing or imputing evil to something referred to: *ill repute.* **5.** promising an unfavourable outcome; unpropitious: *an ill omen.* **6.** harsh; lacking kindness: *ill will.* **7.** not up to an acceptable standard; faulty: *ill manners.* **8. ill at ease.** unable to relax; uncomfortable. ~*n.* **9.** evil or harm; misfortune; trouble. **10.** a mild disease. ~*adv.* **11.** badly: *the title ill befits him.* **12.** with difficulty; hardly: *he can ill afford the money.* **13.** not rightly: *he ill deserves such good fortune.* [C11 (in the sense: evil): from ON *illr* bad]

I'll (aɪl) *contraction of* I will *or* I shall.

ill. *abbrev. for:* **1.** illustrated. **2.** illustration.

ill-advised *adj.* **1.** acting without reasonable care or thought: *you would be ill-advised to sell your house now.* **2.** badly thought out; not or insufficiently considered: *an ill-advised plan of action.* —**ill-advisedly** (,ɪləd'vaɪzɪdlɪ) *adv.*

ill-affected *adj.* (often foll. by *towards*) not well disposed; disaffected.

Illampu (*Spanish* iʎam'pu) *n.* one of the two peaks of Mount **Sorata**.

ill-assorted *adj.* badly matched; incompatible.

illative (ɪ'leɪtɪv) *adj.* **1.** relating to inference; inferential. **2.** *Grammar.* denoting a word or morpheme used to signal inference, for example *so* or *therefore*. **3.** (esp. in

Finnish grammar) denoting a case of nouns expressing a relation of motion or direction, usually translated by *into* or *towards*. ~*n*. **4.** *Grammar.* **a.** the illative case. **b.** an illative word or speech element. [C16: from LL *illātīvus* inferring, concluding] —**il'latively** *adv.*

Illawarra (ˌɪləˈwɒrə) *n.* a coastal district of E Australia, in S New South Wales.

ill-bred *adj.* badly brought up; lacking good manners. —ˌill-'breeding *n.*

ill-considered *adj.* done without due consideration; not thought out: *an ill-considered decision.*

ill-defined *adj.* imperfectly defined; having no clear outline.

ill-disposed *adj.* (often foll. by *towards*) not kindly disposed.

Ille-et-Vilaine (*French* ilevilɛn) *n.* a department of NW France, in E Brittany. Capital: Rennes. Pop.: 749 764 (1982). Area: 6992 sq. km (2727 sq. miles).

illegal (ɪˈliːgəl) *adj.* **1.** forbidden by law; unlawful; illicit. **2.** unauthorized or prohibited by a code of official or accepted rules. —**il'legally** *adv.* —ˌille'gality *n.*

illegible (ɪˈlɛdʒɪbəl) *adj.* unable to be read or deciphered. —il,legi'bility *or* il'legibleness *n.* —il'legibly *adv.*

illegitimate (ˌɪlɪˈdʒɪtɪmɪt) *adj.* **1. a.** born of parents who were not married to each other at the time of birth; bastard. **b.** occurring outside marriage: *of illegitimate birth.* **2.** illegal; unlawful. **3.** contrary to logic; incorrectly reasoned. ~*n.* **4.** an illegitimate person; bastard. —ˌille'gitimacy *or* ˌille'gitimateness *n.* —ˌille'gitimately *adv.*

ill-fated *adj.* doomed or unlucky.

ill-favoured *adj.* **1.** unattractive or repulsive in appearance; ugly. **2.** disagreeable or objectionable. —ˌill-'favouredly *adv.* —ˌill-'favouredness *n.*

ill feeling *n.* hostile feeling; animosity.

ill-founded *adj.* not founded on true or reliable premises; unsubstantiated.

ill-gotten *adj.* obtained dishonestly or illegally (esp. in **ill-gotten gains**).

ill humour *n.* a disagreeable or sullen mood; bad temper. —ˌill-'humoured *adj.* —ˌill-'humouredly *adv.*

illiberal (ɪˈlɪbərəl) *adj.* **1.** narrow-minded; prejudiced; intolerant. **2.** not generous; mean. **3.** lacking in culture or refinement. —il,liber'ality *n.* —il'liberally *adv.*

Illich (ˈɪlɪtʃ) *n.* **Ivan.** born 1926. U.S. teacher and writer, born in Austria. His books include *Deschooling Society* (1971) and *Medical Nemesis* (1975).

illicit (ɪˈlɪsɪt) *adj.* **1.** another word for **illegal**. **2.** not allowed or approved by common custom, rule, or standard: *illicit sexual relations.* —il'licitly *adv.* —il'licitness *n.*

Illimani (*Spanish* iʎiˈmani) *n.* a mountain in W Bolivia, in the Andes near La Paz. Height: 6882 m (22 580 ft.).

illimitable (ɪˈlɪmɪtəbəl) *adj.* limitless; boundless. —il,limita'bility *or* il'limitableness *n.*

Illinois (ˌɪlɪˈnɔɪ) *n.* **1.** a state of the N central U.S., in the Midwest: consists of level prairie crossed by the Illinois and Kaskaskia Rivers; mainly agricultural. Capital: Springfield. Pop.: 11 426 518 (1980). Area: 144 858 sq. km (55 930 sq. miles). Abbrevs.: **Ill.** or (with zip code) **IL 2.** a river in Illinois, flowing SW to the Mississippi. Length: 439 km (273 miles). —**Illinoisan** (ˌɪlɪˈnɔɪən), **Illinoian** (ˌɪlɪˈnɔɪən) *or* **Illinoisian** (ˌɪlɪˈnɔɪzɪən) *n., adj.*

illiterate (ɪˈlɪtərɪt) *adj.* **1.** unable to read and write. **2.** violating accepted standards in reading and writing: *an illiterate scrawl.* **3.** uneducated, ignorant, or uncultured: *scientifically illiterate.* ~*n.* **4.** an illiterate person. —il'literacy *or* il'literateness *n.* —il'literately *adv.*

ill-judged *adj.* rash; ill-advised.

ill-mannered *adj.* having bad manners; rude; impolite. —ˌill-'manneredly *adv.*

ill-natured *adj.* naturally unpleasant and mean. —ˌill-'naturedly *adv.* —ˌill-'naturedness *n.*

illness (ˈɪlnɪs) *n.* **1.** a disease or indisposition; sickness. **2.** a state of ill health.

illogical (ɪˈlɒdʒɪkəl) *adj.* **1.** characterized by lack of logic; senseless or unreasonable. **2.** disregarding logical principles. —illogicality (ɪˌlɒdʒɪˈkælɪtɪ) *or* il'logicalness *n.* —il'logically *adv.*

ill-starred *adj.* unlucky; unfortunate; ill-fated.

ill temper *n.* bad temper; irritability. —ˌill-'tempered *adj.* —ˌill-'temperedly *adv.*

ill-timed *adj.* occurring at or planned for an unsuitable time.

ill-treat *vb.* (*tr.*) to behave cruelly or harshly towards; misuse; maltreat. —ˌill-'treatment *n.*

illuminance (ɪˈluːmɪnəns) *n.* the luminous flux incident on unit area of a surface. Sometimes called: **illumination.** Cf. **irradiance.**

illuminant (ɪˈluːmɪnənt) *n.* **1.** something that provides or gives off light. ~*adj.* **2.** giving off light; illuminating.

illuminate *vb.* (ɪˈluːmɪˌneɪt) **1.** (*tr.*) to throw light in or into; light up. **2.** (*tr.*) to make easily understood; clarify. **3.** to adorn, decorate, or be decorated with lights. **4.** (*tr.*) to decorate (a letter, etc.) by the application of colours, gold, or silver. **5.** (*intr.*) to become lighted up. ~*adj.* (ɪˈluːmɪnɪt, -ˌneɪt). **6.** *Arch.* made clear or bright with light. ~*n.* (ɪˈluːmɪnɪt, -ˌneɪt). **7.** a person who claims to have special enlightenment. [C16: from L *illūmināre* to light up, from *lūmen* light] —il'lumi,nating *adj.* —il'luminative *adj.* —il'lumi,nator *n.*

illuminati (ɪˌluːmɪˈnɑːtiː) *pl. n., sing.* -**to** (-təʊ). **1.** a group of persons claiming exceptional enlightenment on some subject, esp. religion. **2.** (*cap.*) any of several groups of illuminati, esp. in 18th-century France and Bavaria or 16th-century Spain. [C16: from L, lit.: the enlightened ones, from *illūmināre* to ILLUMINATE]

illumination (ɪˌluːmɪˈneɪʃən) *n.* **1.** the act of illuminating or the state of being illuminated. **2.** a source of light. **3.** (*often pl.*) *Chiefly Brit.* a light or lights used as decoration in streets, parks, etc. **4.** spiritual or intellectual enlightenment; insight or understanding. **5.** the act of making understood; clarification. **6.** decoration in colours, gold, or silver used on some manuscripts. **7.** *Physics.* another name (not in technical usage) for **illuminance.**

illumine (ɪˈluːmɪn) *vb.* a literary word for **illuminate.** [C14: from L *illūmināre* to make light] —il'luminable *adj.*

ill-use *vb.* (ˈɪlˈjuːz). **1.** to use badly or cruelly; abuse; maltreat. ~*n.* (ˈɪlˈjuːs), *also* **ill-usage. 2.** harsh or cruel treatment; abuse.

illusion (ɪˈluːʒən) *n.* **1.** a false appearance or deceptive impression of reality: *the mirror gives an illusion of depth.* **2.** a false or misleading perception or belief; delusion. **3.** *Psychol.* a perception that is not true to reality, having been altered subjectively in the mind of the perceiver. See also **hallucination.** [C14: from L *illūsiō* deceit, from *illūdere* to sport with, from *ludus* game] —il'lusionary *or* il'lusional *adj.* —il'lusioned *adj.*

illusionism (ɪˈluːʒəˌnɪzəm) *n.* **1.** *Philosophy.* the doctrine that the external world exists only in illusory sense perceptions. **2.** the use of highly illusory effects in art.

illusionist (ɪˈluːʒənɪst) *n.* **1.** a person given to illusions; visionary; dreamer. **2.** *Philosophy.* a person who believes in illusionism. **3.** an artist who practises illusionism. **4.** a conjuror; magician. —il,lusion'istic *adj.*

illusory (ɪˈluːsərɪ) *or* **illusive** (ɪˈluːsɪv) *adj.* producing or based on illusion; deceptive or unreal. —il'lusorily *adv.* —il'lusoriness *n.*

illust. *or* **illus.** *abbrev. for:* **1.** illustrated. **2.** illustration.

illustrate (ˈɪləˌstreɪt) *vb.* **1.** to clarify or explain by use of examples, analogy, etc. **2.** (*tr.*) to be an example of. **3.** (*tr.*) to explain or decorate (a book, text, etc.) with pictures. [C16: from L, from *lustrāre* to purify, brighten; see LUSTRUM] —'illus,trative *adj.* —'illus,trator *n.*

illustration (ˌɪləˈstreɪʃən) *n.* **1.** pictorial matter used to explain or decorate a text. **2.** an example: *an illustration of his ability.* **3.** the act of illustrating or the state of being illustrated. —,illus'trational *adj.*

illustrious (ɪˈlʌstrɪəs) *adj.* **1.** of great renown; famous and distinguished. **2.** glorious or great: *illustrious deeds.* [C16: from L *illustris* bright, famous, from *illustrāre* to make light; see ILLUSTRATE] —il'lustriously *adv.* —il'lustriousness *n.*

ill will *n.* hostile feeling; enmity; antagonism.

Illyria (ɪˈlɪərɪə) *n.* an ancient region of uncertain boundaries on the E shore of the Adriatic Sea, including parts of present-day Yugoslavia and Albania. —I'llyrian *adj., n.*

Illyricum (ɪˈlɪərɪkəm) *n.* a Roman province founded after 168 B.C., based on the coastal area of Illyria.

Ilmen (ˈɪlmən) *n.* **Lake.** a lake in the NW Soviet Union, in the Novgorod Region: drains through the Volkhov River into Lake Ladoga. Area: between 780 sq. km (300 sq. miles) and 2200 sq. km (850 sq. miles), according to the season.

ILO *abbrev. for* International Labour Organisation.

Iloilo (ˌiːləʊˈiːləʊ) *n.* a port in the W central Philippines, on SE Panay Island. Pop.: 244 827 (1980).

Ilorin (ɪˈlɒrɪn) *n.* a city in W Nigeria, capital of Kwara state: agricultural trade centre. Pop.: 343 900 (1983 est.).

IM *or* **i.m.** *abbrev. for* intramuscular(ly).

I'm (aɪm) *contraction of* I am.

im- *prefix.* a variant of **in-**[1] and **in-**[2] before *b, m,* and *p.*

image (ˈɪmɪdʒ) *n.* **1.** a representation or likeness of a person or thing, esp. in sculpture. **2.** an optically formed reproduction of an object, such as one formed by a lens or mirror. **3.** a person or thing that resembles another closely; double or copy. **4.** a mental picture; idea produced by the imagination. **5.** the personality presented to the public by a person, organization, etc.: *a politician's image.* **6.** the pattern of light that is focused onto the retina. **7.** *Psychol.* the mental experience of something that is not immediately present to the senses, often involving memory. See also **imagery.** **8.** a personification of a specified quality; epitome: *the image of good breeding.* **9.** a mental picture or association of ideas evoked in a literary work. **10.** a figure of speech such as a simile or metaphor. ~*vb.* (*tr.*) **11.** to picture in the mind; imagine. **12.** to make or reflect an image of. **13.** to project or display on a screen, etc. **14.** to portray or describe. **15.** to be an example or epitome of; typify. [C13: from OF *imagene,* from L *imāgō* copy, representation; rel. to L *imitārī* to IMITATE] —**ˈimageable** *adj.* —**ˈimageless** *adj.*

image converter *n.* an electronic device that converts an invisible image, esp. one formed by x-rays, into an image that is visible on a fluorescent screen.

image enhancement *n.* a method of improving the definition of a video picture by a computer program which reduces the lowest grey values to black and the highest to white: used for pictures from microscopes, surveillance cameras, and scanners.

image intensifier *n.* **1.** (in fluoroscopy) a device by which a smaller brighter image is produced by electrons from an x-ray beam released from one screen being focused onto a second fluorescent screen. **2.** a device that concentrates ambient light so as to allow the user to see objects at night.

image orthicon *n.* a television camera tube in which electrons, emitted from a surface in proportion to the intensity of the incident light, are focused onto the target causing secondary emission of electrons.

imagery (ˈɪmɪdʒrɪ, -dʒərɪ) *n., pl.* **-ries. 1.** figurative or descriptive language in a literary work. **2.** images collectively. **3.** *Psychol.* **a.** the materials or general processes of the imagination. **b.** the characteristic kind of mental images formed by a particular individual. See also **image** (sense 7), **imagination** (sense 1).

imaginary (ɪˈmædʒɪnərɪ, -dʒɪnrɪ) *adj.* **1.** existing in the imagination; unreal; illusory. **2.** *Maths.* involving or containing imaginary numbers. —**imˈaginarily** *adv.*

imaginary number *n.* any complex number of the form *a* + *bi,* where *b* is not zero and i = √ − 1.

imagination (ɪˌmædʒɪˈneɪʃən) *n.* **1.** the faculty or action of producing ideas, esp. mental images of what is not present or has not been experienced. **2.** mental creative ability. **3.** the ability to deal resourcefully with unexpected or unusual problems, circumstances, etc.

imaginative (ɪˈmædʒɪnətɪv) *adj.* **1.** produced by or indicative of a creative imagination. **2.** having a vivid imagination. —**imˈaginatively** *adv.* —**imˈaginativeness** *n.*

imagine (ɪˈmædʒɪn) *vb.* **1.** (when *tr., may take a clause as object*) to form a mental image of. **2.** (when *tr., may take a clause as object*) to think, believe, or guess. **3.** (*tr.; takes a clause as object*) to suppose; assume: *I imagine he'll come.* **4.** (*tr.; takes a clause as object*) to believe without foundation: *he imagines he knows the whole story.* [C14: from L *imāginārī* to fancy, picture mentally, from *imāgō* likeness; see IMAGE] —**imˈaginable** *adj.* —**imˈaginably** *adv.* —**imˈaginer** *n.*

imagism (ˈɪmɪˌdʒɪzəm) *n.* an early 20th-century poetic movement, advocating the use of ordinary speech and the precise presentation of images. —**ˈimagist** *n., adj.* —ˌimagˈistic *adj.*

imago (ɪˈmeɪgəʊ) *n., pl.* **imagoes** *or* **imagines** (ɪˈmædʒɪˌniːz). **1.** an adult sexually mature insect. **2.** *Psychoanal.* an idealized image of another person, usually a parent, carried in the unconscious. [C18: NL, from L: likeness]

imam (ɪˈmɑːm) *or* **imaum** (ɪˈmɑːm, ɪˈmɔːm) *n. Islam.* **1.** a leader of congregational prayer in a mosque. **2.** a caliph, as leader of a Muslim community. **3.** any of a succession of Muslim religious leaders regarded by their followers as divinely inspired. [C17: from Ar.: leader.]

imamate (ɪˈmɑːmeɪt) *n. Islam.* **1.** the region or territory governed by an imam. **2.** the office, rank, or period of office of an imam.

imbalance (ɪmˈbæləns) *n.* a lack of balance, as in emphasis, proportion, etc.: *the political imbalance of the programme.*

imbecile (ˈɪmbɪˌsiːl, -ˌsaɪl) *n.* **1.** *Psychol.* a person of very low intelligence (IQ of 25 to 50). **2.** *Inf.* an extremely stupid person; dolt. ~*adj. also* **imbecilic** (ˌɪmbɪˈsɪlɪk). **3.** of or like an imbecile; mentally deficient; feeble-minded. **4.** stupid or senseless: *an imbecile thing to do.* [C16: from L *imbēcillus* feeble (physically or mentally)] —**ˈimbeˌcilely** *or* ˌimbeˈcilically *adv.* —ˌimbeˈcility *n.*

imbed (ɪmˈbɛd) *vb.* **-bedding, -bedded.** a less common spelling of **embed.**

imbibe (ɪmˈbaɪb) *vb.* **1.** to drink (esp. alcoholic drinks). **2.** *Literary.* to take in or assimilate (ideas, etc.): *to imbibe the spirit of the Renaissance.* **3.** (*tr.*) to take in as if by drinking: *to imbibe fresh air.* **4.** to absorb or cause to absorb liquid or moisture; assimilate or saturate. [C14: from L *imbibere,* from *bibere* to drink] —**imˈbiber** *n.*

imbricate *adj.* (ˈɪmbrɪkɪt, -ˌkeɪt), *also* **imbricated. 1.** *Archit.* relating to or having tiles, shingles, or slates that overlap. **2.** (of leaves, scales, etc.) overlapping each other. ~*vb.* (ˈɪmbrɪˌkeɪt). **3.** (*tr.*) to decorate with a repeating pattern resembling scales or overlapping tiles. [C17: from L *imbricāre* to cover with overlapping tiles, from *imbrex* pantile] —**ˈimbricately** *adv.* —ˌimbriˈcation** *n.*

imbroglio (ɪmˈbrəʊlɪˌəʊ) *n., pl.* **-glios. 1.** a confused or perplexing political or interpersonal situation. **2.** *Obs.* a confused heap; jumble. [C18: from It., from *imbrogliare* to confuse, EMBROIL]

Imbros (ˈɪmbrɒs) *n.* a Turkish island in the NE Aegean Sea, west of the Gallipoli Peninsula: occupied by Greece (1912–14) and Britain (1914–23). Area: 280 sq. km (108 sq. miles). Turkish name: **Imroz.**

imbrue (ɪmˈbruː) *vb.* **-bruing, -brued.** (*tr.*) *Rare.* **1.** to stain, esp. with blood. **2.** to permeate or impregnate. [C15: from OF *embreuver,* from L *imbibere* to IMBIBE] —**imˈbruement** *n.*

imbue (ɪmˈbjuː) *vb.* **-buing, -bued.** (*tr.; usually foll. by with*) **1.** to instil or inspire (with ideals, principles, etc.). **2.** *Rare.* to soak, esp. with dye, etc. [C16: from L *imbuere* to stain, accustom] —**imˈbuement** *n.*

IMechE *abbrev. for* Institution of Mechanical Engineers.

IMF *abbrev. for* International Monetary Fund.

imit. *abbrev. for:* **1.** imitation. **2.** imitative.

imitate (ˈɪmɪˌteɪt) *vb.* (*tr.*) **1.** to try to follow the manner, style, etc., of or take as a model: *many writers imitated the language of Shakespeare.* **2.** to pretend to be or to impersonate, esp. for humour; mimic. **3.** to make a copy or reproduction of; duplicate. [C16: from L *imitārī;* see IMAGE] —**imitable** (ˈɪmɪtəbəl) *adj.* —ˌimitaˈbility *n.* —**ˈimiˌtator** *n.*

imitation (ˌɪmɪˈteɪʃən) *n.* **1.** the act or practice of imitating; mimicry. **2.** an instance or product of imitating, such as a copy of the manner of a person; impression. **3. a.** a copy of a genuine article; counterfeit. **b.** (*as modifier*): *imitation jewellery.* **4.** *Music.* the repetition of a phrase or figure in one part after its appearance in another, as in a fugue. —ˌimiˈtational *adj.*

imitative (ˈɪmɪtətɪv) *adj.* **1.** imitating or tending to copy. **2.** characterized by imitation. **3.** copying or reproducing an original, esp. in an inferior manner: *imitative painting.* **4.** another word for **onomatopoeic.** —**ˈimitatively** *adv.* —**ˈimitativeness** *n.*

Imittós (ˌimiˈtɒs) *n.* a transliteration of the Modern Greek name for **Hymettus.**

immaculate (ɪˈmækjʊlɪt) *adj.* **1.** completely clean; extremely tidy: *his clothes were immaculate.* **2.** completely flawless, etc.: *an immaculate rendering of the symphony.* **3.** morally pure; free from sin or corruption. **4.** *Biol.* with no spots or markings. [C15: from L, from IM- (not) + *macula* blemish] —**imˈmaculacy** *or* **imˈmaculateness** *n.* —**imˈmaculately** *adv.*

Immaculate Conception n. Christian theol., R.C. Church. the doctrine that the Virgin Mary was conceived without any stain of original sin.

immanent ('ɪmənənt) adj. **1.** existing, operating, or remaining within; inherent. **2.** (of God) present throughout the universe. [C16: from L immanēre to remain in] —'**immanence** or '**immanency** n. —'**immanently** adv. —'**immanen,tism** n.

▷ **Usage.** See at **imminent.**

Immanuel or **Emmanuel** (ɪ'mænjʊəl) n. Bible. the child whose birth was foretold by Isaiah (Isaiah 7:14) and who in Christian tradition is identified with Jesus. [from Heb. 'immānū'el, lit.: God with us]

immaterial (,ɪmə'tɪərɪəl) adj. **1.** of no real importance; inconsequential. **2.** not formed of matter; incorporeal; spiritual. —,**imma,teri'ality** n. —,**imma'terially** adv.

immaterialism (,ɪmə'tɪərɪə,lɪzəm) n. Philosophy. the doctrine that the material world exists only in the mind. —,**imma'terialist** n.

immature (,ɪmə'tjʊə, -'tʃʊə) adj. **1.** not fully grown or developed. **2.** deficient in maturity; lacking wisdom, insight, emotional stability, etc. —,**imma'turely** adv. —,**imma'turity** or ,**imma'tureness** n.

immeasurable (ɪ'mɛʒərəbᵊl) adj. incapable of being measured, esp. by virtue of great size; limitless. —**im,measura'bility** or **im'measurableness** n. —**im'measurably** adv.

immediate (ɪ'miːdɪət) adj. (usually prenominal) **1.** taking place or accomplished without delay: an immediate reaction. **2.** closest or most direct in effect or relationship: the immediate cause of his downfall. **3.** having no intervening medium; direct in effect: an immediate influence. **4.** contiguous in space, time, or relationship: our immediate neighbour. **5.** present; current: the immediate problem is food. **6.** Philosophy. of or relating to a concept that is directly known or intuited. [C16: from Med. L, from L IM- (not) + mediāre to be in the middle; see MEDIATE] —**im'mediacy** or **im'mediateness** n.

immediately (ɪ'miːdɪətlɪ) adv. **1.** without delay or intervention; at once; instantly. **2.** very closely or directly: this immediately concerns you. **3.** near or close by: somewhere immediately in this area. ~conj. **4.** (subordinating) Chiefly Brit. as; as soon as: immediately he opened the door, there was a gust of wind.

immemorial (,ɪmɪ'mɔːrɪəl) adj. originating in the distant past; ancient (postpositive in time immemorial). [C17: from Med. L, from L IM- (not) + memoria MEMORY] —,**imme'morially** adv.

immense (ɪ'mɛns) adj. **1.** unusually large; huge; vast. **2.** without limits; immeasurable. **3.** Inf. very good; excellent. [C15: from L immensus, lit.: unmeasured, from IM- (not) + mētīrī to measure] —**im'mensely** adv. —**im'menseness** n.

immensity (ɪ'mɛnsɪtɪ) n., pl. **-ties. 1.** the state of being immense; vastness; enormity. **2.** enormous expanse, distance, or volume. **3.** Inf. a huge amount: an immensity of wealth.

immerse (ɪ'mɜːs) vb. (tr.) **1.** (often foll. by in) to plunge or dip into liquid. **2.** (often passive; often foll. by in) to involve deeply; engross: to immerse oneself in a problem. **3.** to baptize by dipping the whole body into water. [C17: from L immergere, from IM- (in) + mergere to dip] —**im'mersible** adj. —**im'mersion** n.

immerser (ɪ'mɜːsə) n. an informal term for **immersion heater.**

immersion heater n. an electrical device, usually thermostatically controlled, for heating the liquid in which it is immersed, esp. as a fixture in a domestic hot-water tank.

immigrant ('ɪmɪgrənt) n. **1. a.** a person who immigrates. **b.** (as modifier): an immigrant community. **2.** Brit. a person who has been settled in a country of which he is not a native for less than ten years.

immigrate ('ɪmɪ,greɪt) vb. **1.** (intr.) to come to a place or country of which one is not a native in order to settle there. **2.** (tr.) to introduce or bring in as an immigrant. [C17: from L immigrāre to go into] —,**immi'gration** n. —'**immi,grator** or '**immi,gratory** adj.

imminent ('ɪmɪnənt) adj. **1.** liable to happen soon; impending. **2.** Obs. overhanging. [C16: from L imminēre to project over; rel. to mons mountain] —'**imminence** n. —'**imminently** adv.

▷ **Usage.** The spelling of imminent should not be confused

with that of immanent, a word used chiefly in religious contexts, and in distinguishing the two it may be helpful to note the etymologies, which show why the spelling differs. Imminent means "likely to happen soon" and is generally used of something dangerous or unpleasant: he believed that war was imminent.

Immingham ('ɪmɪŋəm) n. a port in NE England, in Humberside: docks opened in 1912, principally for the exporting of coal; now handles chiefly bulk materials, esp. imported iron ore. Pop.: 11 630 (1985 est.).

immiscible (ɪ'mɪsɪbᵊl) adj. (of liquids) incapable of being mixed: oil and water are immiscible. —**im,misci'bility** n. —**im'miscibly** adv.

immitigable (ɪ'mɪtɪgəbᵊl) adj. Rare. unable to be mitigated. —**im,mitiga'bility** n. —**im'mitigably** adv.

immobile (ɪ'məʊbaɪl) adj. **1.** not moving; motionless. **2.** not able to move or be moved; fixed. —**immobility** (,ɪməʊ'bɪlɪtɪ) n.

immobilize or **-lise** (ɪ'məʊbɪ,laɪz) vb. (tr.) **1.** to make immobile: to immobilize a car. **2.** Finance. to convert (circulating capital) into fixed capital. —**im,mobili'zation** or **-li'sation** n. —**im'mobi,lizer** or **-,liser** n.

immoderate (ɪ'mɒdərɪt, ɪ'mɒdrɪt) adj. lacking in moderation; excessive: immoderate demands. —**im'moderately** adv. —**im,moder'ation** or **im'moderateness** n.

immodest (ɪ'mɒdɪst) adj. **1.** indecent, esp. with regard to sexual propriety; improper. **2.** bold, impudent, or shameless. —**im'modestly** adv. —**im'modesty** n.

immolate ('ɪməʊ,leɪt) vb. (tr.) **1.** to kill or offer as a sacrifice. **2.** Literary. to sacrifice (something highly valued). [C16: from L immolāre to sprinkle an offering with sacrificial meal, sacrifice; see MILL] —,**immo'lation** n. —'**immo,lator** n.

immoral (ɪ'mɒrəl) adj. **1.** transgressing accepted moral rules; corrupt. **2.** sexually dissolute; profligate or promiscuous. **3.** unscrupulous or unethical: immoral trading. **4.** tending to corrupt or resulting from corruption: immoral earnings. —**im'morally** adv.

▷ **Usage.** See at **amoral.**

immorality (,ɪmə'rælɪtɪ) n., pl. **-ties. 1.** the quality or state of being immoral. **2.** immoral behaviour, esp. in sexual matters; licentiousness; promiscuity. **3.** an immoral act.

immortal (ɪ'mɔːtᵊl) adj. **1.** not subject to death or decay; having perpetual life. **2.** having everlasting fame; remembered throughout time. **3.** everlasting; perpetual; constant. **4.** of or relating to immortal beings or concepts. ~n. **5.** an immortal being. **6.** (often pl.) a person who is remembered enduringly, esp. an author. —,**immor'tality** n. —**im'mortally** adv.

immortalize or **-ise** (ɪ'mɔːtə,laɪz) vb. (tr.) **1.** to give everlasting fame to, as by treating in a literary work: Macbeth was immortalized by Shakespeare. **2.** to give immortality to. —**im,mortali'zation** or **-i'sation** n. —**im'mortal,izer** or **-,iser** n.

immortelle (,ɪmɔː'tɛl) n. any of various composite plants that retain their colour when dried. Also called: **everlasting.** [C19: from F (fleur) immortelle everlasting (flower)]

immovable or **immoveable** (ɪ'muːvəbᵊl) adj. **1.** unable to move or be moved; immobile. **2.** unable to be diverted from one's intentions; steadfast. **3.** unaffected by feeling; impassive. **4.** unchanging; unalterable. **5.** (of feasts, etc.) on the same date every year. **6.** Law. **a.** (of property) not liable to be removed; fixed. **b.** of or relating to immovable property. —**im,mova'bility, im,movea'bility** or **im'movableness, im'moveableness** n. —**im'movably** or **im'moveably** adv.

immune (ɪ'mjuːn) adj. **1.** protected against a specific disease by inoculation or as the result of innate or acquired resistance. **2.** relating to or conferring immunity: an immune body (see **antibody**). **3.** (usually postpositive; foll. by to) unsusceptible (to) or secure (against): immune to inflation. **4.** exempt from obligation, penalty, etc. ~n. **5.** an immune person or animal. [C15: from L immūnis exempt from a public service]

immune response n. the reaction of an organism's body to foreign materials (antigens), including the production of antibodies.

immunity (ɪ'mjuːnɪtɪ) n., pl. **-ties. 1.** the ability of an organism to resist disease, as by producing its own antibodies or as a result of inoculation. **2.** freedom from obligation or duty, esp. exemption from tax, legal liability, etc.

immunize *or* **-nise** ('ɪmjʊˌnaɪz) *vb.* (*tr.*) to make immune, esp. by inoculation. —ˌimmuni'zation *or* -ni'sation *n.* —'immuˌnizer *or* -ˌniser *n.*

immuno- *or before a vowel* **immun-** *combining form.* indicating immunity or immune: *immunology.*

immunodeficiency (ˌɪmjʊnəʊdɪ'fɪʃənsɪ) *n.* a deficiency in or breakdown of a person's immune system.

immunoglobulin (ˌɪmjʊnəʊ'glɒbjʊlɪn) *n.* any of five classes of proteins, all of which show antibody activity.

immunology (ˌɪmjʊ'nɒlədʒɪ) *n.* the branch of biological science concerned with the study of immunity. —**immunologic** (ˌɪmjʊnə'lɒdʒɪk) *or* ˌimmuno'logical *adj.* —ˌimmuno'logically *adv.* —ˌimmu'nologist *n.*

immunoreaction (ɪˌmjʊ:nəʊrɪ'ækʃən) *n.* the reaction between an antigen and its antibody.

immunosuppressive (ˌɪmjʊnəʊsə'prɛsɪv) *n.* **1.** any drug that lessens the body's rejection, esp. of a transplanted organ. ~*adj.* **2.** of or relating to such a drug —ˌimmunosup'pressant *n.*, *adj.*

immunotherapy (ˌɪmjʊnəʊ'θɛrəpɪ) *n.* the treatment of disease by stimulating or modifying the immune response. —**immunotherapeutic** (ˌɪmjʊnəʊˌθɛrə'pju:tɪk) *adj.*

immure (ɪ'mjʊə) *vb.* (*tr.*) **1.** *Arch. or literary.* to enclose within or as if within walls; imprison. **2.** to shut (oneself) away from society. [C16: from Med. L, from L IM-(in) + *mūrus* wall] —**im'murement** *n.*

immutable (ɪ'mju:təbəl) *adj.* unchanging through time; unalterable; ageless: *immutable laws.* —imˌmuta'bility *or* **im'mutableness** *n.*

Imo ('i:məʊ) *n.* a state of SE Nigeria, formed in 1976 from part of East-Central State. Capital: Owerri. Pop.: 6 004 900 (1983 est.). Area: 8720 sq. km (3366 sq. miles).

imp (ɪmp) *n.* **1.** a small demon or devil; mischievous sprite. **2.** a mischievous child. ~*vb.* **3.** (*tr.*) *Falconry.* to insert new feathers in order to repair (the wing of a falcon). [OE *impa* bud, graft, hence offspring, child, from *impian* to graft]

imp. *abbrev. for:* **1.** imperative. **2.** imperfect. **3.** imperial. **4.** impersonal. **5.** import. **6.** importer.

impact *n.* ('ɪmpækt). **1.** the act of one body, etc., striking another; collision. **2.** the force with which one thing hits another. **3.** the impression made by an idea, social group, etc. ~*vb.* (ɪm'pækt). **4.** to drive or press (an object) firmly into (another object, thing, etc.) or (of two objects) to be driven or pressed firmly together. **5.** to have an impact or strong effect (on). [C18: from L *impactus* pushed against, fastened on, from *impingere* to thrust at, from *pangere* to drive in] —**im'paction** *n.*

impacted (ɪm'pæktɪd) *adj.* **1.** (of a tooth) unable to erupt, esp. because of being wedged against another tooth below the gum. **2.** (of a fracture) having the jagged broken ends wedged into each other.

impair (ɪm'pɛə) *vb.* (*tr.*) to reduce or weaken in strength, quality, etc.: *his hearing was impaired by an accident.* [C14: from OF *empeirer* to make worse, from LL, from L *pêior* worse; see PEJORATIVE] —**im'pairable** *adj.* —**im'pairer** *n.* —**im'pairment** *n.*

impala (ɪm'pɑ:lə) *n.*, *pl.* **-las** *or* **-la.** an antelope of southern and eastern Africa, having lyre-shaped horns and able to move with enormous leaps. [from Zulu]

impale *or* **empale** (ɪm'peɪl) *vb.* (*tr.*) **1.** (often foll. by *on*, *upon*, *or with*) to pierce with a sharp instrument: *they impaled his severed head on a spear.* **2.** *Heraldry.* to charge (a shield) with two coats of arms placed side by side. [C16: from Med. L, from L IM- (in) + *pālus* PALE²] —**im'palement** *or* **em'palement** *n.*

impalpable (ɪm'pælpəbəl) *adj.* **1.** imperceptible, esp. to the touch: *impalpable shadows.* **2.** difficult to understand; abstruse. —imˌpalpa'bility *n.* —**im'palpably** *adv.*

impanel (ɪm'pænəl) *vb.* **-elling, -elled** *or U.S.* **-eling, -eled.** a variant spelling (esp. U.S.) of **empanel.** —**im'panelment** *n.*

impart (ɪm'pɑ:t) *vb.* (*tr.*) **1.** to communicate (information, etc.); relate. **2.** to give or bestow (an abstract quality): *to impart wisdom.* [C15: from OF, from L, from IM- (in) + *partīre* to share, from *pars* part] —**im'partable** *adj.* —ˌimpar'tation *or* **im'partment** *n.*

impartial (ɪm'pɑ:ʃəl) *adj.* not prejudiced towards or against any particular side; fair; unbiased. —imˌparti'ality *or* **im'partialness** *n.* —**im'partially** *adv.*

impartible (ɪm'pɑ:təbəl) *adj.* *Law.* (of land, an estate, etc.) incapable of partition; indivisible. —imˌparti'bility *n.* —**im'partibly** *adv.*

impassable (ɪm'pɑ:səbəl) *adj.* (of terrain, roads, etc.) not able to be travelled through or over. —imˌpassa'bility *or* **im'passableness** *n.* —**im'passably** *adv.*

impasse (æm'pɑ:s, 'æmpɑ:s) *n.* a situation in which progress is blocked; an insurmountable difficulty; stalemate. [C19: from F; see IM-, PASS]

impassible (ɪm'pæsɪbəl) *adj. Rare.* **1.** not susceptible to pain or injury. **2.** impassive or unmoved. —imˌpassi'bility *or* **im'passibleness** *n.* —**im'passibly** *adv.*

impassion (ɪm'pæʃən) *vb.* (*tr.*) to arouse the passions of; inflame.

impassioned (ɪm'pæʃənd) *adj.* filled with passion; fiery; inflamed: *an impassioned appeal.* —**im'passionedly** *adv.* —**im'passionedness** *n.*

impassive (ɪm'pæsɪv) *adj.* **1.** not revealing or affected by emotion; reserved. **2.** calm; serene; imperturbable. —**im'passively** *adv.* —**im'passiveness** *or* **impassivity** (ˌɪmpæ'sɪvɪtɪ) *n.*

impasto (ɪm'pæstəʊ) *n.* **1.** paint applied thickly, so that brush marks are evident. **2.** the technique of painting in this way. [C18: from It., from *impastare*, from *pasta* PASTE]

impatience (ɪm'peɪʃəns) *n.* **1.** lack of patience; intolerance of or irritability with anything that impedes or delays. **2.** restless desire for change and excitement.

impatiens (ɪm'peɪʃɪˌɛnz) *n.*, *pl.* **-ens.** a plant with explosive pods, such as balsam, touch-me-not, and busy Lizzie. [C18: NL from L: impatient; from the fact that the ripe pods burst open when touched]

impatient (ɪm'peɪʃənt) *adj.* **1.** lacking patience; easily irritated at delay, etc. **2.** exhibiting lack of patience. **3.** (*postpositive*; foll. by *of*) intolerant (of) or indignant (at): *impatient of indecision.* **4.** (*postpositive*; often foll. by *for*) restlessly eager (for *or* to do something). —**im'patiently** *adv.*

impeach (ɪm'pi:tʃ) *vb.* (*tr.*) **1.** *Criminal law.* to bring a charge or accusation against. **2.** *Brit. criminal law.* to accuse of a crime against the state. **3.** *Chiefly U.S.* to charge (a public official) with an offence committed in office. **4.** to challenge or question (a person's honesty, etc.). [C14: from OF, from LL *impedicāre* to entangle, catch, from L IM-(in) + *pedica* a fetter, from *pēs* foot] —**im'peachable** *adj.* —**im'peachment** *n.*

impeccable (ɪm'pɛkəbəl) *adj.* **1.** without flaw or error; faultless: *an impeccable record.* **2.** *Rare.* incapable of sinning. [C16: from LL *impeccābilis* sinless, from L IM-(not) + *peccāre* to sin] —imˌpecca'bility *n.* —**im'peccably** *adv.*

impecunious (ˌɪmpɪ'kju:nɪəs) *adj.* without money; penniless. [C16: from IM- (not) + from L *pecūniōsus* wealthy, from *pecūnia* money] —ˌimpe'cuniously *adv.* —ˌimpe'cuniousness *or* **impecuniosity** (ˌɪmpɪkjuːnɪ'ɒsɪtɪ) *n.*

impedance (ɪm'pi:dəns) *n.* **1.** a measure of the opposition to the flow of an alternating current equal to the square root of the sum of the squares of the resistance and the reactance, expressed in ohms. **2.** the ratio of the sound pressure in a medium to the rate of alternating flow through a specified surface due to the sound wave. **3.** the ratio of the mechanical force to the velocity of the resulting vibration.

impede (ɪm'pi:d) *vb.* (*tr.*) to restrict or retard in action, progress, etc.; obstruct. [C17: from L *impedīre* to hinder, lit.: shackle the feet, from *pēs* foot] —**im'peder** *n.* —**im'pedingly** *adv.*

impediment (ɪm'pɛdɪmənt) *n.* **1.** a hindrance or obstruction. **2.** a physical defect, esp. one of speech, such as a stammer. **3.** (*pl.* **-ments** *or* **-menta** (-'mɛntə)) *Law.* an obstruction to the making of a contract, esp. one of marriage. —imˌpedi'mental *or* imˌpedi'mentary *adj.*

impedimenta (ɪmˌpɛdɪ'mɛntə) *pl. n.* **1.** any objects that impede progress, esp. the baggage and equipment carried by an army. **2.** a plural of **impediment** (sense 3). [C16: from L, pl. of *impedīmentum* hindrance; see IMPEDE]

impel (ɪm'pɛl) *vb.* **-pelling, -pelled.** (*tr.*) **1.** to urge or force (a person) to an action; constrain or motivate. **2.** to push, drive, or force into motion. [C15: from L *impellere* to push against, drive forward] —**im'pellent** *n.*, *adj.*

impeller (ɪm'pɛlə) *n.* the vaned rotating disc of a centrifugal pump, compressor, etc.

impend (ım'pɛnd) vb. (intr.) **1.** (esp. of something threatening) to be imminent. **2.** (foll. by over) Rare. to be suspended; hang. [C16: from L impendēre to overhang, from pendēre to hang] —**im'pendence** or **im'pendency** n. —**im'pending** adj.

impenetrable (ım'pɛnıtrəb°l) adj. **1.** incapable of being pierced through or penetrated: an impenetrable forest. **2.** incapable of being understood; incomprehensible. **3.** incapable of being seen through: impenetrable gloom. **4.** not susceptible to ideas, influence, etc.: impenetrable ignorance. **5.** Physics. (of a body) incapable of occupying the same space as another body. —**im,penetra'bility** n. —**im'penetrableness** n. —**im'penetrably** adv.

impenitent (ım'pɛnıtənt) adj. not sorry or penitent; unrepentant. —**im'penitence, im'penitency,** or **im'penitentness** n. —**im'penitently** adv.

imper. abbrev. for imperative.

imperative (ım'pɛrətɪv) adj. **1.** extremely urgent or important; essential. **2.** peremptory or authoritative: an imperative tone of voice. **3.** Also: **imperatival** (ım,pɛrə'taɪv°l). Grammar. denoting a mood of verbs used in giving orders, making requests, etc. ~n. **4.** something that is urgent or essential. **5.** an order or command. **6.** Grammar. **a.** the imperative mood. **b.** a verb in this mood. [C16: from LL, from L imperāre to command] —**im'peratively** adv. —**im'perativeness** n.

imperator (,ımpə'rɑːtɔː) n. (in ancient Rome) a title bestowed upon generals and, later, emperors. [C16: from L: commander, from imperāre to command] —**imperatorial** (ım,pɛrə'tɔːrɪəl) adj. —**impe'rator,ship** n.

imperceptible (,ımpə'sɛptıb°l) adj. too slight, subtle, gradual, etc., to be perceived. —**imper,cepti'bility** or **,imper'ceptibleness** n. —**,imper'ceptibly** adv.

imperceptive (,ımpə'sɛptıv) adj., also **impercipient** (,ımpə'sıpıənt). lacking in perception; obtuse. —**,imper'ception** n. —**,imper'ceptively** adv. —**,imper'ceptiveness** or **,imper'cipience** n.

imperf. abbrev. for: **1.** Also: **impf.** imperfect. **2.** (of stamps) imperforate.

imperfect (ım'pɜːfıkt) adj. **1.** exhibiting or characterized by faults, mistakes, etc.; defective. **2.** not complete or finished; deficient. **3.** Grammar. denoting a tense of verbs used most commonly in describing continuous or repeated past actions or events. **4.** Law. legally unenforceable. **5.** Music. **a.** proceeding to the dominant from the tonic, subdominant, or any chord other than the dominant. **b.** of or relating to all intervals other than the fourth, fifth, and octave. Cf. **perfect** (sense 9). ~n. **6.** Grammar. **a.** the imperfect tense. **b.** a verb in this tense. —**im'perfectly** adv. —**im'perfectness** n.

imperfection (,ımpə'fɛkʃən) n. **1.** the condition or quality of being imperfect. **2.** a fault or defect.

imperfective (,ımpə'fɛktıv) Grammar. ~adj. **1.** denoting an aspect of the verb to indicate that the action is in progress without regard to its completion. Cf. **perfective.** ~n. **2. a.** the imperfective aspect of a verb. **b.** a verb in this aspect. —**,imper'fectively** adv.

imperforate (ım'pɜːfərıt, -,reıt) adj. **1.** not perforated. **2.** (of a postage stamp) not provided with perforation or any other means of separation. **3.** Anat. without the normal opening. —**im,perfo'ration** n.

imperial (ım'pıərıəl) adj. **1.** of or relating to an empire, emperor, or empress. **2.** characteristic of an emperor; majestic; commanding. **3.** exercising supreme authority; imperious. **4.** (esp. of products) of a superior size or quality. **5.** (usually prenominal) (of weights, measures, etc.) conforming to standards legally established in Great Britain. ~n. **6.** a book size, esp. 7½ by 11 inches or 11 by 15 inches. **7.** a size of writing paper, 23 by 31 inches (U.S. and Canad.) or 22 by 30 inches (Brit.). **8.** U.S. **a.** the top of a carriage. **b.** a luggage case carried there. **9.** a small tufted beard popularized by the French emperor Napoleon III. [C14: from LL, from L imperium command, authority, empire] —**im'perially** adv. —**im'perialness** n.

imperialism (ım'pıərıə,lızəm) n. **1.** the policy or practice of extending a state's rule over other territories. **2.** the extension or attempted extension of authority, influence, power, etc., by any person, country, institution, etc.: cultural imperialism. **3.** a system of imperial government or rule by an emperor. **4.** the spirit, character, authority, etc., of an empire. —**im'perialist** adj., n. —**im,perial'istic** adj. —**im,perial'istically** adv.

imperil (ım'pɛrıl) vb. **-illing, -illed** or U.S. **-iling, -iled.** (tr.) to place in danger or jeopardy; endanger. —**im'periIment** n.

imperious (ım'pıərıəs) adj. **1.** domineering; overbearing. **2.** Rare. urgent. [C16: from L, from imperium command, power] —**im'periously** adv. —**im'periousness** n.

imperishable (ım'pɛrıʃəb°l) adj. **1.** not subject to decay or deterioration. **2.** not likely to be forgotten: imperishable truths. —**im,perisha'bility** or **im'perishableness** n. —**im'perishably** adv.

impermanent (ım'pɜːmənənt) adj. not permanent; fleeting. —**im'permanence** or **im'permanency** n. —**im'permanently** adv.

impermeable (ım'pɜːmıəb°l) adj. (of a substance) not allowing the passage of a fluid through interstices; not permeable. —**im,permea'bility** or **im'permeableness** n. —**im'permeably** adv.

impermissible (,ımpə'mısıb°l) adj. not permissible; not allowed. —**,imper,missi'bility** n.

impersonal (ım'pɜːsən°l) adj. **1.** without reference to any individual person; objective: an impersonal assessment. **2.** devoid of human warmth or sympathy; cold: an impersonal manner. **3.** not having human characteristics: an impersonal God. **4.** Grammar. (of a verb) having no logical subject: it is raining. **5.** Grammar. (of a pronoun) not denoting a person. —**im,person'ality** n. —**im'personally** adv.

impersonalize or **-ise** (ım'pɜːsənə,laız) vb. (tr.) to make impersonal, esp. to rid of such human characteristics as sympathy, etc.; dehumanize. —**im,personali'zation** or **-i'sation** n.

impersonate (ım'pɜːsə,neıt) vb. (tr.) **1.** to pretend to be (another person). **2.** to imitate the character, mannerisms, etc., of (another person). **3.** Rare. to play the part or character of. **4.** an archaic word for **personify.** —**im,person'ation** n. —**im'person,ator** n.

impertinence (ım'pɜːtınəns) or **impertinency** n. **1.** disrespectful behaviour or language; rudeness; insolence. **2.** an impertinent act, gesture, etc. **3.** Rare. lack of pertinence; irrelevance; inappropriateness.

impertinent (ım'pɜːtınənt) adj. **1.** rude; insolent; impudent. **2.** irrelevant or inappropriate. [C14: from L impertinēns not belonging, from L IM- (not) + pertinēre to be relevant; see PERTAIN] —**im'pertinently** adv.

imperturbable (,ımpə'tɜːbəb°l) adj. not easily perturbed; calm; unruffled. —**,imper,turba'bility** or **,imper'turbableness** n. —**,imper'turbably** adv.

impervious (ım'pɜːvıəs) or **imperviable** adj. **1.** not able to be penetrated, as by water, light, etc.; impermeable. **2.** (often postpositive; foll. by to) not able to be influenced (by) or not receptive (to): impervious to argument. —**im'perviously** adv. —**im'perviousness** n.

impetigo (,ımpı'taıgəʊ) n. a contagious pustular skin disease. [C16: from L: scabby eruption, from impetere to assail; see IMPETUS; for form, cf. VERTIGO] —**impetiginous** (,ımpı'tıdʒınəs) adj.

impetuous (ım'pɛtjʊəs) adj. **1.** liable to act without consideration; rash; impulsive. **2.** resulting from or characterized by rashness or haste. **3.** Poetic. moving with great force or violence; rushing: the impetuous stream hurtled down the valley. [C14: from LL impetuōsus violent; see IMPETUS] —**im'petuously** adv. —**im'petuousness** or **impetuosity** (ım,pɛtjʊ'ɒsıtı) n.

impetus ('ımpıtəs) n., pl. **-tuses. 1.** an impelling movement or force; incentive or impulse; stimulus. **2.** Physics. the force that sets a body in motion or that tends to resist changes in a body's motion. [C17: from L: attack, from impetere to assail, from IM- (in) + petere to make for, seek out]

impf. or **imperf.** abbrev. for imperfect.

Imphal (ım'fɑːl, 'ımfəl) n. a city in NE India, capital of Manipur Territory, on the Manipur River: formerly the seat of the Manipur kings: site of a major Anglo-Indian victory over the Japanese (1944), which was a turning point in the British recovery of Burma. Pop.: 156 622 (1981).

impi ('ımpı) n., pl. **-pi** or **-pies.** a group of Bantu warriors. [C19: from Zulu]

impiety (ım'paııtı) n., pl. **-ties. 1.** lack of reverence or proper respect for a god. **2.** any lack of proper respect. **3.** an impious act.

impinge (ım'pındʒ) vb. **1.** (intr.; usually foll. by on or upon) to encroach or infringe; trespass: to impinge on someone's time. **2.** (intr.; usually foll. by on, against, or *upon*) to collide (with); strike. [C16: from L *impingere* to drive at, dash against, from *pangere* to fasten, drive in] —**im'pingement** *n.* —**im'pinger** *n.*

impious ('ɪmpɪəs) *adj.* **1.** lacking piety or reverence for a god. **2.** lacking respect; undutiful. —'**impiously** *adv.* —'**impiousness** *n.*

impish ('ɪmpɪʃ) *adj.* of or like an imp; mischievous. —'**impishly** *adv.* —'**impishness** *n.*

implacable (ɪm'plækəbªl) *adj.* **1.** incapable of being placated or pacified; unappeasable. **2.** inflexible; intractable. —**im,placa'bility** *n.* —**im'placably** *adv.*

implant *vb.* (ɪm'plɑːnt). (*tr.*) **1.** to inculcate; instil: *to implant sound moral principles.* **2.** to plant or embed; infix; entrench. **3.** *Surgery.* to graft or insert (a tissue, hormone, etc.) into the body. ~*n.* ('ɪmplɑːnt). **4.** anything implanted, esp. surgically, such as a tissue graft. —,**implan'tation** *n.*

implausible (ɪm'plɔːzəbªl) *adj.* not plausible; provoking disbelief; unlikely. —**im,plausi'bility** or **im'plausibleness** *n.* —**im'plausibly** *adv.*

implement *n.* ('ɪmplɪmənt). **1.** a piece of equipment; tool or utensil: *gardening implements.* **2.** a means to achieve a purpose; agent. ~*vb.* ('ɪmplɪ,ment). (*tr.*) **3.** to carry out; put into action: *to implement a plan.* **4.** *Rare.* to supply with tools. [C17: from LL *implēmentum*, lit.: a filling up, from L *implēre* to fill up, satisfy, fulfil] —,**imple'mental** *adj.* —,**implemen'tation** *n.*

implicate ('ɪmplɪ,keɪt) *vb.* (*tr.*) **1.** to show to be involved, esp. in a crime. **2.** to imply: *his protest implicated censure by the authorities.* **3.** *Rare.* to entangle. [C16: from L *implicāre* to involve, from *plicāre* to fold] —**implicative** (ɪm'plɪkətɪv) *adj.* —**im'plicatively** *adv.*

implication (,ɪmplɪ'keɪʃən) *n.* **1.** the act of implicating. **2.** something that is implied. **3.** *Logic.* a relation between two propositions, such that the second can be logically deduced from the first.

implicit (ɪm'plɪsɪt) *adj.* **1.** not explicit; implied; indirect. **2.** absolute and unreserved; unquestioning: *implicit trust.* **3.** (when *postpositive*, foll. by *in*) contained or inherent: *to bring out the anger implicit in the argument.* [C16: from L *implicitus*, var. of *implicātus* interwoven; see IMPLICATE] —**im'plicitly** *adv.* —**im'plicitness** *n.*

implied (ɪm'plaɪd) *adj.* hinted at or suggested; not directly expressed: *an implied criticism.*

implode (ɪm'pləʊd) *vb.* to collapse inwards. Cf. **explode.** [C19: from IM- + (EX)PLODE]

implore (ɪm'plɔː) *vb.* (*tr.*) to beg or ask (someone) earnestly (to do something); plead with; beseech; supplicate. [C16: from L *implōrāre*, from IM- + *plōrāre* to bewail] —,**implo'ration** *n.* —**im'ploratory** *adj.* —**im'ploringly** *adv.*

imply (ɪm'plaɪ) *vb.* -**plying,** -**plied.** (*tr.; may take a clause as object*) **1.** to express or indicate by a hint; suggest. **2.** to suggest or involve as a necessary consequence. [C14: from OF *emplier*, from L; see IMPLICATE]
▷ **Usage.** See at **infer.**

impolder (ɪm'pəʊldə) or **empolder** *vb.* to make into a polder; reclaim (land) from the sea. [C19: from Du. *inpolderen*, see IN-[2], POLDER]

impolite (,ɪmpə'laɪt) *adj.* discourteous; rude. —,**impo'litely** *adv.* —,**impo'liteness** *n.*

impolitic (ɪm'pɒlɪtɪk) *adj.* not politic or expedient; unwise. —**im'politicly** *adv.*

imponderable (ɪm'pɒndərəbªl, -drəbªl) *adj.* **1.** unable to be weighed or assessed. ~*n.* **2.** something difficult or impossible to assess. —**im,pondera'bility** or **im'ponderableness** *n.* —**im'ponderably** *adv.*

import *vb.* (ɪm'pɔːt, 'ɪmpɔːt). **1.** to buy or bring in (goods or services) from a foreign country. **2.** (*tr.*) to bring in from an outside source: *to import foreign words into the language.* **3.** *Rare.* to signify; mean: *to import doom.* ~*n.* ('ɪmpɔːt). **4.** (*often pl.*) **a.** goods or services that are bought from foreign countries. **b.** (*as modifier*): *an import licence.* **5.** importance: *a man of great import.* **6.** meaning. **7.** *Canad. sl.* a sportsman who is not native to the area where he plays. [C15: from L *importāre* to carry in] —**im'portable** *adj.* —**im'porter** *n.*

importance (ɪm'pɔːtªns) *n.* **1.** the state of being important; significance. **2.** social status; standing; esteem: *a man of importance.* **3.** *Obs.* **a.** meaning or signification. **b.** an important matter. **c.** importunity.

important (ɪm'pɔːtªnt) *adj.* **1.** of great significance or value; outstanding. **2.** of social significance; notable; eminent; esteemed: *an important man in the town.* **3.** (when *postpositive*, usually foll. by *to*) of great concern (to); valued highly (by): *your wishes are important to me.* [C16: from OIt., from Med. L *importāre* to signify, be of consequence, from L: to carry in] —**im'portantly** *adv.*
▷ **Usage.** In a sentence such as *he changed the financial structure of the parent company and, more important, he altered its social policy,* careful writers often prefer *more important* to *more importantly,* since the *-ly* ending of the adverb is unnecessary in parenthetical constructions. This is also true of *first, second, last,* etc., which are often preferred to *firstly, secondly, lastly,* etc.: *first, he introduced the sonnet to his homeland; second, he initiated influential poetic experiments; last and most important, he was able to create an atmosphere of sincerity in his poetry.*

importation (,ɪmpɔː'teɪʃən) *n.* **1.** the act, business, or process of importing goods or services. **2.** an imported product or service.

importunate (ɪm'pɔːtjʊnɪt) *adj.* **1.** persistent or demanding; insistent. **2.** *Rare.* troublesome; annoying. —**im'portunately** *adv.* —**im'portunateness** *n.*

importune (ɪm'pɔːtjuːn, ,ɪmpɔː'tjuːn) *vb.* (*tr.*) **1.** to harass with persistent requests; demand of (someone) insistently. **2.** to beg for persistently; request with insistence. [C16: from L *importūnus* tiresome, from *im-* IN-[1] + *-portūnus* as in *opportūnus* OPPORTUNE] —**im'portunely** *adv.* —**im'portuner** *n.* —,**impor'tunity** or **im'portunacy** *n.*

impose (ɪm'pəʊz) *vb.* (usually foll. by *on* or *upon*) **1.** (*tr.*) to establish as something to be obeyed or complied with; enforce. **2.** to force (oneself, one's presence, etc.) on others; obtrude. **3.** (*intr.*) to take advantage, as of a person or quality: *to impose on someone's kindness.* **4.** (*tr.*) *Printing.* to arrange (pages, type, etc.) in a chase so that the pages will be in the correct order. **5.** (*tr.*) to pass off deceptively; foist. [C15: from OF, from L *impōnere* to place upon, from *pōnere* to place, set] —**im'posable** *adj.* —**im'poser** *n.*

imposing (ɪm'pəʊzɪŋ) *adj.* grand or impressive: *an imposing building.* —**im'posingly** *adv.* —**im'posingness** *n.*

imposition (,ɪmpə'zɪʃən) *n.* **1.** the act of imposing. **2.** something imposed unfairly on someone. **3.** a task set as a school punishment. **4.** the arrangement of pages for printing.

impossibility (ɪm,pɒsə'bɪlɪtɪ, ,ɪmpɒs-) *n., pl.* -**ties.** **1.** the state or quality of being impossible. **2.** something that is impossible.

impossible (ɪm'pɒsəbªl) *adj.* **1.** incapable of being done, undertaken, or experienced. **2.** incapable of occurring or happening. **3.** absurd or inconceivable; unreasonable. **4.** *Inf.* intolerable; outrageous: *those children are impossible.* —**im'possibleness** *n.* —**im'possibly** *adv.*

impossible figure *n.* a picture of an object that at first sight looks three-dimensional but cannot be a two-dimensional projection of a real three-dimensional object, for example a picture of a staircase that re-enters itself while appearing to ascend continuously.

impost[1] ('ɪmpəʊst) *n.* **1.** a tax, esp. a customs duty. **2.** the weight that a horse must carry in a handicap race. ~*vb.* **3.** (*tr.*) *U.S.* to classify (imported goods) according to the duty payable on them. [C16: from Med. L *impostus* tax, from L *impositus* imposed; see IMPOSE] —'**imposter** *n.*

impost[2] ('ɪmpəʊst) *n. Archit.* a member at the top of a column that supports an arch. [C17: from F *imposte,* from L *imposita* placed upon; see IMPOSE]

impostor or **imposter** (ɪm'pɒstə) *n.* a person who deceives others, esp. by assuming a false identity; charlatan. [C16: from LL: deceiver; see IMPOSE]

imposture (ɪm'pɒstʃə) *n.* the act or an instance of deceiving others, esp. by assuming a false identity. [C16: from F, from LL, from L *impōnere*; see IMPOSE] —**impostrous** (ɪm'pɒstrəs) or **impostorous** (ɪm'pɒstərəs) *adj.*

impotent ('ɪmpətənt) *adj.* **1.** (when *postpositive*, often takes an infinitive) lacking sufficient strength; powerless. **2.** (esp. of males) unable to perform sexual intercourse. —'**impotence** or '**impotency** *n.* —'**impotently** *adv.*

impound (ɪmˈpaʊnd) vb. (tr.) **1.** to confine (animals, etc.) in a pound. **2.** to take legal possession of (a document, evidence, etc.). **3.** to collect (water) in a reservoir or dam. —**imˈpoundable** adj. —**imˈpoundage** or **imˈpoundment** n. —**imˈpounder** n.

impoverish (ɪmˈpɒvərɪʃ) vb. (tr.) **1.** to make poor or diminish the quality of: to impoverish society by cutting the grant to the arts. **2.** to deprive (soil, etc.) of fertility. [C15: from OF empovrir, from povre POOR] —**imˈpoverishment** n.

impracticable (ɪmˈpræktɪkəbəl) adj. **1.** incapable of being put into practice or accomplished; not feasible. **2.** unsuitable for a desired use; unfit. —**im,practicaˈbility** or **imˈpracticableness** n. —**imˈpracticably** adv.

impractical (ɪmˈpræktɪkəl) adj. **1.** not practical or workable: an impractical solution. **2.** not given to practical matters or gifted with practical skills. —**im,practiˈcality** or **imˈpracticalness** n. —**imˈpractically** adv.

imprecate (ˈɪmprɪˌkeɪt) vb. **1.** (intr.) to swear or curse. **2.** (tr.) to invoke or bring down (evil, a curse, etc.). [C17: from L imprecārī to invoke, from im- IN-² + precārī to PRAY] —**,impreˈcation** n. —**ˈimpre,catory** adj.

imprecise (ˌɪmprɪˈsaɪs) adj. not precise; inexact or inaccurate. —**,impreˈcisely** adv. —**imprecision** (ˌɪmprɪˈsɪʒən) or **,impreˈciseness** n.

impregnable¹ (ɪmˈprɛgnəbəl) adj. **1.** unable to be broken into or taken by force: an impregnable castle. **2.** unshakable: impregnable self-confidence. **3.** incapable of being refuted: an impregnable argument. [C15 imprenable, from OF, from IM- (not) + prenable able to be taken, from prendre to take] —**im,pregnaˈbility** n. —**imˈpregnably** adv.

impregnable² (ɪmˈprɛgnəbəl) or **impregnatable** (ˌɪmprɛgˈneɪtəbəl) adj. able to be impregnated; fertile.

impregnate vb. (ˈɪmprɛgˌneɪt). (tr.) **1.** to saturate, soak, or imbue. **2.** to imbue or permeate; pervade. **3.** to cause to conceive; make pregnant; fertilize. **4.** to make (land, soil, etc.) fruitful. ~adj. (ɪmˈprɛgnɪt, -ˌneɪt). **5.** pregnant or fertilized. [C17: from LL, from L im- IN-² + praegnans PREGNANT] —**,impregˈnation** n. —**imˈpregnator** n.

impresario (ˌɪmprɪˈsɑːrɪˌəʊ) n., pl. **-sarios.** the director or manager of an opera, ballet, etc. [C18: from It., lit.: one who undertakes]

imprescriptible (ˌɪmprɪˈskrɪptəbəl) adj. Law. immune or exempt from prescription. —**,impreˈscriptiˈbility** n. —**,impreˈscriptibly** adv.

impress¹ vb. (ɪmˈprɛs). (tr.) **1.** to make an impression on; have a strong, lasting, or favourable effect on: I am impressed by your work. **2.** to produce (an imprint, etc.) by pressure in or on (something): to impress a seal in wax. **3.** (often foll. by on) to stress (something to a person); urge; emphasize. **4.** to exert pressure on; press. ~n. (ˈɪmprɛs). **5.** the act or an instance of impressing. **6.** a mark, imprint, or effect produced by impressing. [C14: from L imprimere to press into, imprint] —**imˈpresser** n. —**imˈpressible** adj.

impress² vb. (ɪmˈprɛs). **1.** to commandeer or coerce (men or things) into government service; press-gang. ~n. (ˈɪmprɛs). **2.** the act of commandeering or coercing into government service. [C16: see im- IN-², PRESS²]

impression (ɪmˈprɛʃən) n. **1.** an effect produced in the mind by a stimulus; sensation: he gave the impression of wanting to help. **2.** an imprint or mark produced by pressing. **3.** a vague idea, consciousness, or belief: I had the impression we had met before. **4.** a strong, favourable, or remarkable effect. **5.** the act of impressing or the state of being impressed. **6.** Printing. **a.** the act, process, or result of printing from type, plates, etc. **b.** the total number of copies of a publication printed at one time. **7.** an imprint of the teeth and gums for preparing crowns, dentures, etc. **8.** an imitation or impersonation. —**imˈpressional** adj. —**imˈpressionally** adv.

impressionable (ɪmˈprɛʃənəbəl, -ˈprɛʃnə-) adj. easily influenced or characterized by susceptibility to influence: an impressionable age. —**im,pressionaˈbility** or **imˈpressionableness** n.

impressionism (ɪmˈprɛʃəˌnɪzəm) n. (often cap.) a 19th-century movement in French painting, having the aim of objectively recording experience by a system of fleeting impressions, esp. of natural light effects. —**imˈpressionist** n.

impressive (ɪmˈprɛsɪv) adj. capable of impressing, esp. by size, magnificence, etc.; awe-inspiring; commanding. —**imˈpressively** adv. —**imˈpressiveness** n.

imprest (ɪmˈprɛst) n. **1.** a fund of cash from which a department, etc., pays incidental expenses, topped up periodically from central funds. **2.** Chiefly Brit. an advance from government funds for some public business or service. [C16: prob. from It. imprestare to lend, from L in- towards + praestāre to pay, from praestō at hand; see PRESTO]

imprimatur (ˌɪmprɪˈmeɪtə, -ˈmɑː-) n. **1.** sanction or approval for something to be printed. **2.** R.C. Church. a licence certifying the Church's approval. [C17: NL, lit.: let it be printed]

imprint n. (ˈɪmprɪnt). **1.** a mark or impression produced by pressure, printing, or stamping. **2.** a characteristic mark or indication; stamp: the imprint of great sadness on his face. **3. a.** the publisher's name and address, often with the date of publication, printed in a book, usually on the title page or the verso title page. **b.** the printer's name and address on any printed matter. ~vb. (ɪmˈprɪnt). (tr.) **4.** to produce (a mark, impression, etc.) on (a surface) by pressure, printing, or stamping: to imprint a seal on wax. **5.** to establish firmly; impress: to imprint the details on one's mind. **6.** to cause (a young animal) to undergo the process of imprinting: chicks can be imprinted on human beings if the mother is absent.

imprinting (ɪmˈprɪntɪŋ) n. the development in young animals of recognition of and attraction to members of their own species or surrogates.

imprison (ɪmˈprɪzən) vb. (tr.) to confine in or as if in prison. —**imˈprisonment** n.

improbable (ɪmˈprɒbəbəl) adj. not likely or probable; doubtful; unlikely. —**im,probaˈbility** or **imˈprobableness** n. —**imˈprobably** adv.

improbity (ɪmˈprəʊbɪtɪ) n., pl. **-ties.** dishonesty, wickedness, or unscrupulousness.

impromptu (ɪmˈprɒmptjuː) adj. **1.** unrehearsed; spontaneous; extempore. **2.** produced or done without care or planning; improvised. ~adv. **3.** in a spontaneous or improvised way: he spoke impromptu. ~n. **4.** something that is impromptu. **5.** a short piece of instrumental music, sometimes improvisatory in character. [C17: from F, from L in promptū in readiness, from promptus (adj.) ready, PROMPT]

improper (ɪmˈprɒpə) adj. **1.** lacking propriety; not seemly. **2.** unsuitable for a certain use or occasion; inappropriate. **3.** irregular or abnormal. —**imˈproperly** adv. —**imˈproperness** n.

improper fraction n. a fraction in which the numerator is greater than the denominator, as 7/6.

impropriate vb. (ɪmˈprəʊprɪˌeɪt). **1.** (tr.) to transfer (property, rights, etc.) from the Church into lay hands. ~adj. (ɪmˈprəʊprɪɪt, -ˌeɪt). **2.** transferred in this way. [C16: from Med. L impropriāre to make one's own, from L im- IN-² + propriāre to APPROPRIATE] —**im,propriˈation** n. —**imˈpropri,ator** n.

impropriety (ˌɪmprəˈpraɪɪtɪ) n., pl. **-ties. 1.** lack of propriety; indecency; indecorum. **2.** an improper act or use. **3.** the state of being improper.

improve (ɪmˈpruːv) vb. **1.** to make or become better in quality; ameliorate. **2.** (tr.) to make (buildings, land, etc.) more valuable by additions or betterment. **3.** (intr.; usually foll. by on or upon) to achieve a better standard or quality in comparison (with): to improve on last year's crop. [C16: from Anglo-F emprouer to turn to profit, from LL prōde beneficial, from L prōdesse to be advantageous] —**imˈprovable** adj. —**im,provaˈbility** or **imˈprovableness** n. —**imˈprover** n.

improvement (ɪmˈpruːvmənt) n. **1.** the act of improving or the state of being improved. **2.** something that improves, esp. an addition or alteration. **3.** Austral. & N.Z. a building on a piece of land, adding to its value.

improvident (ɪmˈprɒvɪdənt) adj. **1.** not provident; thriftless, imprudent, or prodigal. **2.** heedless or incautious; rash. —**imˈprovidence** n. —**imˈprovidently** adv.

improvise (ˈɪmprəˌvaɪz) vb. **1.** to perform or make quickly from materials and sources available, without previous planning. **2.** to perform (a poem, play, piece of music, etc.), composing as one goes along. [C19: from F, from It., from L imprōvīsus unforeseen, from prōvidēre to foresee; see PROVIDE] —**ˈimpro,viser** n. —**,improviˈsation**

n. —**improvisatory** (,imprə'vaizətəri, -'viz-, ,imprə-vaiz'eitəri) *adj.*

imprudent (im'pru:d³nt) *adj.* not prudent; rash, heedless, or indiscreet. —**im'prudence** *n.* —**im'prudently** *adv.*

impudence ('impjʊdəns) *or* **impudency** *n.* **1.** the quality of being impudent. **2.** an impudent act or statement. [C14: from L *impudēns* shameless]

impudent ('impjʊdənt) *adj.* **1.** mischievous, impertinent, or disrespectful. **2.** *Obs.* immodest. —**'impudently** *adv.* —**'impudentness** *n.*

impugn (im'pju:n) *vb.* (*tr.*) to challenge or attack as false; criticize. [C14: from OF, from L *impugnāre* to fight against, attack] —**im'pugnable** *adj.* —**im'pugnment** *n.* —**im'pugner** *n.*

impulse ('impʌls) *n.* **1.** an impelling force or motion; thrust; impetus. **2.** a sudden desire, whim, or inclination. **3.** an instinctive drive; urge. **4.** tendency; current; trend. **5.** *Physics.* **a.** the product of the average magnitude of a force acting on a body and the time for which it acts. **b.** the change in the momentum of a body as a result of a force acting upon it. **6.** *Physiol.* See **nerve impulse. 7. on impulse.** spontaneously or impulsively. [C17: from L *impulsus* a pushing against, incitement, from *impellere* to strike against; see IMPEL]

impulse buying *n.* the buying of merchandise prompted by a whim. —**impulse buyer** *n.*

impulsion (im'pʌlʃən) *n.* **1.** the act of impelling or the state of being impelled. **2.** motion produced by an impulse; propulsion. **3.** a driving force; compulsion.

impulsive (im'pʌlsiv) *adj.* **1.** characterized by actions based on sudden desires, whims, or inclinations: *an impulsive man.* **2.** based on emotional impulses or whims; spontaneous. **3.** forceful, inciting, or impelling. **4.** (of physical forces) acting for a short time; not continuous. —**im'pulsively** *adv.* —**im'pulsiveness** *n.*

impundulu ('impun,dulu) *n. S. African.* a mythical bird often associated with witchcraft. [from Bantu]

impunity (im'pju:niti) *n., pl.* **-ties. 1.** exemption or immunity from punishment, recrimination, or other unpleasant consequences. **2. with impunity.** with no care or heed for such consequences. [C16: from L, from *impūnis* unpunished, from IM- (not) + *poena* punishment]

impure (im'pjʊə) *adj.* **1.** not pure; combined with something else; tainted or sullied. **2.** (in certain religions) ritually unclean. **3.** (of a colour) mixed with another colour. **4.** of more than one origin or style, as of architecture. —**im'purely** *adv.* —**im'pureness** *n.*

impurity (im'pjʊəriti) *n., pl.* **-ties. 1.** the quality of being impure. **2.** an impure thing, constituent, or element: *impurities in the water.* **3.** *Electronics.* a small quantity of an element added to a pure semiconductor crystal to control its electrical conductivity.

impute (im'pju:t) *vb.* (*tr.*) **1.** to attribute or ascribe (something dishonest or dishonourable) to a person. **2.** to attribute to a source or cause: *I impute your success to nepotism.* **3.** *Commerce.* to give (a notional value) to goods, etc., when the real value is unknown. [C14: from L, from IM- + *putāre* to think, calculate] —**,impu'tation** *n.* —**im'putative** *adj.* —**im'puter** *n.* —**im'putable** *adj.*

Imran Khan ('imra:n'ka:n)*n.* born 1952, Pakistani cricketer: played for Worcestershire (1971–76) and Sussex from 1977; captained Pakistan from 1982.

Imroz ('imrɔz) *n.* the Turkish name for **Imbros.**

IMunE *abbrev. for* Institution of Municipal Engineers.

in (in) *prep.* **1.** inside; within: *no smoking in the auditorium.* **2.** at a place where there is: *in the shade; in the rain.* **3.** indicating a state, situation, or condition: *in silence.* **4.** when (a period of time) has elapsed: *come back in one year.* **5.** using: *written in code.* **6.** concerned with, esp. as an occupation: *in journalism.* **7.** while or by performing the action of: *in crossing the street he was run over.* **8.** used to indicate purpose: *in honour of the president.* **9.** (of certain animals) pregnant with: *in calf.* **10.** a variant of *into: she fell in the water.* **11. have it in one.** (often foll. by an infinitive) to have the ability (to do something). **12. in that** *or* **in so far as.** (*conj.*) because or to the extent that: *I regret my remark in that it upset you.* **13. nothing in it.** no difference or interval between two things. ~*adv.* (*particle*) **14.** in or into a particular place; inward or indoors: *come in.* **15.** so as to achieve

office or power: *the Conservatives got in at the last election.* **16.** so as to enclose: *block in.* **17.** (in certain games) so as to take one's turn of the play: *you have to get the other side out before you go in.* **18.** *N.Z.* competing: *you've got to be in to win.* **19.** *Brit.* (of a fire) alight. **20.** (*in combination*) indicating an activity or gathering: *teach-in; work-in.* **21. in at.** present at (the beginning, end, etc.). **22. in for.** about to be affected by (something, esp. something unpleasant): *you're in for a shock.* **23. in on.** acquainted with or sharing in: *I was in on all his plans.* **24. in with.** associated with; friendly with; regarded highly by. **25. have (got) it in for.** to wish or intend harm towards. ~*adj.* **26.** (*stressed*) fashionable; modish: *the in thing to do.* ~*n.* **27. ins and outs.** intricacies or complications; details. [OE]

In the chemical symbol for indium.

in. *abbrev. for* inch(es).

in-[1], **il-**, **im-**, *or* **ir-** *prefix.* **a.** not; non-: *incredible; illegal; imperfect; irregular.* **b.** lack of: *inexperience.* Cf. **un-.** [from L *in-*; rel. to *ne-, nŏn* not]

in-[2], **il-**, **im-**, *or* **ir-** *prefix.* **1.** in; into; towards; within; on: *infiltrate; immigrate.* **2.** having an intensive or causative function: *inflame; imperil.* [from IN (prep., adv.)]

-in *suffix forming nouns.* **1.** indicating a neutral organic compound, including proteins, glucosides, and glycerides: *insulin; tripalmitin.* **2.** indicating an enzyme in certain nonsystematic names: *pepsin.* **3.** indicating a pharmaceutical substance: *penicillin; aspirin.* **4.** indicating a chemical substance in certain nonsystematic names: *coumarin.* [from NL *-ina*; cf. -INE[2]]

in absentia *Latin.* (in æb'sɛntiə) *adv.* in the absence of (someone indicated).

inaccessible (,inæk'sɛsəb³l) *adj.* not accessible; unapproachable. —**,inac,cessi'bility** *or* **,inac'cessibleness** *n.* —**,inac'cessibly** *adv.*

inaccuracy (in'ækjʊrəsi) *n., pl.* **-cies. 1.** lack of accuracy; imprecision. **2.** an error, mistake, or slip. —**in'accurate** *adj.*

inaction (in'ækʃən) *n.* lack of action; idleness; inertia.

inactivate (in'ækti,veit) *vb.* (*tr.*) to render inactive. —**in,acti'vation** *n.*

inactive (in'æktiv) *adj.* **1.** idle or inert; not active. **2.** sluggish or indolent. **3.** *Mil.* of or relating to persons or equipment not in active service. **4.** *Chem.* (of a substance) having little or no reactivity. —**in'actively** *adv.* —**,inac'tivity** *n.*

inadequate (in'ædikwit) *adj.* **1.** not adequate; insufficient. **2.** not capable; lacking. —**in'adequacy** *n.* —**in'adequately** *adv.*

inadvertence (,inəd'vɜ:t³ns) *or* **inadvertency** *n.* **1.** lack of attention; heedlessness. **2.** an oversight; slip.

inadvertent (,inəd'vɜ:t³nt) *adj.* **1.** failing to act carefully or considerately; inattentive. **2.** resulting from heedless action; unintentional. —**,inad'vertently** *adv.*

-inae *suffix forming plural proper nouns.* occurring in names of zoological subfamilies: *Felinae.* [NL, from L, fem. pl. of *-īnus* -INE[1]]

inalienable (in'eiljənəb³l) *adj.* not able to be transferred to another; not alienable: *the inalienable rights of the citizen.* —**in,aliena'bility** *or* **in'alienableness** *n.* —**in'a-lienably** *adv.*

inalterable (in'ɔ:ltərəb³l) *adj.* not alterable; unalterable. —**in,altera'bility** *or* **in'alterableness** *n.* —**in'altera-bly** *adv.*

inamorata (in,æmə'ra:tə, ,inæmə-) *or* (*masc.*) **inamorato** (in,æmə'ra:təʊ, ,inæmə-) *n., pl.* **-tas** *or* (*masc.*) **-tos.** a person with whom one is in love; lover. [C17: from It., from *innamorare* to cause to fall in love, from *amore* love, from L *amor*]

inane (i'nein) *adj.* **1.** senseless, unimaginative, or empty; unintelligent: *inane remarks.* ~*n.* **2.** *Arch.* something empty or vacant, esp. the void of space. [C17: from L *inānis* empty] —**in'anely** *adv.*

inanimate (in'ænimit) *adj.* **1.** lacking the qualities of living beings; not animate: *inanimate objects.* **2.** lacking any sign of life or consciousness; appearing dead. **3.** lacking vitality; dull. —**in'animately** *adv.* —**in'animateness** *or* **inanimation** (in,æni'meiʃən) *n.*

inanition (,inə'niʃən) *n.* **1.** exhaustion resulting from lack of food. **2.** mental, social, or spiritual weakness or lassitude. [C14: from LL *inānītio* emptiness, from L *inānis* empty; see INANE]

inanity (ɪ'nænɪtɪ) *n.*, *pl.* **-ties. 1.** lack of intelligence or imagination; senselessness; silliness. **2.** a senseless action, remark, etc. **3.** an archaic word for **emptiness.**

inapposite (ɪn'æpəzɪt) *adj.* not appropriate or pertinent; unsuitable. —**in'appositely** *adv.* —**in'appositeness** *n.*

inapt (ɪn'æpt) *adj.* **1.** not apt or fitting; inappropriate. **2.** lacking skill; inept. —**in'apti,tude** *or* **in'aptness** *n.* —**in'aptly** *adv.*

inarch (ɪn'ɑːtʃ) *vb.* (*tr.*) to graft (a plant) by uniting stock and scion while both are still growing independently.

inasmuch as (,ɪnəz'mʌtʃ) *conj.* (*subordinating*) **1.** in view of the fact that; seeing that; since. **2.** to the extent or degree that; in so far as.

inaugural (ɪn'ɔːgjʊrəl) *adj.* **1.** characterizing or relating to an inauguration. ~*n.* **2.** a speech made at an inauguration, esp. by a president of the U.S.

inaugurate (ɪn'ɔːgjʊ,reɪt) *vb.* (*tr.*) **1.** to commence officially or formally; initiate. **2.** to place in office formally and ceremonially; induct. **3.** to open ceremonially; dedicate formally: *to inaugurate a factory.* [C17: from L *inaugurāre*, lit.: to take omens, practise augury, hence to install in office after taking auguries; see IN-², AUGUR] —**in,augu'ration** *n.* —**in'augu,rator** *n.* —**inauguratory** (ɪn'ɔːgjʊrətərɪ, -trɪ) *adj.*

in-between *adj.* intermediate: *he's at the in-between stage, neither a child nor an adult.*

inboard ('ɪn,bɔːd) *adj.* **1.** (esp. of a boat's motor or engine) situated within the hull. **2.** situated between the wing tip of an aircraft and its fuselage: *an inboard engine.* ~*adv.* **3.** towards the centre line of or within a vessel, aircraft, etc.

inborn ('ɪn'bɔːn) *adj.* existing from birth; congenital; innate.

inbred ('ɪn'brɛd) *adj.* **1.** produced as a result of inbreeding. **2.** deeply ingrained; innate: *inbred good manners.*

inbreed ('ɪn'briːd) *vb.* **-breeding, -bred. 1.** to breed from unions between closely related individuals, esp. over several generations. **2.** (*tr.*) to develop within; engender. —**'in'breeding** *n.*, *adj.*

in-built *adj.* built-in, integral.

inc. *abbrev. for:* **1.** including. **2.** inclusive. **3.** income. **4.** increase.

Inc. (esp. U.S.) *abbrev. for* incorporated.

incalculable (ɪn'kælkjʊləbəl) *adj.* beyond calculation; unable to be predicted or determined. —**in,calcula'bility** *n.* —**in'calculably** *adv.*

incandesce (,ɪnkæn'dɛs) *vb.* (*intr.*) to make or become incandescent.

incandescent (,ɪnkæn'dɛsənt) *adj.* emitting light as a result of being heated; red-hot or white-hot. [C18: from L *incandescere* to become hot, glow, from *candēre* to be white; see CANDID] —**,incan'descently** *adv.* —**,incan'descence** *n.*

incandescent lamp *n.* a source of light that contains a heated solid, such as an electrically heated filament.

incantation (,ɪnkæn'teɪʃən) *n.* **1.** ritual recitation of magic words or sounds. **2.** the formulaic words or sounds used; a magic spell. [C14: from LL *incantātiō* an enchanting, from *incantāre* to repeat magic formulas, from L, from IN-² + *cantāre* to sing; see ENCHANT] —**in'can'tational** *or* **in'cantatory** *adj.*

incapacitate (,ɪnkə'pæsɪ,teɪt) *vb.* (*tr.*) **1.** to deprive of power, strength, or capacity; disable. **2.** to deprive of legal capacity or eligibility. —**,inca,paci'tation** *n.*

incapacity (,ɪnkə'pæsɪtɪ) *n.*, *pl.* **-ties. 1.** lack of power, strength, or capacity; inability. **2.** *Law.* legal disqualification or ineligibility.

in-car *adj.* (of hi-fi equipment, etc.) installed inside a car.

incarcerate (ɪn'kɑːsə,reɪt) *vb.* (*tr.*) to confine or imprison. [C16: from Med. L, from IN-² + *carcer* prison] —**in,carcer'ation** *n.* —**in'carcer,ator** *n.*

incarnadine (ɪn'kɑːnə,daɪn) *Arch. or literary.* ~*vb.* **1.** (*tr.*) to tinge with or stain with red. ~*adj.* **2.** of a pinkish or reddish colour similar to that of flesh or blood. [C16: from F *incarnadin* flesh-coloured, from It., from LL *incarnātus* made flesh, INCARNATE]

incarnate *adj.* (ɪn'kɑːnɪt, -neɪt). (*usually immediately postpositive*) **1.** possessing bodily form, esp. the human form: *a devil incarnate.* **2.** personified or typified: *stupidity incarnate.* ~*vb.* (ɪn'kɑːneɪt). (*tr.*) **3.** to give a bodily or concrete form to. **4.** to be representative or typical of. [C14: from LL *incarnāre* to make flesh, from L IN-² + *carō* flesh]

incarnation (,ɪnkɑː'neɪʃən) *n.* **1.** the act of manifesting or state of being manifested in bodily form, esp. human form. **2.** a bodily form assumed by a god, etc. **3.** a person or thing that typifies or represents some quality, idea, etc.

Incarnation (,ɪnkɑː'neɪʃən) *n. Christian theol.* the assuming of a human body by the Son of God.

incarvillea (,ɪnkɑː'vɪlɪə) *n.* any of various perennials with pink flowers and pinnate leaves. Also called: **Chinese trumpet flower.** [C18: after Pierre d'*Incarville*, F missionary in China]

incase (ɪn'keɪs) *vb.* a variant spelling of **encase.** —**in'casement** *n.*

incautious (ɪn'kɔːʃəs) *adj.* not careful or cautious. —**in'cautiously** *adv.* —**in'cautiousness** *or* **in'caution** *n.*

incendiary (ɪn'sɛndɪərɪ) *adj.* **1.** of or relating to the illegal burning of property, goods, etc. **2.** tending to create strife, violence, etc. **3.** (of a substance) capable of catching fire or burning readily. ~*n.*, *pl.* **-aries. 4.** a person who illegally sets fire to property, goods, etc.; arsonist. **5.** (esp. formerly) a person who stirs up civil strife, violence, etc.; agitator. **6.** Also called: **incendiary bomb.** a bomb that is designed to start fires. **7.** an incendiary substance, such as phosphorus. [C17: from L, from *incendium* fire, from *incendere* to kindle] —**in'cendia,rism** *n.*

incense¹ ('ɪnsɛns) *n.* **1.** any of various aromatic substances burnt for their fragrant odour, esp. in religious ceremonies. **2.** the odour or smoke so produced. **3.** any pleasant fragrant odour; aroma. ~*vb.* **4.** to burn incense in honour of (a deity). **5.** (*tr.*) to perfume or fumigate with incense. [C13: from OF *encens*, from Church L *incensum*, from L *incendere* to kindle]

incense² (ɪn'sɛns) *vb.* (*tr.*) to enrage greatly. [C15: from L *incensus* set on fire, from *incendere* to kindle] —**in'censement** *n.*

incensory ('ɪnsɛnsərɪ) *n.*, *pl.* **-ries.** a less common name for **censer.** [C17: from Med. L *incensorium*]

incentive (ɪn'sɛntɪv) *n.* **1.** a motivating influence; stimulus. **2. a.** an additional payment made to employees to increase production. **b.** (*as modifier*): *an incentive scheme.* ~*adj.* **3.** serving to incite to action. [C15: from LL, from L: striking up, setting the tune, from *incinere* to sing]

incept (ɪn'sɛpt) *vb.* (*tr.*) **1.** (of organisms) to ingest (food). **2.** *Brit.* (formerly) to take a master's or doctor's degree at a university. [C19: from L *inceptus* begun, attempted, from *incipere* to begin, take in hand] —**in'ceptor** *n.*

inception (ɪn'sɛpʃən) *n.* the beginning, as of a project or undertaking.

inceptive (ɪn'sɛptɪv) *adj.* **1.** beginning; incipient; initial. **2.** Also called: **inchoative.** *Grammar.* denoting a verb used to indicate the beginning of an action. ~*n.* **3.** *Grammar.* an inceptive verb. —**in'ceptively** *adv.*

incertitude (ɪn'sɜːtɪ,tjuːd) *n.* **1.** uncertainty; doubt. **2.** a state of mental or emotional insecurity.

incessant (ɪn'sɛsənt) *adj.* not ceasing; continual. [C16: from LL, from L IN-¹ + *cessāre* to CEASE] —**in'cessancy** *n.* —**in'cessantly** *adv.*

incest ('ɪnsɛst) *n.* sexual intercourse between two persons who are too closely related to marry. [C13: from L, from IN-¹ + *castus* CHASTE]

incestuous (ɪn'sɛstjʊəs) *adj.* **1.** relating to or involving incest: *an incestuous union.* **2.** guilty of incest. **3.** resembling incest in excessive or claustrophobic intimacy. —**in'cestuously** *adv.* —**in'cestuousness** *n.*

inch¹ (ɪntʃ) *n.* **1.** a unit of length equal to one twelfth of a foot or 0.0254 metre. **2.** *Meteorol.* **a.** an amount of precipitation that would cover a surface with water one inch deep. **b.** a unit of pressure equal to a mercury column one inch high in a barometer. **3.** a very small distance,

in'appetence *n.*	**,inap'preciative** *adj.*	**,inar'tistic** *adj.*	**,inaus'picious** *adj.*
in'applicable *adj.*	**,inap'propriate** *adj.*	**,inat'tentive** *adj.*	**in'capable** *adj.*
,inap'preciable *adj.*	**,inar'ticulate** *adj.*	**in'audible** *adj.*	

degree, or amount. **4. every inch.** in every way; completely: *every inch an aristocrat.* **5. inch by inch.** gradually; little by little. **6. within an inch of one's life.** almost to death. ~*vb.* **7.** to move or be moved very slowly or in very small steps: *the car inched forward.* [OE *ynce;* see OUNCE[1]]

inch[2] (ɪntʃ) *n. Scot. & Irish.* a small island. [C15: from Gaelic *innis* island; cf. Welsh *ynys*]

inchoate *adj.* (ɪn'kəʊeɪt, -'kəʊɪt). **1.** just beginning; incipient. **2.** undeveloped; immature; rudimentary. ~*vb.* (ɪn'kəʊeɪt). (*tr.*) **3.** to begin. [C16: from L *incohāre* to make a beginning, lit.: to hitch up, from IN-[2] + *cohum* yokestrap] **—in'choately** *adv.* **—in'choateness** *n.* **—,incho'ation** *n.* **—inchoative** (ɪn'kəʊətɪv) *adj.*

Inchon *or* **Incheon** ('ɪn'tʃɒn) *n.* a port in W South Korea, on the Yellow Sea: the chief port for Seoul: site of a major strategic amphibious assault by UN troops, liberating Seoul (Sept. 15, 1950). Pop.: 1 387 475 (1985). Former name: **Chemulpo.**

inchworm ('ɪntʃ,wɜːm) *n.* another name for **measuring worm.**

incidence ('ɪnsɪdəns) *n.* **1.** degree, extent, or frequency of occurrence; amount: *a high incidence of death from pneumonia.* **2.** the act or manner of impinging on or affecting by proximity or influence. **3.** *Physics.* the arrival of a beam of light or particles at a surface. See also **angle of incidence. 4.** *Geom.* the partial coincidence of two configurations, such as a point on a circle.

incident ('ɪnsɪdənt) *n.* **1.** a definite occurrence; event. **2.** a minor, subsidiary, or related event. **3.** a relatively insignificant event that might have serious consequences. **4.** a public disturbance. ~*adj.* **5.** (*postpositive;* foll. by *to*) related (to) or dependent (on). **6.** (when *postpositive,* often foll. by *to*) having a subsidiary or minor relationship (with). **7.** (esp. of a beam of light or particles) arriving at or striking a surface. [C15: from Med. L, from L *incidere,* lit.: to fall into, hence befall, happen]

incidental (,ɪnsɪ'dɛnt[ə]l) *adj.* **1.** happening in connection with or resulting from something more important; casual or fortuitous. **2.** (*postpositive;* foll. by *to*) found in connection (with); related (to). **3.** (*postpositive;* foll. by *upon*) caused (by). **4.** occasional or minor: *incidental expenses.* ~*n.* **5.** (*often pl.*) a minor expense, event, or action. **—,inci'dentalness** *n.*

incidentally (,ɪnsɪ'dɛntəlɪ) *adv.* **1.** as a subordinate or chance occurrence. **2.** (*sentence modifier*) by the way.

incidental music *n.* background music for a film, etc.

incinerate (ɪn'sɪnə,reɪt) *vb.* to burn up completely; reduce to ashes. [C16: from Med. L, from L IN-[2] + *cinis* ashes] **—in,ciner'ation** *n.*

incinerator (ɪn'sɪnə,reɪtə) *n.* a furnace or apparatus for incinerating something, esp. refuse.

incipient (ɪn'sɪpɪənt) *adj.* just starting to be or happen; beginning. [C17: from L, from *incipere* to begin, take in hand] **—in'cipience** *or* **in'cipiency** *n.* **—in'cipiently** *adv.*

incise (ɪn'saɪz) *vb.* (*tr.*) to produce (lines, a design, etc.) by cutting into the surface of (something) with a sharp tool. [C16: from L *incīdere* to cut into]

incision (ɪn'sɪʒən) *n.* **1.** the act of incising. **2.** a cut, gash, or notch. **3.** a cut made with a knife during a surgical operation.

incisive (ɪn'saɪsɪv) *adj.* **1.** keen, penetrating, or acute. **2.** biting or sarcastic; mordant: *an incisive remark.* **3.** having a sharp cutting edge: *incisive teeth.* **—in'cisively** *adv.* **—in'cisiveness** *n.*

incisor (ɪn'saɪzə) *n.* a chisel-edged tooth at the front of the mouth.

incite (ɪn'saɪt) *vb.* (*tr.*) to stir up or provoke to action. [C15: from L, from IN-[2] + *citāre* to excite] **—,inci'tation** *n.* **—in'citement** *n.* **—in'citer** *n.* **—in'citingly** *adv.*

incivility (,ɪnsɪ'vɪlɪtɪ) *n., pl.* **-ties. 1.** lack of civility or courtesy; rudeness. **2.** an impolite or uncivil act or remark.

incl. *abbrev. for:* **1.** including. **2.** inclusive.

inclement (ɪn'klɛmənt) *adj.* **1.** (of weather) stormy, severe, or tempestuous. **2.** severe or merciless. **—in'clemency** *n.* **—in'clemently** *adv.*

inclination (,ɪnklɪ'neɪʃən) *n.* **1.** (often foll. by *for, to, towards,* or an infinitive) a particular disposition, esp. a liking; tendency: *I've no inclination for such dull work.* **2.**

the degree of deviation from a particular plane, esp. a horizontal or vertical plane. **3.** a sloping or slanting surface; incline. **4.** the act of inclining or the state of being inclined. **5.** the act of bowing or nodding the head. **6.** another name for **dip** (sense 24). **—,incli'national** *adj.*

incline *vb.* (ɪn'klaɪn). **1.** to deviate from a particular plane, esp. a vertical or horizontal plane; slope or slant. **2.** (when *tr.,* may take an infinitive) to be disposed or cause to be disposed (towards some attitude or to do something): *that does not incline me to think that you are right.* **3.** to bend or lower (part of the body, esp. the head), as in a bow or in order to listen. **4. incline one's ear.** to listen favourably (to). ~*n.* ('ɪnklaɪn, ɪn'klaɪn). **5.** an inclined surface or slope; gradient. [C13: from L *inclināre* to cause to lean, from *clīnāre* to bend; see LEAN[1]] **—in'clined** *adj.* **—in'cliner** *n.*

inclined plane *n.* a plane whose angle to the horizontal is less than a right angle.

inclinometer (,ɪnklɪ'nɒmɪtə) *n.* an aircraft instrument for indicating the angle that an aircraft makes with the horizontal.

inclose (ɪn'kləʊz) *vb.* a less common spelling of **enclose.** **—in'closure** *n.*

include (ɪn'kluːd) *vb.* (*tr.*) **1.** to have as contents or part of the contents; be made up of or contain. **2.** to add as part of something else; put in as part of a set, group, or category. **3.** to contain as a secondary or minor ingredient or element. [C15 (in the sense: to enclose): from L, from IN-[2] + *claudere* to close] **—in'cludable** *or* **in'cludible** *adj.*

▷ **Usage.** See at **comprise.**

include out *vb.* (*tr., adv.*) *Inf.* to exclude: *you can include me out of that deal.*

inclusion (ɪn'kluːʒən) *n.* **1.** the act of including or the state of being included. **2.** something included.

inclusion body *n. Pathol.* any of the small particles found in cells infected with certain viruses.

inclusive (ɪn'kluːsɪv) *adj.* **1.** (*postpositive;* foll. by *of*) considered together (with): *capital inclusive of profit.* **2.** (*postpositive*) including the limits specified: *Monday to Friday inclusive.* **3.** comprehensive. **4.** *Logic.* (of a disjunction) true if at least one of its component propositions is true. **—in'clusively** *adv.* **—in'clusiveness** *n.*

incognito (,ɪnkɒg'niːtəʊ, ɪn'kɒgnɪtəʊ) *or (fem.)* **incognita** *adv., adj.* (*postpositive*) **1.** under an assumed name or appearance; in disguise. ~*n., pl.* **-tos** *or (fem.)* **-tas. 2.** a person who is incognito. **3.** the assumed name or disguise of such a person. [C17: from It., from L *incognitus* unknown]

incognizant (ɪn'kɒgnɪzənt) *adj.* (when *postpositive,* often foll. by *of*) unaware (of). **—in'cognizance** *n.*

incoherent (,ɪnkəʊ'hɪərənt) *adj.* **1.** lacking in clarity or organization; disordered. **2.** unable to express oneself clearly; inarticulate. **—,inco'herence** *or* **,inco'herency** *n.* **—,inco'herently** *adv.*

income ('ɪnkʌm, 'ɪnkəm) *n.* **1.** the amount of monetary or other returns, either earned or unearned, accruing over a given period of time. **2.** receipts; revenue. [C13 (in the sense: arrival, entrance): from OE *incumen* a coming in]

incomer ('ɪnkʌmə) *n.* a person who comes to live in a place in which he was not born.

incomes policy *n.* an economic policy that attempts to reduce or control inflation by limiting incomes.

income support *n.* (in Britain) a social-security payment for the unemployed and people on low incomes, replacing supplementary benefit.

income tax *n.* a personal tax levied on annual income subject to certain deductions.

incoming ('ɪn,kʌmɪŋ) *adj.* **1.** coming in; entering. **2.** about to come into office; succeeding. **3.** (of interest, dividends, etc.) being received; accruing. ~*n.* **4.** the act of coming in; entrance. **5.** (*usually pl.*) income or revenue.

incommensurable (,ɪnkə'mɛnʃərəb[ə]l) *adj.* **1.** incapable of being judged, measured, or considered comparatively. **2.** (*postpositive;* foll. by *with*) not in accordance; incommensurate. **3.** *Maths.* not having a common factor other than 1, such as 2 and √−5. ~*n.* **4.** something incommensurable. **—,incom,mensura'bility** *n.* **—,incom'mensurably** *adv.*

incommensurate (ˌɪnkəˈmɛnʃərɪt) *adj.* **1.** (when *postpositive*, often foll. by *with*) not commensurate; disproportionate. **2.** incommensurable. —ˌincom'mensurately *adv.* —ˌincom'mensurateness *n.*

incommode (ˌɪnkəˈməʊd) *vb.* (*tr.*) to bother, disturb, or inconvenience. [C16: from L *incommodāre* to be troublesome, from *incommodus* inconvenient; see COMMODE]

incommodious (ˌɪnkəˈməʊdɪəs) *adj.* **1.** insufficiently spacious; cramped. **2.** troublesome or inconvenient. —ˌincom'modiously *adv.*

incommodity (ˌɪnkəˈmɒdɪtɪ) *n., pl.* **-ties.** anything that causes inconvenience.

incommunicado (ˌɪnkəˌmjuːnɪˈkɑːdəʊ) *adv., adj.* (*postpositive*) deprived of communication with other people, as while in solitary confinement. [C19: from Sp., from *incomunicar* to deprive of communication; see IN-[1], COMMUNICATE]

incomparable (ɪnˈkɒmpərəbəl, -prəbəl) *adj.* **1.** beyond or above comparison; matchless; unequalled. **2.** lacking a basis for comparison; not having qualities or features that can be compared. —inˌcompara'bility *or* in'comparableness *n.* —in'comparably *adv.*

incompatible (ˌɪnkəmˈpætəbəl) *adj.* **1.** incapable of living or existing together in harmony; conflicting or antagonistic. **2.** opposed in nature or quality; inconsistent. **3.** *Med.* (esp. of two drugs or two types of blood) incapable of being combined or used together; antagonistic. **4.** *Logic.* (of two propositions) unable to be both true at the same time. **5.** (of plants) incapable of self-fertilization. ~*n.* **6.** (*often pl.*) a person or thing that is incompatible with another. —ˌincomˌpati'bility *or* ˌincom'patibleness *n.* —ˌincom'patibly *adv.*

incompetent (ɪnˈkɒmpɪtənt) *adj.* **1.** not possessing the necessary ability, skill, etc., to do or carry out a task; incapable. **2.** marked by lack of ability, skill, etc. **3.** *Law.* not legally qualified: *an incompetent witness.* ~*n.* **4.** an incompetent person. —in'competence *or* in'competency *n.* —in'competently *adv.*

inconceivable (ˌɪnkənˈsiːvəbəl) *adj.* incapable of being conceived, imagined, or considered. —inconˌceiva'bility *or* ˌincon'ceivableness *n.* —ˌincon'ceivably *adv.*

incongruous (ɪnˈkɒŋgrʊəs) *or* **incongruent** *adj.* **1.** (when *postpositive*, foll. by *with* or *to*) incompatible with (what is suitable); inappropriate. **2.** containing disparate or discordant elements or parts. —in'congruously *adv.* —in'congruousness *or* incongruity (ˌɪnkɒŋˈgruːɪtɪ) *n.*

inconnu (ˈɪnkənjuː, ˈɪnkənuː) *n. Canad.* a whitefish of Far Northern waters. [C19: from F, lit: unknown]

inconsequential (ˌɪnkɒnsɪˈkwɛnʃəl, ɪnˌkɒn-) *or* **inconsequent** (ɪnˈkɒnsɪkwənt) *adj.* **1.** not following logically as a consequence. **2.** trivial or insignificant. **3.** not in a logical sequence; haphazard. —ˌinconseˌquenti'ality, or in'consequence *n.* —ˌinconse'quentially *or* in'consequently *adv.*

inconsiderable (ˌɪnkənˈsɪdərəbəl) *adj.* **1.** relatively small. **2.** not worthy of consideration; insignificant. —ˌincon'siderableness *n.* —ˌincon'siderably *adv.*

inconsiderate (ˌɪnkənˈsɪdərɪt) *adj.* lacking in care or thought for others; thoughtless. —ˌincon'siderately *adv.* —ˌincon'siderateness *or* ˌinconˌsider'ation *n.*

inconsistency (ˌɪnkənˈsɪstənsɪ) *n., pl.* **-cies. 1.** lack of consistency or agreement; incompatibility. **2.** an inconsistent feature or quality.

inconsistent (ˌɪnkənˈsɪstənt) *adj.* **1.** lacking in consistency, agreement, or compatibility; at variance. **2.** containing contradictory elements. **3.** irregular or fickle in behaviour or mood. **4.** *Logic.* (of a set of propositions) enabling an explicit contradiction to be validly derived. —ˌincon'sistently *adv.*

inconsolable (ˌɪnkənˈsəʊləbəl) *adj.* incapable of being consoled or comforted; disconsolate. —ˌinconˌso'lability *or* ˌincon'solableness *n.* —ˌincon'solably *adv.*

inconsonant (ɪnˈkɒnsənənt) *adj.* lacking in harmony or compatibility; discordant. —in'consonance *n.* —in'consonantly *adv.*

inconspicuous (ˌɪnkənˈspɪkjʊəs) *adj.* not easily noticed or seen; not prominent or striking. —ˌincon'spicuously *adv.* —ˌincon'spicuousness *n.*

incontinent[1] (ɪnˈkɒntɪnənt) *adj.* **1.** relating to or exhibiting involuntary urination or defecation. **2.** lacking in restraint or control, esp. sexually. **3.** (foll. by *of*) having little or no control (over). **4.** unrestrained; uncontrolled. [C14: from OF, from L, from IN-[1] + *continere* to hold, restrain] —in'continence *n.* —in'continently *adv.*

incontinent[2] (ɪnˈkɒntɪnənt) *or* **incontinently** *adv.* obsolete words for **immediately.** [C15: from LL *in continentī tempore*, lit.: in continuous time, that is, with no interval]

incontrovertible (ˌɪnkɒntrəˈvɜːtəbəl, ɪnˌkɒn-) *adj.* incapable of being contradicted or disputed; undeniable. —inˌcontro'verti'bility *n.* —ˌincontro'vertibly *adv.*

incorporate *vb.* (ɪnˈkɔːpəˌreɪt). **1.** to include or be included as a part or member of a united whole. **2.** to form a united whole or mass; merge or blend. **3.** to form into a corporation or other organization with a separate legal identity. ~*adj.* (ɪnˈkɔːpərɪt, -prɪt). **4.** combined into a whole; incorporated. **5.** formed into or constituted as a corporation. [C14 (in the sense: put into the body of something else): from LL *incorporāre* to embody, from L IN-[2] + *corpus* body] —in'corpoˌrated *adj.* —inˌcorpo'ration *n.* —in'corporative *adj.*

incorporeal (ˌɪnkɔːˈpɔːrɪəl) *adj.* **1.** without material form, body, or substance. **2.** spiritual or metaphysical. **3.** *Law.* having no material existence but existing by reason of its annexation of something material: *an incorporeal hereditament.* —ˌincor'poreally *adv.* —incorporeity (ɪnˌkɔːpəˈriːɪtɪ) *or* ˌincorpore'ality *n.*

incorrigible (ɪnˈkɒrɪdʒəbəl) *adj.* **1.** beyond correction, reform, or alteration. **2.** firmly rooted; ineradicable. ~*n.* **3.** a person or animal that is incorrigible. —inˌcorrigi'bility *or* in'corrigibleness *n.* —in'corrigibly *adv.*

incorruptible (ˌɪnkəˈrʌptəbəl) *adj.* **1.** incapable of being corrupted; honest; just. **2.** not subject to decay or decomposition. —ˌincorˌrupti'bility *n.* —ˌincor'ruptibly *adv.*

incr. *abbrev. for:* **1.** increase. **2.** increased. **3.** increasing.

incrassate *adj.* (ɪnˈkræsɪt, -eɪt), *also* **incrassated. 1.** *Biol.* thickened or swollen. ~*vb.* (ɪnˈkræseɪt). **2.** *Obs.* to make or become thicker. [C17: from LL, from L *crassus* thick, dense] —ˌincras'sation *n.*

increase *vb.* (ɪnˈkriːs). **1.** to make or become greater in size, degree, frequency, etc.; grow or expand. ~*n.* (ˈɪnkriːs). **2.** the act of increasing; augmentation. **3.** the amount by which something increases. **4. on the increase.** increasing, esp. becoming more frequent. [C14: from OF *encreistre*, from L, from IN-[2] + *crēscere* to grow] —in'creasable *adj.* —increasedly (ɪnˈkriːsɪdlɪ) *or* in'creasingly *adv.* —in'creaser *n.*

incredible (ɪnˈkrɛdəbəl) *adj.* **1.** beyond belief or understanding; unbelievable. **2.** *Inf.* marvellous; amazing. —inˌcredi'bility *or* in'credibleness *n.* —in'credibly *adv.*

incredulity (ˌɪnkrɪˈdjuːlɪtɪ) *n.* lack of belief; scepticism.

incredulous (ɪnˈkrɛdjʊləs) *adj.* (often foll. by *of*) not prepared or willing to believe (something); unbelieving. —in'credulously *adv.* —in'credulousness *n.*

increment (ˈɪnkrɪmənt) *n.* **1.** an increase or addition, esp. one of a series. **2.** the act of increasing; augmentation. **3.** *Maths.* a small positive or negative change in a variable or function. [C15: from L *incrēmentum* growth, INCREASE] —**incremental** (ˌɪnkrɪˈmɛntəl) *adj.*

incremental plotter *n.* a device that plots graphs on paper from computer-generated instructions.

incriminate (ɪnˈkrɪmɪˌneɪt) *vb.* (*tr.*) **1.** to imply or suggest the guilt or error of (someone). **2.** to charge with a crime or fault. [C18: from LL *incrīmināre* to accuse, from L *crīmen* accusation; see CRIME] —in'crimi'nation *n.* —in'crimiˌnator *n.* —in'criminatory *adj.*

incrust (ɪnˈkrʌst) *vb.* a variant spelling of **encrust.** —in'crustant *n., adj.* —ˌincrus'tation *n.*

incubate (ˈɪnkjʊˌbeɪt) *vb.* **1.** (of birds) to supply (eggs) with heat for their development, esp. by sitting on them. **2.** to cause (bacteria, etc.) to develop, esp. in an incubator or culture medium. **3.** (*intr.*) (of embryos, etc.) to develop in favourable conditions, esp. in an incubator. **4.**

ˌincom'municable *adj.*
ˌincom'municative *adj.*
ˌincom'mutable *adj.*
ˌincom'plete *adj.*

ˌincompre'hensible *adj.*
ˌincom'pressible *adj.*
ˌincon'clusive *adj.*
in'constant *adj.*

ˌincon'testable *adj.*
ˌincon'venience *n., vb.*
ˌincon'venient *adj.*
ˌincon'vertible *adj.*

ˌincoˌordi'nation *n.*
ˌincor'rect *adj.*
ˌincor'rupt *adj.*

(*intr.*) (of disease germs) to remain inactive in an animal or human before causing disease. **5.** to develop gradually; foment or be fomented. [C18: from L *incubāre* to lie upon, hatch, from IN-² + *cubāre* to lie down] —,incu'bation *n.* —,incu'bational *adj.* —'incu,bative *or* 'in-cu,batory *adj.*

incubation period *n. Med.* the time between exposure to an infectious disease and the appearance of the first signs or symptoms.

incubator ('ɪnkjʊ,beɪtə) *n.* **1.** *Med.* an apparatus for housing prematurely born babies until they are strong enough to survive. **2.** a container in which birds' eggs can be artificially hatched or bacterial cultures grown. **3.** a person, animal, or thing that incubates.

incubus ('ɪnkjʊbəs) *n., pl.* **-bi** (-,baɪ) *or* **-buses. 1.** a demon believed in folklore to have sexual intercourse with sleeping women. Cf. **succubus. 2.** something that oppresses or disturbs greatly, esp. a nightmare or obsession. [C14: from LL, from L *incubāre* to lie upon; see INCUBATE]

inculcate ('ɪnkʌl,keɪt, ɪn'kʌlkeɪt) *vb.* (*tr.*) to instil by insistent repetition. [C16: from L *inculcāre* to tread upon, ram down, from IN-² + *calcāre* to trample, from *calx* heel] —,incul'cation *n.* —'incul,cator *n.*

inculpate ('ɪnkʌl,peɪt, ɪn'kʌlpeɪt) *vb.* (*tr.*) to incriminate; cause blame to be imputed to. [C18: from LL, from L *culpāre* to blame, from *culpa* fault, blame] —,incul'pation *n.* —**inculpative** (ɪn'kʌlpətɪv) *or* **inculpatory** (ɪn'kʌlpətərɪ, -trɪ) *adj.*

incumbency (ɪn'kʌmbənsɪ) *n., pl.* **-cies. 1.** the state or quality of being incumbent. **2.** the office, duty, or tenure of an incumbent.

incumbent (ɪn'kʌmbənt) *adj.* **1.** *Formal.* (often *postpositive* and foll. by *on* or *upon* and an infinitive) morally binding; obligatory: *it is incumbent on me to attend.* **2.** (usually *postpositive* and foll. by *on*) resting or lying (on). **3.** (usually *prenominal*) occupying or holding an office. ~*n.* **4.** a person who holds an office, esp. a clergyman holding a benefice. [C16: from L *incumbere* to lie upon, devote one's attention to]

incunabula (,ɪnkjʊ'næbjʊlə) *pl. n., sing.* **-lum** (-ləm). **1.** any book printed before 1500. **2.** the earliest stages of something; beginnings. [C19: from L, orig.: swaddling clothes, hence beginnings, from IN-² + *cūnābula* cradle] —,incu'nabular *adj.*

incur (ɪn'kɜː) *vb.* **-curring, -curred.** (*tr.*) **1.** to make oneself subject to (something undesirable); bring upon oneself. **2.** to run into or encounter. [C16: from L *incurrere* to run into, from *currere* to run] —**in'currable** *adj.*

incurable (ɪn'kjʊərəbəl) *adj.* **1.** (esp. of a disease) not curable; unresponsive to treatment. ~*n.* **2.** a person having an incurable disease. —,in,cura'bility *or* **in'curable-ness** *n.* —**in'curably** *adv.*

incurious (ɪn'kjʊərɪəs) *adj.* not curious; indifferent or uninterested. —**incuriosity** (ɪn,kjʊərɪ'ɒsɪtɪ) *or* **in'curious-ness** *n.* —**in'curiously** *adv.*

incursion (ɪn'kɜːʃən) *n.* **1.** a sudden invasion, attack, or raid. **2.** the act of running or leaking into; penetration. [C15: from L *incursiō* onset, attack, from *incurrere* to run into; see INCUR] —**incursive** (ɪn'kɜːsɪv) *adj.*

incus ('ɪŋkəs) *n., pl.* **incudes** (ɪn'kjuːdiːz). the central of the three small bones in the middle ear of mammals. Cf. **malleus, stapes.** [C17: from L: anvil, from *incūdere* to forge]

incuse (ɪn'kjuːz) *n.* **1.** a design stamped or hammered onto a coin. ~*vb.* **2.** to impress (a coin) with a design by hammering or stamping. ~*adj.* **3.** stamped or hammered onto a coin. [C19: from L *incūsus* hammered; see INCUS]

ind. *abbrev. for:* **1.** independence. **2.** independent. **3.** index. **4.** indicative. **5.** indirect. **6.** industrial. **7.** industry.

Ind. *abbrev. for:* **1.** Independent. **2.** India. **3.** Indian. **4.** Indies.

indaba (ɪn'dɑːbə) *n.* **1.** (among Bantu peoples of southern Africa) a meeting to discuss a serious topic. **2.** *S. African inf.* a matter of concern or for discussion. [C19: from Zulu: topic]

indebted (ɪn'detɪd) *adj.* (*postpositive*) **1.** owing gratitude for help, favours, etc.; obligated. **2.** owing money. —**in'debtedness** (ɪn'detɪdnɪs) *n.* **1.** the state of being indebted. **2.** the total of a person's debts.

indecency (ɪn'diːsənsɪ) *n., pl.* **-cies. 1.** the state or quality of being indecent. **2.** an indecent act, etc.

indecent (ɪn'diːs³nt) *adj.* **1.** offensive to standards of decency, esp. in sexual matters. **2.** unseemly or improper (esp. in **indecent haste**). —**in'decently** *adv.*

indecent assault *n.* the offence of subjecting a person to a form of sexual activity, other than rape, against his or her will.

indecent exposure *n.* the offence of indecently exposing one's body in public, esp. the genitals.

indecisive (,ɪndɪ'saɪsɪv) *adj.* **1.** (of a person) vacillating; irresolute. **2.** not decisive or conclusive. —,inde'cision *or* ,inde'cisiveness *n.* —,inde'cisively *adv.*

indecorum (,ɪndɪ'kɔːrəm) *n.* lack of decorum; unseemliness. —**in'decorous** *adj.*

indeed (ɪn'diːd) (*sentence connector*). **1.** certainly; actually: *indeed, it may never happen.* ~*adv.* **2.** (intensifier): *that is indeed amazing.* **3.** or rather; what is more: *a comfortable, indeed wealthy family.* ~*interj.* **4.** an expression of doubt, surprise, etc.

indef. *abbrev. for* indefinite.

indefatigable (,ɪndɪ'fætɪgəb³l) *adj.* unable to be tired out; unflagging. [C16: from L, from *fatigāre* to tire] —,inde,fatiga'bility *n.* —,inde'fatigably *adv.*

indefeasible (,ɪndɪ'fiːzəb³l) *adj. Law.* not liable to be annulled or forfeited. —,inde,feasi'bility *n.* —,inde'feasi-bly *adv.*

indefensible (,ɪndɪ'fɛnsəb³l) *adj.* **1.** not justifiable or excusable. **2.** capable of being disagreed with; untenable. **3.** incapable of defence against attack. —,inde,fen-si'bility *n.* —,inde'fensibly *adv.*

indefinite (ɪn'dɛfɪnɪt) *adj.* **1.** not certain or determined; unsettled. **2.** without exact limits; indeterminate: *an indefinite number.* **3.** vague or unclear. **4.** in traditional logic, a proposition in which it is not stated whether the subject is universal or particular, as in *men are mortal.* —**in'definitely** *adv.* —**in'definiteness** *n.*

indefinite article *n. Grammar.* a determiner that expresses nonspecificity of reference, such as *a, an,* or *some.*

indehiscent (,ɪndɪ'hɪs³nt) *adj.* (of fruits, etc.) not dehiscent; not opening to release seeds, etc. —,inde'hiscence *n.*

indelible (ɪn'dɛlɪb³l) *adj.* **1.** incapable of being erased or obliterated. **2.** making indelible marks: *indelible ink.* [C16: from L, from IN-¹ + *dēlēre* to destroy] —**in,deli'bil-ity** *or* **in'delibleness** *n.* —**in'delibly** *adv.*

indelicate (ɪn'dɛlɪkɪt) *adj.* **1.** coarse, crude, or rough. **2.** offensive, embarrassing, or tasteless. —**in'delicacy** *or* **in'delicateness** *n.* —**in'delicately** *adv.*

indemnify (ɪn'dɛmnɪ,faɪ) *vb.* **-fying, -fied.** (*tr.*) **1.** to secure against future loss, damage, or liability; give security for; insure. **2.** to compensate for loss, damage, etc. —**in,demnifi'cation** *n.* —**in'demni,fier** *n.*

indemnity (ɪn'dɛmnɪtɪ) *n., pl.* **-ties. 1.** compensation for loss or damage; reimbursement. **2.** protection or insurance against future loss or damage. **3.** legal exemption from penalties incurred through one's acts or defaults. **4.** *Canad.* the annual salary paid by the government to a member of Parliament or of a provincial legislature. [C15: from LL, from *indemnis* uninjured, from L IN-¹ + *damnum* damage]

indene ('ɪndiːn) *n.* a colourless liquid hydrocarbon obtained from coal tar and used in making synthetic resins. Formula: C_9H_8. [C20: from INDOLE + -ENE]

indent¹ *vb.* (ɪn'dɛnt). (*mainly tr.*) **1.** to place (written matter, etc.) in from the margin. **2.** to cut (a document in duplicate) so that the irregular lines may be matched. **3.** *Chiefly Brit.* (in foreign trade) to place an order for (foreign goods). **4.** (when *intr.*, foll. by *for, on,* or *upon*) *Chiefly Brit.* to make an order on (a source or supply) or for (something). **5.** to notch (an edge, border, etc.); make jagged. **6.** to bind (an apprentice, etc.) by indenture. ~*n.* ('ɪn,dɛnt). *Chiefly Brit.* **7.** (in foreign trade) an order for foreign merchandise. **8.** an official order for goods. [C14: from OF *endenter,* from EN-¹ + *dent* tooth, from L *dēns*] —**in'denter** *or* **in'dentor** *n.*

indent² *vb.* (ɪn'dɛnt). **1.** (*tr.*) to make a dent or depression in. ~*n.* ('ɪn,dɛnt). **2.** a dent or depression. [C15: from IN-² + DENT]

indentation (,ɪndɛn'teɪʃən) *n.* **1.** a hollowed, notched, or cut place, as on an edge or on a coastline. **2.** a series of hollows, notches, or cuts. **3.** the act of indenting or the

,inde'cipherable *adj.*   ,inde'clinable *adj.*   ,inde'finable *adj.*   ,inde'monstrable *adj.*

condition of being indented. **4.** Also: **indention, indent.** the leaving of space or the amount of space left between a margin and the start of an indented line.

indention (ɪnˈdɛnʃən) n. another word for **indentation** (sense 4).

indenture (ɪnˈdɛntʃə) n. **1.** any deed, contract, or sealed agreement between two or more parties. **2.** (formerly) a deed drawn up in duplicate, each part having correspondingly indented edges for identification and security. **3.** (often pl.) a contract between an apprentice and his master. **4.** a less common word for **indentation.** ~vb. **5.** (intr.) to enter into an agreement by indenture. **6.** (tr.) to bind (an apprentice, servant, etc.) by indenture. —**inˈdentureˌship** n.

independence (ˌɪndɪˈpɛndəns) n. the state or quality of being independent. Also: **independency.**

Independence (ˌɪndɪˈpɛndəns) n. a city in W Missouri, near Kansas City: starting point for the Santa Fe, Oregon, and California Trails (1831–44). Pop.: 112 121 (1984 est.).

independency (ˌɪndɪˈpɛndənsɪ) n., pl. **-cies. 1.** a territory or state free from the control of any other power. **2.** another word for **independence.**

independent (ˌɪndɪˈpɛndənt) adj. **1.** free from control in action, judgment, etc.; autonomous. **2.** not dependent on anything else for function, validity, etc.; separate. **3.** not reliant on the support, esp. financial support, of others. **4.** capable of acting for oneself or on one's own: a very independent little girl. **5.** providing a large unearned sum towards one's support (esp. in **independent income, independent means**). **6.** living on an unearned income. **7.** Maths. (of a system of equations) not linearly dependent. See also **independent variable. 8.** Logic. (of two or more propositions) unrelated. ~n. **9.** an independent person or thing. **10.** a person who is not affiliated to or who acts independently of a political party. —ˌindeˈpendently adv.

Independent (ˌɪndɪˈpɛndənt) Christianity. ~n. **1.** (in England) a member of the Congregational Church. ~adj. **2.** of or relating to the Congregational Church.

independent clause n. Grammar. a main or coordinate clause.

independent school n. (in Britain) a school that is neither financed nor controlled by the government or local authorities.

independent variable n. a variable in a mathematical equation or statement whose value determines that of the dependent variable: in $y = f(x)$, x is the independent variable.

in-depth adj. detailed and thorough: an in-depth study.

indescribable (ˌɪndɪˈskraɪbəbəl) adj. beyond description; too intense, extreme, etc., for words. —ˌindeˈscribaˈbility n. —ˌindeˈscribably adv.

indeterminate (ˌɪndɪˈtɜːmɪnɪt) adj. **1.** uncertain in extent, amount, or nature. **2.** not definite; inconclusive: an indeterminate reply. **3.** unable to be predicted, calculated, or deduced. **4.** Maths. **a.** having no numerical meaning, as 0/0. **b.** (of an equation) having more than one variable and an unlimited number of solutions. —ˌindeˈterminacy or ˌindeˈterminateness n. —ˌindeˈterminately adv.

indeterminism (ˌɪndɪˈtɜːmɪˌnɪzəm) n. the philosophical doctrine that behaviour is not entirely determined by motives. —ˌindeˈterminist n., adj. —ˌindeˌterminˈistic adj.

index (ˈɪndɛks) n., pl. **-dexes** or **-dices** (-dɪˌsiːz). **1.** an alphabetical list of persons, subjects, etc., mentioned in a printed work, usually at the back, and indicating where they are referred to. **2.** See **thumb index. 3.** Library science. a systematic list of book titles or authors' names, giving cross-references and the location of each book; catalogue. **4.** an indication, sign, or token. **5.** a pointer, needle, or other indicator, as on an instrument. **6.** Maths. **a.** another name for **exponent** (sense 4). **b.** a number or variable placed as a superscript to the left of a radical sign indicating the root to be extracted, as in $\sqrt[3]{8} = 2$. **7.** a numerical scale by means of which levels of the cost of living can be compared with some base number. **8.** a number or ratio indicating a specific characteristic, property, etc.: refractive index. **9.** Also called: **fist.** a printer's mark, ☞ used to indicate notes, paragraphs, etc. ~vb. (tr.) **10.** to put an index in (a book). **11.** to enter (a word,

item, etc.) in an index. **12.** to point out; indicate. **13.** to make index-linked. **14.** to move (a machine, etc.) so that an operation will be repeated at certain defined intervals. [C16: from L: pointer, hence forefinger, title, index, from indicāre to disclose, show; see INDICATE] —ˈindexer n. —inˈdexical adj.

indexation (ˌɪndɛkˈseɪʃən) or **index-linking** n. the act of making wages, interest rates, etc., index-linked.

index finger n. the finger next to the thumb. Also called: **forefinger.**

Index Librorum Prohibitorum Latin. (ˈɪndɛks laɪˈbrɔːrʊm prəʊˌhɪbɪˈtɔːrʊm) n. R.C. Church. (formerly) an official list of proscribed books. Often called: **the Index.** [C17, lit.: list of forbidden books]

index-linked adj. (of wages, interest rates, etc.) directly related to the cost-of-living index and rising or falling accordingly.

index number n. Statistics. a statistic indicating the relative change occurring in the price or value of a commodity or in a general economic variable, with reference to a previous base period conventionally given the number 100.

India (ˈɪndɪə) n. a republic in S Asia: history dates from the Indus Valley civilization (3rd millennium B.C.); came under British supremacy in 1763 and passed to the British Crown in 1858; nationalist movement arose under Gandhi (1869–1948); Indian subcontinent divided into Pakistan (Muslim) and India (Hindu) in 1947; became a republic within the Commonwealth in 1950. It consists chiefly of the Himalayas, rising over 7500 m (25 000 ft.) in the extreme north, the Ganges plain in the north, the Thar Desert in the northwest, the Chota Nagpur plateau in the northeast, and the Deccan Plateau in the south. Official and administrative languages: Hindi and English; each state has its own language. Religion: Hindu majority. Currency: rupee. Capital: New Delhi. Pop.: 783 940 000 (1986). Area: 3 268 100 sq. km (1 261 813 sq. miles). Hindi name: **Bharat.**

Indiaman (ˈɪndɪəmən) n., pl. **-men.** (formerly) a merchant ship engaged in trade with India.

Indian (ˈɪndɪən) n. **1.** a native or inhabitant of the Republic of India. **2.** an American Indian. **3.** (not in scholarly usage) any of the languages of the American Indians. ~adj. **4.** of or relating to India, its inhabitants, or any of their languages. **5.** of or relating to the American Indians or any of their languages.

Indiana (ˌɪndɪˈænə) n. a state of the N central U.S., in the Midwest: consists of an undulating plain, with sand dunes and lakes in the north and limestone caves in the south. Capital: Indianapolis. Pop.: 5 503 000 (1986 est.). Area: 93 491 sq. km (36 097 sq. miles). Abbrevs.: **Ind.** or (with zip code) **IN** —**Indiˈanian** adj., n.

Indianapolis (ˌɪndɪəˈnæpəlɪs) n. a city in central Indiana: the state capital. Pop.: 719 820 (1986 est.).

Indian club n. a bottle-shaped club, usually used in pairs by gymnasts, jugglers, etc.

Indian corn n. another name for **maize** (sense 1).

Indian Desert n. another name for the **Thar Desert.**

Indian Empire n. British India and the Indian states under indirect British control, which gained independence as India and Pakistan in 1947.

Indian file n. another term for **single file.**

Indian hemp n. another name for **hemp,** esp. the variety *Cannabis indica,* from which several narcotic drugs are obtained.

Indian ink or esp. U.S. & Canad. **India ink** n. **1.** a black pigment made from a mixture of lampblack and a binding agent such as gelatin or glue: usually formed into solid cakes and sticks. **2.** a black liquid ink made from this pigment. ~Also called: **China ink, Chinese ink.**

Indian list n. Inf. (in Canada) a list of persons to whom spirits may not be sold.

Indian meal n. another name for **corn meal.**

Indian Ocean n. an ocean bordered by Africa in the west, Asia in the north, and Australia in the east and merging with the Antarctic Ocean in the south. Average depth: 3900 m (13 000 ft.). Greatest depth (off the Sunda Islands): 7450 m (24 442 ft.). Area: about 73 556 000 sq. km (28 400 000 sq. miles).

Indian rope-trick n. the supposed Indian feat of climbing an unsupported rope.

ˌindeˈstructible adj.   ˌindeˈterminable adj.

Indian States and Agencies *pl. n.* another name for the **Native States.**

Indian summer *n.* **1.** a period of unusually warm weather in the late autumn. **2.** a period of tranquillity or of renewed productivity towards the end of something, esp. a person's life. [orig. U.S.: prob. so named because it was first noted in Amerind regions]

Indian Territory *n.* the territory established in the early 19th century in present-day Oklahoma, where Indians were forced to settle by the U.S. government. The last remnant was integrated into the new state of Oklahoma in 1907.

Indian tobacco *n.* a poisonous North American plant with small pale bell-shaped blue flowers and rounded inflated seed capsules.

India paper *n.* a thin soft opaque printing paper originally made in the Orient.

India rubber *n.* another name for **rubber**¹ (sense 1).

Indic ('ɪndɪk) *adj.* **1.** denoting, belonging to, or relating to a branch of Indo-European consisting of certain languages of India, including Sanskrit, Hindi and Urdu. ~*n.* **2.** this group of languages. ~Also: **Indo-Aryan.**

indicate ('ɪndɪˌkeɪt) *vb.* (*tr.*) **1.** (*may take a clause as object*) to be or give a sign or symptom of; imply: *cold hands indicate a warm heart.* **2.** to point out or show. **3.** (*may take a clause as object*) to state briefly; suggest. **4.** (of instruments) to show a reading of. **5.** (*usually passive*) to recommend or require: *surgery seems to be indicated for this patient.* [C17: from L *indicāre* to point out, from IN-² + *dicāre* to proclaim; cf. INDEX] —'indi,catable *adj.* —indicatory (ɪn'dɪkətərɪ, -trɪ) *adj.*

indication (,ɪndɪ'keɪʃən) *n.* **1.** something that serves to indicate or suggest; sign: *an indication of foul play.* **2.** the degree or quantity represented on a measuring instrument or device. **3.** the action of indicating. **4.** something that is indicated as advisable, necessary, or expedient.

indicative (ɪn'dɪkətɪv) *adj.* **1.** (*usually postpositive*; foll. by *of*) serving as a sign; suggestive: *indicative of trouble ahead.* **2.** *Grammar.* denoting a mood of verbs used chiefly to make statements. ~*n.* **3.** *Grammar.* **a.** the indicative mood. **b.** a verb in the indicative mood. ~Abbrev.: **indic.** —in'dicatively *adv.*

indicator ('ɪndɪˌkeɪtə) *n.* **1.** a device to attract attention, such as the pointer of a gauge or a warning lamp. **2.** an instrument that displays certain operating conditions in a machine, such as a gauge showing temperature, etc. **3.** a device that registers something, such as the movements of a lift, or that shows information, such as train departure times. **4.** Also called: **blinkers** a device for indicating that a motor vehicle is about to turn left or right, esp. two pairs of lights that flash. **5.** a delicate measuring instrument used to determine small differences in the height of mechanical components. **6.** *Chem.* a substance used to indicate the completion of a chemical reaction, usually by a change of colour.

indices ('ɪndɪˌsiːz) *n.* a plural of **index.**

indicia (ɪn'dɪʃɪə) *pl. n., sing.* **-cium** (-ʃɪəm). distinguishing markings or signs; indications. [C17: from L, pl. of *indicium* a notice, from INDEX] —in'dicial *adj.*

indict (ɪn'daɪt) *vb.* (*tr.*) to charge (a person) with crime, esp. formally in writing; accuse. [C14: alteration of *enditen* to INDITE] —indict'ee *n.* —in'dicter *or* in'dictor *n.* —in'dictable *adj.*

indictment (ɪn'daɪtmənt) *n. Criminal law.* **1.** a formal written charge of crime formerly referred to and presented on oath by a grand jury. **2.** any formal accusation of crime. **3.** the act of indicting or the state of being indicted.

indie ('ɪndɪ) *n. Inf.* **a.** an independent record company. **b.** (*as modifier*): *the indie charts.*

Indies ('ɪndɪz) *n.* **the. 1.** the territories of S and SE Asia included in the East Indies, India, and Indochina. **2.** See **East Indies. 3.** See **West Indies.**

indifference (ɪn'dɪfrəns, -fərəns) *n.* **1.** the fact or state of being indifferent; lack of care or concern. **2.** lack of quality; mediocrity. **3.** lack of importance; insignificance.

indifferent (ɪn'dɪfrənt, -fərənt) *adj.* **1.** (often foll. by *to*) showing no care or concern; uninterested: *he was indifferent to my pleas.* **2.** unimportant; immaterial. **3. a.** of only average or moderate size, extent, quality, etc. **b.** not at all good; poor. **4.** showing or having no preferences;

impartial. [C14: from L *indifferēns* making no distinction] —in'differently *adv.*

indifferentism (ɪn'dɪfrən,tɪzəm, -fərən-) *n.* systematic indifference, esp. in matters of religion. —in'differentist *n.*

indigenous (ɪn'dɪdʒɪnəs) *adj.* (when *postpositive*, foll. by *to*) **1.** originating or occurring naturally (in a country, etc.); native. **2.** innate (to); inherent (in). [C17: from L *indigenus*, from *indi*- in + *gignere* to beget] —in'digenously *adv.* —in'digenousness *n.*

indigent ('ɪndɪdʒənt) *adj.* **1.** so poor as to lack even necessities; very needy. **2.** (usually foll. by *of*) *Arch.* lacking (in) or destitute (of). ~*n.* **3.** an impoverished person. [C14: from L *indigēre* to need, from *egēre* to lack] —'indigence *n.* —'indigently *adv.*

indigestible (,ɪndɪ'dʒɛstəbəl) *adj.* **1.** incapable of being digested or difficult to digest. **2.** difficult to understand or absorb mentally: *an indigestible book.* —,indi,gesti'bility *n.* —indi'gestibly *adv.*

indigestion (,ɪndɪ'dʒɛstʃən) *n.* difficulty in digesting food, accompanied by abdominal pain, heartburn, and belching.

indignant (ɪn'dɪɡnənt) *adj.* feeling or showing indignation. [C16: from L *indignārī* to be displeased with] —in'dignantly *adv.*

indignation (,ɪndɪɡ'neɪʃən) *n.* anger aroused by something felt to be unfair, unworthy, or wrong.

indignity (ɪn'dɪɡnɪtɪ) *n., pl.* **-ties.** injury to one's self-esteem or dignity; humiliation.

indigo ('ɪndɪˌɡəʊ) *n., pl.* **-gos** *or* **-goes. 1.** a blue vat dye originally obtained from plants but now made synthetically. **2.** any of various leguminous tropical plants, such as the anil, that yield this dye. **3. a.** any of a group of colours that have the same blue-violet hue; a spectral colour. **b.** (*as adj.*): *an indigo rug.* [C16: from Sp. *indico*, via L from Gk *Indikos* of India] —indigotic (,ɪndɪ'ɡɒtɪk) *adj.*

indigo blue *n., adj.* (**indigo-blue** *when prenominal*). the full name for **indigo** (the colour and the dye).

indirect (,ɪndɪ'rɛkt) *adj.* **1.** deviating from a direct course or line; roundabout; circuitous. **2.** not coming as a direct effect or consequence; secondary: *indirect benefits.* **3.** not straightforward, open, or fair; devious or evasive. —,indi'rectly *adv.* —,indi'rectness *n.*

indirect costs *pl. n.* another name for **overheads.**

indirection (,ɪndɪ'rɛkʃən) *n.* **1.** indirect procedure, courses, or methods. **2.** lack of direction or purpose; aimlessness. **3.** indirect dealing; deceit.

indirect lighting *n.* reflected or diffused light from a concealed source.

indirect object *n. Grammar.* a noun, pronoun, or noun phrase indicating the recipient or beneficiary of the action of a verb and its direct object, as *John* in the sentence *I bought John a newspaper.*

indirect proof *n. Logic, maths.* proof of a conclusion by showing its negation to be self-contradictory. Cf. **direct** (sense 17).

indirect question *n.* a question reported in indirect speech, as in *She asked why you came.*

indirect speech *or esp. U.S.* **indirect discourse** *n.* the reporting of something said or written by conveying what was meant rather than repeating the exact words, as in the sentence *He asked me whether I would go* as opposed to *He asked me, "Will you go?"* Also called: **reported speech.**

indirect tax *n.* a tax levied on goods or services rather than on individuals or companies.

indiscreet (,ɪndɪ'skriːt) *adj.* not discreet; imprudent or tactless. —,indis'creetly *adv.* —,indis'creetness *n.*

indiscrete (,ɪndɪ'skriːt) *adj.* not divisible or divided into parts.

indiscretion (,ɪndɪ'skrɛʃən) *n.* **1.** the characteristic or state of being indiscreet. **2.** an indiscreet act, remark, etc.

indiscriminate (,ɪndɪ'skrɪmɪnɪt) *adj.* **1.** lacking discrimination or careful choice; random or promiscuous. **2.** jumbled; confused. —,indis'criminately *adv.* —,indis'criminateness *n.* —,indis,crimi'nation *n.*

indispensable (,ɪndɪ'spɛnsəbəl) *adj.* **1.** absolutely necessary; essential. **2.** not to be disregarded or escaped: *an indispensable role.* ~*n.* **3.** an indispensable person or

,indis'cernible *adj.*

thing. —**,indis,pensa'bility** or **,indis'pensableness** n. —**,indis'pensably** adv.

indispose (,ındı'spəʊz) vb. (tr.) **1.** to make unwilling or opposed; disincline. **2.** to cause to feel ill. **3.** to make unfit (for something or to do something).

indisposed (,ındı'spəʊzd) adj. **1.** sick or ill. **2.** unwilling. [C15: from L *indispositus* disordered] —**indisposition** (,ındıspə'zıʃən) n.

indissoluble (,ındı'sɒljʊbˀl) adj. incapable of being dissolved or broken; permanent. —**,indis'solubly** adv.

indistinct (,ındı'stıŋkt) adj. incapable of being clearly distinguished, as by the eyes, ears, or mind; not distinct. —**,indis'tinctly** adv. —**,indis'tinctness** n.

indite (ın'daɪt) vb. (tr.) Arch. to write. [C14: from OF *enditer*, from L *indīcere* to declare, from IN-² + *dīcere* to say] —**in'ditement** n. —**in'diter** n.

indium ('ındıəm) n. a rare soft silvery metallic element associated with zinc ores: used in alloys, electronics, and electroplating. Symbol: In; atomic no.: 49; atomic wt.: 114.82. [C19: NL, from INDIGO + -IUM]

individual (,ındı'vɪdjʊəl) adj. **1.** of, relating to, characteristic of, or meant for a single person or thing. **2.** separate or distinct, esp. from others of its kind; particular: *please mark the individual pages.* **3.** characterized by unusual and striking qualities; distinctive. **4.** Obs. indivisible; inseparable. ~n. **5.** a single person, esp. when regarded as distinct from others. **6.** Biol. a single animal or plant, esp. as distinct from a species. **7.** Inf. a person: *a most obnoxious individual.* [C15: from Med. L, from L *indivīduus* indivisible, from IN-¹ + *dīvidere* to DIVIDE] —**,indi'vidually** adv.

▷ **Usage.** In careful speech and writing, the noun *individual* is not loosely used as a synonym of *person*, although it is appropriate in that sense when a single person is being considered in contrast to a group, as in *in mass democracy the rights of the individual must be protected.*

individualism (,ındı'vɪdjʊə,lızəm) n. **1.** the principle of asserting one's independence and individuality; egoism. **2.** an individual quirk. **3.** another word for **laissez faire** (sense 1). **4.** Philosophy. the doctrine that only individual things exist. —**indi'vidualist** n.

individuality (,ındı,vɪdjʊ'ælɪtɪ) n., pl. **-ties. 1.** distinctive or unique character or personality: *a work of great individuality.* **2.** the qualities that distinguish one person or thing from another; identity. **3.** the state or quality of being a separate entity; discreteness.

individualize or **-ise** (,ındı'vɪdjʊə,laɪz) vb. (tr.) **1.** to make or mark as individual or distinctive in character. **2.** to consider or treat individually; particularize. **3.** to make or modify so as to meet the special requirements of a person. —**,indi,viduali'zation** or **-i'sation** n. —**,indi'vidual,izer** or **-,iser** n.

individuate (,ındı'vɪdjʊ,eɪt) vb. (tr.) **1.** to give individuality or an individual form to. **2.** to distinguish from others of the same species or group; individualize. —**,indi'vidu,ator** n.

indivisible (,ındı'vɪzəbˀl) adj. **1.** unable to be divided. **2.** Maths. leaving a remainder when divided by a given number. —**,indi,visi'bility** n. —**,indi'visibly** adv.

Indo- ('ındəʊ) combining form. denoting India or Indian: *Indo-European.*

Indochina or **Indo-China** ('ındəʊ'tʃaɪnə) n. **1.** Also called: **Farther India.** a peninsula in SE Asia, between India and China: consists of Burma, Thailand, Laos, Kampuchea, Vietnam, and Malaysia. **2.** the former French colonial possessions of Cochin China, Annam, Tonkin, Laos, and Kampuchea. —**'Indochi'nese** or **'Indo-Chi'nese** adj., n.

indoctrinate (ın'dɒktrɪ,neɪt) vb. (tr.) **1.** to teach (a person or group of people) systematically to accept doctrines, esp. uncritically. **2.** Rare. to instruct. —**in,doctri'nation** n. —**in'doctri,nator** n.

Indo-European adj. **1.** denoting, belonging to, or relating to a family of languages that includes English: characteristically marked, esp. in the older languages, such as Latin, by inflection showing gender, number, and case. **2.** denoting or relating to the hypothetical parent language of this family, primitive Indo-European. **3.** denoting, belonging to, or relating to any of the peoples speaking these languages. ~n. **4.** the Indo-European family of languages. **5.** the reconstructed hypothetical parent language of this family. ~Also (obs.): **Indo-Germanic.**

Indo-Iranian adj. **1.** of or relating to the Indic and Iranian branches of the Indo-European family of languages. ~n. **2.** this group of languages, sometimes considered as forming a single branch of Indo-European.

indole ('ındəʊl) or **indol** ('ındəʊl, -dɒl) n. a white or yellowish crystalline heterocyclic compound extracted from coal tar and used in perfumery, medicine, and as a flavouring agent. [C19: from IND(IGO) + -OLE¹]

indolent ('ındələnt) adj. **1.** disliking work or effort; lazy; idle. **2.** Pathol. causing little pain: *an indolent tumour.* **3.** (esp. of a painless ulcer) slow to heal. [C17: from L *indolēns* not feeling pain, from IN-¹ + *dolēre* to grieve, cause distress] —**'indolence** n. —**'indolently** adv.

indomitable (ın'dɒmɪtəbˀl) adj. (of courage, pride, etc.) difficult or impossible to defeat or subdue. [C17: from LL, from L *indomitus* untameable, from *domāre* to tame] —**in,domita'bility** or **in'domitableness** n. —**in'domitably** adv.

Indonesia (,ındəʊ'niːzɪə) n. a republic in SE Asia, in the Malay Archipelago, consisting of the main islands of Sumatra, Java and Madura, Bali, Sulawesi (Celebes), Lombok, Sumbawa, Flores, the Moluccas, Timor, part of Borneo (Kalimantan), Irian Jaya, and over 3000 small islands in the Indian and Pacific Oceans: became the Dutch East Indies in 1798; declared independence in 1945; became a republic in 1950. Official language: Bahasa Indonesia. Religion: mostly Muslim. Currency: rupiah. Capital: Jakarta. Pop.: 147 490 298 (1980). Area: 1 907 568 sq. km (736 512 sq. miles). Former names (1798–1945): **Dutch East Indies, Netherlands East Indies.**

Indonesian (,ındəʊ'niːzɪən) adj. **1.** of or relating to Indonesia, its people, or their language. ~n. **2.** a native or inhabitant of Indonesia.

indoor ('ın,dɔː) adj. (prenominal) of, situated in, or appropriate to the inside of a house or other building: *an indoor pool; indoor amusements.*

indoors (,ın'dɔːz) adv., adj. (postpositive) inside or into a house or other building.

Indore (ın'dɔː) n. **1.** a city in central India, in W Madhya Pradesh. Pop.: 827 000 (1981). **2.** a former state of central India: became part of Madhya Bharat in 1948, which in turn became part of Madhya Pradesh in 1956.

indorse (ın'dɔːs) vb. a variant of **endorse.**

Indra ('ındrə) n. Hinduism. the most celebrated god of the Rig-Veda, governing the weather and dispensing rain.

indraught or U.S. **indraft** ('ın,drɑːft) n. **1.** the act of drawing or pulling in. **2.** an inward flow, esp. of air.

indrawn (ın'drɔːn) adj. **1.** drawn or pulled in. **2.** inward-looking or introspective.

Indre (French ɛ̃dr) n. a department of central France in the Centre region. Capital: Châteauroux. Pop.: 243 191 (1982). Area: 6906 sq. km (2693 sq. miles).

Indre-et-Loire (French ɛ̃drəlwar) n. a department of W central France in the Centre region: contains many famous châteaux along the Loire. Capital: Tours. Pop.: 506 097 (1982). Area: 6158 sq. km (2402 sq. miles).

indris ('ındrıs) or **indri** ('ındrı) n., pl. **-dris. 1.** a large Madagascan arboreal lemuroid primate with thick silky fur patterned in black, white, and fawn. **2. woolly indris.** a related nocturnal Madagascan animal with thick greybrown fur and a long tail. [C19: from F: lemur, from native word *indry!* look! mistaken for the animal's name]

indubitable (ın'djuːbɪtəbˀl) adj. incapable of being doubted; unquestionable. [C18: from L, from IN-¹ + *dubitāre* to doubt] —**in'dubitably** adv.

induce (ın'djuːs) vb. (tr.) **1.** (often foll. by an infinitive) to persuade or use influence on. **2.** to cause or bring about. **3.** Med. to initiate or hasten (labour), as by administering a drug to stimulate uterine contractions. **4.** Logic, obs. to assert or establish (a general proposition, etc.) by induction. **5.** to produce (an electromotive force or electrical current) by induction. **6.** to transmit (magnetism) by induction. [C14: from L *indūcere* to lead in] —**in'ducer** n. —**in'ducible** adj.

inducement (ın'djuːsmənt) n. **1.** the act of inducing. **2.** a means of inducing; persuasion; incentive. **3.** Law. the introductory part that leads up to and explains the matter in dispute.

induct (ın'dʌkt) vb. (tr.) **1.** to bring in formally or install in an office, place, etc.; invest. **2.** (foll. by to or into) to initiate in knowledge (of). **3.** U.S. to enlist for military service. **4.** *Physics.* another word for **induce** (senses 5, 6). [C14: from L *inductus* led in, p.p. of *indūcere* to introduce; see INDUCE]

inductance (ɪn'dʌktəns) *n.* **1.** the property of an electric circuit as a result of which an electromotive force is created by a change of current in the same or in a neighbouring circuit. **2.** a component, such as a coil, in an electrical circuit, the main function of which is to produce inductance.

induction (ɪn'dʌkʃən) *n.* **1.** the act of inducting or state of being inducted. **2.** the act of inducing. **3.** (in an internal-combustion engine) the drawing in of mixed air and fuel from the carburettor to the cylinder. **4.** *Logic.* **a.** a process of reasoning by which a general conclusion is drawn from a set of premises, based mainly on experience or experimental evidence. **b.** a conclusion reached by this process of reasoning. **5.** the process by which electrical or magnetic properties are transferred, without physical contact, from one circuit or body to another. See also **inductance**. **6.** *Maths.* a method of proving a proposition P(*n*) by showing that it is true for all preceding values of *n* and for *n* + 1. **7. a.** a formal introduction or entry into an office or position. **b.** (*as modifier*): *induction course.* **8.** *U.S.* the enlistment of a civilian into military service. —**in'ductional** *adj.*

induction coil *n.* a transformer for producing a high voltage from a low voltage. It consists of a cylindrical primary winding of few turns, a concentric secondary winding of many turns, and often a common soft-iron core.

induction heating *n.* the heating of a conducting material as a result of the electric currents induced in it by an externally applied alternating magnetic field.

induction motor *n.* a type of electric motor in which an alternating supply fed to the windings of the stator creates a magnetic field that induces a current in the windings of the rotor. Rotation of the rotor results from the interaction of the magnetic field created by the rotor current with the field of the stator.

inductive (ɪn'dʌktɪv) *adj.* **1.** relating to or operated by electrical or magnetic induction: *an inductive reactance.* **2.** *Logic, maths.* of, relating to, or using induction: *inductive reasoning.* **3.** serving to induce or cause. —**in'ductively** *adv.* —**in'ductiveness** *n.*

inductor (ɪn'dʌktə) *n.* **1.** a person or thing that inducts. **2.** another name for an **inductance** (sense 2).

indue (ɪn'djuː) *vb.* **-duing, -dued.** a variant spelling of **endue.**

indulge (ɪn'dʌldʒ) *vb.* **1.** (when *intr.*, often foll. by *in*) to yield to or gratify (a whim or desire for): *to indulge in new clothes.* **2.** (*tr.*) to yield to the wishes of; pamper: *to indulge a child.* **3.** (*tr.*) to allow (oneself) the pleasure of something: *he indulged himself.* **4.** (*intr.*) *Inf.* to take alcoholic drink, esp. to excess. [C17: from L *indulgēre* to concede] —**in'dulger** *n.* —**in'dulgingly** *adv.*

indulgence (ɪn'dʌldʒəns) *n.* **1.** the act of indulging or state of being indulgent. **2.** a pleasure, habit, etc., indulged in; extravagance. **3.** liberal or tolerant treatment. **4.** something granted as a favour or privilege. **5.** *R.C. Church.* a remission of the temporal punishment for sin after its guilt has been forgiven. **6.** Also called: **Declaration of Indulgence.** a royal grant during the reigns of Charles II and James II of England giving Nonconformists and Roman Catholics a measure of religious freedom.

indulgent (ɪn'dʌldʒənt) *adj.* showing or characterized by indulgence. —**in'dulgently** *adv.*

induna (ɪn'duːnə) *n.* (in South Africa) a Black African overseer in a factory, mine, etc. [C20: from Zulu *nduna* an official]

indurate *vb.* ('ɪndjʊˌreɪt). **1.** to make or become hard or callous. **2.** to make or become hardy. ~*adj.* ('ɪndjʊrɪt). **3.** hardened, callous, or unfeeling. [C16: from L *indūrāre* to make hard; see ENDURE] —ˌ**indu'ration** *n.* —'**induˌra-tive** *adj.*

Indus ('ɪndəs) *n.* a river in S Asia, rising in SW Tibet in the Kailas Range of the Himalayas and flowing northwest through Kashmir, then southwest across Pakistan to the Arabian Sea: important throughout history, esp. for the Indus Civilization (about 3000 to 1500 B.C.), and for irrigation. Length: about 2900 km (1800 miles).

indusium (ɪn'djuːzɪəm) *n., pl.* **-sia** (-zɪə). **1.** a membranous outgrowth on the undersurface of fern leaves that protects the developing spores. **2.** an enveloping membrane, such as the amnion. [C18: NL, from L: tunic, from *induere* to put on] —**in'dusial** *adj.*

industrial (ɪn'dʌstrɪəl) *adj.* **1.** of, relating to, or derived from industry. **2.** employed in industry: *the industrial workforce.* **3.** relating to or concerned with workers in industry: *industrial conditions.* **4.** used in industry: *industrial chemicals.* —**in'dustrially** *adv.*

industrial action *n. Brit.* any action, such as a strike or go-slow, taken by employees in industry to protest against working conditions, etc.

industrial archaeology *n.* the study of industrial machines, works, etc. of the past.

industrial design *n.* the art or practice of designing any object for manufacture. —**industrial designer** *n.*

industrial disease *n.* any disease to which workers in a particular industry are prone.

industrial estate *n. Brit.* an area of land set aside for industry and business. U.S. equivalent: **industrial park.**

industrialism (ɪn'dʌstrɪəˌlɪzəm) *n.* an organization of society characterized by large-scale mechanized manufacturing industry rather than trade, farming, etc.

industrialist (ɪn'dʌstrɪəlɪst) *n.* a person who has a substantial interest in the ownership or control of industrial enterprise.

industrialize *or* **-lise** (ɪn'dʌstrɪəˌlaɪz) *vb.* **1.** (*tr.*) to develop industry on an extensive scale in (a country, region, etc.). **2.** (*intr.*) (of a country, region, etc.) to undergo the development of industry on an extensive scale. —**in,dustriali'zation** *or* **-li'sation** *n.*

industrial relations *n.* **1.** (*functioning as pl.*) relations between the employers and employees in an industrial enterprise. **2.** (*functioning as sing.*) the management of such relations.

Industrial Revolution *n.* **the.** the transformation in the 18th and 19th centuries of Britain and other countries into industrial nations.

industrial tribunal *n.* a tribunal that rules on disputes between employers and employees regarding unfair dismissal, redundancy, etc.

industrious (ɪn'dʌstrɪəs) *adj.* hard-working, diligent, or assiduous. —**in'dustriously** *adv.* —**in'dustriousness** *n.*

industry ('ɪndəstrɪ) *n., pl.* **-tries. 1.** organized economic activity concerned with manufacture, processing of raw materials, or construction. **2.** a branch of commercial enterprise concerned with the output of a specified product: *the steel industry.* **3. a.** industrial ownership and management interests collectively. **b.** manufacturing enterprise collectively, as opposed to agriculture. **4.** diligence; assiduity. [C15: from L *industria* diligence, from *industrius* active, from ?]

indwell (ɪn'dwɛl) *vb.* **-dwelling, -dwelt. 1.** (*tr.*) (of a spirit, principle, etc.) to inhabit; suffuse. **2.** (*intr.*) to dwell; exist. —**in'dweller** *n.*

Indy, d' (*French* dēdi) *n.* **Vincent** (vɛ̃sã). 1851–1931, French composer.

-ine[1] *suffix forming adjectives.* **1.** of, relating to, or belonging to: *saturnine.* **2.** consisting of or resembling: *crystalline.* [from L *-inus*, from Gk *-inos*]

-ine[2] *suffix forming nouns.* **1.** indicating a halogen: *chlorine.* **2.** indicating a nitrogenous organic compound, including amino acids, alkaloids, and certain other bases: *nicotine.* **3.** Also: **-in.** indicating a chemical substance in certain nonsystematic names: *glycerine.* **4.** indicating a mixture of hydrocarbons: *benzine.* **5.** indicating feminine form: *heroine.* [via F from L *-ina* (from *-inus*) and Gk *-inē*]

inebriate *vb.* (ɪn'iːbrɪˌeɪt). (*tr.*) **1.** to make drunk; intoxicate. **2.** to arouse emotionally; make excited. ~*n.* (ɪn'iːbrɪɪt). **3.** a person who is drunk, esp. habitually. ~*adj.* (ɪn'iːbrɪɪt), *also* **inebriated. 4.** drunk, esp. habitually. [C15: from L, from IN-[2] + *ēbriāre* to intoxicate, from *ēbrius* drunk] —**in,ebri'ation** *n.* —**inebriety** (ˌɪnɪ'braɪɪtɪ) *n.*

inedible (ɪn'ɛdɪbʰl) *adj.* not fit to be eaten. —**in,edi'bility** *n.*

▷**Usage.** In careful speech and writing, *inedible* is not synonymous with *uneatable.* *Inedible* implies that something is of a sort not suitable for eating, while *uneatable* implies that it is so disgusting as to be beyond eating.

---

in'ductile *adj.*   **in'edited** *adj.*

ineducable (ɪn'ɛdjʊkəbəl) *adj.* incapable of being educated, esp. on account of mental retardation. —**in,educa'bility** *n.*

ineffable (ɪn'ɛfəbəl) *adj.* **1.** too great or intense to be expressed in words; unutterable. **2.** too sacred to be uttered. **3.** indescribable; indefinable. [C15: from L, from IN-¹+ *effābilis*, from *fārī* to speak] —**in,effa'bility** *or* **in'effableness** *n.* —**in'effably** *adv.*

ineffective (,ɪnɪ'fɛktɪv) *adj.* **1.** having no effect. **2.** incompetent or inefficient. —**,inef'fectively** *adv.* —**,inef'fectiveness** *n.*

ineffectual (,ɪnɪ'fɛktʃʊəl) *adj.* **1.** having no effect or an inadequate effect. **2.** lacking in power or forcefulness; impotent: *an ineffectual ruler.* —**,inef,fectu'ality** *or* **,inef'fectualness** *n.* —**,inef'fectually** *adv.*

inefficacious (,ɪnɛfɪ'keɪʃəs) *adj.* failing to produce the desired effect. —**,ineffi'caciously** *adv.* —**inefficacy** (ɪn'ɛfɪkəsɪ), **,ineffi'caciousness,** *or* **inefficacity** (,ɪnɛfɪ'kæsɪtɪ) *n.*

ineluctable (,ɪnɪ'lʌktəbəl) *adj.* (esp. of fate) incapable of being avoided; inescapable. [C17: from L, from IN-¹+ *ēluctārī* to escape, from *luctārī* to struggle] —**,ine,lucta'bility** *n.* —**,ine'luctably** *adv.*

inept (ɪn'ɛpt) *adj.* **1.** awkward, clumsy, or incompetent. **2.** not suitable, appropriate, or fitting; out of place. [C17: from L *ineptus,* from IN-¹ + *aptus* fitting] —**in'epti,tude** *n.* —**in'eptly** *adv.* —**in'eptness** *n.*

inequable (ɪn'ɛkwəbəl) *adj.* **1.** uneven. **2.** not uniform. **3.** changeable.

inequality (,ɪnɪ'kwɒlɪtɪ) *n., pl.* **-ties. 1.** the state or quality of being unequal; disparity. **2.** an instance of disparity. **3.** lack of smoothness or regularity. **4.** social or economic disparity. **5.** *Maths.* **a.** a statement indicating that the value of one quantity or expression is not equal to another. **b.** the relation of being unequal.

inert (ɪn'ɜːt) *adj.* **1.** having no inherent ability to move or to resist motion. **2.** inactive, lazy, or sluggish. **3.** having only a limited ability to react chemically; unreactive. [C17: from L *iners* unskilled, from IN-¹ + *ars* skill; see ART¹] —**in'ertly** *adv.* —**in'ertness** *n.*

inert gas *n.* **1.** any of the unreactive gaseous elements helium, neon, argon, krypton, xenon, and radon. **2.** (loosely) any gas, such as carbon dioxide, that is nonoxidizing.

inertia (ɪn'ɜːʃə, -ʃɪə) *n.* **1.** the state of being inert; disinclination to move or act. **2.** *Physics.* **a.** the tendency of a body to preserve its state of rest or uniform motion unless acted upon by an external force. **b.** an analogous property of other physical quantities that resist change: *thermal inertia.* —**in'ertial** *adj.*

inertial guidance *or* **navigation** *n.* a method of controlling the flight path of a missile by instruments contained within it.

inertial mass *n.* the mass of a body as determined by its momentum, as opposed to the extent to which it responds to the force of gravity. Cf. **gravitational mass.**

inertia-reel seat belt *n.* a type of car seat belt in which the belt is free to unwind from a metal drum except when the drum locks as a result of rapid deceleration.

inertia selling *n.* the illegal practice of sending unrequested goods to householders, followed by a bill for the goods if they do not return them.

inescapable (,ɪnɪ'skeɪpəbəl) *adj.* incapable of being escaped or avoided. —**,ines'capably** *adv.*

inestimable (ɪn'ɛstɪməbəl) *adj.* **1.** not able to be estimated; immeasurable. **2.** of immeasurable value. —**in,estima'bility** *or* **in'estimableness** *n.* —**in'estimably** *adv.*

inevitable (ɪn'ɛvɪtəbəl) *adj.* **1.** unavoidable. **2.** sure to happen; certain. ~*n.* **3.** (often preceded by *the*) something that is unavoidable. [C15: from L, from IN-¹ + *ēvītāre* to shun, from *vītāre* to avoid] —**in,evita'bility** *or* **in'evitableness** *n.* —**in'evitably** *adv.*

inexhaustible (,ɪnɪg'zɔːstəbəl) *adj.* **1.** incapable of being used up; endless. **2.** incapable or apparently incapable of becoming tired; tireless. —**,inex,hausti'bility** *n.* —**,inex'haustibly** *adv.*

inexorable (ɪn'ɛksərəbəl) *adj.* **1.** not able to be moved by entreaty or persuasion. **2.** relentless. [C16: from L, from IN-¹ + *exōrāre* to prevail upon, from *ōrāre* to pray] —**in,exora'bility** *n.* —**in'exorably** *adv.*

inexpiable (ɪn'ɛkspɪəbəl) *adj.* **1.** incapable of being expiated; unpardonable. **2.** *Arch.* implacable. —**in'expiableness** *n.*

in extenso *Latin.* (ɪn ɪk'stɛnsəʊ) *adv.* at full length.

in extremis *Latin.* (ɪn ɪk'striːmɪs) *adv.* **1.** in extremity; in dire straits. **2.** at the point of death. [lit.: in the furthest reaches]

inextricable (,ɪnɛks'trɪkəbəl) *adj.* **1.** not able to be escaped from: *an inextricable dilemma.* **2.** not able to be disentangled, etc.: *an inextricable knot.* **3.** extremely involved or intricate. —**,inextrica'bility** *or* **,inex'tricableness** *n.* —**,inex'tricably** *adv.*

inf. *abbrev. for:* **1.** Also: **Inf.** infantry. **2.** inferior. **3.** infinitive. **4.** informal. **5.** information.

infallible (ɪn'fæləbəl) *adj.* **1.** not fallible; not liable to error. **2.** not liable to failure; certain; sure: *an infallible cure.* ~*n.* **3.** a person or thing that is incapable of error or failure. —**in,falli'bility** *or* **in'fallibleness** *n.* —**in'fallibly** *adv.*

infamous ('ɪnfəməs) *adj.* **1.** having a bad reputation; notorious. **2.** causing or deserving a bad reputation; shocking: *infamous conduct.* —**'infamously** *adv.* —**'infamousness** *n.*

infamy ('ɪnfəmɪ) *n., pl.* **-mies. 1.** the state or condition of being infamous. **2.** an infamous act or event. [C15: from L *infāmis* of evil repute, from IN-¹ + *fāma* FAME]

infancy ('ɪnfənsɪ) *n., pl.* **-cies. 1.** the state or period of being an infant; childhood. **2.** an early stage of growth or development. **3.** infants collectively. **4.** the period of life prior to attaining legal majority; minority nonage.

infant ('ɪnfənt) *n.* **1.** a child at the earliest stage of its life; baby. **2.** *Law.* another word for **minor** (sense 9). **3.** *Brit.* a young schoolchild. **4.** a person who is beginning or inexperienced in an activity. **5.** (*modifier*) **a.** of or relating to young children or infancy. **b.** designed or intended for young children. ~*adj.* **6.** in an early stage of development; nascent: *an infant science.* **7.** *Law.* of or relating to the legal status of infancy. [C14: from L *infāns,* lit.: speechless, from IN-¹ + *fārī* to speak] —**'infant,hood** *n.*

infanta (ɪn'fæntə) *n.* **1.** (formerly) a daughter of a king of Spain or Portugal. **2.** the wife of an infante. [C17: from Sp. or Port., fem. of INFANTE]

infante (ɪn'fæntɪ) *n.* (formerly) a son of a king of Spain or Portugal, esp. one not heir to the throne. [C16: from Sp. or Port., lit.: INFANT]

infanticide (ɪn'fæntɪ,saɪd) *n.* **1.** the killing of an infant. **2.** the practice of killing newborn infants, still prevalent in some primitive tribes. **3.** a person who kills an infant. —**in,fanti'cidal** *adj.*

infantile ('ɪnfən,taɪl) *adj.* **1.** like a child in action or behaviour; childishly immature; puerile. **2.** of, relating to, or characteristic of infants or infancy. **3.** in an early stage of development. —**infantility** (,ɪnfən'tɪlɪtɪ) *n.*

infantile paralysis *n.* a former name for **poliomyelitis.**

infantilism (ɪn'fæntɪ,lɪzəm) *n.* **1.** *Psychol.* a condition in which an older child or adult is mentally or physically undeveloped. **2.** childish speech; baby talk.

infantry ('ɪnfəntrɪ) *n., pl.* **-tries. a.** soldiers or units of soldiers who fight on foot with small arms. **b.** (*as modifier*): *an infantry unit.* [C16: from It. *infanteria,* from *infante* boy, foot soldier; see INFANT]

infantryman ('ɪnfəntrɪmən) *n., pl.* **-men.** a soldier belonging to the infantry.

infant school *n. Brit.* a school for children aged between 5 and 7.

infarct (ɪn'fɑːkt) *n.* a localized area of dead tissue resulting from obstruction of the blood supply to that part. Also called: **infarction.** [C19: via NL from L *infarctus* stuffed into, from *farcīre* to stuff] —**in'farcted** *adj.*

infatuate *vb.* (ɪn'fætjʊ,eɪt). (*tr.*) **1.** to inspire or fill with foolish, shallow, or extravagant passion. **2.** to cause to act foolishly. ~*n.* (ɪn'fætjʊɪt, -,eɪt). **3.** *Literary.* a person

,inef'faceable *adj.*	in'equitable *adj.*	,inex'cusable *adj.*	in'explicable *adj.*
,inef'ficient *adj.*	in'equity *n.*	,inex'pedient *adj.*	,inex'plicit *adj.*
,ine'lastic *adj.*	,ine'radicable *adj.*	,inex'pensive *adj.*	,inex'pressible *adj.*
in'elegant *adj.*	,ines'sential *adj., n.*	,inex'perience *n.*	,inex'pressive *adj.*
in'eligible *adj.*	,inex'act *adj.*	in'expert *adj.*	,inex'tinguishable *adj.*

who is infatuated. [C16: from L *infatuāre*, from IN-[2] + *fatuus* FATUOUS] —**in,fatu'ation** *n.*

infatuated (ɪnˈfætjʊˌeɪtɪd) *adj.* (often foll. by *with*) possessed by a foolish or extravagant passion, esp. for another person.

infect (ɪnˈfɛkt) *vb.* (*mainly tr.*) **1.** to cause infection in; contaminate (an organism, wound, etc.) with pathogenic microorganisms. **2.** (*also intr.*) to affect or become affected with a communicable disease. **3.** to taint, pollute, or contaminate. **4.** to affect, esp. adversely, as if by contagion. ~*adj.* **5.** *Arch.* contaminated or polluted with or as if with a disease; infected. [C14: from L *inficere* to dip into, stain, from *facere* to make] —**in'fector** *or* **in'fecter** *n.*

infection (ɪnˈfɛkʃən) *n.* **1.** invasion of the body by pathogenic microorganisms. **2.** the resulting condition in the tissues. **3.** an infectious disease. **4.** the act of infecting or state of being infected. **5.** an agent or influence that infects. **6.** persuasion or corruption, as by ideas, perverse influences, etc.

infectious (ɪnˈfɛkʃəs) *adj.* **1.** (of a disease) capable of being transmitted. **2.** (of a disease) caused by microorganisms, such as bacteria, viruses, or protozoa. **3.** causing or transmitting infection. **4.** tending or apt to spread, as from one person to another: *infectious mirth.* —**in'fectiously** *adv.* —**in'fectiousness** *n.*

infectious hepatitis *n.* an acute infectious viral disease characterized by inflammation of the liver, fever, and jaundice.

infectious mononucleosis *n.* an acute infectious disease, caused by a virus (**Epstein-Barr virus**), characterized by fever, sore throat, swollen and painful lymph nodes, and abnormal lymphocytes in the blood. Also called: **glandular fever.**

infective (ɪnˈfɛktɪv) *adj.* **1.** capable of causing infection. **2.** a less common word for **infectious.** —**in'fectively** *adv.* —**in'fectiveness** *n.*

infelicity (ˌɪnfɪˈlɪsɪtɪ) *n., pl.* **-ties. 1.** unhappiness; misfortune. **2.** an instance of bad luck or mischance. **3.** something, esp. a remark or expression, that is inapt or inappropriate. —**,infe'licitous** *adj.*

infer (ɪnˈfɜː) *vb.* **-ferring, -ferred.** (when *tr., may take a clause as object*) **1.** to conclude (a state of affairs, supposition, etc.) by reasoning from evidence; deduce. **2.** (*tr.*) to have or lead to as a necessary or logical consequence; indicate. **3.** (*tr.*) to hint or imply. [C16: from L *inferre* to bring into, from *ferre* to bear, carry] —**in'ferable** *or* **in'ferrable** *adj.* —**in'ferrer** *n.*

▷ **Usage.** The use of *infer* in the sense of *imply* often occurs in both speech and writing but is avoided by all careful speakers and writers of English.

inference (ˈɪnfərəns, -frəns) *n.* **1.** the act or process of inferring. **2.** an inferred conclusion, deduction, etc. **3.** any process of reasoning from premises to a conclusion. **4.** *Logic.* the specific mode of reasoning used.

inferential (ˌɪnfəˈrɛnʃəl) *adj.* of, relating to, or derived from inference. —**,infer'entially** *adv.*

inferior (ɪnˈfɪərɪə) *adj.* **1.** lower in value or quality. **2.** lower in rank, position, or status; subordinate. **3.** not of the best; mediocre; commonplace. **4.** lower in position; situated beneath. **5.** (of a plant ovary) situated below the other floral parts. **6.** *Astron.* **a.** orbiting between the sun and the earth: *an inferior planet.* **b.** lying below the horizon. **7.** *Printing.* (of a character) printed at the foot of an ordinary character. ~*n.* **8.** an inferior person. **9.** *Printing.* an inferior character. [C15: from L: lower, from *inferus* low] —**inferiority** (ɪn,fɪərɪˈɒrɪtɪ) *n.* —**in'feriorly** *adv.*

inferiority complex *n. Psychiatry.* a disorder arising from the conflict between the desire to be noticed and the fear of being humiliated, characterized by aggressiveness or withdrawal into oneself.

infernal (ɪnˈfɜːnəl) *adj.* **1.** of or relating to an underworld of the dead. **2.** deserving or befitting hell; diabolic; fiendish. **3.** *Inf.* irritating; confounded. [C14: from LL, from *infernus* hell, from L (adj.): lower, hellish; rel. to L *inferus* low] —**,infer'nality** *n.* —**in'fernally** *adv.*

infernal machine *n. Arch.* an explosive device (usually disguised) or booby trap.

inferno (ɪnˈfɜːnəʊ) *n., pl.* **-nos. 1.** (*sometimes cap.*; usually preceded by *the*) hell; the infernal region. **2.** any

place or state resembling hell, esp. a conflagration. [C19: from It., from LL *infernus* hell]

infest (ɪnˈfɛst) *vb.* (*tr.*) **1.** to inhabit or overrun in unpleasantly large numbers. **2.** (of parasites such as lice) to invade and live on or in (a host). [C15: from L *infestāre* to molest, from *infestus* hostile] —**,infes'tation** *n.* —**in'fester** *n.*

infeudation (ˌɪnfjuːˈdeɪʃən) *n. History.* **1.** (in feudal society) the act of putting a vassal in possession of a fief. **2.** the granting of tithes to laymen.

infidel (ˈɪnfɪdəl) *n.* **1.** a person who has no religious belief; unbeliever. ~*adj.* **2.** rejecting a specific religion, esp. Christianity or Islam. **3.** of or relating to unbelievers or unbelief. [C15: from Med. L, from L (adj.): unfaithful, from IN-[1] + *fidēlis* faithful; see FEALTY]

infidelity (ˌɪnfɪˈdɛlɪtɪ) *n., pl.* **-ties. 1.** lack of faith or constancy, esp. sexual faithfulness. **2.** lack of religious faith; disbelief. **3.** an act or instance of disloyalty.

infield (ˈɪnˌfiːld) *n.* **1.** *Cricket.* the area of the field near the pitch. **2.** *Baseball.* the area of the playing field enclosed by the base lines. **3.** *Agriculture.* the part of a farm nearest to the farm buildings. —**'in,fielder** *n.*

infighting (ˈɪnˌfaɪtɪŋ) *n.* **1.** *Boxing.* combat at close quarters in which proper blows are inhibited. **2.** intense competition, as between members of an organization. —**'in,fighter** *n.*

infill (ˈɪnfɪl) *or* **infilling** (ˈɪnfɪlɪŋ) *n.* **1.** the act of filling or closing gaps, etc., in something, such as a row of buildings. **2.** material used to fill a cavity, gap, hole, etc.

infiltrate (ˈɪnfɪlˌtreɪt) *vb.* **1.** to undergo the process in which a fluid passes into the pores or interstices of a solid; permeate. **2.** *Mil.* to pass undetected through (an enemy-held line or position). **3.** to gain or cause to gain entrance or access surreptitiously: *they infiltrated the party structure.* ~*n.* **4.** something that infiltrates. [C18: from IN-[2] + FILTRATE] —**,infil'tration** *n.* —**'infil,trative** *adj.* —**'infil,trator** *n.*

infin. *abbrev. for* infinitive.

infinite (ˈɪnfɪnɪt) *adj.* **1. a.** having no limits or boundaries in time, space, extent, or magnitude. **b.** (*as n.*; preceded by *the*): *the infinite.* **2.** extremely or immeasurably great or numerous: *infinite wealth.* **3.** all-embracing, absolute, or total: *God's infinite wisdom.* **4.** *Maths.* having an unlimited or uncountable number of digits, factors, terms, etc. —**'infinitely** *adv.* —**'infiniteness** *n.*

infinitesimal (ˌɪnfɪnɪˈtɛsɪməl) *adj.* **1.** infinitely or immeasurably small. **2.** *Maths.* of, relating to, or involving a small change in the value of a variable that approaches zero as a limit. ~*n.* **3.** *Maths.* an infinitesimal quantity. —**,infini'tesimally** *adv.*

infinitesimal calculus *n.* another name for **calculus** (sense 1).

infinitive (ɪnˈfɪnɪtɪv) *n. Grammar.* a form of the verb not inflected for grammatical categories such as tense and person and used without an overt subject. In English, the infinitive usually consists of the word *to* followed by the verb. —**infinitival** (ˌɪnfɪnɪˈtaɪvəl) *adj.* —**in'finitively** *or* **,infini'tivally** *adv.*

infinitude (ɪnˈfɪnɪˌtjuːd) *n.* **1.** the state or quality of being infinite. **2.** an infinite extent, quantity, degree, etc.

infinity (ɪnˈfɪnɪtɪ) *n., pl.* **-ties. 1.** the state or quality of being infinite. **2.** endless time, space, or quantity. **3.** an infinitely or indefinitely great number or amount. **4.** *Maths.* **a.** the concept of a value greater than any finite numerical value. **b.** the reciprocal of zero. **c.** the limit of an infinite sequence of numbers.

infirm (ɪnˈfɜːm) *adj.* **1. a.** weak in health or body, esp. from old age. **b.** (*as collective n.*; preceded by *the*): *the infirm.* **2.** lacking moral certainty; indecisive or irresolute. **3.** not stable, sound, or secure: *an infirm structure.* **4.** *Law.* (of a law, etc.) lacking legal force; invalid. —**in'firmly** *adv.* —**in'firmness** *n.*

infirmary (ɪnˈfɜːmərɪ) *n., pl.* **-ries.** a place for the treatment of the sick or injured; hospital.

infirmity (ɪnˈfɜːmɪtɪ) *n., pl.* **-ties. 1.** the state or quality of being infirm. **2.** physical weakness or debility; frailty. **3.** a moral flaw or failing.

infix *vb.* (ɪnˈfɪks, ˈɪnˌfɪks). **1.** (*tr.*) to fix firmly in. **2.** (*tr.*) to instil or inculcate. **3.** *Grammar.* to insert (an affix) into the middle of a word. ~*n.* (ˈɪnˌfɪks). **4.** *Grammar.* an

---

affix inserted into the middle of a word. — ‚**infix'ation** *or* **infixion** (ɪn'fɪkʃən) *n*.

in flagrante delicto (ɪn flə'græntɪ dɪ'lɪktəʊ) *adv. Chiefly law.* while committing the offence; red-handed. Also: **flagrante delicto.** [L, lit.: with the crime still blazing]

inflame (ɪn'fleɪm) *vb.* **1.** to arouse or become aroused to violent emotion. **2.** (*tr.*) to increase or intensify; aggravate. **3.** to produce inflammation in (a tissue, organ, or part) or (of a tissue, etc.) to become inflamed. **4.** to set or be set on fire. **5.** (*tr.*) to cause to redden. —**in'flamer** *n*.

inflammable (ɪn'flæməbᵊl) *adj.* **1.** liable to catch fire; flammable. **2.** readily aroused to anger or passion. ~*n.* **3.** something that is liable to catch fire. —**in‚flamma'bility** *or* **in'flammableness** *n*. —**in'flammably** *adv*.
▷ *Usage.* See at **flammable.**

inflammation (‚ɪnflə'meɪʃən) *n.* **1.** the reaction of living tissue to injury or infection, characterized by heat, redness, swelling, and pain. **2.** the act of inflaming or the state of being inflamed.

inflammatory (ɪn'flæmətərɪ, -trɪ) *adj.* **1.** characterized by or caused by inflammation. **2.** tending to arouse violence, strong emotion, etc. —**in'flammatorily** *adv*.

inflatable (ɪn'fleɪtəbᵊl) *n.* **1.** any of various large air-filled objects made of strong plastic or rubber. ~*adj.* **2.** capable of being inflated.

inflate (ɪn'fleɪt) *vb.* **1.** to expand or cause to expand by filling with gas or air. **2.** (*tr.*) to cause to increase excessively; puff up; swell: *to inflate one's opinion of oneself.* **3.** (*tr.*) to cause inflation of (prices, money, etc.). **4.** (*tr.*) to raise in spirits; elate. **5.** (*intr.*) to undergo economic inflation. [C16: from L *inflāre* to blow into, from *flāre* to blow] —**in'flatedly** *adv.* —**in'flatedness** *n.* —**in'flater** *or* **in'flator** *n*.

inflation (ɪn'fleɪʃən) *n.* **1.** the act of inflating or state of being inflated. **2.** *Econ.* a progressive increase in the general level of prices brought about by an expansion in demand or the money supply or by autonomous increases in costs. **3.** *Inf.* the rate of increase of prices. —**in'flationary** *adj*.

inflationary spiral *n.* a self-sustaining form of inflation in which a rise in prices generates a wage demand, causing a further price rise and a further wage demand.

inflationism (ɪn'fleɪʃə‚nɪzəm) *n.* the policy of inflation through expansion of the supply of money and credit. —**in'flationist** *n., adj*.

inflect (ɪn'flɛkt) *vb.* **1.** *Grammar.* to change (the form of a word) by inflection. **2.** (*tr.*) to change (the voice) in tone or pitch; modulate. **3.** (*tr.*) to cause to deviate from a straight or normal line or course; bend. [C15: from L *inflectere* to curve round, alter, from *flectere* to bend] —**in'flectedness** *n.* —**in'flective** *adj.* —**in'flector** *n*.

inflection *or* **inflexion** (ɪn'flɛkʃən) *n.* **1.** modulation of the voice. **2.** *Grammar.* a change in the form of a word, signalling change in such grammatical functions as tense, person, gender, number, or case. **3.** an angle or bend. **4.** the act of inflecting or the state of being inflected. **5.** *Maths.* a change in curvature from concave to convex or vice versa. —**in'flectional** *or* **in'flexional** *adj.* —**in'flectionally** *or* **in'flexionally** *adv.* —**in'flectionless** *or* **in'flexionless** *adj*.

inflict (ɪn'flɪkt) *vb.* (*tr.*) **1.** (often foll. by *on* or *upon*) to impose (something unwelcome, such as pain, oneself, etc.). **2.** to deal out (blows, lashes, etc.). [C16: from L *inflīgere* to strike (something) against, dash against, from *flīgere* to strike] —**in'flictable** *adj.* —**in'flicter** *or* **in'flictor** *n.* —**in'fliction** *n*.

in-flight *adj.* provided during flight in an aircraft: *in-flight entertainment.*

inflorescence (‚ɪnflɔː'rɛsəns) *n.* **1.** the part of a plant that consists of the flower-bearing stalks. **2.** the arrangement of the flowers on the stalks. **3.** the process of flowering; blossoming. [C16: from NL, from LL, from *flōrescere* to bloom] —**‚inflo'rescent** *adj*.

inflow ('ɪn‚fləʊ) *n.* **1.** something, such as a liquid or gas, that flows in. **2.** Also called: **inflowing.** the act of flowing in; influx.

influence ('ɪnfluəns) *n.* **1.** an effect of one person or thing on another. **2.** the power of a person or thing to have such an effect. **3.** power or sway resulting from ability, wealth, position, etc. **4.** a person or thing having influence. **5.** *Astrol.* an ethereal fluid regarded as emanating from the stars and affecting a person's future. **6. under the influence.** *Inf.* drunk. ~*vb.* (*tr.*) **7.** to persuade or induce. **8.** to have an effect upon (actions, events, etc.); affect. [C14: from Med. L *influentia* emanation of power from the stars, from L *influere* to flow into, from *fluere* to flow] —**'influenceable** *adj.* —**'influencer** *n*.

influent ('ɪnfluənt) *adj. also* **inflowing. 1.** flowing in. ~*n.* **2.** something flowing in, esp. a tributary. **3.** *Ecology.* an organism that has a major effect on the nature of its community.

influential (‚ɪnflu'ɛnʃəl) *adj.* having or exerting influence. —‚**influ'entially** *adv*.

influenza (‚ɪnflu'ɛnzə) *n.* a highly contagious viral disease characterized by fever, muscular aches and pains, and inflammation of the respiratory passages. [C18: from It., lit.: INFLUENCE, hence, incursion, epidemic (first applied to influenza in 1743)] —‚**influ'enzal** *adj*.

influx ('ɪn‚flʌks) *n.* **1.** the arrival or entry of many people or things. **2.** the act of flowing in; inflow. **3.** the mouth of a stream or river. [C17: from LL *influxus*, from *influere*; see INFLUENCE]

info ('ɪnfəʊ) *n. Inf.* short for **information.**

infold (ɪn'fəʊld) *vb.* (*tr.*) a variant of **enfold.**

inform (ɪn'fɔːm) *vb.* **1.** (*tr.;* often foll. by *of* or *about*) to give information to; tell. **2.** (*tr.;* often foll. by *of* or *about*) to make conversant (with). **3.** (*intr.;* often foll. by *against* or *on*) to give information regarding criminals, to the police, etc. **4.** (*tr.*) to give form to. **5.** (*tr.*) to impart some essential or formative characteristic to. **6.** (*tr.*) to animate or inspire. [C14: from L *informāre* to give form to, describe, from *formāre* to FORM] —**in'formable** *adj*.

informal (ɪn'fɔːməl) *adj.* **1.** not of a formal, official, or stiffly conventional nature. **2.** appropriate to everyday life or use: *informal clothes.* **3.** denoting or characterized by idiom, vocabulary, etc., appropriate to conversational language rather than to formal written language. **4.** denoting a second-person pronoun in some languages used when the addressee is regarded as a friend or social inferior. —**in'formally** *adv*.

informality (‚ɪnfɔː'mælɪtɪ) *n., pl.* **-ties. 1.** the condition or quality of being informal. **2.** an informal act.

informal vote *n. Austral. & N.Z.* an invalid vote or ballot.

informant (ɪn'fɔːmənt) *n.* a person who gives information.

information (‚ɪnfə'meɪʃən) *n.* **1.** knowledge acquired through experience or study. **2.** knowledge of specific and timely events or situations; news. **3.** the act of informing or the condition of being informed. **4. a.** an office, agency, etc., providing information. **b.** (*as modifier*): *information service.* **5.** a charge or complaint made before justices of the peace, usually on oath, to institute summary criminal proceedings. **6.** *Computers.* **a.** the meaning given to data by the way it is interpreted. **b.** another word for **data** (sense 2). —‚**infor'mational** *adj*.

information retrieval *n. Computers.* the process of recovering information from stored data.

information technology *n.* the production, storage, and communication of information using computers and microelectronics.

information theory *n.* a collection of mathematical theories concerned with coding, transmitting, storing, retrieving, and decoding information.

informative (ɪn'fɔːmətɪv) *or* **informatory** *adj.* providing information; instructive. —**in'formatively** *adv.* —**in'formativeness** *n*.

informed (ɪn'fɔːmd) *adj.* **1.** having much knowledge or education; learned or cultured. **2.** based on information: *an informed judgment.*

informer (ɪn'fɔːmə) *n.* **1.** a person who informs against someone, esp. a criminal. **2.** a person who provides information.

infra- *prefix.* below; beneath; after: *infrasonic.* [from L *infrā*]

infract (ɪn'frækt) *vb.* (*tr.*) to violate or break (a law, etc.). [C18: from L *infractus* broken off; see INFRINGE] —**in'fraction** *n.* —**in'fractor** *n*.

infra dig ('ɪnfrə 'dɪg) *adj.* (*postpositive*) *Inf.* beneath one's dignity. [C19: from L *infrā dignitātem*]

infrangible (ɪn'frændʒɪbᵊl) *adj.* **1.** incapable of being broken. **2.** not capable of being violated or infringed. [C16: from LL, from L IN-¹ + *frangere* to break]

in'flexible *adj*.

—in,frangi'bility *or* in'frangibleness *n.* —in'frangibly *adv.*

infrared (,ınfrə'rɛd) *n.* **1.** the part of the electromagnetic
spectrum with a longer wavelength than light but a
shorter wavelength than radio waves. ~*adj.* **2.** of, relating to, using, or consisting of radiation lying within the
infrared.

infrared photography *n.* photography using film with an
emulsion that is sensitive to infrared light, enabling it to
be used in dark or misty conditions.

infrasound ('ınfrə,saʊnd) *n.* soundlike waves having a
frequency below the audible range, i.e. below about 16 Hz.
—**infrasonic** (,ınfrə'sɒnɪk) *adj.*

infrastructure ('ınfrə,strʌktʃə) *n.* **1.** the basic structure
of an organization, system, etc. **2.** the stock of fixed capital equipment in a country, including factories, roads,
schools, etc., considered as a determinant of economic
growth.

infringe (ın'frındʒ) *vb.* **1.** (*tr.*) to violate or break (a law,
agreement, etc.). **2.** (*intr.*; foll. by *on* or *upon*) to encroach or trespass. [C16: from L *infringere* to break off,
from *frangere* to break] —**in'fringement** *n.*
—**in'fringer** *n.*

infundibular (,ınfʌn'dıbjʊlə) *adj.* funnel-shaped. [C18:
from L *infundibulum* funnel]

infuriate *vb.* (ın'fjʊərɪ,eɪt). **1.** (*tr.*) to anger; annoy. ~*adj.*
(ın'fjʊərɪɪt). **2.** *Arch.* furious. [C17: from Med. L *in-
furiāre* (vb.); see IN-[2], FURY] —**in'furi,ating** *adj.* —**in'furi,atingly** *adv.*

infuse (ın'fjuːz) *vb.* **1.** (*tr.*; often foll. by *into*) to instil or
inculcate. **2.** (*tr.*; foll. by *with*) to inspire; emotionally
charge. **3.** to soak or be soaked in order to extract flavour or other properties. **4.** *Rare.* (foll. by *into*) to pour.
[C15: from L *infundere* to pour into] —**in'fuser** *n.*

infusible[1] (ın'fjuːzəb³l) *adj.* not fusible; not easily melted;
having a high melting point. [C16: from IN-[1] + FUSIBLE]
—**in,fusi'bility** *or* **in'fusibleness** *n.*

infusible[2] (ın'fjuːzəb³l) *adj.* capable of being infused.
[C17: from INFUSE + -IBLE] —**in,fusi'bility** *or* **in'fusibleness** *n.*

infusion (ın'fjuːʒən) *n.* **1.** the act of infusing. **2.** something infused. **3.** an extract obtained by soaking. —**infu-
sive** (ın'fjuːsɪv) *adj.*

infusorian (,ınfjʊ'zɔːrɪən) *Obs.* ~*n.* **1.** any of the microscopic organisms, such as protozoans, found in infusions
of organic material. ~*adj.* **2.** of or relating to infusorians.
[C18: from NL *Infusoria* former class name; see INFUSE]
—**in,fu'sorial** *adj.*

-ing[1] *suffix forming nouns.* **1.** (*from verbs*) the action of,
process of, result of, or something connected with the
verb: *meeting; a wedding; winnings.* **2.** (*from other
nouns*) something used in, consisting of, involving, etc.:
tubing; soldiering. **3.** (*from other parts of speech*): *an
outing.* [OE *-ing, -ung*]

-ing[2] *suffix.* **1.** forming the present participle of verbs:
walking; believing. **2.** forming participial adjectives: *a
growing boy; a sinking ship.* **3.** forming adjectives not
derived from verbs: *swashbuckling.* [ME *-ing, -inde*, from
OE *-ende*]

-ing[3] *suffix forming nouns.* a person or thing having a certain quality or being of a certain kind: *sweeting; whiting.*
[OE *-ing*; rel. to ON *-ingr*]

ingather (ın'gæðə) *vb.* (*tr.*) to gather together or in (a harvest, etc.). —**in'gatherer** *n.*

Inge (ıŋ) *n.* **William Ralph,** known as *the Gloomy Dean.*
1860–1954, English theologian, noted for his pessimism;
dean of St Paul's Cathedral (1911–34).

ingeminate (ın'dʒɛmɪ,neɪt) *vb.* (*tr.*) *Rare.* to repeat; reiterate. [C16: from L *ingemināre* to redouble, from IN-[2] +
gemināre to GEMINATE]

ingenious (ın'dʒiːnjəs, -nɪəs) *adj.* possessing or done
with ingenuity; skilful or clever. [C15: from L, from *ingenium* natural ability; see ENGINE] —**in'geniously** *adv.*
—**in'geniousness** *n.*

ingénue (,ænʒeɪ'njuː) *n.* an artless, innocent, or inexperienced girl or young woman. [C19: from F, fem. of *ingénu*
INGENUOUS]

ingenuity (,ındʒɪ'njuːɪtɪ) *n., pl.* **-ties.** **1.** inventive talent;
cleverness. **2.** an ingenious device, act, etc. **3.** *Arch.*
frankness; candour. [C16: from L *ingenuitās* a freeborn

condition, outlook consistent with such a condition, from
ingenuus native, freeborn (see INGENUOUS); meaning infl.
by INGENIOUS]

ingenuous (ın'dʒɛnjʊəs) *adj.* **1.** naive, artless, or innocent. **2.** candid; frank; straightforward. [C16: from L *ingenuus* freeborn, virtuous, from IN-[2] + *gignere* to beget]
—**in'genuously** *adv.* —**in'genuousness** *n.*

ingest (ın'dʒɛst) *vb.* (*tr.*) to take (food or liquid) into the
body. [C17: from L *ingerere* to put into, from IN-[2] + *gerere*
to carry; see GEST] —**in'gestible** *adj.* —**in'gestion** *n.*
—**in'gestive** *adj.*

ingle ('ıŋg³l) *n. Arch. or dialect.* a fire in a room or a fireplace. [C16: prob. from Scot. Gaelic *aingeal* fire]

Ingleborough ('ıŋg³lbərə, -brə) *n.* a mountain in N England, in North Yorkshire: potholes. Height: 723 m (2373
ft.).

inglenook ('ıŋg³l,nʊk) *n. Brit.* a corner by a fireplace;
chimney corner.

ingoing ('ın,gəʊɪŋ) *adj.* going in; entering.

Ingolstadt (*German* 'ıŋɔlʃtat) *n.* a city in S West Germany, in Bavaria on the River Danube: oil-refining. Pop.:
90 371 (1983 est.).

ingot ('ıŋgət) *n.* a piece of cast metal obtained from a
mould in a form suitable for storage, etc. [C14: ?from
IN-[2] + OE *goten,* p.p. of *geotan* to pour]

ingraft (ın'grɑːft) *vb.* a variant spelling of **engraft.**
—**in'graftment** *or* ,**ingraf'tation** *n.*

ingrain *or* **engrain** *vb.* (ın'greɪn). (*tr.*) **1.** to impress
deeply on the mind or nature; instil. **2.** *Arch.* to dye into
the fibre of (a fabric). ~*adj.* ('ın,greɪn). **3.** (of woven or
knitted articles) made of dyed yarn or of fibre that is dyed
before being spun into yarn. ~*n.* ('ın,greɪn). **4.** a carpet
made from ingrained yarn. [C18: from *dyed in grain* dyed
with kermes through the fibre]

ingrained *or* **engrained** (ın'greɪnd) *adj.* **1.** deeply impressed or instilled. **2.** (*prenominal*) complete or inveterate; utter. **3.** (esp. of dirt) worked into or through the
fibre, grain, pores, etc. —**ingrainedly** *or* **engrainedly**
(ın'greɪnɪdlɪ) *adv.* —**in'grainedness** *or* **en'grainedness**
n.

ingrate ('ıngreɪt, ın'greɪt) *Arch.* ~*n.* **1.** an ungrateful person. ~*adj.* **2.** ungrateful. [C14: from L *ingrātus* (adj.),
from IN-[1] + *grātus* GRATEFUL] —**'ingrately** *adv.*

ingratiate (ın'greɪʃɪ,eɪt) *vb.* (*tr.*; often foll. by *with*) to
place (oneself) purposely in the favour (of another). [C17:
from L, from IN-[2] + *grātia* grace, favour] —**in'grati,at-
ing** *or* **in'gratiatory** *adj.* —**in'grati,atingly** *adv.*
—**in,grati'ation** *n.*

ingredient (ın'griːdɪənt) *n.* a component of a mixture,
compound, etc., esp. in cooking. [C15: from L *ingrediēns*
going into, from *ingredī* to enter; see INGRESS]

Ingres (*French* ɛ̃grə) *n.* **Jean Auguste Dominique** (ʒɑ̃
ogyst dɔminik). 1780–1867, French classical painter,
noted for his draughtsmanship.

ingress ('ıngrɛs) *n.* **1.** the act of going or coming in; an
entering. **2.** a way in; entrance. **3.** the right or permission to enter. [C15: from L *ingressus,* from *ingredī* to go
in, from *gradī* to step, go] —**ingression** (ın'grɛʃən) *n.*

in-group *n. Sociol.* a highly cohesive and relatively closed
social group characterized by the preferential treatment
reserved for its members.

ingrowing ('ın,grəʊɪŋ) *adj.* **1.** (esp. of a toenail) growing
abnormally into the flesh. **2.** growing within or into.
—**'in,growth** *n.*

ingrown ('ın,grəʊn, ın'grəʊn) *adj.* **1.** (esp. of a toenail)
grown abnormally into the flesh; covered by adjacent tissues. **2.** grown within; native; innate.

inguinal ('ıŋgwɪn³l) *adj. Anat.* of or relating to the groin.
[C17: from L *inguinālis,* from *inguen* groin]

ingulf (ın'gʌlf) *vb.* (*tr.*) a variant of **engulf.**

ingurgitate (ın'gɜːdʒɪ,teɪt) *vb.* to swallow (food, etc.)
greedily or in excess. [C16: from L *ingurgitāre* to flood,
from IN-[2] + *gurges* abyss] —**in,gurgi'tation** *n.*

inhabit (ın'hæbɪt) *vb.* (*tr.*) to live or dwell in; occupy.
[C14: from L *inhabitāre,* from *habitāre* to dwell]
—**in'habitable** *adj.* —**in,habita'bility** *n.* —**in,habi'tation** *n.*

inhabitant (ın'hæbɪtənt) *n.* a person or animal that is a
permanent resident of a particular place or region.
—**in'habitancy** *or* **in'habitance** *n.*

---

in'frequent *adj.* in'glorious *adj.* in'grati,tude *n.*

inhalant (ɪn'heɪlənt) *adj.* **1.** (esp. of a medicinal preparation) inhaled for its therapeutic effect. **2.** inhaling. ~*n.* **3.** an inhalant medicinal preparation.

inhale (ɪn'heɪl) *vb.* to draw (breath, etc.) into the lungs; breathe in. [C18: from IN-² + L *halāre* to breathe] —,in-**ha'lation** *n.*

inhaler (ɪn'heɪlə) *n.* **1.** a device for breathing in therapeutic vapours, esp. one for relieving nasal congestion. **2.** a person who inhales.

Inhambane (,ɪnjəm'bɑːnə) *n.* a port in SE Mozambique on an inlet of the Mozambique Channel (**Inhambane Bay**). Pop.: 26 701 (1970).

inhere (ɪn'hɪə) *vb.* (*intr.; foll. by in*) to be an inseparable part (of). [C16: from L *inhaerēre* to stick in, from *haerēre* to stick]

inherent (ɪn'hɪərənt, -'hɛr-) *adj.* existing as an inseparable part; intrinsic. —**in'herently** *adv.*

inherit (ɪn'hɛrɪt) *vb.* **1.** to receive (property, etc.) by succession or under a will. **2.** (*intr.*) to succeed as heir. **3.** (*tr.*) to possess (a characteristic) through genetic transmission. **4.** (*tr.*) to receive (a position, etc.) from a predecessor. [C14: from OF *enheriter*, from LL *inhērēditāre* to appoint an heir, from L *hērēs* HEIR] —**in'herited** *adj.* —**in'heritor** *n.* —**in'heritress** *or* **in'heritrix** *fem. n.*

inheritable (ɪn'hɛrɪtəb³l) *adj.* **1.** capable of being transmitted by heredity from one generation to a later one. **2.** capable of being inherited. **3.** *Rare.* having the right to inherit. —**in,herita'bility** *or* **in'heritableness** *n.* —**in'heritably** *adv.*

inheritance (ɪn'hɛrɪtəns) *n.* **1.** *Law.* **a.** hereditary succession to an estate, title, etc. **b.** the right of an heir to succeed on the death of an ancestor. **c.** something that may legally be transmitted to an heir. **2.** the act of inheriting. **3.** something inherited; heritage. **4.** the derivation of characteristics of one generation from an earlier one by heredity.

inhibit (ɪn'hɪbɪt) *vb.* (*tr.*) **1.** to restrain or hinder (an impulse, desire, etc.). **2.** to prohibit, forbid, or prevent. **3.** to stop, prevent, or decrease the rate of (a chemical reaction). [C15: from L *inhibēre* to restrain, from IN-² + *habēre* to have] —**in'hibitable** *adj.* —**in'hibiter** *or* **in'hibitor** *n.* —**in'hibitive** *or* **in'hibitory** *adj.*

inhibition (,ɪnɪ'bɪʃən, ,ɪnhɪ-) *n.* **1.** the act of inhibiting or the condition of being inhibited. **2.** *Psychol.* a mental state or condition in which the varieties of expression and behaviour of an individual become restricted. **3.** the process of stopping or retarding a chemical reaction. **4.** *Physiol.* the suppression of the function or action of an organ or part, as by stimulation of its nerve supply.

inhibitor (ɪn'hɪbɪtə) *n.* a substance that retards or stops a chemical reaction.

in-house *adj., adv.* within an organization or group: *an in-house job; the job was done in-house.*

inhuman (ɪn'hjuːmən) *adj.* **1.** Also: **inhumane** (,ɪnhjuː'meɪn). lacking humane feelings, such as sympathy, understanding, etc.; cruel; brutal. **2.** not human. —,inhu'manely *adv.* —**in'humanly** *adv.* —**in'humanness** *n.*

inhumanity (,ɪnhjuː'mænɪtɪ) *n., pl.* **-ties. 1.** lack of humane qualities. **2.** an inhumane act, decision, etc.

inhume (ɪn'hjuːm) *vb.* (*tr.*) to inter; bury. [C17: from L, from IN-² + *humus* ground] —,inhu'mation *n.* —**in'humer** *n.*

inimical (ɪ'nɪmɪk³l) *adj.* **1.** adverse or unfavourable. **2.** not friendly; hostile. [C17: from L, from *inimīcus*, from IN-¹ + *amīcus* friendly; see ENEMY] —**in'imically** *adv.* —**in'imicalness** *or* **in,imi'cality** *n.*

inimitable (ɪ'nɪmɪtəb³l) *adj.* incapable of being duplicated or imitated; unique. —**in,imita'bility** *or* **in'imitableness** *n.* —**in'imitably** *adv.*

iniquity (ɪ'nɪkwɪtɪ) *n., pl.* **-ties. 1.** lack of justice or righteousness; wickedness; injustice. **2.** a wicked act; sin. [C14: from L, from *inīquus* unfair, from IN-¹ + *aequus* even, level; see EQUAL] —**in'iquitous** *adj.* —**in'iquitously** *adv.* —**in'iquitousness** *n.*

initial (ɪ'nɪʃəl) *adj.* **1.** of, at, or concerning the beginning. ~*n.* **2.** the first letter of a word, esp. a person's name. **3.** *Printing.* a large letter set at the beginning of a chapter or work. **4.** *Bot.* a cell from which tissues and organs develop by division and differentiation. ~*vb.* **-tialling, -tial-led** *or U.S.* **-tialing, -tialed. 5.** (*tr.*) to sign with one's

initials, esp. to indicate approval; endorse. [C16: from L *initiālis* of the beginning, from *initium* beginning, lit.: an entering upon, from *inīre* to go in] —**in'itialer** *or* **in'i-tialler** *n.* —**in'itially** *adv.*

initialize *or* **-ise** (ɪ'nɪʃə,laɪz) *vb.* (*tr.*) to assign an initial value to (a variable or storage location) in **a computer program.** —**in,itiali'zation** *or* **-i'sation** *n.*

initiate *vb.* (ɪ'nɪʃɪ,eɪt). (*tr.*) **1.** to begin or originate. **2.** to accept (new members) into an organization such as a club, through often secret ceremonies. **3.** to teach fundamentals to. ~*adj.* (ɪ'nɪʃɪɪt, -,eɪt). **4.** initiated; begun. ~*n.* (ɪ'nɪʃɪɪt, -,eɪt). **5.** a person who has been initiated, esp. recently. **6.** a beginner; novice. [C17: from L *initiāre* (vb.), from *initium*; see INITIAL] —**in'iti,ator** *n.* —**in'iti-atory** *adj.*

initiation (ɪ,nɪʃɪ'eɪʃən) *n.* **1.** the act of initiating or the condition of being initiated. **2.** the ceremony, often secret, initiating new members into an organization.

initiative (ɪ'nɪʃɪətɪv, -'nɪʃətɪv) *n.* **1.** the first step or action of a matter; commencing move: *a peace initiative.* **2.** the right or power to begin or initiate something: *he has the initiative.* **3.** the ability or attitude required to begin or initiate something. **4.** *Government.* the right of citizens to introduce legislation, etc., in a legislative body, as in Switzerland. **5. on one's own initiative.** without being prompted. ~*adj.* **6.** of or concerning initiation or serving to initiate; initiatory. —**in'itiatively** *adv.*

inject (ɪn'dʒɛkt) *vb.* (*tr.*) **1.** *Med.* to introduce (a fluid) into the body (of a person or animal) by means of a syringe. **2.** (foll. by *into*) to introduce (a new aspect or element): *to inject humour into a scene.* **3.** to interject (a comment, idea, etc.). [C17: from *injicere* to throw in, from *jacere* to throw] —**in'jectable** *adj.* —**in'jector** *n.*

injection (ɪn'dʒɛkʃən) *n.* **1.** fluid injected into the body, esp. for medicinal purposes. **2.** something injected. **3.** the act of injecting. **4. a.** the act or process of introducing fluid under pressure, such as fuel into the combustion chamber of an engine. **b.** (*as modifier*): *injection moulding.* —**in'jective** *adj.*

injunction (ɪn'dʒʌŋkʃən) *n.* **1.** *Law.* an instruction or order issued by a court to a party to an action, esp. to refrain from some act. **2.** a command, admonition, etc. **3.** the act of enjoining. [C16: from LL, from L *injungere* to ENJOIN] —**in'junctive** *adj.* —**in'junctively** *adv.*

injure ('ɪndʒə) *vb.* (*tr.*) **1.** to cause physical or mental harm or suffering to; hurt or wound. **2.** to offend, esp. by an injustice. [C16: back formation from INJURY] —'**in-jurable** *adj.* —'**injured** *adj.* —'**injurer** *n.*

injurious (ɪn'dʒʊərɪəs) *adj.* **1.** causing damage or harm; deleterious; hurtful. **2.** abusive, slanderous, or libellous. —**in'juriously** *adv.* —**in'juriousness** *n.*

injury ('ɪndʒərɪ) *n., pl.* **-ries. 1.** physical damage or hurt. **2.** a specific instance of this: *a leg injury.* **3.** harm done to a reputation. **4.** *Law.* a violation or infringement of another person's rights that causes him harm and is actionable at law. [C14: from L *injūria* injustice, wrong, from *injūriōsus* acting unfairly, wrongful, from IN-¹ + *jūs* right]

injury time *n. Soccer, rugby, etc.* extra playing time added on to compensate for time spent attending to injured players during the match.

injustice (ɪn'dʒʌstɪs) *n.* **1.** the condition or practice of being unjust or unfair. **2.** an unjust act.

ink (ɪŋk) *n.* **1.** a fluid or paste used for printing, writing, and drawing. **2.** a dark brown fluid ejected into the water for self-concealment by an octopus or related mollusc. ~*vb.* (*tr.*) **3.** to mark with ink. **4.** to coat (a printing surface) with ink. [C13: from OF *enque*, from LL *encaustum* a purplish-red ink, from Gk *enkauston* purple ink, from *enkaustos* burnt in, from *enkaiein* to burn in; see EN-², CAUSTIC] —'**inker** *n.*

inkblot ('ɪŋk,blɒt) *n.* a patch of ink accidentally or deliberately spilled. Ten such patches, of different shapes, are used in the Rorschach test.

ink-cap *n.* any of several saprophytic fungi whose caps disintegrate into a black inky fluid after the spores mature.

Inkerman ('ɪŋkəmən; *Russian* ɪnkɪr'man) *n.* a village in the SW Soviet Union, in the S Crimea east of Sevastopol: scene of a battle during the Crimean War in which British and French forces defeated the Russians (1854).

,inhar'monious *adj.*   in'hospitable *adj.*   ,inhospi'tality *n.*   ,inju'dicious *adj.*

inkhorn ('ıŋk,hɔːn) n. (formerly) a small portable container for ink, usually made from horn.

ink in vb. (adv.) **1.** (tr.) to use ink to go over pencil lines in (a drawing). **2.** to apply ink to (a printing surface) in preparing to print from it.

inkling ('ıŋklıŋ) n. a slight intimation or suggestion; suspicion. [C14: prob. from inclen to hint at]

inkstand ('ıŋk,stænd) n. a stand or tray on which are kept writing implements and containers for ink.

inkwell ('ıŋk,wɛl) n. a small container for pen ink, often let into the surface of a desk.

inky ('ıŋkı) adj. **inkier, inkiest. 1.** resembling ink, esp. in colour; dark or black. **2.** of, containing, or stained with ink. —**'inkiness** n.

INLA abbrev. for Irish National Liberation Army.

inlaid ('ın,leıd, ın'leıd) adj. **1.** set in the surface, as a design in wood. **2.** having such a design or inlay: an inlaid table.

inland adj. ('ınlənd). **1.** of or located in the interior of a country or region away from a sea or border. **2.** Chiefly Brit. operating within a country or region; domestic; not foreign. ~n. ('ın,lænd, -lənd) **3.** the interior of a country or region. ~adv. ('ın,lænd, -lənd). **4.** towards or into the interior of a country or region. —**'inlander** n.

Inland Revenue n. (in Britain and New Zealand) a government board that administers and collects major direct taxes, such as income tax.

Inland Sea n. a sea in SW Japan, between the islands of Honshu, Shikoku, and Kyushu. Japanese name: **Seto Naikai.**

in-law n. **1.** a relative by marriage. ~adj. **2.** (postpositive; in combination) related by marriage: a father-in-law. [C19: back formation from father-in-law, etc.]

inlay vb. (ın'leı), **-laying, -laid.** (tr.) **1.** to decorate (an article, esp. of furniture) by inserting pieces of wood, ivory, etc., into slots in the surface. ~n. ('ın,leı). **2.** Dentistry. a filling inserted into a cavity and held in position by cement. **3.** decoration made by inlaying. **4.** an inlaid article, surface, etc. —**'in,layer** n.

inlet n. ('ın,lɛt). **1.** a narrow inland opening of the coastline. **2.** an entrance or opening. **3.** the act of letting someone or something in. **4.** something let in or inserted. **5. a.** a passage or valve through which a substance, esp. a fluid, enters a machine. **b.** (as modifier): an inlet valve. ~vb. (ın'lɛt), **-letting, -let. 6.** (tr.) to insert or inlay.

inlier ('ın,laıə) n. an outcrop of rocks that is entirely surrounded by younger rocks.

in loco parentis Latin. (ın 'ləʊkəʊ pə'rɛntıs) in place of a parent: said of a person acting in a parental capacity.

inly ('ınlı) adv. Poetic. inwardly; intimately.

inmate ('ın,meıt) n. a person who is confined to an institution such as a prison or hospital.

in medias res Latin. (ın 'miːdı,æs 'reıs) into the middle of events or a narrative. [lit.: into the midst of things, taken from a passage in Horace's Ars Poetica]

in memoriam (ın mı'mɔːrıəm) in memory of: used in obituaries, epitaphs, etc. [L]

inmost ('ın,məʊst) adj. another word for **innermost.**

inn (ın) n. a pub or small hotel providing food and accommodation.

Inn (ın) n. a river in central Europe, rising in Switzerland in Graubünden and flowing northeast through Austria and Bavaria to join the River Danube at Passau: forms part of the border between Austria and West Germany. Length: 514 km (319 miles).

innards ('ınədz) pl. n. Inf. **1.** the internal organs of the body, esp. the viscera. **2.** the interior parts or components of anything, esp. the working parts. [C19: colloquial var. of inwards]

innate ('ıneıt, 'ıneıt) adj. **1.** existing from birth; congenital; inborn. **2.** being an essential part of the character of a person or thing. **3.** instinctive; not learned: innate capacities. **4.** Philosophy. (of ideas) present in the mind before any experience and knowable by pure reason. [C15: from L, from innasci to be born in, from nasci to be born] —**in'nately** adv. —**in'nateness** n.

inner ('ınə) adj. (prenominal) **1.** being or located further inside: an inner room. **2.** happening or occurring inside. **3.** relating to the soul, mind, spirit, etc. **4.** more profound or obscure; less apparent: the inner meaning. **5.** exclusive or private: inner regions of the party. ~n. **6.** Archery. **a.** the red innermost ring on a target. **b.** a shot which hits this ring. —**'innerly** adv. —**'innerness** n.

inner bar n. the. Brit. all Queen's or King's Counsel collectively.

inner city n. **a.** the parts of a city in or near its centre, esp. when associated with poverty, substandard housing, etc. **b.** (as modifier): inner-city schools.

Inner Hebrides pl. n. See **Hebrides.**

inner man or (fem.) **inner woman** n. **1.** the mind or soul. **2.** Jocular. the stomach or appetite.

Inner Mongolia n. an autonomous region of NE China: consists chiefly of the Mongolian plateau, with the Gobi Desert in the north and the Great Wall of China in the south. Capital: Hohhot. Pop.: 19 850 000 (1985). Area: 1 177 500 sq. km (459 225 sq. miles).

innermost ('ınə,məʊst) adj. **1.** being or located furthest within; central. **2.** intimate; private.

inner tube n. an inflatable rubber tube that fits inside a pneumatic tyre casing.

innervate ('ınɜː,veıt) vb. (tr.) **1.** to supply nerves to (a bodily organ or part). **2.** to stimulate (a bodily organ or part) with nerve impulses. —**,inner'vation** n.

innings ('ınıŋz) n. **1.** (functioning as sing.) Cricket, etc. **a.** the batting turn of a player or team. **b.** the runs scored during such a turn. **2.** (sometimes sing.) a period of opportunity or action.

Inniskilling (,ınıs'kılıŋ) n. the former name of **Enniskillen.**

innkeeper ('ın,kiːpə) n. an owner or manager of an inn.

innocence ('ınəsəns) n. the quality or state of being innocent. Archaic word: **innocency** ('ınəsənsı). [C14: from L innocentia harmlessness, from innocēns blameless, from IN-[1] + nocēre to hurt]

innocent ('ınəsənt) adj. **1.** not corrupted or tainted with evil; sinless; pure. **2.** not guilty of a particular crime; blameless. **3.** (postpositive; foll. by of) free (of); lacking: innocent of all knowledge of history. **4. a.** harmless or innocuous: an innocent game. **b.** not cancerous: an innocent tumour. **5.** credulous, naive, or artless. **6.** simple-minded; slow-witted. ~n. **7.** an innocent person, esp. a young child or an ingenuous adult. **8.** a simple-minded person; simpleton. —**'innocently** adv.

Innocent II n. original name Gregorio Papareschi. died 1143, pope (1130–43). He condemned Abelard's teachings.

Innocent III n. original name Giovanni Lotario de' Conti. ?1161–1216, pope (1198–1216), under whom the temporal power of the papacy reached its height. He instituted the Fourth Crusade (1202) and a crusade against the Albigenses (1208), and called the fourth Lateran Council (1215).

Innocent IV n. original name Sinibaldo de' Fieschi. died 1254, pope (1243–54); an unrelenting enemy of Emperor Frederick II and his heirs.

innocuous (ı'nɒkjʊəs) adj. having little or no adverse or harmful effect; harmless. [C16: from L innocuus harmless, from IN-[1] + nocēre to harm] —**in'nocuously** adv. —**in'nocuousness** or **innocuity** (,ınə'kjuːıtı) n.

innominate bone (ı'nɒmınıt) n. either of the two bones that form the sides of the pelvis, consisting of the ilium, ischium, and pubis. Nontechnical name: **hipbone.**

innovate ('ınə,veıt) vb. to invent or begin to apply (methods, ideas, etc.). [C16: from L innovāre to renew, from IN-[2] + novāre to make new, from novus new] —**'inno,vative** or **'inno,vatory** adj. —**'inno,vator** n.

innovation (,ınə'veıʃən) n. **1.** something newly introduced, such as a new method or device. **2.** the act of innovating. —**,inno'vational** adj. —**,inno'vationist** n.

Innsbruck ('ınzbrʊk) n. a city in W Austria, on the River Inn at the foot of the Brenner Pass: tourist centre. Pop.: 117 287 (1981).

innuendo (,ınjʊ'ɛndəʊ) n., pl. **-dos** or **-does. 1.** an indirect or subtle reference, esp. one made maliciously or indicating criticism or disapproval; insinuation. **2.** Law. (in an action for defamation) an explanation of the construction put upon words alleged to be defamatory where this meaning is not apparent. [C17: from L, lit.: by hinting, from innuere to convey by a nod, from IN-[2] + nuere to nod]

Innuit ('ınjʊ,ıt) n. a variant spelling of **Inuit.**

innumerable (ı'njuːmərəbəl, ı'njuːmrəbəl) or **innumerous** adj. so many as to be uncountable; extremely numerous. —**in,numera'bility** or **in'numerableness** n. —**in'numerably** adv.

innumerate (ɪ'njuːmərɪt) *adj.* **1.** having neither knowledge nor understanding of mathematics or science. ~*n.* **2.** an innumerate person. —**in'numeracy** *n.*

inoculate (ɪ'nɒkjʊ,leɪt) *vb.* **1.** to introduce (the causative agent of a disease) into the body in order to induce immunity. **2.** (*tr.*) to introduce (microorganisms, esp. bacteria) into (a culture medium). **3.** (*tr.*) to cause to be influenced or imbued, as with ideas. [C15: from L *inoculāre* to implant, from IN-[2] + *oculus* eye, bud] —**in,ocu'lation** *n.* —**in'oculative** *adj.* —**in'ocu,lator** *n.*

inoculum (ɪ'nɒkjʊləm) *or* **inoculant** *n.*, *pl.* **-la** (-lə) *or* **-lants.** *Med.* the substance used in giving an inoculation. [C20: NL; see INOCULATE]

in-off *n.* *Billiards.* a shot that goes into a pocket after striking another ball.

İnönü ('iːnɜː,nuː, ,ɪnɜː'nuː) *n.* **Ismet** (ɪs'mɛt, 'ɪsmɛt). 1884–1973, Turkish statesman; president of Turkey (1938–50) and prime minister (1923–37; 1961–65).

inoperable (ɪn'ɒpərəb³l, -'ɒprə-) *adj.* **1.** incapable of being implemented or operated. **2.** *Surgery.* not suitable for operation without risk, esp. because of metastasis. —**in,opera'bility** *or* **in'operableness** *n.* —**in'operably** *adv.*

inordinate (ɪn'ɔːdɪnɪt) *adj.* **1.** exceeding normal limits; immoderate. **2.** unrestrained, as in behaviour or emotion; intemperate. **3.** irregular or disordered. [C14: from L *inordinātus* disordered, from IN-[1] + *ordināre* to put in order] —**in'ordinacy** *or* **in'ordinateness** *n.* —**in'ordinately** *adv.*

inorganic (,ɪnɔː'gænɪk) *adj.* **1.** not having the structure or characteristics of living organisms; not organic. **2.** relating to or denoting chemical compounds that do not contain carbon. **3.** not having a system, structure, or ordered relation of parts; amorphous. **4.** not resulting from or produced by growth; artificial. —**,inor'ganically** *adv.*

inorganic chemistry *n.* the branch of chemistry concerned with the elements and all their compounds except those containing carbon.

inosculate (ɪn'ɒskjʊ,leɪt) *vb.* **1.** *Physiol.* (of small blood vessels) to communicate by anastomosis. **2.** to unite or be united so as to be continuous; blend. **3.** to intertwine or cause to intertwine. [C17: from IN-[2] + L *ōsculāre* to equip with an opening, from *ōsculum*, dim. of *ōs* mouth] —**in,oscu'lation** *n.*

inositol (ɪ'nəʊsɪ,tɒl) *n.* a cyclic alcohol, one isomer of which (*i*-inositol) is present in yeast and is a growth factor for some organisms. [C19: from Gk *in-, is* sinew + -OSE[2] + -ITE[1] + -OL[1]]

inpatient ('ɪn,peɪʃənt) *n.* a patient living in the hospital where he is being treated.

in perpetuum Latin. (ɪn pɜː'pɛtjʊəm) for ever.

input ('ɪn,pʊt) *n.* **1.** the act of putting in. **2.** that which is put in. **3.** (*often pl.*) a resource required for industrial production, such as capital goods, etc. **4.** *Electronics.* the signal or current fed into a component or circuit. **5.** *Computers.* the data fed into a computer from a peripheral device. **6.** (*modifier*) of or relating to electronic, computer, or other input: *input program.* ~*vb.* **7.** (*tr.*) to insert (data) into a computer.

input/output *n.* *Computers.* **1.** the data or information passed into or out of a computer. **2.** (*modifier*) concerned with or relating to such passage of data or information.

inquest ('ɪn,kwɛst) *n.* **1.** an inquiry, esp. into the cause of an unexplained, sudden, or violent death, held by a coroner, in certain cases with a jury. **2.** *Inf.* any inquiry or investigation. [C13: from Med. L, from L IN-[2] + *quaesītus* investigation, from *quaerere* to examine]

inquietude (ɪn'kwaɪɪ,tjuːd) *n.* restlessness, uneasiness, or anxiety. —**inquiet** (ɪn'kwaɪət) *adj.* —**in'quietly** *adv.*

inquiline ('ɪnkwɪ,laɪn) *n.* **1.** an animal that lives in close association with another animal without harming it. See also **commensal** (sense 1). ~*adj.* **2.** of or living as an inquiline. [C17: from L *inquilīnus* lodger, from IN-[2] + *colere* to dwell] —**inquilinous** (,ɪnkwɪ'laɪnəs) *adj.*

inquire *or* **enquire** (ɪn'kwaɪə) *vb.* **1. a.** to seek information (about); ask: *she inquired his age; she inquired about rates of pay.* **b.** (*intr.*; foll. by *of*) to ask (a person) for information: *I'll inquire of my aunt when she is coming.* **2.** (*intr.*; often foll. by *into*) to make a search or investigation. [C13: from L *inquīrere*, from IN-[2] + *quaerere* to seek] —**in'quirer** *or* **en'quirer** *n.* —**in'quiry** *or* **en'quiry** *n.*

inquisition (,ɪnkwɪ'zɪʃən) *n.* **1.** the act of inquiring deeply or searchingly; investigation. **2.** a deep or searching inquiry, esp. a ruthless official investigation in order to suppress revolt or root out the unorthodox. **3.** an official inquiry, esp. one held by a jury before an officer of the Crown. [C14: from legal L *inquisītiō*, from *inquīrere* to seek for; see INQUIRE] —**,inqui'sitional** *adj.* —**,inqui'sitionist** *n.*

Inquisition (,ɪnkwɪ'zɪʃən) *n. History.* a judicial institution of the Roman Catholic Church (1232–1820) founded to suppress heresy.

inquisitive (ɪn'kwɪzɪtɪv) *adj.* **1.** excessively curious, esp. about the affairs of others; prying. **2.** eager to learn; inquiring. —**in'quisitively** *adv.* —**in'quisitiveness** *n.*

inquisitor (ɪn'kwɪzɪtə) *n.* **1.** a person who inquires, esp. deeply, searchingly, or ruthlessly. **2.** (*often cap.*) an official of the ecclesiastical court of the Inquisition.

inquisitorial (ɪn,kwɪzɪ'tɔːrɪəl) *adj.* **1.** of, relating to, or resembling inquisition or an inquisitor. **2.** offensively curious; prying. **3.** *Law.* denoting criminal procedure in which one party is both prosecutor and judge, or in which the trial is held in secret. Cf. **accusatorial** (sense 2). —**in,quisi'torially** *adv.* —**in,quisi'torialness** *n.*

inquorate (ɪn'kwɔː,reɪt) *adj. Brit.* not consisting of or being a quorum: *this meeting is inquorate.*

in re (ɪn 'reɪ) *prep.* in the matter of: used esp. in bankruptcy proceedings. [C17: from L]

INRI *abbrev. for* Iesus Nazarenus Rex Iudaeorum (the inscription placed over Christ's head during the Crucifixion). [L: Jesus of Nazareth, King of the Jews]

inro ('ɪnrəʊ) *n.*, *pl.* **inro.** a set of small lacquer boxes formerly worn hung from the belt by Japanese men and used to carry medicines, seals, etc.

inroad ('ɪn,rəʊd) *n.* **1.** an invasion or hostile attack; raid or incursion. **2.** an encroachment or intrusion.

inrush ('ɪn,rʌʃ) *n.* a sudden usually overwhelming inward flow or rush; influx. —**'in,rushing** *n.*, *adj.*

ins. *abbrev. for:* **1.** inches. **2.** insulated. **3.** insurance.

insane (ɪn'seɪn) *adj.* **1. a.** mentally deranged; crazy; of unsound mind. **b.** (*as collective n.; preceded by the*): *the insane.* **2.** characteristic of a person of unsound mind: *an insane stare.* **3.** irresponsible; very foolish; stupid. —**in'sanely** *adv.* —**in'saneness** *n.*

insanitary (ɪn'sænɪtərɪ, -trɪ) *adj.* not sanitary; dirty or infected.

insanity (ɪn'sænɪtɪ) *n.*, *pl.* **-ties. 1.** relatively permanent disorder of the mind; state or condition of being insane. **2.** utter folly; stupidity.

insatiable (ɪn'seɪʃəb³l, -ʃɪə-) *or* **insatiate** (ɪn'seɪʃɪɪt) *adj.* not able to be satisfied; greedy or unappeasable. —**in,satia'bility** *or* **in'satiateness** *n.* —**in'satiably** *or* **in'satiately** *adv.*

inscape ('ɪnskeɪp) *n.* the essential inner nature of a person, object, etc., as expressed in literary or artistic works. [C19: from IN-[2] + *-scape*, as in LANDSCAPE; coined by Gerard Manley HOPKINS]

inscribe (ɪn'skraɪb) *vb.* (*tr.*) **1.** to make, carve, or engrave (writing, letters, etc.) on (a surface such as wood, stone, or paper). **2.** to enter (a name) on a list or in a register. **3.** to sign one's name on (a book, etc.) before presentation to another person. **4.** to draw (a geometric construction) inside another construction so that the two are in contact but do not intersect. [C16: from L *inscrībere*; see INSCRIPTION] —**in'scribable** *adj.* —**in'scribableness** *n.* —**in'scriber** *n.*

inscription (ɪn'skrɪpʃən) *n.* **1.** something inscribed, esp. words carved or engraved on a coin, tomb, etc. **2.** a signature or brief dedication in a book or on a work of art. **3.** the act of inscribing. [C14: from L *inscriptiō* a writing upon, from *inscrībere* to write upon, from IN-[2] + *scrībere* to write] —**in'scriptional** *or* **in'scriptive** *adj.* —**in'scriptively** *adv.*

inscrutable (ɪn'skruːtəb³l) *adj.* mysterious or enigmatic; incomprehensible. [C15: from LL, from L IN-[1] + *scrūtārī* to examine] —**in,scruta'bility** *or* **in'scrutableness** *n.* —**in'scrutably** *adv.*

,**inof'fensive** *adj.*
,**inof'ficious** *adj.*

in'operative *adj.*

in'oppor,tune *adj.*

,**insa'lubrious** *adj.*

insect ('ınsɛkt) n. **1.** any of a class of small air-breathing arthropods, having a body divided into head, thorax, and abdomen, three pairs of legs, and (in most species) two pairs of wings. **2.** (loosely) any similar invertebrate, such as a spider, tick, or centipede. **3.** a contemptible, loathsome, or insignificant person. [C17: from L *insectum* (animal that has been) cut into, insect, from *insecāre*, from IN-² + *secāre* to cut] —**in'sectile** adj. —'**insect-like** adj.

insectarium (,ınsɛk'tɛərɪəm) or **insectary** (ın'sɛktərı) n., pl. **-tariums, -taria** (-'tɛərɪə), or **-taries.** a place where living insects are kept, bred, and studied.

insecticide (ın'sɛktɪ,saɪd) n. a substance used to destroy insect pests. —**in,secti'cidal** adj.

insectivore (ın'sɛktɪ,vɔː) n. **1.** any of an order of placental mammals, being typically small, with simple teeth, and feeding on invertebrates. The group includes shrews, moles, and hedgehogs. **2.** any animal or plant that derives nourishment from insects. —,**insec'tivorous** adj.

insecure (,ınsı'kjʊə) adj. **1.** anxious or afraid; not confident or certain. **2.** not adequately protected: *an insecure fortress.* **3.** unstable or shaky. —,**inse'curely** adv. —,**inse'cureness** n. —,**inse'curity** n.

inselberg ('ınzᵊl,bɜːɡ) n. an isolated rocky hill rising abruptly from a flat plain. [from G, from *Insel* island + *Berg* mountain]

inseminate (ın'sɛmɪ,neɪt) vb. (tr.) **1.** to impregnate (a female) with semen. **2.** to introduce (ideas or attitudes) into the mind of (a person or group). [C17: from L *in-sēmināre*, from IN-² + *sēmināre* to sow, from *sēmen* seed] —**in,semi'nation** n. —**in'semi,nator** n.

insensate (ın'sɛnseɪt, -sɪt) adj. **1.** lacking sensation or consciousness. **2.** insensitive; unfeeling. **3.** foolish; senseless. —**in'sensately** adv. —**in'sensateness** n.

insensible (ın'sɛnsəbᵊl) adj. **1.** lacking sensation or consciousness. **2.** (foll. by *of* or *to*) unaware (of) or indifferent (to): *insensible to suffering.* **3.** thoughtless or callous. **4.** a less common word for **imperceptible.** —**in,sensi'bility** or **in'sensibleness** n. —**in'sensibly** adv.

insentient (ın'sɛnʃɪənt) adj. lacking consciousness or senses; inanimate. —**in'sentience** n.

insert vb. (ın'sɜːt). (tr.) **1.** to put in or between; introduce. **2.** to introduce into text, as in a newspaper; interpolate. ~n. ('ınsɜːt). **3.** something inserted. **4. a.** a folded section placed in another for binding in with a book. **b.** a printed sheet, esp. one bearing advertising, placed loose between the leaves of a book, periodical, etc. [C16: from L *inserere* to plant in, from IN-² + *serere* to join] —**in'sertable** adj. —**in'serter** n.

insertion (ın'sɜːʃən) n. **1.** the act of inserting or something that is inserted. **2.** a word, sentence, correction, etc., inserted into text, such as a newspaper. **3.** a strip of lace, embroidery, etc., between two pieces of material. **4.** *Anat.* the point or manner of attachment of a muscle to the bone that it moves. —**in'sertional** adj.

in-service adj. denoting training that is given to employees during the course of employment: *an in-service course.*

insessorial (,ınsɛ'sɔːrɪəl) adj. **1.** (of feet or claws) adapted for perching. **2.** (of birds) having insessorial feet. [C19: from NL *Insessōrēs* birds that perch, from L: perchers, from *insidēre* to sit upon]

inset vb. (ın'sɛt), **-setting, -set. 1.** (tr.) to set or place in or within; insert. ~n. ('ınsɛt). **2.** something inserted. **3.** *Printing.* **a.** a small map or diagram set within the borders of a larger one. **b.** another name for **insert** (sense 4). **4.** a piece of fabric inserted into a garment, as to shape it or for decoration. —'**in,setter** n.

inshallah (ın'fælə) sentence substitute. *Islam.* if Allah wills it. [C19: from Ar.]

inshore ('ın'ʃɔː) adj. **1.** in or on the water, but close to the shore: *inshore weather.* ~adv., adj. **2.** towards the shore from the water: *an inshore wind; we swam in-shore.*

inside n. ('ın'saɪd). **1.** the interior; inner or enclosed part or surface. **2.** the side of a path away from the road or adjacent to a wall. **3.** (*also pl.*) *Inf.* the internal organs of the body, esp. the stomach and bowels. **4. inside of.** in a period of time less than; within. **5. inside out.** with the inside facing outwards. **6. know (something) inside** out. to know thoroughly or perfectly. ~prep. (,ın'saɪd). **7.** in or to the interior of; within or to within; on the inside of. ~adj. ('ın,saɪd). **8.** on or of an interior; on the inside: *an inside door.* **9.** (*prenominal*) arranged or provided by someone within an organization or building, esp. illicitly: *the raid was an inside job; inside information.* ~adv. (,ın'saɪd). **10.** within or to within a thing or place; indoors. **11.** *Sl.* in or into prison.
▷ **Usage.** See at **outside.**

inside job n. *Inf.* a crime committed with the assistance of someone associated with the victim.

inside lane n. *Athletics.* the inside and advantageous position in a race that uses the curved parts of the track.

insider (,ın'saɪdə) n. **1.** a member of a specified group. **2.** a person with access to exclusive information.

insider dealing or **trading** n. the illegal practice of a person on the Stock Exchange or in some branches of the Civil Service taking advantage of early confidential information in order to deal in shares for personal profit. —**insider dealer** or **trader** n.

insidious (ın'sɪdɪəs) adj. **1.** stealthy, subtle, cunning, or treacherous. **2.** working in a subtle or apparently innocuous way, but nevertheless deadly: *an insidious illness.* [C16: from L *insidiōsus* cunning, from *insidiae* an ambush, from *insidēre* to sit in] —**in'sidiously** adv. —**in'sidiousness** n.

insight ('ın,saɪt) n. **1.** the ability to perceive clearly or deeply; penetration. **2.** a penetrating and often sudden understanding, as of a complex situation or problem. **3.** *Psychol.* the capacity for understanding one's own or another's mental processes. **4.** *Psychiatry.* the ability to understand one's own problems. —'**in,sightful** adj.

insignia (ın'sɪgnɪə) n., pl. **-nias** or **-nia. 1.** a badge or emblem of membership, office, or dignity. **2.** a distinguishing sign or mark. [C17: from L: badges, from *insignis* distinguished by a mark, prominent, from IN-² + *signum* mark]

insignificant (,ınsıg'nıfıkənt) adj. **1.** having little or no importance; trifling. **2.** almost or relatively meaningless. **3.** small or inadequate: *an insignificant wage.* **4.** not distinctive in character, etc. —,**insig'nificance** or ,**insig'nificancy** n. —,**insig'nificantly** adv.

insincere (,ınsın'sıə) adj. lacking sincerity; hypocritical. —,**insin'cerely** adv. —**insincerity** (,ınsın'sɛrıtı) n.

insinuate (ın'sınjʊ,eɪt) vb. **1.** (*may take a clause as object*) to suggest by indirect allusion, hints, innuendo, etc. **2.** (tr.) to introduce subtly or deviously. **3.** (tr.) to cause (someone, esp. oneself) to be accepted by gradual approaches or manoeuvres. [C16: from L *insinuāre* to wind one's way into, from IN-² + *sinus* curve] —**in'sinuative** or **in'sinuatory** adj. —**in'sinu,ator** n.

insinuation (ın,sınjʊ'eɪʃən) n. **1.** an indirect or devious hint or suggestion. **2.** the act or practice of insinuating.

insipid (ın'sıpıd) adj. **1.** lacking spirit or interest; boring. **2.** lacking taste; unpalatable. [C17: from L, from IN-¹ + *sapidus* full of flavour, SAPID] —,**insi'pidity** or **in'sipidness** n. —**in'sipidly** adv.

insist (ın'sıst) vb. (when tr., takes a clause as object; when intr., usually foll. by *on* or *upon*) **1.** to make a determined demand (for): *he insisted on his rights.* **2.** to express a convinced belief (in) or assertion (of). [C16: from L *insistere* to stand upon, urge, from IN-² + *sistere* to stand] —**in'sister** n. —**in'sistingly** adv.

insistent (ın'sıstənt) adj. **1.** making continual and persistent demands. **2.** demanding notice or attention; compelling: *the insistent cry of a bird.* —**in'sistence** or **in'sistency** n. —**in'sistently** adv.

in situ Latin. (ın 'sıtjuː) adv., adj. (*postpositive*) in the natural, original, or appropriate position.

in so far or *U.S.* **insofar** (,ınsəʊ'fɑː) adv. (usually foll. by *as*) to the degree or extent (that).

insolation (,ınsəʊ'leɪʃən) n. **1.** the quantity of solar radiation falling upon a body or planet, esp. per unit area. **2.** exposure to the sun's rays. **3.** another name for **sunstroke.**

insole ('ın,səʊl) n. **1.** the inner sole of a shoe or boot. **2.** a loose additional inner sole used to give extra warmth or to make a shoe fit.

insolent ('ınsələnt) adj. impudent or disrespectful. [C14: from L, from IN-¹ + *solēre* to be accustomed] —'**insolence** n. —'**insolently** adv.

---

in'sensitive adj. **in'separable** adj. ,**inso'briety** n.

insoluble (ɪnˈsɒljʊbᵊl) *adj.* **1.** incapable of being dissolved; incapable of forming a solution, esp. in water. **2.** incapable of being solved. —**in‚solu'bility** *or* **in'soluble-ness** *n.* —**in'solubly** *adv.*

insolvent (ɪnˈsɒlvənt) *adj.* **1.** having insufficient assets to meet debts and liabilities; bankrupt. **2.** of or relating to bankrupts or bankruptcy. ~*n.* **3.** a person who is insolvent; bankrupt. —**in'solvency** *n.*

insomnia (ɪnˈsɒmnɪə) *n.* chronic inability to fall asleep or to enjoy uninterrupted sleep. [C18: from L, from *insomnis* sleepless, from *somnus* sleep] —**in'somni‚ac** *n., adj.* —**in'somnious** *adj.*

insomuch (‚ɪnsəʊˈmʌtʃ) *adv.* **1.** (foll. by *as* or *that*) to such an extent or degree. **2.** (foll. by *as*) because of the fact (that); inasmuch (as).

insouciant (ɪnˈsuːsɪənt) *adj.* carefree or unconcerned; light-hearted. [C19: from F, from IN-¹ + *souciant* worrying, from *soucier* to trouble, from L *sollicitāre*] —**in'souciance** *n.* —**in'souciantly** *adv.*

inspan (ɪnˈspæn) *vb.* -**spanning,** -**spanned.** (*tr.*) *Chiefly S. African.* **1.** to harness (animals) to (a vehicle); yoke. **2.** to press (people) into service. [C19: from Afrik., from MDu. *inspannen*, from *spannen* to stretch]

inspect (ɪnˈspɛkt) *vb.* (*tr.*) **1.** to examine closely, esp. for faults or errors. **2.** to scrutinize officially (a document, military personnel on ceremonial parade, etc.). [C17: from L *inspicere*, from *specere* to look] —**in'spectable** *adj.* —**in'spection** *n.* —**in'spective** *adj.*

inspector (ɪnˈspɛktə) *n.* **1.** a person who inspects, esp. an official who examines for compliance with regulations, standards, etc. **2.** a police officer ranking below a superintendent and above a sergeant. —**in'spectoral** *or* **in'spectorial** (‚ɪnspɛkˈtɔːrɪəl) *adj.* —**in'spector‚ship** *n.*

inspectorate (ɪnˈspɛktərɪt) *n.* **1.** the office, rank, or duties of an inspector. **2.** a body of inspectors. **3.** a district under an inspector.

inspiration (‚ɪnspɪˈreɪʃən) *n.* **1.** stimulation or arousal of the mind, feelings, etc., to special activity or creativity. **2.** the state or quality of being so stimulated or aroused. **3.** someone or something that causes this state. **4.** an idea or action resulting from such a state. **5.** the act or process of inhaling; breathing in.

inspiratory (ɪnˈspaɪərətərɪ, -trɪ) *adj.* of or relating to inhalation or the drawing in of air.

inspire (ɪnˈspaɪə) *vb.* **1.** to exert a stimulating or beneficial effect upon (a person, etc.); animate or invigorate. **2.** (*tr.*; foll. by *with* or *to*; *may take an infinitive*) to arouse (with a particular emotion or to a particular action); stir. **3.** (*tr.*) to prompt or instigate; give rise to. **4.** (*tr.; often passive*) to guide or arouse by divine influence or inspiration. **5.** to take or draw (air, gas, etc.) into the lungs; inhale. **6.** (*tr.*) *Arch.* to breathe into or upon. [C14 (in the sense: to breathe upon, blow into): from L *inspīrāre*, from *spīrāre* to breathe] —**in'spirable** *adj.* —**in'spirative** *adj.* —**in'spirer** *n.* —**in'spiringly** *adv.*

inspirit (ɪnˈspɪrɪt) *vb.* (*tr.*) to fill with vigour; inspire. —**in'spiriter** *n.* —**in'spiriting** *adj.* —**in'spiritment** *n.*

inspissate (ɪnˈspɪseɪt) *vb. Arch.* to thicken, as by evaporation. [C17: from LL *inspissātus* thickened, from L, from *spissus* thick] —‚**inspis'sation** *n.* —**in'spis‚sator** *n.*

inst. *abbrev. for:* **1.** instant (this month). **2.** instantaneous. **3.** instrumental.

Inst. *abbrev. for:* **1.** Institute. **2.** Institution.

install *or* **instal** (ɪnˈstɔːl) *vb.* -**stalling,** -**stalled.** (*tr.*) **1.** to place (equipment) in position and connect and adjust for use. **2.** to put in a position, rank, etc. **3.** to settle (a person, esp. oneself) in a position or state: *she installed herself in an armchair.* [C16: from Med. L *installāre*, from IN-² + *stallum* STALL¹] —**in'staller** *n.*

installation (‚ɪnstəˈleɪʃən) *n.* **1.** the act of installing or the state of being installed. **2.** a large device, system, or piece of equipment that has been installed.

installment plan *or esp.* **Canad. instalment plan** *n.* the U.S. and Canad. name for **hire-purchase.**

instalment *or U.S.* **installment** (ɪnˈstɔːlmənt) *n.* **1.** one of the portions into which a debt is divided for payment at specified intervals over a fixed period. **2.** a portion of something that is issued, broadcast, or published in parts. [C18: from obs. *estallment*, prob. from OF *estaler* to fix, from *estal* something fixed, from OHG *stal* STALL¹]

instance ('ɪnstəns) *n.* **1.** a case or particular example. **2. for instance.** for or as an example. **3.** a specified stage in proceedings; step (in **in the first, second,** etc., **instance**). **4.** urgent request or demand (esp. in **at the instance of**). ~*vb.* (*tr.*) **5.** to cite as an example. [C14 (in the sense: case, example): from Med. L *instantia* example, (in the sense: urgency) from L: a being close upon, from *instāns* urgent; see INSTANT]

instant ('ɪnstənt) *n.* **1.** a very brief time; moment. **2.** a particular moment or point in time: *at the same instant.* **3. on the instant.** immediately; without delay. ~*adj.* **4.** immediate; instantaneous. **5.** (esp. of foods) prepared or designed for preparation with very little time and effort: *instant coffee.* **6.** urgent or imperative. **7.** (*postpositive*) of the present month: *a letter of the 7th instant.* Abbrev.: **inst.** [C15: from L *instāns*, from *instāre* to be present, press closely, from IN-² + *stāre* to stand]

instantaneous (‚ɪnstənˈteɪnɪəs) *adj.* **1.** occurring with almost no delay; immediate. **2.** happening or completed within a moment: *instantaneous death.* —‚**instan'taneously** *adv.* —‚**instan'taneousness** *or* **instantaneity** (ɪn‚stæntəˈniːɪtɪ) *n.*

instanter (ɪnˈstæntə) *adv. Law.* without delay; the same day or within 24 hours. [C17: from L: urgently, from *instans* INSTANT]

instantly ('ɪnstəntlɪ) *adv.* **1.** immediately; at once. **2.** *Arch.* urgently or insistently.

instar ('ɪnstɑː) *n.* the stage in the development of an insect between any two moults. [C19: NL from L: image]

instate (ɪnˈsteɪt) *vb.* (*tr.*) to place in a position or office; install. —**in'statement** *n.*

instead (ɪnˈstɛd) *adv.* **1.** as a replacement, substitute, or alternative. **2. instead of.** (*prep.*) in place of or as an alternative to. [C13: from *in stead* in place]

instep ('ɪn‚stɛp) *n.* **1.** the middle section of the human foot, forming the arch between the ankle and toes. **2.** the part of a shoe, stocking, etc., covering this. [C16: prob. from IN-² + STEP]

instigate ('ɪnstɪ‚geɪt) *vb.* (*tr.*) **1.** to bring about, as by incitement: *to instigate rebellion.* **2.** to urge on to some drastic or unadvisable action. [C16: from L *instigāre* to incite] —‚**insti'gation** *n.* —**'insti‚gative** *adj.* —**'insti‚gator** *n.*

instil *or* **instill** (ɪnˈstɪl) *vb.* -**stilling,** -**stilled.** (*tr.*) **1.** to introduce gradually; implant or infuse. **2.** *Rare.* to pour in or inject in drops. [C16: from L *instillāre* to pour in a drop at a time, from *stillāre* to drip] —**in'stiller** *n.* —**in'stilment, in'stillment,** *or* ‚**instil'lation** *n.*

instinct *n.* ('ɪnstɪŋkt). **1.** the innate capacity of an animal to respond to a given stimulus in a relatively fixed way. **2.** inborn intuitive power. ~*adj.* (ɪn'stɪŋkt). **3.** *Rare.* (*postpositive*; often foll. by *with*) **a.** animated or impelled (by). **b.** imbued or infused (with). [C15: from L *instinctus* roused, from *instinguere* to incite]

instinctive (ɪnˈstɪŋktɪv) *or* **instinctual** *adj.* **1.** of, relating to, or resulting from instinct. **2.** conditioned so as to appear innate: *an instinctive movement in driving.* —**in'stinctively** *or* **in'stinctually** *adv.*

institute ('ɪnstɪ‚tjuːt) *vb.* (*tr.*) **1.** to organize; establish. **2.** to initiate: *to institute a practice.* **3.** to establish in a position or office; induct. ~*n.* **4.** an organization founded for particular work, such as education, promotion of the arts, or scientific research. **5.** the building where such an organization is situated. **6.** something instituted, esp. a rule, custom, or precedent. [C16: from L *instituere*, from *statuere* to place] —**'insti‚tutor** *or* **'insti‚tuter** *n.*

institutes ('ɪnstɪ‚tjuːts) *pl. n.* a digest or summary, esp. of laws.

institution (‚ɪnstɪ'tjuːʃən) *n.* **1.** the act of instituting. **2.** an organization or establishment founded for a specific purpose, such as a hospital or college. **3.** the building where such an organization is situated. **4.** an established custom, law, or relationship in a society or community. **5.** *Inf.* a constant feature or practice: *Jones's drink at the bar was an institution.* **6.** the appointment of an incumbent to an ecclesiastical office or pastoral charge. —‚**in-sti'tutionary** *adj.*

---

in'solvable *adj.*　　　‚**insta'bility** *n.*

institutional (ˌɪnstɪˈtjuːʃənəl) *adj.* **1.** of, relating to, or characteristic of institutions. **2.** dull, routine, and uniform: *institutional meals.* **3.** relating to principles or institutes, esp. of law. —ˌinstiˈtutionally *adv.* —ˌinstiˈtutionaˌlism *n.*

institutionalize *or* **-ise** (ˌɪnstɪˈtjuːʃənəˌlaɪz) *vb.* **1.** (*tr.; often passive*) to subject to the deleterious effects of confinement in an institution. **2.** (*tr.*) to place in an institution. **3.** to make or become an institution. —ˌinstiˌtutionaliˈzation *or* -iˈsation *n.*

in-store *adj.* available within a department store: *in-store banking facilities.*

instruct (ɪnˈstrʌkt) *vb.* (*tr.*) **1.** to direct to do something; order. **2.** to teach (someone) how to do (something). **3.** to furnish with information; apprise. **4.** *Law, chiefly Brit.* (esp. of a client to his solicitor or a solicitor to a barrister) to give relevant facts or information to. [C15: from L *instruere* to construct, equip, teach, from *struere* to build] —inˈstructible *adj.*

instruction (ɪnˈstrʌkʃən) *n.* **1.** a direction; order. **2.** the process or act of imparting knowledge; teaching; education. **3.** *Computers.* a part of a program consisting of a coded command to the computer to perform a specified function. —inˈstructional *adj.*

instructions (ɪnˈstrʌkʃənz) *pl. n.* **1.** directions, orders, or recommended rules for guidance, use, etc. **2.** *Law.* the facts and details relating to a case given by a client to his solicitor or by a solicitor to a barrister.

instructive (ɪnˈstrʌktɪv) *adj.* serving to instruct or enlighten; conveying information. —inˈstructively *adv.* —inˈstructiveness *n.*

instructor (ɪnˈstrʌktə) *n.* **1.** someone who instructs; teacher. **2.** *U.S. & Canad.* a university teacher ranking below assistant professor. —inˈstructorship *n.* —inˈstructress** (ɪnˈstrʌktrɪs) *fem. n.*

instrument *n.* (ˈɪnstrəmənt). **1.** a mechanical implement or tool, esp. one used for precision work. **2.** *Music.* any of various contrivances or mechanisms that can be played to produce musical tones or sounds. **3.** an important factor or agency in something: *her evidence was an instrument in his arrest.* **4.** *Inf.* a person used by another to gain an end; dupe. **5.** a measuring device, such as a pressure gauge. **6. a.** a device or system for use in navigation or control, esp. of aircraft. **b.** (*as modifier*): *instrument landing.* **7.** a formal legal document. ~*vb.* (ˈɪnstrəˌmɛnt). (*tr.*) **8.** another word for **orchestrate** (sense 1). **9.** to equip with instruments. [C13: from L *instrūmentum* tool, from *instruere* to erect, furnish; see INSTRUCT]

instrumental (ˌɪnstrəˈmɛntəl) *adj.* **1.** serving as a means or influence; helpful. **2.** of, relating to, or characterized by an instrument. **3.** played by or composed for musical instruments. **4.** *Grammar.* denoting a case of nouns, etc. indicating the instrument used in performing an action, usually using the prepositions *with* or *by means of.* ~*n.* **5.** a piece of music composed for instruments rather than for voices. **6.** *Grammar.* the instrumental case. —ˌinstrumenˈtality *n.* —ˌinstruˈmentally *adv.*

instrumentalist (ˌɪnstrəˈmɛntəlɪst) *n.* a person who plays a musical instrument.

instrumentation (ˌɪnstrəmɛnˈteɪʃən) *n.* **1.** the instruments specified in a musical score or arrangement. **2.** another word for **orchestration.** **3.** the study of the characteristics of musical instruments. **4.** the use of instruments or tools.

instrument panel *or* **board** *n.* **1.** a panel on which instruments are mounted, as on a car. See also **dashboard.** **2.** an array of instruments, gauges, etc., mounted to display the condition or performance of a machine.

insubordinate (ˌɪnsəˈbɔːdɪnɪt) *adj.* **1.** not submissive to authority; disobedient or rebellious. **2.** not in a subordinate position or rank. ~*n.* **3.** an insubordinate person. —ˌinsubˈordinately *adv.* —ˌinsubˌordiˈnation *n.*

insubstantial (ˌɪnsəbˈstænʃəl) *adj.* **1.** not substantial; flimsy, tenuous, or slight. **2.** imaginary; unreal. —ˌinsubˌstantiˈality *n.* —ˌinsubˈstantially *adv.*

insufferable (ɪnˈsʌfərəbəl) *adj.* intolerable; unendurable. —inˈsufferableness *n.* —inˈsufferably *adv.*

insufficiency (ˌɪnsəˈfɪʃənsɪ) *n.* **1.** Also: ˌinsufˈficience. the state of being insufficient. **2.** *Pathol.* failure in the

functioning of an organ, tissue, etc.: *cardiac insufficiency.*

insufflate (ˈɪnsʌˌfleɪt) *vb.* **1.** (*tr.*) to breathe or blow (something) into (a room, area, etc.). **2.** *Med.* to blow (air, medicated powder, etc.) into a body cavity. **3.** (*tr.*) to breathe or blow upon (someone or something) as a ritual or sacramental act. —ˌinsufˈflation *n.* —ˈinsufˌflator *n.*

insular (ˈɪnsjʊlə) *adj.* **1.** of, relating to, or resembling an island. **2.** remote, detached, or aloof. **3.** illiberal or narrow-minded. **4.** isolated or separated. [C17: from LL, from L *insula* island] —ˈinsularism *or* **insularity** (ˌɪnsjʊˈlærɪtɪ) *n.* —ˈinsularly *adv.*

insulate (ˈɪnsjʊˌleɪt) *vb.* (*tr.*) **1.** to prevent the transmission of electricity, heat, or sound to or from (a body or device) by surrounding with a nonconducting material. **2.** to isolate or detach. [C16: from LL *insulātus* made into an island]

insulation (ˌɪnsjʊˈleɪʃən) *n.* **1.** Also: **insulant.** material used to insulate a body or device. **2.** the act or process of insulating.

insulator (ˈɪnsjʊˌleɪtə) *n.* any material or device that insulates, esp. a material with a very low electrical conductivity or thermal conductivity.

insulin (ˈɪnsjʊlɪn) *n.* a protein hormone, secreted in the pancreas by the islets of Langerhans, that controls the concentration of glucose in the blood. [C20: from NL *insula* islet (of the pancreas) + -IN]

insult *vb.* (ɪnˈsʌlt). (*tr.*) **1.** to treat, mention, or speak to rudely; offend; affront. ~*n.* (ˈɪnsʌlt). **2.** an offensive or contemptuous remark or action; affront; slight. **3.** a person or thing producing the effect of an affront: *some television is an insult to intelligence.* **4.** *Med.* an injury or trauma. [C16: from L *insultāre* to jump upon] —inˈsulter *n.*

insuperable (ɪnˈsuːpərəbəl, -prəbəl, -ˈsjuː-) *adj.* incapable of being overcome; insurmountable. —inˌsuperaˈbility *n.* —inˈsuperably *adv.*

insupportable (ˌɪnsəˈpɔːtəbəl) *adj.* **1.** incapable of being endured; intolerable; insufferable. **2.** incapable of being supported or justified; indefensible. —ˌinsupˈportableness *n.* —ˌinsupˈportably *adv.*

insurance (ɪnˈʃʊərəns, -ˈʃɔː-) *n.* **1. a.** the act, system, or business of providing financial protection against specified contingencies, such as death, loss, or damage. **b.** the state of having such protection. **c.** Also called: **insurance policy.** the policy providing such protection. **d.** the pecuniary amount of such protection. **e.** the premium payable in return for such protection. **f.** (*as modifier*): *insurance agent; insurance broker; insurance company.* **2.** a means of protecting or safeguarding against risk or injury.

insure (ɪnˈʃʊə, -ˈʃɔː) *vb.* **1.** (often foll. by *against*) to guarantee or protect (against risk, loss, etc.). **2.** (often foll. by *against*) to issue (a person) with an insurance policy or take out an insurance policy (on): *his house was heavily insured against fire.* **3.** a variant spelling (esp. U.S.) of **ensure.** ~Also (rare) (for senses 1, 2): **ensure.** —inˈsurable *adj.* —inˌsuraˈbility *n.*

insured (ɪnˈʃʊəd, -ˈʃɔːd) *adj.* **1.** covered by insurance: *an insured risk.* ~*n.* **2.** the person, persons, or organization covered by an insurance policy.

insurer (ɪnˈʃʊərə, -ˈʃɔː-) *n.* **1.** a person or company offering insurance policies in return for premiums. **2.** a person or thing that insures.

insurgence (ɪnˈsɜːdʒəns) *n.* rebellion, uprising, or riot.

insurgent (ɪnˈsɜːdʒənt) *adj.* **1.** rebellious or in revolt, as against a government in power or the civil authorities. ~*n.* **2.** a person who takes part in an uprising or rebellion; insurrectionist. [C18: from L *insurgēns* rising upon or against, from *surgere* to rise] —inˈsurgency *n.*

insurrection (ˌɪnsəˈrekʃən) *n.* the act or an instance of rebelling against a government in power or the civil authorities; insurgency. [C15: from LL *insurrectiō*, from *insurgere* to rise up] —ˌinsurˈrectionary *n., adj.* —ˌinsurˈrectional *adj.* —ˌinsurˈrectionist *n., adj.*

int. *abbrev. for:* **1.** interest. **2.** interior. **3.** internal. **4.** Also: **Int.** international.

intact (ɪnˈtækt) *adj.* untouched or unimpaired; left complete or perfect. [C15: from L *intactus* not touched, from *tangere* to touch] —inˈtactness *n.*

ˌinsufˈficient *adj.*   ˌinsurˈmountable *adj.*   ˌinsusˈceptible *adj.*

intaglio (ɪnˈtɑːlɪˌəʊ) n., pl. **-lios** or **-li** (-ljiː). **1.** a seal, gem, etc., ornamented with a sunken or incised design. **2.** the art or process of incised carving. **3.** a design, figure, or ornamentation carved, engraved, or etched into the surface of the material used. **4.** any of various printing techniques using an etched or engraved plate. **5.** an incised die used to make a design in relief. [C17: from It., from *intagliare* to engrave, from *tagliare* to cut, from LL *tāliāre*; see TAILOR] —**intagliated** (ɪnˈtɑːlɪˌeɪtɪd) adj.

intake (ˈɪnˌteɪk) n. **1.** a thing or a quantity taken in: *an intake of students.* **2.** the act of taking in. **3.** the opening through which fluid enters a duct or channel, esp. the air inlet of a jet engine. **4.** a ventilation shaft in a mine. **5.** a contraction or narrowing: *an intake in a garment.*

intangible (ɪnˈtændʒɪbəl) adj. **1.** incapable of being perceived by touch; impalpable. **2.** imprecise or unclear to the mind: *intangible ideas.* **3.** (of property or a business asset) saleable though not possessing intrinsic productive value. ~n. **4.** something that is intangible. —**in,tangi'bility** n. —**in'tangibly** adv.

intarsia (ɪnˈtɑːsɪə) or **tarsia** n. **1.** a decorative mosaic of inlaid wood of a style developed in the Italian Renaissance. **2.** (in knitting) an individually worked motif. [C19: changed from It. *intarsio*]

integer (ˈɪntɪdʒə) n. **1.** any rational number that can be expressed as the sum or difference of a finite number of units, as 1, 2, 3, etc. **2.** an individual entity or whole unit. [C16: from L: untouched, from *tangere* to touch]

integral (ˈɪntɪɡrəl, ɪnˈtɛɡrəl) adj. **1.** (often foll. by *to*) being an essential part (of); intrinsic (to). **2.** intact; entire. **3.** formed of constituent parts; united. **4.** *Maths.* **a.** of or involving an integral. **b.** involving or being an integer. ~n. **5.** *Maths.* the sum of a large number of infinitesimally small quantities, summed either between stated limits (**definite integral**) or in the absence of limits (**indefinite integral**). **6.** a complete thing; whole. —**integrality** (ˌɪntɪˈɡrælɪtɪ) n. —**'integrally** adv.

integral calculus n. the branch of calculus concerned with the determination of integrals (**integration**) and their application to the solution of differential equations.

integrand (ˈɪntɪˌɡrænd) n. a mathematical function to be integrated. [C19: from L: to be integrated]

integrant (ˈɪntəɡrənt) adj. **1.** part of a whole; integral; constituent. ~n. **2.** an integrant part.

integrate vb. (ˈɪntɪˌɡreɪt). **1.** to make or be made into a whole; incorporate or be incorporated. **2.** (tr.) to designate (a school, park, etc.) for use by all races or groups; desegregate. **3.** to amalgamate or mix (a racial or religious group) with an existing community. **4.** *Maths.* to determine the integral of a function or variable. ~adj. (ˈɪntɪɡrɪt). **5.** made up of parts; integrated. [C17: from L *integrāre*; see INTEGER] —**integrable** (ˈɪntəɡrəbəl) adj. —**integra'bility** n. —**inte'gration** n. —**'inte,grative** adj.

integrated circuit n. a very small electronic circuit consisting of an assembly of elements made from a chip of semiconducting material.

integrity (ɪnˈtɛɡrɪtɪ) n. **1.** adherence to moral principles; honesty. **2.** the quality of being unimpaired; soundness. **3.** unity; wholeness. [C15: from L *integritās*; see INTEGER]

integument (ɪnˈtɛɡjʊmənt) n. any outer protective layer or covering, such as a cuticle, seed coat, rind, or shell. [C17: from L *integumentum*, from *tegere* to cover] —**in,tegu'mental** or **in,tegu'mentary** adj.

intellect (ˈɪntɪˌlɛkt) n. **1.** the capacity for understanding, thinking, and reasoning. **2.** a mind or intelligence, esp. a brilliant one: *his intellect is wasted on that job.* **3.** *Inf.* a person possessing a brilliant mind; brain. [C14: from L *intellectus* comprehension, from *intellegere* to understand; see INTELLIGENCE] —**intel'lective** adj. —**intel'lectively** adv.

intellection (ˌɪntɪˈlɛkʃən) n. **1.** mental activity; thought. **2.** an idea or thought.

intellectual (ˌɪntɪˈlɛktʃʊəl) adj. **1.** of or relating to the intellect. **2.** appealing to or characteristic of people with a developed intellect: *intellectual literature.* **3.** expressing or enjoying mental activity. ~n. **4.** a person who enjoys mental activity and has highly developed tastes in art, etc. **5.** a person who uses his intellect. **6.** a highly intelligent person. —**,intel,lectu'ality** or **,intel'lectualness** n. —**,intel'lectual,ize** or -,**ise** vb. —**,intel'lectually** adv.

intellectualism (ˌɪntɪˈlɛktʃʊəˌlɪzəm) n. **1.** development and exercise of the intellect. **2.** *Philosophy.* the doctrine

that reason is the ultimate criterion of knowledge. —**,intel'lectualist** n., adj. —**,intel,lectual'istic** adj.

intelligence (ɪnˈtɛlɪdʒəns) n. **1.** the capacity for understanding; ability to perceive and comprehend meaning. **2.** *Old-fashioned.* news; information. **3.** military information about enemies, spies, etc. **4.** a group or department that gathers or deals with such information. **5.** (*often cap.*) an intelligent being, esp. one that is not embodied. **6.** (*modifier*) of or relating to intelligence: *an intelligence network.* [C14: from L *intellegentia*, from *intellegere* to discern, lit.: to choose between, from INTER- + *legere* to choose] —**in,telli'gential** adj.

intelligence quotient n. a measure of the intelligence of an individual. The quotient is derived by dividing an individual's mental age by his chronological age and multiplying the result by 100. Abbrev.: **IQ**.

intelligence test n. any of a number of tests designed to measure a person's mental skills.

intelligent (ɪnˈtɛlɪdʒənt) adj. **1.** having or indicating intelligence; clever. **2.** indicating high intelligence; perceptive: *an intelligent guess.* **3.** (of computerized functions, weapons, etc.) able to initiate or modify action in the light of ongoing events. **4.** (*postpositive*; foll. by *of*) *Arch.* having knowledge or information. —**in'telligently** adv.

intelligent card n. a plastic card with a built-in microprocessor, used for processing transaction details.

intelligentsia (ɪn,tɛlɪˈdʒɛntsɪə) n. (usually preceded by *the*) the educated or intellectual people in a society or community. [C20: from Russian *intelligentsiya*, from L *intellegentia* INTELLIGENCE]

intelligible (ɪnˈtɛlɪdʒəbəl) adj. **1.** able to be understood; comprehensible. **2.** *Philosophy.* capable of being apprehended by the mind or intellect alone. [C14: from L *intellegibilis*; see INTELLECT] —**in,telligi'bility** n. —**in'telligibly** adv.

intemperate (ɪnˈtɛmpərɪt, -prɪt) adj. **1.** consuming alcoholic drink habitually or to excess; immoderate. **2.** unrestrained: *intemperate rage.* **3.** extreme or severe: *an intemperate climate.* —**in'temperance** or **in'temperateness** n. —**in'temperately** adv.

intend (ɪnˈtɛnd) vb. **1.** (*may take a clause as object*) to propose or plan (something or to do something); have in mind; mean. **2.** (tr.; often foll. by *for*) to design or destine (for a certain purpose, person, etc.). **3.** (tr.) to mean to express or indicate: *what do his words intend?* **4.** (intr.) to have a purpose as specified; mean: *he intends well.* [C14: from L *intendere* to stretch forth, give one's attention to, from *tendere* to stretch] —**in'tender** n.

intendancy (ɪnˈtɛndənsɪ) n. **1.** the position or work of an intendant. **2.** intendants collectively.

intendant (ɪnˈtɛndənt) n. a senior administrator; superintendent or manager.

intended (ɪnˈtɛndɪd) adj. **1.** planned or future. ~n. **2.** *Inf.* a person whom one is to marry; fiancé or fiancée.

intense (ɪnˈtɛns) adj. **1.** of extreme force, strength, degree, or amount: *intense heat.* **2.** characterized by deep or forceful feelings: *an intense person.* [C14: from L *intensus* stretched, from *intendere* to stretch out] —**in'tensely** adv. —**in'tenseness** n.

intensifier (ɪnˈtɛnsɪˌfaɪə) n. **1.** a person or thing that intensifies. **2.** a word, esp. an adjective or adverb, that serves to intensify the meaning of the word or phrase that it modifies. **3.** a substance, esp. one containing silver or uranium, used to increase the density of a photographic film or plate.

intensify (ɪnˈtɛnsɪˌfaɪ) vb. **-fying, -fied. 1.** to make or become intense or more intense. **2.** (tr.) to increase the density of (a photographic film or plate). —**in,tensifi'cation** n.

intension (ɪnˈtɛnʃən) n. *Logic.* the set of characteristics or properties that distinguish the referent or referents of a given word. —**in'tensional** adj.

intensity (ɪnˈtɛnsɪtɪ) n., pl. **-ties. 1.** the state or quality of being intense. **2.** extreme force, degree, or amount. **3.** *Physics.* **a.** a measure of field strength or of the energy transmitted by radiation. **b.** (of sound in a specified direction) the average rate of flow of sound energy for one period through unit area at right angles to the specified direction.

intensive (ɪnˈtɛnsɪv) adj. **1.** of, relating to, or characterized by intensity: *intensive training.* **2.** (*usually in combination*) using one factor of production proportionately more than others, as specified: *capital-intensive; labour-*

intensive. **3.** *Agriculture*. involving or farmed using large amounts of capital or labour to increase production from a particular area. Cf. **extensive** (sense 3). **4.** denoting or relating to a grammatical intensifier. **5.** denoting or belonging to a class of pronouns used to emphasize a noun or personal pronoun. **6.** of or relating to intension. ~*n*. **7.** an intensifier or intensive pronoun or grammatical construction. —**in'tensively** *adv*. —**in'tensiveness** *n*.

intensive care *n*. **1.** extensive and continuous care provided for an acutely ill patient in a hospital. **2.** the unit in which this care is provided; intensive-care unit.

intent (in'tɛnt) *n*. **1.** something that is intended; aim; purpose; design. **2.** the act of intending. **3.** *Law*. the will or purpose with which one does an act. **4.** implicit meaning; connotation. **5. to all intents and purposes.** for all practical purposes; virtually. ~*adj*. **6.** firmly fixed; determined; concentrated: *an intent look*. **7.** (*postpositive*; usually foll. by *on* or *upon*) having the fixed intention (of); directing one's mind or energy (to): *intent on committing a crime*. [C13 (in the sense: intention): from LL *intentus* aim, from L: a stretching out; see INTEND] —**in'tently** *adv*. —**in'tentness** *n*.

intention (in'tɛnʃən) *n*. **1.** a purpose or goal; aim: *it is his intention to reform*. **2.** *Med*. a natural healing process in which the edges of a wound cling together with no tissue between (**first intention**), or in which the edges adhere with tissue between (**second intention**). **3.** (*usually pl*.) design or purpose with respect to a proposal of marriage (esp. in **honourable intentions**).

intentional (in'tɛnʃənªl) *adj*. **1.** performed by or expressing intention; deliberate. **2.** of or relating to intention or purpose. —**in,tention'ality** *n*. —**in'tentionally** *adv*.

inter (in'tɜː) *vb*. **-terring, -terred.** (*tr*.) to place (a body, etc.) in the earth; bury, esp. with funeral rites. [C14: from OF *enterrer*, from L IN-² + *terra* earth]

inter- *prefix*. **1.** between or among: *international*. **2.** together, mutually, or reciprocally: *interdependent*; *interchange*. [from L]

interact (,intər'ækt) *vb*. (*intr*.) to act on or in close relation with each other.

interaction (,intə'ækʃən) *n*. **1.** a mutual or reciprocal action. **2.** *Physics*. the transfer of energy between elementary particles, between a particle and a field, or between fields. See **fundamental interaction**.

interactive (,intər'æktiv) *adj*. **1.** allowing or relating to continuous two-way transfer of information between a user and the central point of a communication system, such as a computer or television. **2.** (of two or more persons, forces, etc.) acting upon or in close relation with each other; interacting.

inter alia *Latin*. among other things.

interbreed (,intə'briːd) *vb*. **-breeding, -bred. 1.** to breed within a single family or strain so as to produce particular characteristics in the offspring. **2.** another term for **crossbreed** (sense 1).

interbroker dealer (,intə'brəʊkə) *n*. *Stock Exchange*. a specialist who matches the needs of different market makers and facilitates dealings between them.

intercalary (in'tɜːkələri) *adj*. **1.** (of a day, month, etc.) inserted in the calendar. **2.** (of a particular year) having one or more days inserted. **3.** inserted, introduced, or interpolated. [C17: from L *intercalārius*; see INTERCALATE]

intercalate (in'tɜːkə,leit) *vb*. (*tr*.) **1.** to insert (one or more days) into the calendar. **2.** to interpolate or insert. [C17: from L *intercalāre* to insert, proclaim that a day has been inserted, from INTER- + *calāre* to proclaim] —**in,terca'lation** *n*. —**in'tercalative** *adj*.

intercede (,intə'siːd) *vb*. (*intr*.; often foll. by *in*) to come between parties or act as mediator or advocate: *to intercede in the strike*. [C16: from L *intercēdere*, from INTER- + *cēdere* to move] —**,inter'ceder** *n*.

intercensal (,intə'sɛnsəl) *adj*. (of population figures, etc.) estimated at a time between official censuses. [C19: from INTER- + *censal*, irregularly formed from CENSUS]

intercept *vb*. (,intə'sɛpt). (*tr*.) **1.** to stop, deflect, or seize on the way from one place to another; prevent from arriving or proceeding. **2.** *Sport*. to seize or cut off (a pass) on its way from one opponent to another. **3.** *Maths*. to cut off, mark off, or bound (some part of a line, curve, plane, or surface). ~*n*. ('intə,sɛpt). **4.** *Maths*. **a.** a point at which two figures intersect. **b.** the distance from the origin to the point at which a line, curve, or surface cuts a coordinate axis. **5.** *Sport, U.S. & Canad*. the act of intercepting an opponent's pass. [C16: from L *intercipere* to seize before arrival, from INTER- + *capere* to take] —**,inter'ception** *n*. —**,inter'ceptive** *adj*.

interceptor *or* **intercepter** (,intə'sɛptə) *n*. **1.** a person or thing that intercepts. **2.** a fast highly manoeuvrable fighter aircraft used to intercept enemy aircraft.

intercession (,intə'sɛʃən) *n*. **1.** the act or an instance of interceding. **2.** the act of interceding or offering petitionary prayer to God on behalf of others. **3.** such petitionary prayer. [C16: from L *intercessio*; see INTERCEDE] —**,inter'cessional** *or* **,inter'cessory** *adj*. —**,inter'cessor** *n*. —**,interces'sorial** *adj*.

interchange *vb*. (,intə'tʃeindʒ). **1.** to change places or cause to change places; alternate; exchange; switch. ~*n*. ('intə,tʃeindʒ). **2.** the act of interchanging; exchange or alternation. **3.** a motorway junction of interconnecting roads and bridges designed to prevent streams of traffic crossing one another. —**,inter'changeable** *adj*. —**,inter,changea'bility** *or* **,inter'changeableness** *n*. —**,inter'changeably** *adv*.

inter-city *adj*. **1.** (in Britain) denoting a fast rail service between main towns. ~*n*. **2.** such a rail service.

intercom ('intə,kɒm) *n*. *Inf*. an internal telephone system for communicating within a building, aircraft, etc. [C20: short for INTERCOMMUNICATION]

intercommunicate (,intəkə'mjuːni,keit) *vb*. (*intr*.) **1.** to communicate mutually. **2.** to interconnect, as two rooms, etc. —**,intercom'municable** *adj*. —**,intercom,muni'cation** *n*. —**,intercom'municative** *adj*.

intercommunion (,intəkə'mjuːnjən) *n*. association between Churches, involving esp. mutual reception of Holy Communion.

intercostal (,intə'kɒstªl) *adj*. *Anat*. between the ribs: *intercostal muscles*. [C16: via NL from L INTER- + *costa* rib]

intercourse ('intə,kɔːs) *n*. **1.** See **sexual intercourse**. **2.** communication or exchange between individuals; mutual dealings. [C15: from Med. L *intercursus* business, from L *intercurrere* to run between]

intercurrent (,intə'kʌrənt) *adj*. **1.** occurring during or in between; intervening. **2.** *Pathol*. (of a disease) occurring during the course of another disease. —**,inter'currence** *n*.

interdict *n*. ('intə,dikt). **1.** *R.C. Church*. the exclusion of a person in a particular place from certain sacraments, although not from communion. **2.** *Civil law*. any order made by a court or official prohibiting an act. **3.** *Scots Law*. an order having the effect of an injunction. ~*vb*. (,intə'dikt). (*tr*.) **4.** to place under legal or ecclesiastical sanction; prohibit; forbid. **5.** *Mil*. to destroy (an enemy's lines of communication) by firepower. [C13: from L *interdictum* prohibition, from *interdīcere* to forbid, from INTER- + *dīcere* to say] —**,inter'diction** *n*. —**,inter'dictive** *or* **,inter'dictory** *adj*. —**,inter'dictively** *adv*. —**,inter'dictor** *n*.

interdigitate (,intə'didʒi,teit) *vb*. (*intr*.) to interlock like the fingers of clasped hands. [C19: from INTER- + L *digitus* (see DIGIT) + -ATE¹]

interdisciplinary (,intə'disi,plinəri) *adj*. involving two or more academic disciplines.

interest ('intrist, -tərist) *n*. **1.** the sense of curiosity about or concern with something or someone. **2.** the power of stimulating such a sense: *to have great interest*. **3.** the quality of such stimulation. **4.** something in which one is interested; a hobby or pursuit. **5.** (*often pl.*) benefit; advantage: *in one's own interest.* **6.** (*often pl.*) a right, share, or claim, esp. in a business or property. **7. a.** a charge for the use of credit or borrowed money. **b.** such a charge expressed as a percentage per time unit of the sum borrowed or used. **8.** (*often pl.*) a section of a community, etc., whose members have common aims: *the landed interest.* **9. declare an interest.** to make known one's connection, esp. a prejudicial connection, with an affair. ~*vb.* (*tr.*) **10.** to arouse or excite the curiosity or concern of. **11.** to cause to become involved in something; concern. [C15: from L: it concerns, from *interesse,* from INTER- + *esse* to be]

interested ('ɪntrɪstɪd, -tərɪs-) *adj.* **1.** showing or having interest. **2.** (*usually prenominal*) personally involved or implicated: *the interested parties met to discuss the business.* — 'interestedly *adv.* — 'interestedness *n.*

interesting ('ɪntrɪstɪŋ, -tərɪs-) *adj.* inspiring interest; absorbing. — 'interestingly *adv.* — 'interestingness *n.*

interface *n.* ('ɪntə,feɪs). **1.** *Physical chem.* a surface that forms the boundary between two liquids or chemical phases. **2.** a common point or boundary between two things. **3.** an electrical circuit linking one device, esp. a computer, with another. ~*vb.* (,ɪntə'feɪs). **4.** (*tr.*) to design or adapt the input and output configurations of (two electronic devices) so that they may work together compatibly. **5.** to be an interface (with). **6.** to be interactive (with). — **interfacial** (,ɪntə'feɪʃəl) *adj.* — ,inter'facially *adv.*

interfacing ('ɪntə,feɪsɪŋ) *n.* **1.** a piece of fabric sewn beneath the facing of a garment, usually at the inside of the neck, armholes, etc., to give shape and firmness. **2.** another name for **interlining.**

interfere (,ɪntə'fɪə) *vb.* (*intr.*) **1.** (often foll. by *in*) to interpose, esp. meddlesomely or unwarrantedly; intervene. **2.** (often foll. by *with*) to come between or into opposition; hinder. **3.** (foll. by *with*) *Euphemistic.* to assault sexually. **4.** to strike one against the other, as a horse's legs. **5.** *Physics.* to cause or produce interference. [C16: from OF *s'entreferir* to collide, from *entre-* INTER- + *ferir* to strike, from L *ferire*] — ,inter'fering *adj.*

interference (,ɪntə'fɪərəns) *n.* **1.** the act or an instance of interfering. **2.** *Physics.* the process in which two or more coherent waves combine to form a resultant wave in which the displacement at any point is the vector sum of the displacements of the individual waves. **3.** any undesired signal that tends to interfere with the reception of radio waves. — **interferential** (,ɪntəfə'rɛnʃəl) *adj.*

interferometer (,ɪntəfə'rɒmɪtə) *n. Physics.* any acoustic, optical, or microwave instrument that uses interference patterns to make accurate measurements of wavelength, distance, etc. — **interferometric** (,ɪntə,fɛrə'mɛtrɪk) *adj.* — ,inter,fero'metrically *adv.* — ,interfer'ometry *n.*

interferon (,ɪntə'fɪərɒn) *n. Biochem.* any of a family of proteins made by cells in response to virus infection that prevent the growth of the virus. [C20: from INTERFERE + -ON]

interfuse (,ɪntə'fjuːz) *vb.* **1.** to diffuse or mix throughout or become so diffused or mixed; intermingle. **2.** to blend or fuse or become blended or fused. — ,inter'fusion *n.*

interim ('ɪntərɪm) *adj.* **1.** (*prenominal*) temporary, provisional, or intervening: *interim measures to deal with the emergency.* ~*n.* **2.** (*usually preceded by the*) the intervening time; the meantime (esp. in **in the interim**). ~*adv.* **3.** *Rare.* meantime. [C16: from L: meanwhile]

interior (ɪn'tɪərɪə) *n.* **1.** a part, surface, or region that is inside or on the inside: *the interior of Africa.* **2.** inner character or nature. **3.** a film or scene shot inside a building, studio, etc. **4.** a picture of the inside of a room or building, as in a painting or stage design. **5.** the inside of a building or room, with respect to design and decoration. ~*adj.* **6.** of, situated on, or suitable for the inside; inner. **7.** coming or acting from within; internal. **8.** of or involving a nation's domestic affairs; internal. **9.** (esp. of one's spiritual or mental life) secret or private; not observable. [C15: from L (adj.), comp. of *inter* within] — in'teriorly *adv.*

interior angle *n.* an angle of a polygon contained between two adjacent sides.

interior decoration *n.* **1.** the colours, furniture, etc., of the interior of a house, etc. **2.** Also called: **interior design.** the art or business of planning the interiors of houses, etc.

interiorize *or* **-ise** (ɪn'tɪərɪə,raɪz) *vb.* (*tr.*) another word for **internalize.**

interj. *abbrev. for* interjection.

interject (,ɪntə'dʒɛkt) *vb.* (*tr.*) to interpose abruptly or sharply; interrupt with; throw in: *she interjected clever remarks.* [C16: from L *interjicere* to place between, from *jacere* to throw] — ,inter'jector *n.*

interjection (,ɪntə'dʒɛkʃən) *n.* **1.** the act of interjecting. **2.** a word or phrase that is used in syntactic isolation and that expresses sudden emotion; expletive. Abbrev.: **interj.** — ,inter'jectional *or* ,inter'jectory *adj.* — ,inter'jectionally *adv.*

Interlaken ('ɪntə,lɑːkən) *n.* a town and resort in central Switzerland, situated between Lakes Brienz and Thun on the River Aar. Pop.: 13 000 (1985 est.).

interlard (,ɪntə'lɑːd) *vb.* (*tr.*) **1.** to scatter thickly in or between; intersperse: *to interlard one's writing with foreign phrases.* **2.** to occur frequently in; be scattered in or through: *foreign phrases interlard his writings.*

interlay (,ɪntə'leɪ) *vb.* **-laying, -laid.** (*tr.*) to insert (layers) between; interpose: *to interlay gold among the silver; to interlay the silver with gold.*

interleaf ('ɪntə,liːf) *n., pl.* **-leaves.** a blank leaf inserted between the leaves of a book.

interleave (,ɪntə'liːv) *vb.* (*tr.*) **1.** (often foll. by *with*) to intersperse (with), esp. alternately, as the illustrations in a book (with protective leaves). **2.** to provide (a book) with blank leaves for notes, etc., or to protect illustrations.

interleukin (,ɪntə'luːkɪn) *n.* a substance extracted from white blood cells that stimulates their activity against infection and may be used to combat some forms of cancer.

interline[1] (,ɪntə'laɪn) *or* **interlineate** (,ɪntə'lɪnɪ,eɪt) *vb.* (*tr.*) to write or print (matter) between the lines of (a text, book, etc.). — 'inter,lining *or* ,inter,line'ation *n.*

interline[2] (,ɪntə'laɪn) *vb.* (*tr.*) to provide (a part of a garment) with a second lining, esp. of stiffened material. — 'inter,liner *n.*

interlinear (,ɪntə'lɪnɪə) *or* **interlineal** *adj.* **1.** written or printed between lines of text. **2.** written or printed with the text in different languages or versions on alternate lines. — ,inter'linearly *or* ,inter'lineally *adv.*

interlining ('ɪntə,laɪnɪŋ) *n.* the material used to interline parts of garments, now often made of reinforced paper.

interlock *vb.* (,ɪntə'lɒk). **1.** to join or be joined firmly, as by a mutual interconnection of parts. ~*n.* ('ɪntə,lɒk). **2.** the act of interlocking or the state of being interlocked. **3.** a device, esp. one operated electromechanically, used in a logic circuit to prevent an activity being initiated unless preceded by certain events. **4.** a closely knitted fabric. ~*adj.* **5.** closely knitted. — 'inter,locker *n.*

interlocutor (,ɪntə'lɒkjʊtə) *n.* **1.** a person who takes part in a conversation. **2.** the man in the centre of a troupe of minstrels who engages the others in talk or acts as announcer. **3.** *Scots Law.* a decree by a judge. — ,inter'locutress, *or* ,inter'locutrice, *or* ,inter'locutrix *fem. n.*

interlocutory (,ɪntə'lɒkjʊtərɪ, -trɪ) *adj.* **1.** *Law.* pronounced during the course of proceedings; provisional: *an interlocutory injunction.* **2.** interposed, as into a conversation, narrative, etc. **3.** of, relating to, or characteristic of dialogue. — ,inter'locutorily *adv.*

interlope (,ɪntə'ləʊp) *vb.* (*intr.*) **1.** to interfere; meddle; intrude. **2.** to intercept another's trade, esp. illegally. [C17: prob. back formation from *interloper,* from INTER- + *-loper,* from MDu. *loopen* to LEAP] — 'inter,loper *n.*

interlude ('ɪntə,luːd) *n.* **1.** a period of time or different activity between longer periods, processes, or events; episode or interval. **2.** *Theatre.* a short dramatic piece played separately or as part of a longer entertainment, common in 16th-century England. **3.** a brief piece of music, dance, etc., given between the sections of another performance. [C14: from Med. L, from L INTER- + *lūdus* play]

,inter'factional *adj.*
,inter'fibrous *adj.*
,inter'flow *vb.*
,inter'fold *vb.*

,interga'lactic *adj.*
,inter'glacial *adj.*
,inter,govern'mental *adj.*

,inter'group *adj.*
,interi'onic *adj.*
,inter'knit *vb.*

,inter'lace *vb.*
,inter'library *adj.*
,inter'link *vb.*

intermarry (ˌɪntəˈmærɪ) vb. **-rying, -ried.** (intr.) **1.** (of different races, religions, etc.) to become connected by marriage. **2.** to marry within one's own family, clan, group, etc. —**ˌinterˈmarriage** n.

intermediary (ˌɪntəˈmiːdɪərɪ) n., pl. **-aries. 1.** a person who acts as a mediator or agent between parties. **2.** something that acts as a medium or means. ~adj. **3.** acting as an intermediary. **4.** situated, acting, or coming between; intermediate.

intermediate adj. (ˌɪntəˈmiːdɪɪt). **1.** occurring or situated between two points, extremes, places, etc.; in between. ~n. (ˌɪntəˈmiːdɪɪt). **2.** something intermediate. **3.** a substance formed during one of the stages of a chemical process before the desired product is obtained. ~vb. (ˌɪntəˈmiːdɪˌeɪt). **4.** (intr.) to act as an intermediary or mediator. [C17: from Med. L intermediāre to intervene, from L INTER- + medius middle] —**ˌinterˈmediacy** or **ˌinterˈmediateness** n. —**ˌinterˈmediately** adv. —**ˌinterˌmediˈation** n. —**ˌinterˈmediˌator** n.

intermediate frequency n. Electronics. the frequency to which the signal carrier frequency is changed in a superheterodyne receiver and at which most of the amplification takes place.

interment (ɪnˈtɜːmənt) n. burial, esp. with ceremonial rites.

intermezzo (ˌɪntəˈmɛtsəʊ) n., pl. **-zos** or **-zi** (-tsiː). **1.** a short piece of instrumental music composed for performance between the acts or scenes of an opera, drama, etc. **2.** an instrumental piece either inserted between two longer movements in an extended composition or intended for independent performance. [C19: from It., from LL intermedium interval; see INTERMEDIATE]

interminable (ɪnˈtɜːmɪnəbəl) adj. endless or seemingly endless because of monotony or tiresome length. —**inˈterminableness** n. —**inˈterminably** adv.

intermission (ˌɪntəˈmɪʃən) n. **1.** an interval, as between parts of a film, etc. **2.** a period between events or activities; pause. **3.** the act of intermitting or the state of being intermitted. [C16: from L, from intermittere to INTERMIT] —**ˌinterˈmissive** adj.

intermit (ˌɪntəˈmɪt) vb. **-mitting, -mitted.** to suspend (activity) or (of activity) to be suspended temporarily or at intervals. [C16: from L intermittere to leave off, from IN-TER- + mittere to send] —**ˌinterˈmittor** n.

intermittent (ˌɪntəˈmɪtⁿt) adj. occurring occasionally or at regular or irregular intervals; periodic. —**ˌinterˈmittence** or **ˌinterˈmittency** n. —**ˌinterˈmittently** adv.

intermixture (ˌɪntəˈmɪkstʃə) n. **1.** the act of intermixing or state of being intermixed. **2.** an additional constituent or ingredient.

intern vb. **1.** (ɪnˈtɜːn). (tr.) to detain or confine within a country or a limited area, esp. during wartime. **2.** (ˈɪntɜːn). (intr.) Chiefly U.S. to serve or train as an intern. ~n. (ˈɪntɜːn). **3.** another word for **internee. 4.** Also: **interne.** the approximate U.S. and Canad. equivalent of **houseman. 5.** Also: **interne.** Chiefly U.S. a student teacher. **6.** Also: **interne.** Chiefly U.S a student or recent graduate undergoing practical training in a working environment. [C19: from L internus internal] —**inˈternment** n. —**ˈinternship** or **ˈinterneship** n.

internal (ɪnˈtɜːnᵊl) adj. **1.** of, situated on, or suitable for the inside; inner. **2.** coming or acting from within; interior. **3.** involving the spiritual or mental life; subjective. **4.** of or involving a nation's domestic as opposed to foreign affairs. **5.** situated within, affecting, or relating to the inside of the body. ~n. **6.** Euphemistic. a medical examination of the vagina or uterus. [C16: from Med. L, from LL internus inward] —**inˈternality** or **inˈternalness** n. —**inˈternally** adv.

internal-combustion engine n. a heat engine in which combustion occurs within the engine rather than in an external furnace.

internal energy n. the thermodynamic property of a system that changes by an amount equal to the work done on the system when it suffers an adiabatic change.

internalize or **-ise** (ɪnˈtɜːnəˌlaɪz) vb. (tr.) Psychol., sociol. to make internal, esp. to incorporate within oneself (values, attitudes, etc.) through learning or socialization. Also: **interiorize.** —**inˌternaliˈzation** or **-iˈsation** n.

internal medicine n. the branch of medical science concerned with the diagnosis and nonsurgical treatment of disorders of the internal structures of the body.

international (ˌɪntəˈnæʃənᵊl) adj. **1.** of, concerning, or involving two or more nations or nationalities. **2.** established by, controlling, or legislating for several nations: an international court. **3.** available for use by all nations: international waters. ~n. **4.** Sport. **a.** a contest between two national teams. **b.** a member of a national team. —**ˌinterˌnationˈality** n. —**ˌinterˈnationally** adv.

International (ˌɪntəˈnæʃənᵊl) n. **1.** any of several international socialist organizations, esp. **First International** (1864–76) and **Second International** (1889 until World War I). **2.** a member of any of these organizations.

International Court of Justice n. a court established in the Hague, in the Netherlands, to settle disputes brought by members of the United Nations. Also called: **World Court.**

International Date Line n. the line approximately following the 180° meridian from Greenwich on the east side of which the date is one day earlier than on the west.

internationalism (ˌɪntəˈnæʃənəˌlɪzəm) n. **1.** the ideal or practice of cooperation and understanding between nations. **2.** the state or quality of being international. —**internationalist** n.

internationalize or **-ise** (ˌɪntəˈnæʃənəˌlaɪz) vb. (tr.) **1.** to make international. **2.** to put under international control. —**ˌinterˌnationaliˈzation** or **-iˈsation** n.

international law n. the body of rules generally recognized by civilized nations as governing their conduct towards each other.

International Phonetic Alphabet n. a series of signs and letters for the representation of human speech sounds. It is based on the Roman alphabet but supplemented by modified signs or symbols from other writing systems.

International Practical Temperature Scale n. a temperature scale adopted by international agreement in 1968 based on thermodynamic temperature and using experimental values to define 11 fixed points.

international style n. an architectural style of the 1920s that used cubic forms, large windows, and modern materials.

interne (ˈɪntɜːn) n. a variant spelling of **intern** (senses 4, 5, 6).

internecine (ˌɪntəˈniːsaɪn) adj. **1.** mutually destructive or ruinous; maiming both or all sides: internecine war. **2.** of or relating to slaughter or carnage; bloody. **3.** of or involving conflict within a group or organization. [C17: from L internecāre to destroy, from necāre to kill]

internee (ˌɪntɜːˈniː) n. a person who is interned, esp. an enemy citizen in wartime or a terrorism suspect.

internist (ˈɪntɜːnɪst, ɪnˈtɜːnɪst) n. a physician who specializes in internal medicine.

interpellate (ɪnˈtɜːpɛˌleɪt) vb. (tr.) Parliamentary procedure. (in European legislatures) to question (a member of the government) on a point of government policy, often interrupting the business of the day. [C16: from L interpellāre to disturb, from INTER- + pellere to push] —**inˌterpelˈlation** n. —**inˈterpelˌlator** n.

interpenetrate (ˌɪntəˈpɛnɪˌtreɪt) vb. **1.** to penetrate (something) thoroughly; pervade. **2.** to penetrate each other or one another mutually. —**ˌinterˈpenetrable** adj. —**ˌinterˈpenetrant** adj. —**ˌinterˌpeneˈtration** n. —**ˌinterˈpenetratively** adv.

interplay (ˈɪntəˌpleɪ) n. reciprocal and mutual action and reaction, as in circumstances, events, or personal relations.

interpleader (ˌɪntəˈpliːdə) n. Law. **1.** a process by which a person holding money claimed by two or more parties and having no interest in it himself can require the claimants to litigate with each other. **2.** a person who interpleads.

Interpol (ˈɪntəˌpɒl) n. acronym for International Criminal Police Organization, an association of over 100 national police forces, devoted chiefly to fighting international crime.

interpolate (ɪnˈtɜːpəˌleɪt) vb. **1.** to insert or introduce (a comment, passage, etc.) into (a conversation, text, etc.).

ˌinterˈmesh vb.
ˌinterˈmingle vb.
ˌinterˈmix vb.

ˌinterˈmixable adj.
ˌinterˈmuscular adj.
ˌinterˈnuclear adj.

ˌinterˈoffice adj.
ˌinterˈplait vb.

ˌinterˈplanetary adj.
ˌinterˈpolar adj.

2. to falsify or alter (a text, manuscript, etc.) by the later addition of (material, esp. spurious passages). **3.** (*intr.*) to make additions, interruptions, or insertions. **4.** *Maths.* to estimate (a value of a function) between the values already known or determined. Cf. **extrapolate** (sense 1). [C17: from L *interpolāre* to give a new appearance to] —in'terpo,later *or* in'terpo,lator *n.* —in'terpolative *adj.*

interpose (,ɪntə'pəʊz) *vb.* **1.** to put or place between or among other things. **2.** to introduce (comments, questions, etc.) into a speech or conversation; interject. **3.** to exert or use influence or action in order to alter or intervene in (a situation). [C16: from OF, from L *interpōnere*, from INTER- + *pōnere* to put] —,inter'posal *n.* —,inter'poser *n.* —,interpo'sition *n.*

interpret (ɪn'tɜːprɪt) *vb.* **1.** (*tr.*) to clarify or explain the meaning of; elucidate. **2.** (*tr.*) to construe the significance or intention of. **3.** (*tr.*) to convey or represent the spirit or meaning of (a poem, song, etc.) in performance. **4.** (*intr.*) to act as an interpreter; translate orally. [C14: from L *interpretārī*, from *interpres* negotiator, one who explains] —in'terpretable *adj.* —in,terpreta'bility *or* in'terpretableness *n.* —in'terpretably *adv.* —in'terpretive *adj.*

interpretation (ɪn,tɜːprɪ'teɪʃən) *n.* **1.** the act or process of interpreting or explaining; elucidation. **2.** the result of interpreting; an explanation. **3.** a particular view of an artistic work, esp. as expressed by stylistic individuality in its performance. **4.** explanation, as of a historical site, provided by the use of original objects, visual display material, etc. —in,terpre'tational *adj.*

interpreter (ɪn'tɜːprɪtə) *n.* **1.** a person who translates orally from one language into another. **2.** a person who interprets the work of others. **3.** *Computers.* a program that translates a statement in a source program to machine code and executes it before translating and executing the next statement. —in'terpretership *n.* —in'terpretress *fem. n.*

interpretive centre *n.* (at a historical site, etc.) a building that provides interpretation of the site through a variety of media, such as video displays and exhibitions, and, often, includes facilities such as refreshment rooms.

interregnum (,ɪntə'rɛgnəm) *n.*, *pl.* **-nums** *or* **-na** (-nə). **1.** an interval between two reigns, governments, etc. **2.** any period in which a state lacks a ruler, government, etc. **3.** a period of absence of some control, authority, etc. **4.** a gap in a continuity. [C16: from L, from INTER- + *regnum* REIGN] —,inter'regnal *adj.*

interrelate (,ɪntərɪ'leɪt) *vb.* to place in or come into a mutual or reciprocal relationship. —,interre'lation *n.* —,interre'lation,ship *n.*

interrogate (ɪn'tɛrə,geɪt) *vb.* to ask questions (of), esp. to question (a witness in court, spy, etc.) closely. [C15: from L *interrogāre*, from *rogāre* to ask] —in'terro,gator *n.*

interrogation (ɪn,tɛrə'geɪʃən) *n.* **1.** the technique, practice, or an instance of interrogating. **2.** a question or query. **3.** *Telecomm.* the transmission of one or more triggering pulses to a transponder. —in,terro'gational *adj.*

interrogation mark *n.* a less common term for **question mark**.

interrogative (,ɪntə'rɒgətɪv) *adj.* **1.** asking or having the nature of a question. **2.** denoting a form or construction used in asking a question. **3.** denoting or belonging to a class of words, such as *which* and *whom*, that serve to question which individual referent is intended. ~*n.* **4.** an interrogative word, phrase, sentence, or construction. **5.** a question mark. —,inter'rogatively *adv.*

interrogatory (,ɪntə'rɒgətərɪ, -trɪ) *adj.* **1.** expressing or involving a question. ~*n.*, *pl.* **-tories**. **2.** a question or interrogation.

interrupt (,ɪntə'rʌpt) *vb.* **1.** to break the continuity of (an action, event, etc.) or hinder (a person) by intrusion. **2.** (*tr.*) to cease to perform (some action). **3.** (*tr.*) to obstruct (a view, etc.). **4.** to prevent or disturb (a conversation, discussion, etc.) by questions, interjections, or comment. [C15: from L *interrumpere*, from INTER- +

rumpere to break] —,inter'ruptible *adj.* —,inter'ruptive *adj.* —,inter'ruptively *adv.* —,inter'rupted *adj.*

interrupted screw *n.* a screw with a slot cut into the thread, esp. one used in the breech of some guns permitting both engagement and release of the block by a partial turn of the screw.

interrupter *or* **interruptor** (,ɪntə'rʌptə) *n.* **1.** a person or thing that interrupts. **2.** an electromechanical device for opening and closing an electric circuit.

interruption (,ɪntə'rʌpʃən) *n.* **1.** something that interrupts, such as a comment, question, or action. **2.** an interval or intermission. **3.** the act of interrupting or the state of being interrupted.

interscholastic (,ɪntəskə'læstɪk) *adj.* **1.** (of sports events, competitions, etc.) occurring between two or more schools. **2.** representative of various schools.

intersect (,ɪntə'sɛkt) *vb.* **1.** to divide, cut, or mark off by passing through or across. **2.** (esp. of roads) to cross (each other). **3.** *Maths.* (often foll. by *with*) to have one or more points in common (with another configuration). [C17: from L *intersecāre* to divide, from INTER- + *secāre* to cut]

intersection (,ɪntə'sɛkʃən, 'ɪntə,sɛk-) *n.* **1.** a point at which things intersect, esp. a road junction. **2.** the act of intersecting or the state of being intersected. **3.** *Maths.* **a.** a point or set of points common to two or more geometric configurations. **b.** Also called: **product**. the set of elements that are common to two sets. **c.** the operation that yields that set from a pair of given sets. —,inter'sectional *adj.*

intersex ('ɪntə,sɛks) *n. Zool.* an individual with characteristics intermediate between those of a male and a female.

intersexual (,ɪntə'sɛksjʊəl) *adj.* **1.** occurring or existing between the sexes. **2.** relating to or being an intersex. —,inter,sexu'ality *n.* —,inter'sexually *adv.*

interspace *vb.* (,ɪntə'speɪs). **1.** (*tr.*) to make or occupy a space between. ~*n.* ('ɪntə,speɪs). **2.** space between or among things. —**interspatial** (,ɪntə'speɪʃəl) *adj.* —,inter'spatially *adv.*

intersperse (,ɪntə'spɜːs) *vb.* (*tr.*) **1.** to scatter or distribute among, between, or on. **2.** to diversify (something) with other things scattered here and there. [C16: from L *interspargere*, from INTER- + *spargere* to sprinkle] —**interspersedly** (,ɪntə'spɜːsɪdlɪ) *adv.* —**interspersion** (,ɪntə'spɜːʃən) *or* ,inter'spersal *n.*

interstice (ɪn'tɜːstɪs) *n.* (*usually pl.*) **1.** a minute opening or crevice between things. **2.** *Physics.* the space between adjacent atoms in a crystal lattice. [C17: from L *interstitium* interval, from *intersistere*, from INTER- + *sistere* to stand]

interstitial (,ɪntə'stɪʃəl) *adj.* **1.** of or relating to an interstice or interstices. **2.** *Physics.* forming or occurring in an interstice: *an interstitial atom.* **3.** *Anat., zool.* occurring in the spaces between organs, tissues, etc.: *interstitial cells.* ~*n.* **4.** *Chem.* an atom or ion situated in the interstices of a crystal lattice. —,inter'stitially *adv.*

intertrigo (,ɪntə'traɪgəʊ) *n.* chafing between two skin surfaces, as at the armpit. [C18: from INTER- + *-trigo*, from L *terere* to rub]

interval ('ɪntəvəl) *n.* **1.** the period of time between two events, instants, etc. **2.** the distance between two points, objects, etc. **3.** a pause or interlude, as between periods of intense activity. **4.** *Brit.* a short period between parts of a play, etc.; intermission. **5.** *Music.* the difference of pitch between two notes, either sounded simultaneously or in succession as in a musical part. **6.** the ratio of the frequencies of two sounds. **7. at intervals. a.** occasionally or intermittently. **b.** with spaces between. [C13: from L *intervallum*, lit.: space between two palisades, from INTER- + *vallum* palisade] —**intervallic** (,ɪntə'vælɪk) *adj.*

intervene (,ɪntə'viːn) *vb.* (*intr.*) **1.** (often foll. by *in*) to take a decisive or intrusive role (in) in order to determine events. **2.** (foll. by *in* or *between*) to come or be (among or between). **3.** (of a period of time) to occur between events or points in time. **4.** (of an event) to disturb or hinder a course of action. **5.** *Econ.* to take action to affect the market forces of an economy, esp. to maintain the stability of a currency. **6.** *Law.* to interpose and become

,interpro'fessional *adj.*	,interre'ligious *adj.*	,inter'stellar *adj.*	,inter'twine *vb.*
,interpro'vincial *adj.*	,inter'school *adj.*	,inter,terri'torial *adj.*	,inter,uni'versity *adj.*
,inter'racial *adj.*	,interso'cietal *adj.*	,inter'tribal *adj.*	,inter'urban *adj.*
,inter'regional *adj.*	,inter'spinal *adj.*	,inter'tropical *adj.*	,inter'varsity *adj.*

a party to a legal action between others, esp. in order to protect one's interests. [C16: from L *intervenīre* to come between] —,**inter'vener** *or* ,**inter'venor** *n*.

intervention (,ɪntə'vɛnʃən) *n*. **1.** an act of intervening. **2.** any interference in the affairs of others, esp. by one state in the affairs of another. **3.** *Econ.* the action of a central bank in supporting the international value of a currency by buying large quantities of the currency to keep the price up. **4.** *Commerce.* the action of the EEC in buying up surplus produce when the market price drops to a certain value.

interventionist (,ɪntə'vɛnʃənɪst) *adj*. **1.** of, relating to, or advocating intervention, esp. in order to achieve a policy objective. ~*n*. **2.** a person or state that pursues a policy of intervention.

intervertebral disc (,ɪntə'vɜ:tɪbrəl) *n*. any of the cartilaginous discs between individual vertebrae, acting as shock absorbers.

interview ('ɪntə,vju:) *n*. **1.** a conversation with or questioning of a person, usually conducted for television or a newspaper. **2.** a formal discussion, esp. one in which an employer assesses a job applicant. ~*vb*. **3.** to conduct an interview with (someone). [C16: from OF *entrevue*] —,**interview'ee** *n*. —'**inter,viewer** *n*.

inter vivos Latin. ('ɪntə 'vi:vɒs) *adj*. *Law*. between living people: *an inter vivos gift*.

intestate (ɪn'tɛsteɪt, -tɪt) *adj*. **1. a.** (of a person) not having made a will. **b.** (of property) not disposed of by will. ~*n*. **2.** a person who dies without having made a will. [C14: from L *intestātus*, from IN-[1] + *testārī* to bear witness, make a will, from *testis* a witness] —**in'testacy** *n*.

intestine (ɪn'tɛstɪn) *n*. the part of the alimentary canal between the stomach and the anus. See **large intestine, small intestine**. [C16: from L *intestīnum* gut, from *intestīnus* internal, from *intus* within] —**intestinal** (ɪn'tɛstɪnᵊl, ,ɪntɛs'taɪnᵊl) *adj*.

inti ('ɪntɪ) *n*. the standard monetary unit of Peru. [C20: from Quechua]

intimacy ('ɪntɪməsɪ) *n*., *pl*. -**cies**. **1.** close or warm friendship or understanding; personal relationship. **2.** (*often pl.*) *Euphemistic.* sexual relations.

intimate[1] ('ɪntɪmɪt) *adj*. **1.** characterized by a close or warm personal relationship: *an intimate friend*. **2.** deeply personal, private, or secret. **3.** (*often postpositive; foll. by with*) *Euphemistic.* having sexual relations (with). **4.** (*postpositive; foll. by with*) having a deep or unusual knowledge (of). **5.** having a friendly, warm, or informal atmosphere: *an intimate nightclub*. **6.** of or relating to the essential part or nature of something; intrinsic. ~*n*. **7.** a close friend. [C17: from L *intimus* very close friend, from (adj.): innermost, from *intus* within] —'**intimately** *adv*. —'**intimateness** *n*.

intimate[2] ('ɪntɪ,meɪt) *vb*. (*tr.; may take a clause as object*) **1.** to hint; suggest. **2.** to proclaim; make known. [C16: from LL *intimāre* to proclaim, from L *intimus* innermost] —'**inti,mater** *n*. —,**inti'mation** *n*.

intimidate (ɪn'tɪmɪ,deɪt) *vb*. (*tr.*) **1.** to make timid or frightened; scare. **2.** to discourage, restrain, or silence unscrupulously, as by threats. [C17: from Med. L *intimidāre*, from L IN-[2] + *timidus* fearful, from *timor* fear] —,**in'timi,dating** *adj*. —**in,timi'dation** *n*. —**in'timi,dator** *n*.

intinction (ɪn'tɪŋkʃən) *n*. *Christianity.* the practice of dipping the Eucharistic bread into the wine at Holy Communion. [C16: from LL *intinctiō* a dipping in, from L *intingere*, from *tingere* to dip]

intitule (ɪn'tɪtjuːl) *vb*. (*tr.*) *Parliamentary procedure.* (in Britain) to entitle (an Act). [C15: from OF *intituler*, from L *titulus* TITLE]

intl *abbrev. for* international.

into ('ɪntuː; *unstressed* 'ɪntə) *prep*. **1.** to the interior or inner parts of: *to look into a case*. **2.** to the middle or midst of so as to be surrounded by: *into the bushes*. **3.** against; up against: *he drove into a wall*. **4.** used to indicate the result of a change: *he changed into a monster*. **5.** *Maths.* used to indicate a dividend: *three into six is two*. **6.** *Inf.* interested or enthusiastically involved in: *I'm really into Freud*.

intonation (,ɪntəʊ'neɪʃən) *n*. **1.** the sound pattern of phrases and sentences produced by pitch variation in the

voice. **2.** the act or manner of intoning. **3.** an intoned, chanted, or monotonous utterance; incantation. **4.** *Music.* the opening of a piece of plainsong, sung by a soloist. **5.** *Music.* the capacity to play or sing in tune. —,**into'national** *adj*.

intone (ɪn'təʊn) *or* **intonate** *vb*. **1.** to utter, recite, or sing (a chant, prayer, etc.) in a monotonous or incantatory tone. **2.** (*intr.*) to speak with a particular or characteristic intonation or tone. **3.** to sing (the opening phrase of a psalm, etc.) in plainsong. [C15: from Med. L *intonare*, from IN-[2] + TONE] —**in'toner** *n*.

in toto Latin. (ɪn 'təʊtəʊ) *adv*. totally; entirely.

intoxicant (ɪn'tɒksɪkənt) *n*. **1.** anything that causes intoxication. ~*adj*. **2.** causing intoxication.

intoxicate (ɪn'tɒksɪ,keɪt) *vb*. (*tr.*) **1.** (of an alcoholic drink) to produce in (a person) a state ranging from euphoria to stupor; make drunk; inebriate. **2.** to stimulate, excite, or elate so as to overwhelm. **3.** (of a drug, etc.) to poison. [C16: from Med. L, from *intoxicāre* to poison, from L *toxicum* poison; see TOXIC] —**in'toxicable** *adj*. —**in'toxi,cating** *adj*. —**in'toxi,catingly** *adv*.

intoxication (ɪn,tɒksɪ'keɪʃən) *n*. **1.** drunkenness; inebriation. **2.** great elation. **3.** the act of intoxicating. **4.** poisoning.

intr. *abbrev. for* intransitive.

intra- *prefix*. within; inside: *intrastate; intravenous*. [from L *intrā* within; see INTERIOR]

intractable (ɪn'træktəbᵊl) *adj*. **1.** difficult to influence or direct: *an intractable disposition*. **2.** (of a problem, illness, etc.) difficult to solve, alleviate, or cure. —**in,tracta'bility** *or* **in'tractableness** *n*. —**in'tractably** *adv*.

intradermal (,ɪntrə'dɜ:məl) *adj*. within the skin: *an intradermal injection*. Abbrev. (esp. of an injection): **ID, i.d.** —,**intra'dermally** *adv*.

intrados (ɪn'treɪdɒs) *n*., *pl*. -**dos** *or* -**doses**. *Archit.* the inner curve or surface of an arch. [C18: from F, from INTRA- + *dos* back, from L *dorsum*]

intramural (,ɪntrə'mjʊərəl) *adj*. *Education, chiefly U.S. & Canad.* operating within or involving those in a single establishment. —,**intra'murally** *adv*.

intramuscular (,ɪntrə'mʌskjʊlə) *adj*. within a muscle: *an intramuscular injection*. Abbrev. (esp. of an injection): **IM, i.m.** —,**intra'muscularly** *adv*.

intrans. *abbrev. for* intransitive.

intransigent (ɪn'trænsɪdʒənt) *adj*. **1.** not willing to compromise; obstinately maintaining an attitude. ~*n*. **2.** an intransigent person, esp. in politics. [C19: from Sp. *los intransigentes* the uncompromising (ones), a name adopted by certain political extremists, from IN-[1] + *transigir* to compromise, from L *transigere* to settle; see TRANSACT] —**in'transigence** *or* **in'transigency** *n*. —**in'transigently** *adv*.

intransitive (ɪn'trænsɪtɪv) *adj*. **1. a.** denoting a verb that does not require a direct object. **b.** (*as n.*) such a verb. **2.** denoting an adjective or noun that does not require any particular noun phrase as a referent. **3.** having the property that if it holds between one argument and a second, and between the second and a third, it must fail to hold between the first and third: *"being the mother of" is an intransitive relation*. ~Cf. **transitive**. —**in'transitively** *adv*. —**in,transi'tivity** *or* **in'transitiveness** *n*.

intrapreneur (,ɪntrəprə'nɜ:) *n*. a person who while remaining within a larger organization uses entrepreneurial skills to develop a new product or line of business as a subsidiary of the organization. [C20: from INTRA- + (EN-TRE)PRENEUR]

intrauterine (,ɪntrə'ju:təraɪn) *adj*. within the womb.

intrauterine device *n*. a metal or plastic device, in the shape of a loop, coil, or ring, inserted into the uterus to prevent conception. Abbrev.: **IUD.**

intravenous (,ɪntrə'vi:nəs) *adj*. *Anat.* within a vein: *an intravenous injection*. Abbrev. (esp. of an injection): **IV, i.v.** —,**intra'venously** *adv*.

in-tray *n*. a tray for incoming papers, etc., requiring attention.

intrench (ɪn'trɛntʃ) *vb*. a less common spelling of **entrench**. —**in'trencher** *n*. —**in'trenchment** *n*.

intrepid (ɪn'trɛpɪd) *adj*. fearless; daring; bold. [C17: from L *intrepidus*, from IN-[1] + *trepidus* fearful] —,**intre'pidity** *n*. —**in'trepidly** *adv*.

,**inter'vertebral** *adj*.   ,**inter'weave** *vb*.   ,**inter'wrought** *adj*.   **in'tolerance** *n*.
,**inter'war** *adj*.   ,**inter'wind** *vb*.   **in'tolerable** *adj*.   **in'tolerant** *adj*.

intricate ('ɪntrɪkɪt) *adj.* **1.** difficult to understand; obscure; complex; puzzling. **2.** entangled or involved: *intricate patterns*. [C15: from L *intrīcāre* to entangle, perplex, from IN-² + *tricae* trifles, perplexities] —**'intricacy** *or* **'intricateness** *n.* —**'intricately** *adv.*

intrigue *vb.* (ɪn'triːg), **-triguing, -trigued. 1.** (*tr.*) to make interested or curious. **2.** (*intr.*) to make secret plots or employ underhand methods; conspire. **3.** (*intr.*; often foll. by *with*) to carry on a clandestine love affair. ~*n.* (ɪn'triːg, 'ɪntriːg). **4.** the act or an instance of secret plotting, etc. **5.** a clandestine love affair. **6.** the quality of arousing interest or curiosity; beguilement. [C17: from F *intriguer*, from It., from L *intrīcāre*; see INTRICATE] —**in'triguer** *n.* —**in'triguingly** *adv.*

intrinsic (ɪn'trɪnsɪk) *or* **intrinsical** *adj.* **1.** of or relating to the essential nature of a thing; inherent. **2.** *Anat.* situated within or peculiar to a part: *intrinsic muscles*. [C15: from LL *intrinsecus* from L, inwardly, from *intrā* within + *secus* alongside] —**in'trinsically** *adv.*

intro ('ɪntrəʊ) *n., pl.* **-tros.** *Inf.* short for **introduction.**

intro. *or* **introd.** *abbrev. for:* **1.** introduction. **2.** introductory.

intro- *prefix.* in, into, or inward: *introvert*. [from L *intrō* inwardly, within]

introduce (,ɪntrə'djuːs) *vb.* (*tr.*) **1.** (often foll. by *to*) to present (someone) by name (to another person). **2.** (foll. by *to*) to cause to experience for the first time: *to introduce a visitor to beer.* **3.** to present for consideration or approval, esp. before a legislative body: *to introduce a bill in parliament.* **4.** to bring in; establish: *to introduce decimal currency.* **5.** to present (a radio or television programme, etc.) verbally. **6.** (foll. by *with*) to start: *he introduced his talk with some music.* **7.** (often foll. by *into*) to insert or inject: *he introduced the needle into his arm.* **8.** to place (members of a plant or animal species) in a new environment with the intention of producing a resident breeding population. [C16: from L *introdūcere* to bring inside] —**,intro'ducer** *n.* —**,intro'ducible** *adj.*

introduction (,ɪntrə'dʌkʃən) *n.* **1.** the act of introducing or fact of being introduced. **2.** a presentation of one person to another or others. **3.** a means of presenting a person to another person, such as a letter of introduction or reference. **4.** a preliminary part, as of a book. **5.** *Music.* an opening passage in a movement or composition that precedes the main material. **6.** a basic or elementary work of instruction, reference, etc.

introductory (,ɪntrə'dʌktərɪ, -trɪ) *adj.* serving as an introduction; preliminary; prefatory.

introit ('ɪntrɔɪt) *n. R.C. Church, Church of England.* a short prayer said or sung as the celebrant is entering the sanctuary to celebrate Mass or Holy Communion. [C15: from Church L *introitus* introit, from L: entrance, from *introīre* to go in] —**in'troital** *adj.*

intromit (,ɪntrə'mɪt) *vb.* **-mitting, -mitted.** (*tr.*) *Rare.* to enter or insert. [C15: from L *intrōmittere* to send in] —**,intro'missible** *adj.* —**,intro'mission** *n.* —**,intro'mittent** *adj.*

introspection (,ɪntrə'spɛkʃən) *n.* the examination of one's own thoughts, impressions, and feelings. [C17: from L *intrōspicere* to look within] —**,intro'spective** *adj.* —**,intro'spectively** *adv.*

introversion (,ɪntrə'vɜːʃən) *n. Psychol.* the directing of interest inwards towards one's own thoughts and feelings rather than towards the external world or making social contacts. —**,intro'versive** *or* **,intro'vertive** *adj.*

introvert *n.* ('ɪntrə,vɜːt). **1.** *Psychol.* a person prone to introversion. ~*adj.* ('ɪntrə,vɜːt). **2.** Also: **introverted.** characterized by introversion. ~*vb.* (,ɪntrə'vɜːt). **3.** (*tr.*) *Pathol.* to turn (a hollow organ or part) inside out. [C17: see INTRO-, INVERT]

intrude (ɪn'truːd) *vb.* **1.** (often foll. by *into, on,* or *upon*) to put forward or interpose (oneself, one's views, something) abruptly or without invitation. **2.** *Geol.* to force or thrust (molten magma) between solid rocks. [C16: from L *intrūdere* to thrust in] —**in'truder** *n.* —**in'trudingly** *adv.*

intrusion (ɪn'truːʒən) *n.* **1.** the act or an instance of intruding; an unwelcome visit, etc.: *an intrusion on one's privacy.* **2. a.** the movement of magma into spaces in the overlying strata to form igneous rock. **b.** any igneous rock formed in this way. **3.** *Property law.* an unlawful entry onto land by a stranger after determination of a particular estate of freehold. —**in'trusional** *adj.*

intrusive (ɪn'truːsɪv) *adj.* **1.** characterized by intrusion or tending to intrude. **2.** (of igneous rocks) formed by intrusion. **3.** *Phonetics.* relating to or denoting a speech sound that is introduced into a word or piece of connected speech for a phonetic reason. —**in'trusively** *adv.* —**in'trusiveness** *n.*

intrust (ɪn'trʌst) *vb.* a less common spelling of **entrust.**

intubate ('ɪntjʊ,beɪt) *vb.* (*tr.*) *Med.* to insert a tube into (a hollow organ). —**,intu'bation** *n.*

intuit (ɪn'tjuːɪt) *vb.* to know or discover by intuition. —**in'tuitable** *adj.*

intuition (,ɪntjʊ'ɪʃən) *n.* **1.** knowledge or belief obtained neither by reason nor perception. **2.** instinctive knowledge or belief. **3.** a hunch or unjustified belief. [C15: from LL *intuitiō* a contemplation, from L *intuērī* to gaze upon, from *tuērī* to look at] —**,intu'itional** *adj.* —**,intu'itionally** *adv.*

intuitionism (,ɪntjʊ'ɪʃə,nɪzəm) *or* **intuitionalism** *n. Philosophy.* **1.** the doctrine that knowledge is acquired primarily by intuition. **2.** the theory that the solution to moral problems can be discovered by intuition. **3.** the doctrine that external objects are known to be real by intuition. —**,intu'itionist** *or* **,intu'itionalist** *n.*

intuitive (ɪn'tjuːɪtɪv) *adj.* **1.** resulting from intuition: *an intuitive awareness.* **2.** of, characterized by, or involving intuition. —**in'tuitively** *adv.* —**in'tuitiveness** *n.*

intumesce (,ɪntjʊ'mɛs) *vb.* (*intr.*) to swell. [C18: from L *intumescere*, from *tumescere* to begin to swell, from *tumēre* to swell] —**,intu'mescence** *n.*

intussusception (,ɪntəssə'sɛpʃən) *n.* **1.** *Pathol.* the telescoping of one section of the intestinal tract into a lower section. **2.** *Biol.* growth in the surface area of a cell by the deposition of new particles between the existing particles of the cell wall. [C18: from L *intus* within + *susceptiō* a taking up]

Inuit *or* **Innuit** ('ɪnjuːɪt) *n., pl.* **-it** *or* **-its.** an Eskimo of North America or Greenland, as distinguished from one from Asia or the Aleuts. [from Eskimo *inuit* people, pl. of *inuk* a man]

Inuktitut (ɪ'nʊktə,tʊt) *n. Canad.* the language of the Inuit; Eskimo. [from Eskimo *inuk* man + *titut* speech]

inunction (ɪn'ʌŋkʃən) *n.* **1.** the application of an ointment to the skin, esp. by rubbing. **2.** the ointment so used. **3.** the act of anointing; anointment. [C15: from L *inunguere* to anoint, from *unguere*; see UNCTION]

inundate ('ɪnʌn,deɪt) *vb.* (*tr.*) **1.** to cover completely with water; overflow; flood; swamp. **2.** to overwhelm, as if with a flood: *to be inundated with requests.* [C17: from L *inundāre*, from *unda* wave] —**'inundant** *or* **in'undatory** *adj.* —**,inun'dation** *n.* —**'inun,dator** *n.*

inure *or* **enure** (ɪn'njʊə) *vb.* **1.** (*tr.; often passive; often* foll. by *to*) to cause to accept or become hardened to; habituate. **2.** (*intr.*) (esp. of a law, etc.) to come into operation; take effect. [C15 *enuren* to accustom, from *ure* use, from OF *euvre* custom, work, from L *opera* works] —**in'urement** *or* **en'urement** *n.*

in utero Latin. (ɪn'juːtərəʊ) *adj.* in the uterus.

inv. *abbrev. for:* **1.** invented. **2.** inventor. **3.** invoice.

in vacuo Latin. (ɪn 'vækjʊ,əʊ) *adv.* in a vacuum.

invade (ɪn'veɪd) *vb.* **1.** to enter (a country, etc.) by military force. **2.** (*tr.*) to occupy in large numbers; overrun; infest. **3.** (*tr.*) to trespass or encroach upon (privacy, etc.). **4.** (*tr.*) to enter and spread throughout, esp. harmfully; pervade. [C15: from L *invādere*, from *vādere* to go] —**in'vadable** *adj.* —**in'vader** *n.*

invaginate *vb.* (ɪn'vædʒɪ,neɪt). **1.** *Pathol.* to push one section of (a tubular organ or part) back into itself so that it becomes ensheathed. **2.** (*intr.*) (of the outer layer of an organism or part) to undergo this process. ~*adj.* (ɪn'vædʒɪnɪt, -,neɪt). **3.** (of an organ or part) folded back upon itself. [C19: from Med. L *invāgināre*, from L IN-² + *vāgīna* sheath] —**in'vaginable** *adj.* —**in,vagi'nation** *n.*

invalid¹ ('ɪnvə,liːd, -lɪd) *n.* **1. a.** a person suffering from disablement or chronic ill health. **b.** (*as modifier*): *an invalid chair.* ~*adj.* **2.** suffering from or disabled by injury, sickness, etc. ~*vb.* (*tr.*) **3.** to cause to become an invalid; disable. **4.** (*often passive* usually foll. by *out*); *Chiefly Brit.* to require (a member of the armed forces) to retire from active service through wounds or illness. [C17: from L *invalidus* infirm, from IN-¹ + *validus* strong] —**invalidity** (,ɪnvə'lɪdɪtɪ) *n.*

invalid[2] (ɪn'vælɪd) adj. **1.** not valid; having no cogency or legal force. **2.** Logic. (of an argument) having a conclusion that does not follow from the premises. [C16: from Med. L invalidus without legal force; see INVALID[1]] —,in·va'lidity or in'validness n. —in'validly adv.

invalidate (ɪn'vælɪ,deɪt) vb. (tr.) **1.** to render weak or ineffective (an argument). **2.** to take away the legal force or effectiveness of; annul (a contract). —in,vali'dation n. —in'vali,dator n.

invaluable (ɪn'væljuəb³l) adj. having great value that is impossible to calculate; priceless. —in'valuableness n. —in'valuably adv.

Invar (ɪn'vɑː) n. Trademark. an alloy containing iron, nickel, and carbon. It has a very low coefficient of expansion and is used for the balance springs of watches, etc. [C20: shortened from INVARIABLE]

invariable (ɪn'vɛərɪəb³l) adj. **1.** not subject to alteration; unchanging. ~n. **2.** a mathematical quantity having an unchanging value; a constant. —in,varia'bility or in'variableness n. —in'variably adv.

invariant (ɪn'vɛərɪənt) Maths. ~n. **1.** an entity, quantity, etc., that is unaltered by a particular transformation of coordinates. ~adj. **2.** (of a relationship or a property of a function, configuration, or equation) unaltered by a particular transformation of coordinates. —in'variance or in'variancy n.

invasion (ɪn'veɪʒən) n. **1.** the act of invading with armed forces. **2.** any encroachment or intrusion: an invasion of rats. **3.** the onset or advent of something harmful, esp. of a disease. **4.** the movement of plants to an area to which they are not native. —invasive (ɪn'veɪsɪv) adj.

invective (ɪn'vɛktɪv) n. **1.** vehement accusation or denunciation, esp. of a bitterly abusive or sarcastic kind. ~adj. **2.** characterized by or using abusive language, bitter sarcasm, etc. [C15: from LL invectīvus reproachful, from L invectus carried in; see INVEIGH] —in'vectively adv. —in'vectiveness n.

inveigh (ɪn'veɪ) vb. (intr.; foll. by against) to speak with violent or invective language; rail. [C15: from L invehī, lit.: to be carried in, hence, assail physically or verbally] —in'veigher n.

inveigle (ɪn'viːg³l, -'veɪ-) vb. (tr.; often foll. by into or an infinitive) to lead (someone into a situation) or persuade (to do something) by cleverness or trickery; cajole. [C15: from OF avogler to blind, deceive, from avogle blind, from Med. L ab oculis without eyes] —in'veiglement n. —in'veigler n.

invent (ɪn'vɛnt) vb. **1.** to create or devise (new ideas, machines, etc.). **2.** to make up (falsehoods, etc.); fabricate. [C15: from L invenīre to find, come upon] —in'ventable adj.

invention (ɪn'vɛnʃən) n. **1.** the act or process of inventing. **2.** something that is invented. **3.** Patent law. the discovery or production of some new or improved process or machine. **4.** creative power or ability; inventive skill. **5.** Euphemistic. a fabrication; lie. **6.** Music. a short piece consisting of two or three parts usually in imitative counterpoint. —in'ventional adj. —in'ventionless adj.

inventive (ɪn'vɛntɪv) adj. **1.** skilled or quick at contriving; ingenious; resourceful. **2.** characterized by inventive skill: an inventive programme of work. **3.** of or relating to invention. —in'ventively adv. —in'ventiveness n.

inventor (ɪn'vɛntə) n. a person who invents, esp. as a profession. —in'ventress fem. n.

inventory ('ɪnvəntərɪ, -trɪ) n., pl. -tories. **1.** a detailed list of articles, goods, property, etc. **2.** (often pl.) Accounting, chiefly U.S. **a.** the amount or value of a firm's current assets that consist of raw materials, work in progress, and finished goods; stock. **b.** such assets individually. ~vb. -torying, -toried. **3.** (tr.) to enter (items) in an inventory; make a list of. [C16: from Med. L inventōrium; see INVENT] —'inventoriable adj. —,inven'torial adj. —,inven'torially adv.

Invercargill (,ɪnvə'kɑːgɪl) n. a city in New Zealand, on South Island: regional trading centre for sheep and agricultural products. Pop.: 52 400 (1987).

Inverness (,ɪnvə'nɛs) n. **1.** a town in NE Scotland, in the Highland region: tourism and specialized engineering. Pop.: 39 736 (1981). **2.** (sometimes not cap.) an overcoat with a removable cape.

Inverness-shire (,ɪnvə'nɛs,ʃɪə, -ʃə) n. (until 1975) a county of NW Scotland, now part of the Highland region.

inverse (ɪn'vɜːs, 'ɪnvɜːs) adj. **1.** opposite or contrary in effect, sequence, direction, etc. **2.** Maths. **a.** (of a relationship) containing two variables such that an increase in one results in a decrease in the other. **b.** (of an element) operating on a specified member of a set to produce the identity of the set: the additive inverse element of x is −x. **3.** (usually prenominal) upside-down; inverted: in an inverse position. ~n. **4.** Maths. an inverse element. [C17: from L inversus, from invertere to INVERT] —in'versely adv.

inverse function n. a function whose independent variable is the dependent variable of a given trigonometric or hyperbolic function: the inverse function of sin x is arcsin y (also written sin⁻¹y).

inversion (ɪn'vɜːʃən) n. **1.** the act of inverting or state of being inverted. **2.** something inverted, esp. a reversal of order, mutual functions, etc.: an inversion of their previous relationship. **3.** Also: **anastrophe**. Rhetoric. the reversal of a normal order of words. **4.** Chem. **a.** the conversion of a dextrorotatory solution of sucrose into a laevorotatory solution of glucose and fructose by hydrolysis. **b.** any similar reaction in which the optical properties of the reactants are opposite to those of the products. **5.** Music. **a.** the process or result of transposing the notes of a chord such that the root, originally in the bass, is placed in an upper part. **b.** the modification of an interval in which the higher note becomes the lower or the lower one the higher. **6.** Pathol. abnormal positioning of an organ or part, as in being upside down or turned inside out. **7.** Psychiatry. **a.** the adoption of the role or characteristics of the opposite sex. **b.** another word for **homosexuality**. **8.** Meteorol. an abnormal condition in which the layer of air next to the earth's surface is cooler than an overlying layer. **9.** Computers. an operation by which each digit of a binary number is changed to the alternative digit, as 10110 to 01001. —in'versive adj.

invert vb. (ɪn'vɜːt). **1.** to turn or cause to turn upside down or inside out. **2.** (tr.) to reverse in effect, sequence, direction, etc. **3.** (tr.) Phonetics. to turn (the tip of the tongue) up and back to pronounce (a speech sound). ~n. ('ɪnvɜːt). **4.** Psychiatry. **a.** a person who adopts the role of the opposite sex. **b.** another word for **homosexual**. **5.** Archit. **a.** the lower inner surface of a drain, sewer, etc. **b.** an arch that is concave upwards, esp. one used in foundations. [C16: from L invertere, from IN-[2] + vertere to turn] —in'vertible adj. —in,verti'bility n.

invertase (ɪn'vɜːteɪz) n. an enzyme, occurring in the intestinal juice of animals and in yeasts, that hydrolyses sucrose to glucose and fructose.

invertebrate (ɪn'vɜːtɪbrɪt, -,breɪt) n. **1.** any animal lacking a backbone, including all species not classified as vertebrates. ~adj. also **invertebral. 2.** of, relating to, or designating invertebrates.

inverted comma n. another term for **quotation mark**.

inverted mordent n. Music. a melodic ornament consisting of the rapid alternation of a principal note with a note one degree higher.

inverter or **invertor** (ɪn'vɜːtə) n. any device for converting a direct current into an alternating current.

invert sugar n. a mixture of fructose and glucose obtained by the inversion of sucrose.

invest (ɪn'vɛst) vb. **1.** (often foll. by in) to lay out (money or capital in an enterprise) with the expectation of profit. **2.** (tr.; often foll. by in) to devote (effort, resources, etc., to a project). **3.** (tr.; often foll. by in or with) Arch. or ceremonial. to clothe or adorn (in some garment, esp. the robes of an office). **4.** (tr.; often foll. by in) to install formally or ceremoniously (in an official position, rank, etc.). **5.** (tr.; foll. by in or with) to place (power, authority, etc., in) or provide (with power or authority): to invest new rights in the monarchy. **6.** (tr.; usually passive; foll. by in or with) to provide or endow (a person with qualities, characteristics, etc.). **7.** (tr.; foll. by with) Usually poetic. to cover or adorn, as if with a coat or garment: when spring invests the trees with leaves. **8.** (tr.) Rare. to surround with military forces; besiege. **9.** (intr.; foll. by in) Inf. to purchase; buy. [C16: from Med. L investīre to clothe, from L, from vestīre, from vestis a garment] —in'vestable or in'vestible adj. —in'vestor n.

,inve'racity n.

investigate (ɪn'vɛstɪˌgeɪt) vb. to inquire into (a situation or problem, esp. a crime or death) thoroughly; examine systematically, esp. in order to discover the truth. [C16: from L investīgāre to search after, from IN-² + vestīgium track; see VESTIGE] —**in'vesti,gative** or **in'vestigatory** adj. —**in'vesti,gator** n.

investigation (ɪnˌvɛstɪ'geɪʃən) n. the act or process of investigating; a careful search or examination in order to discover facts, etc.

investiture (ɪn'vɛstɪtʃə) n. **1.** the act of presenting with a title or with the robes and insignia of an office or rank. **2.** (in feudal society) the formal bestowal of the possessory right to a fief. —**in'vestitive** adj.

investment (ɪn'vɛstmənt) n. **1. a.** the act of investing money. **b.** the amount invested. **c.** an enterprise, asset, etc., in which money is or can be invested. **2. a.** the act of investing effort, resources, etc. **b.** the amount invested. **3.** Biol. the outer layer or covering of an organ, part, or organism. **4.** a less common word for **investiture** (sense 1). **5.** the act of investing or state of being invested, as with an official robe, specific quality, etc. **6.** Rare. the act of besieging with military forces, works, etc.

investment analyst n. a specialist in forecasting the prices of stocks and shares.

investment trust n. a financial enterprise that invests its subscribed capital in securities for its investors' benefit.

inveterate (ɪn'vɛtərɪt) adj. **1.** long established, esp. so as to be deep-rooted or ingrained: an inveterate feeling of hostility. **2.** (prenominal) confirmed in a habit or practice, esp. a bad one; hardened. [C16: from L inveterātus of long standing, from inveterāre to make old, from IN-² + vetus old] —**in'veteracy** n. —**in'veterately** adv.

invidious (ɪn'vɪdɪəs) adj. **1.** incurring or tending to arouse resentment, unpopularity, etc.: an invidious task. **2.** (of comparisons or distinctions) unfairly or offensively discriminating. [C17: from L invidiōsus full of envy, from invidia ENVY] —**in'vidiously** adv. —**in'vidiousness** n.

invigilate (ɪn'vɪdʒɪˌleɪt) vb. (intr.) **1.** Brit. to watch examination candidates, esp. to prevent cheating. U.S. word: **proctor. 2.** Arch. to keep watch. [C16: from L invigilāre to watch over; see VIGIL] —**in,vigi'lation** n. —**in'vigi,lator** n.

invigorate (ɪn'vɪgəˌreɪt) vb. (tr.) to give vitality and vigour to; animate; brace; refresh: to be invigorated by fresh air. [C17: from IN-² + L vigor VIGOUR] —**in'vigor,ating** adj. —**in,vigor'ation** n. —**in'vigorative** adj. —**in'vigor,ator** n.

invincible (ɪn'vɪnsəb³l) adj. incapable of being defeated; unconquerable. [C15: from LL invincibilis, from L IN-¹ + vincere to conquer] —**in,vinci'bility** or **in'vincibleness** n. —**in'vincibly** adv.

inviolable (ɪn'vaɪələb³l) adj. that must not or cannot be transgressed, dishonoured, or broken; to be kept sacred: an inviolable oath. —**in,viola'bility** n. —**in'violably** adv.

inviolate (ɪn'vaɪəlɪt, -ˌleɪt) adj. **1.** free from violation, injury, disturbance, etc. **2.** a less common word for **inviolable.** —**in'violacy** or **in'violateness** n. —**in'violately** adv.

invisible (ɪn'vɪzəb³l) adj. **1.** not visible; not able to be perceived by the eye: invisible rays. **2.** concealed from sight; hidden. **3.** not easily seen or noticed: invisible mending. **4.** kept hidden from public view; secret. **5.** Econ. of or relating to services, such as insurance and freight, rather than goods: invisible earnings. ~n. **6.** Econ. an invisible item of trade; service. —**in,visi'bility** or **in'visibleness** n. —**in'visibly** adv.

invitation (ˌɪnvɪ'teɪʃən) n. **1. a.** the act of inviting, such as an offer of entertainment or hospitality. **b.** (as modifier): an invitation race. **2.** the act of enticing or attracting; allurement.

invite vb. (ɪn'vaɪt). (tr.) **1.** to ask (a person) in a friendly or polite way (to do something, attend an event, etc.). **2.** to make a request for, esp. publicly or formally: to invite applications. **3.** to bring on or provoke; give occasion for: you invite disaster by your actions. **4.** to welcome or tempt. ~n. ('ɪnvaɪt). **5.** Inf. an invitation. [C16: from L invītāre to invite, entertain] —**in'viter** n.

inviting (ɪn'vaɪtɪŋ) adj. tempting; alluring; attractive. —**in'vitingness** n.

in vitro (ɪn 'viːtrəʊ) adv., adj. (of biological processes or reactions) made to occur outside the body of the organism in an artificial environment: in vitro fertilization. [NL, lit.: in glass]

in vivo (ɪn 'viːvəʊ) adv., adj. (of biological processes or experiments) occurring or carried out in the living organism. [NL, lit.: in a living (thing)]

invocation (ˌɪnvə'keɪʃən) n. **1.** the act of invoking or calling upon some agent for assistance. **2.** a prayer asking God for help, forgiveness, etc. **3.** an appeal for inspiration from a Muse or deity at the beginning of a poem. **4. a.** the act of summoning a spirit from another world by ritual incantation or magic. **b.** the incantation used in this act. —**,invo'cational** adj. —**invocatory** (ɪn'vɒkətərɪ, -trɪ) adj.

invoice ('ɪnvɔɪs) n. **1.** a document issued by a seller to a buyer listing the goods or services supplied and stating the sum of money due. **2.** Rare. a consignment of invoiced merchandise. ~vb. **3.** (tr.) **a.** to present (a customer, etc.) with an invoice. **b.** to list (merchandise sold) on an invoice. [C16: from earlier invoyes, from OF envois, pl. of envoi message; see ENVOY]

invoke (ɪn'vəʊk) vb. (tr.) **1.** to call upon (an agent, esp. God or another deity) for help, inspiration, etc. **2.** to put (a law, penalty, etc.) into use: the union invoked the dispute procedure. **3.** to appeal to (an outside authority) for confirmation, corroboration, etc. **4.** to implore or beg (help, etc.). **5.** to summon (a spirit, etc.); conjure up. [C15: from L invocāre to appeal to, from vocāre to call] —**in'vocable** adj. —**in'voker** n.

involucre ('ɪnvəˌluːkə) or **involucrum** (ˌɪnvə'luːkrəm) n., pl. **-cres** or **-cra** (-krə). a ring of bracts at the base of an inflorescence. [C16 (in the sense: envelope): from NL involucrum, from L: wrapper, from involvere to wrap] —**,invo'lucral** adj. —**,invo'lucrate** adj.

involuntary (ɪn'vɒləntərɪ, -trɪ) adj. **1.** carried out without one's conscious wishes; not voluntary; unintentional. **2.** Physiol. (esp. of a movement or muscle) performed or acting without conscious control. —**in'voluntarily** adv. —**in'voluntariness** n.

involute adj. (ɪn'vəˌluːt), also **involuted. 1.** complex, intricate, or involved. **2.** Bot. (esp. of petals, leaves, etc., in bud) having margins that are rolled inwards. **3.** (of certain shells) closely coiled so that the axis is obscured. ~n. ('ɪnvəˌluːt). **4.** Geom. the curve described by the free end of a thread as it is wound around another curve, the **evolute,** such that its normals are tangential to the evolute. ~vb. (ˌɪnvə'luːt). **5.** (intr.) to become involute. [C17: from L involūtus, from involvere; see INVOLVE] —**'invo,lutely** adv. —**,invo'lutedly** adv.

involution (ˌɪnvə'luːʃən) n. **1.** the act of involving or complicating or the state of being involved or complicated. **2.** something involved or complicated. **3.** Zool. degeneration or structural deformation. **4.** Biol. an involute formation or structure. **5.** Physiol. reduction in size of an organ or part, as of the uterus following childbirth or as a result of ageing. **6.** an algebraic operation in which a number, expression, etc., is raised to a specified power. —**,invo'lutional** adj.

involve (ɪn'vɒlv) vb. (tr.) **1.** to include or contain as a necessary part. **2.** to have an effect on; spread to: the investigation involved many innocent people. **3.** (often passive; usually foll. by in or with) to concern or associate significantly: many people were involved in the crime. **4.** (often passive) to make complicated; tangle. **5.** Rare, often poetic. to wrap or surround. **6.** Maths, obs. to raise to a specified power. [C14: from L involvere to surround, from IN-² + volvere to roll] —**in'volvement** n. —**in'volver** n.

invulnerable (ɪn'vʌlnərəb³l, -'vʌlnrəb³l) adj. **1.** incapable of being wounded, hurt, damaged, etc. **2.** incapable of being damaged or captured: an invulnerable fortress. —**in,vulnera'bility** or **in'vulnerableness** n. —**in'vulnerably** adv.

inward ('ɪnwəd) adj. **1.** going or directed towards the middle of or into something. **2.** situated within; inside. **3.** of, relating to, or existing in the mind or spirit: inward meditation. ~adv. **4.** a variant of **inwards.** ~n. **5.** the inward part; inside. —**'inwardness** n.

inwardly ('ɪnwədlɪ) adv. **1.** within the private thoughts or feelings; secretly. **2.** not aloud: to laugh inwardly. **3.** with reference to the inside or inner part; internally.

inwards *adv.* ('ɪnwədz), *also* **inward. 1.** towards the interior or middle of something. **2.** in, into, or towards the mind or spirit. ~*pl. n.* ('ɪnədz). **3.** a variant of **innards** (sense 1).

inweave (ɪn'wiːv) *vb.* -**weaving, -wove** *or* -**weaved; -woven** *or* -**weaved.** (*tr.*) to weave together into or as if into a design, fabric, etc.

inwrap (ɪn'ræp) *vb.* -**wrapping, -wrapped.** a less common spelling of **enwrap.**

inwrought (ˌɪn'rɔːt) *adj.* **1.** worked or woven into material, esp. decoratively. **2.** *Rare.* blended with other things.

inyala (ɪn'jɑːlə) *n.* a spiral-horned southern African antelope with a fringe of white hairs along the back and neck. [from Zulu]

Io[1] ('aɪəʊ) *n.* *Greek myth.* a maiden loved by Zeus and turned into a white heifer by either Zeus or Hera.

Io[2] the chemical symbol for ionium.

Ioánnina (*Greek* jɔ'anina) *or* **Yanina** *n.* a city in NW Greece: belonged to the Serbs (1349–1430) and then the Turks (until 1913); seat of Ali Pasha, the "Lion of Janina", from 1788 to 1822. Pop.: 44 362 (1981). Serbian name: **Janina.**

iodic (aɪ'ɒdɪk) *adj.* of or containing iodine, esp. in the pentavalent state.

iodide ('aɪəˌdaɪd) *n.* **1.** a salt of hydrogen iodide, containing the iodide ion, I⁻. **2.** a compound containing an iodine atom, such as methyl iodide (iodomethane).

iodine ('aɪəˌdiːn) *n.* a bluish-black element of the halogen group that sublimates into a violet irritating gas. Its compounds are used in medicine and photography and in dyes. The radioisotope **iodine-131** is used in the treatment of thyroid disease. Symbol: I; atomic no.: 53; atomic wt.: 126.90. [C19: from F *iode*, from Gk *iōdēs* rust-coloured, but mistaken as violet-coloured, from *ion* violet]

iodize *or* -**dise** ('aɪəˌdaɪz) *vb.* (*tr.*) to treat or react with iodine or an iodine compound. Also: **iodate.** —ˌiodi'zation *or* -di'sation *n.* —'io,dizer *or* -,diser *n.*

iodoform (aɪ'ɒdəˌfɔːm) *n.* a yellow crystalline solid made by heating alcohol with iodine and an alkali: used as an antiseptic. Formula: CHI₃. Systematic name: **triiodomethane.**

iodopsin (ˌaɪə'dɒpsɪn) *n.* a violet light-sensitive pigment in the cones of the retina of the eye. See also **rhodopsin.**

IOM *abbrev. for* Isle of Man.

ion ('aɪən, -ɒn) *n.* an electrically charged atom or group of atoms formed by the loss or gain of one or more electrons. See also **cation, anion.** [C19: from Gk, lit.: going, from *ienai* to go]

-**ion** *suffix forming nouns.* indicating an action, process, or state: *creation; objection.* Cf. -**ation, -tion.** [from L -*iōn*-, -*io*]

Iona ('aɪəʊnə) *n.* an island off the W coast of Scotland, in the Inner Hebrides: site of St Columba's monastery (founded in 563) and an important early centre of Christianity. Area: 854 ha (2112 acres).

Ionesco (ˌiːə'nɛskəʊ; *French* jɔnɛsko) *n.* **Eugène** (øʒɛn). born 1912, French dramatist, born in Romania; a leading exponent of the theatre of the absurd. His plays include *The Bald Prima Donna* (1950) and *Rhinoceros* (1960).

ion exchange *n.* the process in which ions are exchanged between a solution and an insoluble solid, usually a resin. It is used to soften water.

Ionia (aɪ'əʊnɪə) *n.* an ancient region of W central Asia Minor, including adjacent Aegean islands: colonized by Greeks in about 1100 B.C. —**Ionian** *adj., n.*

Ionian Islands *pl. n.* a group of Greek islands in the Ionian Sea, consisting of Corfu, Cephalonia, Zante, Levkas, Ithaca, Cythera, and Paxos: ceded to Greece in 1864. Pop.: 182 651 (1981). Area: 2307 sq. km (891 sq. miles).

Ionian Sea *n.* the part of the Mediterranean Sea between SE Italy, E Sicily, and Greece.

ionic (aɪ'ɒnɪk) *adj.* of, relating to, or occurring in the form of ions.

Ionic (aɪ'ɒnɪk) *adj.* **1.** of, denoting, or relating to one of the five classical orders of architecture, characterized by fluted columns and capitals with scroll-like ornaments. **2.** of or relating to Ionia, on the coast of Asia Minor, its inhabitants or their dialect of Ancient Greek. ~*n.* **3.** one of four chief dialects of Ancient Greek; the dialect spoken in Ionia.

ionium (aɪ'əʊnɪəm) *n.* *Obs.* a naturally occurring radioisotope of thorium with a mass number of 230. Symbol: Io [C20: from NL]

ionization *or* -**isation** (ˌaɪənaɪ'zeɪʃən) *n.* **a.** the formation of ions as a result of a chemical reaction, high temperature, electrical discharge, or radiation. **b.** (*as modifier*): *ionization temperature.*

ionize *or* -**ise** ('aɪəˌnaɪz) *vb.* to change or become changed into ions. —'ion,izable *or* -,isable *adj.* —'ion,izer *or* -,iser *n.*

ionosphere (aɪ'ɒnəˌsfɪə) *n.* a region of the earth's atmosphere, extending from about 60 to 1000 km above the earth's surface, in which there is a high concentration of free electrons formed as a result of ionizing radiation entering the atmosphere from space. —**ionospheric** (aɪˌɒnə'sfɛrɪk) *adj.*

iota (aɪ'əʊtə) *n.* **1.** the ninth letter in the Greek alphabet (I, ι), a vowel or semivowel. **2.** (*usually used with a negative*) a very small amount; jot (esp. in **not one** *or* **an iota**). [C16: via L from Gk, of Semitic origin]

IOU *n.* a written promise or reminder to pay a debt. [C17: representing *I owe you*]

-**ious** *suffix forming adjectives from nouns.* characterized by or full of: *ambitious; suspicious.* [from L -*ius* & -*iōsus* full of]

IOW *abbrev. for* Isle of Wight.

Iowa ('aɪəʊə) *n.* a state of the N central U.S., in the Midwest: consists of rolling plains crossed by many rivers, with the Missouri forming the western border and the Mississippi the eastern. Capital: Des Moines. Pop.: 2 851 000 (1986 est.). Area: 144 887 sq. km (55 941 sq. miles). Abbrevs.: **Ia.** or (with zip code) **IA** —**Iowan** ('aɪəʊən) *adj., n.*

IPA *abbrev. for* International Phonetic Alphabet.

ipecac ('ɪpɪˌkæk) *or* **ipecacuanha** (ˌɪpɪˌkækjʊ'ænə) *n.* **1.** a low-growing South American shrub. **2.** a drug prepared from the dried roots of this plant, used as a purgative and emetic. [C18: from Port. *ipecacuanha*, from Amerind *ipekaaguéne*, from *ipeh* low + *kaa* leaves + *guéne* vomit]

Iphigenia (ˌɪfɪdʒɪ'naɪə) *n.* *Greek myth.* the daughter of Agamemnon, taken by him to be sacrificed to Artemis, who saved her life and made her a priestess.

Ipoh ('iːpəʊ) *n.* a city in Malaysia, capital of Perak state: tin-mining centre. Pop.: 300 727 (1980).

ipomoea (ˌɪpə'mɪə, ˌaɪ-) *n.* **1.** any tropical or subtropical plant, such as the morning-glory, sweet potato, and jalap, having trumpet-shaped flowers. **2.** the dried root of a Mexican species which yields a cathartic resin. [C18: NL, from Gk *ips* worm + *homoios* like]

Ipsambul (ˌɪpsæm'buːl) *n.* another name for **Abu Simbel.**

ipse dixit *Latin.* ('ɪpseɪ 'dɪksɪt) *n.* an arbitrary and unsupported assertion. [C16, lit.: he himself said it]

ipso facto ('ɪpsəʊ 'fæktəʊ) *adv.* by that very fact or act. [from L]

Ipsus ('ɪpsəs) *n.* an ancient town in Asia Minor, in S Phrygia: site of a decisive battle (301 B.C.) in the Wars of the Diadochi in which Lysimachus and Seleucus defeated Antigonus and Demetrius.

Ipswich ('ɪpswɪtʃ) *n.* a town in E England, administrative centre of Suffolk, at the head of the Orwell estuary: manufactures agricultural and industrial machinery. Pop.: 120 447 (1981).

IQ *abbrev. for* intelligence quotient.

Iqbal ('ɪkbal) *n.* Sir **Muhammad** (mʊ'hæməd). 1875–1938, Indian Muslim poet, philosopher, and political leader, who advocated the establishment of separate nations for Indian Hindus and Muslims and is generally regarded as the originator of Pakistan.

Iquique (*Spanish* i'kike) *n.* a port in N Chile: oil refineries. Pop.: 120 732 (1985 est.).

Iquitos (*Spanish* i'kitɔs) *n.* an inland port in NE Peru, on the Amazon 3703 km (2300 miles) from the Atlantic: head of navigation for large steamers. Pop.: 175 000 (1982 est.).

Ir *the chemical symbol for* iridium.

Ir. *abbrev. for:* **1.** Ireland. **2.** Irish.

ir- *prefix.* a variant of **in-**[1] and **in-**[2] before *r.*

IRA *abbrev. for* Irish Republican Army.

irade (ɪ'rɑːde) *n.* a written edict of a Muslim ruler. [C19: from Turkish: will, from Ar. *irādah*]

Iráklion (*Greek* i'rakliɔn) *n.* a port in Greece, in N Crete: former capital of Crete (until 1841); ruled by Venetians (13th–17th centuries). Pop.: 101 668 (1981). Italian name: **Candia.** Also called: **Heraklion, Herakleion.**

Iran (ɪˈrɑːn) *n.* a republic in SW Asia, between the Caspian Sea and the Persian Gulf: consists chiefly of a high central desert plateau almost completely surrounded by mountains, a semitropical fertile region along the Caspian coast, and a hot and dry area beside the Persian Gulf. Oil is the most important export. Language: Iranian. Religion: chiefly Muslim. Currency: rial. Capital: Tehran. Pop.: 49 700 000 (1987). Area: 1 647 050 sq. km (635 932 sq. miles). Former name (until 1935): **Persia**. Official name: **Islamic Republic of Iran**. See also **Persian Empire**.

Iranian (ɪˈreɪnɪən) *n.* **1.** a native or inhabitant of Iran. **2.** a branch of the Indo-European family of languages, including Persian. **3.** the modern Persian language. ∼*adj.* **4.** relating to or characteristic of Iran, its inhabitants, or their language; Persian. **5.** belonging to or relating to the Iranian branch of Indo-European.

Iraq (ɪˈrɑːk) *n.* a republic in SW Asia, on the Persian Gulf: coextensive with ancient Mesopotamia; became a British mandate in 1920, independent in 1932, and a republic in 1958. It consists chiefly of the mountains of Kurdistan in the northeast, part of the Syrian Desert, and the lower basin of the Rivers Tigris and Euphrates. Oil is the major export. Official language: Arabic; Kurdish is also spoken. Religion: chiefly Muslim. Currency: dinar. Capital: Baghdad. Pop.: 17 093 000 (1987). Area: 438 446 sq. km (169 284 sq. miles). — **Iraqi** (ɪˈrɑːkɪ) *adj., n.*

irascible (ɪˈræsɪbᵊl) *adj.* **1.** easily angered; irritable. **2.** showing irritability: *an irascible action.* [C16: from LL *irascibilis*, from L *īra* anger] — **i,rasci'bility** *or* **i'rascibleness** *n.* — **i'rascibly** *adv.*

irate (aɪˈreɪt) *adj.* **1.** incensed with anger; furious. **2.** marked by extreme anger: *an irate letter.* [C19: from L *īrātus* enraged, from *irascī* to be angry] — **i'rately** *adv.*

Irbid (ˈɪrbɪd) *n.* a town in NW Jordan. Pop.: 131 200 (1983 est.).

Irbil (ˈɪəbɪl) *n.* a variant of **Erbil**.

IRBM *abbrev. for* intermediate range ballistic missile.

ire (aɪə) *n. Literary.* anger; wrath. [C13: from OF, from L *īra*] — **'ireful** *adj.* — **'irefulness** *n.*

Ire. *abbrev. for* Ireland.

Ireland¹ (ˈaɪələnd) *n.* **1.** an island off NW Europe: part of the British Isles, separated from Britain by the North Channel, the Irish Sea, and St George's Channel; contains large areas of peat bog, with mountains that rise over 900 m (3000 ft.) in the southwest and several large lakes. It was conquered by England in the 16th and early 17th centuries and ruled as a dependency until 1801, when it was united with Great Britain until its division in 1921 into the Irish Free State and Northern Ireland. Latin name: **Hibernia**. **2. Republic of.** Also called: **Irish Republic, Southern Ireland.** a republic in NW Europe occupying most of Ireland: established as the Irish Free State (a British dominion) in 1921 and declared a republic in 1949; joined the Common Market in 1973. Languages: English and Gaelic. Currency: punt. Capital: Dublin. Pop.: 3 700 000 (1987). Area: 70 282 sq. km (27 136 sq. miles). Gaelic name: **Eire**. ∼See also **Northern Ireland**.

Ireland² (ˈaɪələnd) *n.* **John.** 1879–1962, English composer, esp. of songs.

Irene (aɪˈriːnɪ) *n. Greek myth.* the goddess of peace.

irenic, eirenic (aɪˈriːnɪk, -ˈrɛn-) *or* **irenical, eirenical** *adj.* tending to conciliate or promote peace. [C19: from Gk *eirēnikos*, from *eirēnē* peace] — **i'renically** *or* **ei'renically** *adv.*

Ireton (ˈaɪətᵊn) *n.* **Henry.** 1611–51, English Parliamentarian general in the Civil War; son-in-law of Oliver Cromwell. His plan for a constitutional monarchy was rejected by Charles I (1647), whose death warrant he signed; lord deputy of Ireland (1650–51).

Irian Barat (ˈɪərɪən ˈbærɑːt) *n.* the former Indonesian name for **Irian Jaya**.

Irian Jaya *n.* the W part of the island of New Guinea: formerly under Dutch rule, becoming a province of Indonesia in 1963. Capital: Jayapura. Pop.: 1 174 000 (1980). Area: 416 990 sq. km (161 000 sq. miles). Former names (until 1963): **Dutch New Guinea, Netherlands New Guinea**. English name: **West Irian**.

iridaceous (,ɪrɪˈdeɪʃəs, ,aɪ-) *adj.* of, relating to, or belonging to the family of monocotyledonous plants, including the iris, having swordlike leaves and showy flowers.

iridescent (,ɪrɪˈdɛsᵊnt) *adj.* displaying a spectrum of colours that shimmer and change due to interference and scattering as the observer's position changes. [C18: from L *irid-* iris + -ESCENT] — **,iri'descence** *n.* — **,iri'descently** *adv.*

iridium (aɪˈrɪdɪəm, ɪˈrɪd-) *n.* a very hard yellowish-white transition element that is the most corrosion-resistant metal known. It occurs in platinum ores and is used as an alloy with platinum. Symbol: Ir; atomic no.: 77; atomic wt.: 192.2. [C19: NL, from L *irid-* iris + -IUM; from its colourful appearance when dissolving in certain acids]

iris (ˈaɪrɪs) *n., pl.* **irises** *or* **irides** (ˈaɪrɪˌdiːz, ˈɪrɪ-). **1.** the coloured muscular diaphragm that surrounds and controls the size of the pupil. **2.** Also called: **fleur-de-lis.** any iridaceous plant having brightly coloured flowers composed of three petals and three drooping sepals. **3.** a poetic word for **rainbow. 4.** short for **iris diaphragm**. [C14: from L: rainbow, iris (flower), crystal, from Gk]

Iris (ˈaɪrɪs) *n.* the goddess of the rainbow along which she travelled to earth as a messenger of the gods.

iris diaphragm *n.* an adjustable diaphragm that regulates the amount of light entering an optical instrument, esp. a camera.

Irish (ˈaɪrɪʃ) *adj.* **1.** of, relating to, or characteristic of Ireland, its people, their Celtic language, or their dialect of English. **2.** *Inf. offens.* ludicrous or illogical. ∼*n.* **3. the Irish.** (*functioning as pl.*) the natives or inhabitants of Ireland. **4.** another name for **Irish Gaelic. 5.** the dialect of English spoken in Ireland.

Irish coffee *n.* hot coffee mixed with Irish whiskey and topped with double cream.

Irish Free State *n.* a former name for the (Republic of) Ireland (1921–37).

Irish Gaelic *n.* the Goidelic language of the Celts of Ireland, now spoken mainly along the west coast; an official language of the Republic of Ireland since 1921.

Irishman (ˈaɪrɪʃmən) *or* (*fem.*) **Irishwoman** *n., pl.* **-men** *or* **-women.** a native or inhabitant of Ireland.

Irish pipes *pl. n.* another name for **uillean pipes**.

Irish Republic *n.* See **Ireland**¹ (sense 2).

Irish Republican Army *n.* a militant organization of Irish nationalists founded with the aim of striving for a united independent Ireland by means of guerrilla warfare. Abbrev.: **IRA**.

Irish Sea *n.* an arm of the North Atlantic Ocean between Great Britain and Ireland.

Irish stew *n.* a stew made of mutton, lamb, or beef, with potatoes, onions, etc.

Irish wolfhound *n.* a large breed of hound with a rough thick coat.

iritis (aɪˈraɪtɪs) *n.* inflammation of the iris of the eye. — **iritic** (aɪˈrɪtɪk) *adj.*

irk (ɜːk) *vb.* (*tr.*) to irritate, vex, or annoy. [C13 *irken* to grow weary]

irksome (ˈɜːksəm) *adj.* causing vexation, annoyance, or boredom; troublesome or tedious. — **'irksomely** *adv.* — **'irksomeness** *n.*

Irkutsk (*Russian* irˈkutsk) *n.* a city in the S Soviet Union: situated on the Trans-Siberian railway; university (1918); one of the largest industrial centres in Siberia, esp. for heavy engineering. Pop.: 609 000 (1987).

IRO *abbrev. for:* **1.** (in Britain) Inland Revenue Office. **2.** International Refugee Organization.

iron (ˈaɪən) *n.* **1. a.** a malleable ductile silvery-white ferromagnetic metallic element. It is widely used for structural and engineering purposes. Symbol: Fe; atomic no.: 26; atomic wt.: 55.847. Related adjs.: **ferric, ferrous.** Related prefix: **ferro-. b.** (*as modifier*): *iron railings.* **2.** any of certain tools or implements made of iron or steel, esp. for use when hot: *a grappling iron; a soldering iron.* **3.** an appliance for pressing fabrics using dry heat or steam, esp. a small electrically heated device with a handle and a weighted flat bottom. **4.** any of various golf clubs with metal heads, numbered from 2 to 10 according to the slant of the face. **5.** a splintlike support for a malformed leg. **6.** great hardness, strength, or resolve: *a will of iron.* **7. strike while the iron is hot.** to act at an opportune moment. ∼*adj.* **8.** very hard, immovable, or implacable: *iron determination.* **9.** very strong; extremely robust: *an iron constitution.* **10.** cruel or unyielding: *he ruled with an iron hand.* ∼*vb.* **11.** to smooth (clothes or fabric) by removing (creases or wrinkles) using a heated iron; press. **12.** (*tr.*) to furnish or clothe with iron. **13.** (*tr.*) *Rare.* to place (a prisoner) in irons. ∼See also **iron out, irons**. [OE *īren*] — **'ironer** *n.* — **'ironless** *adj.* — **'iron,like** *adj.*

Iron Age n. **a.** the period following the Bronze Age characterized by the extremely rapid spread of iron tools and weapons. **b.** (*as modifier*) *an Iron-Age weapon*.

ironbark ('aɪən,bɑːk) n. any of several Australian eucalyptus trees that have hard rough bark.

ironbound ('aɪən,baʊnd) adj. **1.** bound with iron. **2.** unyielding; inflexible. **3.** (of a coast) rocky; rugged.

ironclad adj. (,aɪən'klæd). **1.** covered or protected with iron: *an ironclad warship*. **2.** inflexible; rigid: *an ironclad rule*. ~n. ('aɪən,klæd). **3.** a large wooden 19th-century warship with armoured plating.

Iron Curtain n. **1. a.** the guarded border between the countries of the Soviet bloc and the rest of Europe. **b.** (*as modifier*): *Iron Curtain countries*. **2.** (*sometimes not caps.*) any barrier that separates communities or ideologies.

Iron Gate or **Iron Gates** n. a gorge of the River Danube on the border between Romania and Yugoslavia. Length: 3 km (2 miles). Romanian name: **Porţile de Fier**.

iron hand n. harsh or rigorous control; overbearing or autocratic force.

iron horse n. *Arch.* a steam-driven railway locomotive.

ironic (aɪ'rɒnɪk) or **ironical** adj. of, characterized by, or using irony. —**i'ronically** adv. —**i'ronicalness** n.

ironing ('aɪənɪŋ) n. **1.** the act of ironing washed clothes. **2.** clothes, etc., that are to be or that have been ironed.

ironing board n. a board, usually on legs, with a suitable covering on which to iron clothes.

iron lung n. an airtight metal cylinder enclosing the entire body up to the neck and providing artificial respiration.

iron maiden n. a medieval instrument of torture, consisting of a hinged case (often shaped in the form of a woman) lined with iron spikes, which was forcibly closed on the victim.

iron man n. *Austral.* an event at a surf carnival in which contestants compete at swimming, surfing, running, etc.

ironmaster ('aɪən,mɑːstə) n. *Brit.* a manufacturer of iron.

ironmonger ('aɪən,mʌŋgə) n. *Brit.* a dealer in metal utensils, hardware, locks, etc. U.S. and Canad. equivalent: **hardware dealer.** —**'iron,mongery** n.

iron out vb. (*tr.*, *adv.*) **1.** to smooth, using a heated iron. **2.** to put right or settle (a problem or difficulty) as a result of negotiations or discussions. **3.** *Austral. inf.* to knock unconscious.

iron pyrites ('paɪraɪts) n. another name for **pyrite**.

iron rations pl. n. emergency food supplies, esp. for military personnel in action.

irons ('aɪənz) pl. n. **1.** fetters or chains (often in **in** or **into irons**). **2. have several irons in the fire.** to be involved in many projects, etc.

ironsides ('aɪən,saɪdz) n. **1.** a person with great stamina or resistance. **2.** an ironclad ship. **3.** (*often cap.*) (in the English Civil War) **a.** the cavalry regiment trained and commanded by Oliver Cromwell. **b.** Cromwell's entire army.

ironstone ('aɪən,stəʊn) n. **1.** any rock consisting mainly of an iron-bearing ore. **2.** a tough durable earthenware.

ironware ('aɪən,wɛə) n. domestic articles made of iron.

ironwood ('aɪən,wʊd) n. **1.** any of various trees, such as hornbeam, that have very hard wood. **2.** a Californian rosaceous tree with very hard wood. **3.** the wood of any of these trees.

ironwork ('aɪən,wɜːk) n. **1.** work done in iron, esp. decorative work. **2.** the craft or practice of working in iron.

ironworks ('aɪən,wɜːks) n. (*sometimes functioning as sing.*) a building in which iron is smelted, cast, or wrought.

irony[1] ('aɪrənɪ) n., pl. **-nies. 1.** the humorous or mildly sarcastic use of words to imply the opposite of what they normally mean. **2.** an instance of this, used to draw attention to some incongruity or irrationality. **3.** incongruity between what is expected to be and what actually is, or a situation or result showing such incongruity. **4.** See **dramatic irony. 5.** *Philosophy.* see **Socratic irony.** [C16: from L, from Gk *eirōneia*, from *eirōn* dissembler, from *eirein* to speak]

irony[2] ('aɪənɪ) adj. of, resembling, or containing iron.

Iroquois ('ɪrə,kwɔɪ) n. **1.** (pl. **-quois**) a member of a confederacy of North American Indian tribes formerly living in and around New York State. **2.** any of the languages of these people. —**Iro'quoian** adj.

irradiance (ɪ'reɪdɪəns) n. the radiant flux incident on unit area of a surface. Also called: **irradiation.** Cf. **illuminance.**

irradiate (ɪ'reɪdɪ,eɪt) vb. **1.** (*tr.*) *Physics.* to subject to or treat with light or other electromagnetic radiation or with beams of particles. **2.** (*tr.*) to subject to or treat with atomic radiation. **3.** (*tr.*) to make clear or bright intellectually or spiritually; illumine. **4.** a less common word for **radiate** (sense 1). **5.** (*intr.*) *Obs.* to become radiant. —**ir'radi,ation** n. —**ir'radiative** adj. —**ir'radi,ator** n.

irrational (ɪ'ræʃənəl) adj. **1.** inconsistent with reason or logic; illogical; absurd. **2.** incapable of reasoning. **3. a.** *Maths.* (of an equation, etc.) containing one or more variables in irreducible radical form or raised to a fractional power: $\sqrt{(x^2 + 1)} = x^{5/3}$. **b.** (*as n.*): *an irrational number*. —**ir,ration'ality** n. —**ir'rationally** adv.

irrational number n. any real number that cannot be expressed as the ratio of two integers, such as π.

Irrawaddy (,ɪrə'wɒdɪ) n. the main river in Burma, rising in the north in two headstreams and flowing south through the whole length of Burma, to enter the Andaman Sea by nine main mouths. Length: 2100 km (1300 miles).

irreclaimable (,ɪrɪ'kleɪməbəl) adj. not able to be reclaimed. —**,irre,claima'bility** or **,irre'claimableness** n. —**,irre'claimably** adv.

irreconcilable (ɪ'rɛkən,saɪləbəl, ɪ,rɛkən'saɪ-) adj. **1.** not able to be reconciled; uncompromisingly conflicting; incompatible. ~n. **2.** a person or thing that is implacably hostile or uncompromisingly opposed. **3.** (*usually pl.*) one of various principles, ideas, etc., that are incapable of being brought into agreement. —**ir,recon,cila'bility** or **ir'recon,cilableness** n. —**ir'recon,cilably** adv.

irrecoverable (,ɪrɪ'kʌvərəbəl, -'kʌvrə-) adj. **1.** not able to be recovered or regained. **2.** not able to be remedied or rectified. —**,irre'coverableness** n. —**,irre'coverably** adv.

irrecusable (,ɪrɪ'kjuːzəbəl) adj. not able to be rejected or challenged, as evidence, etc.

irredeemable (,ɪrɪ'diːməbəl) adj. **1.** (of bonds, shares, etc.) without a date of redemption of capital; incapable of being bought back directly or paid off. **2.** (of paper money) not convertible into specie. **3.** (of a loss) not able to be recovered; irretrievable. **4.** not able to be improved or rectified; irreparable. —**,irre,deema'bility** or **,ir-re'deemableness** n. —**,irre'deemably** adv.

irredentist (,ɪrɪ'dɛntɪst) n. **1.** (*sometimes cap.*) a person, esp. a member of a 19th-century Italian association, who favours the acquisition of territory that was once part of his country or is considered to have been. ~adj. **2.** of or relating to irredentists or their policies. [C19: from It. *irredentista*, from *ir-* IN-[1] + *redento* redeemed, from L *redemptus* bought back; see REDEEM] —**,irre'dentism** n.

irreducible (,ɪrɪ'djuːsɪbəl) adj. **1.** not able to be reduced or lessened. **2.** not able to be brought to a simpler or reduced form. **3.** *Maths.* (of a polynomial) unable to be factorized into polynomials of lower degree, as $(x^2 + 1)$. —**,irre,duci'bility** n. —**,irre'ducibly** adv.

irrefragable (ɪ'rɛfrəgəbəl) adj. not able to be denied or refuted. [C16: from LL *irrefrāgābilis*, from L *ir-* + *refrāgārī* to resist] —**ir,refraga'bility** or **ir'refragableness** n. —**ir'refragably** adv.

irrefrangible (,ɪrɪ'frændʒəbəl) adj. **1.** not to be broken or transgressed; inviolable. **2.** *Physics.* incapable of being refracted. —**,irre,frangi'bility** or **,irre'frangibleness** n. —**,irre'frangibly** adv.

irrefutable (ɪ'rɛfjʊtəbəl, ,ɪrɪ'fjuːtəbəl) adj. impossible to deny or disprove; incontrovertible. —**ir,refuta'bility** n. —**ir'refutably** adv.

irreg. *abbrev. for* irregular(ly).

irregular (ɪ'rɛgjʊlə) adj. **1.** lacking uniformity or symmetry; uneven in shape, position, arrangement, etc. **2.** not occurring at expected or equal intervals: *an irregular pulse*. **3.** differing from the normal or accepted practice or routine; unconventional. **4.** (of the formation, inflections, or derivations of a word) not following the usual pattern of formation in a language. **5.** of or relating to guerrillas or volunteers not belonging to regular forces: *irregular troops*. **6.** (of flowers) having any of their petals differing in size, shape, etc. **7.** *U.S.* (of merchandise) not up to the manufacturer's standards or specifications; imperfect. ~n. **8.** a soldier not in a regular army. **9.** (*often pl.*) *U.S.* imperfect or flawed merchandise. —**ir,reg-u'larity** n. —**ir'regularly** adv.

irrelevant (ɪˈrɛləvənt) *adj.* not relating or pertinent to the matter at hand. —**irˈrelevance** *or* **irˈrelevancy** *n.* —**irˈrelevantly** *adv.*

irreligion (ˌɪrɪˈlɪdʒən) *n.* **1.** lack of religious faith. **2.** indifference or opposition to religion. —**ˌirreˈligionist** *n.* —**ˌirreˈligious** *adj.* —**ˌirreˈligiously** *adv.* —**ˌirreˈligiousness** *n.*

irremediable (ˌɪrɪˈmiːdɪəbˀl) *adj.* not able to be remedied; incurable or irreparable. —**ˌirreˈmediableness** *n.* —**ˌirreˈmediably** *adv.*

irremissible (ˌɪrɪˈmɪsəbˀl) *adj.* **1.** unpardonable; inexcusable. **2.** that must be done, as through duty or obligation. —**ˌirreˈmissiˈbility** *or* **ˌirreˈmissibleness** *n.* —**ˌirreˈmissibly** *adv.*

irremovable (ˌɪrɪˈmuːvəbˀl) *adj.* not able to be removed. —**ˌirreˈmovaˈbility** *n.* —**ˌirreˈmovably** *adv.*

irreparable (ɪˈrɛpərəbˀl, ɪˈrɛprəbˀl) *adj.* not able to be repaired or remedied; beyond repair. —**irˌreparaˈbility** *or* **irˈreparableness** *n.* —**irˈreparably** *adv.*

irreplaceable (ˌɪrɪˈpleɪsəbˀl) *adj.* not able to be replaced: *an irreplaceable antique.* —**ˌirreˈplaceably** *adv.*

irrepressible (ˌɪrɪˈprɛsəbˀl) *adj.* not capable of being repressed, controlled, or restrained. —**ˌirreˌpressiˈbility** *or* **ˌirreˈpressibleness** *n.* —**ˌirreˈpressibly** *adv.*

irreproachable (ˌɪrɪˈprəʊtʃəbˀl) *adj.* not deserving reproach; blameless. —**ˌirreˈproachaˈbility** *or* **ˌirreˈproachableness** *n.* —**ˌirreˈproachably** *adv.*

irresistible (ˌɪrɪˈzɪstəbˀl) *adj.* **1.** not able to be resisted or refused; overpowering: *an irresistible impulse.* **2.** very fascinating or alluring: *an irresistible woman.* —**ˌirreˌsistiˈbility** *or* **ˌirreˈsistibleness** *n.* —**ˌirreˈsistibly** *adv.*

irresolute (ɪˈrɛzəˌluːt) *adj.* lacking resolution; wavering; hesitating. —**irˈresoˌlutely** *adv.* —**irˈresoˌluteness** *or* **irˌresoˈlution** *n.*

irrespective (ˌɪrɪˈspɛktɪv) *adj.* **1. irrespective of.** without taking account of; regardless of. ~*adv.* **2.** *Inf.* regardless; without due consideration: *he carried on with his plan irrespective.* —**ˌirreˈspectively** *adv.*

irresponsible (ˌɪrɪˈspɒnsəbˀl) *adj.* **1.** not showing or done with due care for the consequences of one's actions or attitudes; reckless. **2.** not capable of bearing responsibility. —**ˌirreˌsponsiˈbility** *or* **ˌirreˈsponsibleness** *n.* —**ˌirreˈsponsibly** *adv.*

irresponsive (ˌɪrɪˈspɒnsɪv) *adj.* not responsive. —**irreˈsponsively** *adv.* —**ˌirreˈsponsiveness** *n.*

irretrievable (ˌɪrɪˈtriːvəbˀl) *adj.* not able to be retrieved, recovered, or repaired. —**ˌirreˌtrievaˈbility** *n.* —**ˌirreˈtrievably** *adv.*

irreverence (ɪˈrɛvərəns, ɪˈrɛvrəns) *n.* **1.** lack of due respect or veneration; disrespect. **2.** a disrespectful remark or act. —**irˈreverent** *or* **irˌreveˈrential** *adj.* —**irˈreverently** *adv.*

irreversible (ˌɪrɪˈvɜːsəbˀl) *adj.* **1.** not able to be reversed: *the irreversible flow of time.* **2.** not able to be revoked or repealed; irrevocable. **3.** *Chem., physics.* capable of changing or producing a change in one direction only: *an irreversible reaction.* —**ˌirreˌversiˈbility** *or* **ˌirreˈversibleness** *n.* —**ˌirreˈversibly** *adv.*

irrevocable (ɪˈrɛvəkəbˀl) *adj.* not able to be revoked, changed, or undone. —**irˌrevocaˈbility** *or* **irˈrevocableness** *n.* —**irˈrevocably** *adv.*

irrigate (ˈɪrɪˌgeɪt) *vb.* **1.** to supply (land) with water by means of artificial canals, etc., esp. to promote the growth of food crops. **2.** *Med.* to bathe or wash out (a bodily part, cavity, or wound). **3.** (*tr.*) to make fertile, fresh, or vital by or as if by watering. [C17: from L *irrigāre*, from *rigāre* to moisten, conduct water] —**ˈirrigable** *adj.* —**irriˈgation** *n.* —**ˈirriˌgative** *adj.* —**ˈirriˌgator** *n.*

irritable (ˈɪrɪtəbˀl) *adj.* **1.** quickly irritated; easily annoyed; peevish. **2.** (of all living organisms) capable of responding to such stimuli as heat, light, and touch. **3.** *Pathol.* abnormally sensitive. —**ˌirritaˈbility** *n.* —**ˈirritableness** *n.* —**ˈirritably** *adv.*

irritable bowel syndrome *n. Med.* a chronic condition of recurring abdominal pain with constipation or diarrhoea or both.

irritant (ˈɪrɪtənt) *adj.* **1.** causing irritation; irritating. ~*n.* **2.** something irritant. —**ˈirritancy** *n.*

irritate (ˈɪrɪˌteɪt) *vb.* **1.** to annoy or anger (someone). **2.** (*tr.*) *Biol.* to stimulate (an organism or part) to respond in

a characteristic manner. **3.** (*tr.*) *Pathol.* to cause (a bodily organ or part) to become excessively stimulated, resulting in inflammation, tenderness, etc. [C16: from L *irritāre* to provoke] —**ˈirriˌtator** *n.*

irritation (ˌɪrɪˈteɪʃən) *n.* **1.** something that irritates. **2.** the act of irritating or the condition of being irritated. —**ˈirriˌtative** *adj.*

irrupt (ɪˈrʌpt) *vb.* (*intr.*) **1.** to enter forcibly or suddenly. **2.** (of a plant or animal population) to enter a region suddenly and in very large numbers. **3.** (of a population) to increase suddenly and greatly. [C19: from L *irrumpere* to rush into, invade, from *rumpere* to break, burst] —**irˈruption** *n.* —**irˈruptive** *adj.*

Irtysh *or* **Irtish** (ɪəˈtɪʃ) *n.* a river in central Asia, rising in China in the Altai Mountains and flowing west into the Soviet Union, then northwest into the Ob River as its chief tributary. Length: 4444 km (2760 miles).

Irvine (ˈɜːvɪn) *n.* a town on the W coast of Scotland, in Strathclyde region: designated a new town in 1966. Pop.: 56 300 (1985 est.).

Irving (ˈɜːvɪŋ) *n.* **1. Sir Henry.** real name *John Henry Brodribb.* 1838–1905, English actor and manager of the Lyceum Theatre in London (1878–1902). **2. Washington.** 1783–1859, U.S. essayist and short-story writer, noted for *The Sketch Book of Geoffrey Crayon* (1820), which contains the stories *Rip Van Winkle* and *The Legend of Sleepy Hollow.*

is (ɪz) *vb.* (used with *he, she, it,* and with singular nouns) a form of the present tense (indicative mood) of **be.** [OE]

Is. *abbrev. for:* **1.** Also: **Isa.** *Bible.* Isaiah. **2.** Island(s) or Isle(s).

is- *combining form.* a variant of **iso-** before a vowel: *isentropic.*

Isaac (ˈaɪzək) *n.* an Old Testament patriarch, the son of Abraham and Sarah and father of Jacob and Esau (Genesis 17; 21–27).

Isabella I (ˌɪzəˈbɛlə) *n.* known as *Isabella the Catholic.* 1451–1504, queen of Castile (1474–1504) and, with her husband, Ferdinand V, joint ruler of Castile and Aragon (1479–1504).

isagogics (ˌaɪsəˈgɒdʒɪks) *n.* introductory studies, esp. in the history of the Bible. [C19: from L, from Gk, from *eisagein* to introduce, from *eis-* into + *agein* to lead]

Isaiah (aɪˈzaɪə) *n. Old Testament.* **1.** the first of the major Hebrew prophets, who lived in the 8th century B.C. **2.** the book of his and others' prophecies.

isallobar (aɪˈsæləˌbɑː) *n.* a line on a map connecting places with equal pressure changes.

Isar (ˈiːzɑː) *n.* a river in central Europe, rising in W Austria and flowing generally northeast through S West Germany into the Danube. Length: over 260 km (160 miles).

isatin (ˈaɪsətɪn) *or* **isatine** (ˈaɪsəˌtiːn) *n.* a yellowish-red crystalline compound soluble in hot water, used for the preparation of vat dyes. [C19: from L *isatis* woad + -IN] —**ˌisaˈtinic** *adj.*

Isauria (aɪˈsɔːrɪə) *n.* an ancient district of S central Asia Minor, chiefly on the N slopes of the W Taurus Mountains. —**Iˈsaurian** *adj., n.*

ISBN *abbrev. for* International Standard Book Number.

Iscariot (ɪˈskærɪət) *n.* See **Judas** (Iscariot).

ischaemia *or* **ischemia** (ɪˈskiːmɪə) *n. Pathol.* an inadequate supply of blood to an organ part, as from an obstructed blood flow. [C19: from Gk *iskhein* to restrict, + -AEMIA] —**ischaemic** *or* **ischemic** (ɪˈskɛmɪk) *adj.*

Ischia (ˈiːskjɑː, ˈɪskɪə) *n.* a volcanic island in the Tyrrhenian Sea, at the N end of the Bay of Naples. Area: 47 sq. km (18 sq. miles).

ischium (ˈɪskɪəm) *n., pl.* **-chia** (-kɪə). one of the three sections of the hipbone, situated below the ilium. [C17: from L: hip joint, from Gk *iskhion*] —**ˈischial** *adj.*

-ise *suffix forming verbs.* a variant of **-ize.**
▷ **Usage.** See at **-ize.**

isentropic (ˌaɪsɛnˈtrɒpɪk) *adj.* having or taking place at constant entropy.

Isère (*French* izɛr) *n.* **1.** a department of SE France, in Rhône-Alpes region. Capital: Grenoble. Pop.: 936 771 (1982). Area: 7904 sq. km (3083 sq. miles). **2.** a river in SE France, rising in the Graian Alps and flowing west and southwest to join the River Rhône near Valence. Length: 290 km (180 miles).

Iseult, Yseult (ɪˈsuːlt), *or* **Isolde** (ɪˈzəʊldə) *n.* (in Arthurian legend) **1.** an Irish princess wed to Mark, king of

Cornwall, but in love with his knight Tristan. **2.** (in another account) the daughter of the king of Brittany, married to Tristan.

Isfahan (ˌɪsfəˈhɑːn) *or* **Eşfahān** *n.* a city in central Iran: the second largest city in the country; capital of Persia in the 11th century and from 1598 to 1722. Pop.: 1 001 248 (1986). Ancient name: **Aspadana** (æspəˈdɑːnə).

-ish *suffix forming adjectives.* **1.** of or belonging to a nationality: *Scottish.* **2.** *Often derog.* having the manner or qualities of; resembling: *slavish; boyish.* **3.** somewhat; approximately: *yellowish; sevenish.* **4.** concerned or preoccupied with: *bookish.* [OE *-isc*]

Isherwood (ˈɪʃəˌwʊd) *n.* **Christopher,** full name *Christopher William Bradshaw-Isherwood.* 1904–86, U.S. novelist and dramatist, born in England. His works include the novel *Goodbye to Berlin* (1939) and three verse plays written in collaboration with W.H. Auden.

Ishmael (ˈɪʃmeɪəl) *n.* **1.** the son of Abraham and Hagar, Sarah's handmaid: the ancestor of 12 Arabian tribes (Genesis 21:8–21; 25:12–18). **2.** a bandit chieftain, who defied the Babylonian conquerors of Judah and assassinated the governor appointed by Nebuchadnezzar (II Kings 25:25; Jeremiah 40:13–41:18). **3.** *Rare.* an outcast.

Ishtar (ˈɪʃtɑː) *n.* the principal goddess of the Babylonians and Assyrians; divinity of love, fertility, and war.

Isidore of Seville (ˈɪzɪdɔː) *n.* **Saint,** Latin name *Isidorus Hispalensis.* ?560–636 A.D., Spanish archbishop and scholar, noted for his *Etymologies,* an encyclopedia. Feast day: April 4.

isinglass (ˈaɪzɪŋˌglɑːs) *n.* **1.** a gelatin made from the air bladders of freshwater fish, used as a clarifying agent and adhesive. **2.** another name for **mica.** [C16: from MDu. *huysenblase,* lit.: sturgeon bladder; infl. by E GLASS]

Isis[1] (ˈaɪsɪs) *n.* the local name for the River Thames at Oxford.

Isis[2] (ˈaɪsɪs) *n.* an ancient Egyptian fertility goddess, usually depicted as a woman with a cow's horns, between which was the disc of the sun; wife and sister of Osiris.

Iskander Bey (ɪsˈkændə beɪ) *n.* the Turkish name for **Scanderbeg.**

Iskenderun (ɪsˈkɛndəˌruːn) *n.* a port in S Turkey, on the **Gulf of Iskenderun.** Pop.: 124 824 (1980). Former name: **Alexandretta.**

Isl. *abbrev. for:* **1.** Island. **2.** Isle.

Islam (ˈɪzlɑːm) *n.* **1.** Also called: **Islamism.** the religion of Muslims, teaching that there is only one God and that Mohammed is his prophet; Mohammedanism. **2. a.** Muslims collectively and their civilization. **b.** the countries where the Muslim religion is predominant. [C19: from Ar.: surrender (to God), from *aslama* to surrender] —**Isˈlamic** *adj.*

Islamabad (ɪzˈlɑːmɑːˌbɑːd) *n.* the capital of Pakistan, in the north on the Potwar Plateau: site chosen in 1959; surrounded by the Capital Territory of Islamabad for 909 sq. km (351 sq. miles). Pop.: 201 000 (1981).

Islamize *or* **-ise** (ˈɪzləˌmaɪz) *vb.* (*tr.*) to convert or subject to the influence of Islam. —ˌIslamiˈzation *or* -iˈsation *n.*

island (ˈaɪlənd) *n.* **1.** a mass of land that is surrounded by water and is smaller than a continent. **2.** something resembling this, esp. in being isolated, detached, or surrounded: *a traffic island.* **3.** *Anat.* a part, structure, or group of cells distinct in constitution from its immediate surroundings. ~Related adj.: **insular.** ~*vb.* (*tr.*) *Rare.* **4.** to cause to become an island. **5.** to intersperse with islands. **6.** to place on an island; insulate; isolate. [OE *īgland*] —ˈisland-,like *adj.*

islander (ˈaɪləndə) *n.* a native or inhabitant of an island.

Islands (ˈaɪləndz) *pl. n. N.Z.* **the.** the islands of the South Pacific.

Islands of the Blessed *pl. n. Greek myth.* lands where the souls of heroes and good men were taken after death. Also called: **Hesperides.**

island universe *n.* a former name for **galaxy.**

Islay (ˈaɪlə, ˈaɪleɪ) *n.* an island off the W coast of Scotland: the southernmost of the Inner Hebrides; separated from the island of Jura by the **Sound of Islay.** Pop.: 3792 (1981). Area: 606 sq. km (234 sq. miles).

isle (aɪl) *n. Poetic except when cap. and part of place name.* an island, esp. a small one. [C13: from OF, from L *insula* island]

Isle of Dogs *n.* See (Isle of) **Dogs.**

Isle of Man *n.* See (Isle of) **Man.**

Isle of Pines *n.* the former name of the (Isle of) **Youth.**

Isle of Sheppey *n.* See (Isle of) **Sheppey.**

Isle of Wight *n.* See (Isle of) **Wight.**

Isle of Youth *n.* See (Isle of) **Youth.**

Isle Royale (ˈrɔɪəl) *n.* an island in the northeast U.S., in NW Lake Superior: forms, with over 100 surrounding islands, **Isle Royale National Park.** Area: 541 sq. km (209 sq. miles).

islet (ˈaɪlɪt) *n.* a small island. [C16: from OF *islette;* see ISLE]

islets *or* **islands of Langerhans** (ˈlæŋəˌhæns) *pl. n.* small groups of endocrine cells in the pancreas that secrete insulin. [C19: after Paul *Langerhans* (1847–88), G physician]

Islington (ˈɪzlɪŋtən) *n.* a borough of N Greater London. Pop.: 168 000 (1986 est.).

ism (ˈɪzəm) *n. Inf., often derog.* an unspecified doctrine, system, or practice.

-ism *suffix forming nouns.* **1.** indicating an action, process, or result: *criticism.* **2.** indicating a state or condition: *paganism.* **3.** indicating a doctrine, system, or body of principles and practices: *Leninism; spiritualism.* **4.** indicating behaviour or a characteristic quality: *heroism.* **5.** indicating a characteristic usage, esp. of a language: *Scotticism.* [from OF *-isme,* from L *-ismus,* from Gk *-ismos*]

Ismaili *or* **Isma'ili** (ˌɪzmɑːˈiːlɪ) *n. Islam.* **1.** a Shiah sect whose adherents believe that Ismail, son of the sixth imam, was the rightful seventh imam. **2.** a member of this sect.

Ismailia (ˌɪzmaɪˈlɪə) *n.* a city in NE Egypt, on the Suez Canal: founded in 1863 by the former Suez Canal Company; devastated by Israeli troops in the October War (1973). Pop.: 191 700 (1985).

Ismail Pasha (ˌɪzmɑːˈiːl ˈpɑːʃə) *n.* 1830–95, viceroy (1863–66) and khedive (1867–79) of Egypt, who brought his country close to bankruptcy. He was forced to submit to Anglo-French financial control (1876) and to abdicate (1879).

isn't (ˈɪzˀnt) *contraction of* is not.

ISO *abbrev. for:* **1.** International Standards Organization. **2.** Imperial Service Order (a Brit. decoration).

iso- *or before a vowel* **is-** *combining form.* **1.** equal or identical: *isomagnetic.* **2.** indicating that a chemical compound is an isomer of a specified compound: *isobutane.* [from Gk *isos* equal]

isobar (ˈaɪsəʊˌbɑː) *n.* **1.** a line on a map connecting places of equal atmospheric pressure, usually reduced to sea level for purposes of comparison, at a given time or period. **2.** *Physics.* any of two or more atoms that have the same mass number but different atomic numbers. Cf. **isotope.** [C19: from Gk *isobarēs* of equal weight] —ˌisoˈbaric *adj.* —ˈiso,bar,ism *n.*

isocheim *or* **isochime** (ˈaɪsəʊˌkaɪm) *n.* a line on a map connecting places with the same mean winter temperature. Cf. **isothere.** [C19: from ISO- + Gk *kheima* winter weather] —ˌisoˈcheimal *or* ˌisoˈchimal *adj.*

isochronal (aɪˈsɒkrən³l) *or* **isochronous** *adj.* **1.** having the same duration; equal in time. **2.** occurring at equal time intervals; having a uniform period of vibration. [C17: from NL, from Gk *isokhronos,* from ISO- + *khronos* time] —iˈsochronally *or* iˈsochronously *adv.* —iˈsochro,nism *n.*

isoclinal (ˌaɪsəʊˈklaɪn³l) *or* **isoclinic** (ˌaɪsəʊˈklɪnɪk) *adj.* **1.** sloping in the same direction and at the same angle. **2.** *Geol.* (of folds) having limbs that are parallel to each other. ~*n.* **3.** Also: **isocline, isoclinal line.** an imaginary line connecting points on the earth's surface having equal angles of magnetic dip.

isocline (ˈaɪsəʊˌklaɪn) *n.* **1.** a series of rock strata with isoclinal folds. **2.** another name for **isoclinal** (sense 3).

Isocrates (aɪˈsɒkrəˌtiːz) *n.* 436–338 B.C., Athenian rhetorician and teacher.

isodynamic (ˌaɪsəʊdaɪˈnæmɪk) *adj. Physics.* **1.** having equal force or strength. **2.** of or relating to an imaginary line on the earth's surface connecting points of equal magnetic intensity.

isogeotherm (ˌaɪsəʊˈdʒiːəʊˌθɜːm) *n.* an imaginary line below the surface of the earth connecting points of equal temperature. —ˌiso,geoˈthermal *or* ˌiso,geoˈthermic *adj.*

isogloss ('aɪsəʊ,glɒs) *n.* a line drawn on a map around the area in which a linguistic feature is to be found. —,iso'glossal *or* ,iso'glottic *adj.*

isogonic (,aɪsəʊ'gɒnɪk) *or* **isogonal** (aɪ'sɒgənᵊl) *adj.* **1.** *Maths.* having, making, or involving equal angles. ~*n.* **2.** Also called: **isogonic line, isogonal line, isogone.** *Physics.* an imaginary line connecting points on the earth's surface having equal magnetic declination.

isohel ('aɪsəʊ,hɛl) *n.* a line on a map connecting places with an equal period of sunshine. [C20: from ISO- + Gk *hēlios* sun]

isohyet (,aɪsəʊ'haɪɪt) *n.* a line on a map connecting places having equal rainfall. [C19: from ISO- + *-hyet,* from Gk *huetos* rain]

isolate *vb.* ('aɪsə,leɪt). (*tr.*) **1.** to place apart; cause to be alone. **2.** *Med.* to quarantine (a person or animal) having a contagious disease. **3.** to obtain (a compound) in an uncombined form. **4.** to obtain pure cultures of (bacteria, esp. those causing a particular disease). **5.** *Electronics.* to prevent interaction between (circuits, components, etc.); insulate. ~*n.* ('aɪsəlɪt). **6.** an isolated person or group. [C19: back formation from *isolated,* via It. from L *insulātus,* lit.: made into an island] —'**isolable** *adj.* —,**isola'bility** *n.* —'**iso,lator** *n.* —,**iso'lation** *n.*

isolationism (,aɪsə'leɪʃə,nɪzəm) *n.* **1.** a policy of nonparticipation in or withdrawal from international affairs. **2.** an attitude favouring such a policy. —,**iso'lationist** *n., adj.*

Isolde (i'zɔldə) *n.* the German name of **Iseult.**

isomer ('aɪsəmə) *n.* **1.** *Chem.* a compound that exhibits isomerism with one or more other compounds. **2.** *Physics.* a nuclide that exhibits isomerism with one or more other nuclides. —**isomeric** (,aɪsə'mɛrɪk) *adj.*

isomerism (aɪ'sɒmə,rɪzəm) *n.* **1.** the existence of two or more compounds having the same molecular formula but a different arrangement of atoms within the molecule. **2.** the existence of two or more nuclides having the same atomic numbers and mass numbers but different energy states.

isomerous (aɪ'sɒmərəs) *adj.* (of flowers) having floral whorls with the same number of parts.

isometric (,aɪsəʊ'mɛtrɪk) *adj. also* **isometrical. 1.** having equal dimensions or measurements. **2.** *Physiol.* of or relating to muscular contraction that does not produce shortening of the muscle. **3.** (of a crystal or system of crystallization) having three mutually perpendicular equal axes. **4.** (of a method of projecting a drawing in three dimensions) having the three axes equally inclined and all lines drawn to scale. ~*n.* **5.** Also called: **isometric drawing.** a drawing made in this way. [C19: from Gk *isometria*] —,**iso'metrically** *adv.*

isometrics (,aɪsəʊ'mɛtrɪks) *n.* (*functioning as sing.*) physical exercise involving isometric contraction of muscles.

isomorphism (,aɪsəʊ'mɔː,fɪzəm) *n.* **1.** *Biol.* similarity of form, as in different generations of the same life cycle. **2.** *Chem.* the existence of two or more substances of different composition in a similar crystalline form. **3.** *Maths.* a one-to-one correspondence between the elements of two or more sets, such as those of Arabic and Roman numerals. —,**iso,morph** *n.* —,**iso'morphic** *or* ,**iso'morphous** *adj.*

isopleth ('aɪsəʊ,plɛθ) *n.* a line on a map connecting places registering the same amount or ratio of some geographical, etc. phenomenon. [C20: from Gk *isoplēthēs* equal in number, from ISO- + *plēthos* multitude]

isopod ('aɪsəʊ,pɒd) *n.* a crustacean, such as the woodlouse, in which the body is flattened. —**isopodan** (aɪ'sɒpədən) *or* **i'sopodous** *adj.*

isoprene ('aɪsəʊ,priːn) *n.* a colourless volatile liquid with a penetrating odour: used in making synthetic rubbers. Formula: $CH_2:C(CH_3)CH:CH_2$. Systematic name: **2-methylbuta-1,3-diene.** [C20: from ISO- + PR(OPYL) + -ENE]

isosceles (aɪ'sɒsɪ,liːz) *adj.* (of a triangle) having two sides of equal length. [C16: from LL, from Gk, from ISO- + *skelos* leg]

isoseismal (,aɪsəʊ'saɪzməl) *adj.* **1.** of or relating to equal intensity of earthquake shock. ~*n.* **2.** a line on a map connecting points at which earthquake shocks are of equal intensity. ~Also: **isoseismic.**

isostasy (aɪ'sɒstəsɪ) *n.* the state of balance which sections of the earth's lithosphere are thought ultimately to

achieve when the vertical forces upon them remain unchanged. If a section is loaded as by ice, it slowly subsides. If a section is reduced in mass, as by erosion, it slowly rises. [C19: ISO- + *-stasy,* from Gk *stasis* a standing] —**isostatic** (,aɪsəʊ'stætɪk) *adj.*

isothere ('aɪsəʊ,θɪə) *n.* a line on a map linking places with the same mean summer temperature. Cf. **isocheim.** [C19: from ISO- + Gk *theros* summer] —**isotheral** (aɪ'sɒθərəl) *adj.*

isotherm ('aɪsəʊ,θɜːm) *n.* **1.** a line on a map linking places of equal temperature. **2.** *Physics.* a curve on a graph that connects points of equal temperature. ~Also called: **isothermal, isothermal line.**

isothermal (,aɪsəʊ'θɜːməl) *adj.* **1.** (of a process or change) taking place at constant temperature. **2.** of or relating to an isotherm. ~*n.* **3.** another word for **isotherm.** —,**iso'thermally** *adv.*

isotonic (,aɪsəʊ'tɒnɪk) *adj.* **1.** *Physiol.* (of two or more muscles) having equal tension. **2.** Also: **isosmotic.** (of two solutions) having the same osmotic pressure, commonly having physiological osmotic pressure. Cf. **hypertonic, hypotonic.** —**isotonicity** (,aɪsəʊtəʊ'nɪsɪtɪ) *n.*

isotope ('aɪsə,təʊp) *n.* one of two or more atoms with the same atomic number that contain different numbers of neutrons. [C20: from ISO- + Gk *topos* place] —**isotopic** (,aɪsə'tɒpɪk) *adj.* —,**iso'topically** *adv.* —**isotopy** (aɪ'sɒtəpɪ) *n.*

isotropic (,aɪsəʊ'trɒpɪk) *or* **isotropous** (aɪ'sɒtrəpəs) *adj.* **1.** having uniform physical properties in all directions. **2.** *Biol.* not having predetermined axes: *isotropic eggs.* —,**iso'tropically** *adv.* —**i'sotropy** *n.*

I-spy *n.* a game in which one player specifies the initial letter of the name of an object that he can see, which the other players then try to guess.

Israel ('ɪzreɪəl, -rɪəl) *n.* **1.** a republic in SW Asia, on the Mediterranean Sea: established in 1948, in the former British mandate of Palestine, as a Jewish state; sporadic border disputes with Arab neighbours, erupting into full-scale wars in 1949, 1956, 1967 (the Six Day War), and 1973. Official language: Hebrew. Religion: Judaism. Currency: shekel. Capital: Jerusalem. Pop.: 4 399 000 (1987 est.). Area (after 1949 armistice): 20 700 sq. km (7993 sq. miles). After the 1967 cease-fire Israel controlled an area of 89 359 sq. km (34 493 sq. miles). **2. a.** the ancient kingdom of the 12 Hebrew tribes at the SE end of the Mediterranean. **b.** the kingdom in the N part of this region formed by the ten northern tribes of Israel in the 10th century B.C. and destroyed by the Assyrians in 721 B.C.

Israeli (ɪz'reɪlɪ) *n., pl.* **-lis** *or* **-li. 1.** a citizen or inhabitant of the state of Israel. ~*adj.* **2.** of or relating to the state of Israel or its inhabitants.

Israelite ('ɪzrɪə,laɪt, -rə-) *n.* **1.** *Bible.* a member of the ethnic group claiming descent from Jacob; a Hebrew. **2.** a member of any of various Christian sects who regard themselves as God's chosen people. **3.** an archaic word for a **Jew.**

Issachar ('ɪsə,kɑː) *n. Old Testament.* **1.** the fifth son of Jacob by his wife Leah (Genesis 30:17–18). **2.** the tribe descended from this patriarch. **3.** the territory of this tribe.

Issigonis (ɪsɪ'gəʊnɪs) *n.* Sir Alec (**Arnold Constantine**). 1906–88, British car designer born in Smyrna. He is noted for his designs for the Morris Minor (1948) and the Mini (1959).

issuance ('ɪʃjʊəns) *n.* the act of issuing.

issue ('ɪʃjuː) *n.* **1.** the act of sending or giving out something; supply; delivery. **2.** something issued; an edition of stamps, a magazine, etc. **3.** the act of emerging; outflow; discharge. **4.** something flowing out, such as a river. **5.** a place of outflow; outlet. **6.** the descendants of a person; offspring; progeny. **7.** a topic of interest or discussion. **8.** an important subject requiring a decision. **9.** an outcome or consequence; result. **10.** *Pathol.* discharge from a wound. **11.** *Law.* the matter remaining in dispute between the parties to an action after the pleadings. **12.** the yield from or profits arising out of land or other property. **13. at issue. a.** under discussion. **b.** in disagreement. **14. force the issue.** to compel decision on some matter. **15. join issue.** to join in controversy. **16. take issue.** to disagree. ~*vb.* **-suing, -sued. 17.** to come forth or emerge or cause to come forth or emerge. **18.** to publish or deliver (a newspaper, magazine, etc.). **19.** (*tr.*) to make known or announce. **20.** (*intr.*) to originate or proceed. **21.** (*intr.*) to be a consequence; result. **22.** (*intr.*; foll. by *in*) to end or terminate. **23.** (*tr.*) (foll. by *with*) to supply officially (with). [C13: from OF *eissue* way out, from *eissir* to go out, from L *exīre*] —**'issuable** *adj.* —**'issuer** *n.*

Issus ('ɪsəs) *n.* an ancient town in S Asia Minor, in Cilicia north of present-day Iskenderun: scene of a battle (333 B.C.) in which Alexander the Great defeated the Persians.

Issyk-Kul (*Russian* is'sik'kulj) *n.* a lake in the SW Soviet Union, in the NE Kirghiz SSR in the Tian Shan mountains, at an altitude of 1609 m (5280 ft.): one of the largest mountain lakes in the world. Area: 6200 sq. km (2390 sq. miles).

-ist *suffix.* **1.** (*forming nouns*) a person who performs a certain action or is concerned with something specified: *motorist; soloist.* **2.** (*forming nouns*) a person who practises in a specific field: *physicist.* **3.** (*forming nouns and adjectives*) a person who advocates a particular doctrine, system, etc., or relating to such a person or the doctrine advocated: *socialist.* **4.** (*forming nouns and adjectives*) a person characterized by a specified trait, tendency, etc., or relating to such a person or trait: *purist.* [via OF from L *-ista, -istēs*, from Gk *-istēs*]

Istanbul (,ɪstæn'buːl) *n.* a port in NW Turkey, on the western (European) shore of the Bosporus: the largest city in Turkey; founded in about 660 B.C. by Greeks; refounded by Constantine the Great in 330 A.D. as the capital of the Eastern Roman Empire; taken by the Turks in 1453 and remained capital of the Ottoman Empire until 1922; industrial centre for shipbuilding, textiles, etc. Pop.: 5 494 916 (1985). Ancient name: **Byzantium.** Former name (330–1926): **Constantinople.**

isthmian ('ɪsθmɪən) *adj.* relating to or situated in an isthmus.

isthmus ('ɪsməs) *n., pl.* **-muses** *or* **-mi** (-maɪ). **1.** a narrow strip of land connecting two relatively large land areas. **2.** *Anat.* **a.** a narrow band of tissue connecting two larger parts of a structure. **b.** a narrow passage connecting two cavities. [C16: from L, from Gk *isthmos*] —**'isthmoid** *adj.*

-istic *suffix forming adjectives.* equivalent to a combination of **-ist** and **-ic** but in some words having a less specific or literal application and sometimes a mildly pejorative force, as compared with corresponding adjectives ending in **-ist**: *communistic; impressionistic.* [from L *-isticus*, from Gk *istikos*]

istle ('ɪstlɪ) *or* **ixtle** *n.* a fibre obtained from various tropical American agave and yucca trees used in making carpets, cord, etc. [C19: from Mexican Sp. *ixtle*, from Amerind *ichtli*]

Istria ('ɪstrɪə) *n.* a peninsula in the N Adriatic Sea: passed from Italy to Yugoslavia (except for Trieste) in 1947. —**'Istrian** *n., adj.*

it (ɪt) *pron.* (*subjective or objective*) **1.** refers to a nonhuman, animal, plant, or inanimate thing, or sometimes to a small baby: *it looks dangerous; give it a bone.* **2.** refers to an unspecified or implied antecedent or to a previous or understood clause, phrase, etc.: *it is impossible; I knew it.* **3.** used to represent human life or experience in respect of the present situation: *how's it going? I've had it; to brazen it out.* **4.** used as a formal subject (or object), referring to a following clause, phrase, or word: *it helps to know the truth; I consider it dangerous to go on.* **5.** used in the nominative as the formal grammatical subject of impersonal verbs: *it is raining; it hurts.* **6.** (used as complement with *be*) *Inf.* the crucial or ultimate point: *the steering failed and I thought that was it.* **~n. 7.** (in children's games) the player whose turn it is to try to touch another. **8.** *Inf.* **a.** sexual intercourse. **b.** sex appeal. [OE *hit*]

IT *abbrev. for* information technology.

It. *abbrev. for:* **1.** Italian. **2.** Italy.

i.t.a. *or* **ITA** *abbrev. for* initial teaching alphabet, a partly phonetic alphabet used to teach reading.

ital. *abbrev. for* italic.

Ital. *abbrev. for:* **1.** Italian. **2.** Italy.

Italia (i'taːlja) *n.* the Italian name for **Italy.**

Italian (ɪ'tæljən) *n.* **1.** the official language of Italy and one of the official languages of Switzerland. **2.** a native or inhabitant of Italy or a descendant of one. **~adj. 3.** relating to, denoting, or characteristic of Italy, its inhabitants, or their language.

Italianate (ɪ'tæljənɪt, -,neɪt) *or* **Italianesque** *adj.* Italian in style or character.

Italian East Africa *n.* a former Italian territory in E Africa, formed in 1936 from the possessions of Eritrea, Italian Somaliland, and Ethiopia: taken by British forces in 1941.

Italian Somaliland *n.* a former Italian colony in E Africa, united with British Somaliland in 1960 to form the independent republic of Somalia.

italic (ɪ'tælɪk) *adj.* **1.** Also: **Italian.** of, relating to, or denoting a style of handwriting with the letters slanting to the right. **~n. 2.** of, relating to, or denoting a style of printing type modelled on this, chiefly used to indicate emphasis, a foreign word, etc. Cf. **roman.** **3.** (*often pl.*) italic type or print. [C16 (after an edition of Virgil (1501) printed in Venice and dedicated to Italy): from L *Italicus* of Italy, from Gk *Italikos*]

Italic (ɪ'tælɪk) *n.* **1.** a branch of the Indo-European family of languages that includes many of the ancient languages of Italy. **~adj. 2.** denoting, relating to, or belonging to this group of languages, esp. the extinct ones.

italicize *or* **-ise** (ɪ'tælɪ,saɪz) *vb.* **1.** to print (textual matter) in italic type. **2.** (*tr.*) to underline (words, etc.) with a single line to indicate italics. —**i,talici'zation** *or* **-i'sation** *n.*

Italy ('ɪtəlɪ) *n.* a republic in S Europe, occupying a peninsula in the Mediterranean between the Tyrrhenian and the Adriatic Seas, with the islands of Sardinia and Sicily to the west: first united under the Romans but became fragmented into numerous political units in the Middle Ages; united kingdom proclaimed in 1861; under the dictatorship of Mussolini (1922–43); became a republic in 1946; a member of the Common Market. It is generally mountainous, with the Alps in the north and the Apennines running the length of the peninsula. Language: Italian. Religion: Roman Catholic. Currency: lira. Capital: Rome. Pop.: 57 373 000 (1988 est.). Area: 301 247 sq. km (116 312 sq. miles). Italian name: **Italia.**

itch (ɪtʃ) *n.* **1.** an irritation or tickling sensation of the skin causing a desire to scratch. **2.** a restless desire. **3.** any skin disorder, such as scabies, characterized by intense itching. **~vb.** (*intr.*) **4.** to feel or produce an irritating or tickling sensation. **5.** to have a restless desire (to do something). **6. have itchy feet.** to be restless; have a desire to travel. **7. itching palm.** a grasping nature; avarice. [OE *giccean*] —**'itchy** *adj.* —**'itchiness** *n.*

-ite¹ *suffix forming nouns.* **1.** a native or inhabitant of: *Israelite.* **2.** a follower or advocate of; a supporter of a group: *Luddite; labourite.* **3.** (in biology) indicating a division of a body or organ: *somite.* **4.** indicating a mineral or rock: *nephrite; peridotite.* **5.** indicating a commercial product: *vulcanite.* [via L *-ita* from Gk *-itēs* or directly from Gk]

-ite² *suffix forming nouns.* indicating a salt or ester of an acid having a name ending in *-ous: a nitrite is a salt of nitrous acid.* [from F, arbitrary alteration of -ATE¹]

item *n.* ('aɪtəm). **1.** a thing or unit, esp. included in a list or collection. **2.** *Book-keeping.* an entry in an account. **3.** a piece of information, detail, or note: *a news item.* **~vb.** ('aɪtəm). **4.** (*tr.*) *Arch.* to itemize. **~adv.** ('aɪtɛm). **5.** likewise; also. [C14 (adv.) from L: in like manner]

itemize *or* **-ise** ('aɪtə,maɪz) *vb.* (*tr.*) to put on a list or make a list of. —**,itemi'zation** *or* **-i'sation** *n.* —**'item,izer** *or* **-,iser** *n.*

Iténez (i'tenɛθ) *n.* the Spanish name for the **Guaporé.**

iterate ('ɪtə,reɪt) *vb.* (*tr.*) to say or do again. [C16: from L *iterāre*, from *iterum* again] —**'iterant** *adj.* —**,iter'ation** *n.* —**'iterative** *adj.*

Ithaca ('ɪθəkə) *n.* a Greek island in the Ionian Sea, the smallest of the Ionian Islands: regarded as the home of Homer's Odysseus. Area: 93 sq. km (36 sq. miles). Modern Greek name: **Itháki** (i'θaki). —**'Ithacan** *n., adj.*

Ithunn ('iːðʊn) *n.* a variant of **Idun.**

itinerancy (ɪ'tɪnərənsɪ, aɪ-) *or* **itineracy** *n.* **1.** the act of itinerating. **2.** *Chiefly Methodist Church.* the system of appointing a minister to a circuit of churches or chapels. **3.** itinerants collectively.

itinerant (ɪ'tɪnərənt, aɪ-) *adj.* **1.** itinerating. **2.** working for a short time in various places, esp. as a casual labourer. **~n. 3.** an itinerant worker or other person. [C16: from LL *itinerārī* to travel, from L *iter* a journey] —**i'tinerantly** *adv.*

itinerary (aɪˈtɪnərərɪ, ɪ-) *n., pl.* **-aries. 1.** a plan or line of travel; route. **2.** a record of a journey. **3.** a guidebook for travellers. ~*adj.* **4.** of or relating to travel or routes of travel.

itinerate (aɪˈtɪnəˌreɪt, ɪ-) *vb.* (*intr.*) to travel from place to place. —**iˌtinerˈation** *n.*

-itis *suffix forming nouns.* **1.** indicating inflammation of a specified part: *tonsillitis.* **2.** *Inf.* indicating a preoccupation with or imaginery condition of illness caused by: *computeritis; telephonitis.* [NL, from Gk, fem. of *-itēs* belonging to]

it'll (ˈɪt²l) *contraction of* it will *or* it shall.

Ito (ˈiːtəʊ) *n.* Prince **Hirobumi** (ˌhɪərəˈbuːmɪ). 1841–1909, Japanese statesman; premier (1884–88; 1892–96; 1898; 1900–01). He led the movement to modernize Japan and helped to draft the Meiji constitution (1889); assassinated.

ITO *abbrev. for* International Trade Organization.

-itol *suffix forming nouns.* indicating that certain chemical compounds are alcohols containing two or more hydroxyl groups: *inisitol; sorbitol.* [from -ITE² + -OL¹]

its (ɪts) *determiner.* **a.** of, belonging to, or associated in some way with it: *its left rear wheel; I can see its logical consequence.* **b.** (*as pronoun*): *its is over there.*

▷ **Usage.** The possessive adjective and pronoun *its* is never written with an apostrophe: *the cat has hurt its ear.* The contraction of *it is,* (*or* it has) *it's,* always has an apostrophe: *it's a pity that the cat has hurt its ear.*

it's (ɪts) *contraction of* it is *or* it has.

itself (ɪtˈsɛlf) *pron.* **1. a.** the reflexive form of **it. b.** (intensifier): *even the money itself won't convince me.* **2.** (*preceded by a copula*) its normal or usual self: *my cat doesn't seem itself these days.*

▷ **Usage.** See at **myself.**

itsy-bitsy (ˈɪtsɪˈbɪtsɪ) *or* **itty-bitty** (ˈɪtɪˈbɪtɪ) *adj. Inf.* very small; tiny. [C20: baby talk alteration of *little bit*]

ITU *abbrev. for:* **1.** Intensive Therapy Unit. **2.** International Telecommunications Union.

ITV (in Britain) *abbrev. for* Independent Television.

-ity *suffix forming nouns.* indicating state or condition: *technicality.* [from OF *-ite,* from L *-itās*]

IU *abbrev. for:* **1.** immunizing unit. **2.** international unit.

IU(C)D *abbrev. for* intrauterine (contraceptive) device.

Iulus (aɪˈjuːləs) *n.* **1.** another name for **Ascanius. 2.** the son of Ascanius, founder of the Julian gens or clan.

-ium *or sometimes* **-um** *suffix forming nouns.* **1.** indicating a metallic element: *platinum; barium.* **2.** (in chemistry) indicating groups forming positive ions: *ammonium chloride; hydroxonium ion.* **3.** indicating a biological structure: *syncytium.* [NL, from L, from Gk *-ion,* dim. suffix]

i.v. *abbrev. for:* **1.** initial velocity. **2.** Also: **IV.** intravenous(ly).

Ivan III (ˈaɪvən) *n.* known as *Ivan the Great.* 1440–1505, grand duke of Muscovy (1462–1505). He expanded Muscovy by conquest, defeated the Tatars (1480), and assumed the title of Ruler of all Russia (1472).

Ivan IV *n.* known as *Ivan the Terrible.* 1530–84, grand duke of Muscovy (1533–47) and first tsar of Russia (1547–84). He conquered Kazan (1552), Astrakhan (1556), and Siberia (1581), but was defeated by Poland in the Livonian War (1558–82) after which his rule became increasingly oppressive.

Ivanovo (*Russian* ɪˈvanəvə) *n.* a city in the central Soviet Union, on the Uvod River; textile centre. Pop.: 479 000 (1987). Former name (1871–1932): **Ivanovo-Voznesensk** (-vəznɪˈsjɛnsk).

I've (aɪv) *contraction of* I have.

-ive *suffix.* **1.** (*forming adjectives*) indicating a tendency, inclination, character, or quality: *divisive; festive; massive.* **2.** (*forming nouns of adjectival origin*): *detective; expletive.* [from L *-ivus*]

Ives (aɪvz) *n.* **1. Charles Edward.** 1874–1954, U.S. composer, noted for his innovative use of polytonality, polyrhythms, and quarter tones. His works include *Second Piano Sonata: Concord* (1915), five symphonies, chamber music, and songs. **2. Frederick Eugene.** 1856–1937, U.S. inventor of halftone photography.

IVF *abbrev. for* in vitro fertilization.

ivied (ˈaɪvɪd) *adj.* covered with ivy.

Iviza (*Spanish* iˈβiθa) *n.* a variant spelling of **Ibiza.**

ivories (ˈaɪvərɪz, -vrɪz) *pl. n. Sl.* **1.** the keys of a piano. **2.** billiard balls. **3.** another word for **teeth. 4.** another word for **dice.**

ivory (ˈaɪvərɪ, -vrɪ) *n., pl.* **-ries. 1. a.** a hard smooth creamy white variety of dentine that makes up a major part of the tusks of elephants and walruses. **b.** (*as modifier*): *ivory ornaments.* **2.** a tusk made of ivory. **3. a.** a yellowish-white colour; cream. **b.** (*as adj.*): *ivory shoes.* **4.** a substance resembling elephant tusk. **5.** an ornament, etc., made of ivory. **6. black ivory.** *Obs.* Negro slaves collectively. [C13: from OF, from L *evoreus* made of ivory, from *ebur* ivory] —**'ivory-,like** *adj.*

ivory black *n.* a black pigment obtained by grinding charred scraps of ivory in oil.

Ivory Coast *n.* **the.** the former name (until 1986) of **Côte d'Ivoire.**

ivory nut *n.* **1.** the seed of the ivory palm, which contains an ivory-like substance used to make buttons, etc. **2.** any similar seed from other palms. ~Also called: **vegetable ivory.**

ivory tower (ˈtaʊə) *n.* **a.** seclusion or remoteness of attitude regarding problems, everyday life, etc. **b.** (*as modifier*): *ivory-tower aestheticism.* —**,ivory-'towered** *adj.*

IVR *abbrev. for* International Vehicle Registration.

ivy (ˈaɪvɪ) *n., pl.* **ivies. 1.** a woody climbing or trailing plant having lobed evergreen leaves and black berry-like fruits. **2.** any of various other climbing or creeping plants, such as poison ivy and ground ivy. [OE *ifig*] —**'ivy-,like** *adj.*

Iwo (ˈiːwəʊ) *n.* a city in SW Nigeria. Pop.: 261 600 (1983 est.).

Iwo Jima (ˈdʒiːmə) *n.* an island in the W Pacific, about 1100 km (700 miles) south of Japan: one of the Volcano Islands; scene of prolonged fighting between U.S. and Japanese forces until taken by the U.S. in 1945; returned to Japan in 1968. Area: 20 sq. km (8 sq. miles).

IWW *abbrev. for* Industrial Workers of the World.

ixia (ˈɪksɪə) *n.* an iridaceous plant of southern Africa, having showy ornamental funnel-shaped flowers. [C18: NL from Gk *ixos* mistletoe]

Ixion (ɪkˈsaɪən) *n. Greek myth.* a Thessalian king punished by Zeus for his love of Hera by being bound to a perpetually revolving wheel. —**Ixionian** (ˌɪksɪˈəʊnɪən) *adj.*

Ixtaccihuatl *or* **Iztaccihuatl** (ˌiːstækˈsiːwət³l) *n.* a dormant volcano in central Mexico, southeast of Mexico City. Height: (central peak) 5286 m (17 342 ft.).

ixtle (ˈɪkstlɪ, ˈɪst-) *n.* a variant spelling of **istle.**

Iyeyasu *or* **Ieyasu** (ˌiːjeɪˈjɑːsuː) *n.* **Tokugawa** (ˌtɒkuˈɡɑːwə). 1542–1616, Japanese general and statesman; founder of the Tokugawa shogunate (1603–1867).

izard (ˈɪzəd) *n.* (esp. in the Pyrenees) another name for **chamois.**

-ize *or* **-ise** *suffix forming verbs.* **1.** to cause to become, resemble, or agree with: *legalize.* **2.** to become; change into: *crystallize.* **3.** to affect in a specified way; subject to: *hypnotize.* **4.** to act according to some practice, principle, policy, etc.: *economize.* [from OF *-iser,* from LL *-izāre,* from Gk *-izein*]

▷ **Usage.** In Britain and the U.S. *-ize* is the preferred ending for many verbs, but *-ise* is equally acceptable in British English. Certain words (chiefly those not formed by adding the suffix to an existing word) are, however, always spelt with *-ise* in both Britain and the U.S.: *advertise, revise.*

Izhevsk (*Russian* iˈʒɛfsk) *n.* an industrial city in the E Soviet Union, capital of the Udmurt ASSR. Pop.: 631 000 (1987).

Izmir (ˈɪzmɪə) *n.* a port in W Turkey, on the **Gulf of Izmir:** the third largest city in the country; university (1955). Pop.: 1 489 817 (1985). Former name: **Smyrna.**

Izmit (ˈɪzmɪt) *n.* a town in NW Turkey, on the **Gulf of Izmit.** Pop.: 236 144 (1985).

Iznik (ɪzˈnɪk) *n.* the modern Turkish name of **Nicaea.**

Iztaccihuatl (ˌiːstəkˈsiːwət³l) *n.* a variant spelling of **Ixtaccihuatl.**

J

j *or* **J** (dʒeɪ) *n., pl.* **j's, J's,** *or* **Js. 1.** the tenth letter of the English alphabet. **2.** a speech sound represented by this letter.

j *symbol for:* **1.** *Maths.* the unit vector along the *y*-axis. **2.** the imaginary number √−1.

J *symbol for:* **1.** current density. **2.** *Cards.* jack. **3.** joule(s).

J. *abbrev. for:* **1.** Journal. **2.** (*pl.* **JJ.**) Judge. **3.** (*pl.* **JJ.**) Justice.

jab (dʒæb) *vb.* **jabbing, jabbed. 1.** to poke or thrust sharply. **2.** to strike with a quick short blow or blows. ~*n.* **3.** a sharp poke or stab. **4.** a quick short blow. **5.** *Inf.* an injection: *polio jabs.* [C19: orig. Scot. var. of JOB] — **'jabbing** *adj.*

Jabalpur *or* **Jubbulpore** (ˌdʒʌbəl'pʊə) *n.* a city in central India, in central Madhya Pradesh. Pop.: 614 879 (1981).

jabber ('dʒæbə) *vb.* **1.** to speak or say rapidly, incoherently, and without making sense; chatter. ~*n.* **2.** such talk. [C15: imit.]

jabberwocky ('dʒæbə,wɒkɪ) *n.* nonsense verse. [C19: coined by Lewis Carroll as the title of a poem in *Through the Looking Glass* (1871)]

Jabir ibn Hayyan ('dʒɑːbɪə 'iːbən hɑː'jɑːn) *n.* ?721–?815. Arab alchemist, whose many works enjoyed enormous esteem among later alchemists, such as Geber.

jabiru ('dʒæbɪˌruː) *n.* **1.** a large white tropical American stork with a dark naked head and a dark bill. **2.** Also called: **black-necked stork, policeman bird.** a large Australian stork, having a white plumage, dark green back and tail, and red legs. **3.** another name for **saddlebill.** [C18: via Port., of Amerind origin]

jabot ('ʒæbəʊ) *n.* a frill or ruffle on the breast or throat of a garment. [C19: from F: bird's crop, jabot]

jaçana (ˌʒɑːsə'nɑː, ˌdʒæ-) *n.* a bird of tropical and subtropical marshy regions, having long legs and very long toes that enable walking on floating plants. [C18: from Port., of Amerind origin, from *jasanã*]

jacaranda (ˌdʒækə'rændə) *n.* **1.** a tropical American tree having fernlike leaves and pale purple flowers. **2.** the fragrant ornamental wood of this tree. **3.** any of several related or similar trees or their wood. [C18: from Port., of Amerind origin, from *yacarandá*]

jacinth ('dʒæsɪnθ) *n.* another name for **hyacinth** (sense 4). [C13: from Med. L *jacinthus,* from L *hyacinthus* plant, precious stone; see HYACINTH]

jack (dʒæk) *n.* **1.** a man or fellow. **2.** a sailor. **3.** the male of certain animals, esp. of the ass or donkey. **4.** a mechanical or hydraulic device for exerting a large force, esp. to raise a heavy weight such as a motor vehicle. **5.** any of several mechanical devices that replace manpower, such as a contrivance for rotating meat on a spit. **6.** one of four playing cards in a pack, one for each suit; knave. **7.** *Bowls.* a small usually white bowl at which the players aim with their own bowls. **8.** *Electrical engineering.* a female socket designed to receive a male plug. **9.** a flag, esp. a small flag flown at the bow of a ship indicating the ship's nationality. **10.** a part of the action of a harpsichord, consisting of a fork-shaped device on the end of a pivoted lever on which a plectrum is mounted. **11. a.** any of various tropical and subtropical fishes. **b.** an immature pike. **12.** Also called: **jackstone.** one of the pieces used in the game of jacks. **13.** *U.S.* a slang word for **money.** **14. every man jack.** everyone without exception. **15. the jack.** *Austral. sl.* syphilis. ~*adj.* **16.** *Austral. sl.* tired or fed up (esp. in **be jack of something**). ~*vb.* **17.** (*tr.*) to lift or push (an object) with a jack. ~See also **jack in, jack up.** [C16 *jakke,* var. of *Jankin,* dim. of *John*]

Jack (dʒæk) *n.* **I'm all right, Jack.** *Brit. inf.* a remark indicating smug and complacent selfishness.

jackal ('dʒækɔːl) *n.* **1.** any of several African or S Asian mammals closely related to the dog, having long legs and pointed ears and muzzle: they are predators and carrion-eaters. **2.** a person who does menial tasks for another. [C17: from Turkish, from Persian, from Sansk. *srgāla*]

jackanapes ('dʒækə,neɪps) *n.* (*functioning as sing.*) **1.** a conceited impertinent person. **2.** a mischievous child. **3.** *Arch.* a monkey. [C16: var. of *Jakken-apes,* lit.: Jack of the ape, nickname of William de la Pole (1396–1450), first

Duke of Suffolk, whose badge showed an ape's ball and chain]

jackass ('dʒæk,æs) *n.* **1.** a male donkey. **2.** a fool. [C18: from JACK (male) + ASS¹]

jackboot ('dʒæk,buːt) *n.* **1.** an all-leather military boot, extending up to or above the knee. **2.** authoritarian rule or behaviour. —'**jack,booted** *adj.*

jackdaw ('dʒæk,dɔː) *n.* a large Eurasian bird, related to the crow, having a black and dark grey plumage: noted for its thieving habits. [C16: from JACK + *daw,* obs. name for jackdaw]

jackeroo *or* **jackaroo** (ˌdʒækə'ruː) *n., pl.* **-roos.** *Austral. inf.* a novice on a sheep or cattle station. [C19: from JACK + (KANG)AROO]

jacket ('dʒækɪt) *n.* **1.** a short coat, esp. one that is hip-length and has a front opening and sleeves. **2.** something that resembles this: *a life jacket.* **3.** any exterior covering or casing, such as the insulating cover of a boiler. **4.** See **dust jacket. 5. a.** the skin of a baked potato. **b.** (*as modifier*): *jacket potatoes.* **6.** *Oil industry.* the support structure, esp. the legs, of an oil platform. ~*vb.* **7.** (*tr.*) to put a jacket on (someone or something). [C15: from OF *jaquet* short jacket, from *jacque* peasant, from *Jacques* James] —'**jacketed** *adj.*

Jack Frost *n.* a personification of frost.

jack in *vb.* (*tr., adv.*) *Sl.* to abandon or leave (an attempt or enterprise).

jack-in-office *n.* a self-important petty official.

jack-in-the-box *n., pl.* **jack-in-the-boxes** *or* **jacks-in-the-box.** a toy consisting of a figure on a tight spring in a box, which springs out when the lid is opened.

Jack Ketch (kɛtʃ) *n. Brit. arch.* a hangman. [C18: after *John Ketch* (died 1686), public executioner in England]

jackknife ('dʒæk,naɪf) *n., pl.* **-knives. 1.** a knife with the blade pivoted to fold into a recess in the handle. **2.** a former name for a type of dive in which the diver bends at the waist in midair; forward pike dive. ~*vb.* (*intr.*) **3.** (of an articulated lorry) to go out of control in such a way that the trailer swings round at an angle to the tractor.

Jacklin ('dʒæklɪn) *n.* **Tony,** full name *Anthony Jacklin.* Born 1944. English golfer: won the British Open Championship (1969) and the U.S. Open Championship (1970).

jack of all trades *n., pl.* **jacks of all trades.** a person who undertakes many different kinds of work.

jack-o'-lantern *n.* **1.** a lantern made from a hollowed pumpkin, which has holes cut in it to represent a human face. **2.** a will-o'-the-wisp.

jack plane *n.* a carpenter's plane, usually with a wooden body, used for rough planing of timber.

jackpot ('dʒæk,pɒt) *n.* **1.** any large prize, kitty, or accumulated stake that may be won in gambling. **2. hit the jackpot. a.** to win a jackpot. **b.** *Inf.* to achieve great success, esp. through luck. [C20: prob. from JACK (playing card) + POT¹]

jack rabbit *n.* any of various W North American hares having long hind legs and large ears. [C19: shortened from *jackass-rabbit,* referring to its long ears]

Jack Robinson ('rɒbɪnsən) *n.* **before you could** (*or* **can**) **say Jack Robinson.** extremely quickly or suddenly.

Jack Russell ('rʌsªl) *n.* a small short-legged terrier having a white coat with tan, black, or lemon markings. [after John *Russell* (1795-1883), E clergyman who developed the breed]

jacks (dʒæks) *n.* (*functioning as sing.*) a game in which bone or metal pieces (**jackstones**) are thrown and then picked up between bounces or throws of a small ball. [C19: shortened from *jackstones,* var. of *checkstones* pebbles]

jacksnipe ('dʒæk,snaɪp) *n., pl.* **-snipe** *or* **-snipes.** a small Eurasian short-billed snipe.

Jackson¹ ('dʒæksən) *n.* a city in and state capital of Mississippi, on the Pearl River. Pop.: 208 440 (1986 est.).

Jackson² ('dʒæksən) *n.* **1. Andrew.** 1767–1845, U.S. statesman, general, and lawyer; seventh president of the U.S. (1828–36). He became a national hero after successfully defending New Orleans from the British (1815). During his administration the spoils system was introduced and the national debt was fully paid off. **2. Glenda.** born 1936, English stage, film, and television actress. Her films include *Women in Love* (1969) for which she won an Oscar, *The Music Lovers* (1970), *Sunday Bloody Sunday* (1971), and *Hopscotch* (1980). **3. Jesse.** born 1941, U.S. Democrat politician; black campaigner for minority rights. **4. Michael (Joe).** born 1958, U.S. pop singer, lead vocalist with the Jacksons (originally the Jackson 5) from 1969. His solo albums include *Thriller* and *Bad.* **5. Thomas Jonathan,** known as *Stonewall Jackson.* 1824–63, Confederate general in the American Civil War, noted particularly for his command at the first Battle of Bull Run (1861). —**Jacksonian** (dʒækˈsəʊnɪən) *adj., n.*

Jacksonville ('dʒæksən,vɪl) *n.* a port in NE Florida: the leading commercial centre of the southeast. Pop.: 609 614 (1986 est.).

jackstraws ('dʒæk,strɔːz) *n. (functioning as sing.)* another name for **spillikins**.

Jack Tar *n. Now chiefly literary.* a sailor.

Jack the Ripper *n.* an unidentified murderer who killed at least seven prostitutes in London's East End between August and November 1888.

jack up *vb. (adv.)* **1.** (*tr.*) to increase (prices, salaries, etc.). **2.** (*tr.*) to raise an object, such as a car, with or as with a jack. **3.** (*intr.*) *Sl.* to inject oneself with a drug. **4.** (*intr.*) *Austral. inf.* to refuse to comply.

Jacob ('dʒeɪkəb) *n. Old Testament.* the son of Isaac, twin brother of Esau, and father of the twelve patriarchs of Israel.

Jacobean (,dʒækə'bɪən) *adj.* **1.** *History.* relating to James I of England or to the period of his rule (1603–25). **2.** of or relating to the style of furniture current at this time, characterized by the use of dark brown carved oak. **3.** relating to or having the style of architecture used in England during this period. [C18: from NL, from *Jacōbus* James]

Jacobi (dʒə'kəʊbɪ; *German* ja'ko:bi) *n.* **Karl Gustav Jacob** (karl 'gʊstaf 'ja:kɔp). 1804–51, German mathematician. Independently of N. H. Abel, he discovered elliptic functions (1829). He also made important contributions to the study of determinants and differential equations.

Jacobin ('dʒækəbɪn) *n.* **1.** a member of the most radical club founded during the French Revolution, which instituted the Reign of Terror. **2.** an extreme political radical. **3.** a French Dominican friar. ~*adj.* **4.** of or relating to the Jacobins or their policies. [C14: from OF, from Med. L *Jacōbīnus,* from LL *Jacōbus* James; the political club orig. met in the convent near the church of *St Jacques* in 1789] —,**Jaco'binic** *or* ,**Jaco'binical** *adj.* —'**Jacobinism** *n.*

Jacobite ('dʒækə,baɪt) *n. Brit. history.* an adherent of James II after his overthrow in 1688, or of his descendants in their attempts to regain the throne. [C17: from *Jacōbus* James + -ITE¹] —**Jacobitic** (,dʒækə'bɪtɪk) *adj.*

Jacobsen (*Danish* 'jakɔbsən) *n.* **Arne** ('arnə). 1902–71, Danish architect and designer. His buildings include the Town Hall at Rodovre (1955).

Jacob's ladder *n.* **1.** *Old Testament.* the ladder reaching up to heaven that Jacob saw in a dream (Genesis 28:12–17). **2.** a ladder made of wooden or metal steps supported by ropes or chains. **3.** a North American plant with blue flowers and a ladder-like arrangement of leaves.

Jacob's staff *n.* a medieval instrument for measuring heights and distances.

jaconet ('dʒækənɪt) *n.* a light cotton fabric used for clothing, etc. [C18: from Urdu *jagannāthī,* from *Jagannāthpūrī,* India, where orig. made]

Jacquard ('dʒækɑːd, dʒə'kɑːd) *n.* **1.** Also called: **Jacquard weave.** a fabric in which the design is incorporated into the weave. **2.** Also called: **Jacquard loom.** the loom that produces this fabric. [C19: after Joseph M. *Jacquard* (1752–1834), F inventor]

jactation (dʒæk'teɪʃən) *n.* **1.** *Rare.* the act of boasting. **2.** *Pathol.* another word for **jactitation**. [C16: from L *jactātiō* bragging, from *jactāre* to flourish, from *jacere* to throw]

jactitation (,dʒæktɪ'teɪʃən) *n.* **1.** the act of boasting. **2.** a false assertion that one is married to another, formerly actionable at law. **3.** *Pathol.* restless tossing in bed, characteristic of severe fevers. [C17: from Med. L, from L *jacitāre* to utter publicly, from *jactitāre* to toss about; see JACTATION]

Jacuzzi (dʒə'ku:zɪ) *n. Trademark.* **1.** a device which swirls water in a bath. **2.** a bath containing such a device.

jade¹ (dʒeɪd) *n.* **1.** a semiprecious stone which varies in colour from white to green and is used for making ornaments and jewellery. **2. a.** the green colour of jade. **b.** (*as adj.*): *a jade skirt.* [C18: from F, from It. *giada,* from

obs. Sp. *piedra de ijada* colic stone (lit.: stone of the flank, because it was believed to cure renal colic)]

jade² (dʒeɪd) *n.* **1.** an old overworked horse. **2.** *Derog., facetious.* a woman considered to be disreputable. ~*vb.* **3.** to exhaust or make exhausted from work or use. [C14: from ?] —'**jadish** *adj.*

jaded ('dʒeɪdɪd) *adj.* **1.** exhausted or dissipated. **2.** satiated. —'**jadedly** *adv.* —'**jadedness** *n.*

jadeite ('dʒeɪdaɪt) *n.* a green or white mineral, a variety of jade, consisting of sodium aluminium silicate in monoclinic crystalline form.

Jadotville (*French* ʒadovil) *n.* the former name of **Likasi**.

j'adoube *French.* (ʒadub) *interj. Chess.* an expression of an intention to touch a piece in order to adjust its placement rather than to make a move. [lit.: I adjust]

Jael ('dʒeɪəl) *n. Old Testament.* the woman who killed Sisera when he took refuge in her tent (Judges 4:17–21).

Jaén (xa'en) *n.* a city in S Spain. Pop.: 95 783 (1981).

Jaffa ('dʒæfə, 'dʒɑː-) *n.* **1.** a port in W Israel, on the Mediterranean: incorporated into Tel Aviv in 1950; an old Canaanite city. Biblical name: **Joppa.** Hebrew name: **Yafo.** **2.** a large variety of orange, having a thick skin.

Jaffna ('dʒæfnə) *n.* a port in N Sri Lanka: for many centuries the capital of a Tamil kingdom. Pop.: 118 224 (1981).

jag¹ (dʒæg) *vb.* **jagging, jagged. 1.** (*tr.*) to cut unevenly. ~*n., vb.* **2.** an informal word for **jab.** ~*n.* **3.** a jagged notch or projection. [C14: from ?]

jag² (dʒæg) *n. Sl.* **a.** intoxication from drugs or alcohol. **b.** a bout of drinking or drug taking. [C16: ?from OE *ceacga* broom]

jagged ('dʒægɪd) *adj.* having sharp projecting notches. —'**jaggedly** *adv.*

Jagger ('dʒægə) *n.* **Mick,** full name *Michael Philip Jagger.* born 1943, English rock singer and songwriter: lead vocalist with the Rolling Stones, noted for the vigour and overt sexuality of his performances on stage.

jaggy ('dʒægɪ) *adj.* **-gier, -giest. 1.** a less common word for **jagged. 2.** *Scot.* prickly.

jaguar ('dʒægjʊə) *n.* a large feline mammal of S North America, Central America, and S South America, similar to the leopard but with larger spots on its coat. [C17: from Port., from Guarani *yaguara*]

jai alai ('haɪ 'laɪ, 'haɪ ə,laɪ) *n.* a version of pelota played by two or four players. [via Sp. from Basque, from *jai* game + *alai* merry]

jail *or* **gaol** (dʒeɪl) *n.* **1.** a place for the confinement of persons convicted and sentenced to imprisonment or of persons awaiting trial. ~*vb.* **2.** (*tr.*) to confine in prison. [C13: from OF *jaiole* cage, from Vulgar L *caveola* (unattested), from L *cavea* enclosure]

jailbird *or* **gaolbird** ('dʒeɪl,bɜːd) *n.* a person who is or has been confined in a jail, esp. repeatedly; convict.

jailbreak *or* **gaolbreak** ('dʒeɪl,breɪk) *n.* an escape from jail.

jailer, jailor, *or* **gaoler** ('dʒeɪlə) *n.* a person in charge of prisoners in a jail.

Jain (dʒaɪn) *or* **Jaina** ('dʒaɪnə) *n.* **1.** an adherent of Jainism. ~*adj.* **2.** of or relating to Jainism. [C19: from Hindi *jaina* saint, lit.: overcomer, from Sansk.]

Jainism ('dʒaɪ,nɪzəm) *n.* an ancient Hindu religion, characterized by the belief that the material world is progressing endlessly in a series of cycles. —'**Jainist** *n., adj.*

Jaipur (dʒaɪ'pʊə) *n.* a city of great beauty in N India, capital of Rajasthan state: University of Rajasthan (1947). Pop.: 966 677 (1981).

Jakarta *or* **Djakarta** (dʒə'kɑːtə) *n.* the capital of Indonesia, in N West Java: founded in 1619 and ruled by the Dutch until 1945; the chief trading centre of the East in the 17th century; University of Indonesia (1947). Pop.: 7 829 000 (1985). Former name (until 1949): **Batavia.**

jake (dʒeɪk) *adj. Austral. & N.Z. sl.* all right; fine: *she's jake.* [from ?]

jalap *or* **jalop** ('dʒæləp) *n.* **1.** a Mexican climbing plant. **2.** the dried and powdered root of any of these plants, used as a purgative. [C17: from F, from Mexican Sp. *jalapa*] —**jalapic** (dʒə'læpɪk) *adj.*

Jalapa (*Spanish* xa'lapa) *n.* a city in E central Mexico, capital of Veracruz State, at an altitude of 1427 m (4681 ft.): resort. Pop.: 212 769 (1980).

jalapeño (,hɑːlə'peɪnjəʊ) *n., pl.* **-ños.** a type of red capsicum with a hot taste used in Mexican cookery. [Mexican Sp.]

Jalisco (*Spanish* xa'lisko) *n.* a state of W Mexico, on the Pacific: crossed by the Sierra Madre; valuable mineral resources. Capital: Guadalajara. Pop.: 4 293 549 (1980). Area: 80 137 sq. km (30 934 sq. miles).

jalopy *or* **jaloppy** (dʒə'lɒpɪ) *n., pl.* **-lopies** *or* **-loppies.** *Inf.* a dilapidated old car. [C20: from ?]

jalousie ('ʒælʊ,ziː) *n.* **1.** a window blind or shutter constructed from angled slats of wood, etc. **2.** a window made of angled slats of glass. [C19: from OF *gelosie* latticework screen]

jam¹ (dʒæm) *vb.* **jamming, jammed. 1.** (*tr.*) to cram or wedge into or against something: *to jam paper into an incinerator.* **2.** (*tr.*) to crowd or pack: *cars jammed the roads.* **3.** to make or become stuck or locked. **4.** (*tr.;* often foll. by *on*) to activate suddenly (esp. in **jam on the brakes**). **5.** (*tr.*) to block; congest. **6.** (*tr.*) to crush or squeeze. **7.** *Radio.* to prevent the clear reception of (radio communications) by transmitting other signals on the same frequency. **8.** (*intr.*) *Sl.* to play in a jam session. ~*n.* **9.** a crowd or congestion in a confined space: *a traffic jam.* **10.** the act of jamming or the state of being jammed. **11.** *Inf.* a predicament: *to help a friend out of a jam.* **12.** See **jam session.** [C18: prob. imit.] —'**jammer** *n.*

jam² (dʒæm) *n.* **1.** a preserve containing fruit, which has been boiled with sugar until the mixture sets. **2.** *Sl.* something desirable: *you want jam on it.* [C18: ?from JAM¹(the act of squeezing)]

Jam. *Bible. abbrev. for* James.

Jamaica (dʒə'meɪkə) *n.* an island and state of the West Indies in the Caribbean Sea: colonized by the Spanish from 1494 onwards, large numbers of Negro slaves being imported; captured by the British in 1655 and established as a colony in 1866; gained full independence in 1962; a member of the Commonwealth. Exports: chiefly bauxite and alumina, sugar, and bananas. Language: English. Religion: Protestant majority. Currency: Jamaican dollar. Capital: Kingston. Pop.: 2 300 000 (1987 est.). Area: 10 992 sq. km (4244 sq. miles). —**Ja'maican** *n., adj.*

jamb *or* **jambe** (dʒæm) *n.* a vertical side member of a doorframe, window frame, or lining. [C14: from OF *jambe* leg, jamb, from LL *gamba* hoof, from Gk *kampē* joint]

Jambi *or* **Djambi** ('dʒæmbɪ) *n.* a port in W Indonesia, in SE Sumatra on the Hari River. Pop.: 230 373 (1980). Also called: **Telanaipura.**

jamboree (,dʒæmbə'riː) *n.* **1.** a large and often international gathering of Scouts. **2.** a party or spree. [C19: from ?]

James (dʒeɪmz) *n.* **1. Henry.** 1843–1916, British novelist, short-story writer, and critic, born in the U.S. Among his novels are *Washington Square* (1880), *The Portrait of a Lady* (1881), *The Spoils of Poynton* (1897), *The Wings of the Dove* (1902), *The Ambassadors* (1903), and *The Golden Bowl* (1904). **2. Jesse (Woodson).** 1847–82, U.S. outlaw. **3.** P(hyllis) D(orothy). born 1920, British detective novelist. Her books include *Death of an Expert Witness* (1977) and *Taste for Death* (1986). **4. William,** brother of Henry James. 1842–1910, U.S. philosopher and psychologist, whose theory of pragmatism is expounded in *Essays in Radical Empiricism* (1912). His other works include *The Will to Believe* (1897), *The Principles of Psychology* (1890), and *The Varieties of Religious Experience* (1902). **5.** *New Testament.* **a.** known as *James the Great.* one of the twelve apostles, a son of Zebedee and brother to John the apostle (Matthew 4:21). **b.** known as *James the Less.* one of the twelve apostles, son of Alphaeus (Matthew 10:3). **c.** known as *James the brother of the Lord.* a brother or close relative of Jesus (Mark 6:3; Galatians 1:19). **d.** the book ascribed to his authorship (in full **The Epistle of James**).

James I *n.* **1.** 1394–1437, king of Scotland (1406–37), second son of Robert III. **2.** 1566–1625, king of England and Ireland (1603–25) and, as James VI, king of Scotland (1567–1625), in succession to Elizabeth I of England and his mother, Mary Queen of Scots, respectively. He alienated Parliament by his assertion of the divine right of kings, his favourites, esp. the Duke of Buckingham, and his subservience to Spain.

James II *n.* **1.** 1430–60, king of Scotland (1437–60), son of James I. **2.** 1633–1701, king of England, Ireland, and, as James VII, of Scotland (1685–88); son of Charles I. His pro-Catholic sympathies and arbitrary rule caused the Whigs and Tories to unite in inviting William of Orange to take the throne. James was defeated at the Boyne (1690) when he attempted to regain the throne.

James III *n.* 1451–88, king of Scotland (1460–88), son of James II.

James IV *n.* 1473–1513, king of Scotland (1488–1513), son of James III; he invaded England (1496) in support of Perkin Warbeck; he was killed at Flodden.

James V *n.* 1512–42, king of Scotland (1513–42), son of James IV.

James VI *n.* title as king of Scotland of **James I** of England and Ireland.

James VII *n.* title as king of Scotland of **James II** of England and Ireland.

James Bay *n.* the S arm of Hudson Bay, in central Canada. Area: 108 780 sq. km (42 000 sq. miles).

Jameson ('dʒeɪmsⁿn) *n.* Sir **Leander Starr.** 1853–1917, British administrator in South Africa, who led an expedition into the Transvaal in 1895 in an unsuccessful attempt to topple its Boer regime (the **Jameson Raid**); prime minister of Cape Colony (1904–08).

Jamestown ('dʒeɪmz,taʊn) *n.* a ruined village in E Virginia, on **Jamestown Island** (a peninsula in the James River): the first permanent settlement by the English in America (1607); capital of Virginia (1607–98); abandoned in 1699.

Jammu ('dʒʌmuː) *n.* a city in N India, winter capital of the state of Jammu and Kashmir. Pop.: 206 135 (1981).

Jammu and Kashmir *n.* the official name for the part of **Kashmir** under Indian control.

jammy ('dʒæmɪ) *adj.* **-mier, -miest.** *Brit. sl.* **1.** pleasant; desirable. **2.** lucky.

jam-packed *adj.* packed or filled to capacity.

jam session *n.* *Sl.* an unrehearsed or improvised performance by jazz or rock musicians. [C20: prob. from JAM¹]

Jamshedpur (,dʒʌmʃed'puə) *n.* a city in NE India, in SE Bihar: large iron and steel works (1907–11); a major industrial centre. Pop.: 438 781 (1981).

Jamshid *or* **Jamshyd** (dʒæm'ʃiːd) *n. Persian myth.* a ruler of the peris who was punished for bragging that he was immortal by being changed into human form. He then became a great king of Persia. See also **peri.**

Jan. *abbrev. for* January.

Janáček (*Czech* 'jana:tʃɛk) *n.* **Leoš** ('lɛɔʃ). 1854–1928, Czech composer. His music is influenced by Czech folksong and speech rhythms and is remarkable for its integration of melody and language. His works include the operas *Jenufa* (1904) and *The Cunning Little Vixen* (1924), the *Glagolitic Mass* (1927), as well as orchestral and chamber music and songs.

Jandal ('dʒænd²l) *n. N.Z. trademark.* a kind of sandal with a strip of material between the big toe and the other toes and over the foot.

Janet (*French* ʒanɛ) *n.* **Pierre Marie Félix** (pjɛr mari feliks). 1859–1947, French psychologist and neurologist, noted particularly for his work on the origins of hysteria.

jangle ('dʒæŋg²l) *vb.* **1.** to sound or cause to sound discordantly, harshly, or unpleasantly. **2.** (*tr.*) to produce a jarring effect on: *the accident jangled his nerves.* **3.** *Arch.* to wrangle. [C13: from OF *jangler*, of Gmc origin] —'**jangler** *n.*

Janiculum (dʒə'nɪkjʊləm) *n.* a hill in Rome across the River Tiber from the Seven Hills.

Janina ('janiːna) *n.* the Serbian name for **Ioánnina.**

janissary ('dʒænɪsərɪ) *or* **janizary** ('dʒænɪzərɪ) *n., pl.* **-saries** *or* **-zaries.** an infantryman in the Turkish army, originally a member of the sovereign's guard, from the 14th to the 19th century. [C16: from F, from It., from Turkish *yeniçeri*, from *yeni* new + *çeri* soldiery]

janitor ('dʒænɪtə) *n.* **1.** *Scot.* the caretaker of a building, esp. a school. **2.** *Chiefly U.S. & Canad.* a person employed to clean and maintain a building. [C17: L: doorkeeper, from *jānua* door, from *jānus* covered way] —**janitorial** (,dʒænɪ'tɔːrɪəl) *adj.*

Jan Mayen ('jæn 'maɪən) *n.* an island in the Arctic Ocean, between Greenland and N Norway: volcanic, with large glaciers; former site of Dutch whaling stations; annexed to Norway in 1929. Area: 373 sq. km (144 sq. miles).

Jansen ('dʒænsⁿn) *n.* **Cornelis** (kɔː'niːlɪs). Latin name *Cornelius Jansenius.* 1585–1638, Dutch Roman Catholic theologian. In *Augustinus* (1640) he defended the teachings of St. Augustine, esp. on free will, grace, and predestination.

Jansenism ('dʒænsə,nɪzəm) *n. R.C. Church.* the doctrine of Cornelis Jansen and his disciples, who believed in predestination and denied free will. —'**Jansenist** *n., adj.* —,**Jansen'istic** *adj.*

Jansky ('dʒænskɪ) *n., pl.* **-skys.** (in radio astronomy) a unit used to measure the intensity of radio waves. Also called: **flux unit.** [C20: after Karl G. *Jansky* (1905-50), U.S. electrical engineer]

January ('dʒænjʊərɪ) *n., pl.* **-aries.** the first month of the year, consisting of 31 days. [C14: from L *Jānuārius*]

Janus ('dʒeɪnəs) n. the Roman god of doorways, passages, and bridges. In art he is depicted with two heads facing opposite ways. [C16: from L, from *jānus* archway]

japan (dʒə'pæn) n. **1.** a glossy black lacquer originally from the Orient, used on wood, metal, etc. **2.** work decorated and varnished in the Japanese manner. ~vb. **-panning, -panned. 3.** (tr.) to lacquer with japan or any similar varnish.

Japan (dʒə'pæn) n. an archipelago and empire in E Asia, extending for 3200 km (2000 miles) between the Sea of Japan and the Pacific and consisting of the main islands of Hokkaido, Honshu, Shikoku, and Kyushu and over 3000 smaller islands: feudalism abolished in 1871, followed by industrialization and expansion of territories, esp. during World Wars I and II, when most of SE Asia came under Japanese control; dogma of the emperor's divinity abolished in 1946 under a new democratic constitution; rapid economic growth has made Japan the most industrialized nation in the Far East. Language: Japanese. Religion: Buddhist and Shintoist. Currency: yen. Capital: Tokyo. Pop.: 122 053 000 (1987 est.). Area: 369 660 sq. km (142 726 sq. miles). Japanese names: **Nippon, Nihon.**

Japan Current n. a warm ocean current flowing northeastwards off the E coast of Japan towards the North Pacific. Also called: **Kuroshio.**

Japanese (,dʒæpə'niːz) adj. **1.** of or characteristic of Japan, its people, or their language. ~n. **2.** (pl. **-nese**) a native or inhabitant of Japan. **3.** the official language of Japan.

Japanese stranglehold n. a wrestling hold in which an opponent's arms exert pressure on his own windpipe.

jape (dʒeɪp) n. **1.** a jest or joke. ~vb. **2.** to joke or jest (about). [C14: ?from OF *japer* to yap, imit.] —**'japer** n. —**'japery** n.

Japheth ('dʒeɪfɛθ) n. Old Testament. the second son of Noah, traditionally regarded as the ancestor of a number of non-Semitic nations (Genesis 10:1–5).

Japlish ('dʒæplɪʃ) n. the adoption and adaptation of English words into the Japanese language. [C20: from a blend of JAPANESE + ENGLISH]

japonica (dʒə'pɒnɪkə) n. **1.** Also called: **Japanese quince.** a Japanese shrub cultivated for its red flowers and yellowish fruit. **2.** another name for the **camellia.** [C19: from NL, fem. of *japonicus* Japanese, from *Japonia* JAPAN]

Japurá (Portuguese ʒapu'ra) n. a river in NW South America, rising in SW Colombia and flowing southeast across Colombia and Brazil to join the Amazon near Tefé: known as the Caquetá in Colombia. Length: about 2800 km (1750 miles). Spanish name: **Yapurá.**

Jaques-Dalcroze (French ʒakdalkroz) n. **Émile** (emil). 1865–1950, Swiss composer and teacher: invented eurythmics.

jar¹ (dʒɑː) n. **1.** a wide-mouthed container that is usually cylindrical, made of glass or earthenware, and without handles. **2.** Also: **jarful.** the contents or quantity contained in a jar. **3.** Brit. inf. a glass of beer. [C16: from OF *jarre, jarra,* from Ar. *jarrah* large earthen vessel]

jar² (dʒɑː) vb. **jarring, jarred. 1.** to vibrate or cause to vibrate. **2.** to make or cause to make a harsh discordant sound. **3.** (often foll. by *on*) to have a disturbing or painful effect (on the nerves, mind, etc.). **4.** (intr.) to disagree; clash. ~n. **5.** a jolt or shock. **6.** a harsh discordant sound. [C16: prob. imit.] —**'jarring** adj. —**'jarringly** adv.

jar³ (dʒɑː) n. **on a** (or **the**) **jar.** (of a door) slightly open; ajar. [C17 (in the sense: turn): from earlier *char*, from OE *cierran* to turn]

jardinière (,ʒɑːdɪ'njɛə) n. **1.** an ornamental pot or trough for plants. **2.** a garnish of fresh vegetables for a dish of meat. [C19: from F, fem. of *jardinier* gardener, from *jardin* GARDEN]

jargon ('dʒɑːgən) n. **1.** specialized language concerned with a particular subject, culture, or profession. **2.** language characterized by pretentious vocabulary or meaning. **3.** gibberish. [C14: from OF, ? imit.]

jarl (jɑːl) n. Medieval history. a Scandinavian chieftain or noble. [C19: from ON] —**'jarldom** n.

jarrah ('dʒærə) n. an Australian eucalyptus tree that yields a valuable timber. [from Abor.]

Jarrett ('dʒærɪt) n. **Keith.** born 1945, U.S. jazz pianist and composer.

Jarrow ('dʒærəʊ) n. a port in NE England, in Tyne and Wear: ruined monastery where the Venerable Bede lived and died; its unemployed marched on London in the 1930s; shipyards, iron and steel works. Pop.: 27 074 (1981).

Jarry (French ʒari) n. **Alfred** (alfrɛd). 1873–1907, French dramatist and poet, who initiated the theatre of the absurd with his play Ubu Roi (1896).

Jaruzelski (Polish jaru:'ʒɛlski) n. **Wojciech** ('vɔɪtʃɛk). born 1927, Polish statesman and soldier; prime minister (1981–85); First Secretary of the Polish United Workers' Party from 1981; head of state from 1985.

jasmine ('dʒæsmɪn, 'dʒæz-) n. **1.** Also called: **jessamine.** any tropical or subtropical oleaceous shrub or climbing plant widely cultivated for their white, yellow, or red fragrant flowers. **2.** any of several other shrubs with fragrant flowers, such as the Cape jasmine, yellow jasmine, and frangipani (**red jasmine**). [C16: from OF *jasmin,* from Ar., from Persian *yāsmīn*]

Jason ('dʒeɪsⁿn) n. Greek myth. the hero who led the Argonauts in quest of the Golden Fleece. He became the husband of Medea, whom he later abandoned for Glauce.

jaspé ('dʒæspeɪ) adj. resembling jasper; variegated. [C19: from F, from *jasper* to marble]

jasper ('dʒæspə) n. **1.** an opaque impure form of quartz, red, yellow, brown, or dark green in colour, used as a gemstone and for ornamental decoration. **2.** Also called: **jasper ware.** a dense hard stoneware. [C14: from OF *jaspe,* from L *jaspis,* from Gk *iaspis,* of Semitic origin]

Jaspers (German 'jaspərs) n. **Karl** (karl). 1883–1969, German existentialist philosopher.

Jassy ('jasi) n. the German name for **Iaşi.**

jato ('dʒeɪtəʊ) n., pl. **-tos.** Aeronautics. jet-assisted takeoff. [C20: from *j(et-)a(ssisted) t(ake)o(ff)*]

jaundice ('dʒɔːndɪs) n. **1.** Also called: **icterus.** yellowing of the skin due to the abnormal presence of bile pigments in the blood, as in hepatitis. **2.** jealousy, envy, and ill humour. ~vb. **3.** to distort (the judgment, etc.) adversely: *jealousy had jaundiced his mind.* **4.** (tr.) to affect with or as if with jaundice. [C14: from OF *jaunisse,* from *jaune* yellow, from L *galbinus* yellowish]

jaunt (dʒɔːnt) n. **1.** a short pleasurable excursion; outing. ~vb. **2.** (intr.) to go on such an excursion. [C16: from ?]

jaunting car n. a light two-wheeled one-horse car, formerly widely used in Ireland.

jaunty ('dʒɔːntɪ) adj. **-tier, -tiest. 1.** sprightly and cheerful: *a jaunty step.* **2.** smart; trim: *a jaunty hat.* [C17: from F *gentil* noble; see GENTEEL] —**'jauntily** adv. —**'jauntiness** n.

Jaurès (French ʒɔrɛs) n. **Jean Léon** (ʒã leõ). 1859–1914, French politician and writer, who founded the socialist paper l'Humanité (1904), and united the French socialist movement into a single party (1905); assassinated.

Java ('dʒɑːvə) n. an island of Indonesia, south of Borneo, from which it is separated by the **Java Sea:** politically the most important island of Indonesia; it consists chiefly of active volcanic mountains and is densely forested. It came under Dutch control in 1596 and became part of Indonesia in 1949. It is one of the most densely populated areas in the world. Capital: Jakarta. Pop. (with Madura): 91 270 000 (1980). Area: 132 174 sq. km (51 032 sq. miles). —**'Javan** n., adj.

Java man n. a type of primitive man, Homo erectus, that lived in the middle Palaeolithic Age in Java.

Javanese (,dʒɑːvə'niːz) adj. **1.** of or relating to the island of Java. ~n. **2.** (pl. **-nese**) a native or inhabitant of Java. **3.** the Malayo-Polynesian language of Java.

Javari or **Javary** (Portuguese ʒava'ri) n. a river in South America, flowing northeast as part of the border between Peru and Brazil to join the Amazon. Length: about 1050 km (650 miles). Spanish name: **Yavarí.**

javelin ('dʒævlɪn) n. **1.** a long pointed spear thrown as a weapon or in competitive field events. **2. the javelin.** the event or sport of throwing the javelin. [C16: from OF *javeline,* var. of *javelot,* of Celtic origin]

jaw (dʒɔː) n. **1.** the part of the skull of a vertebrate that frames the mouth and holds the teeth. **2.** the corresponding part of an invertebrate, esp. an insect. **3.** a pair or either of a pair of hinged or sliding components of a machine or tool designed to grip an object. **4.** Sl. **a.** impudent talk. **b.** idle conversation. **c.** a lecture. ~vb. **5.** (intr.) Sl. **a.** to chat; gossip. **b.** to lecture. [C14: prob. from OF *joue* cheek]

Jawara ('dʒɑːwərə) n. Sir **Dawda** ('dɔːdə). born 1924, Gambian statesman; president of The Gambia from 1970.

jawbone ('dʒɔː,bəʊn) n. a nontechnical name for **mandible** or (less commonly) **maxilla.**

jawbreaker ('dʒɔː,breɪkə) n. **1.** a device having hinged jaws for crushing rocks and ores. **2.** Inf. a word that is hard to pronounce. —**'jaw,breaking** adj.

jaws (dʒɔːz) *pl. n.* **1.** the narrow opening of some confined place such as a gorge. **2. the jaws.** a dangerously close position: *the jaws of death.*

Jaxartes (dʒæk'sɑːtiːz) *n.* the ancient name for **Syr Darya.**

jay (dʒeɪ) *n.* **1.** a passerine bird related to the crow having a pinkish-brown body, blue-and-black wings, and a black-and-white crest. **2.** a foolish or gullible person. [C13: from OF *jai*, from LL *gāius*, ?from name *Gāius*]

Jay (dʒeɪ) *n.* **John.** 1745–1829, American statesman, jurist, and diplomat; first chief justice of the Supreme Court (1789–95). He negotiated the treaty with Great Britain (**Jay's treaty**, 1794), that settled outstanding disputes.

Jaya ('dʒɑːjə) or **Djaja** *n.* **Mount.** a mountain in E Indonesia, in Irian Jaya in the Sudirman Range: the highest mountain in New Guinea. Height: 5039 m (16 532 ft.). Former names: (Mount) **Carstensz, Sukarno Peak.**

Jayapura (,dʒɑːjɑ'puərə) or **Djajapura** *n.* a port in NE Indonesia, capital of Irian Jaya, on the N coast. Pop.: 149 618 (1980). Former names: **Sukarnapura, Kotabaru, Hollandia.**

Jayawardene (,dʒeɪə'wɑːdɪnə) *n.* **Junius Richard.** born 1906, Sri Lanka statesman; prime minister (1977–78) and first president of Sri Lanka (1978–89).

Jaycee ('dʒeɪ'siː) *n. U.S., Canad., Austral., & N.Z.* a young person who belongs to a junior chamber of commerce. [C20: from *J(unior) C(hamber)*]

jaywalk ('dʒeɪ,wɔːk) *vb.* (*intr.*) to cross or walk in a street recklessly or illegally. [C20: from JAY (sense 2)] — **'jay,walker** *n.* — **'jay,walking** *n.*

jazz (dʒæz) *n.* **1. a.** a kind of music of American Negro origin, characterized by syncopated rhythms, solo and group improvisation, and a variety of harmonic idioms and instrumental techniques. **b.** (*as modifier*): *a jazz band.* **c.** (*in combination*): *a jazzman.* **2.** *Sl.* rigmarole: *legal papers and all that jazz.* ~*vb.* **3.** (*intr.*) to play or dance to jazz music. [C20: from ?] — **'jazzy** *adj.* — **'jazzily** *adv.* — **'jazziness** *n.*

jazz up *vb.* (*tr., adv.*) *Inf.* **1.** to imbue (a piece of music) with jazz qualities, esp. by playing at a quicker tempo. **2.** to make more lively or appealing.

JCB *n. Trademark.* a type of construction machine with a hydraulically operated shovel on the front and an excavator arm on the back. [from the initials of *J(oseph) C(yril) B(amford)* (born 1916), its E manufacturer]

jealous ('dʒeləs) *adj.* **1.** suspicious or fearful of being displaced by a rival. **2.** (often *postpositive* and foll. by *of*) resentful (of) or vindictive (towards). **3.** (often *postpositive* and foll. by *of*) possessive and watchful in the protection (of): *jealous of one's reputation.* **4.** characterized by or resulting from jealousy. **5.** *Obsolete except in Biblical use.* demanding exclusive loyalty: *a jealous God.* [C13: from OF *gelos*, from Med. L, from LL *zēlus* emulation, from Gk *zēlos* ZEAL] — **'jealously** *adv.*

jealousy ('dʒeləsɪ) *n., pl.* **-ousies.** the state or quality of being jealous.

jean (dʒiːn) *n.* a tough twill-weave cotton fabric used for hard-wearing trousers, overalls, etc. [C16: short for *jean fustian*, from *Gene* GENOA]

Jean (*French* ʒɑ̃) *n.* born 1921, grand duke of Luxembourg from 1964.

Jean Baptiste (*French* ʒɑ̃batist) *n. Canad. sl.* a French Canadian. [F: John the Baptist, traditional patron saint of French Canada]

Jean de Meung (*French* ʒɑ̃ də mœ̃) *n.* real name *Jean Clopinel.* ?1250–?1305, French poet, who continued Guillaume de Lorris' *Roman de la Rose.* His portion of the poem consists of some 18 000 lines and contains satirical attacks on women and the Church.

Jeanne d'Arc (ʒan dark) *n.* the French name of **Joan of Arc.**

Jean Paul (*French* ʒɑ̃ pɔl) *n.* real name *Johann Paul Friedrich Richter.* 1763–1825, German novelist.

jeans (dʒiːnz) *pl. n.* trousers for casual wear, made esp. of denim or corduroy. [pl. of JEAN]

Jeans (dʒiːnz) *n.* Sir **James Hopwood.** 1877–1946, English astronomer, physicist, and mathematician, best known for his popular books on astronomy. He made important contributions to the kinetic theory of gases and the theory of stellar evolution.

Jebel Musa ('dʒɛbəl 'musə) *n.* a mountain in NW Morocco, near the Strait of Gibraltar: one of the Pillars of Hercules. Height: 850 m (2790 ft.).

Jedda ('dʒɛdə) *n.* another name for **Jidda.**

Jeep (dʒiːp) *n. Trademark.* a small road vehicle with four-wheel drive. [C20: ?from *GP*, for *general-purpose (vehicle)*, infl. by Eugene the *Jeep*, creature in a comic strip by E. C. Segar]

jeepers or **jeepers creepers** ('dʒiːpəz 'kriːpəz) *interj. U.S. sl.* a mild exclamation of surprise. [C20: euphemism for *Jesus*]

Jeeps (dʒiːps) *n.* **Dickie.** born 1931, English Rugby Union footballer: halfback for England (1956–62) and the British Lions (1959–62).

jeer (dʒɪə) *vb.* **1.** (often foll. by *at*) to laugh or scoff (at a person or thing). ~*n.* **2.** a remark or cry of derision. [C16: from ?] — **'jeerer** *n.* — **'jeering** *adj., n.* — **'jeeringly** *adv.*

Jefferson ('dʒɛfəsᵊn) *n.* **Thomas.** 1743–1826, U.S. statesman: secretary of state (1790–93); third president (1801–09). He was the chief drafter of the Declaration of Independence (1776), the chief opponent of the centralizing policies of the Federalists under Hamilton, and effected the Louisiana Purchase (1803). — **Jeffersonian** (,dʒɛfə'səunɪən) *adj., n.*

Jefferson City *n.* a city in central Missouri, the state capital, on the Missouri River. Pop.: 33 619 (1980).

Jeffrey ('dʒɛfrɪ) *n.* **Francis,** Lord Jeffrey. 1773–1850, Scottish judge and literary critic. As editor of the *Edinburgh Review* (1803–29), he was noted for the severity of his criticism of the romantic poets, esp. Wordsworth.

Jeffreys ('dʒɛfrɪz) *n.* **George,** 1st Baron Jeffreys of Wem. ?1645–89, English judge, notorious for his brutality at the "Bloody Assizes" (1685), where those involved in Monmouth's rebellion were tried.

jehad (dʒɪ'hæd) *n.* a variant spelling of **jihad.**

Jehol (dʒə'hɒl) *n.* a region and former province of NE China, north of the Great Wall: divided among Hebei, Liaoning, and Inner Mongolia in 1956. Area: 192 380 sq. km (74 278 sq. miles).

Jehoshaphat (dʒɪ'hɒʃə,fæt, -'hɒs-) *n. Old Testament.* **1.** the king of Judah (?873–?849 B.C.) (I Kings 22:41–50). **2. Valley of Jehoshaphat.** the site of Jehovah's apocalyptic judgment upon the nations (Joel 4:14).

Jehovah (dʒɪ'həuvə) *n. Old Testament.* the personal name of God, revealed to Moses on Mount Horeb (Exodus 3). [C16: from Med. L, from Heb. YHVH YAHWEH]

Jehovah's Witness *n.* a member of a Christian Church of American origin, the followers of which believe that the end of the present world system of government is near.

Jehu ('dʒiː,hjuː) *n.* **1.** *Old Testament.* the successor to Ahab as king of Israel. **2.** *Humorous.* a reckless driver.

jejune (dʒɪ'dʒuːn) *adj.* **1.** naive; unsophisticated. **2.** insipid; dull. **3.** lacking nourishment. [C17: from L *jējūnus* hungry, empty] — **je'junely** *adv.* — **je'juneness** *n.*

jejunum (dʒɪ'dʒuːnəm) *n.* the part of the small intestine between the duodenum and the ileum. [C16: from L, from *jējūnus* empty; from the belief that the jejunum is empty after death]

Jekyll and Hyde ('dʒɛkᵊl; haɪd) *n.* **a.** a person with two distinct personalities, one good, the other evil. **b.** (*as modifier*): *a Jekyll-and-Hyde personality.* [C19: after the principal character of Robert Louis Stevenson's novel *The Strange Case of Dr Jekyll and Mr Hyde* (1886)]

jell or **gel** (dʒɛl) *vb.* **1.** to make or become gelatinous; congeal. **2.** (*intr.*) to assume definite form: *his ideas have jelled.* [C19: back formation from JELLY¹]

jellaba or **jellabah** ('dʒɛləbə) *n.* a kind of loose cloak with a hood, worn esp. in N Africa. [from Ar. *jallabah, jallābīya*]

Jellicoe ('dʒɛlɪ,kəu) *n.* **John Rushworth,** 1st Earl Jellicoe. 1859–1935, British admiral, who commanded the Grand Fleet at the Battle of Jutland (1916), which incapacitated the German fleet for the rest of World War I.

jellify ('dʒɛlɪ,faɪ) *vb.* **-fying, -fied.** to make into or become jelly. — **jellifi'cation** *n.*

jelly¹ ('dʒɛlɪ) *n., pl.* **-lies. 1.** a fruit-flavoured clear dessert set with gelatin. **2.** a preserve made from the juice of fruit boiled with sugar and used as jam. **3.** a savoury food preparation set with gelatin or with gelatinous stock: *calf's-foot jelly.* ~*vb.* **-lying, -lied. 4.** to jellify. [C14: from OF *gelee* frost, jelly, from *geler* to set hard, from L, from *gelu* frost] — **'jellied** *adj.* — **'jelly-,like** *adj.*

jelly² (dʒɛlɪ) *n. Brit.* a slang name for **gelignite.**

jelly baby *n. Brit.* a small sweet made from a gelatinous substance formed to resemble a baby.

jellyfish ('dʒɛlɪ,fɪʃ) *n., pl.* **-fish** or **-fishes. 1.** any marine coelenterate having a gelatinous umbrella-shaped body with trailing tentacles. **2.** *Inf.* a weak indecisive person.

jelly fungus *n.* a fungus that grows on trees and has a jelly-like consistency when wet.

Jemappes (*French* ʒəmap) *n.* a town in SW Belgium, in Hainaut province west of Mons: scene of a battle (1792) during the French Revolutionary Wars, in which the French defeated the Austrians. Pop.: 18 040 (1970).

jemmy ('dʒɛmɪ) *or U.S.* **jimmy** *n., pl.* **-mies. 1.** a short steel crowbar used, esp. by burglars, for forcing doors and windows. ~*vb.* **-mying, -mied. 2.** (*tr.*) to prise (something) open with a jemmy. [C19: from the pet name for *James*]

Jena (*German* 'jeːna) *n.* a city in S East Germany, in Thuringia: university (1558), at which Hegel and Schiller taught; site of the battle (1806) in which Napoleon Bonaparte defeated the Prussians; optical and precision instrument industry. Pop.: 107 369 (1986).

Jenghis Khan ('dʒɛŋgɪs 'kɑːn) *n.* See **Genghis Khan.**

Jenkins ('dʒɛŋkɪnz) *n.* **Roy (Harris),** Baron Jenkins of Hillhead. born 1920, British Social Democrat politician; president of the Common Market Commission (1977–80); originally a Labour politician; cofounder of the Social Democratic Party (1981); leader of party (1982–83); Chancellor of Oxford University from 1987.

Jenner ('dʒɛnə) *n.* **1. Edward.** 1749–1823, English physician, who discovered vaccination by showing that injections of cowpox virus produce immunity against smallpox (1796). **2.** Sir **William.** 1815–98, English physician and pathologist, who differentiated between typhus and typhoid fevers (1849).

jennet, genet, *or* **gennet** ('dʒɛnɪt) *n.* a small Spanish riding horse. [C15: from OF *genet*, from Catalan *ginet*, horse used by the *Zenete*, from Ar. *Zanātah* the Zenete, a Moorish people renowned for their horsemanship]

jenny ('dʒɛnɪ) *n., pl.* **-nies. 1.** a machine for turning up the edge of a piece of sheet metal in preparation for making a joint. **2.** the female of certain animals or birds, esp. a donkey, ass, or wren. **3.** short for **spinning jenny. 4.** *Billiards, etc.* an in-off. [C17: from name *Jenny*, dim. of *Jane*]

jeopardize *or* **-ise** ('dʒɛpə,daɪz) *vb.* (*tr.*) **1.** to risk; hazard: *he jeopardized his job by being persistently unpunctual.* **2.** to put in danger.

jeopardy ('dʒɛpədɪ) *n.* (usually preceded by *in*) **1.** danger of injury, loss, death, etc.: *his health was in jeopardy.* **2.** *Law.* danger of being convicted and punished for a criminal offence. [C14: from OF *jeu parti*, lit.: divided game, hence uncertain issue, from *jeu* game, from L *jocus* joke, game + *partir* to divide]

Jephthah ('dʒɛfθə) *n. Old Testament.* a judge of Israel, who sacrificed his daughter in fulfilment of a vow (Judges 11:12–40). Douay spelling: **Jephte** ('dʒɛftə).

jequirity (dʒɪ'kwɪrɪtɪ) *n., pl.* **-ties.** a tropical climbing plant with scarlet black-spotted seeds used as beads, and roots used as a substitute for liquorice. Also called: **Indian liquorice.** [C19: from Port. *jequiritī*, of Amerind origin, from *jekiritī*]

Jer. *Bible. abbrev. for* Jeremiah.

Jerba ('dʒɜːbə) *n.* a variant spelling of **Djerba.**

jerbil ('dʒɜːbɪl) *n.* a variant spelling of **gerbil.**

jerboa (dʒɜː'bəʊə) *n.* any small nocturnal burrowing rodent inhabiting dry regions of Asia and N Africa, having long hind legs specialized for jumping. [C17: from NL, from Ar. *yarbū*]

jeremiad (,dʒɛrɪ'maɪəd) *n.* a long mournful lamentation or complaint. [C18: from F *jérémiade*, referring to the Lamentations of Jeremiah in the Old Testament]

Jeremiah (,dʒɛrɪ'maɪə) *n.* **1.** *Old Testament.* **a.** a major prophet of Judah from about 626 to 587 B.C. **b.** the book containing his oracles. **2.** a person who habitually prophesies doom or denounces contemporary society.

jerepigo (,dʒɛrɪ'pɪgəʊ) *n. S. African.* a sweet white or red sherry-type wine. [from Port. *cheripiga* an adulterant of port wine]

Jerez (*Spanish* xe'rɛθ) *n.* a town in SW Spain: famous for the making of sherry. Pop.: 175 653 (1981). Official name: **Jerez de la Frontera** (xe'rɛð ðe la frɔn'tera). Former name: **Xeres.**

Jericho ('dʒɛrɪ,kəʊ) *n.* a village in Jordan near the N end of the Dead Sea, 251 m (825 ft.) below sea level: on the site of an ancient city, the first place to be taken by the Israelites under Joshua after entering the Promised Land in the 14th century B.C. (Joshua 6).

jerk[1] (dʒɜːk) *vb.* **1.** to move or cause to move with an irregular or spasmodic motion. **2.** to throw, twist, pull, or push (something) abruptly or spasmodically. **3.** (*tr.*; often foll. by *out*) to utter (words, etc.) in a spasmodic or

breathless manner. ~*n.* **4.** an abrupt or spasmodic movement. **5.** an irregular jolting motion: *the car moved with a jerk.* **6.** (*pl.*) Also called: **physical jerks.** *Brit. inf.* physical exercises. **7.** *Sl., chiefly U.S. & Canad.* a stupid or ignorant person. [C16: prob. var. of *yerk* to pull stitches tight] —'**jerker** *n.*

jerk[2] (dʒɜːk) *vb.* (*tr.*) **1.** to preserve beef, etc., by cutting into thin strips and drying in the sun. ~*n.* **2.** Also called: **jerky.** jerked meat. [C18: back formation from *jerky*, from Sp. *charqui*, from Quechuan]

jerkin ('dʒɜːkɪn) *n.* **1.** a sleeveless short jacket worn by men or women. **2.** a man's sleeveless fitted jacket, often made of leather, worn in the 16th and 17th centuries. [C16: from ?]

jerky ('dʒɜːkɪ) *adj.* **jerkier, jerkiest.** characterized by jerks. —'**jerkily** *adv.* —'**jerkiness** *n.*

jeroboam (,dʒɛrə'bəʊəm) *n.* a wine bottle holding the equivalent of four normal bottles. [C19: allusion to JERO-BOAM, a "mighty man of valour" (I Kings 11:28) who "made Israel to sin" (I Kings 14:16)]

Jeroboam (,dʒɛrə'bəʊəm) *n. Old Testament.* **1.** the first king of the northern kingdom of Israel (?922–?901 B.C.). **2.** king of the northern kingdom of Israel (?786–?746 B.C.).

Jerome (dʒə'rəʊm) *n.* **1. Saint.** Latin name *Eusebius Hieronymus.* ?347–?420 A.D., Christian monk and scholar, whose outstanding work was the production of the Vulgate. Feast day: Sept. 30. **2. Jerome K(lapka).** 1859–1927, English humorous writer; author of *Three Men in a Boat* (1889).

jerry ('dʒɛrɪ) *n., pl.* **-ries.** *Brit.* an informal word for **chamber pot.**

Jerry ('dʒɛrɪ) *n., pl.* **-ries.** *Brit. sl.* **1.** a German, esp. a German soldier. **2.** the Germans collectively.

jerry-build *vb.* **-building, -built.** (*tr.*) to build (houses, flats, etc.) badly using cheap materials. —'**jerry-,builder** *n.*

jerry can *n.* a flat-sided can with a capacity of between 4.5 and 5 gallons used for storing or transporting liquids, esp. motor fuel. [C20: from JERRY]

jersey ('dʒɜːzɪ) *n.* **1.** a knitted garment covering the upper part of the body. **2. a.** a machine-knitted slightly elastic cloth of wool, silk, nylon, etc., used for clothing. **b.** (*as modifier*): *a jersey suit.* **3.** *Austral. & N.Z.* a football strip. [C16: from JERSEY, from the woollen sweaters worn by the fishermen]

Jersey ('dʒɜːzɪ) *n.* **1.** an island in the English Channel, the largest of the Channel Islands: forms, with two other islands, the bailiwick of Jersey; colonized from Normandy in the 11th century and still officially French-speaking; noted for market gardening, dairy farming, and tourism. Capital: St Helier. Pop.: 80 212 (1986). Area: 116 sq. km (45 sq. miles). **2.** a breed of dairy cattle producing milk with a high butterfat content, originating from the island of Jersey.

Jersey City *n.* an industrial city in NE New Jersey, opposite Manhattan on a peninsula between the Hudson and Hackensack Rivers: part of the Port of New York; site of one of the greatest railway terminals in the world. Pop.: 219 480 (1986).

Jerusalem (dʒə'ruːsələm) *n.* **1.** the capital of Israel, situated in the Judaean hills: became capital of the Hebrew kingdom after its capture by David around 1000 B.C.; destroyed by Nebuchadnezzar of Babylon in 586 B.C.; taken by the Romans in 63 B.C.; devastated in 70 A.D. and 135 A.D. during the Jewish rebellions against Rome; fell to the Arabs in 637 and to the Seljuk Turks in 1071; ruled by Crusaders from 1099 to 1187 and by the Egyptians and Turks until conquered by the British (1917); centre of the British mandate of Palestine from 1920 to 1948, when the Arabs took the old city and the Jews held the new city; unified after the Six Day War (1967) under the Israelis; the holy city of Jews, Christians, and Muslims. Pop.: 468 900 (1986). **2. the New Jerusalem.** *Christianity.* Heaven.

Jerusalem artichoke *n.* **1.** a North American sunflower widely cultivated for its underground edible tubers. **2.** the tuber of this plant, which is eaten as a vegetable. [C17: by folk etymology from It. *girasole articiocco*; see GIRA-SOL]

Jervis Bay ('dʒɑːvɪs) *n.* an inlet of the Pacific in SE Australia, on the coast of S New South Wales: part of the Australian Capital Territory: site of the Royal Australian Naval College.

Jespersen ('jɛspəsˀn, 'dʒɛs-) *n.* **(Jens) Otto (Harry).** 1860–1943, Danish philologist: author of *Modern English Grammar* (1909–31).

jess (dʒɛs) n. Falconry. a short leather strap, one end of which is permanently attached to the leg of a hawk or falcon. [C14: from OF *ges*, from L *jactus* a throw, from *jacere* to throw] —**jessed** adj.

jessamine ('dʒɛsəmɪn) n. another name for **jasmine** (sense 1).

Jesse ('dʒɛsɪ) n. Old Testament. the father of David (I Samuel 16).

Jesselton ('dʒɛsəltən) n. the former name of **Kota Kinabalu.**

jest (dʒɛst) n. **1.** something done or said for amusement; joke. **2.** playfulness; fun: to act in jest. **3.** a jeer or taunt. **4.** an object of derision. ~vb. **5.** to act or speak in an amusing or frivolous way. **6.** to make fun of (a person or thing). [C13: var. of GEST] —'**jesting** adj., n. —'**jestingly** adv.

jester ('dʒɛstə) n. a professional clown employed by a king or nobleman during the Middle Ages.

Jesuit ('dʒɛzjʊɪt) n. **1.** a member of a Roman Catholic religious order (the **Society of Jesus**) founded by Ignatius Loyola in 1534 with the aim of defending Catholicism against the Reformation. **2.** (sometimes not cap.) Inf., offens. a person given to subtle and equivocating arguments. [C16: from NL *Jēsuita*, from LL *Jēsus* + -ita -ITE[1]] —,**Jesu'itical** adj.

Jesus ('dʒi:zəs) n. **1.** Also called: **Jesus Christ, Jesus of Nazareth.** ?4 B.C.–?29 A.D., founder of Christianity, born in Bethlehem and brought up as a Jew. He is believed by Christians to be the Son of God and to have been miraculously conceived by the Virgin Mary, wife of Joseph. After the Last Supper with his disciples, he was betrayed by Judas and crucified. He is believed by Christians to have risen from his tomb after three days, appeared to his disciples several times, and ascended to Heaven after 40 days. **2.** Son of Sirach. 3rd century B.C., author of the Apocryphal book of Ecclesiasticus. ~interj. also **Jesus wept.** **3.** used to express intense surprise, dismay, etc. [via L from Gk *Iēsous*, from Heb. *Yeshūă'*, shortened from *Yehōshūă'* God is help, JOSHUA]

Jesus freak n. Inf. a vociferous Christian, esp. one who is evangelical and belongs to a community.

jet[1] (dʒɛt) n. **1.** a thin stream of liquid or gas forced out of a small aperture. **2.** an outlet or nozzle for emitting such a stream. **3.** a jet-propelled aircraft. ~vb. **jetting, jetted.** **4.** to issue or cause to issue in a jet: water jetted from the hose. **5.** to transport or be transported by jet aircraft. [C16: from OF *jeter* to throw, from L *jactāre* to toss about]

jet[2] (dʒɛt) n. **a.** a hard black variety of lignite that takes a brilliant polish and is used for jewellery, etc. **b.** (as modifier): jet earrings. [C14: from OF *jaiet*, from L, from Gk *lithos gagatēs* stone of *Gagai*, a town in Lycia, Asia Minor]

jet black n. **a.** a deep black colour. **b.** (as adj.): jet-black hair.

jet condenser n. a steam condenser in which steam is condensed by jets of water.

jeté (ʒə'teɪ) n. Ballet. a step in which the dancer springs from one leg and lands on the other. [F, lit.: thrown, from *jeter*; see JET[1]]

jet engine n. a gas turbine, esp. one fitted to an aircraft.

Jethro ('dʒɛθrəʊ) n. Old Testament. a Midianite priest, the father-in-law of Moses (Exodus 3:1; 4:18).

jet lag n. a general feeling of fatigue often experienced by travellers by jet aircraft who cross several time zones in relatively few hours.

jet-propelled adj. **1.** driven by jet propulsion. **2.** Inf. very fast.

jet propulsion n. **1.** propulsion by means of a jet of fluid. **2.** propulsion by means of a gas turbine, esp. when the exhaust gases provide the propulsive thrust.

jetsam ('dʒɛtsəm) n. **1.** that portion of the cargo of a vessel thrown overboard to lighten her, as during a storm. Cf. **flotsam** (sense 1). **2.** another word for **flotsam** (sense 2). [C16: shortened from JETTISON]

jet set n. **a.** a rich and fashionable social set, the members of which travel widely for pleasure. **b.** (as modifier): jet-set travellers. —'**jet,setter** n. —'**jet-,setting** n., adj.

jet stream n. **1.** Meteorol. a narrow belt of high-altitude winds moving east at high speeds. **2.** the jet of exhaust gases produced by a gas turbine, etc.

jettison ('dʒɛtɪsᵊn, -zᵊn) vb. (tr.) **1.** to abandon: to jettison old clothes. **2.** to throw overboard. ~n. **3.** another word for **jetsam** (sense 1). [C15: from OF, ult. from L *jactātiō* a tossing about]

jetton ('dʒɛtᵊn) n. a counter or token, esp. a chip used in such gambling games as roulette. [C18: from F *jeton*, from *jeter* to cast up (accounts); see JET[1]]

jetty ('dʒɛtɪ) n., pl. **-ties.** a pier, dock, groyne, mole, or other structure extending into the water from the shore. [C15: from OF *jetee* projecting part, lit.: something thrown out, from *jeter* to throw]

jeu d'esprit (French ʒø dɛspri) n., pl. **jeux d'esprit** (ʒø dɛspri). a light-hearted display of wit or cleverness, esp. in literature. [lit.: play of spirit]

Jevons ('dʒɛvᵊnz) n. **William Stanley.** 1835–82, English economist and logician: introduced the concept of total or marginal utility in The Theory of Political Economy (1871).

Jew (dʒu:) n. **1.** a member of the Semitic people who are descended from the ancient Israelites. **2.** a person whose religion is Judaism. **3.** (modifier) Offens. Jewish: a Jew boy. **4.** (sometimes not cap.) Offens. **a.** a person who drives a hard bargain. **b.** a miserly person. ~vb. **5.** (tr.; often not cap.) Offens. to drive a hard bargain with. [C12: from OF *juiu*, from L *jūdaeus*, from Gk *ioudaios*, from Heb., from *yehūdāh* JUDAH]

jewel ('dʒu:əl) n. **1.** a precious or semiprecious stone; gem. **2.** a person or thing resembling a jewel in preciousness, brilliance, etc. **3.** a gemstone used as a bearing in a watch. **4.** a piece of jewellery. ~vb. **-elling, -elled** or U.S. **-eling, -eled.** **5.** (tr.) to fit or decorate with a jewel or jewels. [C13: from OF *jouel*, ?from *jeu* game, from L *jocus*]

jewelfish ('dʒu:əl,fɪʃ) n., pl. **-fish** or **-fishes.** a beautifully coloured and popular aquarium fish native to Africa.

jeweller or U.S. **jeweler** ('dʒu:ələ) n. a person whose business is the cutting or setting of gemstones or the making or selling of jewellery.

jeweller's rouge n. a finely powdered form of ferric oxide used as a metal polish.

jewellery or U.S. **jewelry** ('dʒu:əlrɪ) n. objects that are worn for personal adornment, such as rings, necklaces, etc., considered collectively.

Jewess ('dʒu:ɪs) n. a Jewish girl or woman.

jewfish ('dʒu:,fɪʃ) n., pl. **-fish** or **-fishes.** **1.** any of various large dark fishes of warm or tropical seas. **2.** Austral. a freshwater catfish. [C17: from ?]

Jewish ('dʒu:ɪʃ) adj. **1.** of or characteristic of Jews. **2.** Offens. miserly. —'**Jewishly** adv. —'**Jewishness** n.

Jewish Autonomous Region n. an administrative division of the SE Soviet Union, in E Siberia: colonized by Jews in 1928; largely agricultural. Capital: Birobidzhan. Pop.: 211 000 (1986). Area: 36 000 sq. km (13 895 sq. miles). Also called: **Birobidzhan.**

Jew lizard n. a large Australian lizard with spiny scales round its neck.

Jewry ('dʒʊərɪ) n., pl. **-ries. 1. a.** Jews collectively. **b.** the Jewish religion or culture. **2.** a quarter of a town inhabited by Jews.

jew's-ear n. a pinky-red fungus.

jew's-harp n. a musical instrument consisting of a small lyre-shaped metal frame held between the teeth, with a steel tongue plucked with the finger.

Jezebel ('dʒɛzə,bɛl) n. **1.** Old Testament. the wife of Ahab, king of Israel. **2.** (sometimes not cap.) a shameless or scheming woman.

Jezreel ('dʒɛzrɪəl) n. Plain of. another name for **Esdraelon.** —'**Jezreel,ite** n.

Jhansi ('dʒɑ:nsɪ) n. a city in central India, in SW Uttar Pradesh: scene of a mutiny against the British in 1857. Pop.: 281 000 (1981).

Jhelum ('dʒi:ləm) n. a river in Pakistan and Kashmir, rising in W central Kashmir and flowing northwest through the Vale of Kashmir, then southwest into N West Punjab to join the Chenab River: important for irrigation, having the Mangla Dam (Pakistan), completed in 1967. Length: about 720 km (450 miles).

Jiang Qing ('dʒæŋ 'tʃɪŋ) or **Chiang Ch'ing** n. born c. 1913, Chinese Communist actress and politician; widow of Mao Tse-tung. She was a leading member of the Gang of Four.

Jiangsu ('dʒæŋ'su:) or **Kiangsu** n. a province of E China, on the Yellow Sea: consists mostly of the marshy delta of the Yangtze River, with some of China's largest cities and most densely populated areas. Capital: Nanjing. Pop.: 61 710 000 (1985). Area: 102 200 sq. km (39 860 sq. miles).

Jiangxi ('dʒæŋ'ʃi:) or **Kiangsi** n. a province of SE central China, in the basins of the Kan River and the Poyang

Lake: mineral resources include coal and tungsten. Capital: Nanchang. Pop.: 34 210 000 (1985). Area: 164 800 sq. km (64 300 sq. miles).

Jiazhou ('dʒjæ'dʒəʊ) or **Kiaochow** n. a territory of NE China, in SE Shandong province, surrounding **Jiazhou Bay** (an inlet of the Yellow Sea): leased to Germany from 1898 to 1914. Area: about 520 sq. km (200 sq. miles).

jib[1] (dʒɪb) n. **1.** Naut. any triangular sail set forward of the foremast of a vessel. **2. cut of someone's jib.** someone's manner, style, etc. [C17: from ?]

jib[2] (dʒɪb) vb. **jibbing, jibbed.** (intr.) Chiefly Brit. **1.** (often foll. by at) to be reluctant (to). **2.** (of an animal) to stop short and refuse to go forwards. **3.** Naut. a variant of **gybe.** [C19: from ?] — **'jibber** n.

jib[3] (dʒɪb) n. the projecting arm of a crane or the boom of a derrick. [C18: prob. based on GIBBET]

jib boom n. Naut. a spar forming an extension of the bowsprit.

jibe[1] (dʒaɪb) or **jib** (dʒɪb) vb., n. Naut. a variant of **gybe.**

jibe[2] (dʒaɪb) vb. a variant spelling of **gibe**[1].

jibe[3] (dʒaɪb) vb. (intr.) Inf. to agree; accord; harmonize. [C19: from ?]

Jibouti or **Jibuti** (dʒɪ'buːtɪ) n. variant spellings of **Djibouti.**

Jidda ('dʒɪdə) or **Jedda** n. a port in W Saudi Arabia, in the Western Province on the Red Sea: the diplomatic capital of the country; the port of entry for Mecca, 80 km (50 miles) east. Pop.: 1 500 000 (1983).

jiffy ('dʒɪfɪ) or **jiff** n., pl. **jiffies** or **jiffs.** Inf. a very short time: wait a jiffy. [C18: from ?]

Jiffy bag n. Trademark. a large padded envelope.

jig (dʒɪg) n. **1.** any of several old rustic kicking and leaping dances. **2.** a piece of music composed for or in the rhythm of this dance. **3.** a mechanical device designed to hold and locate a component during machining. **4.** Angling. any of various spinning lures that wobble when drawn through the water. **5.** Also called: **jigger.** Mining. a device for separating ore or coal from waste material by agitation in water. ~vb. **jigging, jigged. 6.** to dance (a jig). **7.** to jerk or cause to jerk up and down rapidly. **8.** (often foll. by up) to fit or be fitted in a jig. **9.** (tr.) to drill or cut (a workpiece) in a jig. **10.** (tr.) Mining. to separate ore or coal from waste material using a jig. [C16: from ?]

jigger[1] ('dʒɪgə) n. **1.** a person or thing that jigs. **2.** Golf. (formerly) an iron club, usually No. 4. **3.** any of a number of mechanical devices having a vibratory motion. **4.** a light lifting tackle used on ships. **5.** a small glass, esp. for whisky. **6.** Billiards. another word for **bridge**[1]. **7.** N.Z. a light hand- or power-propelled vehicle used on railway lines.

jigger[2] or **jigger flea** ('dʒɪgə) n. another name for the **chigoe** (sense 1).

jiggered ('dʒɪgəd) adj. (postpositive) Inf. damned; blowed: I'm jiggered if he'll get away with it. [C19: prob. euphemism for buggered; see BUGGER]

jiggermast ('dʒɪgə,mɑːst) n. Naut. any small mast on a sailing vessel.

jiggery-pokery ('dʒɪgərɪ'pəʊkərɪ) n. Inf., chiefly Brit. dishonest or deceitful behaviour. [C19: from Scot. dialect joukery-pawkery]

jiggle ('dʒɪgəl) vb. **1.** to move or cause to move up and down or to and fro with a short jerky motion. ~n. **2.** a short jerky motion. [C19: frequentative of JIG] — **'jiggly** adj.

jigsaw ('dʒɪg,sɔː) n. **1.** a mechanical saw with a fine steel blade for cutting intricate curves in sheets of material. **2.** See **jigsaw puzzle.** [C19: from JIG (to jerk up and down rapidly) + SAW[1]]

jigsaw puzzle n. a puzzle in which the player has to reassemble a picture that has been cut into irregularly shaped interlocking pieces.

jihad or **jehad** (dʒɪ'hæd) n. Islam. a holy war against infidels undertaken by Muslims. [C19: from Ar. jihād a conflict]

Jilin ('dʒiː'lɪn) or **Kirin** n. **1.** a province of NE China, in central Manchuria. Capital: Changchun. Pop.: 22 840 000 (1985). Area: 187 000 sq. km (72 930 sq. miles). **2.** Also called: **Chi-lin** ('tʃiː'lɪn) a river port in NE China, in N central Jilin province on the Songhua River. Pop.: 1 140 000 (1986).

Jilolo (dʒaɪ'ləʊləʊ) n. a variant spelling of **Djailolo.** See **Halmahera.**

Jilong ('dʒiː'lʊŋ) n. the Pinyin transliteration of the Chinese name for **Chilung.**

jilt (dʒɪlt) vb. **1.** (tr.) to leave or reject (a lover), esp. without previous warning. ~n. **2.** a woman who jilts a lover. [C17: from dialect jillet flighty girl, dim. of name Gill]

jim crow ('dʒɪm 'krəʊ) n. (often caps.) U.S. **1. a.** the policy or practice of segregating Negroes. **b.** (as modifier): jim-crow laws. **2.** a derogatory term for **Negro. 3.** an implement for bending iron bars or rails. [C19: from Jim Crow, name of song used as the basis of an act by Thomas Rice (1808–60), American entertainer] — **'jim-'crowism** n.

Jiménez (Spanish xi'menθ) n. **Juan Ramón** (xwan ra'mɔn). 1881–1958, Spanish lyric poet. His most famous work is Platero y yo (1917), a prose poem: Nobel prize for literature 1956.

Jiménez de Cisneros (Spanish xi'meneð ðe θiz'nerɔs) n. **Francisco** (fran'θisko). 1436–1517, Spanish cardinal and statesman; regent of Castile (1506–07) and Spain (1516–17) and grand inquisitor for Castile and León (1507–17). Also called: **Ximenes de Cisneros, Ximenez de Cisneros.**

jimjams ('dʒɪm,dʒæmz) pl. n. **1.** Sl. delirium tremens. **2.** a state of nervous tension or anxiety. [C19: whimsical formation based on JAM[1]]

jimmy ('dʒɪmɪ) n., pl. **-mies,** vb. **-mying, -mied.** a U.S. variant of **jemmy.**

Jinan ('dʒiː'næn), **Chinan,** or **Tsinan** n. an industrial city in NE China, capital of Shandong province; probably over 3000 years old. Pop.: 1 430 000 (1986).

Jingdezhen ('dʒɪŋ'dedʒen), **Fowliang,** or **Fou-liang** n. a city in SE China, in NE Jiangxi province east of Lake Poyang: famous for its porcelain industry, established in the sixth century. Pop.: 559 300 (1985 est.).

Jinghis Khan ('dʒɪŋgɪs 'kɑːn) n. See **Genghis Khan.**

jingle ('dʒɪŋgəl) vb. **1.** to ring or cause to ring lightly and repeatedly. **2.** (intr.) to sound in a manner suggestive of jingling: a jingling verse. ~n. **3.** a sound of metal jingling. **4.** a rhythmical verse, etc., esp. one used in advertising. [C16: prob. imit.] — **'jingly** adj.

jingo ('dʒɪŋgəʊ) n., pl. **-goes. 1.** a loud and bellicose patriot. **2.** jingoism. **3. by jingo.** an exclamation of surprise. [C17: orig. ? euphemism for Jesus; applied to bellicose patriots after the use of by Jingo! in a 19th-cent. song]

jingoism ('dʒɪŋgəʊ,ɪzəm) n. the belligerent spirit or foreign policy of jingoes. — **'jingoist** n., adj. — **jingo'istic** adj.

Jinja ('dʒɪndʒə) n. a town in Uganda, on the N shore of Lake Victoria. Pop.: 45 060 (1980).

Jinjiang ('dʒɪn'dʒɪæn), **Chinkiang,** or **Cheng-chiang** n. a port in E China, in S Jiangsu at the confluence of the Yangtze River and the Grand Canal. Pop.: 150 000 (1982).

jink (dʒɪŋk) vb. **1.** (intr.) to move swiftly or turn in order to dodge. ~n. **2.** a jinking movement. [C18: of Scot. origin, imit. of swift movement]

jinker ('dʒɪŋkə) n. Austral. a vehicle for transporting timber, consisting of a tractor and two sets of wheels for supporting the logs. [from ?]

jinks (dʒɪŋks) pl. n. boisterous or mischievous play (esp. in **high jinks.**) [C18: from ?]

jinn (dʒɪn) n. (often functioning as sing.) the plural of **jinni.**

Jinnah ('dʒɪnə) n. **Mohammed Ali.** 1876–1948, Indian Muslim statesman. He campaigned for the partition of India against Hindu and Muslim states, becoming first governor general of Pakistan (1947–48).

jinni, jinnee, or **djinni** (dʒɪ'niː) n., pl. **jinn** or **djinn** (dʒɪn). a spirit in Muslim mythology who could assume human or animal form and influence man by supernatural powers. [C17: from Ar.]

jinrikisha, jinricksha, or **jinrickshaw** (dʒɪn'rɪkʃɔ:) n. another name for **rickshaw.** [C19: from Japanese, from jin man + riki power + sha carriage]

jinx (dʒɪŋks) n. **1.** an unlucky force, person, or thing. ~vb. **2.** (tr.) to be or put a jinx on. [C20: ?from NL Jynx, genus name of the wryneck, from Gk iunx wryneck, a bird used in magic]

Jinzhou ('dʒɪn'dʒəʊ), **Chin-Chou,** or **Chin-chow** n. a city in NE China, in SW Liaoning province. Pop.: 712 000 (1983 est.). Former name (1913–47): **Chin-hsien.**

jitter ('dʒɪtə) Inf. ~vb. **1.** (intr.) to be anxious or nervous. ~n. **2. the jitters.** nervousness and anxiety. [C20: from ?] — **'jittery** adj. — **'jitteriness** n.

jitterbug ('dʒɪtə,bʌg) n. **1.** a fast jerky American dance, usually to a jazz accompaniment, that was popular in the 1940s. **2.** a person who dances the jitterbug. ~vb. **-bugging, -bugged. 3.** (intr.) to perform such a dance.

jiujitsu *or* **jiujutsu** (dʒuːˈdʒɪtsuː) *n.* a variant spelling of **jujitsu.**

jive (dʒaɪv) *n.* **1.** a style of lively and jerky dance, popular esp. in the 1940s and 1950s. **2.** *Sl., chiefly U.S.* **a.** misleading or deceptive talk. **b.** *(as modifier): jive talk.* ~*vb.* **3.** *(intr.)* to dance the jive. **4.** *Sl., chiefly U.S.* to mislead; tell lies (to). [C20: from ?] — **'jiver** *n.*

Joab ('dʒəʊæb) *n. Old Testament.* the successful commander of King David's forces and the slayer of Abner and Absalom (II Samuel 2:18–23; 3:24–27; 18:14–15).

Joachim *n.* **1.** ('jɔːaxɪm). **Joseph** ('jɔːzɛf). 1831–1907, Hungarian violinist and composer. **2.** ('dʒəʊəkɪm). **Saint.** 1st century B.C., traditionally the father of the Virgin Mary; feast day: July 26.

Joan (dʒəʊn) *n.* known as *the Fair Maid of Kent.* 1328–85, wife of Edward the Black Prince; mother of Richard II.

Joan of Arc *n.* **Saint**, known as *the Maid of Orléans;* French name *Jeanne d'Arc.* ?1412–31, French national heroine, who led the army that relieved Orléans in the Hundred Years' War, enabling Charles VII to be crowned at Reims (1429). After being captured (1430), she was burnt at the stake as a heretic. She was canonized in 1920. Feast day: May 30.

João Pessoa (*Portuguese* 'ʒuəʊm pe'soa) *n.* a port in NE Brazil, capital of Paraíba state. Pop.: 397 715 (1985).

job (dʒɒb) *n.* **1.** an individual piece of work or task. **2.** an occupation. **3.** an object worked on or a result produced from working. **4.** a duty or responsibility: *her job was to cook the dinner.* **5.** *Inf.* a difficult task or problem: *I had a job to contact him.* **6.** a state of affairs: *make the best of a bad job.* **7.** *Inf.* a particular type of something: *a four-wheel drive job.* **8.** *Inf.* a crime, esp. a robbery. **9.** *Computers.* a unit of work for a computer. **10. jobs for the boys.** jobs given to or created for allies or favourites. **11. just the job.** exactly what was required. **12. on the job.** actively engaged in one's employment. ~*vb.* **jobbing, jobbed. 13.** *(intr.)* to work by the piece or at casual jobs. **14.** to make a private profit out of (a public office, etc.). **15.** *(intr.;* usually foll. by *in)* **a.** to buy and sell (goods or services) as a middleman: *he jobs in government surplus.* **b.** *Brit.* to buy and sell stocks and shares as a stockjobber. **16.** *Austral. sl.* to punch. [C16: from ?] — **'jobless** *adj.*

Job (dʒəʊb) *n.* **1.** *Old Testament.* **a.** a Jewish patriarch, who maintained his faith in God in spite of the afflictions sent by God to test him. **b.** the book containing Job's pleas to God under these afflictions, attempted explanations of them by his friends, and God's reply to him. **2.** any person who withstands great suffering without despairing.

jobber ('dʒɒbə) *n.* **1.** *Brit.* short for **stockjobber** (sense 1). See also **market maker. 2.** a person who jobs.

jobbery ('dʒɒbərɪ) *n.* the practice of making private profit out of a public office.

jobbing ('dʒɒbɪŋ) *adj.* working by the piece, not regularly employed: *a jobbing gardener.*

Jobcentre ('dʒɒb,sɛntə) *or* **job centre** *n. Brit.* any of a number of government offices having premises situated in the main shopping area of a town in which people seeking jobs can consult displayed advertisements.

job description *n.* a formal description of the duties and responsibilities involved in a job, esp. as given to applicants for the job.

job lot *n.* **1.** a miscellaneous collection of articles sold as a lot. **2.** a collection of cheap or trivial items.

job satisfaction *n.* the extent to which the desires and hopes of a worker are fulfilled as a result of his work.

Job's comforter *n.* a person who, while purporting to give sympathy, succeeds only in adding to distress.

job sharing *n.* the division of a job between two or more people such that each covers the same job for complementary parts of the day or week. —**job share** *n.*

jobsworth ('dʒɒbz,wɜːθ) *n. Inf.* a person in a position of minor authority who invokes the letter of the law in order to avoid any action requiring initiative, cooperation, etc. [C20: from *it's more than my job's worth to . . .*]

Jocasta (dʒəʊ'kæstə) *n. Greek myth.* a queen of Thebes, the wife of Laius, who married Oedipus without either of them knowing he was her son.

Jochum (*German* 'jɔxʊm) *n.* **Eugen** ('ɔʏgeːn). 1902–87, German orchestral conductor.

jock (dʒɒk) *n. Inf.* short for **jockey** or **jockstrap.**

Jock (dʒɒk) *n.* a slang word or name for a **Scot.**

jockey ('dʒɒkɪ) *n.* **1.** a person who rides horses in races, esp. as a profession. ~*vb.* **2. a.** *(tr.)* to ride (a horse) in a

race. **b.** *(intr.)* to ride as a jockey. **3.** *(intr.:* often foll. by *for)* to try to obtain an advantage by manoeuvring (esp. in **jockey for position**). **4.** to trick or cheat (a person). [C16 (in the sense: lad): from name *Jock* + -EY]

jockstrap ('dʒɒk,stræp) *n.* an elasticated belt with a pouch worn by men, esp. athletes, to support the genitals. Also called: **athletic support.** [C20: from sl. *jock* penis + STRAP]

jocose (dʒə'kəʊs) *adj.* characterized by humour. [C17: from L *jocōsus* given to jesting, from *jocus* joke] —**jo'cosely** *adv.* —**jocosity** (dʒə'kɒsɪtɪ) *n.*

jocular ('dʒɒkjʊlə) *adj.* **1.** characterized by joking and good humour. **2.** meant lightly or humorously. [C17: from L *joculāris,* from *joculus* little JOKE] —**jocularity** (,dʒɒkjʊ'lærɪtɪ) *n.* —**'jocularly** *adv.*

jocund ('dʒɒkənd) *adj.* of a humorous temperament; merry. [C14: from LL *jocundus,* from L *jūcundus* pleasant, from *juvāre* to please] —**jocundity** (dʒəʊ'kʌndɪtɪ) *n.* —**'jocundly** *adv.*

Jodhpur (,dʒɒd'pʊə) *n.* **1.** a former state of NW India, one of the W Rajputana states: now part of Rajasthan. **2.** a walled city in NW India, in W Rajasthan: university (1962). Pop.: 493 609 (1981). —**Jodhpuri** ('dʒɒdpʊrɪ) *adj.*

jodhpurs ('dʒɒdpəz) *pl. n.* riding breeches, loose-fitting around the hips and tight-fitting from the thighs to the ankles. [C19: from JODHPUR]

Joe Blake (bleɪk) *n. Austral. sl.* **1.** a snake. **2. the Joe Blakes.** the DT's.

Joe Bloggs (blɒgz) *n. Brit. sl.* an average or typical man. U.S., Canad., and Austral. equivalent: **Joe Blow.**

Joel ('dʒəʊəl) *n. Old Testament.* **1.** a Hebrew prophet. **2.** the book containing his oracles.

Joe Public *n. Sl.* the general public.

joes (dʒəʊz) *pl. n.* **the.** *Austral. inf.* a fit of depression. [short for *the Joe Blakes*]

joey ('dʒəʊɪ) *n. Austral. inf.* **1.** a young kangaroo. **2.** a young animal or child. [C19: from Abor.]

Joffre (*French* ʒɔfrə) *n.* **Joseph Jacques Césaire** (ʒozɛf ʒak sezɛr). 1852–1931, French marshal. He commanded the French army (1914–16) and was largely responsible for the Allies' victory at the Marne (1914), which halted the German advance on Paris.

jog (dʒɒg) *vb.* **jogging, jogged.** **1.** *(intr.)* to run or move slowly or at a jog trot, esp. for physical exercise. **2.** *(intr.;* foll. by *on* or *along)* to continue in a plodding way. **3.** *(tr.)* to jar or nudge slightly. **4.** *(tr.)* to remind: *jog my memory.* ~*n.* **5.** the act of jogging. **6.** a slight jar or nudge. **7.** a jogging motion; trot. [C14: prob. var. of *shog* to shake]

jogger ('dʒɒgə) *n.* **1.** a person who runs at a jog trot over some distance for exercise. **2.** *N.Z.* a cart with rubber tyres used on farms.

jogging ('dʒɒgɪŋ) *n.* a slow run or trot, esp. as a keep-fit exercise.

joggle ('dʒɒgəl) *vb.* **1.** to shake or move (someone or something) with a slightly jolting motion. **2.** *(tr.)* to join or fasten (two pieces of building material) by means of a joggle. ~*n.* **3.** the act of joggling. **4.** a slight irregular shake. **5.** a joint between two pieces of building material by means of a projection on one piece that fits into a notch in the other. [C16: frequentative of JOG] —**'joggler** *n.*

Jogjakarta (,dʒəʊgjɑː'kɑːtɑː, ,dʒɒg-) a variant spelling of **Yogyakarta.**

jog trot *n.* **1.** an easy bouncy gait, esp. of a horse, midway between a walk and a trot. **2.** a regular way of living or doing something.

Johannesburg (dʒəʊ'hænɪs,bɜːg) *n.* a city in South Africa, in S Transvaal: South Africa's largest city and chief industrial centre; grew with the establishment in 1886 of the gold-mining industry; University of Witwatersrand (1922). Pop.: 1 713 000 (1983).

john (dʒɒn) *n. Chiefly U.S. & Canad.* a slang word for **lavatory.** [C20: special use of the name]

John (dʒɒn) *n.* **1.** *New Testament.* **a.** the apostle John, the son of Zebedee, identified with the author of the fourth Gospel, three epistles, and the book of Revelation. **b.** the fourth Gospel. **c.** any of three epistles (in full **The First, Second,** and **Third Epistles of John**). **2.** See **John the Baptist. 3.** known as *John Lackland.* 1167–1216, king of England (1199–1216); son of Henry II. He succeeded to the throne on the death of his brother Richard I, having previously tried to usurp the throne. In 1215 he was compelled by the barons to sign the Magna Carta. **4. Augustus (Edwin).** 1878–1961, Welsh painter, esp. of portraits. **5. Barry.** born 1945, British Rugby Union footballer: halfback for Wales (1966–72) and the British Lions (1968–71). **6. Elton (Hercules).** original name *Reginald Dwight.* born 1947, English rock pianist, composer, and singer.

John I *n.* called *the Great.* 1357–1433, king of Portugal (1385–1433). He secured independence for Portugal by his victory over Castile (1385) and initiated Portuguese overseas expansion.

John III *n.* surnamed *Sobieski.* 1624–96, king of Poland (1674–96). He raised the Turkish siege of Vienna (1683).

John XXII *n.* original name *Jacques Duèse.* ?1244–1334, pope (1316–34), residing at Avignon; involved in a long conflict with the Holy Roman Emperor Louis IV and opposed the Franciscan Spirituals.

John XXIII *n.* original name *Angelo Giuseppe Roncalli.* 1881–1963, pope (1958–63). He promoted ecumenicalism and world peace and summoned the second Vatican Council (1962–65).

John Barleycorn *n. Usually humorous.* the personification of alcoholic drink.

John Bull *n.* **1.** a personification of England or the English people. **2.** a typical Englishman. [C18: name of a character intended to be representative of the English nation in *The History of John Bull* (1712) by John Arbuthnot]

John Chrysostom ('krɪsəstəm) *n. Saint.* ?345–407 A.D., Greek bishop and theologian; one of the Fathers of the Greek Church, noted for his eloquence. Feast day: Sept. 13.

John Doe *n.* See **Doe.**

John Dory ('dɔːrɪ) *n.* a European dory (the fish), having a deep compressed body and massive mobile jaws. [C18: from name *John* + DORY[1]; on the model of DOE]

John Hop *n. Austral. sl.* a policeman. [rhyming sl. for COP[1]]

johnny ('dʒɒnɪ) *n., pl.* **-nies.** *Brit. inf. (often cap.)* a man or boy; chap.

Johnny Canuck ('dʒɒnɪ kə'nʌk) *n. Canad.* **1.** an informal name for a **Canadian. 2.** a personification of Canada.

Johnny-come-lately *n., pl.* **Johnny-come-latelies** or **Johnnies-come-lately.** *Sl.* a brash newcomer, novice, or recruit.

John of Austria *n.* called *Don John.* 1547–78, Spanish general: defeated the Turks at Lepanto (1571).

John of Damascus *n. Saint.* ?675–749 A.D., Syrian theologian, who defended image worship against the iconoclasts. Feast day: Dec. 4.

John of Gaunt (gɔːnt) *n.* Duke of Lancaster. 1340–99, son of Edward III: virtual ruler of England during the last years of his father's reign and during Richard II's minority. [*Gaunt,* variant of GHENT, where he was born]

John of Leyden ('laɪdⁿn) *n.* original name *Jan Bockelson.* ?1509–36, Dutch Anabaptist leader. He established a theocracy in Münster (1534) but was tortured to death after the city was recaptured (1535) by its prince bishop.

John of Salisbury *n.* died 1180, English ecclesiastic and scholar; bishop of Chartres (1176–80). He supported Thomas à Becket against Henry II.

John of the Cross *n. Saint.* original name *Juan de Yepis y Alvarez.* 1542–91, Spanish Carmelite monk, poet, and mystic. He founded the Discalced Carmelites with Saint Teresa (1568). Feast day: Dec. 14.

John o'Groat's (ə'grəʊts) *n.* a village at the northeasternmost tip of the Scottish mainland: considered to be the northernmost point of the mainland of Great Britain although Dunnet Head, slightly to the west, lies further north. See also **Land's End.**

John Paul I *n.* original name *Albino Luciani.* 1912–78, pope (1978) whose brief 33-day reign was characterized by a simpler papal style and anticipated an emphasis on pastoral rather than administrative priorities.

John Paul II *n.* original name *Karol Wojtyla.* born 1920, pope from 1978, born in Poland: the first non-Italian to be elected since 1522.

Johns (dʒɒnz) *n.* **Jasper.** born 1930, U.S. artist, noted for his collages and constructions.

Johnson ('dʒɒnsⁿn) *n.* **1. Amy.** 1903–41, English flier, who made several record flights, including those to Australia (1930) and to Cape Town and back (1936). **2. Andrew.** 1808–75, U.S. Democrat statesman; 17th president of the U.S. (1865–69). His lenience towards the South after the American Civil War led to strong opposition from radical Republicans, who tried to impeach him. **3. Jack.** 1878–1946, U.S. boxer; world heavyweight champion

(1908–15). **4. Lyndon Baines,** known as *LBJ.* 1908–73, U.S. Democrat statesman; 36th president of the U.S. (1963–69). His administration carried the Civil Rights Acts of 1964 and 1965, but he lost popularity by increasing U.S. involvement in the Vietnam war. **5. Robert.** ?1898–1937, U.S. blues singer and guitarist. **6. Samuel,** known as *Dr. Johnson.* 1709–84, English lexicographer, critic, and conversationalist, whose greatest works are his *Dictionary* (1755), his edition of Shakespeare (1765), and his *Lives of the Most Eminent English Poets* (1779–81). His fame, however, rests as much on Boswell's biography of him as on his literary output.

Johnsonian (dʒɒn'səʊnɪən) *adj.* of, relating to, or characteristic of Samuel Johnson, his works, or his style of writing.

John the Baptist *n. New Testament.* the son of Zacharias and Elizabeth and the cousin and forerunner of Jesus, whom he baptized. He was beheaded by Herod (Matthew 14:1–2).

Johore (dʒəʊ'hɔː) *n.* a state of Malaysia, on the S Malay Peninsula: mostly forested, with large swamps; bauxite- and iron-mining. Capital: Johore Bahru. Pop.: 1 601 504 (1980). Area: 18 984 sq. km (7330 sq. miles).

Johore Bahru ('baːruː) *n.* a city in S Malaysia, capital of Johore state: important trading centre, situated at the sole crossing point of **Johore Strait** (between Malaya and Singapore Island). Pop.: 249 880 (1980).

joie de vivre *French.* (ʒwa də vivrə) *n.* joy of living; enjoyment of life; ebullience.

join (dʒɔɪn) *vb.* **1.** to come or bring together. **2.** to become a member of (a club, etc.). **3.** (*intr.;* often foll. by *with*) to become associated or allied. **4.** (*intr.;* usually foll. by *in*) to take part. **5.** (*tr.*) to meet (someone) as a companion. **6.** (*tr.*) to become part of. **7.** (*tr.*) to unite (two people) in marriage. **8.** (*tr.*) *Geom.* to connect with a straight line or a curve. **9. join hands. a.** to hold one's own hands together. **b.** (of two people) to hold each other's hands. **c.** (usually foll. by *with*) to work together in an enterprise. ~*n.* **10.** a joint; seam. **11.** the act of joining. ~See also **join up.** [C13: from OF, from L *jungere* to yoke]

joinder ('dʒɔɪndə) *n.* **1.** the act of joining, esp. in legal contexts. **2.** *Law.* **a.** (in pleading) the stage at which the parties join issue (**joinder of issue**). **b.** the joining of two or more persons as coplaintiffs or codefendants (**joinder of parties**). [C17: from F *joindre* to JOIN]

joiner ('dʒɔɪnə) *n.* **1.** *Chiefly Brit.* a person skilled in making finished woodwork, such as windows and stairs. **2.** a person or thing that joins. **3.** *Inf.* a person who joins many clubs, etc.

joinery ('dʒɔɪnərɪ) *n.* **1.** the skill or craft of a joiner. **2.** work made by a joiner.

joint (dʒɔɪnt) *n.* **1.** a junction of two or more parts or objects. **2.** *Anat.* the junction between two or more bones. **3.** the point of connection between movable parts in invertebrates. **4.** the part of a plant stem from which a branch or leaf grows. **5.** one of the parts into which a carcass of meat is cut by the butcher, esp. for roasting. **6.** *Geol.* a crack in a rock along which no displacement has occurred. **7.** *Sl.* **a.** a bar or nightclub. **b.** *Often facetious.* a dwelling or meeting place. **8.** *Sl.* a cannabis cigarette. **9. out of joint. a.** dislocated. **b.** out of order. ~*adj.* **10.** shared by or belonging to two or more: *joint property.* **11.** created by combined effort. **12.** sharing with others or with one another: *joint rulers.* ~*vb.* (*tr.*) **13.** to provide with or fasten by a joint or joints. **14.** to plane the edge of (a board, etc.) into the correct shape for a joint. **15.** to cut or divide (meat, etc.) into joints. —'**jointed** *adj.* —'**jointly** *adv.*

joint account *n.* a bank account registered in the name of two or more persons, any of whom may make deposits and withdrawals.

joint stock *n.* capital funds held in common and usually divided into shares.

joint-stock company *n.* **1.** *Brit.* a business enterprise characterized by the sharing of ownership between shareholders, whose liability is limited. **2.** *U.S.* a business enterprise whose owners are issued shares of transferable stock but do not enjoy limited liability.

jointure ('dʒɔɪntʃə) *n. Law.* **a.** provision made by a husband for his wife by settling property upon her at marriage for her use after his death. **b.** the property so settled. [C14: from OF, from L *junctūra* a joining]

join up *vb.* (*adv.*) **1.** (*intr.*) to become a member of a military or other organization; enlist. **2.** (often foll. by *with*) to unite or connect.

Joinville (*French* ʒwɛvil) *n.* **Jean de** (ʒɑ̃ də). ?1224–1317, French chronicler, noted for his *Histoire de Saint Louis* (1309).

joist (dʒɔɪst) *n.* a beam made of timber, steel, or reinforced concrete, used in the construction of floors, roofs, etc. [C14: from OF *giste* beam supporting a bridge, from Vulgar L *jacitum* (unattested) support, from *jacēre* to lie]

jojoba (həʊˈhəʊbə) *n.* a shrub or small tree of SW North America that has edible seeds containing a valuable oil: used in cosmetics.

joke (dʒəʊk) *n.* **1.** a humorous anecdote. **2.** something that is said or done for fun. **3.** a ridiculous or humorous circumstance. **4.** a person or thing inspiring ridicule or amusement. **5. no joke.** something very serious. ~*vb.* **6.** (*intr.*) to tell jokes. **7.** (*intr.*) to speak or act facetiously. **8.** to make fun of (someone). **9. joking apart.** seriously: said after there has been joking in a discussion. [C17: from L *jocus* a jest] —**'jokey** or **'joky** *adj.* —**'jokingly** *adv.*

joker (ˈdʒəʊkə) *n.* **1.** a person who jokes, esp. in an obnoxious manner. **2.** *Sl.* a person. **3.** an extra playing card in a pack, which in many card games can rank above any other card.

Jokjakarta (ˌdʒəʊkjɑːˈkɑːtɑː, ˌdʒɒk-) *n.* a variant spelling of **Yogyakarta**.

Joliot-Curie (*French* ʒɔljɔkyri) *n.* **Jean-Frédéric** (ʒɑ̃frederik), 1900–58, and his wife, **Irène** (irɛn), 1897–1956, French physicists: shared the Nobel prize for chemistry in 1935 for discovering artificial radioactivity.

jollify (ˈdʒɒlɪˌfaɪ) *vb.* **-fying, -fied.** to be or cause to be jolly. —**ˌjollifiˈcation** *n.*

jollity (ˈdʒɒlɪtɪ) *n., pl.* **-ties.** the condition of being jolly.

jolly (ˈdʒɒlɪ) *adj.* **-lier, -liest. 1.** full of good humour. **2.** having or provoking gaiety and merrymaking. **3.** pleasing. ~*adv.* **4.** *Brit.* (intensifier): *you're jolly nice.* ~*vb.* **-lying, -lied.** (*tr.*) *Inf.* **5.** (often foll. by *up* or *along*) to try to make or keep (someone) cheerful. **6.** to make good-natured fun of. [C14: from OF *jolif*, prob. from ON *jól* YULE] —**'jolliness** *n.*

jolly boat *n.* a small boat used as a utility tender for a vessel. [C18 *jolly* prob. from Danish *jolle* YAWL]

Jolly Roger *n.* the traditional pirate flag, consisting of a white skull and crossbones on a black field.

Jolo (həʊˈləʊ) *n.* an island in the SW Philippines: the main island of the Sulu Archipelago. Pop.: 360 588 (1980). Area: 893 sq. km (345 sq. miles).

Jolson (ˈdʒəʊlsən) *n.* **Al,** real name *Asa Yoelson.* 1886–1950, U.S. singer and film actor, born in Russia; star of the first talking picture *The Jazz Singer* (1927).

jolt (dʒəʊlt) *vb.* **1.** (*tr.*) to bump against with a jarring blow. **2.** to move in a jolting manner. **3.** (*tr.*) to surprise or shock. ~*n.* **4.** a sudden jar or blow. **5.** an emotional shock. [C16: prob. blend of dialect *jot* to jerk & dialect *joll* to bump]

Jon. *Bible. abbrev. for* Jonah.

Jonah (ˈdʒəʊnə) *or* **Jonas** (ˈdʒəʊnəs) *n.* **1.** *Old Testament.* a Hebrew prophet who, having been thrown overboard from a ship was swallowed by a great fish and vomited onto dry land. **2.** a person believed to bring bad luck to those around him.

Jonathan *n. Old Testament.* the son of Saul and David's close friend, who was killed in battle (I Samuel 31; II Samuel 1:19–26).

Jones (dʒəʊnz) *n.* **1. Daniel.** 1881–1967, English phonetician. **2. Daniel.** born 1912, Welsh composer. He has written nine symphonies and much chamber music. **3. David.** 1895–1974, English painter, poet, and novelist: his highly original literary works include *In Parenthesis* (1937), a novel of World War I, and the religious poem *The Anathemata* (1952). **4. Inigo** (ˈɪnɪɡəʊ). 1573–1652, English architect and theatrical designer, who introduced Palladianism to England. His buildings include the Banqueting Hall of Whitehall. He also designed the settings for court masques, being the first to use the proscenium arch and movable scenery in England. **5. James Larkin,** known as *Jack Jones.* born 1913, English trades union leader; general secretary of the Transport and General Workers' Union (1969–78). **6. John Paul.** 1747–92, American naval commander in the War of Independence. **7. Robert Tyre,** known as *Bobby Jones.* 1902–71, U.S. golfer.

jongleur (*French* ʒɔ̃glœr) *n.* (in medieval France) an itinerant minstrel. [C18: from OF *jogleour*, from L *joculātor* jester]

Jönköping (*Swedish* ˈjœntʃɔːpiŋ) *n.* a city in S Sweden, on the S shore of Lake Vättern: scene of the conclusion of peace between Sweden and Denmark in 1809. Pop.: 108 235 (1986).

jonquil (ˈdʒɒŋkwɪl) *n.* a Eurasian variety of narcissus with long fragrant yellow or white short-tubed flowers. [C17: from F *jonquille*, from Sp. *junquillo*, dim. of *junco* reed]

Jonson (ˈdʒɒnsən) *n.* **Ben.** 1572–1637, English dramatist and poet, who developed the "comedy of humours", in which each character is used to satirize one particular humour or temperament. His plays include *Volpone* (1606), *The Alchemist* (1610), and *Bartholomew Fair* (1614), and he also wrote court masques.

Joplin (ˈdʒɒplɪn) *n.* **1. Janis.** 1943–70, U.S. rock singer, noted for her hoarse and passionate style. Her albums include *Cheap Thrills* (1968) and *Pearl* (1971). **2. Scott.** 1868–1917, U.S. pianist and composer: creator of ragtime.

Joppa (ˈdʒɒpə) *n.* the biblical name of **Jaffa**, the port from which Jonah embarked (Jonah 1:3).

Jordaens (*Flemish* jɔrˈdɑːns) *n.* **Jacob** (ˈjaːkɔp). 1593–1678, Flemish painter, noted for his naturalistic depiction of peasant scenes.

Jordan (ˈdʒɔːdən) *n.* **1.** a kingdom in SW Asia: coextensive with the biblical Moab, Gilead, and Edom; made a League of Nations mandate and emirate under British control in 1922 and became an independent kingdom in 1946; territories west of the River Jordan and the Jordanian part of Jerusalem were occupied by Israel after the war of 1967. It contains part of the Great Rift Valley and consists mostly of desert. Language: Arabic. Religion: mostly Sunni Muslim. Currency: dinar. Capital: Amman. Pop.: 3 958 000 (1988 est.). Area: 89 185 sq. km (34 434 sq. miles). Official name: **Hashemite Kingdom of Jordan.** Former name (1922–49): **Trans-Jordan. 2.** the chief and only perennial river of Israel and Jordan, rising in several headstreams in Syria and Lebanon, and flowing south through the Sea of Galilee to the Dead Sea: occupies the N end of the Great Rift Valley system and lies mostly below sea level. Length: over 320 km (200 miles). —**Jordanian** (dʒɔːˈdeɪnɪən) *adj., n.*

jorum (ˈdʒɔːrəm) *n.* a large drinking bowl or vessel or its contents. [C18: prob. after *Jorum*, who brought vessels of silver, gold, and brass to King David (II Samuel 8:10)]

Jos (dʒɒs) *n.* a city in central Nigeria, capital of Plateau state on the **Jos Plateau:** major centre of the tin-mining industry. Pop.: 149 000 (1983 est.).

Joseph (ˈdʒəʊzɪf) *n.* **1.** *Old Testament.* **a.** the eleventh son of Jacob and one of the 12 patriarchs of Israel (Genesis 30:2–24). **b.** either or both of two tribes descended from his sons Ephraim and Manasseh. **2.** *New Testament.* the husband of Mary the mother of Jesus (Matthew 1:16–25).

Joseph II *n.* 1741–90, Holy Roman emperor (1765–90); son of Francis I. He ruled Austria jointly with his mother, Maria Theresa, until her death (1780). He reorganized taxation, abolished serfdom, curtailed the feudal power of the nobles, and asserted his independence from the pope.

Joseph Bonaparte Gulf *n.* an inlet of the Timor Sea in N Australia. Width: 360 km (225 miles).

Josephine (ˈdʒəʊzəˌfiːn) *n.* **Empress,** previous name *Joséphine de Beauharnais;* real name *Marie Joséphine Tascher de la Pagerie.* 1763–1814, empress of France as wife of Napoleon Bonaparte (1796–1809).

Joseph of Arimathea (ˌærɪməˈθiːə) *n. New Testament.* a wealthy member of the Sanhedrin, who obtained the body of Jesus after the Crucifixion and laid it in his own tomb (Matthew 27:57–60).

Josephus (dʒəʊˈsiːfəs) *n.* **Flavius** (ˈfleɪvɪəs). real name *Joseph ben Matthias.* ?37–?100 A.D., Jewish historian and general; author of *History of the Jewish War* and *Antiquities of the Jews.*

josh (dʒɒʃ) *Sl., chiefly U.S. & Canad.* ~*vb.* **1.** to tease (someone) in a bantering way. ~*n.* **2.** a teasing joke. [C19: ?from JOKE, infl. by BOSH] —**'josher** *n.*

Josh. *Bible. abbrev. for* Joshua.

Joshua (ˈdʒɒʃʊə) *n. Old Testament.* **1.** Moses' successor, who led the Israelites in the conquest of Canaan. **2.** the book recounting his deeds. Douay spelling: **Josue** (ˈdʒɒsjuɪ).

Josiah (dʒəʊˈsaɪə) *n.* died ?609 B.C., king of Judah (?640–?609). After the discovery of a book of law (probably Deuteronomy) in the Temple he began a programme of religious reform. Douay spelling: **Josias** (dʒəʊˈsaɪəs).

Josquin des Prés (*French* ʒɔskɛ̃ de pre) *n.* See **des Prés.**

joss (dʒɒs) *n.* a Chinese deity worshipped in the form of an idol. [C18: from pidgin E, from Port. *deos* god, from L *deus*]

joss house *n.* a Chinese temple or shrine where an idol or idols are worshipped.

joss stick *n.* a stick of dried perfumed paste, giving off a fragrant odour when burnt as incense.

jostle ('dʒɒsᵊl) *vb.* **1.** to bump or push (someone) roughly. **2.** to come or bring into contact. **3.** to force (one's way) by pushing. ~*n.* **4.** the act of jostling. **5.** a rough bump or push. [C14: see JOUST]

jot (dʒɒt) *vb.* **jotting, jotted. 1.** (*tr.*; usually foll. by *down*) to write a brief note of. ~*n.* **2.** (*used with a negative*) a little bit (in **not care** (*or* **give**) **a jot**). [C16: from L *jota*, from Gk *iōta*, of Semitic origin]

jota (*Spanish* 'xɒta) *n.* a Spanish dance in fast triple time. [Sp., prob. from OSp. *sota*, from *sotar* to dance, from L *saltāre*]

jotter ('dʒɒtə) *n.* a small notebook.

jotting ('dʒɒtɪŋ) *n.* something jotted down.

Jotun *or* **Jotunn** ('jɔːtʊn) *n. Norse myth.* any of a race of giants. [from ON *jötunn* giant; related to EAT]

joual (ʒwɑːl) *n.* nonstandard Canadian French dialect, esp. as associated with ill-educated speakers. [from the pronunciation in this dialect of F *cheval* horse]

joule (dʒuːl) *n.* the derived SI unit of work or energy; the work done when the point of application of a force of 1 newton is displaced through a distance of 1 metre in the direction of the force. Symbol: J [C19: after J. P. JOULE]

Joule (dʒuːl) *n.* **James Prescott.** 1818–89, English physicist, who evaluated the mechanical equivalent of heat and contributed to the study of heat and electricity.

jounce (dʒaʊns) *vb.* **1.** to shake or jolt or cause to shake or jolt. ~*n.* **2.** a shake; bump. [C15: prob. from dialect *joll* to bump + BOUNCE]

journal ('dʒɜːnᵊl) *n.* **1.** a newspaper or periodical. **2.** a book in which a daily record of happenings, etc., is kept. **3.** an official record of the proceedings of a legislative body. **4.** *Book-keeping.* one of several books in which transactions are initially recorded to facilitate subsequent entry in the ledger. **5.** the part of a shaft or axle in contact with or enclosed by a bearing. [C14: from OF: daily, from L *diurnālis*; see DIURNAL]

journal box *n. Machinery.* a case enclosing or supporting a journal.

journalese (,dʒɜːnᵊ'liːz) *n. Derog.* a superficial style of writing regarded as typical of newspapers, etc.

journalism ('dʒɜːnᵊ,lɪzəm) *n.* **1.** the profession or practice of reporting about, photographing, or editing news stories for one of the mass media. **2.** newspapers and magazines collectively.

journalist ('dʒɜːnᵊlɪst) *n.* **1.** a person whose occupation is journalism. **2.** a person who keeps a journal. —**jour-na'listic** *adj.* —**journa'listically** *adv.*

journalize *or* **-lise** ('dʒɜːnᵊ,laɪz) *vb.* to record (daily events) in a journal. —**journali'zation** *or* **-li'sation** *n.*

journey ('dʒɜːnɪ) *n.* **1.** a travelling from one place to another. **2. a.** the distance travelled in a journey. **b.** the time taken to make a journey. ~*vb.* **3.** (*intr.*) to make a journey. [C13: from OF *journee* a day, a day's travelling, from L *diurnum* day's portion] —**'journeyer** *n.*

journeyman ('dʒɜːnɪmən) *n., pl.* **-men. 1.** a craftsman, artisan, etc., who is qualified to work at his trade in the employment of another. **2.** a competent workman. [C15: from JOURNEY (in obs. sense: a day's work) + MAN]

joust (dʒaʊst) *History.* ~*n.* **1.** a combat between two mounted knights tilting against each other with lances. ~*vb.* **2.** (*intr.*; often foll. by *against* or *with*) to encounter or engage in a tournament: *he jousted with five opponents.* [C13: from OF, from *jouster* to fight on horseback, from Vulgar L *juxtāre* (unattested) to come together, from L *juxtā* close] —**'jouster** *n.*

Jove (dʒəʊv) *n.* **1.** another name for **Jupiter**[1]. **2. by Jove.** an exclamation of surprise or excitement. [C14: from OL *Jovis* Jupiter] —**'Jovian** *n.*

jovial ('dʒəʊvɪəl) *adj.* having or expressing convivial humour. [C16: from L *joviālis* of (the planet) Jupiter, considered by astrologers to foster good humour] —**joviality** (,dʒəʊvɪ'ælɪtɪ) *n.* —**'jovially** *adv.*

Jovian ('dʒəʊvɪən) *n.* full name *Flavius Claudius Jovianus.* ?331–364 A.D., Roman emperor (363–64): he made peace with Persia, relinquishing Roman provinces beyond the Tigris, and restored privileges to the Christians.

Jowett ('dʒaʊɪt) *n.* **Benjamin.** 1817–93, English classical scholar and educator: translated the works of Plato.

jowl[1] (dʒaʊl) *n.* **1.** the jaw, esp. the lower one. **2.** (*often pl.*) a cheek. **3. cheek by jowl.** See **cheek.** [OE *ceafl* jaw] —**jowled** *adj.*

jowl[2] (dʒaʊl) *n.* **1.** fatty flesh hanging from the lower jaw. **2.** a similar fleshy part in animals, such as the dewlap of a bull. [OE *ceole* throat]

joy (dʒɔɪ) *n.* **1.** a deep feeling or condition of happiness or contentment. **2.** something causing such a feeling. **3.** an outward show of pleasure or delight. **4.** *Brit. inf.* success; satisfaction: *I went for a loan, but got no joy.* ~*vb. Chiefly poetic.* **5.** (*intr.*) to feel joy. **6.** (*tr.*) to gladden. [C13: from OF, from L *gaudium* joy, from *gaudēre* to be glad]

Joyce (dʒɔɪs) *n.* **1. James (Augustine Aloysius).** 1882–1941, Irish novelist and short-story writer. He profoundly influenced the development of the modern novel by his use of complex narrative techniques, esp. stream of consciousness and parody, and of compound and coined words. His works include the novels *Ulysses* (1922) and *Finnegans Wake* (1939) and the short stories *Dubliners* (1914). **2. William,** known as *Lord Haw-Haw.* 1906–46, British broadcaster of Nazi propaganda to Britain, who was executed for treason. —**Joycean** ('dʒɔɪsɪən) *n., adj.*

joyful ('dʒɔɪfʊl) *adj.* **1.** full of joy; elated. **2.** expressing or producing joy: *a joyful look; a joyful occasion.* —**'joyfully** *adv.* —**'joyfulness** *n.*

joyless ('dʒɔɪlɪs) *adj.* having or producing no joy or pleasure. —**'joylessly** *adv.* —**'joylessness** *n.*

joyous ('dʒɔɪəs) *adj.* **1.** having a happy nature or mood. **2.** joyful. —**'joyously** *adv.*

joy ride *n.* **1.** a ride taken for pleasure in a car, esp. in a stolen car driven recklessly. ~*vb.* **joy-ride, -riding, -rode, -ridden. 2.** (*intr.*) to take such a ride. —**'joy,rider** *n.* —**'joyriding** *n.*

joystick ('dʒɔɪ,stɪk) *n.* **1.** *Inf.* the control stick of an aircraft, machine, etc. **2.** *Computers.* a lever for controlling the movement of a cursor on a screen.

JP *abbrev. for* Justice of the Peace.

Jr *or* **jr** *abbrev. for* junior.

Juan Carlos (*Spanish* xwan 'karlɔs) *n.* born 1938, king of Spain from 1975. He was nominated by Franco as the latter's successor and as the first king of the restored Spanish monarchy that was to follow Franco's death.

Juan de Fuca ('dʒuːən dɪ 'fjuːkə; *Spanish* xwan de 'fuka) *n.* **Strait of.** a strait between Vancouver Island (Canada) and NW Washington (U.S.). Length: about 129 km (80 miles). Width: about 24 km (15 miles).

Juan Fernández Islands ('dʒuːən fə'nændɛz; *Spanish* xwan fɛr'nandeθ) *pl. n.* a group of three islands in the S Pacific Ocean, administered by Chile: volcanic and wooded. Area: about 180 sq. km (70 sq. miles).

Juantorena (*Spanish* xwanto'rena) *n.* **Alberto** (al'βɛrto). born 1951, Cuban runner: won the 400 metres and the 800 metres in the 1976 Olympic Games.

Juárez[1] (*Spanish* 'xwareθ) *n.* short for **Ciudad Juárez.**

Juárez[2] (*Spanish* 'xwareθ) *n.* **Benito Pablo** (be'nito 'paβlo). 1806–72, Mexican statesman. As president (1861–65; 1867–72) he thwarted Napoleon III's attempt to impose an empire under Maximilian and introduced many reforms.

Juba ('dʒuːbə) *n.* a river in NE Africa, rising in S central Ethiopia and flowing south across Somalia to the Indian Ocean: the chief river of Somalia. Length: about 1660 km (1030 miles).

Jubal ('dʒuːbᵊl) *n. Old Testament.* the alleged inventor of musical instruments (Genesis 4:21).

jubbah ('dʒʊbə) *n.* a long loose outer garment with wide sleeves, worn by Muslim men and women, esp. in India. [C16: from Ar.]

Jubbulpore (,dʒʌbᵊl'pʊə) *n.* a variant spelling of **Jabalpur.**

jube (dʒuːb) *n. Austral. & N.Z. inf.* any jelly-like sweet. [C20: shortened from JUJUBE]

jubilant ('dʒuːbɪlənt) *adj.* feeling or expressing great joy. [C17: from L, from *jūbilāre* to give a joyful cry, from *jūbilum* a shout] —**'jubilance** *n.* —**'jubilantly** *adv.*

jubilate ('dʒuːbɪ,leɪt) *vb.* (*intr.*) **1.** to have or express great joy; rejoice. **2.** to celebrate a jubilee. [C17: from L *jūbilāre*; see JUBILANT]

jubilation (,dʒuːbɪ'leɪʃən) *n.* **1.** the act of rejoicing. **2.** a celebration or joyful occasion.

jubilee ('dʒuːbɪ,liː) *n.* **1.** a time or season for rejoicing. **2.** a special anniversary, esp. a 25th or 50th one. **3.** *R.C. Church.* a specially appointed period in which special indulgences are granted. **4.** *Old Testament.* a year that was to be observed every 50th year, during which Hebrew slaves were to be liberated, etc. **5.** a less common word for **jubilation.** [C14: from OF *jubile*, from LL *jubilaeus*, from LGk, from Heb. *yōbhēl* ram's horn, used for the proclamation of the year of jubilee]

Jud. *Bible.* ~*abbrev. for:* **1.** Also: **Judg.** Judges. **2.** Judith.

Judaea *or* **Judea** (dʒuːˈdɪə) *n.* the S division of ancient Palestine, succeeding the kingdom of Judah: a Roman province during the time of Christ. —**Juˈdaean** *or* **Juˈdean** *adj., n.*

Judah (ˈdʒuːdə) *n. Old Testament.* **1.** the fourth son of Jacob, one of whose descendants was to be the Messiah (Genesis 29:35; 49:8–12). **2.** the tribe descended from him. **3.** the tribal territory of his descendants which became the nucleus of David's kingdom and, after the kingdom had been divided into Israel and Judah, the southern kingdom of Judah, with Jerusalem as its centre. Douay spelling: **Juda.**

Judah ha-Levi (hɑːˈliːvaɪ) *n.* ?1075–1141, Jewish poet and philosopher, born in Spain; his major works include the collection in *Diwan* and the prose work *Sefer ha-Kuzari*, which presented his philosophy of Judaism in dialogue form.

Judah ha-Nasi (hɑːnɑːˈsiː) *n.* ?135–?220 A.D., rabbi and patriarch of the Sanhedrin, who compiled the Mishnah.

Judaic (dʒuːˈdeɪɪk) *adj.* of or relating to the Jews or Judaism. —**Juˈdaically** *adv.*

Judaism (ˈdʒuːdeɪˌɪzəm) *n.* **1.** the religion of the Jews, based on the Old Testament and the Talmud and having as its central point a belief in one God. **2.** the religious and cultural traditions of the Jews. —**Juˈdaˈistic** *adj.*

Judaize *or* **-ise** (ˈdʒuːdeɪˌaɪz) *vb.* **1.** to conform or bring into conformity with Judaism. **2.** (*tr.*) to convert to Judaism. —**Judaiˈzation** *or* **-iˈsation** *n.*

Judas (ˈdʒuːdəs) *n.* **1.** *New Testament.* the apostle who betrayed Jesus to his enemies for 30 pieces of silver (Luke 22:3–6, 47–48). Full name: **Judas Iscariot.** **2.** a person who betrays a friend; traitor. **3.** a brother or relative of James and also of Jesus (Matthew 13:55). This figure, Thaddaeus, and Jude were probably identical.

Judas Maccabaeus (ˌmækəˈbiːəs) *n.* Jewish leader, whose revolt (166–161 B.C.) against the Seleucid kingdom of Antiochus IV (Epiphanes) enabled him to recapture Jerusalem and rededicate the Temple.

Judas tree *n.* small Eurasian leguminous tree with pinkish-purple flowers that bloom before the leaves appear.

judder (ˈdʒʌdə) *Inf., chiefly Brit.* ~*vb.* **1.** (*intr.*) to shake or vibrate. **2.** abnormal vibration in a mechanical system. **3.** a juddering motion. [prob. blend of JAR² + SHUDDER]

Jude (dʒuːd) *n.* **1.** a book of the New Testament (in full **The Epistle of Jude**). **2.** Also called: **Judas.** the author of this, stated to be the brother of James (Jude 1) and almost certainly identical with Thaddaeus (Matthew 10:2–4).

Judea (dʒuːˈdɪə) *n.* a variant spelling of **Judaea.**

judge (dʒʌdʒ) *n.* **1.** a public official with authority to hear cases in a court of law and pronounce judgment upon them. **2.** a person who is appointed to determine the result of contests or competitions. **3.** a person qualified to comment critically: *a good judge of antiques.* **4.** a leader of the peoples of Israel from Joshua's death to the accession of Saul. ~*vb.* **5.** to hear and decide upon (a case at law). **6.** (*tr.*) to pass judgment on. **7.** (when *tr.,* may take a clause as object or an infinitive) to decide (something) after inquiry. **8.** to determine the result of (a contest or competition). **9.** to appraise (something) critically. **10.** (*tr.; takes a clause as object*) to believe something to be the case. [C14: from OF, from L *jūdicāre* to pass judgment, from *jūdex* a judge] —**ˈjudge,like** *adj.* —**ˈjudger** *n.* —**ˈjudgeship** *n.*

judge advocate *n., pl.* **judge advocates.** an officer who superintends proceedings at a military court martial.

judges' rules *pl. n.* (in English law) a set of rules, not legally binding, governing the behaviour of police towards suspects.

judgment *or* **judgement** (ˈdʒʌdʒmənt) *n.* **1.** the faculty of being able to make critical distinctions and achieve a balanced viewpoint. **2. a.** the verdict pronounced by a court of law. **b.** an obligation arising as a result of such a verdict, such as a debt. **c.** (*as modifier*): *a judgment debtor.* **3.** the formal decision of one or more judges at a contest or competition. **4.** a particular decision formed in a case in dispute or doubt. **5.** an estimation: *a good judgment of distance.* **6.** criticism or censure. **7. against one's better judgment.** contrary to a preferred course of action. **8. sit in judgment. a.** to preside as judge. **b.** to assume the position of critic.

Judgment (ˈdʒʌdʒmənt) *n.* **1.** the estimate by God of the ultimate worthiness or unworthiness of the individual or of all mankind. **2.** God's subsequent decision determining the final destinies of all individuals.

judgmental *or* **judgemental** (dʒʌdʒˈmɛntəl) *adj.* of or denoting an attitude in which judgments about other people's conduct are made.

Judgment Day *n.* the occasion of the Last Judgment by God at the end of the world. Also called: **Day of Judgment.** See **Last Judgment.**

judicatory (ˈdʒuːdɪkətərɪ) *adj.* **1.** of or relating to the administration of justice. ~*n.* **2.** a court of law. **3.** the administration of justice.

judicature (ˈdʒuːdɪkətʃə) *n.* **1.** the administration of justice. **2.** the office, function, or power of a judge. **3.** the extent of authority of a court or judge. **4.** a body of judges; judiciary. **5.** a court of justice or such courts collectively.

judicial (dʒuːˈdɪʃəl) *adj.* **1.** of or relating to the administration of justice. **2.** of or relating to judgment in a court of law or to a judge exercising this function. **3.** allowed or enforced by a court of law: *judicial separation.* **4.** having qualities appropriate to a judge. **5.** giving or seeking judgment. [C14: from L *jūdiciālis* belonging to the law courts, from *jūdicium* judgment, from *jūdex* a judge] —**juˈdicially** *adv.*

judiciary (dʒuːˈdɪʃɪərɪ) *adj.* **1.** of or relating to courts of law, judgment, or judges. ~*n., pl.* **-aries.** **2.** the branch of the central authority in a state concerned with the administration of justice. **3.** the system of courts in a country. **4.** the judges collectively.

judicious (dʒuːˈdɪʃəs) *adj.* having or proceeding from good judgment. —**juˈdiciously** *adv.* —**juˈdiciousness** *n.*

Judith (ˈdʒuːdɪθ) *n.* **1.** the heroine of one of the books of the Apocrypha, who saved her native town by decapitating Holofernes. **2.** the book recounting this episode.

judo (ˈdʒuːdəʊ) *n.* **a.** the modern sport derived from ju-jitsu, in which the object is to force an opponent to submit using the minimum of physical effort. **b.** (*as modifier*): *a judo throw.* [Japanese, from *jū* gentleness + *dō* art] —**ˈjudoist** *n.*

Judy (ˈdʒuːdɪ) *n., pl.* **-dies.** **1.** the wife of Punch in the children's puppet show *Punch and Judy.* See **Punch. 2.** (*often not cap.*) *Brit. sl.* a girl.

jug (dʒʌg) *n.* **1.** a vessel for holding or pouring liquids, usually having a handle and a lip. U.S. equivalent: **pitcher. 2.** *Austral. & N.Z.* a container in which water is boiled, esp. an electric kettle. **3.** *U.S.* a large vessel with a narrow mouth. **4.** Also called: **jugful.** the amount of liquid held by a jug. **5.** *Brit. inf.* a glass of beer. **6.** *Sl.* jail. ~*vb.* **jugging, jugged. 7.** to stew or boil (meat, esp. hare) in an earthenware container. **8.** (*tr.*) *Sl.* to put in jail. [C16: prob. from *Jug,* nickname from name *Joan*]

jugate (ˈdʒuːgeɪt, -gɪt) *adj.* (esp. of compound leaves) having parts arranged in pairs. [C19: from NL *jugātus* (unattested), from L *jugum* a yoke]

juggernaut (ˈdʒʌgəˌnɔːt) *n.* **1.** any terrible force, esp. one that demands complete self-sacrifice. **2.** *Brit.* a very large heavy lorry. [C17: from Hindi, from Sansk. *Jagannātha* lord of the world: devotees formerly threw themselves under a cart carrying *Juggernaut,* an idol of Krishna]

juggins (ˈdʒʌgɪnz) *n.* (*functioning as sing.*) *Brit. inf.* a silly person. [C19: special use of the surname *Juggins*]

juggle (ˈdʒʌgəl) *vb.* **1.** to throw and catch (several objects) continuously so that most are in the air all the time. **2.** to manipulate (facts, etc.) so as to give a false picture. **3.** (*tr.*) to keep (several activities) in progress, esp. with difficulty. ~*n.* **4.** an act of juggling. [C14: from OF *jogler* to perform as a jester, from L, from *jocus* a jest] —**ˈjuggler** *n.*

Jugoslavia (ˌjuːgəʊˈslɑːvɪə) *n.* a variant spelling of **Yugoslavia.** —**ˈJugoˌslav** *or* **ˌJugoˈslavian** *adj., n.*

jugular (ˈdʒʌgjʊlə) *adj.* **1.** of, relating to, or situated near the throat or neck. ~*n.* **2.** Also called: **jugular vein.** any of the large veins in the neck carrying blood to the heart from the head. [C16: from LL, from L *jugulum* throat]

Jugurtha (dʒuːˈgɜːθə) *n.* died 104 B.C., king of Numidia (?112–104), who waged war against the Romans (the **Jugurthine War,** 112–105) and was defeated and executed.

juice (dʒuːs) *n.* **1.** any liquid that occurs naturally in or is secreted by plant or animal tissue: *the juice of an orange.* **2.** *Inf.* **a.** petrol. **b.** electricity. **c.** alcoholic drink. **3.** vigour or vitality. [C13: from OF *jus,* from L] —**ˈjuiceless** *adj.*

juice up vb. (tr., adv.) U.S. sl. to make lively: to juice up a party.

juicy ('dʒuːsɪ) adj. **juicier, juiciest. 1.** full of juice. **2.** provocatively interesting; spicy: juicy gossip. **3.** profitable: a juicy contract. —**'juicily** adv. —**'juiciness** n.

Juiz de Fora (Portuguese ʒuˈiʃ di 'fɔrɐ) n. a city in SE Brazil, in Minas Gerais state on the Rio de Janeiro–Belo Horizonte railway: textiles. Pop.: 299 728 (1980).

jujitsu, jujutsu, or **jiujutsu** (dʒuːˈdʒɪtsuː) n. the traditional Japanese system of unarmed self-defence perfected by the samurai. See also **judo.** [C19: from Japanese, from jū gentleness + jutsu art]

juju ('dʒuːdʒuː) n. **1.** an object superstitiously revered by certain West African peoples and used as a charm or fetish. **2.** the power associated with a juju. [C19: prob. from Hausa djudju evil spirit, fetish]

jujube ('dʒuːdʒuːb) n. **1.** any of several Old World spiny trees that have small yellowish flowers and dark red edible fruits. **2.** the fruit of any of these trees. **3.** a chewy sweet made of flavoured gelatin and sometimes medicated to soothe sore throats. [C14: from Med. L jujuba, modification of L zizyphum, from Gk zizuphon]

jukebox ('dʒuːk,bɒks) n. an automatic record player, usually in a large case, in which records may be selected by inserting coins and pressing appropriate buttons. [C20: from Gullah (a Negro language) juke bawdy (as in juke house brothel) + BOX¹]

jukskei ('juk,skeɪ) n. a South African game in which a peg is thrown over a fixed distance at a stake driven into the ground. [from Afrik. juk yoke + skei pin]

julep ('dʒuːlɪp) n. **1.** a sweet drink, variously prepared and sometimes medicated. **2.** Chiefly U.S. short for **mint julep.** [C14: from OF, from Ar. julāb, from Persian, from gul rose + āb water]

Julian ('dʒuːljən, -lɪən) n. known as Julian the Apostate; Latin name Flavius Claudius Julianus. 331–363 A.D., Roman emperor (361–363), who attempted to revive paganism in the Roman empire while remaining tolerant to Christians and Jews.

Juliana (,dʒʊlɪˈɑːnə; Dutch jyːliːˈaːna) n. full name Juliana Louise Emma Marie Wilhelmina. born 1909, queen of the Netherlands (1948–80). She abdicated in favour of her eldest daughter Beatrix.

Julian Alps pl. n. a mountain range in NW Yugoslavia, in Slovenia: an E range of the Alps.

Julian calendar n. the calendar introduced by Julius Caesar in 46 B.C., in which leap years occurred every fourth year and in every centenary year. Cf. **Gregorian calendar.**

julienne (,dʒuːlɪˈɛn) adj. **1.** (of vegetables) cut into thin shreds. ~n. **2.** a clear consommé to which such vegetables have been added.

Julius II ('dʒuːljəs, -lɪəs) n. original name Giuliano della Rovere. 1443–1513, pope (1503–13). He completed the restoration of the Papal States to the Church, began the building of St Peter's, Rome (1506), and patronized Michelangelo, Raphael, and Bramante.

Julius Caesar n. See **Caesar.**

Jullundur ('dʒʌləndə) n. a city in NW India, in central Punjab. Pop.: 408 196 (1981).

July (dʒuːˈlaɪ) n., pl. **-lies.** the seventh month of the year, consisting of 31 days. [C13: from Anglo-F julie, from L Jūlius, after Gaius Julius CAESAR, in whose honour it was named]

jumble ('dʒʌmb°l) vb. **1.** to mingle (objects, etc.) in a state of disorder. **2.** (tr.; usually passive) to remember in a confused form. ~n. **3.** a disordered mass, state, etc. **4.** Brit. articles donated for a jumble sale. [C16: from ?] —**'jumbly** adj.

jumble sale n. Brit. a sale of miscellaneous articles, usually second-hand, in aid of charity. U.S. and Canad. equivalent: **rummage sale.**

jumbo ('dʒʌmbəʊ) n., pl. **-bos. 1.** Inf. **a.** a very large person or thing. **b.** (as modifier): a jumbo box of detergent. **2.** See **jumbo jet.** [C19: after a famous elephant exhibited by P. T. Barnum, from Swahili jumbe chief]

jumbo jet n. Inf. a type of large jet-propelled airliner.

jumbo pack n. **1.** the promotion of bulk sales of small unit items, such as confectionery, by packing several in one wrapping, usually with a unit price reduction. **2.** such a package of items.

jumbuck ('dʒʌm,bʌk) n. Austral. an informal word for **sheep.** [C19: from Abor.]

Jumna ('dʒʌmnə) n. a river in N India, rising in Uttar Pradesh in the Himalayas and flowing south and southeast to join the Ganges just below Allahabad (a confluence held sacred by Hindus). Length: 1385 km (860 miles).

jump (dʒʌmp) vb. **1.** (intr.) to leap or spring clear of the ground or other surface by using the muscles in the legs and feet. **2.** (tr.) to leap over or clear (an obstacle): to jump a gap. **3.** (tr.) to cause to leap over an obstacle: to jump a horse over a hedge. **4.** (intr.) to move or proceed hastily (into, onto, out of, etc.): she jumped into a taxi. **5.** (tr.) Inf. to board so as to travel illegally on: he jumped the train as it was leaving. **6.** (intr.) to parachute from an aircraft. **7.** (intr.) to jerk or start, as with astonishment, surprise, etc. **8.** to rise or cause to rise suddenly or abruptly. **9.** to pass or skip over (intervening objects or matter): she jumped a few lines and then continued reading. **10.** (intr.) to change from one thing to another, esp. from one subject to another. **11.** Draughts. to capture (an opponent's piece) by moving one of one's own pieces over it to an unoccupied square. **12.** (intr.) Bridge. to bid in response to one's partner at a higher level than is necessary, to indicate a strong hand. **13.** (tr.) to come off (a track, etc.): the locomotive jumped the rails. **14.** (intr.) (of the stylus of a record player) to be jerked out of the groove. **15.** (intr.) Sl. to be lively: the party was jumping. **16.** (tr.) Inf. to attack without warning: thieves jumped the old man. **17.** (tr.) Inf. (of a driver or a motor vehicle) to pass through (a red traffic light) or move away from (traffic lights) before they change to green. **18. jump down someone's throat.** Inf. to address or reply to someone sharply. **19. jump ship.** to desert, esp. to leave a ship in which one is legally bound to serve. **20. jump the queue.** Inf. to obtain some advantage out of turn or unfairly. **21. jump to it.** Inf. to begin something quickly and efficiently. ~n. **22.** an act or instance of jumping. **23.** a space, distance, or obstacle to be jumped or that has been jumped. **24.** a descent by parachute from an aircraft. **25.** Sport. any of several contests involving a jump: the high jump. **26.** a sudden rise: the jump in prices last month. **27.** a sudden or abrupt transition. **28.** a sudden jerk or involuntary muscular spasm, esp. as a reaction of surprise: one jump ahead. **30.** Draughts. a move that captures an opponent's piece by jumping over it. **31.** Films. **a.** a break in continuity in the normal sequence of shots. **b.** (as modifier): a jump cut. **32. on the jump.** Inf., chiefly U.S. & Canad. **a.** in a hurry. **b.** busy. **33. take a running jump.** Brit. inf. a contemptuous expression of dismissal. ~See also **jump at, jump-off,** etc. [C16: prob. imit.]

jump at vb. (intr., prep.) to be glad to accept: I would jump at the chance of going.

jumped-up adj. Inf. suddenly risen in significance, esp. when appearing arrogant.

jumper¹ ('dʒʌmpə) n. **1.** Chiefly Brit. a knitted or crocheted garment covering the upper part of the body. **2.** the U.S. and Canad. term for **pinafore dress.** [C19: from obs. jump man's loose jacket, var. of jupe, from OF, from Ar. jubbah long cloth coat]

jumper² ('dʒʌmpə) n. **1.** a boring tool that works by repeated impact, such as a steel bit in a drill used in boring rock. **2.** Also called: **jumper cable, jumper lead.** a short length of wire used to make a connection, usually temporarily. **3.** a person or animal that jumps.

jumping bean n. a seed of any of several Mexican plants that contains a moth caterpillar whose movements cause it to jerk about.

jumping jack n. a toy figure of a man with jointed limbs that can be moved by pulling attached strings.

jump jet n. Inf. a fixed-wing jet aircraft that is capable of landing and taking off vertically.

jump jockey n. Brit. inf. a jockey riding in a steeplechase, as opposed to racing on the flat.

jump leads (liːdz) pl. n. two heavy cables fitted with crocodile clips used to start a motor vehicle with a discharged battery by connecting the battery to an external battery.

jump-off n. **1.** an extra round in a showjumping contest when two or more horses are equal first, deciding the winner. ~vb. **jump off. 2.** (intr., adv.) to engage in a jump-off.

jump on vb. (intr., prep.) Inf. to reprimand or attack suddenly and forcefully.

jump seat n. **1.** a folding seat on some aircraft for an additional crew member. **2.** Brit. a folding seat in a motor vehicle.

jump-start vb. **1.** to start the engine of (a car) by pushing or rolling it and then engaging the gears or (of a car) to start in this way. ~*n.* **2.** the act of starting a car in this way. ~Also called (Brit.): **bump-start.**

jump suit *n.* a one-piece garment of combined trousers and jacket or shirt.

jumpy ('dʒʌmpɪ) *adj.* **jumpier, jumpiest. 1.** nervous or apprehensive. **2.** moving jerkily or fitfully. —'**jumpily** *adv.* —'**jumpiness** *n.*

Jun. *abbrev. for:* **1.** June. **2.** Also: **jun.** junior.

junco ('dʒʌŋkəʊ) *n., pl.* **-cos** *or* **-coes.** a North American bunting having a greyish plumage. [C18: from Sp.: a rush, from L *juncus* rush]

junction ('dʒʌŋkʃən) *n.* **1.** a place where several routes, lines, or roads meet, link, or cross each other: *a railway junction.* **2.** a point on a motorway where traffic may leave or join it. **3.** *Electronics.* **a.** a contact between two different metals or other materials: *a thermocouple junction.* **b.** a transition region in a semiconductor. **4.** the act of joining or the state of being joined. [C18: from L *junctiō* a joining, from *jungere* to join]

junction box *n.* an earthed enclosure within which wires or cables can be safely connected.

junction transistor *n.* a bipolar transistor consisting of two p-n junctions combined to form either an n-p-n or a p-n-p transistor.

juncture ('dʒʌŋktʃə) *n.* **1.** a point in time, esp. a critical one (often in **at this juncture**). **2.** *Linguistics.* the set of phonological features signalling a division between words, such as those that distinguish *a name* from *an aim.* **3.** a less common word for **junction.**

Jundiaí (*Portuguese* ʒundiaˈi) *n.* an industrial city in SE Brazil, in São Paulo state. Pop.: 210 015 (1980).

June (dʒuːn) *n.* the sixth month of the year, consisting of 30 days. [OE *iunius,* from L *junius,* prob. from *Junius* name of Roman gens]

Juneau ('dʒuːnəʊ) *n.* a port in SE Alaska: state capital. Pop.: 26 000 (1983 est.).

Jung (jʊŋ) *n.* **Carl Gustav** (karl 'gʊstaf). 1875–1961, Swiss psychologist. His criticism of Freud's emphasis on the sexual instinct ended their early collaboration. He went on to found analytic psychology, developing the concepts of the collective unconscious and its archetypes and of the extrovert and introvert as the two main psychological types. —'**Jungian** *adj.*

Jungfrau (*German* 'jʊŋfrau) *n.* a mountain in S Switzerland, in the Bernese Alps south of Interlaken. Height: 4158 m (13 642 ft.).

Junggar Pendi ('dʒʊŋ'gɛər 'pɛn'diː), **Dzungaria,** *or* **Zungaria** *n.* an arid region of W China, in N Xinjiang Uygur between the Altai Mountains and the Tian Shan.

jungle ('dʒʌŋgəl) *n.* **1.** an equatorial forest area with luxuriant vegetation. **2.** any dense or tangled thicket or growth. **3.** a place of intense or ruthless struggle for survival: *the concrete jungle.* [C18: from Hindi, from Sansk. *jāngala* wilderness] —'**jungly** *adj.*

jungle fever *n.* a serious malarial fever occurring in the East Indies.

jungle fowl *n.* **1.** any small gallinaceous bird of S and SE Asia, the males of which (**junglecock**) have an arched tail and a combed and wattled head. **2.** *Austral.* any of several megapodes.

jungle juice *n. Sl.* alcoholic liquor.

junior ('dʒuːnjə) *adj.* **1.** lower in rank or length of service; subordinate. **2.** younger in years. **3.** of or relating to youth or childhood. **4.** *Brit.* of schoolchildren between the ages of 7 and 11 approximately. **5.** *U.S.* of or designating the third year of a four-year course at college or high school. ~*n.* **6.** *Law.* (in England) any barrister below the rank of Queen's Counsel. **7.** a junior person. **8.** *Brit.* a junior schoolchild. **9.** *U.S.* a junior student. [C17: from L: younger, from *juvenis* young]

Junior ('dʒuːnjə) *adj. Chiefly U.S.* being the younger: usually used after a name to distinguish the son from the father: *Charles Parker, Junior.* Abbrev.: **Jnr, Jr, Jun., Junr.**

junior common room *n.* (in certain universities and colleges) a common room for the use of students.

junior lightweight *n.* **a.** a professional boxer weighing 126–130 pounds (57–59 kg). **b.** (*as modifier*): *a junior-lightweight bout.*

junior middleweight *n.* **a.** a professional boxer weighing 147–154 pounds (66.5–70 kg). **b.** (*as modifier*): *the junior-middleweight championship.*

junior school *n. Brit.* a school for children aged between 7 and 11.

junior technician *n.* a rank in the Royal Air Force comparable to that of private in the army.

junior welterweight *n.* **a.** a professional boxer weighing 135–140 pounds (61–63.5 kg). **b.** (*as modifier*): *a junior-welterweight fight.*

juniper ('dʒuːnɪpə) *n.* a coniferous shrub or small tree of the N hemisphere having purple berry-like cones. The cones of the **common** or **dwarf juniper** are used as a flavouring in making gin. [C14: from L *jūniperus,* from ?]

junk¹ (dʒʌŋk) *n.* **1.** discarded objects, etc., collectively. **2.** *Inf.* **a.** rubbish generally. **b.** nonsense: *the play was absolute junk.* **3.** *Sl.* any narcotic drug, esp. heroin. ~*vb.* **4.** (*tr.*) *Inf.* to discard as junk. [C15 *jonke* old useless rope]

junk² (dʒʌŋk) *n.* a sailing vessel used in Chinese waters and characterized by a very high poop, flat bottom, and square sails supported by battens. [C17: from Port. *junco,* from Javanese *jon*]

Junker ('jʊŋkə) *n.* **1.** *History.* any of the aristocratic landowners of Prussia who were devoted to maintaining their privileges. **2.** an arrogant and tyrannical German army officer or official. **3.** (formerly) a young German nobleman. [C16: from G, from OHG *junchêrro* young lord] —'**Junkerdom** *n.*

Junkers ('jʊŋkəz) *n.* **Hugo.** 1859–1935, German aircraft designer. His military aircraft were used in both World Wars.

junket ('dʒʌŋkɪt) *n.* **1.** a sweet dessert made of flavoured milk set to a curd with rennet. **2.** a feast. **3.** *U.S. & Canad.* an excursion, esp. one made for pleasure at public expense. ~*vb.* **4.** to have or entertain with a feast. **5.** (*intr.*) *U.S. & Canad.* (of a public official, etc.) to go on a junket. [C14 (in the sense: rush basket, hence custard served on rushes): from OF (dialect) *jonquette,* from *jonc* rush, from L *juncus* reed] —'**junketing** *n.*

junk food *n.* food which is eaten in addition to or instead of regular meals, and which often has a low nutritional value.

junkie *or* **junky** ('dʒʌŋkɪ) *n., pl.* **junkies.** an informal word for **drug addict.**

junk mail *n.* unsolicited mail advertising goods or services.

junk shop *n.* a shop selling miscellaneous second-hand goods and sometimes antiques.

Juno ('dʒuːnəʊ) *n.* **1.** (in Roman tradition) the queen of the Olympian gods. Greek counterpart: **Hera.** **2.** a woman of stately bearing and regal beauty.

junta ('dʒʌntə, 'hʊntə) *n.* (*functioning as sing. or pl.*) **1.** a group of military officers holding the power in a country, esp. after a coup d'état. **2.** Also called: **junto.** a small group of men. **3.** a legislative or executive council in some parts of Latin America. [C17: from Sp.: council, from L, from *jungere* to join]

junto ('dʒʊntəʊ) *n., pl.* **-tos.** a variant of **junta** (sense 2). [C17]

Jupiter¹ ('dʒuːpɪtə) *n.* (in Roman tradition) the king and ruler of the Olympian gods.

Jupiter² ('dʒuːpɪtə) *n.* the largest of the planets and the fifth from the sun.

Jura ('dʒʊərə) *n.* **1.** a department of E France, in Franche-Comté region. Capital: Lons-le-Saunier. Pop.: 242 925 (1982). Area: 5055 sq. km (1971 sq. miles). **2.** a canton of Switzerland, bordering the French frontier: formed in 1979 from part of Bern. Capital: Delémont. Pop.: 64 986 (1980). Area: 838 sq. km (323 sq. miles). **3.** an island off the W coast of Scotland, in the Inner Hebrides, separated from the mainland by the **Sound of Jura.** Pop. (with Colonsay): 239 (1981). Area: 381 sq. km (147 sq. miles). **4.** a mountain range in W central Europe, between the Rivers Rhine and Rhône: mostly in E France, extending into W Switzerland. **5.** a range of mountains in the NE quadrant of the moon lying on the N border of the Mare Imbrium.

Jurassic (dʒuˈræsɪk) *adj.* **1.** of or formed in the second period of the Mesozoic era, during which dinosaurs and ammonites flourished. ~*n.* **2. the.** the Jurassic period or rock system. [C19: from F *jurassique,* after the JURA (Mountains)]

jurat ('dʒʊəræt) *n.* **1.** *Law.* a statement at the foot of an affidavit, naming the parties, stating when, where, and before whom it was sworn, etc. **2.** (in England) a municipal officer of the Cinque Ports. **3.** (in France and the Channel Islands) a magistrate. [C16: from Med. L *jūrātus* one who has been sworn, from L *jūrāre* to swear]

juridical (dʒuˈrɪdɪkəl) *adj.* of or relating to law or to the administration of justice; legal. [C16: from L, from *iūs* law + *dicere* to say] —**ju'ridically** *adv.*

jurisdiction (,dʒʊərɪs'dɪkʃən) *n.* **1.** the right or power to administer justice and to apply laws. **2.** the exercise or extent of such right or power. **3.** authority in general. [C13: from L *jūrisdictiō* administration of justice, from *jus* law + DICTION] —**juris'dictional** *adj.*

jurisprudence (,dʒʊərɪs'pruːdʰns) *n.* **1.** the science or philosophy of law. **2.** a system or body of law. **3.** a branch of law: *medical jurisprudence.* [C17: from L *jūris prūdentia,* from *jus* law + PRUDENCE] —**jurisprudential** (,dʒʊərɪspruː'dɛnʃəl) *adj.*

jurist ('dʒʊərɪst) *n.* a person versed in the science of law, esp. Roman or civil law. [C15: from F *juriste,* from Med. L *jūrista*]

juristic (dʒʊ'rɪstɪk) *or* **juristical** *adj.* **1.** of or relating to jurists. **2.** of or characteristic of the study of law or the legal profession.

juror ('dʒʊərə) *n.* **1.** a member of a jury. **2.** a person who takes an oath. [C14: from Anglo-F *jurour,* from OF *jurer* to take an oath, from L *jūrāre*]

Juruá (*Portuguese* ʒu'rua) *n.* a river in South America, rising in E central Peru and flowing northeast across NW Brazil to join the Amazon. Length: 1900 km (1200 miles).

jury[1] ('dʒʊərɪ) *n., pl.* **-ries. 1.** a group of, usually, twelve people sworn to deliver a true verdict according to the evidence upon a case presented in a court of law. **2.** a body of persons appointed to judge a competition and award prizes. [C14: from OF *juree,* from *jurer* to swear]

jury[2] ('dʒʊərɪ) *adj. Chiefly naut.* (*in combination*) makeshift: *jury-rigged.* [C16: from ?]

jury box *n.* an enclosure where the jury sits in court.

juryman ('dʒʊərɪmən) *or (fem.)* **jurywoman** *n., pl.* **-men** *or* **-women.** a member of a jury.

jury-rigged *adj. Chiefly naut.* set up in a makeshift manner.

just *adj.* (dʒʌst). **1. a.** fair or impartial in action or judgment. **b.** (*as collective n.; preceded by the*): *the just.* **2.** conforming to high moral standards; honest. **3.** consistent with justice: *a just action.* **4.** rightly applied or given: *a just reward.* **5.** legally valid; lawful: *a just inheritance.* **6.** well-founded: *just criticism.* **7.** correct or true: *a just account.* ~*adv.* (dʒʌst; *unstressed* dʒəst). **8.** used with forms of *have* to indicate an action performed in the very recent past: *I have just closed the door.* **9.** at this very instant: *he's just coming in to land.* **10.** no more than; only: *just an ordinary car.* **11.** exactly: *that's just what I mean.* **12.** barely: *he just got there in time.* **13. just about. a.** at the point of starting (to do something). **b.** almost: *I've just about had enough.* **14. just a moment, second,** *or* **minute.** an expression requesting the hearer to wait or pause for a brief period of time. **15. just so.** arranged with precision. [C14: from L *jūstus* righteous, from *jūs* justice] —**'justly** *adv.* —**'justness** *n.*

justice ('dʒʌstɪs) *n.* **1.** the quality or fact of being just. **2.** *Ethics.* the principle of fairness that like cases should be treated alike. **3.** the administration of law according to prescribed and accepted principles. **4.** conformity to the law. **5.** a judge of the Supreme Court of Judicature. **6.** short for **justice of the peace. 7.** good reason (esp. in **with justice**). **8. bring to justice.** to capture, try, and usually punish (a criminal, etc.). **9. do justice to. a.** to show to full advantage. **b.** to show full appreciation of by action. **c.** to treat or judge fairly. **10. do oneself justice.** to make full use of one's abilities. [C12: from OF, from L *jūstitia,* from *justus* JUST] —**'justice,ship** *n.*

justice of the peace *n.* a lay magistrate whose function is to preserve the peace in his area and try summarily such cases as are within his jurisdiction.

justiciar (dʒʌ'stɪʃɪ,ɑː) *n. English legal history.* the chief political and legal officer from the time of William I to that of Henry III, who deputized for the king in his absence. Also called: **justiciary.** —**jus'ticiar,ship** *n.*

justiciary (dʒʌ'stɪʃɪərɪ) *adj.* **1.** of or relating to the administration of justice. ~*n., pl.* **-aries. 2.** an officer or administrator of justice; judge.

justifiable ('dʒʌstɪ,faɪəbʰl) *adj.* capable of being justified. —**justi,fia'bility** *n.* —**'justi,fiably** *adv.*

justifiable homicide *n.* lawful killing, as in the execution of a death sentence.

justification (,dʒʌstɪfɪ'keɪʃən) *n.* **1.** reasonable grounds for complaint, defence, etc. **2.** proof, vindication, or exculpation. **3.** *Christian theol.* **a.** the act of justifying. **b.** the process of being justified or the condition of having been justified. —**'justifi,catory** *adj.*

justify ('dʒʌstɪ,faɪ) *vb.* **-fying, -fied.** (*mainly tr.*) **1.** (*often passive*) to prove or see to be just or valid; vindicate. **2.** to show to be reasonable: *his behaviour justifies our suspicion.* **3.** to declare or show to be free from blame or guilt. **4.** *Law.* to show good reason in court for (some action taken). **5.** (*also intr.*) *Printing, computers.* to adjust the spaces between words in (a line of type or data) so that it is of the required length or (of a line of type or data) to fit exactly. **6. a.** *Protestant theol.* to declare righteous by the imputation of Christ's merits to the sinner. **b.** *R.C. theol.* to change from sinfulness to righteousness by the transforming effects of grace. **7.** (*also intr.*) *Law.* to prove (a person) to have sufficient means to act as surety, etc., or (of a person) to qualify to provide bail or surety. [C14: from OF *justifier,* from L *justificāre,* from *jūstus* JUST + *facere* to make] —**'justi,fier** *n.*

Justinian I (dʒʌ'stɪnɪən) *n.* called *the Great;* Latin name *Flavius Anicius Justinianus.* 483–565 A.D., Byzantine emperor (527–565). He recovered North Africa, SE Spain, and Italy, largely owing to the brilliance of generals such as Belisarius. He sponsored the Justinian Code.

Justin Martyr ('dʒʌstɪn) *n.* **Saint.** ?100–?165 A.D., Christian apologist and philosopher. Feast day: June 1.

justle ('dʒʌsʰl) *vb.* a less common word for **jostle.**

jut (dʒʌt) *vb.* **jutting, jutted. 1.** (*intr.;* often foll. by *out*) to stick out or overhang beyond the surface or main part. ~*n.* **2.** something that juts out. [C16: var. of JET[1]] —**'jutting** *adj.*

jute (dʒuːt) *n.* **1.** either of two Old World tropical yellow-flowered herbaceous plants, cultivated for their strong fibre. **2.** this fibre, used in making sacks, rope, etc. [C18: from Bengali *jhuto,* from Sansk. *jūta* braid of hair]

Jutland ('dʒʌtlənd) *n.* a peninsula of N Europe: forms the continental portion of Denmark and geographically includes the N part of the West German province of Schleswig-Holstein, while politically it includes only the mainland of Denmark and the islands north of Limfjorden; a major but inconclusive naval battle was fought off its NW coast in 1916 between the British and German fleets. Danish name: **Jylland.** —**'Jutlander** *n.*

juv. *abbrev. for* juvenile.

Juvenal ('dʒuːvɪnʰl) *n.* Latin name *Decimus Junius Juvenalis.* ?60–?140 A.D., Roman satirist. In his 16 verse satires, he denounced the vices of imperial Rome.

juvenescence (,dʒuːvɪ'nɛsəns) *n.* **1.** youth or immaturity. **2.** the act or process of growing from childhood to youth. —**juve'nescent** *adj.*

juvenile ('dʒuːvɪ,naɪl) *adj.* **1.** young, youthful, or immature. **2.** suitable or designed for young people: *juvenile pastimes.* ~*n.* **3.** a juvenile person, animal, or plant. **4.** an actor who performs youthful roles. **5.** a book intended for young readers. [C17: from L *juvenīlis* youthful, from *juvenis* young] —**'juve,nilely** *adv.*

juvenile court *n.* a court that deals with juvenile offenders and children beyond parental control or in need of care.

juvenile delinquency *n.* antisocial or criminal conduct by juvenile delinquents.

juvenile delinquent *n.* a child or young person guilty of some offence, act of vandalism, or antisocial behaviour and who may be brought before a juvenile court.

juvenilia (,dʒuːvɪ'nɪlɪə) *n.* works of art, literature, or music produced in youth, before the artist, author, or composer has formed a mature style. [C17: from L, lit.: youthful things]

juxtapose (,dʒʌkstə'pəʊz) *vb.* (*tr.*) to place close together or side by side. [C19: back formation from *juxtaposition,* from L *juxta* next to + POSITION] —**juxtapo'sition** *n.* —**juxtapo'sitional** *adj.*

Jylland ('jylan) *n.* the Danish name for **Jutland.**

K

k *or* **K** (keɪ) *n., pl.* **k's, K's,** *or* **Ks.** **1.** the 11th letter and 8th consonant of the English alphabet. **2.** a speech sound represented by this letter, usually a voiceless velar stop, as in *kitten.*

k *symbol for:* **1.** kilo(s). **2.** *Maths.* the unit vector along the *z*-axis.

K *symbol for:* **1.** Kelvin(s). **2.** *Chess.* king. **3.** *Chem.* potassium. [from NL *kalium*] **4.** *Physics.* kaon. **5.** *Currency.* **a.** kina. **b.** kip. **c.** kopeck. **d.** kwacha. **e.** kyat. **6.** one thousand. [from KILO-] **7.** *Computers.* originally or strictly a unit of 1024 words, bits, or bytes.

K *or* **K.** *abbrev. for* Köchel: indicating the serial number in the catalogue of the works of Mozart made by Ludwig von Köchel, 1800–77.

k. *abbrev. for:* **1.** karat. **2.** Also: **K.** king.

K2 *n.* a mountain in the Karakoram Range on the Kashmir-Xinjiang Uygur AR border: the second highest mountain in the world. Height: 8611 m (28 250 ft.). Also called: **Godwin Austen, Dapsang.**

Kaaba *or* **Caaba** ('ka:bə) *n.* a cube-shaped building in Mecca, the most sacred Muslim pilgrim shrine, into which is built the black stone believed to have been given by Gabriel to Abraham. [from Ar. *ka'bah,* from *ka'b* cube]

Kabalega Falls (,ka:bə'leɪgə) *pl. n.* rapids on the lower Victoria Nile, about 35 km (22 miles) east of Lake Albert, where the Nile drops 120 m (400 ft.).

Kabardino-Balkar Autonomous Soviet Socialist Republic (,kæbə'di:nəʊ,bælkə) *n.* an administrative division of the S Soviet Union, on the N side of the Caucasus Mountains. Capital: Nalchik. Pop.: 724 000 (1986). Area: 12 500 sq. km (4825 sq. miles).

kabbala *or* **kabala** (kə'bɑ:lə) *n.* variant spellings of **cabbala.**

kabuki (kæ'bu:kɪ) *n.* a form of Japanese drama based on legends and characterized by elaborate costumes and the use of male actors. [Japanese, from *ka* singing + *bu* dancing + *ki* art]

Kabul (kə'bʊl, 'kɔ:bᵊl) *n.* **1.** the capital of Afghanistan, in the northeast of the country at an altitude of 1800 m (5900 ft.) on the **Kabul River:** over 3000 years old, with a strategic position commanding passes through the Hindu Kush and main routes to the Khyber Pass; destroyed and rebuilt many times; capital of the Mogul Empire from 1504 until 1738 and of Afghanistan from 1773; university (1932). Pop.: 1 179 341 (1984). **2.** a river in Afghanistan and Pakistan, rising in the Hindu Kush and flowing east into the Indus at Attock, Pakistan. Length: 700 km (435 miles).

Kabyle (kə'baɪl) *n.* **1.** (*pl.* **-byles** *or* **-byle**) a member of a Berber people in Tunisia and Algeria. **2.** the dialect of Berber spoken by this people. [C19: from Ar. *qabā'il,* pl. of *qabīlah* tribe]

Kádár ('ka:da:r) *n.* **János** ('ja:noʃ). born 1912, Hungarian statesman; Communist prime minister of Hungary (1956–58; 1961–65) and first secretary of the Communist Party (1956–88).

kadi ('ka:dɪ, 'keɪdɪ) *n., pl.* **-dis.** a variant spelling of **cadi.**

Kaduna (kə'du:nə) *n.* **1.** a state of N Nigeria. Capital: Kaduna. Pop.: 6 868 800 (1984). Area: 68 989 sq. km (26 631 sq. miles). Former name (until 1976): **North-Central State.** **2.** a city in N central Nigeria, capital of Kaduna state on the **Kaduna River** (a principal tributary of the Niger). Pop.: 247 100 (1983).

Kaffir *or* **Kafir** ('kæfə) *n., pl.* **-firs** *or* **-fir.** **1.** *Offens.* **a.** (in southern Africa) any Black African. **b.** (*as modifier*): *Kaffir farming.* **2.** a former name for the **Xhosa** language. [C19: from Ar. *kāfir* infidel, from *kafara* to deny]

kaffir beer *n.* S. *African.* beer made from sorghum (kaffir corn) or millet.

kaffirboom ('kæfə,bʊəm) *n.* a S. African deciduous flowering tree. [from KAFFIR + Afrik. *boom* tree]

kaffir corn *n.* a southern African variety of sorghum, cultivated in dry regions for its grain and as fodder. Sometimes shortened to **kaffir.**

Kaffraria (kæ'frɛərɪə) *n.* a former region of South Africa, in E Cape Province: inhabited chiefly by the Kaffirs; British Kaffraria was a crown colony established in 1853 in the southwest of the region and annexed to Cape Colony in 1865. —**Kaf'frarian** *adj., n.*

Kafir ('kæfə) *n., pl.* **-irs** *or* **-ir.** **1.** a member of a people inhabiting E Afghanistan. **2.** a variant spelling of **Kaffir.** [C19: from Ar.; see KAFFIR]

Kafiristan (,kæfɪrɪ'sta:n) *n.* the former name of **Nuristan.**

Kafka ('kæfkə; *Czech* 'kafka) *n.* **Franz** (frants). 1883–1924, Czech novelist writing in German. In his two main novels *The Trial* (1925) and *The Castle* (1926), published posthumously against his wishes, he portrays man's fear, isolation, and bewilderment in a nightmarish dehumanized world. —**Kafkaesque** (,kæfkə'ɛsk) *adj.*

kaftan *or* **caftan** ('kæftæn) *n.* **1.** a long coatlike garment, usually with a belt, worn in the East. **2.** an imitation of this, worn esp. by women, consisting of a loose dress with long wide sleeves. [C16: from Turkish *qaftān*]

Kagera (kæ'gɛrə) *n.* a river in E Africa, rising in headstreams on the border between Tanzania and Rwanda and flowing east to Lake Victoria: the most remote headstream of the Nile and largest tributary of Lake Victoria. Length: about 480 km (300 miles).

Kagoshima (,kægɒ'ʃi:mə) *n.* a port in SW Japan, on S Kyushu. Pop.: 530 000 (1985).

kagoul (kə'gu:l) *n.* a variant spelling of **cagoule.**

kahawai ('ka:həwaɪ, 'ka:waɪ) *n.* a New Zealand food and game fish. [from Maori]

Kahn (ka:n) *n.* **1. Herman.** 1922–83, U.S. mathematician and futurologist; director of the Hudson Institute (1961–83). **2. Louis I(sadore).** 1901–74, U.S. architect, noted for his art museums at Yale (1951–53), Fort Worth (1966–72), and New Haven (1969–74).

kai (kaɪ) *n. N.Z. inf.* food. [from Maori]

kaiak ('kaɪæk) *n.* a variant spelling of **kayak.**

Kaieteur Falls (,kaɪə'tʊə) *pl. n.* a waterfall in Guyana, on the Potaro River. Height: 226 m (741 ft.). Width: about 107 m (350 ft.).

Kaifeng ('kaɪ'fɛŋ) *n.* a city in E China, in N Henan on the Yellow River: one of the oldest cities in China and its capital (as Pien-liang) from 907 to 1126. Pop.: 447 800 (1985 est.).

kail (keɪl) *n.* a variant spelling of **kale.**

kainite ('kaɪnaɪt) *n.* a white mineral consisting of potassium chloride and magnesium sulphate: a fertilizer and source of potassium salts. [C19: from G *Kainit,* from Gk *kainos* new + -ITE¹]

Kairouan (*French* kɛrwā), **Kairwan,** *or* **Qairwan** (kaɪə'wa:n) *n.* a city in NE Tunisia: one of the holy cities of Islam; pilgrimage and trading centre. Pop.: 72 254 (1984).

Kaiser¹ ('kaɪzə) *n.* (*sometimes not cap.*) *History.* **1.** any of the three German emperors. **2.** *Obs.* any Austro-Hungarian emperor. [C16: from G, ult. from L *Caesar* emperor]

Kaiser² (*German* 'kaizər) *n.* **Georg** ('geːɔrk). 1878–1945, German expressionist dramatist.

Kaiserslautern (*German* kaizərs'lautərn) *n.* a city in West Germany, in S Rhineland-Palatinate. Pop.: 98 700 (1984 est.).

kaka ('ka:kə) *n.* a green New Zealand parrot with a long compressed bill. [C18: from Maori, ? imit. of its call]

kaka beak *n.* a New Zealand shrub with beaklike red flowers. [from KAKA]

kakapo ('ka:kə,pəʊ) *n., pl.* **-pos.** a ground-living nocturnal parrot of New Zealand, resembling an owl. [C19: from Maori, lit.: night kaka]

kakemono (,kækɪ'məʊnəʊ) *n., pl.* **-nos.** a Japanese paper or silk wall hanging, usually long and narrow, with a picture or inscription on it. [C19: from Japanese, from *kake* hanging + *mono* thing]

kala-azar (,ka:ləə'za:) *n.* a tropical infectious disease caused by a protozoan in the liver, spleen, etc. [C19: from Assamese *kālā* black + *āzār* disease]

Kalahari (,kælə'ha:rɪ) *n.* **the.** an extensive arid plateau of South Africa, Namibia (South West Africa), and Botswana: inhabited by Bushmen. Also called: **Kalahari Desert.**

Kalamazoo (ˌkæləmə'zuː) *n.* a city in SW Michigan, midway between Detroit and Chicago. Pop.: 79 722 (1980).

kalashnikov (kə'læʃnɪˌkɒf) *n.* a Russian-made sub-machine-gun, used esp. by terrorists and guerrillas. [C20: from Russian]

Kalat *or* **Khelat** (kə'lɑːt) *n.* a division of SW Pakistan, in S Baluchistan: formerly a princely state ruled by the Khan of Kalat, which joined Pakistan in 1948. Capital: Kalat. Pop.: 333 000 (1981 est.). Area: 65 610 sq. km (25 332 sq. miles).

kale *or* **kail** (keɪl) *n.* **1.** a cultivated variety of cabbage with crinkled leaves. **2.** *Scot.* a cabbage. ~Cf. **sea kale.** [OE *cāl*]

kaleidoscope (kə'laɪdəˌskəʊp) *n.* **1.** an optical toy for producing symmetrical patterns by multiple reflections in inclined mirrors enclosed in a tube. Loose pieces of coloured glass, paper, etc., are placed in the tube between the mirrors. **2.** any complex pattern of frequently changing shapes and colours. [C19: from Gk *kalos* beautiful + *eidos* form + -SCOPE] —**kaleidoscopic** (kəˌlaɪdə'skɒpɪk) *adj.*

kalends ('kælɪndz) *pl. n.* a variant spelling of **calends.**

Kalevala (ˌkɑːlə'vɑːlə) *n. Finnish legend.* **1.** the land of the hero Kaleva, who performed legendary exploits. **2.** the Finnish national epic in which these exploits are recounted. [Finnish, from *kaleva* of a hero + *-la* home]

kaleyard *or* **kailyard** ('keɪlˌjɑːd) *n. Scot.* a vegetable garden. [C19: lit.: cabbage garden]

kaleyard school *or* **kailyard school** *n.* a group of writers who depicted the homely aspects of life in the Scottish Lowlands. The best-known contributor was J. M. Barrie.

Kalgan ('kɑːl'gɑːn) *n.* a former name of **Zhangjiakou.**

Kalgoorlie (kæl'gʊəlɪ) *n.* a city in Western Australia, adjoining the town of Boulder: a centre of the Coolgardie gold rushes of the early 1890s; declining gold resources superseded by the discovery of nickel ore in 1966. Pop.: 23 750 (including Boulder) (1986 est.).

Kali ('kɑːlɪ) *n.* the Hindu goddess of destruction, consort of Siva. Her cult was characterized by savagery and cannibalism.

Kalidasa (ˌkælɪ'dɑːsə) *n.* ?5th century A.D., Indian dramatist and poet, noted for his romantic verse drama *Sakuntala.*

Kalimantan (ˌkælɪ'mæntən) *n.* the Indonesian name for Borneo: applied to the Indonesian part of the island only, excluding the Malaysian states of Sabah and Sarawak and the sultanate of Brunei. Pop.: 6 723 086 (1980).

Kalinin[1] (*Russian* kaˈlinin) *n.* a city in the central Soviet Union, at the confluence of the Volga and Tversta Rivers: chief port of the upper Volga, linked by canal with Moscow. Pop.: 447 000 (1987). Former name (until 1932): **Tver.**

Kalinin[2] (*Russian* kaˈlinin) *n.* **Mikhail Ivanovich** (mixa'il i'vanəvitʃ). 1875–1946, Soviet statesman: titular head of state (1919–46), a founder of *Pravda* (1912).

Kaliningrad (*Russian* kəlinin'grat) *n.* a port in the W Soviet Union, on the Pregolya River: severely damaged in World War II as the chief German naval base on the Baltic; ceded to the Soviet Union in 1945 and is now its chief Baltic naval base. Pop.: 394 000 (1987). Former name (until 1946): **Königsberg.**

Kalisz (*Polish* 'kaliʃ) *n.* a town in central Poland, on an island in the Prosna River: textile industry. Pop.: 104 100 (1986 est.). Ancient name: **Calissia** (kə'lɪsɪə).

Kalmar (*Swedish* 'kalmar) *n.* a port in SE Sweden, partly on the mainland and partly on a small island in the **Sound of Kalmar,** opposite Öland: scene of the signing of the Union of Kalmar, which united Sweden, Denmark, and Norway into a single monarchy (1397–1523). Pop.: 54 554 (1986).

kalmia ('kælmɪə) *n.* an evergreen North American ericaceous shrub having showy clusters of pink or white flowers. [C18: after Peter *Kalm* (1715–79), Swedish botanist and pupil of Linnaeus]

Kalmuck ('kælmʌk) *or* **Kalmyk** ('kælmɪk) *n.* **1.** (*pl.* **-mucks, -muck** *or* **-myks, -myk**) a member of a Mongoloid people of Buddhist tradition, who migrated from NE China to the USSR in the 17th century. **2.** the language of this people.

Kalmuck Autonomous Soviet Socialist Republic *n.* an administrative division of the S Soviet Union, on the Caspian Sea: became subject to Russia in 1646. Capital:

Elista. Pop.: 325 000 (1986). Area: 75 900 sq. km (29 300 sq. miles). Also called: **Kalmyk Autonomous Soviet Socialist Republic.**

kalong ('kɑːlɒŋ) *n.* a fruit bat of the Malay Archipelago; a flying fox. [Javanese]

kalpa ('kælpə) *n.* (in Hindu cosmology) a period in which the universe experiences a cycle of creation and destruction. [C18: Sansk.]

Kaluga (*Russian* ka'lugə) *n.* a city in the central Soviet Union, on the Oka River. Pop.: 307 000 (1987).

Kama[1] (*Russian* 'kamə) *n.* a river in the E Soviet Union, rising in the Ural Mountains and flowing to the River Volga, of which it is the largest tributary. Length: 2030 km (1260 miles).

Kama[2] ('kɑːmə) *n.* the Hindu god of love. [from Sansk.]

Kamakura (ˌkæmə'kʊərə) *n.* a city in central Japan, on S Honshu: famous for its Great Buddha (Daibutsu), a 13th-century bronze, 15 m (49 ft.) high. Pop.: 175 975 (1986 est.).

Kamasutra (ˌkɑːmə'suːtrə) *n.* **the.** an ancient Hindu text on erotic pleasure. [Sansk.: book on love, from *kāma* love + *sūtra* thread]

Kamchatka (*Russian* kam'tʃatkə) *n.* a peninsula in the E Soviet Union, between the Sea of Okhotsk and the Bering Sea. Length: about 1200 km (750 miles). —**Kam'chatkan** *adj., n.*

kame (keɪm) *n.* an irregular mound or ridge of gravel, sand, etc., deposited by water derived from melting glaciers. [C19: Scot. & N English var. of COMB]

Kamensk-Uralski (*Russian* 'kaminsku'raljskij) *n.* an industrial city in the W Soviet Union. Pop.: 204 000 (1987).

Kamerun ('kaməruːn) *n.* the German name for **Cameroon.**

Kamet ('kɑːmɛt, 'kʌmeɪt) *n.* a mountain in N India, in Uttar Pradesh in the Himalayas. Height: 7756 m (25 447 ft.).

kamikaze (ˌkæmɪ'kɑːzɪ) *n.* **1.** (*often cap.*) (in World War II) one of a group of Japanese pilots who performed suicidal missions. **2.** (*modifier*) (of an action) undertaken or (of a person) undertaking an action in the knowledge that it will result in the death of the person performing it in order to inflict maximum damage on an enemy: *a kamikaze attack.* **3.** (*modifier*) extremely foolhardy and possibly self-defeating. [C20: from Japanese, from *kami* divine + *kaze* wind]

Kamloops trout ('kæmluːps) *n.* a variety of rainbow trout common in British Columbia.

Kampala (kæm'pɑːlə) *n.* the capital and largest city of Uganda, in Buganda province on Lake Victoria: Makerere University (1961). Pop.: 458 423 (1980).

kampong ('kæmpɒŋ) *n.* (in Malaysia) a village. [C19: from Malay]

Kampuchea (ˌkæmpʊ'tʃɪə) *n.* a state in SE Asia: became part of French Indochina in 1887; declared independence in 1949; was a republic from 1970 until 1975, when five years of civil war ended with the victory of the Khmer Rouge. Fighting took place against the Vietnamese (1977–78). Vietnamese captured Phnom Penh and ousted Khmer Rouge regime (1979); government in exile led by Prince Sihanouk formed in 1982; contains the central plains of the Mekong River, with the Cardamom Mountains in the southwest. Language: Khmer. Currency: riel. Capital: Phnom Penh. Pop.: 5 756 141 (1981 est.). Area: 181 035 sq. km (69 895 sq. miles). Official name (since 1979): People's Republic of Kampuchea. Former name (until 1976): **Cambodia.** —ˌKampu'chean *adj., n.*

Kanak (kə'næk) *n.* a native or inhabitant of New Caledonia who seeks independence from France. [C20: from Hawaiian: man]

Kanaka (kə'nækə) *n.* **1.** a native Hawaiian. **2.** (*often not cap.*) *Austral.* any native of the South Pacific islands, esp. (formerly) one abducted to work in Australia. [C19: from Hawaiian: man]

Kananga (kə'næŋgə) *n.* a city in SW Zaïre: a commercial centre on the railway from Lubumbashi to Port Francqui. Pop.: 290 898 (1984). Former name (until 1966): **Luluabourg.**

Kanara *or* **Canara** (kə'nɑːrə) *n.* a region of SW India, in Karnataka on the Deccan Plateau and the W Coast. Area: about 155 000 sq. km (60 000 sq. miles).

Kanarese *or* **Canarese** (ˌkænə'riːz) *n.* **1.** (*pl.* **-rese**) a member of a people of S India living chiefly in Kanara. **2.** the language of this people.

Kanazawa (ˌkænəˈzɑːwə) n. a port in central Japan, on W Honshu: textile and porcelain industries. Pop.: 430 000 (1985).

Kanchenjunga (ˌkæntʃənˈdʒʌŋɡə) n. a variant spelling of **Kangchenjunga**.

Kanchipuram (kɑːnˈtʃiːpərəm) n. a city in SE India, in Tamil Nadu: a sacred Hindu town known as "the Benares of the South"; textile industries. Pop.: 145 254 (1981).

Kandahar (ˌkændəˈhɑː) n. a city in S Afghanistan: an important trading centre, built by Ahmad Shah Durrani (1724–73) as his capital on the site of several former cities. Pop.: 203 177 (1984 est.).

Kandinsky (Russian kanˈdinskij) n. **Vasili** (vaˈsilij). 1866–1944, Russian expressionist painter and theorist, regarded as the first to develop an entirely abstract style: a founder of der Blaue Reiter, a group of German expressionist painters formed in 1911.

Kandy (ˈkændɪ) n. a city in central Sri Lanka: capital of the kingdom of Kandy from 1480 until 1815, when occupied by the British; sacred Buddhist temple; University of Sri Lanka. Pop.: 140 000 (1985).

kanga or **khanga** (ˈkæŋɡə) n. a piece of gaily decorated thin cotton cloth used as a woman's garment, originally in E Africa. [from Swahili]

kangaroo (ˌkæŋɡəˈruː) n., pl. **-roos**. a large herbivorous marsupial of Australia and New Guinea, having powerful hind legs used for leaping, and a long thick tail. [C18: prob. from Abor.] — ˌkangaˈrooˌlike adj.

kangaroo closure n. Parliamentary procedure. a form of closure in which the chairman or speaker selects certain amendments for discussion and excludes others.

kangaroo court n. an irregular court, esp. one set up by strikers to judge strikebreakers.

Kangaroo Island n. an island in the Indian Ocean, off South Australia. Area: 4350 sq. km (1680 sq. miles).

kangaroo paw n. any of various Australian plants having green-and-red hairy flowers.

kangaroo rat n. **1.** a small leaping rodent related to the squirrels and inhabiting desert regions of North America, having a stocky body and very long hind legs and tail. **2.** Also called: **kangaroo mouse.** any of several leaping Australian rodents.

Kangchenjunga, Kanchenjunga (ˌkæntʃənˈdʒʌŋɡə), or **Kinchinjunga** n. a mountain on the border between Nepal and Sikkim, in the Himalayas: the third highest mountain in the world. Height: 8598 m (28 208 ft.).

KaNgwane (ˌkɑːˀŋˈɡwɑːneɪ) n. a Bantustan in South Africa, in E Transvaal. Capital: Schoemansdal. Former name: **Swazi Territory.**

kanji (ˈkændʒɪ) n., pl. **-ji** or **-jis**. a Japanese syllabary derived from Chinese orthography. [Japanese, from Chinese, from han Chinese + tsū word]

Kano (ˈkɑːnəʊ, ˈkeɪnəʊ) n. **1.** a state of N Nigeria: consists of wooded savanna in the south and scrub vegetation in the north. Capital: Kano. Pop.: 9 681 000 (1984). Area: 42 593 sq. km (16 442 sq. miles). **2.** a city in N Nigeria, capital of Kano state: transport and market centre. Pop.: 487 100 (1983).

Kanpur (kɑːnˈpʊə) n. an industrial city in NE India, in S Uttar Pradesh on the River Ganges: scene of the massacre by Nana Sahib of British soldiers and European families and his later defeat by British forces in 1857. Pop.: 1 531 345 (1981). Former name: **Cawnpore.**

Kansas (ˈkænzəs) n. a state of the central U.S.: consists of undulating prairie, drained chiefly by the Arkansas, Kansas, and Missouri Rivers; mainly agricultural. Capital: Topeka. Pop.: 2 461 000 (1986 est.). Area: 211 828 sq. km (81 787 sq. miles). Abbrevs.: **Kan., Kans.,** or (with zip code) **KS**

Kansas City n. **1.** a city in W Missouri, at the confluence of the Missouri and Kansas Rivers: important centre of livestock and meat-packing industry. Pop.: 441 170 (1986). **2.** a city in NE Kansas, adjacent to Kansas City, Missouri. Pop.: 161 087 (1980).

Kansu (ˈkænˈsuː) n. a variant transliteration of the Chinese name for **Gansu.**

Kant (kænt; German kant) n. **Immanuel** (ɪˈmɑːnuːel). 1724–1804, German idealist philosopher. He sought to determine the limits of man's knowledge in Critique of Pure Reason (1781) and propounded his system of ethics as guided by the categorical imperative in Critique of Practical Reason (1788). — ˈKantian adj. — ˈKantianˌism or ˈKantism n.

KANU (ˈkɑːnuː) n. acronym for Kenya African National Union.

Kaohsiung or **Kao-hsiung** (ˈkaʊˈʃjʊŋ) n. a port in SW Taiwan, on the South China Sea: the chief port of the island. Pop.: 1 300 000 (1986). Japanese name: **Takao.**

Kaolack (ˈkɑːəʊˌlæk, ˈkaʊlæk) n. a port in SW Senegal, on the Saloum River. Pop.: 126 947 (1984 est.).

kaolin (ˈkeɪəlɪn) n. a fine white clay used for the manufacture of hard-paste porcelain and bone china and in medicine as a poultice. Also called: **china clay.** [C18: from F, from Chinese Kaoling Chinese mountain where supplies for Europe were first obtained] — ˌkaoˈlinic adj.

kaon (ˈkeɪɒn) n. a meson that has a rest mass of about 996 or 964 electron masses. Also called: **K-meson.** [C20 ka representing the letter k + (MES)ON]

kapellmeister (kæˈpɛlˌmaɪstə) n. a variant spelling of **capellmeister.**

Kapfenberg (German ˈkapfənbɛrk) n. an industrial town in E Austria, in Styria. Pop.: 25 719 (1981).

Kapitza (kəˈpitsa) n. **Piotr Leonidovich** (ˈpjɔtᵊr liɒˈnidovitʃ). 1894–1984, Russian physicist. He worked in England and the USSR, doing research in several areas, particularly cryogenics; Nobel prize for physics in 1978.

kapok (ˈkeɪpɒk) n. a silky fibre obtained from the hairs covering the seeds of a tropical tree (**kapok tree**): used for stuffing pillows, etc. [C18: from Malay]

Kaposi's sarcoma (kæˈpəʊsɪz) n. a form of skin cancer found in Africans and more recently in victims of AIDS. [C20: after Moritz Kohn Kaposi (1837–1902), Austrian dermatologist who first described the sores that characterize the disease]

kappa (ˈkæpə) n. the tenth letter in the Greek alphabet (K, κ). [Gk, of Semitic origin]

kaput (kæˈpʊt) adj. (postpositive) Inf. ruined, broken, or not functioning. [C20: from G kaputt done for]

karabiner (ˌkærəˈbiːnə) n. Mountaineering. a metal clip with a spring for attaching to a piton, belay, etc. Also called: **snaplink, krab.** [shortened from G Karabinerhaken, lit.: carbine hook]

Karachai-Cherkess Autonomous Region (kərʌˈtʃaɪtʃɛəˈkɛs) n. an administrative division of the S Soviet Union, on the N side of the Caucasus Mountains. Capital: Cherkessk. Pop.: 396 000 (1986). Area: 14 100 sq. km (5440 sq. miles). Also called: **Karachayevo-Cherkess Autonomous Region** (kɑːrɑːˈtʃaɪɛvəʊtʃɛəˈkɛs).

Karachi (kəˈrɑːtʃɪ) n. a port in S Pakistan, on the Arabian Sea: capital of Pakistan (1947–60); university (1950); chief port: commercial and industrial centre. Pop.: 5 103 000 (1981 est.).

Karafuto (ˌkɑːrɑːˈfuːtɔ) n. transliteration of the Japanese name for **Sakhalin.**

Karaganda (Russian kərəɡanˈda) n. a city in the SW Soviet Union, in the W Kazakh SSR: a major coal-mining and industrial centre. Pop.: 633 000 (1987).

Karajan (German ˈkaːrajan) n. **Herbert von** (ˈhɛrbɛrt fɔn). born 1908, Austrian conductor.

Kara-Kalpak Autonomous Soviet Socialist Republic (kəˈrɑːrɑːˈkalˈpɑːk) n. an administrative division of the S Soviet Union, in the Uzbek SSR, on the Aral Sea: came under Russian rule by stages from 1873 onwards. Capital: Nukus. Pop.: 1 108 000 (1986). Area: 165 600 sq. km (63 900 sq. miles). Also called: **Kara-Kalpakia** (kɑːrɑːkəlˈpɑːkɪə), **Kara-Kalpakistan** (kəˈrɑːkəlˌpɑːkɪ-ˈstæn, -ˈstɑːn).

Karakoram or **Karakorum** (ˌkærəˈkɔːrəm) n. a mountain system in N Kashmir, extending for about 480 km (300 miles) from northwest to southeast: contains the second highest peak in the world (K2); crossed by several high passes, notably the **Karakoram Pass,** 5575 m (18 290 ft.).

Karakorum (ˌkærəˈkɔːrəm) n. a ruined city in the Mongolian People's Republic: founded in 1220 by Ghenghis Khan; destroyed by Kublai Khan when his brother rebelled against him, after Kublai Khan had moved his capital to Peking.

karakul or **caracul** (ˈkærəkˀl) n. **1.** a breed of sheep of central Asia having coarse black, grey, or brown hair: the lambs have soft curled hair. **2.** the fur prepared from these lambs. ~See also **Persian lamb.** [C19: from Russian, from the name of a region in Bokhara where the sheep originated]

Kara Kum (Russian kərə ˈkum) n. a desert in the SW Soviet Union, covering most of the Turkmen SSR: extensive areas now irrigated. Area: about 300 000 sq. km (120 000 sq. miles).

Karamanlis (*Greek* karaman'lis) *n.* **Konstantinos** (kɔnstan'tinɔs). born 1907, Greek statesman; prime minister of Greece (1955–58; 1958–61; 1961–63; 1974–80): president of Greece (1980–85).

Kara Sea ('kɑːrə) *n.* a shallow arm of the Arctic Ocean off the N coast of the Soviet Union: ice-free for about three months of the year.

karat ('kærət) *n.* the usual U.S. and Canad. spelling of **carat** (sense 2).

karate (kə'rɑːtɪ) *n.* **a.** a traditional Japanese system of unarmed combat, employing smashes, chops, kicks, etc., made with the hands, feet, elbows, or legs. **b.** (*as modifier*): *karate chop*. [Japanese, lit.: empty hand]

Karbala ('kɑːbələ) *or* **Kerbela** *n.* a town in central Iraq: the chief holy city of Iraq and centre of Shiah Muslim pilgrimage; burial place of Mohammed's grandson Husain. Pop.: 184 574 (1985 est.).

Karelia (kə'riːlɪə; *Russian* ka'reljə) *n.* a region of NE Europe, formerly in Finland but annexed in several stages by the Soviet Union: corresponds roughly to the Karelian ASSR. —**Ka'relian** *adj., n.*

Karelian Autonomous Soviet Socialist Republic *n.* an administrative division of the NW Soviet Union between the White Sea and Lakes Onega and Ladoga. Capital: Petrozavodsk. Pop.: 787 000 (1986). Area: 172 400 sq. km (66 560 sq. miles).

Karelian Isthmus *n.* a strip of land between the Gulf of Finland and Lake Ladoga: annexed by the Soviet Union after the Russo-Finnish War (1939–40).

Kariba (kə'riːbə) *n.* **Lake.** a lake on the Zambia-Zimbabwe border, created by the building of the **Kariba Dam** across the Zambezi for hydroelectric power. Length: 282 km (175 miles).

Karitane (,kærɪ'tɑːnɛ) *n.* *N.Z.* a nurse for babies; nanny. [from former child-care hospital at *Karitane*, New Zealand]

Karl-Marx-Stadt (*German* karl'marksʃtat) *n.* a city in S East Germany, at the foot of the Erz Mountains: a textile centre; engineering works. Pop.: 314 437 (1986). Former name (until 1953): **Chemnitz.**

Karloff ('kɑːlɒf) *n.* **Boris**, real name *William Pratt.* 1887–1969, English film actor, famous for his roles in horror films, esp. *Frankenstein* (1931).

Karlovy Vary (*Czech* 'karlɔvi 'vari) *n.* a city in W Czechoslovakia, at the confluence of the Tepla and Ohře Rivers: warm mineral springs. Pop.: 59 696 (1983). German name: **Karlsbad** ('karlsbaːt).

Karlsruhe (*German* 'karlsruːə) *n.* a city in West Germany, in Baden-Württemberg: capital of the former Baden state; now the seat of justice of West Germany. Pop.: 267 000 (1986).

karma ('kɑːmə) *n.* **1.** *Hinduism, Buddhism.* the principle of retributive justice determining a person's state of life and the state of his reincarnations as the effect of his past deeds. **2.** destiny or fate. **3.** *Inf.* an aura or quality that a person, place, or thing is felt to have. [C19: from Sansk.: action, effect, from *karoti* he does] —**'karmic** *adj.*

Karnak ('kɑːnæk) *n.* a village in E Egypt, on the Nile: site of the N part of the ruins of ancient Thebes.

Karnataka (kə'nɑːtəkə) *n.* a state of S India, on the Arabian Sea: consists of a narrow coastal plain rising to the South Deccan plateau; mainly agricultural. Capital: Bangalore. Pop.: 37 043 451 (1981). Area: 192 204 sq. km (74 210 sq. miles). Former name (1956–73): **Mysore.**

Kärnten ('kɛrntən) *n.* the German name for **Carinthia.**

karoo *or* **karroo** (kə'ruː) *n., pl.* **-roos.** a dry tableland of southern Africa, with semidesert vegetation. [C18: from Afrik. *karo*, ?from Hottentot *garo* desert]

Karoo *or* **Karroo** (kə'ruː) *n., pl.* **-roos.** (*often not cap.*) any of several high arid plateaus in South Africa, esp. the **Great (Central) Karoo** and the **Little Karoo** in S Cape Province. The High Veld, north of the Great Karoo, is sometimes called the **Northern Karoo.** [C18: from Afrik. *karo*, probably from Hottentot *garo* desert]

kaross (kə'rɒs) *n.* a garment of skins worn by indigenous peoples in southern Africa. [C18: from Afrik. *karos*, ?from Du., from F *cuirasse* CUIRASS]

Karpov (*Russian* 'karpəf) *n.* **Anatoly** (ana'tɔlij). born 1951, Soviet chess player: world champion (1975–85).

karri ('kɑːrɪ) *n., pl.* **-ris. 1.** an Australian eucalyptus tree. **2.** the durable dark red wood of this tree, used for construction, etc. [from Abor.]

karst (kɑːst) *n.* (*modifier*) denoting the characteristic scenery of a limestone region, including underground streams, gorges, etc. [C19: G, from *Karst*, limestone plateau near Trieste]

kart (kɑːt) *n.* a light low-framed vehicle with small wheels and engine used for recreational racing (**karting**). Also called: **go-cart, go-kart.**

karyo- *or* **caryo-** *combining form.* indicating the nucleus of a cell. [from NL, from Gk *karuon* kernel]

Kasai (kɑː'saɪ) *n.* a river in southwestern Africa, rising in central Angola and flowing east then north as part of the border between Angola and Zaïre, continuing northwest through Zaïre to the River Congo. Length: 2154 km (1338 miles).

kasbah *or* **casbah** ('kæzbɑː) *n.* (*sometimes cap.*) **1.** the citadel of various North African cities. **2.** the quarter in which a kasbah is located. [from Ar. *kasba* citadel]

Kashi ('kɑː'ʃiː) *or* **Kashgar** ('kɑːʃ'gɑː) *n.* an oasis city in W China, in W Xinjiang Uygur AR. Pop.: 100 000 (1980 est.).

Kashmir (kæʃ'mɪə) *n.* a region of SW central Asia: from the 16th century ruled by the Moguls, Afghanis, Sikhs, and British successively; since 1947 disputed between India, Pakistan, and China; 84 000 sq. km (33 000 sq. miles) in the northwest are held by Pakistan and known as Azad Kashmir (Free Kashmir); 42 735 sq. km (16 496 sq. miles) in the east are held by China; the remainder was in 1956 officially incorporated into India as the state of Jammu and Kashmir; traversed by the Himalaya and Karakoram mountain ranges and the Rivers Jhelum and Indus; a fruit-growing and cattle-grazing region, with a woollen industry. Capitals: (Azad Kashmir) Muzaffarabad; (Jammu and Kashmir) Srinagar (summer), Jammu (winter). —**Kash'miri** *adj., n.* —**Kash'mirian** *adj., n.*

kashruth *or* ***kashrut*** *Hebrew.* (kaʃ'ruːt) *n.* **1.** the condition of being fit for ritual use in general. **2.** the system of dietary laws which require ritual slaughter, the removal of excess blood from meat, and the complete separation of milk and meat, and prohibit such foods as pork and shell fish. ~See also **kosher** (senses 1, 3). [lit.: appropriateness]

Kasparov ('kæspərɒf) *n.* **Gary** ('gærɪ), real name *Gary Weinstein.* born 1963, Soviet chess player: world champion from 1985.

Kassa ('kɔʃʃɔ) *n.* the Hungarian name for **Košice.**

Kassala (kə'sɑːlə) *n.* a city in the E Sudan: founded as a fort by the Egyptians in 1834. Pop.: 149 000 (1980 est.).

Kassel *or* **Cassel** (*German* 'kasəl) *n.* a city in E West Germany, in Hesse: capital of Westphalia (1807–13) and of the Prussian province of Hesse-Nassau (1866–1945). Pop.: 184 200 (1986).

Kastrop-Rauxel (*German* 'kastrɔp'rauksəl) *n.* a variant spelling of **Castrop-Rauxel.**

kata- *prefix.* a variant of **cata-.**

katabatic (,kætə'bætɪk) *adj.* (of winds) blowing downhill through having become denser with cooling.

Katanga (kə'tæŋgə) *n.* the former name (until 1972) of **Shaba.**

Katar (kæ'tɑː) *n.* a variant spelling of **Qatar.**

Kathiawar (,kætɪə'wɑː) *n.* a large peninsula of W India, in Gujarat between the Gulf of Kutch and the Gulf of Cambay. Area: about 60 690 sq. km (23 430 sq. miles).

Katmai ('kætmaɪ) *n.* **Mount.** a volcano in SW Alaska, in the Aleutian Range: erupted in 1912 forming the Valley of Ten Thousand Smokes, a region with numerous fumaroles; established as **Katmai National Monument,** 10 917 sq. km (4215 sq. miles), in 1918. Height: 2100 m (7000 ft.). Depth of crater: 1130 m (3700 ft.). Width of crater: about 4 km (2.5 miles).

Katmandu *or* **Kathmandu** (,kætmæn'duː) *n.* the capital of Nepal, in the east at the confluence of the Baghmati and Vishnumati Rivers. Pop.: 195 260 (1982 est.).

Katowice (*Polish* katɔ'vitsɛ) *n.* an industrial city in S Poland. Pop.: 363 000 (1985). Former name (1953–56): **Stalinogrod.**

Katrine ('kætrɪn) *n.* **Loch.** a lake in central Scotland, east of Loch Lomond: noted for its associations with Sir Walter Scott's *Lady of the Lake.* Length: about 13 km (8 miles).

Katsina (kæt'si:nə) *n.* a city in N Nigeria, in Kaduna state: a major intellectual and cultural centre of the Hausa people (16th–18th centuries). Pop.: 149 300 (1983 est.).

Kattegat *or* **Cattegat** ('kætɪ,gæt) *n.* a strait between Denmark and Sweden: linked by the Sound, the Great Belt, and the Little Belt with the Baltic Sea and by the Skagerrak with the North Sea.

katydid ('keɪtɪ,dɪd) *n.* a green long-horned grasshopper living among the foliage of trees in North America. [C18: imit.]

Kauai (kɑː'wɑːi:) *n.* a volcanic island in NW Hawaii, northwest of Oahu. Chief town: Lihue. Pop.: 46 100 (1986 est.). Area: 1433 sq. km (553 sq. miles).

Kauffmann ('kaufmən) *n.* **Angelica** (andʒe'li:kə). 1741–1807, Swiss painter, who worked chiefly in England.

Kaunas ('kaunəs) *n.* a city in the S central Lithuanian SSR at the confluence of the Neman and Viliya Rivers: ceded by Poland to Russia in 1795; became the provisional capital of Lithuania (1920–40); incorporated into the Soviet Union in 1944; university (1922). Pop.: 417 000 (1987). Russian name: **Kovno.**

Kaunda (kɑː'undə) *n.* **Kenneth** (**David**). born 1924, Zambian statesman. He led his country into independence and became its first president (1964).

kauri ('kaurɪ) *n.*, *pl.* **-ris.** a New Zealand coniferous tree with oval leaves and round cones, cultivated for wood and resin. [C19: from Maori]

kauri gum *n.* the fossil resin of the kauri tree.

kava ('kɑːvə) *n.* **1.** a Polynesian shrub. **2.** a drink prepared from the aromatic roots of this shrub. [C18: from Polynesian: bitter]

Kaválla (kə'vælə; *Greek* ka'vala) *n.* a port in E Greece, in Macedonia on the **Bay of Kaválla:** an important Macedonian fortress of the Byzantine empire; ceded to Greece by Turkey after the Balkan War (1912–13). Pop.: 56 260 (1981). Ancient name: **Neapolis.**

Kaveri ('kɔ:vərɪ) *n.* a variant spelling of **Cauvery.**

Kavir Desert (kæ'vɪə) *n.* another name for the **Dasht-i-Kavir.**

Kawasaki (,kɑːwə'sɑːkɪ) *n.* a port in central Japan, on SE Honshu, between Tokyo and Yokohama: heavy industries. Pop.: 1 089 000 (1985).

Kay (keɪ) *n.* **Sir.** (in Arthurian legend) the braggart foster brother and steward of King Arthur.

kayak *or* **kaiak** ('kaɪæk) *n.* **1.** a canoe-like boat used by Eskimos, consisting of a frame covered with animal skins. **2.** a fibreglass or canvas-covered canoe of similar design. [C18: from Eskimo]

kayo *or* **KO** ('keɪ'əu) *n.*, *pl.* **kayos,** *vb.* **kayoing, kayoed.** *Boxing, sl.* another term for **knockout** or **knock out.** [C20: from the initial letters of *knock out*]

Kayseri (,kaɪsɛ'ri:; *Turkish* 'kaiseri) *n.* a city in central Turkey: trading centre since ancient times as the chief city of Cappadocia. Pop.: 378 458 (1985). Ancient name: **Caesarea Mazaca.**

Kazakh Soviet Socialist Republic (kə'zɑːk, kɑː-) *n.* an administrative division of the S central Soviet Union, on the Caspian Sea. Capital: Alma-Ata. Pop.: 16 028 000 (1986). Area: 2 715 100 sq. km (1 048 030 sq. miles). Also called: **Kazak Soviet Socialist Republic, Kazakhstan,** *or* **Kazakstan** (,kɑːzɑːk'stæn, -'stɑːn).

Kazan[1] (kə'zæn, -'zɑːn; *Russian* ka'zanj) *n.* a city in the E Soviet Union, capital of the Tatar ASSR on the River Volga: capital of an independent khanate in the 15th century; university (1804); a major industrial centre. Pop.: 1 068 000 (1987).

Kazan[2] (kə'zɑːn) *n.* **Elia** ('i:ljə), real name *Elia Kazanjoglous.* born 1909, U.S. stage and film director and writer, born in Turkey. His films include *Gentleman's Agreement* (1947) and *On the Waterfront* (1954) for both of which he won Oscars, and *East of Eden* (1955).

Kazan Retto (kɑː'zɑːn 'rɛtəu) *n.* transliteration of the Japanese name for the **Volcano Islands.**

Kazantzakis (*Greek* kazan'dzakis) *n.* **Nikos** ('nikɔs). 1885–1957, Greek novelist, poet, and dramatist, noted particularly for his novel *Zorba the Greek* (1946) and his epic poem *The Odyssey* (1938).

Kazbek (kɑːz'bɛk) *n.* **Mount.** an extinct volcano in the S Soviet Union, in the N Georgian SSR in the central Caucasus Mountains. Height: 5047 m (16 558 ft.).

Kaz Daği ('kaz 'dɑj) *n.* the Turkish name for (Mount) **Ida** (sense 2).

kazoo (kə'zu:) *n.*, *pl.* **-zoos.** a cigar-shaped musical instrument of metal or plastic with a membranous diaphragm of thin paper that vibrates with a nasal sound when the player hums into it. [C20: prob. imit.]

KB (in Britain) *abbrev. for:* **1.** King's Bench. **2.** *Computers.* kilobyte.

KBE *abbrev. for* Knight (Commander of the Order) of the British Empire.

kbyte *Computers. abbrev. for* kilobyte.

kc *abbrev. for* kilocycle.

KC (in Britain) *abbrev. for:* **1.** King's Counsel. **2.** Kennel Club.

kcal *abbrev. for* kilocalorie.

KCB *abbrev. for* Knight Commander of the Bath (a Brit. title).

KCMG *abbrev. for* Knight Commander (of the Order) of St Michael and St George (a Brit. title).

KE *abbrev. for* kinetic energy.

kea ('kɛə) *n.* a large New Zealand parrot with brownish-green plumage. [C19: from Maori, imit. of its call]

Kéa ('kɛa) *n.* transliteration of the Modern Greek name for **Keos.**

Kean (ki:n) *n.* **Edmund.** 1789–1833, English actor, noted for his Shakespearean roles.

Keaton ('ki:tⁿn) *n.* **Buster,** real name *Joseph Francis Keaton.* 1895–1966, U.S. film comedian who starred in silent films such as *The Navigator* (1924), *The General* (1926), and *Steamboat Bill Junior* (1927).

Keats (ki:ts) *n.* **John.** 1795–1821, English poet. His finest poetry is contained in *Lamia and other Poems* (1820), which includes *The Eve of St Agnes, Hyperion,* and the odes *On a Grecian Urn, To a Nightingale, To Autumn,* and *To Psyche.*

kebab (kə'bæb) *n.* a dish consisting of small pieces of meat, tomatoes, onions, etc., threaded onto skewers and grilled. Also called: **shish kebab.** [C17: via Urdu from Ar. *kabāb* roast meat]

Keble ('ki:bⁿl) *n.* **John.** 1792–1866, English clergyman. His sermon on national apostasy (1833) is considered to have inspired the Oxford Movement.

Kecskemét (*Hungarian* 'kɛtʃkemeːt) *n.* a city in central Hungary: vineyards and fruit farms. Pop.: 104 000 (1985).

Kedah ('kɛdə) *n.* a state of NW Malaysia: under Thai control until it came under the British in 1909; the chief exports are rice, tin, and rubber. Capital: Alor Star. Pop.: 1 102 200 (1980). Area: 9425 sq. km (3639 sq. miles).

kedge (kɛdʒ) *Naut.* ~*vb.* **1.** to draw (a vessel) along by hauling in on the cable of a light anchor, or (of a vessel) to be drawn in this fashion. ~*n.* **2.** a light anchor, used esp. for kedging. [C15: from *caggen* to tug]

kedgeree (,kɛdʒə'ri:) *n. Chiefly Brit.* a dish consisting of rice, cooked flaked fish, and hard-boiled eggs. [C17: from Hindi, from Sansk. *khiccā*]

Kediri (kɪ'dɪərɪ) *n.* a city in Indonesia, in E Java: commercial centre. Pop.: 221 830 (1980).

Kedron ('kɛdrɒn) *or* **Kidron** *n. Bible.* a ravine under the eastern wall of Jerusalem.

Keegan ('ki:gən) *n.* **Kevin.** born 1951, English footballer.

keek (ki:k) *n.*, *vb.* a Scot. word for **peep**[1]. [C18: prob. from MDu. *kiken* to look]

keel[1] (ki:l) *n.* **1.** one of the main longitudinal structural members of a vessel to which the frames are fastened. **2.** **on an even keel.** well-balanced; steady. **3.** any structure corresponding to or resembling the keel of a ship. **4.** *Biol.* a ridgelike part; carina. ~*vb.* **5.** to capsize. ~*See* also **keel over.** [C14: from ON *kjölr*]

keel[2] (ki:l) *n. Eastern English dialect.* **1.** a flat-bottomed vessel, esp. one used for carrying coal. **2.** a measure of coal. [C14 *kele,* from MDu. *kiel*]

keelhaul ('ki:l,hɔ:l) *vb.* (*tr.*) **1.** to drag (a person) by a rope from one side of a vessel to the other through the water under the keel. **2.** to rebuke harshly. [C17: from Du. *kielhalen;* see KEEL[1], HAUL]

Keeling Islands ('ki:lɪŋ) *pl. n.* another name for the **Cocos Islands.**

keel over *vb.* (*adv.*) **1.** to turn upside down; capsize. **2.** (*intr.*) *Inf.* to collapse suddenly.

keelson ('kɛlsən, 'ki:l-) *or* **kelson** *n.* a longitudinal beam fastened to the keel of a vessel for strength and stiffness. [C17: prob. from Low G *kielswin* keel swine, ult. of Scand. origin]

Keelung ('ki:'luŋ) *n.* another name for **Chilung**.

keen[1] (ki:n) *adj.* **1.** eager or enthusiastic. **2.** (*postpositive;* foll. by *on*) fond (of); devoted (to): *keen on golf.* **3.** intellectually acute: *a keen wit.* **4.** (of sight, smell, hearing, etc.) capable of recognizing fine distinctions. **5.** having a sharp cutting edge or point. **6.** extremely cold and penetrating: *a keen wind.* **7.** intense or strong: *a keen desire.* **8.** *Chiefly Brit.* extremely low so as to be competitive: *keen prices.* [OE *cēne*] —**'keenly** *adv.* —**'keenness** *n.*

keen[2] (ki:n) *vb.* (*intr.*) **1.** to lament the dead. ~*n.* **2.** a dirge or lament for the dead. [C19: from Irish Gaelic *caoine,* from Olrish *coínim* I wail] —**'keener** *n.*

keep (ki:p) *vb.* **keeping, kept. 1.** (*tr.*) to have or retain possession of. **2.** (*tr.*) to have temporary possession or charge of: *keep my watch for me.* **3.** (*tr.*) to store in a customary place: *I keep my books in the desk.* **4.** to remain or cause to remain in a specified state or condition: *keep ready.* **5.** to continue or cause to continue: *keep in step.* **6.** (*tr.*) to have or take charge or care of: *keep the shop for me till I return.* **7.** (*tr.*) to look after or maintain for use, pleasure, etc.: *to keep chickens.* **8.** (*tr.*) to provide for the upkeep or livelihood of. **9.** (*tr.*) to support financially, esp. in return for sexual favours. **10.** to confine or detain or be confined or detained. **11.** to withhold or reserve or admit of withholding or reserving: *your news will keep.* **12.** (*tr.*) to refrain from divulging or violating: *to keep a secret.* **13.** to preserve or admit of preservation. **14.** (*tr.*; sometimes foll. by *up*) to observe with due rites or ceremonies. **15.** (*tr.*) to maintain by writing regular records in: *to keep a diary.* **16.** (when *intr.,* foll. by *in, on, to,* etc.) to stay in, on, or at (a place or position): *keep to the path.* **17.** (*tr.*) to associate with (esp. in **keep bad company**). **18.** (*tr.*) to maintain in existence: *to keep court in the palace.* **19.** (*tr.*) *Chiefly Brit.* to have habitually in stock: *this shop keeps all kinds of wool.* **20. how are you keeping?** how are you? ~*n.* **21.** living or support. **22.** *Arch.* charge or care. **23.** Also called: **dungeon, donjon.** the main tower within the walls of a medieval castle or fortress. **24. for keeps.** *Inf.* **a.** permanently. **b.** for the winner or possessor to keep permanently. ~See also **keep at, keep away,** etc. [OE *cēpan* to observe]

keep at *vb.* (*prep.*) **1.** (*intr.*) to persist in. **2.** (*tr.*) to constrain (a person) to continue doing (a task).

keep away *vb.* (*adv.*; often foll. by *from*) to refrain or prevent from coming (near).

keep back *vb.* (*adv.*; often foll. by *from*) **1.** (*tr.*) to refuse to reveal or disclose. **2.** to prevent or be prevented from advancing, entering, etc.

keep down *vb.* (*adv.,* mainly *tr.*) **1.** to repress. **2.** to restrain or control: *he had difficulty keeping his anger down.* **3.** to cause not to increase or rise. **4.** (*intr.*) to lie low. **5.** not to vomit.

keeper ('ki:pə) *n.* **1.** a person in charge of animals, esp. in a zoo. **2.** a person in charge of a museum, collection, or section of a museum. **3.** a person in charge of other people, such as a warder in a jail. **4.** See **goalkeeper, wicketkeeper, gamekeeper, park keeper. 5.** a person who keeps something. **6.** a bar placed across the poles of a permanent magnet to close the magnetic circuit when it is not in use.

keep fit *n.* exercises designed to promote physical fitness if performed regularly.

keep from *vb.* (*prep.*) **1.** (foll. by a gerund) to prevent or restrain (oneself or another); refrain or cause to refrain. **2.** (*tr.*) to preserve or protect.

keeping ('ki:pɪŋ) *n.* **1.** conformity or harmony (esp. in **in** or **out of keeping**). **2.** charge or care: *valuables in the keeping of a bank.*

keepnet ('ki:p,nɛt) *n.* a net strung on wire hoops and sealed at one end, suspended in water by anglers to keep alive the fish they have caught.

keep off *vb.* **1.** to stay or cause to stay at a distance (from). **2.** (*prep.*) not to eat or drink or to prevent from eating or drinking. **3.** (*prep.*) to avoid or cause to avoid (a topic).

keep on *vb.* (*adv.*) **1.** to continue or persist in (doing something): *keep on running.* **2.** (*tr.*) to continue to wear. **3.** (*tr.*) to continue to employ: *the firm kept on only ten men.* **4.** (*intr.*; foll. by *about*) to persist in talking (about). **5.** (*intr.*; foll. by *at*) to nag (a person).

keep out *vb.* (*adv.*) **1.** to remain or cause to remain outside. **2. keep out of. a.** to remain or cause to remain unexposed to. **b.** to avoid or cause to avoid: *keep out of his way.*

keepsake ('ki:p,seɪk) *n.* a gift that evokes memories of a person or event.

keep to *vb.* (*prep.*) **1.** to adhere to or stand by or cause to adhere to or stand by. **2.** to confine or be confined to. **3. keep oneself to oneself.** to avoid the society of others. **4.** keep **to oneself. a.** (*intr.*) to avoid the society of others. **b.** (*tr.*) to refrain from sharing or disclosing.

keep up *vb.* (*adv.*) **1.** (*tr.*) to maintain (prices, one's morale) at the present level. **2.** (*intr.*; often foll. by *with*) to maintain a pace or rate set by another. **3.** (*intr.*; often foll. by *with*) to remain informed: *to keep up with developments.* **4.** (*tr.*) to maintain in good condition. **5.** (*tr.*) to hinder (a person) from going to bed at night. **6. keep it up.** to continue a good performance. **7. keep up with.** to remain in contact with, esp. by letter. **8. keep up with (the Joneses).** *Inf.* to compete with (one's neighbours) in material possessions, etc.

Keewatin (ki:'weɪtɪn) *n.* an administrative district of the Northwest Territories of Canada stretching from the district of Mackenzie to Hudson Bay: mostly tundra. Pop.: 4327 (1981). Area: 590 930 sq. km (228 160 sq. miles).

kef (kɛf) *n.* a variant spelling of **kif.**

keffiyeh (kɛ'fi:jə), **kaffiyeh,** *or* **kufiyah** *n.* a cotton headdress worn by Arabs. [C19: from Ar., ?from LL *cofea* COIF]

keg (kɛg) *n.* **1.** a small barrel with a capacity of between five and ten gallons. **2.** *Brit.* an aluminium container in which beer is transported and stored. [C17: var. of ME *kag,* of Scand. origin]

Keighley ('ki:θlɪ) *n.* a town in N England, in West Yorkshire on the River Aire: textile industry. Pop.: 57 451 (1981).

Keijo (,keɪ'dʒəʊ) *n.* transliteration of the Japanese name for **Seoul.**

Keitel ('kaɪt°l) *n.* **Wilhelm** ('vɪlhɛlm). 1882–1946, German field marshal; chief of the supreme command of the armed forces (1938–45). He was convicted at the Nuremberg trials and executed.

Kekkonen (*Finnish* 'kɛkkɔnɛn) *n.* **Urho** ('urhɔ). (1900–86), Finnish statesman; president (1956–81).

Kelantan (kɛ'læntən, kɪ,læn'tæn) *n.* a state of NE Malaysia: under Thai control until it came under the British in 1909; produces rice and rubber. Capital: Kota Bharu. Pop.: 877 575 (1980). Area: 14 930 sq. km (5765 sq. miles).

Keller ('kɛlə) *n.* **Helen** (**Adams**). 1880–1968, U.S. author and lecturer. Blind and deaf from infancy, she was taught to read, write, and speak and became noted for her work for the handicapped.

Kelly ('kɛlɪ) *n.* **1. Gene,** full name *Eugene Curran Kelly.* born 1912, U.S. dancer, choreographer, film actor, and director. His many films include *An American in Paris* (1951) and *Singin' in the Rain* (1952). **2. Grace.** 1929–82, U.S. film actress. Her films included *High Noon* (1952) and *High Society* (1956). She married Prince Rainier III of Monaco in 1956 and died following a car crash. **3. Ned.** 1855–80, Australian horse and cattle thief and bushranger, active in Victoria: captured by the police and hanged.

keloid ('ki:lɔɪd) *n. Pathol.* a hard smooth pinkish raised growth of scar tissue at the site of an injury, tending to occur more frequently in dark-skinned races. [C19: from Gk *khēlē* claw]

kelp (kɛlp) *n.* **1.** any large brown seaweed. **2.** the ash of such seaweed, used as a source of iodine and potash. [C14: from ?]

kelpie[1] *or* **kelpy** ('kɛlpɪ) *n., pl.* **-pies.** an Australian breed of sheepdog having a smooth coat of various colours and erect ears. [named after a particular specimen of the breed, c. 1870]

kelpie[2] ('kɛlpɪ) *n.* (in Scottish folklore) a water spirit in the form of a horse. [C18: prob. rel. to Scot. Gaelic *cailpeach* heifer, from ?]

kelson ('kɛlsən) *n.* a variant spelling of **keelson.**

kelt (kɛlt) *n.* a salmon that has recently spawned. [C14: from ?]

Kelt (kɛlt) *n.* a variant spelling of **Celt.**

kelter ('kɛltə) *n.* a variant of **kilter.**

kelvin ('kɛlvɪn) *n.* the basic SI unit of thermodynamic temperature; the fraction 1/273.16 of the thermodynamic temperature of the triple point of water. Symbol: K

Kelvin ('kɛlvɪn) *n.* **William Thomson,** 1st Baron Kelvin. 1824–1907, British physicist, noted for his work in thermodynamics, inventing the Kelvin scale, and in electricity, pioneering undersea telegraphy.

Kelvin scale *n.* a thermodynamic temperature scale in which the zero is absolute zero. Originally the degree was equal to that on the Celsius scale but it is now defined so that the triple point of water is exactly 273.16 kelvins.

Kemal Atatürk (kɛ'maːl 'ætə,tɜːk) *n.* See **Atatürk.** —**Ke'malism** *n.* —**Ke'malist** *n., adj.*

Kemble ('kɛmbªl) *n.* **1. Frances Anne,** known as *Fanny.* 1809–93, English actress, in the U.S. from 1832. **2.** her uncle, **John Philip.** 1757–1823, English actor and theatrical manager.

Kemerovo (*Russian* 'kjemɪrəvə) *n.* a city in the S Soviet Union: a major coal-mining centre of the Kuznetsk Basin, with important chemical plants. Pop.: 520 000 (1987). Former name (until 1932): **Shcheglovsk.**

Kempe (*German* 'kɛmpə) *n.* **Rudolf** ('ruːdɔlf). 1910–76, German orchestral conductor, noted esp. for his interpretations of Wagner.

Kempis ('kɛmpɪs) *n.* **Thomas à.** ?1380–1471, German Augustinian monk, generally regarded as the author of the devotional work *The Imitation of Christ.*

kempt (kɛmpt) *adj.* (of hair) tidy; combed. See also **unkempt.** [C20: back formation from *unkempt;* orig. p.p. of dialect *kemb* to COMB]

ken (kɛn) *n.* **1.** range of knowledge or perception (esp. in **beyond** *or* **in one's ken**). ~*vb.* **kenning, kenned** *or* **kent. 2.** *Scot. & northern English dialect.* to know. **3.** *Scot. & northern English dialect.* to understand. [OE *cennan*]

Kendal ('kɛndªl) *n.* a town in NW England, in Cumbria: a gateway town to the Lake District, with an ancient woollen industry. Pop.: 23 411 (1981).

kendo ('kɛndəʊ) *n.* the Japanese art of fencing with pliable bamboo staves or, sometimes, real swords. [from Japanese]

Kendrew ('kɛndruː) *n.* Sir **John Cowdery.** born 1917, British biochemist. Using x-ray diffraction he discovered the structure of myoglobin, for which he shared a Nobel Prize (1962) with Max Perutz.

Kenilworth ('kɛnɪl,wɜːθ) *n.* a town in central England, in Warwickshire: ruined 12th-century castle, subject of Sir Walter Scott's novel *Kenilworth.* Pop.: 19 315 (1981).

Kénitra (*French* kenitra) *n.* another name for **Mina Hassan Tani.**

Kennedy[1] ('kɛnɪdɪ) *n.* **Cape.** a former name (1963–73) of (Cape) **Canaveral.**

Kennedy[2] ('kɛnɪdɪ) *n.* **1. Edward Moore.** born 1932, U.S. Democrat politician; senator since 1962. **2.** his brother, **John Fitzgerald,** known as *JFK.* 1917–63, U.S. Democrat statesman; 35th president of the U.S. (1961–63), the first Roman Catholic and the youngest man ever to be elected president. He demanded the withdrawal of Soviet missiles from Cuba (1962) and prepared civil rights reforms; assassinated. **3.** his brother, **Robert Francis.** 1925–68, U.S. Democrat statesman; attorney general (1961–64) and senator for New York (1965–68); assassinated.

kennel ('kɛnªl) *n.* **1.** a hutlike shelter for a dog. U.S. name: **doghouse. 2.** (*usually pl.*) an establishment where dogs are bred, trained, boarded, etc. **3.** a hovel. **4.** a pack of hounds. ~*vb.* **-nelling, -nelled** *or U.S.* **-neling, -neled. 5.** to keep or stay in a kennel. [C14: from OF, from Vulgar L *canīle* (unattested), from L *canis* dog]

Kennelly ('kɛnəlɪ) *n.* **Arthur Edwin.** 1861–1939, U.S. electrical engineer: independently of Heaviside, he predicted the existence of an ionized layer in the upper atmosphere, known as the Kennelly-Heaviside layer or E region.

kenning ('kɛnɪŋ) *n.* a conventional metaphoric name for something, esp. in Old Norse and Old English poetry. [C14: from ON, from *kenna;* see KEN]

Kensington and Chelsea ('kɛnzɪŋtən) *n.* a borough of Greater London, on the River Thames: **Kensington Palace** (17th century) and gardens. Pop.: 137 400 (1986 est.).

kenspeckle ('kɛn,spɛkªl) *adj. Scot.* easily seen or recognized. [C18: from dialect *kenspeck,* of Scand. origin]

Kent[1] (kɛnt) *n.* a county of SE England, on the English Channel: the first part of Great Britain to be colonized by the Romans; one of the seven kingdoms of Anglo-Saxon England until absorbed by Wessex in the 9th century A.D.

Apart from the Downs it is mostly low-lying and agricultural, specializing in fruit and hops. There is a small coalfield on the S coast. Administrative centre: Maidstone. Pop.: 1 500 900 (1986 est.). Area: 3731 sq. km (1440 sq. miles). —'**Kentish** *adj.*

Kent[2] (kɛnt) *n.* **William.** ?1685–1748, English painter, architect, and landscape gardener.

Kentucky (kɛn'tʌkɪ) *n.* **1.** a state of the S central U.S.: consists of an undulating plain in the west, the Bluegrass region in the centre, the Tennessee and Ohio River basins in the southwest, and the Appalachians in the east. Capital: Frankfort. Pop.: 3 728 000 (1986 est.). Area: 102 693 sq. km (39 650 sq. miles). Abbrevs.: **Ken., Ky.** or (with zip code) **KY 2.** a river in central Kentucky, rising in the Cumberland Mountains and flowing northwest to the Ohio river. Length: 417 km (259 miles). —**Ken'tuckian** *adj., n.*

Kenya ('kɛnjə, 'kiːnjə) *n.* **1.** a republic in E Africa, on the Indian Ocean: became a British protectorate in 1895 and a colony in 1920; gained independence in 1963 and is a member of the Commonwealth. Coffee constitutes about a third of the total exports. Official languages: English and Swahili. Religions: animist and Christian. Currency: shilling. Capital: Nairobi. Pop.: 23 000 000 (1988 est.). Area: 582 647 sq. km (224 960 sq. miles). **2. Mount.** an extinct volcano in central Kenya: the second highest mountain in Africa; girth at 2400 m (8000 ft.) is about 150 km (95 miles). The regions above 3200 m (10 500 ft.) constitute **Mount Kenya National Park.** Height: 5200 m (17 058 ft.). —'**Kenyan** *adj., n.*

Kenyatta (kɛn'jætə) *n.* **Jomo** ('dʒəʊməʊ). ?1891–1978, Kenyan statesman: imprisoned as a leader of the Mau Mau revolt (1953–59); elected president of the Kenya African National Union (1961); prime minister of independent Kenya (1963) and president (1964–78).

Keos ('keɪɒs) *n.* an island in the Aegean Sea, in the NW Cyclades. Pop.: 1648 (1981). Area: 174 sq. km (67 sq. miles). Italian name: **Zea.** Modern Greek name: **Kéa.**

Kephallinía (,kɛfali'niːa; *English* ,kɛfə'liːnɪə) *n.* transliteration of the Modern Greek name for **Cephalonia.**

kepi ('keɪpiː) *n., pl.* **kepis.** a military cap with a circular top and a horizontal peak. [C19: from F *képi,* from G (Swiss dialect) *käppi* a little cap, from *kappe* CAP]

Kepler ('kɛplə) *n.* **Johan** (joˈhan). 1571–1630, German astronomer. As discoverer of Kepler's laws of planetary motion he is regarded as one of the founders of modern astronomy.

Kepler's laws *pl. n.* three laws of planetary motion published by Johan Kepler between 1609 and 1619. They deal with the shape of a planet's orbit, the constant velocity of the planet in orbit, and the relationship between the length of a planetary year and the distance from the sun.

kept (kɛpt) *vb.* **1.** the past tense and past participle of **keep. 2. kept woman.** *Censorious.* a woman maintained by a man as his mistress.

Kerala ('kɛrələ, kəˈrɑːlə) *n.* a state of SW India, on the Arabian Sea: formed in 1956, it includes the former state of Travancore-Cochin; has the highest population density of any Indian state. Capital: Trivandrum. Pop.: 25 403 217 (1981). Area: 38 855 sq. km (15 153 sq. miles).

keratin ('kɛrətɪn) *n.* a fibrous sulphur-containing protein that occurs in the outer layer of the skin and in hair, nails, hooves, etc.

keratose ('kɛrə,təʊs, -,təʊz) *adj.* (esp. of certain sponges) having a horny skeleton. [C19: from Gk *keras* horn + -OSE[1]]

kerb *or U.S. & Canad.* **curb** (kɜːb) *n.* a line of stone or concrete forming an edge between a pavement and a roadway. [C17: from OF *courbe* bent, from L *curvus;* see CURVE] —'**kerbing** *n.*

kerb crawling *n.* the act of driving slowly beside the pavement seeking to entice someone into the car for sexual purposes. —**kerb crawler** *n.*

kerb drill *n.* a pedestrian's procedure for crossing a road safely, esp. as taught to children.

Kerbela ('kɜːbələ) *n.* a variant of **Karbala.**

kerbstone *or U.S. & Canad.* **curbstone** ('kɜːb,stəʊn) *n.* one of a series of stones that form a kerb.

Kerch (*Russian* kjertʃ) *n.* a port in the SW Soviet Union, in the Ukrainian SSR on the **Kerch Peninsula** and the **Strait of Kerch** (linking the Black Sea with the Sea of Azov): founded as a Greek colony in the 6th century B.C.;

ceded to Russia in 1774; iron-mining and fishing. Pop.: 173 000 (1987).

kerchief ('kɜːtʃɪf) *n.* a piece of cloth worn over the head. [C13: from OF, from *covrir* to COVER + *chef* head] —'**kerchiefed** *adj.*

kerel ('kɛərəl) *n. S. African.* a young man. [from Afrik. *kêrel;* cf. OE *ceorl*]

Kerenski *or* **Kerensky** (kə'rɛnskɪ; *Russian* 'kjerɪnskɪj) *n.* **Aleksandr Fyodorovich** (alɪk'sandr 'fjɔdərəvitʃ). 1881–1970, Russian liberal revolutionary leader; prime minister (July–October 1917): overthrown by the Bolsheviks.

kerf (kɜːf) *n.* the cut made by a saw, an axe, etc. [OE *cyrf* a cutting]

kerfuffle (kə'fʌf²l) *n. Inf., chiefly Brit.* commotion; disorder. [from Scot. *curfuffle, carfuffle,* from Scot. Gaelic *car* twist, turn + *fuffle* to disarrange]

Kerguelen ('kɜːgɪlɪn) *n.* an archipelago in the S Indian Ocean: consists of one large volcanic island (Kerguelen or Desolation Island) and 300 small islands; part of the French Southern and Antarctic Territories.

Kerkrade (*Dutch* 'kɛrkraːdə) *n.* a town in the SE Netherlands, in Limburg: one of the oldest coal-mining centres in Europe. Pop.: 52 827 (1987).

Kérkyra ('kɛrkira) *n.* transliteration of the Modern Greek name for **Corfu.**

Kerman (kə'maːn) *n.* a city in SE Iran: carpet-making centre. Pop.: 254 786 (1986).

Kermanshah (,kɜːmæn'ʃaː) *n.* the former name (until 1987) of **Bakhtaran.**

kermes ('kɜːmɪz) *n.* **1.** the dried bodies of female scale insects used as a red dyestuff. **2.** a small evergreen Eurasian oak tree: the host plant of kermes scale insects. [C16: from F, from Ar. *qirmiz,* from Sansk. *krmija-* red dye, lit.: produced by a worm]

kermis *or* **kirmess** ('kɜːmɪs) *n.* **1.** (formerly, esp. in Holland and northern Germany) an annual country festival. **2.** *U.S. & Canad.* a similar event held to collect money for charity. [C16: from MDu., from *kerc* church + *misse* MASS; orig. a festival held to celebrate the dedication of a church]

kern[1] *or* **kerne** (kɜːn) *n.* the part of the character on a piece of printer's type that projects beyond the body. [C17: from F *carne* corner of type, ult. from L *cardō* hinge]

kern[2] (kɜːn) *n.* **1.** a lightly armed foot soldier in medieval Ireland or Scotland. **2.** *Arch.* a loutish peasant. [C14: from MIrish *cethern* band of foot soldiers, from *cath* battle]

Kern (kɜːn) *n.* **Jerome** (**David**). 1885–1945, U.S. composer of musical comedies, esp. *Show Boat* (1927).

kernel ('kɜːn²l) *n.* **1.** the edible seed of a nut or fruit within the shell or stone. **2.** the grain of a cereal, esp. wheat, consisting of the seed in a hard husk. **3.** the central or essential part of something. [OE *cyrnel* a little seed, from *corn* seed] —'**kernel-less** *adj.*

kerosene *or* **kerosine** ('kɛrə,siːn) *n.* **1.** another name (esp. U.S. and Canad.) for **paraffin** (sense 1). **2.** the general name for paraffin as a fuel for jet aircraft. [C19: from Gk *kēros* wax + -ENE]

Kerouac ('kɛru,æk) *n.* **Jack,** real name *Jean-Louis Lebris de Kérouac.* 1922–69, U.S. novelist and poet of the Beat generation. His works include *On the Road* (1957) and *Big Sur* (1962).

Kerr (kɜː) *n.* **Sir John Robert.** born 1914, Australian public servant. As governor general of Australia (1974–77), he dismissed the Labor prime minister Gough Whitlam (1975) amid great controversy.

Kerry ('kɛrɪ) *n.* a county of SW Ireland, in W Munster province: mostly mountainous (including the highest peaks in Ireland), with a deeply indented coast and many offshore islands. County town: Tralee. Pop.: 123 922 (1986). Area: 4701 sq. km (1815 sq. miles).

Kesey ('kiːsɪ) *n.* **Ken.** born 1935, U.S. novelist, best-known for *One Flew Over the Cuckoo's Nest* (1962).

kersey ('kɜːzɪ) *n.* a twilled woollen cloth with a cotton warp. [C14: prob. from *Kersey,* village in Suffolk]

kerseymere ('kɜːzɪ,mɪə) *n.* a fine soft woollen cloth of twill weave. [C18: from KERSEY + (*cassi*)*mere,* var. of CASHMERE]

Kesselring ('kɛs²lrɪŋ) *n.* **Albert** ('albert). 1885–1960, German field marshal. He commanded the Luftwaffe attacks on Poland, France, and Britain (1939–40), and was

supreme commander in Italy (1943–45) and on the western front (1945).

Kesteven ('kɛstɪvⁿn, kɛ'stiːvⁿn) *n.* **Parts of.** an area in E England constituting a former administrative division of Lincolnshire.

kestrel ('kɛstrəl) *n.* any of several small falcons that feed on small mammals and tend to hover against the wind. [C15: changed from OF *cresserele,* from *cressele* rattle, from Vulgar L *crepicella* (unattested), from L, from *crepāre* to rustle]

Keswick ('kɛzɪk) *n.* a market town in NW England, in Cumbria in the Lake District: tourist centre. Pop.: 5000 (1985 est.).

ketch (kɛtʃ) *n.* a two-masted sailing vessel, fore-and-aft rigged, with a tall mainmast. [C15 *cache,* prob. from *cacchen* to hunt; see CATCH]

ketchup ('kɛtʃəp), **catchup,** *or* **catsup** *n.* any of various sauces containing vinegar: *tomato ketchup.* [C18: from Chinese *kōetsiap* brine of pickled fish, from *kōe* seafood + *tsiap* sauce]

ketone ('kiːtəʊn) *n.* any of a class of compounds with the general formula R'COR, where R and R' are alkyl or aryl groups. [C19: from G, from *Aketon* ACETONE] —**ketonic** (kɪ'tɒnɪk) *adj.*

ketone body *n. Biochem.* any of three compounds produced when fatty acids are broken down in the liver to provide a source of energy. Excess ketone bodies are present in the blood and urine of people unable to use glucose as an energy source, as in diabetes.

Kettering ('kɛtərɪŋ) *n.* a town in central England, in Northamptonshire: footwear industry. Pop.: 45 356 (1981).

kettle ('kɛt²l) *n.* **1.** a metal container with a handle and spout for boiling water. **2.** any of various metal containers for heating liquids, cooking fish, etc. [C13: from ON *ketill,* ult. from L *catillus* a little pot, from *catinus* pot]

kettledrum ('kɛt²l,drʌm) *n.* a percussion instrument of definite pitch, consisting of a hollow bowl-like hemisphere covered with a skin or membrane, supported on a tripod. The pitch may be adjusted by means of screws, which alter the tension of the skin. —'**kettle,drummer** *n.*

kettle hole *n.* a round hollow formed by the melting of a mass of buried ice.

kettle of fish *n.* **1.** a situation; state of affairs (often used ironically in **a pretty** *or* **fine kettle of fish**). **2.** case; matter for consideration: *that's quite a different kettle of fish.*

Kew (kjuː) *n.* part of the Greater London borough of Richmond-upon-Thames, on the River Thames: famous for **Kew Gardens** (the Royal Botanic Gardens), established in 1759 and given to the nation in 1841.

key[1] (kiː) *n.* **1.** a metal instrument, usually of a specifically contoured shape, that is made to fit a lock and, when rotated, operates the lock's mechanism. **2.** any instrument that is rotated to operate a valve, clock winding mechanism, etc. **3.** a small metal peg or wedge inserted to prevent relative motion. **4.** any of a set of levers operating a typewriter, computer, etc. **5.** any of the visible parts of the lever mechanism of a musical keyboard instrument that when depressed cause the instrument to sound. **6. a.** Also called: **tonality.** any of the 24 major and minor diatonic scales considered as a corpus of notes upon which a piece of music draws for its tonal framework. **b.** the main tonal centre in an extended composition: *a symphony in the key of F major.* **7.** something that is crucial in providing an explanation or interpretation. **8.** a means of achieving a desired end: *the key to happiness.* **9.** a means of access or control: *Gibraltar is the key to the Mediterranean.* **10.** a list of explanations of symbols, codes, etc. **11.** a text that explains or gives information about a work of literature, art, or music. **12.** *Electrical engineering.* a hand-operated switch that is pressed to transmit coded signals, esp. Morse code. **13.** the grooving or scratching of a surface or the application of a rough coat of plaster, etc., to provide a bond for a subsequent finish. **14.** pitch: *he spoke in a low key.* **15.** a mood or style: *a poem in a melancholic key.* **16.** short for **keystone** (sense 1). **17.** *Bot.* any dry winged fruit, esp. that of the ash. **18.** (*modifier*) of great importance: *a key issue.* ~*vb.* (*mainly tr.*) **19.** (foll. by *to*) to harmonize (with): *to key one's actions to the prevailing mood.* **20.** to adjust or fasten with a key or some similar device. **21.** to provide with a key or keys. **22.** (*also intr.*) another word for **keyboard** (sense 2). **23.** to include a distinguishing device in (an advertisement, etc.), so that responses to it can be identified. ~See also **key in, key up.** [OE *cǽg*] — '**keyless** *adj.*

key² (ki:) *n.* a variant spelling of **cay.**

keyboard ('ki:,bɔ:d) *n.* **1. a.** a set of keys, usually hand-operated, as on a piano, typewriter, or typesetting machine. **b.** (*as modifier*): *a keyboard instrument.* ~*vb.* **2.** (*tr.*) to set (a text) in type by using a keyboard machine. —'**key,boarder** *n.*

key grip *n.* the person in charge of moving and setting up camera tracks and scenery in a film or television studio.

keyhole ('ki:,həʊl) *n.* an aperture in a door or a lock case through which a key may be passed to engage the lock mechanism.

key in *vb.* (*tr., adv.*) to enter (information or instructions) in a computer or other device by means of a keyboard or keypad.

key money *n.* a fee payment required from a new tenant of a house or flat before he moves in.

Keynes (keɪnz) *n.* **John Maynard,** 1st Baron Keynes. 1883–1946, English economist. In *The General Theory of Employment, Interest and Money* (1936) he argued that unemployment was characteristic of an unregulated market economy and therefore to achieve a high level of employment it was necessary for governments to manipulate the overall level of demand through monetary and fiscal policies (including, when appropriate, deficit financing). He helped to found the International Monetary Fund and the World Bank. —'**Keynesian** *adj., n.* —'**Keynesian,ism** *n.*

keynote ('ki:,nəʊt) *n.* **1. a.** a central or determining principle in a speech, literary work, etc. **b.** (*as modifier*): *a keynote speech.* **2.** the note upon which a scale or key is based; tonic. ~*vb.* (*tr.*) **3.** to deliver a keynote address to (a political convention, etc.).

keypad ('ki:,pæd) *n.* a small panel with a set of buttons for operating a teletext system, electronic calculator, etc.

key punch *n.* **1.** Also called: **card punch.** a device having a keyboard that is operated manually to transfer data onto punched cards, paper tape, etc. ~*vb.* **key-punch. 2.** to transfer (data) by using a key punch.

key signature *n. Music.* a group of sharps or flats appearing at the beginning of each stave line to indicate the key in which a piece, section, etc., is to be performed.

keystone ('ki:,stəʊn) *n.* **1.** the central stone at the top of an arch or the top stone of a dome or vault. **2.** something that is necessary to connect other related things.

key up *vb.* (*tr., adv.*) to raise the intensity, excitement, tension, etc., of.

kg 1. *abbrev. for* **keg.** ~ **2.** *symbol for* **kilogram.**

KG *abbrev. for* Knight of the Order of the Garter (a Brit. title).

KGB *abbrev. for* the Soviet secret police since 1954. [from Russian *Komitet gosudarstvennoi bezopasnosti* State Security Committee]

Khabarovsk (*Russian* xa'barəfsk) *n.* a port in the E Soviet Union, on the Amur River: the administrative centre of the whole Soviet Far Eastern territory until 1938; a major industrial centre. Pop.: 591 000 (1987).

Khachaturian (,ka:tʃə'tʊərɪən; *Russian* xətʃatu'rjan) *n.* **Aram Ilich** ('arəm ilj'jitʃ). 1903–78, Russian composer. His works, which often incorporate Armenian folk tunes, include a piano concerto and the ballets *Gayaneh* (1942) and *Spartacus* (1954).

khaddar ('ka:də) *or* **khadi** ('ka:dɪ) *n.* a cotton cloth of plain weave, produced in India. [from Hindi *khādar*]

Khakass Autonomous Region (kə'kæs) *n.* an administrative division of the S central Soviet Union, in the Krasnoyarsk Territory of the RSFSR: formed in 1930. Capital: Abakan. Pop.: 547 000 (1986). Area: 61 900 sq. km (23 855 sq. miles).

khaki ('ka:kɪ) *n., pl.* **-kis. 1.** a dull yellowish-brown colour. **2. a.** a hard-wearing fabric of this colour, used esp. for military uniforms. **b.** (*as modifier*): *a khaki jacket.* [C19: from Urdu, from Persian: dusty, from *khāk* dust]

Khalid ibn Abdul Aziz ('ka:lɪd 'ɪbᵊn 'æbdʊl ə'zi:z) *n.* 1913–82, king and President of the Council of Ministers of Saudi Arabia (1975–82).

khalif ('keɪlɪf) *n.* a variant spelling of **caliph.**

Khalkidiki (xalkiðikʲkɪ) *n.* transliteration of the Modern Greek name for **Chalcidice.**

Khalkís (xal'kis) *n.* transliteration of the Modern Greek name for **Chalcis.**

Khama ('ka:mə) *n.* Sir **Seretse** (sə'rɛtsɪ). 1921–80, Botswana statesman; the first president of Botswana (1966–80).

khan¹ (ka:n) *n.* **1. a.** (formerly) a title borne by medieval Chinese emperors and Mongol and Turkic rulers. **b.** such a ruler. **2.** a title of respect borne by important personages in Afghanistan and central Asia. [C14: from OF, from Med. L, from Turkish *khān*, contraction of *khāqān* ruler] —'**khanate** *n.*

khan² (ka:n) *n.* an inn in Turkey, etc.; caravanserai. [C14: via Ar. from Persian]

Khaniá (xa'nja) *n.* transliteration of the Modern Greek name for **Canea.**

Kharkov (*Russian* 'xarjkəf) *n.* a city in the S Soviet Union, in the E Ukrainian SSR: capital of the Ukrainian SSR (1917–34); university (1805). Pop.: 1 587 000 (1987).

Khartoum *or* **Khartum** (ka:'tu:m) *n.* the capital of the Sudan, at the junction of the Blue and the White Nile: with adjoining Khartoum North and Omdurman, the largest conurbation in the country; destroyed by the Mahdists in 1885 when General Gordon was killed; seat of the Anglo-Egyptian government of the Sudan until 1954, then capital of the new republic. Pop.: 476 218 (1983).

Khayyam, Omar (ka:'ja:m) *n.* **Omar.** See **Omar Khayyam.**

khedive (kɪ'di:v) *n.* the viceroy of Egypt under Ottoman suzerainty (1867–1914). [C19: from F, from Turkish, from Persian *khidiw* prince] —**khe'dival** *or* **khe'divial** *adj.*

Khelat (kə'la:t) *n.* a variant spelling of **Kalat.**

Kherson (*Russian* xɪr'sɔn) *n.* a port in the SW Soviet Union, in the S Ukrainian SSR on the Dnieper River near the Black Sea: shipyards. Pop.: 358 000 (1987).

Khingan Mountains ('ʃɪŋ'a:n) *pl. n.* a mountain system of NE China, in W Manchuria. Highest peak: 2034 m (6673 ft.).

Khíos ('çɔs) *n.* transliteration of the Modern Greek name for **Chios.**

Khmer (kmɛə) *n.* **1.** a member of a people of Kampuchea, noted for a civilization that flourished from about 800 A.D. to about 1370. **2.** the language of this people: the official language of Kampuchea. ~*adj.* **3.** of or relating to this people or their language. —'**Khmerian** *adj.*

Khmer Republic *n.* the former official name (1970–76) of **Kampuchea.**

Khojent *or* **Khodzhent** (*Russian* xad'ʒɛnt) *n.* the former name (until 1936) of **Leninabad.**

Khomeini ('xɔmeɪ'ni:) *n.* **Ruholla** ('ruhɒ'la:), known as *Ayatollah Khomeini.* born 1900, Iranian Shiite Muslim religious leader. Following the overthrow of the shah of Iran (1979) he returned from exile and instituted an Islamic republic.

Khotan ('kəʊ'ta:n) *n.* another name for **Hotan.**

Khrushchev (kru:s'tʃɒf, 'krʊstʃɒf; *Russian* xru'ʃtʃɔf) *n.* **Nikita Sergeyevich** (ni'kitə sɪr'gjejrvitʃ). 1894–1971, Soviet statesman; premier of the Soviet Union (1958–64). After Stalin's death he became first secretary of the Soviet Communist Party (1953–64) and initiated a policy to remove the influence of Stalin (1956). As premier, he pursued a policy of peaceful coexistence with the West, but alienated Communist China. He was removed from office in 1964.

Khufu ('ku:fu:) *n.* the original name of **Cheops.**

Khulna ('kʊlna:) *n.* a city in S Bangladesh. Pop.: 420 000 (1984 est.).

Khyber Pass ('kaɪbə) *n.* a narrow pass over the Safed Koh Range between Afghanistan and Pakistan, over which came the Persian, Greek, Tatar, Mogul, and Afghan invasions of India; scene of bitter fighting between the British and Afghans (1838–42, 1878–80). Length: about 53 km (33 miles). Highest point: 1072 m (3518 ft.).

kHz *symbol for* kilohertz.

kiang (kɪ'æŋ) *n.* a variety of the wild ass that occurs in Tibet and surrounding regions. [C19: from Tibetan *rkyan*]

Kiangsi ('kjæŋ'si:) *n.* a variant transliteration of the Chinese name for **Jiangxi.**

Kiangsu ('kjæŋ'su:) *n.* a variant transliteration of the Chinese name for **Jiangsu.**

Kiaochow ('kjaʊ'tʃaʊ) *n.* a variant transliteration of the Chinese name for **Jiazhou.**

kia ora (,kɪə 'ɔ:rə) *sentence substitute. N.Z.* greetings! good luck! [Maori, lit.: be well!]

kibble[1] ('kɪbəl) *n. Brit.* a bucket used in wells or in mining for hoisting. [C17: from G *kübel*, ult. from Med. L *cuppa* CUP]

kibble[2] ('kɪbəl) *vb.* (*tr.*) to grind into small pieces. [C18: from ?]

kibbutz (kɪ'buts) *n., pl.* **kibbutzim** (,kɪbut'siːm). a collective agricultural settlement in modern Israel, owned and administered communally by its members. [C20: from Mod. Heb. *qibbūs* gathering, from Heb. *qibbūtz*]

kibe (kaɪb) *n.* a chilblain, esp. an ulcerated one on the heel. [C14: prob. from Welsh *cibi*, from ?]

kiblah ('kɪblɑː) *n. Islam.* the direction of Mecca, to which Muslims turn in prayer. [C18: from Ar. *qiblah* that which is placed opposite]

kibosh ('kaɪ,bɒʃ) *n. Sl.* **put the kibosh on.** to put a stop to; prevent from continuing; halt. [C19: from ?]

kick (kɪk) *vb.* **1.** (*tr.*) to drive or impel with the foot. **2.** (*tr.*) to hit with the foot or feet. **3.** (*intr.*) to strike out or thrash about with the feet, as in fighting or swimming. **4.** (*intr.*) to raise a leg high, as in dancing. **5.** (of a gun, etc.) to recoil or strike in recoiling when fired. **6.** (*tr.*) *Rugby.* to make (a conversion or a drop goal) by means of a kick. **7.** (*tr.*) *Soccer.* to score (a goal) by a kick. **8.** (*intr.*) *Athletics.* to put on a sudden spurt. **9.** (*intr.*) to make a sudden violent movement. **10.** (*intr.*; sometimes foll. by *against*) *Inf.* to object or resist. **11.** (*intr.*) *Inf.* to be active and in good health (esp. in **alive and kicking**). **12.** *Inf.* to change gear in (a car): *he kicked into third.* **13.** (*tr.*) *Inf.* to free oneself of (an addiction, etc.): *to kick the habit.* **14. kick up one's heels.** *Inf.* to enjoy oneself without inhibition. ~*n.* **15.** a thrust or blow with the foot. **16.** any of certain rhythmic leg movements used in swimming. **17.** the recoil of a gun or other firearm. **18.** *Inf.* exciting quality or effect (esp. in **get a kick out of, for kicks**). **19.** *Athletics.* a sudden spurt, acceleration, or boost. **20.** a sudden violent movement. **21.** *Inf.* the sudden stimulating effect of strong alcoholic drink or certain drugs. **22.** *Inf.* power or force. **23. kick in the teeth.** *Sl.* a humiliating rebuff. ~See also **kick about, kick in,** etc. [C14 *kiken,* ?from ON] — **'kickable** *adj.*

kick about *or* **around** *vb.* (*mainly adv.*) *Inf.* **1.** (*tr.*) to treat harshly. **2.** (*tr.*) to discuss (ideas, etc.) informally. **3.** (*intr.*) to wander aimlessly. **4.** (*intr.*) to lie neglected or forgotten.

kickback ('kɪk,bæk) *n.* **1.** a strong reaction. **2.** part of an income paid to a person having influence over the size or payment of the income, esp. by some illegal arrangement. ~*vb.* **kick back.** (*adv.*) **3.** (*intr.*) to have a strong reaction. **4.** (*intr.*) (esp. of a gun) to recoil. **5.** to pay a kickback to (someone).

kickdown ('kɪk,daʊn) *n.* a method of changing gear in a car with automatic transmission, by fully depressing the accelerator.

kicker ('kɪkə) *n.* **1.** a person or thing that kicks. **2.** *U.S. & Canad. sl.* a hidden and disadvantageous factor.

kick in *vb.* (*tr., adv.*) *Austral. inf.* to contribute.

kick off *vb.* (*intr., adv.*) **1.** to start play in a game of football by kicking the ball from the centre of the field. **2.** *Inf.* to commence (a discussion, job, etc.). ~*n.* **kickoff.** **3. a.** a place kick from the centre of the field in a game of football. **b.** the time at which the first such kick is due to take place.

kick on *vb.* (*adv.*) *Austral. inf.* to continue.

kick out *vb.* (*tr., adv.*) *Inf.* to eject or dismiss.

kickshaw ('kɪk,ʃɔː) *or* **kickshaws** *n.* **1.** a valueless trinket. **2.** *Arch.* a small exotic delicacy. [C16: back formation from *kickshaws,* by folk etymology from F *quelque chose* something]

kickstand ('kɪk,stænd) *n.* a short metal bar attached to the frame of a motorcycle or bicycle, which when kicked into a vertical position holds the stationary vehicle upright.

kick-start ('kɪk,stɑːt) *vb.* (*tr.*) to start (an engine, esp. of a motorcycle) by means of a pedal that is kicked downwards. — **'kick-,starter** *n.*

kick up *vb.* (*adv.*) *Inf.* to cause (trouble, etc.).

kick upstairs *vb.* (*tr., adv.*) *Inf.* to promote to a higher but effectively powerless position.

kid[1] (kɪd) *n.* **1.** the young of a goat or of a related animal, such as an antelope. **2.** soft smooth leather made from the hide of a kid. **3.** *Inf.* **a.** a young person; child. **b.** (*modifier*) younger or being still a child: *kid brother.* ~*vb.*

kidding, kidded. 4. (of a goat) to give birth to (young). [C12: from ON] — **'kiddishness** *n.* — **'kid,like** *adj.*

kid[2] (kɪd) *vb.* **kidding, kidded.** *Inf.* (sometimes foll. by *on* or *along*) **1.** (*tr.*) to tease or deceive for fun. **2.** (*intr.*) to behave or speak deceptively for fun. **3.** (*tr.*) to fool (oneself) into believing (something): *don't kid yourself that no-one else knows.* [C19: prob. from KID[1]] — **'kidder** *n.* — **'kiddingly** *adv.*

Kid (kɪd) *n.* **Thomas.** a variant spelling of (Thomas) **Kyd.**

Kidd (kɪd) *n.* **William,** known as *Captain Kidd.* 1645–1701, Scottish privateer, pirate, and murderer; hanged.

Kidderminster ('kɪdə,mɪnstə) *n.* **1.** a town in W central England, in NE Hereford and Worcester on the River Stour: carpet industry. Pop.: 51 261 (1981). **2.** a type of ingrain reversible carpet originally made at Kidderminster.

kiddy *or* **kiddie** ('kɪdɪ) *n., pl.* **-dies.** *Inf.* an affectionate word for **child.**

kid glove *n.* **1.** a glove made of kidskin. **2. handle with kid gloves.** to treat with great tact or caution. ~*adj.* **kidglove.** **3.** overdelicate. **4.** diplomatic; tactful: *a kidglove approach.*

kidnap ('kɪdnæp) *vb.* **-napping, -napped** *or U.S.* **-naping, -naped.** (*tr.*) to carry off and hold (a person), usually for ransom. [C17: KID[1] + obs. *nap* to steal; see NAB] — **'kidnapper** *n.*

kidney ('kɪdnɪ) *n.* **1.** either of two bean-shaped organs at the back of the abdominal cavity in man. They filter waste products from the blood, which are excreted as urine. Related adj.: **renal.** **2.** the corresponding organ in other animals. **3.** the kidneys of certain animals used as food. **4.** class, type, or disposition (esp. in **of the same** *or* **a different kidney**). [C14: from ?]

kidney bean *n.* **1.** any of certain bean plants having kidney-shaped seeds, esp. the scarlet runner. **2.** the seed of any of these beans.

kidney machine *n.* a machine carrying out the functions of a kidney, esp. used in haemodialysis.

kidney stone *n. Pathol.* a hard mass formed in the kidney, usually composed of oxalates, phosphates, and carbonates.

kidology (kɪ'dɒlədʒɪ) *n. Brit. inf.* the practice of bluffing or deception. [C20: from KID[2] + *ology* a science]

Kidron ('kiːdrən) *n.* a variant of **Kedron.**

kidskin ('kɪd,skɪn) *n.* a soft smooth leather made from the hide of a young goat. Often shortened to **kid.**

kids' stuff *n. Sl.* **1.** something considered fit only for children. **2.** something considered easy.

kidstakes ('kɪd,steɪks) *Austral. inf.* ~*pl. n.* **1.** pretence; nonsense: *cut the kidstakes!* ~*interj.* **2.** an exclamation of annoyance or disagreement.

kie kie ('kiːɛ kiːɛ) *n.* a New Zealand climbing plant with edible bracts. [from Maori]

Kiel (kiːl) *n.* a port in N West Germany, capital of Schleswig-Holstein state, on the **Kiel Canal** (connecting the North Sea with the Baltic): joined the Hanseatic League in 1284; became part of Denmark in 1773 and passed to Prussia in 1866; an important naval base in World Wars I and II; shipbuilding and engineering industries. Pop.: 244 700 (1986).

Kielce (*Polish* 'kjɛltsɛ) *n.* an industrial city in S Poland. Pop.: 201 000 (1985).

Kierkegaard ('kɪəkə,gɑːd; *Danish* 'kirgəgɔːr) *n.* **Soren Aabye** ('soːrən 'ɔːby). 1813–55, Danish philosopher and theologian. He rejected organized Christianity and anticipated the existentialists in emphasizing man's moral responsibility and freedom of choice. His works include *Either/Or* (1843), *The Concept of Dread* (1844), and *The Sickness unto Death* (1849). — ,**Kierke'gaardian** *adj.*

kieselguhr ('kiːzəl,gʊə) *n.* an unconsolidated form of diatomite. [C19: from G *Kieselgur,* from *Kiesel* flint + *Gur* loose earthy deposit]

Kiev ('kiːɛf; *Russian* 'kijɪf) *n.* a city in the SW Soviet Union, capital of the Ukrainian SSR, on the Dnieper River: formed the first Russian state by the late 9th century; university (1834). Pop.: 2 554 000 (1987).

kif (kɪf, kiːf), **kef,** *or* **kief** (kiːf) *n.* **1.** another name for **marijuana. 2.** any drug that when smoked is capable of producing a euphoric condition. **3.** the euphoric condition produced by smoking marijuana. [C20: from Ar. *kayf* pleasure]

Kigali (kɪ'gɑːlɪ) *n.* the capital of Rwanda, in the central part. Pop.: 156 650 (1981).

kike (kaɪk) *n. U.S. & Canad. sl.* an offensive word for **Jew.** [C20: prob. var. of *kiki*, reduplication of *-ki*, common name-ending among Jews from Slavic countries]

Kikládhes (ki'klaðes) *n.* transliteration of the Modern Greek name for **Cyclades.**

Kilauea (ˌkiːlɑːuːˈeɪə) *n.* a crater on the E side of Mauna Loa volcano, on SE Hawaii Island: the world's largest active crater. Height: 1247 m (4090 ft.). Width: 3 km (2 miles).

Kildare (kɪl'dɛə) *n.* a county of E Ireland, in Leinster province: mostly low-lying and fertile. County town: Naas. Pop.: 116 015 (1986). Area: 1694 sq. km (654 sq. miles).

kilderkin ('kɪldəkɪn) *n.* **1.** an obsolete unit of liquid capacity equal to 16 or 18 Imperial gallons or of dry capacity equal to 16 or 18 wine gallons. **2.** a cask capable of holding a kilderkin. [C14: from MDu. *kindekijn*, from *kintal* hundredweight, from Med. L *quintale*]

Kilimanjaro (ˌkɪlɪmən'dʒɑːrəʊ) *n.* a volcanic massif in N Tanzania: the highest peak in Africa; extends from east to west for 80 km (50 miles). Height: 5895 m (19 340 ft.).

Kilkenny (kɪl'kɛnɪ) *n.* **1.** a county of SE Ireland, in Leinster province: mostly agricultural. County town: Kilkenny. Pop.: 73 094 (1986). Area: 2062 sq. km (796 sq. miles). **2.** a market town in SE Ireland, county town of Co. Kilkenny: capital of the ancient kingdom of Ossory. Pop.: 9466 (1981).

kill (kɪl) *vb. (mainly tr.)* **1.** (*also intr.;* when *tr.,* sometimes foll. by *off*) to cause the death of (a person or animal). **2.** to put an end to: *to kill someone's interest.* **3.** to make (time) pass quickly, esp. while waiting for something. **4.** to deaden (sound). **5.** *Inf.* to tire out: *the effort killed him.* **6.** *Inf.* to cause to suffer pain or discomfort: *my shoes are killing me.* **7.** *Inf.* to quash or veto: *the bill was killed in the House of Lords.* **8.** *Inf.* to switch off; stop. **9.** (*also intr.*) *Inf.* to overcome with attraction, laughter, surprise, etc.: *she was dressed to kill.* **10.** *Tennis, squash, etc.* to hit (a ball) so hard or so accurately that the opponent cannot return it. **11.** *Soccer.* to bring (a moving ball) under control. **12. kill oneself.** *Inf.* to overexert oneself: *don't kill yourself.* **13. kill two birds with one stone.** to achieve two results with one action. ~*n.* **14.** the act of causing death, esp. at the end of a hunt, bullfight, etc. **15.** the animal or animals killed during a hunt. **16.** *N.Z.* a seasonal tally of the number of stock killed at a meatworks. **17.** the destruction of a battleship, tank, etc. **18. in at the kill.** present at the end of some undertaking. [C13 *cullen;* see QUELL]

Killarney (kɪ'lɑːnɪ) *n.* a town in SW Ireland, in Co. Kerry: a tourist centre near the **Lakes of Killarney.** Pop.: 7693 (1981).

killdeer ('kɪlˌdɪə) *n., pl.* **-deer** *or* **-deers.** a large brown-and-white North American plover with two black breast bands. [C18: imit.]

killer ('kɪlə) *n.* **1. a.** a person or animal that kills, esp. habitually. **b.** (*as modifier*): *a killer shark.* **2.** something, esp. a task or activity, that is particularly taxing or exhausting. **3.** *Austral. & N.Z.* a farm animal selected to be killed for food.

killer bee *n.* an African honeybee, or one of its hybrids originating in Brazil, that is extremely aggressive when disturbed.

killer whale *n.* a ferocious black-and-white toothed whale most common in cold seas.

killick ('kɪlɪk) *or* **killock** ('kɪlək) *n. Naut.* a small anchor, esp. one made of a heavy stone. [C17: from ?]

Killiecrankie (ˌkɪlɪ'kræŋkɪ) *n.* a pass in central Scotland, in the Grampians: scene of a battle (1689) in which the Jacobites defeated William III's forces but lost their leader, Viscount Dundee.

killifish ('kɪlɪˌfɪʃ) *n., pl.* **-fish** *or* **-fishes.** any of various chiefly American minnow-like fishes of fresh and brackish waters: used to control mosquitoes and as anglers' bait. [C19: from MDu. *kille* river + FISH]

killing ('kɪlɪŋ) *Inf. ~adj.* **1.** very tiring: *a killing pace.* **2.** extremely funny. **3.** causing death; fatal. ~*n.* **4.** the act of causing death; slaying. **5.** a sudden stroke of success, usually financial, as in speculations on the stock market (esp. in **make a killing**).

killjoy ('kɪlˌdʒɔɪ) *n.* a person who spoils other people's pleasure.

Kilmarnock (kɪl'mɑːnək) *n.* a town in SW Scotland, in SW Strathclyde region: associations with Robert Burns; engineering and textile industries; whisky blending. Pop.: 52 080 (1981).

kiln (kɪln) *n.* a large oven for burning, drying, or processing something, such as porcelain or bricks. [OE *cylen,* from LL *culīna* kitchen, from L *coquere* to COOK]

kilo ('kiːləʊ) *n., pl.* **kilos.** short for **kilogram** or **kilometre.**

kilo- *prefix.* **1.** denoting 10^3 (1000): *kilometre.* Symbol: k **2.** (in computers) denoting 2^{10} (1024): *kilobyte:* in computer usage, *kilo-* is restricted to sizes of storage (e.g. *kilobit*) when it means 1024; in other computer contexts it retains its usual meaning of 1000. [from F, from Gk *khilioi* thousand]

kilobyte ('kɪləˌbaɪt) *n. Computers.* 1024 bytes. Abbrev.: **KB, kbyte.** See also **kilo-** (sense 2).

kilocalorie ('kɪləʊˌkælərɪ) *n.* another name for **Calorie.**

kilocycle ('kɪləʊˌsaɪkəl) *n.* short for kilocycle per second: a former unit of frequency equal to 1 kilohertz.

kilogram *or* **kilogramme** ('kɪləʊˌɡræm) *n.* **1.** one thousand grams. **2.** the basic SI unit of mass, equal to the mass of the international prototype held by the *Bureau International des Poids et Mesures.* Symbol: kg

kilohertz ('kɪləʊˌhɜːts) *n.* one thousand hertz; one thousand cycles per second. Symbol: kHz

kilolitre ('kɪləˌliːtə) *n.* one thousand litres. Symbol: kl

kilometre *or U.S.* **kilometer** ('kɪləˌmiːtə, kɪ'lɒmɪtə) *n.* one thousand metres. Symbol: km —**kilometric** (ˌkɪləʊ'mɛtrɪk) *adj.*

kiloton ('kɪləʊˌtʌn) *n.* **1.** one thousand tons. **2.** an explosive power, esp. of a nuclear weapon, equal to the power of 1000 tons of TNT. Abbrev.: **kt.**

kilovolt ('kɪləʊˌvəʊlt) *n.* one thousand volts. Symbol: kV

kilowatt ('kɪləʊˌwɒt) *n.* one thousand watts. Symbol: kW

kilowatt-hour *n.* a unit of energy equal to the work done by a power of 1000 watts in one hour. Symbol: kWh

kilt (kɪlt) *n.* **1.** a knee-length pleated skirt, esp. one in tartan, as worn by men in Highland dress. ~*vb.* (*tr.*) **2.** to tuck (the skirt) up around one's body. **3.** to put pleats in (cloth, etc.). [C18: of Scand. origin] — **'kilted** *adj.*

kilter ('kɪltə) *or* **kelter** *n.* working order (esp. in **out of kilter**). [C17: from ?]

Kilung ('kiː'lʊŋ) *n.* another name for **Chilung.**

Kimberley ('kɪmbəlɪ) *n.* **1.** a city in central South Africa, in N Cape Province: besieged (1899–1900) for 126 days during the Boer War; diamond-mining and -marketing centre, with heavy engineering works. Pop.: 144 923 (1980). **2.** Also called: **the Kimberleys.** a plateau region of NW Australia, in N Western Australia: consists of rugged mountains surrounded by grassland. Area: about 360 000 sq. km (140 000 sq. miles).

kimberlite ('kɪmbəˌlaɪt) *n.* an intrusive igneous rock consisting largely of peridotite and often containing diamonds. [C19: from KIMBERLEY + -ITE[1]]

Kim Il Sung (kim il sʌŋ) *n.* born 1912, North Korean statesman and marshal; prime minister (1948–72) and president (from 1972) of North Korea.

kimono (kɪ'məʊnəʊ) *n., pl.* **-nos.** a loose sashed ankle-length garment with wide sleeves, worn in Japan. [C19: from Japanese: clothing, from *ki* to wear + *mono* thing] —**ki'monoed** *adj.*

kin (kɪn) *n.* **1.** a person's relatives collectively. **2.** a class or group with similar characteristics. **3.** See **next of kin.** ~*adj.* **4.** (*postpositive*) related by blood. [OE *cyn*]

-kin *suffix forming nouns.* small: *lambkin.* [from MDu., of West Gmc origin]

Kinabalu (ˌkɪnəbə'luː) *n.* a mountain in Malaysia, on N Borneo in central Sabah: the highest peak in Borneo. Height: 4125 m (13 533 ft.).

kinaesthesia (ˌkɪnɪs'θiːzɪə) *or U.S.* **kinesthesia** *n.* the sensation by which bodily position, weight, muscle tension, and movement are perceived. [C19: from NL, from Gk *kinein* to move + AESTHESIA] —**kinaesthetic** *or U.S.* **kinesthetic** (ˌkɪnɪs'θɛtɪk) *adj.*

Kincardineshire (kɪn'kɑːdɪnˌʃɪə, -ʃə) *n.* (until 1975) a county of E Scotland, now part of Grampian region. Also called: **the Mearns.**

Kinchinjunga (ˌkɪntʃɪn'dʒʌŋɡə) *n.* a variant of **Kangchenjunga.**

kincob ('kɪŋkɒb) *n.* a fine silk fabric embroidered with threads of gold or silver, of a kind made in India. [C18: from Urdu *kimkhāb*]

kind[1] (kaɪnd) *adj.* **1.** having a friendly nature or attitude. **2.** helpful to others or to another: *a kind deed.* **3.** considerate or humane. **4.** cordial; courteous (esp. in **kind regards**). **5.** pleasant; mild: *a kind climate.* **6.** *Inf.* beneficial or not harmful. [OE *gecynde* natural, native]

kind[2] (kaɪnd) *n.* **1.** a class or group having characteristics in common; sort; type: *two of a kind.* **2.** an instance or example of a class or group, esp. a rudimentary one: *heating of a kind.* **3.** essential nature or character: *the difference is one of kind rather than degree.* **4.** *Arch.* nature; the natural order. **5. in kind. a.** (of payment) in goods or produce rather than in money. **b.** with something of the same sort: *to return an insult in kind.* [OE *gecynd* nature]

▷ **Usage.** Careful users of English avoid the mixture of plural and singular constructions frequently used with *kind* and *sort*, as in *those kind* (instead of *kinds*) *of buildings seem badly designed* or *these sort* (instead of *sorts*) *of distinctions are becoming blurred.*

kindergarten ('kɪndə,gɑːt²n) *n.* a class or small school for young children, usually between the ages of four and six. [C19: from G, lit.: children's garden]

kind-hearted *adj.* kindly, readily sympathetic. —,**kind-'heartedly** *adv.* — ,**kind-'heartedness** *n.*

kindle ('kɪnd²l) *vb.* **1.** to set alight or start to burn. **2.** to arouse or be aroused: *the project kindled his interest.* **3.** to make or become bright. [C12: from ON *kynda*, infl. by ON *kyndill* candle] —'**kindler** *n.*

kindling ('kɪndlɪŋ) *n.* material for starting a fire, such as dry wood, straw, etc.

kindly ('kaɪndlɪ) *adj.* **-lier, -liest. 1.** having a sympathetic or warm-hearted nature. **2.** motivated by warm and sympathetic feelings. **3.** pleasant: *a kindly climate.* **4.** *Arch.* natural; normal. ~*adv.* **5.** in a considerate or humane way. **6.** with tolerance: *he kindly forgave my rudeness.* **7.** cordially: *he greeted us kindly.* **8.** please (often used to express impatience or formality): *will you kindly behave yourself!* **9.** *Arch.* appropriately. **10. take kindly.** to react favourably. —'**kindliness** *n.*

kindness ('kaɪndnɪs) *n.* **1.** the practice or quality of being kind. **2.** a kind or helpful act.

kindred ('kɪndrɪd) *adj.* **1.** having similar or common qualities, origin, etc. **2.** related by blood or marriage. **3. kindred spirit.** a person with whom one has something in common. ~*n.* **4.** relationship by blood. **5.** similarity in character. **6.** a person's relatives collectively. [C12 *kinred*, from KIN + -*red*, from OE *ræden* rule, from *rædan* to rule]

kine (kaɪn) *n.* (*functioning as pl.*) an archaic word for cows or cattle. [OE *cyna* of cows, from *cū* COW[1]]

kinematics (,kɪnɪ'mætɪks) *n.* (*functioning as sing.*) the study of the motion of bodies without reference to mass or force. [C19: from Gk *kinēma* movement; see CINEMA, -ICS] —,**kine'matic** *adj.* —,**kine'matically** *adv.*

kinematograph (,kɪnɪ'mætə,grɑːf) *n.* a variant spelling of **cinematograph.**

kinesics (kɪ'niːsɪks) *n.* (*functioning as sing.*) the study of the role of body movements, such as winking, shrugging, etc., in communication.

kinesthesia (,kɪnɪs'θiːzɪə) *n.* the usual U.S. spelling of **kinaesthesia.**

kinetic (kɪ'nɛtɪk) *adj.* relating to or caused by motion. [C19: from Gk *kinētikos*, from *kinein* to move] —**ki'netically** *adv.*

kinetic art *n.* art, esp. sculpture, that moves or has moving parts.

kinetic energy *n.* the energy of motion of a body equal to the work it would do if it were brought to rest. It is equal to the product of the increase of mass caused by motion times the square of the speed of light.

kinetics (kɪ'nɛtɪks, kaɪ-) *n.* (*functioning as sing.*) **1.** another name for **dynamics** (sense 2). **2.** the branch of mechanics, including both dynamics and kinematics, concerned with the study of bodies in motion. **3.** the branch of dynamics that excludes the study of bodies at rest.

kinetic theory (of gases) *n.* **the.** a theory of gases postulating that they consist of particles moving at random and undergoing elastic collisions.

kinfolk ('kɪn,fəʊk) *pl. n. Chiefly U.S. & Canad.* another word for **kinsfolk.**

king (kɪŋ) *n.* **1.** a male sovereign prince who is the official ruler of an independent state; monarch. Related adjs.: **royal, regal. 2. a.** a ruler or chief: *king of the fairies.* **b.** (*in combination*): *the pirate king.* **3.** a person, animal, or thing considered as the best or most important of its kind. **4.** any of four playing cards in a pack, one for each suit, bearing the picture of a king. **5.** the most important chess piece. **6.** *Draughts.* a piece that has moved entirely across the board and has been crowned, after which it may move backwards as well as forwards. **7. king of kings. a.** God. **b.** a title of any of various oriental monarchs. ~*vb.* (*tr.*) **8.** to make (someone) a king. **9. king it.** to act in a superior fashion. [OE *cyning*] —'**king,hood** *n.* — '**king,like** *adj.*

King (kɪŋ) *n.* **1. B.B.,** real name *Riley B. King.* born 1925, U.S. blues singer and guitarist. **2. Billie Jean** (née *Moffitt*). born 1943, U.S. tennis player: Wimbledon champion 1966–68, 1972–73, and 1975; U.S. champion 1967, 1971–72, and 1974. **3. Martin Luther.** 1929–68, U.S. Baptist minister and civil-rights leader. He advocated nonviolence in his campaigns against the segregation of Negroes in the South: assassinated: Nobel Peace Prize 1964. **4. William Lyon Mackenzie.** 1874–1950, Canadian Liberal statesman; prime minister (1921–26; 1926–30; 1935–48).

kingbird ('kɪŋ,bɜːd) *n.* any of several large American flycatchers.

kingbolt ('kɪŋ,bəʊlt) *or* **king rod** *n.* **a.** the pivot bolt that connects the body of a horse-drawn carriage to the front axle and provides the steering joint. **b.** a similar bolt placed between a railway carriage and the bogies.

King Charles spaniel *n.* a toy breed of spaniel with a short turned-up nose and a domed skull. [C17: after Charles II of England, who popularized the breed]

king cobra *n.* a very large venomous tropical Asian snake that extends its neck into a hood when alarmed. Also called: **hamadryad.**

King Country *n.* an area in the centre of North Island, New Zealand. [from *The Maori King*, name given to Maori chief there]

king crab *n.* another name for the **horseshoe crab.**

kingcup ('kɪŋ,kʌp) *n. Brit.* any of several yellow-flowered plants, esp. the marsh marigold.

kingdom ('kɪŋdəm) *n.* **1.** a territory, state, people, or community ruled or reigned over by a king or queen. **2.** any of the three groups into which natural objects may be divided: the animal, plant, and mineral kingdoms. **3.** *Theol.* the eternal sovereignty of God. **4.** an area of activity: *the kingdom of the mind.*

kingdom come *n.* **1.** the next world. **2.** *Inf.* the end of the world (esp. in *until kingdom come*). **3.** *Inf.* unconsciousness.

kingfish ('kɪŋ,fɪʃ) *n., pl.* **-fish** *or* **-fishes. 1.** a marine food and game fish occurring in warm American Atlantic coastal waters. **2.** *Austral.* any of various types of trevally, mulloway, and barracouta. **3.** any of various other large food fishes, esp. the Spanish mackerel.

kingfisher ('kɪŋ,fɪʃə) *n.* a bird which has a greenish-blue and orange plumage, a large head, short tail, and long sharp bill, and feeds on fish. [C15: orig. *king's fisher*]

King James Version *or* **Bible** *n.* **the.** another name for the **Authorized Version.**

kingklip ('kɪŋ,klɪp) *n.* an edible eel-like marine fish. [from Afrik., from Du. *koning* king + *klip* rock]

kinglet ('kɪŋlɪt) *n.* **1.** *Often derog.* the king of a small or insignificant territory. **2.** *U.S. & Canad.* any of various small warblers having a black-edged yellow crown.

kingly ('kɪŋlɪ) *adj.* **-lier, -liest. 1.** appropriate to a king. **2.** royal. ~*adv.* **3.** *Poetic* or *arch.* in a manner appropriate to a king. —'**kingliness** *n.*

kingmaker ('kɪŋ,meɪkə) *n.* a person who has control over appointments to positions of authority.

king-of-arms *n., pl.* **kings-of-arms. 1.** the highest rank of heraldic officer. **2.** a person holding this rank.

king of the castle *n. Chiefly Brit.* a children's game in which each child attempts to stand alone on a mound by pushing other children off it.

king penguin *n.* a large New Zealand subantarctic penguin.

kingpin ('kɪŋ,pɪn) *n.* **1.** the most important person in an organization. **2.** Also called (Brit.): **swivel pin.** a pivot pin that provides a steering joint in a motor vehicle by securing the stub axle to the axle beam. **3.** *Tenpin bowling.* the front pin in the triangular arrangement of the ten pins. **4.** (in ninepins) the central pin in the diamond pattern of the nine pins.

king post n. a vertical post connecting the apex of a triangular roof truss to the tie beam.

King's Bench n. (when the sovereign is male) another name for **Queen's Bench Division.**

King's Counsel n. (when the sovereign is male) another name for **Queen's Counsel.**

King's English n. (esp. when the British sovereign is male) standard Southern British English.

king's evidence n. (when the sovereign is male) another name for **queen's evidence.**

king's evil n. **the.** Pathol. a former name for **scrofula.** [C14: from the belief that the king's touch would heal scrofula]

Kingsford-Smith ('kɪŋzfəd'smɪθ) n. Sir **Charles (Edward).** 1897–1935, Australian aviator and pioneer (with Charles Ulm) of trans-Pacific and trans-Tasman flights.

king's highway n. (in Britain, esp. when the sovereign is male) any public road or right of way.

kingship ('kɪŋʃɪp) n. **1.** the position or authority of a king. **2.** the skill of ruling as a king.

king-size or **king-sized** adj. larger or longer than a standard size.

Kingsley ('kɪŋzlɪ) n. **1. Charles.** 1819–75, English clergyman and author. His works include the historical romances Westward Ho! (1855) and Hereward the Wake (1866) and the children's story The Water Babies (1863). **2.** his brother, **Henry.** 1830–76, English novelist, editor, and journalist, who spent some time in Australia. His works include Ravenshoe (1861) and the Anglo-Australian novels The Recollections of Geoffrey Hamlyn (1859) and The Hillyars and the Burtons (1865).

King's Lynn ('kɪŋz 'lɪn) n. a market town in E England, in Norfolk on the estuary of the Great Ouse near the Wash: a leading port in the Middle Ages. Pop.: 33 340 (1981). Also called: **Lynn, Lynn Regis.**

Kingston ('kɪŋstən) n. **1.** the capital and chief port of Jamaica, on the SE coast: University of the West Indies. Pop.: 100 637 (1983 est.). **2.** a port in SE Canada, in SE Ontario: the chief naval base of Lake Ontario and a large industrial centre; university (1841). Pop.: 52 616 (1981). **3.** short for **Kingston upon Thames.**

Kingston upon Hull n. the official name of **Hull**[1].

Kingston upon Thames n. a borough of SW Greater London, on the River Thames: the administrative centre of Surrey; formed in 1965 by the amalgamation of several former boroughs of Surrey. Pop.: 133 800 (1986 est.).

Kingstown ('kɪŋz,taʊn) n. a port in the West Indies, in the Windward Islands, capital of St Vincent. Pop.: 32 600 (1984 est.).

kinin ('kaɪnɪn) n. **1.** any of a group of polypeptides in the blood that cause dilation of the blood vessels. **2.** a substance that promotes cell division and retards ageing in plants. [C20: from Gk kin(ēma) motion + -IN]

kink (kɪŋk) n. **1.** a sharp twist or bend in a wire, rope, hair, etc. **2.** a crick in the neck or similar muscular spasm. **3.** a flaw or minor difficulty in some undertaking. **4.** a flaw or idiosyncrasy of personality. [C17: from Du.: a curl in a rope]

kinkajou ('kɪŋkə,dʒuː) n. an arboreal fruit-eating mammal of Central and South America, with a long prehensile tail. Also called: **honey bear.** [C18: from F quincajou, from Algonquian]

kinky ('kɪŋkɪ) adj. **kinkier, kinkiest. 1.** Sl. given to unusual, abnormal, or deviant sexual practices. **2.** Inf. exhibiting unusual idiosyncrasies of personality. **3.** Inf. attractive or provocative in a bizarre way: kinky clothes. **4.** tightly looped, as a wire or rope. **5.** tightly curled, as hair. —'**kinkily** adv. —'**kinkiness** n.

Kinnock ('kɪnək) n. **Neil (Gordon).** born 1942, British Labour politician, born in Wales; leader of the Labour Party from 1983.

kino ('kiːnəʊ) n. a dark red resin obtained from various tropical plants, esp. an Indian leguminous tree, used as an astringent and in tanning. [C18: of West African origin]

Kinross-shire (kɪn'rɒs,ʃɪə, -ʃə) n. (until 1975) a county of E central Scotland, now part of Tayside region.

Kinsey ('kɪnzɪ) n. **Alfred Charles.** 1894–1956, U.S. zoologist, who directed a survey of human sexual behaviour.

kinsfolk ('kɪnz,fəʊk) pl. n. one's family or relatives.

Kinshasa (kɪn'ʃɑːzə, -'ʃɑːsə) n. the capital of Zaïre, on the River Congo opposite Brazzaville: became capital of the Belgian Congo in 1929 and of the new republic of Zaïre in 1960; university (1954). Pop.: 2 778 281 (1985). Former name (until 1966): **Léopoldville.**

kinship ('kɪnʃɪp) n. **1.** blood relationship. **2.** the state of having common characteristics.

kinsman ('kɪnzmən) n., pl. -**men.** a blood relation or a relation by marriage. —'**kins,woman** fem. n.

kiosk ('kiːɒsk) n. **1.** a small sometimes movable booth from which cigarettes, newspapers, sweets, etc., are sold. **2.** Chiefly Brit. a telephone box. **3.** (in Turkey, Iran, etc.) a light open-sided pavilion. [C17: from F kiosque bandstand, from Turkish, from Persian kūshk pavilion]

Kioto (kɪ'əʊtəʊ, 'kjəʊ-) n. a variant spelling of **Kyoto.**

kip[1] (kɪp) Brit. sl. ~n. **1.** sleep or slumber: to get some kip. **2.** a bed or lodging. ~vb. **kipping, kipped.** (intr.) **3.** to sleep or take a nap. **4.** (foll. by down) to prepare for sleep. [C18: from ?]

kip[2] (kɪp) or **kipskin** n. the hide of a young animal, esp. a calf or lamb. [C16: from MDu. kipp]

kip[3] (kɪp) n. Austral. a small board used to spin the coins in two-up. [C19: from Brit. dialect kep to catch]

Kipling ('kɪplɪŋ) n. (**Joseph) Rudyard** ('rʌdjəd). 1865–1936, English poet, short-story writer, and novelist, born in India. His works include Barrack-Room Ballads (1892), the two Jungle Books (1894, 1895), Stalky and Co. (1899), Kim (1901), and the Just So Stories (1902): Nobel prize for literature 1907.

kipper ('kɪpə) n. **1.** a fish, esp. a herring, that has been cleaned, salted, and smoked. **2.** a male salmon during the spawning season. ~vb. **3.** (tr.) to cure (herrings, etc.) by salting and smoking. [OE cypera, ?from coper COPPER[1], referring to its colour]

kir (kɜː; French kir) n. a drink made from dry white wine and cassis. [after Canon F. Kir (1876–1968), mayor of Dijon, who is said to have invented it]

kirby grip ('kɜːbɪ) n. Trademark. a type of hairgrip with one straight and one wavy side.

Kirchhoff (German 'kɪrçɔf) n. **Gustav Robert** ('gʊstaf 'roːbɛrt). 1824–87, German physicist. With Bunsen he developed the method of spectrum analysis that led to their discovery of caesium (1860) and rubidium (1861): also worked on electrical networks.

Kirghiz Soviet Socialist Republic ('kɜːgɪz) n. an administrative division of the S central Soviet Union: annexed by Russia in 1864. Capital: Frunze. Pop.: 4 143 000 (1987). Area: 198 500 sq. km (76 460 sq. miles). Also called: **Kirgiz Soviet Socialist Republic** or **Kirghizia, Kirgizia** (kɜː'gɪzɪə).

Kirghiz Steppe n. a vast steppe region of the SW Soviet Union, in the central Kazakh SSR. Also called: (the) **Steppes.**

Kiribati (,kɪrɪ'bætɪ) n. an independent republic in the W Pacific: comprises 33 islands including Banaba (Ocean Island), the Gilbert and Phoenix Islands, and eight of the Line Islands; part of the British colony of the Gilbert and Ellice Islands until 1975; became self-governing in 1977 and gained full independence in 1979 as the Republic of Kiribati; a member of the Commonwealth. Official languages: English and I-Kiribati (Gilbertese). Religion: Christian majority. Currency: Australian dollar. Capital: Tarawa. Pop.: 66 250 (1987). Area: 684 sq. km (264 sq. miles).

Kirin ('kiː'rɪn) n. a variant transliteration of the Chinese name for **Jilin.**

Kiritimati ('kɪrɪtɪ'mɑːtɪ) n. an island in the central Pacific, in Kiribati: one of the Line Islands; the largest atoll in the world. Pop.: 1737 (1985). Former name: **Christmas Island.**

kirk (kɜːk) n. **1.** a Scottish word for **church. 2.** a Scottish church. [C12: from ON kirkja, from OE cirice CHURCH]

Kirk (kɜːk) n. **Norman.** 1923–74, prime minister of New Zealand (1972–74).

Kirkby ('kɜːbɪ) n. a town in NW England, in N Merseyside. Pop.: 50 898 (1981).

Kirkcaldy (kɜː'kɔːdɪ) n. a port in E Scotland, in SE Fife on the Firth of Forth. Pop.: 46 314 (1981).

Kirkcudbrightshire (kɜː'kuːbrɪ,ʃɪə, -ʃə) n. (until 1975) a county of SW Scotland, now part of Dumfries and Galloway region.

Kirkpatrick (kɜːk'pætrɪk) n. **Mount.** a mountain in Antarctica, in S Victoria Land in the Queen Alexandra Range. Height: 4528 m (14 856 ft.).

kirk session n. the lowest court of the Presbyterian Church.

Kirkuk (kɜːˈkʊk, ˈkɜːkʊk) *n.* a city in NE Iraq: centre of a rich oilfield with pipelines to the Mediterranean. Pop.: 500 000 (1979).

Kirkwall (ˈkɜːkˌwɔːl) *n.* a town on the N coast of Mainland in the Orkney Islands: administrative centre of the island authority of Orkney: cathedral built by Norsemen (begun in 1137). Pop.: 6000 (1985).

kirmess (ˈkɜːmɪs) *n.* a variant spelling of **kermis.**

Kirov[1] (*Russian* ˈkirəf) *n.* a city in the W Soviet Union, on the Vyatka River: an early trading centre; engineering industries. Pop.: 421 000 (1987). Former name (1780–1934): **Vyatka.**

Kirov[2] (*Russian* ˈkirəf) *n.* **Sergei Mironovich** (sɪrˈgjej mɪˈrɔnəvɪtʃ). 1888–1934, Soviet politician; one of Stalin's chief aides. His assassination was the starting point for Stalin's purge of the Communist Party (1934–38).

Kirovabad (*Russian* kirəvaˈbat) *n.* a city in the S Soviet Union, in the NW Azerbaijan SSR: annexed by the Russians in 1804; centre of a cotton-growing region. Pop.: 270 000 (1987). Former names: **Gandzha** (until 1813 and 1920–35), **Yelisavetpol** (1813–1920).

Kirovograd (*Russian* kirəvaˈgrat) *n.* a city in the SW Soviet Union, in the S central Ukrainian SSR on the Ingul River: manufacturing centre of a rich agricultural area. Pop.: 269 000 (1987). Former names: **Yelisavetgrad** (until 1924), **Zinovievsk** (1924–36).

Kirsch (kɪəʃ) *or* **Kirschwasser** (ˈkɪəʃˌvaːsə) *n.* a brandy distilled from cherries, made chiefly in the Black Forest in Germany. [G *Kirschwasser* cherry water]

kirtle (ˈkɜːtəl) *n. Arch.* **1.** a woman's skirt or dress. **2.** a man's coat. [OE *cyrtel,* prob. from *cyrtan* to shorten, ult. from L *curtus* cut short]

Kiruna (*Swedish* ˈkiːruna) *n.* a town in N Sweden: iron-mining centre. Pop.: 27 754 (1984 est.).

Kisangani (ˌkɪsæŋˈgɑːnɪ) *n.* a city in N Zaïre, at the head of navigation of the River Congo below Stanley Falls: Université Libre du Congo (1963). Pop.: 282 650 (1984). Former name (until 1966): **Stanleyville.**

Kishinev (*Russian* kɪʃiˈnjɔf) *n.* a city in the SW Soviet Union, capital of the Moldavian SSR on the Byk River: manufacturing centre of a rich agricultural region; university (1945). Pop.: 663 000 (1987). Romanian name: **Chişinău.**

Kismayu (kɪsˈmɑːjuː) *n.* another name for **Chisimaio.**

kismet (ˈkɪzmɛt, ˈkɪs-) *n.* **1.** *Islam.* the will of Allah. **2.** fate or destiny. [C19: from Turkish, from Persian *qismat,* from Ar. *qasama* he divided]

kiss (kɪs) *vb.* **1.** (*tr.*) to touch with the lips or press the lips against as an expression of love, greeting, respect, etc. **2.** (*intr.*) to join lips with another person in an act of love or desire. **3.** to touch (each other) lightly. **4.** *Billiards.* (of balls) to touch (each other) lightly while moving. ~*n.* **5.** a caress with the lips. **6.** a light touch. [OE *cyssan,* from *coss*] —'**kissable** *adj.*

kissagram (ˈkɪsəˌgræm) *n.* a greetings service in which a person is employed to present greetings by kissing the person celebrating. [C20: blend of *kiss* and *telegram*]

kiss curl *n. Brit.* a circular curl of hair pressed flat against the cheek or forehead.

kisser (ˈkɪsə) *n.* **1.** a person who kisses, esp. in a way specified. **2.** a slang word for **mouth** or **face.**

Kissinger (ˈkɪsɪndʒə) *n.* **Henry.** born 1923, U.S. academic and diplomat, born in Germany; assistant to President Nixon for national security affairs (1968–73); Secretary of State (1973–76): shared the Nobel Peace Prize 1973.

kissing gate *n.* a gate set in a U- or V-shaped enclosure, allowing only one person to pass through at a time.

kiss of life *n.* **the.** mouth-to-mouth resuscitation in which a person blows gently into the mouth of an unconscious person, allowing the lungs to deflate after each blow.

kist (kɪst) *n. S. African.* a large wooden chest in which linen is stored, esp. one used to store a bride's trousseau. [from Afrik., from Du.: CHEST]

Kistna (ˈkɪstnə) *n.* another name for the (River) **Krishna.**

Kisumu (kɪˈsuːmuː) *n.* a port in W Kenya, in Nyanza province on the NE shore of Lake Victoria: fishing and trading centre. Pop.: 210 000 (1984 est.).

kit[1] (kɪt) *n.* **1.** a set of tools, supplies, etc., for use together or for a purpose: *a first-aid kit.* **2.** the case or container for such a set. **3.** a set of pieces of equipment sold ready to be assembled. **4.** clothing and other personal effects, esp. those of a traveller or soldier: *safari kit.* ~See also **kit out.** [C14: from MDu. *kitte* tankard]

kit[2] (kɪt) *n. N.Z.* a string bag for shopping. [from Maori *kete*]

Kitakyushu (ˌkiːtəˈkjuːʃuː) *n.* a port in Japan, on N Kyushu: formed in 1963 by the amalgamation of the cities of Wakamatsu, Yahata, Tobata, Kokura, and Moji; one of Japan's largest industrial centres. Pop.: 1 056 000 (1985).

kitbag (ˈkɪtˌbæg) *n.* a canvas or other bag for a serviceman's kit.

kitchen (ˈkɪtʃɪn) *n.* **a.** a room or part of a building equipped for preparing and cooking food. **b.** (*as modifier*): *a kitchen table.* [OE *cycene,* ult. from LL *coquīna,* from L *coquere* to COOK]

kitchen Dutch *n. S. African derog.* an impoverished form of Afrikaans often mixed with words from other languages, such as English.

Kitchener[1] (ˈkɪtʃɪnə) *n.* an industrial town in SE Canada, in S Ontario: founded in 1806 as Dutch Sand Hills, it was renamed Berlin in 1830 and Kitchener in 1916. Pop.: 150 604 (1986).

Kitchener[2] (ˈkɪtʃɪnə) *n.* **Horatio Herbert,** 1st Earl Kitchener of Khartoum. 1850–1916, British field marshal. As head of the Egyptian army (1892–98), he expelled the Mahdi from the Sudan (1898), occupying Khartoum; he also commanded British forces (1900–02) in the Boer War and (1902–09) in India. He conducted the mobilization of the British army for World War I as war minister (1914–16); he was drowned on his way to Russia.

kitchenette (ˌkɪtʃɪˈnɛt) *n.* a small kitchen or part of a room equipped for use as a kitchen.

kitchen garden *n.* a garden where vegetables and sometimes also fruit are grown.

kitchen midden *n. Archaeol.* the site of a large mound of domestic refuse marking a prehistoric settlement.

kitchen sink *n.* **1.** a sink in a kitchen for washing dishes, vegetables, etc. **2.** (*modifier*) denoting a type of drama or painting of the 1950s depicting sordid reality.

kitchen tea *n. Austral. & N.Z.* a party held before a wedding to which guests bring items of kitchen equipment as wedding presents.

kitchenware (ˈkɪtʃɪnˌwɛə) *n.* pots and pans, knives, forks, spoons, etc., used in the kitchen.

kite (kaɪt) *n.* **1.** a light frame covered with a thin material flown in the wind at the end of a length of string. **2.** *Brit. sl.* an aeroplane. **3.** (*pl.*) *Naut.* any of various light sails set in addition to the working sails of a vessel. **4.** a bird of prey having a long forked tail and long broad wings and usually preying on small mammals and insects. **5.** *Arch.* a person who preys on others. **6.** *Commerce.* a negotiable paper drawn without any actual transaction or assets and designed to obtain money on credit. ~*vb.* **7.** to issue (fictitious papers) to obtain credit or money. **8.** (*intr.*) to soar and glide. [OE *cȳta*]

Kite mark *n. Brit.* the official mark of quality and reliability, in the form of a kite, on articles approved by the British Standards Institution.

kith (kɪθ) *n.* **kith and kin.** one's friends and relations. [OE *cȳthth,* from *cūth;* see UNCOUTH]

Kíthira (ˈkiːθira) *n.* transliteration of the Modern Greek name for **Cythera.**

kit out *or* **up** *vb.* **kitting, kitted.** (*tr., adv.*) *Chiefly Brit.* to provide with (a kit of personal effects and necessities).

kitsch (kɪtʃ) *n.* tawdry, vulgarized, or pretentious art, literature, etc., usually with popular appeal. [C20: from G] —'**kitschy** *adj.*

kitten (ˈkɪtən) *n.* **1.** a young cat. **2. have kittens.** *Brit. inf.* to react with disapproval, anxiety, etc.: *she had kittens when she got the bill.* ~*vb.* **3.** (of cats) to give birth to (young). [C14: from OF *caton,* from CAT; prob. infl. by ME *kiteling*]

kittenish (ˈkɪtənɪʃ) *adj.* **1.** like a kitten; lively. **2.** (of a woman) flirtatious, esp. coyly flirtatious.

kittiwake (ˈkɪtɪˌweɪk) *n.* either of two oceanic gulls having pale grey black-tipped wings and a square-cut tail. [C17: imit.]

kitty[1] (ˈkɪtɪ) *n., pl.* **-ties.** a diminutive or affectionate name for a **kitten** or **cat.** [C18]

kitty[2] (ˈkɪtɪ) *n., pl.* **-ties. 1.** the pool of bets in certain gambling games. **2.** any shared fund of money. **3.** (in bowls) the jack. [C19: see KIT[1]]

Kitty Hawk (ˈkɪtɪ hɔːk) *n.* a village in NE North Carolina, near Kill Devil Hill, where the Wright brothers made the first aeroplane flight in the U.S. (1903).

Kitwe ('kɪtweɪ) *n.* a city in N Zambia: commercial centre of the Copper Belt. Pop.: 314 794 (1980).

Kiushu ('kju:ʃu:) *n.* a variant spelling of **Kyushu.**

Kivu ('ki:vu:) *n.* **Lake.** a lake in central Africa, between Zaïre and Rwanda at an altitude of 1460 m (4790 ft.). Area: 2698 sq. km (1042 sq. miles). Depth: (maximum) 475 m (1558 ft.).

kiwi ('ki:wi:) *n., pl.* **kiwis. 1.** a nocturnal flightless New Zealand bird having a long beak, stout legs, and weakly barbed feathers. **2.** *Inf. except in N.Z.* a New Zealander. **3.** *N.Z. inf.* a lottery. [C19: from Maori, imit.: N.Z. sense from the *Golden Kiwi Lottery*]

kiwi fruit *n.* the fuzzy edible fruit of an Asian climbing plant. Also called: **Chinese gooseberry.**

Kizil Irmak (kɪ'zɪl ɪə'mɑːk) *n.* a river in Turkey, rising in the Kizil Dag and flowing southwest, northwest, and northeast to the Black Sea: the longest river in Asia Minor. Length: about 1150 km (715 miles). Ancient name: **Halys** ('heɪlɪs).

KKK *abbrev. for* Ku Klux Klan.

kl. *symbol for* kilolitre.

Klagenfurt (*German* 'klɑːgənfʊrt) *n.* a city in S Austria, capital of Carinthia province: tourist centre. Pop.: 86 221 (1981).

Klaipeda (*Russian* 'klajpɪdə) *n.* a port in the W Soviet Union, in the Lithuanian SSR on the Baltic: shipbuilding. Pop.: 201 000 (1987). German name: **Memel.**

Klan (klæn) *n.* (usually preceded by *the*) short for **Ku Klux Klan.** —'**Klanism** *n.*

Klausenburg ('klauzənbʊrk) *n.* the German name for **Cluj.**

klaxon ('klæksᵊn) *n.* a type of loud horn formerly used on motor vehicles. [C20: former trademark]

Kléber (*French* kleber) *n.* **Jean Baptiste** (ʒɑ̃ batist). 1753–1800, French general, who succeeded Napoleon as commander in Egypt (1799); assassinated.

Klee (*German* kle:) *n.* **Paul** (paul). 1879–1940, Swiss painter and etcher. A founder member of *der Blaue Reiter* (a group of German expressionist painters), he subsequently evolved an intensely personal style of unusual fantasy and wit.

Kleenex ('kli:nɛks) *n., pl.* **-ex** or **-exes.** *Trademark.* a kind of soft paper tissue, used esp. as a handkerchief.

Klein bottle (klaɪn) *n.* *Maths.* a three-dimensional surface that is formed by inserting the smaller end of an open tapered tube through the surface of the tube and making this end stretch to fit the other end. [after Felix *Klein* (1849–1925), G mathematician]

Kleist (klaɪst) *n.* (**Bernd**) **Heinrich** (**Wilhelm**) **von** ('haɪnrɪç fɔn). 1777–1811, German dramatist, poet, and short-story writer. His plays include *The Broken Pitcher* (1808), *Penthesilea* (1808), and *The Prince of Homburg* (published 1821).

Klemperer ('klɛmpərə) *n.* **Otto.** 1885–1973, orchestral conductor, born in Germany. He was best known for his interpretations of Beethoven.

kleptomania (ˌklɛptəʊ'meɪnɪə) *n.* *Psychol.* a strong impulse to steal, esp. when there is no obvious motivation. [C19: *klepto-* from Gk, from *kleptein* to steal + -MANIA] —ˌklepto'mani,ac *n.*

klieg light (kli:g) *n.* an intense carbon-arc light used in producing films. [C20: after John H. *Kliegl* (1869–1959) & his brother Anton (1872–1927), German-born American inventors]

Klimt (klɪmt) *n.* **Gustav** ('gʊstaf). 1862–1918, Austrian painter. He founded the Vienna Sezession (1897), a group of painters influenced by Art Nouveau.

Kline (klaɪn) *n.* **Franz** (frænts). 1910–62, U.S. abstract expressionist painter. His works are characterized by heavy black strokes on a white or grey background.

klipspringer ('klɪp,sprɪŋə) *n.* a small agile antelope inhabiting rocky regions of Africa south of the Sahara. [C18: from Afrik., from Du. *klip* rock + *springer*, from *springen* to SPRING]

Klondike ('klɒndaɪk) *n.* **1.** a region of NW Canada, in the Yukon in the basin of the Klondike River: site of rich gold deposits, discovered in 1896 but largely exhausted by 1910. Area: about 2100 sq. km (800 sq. miles). **2.** a river in NW Canada, rising in the Yukon and flowing west to the Yukon River. Length: about 145 km (90 miles).

kloof (klu:f) *n.* a mountain pass or gorge in southern Africa. [C18: from Afrik., from MDu. *clove* a cleft]

Klopstock (*German* 'klɔpʃtɔk) *n.* **Friedrich Gottlieb** ('fri:drɪç 'gɔtliːp). 1724–1803, German poet, noted for his religious epic *Der Messias* (1748–73) and for his odes.

klystron ('klɪstrɒn) *n.* an electron tube for the amplification or generation of microwaves. [C20: *klys-*, from Gk *kluzein* to wash over + -TRON]

km *symbol for* kilometre.

K-meson *n.* another name for **kaon.**

knack (næk) *n.* **1.** a skilful, ingenious, or resourceful way of doing something. **2.** a particular talent or aptitude, esp. an intuitive one. [C14: prob. var. of *knak* sharp knock, imit.]

knacker ('nækə) *Brit.* ~*n.* **1.** a person who buys up old horses for slaughter. **2.** a person who buys up old buildings and breaks them up for scrap. ~*vb.* **3.** (*tr.; usually passive*) *Sl.* to tire. [C16: prob. from *nacker* saddler, prob. of Scand. origin] —'**knackery** *n.*

knag (næg) *n.* **1.** a knot in wood. **2.** a wooden peg. [C15: ?from Low G *knagge*]

knap (næp) *vb.* **knapping, knapped.** (*tr.*) *Dialect.* to hit or chip. [C15 (in the sense: to strike with a sharp sound): imit.] —'**knapper** *n.*

knapsack ('næp,sæk) *n.* a canvas or leather bag carried strapped on the back or shoulder. [C17: from Low G, prob. from *knappen* to bite + *sack* bag]

knapweed ('næp,wi:d) *n.* any of several plants having purplish thistle-like flowers. [C15 *knopwed*, from *knop* of Gmc origin + WEED]

knar (nɑː) *n.* a variant of **knur.** [C14 *knarre* rough stone, knot on a tree]

knave (neɪv) *n.* **1.** *Arch.* a dishonest man. **2.** another word for **jack** (the playing card). **3.** *Obs.* a male servant. [OE *cnafa*] —'**knavish** *adj.*

knavery ('neɪvərɪ) *n., pl.* **-eries. 1.** a deceitful or dishonest act. **2.** dishonest conduct; trickery.

knead (ni:d) *vb.* (*tr.*) **1.** to work and press (a soft substance, such as bread dough) into a uniform mixture with the hands. **2.** to squeeze or press with the hands. **3.** to make by kneading. [OE *cnedan*] —'**kneader** *n.*

knee (ni:) *n.* **1.** the joint of the human leg connecting the tibia and fibula with the femur and protected in front by the patella. Technical name: **genu. 2. a.** the area surrounding and above this joint. **b.** (*modifier*) reaching or covering the knee: *knee socks.* **3.** the upper surface of a sitting person's thigh: *the child sat on her mother's knee.* **4.** a corresponding or similar part in other vertebrates. **5.** the part of a garment that covers the knee. **6.** anything resembling a knee in action or shape. **7.** any of the hollow rounded protuberances that project upwards from the roots of the swamp cypress. **8. bend** *or* **bow the knee.** to kneel or submit. **9. bring someone to his knees.** to force someone into submission. ~*vb.* **kneeing, kneed. 10.** (*tr.*) to strike, nudge, or push with the knee. [OE *cnēow*]

kneecap ('ni:,kæp) *n.* **1.** *Anat.* a nontechnical name for **patella.** ~*vb.* **-capping, -capped.** (*tr.*) **2.** (esp. of certain terrorist groups) to shoot (a person) in the kneecap.

knee-deep *adj.* **1.** so deep as to reach or cover the knees. **2.** (*postpositive; often foll. by *in*) **a.** sunk or covered to the knees: *knee-deep in sand.* **b.** deeply involved: *knee-deep in work.*

knee-high *adj.* another word for **knee-deep** (sense 1).

kneehole ('ni:,həʊl) *n.* a space for the knees, esp. under a desk.

knee jerk *n.* **1.** *Physiol.* an outward reflex kick of the lower leg caused by a sharp tap on the tendon just below the kneecap. ~*modifier.* **kneejerk. 2.** made or occurring as a predictable and automatic response, without thought: *a kneejerk reaction.*

kneel (ni:l) *vb.* **kneeling, knelt** or **kneeled. 1.** (*intr.*) to rest, fall, or support oneself on one's knees. ~*n.* **2.** the act or position of kneeling. [OE *cnēowlian*; see KNEE] —'**kneeler** *n.*

knees-up *n., pl.* **knees-up.** *Brit. inf.* a lively party. [C20: after popular song *Knees-up, Mother Brown!*]

knell (nɛl) *n.* **1.** the sound of a bell rung to announce a death or a funeral. **2.** something that precipitates or indicates death or destruction. ~*vb.* **3.** (*intr.*) to ring a knell. **4.** (*tr.*) to proclaim by or as if by a tolling bell. [OE *cnyll*]

Kneller ('nɛlə) *n.* **Sir Godfrey.** ?1646–1723, portrait painter at the English court, born in Germany.

knelt (nɛlt) *vb.* a past tense and past participle of **kneel**.

Knesset ('knɛsɪt) *n.* the representative assembly of Israel. [C20: Heb., lit.: gathering]

knew (njuː) *vb.* the past tense of **know**.

knickerbocker glory ('nɪkəˌbɒkə) *n.* a rich confection consisting of layers of ice cream, jelly, cream, and fruit, served in a tall glass.

knickerbockers ('nɪkəˌbɒkəz) *pl. n.* baggy breeches fastened with a band at the knee or above the ankle. Also called (U.S.): **knickers**. [C19: regarded as the traditional dress of the Du. settlers in America; after Diedrich *Knickerbocker*, fictitious author of Washington Irving's *History of New York* (1809)]

knickers ('nɪkəz) *pl. n.* an undergarment for women covering the lower trunk and sometimes the thighs and having separate legs or leg-holes. [C19: contraction of KNICKERBOCKERS]

knick-knack *or* **nick-nack** ('nɪkˌnæk) *n.* **1.** a cheap ornament. **2.** an ornamental article of furniture, dress, etc. [C17: by reduplication from *knack*, in obs. sense: toy]

knife (naɪf) *n., pl.* **knives** (naɪvz). **1.** a cutting instrument consisting of a sharp-edged blade of metal fitted into a handle or onto a machine. **2.** a similar instrument used as a weapon. **3. have one's knife in someone.** to have a grudge against someone. **4. under the knife.** undergoing a surgical operation. ~*vb.* (*tr.*) **5.** to stab or kill with a knife. **6.** to betray or depose in an underhand way. [OE *cnīf*] —'**knife,like** *adj.*

knife edge *n.* **1.** the sharp cutting edge of a knife. **2.** any sharp edge, esp. an arête. **3.** a sharp-edged wedge of hard material on which the beam of a balance pivots. **4.** a critical point.

knight (naɪt) *n.* **1.** (in medieval Europe) **a.** (originally) a person who served his lord as a mounted and heavily armed soldier. **b.** (later) a gentleman with the military and social standing of this rank. **2.** (in modern times) a person invested by a sovereign with a nonhereditary rank and dignity usually in recognition of personal services, achievements, etc. **3.** a chess piece, usually shaped like a horse's head. **4.** a champion of a lady or of a cause or principle. **5.** a member of the Roman class below the senators. ~*vb.* **6.** (*tr.*) to make (a person) a knight. [OE *cniht* servant]

knight errant *n., pl.* **knights errant.** (esp. in medieval romance) a knight who wanders in search of deeds of courage, chivalry, etc. —**knight errantry** *n.*

knighthood ('naɪthʊd) *n.* **1.** the order, dignity, or rank of a knight. **2.** the qualities of a knight.

knightly ('naɪtlɪ) *adj.* of, relating to, resembling, or befitting a knight. —'**knightliness** *n.*

knight of the road *n. Brit. inf. or facetious.* **1.** a tramp. **2.** a commercial traveller. **3.** a lorry driver.

Knights Hospitallers *pl. n.* a military Christian religious order founded about the time of the first crusade (1096–99).

Knight Templar *n., pl.* **Knights Templars** *or* **Knights Templar.** another term for **Templar.**

kniphofia (nɪf'əʊfɪə) *n.* the Latin name for **red-hot poker.** [C19: after Johann Hieronymus *Kniphof* (1704–63), G professor of medicine]

knit (nɪt) *vb.* **knitting, knitted** *or* **knit. 1.** to make (a garment, etc.) by looping and entwining (wool) by hand by means of long eyeless needles (**knitting needles**) or by machine (**knitting machine**). **2.** to join or be joined together closely. **3.** to draw (the brows) together or (of the brows) to come together, as in frowning or concentrating. ~*n.* **4. a.** a fabric made by knitting. **b.** (*in combination*): *a heavy knit.* [OE *cnyttan* to tie in] —'**knitter** *n.*

knitting ('nɪtɪŋ) *n.* knitted work or the process of producing it.

knitwear ('nɪtˌwɛə) *n.* knitted clothes, esp. sweaters.

knives (naɪvz) *n.* the plural of **knife.**

knob (nɒb) *n.* **1.** a rounded projection from a surface, such as a lump on a tree trunk. **2.** a handle of a door, drawer, etc., esp. one that is rounded. **3.** a round hill or knoll. ~*vb.* **knobbing, knobbed. 4.** (*tr.*) to supply or ornament with knobs. **5.** (*intr.*) to bulge. [C14: from MLow G *knobbe* knot in wood] —'**knobbly** *adj.* — '**knobby** *adj.* — '**knob,like** *adj.*

knobkerrie ('nɒbˌkɛrɪ) *n.*, **knobkierie,** *or* **knobstick** *n.* a stick with a round knob at the end, used as a club or missile by South African tribesmen. [C19: from Afrik., from

---

knop knob, from MDu. *cnoppe* + *kierie* stick, from Hottentot *kīrri*]

knock (nɒk) *vb.* **1.** (*tr.*) to give a blow or push to. **2.** (*intr.*) to rap sharply with the knuckles, a hard object, etc.: *to knock at the door.* **3.** (*tr.*) to make or force by striking: *to knock a hole in the wall.* **4.** (*intr.; usually foll. by against*) to collide (with). **5.** (*tr.*) to bring into a certain condition by hitting: *to knock someone unconscious.* **6.** (*tr.*) *Inf.* to criticize adversely. **7.** (*intr.*) Also: **pink.** (of an internal-combustion engine) to emit a metallic noise as a result of faulty combustion. **8.** (*intr.*) (of a bearing, esp. one in an engine) to emit a regular characteristic sound as a result of wear. **9.** *Brit. sl.* to have sexual intercourse with (a person). **10. knock (a person) into the middle of next week.** *Inf.* to hit (a person) with a very heavy blow. **11. knock on the head. a.** to daze or kill (a person) by striking on the head. **b.** to prevent the further development of (a plan). ~*n.* **12. a.** a blow, push, or rap: *he gave the table a knock.* **b.** the sound so caused. **13.** the sound of knocking in an engine or bearing. **14.** *Inf.* a misfortune, rebuff, or setback. **15.** *Inf.* criticism. ~See also **knock about, knock back,** etc. [OE *cnocian,* imit.]

knock about *or* **around** *vb.* **1.** (*intr., adv.*) to wander about aimlessly. **2.** (*intr., prep.*) to travel about, esp. as resulting in varied experience: *he's knocked about the world.* **3.** (*intr., adv.; foll. by with*) to associate. **4.** (*tr., adv.*) to treat brutally: *he knocks his wife about.* **5.** (*tr., adv.*) to consider or discuss informally. ~*adj.* **knockabout. 6.** tough; boisterous: *knockabout farce.*

knock back *vb.* (*tr., adv.*) *Inf.* **1.** to drink, esp. quickly. **2.** to cost. **3.** to reject or refuse. **4.** to shock; disconcert. ~*n.* **knockback. 5.** *Sl.* a refusal or rejection. **6.** *Prison sl.* failure to obtain parole.

knock down *vb.* (*tr., adv.*) **1.** to strike to the ground with a blow, as in boxing. **2.** (in auctions) to declare (an article) sold. **3.** to demolish. **4.** to dismantle for ease of transport. **5.** *Inf.* to reduce (a price, etc.). ~*adj.* **knockdown.** (*prenominal*) **6.** powerful: *a knockdown blow.* **7.** *Chiefly Brit.* cheap: *a knockdown price.* **8.** easily dismantled: *knockdown furniture.*

knocker ('nɒkə) *n.* **1.** an object, usually made of metal, attached to a door by a hinge and used for knocking. **2.** *Inf.* a person who finds fault or disparages. **3.** (*usually pl.*) *Sl.* a female breast. **4.** a person or thing that knocks. **5. on the knocker.** *Inf.* promptly: *you pay on the knocker here.*

knocking copy *n.* publicity material designed to denigrate a competing product.

knocking-shop *n. Brit.* a slang word for **brothel.**

knock-knee *n.* a condition in which the legs are bent inwards causing the knees to touch when standing. —,**knock-'kneed** *adj.*

knock off *vb.* (*mainly adv.*) **1.** (*intr., also prep.*) *Inf.* to finish work: *we knocked off an hour early.* **2.** (*tr.*) *Inf.* to make or do hastily or easily: *to knock off a novel in a week.* **3.** (*tr.; also prep.*) *Inf.* to reduce the price of (an article). **4.** (*tr.*) *Sl.* to kill. **5.** (*tr.*) *Sl.* to rob or steal: *to knock off a bank.* **6.** (*tr.*) *Sl.* to stop doing something, used as a command: *knock it off!*

knock-on *Rugby.* ~*n.* **1.** the infringement of playing the ball forward with the hand or arm. ~*vb.* **knock on.** (*adv.*) **2.** to play (the ball) forward with the hand or arm.

knock-on effect *n.* the indirect result of an action: *the number of redundancies was not great but there were as many again from the knock-on effect.*

knockout ('nɒkˌaʊt) *n.* **1.** the act of rendering unconscious. **2.** a blow that renders an opponent unconscious. **3. a.** a competition in which competitors are eliminated progressively. **b.** (*as modifier*): *a knockout contest.* **4.** *Inf.* a person or thing that is overwhelmingly impressive or attractive: *she's a knockout.* ~*vb.* **knock out.** (*tr., adv.*) **5.** to render unconscious, esp. by a blow. **6.** *Boxing.* to defeat (an opponent) by a knockout. **7.** to destroy or injure badly. **8.** to eliminate, esp. in a knockout competition. **9.** *Inf.* to overwhelm or amaze: *I was knocked out by that new song.* **10. knock the bottom out of.** *Inf.* to invalidate (an argument).

knockout drops *pl. n. Sl.* a drug secretly put into someone's drink to cause stupefaction.

knock up *vb.* (*adv., mainly tr.*) **1.** Also: **knock together.** *Inf.* to assemble quickly: *to knock up a set of shelves.* **2.** *Brit. inf.* to waken; rouse: *to knock someone* up early. **3.** *Sl.* to make pregnant. **4.** *Brit. inf.* to exhaust. **5.** *Cricket.* to score (runs). **6.** (*intr.*) *Tennis, squash, etc.* to practise, esp. before a match. ~*n.* **knock-up. 7.** a practice session at tennis, squash, etc.

knoll (nəʊl) *n.* a small rounded hill. [OE *cnoll*]

Knossos *or* **Cnossus** ('nɒsəs, 'knɒs-) *n.* a ruined city in N central Crete: remains of the Minoan Bronze Age civilization.

knot[1] (nɒt) *n.* **1.** any of various fastenings formed by looping and tying a piece of rope, cord, etc., in upon itself or to another piece of rope. **2.** a prescribed method of tying a particular knot. **3.** a tangle, as in hair or string. **4.** a decorative bow, as of ribbon. **5.** a small cluster or huddled group. **6.** a tie or bond: *the marriage knot.* **7.** a difficult problem. **8. a.** a hard mass of wood where a branch joins the trunk of a tree. **b.** a cross section of this visible on a piece of timber. **9.** a sensation of constriction, caused by tension or nervousness: *his stomach was tying itself in knots.* **10.** *Pathol.* a lump of vessels or fibres formed in a part, as in a muscle. **11.** a unit of speed used by nautical vessels and aircraft, being one nautical mile (about 1.15 statute miles or 1.85 km) per hour. **12.** another term (not in technical use) for **nautical mile.** **13. at a rate of knots.** very fast. **14. tie (someone) in knots.** to completely perplex (someone). ~*vb.* **knotting, knotted.** **15.** (*tr.*) to tie or fasten in a knot. **16.** to form or cause to form into a knot. **17.** (*tr.*) to entangle or become entangled. **18.** (*tr.*) to make (an article or design) by tying thread in ornamental knots. [OE *cnotta*] — 'knotted *adj.* — 'knotter *n.* — 'knotless *adj.*

knot[2] (nɒt) *n.* a small northern sandpiper with a short bill and grey plumage. [C15: from ?]

knot garden *n.* (esp. formerly) a formal garden of intricate design.

knotgrass ('nɒt,grɑːs) *n.* **1.** Also called: **allseed.** a weed whose small green flowers produce numerous seeds. **2.** any of several related plants.

knothole ('nɒt,həʊl) *n.* a hole in a piece of wood where a knot has been.

knotty ('nɒtɪ) *adj.* **-tier, -tiest. 1.** (of wood, rope, etc.) full of or characterized by knots. **2.** extremely difficult or intricate.

knout (naʊt) *n.* a stout whip used formerly in Russia as an instrument of punishment. [C17: from Russian *knut*, of Scand. origin]

know (nəʊ) *vb.* **knowing, knew, known.** (*mainly tr.*) **1.** (*also intr.; may take a clause as object*) to be or feel certain of the truth or accuracy of (a fact, etc.). **2.** to be acquainted or familiar with: *she's known him five years.* **3.** to have a familiarity or grasp of: *he knows French.* **4.** (*also intr.; may take a clause as object*) to understand, be aware of, or perceive (facts, etc.): *he knows the answer now.* **5.** (foll. by *how*) to be sure or aware of (how to be or do something). **6.** to experience, esp. deeply: *to know poverty.* **7.** to be intelligent, informed, or sensible enough (to do something). **8.** (*may take a clause as object*) to be able to distinguish or discriminate. **9.** *Arch.* to have sexual intercourse with. **10. know what's what.** to know how one thing or things in general work. **11. you never know.** things are uncertain. ~*n.* **12. in the know.** *Inf.* aware or informed. [OE *gecnāwan*] — 'knowable *adj.* — 'knower *n.*

know-all *n. Inf., disparaging.* a person who pretends or appears to know a great deal.

know-how *n. Inf.* **1.** ingenuity, aptitude, or skill. **2.** commercial and saleable knowledge of how to do a particular thing.

knowing ('nəʊɪŋ) *adj.* **1.** suggesting secret knowledge. **2.** wise, shrewd, or clever. **3.** deliberate. ~*n.* **4. there is no knowing.** one cannot tell. — 'knowingly *adv.* — 'knowingness *n.*

knowledge ('nɒlɪdʒ) *n.* **1.** the facts or experiences known by a person or group of people. **2.** the state of knowing. **3.** consciousness or familiarity gained by experience or learning. **4.** erudition or informed learning. **5.** specific information about a subject. **6. to my knowledge. a.** as I understand it. **b.** as I know.

knowledgeable *or* **knowledgable** ('nɒlɪdʒəb°l) *adj.* possessing or indicating much knowledge. — 'knowledgeably *or* 'knowledgably *adv.*

known (nəʊn) *vb.* **1.** the past participle of **know.** ~*adj.* **2.** identified: *a known criminal.*

Knox (nɒks) *n.* **John.** ?1514–72, Scottish theologian and historian. After exile in England and on the Continent (1547–59), he returned to Scotland in 1559 and established the Presbyterian Church of Scotland (1560). His chief historical work is the *History of the Reformation in Scotland* (1586).

Knox-Johnston (,nɒks'dʒɒnstən) *n.* **Robin (William Robert Patrick).** born 1939, British yachtsman. He was the first to sail round the world alone nonstop (1968–69).

Knoxville ('nɒksvɪl) *n.* an industrial city in E Tennessee, on the Tennessee River: state capital (1796–1812; 1817–19). Pop.: 173 210 (1986 est.).

knuckle ('nʌk°l) *n.* **1.** a joint of a finger, esp. that connecting a finger to the hand. **2.** a joint of veal, pork, etc., consisting of the part of the leg below the knee joint. **3. near the knuckle.** *Inf.* approaching indecency. ~*vb.* **4.** (*tr.*) to rub or press with the knuckles. **5.** (*intr.*) to keep the knuckles on the ground while shooting a marble. ~See also **knuckle down, knuckle under.** [C14] — 'knuckly *adj.*

knucklebones ('nʌk°l,bəʊnz) *n.* (*functioning as sing.*) a less common name for **jacks** (the game).

knuckle down *vb.* (*intr., adv.*) *Inf.* to apply oneself diligently: *to knuckle down to some work.*

knuckle-duster *n.* (*often pl.*) a metal bar fitted over the knuckles, often with holes for the fingers, for inflicting injury by a blow with the fist.

knucklehead ('nʌk°l,hɛd) *n. Inf.* a fool; idiot. — 'knuckle,headed *adj.*

knuckle under *vb.* (*intr., adv.*) to give way under pressure or authority; yield.

knur, knurr (nɜː), *or* **knar** *n.* a knot or protuberance in a tree trunk or in wood. [C16 *knor*; cf. KNAR]

knurl *or* **nurl** (nɜːl) *vb.* (*tr.*) **1.** to impress with a series of fine ridges or serrations. ~*n.* **2.** a small ridge, esp. one of a series. [C17: prob. from KNUR]

Knut (kə'njuːt) *n.* a variant spelling of **Canute.**

KO *or* **k.o.** ('keɪ'əʊ) *vb.* **KO'ing, KO'd; k.o.'ing, k.o.'d,** *n., pl.* **KO's** *or* **k.o.'s.** a slang term for **knock out** or **knockout.**

koala *or* **koala bear** (kəʊ'ɑːlə) *n.* a slow-moving Australian arboreal marsupial, having dense greyish fur and feeding on eucalyptus leaves. Also called (Austral.): **native bear.** [from Abor.]

koan ('kəʊæn) *n.* (in Zen Buddhism) a problem that admits no logical solution. [from Japanese]

Kobarid ('kəʊbə,riːd; *Serbo-Croatian* 'kɔba,rid) *n.* a village in NW Yugoslavia, in Slovenia on the Isonzo River: part of Italy until 1947; scene of the defeat of the Italians by Austro-German forces (1917). Italian name: **Caporetto.**

Kobe ('kəʊbɪ) *n.* a port in S Japan, on S Honshu on Osaka Bay: formed in 1889 by the amalgamation of Hyogo and Kobe; a major industrial complex, producing ships, steel, and rubber goods. Pop.: 1 411 000 (1985).

Kobenhavn (købən'haun) *n.* the Danish name for **Copenhagen.**

Koblenz *or* **Coblenz** (*German* 'koːblɛnts) *n.* a city in West Germany, in the Rhineland-Palatinate at the confluence of the Rivers Moselle and Rhine: ruled by the archbishop-electors of Trier from 1018 until occupied by the French in 1794; passed to Prussia in 1815, becoming capital of the Rhine Province (1824–1945) and of the Rhineland-Palatinate (1946–50); wine trade centre. Pop.: 110 600 (1986). Latin name: **Confluentes** (,kɒnflu'ɛntiːz).

kobold ('kɒbəʊld) *n. German myth.* **1.** a mischievous household sprite. **2.** a spirit that haunts mines. [C19: from G; see COBALT]

Koch (*German* kɔx) *n.* **Robert** ('roːbɛrt). 1843–1910, German bacteriologist, who isolated the anthrax bacillus (1876), the tubercle bacillus (1882), and the cholera bacillus (1883): Nobel prize for physiology or medicine 1905.

Kochi (kəʊ'tʃiː) *n.* a port in SW Japan, on central Shikoku on Urado Bay. Pop.: 312 000 (1985).

kochia ('kɒ'fiːə) *n.* an annual plant with ornamental foliage that turns purple-red in late summer. [C19: after W.D.J. *Koch*, G botanist]

Kodály (*Hungarian* 'kodɑːj) *n.* **Zoltán** ('zoltɑːn). 1882–1967, Hungarian composer. His works were often inspired by native folk songs and include the comic opera *Háry János* (1926) and *Psalmus Hungaricus* (1923) for chorus and orchestra.

Kodiak ('kəʊdɪˌæk) *n.* an island in S Alaska, in the Gulf of Alaska: site of the first European settlement in Alaska, made by Russians in 1784. Pop.: 13 389 (1984). Area: 8974 sq. km (3465 sq. miles).

Kodiak bear *or* **Kodiak** *n.* a large variety of the brown bear inhabiting the W coast of Alaska and neighbouring islands, esp. Kodiak.

Kodok ('kəʊdɒk) *n.* the modern name for **Fashoda**.

koeksister ('kʊkˌsɪstə) *n. S. African.* a small cake of sweetened dough, usually dipped in syrup. [from Afrik., from Du. *koek* cake + *sissen* to sizzle]

koel ('kəʊəl) *n.* any of several parasitic cuckoos of S and SE Asia and Australia. [C19: from Hindi, from Sansk. *kokila*]

Koestler ('kɜːstlə) *n.* **Arthur.** 1905–83, British writer, born in Hungary. Of his early antitotalitarian novels *Darkness at Noon* (1940) is outstanding. His later works, *The Sleepwalkers* (1959), *The Act of Creation* (1964), and *The Ghost in the Machine* (1967) reflect his interest in science, philosophy, and psychology. He committed suicide.

Kofu ('kəʊfuː) *n.* a city in central Japan, on S Honshu: hot springs. Pop.: 199 272 (1980).

Kohima ('kəʊhɪˌmɑː) *n.* a city in NE India, capital of Nagaland, near the Burmese border: centre of fierce fighting in World War II, when it was surrounded by the Japanese but not captured (1944). Pop.: 21 545 (1971).

kohl (kəʊl) *n.* a cosmetic powder used, originally esp. in Muslim and Asian countries, to darken the area around the eyes. [C18: from Ar. *kohl*; see ALCOHOL]

Kohl (kəʊl) *n.* **Helmut** ('hɛlmuːt). born 1930, West German statesman: chancellor of West Germany from 1982.

Köhler (*German* 'koːlər) *n.* **Wolfgang** ('vɔlfgaŋ). 1887–1967, German psychologist, a leading exponent of Gestalt psychology.

kohlrabi (kəʊl'rɑːbɪ) *n., pl.* **-bies.** a cultivated variety of cabbage whose thickened stem is eaten as a vegetable. Also called: **turnip cabbage.** [C19: from G, from It. *cavoli rape* (pl.), from *cavolo* cabbage (from L *caulis*) + *rapa* turnip (from L)]

koine ('kɔɪniː) *n.* a common language among speakers of different languages; lingua franca. [from Gk *koinē dialektos* common language]

Koine ('kɔɪniː) *n.* (*sometimes not cap.*) **the.** the ancient Greek dialect that was the lingua franca of the empire of Alexander the Great and in Roman times.

Kokand (*Russian* ka'kant) *n.* a city in the SW Soviet Union, in the NE Uzbek SSR. Pop.: 169 000 (1986 est.).

kokanee (kəʊ'kænɪ) *n.* a landlocked salmon of lakes in W North America: a variety of sockeye. [prob. from *Kokanee* Creek, in SE British Columbia]

Koko Nor ('kəʊ'kəʊ 'nɔː) *or* **Kuku Nor** *n.* a lake in W China, in Qinghai province in the NE Tibetan Highlands at an altitude of about 3000 m (10 000 ft.): the largest lake in China. Area: about 4100 sq. km (1600 sq. miles). Chinese name: **Qinghai.**

Kokoschka (*German* ko'kɔʃka, 'kɔkɔʃka) *n.* **Oskar** ('ɔskar). 1886–1980, Austrian expressionist painter and dramatist, noted for his landscapes and portraits.

Kokura (ˌkəʊkə'rɑː) *n.* a former city in SW Japan, on N Kyushu: merged with adjacent townships in 1963 to form the new city of **Kitakyushu.**

kola ('kəʊlə) *n.* a variant spelling of **cola.**

kola nut *n.* a variant spelling of **cola nut.**

Kola Peninsula ('kəʊlə) *n.* a peninsula of the NW Soviet Union, between the Barents and White Seas: forms most of the Murmansk Region of the RSFSR. Area: about 130 000 sq. km (50 000 sq. miles).

Kolar Gold Fields (kəʊ'lɑː) *n.* a city in S India, in SE Karnataka: a major gold-mining centre since 1881. Pop.: 77 679 (1981).

Kolding (*Danish* 'kɔlɛŋ) *n.* a port in Denmark, in E Jutland at the head of **Kolding Fjord** (an inlet of the Little Belt). Pop.: 57 148 (1987).

Kolhapur (ˌkəʊlhɑː'pʊə) *n.* a city in W India, in S Maharashtra: university (1963). Pop.: 346 306 (1981).

kolinsky (kə'lɪnskɪ) *n., pl.* **-skies.** 1. any of various Asian minks. 2. the rich tawny fur of this animal. [C19: from Russian *kolinski* of *Kola*; see KOLA PENINSULA]

kolkhoz (kɒl'hɔːz) *n.* a Russian collective farm. [C20: from Russian, short for *kollektivnoe khozyaistvo* collective farm]

Kollwitz (*German* 'kɔlvɪts) *n.* **Käthe** ('kɛːtə). 1867–1945, German lithographer and sculptress.

Kolmar ('kɔlmar) *n.* the German name for **Colmar.**

Kolmogorov (ˌkɒlmə'gɔːrɒf) *n.* **Andrei Nikolaevich** (an'drjej nika'lajəvitʃ). (1903–87), Soviet mathematician, who made important contributions to the theoretical foundations of probability.

Köln (kœln) *n.* the German name for **Cologne.**

Kol Nidre (kɔːl 'nɪdreɪ) *n. Judaism.* 1. the evening service with which Yom Kippur begins. 2. the opening prayer of that service. [Aramaic *kŏl nidhrē* all the vows; the prayer's opening words]

Kolomna (*Russian* ka'lɒmnə) *n.* a city in the W central Soviet Union, at the confluence of the Moskva and Oka Rivers: railway engineering centre. Pop.: 150 000 (1981 est.).

Kolozsvár (*Russian* 'kolɔʒvaːr) *n.* the Hungarian name for **Cluj.**

Kolyma (*Russian* kəlɪ'ma) *n.* a river in the NE Soviet Union, rising in the Kolyma Mountains north of the Sea of Okhotsk and flowing generally north to the East Siberian Sea. Length: 2600 km (1615 miles).

Kolyma Range *n.* a mountain range in the NE Soviet Union, in NE Siberia, extending about 1100 km (700 miles) between the Kolyma River and the Sea of Okhotsk. Highest peak: 1862 m (6109 ft.).

Komati (kə'mɑːtɪ, 'kəʊmətɪ) *n.* a river in southern Africa, rising in South Africa in SE Transvaal and flowing east through Swaziland and Mozambique to the Indian Ocean at Delagoa Bay. Length: about 800 km (500 miles).

komatik ('kəʊmætɪk) *n.* a sledge having wooden runners and crossbars bound with rawhide, used by Eskimos. [C20: from Eskimo]

Komi Autonomous Soviet Socialist Republic ('kəʊmɪ) *n.* an administrative division of the NW Soviet Union: annexed by the princes of Moscow in the 14th century. Capital: Syktyvkar. Pop.: 1 200 000 (1986). Area: 415 900 sq. km (160 540 sq. miles).

Kommunarsk (*Russian* kəmu'narsk) *n.* a city in the SW Soviet Union, in the E Ukrainian SSR. Pop.: 121 000 (1981 est.).

Kommunizma Peak (*Russian* kəmu'njizmə) *n.* a mountain in the SE Tadzhik SSR in the Pamirs: the highest mountain in the Soviet Union. Height: 7495 m (24 590 ft.). Former name: **Stalin Peak.**

Komsomolsk (*Russian* kəmsa'mɔljsk) *n.* an industrial city in the E Soviet Union, in the S Khabarovsk Territory on the Amur River: built by members of the Komsomol (Communist youth league) in 1932. Pop.: 316 000 (1987).

Konakry *or* **Konakri** (*French* kɔnakri) *n.* variant spellings of **Conakry.**

Kongur Shan ('kʊŋʊə 'ʃæn), **Kungur,** *or* **Qungur** *n.* a mountain in China, in W Xinjiang Uygur: the highest peak in the Pamirs. Height: 7719 m (25 325 ft.).

Kong Zi ('kʊŋ ziː) *n.* the Pinyin transliteration of the Chinese name for **Confucius.**

Königgrätz (kø:nɪç'grɛːts) *n.* the German name for **Hradec Králové.**

Königsberg ('kɜːnɪgzˌbɜːɡ; *German* 'koːnɪçsbɛrk) *n.* the former name (until 1946) of **Kaliningrad.**

Königshütte ('koːnɪçshytə) *n.* the German name for **Chorzów.**

Konstanz ('kɔnstants) *n.* the German name for **Constance.**

Konya *or* **Konia** ('kɔːnjaː) *n.* a city in SW central Turkey: in ancient times a Phrygian city and capital of Lycaonia. Pop.: 438 859 (1985). Ancient name: **Iconium.**

koodoo (kuːduː) *n.* a variant spelling of **kudu.**

kook (kuːk) *n. U.S. & Canad. inf.* an eccentric or foolish person. [C20: prob. from CUCKOO] —'**kooky** *or* '**kookie** *adj.*

kookaburra ('kʊkəˌbʌrə) *n.* a large Australian kingfisher with a cackling cry. Also called: **laughing jackass.** [C19: from Aboriginal]

Kooning ('kuːnɪŋ) *n.* **Willem de** ('wɪləm də). born 1904, U.S. abstract expressionist painter, born in Holland.

Kootenay *or* **Kootenai** ('kuːt²niː, 'kuːtneɪ) *n.* a river in W North America, rising in SE British Columbia and flowing south into NW Montana, then north into Idaho before re-entering British Columbia, broadening into **Kootenay Lake,** then flowing to the Columbia River. Length: 655 km (407 miles).

kopeck *or* **copeck** ('kəʊpɛk) *n.* a Soviet monetary unit worth one hundredth of a rouble. [Russian *kopeika*, from *kopye* lance]

Kopeisk or **Kopeysk** (*Russian* ka'pjejsk) *n.* a city in the W central Soviet Union, in Chelyabinsk Region: lignite mining. Pop.: 135 000 (1981 est.). Former name: **Kopi** ('kɒpi).

koppie or **kopje** ('kɒpɪ) *n.* (in southern Africa) a small hill. [C19: from Afrik., from Du. *kopje*, lit.: a little head, from *kop* head]

Koran (kɔː'rɑːn) *n.* the sacred book of Islam, believed by Muslims to be the infallible word of God dictated to Mohammed. Also: **Qur'an.** [C17: from Ar. *qur'ān* reading, book] —**Ko'ranic** *adj.*

Korbut (*Russian* 'kɔrbut) *n.* **Olga** ('ɔljgə). born 1955, Soviet gymnast: noted for her highly individualistic style, which greatly increased the popularity of the sport, esp. following her performance in the 1972 Olympic Games.

Korçë (*Albanian* 'kortʃə) *n.* a market town in SE Albania. Pop.: 57 000 (1983).

Korchnoi ('kɔːtʃ,nɔɪ) *n.* **Victor.** born 1931, Soviet chess player: Soviet champion 1960, 1962, and 1964: defected to the West in 1976.

Kordofan (,kɔːdəʊ'fæn) *n.* a province of the central Sudan: consists of a plateau with rugged uplands (the Nuba Mountains). Capital: El Obeid. Pop.: 3 093 294 (1983). Area: 380 548 sq. km (146 930 sq. miles).

Korea (kə'riːə) *n.* a former country in E Asia, occupying the peninsula between the Sea of Japan and the Yellow Sea: an isolated vassal of Manchu China for three centuries until the opening of ports to Japanese trade in 1876; gained independence in 1895; annexed to Japan in 1910 and divided in 1945 into two occupation zones (Russian in the north, American in the south), which became North Korea and South Korea in 1948. Japanese name (1910–45): **Chosen.** See **North Korea, South Korea.** —**Ko'rean** *adj., n.*

Korea Strait *n.* a strait between South Korea and SW Japan, linking the Sea of Japan with the East China Sea.

korfball ('kɔːf,bɔːl) *n.* a game similar to basketball, in which each team consists of six men and six women. [C20: from Du. *korfbal* basketball]

Kórinthos ('kɒrinθɒs) *n.* transliteration of the Modern Greek name for **Corinth.**

Kortrijk ('kɔrtrɛik) *n.* the Flemish name for **Courtrai.**

Korzybski (kɔː'zɪbski) *n.* **Alfred (Habdank Skarbek).** 1879–1950, U.S. originator of the theory and study of general semantics, born in Poland.

Kos or **Cos** (kɒs) *n.* an island in the SE Aegean Sea, in the Greek Dodecanese Islands: separated from SW Turkey by the **Kos Channel;** settled in ancient times by Dorians and became famous for literature and medicine. Pop.: 20 350 (1981). Area: 282 sq. km (109 sq. miles).

Kosciusko[1] (,kɒsɪ'ʌskəʊ) *n.* **Mount.** a mountain in Australia, in SE New South Wales in the Australian Alps: the highest peak in Australia. Height: 2230 m (7316 ft.).

Kosciusko[2] (,kɒsɪ'ʌskəʊ) *n.* **Thaddeus,** Polish name *Tadeusz Kościusko.* 1746–1817, Polish general: fought for the colonists in the American War of Independence and led an unsuccessful revolt against the partitioning of Poland (1794).

kosher ('kəʊʃə) *adj.* **1.** *Judaism.* conforming to religious law; fit for use: esp. (of food) prepared in accordance with the dietary laws. **2.** *Inf.* **a.** genuine or authentic. **b.** legitimate. ~*n.* **3.** kosher food. [C19: from Yiddish, from Heb. *kāshēr* proper]

Košice (*Czech* 'kɒʃitsɛ) *n.* a city in SE Czechoslovakia: passed from Hungary to Czechoslovakia in 1920. Pop.: 222 000 (1986). Hungarian name: **Kassa.**

Kosovo-Metohija (*Serbo-Croatian* 'kɔsɔvɔmɛ,tɔhija) *n.* an autonomous region in S central Yugoslavia, in SW Serbia: created in 1946 from parts of Serbia and Montenegro; mainly a plateau. Capital: **Priština.** Pop.: 1 584 558 (1981). Area: 10 350 sq. km (4000 sq. miles).

Kossuth (*Hungarian* 'koʃuːt) *n.* **Lajos** ('lɔjoʃ). 1802–94, Hungarian statesman. He led the revolution against Austria (1848) and was provisional governor (1849), but he fled when the revolt was suppressed (1849).

Kostroma (*Russian* kɒstra'ma) *n.* a city in the W central Soviet Union, on the River Volga: fought over bitterly by Novgorod, Tver, and Moscow, until annexed by Moscow in 1329; textile centre. Pop.: 276 000 (1987).

Kosygin (*Russian* ka'sigin) *n.* **Aleksei Nikolayevich** (alık'sjej nika'lajıvitʃ). 1904–80, Soviet statesman; premier of the Soviet Union (1964–80).

Kota or **Kotah** ('kəʊtə) *n.* a city in NW India, in Rajasthan on the Chambal River: textile industry. Pop.: 346 928 (1981).

Kotabaru ('kəʊtə'bɑːruː) *n.* a former name of **Jayapura.**

Kota Bharu or **Bahru** ('kəʊtə 'bɑːruː) *n.* a port in NE Peninsular Malaysia: capital of Kelantan state on the delta of the Kelantan River. Pop.: 170 559 (1980).

Kota Kinabalu ('kəʊtə ,kɪnəbə'luː) *n.* a port in Malaysia, capital of Sabah state on the South China Sea: exports timber and rubber. Pop.: 59 500 (1980). Former name: **Jesselton.**

koto ('kəʊtəʊ) *n., pl.* **kotos.** a Japanese stringed instrument. [Japanese]

kotuku ('kəʊtuːkuː) *n., pl.* **-ku.** *N.Z.* a white heron having brilliant white plumage, black legs and yellow eyes and bill. [Maori]

Kovno ('kɒvnə) *n.* transliteration of the Russian name for **Kaunas.**

Kovrov (*Russian* kav'rɒf) *n.* a city in the W central Soviet Union, on the Klyazma River: textiles and heavy engineering. Pop.: 146 000 (1981 est.).

Koweit (kəʊ'weɪt) *n.* a variant of **Kuwait.**

kowhai ('kɔːwaɪ) *n., pl.* **-hais.** *N.Z.* a small leguminous tree of New Zealand and Chile with clusters of yellow flowers. [C19: from Maori]

Kowloon ('kaʊ'luːn) *n.* **1.** a peninsula of SE China, opposite Hong Kong Island: part of the British colony of Hong Kong. Area: 10 sq. km (3.75 sq. miles). **2.** a port in Hong Kong, on Kowloon Peninsula. Pop.: 799 000 (1981).

kowtow (,kaʊ'taʊ) *vb.* (*intr.*) **1.** to touch the forehead to the ground as a sign of deference: a former Chinese custom. **2.** (often foll. by *to*) to be servile (towards). ~*n.* **3.** the act of kowtowing. [C19: from Chinese, from *k'o* to strike, knock + *t'ou* head]

Kozhikode (,kəʊʒɪ'kəʊd) *n.* a port in SW India, in W Kerala on the Malabar coast: important European trading post (1511–1765): formerly calico-manufacturing. Pop.: 394 440 (1981). Former name: **Calicut.**

Kr 1. *Currency. symbol for:* **a.** krona. **b.** krone. **2.** *the chemical symbol for* krypton.

kr. *abbrev. for:* **1.** krona. **2.** krone.

Kra (krɑː) *n.* **Isthmus of.** an isthmus of SW Thailand, between the Bay of Bengal and the Gulf of Siam: the narrowest part of the Malay Peninsula. Width: about 56 km (35 miles).

kraal (krɑːl) *n.* *S. African.* **1.** a hut village in southern Africa, esp. one surrounded by a stockade. **2.** an enclosure for livestock. [C18: from Afrik., from Port. *curral* pen]

Krafft-Ebing (*German* 'kraft'eːbɪŋ) *n.* **Richard** ('rɪçart), Baron von Krafft-Ebing. 1840–1902, German neurologist and psychiatrist who pioneered the systematic study of sexual behaviour in *Psychopathia Sexualis* (1886).

kraft (krɑːft) *n.* strong wrapping paper. [G: force]

Kragujevac (*Serbo-Croatian* 'kragujɛvats) *n.* a town in E central Yugoslavia, in Serbia; capital of Serbia (1818–39); automobile industry. Pop.: 164 823 (1981).

krait (kraɪt) *n.* any nonaggressive brightly coloured venomous snake of S and SE Asia. [C19: from Hindi *karait*, from ?]

Krakatoa (,krɑːkə'təʊə, ,krækə'təʊə) or **Krakatau** (,krɑːkə'taʊ, ,krækə'taʊ) *n.* a volcanic island in Indonesia, in the Sunda Strait between Java and Sumatra: partially destroyed by its eruption in 1883, the greatest in recorded history. Further eruptions 44 years later formed a new island, **Anak Krakatau** ("Child of Krakatau"). Also called: **Rakata.**

Krakau ('krɑːkau) *n.* the German name for **Cracow.**

kraken ('krɑːkən) *n.* a legendary sea monster of gigantic size believed to dwell off the coast of Norway. [C18: from Norwegian, from ?]

Kraków ('krakuf) *n.* the Polish name for **Cracow.**

Kramatorsk (*Russian* krəma'tɒrsk) *n.* a city in the SW Soviet Union, in the E Ukrainian SSR: a major industrial centre of the Donets Basin. Pop.: 198 000 (1987).

Kranj (krɑːnj) *n.* the Slovene name for **Carniola.**

krans (krɑːns) *n.* *S. African.* a sheer rock face; precipice. [C18: from Afrik.]

Krasnodar (*Russian* krəsna'dar) *n.* an industrial city in the SW Soviet Union, on the Kuban River. Pop.: 623 000 (1987). Former name (until 1920): **Yekaterinodar.**

Krasnoyarsk (*Russian* krəsna'jarsk) *n.* a city in the E central Soviet Union, on the Yenisei River: the country's largest hydroelectric power station is nearby. Pop.: 899 000 (1987).

Krebs (krɛbz) *n.* Sir **Hans Adolf.** 1900–81, British biochemist, born in Germany, who shared a Nobel prize for physiology or medicine (1953) for the discovery of the **Krebs cycle**, a cycle of metabolic reactions.

Krefeld ('kreɪfɛld; *German* 'kreːfɛlt) *n.* a city in West Germany, in W North Rhine-Westphalia: textile industries. Pop.: 216 700 (1986).

Kreisky (*German* 'kraiski) *n.* **Bruno** ('bruːno). born 1911, Austrian statesman; federal chancellor of Austria (1970–83).

Kreisler (*German* 'kraislər) *n.* **Fritz** (frɪts). 1875–1962, U.S. violinist, born in Austria.

Kremenchug (*Russian* krɪmɪn'tʃuk) *n.* an industrial city in the SW Soviet Union, in the E central Ukrainian SSR on the Dnieper River. Pop.: 230 000 (1987).

kremlin ('krɛmlɪn) *n.* the citadel of any Russian city. [C17: from obs. G *Kremelin*, from Russian *kreml*]

Kremlin ('krɛmlɪn) *n.* **1.** the 12th-century citadel in Moscow, containing the offices of the Soviet government. **2.** the central government of the Soviet Union.

Krems (*German* krɛms) *n.* a town in NE Austria, capital of Lower Austria on the River Danube. Pop.: 23 123 (1981).

Kriemhild ('kriːmhɪlt) *or* **Kriemhilde** ('kriːmˌhɪldə) *n.* (in the *Nibelungenlied*) the wife of Siegfried. She corresponds to Gudrun in Norse mythology.

krill (krɪl) *n., pl.* **krill.** any small shrimplike marine crustacean: the principal food of whalebone whales. [C20: from Norwegian *kril* young fish]

krimmer ('krɪmə) *n.* a tightly curled light grey fur obtained from the skins of lambs from Crimea in the USSR. [C20: from G, from *Krim* Crimea]

kris (krɪs) *n.* a Malayan and Indonesian stabbing or slashing knife with a scalloped edge. Also called: **crease, creese.** [C16: from Malay]

Krishna[1] ('krɪʃnə) *n.* a river in S India, rising in the Western Ghats and flowing generally southeast to the Bay of Bengal. Length: 1300 km (800 miles). Also called: **Kistna.**

Krishna[2] ('krɪʃnə) *n. Hinduism.* the most celebrated of the Hindu deities, whose life story is told in the *Mahabharata.* [via Hindi from Sansk., lit.: dark, black] —'**Krishnaism** *or* **Krishnanism** *n.*

Krishna Menon ('kriːʃnə 'mɛnən) *n.* **Vengalil Krishnan** ('vɛŋɡəlɪl 'kriːʃnən). See (Vengalil Krishnan Krishna) **Menon.**

Kristiania (ˌkrɪstɪ'ɑːnɪə) *n.* a former name (1877–1924) of **Oslo.**

Kristiansand *or* **Christiansand** ('krɪstʃən,sænd; *Norwegian* kristian'san) *n.* a port in S Norway, on the Skagerrak: shipbuilding. Pop.: 63 293 (1987).

Kristianstad ('krɪstʃən,stɑːd; *Swedish* kri'ʃansta:d) *n.* a town in S Sweden: founded in 1614 as a Danish fortress, it was finally acquired by Sweden in 1678. Pop.: 69 941 (1986).

Kríti ('kriti) *n.* transliteration of the Modern Greek name for **Crete.**

Krivoy Rog (*Russian* kri'vɔj 'rɔk) *n.* a city in the SW Soviet Union, in the SE Ukrainian SSR: founded in the 17th century by Cossacks; iron-mining centre; iron- and steelworks. Pop.: 698 000 (1987).

krona ('krəʊnə) *n., pl.* **-nor** (-nə). the standard monetary unit of Sweden.

króna ('krəʊnə) *n., pl.* **-nur** (-nə). the standard monetary unit of Iceland.

krone ('krəʊnə) *n., pl.* **-ner** (-nə). **1.** the standard monetary unit of Denmark. **2.** the standard monetary unit of Norway. [C19: from Danish or Norwegian, ult. from L *corōna* CROWN]

Kronos ('krəʊnɒs) *n.* a variant of **Cronus.**

Kronstadt *n.* **1.** (*Russian* kran'ʃtat). a port in the NW Soviet Union, on Kotlin island in the Gulf of Finland: naval base. Pop.: 39 477 (1970). **2.** ('kro:nʃtat). the German name for **Braşov.**

Kropotkin (*Russian* kra'pɔtkin) *n.* Prince **Peter,** Russian name *Pyotr Alexeyevich.* 1842–1921, Russian anarchist: his books include *Mutual Aid* (1902) and *Modern Science and Anarchism* (1903).

Kruger ('kruːɡə) *n.* **Stephanus Johannes Paulus** ('stɛfənʊs jəʊ'hænɪs 'pɔːlʊs), known as *Oom Paul.* 1825–1904, Boer statesman; president of the Transvaal (1883–1900). His opposition to Cecil Rhodes and his denial of

civil rights to the Uitlanders led to the Boer War (1899–1902).

Kruger National Park *n.* a wildlife sanctuary in NE South Africa, in E Transvaal: the world's largest game reserve. Area: over 21 700 sq. km (8400 sq. miles).

Krugerrand ('kruːɡə,rænd) *n.* a one-ounce gold coin minted in South Africa. [C20: from Paul KRUGER + RAND[1]]

Krugersdorp ('kruːɡəz,dɔːp) *n.* a city in NE South Africa, in S Transvaal on the Witwatersrand, at an altitude of 1722 m (5650 ft.): a gold-, manganese-, and uranium-mining centre. Pop.: 141 100 (1984 est.).

krummhorn ('krʌm,hɔːn) *or* **crumhorn** *n.* a medieval wind instrument consisting of an upward-curving tube blown through a double reed.

Krupp (krʊp, krʌp) *n.* a German family of steel and armaments manufacturers, including **Alfred,** 1812–87, his son **Friedrich Alfred,** 1854–1902, and the latter's son-in-law, **Gustav Krupp von Bohlen und Halbach,** 1870–1950.

Krušné Hory ('kruʃne 'hɔri) *n.* the Czech name for the **Erzgebirge.**

Krym *or* **Krim** (krim) *n.* transliteration of the Russian name for **Crimea.**

krypton ('krɪptɒn) *n.* an inert gaseous element occurring in trace amounts in air and used in fluorescent lights and lasers. Symbol: Kr; atomic no.: 36; atomic wt.: 83.80. [C19: from Gk, from *kruptos* hidden]

Kshatriya ('kʃætrɪə) *n.* a member of the second of the four main Hindu castes, the warrior caste. [C18: from Sansk., from *kshatra* rule]

kt *abbrev. for:* **1.** karat. **2.** *Naut.* knot.

Kt 1. Also: **knt.** *abbrev. for* Knight. **2.** Also: **N.** *Chess. symbol for* knight.

Kuala Lumpur ('kwɑːlə 'lʊmpʊə, -pə) *n.* the capital of Malaysia, in the SW Malay Peninsula: became capital of the Federated Malay States in 1895, and of Malaysia in 1963; capital of Selangor state from 1880 to 1973, when it was made a federal territory. Pop.: 1 103 200 (1985).

Kuban (*Russian* ku'banj) *n.* a river in the S central Soviet Union, rising in the Caucasus Mountains and flowing north and northwest to the Sea of Azov. Length: 906 km (563 miles).

Kubelik (*Czech* 'kubɛliːk) *n.* **Raphael** ('raːfaɛl). born 1914, Czech conductor and composer.

Kublai Khan ('kuːblaɪ 'kɑːn) *n.* ?1216–94, Mongol emperor of China: grandson of Genghis Khan. He completed his grandfather's conquest of China by overthrowing the Sung dynasty (1279) and founded the Yuan dynasty (1279–1368).

Kubrick ('kjuːbrɪk) *n.* **Stanley.** born 1928, U.S. film writer, director, and producer. He directed *Lolita* (1962), *Dr Strangelove* (1963), *2001: A Space Odyssey* (1969), *A Clockwork Orange* (1971), and *The Shining* (1980).

Kuch Bihar ('kuːtʃ bɪ'hɑː) *n.* a variant spelling of **Cooch Behar.**

Kuching ('kuːtʃɪŋ) *n.* a port in E Malaysia, capital of Sarawak state, on the Sarawak River 24 km (15 miles) from its mouth. Pop.: 74 229 (1980).

kudos ('kjuːdɒs) *n.* (*functioning as sing.*) acclaim, glory, or prestige. [C18: from Gk]

kudu *or* **koodoo** ('kuːduː) *n.* either of two spiral-horned antelopes (**greater kudu** or **lesser kudu**), which inhabit the bush of Africa. [C18: from Afrik. *koedoe,* prob. from Xhosa *iqudu*]

Kuenlun ('kʊn'lʊn) *n.* a variant spelling of **Kunlun.**

Kuibyshev *or* **Kuybyshev** (*Russian* 'kujbɪʃəf) *n.* a port in the SW central Soviet Union, on the River Volga: centre of an important industrial complex; oil refining. Pop.: 1 280 000 (1987). Former name (until 1935): **Samara.**

Ku Klux Klan (ˌkuː klʌks 'klæn) *n.* **1.** a secret organization of White Southerners formed after the U.S. Civil War to fight Black emancipation. **2.** a secret organization of White Protestant Americans, mainly in the South, who use violence against Blacks, Jews, etc. [C19 *Ku Klux,* prob. based on Gk *kuklos* CIRCLE + *Klan* CLAN] —**Ku Klux Klanner** ('klænə) *n.*

kukri ('kʊkrɪ) *n., pl.* **-ris.** a knife with a curved blade that broadens towards the point, esp. as used by Gurkhas. [from Hindi]

Kuku Nor ('kuː'kuː 'nɔː) *n.* a variant of **Koko Nor.**

kulak ('kuːlæk) *n.* (in Russia after 1906) a member of the class of peasants who became proprietors of their own farms. In 1929 Stalin initiated their liquidation. [C19: from Russian: fist, hence, tightfisted person]

Kulun ('kuː'luːn) *n.* the Chinese name for **Ulan Bator.**

Kum (kum) *n.* a variant spelling of **Qom.**

Kumamoto (ˌkuməˈməʊtəʊ) *n.* a city in SW Japan, on W central Kyushu: Kumamoto Medical University (1949). Pop.: 556 000 (1985).

Kumasi (kuːˈmæsɪ) *n.* a city in S Ghana: seat of Ashanti kings since 1663; university (1961); market town for a cocoa-producing region. Pop.: 348 880 (1984).

kumera *or* **kumara** ('kuːmərə) *n. N.Z.* the sweet potato. [from Maori]

kumiss *or* **koumiss** ('kuːmɪs) *n.* a drink made from fermented mare's or other milk, drunk by certain Asian tribes. [C17: from Russian *kumys*]

kümmel ('kuməl) *n.* a German liqueur flavoured with aniseed and cumin. [C19: from G, from OHG *kumil*, prob. var. of *kumin* CUMIN]

kumquat *or* **cumquat** ('kʌmkwɒt) *n.* **1.** a small Chinese citrus tree. **2.** the small round orange fruit of such a tree, with a sweet rind, used in preserves and confections. [C17: from Mandarin Chinese *chin chü* golden orange]

Kun (kuːn) *n.* **Béla** ('beːlɔ). 1886–?1937, Hungarian Communist leader, president of the short-lived Communist republic in Hungary (1919). He was forced into exile and died in a Stalinist purge.

kung fu ('kʌŋ 'fuː) *n.* a Chinese martial art combining principles of karate and judo. [from Chinese: martial art]

K'ung Fu-tse ('kʊŋ 'fuːˈtseɪ) *n.* the Chinese name of **Confucius.**

Kungur ('kʊŋɡʊə) *n.* a variant transliteration of the Chinese name for **Kongur Shan.**

Kunlun, Kuenlun, *or* **Kwenlun** ('kʊn'lʊn) *n.* a mountain range in China, between the Tibetan plateau and the Tarim Basin, extending over 1600 km (1000 miles) east from the Pamirs: the largest mountain system of Asia. Highest peak: Ulugh Muztagh, 7723 m (25 338 ft.).

Kunming *or* **K'un-ming** ('kʊn'mɪŋ) *n.* a city in SW China, capital of Yunnan province, near Lake Tien: important during World War II as a Chinese military centre, American air base, and transport terminus for the Burma Road; Yunnan University (1934). Pop.: 1 490 000 (1986).

Kuopio (*Finnish* 'kwɔpjɔ) *n.* a city in S central Finland. Pop.: 78 529 (1986).

Kura (kʊˈrɑː) *n.* a river in W Asia, rising in NE Turkey and flowing into the Soviet Union across the Georgian and Azerbaijan SSRs to the Caspian Sea. Length: 1515 km (941 miles).

kurchatovium (ˌkɜːtʃəˈtəʊvɪəm) *n.* another name for **rutherfordium,** esp. as used in the Soviet Union. [C20: from Russian, after I. V. *Kurchatov* (1903–60), Soviet physicist]

Kurd (kɜːd) *n.* a member of a nomadic people living chiefly in E Turkey, N Iraq, and W Iran.

Kurdish ('kɜːdɪʃ) *n.* **1.** the language of the Kurds. ~*adj.* **2.** of or relating to the Kurds or their language.

Kurdistan, Kurdestan, *or* **Kordestan** (ˌkɜːdɪˈstɑːn) *n.* a large plateau and mountainous region, between the Caspian Sea and the Black Sea, south of the Caucasus. Area: over 29 000 sq. km (74 000 sq. miles).

Kure (kuːˈreɪ) *n.* a port in SW Japan, on SW Honshu: a naval base; shipyards. Pop.: 225 357 (1986 est.).

Kurgan (*Russian* kurˈgan) *n.* a city in the W central Soviet Union, on the Tobol River: industrial centre for an agricultural region. Pop.: 356 000 (1987).

kuri ('kuːrɪ) *n., pl.* **-ris.** *N.Z.* a mongrel dog. Also called: **goorie.** [Maori]

Kuril Islands *or* **Kurile Islands** (kuːˈriːl) *pl. n.* a chain of 56 volcanic islands off the NE coast of Asia, extending for 1200 km (750 miles) from the S tip of the Kamchatka Peninsula to NE Hokkaido. Area: 14 990 sq. km (6020 sq. miles). Japanese name: **Chishima.**

Kurland ('kʊələnd) *n.* a variant spelling of **Courland.**

Kurosawa (ˌkʊərəˈsɑːwə) *n.* **Akira** (əˈkɪərə). born 1910, Japanese film director. His works include *Rashomon* (1950), *Seven Samurai* (1954), *Throne of Blood* (1957), *Kagemusha* (1980), and *Ran* (1985).

Kuroshio (kəˈrəʊʃɪˌəʊ) *n.* another name for **Japan Current.**

kurrajong *or* **currajong** ('kʌrəˌdʒɒŋ) *n.* any of various Australian trees or shrubs, esp. one that yields a tough durable fibre. [C19: from Abor.]

kursaal ('kɜːzəl) *n.* a public room at a health resort. [from G, lit.: cure room]

Kursk (*Russian* kursk) *n.* a city in the W central Soviet Union: industrial centre of an agricultural region. Pop.: 434 000 (1987).

kurtosis (kəˈtəʊsɪs) *n. Statistics.* a measure of the concentration of a distribution around its mean. [from Gk, from *kurtos* arched]

Kurzeme ('kʊrzɛmɛ) *n.* the Latvian name for **Courland.**

Kush (kʌʃ, kuʃ) *n.* a variant spelling of **Cush.**

Kuskokwim ('kʌskəˌkwɪm) *n.* a river in SW Alaska, rising in the Alaska Range and flowing generally southwest to **Kuskokwim Bay,** an inlet of the Bering Sea. Length: about 970 km (600 miles).

Kutaisi (*Russian* kutaˈisi) *n.* an industrial city in the SW Soviet Union, in the W Georgian SSR on the Rioni River: one of the oldest towns of the Caucasus. Pop.: 220 000 (1987).

Kutch *or* **Cutch** (kʌtʃ) *n.* **1.** a former state of W India, on the **Gulf of Kutch** (an inlet of the Arabian Sea): part of Gujarat state since 1960. **2. Rann of.** an extensive salt waste in W central India, and S Pakistan: consists of the Great Rann in the north and the Little Rann in the southeast; seasonal alternation between marsh and desert; some saltworks. In 1968 an international tribunal awarded about 10 per cent of the border area to Pakistan. Area: 23 000 sq. km (9000 sq. miles).

Kutuzov (*Russian* kuˈtuzəf) *n.* Prince **Mikhail Ilarionovich** (mixaˈil ɪlərɪˈɒnəvɪtʃ). 1745–1813, Russian field marshal, who harried the French army under Napoleon throughout their retreat from Moscow (1812–13).

Kuwait (kuˈweɪt) *or* **Koweit** *n.* **1.** a state on the NW coast of the Persian Gulf: came under British protection in 1899 and gained independence in 1961; mainly desert. The economy is dependent on oil. Official language: Arabic. Religion: mostly Muslim. Currency: dinar. Capital: Kuwait. Pop.: 1 771 000 (1986). Area: 24 280 sq. km (9375 sq. miles). **2.** the capital of Kuwait: a port on the Persian Gulf. Pop.: 44 335 (1985). —**Ku'waiti** *or* **ko'waiti** *adj., n.*

Kuznets ('kuznɪtz) *n.* **Simon.** born 1901, U.S. economist born in Russia. His books include *National Income and its Composition (1919–1938)* (1941) and *Economic Growth of Nations* (1971). He was awarded the Nobel Prize for economics in 1971.

Kuznetsk Basin (*Russian* kuzˈnjɛtsk) *or* **Kuzbass** (*Russian* kuzˈbas) *n.* a region of the Soviet Union, in the Kemerovo Region of W Siberia: the richest coalfield in the country, with reserves of iron ore. Chief industrial centre: Novokuznetsk. Area: about 69 900 sq. km (27 000 sq. miles).

Kvaloy (*Norwegian* 'kvaːlœj) *n.* two islands in the Arctic Ocean, off the N coast of Norway: **North Kvaloy,** 329 sq. km (127 sq. miles), and **South Kvaloy,** 735 sq. km (284 sq. miles).

kvass (kvɑːs) *n.* an alcoholic drink of low strength made in the Soviet Union from cereals and stale bread. [C16: from Russian *kvas*]

kW *abbrev. for* kilowatt.

kwacha ('kwɑːtʃɑː) *n.* **1.** the standard monetary unit of Zambia. **2.** the standard monetary unit of Malawi. [from a native word in Zambia]

Kwajalein ('kwɑːdʒəˌleɪn) *n.* an atoll in the W Pacific, in the W Marshall Islands, in the central part of the Ralik Chain. Length: about 125 km (78 miles).

Kwangchow ('kwæŋ'tʃaʊ) *n.* a variant transliteration of the Chinese name for **Canton.**

Kwangchowan ('kwæŋ'tʃaʊ'wɑːn) *n.* a territory of SE China, in SW Kwantung province: leased to France as part of French Indochina from 1898 to 1945. Area: 842 sq. km (325 sq. miles).

Kwangju ('kwæŋ'dʒuː) *n.* a city in SW South Korea: an important military base during the Korean War; cotton textile industry. Pop.: 905 896 (1985).

Kwangsi-Chuang Autonomous Region ('kwæŋ'siː'tʃwæŋ) *n.* a variant transliteration of the Chinese name for **Guangxi Zhuang.**

Kwangtung ('kwæŋ'tʊŋ) *n.* a variant transliteration of the Chinese name for **Guangdong.**

Kwantung Leased Territory (ˌkwæn'tʌŋ) *n.* a strategic territory of NE China, at the S tip of the Liaotung Peninsula of Manchuria: leased forcibly by Russia in 1898; taken over by Japan in 1905; occupied by the Soviet Union in 1945 and subsequently returned to China on the condition of shared administration; made part of Liaoning province by China in 1954. Area: about 3400 sq. km (1300 sq. miles). Also called: **Kuan-tung.**

Kwara ('kwɑːrə) *n.* a state of W Nigeria: mainly wooded savanna. Capital: Ilorin. Pop.: 2 884 400 (1984). Area: 73 400 sq. km (28 334 sq. miles).

kwashiorkor (,kwæʃɪ'ɔːkə) *n.* severe malnutrition of infants and young children, resulting from dietary deficiency of protein. [C20: from native word in Ghana]

Kwazulu (kwɑː'zuːlʊ) *n.* a Bantustan in South Africa, in Natal: consists of ten separate territories. Capital: Ulundi. Pop.: 3 738 334 (1985).

Kweichow *or* **Kueichou** ('kweɪ'tʃaʊ) *n.* a variant transliteration of the Chinese name for **Guizhou.**

Kweilin *or* **Kuei-lin** ('kweɪ'lɪn) *n.* a variant transliteration of the Chinese name for **Guilin.**

Kweisui ('kweɪ'sweɪ) *n.* the former name of **Hohhot.**

Kweiyang *or* **Kuei-yang** ('kweɪ'jæŋ) *n.* a variant transliteration of the Chinese name for **Guiyang.**

kWh *abbrev. for* kilowatt-hour.

KWIC (kwɪk) *n. acronym for* key word in context (esp. in **KWIC index**).

KWOC (kwɒk) *n. acronym for* key word out of context.

Ky (kiː) *n.* **Nguyen Kao** (ᵊŋ'guːjɛn 'kaʊ). born 1930, premier of South Vietnam (1965–67); vice president (1967–69).

kyanite ('kaɪə,naɪt) *n.* a variant spelling of **cyanite.** —**kyanitic** (,kaɪə'nɪtɪk) *adj.*

kyanize *or* **-ise** ('kaɪə,naɪz) *vb.* (*tr.*) to treat (timber) with corrosive sublimate to make it resistant to decay. [C19: after J.H. **Kyan** (died 1850), E inventor of the process] —**,kyani'zation** *or* **-i'sation** *n.*

Kyd *or* **Kid** (kɪd) *n.* **Thomas.** 1558–94, English dramatist, noted for his revenge play *The Spanish Tragedy* (1586).

kyle (kaɪl) *n. Scot.* (esp. in place names) a narrow strait or channel. [C16: from Gaelic *caol* narrow]

kylie *or* **kiley** ('kaɪlɪ) *n. Austral.* a boomerang that is flat on one side and convex on the other. [C19: from Abor.]

kyloe ('kaɪləʊ) *n.* a breed of small long-horned long-haired beef cattle from NW Scotland. [C19: from ?]

kymograph ('kaɪmə,grɑːf) *n.* a rotatable drum for holding paper on which a tracking stylus continuously records variations in sound waves, blood pressure, respiratory movements, etc. [C20: from Gk *kuma* wave + -GRAPH] —**,kymo'graphic** *adj.*

Kymric ('kɪmrɪk) *n., adj.* a variant spelling of **Cymric.**

Kymry ('kɪmrɪ) *pl. n.* a variant spelling of **Cymry.**

Kynewulf ('kɪnə,wʊlf) *n.* a variant spelling of **Cynewulf.**

Kyongsong ('kjɔːŋ'sɔːŋ) *n.* another name for **Seoul.**

Kyoto *or* **Kioto** (kɪ'əʊtəʊ, 'kjəʊ-) *n.* a city in central Japan, on S Honshu: the capital of Japan from 794 to 1868; cultural centre, with two universities (1875, 1897). Pop.: 1 479 000 (1985).

kyphosis (kaɪ'fəʊsɪs) *n. Pathol.* backward curvature of the thoracic spine, of congenital origin or resulting from injury or disease. [C19: from NL, from Gk *kuphōsis,* from *kuphos* humpbacked] —**kyphotic** (kaɪ'fɒtɪk) *adj.*

Kyprianou (,kɪprɪ'ɑːnuː) *n.* **Spyros** ('spɪərɒs). born 1932, Cypriot statesman; president of Cyprus (1977–88).

Kyrie eleison ('kɪriː ə'leɪsᵊn) *n.* **1.** a formal invocation used in the liturgies of the Roman Catholic, Greek Orthodox, and Anglican Churches. **2.** a musical setting of this. Often shortened to **Kyrie.** [C14: via LL from LGk *kurie eleēson* Lord, have mercy]

Kythera ('kɪθɪrə) *n.* a variant spelling of **Cythera.**

kyu (kjuː) *n. Judo.* one of the student grades for inexperienced competitors. [from Japanese]

Kyushu *or* **Kiushu** ('kjuːʃuː) *n.* an island of SW Japan: the southernmost of Japan's four main islands, with over 300 surrounding small islands; contains the country's main coalfield. Chief cities: Fukuoka, Kitakyushu, and Nagasaki. Pop.: 13 276 000 (1985). Area: 35 659 sq. km (13 768 sq. miles).

Kyzyl Kum (*Russian* ki'zil 'kum) *n.* a desert in the SW Soviet Union, in the Kazakh and Uzbek SSRs.

L

l *or* **L** (ɛl) *n.*, *pl.* **l's**, **L's**, *or* **Ls**. **1.** the 12th letter of the English alphabet. **2.** a speech sound represented by this letter. **3. a.** something shaped like an L. **b.** (*in combination*): *an L-shaped room.*

l *symbol for* litre.

L *symbol for:* **1.** lambert(s). **2.** large. **3.** Latin. **4.** (on British motor vehicles) learner driver. **5.** *Physics.* length. **6.** live. **7.** Usually written: ₤ pound. [L *libra*]. **8.** lire. **9.** *Electronics.* inductor (in circuit diagrams). **10.** *Physics.* **a.** latent heat. **b.** self-inductance. **~11.** the Roman numeral for 50. See **Roman numerals**.

L. *or* **l.** *abbrev. for:* **1.** lake. **2.** law. **3.** leaf. **4.** league. **5.** left. **6.** length. **7.** (*pl.* **LL** *or* **ll.**) line. **8.** link. **9.** low.

L. *abbrev. for:* **1.** *Politics.* Liberal. **2.** (in titles) Licentiate. **3.** Linnaeus.

la¹ (lɑː) *n.* *Music.* a variant spelling of **lah.**

la² (lɔː) *interj.* an exclamation of surprise or emphasis. [OE *lā* lo]

La *the chemical symbol for* lanthanum.

laager ('lɑːgə) *n.* **1.** (in Africa) a camp, esp. one defended by a circular formation of wagons. **2.** *Mil.* a place where armoured vehicles are parked. *~vb.* **3.** to form (wagons) into a laager. **4.** (*tr.*) to park (armoured vehicles) in a laager. [C19: from Afrik. *lager*, via G from OHG *legar* bed, lair]

Laaland (*Danish* 'lɔlən) *n.* a variant spelling of **Lolland.**

lab (læb) *n.* *Inf.* short for **laboratory.**

lab. *abbrev. for:* **1.** laboratory. **2.** labour.

Lab. *abbrev. for:* **1.** *Politics.* Labour. **2.** Labrador.

Laban ('leɪbən) *n.* *Old Testament.* the father-in-law of Jacob, father of Leah and Rachel (Genesis 29:16).

Labe ('lɑbɛ) *n.* the Czech name for the (River) **Elbe.**

label ('leɪbªl) *n.* **1.** a piece of paper, card, or other material attached to an object to identify it or give instructions or details concerning its ownership, use, nature, destination, etc.; tag. **2.** a brief descriptive phrase or term given to a person, group, school of thought, etc.: *the label "Romantic" is applied to many different kinds of poetry.* **3.** a word or phrase heading a piece of text to indicate or summarize its contents. **4.** a trademark or company or brand name on certain goods, esp. on gramophone records. **5.** *Computers.* a group of characters appended to a statement in a program to allow it to be identified. **6.** *Chem.* a radioactive element used in a compound to trace the mechanism of a chemical reaction. *~vb.* **-belling, -belled** *or U.S.* **-beling, -beled.** (*tr.*) **7.** to fasten a label to. **8.** to mark with a label. **9.** to describe or classify in a word or phrase: *to label someone a liar.* **10.** to make (one or more atoms in a compound) radioactive, for use in determining the mechanism of a reaction. [C14: from OF, from Gmc] —**'labeller** *n.*

labia ('leɪbɪə) *n.* the plural of **labium.**

labial ('leɪbɪəl) *adj.* **1.** of, relating to, or near lips or labia. **2.** *Music.* producing sounds by the action of an air stream over a narrow liplike fissure, as in a flue pipe of an organ. **3.** *Phonetics.* relating to a speech sound whose articulation involves movement or use of the lips. *~n.* **4.** Also called: **labial pipe.** *Music.* an organ pipe with a liplike fissure. **5.** *Phonetics.* a speech sound such as English *p* or *m*, whose articulation involves movement or use of the lips. [C16: from Med. L *labiālis*, from L *labium* lip] —**'labially** *adv.*

labiate ('leɪbɪˌeɪt, -ɪt) *n.* **1.** any plant of the family *Labiatae*, having square stems, aromatic leaves, and a two-lipped corolla: includes mint, thyme, sage, rosemary, etc. *~adj.* **2.** of, relating to, or belonging to the family *Labiatae*. [C18: from NL *labiātus*, from L *labium* lip]

Labiche (*French* labiʃ) *n.* **Eugène Marin** (øʒɛn marɛ̃). 1815–88, French dramatist, noted for his farces of middle-class life, which include *Le Chapeau de paille d'Italie* (1851) and *Le Voyage de Monsieur Perrichon* (1860).

labile ('leɪbɪl) *adj.* *Chem.* (of a compound) prone to chemical change. [C15: via LL *lābilis*, from L *lābī* to slide] —**lability** (lə'bɪlɪtɪ) *n.*

labiodental (ˌleɪbɪəʊ'dɛntªl) *Phonetics.* *~adj.* **1.** pronounced by bringing the bottom lip into contact with the upper teeth, as for *f* in *fat, puff.* *~n.* **2.** a labiodental consonant. [C17: from L LABIUM + DENTAL]

labium ('leɪbɪəm) *n.*, *pl.* **-bia** (-bɪə). **1.** a lip or liplike structure. **2.** any one of the four lip-shaped folds of the female vulva, comprising an outer pair (**labia majora**) and an inner pair (**labia minora**). [C16: NL, from L.: lip]

laboratory (lə'bɒrətərɪ, -trɪ; *U.S.* 'læbrə,tɔːrɪ) *n.*, *pl.* **-ries. 1. a.** a building or room equipped for conducting scientific research or for teaching practical science. **b.** (*as modifier*): *laboratory equipment.* **2.** a place where chemicals or medicines are manufactured. ~Often shortened to **lab.** [C17: from Med. L *labōrātōrium* workshop, from L *labōrāre* to LABOUR]

Labor Day *n.* **1.** a public holiday in the U.S. and Canada in honour of labour, held on the first Monday in September. **2.** a public holiday in Australia, observed on different days in different states.

laborious (lə'bɔːrɪəs) *adj.* **1.** involving great exertion or long effort. **2.** given to working hard. **3.** (of literary style, etc.) not fluent. —**la'boriously** *adv.* —**la'boriousness** *n.*

Labor Party *n.* one of the two chief political parties of Australia, generally supporting the interests of organized labour.

labour *or U.S.* **labor** ('leɪbə) *n.* **1.** productive work, esp. physical toil done for wages. **2. a.** the people, class, or workers involved in this, esp. as opposed to management, capital, etc. **b.** (*as modifier*): *labour relations.* **3. a.** difficult or arduous work or effort. **b.** (*in combination*): *labour-saving.* **4.** a particular job or task, esp. of a difficult nature. **5. a.** the process or effort of childbirth or the time during which this takes place. **b.** (*as modifier*): *labour pain; labour ward.* *~vb.* **6.** (*intr.*) to perform labour; work. **7.** (*intr.*; foll. by *for*, etc.) to strive or work hard (for something). **8.** (*intr.*; usually foll. by *under*) to be burdened (by) or be at a disadvantage (because of): *to labour under a misapprehension.* **9.** (*intr.*) to make one's way with difficulty. **10.** (*tr.*) to deal with too persistently: *to labour a point.* **11.** (*intr.*) (of a woman) to be in labour. **12.** (*intr.*) (of a ship) to pitch and toss. [C13: via OF from L *labor*]

labour camp *n.* **1.** a penal colony involving forced labour. **2.** a camp for migratory labourers.

Labour Day *n.* a public holiday in many countries in honour of labour, usually held on May 1.

laboured *or U.S.* **labored** ('leɪbəd) *adj.* **1.** (of breathing) performed with difficulty. **2.** showing effort.

labourer *or U.S.* **laborer** ('leɪbərə) *n.* a person engaged in physical work, esp. unskilled work.

labour exchange *n.* *Brit.* a former name for the **employment office.**

labour-intensive *adj.* of or denoting a task, organization, industry, etc., in which a high proportion of the costs are due to wages, salaries, etc.

Labourite ('leɪbə,raɪt) *n.* an adherent of the Labour Party.

Labour Party *n.* **1.** a British political party, formed in 1900 as an amalgam of various trade unions and socialist groups, generally supporting the interests of organized labour. **2.** any similar party in any of various other countries.

Labrador ('læbrə,dɔː) *n.* **1.** Also called: **Labrador-Ungava.** a large peninsula of NE Canada, on the Atlantic, the Gulf of St. Lawrence, Hudson Strait, and Hudson Bay: contains most of the province of Quebec and the mainland part of Newfoundland; geologically part of the Canadian Shield. Area: 1 619 000 sq. km (625 000 sq. miles). **2.** Also called: **Coast of Labrador.** a region of NE Canada, on the Atlantic and consisting of the mainland part of Newfoundland province. **3.** (*often not cap.*) short for **Labrador retriever.**

Labrador retriever *n.* a powerfully-built variety of retriever with a short dense black or golden-brown coat. Often shortened to **Labrador.**

labret ('leɪbrɛt) *n.* a piece of bone, shell, etc., inserted into the lip as an ornament by certain peoples. [C19: from L *labrum* lip]

labrum ('leɪbrəm, 'læb-) *n.*, *pl.* **-bra** (-brə). a lip or liplike part, such as the cuticular plate forming the upper lip of insects. [C19: NL, from L]

La Bruyère (*French* la bryjɛr) *n.* **Jean de** (ʒɑ̃ də). 1645–96, French moralist, noted for his *Caractères* (1688), satirical character studies, including portraits of contemporary public figures.

Labuan (lə'buːən) *n.* an island in Malaysia, off the NW coast of Borneo: part of the Straits Settlements until 1946, when transferred to North Borneo. Chief town: Victoria. Area: 98 sq. km (38 sq. miles).

laburnum (lə'bɜːnəm) *n.* any tree or shrub of a Eurasian genus having clusters of yellow drooping flowers: all parts of the plant are poisonous. [C16: NL, from L]

labyrinth ('læbərɪnθ) *n.* **1.** a mazelike network of tunnels, chambers, or paths, either natural or man-made. **2.** any complex or confusing system of streets, passages, etc. **3.** a complex or intricate situation. **4.** any system of interconnecting cavities, esp. those comprising the internal ear. **5.** *Electronics.* an enclosure behind a high-performance loudspeaker, consisting of a series of air chambers designed to absorb unwanted sound waves. [C16: via L from Gk *laburinthos*, from ?]

labyrinthine (,læbə'rɪnθaɪn) *adj.* **1.** of or relating to a labyrinth. **2.** resembling a labyrinth in complexity.

lac¹ (læk) *n.* a resinous substance secreted by certain insects (**lac insects**), used in the manufacture of shellac. [C16: from Du. *lak* or F *laque*, from Hindi *lākh* resin, ult. from Sansk. *lākshā*]

lac² (lɑːk) *n.* a variant spelling of **lakh.**

Laccadive, Minicoy, and Amindivi Islands ('lækədɪv, 'mɪnɪ,kɔɪ, ,ʌmən'diːviː) *pl. n.* the former name (until 1973) of the **Lakshadweep Islands.**

laccolith ('lækəlɪθ) *or* **laccolite** ('lækə,laɪt) *n.* a dome of igneous rock between two layers of older sedimentary rock. [C19: from Gk *lakkos* cistern + -LITH]

lace (leɪs) *n.* **1.** a delicate decorative fabric made from cotton, silk, etc., woven in an open web of different symmetrical patterns and figures. **2.** a cord or string drawn through eyelets or around hooks to fasten a shoe or garment. **3.** ornamental braid often used on military uniforms, etc. ~*vb.* **4.** to fasten (shoes, etc.) with a lace. **5.** (*tr.*) to draw (a cord or thread) through holes, eyes, etc., as when tying shoes. **6.** (*tr.*) to compress the waist of (someone), as with a corset. **7.** (*tr.*) to add a dash of spirits to (a beverage). **8.** (*tr.; usually passive* and foll. by *with*) to streak or mark with lines or colours: *the sky was laced with red.* **9.** (*tr.*) to intertwine; interlace. **10.** (*tr.*) *Inf.* to give a sound beating to. [C13 *las*, from OF *laz*, from L *laqueus* noose]

lacebark ('leɪsbɑːk) *n.* another name for **ribbonwood.**

Lacedaemon (,læsɪ'diːmən) *n.* another name for **Sparta** or **Laconia.** —**Lacedae'monian** *adj., n.*

lacerate *vb.* ('læsə,reɪt). (*tr.*) **1.** to tear (the flesh, etc.) jaggedly. **2.** to hurt or harrow (the feelings, etc.). ~*adj.* ('læsə,reɪt, -rɪt). **3.** having edges that are jagged: *lacerate leaves.* [C16: from L *lacerāre* to tear, from *lacer* mangled]

lace up *vb.* **1.** (*tr., adv.*) to tighten or fasten (clothes or footwear) with laces. ~*adj.* **lace-up. 2.** (of footwear) to be fastened with laces. ~*n.* **lace-up. 3.** a lace-up shoe or boot.

lacewing ('leɪs,wɪŋ) *n.* any of various insects, esp. the green lacewings and brown lacewings, having lacy wings and preying on aphids and similar pests.

laches ('lætʃɪz) *n.* *Law.* negligence or unreasonable delay in pursuing a legal remedy. [C14 *lachesse*, via OF *lasche* slack, from L *laxus* LAX]

Lachesis ('lækɪsɪs) *n.* *Greek myth.* one of the three Fates. [via L from Gk, from *lakhesis* destiny, from *lakhein* to befall by lot]

Lachlan ('lɒklən) *n.* a river in SE Australia, rising in central New South Wales and flowing northwest then southwest to the Murrumbidgee River. Length: about 1450 km (900 miles). [named after *Lachlan* Macquarie, governor of New South Wales (1809–21)]

lachrymal ('lækrɪməl) *adj.* a variant spelling of **lacrimal.**

lachrymatory ('lækrɪmətərɪ, -trɪ) *n., pl.* **-ries. 1.** a small vessel found in ancient tombs, formerly thought to hold the tears of mourners. ~*adj.* **2.** a variant spelling of **lacrimatory.**

lachrymose ('lækrɪ,məʊs) *adj.* **1.** given to weeping; tearful. **2.** mournful; sad. [C17: from L, from *lacrima* a tear] —'**lachry,mosely** *adv.*

lacing ('leɪsɪŋ) *n.* **1.** *Chiefly Brit.* a course of bricks, stone, etc., for strengthening a rubble or flint wall. **2.** another word for **lace** (senses 2, 3). **3.** *Inf.* a severe beating.

laciniate (lə'sɪnɪ,eɪt, -ɪt) *or* **laciniated** *adj.* **1.** *Biol.* jagged: *a laciniate leaf.* **2.** having a fringe. [C17: from L *lacinia* flap] —**la,cini'ation** *n.*

lack (læk) *n.* **1.** an insufficiency, shortage, or absence of something required or desired. **2.** something that is required but is absent or in short supply. ~*vb.* **3.** (when *intr.*, often foll. by *in* or *for*) to be deficient (in) or have need (of). [C12: rel. to MDu. *laken* to be wanting]

lackadaisical (,lækə'deɪzɪkᵊl) *adj.* **1.** lacking vitality and purpose. **2.** lazy, esp. in a dreamy way. [C18: from earlier *lackadaisy*] —,**lacka'daisically** *adv.*

lackey ('lækɪ) *n.* **1.** a servile follower; hanger-on. **2.** a liveried male servant or valet. **3.** a person who is treated like a servant. ~*vb.* **4.** (*intr.*, often foll. by *for*) to act as a lackey (to). [C16: via F *laquais*, from OF, ?from Catalan *lacayo*, *alacayo*]

lacklustre *or U.S.* **lackluster** ('læk,lʌstə) *adj.* lacking force, brilliance, or vitality.

Laclos (*French* laklo) *n.* **Pierre Choderlos de** (pjɛr ʃɔdɛrlo də). 1741–1803, French soldier and writer, noted for his novel in epistolary form *Les Liaisons dangereuses* (1782).

Laconia (lə'kəʊnɪə) *n.* an ancient country of S Greece, in the SE Peloponnese, of which Sparta was the capital: corresponds to the present-day department of Lakonia. —**La'conian** *n., adj.*

laconic (lə'kɒnɪk) *adj.* (of a person's speech) using few words; terse. [C16: via L from Gk *Lakōnikos*, from *Lakōn* Laconian, Spartan; referring to the Spartans' terseness of speech] —**la'conically** *adv.*

La Coruña (*Spanish* la ko'ruɲa) *n.* a port in NW Spain, on the Atlantic: point of departure for the Spanish Armada (1588); site of the defeat of the French by the English under Sir John Moore in the Peninsular War (1809). Pop.: 239 505 (1986). English name: **Corunna.**

lacquer ('lækə) *n.* **1.** a hard glossy coating made by dissolving cellulose derivatives or natural resins in a volatile solvent. **2.** a black resinous substance, obtained from certain trees (**lacquer trees**), used to give a hard glossy finish to wooden furniture. **3.** Also called: **hair lacquer.** a mixture of shellac and alcohol for spraying onto the hair to hold a style in place. **4.** *Art.* decorative objects coated with such lacquer, often inlaid. ~*vb.* (*tr.*) **5.** to apply lacquer to. [C16: from obs. F *lacre* sealing wax, from Port. *laca* LAC¹] —'**lacquerer** *n.*

lacrimal, lachrymal, *or* **lacrymal** ('lækrɪməl) *adj.* of or relating to tears or to the glands that secrete tears. [C16: from Med. L, from L *lacrima* a tear]

lacrimation (,lækrɪ'meɪʃən) *n.* the secretion of tears.

lacrimatory, lachrymatory, *or* **lacrymatory** ('lækrɪmətərɪ, -trɪ) *adj.* of, causing, or producing tears.

lacrosse (lə'krɒs) *n.* a ball game invented by American Indians, now played by two teams who try to propel a ball into each other's goal by means of long-handled pouched sticks (**lacrosse sticks**). [C19: Canad. F: the hooked stick, crosier]

lactate¹ ('lækteɪt) *n.* an ester or salt of lactic acid. [C18]

lactate² ('lækteɪt) *vb.* (*intr.*) (of mammals) to produce or secrete milk.

lactation (læk'teɪʃən) *n.* **1.** the secretion of milk from the mammary glands after parturition. **2.** the period during which milk is secreted.

lacteal ('læktɪəl) *adj.* **1.** of, relating to, or resembling milk. **2.** (of lymphatic vessels) conveying or containing chyle. ~*n.* **3.** any of the lymphatic vessels conveying chyle from the small intestine to the thoracic duct. [C17: from L *lacteus* of milk, from *lac* milk]

lactescent (læk'tɛsᵊnt) *adj.* **1.** (of plants and certain insects) secreting a milky fluid. **2.** milky or becoming milky. [C18: from L, from *lactescēre* to become milky, from *lact-*, *lac* milk] —**lac'tescence** *n.*

lactic ('læktɪk) *adj.* relating to or derived from milk. [C18: from L *lact-*, *lac* milk]

lactic acid *n.* a colourless syrupy carboxylic acid found in sour milk and many fruits and used as a preservative (**E270**) for foodstuffs. Formula: $CH_3CH(OH)COOH$. Systematic name: **2-hydroxypropanoic acid.**

lactiferous (læk'tɪfərəs) *adj.* producing, conveying, or secreting milk or a milky fluid. [C17: from L *lactifer*, from *lact-*, *lac* milk]

lacto- *or before a vowel* **lact-** *combining form.* indicating milk: *lactobacillus.* [from L *lact-, lac* milk]

lactose ('læktəʊs, -təʊz) *n.* a white crystalline sugar occurring in milk and used in pharmaceuticals and baby foods. Formula: $C_{12}H_{22}O_{11}$.

La Cumbre (lə 'kuːmbreɪ) *n.* another name for the **Uspallata Pass.**

lacuna (lə'kjuːnə) *n., pl.* **-nae** (-niː) *or* **-nas.** **1.** a gap or space, esp. in a book or manuscript. **2.** *Biol.* a cavity or depression, such as any of the spaces in the matrix of bone. [C17: from L *lacūna* pool, cavity, from *lacus* lake] **—la'cunose, la'cunal, la'cunar,** *or* **la'cunary** *adj.*

lacustrine (lə'kʌstraɪn) *adj.* **1.** of or relating to lakes. **2.** living or growing in or on the shores of a lake. [C19: from It. *lacustre,* from L *lacus* lake]

lacy ('leɪsɪ) *adj.* **lacier, laciest.** made of or resembling lace. **—'lacily** *adv.* **—'laciness** *n.*

lad (læd) *n.* **1.** a boy or young man. **2.** *Inf.* a familiar form of address for any male. **3.** a lively or dashing man or youth (esp. in **a bit of a lad**). **4.** *Brit.* a boy or man who looks after horses. [C13 *ladde;* ?from ON]

ladanum ('lædənəm) *n.* a dark resinous juice obtained from various rockroses: used in perfumery. [C16: L from Gk, from *lēdon* rockrose]

ladder ('lædə) *n.* **1.** a portable framework of wood, metal, rope, etc., in the form of two long parallel members connected by rungs or steps fixed to them at right angles, for climbing up or down. **2.** any hierarchy conceived of as having a series of ascending stages, levels, etc.: *the social ladder.* **3.** Also called: **run.** *Chiefly Brit.* a line of connected stitches that have come undone in knitted material, esp. stockings. ~*vb.* **4.** *Chiefly Brit.* to cause a line of interconnected stitches in (stockings, etc.) to undo, as by snagging, or (of a stocking) to come undone in this way. [OE *hlǣdder*]

ladder back *n.* a type of chair in which the back is constructed of horizontal slats between two uprights.

laddie ('lædɪ) *n. Chiefly Scot.* a familiar term for a male, esp. a boy; lad.

lade (leɪd) *vb.* **lading, laded, laden** *or* **laded.** **1.** to put cargo or freight on board (a ship, etc.) or (of a ship, etc.) to take on cargo or freight. **2.** (*tr.; usually passive*) to burden or oppress. **3.** (*tr.; usually passive* and foll. by *with*) to fill or load. **4.** to remove (liquid) with or as if with a ladle. [OE *hladen* to load]

laden ('leɪd'n) **1.** a past participle of **lade.** ~*adj.* **2.** weighed down with a load; loaded. **3.** encumbered; burdened.

la-di-da, lah-di-dah, *or* **la-de-da** (ˌlɑːdiː'dɑː) *adj. Inf.* affecting exaggeratedly genteel manners or speech. [C19: mockingly imit. of affected speech]

ladies *or* **ladies' room** *n.* (*functioning as sing.*) *Inf.* a women's public lavatory.

lading ('leɪdɪŋ) *n.* a load; cargo; freight.

Ladislaus I ('lædɪsˌlɔːs) *or* **Ladislas** ('lædɪsˌlæs) *n.* **Saint.** 1040–95, king of Hungary (1077–95). He extended his country's boundaries and suppressed paganism. Feast day: June 27.

ladle ('leɪd'l) *n.* **1.** a long-handled spoon having a deep bowl for serving or transferring liquids. **2.** a large bucket-shaped container for transferring molten metal. ~*vb.* **3.** (*tr.*) to serve out as with a ladle. [OE *hlǣdel,* from *hladan* to draw out] **—'ladleful** *n.*

ladle out *vb.* (*tr., adv.*) *Inf.* to distribute (money, gifts, etc.) generously.

Ladoga (*Russian* 'ladəgə) *n.* **Lake.** a lake in the NW Soviet Union, in the N Leningrad Region and the SW Karelian ASSR: the largest lake in Europe; drains through the River Neva into the Gulf of Finland. Area: about 18 000 sq. km (7000 sq. miles). Russian name: **Ladozhskoye Ozero** ('ladəʃskəjə 'ɔzırə).

Ladrone Islands (lə'drəʊn) *pl. n.* the former name (1521–1668) of the **Mariana Islands.**

lady ('leɪdɪ) *n., pl.* **-dies.** **1.** a woman regarded as having the characteristics of a good family and high social position. **2. a.** a polite name for a woman. **b.** (*as modifier*): *a lady doctor.* **3.** an informal name for **wife. 4. lady of the house.** the female head of the household. **5.** *History.* a woman with proprietary rights and authority, as over a manor. [OE *hlǣfdige,* from *hlāf* bread + *dīge* kneader, rel. to *dāh* dough]

Lady ('leɪdɪ) *n., pl.* **-dies.** **1.** (in Britain) a title of honour borne by various classes of women of the peerage. **2. my**

lady. a term of address to holders of the title Lady. **3. Our Lady.** a title of the Virgin Mary.

ladybird ('leɪdɪˌbɜːd) *n.* any of various small brightly coloured beetles, esp. one having red elytra with black spots. [C18: after Our *Lady,* the Virgin Mary]

lady bountiful *n.* an ostentatiously charitable woman. [C19: after a character in George Farquhar's play *The Beaux' Stratagem* (1707)]

Lady Chapel *n.* a chapel within a church or cathedral, dedicated to the Virgin Mary.

Lady Day *n.* March 25, the feast of the Annunciation of the Virgin Mary. Also called: **Annunciation Day.**

lady-in-waiting *n., pl.* **ladies-in-waiting.** a lady who attends a queen or princess.

lady-killer *n. Inf.* a man who is, or believes he is, irresistibly fascinating to women.

ladylike ('leɪdɪˌlaɪk) *adj.* like or befitting a lady in manners and bearing; refined and fastidious.

ladylove ('leɪdɪˌlʌv) *n. Now rare.* a beloved woman.

Lady of the Lake *n.* (in Arthurian legend) a mysterious supernatural being sometimes identified with **Vivian.**

lady's bedstraw *n.* a Eurasian plant with clusters of small yellow flowers.

lady's finger *n.* another name for **bhindi.**

Ladyship ('leɪdɪˌʃɪp) *n.* (preceded by *your* or *her*) a title used to address or refer to any peeress except a duchess.

Ladysmith ('leɪdɪˌsmɪθ) *n.* a town in E South Africa, in W Natal: besieged by Boers for four months (1899–1900) during the Boer War. Pop.: 43 200 (1985).

lady's-slipper *n.* any of various orchids having reddish or purple flowers.

lady's-smock *n.* a N temperate plant with white or rose-pink flowers. Also called: **cuckooflower.**

Laënnec (*French* laɛnɛk) *n.* **René Théophile Hyacinthe** (rəne teɔfil jasɛt). 1781–1826, French physician, who invented the stethoscope.

Laertes (leɪ'ɜːtiːz) *n. Greek myth.* the father of Odysseus.

laevo- *or U.S.* **levo-** *combining form.* **1.** on or towards the left: *laevorotatory.* **2.** (in chemistry) denoting a laevorotatory compound. [from L *laevus* left]

laevorotation (ˌliːvəʊrəʊ'teɪʃən) *n.* **1.** a rotation to the left. **2.** an anticlockwise rotation of the plane of polarization of plane-polarized light as a result of its passage through a crystal, liquid, or solution. ~Cf. **dextrorotation.** **—laevorotatory** (ˌliːvəʊ'rəʊtətərɪ) *adj.*

Lafayette *or* **La Fayette** (*French* lafajɛt) *n.* **1. Marie Joseph Paul Yves Roch Gilbert du Motier** (mari ʒɔzɛf pɔl iv rɔk ʒilbɛr dy mɔtje), Marquis de Lafayette. 1757–1834, French general and statesman. He fought on the side of the colonists in the War of American Independence and, as commander of the National Guard (1789–91; 1830), he played a leading part in the French Revolution and the revolution of 1830. **2. Marie-Madeleine** (marimadlɛn), Comtesse de Lafayette. 1634–93, French novelist, noted for her historical romance *La Princesse de Clèves* (1678).

La Fontaine (*French* la fɔtɛn) *n.* **Jean de** (ʒɑ̃ də). 1621–95, French poet, famous for his *Fables* (1668).

Laforgue (*French* lafɔrg) *n.* **Jules** (ʒyl). 1860–87, French symbolist poet. An originator of free verse, his influence on modern poetry was considerable.

lag[1] (læg) *vb.* **lagging, lagged.** (*intr.*) **1.** (often foll. by *behind*) to hang (back) or fall (behind) in movement, progress, development, etc. **2.** to fall away in strength or intensity. ~*n.* **3.** the act or state of slowing down or falling behind. **4.** the interval of time between two events, esp. between an action and its effect. [C16: from ?]

lag[2] (læg) *Sl.* ~*n.* **1.** a convict or ex-convict (esp. in **old lag**). **2.** a term of imprisonment. ~*vb.* **lagging, lagged.** **3.** (*tr.*) to arrest or put in prison. [C19: from ?]

lag[3] (læg) *vb.* **lagging, lagged. 1.** (*tr.*) to cover (a pipe, cylinder, etc.) with lagging to prevent loss of heat. ~*n.* **2.** the insulating casing of a steam cylinder, boiler, etc. **3.** a stave. [C17: of Scand. origin]

lagan ('lægən) *n.* goods or wreckage on the sea bed, sometimes attached to a buoy to permit recovery. [C16: from OF *lagan,* prob. of Gmc origin]

lager ('lɑːgə) *n.* a light-bodied effervescent beer, stored for varying periods before use. [C19: from G *Lagerbier* beer for storing, from *Lager* storehouse]

Lagerkvist (*Swedish* 'lɑːgərkvɪst) *n.* **Pär (Fabian)** (pæːr). 1891–1974, Swedish novelist and dramatist. His works include the novels *The Dwarf* (1944) and *Barabbas* (1950): Nobel prize for literature 1951.

Lagerlöf (*Swedish* 'lɑːgərloːv) *n.* **Selma** ('sɛlma). 1858–1940, Swedish novelist, noted esp. for her children's classic *The Wonderful Adventures of Nils* (1906–07): Nobel prize for literature 1909.

laggard ('lægəd) *n.* **1.** a person who lags behind. ~*adj.* **2.** *Rare.* sluggish, slow, or dawdling. —**'laggardly** *adj.,* *adv.* —**'laggardness** *n.*

lagging ('lægɪŋ) *n.* **1.** insulating material wrapped around pipes, boilers, etc., or laid in a roof loft, to prevent loss of heat. **2.** the act or process of applying lagging.

lagomorph ('lægəʊˌmɔːf) *n.* any placental mammal having two pairs of upper incisors specialized for gnawing, such as rabbits and hares. [C19: via NL from Gk *lagōs* hare; see -MORPH]

lagoon (lə'guːn) *n.* **1.** a body of water cut off from the open sea by coral reefs or sand bars. **2.** any small body of water, esp. one adjoining a larger one. [C17: from It. *laguna*, from L *lacūna* pool; see LACUNA]

Lagoon Islands *pl. n.* a former name of **Tuvalu.**

Lagos ('leɪgɒs) *n.* **1.** the former capital and chief port of Nigeria, on the Bight of Benin: first settled in the sixteenth century; a slave market until the nineteenth century; ceded to Britain (1861); university (1962). Pop.: 1 097 000 (1983 est.). **2.** a state of SW Nigeria. Capital: Ikeja. Pop.: 2 825 200 (1984). Area: 14 712 sq. km (5679 sq. miles).

Lagrange (*French* lagrɑ̃ʒ) *n.* Comte **Joseph Louis** (ʒozɛf lwi). 1736–1813, French mathematician and astronomer, noted particularly for his work on harmonics, mechanics, and the calculus of variations.

La Granja (*Spanish* la 'graŋxa) *n.* another name for **San Ildefonso.**

La Guaira *or* **La Guayra** (*Spanish* la 'gwaira) *n.* the chief seaport of Venezuela, on the Caribbean. Pop.: 20 344 (1971).

La Guardia (lə'gwɑːdɪə) *n.* **Fiorello H(enry)** (ˌfɪə'rɛləʊ). 1882–1947, U.S. politician. As mayor of New York (1933–45), he organized slum-clearance and labour safeguard schemes and suppressed racketeering.

lah (lɑː) *n. Music.* (in tonic sol-fa) the sixth note of any major scale; submediant. [C14: see GAMUT]

lah-di-dah (ˌlɑːdɪ'dɑː) *adj., n. Inf.* a variant spelling of **la-di-da.**

Lahore (lə'hɔː) *n.* a city in NE Pakistan: capital of the former province of West Pakistan (1955–70); University of the Punjab (1882). Pop.: 2 922 000 (1981 est.).

Lahti (*Finnish* 'lahti) *n.* a town in S Finland: site of the main Finnish radio and television stations; furniture industry. Pop.: 94 205 (1986).

Laibach ('laibax) *n.* the German name for **Ljubljana.**

laic ('leɪɪk) *adj. also* **laical. 1.** of or involving the laity; secular. ~*n.* **2.** a rare word for **layman.** [C15: from LL *lāicus* LAY³] —**'laically** *adv.*

laicize *or* **-cise** ('leɪɪˌsaɪz) *vb.* (*tr.*) to withdraw clerical or ecclesiastical character or status from (an institution, building, etc.). —ˌlaici'zation *or* -ci'sation *n.*

laid (leɪd) *vb.* the past tense and past participle of **lay¹.**

laid-back *adj.* relaxed in style or character; easy-going and unhurried.

laid paper *n.* paper with a regular mesh impressed upon it.

lain (leɪn) *vb.* the past participle of **lie².**

Laing (læŋ) *n.* **R(onald) D(avid).** born 1927, English psychiatrist; his best known books include *The Divided Self* (1960), *The Politics of Experience and the Bird of Paradise* (1967), and *Knots* (1970).

Laingian ('læŋɪən) *adj.* **1.** of or based on R. D. Laing's theory that mental illnesses are understandable as natural responses to stress in family and social situations. ~*n.* **2.** a follower or adherent of Laing's teaching.

lair¹ (lɛə) *n.* **1.** the resting place of a wild animal. **2.** *Inf.* a place of seclusion or hiding. ~*vb.* **3.** (*intr.*) (esp. of a wild animal) to retreat to or rest in a lair. **4.** (*tr.*) to drive or place (an animal) in a lair. [OE *leger*]

lair² (lɛə) *Austral. sl.* ~*n.* **1.** a flashy man who shows off. ~*vb.* **2.** (*intr.;* foll. by *up* or *around*) to behave or dress like a lair. [?from LEER]

laird (lɛəd) *n. Scot.* a landowner, esp. of a large estate. [C15: Scot. var. of LORD]

laissez faire *or* **laisser faire** *French.* (ˌlɛseɪ 'fɛə) *n.* **1. a.** Also called: **individualism.** the doctrine of unrestricted freedom in commerce, esp. for private interests.

b. (*as modifier*): *a laissez-faire economy.* **2.** indifference or noninterference, esp. in the affairs of others. [F, lit.: let (them) act]

laissez passer (ˌlɛseɪ 'pæseɪ) *n.* a permit allowing someone to pass, cross a frontier, etc. [F, lit.: let (them) pass]

laity ('leɪɪtɪ) *n.* **1.** laymen, as distinguished from clergymen. **2.** all people not of a specific occupation. [C16: from LAY³]

Laius ('laɪəs) *n. Greek myth.* a king of Thebes, killed by his son Oedipus, who did not know of their relationship.

lake¹ (leɪk) *n.* **1.** an expanse of water entirely surrounded by land and unconnected to the sea except by rivers or streams. Related adj.: **lacustrine. 2.** anything resembling this. **3.** a surplus of a liquid commodity: *a wine lake.* [C13 *lac,* via OF from L *lacus* basin]

lake² (leɪk) *n.* **1.** a bright pigment produced by the combination of an organic colouring matter with an inorganic compound, usually a metallic salt, oxide, or hydroxide. **2.** a red dye obtained by combining a metallic compound with cochineal. [C17: var. of LAC¹]

Lake District *n.* a region of lakes and mountains in NW England, in Cumbria: includes England's largest lake (Windermere) and highest mountain (Scafell Pike); national park; literary associations (the Lake Poets); tourist region. Also called: **Lakeland.**

lake dwelling *n.* a dwelling, esp. in prehistoric villages, constructed on platforms supported by wooden piles driven into the bottom of a lake. —**lake dweller** *n.*

Lakeland ('leɪkˌlænd) *n.* **1.** another name for the **Lake District.** ~*adj.* **2.** of or relating to the Lake District.

Lakeland terrier *n.* a wire-haired breed of terrier, originally from the Lake District.

Lake of the Woods *n.* a lake in N central North America, mostly in W Northern Ontario, Canada: fed chiefly by the Rainy River; drains into Lake Winnipeg by the Winnipeg River; many islands; tourist region. Area: 3846 sq. km (1485 sq. miles).

Lake Poets *pl. n.* the English poets Wordsworth, Coleridge, and Southey, who lived in and drew inspiration from the Lake District at the beginning of the 19th century.

Lake Success *n.* a village in SE New York State, on W Long Island: headquarters of the United Nations Security Council from 1946 to 1951. Pop.: 3254 (1970).

lake trout *n.* a yellow-spotted char of the Great Lakes region of Canada.

lakh *or* **lac** (lɑːk) *n.* (in India) the number 100 000, esp. referring to this sum of rupees. [C17: from Hindi *lākh,* ult. from Sansk. *lakshā* a sign]

Lakshadweep Islands (læk'ʃædwiːp) *pl. n.* a group of 26 coral islands and reefs in the Arabian Sea, off the SW coast of India: a union territory of India since 1956. Administrative centre: Kavaratti Island. Pop.: 40 237 (1981). Area: 28 sq. km (11 sq. miles). Former name (until 1973): **Laccadive, Minicoy, and Amindivi Islands.**

-lalia *n. combining form.* indicating a speech defect or abnormality: *echolalia.* [NL, from Gk *lalia* chatter, from *lalein* to babble]

La Línea (*Spanish* la 'linea) *n.* a town in SW Spain, on the Bay of Gibraltar. Pop.: 56 282 (1981). Official name: **La Línea de la Concepción** (ðe la ˌkonθep'θjon).

Lallans ('lælənz) *or* **Lallan** ('lælən) *n.* **1.** a literary version of the variety of English spoken and written in the Lowlands of Scotland. **2.** (*modifier*) of or relating to the Lowlands of Scotland or their dialects. [Scot. var. of *Lowlands*]

lallation (læ'leɪʃən) *n. Phonetics.* a defect of speech consisting of the pronunciation of (r) as (l). [C17: from L *lallāre* to sing lullaby, imit.]

Lalo ('lɑːləʊ) *n.* (**Victor-Antoine-)Édouard** (edwar). 1823–92, French composer of Spanish descent. His works include the *Symphonie espagnole* (1873) and the ballet *Namouna* (1882).

lam¹ (læm) *vb.* **lamming, lammed.** *Sl.* **1.** (*tr.*) to thrash or beat. **2.** (*intr.*; usually foll. by *into* or *out*) to make a sweeping stroke or blow. [C16: from Scand.]

lam² (læm) *n. U.S. & Canad. sl.* **1.** a sudden flight or escape, esp. to avoid arrest. **2. on the lam.** making an escape. [C19: ?from LAM¹; hence, to be off)]

Lam. *Bible. abbrev. for* Lamentations.

lama ('lɑːmə) *n.* a priest or monk of Lamaism. [C17: from Tibetan *blama*]

Lamaism ('lɑːmə,ɪzəm) n. the Mahayana form of Buddhism of Tibet and Mongolia. —'**Lamaist** n., adj. —,**Lama'istic** adj.

La Mancha (Spanish la 'mantʃa) n. a plateau of central Spain, between the mountains of Toledo and the hills of Cuenca: traditionally associated with episodes in Don Quixote. Average height: 600 m (2000 ft.).

La Manche (French la mɑ̃ʃ) n. See **Manche** (sense 2).

Lamarck (French lamark) n. **Jean Baptiste Pierre Antoine de Monet** (ʒɑ̃ batist pjɛr ɑ̃twan də mɔnɛ), Chevalier de Lamarck. 1744–1829, French naturalist. He outlined his theory of organic evolution (Lamarckism) in Philosophie zoologique (1809). —**La'marckian** adj., n.

Lamarckism (lɑː'mɑːkɪzəm) n. the theory of organic evolution proposed by Lamarck, based on the principle that characteristics of an organism modified during its lifetime are inheritable.

Lamartine (French lamartin) n. **Alphonse Marie Louis de Prat de** (alfɔ̃s mari lwi də pra də). 1790–1869, French romantic poet, historian, and statesman: his works include Méditations poétiques (1820) and Histoire des Girondins (1847).

lamasery ('lɑːməsərɪ) n., pl. -**series**. a monastery of lamas. [C19: from F lamaserie, from LAMA + F -serie, from Persian serāi palace]

lamb (læm) n. **1.** the young of a sheep. **2.** the meat of a young sheep. **3.** a person, esp. a child, who is innocent, meek, good, etc. **4.** a person easily deceived. ~vb. **5.** (intr.) (of a ewe) to give birth. **6.** (intr.) (of a shepherd) to tend the ewes and newborn lambs at lambing time. [OE lamb, from Gmc] —'**lamb,like** adj.

Lamb[1] (læm) n. **the.** a title given to Christ in the New Testament.

Lamb[2] (læm) n. **1. Charles,** pen name Elia. 1775–1834, English essayist and critic. He collaborated with his sister Mary on Tales from Shakespeare (1807). His other works include Specimens of English Dramatic Poets (1808) and the largely autobiographical essays collected in Essays of Elia (1823; 1833). **2. William.** See (2nd Viscount) **Melbourne. 3. Willis Eugene.** born 1913, U.S. physicist. He detected the small difference in energy between two states of the hydrogen atom (**Lamb shift**). Nobel prize for physics 1955.

Lambaréné (French lābarene) n. a town in W Gabon on the Ogooué River: site of the hospital built by Albert Schweitzer, who died and was buried there (1965). Pop.: 26 257 (1978 est.).

lambaste (læm'beɪst) or **lambast** (læm'bæst) vb. (tr.) **1.** to beat or whip severely. **2.** to reprimand or scold. [C17: ?from LAM[1] + BASTE[3]]

lambda ('læmdə) n. the 11th letter of the Greek alphabet (Λ, λ). [C14: from Gk, from Semitic]

lambent ('læmbənt) adj. **1.** (esp. of a flame) flickering softly over a surface. **2.** glowing with soft radiance. **3.** (of wit or humour) light or brilliant. [C17: from the present participle of L lambere to lick] —'**lambency** n. —'**lambently** adv.

lambert ('læmbət) n. the cgs unit of illumination, equal to 1 lumen per square centimetre. Symbol: L [C20: after J. H. Lambert (1728–77), G mathematician & physicist]

Lambert ('læmbət) n. **Constant.** 1905–51, English composer and conductor. His works include much ballet music and The Rio Grande (1929), a work for chorus, orchestra, and piano, using jazz idioms.

Lambeth ('læmbəθ) n. a borough of S Greater London, on the Thames: contains **Lambeth Palace** (the London residence of the Archbishop of Canterbury). Pop.: 245 000 (1986 est.).

lambing ('læmɪŋ) n. **1.** the birth of lambs. **2.** the shepherd's work of tending the ewes and newborn lambs at this time.

lambkin ('læmkɪn) n. **1.** a small lamb. **2.** a term of affection for a small endearing child.

Lamb of God n. a title given to Christ in the New Testament, probably with reference to his sacrificial death.

lambrequin ('læmbrɪkɪn, 'læmbə-) n. **1.** an ornamental hanging covering the edge of a shelf or the upper part of a window or door. **2.** (often pl.) a scarf worn over a helmet. [C18: from F, from Du. lamperkin (unattested), dim. of lamper veil]

lambskin ('læm,skɪn) n. **1.** the skin of a lamb, esp. with the wool still on. **2.** a material or garment prepared from this skin.

lamb's lettuce n. another name for **corn salad.**

lamb's tails pl. n. the pendulous catkins of the hazel tree.

lame (leɪm) adj. **1.** disabled or crippled in the legs or feet. **2.** painful or weak: a lame back. **3.** weak; unconvincing: a lame excuse. **4.** not effective or enthusiastic: a lame try. **5.** U.S. sl. conventional or uninspiring. ~vb. **6.** (tr.) to make lame. [OE lama] —'**lamely** adv. —'**lameness** n.

lamé ('lɑːmeɪ) n. a fabric of silk, cotton, or wool interwoven with threads of metal. [C20: from F, from OF lame gold or silver thread, thin plate, from L lāmina thin plate]

lame duck n. **1.** a person or thing that is disabled or ineffectual. **2.** Stock Exchange. a speculator who cannot discharge his liabilities. **3.** U.S. an elected official or body of officials remaining in office in the interval between the election and inauguration of a successor.

lamella (lə'mɛlə) n., pl. -**lae** (-liː) or -**las.** a thin layer, plate, or membrane, esp. any of the calcified layers of which bone is formed. [C17: NL, from L, dim. of lāmina thin plate] —**la'mellar, lamellate** ('læmɪ,leɪt, -lɪt), or **lamellose** (lə'mɛləus, 'læmɪ,ləus) adj.

lamellibranch (lə'mɛlɪ,bræŋk) n., adj. another word for **bivalve.** [C19: from NL lamellibranchia plate-gilled (animals)]

lamellicorn (lə'mɛlɪ,kɔːn) n. **1.** any beetle having flattened terminal plates to the antennae, such as the scarabs and stag beetles. ~adj. **2.** designating antennae with platelike terminal segments. [C19: from NL Lamellicornia plate-horned (animals)]

lament (lə'mɛnt) vb. **1.** to feel or express sorrow, remorse, or regret (for or over). ~n. **2.** an expression of sorrow. **3.** a poem or song in which a death is lamented. [C16: from L lāmentum] —**la'menter** n. —**la'mentingly** adv.

lamentable ('læməntəb°l) adj. **1.** wretched, deplorable, or distressing. **2.** an archaic word for **mournful.** —'**lamentably** adv.

lamentation (,læmɛn'teɪʃən) n. **1.** a lament; expression of sorrow. **2.** the act of lamenting.

lamented (lə'mɛntɪd) adj. grieved for or regretted (often in **late lamented**): our late lamented employer. —**la'mentedly** adv.

lamina ('læmɪnə) n., pl. -**nae** (-,niː) or -**nas. 1.** a thin plate, esp. of bone or mineral. **2.** Bot. the flat blade of a leaf. [C17: NL, from L: thin plate] —'**laminar** or **laminose** ('læmɪ,nəus, -,nəuz) adj.

laminar flow n. nonturbulent motion of a fluid in which parallel layers have different velocities relative to each other.

laminate vb. ('læmɪ,neɪt). **1.** (tr.) to make (material in sheet form) by bonding together two or more thin sheets. **2.** to split or be split into thin sheets. **3.** (tr.) to beat, form, or press (material, esp. metal) into thin sheets. **4.** (tr.) to cover or overlay with a thin sheet of material. ~n. ('læmɪ,neɪt, -nɪt). **5.** a material made by bonding together two or more sheets. ~adj. ('læmɪ,neɪt, -nɪt). **6.** having or composed of lamina; laminated. [C17: from NL lāminātus plated] —**laminable** ('læmɪnəb°l) adj. —,**lami'nation** n. —'**lami,nator** n.

laminated ('læmɪ,neɪtɪd) adj. **1.** composed of many layers of plastic, wood, etc., bonded together. **2.** covered with a thin protective layer of plastic, etc.

lamington ('læmɪŋtən) n. Austral. & N.Z. a cube of sponge cake coated in chocolate and dried coconut. [C20 (in the earlier sense: a homburg hat): after Lady Lamington, wife of Baron Lamington, governor of Queensland (1896–1901)]

Lammas ('læməs) n. **1.** R.C. Church. Aug. 1, held as a feast, commemorating St Peter's miraculous deliverance from prison. **2.** Also called: **Lammas Day.** the same day formerly observed in England as a harvest festival. [OE hlāfmæsse loaf mass]

lammergeier or **lammergeyer** ('læmə,gaɪə) n. a rare vulture of S Europe, Africa, and Asia, with dark wings, a pale breast, and black feathers around the bill. [C19: from G Lämmergeier, from Lämmer lambs + Geier vulture]

lamp (læmp) n. **1. a.** any of a number of devices that produce illumination: an electric lamp; a gas lamp; an oil lamp. **b.** (in combination): lampshade. **2.** a device for holding one or more electric light bulbs: a table lamp. **3.** a vessel in which a liquid fuel is burned to supply illumination. **4.** any of a variety of devices that produce radiation, esp. for therapeutic purposes: an ultraviolet lamp.

[C13 *lampe*, via OF from L *lampas*, from Gk, from *lampein* to shine]

lampblack ('læmp,blæk) *n.* a finely divided form of almost pure carbon produced by the incomplete combustion of organic compounds, such as natural gas, used in making carbon electrodes and dynamo brushes and as a pigment.

lamp chimney *n.* a glass tube that surrounds the wick in an oil lamp.

Lampedusa[1] (,læmpɪ'djuːzə) *n.* an island in the Mediterranean, between Malta and Tunisia. Area: about 21 sq. km (8 sq. miles).

Lampedusa[2] (,læmpɪ'djuːzə) *n.* **Giuseppe Tomasi di.** 1896–1957, Italian novelist: author of the historical novel *The Leopard* (1958).

lamplight ('læmp,laɪt) *n.* the light produced by a lamp or lamps.

lamplighter ('læmp,laɪtə) *n.* **1.** (formerly) a person who lit and extinguished street lamps, esp. gas ones. **2.** *Chiefly U.S. & Canad.* any of various devices used to light lamps.

lampoon (læm'puːn) *n.* **1.** a satire in prose or verse ridiculing a person, literary work, etc. ~*vb.* **2.** (*tr.*) to attack or satirize in a lampoon. [C17: from F *lampon*, ?from *lampons* let us drink (frequently used as a refrain in poems)] —**lam'pooner** *or* **lam'poonist** *n.* —**lam'poonery** *n.*

lamppost ('læmp,pəʊst) *n.* a post supporting a lamp, esp. in a street.

lamprey ('læmprɪ) *n.* any eel-like vertebrate having a round sucking mouth for clinging to and feeding on the blood of other animals. Also called: **lamper eel**. [C13: from OF *lamproie*, from LL *lamprēda*, from ?]

Lanai (lɑː'nɑːɪ, lə'naɪ) *n.* an island in central Hawaii, west of Maui Island. Pop.: 2200 (1986 est.). Area: 363 sq. km. (140 sq. miles).

Lanarkshire ('lænək,ʃɪə, -ʃə) *n.* (until 1975) a county of S Scotland, now part of Strathclyde region.

Lancashire ('læŋkə,ʃɪə, -ʃə) *n.* **1.** a county of NW England, on the Irish Sea: became a county palatine in 1351 and a duchy attached to the Crown; much reduced in size after the 1974 boundary changes, losing the Furness district to Cumbria and much of the south to Greater Manchester, Merseyside, and Cheshire. It was traditionally a cotton textiles manufacturing region. Administrative centre: Preston. Pop.: 1 380 700 (1986 est.). Area: 3063 sq. km (1182 sq. miles). Abbrev.: **Lancs**. **2.** a mild whitish-coloured cheese with a crumbly texture.

Lancaster[1] ('læŋkəstə, 'læŋ,kæstə) *n.* the English royal house that reigned from 1399 to 1461.

Lancaster[2] ('læŋkəstə) *n.* a city in NW England, former county town of Lancashire, on the River Lune: castle (built on the site of a Roman camp); university (1964). Pop.: 46 321 (1981).

Lancastrian (læŋ'kæstrɪən) *n.* **1.** a native or resident of Lancashire or Lancaster. **2.** an adherent of the house of Lancaster in the Wars of the Roses. ~*adj.* **3.** of or relating to Lancashire or Lancaster. **4.** of or relating to the house of Lancaster.

lance (lɑːns) *n.* **1.** a long weapon with a pointed head used by horsemen. **2.** a similar weapon used for hunting, whaling, etc. **3.** *Surgery.* another name for **lancet.** ~*vb.* (*tr.*) **4.** to pierce (an abscess or boil) with a lancet. **5.** to pierce with or as with a lance. [C13 *launce*, from OF *lance*, from L *lancea*]

lance corporal *n.* a noncommissioned officer of the lowest rank in the British Army.

lancelet ('lɑːnslɪt) *n.* any of several marine animals closely related to the vertebrates: they burrow in sand. Also called: **amphioxus**. [C19: referring to the slender shape]

Lancelot ('lɑːnslət) *n.* (in Arthurian legend) one of the Knights of the Round Table; the lover of Queen Guinevere.

lanceolate ('lɑːnsɪə,leɪt, -lɪt) *adj.* narrow and tapering to a point at each end: *lanceolate leaves.* [C18: from LL *lanceolātus*, from *lanceola* small LANCE]

lancer ('lɑːnsə) *n.* **1.** (formerly) a cavalryman armed with a lance. **2.** a member of a regiment retaining such a title.

lancers ('lɑːnsəz) *n.* (*functioning as sing.*) **1.** a quadrille for eight or sixteen couples. **2.** a piece of music composed for or in the rhythm of this dance.

lancet ('lɑːnsɪt) *n.* **1.** Also called: **lance**. a pointed surgical knife with two sharp edges. **2.** short for **lancet arch** or **lancet window**. [C15 *lancette*, from OF: small LANCE]

lancet arch *n.* a narrow acutely pointed arch.

lancet window *n.* a narrow window having a lancet arch.

lancewood ('lɑːns,wʊd) *n.* a New Zealand tree with slender leaves showing different configurations in youth and maturity.

Lanchow *or* **Lan-chou** ('læn'tʃaʊ) *n.* a variant transliteration of the Chinese name for **Lanzhou.**

Lancs (læŋks) *abbrev. for* Lancashire.

land (lænd) *n.* **1.** the solid part of the surface of the earth as distinct from seas, lakes, etc. Related adj.: **terrestrial**. **2.** ground, esp. with reference to its use, quality, etc. **3.** rural or agricultural areas as contrasted with urban ones. **4.** farming as an occupation or way of life. **5.** *Law.* any tract of ground capable of being owned as property. **6. a.** a country, region, or area. **b.** the people of a country, etc. **7.** *Econ.* the factor of production consisting of all natural resources. ~*vb.* **8.** to transfer (something) or go from a ship or boat to the shore: *land the cargo.* **9.** (*intr.*) to come to or touch shore. **10.** (*intr.*) (in Canada) to be legally admitted to the country, as an immigrant or **landed immigrant. 11.** to come down or bring (something) down to earth after a flight or jump. **12.** to come or bring to some point, condition, or state. **13.** (*tr.*) *Angling.* to retrieve (a hooked fish) from the water. **14.** (*tr.*) *Inf.* to win or obtain: *to land a job.* **15.** (*tr.*) *Inf.* to deliver (a blow). ~See also **land up**. [OE] —**landless** *adj.*

Land (lænd) *n.* **Edwin Herbert.** born 1909, U.S. inventor of the Polaroid Land camera.

land agent *n.* **1.** a person who administers a landed estate and its tenancies. **2.** a person who acts as an agent for the sale of land. —**land agency** *n.*

landau ('lændɔː) *n.* a four-wheeled horse-drawn carriage with two folding hoods over the passenger compartment. [C18: after *Landau* (a town in Germany), where first made]

Landau (*Russian* lan'dau) *n.* **Lev Davidovich** (ljef da'vidəvitʃ). 1908–68, Soviet physicist, noted for his researches into quantum theory and his work on the theories of solids and liquids: Nobel prize for physics 1962.

landaulet (,lændɔː'let) *n.* **1.** a small landau. **2.** *U.S.* an early type of car with a folding hood over the passenger seats.

landed ('lændɪd) *adj.* **1.** owning land: *landed gentry.* **2.** consisting of or including land: *a landed estate.*

Landes (*French* lãd) *n.* **1.** a department of SW France, in Aquitaine region. Capital: Mont-de-Marsan. Pop.: 297 424 (1982). Area: 9364 sq. km (3652 sq. miles). **2.** a region of SW France, on the Bay of Biscay: occupies most of the Landes department and parts of Gironde and Lot-et-Garonne; consists chiefly of the most extensive forest in France. Area: 14 000 sq. km (5400 sq. miles).

landfall ('lænd,fɔːl) *n.* **1.** the act of sighting or nearing land, esp. from the sea. **2.** the land sighted or neared.

landfill ('lænd,fɪl) *adj.* of or denoting low-lying sites or tips being filled up with alternate layers of rubbish and earth.

landform ('lænd,fɔːm) *n.* *Geol.* any natural feature of the earth's surface.

land girl *n.* a girl or woman who does farm work, esp. in wartime.

landgrave ('lænd,greɪv) *n.* *German history.* **1.** (from the 13th century to 1806) a count who ruled over a specified territory. **2.** (after 1806) the title of any of various sovereign princes. [C16: via G, from MHG *lantgrāve*, from *lant* land + *grāve* count]

land-holder *n.* a person who owns or occupies land. —**'land-,holding** *adj.*, *n.*

landing ('lændɪŋ) *n.* **1. a.** the act of coming to land, esp. after a sea voyage. **b.** (*as modifier*): *landing place.* **2.** a place of disembarkation. **3.** the floor area at the top of a flight of stairs.

landing craft *n.* *Mil.* any small vessel designed for the landing of troops and equipment on beaches.

landing field *n.* an area of land on which aircraft land and from which they take off.

landing gear *n.* another name for **undercarriage.**

landing net *n.* *Angling.* a loose long-handled net for lifting hooked fish from the water.

landing stage *n.* a platform used for landing goods and passengers from a vessel.

landing strip *n.* another name for **airstrip**.

landlady ('lænd,leɪdɪ) *n.*, *pl.* **-dies**. **1.** a woman who owns and leases property. **2.** a woman who owns or runs a lodging house, pub, etc.

ländler (*German* 'lɛntlər) *n.* **1.** an Austrian country dance in which couples spin and clap. **2.** a piece of music composed for or in the rhythm of this dance, in three-four time. [G, from dialect *Landl* Upper Austria]

land line *n.* a telecommunications wire or cable laid over land.

landlocked ('lænd,lɒkt) *adj.* **1.** (esp. of lakes) completely surrounded by land. **2.** (esp. of certain salmon) living in fresh water that is permanently isolated from the sea.

landlord ('lænd,lɔːd) *n.* **1.** a man who owns and leases property. **2.** a man who owns or runs a lodging house, pub, etc.

landlubber ('lænd,lʌbə) *n. Naut.* any person having no experience at sea.

landmark ('lænd,mɑːk) *n.* **1.** a prominent or well-known object in or feature of a particular landscape. **2.** an important or unique decision, event, fact, discovery, etc. **3.** a boundary marker.

landmass ('lænd,mæs) *n.* a large continuous area of land, as opposed to seas or islands.

land mine *n. Mil.* an explosive charge placed in the ground, usually detonated by stepping or driving on it.

land of milk and honey *n.* **1.** *Old Testament.* the land of natural fertility promised to the Israelites by God. (Ezekiel 20:6) **2.** any fertile land, state, etc.

land of Nod *n.* **1.** *Old Testament.* a region to the east of Eden to which Cain went after he had killed Abel (Genesis 4:14). **2.** an imaginary land of sleep.

Landor ('lændɔː) *n.* **Walter Savage**. 1775–1864, English poet, noted also for his prose works, including *Imaginary Conversations* (1824–29).

landowner ('lænd,əʊnə) *n.* a person who owns land. — '**land,owner,ship** *n.* — '**land,owning** *n.*, *adj.*

Landowska (*Polish* lan'dɔfska) *n.* **Wanda** ('vanda). 1877–1959, U.S. harpsichordist, born in Poland.

land rail *n.* another name for **corncrake**.

land reform *n.* the redistributing of large agricultural holdings among the landless.

landscape ('lænd,skeɪp) *n.* **1.** an extensive area of scenery as viewed from a single aspect. **2.** a painting, drawing, photograph, etc., depicting natural scenery. **3.** the genre including such pictures. ~*vb.* **4.** (*tr.*) to improve the natural features of (a garden, park, etc.), as by creating contoured features and planting trees. **5.** (*intr.*) to work as a landscape gardener. [C16 *landskip* (orig. a term in painting), from MDu. *lantscap* region]

landscape gardening *n.* the art of laying out grounds in imitation of natural scenery. Also called: **landscape architecture.** — **landscape gardener** *n.*

landscapist ('lænd,skeɪpɪst) *n.* a painter of landscapes.

Landseer ('lænsɪə) *n.* Sir **Edwin Henry**. 1802–73, English painter, noted for his studies of animals.

Land's End *n.* a granite headland in SW England, on the SW coast of Cornwall: the westernmost point of England.

Landshut (*German* 'lantshuːt) *n.* a city in SE West Germany, in Bavaria: Trausnitz castle (13th century); manufacturing centre for machinery and chemicals. Pop.: 56 400 (1984 est.).

landslide ('lænd,slaɪd) *n.* **1.** Also called: **landslip. a.** the sliding of a large mass of rock material, soil, etc., down the side of a mountain or cliff. **b.** the material dislodged in this way. **2.** an overwhelming electoral victory.

landsman ('lændzmən) *n.*, *pl.* **-men.** a person who works or lives on land, as distinguished from a seaman.

land up *vb.* (*adv., usually intr.*) to arrive or cause to arrive at a final point or condition.

landward ('lændwəd) *adj.* **1.** lying, facing, or moving towards land. **2.** in the direction of the land. ~*adv.* **3.** a variant of **landwards**.

landwards ('lændwədz) *or* **landward** *adv.* towards land.

lane (leɪn) *n.* **1.** a narrow road or way between buildings, hedges, fences, etc. **2.** any narrow well-defined track or course, as for lines of traffic in a road, or for ships or aircraft. **3.** one of the parallel strips into which a running track or swimming bath is divided for races. **4.** the long strip of wooden flooring down which balls are bowled in a bowling alley. [OE *lane, lanu*]

Lanfranc ('lænfræŋk) *n.* ?1005–89, Italian ecclesiastic and scholar; archbishop of Canterbury (1070–89) and adviser to William the Conqueror. He instituted many reforms in the English Church.

Lang (læŋ) *n.* **1. Cosmo Gordon,** 1st Baron Lang of Lambeth. 1864–1945, British churchman; archbishop of Canterbury (1928–42). **2. Fritz**. 1890–1976, Austrian film director, later in the U.S., most notable for his silent films, such as *Metropolis* (1926), *M* (1931), and *The Testament of Dr. Mabuse* (1932). **3. Jack (John Thomas)**. 1876–1975, controversial Labor premier of New South Wales from 1925–27 and from 1930–32, who introduced much social welfare legislation and was dismissed by the governor, Sir Philip Game, in 1932 for acting unconstitutionally.

lang. *abbrev. for* language.

Lange ('lɒŋɪ) *n.* **David.** born 1942, New Zealand statesman: prime minister from 1984.

Langer ('læŋə) *n.* **Bernhard** ('bernhart). born 1957, West German professional golfer: won the U.S. Masters Championship (1985).

Langland ('læŋlənd) *or* **Langley** *n.* **William.** ?1332–?1400, English poet. The allegorical religious poem in alliterative verse, *The Vision of William concerning Piers the Plowman*, is attributed to him.

langlauf ('lɑː,laʊf) *n.* cross-country skiing. [G, lit.: long run] —**langläufer** ('lɑː,lɔɪfə) *n.*

Langley ('læŋlɪ) *n.* **1. Samuel Pierpont,** 1834–1906, U.S. astronomer and physicist: invented the bolometer (1878) and pioneered the construction of heavier-than-air flying machines. **2. William**. See **Langland**.

Langmuir ('læŋmjʊə) *n.* **Irving**. 1881–1957, U.S. chemist. He developed the gas-filled tungsten lamp and the atomic hydrogen welding process: Nobel prize for chemistry 1932.

langouste ('lɒŋguːst, lɒŋ'guːst) *n.* another name for the **spiny lobster**. [F, from OProvençal *langosta*, ? from L *lŏcusta* lobster, locust]

langoustine (,lɒŋguː'stiːn) *n.* a large prawn or small lobster. [from F, dim. of LANGOUSTE]

Langres Plateau (*French* lɑ̃grə) *n.* a calcareous plateau of E France north of Dijon between the Seine and the Saône, reaching over 580 m (1900 ft.): forms a watershed between rivers flowing to the Mediterranean and to the English Channel.

langsam ('læŋzæm) *adj. Music.* slow. [G]

langsyne (,læŋ'saɪn) *Scot.* ~*adv.* **1.** long ago; long since. ~*n.* **2.** times long past, esp. those fondly remembered. [C16: Scot.: long since]

Langton ('læŋtən) *n.* **Stephen.** ?1150–1228, English cardinal; archbishop of Canterbury (1213–28). He was consecrated archbishop by Pope Innocent III in 1207 but was kept out of his see by King John until 1213. He was partly responsible for the Magna Carta (1215).

Langtry ('læŋtrɪ) *n.* **Lillie**, known as *the Jersey Lily*, real name *Émilie Charlotte le Breton*. 1852–1929, English actress, noted for her beauty and for her friendship with Edward VII.

language ('læŋgwɪdʒ) *n.* **1.** a system for the expression of thoughts, feelings, etc., by the use of spoken sounds or conventional symbols. **2.** the faculty for the use of such systems, which is a distinguishing characteristic of man as compared with other animals. **3.** the language of a particular nation or people. **4.** any other means of communicating, such as gesture or animal sounds: *the language of love*. **5.** the specialized vocabulary used by a particular group: *medical language*. **6.** a particular manner or style of verbal expression: *your language is disgusting*. **7.** *Computers*: See **programming language**. [C13: from OF *language*, ult. from L *lingua* tongue]

language laboratory *n.* a room equipped with tape recorders, etc., for learning foreign languages.

langue (lɑːŋg) *n. Linguistics.* language considered as an abstract system or a social institution, being the common possession of a speech community. [C19: from F: language]

langue d'oc *French.* (lɑ̃g dɔk) *n.* the group of medieval French dialects spoken in S France: often regarded as including Provençal. [lit.: language of *oc* (form for the Provençal *yes*), ult. from L *hoc* this]

Languedoc (*French* lɑ̃gdɔk) *n.* a former province of S France, lying between the foothills of the Pyrenees and the River Rhône: formed around the countship of Toulouse in the 13th century; important production of bulk wines.

Languedoc-Roussillon (*French* lāgdɔkrusijɔ̃) *n.* a region of S France, on the Gulf of Lions: consists of the departments of Lozère, Gard, Hérault, Aude, and Pyrénées-Orientales; mainly mountainous with a coastal plain.

langue d'oïl *French.* (lāg dɔj) *n.* the group of medieval French dialects spoken in France north of the Loire; the medieval basis of modern French. [lit.: language of *oïl* (the northern form for *yes*), ult. from L *hoc ille* (*fecit*) this he (did)]

languid ('læŋgwɪd) *adj.* **1.** without energy or spirit. **2.** without interest or enthusiasm. **3.** sluggish; inactive. [C16: from L *languidus*, from *languēre* to languish] —'**languidly** *adv.* —'**languidness** *n.*

languish ('læŋgwɪʃ) *vb.* (*intr.*) **1.** to lose or diminish in strength or energy. **2.** (often foll. by *for*) to be listless with desire; pine. **3.** to suffer deprivation, hardship, or neglect: *to languish in prison.* **4.** to put on a tender, nostalgic, or melancholic expression. [C14 *languishen*, from OF *languiss-*, stem of *languir*, ult. from L *languēre*] —'**languishing** *adj.* —'**languishingly** *adv.* —'**languishment** *n.*

languor ('læŋgə) *n.* **1.** physical or mental laziness or weariness. **2.** a feeling of dreaminess and relaxation. **3.** oppressive silence or stillness. [C14 *langour*, via OF from L *languor*, from *languēre* to languish; the modern spelling is directly from L] —'**languorous** *adj.*

langur (lʌŋ'gʊə) *n.* any of various agile arboreal Old World monkeys of S and SE Asia having a long tail and long hair surrounding the face. [Hindi]

laniard ('lænjəd) *n.* a variant spelling of **lanyard.**

laniary ('læniərɪ) *adj.* **1.** (esp. of canine teeth) adapted for tearing. ~*n.*, *pl.* **-aries. 2.** a tooth adapted for tearing. [C19: from L *lanius* butcher, from *laniāre* to tear]

laniferous (lə'nɪfərəs) *or* **lanigerous** (lə'nɪdʒərəs) *adj.* *Biol.* bearing wool or fleecy hairs resembling wool. [C17: from L *lānifer*, from *lāna* wool]

lank (læŋk) *adj.* **1.** long and limp. **2.** thin or gaunt. [OE *hlanc* loose] —'**lankly** *adv.* —'**lankness** *n.*

Lankester ('læŋkɪstə) *n.* Sir **Edwin Ray.** 1847–1929, English zoologist, noted particularly for his work in embryology and study of protozoans.

lanky ('læŋkɪ) *adj.* **lankier, lankiest.** tall, thin, and loose-jointed. —'**lankily** *adv.* —'**lankiness** *n.*

lanner ('lænə) *n.* **1.** a large falcon of Mediterranean regions, N Africa, and S Asia. **2.** *Falconry.* the female of this falcon. The male is called **lanneret.** [C15: from OF (*faucon*) *lanier* cowardly (falcon), from L *lanārius* wool worker, coward; referring to its sluggish flight and timid nature]

lanolin ('lænəlɪn) *or* **lanoline** ('lænəlɪn, -,liːn) *n.* a yellowish viscous substance extracted from wool: used in some ointments. [C19: via G from L *lāna* wool + *oleum* oil; see -IN]

Lansing ('lænsɪŋ) *n.* a city in S Michigan, on the Grand River: the state capital. Pop.: 128 980 (1986 est.).

lantern ('læntən) *n.* **1.** a light with a transparent protective case. **2.** a structure on top of a dome or roof having openings or windows to admit light or air. **3.** the upper part of a lighthouse that houses the light. [C13: from L *lanterna*, from Gk *lamptēr* lamp, from *lampein* to shine]

lantern jaw *n.* (when *pl.*, refers to upper and lower jaw; when *sing.*, usually to lower jaw) a long hollow jaw that gives the face a drawn appearance. —'**lantern-,jawed** *adj.*

lantern slide *n.* (formerly) a photographic slide for projection, used in a magic lantern.

lanthanide ('lænθə,naɪd) *or* **lanthanoid** ('lænθə,nɔɪd) *n.* any of a class of 15 chemically related elements with atomic numbers from 57 (lanthanum) to 71 (lutetium).

lanthanum ('lænθənəm) *n.* a silvery-white ductile metallic element of the lanthanide series: used in pyrophoric alloys, electronic devices, and in glass manufacture. Symbol: La; atomic no.: 57; atomic wt.: 138.91. [C19: NL, from Gk *lanthanein* to lie unseen]

lanthorn ('lænt,hɔːn, 'læntən) *n.* an archaic word for **lantern.**

lanugo (lə'njuːgəʊ) *n.*, *pl.* **-gos.** a layer of fine hairs, esp. the covering of the human fetus before birth. [C17: from L: down, from *lāna* wool]

Lanús (*Spanish* la'nus) *n.* a city in E Argentina: a S suburb of Buenos Aires. Pop.: 465 891 (1980).

lanyard *or* **laniard** ('lænjəd) *n.* **1.** a cord, esp. one worn around the neck, to hold a whistle, knife, etc. **2.** a cord used in firing certain types of cannon. **3.** *Naut.* a line for extending or tightening standing rigging. [C15 *lanyer*, from F *lanière*, from *lasne* strap, prob. of Gmc origin]

Lanzhou, Lanchow, *or* **Lan-chou** ('læn'dʒəʊ) *n.* a city in N China, capital of Gansu province, on the Yellow River: situated on the main route between China and the West. Pop.: 1 350 000 (1986).

Laoag (lɑː'wɑːg) *n.* a city in the N Philippines, on NW Luzon: trade centre for an agricultural region. Pop.: 61 727 (1970).

Laocoon (leɪ'ɒkəʊ,ɒn) *n. Greek myth.* a priest of Apollo at Troy who warned the Trojans against the wooden horse left by the Greeks; killed with his twin sons by two sea serpents.

Laodicea (,leɪəʊdɪ'sɪə) *n.* the ancient name of several Greek cities in W Asia, notably of **Latakia.**

laodicean (,leɪəʊdɪ'sɪən) *adj.* **1.** lukewarm and indifferent, esp. in religious matters. ~*n.* **2.** a person having a lukewarm attitude towards religious matters. [C17: referring to the early Christians of Laodicea (Revelation 3:14–16)]

Laoighis ('leɪɪʃ) *n.* a county of central Ireland, in Leinster province: formerly boggy but largely reclaimed for agriculture. County town: Portlaoise. Pop.: 53 270 (1986). Area: 1719 sq. km (664 sq. miles). Also called: **Leix.** Former name: **Queen's County.**

Laomedon (leɪ'ɒmɪ,dɒn) *n. Greek myth.* the founder and ruler of Troy, who cheated Apollo and Poseidon of their wage for constructing the city's walls; the father of Priam.

Laos (lauz, laus) *n.* a republic in SE Asia: first united as the kingdom of Lan Xang ("million elephants") in 1353, after being a province of the Khmer Empire for about four centuries; made part of French Indochina in 1893 and gained independence in 1949; became a republic in 1975. It is generally forested and mountainous, with the Mekong River running almost the whole length of the W border. Official language: Lao. Currency: kip. Capital: Vientiane. Pop.: 4 322 000 (1987 est.). Area: 236 000 sq. km (91 000 sq. miles). Official name: **People's Democratic Republic of Laos.** —**Laotian** ('lauʃɪən) *adj.*, *n.*

Lao Zi ('lau'zɪ) *or* **Lao-tzu** ('lau'tsuː) *n.* ?604–?531 B.C., Chinese philosopher, traditionally regarded as the founder of Taoism and the author of the *Tao-te Ching.*

lap¹ (læp) *n.* **1.** the area formed by the upper surface of the thighs of a seated person. **2.** Also called: **lapful.** the amount held in one's lap. **3.** a protected place or environment: *in the lap of luxury.* **4.** the part of one's clothing that covers the lap. **5. drop in someone's lap.** give someone the responsibility of. [OE *læppa* flap]

lap² (læp) *n.* **1.** one circuit of a racecourse or track. **2.** a stage or part of a journey, race, etc. **3. a.** an overlapping part or projection. **b.** the extent of overlap. **4.** the length of material needed to go around an object. **5.** a rotating disc coated with fine abrasive for polishing gemstones. ~*vb.* **lapping, lapped. 6.** (*tr.*) to wrap or fold (around or over): *he lapped a bandage around his wrist.* **7.** (*tr.*) to enclose or envelop in: *he lapped his wrist in a bandage.* **8.** to place or lie partly or completely over or project beyond. **9.** (*tr.*; *usually passive*) to envelop or surround with comfort, love, etc.: *lapped in luxury.* **10.** (*intr.*) to be folded. **11.** (*tr.*) to overtake (an opponent) in a race so as to be one or more circuits ahead. **12.** (*tr.*) to polish or cut (a workpiece, gemstone, etc.) with a fine abrasive. [C13 (in the sense: to wrap): prob. from LAP¹] —'**lapper** *n.*

lap³ (læp) *vb.* **lapping, lapped. 1.** (of small waves) to wash against (a shore, boat, etc.), usually with light splashing sounds. **2.** (often foll. by *up*) (esp. of animals) to scoop (a liquid) into the mouth with the tongue. ~*n.* **3.** the act or sound of lapping. **4.** a thin food for dogs or other animals. ~See also **lap up.** [OE *lapian*] —'**lapper** *n.*

La Palma (*Spanish* la 'palma) *n.* an island in the N Atlantic, in the NW Canary Islands: administratively part of Spain. Chief town: Santa Cruz de la Palma. Pop.: 76 426 (1981). Area: 725 sq. km (280 sq. miles).

laparoscope ('læpərə,skəʊp) *n.* a medical instrument consisting of a tube that is inserted through the abdominal wall and illuminated to enable a doctor to view the internal organs. [C19 (applied to various instruments used to examine the abdomen) and C20 (in the specific modern sense): from Gk *lapara* (see LAPAROTOMY) + -SCOPE] —,**lapa'roscopy** *n.*

laparotomy (,læpə'rɒtəmɪ) *n., pl.* -**mies**. surgical incision through the abdominal wall. [C19: from Gk *lapara* flank, from *laparos* soft + -TOMY]

La Paz (læ 'pæz; *Spanish* la 'paθ) *n.* a city in W Bolivia, at an altitude of 3600 m (12 000 ft.): seat of government since 1898 (though Sucre is still the official capital); the country's largest city; founded in 1548 by the Spaniards; university (1830). Pop.: 992 600 (1985).

lap dissolve *n. Films.* the transposing from one picture to another by reducing one picture in brightness and amplitude while increasing the other until it replaces the first.

lapdog ('læp,dɒg) *n.* a pet dog small and docile enough to be cuddled in the lap.

lapel (lə'pɛl) *n.* the continuation of the turned or folded back collar on a suit, coat, jacket, etc. [C18: from LAP[1]] —**la'pelled** *adj.*

lapheld ('læp,hɛld) *adj.* (esp. of a personal computer) small enough to be used on one's lap; portable.

lapidary ('læpɪdərɪ) *n., pl.* -**daries**. **1.** a person whose business is to cut, polish, set, or deal in gemstones. ~*adj.* **2.** of or relating to gemstones or the work of a lapidary. **3.** Also: **lapidarian** (,læpɪ'dɛərɪən). engraved, cut, or inscribed in a stone or gemstone. **4.** of sufficiently high quality to be engraved on a stone: *a lapidary inscription.* [C14: from L *lapidārius*, from *lapid-*, *lapis* stone]

lapillus (lə'pɪləs) *n., pl.* -**li** (-laɪ). a small piece of lava thrown from a volcano. [C18: L: little stone]

lapis lazuli ('læpɪs 'læzjʊ,laɪ) *n.* **1.** a brilliant blue mineral used as a gemstone. **2.** the deep blue colour of lapis lazuli. [C14: from L *lapis* stone + Med. L *lazulī*, from Ar. *lāzaward*, from Persian *lāzhuward*, from ?]

Lapith ('læpɪθ) *n., pl.* **Lapithae** ('læpɪ,θiː) *or* **Lapiths**. *Greek myth.* a member of a people in Thessaly who at the wedding of their king, Pirithoüs, fought the drunken centaurs.

lap joint *n.* a joint made by placing one member over another and fastening them together. Also called: **lapped joint**. —'**lap-,jointed** *adj.*

Laplace (*French* laplas) *n.* **Pierre Simon** (pjɛr sim5), Marquis de Laplace. 1749–1827, French mathematician, physicist, and astronomer. He formulated the nebular hypothesis (1796). He also developed the theory of probability.

Laplace operator *n. Maths.* the operator $\partial^2/\partial x^2 + \partial^2/\partial y^2 + \partial^2/\partial z^2$, used in differential analysis. Symbol: ∇^2

Lapland ('læp,lænd) *n.* an extensive region of N Europe, mainly within the Arctic Circle: consists of the N parts of Norway, Sweden, Finland, and the Kola Peninsula of the extreme NW Soviet Union. Also called (informal): **Land of the Midnight Sun**. —'**Lap,lander** *n.*

La Plata (*Spanish* la 'plata) *n.* **1.** a port in E Argentina, near the Río de la Plata estuary: founded in 1882 and modelled on Washington DC; university (1897). Pop.: 455 000 (1980). **2.** See (Río de la) **Plata**.

lap of honour *n.* a ceremonial circuit of a racing track, etc., by the winner of a race.

Lapp (læp) *n.* **1.** Also **Laplander**. a member of a nomadic people living chiefly in N Scandinavia and the Kola Peninsula of the Soviet Union. The language of this people. ~*adj.* **3.** of or relating to this people or their language. —'**Lappish** *adj.*, *n.*

lappet ('læpɪt) *n.* **1.** a small hanging flap or piece of lace, etc. **2.** *Zool.* a lobelike hanging structure, such as the wattle on a bird's head. [C16: from LAP[1] + -ET]

lapse (læps) *n.* **1.** a drop in standard of an isolated or temporary nature: *a lapse of justice.* **2.** a break in occurrence, usage, etc.: *a lapse of five weeks between letters.* **3.** a gradual decline or a drop to a lower degree, condition, or state: *a lapse from high office.* **4.** a moral fall. **5.** *Law.* the termination of some right, interest, or privilege, as by neglecting to exercise it or through failure of some contingency. **6.** *Insurance.* the termination of coverage following a failure to pay the premiums. ~*vb.* (*intr.*) **7.** to drop in standard or fail to maintain a norm. **8.** to decline gradually or fall in status, condition, etc. **9.** to be discontinued, esp. through negligence or other failure. **10.** (usually foll. by *into*) to drift or slide (into a condition): *to lapse into sleep.* **11.** (often foll. by *from*) to turn away (from beliefs or norms). **12.** (of time) to slip away. [C15: from L

lāpsus error, from *lābī* to glide] —'**lapsable** *or* '**lapsible** *adj.* —**lapsed** *adj.* —'**lapser** *n.*

lapse rate *n.* the rate of change of any meteorological factor with altitude, esp. atmospheric temperature.

Laptev Sea ('læptɪf) *n.* a shallow arm of the Arctic Ocean, along the N coast of the Soviet Union between the Taimyr Peninsula and the New Siberian Islands. Former name: **Nordenskjöld Sea**.

laptop ('læp,tɒp) *adj.* (of a computer) small and light enough to be held on the user's lap.

lap up *vb.* (*tr., adv.*) **1.** to eat or drink. **2.** to relish or delight in: *he laps up horror films.* **3.** to believe or accept eagerly and uncritically: *he laps up stories.*

lapwing ('læp,wɪŋ) *n.* any of several plovers, typically having a crested head, wattles, and spurs. Also called: **green plover, peewit**. [C17: altered form of OE *hlēapewince* plover]

larboard ('lɑ:bəd) *n., adj. Naut.* a former word for **port**[2]. [C14 *laddeborde* (changed to *larboard* by association with *starboard*), from *laden* to load + *borde* BOARD]

larceny ('lɑ:sɪnɪ) *n., pl.* -**nies**. *Law.* (formerly) a technical word for **theft**. [C15: from OF *larcin*, from L *lātrocinium* robbery, from *latrō* robber] —'**larcenist** *or* '**larcener** *n.* —'**larcenous** *adj.*

larch (lɑ:tʃ) *n.* **1.** any coniferous tree having deciduous needle-like leaves and egg-shaped cones. **2.** the wood of any of these trees. [C16: from G *Lärche*, ult. from L *larix*]

lard (lɑ:d) *n.* **1.** the rendered fat from a pig, used in cooking. ~*vb.* (*tr.*) **2.** to prepare (lean meat, poultry, etc.) by inserting small strips of bacon or fat before cooking. **3.** to cover or smear (foods) with lard. **4.** to add extra material to (speech or writing); embellish. [C15: via OF from L *lāridum* bacon fat] —'**lardy** *adj.*

larder ('lɑ:də) *n.* a room or cupboard, used as a store for food. [C14: from OF *lardier*, from LARD]

lardon ('lɑ:d[ə]n) *or* **lardoon** (lɑ:'du:n) *n.* a strip of fat used in larding meat. [C15: from OF, from LARD]

lardy cake ('lɑ:dɪ) *n. Brit.* a rich sweet cake made of bread dough, lard, sugar, and dried fruit.

lares and penates ('lɛərɪ:z, 'lɑ:-) *pl. n.* **1.** *Roman myth.* **a.** household gods. **b.** statues of these gods kept in the home. **2.** the valued possessions of a household. [from L]

large (lɑ:dʒ) *adj.* **1.** having a relatively great size, quantity, extent, etc.; big. **2.** of wide or broad scope, capacity, or range; comprehensive. **3.** having or showing great breadth of understanding. ~*n.* **4. at large. a.** (esp. of a dangerous criminal or wild animal) free; not confined. **b.** roaming freely, as in a foreign country. **c.** as a whole; in general. **d.** in full detail; exhaustively. **e. ambassador at large.** See **ambassador** (sense 4). [C12 (orig.: generous): via OF from L *largus* ample] —'**largeness** *n.*

large intestine *n.* the part of the alimentary canal consisting of the caecum, colon, and rectum.

largely ('lɑ:dʒlɪ) *adv.* **1.** principally; to a great extent. **2.** on a large scale or in a large manner.

larger-than-life *adj.* exceptionally striking or colourful.

large-scale *adj.* **1.** wide-ranging or extensive. **2.** (of maps and models) constructed or drawn to a big scale.

largess *or* **largesse** (lɑ:'dʒɛs) *n.* **1.** the generous bestowal of gifts, favours, or money. **2.** the things so bestowed. **3.** generosity of spirit or attitude. [C13: from OF, from LARGE]

larghetto (lɑ:'gɛtəʊ) *Music.* ~*adj., adv.* **1.** to be performed moderately slowly. ~*n., pl.* -**tos**. **2.** a piece or passage to be performed in this way. [It.: dim. of LARGO]

largish ('lɑ:dʒɪʃ) *adj.* fairly large.

largo ('lɑ:gəʊ) *Music.* ~*adj., adv.* **1.** to be performed slowly and broadly. ~*n., pl.* -**gos**. **2.** a piece or passage to be performed in this way. [C17: from It., from L *largus* large]

lariat ('lærɪət) *n. U.S. & Canad.* **1.** another word for **lasso**. **2.** a rope for tethering animals. [C19: from Sp. *la reata* the rope]

Larisa *or* **Larissa** (lə'rɪsə; *Greek* 'larisa) *n.* a city in E Greece, in E Thessaly: fortified by Justinian; annexed to Greece in 1881. Pop.: 103 263 (1981).

lark[1] (lɑ:k) *n.* **1.** any brown bird of a predominantly Old World family of songbirds, esp. the skylark: noted for their singing. **2.** short for **titlark**. [OE *lāwerce*, *lǣwerce*, from Gmc origin]

lark[2] (lɑ:k) *Inf.* ~*n.* **1.** a carefree adventure or frolic. **2.** a harmless piece of mischief. ~*vb.* (*intr.*) **3.** (often foll. by *about*) to have a good time by frolicking. **4.** to play a prank. [C19: orig. sl.] —**'larkish** *or* **'larky** *adj.*

Larkin ('lɑːkɪn) *n.* **Philip.** 1922–85, English poet: his verse collections include *The Less Deceived* (1955) and *The Whitsun Weddings* (1964).

larkspur ('lɑːk,spɜː) *n.* any of various plants related to the delphinium, with spikes of blue, pink, or white irregular spurred flowers. [C16: LARK¹ + SPUR]

larn (lɑːn) *vb. Not standard.* **1.** *Facetious.* to learn. **2.** (*tr.*) to teach (someone) a lesson: *that'll larn you!* [C18: from a dialect form of LEARN]

La Rochefoucauld (*French* la rɔʃfuko) *n.* **François** (frɑ̃swa), Duc de La Rochefoucauld. 1613–80, French writer. His best-known work is *Réflexions ou sentences et maximes morales* (1665), a collection of epigrammatic and cynical observations on human nature.

La Rochelle (*French* la rɔʃɛl) *n.* a port in W France, on the Bay of Biscay: a Huguenot stronghold until its submission through famine to Richelieu's forces after a long siege (1627–28). Pop.: 78 500 (1983 est.).

Larousse (*French* larus) *n.* **Pierre Athanase** (pjɛr atanɑz). 1817–75, French grammarian, lexicographer, and encyclopedist. He edited and helped to compile the *Grand Dictionnaire universel du XIX siècle* (1866–76).

larrigan ('lærɪɡən) *n.* a knee-high oiled leather moccasin boot worn by trappers, etc. [C19: from ?]

larrikin ('lærɪkɪn) *n. Austral. & N.Z. sl.* **a.** a hooligan. **b.** (*as modifier*): *a larrikin bloke.* [C19: from E dialect: a mischievous youth]

larrup ('lærəp) *vb.* (*tr.*) *Dialect.* to beat or flog. [C19: from ?] —**'larruper** *n.*

Larry ('lærɪ) *n. Inf., chiefly Austral.* **happy as Larry.** very happy.

larva ('lɑːvə) *n., pl.* **-vae** (-viː). an immature free-living form of many animals that develops into a different adult form by metamorphosis. [C18: (C17 in the orig. L sense: ghost): NL] —**'larval** *adj.*

Larwood ('lɑːwʊd) *n.* **Harold.** born 1904, English cricketer. An outstanding fast bowler, he played 21 times for England between 1926 and 1932.

laryngeal (,lærɪn'dʒiːəl, lə'rɪndʒɪəl) *or* **laryngal** (lə'rɪŋɡ°l) *adj.* **1.** of or relating to the larynx. **2.** *Phonetics.* articulated at the larynx; glottal. [C18: from NL *laryngeus* of the LARYNX]

laryngitis (,lærɪn'dʒaɪtɪs) *n.* inflammation of the larynx. —**laryngitic** (,lærɪn'dʒɪtɪk) *adj.*

laryngo- *or before a vowel* **laryng-** *combining form.* indicating the larynx: *laryngoscope.*

laryngoscope (lə'rɪŋɡə,skəʊp) *n.* a medical instrument for examining the larynx. —**,laryn'goscopy** *n.*

laryngotomy (,lærɪŋ'ɡɒtəmɪ) *n., pl.* **-mies.** surgical incision into the larynx to facilitate breathing.

larynx ('lærɪŋks) *n., pl.* **larynges** (lə'rɪndʒiːz) *or* **larynxes.** a cartilaginous and muscular hollow organ forming part of the air passage to the lungs: in higher vertebrates it contains the vocal cords. [C16: from NL, from Gk *larunx*]

lasagne *or* **lasagna** (lə'zænjə, -'sæn-) *n.* **1.** a form of pasta consisting of wide flat sheets. **2.** any of several dishes made from layers of lasagne and meat, cheese, etc. [from It. *lasagna*, from L *lasanum* cooking pot]

La Salle¹ (lə 'sæl) *n.* a city in SE Canada, in Quebec: a S suburb of Montreal. Pop.: 76 299 (1981).

La Salle² (*French* la 'sal) *n.* Sieur **Robert Cavelier de** (rɔbɛr kavəlje də). 1643–87, French explorer and fur trader in North America; founder of Louisiana (1682).

La Scala (la 'skɑːla) *n.* the chief opera house in Italy, in Milan (opened 1776).

lascar ('læskə) *n.* a sailor from the East Indies. [C17: from Urdu *lashkar* soldier, from Persian: the army]

lascivious (lə'sɪvɪəs) *adj.* **1.** lustful; lecherous. **2.** exciting sexual desire. [C15: from LL *lascīviōsus*, from L *lascīvia* wantonness, from *lascīvus*] —**las'civiously** *adv.* —**las'civiousness** *n.*

Lasdun ('læsdən) *n.* Sir **Denys.** born 1914, British architect. He is best known for the University of East Anglia (1968) and the National Theatre in London (1976).

lase (leɪz) *vb.* (*intr.*) (of a substance, such as carbon dioxide or ruby) to be capable of acting as a laser.

laser ('leɪzə) *n.* **1.** Also called: **optical maser.** a device for converting light of mixed frequencies into an intense narrow monochromatic beam of coherent light. **2.** any

similar device for producing a beam of any electromagnetic radiation, such as infrared or microwave radiation. [C20: from *light amplification by stimulated emission of radiation*]

laser printer *n.* a quiet high-quality computer printer that uses a laser beam shining on a photoconductive drum to produce characters, which are then transferred to paper.

lash¹ (læʃ) *n.* **1.** a sharp cutting blow from a whip or other flexible object. **2.** the flexible end or ends of a whip. **3.** a cutting or hurtful blow to the feelings, as one caused by ridicule or scolding. **4.** a forceful beating or impact, as of wind, rain, or waves against something. **5.** **have a lash at.** *Austral. & N.Z. inf.* to make an attempt at or take part in (something). **6.** See **eyelash.** ~*vb.* (*tr.*) **7.** to hit (a person or thing) sharply with a whip, rope, etc., esp., formerly, as punishment. **8.** (of rain, waves, etc.) to beat forcefully against. **9.** to attack with words, ridicule, etc. **10.** to flick or wave sharply to and fro: *the panther lashed his tail.* **11.** to urge or drive as with a whip: *to lash the audience into a violent mood.* ~See also **lash out.** [C14: ? imit.] —**'lasher** *n.*

lash² (læʃ) *vb.* (*tr.*) to bind or secure with rope, string, etc. [C15: from OF *lachier*, ult. from L *laqueāre* to ensnare, from *laqueus* noose]

-lashed *adj.* having eyelashes as specified: *long-lashed.*

lashing¹ ('læʃɪŋ) *n.* **1.** a whipping; flogging. **2.** a scolding. **3.** (*pl.;* usually foll. by *of*) *Brit. inf.* large amounts; lots.

lashing² ('læʃɪŋ) *n.* rope, cord, etc., used for binding or securing.

Lashio ('læʃɪ,əʊ) *n.* a town in NE central Burma: starting point of the Burma Road to Chongqing, China.

Lashkar ('lʌʃkə) *n.* a former city in N India, in Madhya Pradesh: capital of the former states of Gwalior and Madhya Bharat; now part of the city of Gwalior.

lash out *vb.* (*intr., adv.*) **1.** to burst into or resort to verbal or physical attack. **2.** *Inf.* to be extravagant, as in spending.

lash-up *n.* a temporary connection of equipment for experimental or emergency use.

Lasker ('læskə) *n.* **Emanuel.** 1868–1941, German chess player: world champion (1894–1921).

Laski ('læskɪ) *n.* **Harold Joseph.** 1893–1950, English political scientist and socialist leader.

Las Palmas (*Spanish* las 'palmas) *n.* a port in the central Canary Islands, on NE Grand Canary: a major fuelling port on the main shipping route between Europe and South America. Pop.: 360 098 (1981).

La Spezia (*Italian* la 'spɛttsia) *n.* a port in NW Italy, in Liguria, on the **Gulf of Spezia:** the chief naval base in Italy. Pop.: 108 937 (1986).

lass (læs) *n.* a girl or young woman. [C13: from ?]

Lassa ('lɑːsə) *n.* a variant spelling of **Lhasa.**

Lassa fever ('læsə) *n.* a serious viral disease of Central West Africa, characterized by high fever and muscular pains. [from *Lassa*, the Nigerian village where it was first identified]

Lassalle (*German* la'sal) *n.* **Ferdinand** ('fɛrdinant). 1825–64, German socialist and writer: a founder of the first German workers' political party (1863), which later became the Social Democratic Party.

Lassen Peak ('læs°n) *n.* a volcano in S California, in the S Cascade Range. An area of 416 sq. km (161 sq. miles) established as **Lassen Volcanic National Park** in 1916. Height: 3187 m (10 457 ft.).

lassie ('læsɪ) *n. Inf.* a little lass; girl.

lassitude ('læsɪ,tjuːd) *n.* physical or mental weariness. [C16: from L *lassitūdō*, from *lassus* tired]

lasso (læ'suː, 'læsəʊ) *n., pl.* **-sos** *or* **-soes. 1.** a long rope or thong with a running noose at one end, used (esp. in America) for roping horses, cattle, etc.; lariat. ~*vb.* **-soing, -soed. 2.** (*tr.*) to catch as with a lasso. [C19: from Sp. *lazo*, ult. from L *laqueus* noose] —**las'soer** *n.*

Lassus ('læsəs) *n.* **Roland de.** Italian name *Orlando di Lasso.* ?1532–94, Flemish composer, noted for his mastery in both sacred and secular music.

last¹ (lɑːst) *adj.* (*often prenominal*) **1.** being, happening, or coming at the end or after all others: *the last horse in the race.* **2.** being or occurring just before the present; most recent: *last Thursday.* **3.** only remaining: *one's last cigarette.* **4.** most extreme; utmost. **5.** least suitable, appropriate, or likely: *he was the last person I would have chosen.* **6.** (esp. relating to the end of a person's life or of the world) final or ultimate: *last rites.* ~*adv.* **7.** after all others; at or in the end: *he came last.* **8.** most recently: *he was last seen in the mountains.* **9.** (*sentence modifier*) as the last or latest item. ~*n.* **10. the last. a.** a person or thing that is last. **b.** the final moment; end. **11.** one's last moments before death. **12.** the final appearance, mention, or occurrence: *we've seen the last of him.* **13. at last.** in the end; finally. **14. at long last.** finally, after difficulty, delay, or irritation. [var. of OE *latest, lætest,* sup. of LATE]

last[2] (lɑːst) *vb.* **1.** (when *intr.*, often foll. by *for*) to remain in being (for a length of time); continue: *his hatred lasted for several years.* **2.** to be sufficient for the needs of (a person) for (a length of time): *it will last us until Friday.* **3.** (when *intr.*, often foll. by *for*) to remain fresh, uninjured, or unaltered (for a certain time). ~See also **last out.** [OE *læstan*] — **'laster** *n.*

last[3] (lɑːst) *n.* **1.** the wooden or metal form on which a shoe or boot is fashioned or repaired. ~*vb.* **2.** (*tr.*) to fit (a shoe or boot) on a last. [OE *lǣste,* from *lǣst* footprint] — **'laster** *n.*

last-ditch *n.* **a.** a last resort or place of last defence. **b.** (*as modifier*): *a last-ditch effort.*

last-gasp *n.* (*modifier*) done in desperation at the last minute: *a last-gasp attempt to save the talks.*

lasting ('lɑːstɪŋ) *adj.* permanent or enduring. — **'lastingly** *adv.* — **'lastingness** *n.*

Last Judgment *n.* **the.** the occasion, after the resurrection of the dead at the end of the world, when, according to biblical tradition, God will decree the final destinies of all men according to the good and evil in their earthly lives. Also called: **the Last Day, Doomsday, Judgment Day.**

lastly ('lɑːstlɪ) *adv.* **1.** at the end or at the last point. ~*sentence connector.* **2.** finally.

last name *n.* another term for **surname.**

last out *vb.* (*intr., adv.*) **1.** to be sufficient for one's needs: *how long will our supplies last out?* **2.** to endure or survive: *some old people don't last out the winter.*

last post *n.* (in the British military services) **1.** a bugle call that orders men to retire for sleep. **2.** a similar call sounded at military funerals.

last rites *pl. n. Christianity.* religious rites prescribed for those close to death.

Last Supper *n.* **the.** the meal eaten by Christ with his disciples on the night before his Crucifixion.

Las Vegas (læs 'veɪɡəs) *n.* a city in SE Nevada: famous for luxury hotels and casinos. Pop.: 201 500 (1986 est.).

lat. *abbrev. for* latitude.

Lat. *abbrev. for* Latin.

Latakia *or* **Lattakia** (ˌlætəˈkiːə) *n.* the chief port of Syria, in the northwest: tobacco industry. Pop.: 241 000 (1987 est.). Latin name: **Laodicea ad Mare.**

latch (lætʃ) *n.* **1.** a fastening for a gate or door that consists of a bar that may be slid or lowered into a groove, hole, etc. **2.** a spring-loaded door lock that can be opened by a key from outside. **3.** Also called: **latch circuit.** *Electronics.* a logic circuit that transfers the input states to the output states when signalled. ~*vb.* **4.** to fasten, fit, or be fitted as with a latch. [OE *læccan* to seize, of Gmc origin]

latchkey ('lætʃˌkiː) *n.* **1.** a key for an outside door or gate, esp. one that lifts a latch. **2.** a supposed freedom from restrictions.

latchkey child *n.* a child who has to let himself in at home on returning from school, as his parents are out at work.

latch on *vb.* (*intr., adv.; often foll. by to*) *Inf.* **1.** to attach oneself (to). **2.** to understand.

latchstring ('lætʃˌstrɪŋ) *n.* a length of string fastened to a latch and passed through a hole in the door so that it can be opened from the other side.

late (leɪt) *adj.* **1.** occurring or arriving after the correct or expected time: *the train was late.* **2.** (*prenominal*) occurring at, scheduled for, or being at a relatively advanced time: *a late marriage.* **3.** (*prenominal*) towards or near the end: *the late evening.* **4.** at an advanced time in the evening or at night: *it was late.* **5.** (*prenominal*) occurring or being just previous to the present time: *his late remarks on industry.* **6.** (*prenominal*) having died, esp. recently: *my late grandfather.* **7.** (*prenominal*) just preceding the present or existing person or thing; former: *the late manager of this firm.* **8. of late.** recently; lately.

~*adv.* **9.** after the correct or expected time: *he arrived late.* **10.** at a relatively advanced age: *she married late.* **11.** recently; lately: *as late as yesterday he was selling books.* **12. late in the day. a.** at a late or advanced stage. **b.** too late. [OE *læt*] — **'lateness** *n.*

lateen (ləˈtiːn) *adj. Naut.* denoting a rig with a triangular sail (**lateen sail**) bent to a yard hoisted to the head of a low mast, used esp. in the Mediterranean. [C18: from F *voile latine* Latin sail]

Late Greek *n.* the Greek language from about the 3rd to the 8th centuries A.D.

Late Latin *n.* the form of written Latin used from the 3rd to the 7th centuries A.D.

lately ('leɪtlɪ) *adv.* in recent times; of late.

La Tène (læ 'tɛn) *adj.* of or relating to a Celtic culture in Europe from about the 5th to the 1st centuries B.C., characterized by a distinctive type of curvilinear decoration. [C20: from *La Tène,* a part of Lake Neuchâtel, Switzerland, where remains of this culture were first discovered]

latent ('leɪt³nt) *adj.* **1.** potential but not obvious or explicit. **2.** (of buds, spores, etc.) dormant. **3.** *Pathol.* (esp. of an infectious disease) not yet revealed or manifest. [C17: from L *latent-,* from *latēre* to lie hidden] — **'latency** *n.* — **'latently** *adv.*

latent heat *n.* (*no longer in technical usage*) the heat evolved or liberated when a substance changes phase without any change in its temperature.

latent image *n. Photog.* the invisible image produced by the action of light, etc., on silver halide crystals suspended in the emulsion of a photographic material. It becomes visible after development.

later ('leɪtə) *adj., adv.* **1.** the comparative of **late.** ~*adv.* **2.** afterwards; subsequently.

lateral ('lætərəl) *adj.* **1.** of or relating to the side or sides: *a lateral blow.* ~*n.* **2.** a lateral object, part, passage, or movement. [C17: from L *laterālis,* from *latus* side] — **'laterally** *adv.*

lateral thinking *n.* a way of solving problems by employing unorthodox and apparently illogical means.

laterite ('lætəˌraɪt) *n.* any of a group of residual insoluble deposits of ferric and aluminium oxides: formed by weathering of rocks in tropical regions. [C19: from L *later* brick]

latest ('leɪtɪst) *adj., adv.* **1.** the superlative of **late.** ~*adj.* **2.** most recent, modern, or new: *the latest fashions.* ~*n.* **3. at the latest.** no later than the time specified. **4. the latest.** *Inf.* the most recent fashion or development.

latex ('leɪtɛks) *n., pl.* **latexes** *or* **latices** ('læti,siːz). **1.** a whitish milky fluid containing protein, starch, alkaloids, etc., that is produced by many plants. Latex from the rubber tree is used in the manufacture of rubber. **2.** a suspension of synthetic rubber or plastic in water, used in the manufacture of synthetic rubber products, etc. [C19: NL, from L: liquid]

lath (lɑːθ) *n., pl.* **laths** (lɑːðz, lɑːθs). **1.** one of several thin narrow strips of wood used to provide a supporting framework for plaster, tiles, etc. **2.** expanded sheet metal, wire mesh, etc., used to provide backing for plaster or rendering. **3.** any thin strip of wood. ~*vb.* **4.** (*tr.*) to attach laths to (a ceiling, roof, floor, etc.). [OE *lætt*]

lathe (leɪð) *n.* **1.** a machine for shaping or boring metal, wood, etc., in which the workpiece is turned about a horizontal axis against a fixed tool. ~*vb.* **2.** (*tr.*) to shape or bore (a workpiece) on a lathe. [? C15 *lath* a support, from ON]

lather ('lɑːðə) *n.* **1.** foam formed by the action of soap or a detergent in water. **2.** foam formed by other liquid, such as the saliva of a horse. **3.** *Inf.* a state of agitation. ~*vb.* **4.** to coat or become coated with lather. **5.** (*intr.*) to form a lather. **6.** (*tr.*) *Inf.* to beat; flog. [OE *lēathor* soap] — **'lathery** *adj.*

lathi ('lɑːtɪ) *n., pl.* **-this.** a long heavy wooden stick used as a weapon in India, esp. by the police. [Hindi]

Latimer ('lætɪmə) *n.* **Hugh.** ?1485–1555, English Protestant bishop: burnt at the stake for heresy under Mary I.

Latin ('lætɪn) *n.* **1.** the language of ancient Rome and the Roman Empire and of the educated in medieval Europe. Having originally been the language of Latium in W central Italy, belonging to the Italic branch of the Indo-European family, it later formed the basis of the Romance group. **2.** a member of any of those peoples whose languages are derived from Latin. **3.** an inhabitant of ancient Latium. ~*adj.* **4.** of or relating to the Latin language, the ancient Latins, or Latium. **5.** characteristic of or relating to those peoples whose languages are derived from Latin. **6.** of or relating to the Roman Catholic Church. [OE *latin* and *læden* Latin, language, from L *Latīnus* of Latium]

Latina (*Italian* la'ti:na) *n.* a city in W central Italy, in Lazio: built as a planned town in 1932 on reclaimed land of the Pontine Marshes. Pop.: 93 799 (1981). Former name (until 1947): **Littoria.**

Latin America *n.* those areas of America whose official languages are Spanish and Portuguese, derived from Latin: South America, Central America, Mexico, and certain islands in the Caribbean. —**Latin American** *n., adj.*

Latinate ('lætɪˌneɪt) *adj.* (of writing, vocabulary, etc.) imitative of or derived from Latin.

Latinism ('lætɪˌnɪzəm) *n.* a word, idiom, or phrase borrowed from Latin.

Latinist ('lætɪnɪst) *n.* a person who studies or is proficient in Latin.

Latinize *or* **-ise** ('lætɪˌnaɪz) *vb.* (*tr.*) **1.** to translate into Latin or Latinisms. **2.** to cause to acquire Latin style or customs. **3.** to bring Roman Catholic influence to bear upon (the form of religious ceremonies, etc.). —,**Latini'zation** *or* **-i'sation** *n.* —'**Latin,izer** *or* -,**iser** *n.*

Latin Quarter *n.* an area of Paris, on the S bank of the River Seine: contains the city's main educational establishments; centre for students and artists.

latish ('leɪtɪʃ) *adj., adv.* rather late.

latitude ('lætɪˌtjuːd) *n.* **1. a.** an angular distance measured in degrees north or south of the equator (latitude 0°). **b.** (*often pl.*) a region considered with regard to its distance from the equator. **2.** scope for freedom of action, thought, etc.; freedom from restriction: *his parents gave him a great deal of latitude.* [C14: from L *lātitūdō,* from *lātus* broad] —,**lati'tudinal** *adj.* —,**lati'tudinally** *adv.*

latitudinarian (,lætɪˌtjuːdɪ'nɛərɪən) *adj.* **1.** permitting or marked by freedom of attitude or behaviour, esp. in religious matters. ~*n.* **2.** a person with latitudinarian views. [C17: from L *lātitūdō* breadth, infl. in form by TRINITARIAN] —,**lati,tudi'narianism** *n.*

Latium ('leɪʃɪəm) *n.* a region of W central Italy, on the Tyrrhenian Sea: less extensive ancient territory inhabited by the Latin people from the 10th century B.C. until dominated by Rome (4th century B.C.); includes the plain of the lower Tiber, the reclaimed Pontine Marshes, and Campagna. Capital: Rome. Pop.: 5 116 125 (1986 est.). Area: 17 203 sq. km (6709 sq. miles). Italian name: **Lazio.**

Latona (lə'təʊnə) *n.* the Roman name of **Leto.**

Latour (*French* latur) *n.* **Maurice Quentin de** (mɔris kɑ̃tɛ̃ də) 1704–88, French pastellist noted for the vivacity of his portraits.

La Tour (*French* la tur) *n.* **Georges de** (ʒɔrʒ də). ?1593–1652, French painter, esp. of candlelit religious scenes.

latria (lə'traɪə) *n. R.C. Church, theol.* the adoration that may be offered to God alone. [C16: via L from Gk *latreia* worship]

latrine (lə'triːn) *n.* a lavatory, as in a barracks, camp, etc. [C17: from F, from L *lātrīna,* shortened form of *lavātrīna* bath, from *lavāre* to wash]

-latry *n. combining form.* indicating worship of or excessive veneration of: *idolatry; Mariolatry.* [from Gk *-latria,* from *latreia* worship] —**-latrous** *adj. combining form.*

latter ('lætə) *adj.* (*prenominal*) **1. a.** denoting the second or second mentioned of two: distinguished from *former.* **b.** (*as n.; functioning as sing. or pl.*): *the latter is not important.* **2.** near or nearer the end: *the latter part of a film.* **3.** more advanced in time or sequence; later. [OE *lætra*]

▷ **Usage.** In careful usage, *latter* is used when only two items are in question: *he gave the money to Christopher and not to John, the latter being less in need of it. Last-named* is used to refer to the last-named of three or more items.

latter-day *adj.* present-day; modern.

Latter-day Saint *n.* a more formal name for a **Mormon.**

latterly ('lætəlɪ) *adv.* recently; lately.

lattice ('lætɪs) *n.* **1.** Also called: **latticework.** an open framework of strips of wood, metal, etc., arranged to form an ornamental pattern. **2. a.** a gate, screen, etc., formed of such a framework. **b.** (*as modifier*): *a lattice window.* **3.** something, such as a decorative or heraldic device, resembling such a framework. **4.** an array of objects or

points in a periodic pattern in two or three dimensions, esp. an array of atoms, ions, etc., in a crystal or an array of points indicating their positions in space. ~*vb.* **5.** to make, adorn, or supply with a lattice or lattices. [C14: from OF *lattis,* from *latte* LATH] —'**latticed** *adj.*

Latvia ('lætvɪə) *n.* the unofficial name of **Latvian Soviet Socialist Republic.**

Latvian ('lætvɪən) *adj.* **1.** of or relating to Latvia, its people, or their language. ~*n.* **2.** Also called: **Lettish.** an official language of the Latvian SSR. **3.** a native or inhabitant of Latvia.

Latvian Soviet Socialist Republic *n.* an administrative division of the W Soviet Union, on the Gulf of Riga and the Baltic Sea. Capital: Riga. Pop.: 2 600 000 (1987). Area: 63 700 sq. km (25 590 sq. miles).

laud (lɔːd) *Literary.* ~*vb.* **1.** (*tr.*) to praise or glorify. ~*n.* **2.** praise or glorification. [C14: vb. from L *laudāre;* n. from *laudēs,* pl. of L *laus* praise]

Laud (lɔːd) *n.* **William.** 1573–1645, English prelate; archbishop of Canterbury (1633–45). His persecution of Puritans and his High Church policies in England and Scotland were a cause of the Civil War; he was impeached by the Long Parliament (1640) and executed. —'**Laudian** *adj.*

Lauda (*German* 'lauda) *n.* **Niki** ('nɪkɪ). born 1949, Austrian motor-racing driver.

laudable ('lɔːdəbəl) *adj.* deserving or worthy of praise; admirable; commendable. —'**laudableness** *or* ,**lauda'bility** *n.* —'**laudably** *adv.*

laudanum ('lɔːdənəm) *n.* **1.** a tincture of opium. **2.** (formerly) any medicine of which opium was the main ingredient. [C16: NL, name chosen by Paracelsus for a preparation prob. containing opium]

laudation (lɔː'deɪʃən) *n.* a formal word for **praise.**

laudatory ('lɔːdətərɪ, -trɪ) *or* **laudative** *adj.* expressing or containing praise; eulogistic.

Lauder ('lɔːdə) *n.* **Sir Harry.** real name *Hugh MacLennan.* 1870–1950, Scottish ballad singer and music-hall comedian.

lauds (lɔːdz) *n.* (*functioning as sing. or pl.*) *Chiefly R.C. Church.* the traditional morning prayer, constituting with matins the first of the seven canonical hours. [C14: see LAUD]

Laue (*German* 'lauə) *n.* **Max Theodor Felix von** (maks 'teːodoːr 'feːlɪks fɔn). 1879–1960, German physicist. He pioneered the technique of measuring the wavelengths of x-rays by their diffraction by crystals and contributed to the theory of relativity: Nobel prize for physics 1914.

laugh (lɑːf) *vb.* **1.** (*intr.*) to express or manifest emotion, esp. mirth or amusement, typically by expelling air from the lungs in short bursts to produce an inarticulate voiced noise, with the mouth open. **2.** (*intr.*) (esp. of certain mammals or birds) to make a noise resembling a laugh. **3.** (*tr.*) to utter or express with laughter: *he laughed his derision at the play.* **4.** (*tr.*) to bring or force (someone, esp. oneself) into a certain condition by laughter: *he laughed himself sick.* **5.** (*intr.; foll. by at*) to make fun (of); jeer (at). **6. laugh up one's sleeve.** to laugh or have grounds for amusement, self-satisfaction, etc., secretly. **7. laugh on the other side of one's face.** to show sudden disappointment or shame after appearing cheerful or confident. ~*n.* **8.** the act or an instance of laughing. **9.** a manner of laughter. **10.** *Inf.* a person or thing that causes laughter: *that holiday was a laugh.* **11. the last laugh.** the final success in an argument, situation, etc., after previous defeat. ~See also **laugh off.** [OE *lœhan, hliehhen*] —'**lom laugher** *n.* —'**laughing** *n., adj.* —'**laughingly** *adv.*

laughable ('lɑːfəbəl) *adj.* **1.** producing scorn; ludicrous: *he offered me a laughable sum for the picture.* **2.** arousing laughter. —'**laughableness** *n.* —'**laughably** *adv.*

laughing gas *n.* another name for **nitrous oxide.**

laughing jackass *n.* another name for the **kookaburra.**

laughing stock *n.* an object of humiliating ridicule.

laugh off *vb.* (*tr., adv.*) to treat or dismiss lightly, esp. with stoicism.

laughter ('lɑːftə) *n.* **1.** the action of or noise produced by laughing. **2.** the experience or manifestation of mirth, amusement, scorn, or joy. [OE *hleahtor*]

Laughton ('lɔːtən) *n.* **Charles.** 1899–1962, U.S. actor, born in England: noted esp. for his films of the 1930s, such as *The Private Life of Henry VIII* (1933), for which he won an Oscar, and *Mutiny on the Bounty* (1935).

Launceston ('lɔːnsəstən) *n.* a city in Australia, the chief port of the island state of Tasmania on the Tamar River, 64 km (40 miles) from Bass Strait. Pop.: 88 486 (1986).

launch[1] (lɔːntʃ) *vb.* **1.** to move (a vessel) into the water. **2.** to move (a newly built vessel) into the water for the first time. **3.** (*tr.*) **a.** to start off or set in motion: *to launch a scheme.* **b.** to put (a new product) on the market. **4.** (*tr.*) to propel with force. **5.** to involve (oneself) totally and enthusiastically: *to launch oneself into work.* **6.** (*tr.*) to set (a missile, spacecraft, etc.) into motion. **7.** (*intr.; foll. by into*) to start talking or writing (about): *he launched into a story.* **8.** (*intr.; usually foll. by out*) to start (out) on a fresh course. ~*n.* **9.** an act or instance of launching. [C14: from Anglo-F *lancher*, from LL *lanceāre* to use a lance, hence, to set in motion. See LANCE] — '**launcher** *n.*

launch[2] (lɔːntʃ) *n.* **1.** a motor driven boat used chiefly as a transport boat. **2.** the largest of the boats of a man-of-war. [C17: via Sp. *lancha* and Port. from Malay *lancharan* boat, from *lanchar* speed]

launching pad *or* **launch pad** *n.* a platform from which a spacecraft, rocket, etc., is launched.

launch window *n.* the limited period during which a spacecraft can be launched on a particular mission.

launder ('lɔːndə) *vb.* **1.** to wash and often also iron (clothes, linen, etc.). **2.** (*intr.*) to be capable of being laundered without shrinking, fading, etc. **3.** (*tr.*) to make (money illegally obtained) appear to be legally gained by passing it through foreign banks or legitimate enterprises. [C14 (*n.*, meaning: a person who washes linen): changed from *lavender* washerwoman, from OF *lavandiere*, ult. from L *lavāre* to wash] — '**launderer** *n.*

Launderette (,lɔːndə'rɛt, lɔːn'drɛt) *Brit. & N.Z. trademark.* a commercial establishment where clothes can be washed and dried, using coin-operated machines. Also called (U.S., Canad., and N.Z.): **Laundromat.**

laundress ('lɔːndrɪs) *n.* a woman who launders clothes, sheets, etc., for a living.

laundry ('lɔːndrɪ) *n., pl.* **-dries. 1.** a place where clothes and linen are washed and ironed. **2.** the clothes or linen washed and ironed. **3.** the act of laundering. [C16: changed from C14 *lavendry*; see LAUNDER]

laundryman ('lɔːndrɪmən) *or* (*fem.*) **laundrywoman** *n., pl.* **-men** *or* **-women. 1.** a person who collects or delivers laundry. **2.** a person who works in a laundry.

Laurasia (lɔː'reɪʃə) *n.* one of the two ancient supercontinents comprising what are now North America, Greenland, Europe, and Asia (excluding India). [C20: from NL *Laur(entia)* (referring to the ancient N American landmass, from *Laurentian* strata of the Canadian Shield) + (*Eur)asia*]

laureate ('lɔːrɪɪt) *adj.* (*usually immediately postpositive*) **1.** *Literary.* crowned with laurel leaves as a sign of honour. ~*n.* **2.** short for **poet laureate. 3.** a person honoured with an award for art or science: *a Nobel laureate.* **4.** *Rare.* a person honoured with the laurel crown or wreath. [C14: from L *laureātus*, from *laurea* LAUREL] — '**laureate,ship** *n.*

laurel ('lɒrəl) *n.* **1.** Also called: **bay, bay laurel, sweet bay, true laurel.** a small Mediterranean evergreen tree with glossy aromatic leaves, used for flavouring in cooking, and small blackish berries. **2.** a similar and related tree of the Canary Islands and Azores. **3.** short for **mountain laurel. 4. spurge laurel.** a European evergreen shrub, *Daphne laureola,* with glossy leaves and small green flowers. **5.** (*pl.*) a wreath of true laurel, worn on the head as an emblem of victory or honour in classical times. **6.** (*pl.*) honour, distinction, or fame. **7. look to one's laurels.** to be on guard against one's rivals. **8. rest on one's laurels.** to be satisfied with distinction won by past achievements and cease to strive for further achievements. ~*vb.* **-relling, -relled** *or U.S.* **-reling, -reled. 9.** (*tr.*) to crown with laurels. [C13 *lorer,* from OF *lorier* laurel tree, ult. from L *laurus*]

Laurel and Hardy ('lɔrəl; 'hɑːdɪ) *n.* a team of U.S. film comedians, **Stan Laurel,** 1890–1965, born in Britain, the thin one, and his partner, **Oliver Hardy,** 1892–1957, the fat one.

Laurentian (lɔː'rɛnʃən) *adj.* Also: **Lawrentian.** of or resembling the style of D. H. or T. E. Lawrence. **2.** of, relating to, or situated near the St Lawrence River.

Laurentian Mountains *pl. n.* a range of low mountains in E Canada, in Quebec between the St Lawrence River

and Hudson Bay. Highest point: 1191 m (3905 ft.). Also called: **Laurentides** ('lɔːrən,taɪdz).

Laurentian Shield *n.* another name for the **Canadian Shield.** Also: **Laurentian Plateau.**

Laurier ('lɒrɪə) *n.* Sir **Wilfrid.** 1841–1919, Canadian Liberal statesman; the first French-Canadian prime minister (1896–1911).

laurustinus (,lɔːrə'staɪnəs) *n.* a Mediterranean shrub with glossy evergreen leaves and white or pink fragrant flowers. [C17: from NL, from L *laurus* laurel]

Lausanne (ləʊ'zæn; *French* lozan) *n.* a city in W Switzerland, capital of Vaud canton, on Lake Geneva; cultural and commercial centre; university (1537). Pop.: 125 000 (1985).

Lautrec (*French* lo'trɛk) *n.* See (Henri de) **Toulouse-Lautrec.**

lav (læv) *n. Brit. inf.* short for **lavatory.**

lava ('lɑːvə) *n.* **1.** magma emanating from volcanoes. **2.** any extrusive igneous rock formed by the solidification of lava. [C18: from It., from L *lavāre* to wash]

lavabo (lə'veɪbəʊ) *n., pl.* **-boes** *or* **-bos.** *Chiefly R.C. Church.* **1. a.** the ritual washing of the celebrant's hands after the offertory at Mass. **b.** (*as modifier*): *lavabo basin; lavabo towel.* **2.** another name for **washbasin. 3.** a trough for washing in a convent or monastery. [C19: from L: I shall wash, the opening of Psalm 26:6]

lavage ('lævɪdʒ, læ'vɑːʒ) *n. Med.* the washing out of a hollow organ by flushing with water. [C19: via F, from L *lavāre* to wash]

Laval[1] (lə'væl) *n.* a city in SE Canada, in Quebec: a NW suburb of Montreal. Pop.: 284 164 (1986).

Laval[2] (*French* laval) *n.* **Pierre** (pjɛr). 1883–1945, French statesman. He was premier of France (1931–32; 1935–36) and premier of the Vichy government (1942–44). He was executed for collaboration with Germany.

lavatorial (,lævə'tɔːrɪəl) *adj.* characterized by excessive mention of the excretory functions; vulgar or scatological: *lavatorial humour.*

lavatory ('lævətərɪ, -trɪ) *n., pl.* **-ries. a.** a sanitary installation for receiving and disposing of urine and faeces, consisting of a bowl fitted with a water-flushing device and connected to a drain. **b.** a room containing such an installation. Also called: **toilet, water closet, WC.** [C14: from LL *lavātōrium,* from L *lavāre* to wash]

lavatory paper *n. Brit.* another name for **toilet paper.**

lave (leɪv) *vb.* an archaic word for **wash.** [OE *lafian,* ?from L *lavāre* to wash]

lavender ('lævəndə) *n.* **1.** any of various perennial shrubs or herbaceous plants of the labiate family, esp. *Lavandula vera,* cultivated for its mauve or blue flowers and as the source of a fragrant oil (**oil of lavender**). **2.** the dried parts of *L. vera,* used to perfume clothes. **3.** a pale or light bluish-purple colour. **4.** perfume scented with lavender. [C13 *lavendre,* via F from Med. L *lavendula,* from ?]

laver ('leɪvə) *n. Old Testament.* a large basin of water used by the priests for ritual ablutions. [C14: from OF *laveoir,* from LL *lavātōrium* washing place]

Laver ('leɪvə) *n.* **Rod(ney).** born 1938, Australian tennis player: Wimbledon champion 1961, 1962, 1968, 1969; U.S. champion 1962, 1969.

lavish ('lævɪʃ) *adj.* **1.** prolific, abundant, or profuse. **2.** generous; unstinting; liberal. **3.** extravagant; prodigal; wasteful: *lavish expenditure.* ~*vb.* **4.** (*tr.*) to give, expend, or apply abundantly, generously, or in profusion. [C15: adj. use of *lavas* profusion, from OF *lavasse* torrent, from L *lavāre* to wash] — '**lavisher** *n.* — '**lavishly** *adv.* — '**lavishness** *n.*

Lavoisier (*French* lavwazje) *n.* **Antoine Laurent** (ɑ̃twan lɔrɑ̃). 1743–94, French chemist; one of the founders of modern chemistry. He disproved the phlogiston theory, named oxygen, and discovered its importance in respiration and combustion.

law (lɔː) *n.* **1.** a rule or set of rules, enforceable by the courts regulating the relationship between the state and its subjects, and the conduct of subjects towards one another. **2. a.** a rule or body of rules made by the legislature. See **statute law. b.** a rule or body of rules made by a municipal or other authority. See **bylaw. 3. a.** the condition and control enforced by such rules. **b.** (*in combination*): *lawcourt.* **4. law and order. a.** the policy of strict enforcement of the law, esp. against crime and violence. **b.** (*as modifier*): *law-and-order candidate.* **5.** a rule of conduct: *a law of etiquette*. **6.** one of a set of rules governing a particular field of activity: *the laws of tennis*. **7. the law. a.** the legal or judicial system. **b.** the profession or practice of law. **c.** *Inf.* the police or a policeman. **8.** Also called: **law of nature.** a generalization based on a recurring fact or event. **9.** the science or knowledge of law; jurisprudence. **10.** the principles originating and formerly applied only in courts of common law. Cf. **equity** (sense 3). **11.** a general principle, formula, or rule describing a phenomenon in mathematics, science, philosophy, etc.: *the laws of thermodynamics*. **12.** Also called: **Law of Moses.** (*often cap.; preceded by the*) the body of laws contained in the first five books of the Old Testament. **13. go to law.** to resort to legal proceedings on some matter. **14. lay down the law.** to speak in an authoritative or dogmatic manner. ~Related adjs.: **judicial, juridical, legal.** [OE *lagu*, from ON]

Law (lɔː) *n.* **1. Andrew Bonar** ('bɒnə). 1858–1923, British Conservative statesman, born in Canada; prime minister (1922–23). **2. John.** 1671–1729, Scottish financier. He founded the first bank in France (1716) and the Mississippi Scheme for the development of Louisiana (1717), which collapsed due to excessive speculation.

law-abiding *adj.* adhering more or less strictly to the laws: *a law-abiding citizen.*

law agent *n.* (in Scotland) a solicitor entitled to appear for a client in any Sheriff Court.

lawbreaker ('lɔːˌbreɪkə) *n.* a person who breaks the law. — **'law,breaking** *n., adj.*

law centre *n. Brit.* an independent service financed by a local authority, which provides free legal advice and information to the general public.

Lawes (lɔːz) *n.* **1. Henry.** 1596–1662, English composer, noted for his music for Milton's masque *Comus* (1634) and for his settings of some of Robert Herrick's poems. **2.** his brother, **William.** 1602–45, English composer, noted for his harmonically experimental instrumental music.

lawful ('lɔːfʊl) *adj.* allowed, recognized, or sanctioned by law; legal. — **'lawfully** *adv.* — **'lawfulness** *n.*

lawgiver ('lɔːˌgɪvə) *n.* **1.** the giver of a code of laws. **2.** Also called: **lawmaker.** a maker of laws. — **'law,giving** *n., adj.*

lawks (lɔːks) *interj. Brit.* an expression of surprise or dismay. [C18: var. of *Lord!*, prob. infl. in form by ALACK]

lawless ('lɔːlɪs) *adj.* **1.** without law. **2.** disobedient to the law. **3.** contrary to or heedless of the law. **4.** uncontrolled; unbridled: *lawless rage*. — **'lawlessly** *adv.* — **'lawlessness** *n.*

Law Lords *pl. n.* members of the House of Lords who sit as the highest court of appeal.

lawn[1] (lɔːn) *n.* a flat and usually level area of mown and cultivated grass. [C16: changed form of C14 *launde*, from OF *lande*, of Celtic origin] — **'lawny** *adj.*

lawn[2] (lɔːn) *n.* a fine linen or cotton fabric, used for clothing. [C15: prob. from *Laon*, town in France where made] — **'lawny** *adj.*

lawn mower *n.* a hand-operated or power-operated machine for cutting grass on lawns.

lawn tennis *n.* **1.** tennis played on a grass court. **2.** the formal name for **tennis.**

law of averages *n.* (popularly) the expectation that a possible event is bound to occur regularly with a frequency approximating to its probability.

law of supply and demand *n.* the theory that the price of an article or service is determined by the interaction of supply and demand.

law of the jungle *n.* a state of ruthless competition or self-interest.

law of thermodynamics *n.* any of three principles governing the relationships between different forms of energy. The **first law** (conservation of energy) states that energy can be transformed but not destroyed. The **second law** states that in any irreversible process entropy always increases. The **third law** states that it is impossible to reduce the temperature of a system to absolute zero in a finite number of steps.

Lawrence ('lɒrəns) *n.* **1. D(avid) H(erbert).** 1885–1930, English novelist, poet, and short-story writer. Many of his works deal with the destructiveness of modern industrial society, contrasted with the beauty of nature and instinct, esp. the sexual impulse. His novels include *Sons and Lovers* (1913), *The Rainbow* (1915), *Women in Love* (1920),

and *Lady Chatterley's Lover* (1928). **2. Ernest Orlando.** 1901–58, U.S. physicist, who invented the cyclotron (1931): Nobel prize for physics 1939. **3. Gertrude.** 1898–1952, English actress, noted esp. for her roles in comedies such as Noël Coward's *Private Lives* (1930). **4.** Sir **Thomas.** 1769–1830, English portrait painter. **5.** **T(homas) E(dward),** known as *Lawrence of Arabia*. 1888–1935, British soldier and writer. He took a major part in the Arab revolt against the Turks (1916–18), proving himself an outstanding guerrilla leader. He described his experiences in *The Seven Pillars of Wisdom* (1926).

lawrencium (lɒ'rɛnsɪəm) *n.* an element artificially produced from californium. Symbol: Lr; atomic no.: 103; half-life of most stable isotope, ^{256}Lr: 35 seconds. [C20: after Ernest O. LAWRENCE]

Lawrentian (lɔː'rɛnʃən) *adj.* a variant spelling of **Laurentian** (sense 1).

Lawson ('lɔːsən) *n.* **1. Henry Archibald.** 1867–1922, Australian poet and short-story writer, whose work is taken as being most representative of the Australian outback, esp. in *While the Billy Boils* (1896) and *Joe Wilson and his Mates* (1901). **2. Nigel.** born 1932, British Conservative politician; Chancellor of the Exchequer from 1983.

lawsuit ('lɔːˌsuːt) *n.* a proceeding in a court of law brought by one party against another, esp. a civil action.

law term *n.* **1.** an expression or word used in law. **2.** any of various periods of time appointed for the sitting of law courts.

lawyer ('lɔːjə, 'lɔɪə) *n.* a member of the legal profession, esp. a solicitor. [C14: from LAW]

lax (læks) *adj.* **1.** lacking firmness; not strict. **2.** lacking precision or definition. **3.** not taut. **4.** *Phonetics.* (of a speech sound) pronounced with little muscular effort. [C14 (orig. used with reference to the bowels): from L *laxus* loose] — **'laxly** *adv.* — **'laxity** or **'laxness** *n.*

laxative ('læksətɪv) *n.* **1.** an agent stimulating evacuation of faeces. ~*adj.* **2.** stimulating evacuation of faeces. [C14 (orig.: relaxing): from Med. L *laxātīvus*, from L *laxāre* to loosen]

lay[1] (leɪ) *vb.* **laying, laid.** (*mainly tr.*) **1.** to put in a low or horizontal position; cause to lie: *to lay a cover on a bed*. **2.** to place, put, or be in a particular state or position: *he laid his finger on his lips*. **3.** (*intr.*) *Dialect or not standard*. to be in a horizontal position; lie: *he often lays in bed all the morning*. **4.** (sometimes foll. by *down*) to establish as a basis: *to lay a foundation for discussion*. **5.** to place or dispose in the proper position: *to lay a carpet*. **6.** to arrange (a table) for eating a meal. **7.** to prepare (a fire) for lighting by arranging fuel in the grate. **8.** (*also intr.*) (of birds, esp. the domestic hen) to produce (eggs). **9.** to present or put forward: *he laid his case before the magistrate*. **10.** to impute or attribute: *all the blame was laid on him*. **11.** to arrange, devise, or prepare: *to lay a trap*. **12.** to place, set, or locate: *the scene is laid in London*. **13.** to make (a bet) with (someone): *I lay you five to one on Prince*. **14.** to cause to settle: *to lay the dust*. **15.** to allay; suppress: *to lay a rumour*. **16.** to bring down forcefully: *to lay a whip on someone's back*. **17.** *Taboo sl.* to have sexual intercourse with. **18.** to press down or make smooth: *to lay the nap of cloth*. **19.** (*intr.*) *Naut.* to move or go, esp. into a specified position or direction: *to lay close to the wind*. **20. lay bare.** to reveal or explain: *he laid bare his plans*. **21. lay hold of.** to seize or grasp. **22. lay oneself open.** to make oneself vulnerable (to criticism, attack, etc.). **23. lay open.** to reveal or disclose. ~*n.* **24.** the manner or position in which something lies or is placed. **25.** *Taboo sl.* **a.** an act of sexual intercourse. **b.** a sexual partner. ~See also **layabout, lay aside,** etc. [OE *lecgan*]

▷ **Usage.** In careful English, the verb *lay* is used with an object and *lie* without one: *the soldier laid down his arms; the book was lying on the table*. All careful writers and speakers observe this distinction even in informal contexts.

lay[2] (leɪ) *vb.* the past tense of **lie**[2].

lay[3] (leɪ) *adj.* **1.** of, involving, or belonging to people who are not clergymen. **2.** nonprofessional or nonspecialist; amateur. [C14: from OF *lai*, from LL *lāicus*, ult. from Gk *laos* people]

lay[4] (leɪ) *n.* **1.** a ballad or short narrative poem, esp. one intended to be sung. **2.** a song or melody. [C13: from OF *lai*, ? of Gmc origin]

layabout ('leɪə,baʊt) *n.* a lazy person; loafer.
Layamon ('laɪəmən) *or* **Lawman** ('lɔːmən) *n.* 12th-century English poet and priest; author of the *Brut*, a chronicle providing the earliest version of the Arthurian story in English.
lay analyst *n.* a person without medical qualifications who practises psychoanalysis.
Layard (lɛəd) *n.* Sir **Austen Henry.** 1817–94, English archaeologist, noted for his excavations at Nimrud and Nineveh.
lay aside *vb. (tr., adv.)* **1.** to abandon or reject. **2.** to store or reserve for future use.
lay brother *n.* a man who has taken the vows of a religious order but is not ordained.
lay-by *n.* **1.** *Brit.* a place for drivers to stop at the side of a main road. **2.** *Naut.* an anchorage in a narrow waterway, away from the channel. **3.** a small railway siding where rolling stock may be stored or parked. **4.** *Austral. & N.Z.* a system of payment whereby a buyer pays a deposit on an article, which is reserved for him until he has paid the full price. ~*vb.* **lay by.** *(tr., adv.)* **5.** to set aside or save for future needs.
lay days *pl. n.* **1.** *Commerce.* the number of days permitted for the loading or unloading of a ship without payment of demurrage. **2.** *Naut.* the time during which a ship is kept from sailing because of loading, bad weather, etc.
lay down *vb. (tr., adv.)* **1.** to place on the ground, etc. **2.** to relinquish or discard: *to lay down one's life.* **3.** to formulate (a rule, principle, etc.). **4.** to build or begin to build: *the railway was laid down as far as Chester.* **5.** to record (plans) on paper. **6.** to convert (land) into pasture. **7.** to store or stock: *to lay down wine.* **8.** *Inf.* to wager or bet. **9.** *Inf.* to record (tracks) in a studio.
layer ('leɪə) *n.* **1.** a thickness of some homogeneous substance, such as a stratum or a coating on a surface. **2.** a laying hen. **3.** *Horticulture.* a shoot or branch rooted during layering. ~*vb.* **4.** to form or make a layer of (something). **5.** to take root or cause to take root by layering. [C14 *leyer, legger,* from LAY[1] + -ER[1]]
layering ('leɪərɪŋ) *n. Horticulture.* a method of propagation that induces a shoot to take root while it is still attached to the parent plant.
layette (leɪ'ɛt) *n.* a complete set of articles, including clothing, bedclothes, and other accessories, for a newborn baby. [C19: from F, from OF, from *laie,* from MDu. *laege* box]
lay figure *n.* **1.** an artist's jointed dummy, used in place of a live model, esp. for studying effects of drapery. **2.** a person considered to be subservient or unimportant. [C18: from obs. *layman,* from Du. *leeman,* lit.: joint-man]
lay in *vb. (tr., adv.)* to accumulate and store: *we must lay in food for the party.*
lay into *vb. (intr., prep.) Inf.* **1.** to attack forcefully. **2.** to berate severely.
layman ('leɪmən) *or (fem.)* **laywoman** *n., pl.* **-men** *or* **-women.** **1.** a person who is not a clergyman. **2.** a person who does not have specialized or professional knowledge of a subject: *science for the layman.*
lay off *vb.* **1.** *(tr., adv.)* to suspend from work with the intention of re-employing later: *the firm had to lay off 100 men.* **2.** *(intr.) Inf.* to leave (a person, thing, or activity) alone: *lay off me, will you!* **3.** *(tr., adv.)* to mark off the boundaries of. ~*n.* **lay-off. 4.** the act of suspending employees. **5.** a period of imposed unemployment.
lay on *vb. (tr., adv.)* **1.** to provide or supply: *to lay on entertainment.* **2.** *Brit.* to install: *to lay on electricity.* **3. lay it on.** *Sl.* **a.** to exaggerate, esp. when flattering. **b.** to charge an exorbitant price. **c.** to punish or strike harshly.
lay out *vb. (tr., adv.)* **1.** to arrange or spread out. **2.** to prepare (a corpse) for burial. **3.** to plan or contrive. **4.** *Inf.* to spend (money), esp. lavishly. **5.** *Inf.* to knock unconscious. ~*n.* **layout. 6.** the arrangement or plan of something, such as a building. **7.** the arrangement of written material, photographs, or other artwork on an advertisement or page in a book, newspaper, etc. **8.** a preliminary plan indicating this. **9.** a drawing showing the relative disposition of parts in a machine, etc. **10.** the act of laying out. **11.** something laid out.
lay over *U.S.* ~*vb. (adv.)* **1.** *(tr.)* to postpone for future action. **2.** *(intr.)* to make a temporary stop in a journey. ~*n.* **layover. 3.** a break in a journey, esp. in waiting for a connection.

lay reader *n.* **1.** *Church of England.* a person licensed by a bishop to conduct religious services other than the Eucharist. **2.** *R.C. Church.* a layman chosen from among the congregation to read the epistle at Mass.
lay up *vb. (tr., adv.)* **1.** to store or reserve for future use. **2.** *(usually passive) Inf.* to incapacitate or confine through illness.
lazar ('læzə) *n.* an archaic word for **leper.** [C14: via OF and Med. L, after LAZARUS]
lazaretto (,læzə'rɛtəʊ), **lazaret,** *or* **lazarette** (,læzə'rɛt) *n., pl.* **-rettos, -rets,** *or* **-rettes. 1.** Also called: **glory hole.** *Naut.* a small locker at the stern of a boat or a storeroom between decks of a ship. **2.** Also called: **lazar house, pesthouse.** (formerly) a hospital for persons with infectious diseases, esp. leprosy. [C16: It., from *lazzaro* LAZAR]
Lazarus ('læzərəs) *n. New Testament.* **1.** the brother of Mary and Martha, whom Jesus restored to life (John 11–12). **2.** the beggar who lay at the gate of the rich man Dives in Jesus' parable (Luke 16:19–31).
laze (leɪz) *vb.* **1.** *(intr.)* to be indolent or lazy. **2.** *(tr.; often foll. by away)* to spend (time) in indolence. ~*n.* **3.** the act or an instance of idling. [C16: back formation from LAZY]
Lazio ('lattsjo) *n.* the Italian name for **Latium.**
lazy ('leɪzɪ) *adj.* **lazier, laziest. 1.** not inclined to work or exertion. **2.** conducive to or causing indolence. **3.** moving in a languid or sluggish manner: *a lazy river.* [C16: from ?] —**'lazily** *adv.* —**'laziness** *n.*
lazybones ('leɪzɪ,bəʊnz) *n. Inf.* a lazy person.
lazy Susan *n.* a revolving tray, often divided into sections, for holding condiments, etc.
lb *abbrev. for:* **1.** pound (weight). [L: *libra*] **2.** *Cricket.* leg bye.
lbw *Cricket. abbrev. for* leg before wicket.
lc *abbrev. for:* **1.** left centre (of a stage, etc.). **2.** loco citato. [L: in the place cited] **3.** *Printing.* lower case.
L/C, l/c, *or* **lc** *abbrev. for* letter of credit.
LCD *abbrev. for:* **1.** liquid-crystal display. **2.** Also: **lcd.** lowest common denominator.
LCJ (in Britain) *abbrev. for* Lord Chief Justice.
lcm *or* **LCM** *abbrev. for* lowest common multiple.
L/Cpl *abbrev. for* lance corporal.
LDS *abbrev. for:* **1.** Latter-day Saints. **2.** laus Deo semper. [L: praise be to God for ever] **3.** (in Britain) Licentiate in Dental Surgery.
lea (liː) *n.* **1.** *Poetic.* a meadow or field. **2.** land that has been sown with grass seed. [OE *lēah*]
LEA (in Britain) *abbrev. for* Local Education Authority.
leach (liːtʃ) *vb.* **1.** to remove or be removed from a substance by a percolating liquid. **2.** to lose or cause to lose soluble substances by the action of a percolating liquid. ~*n.* **3.** the act or process of leaching. **4.** a substance that is leached or the constituents removed by leaching. **5.** a porous vessel for leaching. [C17: var. of obs. *letch* to wet, ?from OE *leccan* to water] —**'leacher** *n.*
Leach (liːtʃ) *n.* **Bernard (Howell).** 1887–1979, British potter, born in Hong Kong.
Leacock ('liːkɒk) *n.* **Stephen Butler.** 1869–1944, Canadian humorist and economist: his comic works include *Literary Lapses* (1910) and *Frenzied Fiction* (1917).
lead[1] (liːd) *vb.* **leading, led. 1.** to show the way to (an individual or a group) by going with or ahead: *lead the party into the garden.* **2.** to guide or be guided by holding, pulling, etc.: *he led the horse by its reins.* **3.** *(tr.)* to cause to act, feel, think, or behave in a certain way; induce: *he led me to believe that he would go.* **4.** (when *intr.,* foll. by *to*) (of a road, route, etc.) to serve as the means of reaching a place. **5.** *(tr.)* to go ahead so as to indicate (esp. in **lead the way**). **6.** to guide, control, or direct: *to lead an army.* **7.** *(tr.)* to direct the course of or conduct (water, a rope, or wire, etc.) along or as if along a channel. **8.** to initiate the action of (something); have the principal part in (something): *to lead a discussion.* **9.** to go at the head of or have the top position in (something): *he leads his class in geography.* **10.** *(intr.;* foll. by *with)* to have as the first or principal item: *the newspaper led with the royal birth.* **11.** *Music, Brit.* to play first violin in (an orchestra). **12.** to direct and guide (one's partner) in a dance. **13.** *(tr.)* **a.** to pass or spend: *I lead a miserable life.* **b.** to cause to pass a life of a particular kind: *to lead a person a dog's life.* **14.** *(intr.;* foll. by *to)* to tend (to) or result (in): *this will only lead to misery.* **15.** to

initiate a round of cards by putting down (the first card) or to have the right to do this: *she led a diamond.* **16.** (*intr.*) *Boxing.* to make an offensive blow, esp. as one's habitual attacking punch. ~*n.* **17. a.** the first, foremost, or most prominent place. **b.** (*as modifier*): *lead singer.* **18.** example, precedence, or leadership: *the class followed the teacher's lead.* **19.** an advance or advantage held over others: *the runner had a lead of twenty yards.* **20.** anything that guides or directs; indication; clue. **21.** another name for **leash. 22.** the act or prerogative of playing the first card in a round of cards or the card so played. **23.** the principal role in a play, film, etc., or the person playing such a role. **24. a.** the principal news story in a newspaper: *the scandal was the lead in the papers.* **b.** (*as modifier*): *lead story.* **25.** *Music.* an important entry assigned to one part. **26.** a wire, cable, or other conductor for making an electrical connection. **27.** *Boxing.* **a.** one's habitual attacking punch. **b.** a blow made with this. **28.** a deposit of metal or ore; lode. ~See also **lead off, lead on,** etc. [OE *lǣdan;* rel. to *līthan* to travel]

lead[2] (lɛd) *n.* **1.** a heavy toxic bluish-white metallic element that is highly malleable: used in alloys, accumulators, cable sheaths, paints, and as a radiation shield. Symbol: Pb; atomic no.: 82; atomic wt.: 207.2. **2.** a lead weight suspended on a line used to take soundings of the depth of water. **3.** lead weights or shot, as used in cartridges, fishing lines, etc. **4.** a thin grooved strip of lead for holding small panes of glass or pieces of stained glass. **5.** (*pl.*) **a.** thin sheets or strips of lead used as a roof covering. **b.** a flat or low-pitched roof covered with such sheets. **6.** Also called: **leading.** *Printing.* a thin strip of type metal used for spacing between lines. **7. a.** graphite used for drawing. **b.** a thin stick of this material, esp. the core of a pencil. **8.** (*modifier*) of, consisting of, relating to, or containing lead. ~*vb.* (*tr.*) **9.** to fill or treat with lead. **10.** to surround, cover, or secure with lead or leads. **11.** *Printing.* to space (type) by use of leads. [OE]

lead acetate (lɛd) *n.* a white crystalline toxic solid used in dyeing cotton and in making varnishes and enamels. Formula: Pb(CH₃COOH)₂. Systematic name: **lead ethanoate.**

Leadbelly ('lɛd,bɛli) *n.*, real name *Huddie Ledbetter.* 1888–1949, U.S. blues singer and guitarist.

leaded ('lɛdɪd) *adj.* (of windows) composed of small panes of glass held in place by thin grooved strips of lead: *leaded lights.*

leaden ('lɛdᵊn) *adj.* **1.** heavy and inert. **2.** laboured or sluggish: *leaden steps.* **3.** gloomy, spiritless, or lifeless. **4.** made partly or wholly of lead. **5.** of a dull greyish colour: *a leaden sky.* —'**leadenly** *adv.* —'**leadenness** *n.*

leader ('li:də) *n.* **1.** a person who rules, guides, or inspires others; head. **2.** *Music.* a. Also called (esp. U.S. and Canad.): **concertmaster.** the principal first violinist of an orchestra, who plays solo parts, and acts as the conductor's deputy and spokesman for the orchestra. **b.** *U.S.* a conductor or director of an orchestra or chorus. **3. a.** the leading horse or dog in a team. **b.** the first man on a climbing rope. **4.** *Chiefly Brit.* the leading editorial in a newspaper. Also: **leading article. 5.** *Angling.* another word for **trace**[2]. **6.** a strip of blank film or tape used to facilitate threading a projector, developing machine, etc. **7.** (*pl.*) *Printing.* rows of dots or hyphens used to guide the reader's eye across a page, as in a table of contents. **8.** *Bot.* any of the long slender shoots that grow from the stem or branch of a tree. **9.** *Brit.* a member of the Government having primary authority in initiating legislative business (esp. in **Leader of the House of Commons** and **Leader of the House of Lords**). —'**leaderless** *adj.* —'**leader,ship** *n.*

lead-free ('lɛd,fri:) *adj.* See **unleaded.**

lead glass (lɛd) *n.* glass that contains lead oxide as a flux.

lead-in ('li:d,ɪn) *n.* **1.** an introduction to a subject. **2.** the connection between a radio transmitter, receiver, etc., and the aerial or transmission line.

leading[1] ('li:dɪŋ) *adj.* **1.** capable of guiding, directing, or influencing. **2.** (*prenominal*) principal or primary. **3.** in the first position.

leading[2] ('lɛdɪŋ) *n.* *Printing.* another name for **lead**[2](sense 6).

leading aircraftman ('li:dɪŋ) *n.* *Brit. airforce.* the rank above aircraftman. —**leading aircraftwoman** *fem. n.*

leading edge ('li:dɪŋ) *n.* **1.** the forward edge of a propeller blade, wing, or aerofoil. Cf. **trailing edge.** ~*modifier.* **leading-edge. 2.** advanced; foremost: *leading-edge technology.*

leading light ('li:dɪŋ) *n.* an important or outstanding person, esp. in an organization.

leading note ('li:dɪŋ) *n.* *Music.* **1.** another word for **subtonic. 2.** (esp. in cadences) a note that tends most naturally to resolve to the note lying one semitone above it.

leading question ('li:dɪŋ) *n.* a question phrased in a manner that tends to suggest the desired answer, such as *What do you think of the horrible effects of pollution?*

leading rating ('li:dɪŋ) *n.* a rank in the Royal Navy comparable but junior to that of a corporal in the army.

leading reins *or U.S. & Canad.* **leading strings** ('li:dɪŋ) *pl. n.* **1.** straps or a harness and strap used to assist and control a child who is learning to walk. **2.** excessive guidance or restraint.

lead monoxide (lɛd) *n.* a poisonous insoluble oxide of lead existing in red and yellow forms: used in making glass, glazes, and cements, and as a pigment. Formula: PbO. Systematic name: **lead(II) oxide.**

lead off (li:d) *vb.* (*adv.*) **1.** to initiate the action of (something); begin. ~*n.* **lead-off. 2.** an initial move or action.

lead on (li:d) *vb.* (*tr., adv.*) to lure or entice, esp. into trouble or wrongdoing.

lead pencil (lɛd) *n.* a pencil containing a thin stick of a graphite compound.

lead poisoning (lɛd) *n.* **1.** acute or chronic poisoning by lead, characterized by abdominal pain, vomiting, convulsions, and coma. **2.** *U.S. sl.* death or injury resulting from being shot with bullets.

lead screw (li:d) *n.* a threaded rod that drives the tool carriage in a lathe.

lead tetraethyl (lɛd) *n.* another name for **tetraethyl lead.**

lead time (li:d) *n.* **1.** *Manufacturing, chiefly U.S.* the time between the design of a product and its production. **2.** *Commerce.* the time from the placing of an order to the delivery of the goods.

lead up to (li:d) *vb.* (*intr., adv. + prep.*) **1.** to act as a preliminary or introduction to. **2.** to approach (a topic) gradually or cautiously.

leaf (li:f) *n., pl.* **leaves** (li:vz). **1.** the main organ of photosynthesis and transpiration in higher plants, usually consisting of a flat green blade attached to the stem directly or by a stalk. **2.** foliage collectively. **3. in leaf.** (of shrubs, trees, etc.) having a full complement of foliage leaves. **4.** one of the sheets of paper in a book. **5.** a hinged, sliding, or detachable part, such as an extension to a table. **6.** metal in the form of a very thin flexible sheet: *gold leaf.* **7. take a leaf out of** (*or* from) **someone's book.** to imitate someone, esp. in one particular course of action. **8. turn over a new leaf.** to begin a new and improved course of behaviour. ~*vb.* **9.** (when *intr.,* usually foll. by *through*) to turn (through pages, sheets, etc.) cursorily. **10.** (*intr.*) (of plants) to produce leaves. [OE] —'**leafless** *adj.* —'**leaf,like** *adj.*

leafage ('li:fɪdʒ) *n.* a less common word for **foliage.**

leaflet ('li:flɪt) *n.* **1.** a printed and usually folded sheet of paper for distribution, usually free, esp. for advertising, giving information about a charity, etc. **2.** any of the subdivisions of a compound leaf such as a fern leaf. **3.** any small leaf or leaflike part. ~*vb.* **4.** to distribute leaflets (to).

leaf miner *n.* **1.** any of various insect larvae that bore into and feed on leaf tissue. **2.** the adult insect of any of these larvae.

leaf mould *n.* **1.** a nitrogen-rich material consisting of decayed leaves, etc., used as a fertilizer. **2.** any of various fungus diseases affecting the leaves of certain plants.

leaf spring *n.* **1.** one of a number of metal strips bracketed together in length to form a spring. **2.** the compound spring so formed.

leafstalk ('li:f,stɔ:k) *n.* the stalk attaching a leaf to a stem or branch. Technical name: **petiole.**

leafy ('li:fɪ) *adj.* **leafier, leafiest. 1.** covered with or having leaves. **2.** resembling a leaf or leaves. —'**leafiness** *n.*

league[1] (li:g) *n.* **1.** an association or union of persons, nations, etc., formed to promote the interests of its members. **2.** an association of sporting clubs that organizes matches between member teams. **3.** a class, category, or level: *he is not in the same league.* **4. in league** (with).

working or planning together with. **5.** (*modifier*) of, involving, or belonging to a league: *a league game; a league table.* ~*vb.* **leaguing, leagued. 6.** to form or be formed into a league. [C15: from OF *ligue,* from It. *liga,* ult. from L *ligāre* to bind]

league[2] (li:g) *n.* an obsolete unit of distance of varying length. It is commonly equal to 3 miles. [C14 *leuge,* from LL *leuga, leuca,* of Celtic origin]

league football *n.* **1.** Also called: **league.** *Chiefly Austral.* rugby league football. Cf. **rugby union. 2.** *Austral.* an Australian Rules competition conducted within a league. Cf. **association football.**

leaguer ('li:gə) *n. Chiefly U.S. & Canad.* a member of a league.

league table *n.* **1.** a list of sports clubs ranked in order according to their performance. **2.** a comparison of performance in any sphere.

Leah ('li:ə) *n. Old Testament.* the first wife of Jacob and elder sister of Rachel, his second wife (Genesis 29).

leak (li:k) *n.* **1. a.** a crack, hole, etc., that allows the accidental escape or entrance of fluid, light, etc. **b.** such escaping or entering fluid, light, etc. **2. spring a leak.** to develop a leak. **3.** something resembling this in effect: *a leak in the defence system.* **4.** the loss of current from an electrical conductor because of faulty insulation, etc. **5.** a disclosure of secret information. **6.** the act or an instance of leaking. **7.** a slang word for *urination.* ~*vb.* **8.** to enter or escape or allow to enter or escape through a crack, hole, etc. **9.** (when *intr.,* often foll. by *out*) to disclose (secret information) or (of secret information) to be disclosed. **10.** (*intr.*) a slang word for **urinate.** [C15: from ON] — **'leaker** *n.*

leakage ('li:kɪdʒ) *n.* **1.** the act or an instance of leaking. **2.** something that escapes or enters by a leak. **3.** *Physics.* an undesired flow of electric current, neutrons, etc.

Leakey ('li:kɪ) *n.* **1. Louis Seymour Bazett** ('bæzɪt). 1903–72, British anthropologist and archaeologist, settled in Kenya. He discovered fossil remains of manlike apes in E Africa. **2.** his son **Richard.** born 1944, Kenyan anthropologist, who discovered the remains of primitive man over 2 million years old in E Africa.

leaky ('li:kɪ) *adj.* **leakier, leakiest.** leaking or tending to leak. — **'leakiness** *n.*

leal (li:l) *adj. Arch. or Scot.* loyal; faithful. [C13: from OF *leial,* from L *lēgālis* LEGAL; rel. to LOYAL] — **'leally** *adv.* — **lealty** ('li:əltɪ) *n.*

Leamington Spa ('lemɪŋtən) *n.* a town in central England, in central Warwickshire: saline springs. Pop.: 56 538 (1985 est.). Official name: **Royal Leamington Spa.**

lean[1] (li:n) *vb.* **leaning; leant** *or* **leaned. 1.** (foll. by *against, on,* or *upon*) to rest or cause to rest against a support. **2.** to incline or cause to incline from a vertical position. **3.** (*intr.;* foll. by *to* or *towards*) to have or express a tendency or leaning. ~*n.* **4.** the condition of inclining from a vertical position. [OE *hleonian, hlinian*]

lean[2] (li:n) *adj.* **1.** (esp. of a person or animal) having no surplus flesh or bulk; not fat. **2.** not bulky or full. **3.** (of meat) having little or no fat. **4.** not rich, abundant, or satisfying. **5.** (of mixture of fuel and air) containing insufficient fuel and too much air. ~*n.* **6.** the part of meat that contains little or no fat. [OE *hlǣne,* of Gmc origin] — **'leanly** *adv.* — **'leanness** *n.*

Lean (li:n) *n.* Sir **David.** born 1908, English film director. His films include *In Which We Serve* (1942), *Blithe Spirit* (1945), *Brief Encounter* (1946), *Great Expectations* (1946), *Oliver Twist* (1948), *The Bridge on the River Kwai* (1957), *Lawrence of Arabia* (1962), *Dr Zhivago* (1965), and *A Passage to India* (1984).

lean-burn *adj.* (esp. of an internal-combustion engine) designed to use a lean mixture of fuel and air in order to reduce petrol consumption and exhaust emissions.

Leander (lɪ'ændə) *n.* (in Greek legend) a youth of Abydos, who drowned in the Hellespont in a storm on one of his nightly visits to Hero, his beloved. See also **Hero**[1].

leaning ('li:nɪŋ) *n.* a tendency or inclination.

leant (lɛnt) *vb.* a past tense and past participle of **lean**[1].

lean-to *n., pl.* **-tos. 1.** a roof that has a single slope adjoining a wall or building. **2.** a shed or outbuilding with such a roof.

leap (li:p) *vb.* **leaping; leapt** *or* **leaped. 1.** (*intr.*) to jump suddenly from one place to another. **2.** (*intr.;* often foll. by *at*) to move or react quickly. **3.** (*tr.*) to jump over. **4.** to come into prominence rapidly: *the thought leapt into*

his mind. **5.** (*tr.*) to cause (an animal, esp. a horse) to jump a barrier. ~*n.* **6.** the act of jumping. **7.** a spot from which a leap was or may be made. **8.** an abrupt change or increase. **9. a leap in the dark.** an action performed without knowledge of the consequences. **10. by leaps and bounds.** with unexpectedly rapid progress. [OE *hlēapan*] — **'leaper** *n.*

leapfrog ('li:p,frɒg) *n.* **1.** a children's game in which each player in turn leaps over the others' bent backs. ~*vb.* **-frogging, -frogged.** **2. a.** (*intr.*) to play leapfrog. **b.** (*tr.*) to leap in this way over (something). **3.** to advance or cause to advance by jumps or stages.

leapt (lept, li:pt) *vb.* a past tense and past participle of **leap.**

leap year *n.* a calendar year of 366 days, February 29 (**leap day**) being the additional day, that occurs every four years (those whose number is divisible by four) except for century years whose number is not divisible by 400.

Lear (lɪə) *n.* **Edward.** 1812–88, English humorist and painter, noted for his illustrated nonsense poems and limericks.

learn (lɜːn) *vb.* **learning; learnt** *or* **learned** (lɜːnd). **1.** (when *tr., may take a clause as object*) to gain knowledge of (something) or acquire skill in (some art or practice). **2.** (*tr.*) to commit to memory. **3.** (*tr.*) to gain by experience, example, etc. **4.** (*intr.;* often foll. by *of* or *about*) to become informed; know. **5.** *Not standard.* to teach. [OE *leornian*] — **'learnable** *adj.* — **'learner** *n.*

▷ **Usage.** Educated writers and speakers of English do not use *learn* for *teach: that will teach* (not *learn*) *him a lesson.*

learned ('lɜːnɪd) *adj.* **1.** having great knowledge or erudition. **2.** involving or characterized by scholarship. **3.** (*prenominal*) a title applied in referring to a member of the legal profession, esp. to a barrister: *my learned friend.* — **'learnedly** *adv.* — **'learnedness** *n.*

learning ('lɜːnɪŋ) *n.* **1.** knowledge gained by study; instruction or scholarship. **2.** the act of gaining knowledge.

learnt (lɜːnt) *vb.* a past tense and past participle of **learn.**

lease (li:s) *n.* **1.** a contract by which property is conveyed to a person for a specified period, usually for rent. **2.** the instrument by which such property is conveyed. **3.** the period of time for which it is conveyed. **4.** a prospect of renewed health, happiness, etc.: *a new lease of life.* ~*vb.* (*tr.*) **5.** to grant possession of (land, buildings, etc.) by lease. **6.** to take a lease of (property); hold under a lease. [C15: via Anglo-F from OF *lais* (n.), from *laissier* to let go, from L *laxāre* to loosen] — **'leasable** *adj.* — **'leaser** *n.*

leaseback ('li:s,bæk) *n.* a transaction in which the buyer leases the property to the seller.

leasehold ('li:s,həʊld) *n.* **1.** land or property held under a lease. **2.** the tenure by which such property is held. **3.** (*modifier*) held under a lease. — **'lease,holder** *n.*

leash (li:ʃ) *n.* **1.** a line or rope used to walk or control a dog or other animal; lead. **2.** something resembling this in function: *he kept a tight leash on his emotions.* **3. straining at the leash.** eagerly impatient to begin something. ~*vb.* **4.** (*tr.*) to control or secure as by a leash. [C13: from OF *laisse,* from *laissier* to loose (hence, to let a dog run on a leash), ult. from L *laxus* lax]

least (li:st) *determiner.* **1. a. the.** the superlative of **little:** *you have the least talent of anyone.* **b.** (*as pronoun; functioning as sing.*): *least isn't necessarily worst.* **2. at least. a.** if nothing else: *you should at least try.* **b.** at the least. **3. at the least.** Also: **at least.** at the minimum: *at the least you should earn a hundred pounds.* **4. in the least.** (*usually used with a negative*) in the slightest degree; at all: *I don't mind in the least.* ~*adv.* **5. the least.** superlative of **little:** *they travel the least.* ~*adj.* **6.** of very little importance. [OE *lǣst,* sup. of *lǣssa* less]

least common denominator *n.* another name for **lowest common denominator.**

least common multiple *n.* another name for **lowest common multiple.**

least squares *n.* a method for determining the best value of an unknown quantity relating one or more sets of observations or measurements, esp. to find a curve that best fits a set of data.

leastways ('li:st,weɪz) *or U.S. & Canad.* **leastwise** *adv. Inf.* at least; anyway; at any rate.

leather ('lɛðə) n. **1. a.** a material consisting of the skin of an animal made smooth and flexible by tanning, removing the hair, etc. **b.** (as modifier): leather goods. **2.** something, such as a garment, made of leather. ~vb. (tr.) **3.** to cover with leather. **4.** to whip as with a leather strap. [OE lether- (in compound words)]

Leatherhead ('lɛðə,hɛd) n. a town in S England, in Surrey. Pop.: 40 300 (1985 est.).

leatherjacket ('lɛðə,dʒækɪt) n. **1.** any of various tropical fishes having a leathery skin. **2.** the greyish-brown toughskinned larva of certain craneflies, which destroy the roots of grasses, etc.

leathern ('lɛðən) adj. Arch. made of or resembling leather.

leatherneck ('lɛðə,nɛk) n. Sl. a member of the U.S. Marine Corps. [from the custom of facing the neckband of their uniform with leather]

leathery ('lɛðərɪ) adj. having the appearance or texture of leather, esp. in toughness. —'**leatheriness** n.

leave[1] (liːv) vb. **leaving, left.** (mainly tr.) **1.** (also intr.) to go or depart (from a person or place). **2.** to cause to remain behind, often by mistake, in a place: he often leaves his keys in his coat. **3.** to cause to be or remain in a specified state: paying the bill left him penniless. **4.** to renounce or abandon: to leave a political movement. **5.** to refrain from consuming or doing something: the things we have left undone. **6.** to result in; cause: childhood problems often leave emotional scars. **7.** to entrust or commit: leave the shopping to her. **8.** to pass in a specified direction: flying out of the country, we left the cliffs on our left. **9.** to be survived by (members of one's family): he leaves a wife and two children. **10.** to bequeath: he left his investments to his children. **11.** (tr.) to have as a remainder: 37 − 14 leaves 23. **12.** Not standard. to permit; let. **13. leave (someone) alone. a.** Also: **let alone.** See let[1] (sense 6). **b.** to permit to stay or be alone. [OE læfan; rel. to belīfan to be left as a remainder] ~See also **leave off, leave out.** —'**leaver** n.
▷ **Usage.** In educated usage, leave is not used in the sense of let (allow): let him go, not leave him go.

leave[2] (liːv) n. **1.** permission to do something: he was granted leave to speak. **2. by** or **with your leave.** with your permission. **3.** permission to be absent, as from a place of work. **4.** the duration of such absence: ten days' leave. **5.** a farewell or departure (esp. in **take (one's) leave). 6. on leave.** officially excused from work or duty. **7. take leave (of).** to say farewell (to). [OE lēaf; rel. to alȳfan to permit]

leave[3] (liːv) vb. **leaving, leaved.** (intr.) to produce or grow leaves.

leaved (liːvd) adj. **a.** having a leaf or leaves; leafed. **b.** (in combination): a five-leaved stem.

leaven ('lɛvⁿn) n. also **leavening. 1.** any substance that produces fermentation in dough or batter, such as yeast, and causes it to rise. **2.** a piece of such a substance kept to ferment a new batch of dough. **3.** an agency or influence that produces a gradual change. ~vb. (tr.) **4.** to cause fermentation in (dough or batter). **5.** to pervade, causing a gradual change, esp. with some moderating or enlivening influence. [C14: via OF ult. from L levāmen relief, (hence, raising agent), from levāre to raise]

Leavenworth ('lɛvⁿn,wɜːθ, -wəθ) n. a city in NE Kansas, on the Missouri River: the state's oldest city, founded in 1854 by proslavery settlers from Missouri. Pop.: 33 656 (1980).

leave off vb. **1.** (intr.) to stop; cease. **2.** (tr., adv.) to stop wearing or using.

leave out vb. (tr., adv.) **1.** to cause to remain in the open. **2.** to omit or exclude.

leaves (liːvz) n. the plural of **leaf.**

leave-taking n. the act of departing; a farewell.

leavings ('liːvɪŋz) pl. n. something remaining, such as food on a plate, residue, refuse, etc.

Leavis ('liːvɪs) n. **F**(rank) **R**(aymond). 1895–1978, English literary critic. He edited Scrutiny (1932–53) and his books include The Great Tradition (1948) and The Common Pursuit (1952). —'**Leavis,ite** adj., n.

Lebanon ('lɛbənən) n. (sometimes preceded by the) a republic in W Asia, on the Mediterranean: an important centre of the Phoenician civilization in the third millennium B.C.; part of the Ottoman Empire from 1516 until 1919;

gained independence in 1941 (effective by 1945). Official language: Arabic; French and English are also widely spoken. Religion: Muslim and Christian. Currency: Lebanese pound. Capital: Beirut. Pop.: 2 762 000 (1987). Area: 10 400 sq. km (4015 sq. miles). —**Lebanese** (,lɛbə'niːz) adj., n.

Lebanon Mountains pl. n. a mountain range in central Lebanon, extending across the whole country parallel with the Mediterranean coast. Highest peak: 3104 m (10 184 ft.). Arabic name: **Jebel Liban** ('dʒɛbⁿl 'liːbɑːn).

Lebensraum ('leɪbənz,raʊm) n. territory claimed by a nation or state as necessary for survival or growth. [G, lit.: living space]

Leblanc (French ləblã) n. **Nicolas** (nikɔla). ?1742–1806, French chemist, who invented a process for the manufacture of soda from common salt.

Lebowa (lə'baʊə) n. a Bantustan in South Africa, in N Transvaal: consists of three separate territories with several smaller exclaves.

Lebrun (French ləbrœ̃) n. **1. Albert** (albɛr). 1871–1950, French statesman; president (1932–40). **2.** Also: **Le Brun. Charles** (ʃarl). 1619–90, French historical painter. He was court painter to Louis XIV and executed much of the decoration of the palace of Versailles.

Le Carré (lə 'kæreɪ) n. **John,** real name David John Cornwell. born 1931, English novelist, esp. of spy thrillers such as The Spy who came in from the Cold (1963), Tinker, Tailor, Soldier, Spy (1974), Smiley's People (1980), and A Perfect Spy (1986).

Lecce (Italian 'lettʃe) n. a walled city in SE Italy, in Puglia: Greek and Roman remains. Pop.: 100 981 (1986).

lech (lɛtʃ) Inf. ~vb. **1.** (intr.; usually foll. by after) to behave lecherously (towards); lust (after). ~n. **2.** a lecherous act or indulgence. [C19: back formation from LECHER]

Lech (lɛk; German lɛç) n. a river in central Europe, rising in SW Austria and flowing generally north through S West Germany to the River Danube. Length: 285 km (177 miles).

lecher ('lɛtʃə) n. a promiscuous or lewd man. [C12: from OF lecheor, from lechier to lick, of Gmc origin]

lecherous ('lɛtʃərəs) adj. characterized by or inciting lechery. —'**lecherously** adv.

lechery ('lɛtʃərɪ) n., pl. -**eries.** unrestrained and promiscuous sexuality.

lecithin ('lɛsɪθɪn) n. Biochem. any of a group of yellowbrown compounds that are found in many plant and animal tissues, esp. egg yolk: used in making candles, cosmetics, and inks, and as an emulsifier and stabilizer (**E322**) in foods. [C19: from Gk lekithos egg yolk]

Lecky ('lɛkɪ) n. **William Edward Hartpole** ('hɑːt,pəʊl). 1838–1903, Irish historian; author of The History of England in the 18th Century (1878–90).

Leconte de Lisle (French ləkɔ̃t də lil) n. **Charles Marie René** (ʃarl mari rəne). 1818–94, French Parnassian poet.

Le Corbusier (French lə kɔrbyzje) n., real name Charles Edouard Jeanneret. 1887–1965, French architect and town planner, born in Switzerland. He is noted for his use of reinforced concrete and for his modular system, which used units of a standard size. His works include Unité d'Habitation at Marseilles (1946–52) and the city of Chandigarh, India (1954).

Le Creusot (French lə krozo) n. a town in E central France: metal, machinery, and armaments industries. Pop.: 33 274 (1983 est.).

lectern ('lɛktən) n. **1.** a reading desk in a church. **2.** any similar desk or support. [C14: from OF lettrun, from LL lectrum, ult. from legere to read]

lectionary ('lɛkʃənərɪ) n., pl. -**aries.** a book containing readings appointed to be read at divine services. [C15: from Church L lectiōnārium, from lectio a reading, from legere to read]

lector ('lɛktɔː) n. **1.** a lecturer or reader in certain universities. **2.** R.C. Church. **a.** a person appointed to read lessons at certain services. **b.** (in convents or monastic establishments) a member of the community appointed to read aloud during meals. [C15: from L, from legere to read]

lecture ('lɛktʃə) n. **1.** a discourse on a particular subject given or read to an audience. **2.** the text of such a discourse. **3.** a method of teaching by formal discourse. **4.** a lengthy reprimand or scolding. ~vb. **5.** to give or read a lecture (to an audience or class). **6.** (tr.) to reprimand at length. [C14: from Med. L lectūra reading, from legere to read] —'**lecturer** n. —'**lectureship** n.

led (lɛd) *vb.* the past tense and past participle of **lead**[1].

LED *Electronics. abbrev. for* light-emitting diode.

Leda ('li:də) *n. Greek myth.* a queen of Sparta who was the mother of Helen and Pollux by Zeus, who visited her in the form of a swan.

lederhosen ('leɪdə,həʊzⁿn) *pl. n.* leather shorts with H-shaped braces, worn by men in Austria, Bavaria, etc. [G]

ledge (lɛdʒ) *n.* **1.** a narrow horizontal surface resembling a shelf and projecting from a wall, window, etc. **2.** a layer of rock that contains an ore; vein. **3.** a ridge of rock that lies beneath the surface of the sea. **4.** a narrow shelflike projection on a cliff or mountain. [C14 *legge*, ?from *leggen* to LAY[1]] —'**ledgy** *or* **ledged** *adj.*

ledger ('lɛdʒə) *n.* **1.** *Book-keeping.* the principal book in which the commercial transactions of a company are recorded. **2.** *Angling.* a wire trace that allows the weight to rest on the bottom and the bait to float freely. ~*vb.* **3.** (*intr.*) *Angling.* to fish using a ledger. [C15 *legger* book retained in a specific place, prob. from *leggen* to LAY[1]]

ledger line *n. Music.* a short line placed above or below the staff to accommodate notes representing pitches above or below the staff.

lee (li:) *n.* **1.** a sheltered part or side; the side away from the direction from which the wind is blowing. ~*adj.* **2.** (*prenominal*) *Naut.* on, at, or towards the side or part away from the wind: *on a lee shore.* Cf. **weather** (sense 4). [OE *hlēow* shelter]

Lee (li:) *n.* a river in SW Ireland, flowing east into Cork Harbour. Length: about 80 km (50 miles).

Lee[2] (li:) *n.* **1. Laurie** ('lɒrɪ). born 1914, British novelist and poet, who is best known for the autobiographical novel *Cider with Rosie* (1959) and several volumes of poetry. **2. Richard Henry.** 1732–94, American Revolutionary statesman, who moved the resolution in favour of American independence (1776). **3. Robert E(dward).** 1807–70, American general; commander-in-chief of the Confederate armies in the Civil War. **4. T(sung)-D(ao)** (tsu:ŋ daʊ). born 1926, U.S. physicist, born in China. With Yang he disproved the principle that parity is always conserved and shared the Nobel prize for physics in 1957.

leech[1] (li:tʃ) *n.* **1.** an annelid worm which has a sucker at each end of the body and feeds on the blood or tissues of other animals. **2.** a person who clings to or preys on another person. **3. a.** an archaic word for **physician. b.** (*in combination*): *leechcraft.* ~*vb.* (*tr.*) **4.** to use leeches to suck the blood of (a person), as a method of medical treatment. [OE *lǣce, lȳce*]

leech[2] (li:tʃ) *n. Naut.* the after edge of a fore-and-aft sail or either of the vertical edges of a squaresail. [C15: of Gmc origin]

Leeds (li:dz) *n.* a city in N England, in West Yorkshire on the River Aire: linked with Liverpool and Goole by canals; a chief centre of the clothing industry; university (1904). Pop.: 448 528 (1981).

leek (li:k) *n.* **1.** a vegetable with a slender white bulb, cylindrical stem, and broad flat overlapping leaves. **2.** a leek, or a representation of one, as a national emblem of Wales. [OE *lēac*]

Lee Kuan Yew (li: 'kwɑ:n 'ju:) *n.* born 1923, Singapore statesman; prime minister from 1959.

leer (lɪə) *vb.* **1.** (*intr.*) to give an oblique, sneering, or suggestive look or grin. ~*n.* **2.** such a look. [C16: ? verbal use of obs. *leer* cheek, from OE *hlēor*] —'**leering** *adj., n.* —'**leeringly** *adv.*

leery ('lɪərɪ) *adj.* **leerier, leeriest 1.** *Now chiefly dialect.* knowing or sly. **2.** *Sl.* (foll. by *of*) suspicious or wary. [C18: ?from obs. sense (to look askance) of LEER] —'**leeriness** *n.*

lees (li:z) *pl. n.* the sediment from an alcoholic drink. [C14: pl. of obs. *lee*, from OF, prob. from Celtic]

leet (li:t) *n. Scot.* a list of candidates for an office. [C15: ?from Anglo-F *litte*, var. of LIST[1]]

Leeuwarden (*Dutch* 'le:wardə) *n.* a city in the N Netherlands, capital of Friesland province. Pop.: 85 191 (1987).

Leeuwenhoek ('leɪvⁿn,hu:k, *Dutch* 'le:wənhu:k) *n.* **Anton van** ('ɑntɔn vɑn). 1632–1723, Dutch microscopist, whose microscopes enabled him to give the first accurate description of blood corpuscles, spermatozoa, and microbes.

leeward ('li:wəd; *Naut.* 'lu:əd) *Chiefly naut.* ~*adj.* **1.** of, in, or moving to the quarter towards which the wind blows. ~*n.* **2.** the point or quarter towards which the

wind blows. **3.** the side towards the lee. ~*adv.* **4.** towards the lee. ~Cf. **windward.**

Leeward Islands ('li:wəd) *pl. n.* **1.** a group of islands in the West Indies, in the N Lesser Antilles between Puerto Rico and Martinique. **2.** a former British colony in the E West Indies (1871–1956), consisting of Antigua, Barbuda, Redonda, St. Kitts, Nevis, Anguilla, Montserrat, and the British Virgin Islands. **3.** a group of islands in the S Pacific, in French Polynesia in the W Society Archipelago: Huahiné, Raiatéa, Tahaa, Bora-Bora, and Maupiti. Pop.: 15 718 (1970). French name: **Îles sous le Vent.**

leeway ('li:,weɪ) *n.* **1.** room for free movement within limits, as in action or expenditure. **2.** sideways drift of a boat or aircraft.

left[1] (lɛft) *adj.* **1.** (*usually prenominal*) of or designating the side of something or someone that faces west when the front is turned towards the north. **2.** (*usually prenominal*) worn on a left hand, foot, etc. **3.** (*sometimes cap.*) of or relating to the political left. **4.** (*sometimes cap.*) radical or progressive. ~*adv.* **5.** on or in the direction of the left. ~*n.* **6.** a left side, direction, position, area, or part. Related adjs.: **sinister, sinistral. 7.** (*often cap.*) the supporters or advocates of varying degrees of social, political, or economic change, reform, or revolution. **8.** *Boxing.* **a.** a blow with the left hand. **b.** the left hand. [OE *left* idle, weak, var. of *lyft-* (in *lyftādl* palsy, lit.: left-disease)]

left[2] (lɛft) *vb.* the past tense and past participle of **leave**[1].

Left Bank *n.* a district of Paris, on the S bank of the River Seine; frequented by artists, students, etc.

left-hand *adj.* (*prenominal*) **1.** of, relating to, located on, or moving towards the left. **2.** for use by the left hand; left-handed.

left-handed *adj.* **1.** using the left hand with greater ease than the right. **2.** performed with the left hand. **3.** designed or adapted for use by the left hand. **4.** awkward or clumsy. **5.** ironically ambiguous: *a left-handed compliment.* **6.** turning from right to left; anticlockwise. ~*adv.* **7.** with the left hand. —,**left-'handedly** *adv.* —,**left-'handedness** *n.* —,**left-'hander** *n.*

leftist ('lɛftɪst) *adj.* **1.** of, tending towards, or relating to the political left or its principles. ~*n.* **2.** a person who supports or belongs to the political left. —'**leftism** *n.*

left-luggage office *n. Brit.* a place at a railway station, etc., where luggage may be left for a small charge. U.S. and Canad. name: **checkroom.**

leftover ('lɛft,əʊvə) *n.* **1.** (*often pl.*) an unused portion or remnant, as of material or of cooked food. ~*adj.* **2.** left as an unused portion.

leftward ('lɛftwəd) *adj.* **1.** on or towards the left. ~*adv.* **2.** a variant of **leftwards.**

leftwards ('lɛftwədz) *or* **leftward** *adv.* towards or on the left.

left wing *n.* **1.** (*often cap.*) the leftist faction of an assembly, party, group, etc.; the radical or progressive wing. **2.** *Sports.* **a.** the left-hand side of the field of play from the point of view of either team facing its opponents' goal. **b.** a player positioned in this area in certain games. ~*adj.* **left-wing. 3.** of, belonging to, or relating to the political left wing. —,**left-'winger** *n.*

lefty ('lɛftɪ) *n., pl.* **lefties.** *Inf.* **1.** a left-winger. **2.** *Chiefly U.S. & Canad.* a left-handed person.

leg (lɛg) *n.* **1.** either of the two lower limbs in humans, or any similar or analogous structure in animals that is used for locomotion or support. **2.** this part of an animal, esp. the thigh, used for food: *leg of lamb.* **3.** something similar to a leg in appearance or function, such as one of the four supporting members of a chair. **4.** a branch, limb, or part of a forked or jointed object. **5.** the part of a garment that covers the leg. **6.** a section or part of a journey or course. **7.** a single stage, lap, length, etc., in a relay race. **8.** either the opposite or adjacent side of a right-angled triangle. **9.** one of a series of games, matches, or parts of games. **10.** *Austral. & N.Z.* either one of two races on which a cumulative bet has been placed. **11.** *Cricket.* **a.** the side of the field to the left of and behind a right-handed batsman as he faces the bowler. **b.** (*as modifier*): *a leg slip; leg stump.* **12. not have a leg to stand on.** *Inf.* to have no reasonable or logical basis for an opinion or argument. **13. on his, its,** etc., **last legs.** (of a person or thing) worn out; exhausted. **14. pull (someone's) leg.** *Inf.* to tease, fool, or make fun of (someone). **15. shake a leg.** *Inf.* to hurry up: usually used in the imperative. **16. stretch**

one's legs. to stand up or walk around, esp. after sitting for some time. ~*vb.* **legging, legged. 17. leg it.** *Inf.* to walk, run, or hurry. [C13: from ON *leggr*, from ?]

leg. *abbrev. for:* **1.** legal. **2.** legate. **3.** legato. **4.** legislation. **5.** legislative. **6.** legislature.

legacy ('lɛgəsɪ) *n., pl.* **-cies. 1.** a gift by will, esp. of money or personal property. **2.** something handed down or received from an ancestor or predecessor. [C14 (meaning: office of a legate), C15 (meaning: bequest): from Med. L *lēgātia* commission; see LEGATE]

legal ('li:gəl) *adj.* **1.** established by or founded upon law; lawful. **2.** of or relating to law. **3.** recognized, enforceable, or having a remedy at law rather than in equity. **4.** relating to or characteristic of the profession of law. [C16: from L *lēgālis*, from *lēx* law] — **'legally** *adv.*

legal aid *n.* financial assistance available to persons unable to meet the full cost of legal proceedings.

legalese (,li:gə'li:z) *n.* the conventional language in which legal documents are written.

legalism ('li:gə,lɪzəm) *n.* strict adherence to the law, esp. the letter of the law rather than its spirit. — **'legalist** *n.*, *adj.* — ,legal'istic *adj.*

legality (lɪ'gælɪtɪ) *n., pl.* **-ties. 1.** the state or quality of being legal or lawful. **2.** adherence to legal principles.

legalize *or* **-ise** ('li:gə,laɪz) *vb.* (*tr.*) to make lawful or legal. — ,legali'zation *or* -i'sation *n.*

legal tender *n.* currency that a creditor must by law accept in redemption of a debt.

Legaspi (lɛ'gæspɪ) *n.* a port in the Philippines, on SE Luzon on the Gulf of Albay. Pop.: 108 864 (1984 est.).

legate ('lɛgɪt) *n.* **1.** a messenger, envoy, or delegate. **2.** *R.C. Church.* an emissary representing the Pope. [OE, via OF from L *lēgātus* deputy, from *lēgāre* to delegate; rel. to *lēx* law] — **'legate,ship** *n.*

legatee (,lɛgə'ti:) *n.* a person to whom a legacy is bequeathed.

legation (lɪ'geɪʃən) *n.* **1.** a diplomatic mission headed by a minister. **2.** the official residence and office of a diplomatic minister. **3.** the act of sending forth a diplomatic envoy. **4.** the mission of a diplomatic envoy. **5.** the rank or office of a legate. [C15: from L *lēgātiō*, from *lēgātus* LEGATE]

legato (lɪ'gɑ:təʊ) *Music.* ~*adj., adv.* **1.** to be performed smoothly and connectedly. ~*n., pl.* **-tos. 2. a.** a style of playing with no perceptible gaps between notes. **b.** (*as modifier*): *a legato passage.* [C19: from It., lit.: bound]

leg before wicket *n. Cricket.* a manner of dismissal on the grounds that a batsman has been struck on the leg by a bowled ball that otherwise would have hit the wicket. Abbrev.: **lbw.**

leg break *n. Cricket.* a bowled ball that spins from leg to off on pitching.

legend ('lɛdʒənd) *n.* **1.** a popular story handed down from earlier times whose truth has not been ascertained. **2.** a group of such stories: *the Arthurian legend.* **3.** a modern story that has the characteristics of a traditional tale. **4.** a person whose fame or notoriety makes him a source of exaggerated or romanticized tales. **5.** an inscription or title, as on a coin or beneath a coat of arms. **6.** explanatory matter accompanying a table, map, chart, etc. [C14 (in the sense: a saint's life): from Med. L *legenda* passages to be read, from L *legere* to read]

legendary ('lɛdʒəndərɪ, -drɪ) *adj.* **1.** of or relating to legend. **2.** celebrated or described in a legend or legends. **3.** very famous or notorious.

Legendre (*French* ləʒɑ̃drə) *n.* **Adrien Marie** (adriɛ̃ mari). 1752–1833, French mathematician, noted for his work on the theory of numbers, the theory of elliptical functions, and the method of least squares.

Léger (*French* leʒe) *n.* **Fernand** (fɛrnɑ̃). 1881–1955, French cubist painter, influenced by industrial technology.

legerdemain (,lɛdʒədə'meɪn) *n.* **1.** another name for **sleight of hand. 2.** cunning deception or trickery. [C15: from OF: light of hand]

leger line ('lɛdʒə) *n.* a variant spelling of **ledger line.**

legged ('lɛgɪd, lɛgd) *adj.* **a.** having a leg or legs. **b.** (*in combination*): *three-legged; long-legged.*

leggiero (lɛdʒ'ɛərəʊ) *adj., adv. Music.* to be performed lightly and nimbly. [It.]

leggings ('lɛgɪŋz) *pl. n.* **1.** an extra outer covering for the lower legs. **2.** children's closefitting trousers, usually with a strap under the instep, worn for warmth in winter. **3.** a fashion garment for women consiting of closefitting trousers.

leggy ('lɛgɪ) *adj.* **-gier, -giest. 1.** having unusually long legs. **2.** (of a woman) having long and shapely legs. **3.** (of a plant) having an unusually long and weak stem. — **'legginess** *n.*

leghorn ('lɛg,hɔ:n) *n.* **1.** a type of Italian wheat straw that is woven into hats. **2.** any hat made from this straw. [C19: after LEGHORN (Livorno)]

Leghorn *n.* **1.** ('lɛg,hɔ:n). the English name for **Livorno. 2.** (lɛ'gɔ:n). a breed of domestic fowl.

legible ('lɛdʒəbəl) *adj.* (of handwriting, print, etc.) able to be read or deciphered. [C14: from LL *legibilis*, from L *legere* to read] — ,legi'bility *n.* — **'legibly** *adv.*

legion ('li:dʒən) *n.* **1.** a unit in the ancient Roman army of infantry with supporting cavalry of three to six thousand men. **2.** any large military force: *the French Foreign Legion.* **3.** (*usually cap.*) an association of ex-servicemen: *the British Legion.* **4.** (*often pl.*) any very large number. ~*adj.* **5.** (*usually postpositive*) very numerous. [C13: from OF, from L *legio*, from *legere* to choose]

legionary ('li:dʒənərɪ) *adj.* **1.** of a legion. ~*n., pl.* **-aries. 2.** a soldier belonging to a legion.

legionnaire (,li:dʒə'nɛə) *n.* (*often cap.*) a member of certain military forces or associations.

Legionnaire's disease (,li:dʒə'nɛəz) *n.* a serious, sometimes fatal infection, caused by bacteria (**legionella**), which has symptoms similar to those of pneumonia. [C20: after the outbreak at a meeting of the American Legion in Philadelphia in 1976]

legislate ('lɛdʒɪs,leɪt) *vb.* **1.** (*intr.*) to make or pass laws. **2.** (*tr.*) to bring into effect by legislation. [C18: back formation from LEGISLATOR]

legislation (,lɛdʒɪs'leɪʃən) *n.* **1.** the act or process of making laws. **2.** the laws so made.

legislative ('lɛdʒɪslətɪv) *adj.* **1.** of or relating to legislation. **2.** having the power or function of legislating: *a legislative assembly.* **3.** of or relating to a legislature. — **'legislatively** *adv.*

legislative assembly *n.* (*often cap.*) **1.** the bicameral legislature in 28 states of the U.S. **2.** the unicameral legislature in most Canadian provinces. **3.** the lower chamber of the bicameral state legislatures in several other Commonwealth countries, such as Australia. **4.** any assembly with legislative powers.

legislative council *n.* (*often cap.*) **1.** the upper chamber of certain bicameral legislatures, such as those of the Indian and Australian states (except Queensland). **2.** the unicameral legislature of certain colonies or dependent territories. **3.** (in the U.S.) a committee of members of both chambers of a state legislature that discusses problems, constructs a legislative programme, etc.

legislator ('lɛdʒɪs,leɪtə) *n.* **1.** a person concerned with the making of laws. **2.** a member of a legislature. [C17: from L *lēgis lātor*, from *lēx* law + *lātor* from *lātus*, p.p. of *ferre* to bring]

legislature ('lɛdʒɪs,leɪtʃə) *n.* a body of persons vested with power to make and repeal laws.

legit (lɪ'dʒɪt) *Sl.* ~*adj.* **1.** short for **legitimate.** ~*n.* **2.** legitimate drama.

legitimate *adj.* (lɪ'dʒɪtɪmɪt). **1.** born in lawful wedlock. **2.** conforming to established standards of usage, behaviour, etc. **3.** based on correct or acceptable principles of reasoning. **4.** authorized by or in accordance with law. **5.** of, relating to, or ruling by hereditary right: *a legitimate monarch.* **6.** of or relating to serious drama as distinct from films, television, vaudeville, etc. ~*vb.* (lɪ'dʒɪtɪ,meɪt). **7.** (*tr.*) to make, pronounce, or show to be legitimate. [C15: from Med. L *lēgitimātus* made legal, from *lēx* law] — **le'gitimacy** *n.* — **le'gitimately** *adv.* — **le,giti'mation** *n.*

legitimatize, -tise (lɪ'dʒɪtɪmə,taɪz) *or* **legitimize, -mise** (lɪ'dʒɪtɪ,maɪz) *vb.* (*tr.*) to make legitimate; legalize. — **le,gitimati'zation, -ti'sation** *or* **le,gitimi'zation, -mi'sation** *n.*

legitimist (lɪ'dʒɪtɪmɪst) *n.* a monarchist who supports the rule of a legitimate dynasty or of its senior branch. — **le'gitimism** *n.*

legless ('lɛglɪs) *adj.* **1.** without legs. **2.** *Inf.* very drunk.

Legnica (*Polish* lɛg'nitsa) *n.* an industrial town in SW Poland. Pop.: 91 400 (1982 est.). German name: **Liegnitz.**

Lego ('lɛgəʊ) n. Trademark. a construction toy consisting of plastic bricks that fit together with studs. [C20: from Danish leg godt play well]

leg-of-mutton or **leg-o'-mutton** n. (modifier) (of a sail, sleeve, etc.) tapering sharply.

leg-pull n. Brit. inf. a practical joke or mild deception.

legroom ('lɛg,ruːm) n. room to move one's legs comfortably, as in a car.

leg rope n. Austral. & N.Z. a rope used to secure an animal by its hind leg.

leguan ('lɛgu,ɑːn) n. a large amphibious S African lizard. [from Du. leguaan]

legume ('lɛgjuːm, lɪ'gjuːm) n. 1. the long dry fruit produced by leguminous plants; a pod. 2. any of various table vegetables, esp. beans or peas. 3. any leguminous plant. [C17: from F légume, from L legūmen bean, from legere to pick (a crop)]

leguminous (lɪ'gjuːmɪnəs) adj. of, relating to, or belonging to any family of flowering plants having pods (or legumes) as fruits and root nodules enabling storage of nitrogen-rich material. [C17: from L legūmen; see LEGUME]

legwarmer ('lɛg,wɔːmə) n. one of a pair of garments resembling stockings without feet, often worn over jeans, tights, etc., or during exercise.

legwork ('lɛg,wɜːk) n. Inf. work that involves travelling on foot or as if on foot.

Lehár ('leɪhɑː, lɪ'hɑː) n. Franz (frants). 1870–1948, Hungarian composer of operettas, esp. The Merry Widow (1905).

Le Havre (lə 'hɑːvrə; French lə avrə) n. a port in N France, on the English Channel at the mouth of the River Seine: transatlantic trade; oil refining. Pop.: 217 325 (1983 est.).

Lehmann ('leɪmən) n. 1. **Lilli** ('lɪlɪ). 1848–1929, German soprano. 2. **Lotte** ('lɒtə). 1888–1976, U.S. soprano, born in Germany. 3. **Rosamond (Nina).** born 1903, British novelist. Her books include Dusty Answer (1927), Invitation to the Waltz (1932), and The Echoing Grove (1953).

Lehmbruck (German 'leːmbrʊk) n. **Wilhelm** ('vɪlhɛlm). 1881–1919, German sculptor and graphic artist.

lei (leɪ) n. (in Hawaii) a garland of flowers, worn around the neck. [from Hawaiian]

Leibnitz or **Leibniz** ('laɪbnɪts) n. Baron **Gottfried Wilhelm von** ('gɒtfriːt 'vɪlhɛlm fɔn). 1646–1716, German rationalist philosopher and mathematician. He conceived of the universe as a hierarchy of independent units or monads, synchronized by pre-established harmony. His works include Théodicée (1710) and Monadologia (1714). He also devised a system of calculus, independently of Newton. —**Leib'nitzian** adj.

Leicester[1] ('lɛstə) n. 1. a city in central England, administrative centre of Leicestershire, on the River Soar: Roman remains and a ruined Norman castle; university (1918); light engineering, hosiery, and footwear industries. Pop.: 282 300 (1983 est.). 2. a fairly mild dark orange whole-milk cheese, similar to Cheddar but looser and more moist.

Leicester[2] ('lɛstə) n. **Earl of.** title of Robert Dudley. ?1532–88, English courtier; favourite of Elizabeth I. He led an unsuccessful expedition to the Netherlands (1585–87).

Leicestershire ('lɛstə,ʃɪə, -ʃə) n. a county of central England, including (since 1974) the former county of Rutland: largely agricultural. Administrative centre: Leicester. Pop.: 875 000 (1986 est.). Area: 2553 sq. km (986 sq. miles). Shortened form: **Leicester.** Abbrev.: **Leics.**

Leichhardt ('laɪk,hɑːt; German 'laɪçhart) n. **Friedrich Wilhelm Ludwig** ('friːdrɪç 'vɪlhɛlm 'luːtvɪç). 1813–48, Australian explorer, born in Prussia. He disappeared during an attempt to cross Australia from East to West.

Leics abbrev. for Leicestershire.

Leiden or **Leyden** ('laɪdən; Dutch 'lɛɪdə) n. a city in the W Netherlands, in South Holland province: residence of the Pilgrim Fathers for 11 years before they sailed for America in 1620; university (1575). Pop.: 106 808 (1987).

Leif Ericson ('liːf 'ɛrɪksən) n. See **Ericson.**

Leigh[1] (liː) n. a town in NW England, in Greater Manchester: engineering industries. Pop.: 45 341 (1981).

Leigh[2] (liː) n. **Vivien,** real name Vivien Hartley. 1913–67, English stage and film actress. Her films include Gone with the Wind (1939) and A Streetcar Named Desire (1951), for both of which she won Oscars.

Leinster ('lɛnstə) n. a province of E and SE Ireland: it consists of the counties of Carlow, Dublin, Kildare,

Kilkenny, Laoighis, Longford, Louth, Meath, Offaly, Westmeath, Wexford, and Wicklow. Pop.: 1 851 134 (1986). Area: 19 632 sq. km (7580 sq. miles).

Leipzig ('laɪpsɪg; German 'laɪptsɪç) n. a city in S East Germany: famous fairs, begun about 1170; publishing and music centre; university (1409); scene of a decisive defeat for Napoleon Bonaparte in 1813. Pop.: 552 133 (1986).

Leiria (Portuguese leiˈriɐ) n. a city in central Portugal: site of the first printing press in Portugal (1466). Pop.: 96 583 (1981).

leishmaniasis (,liːʃməˈnaɪəsɪs) or **leishmaniosis** (liːʃ,meɪnɪˈəʊsɪs, -,mæn-) n. any disease, such as kalaazar, caused by protozoa of the genus Leishmania. [C20: NL, after Sir W. B. Leishman (1865-1926), Scot. bacteriologist]

leister ('liːstə) n. 1. a spear with three or more prongs for spearing fish, esp. salmon. ~vb. 2. (tr.) to spear (a fish) with a leister. [C16: from Scand.]

leisure ('lɛʒə) n. 1. a. time or opportunity for ease, relaxation, etc. b. (as modifier): leisure activities. 2. ease or leisureliness. 3. at leisure. a. having free time. b. not occupied or engaged. c. without hurrying. 4. at one's leisure. when one has free time. [C14: from OF leisir; ult. from L licēre to be allowed] —**'leisured** adj.

leisure centre n. a building designed to provide facilities for a range of leisure pursuits, such as a library, sports hall, café, and rooms for meetings.

leisurely ('lɛʒəlɪ) adj. 1. unhurried; relaxed. ~adv. 2. without haste; in a relaxed way. —**'leisureliness** n.

Leith (liːθ) n. a port in SE Scotland, on the Firth of Forth: part of Edinburgh since 1920.

leitmotiv or **leitmotif** ('laɪtməʊ,tiːf) n. 1. Music. a recurring short melodic phrase used, esp. in Wagnerian music dramas, to suggest a character, thing, etc. 2. an often repeated image or theme in a literary work. [C19: from G: leading motif]

Leitrim ('liːtrɪm) n. a county of N Ireland in Connacht province, on Donegal Bay: agricultural. County town: Carrick-on-Shannon. Pop.: 27 000 (1986). Area: 1525 sq. km (589 sq. miles).

Leix (liːʃ) n. another name for **Laoighis.**

Leizhou ('leɪ'dʒəʊ) or **Luichow Peninsula** n. a peninsula of SE China, in SW Guangdong province, separated from Hainan Island by Hainan Strait.

lek (lɛk) n. a small area in which birds of certain species, notably the black grouse, gather for sexual display and courtship. [C19: ?from dialect lake (vb.) from OE lácan to frolic, fight, or ?from Swedish leka to play]

lekker ('lɛkə) adj. S. African sl. pleasing, enjoyable, or likeable. [from Afrik., from Du.]

Lely ('liːlɪ) n. Sir **Peter.** Dutch name Pieter van der Faes. 1618–80, Dutch portrait painter in England.

LEM (lɛm) n. acronym for lunar excursion module.

Léman (lemɑ̃) n. **Lac.** the French name for (Lake) **Geneva.**

Le Mans (French lə mɑ̃) n. a city in NW France: scene of the first experiments in motoring and flying; annual motor race. Pop.: 151 259 (1983 est.).

Lemberg ('lɛmbɛrk) n. the German name for **Lvov.**

lemma ('lɛmə) n., pl. **-mas** or **-mata** (-mətə). 1. a subsidiary proposition, assumed to be valid, that is used in the proof of another proposition. 2. an argument or theme, esp. when used as the subject or title of a composition. 3. Linguistics. a word considered as its citation form together with all the inflected forms. [C16 (meaning: proposition), C17 (meaning: title, theme): via L from Gk: premise, from lambanein to take (for granted)]

lemming ('lɛmɪŋ) n. 1. any of various volelike rodents of northern and arctic regions of Europe, Asia, and North America. 2. a member of any group following an unthinking course towards destruction. [C17: from Norwegian] —**'lemming-,like** adj.

Lemnos ('lɛmnɒs) n. a Greek island in the N Aegean Sea: famous for its medicinal earth (**Lemnian seal**). Chief town: Kastron. Pop.: 15 721 (1981). Area: 477 sq. km (184 sq. miles). Modern Greek name: **Límnos.** —**Lemnian** ('lɛmnɪən) adj., n.

lemon ('lɛmən) n. 1. a small Asian evergreen tree widely cultivated in warm and tropical regions for its edible fruits. Related adjs.: **citric, citrine, citrous.** 2. a. the yellow oval fruit of this tree, having juicy acidic flesh. b. (as modifier): a lemon jelly. 3. Also called: **lemon yellow.** a. a greenish-yellow or pale yellow colour. b. (as adj.):

lemon wallpaper. **4.** a distinctive tart flavour made from or in imitation of the lemon. **5.** *Sl.* a person or thing considered to be useless or defective. [C14: from Med. L *lemōn-*, from Ar. *laymūn*] —**'lemony** *adj.*

lemonade (ˌlɛmə'neɪd) *n.* a drink made from lemon juice, sugar, and water or from carbonated water, citric acid, etc.

lemon balm *n.* the full name of **balm.**

lemon cheese *or* **curd** *n.* a soft spread made from lemons, sugar, eggs, and butter.

lemon grass *n.* a perennial grass with a large flower spike: grown in tropical regions as the source of an aromatic oil (**lemon grass oil**).

lemon sole *n.* a European flatfish with a variegated brown body: highly valued as a food fish.

lemon squash *n. Brit.* a drink made from a sweetened lemon concentrate and water.

lemur ('liːmə) *n.* **1.** any of a family of Madagascan prosimian primates such as the ring-tailed lemur. They are typically arboreal, having foxy faces and long tails. **2.** any similar or closely related animal, such as a loris or indris. [C18: NL, adapted from L *lemurēs* ghosts; so named for its ghost-like face and nocturnal habits] —**lemuroid** ('lɛmjʊˌrɔɪd) *n., adj.*

Lena ('liːnə; *Russian* 'ljɛnə) *n.* a river in the E Soviet Union, rising in S Siberia and flowing generally north through the Yakut ASSR to the Laptev Sea by an extensive delta: the longest river in the Soviet Union. Length: 4271 km (2653 miles).

lend (lɛnd) *vb.* **lending, lent. 1.** (*tr.*) to permit the use of (something) with the expectation of its return. **2.** to provide (money) temporarily, often at interest. **3.** (*intr.*) to provide loans, esp. as a profession. **4.** (*tr.*) to impart or contribute (something, esp. some abstract quality): *her presence lent beauty.* **5. lend an ear.** to listen. **6. lend oneself** *or* **itself.** to possess the right characteristics or qualities for: *the novel lends itself to serialization.* [C15 *lende* (orig. the past tense), from OE *lǣnan*, from *lǣn* loan] —**'lender** *n.*

▷**Usage.** Although the use of *loan* as a verb equivalent to *lend* is widespread, it is avoided by careful speakers and writers except when referring to the formal lending of money: *the bank loaned him the money.*

lending library *n.* **1.** Also called (esp. U.S.): **circulating library.** the department of a public library providing books for use outside the building. **2.** a small commercial library.

Lendl (lɛndl) *n.* **Ivan** (iː'væn, -'vɑːn). born 1960, Czech tennis player: US Open champion (1985).

lend-lease *n.* (during World War II) the system organized by the U.S. in 1941 by which equipment and services were provided for countries fighting Fascism.

Lenglen (*French* lãglã) *n.* **Suzanne** (syzan). 1899–1938, French tennis player: Wimbledon champion (1919-25).

length (lɛŋkθ, lɛŋθ) *n.* **1.** the linear extent or measurement of something from end to end, usually being the longest dimension. **2.** the extent of something from beginning to end, measured in some more or less regular units or intervals: *the book was 600 pages in length.* **3.** a specified distance, esp. between two positions: *the length of a race.* **4.** a period of time, as between specified limits or moments. **5.** a piece or section of something narrow and long: *a length of tubing.* **6.** the quality, state, or fact of being long rather than short. **7.** (*usually pl.*) the amount of trouble taken in pursuing or achieving something (esp. in **to great lengths**). **8.** (*often pl.*) the extreme or limit of action (esp. in **to any length(s)**). **9.** *Prosody, phonetics.* the metrical quantity or temporal duration of a vowel or syllable. **10.** the distance from one end of a rectangular swimming bath to the other. **11. at length. a.** in depth; fully. **b.** eventually. **c.** interminably. [OE *lengthu*]

lengthen ('lɛŋkθən, 'lɛŋθən) *vb.* to make or become longer. —**'lengthener** *n.*

lengthways ('lɛŋkθˌweɪz, 'lɛŋθ-) *or* **lengthwise** *adv., adj.* in, according to, or along the direction of length.

lengthy ('lɛŋkθɪ, 'lɛŋθɪ) *adj.* **lengthier, lengthiest.** of relatively great or tiresome extent or duration. —**'lengthily** *adv.* —**'lengthiness** *n.*

lenient ('liːnɪənt) *adj.* showing or characterized by mercy or tolerance. [C17: from L *lēnīre* to soothe, from *lēnis* soft] —**'leniency** *or* **'lenience** *n.* —**'leniently** *adv.*

Lenin ('lɛnɪn) *n.* **Vladimir Ilyich** (vla'dimir ilj'jitʃ), original surname *Ulyanov.* 1870–1924, Russian statesman and Marxist theoretician; first premier of the Soviet Union. He formed the Bolsheviks (1903) and led them in the October Revolution (1917), which established the Soviet Government. He adopted the New Economic Policy (1921) after the Civil War had led to the virtual collapse of the Russian economy, formed the Comintern (1919), and was the originator of the guiding doctrine of the Soviet Union, Marxism-Leninism.

Leninabad (*Russian* lnina'bat) *n.* a town in the S central Soviet Union, in the Tadzhik SSR on the Syr Darya River: one of the oldest towns in central Asia; textile industries. Pop.: 153 000 (1987). Former name (until 1936): **Khojent** ('xojent).

Leninakan (*Russian* lnina'kan) *n.* a city in the SW Soviet Union, in the NW Armenian SSR: textile centre. Pop.: 228 000 (1987). Former name (1840–1924): **Aleksandropol.**

Leningrad ('lɛnɪnˌgræd; *Russian* lnin'grat) *n.* a city and port in the NW Soviet Union, on the Gulf of Finland at the mouth of the Neva River: founded by Peter the Great in 1703 and built on low-lying marshes subject to frequent flooding; capital of Russia from 1712 to 1918; a cultural and educational centre, with a university (1819); a major industrial centre, with engineering, shipbuilding, chemical, textile, and printing industries. Pop.: 4 948 000 (1987). Former names: **Saint Petersburg** (1703–1914), **Petrograd** (1914–24).

Leninism ('lɛnɪˌnɪzəm) *n.* the political and economic theories of Lenin. —**'Leninist** *n., adj.*

Lenin Peak *n.* a mountain in the S central Soviet Union, in the NE Tadzhik SSR: the highest peak in the Trans Alai Range and the second highest in the Soviet Union. Height: 7134 m (23 406 ft.).

lenitive ('lɛnɪtɪv) *adj.* **1.** soothing or alleviating pain or distress. ~*n.* **2.** a lenitive drug. [C16: from Med. L *lēnītīvus*, from L *lēnīre* to soothe]

lenity ('lɛnɪtɪ) *n., pl.* **-ties.** the state or quality of being lenient. [C16: from L *lēnitās* gentleness, from *lēnis* soft]

Lennon ('lɛnən) *n.* **John** (**Winston Ono**), original name *John Winston Lennon.* 1940–80, English rock guitarist, singer, and songwriter: member of the Beatles (1962–70). His subsequent recordings, many in collaboration with his wife Yoko Ono, include "Instant Karma" (1970), *Imagine* (1971), and *Double Fantasy* (1980). He was assassinated.

leno ('liːnəʊ) *n., pl.* **-nos. 1.** (in textiles) a weave in which the warp yarns are twisted together in pairs between the weft or filling yarns. **2.** a fabric of this weave. [C19: prob. from F *linon* lawn, from *lin* flax, from L *līnum*]

lens (lɛnz) *n.* **1.** a piece of glass or other transparent material, used to converge or diverge transmitted light and form optical images. **2.** Also called: **compound lens.** a combination of such lenses for forming images or concentrating a beam of light. **3.** a device that diverges or converges a beam of electromagnetic radiation, sound, or particles. **4.** *Anat.* See **crystalline lens.** [C17: from L *lēns* lentil, referring to the similarity of a lens to the shape of a lentil]

lent (lɛnt) *vb.* the past tense and past participle of **lend.**

Lent (lɛnt) *n. Christianity.* the period of forty weekdays lasting from Ash Wednesday to Holy Saturday, observed as a time of penance and fasting commemorating Jesus' fasting in the wilderness. [OE *lencten, lengten* spring, lit.: lengthening (of hours of daylight)]

lentamente (ˌlɛntə'mɛnteɪ) *adv. Music.* slowly. [It.]

lenten ('lɛntən) *adj.* **1.** (*often cap.*) of or relating to Lent. **2.** *Arch.* or *literary.* spare, plain, or meagre: *lenten fare.*

lenticel ('lɛntɪˌsɛl) *n.* any of numerous pores in the stem of a woody plant allowing exchange of gases between the plant and the exterior. [C19: from NL *lenticella*, from L *lenticula* dim. of *lēns* lentil]

lenticular (lɛn'tɪkjʊlə) *adj.* **1.** shaped like a biconvex lens. **2.** of or concerned with a lens or lenses. **3.** shaped like a lentil seed. [C17: from L *lenticulāris* like a LENTIL]

lentil ('lɛntɪl) *n.* **1.** a small annual leguminous plant of the Mediterranean region and W Asia, having edible convex seeds. **2.** any of the seeds of this plant, which are cooked and eaten in soups, etc. [C13: from OF *lentille*, from L *lenticula*, dim. of *lēns* lentil]

lentivirus ('lɛntɪˌvaɪrəs) *n.* another name for **slow virus.** [C20: NL, from L *lentus* slow + VIRUS]

lent lily *n.* another name for the **daffodil.**

lento ('lɛntəʊ) *Music.* ~*adj.*, *adv.* **1.** to be performed slowly. ~*n.*, *pl.* **-tos.** **2.** a movement or passage performed in this way. [C18: It., from L *lentus* slow]

Lent term *n.* the spring term at Cambridge University and some other educational establishments.

Leo ('li:əʊ) *n.*, *Latin genitive* **Leonis** (li:'əʊnɪs). **1.** *Astron.* a zodiacal constellation in the N hemisphere, lying between Cancer and Virgo. **2.** *Astrol.* Also called: the **Lion.** the fifth sign of the zodiac. The sun is in this sign between about July 23 and Aug. 22.

Leo I ('li:əʊ) *n.* **Saint,** known as *Leo the Great.* ?390–461 A.D., pope (440–461). He extended the authority of the papacy in the West and persuaded Attila not to attack Rome (452). Feast day: Nov. 10.

Leo III *n.* **Saint.** ?750–816 A.D., pope (795–816). He crowned Charlemagne emperor of the Romans (800). Feast day: June 12.

Leo X *n.* original name *Giovanni de' Medici.* 1475–1521, pope (1513–21): noted for his patronage of Renaissance art and learning; excommunicated Luther (1521).

Leo XIII *n.* original name *Gioacchino Pecci.* 1810–1903, pope (1878–1903). His many important encyclicals include *Rerum novarum* (1891) on the need for Catholic action on social problems.

Leoben (*German* le'o:bən) *n.* a city in E central Austria, in Styria on the Mur River: lignite mining. Pop.: 32 006 (1981).

León (*Spanish* le'ɔn) *n.* **1.** a region and former kingdom of NW Spain, which united with Castile in 1230. **2.** a city of NW Spain: capital of the kingdom of León (10th century). Pop.: 127 095 (1981). **3.** a city in central Mexico, in W Guanajuato state: commercial centre of a rich agricultural region. Pop.: 655 809 (1980). Official name **León de los Aldamas** (de los 'aldamas). **4.** a city in W Nicaragua: one of the oldest towns of Central America, founded in 1524; capital of Nicaragua until 1855; university (1812). Pop.: 100 982 (1985).

Leonardo da Vinci (ˌli:ə'nɑ:dəʊ də 'vɪntʃɪ) *n.* 1452–1519, Italian painter, sculptor, architect, and engineer: the most versatile talent of the Italian Renaissance. His most famous paintings include *The Virgin of the Rocks* (1483–85), the *Mona Lisa* (or *La Gioconda*, 1503), and the *Last Supper* (?1495–97). His numerous drawings, combining scientific precision in observation with intense imaginative power, reflect the breadth of his interests, which ranged over biology, physiology, hydraulics, and aeronautics. He invented the first armoured tank and foresaw the invention of aircraft and submarines. — **Leonardesque** (ˌli:ənɑ:'dɛsk) *adj.*

Leoncavallo (*Italian* leoŋka'vallo) *n.* **Ruggiero** (rud-'dʒɛːro). 1858–1919, Italian composer of operas, notably *I Pagliacci* (1892).

Leonid ('li:ənɪd) *n.*, *pl.* **Leonids** *or* **Leonides** (lɪ'ɒnɪˌdi:z). any member of a meteor shower appearing to radiate from the constellation Leo. [C19: from NL *Leōnidēs*, from *leō* lion]

Leonidas (lɪ'ɒnɪˌdæs) *n.* died 480 B.C., king of Sparta (?490–480), hero of the Battle of Thermopylae, in which he was killed by the Persians under Xerxes.

leonine ('li:əˌnaɪn) *adj.* of, characteristic of, or resembling a lion. [C14: from L *leōnīnus*, from *leō* lion]

Leonine ('li:əˌnaɪn) *adj.* **1.** connected with one of the popes called Leo: an epithet applied to a district of Rome fortified by Pope Leo IV (**Leonine City**). **2.** **Leonine verse. a.** a type of medieval hexameter or elegiac verse having internal rhyme. **b.** a type of English verse with internal rhyme.

leopard ('lɛpəd) *n.* **1.** Also called: **panther.** a large feline mammal of forests of Africa and Asia, usually having a tawny yellow coat with black rosette-like spots. **2.** any of several similar felines, such as the snow leopard and cheetah. **3.** *Heraldry.* a stylized leopard, painted as a lion with the face turned towards the front. [C13: from OF *lepart*, from LL, from LGk *leópardos*, from *león* lion + *pardos* PARD (the leopard was thought to be the result of cross-breeding)] — **'leopardess** *fem. n.*

Leopardi (*Italian* leo'pardi) *n.* Count **Giacomo** ('dʒaːkomo). 1798–1837, Italian poet and philosopher, noted esp. for his lyrics, collected in *I Canti* (1831).

Leopold I ('lɪəˌpəʊld) *n.* **1.** 1640–1705, Holy Roman Emperor (1658–1705). His reign was marked by wars with

Louis XIV of France and with the Turks. **2.** 1790–1865, first king of the Belgians (1831–65).

Leopold II *n.* **1.** 1747–92, Holy Roman Emperor (1790–92). He formed an alliance with Prussia against France (1792) after the downfall of his brother-in-law Louis XVI. **2.** 1835–1909, king of the Belgians (1865–1909); son of Leopold I. He financed Stanley's explorations in Africa, becoming first sovereign of the Congo Free State (1885).

Leopold III *n.* 1901–83, king of the Belgians (1934–51); son of Albert I. His surrender to the Nazis (1940) forced his eventual abdication in favour of his son, Baudouin.

Léopoldville ('lɪəˌpəʊldˌvɪl; *French* leɔpɔlvil) *n.* the former name (until 1966) of **Kinshasa.**

leotard ('lɪəˌtɑːd) *n.* a tight-fitting garment covering the body from the shoulders down to the thighs and worn by acrobats, ballet dancers, etc. [C19: after Jules *Léotard*, F acrobat]

Lepanto (*Italian* 'lɛːpanto) *n.* **1.** (*Italian* 'lɛːpanto) a port in W Greece, between the Gulfs of Corinth and Patras: scene of a naval battle (1571) in which the Turkish fleet was defeated by the fleets of the Holy League. Pop.: 8170 (1971). Greek name: **Návpaktos. 2.** (lɪ'pæntəʊ). **Gulf of.** another name for the (Gulf of) **Corinth.**

Lepaya (lɪ'pɑːjə) *n.* a variant spelling of **Liepāja.**

leper ('lɛpə) *n.* **1.** a person who has leprosy. **2.** a person who is ignored or despised. [C14: via LL from Gk *lepra*, n. use of *lepros* scaly, from *lepein* to peel]

lepido- *or before a vowel* **lepid-** *combining form.* scale or scaly: *lepidopterous.* [from Gk *lepis* scale; see LEPER]

lepidopteran (ˌlɛpɪ'dɒptərən) *n.*, *pl.* **-terans** *or* **-tera** (-tərə). **1.** any of a large order of insects typically having two pairs of wings covered with fragile scales: comprises the butterflies and moths. ~*adj. also* **lepidopterous. 2.** of, relating to, or belonging to this order. [C19: from NL, from LEPIDO- + Gk *pteron* wing]

lepidopterist (ˌlɛpɪ'dɒptərɪst) *n.* a person who studies or collects moths and butterflies.

Lepidus ('lɛpɪdəs) *n.* **Marcus Aemilius** ('maːkəs i:'mɪlɪəs). died ?13 B.C., Roman statesman: formed the Second Triumvirate with Octavian (later Augustus) and Mark Antony.

Lepontine Alps (lɪ'pɒntaɪn) *pl. n.* a range of the S central Alps, in S Switzerland and N Italy. Highest peak: Monte Leone, 3553 m (11 657 ft.).

leprechaun ('lɛprəˌkɔːn) *n.* (in Irish folklore) a mischievous elf, often believed to have a treasure hoard. [C17: from Irish Gaelic *leipreachān*, from MIrish *lúchorpān*, from *lū* small + *corp* body, from L *corpus* body]

leprosy ('lɛprəsɪ) *n.* *Pathol.* a chronic infectious disease occurring mainly in tropical and subtropical regions, characterized by the formation of painful inflamed nodules beneath the skin and disfigurement and wasting of affected parts. [C16: from LEPROUS + -Y³]

leprous ('lɛprəs) *adj.* **1.** having leprosy. **2.** relating to or resembling leprosy. [C13: from OF, from LL *leprosus*, from *lepra* LEPER]

-lepsy *or sometimes* **-lepsia** *n. combining form.* indicating a seizure: *catalepsy.* [from NL *-lepsia*, from Gk, from *lēpsis* a seizure, from *lambanein* to seize] —**-leptic** *adj. combining form.*

lepton¹ ('lɛptɒn) *n.*, *pl.* **-ta** (-tə). **1.** a Greek monetary unit worth one hundredth of a drachma. **2.** a small coin of ancient Greece. [from Gk *lepton* (*nomisma*) small (coin)]

lepton² ('lɛptɒn) *n.* *Physics.* any of a group of elementary particles and their antiparticles, such as an electron, muon, or neutrino, that participate in electromagnetic and weak interactions. [C20: from Gk *leptos* thin, from *lepein* to peel + -ON]

lepton number *n.* *Physics.* a quantum number describing the behaviour of elementary particles, equal to the number of leptons present minus the number of antileptons. It is thought to be conserved in all processes.

leptospirosis (ˌlɛptəʊspaɪ'rəʊsɪs) *n.* any of several infectious diseases caused by bacteria, transmitted to man by animals and characterized by jaundice, meningitis, and kidney failure. [C20: from NL *Leptospira* (from Gk *leptos* thin + *speira* coil + -OSIS)]

Lérida (*Spanish* 'leriða) *n.* a city in NE Spain, in Catalonia: commercial centre of an agricultural region. Pop.: 106 814 (1981).

Lermontov (*Russian* 'ljɛrməntəf) *n.* **Mikhail Yurievich** (mixa'il 'jurjɪvitʃ). 1814–41, Russian novelist and poet: noted esp. for the novel *A Hero of Our Time* (1840).

Lerner ('lɜːnə) n. **Alan Jay.** 1914–86, U.S. songwriter and librettist. With Frederick Loewe he wrote *My Fair Lady* (1956) and *Camelot* (1960) as well as a number of film scripts, including *Gigi* (1958).

Lerwick ('lɜːwɪk) n. a town in Shetland, administrative centre of the island authority of Shetland, on the island of Mainland: the most northerly town in the British Isles; knitwear, oil refining. Pop.: 8000 (1985 est.).

Le Sage *or* **Lesage** (*French* lə saʒ) n. **Alain-René** (alɛ̃rəne). 1668–1747, French novelist and dramatist, author of the picaresque novel *Gil Blas* (1715–35).

lesbian ('lɛzbɪən) n. **1.** a female homosexual. ~*adj.* **2.** of or characteristic of lesbians. [C19: from the homosexuality attributed to Sappho] —'**lesbianism** n.

Lesbos ('lɛzbɒs) n. an island in the E Aegean, off the NW coast of Turkey: a centre of lyric poetry, led by Alcaeus and Sappho (6th century B.C.); annexed to Greece in 1913. Chief town: Mytilene. Pop.: 104 620 (1981). Area: 1630 sq. km (630 sq. miles). Modern Greek name: **Lésvos.** Former name: **Mytilene.** — '**Lesbian** adj., n.

Les Cayes (le 'keɪ; *French* le kaj) n. a port in SW Haiti, on the S Tiburon Peninsula. Pop.: 34 090 (1982). Also called: **Cayes.** Former name: **Aux Cayes.**

lese-majesty ('liːz'mædʒɪstɪ) n. **1.** any of various offences committed against the sovereign power in a state; treason. **2.** an attack on authority or position. [C16: from F *lèse majesté*, from L *laesa mājestās* wounded majesty]

lesion ('liːʒən) n. **1.** any structural change in a bodily part resulting from injury or disease. **2.** an injury or wound. [C15: via OF from LL *laesiō* injury, from L *laedere* to hurt]

Lesotho (lɪ'suːtʊ, lə'səʊtəʊ) n. a kingdom in southern Africa, forming an enclave in the Republic of South Africa: annexed to British Cape Colony in 1871; made a protectorate in 1884; gained independence in 1966; a member of the Commonwealth. It is generally mountainous, with temperate grasslands throughout. Languages: Sesotho and English. Religion: Christian majority. Currency: loti. Capital: Maseru. Pop.: 1 626 500 (1987 est.). Area: 30 344 sq. km (11 716 sq. miles). Former name (1884–1966): **Basutoland.**

less (lɛs) determiner. **1. a.** the comparative of **little** (sense 1): *less sugar; less spirit than before.* **b.** (*as pronoun; functioning as sing. or pl.*): *she has less than she needs; the less you eat, the less you want.* **2.** (usually preceded by *no*) lower in rank or importance: *no less a man than the president.* **3. less of.** to a smaller extent or degree: *we see less of John these days; less of a success than I'd hoped.* ~*adv.* **4.** the comparative of *a little: she walks less than she should; less quickly; less beautiful.* ~*prep.* **5.** subtracting; minus: *three weeks less a day.* [OE *lǣssa* (adj.), *lǣs* (adv., n.)]

▷ **Usage.** *Less* should not be confused with *fewer. Less* refers only to quantity and not to number: *there is less water than before. Fewer* means smaller in number: *there are fewer people than before.*

-less *suffix forming adjectives.* **1.** without; lacking: *speechless.* **2.** not able to (do something) or not able to be (done, performed, etc.): *countless.* [OE *-lās*, from *lēas* lacking]

lessee (lɛ'siː) n. a person to whom a lease is granted; a tenant under a lease. [C15: via Anglo-F from OF *lessé*, from *lesser* to LEASE]

lessen ('lɛsən) vb. **1.** to make or become less. **2.** (tr.) to make little of.

Lesseps ('lɛsəps; *French* lɛsɛps) n. Vicomte **Ferdinand Marie de** (fɛrdinɑ̃ mari də). 1805–94, French diplomat: directed the construction of the Suez Canal (1859–69) and the unsuccessful first attempt to build the Panama Canal (1881–89).

lesser ('lɛsə) adj. not as great in quantity, size, or worth.

Lesser Antilles pl. n. the group of islands in the West Indies, including the Leeward Islands, the Windward Islands, Barbados, and the Netherlands Antilles. Also called: **Caribbees.**

lesser celandine n. a Eurasian plant, related to the buttercup, having yellow flowers and heart-shaped leaves.

lesser panda n. See **panda** (sense 2).

Lesser Sunda Islands pl. n. the former name of **Nusa Tenggara.**

Lessing ('lɛsɪŋ) n. **1. Doris (May).** born 1919, English novelist and short-story writer, brought up in Rhodesia:

her novels include the five-novel sequence *Children of Violence* (1952–69), *The Golden Notebook* (1962), *Memoirs of a Survivor* (1974), a series of science-fiction works (1979–83), and *The Good Terrorist* (1985). **2. Gotthold Ephraim** ('gɔthɔlt 'eːfraɪm). 1729–81, German dramatist and critic. His plays include *Miss Sara Sampson* (1755), the first German domestic tragedy, and *Nathan der Weise* (1779). He is noted for his criticism of French classical dramatists, and for his treatise on aesthetics *Laokoon* (1766).

lesson ('lɛsən) n. **1. a.** a unit, or single period of instruction in a subject; class: *an hour-long music lesson.* **b.** the content of such a unit. **2.** material assigned for individual study. **3.** something from which useful knowledge or principles can be learned; example. **4.** the principles, knowledge, etc., gained. **5.** a reprimand or punishment intended to correct. **6.** a portion of Scripture appointed to be read at divine service. [C13: from OF *leçon*, from L *lĕctiō*, from *legere* to read]

lessor ('lɛsɔː, lɛ'sɔː) n. a person who grants a lease of property.

lest (lɛst) conj. (subordinating; takes a subjunctive vb.) **1.** so as to prevent any possibility that: *keep down lest anyone see us.* **2.** (after vbs. or phrases expressing fear, worry, anxiety, etc.) for fear that; in case: *he was alarmed lest she should find out.* [OE *the lǣste,* earlier *thȳ lǣs the,* lit.: whereby less that]

Lésvos ('lɛzvɒs) n. transliteration of the Modern Greek name for **Lesbos.**

let[1] (lɛt) vb. **letting, let.** (tr.; usually takes an infinitive without *to* or an implied infinitive) **1.** to permit; allow: *she lets him roam around.* **2.** (imperative or dependent imperative) **a.** used as an auxiliary to express a request, proposal, or command, or to convey a warning or threat: *let's get on; just let me catch you here again!* **b.** (in mathematical or philosophical discourse) used as an auxiliary to express an assumption or hypothesis: *let "a" equal "b".* **c.** used as an auxiliary to express resigned acceptance of the inevitable: *let the worst happen.* **3. a.** to allow the occupation of (accommodation) in return for rent. **b.** to assign (a contract for work). **4.** to allow or cause the movement of (something) in a specified direction: *to let air out of a tyre.* **5. let alone.** (conj.) much less; not to mention: *I can't afford wine, let alone champagne.* **6. let** *or* **leave alone** *or* **be.** refrain from annoying or interfering with: *let the poor cat alone.* **7. let go.** See **go**[1] (sense 45). **8. let loose.** to set free. ~*n.* **8.** *Brit.* the act of letting property or accommodation. ~See also **let down, let off,** etc. [OE *lǣtan* to permit]

let[2] (lɛt) n. **1.** an impediment or obstruction (esp. in **without let or hindrance**). **2.** *Tennis, squash, etc.* **a.** a minor infringement or obstruction of the ball, requiring a point to be replayed. **b.** the point so replayed. ~*vb.* **letting, letted** *or* **let.** **3.** (tr.) *Arch.* to hinder; impede. [OE *lettan* to hinder, from *lǣt* late]

-let *suffix forming nouns.* **1.** small or lesser: *booklet.* **2.** an article of attire or ornament worn on a specified part of the body: *anklet.* [from OF *-elet,* from L *-āle,* from L *-ellus,* dim. suffix]

Letchworth ('lɛtʃwəθ, -,wɜːθ) n. a town in SE England, in N Hertfordshire: the first garden city in Great Britain (founded in 1903). Pop.: 31 835 (1981).

let down vb. (tr., mainly adv.) **1.** (also prep.) to lower. **2.** to fail to fulfil the expectations of (a person); disappoint. **3.** to undo, shorten, and resew (the hem) so as to lengthen (a dress, skirt, etc.). **4.** to untie (long hair that is bound up) and allow to fall loose. **5.** to deflate: *to let down a tyre.* ~*n.* **letdown. 6.** a disappointment.

lethal ('liːθəl) adj. **1.** able to cause or causing death. **2.** of or suggestive of death. [C16: from L *lēthālis,* from *lētum* death] —**lethality** (liː'θælɪtɪ) n. —'**lethally** adv.

lethargy ('lɛθədʒɪ) n., pl. **-gies. 1.** sluggishness, slowness, or dullness. **2.** an abnormal lack of energy. [C14: from LL *lēthargīa,* from Gk *lēthargos* drowsy, from *lēthē* forgetfulness] —**lethargic** (lɪ'θɑːdʒɪk) adj. —**le'thargically** adv.

Lethbridge ('lɛθbrɪdʒ) n. a city in Canada, in S Alberta: coal-mining. Pop.: 60 610 (1987).

Lethe ('liːθɪ) n. **1.** *Greek myth.* a river in Hades that caused forgetfulness in those who drank its waters. **2.** forgetfulness. [C16: via L from Gk, from *lēthē* oblivion] —**Lethean** (lɪ'θiːən) adj.

Leto ('li:təʊ) *n.* the mother by Zeus of Apollo and Artemis. Roman name: **Latona.**

let off *vb.* (*tr., mainly adv.*) **1.** (*also prep.*) to allow to disembark or leave. **2.** to explode or fire (a bomb, gun, etc.). **3.** (*also prep.*) to excuse from (work or other responsibilities): *I'll let you off for a week.* **4.** *Inf.* to allow to get away without the expected punishment, work, etc. **5.** to let (accommodation) in portions. **6.** to release (liquid, air, etc.).

let on *vb.* (*adv.*; when *tr.*, takes a clause as object) *Inf.* **1.** to allow (something, such as a secret) to be known; reveal: *he never let on that he was married.* **2.** (*tr.*) to cause or encourage to be believed; pretend.

let out *vb.* (*adv., mainly tr.*) **1.** to give vent to; emit: *to let out a howl.* **2.** to allow to go or run free; release. **3.** (*may take a clause as object*) to reveal (a secret). **4.** to make available to tenants, hirers, or contractors. **5.** to permit to flow out: *to let air out of the tyres.* **6.** to make (a garment) larger, as by unpicking (the seams) and sewing nearer the outer edge. ~*n.* **let-out. 7.** a chance to escape.

let's (lɛts) *contraction of* let us: used to express a suggestion, command, etc., by the speaker to himself and his hearers.

Lett (lɛt) *n.* another name for a **Latvian.**

letter ('lɛtə) *n.* **1.** any of a set of conventional symbols used in writing or printing a language, each symbol being associated with a group of phonetic values; character of the alphabet. **2.** a written or printed communication addressed to a person, company, etc., usually sent by post. **3.** (often preceded by *the*) the strict legalistic or pedantic interpretation of the meaning of an agreement, document, etc.; exact wording as distinct from actual intention (esp. in **the letter of the law**). **4. to the letter. a.** following the literal interpretation or wording exactly. **b.** attending to every detail. ~*vb.* **5.** to write or mark letters on (a sign, etc.), esp. by hand. **6.** (*tr.*) to set down or print using letters. [C13: from OF *lettre*, from L *littera* letter of the alphabet] —'**letterer** *n.*

letter bomb *n.* an explosive device in an envelope, detonated when the envelope is opened.

letter box *n. Chiefly Brit.* **1. a.** a slot through which letter, etc. are delivered to a building. **b.** a private box into which letters, etc., are delivered. **2.** Also: **postbox.** a public box into which letters, etc., are put for collection.

lettered ('lɛtəd) *adj.* **1.** well educated in literature, the arts, etc. **2.** literate. **3.** of or characterized by learning or culture. **4.** printed or marked with letters.

letterhead ('lɛtə,hɛd) *n.* a sheet of writing paper printed with one's address, name, etc.

lettering ('lɛtərɪŋ) *n.* **1.** the act, art, or technique of inscribing letters on to something. **2.** the letters so inscribed.

letter of credit *n.* a letter issued by a bank entitling the bearer to draw funds up to a specified maximum from that bank or its agencies.

letter of marque *or* **letters of marque** *n.* (formerly) a licence granted by a state to a private citizen to arm a ship and seize merchant vessels of another nation. Also called: **letter of marque and reprisal.**

letter-perfect *adj.* another term (esp. U.S.) for **word-perfect.**

letterpress ('lɛtə,prɛs) *n.* **1. a.** a method of printing in which ink is transferred from raised surfaces to paper by pressure. **b.** matter so printed. **2.** text matter as distinct from illustrations.

letters ('lɛtəz) *n.* (*functioning as sing. or pl.*) **1.** literary knowledge, ability, or learning: *a man of letters.* **2.** literary culture in general. **3.** an official title, degree, etc., indicated by an abbreviation: *letters after one's name.*

letters patent *pl. n.* See **patent** (senses 1, 4).

Lettish ('lɛtɪʃ) *n., adj.* another word for **Latvian.**

lettuce ('lɛtɪs) *n.* **1.** any of various plants of the composite family cultivated in many varieties for their large edible leaves. **2.** the leaves of any of these varieties, which are eaten in salads. **3.** any of various plants that resemble true lettuce, such as lamb's lettuce. [C13: prob. from OF *laitues*, from L *lactūca*, from *lac-* milk, because of its milky juice]

let up *vb.* (*intr., adv.*) **1.** to diminish, slacken, or stop. **2.** (foll. by *on*) *Inf.* to be less harsh (towards someone). ~*n.* **let-up. 3.** *Inf.* a lessening or abatement.

Leucas ('lu:kəs) *n.* a variant spelling of **Leukas.**

Leucippus (lu:'sɪpəs) *n.* 5th century B.C. Greek philosopher, who originated the atomist theory of matter, developed by his disciple, Democritus.

leuco-, leuko- *or before a vowel* **leuc-, leuk-** *combining form.* white or lacking colour: *leucocyte; leukaemia.* [from Gk *leukos* white]

leucocyte *or esp. U.S.* **leukocyte** ('lu:kə,saɪt) *n.* any of the various large unpigmented cells in the blood of vertebrates. Also called: **white blood cell, white (blood) corpuscle.** —**leucocytic** *or esp. U.S.* **leukocytic** (,lu:kə'sɪtɪk) *adj.*

leucoma (lu:'kəʊmə) *n. Pathol.* a white opaque scar of the cornea.

leucotomy (lu:'kɒtəmɪ) *n., pl.* **-mies,** the surgical operation of cutting some of the nerve fibres in the frontal lobes of the brain for treating intractable mental disorders.

Leuctra ('lu:ktrə) *n.* an ancient town in Greece southwest of Thebes in Boeotia: site of a victory of Thebes over Sparta (371 B.C.), which marked the end of Spartan military supremacy in Greece.

leukaemia *or esp. U.S.* **leukemia** (lu:'ki:mɪə) *n.* an acute or chronic disease characterized by a gross proliferation of leucocytes, which crowd into the bone marrow, spleen, lymph nodes, etc., and suppress the blood-forming apparatus. [C19: from LEUCO- + Gk *haima* blood]

Leukas *or* **Leucas** ('lu:kəs) *n.* another name for **Levkás.**

Leuven ('lɔːvə) *n.* the Flemish name for **Louvain.**

Lev. *Bible. abbrev. for* Leviticus.

levant (lɪ'vænt) *n.* a type of leather made from the skins of goats, sheep, or seals, having a pattern of irregular creases. [C19: shortened from *Levant morocco* (type of leather)]

Levant (lɪ'vænt) *n.* **the.** a former name for the area of the E Mediterranean now occupied by Lebanon, Syria, and Israel. [C15: from OF, from *lever* to raise (referring to the rising of the sun in the east), from L *levāre*] —**Levantine** ('lɛvən,taɪn) *adj., n.*

levanter (lɪ'væntə) *n.* (*sometimes cap.*) **1.** an easterly wind in the W Mediterranean area. **2.** an inhabitant of the Levant.

levator (lɪ'veɪtə, -tɔː) *n. Anat.* any of various muscles that raise a part of the body. [C17: NL, from L *levāre* to raise]

levee[1] ('lɛvɪ) *n. U.S.* **1.** an embankment alongside a river, produced naturally by sedimentation or constructed by man to prevent flooding. **2.** an embankment that surrounds a field that is to be irrigated. **3.** a landing place on a river; quay. [C18: from F, from Med. L *levāta* from L *levāre* to raise]

levee[2] ('lɛvɪ, 'lɛveɪ) *n.* **1.** a formal reception held by a sovereign just after rising from bed. **2.** (in Britain) a public court reception for men. [C17: from F, var. of *lever* a rising, from L *levāre* to raise]

level ('lɛvəl) *adj.* **1.** on a horizontal plane. **2.** having a surface of completely equal height. **3.** being of the same height as something else. **4.** (of quantities to be measured, as in recipes) even with the top of the cup, spoon, etc. **5.** equal to or even with (something or someone else). **6.** not having or showing inconsistency or irregularities. **7.** Also: **level-headed.** even-tempered; steady. **8. one's level best.** the best one can do. ~*vb.* **-elling, -elled** *or U.S.* **-eling, -eled. 9.** (*tr.*; sometimes foll. by *off*) to make (a surface) horizontal, level, or even. **10.** to make (two or more people or things) equal, as in position or status. **11.** (*tr.*) to raze to the ground. **12.** (*tr.*) to knock (a person) down as by a blow. **13.** (*tr.*) to direct (a gaze, criticism, etc.) emphatically at someone. **14.** (*intr.*; often foll. by *with*) *Inf.* to be straightforward and frank. **15.** (*intr.*; foll. by *off* or *out*) to manoeuvre an aircraft into a horizontal flight path after a dive, climb, or glide. **16.** (often foll. by *at*) to aim (a weapon) horizontally. ~*n.* **17.** a horizontal datum line or plane. **18.** a device, such as a spirit level, for determining whether a surface is horizontal. **19.** a surveying instrument used for measuring relative heights of land. **20.** position or status in a scale of values. **21.** amount or degree of progress; stage. **22.** a specified vertical position; altitude. **23.** a horizontal line or plane with respect to which measurement of elevation is based: *sea level.* **24.** a flat even surface or area of land. **25.** *Physics.* the ratio of the magnitude of a physical quantity to an arbitrary magnitude: *sound-pressure level.* **26. on the level.** *Inf.* sincere or genuine. [C14: from OF *livel*, from Vulgar L *libellum* (unattested), from L *lībella*, dim.

of *lībra* scales] — 'leveller *or U.S.* 'leveler *n.* — 'levelly *adv.* — 'levelness *n.*

level crossing *n. Brit.* a point at which a railway and a road cross, esp. one with barriers that close the road when a train is due to pass.

level-headed *adj.* even-tempered, balanced, and reliable; steady. — ,level-'headedly *adv.* — ,level-'headedness *n.*

level pegging *Brit. inf.* ~*n.* **1.** equality between two contestants. ~*adj.* **2.** (of two contestants) equal.

Leven ('li:vᵊn) *n.* Loch. **1.** a lake in E central Scotland: one of the shallowest of Scottish lochs, with seven islands, on one of which Mary Queen of Scots was imprisoned (1567–8). Length: 6 km (3·7miles). Width: 4 km (2·5miles). **2.** a sea loch in W Scotland, extending for about 14 km (9 miles) east from Loch Linnhe.

lever ('li:və) *n.* **1.** a rigid bar pivoted about a fulcrum, used to transfer a force to a load and usually to provide a mechanical advantage. **2.** any of a number of mechanical devices employing this principle. **3.** a means of exerting pressure in order to accomplish something. ~*vb.* **4.** to prise or move (an object) with a lever. [C13: from OF *leveour*, from *lever* to raise, from L *levāre* from *levis* light]

leverage ('li:vərɪdʒ, -vrɪdʒ) *n.* **1.** the action of a lever. **2.** the mechanical advantage gained by employing a lever. **3.** strategic advantage.

leveret ('lɛvərɪt, -vrɪt) *n.* a young hare, esp. one less than one year old. [C15: from Norman F *levrete*, dim. of *levre*, from L *lepus* hare]

Leverhulme ('li:və,hju:m) *n.* William Hesketh, 1st Viscount. 1851-1925, English soap manufacturer and philanthropist, who founded (1881) the model industrial town Port Sunlight.

Leverkusen (*German* 'le:vər,ku:zən) *n.* a town in West Germany, in North Rhine-Westphalia on the Rhine: chemical industries. Pop.: 154 700 (1986).

Leverrier (*French* lǝvɛrje) *n.* Urbain Jean Joseph (yrbɛ̃ ʒɑ̃ ʒozɛf). 1811–77, French astronomer: calculated the existence and position of the planet Neptune.

Levi [1]('li:vaɪ) *n.* **1.** *Old Testament.* **a.** the third son of Jacob and Leah and the ancestor of the tribe of Levi (Genesis 29:34). **b.** the priestly tribe descended from this patriarch (Numbers 18:21–24). **2.** *New Testament.* another name for **Matthew** (the apostle).

Levi [2] (*Italian* 'levi) *n.* **1.** Carlo. 1902–75, Italian physician, painter, and writer. Best known for his novel *Christ Stopped at Eboli* (1947), his other works include *The Watch* (1952) and *Words are Stones* (1958). **2.** Primo ('pri:mǝʊ). 1919–87, Italian novelist. His book *If This is a Man* (1947) relates his experiences in Auschwitz. Other books include *The Periodic Table* (1956) and *The Drowned and the Saved* (1988), published after his suicide.

leviable ('lɛvɪǝbᵊl) *adj.* **1.** (of taxes, etc.) liable to be levied. **2.** (of goods, etc.) liable to bear a levy; taxable.

leviathan (lɪ'vaɪǝθǝn) *n.* **1.** *Bible.* a monstrous beast, esp. a sea monster. **2.** any huge or powerful thing. [C14: from LL, ult. from Heb. *liwyāthān*, from ?]

levigate ('lɛvɪ,geɪt) *vb. Chem.* **1.** (*tr.*) to grind into a fine powder or a smooth paste. **2.** to form or cause to form a homogeneous mixture, as in the production of gels. **3.** (*tr.*) to suspend (fine particles) by grinding in a liquid, esp. as a method of separating fine from coarse particles. [C17: from L *lēvigāre*, from *lēvis* smooth] — ,levi'gation *n.*

Levis ('li:vaɪz) *pl. n. Trademark.* jeans, usually blue and made of denim.

Lévi-Strauss ('lɛvɪ'straʊs; *French* levistros) *n.* Claude (klod). born 1908, French anthropologist, leading exponent of structuralism. His books include *The Elementary Structures of Kinship* (1969), *Totemism* (1962), *The Savage Mind* (1966), and *Mythologies* (1964–71).

levitate ('lɛvɪ,teɪt) *vb.* to rise or cause to rise and float in the air, usually attributed to supernatural intervention. [C17: from L *levis* light + *-tate*, as in *gravitate*] — ,levi'tation *n.* — 'levi,tator *n.*

levity ('lɛvɪtɪ) *n., pl.* **-ties. 1.** inappropriate lack of seriousness. **2.** fickleness or instability. **3.** *Arch.* lightness in weight. [C16: from L *levitās* lightness, from *levis* light]

Levkás (lɛf'kæs), **Leukas** *or* **Leucas** *n.* a Greek island in the Ionian Sea, in the Ionian Islands. Pop.: 21 863 (1981). Area: 295 sq. km (114 sq. miles). Italian name: **Santa Maura.**

levy ('lɛvɪ) *vb.* **levying, levied.** (*tr.*) **1.** to impose and collect (a tax, tariff, fine, etc.). **2.** to conscript troops for service. **3.** to seize or attach (property) in accordance with the judgment of a court. ~*n., pl.* **levies. 4. a.** the act of imposing and collecting a tax, tariff, etc. **b.** the money so raised. **5. a.** the conscription of troops for service. **b.** a person conscripted in this way. [C15: from OF *levée* a raising, from *lever*, from L *levāre* to raise]

lewd (lu:d) *adj.* characterized by or intended to excite crude sexual desire; obscene. [C14: from OE *lǣwde* ignorant] — 'lewdly *adv.* — 'lewdness *n.*

Lewes ('lu:ɪs) *n.* a market town in S England, administrative centre of East Sussex, on the River Ouse: site of a battle (1264) in which Henry III was defeated by Simon de Montfort. Pop.: 13 770 (1981).

lewis ('lu:ɪs) *n.* a lifting device for heavy stone blocks consisting of a number of curved pieces of metal fitting into a dovetailed recess cut into the stone. [C18: ?from the name of the inventor]

Lewis [1] ('lu:ɪs) *n.* the N part of the island of Lewis with Harris, in the Outer Hebrides. Area: 1634 sq. km (631 sq. miles).

Lewis [2] ('lu:ɪs) *n.* **1.** Carl. full name *Frederick Carleton Lewis.* born 1961, U.S. athlete; winner of the long jump, 100 metres, 200 metres, and 4 × 100 metres relay at the 1984 Olympic Games; winner of the 100 metres in the 1988 Olympic Games. **2.** See (Cecil) **Day-Lewis. 3.** C(live) S(taples). 1898–1963, English novelist, critic, and Christian apologist, noted for his critical work, *Allegory of Love* (1936), his theological study, *The Screwtape Letters* (1942), and for his children's books chronicling the land of Narnia. **4. (Harry) Sinclair.** 1885–1951, U.S. novelist. He satirized the complacency and philistinism of American small-town life, esp. in *Main Street* (1920) and *Babbitt* (1922): Nobel prize for literature 1930. **5.** Matthew Gregory, known as *Monk Lewis.* 1775–1818, English novelist and dramatist, noted for his Gothic horror story *The Monk* (1796). **6. Meriwether.** 1774–1807, American explorer who, with William Clark, led an overland expedition from St. Louis to the Pacific Ocean (1804–06). **7. (Percy) Wyndham.** 1884–1957, British painter, novelist, and critic, born in the U.S. A founder of vorticism, his writings include *Time and Western Man* (1927), *The Apes of God* (1930), and the trilogy *The Human Age* (1928–55).

Lewis acid *n.* a substance capable of accepting a pair of electrons from a base to form a covalent bond. Cf. **Lewis base.** [C20: after G. N. *Lewis* (1875–1946), U.S. chemist]

Lewis base *n.* a substance capable of donating a pair of electrons to an acid to form a covalent bond. Cf. **Lewis acid.** [C20: after G. N. *Lewis*; see LEWIS ACID]

Lewis gun *n.* a light air-cooled gas-operated machine gun used chiefly in World Wars I and II. [C20: after I. N. *Lewis* (1858–1931), U.S. soldier]

Lewisham ('lu:ɪʃǝm) *n.* a borough of S Greater London, on the River Thames. Pop.: 232 000 (1986 est.).

lewisite ('lu:ɪ,saɪt) *n.* a colourless oily poisonous liquid having a powerful blistering action and used as a war gas. Formula: ClCH:CHAsCl₂. Systematic name: **1-chloro-2dichloroarsinoethene.** [C20: after W. L. *Lewis* (1878–1943), U.S. chemist]

Lewis with Harris *or* **Lewis and Harris** *n.* an island in the Outer Hebrides, separated from the NW coast of Scotland by the Minch: consists of Lewis in the north and Harris in the south; many lakes and peat moors; economy based chiefly on the Harris tweed industry, with some fishing. Chief town: Stornoway. Pop.: 23 390 (1981). Area: 2134 sq. km (824 sq. miles).

lexeme ('lɛksi:m) *n. Linguistics.* a minimal meaningful unit that cannot be understood from the meanings of its component morphemes. [C20: from LEX(ICON) + -EME]

lexical ('lɛksɪkᵊl) *adj.* **1.** of or relating to items of vocabulary in a language. **2.** of or relating to a lexicon. — 'lexically *adv.*

lexicography (,lɛksɪ'kɒɡrǝfɪ) *n.* the process or profession of writing or compiling dictionaries. — ,lexi'cographer *n.* — lexicographic (,lɛksɪkǝ'ɡræfɪk) *or* ,lexico'graphical *adj.*

lexicon ('lɛksɪkǝn) *n.* **1.** a dictionary, esp. one of an ancient language such as Greek or Hebrew. **2.** a list of terms relating to a particular subject. **3.** the vocabulary of a language or of an individual. **4.** *Linguistics.* the set of all the morphemes of a language. [C17: NL, from Gk *lexikon* n. use of *lexikos* relating to words, from Gk *lexis* word, from *legein* to speak]

lexigraphy (lɛk'sɪgrəfɪ) n. a system of writing in which each word is represented by a sign. [C19: from Gk *lexis* word + -GRAPHY]

Lexington ('lɛksɪŋtən) n. **1.** a city in NE central Kentucky, in the bluegrass region: major centre for horse-breeding. Pop.: 213 600 (1986 est.). **2.** a city in Massachusetts, northwest of Boston: site of the first action (1775) of the War of American Independence. Pop.: 29 479 (1981).

lexis ('lɛksɪs) n. the totality of vocabulary items in a language. [C20: from Gk *lexis* word]

ley (leɪ, liː) n. **1.** arable land temporarily under grass. **2.** Also: **ley line.** a line joining two prominent points in the landscape, thought to be the line of a prehistoric track. [C14: var. of LEA]

Leyden¹ ('laɪdᵊn; *Dutch* 'lɛɪdə) n. a variant spelling of **Leiden.**

Leyden² ('laɪdᵊn) n. See **Lucas van Leyden.**

Leyden jar n. *Physics.* an early type of capacitor consisting of a glass jar with the lower part of the inside and outside coated with tin foil. [C18: first made in Leiden]

Leyte ('leɪteɪ) n. an island in the central Philippines, in the Visayan Islands. Chief town: Tacloban. Pop.: 1 302 648 (1980). Area: 7215 sq. km (2786 sq. miles).

Leyte Gulf n. an inlet of the Pacific in the E Philippines, east of Leyte and south of Samar: scene of a battle (Oct. 23–26, 1944) during World War II, in which the Americans defeated almost the entire Japanese navy, thereby ensuring ultimate Allied victory.

lf *Printing. abbrev. for* light face.

LF *Radio. abbrev. for* low frequency.

LG *abbrev. for* Low German.

lh *or* **LH** *abbrev. for* left hand.

Lhasa *or* **Lassa** ('lɑːsə) n. a city in SW China, capital of Tibet AR, at an altitude of 3606 m (11 830 ft.): for centuries the sacred city of Lamaism and residence of the Dalai Lamas from the 17th century until 1950; known as the Forbidden City because it was closed to Westerners until the beginning of the 20th century; annexed by China in 1951. The Dalai Lama fled after an unsuccessful revolt against Chinese rule in 1959. Pop.: 110 000 (1982 est.).

Li *the chemical symbol for* lithium.

liabilities (ˌlaɪə'bɪlɪtɪz) pl. n. *Accounting.* business obligations not discharged and shown as balanced against assets on the balance sheet.

liability (ˌlaɪə'bɪlɪtɪ) n., pl. **-ties. 1.** the state of being liable. **2.** a financial obligation. **3.** a hindrance or disadvantage.

liable ('laɪəbᵊl) adj. (*postpositive*) **1.** legally obliged or responsible; answerable. **2.** susceptible or exposed; subject. **3.** probable or likely: *it's liable to happen soon.* [C15: ? from Anglo-F, from OF *lier* to bind, from L *ligāre*]

▷ **Usage.** Careful users of English take *liable* to mean *responsible for* and *subject to* in sentences such as *he was liable for his employees' accidents* and *he was liable to accidents.* The use of *liable* in the sense of *likely* is avoided: *he was likely* (not *liable*) *to have accidents.*

liaise (lɪ'eɪz) vb. (*intr.*; usually foll. by *with*) to communicate and maintain contact (with). [C20: back formation from LIAISON]

liaison (lɪ'eɪzɒn) n. **1.** communication and contact between groups or units. **2.** a secretive or adulterous sexual relationship. **3.** the relationship between military units necessary to ensure unity of purpose. **4.** (esp. in French) the pronunciation of a normally silent consonant at the end of a word immediately before another word commencing with a vowel, in such a way that the consonant is taken over as the initial sound of the following word, as in *ils ont* (ilzɔ̃). **5.** any thickening for soups, sauces, etc., such as egg yolks or cream. [C17: via F from OF, from *lier* to bind, from L *ligāre*]

Liákoura ('ljakura) n. transliteration of the Modern Greek name for (Mount) **Parnassus.**

liana (lɪ'ɑːnə) *or* **liane** (lɪ'ɑːn) n. any of various woody climbing plants of tropical forests. [C19: changed from earlier *liane* (through infl. of F *lier* to bind), from F, from ?]

Lianyungang ('ljæn'jʊŋ'gæŋ), **Sinhailien,** *or* **Hsin-hai-lien** n. a city in E China, near the coast of Jiangsu. Pop.: 446 100 (1984 est.).

Liao (ljaʊ) n. a river in NE China, rising in SE Inner Mongolia and flowing northeast then southwest to the Gulf of Liaodong. Length: about 1100 km (700 miles).

Liaodong ('ljaʊ'dʊŋ) *or* **Liaotung** ('ljaʊ'tʊŋ) n. **1.** a peninsula of NE China, in S Manchuria extending south into the Yellow Sea: forms the S part of Liaoning province. **2.** **Gulf of.** the N part of the Gulf of Chihli, west of the peninsula of Liaodong.

Liaoning ('ljaʊ'nɪŋ) n. a province of NE China, in S Manchuria. Capital: Shenyang. Pop.: 36 550 000 (1985). Area: 150 000 sq. km (58 500 sq. miles).

Liaoyang ('ljaʊ'jæŋ) n. a city in NE China, in S Manchuria, in Liaoning province: a regional capital in the early dynasties. Pop.: 430 100 (1985 est.).

liar ('laɪə) n. a person who tells lies.

Liard ('liːɑːd, liː'ɑːd, -'ɑː) n. a river in W Canada, rising in the SE Yukon and flowing east and then northwest to the Mackenzie River. Length: 885 km (550 miles).

Lias ('laɪəs) n. the lowest series of rocks of the Jurassic system. [C15 (referring to a kind of limestone), C19 (geological sense): from OF *liois*, ?from *lie* dregs, so called from its appearance] —**Liassic** (laɪ'æsɪk) adj.

lib (lɪb) n. *Inf., sometimes derog.* short for **liberation.**

lib. *abbrev. for:* **1.** liber. [L: book] **2.** librarian. **3.** library.

Lib. *abbrev. for* Liberal.

libation (laɪ'beɪʃən) n. **1. a.** the pouring-out of wine, etc., in honour of a deity. **b.** the liquid so poured out. **2.** *Usually facetious.* an alcoholic drink. [C14: from L *lībātiō*, from *lībāre* to pour an offering of drink]

Libau ('liːbaʊ) n. the German name for **Liepāja.**

Libava (lɪ'bavə) n. transliteration of the Russian name for **Liepāja.**

Libby ('lɪbɪ) n. **Willard Frank.** 1908–80, U.S. chemist, who devised the technique of radiocarbon dating: Nobel prize for chemistry 1960.

libel ('laɪbᵊl) n. **1.** *Law.* **a.** the publication of defamatory matter in permanent form, as by a written or printed statement, picture, etc. **b.** the act of publishing such matter. **2.** any defamatory or unflattering representation or statement. ~vb. **-belling, -belled** *or U.S.* **-beling, -beled.** (*tr.*) **3.** *Law.* to make or publish a defamatory statement or representation about (a person). **4.** to misrepresent injuriously. [C13 (in the sense: written statement), hence C14 legal sense: a plaintiff's statement, via OF from L *libellus* a little book] —**'libeller** *or* **'libelist** n. —**'libellous** *or* **'libelous** adj.

liberal ('lɪbərəl, 'lɪbrəl) adj. **1.** relating to or having social and political views that favour progress and reform. **2.** relating to or having policies or views advocating individual freedom. **3.** giving and generous in temperament or behaviour. **4.** tolerant of other people. **5.** abundant; lavish: *a liberal helping of cream.* **6.** not strict; free: *a liberal translation.* **7.** of or relating to an education that aims to develop general cultural interests and intellectual ability. ~n. **8.** a person who has liberal ideas or opinions. [C14: from L *līberālis* of freedom, from *līber* free] —**'liberally** adv. —**'liberalness** n.

Liberal ('lɪbərəl, 'lɪbrəl) n. **1.** a member or supporter of a Liberal Party. ~adj. **2.** of or relating to a Liberal Party.

liberal arts pl. n. the fine arts, humanities, sociology, languages, and literature. Often shortened to **arts.**

liberalism ('lɪbərəˌlɪzəm, 'lɪbrə-) n. liberal opinions, practices, or politics.

liberality (ˌlɪbə'rælɪtɪ) n., pl. **-ties. 1.** generosity; bounty. **2.** the quality or condition of being liberal.

liberalize *or* **-ise** ('lɪbərəˌlaɪz, 'lɪbrə-) vb. to make or become liberal. —ˌliberali'zation *or* -i'sation n. —'liberalˌizer *or* -ˌiser n.

Liberal Party n. **1.** one of the former major political parties in Britain; merged with the Social Democrat Party to form the Social and Liberal Democrat Party. **2.** one of the major political parties in Australia, a conservative party, generally opposed to the Labor Party. **3.** any other party supporting liberal policies.

liberal studies n. (*functioning as sing.*) *Brit.* a supplementary arts course for those specializing in scientific, technical, or professional studies.

liberate ('lɪbəˌreɪt) vb. (*tr.*) **1.** to give liberty to; make free. **2.** to release (something, esp. a gas) from chemical combination. **3.** to release from occupation or subjugation by a foreign power. **4.** to free from social prejudices or injustices. **5.** *Euphemistic or facetious.* to steal. —'liberˌator n.

liberated ('lɪbə,reɪtɪd) *adj.* **1.** given liberty; freed; released. **2.** released from occupation or subjugation by a foreign power. **3.** (esp. in feminist theory) not bound by traditional sexual and social roles.

liberation (,lɪbə'reɪʃən) *n.* **1.** a liberating or being liberated. **2.** the seeking of equal status or just treatment for or on behalf of any group believed to be discriminated against: *women's liberation; animal liberation.* —,liber'ationist *n., adj.*

liberation theology *n.* the belief that Christianity involves not only faith in the Church but a commitment to change social and political conditions where it is considered exploitation and oppression exist: applied esp. to South America.

Liberec (*Czech* 'lɪbɛrɛts) *n.* a city in NW Czechoslovakia, on the Neisse River: a centre of the German Sudeten movement in 1938. Pop.: 101 000 (1986). German name: **Reichenberg.**

Liberia (laɪ'bɪərɪə) *n.* a republic in W Africa, on the Atlantic: originated in 1822 as a home for freed Afro-American slaves, with land purchased by the American Colonization Society; republic declared in 1847; exports are predominantly rubber and iron ore. Official language: English. Religion: mostly animist. Currency: U.S. dollar. Capital: Monrovia. Pop.: 2 500 000 (1987 est.). Area: 111 400 sq. km (43 000 sq. miles). —**Li'berian** *adj., n.*

libertarian (,lɪbə'tɛərɪən) *n.* **1.** a believer in freedom of thought, expression, etc. **2.** a believer in the doctrine of free will. ~*adj.* **3.** of, relating to, or characteristic of a libertarian. [C18: from LIBERTY] —,liber'tarianism *n.*

libertine ('lɪbə,tiːn, -,taɪn) *n.* **1.** a morally dissolute person. ~*adj.* **2.** morally dissolute. [C14 (in the sense: freedman, dissolute person): from L *libertīnus* freedman, from *lībertus* freed, from *līber* free] —'liber,tinage *or* 'libertin,ism *n.*

liberty ('lɪbətɪ) *n., pl.* **-ties. 1.** the power of choosing, thinking, and acting for oneself; freedom from control or restriction. **2.** the right or privilege of access to a particular place; freedom. **3.** (*often pl.*) a social action regarded as being familiar, forward, or improper. **4.** (*often pl.*) an action that is unauthorized: *he took liberties with the translation.* **5. a.** authorized leave granted to a sailor. **b.** (*as modifier*): *liberty man; liberty boat.* **6. at liberty.** free, unoccupied, or unrestricted. **7. take liberties (with).** to be overfamiliar or overpresumptuous. [C14: from OF *liberté*, from L *lībertās*, from *līber* free]

liberty bodice *n.* a sleeveless vestlike undergarment covering the upper part of the body, formerly worn esp. by young children.

liberty hall *n.* (*sometimes caps.*) *Inf.* a place or condition of complete liberty.

Liberty Island *n.* a small island in upper New York Bay: site of the Statue of Liberty. Area: 5 hectares (12 acres). Former name (until 1956): **Bedloe's Island.**

Libia ('liːbja) *n.* the Italian name for **Libya.**

libidinous (lɪ'bɪdɪnəs) *adj.* characterized by excessive sexual desire. —**li'bidinously** *adv.* —**li'bidinousness** *n.*

libido (lɪ'biːdəʊ) *n., pl.* **-dos. 1.** *Psychoanal.* psychic energy emanating from the id. **2.** sexual urge or desire. [C20 (in psychoanalysis): from L: desire] —**libidinal** (lɪ'bɪdɪnəl) *adj.* —**li'bidinally** *adv.*

libra ('laɪbrə) *n., pl.* **-brae** (-briː). an ancient Roman unit of weight corresponding to 1 pound. [C14: from L, lit.: scales]

Libra ('liːbrə) *n., Latin genitive* **Librae** ('liːbriː). **1.** *Astron.* a small faint zodiacal constellation in the S hemisphere, lying between Virgo and Scorpius. **2.** Also called: the **Scales,** the **Balance.** *Astrol.* the seventh sign of the zodiac. The sun is in this sign between about Sept. 23 and Oct. 22.

librarian (laɪ'brɛərɪən) *n.* a person in charge of or assisting in a library. —**li'brarian,ship** *n.*

library ('laɪbrərɪ) *n., pl.* **-braries. 1.** a room or set of rooms where books and other literary materials are kept. **2.** a collection of literary materials, films, tapes, gramophone records, etc., kept for borrowing or reference. **3.** the building or institution that houses such a collection: *a public library.* **4.** a set of books published as a series, often in a similar format. **5.** *Computers.* a collection of standard programs and subroutines, usually stored on disk. **6.** a collection of specific items for reference or checking against: *a library of genetic material.* [C14: from OF *librairie*, from Med. L *librāris*, n. use of L *librārius* relating to books, from *liber* book]

libration (laɪ'breɪʃən) *n.* **1.** the act of oscillating. **2.** a real or apparent oscillation of the moon enabling approximately nine per cent of the surface facing away from earth to be seen. [C17: from L, from *librāre* to balance]

librettist (lɪ'brɛtɪst) *n.* the author of a libretto.

libretto (lɪ'brɛtəʊ) *n., pl.* **-tos** *or* **-ti** (-tiː). a text written for and set to music in an opera, etc. [C18: from It., dim. of *libro* book]

Libreville (*French* librəvil) *n.* the capital of Gabon, in the west on the estuary of the Gabon River: founded as a French trading post in 1843 and expanded with the settlement of freed slaves in 1848. Pop.: 350 000 (1985 est.).

Librium ('lɪbrɪəm) *n. Trademark.* a preparation of the drug chlordiazepoxide used as a tranquillizer. See also **benzodiazepine.**

Libya ('lɪbɪə) *n.* a republic in N Africa, on the Mediterranean: became an Italian colony in 1912; divided after World War II into Tripolitania and Cyrenaica (under British administration) and Fezzan (under French); gained independence in 1951; monarchy overthrown by a military junta in 1969. It consists almost wholly of desert and is a major exporter of oil. Language: Arabic. Religion: mostly Sunni Muslim. Currency: Libyan dinar. Capital: Tripoli. Pop.: 3 883 000 (1987 est.). Area: 1 760 000 sq. km (680 000 sq. miles). Official name: **Al-Jumhuria al-Arabia allibya** (-,dʒæmə'hriːjθ). —'**Libyan** *adj., n.*

Libyan Desert *n.* a desert in N Africa, in E Libya, W Egypt, and the NW Sudan: the NE part of the Sahara.

lice (laɪs) *n.* the plural of **louse.**

licence *or U.S.* **license** ('laɪsəns) *n.* **1.** a certificate, tag, document, etc., giving official permission to do something. **2.** formal permission or exemption. **3.** liberty of action or thought; freedom. **4.** intentional disregard of conventional rules to achieve a certain effect: *poetic licence.* **5.** excessive freedom. [C14: via OF and Med. L *licentia* permission, from L: freedom, from *licet* it is allowed]

license ('laɪsəns) *vb.* (*tr.*) **1.** to grant or give a licence for (something, such as the sale of alcohol). **2.** to give permission to or for. —'**licensable** *adj.* —'**licenser** *or* 'li**censor** *n.*

licensee (,laɪsən'siː) *n.* a person who holds a licence, esp. one to sell alcoholic drink.

licentiate (laɪ'sɛnʃɪɪt) *n.* **1.** a person who holds a formal attestation of competence to practise a certain profession. **2.** a higher degree awarded by certain, chiefly European, universities. **3.** a person who holds this degree. **4.** *Chiefly Presbyterian Church.* a person holding a licence to preach. [C15: from Med. L *licentiātus*, from *licentiāre* to permit] —**li'centiate,ship** *n.*

licentious (laɪ'sɛnʃəs) *adj.* **1.** sexually unrestrained or promiscuous. **2.** *Now rare.* showing disregard for convention. [C16: from L *licentiōsus* capricious, from *licentia* LICENCE] —**li'centiously** *adv.* —**li'centiousness** *n.*

lichee (,laɪ'tʃiː) *n.* a variant spelling of **litchi.**

lichen ('laɪkən, 'lɪtʃən) *n.* any of various small plants which are formed by the symbiotic association of a fungus and an alga and occur as crusty patches or bushy growths on tree trunks, bare ground, etc. [C17: via L from Gk *leikhēn*, from *leikhein* to lick] —'**lichened** *adj.* —'**lichenous** *adj.*

Lichfield ('lɪtʃ,fiːld) *n.* a city in central England, in SE Staffordshire: cathedral with three spires (13th-14th century); birthplace of Samuel Johnson, during whose lifetime the **Lichfield Group** (a literary circle) flourished. Pop.: 26 310 (1981).

lich gate *or* **lych gate** (lɪtʃ) *n.* a roofed gate to a churchyard, formerly used as a temporary shelter for the bier. [C15: *lich*, from OE *līc* corpse]

Lichtenstein ('lɪktən,staɪn) **Roy.** born 1923, U.S. pop artist.

licit ('lɪsɪt) *adj.* a less common word for **lawful.** [C15: from L *licitus*, from *licēre* to be permitted] —'**licitly** *adv.* —'**licitness** *n.*

lick (lɪk) *vb.* **1.** (*tr.*) to pass the tongue over, esp. in order to taste or consume. **2.** to flicker or move lightly over or round (something): *the flames licked around the door.* **3.** (*tr.*) *Inf.* **a.** to defeat or vanquish. **b.** to flog or thrash. **c.** to be or do much better than. **4. lick into shape.** to put into a satisfactory condition. **5. lick one's wounds.** to retire after a defeat. ~*n.* **6.** an instance of passing the tongue over something. **7.** a small amount: *a lick of paint.* **8.** short for **salt lick. 9.** *Inf.* a hit; blow. **10.** *Sl.* a short musical phrase, usually on one instrument. **11.** *Inf.* rate of movement; speed. **12. a lick and a promise.** something hastily done, esp. a hurried wash. [OE *liccian*] — **'licker** *n.*

lickerish *or* **liquorish** ('lıkərıʃ) *adj. Arch.* **1.** lecherous or lustful. **2.** greedy; gluttonous. **3.** appetizing or tempting. [C16: changed from C13 *lickerous*, from OF *lechereus* lecherous; see LECHER]

lickety-split ('lıkıtı'splıt) *adv. U.S. & Canad. inf.* very quickly; speedily. [C19: from LICK + SPLIT]

licking ('lıkıŋ) *n. Inf.* **1.** a beating. **2.** a defeat.

lickspittle ('lık,spıtᵊl) *n.* a flattering or servile person.

licorice ('lıkərıs) *n.* the usual U.S. and Canad. spelling of **liquorice.**

lictor ('lıktə) *n.* one of a group of ancient Roman officials, usually bearing fasces, who attended magistrates, etc. [C16 *lictor*, C14 *littour*, from L *ligāre* to bind]

lid (lıd) *n.* **1.** a cover, usually removable or hinged, for a receptacle: *a saucepan lid; a desk lid.* **2.** short for **eyelid. 3. put the lid on.** *Inf.* **a.** *Brit.* to be the final blow to. **b.** to curb, prevent, or discourage. [OE *hlid*] — **'lidded** *adj.* — **'lidless** *adj.*

Liddell Hart ('lıdᵊl 'hɑːt) *n.* Sir **Basil Henry.** 1895–1970, English military strategist and historian: he advocated the development of mechanized warfare before World War II.

Lidice (*Czech* 'lıdjıtsɛ) *n.* a mining village in Czechoslovakia, in W central Bohemia: destroyed by the Germans in 1942 in reprisal for the assassination of Reinhard Heydrich; rebuilt as a national memorial.

lido ('liːdəʊ) *n., pl.* **-dos.** *Brit.* a public place of recreation, including a swimming pool. [C20: after the *Lido,* island bathing beach near Venice, from L *litus* shore]

lie¹ (laı) *vb.* **lying, lied. 1.** (*intr.*) to speak untruthfully with intent to mislead or deceive. **2.** (*intr.*) to convey a false impression or practise deception: *the camera does not lie.* ~*n.* **3.** an untrue or deceptive statement deliberately used to mislead. **4.** something that is deliberately intended to deceive. **5. give the lie to. a.** to disprove. **b.** to accuse of lying. ~Related *adj.*: **mendacious.** [OE *lyge* (n.), *lēogan* (vb.)]

lie² (laı) *vb.* **lying, lay, lain.** (*intr.*) **1.** (often foll. by *down*) to place oneself or be in a prostrate position, horizontal to the ground. **2.** to be situated, esp. on a horizontal surface: *the pencil is lying on the desk; India lies to the south of Russia.* **3.** to be buried: *here lies Jane Brown.* **4.** (*copula*) to be and remain (in a particular state or condition): *to lie dormant.* **5.** to stretch or extend: *the city lies before us.* **6.** (usually foll. by *on* or *upon*) to rest or weigh: *my sins lie heavily on my mind.* **7.** (usually foll. by *in*) to exist or consist inherently: *strength lies in unity.* **8.** (foll. by *with*) **a.** to be or rest (with): *the ultimate decision lies with you.* **b.** *Arch.* to have sexual intercourse (with). **9.** (of an action, claim, appeal, etc.) to subsist; be maintainable or admissible. **10.** *Arch.* to stay temporarily. ~*n.* **11.** the manner, place, or style in which something is situated. **12.** the hiding place or lair of an animal. **13. lie of the land. a.** the topography of the land. **b.** the way in which a situation is developing. ~See also **lie down, lie in,** etc. [OE *licgan* akin to OHG *ligen* to lie, L *lectus* bed]

▷ **Usage.** See at **lay.**

Lie (liː) *n.* **Trygve Halvdan** ('trygvə 'halðan). 1896–1968, Norwegian statesman; first secretary-general of the United Nations (1946–52).

Liebig (*German* 'liːbıç) *n.* **Justus** ('jʊstʊs), Baron von Liebig. 1803–73, German chemist, who founded agricultural chemistry. He also contributed to organic chemistry, esp. to the concept of radicals, and he discovered chloroform.

Liebknecht (*German* 'liːpknɛçt) *n.* **1. Karl** (karl). 1871–1919, German socialist leader: with Rosa Luxemburg he led an unsuccessful Communist revolt (1919) and was assassinated. **2.** his father, **Wilhelm** ('vılhɛlm). 1826–1900, German socialist leader and journalist, a founder (1869) of what was to become (1891) the German Social Democratic Party.

Liechtenstein ('lıktən,staın; *German* 'lıçtənʃtaın) *n.* a small mountainous principality in central Europe on the Rhine: formed in 1719 by the uniting of the lordships of Schellenburg and Vaduz, which had been purchased by the Austrian family of Liechtenstein; customs union

formed with Switzerland in 1924. Language: German. Religion: mostly Roman Catholic. Currency: Swiss franc. Capital: Vaduz. Pop.: 28 000 (1986). Area: 160 sq. km (62 sq. miles).

lied (liːd; *German* liːt) *n., pl.* **lieder** ('liːdə; *German* 'liːdər). *Music.* any of various musical settings for solo voice and piano of a romantic or lyrical poem. [from G: song]

lie detector *n. Inf.* a polygraph used esp. by a police interrogator to detect false or devious answers to questions, a sudden change in one or more involuntary physiological responses being considered a manifestation of guilt, fear, etc.

lie down *vb.* (*intr., adv.*) **1.** to place oneself or be in a prostrate position in order to rest. **2.** to accept without protest or opposition (esp. in **take something lying down**). ~*n.* **lie-down. 3.** a rest.

lief (liːf) *adv.* **1.** *Now rare.* gladly; willingly: *I'd as lief go today as tomorrow.* ~*adj.* **2.** *Arch.* **a.** ready; glad. **b.** dear; beloved. [OE *leof;* rel. to *lufu* love]

liege (liːdʒ) *adj.* **1.** (of a lord) owed feudal allegiance (esp. in **liege lord**). **2.** (of a vassal or servant) owing feudal allegiance: *a liege subject.* **3.** faithful; loyal. ~*n.* **4.** a liege lord. **5.** a liegeman or true subject. [C13: from OF *lige*, from Med. L *liticus*, from *litus, laetus* serf, of Gmc origin]

Liège (lı'eıʒ; *French* ljɛʒ) *n.* **1.** a province of E Belgium: formerly a principality of the Holy Roman Empire, much larger than the present-day province. Pop.: 998 007 (1981 est.). Area: 3877 sq. km (1497 sq. miles). **2.** a city in E Belgium, capital of Liège province: the largest French-speaking city in Belgium; river port and industrial centre. Pop.: 200 891 (1987 est.). ~Flemish name: **Luik.**

liegeman ('liːdʒ,mæn) *n., pl.* **-men. 1.** (formerly) a vassal. **2.** a loyal follower.

Liegnitz ('liːgnıts) *n.* the German name for **Legnica.**

lie in *vb.* (*intr., adv.*) **1.** to remain in bed late in the morning. **2.** to be confined in childbirth. ~*n.* **lie-in. 3.** a long stay in bed in the morning.

lien ('liːən, liːn) *n. Law.* a right to retain possession of another's property pending discharge of a debt. [C16: via OF from L *ligāmen* bond, from *ligāre* to bind]

Liepāja *or* **Lepaya** (lı'pɑːjə) *n.* a port in the W Soviet Union, in the W Latvian SSR on the Baltic Sea: a naval and industrial centre, with a fishing fleet. Pop.: 113 000 (1986 est.). Russian name: **Libava.** German name: **Libau.**

lierne (lı'ɜːn) *n. Archit.* a short rib that connects the intersections of the primary ribs, esp. in Gothic vaulting. [C19: from F, ? rel. to *lier* to bind]

Liestal (*German* 'liːstɑːl) *n.* a city in NW Switzerland, capital of Basel-Land demicanton. Pop.: 12 158 (1980).

lie to *vb.* (*intr., adv.*) *Naut.* (of a vessel) to be hove to with little or no swinging.

Lietuva (lıə'tuːvə) *n.* the Lithuanian name for **Lithuanian Soviet Socialist Republic.**

lieu (ljuː, luː) *n.* stead; place (esp. in **in lieu, in lieu of**). [C13: from OF, ult. from L *locus* place]

lieutenant (lɛf'tɛnənt; *U.S.* luː'tɛnənt) *n.* **1.** a military officer holding commissioned rank immediately junior to a captain. **2.** a naval officer holding commissioned rank immediately junior to a lieutenant commander. **3.** *U.S.* an officer in a police or fire department ranking immediately junior to a captain. **4.** a person who holds an office in subordination to or in place of a superior. [C14: from OF, lit.: place-holding] — **lieu'tenancy** *n.*

lieutenant colonel *n.* an officer holding commissioned rank immediately junior to a colonel in certain armies, air forces, and marine corps.

lieutenant commander *n.* an officer holding commissioned rank in certain navies immediately junior to a commander.

lieutenant general *n.* an officer holding commissioned rank in certain armies, air forces, and marine corps immediately junior to a general.

lieutenant governor *n.* **1.** a deputy governor. **2.** (in the U.S.) an elected official who acts as deputy to a state governor. **3.** (in Canada) the representative of the Crown in a province: appointed by the federal government.

life (laıf) *n., pl.* **lives** (laıvz). **1.** the state or quality that distinguishes living beings or organisms from dead ones and from inorganic matter, characterized chiefly by metabolism, growth, and the ability to reproduce and respond to stimuli. Related *adj.*: **animate. 2.** the period between birth and death. **3.** a living person or being: *to save a life.* **4.** the time between birth and the present time. **5. a.** the remainder or extent of one's life. **b.** (*as modifier*): *a life sentence; life membership; life work.* **6.** *Inf.* a sentence of imprisonment for life. **7.** the amount of time that something is active or functioning: *the life of a battery.* **8.** a present condition, state, or mode of existence: *my life is very dull here.* **9. a.** a biography. **b.** (*as modifier*): *a life story.* **10.** a characteristic state or mode of existence: *town life.* **11.** the sum or course of human events and activities. **12.** liveliness or high spirits: *full of life.* **13.** a source of strength, animation, or vitality: *he was the life of the show.* **14.** all living things, taken as a whole: *there is no life on Mars; plant life.* **15.** (*modifier*) *Arts.* drawn or taken from a living model: *life drawing.* **16.** (in certain games) one of a number of opportunities for participation. **17. a matter of life and death.** a matter of extreme urgency. **18. as large as life.** *Inf.* real and living. **19. for the life of me** (**him, her,** etc.) though trying desperately. **20. not on your life.** *Inf.* certainly not. **21. the life and soul.** *Inf.* a person regarded as the main source of merriment and liveliness: *the life and soul of the party.* **22. to the life.** (of a copy or image) resembling the original exactly. **23. true to life.** faithful to reality. [OE *līf*]

life assurance *n.* a form of insurance providing for the payment of a specified sum to a named beneficiary on the death of the policyholder. Also called: **life insurance.**

life belt *n.* a buoyant ring used to keep a person afloat when in danger of drowning.

lifeblood ('laɪf,blʌd) *n.* **1.** the blood, considered as vital to life. **2.** the essential or animating force.

lifeboat ('laɪf,bəʊt) *n.* a boat used for rescuing people at sea, escaping from a sinking ship, etc.

life buoy *n.* any of various kinds of buoyant device for keeping people afloat in an emergency.

life cycle *n.* the series of changes occurring in an animal or plant between one stage and the identical stage in the next generation.

life expectancy *n.* the statistically determined average number of years of life remaining after a specified age.

lifeguard ('laɪf,gɑːd) *n.* a person at a beach or pool to guard people against the risk of drowning.

life jacket *n.* an inflatable sleeveless jacket worn to keep a person afloat when in danger of drowning.

lifeless ('laɪflɪs) *adj.* **1.** without life; inanimate; dead. **2.** not sustaining living organisms. **3.** having no vitality or animation. **4.** unconscious. — '**lifelessly** *adv.* — '**lifelessness** *n.*

lifelike ('laɪf,laɪk) *adj.* closely resembling or representing life. — '**life,likeness** *n.*

lifeline ('laɪf,laɪn) *n.* **1.** a line thrown or fired aboard a vessel for hauling in a hawser for a breeches buoy. **2.** a line by which a deep-sea diver is raised or lowered. **3.** a single means of contact, communication, or support on which a person or an area, etc., relies.

lifelong ('laɪf,lɒŋ) *adj.* lasting for or as if for a lifetime.

life peer *n. Brit.* a peer whose title lapses at his death.

life preserver *n.* **1.** *Brit.* a club or bludgeon, esp. one kept for self-defence. **2.** *U.S. & Canad.* a life belt or life jacket.

lifer ('laɪfə) *n. Inf.* a prisoner sentenced to imprisonment for life.

life raft *n.* a raft for emergency use at sea.

life-saver *n.* **1.** the saver of a person's life. **2.** *Austral.* an expert swimmer, esp. a member of a surf life-saving club at a surfing beach, who rescues surfers or swimmers from drowning. **3.** *Inf.* a person or thing that gives help in time of need. — '**life-,saving** *adj., n.*

life science *n.* any one of the branches of science concerned with the structure and behaviour of living organisms, such as biology, botany, zoology, physiology, or biochemistry.

life-size *or* **life-sized** *adj.* representing actual size.

life span *n.* the period of time during which a human being, animal, machine, etc., may be expected to live or function.

lifestyle ('laɪf,staɪl) *n.* **1.** a set of attitudes, habits, or possessions associated with a particular person or group. **2.** such attitudes, etc., regarded as fashionable or desirable.

life-support *adj.* of, providing, or relating to the equipment or treatment necessary to keep a person alive.

lifetime ('laɪf,taɪm) *n.* **1. a.** the length of time a person or animal is alive. **b.** (*as modifier*): *a lifetime supply.* **2.** the length of time that something functions, is useful, etc. **3.** Also called: **life.** *Physics.* the average time of existence of an unstable or reactive entity.

Liffey ('lɪfɪ) *n.* a river in E Ireland, rising in the Wicklow Mountains and flowing west, then northeast through Dublin into Dublin Bay. Length: 80 km (50 miles).

lift (lɪft) *vb.* **1.** to rise or cause to rise upwards from the ground or another support to a higher place: *to lift a sack.* **2.** to move or cause to move upwards: *to lift one's eyes.* **3.** (*tr.*) to take hold of in order to carry or remove: *to lift something down from a shelf.* **4.** (*tr.*) to raise in status, spirituality, estimation, etc.: *his position lifted him from the common crowd.* **5.** (*tr.*) to revoke or rescind: *to lift tax restrictions.* **6.** (*tr.*) to take (plants or underground crops) out of the ground for transplanting or harvesting. **7.** (*intr.*) to disappear by lifting or as if by lifting: *the fog lifted.* **8.** (*tr.*) *Inf.* to take unlawfully or dishonourably; steal. **9.** (*tr.*) *Inf.* to plagiarize. **10.** (*tr.*) *Sl.* to arrest. **11.** (*tr.*) to perform a face-lift on. ~*n.* **12.** the act or an instance of lifting. **13.** the power or force available or used for lifting. **14. a.** *Brit.* a platform, compartment, or cage raised or lowered in a vertical shaft to transport persons or goods in a building. U.S. and Canad. word: **elevator. b.** See **chair lift, ski lift. 15.** the distance or degree to which something is lifted. **16.** a ride in a car or other vehicle for part or all of a passenger's journey. **17.** a rise in the height of the ground. **18.** a rise in morale or feeling of cheerfulness usually caused by some specific thing or event. **19.** the force required to lift an object. **20.** a layer inserted in the heel of a shoe, etc., to give the wearer added height. **21.** aid; help. **22.** the component of the aerodynamic forces acting on a wing, etc., at right angles to the airflow and opposing gravity. [C13: from ON] — '**lifter** *n.*

liftoff ('lɪft,ɒf) *n.* **1.** the initial movement of a rocket from its launching pad. **2.** the instant at which this occurs. ~*vb.* **lift off. 3.** (*intr., adv.*) (of a rocket) to leave its launching pad.

lift pump *n.* a pump that raises a fluid to a higher level. Cf. **force pump.**

ligament ('lɪgəmənt) *n.* **1.** *Anat.* any one of the bands of tough fibrous connective tissue that restrict movement in joints, connect various bones or cartilages, support muscles, etc. **2.** any physical or abstract bond. [C14: from Med. L *ligāmentum*, from L (in the sense: bandage), from *ligāre* to bind]

ligand ('lɪgənd, 'laɪ-) *n. Chem.* an atom, molecule, radical, or ion forming a complex with a central atom. [C20: from L *ligandum*, from *ligāre* to bind]

ligate ('laɪgeɪt) *vb.* (*tr.*) to tie up or constrict (something) with a ligature. [C16: from L *ligātus*, from *ligāre* to bind] — **li'gation** *n.*

ligature ('lɪgətʃə, -,tʃʊə) *n.* **1.** the act of binding or tying up. **2.** something used to bind. **3.** a link, bond, or tie. **4.** *Surgery.* a thread or wire for tying around a vessel, duct, etc., as for constricting the flow of blood. **5.** *Printing.* a character of two or more joined letters, such as **ff, fi, fl**, **ffi**. **6.** *Music.* a slur or the group of notes connected by it. ~*vb.* **7.** (*tr.*) to bind with a ligature; ligate. [C14: from LL *ligātūra*, ult. from L *ligāre* to bind]

liger ('laɪgə) *n.* the hybrid offspring of a female tiger and a male lion.

Ligeti (*Hungarian* 'lɪgɛti) *n.* **György** (djɔrdj). born 1923, Hungarian composer, resident in Vienna. His works, noted for their experimentalism, include *Atmospheres* (1961) for orchestra, *Volumina* (1962) for organ, and a requiem mass (1965).

ligger ('lɪgə) *n. Sl.* (esp. in the media) a person who habitually takes advantage of what is freely available. [C20: from ?] — '**ligging** *n.*

light[1] (laɪt) *n.* **1.** the medium of illumination that makes sight possible. **2.** Also called: **visible radiation.** electromagnetic radiation that is capable of causing a visual sensation. **3.** (*not in technical usage*) electromagnetic radiation that has a wavelength outside this range, esp. ultraviolet radiation: *ultraviolet light.* **4.** the sensation experienced when electromagnetic radiation within the visible spectrum falls on the retina of the eye. **5.** anything that illuminates, such as a lamp or candle. **6.** See **traffic light. 7.** a particular quality or type of light: *a good light for reading.* **8. a.** illumination from the sun during the day; daylight. **b.** the time this appears; daybreak; dawn. **9.** anything that allows the entrance of light, such as a window or compartment of a window. **10.** the condition of being visible or known (esp. in **bring** or **come to light**). **11.** an aspect or view: *he saw it in a different light.* **12.** mental understanding or spiritual insight. **13.** a person considered to be an authority or leader. **14.** brightness of countenance, esp. a sparkle in the eyes. **15. a.** the act of igniting or kindling something, such as a cigarette. **b.** something that ignites or kindles, esp. in a specified manner, such as a spark or flame. **c.** something used for igniting or kindling, such as a match. **16.** See **lighthouse.** **17. in (the) light of.** in view of; taking into account; considering. **18. see the light.** to acquire insight. **19. see the light (of day). a.** to come into being. **b.** to come to public notice. **20. strike a light. a.** (*vb.*) to ignite something, esp. a match, by friction. **b.** (*interj.*) *Brit.* an exclamation of surprise. ~*adj.* **21.** full of light; well-lighted. **22.** (of a colour) reflecting or transmitting a large amount of light: *light yellow.* ~*vb.* **lighting, lighted** or **lit.** **23.** to ignite or cause to ignite. **24.** (often foll. by *up*) to illuminate or cause to illuminate. **25.** to make or become cheerful or animated. **26.** (*tr.*) to guide or lead by light. ~See also **lights**[1], **light up.** [OE *lēoht*] — **'lightish** *adj.* — **'lightless** *adj.*

light[2] (laɪt) *adj.* **1.** not heavy; weighing relatively little. **2.** having relatively low density: *magnesium is a light metal.* **3.** lacking sufficient weight; not agreeing with standard or official weights. **4.** not great in degree, intensity, or number: *light rain.* **5.** without burdens, difficulties, or problems; easily borne or done: *a light heart; light work.* **6.** graceful, agile, or deft: *light fingers.* **7.** not bulky or clumsy. **8.** not serious or profound; entertaining: *light music; light verse.* **9.** without importance or consequence; insignificant: *no light matter.* **10.** frivolous or capricious. **11.** loose in morals. **12.** dizzy or unclear: *a light head.* **13.** (of bread, cake, etc.) spongy or well leavened. **14.** easily digested: *a light meal.* **15.** relatively low in alcoholic content: *a light wine.* **16.** (of a soil) having a crumbly texture. **17.** (of a vessel, lorry, etc.) **a.** designed to carry light loads. **b.** not loaded. **18.** carrying light arms or equipment: *light infantry.* **19.** (of an industry) engaged in the production of small consumer goods using light machinery. **20.** *Phonetics, prosody.* (of a syllable, vowel, etc.) unaccented or weakly stressed; short. **21. light on.** *Inf.* lacking a sufficient quantity of (something). **22. make light of.** to treat as insignificant or trifling. ~*adv.* **23.** a less common word for **lightly.** **24.** with little equipment, baggage, etc.: *to travel light.* ~*vb.* **lighting, lighted** or **lit.** (*intr.*) **25.** (esp. of birds) to settle or land after flight. **26.** to get down from a horse, vehicle, etc. **27.** (foll. by *on* or *upon*) to come upon unexpectedly. **28.** to strike or fall on: *the choice lighted on me.* ~See also **light into, light out, lights**[2]. [OE *lēoht*] — **'lightish** *adj.* — **'lightly** *adv.* — **'lightness** *n.*

light air *n.* very light air movement of force one (1–3 mph) on the Beaufort scale.

light breeze *n.* a very light wind of force two (4–7 mph) on the Beaufort scale.

light bulb *n.* a glass bulb containing a gas at low pressure and enclosing a thin metal filament that emits light when an electric current is passed through it. Sometimes shortened to **bulb.**

light-emitting diode *n.* a semiconductor that emits light when an electric current is applied to it: used in electronic calculators, digital watches, etc.

lighten[1] ('laɪt³n) *vb.* **1.** to become or make light. **2.** (*intr.*) to shine; glow. **3.** (*intr.*) (of lightning) to flash. **4.** (*tr.*) *Arch.* to cause to flash.

lighten[2] ('laɪt³n) *vb.* **1.** to make or become less heavy. **2.** to make or become less burdensome or oppressive; mitigate. **3.** to make or become more cheerful or lively.

lighter[1] ('laɪtə) *n.* **1.** a small portable device for providing a naked flame to light cigarettes, etc. **2.** a person or thing that ignites something.

lighter[2] ('laɪtə) *n.* a flat-bottomed barge used for transporting cargo, esp. in loading or unloading a ship. [C15: prob. from MDu.]

lighterage ('laɪtərɪdʒ) *n.* **1.** the conveyance or loading and unloading of cargo by means of a lighter. **2.** the charge for this service.

light face *n.* **1.** *Printing.* a weight of type characterized by light thin lines. ~*adj.* also **light-faced.** **2.** (of type) having this weight.

light-fingered *adj.* having nimble or agile fingers, esp. for thieving or picking pockets.

light flyweight *n.* **1.** an amateur boxer weighing not more than 48 kg (106 pounds). **2.** an amateur wrestler weighing not more than 48 kg (106 pounds).

light-footed *adj.* having a light or nimble tread. — **,light-'footedly** *adv.*

light-headed *adj.* **1.** frivolous. **2.** giddy; feeling faint or slightly delirious. — **,light-'headedly** *adv.* — **,light-'headedness** *n.*

light-hearted *adj.* cheerful or carefree in mood or disposition. — **,light-'heartedly** *adv.* — **,light-'heartedness** *n.*

light heavyweight *n.* **1.** Also (in Britain): **cruiserweight. a.** a professional boxer weighing 160–175 pounds (72.5–79.5 kg). **b.** an amateur boxer weighing 75–81 kg (165–179 pounds). **2. a.** a professional wrestler weighing not more than 198 pounds (90 kg). **b.** an amateur wrestler weighing not more than 90 kg (198 pounds).

lighthouse ('laɪt,haʊs) *n.* a fixed structure in the form of a tower equipped with a light visible to mariners for warning them of obstructions, etc.

lighting ('laɪtɪŋ) *n.* **1.** the act or quality of illumination or ignition. **2.** the apparatus for supplying artificial light effects to a stage, film, or television set. **3.** the distribution of light on an object or figure, as in painting, photography, etc.

lighting-up time *n.* the time when vehicles are required by law to have their lights on.

light into *vb.* (*tr., prep.*) *Inf.* to assail physically or verbally.

light middleweight *n.* an amateur boxer weighing 67–71 kg (148–157 pounds).

lightness ('laɪtnɪs) *n.* the attribute of an object or colour that enables an observer to judge the extent to which the object or colour reflects or transmits incident light.

lightning ('laɪtnɪŋ) *n.* **1.** a flash of light in the sky, occurring during a thunderstorm and caused by a discharge of electricity, either between clouds or between a cloud and the earth. **2.** (*modifier*) fast and sudden: *a lightning raid.* [C14: var. of *lightening*]

lightning conductor or **rod** *n.* a metal strip terminating in sharp points, attached to the highest part of a building, etc., to provide a safe path to earth for lightning discharges.

light opera *n.* another term for **operetta.**

light out *vb.* (*intr., adv.*) *Inf.* to depart quickly, as if being chased.

light pen *n. Computer technol.* **a.** a rodlike device which, when applied to the screen of a cathode-ray tube, can detect the time of passage of the illuminated spot across that point thus enabling a computer to determine the position on the screen being pointed at. **b.** a penlike device, used to read bar codes, that emits light and determines the intensity of that light as reflected from a small area of an adjacent surface.

lights[1] (laɪts) *pl. n.* a person's ideas, knowledge, or understanding: *he did it according to his lights.*

lights[2] (laɪts) *pl. n.* the lungs, esp. of sheep, bullocks, and pigs, used esp. for feeding pets. [C13: pl. n. use of LIGHT[2], referring to the light weight of the lungs]

lightship ('laɪt,ʃɪp) *n.* a ship equipped as a lighthouse and moored where a fixed structure would prove impracticable.

light show *n.* a kaleidoscopic display of moving lights, etc., projected onto a screen, esp. during pop concerts.

lightsome ('laɪtsəm) *adj. Arch.* or *poetic.* **1.** light-hearted or gay. **2.** airy or buoyant. **3.** not serious; frivolous.

lights out *n.* **1.** the time when those resident at an institution, such as soldiers in barracks or children at a boarding school, are expected to retire to bed. **2.** a signal indicating this.

light up *vb.* (*adv.*) **1.** to light a cigarette, pipe, etc. **2.** to illuminate or cause to illuminate. **3.** to make or become cheerful or animated.

lightweight ('laɪt,weɪt) *adj.* **1.** of a relatively light weight. **2.** not serious; trivial. ~*n.* **3.** a person or animal of a relatively light weight. **4. a.** a professional boxer weighing

130–135 pounds (59–61 kg). **b.** an amateur boxer weighing 57–60 kg (126–132 pounds). **5. a.** a professional wrestler weighing not more than 154 pounds (70 kg). **b.** an amateur wrestler weighing not more than 68 kg (150 pounds). **6.** *Inf.* a person of little importance or influence.

light welterweight *n.* an amateur boxer weighing 60–63.5 kg (132–140 pounds).

light year *n.* a unit of distance used in astronomy, equal to the distance travelled by light in one mean solar year, i.e. 9.4607×10^{15} metres or 5.8784×10^{12} miles.

ligneous ('lɪgnɪəs) *adj.* of or resembling wood. [C17: from L *ligneus*, from *lignum* wood]

lignin ('lɪgnɪn) *n.* a complex polymer occurring in certain plant cell walls making the plant rigid. [C19: from L *lignum* wood + -IN]

lignite ('lɪgnaɪt) *n.* a brown carbonaceous sedimentary rock with woody texture that consists of accumulated layers of partially decomposed vegetation: used as a fuel. Also called: **brown coal.** —**lignitic** (lɪg'nɪtɪk) *adj.*

lignum vitae ('lɪgnəm 'vaɪtɪ) *n.* **1.** either of two tropical American trees having blue or purple flowers. **2.** the heavy resinous wood of either of these trees. ~See also **guaiacum.** [NL, from LL, lit.: wood of life]

ligroin ('lɪgrəʊɪn) *n.* a volatile fraction of petroleum: used as a solvent. [from ?]

Liguria (lɪ'gjʊərɪə) *n.* a region of NW Italy, on the **Ligurian Sea** (an arm of the Mediterranean): the third smallest of the regions of Italy. Pop.: 1 758 961 (1986 est.). Area: 5410 sq. km (2089 sq. miles). —**Li'gurian** *adj.*, *n.*

likable *or* **likeable** ('laɪkəbᵊl) *adj.* easy to like; pleasing. —'**likableness** *or* '**likeableness** *n.*

Likasi (lɪ'kɑːsɪ) *n.* a city in S Zaïre, in Shaba province: a centre of copper and cobalt production. Pop.: 194 465 (1984). Former name: **Jadotville.**

like[1] (laɪk) *adj.* **1.** (*prenominal*) similar; resembling. ~*prep.* **2.** similar to; similarly to; in the manner of: *acting like a maniac; he's so like his father.* **3.** used correlatively to express similarity: *like mother, like daughter.* **4.** such as: *there are lots of games—like draughts, for instance.* ~*adv.* **5.** a dialect word for **likely.** ~*conj.* **6.** *Not standard.* as though; as if: *you look like you've just seen a ghost.* **7.** in the same way as; in the same way that: *she doesn't dance like you do.* ~*n.* **8.** the equal or counterpart of a person or thing. **9. the like.** similar things: *dogs, foxes, and the like.* **10. the likes** (*or* **like**) **of.** people or things similar to (someone or something specified): *we don't want the likes of you around here.* [shortened from OE *gelīc*]

▷ **Usage.** The use of *like* as a conjunction (*he behaves like his father did*) is avoided in good usage, *as*, *as if*, or *as though* being preferred. Many careful writers and speakers do accept, however, the use of *like* as a preposition in constructions where no verb is expressed: *he looks like his father.*

like[2] (laɪk) *vb.* **1.** (*tr.*) to find (something) enjoyable or agreeable or find it enjoyable or agreeable (to do something): *he likes boxing; he likes to hear music.* **2.** (*tr.*) to be fond of. **3.** (*tr.*) to prefer or wish (to do something): *we would like you to go.* **4.** (*tr.*) to feel towards; consider; regard: *how did she like it?* **5.** (*intr.*) to feel disposed or inclined; choose; wish. ~*n.* **6.** (*usually pl.*) a favourable feeling, desire, preference, etc. (esp. in **likes and dislikes**). [OE *lician*]

-like *suffix forming adjectives.* **1.** resembling or similar to: *lifelike.* **2.** having the characteristics of: *childlike.* [from LIKE[1] (prep.)]

likelihood ('laɪklɪˌhʊd) *or* **likeliness** *n.* **1.** the condition of being likely or probable; probability. **2.** something that is probable.

likely ('laɪklɪ) *adj.* **1.** (usually foll. by an infinitive) tending or inclined; apt: *likely to rain.* **2.** probable: *a likely result.* **3.** believable or feasible; plausible. **4.** appropriate for a purpose or activity. **5.** having good possibilities of success: *a likely candidate.* ~*adv.* **6.** probably or presumably. **7. as likely as not.** very probably. [C14: from ON *líkligr*]

like-minded *adj.* agreeing in opinions, goals, etc. — ,**like-'mindedly** *adv.* — ,**like-'mindedness** *n.*

liken ('laɪkən) *vb.* (*tr.*) to see or represent as the same or similar; compare. [C14: from LIKE[1] (adj.)]

likeness ('laɪknɪs) *n.* **1.** the condition of being alike; similarity. **2.** a painted, carved, moulded, or graphic image of a person or thing. **3.** an imitative appearance; semblance.

likewise ('laɪkˌwaɪz) *adv.* **1.** in addition; moreover; also. **2.** in like manner; similarly.

liking ('laɪkɪŋ) *n.* **1.** the feeling of a person who likes; fondness. **2.** a preference, inclination, or pleasure.

lilac ('laɪlək) *n.* **1.** any of various Eurasian shrubs or small trees of the olive family which have large sprays of purple or white fragrant flowers. **2. a.** a light or moderate purple colour. **b.** (*as adj.*): *a lilac carpet.* [C17: via F from Sp., from Ar. *līlak*, changed from Persian *nīlak* bluish, from *nīl* blue]

Lilburne ('lɪlˌbɜːn) *n.* **John.** ?1614-57, English Puritan pamphleteer and leader of the Levellers, a radical group prominent during the Civil War.

liliaceous (ˌlɪlɪ'eɪʃəs) *adj.* of, relating to, or belonging to a family of plants having showy flowers and a bulb or bulb-like organ: includes the lily, tulip, bluebell, and onion. [C18: from LL *līliāceus*, from *lilium* lily]

Lilienthal (*German* 'liːliəntaːl) *n.* **Otto** ('ɔto). 1848–96, German aeronautical engineer, a pioneer of glider design.

Lilith ('lɪlɪθ) *n.* **1.** (in the Old Testament and in Jewish folklore) a female demon, who attacks children. **2.** (in Talmudic literature) Adam's first wife. **3.** a witch notorious in medieval demonology.

Liliuokalani (liːˌliːʊəʊkɑː'lɑːniː) *n.* **Lydia Kamekeha** (ˌkɑːmeɪ'keɪhɑː). 1838–1917, queen and last sovereign of the Hawaiian Islands (1891–95).

Lille (*French* lil) *n.* an industrial city in N France: the medieval capital of Flanders; forms with Roubaix and Tourcoing one of the largest conurbations in France. Pop.: 189 555 (1983 est.).

Lille Bælt ('lilə 'bɛld) *n.* the Danish name for the **Little Belt.**

Lillee ('lɪlɪ) *n.* **Dennis (Keith).** born 1949, Australian cricketer who, by the end of the 1982–83 season, had taken a total of 355 wickets in 65 tests which is a world record.

Lilliputian (ˌlɪlɪ'pjuːʃɪən) *n.* **1.** a tiny person or being. ~*adj.* **2.** tiny; very small. **3.** petty or trivial. [C18: from *Lilliput,* an imaginary country of tiny inhabitants in Swift's *Gulliver's Travels* (1726)]

Lilo ('laɪˌləʊ) *n., pl.* **-los.** *Trademark.* a type of inflatable plastic or rubber mattress.

Lilongwe (lɪ'lɒŋwɪ) *n.* the capital of Malawi, in the central part west of Lake Malawi. Pop.: 186 800 (1985 est.).

lilt (lɪlt) *n.* **1.** (in music) a jaunty rhythm. **2.** a buoyant motion. ~*vb.* (*intr.*) **3.** (of a melody) to have a lilt. **4.** to move in a buoyant manner. [C14 *lulten,* from ?] — '**lilting** *adj.*

lily ('lɪlɪ) *n., pl.* **lilies. 1.** any perennial plant of a N temperate genus, such as the tiger lily, having scaly bulbs and showy typically pendulous flowers. **2.** the bulb or flower of any of these plants. **3.** any of various similar or related plants, such as the water lily. [OE, from L *lilium;* rel. to Gk *leirion* lily] — '**lily-**,**like** *adj.*

lily-livered *adj.* cowardly; timid.

lily of the valley *n., pl.* **lilies of the valley.** a small liliaceous plant of Eurasia and North America cultivated for its spikes of fragrant white bell-shaped flowers.

lily-white *adj.* **1.** of a pure white: *lily-white skin.* **2.** *Inf.* pure; irreproachable.

Lima ('liːmə) *n.* the capital of Peru, near the Pacific coast on the Rímac River: the centre of Spanish colonization in South America; university founded in 1551 (the oldest in South America); an industrial centre with a port at nearby Callao. Pop.: 5 258 600 (1983).

lima bean ('laɪmə) *n.* **1.** any of several varieties of the bean plant native to tropical America, cultivated for its flat pods containing pale green edible seeds. **2.** the seed of such a plant. [C19: after LIMA]

Limassol ('lɪməˌsɒl) *n.* a port in S Cyprus: trading centre. Pop.: 113 600 (1986 est.). Ancient name: **Lemessus** (lə'mɛsəs).

limb[1] (lɪm) *n.* **1.** an arm or leg, or the analogous part on an animal, such as a wing. **2.** any of the main branches of a tree. **3.** a branching or projecting section or member; extension. **4.** a person or thing considered to be a member, part, or agent of a larger group or thing. **5.** *Chiefly Brit.* a mischievous child (esp. in **limb of Satan,** etc.).

6. out on a limb. a. in a precarious or questionable position. **b.** *Brit.* isolated, esp. because of unpopular opinions. [OE *lim*] — **'limbless** *adj.*

limb² (lɪm) *n.* **1.** the edge of the apparent disc of the sun, a moon, or a planet. **2.** a graduated arc attached to instruments, such as the sextant, used for measuring angles. **3.** *Bot.* the expanded part of a leaf, petal, or sepal. [C15: from L *limbus* edge]

limbed (lɪmd) *adj.* **a.** having limbs. **b.** (*in combination*): *short-limbed; strong-limbed.*

limber¹ ('lɪmbə) *adj.* **1.** capable of being easily bent or flexed; pliant. **2.** able to move or bend freely; agile. [C16: from ?] — **'limberness** *n.*

limber² ('lɪmbə) *n.* **1.** part of a gun carriage, consisting of an axle, pole, and two wheels. ~*vb.* **2.** (usually foll. by *up*) to attach the limber (to a gun, etc.). [C15 *lymour* shaft of a gun carriage, from ?]

limber up *vb.* (*intr., adv.*) (esp. in sports) to exercise in order to be limber and agile.

limbic system ('lɪmbɪk) *n.* the part of the brain concerned with basic emotion, hunger, and sex. [C19 *limbic*, from F, from *limbe*, from NL *limbus*, from L: border]

limbo¹ ('lɪmbəʊ) *n., pl.* **-bos. 1.** (*often cap.*) *Christianity.* the supposed abode of infants dying without baptism and the just who died before Christ. **2.** an imaginary place for lost, forgotten, or unwanted persons or things. **3.** an unknown intermediate place or condition between two extremes: *in limbo.* [C14: from Med. L *in limbo* on the border (of hell)]

limbo² ('lɪmbəʊ) *n., pl.* **-bos.** a West Indian dance in which dancers pass, while leaning backwards, under a bar. [C20: from ?]

Limbourg (lɛ̄bur) *n.* the French name for **Limburg** (sense 3).

Limburg ('lɪmbɜːg; *Dutch* 'lɪmbyrx) *n.* **1.** a medieval duchy of W Europe: divided between the Netherlands and Belgium in 1839. **2.** a province of the SE Netherlands: contains a coalfield and industrial centres. Capital: Maastricht. Pop.: 1 091 553 (1987 est.). Area: 2253 sq. km (809 sq. miles). **3.** a province of NE Belgium: contains the industrial regions of the Kempen coalfield. Capital: Hassett. Pop.: 734 382 (1986 est.). Area: 2422 sq. km (935 sq. miles). French name: **Limbourg.**

Limburger ('lɪm,bɜːgə) *n.* a semihard white cheese of very strong smell and flavour. Also called: **Limburg cheese.**

lime¹ (laɪm) *n.* **1.** short for **quicklime, birdlime, slaked lime. 2.** *Agriculture.* any of certain calcium compounds, esp. calcium hydroxide, spread as a dressing on lime-deficient land. ~*vb.* (*tr.*) **3.** to spread (twigs, etc.) with birdlime. **4.** to spread a calcium compound upon (land) to improve plant growth. **5.** to catch (animals, esp. birds) as with birdlime. **6.** to whitewash (a wall, ceiling, etc.) with a mixture of lime and water (**limewash**). [OE *līm*]

lime² (laɪm) *n.* **1.** a small Asian citrus tree with stiff sharp spines and small round or oval greenish fruits. **2. a.** the fruit of this tree, having acid fleshy pulp rich in vitamin C. **b.** (*as modifier*): *lime juice.* ~*adj.* **3.** having the flavour of lime fruit. [C17: from F, from Ar. *līmah*]

lime³ (laɪm) *n.* a European linden tree planted in many varieties for ornament. [C17: changed from obs. *line*, from OE *lind* LINDEN]

limeade (,laɪm'eɪd) *n.* a drink made from sweetened lime juice and plain or carbonated water.

lime green *n.* **a.** a moderate greenish-yellow colour. **b.** (*as adj.*): *a lime-green dress.*

limekiln ('laɪm,kɪln) *n.* a kiln in which calcium carbonate is calcined to produce quicklime.

limelight ('laɪm,laɪt) *n.* **1. the.** a position of public attention or notice (esp. in **in the limelight**). **2. a.** a type of lamp, formerly used in stage lighting, in which light is produced by heating lime to white heat. **b.** Also called: **calcium light.** brilliant white light produced in this way.

limerick ('lɪmərɪk) *n.* a form of comic verse consisting of five anapaestic lines. [C19: allegedly from *will you come up to Limerick?*, a refrain sung between nonsense verses at a party]

Limerick ('lɪmərɪk) *n.* **1.** a county of SW Ireland, in N Munster province: consists chiefly of an undulating plain with rich pasture and mountains in the south. County town: Limerick. Pop.: 164 204 (1986). Area: 2686 sq. km (1037 sq. miles). **2.** a port in SW Ireland, county town of

Limerick, at the head of the Shannon estuary. Pop.: 75 520 (1981).

limestone ('laɪm,stəʊn) *n.* a sedimentary rock consisting mainly of calcium carbonate: used as a building stone and in making cement, lime, etc.

limewater ('laɪm,wɔːtə) *n.* **1.** a clear colourless solution of calcium hydroxide in water, sometimes used in medicine as an antacid. **2.** water that contains dissolved lime or calcium salts, esp. calcium carbonate or calcium sulphate.

limey ('laɪmɪ) *U.S. & Canad. sl.* ~*n.* **1.** a British person. **2.** a British sailor or ship. ~*adj.* **3.** British. [abbrev. from C19 *lime-juicer*, because British sailors drank lime juice as a protection against scurvy]

limit ('lɪmɪt) *n.* **1.** (*sometimes pl.*) the ultimate extent, degree, or amount of something: *the limit of endurance.* **2.** (*often pl.*) the boundary or edge of a specific area: *the city limits.* **3.** (*often pl.*) the area of premises within specific boundaries. **4.** the largest quantity or amount allowed. **5.** *Maths.* **a.** a value to which a function approaches as the independent variable approaches a specified value or infinity. **b.** a value to which a sequence a_n approaches as n approaches infinity. **c.** the limit of a sequence of partial sums of a convergent infinite series. **6.** *Maths.* one of the two specified values between which a definite integral is evaluated. **7. the limit.** *Inf.* a person or thing that is intolerably exasperating. ~*vb.* (*tr.*) **8.** to restrict or confine, as to area, extent, time, etc. [C14: from L *līmes* boundary] — **'limitable** *adj.* — **'limitless** *adj.* — **'limitlessly** *adv.* — **'limitlessness** *n.*

limitary ('lɪmɪtərɪ, -trɪ) *adj.* **1.** of, involving, or serving as a limit. **2.** restricted or limited.

limitation (,lɪmɪ'teɪʃən) *n.* **1.** something that limits a quality or achievement. **2.** the act of limiting or the condition of being limited. **3.** *Law.* a certain period of time, legally defined, within which an action, claim, etc., must be commenced.

limited ('lɪmɪtɪd) *adj.* **1.** having a limit; restricted; confined. **2.** without fullness or scope; narrow. **3.** (of governing powers, sovereignty, etc.) restricted or checked, by or as if by a constitution, laws, or an assembly: *limited government.* **4.** *Chiefly Brit.* (of a business enterprise) owned by shareholders whose liability for the enterprise's debts is restricted. — **'limitedly** *adv.* — **'limitedness** *n.*

limited liability *n. Brit.* liability restricted to the unpaid portion (if any) of the par value of the shares of a limited company.

limiter ('lɪmɪtə) *n.* an electronic circuit that produces an output signal whose positive or negative amplitude, or both, is limited to some predetermined value above which the peaks become flattened. Also called: **clipper.**

limn (lɪm) *vb.* (*tr.*) **1.** to represent in drawing or painting. **2.** *Arch.* to describe in words. [C15: from OF *enluminer* to illumine (a manuscript) from L *inlūmināre* to brighten, from *lūmen* light] — **limner** ('lɪmnə) *n.*

limnology (lɪm'nɒlədʒɪ) *n.* the study of bodies of fresh water with reference to their plant and animal life, physical properties, geographical features, etc. [C20: from Gk *limnē* lake] — **limnological** (,lɪmnə'lɒdʒɪkᵊl) *adj.* — **lim'nologist** *n.*

Límnos ('lɪmnɒs) *n.* transliteration of the Modern Greek name for **Lemnos.**

Limoges (lɪ'məʊʒ; *French* limɔʒ) *n.* a city in S central France, on the Vienne River: a centre of the porcelain industry since the 18th century. Pop.: 141 865 (1983 est.).

Limousin (*French* limuzɛ̄) *n.* a region and former province of W central France, in the W part of the Massif Central.

limousine ('lɪmə,ziːn, ,lɪmə'ziːn) *n.* any large and luxurious car, esp. one that has a glass division between the driver and passengers. [C20: from F, lit.: cloak (orig. one worn by shepherds in *Limousin*), hence later applied to the car]

limp¹ (lɪmp) *vb.* (*intr.*) **1.** to walk with an uneven step, esp. with a weak or injured leg. **2.** to advance in a labouring or faltering manner. ~*n.* **3.** an uneven walk or progress. [C16: prob. a back formation from obs. *limphalt* lame, from OE *lemphealt*] — **'limper** *n.* — **'limping** *adj.*, *n.*

limp² (lɪmp) *adj.* **1.** not firm or stiff. **2.** not energetic or vital. **3.** (of the binding of a book) not stiffened with boards. [C18: prob. of Scand. origin] — **'limply** *adv.* — **'limpness** *n.*

limpet ('lɪmpɪt) *n.* **1.** any of numerous marine gastropods, such as the common limpet and keyhole limpet, that have a conical shell and are found clinging to rocks. **2.** (*modifier*) relating to or denoting certain weapons that are attached to their targets by magnetic or adhesive properties and resist removal: *limpet mines.* [OE *lempedu,* from L *lepas,* from Gk]

limpid ('lɪmpɪd) *adj.* **1.** clear or transparent. **2.** (esp. of writings, style, etc.) free from obscurity. **3.** calm; peaceful. [C17: from F *limpide,* from L *limpidus* clear] — **lim'pidity** *or* **'limpidness** *n.* — **'limpidly** *adv.*

Limpopo (lɪm'pəʊpəʊ) *n.* a river in SE Africa, rising in South Africa in S Transvaal and flowing northeast, then southeast as the border between South Africa and Zimbabwe and through Mozambique to the Indian Ocean. Length: 1770 km (1100 miles). Also called (esp. in its upper course): **Crocodile River.**

limp-wristed *adj.* ineffectual; effete.

limy[1] ('laɪmɪ) *adj.* **limier, limiest.** of, like, or smeared with birdlime. — **'liminess** *n.*

limy[2] ('laɪmɪ) *adj.* **limier, limiest.** of or tasting of lime (the fruit).

Linacre ('lɪnəkə) *n.* **Thomas.** ?1460–1524, English humanist and physician: founded the Royal College of Physicians (1518).

linage ('laɪnɪdʒ) *n.* **1.** the number of lines in a piece of written or printed matter. **2.** payment for written material calculated according to the number of lines.

Linares (*Spanish* li'nares) *n.* a city in S Spain: site of Scipio Africanus' defeat of the Carthaginians (208 B.C.); lead mines. Pop.: 54 549 (1981).

linchpin ('lɪntʃˌpɪn) *n.* **1.** a pin placed transversely through an axle to keep a wheel in position. **2.** a person or thing regarded as an essential or coordinating element: *the linchpin of the company.* [C14 *lynspin,* from OE *lynis*]

Lincoln[1] ('lɪŋkən) *n.* **1.** a city in E central England, administrative centre of Lincolnshire: an important ecclesiastical and commercial centre in the Middle Ages; Roman ruins, a castle (founded by William the Conqueror) and a famous cathedral (begun in 1086). Pop.: 78 000 (1983 est.). Latin name: **Lindum** ('lɪndəm). **2.** a city in SE Nebraska: state capital; University of Nebraska (1869). Pop.: 183 050 (1986 est.).

Lincoln[2] ('lɪŋkən) *n.* **Abraham.** 1809–65, U.S. Republican statesman; 16th president of the U.S. His fame rests on his success in saving the Union in the Civil War (1861–65) and on his emancipation of slaves (1863); assassinated by Booth.

Lincoln green *n.* **1. a.** a yellowish-green or brownish-green colour. **b.** (*as adj.*): *a Lincoln-green suit.* **2.** a cloth of this colour. [C16: after a green fabric formerly made at LINCOLN]

Lincolnshire ('lɪŋkənˌʃɪə, -ʃə) *n.* a county of E England, on the North Sea and the Wash: mostly low-lying and fertile, with fenland around the Wash and hills (the **Lincoln Wolds**) in the east; one of the main agricultural counties of Great Britain. Administrative centre: Lincoln. Pop.: 567 300 (1986 est.). Area: 5915 sq. km (2283 sq. miles). Abbrev.: **Lincs.**

Lincs (lɪŋks) *abbrev. for* Lincolnshire.

linctus ('lɪŋktəs) *n., pl.* **-tuses.** a syrupy medicinal preparation, taken to relieve coughs and sore throats. [C17 (in the sense: medicine to be licked with the tongue): from L, p.p. of *lingere* to lick]

Lind (lɪnd) *n.* **Jenny.** Swedish name *Johanna Maria Lind Goldschmidt.* 1820–87, Swedish coloratura soprano.

lindane ('lɪndeɪn) *n.* a white poisonous crystalline powder: used as an insecticide and weedkiller. [C20: after T. van der *Linden,* Du. chemist]

Lindbergh ('lɪndbɜːg, 'lɪnbɜːg) *n.* **Charles Augustus.** 1902–74, U.S. aviator, who made the first solo nonstop flight across the Atlantic (1927).

linden ('lɪndən) *n.* any of various deciduous trees of a N temperate genus having heart-shaped leaves and small fragrant yellowish flowers: cultivated for timber and as shade trees. See also **lime**[3]. [C16: n. use of obs. adj. *linden,* from OE *linde* lime tree]

Lindesnes ('lɪndɪsˌnɛs) *n.* a cape at the S tip of Norway, projecting into the North Sea. Also called: (the) **Naze.**

Lindisfarne ('lɪndɪsˌfɑːn) *n.* another name for **Holy Island.**

Lindsey ('lɪndzɪ) *n.* **Parts of.** an area in E England constituting a former administrative division of Lincolnshire.

Lindwall ('lɪndˌwɔːl) *n.* **Ray(mond Russell).** born 1921, Australian cricketer. A fast bowler, he played for Australia 61 times between 1946 and 1958.

line[1] (laɪn) *n.* **1.** a narrow continuous mark, as one made by a pencil, pen, or brush across a surface. **2.** such a mark cut into or raised from a surface. **3.** a thin indented mark or wrinkle. **4.** a straight or curved continuous trace having no breadth that is produced by a moving point. **5.** *Maths.* **a.** any straight one-dimensional geometrical element whose identity is determined by two points. A **line segment** lies between any two points on a line. **b.** a set of points (*x, y*) that satisfies the equation $y = mx + c$, where *m* is the gradient and *c* is the intercept with the *y*-axis. **6.** a border or boundary: *the county line.* **7.** *Sport.* **a.** a white or coloured band indicating a boundary or division on a field, track, etc. **b.** a mark or imaginary mark at which a race begins or ends. **8.** *American football.* **a.** See **line of scrimmage. b.** the players arranged in a row on either side of the line of scrimmage at the start of each play. **9.** a specified point of change or limit: *the dividing line between sanity and madness.* **10. a.** the edge or contour of a shape. **b.** the sum or type of such contours, characteristic of a style or design: *the line of a building.* **11.** anything long, flexible, and thin, such as a wire or string: *a washing line; a fishing line.* **12.** a telephone connection: *a direct line to New York.* **13.** a conducting wire, cable, or circuit for making connections between pieces of electrical apparatus, such as a cable for electric-power transmission, telecommunications, etc. **14.** a system of travel or transportation, esp. over agreed routes: *a shipping line.* **15.** a company operating such a system. **16.** a route between two points on a railway. **17.** *Chiefly Brit.* a railway track, including the roadbed, sleepers, etc. **18.** a course or direction of movement or advance: *the line of flight of a bullet.* **19.** a course or method of action, behaviour, etc.: *take a new line with him.* **20.** a policy or prescribed course of action or way of thinking (often in **bring** *or* **come into line**). **21.** a field of study, interest, occupation, trade, or profession: *this book is in your line.* **22.** alignment; true (esp. in **in line, out of line**). **23.** one kind of product or article: *a nice line in hats.* **24.** a row of persons or things: *a line of cakes on the conveyor belt.* **25.** a chronological or ancestral series, esp. of people: *a line of prime ministers.* **26.** a row of words printed or written across a page or column. **27.** a unit of verse consisting of the number of feet appropriate to the metre being used and written or printed with the words in a single row. **28.** a short letter; note: *just a line to say thank you.* **29.** a piece of useful information or hint about something: *give me a line on his work.* **30.** one of a number of narrow horizontal bands forming a television picture. **31.** a narrow band in an electromagnetic spectrum, resulting from a transition in an atom of a gas. **32.** *Music.* **a.** any of the five horizontal marks that make up the stave. **b.** the musical part or melody notated on one such set. **c.** a discernible shape formed by sequences of notes or musical sounds: *a meandering melodic line.* **d.** (in polyphonic music) a set of staves that are held together with a bracket or brace. **33.** a defensive or fortified position, esp. one that marks the most forward position in war or a national boundary: *the front line.* **34.** a formation adopted by a body or a number of military units when drawn up abreast. **35.** the combatant forces of certain armies and navies, excluding supporting arms. **36. a.** the equator (esp. in **crossing the line**). **b.** any circle or arc on the terrestrial or celestial sphere. **37.** a U.S. and Canad. word for **queue. 38.** *Sl.* a portion of a powdered drug for snorting. **39.** *Sl.* something said for effect, esp. to solicit for money, sex, etc. **40. all along the line. a.** at every stage in a series. **b.** in every detail. **41. draw the line (at).** to object (to) or set a limit (on): *her father draws the line at her coming in after midnight.* **42. get a line on.** *Inf.* to obtain information about. **43. hold the line. a.** to keep a telephone line open. **b.** *Football.* to prevent the opponents from taking the ball forward. **c.** (of soldiers) to keep formation, as when under fire. **44. in line for.** in the running for; a candidate for: *he's in line for a directorship.* **45. in line with.** conforming to. **46. lay** *or* **put on the line. a.** to pay money. **b.** to speak frankly and directly. **c.** to risk (one's career, reputation, etc.) on something. ~*vb.* **47.** (*tr.*) to mark with a line or lines. **48.** (*tr.*) to draw or represent with a line or lines. **49.** (*tr.*) to be or put as a border to: *tulips lined the lawns.* **50.** to place in or form a row, series, or alignment. ~See also **lines, line-up.** [C13: partly from OF *ligne*, ult. from L *līnea*, n. use of *līneus* flaxen, from *līnum* flax; partly from OE *līn*, ult. also from L *līnum* flax] —**'linable** or **'line- able** *adj.* —**lined** *adj.*

line² (laɪn) *vb.* (*tr.*) **1.** to attach an inside covering to (a garment, curtain, etc.), as for protection, to hide the seam- ing, or so that it should hang well. **2.** to cover or fit the inside of: *to line the walls with books.* **3.** to fill plentifully: *a purse lined with money.* [C14: ult. from L *līnum* flax, since linings were often of linen]

lineage¹ ('lɪnɪɪdʒ) *n.* direct descent from an ancestor, esp. a line of descendants from one ancestor. [C14: from OF *lignage*, ult. from L *līnea* LINE¹]

lineage² ('laɪnɪdʒ) *n.* a variant spelling of **linage.**

lineal ('lɪnɪəl) *adj.* **1.** being in a direct line of descent from an ancestor. **2.** of, involving, or derived from direct descent. **3.** a less common word for **linear.** [C14: via OF from LL *līneālis*, from L *līnea* LINE¹] —**'lineally** *adv.*

lineament ('lɪnɪəmənt) *n.* (*often pl.*) **1.** a facial outline or feature. **2.** a distinctive feature. [C15: from L: line, from *līneāre* to draw a line]

linear ('lɪnɪə) *adj.* **1.** of, in, along, or relating to a line. **2.** of or relating to length. **3.** resembling, represented by, or consisting of a line or lines. **4.** having one dimension. **5.** designating a style in the arts, esp. painting, that obtains its effects through line rather than colour or light. **6.** *Maths.* of or relating to the first degree: *a linear equation.* **7.** narrow and having parallel edges: *a linear leaf.* **8.** *Electronics.* **a.** (of a circuit, etc.) having an output that is directly proportional to input: *linear amplifier.* **b.** hav- ing components arranged in a line. [C17: from L *līneāris* of lines] —**linearity** (ˌlɪnɪ'ærɪtɪ) *n.* —**'linearly** *adv.*

linear accelerator *n.* an accelerator in which charged particles are accelerated along a linear path by potential differences applied to a number of electrodes along their path.

Linear B *n.* an ancient system of writing found on clay tablets and jars of the second millennium B.C. excavated in Crete and on the Greek mainland. The script is appar- ently a modified form of the earlier and hitherto un- deciphered **Linear A** and is generally accepted as being an early representation of Mycenaean Greek.

linear measure *n.* a unit or system of units for the mea- surement of length.

linear motor *n.* a form of electric motor in which the stator and the rotor are linear and parallel. It can be used to drive a train, one part of the motor being in the locomo- tive, the other in the track.

linear programming *n.* *Maths.* a technique used in eco- nomics, etc., for determining the maximum or minimum of a linear function of non-negative variables subject to constraints expressed as linear equalities or inequalities.

lineation (ˌlɪnɪ'eɪʃən) *n.* **1.** the act of marking with lines. **2.** an arrangement of or division into lines.

line drawing *n.* a drawing made with lines only.

Line Islands *pl. n.* a group of coral islands in the central Pacific, including Tabuaeran, Teraina, and Kiritimati: part of Kiribati, with Palmyra and Jarvis administered by the U.S.

lineman ('laɪnmən) *n.*, *pl.* **-men. 1.** another name for **platelayer. 2.** a person who does the chaining, taping, or marking of points for a surveyor. **3.** *Austral. & N.Z.* the member of a beach life-saving team who controls the line used to help drowning swimmers and surfers. **4.** *Ameri- can football.* a member of a line. **5.** *U.S. & Canad.* an- other word for **linesman** (sense 2).

line management *n.* the managers in charge of specific functions and concerned in the day-to-day operations of a company.

linen ('lɪnɪn) *n.* **1. a.** a hard-wearing fabric woven from the spun fibres of flax. **b.** (*as modifier*): *a linen table- cloth.* **2.** yarn or thread spun from flax fibre. **3.** clothes, sheets, tablecloths, etc., made from linen cloth or from cotton. [OE *linnen*, ult. from L *līnum* flax]

line of battle *n.* a formation adopted by a military or naval force when preparing for action.

line of fire *n.* the flight path of a missile discharged or to be discharged from a firearm.

line of force *n.* a line in a field of force, such as an electric or magnetic field, for which the tangent at any point is the direction of the force at that point.

line of scrimmage *n.* *American football.* an imaginary line, parallel to the goal lines, on which the ball is placed at the start of each play and on either side of which the teams line up.

line-out *n.* *Rugby Union.* the method of restarting play when the ball goes into touch, the forwards forming two parallel lines at right angles to the touchline and jumping for the ball when it is thrown in.

line printer *n.* an electromechanical device that prints a line of characters at a time: used in printing and in com- puter systems.

liner¹ ('laɪnə) *n.* **1.** a passenger ship or aircraft, esp. one that is part of a commercial fleet. **2.** See **freightliner. 3.** Also called: **eyeliner.** a cosmetic used to outline the eyes. **4.** a person or thing that uses lines, esp. in drawing or cop- ying.

liner² ('laɪnə) *n.* **1.** a material used as a lining. **2.** a person who supplies or fits linings.

lines (laɪnz) *pl. n.* **1.** general appearance or outline: *a car with fine lines.* **2.** a plan of procedure or construction: *built on traditional lines.* **3. a.** the spoken words of a theatrical presentation. **b.** the words of a particular role: *he forgot his lines.* **4.** *Inf., chiefly Brit.* a marriage certif- icate: *marriage lines.* **5.** a defensive position, row of trenches, or other fortification: *we broke through the en- emy lines.* **6.** a school punishment of writing the same sentence or phrase out a specified number of times. **7. read between the lines.** to understand or find an im- plicit meaning in addition to the obvious one.

linesman ('laɪnzmən) *n.*, *pl.* **-men. 1.** an official who helps the referee or umpire in various sports, esp. by indi- cating when the ball has gone out of play. **2.** *Chiefly Brit.* a person who installs, maintains, or repairs telephone or electric-power lines. U.S. and Canad. name: **lineman.**

line-up *n.* **1.** a row or arrangement of people or things assembled for a particular purpose: *the line-up for the football match.* **2.** the members of such a row or arrange- ment. ~*vb.* **line up.** (*adv.*) **3.** to form, put into, or organ- ize a line-up. **4.** (*tr.*) to produce, organize, and assemble: *they lined up some questions.* **5.** (*tr.*) to align.

ling¹ (lɪŋ) *n.*, *pl.* **ling** or **lings. 1.** any of several northern coastal food fishes having an elongated body with long fins. **2.** another name for **burbot** (a fish). [C13: prob. from Low G]

ling² (lɪŋ) *n.* another name for **heather.** [C14: from ON *lyng*]

-ling¹ *suffix forming nouns.* **1.** *Often disparaging.* a per- son or thing belonging to or associated with the group, activity, or quality specified: *nestling; underling.* **2.** used as a diminutive: *duckling.* [OE *-ling*, of Gmc origin]

-ling² *suffix forming adverbs.* in a specified condition, manner, or direction: *darkling.* [OE *-ling*, adv. suffix]

ling. *abbrev. for* linguistics.

lingam ('lɪŋgəm) *or* **linga** ('lɪŋgə) *n.* the Hindu phallic im- age of the god Siva. [C18: from Sansk.]

Lingayen Gulf ('lɪŋgɑː'jɛn) *n.* a large inlet of the South China Sea in the Philippines, on the NW coast of Luzon: site of Japanese landing in 1941 invasion.

linger ('lɪŋgə) *vb.* (*mainly intr.*) **1.** to delay or prolong departure. **2.** to go in a slow or leisurely manner; saunter. **3.** to remain just alive for some time prior to death. **4.** to persist or continue, esp. in the mind. **5.** to be slow to act; dither. [C13 (northern dialect) *lengeren* to dwell, from *lengen* to prolong, from OE *lengan*] —**'lingerer** *n.* —**'lin- gering** *adj.* —**'lingeringly** *adv.*

lingerie ('læn̄ʒərɪ) *n.* women's underwear and nightwear. [C19: from F, from *linge*, from L *līneus* linen, from *līnum* flax]

lingo ('lɪŋgəʊ) *n.*, *pl.* **-goes.** *Inf.* any foreign or unfamiliar language, jargon, etc. [C17: ?from LINGUA FRANCA]

lingua franca ('lɪŋgwə 'fræŋkə) *n.*, *pl.* **lingua francas** *or* **linguae francae** ('lɪŋgwiː 'frænsiː). **1.** a language used for communication among people of different mother tongues. **2.** a hybrid language containing elements from several different languages used in this way. **3.** any sys- tem of communication providing mutual understanding. [C17: It., lit.: Frankish tongue]

Lingua Franca *n.* a particular lingua franca spoken from the Crusades to the 18th century in the ports of the Mediterranean, based on Italian, Spanish, French, Arabic, Greek, and Turkish.

lingual ('lɪŋgwəl) *adj.* **1.** *Anat.* of or relating to the tongue. **2. a.** *Rare.* of or relating to language or languages. **b.** (*in combination*): *polylingual.* **3.** articulated with the tongue. ~*n.* **4.** a lingual consonant, such as Scots (r). —'**lingually** *adv.*

linguiform ('lɪŋgwɪˌfɔːm) *adj.* shaped like a tongue.

linguist ('lɪŋgwɪst) *n.* **1.** a person who is skilled in foreign languages. **2.** a person who studies linguistics. [C16: from L *lingua* tongue]

linguistic (lɪŋ'gwɪstɪk) *adj.* **1.** of or relating to language. **2.** of or relating to linguistics. —**lin**'**guistically** *adv.*

linguistic atlas *n.* an atlas showing the distribution of distinctive linguistic features.

linguistics (lɪŋ'gwɪstɪks) *n.* (*functioning as sing.*) the scientific study of language.

liniment ('lɪnɪmənt) *n.* a medicated liquid, usually containing alcohol, camphor, and an oil, applied to the skin to relieve pain, stiffness, etc. [C15: from LL *linimentum*, from *linere* to smear]

lining ('laɪnɪŋ) *n.* **1.** material used to line a garment, curtain, etc. **2.** any material used as an interior covering.

link[1] (lɪŋk) *n.* **1.** any of the separate rings, loops, or pieces that connect or make up a chain. **2.** something that resembles such a ring, loop, or piece. **3.** a connecting part or episode. **4.** a connecting piece in a mechanism. **5.** Also called: **radio link.** a system of transmitters and receivers that connect two locations by means of radio and television signals. **6.** a unit of length equal to one hundredth of a chain. 1 link of a Gunter's chain is equal to 7.92 inches, and of an engineer's chain to 1 foot. ~*vb.* **7.** (often foll. by *up*) to connect or be connected with or as if with links. **8.** (*tr.*) to connect by association, etc. [C14: from ON]

link[2] (lɪŋk) *n.* (formerly) a torch used to light dark streets. [C16: ?from L *lychnus*, from Gk *lukhnos* lamp]

linkage ('lɪŋkɪdʒ) *n.* **1.** the act of linking or the state of being linked. **2.** a system of interconnected levers or rods for transmitting or regulating the motion of a mechanism. **3.** *Electronics.* the product of the total number of lines of magnetic flux and the number of turns in a coil or circuit through which they pass. **4.** *Genetics.* the occurrence of two genes close together on the same chromosome so that they tend to be inherited as a single unit.

linkman ('lɪŋkmən) *n.*, *pl.* **-men.** a presenter of a television or radio programme, esp. a sports transmission, consisting of a number of outside broadcasts from different locations.

Linköping (*Swedish* 'lintçøːpiŋ) *n.* a city in S Sweden: a political and ecclesiastical centre in the Middle Ages; engineering industry. Pop.: 117 835 (1986).

links (lɪŋks) *pl. n.* **1. a.** short for **golf links. b.** (*as modifier*): *a links course.* See **golf course. 2.** *Chiefly Scot.* undulating sandy ground near the shore. [OE *hlincas* pl. of *hlinc* ridge]

link-up *n.* a joining or linking together of two factions, objects, etc.

Linlithgow (lɪn'lɪθgəʊ) *n.* **1.** a town in SE Scotland, in Lothian region: ruined palace, residence of Scottish kings and birthplace of Mary Queen of Scots. Pop.: 10 000 (1984 est.). **2.** the former name of **West Lothian.**

linn (lɪn) *n. Chiefly Scot.* **1.** a waterfall or a pool at the foot of it. **2.** a ravine or precipice. [C16: prob. from a confusion of two words, Scot. Gaelic *linne* pool and OE *hlynn* torrent]

Linnaeus (lɪ'niːəs, -'neɪ-) *n.* **Carolus** ('kærələs), original name *Carl von Linné.* 1707–78, Swedish botanist, who established the binomial system of biological nomenclature that forms the basis of modern classification. —**Lin**'**nean** *or* **Lin**'**naean** *adj.*

linnet ('lɪnɪt) *n.* a brownish Old World finch: the male has a red breast and forehead. [C16: from OF *linotte*, ult. from L *linum* flax (because the bird feeds on flaxseeds)]

Linnhe ('lɪnɪ) *n.* **Loch.** a sea loch of W Scotland, at the SW end of the Great Glen. Length: about 32 km (20 miles).

lino ('laɪnəʊ) *n.* short for **linoleum.**

linocut ('laɪnəʊˌkʌt) *n.* **1.** a design cut in relief on a block of linoleum. **2.** a print made from such a block.

linoleum (lɪ'nəʊlɪəm) *n.* a sheet material made of hessian, jute, etc., coated with a mixture of powdered cork, linseed oil, rosin, and pigment, used as a floor covering. Often shortened to **lino.** [C19: from L *linum* flax + *oleum* oil]

Linotype ('laɪnəʊˌtaɪp) *n.* **1.** *Trademark.* a typesetting machine, operated by a keyboard, that casts an entire line on one solid slug of metal. **2.** type produced by such a machine.

Lin Piao ('lɪn 'pjaʊ) *n.* 1908–71, Chinese Communist general and statesman. He became minister of defence (1959) and second in rank to Mao Tse-tung (1966). He fell from grace and is reported to have died in an air crash while attempting to flee to the Soviet Union.

linseed ('lɪnˌsiːd) *n.* another name for **flaxseed.** [OE *linsǣd*, from *lin* flax + *sǣd* seed]

linseed oil *n.* a yellow oil extracted from seeds of the flax plant. It is used in making oil paints, printer's ink, linoleum, etc.

linsey-woolsey ('lɪnzɪ'wʊlzɪ) *n.* **1.** a thin rough fabric of linen warp and coarse wool or cotton filling. **2.** a strange nonsensical mixture or confusion. [C15: prob. from *Lindsey*, village in Suffolk where first made + WOOL (with rhyming suffix *-sey*)]

lint (lɪnt) *n.* **1.** an absorbent cotton or linen fabric with the nap raised on one side, used to dress wounds, etc. **2.** shreds of fibre, yarn, etc. [C14: prob. from L *linteus* made of linen, from *linum* flax] —'**linty** *adj.*

lintel ('lɪntˀl) *n.* a horizontal beam, as over a door or window. [C14: via OF prob. from LL *limitāris* (unattested) of the boundary, infl. by *liminaris* (of the threshold)]

linter ('lɪntə) *n.* **1.** a machine for stripping the short fibres of ginned cotton seeds. **2.** (*pl.*) the fibres so removed.

Linz (lɪnts) *n.* a port in N Austria, capital of Upper Austria, on the River Danube: cultural centre; steelworks. Pop.: 199 910 (1983 est.). Latin name: **Lentia** ('lɛntɪə, 'lensɪə).

lion ('laɪən) *n.* **1.** a large gregarious predatory feline mammal of open country in parts of Africa and India, having a tawny yellow coat and, in the male, a shaggy mane. Related adj.: **leonine. 2.** a conventionalized lion, the principal beast used as an emblem in heraldry. **3.** a courageous, strong, or bellicose person. **4.** a celebrity or idol who attracts much publicity and a large following. **5.** the **lion's share.** the largest portion. [OE *lio, leo* (ME *lioun,* from Anglo-F *liun*), both from L *leo,* Gk *leon*] —'**lioness** *fem. n.*

Lion ('laɪən) *n.* **the.** the constellation Leo, the fifth sign of the zodiac.

lion-hearted *adj.* very brave; courageous.

lionize *or* **-ise** ('laɪəˌnaɪz) *vb.* (*tr.*) to treat as or make into a celebrity. —ˌ**lioni**'**zation** *or* **-i**'**sation** *n.* —'**lion**ˌ**izer** *or* **-ˌiser** *n.*

Lions ('laɪənz) *n.* **Gulf of.** a wide bay of the Mediterranean off the S coast of France, between the Spanish border and Toulon. French name: **Golfe du Lion** (gɔlf dy ljɔ̃).

lip (lɪp) *n.* **1.** *Anat.* **a.** either of the two fleshy folds surrounding the mouth. Related adj.: **labial. b.** (*as modifier*): *lip salve.* **2.** the corresponding part in animals, esp. mammals. **3.** any structure resembling a lip, such as the rim of a crater, the margin of a gastropod shell, etc. **4.** a nontechnical word for **labium. 5.** *Sl.* impudent talk or backchat. **6. bite one's lip. a.** to stifle one's feelings. **b.** to be annoyed or irritated. **7. keep a stiff upper lip.** to maintain one's courage or composure during a time of trouble. **8. lick** *or* **smack one's lips.** to anticipate or recall something with glee or relish. ~*vb.* **lipping, lipped. 9.** (*tr.*) to touch with the lip or lips. **10.** (*tr.*) to form or be a lip or lips for. **11.** (*tr.*) *Rare.* to murmur or whisper. **12.** (*intr.*) to use the lips in playing a wind instrument. [OE *lippa*] —'**lipless** *adj.* —'**lip**ˌ**like** *adj.*

Lipari Islands ('lɪpərɪ) *pl. n.* a group of volcanic islands under Italian administration off the N coast of Sicily: remains that form a continuous record from Neolithic times. Chief town: Lipari. Pop.: 10 208 (1981 est.). Area: 114 sq. km (44 sq. miles). Also called: **Aeolian Islands.** Italian name: **Isole Eolie** ('iːzole e'ɔːlje).

lipase ('laɪpeɪs, 'lɪpeɪs) *n.* any of a group of fat-digesting enzymes produced in the stomach, pancreas, and liver. [C19: from Gk *lipos* fat + -ASE]

Lipchitz ('lɪpˌʃɪts) *n.* **Jacques** (ʒɑːk). 1891–1973, U.S. sculptor, born in Lithuania: he pioneered cubist sculpture.

Lipetsk (*Russian* 'lipɪtsk) *n.* a city in the central Soviet Union, on the Voronezh River: steelworks. Pop.: 465 000 (1987).

lip gloss *n.* a cosmetic applied to the lips to give a sheen.
lipid *or* **lipide** ('laɪpɪd, 'lɪpɪd) *n. Biochem.* any of a large group of organic compounds that are esters of fatty acids or closely related substances. They are important structural materials in living organisms. Former name: **lipoid**. [C20: from F *lipide*, from Gk *lipos* fat]
Li Po *or* **Li T'ai-po** ('liː 'taɪ 'pəʊ) *n.* ?700–762 A.D., Chinese poet. His lyrics deal mostly with wine, nature, and women and are remarkable for their imagery.
lipo- *or before a vowel* **lip-** *combining form.* fat or fatty: *lipoprotein.* [from Gk *lipos* fat]
lipography (lɪ'pɒɡrəfɪ) *n.* the accidental omission of words or letters in writing. [C19: from Gk *lip-*, stem of *leipein* to omit + -GRAPHY]
lipoid ('lɪpɔɪd, 'laɪ-) *adj. also* **lipoidal.** **1.** resembling fat; fatty. ~*n.* **2.** a fatlike substance, such as wax. **3.** *Biochem.* a former name for **lipid.**
liposuction ('lɪpəʊ,sʌkʃən) *n.* a cosmetic surgical operation in which subcutaneous fat is removed from the body by suction.
Lippe ('lɪpə) *n.* **1.** a former state of NW Germany: now part of the West German state of North Rhine-Westphalia. **2.** a river in W West Germany, flowing west to the Rhine. Length: about 240 km (150 miles).
-lipped *adj.* having a lip or lips as specified: *tight-lipped.*
Lippi (*Italian* 'lippi) *n.* **1.** **Filippino** (filip'piːno). ?1457–1504, Italian painter of the Florentine school. **2.** his father, **Fra Filippo** (fra fi'lippo). ?1406–69, Italian painter of the Florentine school, noted particularly for his frescoes at Prato Cathedral (1452–64).
Lippizaner (,lɪpɪt'saːnə) *n.* a breed of riding and carriage horse used by the Spanish Riding School in Vienna and usually white or grey in colour. [G, after *Lippiza*, Yugoslavia, where bred]
Lippmann ('lɪpmən; *French* lipman) *n.* **Gabriel** (gabriɛl). 1845–1921, French physicist. He devised the earliest process of colour photography: Nobel prize for physics 1908.
lip-read ('lɪp,riːd) *vb.* **-reading, -read** (-'rɛd). to interpret (words) by lip-reading.
lip-reading *n.* a method used by the deaf to comprehend spoken words by interpreting movements of the speaker's lips. Also called: **speech-reading.** — **'lip-,reader** *n.*
lip service *n.* insincere support or respect expressed but not practised.
lipstick ('lɪp,stɪk) *n.* a cosmetic for colouring the lips, usually in the form of a stick.
lip-synch *or* **lip-sync** ('lɪp,sɪŋk) *vb.* to mouth (the words of a prerecorded song) on television or film.
liq. *abbrev. for:* **1.** liquid. **2.** liquor.
liquefacient (,lɪkwɪ'feɪʃənt) *n.* a substance that liquefies or causes liquefaction. ~*adj.* **2.** becoming or causing to become liquid. [C19: from L *liquefacere* to make LIQUID]
liquefied natural gas *n.* a mixture of various gases, esp. methane, liquefied under pressure for transportation and used as an engine fuel. Abbrev.: **LNG.**
liquefied petroleum gas *n.* a mixture of various petroleum gases, esp. propane and butane, stored as a liquid under pressure and used as an engine fuel. Abbrev.: **LPG** *or* **LP gas.**
liquefy ('lɪkwɪ,faɪ) *vb.* **-fying, -fied.** (esp. of a gas) to become or cause to become liquid. [C15: via OF from L *liquefacere* to make liquid] —**lique,fiable** *adj.* —**'lique,fier** *n.*
liquescent (lɪ'kwɛsᵊnt) *adj.* (of a solid or gas) becoming or tending to become liquid. [C18: from L *liquescere*] —**li'quescence** *or* **li'quescency** *n.*
liqueur (lɪ'kjʊə; *French* likœr) *n.* **1. a.** any of several highly flavoured sweetened spirits such as kirsch or cointreau, intended to be drunk after a meal. **b.** (*as modifier*): *liqueur glass.* **2.** a small hollow chocolate sweet containing liqueur. [C18: from F; see LIQUOR]
liquid ('lɪkwɪd) *n.* **1.** a substance in a physical state in which it does not resist change of shape but does resist change of size. Cf. **gas** (sense 1), **solid** (sense 1). **2.** a substance that is a liquid at room temperature and atmospheric pressure. **3.** *Phonetics.* a frictionless continuant, esp. (l) or (r). ~*adj.* **4.** of, concerned with, or being a liquid or having the characteristic state of liquids: *liquid wax.* **5.** shining, transparent, or brilliant. **6.** flowing, fluent, or smooth. **7.** (of assets) in the form of money or easily convertible into money. [C14: via OF from L *liquidus*, from *liquēre* to be fluid] —**li'quidity** *or* **'liquidness** *n.* —**'liquidly** *adv.*

liquid air *n.* air that has been liquefied by cooling: used in the production of pure oxygen, nitrogen, and as a refrigerant.
liquidambar (,lɪkwɪd'æmbə) *n.* **1.** a deciduous tree of Asia and North and Central America, with star-shaped leaves, and exuding a yellow aromatic balsam. **2.** the balsam of this tree, used in medicine. [C16: NL, from L *liquidus* liquid + Med. L *ambar* AMBER]
liquidate ('lɪkwɪ,deɪt) *vb.* **1.** to settle or pay off (a debt, claim, etc.). **2. a.** to terminate the operations of (a commercial firm, bankrupt estate, etc.) by assessment of liabilities and appropriation of assets for their settlement. **b.** (of a commercial firm, etc.) to terminate operations in this manner. **3.** (*tr.*) to convert (assets) into cash. **4.** (*tr.*) to eliminate or kill. —**'liqui,dator** *n.*
liquidation (,lɪkwɪ'deɪʃən) *n.* **1. a.** the process of terminating the affairs of a business firm, etc., by realizing its assets to discharge its liabilities. **b.** the state of a business firm, etc., having its affairs so terminated (esp. in **to go into liquidation**). **2.** destruction; elimination.
liquid-crystal display *n.* a display of numbers, esp. in an electronic calculator, using cells containing a liquid with crystalline properties (**liquid crystal**), that change their reflectivity or optical polarization when an electric field is applied to them.
liquidize *or* **-dise** ('lɪkwɪ,daɪz) *vb.* **1.** to make or become liquid; liquefy. **2.** (*tr.*) to pulverize (food) in a liquidizer so as to produce a fluid.
liquidizer *or* **-diser** ('lɪkwɪ,daɪzə) *n.* a kitchen appliance with blades for puréeing vegetables, blending liquids, etc. Also called: **blender.**
liquid measure *n.* a unit or system of units for measuring volumes of liquids or their containers.
liquid oxygen *n.* the clear pale blue liquid state of oxygen produced by liquefying air and allowing the nitrogen to evaporate: used in rocket fuels. Also called: **lox.**
liquid paraffin *n.* an oily liquid obtained by petroleum distillation and used as a laxative. Also called (esp. U.S. and Canad.): **mineral oil.**
liquor ('lɪkə) *n.* **1.** any alcoholic drink, esp. spirits, or such drinks collectively. **2.** any liquid substance, esp. that in which food has been cooked. **3.** *Pharmacol.* a solution of a pure substance in water. **4. in liquor.** drunk. [C13: via OF from L, from *liquēre* to be liquid]
liquorice *or U.S. & Canad.* **licorice** ('lɪkərɪs, -ərɪʃ) *n.* **1.** a perennial Mediterranean leguminous shrub. **2.** the dried root of this plant, used as a laxative and in confectionery. **3.** a sweet having a liquorice flavour. [C13: via Anglo-Norman and OF from LL *liquiritia*, from L *glycyrrhiza*, from Gk *glukurrhiza*, from *glukus* sweet + *rhiza* root]
lira ('lɪərə; *Italian* 'liːra) *n., pl.* **lire** ('lɪərɪ; *Italian* 'liːre) *or* **liras.** **1.** the standard monetary unit of Italy. **2.** Also called: **pound.** the standard monetary unit of Turkey. [It., from L *libra* pound]
liriodendron (,lɪrɪəʊ'dɛndrən) *n., pl.* **-drons** *or* **-dra** (-drə). a deciduous tulip tree of N America or a similar Chinese tree. [C18: NL, from Gk *leiron* lily + *dendron* tree]
Lisbon ('lɪzbən) *n.* the capital and chief port of Portugal, in the southwest on the Tagus estuary: became capital in 1256; subject to earthquakes and severely damaged in 1755; university (1911). Pop.: 827 800 (1985 est.). Portuguese name: **Lisboa** (liʒ'boə).
Lisieux (*French* lizjø) *n.* a town in NW France: Roman Catholic pilgrimage centre, for its shrine of St. Thérèse, who lived there. Pop.: 25 823 (1982).
lisle (laɪl) *n.* **a.** a strong fine cotton thread or fabric. **b.** (*as modifier*): *lisle stockings.* [C19: after *Lisle* (now Lille), town in France where this thread was orig. manufactured]
lisp (lɪsp) *n.* **1.** the articulation of *s* and *z* like or nearly like the *th* sounds in English *thin* and *then* respectively. **2.** the habit or speech defect of pronouncing *s* and *z* in this manner. **3.** the sound of a lisp in pronunciation. ~*vb.* **4.** to use a lisp in the pronunciation of (speech). **5.** to speak or pronounce imperfectly or haltingly. [OE *āwlispian*, from *wlisp* lisping (adj.), imit.] —**'lisper** *n.* —**'lisping** *adj., n.* —**'lispingly** *adv.*
lissom *or* **lissome** ('lɪsəm) *adj.* **1.** supple in the limbs or body; lithe; flexible. **2.** agile; nimble. [C19: var. of *lithesome*, LITHE + -SOME[1]] —**'lissomly** *or* **'lissomely** *adv.* —**'lissomness** *or* **'lissomeness** *n.*

list[1] (lıst) n. **1.** an item-by-item record of names or things, usually written or printed one under the other. **2.** *Computers.* a linearly ordered data structure. ~vb. **3.** (tr.) to make a list of. **4.** (tr.) to include in a list. **5.** (tr.) *Brit.* to declare to be a listed building. **6.** (tr.) *Stock Exchange.* to obtain an official quotation for (a security) so that it may be traded on the recognized market. **7.** an archaic word for **enlist**. [C17: from F, ult. rel. to LIST[2]] —'**listable** adj. —'**listing** n.

list[2] (lıst) n. **1.** a border or edging strip, esp. of cloth. **2.** a less common word for **selvage**. ~vb. (tr.) **3.** to border with or as if with a list or lists. ~See also **lists**. [OE *līst*]

list[3] (lıst) vb. **1.** (esp. of ships) to lean over or cause to lean over to one side. ~n. **2.** the act or an instance of leaning to one side. [C17: from ?]

list[4] (lıst) *Arch.* ~vb. **1.** to be pleasing to (a person). **2.** (tr.) to desire or choose. ~n. **3.** a liking or desire. [OE *lystan*]

list[5] (lıst) vb. an archaic or poetic word for **listen**. [OE *hlystan*]

listed building n. (in Britain) a building officially recognized as having special historical or architectural interest and therefore protected from demolition or alteration.

listen ('lıs³n) vb. (intr.) **1.** to concentrate on hearing something. **2.** to take heed; pay attention: *I warned you but you wouldn't listen.* [OE *hlysnan*] —'**listener** n.

listen in vb. (intr., adv.; often foll. by *to*) **1.** to listen to the radio. **2.** to intercept radio communications. **3.** to listen but not contribute (to a discussion), esp. surreptitiously.

listening post n. **1.** *Mil.* a forward position set up to obtain early warning of enemy movement. **2.** any strategic position for obtaining information about another country or area.

lister ('lıstə) n. *U.S. & Canad. agriculture.* a plough with a double mouldboard designed to throw soil to either side of a central furrow. [C19: from LIST[2]]

Lister ('lıstə) n. **Joseph,** 1st Baron Lister. 1827–1912, English surgeon, who introduced the use of antiseptics.

listeriosis (lı,stıərı'əusıs) n. a serious form of food poisoning, caused by bacteria of the genus *Listeria.* Its symptoms can include meningitis. [after Joseph LISTER]

listless ('lıstlıs) adj. having or showing no interest; lacking vigour or energy. [C15: from *list* desire + -LESS] —'**listlessly** adv. —'**listlessness** n.

list price n. the selling price of merchandise as quoted in a catalogue or advertisement.

lists (lısts) pl. n. **1.** *History.* **a.** the enclosed field of combat at a tournament. **b.** the barriers enclosing the field at a tournament. **2.** any arena or scene of conflict, controversy, etc. **3. enter the lists.** to engage in a conflict, controversy, etc. [C14: pl. of LIST[2] (border)]

Liszt (lıst) n. **Franz** (frants). 1811–86, Hungarian composer and pianist. The greatest piano virtuoso of the 19th century, he originated the symphonic poem, pioneered the one-movement sonata form, and developed new harmonic combinations. His works include the symphonies *Faust* (1861) and *Dante* (1867), piano compositions and transcriptions, songs, and church music.

lit (lıt) vb. **1.** a past tense and past participle of **light**[1]. **2.** a past tense and past participle of **light**[2].

lit. abbrev. for: **1.** literal(ly). **2.** literary. **3.** literature. **4.** litre.

Li T'ai-po ('li: 'taı'pəu) n. See **Li Po.**

litany ('lıtənı) n., pl. -**nies.** **1.** *Christianity.* **a.** a form of prayer consisting of a series of invocations, each followed by an unvarying response. **b. the Litany.** the general supplication in this form in the Book of Common Prayer. **2.** any tedious recital. [C13: via OF from Med. L *litania* from LGk *litaneia* prayer, ult. from Gk *litē* entreaty]

litchi, lichee, or **lychee** (,laı'tʃiː) n. **1.** a Chinese tree cultivated for its round edible fruits. **2.** the fruit of this tree, which has whitish juicy pulp. [C16: from Cantonese *lai chi*]

-lite n. combining form. (in names of minerals) stone: *chrysolite.* [from F -*lite* or -*lithe,* from Gk *lithos* stone]

liter ('liːtə) n. the U.S. spelling of **litre.**

literacy ('lıtərəsı) n. **1.** the ability to read and write. **2.** the ability to use language proficiently.

literal ('lıtərəl) adj. **1.** in exact accordance with or limited to the primary or explicit meaning of a word or text. **2.** word for word. **3.** dull, factual, or prosaic. **4.** consisting of, concerning, or indicated by letters. **5.** true; actual.

~n. **6.** Also called: **literal error.** a misprint or misspelling in a text. [C14: from LL *litterālis* concerning letters, from L *littera* letter] —'**literally** adv. —'**literalness** or **literality** (,lıtə'rælıtı) n.

literalism ('lıtərə,lızəm) n. **1.** the disposition to take words and statements in their literal sense. **2.** literal or realistic portrayal in art or literature. —'**literalist** n. —,**literal'istic** adj.

literary ('lıtərərı, 'lıtrərı) adj. **1.** of, relating to, concerned with, or characteristic of literature or scholarly writing: *a literary style.* **2.** versed in or knowledgeable about literature. **3.** (of a word) formal; not colloquial. [C17: from L *litterārius* concerning reading & writing. See LETTER] —'**literarily** adv. —'**literariness** n.

literate ('lıtərıt) adj. **1.** able to read and write. **2.** educated; learned. ~n. **3.** a literate person. [C15: from L *litterātus* learned. See LETTER] —'**literately** adv.

literati (,lıtə'rɑːtiː) pl. n. literary or scholarly people. [C17: from L]

literature ('lıtərıtʃə, 'lıtrı-) n. **1.** written material such as poetry, novels, essays, etc. **2.** the body of written work of a particular culture or people: *Scandinavian literature.* **3.** written or printed matter of a particular type or genre: *scientific literature.* **4.** the art or profession of a writer. **5.** *Inf.* printed matter on any subject. [C14: from L *litterātūra* writing; see LETTER]

-lith n. combining form. indicating stone or rock: *megalith.* [from Gk *lithos* stone]

lith. abbrev. for: **1.** lithograph. **2.** lithography.

Lith. abbrev. for Lithuania(n).

litharge ('lıθɑːdʒ) n. another name for **lead monoxide.** [C14: via OF from L *lithargyrus,* from Gk, from *lithos* stone + *arguros* silver]

lithe (laıð) adj. flexible or supple. [OE (in the sense: gentle; C15: supple)] —'**lithely** adv. —'**litheness** n.

lithia ('lıθıə) n. **1.** another name for **lithium oxide. 2.** lithium present in mineral waters as lithium salts. [C19: NL, ult. from Gk *lithos* stone]

lithic ('lıθık) adj. **1.** of, relating to, or composed of stone. **2.** *Pathol.* of or relating to a calculus or calculi. **3.** of or containing lithium. [C18: from Gk *lithikos* stony]

-lithic n. and adj. combining form. relating to the use of stone implements in a specified cultural period: *Neolithic.* [from Gk *lithikos,* from *lithos* stone]

lithium ('lıθıəm) n. a soft silvery element of the alkali metal series: the lightest known metal, used as an alloy hardener, as a reducing agent, and in batteries. Symbol: Li; atomic no.: 3; atomic wt.: 6.941. [C19: NL, from LITHO- + -IUM]

lithium oxide n. a white crystalline compound. It absorbs carbon dioxide and water vapour. Formula: Li_2O.

litho ('laıθəu) n., pl. -**thos,** adj., adv. short for **lithography, lithograph, lithographic,** or **lithographically.**

litho- or before a vowel **lith-** combining form. stone: *lithograph.* [from L, from Gk, from *lithos* stone]

lithograph ('lıθə,grɑːf) n. **1.** a print made by lithography. ~vb. **2.** (tr.) to reproduce (pictures, text, etc.) by lithography. —**lithographic** (,lıθə'græfık) adj. —,**litho'graphically** adv.

lithography (lı'θɒgrəfı) n. a method of printing from a metal or stone surface on which the printing areas are not raised but made ink-receptive as opposed to ink-repellent. [C18: from NL *lithographia*] —**li'thographer** n.

lithology (lı'θɒlədʒı) n. **1.** the physical characteristics of a rock, including colour, composition, and texture. **2.** the study of rocks.

lithophyte ('lıθə,faıt) n. **1.** a plant that grows on stony ground. **2.** an organism, such as a coral, that is partly composed of stony material.

lithosphere ('lıθə,sfıə) n. the rigid outer layer of the earth, comprising the earth's crust and the solid upper part of the mantle.

lithotomy (lı'θɒtəmı) n., pl. -**mies.** the surgical removal of a calculus, esp. one in the urinary bladder. [C18: via LL from Gk]

Lithuanian (,lıθjʊ'eınıən) adj. **1.** of, relating to, or characteristic of the Lithuanian SSR, its people, or their language. ~n. **2.** an official language of the Lithuanian SSR. **3.** a native or inhabitant of the Lithuanian SSR.

Lithuanian Soviet Socialist Republic n. an administrative division of the W Soviet Union, on the Baltic Sea: a grand duchy in medieval times. Capital: Vilnius. Pop.:

3 603 000 (1986). Area: 65 200 sq. km (25 174 sq. miles). Also called: **Lithuania.** Lithuanian name: **Lietuva.**

litigable ('lɪtɪgəbʰl) *adj. Law.* that may be the subject of litigation.

litigant ('lɪtɪgənt) *n.* **1.** a party to a lawsuit. ~*adj.* **2.** engaged in litigation.

litigate ('lɪtɪ,geɪt) *vb.* **1.** to bring or contest (a claim, action, etc.) in a lawsuit. **2.** (*intr.*) to engage in legal proceedings. [C17: from L *litigāre*, from *lit-*, stem of *lis* lawsuit + *agere* to carry on] —'**liti,gator** *n.*

litigation (,lɪtɪ'geɪʃən) *n.* **1.** the act or process of bringing or contesting a lawsuit. **2.** a judicial proceeding or contest.

litigious (lɪ'tɪdʒəs) *adj.* **1.** excessively ready to go to law. **2.** of or relating to litigation. **3.** inclined to dispute or disagree. [C14: from L *litigiōsus* quarrelsome, from *litigium* strife] —**li'tigiously** *adv.* —**li'tigiousness** *n.*

litmus ('lɪtməs) *n.* a soluble powder obtained from certain lichens. It turns red under acid conditions and blue under basic conditions. Absorbent paper treated with it (**litmus paper**) is used as an indicator. [C16: ?from Scand.]

litotes ('laɪtəʊ,tiːz) *n., pl.* **-tes.** understatement for rhetorical effect, esp. using negation with a term in place of using an antonym of that term, as in "She was not a little upset" for "She was extremely upset." [C17: from Gk, from *litos* small]

litre *or U.S.* **liter** ('liːtə) *n.* **1.** one cubic decimetre. **2.** (formerly) the volume occupied by 1 kilogram of pure water. This is equivalent to 1.000 028 cubic decimetres or about 1.76 pints. [C19: from F, from Med. L *litra*, from Gk: a unit of weight]

LittD *or* **LitD** *abbrev. for* Doctor of Letters *or* Doctor of Literature. [L: *Litterarum Doctor*]

litter ('lɪtə) *n.* **1. a.** small refuse or waste materials carelessly dropped, esp. in public places. **b.** (*as modifier*): *litter bin.* **2.** a disordered or untidy condition or a collection of objects in this condition. **3.** a group of offspring produced at one birth by a mammal such as a sow. **4.** a layer of partly decomposed leaves, twigs, etc., on the ground in a wood or forest. **5.** straw, hay, or similar material used as bedding, protection, etc., by animals or plants. **6.** a means of conveying people, esp. sick or wounded people, consisting of a light bed or seat held between parallel sticks. **7.** see **cat litter.** ~*vb.* **8.** to make (a place) untidy by strewing (refuse). **9.** to scatter (objects, etc.) about or (of objects) to lie around or upon (anything) in an untidy fashion. **10.** (of pigs, cats, etc.) to give birth to (offspring). **11.** (*tr.*) to provide (an animal or plant) with straw or hay for bedding, protection, etc. [C13 (in the sense: bed): via Anglo-F, ult. from L *lectus* bed]

littérateur (,lɪtərə'tɜː; *French* literatœr) *n.* an author, esp. a professional writer. [C19: from F from L *litterātor* a grammarian]

litter lout *or U.S. & Canad.* **litterbug** ('lɪtə,bʌg) *n. Sl.* a person who tends to drop refuse in public places.

little ('lɪtʰl) *determiner.* **1.** (often preceded by *a*) **a.** a small quantity, extent, or duration of: *the little hope there is left; very little milk.* **b.** (*as pronoun*): *save a little for me.* **2.** not much: *little damage was done.* **3. make little of.** to regard or treat as insignificant; dismiss. **4. not a little. a.** very. **b.** a lot. **5. think little of.** to have a low opinion of. ~*adj.* **6.** of small or less than average size. **7.** young: *a little boy.* **8.** endearingly familiar; dear: *my husband's little ways.* **9.** contemptible, mean, or disagreeable: *your filthy little mind.* ~*adv.* **10.** (usually preceded by *a*) in a small amount; to a small extent or degree; not a lot: *to laugh a little.* **11.** (used preceding a verb) not at all, or hardly: *he little realized his fate.* **12.** not much or often: *we go there very little now.* **13. little by little.** by small degrees. ~See also **less, lesser, least.** [OE *lȳtel*]

Little Bear *n.* the. the English name for **Ursa Minor.**

Little Belt *n.* a strait in Denmark, between Jutland and Fyn Island, linking the Kattegat with the Baltic. Length: about 48 km (30 miles). Width: up to 29 km (18 miles). Danish name: **Lille Bælt.**

Little Bighorn *n.* a river in the W central U.S., rising in N Wyoming and flowing north to the Bighorn River. Its banks were the scene of the defeat (1876) and killing of General Custer and his command by Indians.

Little Diomede *n.* the smaller of the two Diomede Islands in the Bering Strait: administered by the U.S. Area: about 10 sq. km (4 sq. miles).

Little Dipper *n.* the. a U.S. name for **Ursa Minor.**

Little John *n.* one of Robin Hood's companions, noted for his great size and strength.

little people *pl. n. Folklore.* small supernatural beings, such as elves or leprechauns.

Little Rock *n.* a city in central Arkansas, on the Arkansas River: state capital. Pop.: 181 030 (1986 est.).

Little Russia *n.* a region of the SW Soviet Union, consisting chiefly of the Ukrainian SSR.

little slam *n. Bridge, etc.* the winning of all tricks except one. Also called: **small slam.**

Little St Bernard Pass *n.* a pass over the Savoy Alps, between Bourg-Saint-Maurice, France, and La Thuile, Italy: 11th-century hospice. Height: 2187 m (7177 ft.).

littoral ('lɪtərəl) *adj.* **1.** of or relating to the shore of a sea, lake, or ocean. ~*n.* **2.** a coastal or shore region. [C17: from LL *littorālis*, from *litus* shore]

Littoria (*Italian* lit'tɔːrja) *n.* the former name (until 1947) of **Latina.**

liturgical (lɪ'tɜːdʒɪkʰl) *adj.* **1.** of or relating to public worship. **2.** of or relating to the liturgy. —**li'turgically** *adv.*

liturgy ('lɪtədʒɪ) *n., pl.* **-gies. 1.** the forms of public services officially prescribed by a Church. **2.** (*often cap.*) Also called: **Divine Liturgy.** *Chiefly Eastern Churches.* the Eucharistic celebration. **3.** a particular order or form of public service laid down by a Church. [C16: via Med. L, from Gk *leitourgia*, from *leitourgos* minister, from *leit-* people + *ergon* work]

Liturgy of the Hours *n. Christianity.* another name for **divine office.**

Liu Shao Qi *or* **Liu Shao-ch'i** ('lju: 'ʃaʊ'tʃiː) *n.* 1898– 1974, Chinese Communist statesman; chairman of the People's Republic of China (1959–68); deposed during the Cultural Revolution.

livable *or* **liveable** ('lɪvəbʰl) *adj.* **1.** (of a room, house, etc.) suitable for living in. **2.** worth living; tolerable. **3.** (foll. by *with*) pleasant to live (with). —'**livableness,** '**liveableness** *or* ,**liva'bility,** ,**livea'bility** *n.*

live¹ (lɪv) *vb.* (*mainly intr.*) **1.** to show the characteristics of life; be alive. **2.** to remain alive or in existence. **3.** to exist in a specified way: *to live poorly.* **4.** (usually foll. by *in* or *at*) to reside or dwell: *to live in London.* **5.** (often foll. by *on*) to continue or last: *the pain still lives in her memory.* **6.** (usually foll. by *by*) to order one's life (according to a certain philosophy, religion, etc.). **7.** (foll. by *on, upon,* or *by*) to support one's style of life; subsist: *to live by writing.* **8.** (foll. by *with*) to endure the effects (of a crime, mistake, etc.). **9.** (foll. by *through*) to experience and survive: *he lived through the war.* **10.** (*tr.*) to pass or spend (one's life, etc.). **11.** to enjoy life to the full: *he knows how to live.* **12.** (*tr.*) to put into practice in one's daily life; express: *he lives religion every day.* **13. live and let live.** to refrain from interfering in others' lives; be tolerant. ~See also **live down, live in,** etc. [OE *libban, lifian*]

live² (laɪv) *adj.* **1.** (*prenominal*) showing the characteristics of life. **2.** (*usually prenominal*) of, relating to, or abounding in life: *the live weight of an animal.* **3.** (*usually prenominal*) of current interest; controversial: *a live issue.* **4.** actual: *a real live cowboy.* **5.** *Inf.* full of life and energy. **6.** (of a coal, ember, etc.) glowing or burning. **7.** (esp. of a volcano) not extinct. **8.** loaded or capable of exploding: *a live bomb.* **9.** *Radio, television, etc.* transmitted or present at the time of performance, rather than being a recording: *a live show.* **10.** (of a record) **a.** recorded in concert. **b.** recorded in one studio take. **11.** connected to a source of electric power: *a live circuit.* **12.** being in a state of motion or transmitting power. **13.** acoustically reverberant. ~*adv.* **14.** during, at, or in the form of a live performance. [C16: from *on live* ALIVE]

-lived (-lɪvd) *adj.* having or having had a life as specified: *short-lived.*

lived-in *adj.* having a comfortable, natural, or homely appearance.

live down (lɪv) *vb.* (*tr., adv.*) to withstand the effects of (a crime, mistake, etc.) by waiting until others forget or forgive it.

live in (lɪv) *vb.* (*intr., adv.*) **1.** (of an employee) to dwell at one's place of employment, as in a hotel, etc. ~*adj.* **live-in. 2.** resident: *a live-in nanny; a live-in lover.*

livelihood ('laɪvlɪ,hʊd) *n.* occupation or employment.

livelong ('lɪv,lɒŋ) *adj. Chiefly poetic.* **1.** (of time) long or seemingly long (esp. in **all the livelong day**). **2.** whole; entire.

lively ('laɪvlɪ) *adj.* **-lier, -liest. 1.** full of life or vigour. **2.** vivacious or animated, esp. when in company. **3.** busy; eventful. **4.** characterized by mental or emotional intensity; vivid. **5.** having a striking effect on the mind or senses. **6.** refreshing or invigorating: *a lively breeze.* **7.** springy or bouncy or encouraging springiness: *a lively ball.* ~*adv.* also **livelily. 8.** in a brisk or lively manner: *step lively.* —**'liveliness** *n.*

liven ('laɪv°n) *vb.* (usually foll. by *up*) to make or become lively; enliven. —**'livener** *n.*

live oak (laɪv) *n.* a hard-wooded evergreen oak of S North America: used for shipbuilding.

live out (lɪv) *vb.* (*intr., adv.*) (of an employee, as in a hospital or hotel) to dwell away from one's place of employment.

liver[1] ('lɪvə) *n.* **1.** a large highly vascular reddish-brown glandular organ in the human abdominal cavity. Its main function is the metabolic transformation of nutrients. It also secretes bile, stores glycogen, and detoxifies certain poisons. Related adj.: **hepatic. 2.** the corresponding organ in animals. **3.** the liver of certain animals used as food. **4.** a reddish-brown colour. [OE *lifer*]

liver[2] ('lɪvə) *n.* a person who lives in a specified way: *a fast liver.*

liveried ('lɪvərɪd) *adj.* (esp. of servants or footmen) wearing livery.

liverish ('lɪvərɪʃ) *adj.* **1.** *Inf.* having a disorder of the liver. **2.** disagreeable; peevish. —**'liverishness** *n.*

Liverpool[1] ('lɪvə,puːl) *n.* a city in NW England, administrative centre of Merseyside, on the Mersey estuary: second largest seaport in Great Britain; developed chiefly in the 17th century with the industrialization of S Lancashire; university (1881). Pop.: 476 500 (1987 est.).

Liverpool[2] ('lɪvə,puːl) *n.* **Robert Banks Jenkinson**, 2nd Earl of Liverpool. 1770–1828, British Tory statesman; prime minister (1812–27). His government was noted for its repressive policies until about 1822, when more liberal measures were introduced by such men as Peel and Canning.

Liverpudlian (,lɪvə'pʌdlɪən) *n.* **1.** a native or inhabitant of Liverpool. ~*adj.* **2.** of or relating to Liverpool. [C19: from LIVERPOOL, with humorous alteration of *pool* to *puddle*]

liver salts *pl. n.* a preparation of mineral salts used to treat indigestion.

liver sausage or esp. U.S. **liverwurst** ('lɪvə,wɜːst) *n.* a sausage containing liver.

liverwort ('lɪvə,wɜːt) *n.* any of a class of plants growing in wet places and resembling green seaweeds or leafy mosses. [late OE *liferwyrt*]

livery ('lɪvərɪ) *n., pl.* **-eries. 1.** the identifying uniform, badge, etc., of a member of a guild or one of the servants of a feudal lord. **2.** a uniform worn by some menservants. **3.** an individual or group that wears such a uniform. **4.** distinctive dress or outward appearance. **5. a.** the stabling, keeping, or hiring out of horses for money. **b.** (*as modifier*): *a livery horse.* **6. at livery.** being kept in a livery stable. [C14: via Anglo-F from OF *livrée* allocation, from *livrer* to hand over, from L *liberāre* to set free]

livery company *n. Brit.* one of the chartered companies of the City of London originating from the craft guilds.

liveryman ('lɪvərɪmən) *n., pl.* **-men. 1.** *Brit.* a member of a livery company. **2.** a worker in a livery stable.

livery stable *n.* a stable where horses are accommodated and from which they may be hired out.

lives (laɪvz) *n.* the plural of **life.**

livestock ('laɪv,stɒk) *n.* (*functioning as sing. or pl.*) cattle, horses, and similar animals kept for domestic use but not as pets, esp. on a farm.

live together (lɪv) *vb.* (*intr., adv.*) (esp. of an unmarried couple) to dwell in the same house or flat; cohabit.

live up (lɪv) *vb.* **1.** (*intr., adv.;* foll. by *to*) to fulfil (an expectation, obligation, principle, etc.). **2. live it up.** *Inf.* to enjoy oneself, esp. flamboyantly.

live wire (laɪv) *n.* **1.** *Inf.* an energetic or enterprising person. **2.** a wire carrying an electric current.

live with (lɪv) *vb.* (*tr., prep.*) to dwell with (a person to whom one is not married).

livid ('lɪvɪd) *adj.* **1.** (of the skin) discoloured, as from a bruise or contusion. **2.** of a greyish tinge or colour. **3.** *Inf.* angry or furious. [C17: via F from L *lividus*, from *livēre* to be black and blue] —**'lividly** *adv.* —**'lividness** *or* **li'vidity** *n.*

living ('lɪvɪŋ) *adj.* **1. a.** possessing life; not dead. **b.** (*as collective n.* preceded by *the*): *the living.* **2.** having the characteristics of life (used esp. to distinguish organisms from nonliving matter). **3.** currently in use or valid: *living language.* **4.** seeming to be real: *a living image.* **5.** (of animals or plants) existing in the present age. **6.** presented by actors before a live audience: *living theatre.* **7.** (*prenominal*) (intensifier): *the living daylights.* ~*n.* **8.** the condition of being alive. **9.** the manner in which one conducts one's life: *fast living.* **10.** the means, esp. the financial means, whereby one lives. **11.** *Church of England.* another term for **benefice. 12.** (*modifier*) of, involving, or characteristic of everyday life: *living area.* **13.** (*modifier*) of or involving those now alive (esp. in **living memory**).

living death *n.* a life or lengthy experience of constant misery.

living room *n.* a room in a private house or flat used for relaxation and entertainment.

Livingston ('lɪvɪŋstən) *n.* a town in SE Scotland, in W Lothian region: founded as a new town in 1962. Pop.: 40 000 (1985).

Livingstone ('lɪvɪŋstən) *n.* **David.** 1813–73, Scottish missionary and explorer in Africa. After working as a missionary in Botswana, he led a series of expeditions, discovering Lake Ngami (1849), the Zambezi River (1851), the Victoria Falls (1855), and Lake Malawi (1859). In 1866 he set out to search for the source of the Nile and was found in dire straits and rescued (1871) by the journalist H. M. Stanley.

living wage *n.* a wage adequate to maintain a person and his family in reasonable comfort.

Livonia (lɪ'vəʊnɪə) *n.* **1.** a former Russian province on the Baltic, north of Lithuania: became Russian in 1721; divided between Estonia and Latvia in 1918. **2.** a city in SE Michigan, west of Detroit. Pop.: 104 814 (1980). —**Li'vonian** *adj., n.*

Livorno (*Italian* li'vorno) *n.* a port in W central Italy, in Tuscany on the Ligurian Sea: shipyards; oil-refining. Pop.: 174 065 (1986). English name: **Leghorn.**

Livy ('lɪvɪ) *n.* Latin name *Titus Livius.* 59 B.C.–17 A.D., Roman historian, famous for his history of Rome in 142 books of which only 35 survive.

lizard ('lɪzəd) *n.* any of a group of reptiles typically having an elongated body, four limbs, and a long tail: includes the geckos, iguanas, chameleons, monitors, and slowworms. [C14: via OF from L *lacerta*]

Lizard ('lɪzəd) *n.* **the.** a promontory in SW England, in SW Cornwall: the southernmost point in Great Britain. Also called: **Lizard Head, Lizard Peninsula.**

LJ (in Britain) *abbrev. for* Lord Justice.

Ljubljana (luː'bljaːnə) *n.* a city in NW Yugoslavia, capital of Slovenia: capital of Illyria (1816–49); became part of Yugoslavia in 1918; university (1595). Pop.: 326 467 (1983 est.). German name: **Laibach.**

LL *abbrev. for:* **1.** Late Latin. **2.** Low Latin. **3.** Lord Lieutenant.

ll. *abbrev. for* lines (of written matter).

llama ('laːmə) *n.* **1.** a domesticated South American cudchewing mammal of the camel family, that is used as a beast of burden and is valued for its hair, flesh, and hide. **2.** the cloth made from the wool of this animal. [C17: via Sp. from Amerind]

Llandaff ('lændəf, -dæf) *or* **Llandaf** (*Welsh* ɬan'dav) *n.* a town in SE Wales, in South Glamorgan: a suburb of Cardiff; the oldest bishopric in Wales (6th century).

Llandudno (læn'dɪdnəʊ; *Welsh* ɬan'dɪdnɔ) *n.* a town and resort in NW Wales, in NE Gwynedd on the Irish Sea. Pop.: 18 991 (1981).

Llanelli *or* **Llanelly** (θlæ'nɛθlɪ; *Welsh* ɬa'nɛɬlɪ) *n.* an industrial town in S Wales, in S Dyfed on an inlet of Carmarthen Bay. Pop.: 24 079 (1981).

Llanfairpwllgwyngyll (*Welsh* ɬan,vaɪrpʊɬ'gwɪŋgɪɬ), **Llanfairpwll,** *or* **Llanfair P. G.** *n.* a village in NW Wales, in SE Anglesey: reputed to be the longest place name in Great Britain when unabbreviated; means: St. Mary's Church in the hollow of the white hazel near the rapid whirlpool of Llandysilio of the red cave. Full name: **Llan-fairpwllgwyngyllgogerychwyrndrobwllllantysiliogog-ogoch** (*Welsh* ɬanˈvairpʊɬˈgwɪŋɪɬgɔˈgɛrəxwɪrnˈdrɔˈbʊɬˈɬlantəˈsɪljɔˈgɔgɔˈgɔx).

Llangollen (*Welsh* ɬanˈgɔɬlɛn) *n.* a town in NE Wales, in Clwyd on the River Dee: International Musical Eisteddfod held annually since 1946. Pop.: 3058 (1981).

llano (ˈlɑːnəʊ; *Spanish* ˈʎano) *n.*, *pl.* **-nos** (-nəʊz; *Spanish* -nɔs). an extensive grassy treeless plain, esp. in South America. [C17: Sp., from L *plānum* level ground]

Llano Estacado (ˈlɑːnəʊ ˌɛstəˈkɑːdəʊ) *n.* the S part of the Great Plains of the U.S., extending over W Texas and E New Mexico: oil and natural gas resources. Chief towns: Lubbock and Amarillo. Area: 83 700 sq. km (30 000 sq. miles). Also called: **Staked Plain.**

LLB *abbrev. for* Bachelor of Laws. [L: *Legum Baccalaureus*]

LLD *abbrev. for* Doctor of Laws. [L: *Legum Doctor*]

Llewellyn (luːˈɛlɪn) *n.* Colonel **Harry.** born 1911, Welsh show-jumping rider: on Foxhunter, he was a member of the British team that won the gold medal at the 1952 Olympic Games.

Lleyn Peninsula (*Welsh* hliːn) *n.* a peninsula in NW Wales between Cardigan Bay and Caernarvon Bay.

LLM *abbrev. for* Master of Laws. [L: *Legum Magister*]

Lloyd (lɔɪd) *n.* **1. Clive (Hubert).** born 1944, West Indian cricketer; captained West Indies (1974–78; 1979–85). **2. Harold (Clayton).** 1893–1971, U.S. comic film actor. **3. Marie,** real name *Matilda Alice Victoria Wood.* 1870–1922, English music-hall comedienne.

Lloyd George *n.* **David,** 1st Earl Lloyd George of Dwyfor. 1863–1945, British Liberal statesman: prime minister (1916–22). As chancellor of the exchequer (1908–15) he introduced old age pensions (1908), a radical budget (1909), and an insurance scheme (1911).

Lloyd's (lɔɪdz) *n.* an association of London underwriters, set up in the late 17th century. Originally concerned with marine insurance and shipping information, it now subscribes a variety of insurance policies and publishes a daily list (**Lloyd's List**) of shipping data and news. [C17: after Edward *Lloyd* (died ?1726) at whose coffee house in London the underwriters orig. carried on their business]

Lloyd Webber (ˈwɛbə) *n.* **Andrew.** born 1948, English composer. His musicals include *Joseph and the Amazing Technicolour Dreamcoat* (1968), *Jesus Christ Superstar* (1970), and *Evita* (1978), all with lyrics by Tim Rice, and *Cats* (1981), *Starlight Express* (1984), and *Phantom of the Opera* (1986).

lm *symbol for* lumen.

LNG *abbrev. for* liquefied natural gas.

lo (ləʊ) *interj.* look! see! (now often in **lo and behold**). [OE *lā*]

loach (ləʊtʃ) *n.* a carplike freshwater fish of Eurasia and Africa, having a long narrow body with barbels around the mouth. [C14: from OF *loche*, from ?]

load (ləʊd) *n.* **1.** something to be borne or conveyed; weight. **2. a.** the usual amount borne or conveyed. **b.** (*in combination*): *a carload.* **3.** something that weighs down, oppresses, or burdens: *that's a load off my mind.* **4.** a single charge of a firearm. **5.** the weight that is carried by a structure. **6.** *Electrical engineering, electronics.* **a.** a device that receives or dissipates the power from an amplifier, oscillator, generator, or some other source of signals. **b.** the power delivered by a machine, generator, circuit, etc. **7.** the resistance overcome by an engine or motor when it is driving a machine, etc. **8.** an external force applied to a component or mechanism. **9. a load of.** *Inf.* a quantity of: *a load of nonsense.* **10. get a load of.** *Inf.* pay attention to. **11. have a load on.** *U.S. & Canad. sl.* to be intoxicated. ~*vb.* (*mainly tr.*) **12.** (*also intr.*) to place or receive (cargo, goods, etc.) upon (a ship, lorry, etc.). **13.** to burden or oppress. **14.** to supply in abundance: *load with gifts.* **15.** to cause to be biased: *to load a question.* **16.** (*also intr.*) to put an ammunition charge into (a firearm). **17.** *Photog.* to position (a film, cartridge, or plate) in (a camera). **18.** to weight or bias (a roulette wheel, dice, etc.). **19.** *Insurance.* to increase (a premium) to cover expenses, etc. **20.** *Computers.* to transfer (a program) to a memory. **21. load the dice. a.** to add weights to dice in order to bias them. **b.** to arrange to have a favourable or unfavourable position. [OE *lād* course; in meaning, infl. by LADE] ~See also **loads.** — **ˈloader** *n.*

loaded (ˈləʊdɪd) *adj.* **1.** carrying a load. **2.** (of dice, a roulette wheel, etc.) weighted or otherwise biased. **3.** (of a question or statement) containing a hidden trap or implication. **4.** charged with ammunition. **5.** (of concrete) containing heavy metals, esp. iron or lead, for use in making radiation shields. **6.** *Sl.* wealthy. **7.** (*postpositive*) *Sl., chiefly U.S. & Canad.* **a.** drunk. **b.** drugged.

loading (ˈləʊdɪŋ) *n.* **1.** a load or burden; weight. **2.** the addition of an inductance to electrical equipment, such as a transmission line or aerial, to improve its performance. **3.** *Austral. & N.Z.* a payment made in addition to a basic wage or salary to reward special skills, compensate for unfavourable conditions, etc.

load line *n.* a pattern of lines painted on the hull of a ship, approximately midway between the bow and the stern, indicating the various levels that the water line should reach if the ship is properly loaded in different conditions.

loads (ləʊdz) *Inf.* ~*pl. n.* **1.** (often foll. by *of*) a lot. ~*adv.* **2.** (intensifier): *loads better.*

loadstar (ˈləʊdˌstɑː) *n.* a variant spelling of **lodestar.**

loadstone (ˈləʊdˌstəʊn) *n.* a variant spelling of **lodestone.**

loaf[1] (ləʊf) *n.*, *pl.* **loaves** (ləʊvz). **1.** a shaped mass of baked bread. **2.** any shaped or moulded mass of food, such as sugar, cooked meat, etc. **3.** *Sl.* the head; sense: *use your loaf!* [OE *hlāf*]

loaf[2] (ləʊf) *vb.* **1.** (*intr.*) to loiter or lounge around in an idle way. **2.** (*tr.*; foll. by *away*) to spend (time) idly: *he loafed away his life.* [C19: ? back formation from LOAFER]

loafer (ˈləʊfə) *n.* **1.** a person who avoids work; idler. **2.** *Chiefly U.S. & Canad.* a moccasin-like shoe. [C19: ?from G *Landläufer* vagabond]

loam (ləʊm) *n.* **1.** rich soil consisting of a mixture of sand, clay, and decaying organic material. **2.** a paste of clay and sand used for making moulds in a foundry, plastering walls, etc. ~*vb.* **3.** (*tr.*) to cover, treat, or fill with loam. [OE *lām*] — **ˈloamy** *adj.* — **ˈloaminess** *n.*

loan (ləʊn) *n.* **1.** the act of lending: *the loan of a car.* **2.** property lent, esp. money lent at interest for a period of time. **3.** the adoption by speakers of one language of a form current in another language. **4.** short for **loan word. 5. on loan.** lent out; borrowed. ~*vb.* **6.** to lend (something, esp. money). [C13 *loon, lan,* from ON *lān*] — **ˈloaner** *n.*

▷ *Usage.* See at **lend.**

Loanda (ləʊˈændə) *n.* a variant spelling of **Luanda.**

loan shark *n.* *Inf.* a person who lends funds at illegal or exorbitant rates of interest.

loan translation *n.* the adoption by one language of a phrase or compound word whose components are literal translations of the components of a corresponding phrase or compound in a foreign language: *English "superman" from German "Übermensch".* Also called: **calque.**

loan word *n.* a word adopted, often in a modified form, from one language into another.

loath or **loth** (ləʊθ) *adj.* **1.** (usually foll. by *to*) reluctant or unwilling. **2. nothing loath.** willing. [OE *lāth* (in the sense: hostile)]

loathe (ləʊð) *vb.* (*tr.*) to feel strong hatred or disgust for. [OE *lāthian,* from LOATH] — **ˈloather** *n.*

loathing (ˈləʊðɪŋ) *n.* abhorrence; disgust.

loathly[1] (ˈləʊðlɪ) *adv.* with reluctance; unwillingly.

loathly[2] (ˈləʊðlɪ) *adj.* an archaic word for **loathsome.**

loathsome (ˈləʊðsəm) *adj.* causing loathing; abhorrent. — **ˈloathsomely** *adv.* — **ˈloathsomeness** *n.*

loaves (ləʊvz) *n.* the plural of **loaf**[1].

lob (lɒb) *Sport.* ~*n.* **1.** a ball struck in a high arc. **2.** *Cricket.* a ball bowled in a slow high arc. ~*vb.* **lobbing, lobbed. 3.** to hit or kick (a ball) in a high arc. **4.** *Inf.* to throw, esp. in a high arc. [C14: prob. from Low G, orig. in the sense: something dangling]

Lobachevsky (*Russian* ləbaˈtʃɛfskij) *n.* **Nikolai Ivanovich** (nikaˈlaj iˈvanəvitʃ). 1793–1856, Russian mathematician; a founder of non-Euclidean geometry.

lobar (ˈləʊbə) *adj.* of, relating to, or affecting a lobe.

lobate (ˈləʊbeɪt) *adj.* **1.** having or resembling lobes. **2.** (of birds) having separate toes that are each fringed with a weblike lobe. — **ˈlobately** *adv.* — **loˈbation** *n.*

lobby (ˈlɒbɪ) *n.*, *pl.* **-bies. 1.** a room or corridor used as an entrance hall, vestibule, etc. **2.** *Chiefly Brit.* a hall in a legislative building used for meetings between the legislators and members of the public. **3.** Also called: **division lobby.** *Chiefly Brit.* one of two corridors in a legislative building in which members vote. **4.** a group of persons who attempt to influence legislators on behalf of a particular interest. ~*vb.* **-bying, -bied. 5.** to attempt to influence (legislators, etc.) in the formulation of policy. **6.** (*intr.*) to act in the manner of a lobbyist. **7.** (*tr.*) to apply pressure for the passage of (a bill, etc.). [C16: from Med. L *lobia* portico, from OHG *lauba* arbor, from *laub* leaf] — '**lobbyer** *n.*

lobbyist ('lɒbɪɪst) *n.* a person employed by a particular interest to lobby. — '**lobby,ism** *n.*

lobe (ləʊb) *n.* **1.** any rounded projection forming part of a larger structure. **2.** any of the subdivisions of a bodily organ or part, delineated by shape or connective tissue. **3.** Also called: **ear lobe.** the fleshy lower part of the external ear. **4.** any of the parts, not entirely separate from each other, into which a flattened plant part, such as a leaf, is divided. [C16: from LL *lobus*, from Gk *lobos* lobe of the ear or of the liver]

lobectomy (ləʊ'bɛktəmɪ) *n., pl.* **-mies.** surgical removal of a lobe from any organ or gland in the body.

lobelia (ləʊ'biːlɪə) *n.* any of a genus of plants having red, blue, white, or yellow five-lobed flowers with the three lower lobes forming a lip. [C18: from NL, after Matthias de *Lobel* (1538–1616), Flemish botanist]

Lobengula (,ləʊbən'gjuːlə) *n.* ?1836–94, last Matabele king (1870–93); his kingdom was destroyed by the British.

Lobito (*Portuguese* lu'βitu) *n.* the chief port in Angola, in the west on **Lobito Bay:** terminus of the railway through Benguela to Mozambique. Pop.: 70 000 (1976 est.).

loblolly ('lɒb,lɒlɪ) *n., pl.* **-lies.** a southern U.S. pine tree with bright reddish-brown bark, green needle-like leaves, and reddish-brown cones. [C16: ?from dialect *lob* to boil + obs. dialect *lolly* thick soup]

lobola *or* **lobolo** (lɔː'bɔːlə, lə'bəʊ-) *n.* (in southern Africa) an African custom by which a bridegroom's family makes a payment in cattle or cash to the bride's family shortly before the marriage. [from Zulu]

lobotomy (ləʊ'bɒtəmɪ) *n., pl.* **-mies. 1.** surgical incision into a lobe of any organ. **2.** Also called: **prefrontal leucotomy.** surgical interruption of one or more nerve tracts in the frontal lobe of the brain: used in the treatment of intractable mental disorders. [C20: from LOBE + -TOMY]

lobscouse ('lɒb,skaʊs) *n.* a sailor's stew of meat, vegetables, and hardtack. [C18: ?from dialect *lob* to boil + *scouse* broth]

lobster ('lɒbstə) *n., pl.* **-sters** *or* **-ster. 1.** any of several large marine decapod crustaceans occurring on rocky shores and having the first pair of limbs modified as large pincers. **2.** any of several similar crustaceans, esp. the spiny lobster. **3.** the flesh of any of these crustaceans, eaten as a delicacy. [OE *loppestre*, from *loppe* spider]

lobster pot *or* **trap** *n.* a round basket or trap made of open slats used to catch lobsters.

lobule ('lɒbjuːl) *n.* a small lobe or a subdivision of a lobe. [C17: from NL *lobulus*, from LL *lobus* LOBE] — **lobular** ('lɒbjʊlə) *or* **lobulate** ('lɒbjʊlɪt) *adj.*

lobworm ('lɒb,wɜːm) *n.* **1.** another name for **lugworm. 2.** a large earthworm used as bait in fishing. [C17: from obs. *lob* lump + WORM]

local ('ləʊkəl) *adj.* **1.** characteristic of or associated with a particular locality or area. **2.** of, concerned with, or relating to a particular place or point in space. **3.** *Med.* of, affecting, or confined to a limited area or part. **4.** (of a train, bus, etc.) stopping at all stations or stops. ~*n.* **5.** a train, bus, etc., that stops at all stations or stops. **6.** an inhabitant of a specified locality. **7.** *Brit. inf.* a pub close to one's home or place of work. **8.** *Med.* short for **local anaesthetic** (see **anaesthesia**). **9.** *U.S. & Canad.* an item of local interest in a newspaper. [C15: via OF from LL *localis*, from L *locus* place] — '**locally** *adv.* — '**localness** *n.*

local anaesthetic *n. Med.* See **anaesthesia.**

local authority *n. Brit. & N.Z.* the governing body of a county, district, etc. U.S. equivalent: **local government.**

locale (ləʊ'kaːl) *n.* a place or area, esp. with reference to events connected with it. [C18: from F *local* (n. use of adj.); see LOCAL]

local government *n.* **1.** government of the affairs of counties, towns, etc., by locally elected political bodies. **2.** the U.S. equivalent of **local authority.**

localism ('ləʊkə,lɪzəm) *n.* **1.** a pronunciation, phrase, etc., peculiar to a particular locality. **2.** another word for **provincialism.**

locality (ləʊ'kælɪtɪ) *n., pl.* **-ties. 1.** a neighbourhood or area. **2.** the site or scene of an event. **3.** the fact or condition of having a location or position in space.

localize *or* **-ise** ('ləʊkə,laɪz) *vb.* **1.** to make or become local in attitude, behaviour, etc. **2.** (*tr.*) to restrict or confine (something) to a particular area or part. **3.** (*tr.*) to assign or ascribe to a particular region. — '**local,izable** *or* -,**isable** *adj.* —,**locali'zation** *or* **-i'sation** *n.*

local option *n.* (esp. in Scotland, New Zealand, and the U.S.) the privilege of a municipality, county, etc., to determine by referendum whether a particular activity, esp. the sale of liquor, shall be permitted there.

Locarno (*Italian* lo'karno) *n.* a town in S Switzerland, in Ticino canton at the N end of Lake Maggiore: tourist resort. Pop.: 14 224 (1983 est.).

locate (ləʊ'keɪt) *vb.* **1.** (*tr.*) to discover the position, situation, or whereabouts of; find. **2.** (*tr.; often passive*) to situate or place: *located on the edge of the city.* **3.** (*intr.*) *U.S. & Canad.* to become established or settled. —**lo'cater** *n.*

▷ **Usage.** *Locate* is often used to mean "find", but many careful users of English prefer to restrict it to its more precise meaning "to find the exact position of": *she located the town on the map.*

location (ləʊ'keɪʃən) *n.* **1.** a site or position; situation. **2.** the act or process of locating or the state of being located. **3.** a place outside a studio where filming is done: *shot on location.* **4.** (in South Africa) **a.** a Black African or Coloured township, usually located near a small town. **b.** a Black African tribal reserve in the E Cape Province. **5.** *Computers.* a position in a memory capable of holding a unit of information, such as a word, and identified by its address. [C16: from L *locatio*, from *locare* to place]

locative ('lɒkətɪv) *Grammar.* ~*adj.* **1.** (of a word or phrase) indicating place or direction. **2.** denoting a case of nouns, etc., that refers to the place at which the action described by the verb occurs. ~*n.* **3. a.** the locative case. **b.** a word or speech element in this case. [C19: LOCATE + -IVE, on the model of *vocative*]

loc. cit. (in textual annotation) *abbrev. for* loco citato. [L: in the place cited]

loch (lɒx, lɒk) *n.* **1.** a Scot. word for **lake**[1]. **2.** Also: **sea loch.** a long narrow bay or arm of the sea in Scotland. [C14: from Gaelic]

lochia ('lɒkɪə) *n.* a vaginal discharge of cellular debris, mucus, and blood following childbirth. [C17: NL from Gk *lokhia*, from *lokhos* childbirth] — '**lochial** *adj.*

loci ('ləʊsaɪ) *n.* the plural of **locus.**

lock[1] (lɒk) *n.* **1.** a device fitted to a gate, door, drawer, lid, etc., to keep it firmly closed. **2.** a similar device attached to a machine, vehicle, etc. **3. a.** a section of a canal or river that may be closed off by gates to control the water level and the raising and lowering of vessels that pass through it. **b.** (*as modifier*): *a lock gate; a lock keeper.* **4.** the jamming, fastening, or locking together of parts. **5.** *Brit.* the extent to which a vehicle's front wheels will turn: *this car has a good lock.* **6.** a mechanism that detonates the charge of a gun. **7. lock, stock, and barrel.** completely; entirely. **8.** any wrestling hold in which a wrestler seizes a part of his opponent's body. **9.** Also called: **lock forward.** *Rugby.* **a.** a player in the second row of the scrum. **b.** this position. **10.** a gas bubble in a hydraulic system or a liquid bubble in a pneumatic system that stops the fluid flow in a pipe, capillary, etc.: *an air lock.* ~*vb.* **11.** to fasten (a door, gate, etc.) or (of a door, etc.) to become fastened with a lock, bolt, etc., so as to prevent entry or exit. **12.** (*tr.*) to secure (a building) by locking all doors, windows, etc. **13.** to fix or become fixed together securely or inextricably. **14.** to become or cause to become rigid or immovable: *the front wheels of the car locked.* **15.** (when *tr.*, *often passive*) to clasp or entangle (someone or each other) in a struggle or embrace. **16.** (*tr.*) to furnish (a canal) with locks. **17.** (*tr.*) to move (a vessel) through a system of locks. ~See also **lock out, lock up.** [OE *loc*] — '**lockable** *adj.*

lock[2] (lɒk) *n.* **1.** a strand, curl, or cluster of hair. **2.** a tuft or wisp of wool, cotton, etc. **3.** (*pl.*) *Chiefly literary.* hair, esp. when curly or fine. [OE *loc*]

Locke (lɒk) *n.* **1. John.** 1632–1704, English philosopher, who discussed the concept of empiricism in his *Essay*

Concerning Human Understanding (1690). He influenced political thought, esp. in France and America, with his *Two Treatises on Government* (1690), in which he sanctioned the right to revolt. **2. Matthew.** ?1630–77, English composer, esp. of works for the stage.

locker ('lɒkə) *n.* **1. a.** a small compartment or drawer that may be locked, as one of several in a gymnasium, etc., for clothes and valuables. **b.** (*as modifier*): *a locker room.* **2.** a person or thing that locks.

locket ('lɒkɪt) *n.* a small ornamental case, usually on a necklace or chain, that holds a picture, keepsake, etc. [C17: from F *loquet* latch, dim. of *loc* LOCK¹]

lockjaw ('lɒk,dʒɔː) *n. Pathol.* a nontechnical name for **trismus** and (often) **tetanus.**

lock out *vb.* (*tr., adv.*) **1.** to prevent from entering by locking a door. **2.** to prevent (employees) from working during an industrial dispute, as by closing a factory. ~*n.* **lockout. 3.** the closing of a place of employment by an employer, in order to bring pressure on employees to agree to terms.

locksmith ('lɒk,smɪθ) *n.* a person who makes or repairs locks.

lock step *n.* a method of marching such that the men follow one another as closely as possible.

lock up *vb.* (*adv.*) **1.** (*tr.*) Also: **lock in, lock away.** to imprison or confine. **2.** to lock or secure the doors, windows, etc., of (a building). **3.** (*tr.*) to keep or store securely: *secrets locked up in history.* **4.** (*tr.*) to invest (funds) so that conversion into cash is difficult. ~*n.* **lockup. 5.** the action or time of locking up. **6.** a jail or block of cells. **7.** *Brit.* a small shop with no attached quarters for the owner. **8.** *Brit.* a garage or storage place separate from the main premises. ~*adj.* **lock-up. 9.** *Brit. & N.Z.* (of premises) without living quarters: *a lock-up shop.*

Lockyer ('lɒkjə) *n.* Sir **Joseph Norman.** 1836–1920, English astronomer: a pioneer in solar spectroscopy, he was the first to observe helium in the sun's atmosphere (1868).

loco¹ ('ləʊkəʊ) *n. Inf.* short for **locomotive.**

loco² ('ləʊkəʊ) *adj.* **1.** *Sl., chiefly U.S.* insane. **2.** (of an animal) affected with loco disease. ~*n., pl.* **-cos. 3.** *U.S.* short for **locoweed.** ~*vb.* **locoed, locoing.** (*tr.*) **4.** to poison with locoweed. **5.** *U.S. sl.* to make insane. [C19: via Mexican Sp. from Sp.: crazy]

loco disease *n.* a disease of cattle, sheep, and horses characterized by paralysis and faulty vision, caused by ingestion of locoweed.

locomotion (,ləʊkə'məʊʃən) *n.* the act, fact, ability, or power of moving. [C17: from L *locō* from a place, ablative of *locus* place + MOTION]

locomotive (,ləʊkə'məʊtɪv) *n.* **1. a.** Also called: **locomotive engine.** a self-propelled engine driven by steam, electricity, or diesel power and used for drawing trains along railway tracks. **b.** (*as modifier*): *a locomotive shed; a locomotive works.* ~*adj.* **2.** of or relating to locomotion. **3.** moving or able to move, as by self-propulsion.

locomotor (,ləʊkə'məʊtə) *adj.* of or relating to locomotion. [C19: from L *locō* from a place + MOTOR (mover)]

locomotor ataxia *n. Pathol.* another name for **tabes dorsalis.**

locoweed ('ləʊkəʊ,wiːd) *n.* any of several perennial leguminous plants of W North America that cause loco disease in horses, cattle, and sheep.

Locris *or* **Lokris** ('ləʊkrɪs, 'lɒk-) *n.* an ancient region of central Greece. — **'Locrian** *or* **'Lokrian** *adj., n.*

loculus ('lɒkjʊləs) *n., pl.* **loculi** ('lɒkjʊ,laɪ). **1.** *Bot.* any of the chambers of an ovary or anther. **2.** *Biol.* any small cavity or chamber. [C19: NL, from L: compartment, from *locus* place] — **'locular** *adj.*

locum tenens ('ləʊkəm 'tiːnɛnz) *n., pl.* **locum tenentes** (təˈnɛntiːz). *Chiefly Brit.* a person who stands in temporarily for another member of the same profession, esp. for a physician, chemist, or clergyman. Often shortened to **locum.** [C17: Med. L: (someone) holding the place (of another)]

locus ('ləʊkəs) *n., pl.* **loci. 1.** (in many legal phrases) a place or area, esp. the place where something occurred. **2.** *Maths.* a set of points or lines whose location satisfies or is determined by one or more specified conditions: *the locus of points equidistant from a given point is a circle.* **3.** *Genetics.* the position of a particular gene on a chromosome. [C18: L]

locust ('ləʊkəst) *n.* **1.** any of numerous insects, related to the grasshopper, of warm and tropical regions of the Old World, which travel in vast swarms, stripping large areas of vegetation. **2.** Also called: **locust tree.** a North American leguminous tree having prickly branches, hanging clusters of white fragrant flowers, and reddish-brown seed pods. **3.** the yellowish durable wood of this tree. **4.** any of several similar trees, such as the honey locust and carob. [C13 (the insect): from L *locusta*; applied to the tree (C17) because the pods resemble locusts]

locution (ləʊ'kjuːʃən) *n.* **1.** a word, phrase, or expression. **2.** manner or style of speech. [C15: from L *locūtiō* an utterance, from *loquī* to speak]

Lod (lɒd) *n.* a town in central Israel, southeast of Tel Aviv: Israel's chief airport. Pop.: 40 700 (1982 est.). Also called: **Lydda.**

lode (ləʊd) *n.* **1.** a deposit of valuable ore occurring between definite limits in the surrounding rock; vein. **2.** a deposit of metallic ore filling a fissure in the surrounding rock. [OE *lād* course]

loden ('ləʊdⁿn) *n.* **1.** a thick heavy waterproof woollen cloth with a short pile, used for coats. **2.** a dark bluish-green colour, in which the cloth is often made. [G, from OHG *lodo* thick cloth]

lodestar *or* **loadstar** ('ləʊd,stɑː) *n.* **1.** a star, esp. the North Star, used in navigation or astronomy as a point of reference. **2.** something that serves as a guide or model. [C14: lit.: guiding star]

lodestone *or* **loadstone** ('ləʊd,stəʊn) *n.* **1. a.** magnetite that is naturally magnetic. **b.** a piece of this, which can be used as a magnet. **2.** a person or thing regarded as a focus of attraction. [C16: lit.: guiding stone]

lodge (lɒdʒ) *n.* **1.** *Chiefly Brit.* a small house at the entrance to the grounds of a country mansion, usually occupied by a gatekeeper or gardener. **2.** a house or cabin used occasionally, as for some seasonal activity. **3.** (*cap. when part of a name*) a large house or hotel. **4.** a room for the use of porters in a university, college, etc. **5.** a local branch or chapter of certain societies. **6.** the building used as the meeting place of such a society. **7.** the dwelling place of certain animals, esp. beavers. **8.** a hut or tent of certain North American Indian peoples. ~*vb.* **9.** to provide or be provided with accommodation or shelter, esp. rented accommodation. **10.** (*intr.*) to live temporarily, esp. in rented accommodation. **11.** to implant, embed, or fix or be implanted, embedded, or fixed. **12.** (*tr.*) to deposit or leave for safety, storage, etc. **13.** (*tr.*) to bring (a charge or accusation) against someone. **14.** (*tr.*; often foll. by *in* or *with*) to place (authority, power, etc.) in the control (of someone). [C15: from OF *loge*, ?from OHG *louba* bower]

Lodge (lɒdʒ) *n.* **1. David (John).** born 1935, British novelist. His books include *Changing Places* (1975), *Small World* (1984), and *Nice Work* (1988). **2.** Sir **Oliver (Joseph).** 1851–1940, English physicist, who made important contributions to electromagnetism, radio reception, and attempted to detect the ether. He also studied allegedly psychic phenomena. **3. Thomas.** ?1558–1625, English writer. His romance *Rosalynde* (1590) supplied the plot for Shakespeare's *As You Like It.*

lodger ('lɒdʒə) *n.* a person who pays rent in return for accommodation in someone else's house.

lodging ('lɒdʒɪŋ) *n.* **1.** a temporary residence. **2.** (*sometimes pl.*) sleeping accommodation.

lodging house *n.* a private home providing accommodation and meals for lodgers.

lodgings ('lɒdʒɪŋz) *pl. n.* a rented room or rooms, esp. in another person's house.

lodgment *or* **lodgement** ('lɒdʒmənt) *n.* **1.** the act of lodging or the state of being lodged. **2.** a blockage or accumulation. **3.** a small area gained and held in enemy territory.

Lodi (*Italian* 'lɔːdi) *n.* a town in N Italy, in Lombardy: scene of Napoleon's defeat of the Austrians in 1796. Pop.: 35 221 (1980).

Łódź (*Polish* wutʃ) *n.* a city in central Poland: the country's second largest city; major centre of the textile industry; university (1945). Pop.: 849 000 (1985).

Loeb (lɜːb; *German* loːp) *n.* **Jacques** (ʒɑːk). 1859–1924, U.S. physiologist, born in Germany, noted esp. for his pioneering work on artificial parthenogenesis.

loess ('ləʊɪs) *n.* a light-coloured fine-grained accumulation of clay and silt deposited by the wind. [C19: from G

Löss, from Swiss G dialect *lösch* loose] —**loessial** (lǝʊˈɛsɪǝl) *adj.*

Loewe (lǝʊ) *n.* **Frederick**. 1904–88, U.S. composer of such musical comedies as *Brigadoon* (1947), *My Fair Lady* (1956), and *Camelot* (1960), all with librettos by Alan Jay Lerner.

Loewe *or* **Löwe** (German ˈloːvǝ) *n.* (**Johann**) **Karl** (**Gottfried**). 1796–1869, German composer, esp. of songs, such as *Der Erlkönig* (1818).

Loewi (ˈlǝʊɪ) *n.* **Otto**. 1873–1961, U.S. pharmacologist, born in Germany. He shared a Nobel prize for physiology or medicine (1936) with Dale for their work on the chemical transmission of nerve impulses.

Lofoten and Vesterålen (Norwegian ˈluːfutǝn; ˈvɛstǝrɔːlǝn) *pl. n.* a group of islands off the NW coast of Norway, within the Arctic Circle. Largest island: Hinny. Pop.: 60 000 (1979 est.). Area: about 5130 sq. km (1980 sq. miles).

loft (lɒft) *n.* **1.** the space inside a roof. **2.** a gallery, esp. one for the choir in a church. **3.** a room over a stable used to store hay. **4.** *U.S.* an upper storey of a warehouse or factory. **5.** a raised house or coop in which pigeons are kept. **6.** *Sport.* **a.** (in golf) the angle from the vertical made by the club face to give elevation to a ball. **b.** elevation imparted to a ball. **c.** a lofting stroke or shot. ∼*vb.* (*tr.*) **7.** *Sport.* to strike or kick (a ball) high in the air. **8.** to store or place in a loft. **9.** *Golf.* to slant (the face of a golf club). [OE, from ON *lopt* air, ceiling]

lofty (ˈlɒftɪ) *adj.* **loftier, loftiest. 1.** of majestic or imposing height. **2.** exalted or noble in character or nature. **3.** haughty or supercilious. **4.** elevated, eminent, or superior. —**ˈloftily** *adv.* —**ˈloftiness** *n.*

log[1] (lɒg) *n.* **1. a.** a section of the trunk or a main branch of a tree, when stripped of branches. **b.** (*modifier*) constructed out of logs: *a log cabin.* **2. a.** a detailed record of a voyage of a ship or aircraft. **b.** a record of the hours flown by pilots and aircrews. **c.** a book in which these records are made; logbook. **3.** a written record of information about transmissions kept by radio stations, amateur radio operators, etc. **4.** Also called: **chip log.** a device consisting of a float with an attached line, formerly used to measure the speed of a ship. **5. like a log.** without stirring or being disturbed (in **sleep like a log**). ∼*vb.* **logging, logged. 6.** (*tr.*) to fell the trees of (a forest, area, etc.) for timber. **7.** (*tr.*) to saw logs from (trees). **8.** (*intr.*) to work at the felling of timber. **9.** (*tr.*) to enter (a distance, event, etc.) in a logbook or log. **10.** (*tr.*) to travel (a specified distance or time) or move at (a specified speed). [C14: from ?]

log[2] (lɒg) *n.* short for **logarithm.**
▷**Usage.** In mathematical usage *log* is followed by a subscript number indicating the base. The absence of this number implies that the logarithm is a common logarithm.

-log *combining form.* a U.S. variant of **-logue.**

logan (ˈlǝʊgǝn) *n. Canad.* another name for **bogan** (a backwater).

Logan (ˈlǝʊgǝn) *n.* **Mount.** a mountain in NW Canada, in SW Yukon in the St. Elias Range: the highest peak in Canada and the second highest in North America. Height: 6050 m (19 850 ft.).

loganberry (ˈlǝʊgǝnbǝrɪ, -brɪ) *n., pl.* **-ries. 1.** a trailing prickly hybrid plant of the rose family, cultivated for its edible fruit. **2.** the purplish-red acid fruit of this plant. [C19: after James H. *Logan* (1841–1928), American judge and horticulturist who first grew it (1881)]

logarithm (ˈlɒgǝˌrɪðǝm) *n.* the exponent indicating the power to which a fixed number, the base, must be raised to obtain a given number or variable. It is used esp. to simplify multiplication and division. Often shortened to **log.** [C17: from NL *logarithmus*, coined 1614 by John NAPIER, from Gk *logos* ratio + *arithmos* number] —**logarithmic** (ˌlɒgǝˈrɪðmɪk) *adj.*

logarithmic function *n.* **a.** the mathematical function *y* = log *x*. **b.** a function that can be expressed in terms of this function.

logbook (ˈlɒgˌbʊk) *n.* **1.** a book containing the official record of trips made by a ship or aircraft. **2.** *Brit.* a former name for **registration document.**

log chip *n. Naut.* the wooden chip of a chip log. See **log** (sense 4).

loge (lǝʊʒ) *n.* a small enclosure or box in a theatre or opera house. [C18: F; see LODGE]

logger (ˈlɒgǝ) *n.* another word for **lumberjack.**

loggerhead (ˈlɒgǝˌhɛd) *n.* **1.** Also called: **loggerhead turtle.** a large-headed turtle occurring in most seas. **2.** a tool consisting of a large metal sphere attached to a long handle, used for warming liquids, melting tar, etc. **3.** *Arch. or dialect.* a blockhead; dunce. **4. at loggerheads.** engaged in dispute or confrontation. [C16: prob. from dialect *logger* wooden block + HEAD]

loggia (ˈlɒdʒǝ, ˈlɒdʒɪǝ) *n., pl.* **-gias** *or* **-gie** (-dʒɛ). a covered area on the side of a building. [C17: It., from F *loge.* See LODGE]

logging (ˈlɒgɪŋ) *n.* the work of felling, trimming, and transporting timber.

logic (ˈlɒdʒɪk) *n.* **1.** the branch of philosophy concerned with analysing the patterns of reasoning by which a conclusion is properly drawn from a set of premises, without reference to meaning or context. **2.** any formal system in which are defined axioms and rules of inference. **3.** the system and principles of reasoning used in a specific field of study. **4.** a particular method of argument or reasoning. **5.** force or effectiveness in argument or dispute. **6.** reasoned thought or argument, as distinguished from irrationality. **7.** the relationship and interdependence of a series of events, facts, etc. **8.** *Electronics, computers.* the principles underlying the units in a computer system that perform arithmetical and logical operations. See also **logic circuit.** [C14: from OF *logique* from Med. L *logica*, from Gk *logikos* concerning speech or reasoning]

logical (ˈlɒdʒɪkᵊl) *adj.* **1.** relating to, used in, or characteristic of logic: *logical connective.* **2.** using, according to, or deduced from the principles of logic: *a logical conclusion.* **3.** capable of or characterized by clear or valid reasoning. **4.** reasonable or necessary because of facts, events, etc.: *the logical candidate.* **5.** *Computers.* of, performed by, used in, or relating to the logic circuits in a computer. —**ˌlogiˈcality** *or* **ˈlogicalness** *n.* —**ˈlogically** *adv.*

logical form *n.* the structure of an argument by virtue of which it can be shown to be formally valid.

logical positivism *or* **empiricism** *n.* a philosophical theory which holds that the only meaningful statements are those that are analytic or can be tested empirically, and so rejects theology, metaphysics, etc., as meaningless.

logic circuit *n.* an electronic circuit used in computers to perform a logical operation on its two or more input signals.

logician (lɒˈdʒɪʃǝn) *n.* a person who specializes in or is skilled at logic.

logistics (lɒˈdʒɪstɪks) *n.* (*functioning as sing. or pl.*) **1.** the science of the movement and maintenance of military forces. **2.** the management of materials flow through an organization. **3.** the detailed planning and organization of any large complex operation. [C19: from F *logistique*, from *loger* to LODGE] —**loˈgistical** *adj.*

log jam *n. Chiefly U.S. & Canad.* **1.** blockage caused by the crowding together of a number of logs floating in a river. **2.** a deadlock; standstill.

loglog (ˈlɒglɒg) *n.* the logarithm of a logarithm (in equations, etc.).

logo (ˈlǝʊgǝʊ, ˈlɒg-) *n., pl.* **-os.** short for **logotype** (sense 2).

logo- *combining form.* indicating word or speech: *logogram.* [from Gk *logos* word, from *legein* to speak]

logogram (ˈlɒgǝˌgræm) *n.* single symbol representing an entire morpheme, word, or phrase, as for example the symbol (%) meaning *per cent.*

logorrhoea *or esp. U.S.* **logorrhea** (ˌlɒgǝˈrɪǝ) *n.* uncontrollable or incoherent talkativeness.

logos (ˈlɒgɒs) *n.* **1.** *Philosophy.* reason, regarded as the controlling principle of the universe. **2.** (*cap.*) the divine Word; the second person of the Trinity. [C16: Gk: word, reason]

logotype (ˈlɒgǝʊˌtaɪp) *n.* **1.** *Printing.* a piece of type with several uncombined characters cast on it. **2.** Also called: **logo.** a trademark, company emblem, or similar device.

logroll (ˈlɒgˌrǝʊl) *vb. Chiefly U.S.* to use logrolling in order to procure the passage of (legislation). —**ˈlogˌroller** *n.*

logrolling (ˈlɒgˌrǝʊlɪŋ) *n.* **1.** *U.S.* the practice of undemocratic agreements between politicians involving mutual favours, the trading of votes, etc. **2.** another name for **birling.** See **birl.**

Logroño (*Spanish* lo'ɣroɲo) *n.* a walled city in N Spain, on the Ebro River: trading centre of an agricultural region noted for its wine. Pop.: 109 536 (1981).

-logue *or U.S.* **-log** *n. combining form.* indicating speech or discourse of a particular kind: *travelogue; monologue.* [from F, from Gk *-logos*]

logwood ('lɒg,wʊd) *n.* **1.** a leguminous tree of the West Indies and Central America. **2.** the heavy reddish-brown wood of this tree, yielding a dye.

-logy *n. combining form.* **1.** indicating the science or study of: *musicology.* **2.** indicating writing, discourse, or body of writings: *trilogy; phraseology; martyrology.* [from L *-logia*, from Gk, from *logos* word] —**logical** *or* **-logic** *adj. combining form.* —**logist** *n. combining form.*

Lohengrin ('ləʊɪŋgrɪn) *n.* (in German legend) a son of Parzival and knight of the Holy Grail.

loin (lɔɪn) *n.* **1.** *Anat.* the lower back and sides between the pelvis and the ribs. Related adj.: **lumbar. 2.** a cut of meat from this part of an animal. ~See also **loins.** [C14: from OF *loigne*, ?from Vulgar L *lumbra* (unattested), from L *lumbus* loin]

loincloth ('lɔɪn,klɒθ) *n.* a piece of cloth worn round the loins. Also called: **breechcloth.**

loins (lɔɪnz) *pl. n.* **1.** the hips and the inner surface of the legs where they join the trunk of the body; crotch. **2.** *Euphemistic.* the reproductive organs.

Loire (*French* lwar) *n.* **1.** a department of E central France, in Rhône-Alpes region. Capital: St. Étienne. Pop.: 739 521 (1982). Area: 4799 sq. km (1872 sq. miles). **2.** a river in France, rising in the Massif Central and flowing north and west in a wide curve to the Bay of Biscay: the longest river in France. Its valley is famous for its wines and châteaux. Length: 1020 km (634 miles). Ancient name: **Liger.**

Loire-Atlantique (*French* lwaratlɑ̃tik) *n.* a department of W France, in Pays de la Loire region. Capital: Nantes. Pop.: 995 498 (1982). Area: 6980 sq. km (2722 sq. miles).

Loiret (*French* lwarɛ) *n.* a department of central France, in Centre region. Capital: Orléans. Pop.: 535 669 (1982). Area: 6812 sq. km (2657 sq. miles).

Loir-et-Cher (*French* lwarɛʃɛr) *n.* a department of N central France, in Centre region. Capital: Blois. Pop.: 296 220 (1982). Area: 6422 sq. km (2505 sq. miles).

loiter ('lɔɪtə) *vb.* (*intr.*) to stand or act aimlessly or idly. [C14: ?from MDu. *löteren* to wobble] —**'loiterer** *n.* —**'loitering** *n., adj.*

Loki ('ləʊkɪ) *n. Norse myth.* the god of mischief and destruction.

loll (lɒl) *vb.* **1.** (*intr.*) to lie, lean, or lounge in a lazy or relaxed manner. **2.** to hang or allow to hang loosely. ~*n.* **3.** an act or instance of lolling. [C14: ? imit.] —**'loller** *n.* —**'lolling** *adj.*

Lolland *or* **Laaland** (*Danish* 'lɔlan) *n.* an island of Denmark in the Baltic Sea, south of Sjælland. Pop.: 77 957 (1976). Area: 1240 sq. km (480 sq. miles).

Lollard ('lɒləd) *n. English history.* a follower of John Wycliffe during the 14th, 15th, and 16th centuries. [C14: from MDu.; mutterer, from *lollen* to mumble (prayers)] —**'Lollardism** *n.*

lollipop ('lɒlɪ,pɒp) *n.* **1.** a boiled sweet or toffee stuck on a small wooden stick. **2.** *Brit.* another word for **ice lolly.** [C18: ?from N. English dialect *lolly* the tongue + POP¹]

lollipop man *or* **lady** *n. Brit. inf.* a person holding a circular sign on a pole who stops traffic so that children may cross the road.

lollop ('lɒləp) *vb.* (*intr.*) *Chiefly Brit.* **1.** to walk or run with a clumsy or relaxed bouncing movement. **2.** a less common word for **lounge.** [C18: prob. from LOLL + *-op* as in GALLOP, to emphasize the contrast in meaning]

lolly ('lɒlɪ) *n., pl.* **-lies. 1.** an informal word for **lollipop. 2.** *Brit.* short for **ice lolly. 3.** *Brit., Austral. & N.Z.* a slang word for **money. 4.** *Austral. & N.Z. inf.* a sweet, esp. a boiled one. **5. do the** (*or* **one's**) **lolly.** *Austral. inf.* to lose one's temper. [shortened from LOLLIPOP]

Lomax ('ləʊmæks) *n.* **Alan.** born 1915, and his father **John Avery** ('eɪvərɪ) (1867–1948), U.S. folklorists.

Lombard¹ ('lɒmbəd, -bɑːd, 'lʌm-) *n.* **1.** a native or inhabitant of Lombardy. **2.** a member of an ancient Germanic people who settled in N Italy after 568 A.D. ~*adj. also* **Lombardic. 3.** of or relating to Lombardy or the Lombards.

Lombard² ('lɒmbəd, -bɑːd, 'lʌm-) *n.* **Peter.** ?1100–?60, Italian theologian, noted for his *Sententiarum libri quatuor.*

Lombard Street *n.* the British financial and banking world. [C16: from a street in London once occupied by Lombard bankers]

Lombardy ('lɒmbədɪ, 'lʌm-) *n.* a region of N central Italy, bordering on the Alps: dominated by prosperous lordships and city-states during the Middle Ages; later ruled by Spain and then by Austria before becoming part of Italy in 1859; intensively cultivated and in parts highly industrialized. Pop.: 8 876 787 (1986 est.). Area: 23 804 sq. km (9284 sq. miles). Italian name: **Lombardia** (,lombar'diːa).

Lombardy poplar *n.* an Italian poplar tree with upwardly pointing branches giving it a columnar shape.

Lombok ('lɒmbɒk) *n.* an island of Indonesia, in the Nusa Tenggara Islands east of Java: came under Dutch rule in 1894; important biologically as being transitional between Asian and Australian in flora and fauna, the line of demarcation beginning at **Lombok Strait** (a channel between Lombok and Bali, connecting the Flores Sea with the Indian Ocean). Chief town: Mataram. Pop.: 1 957 128 (1980). Area: 4730 sq. km (1826 sq. miles).

Lombroso (*Italian* lom'broːso) *n.* **Cesare** ('tʃeːzare). 1836–1909, Italian criminologist: he postulated the existence of a criminal type. —**Lombrosian** (lɒm'brəʊzɪən) *adj.*

Lomé (*French* lɔme) *n.* the capital and chief port of Togo, on the Bight of Benin. Pop.: 366 476 (1983).

Lomond ('ləʊmənd) *n.* **1. Loch.** a lake in W Scotland, north of Glasgow: the largest Scottish lake. Length: about 38 km (24 miles). Width: up to 8 km (5 miles). **2.** See **Ben Lomond.**

London¹ ('lʌndən) *n.* **1.** the capital of the United Kingdom, a port in S England on the River Thames near its estuary on the North Sea: consists of the **City** (the financial quarter), the **West End** (the entertainment and major shopping centre), the **East End** (the industrial and dock area), and extensive suburbs. Latin name: **Londinium.** See also **City. 2. Greater.** the administrative area of London, consisting of the City of London and 32 boroughs (13 Inner London boroughs and 19 Outer London boroughs): formed in 1965 from the City, parts of Surrey, Kent, Essex, and Hertfordshire, and almost all of Middlesex. Pop.: 6 775 200 (1986). Area: 1579 sq. km (610 sq. miles). **3.** a city in SE Canada, in SE Ontario on the Thames River: University of Western Ontario (1878). Pop.: 269 140 (1986). —**'Londoner** *n.*

London² ('lʌndən) *n.* **Jack,** full name *John Griffith London.* 1876–1916, U.S. novelist, short-story writer, and adventurer. His works include *Call of the Wild* (1903), *The Sea Wolf* (1904), *The Iron Heel* (1907), and the semiautobiographical *John Barleycorn* (1913).

Londonderry ('lʌndən,derɪ) *or* **Derry** *n.* **1.** a district (former county) of Northern Ireland, on the Atlantic. Pop.: 95 700 (1986 est.). Area: 372 sq. km (144 sq. miles). **2.** a port in N Northern Ireland, second city of Northern Ireland: given to the City of London in 1613 to be colonized by Londoners; besieged by James II's forces (1688–89). Pop.: 96 100 (1983 est.).

London pride *n.* a type of saxifrage plant having a basal rosette of leaves and pinkish-white flowers.

Londrina (*Portuguese* lon'drina) *n.* a city in S Brazil, in Paraná: centre of a coffee-growing area. Pop.: 349 200 (1980).

lone (ləʊn) *adj.* (*prenominal*) **1.** unaccompanied; solitary. **2.** single or isolated: *a lone house.* **3.** a literary word for **lonely. 4.** *Rare.* unmarried or widowed. [C14: from the mistaken division of ALONE into *a lone*] —**'loneness** *n.*

lonely ('ləʊnlɪ) *adj.* **-lier, -liest. 1.** unhappy as a result of being without companions. **2.** causing or resulting from the state of being alone. **3.** isolated, unfrequented, or desolate. **4.** without companions; solitary. —**'loneliness** *n.*

lonely hearts *adj.* (*often caps.*) of or for people who wish to meet a congenial companion or marriage partner: *a lonely hearts advertisement.*

loner ('ləʊnə) *n. Inf.* a person who avoids the company of others or prefers to be alone.

lonesome ('ləʊnsəm) *adj.* **1.** *Chiefly U.S. & Canad.* another word for **lonely.** ~*n.* **2. on** *or U.S.* **by one's lonesome.** *Inf.* on one's own. —'**lonesomely** *adv.* —'**lonesomeness** *n.*

long[1] (lɒŋ) *adj.* **1.** having relatively great extent in space or duration in time. **2. a.** (*postpositive*) of a specified number of units in extent or duration: *three hours long.* **b.** (*in combination*): *a two-foot-long line.* **3.** having or consisting of a relatively large number of items or parts: *a long list.* **4.** having greater than the average or expected range, extent, or duration: *a long match.* **5.** seeming to occupy a greater time than is really so: *she spent a long afternoon waiting.* **6. a.** (of drinks) containing a large quantity of nonalcoholic beverage. **b.** beer as opposed to spirits. **7.** (of a garment) reaching to the wearer's ankles. **8.** *Inf.* (foll. by *on*) plentifully supplied or endowed (with): *long on good ideas.* **9.** *Phonetics.* (of a speech sound, esp. a vowel) **a.** of relatively considerable duration. **b.** (in popular usage) denoting the qualities of the five English vowels in such words as *mate, mete, mite, moat, moot,* and *mute.* **10.** from end to end; lengthwise. **11.** unlikely to win, happen, succeed, etc.: *a long chance.* **12.** *Prosody.* **a.** denoting a vowel of relatively great duration. **b.** denoting a syllable containing such a vowel. **c.** carrying the emphasis. **13.** *Finance.* having or characterized by large holdings of securities or commodities in anticipation of rising prices. **14.** *Cricket.* (of a fielding position) near the boundary: *long leg.* **15. in the long run.** ultimately; after or over a period of time. ~*adv.* **16.** for a certain time or period: *how long will it last?* **17.** for or during an extensive period of time: *long into the next year.* **18.** at a distant time; quite a bit of time: *long before I met you; long ago.* **19.** *Finance.* into a position with more security or commodity holdings than are required by sale contracts and therefore dependent on rising prices for profit: *to go long.* **20. as** (*or* **so**) **long as. a.** for or during just the length of time that. **b.** inasmuch as; since. **c.** provided that; if. **21. no longer.** not any more; formerly but not now. ~*n.* **22.** a long time (esp. in **for long**). **23.** a relatively long thing, such as a signal in Morse code. **24.** *Phonetics.* a long vowel or syllable. **25.** *Finance.* a person with large holdings of a security or commodity in expectation of a rise in its price; bull. **26. before long.** soon. **27. the long and the short of it.** the essential points or facts. ~See also **longs.** [OE *lang*]

long[2] (lɒŋ) *vb.* (*intr.*; foll. by *for* or an infinitive) to have a strong desire. [OE *langian*]

Long (lɒŋ) *n.* **Crawford Williamson.** 1815–78, U.S. surgeon. He was the first to use ether as an anaesthetic.

long. *abbrev. for* longitude.

long- *adv.* (*in combination*) for or lasting a long time: *long-awaited; long-established; long-lasting.*

Long Beach *n.* a city in SW California, on San Pedro Bay: resort and naval base; oil-refining. Pop.: 396 280 (1986 est.).

Longbenton (,lɒŋ'bɛntən) *n.* a town in N England, in Tyne and Wear near Newcastle. Pop.: 50 646 (1981).

longboat ('lɒŋ,bəʊt) *n.* the largest boat carried aboard a commercial sailing vessel.

longbow ('lɒŋ,bəʊ) *n.* a large powerful hand-drawn bow, esp. as used in medieval England.

longcase clock ('lɒŋ,keɪs) *n.* another name for **grandfather clock.**

longcloth ('lɒŋ,klɒθ) *n.* a fine plain-weave cotton cloth made in long strips.

long-dated *adj.* (of a gilt-edged security) having more than 15 years to run before redemption. Cf. **medium-dated, short-dated.**

long-day *adj.* (of certain plants) able to mature and flower only if exposed to long periods of daylight. Cf. **short-day.**

long-distance *n.* **1.** (*modifier*) covering relatively long distances: *a long-distance driver.* **2.** (*modifier*) (of telephone calls, lines, etc.) connecting points a relatively long way apart. **3.** *Chiefly U.S.* a long-distance telephone call. **4.** a long-distance telephone system or its operator. ~*adv.* **5.** by a long-distance telephone line: *he phoned long-distance.*

long-drawn-out *adj.* overprolonged or extended.

Long Eaton ('iːtᵊn) *n.* a town in N central England, in SE Derbyshire. Pop.: 32 895 (1981).

longeron ('lɒndʒərən) *n.* a main longitudinal structural member of an aircraft. [C20: from F: side support, ult. from L *longus* LONG[1]]

longevity (lɒn'dʒɛvɪtɪ) *n.* **1.** long life. **2.** relatively long duration of employment, service, etc. [C17: from LL *longaevitās,* from L *longaevus* long-lived, from *longus* LONG[1] + *aevum* age]

long face *n.* a disappointed, solemn, or miserable facial expression. —,**long-'faced** *adj.*

Longfellow ('lɒŋ,fɛləʊ) *n.* **Henry Wadsworth.** 1807–82, U.S. poet, noted particularly for his long narrative poems *Evangeline* (1847) and *The Song of Hiawatha* (1855).

Longford ('lɒŋfəd) *n.* **1.** a county of N Ireland, in Leinster province. County town: Longford. Pop.: 31 491 (1986). Area: 1043 sq. km (403 sq. miles). **2.** a town in N Ireland, county town of Co. Longford. Pop.: 6548 (1981).

longhand ('lɒŋ,hænd) *n.* ordinary handwriting in which letters, words, etc., are set down in full, as opposed to typing or to shorthand.

long haul *n.* **1.** a journey over a long distance, esp. one involving the transport of goods. **2.** a lengthy job.

long-headed *adj.* astute; shrewd; sagacious. —,**long-'headedly** *adv.* —,**long-'headedness** *n.*

longhorn ('lɒŋ,hɔːn) *n.* **1.** a long-horned breed of beef cattle, formerly common in the southwestern U.S. **2.** a British breed of beef cattle with long curved horns.

longing ('lɒŋɪŋ) *n.* **1.** a prolonged unfulfilled desire or need. ~*adj.* **2.** having or showing desire or need: *a longing look.* —'**longingly** *adv.*

Longinus (lɒn'dʒaɪnəs) *n.* **Dionysius** (,daɪə'nɪsɪəs). ?2nd century A.D., supposed author of the famous Greek treatise on literary criticism, *On the Sublime.* —**Longinean** (lɒn'dʒɪnɪən) *adj.*

longish ('lɒŋɪʃ) *adj.* rather long.

Long Island *n.* an island in SE New York State, separated from the S shore of Connecticut by **Long Island Sound** (an arm of the Atlantic): contains the New York City boroughs of Brooklyn and Queens in the west, many resorts (notably Coney Island), and two large airports (La Guardia and John F. Kennedy). Area: 4462 sq. km (1723 sq. miles).

longitude ('lɒndʒɪ,tjuːd, 'lɒŋgɪ-) *n.* distance in degrees east or west of the prime meridian at 0° measured by the angle between the plane of the prime meridian and that of the meridian through the point in question, or by the time difference. [C14: from L *longitūdō* length, from *longus* LONG[1]]

longitudinal (,lɒndʒɪ'tjuːdɪnᵊl, ,lɒŋgɪ-) *adj.* **1.** of or relating to longitude or length. **2.** placed or extended lengthways. —,**longi'tudinally** *adv.*

longitudinal wave *n.* a wave that is propagated in the same direction as the displacement of the transmitting medium.

long johns *pl. n. Inf.* underpants with long legs.

long jump *n.* an athletic contest in which competitors try to cover the farthest distance possible with a running jump from a fixed board or mark. U.S. and Canad. equivalent: **broad jump.**

long-lived *adj.* having long life, existence, or currency. —,**long-'livedness** *n.*

long-playing *adj.* of or relating to an LP (long player).

long-range *adj.* **1.** of or extending into the future: *a long-range weather forecast.* **2.** (of vehicles, aircraft, etc.) capable of covering great distances without refuelling. **3.** (of weapons) made to be fired at a distant target.

longs (lɒŋz) *pl. n.* **1.** full-length trousers. **2.** long-dated gilt-edged securities.

longship ('lɒŋ,ʃɪp) *n.* a narrow open vessel with oars and a square sail, used esp. by the Vikings.

longshore ('lɒŋ,ʃɔː) *adj.* situated on, relating to, or along the shore. [C19: short form of *alongshore*]

longshore drift *n.* the process whereby beach material is gradually shifted laterally.

longshoreman ('lɒŋ,ʃɔːmən) *n., pl.* **-men.** a U.S. and Canad. word for **docker**[1].

long shot *n.* **1.** a competitor, as in a race, considered to be unlikely to win. **2.** a bet against heavy odds. **3.** an undertaking, guess, or possibility with little chance of success. **4.** *Films, television.* a shot where the camera is or appears to be distant from the object to be photographed. **5. by a long shot.** by any means: *he still hasn't finished by a long shot.*

long-sighted adj. **1.** related to or suffering from hyperopia. **2.** able to see distant objects in focus. **3.** another term for **far-sighted.** — ,long-'sightedly adv. — ,long-'sightedness n.

Longs Peak n. a mountain in N Colorado, in the Front Range of the Rockies: the highest peak in the Rocky Mountain National Park. Height: 4345 m (14 255 ft.).

long-standing adj. existing for a long time.

long-suffering adj. **1.** enduring pain, unhappiness, etc., without complaint. ~n. **2.** long and patient endurance. — ,long-'sufferingly adv.

long suit n. **1. a.** the longest suit in a hand of cards. **b.** a holding of four or more cards of a suit. **2.** Inf. an outstanding advantage, personal quality, or talent.

long-term adj. **1.** lasting or extending over a long time: long-term prospects. **2.** Finance. maturing after a long period: a long-term bond.

longtime ('lɒŋ,taɪm) adj. of long standing.

long ton n. the full name for **ton**[1] (sense 1).

Longueuil (lɒŋ'geɪl; French lɔ̃gœj) n. a city in SE Canada, in S Quebec: a suburb of Montreal. Pop.: 124 320 (1981).

longueur (French lɔ̃gœr) n. a period of boredom or dullness. [lit.: length]

Longus ('lɒŋgəs) n. ?3rd century A.D., Greek author of the prose romance Daphnis and Chloe.

long vacation n. the long period of holiday in the summer during which universities, law courts, etc., are closed.

long wave n. **a.** a radio wave with a wavelength greater than 1000 metres. **b.** (as modifier): a long-wave broadcast.

longways ('lɒŋ,weɪz) or U.S. & Canad. **longwise** adv. another word for **lengthways.**

long weekend n. a weekend holiday extended by a day or days on either side.

long-winded (,lɒŋ'wɪndɪd) adj. **1.** tiresomely long. **2.** capable of energetic activity without becoming short of breath. — ,long-'windedly adv. — ,long-'windedness n.

Longyearbyen ('lɒŋjɪə,bjɛn) n. a village on Spitsbergen island, administrative centre of the Svalbard archipelago: coal-mining.

lonicera (lɒ'nɪsərə) n. See **honeysuckle.**

Lons-le-Saunier (French lɔ̃ləsonje) n. a town in E France: saline springs; manufactures sparkling wines. Pop.: 19 996 (1982).

loo[1] (luː) n., pl. **loos.** Brit. an informal word for **lavatory.** [C20: ?from F lieux d'aisance water closet]

loo[2] (luː) n., pl. **loos. 1.** a gambling card game. **2.** a stake used in this game. [C17: shortened from lanterloo, via Du. from F lanterelu, orig. a nonsense word from the refrain of a popular song]

loofah ('luːfə) n. the fibrous interior of the fruit of a type of gourd, which is dried and used as a bath sponge or for scrubbing. Also (esp. U.S.): **loofa, luffa.** [C19: from NL luffa, from Ar. lūf]

look (lʊk) vb. (mainly intr.) **1.** (often foll. by at) to direct the eyes (towards): to look at the sea. **2.** (often foll. by at) to direct one's attention (towards): let's look at the circumstances. **3.** (often foll. by to) to turn one's interests or expectations (towards): to look to the future. **4.** (copula) to give the impression of being by appearance to the eye or mind; seem: that looks interesting. **5.** to face in a particular direction: the house looks north. **6.** to expect or hope (to do something): I look to hear from you soon. **7.** (foll. by for) **a.** to search or seek: I looked for you everywhere. **b.** to cherish the expectation (of); hope (for): I look for success. **8.** (foll. by to) **a.** to be mindful (of): to look to the promise one has made. **b.** to have recourse (to): look to your swords, men! **9.** (foll. by into) to carry out an investigation. **10.** (tr.) to direct a look at (someone) in a specified way: she looked her rival up and down. **11.** (tr.) to accord in appearance with (something): to look one's age. **12. look alive, lively, sharp,** or **smart,** to hurry up; get busy. **13. look here.** an expression used to attract someone's attention, add emphasis to a statement, etc. ~n. **14.** the act or an instance of looking: a look of despair. **15.** a view or sight (of something): let's have a look. **16.** (often pl.) appearance to the eye or mind; aspect: the look of innocence; I don't like the looks of this place. **17.** style; fashion: the new look for spring. ~sentence connector. **18.** an expression demanding attention or showing annoyance, determination, etc.: look, I've had

enough of this. ~See also **look after, look back,** etc. [OE lōcian] — 'looker n.

▷ Usage. See at **feel.**

look after vb. (intr., prep.) **1.** to take care of; be responsible for. **2.** to follow with the eyes.

lookalike ('lʊkə,laɪk) n. **a.** a person or thing that is the double of another, often well known, person or thing. **b.** (as modifier): a lookalike Minister; a lookalike newspaper.

look back vb. (intr., adv.) **1.** to cast one's mind to the past. **2.** (usually used with a negative) to cease to make progress: after his first book was published, he never looked back.

look down vb. (intr., adv.; foll. by on or upon) to express or show contempt or disdain (for).

look forward to vb. (intr., adv. + prep.) to wait or hope for, esp. with pleasure.

look-in Inf. ~n. **1.** a chance to be chosen, participate, etc. **2.** a short visit. ~vb. **look in. 3.** (intr., adv.; often foll. by on) to pay a short visit.

looking glass n. a mirror.

look on vb. (intr.) **1.** (adv.) to be a spectator at an event or incident. **2.** (prep.) Also: **look upon.** to consider or regard: she looked on the whole affair as a joke. — ,looker-'on n.

lookout ('lʊk,aʊt) n. **1.** the act of keeping watch against danger, etc. **2.** a person or persons instructed or employed to keep such a watch, esp. on a ship. **3.** a strategic point from which a watch is kept. **4.** Inf. worry or concern: that's his lookout. **5.** Chiefly Brit. outlook, chances, or view. ~vb. **look out.** (adv., mainly intr.) **6.** to heed one's behaviour; be careful. **7.** to be on the watch: look out for my mother at the station. **8.** (tr.) to search for and find. **9.** (foll. by on or over) to face in a particular direction: the house looks out over the moor.

look over vb. **1.** (intr., prep.) to inspect by making a tour of (a factory, house, etc.). **2.** (tr., adv.) to examine (a document, letter, etc.). ~n. **look-over. 3.** an inspection.

look-see n. Sl. a brief inspection or look.

look up vb. (adv.) **1.** (tr.) to discover (something required to be known) by resorting to a work of reference, such as a dictionary. **2.** (intr.) to increase, as in quality or value: things are looking up. **3.** (intr.; foll. by to) to have respect (for): I've always wanted a girlfriend I could look up to. **4.** (tr.) to visit or make contact with (a person): I'll look you up when I'm in town.

loom[1] (luːm) n. an apparatus, worked by hand or mechanically (**power loom**), for weaving yarn into a textile. [C13 (meaning any kind of tool): var. of OE gelōma tool]

loom[2] (luːm) vb. (intr.) **1.** to come into view indistinctly with an enlarged and often threatening aspect. **2.** (of an event) to seem ominously close. **3.** (often foll. by over) (of large objects) to dominate or overhang. ~n. **4.** a rising appearance, as of something far away. [C16: ?from East Frisian lomen to move slowly]

loon[1] (luːn) n. the U.S. and Canad. name for **diver** (the bird). [C17: of Scand. origin]

loon[2] (luːn) n. **1.** Inf. a simple-minded or stupid person. **2.** Arch. a person of low rank or occupation. [C15: from ?]

loony or **looney** ('luːnɪ) Sl. ~adj. **loonier, looniest. 1.** lunatic; insane. **2.** foolish or ridiculous. ~n., pl. **loonies** or **looneys. 3.** a foolish or insane person. — 'looniness n.

loony bin n. Sl. a mental hospital or asylum.

loop (luːp) n. **1.** the round or oval shape formed by a line, string, etc., that curves around to cross itself. **2.** any round or oval-shaped thing that is closed or nearly closed. **3.** an intrauterine contraceptive device in the shape of a loop. **4.** Electronics. a closed electric or magnetic circuit through which a signal can circulate, as in a feedback control system. **5.** a flight manoeuvre in which an aircraft flies one complete circle in the vertical plane. **6.** Also called: **loop line.** Chiefly Brit. a railway branch line which leaves the main line and rejoins it after a short distance. **7.** Maths, physics. a closed curve on a graph: hysteresis loop. **8.** a continuous strip of cinematographic film. **9.** Computers. a series of instructions in a program, performed repeatedly until some specified condition is satisfied. ~vb. **10.** (tr.) to make a loop in or of (a line, string, etc.). **11.** (tr.) to fasten or encircle with a loop or something like a loop. **12.** Also: **loop the loop.** to cause (an aircraft) to perform a loop or (of an aircraft) to perform a loop. **13.** (*intr.*) to move in loops or in a path like a loop. [C14 *loupe*, from ?] — **'looper** *n.*

loophole ('lu:p,həʊl) *n.* **1.** an ambiguity, omission, etc., as in a law, by which one can avoid a penalty or responsibility. **2.** a small gap or hole in a wall, esp. one in a fortified wall. ~*vb.* **3.** (*tr.*) to provide with loopholes.

loopy ('lu:pɪ) *adj.* **loopier, loopiest.** **1.** full of loops; curly or twisted. **2.** *Inf.* slightly mad, crazy.

loose (lu:s) *adj.* **1.** free or released from confinement or restraint. **2.** not close, compact, or tight in structure or arrangement. **3.** not fitted or fitting closely: *loose clothing is cooler.* **4.** not bundled, packaged, fastened, or put in a container: *loose nails.* **5.** inexact; imprecise: *a loose translation.* **6.** (of funds, cash, etc.) not allocated or locked away; readily available: *loose change.* **7. a.** (esp. of women) promiscuous or easy. **b.** (of attitudes, ways of life, etc.) immoral or dissolute. **8. a.** lacking a sense of responsibility or propriety: *loose talk.* **b.** (*in combination*): *loosetongued.* **9. a.** (of the bowels) emptying easily, esp. excessively. **b.** (of a cough) accompanied by phlegm, mucus, etc. **10.** *Inf., chiefly U.S. & Canad.* very relaxed; easy. ~*n.* **11. the loose.** *Rugby.* the part of play when the forwards close round the ball in a ruck or loose scrum. **12. on the loose. a.** free from confinement or restraint. **b.** *Inf.* on a spree. ~*adv.* **13. a.** in a loose manner; loosely. **b.** (*in combination*): *loose-fitting.* ~*vb.* **14.** (*tr.*) to set free or release, as from confinement, restraint, or obligation. **15.** (*tr.*) to unfasten or untie. **16.** to make or become less strict, tight, firmly attached, compact, etc. **17.** (when *intr.*, often foll. by *off*) to let fly (a bullet, arrow, or other missile). [C13 (in the sense: not bound): from ON *lauss* free] — **'loosely** *adv.* — **'looseness** *n.*

loosebox ('lu:s,bɒks) *n.* an enclosed stall with a door in which an animal can be confined.

loose cover *n.* a fitted but easily removable cloth cover for a chair, sofa, etc.

loose end *n.* **1.** a detail that is left unsettled, unexplained, or incomplete. **2. at a loose end.** without purpose or occupation.

loose-jointed *adj.* **1.** supple and easy in movement; loosely built; with ill-fitting joints. — **loose-'jointedness** *n.*

loose-leaf *adj.* (of a binder, album, etc.) capable of being opened to allow removal and addition of pages.

loosen ('lu:s°n) *vb.* **1.** to make or become less tight, fixed, etc. **2.** (often foll. by *up*) to make or become less firm, compact, or rigid. **3.** (*tr.*) to untie. **4.** (*tr.*) to let loose; set free. **5.** (often foll. by *up*) to make or become less strict, severe, etc. **6.** (*tr.*) to rid or relieve (the bowels) of constipation. [C14: from LOOSE] — **'loosener** *n.*

loosestrife ('lu:s,straɪf) *n.* **1.** any of a genus of plants, esp. the yellow-flowered yellow loosestrife. **2. purple loosestrife.** a purple-flowered marsh plant. [C16: LOOSE + STRIFE, an erroneous translation of L *lysimachia*, as if from Gk *lusimakhos* ending strife, instead of from the name of the supposed discoverer, *Lusimakhos*]

loot (lu:t) *n.* **1.** goods stolen during pillaging, as in wartime, during riots, etc. **2.** goods, money, etc., obtained illegally. **3.** *Inf.* money or wealth. ~*vb.* **4.** to pillage (a city, etc.) during war or riots. **5.** to steal (money or goods), esp. during pillaging. [C19: from Hindi *lūt*] — **'looter** *n.*

lop[1] (lɒp) *vb.* **lopping, lopped.** (*tr.*; usually foll. by *off*) **1.** to sever (parts) from a tree, body, etc., esp. with swift strokes. **2.** to cut out or eliminate from as excessive. ~*n.* **3.** a part or parts lopped off, as from a tree. [C15 *loppe* branches cut off] — **'lopper** *n.*

lop[2] (lɒp) *vb.* **lopping, lopped.** **1.** to hang or allow to hang loosely. **2.** (*intr.*) to slouch about or move awkwardly. [C16: ? rel. to LOP[1]]

lope (ləʊp) *vb.* **1.** (*intr.*) (of a person) to move or run with a long swinging stride. **2.** (*intr.*) (of four-legged animals) to run with a regular bounding movement. **3.** to cause (a horse) to canter with a long easy stride or (of a horse) to canter in this manner. ~*n.* **4.** a long steady gait or stride. [C15: from ON *hlaupa* to LEAP]

lop-eared *adj.* (of animals) having ears that droop.

Lope de Vega (*Spanish* 'lope ðe 'βeɣa) *n.* full name *Lope Felix de Vega Carpio.* 1562–1635, Spanish dramatist, novelist, and poet. He established the classic form of Spanish drama and was a major influence on European, esp. French, literature. Some 500 of his 1800 plays are extant.

lopsided (,lɒp'saɪdɪd) *adj.* **1.** leaning to one side. **2.** greater in weight, height, or size on one side. — ,lop'sidedly *adv.* — ,lop'sidedness *n.*

loquacious (lɒ'kweɪʃəs) *adj.* characterized by or showing a tendency to talk a great deal. [C17: from L *loquāx* from *loquī* to speak] — lo'quaciously *adv.* — loquacity (lɒ'kwæsɪtɪ) *or* lo'quaciousness *n.*

loquat ('ləʊkwɒt, -kwət) *n.* **1.** an ornamental evergreen tree of China and Japan, having reddish woolly branches, white flowers, and small yellow edible plumlike fruits. **2.** the fruit of this tree. [C19: from Chinese (Cantonese) *lō kwat*, lit.: rush orange]

lor (lɔ:) *interj. Not standard.* an exclamation of surprise or dismay. [from LORD (interj.)]

loran ('lɔ:rən) *n.* a radio navigation system operating over long distances. Synchronized pulses are transmitted from widely spaced radio stations to aircraft or shipping, the time of arrival of the pulses being used to determine position. [C20: *lo(ng-)ra(nge) n(avigation)*]

Lorca[1] (*Spanish* 'lɔrka) *n.* a town in SE Spain, on the Guadalentín River. Pop.: 60 627 (1981).

Lorca[2] (*Spanish* 'lɔrka) *n.* **Federico García** (feðe'riko gar'θia). 1899–1936, Spanish poet and dramatist. His poetry, such as *Romancero gitano* (1928), shows his debt to Andalusian folk poetry. His plays include the trilogy *Bodas de sangre* (1933), *Yerma* (1935), and *La Casa de Bernarda Alba* (1936).

lord (lɔ:d) *n.* **1.** a person who has power or authority over others, such as a monarch or master. **2.** a male member of the nobility, esp. in Britain. **3.** (in medieval Europe) a feudal superior, esp. the master of a manor. **4.** a husband considered as head of the household (archaic except in the facetious phrase **lord and master**). **5. my lord.** a respectful form of address used to a judge, bishop, or nobleman. ~*vb.* **6.** (*tr.*) *Now rare.* to make a lord of (a person). **7.** to act in a superior manner towards (esp. in **lord it over**). [OE *hlāford* bread keeper] — **'lordless** *adj.* — **'lord,like** *adj.*

Lord (lɔ:d) *n.* **1.** a title given to God or Jesus Christ. **2.** *Brit.* **a.** a title given to men of high birth, specifically to an earl, marquess, baron, or viscount. **b.** a courtesy title given to the younger sons of a duke or marquess. **c.** the ceremonial title of certain high officials or of a bishop or archbishop: *Lord Mayor; Lord Bishop of Durham.* ~*interj.* **3.** (*sometimes not cap.*) an exclamation of dismay, surprise, etc.: *Good Lord!*

Lord Chancellor *n. Brit. government.* the cabinet minister who is head of the judiciary in England and Wales, and Speaker of the House of Lords.

Lord Chief Justice *n.* the judge who is second only to the Lord Chancellor in the English legal hierarchy; president of one division of the High Court of Justice.

Lord High Chancellor *n.* another name for the **Lord Chancellor.**

Lord Howe Island *n.* an island in the Tasman Sea, southeast of Australia: part of New South Wales. Area: 17 sq. km (6 sq. miles). Pop.: 300 (1981 est.).

Lord Lieutenant *n.* **1.** (in Britain) the representative of the Crown in a county. **2.** (formerly) the British viceroy in Ireland.

lordly ('lɔ:dlɪ) *adj.* **-lier, -liest.** **1.** haughty; arrogant; proud. **2.** of or befitting a lord. ~*adv.* **3.** *Arch.* in the manner of a lord. — **'lordliness** *n.*

Lord Mayor *n.* the mayor in the City of London and in certain other boroughs.

Lord of Misrule *n.* (formerly, in England) a person appointed master of revels at a Christmas celebration.

lordosis (lɔ:'dəʊsɪs) *n. Pathol.* forward curvature of the lumbar spine. [C18: NL from Gk, from *lordos* bent backwards] — **lordotic** (lɔ:'dɒtɪk) *adj.*

Lord President of the Council *n.* (in Britain) the cabinet minister who presides at meetings of the Privy Council.

Lord Privy Seal *n.* (in Britain) the senior cabinet minister without official duties.

Lord Protector *n.* See **Protector.**

Lord Provost *n.* the provost of one of the major Scottish cities.

Lords (lɔ:dz) *n.* **the.** short for **House of Lords.**

Lord's (lɔ:dz) *n.* a cricket ground in N London; headquarters of the MCC.

lords-and-ladies *n.* (*functioning as sing.*) another name for **cuckoopint.**

Lord's Day *n.* **the.** the Christian Sabbath; Sunday.

lordship ('lɔːdʃɪp) *n.* the position or authority of a lord.

Lordship ('lɔːdʃɪp) *n.* (preceded by *Your* or *His*) *Brit.* a title used to address or refer to a bishop, a judge of the high court, or any peer except a duke.

Lord's Prayer *n.* **the.** the prayer taught by Jesus Christ to his disciples, in Matthew 6:9–13, Luke 11:2–4. Also called: **Our Father, Paternoster** (esp. Latin version).

Lords Spiritual *pl. n.* the Anglican archbishops and senior bishops of England and Wales who are members of the House of Lords.

Lord's Supper *n.* **the.** another term for **Holy Communion** (I Corinthians 11:20).

Lords Temporal *pl. n.* **the.** (in Britain) peers other than bishops in their capacity as members of the House of Lords.

lore (lɔː) *n.* **1.** collective knowledge or wisdom on a particular subject, esp. of a traditional nature. **2.** knowledge or learning. [OE *lār*; rel. to *leornian* to LEARN]

Lorelei ('lɒrəˌlaɪ) *n.* (in German legend) a siren, said to dwell on a rock at the edge of the Rhine south of Koblenz, who lures boatmen to destruction. [C19: from G *Lurlei* name of the rock; from a poem by Clemens Brentano (1778–1842)]

Loren (*Italian* 'lɔːren) *n.* **Sophia** (so'fia), real name *Sophia Scicolone*. born 1934, Italian film actress. Her films include *Two Women* (1961) for which she won an Oscar, *The Millionairess* (1961), *Man of La Mancha* (1972), and *The Cassandra Crossing* (1977).

Lorentz (*Dutch* 'lɔːrənts) *n.* **Hendrik Antoon** ('hɛndrɪk 'antoːn). 1853–1928, Dutch physicist: shared the Nobel prize for physics (1902) with Zeeman for their work on electromagnetic theory.

Lorenz (*German* 'loːrɛnts) *n.* **Konrad Zacharias** ('kɔnraːt tsaxa'riːas) 1903–89, Austrian zoologist, who founded ethology. His works include *On Aggression* (1966): shared the Nobel prize for physiology or medicine 1973.

lorgnette (lɔː'njɛt) *n.* a pair of spectacles or opera glasses mounted on a handle. [C19: from F, from *lorgner* to squint, from OF *lorgne* squinting]

Lorient (*French* lɔrjɑ̃) *n.* a port in W France, on the Bay of Biscay. Pop.: 64 675 (1982).

lorikeet ('lɒrɪˌkiːt, ˌlɒrɪ'kiːt) *n.* any of various small lories, such as the varied lorikeet or rainbow lorikeet. [C18: from LORY + *-keet*, as in PARAKEET]

loris ('lɔːrɪs) *n.*, *pl.* **-ris.** any of several omnivorous nocturnal slow-moving prosimian primates of S and SE Asia, esp. the slow loris and slender loris, having vestigial sight and no tails. [C18: from F; from ?]

lorn (lɔːn) *adj. Poetic.* forsaken or wretched. [OE *loren*, p.p. of *-lēosan* to lose]

Lorrain (*French* lɔrɛ̃) *n.* See **Claude Lorrain.**

Lorraine (lɒ'reɪn; *French* lɔrɛn) *n.* **1.** a region and former province of E France; ceded to Germany in 1871 after the Franco-Prussian war and regained by France in 1919; rich iron-ore deposits. German name: **Lothringen.** **2. Kingdom of.** an early medieval kingdom on the Meuse, Moselle, and Rhine rivers: later a duchy. **3.** a former duchy in E France, once the S half of this kingdom.

Lorris (*French* lɔris) *n.* See **Guillaume de Lorris.**

lorry ('lɒrɪ) *n.*, *pl.* **-ries. 1.** a large motor vehicle designed to carry heavy loads, esp. one with a flat platform. U.S. and Canad. name: **truck. 2. off the back of a lorry.** *Brit. inf.* a phrase used humorously to indicate that something has been dishonestly acquired. **3.** any of various vehicles with a flat load-carrying surface, esp. one designed to run on rails. [C19: ? rel. to northern English dialect *lurry* to pull]

lory ('lɔːrɪ), **lowry,** or **lowrie** ('laʊrɪ) *n.*, *pl.* **-ries.** any of various small brightly coloured parrots of Australia and Indonesia, having a brush-tipped tongue with which to feed on nectar and pollen. [C17: via Du. from Malay *lūri*, var. of *nūrī*]

Los Angeles (lɒs 'ændʒɪ,liːz) *n.* a city in SW California, on the Pacific: the third largest city in the U.S., having absorbed many adjacent townships; industrial centre and port, with several universities. Pop.: 3 259 300 (1986 est.). Abbrev.: **LA.**

lose (luːz) *vb.* **losing, lost.** (*mainly tr.*) **1.** to part with or come to be without, as through theft, accident, negligence, etc. **2.** to fail to keep or maintain: *to lose one's balance.* **3.** to suffer the loss or deprivation of: *to lose a parent.* **4.** to cease to have or possess. **5.** to fail to get or make use of: *to lose a chance.* **6.** (*also intr.*) to fail to gain or win (a contest, game, etc.): *to lose the match.* **7.** to fail to see, hear, perceive, or understand: *I lost the gist of his speech.* **8.** to waste: *to lose money gambling.* **9.** to wander from so as to be unable to find: *to lose one's way.* **10.** to cause the loss of: *his delay lost him the battle.* **11.** to allow to go astray or out of sight: *we lost him in the crowd.* **12.** (*usually passive*) to absorb or engross: *he was lost in contemplation.* **13.** (*usually passive*) to cause the death or destruction of: *two men were lost in the attack.* **14.** to outdistance or elude: *he soon lost his pursuers.* **15.** (*intr.*) to decrease or depreciate in value or effectiveness: *poetry always loses in translation.* **16.** (*also intr.*) (of a timepiece) to run slow (by a specified amount). **17.** (of a woman) to fail to give birth to (a viable baby), esp. as the result of a miscarriage. [OE *losian* to perish] —**losable** *adj.*

lose out *vb. Inf.* **1.** (*intr., adv.*) to be defeated or unsuccessful. **2. lose out on.** to fail to secure or make use of: *we lost out on the sale.*

loser ('luːzə) *n.* **1.** a person or thing that loses. **2.** *Inf.* a person or thing that seems destined to be taken advantage of, fail, etc.: *a born loser.*

Losey ('ləʊsɪ) *n.* **Joseph.** 1909–84, U.S. film director, in Britain since 1952. His films include *The Servant* (1963), *Accident* (1967), *Secret Ceremony* (1968), and *The Go-Between* (1971).

losing ('luːzɪŋ) *adj.* unprofitable; failing: *the business was a losing concern.*

losings ('luːzɪŋz) *pl. n.* losses, esp. in gambling.

loss (lɒs) *n.* **1.** the act or an instance of losing. **2.** the disadvantage or deprivation resulting from losing: *a loss of reputation.* **3.** the person, thing, or amount lost: *a large loss.* **4.** (*pl.*) military personnel lost by death or capture. **5.** (*sometimes pl.*) the amount by which the costs of a business transaction or operation exceed its revenue. **6.** *Insurance.* **a.** an occurrence of something that has been insured against, thus giving rise to a claim by a policyholder. **b.** the amount of the resulting claim. **7. at a loss. a.** uncertain what to do; bewildered. **b.** rendered helpless (for lack of something): *at a loss for words.* **c.** with income less than outlay: *the firm was running at a loss.* [C14: n. prob. formed from *lost*, p.p. of *losen* to perish, from OE *lōsian* to be destroyed, from *los* destruction]

loss adjuster *n. Insurance.* a person qualified to adjust losses incurred through fire, theft, natural disaster, etc., to agree the loss and the compensation to be paid.

loss leader *n.* an article offered below cost to attract customers.

lost (lɒst) *adj.* **1.** unable to be found or recovered. **2.** unable to find one's way or ascertain one's whereabouts. **3.** confused, bewildered, or helpless: *he is lost in discussions of theory.* **4.** (sometimes foll. by *on*) not utilized, noticed, or taken advantage of (by): *rational arguments are lost on her.* **5.** no longer possessed or existing because of defeat, misfortune, or the passage of time: *a lost art.* **6.** destroyed physically: *the lost platoon.* **7.** (foll. by *to*) no longer available or open (to). **8.** (foll. by *to*) insensible or impervious (to a sense of shame, justice, etc.). **9.** (foll. by *in*) engrossed (in): *he was lost in his book.* **10.** morally fallen: *a lost woman.* **11.** damned: *a lost soul.*

Lost Generation *n.* (*sometimes not cap.*) **1.** the large number of talented young men killed in World War I. **2.** the generation of writers, esp. American authors, active after World War I.

lot (lɒt) *pron.* **1.** (*functioning as sing. or pl.; preceded by a*) a great number or quantity: *a lot to do; a lot of people.* ∼*n.* **2.** a collection of objects, items, or people: *a nice lot of youngsters.* **3.** portion in life; destiny; fortune: *it falls to my lot to be poor.* **4.** any object, such as a straw or slip of paper, drawn from others at random to make a selection or choice (esp. in **draw** or **cast lots**). **5.** the use of lots in making a selection or choice (esp. in **by lot**). **6.** an assigned or apportioned share. **7.** an item or set of items for sale in an auction. **8.** *Chiefly U.S. & Canad.* an area of land: *a parking lot.* **9.** *Chiefly U.S. & Canad.* a film studio. **10. a bad lot.** an unpleasant or disreputable person. **11. cast** or **throw in one's lot with.** to join with voluntarily and share the fortunes of. **12. the lot.** the entire amount or number. ~*adv.* (preceded by *a*) *Inf.* **13.** to a considerable extent, degree, or amount; very much: *to delay a lot.* **14.** a great deal of the time or often: *to sing madrigals a lot.* ~*vb.* **lotting, lotted. 15.** to draw lots for (something). **16.** (*tr.*) to divide (land, etc.) into lots. **17.** (*tr.*) another word for **allot.** ~See also **lots.** [OE *hlot*]

Lot[1] (lɒt) *n.* **1.** a department of S central France, in Midi-Pyrénées region. Capital: Cahors. Pop.: 154 533 (1982). Area: 5226 sq. km (2038 sq. miles). **2.** a river in S France, rising in the Cevennes and flowing west into the Garonne River. Length: about 483 km (300 miles).

Lot[2] (lɒt) *n. Old Testament.* Abraham's nephew: he escaped the destruction of Sodom, but his wife was changed into a pillar of salt for looking back as they fled (Genesis 19).

Lot-et-Garonne (*French* lɔtegarɔn) *n.* a department of SW France, in Aquitaine. Capital: Agen. Pop.: 298 522 (1982). Area: 5385 sq. km (2100 sq. miles).

loth (ləʊθ) *adj.* a variant spelling of **loath.**

Lothair I (ləʊ'θɛə) *n.* ?795–855 A.D., German king (840–43) and Holy Roman Emperor (840–55); son of Louis I.

Lothair II *n.* called *the Saxon.* ?1070–1137, German king (1125–37) and Holy Roman Emperor (1133–37). He was elected German king over the hereditary Hohenstaufen claimant.

Lothario (ləʊ'θɑːrɪˌəʊ) *n., pl.* **-os.** (*sometimes not cap.*) a rake, libertine, or seducer. [C18: after a seducer in Nicholas Rowe's tragedy *The Fair Penitent* (1703)]

Lothian Region (ˈləʊðɪən) *n.* a local government region in SE central Scotland, formed in 1975 from East Lothian, most of Midlothian, and West Lothian. Administrative centre: Edinburgh. Pop.: 741 910 (1986 est.). Area: 1756 sq. km (678 sq. miles).

Lothians (ˈləʊðɪənz) *pl. n.* **the.** three former counties of SE central Scotland: East Lothian, West Lothian, and Midlothian.

Lothringen (ˈloːtrɪŋən) *n.* the German name for **Lorraine.**

lotion (ˈləʊʃən) *n.* a liquid preparation having a soothing, cleansing, or antiseptic action, applied to the skin, eyes, etc. [C14: via OF from L *lōtiō* a washing, from *lōtus* p.p. of *lavāre* to wash]

lots (lɒts) *Inf.* ~*pl. n.* **1.** (often foll. by *of*) great numbers or quantities: *lots of people; to eat lots.* ~*adv.* **2.** a great deal. **3.** (intensifier): *the journey is lots quicker by train.*

lottery (ˈlɒtərɪ) *n., pl.* **-teries. 1.** a game of chance in which tickets are sold, which may later qualify the holder for a prize. **2.** an endeavour, the success of which is regarded as a matter of luck. [C16: from OF *loterie*, from MDu. *loterije*]

lotto (ˈlɒtəʊ) *n.* a children's game in which numbered discs are drawn at random and called out, while the players cover the corresponding numbers on cards, the winner being the first to cover all the numbers, a particular row, etc. [C18: from It., from OF *lot*, from Gmc]

lotus (ˈləʊtəs) *n.* **1.** (in Greek mythology) a fruit that induces forgetfulness and a dreamy languor in those who eat it. **2.** any of several water lilies of tropical Africa and Asia, esp. the **white lotus,** which was regarded as sacred in ancient Egypt. **3.** a related plant which is the sacred lotus of India, China, and Tibet. **4.** a representation of such a plant, common in Hindu, Buddhist, and ancient Egyptian art. **5.** any of a genus of leguminous plants of the legume family of the Old World and North America, having yellow, pink, or white pealike flowers. ~Also (rare): **lotos.** [C16: via L from Gk *lōtos*, from Semitic]

lotus-eater *n. Greek myth.* one of a people encountered by Odysseus in North Africa who lived in indolent forgetfulness, drugged by the fruit of the legendary lotus.

lotus position *n.* a seated cross-legged position used in yoga, meditation, etc.

loud (laʊd) *adj.* **1.** (of sound) relatively great in volume: *a loud shout.* **2.** making or able to make sounds of relatively great volume: *a loud voice.* **3.** clamorous, insistent, and emphatic: *loud protests.* **4.** (of colours, designs, etc.) offensive or obtrusive to look at. **5.** characterized by noisy, vulgar, and offensive behaviour. ~*adv.* **6.** in a loud manner. **7. out loud.** audibly, as distinct from silently. [OE *hlūd*] — **ˈloudish** *adj.* — **ˈloudly** *adv.* — **ˈloudness** *n.*

louden (ˈlaʊdᵊn) *vb.* to make or become louder.

loud-hailer *n.* a portable loudspeaker having a built-in amplifier and microphone. Also (U.S. and Canad.): **bull-horn.**

loudmouth (ˈlaʊd,maʊθ) *n. Inf.* a person who brags or talks too loudly. —**loudmouthed** (ˈlaʊd,maʊðd, -,maʊθt) *adj.*

loudspeaker (ˌlaʊd'spiːkə) *n.* a device for converting audio-frequency signals into sound waves. Often shortened to **speaker.**

lough (lɒx, lɒk) *n.* **1.** an Irish word for **lake**[1]. **2.** a long narrow bay or arm of the sea in Ireland. [C14: from Irish *loch* lake]

Loughborough (ˈlʌfbərə, -brə) *n.* a town in central England, in N Leicestershire: university (1966). Pop.: 47 647 (1981).

Louis I (ˈluːɪ; *French* lwi) *n.* known as *Louis the Pious* or *Louis the Debonair.* 778–840 A.D., king of France and Holy Roman Emperor (814–40).

Louis II *n.* **1.** known as *Louis the German.* ?804–876 A.D., king of Germany (843–76); son of Louis I. **2. de Bourbon.** See (Prince de) **Condé.**

Louis IV *n.* known as *Louis the Bavarian.* ?1287–1347, king of Germany (1314–47) and Holy Roman Emperor (1328–47).

Louis V *n.* known as *Louis le Fainéant.* ?967–987 A.D., last Carolingian king of France (986–87).

Louis IX *n.* known as *Saint Louis.* 1214–70, king of France (1226–70): led the Sixth Crusade (1248–54) and was held to ransom (1250); died at Tunis while on another crusade.

Louis XI *n.* 1423–83, king of France (1461–83): involved in a struggle with his vassals, esp. the duke of Burgundy, in his attempt to unite France under an absolute monarchy.

Louis XII *n.* 1462–1515, king of France (1498–1515), who fought a series of unsuccessful wars in Italy.

Louis XIII *n.* 1601–43, king of France (1610–43). His mother (Marie de Médicis) was regent until 1617; after 1624 he was influenced by his chief minister Richelieu.

Louis XIV *n.* known as *le roi soleil* (the Sun King). 1638–1715, king of France (1643–1715); son of Louis XIII and Anne of Austria. Effective ruler from 1661, he established an absolute monarchy. His attempt to establish French supremacy in Europe, waging almost continual wars from 1667 to 1714, ultimately failed. But his reign is regarded as a golden age of French literature and art.

Louis XV *n.* 1710–74, king of France (1715–74); great-grandson of Louis XIV. He engaged France in a series of wars, esp. the disastrous Seven Years' War (1756–63), which undermined the solvency and authority of the crown.

Louis XVI *n.* 1754–93, king of France (1774–92); grandson of Louis XV. He married Marie Antoinette in 1770 and they were guillotined during the French Revolution.

Louis XVII *n.* 1785–95, titular king of France (1793–95) during the Revolution, after the execution of his father Louis XVI; he died in prison.

Louis XVIII *n.* 1755–1824, king of France (1814–24); younger brother of Louis XVI. He became titular king after the death of Louis XVII (1795) and ascended the throne at the Bourbon restoration in 1814. He was forced to flee during the Hundred Days.

Louis (ˈluːɪs) *n.* Joe, real name *Joseph Louis Barrow*, nicknamed *the Brown Bomber.* 1914–81, U.S. boxer; world heavyweight champion (1937–49).

louis d'or (ˌluːɪ 'dɔː) *n., pl.* **louis d'or** (ˌluːɪz 'dɔː). **1.** a former French gold coin worth 20 francs. **2.** an old French coin minted in the reign of Louis XIII. ~Often shortened to **louis.** [C17: from F: golden louis, after Louis XIII]

Louisiana (luːˌiːzɪ'ænə) *n.* a state of the southern U.S., on the Gulf of Mexico: originally a French colony; bought by the U.S. in 1803 as part of the Louisiana Purchase; chiefly low-lying. Capital: Baton Rouge. Pop.: 4 481 000 (1985 est.). Area: 116 368 sq. km (44 930 sq. miles). Abbrevs.: **La.** or (with zip code) **LA**

Louis Napoleon *n.* the original name of **Napoleon III.**

Louis Philippe (*French* filip) *n.* known as the *Citizen King.* 1773–1850, king of the French (1830–48). His régime became excessively identified with the bourgeoisie and he was forced to abdicate by the revolution of 1848.

Louisville ('luːɪ,vɪl) *n.* a port in N Kentucky, on the Ohio River: site of the annual Kentucky Derby; university (1837). Pop.: 287 460 (1986 est.).

lounge (laʊndʒ) *vb.* **1.** (*intr.; often foll. by about or around*) to sit, lie, walk, or stand in a relaxed manner. **2.** to pass (time) lazily or idly. ~*n.* **3.** a communal room in a hotel, ship, etc., used for waiting or relaxing in. **4.** *Chiefly Brit.* a living room in a private house. **5.** Also called: **lounge bar, saloon bar.** *Brit.* a more expensive bar in a pub or hotel. **6.** a sofa or couch. **7.** the act or an instance of lounging. [C16: from ?]

lounger ('laʊndʒə) *n.* **1.** a comfortable couch or extending chair designed for someone to relax on. **2.** a loose comfortable leisure garment. **3.** a person who lounges.

lounge suit *n.* a man's suit of matching jacket and trousers worn for the normal business day.

loupe (luːp) *n.* a magnifying glass used by jewellers, horologists, etc. [C20: from F (formerly an imperfect precious stone), from OF, from ?]

lour *or* **lower** ('laʊə) *vb.* (*intr.*) **1.** (esp. of the sky, weather, etc.) to be overcast, dark, and menacing. **2.** to scowl or frown. ~*n.* **3.** a menacing scowl or appearance. [C13 *louren* to scowl] —'**louring** *or* '**lowering** *adj.*

Lourdes (*French* lurd) *n.* a town in SW France: a leading place of pilgrimage for Roman Catholics after a peasant girl, Bernadette Soubirous, had visions of the Virgin Mary in 1858. Pop.: 17 619 (1982).

Lourenço Marques (lə'rɛnsəʊ 'maːk, 'maːks; *Portuguese* lo'resu 'markɪʃ) *n.* the former name (until 1975) of **Maputo.**

lourie ('laʊrɪ) *n.* a type of African bird with bright plumage. [from Afrik.]

louse (laʊs) *n., pl.* **lice. 1.** a wingless bloodsucking insect, such as the head louse, body louse, and crab louse, all of which infest man. **2. biting** *or* **bird louse.** a wingless insect, such as the chicken louse: external parasites of birds and mammals, with biting mouthparts. **3.** any of various similar but unrelated insects. **4.** (*pl.* **louses**) *Sl.* an unpleasant or mean person. ~*vb.* (*tr.*) **5.** to remove lice from. **6.** (foll. by *up*) *Sl.* to ruin or spoil. [OE *lūs*]

lousewort ('laʊs,wɜːt) *n.* any of various N temperate plants having spikes of white, yellow, or mauve flowers.

lousy ('laʊzɪ) *adj.* **lousier, lousiest. 1.** *Sl.* very mean or unpleasant. **2.** *Sl.* inferior or bad. **3.** infested with lice. **4.** (foll. by *with*) *Sl.* provided with an excessive amount (of): *he's lousy with money.* —'**lousily** *adv.* — '**lousiness** *n.*

lout (laʊt) *n.* a crude or oafish person; boor. [C16: ? from OE *lūtan* to stoop] —'**loutish** *adj.*

Louth (laʊθ) *n.* a county of NE Ireland, in Leinster province on the Irish Sea: the smallest of the counties. County town: Dundalk. Pop.: 91 698 (1986). Area: 821 sq. km (317 sq. miles).

Louvain (*French* luvɛ̃) *n.* a town in central Belgium, in Brabant province: capital of the duchy of Brabant (11th–15th centuries) and centre of the cloth trade; university (1426). Pop.: 84 583 (1987 est.). Flemish name: **Leuven.**

louvre *or U.S.* **louver** ('luːvə) *n.* **1. a.** any of a set of horizontal parallel slats in a door or window, sloping outwards to throw off rain and admit air. **b.** Also called: **louvre boards.** the slats and frame supporting them. **2.** *Archit.* a turret that allows smoke to escape. [C14: from OF *lovier*, from ?] —'**louvred** *or U.S.* '**louvered** *adj.*

Louvre (*French* luvrə) *n.* the national museum and art gallery of France, in Paris: formerly a royal palace, begun in 1546; used for its present purpose since 1793.

lovable *or* **loveable** ('lʌvəbᵊl) *adj.* attracting or deserving affection. — ,**lova'bility,** ,**love'bility** *or* '**lovableness,** '**loveableness** *n.* —'**lovably** *or* '**loveably** *adv.*

lovage ('lʌvɪdʒ) *n.* a European umbelliferous plant with greenish-white flowers and aromatic fruits, which are used for flavouring food. [C14 *loveache,* from OF *luvesche,* from LL *levisticum,* from L *ligusticum,* lit.: Ligurian (plant)]

love (lʌv) *vb.* **1.** (*tr.*) to have a great attachment to and affection for. **2.** (*tr.*) to have passionate desire, longing, and feelings for. **3.** (*tr.*) to like or desire (to do something) very much. **4.** (*tr.*) to make love to. **5.** (*intr.*) to be in love. ~*n.* **6. a.** an intense emotion of affection, warmth, fondness, and regard towards a person or thing. **b.** (*as modifier*): *love story.* **7.** a deep feeling of sexual attraction and desire. **8.** wholehearted liking for or pleasure in something. **9.** *Christianity.* God's benevolent attitude towards man. **10.** Also: **my love.** a beloved person: used esp. as an endearment. **11.** *Brit. inf.* a term of address, not necessarily for a person regarded as likable. **12.** (in tennis, squash, etc.) a score of zero. **13. fall in love.** to become in love. **14. for love.** without payment. **15. for love or money.** by any means. **16. for the love of.** for the sake of. **17. in love.** in a state of strong emotional attachment and usually sexual attraction. **18. make love (to). a.** to have sexual intercourse (with). **b.** *Now arch.* to court. [OE *lufu*]

love affair *n.* a romantic or sexual relationship, esp. temporary, between two people.

love apple *n.* an archaic name for **tomato.**

lovebird ('lʌv,bɜːd) *n.* any of several small African parrots often kept as cagebirds.

lovebite ('lʌv,baɪt) *n.* a temporary red mark left on a person's skin by a partner's biting or sucking it during love-making.

love child *n.* *Euphemistic.* an illegitimate child; bastard.

love-in-a-mist *n.* an erect S European plant, cultivated as a garden plant, having finely cut leaves and white or pale blue flowers.

Lovelace ('lʌv,leɪs) *n.* **1. Ada Augusta King,** Countess of Lovelace. 1815–52, English mathematician and personal assistant to Charles Babbage: daughter of Lord Byron. She wrote the first computer program. **2. Richard.** 1618–58, English Cavalier poet, noted for *To Althea from Prison* (1642) and *Lucasta* (1649).

loveless ('lʌvlɪs) *adj.* **1.** without love: *a loveless marriage.* **2.** receiving or giving no love. —'**lovelessly** *adv.* —'**lovelessness** *n.*

love-lies-bleeding *n.* any of several plants having drooping spikes of small red flowers.

Lovell ('lʌvəl) *n.* Sir **Bernard.** born 1913, English radio astronomer; founder (1951) and director of Jodrell Bank.

lovelock ('lʌv,lɒk) *n.* a long lock of hair worn on the forehead.

lovelorn ('lʌv,lɔːn) *adj.* miserable because of unrequited love or unhappiness in love.

lovely ('lʌvlɪ) *adj.* **-lier, -liest. 1.** very attractive or beautiful. **2.** highly pleasing or enjoyable: *a lovely time.* **3.** inspiring love; lovable. ~*n., pl.* **-lies. 4.** *Sl.* a lovely woman. —'**loveliness** *n.*

lovemaking ('lʌv,meɪkɪŋ) *n.* **1.** sexual play and activity between lovers, esp. including sexual intercourse. **2.** an archaic word for **courtship.**

love potion *n.* any drink supposed to arouse sexual love in the one who drinks it.

lover ('lʌvə) *n.* **1.** a person, now esp. a man, who has an extramarital or premarital sexual relationship with another person. **2.** (*often pl.*) either of the two people involved in a love affair. **3. a.** someone who loves a specified person or thing: *a lover of music.* **b.** (*in combination*): *a music-lover; a cat-lover.*

love seat *n.* a small upholstered sofa for two people.

lovesick ('lʌv,sɪk) *adj.* pining or languishing because of love. —'**love,sickness** *n.*

lovey-dovey (,lʌvɪ'dʌvɪ) *adj.* making an excessive or ostentatious display of affection.

loving ('lʌvɪŋ) *adj.* feeling or showing love and affection. —'**lovingly** *adv.* —'**lovingness** *n.*

loving cup *n.* **1.** a large vessel, usually two-handled, out of which people drink in turn at a banquet. **2.** a similar cup awarded to the winner of a competition.

low[1] (ləʊ) *adj.* **1.** having a relatively small distance from base to top; not tall or high: *a low hill; a low building.* **2. a.** situated at a relatively short distance above the ground, sea level, the horizon, or other reference position: *low cloud.* **b.** (*in combination*): *low-lying.* **3.** of less than usual height, depth, or degree: *low temperature.* **4. a.** (of numbers) small. **b.** (of measurements) expressed in small numbers. **5. a.** involving or containing a relatively small amount of something: *a low supply.* **b.** (*in combination*): *low-pressure.* **6. a.** having little value or quality. **b.** (*in combination*): *low-grade.* **7.** coarse or vulgar: *a low conversation.* **8. a.** inferior in culture or status. **b.** (*in combination*): *low-class.* **9.** in a physically or mentally depressed or weakened state. **10.** low-necked: *a low dress.* **11.** with a hushed tone; quiet or soft: *a low whisper.* **12.** of relatively small price or monetary value:

low cost. **13.** *Music.* relating to or characterized by a relatively low pitch. **14.** (of latitudes) situated not far north or south of the equator. **15.** having little or no money. **16.** abject or servile. **17.** unfavourable: *a low opinion.* **18.** not advanced in evolution: *a low form of plant life.* **19.** deep: *a low bow.* **20.** *Phonetics.* of, relating to, or denoting a vowel whose articulation is produced by moving the back of the tongue away from the soft palate, such as for the *a* in English *father.* **21.** (of a gear) providing a relatively low forward speed for a given engine speed. **22.** (*usually cap.*) of or relating to the Low Church. ~*adv.* **23.** in a low position, level, degree, intensity, etc.: *to bring someone low.* **24.** at a low pitch; deep: *to sing low.* **25.** at a low price; cheaply: *to buy low.* **26.** **lay low. a.** to cause to fall by a blow. **b.** to overcome, defeat, or destroy. **27.** **lie low. a.** to keep or be concealed or quiet. **b.** to wait for a favourable opportunity. ~*n.* **28.** a low position, level, or degree: *an all-time low.* **29.** an area of relatively low atmospheric pressure, esp. a depression. [C12 *lāh,* from ON *lágr*] — **'lowness** *n.*

low[2] (ləʊ) *n. also* **lowing. 1.** the sound uttered by cattle; moo. ~*vb.* **2.** to make or express by a low or moo. [OE *hlōwan*]

Low (ləʊ) *n.* Sir **David.** 1891–1963, British political cartoonist, born in New Zealand: created Colonel Blimp. See **blimp**[2].

lowan ('ləʊən) *n.* another name for **mallee fowl.** [from Abor.]

Low Archipelago *n.* another name for the **Tuamotu Archipelago.**

lowborn (,ləʊ'bɔːn) *or* **lowbred** (,ləʊ'brɛd) *adj. Now rare.* of ignoble or common parentage.

lowbrow ('ləʊ,braʊ) *Disparaging.* ~*n.* **1.** a person who has uncultivated or nonintellectual tastes. ~*adj. also* **low-browed. 2.** of or characteristic of such a person.

Low Church *n.* **1.** the school of thought in the Church of England stressing evangelical beliefs and practices. ~*adj.* **Low-Church. 2.** of or relating to this school.

low comedy *n.* comedy characterized by slapstick and physical action.

Low Countries *pl. n.* the lowland region of W Europe, on the North Sea: consists of Belgium, Luxembourg, and the Netherlands.

low-down *Inf.* ~*adj.* **1.** mean, underhand, or despicable. ~*n.* **lowdown. 2. the.** information.

Löwe (*German* 'lɔːvə) *n.* See (Karl) **Loewe.**

Lowell ('ləʊəl) *n.* **1. Amy (Lawrence).** 1874–1925, U.S. imagist poet and critic. **2. James Russell.** 1819–91, U.S. poet, essayist, and diplomat, noted for his series of poems in Yankee dialect, *Biglow Papers* (1848; 1867). **3. Robert.** 1917–77, U.S. poet. His volumes of verse include *Lord Weary's Castle* (1946), *Life Studies* (1959), and *For the Union Dead* (1964). He also wrote a trilogy of verse dramas, *The Old Glory* (1968), and a book of free translations of European poems, *Imitations* (1961).

lower[1] ('ləʊə) *adj.* **1.** being below one or more other things: *the lower shelf.* **2.** reduced in amount or value: *a lower price.* **3.** *Maths.* (of a limit or bound) less than or equal to one or more numbers or variables. **4.** (sometimes cap.) *Geol.* denoting the early part of a period, formation, etc.: *Lower Silurian.* ~*vb.* **5.** (*tr.*) to cause to become lower or on a lower level; bring, put, or cause to move down. **6.** (*tr.*) to reduce or bring down in estimation, dignity, value, etc.: *to lower oneself.* **7.** to reduce or be reduced: *to lower one's confidence.* **8.** (*tr.*) to make quieter: *to lower the radio.* **9.** (*tr.*) to reduce the pitch of. **10.** (*intr.*) to diminish or become less. [C12 (comp. of LOW[1]); C17 (vb.)]

lower[2] ('ləʊə) *vb.* a variant of **lour.**

Lower Austria *n.* a province of NE Austria: the largest Austrian province, containing most of the Vienna basin. Capital: Krems. Pop.: 1 439 137 (1981). Area: 19 170 sq. km (7476 sq. miles). German name: **Niederösterreich.**

Lower Burma *n.* the coastal region of Burma.

Lower California *n.* a mountainous peninsula of NW Mexico, between the Pacific and the Gulf of California: administratively divided into the states of Baja California and Baja California Sur. Spanish name: **Baja California.**

Lower Canada *n.* (from 1791 to 1841) the official name of the S region of the present-day province of Quebec.

lower case *n.* **1.** the bottom half of a compositor's type case, in which the small letters are kept. ~*adj.* **lower-**

case. 2. of or relating to small letters. ~*vb.* **lower-case. 3.** (*tr.*) to print with lower-case letters.

lower class *n.* **1.** the social stratum having the lowest position in the social hierarchy. ~*adj.* **lower-class. 2.** of or relating to the lower class. **3.** inferior or vulgar.

lower deck *n.* **1.** the deck of a ship situated immediately above the hold. **2.** *Inf.* the petty officers and seamen of a ship collectively.

Lower Egypt *n.* one of the two main administrative districts of Egypt: consists of the Nile Delta.

lower house *n.* one of the houses of a bicameral legislature: usually the larger and more representative. Also called: **lower chamber.**

Lower Hutt (hʌt) *n.* an industrial town in New Zealand on the S coast of North Island. Pop.: 62 900 (1983).

Lower Lakes *pl. n. Chiefly Canadian.* Lakes Erie and Ontario.

lowermost ('ləʊə,məʊst) *adj.* lowest.

lower regions *pl. n.* (usually preceded by *the*) hell.

Lower Saxony *n.* a state of N West Germany, on the North Sea and including the E Frisian Islands; a leading European producer of petroleum. Capital: Hanover. Pop.: 7 149 300 (1986). Area: 47 408 sq. km (18 489 sq. miles). German name: **Niedersachsen.**

lower world *n.* **1.** the earth as opposed to heaven. **2.** another name for **hell.**

lowest common denominator *n.* the smallest integer or polynomial that is exactly divisible by each denominator of a set of fractions. Abbrevs.: **lcd, LCD.** Also called: **least common denominator.**

lowest common multiple *n.* the smallest number or quantity that is exactly divisible by each member of a set of numbers or quantities. Abbrevs.: **lcm, LCM.** Also called: **least common multiple.**

Lowestoft ('ləʊstɒft) *n.* a fishing port and resort in E England, in NE Suffolk on the North Sea. Pop.: 57 000 (1985 est.).

low frequency *n.* a radio-frequency band or a frequency lying between 300 and 30 kilohertz.

Low German *n.* a language of N Germany, spoken esp. in rural areas: more closely related to Dutch than to standard High German. Abbrev.: **LG.** Also called: **Platt-deutsch.**

low-key *or* **low-keyed** *adj.* **1.** having a low intensity or tone. **2.** restrained or subdued.

lowland ('ləʊlənd) *n.* **1.** relatively low ground. **2.** (*often pl.*) a low generally flat region. ~*adj.* **3.** of or relating to a lowland or lowlands. —'**lowlander** *n.*

Lowland ('ləʊlənd) *adj.* of or relating to the Lowlands of Scotland or the dialects of English spoken there.

Lowlands ('ləʊləndz) *pl. n.* **the.** a low, generally flat region of S central Scotland. —'**Lowlander** *n.*

Low Latin *n.* any form of Latin other than the classical, such as Medieval Latin.

low-level language *n.* a computer programming language that is closer to machine language than to human language.

lowlife ('ləʊ,laɪf) *n., pl.* **-lifes.** *Sl.* a member or members of the criminal underworld.

low-loader *n.* a road or rail vehicle with a low platform for ease of access.

lowly ('ləʊlɪ) *adj.* **-lier, -liest. 1.** humble or low in position, rank, status, etc. **2.** full of humility; meek. **3.** simple, unpretentious, or plain. ~*adv.* **4.** in a low or lowly manner. — '**lowliness** *n.*

Low Mass *n.* a Mass that has a simplified ceremonial form and is spoken rather than sung.

low-minded *adj.* having a vulgar or crude mind and character. — ,**low-'mindedly** *adv.* — ,**low-'mindedness** *n.*

low-pass filter *n. Electronics.* a filter that transmits all frequencies below a specified value, attenuating frequencies above this value.

low-pitched *adj.* **1.** pitched low in tone. **2.** (of a roof) having sides with a shallow slope.

low-pressure *adj.* **1.** having, using, or involving a pressure below normal: *a low-pressure gas.* **2.** relaxed or calm.

low profile *n.* **1.** a position or attitude characterized by a deliberate avoidance of prominence or publicity. ~*adj.* **low-profile. 2.** (of a tyre) wide in relation to its height.

low-rise *adj.* **1.** of or relating to a building having only a few storeys. ~*n.* **2.** such a building.

lowry *or* **lowrie** ('lauri) *n.* variant spellings of **lory.**

Lowry ('lauri) *n.* **L(awrence) S(tephen).** 1887–1976, English painter, noted for his bleak northern industrial scenes, often containing primitive or stylized figures.

low-spirited *adj.* depressed or dejected. —,**low-'spiritedly** *adv.* —,**low-'spiritedness** *n.*

low tech *n.* **1.** short for **low technology. 2.** a style of interior design using items associated with low technology. ~*adj.* **low-tech. 3.** of or using low technology. **4.** of or in the interior design style. ~Cf. **high tech.**

low technology *n.* simple unsophisticated technology that is limited to the production of basic necessities.

low-tension *adj.* subjected to, carrying, or operating at a low voltage. Abbrev.: **LT.**

low tide *n.* **1.** the tide when it is at its lowest level or the time at which it reaches this. **2.** a lowest point.

Lowveld ('lou,fɛlt, -,vɛlt) *n.* **the.** another name for **Bushveld.**

low water *n.* **1.** another name for **low tide. 2.** the state of any stretch of water at its lowest level.

low-water mark *n.* **1.** the level reached at low tide. **2.** the lowest point or level; nadir.

lox[1] (lɒks) *n.* a kind of smoked salmon. [C19: from Yiddish *laks*, from MHG *lahs* salmon]

lox[2] (lɒks) *n.* short for **liquid oxygen,** esp. when used as an oxidizer for rocket fuels.

loyal ('lɔɪəl) *adj.* **1.** showing allegiance. **2.** faithful to one's country, government, etc. **3.** of or expressing loyalty. [C16: from OF *loial, leial*, from L *lēgālis* LEGAL] —'**loyally** *adv.*

loyalist ('lɔɪəlɪst) *n.* a patriotic supporter of his sovereign or government. —'**loyalism** *n.*

Loyalist ('lɔɪəlɪst) *n.* **1.** (in Northern Ireland) any of the Protestants wishing to retain Ulster's link with Britain. **2.** (in North America) an American colonist who supported Britain during the War of American Independence. **3.** (in Canada) short for **United Empire Loyalist. 4.** (during the Spanish Civil War) a supporter of the republican government.

loyalty ('lɔɪəltɪ) *n., pl.* **-ties. 1.** the state or quality of being loyal. **2.** (*often pl.*) allegiance.

Loyang ('ləu'jæŋ) *n.* a variant transliteration of the Chinese name for **Luoyang.**

Loyola (lɔɪ'əulə) *n.* See (Saint) **Ignatius Loyola.**

lozenge ('lɒzɪndʒ) *n.* **1.** *Med.* a medicated tablet held in the mouth until it has dissolved. **2.** *Geom.* another name for **rhombus. 3.** *Heraldry.* a diamond-shaped charge. [C14: from OF *losange* of Gaulish origin] —'**lozenged** *or* '**lozengy** *adj.*

Lozère (*French* lɔzɛr) *n.* a department of S central France, in Languedoc-Roussillon region. Capital: Mende. Pop.: 74 294 (1982). Area: 5180 sq. km (2020 sq. miles).

LP[1] *n.* **a.** Also called: **long player.** a long-playing gramophone record, usually 12 inches (30 cm) in diameter, designed to rotate at 33⅓ revolutions per minute. **b.** (*as modifier*): *an LP sleeve.*

LP[2] *abbrev. for:* **1.** (in Britain) Lord Provost. **2.** Also: **lp.** low pressure.

L/P *Printing. abbrev. for* letterpress.

LPG *or* **LP gas** *abbrev. for* liquefied petroleum gas.

L-plate *n. Brit.* a white rectangle with a red "L" sign fixed to the back and front of a motor vehicle to show that the driver has not passed the driving test.

Lr *the chemical symbol for* lawrencium.

LSD *n.* lysergic acid diethylamide; a crystalline compound prepared from lysergic acid, used in experimental medicine and taken illegally as a hallucinogenic drug. Informal name: **acid.**

L.S.D., £.s.d., *or* **l.s.d.** (in Britain, esp. formerly) *abbrev. for* librae, solidi, denarii. [L: pounds, shillings, pence]

LSE *abbrev. for* London School of Economics.

LSO *abbrev. for* London Symphony Orchestra.

Lt *abbrev. for* Lieutenant.

Ltd *or* **ltd** *abbrev. for* limited (liability). U.S. equivalent: **Inc.**

Lu *the chemical symbol for* lutetium.

Lualaba (,luːəˈlɑːbə) *n.* a river in SE Zaïre, rising in Shaba province and flowing north as the W headstream of the River Congo. Length: about 1800 km (1100 miles).

Luanda (luˈændə) *or* **Loanda** *n.* the capital of Angola, a port in the west, on the Atlantic: founded in 1576, it became a centre of the slave trade to Brazil in the 17th and 18th centuries; oil refining. Pop.: 1 134 000 (1987 est.). Official name: **São Paulo de Loanda.**

Luang Prabang (luˈæŋ prɑːˈbæŋ) *n.* a market town in N Laos, on the Mekong River: residence of the monarch of Laos (1946–75). Pop.: 44 244 (1984 est.).

luau (luːˈɑːu, ˈluːaʊ) *n.* a feast of Hawaiian food. [from Hawaiian *lu'au*]

lubber ('lʌbə) *n.* **1.** a big, awkward, or stupid person. **2.** short for **landlubber.** [C14 *lobre*, prob. from ON] —'**lubberly** *adj., adv.* —'**lubberliness** *n.*

lubber line *n.* a mark on a ship's compass that designates the fore-and-aft axis of the vessel. Also called: **lubber's line.**

Lubbock ('lʌbək) *n.* a city in NW Texas: cotton market. Pop.: 186 400 (1986 est.).

Lübeck (*German* 'lyːbɛk) *n.* a port in N West Germany, in Schleswig-Holstein: the leading member of the Hanseatic League, and a major European commercial centre until the 15th century; West Germany's chief Baltic port, with large shipyards and many industries. Pop.: 209 800 (1986).

Lublin (*Polish* 'lublin) *n.* an industrial city in E Poland: provisional seat of the government in 1918 and 1944. Pop.: 324 000 (1985). Russian name: **Lyublin.**

lubra ('luːbrə) *n. Austral.* an Aboriginal woman. [C19: from Abor.]

lubricant ('luːbrɪkənt) *n.* **1.** a lubricating substance, such as oil. ~*adj.* **2.** serving to lubricate. [C19: from L *lūbricāns*, present participle of *lūbricāre*]

lubricate ('luːbrɪˌkeɪt) *vb.* **1.** (*tr.*) to cover or treat with an oily substance so as to lessen friction. **2.** (*tr.*) to make greasy, slippery, or smooth. **3.** (*intr.*) to act as a lubricant. [C17: from L *lūbricāre*, from *lūbricus* slippery] —,**lubri'cation** *n.* —'**lubri,cative** *adj.* —'**lubri,cator** *n.*

lubricity (luːˈbrɪsɪtɪ) *n.* **1.** *Formal or literary.* lewdness or salaciousness. **2.** *Rare.* smoothness or slipperiness. [C15 (lewdness), C17 (slipperiness): from OF *lubricité*, from Med. L *lubricitās*, from L, from *lūbricus* slippery] —**lubricious** (luːˈbrɪʃəs) *or* **lubricous** ('luːbrɪkəs) *adj.*

Lubumbashi (,luːbumˈbæʃɪ) *n.* a city in S Zaïre, capital of Shaba province: founded in 1910 as a copper-mining centre; university (1955). Pop.: 543 268 (1984). Former name (until 1966): **Elisabethville.**

Lucan ('luːkən) *n.* Latin name *Marcus Annaeus Lucanus.* 39–65 A.D., Roman poet. His epic poem *Pharsalia* describes the civil war between Caesar and Pompey.

Lucania (luːˈkeɪnɪə) *n.* the Latin name for **Basilicata.**

Lucas van Leyden ('luːkəs væn 'laɪdən) *n.* ?1494–1533, Dutch painter and engraver.

Lucca (*Italian* 'lukka) *n.* a city in NW Italy, in Tuscany: centre of a rich agricultural region, noted for the production of olive oil. Pop.: 90 686 (1983 est.). Ancient name: **Luca** ('luːkə).

luce (luːs) *n.* another name for the **pike** (the fish). [C14: from OF *lus*, from LL *lūcius* pike]

lucent ('luːsᵊnt) *adj.* brilliant, shining, or translucent. [C16: from L *lūcēns*, present participle of *lūcēre* to shine] —'**lucency** *n.* —'**lucently** *adv.*

lucerne (luːˈsɜːn) *n. Brit.* another name for **alfalfa.**

Lucerne (luːˈsɜːn; *French* lysɛrn) *n.* **1.** a canton in central Switzerland, northwest of Lake Lucerne: joined the Swiss Confederacy in 1332. Pop.: 296 159 (1980). Area: 1494 sq. km (577 sq. miles). **2.** a city in central Switzerland, capital of Lucerne canton, on Lake Lucerne: tourist centre. Pop.: 63 278 (1980). **3. Lake.** a lake in central Switzerland: fed and drained chiefly by the River Reuss. Area: 115 sq. km (44 sq. miles). German name: **Vierwaldstättersee.** ~German name (for senses 1 and 2): **Luzern.**

Lucian ('luːsɪən) *n.* 2nd century A.D., Greek writer, noted esp. for his satirical *Dialogues of the Gods* and *Dialogues of the Dead.*

lucid ('luːsɪd) *adj.* **1.** readily understood; clear. **2.** shining or glowing. **3.** of or relating to a period of normality between periods of insane behaviour. [C16: from L *lūcidus* full of light, from *lūx* light] —**lu'cidity** *or* '**lucidness** *n.* —'**lucidly** *adv.*

lucifer ('luːsɪfə) *n.* a friction match: originally a trade name.

Lucifer ('luːsɪfə) *n.* **1.** the leader of the rebellion of the angels; Satan. **2.** the planet Venus when it rises as the morning star. [OE, from L *Lūcifer* light-bearer, from *lūx* light + *ferre* to bear]

Lucilius (luːˈsɪlɪəs) *n.* **Gaius** ('gaɪəs). ?180–102 B.C., Roman satirist, regarded as the originator of poetical satire.

Lucina (luːˈsaɪnə) *n. Roman myth.* a title or name given to Juno as goddess of childbirth. [C14: from L *lūcīnus* bringing to the light, from *lūx* light]

luck (lʌk) *n.* **1.** events that are beyond control and seem subject to chance; fortune. **2.** success or good fortune. **3.** something considered to bring good luck. **4. down on one's luck.** having little or no good luck to the point of suffering hardships. **5. no such luck.** *Inf.* unfortunately not. **6. try one's luck.** to attempt something that is uncertain. [C15: from MDu. *luc*]

luckless (ˈlʌklɪs) *adj.* having no luck; unlucky. —**'lucklessly** *adv.* —**'lucklessness** *n.*

Lucknow (ˈlʌknaʊ) *n.* a city in N India, capital of Uttar Pradesh: capital of Oudh (1775–1856); the British residency was besieged (1857) during the Indian Mutiny. Pop.: 895 947 (1981).

lucky (ˈlʌkɪ) *adj.* **luckier, luckiest. 1.** having or bringing good fortune. **2.** happening by chance, esp. as desired. —**'luckily** *adv.* —**'luckiness** *n.*

lucky dip *n. Brit.* **1.** a box filled with sawdust containing small prizes for which children search. **2.** *Inf.* an undertaking of uncertain outcome.

lucrative (ˈluːkrətɪv) *adj.* producing a profit; profitable. [C15: from OF *lucratif*; see LUCRE] —**'lucratively** *adv.* —**'lucrativeness** *n.*

lucre (ˈluːkə) *n. Usually facetious.* money or wealth (esp. in **filthy lucre**). [C14: from L *lucrum* gain]

Lucretia (luːˈkriːʃɪə) *n.* (in Roman legend) a Roman woman who killed herself after being raped by a son of Tarquin the Proud.

Lucretius (luːˈkriːʃɪəs) *n.* full name *Titus Lucretius Carus.* ?96–55 B.C., Roman poet and philosopher. In his didactic poem *De rerum natura*, he expounds Epicurus' atomist theory of the universe. —**Lu'cretian** *adj.*

lucubrate (ˈluːkjʊˌbreɪt) *vb.* (*intr.*) to write or study, esp. at night. [C17: from L *lūcubrāre* to work by lamplight] —**'lucu,brator** *n.*

lucubration (ˌluːkjʊˈbreɪʃən) *n.* **1.** laborious study, esp. at night. **2.** (*often pl.*) a solemn literary work.

Lucullus (luːˈkʌləs) *n.* **Lucius Licinius** (ˈluːsɪəs lɪˈsɪnɪəs). ?110–56 B.C., Roman general and consul, famous for his luxurious banquets. He fought Mithradates VI (74–66). —**Lu'cullan, Lucullean** (ˌluːkʌˈliːən), *or* ˌLucul'lian *adj.*

Lucy (ˈluːsɪ) *n.* **Saint.** died ?303 A.D., a virgin martyred by Diocletian in Syracuse. Feast day: Dec 13.

lud (lʌd) *n. Brit.* lord (in **my lud, m'lud**): used when addressing a judge in court.

Lüda (ˈluːˈdɑː) *or* **Lü-ta** *n.* a port in NE China, in S Liaoning province, adjoining Lü-shun at the S end of the Liaodong peninsula: the chief northern port. Pop.: 4 500 000 (1983 est.). Former name: **Dairen.**

Luddite (ˈlʌdaɪt) *n. English history.* **1.** any of the textile workers opposed to mechanization, believing that its use led to unemployment, who organized machine-breaking between 1811 and 1816. **2.** any opponent of industrial change or innovation. ~*adj.* **3.** of or relating to the Luddites. [C19: alleged to be after Ned *Ludd*, an 18th-century Leicestershire workman, who destroyed industrial machinery]

Ludendorff (German ˈluːdəndɔrf) *n.* **Erich Friedrich Wilhelm von** (ˈeːrɪç ˈfriːdrɪç ˈvɪlhɛlm fɔn). 1865–1937, German general, Hindenburg's aide in World War I.

Lüdenscheid (German ˈlyːdənʃaɪt) *n.* a city in NW West Germany, in North Rhine-Westphalia: manufacturing centre for aluminium and plastics. Pop.: 73 292 (1986 est.).

Lüderitz (German ˈlyːdərɪts) *n.* a port in Namibia (South West Africa): diamond-mining centre. Pop.: 6460 (1978 est.).

Ludhiana (ˌlʊdɪˈɑːnə) *n.* a city in N India, in the central Punjab: Punjab Agricultural University (1962). Pop.: 606 250 (1981).

ludicrous (ˈluːdɪkrəs) *adj.* absurd or incongruous to the point of provoking laughter. [C17: from L *lūdicrus* done in sport, from *lūdus* game] —**'ludicrously** *adv.* —**'ludicrousness** *n.*

Ludlow (ˈlʌdləʊ) *n.* a market town in W central England, in Shropshire: castle (11th–16th century). Pop.: 8130 (1983 est.).

ludo (ˈluːdəʊ) *n. Brit.* a simple board game in which players advance counters by throwing dice. [C19: from L: I play]

Ludwigsburg (German ˈluːtvɪçsbʊrk) *n.* a city in SW West Germany, in Baden-Württemberg northeast of Stuttgart: expanded in the 18th century around the palace of the dukes of Württemberg. Pop.: 79 676 (1983 est.).

Ludwigshafen (German ˈluːtvɪçshaːfən) *n.* a city in SW West Germany, in the Rhineland-Palatinate, on the Rhine: chemical industry. Pop.: 153 000 (1986).

luff (lʌf) *n. Naut.* the leading edge of a fore-and-aft sail. ~*vb.* **2.** *Naut.* to head (a sailing vessel) into the wind so that her sails flap. **3.** (*intr.*) *Naut.* (of a sail) to flap when the wind is blowing equally on both sides. **4.** to move the jib (of a crane) in order to shift a load. [C13 (in the sense: steering gear): from OF *lof*, ?from MDu. *loef* peg of a tiller]

lug[1] (lʌg) *vb.* **lugging, lugged. 1.** to carry or drag (something heavy) with great effort. **2.** (*tr.*) to introduce (an irrelevant topic) into a conversation or discussion. ~*n.* **3.** the act or an instance of lugging. [C14: prob. from ON]

lug[2] (lʌg) *n.* **1.** a projecting piece by which something is connected, supported, or lifted. **2.** a box or basket for vegetables or fruit. **3.** *Inf. or Scot.* another word for **ear**[1]. **4.** *Sl.* a man, esp. a stupid or awkward one. [C15 (Scots dialect) *lugge* ear]

lug[3] (lʌg) *n. Naut.* short for **lugsail.**

Lugansk (*Russian* luˈgansk) *n.* the former name (until 1935) of **Voroshilovgrad.**

luge (luːʒ) *n.* **1.** a light one-man toboggan. ~*vb.* **2.** (*intr.*) to ride or race on a luge. [C20: from F]

Luger (ˈluːgə) *n. Trademark.* a German 9 mm calibre automatic pistol.

luggage (ˈlʌgɪdʒ) *n.* suitcases, trunks, etc. [C16: ? from LUG[1], infl. in form by BAGGAGE]

luggage van *n. Brit.* a railway carriage used to transport passengers' luggage, bicycles, etc.

lugger (ˈlʌgə) *n. Naut.* a small working boat rigged with a lugsail. [C18: from LUGSAIL]

Lugo (*Spanish* ˈluɣo) *n.* a city in NW Spain: Roman walls; Romanesque cathedral. Pop.: 72 574 (1981). Latin name: **Lucus Augusti** (ˈluːkəs ɔːˈgʌstaɪ, ɔːˈgaːstiː).

lugsail (ˈlʌgseɪl) *n. Naut.* a four-sided sail bent and hoisted on a yard. [C17: ?from ME (now dialect) *lugge* pole, or from *lugge* ear]

lug screw *n.* a small screw without a head.

lugubrious (lʊˈguːbrɪəs) *adj.* excessively mournful; doleful. [C17: from L *lūgubris* mournful, from *lūgēre* to grieve] —**lu'gubriously** *adv.* —**lu'gubriousness** *n.*

lugworm (ˈlʌgˌwɜːm) *n.* a worm living in burrows on sandy shores and having tufted gills: much used as bait. Sometimes shortened to **lug.**

Luichow Peninsula (ˈluːˈtʃaʊ) *n.* a variant transliteration of the Chinese name for **Leizhou Peninsula.**

Luik (lœik) *n.* the Flemish name for **Liège.**

Lukács (ˈluːkætʃ) *n.* **Georg** (ˈgeɪɔːk), original name *György.* 1885–1971, Hungarian Marxist philosopher and literary critic, whose works include *History and Class Consciousness* (1923), *Studies in European Realism* (1946), and *The Historical Novel* (1955).

Luke (luːk) *n. New Testament.* **1.** the Evangelist, a fellow worker of Paul and a physician (Colossians 4:14). **2.** the third Gospel, traditionally ascribed to Luke. Related adj.: **Lucan.**

lukewarm (ˌluːkˈwɔːm) *adj.* **1.** (esp. of water) moderately warm; tepid. **2.** having or expressing little enthusiasm or conviction. [C14 *luke* prob. from OE *hlēow* warm] —**ˌluke'warmly** *adv.* —**ˌluke'warmness** *n.*

Luleå (*Swedish* ˈluːləɔ) *n.* a port in N Sweden, on the Gulf of Bothnia: industrial and shipbuilding centre; icebound in winter. Pop.: 66 526 (1986).

lull (lʌl) *vb.* (*tr.*) **1.** to soothe (a person or animal) by soft sounds or motions (esp. in **lull to sleep**). **2.** to calm (someone or someone's fears, suspicions, etc.), esp. by deception. ~*n.* **3.** a short period of calm or diminished activity. [C14: ? imit. of crooning sounds; rel. to MLow G *lollen* to soothe, MDu. *lollen* to talk drowsily, mumble]

lullaby (ˈlʌləˌbaɪ) *n., pl.* **-bies. 1.** a quiet song to lull a child to sleep. ~*vb.* **-bying, -bied. 2.** (*tr.*) to quiet or soothe as with a lullaby. [C16: ? a blend of LULL + GOODBYE]

Lully *n.* **1.** (*French* lyli). **Jean Baptiste** (ʒɑ̃ batist), Italian name *Giovanni Battista Lulli.* 1632–87, French composer, born in Italy; founder of French opera. With Philippe Quinault as librettist, he wrote operas such as *Alceste* (1674) and *Armide* (1686); as superintendent of music at the court of Louis XIV, he wrote incidental music to comedies by Molière. **2.** ('lʌlɪ). Also: **Lull** (*Spanish* lul). **Raymond** *or* **Ramón** (ra'mɔn). ?1235–1315, Spanish philosopher, mystic, and missionary. His chief works are *Ars generalis sive magna* and the Utopian novel *Bla-querna.*

Luluabourg (lu:'lu:ə,buə) *n.* the former name (until 1966) of **Kananga.**

lumbago (lʌm'beɪgəʊ) *n.* pain in the lower back; back-ache. [C17: from LL, from L *lumbus* loin]

lumbar ('lʌmbə) *adj.* of, near, or relating to the part of the body between the lowest ribs and the hipbones. [C17: from NL *lumbāris*, from L *lumbus* loin]

lumbar puncture *n. Med.* insertion of a hollow needle into the lower spinal cord to withdraw cerebrospinal fluid, introduce drugs, etc.

lumber[1] ('lʌmbə) *n.* **1.** *Chiefly U.S. & Canad.* **a.** logs; sawn timber. **b.** (*as modifier*): *the lumber trade.* **2.** *Brit.* **a.** useless household articles that are stored away. **b.** (*as modifier*): *lumber room.* ~*vb.* **3.** (*tr.*) to pile together in a disorderly manner. **4.** (*tr.*) to fill up or encumber with useless household articles. **5.** *Chiefly U.S. & Canad.* to convert (the trees) of (a forest) into marketable timber. **6.** (*tr.*) *Brit. inf.* to burden with something unpleasant, tedious, etc. [C17: ?from a n. use of LUMBER[2]] —'**lum-berer** *n.* —'**lumbering** *n.*

lumber[2] ('lʌmbə) *vb.* (*intr.*) **1.** to move or proceed in an awkward heavy manner. **2.** an obsolete word for **rum-ble.** [C14 *lomeren*] —'**lumbering** *adj.*

lumberjack ('lʌmbə,dʒæk) *n.* (esp. in North America) a person whose work involves felling trees, transporting the timber, etc. [C19: from LUMBER[1] + JACK[1] (man)]

lumberjacket ('lʌmbə,dʒækɪt) *n.* a boldly coloured, usu-ally checked jacket in warm cloth.

lumberyard ('lʌmbə,jɑːd) *n.* the U.S. and Canad word for **timberyard.**

lumen ('lu:mɪn) *n., pl.* **-mens** *or* **-mina** (-mɪnə). **1.** the derived SI unit of luminous flux; the flux emitted in a solid angle of 1 steradian by a point source having a uniform intensity of 1 candela. Symbol: lm **2.** *Anat.* a passage, duct, or cavity in a tubular organ. **3.** a cavity within a plant cell. [C19: NL, from L: light, aperture] —'**luminal** *adj.*

Lumière (*French* lymjɛr) *n.* **Auguste Marie Louis Nico-las** (ogyst mari lwi nikɔla). 1862–1954, and his brother, **Louis Jean** (lwi ʒɑ̃), 1864–1948, French chemists and cinema pioneers, who invented a cinematograph and a process of colour photography.

luminance ('lu:mɪnəns) *n.* **1.** a state or quality of radiat-ing or reflecting light. **2.** a measure (in candelas per square metre) of the brightness of a point on a surface that is radiating or reflecting light. Symbol: *L* [C19: from L *lūmen* light]

luminary ('lu:mɪnərɪ) *n., pl.* **-naries. 1.** a person who en-lightens or influences others. **2.** a famous person. **3.** *Lit-erary.* something, such as the sun or moon, that gives off light. [C15: via OF, from L *lūmināre* lamp, from *lūmen* light]

luminesce (,lu:mɪ'nɛs) *vb.* (*intr.*) to exhibit lumines-cence. [back formation from LUMINESCENT]

luminescence (,lu:mɪ'nɛsəns) *n. Physics.* the emission of light at low temperatures by any process other than in-candescence. [C19: from L *lūmen* light] —,lumi'**nescent** *adj.*

luminous ('lu:mɪnəs) *adj.* **1.** radiating or reflecting light; shining; glowing: *luminous colours.* **2.** (*not in technical use*) exhibiting luminescence: *luminous paint.* **3.** full of light; well-lit. **4.** (of a physical quantity in photometry) evaluated according to the visual sensation produced in an observer rather than by absolute energy measure-ments: *luminous intensity.* **5.** easily understood; lucid; clear. **6.** enlightening or wise. [C15: from L *lūminōsus* full of light, from *lūmen* light] —**luminosity** (,lu:mɪ'nɒsɪtɪ) *n.* —'**luminously** *adv.* —'**luminousness** *n.*

luminous flux *n.* a measure of the rate of flow of lumi-nous energy, evaluated according to its ability to produce a visual sensation. It is measured in lumens.

luminous intensity *n.* a measure of the amount of light that a point source radiates in a given direction.

lumme *or* **lummy** ('lʌmɪ) *interj. Brit.* an exclamation of surprise or dismay. [C19: alteration of *Lord love me*]

lummox ('lʌməks) *n. Inf.* a clumsy or stupid person. [C19: from ?]

lump[1] (lʌmp) *n.* **1.** a small solid mass without definite shape. **2.** *Pathol.* any small swelling or tumour. **3.** a col-lection of things; aggregate. **4.** *Inf.* an awkward, heavy, or stupid person. **5. the lump.** *Brit.* self-employed workers in the building trade considered collectively. **6.** (*modi-fier*) in the form of a lump or lumps: *lump sugar.* **7. a lump in one's throat.** a tight dry feeling in one's throat, usually caused by great emotion. **8. in the lump.** collec-tively; en masse. **9.** (*tr.*; often foll. by *together*) to collect into a mass or group. **10.** (*intr.*) to grow into lumps or become lumpy. **11.** (*tr.*) to consider as a single group, often without justification. **12.** (*tr.*) to make or cause lumps in or on. **13.** (*intr.*; often foll. by *along*) to move in a heavy manner. [C13: prob. rel. to early Du. *lompe* piece, Scand. dialect *lump* block, MHG *lumpe* rag]

lump[2] (lʌmp) *vb.* (*tr.*) *Inf.* to tolerate or put up with; en-dure (in **lump it**). [C16: from ?]

lumpectomy (lʌm'pɛktəmɪ) *n., pl.* **-mies.** the surgical re-moval of a tumour in a breast. [C20: from LUMP[1] + -ECTOMY]

lumpen ('lʌmpᵊn) *adj. Inf.* stupid or unthinking. [from G *Lump* vagabond, infl. by *Lumpen* rags, as in LUMPEN-PROLETARIAT]

lumpenproletariat (,lʌmpən,prəʊlɪ'tɛərɪət) *n.* (esp. in Marxist theory) the urban social group below the proleta-riat, consisting of criminals, tramps, etc. [G, lit.: ragged proletariat]

lumpfish ('lʌmp,fɪʃ) *n., pl.* **-fish** *or* **-fishes.** a North Atlan-tic fish having a globular body covered with tubercles, pelvic fins fused into a sucker, and an edible roe. Also called: '**lump,sucker.** [C16 *lump* (now obs.) lumpfish, from MDu. *lumpe*, ? rel. to LUMP[1]]

lumpish ('lʌmpɪʃ) *adj.* **1.** resembling a lump. **2.** stupid, clumsy, or heavy. —'**lumpishly** *adv.* —'**lumpishness** *n.*

lump sum *n.* a relatively large sum of money, paid at one time, esp. in cash.

lumpy ('lʌmpɪ) *adj.* **lumpier, lumpiest. 1.** full of or hav-ing lumps. **2.** (esp. of the sea) rough. **3.** (of a person) heavy or bulky. —'**lumpily** *adv.* —'**lumpiness** *n.*

Lumumba (lʊ'mʊmbə) *n.* **Patrice** (pə'tri:s). 1925–61, Congolese statesman; first prime minister of the Demo-cratic Republic of the Congo (now Zaïre) (1960); assassi-nated.

Luna ('lu:nə) *n.* the Roman goddess of the moon. [from L: moon]

lunacy ('lu:nəsɪ) *n., pl.* **-cies. 1.** (formerly) any severe mental illness. **2.** foolishness.

luna moth *n.* a large American moth having light green wings with a yellow crescent-shaped marking on each forewing. [C19: from the markings on its wings]

lunar ('lu:nə) *adj.* **1.** of or relating to the moon. **2.** occur-ing on or used on the moon: *lunar module.* **3.** relating to, caused by, or measured by the position or orbital motion of the moon. [C17: from L *lūnāris*, from *lūna* the moon]

lunar eclipse *n.* See **eclipse.**

lunar module *n.* the module used to carry astronauts on a spacecraft to the surface of the moon and back to the spacecraft.

lunar month *n.* another name for **synodic month.** See **month** (sense 6).

lunar year *n.* See **year** (sense 6).

lunate ('lu:neɪt) *or* **lunated** *adj. Anat., bot.* shaped like a cresent. [C18: from L *lūnātus* crescent-shaped, from *lūna* moon]

lunatic ('lu:nətɪk) *adj.* **1.** an archaic word for **insane. 2.** foolish; eccentric. ~*n.* **3.** a person who is insane. [C13 (adj.): via OF from LL *lūnāticus* crazy, moonstruck, from L *lūna* moon]

lunatic asylum *n.* another name, usually regarded as of-fensive, for an institution for the mentally ill.

lunatic fringe *n.* the members of a society who adopt views regarded as fanatical.

lunch (lʌntʃ) *n.* **1.** a meal eaten during the middle of the day. ~*vb.* **2.** (*intr.*) to eat lunch. **3.** (*tr.*) to provide or buy lunch for. [C16: prob. short form of LUNCHEON] —'**luncher** *n.*

luncheon ('lʌntʃən) *n.* a lunch, esp. a formal one. [C16: prob. var. of *nuncheon*, from ME *noneschench*, from *none* NOON + *schench* drink]

luncheon meat *n.* a ground mixture of meat (often pork) and cereal, usually tinned.

luncheon voucher *n.* a voucher worth a specified amount issued to employees and redeemable at a restaurant for food. Abbrev.: **LV.**

lunchroom ('lʌntʃˌruːm, -ˌrʊm) *n. Chiefly Canad.* a room where lunch is served or where students, employees, etc., may eat lunches they bring.

Lund (lʊnd) *n.* a city in SE Sweden, northeast of Malmö: founded in about 1020 by the Danish King Canute; the archbishopric for all Scandinavia in the Middle Ages; university (1668). Pop.: 83 391 (1986).

Lüneburg (*German* 'lyːnəbʊrk) *n.* a city in N West Germany, in Lower Saxony: capital of the duchy of Brunswick-Lüneburg from 1235 to 1369; prominent Hanse town; saline springs. Pop.: 61 000 (1985 est.).

lunette (luːˈnɛt) *n.* **1.** anything that is shaped like a crescent. **2.** an oval or circular opening to admit light in a dome. **3.** a semicircular panel containing a window, mural, or sculpture. **4.** a type of fortification like a detached bastion. **5.** Also called: **lune.** *R.C. Church.* a case fitted with a bracket to hold the consecrated host. [C16: from F: crescent, from *lune* moon, from L *lūna*]

Lunéville (*French* lynevil) *n.* a city in NE France: scene of the signing of the **Peace of Lunéville** between France and Austria (1801). Pop.: 21 200 (1982).

lung (lʌŋ) *n.* **1.** either one of a pair of spongy saclike respiratory organs within the thorax of higher vertebrates, which oxygenate the blood and remove its carbon dioxide. **2. at the top of one's lungs.** in one's loudest voice; yelling. [OE *lungen*]

lunge[1] (lʌndʒ) *n.* **1.** a sudden forward motion. **2.** *Fencing.* a thrust made by advancing the front foot and straightening the back leg, extending the sword arm forwards. ~*vb.* **3.** to move or cause to move with a lunge. **4.** (*intr.*) *Fencing.* to make a lunge. [C18: short form of obs. C17 *allonge*, from F *allonger* to stretch out (one's arm) from LL *ēlongāre* to lengthen] — **'lunger** *n.*

lunge[2] (lʌndʒ) *n.* **1.** a rope used in training or exercising a horse. ~*vb.* **2.** to exercise or train (a horse) on a lunge. [C17: from OF *longe*, shortened from *allonge*, ult. from L *longus* long]

lungfish ('lʌŋˌfɪʃ) *n., pl.* **-fish** *or* **-fishes.** a freshwater bony fish having an air-breathing lung, fleshy paired fins, and an elongated body.

Lungki *or* **Lung-chi** ('lʊŋ'kiː) *n.* the former name of **Zhangzhou.**

lungwort ('lʌŋˌwɜːt) *n.* **1.** any of several Eurasian plants which have spotted leaves and clusters of blue or purple flowers: formerly used to treat lung diseases. **2.** See **oyster plant.**

lunula ('luːnjʊlə) *n., pl.* **-nulae** (-njʊˌliː). the white crescent-shaped area at the base of the human fingernail. Nontechnical name: **half-moon.** [C16: from L: small moon, from *lūna*]

Luoyang *or* **Loyang** ('ləʊ'jæŋ) *n.* a city in E China, in N Henan province on the Luo River near its confluence with the Yellow River; an important Buddhist centre in the 5th and 6th centuries; a commercial and industrial centre. Pop.: 1 050 000 (1986).

Lupercalia (ˌluːpɜːˈkeɪlɪə) *n., pl.* **-lia** *or* **-lias.** an ancient Roman festival of fertility, celebrated on Feb. 15. [L, from *Lupercālis* belonging to *Lupercus*, a Roman god of the flocks] — **Luperˈcalian** *adj.*

lupin *or U.S.* **lupine** ('luːpɪn) *n.* a leguminous plant of North America, Europe, and Africa, with large spikes of brightly coloured flowers and flattened pods. [C14: from L *lupīnus* wolfish (see LUPINE); from the belief that the plant ravenously exhausted the soil]

lupine ('luːpaɪn) *adj.* of, relating to, or resembling a wolf. [C17: from L *lupīnus*, from *lupus* wolf]

lupus ('luːpəs) *n.* any of various ulcerative skin diseases. [C16: via Med. L from L: wolf; so called because it rapidly eats away the affected part]

lupus vulgaris (vʌlˈgɛərɪs) *n.* tuberculosis of the skin, esp. of the face. Sometimes shortened to **lupus.**

lurch[1] (lɜːtʃ) *vb.* (*intr.*) **1.** to lean or pitch suddenly to one side. **2.** to stagger. ~*n.* **3.** the act or an instance of lurching. [C19: from ?]

lurch[2] (lɜːtʃ) *n.* **1. leave (someone) in the lurch.** to desert (someone) in trouble. **2.** *Cribbage.* the state of a losing player with less than 30 points at the end of a game. [C16: from F *lourche* a game similar to backgammon, from *lourche* (adj.) deceived, prob. of Gmc origin]

lurch[3] (lɜːtʃ) *vb.* (*intr.*) *Arch. or dialect.* to prowl suspiciously. [C15: ? a var. of LURK]

lurcher ('lɜːtʃə) *n.* **1.** a crossbred hunting dog, esp. one trained to hunt silently. **2.** *Arch.* a person who prowls or lurks. [C16: from LURCH[3]]

lure (lʊə) *vb.* (*tr.*) **1.** (sometimes foll. by *away* or *into*) to tempt or attract by the promise of some type of reward. **2.** *Falconry.* to entice (a hawk or falcon) from the air to the falconer by a lure. ~*n.* **3.** a person or thing that lures. **4.** *Angling.* any of various types of brightly coloured artificial spinning baits. **5.** *Falconry.* a feathered decoy to which small pieces of meat can be attached. [C14: from OF *loirre* falconer's lure, from Gmc] — **'lurer** *n.*

Lurex ('lʊərɛks) *n.* **1.** *Trademark.* a thin metallic thread coated with plastic. **2.** fabric containing such thread, which makes it glitter.

lurid ('lʊərɪd) *adj.* **1.** vivid in shocking detail; sensational. **2.** horrible in savagery or violence. **3.** pallid in colour; wan. **4.** glowing with an unnatural glare. [C17: from L *lūridus* pale yellow] — **'luridly** *adv.* — **'luridness** *n.*

lurk (lɜːk) *vb.* (*intr.*) **1.** to move stealthily or be concealed, esp. for evil purposes. **2.** to be present in an unobtrusive way; be latent. ~*n.* **3.** *Austral. & N.Z. sl.* a scheme for success. [C13: prob. frequentative of LOUR] — **'lurker** *n.*

lurking ('lɜːkɪŋ) *adj.* lingering but almost unacknowledged: *a lurking suspicion.*

Lusaka (luːˈzɑːkə, -ˈsɑːkə) *n.* the capital of Zambia, in the southeast at an altitude of 1280 m (4200 ft.): became capital of Northern Rhodesia in 1932 and of Zambia in 1964; University of Zambia (1966). Pop.: 641 000 (1980 est.).

Lusatia (luːˈseɪʃɪə) *n.* a region of central Europe, lying between the upper reaches of the Elbe and Oder Rivers: now mostly in S East Germany, extending into SW Poland; inhabited chiefly by Sorbs. — **Luˈsatian** *adj., n.*

luscious ('lʌʃəs) *adj.* **1.** extremely pleasurable, esp. to the taste or smell. **2.** very attractive. **3.** *Arch.* cloying. [C15 *lucius, licius,* ? short for DELICIOUS] — **'lusciously** *adv.* — **'lusciousness** *n.*

lush[1] (lʌʃ) *adj.* **1.** (of vegetation) abounding in lavish growth. **2.** (esp. of fruits) succulent and fleshy. **3.** luxurious, elaborate, or opulent. [C15: prob. from OF *lasche* lazy, from L *laxus* loose] — **'lushly** *adv.* — **'lushness** *n.*

lush[2] (lʌʃ) *Sl.* ~*n. Chiefly U.S. & Canad.* **1.** a heavy drinker, esp. an alcoholic. **2.** *U.S. & Canad.* alcoholic drink. ~*vb.* **3.** *U.S. & Canad.* to drink (alcohol) to excess. [C19: from ?]

Lüshun ('luːˈʃʊn) *n.* a port in NE China, in S Liaoning province, adjoining Lüda at the S end of the Liaodong peninsula: jointly held by China and the Soviet Union (1945–55). Former name: **Port Arthur.**

Lusitania (ˌluːsɪˈteɪnɪə) *n.* an ancient region of the W Iberian Peninsula: a Roman province from 27 B.C. to the late 4th century A.D.; corresponds to most of present-day Portugal and the Spanish provinces of Salamanca and Cáceres. — **Lusiˈtanian** *adj.*

lust (lʌst) *n.* **1.** a strong desire for sexual gratification. **2.** a strong desire or drive. ~*vb.* **3.** (*intr.; often foll. by *after* or *for*) to have a lust (for). [OE] — **'lustful** *adj.* — **'lustfully** *adv.* — **'lustfulness** *n.*

lustral ('lʌstrəl) *adj.* of or relating to a ceremony of purification. [C16: from L *lūstrālis* (adj.) from LUSTRUM]

lustrate ('lʌstreɪt) *vb.* (*tr.*) to purify by means of religious rituals or ceremonies. [C17: from L *lūstrāre* to brighten] — **lusˈtration** *n.*

lustre *or U.S.* **luster** ('lʌstə) *n.* **1.** reflected light; sheen; gloss. **2.** radiance or brilliance of light. **3.** great splendour of accomplishment, beauty, etc. **4.** a dress fabric of cotton and wool with a glossy surface. **5.** a vase or chandelier from which hang cut-glass drops. **6.** a drop-shaded piece of cut glass or crystal used as such a decoration. **7.** a shiny metallic surface on some pottery and porcelain. **8.** *Mineralogy.* the way in which light is reflected from the surface of a mineral. ~*vb.* **9.** to make, be, or become lustrous. [C16: from OF, from OIt. *lustro,* from L *lūstrāre* to make bright] — **'lustreless** *or U.S.* **'lusterless** *adj.* — **'lustrous** *adj.*

lustreware *or U.S.* **lusterware** ('lʌstəˌwɛə) *n.* pottery with lustre decoration.

lustrum ('lʌstrəm) *or* **lustre** *n., pl.* **-trums** *or* **-tra** (-trə). a period of five years. [C16: from L: ceremony of purification, from *lūstrāre* to brighten, purify]

lusty ('lʌstɪ) *adj.* **lustier, lustiest. 1.** having or characterized by robust health. **2.** strong or invigorating. —'**lustily** *adv.* —'**lustiness** *n.*

Lü-ta ('luː'taː) *n.* a variant transliteration of the Chinese name for **Lüda.**

lute[1] (luːt) *n.* an ancient plucked stringed instrument with a long fretted fingerboard and a body shaped like a sliced pear. [C14: from OF *lut*, from Ar. *al 'ūd*, lit.: the wood]

lute[2] (luːt) *n.* **1.** a mixture of cement and clay used to seal the joints between pipes, etc. ~*vb.* **2.** (*tr.*) to seal (a joint or surface) with lute. [C14: via OF ult. from L *lutum* clay]

luteinizing hormone ('luːtɪɪ,naɪzɪŋ) *n.* a hormone secreted by the anterior lobe of the pituitary gland. In female vertebrates it stimulates ovulation, and in mammals it also induces the conversion of the ruptured follicle into the corpus luteum. In male vertebrates it promotes maturation of the interstitial cells of the testes and stimulates androgen secretion. [C19: from L *lūteum* egg yolk, from *lūteus* yellow]

lutenist, lutanist, ('luːtənɪst) *or U.S. & Canad.* (*sometimes*) **lutist** ('luːtɪst) *n.* a person who plays the lute. [C17: from Med. L *lūtānista*, from *lūtāna*, apparently from OF *lut* LUTE[1]]

Lutetia *or* **Lutetia Parisiorum** (luː'tiːʃəpə,rɪzɪ'ɔːrəm) *n.* an ancient name for **Paris** (the French city).

lutetium *or* **lutecium** (lʊ'tiːʃɪəm) *n.* a silvery-white metallic element of the lanthanide series. Symbol: Lu; atomic no.: 71; atomic wt.: 174.97. [C19: NL, from L *Lūtētia* ancient name of Paris, home of G. Urbain (1872–1938), F chemist, who discovered it]

Luther ('luːθə) *n.* **Martin.** 1483–1546, German leader of the Protestant Reformation. As professor of biblical theology at Wittenberg University from 1511, he began preaching the crucial doctrine of justification by faith rather than by works, and in 1517 he nailed 95 theses to the church door at Wittenberg, attacking Tetzel's sale of indulgences. He was excommunicated and outlawed by the Diet of Worms (1521) as a result of his refusal to recant, but he was protected in Wartburg Castle by Frederick III of Saxony (1521–22). He translated the Bible into German (1521–34) and approved Melanchthon's Augsburg Confession (1530), defining the basic tenets of Lutheranism. —'**Lutherism** *n.*

Lutheran ('luːθərən) *n.* **1.** a follower of Luther or a member of a Lutheran Church. ~*adj.* **2.** of or relating to Luther or his doctrines. **3.** of or denoting any of the Churches that follow Luther's doctrines. —'**Lutheranism** *n.*

Luthuli *or* **Lutuli** (luː'tuːlɪ) *n.* Chief **Albert John.** 1899–1967, South African political leader. As president of the African National Congress (1952–60), he campaigned for nonviolent resistance to apartheid: Nobel peace prize 1961.

Lutine bell ('luːtiːn, luː'tiːn) *n.* a bell, taken from the ship *Lutine*, kept at Lloyd's in London and rung before important announcements, esp. the loss of a vessel.

Luton ('luːtᵊn) *n.* a town in SE central England, in S Bedfordshire: airport; motor-vehicle industries. Pop.: 165 000 (1985 est.).

Lutoslawski (*Polish* luto'slavski) *n.* **Witold** ('vitɔlt). born 1913, Polish composer, whose works frequently juxtapose aleatoric and notated writing.

Lutyens ('lʌtʃənz) *n.* **1.** Sir **Edwin.** 1869–1944, English architect, noted for his neoclassical country houses and his planning of New Delhi, India. **2.** his daughter, **Elisabeth.** 1906–83, English composer.

Lützen (*German* 'lytsən) *n.* a town near Leipzig in East Germany: site of a battle (1632) in the Thirty Years' War in which the Imperialists under Wallenstein were defeated by the Swedes under Gustavus Adolphus, who died in the battle.

Lützow-Holm Bay ('lʊtsəʊ'həʊm) *n.* an inlet of the Indian Ocean on the coast of Antarctica, between Enderby Land and Queen Maud Land.

lux (lʌks) *n., pl.* **lux.** the derived SI unit of illumination equal to a luminous flux of 1 lumen per square metre. [C19: from L: light]

luxate ('lʌkseɪt) *vb.* (*tr.*) *Pathol.* to put (a shoulder, knee, etc.) out of joint; dislocate. [C17: from L *luxāre* to displace, from *luxus* dislocated] —**lux'ation** *n.*

luxe (lʌks, lʊks; *French* lyks) *n.* See **de luxe.** [C16: from F from L *luxus* extravagance]

Luxembourg ('lʌksəm,bɜːg; *French* lyksābur) *n.* **1.** a grand duchy in W Europe: formed the Benelux customs union with Belgium and the Netherlands in 1948 and is now a member of the Common Market. Languages: French and German. Religion: mostly Roman Catholic. Currency: (Belgian) franc. Capital: Luxembourg. Pop.: 369 500 (1987 est.). Area: 2586 sq. km (999 sq. miles). **2.** the capital of Luxembourg, on the Alzette River: an industrial centre. Pop.: 76 640 (1987 est.). **3.** a province in SE Belgium, in the Ardennes. Capital: Arlon. Pop.: 225 563 (1986 est.). Area: 4416 sq. km (1705 sq. miles).

Luxemburg (*German* 'luksəmburk) *n.* **Rosa** ('roːza). 1871–1919, German socialist theoretician and leader, involved with Karl Liebknecht in an unsuccessful Communist revolt (1919) and assassinated.

Luxor ('lʌksɔː) *n.* a town in S Egypt, on the River Nile: the southern part of the site of ancient Thebes; many ruins and tombs, notably the temple built by Amenhotep III (about 1411–1375 B.C.). Pop.: 137 300 (1985).

luxuriant (lʌg'zjʊərɪənt) *adj.* **1.** rich and abundant; lush. **2.** very elaborate or ornate. **3.** extremely productive or fertile. [C16: from L *luxuriāns*, present participle of *luxuriāre* to abound to excess] —**lux'uriance** *n.* —**lux'uriantly** *adv.*

luxuriate (lʌg'zjʊərɪ,eɪt) *vb.* (*intr.*) **1.** (foll. by *in*) to take voluptuous pleasure; revel. **2.** to flourish profusely. **3.** to live in a sumptuous way. [C17: from L *luxuriāre*] —**lux,u-ri'ation** *n.*

luxurious (lʌg'zjʊərɪəs) *adj.* **1.** characterized by luxury. **2.** enjoying or devoted to luxury. [C14: via OF from L *luxuriōsus* excessive] —**lux'uriously** *adv.* —**lux'uriousness** *n.*

luxury ('lʌkʃərɪ) *n., pl.* **-ries. 1.** indulgence in and enjoyment of rich, comfortable, and sumptuous living. **2.** (*sometimes pl.*) something considered an indulgence rather than a necessity. **3.** (*modifier*) relating to, indicating, or supplying luxury: *a luxury liner.* [C14 (in the sense: lechery): via OF from L *luxuria* excess, from *luxus* extravagance]

Luzern (luː'tsɛrn) *n.* the German name for **Lucerne.**

Luzon (luː'zɒn) *n.* the main and largest island of the Philippines, in the N part of the archipelago, separated from the other islands by the Sibuyan Sea: important agriculturally, producing most of the country's rice, with large forests and rich mineral resources; industrial centres at Manila and Batangas. Capital: Quezon City. Pop.: 23 900 796 (1980). Area: 108 378 sq. km (41 845 sq. miles).

LV *abbrev. for* luncheon voucher.

Lvov (*Russian* ljvɔf) *n.* an industrial city in the SW Soviet Union, in the W Ukrainian SSR: belonging to Poland from 1340 until 1772 and to Austria until 1918; annexed to the Soviet Union in 1945; Ukrainian cultural centre, with a university (1661). Pop.: 767 000 (1987). Ukrainian name: **Lviv** (lvif). Polish name: **Lwów.** German name: **Lemberg.**

LW *abbrev. for:* **1.** *Radio.* long wave. **2.** low water.

Lwów (lvuf) *n.* the Polish name for **Lvov.**

lx *Physics. symbol for* lux.

LXX *symbol for* Septuagint.

-ly[1] *suffix forming adjectives.* **1.** having the nature or qualities of: *godly.* **2.** occurring at certain intervals; every: *daily.* [OE *-lic*]

-ly[2] *suffix forming adverbs.* in a certain manner; to a certain degree: *quickly; recently; chiefly.* [OE *-lice*, from *-lic* -LY[1]]

Lyallpur (,laɪəl'pʊə) *n.* the former name (until 1979) of **Faisalabad.**

Lyautey (*French* ljotɛ) *n.* **Louis Hubert Gonzalve** (lwi ybɛr gōzalv). 1854–1934, French marshal and colonial administrator; resident general in Morocco (1912–25).

lycanthropy (laɪ'kænθrəpɪ) *n.* **1.** the supposed magical transformation of a human being into a wolf. **2.** *Psychiatry.* a delusion in which a person believes that he is a wolf. [C16: from Gk *lukánthropía*, from *lukos* wolf + *anthrōpos* man] —**lycanthrope** ('laɪkən,θrəʊp) *n.* —**lycanthropic** (,laɪkən'θrɒpɪk) *adj.*

Lycaon (laɪ'keɪɒn) *n. Greek myth.* a king of Arcadia said to have offered Zeus a plate of human flesh to learn whether the god was omniscient.

Lycaonia (,lɪkə'əʊnɪə) *n.* an ancient region of S Asia Minor, north of the Taurus Mountains; corresponds to present-day S central Turkey.

lycée ('li:seɪ) *n., pl.* **-cées** (-seɪz). *Chiefly French.* a secondary school. [C19: F, from L: *Lyceum* a school in ancient Athens]

lyceum (laɪ'sɪəm) *n.* (now chiefly in the names of buildings) **1.** a public building for concerts, lectures, etc. **2.** *U.S.* a cultural organization responsible for presenting concerts, lectures, etc.

lychee (ˌlaɪ'tʃiː) *n.* a variant spelling of **litchi.**

lych gate (lɪtʃ) *n.* a variant spelling of **lich gate.**

lychnis ('lɪknɪs) *n.* any of a genus of plants having red, pink, or white five-petalled flowers: includes ragged robin. [C17: NL, via L, from Gk *lukhnis* a red flower]

Lycia ('lɪsɪə) *n.* an ancient region on the coast of SW Asia Minor: a Persian, Rhodian, and Roman province. —**'Lycian** *adj., n.*

lycopodium (ˌlaɪkə'pəʊdɪəm) *n.* **1.** any of a genus of club moss resembling moss but having woody tissue and spore-bearing cones. **2.** a flammable yellow powder from the spores of this plant, used in medicine and in making fireworks. [C18: NL, from Gk, from *lukos* wolf + *pous* foot]

Lycra ('laɪkrə) *n. Trademark.* a type of synthetic elastic fabric and fibre used for tight-fitting garments, such as swimming costumes.

Lycurgus (laɪ'kɜːgəs) *n.* 9th century B.C., Spartan lawgiver. He is traditionally regarded as the founder of the Spartan constitution, military institutions, and educational system.

Lydda ('lɪdə) *n.* another name for **Lod.**

lyddite ('lɪdaɪt) *n.* an explosive consisting chiefly of fused picric acid. [C19: after *Lydd*, town in Kent near which the first tests were made]

Lydgate ('lɪdˌgeɪt) *n.* **John.** ?1370–?1450, English poet and monk. His vast output includes devotional works and translations, such as that of a French version of Boccaccio's *The Fall of Princes* (1430–38).

Lydia ('lɪdɪə) *n.* an ancient region on the coast of W Asia Minor: a powerful kingdom in the century and a half before the Persian conquest (546 B.C.). Chief town: Sardis. —**'Lydian** *adj., n.*

lye (laɪ) *n.* **1.** any solution obtained by leaching, such as the caustic solution obtained by leaching wood ash. **2.** a concentrated solution of sodium hydroxide or potassium hydroxide. [OE *lēag*]

Lyell ('laɪəl) *n.* Sir **Charles.** 1797–1875, Scottish geologist. In *Principles of Geology* (1830–33) he advanced the theory of uniformitarianism, refuting the doctrine of catastrophism.

lying[1] ('laɪɪŋ) *vb.* the present participle and gerund of **lie**[1].

lying[2] ('laɪɪŋ) *vb.* the present participle and gerund of **lie**[2].

lying-in *n., pl.* **lyings-in.** confinement in childbirth

lyke-wake ('laɪk,weɪk) *n. Brit.* a watch held over a dead person, often with festivities. [C16: ?from ON]

Lyle (laɪl) *n.* **Sandy,** full name *Alexander Walter Barr Lyle.* born 1958, Scottish professional golfer: won the British Open Championship (1985).

Lyly ('lɪlɪ) *n.* **John.** ?1554–1606, English dramatist and novelist, noted for his two romances, *Euphues, or the Anatomy of Wit* (1578) and *Euphues and his England* (1580), written in an elaborate style. See also **euphuism.**

Lymington ('lɪmɪŋtən) *n.* a market town in S England, in SW Hampshire on the Solent: yachting centre and holiday resort. Pop.: 38 698 (1981).

lymph (lɪmf) *n.* the almost colourless fluid, containing chiefly white blood cells, that is collected from the tissues of the body and transported in the lymphatic system. [C17: from L *lympha* water, from earlier *limpa*, infl. in form by Gk *numphē* nymph]

lymphatic (lɪm'fætɪk) *adj.* **1.** of, relating to, or containing lymph. **2.** of or relating to the lymphatic system. **3.** sluggish or lacking vigour. ~*n.* **4.** a lymphatic vessel. [C17 (meaning: mad): from L *lymphāticus*. Original meaning ?from a confusion between *nymph* and LYMPH]

lymphatic system *n.* an extensive network of capillary vessels that transports the interstitial fluid of the body as lymph to the venous blood circulation.

lymph gland *n.* a former name for **lymph node.**

lymph node *n.* any of numerous bean-shaped masses of tissue, situated along the course of lymphatic vessels, that help to protect against infection and are a source of lymphocytes.

lympho- or *before a vowel* **lymph-** *combining form.* indicating lymph or the lymphatic system: *lymphocyte.*

lymphocyte ('lɪmfəʊ,saɪt) *n.* a type of white blood cell formed in lymphoid tissue. —**lymphocytic** (ˌlɪmfəʊ'sɪtɪk) *adj.*

lymphoid ('lɪmfɔɪd) *adj.* of or resembling lymph or lymphatic tissue, or relating to the lymphatic system.

lymphoma (lɪm,fəʊmə) *n.* cancer of the lymphoid tissue. Also called: **lymphosarcoma** (ˌlɪmfəʊsɑː'kəʊmə).

lynch (lɪntʃ) *vb.* (*tr.*) (of a mob) to punish (a person) for some supposed offence by hanging without a trial. [orig. *Lynch's law;* ? after Capt. William *Lynch* (1742–1820) of Virginia, USA] —**'lyncher** *n.* —**'lynching** *n.*

Lynch (lɪntʃ) *n.* **John,** known as *Jack Lynch.* born 1917, Irish statesman; prime minister of the Republic of Ireland (1966–73; 1977–79).

lynchet ('lɪntʃɪt) *n.* a terrace or ridge formed in prehistoric or medieval times by ploughing a hillside. [OE *hlinc* ridge]

lynch law *n.* the practice of punishing a person by mob action without a proper trial.

Lynn (lɪn) *n.* another name for **King's Lynn.** Also called: **Lynn Regis** ('riːdʒɪs).

lynx (lɪŋks) *n., pl.* **lynxes** or **lynx. 1.** a feline mammal of Europe and North America, with grey-brown mottled fur, tufted ears, and a short tail. **2.** the fur of this animal. **3. bay lynx.** another name for **bobcat. 4. desert lynx.** another name for **caracal.** [C14: via L from Gk *lunx*] —**'lynx,like** *adj.*

lynx-eyed *adj.* having keen sight.

Lyon (*French* ljɔ̃) *n.* a city in SE central France, capital of Rhône department, at the confluence of the Rivers Rhône and Saône: the third largest city in France; a major industrial centre and river port. Pop.: 454 366 (1983 est.). English name: **Lyons** ('laɪənz). Ancient name: **Lugdunum** (lʊg'duːnəm).

Lyon King of Arms ('laɪən) *n.* the chief herald of Scotland. Also called: **Lord Lyon.** [C14: archaic spelling of LION, referring to the figure on the royal shield]

Lyonnais (*French* ljɔnɛ) *n.* a former province of E central France, on the Rivers Rhône and Saône: occupied by the present-day departments of Rhône and Loire. Chief town: Lyon.

Lyonnesse (ˌlaɪə'nɛs) *n.* (in Arthurian legend) the mythical birthplace of Sir Tristram, situated in SW England and believed to have been submerged by the sea.

Lyons ('laɪənz) *n.* **Joseph Aloysius.** 1879–1939, Australian statesman; prime minister of Australia (1931–39).

lyrate ('laɪərɪt) *adj.* **1.** shaped like a lyre. **2.** (of leaves) having a large terminal lobe and smaller lateral lobes. [C18: from NL *lyrātus, from* L *lyra* LYRE]

lyre ('laɪə) *n.* an ancient Greek stringed instrument consisting of a resonating tortoise shell to which a crossbar was attached by two projecting arms. It was plucked with a plectrum and used for accompanying songs. [C13: via OF from L *lyra, from* Gk *lura*]

lyrebird ('laɪə,bɜːd) *n.* either of two pheasant-like Australian birds: during courtship displays, the male spreads its tail into the shape of a lyre.

lyric ('lɪrɪk) *adj.* **1.** (of poetry) **a.** expressing the writer's personal feelings and thoughts. **b.** having the form and manner of a song. **2.** of or relating to such poetry. **3.** (of a singing voice) having a light quality and tone. **4.** intended for singing, esp. (in classical Greece) to the accompaniment of the lyre. ~*n.* **5.** a short poem of songlike quality. **6.** (*pl.*) the words of a popular song. ~Also (for senses 1–3): **lyrical.** [C16: from L *lyricus, from* Gk *lurikos, from* *lura* lyre] —**'lyrically** *adv.* —**'lyricalness** *n.*

lyrical ('lɪrɪk[ə]l) *adj.* **1.** another word for **lyric** (senses 1–3). **2.** enthusiastic; effusive.

lyricism ('lɪrɪ,sɪzəm) *n.* **1.** the quality or style of lyric poetry. **2.** emotional outpouring.

lyricist ('lɪrɪsɪst) *n.* **1.** a person who writes the words for a song, opera, or musical play. **2.** Also called: **lyrist.** a lyric poet.

Lysander (laɪ'sændə) *n.* died 395 B.C., Spartan naval commander of the Peloponnesian War.

lyse (laɪs, laɪz) *vb.* to undergo or cause to undergo lysis.

Lysenko (lɪ'sɛŋkəʊ; *Russian* li'sjɛnkə) *n.* **Trofim Denisovich** (tra'fim dɪ'nisəvitʃ). 1898–1976, Russian biologist and geneticist.

lysergic acid diethylamide (lɪ'sɜːdʒɪk; daɪ,ɛθɪl'eɪmaɪd) *n.* See **LSD.**

Lysias ('lɪsɪˌæs) *n.* ?450–?380 B.C., Athenian orator.

Lysimachus (laɪˈsɪməkəs) *n.* ?360–281 B.C., Macedonian general under Alexander the Great; king of Thrace (323–281); killed in battle by Seleucus I.

lysin ('laɪsɪn) *n.* any of a group of antibodies that cause dissolution of cells.

Lysippus (laɪˈsɪpəs) *n.* 4th century B.C., Greek sculptor. He introduced a new naturalism into Greek sculpture.

lysis ('laɪsɪs) *n., pl.* **-ses** (-siːz). **1.** the destruction of cells by the action of a particular lysin. **2.** *Med.* the gradual reduction in the symptoms of a disease. [C19: NL, from Gk, from *luein* to release]

-lysis *n. combining form.* indicating a loosening, decomposition, or breaking down: *electrolysis; paralysis.* [from Gk, from *lusis* a loosening; see LYSIS]

Lysol ('laɪsɒl) *n. Trademark.* a solution containing a mixture of cresols in water, used as an antiseptic and disinfectant.

-lyte *n. combining form.* indicating a substance that can be decomposed or broken down: *electrolyte.* [from Gk *lutos* soluble, from *luein* to loose]

Lytham Saint Anne's ('lɪðəm sənt 'ænz) *n., usually abbreviated to* **Lytham St Anne's.** a resort in NW England, in Lancashire on the Irish Sea. Pop.: 39 707 (1981).

-lytic *adj. combining form.* indicating a loosening or dissolving: *paralytic.* [from Gk, from *lusis;* see -LYSIS]

Lytton ('lɪtⁿn) *n.* **1st Baron,** title of *Edward George Earle Lytton Bulwer-Lytton.* 1803–73, English novelist, dramatist, and statesman, noted particularly for his historical romances.

Lyublin ('ljublɪn) *n.* transliteration of the Russian name for **Lublin.**

M

m *or* **M** (ɛm) *n.*, *pl.* **m's, M's,** *or* **Ms.** **1.** the 13th letter of the English alphabet. **2.** a speech sound represented by this letter, as in *mat.*

m *symbol for:* **1.** metre(s). **2.** mile(s). **3.** milli-. **4.** minute(s).

M *symbol for:* **1.** mach. **2.** *Currency.* mark(s). **3.** medium. **4.** mega-. **5.** million. **6.**(in Britain) motorway. ~ **7.** *the Roman numeral for* 1000.

m. *abbrev. for:* **1.** *Cricket.* maiden (over). **2.** male. **3.** mare. **4.** married. **5.** masculine. **6.** meridian. **7.** month.

M. *abbrev. for:* **1.** Majesty. **2.** Master. **3.** Medieval. **4.** (in titles) Member. **5.** million. **6.** (*pl.* **MM.** *or* **MM**) Also: **M** French. Monsieur. [F equivalent of *Mr*]

M'- *prefix.* a variant of **Mac-**.

ma (mɑː) *n.* an informal word for **mother.**

MA *abbrev. for:* **1.** Master of Arts. **2.** Military Academy.

ma'am (mæm, mɑːm; *unstressed* məm) *n.* short for **madam:** used as a title of respect, esp. for female royalty.

Maarianhamina (ˈmɑːriɑnhɑminɑ) *n.* the Finnish name for **Mariehamn.**

Maas (mɑːs) *n.* the Dutch name for the **Meuse.**

Maastricht *or* **Maestricht** (ˈmɑːstrɪxt; *Dutch* mɑːˈstrɪxt) *n.* a city in the SE Netherlands near the Belgian and German borders: capital of Limburg province, on the River Maas (Meuse); formerly a strategic fortress. Pop.: 115 272 (1987).

Mabuse (məˈbjuːz; *French* mabyz) *n.* **Jan** (jɑn). original name *Jan Gossaert.* ?1478–?1533, Flemish painter.

mac *or* **mack** (mæk) *n. Brit. inf.* short for **mackintosh** (senses 1, 3).

Mac (mæk) *n. Chiefly U.S. & Canad.* an informal term of address to a man. [C20: abstracted from MAC-]

Mac-, Mc-, *or* **M'-** *prefix.* (in surnames of Scottish or Irish Gaelic origin) son of: *MacDonald.* [from Goidelic *mac* son of]

macabre (məˈkɑːbə, -brə) *adj.* gruesome; ghastly; grim. [C15: from OF *danse macabre* dance of death, prob. from *macabé* relating to the Maccabees, who were associated with death because of the doctrines and prayers for the dead in II Macc. (12:43–46)]

macadam (məˈkædəm) *n.* a road surface made of compressed layers of small broken stones, esp. one that is bound together with tar or asphalt. [C19: after John *McAdam* (1756–1836), Scot. engineer, the inventor]

macadamia (ˌmækəˈdeɪmɪə) *n.* **1.** an Australian tree having clusters of small white flowers and edible nutlike seeds. **2. macadamia nut.** the seed. [C19: NL, after John *Macadam* (died 1865), Australian chemist]

macadamize *or* **-ise** (məˈkædəˌmaɪz) *vb.* (*tr.*) to construct or surface (a road) with macadam. —**mac,adam i'zation** *or* **-i'sation** *n.* —**mac'adam,izer** *or* -**,iser** *n.*

Macao (məˈkaʊ) *n.* a Portuguese overseas province and city on the coast of S China, across the estuary of the Zhu Jiang from Hong Kong: chief centre of European trade with China in the 18th century; attained partial autonomy in 1976; sovereignty will pass to China in 1999; transit trade with China; tourism. Pop.: 426 400 (1986 est.). Area: 16 sq. km (6 sq. miles). Portuguese name: **Macáu.**

Macapá (*Portuguese* makaˈpa) *n.* a town in NE Brazil, capital of the federal territory of Amapá, on the Canal do Norte of the Amazon delta. Pop.: 115 000 (1984 est.).

macaque (məˈkɑːk) *n.* any of various Old World monkeys of Asia and Africa. Typically the tail is short or absent and cheek pouches are present. [C17: from F, from Port. *macaco*, from W African *makaku*, from *kaku* monkey]

macaroni *or* **maccaroni** (ˌmækəˈrəʊnɪ) *n.*, *pl.* **-nis** *or* **-nies. 1.** pasta tubes made from wheat flour. **2.** (in 18th-century Britain) a dandy who affected foreign manners and style. [C16: from It. (dialect) *maccarone*, prob. from Gk *makaria* food made from barley]

macaroon (ˌmækəˈruːn) *n.* a kind of sweet biscuit made of ground almonds, sugar, and egg whites. [C17: via F *macaron* from It. *maccarone* MACARONI]

Macarthur (məˈkɑːθə) *n.* **John.** 1767–1834, Australian military officer, pastoralist, and entrepreneur, born in England. He established the breeding of merino sheep in Australia and was influential in founding the Australian wool industry.

MacArthur (məˈkɑːθə) *n.* **Douglas.** 1880–1964, U.S. general. During World War II he became commanding general of U.S. armed forces in the Pacific (1944) and accepted the surrender of Japan, the Allied occupation of which he commanded (1945–51). He was commander in chief of United Nations forces in Korea (1950–51) until dismissed by President Truman.

Macassar (məˈkæsə) *n.* a variant spelling of **Makasar.**

Macassar oil *n.* an oily preparation formerly put on the hair to make it smooth and shiny. [C19: MAKASAR]

Macáu (məˈkau) *n.* the Portuguese name for **Macao.**

Macaulay (məˈkɔːlɪ) *n.* **1.** Dame **Rose.** 1881–1958, British novelist. Her books include *Dangerous Ages* (1921) and *The Towers of Trebizond* (1956). **2. Thomas Babington,** 1st Baron Macaulay. 1800–59, English historian, essayist, and statesman. His *History of England from the Accession of James the Second* (1848–61) is regarded as a classic of the Whig interpretation of history.

macaw (məˈkɔː) *n.* a large tropical American parrot having a long tail and brilliant plumage. [C17: from Port. *macau*, from ?]

Macbeth (məkˈbɛθ, mæk-) *n.* died 1057, king of Scotland (1040–57): succeeded Duncan, whom he killed in battle; defeated and killed by Duncan's son Malcolm III.

MacBride (məkˈbraɪd) *n.* **Sean** (ʃɔːn). 1904–88, Irish statesman; minister for external affairs (1948–51); chairman of Amnesty International (1961–75); Nobel Peace Prize 1974; UN commissioner for Namibia (1974–76).

McBride (məkˈbraɪd) *n.* **Willie John.** born 1940, Irish Rugby Union footballer. A forward, he played for Ireland (1962–75) and the British Lions (1962–74).

Macc. *abbrev. for* Maccabees (books of the Apocrypha).

McCarthy (məˈkɑːθɪ) *n.* **1. Eugene Joseph.** born 1916, U.S. senator, a leader of the movement against the Vietnam war and a contender for the Democratic presidential nomination in 1968. **2. Joseph R(aymond).** 1908–57, U.S. Republican senator, who led (1950–54) the notorious investigations of alleged Communist infiltration into the U.S. government. **3. Mary (Therese).** born 1912, U.S. novelist and critic; her works include *The Group* (1963).

McCarthyism (məˈkɑːθɪˌɪzəm) *n. Chiefly U.S.* **1.** the practice of making unsubstantiated accusations of disloyalty or Communist leanings. **2.** the use of unsupported accusations for any purpose. [C20: after Senator Joseph MCCARTHY] —**Mc'Carthyist** *n.*, *adj.*

McCartney (məˈkɑːtnɪ) *n.* **Paul.** born 1942, English rock musician and songwriter; member of the Beatles (1961–70); leader of Wings (1971–81). His recordings include *Band on the Run* (1973), "Mull of Kintyre" (1977), and *Tug of War* (1982). See also **Beatles.**

Macclesfield (ˈmækəlzˌfiːkld) *n.* a market town in NW England, in Cheshire: silk industry. Pop.: 46 832 (1981).

McCormack (məˈkɔːmæk) *n.* **John.** 1884–1945, Irish tenor: became U.S. citizen 1919.

McCormick (məˈkɔːmɪk) *n.* **Cyrus Hall.** 1809–84, U.S. inventor of the reaping machine (1831).

McCoy (məˈkɔɪ) *n. Sl.* the genuine person or thing (esp. in **the real McCoy**). [C20: ? after Kid *McCoy*, professional name of Norman Selby (1873–1940), American boxer, who was called "the real McCoy" to distinguish him from another boxer of that name]

McCullers (məˈkʌləz) *n.* **Carson.** 1917–67, U.S. writer, whose novels include *The Heart is a Lonely Hunter* (1940).

McDiarmid (mˈəkˈdɛəmɪd) *n.* **Hugh,** pen name of *Christopher Murray Grieve.* 1892–1978, Scottish poet; a founder of the Scottish National Party. His *Complete Poems* were published in 1978.

Macdonald (məkˈdɒnəld) *n.* **1. Flora.** 1722–90, Scottish heroine, who helped the Young Pretender to escape to Skye after his defeat at the battle of Culloden (1746). **2.** Sir **John Alexander.** 1815–91, Canadian statesman, born in Scotland, who was the first prime minister of the Dominion of Canada (1867–73; 1878–91).

MacDonald (mək'dɒnəld) n. (**James**) **Ramsay**. 1866–1937, British statesman, who led the first and second Labour Governments (1924 and 1929–31). He also led a coalition (1931–35), which the majority of the Labour Party refused to support.

Macdonnell Ranges (mək'dɒnəl) pl. n. a mountain system of central Australia, in S central Northern Territory, extending about 160 km (100 miles) east and west of Alice Springs. Highest peak: Mount Ziel, 1510 m (4955 ft.).

mace[1] (meɪs) n. 1. a club, usually having a spiked metal head, used esp. in the Middle Ages. 2. a ceremonial staff carried by certain officials. 3. See **macebearer**. 4. an early form of billiard cue. [C13: from OF, prob. from Vulgar L *mattea* (unattested); apparently rel. to L *mateola* mallet]

mace[2] (meɪs) n. a spice made from the dried aril round the nutmeg seed. [C14: formed as a singular from OF *macis* (wrongly assumed to be pl.), from L *macir* an oriental spice]

macebearer ('meɪs,bɛərə) n. a person who carries a mace in processions or ceremonies.

macedoine (,mæsɪ'dwɑːn) n. 1. a mixture of diced vegetables. 2. a mixture of fruit in a syrup or in jelly. 3. any mixture; medley. [C19: from F, lit.: Macedonian, alluding to the mixture of nationalities in Macedonia]

Macedon ('mæsɪ,dɒn) or **Macedonia** n. a region of the S Balkans, now divided among Greece, Bulgaria, and Yugoslavia. As a kingdom in the ancient world it achieved prominence under Philip II (359–336 B.C.) and his son Alexander the Great.

Macedonia (,mæsɪ'dəʊnɪə) n. 1. a division of N Greece. Pop.: 2 121 953 (1981). Area: 34 203 sq. km (13 339 sq. miles). Modern Greek name: **Makedhonia**. 2. a constituent republic of S Yugoslavia. Capital: Skopje. Pop.: 1 913 571 (1981). Area: 25 713 sq. km (10 028 sq. miles). Serbian name: ,**Makedo'nija**. 3. a district of SW Bulgaria, now occupied by Blagoevgrad province. Area: 6465 sq. km (2496 sq. miles). — ,**Mace'donian** adj., n.

Maceió (mase'jɔ) n. a port in NE Brazil, capital of Alagôas state, on the Atlantic. Pop.: 376 479 (1980).

McEnroe ('mækⁿ,rəʊ) n. **John** (**Patrick Jr**) born 1959, U.S. tennis player: U.S. singles champion (1979–81) and doubles champion (1979): Wimbledon singles champion (1981; 1983) and doubles champion (1979; 1981; 1983; 1984).

macerate ('mæsə,reɪt) vb. 1. to soften or separate or be softened or separated as a result of soaking. 2. to become or cause to become thin. [C16: from L *mācerāre* to soften] — ,**macer'ation** n. — '**macer,ator** n.

McGonagall (mə'gɒnəgəl) n. **William**. 1830–?1902, Scottish writer of doggerel, noted for its bathos, repetitive rhymes, poor scansion, and ludicrous effect.

Mach[1] (mæk) n. short for **Mach number**.

Mach[2] (German max) n. **Ernst** (ɛrnst). 1838–1916, Austrian physicist and philosopher. He devised the system of speed measurement using the Mach number. He also founded logical positivism, asserting that the validity of a scientific law is proved only after empirical testing.

mach. abbrev. for: 1. machine. 2. machinery. 3. machinist.

Machado (Portuguese ma'ʃadu) n. **Joaquim Maria** (ʒuaˈki maˈria). 1839–1908, Brazilian author of novels and short stories, whose novels include *Epitaph of a Small Winner* (1881) and *Dom Casmurro* (1899).

machair ('mæxər) n. Scot. (in the western Highlands and islands of Scotland) a strip of sandy, grassy land just above the shore: used as grazing or arable land. [C17: from Scot. Gaelic]

Machel (mə'ʃɛl) n. **Samora** (**Moises**) (sə'mɔːrə). 1933–86, Mozambique statesman; president of Mozambique from 1975–86.

machete (mə'ʃɛtɪ, -'tʃeɪ-) n. a broad heavy knife used for cutting or as a weapon, esp. in parts of Central and South America. [C16 *macheto*, from Sp. *machete*, from *macho* club, ?from Vulgar L *mattea* (unattested) club]

Machiavelli (,mækɪə'vɛlɪ) n. **Niccolò** (nikkoˈlɔ). 1469–1527, Florentine statesman and political philosopher; secretary to the war council of the Florentine republic (1498–1512). His most famous work is *Il Principe* (*The Prince*, 1532).

Machiavellian (,mækɪə'vɛlɪən) adj. 1. of or relating to the alleged political principles of Machiavelli; cunning, amoral, and opportunist. ~n. 2. a cunning, amoral, and

opportunist person, esp. a politician. — ,**Machia'vellian,ism** n.

machicolate (mə'tʃɪkəʊ,leɪt) vb. (tr.) to construct machicolations at the top of (a wall). [C18: from OF *machicoller*, ult. from Provençal *machacol*, from *macar* to crush + *col* neck]

machicolation (mə,tʃɪkəʊ'leɪʃən) n. 1. (esp. in medieval castles) a projecting gallery or parapet having openings through which missiles could be dropped. 2. any such opening.

machinate ('mækɪ,neɪt) vb. (usually tr.) to contrive, plan, or devise (schemes, plots, etc.). [C17: from L *māchinārī* to plan, from *māchina* MACHINE] — '**machi,nator** n.

machination (,mækɪ'neɪʃən) n. 1. a plot or scheme. 2. the act of devising plots or schemes.

machine (mə'ʃiːn) n. 1. an assembly of interconnected components arranged to transmit or modify force in order to perform useful work. 2. a device for altering the magnitude or direction of a force, such as a lever or screw. 3. a mechanically operated device or means of transport, such as a car or aircraft. 4. any mechanical or electrical device that automatically performs tasks or assists in performing tasks. 5. any intricate structure or agency. 6. a mechanically efficient, rigid, or obedient person. 7. an organized body of people that controls activities, policies, etc. ~vb. 8. (tr.) to shape, cut, or remove (excess material) from (a workpiece) using a machine tool. 9. to use a machine to carry out a process on (something). [C16: via F from L *māchina* machine, engine, from Doric Gk *makhana* pulley] — **ma'chinable** or **ma'chineable** adj. — **ma,china'bility** n.

machine-down time n. a period during which a machine, computer, etc., is out of service, because it is out of order or being serviced.

machine gun n. 1. a. a rapid-firing automatic gun, using small-arms ammunition. b. (as modifier): machine-gun fire. ~vb. **machine-gun**, -**gunning**, -**gunned**. 2. (tr.) to shoot or fire at with a machine gun. — **machine gunner** n.

machine language or **code** n. instructions for a computer in binary or hexadecimal code.

machine learning n. a branch of artificial intelligence in which a computer generates rules underlying or based on raw data that has been fed into it.

machinery (mə'ʃiːnərɪ) n., pl. -**eries**. 1. machines, machine parts, or machine systems collectively. 2. a particular machine system or set of machines. 3. a system similar to a machine.

machine shop n. a workshop in which machine tools are operated.

machine tool n. a power-driven machine, such as a lathe, for cutting, shaping, and finishing metals, etc. — **machine-,tooled** adj.

machinist (mə'ʃiːnɪst) n. 1. a person who operates machines to cut or process materials. 2. a maker or repairer of machines.

machismo (mæ'kɪzməʊ, -'tʃɪz-) n. strong or exaggerated masculinity. [Mexican Sp., from Sp. *macho* male, from L *masculus* MASCULINE]

Mach number n. (often not cap.) the ratio of the speed of a body in a particular medium to the speed of sound in that medium. Mach number 1 corresponds to the speed of sound. [C19: after Ernst MACH]

macho ('mætʃəʊ) adj. 1. strongly or exaggeratedly masculine. ~n., pl. **machos**. adj. 2. a strong virile man. [see MACHISMO]

Machu Picchu ('mɑːtʃuː 'piːktʃuː) n. a ruined Incan city in S central Peru.

Macías Nguema (mə'siːəs ²ŋ'gweɪmə) n. the former name (until 1979) of **Bioko**.

mack (mæk) n. Brit. inf. short for **mackintosh** (senses 1, 3).

Mackay (mə'kaɪ) n. a port in E Australia, in Queensland: artificial harbour. Pop.: 35 361 (1981).

Mackellar (mə'kɛlə) n. **Dorothea**. 1885–1968, Australian poet, who wrote "My Country", Australia's best known poem.

Mackenzie[1] (mə'kɛnzɪ) n. 1. an administrative district of the Northwest Territories of Canada: includes the W edge of the Canadian Shield, lowlands, and mountains. Pop.: 29 869 (1981). Area: 1 366 199 sq. km (527 490 sq. miles). 2. a river in NW Canada, in the Northwest Territories, flowing northwest from Great Slave Lake to the Beaufort

Sea: the longest river in Canada; navigable in summer. Length: 1770 km (1100 miles).

Mackenzie[2] (məˈkɛnzɪ) *n.* **1. Sir Alexander.** ?1755–1820, Scottish explorer and fur trader in Canada. He explored the Mackenzie River (1789) and was the first European to cross America north of Mexico (1793). **2. Alexander.** 1822–92, Canadian statesman; first Liberal prime minister (1873–78). **3. Sir Compton.** 1883–1972, English author. His works include *Sinister Street* (1913–14) and the comic novel *Whisky Galore* (1947). **4. Sir Thomas.** 1854–1930, New Zealand statesman born in Scotland: prime minister of New Zealand (1912). **5. William Lyon.** 1795–1861, Canadian journalist and politician, born in Scotland. He led an unsuccessful rebellion against the oligarchic Family Compact (1837).

mackerel (ˈmækrəl) *n., pl.* **-rel** *or* **-rels. 1.** a spiny-finned food fish occurring in northern coastal regions of the Atlantic and in the Mediterranean. It has a deeply forked tail and a greenish-blue body marked with wavy dark bands on the back. **2.** any of various related fishes. [C13: from Anglo-F, from OF *maquerel*, from ?]

mackerel sky *n.* a sky patterned with cirrocumulus or small altocumulus clouds. [from similarity to pattern on mackerel's back]

Mackerras (məˈkɛrəs) *n.* **Charles.** born 1925, Australian conductor, esp. of opera; resident in England.

Mackinac (ˈmækɪˌnɔː, -ˌnæk) *n.* a wooded island in N Michigan, in the **Straits of Mackinac** (a channel between the lower and upper peninsulas of Michigan): an ancient Indian burial ground; state park. Length: 5 km (3 miles).

McKinley[1] (məˈkɪnlɪ) *n.* **Mount.** a mountain in S central Alaska, in the Alaska Range: the highest peak in North America. Height: 6194 m (20 320 ft.).

McKinley[2] (məˈkɪnlɪ) *n.* **William.** 1843–1901, 25th president of the U.S. (1897–1901). His administration was marked by the highest tariffs in American history and by expansionist policies. He was assassinated.

mackintosh *or* **macintosh** (ˈmækɪnˌtɒʃ) *n.* **1.** a waterproof raincoat made of rubberized cloth. **2.** such cloth. **3.** any raincoat. [C19: after Charles *Macintosh* (1760–1843), who invented it]

Mackintosh (ˈmækɪnˌtɒʃ) *n.* **Charles Rennie.** 1868–1928, Scottish architect and artist, exponent of the Art Nouveau style; designer of the Glasgow School of Art (1896).

Maclean (məˈkleɪn) *n.* **1. Donald.** 1913–83, British civil servant, who spied for the Russians: fled to the Soviet Union (with Guy Burgess) in 1951. **2. Sorley** (ˈsɔːlɪ). born 1911, Scottish Gaelic poet. His works include *Dàin do Eimhir agus Dàin Eile* (1943) and *Spring Tide and Neap Tide* (1977).

Macleod (məˈklaʊd) *n.* **John James Rickard.** 1876–1935, Scottish physiologist: shared the Nobel prize for physiology or medicine (1923) with Banting for their part in discovering insulin.

McLuhan (məˈkluːən) *n.* **(Herbert) Marshall.** 1911–81, Canadian author of works analysing the mass media, including *Understanding Media* (1964) and *The Medium is the Message* (1967).

Macmahon (*French* makmaɔ̃) *n.* **Marie Edme Patrice Maurice** (mari ɛdmə patris mɔris), Comte de Macmahon. 1808–93, French military commander. He commanded the troops that suppressed the Paris Commune (1871) and was elected president of the Third Republic (1873–79).

McMahon (məkˈmaːən) *n.* **Sir William.** 1908–88, Australian statesman; prime minister of Australia (1971–72).

Macmillan (məkˈmɪlən) *n.* **(Maurice) Harold,** 1st Earl of Stockton. 1894–1986, British statesman; Conservative prime minister (1957–63).

Mcmurdo Sound (məkˈmɜːdəʊ) *n.* an inlet of the Ross Sea in Antarctica, north of Victoria Land.

McNaughten Rules *or* **McNaghten Rules** (məkˈnɔːtⁿn) *pl. n.* (in English law) a set of rules established by the case of Regina *v.* McNaughten (1843) by which legal proof of criminal insanity depends on the accused being shown to be incapable of understanding what he has done.

MacNeice (məkˈniːs) *n.* **Louis.** 1907–63, British poet, born in Northern Ireland. His works include the poems in *Autumn Sequel* (1954) and *Solstices* (1961) and a translation of the *Agamemnon* of Aeschylus (1936).

Macon (ˈmeɪkən) *n.* a city in central Georgia, on the Ocmulgee River. Pop.: 118 420 (1986 est.).

Mâcon (*French* makɔ̃) *n.* a city in E central France, in the Saône valley: a centre of the wine-producing region of lower Burgundy. Pop.: 39 242 (1983 est.).

Macpherson (məkˈfɜːsⁿn) *n.* **James.** 1736–96, Scottish poet and translator. He published verse, which he claimed to be translations of the legendary Gaelic poet Ossian.

Macquarie[1] (məˈkwɒrɪ) *n.* **Lachlan.** 1762–1824, Australian colonial administrator; Governor of New South Wales (1809–21), noted for his reformist policies towards ex-convicts and for his record in public works such as road-building in the colony.

Macquarie[2] (məˈkwɒrɪ) *n.* **1.** an Australian island in the Pacific, southeast of Tasmania: noted for its species of albatross and penguin. Area: about 168 sq. km (65 sq. miles). **2.** a river in SE Australia, in E central New South Wales, rising in the Blue Mountains and flowing northwest to the Darling. Length: about 1200 km (750 miles).

McQueen (məˈkwiːn) *n.* **Steve.** 1930–80, U.S. film actor, noted for his portrayal of tough characters.

macramé (məˈkrɑːmɪ) *n.* a type of ornamental work made by knotting and weaving coarse thread. [C19: via F & It. from Turkish *makrama* towel, from Ar. *migraman* striped cloth]

Macready (məˈkriːdɪ) *n.* **William Charles.** 1793–1873, English actor and theatre manager.

macro- *or before a vowel* **macr-** *combining form.* **1.** large, long, or great in size or duration: *macroscopic.* **2.** *Pathol.* indicating abnormal enlargement or overdevelopment: *macrocephaly.* [from Gk *makros* large]

macrobiotics (ˌmækrəʊbaɪˈɒtɪks) *n.* (*functioning as sing.*) a dietary system which advocates whole grains and vegetables grown without chemical additives. [C20: from MACRO- + Gk *biotos* life + -ICS] —**macrobiˈotic** *adj.*

macrocarpa (ˌmækrəʊˈkɑːpə) *n.* a large New Zealand coniferous tree, used to form shelter belts on farms and for rough timber. [C19: from NL, from MACRO- + Gk *karpos* fruit]

macrocephaly (ˌmækrəʊˈsɛfəlɪ) *n.* the condition of having an abnormally large head or skull. —**macrocephalic** (ˌmækrəʊsɪˈfælɪk) *or* **ˌmacroˈcephalous** *adj.*

macroclimate (ˈmækrəʊˌklaɪmɪt) *n.* the predominant climate over a large area.

macrocosm (ˈmækrəˌkɒzəm) *n.* a complex structure, such as the universe or society, regarded as an entirety. Cf. **microcosm.** [C16: via F & L from Gk *makros kosmos* great world] —**ˌmacroˈcosmic** *adj.* —**ˌmacroˈcosmically** *adv.*

macroeconomics (ˌmækrəʊˌiːkəˈnɒmɪks, -ˌɛk-) *n.* (*functioning as sing.*) the branch of economics concerned with aggregates, such as national income, consumption, and investment. —**ˌmacroeˈnomic** *adj.*

macromolecule (ˌmækrəʊˈmɒlɪˌkjuːl) *n.* any very large molecule, such as a protein or synthetic polymer.

macron (ˈmækrɒn) *n.* a diacritical mark (ˉ) placed over a letter to represent a long vowel. [C19: from Gk *makron* something long, from *makros* long]

macroscopic (ˌmækrəʊˈskɒpɪk) *adj.* **1.** large enough to be visible to the naked eye. **2.** comprehensive; concerned with large units. [C19: see MACRO-, -SCOPIC] —**ˌmacroˈscopically** *adv.*

macula (ˈmækjʊlə) *or* **macule** (ˈmækjuːl) *n., pl.* **-ulae** (-jʊˌliː) *or* **-ules.** *Anat.* **1.** a small spot or area of distinct colour, esp. the macula lutea. **2.** any small discoloured spot or blemish on the skin, such as a freckle. [C14: from L] —**ˈmacular** *adj.* —**ˌmacuˈlation** *n.*

macula lutea (ˈluːtɪə) *n., pl.* **maculae luteae** (ˈluːtɪˌiː). a small yellowish oval-shaped spot on the retina of the eye, where vision is especially sharp. [NL, lit.: yellow spot]

mad (mæd) *adj.* **madder, maddest. 1.** mentally deranged; insane. **2.** senseless; foolish. **3.** (often foll. by *at*) *Inf.* angry; resentful. **4.** (foll. by *about, on,* or *over;* often *postpositive*) wildly enthusiastic (about) or fond (of). **5.** extremely excited or confused; frantic: *a mad rush.* **6.** wildly gay: *a mad party.* **7.** temporarily overpowered by violent reactions, emotions, etc.: *mad with grief.* **8.** (of animals) **a.** unusually ferocious: *a mad buffalo.* **b.** afflicted with rabies. **9. like mad.** *Inf.* with great energy, enthusiasm, or haste. ~*vb.* **madding, madded. 10.** *U.S. or arch.* to make or become mad; act or cause to act as if mad. [OE *gemǣded,* p.p. of *gemǣdan* to render insane]

Madagascar (ˌmædəˈgæskə) *n.* an island republic in the Indian Ocean, off the E coast of Africa: made a French protectorate in 1895; became autonomous in 1958 and fully independent in 1960; contains unique flora and fauna. Language: Malagasy. Religions: animist and Christian. Currency: franc. Capital: Antananarivo. Pop.: 10 568 000 (1987 UN est.). Area: 587 041 sq. km (266 657 sq. miles). Official name (since 1975): **Democratic Republic of Madagascar**. Former name (1958–75): **Malagasy Republic**. —,**Mada'gascan** n., adj.

madam ('mædəm) n., pl. **madams** or (for sense 1) **mesdames**. **1.** a polite term of address for a woman, esp. one of relatively high social status. **2.** a woman who runs a brothel. **3.** Brit. inf. a precocious or pompous little girl. [C13: from OF ma dame my lady]

madame ('mædəm) n., pl. **mesdames**. a married Frenchwoman: used as a title equivalent to Mrs, and sometimes extended to older unmarried women to show respect. [C17: from F; see MADAM]

madcap ('mæd,kæp) adj. **1.** impulsive, reckless, or lively. ~n. **2.** an impulsive, reckless, or lively person.

madden ('mæd³n) vb. to make or become mad or angry. —'**maddening** adj. —'**maddeningly** adv.

madder ('mædə) n. **1.** a plant having small yellow flowers and a red fleshy root. **2.** this root. **3.** a dark reddish-purple dye formerly obtained from this root. **4.** a red lake obtained from alizarin and an inorganic base; used as a pigment in inks and paints. [OE mædere]

madding ('mædɪŋ) adj. Arch. **1.** acting or behaving as if mad: the madding crowd. **2.** making mad; maddening. —'**maddingly** adv.

made (meɪd) vb. **1.** the past tense and past participle of **make**. ~adj. **2.** artificially produced. **3.** (in combination) produced or shaped as specified: handmade. **4.** get or **have it made**. Inf. to be assured of success.

Madeira (mə'dɪərə; Portuguese mə'ðəirə) n. **1.** a group of volcanic islands in the N Atlantic, west of Morocco: constitutes the Portuguese administrative district of Funchal; consists of the chief island, Madeira, Pôrto Santo, and the uninhabited Deserta and Selvagen Islands; gained partial autonomy in 1976. Capital: Funchal. Pop.: 257 822 (1981). Area: 797 sq. km (311 sq. miles). **2.** a river in W Brazil, flowing northeast to the Amazon below Manaus. Length: 3241 km (2013 miles). **3.** a rich strong fortified white wine made on Madeira.

madeleine ('mædəlɪn, -,leɪn) n. a small fancy sponge cake. [C19: ? after Madeleine Paulmier, F pastry cook]

mademoiselle (,mædmwə'zɛl) n., pl. **mesdemoiselles**. **1.** a young unmarried French girl or woman: used as a title equivalent to Miss. **2.** a French teacher or governess. [C15: F, from ma my + demoiselle DAMSEL]

made-up adj. **1.** invented; fictional. **2.** wearing make-up. **3.** put together. **4.** (of a road) surfaced with tarmac, concrete, etc.

madhouse ('mæd,haʊs) n. Inf. **1.** a mental hospital or asylum. **2.** a state of uproar or confusion.

Madhya Bharat ('mʌdjə 'baːrət) n. a former state of central India: part of Madhya Pradesh since 1956.

Madhya Pradesh ('mʌdjə praː'dɛʃ) n. a state of central India, situated on the Deccan Plateau: the largest Indian state; rich in mineral resources, with several industrial cities. Capital: Bhopal. Pop.: 52 138 467 (1981). Area: 443 452 sq. km (171 217 sq. miles).

Madison[1] ('mædɪs³n) n. a city in S central Wisconsin, on an isthmus between Lakes Mendota and Monona: the state capital. Pop.: 175 850 (1986 est.).

Madison[2] ('mædɪs³n) n. James. 1751–1836, U.S. statesman; 4th president of the U.S. (1809–17). He helped to draft the U.S. Constitution and Bill of Rights. His presidency was dominated by the War of 1812.

madly ('mædlɪ) adv. **1.** in an insane or foolish manner. **2.** with great speed and energy. **3.** Inf. extremely or excessively: I love you madly.

madman ('mædmən) or (fem.) **madwoman** n., pl. -**men** or -**women**. a person who is insane.

madness ('mædnɪs) n. **1.** insanity; lunacy. **2.** extreme anger, excitement, or foolishness. **3.** a nontechnical word for **rabies**.

Madonna (mə'dɒnə) n. **1.** Chiefly R.C. Church. a designation of the Virgin Mary. **2.** (sometimes not cap.) a picture or statue of the Virgin Mary. [C16: It., from ma my + donna lady]

Madonna lily n. a perennial widely cultivated Mediterranean lily plant with white trumpet-shaped flowers.

madras ('mædrəs, mə'drɑːs) n. a strong fine cotton or silk fabric, usually with a woven stripe. [from MADRAS]

Madras (mə'drɑːs, -'dræs) n. **1.** a port in SE India, capital of Tamil Nadu, on the Bay of Bengal: founded in 1639 by the English East India Company as **Fort St George**; traditional burial place of St Thomas; university (1857). Pop.: 3 266 034 (1981). **2.** the former name (until 1968) for the state of **Tamil Nadu**.

Madre de Dios (Spanish 'maðre ðe 'ðiɔs) n. a river in NE South America, rising in SE Peru and flowing northeast to the Beni River in N Bolivia. Length: about 965 km (600 miles).

madrepore (,mædrɪ'pɔː) n. any coral of the genus Madrepora, many of which occur in tropical seas and form large coral reefs. [C18: via F from It. madrepora mother-stone] —,**madre'poral**, **madreporic** (,mædrɪ'pɒrɪk), or ,**madre'porian** adj.

Madrid (mə'drɪd) n. the capital of Spain, situated centrally in New Castile: the highest European capital, at an altitude of about 700 m (2300 ft.); a Moorish fortress in the 10th century, captured by Castile in 1083 and made capital of Spain in 1561; university (1836). Pop.: 3 053 101 (1986 est.).

madrigal ('mædrɪg³l) n. **1.** Music. a type of 16th- or 17th-century part song for unaccompanied voices, with an amatory or pastoral text. **2.** a short love poem. [C16: from It., from Med. L mātricāle primitive, apparently from L mātricālis, from matrix womb] —'**madrigal,esque** adj. —**madrigalian** (,mædrɪ'gælɪən, -'geɪ-) adj. —'**madrigalist** n.

Madura (mə'dʊərə) n. an island in Indonesia, off the NE coast of Java: extensive forests and saline springs. Capital: Pamekasan. Area: 5472 sq. km (2113 sq. miles). —**Madurese** (,mædjʊə'riːz) adj., n.

Madurai ('mædjʊˌraɪ) n. a city in S India, in S Tamil Nadu: centre of Dravidian culture for over 2000 years; cotton industry. Pop.: 904 000 (1981). Former name: **Madura**.

Maeander (miː'ændə) n. ancient name of the river **Menderes** (sense 1). Also spelled: **Meander**.

Maebashi ('maːɛ'baːʃi) n. a city in central Japan, on central Honshu: centre of sericulture and silk-spinning; university (1949). Pop.: 265 171 (1980).

Maecenas (miː'siːnæs) n. **1.** Gaius ('gaɪəs). ?70–8 B.C., Roman statesman; adviser to Augustus and patron of Horace and Virgil. **2.** a wealthy patron of the arts.

maelstrom ('meɪlstrəʊm) n. **1.** a large powerful whirlpool. **2.** any turbulent confusion. [C17: from obs. Du. maelstroom, from malen to whirl round + stroom STREAM]

Maelstrom ('meɪlstrəʊm) n. a strong tidal current in a restricted channel in the Lofoten Islands off the NW coast of Norway.

maenad ('miːnæd) n. **1.** Classical history. a woman participant in the orgiastic rites of Dionysus, Greek god of wine. **2.** a frenzied woman. [C16: from L Maenas, from Gk mainas madwoman] —**mae'nadic** adj.

maestoso (maɪ'stəʊsəʊ) Music. ~adj., adv. **1.** to be performed majestically. ~n., pl. -**sos**. **2.** a piece or passage directed to be played in this way. [C18: It.: majestic, from L māiestās MAJESTY]

Maestricht ('maːstrɪxt; Dutch maː'strɪxt) n. an obsolete spelling of **Maastricht**.

maestro ('maɪstrəʊ) n., pl. -**tri** (-trɪ) or -**tros**. **1.** a distinguished music teacher, conductor, or musician. **2.** any master of an art: often used as a term of address. [C18: It.: master]

Maeterlinck ('meɪtəˌlɪŋk; French mɛtɛrlɛ̃k) n. Comte **Maurice** (mɔrɪs). 1862–1949, Belgian poet and dramatist, noted particularly for his symbolist plays, such as Pelléas et Mélisande (1892), which served as the basis for an opera by Debussy, and L'Oiseau bleu (1909). Nobel prize for literature 1911.

mae west (meɪ) n. Sl. an inflatable life jacket, esp. as issued to the U.S. armed forces. [C20: after Mae West (1892–1980), American actress, renowned for her generous bust]

Maewo (maː'eɪwəʊ) n. an almost uninhabited island in Vanuatu. Also called: **Aurora**.

Mafeking ('mæfɪˌkɪŋ) n. the former name (until 1980) of **Mafikeng**.

Mafia ('mæfɪə) n. **1.** the. an international secret criminal organization founded in Sicily, and carried to the U.S. by Italian immigrants. **2.** any group considered to resemble the Mafia. [C19: from Sicilian dialect of It., lit.: hostility to the law, ?from Ar. mahyah bragging]

Mafikeng ('mæfɪˌkɛŋ) n. a town in South Africa, in Bophuthatswana: besieged by the Boers for 217 days (1899–1900) during the second Boer War: administrative headquarters of the British protectorate of Bechuanaland until 1965, although outside its borders: in Cape Province until 1980, when officially surrendered to Bophuthatswana by South Africa. Pop.: 6775 (1980). Former name (until 1980): **Mafeking.**

mafioso (ˌmæfɪˈəʊsəʊ) n., pl. **-sos** or **-si** (-sɪ). a person belonging to the Mafia.

mag. abbrev. for: **1.** magazine. **2.** magnesium. **3.** magnetic. **4.** magnetism. **5.** magnitude.

Magallanes (Spanish maɣaˈʎanes) n. the former name of **Punta Arenas.**

magazine (ˌmægəˈziːn) n. **1.** a periodic paperback publication containing articles, fiction, photographs, etc. **2. a.** a metal case holding several cartridges used in some automatic firearms. **b.** this compartment itself. **3.** a building or compartment for storing weapons, explosives, military provisions, etc. **4.** a stock of ammunition. **5.** Photog. another name for **cartridge** (sense 3). **6.** a rack for automatically feeding slides through a projector. [C16: via F magasin from It. magazzino, from Ar. makhāzin, pl. of makhzan storehouse, from khazana to store away]

magdalen ('mægdəlɪn) or **magdalene** ('mægdəˌliːn) n. **1.** Literary. a reformed prostitute. **2.** Rare. a reformatory for prostitutes. [from Mary MAGDALENE]

Magdalena (ˌmægdəˈleɪnə, -ˈliː-; Spanish maɣðaˈlena) n. a river in SW Colombia, rising on the E slopes of the Andes and flowing north to the Caribbean near Barranquilla. Length: 1540 km (956 miles).

Magdalena Bay n. an inlet of the Pacific on the coast of NW Mexico, in Lower California.

Magdalene ('mægdəˌliːn, ˌmægdəˈliːnɪ) n. See **Mary Magdalene.**

Magdalenian (ˌmægdəˈliːnɪən) adj. **1.** of or relating to the latest Palaeolithic culture in Europe, which ended about 10 000 years ago. ~n. **2. the.** the Magdalenian culture. [C19: from F magdalénien, after La Madeleine, village in Dordogne, France, near which artefacts of the culture were found]

Magdeburg ('mægdəˌbɜːg; German 'makdəbʊrk) n. an industrial city and port in W East Germany, on the River Elbe: a leading member of the Hanseatic League, whose local laws, the **Magdeburg Laws,** were adopted by many European cities. Pop.: 288 798 (1981 est.).

Magellan[1] (məˈgɛlən) n. **Strait of.** a strait between the mainland of S South America and Tierra del Fuego, linking the S Pacific with the S Atlantic. Length: 600 km (370 miles). Width: up to 32 km (20 miles).

Magellan[2] (məˈgɛlən) n. **Ferdinand.** Portuguese name Fernão de Magalhães. ?1480–1521, Portuguese navigator in the service of Spain. He commanded an expedition of five ships that set out to sail to the East Indies via the West. He discovered the Strait of Magellan (1520), crossed the Pacific, and reached the Philippines (1521), where he was killed by natives. One of his ships reached Spain (1522) and was therefore the first to circumnavigate the world.

Magellanic cloud (ˌmægɪˈlænɪk) n. either of two small irregular galaxies situated near the S celestial pole at a distance of 160 000 light years.

magenta (məˈdʒɛntə) n. **1. a.** a deep purplish red. **b.** (as adj.): a magenta filter. **2.** another name for **fuchsin.** [C19: after Magenta, Italy, alluding to the blood shed in a battle there (1859)]

Maggiore (ˌmædʒɪˈɔːrɪ; Italian madˈdʒore) n. **Lake.** a lake in N Italy and S Switzerland, in the S Lepontine Alps.

maggot ('mægət) n. **1.** the limbless larva of dipterous insects, esp. the housefly and blowfly. **2.** Rare. a fancy or whim. [C14: from earlier mathek; rel. to ON mathkr worm, OE matha, OHG mado grub]

maggoty ('mægətɪ) adj. **1.** of, like, or ridden with maggots. **2.** Austral. sl. angry.

Maghreb or **Maghrib** ('mʌgrəb) n. NW Africa, including Morocco, Algeria, Tunisia, and sometimes Libya. [from Ar., lit.: the West] —**Maghrebi** or **Maghribi** adj., n.

magi ('meɪdʒaɪ) pl. n., sing. **magus** ('meɪgəs). **1.** See **magus.** **2. the three Magi.** the wise men from the East who came to do homage to the infant Jesus (Matthew 2:1–12). [see MAGUS] —**magian** ('meɪdʒɪən) adj.

magic ('mædʒɪk) n. **1.** the art that, by use of spells, supposedly invokes supernatural powers to influence events;

sorcery. **2.** the practice of this art. **3.** the practice of illusory tricks to entertain; conjuring. **4.** any mysterious or extraordinary quality or power. **5.** like **magic.** very quickly. ~adj. also **magical.** **6.** of or relating to magic. **7.** possessing or considered to possess mysterious powers. **8.** unaccountably enchanting. **9.** Inf. wonderful; marvellous. ~vb. **-icking, -icked.** (tr.) **10.** to transform or produce by or as if by magic. **11.** (foll. by away) to cause to disappear as if by magic. [C14: via OF magique, from Gk magikē witchcraft, from magos MAGUS] —**magically** adv.

magic eye n. a miniature cathode-ray tube in some radio receivers, on the screen of which a pattern is displayed to assist tuning. Also called: **electric eye.**

magician (məˈdʒɪʃən) n. **1.** another term for **conjurer.** **2.** a person who practises magic. **3.** a person with extraordinary skill, influence, etc.

magic lantern n. an early type of slide projector.

magic mushroom n. Inf. any of various types of fungi that contain a hallucinogenic substance.

magic realism or **magical realism** n. a style of painting or writing that depicts images or scenes of surreal fantasy in a representational or realistic way. —**magic realist** or **magical realist** n.

magic square n. a square array of rows of integers arranged so that the sum of the integers is the same when taken vertically, horizontally, or diagonally.

Maginot line ('mæʒɪˌnəʊ) n. **1.** a line of fortifications built by France to defend its border with Germany prior to World War II; it proved ineffective. **2.** any line of defence in which blind confidence is placed. [after André Maginot (1877–1932), F minister of war when the fortifications were begun in 1929]

magisterial (ˌmædʒɪˈstɪərɪəl) adj. **1.** commanding; authoritative. **2.** domineering; dictatorial. **3.** of or relating to a teacher or person of similar status. **4.** of or relating to a magistrate. [C17: from LL magisteriālis, from magister master] —**magis'terially** adv.

magistracy ('mædʒɪstrəsɪ) or **magistrature** ('mædʒɪstrəˌtjʊə) n., pl. **-cies** or **-tures. 1.** the office or function of a magistrate. **2.** magistrates collectively. **3.** the district under the jurisdiction of a magistrate.

magistral (məˈdʒɪstrəl) adj. **1.** Pharmacol. made up according to a special prescription. **2.** of a master; masterly. [C16: from L magistrālis, from magister master] —**magistrality** (ˌmædʒɪˈstrælɪtɪ) n.

magistrate ('mædʒɪˌstreɪt, -strɪt) n. **1.** a public officer concerned with the administration of law. **2.** another name for **justice of the peace.** [C17: from L magistrātus, from magister master] —**'magis,trateship** n.

magistrates' court n. (in England) a court held before two or more justices of the peace or a stipendiary magistrate to deal with minor crimes, certain civil actions, and preliminary hearings.

Maglemosian or **Maglemosean** (ˌmægləˈməʊzɪən) n. **1.** the first Mesolithic culture of N Europe, dating from 8000 B.C. to about 5000 B.C. ~adj. **2.** designating or relating to this culture. [C20: after the site at Maglemose, Denmark, where the culture was first classified]

magma ('mægmə) n., pl. **-mas** or **-mata** (-mətə). **1.** a paste or suspension consisting of a finely divided solid dispersed in a liquid. **2.** hot molten rock within the earth's crust which sometimes finds its way to the surface where it solidifies to form igneous rock. [C15: from L: dregs (of an ointment), from Gk: salve made by kneading, from massein to knead] —**magmatic** (mægˈmætɪk) adj.

Magna Carta or **Magna Charta** ('mægnə 'kɑːtə) n. English history. the charter granted by King John at Runnymede in 1215, recognizing the rights and privileges of the barons, church, and freemen. [Med. L: great charter]

Magna Graecia ('mægnə 'griːʃɪə) n. (in the ancient world) S Italy, where numerous colonies were founded by Greek cities. [L: Great Greece]

magnanimity (ˌmægnəˈnɪmɪtɪ) n., pl. **-ties.** generosity. [C14: via OF from L magnanimitās, from magnus great + animus soul]

magnanimous (mægˈnænɪməs) adj. generous and noble. [C16: from L magnanimus great-souled] —**mag'nanimously** adv.

magnate ('mægneɪt, -nɪt) n. **1.** a person of power and rank, esp. in industry. **2.** History. a great nobleman. [C15: back formation from earlier magnates, from LL: great men, from L magnus great] —**'magnate,ship** n.

magnesia (mæg'niːʃə) n. another name for **magnesium oxide**. [C14: via Med. L from Gk *Magnēsia*, of *Magnēs*, ancient mineral-rich region] —**mag'nesian** or **magnesic** (mæg'niːsɪk) adj.

magnesium (mæg'niːzɪəm) n. a light silvery-white metallic element of the alkaline earth series that burns with an intense white flame: used in light structural alloys, flashbulbs, flares, and fireworks. Symbol: Mg; atomic no.: 12; atomic wt.: 24.312. [C19: NL, from MAGNESIA]

magnesium oxide n. a white tasteless substance used as an antacid and laxative and in refractory materials. Formula: MgO. Also called: **magnesia.**

magnet ('mægnɪt) n. **1.** a body that can attract certain substances, such as iron or steel, as a result of a magnetic field; a piece of ferromagnetic substance. See also **electromagnet. 2.** a person or thing that exerts a great attraction. [C15: via L from Gk *magnēs*, shortened from *ho Magnēs lithos* the Magnesian stone. See MAGNESIA]

magnetic (mæg'nɛtɪk) adj. **1.** of, producing, or operated by means of magnetism. **2.** of or concerned with a magnet. **3.** of or concerned with the magnetism of the earth: *the magnetic equator.* **4.** capable of being magnetized. **5.** exerting a powerful attraction: *a magnetic personality.* —**mag'netically** adv.

magnetic constant n. the magnetic permeability of free space; it has the value $4\pi \times 10^{-7}$ H m^{-1}.

magnetic declination n. the angle that a compass needle makes with the direction of the geographical north pole at any given point on the earth's surface.

magnetic dip or **inclination** n. another name for **dip** (sense 27).

magnetic dipole moment n. a measure of the magnetic strength of a magnet or current-carrying coil, expressed as the torque produced when the magnet or coil is set with its axis perpendicular to unit magnetic field.

magnetic disk n. another name for **disk** (sense 2).

magnetic equator n. an imaginary line on the earth's surface, near the equator, at all points on which there is no magnetic dip.

magnetic field n. a field of force surrounding a permanent magnet or a moving charged particle, in which another permanent magnet or moving charge experiences a force.

magnetic flux n. a measure of the strength of a magnetic field over a given area, equal to the product of the area and the magnetic flux density through it. Symbol: ϕ

magnetic mine n. a mine designed to activate when a magnetic field such as that generated by the metal of a ship's hull is detected.

magnetic needle n. a slender magnetized rod used in certain instruments, such as the magnetic compass, for indicating the direction of a magnetic field.

magnetic north n. the direction in which a compass needle points, at an angle (the declination) from the direction of true (geographic) north.

magnetic pick-up n. a type of record-player pick-up in which the stylus moves an iron core in a coil, causing a changing magnetic field that produces the current.

magnetic pole n. **1.** either of two regions in a magnet where the magnetic induction is concentrated. **2.** either of two variable points on the earth's surface towards which a magnetic needle points, where the lines of force of the earth's magnetic field are vertical.

magnetic resonance n. the response by atoms, molecules, or nuclei subjected to a magnetic field to radio waves or other forms of energy: used in medicine for scanning.

magnetic storm n. a sudden severe disturbance of the earth's magnetic field, caused by emission of charged particles from the sun.

magnetic stripe n. (across the back of various types of bank card, credit card, etc.) a dark stripe of magnetic material consisting of several tracks onto which information may be coded and which may be read or written to electronically.

magnetic tape n. a long narrow plastic or metal strip coated or impregnated with iron oxide, chrome dioxide, etc., used to record sound or video signals or to store information in computers.

magnetism ('mægnɪ,tɪzəm) n. **1.** the property of attraction displayed by magnets. **2.** any of a class of phenomena in which a field of force is caused by a moving electric charge. **3.** the branch of physics concerned with magnetic phenomena. **4.** powerful attraction.

magnetite ('mægnɪ,taɪt) n. a black magnetizable mineral that is an important source of iron.

magnetize or **-ise** ('mægnɪ,taɪz) vb. (tr.) **1.** to make (a substance or object) magnetic. **2.** to attract strongly. —,**magnet'izable** or **-'isable** adj. —,**magneti'zation** or **-i'sation** n. — '**magnet,izer** or **-,iser** n.

magneto (mæg'niːtəʊ) n., pl. **-tos.** a small electric generator in which the magnetic field is produced by a permanent magnet, esp. one for providing the spark in an internal-combustion engine. [C19: short for *magnetoelectric generator*]

magneto- *combining form.* indicating magnetism or magnetic properties: *magnetosphere.*

magnetoelectricity (mæg,niːtəʊɪlɛk'trɪsɪtɪ) n. electricity produced by the action of magnetic fields. —**mag,neto-e'lectric** or **mag,netoe'lectrical** adj.

magnetometer (,mægnɪ'tɒmɪtə) n. any instrument for measuring the intensity or direction of a magnetic field, esp. the earth's field. —,**magne'tometry** n.

magnetomotive (mæg,niːtəʊ'məʊtɪv) adj. causing a magnetic flux.

magnetosphere (mæg'niːtəʊ,sfɪə) n. the region surrounding the earth in which the behaviour of charged particles is dominated by the earth's magnetic field.

magnetron ('mægnɪ,trɒn) n. a two-electrode electronic valve used with an applied magnetic field to generate high-power microwave oscillations, esp. for use in radar. [C20: from MAGNET + ELECTRON]

Magnificat (mæg'nɪfɪ,kæt) n. *Christianity.* the hymn of the Virgin Mary (Luke 1:46-55), used as a canticle. [from the opening phrase, *Magnificat anima mea Dominum* (my soul doth magnify the Lord)]

magnification (,mægnɪfɪ'keɪʃən) n. **1.** the act of magnifying or the state of being magnified. **2.** the degree to which something is magnified. **3.** a magnified copy, photograph, drawing, etc., of something. **4.** a measure of the ability of a lens or other optical instrument to magnify.

magnificence (mæg'nɪfɪsəns) n. the quality of being magnificent. [C14: via F from L *magnificentia*]

magnificent (mæg'nɪfɪsənt) adj. **1.** splendid or impressive in appearance. **2.** superb or very fine. **3.** (esp. of ideas) noble or elevated. [C16: from L *magnificentior*, irregular comp. of *magnificus* great in deeds, from *magnus* great + *facere* to do] —**mag'nificently** adv.

magnifico (mæg'nɪfɪkəʊ) n., pl. **-coes.** a magnate; grandee. [C16: It. from L *magnificus;* see MAGNIFICENT]

magnify ('mægnɪ,faɪ) vb. **-fying, -fied. 1.** to increase, cause to increase, or be increased in apparent size, as through the action of a lens, microscope, etc. **2.** to exaggerate or become exaggerated in importance: *don't magnify your troubles.* **3.** (tr.) *Arch.* to glorify. [C14: via OF from L *magnificāre* to praise] — '**magni,fiable** adj.

magnifying glass or **magnifier** n. a convex lens used to produce an enlarged image of an object.

magniloquent (mæg'nɪləkwənt) adj. (of speech) lofty in style; grandiloquent. [C17: from L *magnus* great + *loquī* to speak] —**mag'niloquence** n. —**mag'niloquently** adv.

Magnitogorsk (*Russian* məgnita'gɔrsk) n. a city in the central Soviet Union, on the Ural River: founded in 1930 to exploit local magnetite ores; site of one of the world's largest metallurgical plants. Pop.: 430 000 (1987).

magnitude ('mægnɪ,tjuːd) n. **1.** relative importance or significance: *a problem of the first magnitude.* **2.** relative size or extent. **3.** *Maths.* a number assigned to a quantity as a basis of comparison for the measurement of similar quantities. **4.** Also called: **apparent magnitude.** *Astron.* the apparent brightness of a celestial body expressed on a numerical scale on which bright stars have a low value. **5.** Also called: **earthquake magnitude.** *Geol.* a measure of the size of an earthquake based on the quantity of energy released. [C14: from L *magnitūdō* size, from *magnus* great]

magnolia (mæg'nəʊlɪə) n. **1.** any tree or shrub of the genus *Magnolia* of Asia and North America: cultivated for their white, pink, purple, or yellow showy flowers. **2.** the flower of any of these plants. **3. a.** a very pale pinkish-white colour. **b.** (*as adj.*): *magnolia walls.* [C18: NL, after Pierre *Magnol* (1638–1715), F botanist]

magnox ('mægnɒks) *n.* an alloy consisting mostly of magnesium with small amounts of aluminium, used in fuel elements of nuclear reactors. [C20: from *mag(nesium) n(o) ox(idation)*]

magnox reactor *n.* a nuclear reactor using carbon dioxide as the coolant, graphite as the moderator, and uranium cased in magnox as the fuel.

magnum ('mægnəm) *n., pl.* **-nums.** a wine bottle holding the equivalent of two normal bottles (approximately 52 fluid ounces). [C18: from L: a big thing, from *magnus* large]

magnum opus *n.* a great work of art or literature, esp. the greatest single work of an artist. [L]

Magog ('meigɒg) *n.* See **Gog and Magog**.

magpie ('mæg,pai) *n.* **1.** any of various birds having a black-and-white plumage, long tail, and a chattering call. **2.** any of various similar birds of Australia. **3.** *Brit.* a person who hoards small objects. **4.** a person who chatters. **5. a.** the outmost ring but one on a target. **b.** a shot that hits this ring. [C17: from *Mag*, dim. of *Margaret*, used to signify a chatterbox + PIE²]

Magritte (*French* magrit) *n.* **René** (rəne). 1898–1967, Belgian surrealist painter. By juxtaposing incongruous objects, depicted with meticulous realism, his works create a bizarre and disturbing impression.

maguey ('mægwei) *n.* **1.** any of various tropical American agave plants, esp. one that yields a fibre or is used in making an alcoholic beverage. **2.** the fibre from any of these plants, used esp. for rope. [C16: Sp., of Amerind origin]

magus ('meigəs) *n., pl.* **magi. 1.** a Zoroastrian priest. **2.** an astrologer, sorcerer, or magician of ancient times. [C14: from L, from Gk *magos*, from OPersian *magus* magician]

Magus ('meigəs) *n.* **Simon.** *New Testament.* a sorcerer who tried to buy spiritual powers from the apostles (Acts 8:9-24).

Magyar ('mægjɑː) *n.* **1.** (*pl.* **-yars**) a member of the predominant ethnic group of Hungary. **2.** the Hungarian language. ~*adj.* **3.** of or relating to the Magyars or their language. **4.** *Sewing.* of or relating to a style of sleeve cut in one piece with the bodice.

Magyarország ('mɔdjɔrorsɑːg) *n.* the Hungarian name for **Hungary**.

Mahabharata (,mɑːhəˈbɑːrətə), **Mahabharatam,** *or* **Mahabharatum** (,mɑːhəˈbɑːrətəm) *n.* an epic Sanskrit poem of India of which the *Bhagavad-Gita* forms a part. [Sansk., from *mahā* great + *bhārata* story]

Mahajanga (,mæhəˈdʒæŋgə) *n.* a port in NW Madagascar, on Bombetoka Bay. Pop.: 80 881 (1982). Former name: **Majunga.**

Mahalla el Kubra (məˈhɑːlə ɛl ˈkuːbrə) *n.* a city in N Egypt, on the Nile delta: one of the largest diversified textile centres in Egypt. Pop.: 362 700 (1985).

Mahanadi (məˈhɑːnədi) *n.* a river in E India, rising in S Madhya Pradesh and flowing north, then south and east to the Bay of Bengal. Length: 885 km (550 miles).

maharajah *or* **maharaja** (,mɑːhəˈrɑːdʒə) *n.* any of various Indian princes, esp. any of the rulers of the former native states. [C17: Hindi, from *mahā* great + RAJAH]

maharani *or* **maharanee** (,mɑːhəˈrɑːniː) *n.* **1.** the wife of a maharajah. **2.** a woman holding the rank of maharajah. [C19: from Hindi, from *mahā* great + RANI]

Maharashtra (,mɑːhəˈræʃtrə) *n.* a state of W central India, formed in 1960 from the Marathi-speaking S and E parts of former Bombay state: lies mainly on the Deccan plateau; mainly agricultural. Capital: Bombay. Pop.: 62 715 300 (1981). Area: 306 345 sq. km (119 475 sq. miles).

maharishi (,mɑːhəˈriːʃi, məˈhɑːriːʃi) *n. Hinduism.* a Hindu teacher of religious and mystical knowledge. [from Hindi, from *mahā* great + *rishi* sage]

mahatma (məˈhɑːtmə) *n.* (*sometimes cap.*) **1.** *Hinduism.* a Brahman sage. **2.** *Theosophy.* an adept or sage. [C19: from Sansk. *mahātman*, from *mahā* great + *ātman* soul]

Mahayana (,mɑːhəˈjɑːnə) *n.* **a.** a liberal Buddhist school of Tibet, China, and Japan, whose adherents seek enlightenment for all sentient beings. **b.** (*as modifier*): *Mahayana Buddhism.* [from Sansk., from *mahā* great + *yāna* vehicle]

Mahdi ('mɑːdi) *n.* **1.** the title assumed by *Mohammed Ahmed.* ?1843–85, Sudanese military leader, who led a revolt against Egypt (1881) and captured Khartoum (1885). **2.**

Islam. any of a number of Muslim messiahs expected to forcibly convert all mankind to Islam. [Ar. *mahdīy* one who is guided, from *madā* to guide aright] —**'Mahdism** *n.* —**'Mahdist** *n., adj.*

Mahé (mɑːˈhei) *n.* an island in the Indian Ocean, the chief island of the Seychelles. Capital: Victoria. Pop.: 59 500 (1987). Area: 147 sq. km (57 sq. miles).

mahjong *or* **mah-jongg** (,mɑːˈdʒɒŋ) *n.* a game of Chinese origin, usually played by four people, using tiles bearing various designs. [from Chinese, lit.: sparrows]

Mahler ('mɑːlə) *n.* **Gustav** ('gustaf). 1860–1911, Austrian composer and conductor, whose music links the romantic tradition of the 19th century with the music of the 20th century. His works include nine complete symphonies for large orchestras, the symphonic song cycle *Das Lied von der Erde* (1908), and the song cycle *Kindertotenlieder* (1902).

mahlstick ('mɔːl,stik) *n.* a variant spelling of **maulstick**.

mahogany (məˈhɒgəni) *n., pl.* **-nies. 1.** any of various tropical American trees valued for their hard reddish-brown wood. **2.** any of several trees with similar wood, such as African mahogany and Philippine mahogany. **3. a.** the wood of any of these trees. **b.** (*as modifier*): *a mahogany table.* **4. a.** a reddish-brown colour. **b.** (*as adj.*): *mahogany skin.* [C17: from ?]

Mahomet (məˈhɒmit) *n.* a variant of **Mohammed**.

mahonia (məˈhəʊniə) *n.* any evergreen shrub of the Asian and American genus *Mahonia*: cultivated for their ornamental spiny divided leaves and clusters of small yellow flowers. [C19: NL, after Bernard *McMahon* (died 1816), American botanist]

Mahound (məˈhaʊnd, -ˈhuːnd) *n.* an archaic name for **Mohammed**. [C16: from OF *Mahun*]

mahout (məˈhaʊt) *n.* (in India and the East Indies) an elephant driver or keeper. [C17: Hindi *mahāut*, from Sansk. *mahāmātra* of great measure, orig. a title]

Mähren ('mɛːrən) *n.* the German name for **Moravia**.

mahseer (məˈsiə) *n.* any of various large freshwater Indian cyprinid fishes. [from Hindi]

Maia ('maiə) *n. Greek myth.* the eldest of the seven Pleiades, mother by Zeus of Hermes.

maid (meid) *n.* **1.** *Arch. or literary.* a young unmarried girl; maiden. **2. a.** a female servant. **b.** (*in combination*): *a housemaid.* **3.** a spinster. [C12: form of MAIDEN]

maiden ('meidᵊn) *n.* **1.** *Arch. or literary.* **a.** a young unmarried girl, esp. a virgin. **b.** (*as modifier*): *a maiden blush.* **2.** *Horse racing.* **a.** a horse that has never won a race. **b.** (*as modifier*): *a maiden race.* **3.** *Cricket.* See **maiden over. 4.** (*modifier*) of or relating to an older unmarried woman: *a maiden aunt.* **5.** (*modifier*) of or involving an initial experience or attempt: *a maiden voyage.* **6.** (*modifier*) (of a person or thing) untried; unused. **7.** (*modifier*) (of a place) never trodden, penetrated, or captured. [OE *mægden*] —**'maidenish** *adj.* —**'maiden,like** *adj.*

maidenhair fern *or* **maidenhair** ('meidᵊn,hɛə) *n.* any of various ferns of tropical and warm regions, having delicate fan-shaped fronds with small pale green leaflets. [C15: from the hairlike appearance of its fronds]

maidenhair tree *n.* another name for **ginkgo**.

maidenhead ('meidᵊn,hɛd) *n.* **1.** a nontechnical word for the **hymen. 2.** virginity; maidenhood. [C13: from *maiden* + *-hed*, var. of -HOOD]

Maidenhead ('meidᵊn,hɛd) *n.* a town in S England, in Berkshire on the River Thames. Pop.: 48 473 (1983 est.).

maidenhood ('meidᵊn,hʊd) *n.* **1.** the time during which a woman is a maiden or virgin. **2.** the condition of being a maiden or virgin.

maidenly ('meidᵊnli) *adj.* of or befitting a maiden. —**'maidenliness** *n.*

maiden name *n.* a woman's surname before marriage.

maiden over *n. Cricket.* an over in which no runs are scored.

maid of honour *n.* **1.** *U.S. & Canad.* the principal unmarried attendant of a bride. **2.** *Brit.* a small tart with an almond-flavoured filling. **3.** an unmarried lady attending a queen or princess.

Maid of Orléans *n.* **the.** another name for **Joan of Arc**.

maidservant ('meid,sɜːvənt) *n.* a female servant.

Maidstone ('meidstən, -,stəʊn) *n.* a town in SE England, administrative centre of Kent, on the River Medway. Pop.: 71 800 (1983 est.).

Maiduguri (ˌmaɪdʊˈɡʊːrɪ) *n.* a city in NE Nigeria, capital of Bornu State; agricultural trade centre. Pop. (with Yerwa) 230 900 (1983 est.). Also called: **Yerwa-Maiduguri.**

maihem ('meɪhɛm) *n.* a variant spelling of **mayhem.**

Maikop (*Russian* maj'kɔp) *n.* a city in the SW Soviet Union, capital of the Adygei AR: extensive oilfields to the southwest; mineral springs. Pop.: 142 000 (1986 est.).

mail¹ (meɪl) *n.* **1.** Also called (esp. Brit.): **post.** letters, packages, etc., that are transported and delivered by the post office. **2.** the postal system. **3.** a single collection or delivery of mail. **4.** a train, ship, or aircraft that carries mail. **5.** (*modifier*) of, involving, or used to convey mail: *a mail train.* ~*vb.* **6.** (*tr.*) *Chiefly U.S. & Canad.* to send by mail. [C13: from OF *male* bag, prob. from OHG *malha* wallet] —'**mailable** *adj.*

mail² (meɪl) *n.* **1.** a type of flexible armour consisting of riveted metal rings or links. **2.** the hard protective shell of such animals as the turtle and lobster. ~*vb.* **3.** (*tr.*) to clothe or arm with mail. [C14: from OF *maille* mesh, from L *macula* spot]

mailbag ('meɪlˌbæɡ) *or* **mailsack** *n.* a large bag for transporting or delivering mail.

mailbox ('meɪlˌbɒks) *n.* another name (esp. U.S. and Canad.) for **letter box.**

Mailer ('meɪlə) *n.* **Norman.** born 1923, U.S. author. His works, which are frequently critical of modern American society, include the war novel *The Naked and the Dead* (1948), *The American Dream* (1965), his account of the 1967 peace march on Washington *The Armies of the Night* (1968), and *Why Are We In Vietnam* (1988).

mailing list *n.* a register of names and addresses to which advertising matter, etc., is sent by post.

Maillol (*French* majɔl) *n.* **Aristide** (aristid). 1861–1944, French sculptor, esp. of monumental female nudes.

maillot (mæˈjəʊ) *n.* **1.** tights worn for ballet, gymnastics, etc. **2.** a woman's swimsuit. **3.** a jersey. [from F]

mailman ('meɪlˌmæn) *n., pl.* -men. *Chiefly U.S. & Canad.* another name for **postman.**

mail order *n.* **1.** an order for merchandise sent by post. **2. a.** a system of buying and selling merchandise through the post. **b.** (*as modifier*): *a mail-order firm.*

mailshot ('meɪlˌʃɒt) *n.* a circular, leaflet, or other advertising material sent by post, or the posting of such material to a large group of people at one time.

maim (meɪm) *vb.* (*tr.*) **1.** to mutilate, cripple, or disable a part of the body of (a person or animal). **2.** to make defective. [C14: from OF *mahaignier* to wound, prob. of Gmc origin]

mai mai (maɪ maɪ) *n. N.Z.* a duck shooter's shelter; hide. [from Maori]

Maimonides (maɪˈmɒnɪˌdiːz) *n.* also called Rabbi *Moses ben Maimon.* 1135–1204, Jewish philosopher, physician, and jurist, born in Spain. He codified Jewish law in *Mishneh Torah* (1180). —**Mai̲moni'dean** *adj., n.*

main¹ (meɪn) *adj.* (*prenominal*) **1.** chief or principal. **2.** sheer or utmost (esp. in **by main force**) . **3.** *Naut.* of, relating to, or denoting any gear, such as a stay or sail, belonging to the mainmast. ~*n.* **4.** a principal pipe, conduit, duct, or line in a system used to distribute water, electricity, etc. **5.** (*pl.*) **a.** the main distribution network for water, gas, or electricity. **b.** (*as modifier*): *mains voltage.* **6.** the chief or most important part or consideration. **7.** great strength or force (now esp. in **might and main**) . **8.** *Literary.* the open ocean. **9.** *Arch.* short for **Spanish Main. 10.** *Arch.* short for **mainland. 11. in** (*or* **for**) **the main.** on the whole; for the most part. [C13: from OE *mægen* strength]

main² (meɪn) *n.* **1.** a throw of the dice in dice games. **2.** a cockfighting contest. **3.** a match in archery, boxing, etc. [C16: from ?]

Main (meɪn; *German* main) *n.* a river in central and W West Germany, flowing west through Würzburg and Frankfurt to the Rhine. Length: about 515 km (320 miles).

mainbrace ('meɪnˌbreɪs) *n. Naut.* **1.** a brace attached to the main yard. **2. splice the mainbrace. See splice.**

main clause *n. Grammar.* a clause that can stand alone as a sentence.

Maine (meɪn) *n.* a state of the northeastern U.S., on the Atlantic: chiefly hilly, with many lakes, rivers, and forests. Capital: Augusta. Pop.: 1 174 000 (1986 est.). Area: 80 082 sq. km (30 920 sq. miles). Abbrev. (with zip code): **ME**

Maine-et-Loire (*French* mɛnelwar) *n.* a department of W France, in Pays de la Loire region. Capital: Angers. Pop.: 675 321 (1982). Area: 7218 sq. km (2815 sq. miles).

mainframe ('meɪnˌfreɪm) *Computers.* ~*adj.* **1.** denoting a high-speed general-purpose computer, usually with a large store capacity. ~*n.* **2.** such a computer. **3.** the central processing unit of a computer.

mainland ('meɪnlənd) *n.* the main part of a land mass as opposed to an island or peninsula. —'**mainlander** *n.*

Mainland ('meɪnlənd) *n.* **1.** an island off N Scotland: the largest of the Shetland Islands. Chief town: Lerwick. Pop.: 19 236 (1986). Area: about 583 sq. km (225 sq. miles). **2.** Also called: **Pomona.** an island off N Scotland: the largest of the Orkney Islands. Chief town: Kirkwall. Pop.: 14 279 (1981). Area: 492 sq. km (190 sq. miles). **3. the Mainland.** *N.Z.* a South Islanders' name for **South Island.**

main line *n.* **1.** *Railways.* **a.** the trunk route between two points, usually fed by branch lines. **b.** (*as modifier*): *a main-line station.* **2.** *U.S.* a main road. ~*vb.* **3.** (*intr.*) *Sl.* to inject a drug into a vein. ~*adj.* **mainline.** **4.** having an important position. —'**main̲line** *n.*

mainly ('meɪnlɪ) *adv.* for the most part; to the greatest extent; principally.

mainmast ('meɪnˌmɑːst) *n. Naut.* the chief mast of a sailing vessel with two or more masts.

mainsail ('meɪnˌseɪl; *Naut.* 'meɪnsəl) *n. Naut.* the largest and lowermost sail on the mainmast.

mainsheet ('meɪnˌʃiːt) *n. Naut.* the line used to control the angle of the mainsail to the wind.

mainspring ('meɪnˌsprɪŋ) *n.* **1.** the principal spring of a mechanism, esp. in a watch or clock. **2.** the chief cause or motive of something.

mainstay ('meɪnˌsteɪ) *n.* **1.** *Naut.* the forestay that braces the mainmast. **2.** a chief support.

mainstream ('meɪnˌstriːm) *n.* **1.** the main current (of a river, cultural trend, etc.). ~*adj.* **2.** of or relating to the style of jazz that lies between the traditional and the modern.

mainstreeting ('meɪnˌstriːtɪŋ) *n. Canad.* the practice of a politician walking about the streets of a town or city to gain votes and greet supporters.

maintain (meɪn'teɪn) *vb.* (*tr.*) **1.** to continue or retain; keep in existence. **2.** to keep in proper or good condition. **3.** to enable (a person) to support a style of living: *the money maintained us for a month.* **4.** (*takes a clause as object*) to state or assert. **5.** to defend against contradiction; uphold: *she maintained her innocence.* **6.** to defend against physical attack. [C13: from OF *maintenir*, ult. from L *manū tenēre* to hold in the hand] —**main'tainable** *adj.* —**main'tainer** *n.*

maintenance ('meɪntɪnəns) *n.* **1.** the act of maintaining or the state of being maintained. **2.** a means of support; livelihood. **3.** (*modifier*) of or relating to the maintaining of buildings, machinery, etc.: *maintenance man.* **4.** *Law.* the interference in a legal action by a person having no interest in it, as by providing funds to continue the action. **5.** *Law.* a provision ordered to be made by way of periodical payments or a lump sum, as for a spouse after a divorce. [C14: from OF; see MAINTAIN]

Maintenon (*French* mɛ̃tnɔ̃) *n.* **Marquise de,** title of *Françoise d'Aubigné.* 1635–1719, the mistress and, from about 1685, second wife of Louis XIV.

maintop ('meɪnˌtɒp) *n.* a top or platform at the head of the mainmast.

main-topmast *n. Naut.* the mast immediately above the mainmast.

maintopsail (ˌmeɪn'tɒpseɪl; *Naut.* ˌmeɪn'tɒpsəl) *n. Naut.* a topsail on the mainmast.

main yard *n. Naut.* a yard for a square mainsail.

Mainz (*German* maints) *n.* a port in W West Germany, capital of the Rhineland-Palatinate, at the confluence of the Main and Rhine: an archbishopric from about 780 until 1801; important in the 15th century for the development of printing (by Johann Gutenberg). Pop.: 188 500 (1986). French name: **Mayence.**

maiolica (məˈjɒlɪkə) *n.* a variant of **majolica.**

maisonette *or* **maisonnette** (ˌmeɪzə'nɛt) *n.* self-contained living accommodation often occupying two floors of a larger house and having its own outside entrance. [C19: from F, dim. of *maison* house]

Maitland¹ ('meɪtlənd) *n.* a town in SE Australia, in E New South Wales: industrial centre of an agricultural region. Pop.: 38 863 (1981).

Maitland[2] ('meɪtlənd) n. **Frederic William.** 1850–1906, English legal historian.

maître d'hôtel (ˌmɛtrə dəu'tɛl) n., pl. **maîtres d'hôtel.** 1. a head waiter or steward. 2. the manager or owner of a hotel. [C16: from F: master of (the) hotel]

maize (meɪz) n. 1. Also called: **sweet corn, Indian corn.** a. a tall annual grass cultivated for its yellow edible grains, which develop on a spike. b. the grain of this plant, used for food, for fodder, and as a source of oil. 2. a. a yellow colour. b. (as adj.): a maize gown. [C16: from Sp. maiz, from Taino mahiz]

Maj. abbrev. for Major.

majestic (mə'dʒɛstɪk) adj. having or displaying majesty or great dignity; grand; lofty. —**ma'jestically** adv.

majesty ('mædʒɪstɪ) n. 1. great dignity of bearing; loftiness; grandeur. 2. supreme power or authority. [C13: from OF, from L mājestās; rel. to L major, comp. of magnus great]

Majesty ('mædʒɪstɪ) n., pl. **-ties.** (preceded by Your, His, Her, or Their) a title used to address or refer to a sovereign or the wife or widow of a sovereign.

majolica (mə'dʒɒlɪkə, mə'jɒl-) or **maiolica** n. a type of porous pottery glazed with bright metallic oxides that was originally imported into Italy via Majorca and was extensively made in Renaissance Italy. [C16: from It., from LL Mājorica Majorca]

major ('meɪdʒə) n. 1. Mil. an officer immediately junior to a lieutenant colonel. 2. a person who is superior in a group or class. 3. (often preceded by the) Music. a major key, chord, mode, or scale. 4. U.S., Canad., Austral., & N.Z. a. the principal field of study of a student. b. a student who is studying a particular subject as his principal field: a sociology major. 5. a person who has reached the age of legal majority. 6. a principal or important record company, film company, etc. 7. Logic. a major term or premise. ~adj. 8. larger in extent, number, etc. 9. of greater importance or priority. 10. very serious or significant. 11. main, chief, or principal. 12. of, involving, or making up a majority. 13. Music. a. (of a scale or mode) having notes separated by a whole tone, except for the third and fourth degrees, and seventh and eighth degrees, which are separated by a semitone. b. relating to or employing notes from the major scale: a major key. c. (postpositive) denoting a specified key or scale as being major: C major. d. denoting a chord or triad having a major third above the root. e. (in jazz) denoting a major chord with a major seventh added above the root. 14. Logic. constituting the major term or major premise of a syllogism. 15. Chiefly U.S., Canad., Austral., & N.Z. of or relating to a student's principal field of study at a university, etc. 16. Brit. the elder: used after a schoolboy's surname if he has one or more younger brothers in the same school: Price major. 17. of full legal age. ~vb. 18. (intr.; usually foll. by in) U.S., Canad., Austral., & N.Z. to do one's principal study (in a particular subject): to major in English literature. 19. (intr.; usually foll. by on) to take or deal with as the main area of interest: the book majors on peasant dishes. [C15 (adj.): from L, comp. of magnus great; C17 (n., in military sense): from F, short for SERGEANT MAJOR] —'**majorship** n.

▷ **Usage.** The overuse of major in examples like the major reason, the major differences, a major factor, where a comparative is not really implied, is avoided by careful writers and speakers of English.

Majorca (mə'jɔːkə, -'dʒɔː-) n. an island in the W Mediterranean: the largest of the Balearic Islands; tourism. Capital: Palma. Pop.: 534 511 (1981). Area: 3639 sq. km (1465 sq. miles). Spanish name: **Mallorca.**

major-domo (-'dəuməu) n., pl. **-mos.** 1. the chief steward or butler of a great household. 2. Facetious. a steward or butler. [C16: from Sp. mayordomo, from Med. L mājor domūs head of the household]

majorette (ˌmeɪdʒə'rɛt) n. 1. one of a group of girls who practise formation marching and baton twirling. 2. See **drum majorette.**

major general n. Mil. an officer immediately junior to a lieutenant general. —**major-'generalship** or **major-'generalcy** n.

majority (mə'dʒɒrɪtɪ) n., pl. **-ties.** 1. the greater number or part of something. 2. (in an election) the number of votes or seats by which the strongest party or candidate beats the combined opposition or the runner-up. 3. the largest party or group that votes together in a legislative or deliberative assembly. 4. the time of reaching or state of having reached full legal age. 5. the rank, office, or commission of major. 6. Euphemistic. the dead (esp. in **join the majority, go** or **pass over to the majority**). 7. (modifier) of, involving, or being a majority: a majority decision. 8. **in the majority.** forming or part of the greater number of something. [C16: from Med. L mājoritās, from MAJOR (adj.)]

major league n. U.S. & Canad. a league of highest classification in baseball, football, hockey, etc.

major orders pl. n. R.C. Church. the three higher degrees of holy orders: bishop, priest, and deacon.

major premise n. Logic. the premise of a syllogism containing the predicate of its conclusion.

major term n. Logic. the predicate of the conclusion of a syllogism.

Majunga (French maʒ̃ɛga) n. the former name of **Mahajanga.**

majuscule ('mædʒə,skjuːl) n. 1. a large letter, either capital or uncial, used in printing or writing. ~adj. 2. relating to, printed, or written in such letters. ~Cf. **minuscule.** [C18: via F from L mājusculus, dim. of mājor bigger] —**majuscular** (mə'dʒʌskjulə) adj.

Makalu ('mʌkə,luː) n. a massif in NE Nepal, on the border with Tibet in the Himalayas.

Makarios III (mə'kɑːrɪ,ɒs) n. original name Mikhail Christodoulou Mouskos. 1913–77, Cypriot archbishop, patriarch, and statesman; first president of the republic of Cyprus (1960–74; 1974–77).

Makasar, Makassar, or **Macassar** (mə'kæsə, -'kɑː-) n. another name for **Ujung Pandang.**

make (meɪk) vb. **making, made.** (mainly tr.) 1. to bring into being by shaping, changing, or combining materials, ideas, etc.; form or fashion. 2. to draw up, establish, or form: to make one's will. 3. to cause to exist, bring about, or produce: don't make a noise. 4. to cause, compel, or induce: please make him go away. 5. to appoint or assign: they made him chairman. 6. to constitute: one swallow doesn't make a summer. 7. (also intr.) to come or cause to come into a specified state or condition: to make merry. 8. (copula) to be or become through development: he will make a good teacher. 9. to cause or ensure the success of: your news has made my day. 10. to amount to: twelve inches make a foot. 11. to serve as or be suitable for: that piece of cloth will make a coat. 12. to prepare or put into a fit condition for use: to make a bed. 13. to be the essential element in or part of: charm makes a good salesman. 14. to carry out, effect, or do. 15. (intr.; foll. by to, as if to, or as though to) to act with the intention or a show of doing something: he made as if to hit her. 16. to use for a specified purpose: I will make this town my base. 17. to deliver or pronounce: to make a speech. 18. to give information or an opinion: what time do you make it? 19. to cause to seem or represent as being. 20. to earn, acquire, or win for oneself: to make friends. 21. to engage in: to make war. 22. to traverse or cover (distance) by travelling: we can make a hundred miles by nightfall. 23. to arrive in time for: he didn't make the first act of the play. 24. Cards. a. to win a trick with (a specified card). b. to shuffle (the cards). c. Bridge. to fulfil (a contract) by winning the necessary number of tricks. 25. Cricket. to score (runs). 26. Electronics. to close (a circuit) permitting a flow of current. 27. (intr.) to increase in depth: the water in the hold was making a foot a minute. 28. Inf. to gain a place or position on or in: to make the headlines. 29. Inf., chiefly U.S. to achieve the end of. 30. Taboo sl. to seduce. 31. **make a book.** to take bets on a race or another contest. 32. **make a day, night,** etc., **of it.** to cause an activity to last a day, night, etc. 33. **make do.** See **do**[1](sense 31). 34. **make eyes at.** to flirt with or ogle. 35. **make it. a.** Inf. to be successful in doing something. b. (foll. by with) Taboo sl. to have sexual intercourse. 36. **make like.** Sl., chiefly U.S. & Canad. a. to imitate. b. to pretend. ~n. 37. brand, type, or style. 38. the manner or way in which something is made. 39. disposition or character; make-up. 40. the act or process of making. 41. the amount or number made. 42. Cards. a player's turn to shuffle. 43. **on the make.** Sl. a. out for profit or conquest. b. in search of a sexual partner. ~See also **make away, make for,** etc. [OE macian] —'**makable** adj.

make away vb. (intr., adv.) **1.** to depart in haste. **2. make away with. a.** to steal or abduct. **b.** to kill, destroy, or get rid of.

make believe vb. **1.** to pretend or enact a fantasy. ~n. **make-believe. 2. a.** a fantasy or pretence. **b.** (as modifier): a make-believe world.

Makedhonia (ˌmakɛðɔˈnia) n. transliteration of the Modern Greek name for **Macedonia** (sense 1).

make for vb. (intr., prep.) **1.** to head towards. **2.** to prepare to attack. **3.** to help bring about.

make of vb. (tr., prep.) **1.** to interpret as the meaning of. **2.** to produce or construct from: houses made of brick. **3. make little, much,** etc., **of. a.** to gain little, much, etc., benefit from. **b.** to attribute little, much, etc., significance to.

make off vb. **1.** (intr., adv.) to go or run away in haste. **2. make off with.** to steal or abduct.

make out vb. (adv.) **1.** (tr.) to discern or perceive. **2.** (tr.) to understand or comprehend. **3.** (tr.) to write out: he made out a cheque. **4.** (tr.) to attempt to establish or prove: he made me out to be a liar. **5.** (intr.) to pretend: he made out that he could cook. **6.** (intr.) to manage or fare.

maker (ˈmeɪkə) n. a person who executes a legal document, esp. one who signs a promissory note.

Maker (ˈmeɪkə) n. **1.** a title given to God (as Creator). **2. (go to) meet one's Maker.** to die.

makeshift (ˈmeɪkˌʃɪft) adj. **1.** serving as a temporary or expedient means. ~n. **2.** something serving in this capacity.

make-up n. **1.** cosmetics, such as powder, lipstick, etc., applied to the face. **2. a.** the cosmetics, false hair, etc., used by an actor to adapt his appearance. **b.** the art or result of applying such cosmetics. **3.** the manner of arrangement of the parts or qualities of someone or something. **4.** the arrangement of type matter and illustrations on a page or in a book. **5.** mental or physical constitution. ~vb. **make up.** (adv.) **6.** (tr.) to form or constitute: these arguments make up the case for the defence. **7.** (tr.) to devise, construct, or compose, sometimes with the intent to deceive: to make up an excuse. **8.** (tr.) to supply what is lacking or deficient in; complete: these extra people will make up our total. **9.** (tr.) to put in order, arrange, or prepare: to make up a bed. **10.** (intr.; foll. by for) to compensate or atone (for). **11.** to settle (differences) amicably (often in **make it up**). **12.** to apply cosmetics to (the face) to enhance one's appearance or for a theatrical role. **13.** to assemble (type and illustrations) into (columns or pages). **14.** (tr.) to surface (a road) with tarmac, concrete, etc. **15. make up to.** Inf. **a.** to make friendly overtures to. **b.** to flirt with.

makeweight (ˈmeɪkˌweɪt) n. **1.** something put on a scale to make up a required weight. **2.** an unimportant person or thing added to make up a lack.

Makeyevka (Russian maˈkjejɪfkə) n. a city in the SW Soviet Union, in the SE Ukrainian SSR: coal-mining centre. Pop.: 455 000 (1987).

Makhachkala (Russian məxətʃkaˈla) n. a port in the S Soviet Union, capital of the Dagestan SSR, on the Caspian Sea: fishing fleet; oil refining. Pop.: 320 000 (1987). Former name (until 1921): **Petrovsk.**

making (ˈmeɪkɪŋ) n. **1. a.** the act of a person or thing that makes or the process of being made. **b.** (in combination): watchmaking. **2. be the making of.** to cause the success of. **3. in the making.** in the process of becoming or being made. **4.** something made or the quantity of something made at one time.

makings (ˈmeɪkɪŋz) pl. n. **1.** potentials, qualities, or materials: he had the makings of a leader. **2.** Also called: **rollings.** Sl. the tobacco and cigarette paper used for rolling a cigarette. **3.** profits; earnings.

Makkah or **Makah** (ˈmækə, -kɑ:) n. transliteration of the Arabic name for **Mecca.**

mako[1] (ˈmɑːkəʊ) n., pl. **-kos.** a blue-pointer game shark. [from Maori]

mako[2] (ˈmɑːkəʊ) n., pl. **-kos.** a small evergreen New Zealand tree. [from Maori]

Makurdi (məˈkɜːdɪ) n. a port in E central Nigeria, capital of Benue State on the Benue River: agricultural trade centre. Pop.: 89 000 (1983 est.).

Mal. abbrev. for: **1.** Bible. Malachi. **2.** Malay(an).

mal- combining form. bad or badly; wrong or wrongly; imperfect or defective: maladjusted; malfunction. [OF, from L malus bad, male badly]

Malabar Coast or **Malabar** (ˈmælə,bɑː) n. a region along the SW coast of India, extending from Goa to Cape Comorin: includes most of Kerala state.

Malabo (məˈlɑːbəʊ) n. the capital and chief port of Equatorial Guinea, on the island of Bioko in the Gulf of Guinea. Pop.: 10 000 (1986). Former name (until 1973): **Santa Isabel.**

malabsorption (ˌmæləbˈsɔːpʃən) n. a failure of absorption, esp. by the small intestine in coeliac disease, cystic fibrosis, etc.

malacca or **malacca cane** (məˈlækə) n. **1.** the stem of the rattan palm. **2.** a walking stick made from this stem.

Malacca (məˈlækə) n. a state of SW Peninsular Malaysia: rubber plantations. Capital: Malacca. Pop.: 453 153 (1980). Area: 1650 sq. km (637 sq. miles).

Malachi (ˈmælə,kaɪ) n. Old Testament. **1.** a Hebrew prophet of the 5th century B.C. **2.** the book containing his oracles. Douay spelling: **Malachias** (ˌmæləˈkaɪəs).

malachite (ˈmælə,kaɪt) n. a green mineral consisting of hydrated basic copper carbonate: a source of copper, also used for making ornaments. [C16: via OF from L molochītēs, from Gk molokhitis mallow-green stone, from molokhē mallow]

maladjustment (ˌmælədˈdʒʌstmənt) n. **1.** Psychol. a failure to meet the demands of society, such as coping with problems and social relationships. **2.** faulty or bad adjustment. — **,malad'justed** adj.

maladminister (ˌmælədˈmɪnɪstə) vb. (tr.) to administer badly, inefficiently, or dishonestly. — **,malad,minis'tration** n.

maladroit (ˌmælə'drɔɪt) adj. **1.** clumsy; not dexterous. **2.** tactless and insensitive. [C17: from F, from mal badly + ADROIT] — **,mala'droitly** adv. — **,mala'droitness** n.

malady (ˈmælədɪ) n., pl. **-dies. 1.** any disease or illness. **2.** any unhealthy, morbid, or desperate condition. [C13: from OF, from Vulgar L male habitus (unattested) in poor condition, from L male badly + habitus, from habēre to have]

Málaga (ˈmæləgə; Spanish ˈmalaɣa) n. **1.** a port and resort in S Spain, in Andalusia on the Mediterranean. Pop.: 566 480 (1981). **2.** a sweet fortified dessert wine from Málaga.

Malagasy (ˌmæləˈgæsɪ) n. **1.** (pl. **-gasy** or **-gasies**) a native or inhabitant of Madagascar. **2.** the official language of Madagascar. ~adj. **3.** of or relating to Madagascar, its people, or their language.

Malagasy Republic n. the former name (1958–75) of **Madagascar.**

malaise (mæˈleɪz) n. a feeling of unease, mild sickness, or depression. [C18: from OF, from mal bad + aise EASE]

malamute or **malemute** (ˈmælə,mjuːt) n. an Alaskan Eskimo dog of the spitz type. [from the name of an Eskimo tribe]

Malang (ˈmælæŋ) n. a city in S Indonesia, on E Java: commercial centre. Pop.: 510 000 (1980 est.).

malapropism (ˈmæləprɒp,ɪzəm) n. **1.** the unintentional misuse of a word by confusion with one of similar sound, esp. when creating a ridiculous effect, as in under the affluence of alcohol. **2.** the habit of misusing words in this manner. [C18: after Mrs Malaprop in Sheridan's play The Rivals (1775), a character who misused words, from MAL-APROPOS]

malapropos (ˌmæləprəˈpəʊ) adj. **1.** inappropriate or misapplied. ~adv. **2.** in an inappropriate way or manner. ~n. **3.** something inopportune or inappropriate. [C17: from F mal à propos not to the purpose]

Mälar (ˈmeɪlə) n. Lake. a lake in S Sweden, extending 121 km (75 miles) west from Stockholm, where it joins with an inlet of the Baltic Sea (the **Saltsjön**). Area: 1140 sq. km (440 sq. miles). Swedish name: **Mälaren** (ˈmelaren).

malaria (məˈlɛərɪə) n. an infectious disease characterized by recurring attacks of chills and fever, caused by the bite of an anopheles mosquito infected with any of certain protozoans. [C18: from It. mala aria bad air, from the belief that the disease was caused by the unwholesome air in swampy districts] — **ma'larial, ma'larian,** or **ma'larious** adj.

malarkey or **malarky** (məˈlɑːkɪ) n. Sl. nonsense; rubbish. [C20: from ?]

Malatesta (*Italian* mala'tɛsta) *n.* an Italian family that ruled Rimini from the 13th to the 16th century.

Malathion (ˌmælə'θaɪɒn) *n. Trademark.* an insecticide consisting of an organic phosphate. [C20: from (*diethyl*) MAL(EATE) + THIO- + -ON]

Malatya (ˌmɑːlɑː'tjɑː) *n.* a city in E central Turkey: nearby is the ruined Roman and medieval city of Melitene (Old Malatya). Pop.: 251 257 (1985).

Malawi (mə'lɑːwɪ) *n.* **1.** a republic in E central Africa: established as a British protectorate in 1891; became independent in 1964 and a republic, within the Commonwealth, in 1966; lies along the Great Rift Valley, with Lake Nyasa (Malawi) along the E border, the Nyika Plateau in the northwest, and the Shiré Highlands in the southeast. Languages: English and various Bantu languages. Religion: Christian, Muslim, and animist. Currency: kwacha. Capital: Lilongwe. Pop.: 7 058 800 (1985 UN est.). Area: 117 050 sq. km (45 193 sq. miles). Former name: **Nyasaland. 2. Lake.** the Malawi name for (Lake) **Nyasa.**

Malay (mə'leɪ) *n.* **1.** a member of a people living chiefly in Malaysia and Indonesia. **2.** the language of this people. ~*adj.* **3.** of or relating to the Malays or their language.

Malaya (mə'leɪə) *n.* **1. States of the Federation of.** part of Malaysia, in the S Malay Peninsula, constituting Peninsular Malaysia: consists of the former Federated Malay States, the former Unfederated Malay States, and the former Straits Settlements. Capital: Kuala Lumpur. Pop.: 11 128 227 (1980). Area: 131 587 sq. km (50 806 sq. miles). **2. Federation of.** a federation of the nine Malay States of the Malay Peninsula and two of the Straits Settlements (Malacca and Penang): formed in 1948: became part of the British Commonwealth in 1957 and joined Malaysia in 1963. —**Ma'layan** *adj., n.*

Malayalam *or* **Malayalaam** (ˌmælɪ'ɑːləm) *n.* a language of SW India.

Malay Archipelago *n.* a group of islands in the Indian and Pacific Oceans, between SE Asia and Australia: the largest group of islands in the world; includes over 3000 Indonesian islands, about 7000 islands of the Philippines, and, sometimes, New Guinea.

Malayo-Polynesian *n.* **1.** Also called: **Austronesian.** a family of languages extending from Madagascar to the central Pacific. ~*adj.* **2.** of or relating to this family of languages.

Malay Peninsula *n.* a peninsula of SE Asia, extending south from the Isthmus of Kra in Thailand to Cape Tanjong Piai in Malaysia: consists of SW Thailand and the states of Malaya (Peninsular Malaysia). Ancient name: **Chersonesus Aurea** (ˌkɜːsə'niːsəs 'ɔːrɪə).

Malaysia (mə'leɪzɪə) *n.* a federation in SE Asia (within the Commonwealth), consisting of **Peninsular Malaysia,** on the Malay Peninsula, and **East Malaysia** (Sabah and Sarawak), occupying the N part of the island of Borneo: formed in 1963 as a federation of Malaya, Sarawak, Sabah, and Singapore (the latter seceded in 1965); densely forested and mostly mountainous. Languages: Malay and English, with various Chinese and Indian minority languages. Religion: mostly Muslim. Currency: ringgit. Capital: Kuala Lumpur. Pop.: 16 527 000 (1987 UN est.). Area: 333 403 sq. km (128 727 sq. miles). —**Ma'laysian** *adj., n.*

Malay States *pl. n.* the former states of the Malay Peninsula that, together with Penang and Malacca, formed the Union of Malaya (1946) and the Federation of Malaya (1948). Perak, Selangor, Negri Sembilan, and Pahang were established as the **Federated Malay States** by the British in 1895 and Perlis, Kedah, Kelantan, and Trengannu as the **Unfederated Malay States** in 1909 (joined by Johore in 1914).

Malcolm ('mælkəm) *n.* **George.** born 1917, British harpsichordist.

Malcolm III *n.* died 1093, king of Scotland (1057–93). He became king after Macbeth.

Malcolm X (ɛks) *n.* original name *Malcolm Little.* 1925–65, U.S. Negro leader: assassinated.

malcontent ('mælkən,tɛnt) *adj.* **1.** disgusted or discontented. ~*n.* **2.** a person who is malcontent. [C16: from OF]

mal de mer French. (mal də mɛr) *n.* seasickness.

Maldives ('mɔːldaɪvz) *pl. n.* **Republic of.** a republic occupying an archipelago of 1087 coral islands in the Indian Ocean, southwest of Sri Lanka: came under British protection in 1887; became independent in 1965 and a republic in 1968. Language: Divehi. Religion: Sunni Muslim.

Currency: rufiya. Capital: Malé. Pop.: 195 000 (1986 est.). Area: 298 sq. km (115 sq. miles). Also called: **Maldive Islands.** —**Maldivian** (mɔːl'dɪvɪən) *or* **Maldivan** ('mɔːldaɪvⁿn, -dɪ-) *adj., n.*

Maldon ('mɔːldən) *n.* a market town in SE England, in Essex; scene of a battle (991) between the East Saxons and the victorious Danes, celebrated in *The Battle of Maldon,* an Old English poem. Pop.: 15 250 (1981).

male (meɪl) *adj.* **1.** of, relating to, or designating the sex producing gametes (spermatozoa) that can fertilize female gametes (ova). **2.** of, relating to, or characteristic of a man. **3.** for or composed of men or boys: *a male choir.* **4.** (of gametes) capable of fertilizing an egg cell. **5.** (of reproductive organs) capable of producing male gametes. **6.** (of flowers) bearing stamens but lacking a functional pistil. **7.** *Electronics, engineering.* having a projecting part or parts that fit into a female counterpart: *a male plug.* ~*n.* **8.** a male person, animal, or plant. [C14: via OF from L *masculus* MASCULINE] —'**maleness** *n.*

Malé ('mɑːleɪ) *n.* the capital of the Republic of Maldives, on Malé Island in the centre of the island group. Pop.: 46 334 (1985).

maleate ('mælɪˌeɪt) *n.* any salt or ester of maleic acid. [C19: from MALE(IC) ACID + -ATE¹]

Malebranche (*French* malbrɑ̃ʃ) *n.* **Nicolas** (nikɔla). 1638–1715, French philosopher. Originally a follower of Descartes, he developed the philosophy of occasionalism, esp. in *De la recherche de la vérité* (1674).

male chauvinism *n.* the belief, held or alleged to be held by certain men, that men are superior to women. —**male chauvinist** *n., adj.*

malediction (ˌmælɪ'dɪkʃən) *n.* **1.** the utterance of a curse against someone or something. **2.** a slanderous accusation or comment. [C15: from L *maledictiō* a reviling, from *male* ill + *dīcere* to speak] —ˌ**male'dictive** *or* ˌ**male'dictory** *adj.*

malefactor (ˌmælɪ,fæktə) *n.* a criminal; wrongdoer. [C15: via OF from L, from *malefacere* to do evil] —'**male,faction** *n.*

maleficent (mə'lɛfɪsənt) *adj.* causing evil or mischief; harmful or baleful. [C17: from L, from *maleficus* wicked, from *malum* evil] —**ma'lefic** *adj.* —**ma'leficence** *n.*

maleic acid (mə'leɪɪk) *n.* a colourless soluble crystalline substance used to synthesize other compounds, such as polyester resins. Formula: HOOCCH:CHCOOH. Systematic name: *cis-butenedioic acid.* [C19: from F *maléique,* altered form of *malique;* see MALIC ACID]

male menopause *n.* a period in a man's later middle age in which he may experience an identity crisis as he feels age overtake his sexual powers.

Malevich (*Russian* 'malɪvitʃ) *n.* **Kasimir** (kəzi'mir). 1878–1935, Russian painter. He founded the abstract art movement known as Suprematism.

malevolent (mə'lɛvələnt) *adj.* wishing or appearing to wish evil to others; malicious. [C16: from L *malevolens,* from *male* ill + *volens,* present participle of *velle* to wish] —**ma'levolence** *n.* —**ma'levolently** *adv.*

malfeasance (mæl'fiːzⁿns) *n. Law.* the doing of a wrongful or illegal act, esp. by a public official. Cf. **misfeasance, nonfeasance.** [C17: from OF *mal faisant,* from *mal* evil + *faisant,* from *faire* to do, from L *facere*] —**mal'feasant** *n., adj.*

malformation (ˌmælfɔː'meɪʃən) *n.* **1.** the condition of being faulty or abnormal in form or shape. **2.** *Pathol.* a deformity, esp. when congenital. —**mal'formed** *adj.*

malfunction (mæl'fʌŋkʃən) *vb.* **1.** (*intr.*) to function imperfectly or fail to function. ~*n.* **2.** failure to function or defective functioning.

Malherbe (*French* malɛrb) *n.* **François de** (frɑ̃swa də). 1555–1628, French poet and critic. He advocated the classical ideals of clarity and concision of meaning.

Mali ('mɑːlɪ) *n.* a landlocked republic in West Africa: conquered by the French by 1898 and incorporated (as French Sudan) into French West Africa; became independent in 1960; settled chiefly in the basins of the Rivers Senegal and Niger in the south. Official language: French. Religion: Muslim and animist. Currency: franc. Capital: Bamako. Pop.: 8 730 000 (1987 UN est.). Area: 1 239 710 sq. km (478 764 sq. miles). Former name (1898–1959): **French Sudan.**

malic acid ('mælɪk, 'meɪ-) *n.* a colourless crystalline compound occurring in apples and other fruits. [C18 *malic,* via F *malique* from L *mālum* apple]

malice ('mælɪs) *n*. **1.** the desire to do harm or mischief. **2.** evil intent. **3.** *Law*. the state of mind with which an act is committed and from which the intent to do wrong may be inferred. [C13: via OF from L *malitia*, from *malus* evil]

malice aforethought *n*. *Law*. **1.** the predetermination to do an unlawful act, esp. to kill or seriously injure. **2.** the intent with which an unlawful killing is effected, which must be proved for the crime to constitute murder.

malicious (mə'lɪʃəs) *adj*. **1.** characterized by malice. **2.** motivated by wrongful, vicious, or mischievous purposes. —**ma'liciously** *adv*. —**ma'liciousness** *n*.

malign (mə'laɪn) *adj*. **1.** evil in influence, intention, or effect. ~*vb*. **2.** (*tr*.) to slander or defame. [C14: via OF from L *malignus* spiteful, from *malus* evil] —**ma'ligner** *n*. —**ma'lignly** *adv*.

malignancy (mə'lɪgnənsɪ) *n*., *pl.* **-cies**. **1.** the state or quality of being malignant. **2.** *Pathol.* a cancerous growth.

malignant (mə'lɪgnənt) *adj*. **1.** having or showing desire to harm others. **2.** tending to cause great harm; injurious. **3.** *Pathol.* (of a tumour) uncontrollable or resistant to therapy. [C16: from LL *malignāre* to behave spitefully, from L *malignus* MALIGN] —**ma'lignantly** *adv*.

malignity (mə'lɪgnɪtɪ) *n*., *pl.* **-ties**. **1.** the condition or quality of being malign or deadly. **2.** (*often pl.*) a malign or malicious act or feeling.

malines (mə'liːn) *n*. **1.** a type of silk net used in dressmaking. **2.** another name for **Mechlin lace**. [C19: from F *Malines* (Mechelen), where this lace was traditionally made]

Malines (malin) *n*. the French name for **Mechelen**.

malinger (mə'lɪŋgə) *vb*. (*intr.*) to pretend or exaggerate illness, esp. to avoid work. [C19: from F *malingre* sickly, ?from *mal* badly + OF *haingre* feeble] —**ma'lingerer** *n*.

Malinowski (ˌmælɪ'nɒfskɪ) *n*. **Bronislaw Kasper** (brɔ'nislaf 'kaspɛr). 1884–1942, Polish anthropologist in England and the U.S., who researched into the sexual behaviour of primitive people in New Guinea and Melanesia.

mall (mɔːl, mæl) *n*. **1.** a shaded avenue, esp. one open to the public. **2.** a street or area lined with shops and closed to vehicles. **3.** See **pall-mall**. [C17: after *the* Mall, in St James's Park, London]

mallard ('mælɑːd) *n*., *pl.* **-lard** or **-lards**. a duck common over most of the N hemisphere, the male of which has a dark green head and reddish-brown breast: the ancestor of all domestic breeds of duck. [C14: from OF *mallart*, ?from *maslart* (unattested); see MALE, -ARD]

Mallarmé (*French* malarme) *n*. **Stéphane** (stefan). 1842–98, French symbolist poet, noted for his free verse, in which he chooses words for their evocative qualities; his works include *L'Après-midi d'un Faune* (1876), *Vers et Prose* (1893), and *Divagations* (1897).

malleable ('mælɪəbᵊl) *adj*. **1.** (esp. of metal) able to be worked, hammered, or shaped under pressure or blows without breaking. **2.** able to be influenced; pliable or tractable. [C14: via OF from Med. L *malleābilis*, from L *malleus* hammer] —**ˌmallea'bility** or (*less commonly*) **'malleableness** *n*. —**'malleably** *adv*.

mallee ('mælɪ) *n*. **1.** any of several low shrubby eucalyptus trees in desert regions of Australia. **2.** (usually preceded by *the*) *Austral.* another name for the **bush** (sense 4). [C19: Abor.]

Mallee ('mælɪ) *n*. a region in NW Victoria, Australia.

mallee fowl *n*. an Australian megapode.

malleolus (mə'liːələs) *n*., *pl.* **-li** (-ˌlaɪ). either of two rounded bony projections, one on each side of the ankle. [C17: dim. of L *malleus* hammer]

mallet ('mælɪt) *n*. **1.** a tool resembling a hammer but having a large head of wood, copper, lead, leather, etc., used for driving chisels, beating sheet metal, etc. **2.** a long stick with a head like a hammer used to strike the ball in croquet or polo. [C15: from OF *maillet* wooden hammer, dim. of *mail* MAUL (*q.v.*)]

malleus ('mælɪəs) *n*., *pl.* **-lei** (-lɪˌaɪ). the outermost and largest of the three small bones in the middle ear of mammals. See also **incus, stapes**. [C17: from L: hammer]

Mallorca (ma'ʎɔrka) *n*. the Spanish name for **Majorca**.

mallow ('mæləʊ) *n*. **1.** any of several malvaceous plants of Europe, having purple, pink, or white flowers. **2.** any of various related plants, such as the marsh mallow. [OE *mealuwe*, from L *malva*]

malm (mɑːm) *n*. **1.** a soft greyish limestone that crumbles easily. **2.** a chalky soil formed from this. **3.** an artificial

mixture of clay and chalk used to make bricks. [OE *mealm-* (in compound words)]

Malmédy (*French* malmedi) *n*. See **Eupen and Malmédy**.

Malmö ('mælməʊ; *Swedish* 'malmɔː) *n*. a port in S Sweden, on the Sound: part of Denmark until 1658; industrial centre. Pop.: 230 056 (1986).

malmsey ('mɑːmzɪ) *n*. a sweet Madeira wine. [C15: from Med. L *Malmasia*, corruption of Gk *Monembasia*, Gk port from which the wine was shipped]

malnutrition (ˌmælnjuː'trɪʃən) *n*. lack of adequate nutrition resulting from insufficient food, unbalanced diet, or defective assimilation.

malodorous (mæl'əʊdərəs) *adj*. having a bad smell.

Malory ('mælərɪ) *n*. **Sir Thomas**. 15th-century English author of *Le Morte d'Arthur* (?1470), a prose collection of Arthurian legends, translated from the French.

Malpighi (*Italian* mal'piːgi) *n*. **Marcello** (mar'tʃɛllo). 1628–94, Italian physiologist. A pioneer in microscopic anatomy, he identified the capillary system (1661). —**Malpighian** (mæl'pɪgɪən) *adj*.

malpractice (mæl'præktɪs) *n*. **1.** immoral, illegal, or unethical professional conduct or neglect of professional duty. **2.** any instance of improper professional conduct.

Malraux (*French* malro) *n*. **André** (ɑ̃dre). 1901–76, French writer and statesman. His novels include *La Condition humaine* (1933) on the Kuomintang revolution (1927–28) and *L'Espoir* (1937) on the Spanish Civil War, in both of which events he took part. He also wrote on art, notably in *Les Voix du silence* (1951).

malt (mɔːlt) *n*. **1.** cereal grain, such as barley, that is kiln-dried after it has germinated by soaking in water. **2.** See **malt liquor, malt whisky**. ~*vb*. **3.** to make into or become malt. **4.** to make (something, esp. liquor) with malt. [OE *mealt*] —**'malty** *adj*.

Malta ('mɔːltə) *n*. a republic occupying the islands of Malta, Gozo, and Comino, in the Mediterranean south of Sicily: governed by the Knights Hospitallers from 1530 until Napoleon's conquest in 1798; French driven out, with British help, 1800; became British dependency 1814; suffered severely in World War II; became independent in 1964 and a republic in 1974; a member of the Commonwealth. Languages: Maltese and English. Religion: Roman Catholic. Currency: Maltese pound. Capital: Valletta. Pop.: 343 334 (1986 UN est.). Area: 316 sq. km (122 sq. miles).

malted milk *n*. **1.** a soluble powder made from dehydrated milk and malted cereals. **2.** a drink made from this powder.

Maltese (mɔːl'tiːz) *adj*. **1.** of or relating to Malta, its inhabitants, or their language. ~*n*. **2.** (*pl.* **-tese**) a native or inhabitant of Malta. **3.** the official language of Malta, a form of Arabic with borrowings from Italian, etc.

Maltese cross *n*. a cross with triangular arms that taper towards the centre, sometimes having indented outer sides.

malt extract *n*. a sticky substance obtained from an infusion of malt.

Malthus ('mælθəs) *n*. **Thomas Robert**. 1766–1834, English economist. He propounded his population theory in *An Essay on the Principle of Population* (1798).

Malthusian (mæl'θjuːzɪən) *adj*. **1.** of or relating to the theory of Malthus stating that increases in population tend to exceed increases in the means of subsistence and that therefore sexual restraint should be exercised. ~*n*. **2.** a supporter of this theory. —**Mal'thusianism** *n*.

malting ('mɔːltɪŋ) *n*. a building in which malt is made or stored. Also called: **malt house**.

malt liquor *n*. any alcoholic drink brewed from malt.

maltose ('mɔːltəʊz) *n*. a sugar formed by the enzymic hydrolysis of starch. [C19: from MALT + -OSE²]

maltreat (mæl'triːt) *vb*. (*tr*.) to treat badly, cruelly, or inconsiderately. [C18: from F *maltraiter*] —**mal'treater** *n*. —**mal'treatment** *n*.

maltster ('mɔːltstə) *n*. a person who makes or deals in malt.

malt whisky *n*. whisky made from malted barley.

Maluku (mɑː'luːkuː) *n*. the Indonesian name for the **Moluccas**.

malvaceous (mæl'veɪʃəs) *adj*. of, relating to, or belonging to a family of plants that includes mallow, cotton, okra, althaea, and abutilon. [C17: from L *malvāceus*, from *malva* MALLOW]

Malvern ('mɔːlvən) *n*. a town and resort in W England, in Hereford and Worcester on the E slopes of the **Malvern**

Hills: annual dramatic festival; mineral springs. Pop.: 30 187 (1981).

malversation (ˌmælvɜːˈseɪʃən) n. Rare. professional or public misconduct. [C16: from F, from malverser to behave badly, from L male versāri]

Malvinas (Spanish malˈβinas) pl. n. **Islas** (ˈizlas). the Argentine name for the **Falkland Islands.**

mam (mæm) n. Inf. or dialect. another word for **mother.**

mama or esp. U.S. **mamma** (məˈmɑː) n. Old-fashioned. an informal word for **mother**[1]. [C16: reduplication of childish syllable ma]

mamba (ˈmæmbə) n. any of various partly arboreal tropical African venomous snakes, esp. the **green** and **black** mambas. [from Zulu im-amba]

mambo (ˈmæmbəʊ) n., pl. **-bos. 1.** a modern Latin American dance, resembling the rumba. ~vb. **2.** (intr.) to perform this dance. [American Sp., prob. from Haitian Creole: voodoo priestess]

Mameluke or **Mamaluke** (ˈmæmɪˌluːk) n. **1.** a member of a military class, originally of Turkish slaves, ruling in Egypt from about 1250 to 1517 and remaining powerful until 1811. **2.** (in Muslim countries) a slave. [C16: via F, ult. from Ar. mamlūk slave, from malaka to possess]

mamilla or U.S. **mammilla** (mæˈmɪlə) n., pl. **-lae** (-liː). **1.** a nipple or teat. **2.** any nipple-shaped prominence. [C17: from L, dim. of mamma breast] —**'mamillary** or U.S. **'mammillary** adj.

mamma (ˈmæmə) n., pl. **-mae** (-miː). the milk-secreting organ of female mammals: the breast in women, the udder in cows, sheep, etc. [C17: from L: breast] —**'mammary** adj.

mammal (ˈmæməl) n. any animal of the Mammalia, a large class of warm-blooded vertebrates having mammary glands in the female. [C19: via NL from L mamma breast] —**mammalian** (mæˈmeɪlɪən) adj., n.

mammary gland n. any of the milk-producing glands in mammals.

mammogram (ˈmæməʊˌgræm) n. an x-ray photograph of the breast.

mammography (mæˈmɒgrəfɪ) n. examination of the breasts by x-ray, esp. to detect early signs of cancer.

mammon (ˈmæmən) n. riches or wealth regarded as a source of evil and corruption. [C14: via LL from New Testament Gk mammōnas, from Aramaic māmōnā wealth] —**'mammonish** adj. —**'mammonism** n. —**'mammonist** or **'mammonite** n.

Mammon (ˈmæmən) n. Bible. the personification of riches and greed in the form of a false god.

mammoth (ˈmæməθ) n. **1.** any large extinct elephant of the Pleistocene epoch, such as the **woolly mammoth,** having a hairy coat and long curved tusks. ~adj. **2.** of gigantic size or importance. [C18: from Russian mamot, from Tartar mamont, ?from mamma earth, because of a belief that the animal made burrows]

mammy or **mammie** (ˈmæmɪ) n., pl. **-mies. 1.** a child's word for **mother**[1]. **2.** Chiefly southern U.S. a Black woman employed as a nurse or servant to a White family.

Mamoré (Spanish mamoˈre) n. a river in central Bolivia, flowing north to the Beni River to form the Madeira River. Length: about 1500 km (930 miles).

man (mæn) n., pl. **men. 1.** an adult male human being, as distinguished from a woman. **2.** (modifier) male; masculine: a man child. **3.** a human being, considered as representative of mankind. **4.** human beings collectively; mankind. **5.** Also called: **modern man. a.** a member of any of the living races of Homo sapiens, characterized by erect bipedal posture, a highly developed brain, and powers of articulate speech, abstract reasoning, and imagination. **b.** any extinct member of the species Homo sapiens, such as Cro-Magnon man. **6.** a member of any of the extinct species of the genus Homo, such as Java man. **7.** an adult male human being with qualities associated with the male, such as courage or virility: be a man. **8.** manly qualities or virtues: the man in him was outraged. **9. a.** a subordinate, servant, or employee. **b.** (in combination): the man-days required to complete a job. **10.** (usually pl.) a member of the armed forces who does not hold commissioned, warrant, or noncommissioned rank (as in **officers and men**). **11.** a member of a group, team, etc. **12.** a husband, boyfriend, etc. **13.** an expression used parenthetically to indicate an informal relationship between speaker and hearer. **14.** a movable piece in various games, such as draughts. **15.** a vassal of a feudal

lord. **16.** S. African sl. any person. **17. as one man.** with unanimous action or response. **18. be one's own man.** to be independent or free. **19. he's your man.** he's the person needed. **20. man and boy.** from childhood. **21. sort out** or **separate the men from the boys.** to separate the experienced from the inexperienced. **22. to a man.** without exception. ~interj. **23.** Inf. an exclamation or expletive, often indicating surprise or pleasure. ~vb. **manning, manned.** (tr.) **24.** to provide with sufficient men for operation, defence, etc. **25.** to take one's place at or near in readiness for action. [OE mann]

Man (mæn) n. **Isle of.** an island in the British Isles, in the Irish Sea between Cumbria and Northern Ireland: a Crown possession with its own parliament, the Court of Tynwald; a dependency of Norway until 1266, when it came under Scottish rule; its own language, Manx, is now almost extinct. Capital: Douglas. Pop.: 55 482 (1986). Area: 588 sq. km (227 sq. miles).

-man n. combining form. indicating a person who has a role, works in a place, or operates equipment as specified: salesman; barman; cameraman.

▷ **Usage.** The use of words ending in -man is avoided as implying a male in job advertisements, where sexual discrimination is illegal, and in many other contexts where a term that is not gender-specific is available, such as salesperson, barperson, camera operator.

Man. abbrev. for: **1.** Manila paper. **2.** Manitoba.

mana (ˈmɑːnə) n. Anthropol. **1.** (in Polynesia, Melanesia, etc.) a concept of a life force associated with high social status and ritual power. **2.** any power achieved by ritual means; prestige; authority. [of Polynesian origin]

man about town n. a fashionable sophisticate, esp. one in a big city.

manacle (ˈmænəkəl) n. **1.** (usually pl.) a shackle, handcuff, or fetter, used to secure the hands of a prisoner, convict, etc. ~vb. (tr.) **2.** to put manacles on. **3.** to confine or constrain. [C14: via OF from L manicula, dim. of manus hand]

Manado (məˈnɑːdəʊ) n. a variant of **Menado.**

manage (ˈmænɪdʒ) vb. (mainly tr.) **1.** (also intr.) to be in charge (of); administer: to manage a shop. **2.** to succeed in being able (to do something); contrive. **3.** to have room, time, etc., for: can you manage dinner tomorrow? **4.** to exercise control or domination over. **5.** (intr.) to contrive to carry on despite difficulties, esp. financial ones. **6.** to wield or handle (a weapon). [C16: from It. maneggiare to train (esp. horses), ult. from L manus hand]

manageable (ˈmænɪdʒəbəl) adj. able to be managed or controlled. —**managea'bility** or **'manageableness** n. —**'manageably** adv.

managed bonds pl. n. investment in a combination of funds, such as fixed-interest securities and property shares, in which the amount invested in each fund is dependent on the expected returns.

managed currency n. a currency subject to governmental control with respect to the amount in circulation and rate of exchange.

management (ˈmænɪdʒmənt) n. **1.** the members of the executive or administration of an organization or business. **2.** managers or employers collectively. **3.** the technique, practice, or science of managing or controlling. **4.** the skilful or resourceful use of materials, time, etc. **5.** the specific treatment of a disease, etc.

manager (ˈmænɪdʒə) n. **1.** a person who directs or manages an organization, industry, shop, etc. **2.** a person who controls the business affairs of an actor, entertainer, etc. **3.** a person who controls the training of a sportsman or team. **4.** a person who has a talent for managing efficiently. **5.** (in Britain) a member of either House of Parliament appointed to arrange a matter in which both Houses are concerned. —**'managership** n.

manageress (ˌmænɪdʒəˈrɛs) n. a woman who is in charge of a shop, department, etc.

managerial (ˌmænɪˈdʒɪərɪəl) adj. of or relating to a manager or management. —**mana'gerially** adv.

managing (ˈmænɪdʒɪŋ) adj. having administrative control or authority: a managing director.

Managua (məˈnægwə; Spanish maˈnaɣwa) n. **1.** the capital of Nicaragua, on the S shore of Lake Managua: chosen as capital in 1857. Pop.: 682 111 (1985). **2. Lake.** a lake in W Nicaragua: drains into Lake Nicaragua by the Tipitapa

River. Length: 61 km (38 miles). Width: about 26 km (16 miles).

Manama (mə'nɑːmə) n. the capital of Bahrain, at the N end of Bahrain Island: transit port. Pop.: 121 986 (1987).

mañana Spanish. (mə'njɑːnə) n., adv. **a.** tomorrow. **b.** some other and later time.

Manáos (Portuguese mə'naus) n. a variant spelling of **Manaus**.

Manassas (mə'næsəs) n. a town in NE Virginia, west of Alexandria: site of the victory of Confederate forces in the Battles of Bull Run, or First and Second Manassas (1861; 1862) during the American Civil War. Pop.: 15 438 (1980).

Manasseh (mə'næsɪ) n. Old Testament. **1.** the elder son of Joseph (Genesis 41:51). **2.** the Israelite tribe descended from him. **3.** the territory of this tribe, in the upper Jordan valley. Douay spelling: **Manases** (mə'næsiːz).

man-at-arms n., pl. **men-at-arms.** a soldier, esp. a heavily armed mounted soldier in medieval times.

manatee (ˌmænə'tiː) n. a sirenian mammal occurring in tropical coastal waters of America, the West Indies, and Africa, having a prehensile upper lip and a broad flattened tail. [C16: via Sp. from Carib *Manattouī*]

Manaus or **Manáos** (Portuguese mə'naus) n. a port in N Brazil, capital of Amazonas state, on the Rio Negro 19 km (12 miles) above its confluence with the Amazon: chief commercial centre of the Amazon basin. Pop.: 613 068 (1980).

Manche (French mɑ̃ʃ) n. **1.** a department of NW France, in Basse-Normandie region. Capital: St Lô. Pop.: 465 948 (1982). Area: 6412 sq. km (2501 sq. miles). **2. La.** the French name for the **English Channel.**

manchester ('mæntʃɪstə) n. Austral. & N.Z. **1.** goods, such as sheets and pillowcases, which are, or were originally, made of cotton. **2. manchester department.** a section of a store which sells such goods. [from MANCHESTER, England]

Manchester ('mæntʃɪstə) n. a city in NW England, linked to the Mersey estuary by the **Manchester Ship Canal:** commercial and industrial centre, esp. of the cotton and textile trades; university (1846). Pop.: 451 000 (1985). Latin name: **Man'cunium.**

manchineel (ˌmæntʃɪ'niːl) n. a tropical American tree having fruit and milky highly caustic poisonous sap, which causes skin blisters. [C17: via F from Sp. MANZANILLA]

Manchu (mæn'tʃuː) n. **1.** (pl. **-chus** or **-chu**) a member of a Mongoloid people of Manchuria, a region of NE China, who conquered China in the 17th century, establishing a dynasty that lasted until 1912. **2.** the language of this people. ~adj. **3.** Also: **Ching.** of or relating to the dynasty of the Manchus. [from Manchu, lit.: pure]

Manchukuo or **Manchoukuo** ('mæn'tʃuː'kwəu) n. a former state of E Asia (1932–45), consisting of the three provinces of old Manchuria and Jehol.

Manchuria (mæn'tʃʊərɪə) n. a region of NE China, historically the home of the Manchus, rulers of China from 1644 to 1912: includes part of the Inner Mongolian AR and the provinces of Heilongjiang, Jilin, and Liaoning. Area: about 1 300 000 sq. km (502 000 sq. miles). —**Man'churian** adj., n.

manciple ('mænsɪpəl) n. a steward who buys provisions, esp. in an Inn of Court. [C13: via OF from L *mancipium* purchase, from *manceps* purchaser, from *manus* hand + *capere* to take]

Mancunian (mæŋ'kjuːnɪən) n. **1.** a native or inhabitant of Manchester. ~adj. **2.** of or relating to Manchester. [from Med. L *Mancunium* Manchester]

-mancy n. combining form. indicating divination of a particular kind: *chiromancy.* [from OF *-mancie*, from L *-mantia*, from Gk *manteia* soothsaying] —**-mantic** adj. combining form.

mandala ('mændələ, mæn'dɑːlə) n. Hindu & Buddhist art. any of various designs symbolizing the universe, usually circular. [Sansk.: circle]

Mandalay (ˌmændə'leɪ) n. a city in central Burma, on the Irrawaddy River: the second largest city in the country and former capital of Burma and of Upper Burma; Buddhist religious centre. Pop.: 417 266 (1983).

mandamus (mæn'deɪməs) n., pl. **-muses.** Law. (formerly) a writ from, now an order of, a superior court commanding an inferior tribunal, public official, etc., to carry out a public duty. [C16: L, lit.: we command, from *mandāre*]

mandarin ('mændərɪn) n. **1.** (in the Chinese Empire) a member of a senior grade of the bureaucracy. **2.** a high-ranking official whose powers were extensive and thought to be outside political control. **3.** a person of standing and influence, as in literary or intellectual circles, esp. one regarded as conservative or reactionary. **4. a.** a small citrus tree cultivated for its edible fruit. **b.** the fruit, resembling the tangerine. [C16: from Port. via Malay from Sansk. *mantrin* counsellor, from *mantra* counsel] —'**mandarinate** n.

Mandarin Chinese or **Mandarin** n. the official language of China since 1917.

Mandarin collar n. a high stiff round collar.

mandarin duck n. an Asian duck, the male of which has a distinctive brightly coloured and patterned plumage and crest.

mandate n. ('mændeɪt, -dɪt). **1.** an official or authoritative instruction or command. **2.** Politics. the support or commission given to a government and its policies or an elected representative and his policies through an electoral victory. **3.** (often cap.) Also called: **mandated territory.** (formerly) any of the territories under the trusteeship of the League of Nations administered by one of its member states. **4. a.** Roman law. a contract by which one person commissions another to act for him gratuitously. **b.** Contract law. a contract under which a party entrusted with goods undertakes to perform gratuitously some service in respect of such goods. **c.** Scots Law. a contract by which a person is engaged to act in the management of the affairs of another. ~vb. ('mændeɪt). (tr.) **5.** to assign (territory) to a nation under a mandate. **6.** to delegate authority to. [C16: from L *mandātum* something commanded, from *mandāre* to command, ?from *manus* hand + *dāre* to give] —'**mandator** n.

mandatory ('mændətərɪ, -trɪ) adj. **1.** having the nature or powers of a mandate. **2.** obligatory; compulsory. **3.** (of a state) having received a mandate over some territory. ~n., pl. **-ries.** also **mandatary. 4.** a person or state holding a mandate. —'**mandatorily** adv.

Mandela (mæn'delə) n. **Nelson (Rolihlahla).** born 1918, Black South African lawyer and civil rights leader: leader of the banned African National Congress: jailed in 1962 for 5 years and, in 1964, for life.

Mandeville ('mændəvɪl) n. **1. Bernard de.** ?1670–1733, English author, born in Holland, noted for his satire The Fable of the Bees (1723). **2. Sir John.** 14th century, English author of The Travels of Sir John Mandeville. The book claims to be an account of the author's journeys in the East but is largely a compilation from other works.

mandible ('mændɪbəl) n. **1.** the lower jawbone in vertebrates. **2.** either of a pair of mouthparts in insects and other arthropods that are usually used for biting and crushing food. **3.** Ornithol. either part of the bill, esp. the lower part. [C16: via OF from LL *mandibula* jaw, from *mandere* to chew] —**mandibular** (mæn'dɪbjʊlə) adj. —**mandibulate** (mæn'dɪbjʊlɪt, -ˌleɪt) n., adj.

mandolin or **mandoline** (ˌmændə'lɪn) n. a plucked stringed instrument having four pairs of strings stretched over a small light body with a fretted fingerboard: usually played with a plectrum. [C18: via F from It. *mandolino*, dim. of *mandora* lute, ult. from Gk *pandoura* musical instrument with three strings] —ˌmando'linist n.

mandrake ('mændreɪk) or **mandragora** (mæn'drægərə) n. **1.** a Eurasian plant with purplish flowers and a forked root. It was formerly thought to have magic powers and a narcotic was prepared from its root. **2.** another name for the **May apple.** [C14: prob. via MDu. from L *mandragoras*, from Gk. The form *mandrake* was prob. adopted through folk etymology, because of the allegedly human appearance of the root and because *drake* (dragon) suggested magical powers]

mandrel or **mandril** ('mændrəl) n. **1.** a spindle on which a workpiece is supported during machining operations. **2.** a shaft or arbor on which a machining tool is mounted. [C16: ? rel. to F *mandrin* lathe]

mandrill ('mændrɪl) n. an Old World monkey of W Africa. It has a short tail and brown hair, and the ridged muzzle, nose, and hindquarters are red and blue. [C18: from MAN + DRILL⁴]

mane (meɪn) n. **1.** the long coarse hair that grows from the crest of the neck in such mammals as the lion and horse. **2.** long thick human hair. [OE *manu*] —**maned** adj.

manège *or* **manege** (mæ'neɪʒ) *n.* **1.** the art of training horses and riders. **2.** a riding school. [C17: via F from It. *maneggio*, from *maneggiare* to MANAGE]

manes ('mɑːneɪz) *pl. n.* (*sometimes cap.*) (in Roman legend) **1.** the spirits of the dead, often revered as minor deities. **2.** (*functioning as sing.*) the shade of a dead person. [C14: from L, prob.: the good ones, from OL *mānus* good]

Manes ('meɪniːz) *n.* See **Mani.**

Manet (*French* manε) *n.* **Edouard** (edwar). 1832–83, French painter. His painting *Le Déjeuner sur l'herbe* (1863), which was condemned by the Parisian establishment, was acclaimed by the impressionists, whom he decisively influenced.

maneuver (mə'nuːvə) *n., vb.* the usual U.S. spelling of **manoeuvre**.

man Friday *n.* **1.** a loyal male servant or assistant. **2.** Also: **girl Friday, person Friday.** any factotum, esp. in an office. [after the native in Daniel Defoe's novel *Robinson Crusoe* (1719)]

manful ('mænful) *adj.* resolute, strong; manly. —'**manfully** *adv.* —'**manfulness** *n.*

mangabey ('mæŋɡə,beɪ) *n.* any of several large agile arboreal Old World monkeys of central Africa, having long limbs and tail. [C18: after a region in Madagascar]

Mangalore (,mæŋɡə'lɔː) *n.* a port in S India, in Karnataka on the Malabar Coast. Pop.: 306 000 (1981).

manganese ('mæŋɡə,niːz) *n.* a brittle greyish-white metallic element: used in making steel and ferromagnetic alloys. Symbol: Mn; atomic no.: 25; atomic wt.: 54.938. [C17: via F from It., prob. altered form of Med. L MAGNESIA]

mange (meɪndʒ) *n.* an infectious disorder mainly affecting domestic animals, characterized by itching and loss of hair: caused by parasitic mites. [C14: from OF *mangeue* itch, from *mangier* to eat]

mangelwurzel ('mæŋɡ³l,wɜːz³l) *or* **mangoldwurzel** ('mæŋɡəʊld,wɜːz³l) *n.* a Eurasian variety of beet, cultivated as a cattle food, having a large yellowish root. [C18: from G *Mangoldwurzel*, from *Mangold* beet + *Wurzel* root]

manger ('meɪndʒə) *n.* a trough or box in a stable, barn, etc., from which horses or cattle feed. [C14: from OF *maingeure* food trough, from *mangier* to eat, ult. from L *mandūcāre* to chew]

mangetout ('mɑʒ'tuː) *n.* a variety of garden pea in which the pod is also edible. Also called: **sugar pea.** [C20: from F: eat all]

mangle[1] ('mæŋɡ³l) *vb.* (*tr.*) **1.** to mutilate, disfigure, or destroy by cutting, crushing, or tearing. **2.** to ruin, spoil, or mar. [C14: from Norman F *mangler*, prob. from OF *mahaignier* to maim] —'**mangled** *adj.* —'**mangler** *n.*

mangle[2] ('mæŋɡ³l) *n.* **1.** Also called: **wringer.** a machine for pressing or drying textiles, clothes, etc., consisting of two heavy rollers between which the cloth is passed. ~*vb.* (*tr.*) **2.** to press or dry in a mangle. [C18: from Du. *mangel*, ult. from LL *manganum*. See MANGONEL]

mango ('mæŋɡəʊ) *n., pl.* -**goes** *or* -**gos.** **1.** a tropical Asian evergreen tree, cultivated in the tropics for its fruit. **2.** the ovoid edible fruit of this tree, having a smooth rind and sweet juicy flesh. [C16: via Port. from Malay *mangā*, from Tamil *mānkāy*, from *mān* mango tree + *kāy* fruit]

mangonel ('mæŋɡə,nεl) *n. History.* a war engine for hurling stones. [C13: via OF from Med. L *manganellus*, ult. from Gk *manganon*]

mangrove ('mæŋɡrəʊv, 'mæn-) *n.* any of various tropical evergreen trees or shrubs, having stiltlike intertwining aerial roots and forming dense thickets along coasts. [C17 *mangrow* (changed through infl. of *grove*), from Port. *mangue*, ult. from Taino]

mangy *or* **mangey** ('meɪndʒɪ) *adj.* -**gier, -giest.** **1.** having or caused by mange. **2.** scruffy or shabby. —'**mangily** *adv.* —'**manginess** *n.*

manhandle (mæn,hænd³l, ,mæn'hænd³l) *vb.* (*tr.*) **1.** to handle or push (someone) about roughly. **2.** to move or do by manpower rather than by machinery.

Manhattan (mæn'hæt³n, mən-) *n.* **1.** an island at the N end of New York Bay, between the Hudson, East, and Harlem Rivers: administratively (with adjacent islets) a borough of New York City; a major financial, commercial, and cultural centre. Pop.: 1 428 285 (1980). Area: 47 sq. km (22 sq. miles). **2.** a mixed drink consisting of four parts whisky, one part vermouth, and a dash of bitters.

manhole ('mæn,həʊl) *n.* **1.** Also called: **inspection chamber.** a shaft with a removable cover that leads down to a sewer or drain. **2.** a hole, usually with a detachable cover, through which a man can enter a boiler, tank, etc.

manhood ('mænhʊd) *n.* **1.** the state or quality of being a man or being manly. **2.** men collectively. **3.** the state of being human.

man-hour *n.* a unit of work in industry, equal to the work done by one man in one hour.

manhunt ('mæn,hʌnt) *n.* an organized search, usually by police, for a wanted man or fugitive.

Mani ('mɑːnɪ) *n.* ?216–?276 A.D., Persian prophet who founded Manichaeism. Also called: **Manes, Manichaeus.**

mania ('meɪnɪə) *n.* **1.** a mental disorder characterized by great excitement and occasionally violent behaviour. **2.** obsessional enthusiasm or partiality. [C14: via LL from Gk: madness]

-mania *n. combining form.* indicating extreme desire or pleasure of a specified kind or an abnormal excitement aroused by something: *kleptomania; nymphomania; pyromania.* [from MANIA] —**maniac** *n. and adj. combining form.*

maniac ('meɪnɪ,æk) *n.* **1.** a wild disorderly person. **2.** a person who has a great craving or enthusiasm for something. **3.** *Psychiatry, obs.* a person afflicted with mania. [C17: from LL *maniacus* belonging to madness, from Gk]

maniacal (mə'naɪək³l) *or* **maniac** *adj.* **1.** affected with or characteristic of mania. **2.** characteristic of or befitting a maniac: *maniacal laughter.* —ma'**niacally** *adv.*

manic ('mænɪk) *adj.* **1.** characterizing, denoting, or affected by mania. ~*n.* **2.** a person afflicted with mania. [C19: from Gk, from MANIA]

manic-depressive *Psychiatry.* ~*adj.* **1.** denoting a mental disorder characterized by an alternation between extreme euphoria and deep depression. ~*n.* **2.** a person afflicted with this disorder.

Manichaeism *or* **Manicheism** ('mænɪkiː,ɪzəm) *n.* the system of religious doctrines taught by the Persian prophet Mani about the 3rd century A.D. It was based on a supposed primordial conflict between light and darkness or goodness and evil. [C14: from LL *Manichaeus*, from LGk *Manikhaios* of Mani] —,**Mani'chaean** *or* ,**Man**i'**chean** *adj., n.* —'**Manichee** *n.*

Manichaeus *or* **Manicheus** (,mænɪ'kiːəs) *n.* See **Mani.**

manicure ('mænɪ,kjʊə) *n.* **1.** care of the hands and fingernails, involving shaping the nails, removing cuticles, etc. **2.** Also called: **manicurist.** a person who gives manicures, esp. as a profession. ~*vb.* **3.** to care for (the hands and fingernails) in this way. [C19: from F, from L *manus* hand + *cūra* care]

manifest ('mænɪ,fεst) *adj.* **1.** easily noticed or perceived; obvious. ~*vb.* **2.** (*tr.*) to show plainly; reveal or display. **3.** (*tr.*) to prove beyond doubt. **4.** (*intr.*) (of a disembodied spirit) to appear in visible form. ~*n.* **5.** a customs document containing particulars of a ship, its cargo, and its destination. **6. a.** a list of cargo, passengers, etc., on an aeroplane. **b.** a list of railway trucks or their cargo. [C14: from L *manifestus* plain, lit.: struck with the hand] —'**mani,festable** *adj.* —'**mani,festly** *adv.*

manifestation (,mænɪfε'steɪʃən) *n.* **1.** the act of demonstrating; display. **2.** the state of being manifested. **3.** an indication or sign. **4.** a public demonstration of feeling. **5.** the materialization of a disembodied spirit. —,**man**i'**festative** *adj.*

manifesto (,mænɪ'fεstəʊ) *n., pl.* -**toes** *or* -**tos.** a public declaration of intent, policy, aims, etc., as issued by a political party, government, or movement. [C17: from It., from *manifestare* to MANIFEST]

manifold ('mænɪ,fəʊld) *adj. Formal.* **1.** of several different kinds; multiple. **2.** having many different forms, features, or elements. ~*n.* **3.** something having many varied parts, forms, or features. **4.** a chamber or pipe with a number of inlets or outlets used to collect or distribute a fluid. In an internal-combustion engine the **inlet manifold** carries the vaporized fuel from the carburettor to the inlet ports and the **exhaust manifold** carries the exhaust gases away. ~*vb.* (*tr.*) **5.** to duplicate (a page, book, etc.). **6.** to make manifold; multiply. [OE *manigfeald*. See MANY, -FOLD] —'**mani,foldly** *adv.* —'**mani,foldness** *n.*

manikin *or* **mannikin** ('mænɪkɪn) *n.* **1.** a little man; dwarf or child. **2.** an anatomical model of the body or a part of the body, esp. for use in medical or art instruction.

3. a variant of **mannequin.** [C17: from Du. *manneken*, dim. of MAN]

Manila (mə'nɪlə) *n.* **1.** the chief port of the Philippines, on S Luzon on Manila Bay: capital of the republic until 1948 and from 1976; seat of the Far Eastern University and the University of Santo Tomas (1611). Pop.: 1 728 441 (1984 est.). **2.** a type of cigar made in this city. **3.** short for **Manila hemp, Manila paper.**

Manila Bay *n.* an almost landlocked inlet of the South China Sea in the Philippines, in W Luzon: mostly forms Manila harbour. Area: 1994 sq. km (770 sq. miles).

Manila hemp *or* **Manila hemp** *n.* a fibre obtained from the abaca plant, used for rope, paper, etc.

Manila paper *or* **Manilla paper** *n.* a strong usually brown paper made from Manila hemp or similar fibres.

manilla (mə'nɪlə) *n.* an early form of currency in W Africa in the pattern of a small bracelet. [from Sp.: bracelet, dim. of *mano* hand, from L *manus*]

man in the street *n.* the typical or ordinary person.

manioc ('mænɪˌɒk) *or* **manioca** (ˌmænɪ'əʊkə) *n.* another name for **cassava** (sense 1). [C16: from Tupi *mandioca*]

manipulate (mə'nɪpjʊˌleɪt) *vb.* **1.** (*tr.*) to handle or use, esp. with some skill. **2.** to control or influence (something or someone) cleverly, deviously, or skilfully. **3.** to falsify (a bill, accounts, etc.) for one's own advantage. **4.** (in physiotherapy) to examine or treat manually, as in loosening a joint. [C19: back formation from *manipulation*, from L *manipulus* handful] —**manipulability** (mə,nɪpjʊlə'bɪlɪtɪ) *n.* —**ma'nipu,latable** *or* **ma'nipulable** *adj.* —**ma,nipu'lation** *n.* —**ma'nipulative** *adj.* —**ma'nipu,lator** *n.* —**ma'nipulatory** *adj.*

Manipur (ˌmʌnɪ'pʊə) *n.* a state in NE India: largely densely forested mountains. Capital: Imphal. Pop.: 1 411 375 (1981). Area: 20 793 sq. km (8109 sq. miles).

Manisa ('mɑːnɪˌsɑː) *n.* a city in W Turkey: the Byzantine seat of government (1204–1313). Pop.: 126 319 (1985).

Manitoba (ˌmænɪ'təʊbə) *n.* **1.** a province of W Canada: consists of prairie in the southwest, with extensive forests in the north and tundra near Hudson Bay in the northeast. Capital: Winnipeg. Pop.: 1 063 016 (1986). Area: 650 090 sq. km (251 000 sq. miles). Abbrev.: **MB. 2. Lake.** a lake in W Canada, in S Manitoba: fed by the outflow from Lake Winnipegosis; drains into Lake Winnipeg. Area: 4706 sq. km (1817 sq. miles). —**Mani'toban** *n.*, *adj.*

manitou, manitu ('mænɪˌtuː), *or* **manito** ('mænɪˌtəʊ) *n.*, *pl.* **-tous, -tus, -tos** *or* **-tou, -tu, -to.** (among the Algonquian Indians) a deified spirit or force. [C17: of Amerind origin]

Manitoulin Island (ˌmænɪ'tuːlɪn) *n.* an island in N Lake Huron in Ontario: the largest freshwater island in the world. Length: 129 km (80 miles). Width: up to 48 km (30 miles).

Manizales (ˌmænɪ'zɑːlɛs; *Spanish* mani'θales) *n.* a city in W Colombia, in the Cordillera Central of the Andes at an altitude of 2100 m (7000 ft.): commercial centre of a rich coffee-growing area. Pop.: 309 821 (1985).

man jack *n. Inf.* a single individual (in **every man jack, no man jack**).

mankind (ˌmæn'kaɪnd) *n.* **1.** human beings collectively; humanity. **2.** men collectively, as opposed to womankind.

Manley ('mænlɪ) *n.* **Michael Norman.** born 1924, Jamaican statesman; prime minister of Jamaica (1972–80).

manlike ('mæn,laɪk) *adj.* resembling or befitting a man.

manly ('mænlɪ) *adj.* **-lier, -liest. 1.** possessing qualities, such as vigour or courage, generally regarded as appropriate to or typical of a man; masculine. **2.** characteristic of or befitting a man. —'**manliness** *n.*

man-made *adj.* made by man; artificial.

Mann (*German* man) *n.* **1. Heinrich** ('haɪnrɪç). 1871–1950, German novelist: works include *Professor Unrat* (1905), which was filmed as *The Blue Angel* (1928), and *Man of Straw* (1918). **2.** his brother, **Thomas** ('toːmas). 1875–1955, German novelist, in the U.S. after 1937. His works deal mainly with the problem of the artist in bourgeois society and include the short story *Death in Venice* (1913) and the novels *Buddenbrooks* (1900), *The Magic Mountain* (1924), and *Doctor Faustus* (1947): Nobel prize for literature 1929.

manna ('mænə) *n.* **1.** *Old Testament.* the miraculous food which sustained the Israelites in the wilderness (Exodus 16:14–36). **2.** any spiritual or divine nourishment. **3.** a windfall (esp. in **manna from heaven**). **4.** a sweet

substance obtained from various plants, esp. from the **manna** or **flowering ash** of S Europe, used as a mild laxative. [OE via LL from Gk, from Heb. *mān*]

Mannar (mə'nɑː) *n.* **Gulf of.** the part of the Indian Ocean between SE India and the island of Sri Lanka: pearl fishing.

manned (mænd) *adj.* **1.** supplied or equipped with men, esp. soldiers. **2.** (of spacecraft, etc.) having a human crew.

mannequin ('mænɪkɪn) *n.* **1.** a woman who wears the clothes displayed at a fashion show; model. **2.** a life-size dummy of the human body used to fit or display clothes. [C18: via F from Du. *manneken* MANIKIN]

manner ('mænə) *n.* **1.** a way of doing or being. **2.** a person's bearing and behaviour. **3.** the style or customary way of doing or accomplishing something. **4.** type or kind. **5.** mannered style, as in art; mannerism. **6. in a manner of speaking.** in a way; so to speak. **7. to the manner born.** naturally fitted to a specified role or activity. [C12: via Norman F from OF *maniere*, from Vulgar L *manuāria* (unattested) a way of handling something, noun use of L *manuārius* belonging to the hand, from *manus* hand]

mannered ('mænəd) *adj.* **1.** having idiosyncrasies or mannerisms; affected. **2.** (*in combination*) having manners as specified: *ill-mannered.*

Mannerheim ('mænə,heɪm) *n.* Baron **Carl Gustaf Emil.** 1867–1951, Finnish soldier and statesman; president of Finland (1944–46).

mannerism ('mænə,rɪzəm) *n.* **1.** a distinctive and individual gesture or trait. **2.** (*often cap.*) a principally Italian movement in art and architecture between the High Renaissance and Baroque periods (1520–1600), using distortion and exaggeration of human proportions, perspective, etc. **3.** adherence to a distinctive or affected manner, esp. in art or literature. —'**mannerist** *n.*, *adj.* —,**manner'istic** *adj.* —,**manner'istically** *adv.*

mannerless ('mænəlɪs) *adj.* having bad manners; boorish. —'**mannerlessness** *n.*

mannerly ('mænəlɪ) *adj.* **1.** well-mannered; polite. ~*adv.* **2.** *Now rare.* with good manners; politely. —'**mannerliness** *n.*

manners ('mænəz) *pl. n.* **1.** social conduct. **2.** a socially acceptable way of behaving.

Mannheim ('mænhaɪm; *German* 'manhaɪm) *n.* a city in SW West Germany, in Baden-Württemberg at the confluence of the Rhine and Neckar: one of Europe's largest inland harbours; a cultural and musical centre. Pop.: 295 500 (1986).

mannikin ('mænɪkɪn) *n.* a variant spelling of **manikin.**

Manning ('mænɪŋ) *n.* **Henry Edward.** 1808–92, English churchman. Originally an Anglican, he was converted to Roman Catholicism (1851) and made archbishop of Westminster (1865) and cardinal (1875).

mannish ('mænɪʃ) *adj.* **1.** (of a woman) displaying qualities regarded as typical of a man. **2.** of or resembling a man. —'**mannishly** *adv.* —'**mannishness** *n.*

manoeuvre *or U.S.* **maneuver** (mə'nuːvə) *n.* **1.** a contrived, complicated, and possibly deceptive plan or action. **2.** a movement or action requiring dexterity and skill. **3. a.** a tactic or movement of a military or naval unit. **b.** (*pl.*) tactical exercises, usually on a large scale. **4.** a planned movement of an aircraft in flight. **5.** any change from the straight steady course of a ship. ~*vb.* **6.** (*tr.*) to contrive or accomplish with skill or cunning. **7.** (*intr.*) to manipulate situations, etc., in order to gain some end. **8.** (*intr.*) to perform a manoeuvre or manoeuvres. **9.** to move or deploy or be moved or deployed, as military units, etc. [C15: from F, from Med. L *manuopera* manual work, from L *manū operāre* to work with the hand] —**ma'noeuvrable** *or U.S.* **ma'neuverable** *adj.* —**ma,noeuvra'bility** *or U.S.* **ma,neuvera'bility** *n.* —**ma'noeuvrer** *or U.S.* **ma'neuverer** *n.*

man of God *n.* **1.** a saint or prophet. **2.** a clergyman.

man of straw *n.* **1.** a man who cannot be relied upon to honour his financial commitments, esp. because of his limited resources. **2.** any weak or vulnerable man.

man-of-war *or* **man o' war** *n.*, *pl.* **men-of-war** *or* **men o' war. 1.** a warship. **2.** See **Portuguese man-of-war.**

man-of-war bird *or* **man-o'-war bird** *n.* another name for **frigate bird.**

Manolete (*Spanish* mano'lete) *n.* original name *Manuel Rodríguez y Sánchez.* 1917–47, Spanish bullfighter.

manometer (mə'nɒmɪtə) n. an instrument for comparing pressures. [C18: from F manomètre, from Gk manos sparse + metron measure] —**manometric** (ˌmænəʊ'mɛtrɪk) or ˌmano'metrical adj.

manor ('mænə) n. 1. (in medieval Europe) the manor house of a lord and the lands attached to it. 2. a manor house. 3. a landed estate. 4. Brit. sl. a police district. [C13: from OF manoir dwelling, from maneir to dwell, from L manēre to remain] —**manorial** (mə'nɔːrɪəl) adj.

manor house n. (esp. formerly) the house of the lord of a manor.

manpower ('mæn,paʊə) n. 1. power supplied by men. 2. a unit of power based on the rate at which a man can work; roughly 75 watts. 3. the number of people needed or available for a job.

manqué French. ('mɒŋkeɪ) adj. (postpositive) unfulfilled; potential; would-be: the manager is an actor manqué. [C19: lit.: having missed]

Manresa (Spanish man'rɛsa) n. a city in NE Spain: contains a cave used as the spiritual retreat of St. Ignatius Loyola. Pop.: 67 014 (1981).

mansard ('mænsɑːd, -səd) n. a roof having two slopes on both sides and both ends, the lower slopes being steeper than the upper. Also called: **mansard roof**. [C18: from F mansarde, after François MANSART]

Mansart (French mɑ̃sar) n. 1. François (frɑ̃swa). 1598–1666, French architect, who established the classical style in French architecture. 2. his great-nephew, **Jules Hardouin** (ʒyl ardwɛ̃). 1646–1708, French architect, who completed the Palace of Versailles.

manse (mæns) n. (in certain religious denominations) the house provided for a minister. [C15: from Med. L mansus dwelling, from p.p. of L manēre to stay]

Mansell ('mænsəl) n. Nigel. born 1954, English motor-racing driver.

manservant ('mæn,sɜːvənt) n., pl. menservants. a male servant, esp. a valet.

Mansfield[1] ('mæns,fiːld) n. a town in central England, in W Nottinghamshire: former coal-mining and cotton-textiles industries. Pop.: 58 949 (1981).

Mansfield[2] ('mæns,fiːld) n. **Katherine**, real name Kathleen Mansfield Beauchamp. 1888–1923, British writer, born in New Zealand, noted for her short stories, such as those in Bliss (1920) and The Garden Party (1922).

Mansholt (Dutch 'mansholt) n. **Sicco Leendert** ('sɪkɒ 'leːndərt). born 1908, Dutch economist and politician; vice president (1958–72) and president (1972–73) of the Common Market Commission. He was the author of the Mansholt Plan for the agricultural organization of the Common Market.

mansion ('mænʃən) n. 1. Also called: **mansion house**. a large and imposing house. 2. a less common word for **manor house**. 3. (pl.) Brit. a block of flats. [C14: via OF from L mansio a remaining, from mansus; see MANSE]

Mansion House n. the. the residence of the Lord Mayor of London.

man-sized adj. 1. of a size appropriate for or convenient for a man. 2. Inf. big; large.

manslaughter ('mæn,slɔːtə) n. 1. Law. the unlawful killing of one human being by another without malice aforethought. Cf. **murder**. 2. (loosely) the killing of a human being.

Mansûra (mæn'suərə) n. See El Mansûra.

manta ('mæntə) n. 1. Also called: **manta ray, devilfish, devil ray**. any large ray (fish), having very wide winglike pectoral fins and feeding on plankton. 2. a rough cotton cloth made in Spain and Spanish America. 3. a piece of this used as a blanket or shawl. [Sp.: cloak, from Vulgar L; see MANTLE]

manteau ('mæntəʊ) n., pl. -teaus (-təʊz) or -teaux (-təʊ). a cloak or mantle. [C17: via F from L mantellum MANTLE]

Mantegna (Italian man'tɛɲɲa) n. **Andrea** (an'drɛːa). 1431–1506, Italian painter and engraver, noted esp. for his frescoes, such as those in the Ducal Palace, Mantua.

mantel ('mæntˀl) n. 1. a wooden or stone frame around the opening of a fireplace, together with its decorative facing. 2. Also called: **mantel shelf**. a shelf above this frame. [C15: from F, var. of MANTLE]

mantelet ('mæntˀ,lɛt) or **mantlet** n. 1. a woman's short mantle, worn in the mid-19th century. 2. a portable bulletproof screen or shelter. [C14: from OF, dim. of mantel MANTLE]

mantelpiece ('mæntˀl,piːs) n. 1. Also called: **mantel shelf, chimneypiece**. a shelf above a fireplace often forming part of the mantel. 2. another word for **mantel** (sense 1).

mantic ('mæntɪk) adj. 1. of or relating to divination and prophecy. 2. having divining or prophetic powers. [C19: from Gk mantikos prophetic, from mantis seer] —'**mantically** adv.

-mantic adj. combining form. forming adjectives from nouns ending in **-mancy**.

mantilla (mæn'tɪlə) n. a woman's lace or silk scarf covering the shoulders and head, worn esp. in Spain. [C18: Sp., dim. of manta cloak]

Mantinea or **Mantineia** (ˌmæntɪ'neɪə) n. (in ancient Greece) a city in E Arcadia; site of several battles.

mantis ('mæntɪs) n., pl. -tises or -tes (-tiːz). any carnivorous typically green insect of warm and tropical regions, having a long body and large eyes and resting with the first pair of legs raised as if in prayer. Also called: **praying mantis**. [C17: NL, from Gk: prophet, alluding to its praying posture]

mantissa (mæn'tɪsə) n. the fractional part of a common logarithm representing the digits of the associated number but not its magnitude: the mantissa of 2.4771 is .4771. [C17: from L: something added]

mantle ('mæntˀl) n. 1. Arch. a loose wrap or cloak. 2. anything that covers completely or envelops. 3. a small dome-shaped or cylindrical mesh, used to increase illumination in a gas or oil lamp by becoming incandescent. 4. Zool. a protective layer of epidermis in molluscs and brachiopods that secretes a substance forming the shell. 5. Ornithol. the feathers of the folded wings and back, esp. when of a different colour from the remaining feathers. 6. Geol. the part of the earth between the crust and the core. 7. a less common spelling of **mantel**. ~vb. 8. (tr.) to envelop or supply with a mantle. 9. (tr.) to spread over or become spread over. 10. (intr.) to blush; flush. [C13: via OF from L mantellum, dim. of mantum cloak]

mantle rock n. the loose rock material, including glacial drift, soils, etc., that covers the bedrock and forms the land surface.

Mantova ('mantova) n. the Italian name for **Mantua**.

mantra ('mæntrə, 'mʌn-) n. 1. Hinduism. any of those parts of the Vedic literature which consist of the metrical psalms of praise. 2. Hinduism, Buddhism. any sacred word or syllable used as an object of concentration. [C19: from Sansk., lit.: speech, instrument of thought, from man to think]

mantua ('mæntjʊə) n. a woman's loose gown of the 17th and 18th centuries. [C17: changed from MANTEAU, through the infl. of MANTUA]

Mantua ('mæntjʊə) n. a city in N Italy, in E Lombardy, surrounded by lakes: birthplace of Virgil. Pop.: 60 468 (1983 est.). Italian name: **Mantova**.

manual ('mænjʊəl) adj. 1. of or relating to a hand or hands. 2. operated or done by hand. 3. physical, as opposed to mental or mechanical: manual labour. 4. by human labour rather than automatic or computer-aided means. ~n. 5. a book, esp. of instructions or information. 6. Music. one of the keyboards played by hand on an organ. 7. Mil. the prescribed drill with small arms. [C15: via OF from L manuālis, from manus hand] —'**manually** adv.

manufactory (ˌmænjʊ'fæktərɪ, -trɪ) n., pl. -ries. an obsolete word for **factory**. [C17: from obs. manufact; see MANUFACTURE]

manufacture (ˌmænjʊ'fæktʃə) vb. 1. to process or make (a product) from a raw material, esp. as a large-scale operation using machinery. 2. (tr.) to invent or concoct. ~n. 3. the production of goods, esp. by industrial processes. 4. a manufactured product. 5. the creation or production of anything. [C16: from obs. manufact handmade, from LL manūfactus, from L manus hand + facere to make] —ˌmanu'facturing n., adj.

manufacturer (ˌmænjʊ'fæktʃərə) n. a person or business concern that manufactures goods or owns a factory.

manuka ('mɑːnʊkə) n. a New Zealand tree with strong elastic wood and aromatic leaves. Also called: **tea tree**. [from Maori]

Manukau ('mɑːnʊ,kaʊ) n. a city in New Zealand, on **Manukau Harbour** (an inlet of the Tasman Sea) near Auckland on NW North Island. Pop.: 177 248 (1986).

manumit (ˌmænjʊˈmɪt) *vb.* **-mitting, -mitted.** (*tr.*) to free from slavery, servitude, etc.; emancipate. [C15: from L *manūmittere* to release, from *manū* from one's hand + *ēmittere* to send away] —**manumission** (ˌmænjʊˈmɪʃən) *n.*

manure (məˈnjʊə) *n.* **1.** animal excreta, usually from straw, etc., used to fertilize land. **2.** *Chiefly Brit.* any material, esp. chemical fertilizer, used to fertilize land. ~*vb.* **3.** (*tr.*) to spread manure upon (fields or soil). [C14 (verb): from Anglo-F *mainoverer;* see MANOEUVRE] —**ma'nurer** *n.*

manus (ˈmeɪnəs) *n., pl.* **-nus. 1.** *Anat.* the wrist and hand. **2.** the corresponding part in other vertebrates. [C19: L: hand]

manuscript (ˈmænjʊˌskrɪpt) *n.* **1.** a book or other document written by hand. **2.** the original handwritten or typed version of a book, article, etc., as submitted by an author for publication. **3.** handwriting, as opposed to printing. [C16: from Med. L *manūscriptus,* from L *manus* hand + *scribere* to write]

Manutius (məˈnjuːʃɪəs) *n.* See **Aldus Manutius.**

Manx (mæŋks) *adj.* **1.** of or relating to the Isle of Man (an island in the Irish Sea), its inhabitants, their language, or their dialect of English. ~*n.* **2.** an almost extinct language of the Isle of Man, closely related to Scottish Gaelic. **3. the Manx.** (*functioning as pl.*) the people of the Isle of Man. [C16: earlier *Maniske,* of Scand. origin, from *Mana* Isle of Man + *-iske* -ISH]

Manx cat *n.* a short-haired tailless variety of cat, believed to originate on the Isle of Man.

Manxman (ˈmæŋksmən) *or* (*fem.*) **Manxwoman** (ˈmæŋksˌwʊmən) *n., pl.* **-men** *or* **-women.** a native or inhabitant of the Isle of Man.

many (ˈmɛnɪ) *determiner.* **1.** (sometimes preceded by *a great* or *a good*) **a.** a large number of: *many times.* **b.** (*as pron.; functioning as pl.*): *many are seated already.* **2.** (foll. by *a, an,* or *another,* and a sing. noun) each of a considerable number of: *many a man.* **3.** (preceded by *as, too, that,* etc.) **a.** a great number of: *as many apples as you like.* **b.** (*as pron.; functioning as pl.*): *I have as many as you.* ~*n.* **4. the many.** the majority of mankind, esp. the common people. [OE *manig*]

many-sided *adj.* having many sides, aspects, etc. —ˌmany-'sidedness *n.*

many-valued logic *n.* any of various logics in which the truth-values that a proposition may have are not restricted to truth and falsity.

manzanilla (ˌmænzəˈnɪlə) *n.* a very dry pale sherry. [C19: from Sp.: camomile (referring to its bouquet)]

Manzoni (*Italian* manˈdzoːni) *n.* **Alessandro** (alesˈsandro). 1785–1873, Italian romantic novelist and poet, famous for his historical novel *I Promessi sposi* (1825–27).

Maoism (ˈmaʊɪzəm) *n.* **1.** Marxism-Leninism as interpreted by Mao Tse-tung: distinguished by its theory of guerrilla warfare and its emphasis on the revolutionary potential of the peasantry. **2.** adherence to or reverence for Mao Tse-tung and his teachings. —'Maoist *n., adj.*

Maori (ˈmaʊrɪ) *n.* **1.** (*pl.* **-ris** *or* **-ri**) a member of the people of Polynesian origin living in New Zealand and the Cook Islands since before the arrival of European settlers. **2.** the language of this people, belonging to the Malayo-Polynesian family. ~*adj.* **3.** of or relating to this people or their language.

Maoriland (ˈmaʊrɪˌlænd) *n.* an obsolete name for **New Zealand.** —'Maoriˌlander *n.*

Mao Tse-tung (ˈmaʊ tseɪˈtʊŋ) *or* **Mao Ze Dong** *n.* 1893– 1976, Chinese Marxist theoretician and statesman. The son of a peasant farmer, he helped to found the Chinese Communist Party (1921) and established a soviet republic in SE China (1931–34). He led the retreat of Communist forces to NW China known as the Long March (1935–36), emerging as leader of the party. In opposing the Japanese in World War II, he united with the Kuomintang regime, which he then defeated in the ensuing civil war. He founded the People's Republic of China (1949) of which he was chairman until 1959. As party chairman until his death, he instigated the Cultural Revolution in 1966.

map (mæp) *n.* **1.** a diagrammatic representation of the earth's surface or part of it, showing the geographical distributions, positions, etc., of features such as roads, towns, relief, rainfall, etc. **2.** a diagrammatic representation of the stars or of the surface of a celestial body. **3.** a maplike drawing of anything. **4.** *Maths.* another name for

function (sense 4b). **5.** a slang word for **face** (sense 1). **6. off the map.** no longer important; out of existence (esp. in **wipe off the map**). **7. put on the map.** to make (a town, company, etc.) well-known. ~*vb.* **mapping, mapped.** (*tr.*) **8.** to make a map of. **9.** *Maths.* to represent or transform (a function, figure, set, etc.). ~See also **map out.** [C16: from Med. L *mappa* (*mundi*) map (of the world), from L *mappa* cloth]

Map (mæp) *or* **Mapes** (mæps, ˈmeɪpiːz) *n.* **Walter.** ?1140–?1209, Welsh ecclesiastic and satirical writer. His chief work is the miscellany *De Nugis curialium.*

maple (ˈmeɪpəl) *n.* **1.** any tree or shrub of a N temperate genus, having winged seeds borne in pairs and lobed leaves. **2.** the hard wood of any of these trees, used for furniture and flooring. **3.** the flavour of the sap of the sugar maple. ~See also **sugar maple.** [C14: from OE *mapel-,* as in *mapeltrēow* maple tree]

maple leaf *n.* the leaf of the maple tree, the national emblem of Canada.

maple sugar *n.* *U.S. & Canad.* sugar made from the sap of the sugar maple.

maple syrup *n.* *Chiefly U.S. & Canad.* a very sweet syrup made from the sap of the sugar maple.

map out *vb.* (*tr., adv.*) to plan or design.

mapping (ˈmæpɪŋ) *n.* *Maths.* another name for **function** (sense 4b).

map projection *n.* a means of representing or a representation of a globe or celestial sphere or part of it on a flat map.

Maputo (məˈpuːtəʊ) *n.* the capital and chief port of Mozambique, in the south on Delagoa Bay: became capital in 1907; the nearest port to the Rand gold-mining and industrial region of South Africa. Pop.: 882 800 (1986). Former name (until 1975): **Lourenço Marques.**

maquette (mæˈkɛt) *n.* a sculptor's small preliminary model or sketch. [C20: from F, from It. *macchietta* a little sketch, from *macchiare,* from L *macula* blemish]

maquis (mɑːˈkiː) *n., pl.* **-quis** (-ˈkiː). **1.** shrubby, mostly evergreen, vegetation found in coastal regions of the Mediterranean. **2.** (*often cap.*) **a.** the French underground movement that fought against the German occupying forces in World War II. **b.** a member of this movement. [C20: from F, from It. *macchia* thicket, from L *macula* spot]

mar (mɑː) *vb.* **marring, marred.** (*tr.*) to cause harm to; spoil or impair. [OE *merran*] —'marrer *n.*

mar. *abbrev. for:* **1.** maritime. **2.** married.

Mar. *abbrev. for* March.

marabou (ˈmærəˌbuː) *n.* **1.** a large black-and-white African carrion-eating stork. **2.** a down feather of this bird, used to trim garments. [C19: from F, from Ar. *murābit* MARABOUT: the stork is considered a holy bird in Islam]

marabout (ˈmærəˌbuː) *n.* **1.** a Muslim holy man or hermit of North Africa. **2.** a shrine of the grave of a marabout. [C17: via F & Port. *marabuto,* from Ar. *murābit*]

maraca (məˈrækə) *n.* a percussion instrument, usually one of a pair, consisting of a gourd or plastic shell filled with dried seeds, pebbles, etc. [C20: Brazilian Port., of Amerind origin]

Maracaibo (ˌmærəˈkaɪbəʊ; *Spanish* maraˈkaiβo) *n.* **1.** a port in NW Venezuela, on the channel from Lake Maracaibo to the Gulf of Venezuela: the second largest city in the country; University of Zulia (1891); major oil centre. Pop.: 1 124 432 (1987 est.). **2. Lake.** a lake in NW Venezuela, linked with the Gulf of Venezuela by a dredged channel: centre of the Venezuelan and South American oil industry. Area: about 13 000 sq. km (5000 sq. miles).

Maracanda (ˌmærəˈkændə) *n.* the ancient name for **Samarkand.**

Maracay (*Spanish* maraˈkai) *n.* a city in N central Venezuela: developed greatly as the headquarters of Juan Vicente Gómez during his dictatorship; textile industries. Pop.: 496 662 (1987 est.).

Maradona (ˌmærəˈdɒnə) *n.* **Diego** (dɪˈeɪɡəʊ). born 1960, Argentinian footballer.

marae (məˈraɪ) *n.* *N.Z.* a traditional Maori tribal meeting place, originally one in the open air, now frequently a purpose-built building. [from Maori]

Marajó (*Portuguese* maraˈʒɔ) *n.* an island in N Brazil, at the mouth of the Amazon. Area: 38 610 sq. km (15 444 sq. miles).

Maranhão (*Portuguese* maraˈɲəu) *n.* a state of NE Brazil, on the Atlantic: forested and humid in the northwest, with high plateaus in the east and south. Capital: São Luís. Pop.: 4 751 000 (1986 est.). Area: 328 666 sq. km (128 179 sq. miles).

Marañón (*Spanish* maraˈɲɔn) *n.* a river in NE Peru, rising in the Andes and flowing northwest into the Ucayali River, forming the Amazon. Length: about 1450 km (900 miles).

maranta (məˈræntə) *n.* any of various tropical monocotyledons with ornamental leaves. [C19: after B. *Maranta* 16th-century Venetian botanist]

marasca (məˈræskə) *n.* a European cherry tree with red acid-tasting fruit. [C19: from It., var. of *amarasca*, ult. from L *amārus* bitter]

maraschino (ˌmærəˈskiːnəʊ, -ˈʃiːnəʊ) *n.* a liqueur made from marasca cherries, having a taste like bitter almonds. [C18: from It.; see MARASCA]

maraschino cherry *n.* a cherry preserved in maraschino or an imitation of this liqueur.

marasmus (məˈræzməs) *n. Pathol.* general emaciation, esp. of infants, thought to be associated with severe malnutrition or impaired utilization of nutrients. [C17: from NL, from Gk *marasmos*, from *marainein* to waste] —**maˈrasmic** *adj.*

Marat (*French* mara) *n.* **Jean Paul** (ʒɑ̃ pɔl). 1743–93, French revolutionary leader and journalist. He founded the radical newspaper *L'Ami du peuple* and was elected to the National Convention (1792). He was instrumental in overthrowing the Girondists (1793); he was stabbed to death in his bath by Charlotte Corday.

marathon (ˈmærəθən) *n.* **1.** a race on foot of 26 miles 385 yards (42.195 kilometres). **2. a.** any long or arduous task, etc. **b.** (*as modifier*): *a marathon effort.* [referring to the feat of the messenger who ran 26 miles from Marathon to Athens to bring the news of victory in 490 B.C.]

Marathon (ˈmærəθən) *n.* a plain in Attica northeast of Athens: site of a victory of the Athenians and Plataeans over the Persians (490 B.C.).

maraud (məˈrɔːd) *vb.* to wander or raid in search of plunder. [C18: from F *marauder* to prowl, from *maraud* vagabond] —**maˈrauder** *n.* —**maˈrauding** *adj.*

marble (ˈmɑːbᵊl) *n.* **1. a.** a hard crystalline metamorphic rock resulting from the recrystallization of a limestone. **b.** (*as modifier*): *a marble bust.* **2.** a block or work of art of marble. **3.** a small round glass or stone ball used in playing marbles. ~*vb.* **4.** (*tr.*) to mottle with variegated streaks in imitation of marble. [C12: via OF from L *marmor*, from Gk *marmaros*, rel. to Gk *marmairein* to gleam] —**ˈmarbled** *adj.*

marbles (ˈmɑːbᵊlz) *n.* **1.** (*functioning as sing.*) a game in which marbles are rolled at one another, similar to bowls. **2.** (*functioning as pl.*) *Inf.* wits: *to lose one's marbles.*

marbling (ˈmɑːblɪŋ) *n.* **1.** a mottled effect or pattern resembling marble. **2.** such an effect obtained by transferring floating colours from a gum solution. **3.** the streaks of fat in lean meat.

Marburg (ˈmɑːˌbɜːg; *German* ˈmaːrbʊrk) *n.* **1.** a city in central West Germany, in Hesse; famous for the religious debate between Luther and Zwingli in 1529; Europe's first Protestant university (1527). Pop.: 77 300 (1984 est.). **2.** the German name for **Maribor**.

marc (mɑːk) *n.* **1.** the remains of grapes or other fruit that have been pressed for wine-making. **2.** a brandy distilled from these. [C17: from F, from OF *marchier* to trample (grapes)]

Marc (*German* mark) *n.* **Franz** (frants). 1880–1916, German expressionist painter; cofounder with Kandinsky of the *Blaue Reiter* group (1911). He is noted for his symbolic compositions of animals.

marcasite (ˈmɑːkəˌsaɪt) *n.* **1.** a metallic pale yellow mineral consisting of iron pyrites in crystalline form used in jewellery. **2.** a cut and polished form of steel or any white metal used for making jewellery. [C15: from Med. L *marcasīta*, from Ar. *marqashītā*, ?from Persian]

marcato (mɑːˈkɑːtəʊ) *adj., adv. Music.* with each note heavily accented. [from It.: marked]

Marceau (*French* marso) *n.* **Marcel** (marsɛl). born 1923, French mime artist.

Marcellus (mɑːˈsɛləs) *n.* **Marcus Claudius** (ˈmɑːkəs ˈklɔːdɪəs). ?268–208 B.C., Roman general and consul, who captured Syracuse (212) in the Second Punic War.

march[1] (mɑːtʃ) *vb.* **1.** (*intr.*) to walk or proceed with stately or regular steps, usually in a procession or military formation. **2.** (*tr.*) to make (a person or group) proceed.

3. (*tr.*) to traverse or cover by marching. ~*n.* **4.** the act or an instance of marching. **5.** a regular stride. **6.** a long or exhausting walk. **7.** advance; progression (of time, etc.). **8.** a distance or route covered by marching. **9.** a piece of music, as for a march. **10. steal a march on.** to gain an advantage over, esp. by a secret enterprise or trick. [C16: from OF *marchier* to tread, prob. of Gmc origin] —**ˈmarcher** *n.*

march[2] (mɑːtʃ) *n.* **1.** a frontier, border, or boundary or the land lying along it, often of disputed ownership. ~*vb.* **2.** (*intr.*; often foll. by *upon* or *with*) to share a common border (with). [C13: from OF *marche*, of Gmc origin]

March[1] (mɑːtʃ) *n.* the third month of the year, consisting of 31 days. [from OF, from L *Martius* (month) of Mars]

March[2] (març) *n.* the German name for the **Morava** (sense 1).

Marche (*French* marʃ) *n.* a former province of central France.

Marches (ˈmɑːtʃɪz) *n.* **the.** **1.** the border area between England and Wales or Scotland, both characterized by continual feuding (13th–16th centuries). **2.** a region of central Italy. Capital: Ancona. Pop.: 1 426 965 (1986 est.). Area: 9692 sq. km (3780 sq. miles). Italian name: **Le Marche** (le ˈmarke). **3.** any of various other border regions.

March hare *n.* a hare during its breeding season in March, noted for its wild and excitable behaviour (esp. in **mad as a March hare**).

marching orders *pl. n.* **1.** military orders, esp. to infantry, giving instructions about a march, its destination, etc. **2.** *Inf.* any dismissal, esp. notice of dismissal from employment.

marchioness (ˈmɑːʃənɪs, ˌmɑːʃəˈnɛs) *n.* **1.** the wife or widow of a marquis. **2.** a woman who holds the rank of marquis. [C16: from Med. L *marchionissa*, fem. of *marchiō* MARQUIS]

marchpane (ˈmɑːtʃˌpeɪn) *n.* an archaic word for **marzipan.** [C16: from F]

Marciano (ˌmɑːsɪˈænəʊ, -ˈɑːnəʊ) *n.* **Rocky.** original name *Rocco Francis Marchegiano.* 1923–69, U.S. heavyweight boxer; world heavyweight champion, 1952–56.

Marconi (mɑːˈkəʊnɪ) *n.* **Guglielmo** (guʌˈʎɛlmo). 1874–1937, Italian physicist, who developed radio telegraphy and succeeded in transmitting signals across the Atlantic (1901): Nobel prize for physics 1909.

Marco Polo (ˈmɑːkəʊ ˈpəʊləʊ) *n.* See (Marco) **Polo.**

Marcos (ˈmɑːkɒs) *n.* **Ferdinand** (**Edralin**). born 1917, Filipino statesman; president of the Philippines from 1965, deposed and exiled in 1986.

Marcus Aurelius Antoninus (ˈmɑːkəs ɔːˈriːlɪəs ˌæntəˈnaɪnəs) *n.* original name *Marcus Annius Verus.* 121–180 A.D., Roman emperor (161–180) noted particularly for his *Meditations*, propounding his stoic view of life.

Marcuse (mɑːˈkuːzə) *n.* **Herbert.** 1898–1979, U.S. philosopher, born in Germany. In his later works he analysed the situation of man under monopoly capitalism and the dehumanizing effects of modern technology. His works include *Eros and Civilization* (1958) and *One Dimensional Man* (1964).

Mar del Plata (*Spanish* ˈmar ðɛl ˈplata) *n.* a city and resort in E Argentina, on the Atlantic: fishing port. Pop.: 350 000 (1984 est.).

Mardi Gras (ˈmɑːdɪ ˈɡrɑː) *n.* the festival of Shrove Tuesday, celebrated in some cities with great revelry. [F: fat Tuesday]

Marduk (ˈmɑːduk) *n.* the chief god of the Babylonian pantheon.

mare[1] (mɛə) *n.* the adult female of a horse or zebra. [C12: from OE, of Gmc origin]

mare[2] (ˈmɑːreɪ) *n., pl.* **maria.** **1.** (*cap. when part of a name*) any of a large number of huge dry plains on the surface of the moon, visible as dark markings and once thought to be seas. **2.** a similar area on the surface of Mars. [from L: sea]

Marengo (məˈrɛŋɡəʊ; *Italian* maˈreŋɡo) *n.* a village in NW Italy: site of a major battle in which Napoleon decisively defeated the Austrians (1800).

Marenzio (*Italian* maˈrɛntsjo) *n.* **Luca** (ˈluːka). 1553–99, Italian composer of madrigals.

mare's-nest (ˈmɛəzˌnɛst) *n.* **1.** a discovery imagined to be important but proving worthless. **2.** a disordered situation.

mare's-tail ('mɛəz,teɪl) *n.* **1.** a wisp of trailing cirrus cloud, indicating strong winds at high levels. **2.** an erect pond plant with minute flowers and crowded whorls of narrow leaves.

Margaret ('mɑːgrət) *n.* **Princess.** born 1930, younger sister of Queen Elizabeth II of Great Britain and Northern Ireland.

Margaret of Anjou *n.* 1430–82, queen of England. She married the mentally unstable Henry VI of England in 1445 to confirm the truce with France during the Hundred Years' War. She became a leader of the Lancastrians in the Wars of the Roses and was defeated at Tewkesbury (1471) by Edward IV.

Margaret of Navarre *n.* 1492–1549, queen of Navarre (1544–49) by marriage to Henry II of Navarre; sister of Francis I of France. She was a poet and a patron of humanism.

Margaret of Valois *n.* 1553–1615, daughter of Henry II of France and Catherine de' Medici; queen of Navarre (1572) by marriage to Henry of Navarre. The marriage was dissolved (1599) after his accession as Henry IV of France: noted for her *Mémoires.*

margaric (mɑː'gærɪk) *or* **margaritic** *adj.* of or resembling pearl. [C19: from Gk *margaron* pearl]

margarine (,mɑːdʒə'riːn, ,mɑːg-) *n.* a substitute for butter, prepared from vegetable and animal fats with added small amounts of milk, salt, vitamins, colouring matter, etc. [C19: from MARGARIC]

Margarita (,mɑːgə'riːtə) *n.* an island in the Caribbean, off the NE coast of Venezuela: pearl fishing. Capital: La Asunción.

Margate ('mɑːgeɪt) *n.* a town and resort in SE England, in E Kent on the Isle of Thanet. Pop.: 53 280 (1981).

marge[1] (mɑːdʒ) *n. Brit. inf.* short for **margarine.**

marge[2] (mɑːdʒ) *n. Arch.* a margin. [C16: from F]

margin ('mɑːdʒɪn) *n.* **1.** an edge or rim, and the area immediately adjacent to it; border. **2.** the blank space surrounding the text on a page. **3.** a vertical line on a page delineating this space. **4.** an additional amount or one beyond the minimum necessary: *a margin of error.* **5.** *Chiefly Austral.* a payment made in addition to a basic wage, esp. for special skill or responsibility. **6.** a bound or limit. **7.** the amount by which one thing differs from another. **8.** *Commerce.* the profit on a transaction. **9.** *Econ.* the minimum return below which an enterprise becomes unprofitable. **10.** *Finance.* collateral deposited by a client with a broker as security. ~Also (archaic): **margent** ('mɑːdʒənt). ~*vb.* (*tr.*) **11.** to provide with a margin; border. **12.** *Finance.* to deposit a margin upon. [C14: from L *margō* border]

marginal ('mɑːdʒɪnᵊl) *adj.* **1.** of, in, on, or constituting a margin. **2.** close to a limit, esp. a lower limit: *marginal legal ability.* **3.** not considered central or important; insignificant. **4.** *Econ.* relating to goods or services produced and sold at the margin of profitability: *marginal cost.* **5.** *Politics, chiefly Brit. & N.Z.* of or designating a constituency in which elections tend to be won by small margins: *a marginal seat.* **6.** designating agricultural land on the margin of cultivated zones. ~*n.* **7.** *Politics, chiefly Brit. & N.Z.* a marginal constituency. —**marginality** (,mɑːdʒɪ'nælɪtɪ) *n.* —**marginally** *adv.*

marginalia (,mɑːdʒɪ'neɪlɪə) *pl. n.* notes in the margin of a book, manuscript, or letter. [C19: NL, noun (neuter pl.) from *marginālis* marginal]

marginate ('mɑːdʒɪ,neɪt) *vb.* **1.** (*tr.*) to provide with a margin or margins. ~*adj.* **2.** *Biol.* having a margin of a distinct colour or form. [C18: from L *margināre*] —,**margin'ation** *n.*

margrave ('mɑː,greɪv) *n.* a German nobleman ranking above a count. Margraves were originally counts appointed to govern frontier provinces, but all eventually became princes of the Holy Roman Empire. [C16: from MDu. *markgrave*, lit.: count of the MARCH[2]] —**margravate** ('mɑːgrəvɪt) *n.*

margravine ('mɑːgrə,viːn) *n.* **1.** the wife or widow of a margrave. **2.** a woman who holds the rank of margrave. [C17: from MDu., fem. of MARGRAVE]

Margrethe II (*Danish* mar'greːdə) *n.* born 1940, queen of Denmark from 1972.

marguerite (,mɑːgə'riːt) *n.* **1.** a cultivated garden plant whose flower heads have white or pale yellow rays around a yellow disc. **2.** any of various related plants

with daisy-like flowers. [C19: from F: daisy, pearl, from L, from Gk, from *margaron*]

maria ('mɑːrɪə) *n.* the plural of **mare**[2].

mariachi (,mɑːrɪ'ɑːtʃɪ) *n.* a small ensemble of street musicians in Mexico. [C20: from Mexican Sp.]

Maria de' Medici (*Italian* ma'riːa de 'mɛːditʃi) *n.* French name *Marie de Médicis.* 1573–1642, queen of France (1600–10) by marriage to Henry IV of France; daughter of Francesco, grand duke of Tuscany. She became regent for her son (later Louis XIII) but continued to wield power after he came of age (1614). She was finally exiled from France in 1631 after plotting to undermine Richelieu's influence at court.

Mariana Islands (,mærɪ'ɑːnə) *pl. n.* a chain of volcanic and coral islands in the W Pacific, east of the Philippines and north of New Guinea: divided politically into Guam and the islands north of Guam constituting the Commonwealth of the Northern Mariana Islands. Pop.: 135 391 (1984 est.). Area: 958 sq. km (370 sq. miles). Former name (1521–1668): **Ladrone Islands.**

Marianao (*Spanish* marja'nao) *n.* a city in NW Cuba, adjacent to W Havana city: the chief Cuban military base. Pop.: 127 563 (1981).

Mariánské Lázně (*Czech* 'marjanskɛː 'laːznjɛ) *n.* a town in W Czechoslovakia: a fashionable spa in the 18th and 19th centuries. Pop.: 17 950 (1981 est.). German name: **Marienbad.**

Maria Theresa (mə'riːə tə'reɪzə) *n.* 1717–80, archduchess of Austria and queen of Hungary and Bohemia (1740–80); the daughter and heiress of Emperor Charles VI of Austria; the wife of Emperor Francis I; the mother of Emperor Joseph II. In the War of the Austrian Succession (1740–48) she was confirmed in all her possessions except Silesia, which she attempted unsuccessfully to regain in the Seven Years' War (1756–63).

Mari Autonomous Soviet Socialist Republic ('mɑːrɪ) *n.* an administrative division of the W central Soviet Union, in the middle Volga basin. Capital: Yoshkar-Ola. Pop.: 731 000 (1986). Area: 23 200 sq. km (8955 sq. miles).

Maribor ('mærɪbɔː) *n.* an industrial city in N Yugoslavia, in Slovenia on the Drava River: a flourishing Hapsburg trading centre in the 13th century; resort. Pop.: 185 699 (1981). German name: **Marburg.**

Marie Antoinette (*French* mari ãtwanɛt) *n.* 1755–93, queen of France (1774–93) by marriage to Louis XVI of France. Her opposition to reform during the Revolution contributed to the overthrow of the monarchy; guillotined.

Marie Byrd Land ('mɑːrɪ 'bɜːd) *n.* the former name of Byrd Land.

Marie Galante (*French* mari galãt) *n.* an island in the E West Indies southeast of Guadeloupe, of which it is a dependency. Chief town: Grand Bourg. Pop.: 13 757 (1981 est.). Area: 155 sq. km (60 sq. miles).

Mariehamn (maria'hamn) *n.* a city in SW Finland, chief port of the Åland Islands. Pop.: 9824 (1985 est.). Finnish name: **Maarianhamina.**

Marie Louise (*French* mari lwiz) *n.* 1791–1847, empress of France (1811–15) as the second wife of Napoleon I; daughter of Francis I of Austria. On Napoleon's abdication (1815) she became Duchess of Parma.

Marienbad ('mærɪən,bæd; *German* ma'riːənbaːt) *n.* the German name for **Mariánské Lázně.**

marigold ('mærɪ,gəʊld) *n.* **1.** any of various tropical American plants cultivated for their yellow or orange flower heads and strongly scented foliage. **2.** any of various similar or related plants, such as the marsh marigold. [C14: from *Mary* (the Virgin) + GOLD]

marijuana *or* **marihuana** (,mærɪ'hwɑːnə) *n.* **1.** the dried leaves and flowers of the hemp plant, used as a narcotic, esp. in cigarettes. See also **cannabis. 2.** another name for **hemp** (the plant). [C19: from Mexican Sp.]

marimba (mə'rɪmbə) *n.* a Latin American percussion instrument consisting of a set of hardwood plates placed over tuned metal resonators, played with two soft-headed sticks in each hand. [C18: of West African origin]

Marin ('mɑːrɪn) *n.* **John.** 1870–1953, U.S. painter, noted esp. for his watercolour landscapes and seascapes.

marina (mə'riːnə) *n.* an elaborate docking facility for yachts and other pleasure boats. [C19: via It. & Sp. from L: MARINE]

marinade *n.* (,mærɪ'neɪd). **1.** a spiced liquid mixture of oil, wine, vinegar, etc., in which meat or fish is soaked before cooking. **2.** meat or fish soaked in this. ~*vb.* ('mærɪ,neɪd). **3.** a variant of **marinate**. [C17: from F, from Sp., from *marinar* to MARINATE]

marinate ('mærɪ,neɪt) *vb.* to soak in marinade. [C17: prob. from It. *marinato*, from *marinare* to pickle, ult. from L *marīnus* MARINE] —,**mari'nation** *n.*

Marinduque (,mɑːrɪn'duːkeɪ) *n.* an island of the central Philippines, east of Mindoro: forms, with offshore islets, a province of the Philippines. Capital: Boac. Pop.: 173 715 (1980). Area: 960 sq. km (370 sq. miles).

marine (mə'riːn) *adj.* (*usually prenominal*) **1.** of, found in, or relating to the sea. **2.** of or relating to shipping, navigation, etc. **3.** of or relating to a body of seagoing troops: *marine corps.* **4.** of or relating to a government department concerned with maritime affairs. **5.** used or adapted for use at sea. ~*n.* **6.** shipping and navigation in general. **7.** (*cap. when part of a name*) a member of a marine corps or similar body. **8.** a picture of a ship, seascape, etc. **9. tell it to the marines.** *Inf.* an expression of disbelief. [C15: from OF *marin*, from L *marinus*, from *mare* sea]

mariner ('mærɪnə) *n.* a formal or literary word for **seaman**. [C13: from Anglo-F, ult. from L *marīnus* MARINE]

Marinetti (*Italian* mari'netti) *n.* **Filippo Tommaso** (fiˈlippo tomˈmaːzo). 1876–1944, Italian poet; founder of futurism (1909).

Mariolatry (,mɛərɪ'ɒlətrɪ) *n. Derog.* devotion to the Virgin Mary, considered as excessive. —,**Mari'olater** *n.* —,**Mari'olatrous** *adj.*

marionette (,mærɪə'nɛt) *n.* a puppet or doll whose jointed limbs are moved by strings. [C17: from F, from *Marion*, dim. of *Marie* Mary + -ETTE]

Marist ('mɛərɪst) *n. R.C. Church.* a member of the Society of Mary, a religious congregation founded in 1824. [C19: from F *Mariste*, from *Marie* Mary (the Virgin)]

Maritain (*French* mariˈtɛ̃) *n.* **Jacques** (ʒak). 1882–1973, French neo-Thomist Roman Catholic philosopher.

marital ('mærɪtᵊl) *adj.* **1.** of or relating to marriage. **2.** of or relating to a husband. [C17: from L *maritālis*, from *maritus* married (adj.), husband (n.)] —'**maritally** *adv.*

maritime ('mærɪ,taɪm) *adj.* **1.** of or relating to navigation, shipping, etc. **2.** of, relating to, near, or living near the sea. **3.** (of a climate) having small temperature differences between summer and winter. [C16: from L *maritimus*, from *mare* sea]

Maritime Alps *pl. n.* a range of the W Alps in SE France and NW Italy. Highest peak: Argentera, 3297 m (10 817 ft.).

Maritime Provinces *or* **Maritimes** *pl. n.* **the. the Atlantic Provinces** of Canada, often excluding Newfoundland.

Maritimer ('mærɪ,taɪmə) *n.* a native or inhabitant of the Maritime Provinces of Canada.

Maritsa (*Bulgarian* ma'ritsa) *n.* a river in S Europe, rising in S Bulgaria and flowing east into Turkey, then south from Edirne as part of the border between Turkey and Greece to the Aegean. Length: 483 km (300 miles). Turkish name: **Meriç.** Greek name: **Évros.**

Mariupol (*Russian* məri'upəlj) *n.* the former name (until 1948) of **Zhdanov.**

Marius ('mɛərɪəs, 'mærɪəs) *n.* **Gaius** ('gaɪəs). ?155–86 B.C., Roman general and consul. He defeated Jugurtha, the Cimbri, and the Teutons (107–101), but his rivalry with Sulla caused civil war (88). He was exiled but returned (87) and took Rome.

Marivaux (*French* marivo) *n.* **Pierre Carlet de Chamblain de** (pjɛr karlɛ də ʃɑ̃blɛ̃ də). 1688–1763, French dramatist and novelist, noted particularly for his comedies, such as *Le jeu de l'amour et du hasard* (1730) and *La Vie de Marianne* (1731–41).

marjoram ('mɑːdʒərəm) *n.* **1.** Also called: **sweet marjoram.** an aromatic Mediterranean plant with sweet-scented leaves, used for seasoning food and in salads. **2.** Also called: **wild marjoram, pot marjoram, origan.** a similar and related European plant. See also **oregano.** [C14: via OF *majorane*, from Med. L *marjorana*]

mark¹ (mɑːk) *n.* **1.** a visible impression, stain, etc., on a surface, such as a spot or scratch. **2.** a sign, symbol, or other indication that distinguishes something. **3.** a cross or other symbol made instead of a signature. **4.** a written or printed sign or symbol, as for punctuation. **5.** a letter, number, or percentage used to grade academic work. **6.** a thing that indicates position or directs; marker. **7.** a desired or recognized standard: *up to the mark.* **8.** an indication of some quality, feature, or prowess. **9.** quality or

importance: *a person of little mark.* **10.** a target or goal. **11.** impression or influence. **12.** *Sl.* a suitable victim, esp. for swindling. **13.** (*often cap.*) (in trade names) a model, brand, or type. **14.** *Naut.* one of the intervals distinctively marked on a sounding lead. **15.** *Rugby.* an action in which a player standing with both feet on the ground within his own 22 m line catches a forward kick, throw, or knock by an opponent and shouts "mark", which entitles him to a free kick. **16.** *Australian Rules football.* **a.** a catch of the ball from a kick of at least 10 yards, after which a free kick is taken. **b.** the spot where this occurs. **17.** (in medieval England and Germany) a piece of land held in common by the free men of a community. **18. the mark.** *Boxing.* the middle of the stomach. **19. make one's mark.** to succeed or achieve recognition. **20. on your mark** *or* **marks.** a command given to runners in a race to prepare themselves at the starting line. ~*vb.* **21.** to make or receive (a visible impression, trace, or stain) on (a surface). **22.** (*tr.*) to characterize or distinguish. **23.** (often foll. by *off* or *out*) to set boundaries or limits (on). **24.** (*tr.*) to select, designate, or doom by or as if by a mark: *to mark someone as a criminal.* **25.** (*tr.*) to put identifying or designating labels, stamps, etc., on, esp. to indicate price. **26.** (*tr.*) to pay heed or attention to: *mark my words.* **27.** to observe; notice. **28.** to grade or evaluate (scholastic work). **29.** *Brit. football, etc.* to stay close to (an opponent) to hamper his play. **30.** to keep (score) in some games. **31. mark time. a.** to move the feet alternately as in marching but without advancing. **b.** to act in a mechanical and routine way. **c.** to halt progress temporarily. ~See also **markdown, mark-up.** [OE *mearc* mark] —'**marker** *n.*

mark² (mɑːk) *n.* **1.** See **Deutschmark, markka, Reichsmark, ostmark. 2.** a former monetary unit and coin in England and Scotland worth two thirds of a pound sterling. **3.** a silver coin of Germany until 1924. [OE *marc* unit of weight of precious metal, ?from the marks on metal bars; apparently of Gmc origin and rel. to MARK¹]

Mark (mɑːk) *n. New Testament.* **1.** one of the four Evangelists. Feast day: April 25. **2.** the second Gospel, traditionally ascribed to him.

Mark Antony *n.* See (Mark) **Antony.**

markdown ('mɑːk,daʊn) *n.* **1.** a price reduction. ~*vb.* **mark down. 2.** (*tr., adv.*) to reduce in price.

marked (mɑːkt) *adj.* **1.** obvious, evident, or noticeable. **2.** singled out, esp. as the target of attack: *a marked man.* **3.** *Linguistics.* distinguished by a specific feature, as in phonology. For example, of the two phonemes /t/ and /d/, the /d/ is marked because it exhibits the feature of voice. —**markedly** ('mɑːkɪdlɪ) *adv.* —'**markedness** *n.*

market ('mɑːkɪt) *n.* **1. a.** an event or occasion, usually held at regular intervals, at which people meet to buy and sell merchandise. **b.** (*as modifier*): *market day.* **2.** a place at which a market is held. **3.** a shop that sells a particular merchandise: *an antique market.* **4.** the trading or selling opportunities provided by a particular group of people: *the foreign market.* **5.** demand for a particular product or commodity. **6.** See **stock market. 7.** See **market price, market value. 8. be in the market for.** to wish to buy or acquire. **9. on the market.** available for purchase. **10. seller's** (*or* **buyer's**) **market.** a market characterized by excess demand (or supply) and thus favourable to sellers (or buyers). **11. the market.** business or trade in a commodity as specified: *the sugar market.* ~*vb.* **12.** (*tr.*) to offer or produce for sale. **13.** (*intr.*) to buy or deal in a market. [C12: from L *mercātus*, from *mercāri* to trade, from *merx* merchandise] —'**marketable** *adj.* —'**marketer** *n.*

market garden *n. Chiefly Brit.* an establishment where fruit and vegetables are grown for sale. —**market gardener** *n.* —**market gardening** *n.*

marketing ('mɑːkɪtɪŋ) *n.* the provision of goods or services to meet consumer needs.

market maker *n. Stock Exchange.* a principal who uses his firm's money to create a market for a stock: formerly done by a jobber, the difference being that the market maker, since Big Bang, can deal direct with the public.

marketplace ('mɑːkɪt,pleɪs) *n.* **1.** a place where a public market is held. **2.** any centre where ideas, opinions, etc., are exchanged. **3.** the commercial world of buying and selling.

market price *n.* the prevailing price, as determined by supply and demand, at which goods, services, etc., may be bought or sold.

market research *n.* the study of influences upon customer behaviour and the analysis of market characteristics and trends.

market town *n. Chiefly Brit.* a town that holds a market, esp. an agricultural centre.

market value *n.* the amount obtainable on the open market for the sale of property, financial assets, or goods and services.

Markham ('mɑːkəm) *n.* **Mount.** a mountain in Antarctica, in Victoria Land. Height: 4350 m (14 272 ft.).

markhor ('mɑːkɔː) *or* **markhoor** ('mɑːkʊə) *n., pl.* **-khors, -khor** *or* **-khoors, -khoor.** a large wild Himalayan goat with large spiralled horns. [C19: from Persian, lit.: snake-eater]

marking ('mɑːkɪŋ) *n.* **1.** a mark or series of marks. **2.** the arrangement of colours on an animal, plant, etc. **3.** assessment and correction of pupils' or students' written work by teachers.

markka ('mɑːkɑː, -kə) *n., pl.* **-kaa** (-kɑː). the standard monetary unit of Finland. [Finnish; see MARK²]

Markova (mɑːˈkəʊvə) *n.* Dame **Alicia.** real name *Lilian Alicia Marks.* born 1910, English ballerina.

marksman ('mɑːksmən) *n., pl.* **-men. 1.** a person skilled in shooting. **2.** a serviceman selected for his skill in shooting. —'**marksmanship** *n.*

mark-up *n.* **1.** an amount added to the cost of a commodity to provide the seller with a profit. **2. a.** an increase in the price of a commodity. **b.** the amount of this. ~*vb.* **mark up.** (*tr., adv.*) **3.** to add a percentage for profit, etc., to the cost of (a commodity). **4.** to increase the price of.

marl (mɑːl) *n.* **1.** a fine-grained sedimentary rock consisting of clay minerals, calcium carbonate, and silt: used as a fertilizer. ~*vb.* **2.** (*tr.*) to fertilize (land) with marl. [C14: via OF, from LL *margila,* dim. of L *marga*] —'**marly** *adj.*

Marlborough¹ ('mɑːlbərə, -brə, 'mɔːl-) *n.* a town in S England, in Wiltshire: besieged and captured by Royalists in the Civil War (1642); site of Marlborough College, a public school founded in 1843. Pop.: 6900 (1985 est.).

Marlborough² ('mɑːlbərə, -brə, 'mɔːl-) *n.* **1st Duke of,** title of *John Churchill.* 1650–1722, English general; commander of British forces in the War of the Spanish Succession (1701-14), in which he won victories at Blenheim (1704), Ramillies (1706), Oudenaarde (1708), and Malplaquet (1709).

Marley ('mɑːlɪ) *n.* **Bob,** full name *Robert Nesta Marley.* 1945–81, Jamaican reggae singer, guitarist, and songwriter. With his group, the Wailers, his albums included *Burnin'* (1973), *Natty Dread* (1975), *Rastaman Vibration* (1976), and *Exodus* (1977).

marlin ('mɑːlɪn) *n., pl.* **-lin** *or* **-lins.** any of several large food and game fishes of warm and tropical seas, having a very long upper jaw. [C20: from MARLINESPIKE, from shape of the beak]

marline *or* **marlin** ('mɑːlɪn) *n. Naut.* a light rope, usually tarred, made of two strands laid left-handed. [C15: from Du. *marlijn,* from *marren* to tie + *lijn* line]

marlinespike *or* **marlinspike** ('mɑːlɪnˌspaɪk) *n. Naut.* a pointed metal tool used in separating strands of rope, etc.

marlite ('mɑːlaɪt) *or* **marlstone** ('mɑːlˌstəʊn) *n.* a type of marl that is resistant to the decomposing action of air.

Marlowe ('mɑːləʊ) *n.* **Christopher.** 1564–93, English dramatist and poet, who established blank verse as a creative form of dramatic expression. His plays include *Tamburlaine the Great* (1590), *Edward II* (?1592), and *Dr. Faustus* (1604). He was stabbed to death in a tavern brawl.

marmalade ('mɑːməˌleɪd) *n.* a preserve made by boiling the pulp and rind of citrus fruits, esp. oranges, with sugar. [C16: via F from Port. *marmelada,* from *marmelo* quince, from L, from Gk *melimēlon,* from *meli* honey + *mēlon* apple]

Marmara *or* **Marmora** ('mɑːmərə) *n.* **Sea of.** a deep inland sea in NW Turkey, linked with the Black Sea by the Bosporus and with the Aegean by the Dardanelles: separates Turkey in Europe from Turkey in Asia. Area: 11 471 sq. km (4429 sq. miles). Ancient name: **Propontis.**

marmite ('mɑːmaɪt) *n.* a large cooking pot. [from F: pot]

Marmite ('mɑːmaɪt) *n. Brit. trademark.* a yeast and vegetable extract used as a spread, flavouring, etc.

Marmolada (*Italian* marmo'lɑːda) *n.* a mountain in NE Italy: highest peak in the Dolomites. Height: 3342 m (10 965 ft.).

marmoreal (mɑːˈmɔːrɪəl) *adj.* of, relating to, or resembling marble. [C18: from L *marmoreus,* from *marmor* marble]

marmoset ('mɑːməˌzɛt) *n.* **1.** any of various small South American monkeys having long hairy tails. **2. pygmy marmoset.** a related form: the smallest monkey, inhabiting tropical forests of the Amazon. [C14: from OF *marmouset* grotesque figure, from ?]

marmot ('mɑːmət) *n.* **1.** any of various burrowing rodents of Europe, Asia, and North America. They are heavily built and have coarse fur. **2. prairie marmot.** another name for **prairie dog.** [C17: from F *marmotte,* ? ult. from L *mūr-* (stem of *mūs*) mouse + *montis* of the mountain]

Marne (*French* marn) *n.* **1.** a department of NE France, in Champagne-Ardenne region. Capital: Châlons-sur-Marne. Pop.: 543 627 (1982). Area: 8205 sq. km (3200 sq. miles). **2.** a river in NE France, rising on the plateau of Langres and flowing north, then west to the River Seine, north of Paris: linked by canal with the Rivers Saône, Rhine, and Aisne; scene of two unsuccessful German offensives (1914, 1918) during World War I. Length: 525 km (326 miles).

Maroc (marɔk) *n.* the French name for **Morocco.**

marocain ('mærəˌkeɪn) *n.* **1.** a fabric of ribbed crepe. **2.** a garment made from this fabric. [C20: from F *maroquin* Moroccan]

maroon¹ (məˈruːn) *vb.* (*tr.*) **1.** to abandon ashore, esp. on an island. **2.** to isolate without resources. ~*n.* **3.** a descendant of a group of runaway slaves living in the remoter areas of the West Indies or Guyana. [C17 (applied to fugitive slaves): from American Sp. *cimarrón* wild, lit.: dwelling on peaks, from Sp. *cima* summit]

maroon² (məˈruːn) *n.* **1. a.** a dark red to purplish-red colour. **b.** (*as adj.*): *a maroon carpet.* **2.** an exploding firework, esp. one used as a warning signal. [C18: from F, lit.: chestnut]

Maros ('mɒrɒʃ) *n.* the Hungarian name for the **Mureş.**

Marprelate ('mɑːprɛlɪt) *n.* **Martin,** the pen name of the anonymous author or authors of a series of satirical Puritan tracts (1588–89), attacking the bishops of the Church of England.

Marq. *abbrev. for:* **1.** Marquess. **2.** Marquis.

Marquand (mɑːˈkwɒnd) *n.* **J(ohn) P(hillips).** 1893–1960, U.S. novelist, noted for his stories featuring the Japanese detective Mr Moto and for his satirical comedies of New England life, such as *The Late George Apley* (1937).

marque (mɑːk) *n.* **1.** a brand of product, esp. of a car. **2.** See **letter of marque.** [from F, from *marquer* to MARK¹]

marquee (mɑːˈkiː) *n.* **1.** a large tent used for entertainment, exhibition, etc. **2.** Also called: **marquise.** *Chiefly U.S. & Canad.* a canopy over the entrance to a theatre, hotel, etc. [C17 (orig. an officer's tent): invented sing. form of MARQUISE, erroneously taken to be pl.]

Marquesas Islands (mɑːˈkeɪsæs) *pl. n.* a group of volcanic islands in the S Pacific, in French Polynesia. Pop.: 6548 (1984). Area: 1287 sq. km (497 sq. miles). French name: **Îles Marquises** (il markiz).

marquess ('mɑːkwɪs) *n.* **1.** (in the British Isles) a nobleman ranking between a duke and an earl. **2.** See **marquis.**

marquetry *or* **marqueterie** ('mɑːkɪtrɪ) *n., pl.* **-quetries** *or* **-queteries.** a pattern of inlaid veneers of wood, brass, ivory, etc., used chiefly as ornamentation in furniture. [C16: from OF, from *marqueter* to inlay, from *marque* MARK¹]

Marquette (mɑːˈkɛt) *n.* **Jacques** (ʒak), known as *Père Marquette.* 1637–75, French Jesuit missionary and explorer, with Louis Jolliet, of the Mississippi river.

marquis ('mɑːkwɪs, mɑːˈkiː) *n., pl.* **-quises** *or* **-quis.** (in various countries) a nobleman ranking above a count, corresponding to a British marquess. The title of marquis is often used in place of that of marquess. [C14: from OF *marchis,* lit.: count of the march, from *marche* MARCH²]

Marquis ('mɑːkwɪs) *n.* **Don(ald Robert Perry).** 1878–1937, U.S. humorist; author of *archy and mehitabel* (1927).

marquise (mɑːˈkiːz) *n.* **1.** (in various countries) another word for **marchioness. 2. a.** a gemstone, esp. a diamond, cut in a pointed oval shape and usually faceted. **b.** a piece of jewellery, esp. a ring, set with such a stone or with an oval cluster of stones. **3.** another name for **marquee** (sense 2). [C18: from F, fem. of MARQUIS]

marquisette (ˌmɑːkɪˈzɛt, -kwɪ-) n. a leno-weave fabric of cotton, silk, etc. [C20: from F, dim. of MARQUISE]

Marrakech or **Marrakesh** (məˈrækɛʃ, ˌmærəˈkɛʃ) n. a city in W central Morocco: several times capital of Morocco; tourist centre. Pop.: 439 728 (1982).

marram grass (ˈmærəm) n. any of several grasses that grow on sandy shores: often planted to stabilize sand dunes. [C17 marram, from ON marálmr, from marr sea + hálmr HAULM]

marri (ˈmærɪ) n. a species of eucalyptus of Western Australia, widely cultivated for its coloured flowers. [C19: from Abor.]

marriage (ˈmærɪdʒ) n. **1.** the state or relationship of being husband and wife. **2. a.** the legal union or contract made by a man and woman to live as husband and wife. **b.** (as modifier): marriage certificate. **3.** the ceremony formalizing this union; wedding. **4.** a close or intimate union, relationship, etc. [C13: from OF; see MARRY¹, -AGE]

marriageable (ˈmærɪdʒəbᵊl) adj. (esp. of women) suitable for marriage, usually with reference to age. —ˌmarriageaˈbility n.

marriage guidance n. advice given to couples who have problems in their married life.

married (ˈmærɪd) adj. **1.** having a husband or wife. **2.** joined in marriage. **3.** of or involving marriage or married persons. **4.** closely or intimately united. ~n. **5.** (usually pl.) a married person (esp. in **young marrieds**).

marrons glacés French. (marɔ̃ glase) pl. n. chestnuts cooked in syrup and glazed.

marrow (ˈmærəʊ) n. **1.** the fatty network of connective tissue that fills the cavities of bones. **2.** the vital part; essence. **3.** Brit. short for **vegetable marrow**. [OE mærg] —ˈmarrowy adj.

marrowbone (ˈmærəʊˌbəʊn) n. **a.** a bone containing edible marrow. **b.** (as modifier): marrowbone jelly.

marrowfat (ˈmærəʊˌfæt) or **marrow pea** n. **1.** any of several varieties of pea plant that have large seeds. **2.** the seed of such a plant.

marry¹ (ˈmærɪ) vb. **-rying, -ried. 1.** to take (someone as one's husband or wife) in marriage. **2.** (tr.) to join or give in marriage. **3.** to unite closely or intimately. **4.** (tr.; sometimes foll. by up) to fit together or align (two things); join. **5.** (tr.) Naut. to match up (the strands of ropes) before splicing. [C13: from OF marier, from L maritāre, from maritus married (man), ?from mās male]

marry² (ˈmærɪ) interj. Arch. An exclamation of surprise, anger, etc. [C14: euphemistic for the Virgin Mary]

Marryat (ˈmærɪət) n. **Frederick,** known as Captain Marryat. 1792–1848, English novelist and naval officer; author of novels of sea life, such as Mr Midshipman Easy (1836), and children's stories, such as The Children of the New Forest (1847).

marry off vb. (tr., adv.) to find a husband or wife for (a person, esp. one's son or daughter).

Mars¹ (mɑːz) n. the Roman god of war.

Mars² (mɑːz) n. the fourth planet from the sun.

Marsala (mɑːˈsɑːlə) n. **1.** a port in W Sicily: landing place of Garibaldi at the start of his Sicilian campaign (1860). Pop.: 79 093 (1981). **2.** a dark sweet dessert wine made in Sicily.

Marsalis (mɑːˈsɑːlɪs) n. **Wynton.** born 1962, U.S. classical and jazz trumpeter.

Marseillaise (ˌmɑːseɪˈjeɪz, -səˈleɪz) n. **the.** the French national anthem. [C18: from F (chanson) marseillaise song of Marseilles (first sung in Paris by the battalion of Marseilles)]

marseille (mɑːˈseɪl) or **marseilles** (mɑːˈseɪlz) n. a strong cotton fabric with a raised pattern, used for bedspreads, etc. [C18: from Marseille quilting, made in Marseilles]

Marseille (French marsɛj) n. a port in SE France, on the Gulf of Lions: second largest city in the country and a major port; founded in about 600 B.C. by Greeks from Phocaea; oil refining. Pop.: 903 211 (1983 est.). Ancient name: **Mas'silia.** English name: **Marseilles** (mɑːˈseɪ, -ˈseɪlz).

marsh (mɑːʃ) n. low poorly drained land that is sometimes flooded and often lies at the edge of lakes, etc. Cf. **swamp** (sense 1). [OE merisc]

Marsh (mɑːʃ) n. **Rodney (William).** born 1947, Australian cricketer. By the end of the 1982–83 season he held the world record for Test match dismissals (334).

marshal (ˈmɑːʃəl) n. **1.** (in some armies and air forces) an officer of the highest rank. **2.** (in England) an officer who accompanies a judge on circuit and performs secretarial duties. **3.** (in the U.S.) **a.** a Federal court officer assigned to a judicial district whose functions are similar to those of a sheriff. **b.** (in some states) the chief police or fire officer. **4.** an officer who organizes or conducts ceremonies, parades, etc. **5.** Also called: **knight marshal.** (formerly in England) an officer of the royal family or court, esp. one in charge of protocol. ~vb. **-shalling, -shalled** or U.S. **-shaling, -shaled.** (tr.) **6.** to arrange in order: to marshal the facts. **7.** to assemble and organize (troops, vehicles, etc.) prior to onward movement. **8.** to guide or lead, esp. in a ceremonious way. **9.** to combine (coats of arms) on one shield. [C13: from OF mareschal; rel. to OHG marahscalc, from marah horse + scalc servant] —ˈmarshalcy or ˈmarshalship n.

Marshall (ˈmɑːʃəl) n. **1. Alfred.** 1842–1924, English economist, author of Principles of Economics (1890). **2. George Catlett.** 1880–1959, U.S. general and statesman. He was chief of staff of the U.S. army (1939–45) and, as secretary of state (1947–49), he proposed the Marshall Plan (1947), later called the European Recovery Programme: Nobel peace prize 1953. **3. John.** 1755–1835, U.S. jurist and statesman. As chief justice of the Supreme Court (1801–35), he established the principles of U.S. constitutional law. **4.** Sir **John Ross.** born 1912, New Zealand politician; prime minister (1972).

marshalling yard n. Railways. a place or depot where railway wagons are shunted and made up into trains.

Marshall Islands pl. n. a group of 34 coral islands in the W central Pacific, in E Micronesia: administratively part of the Trust Territory of the Pacific Islands (1947–87); status of free association with the U.S. from 1982; consists of two parallel chains, Ralik and Ratak. Pop.: 31 041 (1980). Area: (land) 158 sq. km (61 sq. miles); (lagoon) 11 655 sq. km (4500 sq. miles).

Marshal of the Royal Air Force n. a rank in the Royal Air Force comparable to that of a field marshal in the army.

marsh fever n. another name for **malaria.**

marsh gas n. a hydrocarbon gas largely composed of methane formed when organic material decays in the absence of air.

marshmallow (ˌmɑːʃˈmæləʊ) n. **1.** a spongy sweet containing gum arabic or gelatin, sugar, etc. **2.** a sweetened paste or confection made from the root of the marsh mallow.

marsh mallow n. a malvaceous plant, that grows in salt marshes and has pale pink flowers. The roots yield a mucilage formerly used to make marshmallows.

marsh marigold n. a yellow-flowered plant that grows in swampy places.

marshy (ˈmɑːʃɪ) adj. **marshier, marshiest.** of, involving, or like a marsh. —ˈmarshiness n.

Marsilius of Padua (mɑːˈsɪlɪəs) n. Italian name Marsiglio dei Mainardini. ?1290–?1343, Italian political philosopher, best known as the author of the Defensor pacis (1324), which upheld the power of the temporal ruler over that of the church.

Marston (ˈmɑːstən) n. **John.** ?1576–1634, English dramatist and satirist. His works include the revenge tragedies Antonio and Mellida (1602) and Antonio's Revenge (1602) and the satirical comedy The Malcontent (1604).

Marston Moor n. a flat low-lying area in NE England, west of York: scene of a battle (1644) in which the Parliamentarians defeated the Royalists.

marsupial (mɑːˈsjuːpɪəl, -ˈsuː-) n. **1.** any mammal of an order in which the young are born in an immature state and continue development in the marsupium. The order occurs mainly in Australia and South and Central America and includes the opossums and kangaroos. ~adj. **2.** of, relating to, or belonging to marsupials. **3.** of or relating to a marsupium. [C17: see MARSUPIUM]

marsupium (mɑːˈsjuːpɪəm, -ˈsuː-) n., pl. **-pia** (-pɪə). an external pouch in most female marsupials within which the newly born offspring complete their development. [C17: NL, from L: purse, from Gk, dim. of marsipos]

mart (mɑːt) n. a market or trading centre. [C15: from MDu.: MARKET]

Martaban (ˌmɑːtɑːˈbɑːn) n. **Gulf of.** an inlet of the Bay of Bengal in Lower Burma.

martagon or **martagon lily** ('mɑːtəgən) n. a Eurasian lily plant cultivated for its mottled purplish-red flowers with reflexed petals. [C15: from F, from Turkish *martagān* a type of turban]

Martel (mɑːˈtɛl) n. See **Charles Martel**.

Martello tower (mɑːˈtɛləʊ) n. a small circular tower for coastal defence. [C18: after Cape *Mortella* in Corsica, where the British navy captured a tower of this type in 1794]

marten ('mɑːtɪn) n., pl. **-tens** or **-ten**. 1. any of several agile arboreal mammals of Europe, Asia, and North America, having bushy tails and golden-brown to blackish fur. See also **pine marten**. 2. the highly valued fur of these animals. ~See also **sable** (sense 1). [C15: from MDu. *martren*, from OF (*peau*) *martrine* skin of a marten, from *martre*, prob. of Gmc origin]

Martha ('mɑːθə) n. *New Testament*. a sister of Mary and Lazarus, who lived at Bethany and ministered to Jesus (Luke 10:38–42).

martial ('mɑːʃəl) adj. of, relating to, or characteristic of war, soldiers, or the military life. [C14: from L *martiālis* of MARS[1]] —**'martialism** n. —**'martialist** n. —**'martially** adv.

Martial ('mɑːʃəl) n. full name *Marcus Valerius Martialis*. ?40–?104 A.D., Latin epigrammatist and poet, born in Spain.

martial art n. any of various philosophies of self-defence and techniques of single combat, such as judo or karate, originating in the Far East.

martial law n. rule of law maintained by the military in the absence of civil law.

Martian ('mɑːʃən) adj. 1. of, occurring on, or relating to the planet Mars. ~n. 2. an inhabitant of Mars, esp. in science fiction.

martin ('mɑːtɪn) n. any of various birds of the swallow family, having a square or slightly forked tail. See also **house martin**. [C15: ?from St MARTIN, because the birds were believed to migrate at the time of Martinmas]

Martin (*French* martɛ̃) n. 1. **Frank**. 1890–1974, Swiss composer. He used a modified form of the twelve-note technique in some of his works, which include *Petite Symphonie Concertante* (1946) and the oratorio *Golgotha* (1949). 2. **Saint**, called *Saint Martin of Tours*. ?316–?397 A.D., bishop of Tours (?371–?397); a patron saint of France. He furthered monasticism in Gaul. Feast day: Nov. 11.

Martin du Gard (*French* martɛ̃ dy gar) n. **Roger** (rɔʒe). 1881–1958, French novelist, noted for his series of novels, *Les Thibault* (1922–40): Nobel prize for literature 1937.

Martineau ('mɑːtɪˌnəʊ) n. 1. **Harriet**. 1802–76, English author of books on political economy and of novels and childrens stories. 2. her brother, **James**. 1805–1900, English Unitarian theologian and minister.

martinet (ˌmɑːtɪˈnɛt) n. a person who maintains strict discipline, esp. in a military force. [C17: from F, from General *Martinet*, drillmaster under Louis XIV]

martingale ('mɑːtɪŋˌgeɪl) n. 1. a strap from the reins to the girth of a horse, preventing it from carrying its head too high. 2. any gambling system in which the stakes are raised, usually doubled, after each loss. 3. *Naut.* a chain or cable running from a jib boom to the stern or stem. [C16: from F, from ?]

martini (mɑːˈtiːnɪ) n. 1. (*often cap.*) *Trademark*. an Italian vermouth. 2. a cocktail of gin and vermouth. [C19 (sense 2): ?from the name of the inventor]

Martini (*Italian* marˈtiːni) n. **Simone** (siˈmoːne). ?1284–1344, Sienese painter.

Martinique (ˌmɑːtɪˈniːk) n. an island in the E Caribbean, in the Windward Islands of the Lesser Antilles: administratively an overseas region of France. Capital: Fort-de-France. Pop: 328 500 (1987 est.). Area: 1090 sq. km (420 sq. miles). —ˌMarti'nican n., adj.

Martinmas ('mɑːtɪnməs) n. the feast of St Martin on Nov. 11; a quarter day in Scotland.

Martinů ('mɑːtɪˌnuː; *Czech* 'martjinuː) n. **Bohuslav** ('bɔhuslaf). 1890–1959, Czech composer.

martyr ('mɑːtə) n. 1. a person who suffers death rather than renounce his religious beliefs. 2. a person who suffers greatly or dies for a cause, belief, etc. 3. a person who suffers from poor health, misfortune, etc.: *a martyr to rheumatism*. ~vb. also **'martyrize** or **-ise**. (tr.) 4. to kill as a martyr. 5. to make a martyr of. [OE *martir*, from

Church L *martyr*, from LGk *martur-*, *martus* witness] —**'martyrdom** n. —ˌmartyri'zation or **-i'sation** n.

martyrology (ˌmɑːtəˈrɒlədʒɪ) n., pl. **-gies**. 1. an official list of martyrs. 2. *Christianity*. the study of the lives of the martyrs. 3. a historical account of the lives of martyrs. —ˌmartyr'ologist n.

marvel ('mɑːvəl) vb. **-velling**, **-velled** or U.S. **-veling**, **-veled**. 1. (when *intr.*, often foll. by *at* or *about*; when *tr.*, takes a clause as object) to be filled with surprise or wonder. ~n. 2. something that causes wonder. 3. *Arch.* astonishment. [C13: from OF *merveille*, from LL *mīrābilia*, from L *mīrābilis* from *mīrārī* to wonder at]

Marvell ('mɑːvəl) n. **Andrew**. 1621–78, English poet and satirist. He is noted for his lyrical poems and verse and prose satires attacking the government after the Restoration.

marvellous or U.S. **marvelous** ('mɑːvələs) adj. 1. causing great wonder, surprise, etc.; extraordinary. 2. improbable or incredible. 3. excellent; splendid. —**'marvellously** or U.S. **'marvelously** adv. —**'marvellousness** or U.S. **'marvelousness** n.

marvel-of-Peru n., pl. **marvels-of-Peru**. another name for **four-o'clock** (the plant). [C16: first found in Peru]

Marx (mɑːks) n. **Karl** (kɑːl). 1818–83, German founder of modern communism, in England from 1849. With Engels, he wrote *The Communist Manifesto* (1848). He developed his theories of the class struggle and the economics of capitalism in *Das Kapital* (1867; 1885; 1895). He was one of the founders of the International Workingmen's Association (First International) (1864). —**'Marxian** adj.

Marx Brothers (mɑːks) n. **the**. a U.S. family of film comedians, esp. **Arthur Marx**, known as *Harpo* (1893–1964), **Herbert Marx**, known as *Zeppo* (1901–79), **Julius Marx**, known as *Groucho* (1895–1977), and **Leonard Marx**, known as *Chico* (1891–1961). Their films include *Animal Crackers* (1930), *Monkey Business* (1931), *Horsefeathers* (1932), *Duck Soup* (1933), and *A Day at the Races* (1937).

Marxism ('mɑːksɪzəm) n. the economic and political theory and practice originated by Karl Marx and Friedrich Engels. It holds that actions and human institutions are economically determined, that the class struggle is the basic agency of historical change, and that capitalism will ultimately be superseded by communism. —**'Marxist** n., adj.

Marxism-Leninism n. the modification of Marxism by Lenin stressing that imperialism is the highest form of capitalism. —**'Marxist-'Leninist** n., adj.

Mary ('mɛərɪ) n. 1. *New Testament*. a. Also called: the **Virgin Mary**. the mother of Jesus, believed to have conceived and borne him while still a virgin; she was married to Joseph (Matthew 1:18–25). b. the sister of Martha and Lazarus (Luke 10:38–42; John 11:1–2). 2. original name *Princess Mary of Teck*. 1867–1953, queen of Great Britain and Northern Ireland (1910–36) by marriage to George V. 3. (pl. **'Maries**) *Austral. Sl.* an Aboriginal woman or girl.

Mary I n. family name *Tudor*, known as *Bloody Mary*. 1516–58, queen of England (1553–58). The daughter of Henry VIII and Catherine of Aragon, she married Philip II of Spain in 1554. She restored Roman Catholicism to England and about 300 Protestants were burnt at the stake as heretics.

Mary II n. 1662–94, queen of England, Scotland, and Ireland (1689–94), ruling jointly with her husband William III. They were offered the crown by the opposition to the arbitrary rule of her father James II.

Maryland ('mɛərɪˌlænd, 'mɛrɪlənd) n. a state of the eastern U.S., on the Atlantic: divided into two unequal parts by Chesapeake Bay: mostly low-lying, with the Alleghenies in the northwest. Capital: Annapolis. Pop: 4 463 000 (1986 est.). Area: 31 864 sq. km (12 303 sq. miles). Abbrevs.: **Md.** or (with zip code) **MD**

Mary Magdalene n. *New Testament*. a woman of **Magdala** ('mægdələ) in Galilee whom Jesus cured of evil spirits (Luke 8:2) and who is often identified with the sinful woman of Luke 7:36–50. In Christian tradition she is usually taken to have been a prostitute. See **magdalen**.

Mary, Queen of Scots n. family name *Stuart*. 1542–87, queen of Scotland (1542–67); daughter of James V of Scotland and Mary of Guise. She was married to Francis II of France (1558–60), her cousin Lord Darnley (1565–67), and the Earl of Bothwell (1567–71), who was commonly regarded as Darnley's murderer. She was forced to abdicate in favour of her son (later James VI of Scotland) and fled to England. Imprisoned by Elizabeth I until 1587, she was beheaded for plotting against the English crown.

marzipan ('mɑːzɪ,pæn) *n.* a paste made from ground almonds, sugar, and egg whites, used to coat fruit cakes or moulded into sweets. [C19: via G from It. *marzapane*]

-mas *n. combining form.* indicating a Christian festival: *Christmas; Michaelmas.* [from MASS]

Masaccio (*Italian* ma'zattʃo) *n.* original name *Tommaso Guidi.* 1401–28, Florentine painter. He was the first to apply to painting the laws of perspective discovered by Brunelleschi. His chief work is the frescoes in the Brancacci chapel in the church of Sta. Maria del Carmine, Florence.

Masada (mə'sɑːdə) *n.* an ancient mountaintop fortress in Israel, 400 m (1300 ft.) above the W shore of the Dead Sea: the last Jewish stronghold during a revolt in Judaea (66–73 A.D.). Besieged by the Romans for a year, almost all of the inhabitants killed themselves rather than surrender. The site is an Israeli national monument.

Masai ('mɑːsaɪ, mɑː'saɪ) *n.* **1.** (*pl.* **-sais** *or* **-sai**) a member of a Nilotic people, formerly noted as warriors, living chiefly in Kenya and Tanzania. **2.** the language of this people.

Masan ('mɑː,sɑːn) *n.* a port in SE South Korea, on an inlet of the Korea Strait: first opened to foreign trade in 1899. Pop.: 386 773 (1980).

Masaryk ('mæsərɪk; *Czech* 'masarik) *n.* **1. Jan** (jan). 1886–1948, Czech statesman; foreign minister (1941–48). He died in mysterious circumstances after the Communists took control of the government. **2.** his father, **Tomáš Garrigue** ('tɔmaːʃ 'garik). 1850–1937, Czech philosopher and statesman; a founder of Czechoslovakia (1918) and its first president (1918–35).

Masbate (mæs'baːtɪ) *n.* **1.** an island in the central Philippines, between Negros and SE Luzon: agricultural, with resources of gold, copper, and manganese. Pop.: 492 908 (1970). Area: 4045 sq. km (1562 sq. miles). **2.** the capital of this island, a port in the northeast. Pop.: 52 944 (1980).

masc. *abbrev. for* masculine.

Mascagni (*Italian* mas'kaɲɲi) *n.* **Pietro** ('piɛːtro). 1863–1945, Italian composer of operas, including *Cavalleria rusticana* (1890).

mascara (mæ'skɑːrə) *n.* a cosmetic for darkening the eyelashes. [C20: from Sp.: mask]

Mascarene Islands (,mæskə'riːn) *pl. n.* a group of volcanic islands in the W Indian Ocean, east of Madagascar: consists of the islands of Réunion, Mauritius, and Rodrigues. French name: **Îles Mascareignes.**

mascon ('mæskɒn) *n.* any of several lunar regions of high gravity. [C20: from MAS(S) + CON(CENTRATION)]

mascot ('mæskət) *n.* a person, animal, or thing considered to bring good luck. [C19: from F *mascotte*, from Provençal *mascotto* charm, from *masco* witch]

masculine ('mæskjʊlɪn) *adj.* **1.** possessing qualities or characteristics considered typical of or appropriate to a man; manly. **2.** unwomanly. **3.** *Grammar.* denoting a gender of nouns that includes all kinds of referents as well as some male animate referents. **4.** *Prosody.* denoting an ending consisting of a single stressed syllable. **5.** *Prosody.* denoting a rhyme between pairs of single final stressed syllables. [C14: via F from L *masculīnus*, from *masculus* male, from *mās* a male] —**'masculinely** *adv.* —,**mascu'linity** *n.*

masculinize *or* **-ise** ('mæskjʊlɪn,aɪz) *vb.* to make or become masculine, esp. to cause (a woman) to show male secondary characteristics as a result of taking steroids. —,**masculini'zation** *or* **-i'sation** *n.*

Masefield ('meɪs,fiːld) *n.* **John.** 1878–1967, English poet, novelist, and critic; poet laureate (1930–67).

maser ('meɪzə) *n.* a device for amplifying microwaves, working on the same principle as a laser. [C20: m(icrowave) a(mplification by) s(timulated) e(mission of) r(adiation)]

Maseru (mə'sɛəruː) *n.* the capital of Lesotho, in the northwest near the W border with South Africa; established as capital of Basutoland in 1869. Pop.: 109 382 (1986).

mash (mæʃ) *n.* **1.** a soft pulpy mass or consistency. **2.** *Agriculture.* a feed of bran, meal, or malt mixed with water and fed to horses, cattle, or poultry. **3.** (esp. in

brewing) a mixture of mashed malt grains and hot water, from which malt is extracted. **4.** *Brit. inf.* mashed potatoes. ~*vb.* (*tr.*) **5.** to beat or crush into a mash. **6.** to steep (malt grains) in hot water in order to extract malt. **7.** *Scot. & N English dialect.* to brew (tea). [OE *mæsc-* (in compound words)] —**mashed** *adj.* —'**masher** *n.*

Masharbrum *or* **Masherbrum** ('mʌʃə,brum) *n.* a mountain in N India, in N Kashmir in the Karakoram Range of the Himalayas. Height: 7822 m (25 660 ft.).

Mashhad (mæʃ'hæd) *or* **Meshed** *n.* a city in NE Iran: the holy city of Shi'ite Muslims; carpet manufacturing. Pop.: 1 103 300 (1985 est.).

mashie *or* **mashy** ('mæʃɪ) *n., pl.* **mashies.** *Golf.* (formerly) an iron for lofting shots, usually No. 5. [C19: ?from F *massue* club, ult. from L *mateola* mallet]

Masinissa *or* **Massinissa** (,mæsɪ'nɪsə) *n.* ?238–?149 B.C., king of Numidia (?210–149), who fought as an ally of Rome against Carthage in the Second Punic War.

mask (mɑːsk) *n.* **1.** any covering for the whole or a part of the face worn for amusement, protection, disguise, etc. **2.** a fact, action, etc., that conceals something. **3.** another name for **masquerade.** **4.** a likeness of a face or head, either sculpted or moulded, such as a death mask. **5.** an image of a face worn by an actor, esp. in classical drama, in order to symbolize a character. **6.** a variant spelling of **masque.** **7.** *Surgery.* a sterile gauze covering for the nose and mouth worn to minimize the spread of germs. **8.** *Sport.* a protective covering for the face worn for fencing, ice hockey, etc. **9.** a carving in the form of a face or head, used as an ornament. **10.** a device placed over the nose and mouth to facilitate or prevent inhalation of a gas. **11.** *Photog.* a shield of paper, paint, etc., placed over an area of unexposed photographic surface to stop light falling on it. **12.** the face or head of an animal, such as a fox. **13.** *Rare.* a person wearing a mask. ~*vb.* **14.** to cover with or put on a mask. **15.** (*tr.*) to conceal; disguise: *to mask an odour.* **16.** (*tr.*) *Photog.* to shield a particular area of (an unexposed photographic surface) to prevent or reduce the action of light there. [C16: from It. *maschera,* ult. from Ar. *maskharah* clown, from *sakhira* mockery] —**masked** *adj.* —'**masker** *n.*

masked ball *n.* a ball at which masks are worn.

masking tape *n.* an adhesive tape used to protect surfaces surrounding an area to be painted.

maskinonge ('mæskə,nɒndʒ) *n.* another name for **muskellunge.**

masochism ('mæsə,kɪzəm) *n.* **1.** *Psychiatry.* an abnormal condition in which pleasure, esp. sexual pleasure, is derived from pain or from humiliation, domination, etc., by another person. **2.** a tendency to take pleasure from one's own suffering. Cf. **sadism.** [C19: after Leopold von Sacher *Masoch* (1836–95), Austrian novelist, who described it] —'**masochist** *n., adj.* —,**maso'chistic** *adj.* —,**maso'chistically** *adv.*

mason ('meɪsᵊn) *n.* **1.** a person skilled in building with stone. **2.** a person who dresses stone. ~*vb.* **3.** (*tr.*) to construct or strengthen with masonry. [C13: from OF *masson,* of Frankish origin; ? rel. to OE *macian* to make]

Mason ('meɪsᵊn) *n.* short for **Freemason.**

Mason-Dixon Line (-'dɪksən) *n.* in the U.S.A., the state boundary between Maryland and Pennsylvania: surveyed between 1763 and 1767 by Charles Mason and Jeremiah Dixon; popularly regarded as the dividing line between North and South.

masonic (mə'sɒnɪk) *adj.* **1.** (*often cap.*) of or relating to Freemasons or Freemasonry. **2.** of or relating to masons or masonry. —**ma'sonically** *adv.*

Masonite ('meɪsənaɪt) *n. Austral. trademark.* a kind of dark brown hardboard.

masonry ('meɪsənrɪ) *n., pl.* **-ries. 1.** the craft of a mason. **2.** work that is built by a mason; stonework or brickwork. **3.** (*often cap.*) short for **Freemasonry.**

Masqat ('mʌskət, -kæt) *n.* a transliteration of the Arabic name for **Muscat.**

masque *or* **mask** (mɑːsk) *n.* **1.** a dramatic entertainment of the 16th to 17th centuries, consisting of pantomime, dancing, dialogue, and song. **2.** the words and music for this. **3.** short for **masquerade.** [C16: var. of MASK]

masquerade (,mæskə'reɪd) *n.* **1.** a party or other gathering at which the guests wear masks and costumes. **2.** the disguise worn at such a function. **3.** a pretence or disguise. ~*vb.* (*intr.*) **4.** to participate in a masquerade; disguise oneself. **5.** to dissemble. [C16: from Sp. *mascarada*, from *mascara* MASK] —,**masquer'ader** *n.*

mass (mæs) *n.* **1.** a large coherent body of matter without a definite shape. **2.** a collection of the component parts of something. **3.** a large amount or number, as of people. **4.** the main part or majority. **5. in the mass.** in the main; collectively. **6.** the size of a body; bulk. **7.** *Physics.* a physical quantity expressing the amount of matter in a body. It is a measure of a body's resistance to changes in velocity (**inertial mass**) and also of the force experienced in a gravitational field (**gravitational mass**). **8.** (in painting, drawing, etc.) an area of unified colour, shade, or intensity, usually denoting a solid form or plane. ~(*modifier*) **9.** done or occurring on a large scale: *mass hysteria.* **10.** consisting of a mass or large number, esp. of people: *a mass meeting.* ~*vb.* **11.** to form (people or things) or (of people or things) to join together into a mass. ~See also **masses.** [C14: from OF *masse*, from L *massa* that which forms a lump, from Gk *maza* barley cake]

Mass (mæs, mɑːs) *n.* **1.** (in the Roman Catholic Church and certain Protestant Churches) the celebration of the Eucharist. See also **High Mass, Low Mass. 2.** a musical setting of those parts of the Eucharistic service sung by choir or congregation. [OE *mæsse*, from Church L *missa*, ult. from L *mittere* to send away; ?from the concluding dismissal in the Roman Mass, *Ite, missa est* Go, it is the dismissal]

Massa (*Italian* 'massa) *n.* a town in W Italy, in NW Tuscany. Pop.: 65 687 (1981).

Massachusetts (,mæsə'tʃuːsɪts) *n.* a state of the northeastern U.S., on the Atlantic: a centre of resistance to English colonial policy during the War of American Independence; consists of a coastal plain rising to mountains in the west. Capital: Boston. Pop.: 5 741 000 (1984). Area: 20 269 sq. km (7826 sq. miles). Abbrevs.: **Mass.** or (with zip code) **MA**

Massachusetts Bay *n.* an inlet of the Atlantic on the E coast of Massachusetts.

massacre ('mæsəkə) *n.* **1.** the wanton or savage killing of large numbers of people, as in battle. **2.** *Inf.* an overwhelming defeat, as in a game. ~*vb.* (*tr.*) **3.** to kill indiscriminately or in large numbers. **4.** *Inf.* to defeat overwhelmingly. [C16: from OF]

massage ('mæsɑːʒ, -sɑːdʒ) *n.* **1.** the act of kneading, rubbing, etc., parts of the body to promote circulation, suppleness, or relaxation. ~*vb.* (*tr.*) **2.** to give a massage to. **3.** to treat (stiffness, etc.) by a massage. **4.** to manipulate (statistics, etc.) to produce a desired result; doctor. [C19: from F, from *masser* to rub]

massasauga (,mæsə'sɔːgə) *n.* a North American venomous snake that has a horny rattle at the end of the tail. [C19: after the *Missisauga* River, Ontario, Canada, where it was first found]

Massasoit ('mæsə,sɔɪt) *n.* died 1661, Wampanoag Indian chief, who negotiated peace with the Pilgrim Fathers (1621).

Massawa or **Massaua** (mə'sɑːwə) *n.* a port in N Ethiopia, on the Red Sea: capital of the Italian colony of Eritrea from 1885 until 1900. Pop.: 36 839 (1982 est.).

mass defect *n. Physics.* the amount by which the mass of a particular nucleus is less than the total mass of its constituent particles.

massé or **massé shot** ('mæsɪ) *n. Billiards.* a stroke made by hitting the cue ball off centre with the cue held nearly vertically, esp. so as to make the ball move in a curve. [C19: from F, from *masser*, from *masse* sledgehammer, from OF *mace* MACE¹]

Masséna (*French* masena) *n.* **André** (ɑ̃dre), Prince d'Essling. 1758–1817, French marshal under Napoleon I: victories at Saorgio (1794), Loano (1795), Rivoli (1797), Zürich (1799), and Caldiero (1805): defeated by Wellington in the Peninsular War (1810–11).

Massenet (,mæsə,neı; *French* masnɛ) *n.* **Jules Émile Frédéric** (ʒyl emil frederik). 1842–1912, French composer of operas, including *Manon* (1884), *Werther* (1892), and *Thaïs* (1894).

masses ('mæsɪz) *pl. n.* **1.** (preceded by *the*) the body of common people. **2.** (often foll. by *of*) *Inf., chiefly Brit.* great numbers or quantities: *masses of food.*

masseur (mæ'sɜː) or (*fem.*) **masseuse** (mæ'sɜːz) *n.* a person who gives massages, esp. as a profession. [C19: from F *masser* to MASSAGE]

Massey ('mæsɪ) *n.* **1. Raymond.** 1896–1983, Canadian actor and film star. His films include *The Scarlet Pimpernel* (1934) and *East of Eden* (1955). He also appeared in the television series *Dr Kildare* (1961–65). **2. Vincent.** 1887–1967, Canadian statesman: first Canadian governor general of Canada (1952–59). **3. William Ferguson.** 1856–1925, New Zealand statesman, born in Ireland: prime minister of New Zealand (1912–25).

massif ('mæsiːf) *n.* a mass of rock or a series of connected masses forming a mountain range. [C19: from F, noun use of *massif* MASSIVE]

Massif Central (*French* masif sɑ̃tral) *n.* a mountainous plateau region of S central France, occupying about one sixth of the country: contains several extinct volcanic cones, notably Puy de Dôme, 1465 m (4806 ft.). Highest point: Puy de Sancy, 1886 m (6188 ft.). Area: about 85 000 sq. km (33 000 sq. miles).

Massine (mɑ'siːn) *n.* **Léonide** (leɔnid). 1896–1979, U.S. ballet dancer and choreographer, born in Russia.

Massinger ('mæsɪndʒə) *n.* **Philip.** 1583–?1640, English dramatist, noted esp. for his comedy *A New Way to pay Old Debts* (1633).

Massinissa (,mæsɪ'nɪsə) *n.* a variant spelling of **Masinissa.**

massive ('mæsɪv) *adj.* **1.** (of objects) large in mass; bulky, heavy, and usually solid. **2.** impressive or imposing. **3.** relatively intensive or large; considerable: *a massive dose.* **4.** *Geol.* **a.** (of igneous rocks) having no stratification, cleavage, etc.; homogeneous. **b.** (of sedimentary rocks) arranged in thick poorly defined strata. **5.** *Mineralogy.* without obvious crystalline structure. [C15: from F *massif*, from *masse* MASS] —'**massively** *adv.* —'**massiveness** *n.*

▷ **Usage.** *Massive* has in journalistic and media usage become something of a stock adjective applied to anything serious, significant, large, or important: *a massive heart attack; a massive response to the strike call.* While in some instances it is undoubtedly suitable, careful users of English should consider its applicability to the noun and avoid its use if a more appropriate adjective can be found.

mass-market *adj.* of, for, or appealing to a large number of people; popular: *mass-market paperbacks.*

mass media *pl. n.* the means of communication that reach large numbers of people, such as television, newspapers, magazines, and radio.

mass noun *n.* a noun that refers to an extended substance rather than to each of a set of objects, e.g., *water* as opposed to *lake.* In English when used indefinitely they are characteristically preceded by *some* rather than *a* or *an;* they do not have normal plural forms. Cf. **count noun.**

mass number *n.* the total number of neutrons and protons in the nucleus of a particular atom.

mass observation *n.* (*sometimes cap.*) *Chiefly Brit.* the study of the social habits of people through observation, interviews, etc.

mass-produce *vb.* (*tr.*) to manufacture (goods) to a standardized pattern on a large scale by means of extensive mechanization and division of labour. —,**mass pro'duced** *adj.* —,**mass-pro'ducer** *n.* —**mass production** *n.*

mass spectrometer or **spectroscope** *n.* an instrument in which ions, produced from a sample, are separated by electric or magnetic fields according to their ratios of charge to mass. A record is produced (**mass spectrum**) of the types of ion present and their amounts.

mast¹ (mɑːst) *n.* **1.** *Naut.* any vertical spar for supporting sails, rigging, flags, etc., above the deck of a vessel. **2.** any sturdy upright pole used as a support. **3. before the mast.** *Naut.* as an apprentice seaman. ~*vb.* **4.** (*tr.*) *Naut.* to equip with a mast or masts. [OE *mæst;* rel. to MDu. *mast* & L *mālus* pole]

mast² (mɑːst) *n.* the fruit of forest trees, such as beech, oak, etc., used as food for pigs. [OE *mæst;* rel. to OHG *mast* food]

mastaba or **mastabah** ('mæstəbə) *n.* a mudbrick superstructure above tombs in ancient Egypt. [from Ar.: bench]

mast cell *n.* any of a number of cells in connective tissue that release heparin, histamine, and serotonin during inflammation and allergic reactions.

mastectomy (mæ'stɛktəmɪ) *n., pl.* **-mies.** the surgical removal of a breast.

master ('mɑːstə) *n.* **1.** the man in authority, such as the head of a household, the employer of servants, or the owner of slaves or animals. **2. a.** a person with exceptional skill at a certain thing. **b.** (*as modifier*): *a master thief.* **3.** (*often cap.*) a great artist, esp. an anonymous but influential one. **4. a.** a person who has complete control of a situation, etc. **b.** an abstract thing regarded as having power or influence: *they regarded fate as the master of their lives.* **5. a.** a workman or craftsman fully qualified to practise his trade and to train others. **b.** (*as modifier*): *master carpenter.* **6. a.** an original copy, stencil, tape, etc., from which duplicates are made. **b.** (*as modifier*): *master copy.* **7.** a player of a game, esp. chess or bridge, who has won a specified number of tournament games. **8.** the principal of some colleges. **9.** a highly regarded teacher or leader. **10.** a graduate holding a master's degree. **11.** the chief executive officer aboard a merchant ship. **12.** a person presiding over a function, organization, or institution. **13.** *Chiefly Brit.* a male teacher. **14.** an officer of the Supreme Court of Judicature subordinate to a judge. **15.** the superior person or side in a contest. **16.** (*often cap.*) the heir apparent of a Scottish viscount or baron. ~(*modifier*) **17.** overall or controlling: *master plan.* **18.** designating a device or mechanism that controls others: *master switch.* **19.** main; principal: *master bedroom.* ~*vb.* (*tr.*) **20.** to become thoroughly proficient in. **21.** to overcome; defeat. **22.** to rule or control as master. [OE *magister* teacher]

Master ('mɑːstə) *n.* **1.** a title of address for a boy. **2.** a term of address, esp. as used by disciples addressing or referring to a religious teacher. **3.** an archaic equivalent of **Mr.**

master aircrew *n.* a warrant rank in the Royal Air Force, equal to but before a warrant officer.

master-at-arms *n., pl.* **masters-at-arms.** the senior rating in a naval unit responsible for discipline and police duties.

master builder *n.* **1.** a person skilled in the design and construction of buildings, esp. before the foundation of the the profession of architecture. **2.** a self-employed builder who employs labour.

master class *n.* a class for trained musicians, either in private or on television, conducted by a virtuoso player.

masterful ('mɑːstəfʊl) *adj.* **1.** having or showing mastery. **2.** fond of playing the master; imperious. —'**masterfully** *adv.* —'**masterfulness** *n.*

master key *n.* a key that opens all the locks of a set. Also called: **passkey.**

masterly ('mɑːstəlɪ) *adj.* of the skill befitting a master. —'**masterliness** *n.*

master mason *n.* **1.** see **master** (sense 4a). **2.** a Freemason who has reached the rank of third degree.

mastermind ('mɑːstəˌmaɪnd) *vb.* **1.** (*tr.*) to plan and direct (a complex undertaking). ~*n.* **2.** a person of great intelligence or executive talent, esp. one who directs an undertaking.

Master of Arts *n.* a degree, usually postgraduate and in a nonscientific subject, or the holder of this degree. Abbrev.: **MA.**

master of ceremonies *n.* a person who presides over a public ceremony, formal dinner, or entertainment, introducing the events, performers, etc.

Master of the Rolls *n.* (in England) a judge of the court of appeal: the senior civil judge in the country and the Keeper of the Records at the Public Record Office.

masterpiece ('mɑːstəˌpiːs) *or* (*less commonly*) **masterwork** ('mɑːstəˌwɜːk) *n.* **1.** an outstanding work or performance. **2.** the most outstanding piece of work of a creative artist, craftsman, etc. [C17: cf. Du. *meesterstuk*, G *Meisterstück*, a sample of work submitted to a guild by a craftsman in order to qualify for the rank of master]

masterstroke ('mɑːstəˌstrəʊk) *n.* an outstanding piece of strategy, skill, talent, etc.

mastery ('mɑːstərɪ) *n., pl.* **-teries. 1.** full command or understanding of a subject. **2.** outstanding skill; expertise. **3.** the power of command; control. **4.** victory or superiority.

masthead ('mɑːstˌhɛd) *n.* **1.** *Naut.* the head of a mast. **2.** the name of a newspaper or periodical, its proprietors, staff, etc., printed at the top of the front page. ~*vb.* (*tr.*)

3. to send (a sailor) to the masthead as a punishment. **4.** to raise (a sail) to the masthead.

mastic ('mæstɪk) *n.* **1.** an aromatic resin obtained from the mastic tree and used as an astringent and to make varnishes and lacquers. **2. mastic tree.** a small Mediterranean evergreen tree that yields the resin mastic. **3.** any of several putty-like substances used as a filler, adhesive, or seal in wood, plaster, or masonry. **4.** a liquor flavoured with mastic gum. [C14: via OF from LL *masticum*, from L from Gk *mastikhē* resin used as chewing gum]

masticate ('mæstɪˌkeɪt) *vb.* **1.** to chew (food). **2.** to reduce (materials such as rubber) to a pulp by crushing, grinding, or kneading. [C17: from LL *masticāre*, from Gk *mastikhan* to grind the teeth] —ˌmasti'cation *n.* —'masti,cator *n.*

masticatory ('mæstɪkətərɪ, -trɪ) *adj.* **1.** of, relating to, or adapted to chewing. ~*n., pl.* **-tories. 2.** a medicinal substance chewed to increase the secretion of saliva.

mastiff ('mæstɪf) *n.* a breed of large powerful short-haired dog, usually fawn or brindled. [C14: from OF, ult. from L *mansuētus* tame]

mastitis (mæ'staɪtɪs) *n.* inflammation of a breast or an udder.

masto- *or before a vowel* **mast-** *combining form.* indicating the breast, mammary glands, or something resembling a breast or nipple: *mastodon; mastoid.* [from Gk *mastos* breast]

mastodon ('mæstəˌdɒn) *n.* an extinct elephant-like mammal common in Pliocene times. [C19: from NL, lit.: breast-tooth, referring to the nipple-shaped projections on the teeth]

mastoid ('mæstɔɪd) *adj.* **1.** shaped like a nipple or breast. **2.** designating or relating to a nipple-like process of the temporal bone behind the ear. ~*n.* **3.** the mastoid process. **4.** *Inf.* mastoiditis.

mastoiditis (ˌmæstɔɪ'daɪtɪs) *n.* inflammation of the mastoid process.

masturbate ('mæstəˌbeɪt) *vb.* to stimulate the genital organs of (oneself or another) to achieve sexual pleasure. [C19: from L *masturbārī*, from ?; formerly thought to be derived from *manus* hand + *stuprāre* to defile] —ˌmastur'bation *n.* —'mastur,bator *n.* —**masturbatory** ('mæstəˌbeɪtərɪ) *adj.*

Masuria (mə'sjʊərɪə) *n.* a region of NE Poland: until 1945 part of East Prussia: includes the **Masurian Lakes,** scene of Russian defeats by the Germans (1914, 1915) during World War I. —**Ma'surian** *adj., n.*

mat¹ (mæt) *n.* **1.** a thick flat piece of fabric used as a floor covering, a place to wipe one's shoes, etc. **2.** a smaller pad of material used to protect a surface from the heat, scratches, etc., of an object placed upon it. **3.** a large piece of thick padded material put on the floor as a surface for wrestling, judo, etc. **4.** any surface or mass that is densely interwoven or tangled: *a mat of weeds.* ~*vb.* **matting, matted. 5.** to tangle or weave or become tangled or woven into a dense mass. **6.** (*tr.*) to cover with a mat or mats. [OE *matte*]

mat² (mæt) *n.* **1.** a border of cardboard, cloth, etc., placed around a picture as a frame or between picture and frame. ~*adj.* **2.** having a dull, lustreless, or roughened surface. ~*vb.* **matting, matted.** (*tr.*) **3.** to furnish (a picture) with a mat. **4.** to give (a surface) a mat finish. ~Also (for senses 2 & 4): **matt.** [C17: from F, lit.: dead]

mat³ (mæt) *n. Printing, inf.* short for **matrix** (sense 4).

mat. *abbrev. for* matinée.

Matabeleland (ˌmætə'biːlɪˌlænd, -'bɛlɪ-) *n.* a region of W Zimbabwe, between the Rivers Limpopo and Zambezi: rich gold deposits. Chief town: Bulawayo. Area: 181 605 sq. km (70 118 sq. miles).

Matadi (mə'tɑːdɪ) *n.* the chief port of Zaïre, in the west at the mouth of the River Congo. Pop.: 144 742 (1984).

matador ('mætəˌdɔː) *n.* **1.** the principal bullfighter who kills the bull. **2.** (in some card games) one of the highest cards. **3.** a game played with dominoes in which the dots on adjacent halves must total seven. [C17: from Sp., from *matar* to kill]

matagouri (ˌmætə'gʊərɪ) *n.* a New Zealand thorny bush which forms thickets in open country. Also called: **wild Irishman.** [from Maori *tumatakuru*]

Mata Hari ('mɑːtə 'hɑːrɪ) *n.* real name *Gertrud Margarete Zelle.* 1876–1917, Dutch dancer in France, who was executed as a German spy in World War I.

matai ('mɑːtaɪ) *n.* a New Zealand tree, the black pine, the wood of which is used as building timber. Also called: **black pine**. [from Maori]

Matamoros (ˌmætə'mɔːrəs; *Spanish* mata'morɔs) *n.* a port in NE Mexico, on the Río Grande: scene of bitter fighting during the U.S.–Mexican War; centre of a cotton-growing area. Pop.: 238 840 (1980 est.).

Matanzas (mə'tænzəs; *Spanish* ma'tanθas) *n.* a port in W central Cuba: founded in 1693 and developed into the second city of Cuba in the mid-19th century; exports chiefly sugar. Pop.: 105 430 (1986 est.).

Matapan ('mætəˌpæn, ˌmætə'pæn) *n.* **Cape.** a cape in S Greece, at the S central tip of the Peloponnese: the southern point of the mainland of Greece. Modern Greek name: **Taínaron**.

match[1] (mætʃ) *n.* **1.** a formal game or sports event in which people, teams, etc., compete. **2.** a person or thing able to provide competition for another: *she's met her match.* **3.** a person or thing that resembles, harmonizes with, or is equivalent to another in a specified respect. **4.** a person or thing that is an exact copy or equal of another. **5. a.** a partnership between a man and a woman, as in marriage. **b.** an arrangement for such a partnership. **6.** a person regarded as a possible partner, as in marriage. ~*vb. (mainly tr.)* **7.** to fit (parts) together. **8.** *(also intr.;* sometimes foll. by *up)* to resemble, harmonize with, or equal (one another or something else). **9.** (sometimes foll. by *with* or *against*) to compare in order to determine which is the superior. **10.** (often foll. by *to* or *with*) to adapt so as to correspond with: *to match hope with reality.* **11.** (often foll. by *with* or *against*) to arrange a competition between. **12.** to find a match for. **13.** *Electronics.* to connect (two circuits) so that their impedances are equal, to produce a maximum transfer of energy. [OE *gemœcca* spouse] —**'matchable** *adj.* —**'matching** *adj.*

match[2] (mætʃ) *n.* **1.** a thin strip of wood or cardboard tipped with a chemical that ignites by friction on a rough surface or a surface coated with a suitable chemical (see **safety match**). **2.** a length of cord or wick impregnated with a chemical so that it burns slowly. It is used to fire cannons, explosives, etc. [C14: from OF *meiche,* ?from L *myxa* wick, from Gk *muxa* lamp nozzle]

matchboard ('mætʃˌbɔːd) *n.* a long flimsy board tongued and grooved for lining work.

matchbox ('mætʃˌbɒks) *n.* a small box for holding matches.

matchless ('mætʃlɪs) *adj.* unequalled; incomparable; peerless. —**'matchlessly** *adv.*

matchlock ('mætʃˌlɒk) *n.* **1.** an obsolete type of gunlock igniting the powder by means of a slow match. **2.** a gun having such a lock.

matchmaker ('mætʃˌmeɪkə) *n.* **1.** a person who brings together suitable partners for marriage. **2.** a person who arranges competitive matches. —**'match,making** *n., adj.*

match play *n. Golf.* scoring according to the number of holes won and lost. Cf. **stroke play.** —**match player** *n.*

match point *n.* **1.** *Tennis, squash, etc.* the final point needed to win a match. **2.** *Bridge.* the unit used for scoring in tournaments.

matchstick ('mætʃˌstɪk) *n.* **1.** the wooden part of a match. ~*adj.* **2.** made with or as if with matchsticks. **3.** (esp. of drawn figures) thin and straight: *matchstick men.*

matchwood ('mætʃˌwʊd) *n.* **1.** wood suitable for making matches. **2.** splinters or fragments.

mate[1] (meɪt) *n.* **1.** the sexual partner of an animal. **2.** a marriage partner. **3. a.** *Inf., chiefly Brit., Austral. & N.Z.* a friend, usually of the same sex: often used to any male in direct address. **b.** *(in combination)* an associate, colleague, fellow sharer, etc.: *a classmate.* **4.** one of a pair of matching items. **5.** *Naut.* **a.** short for **first mate. b.** any officer below the master on a commercial ship. **6.** (in some trades) an assistant: *a plumber's mate.* ~*vb.* **7.** to pair (a male and female animal) or (of animals) to pair for reproduction. **8.** to marry or join in marriage. **9.** *(tr.)* to join as a pair. [C14: from MLow G; rel. to OE *gemetta* table-guest, from *mete* MEAT]

mate[2] (meɪt) *n., vb. Chess.* See **checkmate.**

maté *or* **mate** ('mɑːteɪ) *n.* **1.** an evergreen tree cultivated in South America for its leaves, which contain caffeine. **2.** a stimulating milky beverage made from the dried leaves of this tree. ~Also called: **Paraguay tea, yerba, yerba maté.** [C18: from American Sp. (orig. referring to

the vessel in which the drink was brewed), from Quechua *máti* gourd]

matelot, matlo, *or* **matlow** ('mætləʊ) *n. Sl., chiefly Brit.* a sailor. [C20: from F]

mater ('meɪtə) *n. Brit. sl.* a word for **mother:** often used facetiously. [C16: from L]

material (mə'tɪərɪəl) *n.* **1.** the substance of which a thing is made or composed; component or constituent matter. **2.** facts, notes, etc., that a finished work may be based on or derived from. **3.** cloth or fabric. **4.** a person who has qualities suitable for a given occupation, training, etc.: *that boy is university material.* ~*adj.* **5.** of, relating to, or composed of physical substance. **6.** of, relating to, or affecting economic or material wellbeing: *material ease.* **7.** of or concerned with physical rather than spiritual interests. **8.** of great import or consequence: *material benefit.* **9.** (often foll. by *to*) relevant. **10.** *Philosophy.* of or relating to matter as opposed to form. ~See also **materials.** [C14: via F from LL *māteriālis,* from L *māteria* MATTER] —**ma,teri'ality** *n.*

material implication *n. Logic.* a form of implication in which the proposition "if A then B" is true except when A is true and B is false.

materialism (mə'tɪərɪəˌlɪzəm) *n.* **1.** interest in and desire for money, possessions, etc., rather than spiritual or ethical values. **2.** *Philosophy.* the doctrine that matter is the only reality and that the mind, the emotions, etc., are merely functions of it. Cf. **idealism, dualism. 3.** *Ethics.* the rejection of any religious or supernatural account of things. —**ma'terialist** *n.* —**ma,terial'istic** *adj.* —**ma,terial'istically** *adv.*

materialize *or* **-ise** (mə'tɪərɪəˌlaɪz) *vb.* **1.** *(intr.)* to become fact; actually happen. **2.** to invest or become invested with a physical shape or form. **3.** to cause (a spirit, as of a dead person) to appear in material form or (of a spirit) to appear in such form. **4.** *(intr.)* to take shape; become tangible. —**ma,teriali'zation** *or* **-i'sation** *n.* —**ma'terial,izer** *or* **-,iser** *n.*

▷ **Usage.** Careful writers and speakers avoid using *materialize* to mean *happen* or *occur,* esp. in formal contexts: *they talked for several hours but nothing happened* (not *materialized*). The word is often used, however, in the sense of taking shape: *after many hours of discussion, the project finally began to materialize.*

materially (mə'tɪərɪəlɪ) *adv.* **1.** to a significant extent; considerably. **2.** with respect to material objects. **3.** *Philosophy.* with respect to substance as distinct from form.

materials (mə'tɪərɪəlz) *pl. n.* the equipment necessary for a particular activity.

materia medica (mə'tɪərɪə 'mɛdɪkə) *n.* **1.** the branch of medical science concerned with the study of drugs used in the treatment of disease. **2.** the drugs used in the treatment of disease. [C17: from Med. L: medical matter]

materiel *or* **matériel** (mə,tɪərɪ'ɛl) *n.* the materials and equipment of an organization, esp. of a military force. [C19: from F: MATERIAL]

maternal (mə'tɜːnəl) *adj.* **1.** of, relating to, or characteristic of a mother. **2.** related through the mother's side of the family: *his maternal uncle.* [C15: from Med. L *māternālis,* from L *māternus,* from *māter* mother] —**ma'ternalism** *n.* —**ma,ternal'istic** *adj.* —**ma'ternally** *adv.*

maternity (mə'tɜːnɪtɪ) *n.* **1.** motherhood. **2.** the characteristics associated with motherhood; motherliness. **3.** *(modifier)* relating to pregnant women or women at the time of childbirth: *a maternity ward.*

mateship ('meɪtʃɪp) *n. Austral.* friendly egalitarian comradeship.

mate's rates *pl. n. N.Z. inf.* discounted or preferential rates of payment offered to a friend or colleague: *he got the job done cheaply by a plumber friend at mate's rates.*

matey *or* **maty** ('meɪtɪ) *Brit. inf.* ~*adj.* **1.** friendly or intimate. ~*n.* **2.** friend or fellow: usually used in direct address. —**'mateyness** *or* **'matiness** *n.*

math (mæθ) *n. U.S. & Canad. inf.* short for **mathematics.** Brit. equivalent: **maths.**

mathematical (ˌmæθə'mætɪkəl) *or* **mathematic** *adj.* **1.** of, used in, or relating to mathematics. **2.** characterized by or using the precision of mathematics. **3.** using, determined by, or in accordance with the principles of mathematics. —**mathe'matically** *adv.*

mathematical logic *n.* symbolic logic, esp. when concerned with the foundations of mathematics.

mathematician (ˌmæθəmə'tɪʃən) *n.* an expert or specialist in mathematics.
mathematics (ˌmæθə'mætɪks) *n.* **1.** (*functioning as sing.*) a group of related sciences, including algebra, geometry, and calculus, concerned with the study of number, quantity, shape, and space and their interrelationships by using a specialized notation. **2.** (*functioning as sing. or pl.*) mathematical operations and processes involved in the solution of a problem or study of some scientific field. [C14 *mathematik* (n.), via L from Gk (adj.), from *mathēma* a science; rel. to *manthanein* to learn]
maths (mæθs) *n.* (*functioning as sing.*) *Brit. inf.* short for **mathematics**. U.S. and Canad. equivalent: **math.**
Mathura ('mʌtuərə, mʌ'θuərə) *n.* a city in N India, in W Uttar Pradesh on the Jumna River: a place of Hindu pilgrimage, revered as the birthplace of Krishna. Pop.: 159 458 (1981). Former name: **Muttra.**
Matilda[1] (mə'tɪldə) *n. Austral. inf.* **1.** a bushman's swag. **2. waltz Matilda.** to travel as a bushman carrying one's swag. [C20: from the Christian name]
Matilda[2] (mə'tɪldə) *n.* known as *the Empress Maud.* 1102–67, only daughter of Henry I of England and wife of Geoffrey of Anjou. After her father's death (1135) she unsuccessfully waged a civil war with Stephen for the English throne; her son succeeded as Henry II.
matin, mattin ('mætɪn), *or* **matinal** *adj.* of or relating to matins. [C14: see MATINS]
matinée ('mætɪˌneɪ) *n.* a daytime, esp. afternoon, performance of a play, concert, etc. [C19: from F; see MATINS]
matinée coat *or* **jacket** *n.* a short coat for a baby.
matins *or* **mattins** ('mætɪnz) *n.* (*functioning as sing. or pl.*) **1. a.** *Chiefly R.C. Church.* the first of the seven canonical hours of prayer. **b.** the service of morning prayer in the Church of England. **2.** *Literary.* a morning song, esp. of birds. [C13: from OF, ult. from L *mātūtīnus* of the morning, from *Mātūta* goddess of dawn]
Matisse (*French* matis) *n.* **Henri** (ãri). 1869–1954, French painter and sculptor; leader of Fauvism.
matlo *or* **matlow** ('mætləʊ) *n.* variant spellings of **matelot.**
Matlock ('mætˌlɒk) *n.* a town in N England, on the River Derwent, administrative centre of Derbyshire: mineral springs. Pop.: 20 750 (1981).
Mato Grosso *or* **Matto Grosso** ('mætəʊ 'grɒsəʊ; *Portuguese* 'matu 'grosu) *n.* **1.** a high plateau of SW Brazil: forms the watershed separating the Amazon and Plata river systems. **2.** a state of W central Brazil: mostly on the Mato Grosso Plateau, with the Amazon basin to the north; valuable mineral resources. Capital: Cuiabá. Pop.: 1 138 866 (1980). Area: 881 001 sq. km (340 083 sq. miles).
Mato Grosso do Sul ('duː sul) *n.* a state of W central Brazil: formed in 1979 from part of Mato Grosso state. Capital: Campo Grande. Pop.: 1 367 197 (1980). Area: 350 548 sq. km (135 318 sq. miles).
Matopo Hills (mə'təʊpə) *or* **Matopos** *pl. n.* the granite hills south of Bulawayo, Zimbabwe, where Cecil Rhodes chose to be buried.
Matozinhos (*Portuguese* mətu'ziɲuʃ) *n.* a port in N Portugal, on the estuary of the Leça River north of Oporto: fishing industry. Pop.: 26 426 (1981).
matrass ('mætrəs) *n. Chem., obs.* a long-necked glass flask, used for distilling, dissolving substances, etc. [C17: from F, ? rel. to L *mētiri* to measure]
matri- *combining form.* mother or motherhood: *matriarchy.* [from L *māter* mother]
matriarch ('meɪtrɪˌɑːk) *n.* **1.** a woman who dominates an organization, community, etc. **2.** the female head of a tribe or family. **3.** a very old or venerable woman. [C17: from MATRI- + -ARCH, by false analogy with PATRIARCH] —'**matri**ˌarchal *or* '**matri**ˌarchic *adj.*
matriarchy ('meɪtrɪˌɑːkɪ) *n., pl.* **-chies. 1.** a form of social organization in which a female is head of the family or society, and descent and kinship are traced through the female line. **2.** any society dominated by women.
matric (mə'trɪk) *n. Brit.* short for **matriculation** (see **matriculate**).
matrices ('meɪtrɪˌsiːz, 'mæ-) *n.* a plural of **matrix.**
matricide ('mætrɪˌsaɪd, 'meɪ-) *n.* **1.** the act of killing one's own mother. **2.** a person who kills his mother. [C16: from L *mātrīcīdium* (the act), *mātrīcīda* (the agent). See MATRI-, -CIDE] —ˌmatri'cidal *adj.*
matriculate (mə'trɪkjuˌleɪt) *vb.* **1.** to enrol or be enrolled in an institution, esp. a college or university. **2.** (*intr.*) to

attain the academic standard required for a course at such an institution. [C16: from Med. L *mātrīculāre* to register, from *mātrīcula*, dim. of *matrix* list] —maˌtricu'lation *n.*
matrilineal (ˌmætrɪ'lɪnɪəl, ˌmeɪ-) *adj.* relating to descent or kinship through the female line.
matrimony ('mætrɪmənɪ) *n., pl.* **-nies. 1.** the state or condition of being married. **2.** the ceremony of marriage. **3. a.** a card game in which the king and queen together are a winning combination. **b.** such a combination. [C14: via Norman F from L *mātrimōnium* wedlock, from *māter* mother] —ˌmatri'monial *adj.*
matrix ('meɪtrɪks, 'mæ-) *n., pl.* **matrices** *or* **matrixes. 1.** a substance, situation, or environment in which something has its origin, takes form, or is enclosed. **2.** the intercellular substance of bone, cartilage, connective tissue, etc. **3.** the rock in which fossils, pebbles, etc., are embedded. **4.** *Printing.* **a.** a metal mould for casting type. **b.** a papier-mâché or plastic mould impressed from the forme and used for stereotyping. **5.** a mould used in the production of gramophone records. **6.** a bed of perforated material placed beneath a workpiece in a press or stamping machine against which the punch operates. **7.** *Maths.* a rectangular array of elements set out in rows and columns, used to facilitate the solution of problems, such as transformation of coordinates. **8.** *Obs.* the womb. [C16: from L: womb, female animal used for breeding, from *māter* mother]
matron ('meɪtrən) *n.* **1.** a married woman regarded as staid or dignified. **2.** a woman in charge of the domestic or medical arrangements in an institution. **3.** *U.S.* a wardress in a prison. **4.** *Brit.* the administrative head of the nursing staff in a hospital. Official name: **nursing officer.** [C14: via OF from L *mātrōna*, from *māter* mother] —'**ma**tronal *or* '**matron**ly *adj.* —'**matron**ˌhood *or* '**matron**ship *n.*
matron of honour *n., pl.* **matrons of honour.** a married woman serving as chief attendant to a bride.
Matsu *or* **Mazu** (mæt'suː) *n.* an island group in Formosa Strait, off the SE coast of mainland China: belongs to Taiwan. Pop.: 8199 (1982 est.). Area: 44 sq. km (17 sq. miles).
Matsuyama (ˌmætsʊ'jɑːmə) *n.* a port in SW Japan, on NW Shikoku: textile and chemical industries; Ehime University (1949). Pop.: 427 000 (1985).
matt *or* **matte** (mæt) *adj., n., vb.* variant spellings of **mat**[2] (senses 2 & 4).
Matt. *Bible. abbrev. for* Matthew.
mattamore ('mætəˌmɔː) *n.* a subterranean storehouse or dwelling. [C17: from F, from Ar. *matmurā*, from *tamara* to store, bury]
matted ('mætɪd) *adj.* **1.** tangled into a thick mass. **2.** covered with or formed of matting.
matter ('mætə) *n.* **1.** that which makes up something, esp. a physical object; material. **2.** substance that occupies space and has mass, as distinguished from substance that is mental, spiritual, etc. **3.** substance of a specified type: *vegetable matter.* **4.** (sometimes foll. by *of* or *for*) thing; affair; concern; question: *a matter of taste.* **5.** a quantity or amount: *a matter of a few pence.* **6.** the content of written or verbal material as distinct from its style or form. **7.** (*used with a negative*) importance; consequence. **8.** *Philosophy.* **a.** (in the writings of Aristotle and the Scholastics) that which is itself formless but can receive form and become substance. **b.** that which is organized into chemical substances and living things. **9.** *Philosophy.* (in the Cartesian tradition) one of two basic modes of existence, the other being mind. **10.** *Printing.* **a.** type set up. **b.** copy to be set in type. **11.** a secretion or discharge, such as pus. **12.** *Law.* **a.** something to be proved. **b.** statements or allegations to be considered by a court. **13. for that matter.** as regards that. **14. no matter. a.** regardless of; irrespective of: *no matter what the excuse, you must not be late.* **b.** (*sentence substitute*) it is unimportant. **15. the matter.** wrong; the trouble: *there's nothing the matter.* ~*vb.* (*intr.*) **16.** to be of consequence or importance. **17.** to form and discharge pus. [C13 (n.), C16 (vb.): from L *māteria* cause, substance, esp. wood, or a substance that produces something else]
Matterhorn ('mætəˌhɔːn) *n.* a mountain on the border between Italy and Switzerland, in the Pennine Alps. Height: 4477 m (14 688 ft.). French name: **Mont Cervin.** Italian name: **Monte Cervino** ('monte tʃer'viːno).

matter of course *n.* **1.** an event or result that is natural or inevitable. ~*adj.* **matter-of-course. 2.** (*usually post-positive*) occurring as a matter of course. **3.** accepting things as inevitable or natural: *a matter-of-course attitude.*

matter of fact *n.* **1.** a fact that is undeniably true. **2.** *Law.* a statement of facts the truth of which the court must determine on the basis of the evidence before it. **3. as a matter of fact.** actually; in fact. ~*adj.* **matter-of-fact. 4.** unimaginative or emotionless: *he gave a matter-of-fact account of the murder.*

Matthew ('mæθjuː) *n. New Testament.* **1.** Also called: **Levi.** a tax collector of Capernaum called by Christ to be one of the 12 apostles (Matthew 9:9–13; 10:3). **2.** the first Gospel, traditionally ascribed to him.

Matthew Paris *n.* See (Matthew) **Paris**[2] (sense 2).

Matthews ('mæθjuːz) *n.* Sir **Stanley.** born 1915, English footballer.

Matthias (mə'θaɪəs) *n. New Testament.* the disciple chosen by lot to replace Judas as one of the 12 apostles (Acts 1:15–26).

Matthias I Corvinus (kɔː'vaɪnəs) *n.* ?1440–90, king of Hungary (1458–90): built up the most powerful kingdom in Central Europe. A patron of Renaissance art, he founded the Corvina library, one of the finest in Europe. Hungarian name: **Mátyás Hollós** ('maːtjaːʃ 'hɔlɔʃ).

matting[1] ('mætɪŋ) *n.* **1.** a coarsely woven fabric, usually made of a natural fibre such as straw or hemp and used as a floor covering, packing material, etc. **2.** the act or process of making mats. **3.** material for mats.

matting[2] ('mætɪŋ) *n.* **1.** another word for **mat**[2](sense 1). **2.** the process of producing a mat finish.

mattins ('mætɪnz) *n.* a variant spelling of **matins.**

mattock ('mætək) *n.* a type of large pick that has one end of its blade shaped like an adze, used for loosening soil, cutting roots, etc. [OE *mattuc*, from ?; rel. to L *mateola* club, mallet]

Matto Grosso ('mætəʊ 'ɡrɒsəʊ) *n.* a variant spelling of **Mato Grosso.**

mattress ('mætrɪs) *n.* **1.** a large flat pad with a strong cover, filled with straw, foam rubber, etc., and often incorporating coiled springs, used as a bed or as part of a bed. **2.** a woven mat of brushwood, poles, etc., used to protect an embankment, dyke, etc., from scour. **3.** a concrete or steel raft or slab used as a foundation or footing. [C13: via OF from It. *materasso*, from Ar. *almatrah* place where something is thrown]

maturate ('mætjʊˌreɪt, 'mætʃʊ-) *vb.* **1.** to mature or bring to maturity. **2.** a less common word for **suppurate.** —ˌmatu'ration *n.* —maturative (mə'tjʊərətɪv, mə'tʃʊə-) *adj.*

mature (mə'tjʊə, -'tʃʊə) *adj.* **1.** relatively advanced physically, mentally, etc.; grown-up. **2.** (of plans, theories, etc.) fully considered; perfected. **3.** due or payable: *a mature debenture.* **4.** *Biol.* **a.** fully developed or differentiated: *a mature cell.* **b.** fully grown; adult: *a mature animal.* **5.** (of fruit, wine, cheese, etc.) ripe or fully aged. ~*vb.* **6.** to make or become mature. **7.** (*intr.*) (of notes, bonds, etc.) to become due for payment or repayment. [C15: from L *mātūrus* early, developed] —ma'turely *adv.* —ma'tureness *n.*

mature student *n.* a student at a college or university who has passed the usual age for formal education.

maturity (mə'tjʊərɪtɪ, -'tʃʊə-) *n.* **1.** the state or quality of being mature; full development. **2.** *Finance.* **a.** the date upon which a bond, note, etc., becomes due for repayment. **b.** the state of a bill, note, etc., when due.

matutinal (ˌmætjʊ'taɪnᵊl) *adj.* of, occurring in, or during the morning. [C17: from LL *mātūtinālis*, from L, from *Mātūta* goddess of the dawn]

matzo, matzoh ('mætsəʊ) *or* **matza, matzah** ('mætsə) *n., pl.* **matzos, matzohs, matzas, matzahs,** *or* **matzoth** (*Hebrew* ma'tsɔt). a large very thin biscuit of unleavened bread, traditionally eaten during Passover. [from Heb. *matsāh*]

Maubeuge (*French* mobɔʒ) *n.* an industrial town in N France, near the border with Belgium. Pop.: 35 380 (1983 est.).

maudlin ('mɔːdlɪn) *adj.* foolishly tearful or sentimental, as when drunk. [C17: from ME *Maudelen* Mary Magdalene, typically portrayed as a tearful penitent]

Maugham ('mɔːm) *n.* **W(illiam) Somerset.** 1874–1965, English writer. His works include the novels *Of Human*

Bondage (1915) and *Cakes and Ale* (1930), short stories, and comedies.

maugre *or* **mauger** ('mɔːɡə) *prep. Obs.* in spite of. [C13 (meaning: ill will): from OF *maugre*, lit.: bad pleasure]

Maui ('maʊi) *n.* a volcanic island in S central Hawaii: the second largest of the Hawaiian Islands. Pop.: 78 700 (1986 est.). Area: 1885 sq. km (728 sq. miles).

maul (mɔːl) *vb.* (*tr.*) **1.** to handle clumsily; paw. **2.** to batter or lacerate. ~*n.* **3.** a heavy two-handed hammer. **4.** *Rugby.* a loose scrum. [C13: from OF *mail*, from L *malleus* hammer] —'mauler *n.*

Maulmain (maʊl'meɪn) *n.* a variant spelling of **Moulmein.**

maulstick *or* **mahlstick** ('mɔːl,stɪk) *n.* a long stick used by artists to steady the hand holding the brush. [C17: partial translation of Du. *maalstok*, from obs. *malen* to paint + *stok* STICK]

Mauna Kea ('maʊnə 'keɪə) *n.* an extinct volcano in Hawaii, on N central Hawaii Island: the highest island mountain in the world. Height: 4206 m (13 799 ft.).

Mauna Loa ('maʊnə 'ləʊə) *n.* an active volcano in Hawaii, on S central Hawaii Island. Height: 4171 m (13 684 ft.).

maunder ('mɔːndə) *vb.* (*intr.*) to move, talk, or act aimlessly or idly. [C17: ?from obs. *maunder* to beg, from L *mendīcāre*]

maundy ('mɔːndɪ) *n., pl.* **maundies.** *Christianity.* the ceremonial washing of the feet of poor persons in commemoration of Jesus' washing of his disciples' feet. [C13: from OF *mandé* something commanded, from L, ult. from Christ's words: *Mandātum novum dō vōbīs* A new commandment give I unto you]

Maundy money *n.* specially minted coins distributed by the British sovereign on the Thursday before Easter (**Maundy Thursday**).

Maupassant (*French* mopasɑ̃) *n.* (**Henri René Albert) Guy de** (gi də). 1850–93, French writer, noted esp. for his short stories, such as *Boule de suif* (1880), *La Maison Tellier* (1881), and *Mademoiselle Fifi* (1883). His novels include *Bel Ami* (1885) and *Pierre et Jean* (1888).

Maupertuis (*French* mopɛrtɥi) *n.* **Pierre Louis Moreau de** (pjɛr lwi mɔro də). 1698–1759, French mathematician, who originated the principle of least action (or Maupertuis principle).

Mauretania (ˌmɒrɪ'teɪnɪə) *n.* an ancient region of N Africa, corresponding approximately to the N parts of modern Algeria and Morocco. —ˌMaure'tanian *adj., n.*

Mauriac (*French* mɔrjak) *n.* **François** (frɑ̃swa). 1885–1970, French novelist, noted esp. for his psychological studies of the conflict between religious belief and human desire. His works include *Le désert de l'amour* (1925), *Thérèse Desqueyroux* (1927), and *Le noeud de vipères* (1932): Nobel prize for literature 1952.

Maurice ('mɒrɪs) *n.* **1.** 1521–53, duke of Saxony (1541–53) and elector of Saxony (1547–53). He was instrumental in gaining recognition of Protestantism in Germany. **2.** known as *Maurice of Nassau.* 1567–1625, prince of Orange and count of Nassau; the son of William the Silent, after whose death he led the United Provinces of the Netherlands in their struggle for independence from Spain (achieved by 1609). **3. Frederick Denison.** 1805–72, English Anglican theologian and pioneer of Christian socialism.

Mauritania (ˌmɒrɪ'teɪnɪə) *n.* a republic in NW Africa, on the Atlantic: established as a French protectorate in 1903 and a colony in 1920; gained full independence in 1960; lies mostly in the Sahara; contains rich resources of iron ore. Official languages: Arabic and French. Religion: Muslim. Currency: franc. Capital: Nouakchott. Pop.: 2 015 000 (1987 UN est.). Area: 1 085 805 sq. km (419 232 sq. miles). Official name: **Islamic Republic of Mauritania.** —ˌMauri'tanian *adj., n.*

Mauritius (mə'rɪʃəs) *n.* an island and state in the Indian Ocean, east of Madagascar: originally uninhabited, it was settled by the Dutch (1638–1710) then abandoned; taken by the French in 1715 and the British in 1810; became an independent member of the Commonwealth in 1968. It is economically dependent on sugar. Official language: English; a French creole is widely spoken. Religion: mostly Hindu and Christian. Currency: rupee. Capital: Port Louis. Pop.: 1 041 000 (1987 UN est.). Area: 1865 sq. km (720 sq. miles). Former name (1715–1810): **Île-de-France.** —**Mau'ritian** *adj., n.*

Maurois (*French* mɔrwa) *n.* André (ādre), pen name of *Emile Herzog*. 1885–1967, French writer, best known for his biographies, such as those of Shelley, Byron, and Proust.

Maury ('mɔːrɪ) *n.* **Matthew Fontaine**. 1806–73, U.S. pioneer hydrographer and oceanographer.

mausoleum (,mɔːsə'lɪəm) *n., pl.* **-leums** *or* **-lea** (-'lɪə). a large stately tomb. [C16: via L from Gk *mausōleion*, the tomb of *Mausolus*, king of Caria; built at Halicarnassus in the 4th cent. B.C.]

mauve (məʊv) *n.* **1. a.** any of various pale to moderate pinkish-purple or bluish-purple colours. **b.** (*as adj.*): *a mauve flower*. **2.** a reddish-purple aniline dye. [C19: from F, from L *malva* MALLOW]

maverick ('mævərɪk) *n.* **1.** (in the U.S. and Canada) an unbranded animal, esp. a stray calf. **2. a.** a person of independent or unorthodox views. **b.** (*as modifier*): *a maverick politician*. [C19: after Samuel A. *Maverick* (1803–70), Texas rancher, who did not brand his cattle]

mavis ('meɪvɪs) *n.* a popular name for the **song thrush**. [C14: from OF *mauvis* thrush; from ?]

maw (mɔː) *n.* **1.** the mouth, throat, crop, or stomach of an animal, esp. of a voracious animal. **2.** *Inf.* the mouth or stomach of a greedy person. [OE *maga*]

mawkish ('mɔːkɪʃ) *adj.* **1.** falsely sentimental, esp. in a weak or maudlin way. **2.** nauseating or insipid. [C17: from obs. *mawk* MAGGOT + -ISH] —'**mawkishly** *adv.* —'**mawkishness** *n.*

Mawson ('mɔːsən) *n.* Sir **Douglas**. 1882–1958, Australian Antarctic explorer, born in England.

max. *abbrev. for* maximum.

maxi ('mæksɪ) *adj.* **1. a.** (of a garment) reaching the ankle. **b.** (*as n.*): *she wore a maxi*. **c.** (*in combination*): *a maxidress*. **2.** large or considerable. [C20: from MAXI-MUM]

maxilla (mæk'sɪlə) *n., pl.* **-lae** (-liː). **1.** the upper jawbone in vertebrates. **2.** any member of one or two pairs of mouthparts in insects and other arthropods. [C17: NL, from L: jaw] —**max'illary** *adj.*

maxim ('mæksɪm) *n.* a brief expression of a general truth, principle, or rule of conduct. [C15: via F from Med. L, from *maxima*, in the phrase *maxima prōpositio* basic axiom (lit.: greatest proposition)]

Maxim ('mæksɪm) *n.* Sir **Hiram Stevens**. 1840–1916, British inventor of the first automatic machine gun (1884), born in the U.S.

maxima ('mæksɪmə) *n.* a plural of **maximum**.

maximal ('mæksɪməl) *adj.* of, relating to, or achieving a maximum; being the greatest or best possible. —'**maximally** *adv.*

Maximilian (,mæksɪ'mɪlɪən) *n.* full name *Ferdinand Maximilian Joseph*. 1832–67, archduke of Austria and emperor of Mexico (1864–67). After the French had partially conquered Mexico, he was offered the throne but was defeated and shot by the Mexicans under Juárez.

Maximilian I *n.* 1459–1519, king of Germany (1486–1519) and Holy Roman Emperor (1493–1519).

maximin ('mæksɪ,mɪn) *n.* **1.** *Maths.* the highest of a set of minimum values. **2.** (in game theory, etc.) the procedure of choosing the strategy that most benefits the least advantaged member of a group. Cf. **minimax**. [C20: from MAXI(MUM) MIN(IMUM)]

maximize *or* **-ise** ('mæksɪ,maɪz) *vb.* (*tr.*) to make as high or great as possible; increase to a maximum. —,**maxi'zation** *or* **-i'sation** *n.* —'**maxi,mizer** *or* **-iser** *n.*

maximum ('mæksɪməm) *n., pl.* **-mums** *or* **-ma**. **1.** the greatest possible amount, degree, etc. **2.** the highest value of a variable quantity. ~*adj.* **3.** of, being, or showing a maximum or maximums. ~*Abbrev.*: **max.** [C18: from L: greatest (neuter form used as noun), from *magnus* great]

Max Müller (*German* maks 'mylər) *n.* See (Friedrich Max) **Müller**.

maxwell ('mækswəl) *n.* the cgs unit of magnetic flux equal to the flux through one square centimetre normal to a field of one gauss. It is equivalent to 10^{-8} weber. Symbol: Mx [C20: after J. C. MAXWELL]

Maxwell ('mækswəl) *n.* **James Clerk**. 1831–79, Scottish physicist. He made major contributions to the electromagnetic theory, developing the equations (**Maxwell equations**) upon which classical theory is based. He also contributed to the kinetic theory of gases, and colour vision.

may[1] (meɪ) *vb. past* **might**. (takes an infinitive without *to* or an implied infinitive) used as an auxiliary: **1.** to indicate that permission is requested by or granted to someone: *he may go*. **2.** (often foll. by *well*) to indicate possibility: *the rope may break*. **3.** to indicate ability or capacity, esp. in questions: *may I help you?* **4.** to express a strong wish: *long may she reign*. **5.** to indicate result or purpose: used only in clauses introduced by *that* or *so that*: *he writes so that the average reader may understand*. **6.** to express courtesy in a question: *whose child may this little girl be?* **7. be that as it may**. in spite of that: a sentence connector conceding the possible truth of a previous statement and introducing an adversative clause: *be that as it may, I still think he should come*. **8. come what may**. whatever happens. **9. that's as may be**. (foll. by a clause introduced by *but*) that may be so. [OE *mæg*, from *magan*]

▷**Usage.** In careful written usage, *may* is used rather than *can* when reference is made to permission rather than to capability. *He may do it* is, for this reason, more appropriate than *he can do it* when the desired sense is *he is allowed to do it*. In spoken English, however, *can* is often used where the correct use of *may* results in forms that are considered to be awkward. *Can't I?* is preferred on this ground to *mayn't I?* in speech. The difference between *may* and *might* is one of emphasis: *he might be coming* usually indicates less certainty than *he may be coming*. Similarly, *might I have it?* is felt to be more hesitant than *may I have it?*

may[2] *or* **may tree** (meɪ) *n.* a Brit. name for **hawthorn**. [C16: from MAY]

May (meɪ) *n.* the fifth month of the year, consisting of 31 days. [from OF, from L *Maius* (month) of *Maia*, Roman goddess]

Maya[1] ('maɪə) *n.* **1.** (*pl.* **-ya** *or* **-yas**) Also called: **Mayan**. a member of an American Indian people of Yucatán, Belize, and N Guatemala, once having an advanced civilization. **2.** the language of this people.

Maya[2] ('maɪə, 'mɑːjə, 'mɑːjɑː) *n.* the Hindu goddess of illusion, the personification of the power of maya. —'**Mayan** *adj.*

Mayagüez (*Spanish* maja'γwɛθ) *n.* a port in W Puerto Rico; needlework industry. Pop.: 82 703 (1980).

Mayakovski *or* **Mayakovsky** (*Russian* məjɪ'kɔfskɪj) *n.* **Vladimir Vladimirovich** (vla'dimir vla'dimirəvitʃ). 1893–1930, Russian Futurist poet and dramatist. His poems include *150 000 000* (1921) and *At the Top of my Voice* (1930); his plays include *Vladimir Mayakovsky—a Tragedy* (1913) and *The Bedbug* (1929).

May apple *n.* **1.** an American plant with edible yellowish egg-shaped fruit. **2.** the fruit.

maybe ('meɪ,biː) *adv.* **1.** perhaps. ~*sentence substitute*. **2.** possibly; neither yes nor no.

May beetle *or* **bug** *n.* another name for **cockchafer**.

Mayday ('meɪ,deɪ) *n.* the international radiotelephone distress signal. [C20: phonetic spelling of F *m'aider* help me]

May Day *n.* the first day of May, traditionally a celebration of the coming of spring: in some countries now observed as a holiday in honour of workers.

Mayence (majɑ̃s) *n.* the French name for **Mainz**.

Mayenne (*French* majɛn) *n.* a department of NW France, in Pays de la Loire region. Capital: Laval. Pop.: 271 784 (1982). Area: 5212 sq. km (2033 sq. miles).

Mayer (*German* 'maɪər) *n.* **Julius Robert von** ('juːlius 'roːbɛrt fɔn). 1814–78, German physicist whose research in thermodynamics (1842) contributed to the discovery of the law of conservation of energy.

mayest ('meɪɪst) *vb.* a variant of **mayst**.

Mayfair ('meɪ,fɛə) *n.* a fashionable district of west central London.

mayflower ('meɪ,flaʊə) *n.* **1.** any of various plants that bloom in May. **2.** *Brit.* another name for **hawthorn**, **cowslip**, or **marsh marigold**.

Mayflower ('meɪ,flaʊə) *n.* **the.** the ship in which the Pilgrim Fathers sailed from Plymouth to America in 1620.

mayfly ('meɪ,flaɪ) *n., pl.* **-flies.** any of an order of short-lived insects having large transparent wings.

mayhap ('meɪ,hæp) *adv.* an archaic word for **perhaps**. [C16: shortened from *it may hap*]

mayhem *or* **maihem** ('meɪhɛm) *n.* **1.** *Law.* the wilful and unlawful infliction of injury upon a person, esp. (formerly) the injuring or removing of a limb rendering him less capable of defending himself against attack. **2.** any violent destruction or confusion. [C15: from Anglo-F *mahem* injury, of Gmc origin]

Maying ('meɪɪŋ) *n.* the traditional celebration of May Day.

mayn't ('meɪənt, meɪnt) *contraction of* may not.

Mayo ('meɪəʊ) *n.* a county of NW Ireland, in NW Connacht province, on the Atlantic: has many offshore islands and several large lakes. County town: Castlebar. Pop.: 115 016 (1986). Area: 5397 sq. km (2084 sq. miles).

Mayon (maːˈjɔːn) *n.* a volcano in the Philippines, on SE Luzon: Height: 2421 m (7943 ft.).

mayonnaise (ˌmeɪəˈneɪz) *n.* a thick creamy sauce made from egg yolks, oil, and vinegar or lemon juice. [C19: from F, ?from *mahonnais* of *Mahón*, a port in Minorca]

mayor (mɛə) *n.* the civic head of a municipal corporation in many countries. Scot. equivalent: **provost.** [C13: from OF *maire*, from L *maior* greater] —'**mayoral** *adj.* —'**mayorship** *n.*

mayoralty ('mɛərəltɪ) *n., pl.* -ties. the office or term of office of a mayor. [C14: from OF *mairalté*]

mayoress ('mɛərɪs) *n.* 1. *Chiefly Brit.* the wife of a mayor. 2. a female mayor.

Mayotte (*French* majɔt) *n.* an island in the Indian Ocean, northwest of Madagascar; administered by France. Pop. (including Pamanzi): 73 900 (1987 est.). Area: 374 sq. km (146 sq. miles).

maypole ('meɪˌpəʊl) *n.* a tall pole around which people dance during May-Day celebrations.

May queen *n.* a girl chosen, esp. for her beauty, to preside over May-Day celebrations.

mayst (meɪst) *or* **mayest** *vb. Arch.* (used with *thou* or its relative equivalent) a singular form of the present tense of **may**[1].

mayweed ('meɪˌwiːd) *n.* 1. Also called: **dog fennel, stinking mayweed.** a widespread Eurasian weedy plant having evil-smelling leaves and daisy-like flower heads. 2. scentless mayweed. a similar and related plant, with scentless leaves. [C16: changed from OE *mægtha* mayweed + WEED]

Mazarin ('mæzərɪn; *French* mazarɛ̃) *n.* **Jules** (ʒyl), original name *Giulio Mazarini.* 1602–61, French cardinal and statesman, born in Italy. He succeeded Richelieu (1642) as chief minister to Louis XIII and under the regency of Anne of Austria (1643–61). Despite the disturbances of the Fronde (1648–53), he strengthened the power of France in Europe.

Mazatlán (*Spanish* maθaˈtlan) *n.* a port in W Mexico, in S Sinaloa on the Pacific: situated opposite the tip of the peninsula of Lower California, for which it is the chief link with the mainland. Pop.: 174 000 (1984 est.).

maze (meɪz) *n.* 1. a complex network of paths or passages, esp. one with high hedges in a garden, designed to puzzle those walking through it. 2. a similar system represented diagrammatically as a pattern of lines. 3. any confusing network of streets, paths, etc. 4. a state of confusion. ~*vb.* 5. an archaic or dialect word for **amaze.** [C13: see AMAZE] —'**mazement** *n.* —'**mazy** *adj.*

Mazu ('mæˈzuː) *n.* the Pinyin transliteration of the Chinese name for **Matsu.**

mazurka *or* **mazourka** (məˈzɜːkə) *n.* 1. a Polish national dance in triple time. 2. a piece of music composed for this dance. [C19: from Polish: (dance) of *Mazur* (Mazovia) province in Poland]

Mazzini (*Italian* matˈtsiːni) *n.* **Giuseppe** (dʒuˈzɛppe). 1805–72, Italian nationalist. In 1831, in exile, he established the Young Italy association in Marseille, which sought to unite Italy as a republic. In 1849 he was one of the triumvirate that ruled the short-lived Roman republic.

MB *abbrev. for:* 1. Bachelor of Medicine. 2. *Computers.* megabyte.

MBA *abbrev. for* Master of Business Administration.

Mbabane (ᵊmbaːˈbaːnɪ) *n.* the capital of Swaziland, in the northwest: administrative and financial centre, with a large iron mine nearby. Pop.: 23 109 (1984 est.).

MBE *abbrev. for* Member of the Order of the British Empire (a Brit. title).

Mbujimayi (ᵊmˈbuːdʒɪˌmaɪi) *n.* a city in S Zaïre: diamond mining. Pop.: 423 363 (1984).

MC *abbrev. for:* 1. Master of Ceremonies. 2. (in the U.S.) Member of Congress. 3. (in Britain) Military Cross.

Mc- *prefix.* a variant of **Mac-.** For entries beginning with this prefix, see under **Mac-.**

MCC (in Britain) *abbrev. for* Marylebone Cricket Club.

MCh *abbrev. for* Master of Surgery. [L *Magister Chirurgiae*]

MCP *Inf. abbrev. for* male chauvinist pig.

Md *the chemical symbol for* mendelevium.

MD *abbrev. for:* 1. Doctor of Medicine. [from L *Medicinae Doctor*] 2. Managing Director. 3. mentally deficient.

MDMA *abbrev. for* 3,4-methylenedioxymethamphetamine.

MDT (in the U.S. and Canada) *abbrev. for* Mountain Daylight Time.

me (*mi*; *unstressed* mɪ) *pron.* (*objective*) 1. refers to the speaker or writer: *that shocks me.* ~*n.* 2. *Inf.* the personality of the speaker or writer or something that expresses it: *the real me.* [OE *mē* (dative)]

▷**Usage.** Although the nominative case is traditionally required after the verb *to be*, even careful speakers say *it is me* (or *him, her,* etc.) rather than *it is I* in informal contexts. The use of *me,* etc., before an -*ing* form of the verb (*he disapproved of me coming*) is common, but careful speakers and writers use the possessive form: *he disapproved of my coming.*

ME *abbrev. for:* 1. Marine Engineer. 2. Mechanical Engineer. 3. Methodist Episcopal. 4. Middle English. 5. Mining Engineer. 6. (in titles) Most Excellent. 7. myalgic encephalomyelitis.

mea culpa *Latin.* ('meɪɑ ˈkʊlpɑ) an acknowledgment of guilt. [lit.: my fault]

mead[1] (miːd) *n.* a wine made by fermenting a solution of honey, often with spices added. [OE *meodu*]

mead[2] (miːd) *n.* an archaic or poetic word for **meadow.** [OE *mæd*]

Mead[1] (miːd) *n.* Lake. a reservoir in NW Arizona and SE Nevada, formed by the Hoover Dam across the Colorado River: one of the largest man-made lakes in the world. Area: 588 sq. km (227 sq. miles).

Mead[2] (miːd) *n.* **Margaret.** 1901–78, U.S. anthropologist. Her works include *Coming of Age in Samoa* (1928) and *Male and Female* (1949).

Meade (miːd) *n.* **George Gordon.** 1815–72, Union general in the American Civil War. He commanded the Army of the Potomac, defeating the Confederates at Gettysburg (1863).

meadow ('mɛdəʊ) *n.* 1. an area of grassland, often used for hay or for grazing of animals. 2. a low-lying piece of grassland, often boggy and near a river. [OE *mædwe,* from *mæd* MEAD[2]] —'**meadowy** *adj.*

meadow grass *n.* a perennial grass that grows in meadows and similar places in N temperate regions.

meadow saffron *n.* another name for **autumn crocus.**

meadowsweet ('mɛdəʊˌswiːt) *n.* 1. a Eurasian plant with dense heads of small fragrant cream-coloured flowers. 2. any of several related North American plants.

Meads (miːdz) *n.* **Colin.** born 1935, New Zealand Rugby Union footballer. A forward, he played for the All Blacks (1957–71).

meagre *or U.S.* **meager** ('miːgə) *adj.* 1. deficient in amount, quality, or extent. 2. thin or emaciated. 3. lacking in richness or strength. [C14: from OF *maigre,* from L *macer* lean, poor] —'**meagrely** *adv.* —'**meagreness** *n.*

meal[1] (miːl) *n.* 1. a. any of the regular occasions, such as breakfast, lunch, dinner, etc., when food is served and eaten. b. (*in combination*): *mealtime.* 2. the food served and eaten. 3. **make a meal of.** *Inf.* to perform (a task) with unnecessarily great effort. [OE *mæl* measure, set time, meal]

meal[2] (miːl) *n.* 1. the edible part of a grain or pulse (excluding wheat) ground to a coarse powder. 2. *Scot.* oatmeal. 3. *Chiefly U.S.* maize flour. [OE *melu*]

mealie ('miːlɪ) *n.* (*often pl.*) a S. African word for **maize.** [C19: from Afrik. *milie,* from Port. *milho,* from L *milium* millet]

mealie-meal *n. S. African.* meal made from finely ground maize.

meals-on-wheels *n.* (*functioning as sing.*) (in Britain) a service taking hot meals to the elderly, infirm, etc., in their own homes.

meal ticket *n. Sl.* a person, situation, etc., providing a source of livelihood or income. [from orig. U.S. sense of ticket entitling holder to a meal]

mealworm ('miːlˌwɜːm) *n.* the larva of various beetles feeding on stored foods, esp. meal and flour.

mealy ('miːlɪ) *adj.* **mealier, mealiest.** 1. resembling meal; powdery. 2. containing or consisting of meal or grain. **3.** sprinkled or covered with meal or similar granules. **4.** (esp. of horses) spotted; mottled. **5.** pale in complexion. **6.** short for **mealy-mouthed**. — **'mealiness** *n.*

mealy bug *n.* any of various plant-eating insects coated with a powdery waxy secretion: some species are pests of citrus fruits and greenhouse plants.

mealy-mouthed *adj.* hesitant or afraid to speak plainly; not outspoken. [C16: from MEALY (in the sense: soft, soft-spoken)]

mean[1] (miːn) *vb.* **meaning, meant.** (*mainly tr.*) **1.** (*may take a clause as object or an infinitive*) to intend to convey or express. **2.** (*may take a clause as object or an infinitive*) to intend: *she didn't mean to hurt it.* **3.** (*may take a clause as object*) to say or do in all seriousness: *the boss means what he says.* **4.** (*often passive;* often foll. by *for*) to destine or design (for a certain person or purpose): *she was meant for greater things.* **5.** (*may take a clause as object*) to denote or connote; signify; represent. **6.** (*may take a clause as object*) to produce; cause: *the weather will mean long traffic delays.* **7.** (*may take a clause as object*) to foretell; portend: *those dark clouds mean rain.* **8.** to have the importance of: *money means nothing to him.* **9.** (*intr.*) to have the intention of behaving or acting (esp. in **mean well** *or* **mean ill**). [OE *mænan*]

mean[2] (miːn) *adj.* **1.** *Chiefly Brit.* miserly, ungenerous, or petty. **2.** despicable, ignoble, or callous: *a mean action.* **3.** poor or shabby: *a mean abode.* **4.** *Inf., chiefly U.S. & Canad.* bad-tempered; vicious. **5.** *Inf.* ashamed: *he felt mean about not letting the children stay out late.* **6.** *Sl.* excellent; skilful: *he plays a mean trombone.* **7. no mean. a.** of high quality: *no mean performer.* **b.** difficult: *no mean feat.* [C12: from OE *gemǣne* common] — **'meanly** *adv.* — **'meanness** *n.*

mean[3] (miːn) *n.* **1.** the middle point, state, or course between limits or extremes. **2.** moderation. **3.** *Maths.* **a.** the second and third terms of a proportion, as *b* and *c* in *a/b = c/d.* **b.** another name for **average** (sense 2). **4.** *Statistics.* a statistic obtained by multiplying each possible value of a variable by its probability and then taking the sum or integral over the range of the variable. ~*adj.* **5.** intermediate or medium in size, quantity, etc. **6.** occurring halfway between extremes or limits; average. [C14: via Anglo-Norman from OF *moien*, from LL *mediānus* MEDIAN]

meander (mɪˈændə) *vb.* (*intr.*) **1.** to follow a winding course. **2.** to wander without definite aim or direction. ~*n.* **3.** (*often pl.*) a curve or bend, as in a river. **4.** (*often pl.*) a winding course or movement. **5.** an ornamental pattern, esp. as used in ancient Greek architecture. [C16: from L *maeander*, from Gk *Maiandros* the River Maeander; see MENDERES (sense 1)] — **meˈandering** *adj.*

Meander (mɪˈændə) *n.* a variant spelling of **Maeander.**

mean deviation *n. Statistics.* **1.** the difference between an observed value of a variable and its mean. **2.** Also called: **mean deviation from the mean** (*or* **median**), **average deviation.** a measure of dispersion derived by computing the mean of the absolute values of the differences between observed values of a variable and the variable's mean.

meanie *or* **meany** (ˈmiːnɪ) *n. Inf.* **1.** *Chiefly Brit.* a miserly or stingy person. **2.** *Chiefly U.S.* a nasty ill-tempered person.

meaning (ˈmiːnɪŋ) *n.* **1.** the sense or significance of a word, sentence, symbol, etc.; import. **2.** the purpose behind speech, action, etc. **3.** the inner, symbolic, or true interpretation, value, or message. **4.** valid content; efficacy. ~*adj.* **5.** expressive of some sense, intention, criticism, etc.: *a meaning look.* ~See also **well-meaning.**

meaningful (ˈmiːnɪŋfʊl) *adj.* **1.** having great meaning or validity. **2.** eloquent; expressive: *a meaningful silence.* — **'meaningfully** *adv.* — **'meaningfulness** *n.*

▷ **Usage.** *Meaningful* has become something of a vogue word and is well established in collocations such as *a meaningful experience; a meaningful relationship.* Careful writers and speakers of English, however, do not use *meaningful* in instances where other adjectives, such as real, fruitful, useful, or significant may be more exact. Examples are: *delighted to have an apparently meaningful task to perform; computers could never play any meaningful role in the lives of ordinary people.* Often, *meaningful* can be omitted without any loss of sense: *to implement meaningful reform of housing tenures.*

meaningless (ˈmiːnɪŋlɪs) *adj.* futile or empty of meaning. — **'meaninglessly** *adv.* — **'meaninglessness** *n.*

mean life *n. Physics.* the average time of existence of an unstable or reactive entity, such as a nucleus, elementary particle, etc.

means (miːnz) *n.* **1.** (*functioning as sing. or pl.*) the medium, method, or instrument used to obtain a result or achieve an end: *a means of communication.* **2.** (*functioning as pl.*) resources or income. **3.** (*functioning as pl.*) considerable wealth or income: *a man of means.* **4. by all means.** without hesitation or doubt; certainly. **5. by means of.** with the use or help of. **6. by no manner of means.** definitely not. **7. by no** (*or* **not by any**) **means.** on no account; in no way.

means test *n.* the checking of a person's income to determine whether he qualifies for financial or social aid from a government.

mean sun *n.* an imaginary sun moving along the celestial equator at a constant speed and completing its annual course in the same time as the sun takes to move round the ecliptic at a varying speed. It is used in the measurement of mean solar time.

meant (mɛnt) *vb.* the past tense and past participle of **mean**[1].

meantime (ˈmiːnˌtaɪm) *or* **meanwhile** (ˈmiːnˌwaɪl) *n.* **1.** the intervening time or period (esp. in **in the meantime**). ~*adv.* **2.** during the intervening time or period. **3.** at the same time, esp. in another place.

▷ **Usage.** In formal usage, *in the meantime* is preferred to *meantime*, although *meantime* is very common in informal spoken English. The most usual one-word form of the adverb in written English is *meanwhile: in the meantime* (or *meanwhile* not *meantime*), *the king had not been idle.*

mean time *or* **mean solar time** *n.* the times, at a particular place, measured in terms of the passage of the mean sun, giving 24-hour days (mean solar days) throughout a year.

meany (ˈmiːnɪ) *n., pl.* **meanies.** a variant of **meanie.**

Mearns (mɛənz) *n.* **the.** another name for **Kincardineshire.**

measles (ˈmiːzəlz) *n.* (*functioning as sing.*) **1.** a highly contagious viral disease common in children, characterized by fever, profuse nasal discharge of mucus, conjunctivitis, and a rash of small red spots. See also **German measles. 2.** a disease of cattle, sheep, and pigs, caused by infestation with tapeworm larvae. [C14: from MLow G *masele* spot on the skin; infl. by ME *mesel* leper, from L *misellus*, dim. of *miser* wretched]

measly (ˈmiːzlɪ) *adj.* **-slier, -sliest. 1.** *Inf.* meagre in quality or quantity. **2.** (of meat) infested with tapeworm larvae. **3.** having or relating to measles. [C17: see MEASLES]

measurable (ˈmɛʒərəb[ə]l) *adj.* able to be measured; perceptible or significant. — **'measurably** *adv.*

measure (ˈmɛʒə) *n.* **1.** the extent, quantity, amount, or degree of something, as determined by measurement or calculation. **2.** a device for measuring distance, volume, etc., such as a graduated scale or container. **3.** a system of measurement: *metric measure.* **4.** a standard used in a system of measurements. **5.** a specific or standard amount of something: *a measure of grain; full measure.* **6.** a basis or standard for comparison. **7.** reasonable or permissible limit or bounds: *within measure.* **8.** degree or extent (often in **in some measure, in a measure,** etc.): *a measure of freedom.* **9.** (*often pl.*) a particular action intended to achieve an effect. **10.** a legislative bill, act, or resolution. **11.** *Music.* another word for **bar**[1] (sense 15). **12.** *Prosody.* poetic rhythm or cadence; metre. **13.** a metrical foot. **14.** *Poetic.* a melody or tune. **15.** the act of measuring; measurement. **16.** *Arch.* a dance. **17.** *Printing.* the width of a page or column of type. **18. for good measure.** as an extra precaution or beyond requirements. **19. made to measure.** (of clothes) made to fit an individual purchaser. ~*vb.* **20.** (*tr.; often foll. by up*) to determine the size, amount, etc., of by measurement. **21.** (*intr.*) to make a measurement. **22.** (*tr.*) to estimate or determine. **23.** (*tr.*) to function as a measurement of: *the ohm measures electrical resistance.* **24.** (*tr.*) to bring into competition or conflict with: *he measured his strength against that of his opponent.* **25.** (*intr.*) to be as specified in extent, amount, etc.: *the room measures six feet.* **26.** (*tr.*) to travel or move over as if measuring. ~See also **measure up**. [C13: from OF, from L *mēnsūra*, from *mēnsus*, p.p. of *mētīri* to measure]

measured ('mɛʒəd) *adj.* **1.** determined by measurement. **2.** slow or stately. **3.** carefully considered; deliberate. —'**measuredly** *adv.*

measureless ('mɛʒəlɪs) *adj.* limitless, vast, or infinite. —'**measurelessly** *adv.*

measurement ('mɛʒəmənt) *n.* **1.** the act or process of measuring. **2.** an amount, extent, or size determined by measuring. **3.** a system of measures based on a particular standard.

measures ('mɛʒəz) *pl. n.* rock strata that are characterized by a particular type of sediment or deposit: *coal measures.*

measure up *vb.* **1.** (*adv.*) to determine the size of (something) by measurement. **2. measure up to.** to fulfil (expectations, standards, etc.).

measuring jug *n.* a graduated jug used in cooking to measure ingredients.

measuring worm *n.* the larva of a geometrid moth: it moves in a series of loops. Also called: **inchworm.**

meat (miːt) *n.* **1.** the flesh of mammals used as food. **2.** anything edible, esp. flesh with the texture of meat: *crab meat.* **3.** food, as opposed to drink. **4.** the essence or gist. **5.** an archaic word for **meal**[1]. **6. meat and drink.** a source of pleasure. [OE *mete*] —'**meatless** *adj.*

meatball ('miːt,bɔːl) *n.* **1.** minced beef, shaped into a ball before cooking. **2.** *U.S. & Canad. sl.* a stupid or boring person.

Meath (miːð, miːθ) *n.* a county of E Ireland, in Leinster province on the Irish Sea: formerly a kingdom much larger than the present county; livestock farming. County town: Trim. Pop.: 103 762 (1986). Area: 2338 sq. km (903 sq. miles).

meatus (mɪ'eɪtəs) *n., pl.* **-tuses** *or* **-tus.** *Anat.* a natural opening or channel, such as the canal leading from the outer ear to the eardrum. [C17: from L: passage, from *meāre* to pass]

meaty ('miːtɪ) *adj.* **meatier, meatiest. 1.** of, relating to, or full of meat. **2.** heavily built; fleshy or brawny. **3.** full of import or interest: *a meaty discussion.* —'**meatily** *adv.* —'**meatiness** *n.*

Mecca *or* **Mekka** ('mɛkə) *n.* **1.** a city in W Saudi Arabia, joint capital (with Riyadh) of Saudi Arabia: birthplace of Mohammed; the holiest city of Islam, containing the Kaaba. Pop.: 550 000 (1980). Arabic name: **Makkah. 2.** (*sometimes not cap.*) a place that attracts many visitors: *Athens is a Mecca for tourists.*

Meccano (mɪ'kɑːnəʊ) *n. Trademark.* a construction set of miniature metal parts from which mechanical models can be made.

mech. *abbrev. for:* **1.** mechanical. **2.** mechanics. **3.** mechanism.

mechanic (mɪ'kænɪk) *n.* a person skilled in maintaining or operating machinery, motors, etc. [C14: from L *mēchanicus,* from Gk, from *mēkhanē* MACHINE]

mechanical (mɪ'kænɪk³l) *adj.* **1.** made, performed, or operated by or as if by a machine or machinery. **2.** concerned with machines or machinery. **3.** relating to or controlled or operated by physical forces. **4.** of or concerned with mechanics. **5.** (of a gesture, etc.) automatic; lacking thought, feeling, etc. **6.** *Philosophy.* accounting for phenomena by physically determining forces. —**me'chanicalism** *n.* —**me'chanically** *adv.* —**me'chanicalness** *n.*

mechanical advantage *n.* the ratio of the working force exerted by a mechanism to the applied effort.

mechanical drawing *n.* a drawing to scale of a machine, machine component, architectural plan, etc., from which dimensions can be taken.

mechanical engineering *n.* the branch of engineering concerned with the design, construction, and operation of machines.

mechanical equivalent of heat *n. Physics.* a factor for converting units of energy into heat units.

mechanician (,mɛkə'nɪʃən) *or* **mechanist** *n.* a person skilled in making machinery and tools; technician.

mechanics (mɪ'kænɪks) *n.* **1.** (*functioning as sing.*) the branch of science, divided into statics, dynamics, and kinematics, concerned with the equilibrium or motion of bodies in a particular frame of reference. **2.** (*functioning*

as sing.) the science of designing, constructing, and operating machines. **3.** the working parts of a machine. **4.** the technical aspects of something.

mechanism ('mɛkə,nɪzəm) *n.* **1.** a system or structure of moving parts that performs some function, esp. in a machine. **2.** something resembling a machine in the arrangement and working of its parts. **3.** any mechanical device or part of such a device. **4.** a process or technique: *the mechanism of novel writing.* **5.** *Philosophy.* the doctrine that human action can be explained in purely physical terms. **6.** *Psychoanal.* **a.** the ways in which psychological forces interact and operate. **b.** a structure having an influence on the behaviour of a person, such as a defence mechanism.

mechanistic (,mɛkə'nɪstɪk) *adj.* **1.** *Philosophy.* of or relating to the theory of mechanism. **2.** *Maths.* of or relating to mechanics. —'**mechanist** *n.* —,**mecha'nistically** *adv.*

mechanize *or* **-ise** ('mɛkə,naɪz) *vb.* (*tr.*) **1.** to equip (a factory, industry, etc.) with machinery. **2.** to make mechanical, automatic, or monotonous. **3.** to equip (an army, etc.) with motorized or armoured vehicles. —,**mechani'zation** *or* **-i'sation** *n.* —'**mecha,nizer** *or* **-iser** *n.*

mechanotherapy (,mɛkənəʊ'θɛrəpɪ) *n.* the treatment of disorders or injuries by means of mechanical devices, esp. devices that provide exercise for feeble parts.

Mechelen ('mɛxələn) *n.* a city in N Belgium, in Antwerp province: capital of the Netherlands from 1507 to 1530; formerly famous for lace-making; now has an important vegetable market. Pop.: 75 808 (1987 est.). French name: **Malines.** English name: **Mechlin.**

Mechlin ('mɛklɪn) *n.* the English name for **Mechelen.**

Mechlin lace *n.* bobbin lace made at Mechlin, characterized by patterns outlined by a heavier flat thread. Also called: **malines.**

Mecklenburg ('mɛklən,bɜːg; *German* 'meːklənbʊrk) *n.* a region and former state of NE Germany, along the Baltic coast: divided in 1952 into the East German administrative districts of Rostock, Schwerin, and Neubrandenburg.

meconium (mɪ'kəʊnɪəm) *n.* the first faeces of a newborn infant. [C17: from NL, from L: poppy juice, from Gk, from *mēkōn* poppy]

meconopsis (,miːkən'ɒpsɪs) *n.* any of various mainly Asiatic poppies. [C19: from Gk *mekon* poppy + -OPSIS]

Med (mɛd) *n. Inf.* the Mediterranean region.

MEd *abbrev. for* Master of Education.

med. *abbrev. for:* **1.** medical. **2.** medicine. **3.** medieval. **4.** medium.

médaillons (*French* medajɔ̃) *pl. n. Cookery.* small round pieces of meat, fish, vegetables, etc. Also called: **medallions.**

medal ('mɛd³l) *n.* a small flat piece of metal bearing an inscription or image, given as an award or commemoration of some outstanding event, etc. [C16: from F *médaille,* prob. from It. *medaglia,* ult. from L *metallum* METAL]

medallion (mɪ'dæljən) *n.* **1.** a large medal. **2.** an oval or circular decorative device resembling a medal, usually bearing a portrait or relief moulding, used in architecture and textile design. [C17: from F, from It., from *medaglia* MEDAL]

medallist *or U.S.* **medalist** ('mɛd³lɪst) *n.* **1.** a designer, maker, or collector of medals. **2.** *Chiefly sport.* a recipient of a medal or medals.

medal play *n. Golf.* another name for **stroke play.**

Medan ('mɛdɑːn) *n.* a city in Indonesia, in NE Sumatra: seat of the University of North Sumatra (1952) and the Indonesian Islam University (1952). Pop.: 1 378 955 (1980).

Medawar ('mɛdəwə) *n.* Sir **Peter Brian.** 1915–87, English zoologist, who shared the Nobel prize for physiology or medicine (1960) with Sir Macfarlane Burnet for work on immunology.

meddle ('mɛd³l) *vb.* (*intr.*) **1.** (usually foll. by *with*) to interfere officiously or annoyingly. **2.** (usually foll. by *in*) to involve oneself unwarrantedly. [C14: from OF *medler,* ult. from L *miscēre* to mix] —'**meddler** *n.* —'**meddling** *adj.*

meddlesome ('mɛd³lsəm) *adj.* intrusive or meddling. —'**meddlesomely** *adv.* —'**meddlesomeness** *n.*

Mede (miːd) n. a member of an Indo-European people who established an empire in SW Asia in the 7th and 6th centuries B.C. —'**Median** n., adj.

Medea (mɪˈdɪə) n. Greek myth. a princess of Colchis, who assisted Jason in obtaining the Golden Fleece from her father.

Medellín (Spanish meðeˈʎin) n. a city in W Colombia, at an altitude of 1554 m (5100 ft.): the second largest city in the country, with three universities; important coffee centre, with large textile mills. Pop.: 1 506 050 (1985).

media (ˈmiːdɪə) n. 1. a plural of **medium**. 2. the mass media collectively.

Media (ˈmiːdɪə) n. an ancient country of SW Asia, south of the Caspian Sea: inhabited by the Medes; overthrew the Assyrian Empire in 612 B.C. in alliance with Babylonia; conquered by Cyrus the Great in 550 B.C.; corresponds to present-day NW Iran.

mediaeval (ˌmɛdɪˈiːvəl) adj. a variant spelling of **medieval**.

media event n. an event that is staged for or exploited by the mass media.

medial (ˈmiːdɪəl) adj. 1. of or situated in the middle. 2. ordinary or average in size. 3. Maths. relating to an average. 4. another word for **median** (senses 1, 2). [C16: from LL mediālis, from medius middle] —'**medially** adv.

median (ˈmiːdɪən) adj. 1. of, relating to, situated in, or directed towards the middle. 2. Statistics. of or relating to the median. ~n. 3. a middle point, plane, or part. 4. Geom. **a.** a straight line joining one vertex of a triangle to the midpoint of the opposite side. **b.** a straight line joining the midpoints of the nonparallel sides of a trapezium. 5. Statistics. the middle value in a frequency distribution, below and above which lie values with equal total frequencies. 6. Statistics. the middle number or average of the two middle numbers in an ordered sequence of numbers. [C16: from L mediānus, from medius middle] —'**medianly** adv.

mediant (ˈmiːdɪənt) n. Music. **a.** the third degree of a minor scale. **b.** (as modifier): a mediant chord. [C18: from It. mediante, from LL mediāre to be in the middle]

mediastinum (ˌmiːdɪəˈstaɪnəm) n., pl. **-na** (-nə). Anat. 1. a membrane between two parts of an organ or cavity such as the pleural tissue between the two lungs. 2. the part of the thoracic cavity that lies between the lungs, containing the heart, trachea, etc. [C16: from Medical L, neuter of Med. L mediastīnus median, from L: low grade of servant, from medius mean] —ˌmedias'**tinal** adj.

mediate vb. (ˈmiːdɪˌeɪt). 1. (intr.; usually foll. by between or in) to intervene (between parties or in a dispute) in order to bring about agreement. 2. to bring about (an agreement) between parties in a dispute. 3. to resolve (differences) by mediation. 4. (intr.) to be in an intermediate position. 5. (tr.) to serve as a medium for causing (a result) or transmitting (objects, information, etc.). ~adj. (ˈmiːdɪɪt). 6. occurring as a result of or dependent upon mediation. [C16: from LL mediāre to be in the middle] —'**mediately** adv. —'**medi,ator** n.

mediation (ˌmiːdɪˈeɪʃən) n. the act of mediating; intercession between people, states, etc. in an attempt to reconcile disputed matters.

Medibank (ˈmɛdɪbæŋk) n. (in Australia), a government-run health insurance scheme.

medic[1] (ˈmɛdɪk) n. Inf. a doctor, medical orderly, or medical student. [C17: from MEDICAL]

medic[2] (ˈmɛdɪk) n. the usual U.S. spelling of **medick**.

medicable (ˈmɛdɪkəbəl) adj. potentially able to be treated or cured medically.

medical (ˈmɛdɪkəl) adj. 1. of or relating to the science of medicine or to the treatment of patients by drugs, etc., as opposed to surgery. 2. Inf. a medical examination. [C17: from Med. L medicālis, from L medicus physician, surgeon, from medērī to heal] —'**medically** adv.

medical certificate n. 1. a document stating the result of a satisfactory medical examination. 2. a doctor's certificate giving evidence of a person's unfitness for work.

medical jurisprudence n. another name for **forensic medicine**.

medicament (mɪˈdɪkəmənt, ˈmɛdɪ-) n. a medicine or remedy. [C16: via F from L medicāmentum, from medicāre to cure]

medicate (ˈmɛdɪˌkeɪt) vb. (tr.) 1. to cover or impregnate (a wound, etc.) with an ointment, etc. 2. to treat (a patient) with a medicine. 3. to add a medication to (a bandage, shampoo, etc.). [C17: from L medicāre to heal] —'**medicative** adj.

medication (ˌmɛdɪˈkeɪʃən) n. 1. treatment with drugs or remedies. 2. a drug or remedy.

Medici (ˈmɛdɪtʃɪ, məˈdiːtʃɪ; Italian ˈmɛːdɪtʃi) n. 1. an Italian family of bankers, merchants, and rulers of Florence and Tuscany, prominent in Italian political and cultural history in the 15th, 16th, and 17th centuries, including: 2. **Catherine de'** (kaˈtriːn de). See **Catherine de' Medici. 3. Cosimo I** (ˈkɔːzimo), known as Cosimo the Great. 1519–74, duke of Florence and first grand duke of Tuscany (1569–74). 4. **Cosimo de',** known as Cosimo the Elder. 1389–1464, Italian banker, statesman, and patron of arts, who established the political power of the family in Florence (1434). 5. **Giovanni de',** (dʒoˈvanni de). See **Leo X. 6. Giulio de'** (ˈdʒuːljo de). See **Clement VII. 7. Lorenzo de'** (loˈrɛntso de), known as Lorenzo the Magnificent. 1449–92, Italian statesman, poet, and scholar; ruler of Florence (1469–92) and first patron of Michelangelo. 8. **Maria de'** (maˈriːa de). See **Maria de' Medici.** ~French name: **Médicis** (medisis). —**Medicean** (ˌmɛdɪˈsiːən, -ˈfiː-) adj.

medicinal (mɛˈdɪsɪnəl) adj. 1. relating to or having therapeutic properties. ~n. 2. a medicinal substance. —me'**dicinally** adv.

medicine (ˈmɛdɪsɪn, ˈmɛdsɪn) n. 1. any drug or remedy for use in treating, preventing, or alleviating the symptoms of disease. 2. the science of preventing, diagnosing, alleviating, or curing disease. 3. any nonsurgical branch of medical science. 4. the practice or profession of medicine. 5. something regarded by primitive people as having magical or remedial properties. **6. a taste** (or dose) **of one's own medicine.** an unpleasant experience in retaliation for a similar unkind or aggressive act. **7. take one's medicine.** to accept a deserved punishment. [C13: via OF from L medicīna (ars) (art) of healing, from medicus doctor, from medērī to heal]

medicine ball n. a heavy ball used for physical training.

medicine man n. (among certain peoples, esp. North American Indians) a person believed to have supernatural powers of healing; a magician or sorcerer.

medick or U.S. **medic** (ˈmɛdɪk) n. any of various small plants having yellow or purple flowers and trifoliate leaves. [C15: from L mēdica, from Gk mēdikē (poa) Median (grass), a type of clover]

medico (ˈmɛdɪˌkəʊ) n., pl. **-cos.** Inf. a doctor or medical student. [C17: via It. from L medicus]

medieval or **mediaeval** (ˌmɛdɪˈiːvəl) adj. 1. of, relating to, or in the style of the Middle Ages. 2. Inf. old-fashioned; primitive. [C19: from NL medium aevum the middle age]

Medieval Greek n. the Greek language from the 7th century A.D. to shortly after the sacking of Constantinople in 1204. Also called: **Middle Greek, Byzantine Greek.**

medievalism or **mediaevalism** (ˌmɛdɪˈiːvəˌlɪzəm) n. 1. the beliefs, life, or style of the Middle Ages or devotion to those. 2. a belief, custom, or point of style copied or surviving from the Middle Ages.

medievalist or **mediaevalist** (ˌmɛdɪˈiːvəlɪst) n. a student or devotee of the Middle Ages.

Medieval Latin n. the Latin language as used throughout Europe in the Middle Ages.

Medina (mɛˈdiːnə) n. a city in W Saudi Arabia, in Hejaz province: the second most holy city of Islam (after Mecca), with the tomb of Mohammed; university (1960). Pop.: 290 000 (1980 est.). Arabic name: **Al Madinah.**

mediocre (ˌmiːdɪˈəʊkə) adj. Often derog. average or ordinary in quality. [C16: via F from L mediocris moderate, lit.: halfway up the mountain, from medius middle + ocris stony mountain]

mediocrity (ˌmiːdɪˈɒkrɪtɪ, ˌmɛd-) n., pl. **-ties. 1.** the state or quality of being mediocre. 2. a mediocre person or thing.

Medit. abbrev. for Mediterranean.

meditate (ˈmɛdɪˌteɪt) vb. 1. (intr.; foll. by on or upon) to think about something deeply. 2. (intr.) to reflect deeply on spiritual matters, esp. as a religious act. 3. (tr.) to plan, consider, or think of doing (something). [C16: from L meditārī to reflect upon] —'**meditative** adj. —'**meditatively** adv. —'**medi,tator** n.

meditation (ˌmɛdɪ'teɪʃən) n. 1. the act of meditating; reflection. 2. contemplation of spiritual matters, esp. as a religious practice.

Mediterranean (ˌmɛdɪtə'reɪnɪən) n. 1. short for the **Mediterranean Sea**. 2. a native or inhabitant of a Mediterranean country. ~adj. 3. of, relating to, situated or dwelling near the Mediterranean Sea. 4. denoting a postulated subdivision of the Caucasoid race, characterized by slender build and dark complexion. 5. Meteorol. (of a climate) characterized by hot summers and relatively warm winters when most of the annual rainfall occurs. 6. (often not cap.) Obs. situated in the middle of a landmass; inland. [C16: from L mediterrāneus, from medius middle + -terrāneus, from terra land]

Mediterranean Sea n. a large inland sea between S Europe, N Africa, and SW Asia: linked with the Atlantic by the Strait of Gibraltar, with the Red Sea by the Suez Canal, and with the Black Sea by the Dardanelles, Sea of Marmara, and Bosporus; many ancient civilizations developed around its shores. Greatest depth: 4770 m (15 900 ft.). Length: (west to east) over 3700 km (2300 miles). Greatest width: about 1368 km (850 miles). Area: (excluding the Black Sea) 2 512 300 sq. km (970 000 sq. miles). Ancient name: **Mare Internum**.

medium ('miːdɪəm) adj. 1. midway between extremes; average. ~n., pl. **-dia** or **-diums**. 2. an intermediate or middle state, degree, or condition; mean: the happy medium. 3. an intervening substance or agency for transmitting or producing an effect; vehicle. 4. a means or agency for communicating or diffusing information, news, etc., to the public. 5. a person supposedly used as a spiritual intermediary between the dead and the living. 6. the substance in which specimens of animals and plants are preserved or displayed. 7. Biol. Also called: **culture medium**. a nutritive substance in which cultures of bacteria or fungi are grown. 8. the substance or surroundings in which an organism naturally lives or grows. 9. Art. a. the category of a work of art, as determined by its materials and methods of production. b. the materials used in a work of art. 10. any solvent in which pigments are mixed and thinned. [C16: from L: neuter sing. of medius middle]
▷ Usage. Careful writers and speakers do not use media as a singular noun when referring to a medium of mass communication: television is a valuable medium (not media) for advertising.

medium-dated adj. (of a gilt-edged security) having between five and fifteen years to run before redemption. Cf. **long-dated, short-dated**.

medium frequency n. a radio-frequency band or radio frequency lying between 3000 and 300 kilohertz. Abbrev: **MF**.

medium wave n. a. a radio wave with a wavelength between 100 and 1000 metres. b. (as modifier): a medium-wave broadcast.

medlar ('mɛdlə) n. 1. a small Eurasian tree. 2. its fruit, which resembles the crab apple and is not edible until it has begun to decay. [C14: from OF medlier, from L mespilum medlar fruit, from Gk mespilon]

medley ('mɛdlɪ) n. 1. a mixture of various types or elements. 2. a musical composition consisting of various tunes arranged as a continuous whole. 3. Also called: **medley relay. a.** Swimming. a race in which a different stroke is used for each length. b. Athletics. a relay race in which each leg has a different distance. [C14: from OF medlee, from medler to mix, quarrel]

Médoc (meɪ'dɒk, 'mɛdɒk; French medɔk) n. a district of SW France, on the left bank of the Gironde estuary: famous vineyards.

medulla (mɪ'dʌlə) n., pl. **-las** or **-lae** (-liː). 1. Anat. a. the innermost part of an organ or structure. b. short for **medulla oblongata**. 2. Bot. another name for **pith** (sense 4). [C17: from L: marrow, prob. from medius middle] —**me'dullary** or **me'dullar** adj.

medulla oblongata (ˌɒblɒŋ'gɑːtə) n., pl. **medulla oblongatas** or **medullae oblongatae** (mɪ'dʌliː ˌɒblɒŋ'gɑːtiː). the lower stalklike section of the brain, continuous with the spinal cord, containing control centres for the heart and lungs. [C17: NL: oblong-shaped medulla]

medusa (mɪ'djuːzə) n., pl. **-sas** or **-sae** (-ziː). another name for **jellyfish** (sense 1). [C18: from the likeness of its tentacles to the snaky locks of Medusa] —**me'dusoid** adj., n.

Medusa (mɪ'djuːzə) n. Greek myth. a mortal woman who was transformed by Athena into one of the three Gorgons. Her appearance was so hideous that those who looked directly at her were turned to stone. Perseus eventually slew her. See also **Pegasus**[1]. —**Me'dusan** adj.

Medway ('mɛdˌweɪ) n. a river in SE England, flowing through Kent and the **Medway towns** (Rochester, Chatham, and Gillingham) to the Thames estuary. Length: 110 km (70 miles).

meed (miːd) n. Arch. a recompense; reward. [OE: wages]

meek (miːk) adj. 1. patient, long-suffering, or submissive; humble. 2. spineless or spiritless; compliant. [C12: rel. to ON mjūkr amenable] —**'meekly** adv. —**'meekness** n.

meerkat ('mɪəˌkæt) n. any of several South African mongooses, esp. the slender-tailed meerkat or suricate, which has a lemur-like face and four-toed feet. [C19: from Du.: sea-cat]

meerschaum ('mɪəʃəm) n. 1. a white, yellowish, or pink compact earthy mineral consisting of hydrated magnesium silicate: used to make tobacco pipes and as a building stone. 2. a tobacco pipe having a bowl made of this mineral. [C18: from G Meerschaum lit.: sea foam]

Meerut ('mɪərət) n. an industrial city in N India, in W Uttar Pradesh: founded as a military base by the British in 1806 and scene of the first uprising (1857) of the Indian Mutiny. Pop.: 417 288 (1981).

meet[1] (miːt) vb. **meeting, met.** 1. (sometimes foll. by up or (U.S.) with) to come together (with), either by design or by accident; encounter. 2. to come into or be in conjunction or contact with (something or each other). 3. (tr.) to come to or be at the place of arrival of: to meet a train. 4. to make the acquaintance of or be introduced to (someone or each other). 5. to gather in the company of (someone or each other). 6. to come into the presence of (someone or each other) as opponents. 7. (tr.) to cope with effectively; satisfy: to meet someone's demands. 8. (tr.) to be apparent to (esp. in **meet the eye**). 9. (tr.) to return or counter: to meet a blow with another. 10. to agree with (someone or each other): we met him on the price he suggested. 11. (tr.; sometimes foll. by with) to experience; suffer: he met his death in a road accident. 12. (intr.) to occur together: courage and kindliness met in him. ~n. 13. the assembly of hounds, huntsmen, etc., prior to a hunt. 14. a meeting, esp. a sports meeting. [OE mētan] —**'meeter** n.

meet[2] (miːt) adj. Arch. proper, fitting, or correct. [C13: from var. of OE gemǣte] —**'meetly** adv.

meeting ('miːtɪŋ) n. 1. an act of coming together; encounter. 2. an assembly or gathering. 3. a conjunction or union. 4. a sporting competition, as of athletes, or of horse racing.

meeting house n. the place in which certain religious groups, esp. Quakers, hold their meetings for worship.

mega ('mɛgə) adj. Sl. extremely good, great, or successful. [C20: prob. independent use of MEGA-]

mega- combining form. 1. denoting 10[6]: megawatt. Symbol: M 2. (in computer technology) denoting 2[20] (1 048 576): megabyte. 3. large or great: megalith. 4. Inf. greatest: megastar. [from Gk megas huge, powerful]

megabit ('mɛgəˌbɪt) n. Computers. 1. one million bits. 2. 2[20] bits.

megabuck ('mɛgəˌbʌk) n. U.S. & Canad. sl. a million dollars.

megacephaly (ˌmɛgə'sɛfəlɪ) or **megalocephaly** n. the condition of having an unusually large head or cranial capacity. —**megacephalic** (ˌmɛgəsɪ'fælɪk), **mega'cephalous**, **megaloce'phalic**, or **megalo'cephalous** adj.

megacycle ('mɛgəˌsaɪkl) n. a former unit of frequency equal to one million cycles per second; megahertz.

megadeath ('mɛgəˌdɛθ) n. the death of a million people, esp. in a nuclear war or attack.

Megaera (mɪ'dʒɪərə) n. Greek myth. one of the three Furies; the others are Alecto and Tisiphone.

megaflop ('mɛgəˌflɒp) n. Computers. a measure of processing speed, consisting of a million floating-point operations a second. [C20: from MEGA- + flo(ating) p(oint)]

megahertz ('mɛgəˌhɜːts) n., pl. **megahertz**. one million hertz. Former name: **megacycle**.

megalith ('mɛgəlɪθ) n. a stone of great size, esp. one forming part of a prehistoric monument. —**mega'lithic** adj.

megalo- or before a vowel **megal-** combining form. indicating greatness or abnormal size: megalopolis. [from Gk megas great]

megalomania (ˌmɛgələʊ'meɪnɪə) n. 1. a mental illness characterized by delusions of grandeur, power, wealth, etc. 2. *Inf.* a lust or craving for power. —ˌmegalo'maniac *adj., n.* —**megalomaniacal** (ˌmɛgələʊmə'naɪəkˀl) *adj.*

megalopolis (ˌmɛgə'lɒpəlɪs) n. an urban complex, usually comprising several large towns. [C20: MEGALO- + Gk *polis* city] —**megalopolitan** (ˌmɛgələ'pɒlɪtˀn) *adj., n.*

megalosaur (ˈmɛgələʊˌsɔː) n. any very large Jurassic or Cretaceous bipedal carnivorous dinosaur. [C19: from NL *megalosaurus*, from MEGALO- + Gk *sauros* lizard]

megaphone (ˈmɛgəˌfəʊn) n. a funnel-shaped instrument used to amplify the voice. See also **loud-hailer**. —**megaphonic** (ˌmɛgə'fɒnɪk) *adj.*

megapode (ˈmɛgəˌpəʊd) n. any of various ground-living gallinaceous birds of Australia, New Guinea, and adjacent islands. Their eggs incubate in mounds of sand, rotting vegetation, etc., by natural heat.

Megara (ˈmɛgərə) n. a town in E central Greece: an ancient trading city, founding many colonies in the 7th and 8th centuries B.C. Pop.: 17 719 (1981).

megathere (ˈmɛgəˌθɪə) n. any of various gigantic extinct American sloths, common in late Cenozoic times. [C19: from NL *megathērium*, from MEGA- + *-there*, from Gk *thērion* wild beast]

megaton (ˈmɛgəˌtʌn) n. 1. one million tons. 2. an explosive power, esp. of a nuclear weapon, equal to the power of one million tons of TNT.

megawatt (ˈmɛgəˌwɒt) n. one million watts.

Me generation n. **the.** the generation, originally in the 1970s, characterized by self-absorption; latterly, in the 1980s, characterized by material greed.

Megger (ˈmɛgə) n. *Trademark.* an instrument that generates a high voltage in order to test the resistance of insulation, etc.

Meghalaya (ˌmeɪgə'leɪə) n. a state of NE India, created in 1969 from part of Assam. Capital: Shillong. Pop.: 1 328 343 (1981). Area: 22 445 sq. km (7800 sq. miles).

Megiddo (mə'gɪdəʊ) n. an ancient town in N Palestine, strategically located on a route linking Egypt to Mesopotamia: site of many battles, including an important Egyptian victory over rebel chieftains in 1469 or 1468 B.C. See also **Armageddon**.

megilp *or* **magilp** (mə'gɪlp) n. an oil-painting medium of linseed oil mixed with mastic varnish or turpentine. [C18: from ?]

megohm (ˈmɛgˌəʊm) n. one million ohms.

megrim (ˈmiːgrɪm) n. *Arch.* 1. a caprice. 2. a migraine. 3. (*pl.*) *Rare.* a fit of depression. 4. (*pl.*) a disease of horses and cattle; staggers. [C14: see MIGRAINE]

Mehemet Ali (mɪ'hɛmɪt 'ɑːlɪ) *or* **Mohammed Ali** n. 1769–1849, Albanian commander in the service of Turkey. He was made viceroy of Egypt (1805) and its hereditary ruler (1841), founding a dynasty that ruled until 1952.

Meilhac (*French* mɛjak) n. **Henri** (ãri). 1831–97, French dramatist, who collaborated with Halévy on opera libretti, esp. Offenbach's *La Belle Hélène* (1865) and *La Vie parisienne* (1867).

meiosis (maɪ'əʊsɪs) n., *pl.* **-ses** (-ˌsiːz). 1. a type of cell division in which a nucleus divides into four daughter nuclei, each containing half the chromosome number of the parent nucleus. 2. *Rhetoric.* another word for **litotes**. [C16: via NL from Gk, from *meioun* to diminish, from *meiōn* less] —**meiotic** (maɪ'ɒtɪk) *adj.* —**mei'otically** *adv.*

Meir (meɪ'ɪə) n. **Golda** ('gəʊldə) 1898–1978, Israeli statesman, born in Russia; prime minister (1969–74).

Meissen (*German* 'maɪsən) n. a town in SE East Germany, in Dresden district on the River Elbe: famous for its porcelain (Dresden china), begun here in 1710. Pop.: 38 908 (1983 est.).

Meistersinger (ˈmaɪstəˌsɪŋə) n., *pl.* **-singer** *or* **-singers**. a member of one of the German guilds organized to compose and perform poetry and music, esp. in the 15th and 16th centuries. [C19: from G *Meistersinger* master singer]

Meitner (*German* 'maɪtnər) n. **Lise** ('liːzə). 1878–1968, Austrian nuclear physicist. With Hahn, she discovered protactinium (1918), and they demonstrated with F. Strassmann the fission of uranium.

Méjico ('mɛxiko) n. the Spanish name for **Mexico**.

Mekka ('mɛkə) n. a variant spelling of **Mecca**.

Meknès (mɛk'nɛs) n. a city in N central Morocco, in the Middle Atlas Mountains: noted for the making of carpets. Pop.: 319 783 (1982).

Mekong (ˌmiː'kɒŋ) n. a river in SE Asia, rising in SW China in Qinghai province: flows southeast forming the border between Laos and Burma, and part of the border between Laos and Thailand, then continues south across Kampuchea and Vietnam to the South China Sea by an extensive delta, one of the greatest rice-growing areas in Asia. Length: about 4025 km (2500 miles).

melaleuca (ˌmɛlə'luːkə) n. any shrub or tree of the mostly Australian genus *Melaleuca*, found in sandy or swampy regions. [C19: NL from Gk *melas* black + *leukos* white, from its black trunk and white branches]

melamine (ˈmɛləˌmiːn) n. 1. a colourless crystalline compound used in making synthetic resins. Formula: $C_3N_6H_6$. 2. a resin produced from melamine (**melamine resin**) or a material made from this resin. [C19: from G *Melamin*, from *Melam* distillate of ammonium thiocyanate, with *-am* representing *ammonia*]

melancholia (ˌmɛlən'kəʊlɪə) n. a former name for **depression** (sense 3). —ˌmelan'choli,ac *adj., n.*

melancholy (ˈmɛlənkəlɪ) n., *pl.* **-cholies**. 1. a tendency to gloominess or depression. 2. a sad thoughtful state of mind. 3. *Arch.* a. a gloomy character. b. one of the four bodily humours; black bile. ~*adj.* 4. characterized by, causing, or expressing sadness, dejection, etc. [C14: via OF from LL *melancholia*, from Gk, from *melas* black + *kholē* bile] —ˈmelanˌcholic *adj., n.*

Melanchthon (mə'læŋkθən; *German* me'laŋçtɔn) n. **Philipp** ('fiːlɪp). original surname *Schwarzerd*. 1497–1560, German Protestant reformer. His *Loci Communes* (1521) was the first systematic presentation of Protestant theology and in the Augsburg Confession (1530) he stated the faith of the Lutheran churches. He also reformed the German educational system.

Melanesia (ˌmɛlə'niːzɪə) n. one of the three divisions of islands in the Pacific (the others being Micronesia and Polynesia): the SW division of Oceania: includes Fiji, New Caledonia, Vanuatu, the Bismarck Archipelago, and the Louisiade, Solomon, Santa Cruz, and Loyalty Islands, which all lie northeast of Australia. [C19: from Gk *melas* black + *nēsos* island; with reference to the dark skins of the inhabitants; on the model of *Polynesia*]

Melanesian (ˌmɛlə'niːʒən, -ʒɪən) *adj.* 1. of or relating to Melanesia, its people, or their languages. ~n. 2. a native or inhabitant of Melanesia: generally Negroid with frizzy hair and small stature. 3. a group or branch of languages spoken in Melanesia.

melange *or* **mélange** (meɪ'lɑːnʒ) n. a mixture; confusion. [C17: from F *mêler* to mix]

melanin (ˈmɛlənɪn) n. any of a group of black or dark brown pigments present in the hair, skin, and eyes of man and animals: produced in excess in certain skin diseases and in melanomas.

melanism (ˈmɛləˌnɪzəm) n. 1. the condition in man and animals of having dark-coloured or black skin, feathers, etc. 2. another name for **melanosis**. —ˌmela'nistic *adj.*

melano- *or before a vowel* **melan-** *combining form.* black or dark: *melanin; melanism; melanoma.* [from Gk *melas* black]

melanoma (ˌmɛlə'nəʊmə) n., *pl.* **-mas** *or* **-mata** (-mətə). *Pathol.* a tumour composed of darkly pigmented cells.

melanosis (ˌmɛlə'nəʊsɪs) *or* **melanism** (ˈmɛləˌnɪzəm) n. *Pathol.* a skin condition characterized by excessive deposits of melanin. —**melanotic** (ˌmɛlə'nɒtɪk) *adj.*

Melba ('mɛlbə) n. 1. Dame **Nellie**, stage name of *Helen Porter Mitchell*. 1861–1931, Australian operatic soprano. 2. **do a Melba**. *Austral sl.* to make repeated farewell appearances.

Melba toast n. very thin crisp toast. [C20: after Dame Nellie MELBA]

Melbourne[1] ('mɛlbən) n. a port in SE Australia, capital of Victoria, on Port Phillip Bay: the second largest city in the country; settled in 1835 and developed rapidly with the discovery of rich goldfields in 1851; three universities. Pop.: 2 832 893 (1986). —**Melburnian** (mɛl'bɜːnɪən) n., *adj.*

Melbourne[2] ('mɛlbən) n. **William Lamb,** 2nd Viscount. 1779–1848; Whig prime minister (1834; 1835–41). He was the chief political adviser to the young Queen Victoria.

Melchior ('mɛlkɪˌɔ:) n. **1.** (in Christian tradition) one of the Magi, the others being Balthazar and Caspar. **2. Lauritz** ('laurɪts). 1890–1973, U.S. operatic tenor, born in Denmark.

Melchizedek (mɛl'kɪzəˌdɛk) n. Old Testament. the priest-king of Salem who blessed Abraham (Genesis 14:18-19) and was taken as a prototype of Christ's priesthood (Hebrews 7). Douay spelling: **Melchisedech.**

meld[1] (mɛld) vb. to blend or become blended; combine. [C20: blend of MELT + WELD[1]]

meld[2] (mɛld) vb. **1.** (in some card games) to declare or lay down (cards), which then score points. ~n. **2.** the act of melding. **3.** a set of cards for melding. [C19: from G melden to announce]

Meleager (ˌmɛlɪ'eɪgə) n. Greek myth. one of the Argonauts, slayer of the Calydonian boar.

melee or **mêlée** ('mɛleɪ) n. a noisy riotous fight or brawl. [C17: from F mêlée, from mêler to mix]

Méliès (French meljɛs) n. **Georges** (ʒɔrʒ). 1861–1938, French pioneer film director.

Melilla (French melija) n. the chief town of a Spanish enclave in Morocco, on the Mediterranean coast: founded by the Phoenicians; exports iron ore. Pop.: 58 449 (1970).

meliorate ('mi:lɪəˌreɪt) vb. a variant of **ameliorate.** —ˌmelio'ration n. —**meliorative** ('mi:lɪərətɪv) adj., n.

melisma (mɪ'lɪzmə) n., pl. **-mata** (-mətə) or **-mas.** Music. an expressive vocal phrase or passage consisting of several notes sung to one syllable [C19: from Gk: melody]

Melitopol (Russian mɪlɪ'tɔpəlj) n. a city in the SW Soviet Union, in the SE Ukrainian SSR. Pop.: 174 000 (1987).

melliferous (mɪ'lɪfərəs) or **mellific** (mɪ'lɪfɪk) adj. forming or producing honey. [C17: from L mellifer, from mel honey + ferre to bear]

mellifluous (mɪ'lɪfluəs) or **mellifluent** adj. (of sounds or utterances) smooth or honeyed; sweet. [C15: from LL mellifluus, from L mel honey + fluere to flow] —**mel'lifluously** adv. —**mel'lifluousness** or **mel'lifluence** n.

mellow ('mɛləu) adj. **1.** (esp. of fruits) full-flavoured; sweet; ripe. **2.** (esp. of wines) well-matured. **3.** (esp. of colours or sounds) soft or rich. **4.** kind-hearted, esp. through maturity or old age. **5.** genial, as through the effects of alcohol. **6.** (of soil) soft and loamy. ~vb. **7.** to make or become mellow. [C15: ?from OE meru soft (as through ripeness)] —**'mellowness** n.

melodeon or **melodion** (mɪ'ləudɪən) n. Music. **1.** a type of small accordion. **2.** a type of keyboard instrument similar to the harmonium. [C19: from G, from Melodie melody]

melodic (mɪ'lɒdɪk) adj. **1.** of or relating to melody. **2.** of or relating to a part in a piece of music. **3.** melodious. —me'lodically adv.

melodic minor scale n. Music. a minor scale modified from the natural by the sharpening of the sixth and seventh when taken in ascending order and the restoration of their original pitches when taken in descending order.

melodious (mɪ'ləudɪəs) adj. **1.** having a tune that is pleasant to the ear. **2.** of or relating to melody; melodic. —me'lodiously adv. —me'lodiousness n.

melodist ('mɛlədɪst) n. **1.** a composer of melodies. **2.** a singer.

melodize or **-ise** ('mɛləˌdaɪz) vb. **1.** (tr.) to provide with a melody. **2.** (tr.) to make melodious. **3.** (intr.) to sing or play melodies. —**'melo,dizer** or **-iser** n.

melodrama ('mɛləˌdrɑ:mə) n. **1.** a play, film, etc., characterized by extravagant action and emotion. **2.** (formerly) a romantic drama characterized by sensational incident, music, and song. **3.** overdramatic emotion or behaviour. [C19: from F mélodrame, from Gk melos song + drame DRAMA] —**melodramatist** (ˌmɛlə'dræmətɪst) n. —**melodramatic** (ˌmɛlədrə'mætɪk) adj. —ˌmelodra'matics pl. n. —ˌmelodra'matically adv.

melody ('mɛlədɪ) n., pl. **-dies.** Music. **a.** a succession of notes forming a distinctive sequence; tune. **b.** the horizontally represented aspect of the structure of a piece of music. Cf. harmony (sense 4b). **2.** sounds that are pleasant because of tone or arrangement, esp. words of poetry. [C13: from OF, from LL melōdia, from Gk melōidia, from melos song + ōidein to sing]

melon ('mɛlən) n. **1.** any of several varieties of trailing plants (see **muskmelon, watermelon**), cultivated for their edible fruit. **2.** the fruit of any of these plants, which has a hard rind and juicy flesh. [C14: via OF from LL mēlo,

form of mēlopepō, from Gk, from mēlon apple + pepōn gourd]

Melos ('mi:lɒs) n. an island in the SW Aegean Sea, in the Cyclades: of volcanic origin, with hot springs; centre of early Aegean civilization, where the Venus de Milo was found. Pop.: 4554 (1981). Area: 132 sq. km (51 sq. miles). Modern Greek name: **Mílos.**

Melpomene (mɛl'pɒmɪnɪ) n. Greek myth. the Muse of tragedy.

melt (mɛlt) vb. **melting, melted; melted** or **molten.** **1.** to liquefy (a solid) or (of a solid) to become liquefied, as a result of the action of heat. **2.** to become or make liquid; dissolve. **3.** (often foll. by away) to disappear; fade. **4.** (foll. by down) to melt (metal scrap) for reuse. **5.** (often foll. by into) to blend or cause to blend gradually. **6.** to make or become emotional or sentimental; soften. ~n. **7.** the act or process of melting. **8.** something melted or an amount melted. [OE meltan to digest] —**'meltable** adj. —**'melter** n. —**'meltingly** adv.

meltdown ('mɛlt,daun) n. **1.** (in a nuclear reactor) the melting of the fuel rods as a result of a defect in the cooling system, with the possible escape of radiation. **2.** Inf. a sudden disastrous failure with potential for widespread harm, as a stock-exchange crash.

melting point n. the temperature at which a solid turns into a liquid.

melting pot n. **1.** a pot in which metals or other substances are melted, esp. in order to mix them. **2.** an area in which many races, ideas, etc., are mixed.

melton ('mɛltən) n. a heavy smooth woollen fabric with a short nap. Also called: **melton cloth.** [C19: from Melton Mowbray, Leicestershire, a former centre for making this]

meltwater ('mɛlt,wɔ:tə) n. melted snow or ice.

Melville ('mɛlvɪl) n. **Herman.** 1819–91, U.S. novelist and short-story writer. Among his works, Moby Dick (1851) and Billy Budd (written 1891, published 1924) are outstanding.

Melville Island n. **1.** an island in the Arctic Ocean, north of Victoria Island: administratively part of the Northwest Territories of Canada. Area: 41 865 sq. km (16 164 sq. miles). **2.** an island in the Arafura Sea, off the N central coast of Australia, separated from the mainland by Clarence Strait. Area: 6216 sq. km (2400 sq. miles).

Melville Peninsula n. a peninsula of N Canada, in the Northwest Territories, between the Gulf of Boothia and Foxe Basin.

mem. abbrev. for: **1.** member. **2.** memoir. **3.** memorandum. **4.** memorial.

member ('mɛmbə) n. **1.** a person who belongs to a club, political party, etc. **2.** any individual plant or animal in a taxonomic group. **3.** any part of an animal body, such as a limb. **4.** any part of a plant, such as a petal, root, etc. **5.** Maths, logic. any individual object belonging to a set or logical class. **6.** a component part of a building or construction. [C13: from L membrum limb, part] —**'memberless** adj.

Member ('mɛmbə) n. (sometimes not cap.) **1.** short for **Member of Parliament. 2.** short for **Member of Congress. 3.** a member of some other legislative body.

Member of Congress n. a member of the U.S. Congress, esp. of the House of Representatives.

Member of Parliament n. a member of the House of Commons or similar legislative body, as in many Commonwealth countries.

membership ('mɛmbəʃɪp) n. **1.** the members of an organization collectively. **2.** the state of being a member.

membrane ('mɛmbreɪn) n. **1.** any thin pliable sheet of material. **2.** a pliable sheetlike usually fibrous tissue that covers, lines, or connects plant and animal organs or cells. [C16: from L membrāna skin covering a part of the body, from membrum MEMBER] —**membranous** ('mɛmbrənəs) or **membraneous** (mɛm'breɪnɪəs) adj.

Memel ('me:məl) n. **1.** the German name for **Klaipeda. 2.** the lower course of the Neman River.

memento (mɪ'mɛntəu) n., pl. **-tos** or **-toes.** something that reminds one of past events; a souvenir. [C15: from L, imperative of meminisse to remember]

memento mori ('mɔ:ri:) n., pl. **memento mori.** an object, such as a skull, intended to remind people of death. [C16: L: remember you must die]

Memling ('mɛmlɪŋ) or **Memlinc** ('mɛmlɪŋk) n. **Hans** (hans). ?1430–94, Flemish painter of religious works and portraits.

Memnon ('mɛmnɒn) n. **1.** *Greek myth.* a king of Ethiopia, son of Eos: slain by Achilles in the Trojan War. **2.** a colossal statue of Amenhotep III at Thebes in ancient Egypt, which emitted a sound thought by the Greeks to be the voice of Memnon. —**Memnonian** (mɛm'nəʊnɪən) *adj.*

memo ('mɛməʊ, 'miːməʊ) n., pl. **memos.** short for **memorandum.**

memoir ('mɛmwɑː) n. **1.** a biography or historical account, esp. one based on personal knowledge. **2.** an essay, as on a specialized topic. [C16: from F, from L *memoria* MEMORY] —'**memoirist** n.

memoirs ('mɛmwɑːz) pl. n. **1.** a collection of reminiscences about a period, series of events, etc., written from personal experience or special sources. **2.** an autobiographical record. **3.** a record, as of transactions of a society, etc.

memorabilia (,mɛmərə'bɪlɪə) pl. n., sing. -**rabile** (-'ræbɪlɪ). **1.** memorable events or things. **2.** objects connected with famous people or events. [C17: from L, from *memorābilis* MEMORABLE]

memorable ('mɛmərəb³l) adj. worth remembering or easily remembered. [C15: from L *memorābilis*, from *memorāre* to recall, from *memor* mindful] —,**memora'bility** n. —'**memorably** adv.

memorandum (,mɛmə'rændəm) n., pl. -**dums** or -**da** (-də). **1.** a written statement, record, or communication. **2.** a note of things to be remembered. **3.** an informal diplomatic communication. **4.** *Law.* a short written summary of the terms of a transaction. ~Often (esp. for senses 1, 2) shortened to **memo.** [C15: from L: (something) to be remembered]

memorial (mɪ'mɔːrɪəl) adj. **1.** serving to preserve the memory of the dead or a past event. **2.** of or involving memory. ~n. **3.** something serving as a remembrance. **4.** a written statement of facts submitted to a government, authority, etc., in conjunction with a petition. **5.** an informal diplomatic paper. [C14: from LL *memoriāle* a reminder, neuter of *memoriālis*] —me'**morially** adv.

memorialize or -**ise** (mɪ'mɔːrɪə,laɪz) vb. (tr.) **1.** to honour or commemorate. **2.** to present or address a memorial to.

memorize or -**ise** ('mɛmə,raɪz) vb. (tr.) to commit to memory; learn so as to remember.

memory ('mɛmərɪ) n., pl. -**ries.** **1. a.** the ability of the mind to store and recall past sensations, thoughts, knowledge, etc.: *he can do it from memory.* **b.** the part of the brain that appears to have this function. **2.** the sum of everything retained by the mind. **3.** a particular recollection of an event, person, etc. **4.** the time over which recollection extends: *within his memory.* **5.** commemoration or remembrance: *in memory of our leader.* **6.** the state of being remembered, as after death. **7.** Also called: **store.** a part of a computer in which information is stored for immediate use by the central processing unit. [C14: from OF *memorie*, from L *memoria*, from *memor* mindful]

Memphis ('mɛmfɪs) n. **1.** a port in SW Tennessee, on the Mississippi River: the largest city in the state; a major cotton and timber market; Memphis State University (1909). Pop.: 646 356 (1980). **2.** a ruined city in N Egypt, the ancient centre of Lower Egypt, on the Nile: administrative and artistic centre, sacred to the worship of Ptah. —'**Memphian** adj., n.

Memphremagog (,mɛmfriː'meɪgɒg) n. **Lake.** a lake on the border between the U.S. and Canada, in N Vermont and S Quebec. Length: about 43 km (27 miles). Width: up to 6 km (4 miles).

memsahib ('mɛm,sɑːɪb, -hɪb) n. (formerly, in India) a term of respect used for a European married woman. [C19: from MA'AM + SAHIB]

men (mɛn) n. the plural of **man.**

menace ('mɛnɪs) vb. **1.** to threaten with violence, danger, etc. ~n. **2.** *Literary.* a threat. **3.** something menacing; a source of danger. **4.** *Inf.* a nuisance. [C13: ult. rel. to L *minax* threatening, from *mināri* to threaten] —'**menacer** n. —'**menacing** adj. —'**menacingly** adv.

Menado (mɛ'nɑːdəʊ) or **Manado** n. a port in NE Indonesia, on NE Sulawesi: founded by the Dutch in 1657. Pop.: 217 159 (1980).

ménage (meɪ'nɑːʒ) n. the persons of a household. [C17: from F, from Vulgar L (unattested) *mansiōnāticum* household]

ménage à trois *French.* (menaʒ a trwɑ) n., pl. **ménages à trois** (menaʒ a trwɑ). a sexual arrangement involving a married couple and the lover of one of them. [lit.: household of three]

menagerie (mɪ'nædʒərɪ) n. **1.** a collection of wild animals kept for exhibition. **2.** the place where such animals are housed. [C18: from F: household management, which formerly included care of domestic animals]

Menai Strait ('mɛnaɪ) n. a channel of the Irish Sea between the island of Anglesey and the mainland of NW Wales: famous suspension bridge (1819–26) designed by Thomas Telford and tubular bridge (1846–50) by Robert Stephenson. Length: 24 km (15 miles). Width: up to 3 km (2 miles).

Menam (miː'næm) n. another name for the **Chao Phraya.**

Menander (mə'nændə) n. ?342–?292 B.C., Greek comic dramatist. The *Dyskolos* is his only complete extant comedy but others survive in adaptations by Terence and Plautus.

Mencius ('mɛnʃɪəs, -ʃəs) n. Chinese name *Mengzi* or *Meng-tze.* ?372–?289 B.C., Chinese philosopher, who propounded the ethical system of Confucius.

Mencken ('mɛŋkən) n. **H(enry) L(ouis)** . 1880–1956, U.S. journalist and literary critic, noted for *The American Language* (1919): editor of the *Smart Set* and the *American Mercury*, which he founded (1924).

mend (mɛnd) vb. **1.** (tr.) to repair (something broken or unserviceable). **2.** to improve or undergo improvement; reform (often in **mend one's ways**) . **3.** (intr.) to heal or recover. **4.** (intr.) (of conditions) to improve; become better. ~n. **5.** the act of repairing. **6.** a mended area, esp. on a garment. **7. on the mend.** becoming better, esp. in health. [C12: from AMEND] —'**mendable** adj. —'**mender** n.

mendacity (mɛn'dæsɪtɪ) n., pl. -**ties.** **1.** the tendency to be untruthful. **2.** a falsehood. [C17: from LL *mendācitās*, from L *mendāx* untruthful] —**mendacious** (mɛn'deɪʃəs) adj. —**men'daciously** adv.

Mendel ('mɛnd³l) n. **Gregor Johann** ('greːgɔr jo'han). 1822–84, Austrian monk and botanist; founder of the science of genetics. He developed his theory of organic inheritance from his experiments on the hybridization of green peas. His findings were published (1865) but remained unrecognized until 1900. See **Mendel's laws.**

mendelevium (,mɛndɪ'liːvɪəm) n. a transuranic element artificially produced by bombardment of einsteinium. Symbol: Md; atomic no.: 101; half-life of most stable isotope, ^{258}Md: 60 days (approx.). [C20: after D. I. MENDELEYEV]

Mendeleyev or **Mendeleev** (*Russian* mɪndɪ'ljejɪf) n. **Dmitri Ivanovich** ('dmitrij i'vanəvitʃ). 1834–1907, Russian chemist. He devised the first form of the periodic table of the chemical elements (1869).

Mendel's laws pl. n. the principles of heredity proposed by Gregor Mendel (1822–84). The **Law of Segregation** states that every somatic cell of an individual carries a pair of hereditary units for each character: the pairs separate during meiosis so that each gamete carries only one unit of each pair. The **Law of Independent Assortment** states that the separation of the units of each pair is not influenced by that of any other pair.

Mendelssohn ('mɛnd³lsən; *German* 'mɛndəlzoːn) n. **1. Felix** ('feːlɪks), full name *Jacob Ludwig Felix Mendelssohn-Bartholdy.* 1809–47, German romantic composer. His works include the overtures *A Midsummer Night's Dream* (1826) and *Fingal's Cave* (1832), five symphonies, the oratorio *Elijah* (1846), piano pieces, and songs. He was instrumental in the revival of the music of J. S. Bach in the 19th century. **2.** his grandfather, **Moses** ('moːzəs). 1729–86, German Jewish philosopher. His best-known work is *Jerusalem* (1783), in which he defends Judaism and appeals for religious toleration.

Menderes (,mɛndə'rɛs) n. **1.** a river in SW Turkey flowing southwest, then west to the Aegean. Length: about 386 km (240 miles). Ancient name: **Maeander. 2.** a river in NW Turkey flowing west and northwest to the Dardanelles. Length: 104 km (65 miles). Ancient name: **Scamander.**

Mendès-France (*French* mɛdɛsfrɑ̃s) n. **Pierre** (pjɛr). 1907–82, French statesman; prime minister (1954–55). He concluded the war in Indochina and granted independence to Tunisia.

mendicant ('mɛndɪkənt) *adj.* **1.** begging. **2.** (of a member of a religious order) dependent on alms for sustenance. ~*n.* **3.** a mendicant friar. **4.** a less common word for **beggar**. [C16: from L *mendicāre*, from *mendicus* beggar, from *mendus* flaw] —'**mendicancy** *or* **mendicity** (mɛn'dɪsɪtɪ) *n.*

Mendips ('mɛndɪps) *pl. n.* a range of limestone hills in SW England, in N Somerset: includes the Cheddar Gorge and numerous caves. Highest point: 325 m (1068 ft.). Also called: **Mendip Hills.**

Mendoza[1] (mɛn'dəʊzə; *Spanish* men'doθa) *n.* a city in W central Argentina, in the foothills of the Sierra de los Paramillos: largely destroyed by an earthquake in 1861; commercial centre of an intensively cultivated irrigated region; University of Cuyo (1939). Pop.: 597 000 (1980).

Mendoza[2] (*Spanish* men'doθa) *n.* **Pedro de** ('peðro de). died 1537, Spanish soldier and explorer; founder of Buenos Aires (1536).

meneer (mə'nɪə) *n.* a S. African title of address equivalent to *sir* when used alone or *Mr* when placed before a name. [Afrik.]

Menelaus (,mɛnɪ'leɪəs) *n. Greek myth.* a king of Sparta and the brother of Agamemnon. He was the husband of Helen, whose abduction led to the Trojan War.

Menelik II ('mɛnɪlɪk) *n.* 1844–1913, emperor of Abyssinia (1889–1910). He defeated the Italians at Aduwa (1896), maintaining the independence of Abyssinia in an era of European expansion in Africa.

Menes ('miːniːz) *n.* the first king of the first dynasty of Egypt (?3100 B.C.). He is said to have united Upper and Lower Egypt and founded Memphis.

menfolk ('mɛn,fəʊk) *pl. n.* men collectively, esp. the men of a particular family.

Mengelberg ('mɛŋgəl,bɜːg; *Dutch* 'mɛŋəlberx) *n.* (**Josef**) **Willem** ('wɪləm). 1871–1951, Dutch orchestral conductor, noted for his performances of the music of Mahler.

Mengistu Haile Mariam (mɛŋ'gɪstu: 'haɪlɪ 'mɑːrɪəm) *n.* born 1937, Ethiopian soldier and statesman; head of state from 1977.

Mengzi *or* **Meng-tze** ('mɛŋ'tseɪ) *n.* the Chinese name for **Mencius.**

menhaden (mɛn'heɪdᵊn) *n., pl.* **-den.** a marine North American fish: source of fish meal, fertilizer, and oil. [C18: from Algonquian; prob. rel. to another Amerind word, *munnawhatteaig* fertilizer]

menhir ('mɛnhɪə) *n.* a single standing stone, dating from prehistoric times. [C19: from Breton *men* stone + *hir* long]

menial ('miːnɪəl) *adj.* **1.** consisting of or occupied with work requiring little skill, esp. domestic duties. **2.** of, involving, or befitting servants. **3.** servile. ~*n.* **4.** a domestic servant. **5.** a servile person. [C14: from Anglo-Norman *meignial*, from OF *meinie* household]

meninges (mɪ'nɪndʒiːz) *pl. n., sing.* **meninx** ('miːnɪŋks). the three membranes (**dura mater, arachnoid, pia mater**) that envelop the brain and spinal cord. [C17: from Gk, pl. of *meninx* membrane] —**meningeal** (mɪ'nɪndʒɪəl) *adj.*

meningitis (,mɛnɪn'dʒaɪtɪs) *n.* inflammation of the membranes that surround the brain or spinal cord, caused by infection. —**meningitic** (,mɛnɪn'dʒɪtɪk) *adj.*

meningococcus (mɛ,nɪŋgəʊ'kɒkəs) *n., pl.* **-cocci** (-'kɒksaɪ). the bacterium that causes cerebrospinal meningitis. — **me,ningo'coccal** *adj.*

meniscus (mɪ'nɪskəs) *n., pl.* **-nisci** (-'nɪsaɪ) *or* **-niscuses.** **1.** the curved upper surface of a liquid standing in a tube, produced by the surface tension. **2.** a crescent-shaped lens; a concavo-convex or convexo-concave lens. [C17: from NL, from Gk *mēniskos* crescent, dim. of *mēnē* moon] —**me'niscoid** *adj.*

Mennonite ('mɛnə,naɪt) *n.* a member of a Protestant sect that rejects infant baptism and Church organization, and in most cases refuses military service, public office, and the taking of oaths. [C16: from G *Mennonit*, after *Menno Simons* (1496–1561), Frisian religious leader] —'**Mennonitism** *n.*

meno ('mɛnəʊ) *adv. Music.* to be played less quickly, less softly, etc. [from It., from L *minus* less]

meno- *combining form.* menstruation. [from Gk *mēn* month]

Menon ('mɛnən) *n.* **Vengalil Krishnan Krishna** ('vɛŋgəlɪl 'kriːʃnən 'kriːʃnə). 1897–1974, Indian diplomat

and politician, who was a close associate of Nehru and played a key role in the Indian nationalist movement.

menopause ('mɛnəʊ,pɔːz) *n.* the period during which a woman's menstrual cycle ceases, normally at an age of 45 to 50. [C19: from F, from Gk *mēn* month + *pausis* halt] —,meno'pausal *adj.*

menorah (mɪ'nɔːrə) *n. Judaism.* **1.** a seven-branched candelabrum used in the Temple and now an emblem of Judaism and the badge of the state of Israel. **2.** a similar lamp lit during the Chanukah festival. [from Heb.: candlestick]

Menorca (me'nɔrka) *n.* the Spanish name for **Minorca** (sense 1).

menorrhagia (,mɛnɔ'reɪdʒɪə) *n.* excessive bleeding during menstruation.

menorrhoea (,mɛnə'rɪə) *n.* normal bleeding in menstruation.

Menotti (mə'nɒtɪ; *Italian* me'nɔtti) *n.* **Gian Carlo** (dʒan 'karlo). born 1911, Italian composer, in the U.S. from 1928. His works include the operas *The Medium* (1946), *The Consul* (1950), and *Amahl and the Night Visitors* (1951).

menses ('mɛnsiːz) *n., pl.* **menses.** **1.** another name for **menstruation. 2.** the period of time during which one menstruation occurs. **3.** the matter discharged during menstruation. [C16: from L, pl. of *mensis* month]

Menshevik ('mɛnʃɪvɪk) *or* **Menshevist** *n.* a member of the moderate wing of the Russian Social Democratic Party. Cf. **Bolshevik.** [C20: from Russian, lit.: minority, from *menshe* less, from *malo* few] —'**Menshevism** *n.*

menstruate ('mɛnstrʊ,eɪt) *vb.* (*intr.*) to undergo menstruation. [C17: from L *menstruāre*, from *mensis* month]

menstruation (,mɛnstrʊ'eɪʃən) *n.* the approximately monthly discharge of blood and cellular debris from the uterus by nonpregnant women from puberty to the menopause. —'**menstrual** *or* '**menstruous** *adj.*

menstruum ('mɛnstrʊəm) *n., pl.* **-struums** *or* **-strua** (-strʊə). a solvent, esp. one used in the preparation of a drug. [C17 (meaning: solvent), C14 (menstrual discharge): from Med. L, from L *mēnstruus* monthly, from *mēnsis* month; from alchemical comparison between a base metal being transmuted into gold and the supposed action of the menses]

mensurable ('mɛnsjʊrəbᵊl, -ʃə-) *adj.* a less common word for **measurable.** [C17: from LL *mēnsūrābilis*, from *mēnsūra* MEASURE] —,**mensura'bility** *n.*

mensural ('mɛnʃərəl) *adj.* **1.** of or involving measure. **2.** *Music.* of or relating to music in which notes have fixed values. [C17: from LL *mēnsūrālis*, from *mēnsūra* MEASURE]

mensuration (,mɛnʃə'reɪʃən) *n.* **1.** the study of the measurement of geometric magnitudes such as length. **2.** the act or process of measuring. —**mensurative** ('mɛnʃərətɪv) *adj.*

-ment *suffix forming nouns, esp. from verbs.* **1.** indicating state, condition, or quality: *enjoyment.* **2.** indicating the result or product of an action: *embankment.* **3.** indicating process or action: *management.* [from F, from L *-mentum*]

mental ('mɛntᵊl) *adj.* **1.** of or involving the mind. **2.** occurring only in the mind: *mental arithmetic.* **3.** affected by mental illness: *a mental patient.* **4.** concerned with mental illness: *a mental hospital.* **5.** *Sl.* insane. [C15: from LL *mentālis*, from L *mēns* mind] —'**mentally** *adv.*

mental handicap *n.* any intellectual disability resulting from injury to the brain or from abnormal neurological development. —**mentally handicapped** *adj.*

mental healing *n.* the healing of a disorder by mental concentration or suggestion.

mentalism ('mɛntᵊ,lɪzəm) *n. Philosophy.* the doctrine that mind is the fundamental reality and that objects of knowledge exist only as aspects of the subject's consciousness. —,**mental'istic** *adj.*

mentality (mɛn'tælɪtɪ) *n., pl.* **-ties. 1.** the state or quality of mental or intellectual ability. **2.** a way of thinking; mental inclination or character.

mental reservation *n.* a tacit withholding of full assent or an unexpressed qualification made when taking an oath, making a statement, etc.

menthol ('mɛnθɒl) *n.* an organic compound found in peppermint oil and used as an antiseptic, in inhalants, and as an analgesic. Formula: $C_{10}H_{19}OH$. [C19: from G, from L *mentha* MINT[1]]

mentholated ('mɛnθə,leɪtɪd) *adj.* containing, treated with, or impregnated with menthol.

mention ('mɛnʃən) *vb.* (*tr.*) **1.** to refer to or speak about briefly or incidentally. **2.** to acknowledge or honour. **3.** not to mention (something). to say nothing of (something too obvious to mention). ~*n.* **4.** a recognition or acknowledgment. **5.** a slight reference or allusion. **6.** the act of mentioning. [C14: via OF from L *mentiō* a calling to mind, from *mēns* mind] — 'mentionable *adj.*

Menton (mɛn'tɔ̃n; *French* mɑ̃tɔ̃) *n.* a town and resort in SE France, on the Mediterranean: belonged to Monaco from the 14th century until 1848, then an independent republic until purchased by France in 1860. Pop.: 25 449 (1982).

mentor ('mɛntɔ:) *n.* a wise or trusted adviser or guide. [C18: from MENTOR]

Mentor ('mɛntɔ:) *n.* the friend whom Odysseus put in charge of his household when he left for Troy. He was the adviser of the young Telemachus.

menu ('mɛnju:) *n.* **1.** a list of dishes served at a meal or that can be ordered in a restaurant. **2.** a list of options displayed on a visual display unit from which the operator selects an action to be carried out. [C19: from F *menu* small, detailed (list), from L *minūtus* MINUTE²]

menuetto (mɛnjʊ'ɛtəʊ) *n., pl.* **-tos.** *Music.* another term for **minuet.** [from It.]

Menuhin ('mɛnjʊɪn) *n.* Sir **Yehudi** (jɛ'huːdɪ). born 1916, British violinist, born in the U.S.

Menzies ('mɛnzɪz) *n.* Sir **Robert Gordon.** 1894–1978, Australian statesman; prime minister (1939–41; 1949–66).

meow, miaou, miaow (mɪ'aʊ, mjaʊ), *or* **miaul** (mɪ'aʊl, mjaʊl) *vb.* **1.** (*intr.*) (of a cat) to make a characteristic crying sound. ~*interj.* **2.** an imitation of this sound.

MEP (in Britain) *abbrev. for* Member of the European Parliament.

mepacrine ('mɛpəkrɪn) *n. Brit.* a drug formerly widely used to treat malaria. [C20: from ME(THYL) + PA(LUDISM + A)CR(ID)INE]

meperidine (mə'pɛrɪ,diːn, -dɪn) *n.* the U.S. name for **pethidine.** [C20: from METHYL PIPERIDINE]

Mephistopheles (,mɛfɪ'stɒfɪ,liːz) *or* **Mephisto** (mə'fɪstəʊ) *n.* a devil in medieval mythology and the one to whom Faust sold his soul in German legend. —**Mephistophelean** *or* **Mephistophelian** (,mɛfɪstə'fiːlɪən) *adj.*

mephitic (mɪ'fɪtɪk) *or* **mephitical** *adj.* **1.** poisonous; foul. **2.** foul-smelling; putrid. [C17: from LL *mephīticus* pestilential]

meprobamate (mə'prəʊbə,meɪt, ,mɛprəʊ'bæmeɪt) *n.* a white bitter powder used as a tranquillizer. [C20: from ME(THYL) + PRO(PYL + *car*)bamate a salt or ester of an amide of carbonic acid]

-mer *suffix forming nouns. Chem.* denoting a substance of a particular class: *monomer; polymer.* [from Gk *meros* part]

Merano (mə'rɑːnəʊ; *Italian* me'raːno) *n.* a town and resort in NE Italy, in the foothills of the central Alps: capital of the Tyrol (12th–15th century); under Austrian rule until 1919. Pop.: 33 508 (1981). German name: **Meran** (me'raːn).

Merca ('mɛəkə) *n.* a port in S Somalia on the Indian Ocean. Pop.: 60 000 (1980 est.).

mercantile ('mɜːkən,taɪl) *adj.* **1.** of, relating to, or characteristic of trade or traders; commercial. **2.** of or relating to mercantilism. [C17: from F, from It., from *mercante* MERCHANT]

mercantilism ('mɜːkəntɪ,lɪzəm) *n. Econ.* a theory prevalent in Europe during the 17th and 18th centuries asserting that the wealth of a nation depends on possession of precious metals and therefore that a government must maximize foreign trade surplus and foster national commercial interests, a merchant marine, the establishment of colonies, etc. — 'mercantilist *n., adj.*

mercaptan (mɜː'kæptæn) *n.* another name (not in technical use) for **thiol.** [C19: from G, from Med. L *mercurium captans*, lit.: seizing quicksilver]

Mercator (mɜː'keɪtə) *n.* **Gerardus** (dʒə'rɑːdəs). Latinized name of *Gerhard Kremer.* 1512–94, Flemish cartographer and mathematician.

Mercator projection *n.* an orthomorphic map projection on which parallels and meridians form a rectangular grid, scale being exaggerated with increasing distance from the equator. Also called: **Mercator's projection.** [C17: after G. MERCATOR]

mercenary ('mɜːsɪnərɪ, -sɪnrɪ) *adj.* **1.** influenced by greed or desire for gain. **2.** of or relating to a mercenary or mercenaries. ~*n., pl.* **-naries. 3.** a man hired to fight for a foreign army, etc. **4.** *Rare.* any person who works solely for pay. [C16: from L *mercēnārius*, from *mercēs* wages]

mercer ('mɜːsə) *n. Brit.* a dealer in textile fabrics and fine cloth. [C13: from OF *mercier* dealer, from Vulgar L, from L *merx* wares] — 'mercery *n.*

mercerize *or* **-ise** ('mɜːsə,raɪz) *vb.* (*tr.*) to treat (cotton yarn) with an alkali to increase its strength and reception to dye and impart a lustrous silky appearance. [C19: after John *Mercer* (1791–1866), E maker of textiles]

merchandise *n.* ('mɜːtʃən,daɪs, -,daɪz). **1.** commercial goods; commodities. ~*vb.* ('mɜːtʃən,daɪz). **2.** to engage in the commercial purchase and sale of (goods or services); trade. [C13: from OF; see MERCHANT]

merchant ('mɜːtʃənt) *n.* **1.** a person engaged in the purchase and sale of commodities for profit; trader. **2.** *Chiefly Scot., U.S., & Canad.* a person engaged in retail trade. **3.** (esp. in historical contexts) any trader. **4.** *Derog.* a person dealing or involved in something undesirable: *a gossip merchant.* **5.** (*modifier*) **a.** of the merchant navy: *a merchant sailor.* **b.** of or concerned with trade: *a merchant ship.* ~*vb.* **6.** (*tr.*) to conduct trade in; deal in. [C13: from OF, prob. from Vulgar L, from L *mercārī* to trade, from *merx* wares]

merchantable ('mɜːtʃəntəbᵊl) *adj.* suitable for trading.

merchant bank *n. Brit.* a financial institution engaged primarily in accepting foreign bills and underwriting new security issues. —**merchant banker** *n.*

merchantman ('mɜːtʃəntmən) *n., pl.* **-men.** a merchant ship.

merchant navy *or* **marine** *n.* the ships or crew engaged in a nation's commercial shipping.

Mercia ('mɜːʃɪə) *n.* a kingdom and earldom of central and S England during the Anglo-Saxon period that reached its height under King Offa (757–96).

Mercian ('mɜːʃɪən) *adj.* **1.** of or relating to Mercia, or its dialect. ~*n.* **2.** the dialect of Old and Middle English spoken in Mercia. **3.** a native or inhabitant of Mercia.

merciful ('mɜːsɪful) *adj.* showing or giving mercy; compassionate. — 'mercifully *adv.* — 'mercifulness *n.*

merciless ('mɜːsɪlɪs) *adj.* without mercy; pitiless, cruel, or heartless. — 'mercilessly *adv.* — 'mercilessness *n.*

Mercouri (mɜː'kuːrɪ) *n.* **Melina** (mə'liːnə). born 1923, Greek actress and politician: her films include *Never on Sunday* (1960); minister of culture and science from 1981.

mercurial (mɜː'kjʊərɪəl) *adj.* **1.** of, like, containing, or relating to mercury. **2.** volatile; lively: *a mercurial temperament.* **3.** (*sometimes cap.*) of, like, or relating to the god or the planet Mercury. ~*n.* **4.** *Med.* any salt of mercury for use as a medicine. [C14: from L *mercuriālis*] —mer,curi'ality *n.* —mer'curially *adv.*

mercuric (mɜː'kjʊərɪk) *adj.* of or containing mercury in the divalent state; denoting a mercury(II) compound.

mercuric chloride *n.* a white poisonous crystalline substance used as a pesticide, antiseptic, and preservative for wood. Formula: $HgCl_2$.

Mercurochrome (mə'kjʊərə,krəʊm) *n. Trademark.* a solution of a crystalline compound, used as tropical antibacterial agent.

mercurous ('mɜːkjʊrəs) *adj.* of or containing mercury in the monovalent state; denoting a mercury(I) compound.

mercury ('mɜːkjʊrɪ) *n., pl.* **-ries. 1.** Also called: **quicksilver.** a heavy silvery-white toxic liquid metallic element: used in thermometers, barometers, mercury-vapour lamps, and dental amalgams. Symbol: Hg; atomic no.: 80; atomic wt.: 200.59. **2.** any plant of the genus *Mercurialis.* **3.** *Arch.* a messenger or courier. [C14: from L *Mercurius*, messenger of Jupiter, god of commerce; rel. to *merx* merchandise]

Mercury[1] ('mɜːkjʊrɪ) *n. Roman myth.* the messenger of the gods.

Mercury[2] ('mɜːkjʊrɪ) *n.* the second smallest planet and the nearest to the sun.

mercury-vapour lamp *n.* a lamp in which an electric discharge through mercury vapour is used to produce a greenish-blue light.

mercy ('mɜːsɪ) *n., pl.* **-cies. 1.** compassionate treatment of or attitude towards an offender, adversary, etc., who is in one's power or care; clemency; pity. **2.** the power to show mercy. **3.** a relieving or welcome occurrence or state of affairs. **4. at the mercy of.** in the power of. [C12: from OF, from L *mercēs* recompense, from *merx* goods]

mercy flight *n.* an aircraft flight to bring a seriously ill or injured person to hospital from an isolated community.

mercy killing *n.* another term for **euthanasia.**

mere[1] (mɪə) *adj.* being nothing more than something specified: *a mere child.* [C15: from L *merus* pure] —**'merely** *adv.*

mere[2] (mɪə) *n.* **1.** *Dialect or arch.* a lake or marsh. **2.** *Obs.* the sea or an inlet of it. [OE *mere* sea, lake]

mere[3] ('mɛrɪ) *n.* a short flat Maori striking weapon. [from Maori]

-mere *n. combining form.* indicating a part or division. [from Gk *meros* part] —**-meric** *adj. combining form.*

Meredith ('mɛrɪdɪθ) *n.* **George.** 1828–1909, English novelist and poet. His works, notable for their social satire and analysis of character, include the novels *Beauchamp's Career* (1876) and *The Egoist* (1879) and the long tragic poem *Modern Love* (1862).

meretricious (,mɛrɪ'trɪʃəs) *adj.* **1.** superficially or garishly attractive. **3.** insincere. **3.** *Arch.* of, like, or relating to a prostitute. [C17: from L *merētrīcius,* from *merētrīx* prostitute, from *merēre* to earn money] —**,mere'triciously** *adv.* —**,mere'triciousness** *n.*

merganser (mɜː'gænsə) *n., pl.* **-sers** *or* **-ser.** any of several typically crested large marine diving ducks, having a long slender hooked bill with serrated edges. [C18: from NL, from L *mergus* waterfowl, from *mergere* to plunge + *anser* goose]

merge (mɜːdʒ) *vb.* **1.** to meet and join or cause to meet and join. **2.** to blend or cause to blend; fuse. [C17: from L *mergere* to plunge] —**'mergence** *n.*

merger ('mɜːdʒə) *n.* **1.** *Commerce.* the combination of two or more companies. **2.** *Law.* the absorption of an estate, interest, offence, etc., into a greater one. **3.** the act of merging or the state of being merged.

Mergui Archipelago (mɜː'gwiː) *n.* a group of over 200 islands in the Andaman Sea, off the Tenasserim coast of S Burma: mountainous and forested.

Meriç (mə'riːtʃ) *n.* the Turkish name for the **Maritsa.**

Mérida (*Spanish* 'meriða) *n.* **1.** a city in SE Mexico, capital of Yucatán state: founded in 1542 on the site of the ancient Mayan city of T'ho; centre of the henequen industry; university. Pop.: 285 000 (1984 est.). **2.** a city in W Venezuela: founded in 1558 by Spanish conquistadores; University of Los Andes (1785). Pop.: 142 752 (1981). **3.** a market town in W Spain, in Estremadura, on the Guadiana River: founded in 25 B.C.; became the capital of Lusitania and one of the chief cities of Iberia. Pop.: 41 783 (1981). Latin name: **Au'gusta E'merita.**

meridian (mə'rɪdɪən) *n.* **1. a.** one of the imaginary lines joining the north and south poles at right angles to the equator, designated by degrees of longitude from 0° at Greenwich to 180°. **b.** the great circle running through both poles. **2.** *Astron.* the great circle on the celestial sphere passing through the north and south celestial poles and the zenith and nadir of the observer. **3.** the peak; zenith: *the meridian of his achievements.* **4.** *Obs.* noon. ~*adj.* **5.** along or relating to a meridian. **6.** of or happening at noon. **7.** relating to the peak of something. [C14: from L *merīdiānus* of midday, from *merīdiēs* midday, from *medius* MID[1] + *diēs* day]

meridional (mə'rɪdɪənᵊl) *adj.* **1.** along, relating to, or resembling a meridian. **2.** characteristic of or located in the south, esp. of Europe. ~*n.* **3.** an inhabitant of the south, esp. of France. [C14: from LL *merīdiōnālis* southern; see MERIDIAN]

Mérimée (*French* merime) *n.* **Prosper** (prɔspɛr). 1803–70, French novelist, dramatist, and short-story writer, noted particularly for his short novels *Colomba* (1840) and *Carmen* (1845), on which Bizet's opera was based.

meringue (mə'ræŋ) *n.* **1.** stiffly beaten egg whites mixed with sugar and baked. **2.** a small cake or shell of this mixture, often filled with cream. [C18: from F, from ?]

merino (mə'riːnəu) *n., pl.* **-nos. 1.** a breed of sheep originating in Spain. **2.** the long fine wool of this sheep. **3.** the yarn made from this wool, often mixed with cotton. ~*adj.* **4.** made from merino wool. [C18: from Sp., from ?]

Merionethshire (,mɛrɪ'ɒnɪθ,ʃɪə, -ʃə) *n.* (until 1974) a county of N Wales, now part of Gwynedd.

meristem ('mɛrɪ,stɛm) *n.* a plant tissue responsible for growth, whose cells divide and differentiate to form the tissues and organs of the plant. [C19: from Gk *meristos* divided, from *merizein,* from *meris* portion] —**meristematic** (,mɛrɪstɪ'mætɪk) *adj.*

merit ('mɛrɪt) *n.* **1.** worth or superior quality; excellence. **2.** (*often pl.*) a deserving or commendable quality or act. **3.** *Christianity.* spiritual credit granted or received for good works. **4.** the fact or state of deserving; desert. ~*vb.* **5.** (*tr.*) to be worthy of; deserve. [C13: via OF from L *meritum* reward, from *merēre* to deserve]

meritocracy (,mɛrɪ'tɒkrəsɪ) *n., pl.* **-cies. 1.** rule by persons chosen for their superior talents or intellect. **2.** the persons constituting such a group. **3.** a social system formed on such a basis. —**meritocratic** (,mɛrɪtə'krætɪk) *adj.*

meritorious (,mɛrɪ'tɔːrɪəs) *adj.* praiseworthy; showing merit. [C15: from L *meritōrius* earning money] —**,meri'toriously** *adv.* —**,meri'toriousness** *n.*

merits ('mɛrɪts) *pl. n.* **1.** the actual and intrinsic rights and wrongs of an issue, esp. in a law case. **2. on its** (**his, her,** etc.) **merits.** on the intrinsic qualities or virtues.

merle *or* **merl** (mɜːl) *n. Scot.* another name for the (European) **blackbird.** [C15: via OF from L *merula*]

Merleau-Ponty (*French* mɛrlopɔ̃ti) *n.* **Maurice** (mɔris). 1908–61, French phenomenological philosopher.

merlin ('mɜːlɪn) *n.* a small falcon that has a dark plumage with a black-barred tail. [C14: from OF *esmerillon,* from *esmeril,* of Gmc origin]

mermaid ('mɜː,meɪd) *n.* an imaginary sea creature fabled to have a woman's head and upper body and a fish's tail. [C14: from MERE[2] + MAID]

merman ('mɜː,mæn) *n., pl.* **-men.** a male counterpart of the mermaid. [C17: see MERMAID]

Meroë ('mɛrəu,iː) *n.* an ancient city in N Sudan, on the Nile; capital of a kingdom that flourished from about 700 B.C. to about 350 A.D.

-merous *adj. combining form.* (in biology) having a certain number or kind of parts. [from Gk *meros* part]

Merovingian (,mɛrəu'vɪndʒɪən) *adj.* **1.** of or relating to a Frankish dynasty which ruled Gaul and W Germany from about 500 to 751 A.D. ~*n.* **2.** a member or supporter of this dynasty. [C17: from F, from Med. L *Merovingi* offspring of *Merovaeus,* L form of *Merowig,* traditional founder of the line]

merriment ('mɛrɪmənt) *n.* gaiety, fun, or mirth.

merry ('mɛrɪ) *adj.* **-rier, -riest. 1.** cheerful; jolly. **2.** very funny; hilarious. **3.** *Brit. inf.* slightly drunk. **4. make merry.** to revel; be festive. **5. play merry hell with.** *Inf.* to disturb greatly; disrupt. [OE *merige* agreeable] —**'merrily** *adv.* —**'merriness** *n.*

merry-andrew (-'ændruː) *n.* a joker, clown, or buffoon. [C17: from ?]

merry-go-round *n.* **1.** another name for **roundabout** (sense 1). **2.** a whirl of activity.

merrymaking ('mɛrɪ,meɪkɪŋ) *n.* fun, revelry, or festivity. —**'merry,maker** *n.*

merrythought ('mɛrɪ,θɔːt) *n. Brit.* a less common word for **wishbone.**

Merse (mɜːs; *Scot.* mɛrs) *n.* **the.** a fertile lowland area of SE Scotland, in the Borders region, north of the Tweed.

Merseburg (*German* 'mɛrzəburk) *n.* a city in S East Germany, on the Saale River: residence of the dukes of Saxe-Merseburg (1656–1738); chemical industry. Pop.: 50 078 (1983 est.).

Mersey ('mɜːzɪ) *n.* a river in W England, rising in N Derbyshire and flowing northwest and west to the Irish Sea through a large estuary on which is situated the port of Liverpool. Length: about 112 km (70 miles).

Merseyside ('mɜːzɪ,saɪd) *n.* a metropolitan county of NW England, comprising the districts of Sefton, Liverpool, St. Helens, Knowsley, and Wirral. Administrative centre: Liverpool. Pop.: 1 467 600 (1986 est.). Area: 652 sq. km (252 sq. miles).

Mersin (mɛə'siːn) *n.* a port in S Turkey, on the Mediterranean: oil refinery. Pop.: 216 308 (1980). Also called: **İçel.**

Merthyr Tydfil ('mɜːθə 'tɪdvɪl) *n.* a town in SE Wales, in Mid Glamorgan: situated on the S Wales coalfield. Pop.: 53 843 (1981).

Merton ('mɜːtᵊn) *n.* a borough in SW Greater London. Pop.: 164 912 (1981).

mesa ('meɪsə) *n.* a flat tableland with steep edges, common in the southwestern U.S. [from Sp.: table]

mésalliance (mɛˈzælɪəns) n. a marriage with a person of lower social status. [C18: from F: MISALLIANCE]

Mesa Verde (ˈmeɪsə ˈvɜːd) n. a high plateau in SW Colorado: remains of numerous prehistoric cliff dwellings, inhabited by the Pueblo Indians.

mescal (mɛˈskæl) n. **1.** Also called: **peyote.** a spineless globe-shaped cactus of Mexico and the southwestern U.S. Its button-like tubercles (**mescal buttons**) are chewed by certain Indian tribes for their hallucinogenic effects. **2.** a colourless alcoholic spirit distilled from the fermented juice of certain agave plants. [C19: from American Sp., from Nahuatl *mexcalli* the liquor, from *metl* MAGUEY + *ixcalli* stew]

mescaline *or* **mescalin** (ˈmɛskəˌliːn, -lɪn) n. a hallucinogenic drug derived from mescal buttons.

mesdames (ˈmeɪˌdæm) n. the plural of **madame** and **madam** (sense 1).

mesdemoiselles (ˌmeɪdmwəˈzɛl) n. the plural of **mademoiselle.**

meseems (mɪˈsiːmz) vb. (tr.; takes a clause as object) Arch. it seems to me.

mesembryanthemum (mɪzˌɛmbrɪˈænθɪməm) n. any of a genus of plants with succulent leaves and bright flowers with rayed petals which typically open at midday. [C18: NL, from Gk *mesēmbria* noon + *anthemon* flower]

mesencephalon (ˌmɛsɛnˈsɛfəˌlɒn) n. the part of the brain that develops from the middle portion of the embryonic neural tube. Nontechnical name: **midbrain.**

mesentery (ˈmɛsəntərɪ, ˈmɛz-) n., pl. **-teries.** the double layer of peritoneum that is attached to the back wall of the abdominal cavity and supports most of the small intestine. [C16: from NL *mesenterium*, from MESO- + Gk *enteron* intestine] — **,mesen'teric** adj. — **mesenteritis** (mɛsˌɛntəˈraɪtɪs) n.

mesh (mɛʃ) n. **1.** a network; net. **2.** an open space between the strands of a network. **3.** (often pl.) the strands surrounding these spaces. **4.** anything that ensnares, or holds like a net. **5.** the engagement of teeth on interacting gearwheels: *the gears are in mesh.* ~vb. **6.** to entangle or become entangled. **7.** (of gear teeth) to engage or cause to engage. **8.** (intr.; often foll. by *with*) to coordinate (with). **9.** to work or cause to work in harmony. [C16: prob. from Du. *maesche*]

Meshach (ˈmiːʃæk) n. Old Testament. one of Daniel's three companions who, together with Shadrach and Abednego, was miraculously saved from destruction in Nebuchadnezzar's fiery furnace (Daniel 3:12-30).

Meshed (mɛˈʃɛd) n. a variant of **Mashhad.**

mesial (ˈmiːzɪəl) adj. Anat. another word for **medial** (sense 1). [C19: from MESO- + -IAL]

mesmerism (ˈmɛzməˌrɪzəm) n. Psychol. **1.** a hypnotic state induced by the operator's imposition of his will on that of the patient. **2.** an early doctrine concerning this. [C19: after F. A. *Mesmer* (1734–1815), Austrian physician] — **mesmeric** (mɛzˈmɛrɪk) adj. — **'mesmerist** n.

mesmerize *or* **-ise** (ˈmɛzməˌraɪz) vb. (tr.) **1.** a former word for **hypnotize.** **2.** to hold (someone) as if spellbound. — **,mesmeri'zation** *or* **-i'sation** n. — **'mesmer,izer** *or* **-,iser** n.

mesne (miːn) adj. Law. **1.** intermediate or intervening: *a mesne assignment of property.* **2. mesne profits.** rents or profits accruing during the rightful owner's exclusion from his land. [C15: from legal F *meien* in the middle]

meso- *or before a vowel* **mes-** combining form. middle or intermediate: *mesomorph.* [from Gk *misos* middle]

mesoblast (ˈmɛsəʊˌblæst) n. another name for **mesoderm.** — **,meso'blastic** adj.

mesocarp (ˈmɛsəʊˌkɑːp) n. the middle layer of the pericarp of a fruit, such as the flesh of a peach.

mesocephalic (ˌmɛsəʊsɪˈfælɪk) Anat. ~adj. **1.** having a medium-sized head. ~n. **2.** an individual with such a head. — **mesocephaly** (ˌmɛsəʊˈsɛfəlɪ) n.

mesoderm (ˈmɛsəʊˌdɜːm) n. the middle germ layer of an animal embryo, giving rise to muscle, blood, bone, connective tissue, etc. — **,meso'dermal** *or* **,meso'dermic** adj.

Mesolithic (ˌmɛsəʊˈlɪθɪk) n. **1.** the period between the Palaeolithic and the Neolithic, in Europe from about 12 000 to 3000 B.C. ~adj. **2.** of or relating to the Mesolithic.

Mesolonghi (ˌmɛsəˈlɒŋgɪ) n. a variant of **Missolonghi.**

Mesolóngion (ˌmɛsəˈlɒŋgɪˌɒn) n. transliteration of the Modern Greek name for **Missolonghi.**

mesomorph (ˈmɛsəʊˌmɔːf) n. a type of person having a muscular body build with a relatively prominent underlying bone structure.

mesomorphic (ˌmɛsəʊˈmɔːfɪk) adj. **1.** Chem. existing in or concerned with an intermediate state of matter between a true liquid and a true solid. **2.** relating to or being a mesomorph. ~Also: **mesomorphous.** — **,meso'morphism** n.

meson (ˈmiːzɒn) n. any of a group of elementary particles that has a rest mass between those of an electron and a proton, and an integral spin. [C20: from MESO- + -ON] — **me'sonic** *or* **'mesic** adj.

mesophyte (ˈmɛsəʊˌfaɪt) n. any plant that grows in surroundings receiving an average supply of water.

Mesopotamia (ˌmɛsəpəˈteɪmɪə) n. a region of SW Asia between the lower and middle reaches of the Tigris and Euphrates rivers: site of several ancient civilizations. [L, from Gk *mesopotamia (khora)* (the land) between rivers] — **,Mesopo'tamian** n., adj.

mesosphere (ˈmɛsəʊˌsfɪə) n. the atmospheric layer lying between the stratosphere and the thermosphere.

Mesozoic (ˌmɛsəʊˈzəʊɪk) adj. **1.** of, denoting, or relating to an era of geological time that began 225 000 000 years ago and lasted about 155 000 000 years. ~n. **2. the.** the Mesozoic era.

mesquite *or* **mesquit** (mɛˈskiːt, ˈmɛskiːt) n. any of various small trees, esp. a tropical American variety, whose sugary pods (**mesquite beans**) are used as animal fodder. [C19: from Mexican Sp., from Nahuatl *mizquitl*]

mess (mɛs) n. **1.** a state of confusion or untidiness, esp. if dirty or unpleasant. **2.** a chaotic or troublesome state of affairs; muddle. **3.** Inf. a dirty or untidy person or thing. **4.** Arch. a portion of food, esp. soft or semiliquid food. **5.** a place where service personnel eat or take recreation. **6.** a group of people, usually servicemen, who eat together. **7.** the meal so taken. ~vb. **8.** (tr.; often foll. by *up*) to muddle or dirty. **9.** (intr.) to make a mess. **10.** (intr.; often foll. by *with*) to interfere; meddle. **11.** (intr.; often foll. by *with* or *together*) Mil. to group together, esp. for eating. [C13: from OF *mes* dish of food, from LL *missus* course (at table), from L *mittere* to send forth]

mess about *or* **around** vb. (adv.) **1.** (intr.) to occupy oneself trivially; potter. **2.** (when intr., often foll. by *with*) to interfere or meddle (with). **3.** (intr.; sometimes foll. by *with*) Chiefly U.S. to engage in adultery.

message (ˈmɛsɪdʒ) n. **1.** a communication, usually brief, from one person or group to another. **2.** an implicit meaning, as in a work of art. **3.** a formal communiqué. **4.** an inspired communication of a prophet or religious leader. **5.** a mission; errand. **6. get the message.** Inf. to understand. ~vb. **7.** (tr.) to send as a message. [C13: from OF, from Vulgar L *missāticum* (unattested) something sent, from L *missus*, p.p. of *mittere*]

Messager (French mɛsaʒe) n. **André** (**Charles Prosper**) (ɑ̃dre). 1853–1929, French composer and conductor.

messages (ˈmɛsɪdʒɪz) pl. n. Scot. & NE English dialect. household shopping.

message stick n. a stick bearing carved symbols, carried by an Australian Aborigine as identification.

Messalina (ˌmɛsəˈliːnə) n. **Valeria** (vəˈlɪərɪə). died 48 A.D., wife of the Roman emperor Claudius, notorious for her debauchery and cruelty.

Messene (mɛˈsiːnɪ) n. an ancient Greek city in the SW Peloponnese: founded in 369 B.C. as the capital of Messenia.

messenger (ˈmɛsɪndʒə) n. **1.** a person who takes messages from one person or group to another. **2.** a person who runs errands. **3.** a carrier of official dispatches; courier. [C13: from OF *messagier*, from MESSAGE]

messenger RNA n. Biochem. a form of RNA, transcribed from a single strand of DNA, that carries genetic information required for protein synthesis from DNA to the ribosomes.

Messenia (məˈsiːnɪə) n. the southwestern area of the Peloponnese in S Greece.

mess hall n. a military dining room.

Messiaen (French mɛsjɑ̃) n. **Olivier** (ɔlivje). born 1908, French composer and organist. His music is distinguished by its rhythmic intricacy and is influenced by Hindu and Greek rhythms and bird song.

Messiah (mɪˈsaɪə) n. **1.** Judaism. the awaited king of the Jews, to be sent by God to free them. **2.** Jesus Christ, when regarded in this role. **3.** an exceptional or hoped-for liberator of a country or people. [C14: from OF *Messie*, ult. from Heb. *māshīah* anointed] —**Mes'siahship** *n.* —**Messianic** *or* **messianic** (ˌmɛsɪˈænɪk) *adj.*

messieurs ('mɛsəz) *n.* the plural of **monsieur**.

Messina (mɛ'siːnə) *n.* a port in NE Sicily, on the **Strait of Messina**: colonized by Greeks around 730 B.C.; under Spanish rule (1282–1676 and 1678–1713); university (1549). Pop.: 268 896 (1986).

mess jacket *n.* a waist-length jacket, worn by officers in the mess for formal dinners.

mess kit *n. Mil.* **1.** *Brit.* formal evening wear for officers. **2.** Also called: **mess gear**. eating utensils used esp. in the field.

messmate ('mɛsˌmeɪt) *n.* a person with whom one shares meals in a mess, esp. in the army.

Messner ('mɛsnə) *n.* **Zbigniew** ('zbignjɛf). born 1928, Polish statesman; prime minister (1985–88).

Messrs ('mɛsəz) *n.* the plural of **Mr.** [C18: abbrev. from F *messieurs*, pl. of MONSIEUR]

messy ('mɛsɪ) *adj.* **messier, messiest.** dirty, confused, or untidy. —**'messily** *adv.* —**'messiness** *n.*

mestizo (mɛ'stiːzəʊ, mɪ-) *n., pl.* **-zos** *or* **-zoes.** a person of mixed parentage, esp. the offspring of a Spanish American and an American Indian. [C16: from Sp., ult. from L *miscēre* to mix] —**mestiza** (mɛ'stiːzə) *fem. n.*

mestranol ('mɛstrəˌnɒl, -ˌnəʊl) *n.* a synthetic oestrogen used in combination with progesterones as an oral contraceptive. [C20: from M(ETHYL) + (O)ESTR(OGEN) + (*pregn*)*an*(*e*) (C₂₁H₃₆) + -OL]

Meštrović (*Serbo-Croatian* 'mɛʃtrɒvitʃ) *n.* **Ivan** ('ivan). 1883–1962, U.S. sculptor, born in Austria: his works include portraits of Sir Thomas Beecham and Pope Pius XI.

met (mɛt) *vb.* the past tense and past participle of **meet**[1].

met. *abbrev. for:* **1.** meteorological. **2.** meteorology. **3.** metropolitan.

Meta ('meɪtə; *Spanish* 'meta) *n.* a river in Colombia, rising in the Andes and flowing northeast and east, forming part of the border between Colombia and Venezuela, to join the Orinoco River. Length: about 1000 km (620 miles).

meta- *or sometimes before a vowel* **met-** *prefix.* **1.** indicating change or alternation: *metabolism; metamorphosis.* **2.** (of an academic discipline) concerned with the concepts and results of that discipline: *metamathematics.* **3.** occurring or situated behind or after: *metaphysics.* **4.** (*often in italics*) denoting that an organic compound contains a benzene ring with substituents in the 1,3-positions: *meta-cresol.* **5.** denoting an isomer, polymer, or compound related to a specified compound: *metaldehyde.* **6.** denoting an oxyacid that is the least hydrated form of the anhydride or a salt of such an acid: *metaphosphoric acid.* [from Gk (prep.)]

metabolism (mɪ'tæbəˌlɪzəm) *n.* **1.** the sum total of the chemical processes that occur in living organisms, resulting in growth, production of energy, elimination of waste, etc. **2.** the sum total of the chemical processes affecting a particular substance in the body: *carbohydrate metabolism.* [C19: from Gk *metabolē* change, from *metaballein*, from META- + *ballein* to throw] —**metabolic** (ˌmɛtə-'bɒlɪk) *adj.* —ˌmeta'bolically *adv.*

metabolize *or* **-ise** (mɪ'tæbəˌlaɪz) *vb.* to produce or be produced by metabolism.

metacarpus (ˌmɛtə'kɑːpəs) *n., pl.* **-pi** (-paɪ). **1.** the skeleton of the hand between the wrist and the fingers, consisting of five long bones. **2.** the corresponding bones in other vertebrates. —ˌmeta'carpal *adj., n.*

metacentre *or U.S.* **metacenter** ('mɛtəˌsɛntə) *n.* the intersection of a vertical line through the centre of buoyancy of a floating body at equilibrium with a vertical line through the centre of buoyancy when the body is tilted. —ˌmeta'centric *adj.*

metage ('miːtɪdʒ) *n.* **1.** the official measuring of weight or contents. **2.** a charge for this. [C16: from METE[1]]

metal ('mɛtəl) *n.* **1. a.** any of a number of chemical elements, such as iron or copper, that are often lustrous ductile solids, have basic oxides, form positive ions, are good conductors of heat and electricity. **b.** an alloy, such as brass or steel, containing one or more of these elements. **2.** the substance of glass in a molten state or as the finished product. **3.** short for **road metal**. **4.** *Heraldry*. gold or silver. **5.** the basic quality of a person or thing; stuff. **6.** (*pl.*) the rails of a railway. ~*adj.* **7.** made of metal. ~*vb.* **-alling, -alled** *or U.S.* **-aling, -aled.** (*tr.*) **8.** to fit or cover with metal. **9.** to make or mend (a road)

with **road metal**. [C13: from L *metallum* mine, product of a mine, from Gk *metallon*] —**'metalled** *adj.*

metal. *or* **metall.** *abbrev. for:* **1.** metallurgical. **2.** metallurgy.

metalanguage ('mɛtəˌlæŋgwɪdʒ) *n.* a language or system of symbols used to discuss another language or system. Cf. **object language.**

metallic (mɪ'tælɪk) *adj.* **1.** of, concerned with, or consisting of metal or a metal. **2.** suggestive of a metal: *a metallic click; metallic lustre.* **3.** *Chem.* (of a metal element) existing in the free state rather than in combination: *metallic copper.*

metallic soap *n.* any one of a number of salts or esters containing a metal, such as aluminium, calcium, magnesium, iron, and zinc. They are used as bases for ointments, fungicides, fireproofing and waterproofing agents, and dryers for paints and varnishes.

metalliferous (ˌmɛtəˈlɪfərəs) *adj.* containing a metallic element. [C17: from L *metallifer* yielding metal, from *metallum* metal + *ferre* to bear]

metallize, -ise, *or U.S.* **metalize** ('mɛtəˌlaɪz) *vb.* (*tr.*) to make metallic or to coat or treat with metal. —ˌmetalli'zation, -i'sation, *or U.S.* ˌmetali'zation *n.*

metallography (ˌmɛtə'lɒgrəfɪ) *n.* the branch of metallurgy concerned with the composition and structure of metals and alloys. —**metallographic** (mɪˌtælə'græfɪk) *adj.*

metalloid ('mɛtəˌlɔɪd) *n.* **1.** a nonmetallic element, such as arsenic or silicon, that has some of the properties of a metal. ~*adj. also* ˌmetal'loidal. **2.** of or being a metalloid. **3.** resembling a metal.

metallurgy (mɛ'tælədʒɪ) *n.* the scientific study of the extraction, refining, alloying, and fabrication of metals and of their structure and properties. —**metallurgic** (ˌmɛtə-'lɜːdʒɪk) *or* ˌmetal'lurgical *adj.* —**metallurgist** (mɛ'tælədʒɪst, 'mɛtəˌlɜːdʒɪst) *n.*

metal tape *n.* a magnetic recording tape coated with pure iron: it gives enhanced recording quality.

metalwork ('mɛtəlˌwɜːk) *n.* **1.** the craft of working in metal. **2.** work in metal or articles made from metal.

metalworking ('mɛtəlˌwɜːkɪŋ) *n.* the processing of metal to change its shape, size, etc. —'metalˌworker *n.*

metamere ('mɛtəˌmɪə) *n.* one of the similar body segments into which earthworms, crayfish, and similar animals are divided longitudinally. —**metameral** (mɪ'tæmərəl) *adj.*

metamerism (mɪ'tæməˌrɪzəm) *n.* **1.** Also called: (**metameric**) **segmentation.** the division of an animal into metameres. **2.** *Chem.* a type of isomerism in which molecular structures differ by the attachment of different groups to the same atom. —**metameric** (ˌmɛtə'mɛrɪk) *adj.*

metamict ('mɛtəˌmɪkt) *adj.* of or denoting the amorphous state of a substance that has lost its crystalline structure as a result of the radioactivity of uranium or thorium within it. —ˌmetamicti'zation *or* ˌmetamicti'sation *n.*

metamorphic (ˌmɛtə'mɔːfɪk) *or* **metamorphous** *adj.* **1.** relating to or resulting from metamorphosis or metamorphism. **2.** (of rocks) altered considerably from the original structure and composition by pressure and heat.

metamorphism (ˌmɛtə'mɔːfɪzəm) *n.* **1.** the process by which metamorphic rocks are formed. **2.** a variant of **metamorphosis.**

metamorphose (ˌmɛtə'mɔːfəʊz) *vb.* to undergo or cause to undergo metamorphosis or metamorphosis.

metamorphosis (ˌmɛtə'mɔːfəsɪs) *n., pl.* **-ses** (-ˌsiːz). **1.** a complete change of physical form or substance. **2.** a complete change of character, appearance, etc. **3.** a person or thing that has undergone metamorphosis. **4.** *Zool.* the rapid transformation of a larva into an adult that occurs in certain animals, for example the stage between chrysalis and butterfly. [C16: via L from Gk: transformation, from META- + *morphē* form]

metaphor ('mɛtəfə, -ˌfɔː) *n.* a figure of speech in which a word or phrase is applied to an object or action that it does not literally denote in order to imply a resemblance, for example *he is a lion in battle.* Cf. **simile.** [C16: from L, from Gk *metaphora*, from *metapherein* to transfer, from META-+ *pherein* to bear] —**metaphoric** (ˌmɛtə'fɒrɪk) *or* ˌmeta'phorical *adj.* —ˌmeta'phorically *adv.*

metaphrase ('mɛtəˌfreɪz) *n.* **1.** a literal translation. ~*vb.* (*tr.*) **2.** to alter or manipulate the wording of. **3.** to translate literally. [C17: from Gk *metaphrazein* to translate]

metaphrast ('mɛtə,fræst) n. a person who metaphrases, esp. one who changes the form of a text, as by rendering verse into prose. [C17: from Med. Gk *metaphrastēs* translator] —,meta'phrastic *or* ,meta'phrastical *adj.* —,meta'phrastically *adv.*

metaphysic (,mɛtə'fɪzɪk) n. the system of first principles and assumptions underlying an inquiry or philosophical theory.

metaphysical (,mɛtə'fɪzɪkəl) *adj.* **1.** of or relating to metaphysics. **2.** (of a statement or theory) having an empirical form but in fact immune from empirical testing. **3.** (popularly) abstract, abtruse, or unduly theoretical. **4.** incorporeal; supernatural. —,meta'physically *adv.*

Metaphysical (,mɛtə'fɪzɪkəl) *adj.* **1.** denoting or relating to certain 17th-century poets who combined intense feeling with elaborate imagery. ~n. **2.** a poet of this group.

metaphysics (,mɛtə'fɪzɪks) n. (*functioning as sing.*) **1.** the branch of philosophy that deals with first principles, esp. of being and knowing. **2.** the philosophical study of the nature of reality. **3.** (popularly) abstract or subtle discussion or reasoning. [C16: from Med. L, from Gk *ta meta ta phusika* the things after the physics, from the arrangement of subjects treated in the works of Aristotle] —**metaphysician** (,mɛtəfɪ'zɪʃən) *or* **metaphysicist** (,mɛtə'fɪzɪsɪst) n.

metapsychology (,mɛtəsaɪ'kɒlədʒɪ) n. *Psychol.* **1.** the study of philosophical questions, such as the relation between mind and body, that go beyond the laws of experimental psychology. **2.** any attempt to state the general laws of psychology. **3.** another word for **parapsychology.** —**metapsychological** (,mɛtə,saɪkə'lɒdʒɪkəl) *adj.*

metastable (,mɛtə'steɪbəl) *adj. Physics.* (of a body or system) having a state of apparent equilibrium although capable of changing to a more stable state. —,metasta'bility n.

metastasis (mɪ'tæstəsɪs) n., pl. **-ses** (-,siːz). *Pathol.* the spreading of a disease organism, esp. cancer cells, from one part of the body to another. [C16: via L from Gk: transition] —**metastatic** (,mɛtə'stætɪk) *adj.* —,meta'statically *adv.*

metastasize *or* **-ise** (mɪ'tæstə,saɪz) vb. (*intr.*) *Pathol.* (esp. of cancer cells) to spread to a new site in the body via blood or lymph vessels.

metatarsus (,mɛtə'tɑːsəs) n., pl. **-si** (-saɪ). **1.** the skeleton of the human foot between the toes and the tarsus, consisting of five long bones. **2.** the corresponding skeletal part in other vertebrates. —,meta'tarsal *adj., n.*

metathesis (mɪ'tæθəsɪs) n., pl. **-ses** (-,siːz). the transposition of two sounds or letters in a word or of two words in a sentence. [C16: from LL, from Gk, from *metatithenai* to transpose] —**metathetic** (,mɛtə'θɛtɪk) *or* ,meta'thetical *adj.*

metazoan (,mɛtə'zəʊən) n. **1.** any animal having a body composed of many cells: includes all animals except sponges and protozoans. ~adj. *also* **metazoic.** **2.** of or relating to the metazoans. [C19: from NL *Metazoa*; see META-, -ZOA]

Metchnikoff (*French* mɛtʃnikɔf; *Russian* 'mjetʃnikəf) n. **Élie** (eli). 1845–1916, Russian bacteriologist in France. He formulated the theory of phagocytosis and shared the Nobel prize for physiology or medicine 1908.

mete[1] (miːt) vb. (*tr.*) **1.** (usually foll. by *out*) *Formal.* to distribute or allot (something, often unpleasant). **2.** *Poetic, dialect.* to measure. [OE *metan*]

mete[2] (miːt) n. *Rare.* a mark, limit, or boundary (esp. in **metes and bounds**). [C15: from OF, from L *mēta* goal, turning post (in race)]

metempsychosis (,mɛtəmsaɪ'kəʊsɪs) n., pl. **-ses** (-siːz). the migration of a soul from one body to another. [C16: via LL from Gk, from *metempsukhousthai*, from META- + -em-in + *psukhē* soul] —,metempsy'chosist n.

meteor ('miːtɪə) n. **1.** a very small meteoroid that has entered the earth's atmosphere. **2.** Also called: **shooting star, falling star.** the bright streak of light appearing in the sky due to the incandescence of such a body heated by friction at its surface. [C15: from Med. L *meteōrum*, from Gk *meteōros*, from *meteōros* lofty, from *meta-* (intensifier) + *aeirein* to raise]

meteoric (,miːtɪ'ɒrɪk) *adj.* **1.** of, formed by, or relating to meteors. **2.** like a meteor in brilliance, speed, or transience. **3.** *Rare.* of weather; meteorological. —,mete'orically *adv.*

meteorite ('miːtɪə,raɪt) n. a rocklike object consisting of the remains of a meteoroid that has fallen on earth. —**meteoritic** (,miːtɪə'rɪtɪk) *adj.*

meteoroid ('miːtɪə,rɔɪd) n. any of the small celestial bodies that are thought to orbit the sun. When they enter the earth's atmosphere, they become visible as meteors. —,meteor'oidal *adj.*

meteorol. *or* **meteor.** *abbrev for:* **1.** meteorological. **2.** meteorology.

meteorology (,miːtɪə'rɒlədʒɪ) n. the study of the earth's atmosphere, esp. of weather-forming processes and weather forecasting. [C17: from Gk; see METEOR, -LOGY] —**meteorological** (,miːtɪərə'lɒdʒɪkəl) *or* ,meteoro'logic *adj.* —,meteoro'logically *adv.* —,meteor'ologist n.

meteor shower n. a transient rain of meteors occurring at regular intervals and coming from a particular region in the sky.

meter[1] ('miːtə) n. **1.** any device that measures and records a quantity, such as of gas, current, voltage, etc., that has passed through it during a specified period. **2.** See **parking meter.** ~vb. (*tr.*) **3.** to measure (a rate of flow) with a meter. [C19: see METE[1]]

meter[2] ('miːtə) n. the U.S. spelling of **metre**[1].

meter[3] ('miːtə) n. the U.S. spelling of **metre**[2].

-meter n. *combining form.* **1.** indicating an instrument for measuring: *barometer.* **2.** *Prosody.* indicating a verse having a specified number of feet: *pentameter.* [from Gk *metron* measure]

Meth. *abbrev. for* Methodist.

meth- *combining form.* indicating a chemical compound derived from methane or containing methyl groups: *methacrylic acid.*

methacrylic acid (,mɛθə'krɪlɪk) n. a colourless crystalline water-soluble substance used in the manufacture of acrylic resins.

methadone ('mɛθə,dəʊn) *or* **methadon** ('mɛθə,dɒn) n. a narcotic analgesic drug similar to morphine but less habit-forming. [C20: from (*di*)*meth*(*yl*) + A (MINO) + *d*(*iphenyl*) + -ONE]

methanal ('mɛθə,næl) n. the systematic name for **formaldehyde.**

methane ('miːθeɪn) n. a colourless odourless flammable gas, the main constituent of natural gas: used as a fuel. Formula: CH_4.

methane series n. another name for **alkane series.**

methanoic acid ('mɛθə,nəʊɪk) n. the systematic name for **formic acid.**

methanol ('mɛθə,nɒl) n. a colourless volatile poisonous liquid compound used as a solvent and fuel. Formula: CH_3OH. Also called: **methyl alcohol, wood alcohol.** [C20: from METHANE -OL[1]]

methinks (mɪ'θɪŋks) vb. past **methought.** (*tr.; takes a clause as object*) *Arch.* it seems to me.

metho ('mɛθəʊ) n. *Austral. inf.* **1.** another name for **methylated spirits. 2.** (*pl.* **methos**) a drinker of methylated spirits.

method ('mɛθəd) n. **1.** a way of proceeding or doing something, esp. a systematic or regular one. **2.** orderliness of thought, action, etc. **3.** (*often pl.*) the techniques or arrangement of work for a particular field or subject. [C16: via F from L, from Gk *methodos*, lit.: a going after, from *meta-*after + *hodos* way]

Method ('mɛθəd) n. (*sometimes not cap.*) **a.** a technique of acting in which the actor bases his role on the inner motivation of the character played. **b.** (*as modifier*): *a Method actor.*

methodical (mɪ'θɒdɪkəl) *or* (*less commonly*) **methodic** *adj.* characterized by method or orderliness; systematic. —me'thodically *adv.*

Methodism ('mɛθə,dɪzəm) n. the system and practices of the Methodist church.

Methodist ('mɛθədɪst) n. **1.** a member of any of the Nonconformist denominations that derive from the system of faith and practice initiated by John Wesley and his followers. ~adj. *also* ,Method'istic *or* ,Method'istical. **2.** of or relating to Methodism or the Church embodying it (the **Methodist Church**).

Methodius (mɛ'θəʊdɪəs) n. **Saint,** with his younger brother Saint Cyril called *the Apostles of the Slavs.* 815–885 A.D., Greek Christian theologian sent as a missionary to the Moravians. Feast day: July 7.

methodize or **-ise** ('mεθə,daɪz) vb. (tr.) to organize according to a method; systematize — '**method,izer** or -,**iser** n.

methodology (,mεθə'dɒlədʒɪ) n., pl. **-gies. 1.** the system of methods and principles used in a particular discipline. **2.** the branch of philosophy concerned with the science of method. — **methodological** (,mεθədə'lɒdʒɪkəl) adj. — ,**methodo'logically** adv. — ,**method'olo- gist** n.

methought (mɪ'θɔːt) vb. Arch. the past tense of **me- thinks.**

meths (mεθs) n. Chiefly Brit., Austral., & N.Z. an informal name for **methylated spirits.**

Methuselah (mɪ'θjuːzələ) n. Old Testament. a patriarch supposed to have lived 969 years (Genesis 5:21–27) who has come to be regarded as a type of longevity. Douay spelling: **Mathusala.**

methyl ('miːθaɪl, 'mεθɪl) n. **1.** (modifier) of, consisting of, or containing the monovalent group of atoms CH_3. **2.** a compound in which methyl groups are bound directly to a metal atom. [C19: from F méthyle, back formation from METHYLENE] — **methylic** (mə'θɪlɪk) adj.

methyl acetate n. a colourless volatile flammable liquid ester used as a solvent, esp. in paint removers. Formula: CH_3COOCH_3. Systematic name: **methyl ethanoate.**

methyl alcohol n. another name for **methanol.**

methylate ('mεθɪ,leɪt) vb. (tr.) to mix with methanol.

methylated spirits n. (functioning as sing. or pl.) alcohol that has been denatured by the addition of methanol and pyridine and a violet dye. Also: **methylated spirit.**

methyl chloride n. a colourless gas with an ether-like odour, used as a refrigerant and anaesthetic. Formula: CH_3Cl. Systematic name: **chloromethane.**

methylene ('mεθɪ,liːn) n. (modifier) of, consisting of, or containing the divalent group of atoms $=CH_2$: a methylene group or radical. [C19: from F méthylène, from Gk methu wine + hulē wood + -ENE: orig. referring to a substance distilled from wood]

meticulous (mɪ'tɪkjʊləs) adj. very precise about details; painstaking. [C16 (meaning: timid): from L meticulōsus fearful, from metus fear] — **me'ticulously** adv. — **me'ticulousness** n.

métier ('mεtɪeɪ) n. **1.** a profession or trade. **2.** a person's strong point or speciality. [C18: from F, ult. from L ministerium service]

Métis (mε'tiːs) n., pl. **-tis** (-'tiːs, -'tiːz). a person of mixed parentage, esp. the offspring of a French Canadian and a North American Indian. [C19: from F, from Vulgar L mixtīcius (unattested) of mixed race] — **Métisse** (mε'tiːs) fem. n.

metol ('miːtɒl) n. a colourless soluble organic substance used, in the form of its sulphate, as a photographic developer. [C20: from G, arbitrary coinage]

Metonic cycle (mɪ'tɒnɪk) n. a cycle of 235 synodic months after which the phases of the moon recur on the same day of the month. [C17: after Meton, 5th-cent. B.C. Athenian astronomer]

metonymy (mɪ'tɒnɪmɪ) n., pl. **-mies.** the substitution of a word referring to an attribute for the thing that is meant, e.g. the crown, used to refer to a monarch. Cf. **synecdo- che.** [C16: from LL, from Gk, from meta- (indicating change) + onoma name] — **metonymical** (,mεtə- 'nɪmɪkəl) or ,**meto'nymic** adj.

metope ('mεtəʊp, 'mεtəpɪ) n. Archit. a square space between triglyphs in a Doric frieze. [C16: via L from Gk, from meta between + opē one of the holes for the beam-ends]

metre[1] or U.S. **meter** ('miːtə) n. **1.** a metric unit of length equal to approximately 1.094 yards. **2.** the basic SI unit of length; the length of the path travelled by light in free space during a time interval of 1/299 792 458 of a second. Symbol: m [C18: from F; see METRE[2]]

metre[2] or U.S. **meter** ('miːtə) n. **1.** Prosody. the rhythmic arrangement of syllables in verse, usually according to the number and kind of feet in a line. **2.** Music. another word (esp. U.S.) for **time** (sense 22). [C14: from L metrum, from Gk metron measure]

metre-kilogram-second n. See **mks units.**

metric ('mεtrɪk) adj. of or relating to the metre or metric system.

metrical ('mεtrɪkəl) or **metric** adj. **1.** of or relating to measurement. **2.** of or in poetic metre. — '**metrically** adv.

metricate ('mεtrɪ,keɪt) vb. to convert (a measuring system, instrument, etc.) from nonmetric to metric units. — ,**metri'cation** n.

metric system n. any decimal system of units based on the metre. For scientific purposes SI units are used.

metric ton n. another name (not in technical use) for **tonne.**

metro ('mεtrəʊ) or **métro** French. (metro) n., pl. **-ros.** an underground, or largely underground, railway system in certain cities, such as that in Paris. [C20: from F, chemin de fer métropolitain metropolitan railway]

Metro ('mεtrəʊ) n. Canad. a metropolitan city administration, esp. Metropolitan Toronto.

metronome ('mεtrə,nəʊm) n. a device which indicates the tempo of music by producing a clicking sound from a pendulum with an adjustable period of swing. [C19: from Gk metron measure + nomos law] — **metronomic** (,mεtrə'nɒmɪk) adj.

metronymic (,mεtrəʊ'nɪmɪk) adj. **1.** (of a name) derived from the name of the mother or other female ancestor. ~n. **2.** a metronymic name. [C19: from Gk mē- tronumikos, from mētēr mother + onoma name]

metropolis (mɪ'trɒpəlɪs) n., pl. **-lises. 1.** the main city, esp. of a country or region. **2.** a centre of activity. **3.** the chief see in an ecclesiastical province. [C16: from LL from Gk, from mētēr mother + polis city]

metropolitan (,mεtrə'pɒlɪtən) adj. **1.** of or characteristic of a metropolis. **2.** constituting a city and its suburbs. **3.** of, relating to, or designating an ecclesiastical metropolis. **4.** of or belonging to the home territories of a country, as opposed to overseas territories: metropolitan France. ~n. **5. a.** Eastern Churches. the head of an ecclesiastical province, ranking between archbishop and patriarch. **b.** Church of England. an archbishop. **c.** R.C. Church. an archbishop or bishop having authority over the dioceses in his province. — ,**metro'politanism** n.

metropolitan county n. (in England 1974–86) any of the six conurbations with elected councils possessing powers resembling those of counties.

metropolitan district n. (in England since 1974) any of the districts into which the metropolitan county areas are divided.

metrorrhagia (,miːtrɔː'reɪdʒɪə, ,mεt-) n. abnormal bleeding from the uterus. [C19: NL, from Gk mētra womb + -rrhagia a breaking forth]

-metry n. combining form. indicating the process or science of measuring: geometry. [from OF -metrie, from L, ult. from Gk metron measure] — **-metric** adj. combining form.

Metternich (German 'mεtərnɪç) n. **Klemens** ('kleːməns). 1773–1859, Austrian statesman. He became foreign minister (1809) and made a significant contribution to the Congress of Vienna (1815). From 1821 to 1848 he was both foreign minister and chancellor of Austria and is noted for his defence of autocracy in Europe.

mettle ('mεtəl) n. **1.** courage; spirit. **2.** character. **3. on one's mettle.** roused to making one's best efforts. [C16: orig. var. of METAL]

mettled ('mεtəld) or **mettlesome** ('mεtəlsəm) adj. courageous, spirited, or valiant.

Metz (mεts; French mεs) n. a city in NE France on the River Moselle: a free imperial city in the 13th century; annexed by France in 1552; part of Germany (1871–1918); centre of the Lorraine iron-mining region. Pop.: 111 098 (1983 est.).

Meung (French mœ̃) n. See **Jean de Meung.**

Meurthe-et-Moselle (French mœrtemɔzεl) n. a department of NE France, in Lorraine region. Capital: Nancy. Pop.: 716 846 (1982). Area: 5280 sq. km (2059 sq. miles).

Meuse (mɜːz; French mœz) n. **1.** a department of N France, in Lorraine region: heavy fighting occurred here in World War I. Capital: Bar-le-Duc. Pop.: 200 101 (1982). Area: 6241 sq. km (2434 sq. miles). **2.** a river in W Europe, rising in NE France and flowing north across E Belgium and the S Netherlands to join the Waal River before entering the North Sea. Length: 926 km (575 miles). Dutch name: **Maas.**

MeV symbol for million electronvolts (10^6 electronvolts).

mevrou (mə'frəʊ) n. a S. African title of address equivalent to Mrs when placed before a surname or madam when used alone. [Afrik.]

mew[1] (mjuː) *vb.* **1.** (*intr.*) (esp. of a cat) to make a characteristic high-pitched cry. ~*n.* **2.** such a sound. [C14: imit.]

mew[2] (mjuː) *n.* any seagull, esp. the common gull. [OE *mǣw*]

mew[3] (mjuː) *n.* **1.** a room or cage for hawks, esp. while moulting. ~*vb.* (*tr.*) **2.** (often foll. by *up*) to confine (hawks or falcons) in a shelter, cage, etc. **3.** to confine; conceal. [C14: from OF *mue*, from *muer* to moult, from L *mūtāre* to change]

Mewar (mɛ'wɑː) *n.* another name for **Udaipur** (sense 1).

mewl (mjuːl) *vb.* **1.** (*intr.*) (esp. of a baby) to cry weakly; whimper. ~*n.* **2.** such a cry. [C17: imit.]

mews (mjuːz) *n.* (*functioning as sing. or pl.*) *Chiefly Brit.* **1.** a yard or street lined by buildings originally used as stables but now often converted into dwellings. **2.** the buildings around a mews. [C14: pl. of MEW[3], orig. referring to royal stables built on the site of hawks' mews at Charing Cross in London]

Mex. *abbrev. for:* **1.** Mexican. **2.** Mexico.

Mexicali (ˌmɛksɪ'kɑːlɪ; *Spanish* mɛxi'kali) *n.* a city in NW Mexico, capital of Baja California state, on the border with the U.S. adjoining Calexico, California: centre of a rich irrigated agricultural region. Pop.: 500 000 (1984 est.).

Mexico ('mɛksɪˌkəʊ) *n.* **1.** a republic in North America, on the Gulf of Mexico and the Pacific: early Mexican history includes the Maya, Toltec, and Aztec civilizations; conquered by the Spanish between 1519 and 1525 and achieved independence in 1821; lost Texas to the U.S. in 1836 and California and New Mexico in 1848. It is generally mountainous with three ranges of the Sierra Madre (east, west, and south) and a large central plateau. Official language: Spanish. Religion: chiefly Roman Catholic. Currency: peso. Capital: Mexico City. Pop.: 76 000 000 (1987 est.). Area: 1 967 183 sq. km (761 530 sq. miles). Official name: **United Mexican States.** Spanish name: **Méjico.** **2.** a state of Mexico, on the central plateau surrounding Mexico City, which is not administratively part of the state. Capital: Toluca. Pop.: 7 545 692 (1980). Area: 21 460 sq. km (8287 sq. miles). **3.** **Gulf of.** an arm of the Atlantic, bordered by the U.S., Cuba, and Mexico: linked with the Atlantic by the Florida Strait and with the Caribbean by the Yucatán Channel. Area: about 1 600 000 sq. km (618 000 sq. miles). —**Mexican** ('mɛksɪkən) *adj., n.*

Mexico City *n.* the capital of Mexico, on the central plateau at an altitude of 2240 m (7350 ft.): founded as the Aztec capital (Tenochtitlán) in about 1300; conquered and rebuilt by the Spanish in 1521; forms, with its suburbs, the federal district of Mexico; the largest industrial complex in the country. Pop.: 15 667 000 (1985).

Meyerbeer (*German* 'maiərbeːr) *n.* **Giacomo** ('dʒaːkomo), real name *Jakob Liebmann Beer.* 1791–1864, German composer, esp. of operas, such as *Robert le diable* (1831) and *Les Huguenots* (1836).

Meyerhof (*German* 'maiərhoːf) *n.* **Otto** (**Fritz**) ('ɔto). 1884–1951, German physiologist, noted for his work on the metabolism of muscles. He shared the Nobel prize for physiology or medicine 1922.

MEZ *abbrev. for* Central European Time. [from G *Mitteleuropäische Zeit*]

mezcal (mɛ'skæl) *n.* a variant spelling of **mescal.**

mezcaline ('mɛskəˌliːn) *n.* a variant spelling of **mescaline.**

Mézières (*French* mezjɛr) *n.* a town in NE France, on the River Meuse opposite Charleville. See **Charleville-Mézières.**

mezuzah (mə'zʊzə) *n., pl.* **-zuzahs** or **-zuzoth** (*Hebrew* məzu'zɔt). *Judaism.* **1.** a piece of parchment inscribed with biblical passages and fixed to the doorpost of a Jewish house. **2.** a metal case for such a parchment, sometimes worn as an ornament. [from Heb., lit.: doorpost]

mezzanine ('mɛzəˌniːn, 'mɛtsəˌniːn) *n.* **1.** Also called: **mezzanine floor.** an intermediate storey, esp. a low one between the ground and first floor of a building. **2.** *Theatre, U.S. & Canad.* the first balcony. **3.** *Theatre, Brit.* a room or floor beneath the stage. [C18: from F, from It., dim. of *mezzano* middle, from L *mediānus* MEDIAN]

mezzo ('mɛtsəʊ) *adv. Music.* moderately; quite: *mezzo piano.* [C19: from It., lit.: half, from L *medius* middle]

mezzo-soprano *n., pl.* **-nos.** **1.** a female voice intermediate between a soprano and contralto. **2.** a singer with such a voice.

mezzotint ('mɛtsəʊˌtɪnt) *n.* **1.** a method of engraving a copper plate by scraping and burnishing the roughened surface. **2.** a print made from a plate so treated. ~*vb.* **3.** (*tr.*) to engrave (a copper plate) in this fashion. [C18: from It. *mezzotinto* half tint]

mf *Music. symbol for* mezzo forte. [It.: moderately loud]

MF *abbrev. for:* **1.** *Radio.* medium frequency. **2.** Middle French.

mfd *abbrev. for* manufactured.

mfg *abbrev. for* manufacturing.

MFH *Hunting. abbrev. for* Master of Foxhounds.

mfr *abbrev. for:* **1.** manufacture. **2.** manufacturer.

mg *symbol for* milligram.

Mg *the chemical symbol for* magnesium.

M. Glam *abbrev. for* Mid Glamorgan.

Mgr *abbrev. for:* **1.** manager. **2.** Monseigneur. **3.** Monsignor.

MHA (in Australia) *abbrev. for* Member of the House of Assembly.

MHG *abbrev. for* Middle High German.

mho (məʊ) *n., pl.* **mhos.** the former name for **siemens.** [C19: formed by reversing the letters of OHM (first used by Lord Kelvin)]

MHR (in the U.S. and Australia) *abbrev. for* Member of the House of Representatives.

MHz *symbol for* megahertz.

mi *or* **me** (miː) *n. Music.* (in tonic sol-fa) the third degree of any major scale; a mediant. [C16: see GAMUT]

MI *abbrev. for* Military Intelligence.

mi. *abbrev. for* mile.

MI5 *abbrev. for* Military Intelligence, section five; a former official and current popular name for the counterintelligence agency of the British Government.

MI6 *abbrev. for* Military Intelligence, section six; a former official and current popular name for the intelligence and espionage agency of the British Government.

Miami (mai'æmi) *n.* a city and resort in SE Florida, on Biscayne Bay: developed chiefly after 1896, esp. with the Florida land boom of the 1920s; centre of an extensive tourist area. Pop.: 371 975 (1986 est.).

Miami Beach *n.* a resort in SE Florida, on an island separated from Miami by Biscayne Bay. Pop.: 96 298 (1980).

miaou *or* **miaow** (miː'aʊ, mjaʊ) *vb., interj.* variant spellings of **meow.**

miasma (mɪ'æzmə) *n., pl.* **-mata** (-mətə) *or* **-mas.** **1.** an unwholesome or foreboding atmosphere. **2.** pollution in the atmosphere, esp. noxious vapours from decomposing organic matter. [C17: NL, from Gk: defilement, from *miainein* to defile] —**mi'asmal** *or* **miasmatic** (ˌmiːəz'mætɪk) *adj.*

Mic. *Bible. abbrev. for* Micah.

mica ('maɪkə) *n.* any of a group of minerals consisting of hydrous silicates of aluminium, potassium, etc., in monoclinic crystalline form, occurring in igneous and metamorphic rock. Because of their resistance to electricity and heat they are used as dielectrics, in heating elements, etc. Also called: **isinglass.** [C18: from L: crumb] —**micaceous** (maɪ'keɪʃəs) *adj.*

Micah ('maɪkə) *n. Old Testament.* **1.** a Hebrew prophet of the late 8th century B.C. **2.** the book containing his prophecies. Douay spelling: **Micheas** (maɪ'kiːəs).

mice (maɪs) *n.* the plural of **mouse.**

micelle, micell (mɪ'sɛl), *or* **micella** (mɪ'sɛlə) *n. Chem.* **a.** a charged aggregate of molecules of colloidal size in a solution. **b.** any molecular aggregate of colloidal size. [C19: from NL *micella*, dim. of L *mica* crumb]

Mich. *abbrev. for:* **1.** Michaelmas. **2.** Michigan.

Michaelmas ('mɪkəlməs) *n.* Sept. 29, the feast of St Michael the archangel; in England, Ireland, and Wales, one of the four quarter days.

Michaelmas daisy *n. Brit.* any of various composite plants that have small autumn-blooming purple, pink, or white flowers.

Michaelmas term *n.* the autumn term at Oxford and Cambridge Universities and some other educational establishments.

Michelangelo (ˌmaɪkəl'ændʒɪˌləʊ) *n.* full name *Michelangelo Buonarroti.* 1475–1564, Florentine sculptor, painter, architect, and poet; one of the outstanding figures of the Renaissance. Among his creations are the sculptures of *David* (1504) and of *Moses* which was commissioned for the tomb of Julius II, for whom he also painted the ceiling of the Sistine Chapel (1508–12). *The Last Judgment*

(1533–41), also in the Sistine, includes a torturous vision of Hell and a disguised self-portrait. His other works include the design of the Laurentian Library (1523–29) and of the dome of St. Peter's, Rome.

Michelozzo (*Italian* mike'lɔttso) *n.* full name *Michelozzo di Bartolommeo.* 1396–1472, Italian architect and sculptor. His most important design was the Palazzo Riccardo for the Medici family in Florence (1444–59).

Michelson ('maɪkᵊlsᵊn) *n.* **Albert Abraham.** 1852–1931, U.S. physicist, born in Germany: noted for his part in the Michelson-Morley experiment: Nobel prize for physics 1907.

Michigan ('mɪʃɪɡən) *n.* **1.** a state of the N central U.S., occupying two peninsulas between Lakes Superior, Huron, Michigan, and Erie: generally low-lying. Capital: Lansing. Pop.: 9 145 000 (1986 est.). Area: 147 156 sq. km (56 817 sq. miles). Abbrevs.: **Mich.** or (with zip code) **MI 2. Lake.** a lake in the N central U.S. between Wisconsin and Michigan: the third largest of the five Great Lakes and the only one wholly in the U.S.: linked with Lake Huron by the Straits of Mackinac. Area: 58 000 sq. km (22 400 sq. miles). —**Michigander** (,mɪʃɪ'ɡændə) *n.* —'**Michigan,ite** *adj., n.*

Michoacán (*Spanish* mitʃoa'kan) *n.* a state of SW Mexico, on the Pacific: rich mineral resources. Capital: Morelia. Pop.: 3 048 704 (1980). Area: 59 864 sq. km (23 114 sq. miles).

Mick (mɪk) *n.* (*sometimes not cap.*) **1.** Also: **Mickey.** *Derog.* a slang name for an **Irishman** or a **Roman Catholic. 2.** *Austral.* the tails side of a coin. [C19: from nickname for *Michael*]

mickey or **micky** ('mɪkɪ) *n. Inf.* **take the mickey out of.** to tease. [C20: from ?]

Mickey Finn *n. Sl.* **a.** a drink containing a drug to make the drinker unconscious. **b.** the drug itself. ~Often shortened to **Mickey.** [C20: from ?]

Mickiewicz (*Polish* mits'kjevitʃ) *n.* **Adam** ('adam). 1798–1855, Polish poet, whose epic *Thaddeus* (1834) is regarded as a masterpiece of Polish literature.

mickle ('mɪkᵊl) or **muckle** ('mʌkᵊl) *Arch.* or *Scot. & N English dialect.* ~*adj.* **1.** great or abundant. ~*adv.* **2.** much; greatly. ~*n.* **3.** a great amount, esp. in the proverb, *many a little makes a mickle.* **4.** *Scot.* a small amount, esp. in the proverb *mony a mickle makes a muckle.* [C13 *mikel,* from ON *mikell,* replacing OE *micel* MUCH]

micro ('maɪkrəʊ) *adj.* **1.** very small. ~*n., pl.* **-cros. 2.** short for **microcomputer, microprocessor.**

micro- or **micr-** *combining form.* **1.** small or minute: *microdot.* **2.** involving the use of a microscope: *microscopy.* **3.** indicating a method or instrument for dealing with small quantities: *micrometer.* **4.** (in pathology) indicating abnormal smallness or underdevelopment: *microcephaly.* **5.** denoting 10⁻⁶: *microsecond.* Symbol: μ [from Gk *mikros* small]

microbe ('maɪkrəʊb) *n.* any microscopic organism, esp. a disease-causing bacterium. [C19: from F, from MICRO- + Gk *bios* life] —**mi'crobial** or **mi'crobic** *adj.*

microbiology (,maɪkrəʊbaɪ'ɒlədʒɪ) *n.* the branch of biology involving the study of microorganisms. —**microbiological** (,maɪkrəʊ,baɪə'lɒdʒɪkᵊl) or ,**micro,bio'logic** *adj.* —,**micro,bio'logically** *adv.* —**microbi'ologist** *n.*

microcephaly (,maɪkrəʊ'sɛfəlɪ) *n.* the condition of having an abnormally small head or cranial capacity. —**microcephalic** (,maɪkrəʊsɪ'fælɪk) *adj., n.* —,**micro'cephalous** *adj.*

microchemistry (,maɪkrəʊ'kɛmɪstrɪ) *n.* chemical experimentation with minute quantities of material. —,**micro'chemical** *adj.*

microchip ('maɪkrəʊ,tʃɪp) *n.* another word for **chip** (sense 7).

microcircuit ('maɪkrəʊ,sɜːkɪt) *n.* a miniature electronic circuit, esp. one in which a number of permanently connected components are contained in one small chip of semiconducting material. See **integrated circuit.** —,**micro'circuitry** *n.*

microclimate ('maɪkrəʊ,klaɪmɪt) *n. Ecology.* the atmospheric conditions affecting an individual or a small group of organisms, esp. when they differ from the climate of the rest of the community. —**microclimatic** (,maɪkrəʊ-klaɪ'mætɪk) *adj.* —,**micro,clima'tology** *n.*

microcomputer (,maɪkrəʊkəm'pjuːtə) *n.* a computer in which the central processing unit is contained in one or more silicon chips.

microcosm ('maɪkrəʊ,kɒzəm) or **microcosmos** (,maɪkrəʊ'kɒzmɒs) *n.* **1.** a miniature representation of something. **2.** man regarded as epitomizing the universe. ~Cf. **macrocosm.** [C15: via Med. L from Gk *mikros kosmos* little world] —,**micro'cosmic** or ,**micro'cosmical** *adj.*

microdot ('maɪkrəʊ,dɒt) *n.* **1.** a greatly reduced photographic copy (about the size of a pinhead) of a document, etc., used esp. in espionage. **2.** a tiny tablet containing LSD.

microeconomics (,maɪkrəʊ,iːkə'nɒmɪks, -,ɛkə-) *n.* (*functioning as sing.*) the branch of economics concerned with particular commodities, firms, or individuals and the economic relationships between them. —,**micro,eco'nomic** *adj.*

microelectronics (,maɪkrəʊɪlɛk'trɒnɪks) *n.* (*functioning as sing.*) the branch of electronics concerned with microcircuits.

microfiche ('maɪkrəʊ,fiːʃ) *n.* a sheet of film, usually the size of a filing card, on which books, newspapers, documents, etc., can be recorded in miniaturized form. [C20: from F, from MICRO- + *fiche* small card]

microfilm ('maɪkrəʊ,fɪlm) *n.* **1.** a strip of film on which books, documents, etc., can be recorded in miniaturized form. ~*vb.* **2.** to photograph (a page, document, etc.) on microfilm.

microgravity ('maɪkrəʊ,ɡrævɪtɪ) *n.* another name for **weightlessness.**

microhabitat (,maɪkrəʊ'hæbɪtæt) *n. Ecology.* the smallest part of the environment that supports a distinct flora and fauna, such as a fallen log in a forest.

microlight ('maɪkrəʊ,laɪt) *n.* a small private aircraft carrying no more than two people, with a wing area not less than 10 square metres: used in pleasure flying and racing.

microlith ('maɪkrəʊ,lɪθ) *n. Archaeol.* a small Mesolithic flint tool which formed part of a hafted tool. —,**micro'lithic** *adj.*

micrometer (maɪ'krɒmɪtə) *n.* **1.** any of various instruments or devices for the accurate measurement of distances or angles. **2.** Also called: **micrometer gauge, micrometer calliper.** a type of gauge for the accurate measurement of small distances, thicknesses, etc. The gap between its measuring faces is adjusted by a fine screw (**micrometer screw**). —**micrometric** (,maɪkrəʊ'mɛtrɪk) or ,**micro'metrical** *adj.* —**mi'crometry** *n.*

microminiaturization or **-isation** (,maɪkrəʊ,mɪnɪtʃəraɪ-'zeɪʃən) *n.* the production and application of very small components and the circuits and equipment in which they are used.

micron ('maɪkrɒn) *n., pl.* **-crons** or **-cra** (-krə). a unit of length equal to 10⁻⁶ metre. It is being replaced by the micrometre, the equivalent SI unit. [C19: NL, from Gk *mikros* small]

Micronesia (,maɪkrəʊ'niːzɪə) *n.* **1.** one of the three divisions of islands in the Pacific (the others being Melanesia and Polynesia); the NW division of Oceania: includes the Mariana, Caroline, Marshall, and Kiribati island groups, and Nauru Island. **2. Federated States of.** an island group in the W Pacific, formerly within the United States Trust Territory of the Pacific Islands: comprises the islands of Truk, Yap, Ponape, and Kosrae: formed in 1979 when the islands became self-governing: status of free association with the U.S. from 1982. Pop.: 88 375 (1984 est.). Capital: Kolonia, on Ponape. [C19: from MICRO- + Greek *nēsos* island; so called from the small size of many of the islands; on the model of *Polynesia*]

Micronesian (,maɪkrəʊ'niːʒən, -ʒɪən) *adj.* **1.** of or relating to Micronesia, its inhabitants, or their languages. ~*n.* **2.** a native or inhabitant of Micronesia. **3.** a group of languages spoken in Micronesia.

microorganism (,maɪkrəʊ'ɔːɡə,nɪzəm) *n.* any organism, such as a virus, of microscopic size.

microphone ('maɪkrə,fəʊn) *n.* a device used in sound-reproduction systems for converting sound into electrical energy. —**microphonic** (,maɪkrə'fɒnɪk) *adj.*

microprint ('maɪkrəʊ,prɪnt) *n.* a greatly reduced photographic copy of print, read by a magnifying device. It is used in order to reduce the size of large books, etc.

microprocessor (,maɪkrəʊ'prəʊsɛsə) *n. Computers.* a single integrated circuit performing the basic functions of the central processing unit in a small computer.

microscope ('maɪkrə,skəʊp) *n.* **1.** an optical instrument that uses a lens or combination of lenses to produce a magnified image of a small, close object. **2.** any instrument, such as the electron microscope, for producing a magnified visual image of a small object.

microscopic (ˌmaɪkrəˈskɒpɪk) or (less commonly) **microscopical** adj. **1.** not large enough to be seen with the naked eye but visible under a microscope. **2.** very small; minute. **3.** of, concerned with, or using a microscope. —ˌmicro'scopically adv.

microscopy (maɪˈkrɒskəpɪ) n. **1.** the study, design, and manufacture of microscopes. **2.** investigation by use of a microscope. —**microscopist** (maɪˈkrɒskəpɪst) n.

microsecond ('maɪkrəʊˌsɛkənd) n. one millionth of a second.

microstructure ('maɪkrəʊˌstrʌktʃə) n. structure on a microscopic scale, esp. the structure of an alloy as observed by etching, polishing, and observation under a microscope.

microsurgery (ˌmaɪkrəʊˈsɜːdʒərɪ) n. intricate surgery performed on cells, tissues, etc., using a specially designed operating microscope and miniature precision instruments.

microtome ('maɪkrəʊˌtəʊm) n. an instrument used for cutting thin sections for microscopical examination. —**microtomy** (maɪˈkrɒtəmɪ) n.

microwave ('maɪkrəʊˌweɪv) n. **1. a.** electromagnetic radiation in the wavelength range 0.3 to 0.001 metres: used in radar, cooking, etc. **b.** (as modifier): microwave oven. **2.** short for **microwave oven.** ~vb. (tr.) **3.** to cook in a microwave oven.

microwave background n. a background of microwave electromagnetic radiation discovered in space in 1965, believed to have emanated from the big bang with which the universe began.

microwave detector n. N.Z. a device for recording the speed of a motorist.

microwave oven n. an oven in which food is cooked by microwaves. Often shortened to **microwave.**

microwave spectroscopy n. a type of spectroscopy in which information is obtained on the structure and chemical bonding of molecules and crystals by measurements of the wavelengths of microwaves emitted or absorbed by the sample. —**microwave spectroscope** n.

micturate ('mɪktjʊˌreɪt) vb. (intr.) a less common word for **urinate.** [C19: from L micturire to desire to urinate, from mingere to urinate] —**micturition** (ˌmɪktjʊˈrɪʃən) n.

mid[1] (mɪd) adj. **1.** Phonetics. of, relating to, or denoting a vowel whose articulation lies approximately halfway between high and low, such as e in English bet. ~n. **2.** an archaic word for **middle.** [C12 midre (inflected form of midd, unattested)]

mid[2] or **'mid** (mɪd) prep. a poetic word for **amid.**

mid- combining form. indicating a middle part, point, time, or position: midday; mid-April; mid-Victorian. [OE; see MIDDLE, MID[1]]

midair (ˌmɪdˈɛə) n. **a.** some point above ground level, in the air. **b.** (as modifier): a midair collision of aircraft.

Midas ('maɪdəs) n. **1.** Greek legend. a king of Phrygia given the power by Dionysus of turning everything he touched to gold. **2. the Midas touch.** ability to make money.

mid-Atlantic adj. characterized by a blend of British and American styles, elements, etc.: a mid-Atlantic accent.

midbrain ('mɪdˌbreɪn) n. the nontechnical name for **mesencephalon.**

midday ('mɪdˈdeɪ) n. **a.** the middle of the day; noon. **b.** (as modifier): a midday meal.

Middelburg ('mɪdˀlˌbɜːɡ; Dutch 'mɪdəlbyrx) n. a city in the SW Netherlands, capital of Zeeland province, on Walcheren Island: an important trading centre in the Middle Ages and member of the Hanseatic League; 12th-century abbey; market town. Pop.: 39 044 (1987).

middelskot ('mɪdˀlˌskɒt) n. (in South Africa) an intermediate payment to a farmers' cooperative for a crop or wool clip. [from Afrik. middel middle + skot payment]

midden ('mɪdˀn) n. **1. a.** Arch. or dialect. a dunghill or pile of refuse. **b.** Dialect. a dustbin. **2.** See **kitchen midden.** [C14: from ON]

middle ('mɪdˀl) adj. **1.** equally distant from the ends or periphery of something; central. **2.** intermediate in status, situation, etc. **3.** located between the early and late parts of a series, time sequence, etc. **4.** not extreme, esp. in size; medium. **5.** (esp. in Greek and Sanskrit grammar)

denoting a voice of verbs expressing reciprocal or reflexive action. **6.** (usually cap.) (of a language) intermediate between the earliest and the modern forms. ~n. **7.** an area or point equal in distance from the ends or periphery or in time between the early and late parts. **8.** an intermediate part or section, such as the waist. **9.** Grammar. the middle voice. **10.** Logic. See **middle term.** ~vb. (tr.) **11.** to place in the middle. **12.** Naut. to fold in two. **13.** Cricket. to hit (the ball) with the middle of the bat. [OE middel]

middle age n. the period of life between youth and old age, usually (in man) considered to occur approximately between the ages of 40 and 60. —ˌmiddle-'aged adj.

Middle Ages n. the. European history. **1.** (broadly) the period from the deposition of the last W Roman emperor in 476 A.D. to the Italian Renaissance (or the fall of Constantinople in 1453). **2.** (narrowly) the period from about 1000 A.D. to the 15th century. Cf. **Dark Ages.**

Middle America n. **1.** the territories between the U.S. and South America: Mexico, Central America, and the Antilles. **2.** the U.S. middle class, esp. those groups that are politically conservative. —**Middle American** adj., n.

Middle Atlantic States or **Middle States** pl. n. the states of New York, Pennsylvania, and New Jersey.

middlebrow ('mɪdˀlˌbraʊ) Disparaging. **1.** a person with conventional tastes and limited cultural appreciation. ~adj. also **middlebrowed.** **2.** of or appealing to middlebrows.

middle C n. Music. the note written on the first ledger line below the treble staff or the first ledger line above the bass staff.

middle class n. **1.** Also called: **bourgeoisie.** a social stratum between the lower and upper classes. It consists of businessmen, professional people, etc., along with their families, and is marked by bourgeois values. ~adj. **middle-class.** **2.** of, relating to, or characteristic of the middle class.

Middle Congo n. one of the four territories of former French Equatorial Africa, in W central Africa: became an autonomous member of the French Community, as the Republic of the Congo, in 1958.

middle ear n. the sound-conducting part of the ear, containing the malleus, incus, and stapes.

Middle East n. **1.** (loosely) the area around the E Mediterranean, esp. Israel and the Arab countries from Turkey to North Africa and eastwards to Iran. **2.** (formerly) the area extending from the Tigris and Euphrates to Burma. —**Middle Eastern** adj.

Middle English n. the English language from about 1100 to about 1450.

middle game n. Chess. the central phase between the opening and the endgame.

Middle High German n. High German from about 1200 to about 1500.

Middle Low German n. Low German from about 1200 to about 1500.

middleman ('mɪdˀlˌmæn) n., pl. **-men. 1.** a trader engaged in the distribution of goods from producer to consumer. **2.** an intermediary.

middlemost ('mɪdˀlˌməʊst) adj. another word for **midmost.**

middle name n. **1.** a name between a person's first name and surname. **2.** a characteristic quality for which a person is known: caution is my middle name.

middle-of-the-road adj. **1.** not extreme, esp. in political views; moderate. **2.** of, denoting, or relating to popular music having a wide general appeal.

middle passage n. the. History. the journey across the Atlantic Ocean from the W coast of Africa to the West Indies: the longest part of the journey of the slave ships.

Middlesbrough ('mɪdˀlzbrə) n. an industrial town in NE England, on the Tees estuary, administrative centre of Cleveland. Pop.: 148 400 (1983 est.).

middle school n. Brit. a school for children aged between 8 or 9 and 12 or 13.

Middlesex ('mɪdˀlˌsɛks) n. a former county of SE England: became mostly part of N and W Greater London in 1965. Abbrev.: **Middx.**

Middle States n. another name for the **Middle Atlantic States.**

middle term n. Logic. the term that appears in both minor and major premises but not in the conclusion of a syllogism.

Middleton[1] ('mɪdᵊltən) *n.* a town in NW England, in Greater Manchester. Pop.: 51 696 (1981).

Middleton[2] ('mɪdᵊltən) *n.* **Thomas.** ?1570–1627, English dramatist. His plays include the tragedies *Women beware Women* (1621) and, in collaboration with William Rowley (?1585–?1642), *The Changeling* (1622) and the political satire *A Game at Chess* (1624).

middle watch *n. Naut.* the watch between midnight and 4 a.m.

middleweight ('mɪdᵊl,weɪt) *n.* **1. a.** a professional boxer weighing 154–160 pounds (70–72.5 kg). **b.** an amateur boxer weighing 71–75 kg (157–165 pounds). **2. a.** a professional wrestler weighing 166–176 pounds (76–80 kg). **b.** an amateur wrestler weighing 75–82 kg (162–180 pounds).

Middle West *n.* another name for the **Midwest.** —**Middle Western** *adj.* —**Middle Westerner** *n.*

middling ('mɪdlɪŋ) *adj.* **1.** mediocre in quality, size, etc.; neither good nor bad, esp. in health (often in **fair to middling**). ~*adv.* **2.** *Inf.* moderately: *middling well.* [C15 (N English & Scot.): from MID[1] + -LING[2]] —'**middlingly** *adv.*

Middx. *abbrev. for* Middlesex.

middy ('mɪdɪ) *n., pl.* **-dies. 1.** *Inf.* See **midshipman** (sense 1). **2.** *Austral.* **a.** a glass of middling size, used for beer. **b.** the measure of beer it contains.

Mideast (,mɪd'iːst) *n. Chiefly U.S.* another name for **Middle East.**

midfield (,mɪd'fiːld) *n. Soccer.* **a.** the general area between the two opposing defences. **b.** (*as modifier*): *a midfield player.*

midge (mɪdʒ) *n.* **1.** a mosquito-like dipterous insect occurring in dancing swarms, esp. near water. **2.** a small or diminutive person or animal. [OE *mycge*] —'**midgy** *adj.*

midget ('mɪdʒɪt) *n.* **1.** a dwarf whose skeleton and features are of normal proportions. **2. a.** something small of its kind. **b.** (*as modifier*): *a midget car.* [C19: from MIDGE + -ET]

Mid Glamorgan *n.* a county in S Wales, formed in 1974 from parts of Breconshire, Glamorgan, and Monmouthshire. Administrative centre: Cardiff. Pop.: 534 500 (1986 est.). Area: 1000 sq. km (393 sq. miles). Abbrev.: **M Glam.**

midgut ('mɪd,gʌt) *n.* **1.** the middle part of the digestive tract of vertebrates, including the small intestine. **2.** the middle part of the digestive tract of arthropods.

mid-heavyweight *n.* **a.** a professional wrestler weighing 199–209 pounds (91–95 kg). **b.** an amateur wrestler weighing 91–100 kg (199–220 pounds).

midi ('mɪdɪ) *adj.* (formerly) **a.** (of a skirt, coat, etc.) reaching to below the knee or midcalf. **b.** (*as n.*): *she wore her new midi.* [C20: from MID-, on the model of MINI]

Midi (*French* mi'di) *n.* **1.** the south of France. **2. Canal du.** a canal in S France, extending from the River Garonne at Toulouse to the Mediterranean at Sète and providing a link between the Mediterranean and Atlantic coasts: built between 1666 and 1681. Length: 181 km (150 miles).

midi- *combining form.* of medium or middle size, length, etc.: *midibus; midi system.*

Midian ('mɪdɪən) *n. Old Testament.* **1.** a son of Abraham (Genesis 25:1–2). **2.** a nomadic nation claiming descent from him. —'**Midian,ite** *n., adj.* —'**Midian,itish** *adj.*

midinette (,mɪdɪ'nɛt) *n.* a Parisian seamstress or salesgirl in a clothes shop. [C20: from F, from *midi* noon + *dinette* light meal; the girls had time for only a snack at midday]

Midi-Pyrénées (*French* midipirene) *n.* a region of SW France: consists of N slopes of the Pyrenees in the south, a fertile lowland area in the west crossed by the River Garonne, and the edge of the Massif Central in the north and east.

midiron ('mɪd,aɪən) *n. Golf.* a club, a No. 2 iron, used for approach shots.

midi system *n.* a complete set of hi-fi sound equipment designed as a single unit that is more compact than the standard equipment.

midland ('mɪdlənd) *n.* **a.** the central or inland part of a country. **b.** (*as modifier*): *a midland region.*

Midlands ('mɪdləndz) *n.* (*functioning as pl. or sing.*) **the.** the central counties of England: characterized by manufacturing industries. —'**Midlander** *n.*

midlife crisis *n.* a crisis that may be experienced in middle age involving frustration, panic, and feelings of pointlessness, sometimes resulting in radical and often ill-advised changes of lifestyle.

Midlothian (mɪd'ləʊðɪən) *n.* (until 1975) a county of SE central Scotland, now part of Lothian region.

midmost ('mɪd,məʊst) *adj., adv.* in the middle or midst.

midnight ('mɪd,naɪt) *n.* **1. a.** the middle of the night; 12 o'clock at night. **b.** (*as modifier*): *the midnight hour.* **2. burn the midnight oil.** to work or study late into the night.

midnight sun *n.* the sun visible at midnight during the summer inside the Arctic and Antarctic circles.

mid-off *n. Cricket.* the fielding position on the off side closest to the bowler.

mid-on *n. Cricket.* the fielding position on the on side closest to the bowler.

midpoint ('mɪd,pɔɪnt) *n.* **1.** the point on a line that is at an equal distance from either end. **2.** a point in time halfway between the beginning and end of an event.

midrib ('mɪd,rɪb) *n.* the main vein of a leaf, running down the centre of the blade.

midriff ('mɪdrɪf) *n.* **1. a.** the middle part of the human body, esp. between waist and bust. **b.** (*as modifier*): *midriff bulge.* **2.** *Anat.* another name for the **diaphragm** (sense 1). **3.** the part of a woman's garment covering the midriff. [OE *midhrif*, from MID[1] + *hrif* belly]

midship ('mɪd,ʃɪp) *Naut.* ~*adj.* **1.** in, of, or relating to the middle of a vessel. ~*n.* **2.** the middle of a vessel.

midshipman ('mɪd,ʃɪpmən) *n., pl.* **-men.** a probationary rank held by young naval officers under training, or an officer holding such a rank.

midships ('mɪd,ʃɪps) *adv., adj. Naut.* See **amidships.**

midst[1] (mɪdst) *n.* **1. in our midst.** among us. **2. in the midst of.** surrounded or enveloped by; at a point during. [C14: back formation from *amiddes* AMIDST]

midst[2] (mɪdst) *prep. Poetic.* See **amidst, amid.**

midsummer ('mɪd'sʌmə) *n.* **1. a.** the middle or height of the summer. **b.** (*as modifier*): *a midsummer carnival.* **2.** another name for **summer solstice.**

Midsummer Day *or* **Midsummer's Day** *n.* June 24, the feast of St John the Baptist; in England, Ireland, and Wales, one of the four quarter days. See also **summer solstice.**

midterm ('mɪd'tɜːm) *n.* **1. a.** the middle of a term in a school, university, etc. **b.** (*as modifier*): *midterm exam.* **2.** *U.S. politics.* **a.** the middle of a term of office, esp. of a presidential term, when congressional and local elections are held. **b.** (*as modifier*): *midterm elections.* **3. a.** the middle of the gestation period. **b.** (*as modifier*): *midterm pregnancy.* See **term** (sense 6).

mid-Victorian *adj.* **1.** *Brit. history.* of or relating to the middle period of the reign of Queen Victoria (1837–1901). ~*n.* **2.** a person of the mid-Victorian era.

midway ('mɪd,weɪ *or, for adv., n.* ,mɪd'weɪ) *adj.* **1.** in or at the middle of the distance; halfway. ~*adv.* **2.** to the middle of the distance. ~*n.* **3.** *Obs.* a middle place, way, etc.

Midway Islands *pl. n.* an atoll in the central Pacific, about 2100 km (1300 miles) northwest of Honolulu: annexed by the U.S. in 1867: scene of a decisive battle (June, 1942), in which the U.S. combined fleets destroyed Japan's carrier fleet. Pop.: 453 (1980). Area: 5 sq. km (2 sq. miles).

midweek ('mɪd'wiːk) *n.* **a.** the middle of the week. **b.** (*as modifier*): *a midweek holiday.*

Midwest ('mɪd'wɛst) *or* **Middle West** *n.* the N central part of the U.S.; the states from Ohio westwards that border on the Great Lakes, and often the upper Mississippi and Missouri valleys. —'**Mid'western** *adj.* —'**Mid'westerner** *n.*

mid-wicket *n. Cricket.* the fielding position on the on side, midway between square leg and mid-on.

midwife ('mɪd,waɪf) *n., pl.* **-wives** (-,waɪvz). **1.** a nurse qualified to deliver babies and to care for women before, during, and after childbirth. **2.** a woman skilled in aiding in the delivery of babies. [C14: from OE *mid* with + *wif* woman]

midwifery ('mɪd,wɪfərɪ) *n.* the training, art, or practice of a midwife; obstetrics.

midwinter ('mɪd'wɪntə) *n.* **1. a.** the middle or depth of the winter. **b.** (*as modifier*): *a midwinter festival.* **2.** another name for **winter solstice.**

midyear ('mɪd'jɪə) *n.* the middle of the year.

mien (miːn) *n. Literary.* a person's manner, bearing, or appearance. [C16: prob. var. of obs. *demean* appearance; rel. to F *mine* aspect]

Mieres (*Spanish* 'mjeres) *n.* a city in N Spain, south of Oviedo: steel and chemical industries; iron and coal mines. Pop.: 58 098 (1981).

Mies van der Rohe ('mi:z væn də 'rəuə) *n.* **Ludwig.** 1886–1969, U.S. architect, born in Germany. He directed the Bauhaus (1929–33) and developed a rational functional style, characterized by pure geometrical design. His works include the Seagram building, New York (1958).

miff (mɪf) *Inf.* ~*vb.* **1.** to take offence or to offend. ~*n.* **2.** a petulant mood. **3.** a petty quarrel. [C17: ? an imitative expression of bad temper] —'**miffy** *adj.*

might[1] (maɪt) *vb.* (takes an implied infinitive or an infinitive without *to*) used as an auxiliary: **1.** making the past tense or subjunctive mood of **may**[1]: *he might have come.* **2.** (often foll. by *well*) expressing possibility: *he might well come.* In this sense *might* looks to the future and functions as a weak form of *may.* See **may**[1] (sense 2). [OE *miht*]
▷**Usage.** See at **may**[1].

might[2] (maɪt) *n.* **1.** power, force, or vigour, esp. of a great or supreme kind. **2.** physical strength. **3. (with) might and main.** See **main**[1] (sense 7). [OE *miht*]

mighty ('maɪtɪ) *adj.* **mightier, mightiest. 1. a.** having or indicating might; powerful or strong. **b.** (*as collective n.; preceded by the*): *the mighty.* **2.** very large; vast. **3.** very great in extent, importance, etc. ~*adv.* **4.** *Inf., chiefly U.S. & Canad.* (intensifier): *mighty tired.* —'**mightily** *adv.* —'**mightiness** *n.*
▷**Usage.** *Mighty* is used by many speakers, esp. in the south of the U.S. and in various dialects, as an intensifier equivalent to *very.* This use of *mighty* is nevertheless avoided outside informal speech by careful users of English.

mignon ('mɪnjɒn) *adj.* small and pretty; dainty. [C16: from F, from OF *mignot* dainty] —**mignonne** ('mɪnjɒn) *fem. n.*

mignonette (ˌmɪnjə'nɛt) *n.* **1.** any of various mainly Mediterranean plants, such as **garden mignonette**, that have spikes of small greenish-white flowers. **2.** a type of fine pillow lace. **3. a.** a greyish-green colour. **b.** (*as adj.*): *mignonette ribbons.* [C18: from F, dim. of MIGNON]

migraine ('mi:greɪn, 'maɪ-) *n.* a throbbing headache usually affecting only one side of the head and commonly accompanied by nausea and visual disturbances. [C18: (earlier form, C14 *mygrame* MEGRIM): from F, from LL *hēmicrānia* pain in half of the head, from Gk, from HEMI- + *kranion* CRANIUM] —'**migrainous** *adj.*

migrant ('maɪgrənt) *n.* **1.** a person or animal that moves from one region, place, or country to another. **2.** an itinerant agricultural worker. ~*adj.* **3.** moving from one region, place, or country to another; migratory.

migrate (maɪ'greɪt) *vb.* (*intr.*) **1.** to go from one place to settle in another, esp. in a foreign country. **2.** (of birds, fishes, etc.) to journey between different habitats at specific times of the year. [C17: from L *migrāre* to change one's abode] —**mi'grator** *n.*

migration (maɪ'greɪʃən) *n.* **1.** the act or an instance of migrating. **2.** a group of people, birds, etc., migrating in a body. **3.** *Chem.* a movement of atoms, ions, or molecules, such as the motion of ions in solution under the influence of electric fields. —**mi'grational** *adj.*

migratory ('maɪgrətərɪ, -trɪ) *adj.* **1.** of or characterized by migration. **2.** nomadic; itinerant.

mihrab ('mi:ræb, -rəb) *n. Islam.* the niche in a mosque showing the direction of Mecca. [from Ar.]

mikado (mɪ'kɑːdəʊ) *n., pl.* -**dos.** (*often cap.*) *Arch.* the Japanese emperor. [C18: from Japanese, from *mi*-honourable + *kado* door, palace gate]

mike[1] (maɪk) *n. Inf.* short for **microphone.**

mike[2] (maɪk) *Brit. sl.* ~*vb.* (*intr.*) **1.** to idle; wait about. ~*n.* **2.** an evasion of work: *to do a mike.* [C19: from ?]

mil (mɪl) *n.* **1.** a unit of length equal to one thousandth of an inch. **2.** a unit of angular measure, used in gunnery, equal to one six-thousand-four-hundredth of a circumference. **3.** *Photog.* short for **millimetre**: *35-mil film.* [C18: from L *millēsimus* thousandth]

mil. *abbrev. for:* **1.** military. **2.** militia.

milady *or* **miladi** (mɪ'leɪdɪ) *n., pl.* -**dies.** (formerly) a continental title used for an English gentlewoman.

Milan (mɪ'læn) *n.* a city in N Italy, in central Lombardy: Italy's second largest city and chief financial and industrial centre; a centre of the Renaissance under the Visconti and Sforza families. Pop.: 1 495 260 (1986). Italian name: **Milano** (mi'la:no). —ˌMila'**nese** *adj., n.*

Milazzo (*Italian* mi'lattso) *n.* a port in NE Sicily: founded in the 8th century B.C.; scene of a battle (1860), in which Garibaldi defeated the Bourbon forces. Pop.: 31 497 (1984 est.). Ancient name: **Mylae** ('maɪ,li:).

milch (mɪltʃ) *n.* **1.** (*modifier*) (esp. of cattle) yielding milk. **2. milch cow.** *Inf.* a source of easy income, esp. a person. [C13: from OE -*milce* (in compounds); rel. to OE *melcan* to milk]

mild (maɪld) *adj.* **1.** (of a taste, sensation, etc.) not powerful or strong; bland. **2.** gentle or temperate in character, climate, behaviour, etc. **3.** not extreme; moderate. **4.** feeble; unassertive. ~*n.* **5.** *Brit.* draught beer, of darker colour than bitter and flavoured with fewer hops. [OE *milde*] —'**mildly** *adv.* —'**mildness** *n.*

mildew ('mɪl,dju:) *n.* **1.** any of various diseases of plants that affect mainly the leaves and are caused by parasitic fungi. **2.** any fungus causing this. **3.** another name for **mould**[2] . ~*vb.* **4.** to affect or become affected with mildew. [OE *mildēaw*, from *mil*- honey + *dēaw* DEW] —'**mil,dewy** *adj.*

mild steel *n.* any of a class of strong tough steels that contain a low quantity of carbon.

mile (maɪl) *n.* **1.** Also called: **statute mile.** a unit of length used in English-speaking countries, equal to 1760 yards. 1 mile is equivalent to 1.60934 kilometres. **2.** See **nautical mile. 3.** the Roman mile, equivalent to 1620 yards. **4.** (*often pl.*) *Inf.* a great distance; great deal: *he missed by a mile.* **5.** a race extending over a mile. ~*adv.* **6. miles.** (intensifier): *that's miles better.* [OE *mīl*, from L *mīlia* (*passuum*) a thousand (paces)]

mileage *or* **milage** ('maɪlɪdʒ) *n.* **1.** a distance expressed in miles. **2.** the total number of miles that a motor vehicle has travelled. **3.** allowance for travelling expenses, esp. as a fixed rate per mile. **4.** the number of miles a motor vehicle will travel on one gallon of fuel. **5.** *Inf.* use, benefit, or service provided by something. **6.** *Inf.* grounds, substance, or weight: *some mileage in their arguments.*

mileometer *or* **milometer** (maɪ'lɒmɪtə) *n.* a device that records the number of miles that a bicycle or motor vehicle has travelled.

milepost ('maɪl,pəʊst) *n.* **1.** *Horse racing.* a marking post on a racecourse a mile before the finishing line. **2.** *Chiefly U.S. & Canad.* a signpost that shows the distance in miles to or from a place.

miler ('maɪlə) *n.* an athlete, horse, etc., that runs or specializes in races of one mile.

Miles (maɪlz) *n.* **Bernard,** Baron Miles of Blackfriars. born 1907, British actor and theatre manager. He founded the Mermaid Theatre in Blackfriars, London, and is known as a character actor.

milestone ('maɪl,stəʊn) *n.* **1.** a stone pillar that shows the distance in miles to or from a place. **2.** a significant event in life, history, etc.

Miletus (mɪ'li:təs) *n.* an ancient city on the W coast of Asia Minor: a major Ionian centre of trade and learning in the ancient world. —**Mi'lesian** *adj., n.*

milfoil ('mɪl,fɔɪl) *n.* **1.** another name for **yarrow. 2.** See **water milfoil.** [C13: from OF, from L *milifolium*, from *mille* thousand + *folium* leaf]

Milford Haven ('mɪlfəd) *n.* a port in SW Wales, in Dyfed on **Milford Haven** (a large inlet of St George's Channel): major oil port. Pop.: 14 000 (1985 est.).

Milhaud (*French* mijo) *n.* **Darius** (darjys). 1892–1974, French composer; member of Les Six. A notable exponent of polytonality, his large output includes operas, symphonies, ballets, string quartets, and songs.

miliaria (ˌmɪlɪ'ɛərɪə) *n.* an acute itching eruption of the skin, caused by blockage of the sweat glands. [C19: from NL, from L *miliārius* MILIARY]

miliary ('mɪlɪərɪ) *adj.* **1.** resembling or relating to millet seeds. **2.** (of a disease or skin eruption) characterized by small lesions resembling millet seeds: *miliary fever.* [C17: from L *miliārius*, from *milium* MILLET]

milieu ('mi:ljɜː) *n., pl.* **milieus** *or French* **milieux** (miljø). surroundings, location, or setting. [C19: from F, from *mi*- MID[1] + *lieu* place]

militant ('mɪlɪtənt) *adj.* **1.** aggressive or vigorous, esp. in the support of a cause. **2.** warring; engaged in warfare. ~*n.* **3.** a militant person. [C15: from L *mīlitāre* to be a soldier, from *mīles* soldier] —'**militancy** *n.* —'**militantly** *adv.*

militarism ('mɪlɪtəˌrɪzəm) *n.* **1.** military spirit; pursuit of military ideals. **2.** domination by the military, esp. on a

political level. **3.** a policy of maintaining a strong military organization in aggressive preparedness for war. —'**militarist** n.
militarize or **-ise** ('mɪlɪtə,raɪz) vb. (tr.) **1.** to convert to military use. **2.** to imbue with militarism. —,**militari'zation** or **-i'sation** n.
military ('mɪlɪtərɪ, -trɪ) adj. **1.** of or relating to the armed forces, warlike matters, etc. **2.** of or characteristic of soldiers. ~n., pl. **-taries** or **-tary**. **3.** (preceded by the) the armed services, esp. the army. [C16: via F from L mīlitāris, from mīles soldier] —'**militarily** adv.
military police n. a corps within an army that performs police and disciplinary duties. —**military policeman** n.
militate ('mɪlɪ,teɪt) vb. (intr.; usually foll. by against or for) (of facts, etc.) to have influence or effect: the evidence militated against his release. [C17: from L mīlitātus, from mīlitāre to be a soldier]
▷ **Usage.** Confusion sometimes arises between militate and mitigate. Militate, which comes from the same Latin root as military, is an intransitive verb meaning "to have influence or effect". While it can be used in a positive sense with for, as in any act that militates for peaceful cooperation, it is typically used in a negative sense with against (see definition, above). Mitigate comes from Latin mītis mild and is typically used transitively. It means "to moderate; make less severe, unpleasant, etc.", and is generally restricted to formal speech or writing: governments should endeavour to mitigate distress.
militia (mɪ'lɪʃə) n. **1.** a body of citizen (as opposed to professional) soldiers. **2.** an organization containing men enlisted for service in emergency only. [C16: from L: soldiery, from mīles soldier] —**mi'litiaman** n.
milk (mɪlk) n. **1. a.** a whitish fluid secreted by the mammary glands of mature female mammals and used for feeding their young until weaned. **b.** the milk of cows, goats, etc., used by man as a food or in the production of butter, cheese, etc. **2.** any similar fluid in plants, such as the juice of a coconut. **3.** a milklike pharmaceutical preparation, such as milk of magnesia. **4. cry over spilt milk.** to lament something that cannot be altered. ~vb. **5.** to draw milk from the udder of (an animal). **6.** (intr.) (of animals) to yield milk. **7.** (tr.) to draw off or tap in small quantities: to milk the petty cash. **8.** (tr.) to extract as much money, help, etc., as possible from: to milk a situation of its news value. **9.** (tr.) to extract venom, sap, etc., from. [OE milc] —'**milker** n.
milk-and-water adj. (milk and water when postpositive). weak, feeble, or insipid.
milk bar n. **1.** a snack bar at which milk drinks and light refreshments are served. **2.** (in Australia) a shop selling, in addition to milk, basic provisions and other items.
milk chocolate n. chocolate that has been made with milk, having a creamy taste.
milk float n. Brit. a small motor vehicle used to deliver milk to houses.
milk leg n. inflammation and thrombosis of the femoral vein following childbirth, characterized by painful swelling of the leg.
milkmaid ('mɪlk,meɪd) n. a girl or woman who milks cows.
milkman ('mɪlkmən) n., pl. **-men.** a man who delivers or sells milk.
milk of magnesia n. a suspension of magnesium hydroxide in water, used as an antacid and laxative.
milk pudding n. Chiefly Brit. a pudding made by boiling or baking milk with a grain, esp. rice.
milk round n. Brit. **1.** a route along which a milkman regularly delivers milk. **2.** a regular series of visits, esp. as made by recruitment officers from industry to universities.
milk run n. Aeronautics, inf. a routine and uneventful flight. [C20: from a milkman's safe and regular routine]
milk shake n. a cold frothy drink made of milk, flavouring, and sometimes ice cream, whisked or beaten together.
milksop ('mɪlk,sɒp) n. a feeble or ineffectual man or youth.
milk sugar n. another name for **lactose.**
milk tooth n. any of the first teeth to erupt; a deciduous tooth. Also called: **baby tooth.**
milkwort ('mɪlk,wɜːt) n. any of several plants having small blue, pink, or white flowers. They were formerly believed to increase milk production in nursing women.

milky ('mɪlkɪ) adj. **milkier, milkiest. 1.** resembling milk, esp. in colour or cloudiness. **2.** of or containing milk. **3.** spiritless or spineless. —'**milkily** adv. —'**milkiness** n.
Milky Way n. **the.** the diffuse band of light stretching across the night sky that consists of millions of faint stars, nebulae, etc., and forms part of the Galaxy. [C14: translation of L via lactea]
mill (mɪl) n. **1.** a building fitted with machinery for processing materials, manufacturing goods, etc.; factory. **2.** a machine that processes materials, manufactures goods, etc., by performing a continuous or repetitive operation, such as a machine to grind flour, pulverize solids, or press fruit. **3.** a machine that tools or polishes metal. **4.** a small machine for grinding solids: a pepper mill. **5.** a system, institution, etc., that influences people or things in the manner of a factory: the educational mill. **6.** an unpleasant experience; ordeal (esp. in **go** or **be put through the mill**). **7.** a fist fight. ~vb. **8.** (tr.) to grind, press, or pulverize in or as if in a mill. **9.** (tr.) to process or produce in or with a mill. **10.** to cut or roll (metal) with or as if with a milling machine. **11.** (tr.) to groove or flute the edge of (a coin). **12.** (intr.; often foll. by about or around) to move about in a confused manner. **13.** Arch. sl. to fight, esp. with the fists. [OE mylen from LL molīna a mill, from L mola mill, from molere to grind] —'**millable** adj. —**milled** adj.
Mill (mɪl) n. **1. James.** 1773–1836, Scottish philosopher, historian, and economist. He expounded Bentham's utilitarian philosophy in Elements of Political Economy (1821) and Analysis of the Phenomena of the Human Mind (1829) and also wrote a History of British India (1817–18). **2.** his son, **John Stuart.** 1806–73, English philosopher and economist. He modified Bentham's utilitarian philosophy in Utilitarianism (1861) and in his treatise On Liberty (1859) he defended the rights and freedom of the individual. Other works include A System of Logic (1843) and Principles of Political Economy (1848).
Millais (mɪ'leɪ) n. Sir **John Everett.** 1829–96, English painter, who was a founder of the Pre-Raphaelite Brotherhood. His works include The Order of Release (1853) and The Blind Girl (1856).
millboard ('mɪl,bɔːd) n. strong pasteboard, used esp. in book covers. [C18: from milled board]
milldam ('mɪl,dæm) n. a dam built in a stream to raise the water level sufficiently for it to turn a millwheel.
millefeuille French. (milfœj) n. Brit. a small iced cake made of puff pastry filled with jam and cream. [lit.: thousand leaves]
millefleurs ('miːl,flɜː) n. (functioning as sing.) a design of stylized floral patterns, used in textiles, paperweights, etc. [F: thousand flowers]
millenarian (,mɪlɪ'nɛərɪən) adj. **1.** of or relating to a thousand or to a thousand years. **2.** of or relating to the millennium or millenarianism. ~n. **3.** an adherent of millenarianism.
millenarianism (,mɪlɪ'nɛərɪə,nɪzəm) n. **1.** Christianity. the belief in a future millennium during which Christ will reign on earth: based on Revelation 20:1–5. **2.** any belief in a future period of ideal peace and happiness.
millenary (mɪ'lɛnərɪ) n., pl. **-naries. 1.** a sum or aggregate of one thousand. **2.** another word for a **millennium.** ~adj., n. **3.** another word for **millenarian.** [C16: from LL millēnārius containing a thousand, from L mille thousand]
millennium (mɪ'lɛnɪəm) n., pl. **-niums** or **-nia** (-nɪə). **1. the.** Christianity. the period of a thousand years of Christ's awaited reign upon earth. **2.** a period or cycle of one thousand years. **3.** a time of peace and happiness, esp. in the distant future. [C17: from NL, from L mille thousand + annus year] —**mil'lennial** adj. —**mil'lennialist** n.
millepede ('mɪlɪ,piːd) or **milleped** n. variants of **millipede.**
millepore ('mɪlɪ,pɔː) n. any of a genus of tropical colonial coral-like hydrozoans, having a calcareous skeleton. [C18: from NL, from L mille thousand + porus hole]
miller ('mɪlə) n. **1.** a person who keeps, operates, or works in a mill, esp. a corn mill. **2.** another name for **milling machine. 3.** a person who operates a milling machine.
Miller ('mɪlə) n. **1. Arthur.** born 1915, U.S. dramatist. His plays include Death of a Salesman (1949), The Crucible

(1953), and *A View from the Bridge* (1955). **2. Glenn.** 1904–44, U.S. composer, trombonist, and band leader. His popular compositions include "Moonlight Serenade". During World War II he was leader of the U.S. Air Force band in Europe. He disappeared without trace on a flight between England and France. **3. Henry.** 1891–1980, U.S. novelist, author of *Tropic of Cancer* (1934) and *Tropic of Capricorn* (1938). **4. Hugh** 1802–56, Scottish geologist and writer. **5. Jonathan (Wolfe).** born 1934, British doctor, actor, and theatre director. His productions include Shakespeare, Ibsen, and Chekhov as well as several operas. He has also presented many television medical programmes.

miller's thumb *n.* any of several small freshwater European fishes having a flattened body. [C15: from the alleged likeness of the fish's head to a thumb]

millesimal (mɪ'lɛsɪməl) *adj.* **1. a.** denoting a thousandth. **b.** (*as n.*): *a millesimal.* **2.** of, consisting of, or relating to a thousandth. [C18: from L *millēsimus*]

millet ('mɪlɪt) *n.* **1.** a cereal grass cultivated for grain and animal fodder. **2. a.** an Indian annual grass cultivated for grain and forage, having pale round shiny seeds. **b.** the seed of this plant. **3.** any of various similar or related grasses. [C14: via OF from L *milium*]

Millet (*French* mile) *n.* **Jean François** (ʒɑ̃ frɑ̃swa). 1814–75, French painter of the Barbizon school, noted for his studies of peasants at work.

milli- *prefix.* denoting 10^{-3}: *millimetre.* Symbol: m [from F, from L *mille* thousand]

milliard ('mɪlɪ,ɑːd, 'mɪljɑːd) *n.* Brit. (no longer in technical use) a thousand million. U.S. & Canad. equivalent: **billion.** [C19: from F]

millibar ('mɪlɪ,bɑː) *n.* a cgs unit of atmospheric pressure equal to 10^{-3} bar, 100 newtons per square metre or 0.7500617 millimetre of mercury.

Milligan ('mɪlɪɡən) *n.* **Spike,** real name *Terence Alan Milligan.* born 1918, Irish radio, stage, and film comedian and author, born in India. He appeared on *The Goon Show* (with Peter Sellers and Harry Secombe; BBC Radio, 1952–60) and his films include *Postman's Knock* (1962), *Adolf Hitler, My Part in his Downfall* (1972), *The Three Musketeers* (1974), and *The Last Remake of Beau Geste* (1977).

milligram *or* **milligramme** ('mɪlɪ,ɡræm) *n.* one thousandth of a gram. [C19: from F]

Millikan ('mɪlɪkən) *n.* **Robert Andrews.** 1868–1953, U.S. physicist. He measured the change of electron (1910), verified Einstein's equation for the photoelectric effect (1916), and studied cosmic rays; Nobel prize for physics 1923.

millilitre *or U.S.* **milliliter** ('mɪlɪ,liːtə) *n.* one thousandth of a litre.

millimetre *or U.S.* **millimeter** ('mɪlɪ,miːtə) *n.* one thousandth of a metre.

millimicron ('mɪlɪ,maɪkrɒn) *n.* an obsolete name for a **nanometre.**

milliner ('mɪlɪnə) *n.* a person who makes or sells women's hats. [C16: orig. *Milaner,* a native of *Milan,* at that time famous for its fancy goods]

millinery ('mɪlɪnərɪ, -ɪnrɪ) *n.* **1.** hats, trimmings, etc., sold by a milliner. **2.** the business or shop of a milliner.

milling ('mɪlɪŋ) *n.* **1.** the act or process of grinding, pressing, or crushing in a mill. **2.** the grooves or fluting on the edge of a coin, etc.

milling machine *n.* a machine tool in which a horizontal arbor or vertical spindle rotates a cutting tool above a horizontal table.

million ('mɪljən) *n., pl.* **-lions** *or* **-lion.** **1.** the cardinal number that is the product of 1000 multiplied by 1000. **2.** a numeral, 1 000 000, 10^6, M̲, etc., representing this number. **3.** (*often pl.*) *Inf.* an extremely large but unspecified number or amount: *I have millions of things to do.* ~*determiner.* **4.** (preceded by *a* or by a numeral) **a.** amounting to a million: *a million light years.* **b.** (*as pron.*): *I can see a million.* [C17: via OF from early It. *millione,* from *mille* thousand, from L]

millionaire (,mɪljə'nɛə) *n.* a person whose assets are worth at least a million of the standard monetary units of his country. —,**million'airess** *fem. n.*

millionth ('mɪljənθ) *n.* **1. a.** one of 1 000 000 equal parts of something. **b.** (*as modifier*): *a millionth part.* **2.** one of 1 000 000 equal divisions of a scientific quantity. **3.** the fraction one divided by 1 000 000. ~*adj.* **4.** (*usually prenominal*) **a.** being the ordinal number of 1 000 000 in

numbering or counting order, etc. **b.** (*as n.*): *the millionth to be manufactured.*

millipede, millepede ('mɪlɪ,piːd), *or* **milleped** ('mɪlɪ,pɛd) *n.* any of various terrestrial herbivorous arthropods, having a cylindrical segmented body, each segment of which bears two pairs of legs. [C17: from L, from *mille* thousand + *pēs* foot]

millisecond ('mɪlɪ,sɛkənd) *n.* one thousandth of a second.

millpond ('mɪl,pɒnd) *n.* **1.** a pool formed by damming a stream to provide water to turn a mill-wheel. **2.** any expanse of calm water.

millrace ('mɪl,reɪs) *or* **millrun** *n.* **1.** the current of water that turns a millwheel. **2.** the channel for this water.

Mills (mɪlz) *n.* **1. Hayley.** born 1946, British actress. Her films include *Pollyanna* (1960) and *The Parent Trap* (1961). **2.** her father, Sir **John.** born 1908, British actor. His films include *This Happy Breed* (1944) and *Ryan's Daughter* (1971).

Mills bomb (mɪlz) *n.* a type of high-explosive hand grenade. [C20: after Sir William *Mills* (1856–1932), E inventor]

millstone ('mɪl,stəʊn) *n.* **1.** one of a pair of heavy flat disc-shaped stones that are rotated one against the other to grind grain. **2.** a heavy burden, such as a responsibility or obligation.

millstream ('mɪl,striːm) *n.* a stream of water used to turn a millwheel.

millwheel ('mɪl,wiːl) *n.* a wheel, esp. a waterwheel, that drives a mill.

millwork ('mɪl,wɜːk) *n.* work done in a mill.

millwright ('mɪl,raɪt) *n.* a person who designs, builds, or repairs grain mills or mill machinery.

Milne (mɪln) *n.* **A(lan) A(lexander) .** 1882–1956, English writer, noted for his books and verse for children, including *When We Were Very Young* (1924) and *Winnie the Pooh* (1926).

milometer (maɪ'lɒmɪtə) *n.* a variant spelling of **mileometer.**

milord (mɪ'lɔːd) *n.* (formerly) a continental title used for an English gentleman. [C19: via F from E *my lord*]

Mílos ('miːlɒs) *n.* transliteration of the Modern Greek name for **Melos.**

Milstein ('mɪlstaɪn) *n.* **Nathan.** born 1904, U.S. violinist, born in Russia.

milt (mɪlt) *n.* **1.** the testis of a fish. **2.** the spermatozoa and seminal fluid produced by a fish. **3.** *Rare.* the spleen, esp. of fowls and pigs. ~*vb.* **4.** to fertilize (fish roe) with milt, esp. artificially. [OE *milte* spleen; in the sense: fish sperm, prob. from MDu. *milte*] —'**milter** *n.*

Miltiades (mɪl'taɪə,diːz) *n.* ?540–?489 B.C., Athenian general, who defeated the Persians at Marathon (490).

Milton ('mɪltən) *n.* **John.** 1608–74, English poet. His early works, notably *L'Allegro* and *Il Penseroso* (1632), the masque *Comus* (1634), and the elegy *Lycidas* (1637), show the influence of his Christian humanist education and his love of Italian Renaissance poetry. A staunch Parliamentarian and opponent of episcopacy, he published many pamphlets during the Civil War period, including *Areopagitica* (1644), which advocated freedom of the press. His greatest works were the epic poems *Paradise Lost* (1667; 1674), and *Paradise Regained* (1671) and the verse drama *Samson Agonistes* (1671). —**Mil'tonic** *or* **Mil'tonian** *adj.*

Milton Keynes ('mɪltən 'kiːnz) *n.* a new town in N Buckinghamshire, founded in 1967. Pop.: 146 000 (1983 est.).

Milwaukee (mɪl'wɔːkiː) *n.* a port in SE Wisconsin, on Lake Michigan: the largest city in the state; established as a trading post in the 18th century; an important industrial centre. Pop.: 605 090 (1986 est.). —**Mil'waukeean** *adj., n.*

mim (mɪm) *adj. Dialect.* prim, modest, or demure. [C17: ? imit. of lip-pursing]

mime (maɪm) *n.* **1.** the theatrical technique of expressing an idea or mood or portraying a character entirely by gesture and bodily movement without the use of words. **2.** Also called: **mime artist.** a performer specializing in this. **3.** a dramatic presentation using such a technique. **4.** (in the classical theatre) **a.** a comic performance with exaggerated gesture and physical action. **b.** an actor in such a performance. ~*vb.* **5.** to express (an idea, etc.) in actions or gestures without speech. **6.** (of singers or musicians) to perform as if singing a song or playing a piece of music that is actually prerecorded. [OE *mīma*, from L *mīmus* mimic actor, from Gk *mimos* imitator] —'**mimer** *n.*

Mimeograph ('mɪmɪə,grɑːf) *n.* **1.** *Trademark.* an office machine for printing multiple copies of text or line drawings from a stencil. **2.** a copy produced by this. ~*vb.* **3.** to print copies from (a prepared stencil) using this machine.

mimesis (mɪ'miːsɪs) *n.* **1.** *Art, literature.* the imitative representation of nature or human behaviour. **2.** *Biol.* another name for **mimicry** (sense 2). **3.** *Rhetoric.* representation of another person's alleged words in a speech. [C16: from Gk, from *mimeisthai* to imitate]

mimetic (mɪ'mɛtɪk) *adj.* **1.** of, resembling, or relating to mimesis or imitation, as in art, etc. **2.** *Biol.* of or exhibiting mimicry. —**mi'metically** *adv.*

mimic ('mɪmɪk) *vb.* **-icking, -icked.** (*tr.*) **1.** to imitate (a person, a manner, etc.), esp. for satirical effect; ape. **2.** to take on the appearance of: *certain flies mimic wasps.* **3.** to copy closely or in a servile manner. ~*n.* **4.** a person or an animal, such as a parrot, that is clever at mimicking. **5.** an animal that displays mimicry. ~*adj.* **6.** of, relating to, or using mimicry. **7.** simulated, make-believe, or mock. [C16: from L *mimicus*, from Gk *mimikos*, from *mimos* MIME] —'**mimicker** *n.*

mimicry ('mɪmɪkrɪ) *n., pl.* **-ries. 1.** the act or art of copying or imitating closely; mimicking. **2.** the resemblance shown by one animal species to another, which protects it from predators.

MIMinE *abbrev. for* Member of the Institute of Mining Engineers.

Mimir ('miːmɪə) *n. Norse myth.* a giant who guarded the well of wisdom near the roots of Yggdrasil.

mimosa (mɪ'məʊsə, -zə) *n.* any of various tropical shrubs or trees having ball-like clusters of typically yellow flowers and leaves that are often sensitive to touch or light. See also **sensitive plant.** [C18: from NL, prob. from L *mimus* MIME, because the plant's sensitivity to touch imitates the similar reaction of animals]

mimulus ('mɪmjʊləs) *n.* any of a genus of flowering plants of temperate regions. See **monkey flower.** [C19: Med. L, from L *mimus* MIME, alluding to masklike flowers]

min. *abbrev. for:* **1.** mineralogy. **2.** minimum. **3.** mining. **4.** minute *or* minutes.

Min. *abbrev. for:* **1.** Minister. **2.** Ministry.

mina ('maɪnə) *n.* a variant spelling of **myna.**

Mina Hassan Tani ('miːnə hɑː'sɑːn 'tɑːnɪ) *n.* a port in NW Morocco, on the Sebou River 16 km (10 miles) from the Atlantic. Pop.: 135 960 (1973 est.). Also called: **Kénitra.** Former name (1932–56): **Port Lyautey.**

minaret (,mɪnə'rɛt, 'mɪnə,rɛt) *n.* a slender tower of a mosque having one or more balconies. [C17: from F, from Turkish, from Ar. *manārat* lamp, from *nār* fire] —,**mina'reted** *adj.*

Minas Basin ('maɪnəs) *n.* a bay in E Canada, in central Nova Scotia: the NE arm of the Bay of Fundy, with which it is linked by **Minas Channel.**

Minas Gerais (Portuguese 'minaʒ ʒe'rais) *n.* an inland state of E Brazil: situated on the high plateau of the Brazilian Highlands; large reserves of iron ore and manganese. Capital: Belo Horizonte. Pop.: 13 389 605 (1980). Area: 587 172 sq. km (226 707 sq. miles).

minatory ('mɪnətərɪ, -trɪ) *or* **minatorial** *adj.* threatening or menacing. [C16: from LL *minātōrius*, from L *minārī* to threaten]

mince (mɪns) *vb.* **1.** (*tr.*) to chop, grind, or cut into very small pieces. **2.** (*tr.*) to soften or moderate: *I didn't mince my words.* **3.** (*intr.*) to walk or speak in an affected dainty manner. ~*n.* **4.** *Chiefly Brit.* minced meat. [C14: from OF *mincier*, ult. from LL *minūtia*; see MINUTIAE] —'**mincer** *n.*

mincemeat ('mɪns,miːt) *n.* **1.** a mixture of dried fruit, spices, etc., used esp. for filling pies. **2.** **make mincemeat of.** *Inf.* to defeat completely.

mince pie *n.* a small round pastry tart filled with mincemeat.

Minch (mɪntʃ) *n.* **the.** a channel of the Atlantic divided into the **North Minch,** between the mainland of Scotland and the Isle of Lewis, and the **Little Minch,** between the Isle of Skye and Harris and North Uist.

mincing ('mɪnsɪŋ) *adj.* (of a person) affectedly elegant in gait, manner, or speech. —'**mincingly** *adv.*

mind (maɪnd) *n.* **1.** the part of a person responsible for thought, feelings, intention, etc. **2.** intelligence or the intellect, esp. as opposed to feelings or wishes. **3.** recollection or remembrance: *it comes to mind.* **4.** the faculty of original or creative thought; imagination: *it's all in the mind.* **5.** a person considered as an intellectual being: *great minds.* **6.** condition, state, or manner of feeling or thought: *his state of mind.* **7.** an inclination, desire, or purpose: *I have a mind to go.* **8.** attention or thoughts: *keep your mind on your work.* **9.** a sound mental state; sanity (esp. in **out of one's mind**). **10.** (in Cartesian philosophy) one of two basic modes of existence, the other being matter. **11. blow someone's mind.** *Sl.* **a.** (of a drug) to alter someone's mental state. **b.** to astound or surprise someone. **12. change one's mind.** to alter one's decision or opinion. **13. in** *or* **of two minds.** undecided; wavering. **14. give** (**someone**) **a piece of one's mind.** to criticize or censure (someone) frankly or vehemently. **15. make up one's mind.** to decide (something or to do something). **16. on one's mind.** in one's thoughts. ~*vb.* **17.** (when *tr., may take a clause as object*) to take offence at: *do you mind if I smoke?* **18.** to pay attention to (something); heed; notice: *to mind one's own business.* **19.** (*tr.; takes a clause as object*) to make certain; ensure: *mind you tell her.* **20.** (*tr.*) to take care of; have charge of: *to mind the shop.* **21.** (when *tr., may take a clause as object*) to be cautious or careful about (something): *mind how you go.* **22.** (*tr.*) to obey (someone or something); heed: *mind your father!* **23.** to be concerned (about); be troubled (about): *never mind about your hat.* **24. mind you.** an expression qualifying a previous statement: *Dogs are nice. Mind you, I don't like all dogs.* ~*Related adj.:* **mental.** ~See also **mind out.** [OE *gemynd* mind]

Mindanao (,mɪndə'naʊ) *n.* the second largest island of the Philippines, in the S part of the archipelago: mountainous and volcanic. Chief towns: Davao, Zamboanga. Pop.: 13 093 000 (1987 est.). Area: (including offshore islands) 94 631 sq. km (36 537 sq. miles).

mind-bending *adj. Inf.* **1.** causing mental aberration, esp. as a result of excessive drinking or of drugs. **2.** reaching the limit of credibility: *they offered a mind-bending salary.* Also: **mind-blowing.**

mind-boggling *adj. Inf.* astonishing; bewildering.

minded ('maɪndɪd) *adj.* **1.** having a mind, inclination, intention, etc., as specified: *politically minded.* **2.** (*in combination*): *money-minded.*

minder ('maɪndə) *n.* **1.** someone who looks after someone or something. **2.** short for **child minder. 3.** *Sl.* an aide to someone in public life who keeps control of press and public relations. **4.** *Sl.* someone acting as a bodyguard or assistant, esp. in the criminal underworld.

mindful ('maɪndfʊl) *adj.* (usually *postpositive* and foll. by *of*) keeping aware; heedful: *mindful of your duty.* —'**mindfully** *adv.* —'**mindfulness** *n.*

mindless ('maɪndlɪs) *adj.* **1.** stupid or careless. **2.** requiring little or no intellectual effort. —'**mindlessly** *adv.* —'**mindlessness** *n.*

Mindoro (mɪn'dɔːrəʊ) *n.* a mountainous island in the central Philippines, south of Luzon. Pop.: 669 369 (1980). Area: 9736 sq. km (3759 sq. miles).

mind out *vb.* (*intr., adv.*) *Brit.* to be careful or pay attention.

mind-reader *n.* a person seemingly able to discern the thoughts of another. —'**mind-,reading** *n.*

mind's eye *n.* the visual memory or the imagination.

Mindszenty ('mɪndsɛntɪ) *n.* **Joseph.** 1892–1975, Hungarian cardinal. He was sentenced to life imprisonment on a charge of treason (1949) but released during the 1956 Revolution.

mine[1] (maɪn) *pron.* **1.** something or someone belonging to or associated with me: *mine is best.* **2. of mine.** belonging to or associated with me. ~*determiner.* **3.** (*preceding a vowel*) an archaic word for **my**: *mine eyes; mine host.* [OE *mīn*]

mine[2] (maɪn) *n.* **1.** a system of excavations made for the extraction of minerals, esp. coal, ores, or precious stones. **2.** any deposit of ore or minerals. **3.** a lucrative source or abundant supply: *a mine of information.* **4.** a device containing explosive designed to destroy ships, vehicles, or personnel, usually laid beneath the ground or in water. **5.** a tunnel dug to undermine a fortification, etc. ~*vb.* **6.** to dig into (the earth) for (minerals). **7.** to make (a hole, tunnel, etc.) by digging or boring. **8.** to place explosive mines in position below the surface of (the sea or land). **9.** to undermine (a fortification, etc.) by digging mines. **10.** another word for **undermine**. [C13: from OF, prob. of Celtic origin]

mine detector *n.* an instrument designed to detect explosive mines. —**mine detection** *n.*

mine-dump *n. S. African.* a large mound of residue esp. from gold-mining operations.

minefield ('main,fiːld) *n.* **1.** an area of ground or water containing explosive mines. **2.** a subject, situation, etc., beset with hidden problems.

minelayer ('main,leɪə) *n.* a warship or aircraft designed for the carrying and laying of mines.

miner ('mainə) *n.* **1.** a person who works in a mine. **2.** any of various insects or insect larvae that bore into and feed on plant tissues. See also **leaf miner**. **3.** *Austral.* any of several honeyeaters.

mineral ('minərəl, 'minrəl) *n.* **1.** any of a class of naturally occurring solid inorganic substances with a characteristic crystalline form and a homogeneous chemical composition. **2.** any inorganic matter. **3.** any substance obtained by mining, esp. a metal ore. **4.** (*often pl.*) *Brit.* short for **mineral water**. **5.** *Brit.* a soft drink containing carbonated water and flavourings. ~*adj.* **6.** of, relating to, containing, or resembling minerals. [C15: from Med. L *minerāle* (n.), from *minerālis* (adj.); rel. to *minera* mine, ore, from ?]

mineral. *abbrev. for* mineralogy *or* mineralogical.

mineralize *or* **-ise** ('minərə,laɪz) *vb.* (*tr.*) **1. a.** to impregnate (organic matter, water, etc.) with a mineral substance. **b.** to convert (such matter) into a mineral; petrify. **2.** (of gases, vapours, etc., in magma) to transform (a metal) into an ore. —**minerali'zation** *or* **-i'sation** *n.* —**'minera,lizer** *or* **-iser** *n.*

mineralogy (,minə'rælədʒɪ) *n.* the branch of geology concerned with the study of minerals. —**mineralogical** (,minərə'lɒdʒɪkəl) *or* **,mineral'ogic** *adj.* —**,miner'alogist** *n.*

mineral oil *n. Brit.* any oil of mineral origin, esp. petroleum.

mineral water *n.* water containing dissolved mineral salts or gases, usually having medicinal properties.

mineral wool *n.* a fibrous material made by blowing steam or air through molten slag and used for packing and insulation.

miner's right *n. Austral.* a licence to prospect for and mine gold, etc.

Minerva (mɪ'nɜːvə) *n.* the Roman goddess of wisdom. Greek counterpart: **Athena**.

minestrone (,mini'strəʊni) *n.* a soup made from a variety of vegetables and pasta. [from It., from *minestrare* to serve]

minesweeper ('main,swiːpə) *n.* a naval vessel equipped to clear mines. —**'mine,sweeping** *n.*

Ming (mɪŋ) *n.* **1.** the imperial dynasty of China from 1368 to 1644. ~*adj.* **2.** of or relating to Chinese porcelain from the Ming dynasty.

mingle ('mɪŋgəl) *vb.* **1.** to mix or cause to mix. **2.** (*intr.; often foll. by with*) to come into close association. [C15: from OE *mengan* to mix] —**'mingler** *n.*

Mingus ('mɪŋgəs) *n.* **Charles**, known as *Charlie Mingus.* 1922–79, U.S. jazz double bassist, composer, and band leader.

mingy ('mɪndʒɪ) *adj.* **-gier, -giest.** *Brit. inf.* miserly, stingy, or niggardly. [C20: prob. a blend of MEAN² + STINGY¹]

Minho ('miːnju) *n.* the Portuguese name for the **Miño**.

mini ('mɪnɪ) *adj.* **1.** (of a woman's dress, skirt, etc.) very short; thigh-length. **2.** (*prenominal*) small; miniature. ~*n., pl.* **minis. 3.** something very small of its kind, esp. a small car or a miniskirt.

mini- *combining form.* smaller or shorter than the standard size: *minibus; miniskirt.* [C20: from MINIATURE & MINIMUM]

miniature ('mɪnɪtʃə) *n.* **1.** a model, copy, or representation on a very small scale. **2.** anything that is very small of its kind. **3.** a very small painting, esp. a portrait. **4.** an illuminated decoration in a manuscript. **5. in miniature.** on a small scale. ~*adj.* **6.** greatly reduced in size, etc. **7.** on a small scale; minute. [C16: from It., from Med. L, from *miniāre* to paint red (in illuminating manuscripts), from *minium* red lead] —**'miniaturist** *n.*

miniaturize *or* **-ise** ('mɪnɪtʃə,raɪz) *vb.* (*tr.*) to make or construct (something, esp. electronic equipment) on a very small scale; reduce in size. —,**miniaturi'zation** *or* **-i'sation** *n.*

minibus ('mɪnɪ,bʌs) *n.* a small bus able to carry approximately ten passengers.

minicab ('mɪnɪ,kæb) *n. Brit.* a small saloon car used as a taxi.

minicomputer (,mɪnɪkəm'pjuːtə) *n.* a small comparatively cheap digital computer.

minim ('mɪnɪm) *n.* **1.** a unit of fluid measure equal to one sixtieth of a drachm. It is approximately equal to one drop. Symbol: M, ♏ **2.** *Music.* a note having the time value of half a semibreve. **3.** a small or insignificant thing. **4.** a downward stroke in calligraphy. [C15 (*Music.*): from L *minimus* smallest]

minimal art *n.* abstract painting or sculpture in which expressiveness and illusion are minimized by the use of simple geometric shapes, flat colour, and arrangements of ordinary objects. —**minimal artist** *n.*

minimalism ('mɪnɪmə,lɪzəm) *n.* **1.** another name for **minimal art**. **2.** a type of music based on simple elements and avoiding elaboration or embellishment. **3.** design or style in which the simplest and fewest elements are used to create the maximum effect. —**'minimalist** *adj., n.*

minimax ('mɪnɪ,mæks) *n.* **1.** *Maths.* the lowest of a set of maximum values. **2.** (in game theory, etc.) the procedure of choosing the strategy that least benefits the most advantaged member of a group. Cf. **maximin**. [C20: from MINI(MUM) + MAX(IMUM)]

minimize *or* **-ise** ('mɪnɪ,maɪz) *vb.* (*tr.*) **1.** to reduce to or estimate at the least possible degree or amount. **2.** to rank or treat at less than the true worth; belittle. —**mini-mi'zation** *or* **-i'sation** *n.* —**'mini,mizer** *or* **-iser** *n.*

minimum ('mɪnɪməm) *n., pl.* **-mums** *or* **-ma** (-mə). **1.** the least possible amount, degree, or quantity. **2.** the least amount recorded, allowed, or reached. **3.** (*modifier*) being the least possible, recorded, allowed, etc.: *minimum age.* ~*adj.* **4.** of or relating to a minimum or minimums. [C17: from L: smallest thing, from *minimus* least] —**'minimal** *adj.* —**'minimally** *adv.*

minimum lending rate *n.* the minimum rate at which a central bank, such as the Bank of England, will lend money to a customer whose credit is first class.

minimum wage *n.* the lowest wage that an employer is permitted to pay by law or union contract.

mining ('maɪnɪŋ) *n.* **1.** the act, process, or industry of extracting coal, ores, etc., from the earth. **2.** *Mil.* the process of laying mines.

minion ('mɪnjən) *n.* **1.** a favourite or dependant, esp. a servile or fawning one. **2.** a servile agent. [C16: from F *mignon*, from OF *mignot*, of Gaulish origin]

minipill ('mɪnɪ,pɪl) *n.* a low-dose oral contraceptive containing progesterone only.

miniseries ('mɪnɪ,sɪəriːz) *n., pl.* **-series.** a television programme in several parts that is shown on consecutive days for a short period.

miniskirt ('mɪnɪ,skɜːt) *n.* a very short skirt, originally in the 1960s, one at least four inches above the knee. Often shortened to **mini**.

minister ('mɪnɪstə) *n.* **1.** (esp. in Presbyterian and some Nonconformist Churches) a clergyman. **2.** a head of a government department. **3.** any diplomatic agent accredited to a foreign government or head of state. **4.** Also called: **minister plenipotentiary**. See **envoy**¹ (sense 1). **5.** Also called: **minister resident**. a diplomat ranking after an envoy. **6.** a person who attends to the needs of others, esp. in religious matters. **7.** a person who acts as the agent or servant of a person or thing. ~*vb.* **8.** (*intr.; often foll. by to*) to attend to the needs (of); take care (of). **9.** (*tr.*) *Arch.* to provide; supply. [C13: via OF from L: servant; rel. to *minus* less]

ministerial (,mɪnɪ'stɪərɪəl) *adj.* **1.** of or relating to a minister of religion or his office. **2.** of or relating to a government minister or ministry. **3.** (*often cap.*) of or supporting the ministry against the opposition. **4.** *Law.* relating to or possessing delegated executive authority. **5.** acting as an agent or cause; instrumental. —,**minis'terially** *adv.*

minister of state *n.* **1.** (in the British Parliament) a minister, usually below cabinet rank, appointed to assist a senior minister. **2.** any government minister.

Minister of Crown *n. Brit.* any Government minister of cabinet rank.

minister plenipotentiary *n., pl.* **ministers plenipotentiary.** another term for **envoy**[1] (sense 1).

ministrant ('mɪnɪstrənt) *adj.* **1.** ministering or serving as a minister. *~n.* **2.** a person who ministers. [C17: from L *ministrans*, from *ministrāre* to wait upon]

ministration (,mɪnɪ'streɪʃən) *n.* **1.** the act or an instance of serving or giving aid. **2.** the act or an instance of ministering religiously. [C14: from L *ministrātiō*, from *ministrāre* to wait upon] —**ministrative** ('mɪnɪstrətɪv) *adj.*

ministry ('mɪnɪstrɪ) *n., pl.* **-tries. 1. a.** the profession or duties of a minister of religion. **b.** the performance of these duties. **2.** ministers of religion or government ministers considered collectively. **3.** the tenure of a minister. **4. a.** a government department headed by a minister. **b.** the buildings of such a department. [C14: from L *ministerium* service; see MINISTER]

miniver ('mɪnɪvə) *n.* white fur, used in ceremonial costumes. [C13: from OF *menu vair*, from *menu* small + *vair* variegated fur]

mink (mɪŋk) *n., pl.* **mink** *or* **minks. 1.** any of several mammals of Europe, Asia, and North America, having slightly webbed feet. **2.** their highly valued fur, esp. that of the American mink. **3.** a garment made of this, esp. a woman's coat or stole. [C15: from ON]

Minna ('mɪnə) *n.* a city in W central Nigeria, capital of Niger state. Pop.: 98 900 (1983).

Minneapolis (,mɪnɪ'æpəlɪs) *n.* a city in SE Minnesota, on the Mississippi River adjacent to St Paul: the largest city in the state; important centre for the grain trade. Pop.: 356 840 (1986 est.).

minneola (,mɪnɪ'əʊlə) *n.* a juicy citrus fruit that is a cross between a tangerine and a grapefruit. [C20: ?from *Mineola*, Texas]

minnesinger ('mɪnɪ,sɪŋə) *n.* one of the German lyric poets and musicians of the 12th to 14th centuries. [C19: from G *Minnesinger* love-singer]

Minnesota (,mɪnɪ'səʊtə) *n.* **1.** a state of the N central U.S.: chief U.S. producer of iron ore. Capital: St Paul. Pop.: 4 214 013 (1986 est.). Area: 218 600 sq. km (84 402 sq. miles). Abbrevs.: **Minn.** or (with zip code) **MN 2.** a river in S Minnesota, flowing southeast and northeast to the Mississippi River near St Paul. Length: 534 km (332 miles). —,**Minne'sotan** *adj., n.*

minnow ('mɪnəʊ) *n., pl.* **-nows** *or* **-now. 1.** a small slender European freshwater cyprinid fish. **2.** a small or insignificant person. [C15: rel. to OE *myne* minnow]

Miño (*Spanish* 'miɲo) *n.* a river in SW Europe, rising in NW Spain and flowing southwest (as part of the border between Spain and Portugal) to the Atlantic. Length: 338 km (210 miles). Portuguese name: **Minho.**

Minoan (mɪ'nəʊən) *adj.* **1.** of or denoting the Bronze Age culture of Crete from about 3000 B.C. to about 1100 B.C. *~n.* **2.** a Cretan belonging to the Minoan culture. [C19: after MINOS from the excavations at his supposed palace at Knossos]

minor ('maɪnə) *adj.* **1.** lesser or secondary in amount, importance, etc. **2.** of or relating to the minority. **3.** below the age of legal majority. **4.** *Music.* **a.** (of a scale) having a semitone between the second and third and fifth and sixth degrees (**natural minor**). **b.** (of a key) based on the minor scale. **c.** (*postpositive*) denoting a specified key based on the minor scale: *C minor.* **d.** (of an interval) reduced by a semitone from the major. **e.** (of a chord, esp. a triad) having a minor third above the root. **f.** (esp. in jazz) of or relating to a chord built upon a minor triad and containing a minor seventh: *a minor ninth.* **5.** *Logic.* (of a term or premise) having less generality or scope than another term or proposition. **6.** *U.S. education.* of or relating to an additional secondary subject taken by a student. **7.** (*immediately postpositive*) *Brit.* the younger or junior: sometimes used after the surname of a schoolboy if he has an older brother in the same school. *~n.* **8.** a person or thing that is lesser or secondary. **9.** a person below the age of legal majority. **10.** *U.S. & Canad. education.* a subsidiary subject. **11.** *Music.* a minor key, chord, mode, or scale. **12.** *Logic.* a minor term or premise. *~vb.* **13.** (*intr.*; usually foll. by *in*) *U.S. education.* to take a minor. [C13: from L: less, smaller]

minor axis *n.* the shorter or shortest axis of an ellipse or ellipsoid.

Minorca (mɪ'nɔːkə) *n.* an island in the W Mediterranean, northeast of Majorca: the second largest of the Balearic Islands. Chief town: Mahón. Pop.: 55 500 (1985). Area: 702 sq. km (271 sq. miles). Spanish name: **Menorca.** —**Mi'norcan** *adj., n.*

minority (maɪ'nɒrɪtɪ, mɪ-) *n., pl.* **-ties. 1.** the smaller of two parts, factions, or groups. **2.** a group that is different racially, politically, etc., from a larger group of which it is a part. **3. a.** the state of being a minor. **b.** the period during which a person is below legal age. **4.** (*modifier*) relating to or being a minority: *a minority opinion.* [C16: from Med. L *minōritās*, from L MINOR]

minor league *n. U.S. & Canad.* any professional league in baseball other than a major league.

minor orders *pl. n. R.C. Church.* the four lower degrees of holy orders, namely porter, exorcist, lector, and acolyte.

minor premise *n. Logic.* the premise of a syllogism containing the subject of its conclusion.

minor term *n. Logic.* the subject of the conclusion of a syllogism.

Minos ('maɪnɒs) *n. Greek myth.* a king of Crete for whom Daedalus built the Labyrinth to contain the Minotaur.

Minotaur ('maɪnətɔː) *n. Greek myth.* a monster with the head of a bull and the body of a man. It was kept in the Labyrinth in Crete, feeding on human flesh, until destroyed by Theseus. [C14: via L from Gk *Minōtauros*, from MINOS + *tauros* bull]

Minsk (mɪnsk) *n.* an industrial city in the W Soviet Union, capital of the Byelorussian SSR: educational and cultural centre, with a university (1921). Pop.: 1 543 000 (1987).

minster ('mɪnstə) *n. Brit.* any of certain cathedrals and large churches, usually originally connected to a monastery. [OE *mynster*, prob. from Vulgar L *monisterium* (unattested), var. of Church L *monastērium* MONASTERY]

minstrel ('mɪnstrəl) *n.* **1.** a medieval musician who performed songs or recited poetry with instrumental accompaniment. **2.** a performer in a minstrel show. **3.** *Arch. or poetic.* any poet, musician, or singer. [C13: from OF *menestral*, from LL *ministeriālis* an official, from L MINISTER]

minstrel show *n.* a theatrical entertainment consisting of songs, dances, etc., performed by actors wearing black face make-up.

minstrelsy ('mɪnstrəlsɪ) *n., pl.* **-sies. 1.** the art of a minstrel. **2.** the poems, music, or songs of a minstrel. **3.** a troupe of minstrels.

mint[1] (mɪnt) *n.* **1.** any N temperate plant of a genus having aromatic leaves. The leaves of some species are used for seasoning and flavouring. See also **peppermint, spearmint. 2.** a sweet flavoured with mint. [OE *minte*, from L *mentha*, from Gk *minthē*] —'**minty** *adj.*

mint[2] (mɪnt) *n.* **1.** a place where money is coined by governmental authority. **2.** a very large amount of money. *~adj.* **3.** (of coins, postage stamps, etc.) in perfect condition as issued. **4. in mint condition.** in perfect condition; as if new. *~vb.* **5.** to make (coins) by stamping metal. **6.** (*tr.*) to invent (esp. phrases or words). [OE *mynet*, from L *monēta* money, mint, from the temple of Juno *Monēta*, used as a mint in ancient Rome] —'**minter** *n.*

mintage ('mɪntɪdʒ) *n.* **1.** the process of minting. **2.** the money minted. **3.** a fee paid for minting a coin. **4.** an official impression stamped on a coin.

mint julep *n. Chiefly U.S.* a long drink consisting of bourbon whiskey, crushed ice, sugar, and sprigs of mint.

Mintoff ('mɪntɒf) *n.* **Dom(inic).** 1916–84, Maltese statesman; prime minister of Malta (1955–58; 1971–84).

minuend ('mɪnjʊ,ɛnd) *n.* the number from which another number, the **subtrahend,** is to be subtracted. [C18: from L *minuendus* (*numerus*) (the number) to be diminished]

minuet (,mɪnjʊ'ɛt) *n.* **1.** a stately court dance of the 17th and 18th centuries in triple time. **2.** a piece of music composed for or in the rhythm of this dance. [C17: from F *menuet* dainty, from *menu* small]

minus ('maɪnəs) *prep.* **1.** reduced by the subtraction of: *four minus two* (written 4 − 2). **2.** *Inf.* deprived of; lacking: *minus the trimmings.* *~adj.* **3. a.** indicating or involving subtraction: *a minus sign.* **b.** Also: **negative.** having a value or designating a quantity less than zero: *a minus number.* **4.** involving a disadvantage, harm, etc.: *a* *minus factor.* **5.** (*postpositive*) *Education.* slightly below the standard of a particular grade: *a B minus.* **6.** denoting a negative electric charge. ~*n.* **7.** short for **minus sign. 8.** a negative quantity. **9.** a disadvantage, loss, or deficit. **10.** *Inf.* something detrimental or negative. ~Mathematical symbol: − [C15: from L, neuter of MINOR]

minuscule ('mɪnə,skju:l) *n.* **1.** a lower-case letter. **2.** writing using such letters. **3.** a small cursive 7th-century style of lettering. ~*adj.* **4.** relating to, printed in, or written in small letters. Cf. **majuscule. 5.** very small. **6.** (of letters) lower-case. [C18: from F, from L (*littera*) *minuscula* very small (letter), dim. of MINOR] —**minuscular** (mɪ'nʌskjʊlə) *adj.*

minus sign *n.* the symbol −, indicating subtraction or a negative quantity.

minute[1] ('mɪnɪt) *n.* **1.** a period of time equal to 60 seconds; one sixtieth of an hour. **2.** Also called: **minute of arc.** a unit of angular measure equal to one sixtieth of a degree. Symbol: '. **3.** any very short period of time; moment. **4.** a short note or memorandum. **5.** the distance that can be travelled in a minute: *it's only two minutes away.* **6. up to the minute** (**up-to-the-minute** *when prenominal*). the very latest or newest. ~*vb.* (*tr.*) **7.** to record in minutes: *to minute a meeting.* **8.** to time in terms of minutes. ~See also **minutes.** [C14: from OF, from Med. L *minūta,* n. use of L *minūtus* MINUTE[2]] —**minutely** ('mɪnɪtlɪ) *adv.*

minute[2] (maɪ'nju:t) *adj.* **1.** very small; diminutive; tiny. **2.** unimportant; petty. **3.** precise or detailed. [C15: from L *minūtus,* p.p. of *minuere* to diminish] —**mi'nuteness** *n.* —**mi'nutely** *adv.*

minute gun ('mɪnɪt) *n.* a gun fired at one-minute intervals as a sign of distress or mourning.

minute hand ('mɪnɪt) *n.* the pointer on a timepiece that indicates minutes.

Minuteman ('mɪnɪt,mæn) *n., pl.* **-men. 1.** (*sometimes not cap.*) (in the War of American Independence) a colonial militiaman who promised to be ready to fight at one minute's notice. **2.** a U.S. three-stage intercontinental ballistic missile.

minutes ('mɪnɪts) *pl. n.* an official record of the proceedings of a meeting, conference, etc.

minute steak ('mɪnɪt) *n.* a small piece of steak that can be cooked quickly.

minutiae (mɪ'nju:ʃɪ,i:) *pl. n., sing.* **-tia** (-ʃɪə). small, precise, or trifling details. [C18: pl. of LL *minūtia* smallness, from L *minūtus* MINUTE[2]]

minx (mɪŋks) *n.* a bold, flirtatious, or scheming woman. [C16: from ?]

Minya ('mɪnjə) *n.* See **El Minya.**

Miocene ('maɪə,si:n) *adj.* **1.** of or denoting the fourth epoch of the Tertiary period. ~*n.* **2. the.** this epoch or rock series. [C19: Gk *meiōn* less + -CENE]

miosis *or* **myosis** (maɪ'əʊsɪs) *n., pl.* **-ses** (-si:z). **1.** excessive contraction of the pupil of the eye. **2.** a variant spelling of **meiosis** (sense 1). [C20: from Gk *muein* to shut the eyes + -OSIS] —**miotic** *or* **myotic** (maɪ'ɒtɪk) *adj., n.*

Miquelon ('mi:kə,lɒn; *French* miklɔ̃) *n.* a group of islands in the French territory of **Saint Pierre and Miquelon.**

Mir (mɪə) *n.* the Soviet orbiting space station. [Russian]

Mirabeau (*French* mirabo) *n.* **Comte de,** title of *Honoré-Gabriel Riqueti.* 1749–91, French Revolutionary politician.

miracle ('mɪrək²l) *n.* **1.** an event contrary to the laws of nature and attributed to a supernatural cause. **2.** any amazing or wonderful event. **3.** a marvellous example of something: *a miracle of engineering.* **4.** short for **miracle play. 5.** (*modifier*) being or seeming a miracle: *a miracle cure.* [C12: from L *mīrāculum,* from *mīrārī* to wonder at]

miracle play *n.* a medieval play based on a biblical story or the life of a saint. Cf. **mystery play.**

miraculous (mɪ'rækjʊləs) *adj.* **1.** of, like, or caused by a miracle; marvellous. **2.** surprising. **3.** having the power to work miracles. —**mi'raculously** *adv.* —**mi'raculousness** *n.*

Miraflores (,mɪrə'flɔ:rəs; *Spanish* mira'flores) *n.* **Lake.** an artificial lake in Panama, in the S Canal Zone of the Panama Canal.

mirage (mɪ'rɑːʒ) *n.* **1.** an image of a distant object or sheet of water, often inverted or distorted, caused by atmospheric refraction by hot air. **2.** something illusory. [C19: from F, from (*se*) *mirer* to be reflected]

mire ('maɪə) *n.* **1.** a boggy or marshy area. **2.** mud, muck, or dirt. ~*vb.* **3.** to sink or cause to sink in a mire. **4.** (*tr.*) to make dirty or muddy. **5.** (*tr.*) to involve, esp. in difficulties. [C14: from ON *mýrr*]

mirepoix (mɪə'pwɑː) *n.* a mixture of sautéed root vegetables used as a base for braising meat or for various sauces. [F, prob. after Duke of *Mirepoix,* 18th-cent. F general]

Miriam ('mɪrɪəm) *n. Old Testament.* the sister of Moses and Aaron. (Numbers 12:1–15). Douay name: **Mary.**

mirk (mɜːk) *n.* a variant spelling of **murk.** —**'mirky** *adj.* —**'mirkily** *adv.* —**'mirkiness** *n.*

Miró (*Spanish* mi'ro) *n.* **Joan** (xwan). 1893–1983, Spanish surrealist painter.

mirror ('mɪrə) *n.* **1.** a surface, such as polished metal or glass coated with a metal film, that reflects an image of an object placed in front of it. **2.** such a reflecting surface mounted in a frame. **3.** any reflecting surface. **4.** a thing that reflects or depicts something else. ~*vb.* **5.** (*tr.*) to reflect, represent, or depict faithfully: *he mirrors his teacher's ideals.* [C13: from OF from *mirer* to look at, from L *mīrārī* to wonder at]

mirror ball *n.* a large revolving ball covered with small pieces of mirror glass so that it reflects light in changing patterns: used in discos and ballrooms.

mirror carp *n.* a variety of carp with a smooth shiny body surface.

mirror image *n.* **1.** an image as observed in a mirror. **2.** an object that corresponds to another but has left and right reversed as if seen in a mirror.

mirror writing *n.* backward writing that forms a mirror image of normal writing.

mirth (mɜːθ) *n.* laughter, gaiety, or merriment. [OE *myrgth*] —**'mirthful** *adj.* —**'mirthfulness** *n.* —**'mirthless** *adj.* —**'mirthlessness** *n.*

MIRV (mɜːv) *n.* acronym for multiple independently targeted re-entry vehicle: a missile that has several warheads, each one being directed to a different enemy target.

mis- *prefix.* **1.** wrong or bad; wrongly or badly: *misunderstanding; misfortune; mistreat; mislead.* **2.** lack of; not: *mistrust.* [OE *mis*(*se*)-]

misadventure (,mɪsəd'vɛntʃə) *n.* **1.** an unlucky event; misfortune. **2.** *Law.* accidental death not due to crime or negligence.

misalliance (,mɪsə'laɪəns) *n.* an unsuitable alliance or marriage. —**,misal'ly** *vb.*

misanthrope ('mɪzən,θrəʊp) *or* **misanthropist** (mɪ'zænθrəpɪst) *n.* a person who dislikes or distrusts other people or mankind in general. [C17: from Gk *misanthrōpos,* from *misos* hatred + *anthrōpos* man] —**misanthropic** (,mɪzən'θrɒpɪk) *or* **,misan'thropical** *adj.* —**misanthropy** (mɪ'zænθrəpɪ) *n.*

misapply (,mɪsə'plaɪ) *vb.* **-plying, -plied.** (*tr.*) **1.** to apply wrongly or badly. **2.** another word for **misappropriate.** —**misapplication** (,mɪsæplɪ'keɪʃən) *n.*

misapprehend (,mɪsæprɪ'hɛnd) *vb.* (*tr.*) to misunderstand. —**misapprehension** (,mɪsæprɪ'hɛnʃən) *n.* —**,misappre'hensive** *adj.* —**,misappre'hensiveness** *n.*

misappropriate (,mɪsə'prəʊprɪ,eɪt) *vb.* (*tr.*) to appropriate for a wrong or dishonest use; embezzle or steal. —**,misap,propri'ation** *n.*

misbecome (,mɪsbɪ'kʌm) *vb.* **-coming, -came.** (*tr.*) to be unbecoming to or unsuitable for.

misbegotten (,mɪsbɪ'gɒt³n) *adj.* **1.** unlawfully obtained. **2.** badly conceived, planned, or designed. **3.** *Literary and dialect.* illegitimate; bastard.

misbehave (,mɪsbɪ'heɪv) *vb.* to behave (oneself) badly. —**,misbe'haver** *n.* —**misbehaviour** *or U.S.* **misbehavior** (,mɪsbɪ'heɪvjə) *n.*

misbelief (,mɪsbɪ'li:f) *n.* a false or unorthodox belief. —**,misbe'liever** *n.*

misc. *abbrev. for:* **1.** miscellaneous. **2.** miscellany.

miscalculate (,mɪs'kælkjʊ,leɪt) *vb.* (*tr.*) to calculate wrongly. —**,miscalcu'lation** *n.*

miscall (ˌmɪsˈkɔːl) vb. (tr.) **1.** to call by the wrong name. **2.** Dialect. to abuse or malign. — ˌmis'caller n.

miscarriage (mɪsˈkærɪdʒ) n. **1.** (also 'mɪskær-). spontaneous expulsion of a fetus from the womb, esp. prior to the 20th week of pregnancy. **2.** an act of mismanagement or failure: a miscarriage of justice. **3.** Brit. the failure of freight to reach its destination.

miscarry (mɪsˈkærɪ) vb. -rying, -ried. (intr.) **1.** to expel a fetus prematurely from the womb; abort. **2.** to fail. **3.** Brit. (of freight, mail, etc.) to fail to reach a destination.

miscast (ˌmɪsˈkɑːst) vb. -casting, -cast. (tr.) **1.** to cast badly. **2.** (often passive) **a.** to cast (a role) in (a play, film, etc.) inappropriately: Falstaff was miscast. **b.** to assign an inappropriate role to: he was miscast as Othello.

miscegenation (ˌmɪsɪdʒɪˈneɪʃən) n. interbreeding of races, esp. where differences of pigmentation are involved. [C19: from L miscēre to mingle + genus race]

miscellanea (ˌmɪsəˈleɪnɪə) pl. n. a collection of miscellaneous items, esp. literary works. [C16: from L: neuter pl. of miscellāneus MISCELLANEOUS]

miscellaneous (ˌmɪsəˈleɪnɪəs) adj. **1.** composed of or containing a variety of things; mixed. **2.** having varied capabilities, sides, etc. [C17: from L miscellāneus, from miscellus mixed, from miscēre to mix] — ˌmiscel'laneously adv. — ˌmiscel'laneousness n. — miscellanist (mɪˈsɛlənɪst) n.

miscellany (mɪˈsɛlənɪ; U.S. ˈmɪsəˌleɪnɪ) n., pl. -nies. (sometimes pl.) a miscellaneous collection of items, esp. essays, poems, etc. [C16: from F miscellanées (pl.) MISCELLANEA]

mischance (mɪsˈtʃɑːns) n. **1.** bad luck. **2.** a stroke of bad luck.

mischief (ˈmɪstʃɪf) n. **1.** wayward but not malicious behaviour, usually of children, that causes trouble, irritation, etc. **2.** a playful inclination to behave in this way or to tease or disturb. **3.** a person who causes mischief. **4.** injury or harm caused by a person or thing. **5.** a source of trouble, difficulty, etc. [C13: from OF meschief, from meschever to meet with calamity; from mes- MIS- + chever, from chef end]

mischievous (ˈmɪstʃɪvəs) adj. **1.** inclined to acts of mischief. **2.** teasing; slightly malicious. **3.** causing or intended to cause harm. — ˈmischievously adv. — ˈmischievousness n.

miscible (ˈmɪsɪbəl) adj. capable of mixing: miscible with water. [C16: from Med. L miscibilis, from miscēre to mix] — ˌmisci'bility n.

misconceive (ˌmɪskənˈsiːv) vb. to have the wrong idea; fail to understand. — ˌmiscon'ceiver n.

misconception (ˌmɪskənˈsɛpʃən) n. a false or mistaken view, opinion, or attitude.

misconduct n. (mɪsˈkɒndʌkt). **1.** behaviour, such as adultery or professional negligence, that is regarded as immoral or unethical. ~vb. (ˌmɪskənˈdʌkt). (tr.) **2.** to conduct (oneself) in such a way. **3.** to manage (something) badly.

misconstrue (ˌmɪskənˈstruː) vb. -struing, -strued. (tr.) to interpret mistakenly. — ˌmiscon'struction n.

miscreant (ˈmɪskrɪənt) n. **1.** a wrongdoer or villain. **2.** Arch. an unbeliever or heretic. ~adj. **3.** evil or villainous. **4.** Arch. unbelieving or heretical. [C14: from OF mescreant unbelieving, from mes- MIS- + creant, ult. from L credere to believe]

miscue (ˌmɪsˈkjuː) n. **1.** Billiards, etc. a faulty stroke in which the cue tip slips off the cue ball or misses it. **2.** Inf. a blunder or mistake. ~vb. -cuing, -cued. (intr.) **3.** Billiards. to make a miscue. **4.** Theatre. to fail to answer one's cue.

misdate (mɪsˈdeɪt) vb. (tr.) to date (a letter, event, etc.) wrongly.

misdeal (mɪsˈdiːl) vb. -dealing, -dealt. **1.** (intr.) to deal out cards incorrectly. ~n. **2.** a faulty deal. — ˌmis'dealer n.

misdeed (ˌmɪsˈdiːd) n. an evil or illegal action.

misdemean (ˌmɪsdɪˈmiːn) vb. a rare word for misbehave.

misdemeanour or U.S. **misdemeanor** (ˌmɪsdɪˈmiːnə) n. **1.** Criminal law. (formerly) an offence generally less

heinous than a felony. **2.** any minor offence or transgression.

misdirect (ˌmɪsdɪˈrɛkt) vb. (tr.) **1.** to give (a person) wrong directions or instructions. **2.** to address (a letter, parcel, etc.) wrongly. — ˌmisdi'rection n.

misdoubt (mɪsˈdaʊt) vb. an archaic word for doubt or suspect.

mise en scène French. (miz ɑ̃ sɛn) n. **1. a.** the arrangement of properties, scenery, etc., in a play. **b.** the objects so arranged; stage setting. **2.** the environment of an event.

Miseno (Italian miˈzɛːno) n. a cape in SW Italy, on the N shore of the Bay of Naples: remains of the town of Misenum, a naval base constructed by Agrippa in 31 B.C.

miser (ˈmaɪzə) n. **1.** a person who hoards money or possessions, often living miserably. **2.** a selfish person. [C16: from L: wretched]

miserable (ˈmɪzərəbəl) adj. **1.** unhappy or depressed; wretched. **2.** causing misery, discomfort, etc.: a miserable life. **3.** contemptible: a miserable villain. **4.** sordid or squalid: miserable living conditions. **5.** mean; stingy. [C16: from OF, from L miserābilis, from miserāri to pity, from miser wretched] — ˈmiserableness n. — ˈmiserably adv.

misère (mɪˈzɛə) n. **1.** a call in solo whist, etc. declaring a hand that will win no tricks. **2.** a hand that will win no tricks. [C19: from F: misery]

Miserere (ˌmɪzəˈrɛərɪ, -ˈrɪərɪ) n. the 51st psalm, the Latin version of which begins "Miserere mei, Deus" ("Have mercy on me, O God").

misericord or **misericorde** (mɪˈzɛrɪˌkɔːd) n. **1.** a ledge projecting from the underside of the hinged seat of a choir stall in a church, on which the occupant can support himself while standing. **2.** Christianity. **a.** a relaxation of certain monastic rules for infirm or aged monks or nuns. **b.** a monastery or room where this can be enjoyed. **3.** a medieval dagger used to give the death stroke to a wounded foe. [C14: from OF, from L misericordia compassion, from miserēre to pity + cor heart]

miserly (ˈmaɪzəlɪ) adj. of or resembling a miser; avaricious. — ˈmiserliness n.

misery (ˈmɪzərɪ) n., pl. -eries. **1.** intense unhappiness, suffering, etc. **2.** a cause of such unhappiness, etc. **3.** squalid or poverty-stricken conditions. **4.** Brit. inf. a person who is habitually depressed: he is such a misery. [C14: via Anglo-Norman from L miseria, from miser wretched]

misfeasance (mɪsˈfiːzəns) n. Law. the improper performance of an act that is lawful in itself. Cf. malfeasance, nonfeasance. [C16: from OF mesfaisance, from mesfaire to perform misdeeds]

misfile (ˌmɪsˈfaɪl) vb. to file (papers, records, etc.) wrongly.

misfire (ˌmɪsˈfaɪə) vb. (intr.) **1.** (of a firearm or its projectile) to fail to fire or explode as expected. **2.** (of a motor engine or vehicle, etc.) to fail to fire at the appropriate time. **3.** to fail to operate or occur as intended. ~n. **4.** the act or an instance of misfiring.

misfit n. (ˈmɪsˌfɪt). **1.** a person not suited to a particular social environment. **2.** something that does not fit or fits badly. ~vb. (ˌmɪsˈfɪt), -fitting, -fitted. (intr.) **3.** to fail to fit or be fitted.

misfortune (mɪsˈfɔːtʃən) n. **1.** evil fortune; bad luck. **2.** an unfortunate or disastrous event.

misgive (mɪsˈgɪv) vb. -giving, -gave, -given. to make or be apprehensive or suspicious.

misgiving (mɪsˈgɪvɪŋ) n. (often pl.) a feeling of uncertainty, apprehension, or doubt.

misguide (ˌmɪsˈgaɪd) vb. (tr.) to guide or direct wrongly or badly.

misguided (ˌmɪsˈgaɪdɪd) adj. foolish or unreasonable, esp. in action or behaviour. — ˌmis'guidedly adv.

mishandle (ˌmɪsˈhændəl) vb. (tr.) to handle or treat badly or inefficiently.

mishap (ˈmɪshæp) n. **1.** an unfortunate accident. **2.** bad luck.

Mishima (ˈmɪʃɪmə) n. **Yukio** (ˈjuːkɪəʊ). 1925–70, Japanese novelist and short-story writer, whose works reflect a preoccupation with homosexuality and death. He committed harakiri in protest at the decline of traditional Japanese values.

mishit *Sport.* ~*n.* ('mɪs,hɪt). **1.** a faulty shot or stroke. ~*vb.* (,mɪs'hɪt), **-hitting, -hit. 2.** to hit (a ball) with a faulty stroke.

mishmash ('mɪʃ,mæʃ) *n.* a confused collection or mixture. [C15: reduplication of MASH]

Mishna ('mɪʃnə) *n., pl.* **Mishnayoth** (mɪʃ'nɑːjəʊt). *Judaism.* a compilation of precepts collected in the late second century A.D. It forms the earlier part of the Talmud. [C17: from Heb., from *shānāh* to repeat] —**Mishnaic** (mɪʃ'neɪɪk) *or* **'Mishnic** *adj.*

misinform (,mɪsɪn'fɔːm) *vb.* (*tr.*) to give incorrect information to. —**misinformation** (,mɪsɪnfə'meɪʃən) *n.*

misinterpret (,mɪsɪn'tɜːprɪt) *vb.* (*tr.*) to interpret badly, misleadingly, or incorrectly. —**,misin'terpreter** *n.* —**,misin'terpretation** *n.*

misjudge (,mɪs'dʒʌdʒ) *vb.* to judge (a person or persons) wrongly or unfairly. —**mis'judger** *n.* —**mis'judgment** *or* **,mis'judgement** *n.*

Miskolc (*Hungarian* 'mɪʃkolts) *n.* a city in NE Hungary: the second most important industrial centre in Hungary; iron and steel industries. Pop.: 211 000 (1985).

mislay (mɪs'leɪ) *vb.* **-laying, -laid.** (*tr.*) **1.** to lose (something) temporarily, esp. by forgetting where it is. **2.** to lay (something) badly.

mislead (mɪs'liːd) *vb.* **-leading, -led.** (*tr.*) **1.** to give false or confusing information to. **2.** to lead or guide in the wrong direction. —**mis'leader** *n.* —**mis'leading** *adj.*

mismatch (,mɪs'mætʃ) *vb.* **1.** to match badly, esp. in marriage. ~*n.* **2.** a bad match.

misnomer (,mɪs'nəʊmə) *n.* **1.** an incorrect or unsuitable name for a person or thing. **2.** the act of referring to a person by the wrong name. [C15: via Anglo-Norman from OF *mesnommer* to misname, from L *nōmināre* to call by name]

miso- *or before a vowel* **mis-** *combining form.* indicating hatred: *misogyny.* [from Gk *misos* hatred]

misogamy (mɪ'sɒgəmɪ, maɪ-) *n.* hatred of marriage. —**mi'sogamist** *n.*

misogyny (mɪ'sɒdʒɪnɪ, maɪ-) *n.* hatred of women. [C17: from Gk, from MISO- + *gunē* woman] —**mi'sogynist** *n.* —**mi'sogynous** *adj.*

misplace (,mɪs'pleɪs) *vb.* (*tr.*) **1.** to put (something) in the wrong place, esp. to lose (something) temporarily by forgetting where it was placed. **2.** (*often passive*) to bestow (trust, affection, etc.) unadvisedly. —**mis'placement** *n.*

misplaced modifier *n. Grammar.* a participle intended to modify a noun but having the wrong grammatical relationship to it, for example *having left* in the sentence *Having left Europe for good, Peter's future seemed bleak.*

misplay (,mɪs'pleɪ) *vb.* **1.** (*tr.*) to play badly or wrongly in games or sports. ~*n.* **2.** a wrong or unskilful play.

misprint *n.* ('mɪs,prɪnt). **1.** an error in printing, made through damaged type, careless reading, etc. ~*vb.* (,mɪs'prɪnt). **2.** (*tr.*) to print (a letter) incorrectly.

misprision[1] (mɪs'prɪʒən) *n.* **a.** a failure to inform the authorities of the commission of an act of treason. **b.** the deliberate concealment of the commission of a felony. [C15: via Anglo-F from OF *mesprision* error, from *mesprendre* to mistake, from *mes-* MIS- + *prendre* to take]

misprision[2] (mɪs'prɪʒən) *n. Arch.* **1.** contempt. **2.** failure to appreciate the value of something. [C16: from MISPRIZE]

misprize *or* **-ise** (mɪs'praɪz) *vb.* to fail to appreciate the value of; disparage. [C15: from OF *mesprisier*, from *mes-* MIS- + *prisier* to PRIZE[2]]

mispronounce (,mɪsprə'naʊns) *vb.* to pronounce (a word) wrongly. —**mispronunciation** (,mɪsprə,nʌnsɪ'eɪʃən) *n.*

misquote (,mɪs'kwəʊt) *vb.* to quote (a text, speech, etc.) inaccurately. —**misquo'tation** *n.*

misread (,mɪs'riːd) *vb.* **-reading, -read** (-'rɛd). (*tr.*) **1.** to read incorrectly. **2.** to misinterpret.

misrepresent (,mɪsrɛprɪ'zɛnt) *vb.* (*tr.*) to represent wrongly or inaccurately. —**,misrepresen'tation** *n.* —**,misrepre'sentative** *adj.*

misrule (,mɪs'ruːl) *vb.* **1.** (*tr.*) to govern inefficiently or without justice. ~*n.* **2.** inefficient or unjust government. **3.** disorder.

miss[1] (mɪs) *vb.* **1.** to fail to reach, hit, meet, find, or attain (some aim, target, etc.). **2.** (*tr.*) to fail to attend or be present for: *to miss an appointment.* **3.** (*tr.*) to fail to see, hear, understand, or perceive. **4.** (*tr.*) to lose, overlook, or fail to take advantage of: *to miss an opportunity.* **5.** (*tr.*) to leave out; omit: *to miss an entry in a list.* **6.** (*tr.*) to discover or regret the loss or absence of: *she missed him.* **7.** (*tr.*) to escape or avoid (something, esp. a danger), usually narrowly: *he missed death by inches.* ~*n.* **8.** a failure to reach, hit, etc. **9. give (something) a miss.** *Inf.* to avoid (something): *give the pudding a miss.* ~See also **miss out.** [OE *missan* (meaning: to fail to hit)]

miss[2] (mɪs) *n. Inf.* **1.** an unmarried woman or girl. **2.** (in the fashion trade) a size in young women's clothes. [C17: from MISTRESS]

Miss (mɪs) *n.* a title of an unmarried woman or girl, usually used before the surname or sometimes alone in direct address. [C17: shortened from MISTRESS]

▷ *Usage.* When reference is made to two or more unmarried women with the same surname, *the Misses Smith* is more formal than *the Miss Smiths.* See also **Ms.**

missal ('mɪsəl) *n. R.C. Church.* a book containing the prayers, rites, etc., of the Masses for a complete year. [C14: from Church L *missale* (n.), from *missālis* concerning the MASS]

misshape *vb.* (,mɪs'ʃeɪp). **-shaping, -shaped** *or* **-shapen. 1.** (*tr.*) to shape badly; deform. ~*n.* ('mɪs,ʃeɪp). **2.** something that is badly shaped.

misshapen (,mɪs'ʃeɪp²n) *adj.* badly shaped; deformed. —**,mis'shapenness** *n.*

missile ('mɪsaɪl) *n.* **1.** any object or weapon that is thrown at a target or shot from an engine, gun, etc. **2.** a rocket-propelled weapon that flies either in a fixed trajectory (**ballistic missile**) or in a trajectory controlled during flight (**guided missile**). [C17: from L *missilis*, from *mittere* to send]

missilery *or* **missilry** ('mɪsaɪlrɪ) *n.* **1.** missiles collectively. **2.** the design, operation, or study of missiles.

missing ('mɪsɪŋ) *adj.* **1.** not present; absent or lost. **2.** not able to be traced and not known to be dead: *nine men were missing after the attack.* **3. go missing.** to become lost or disappear.

missing link *n.* **1.** (*sometimes cap.; usually preceded by the*) a hypothetical extinct animal, formerly thought to be intermediate between the anthropoid apes and man. **2.** any missing section or part in a series.

mission ('mɪʃən) *n.* **1.** a specific task or duty assigned to a person or group of people. **2.** a person's vocation (often in **mission in life**) . **3.** a group of persons representing or working for a particular country, business, etc., in a foreign country. **4.** a special embassy sent to a foreign country for a specific purpose. **5. a.** a group of people sent by a religious body, esp. a Christian church, to a foreign country to do missionary and social work. **b.** the campaign undertaken by such a group. **6. a.** a building in which missionary work is performed. **b.** the area assigned to a particular missionary. **7.** the dispatch of aircraft or spacecraft to achieve a particular task. **8.** a charitable centre that offers shelter or aid to the destitute or underprivileged. **9.** (*modifier*) of or relating to an ecclesiastical mission: *a mission station.* ~*vb.* **10.** (*tr.*) to direct a mission to or establish a mission in (a given region). [C16: from L *missiō*, from *mittere* to send]

missionary ('mɪʃənərɪ) *n., pl.* **-aries. a.** Also called: **missioner.** a member of a religious mission. **b.** (*as modifier*): *missionary work.*

missionary position *n. Inf.* a position for sexual intercourse in which the man lies on top of the woman and they are face to face. [C20: from the belief that missionaries advocated this as the proper position to primitive peoples among whom it was unknown]

Missionary Ridge *n.* a ridge in NW Georgia and SE Tennessee: site of a battle (1863) during the Civil War: Northern victory leading to the campaign in Georgia.

missis *or* **missus** ('mɪsɪz, -ɪs) *n.* **1.** (usually preceded by *the*) *Inf.* one's wife or the wife of the person addressed or referred to. **2.** an informal term of address for a woman. [C19: spoken version of MISTRESS]

Mississauga (,mɪsə'sɔːgə) *n.* a town in SE Ontario: a SW suburb of Toronto. Pop.: 315 056 (1981).

Mississippi (,mɪsɪ'sɪpɪ) *n.* **1.** a state of the southeastern U.S., on the Gulf of Mexico: consists of a largely forested undulating plain, with swampy regions in the northwest and on the coast, the Mississippi river forming the W border; cotton, rice, and oil. Capital: Jackson. Pop.: 2 656 600 (1985 est.). Area: 122 496 sq. km (47 296 sq. miles). Abbrevs.: **Miss.** or (with zip code) **MS** **2.** a river in the central U.S., rising in NW Minnesota and flowing generally south to the Gulf of Mexico through several mouths, known as the Passes: the second longest river in North America (after its tributary, the Missouri), with the third largest drainage basin in the world (after the Amazon and the Congo). Length: 3780 km (2348 miles).

Mississippian (,mɪsɪ'sɪpɪən) *adj.* **1.** of or relating to the state of Mississippi, or the Mississippi river. **2.** (in North America) of or denoting the lower of two subdivisions of the Carboniferous period (see also **Pennsylvanian** (sense 2)). ~*n.* **3.** an inhabitant or native of the state of Mississippi. **4. the.** the Mississippian period or rock system.

missive ('mɪsɪv) *n.* **1.** a formal or official letter. **2.** a formal word for **letter.** [C15: from Med. L *missivus*, from *mittere* to send]

Missolonghi (,mɪsə'lɒŋgɪ) *or* **Mesolonghi** *n.* a town in W Greece, near the Gulf of Patras: famous for its defence against the Turks in 1822–23 and 1825–26 and for its association with Lord Byron, who died here in 1824. Pop.: 11 275 (1981). Modern Greek name: **Mesolóngion.**

Missouri (mɪ'zʊərɪ) *n.* **1.** a state of the central U.S.: consists of rolling prairies in the north, the Ozark Mountains in the south, and part of the Mississippi flood plain in the southeast, with the Mississippi forming the E border; chief U.S. production of lead and barytes. Capital: Jefferson City. Pop.: 5 066 000 (1986 est.). Area: 178 699 sq. km (68 995 sq. miles). Abbrevs.: **Mo.** or (with zip code) **MO** **2.** a river in the W and central U.S., rising in SW Montana: flows north, east, and southeast to join the Mississippi above St Louis; the longest river in North America; chief tributary of the Mississippi. Length: 3970 km (2466 miles). —**Mis'sourian** *n., adj.*

miss out *vb.* (*adv.*) **1.** (*tr.*) to leave out; overlook. **2.** (*intr.; often foll. by on*) to fail to experience: *you missed out on the celebrations.*

misspell (,mɪs'spɛl) *vb.* **-spelling, -spelt** *or* **-spelled.** to spell (a word or words) wrongly.

misspelling (,mɪs'spɛlɪŋ) *n.* a wrong spelling.

misspend (,mɪs'spɛnd) *vb.* **-spending, -spent.** to spend thoughtlessly or wastefully.

misstep (,mɪs'stɛp) *n.* **1.** a false step. **2.** an error.

missy ('mɪsɪ) *n., pl.* **missies.** *Inf.* an affectionate or disparaging form of address to a young girl.

mist (mɪst) *n.* **1.** a thin fog resulting from condensation in the air near the earth's surface. **2.** *Meteorol.* such an atmospheric condition with a horizontal visibility of 1–2 kilometres. **3.** a fine spray of liquid, such as that produced by an aerosol container. **4.** condensed water vapour on a surface. **5.** something that causes haziness or lack of clarity, such as a film of tears. ~*vb.* **6.** to cover or be covered with or as if with mist. [OE]

mistake (mɪ'steɪk) *n.* **1.** an error or blunder in action, opinion, or judgment. **2.** a misconception or misunderstanding. ~*vb.* **-taking, -took, -taken. 3.** (*tr.*) to misunderstand; misinterpret: *she mistook his meaning.* **4.** (*tr.;* foll. by *for*) to take (for), interpret (as), or confuse (with): *she mistook his direct manner for honesty.* **5.** (*tr.*) to choose badly or incorrectly: *he mistook his path.* **6.** (*intr.*) to make a mistake. [C13 (meaning: to do wrong, err): from ON *mistaka* to take erroneously] —**mis'takable** *adj.*

mistaken (mɪ'steɪkən) *adj.* **1.** (*usually predicative*) wrong in opinion, judgment, etc. **2.** arising from error in opinion, judgment, etc.: *a mistaken viewpoint.* —**mis'takenly** *adv.* —**mis'takenness** *n.*

Mistassini (,mɪstə'siːnɪ) *n. Lake.* a lake in E Canada, in N Quebec: the largest lake in the province; drains through the Rupert River into James Bay. Area: 2175 sq. km (840 sq. miles). Length: about 160 km (100 miles).

mister ('mɪstə) (*sometimes cap.*) ~*n.* **1.** an informal form of address for a man. **2.** *Naval.* **a.** the official form of address for subordinate or senior warrant officers. **b.** the official form of address for all officers in a merchant ship, other than the captain. **3.** *Brit.* the form of address for a surgeon. **4.** the form of address for officials holding certain positions: *mister chairman.* ~*vb.* **5.** (*tr.*) *Inf.* to call (someone) mister. [C16: var. of MASTER]

Mister ('mɪstə) *n.* the full form of **Mr.**

misterioso (mɪ,stɛrɪ'əʊsəʊ) *adv. Music.* in a mysterious manner; mysteriously. [It.]

Misti (*Spanish* 'misti) *n.* See **El Misti.**

mistigris ('mɪstɪgrɪ) *n.* **1.** the joker or a blank card used as a wild card in a variety of draw poker. **2.** the game. [C19: from F: jack of clubs, game in which this card was wild]

mistime (,mɪs'taɪm) *vb.* (*tr.*) to time (an action, utterance, etc.) wrongly.

mistle thrush *or* **missel thrush** ('mɪsᵊl) *n.* a large European thrush with a brown back and spotted breast, noted for feeding on mistletoe berries. [C18: from OE *mistel* MISTLETOE]

mistletoe ('mɪsᵊl,təʊ) *n.* **1.** a Eurasian evergreen shrub with waxy white berries: grows as a partial parasite on various trees: used as a Christmas decoration. **2.** any of several similar and related American plants. [OE *misteltān*, from *mistel* mistletoe + *tān* twig; rel. to ON *misteinn*]

mistook (mɪ'stʊk) *vb.* the past tense of **mistake.**

mistral ('mɪstrəl, mɪ'strɑːl) *n.* a strong cold dry wind that blows through the Rhône valley and S France to the Mediterranean coast, mainly in the winter. [C17: via F from Provençal, from L *magistrālis* MAGISTRAL]

Mistral *n.* **1.** (*French* mistral). **Frédéric** (frederik). 1830–1914, French Provençal poet, who led a movement to revive Provençal language and literature: shared the Nobel prize for literature 1904. **2.** (*Spanish* mis'tral). **Gabriela** (ga'βrjela), pen name of *Lucila Godoy de Alcayaga.* 1889–1957, Chilean poet, educationalist, and diplomatist. Her poetry includes the collection *Desolación* (1922): Nobel prize for literature 1945.

mistreat (,mɪs'triːt) *vb.* (*tr.*) to treat badly. —**mis'treatment** *n.*

mistress ('mɪstrɪs) *n.* **1.** a woman who has a continuing extramarital sexual relationship with a man. **2.** a woman in a position of authority, ownership, or control. **3.** a woman having control over something specified: *mistress of her own destiny.* **4.** *Chiefly Brit.* short for **schoolmistress. 5.** an archaic or dialect word for **sweetheart.** [C14: from OF; see MASTER, -ESS]

Mistress ('mɪstrɪs) *n.* an archaic or dialect title equivalent to **Mrs.**

Mistress of the Robes *n.* (in Britain) a lady of high rank in charge of the Queen's wardrobe.

mistrial (mɪs'traɪəl) *n.* **1.** a trial made void because of some error. **2.** *U.S.* an inconclusive trial, as when a jury cannot agree on a verdict.

mistrust (,mɪs'trʌst) *vb.* **1.** to have doubts or suspicions about (someone or something). ~*n.* **2.** distrust. —,**mis'trustful** *adj.* —,**mis'trustfully** *adv.* —,**mis'trustfulness** *n.*

misty ('mɪstɪ) *adj.* **-tier, -tiest. 1.** consisting of or resembling mist. **2.** obscured as by mist. **3.** indistinct; blurred. —'**mistily** *adv.* —'**mistiness** *n.*

misunderstand (,mɪsʌndə'stænd) *vb.* **-standing, -stood.** to fail to understand properly.

misunderstanding (,mɪsʌndə'stændɪŋ) *n.* **1.** a failure to understand properly. **2.** a disagreement.

misunderstood (,mɪsʌndə'stʊd) *adj.* not properly or sympathetically understood: *a misunderstood adolescent.*

misuse *n.* (,mɪs'juːs), *also* **misusage. 1.** erroneous, improper, or unorthodox use: *misuse of words.* **2.** cruel or inhumane treatment. ~*vb.* (,mɪs'juːz). (*tr.*) **3.** to use wrongly. **4.** to treat badly or harshly. —,**mis'user** *n.*

,**mis'state** *vb.* ,**mis'statement** *n.* **mis'title** *vb.* **mis'type** *vb.*

Mitchell ('mɪtʃəl) n. **1. Margaret.** 1900–49, U.S. novelist; author of *Gone with the Wind* (1936). **2. Reginald Joseph.** 1895–1937, English aeronautical engineer; designer of the Spitfire fighter. **3. Sir Thomas Livingstone,** known as *Major Mitchell.* 1792–1855, Australian explorer born in Scotland.

Mitchum ('mɪtʃəm) n. **Robert.** born 1917, U.S. film actor. His many films include *Night of the Hunter* (1955) and *Farewell my Lovely* (1975).

mite[1] (maɪt) n. any of numerous small terrestrial or aquatic free-living or parasitic arachnids. [OE *mite*]

mite[2] (maɪt) n. **1.** a very small particle, creature, or object. **2.** a very small contribution or sum of money. See also **widow's mite. 3.** a former Flemish coin of small value. **4. a mite.** *Inf.* somewhat: *he's a mite foolish.* [C14: from MLow G, MDu. *mite*]

Mithgarthr ('mɪθˌgɑːðə) n. a variant of **Midgard.**

Mithraism ('mɪθreɪˌɪzəm) or **Mithraicism** (mɪθ'reɪɪˌsɪzəm) n. the ancient religion of Mithras. —**Mithraic** (mɪθ'reɪɪk) adj. —'**Mithraist** n., adj.

Mithras ('mɪθræs) or **Mithra** ('mɪθrə) n. *Persian myth.* the god of light, identified with the sun, who slew a primordial bull and fertilized the world with its blood.

Mithridates VI or **Mithradates VI** (ˌmɪθrɪ'deɪtiːz) n. called *the Great.* ?132–63 B.C., king of Pontus (?120–63). He waged three wars against Rome (88–84; 83–81; 74–64) and was finally defeated by Pompey: committed suicide.

mithridatism ('mɪθrɪdeɪˌtɪzəm) n. immunity to large doses of poison by prior ingestion of gradually increased doses. —**mithridatic** (ˌmɪθrɪ'dætɪk, -'deɪ-) adj.

mitigate ('mɪtɪˌgeɪt) vb. to make or become less severe or harsh; moderate. [C15: from L *mītigāre,* from *mītis* mild + *agere* to make] —**mitigable** ('mɪtɪgəb°l) adj. —ˌ**mitigation** n. —'**mitiˌgative** or '**mitiˌgatory** adj. —'**mitiˌgator** n.

▷ *Usage.* See at **militate.**

Mitilini (miti'lini) n. transliteration of the Modern Greek name for **Mytilene** (sense 1).

mitochondrion (ˌmaɪtəʊ'kɒndrɪən) n., pl. **-dria** (-drɪə). a small spherical or rodlike body, in the cytoplasm of most cells: contains enzymes responsible for energy production. [C19: NL, from Gk *mitos* thread + *khondrion* small grain]

mitosis (maɪ'təʊsɪs, mɪ-) n. a method of cell division, in which the nucleus divides into daughter nuclei, each containing the same number of chromosomes as the parent nucleus. [C19: from NL, from Gk *mitos* thread] —**mitotic** (maɪ'tɒtɪk, mɪ-) adj.

mitral ('maɪtrəl) adj. **1.** of or like a mitre. **2.** *Anat.* of or relating to the mitral valve.

mitral valve n. the valve between the left atrium and the left ventricle of the heart.

mitre or *U.S.* **miter** ('maɪtə) n. **1.** *Christianity.* the liturgical headdress of a bishop or abbot, consisting of a tall pointed cleft cap with two bands hanging down at the back. **2.** Also called: **mitre joint.** a corner joint formed by cutting bevels of equal angles at the ends of each piece of material. **3.** a bevelled surface of a mitre joint. ~vb. (tr.) **4.** to make a mitre joint between (two pieces of material). **5.** to confer a mitre upon: *a mitred abbot.* [C14: from OF, from L *mitra,* from Gk: turban]

mitre box n. an open-ended box with sides slotted to guide a saw in cutting mitre joints.

mitt (mɪt) n. **1.** any of various glovelike hand coverings, such as one that does not cover the fingers. **2.** short for **mitten** (sense 1). **3.** *Baseball.* a large round thickly padded leather mitten worn by the catcher. **4.** (often pl.) a slang word for **hand. 5.** *Sl.* a boxing glove. [C18: from MITTEN]

Mittelland Canal (German 'mɪtəllant) n. a canal in West Germany, linking the Rivers Rhine and Elbe. Length: 325 km (202 miles).

mitten ('mɪt°n) n. **1.** a glove having one section for the thumb and a single section for the other fingers. Sometimes shortened to **mitt. 2.** *Sl.* a boxing glove. [C14: from OF *mitaine,* from ?]

Mitterrand (French mitɛrɑ̃) n. **François Maurice Marie** (frɑ̃swa mɔris mari). born 1916, French politician; first secretary of the socialist party from 1971; president from 1981.

mittimus ('mɪtɪməs) n., pl. **-muses.** *Law.* a warrant of commitment to prison or a command to a jailer to hold someone in prison. [C15: from L: we send, the first word of such a command]

mix (mɪks) vb. **1.** (tr.) to combine or blend (ingredients, liquids, objects, etc.) together into one mass. **2.** (intr.) to become or have the capacity to become combined, joined, etc.: *some chemicals do not mix.* **3.** (tr.) to form (something) by combining constituents: *to mix cement.* **4.** (tr.; often foll. by *in* or *into*) to add as an additional element (to a mass or compound): *to mix flour into a batter.* **5.** (tr.) to do at the same time: *to mix study and pleasure.* **6.** (tr.) to consume (different alcoholic drinks) in close succession. **7.** to come or cause to come into association socially: *Pauline mixed well.* **8.** (intr.; often foll. by *with*) to go together; complement. **9.** (tr.) to crossbreed (differing strains of plants or breeds of livestock), esp. more or less at random. **10.** *Music.* to balance and adjust (individual performers' parts) to make an overall sound by electronic means. **11. mix it.** *Inf.* to cause mischief or trouble, often for a person named: *she tried to mix it for John.* ~n. **12.** the act or an instance of mixing. **13.** the result of mixing; mixture. **14.** a mixture of ingredients, esp. one commercially prepared for making a cake, bread, etc. **15.** *Inf.* a state of confusion. **16.** *Music.* the sound produced by mixing. ~See also **mix-up.** [C15: back formation from *mixt* mixed, via OF from L *mixtus,* from *miscēre* to mix] —'**mixable** adj.

mixed (mɪkst) adj. **1.** formed or blended together by mixing. **2.** composed of different elements, races, sexes, etc.: *a mixed school.* **3.** consisting of conflicting elements, thoughts, attitudes, etc.: *mixed feelings.* **4.** *Maths.* (of a number) consisting of the sum of an integer and a fraction or a decimal fraction, as $5\frac{1}{2}$ or 17.43. —**mixedness** ('mɪksɪdnɪs) n.

mixed bag n. *Inf.* something composed of diverse elements, characteristics, people, etc.

mixed blessing n. an event, situation, etc., having both advantages and disadvantages.

mixed doubles pl. n. *Tennis.* a doubles game with a man and a woman as partners on each side.

mixed economy n. an economic system in which the public and private sectors coexist.

mixed farming n. combined arable and livestock farming (on **mixed farms**) .

mixed marriage n. a marriage between persons of different races or religions.

mixed metaphor n. a combination of incongruous metaphors, as *when the Nazi jackboots sing their swan song.*

mixed-up adj. in a state of mental confusion.

mixer ('mɪksə) n. **1.** a person or thing that mixes. **2.** *Inf.* **a.** a person considered in relation to his ability to mix socially. **b.** a person who creates trouble for others. **3.** a kitchen appliance, usually electrical, used for mixing foods, etc. **4.** a drink such as ginger ale, fruit juice, etc., used in preparing cocktails. **5.** *Electronics.* a device in which two or more input signals are combined to give a single output signal.

mixer tap n. a tap in which hot and cold water supplies have a joint outlet but are controlled separately.

mixture ('mɪkstʃə) n. **1.** the act of mixing or state of being mixed. **2.** something mixed; a result of mixing. **3.** *Chem.* a substance consisting of two or more substances mixed together without any chemical bonding between them. **4.** *Pharmacol.* a liquid medicine in which an insoluble compound is suspended in the liquid. **5.** *Music.* an organ stop that controls several ranks of pipes. **6.** the mixture of petrol vapour and air in an internal-combustion engine. [C16: from L *mixtūra,* from *mixtus,* p.p. of *miscere* to mix]

mix-up n. **1.** a confused condition or situation. **2.** *Inf.* a fight. ~vb. **mix up.** (tr., adv.) **3.** to make into a mixture. **4.** to confuse or confound: *Tom mixes John up with Bill.* **5.** (often passive) to put (someone) into a state of confusion: *I'm all mixed up.* **6.** (foll. by *in* or *with; usually passive*) to involve (in an activity or group, esp. one that is illegal): *mixed up in the drugs racket.*

Mizoguchi (ˌmiːtsə'guːtʃi) n. **Kenji** ('kɛndʒi). 1898–1956, Japanese film director. His films include *A Paper Doll's Whisper of Spring* (1925), *Woman of Osaka* (1940), and *Ugetsu Monogatari* (1952).

Mizoram (mɪ'zɔːrəm) n. a state (since 1986) in NE India, created in 1972 from the former Mizo Hills District of Assam. Capital: Aijal. Pop.: 487 774 (1981). Area: about 21 087 sq. km (8140 sq. miles).

mizzen *or* **mizen** ('mɪzᵊn) *Naut.* ~*n.* **1.** a sail set on a mizzenmast. **2.** short for **mizzenmast.** ~*adj.* **3.** of or relating to a mizzenmast: *a mizzen staysail.* [C15: from F *misaine*, from It. *mezzana, mezzano* middle]

mizzenmast *or* **mizenmast** ('mɪzᵊn,mɑːst; *Naut.* 'mɪzᵊnməst) *n. Naut.* (on a vessel with three or more masts) the third mast from the bow.

mizzle¹ ('mɪzᵊl) *vb., n.* a dialect word for **drizzle.** [C15: ?from Low G *miseln* to drizzle] —'**mizzly** *adj.*

mizzle² ('mɪzᵊl) *vb.* (*intr.*) *Brit. sl.* to decamp. [C18: from ?]

mk *Currency. symbol for:* **1.** mark. **2.** markka.

mks units *pl. n.* a metric system of units based on the metre, kilogram, and second as the units of length, mass, and time; it forms the basis of the SI units.

mkt *abbrev. for* market.

ml *symbol for:* **1.** mile. **2.** millilitre.

ML *abbrev. for* Medieval Latin.

MLA *abbrev. for:* **1.** Member of the Legislative Assembly. **2.** Modern Language Association (of America).

MLC (in Australia and India) *abbrev. for* Member of the Legislative Council.

MLitt *abbrev. for* Master of Letters. [L *Magister Litterarum*]

Mlle *or* **Mlle.** *pl.* **Mlles** *or* **Mlles.** the French equivalent of **Miss.** [from F *Mademoiselle*]

MLR *abbrev. for* minimum lending rate.

mm *symbol for* millimetre.

MM **1.** the French equivalent of **Messrs.** [from F *Messieurs*] **2.** *abbrev. for* Military Medal.

Mme *pl.* **Mmes** the French equivalent of **Mrs.** [from F *Madame, Mesdames*]

MMus *abbrev. for* Master of Music.

Mn *the chemical symbol for* manganese.

MNA (in Canada) *abbrev. for* Member of the National Assembly (of Quebec).

mnemonic (nɪ'mɒnɪk) *adj.* **1.** aiding or meant to aid one's memory. **2.** of or relating to memory or mnemonics. ~*n.* **3.** something, such as a verse, to assist memory. [C18: from Gk *mnēmonikos*, from *mnēmōn* mindful, from *mnasthai* to remember] —**mne'monically** *adv.*

mnemonics (nɪ'mɒnɪks) *n.* (*usually functioning as sing.*) **1.** the art or practice of improving or of aiding the memory. **2.** a system of rules to aid the memory.

Mnemosyne (niː'mɒzɪ,niː, -'mɒs-) *n. Greek myth.* the goddess of memory and mother by Zeus of the Muses.

mo (məʊ) *n. Inf.* **1.** *Chiefly Brit.* short for **moment** (sense 1) (esp. in **half a mo**). **2.** *Austral.* short for **moustache** (sense 1).

Mo *the chemical symbol for* molybdenum.

MO *abbrev. for* Medical Officer.

m.o. *or* **MO** *abbrev. for:* **1.** mail order. **2.** money order.

-mo *suffix forming nouns.* (in bookbinding) indicating book size by specifying the number of leaves formed by folding one sheet of paper: *16mo* or *sixteenmo.* [abstracted from DUODECIMO]

moa ('məʊə) *n.* any of various recently extinct large flightless birds of New Zealand (see **ratite**) . [C19: from Maori]

Moab ('məʊæb) *n. Old Testament.* an ancient kingdom east of the Dead Sea, in what is now the SW part of Jordan: flourished mainly from the 9th to the 6th centuries B.C. —**Moabite** ('məʊə,baɪt) *adj., n.*

moa hunter *n. N.Z.* an anthropologists' term for an early Maori.

moan (məʊn) *n.* **1.** a low prolonged mournful sound expressive of suffering or pleading. **2.** any similar mournful sound, esp. that made by the wind. **3.** *Inf.* a grumble or complaint. ~*vb.* **4.** to utter (words, etc.) in a low mournful manner. **5.** (*intr.*) to make a sound like a moan. **6.** (*usually intr.*) *Inf.* to grumble or complain. [C13: rel. to OE *mǽnan* to grieve over] —'**moaner** *n.* —'**moanful** *adj.* —'**moaning** *n., adj.*

moat (məʊt) *n.* **1.** a wide water-filled ditch surrounding a fortified place, such as a castle. ~*vb.* **2.** (*tr.*) to surround with or as if with a moat. [C14: from OF *motte* mound]

mob (mɒb) *n.* **1. a.** a riotous or disorderly crowd of people; rabble. **b.** (*as modifier*): *mob law.* **2.** *Often derog.* a group or class of people, animals, or things. **3.** *Often derog.* the masses. **4.** *Sl.* a gang of criminals. **5.** *Austral. & N.Z.* a large number of anything. **6.** *Austral. & N.Z.* a flock or herd of animals. **7. mobs of.** *Austral. & N.Z. inf.* lots of. ~*vb.* **mobbing, mobbed.** (*tr.*) **8.** to attack in a group resembling a mob. **9.** to surround, esp. in order to

acclaim. **10.** to crowd into (a building, etc.). [C17: shortened from L *mōbile vulgus* the fickle populace]

mobcap ('mɒb,kæp) *n.* a woman's large cotton cap with a pouched crown, worn esp. during the 18th century. [C18: from obs. *mob* woman, esp. loose-living, + CAP]

mobile ('məʊbaɪl) *adj.* **1.** having freedom of movement; movable. **2.** changing quickly in expression: *a mobile face.* **3.** *Sociol.* (of individuals or social groups) moving within and between classes, occupations, and localities. **4.** (of military forces) able to move freely and quickly. **5.** (*postpositive*) *Inf.* having transport available: *are you mobile?* ~*n.* **6. a.** a sculpture suspended in midair with delicately balanced parts that are set in motion by air currents. **b.** (*as modifier*): *mobile sculpture.* [C15: via OF from L *mōbilis*, from *movēre* to move] —**mobility** (məʊ'bɪlɪtɪ) *n.*

Mobile ('məʊbiːl, məʊ'biːln) *n.* a port in SW Alabama, on **Mobile Bay** (an inlet of the Gulf of Mexico): the state's only port and its first permanent settlement, made by French colonists in 1711. Pop.: 203 260 (1986 est.).

-mobile (məʊ,biːl) *suffix forming nouns.* indicating a vehicle designed for a particular person or purpose: *Popemobile.*

mobile home *n.* living quarters mounted on wheels and capable of being towed by a motor vehicle.

mobilize *or* **-lise** ('məʊbɪ,laɪz) *vb.* **1.** to prepare for war or another emergency by organizing (national resources, the armed services, etc.). **2.** (*tr.*) to organize for a purpose. **3.** (*tr.*) to put into motion or use. —'**mobi,lizable** *or* **-lisable** *adj.* —,**mobili'zation** *or* **-li'sation** *n.*

Möbius strip ('mɜːbɪəs) *n. Maths.* a one-sided continuous surface, formed by twisting a long narrow rectangular strip of material through 180° and joining the ends. [C19: after August *Möbius* (1790–1868), G mathematician]

mobocracy (mɒ'bɒkrəsɪ) *n., pl.* **-cies.** **1.** rule or domination by a mob. **2.** the mob that rules.

mobster ('mɒbstə) *n.* a U.S. slang word for **gangster.**

Mobutu¹ (mə'buːtuː) *n. Lake.* a lake in E Africa, between Zaïre and Uganda in the Great Rift Valley, 660 m (2200 ft.) above sea level: a source of the Nile, fed by the Victoria Nile, which leaves as the Albert Nile. Area: 5345 sq. km (2064 sq. miles). Former name: **Lake Albert.**

Mobutu² (mə'buːtuː) *n. Sese Seko* ('sɛsɛ 'sɛkəʊ), original name *Joseph.* born 1930, Zaïrese statesman; president of Zaïre from 1970.

Moçambique (musəm'bikə) *n.* the Portuguese name for **Mozambique.**

moccasin ('mɒkəsɪn) *n.* **1.** a shoe of soft leather, esp. deerskin, worn by North American Indians. **2.** any soft shoe resembling this. **3.** short for **water moccasin.** [C17: of Amerind origin]

moccasin flower *n.* any of several North American orchids with a pink solitary flower. See also **lady's-slipper, cypripedium.**

mocha ('mɒkə) *n.* **1.** a dark brown coffee originally imported from the port of Mocha in Arabia. **2.** a flavouring made from coffee and chocolate. **3.** a soft glove leather, made from goatskin or sheepskin. **4. a.** a dark brown colour. **b.** (*as adj.*): *mocha shoes.*

Mocha *or* **Mokha** ('mɒkə) *n.* a port in SW North Yemen, on the Red Sea: formerly important for the export of Arabian coffee. Pop.: about 8000 (1985 est.).

mock (mɒk) *vb.* **1.** (when *intr.*, often foll. by *at*) to behave with scorn or contempt (towards); show ridicule (for). **2.** (*tr.*) to imitate, esp. in fun; mimic. **3.** (*tr.*) to deceive, disappoint, or delude. **4.** (*tr.*) to defy or frustrate. ~*n.* **5.** the act of mocking. **6.** a person or thing mocked. **7.** a counterfeit; imitation. **8.** (*often pl.*) *Inf.* (in England and Wales) school examinations taken as practice before public exams. ~*adj.* (*prenominal*) **9.** sham or counterfeit. **10.** serving as an imitation or substitute, esp. for practice purposes: *a mock battle.* ~See also **mock-up.** [C15: from OF *mocquer*] —'**mocker** *n.* —'**mocking** *n., adj.* —'**mockingly** *adv.*

mockers ('mɒkəz) *pl. n. Inf.* **put the mockers on.** to ruin the chances of success of. [C20: ?from MOCK]

mockery ('mɒkərɪ) *n., pl.* **-eries.** **1.** ridicule, contempt, or derision. **2.** a derisive action or comment. **3.** an imitation or pretence, esp. a derisive one. **4.** a person or thing that is mocked. **5.** a person, thing, or action that is inadequate.

mock-heroic *adj.* **1.** (of a literary work, esp. a poem) imitating the style of heroic poetry in order to satirize an unheroic subject. ~*n.* **2.** burlesque imitation of the heroic style.

mockingbird ('mɒkɪŋ,bɜːd) *n.* any of various American songbirds, noted for their ability to mimic the song of other birds.

mock orange *n.* **1.** Also called: **syringa, philadelphus.** a shrub with white fragrant flowers resembling those of the orange. **2.** an Australian shrub with white flowers and dark shiny leaves.

mock turtle soup *n.* an imitation turtle soup made from a calf's head.

mock-up *n.* **1.** a working full-scale model of a machine, apparatus, etc., for testing, research, etc. **2.** a layout of printed matter. ~*vb.* **mock up. 3.** (*tr., adv.*) to build or make a mock-up of.

mod[1] (mɒd) *n. Brit.* **a.** a member of a group of teenagers, originally in the mid-1960s, noted for their clothes-consciousness. **b.** a member of a revived group of this type in the late 1970s and early 1980s. [C20: from MODERNIST]

mod[2] (mɒd) *n.* an annual Highland Gaelic meeting with musical and literary competitions. [C19: from Gaelic *mòd* assembly, from ON]

MOD (in Britain) *abbrev. for* Ministry of Defence.

mod. *abbrev. for:* **1.** moderate. **2.** moderato. **3.** modern.

modal ('məʊd[ə]l) *adj.* **1.** of or relating to mode or manner. **2.** *Grammar.* (of a verb form or auxiliary verb) expressing a distinction of mood, such as that between possibility and actuality. **3.** qualifying, or expressing a qualification of, the truth of some statement. **4.** *Metaphysics.* of or relating to the form of a thing as opposed to its attributes, substance, etc. **5.** *Music.* of or relating to a mode. **6.** of or relating to a statistical mode. —**mo'dality** *n.* —**'modally** *adv.*

modal logic *n.* **1.** the logical study of such philosophical concepts as necessity, possibility, contingency, etc. **2.** the logical study of concepts whose formal properties resemble certain moral, epistemological, and psychological concepts.

mod cons *pl. n. Inf.* modern conveniences; the usual installations of a modern house, such as hot water, heating, etc.

mode (məʊd) *n.* **1.** a manner or way of doing, acting, or existing. **2.** the current fashion or style. **3.** *Music.* **a.** any of the various scales of notes within one octave, esp. any of the twelve natural diatonic scales taken in ascending order used in plainsong, folk song, and art music until 1600. **b.** (in the music of classical Greece) any of the descending diatonic scales from which the liturgical modes evolved. **c.** either of the two main scale systems in music since 1600: *major mode; minor mode.* **4.** *Logic, linguistics.* another name for **mood**[2]. **5.** *Philosophy.* a complex combination of ideas which is not simply the sum of its component ideas. **6.** the predominating value in a set of values as determined from statistical data or by observation. [C14: from L *modus* manner]

model ('mɒd[ə]l) *n.* **1. a.** a representation, usually on a smaller scale, of a device, structure, etc. **b.** (*as modifier*): *a model train.* **2. a.** a standard to be imitated. **b.** (*as modifier*): *a model wife.* **3.** a representative form, style, or pattern. **4.** a person who poses for a sculptor, painter, or photographer. **5.** a person who wears clothes to display them to prospective buyers; mannequin. **6.** a preparatory sculpture in clay, wax, etc., from which the finished work is copied. **7.** a design or style of a particular product. ~*vb.* **-elling, -elled** *or U.S.* **-eling, -eled. 8.** to make a model of (something or someone). **9.** to form in clay, wax, etc.; mould. **10.** to display (clothing and accessories) as a mannequin. **11.** to plan or create according to a model or models. [C16: from OF *modelle*, from It., from L *modulus*, dim. of *modus* MODE] —**'modeller** *or U.S.* **'modeler** *n.*

modem ('məʊdɛm) *n. Computers.* a device for connecting two computers by a telephone line, consisting of a modulator that converts computer signals into audio signals and a corresponding demodulator. [C20: from *mo(dulator) dem(odulator)*]

Modena (*Italian* 'mɔːdena) *n.* a city in N Italy, in Emilia-Romagna: ruled by the Este family (18th–19th century); university (1678). Pop.: 176 880 (1986). Ancient name: **Mutina.**

moderate *adj.* ('mɒdərɪt). **1.** not extreme or excessive. **2.** not violent; mild or temperate. **3.** of average quality or extent: *moderate success.* ~*n.* ('mɒdərɪt). **4.** a person who holds moderate views, esp. in politics. ~*vb.* ('mɒdə,reɪt). **5.** to become or cause to become less extreme or violent. **6.** (when *intr.*, often foll. by *over*) to preside over a meeting, discussion, etc. **7.** *Physics.* to slow down (neutrons), esp. by using a moderator. [C14: from L *moderātus*, from *moderāri* to restrain]

moderate breeze *n.* a wind of force 4 on the Beaufort scale, reaching speeds of 13 to 18 mph.

moderation (,mɒdə'reɪʃən) *n.* **1.** the state or an instance of being moderate. **2.** the act of moderating. **3. in moderation.** within moderate or reasonable limits.

moderato (,mɒdə'rɑːtəʊ) *adv. Music.* **1.** at a moderate tempo. **2.** a direction indicating that the tempo specified is to be used with moderation: *allegro moderato.* [It.]

moderator ('mɒdə,reɪtə) *n.* **1.** a person or thing that moderates. **2.** *Presbyterian Church.* a minister appointed to preside over a Church court, synod, or general assembly. **3.** a presiding officer at a public or legislative assembly. **4.** a material, such as heavy water, used for slowing down neutrons in nuclear reactors. **5.** an examiner at Oxford or Cambridge Universities in first public examinations. **6.** (in Britain and New Zealand) one who is responsible for consistency of standards in the grading of some public examinations. —**'moder,atorship** *n.*

modern ('mɒdən) *adj.* **1.** of, involving, or befitting the present or a recent time; contemporary. **2.** of, relating to, or characteristic of contemporary styles or schools of art, literature, music, etc., esp. those of an experimental kind. **3.** belonging or relating to the period in history from the end of the Middle Ages to the present. ~*n.* **4.** a contemporary person. [C16: from OF, from LL *modernus*, from *modō* (adv.) just recently, from *modus* MODE] —**mo'dernity** *or* **'modernness** *n.*

Modern English *n.* the English language since about 1450.

Modern Hebrew *n.* the official language of Israel; a revived form of ancient Hebrew.

modernism ('mɒdə,nɪzəm) *n.* **1.** modern tendencies, thoughts, etc., or the support of these. **2.** something typical of contemporary life or thought. **3.** (*cap.*) *R.C. Church.* the movement at the end of the 19th and beginning of the 20th centuries that sought to adapt doctrine to modern thought. —**'modernist** *n., adj.* —**,modern'istic** *adj.* —**,modern'istically** *adv.*

modern pentathlon *n.* an athletic contest consisting of five different events: horse riding with jumps, fencing with electric épée, freestyle swimming, pistol shooting, and cross-country running.

modernize *or* **-ise** ('mɒdə,naɪz) *vb.* **1.** (*tr.*) to make modern in appearance or style. **2.** (*intr.*) to adopt modern ways, ideas, etc. —**,moderni'zation** *or* **-i'sation** *n.* —**'modern,izer** *or* **-,iser** *n.*

modest ('mɒdɪst) *adj.* **1.** having or expressing a humble opinion of oneself or one's accomplishments or abilities. **2.** reserved or shy. **3.** not ostentatious or pretentious. **4.** not extreme or excessive. **5.** decorous or decent. [C16: via OF from L *modestus* moderate, from *modus* MODE] —**'modestly** *adv.*

modesty ('mɒdɪstɪ) *n., pl.* **-ties.** the quality or condition of being modest.

modicum ('mɒdɪkəm) *n.* a small amount or portion. [C15: from L a little way, from *modicus* moderate]

modification (,mɒdɪfɪ'keɪʃən) *n.* **1.** the act of modifying or the condition of being modified. **2.** something modified. **3.** a small change or adjustment. **4.** *Grammar.* the relation between a modifier and the word or phrase that it modifies. —**'modifi,catory** *or* **'modifi,cative** *adj.*

modifier ('mɒdɪ,faɪə) *n.* **1.** Also called: **qualifier.** *Grammar.* a word or phrase that qualifies the sense of another word; for example, the noun *alarm* is a modifier of *clock* in *alarm clock* and the phrase *every day* is an adverbial modifier of *walks* in *he walks every day.* **2.** a person or thing that modifies.

▷**Usage.** Nouns are frequently used in English to modify other nouns: *police officer; chicken farm.* They should be used with restraint, however, esp. when the appropriate adjective can be used: *lunar research* (not *moon research*); *educational system* (not *education system*).

modify ('mɒdɪ,faɪ) *vb.* **-fying, -fied.** (*mainly tr.*) **1.** to change the structure, character, intent, etc., of. **2.** to make less extreme or uncompromising. **3.** *Grammar.* (of a word or phrase) to bear the relation of modifier to (another word or phrase). **4.** *Linguistics.* to change (a vowel) by umlaut. **5.** (*intr.*) to be or become modified. [C14: from OF *modifier*, from L *modificāre* to limit, from *modus* measure + *facere* to make] —'**modi,fiable** *adj.*

Modigliani (*Italian* modiʎˈʎaːni) *n.* **Amedeo** (ameˈdɛːo). 1884–1920, Italian painter and sculptor, noted esp. for the elongated forms of his portraits.

modish ('məʊdɪʃ) *adj.* in the current fashion or style. —'**modishly** *adv.* —'**modishness** *n.*

modiste (məʊˈdiːst) *n.* a fashionable dressmaker or milliner. [C19: from F, from *mode* fashion]

modular ('mɒdjʊlə) *adj.* of, consisting of, or resembling a module or modulus.

modulate ('mɒdjʊ,leɪt) *vb.* **1.** (*tr.*) to change the tone, pitch, or volume of. **2.** (*tr.*) to adjust or regulate the degree of. **3.** *Music.* **a.** to change or cause to change from one key to another. **b.** (often foll. by *to*) to make or become in tune (with a pitch, key, etc.). **4.** *Physics, electronics.* to superimpose the amplitude, frequency, phase, etc., of a wave or signal onto another wave or signal or onto an electron beam. [C16: from L *modulātus* in due measure, melodious, from *modulāri*, from *modus* measure] —,**modu'lation** *n.* —'**modu,lator** *n.*

module ('mɒdjuːl) *n.* **1.** a standard unit of measure, esp. one used to coordinate the dimensions of buildings and components. **2.** a standard self-contained unit or item, such as an assembly of electronic components, or a standardized piece of furniture, that can be used in combination with other units. **3.** *Astronautics.* any of several self-contained separable units making up a spacecraft or launch vehicle, each of which has one or more specified tasks. **4.** *Education.* a short course of study that together with other such courses counts towards a qualification. [C16: from L *modulus*, dim. of *modus* MODE]

modulus ('mɒdjʊləs) *n.*, *pl.* -**li** (-,laɪ). **1.** *Physics.* a coefficient expressing a specified property of a specified substance. See **modulus of elasticity**. **2.** *Maths.* another name for the **absolute value** of a complex number. **3.** *Maths.* the number by which a logarithm to one base is multiplied to give the corresponding logarithm to another base. **4.** *Maths.* an integer that can be divided exactly into the difference between two other integers: *7 is a modulus of 25 and 11.* [C16: from L, dim. of *modus* measure]

modulus of elasticity *n.* the ratio of the stress applied to a body or substance to the resulting strain within the elastic limit. Also called: **elastic modulus**.

modus operandi ('məʊdəs ,ɒpəˈrændiː, -'rændaɪ) *n.*, *pl.* **modi operandi** ('məʊdi: ,ɒpəˈrændi:, 'məʊdaɪ ,ɒpəˈrændaɪ). procedure; method of operating. [C17: L]

modus vivendi ('məʊdəs vɪˈvɛndi:, -'vɛndaɪ) *n.*, *pl.* **modi vivendi** ('məʊdi: vɪˈvɛndi:, 'məʊdaɪ vɪˈvɛndaɪ). a working arrangement between conflicting interests; practical compromise. [C19: L: way of living]

mog (mɒg) *or* **moggy** *n.*, *pl.* **mogs** *or* **moggies**. *Brit.* a slang name for **cat**. [C20: dialect, orig. a pet name for a cow]

Mogadiscio (,mɒgəˈdɪʃɪ,əʊ, -'dɪʃəʊ) *or* **Mogadishu** (,mɒgəˈdɪʃuː) *n.* the capital and chief port of Somalia, on the Indian Ocean: founded by Arabs around the 10th century; taken by the Sultan of Zanzibar in 1871 and sold to Italy in 1905. Pop.: 1 000 000 (1987 est.).

Mogadon ('mɒgə,dɒn) *n.* *Trademark.* a minor tranquillizer used to treat insomnia.

Mogador (,mɒgəˈdɔː; *French* mɔgadɔr) *n.* the former name (until 1956) of **Essaouira**.

Mogilev (*Russian* məgɪˈljɔf) *or* **Mohilev** *n.* an industrial city in the W Soviet Union, in the E Byelorussian SSR on the Dnieper River: passed to Russia in 1772 after Polish rule. Pop.: 359 000 (1987).

mogul ('məʊgʌl, məʊˈgʌl) *n.* an important or powerful person. [C18: from MOGUL]

Mogul ('məʊgʌl, məʊˈgʌl) *n.* **1.** a member of the Muslim dynasty of Indian emperors established in 1526. **2.** a Muslim Indian, Mongol, or Mongolian. ~*adj.* **3.** of or relating to the Moguls or their empire. [C16: from Persian *mughul* Mongolian]

MOH (in Britain) *abbrev. for* Medical Officer of Health.

mohair ('məʊ,hɛə) *n.* **1.** Also called: **angora**. the long soft silky hair of the Angora goat. **2. a.** a fabric made from the yarn of this hair and cotton or wool. **b.** (*as modifier*): *a mohair suit.* [C16: (infl. by *hair*), ult. from Ar. *mukhayyar*, lit.: choice]

Moham. *abbrev. for* Mohammedan.

Mohammed (məʊˈhæmɪd) *or* **Muhammad** *n.* ?570–632 A.D., the prophet and founder of Islam. He began to teach in Mecca in 610 but persecution forced him to flee with his followers to Medina in 622. After several battles, he conquered Mecca (630), establishing the principles of Islam (embodied in the Koran) over all Arabia. Other names: **Mahomet**, (*archaic*) **Mahound**.

Mohammed II *n.* ?1430–81, Ottoman sultan of Turkey (1451–81). He captured Constantinople (1453) and conquered large areas of the Balkans.

Mohammed Ahmed (məʊˈhæmɪd 'ɑːmɛd) *n.* the original name of the **Mahdi**.

Mohammed Ali *n.* **1.** See **Mehemet Ali**. **2.** See **Muhammad Ali**.

Mohammedan (məʊˈhæmɪdən) *n.*, *adj.* another word (not in Muslim use) for **Muslim**.

Mohammedanism (məʊˈhæmɪdə,nɪzəm) *n.* another word (not in Muslim use) for **Islam**.

Mohave Desert *or* **Mojave Desert** *n.* a desert in S California, south of the Sierra Nevada: part of the Great Basin. Area: 38 850 sq. km (15 000 sq. miles).

Mohawk¹ ('məʊhɔːk) *n.* **1.** (*pl.* -**hawks** *or* -**hawk**) a member of a North American Indian people formerly living along the Mohawk River. **2.** the Iroquoian language of this people.

Mohawk² ('məʊhɔːk) *n.* a river in E central New York State, flowing south and east to the Hudson River at Cohoes: the largest tributary of the Hudson. Length: 238 km (148 miles).

Mohenjo-Daro (mə'hɛndʒəʊ'dɑːrəʊ) *n.* an excavated city in SE Pakistan, southwest of Sukkur near the River Indus: flourished during the third millennium B.C.

mohican (məʊˈhiːkən) *n.* a punk hairstyle in which the head is shaved at the sides and the remaining strip of hair is worn stiffly erect and sometimes brightly coloured.

Moholy-Nagy ('məʊhɔɪ'nɒdj) *n.* **Laszlo** ('læzləʊ) *or* **Ladislaus** ('lɑːdɪs,laʊs). 1895–1946, U.S. painter and teacher, born in Hungary. He worked at the Bauhaus (1923–29).

moidore ('mɔɪdɔː) *n.* a former Portuguese gold coin. [C18: from Port. *moeda de ouro* money of gold]

moiety ('mɔɪɪtɪ) *n.*, *pl.* -**ties**. **1.** a half. **2.** one of two parts or divisions of something. [C15: from OF *moitié*, from L *mediētās* middle, from *medius*]

moil (mɔɪl) *Arch. or dialect.* ~*vb.* **1.** to moisten or soil or become moist, soiled, etc. **2.** (*intr.*) to toil or drudge (esp. in **toil and moil**). ~*n.* **3.** toil; drudgery. **4.** confusion; turmoil. [C14 (to moisten; later: to work hard in unpleasantly wet conditions) from OF *moillier*, ult. from L *mollis* soft]

Moirai ('mɔɪriː) *pl. n.*, *sing.* **Moira** ('mɔɪrə), **the.** the Greek goddesses of fate. Roman counterparts: the **Parcae**. See **Fates**.

moire (mwɑː) *n.* a fabric, usually silk, having a watered effect. [C17: from F, earlier *mouaire*, from MOHAIR]

moiré ('mwɑːreɪ) *adj.* **1.** having a watered or wavelike pattern. ~*n.* **2.** such a pattern, impressed on fabrics by means of engraved rollers. **3.** any fabric having such a pattern; moire. **4.** Also: **moiré pattern**. a pattern seen when two geometrical patterns, such as grids, are visually superimposed. [C17: from F, from *moire* MOHAIR]

moist (mɔɪst) *adj.* **1.** slightly damp or wet. **2.** saturated with or suggestive of moisture. [C14: from OF, ult. rel. to L *mūcidus* musty] —'**moistly** *adv.* —'**moistness** *n.*

moisten ('mɔɪsən) *vb.* to make or become moist.

moisture ('mɔɪstʃə) *n.* water or other liquid diffused as vapour or condensed on or in objects.

moisturize *or* -**ise** ('mɔɪstʃə,raɪz) *vb.* (*tr.*) to add moisture to (the air, the skin, etc.). —'**moistur,izer** *or* -,**iser** *n.*

moke (məʊk) *n.* *Brit. sl.* a donkey. [C19: from ?]

Mokha ('məʊkə, 'mɒk-) *n.* a variant of **Mocha**.

Mokpo (,məʊk'pəʊ) *n.* a port in SW South Korea, on the Yellow Sea. Pop.: 221 856 (1980).

mol *Chem. symbol for* mole³.

mol. *abbrev. for:* **1.** molecular. **2.** molecule.

molal ('məʊləl) *adj. Chem.* of or consisting of a solution containing one mole of solute per thousand grams of solution. [C20: from MOLE³ + -AL¹]

molar¹ ('məʊlə) *n.* **1.** any of the 12 grinding teeth in man. **2.** a corresponding tooth in other mammals. ~*adj.* **3.** of or relating to any of these teeth. **4.** used for or capable of grinding. [C16: from L *molāris*, from *mola* millstone]

molar[2] ('məʊlə) *adj.* **1.** (of a physical quantity) per unit amount of substance: *molar volume.* **2.** (not recommended in technical usage) (of a solution) containing one mole of solute per litre of solution. [C19: from L *mōlēs* a mass]

molasses (mə'læsɪz) *n.* (*functioning as sing.*) **1.** the thick brown uncrystallized bitter syrup obtained from sugar during refining. **2.** the U.S. and Canad. name for **treacle** (sense 1). [C16: from Port. *melaço*, from LL *mellāceum* must, from L *mel* honey]

mold (məʊld) *n., vb.* the U.S. spelling of **mould.**

Moldau ('mɔldaʊ) *n.* **1.** the German name for **Moldavia. 2.** the German name for the **Vltava.**

Moldavia (mɔl'deɪvɪə) *n.* **1.** a former principality of E Europe, consisting of the basins of the Rivers Prut and Dniester: in 1940 the E part (Bessarabia) was ceded to the Soviet Union and became the Moldavian SSR; the W part remains a province of Romania. Romanian name: **Moldova** (mɔl'dova). German name: **Moldau. 2.** another name for the **Moldavian SSR. —Mol'davian** *adj., n.*

Moldavian Soviet Socialist Republic *n.* an administrative division of the SW Soviet Union, bordering on Romania, by which it was ceded to the Soviet Union in 1940. Capital: Kishinev. Pop.: 4 185 000 (1987). Area: 33 700 sq. km (13 012 sq. miles). Also called: **Moldavia, Bessarabia.**

moldboard ('məʊld‚bɔːd) *n.* the U.S. spelling of **mouldboard.**

molder ('məʊldə) *vb.* the U.S. spelling of **moulder.**

molding ('məʊldɪŋ) *n.* the U.S. spelling of **moulding.**

moldy ('məʊldɪ) *adj.* the U.S. spelling of **mouldy.**

mole[1] (məʊl) *n. Pathol.* a nontechnical name for **naevus.** [OE *māl*]

mole[2] (məʊl) *n.* **1.** any small burrowing mammal of a family of Europe, Asia, and North and Central America. They have velvety, typically dark fur and forearms specialized for digging. **2.** *Inf.* a spy who has infiltrated an organization and become a trusted member of it. [C14: from MDu. *mol*, of Gmc origin]

mole[3] (məʊl) *n.* the basic SI unit of amount of substance; the amount that contains as many elementary entities as there are atoms in 0.012 kilogram of carbon-12. The entity may be an atom, a molecule, an ion, a radical, etc. Symbol: mol [C20: from G *Mol*, short for *Molekül* MOLECULE]

mole[4] (məʊl) *n.* **1.** a breakwater. **2.** a harbour protected by a breakwater. [C16: from F *môle*, from L *mōlēs* mass]

Molech ('məʊlɛk) *n. Old Testament.* a variant of **Moloch.**

molecular (məʊ'lɛkjʊlə, mə-) *adj.* of or relating to molecules. **—mo'lecularly** *adv.*

molecular biology *n.* the study of the structure and function of biological molecules, esp. nucleic acids and proteins.

molecular formula *n.* a chemical formula indicating the numbers and types of atoms in a molecule: H_2SO_4 *is the molecular formula of sulphuric acid.*

molecular weight *n.* the sum of all the atomic weights (relative atomic masses) of the atoms in a molecule; the ratio of the average mass per molecule of a specified isotopic composition of a substance to 1/12 the mass of an atom of carbon-12. Abbrev.: **mol. wt.** Also called: **relative molecular mass.**

molecule ('mɔlɪ‚kjuːl) *n.* **1.** the simplest unit of a chemical compound that can exist, consisting of two or more atoms held together by chemical bonds. **2.** a very small particle. [C18: via F from NL *mōlēcula,* dim. of L *mōlēs* mass]

molehill ('məʊl‚hɪl) *n.* **1.** the small mound of earth thrown up by a burrowing mole. **2. make a mountain out of a molehill.** to exaggerate an unimportant matter out of all proportion.

moleskin ('məʊl‚skɪn) *n.* **1.** the dark grey dense velvety pelt of a mole, used as a fur. **2.** a hard-wearing cotton fabric of twill weave. **3.** (*modifier*): *a moleskin waistcoat.*

molest (mə'lɛst) *vb.* (*tr.*) **1.** to disturb or annoy by malevolent interference. **2.** to accost or attack, esp. with the intention of assaulting sexually. [C14: from L *molestāre* to annoy, from *molestus* troublesome, from *mōlēs* mass] **—molestation** (‚məʊlɛ'steɪʃən) *n.* **—mo'lester** *n.*

Molière (*French* mɔljɛr) *n.* real name *Jean-Baptiste Poquelin.* 1622–73, French dramatist, regarded as the greatest French writer of comedy. His works include *Tartuffe*

(1664), *Le Misanthrope* (1666), *L'Avare* (1668), *Le Bourgeois gentilhomme* (1670), and *Le Malade imaginaire* (1673).

Molina (*Spanish* mo'lina) *n.* See **Tirso de Molina.**

Molise (*Italian* mo'liːze) *n.* a region of S central Italy, the second smallest of the regions: separated from **Abruzzi e Molise** in 1965. Capital: Campobasso. Pop.: 332 500 (1984). Area: 4438 sq. km (1731 sq. miles).

moll (mɔl) *n. Sl.* **1.** the female accomplice of a gangster. **2.** a prostitute. [C17: from *Moll,* familiar form of *Mary*]

mollify ('mɔlɪ‚faɪ) *vb.* **-fying, -fied.** (*tr.*) **1.** to pacify; soothe. **2.** to lessen the harshness or severity of. [C15: from OF *mollifier,* via LL, from L *mollis* soft + *facere* to make] **—'molli‚fiable** *adj.* **—‚mollifi'cation** *n.* **—'molli‚fier** *n.*

mollusc *or U.S.* **mollusk** ('mɔləsk) *n.* any of various invertebrates having a soft unsegmented body and often a shell, secreted by a fold of skin (the mantle). The group includes the gastropods (snails, slugs, etc.), bivalves (clams, mussels, etc.), and cephalopods (squid, octopuses, etc.). [C18: via NL from L *molluscus,* from *mollis* soft] **—molluscan** *or U.S.* **molluskan** (mə'lʌskən) *adj., n.*

molly ('mɔlɪ) *n., pl.* **-lies.** any of various brightly coloured tropical or subtropical American freshwater fishes. [C19: from NL *Molienisia,* from Comte F. N. *Mollien* (1758–1850), F statesman]

mollycoddle ('mɔlɪ‚kɒdə̩l) *vb.* **1.** (*tr.*) to treat with indulgent care; pamper. ~*n.* **2.** a pampered person. [C19: from obs. sl. *molly* an effeminate boy, from *Molly* girl's name + CODDLE]

Molnár (*Hungarian* 'molnaːr) *n.* **Ferenc** ('fɛrɛnts). 1878–1952, Hungarian dramatist and novelist. His works include the play *Liliom* (1909).

Moloch ('məʊlɒk) *or* **Molech** ('məʊlɛk) *n. Old Testament.* a Semitic deity to whom parents sacrificed their children.

Molokai (‚məʊləʊ'kaːɪ) *n.* an island in central Hawaii. Pop.: 6700 (1986 est.). Area: 676 sq. km (261 sq. miles).

Molopo (mə'ləʊpəʊ) *n.* a seasonal river in South Africa, rising in N Cape Province and flowing west and southwest to the Orange river. Length: about 1000 km (600 miles).

Molotov[1] ('mɔlə‚tɒf; *Russian* 'mɔlətəf) *n.* the former name (1940–62) for **Perm.**

Molotov[2] ('mɔlə‚tɒf; *Russian* 'mɔlətəf) *n.* **Vyacheslav Mikhailovich** (vɪtʃɪ'slaf mi'xajləvɪtʃ), original surname *Skriabin.* 1890–1986, Soviet statesman. As commissar and later minister for foreign affairs (1939–49; 1953–56) he negotiated the nonaggression pact with Nazi Germany and attended the founding conference of the United Nations and the Potsdam conference (1945).

Molotov cocktail *n.* an elementary incendiary weapon, usually a bottle of petrol with a short delay fuse or wick; petrol bomb. [C20: after V. M. MOLOTOV]

molt (məʊlt) *vb., n.* the usual U.S. spelling of **moult.** **—'molter** *n.*

molten ('məʊltən) *adj.* **1.** liquefied; melted. **2.** made by having been melted: *molten casts.* ~*vb.* **3.** the past participle of **melt.**

Moltke (*German* 'mɔltkə) *n.* **1.** Count **Helmuth Johannes Ludwig von** ('hɛlmuːt jo'hanəs 'luːtvɪç fɔn). 1848–1916, German general; chief of the German general staff (1906–14). **2.** his uncle Count **Helmuth Karl Bernhard von** ('hɛlmuːt karl 'bɛrnhart fɔn). 1800–91, German field marshal; chief of the Prussian general staff (1858–88).

molto ('mɔltəʊ) *adv. Music.* very: *allegro molto; molto adagio.* [from It., from L *multum* (adv.) much]

Moluccas (məʊ'lʌkəz, mə-) *or* **Molucca Islands** *pl. n.* a group of islands in the Malay Archipelago, between Sulawesi (Celebes) and New Guinea. Capital: Amboina. Pop.: 1 411 000 (1980). Area: about 74 505 sq. km (28 766 sq. miles). Indonesian name: **Maluku.** Former name: **Spice Islands.**

mol. wt. *abbrev. for* molecular weight.

moly ('məʊlɪ) *n., pl.* **-lies. 1.** *Greek myth.* a magic herb given by Hermes to Odysseus to nullify the spells of Circe. **2.** a variety of wild garlic of S Europe having yellow flowers. [C16: from L *mōly,* from Gk *mōlu*]

molybdenite (mɒ'lɪbdɪ‚naɪt) *n.* a soft grey mineral consisting of molybdenum sulphide in hexagonal crystalline form with rhenium as an impurity. Formula: MoS_2.

molybdenum (mɒ'lɪbdɪnəm) *n.* a very hard silvery-white metallic element occurring principally in molybdenite:

used in alloys, esp. to harden and strengthen steels. Symbol: Mo; atomic no.: 42; atomic wt.: 95.94. [C19: from NL, from L *molybdaena* galena, from Gk, from *molubdos* lead]

mom (mɒm) *n. Chiefly U.S. & Canad.* an informal word for **mother**[1].

Mombasa (mɒm'bæsə) *n.* a port in S Kenya, on a coral island in a bay of the Indian Ocean: the chief port for Kenya, Uganda, and NE Tanzania; became British in 1887, capital of the East African Protectorate until 1907. Pop.: 481 000 (1984).

moment ('məʊmənt) *n.* **1.** a short indefinite period of time. **2.** a specific instant or point in time: *at that moment the phone rang.* **3. the moment.** the present point of time: *at the moment it's fine.* **4.** import, significance, or value: *a man of moment.* **5.** *Physics.* **a.** a tendency to produce motion, esp. rotation about a point or axis. **b.** the product of a physical quantity, such as force or mass, and its distance from a fixed reference point. See also **moment of inertia.** [C14: from OF, from L *mōmentum*, from *movēre* to move]

momentarily ('məʊməntərəlɪ, -trɪlɪ) *adv.* **1.** for an instant; temporarily. **2.** from moment to moment; every instant. ~*adv.* **3.** *U.S. & Canad.* very soon. Also (for senses 1, 2): **momently.**

momentary ('məʊməntərɪ, -trɪ) *adj.* **1.** lasting for only a moment; temporary. **2.** *Rare.* occurring or present at each moment. — '**momentariness** *n.*

moment of inertia *n.* the tendency of a body to resist angular acceleration, expressed as the sum of the products of the mass of each particle in the body and the square of its perpendicular distance from the axis of rotation.

moment of truth *n.* **1.** a moment when a person or thing is put to the test. **2.** the point in a bullfight when the matador is about to kill the bull.

momentous (məʊ'mɛntəs) *adj.* of great significance. — **mo'mentously** *adv.* — **mo'mentousness** *n.*

momentum (məʊ'mɛntəm) *n., pl.* **-ta** (-tə) *or* **-tums.** **1.** *Physics.* the product of a body's mass and its velocity. **2.** the impetus of a body resulting from its motion. **3.** driving power or strength. [C17: from L: movement; see MOMENT]

momma ('mɒmə) *n. Chiefly U.S.* **1.** an informal or childish word for **mother**[1]. **2.** *Inf.* a buxom and voluptuous woman.

Mommsen (German 'mɔmzən) *n.* **Theodor** ('teːodoːr). 1817–1903, German historian, noted esp. for *The History of Rome* (1854–56): Nobel prize for literature 1902.

Momus ('məʊməs) *n., pl.* **-muses** *or* **-mi** (-maɪ). **1.** *Greek myth.* the god of blame and mockery. **2.** a cavilling critic.

mon. *abbrev. for* monetary.

Mon. *abbrev. for* Monday.

mon- *combining form.* a variant of **mono-** before a vowel.

Monaco ('mɒnə,kəʊ, mə'nɑːkəʊ; *French* mɔnako) *n.* a principality in SW Europe, on the Mediterranean and forming an enclave in SE France: the second smallest sovereign state in the world (after the Vatican); consists of **Monaco-Ville** (the capital) on a rocky headland, **La Condamine** (a business area and port), **Monte Carlo** (the resort centre), and **Fontvieille**, a light industrial area. Language: French. Religion: Roman Catholic. Currency: franc. Pop.: 28 000 (1985). Area: 189 hectares (476 acres). Related adj.: **Monegasque.** — **Monacan** ('mɒnəkən, mə'nɑː-) *n., adj.*

monad ('mɒnæd, 'məʊ-) *n.* **1.** (*pl.* **-ads** *or* **-ades** (-ə,diːz)). *Philosophy.* any fundamental singular metaphysical entity, esp. if autonomous. **2.** a single-celled organism. **3.** an atom, ion, or radical with a valency of one. ~Also (for senses 1, 2): **monas.** [C17: from LL *monas*, from Gk: unit, from *monos* alone] — **monadic** (mɒ'nædɪk) *adj.*

monadelphous (,mɒnə'dɛlfəs) *adj.* **1.** (of stamens) having united filaments forming a tube around the style. **2.** (of flowers) having monadelphous stamens. [C19: from MONO- + Gk *adelphos* brother]

monadnock (mə'nædnɒk) *n.* a residual hill of hard rock in an otherwise eroded area. [C19: after Mount *Monadnock*, New Hampshire, U.S.]

Monaghan ('mɒnəhən) *n.* **1.** a county of NE Ireland, in Ulster province: many small lakes. County town: Monaghan. Pop.: 52 332 (1986). Area: 1292 sq. km (499 sq. miles). **2.** a town in NE Ireland, county town of Co. Monaghan. Pop.: 5256 (1971).

monandrous (mɒ'nændrəs) *adj.* **1.** having only one male sexual partner over a period of time. **2.** (of plants) having flowers with only one stamen. **3.** (of flowers) having only one stamen. [C19: from MONO- + -ANDROUS] — **mo'nandry** *n.*

Mona Passage ('məʊnə) *n.* a strait between Puerto Rico and the Dominican Republic, linking the Atlantic with the Caribbean.

monarch ('mɒnək) *n.* **1.** a sovereign head of state, esp. a king, queen, or emperor, who rules usually by hereditary right. **2.** a supremely powerful or pre-eminent person or thing. **3.** Also called: **milkweed.** a large migratory orange-and-black butterfly that feeds on the milkweed plant. [C15: from LL *monarcha*, from Gk; see MONO-, -ARCH] — **monarchal** (mɒ'nɑːkəl) *or* **mo'narchial** *adj.* — **monarchical** *or* **mo'narchic** *adj.* — **monarchism** *n.* — '**monarchist** *n., adj.* — ,**monar'chistic** *adj.*

monarchy ('mɒnəkɪ) *n., pl.* **-chies.** **1.** a form of government in which supreme authority is vested in a single and usually hereditary figure, such as a king. **2.** a country reigned over by a monarch.

monarda (mɒ'nɑːdə) *n.* any of various mintlike North American plants. [C19: from NL, after N. *Monardés* (1493–1588), Sp. botanist]

monastery ('mɒnəstərɪ) *n., pl.* **-teries.** the residence of a religious community, esp. of monks, living in seclusion from secular society and bound by religious vows. [C15: from Church L *monastērium*, ult. from Gk *monazein* to live alone, from *monos* alone] — **monasterial** (,mɒnə'stɪərɪəl) *adj.*

monastic (mə'næstɪk) *adj.* **1.** of or relating to monasteries or monks, nuns, etc. **2.** resembling this sort of life. ~*n.* **3.** a person committed to this way of life, esp. a monk.

monasticism (mə'næstɪ,sɪzəm) *n.* the monastic system, movement, or way of life.

monatomic (,mɒnə'tɒmɪk) *or* **monoatomic** (,mɒnəʊə'tɒmɪk) *adj. Chem.* **1.** (of an element) having or consisting of single atoms. **2.** (of a compound or molecule) having only one atom or group that can be replaced in a chemical reaction.

monaural (mɒ'nɔːrəl) *adj.* **1.** relating to, having, or hearing with only one ear. **2.** another word for **monophonic.** — **mon'aurally** *adv.*

monazite ('mɒnə,zaɪt) *n.* a yellow to reddish-brown mineral consisting of a phosphate of thorium, cerium, and lanthanum in monoclinic crystalline form. [C19: from G, from Gk *monazein* to live alone, so called because of its rarity]

Mönchen-Gladbach (German mœnçən'glatbax) *n.* a city in West Germany, in W North Rhine-Westphalia: headquarters of NATO forces in N central Europe; textile industry. Pop.: 254 700 (1986). Former name: **München-Gladbach.**

Monck (mʌŋk) *n.* **George.** 1st duke of Albemarle. 1608–70, English general. In the Civil War he was a Royalist until captured (1644) and persuaded to support the Commonwealth. After Cromwell's death he was instrumental in the restoration of Charles II (1660).

Moncton ('mɒŋktən) *n.* a city in E Canada, in SE New Brunswick. Pop.: 55 468 (1986).

Mondale ('mɒn,deɪl) *n.* **Walter (Frederick).** born 1928, U.S. Democratic politician; vice president of the U.S. (1977–81).

Monday ('mʌndɪ) *n.* the second day of the week; first day of the working week. [OE *mōnandæg* moon's day, translation of LL *lūnae diēs*]

Mondrian (Dutch 'mɔndriːaːn) *n.* **Piet** (piːt). 1872–1944, Dutch painter, noted esp. as an exponent of the abstract art movement De Stijl.

monecious (mɒ'niːʃəs) *adj.* a variant spelling of **monoecious.**

Monel metal *or* **Monell metal** (mɒ'nɛl) *n. Trademark.* any of various silvery corrosion-resistant alloys. [C20: after A. *Monell* (died 1921), president of the International Nickel Co., New York, which introduced the alloys]

Monet (French mɔnɛ) *n.* **Claude** (klod). 1840–1926, French landscape painter; the leading exponent of impressionism. His interest in the effect of light on colour led him to paint series of pictures of the same subject at different times of day. These include *Haystacks* (1889–93), *Rouen Cathedral* (1892–94), the *Thames* (1899–1904), and *Water Lilies* (1899–1906).

monetarism ('mʌnɪtə,rɪzəm) n. 1. the theory that inflation is caused by an excess quantity of money in an economy. 2. an economic policy based on this theory and on a belief in the efficiency of free market forces. —'monetarist n., adj.

monetary ('mʌnɪtərɪ, -trɪ) adj. of or relating to money or currency. [C19: from LL monētārius, from L monēta MONEY] —'monetarily adv.

monetize or **-ise** ('mʌnɪ,taɪz) vb. (tr.) 1. to establish as legal tender. 2. to give a legal value to (a coin). —,moneti'zation or -i'sation n.

money ('mʌnɪ) n. 1. a medium of exchange that functions as legal tender. 2. the official currency, in the form of banknotes, coins, etc., issued by a government or other authority. 3. a particular denomination or form of currency: silver money. 4. (Law or arch. pl. moneys or monies) a pecuniary sum or income. 5. an unspecified amount of paper currency or coins: money to lend. 6. for one's money. in one's opinion. 7. in the money. Inf. well-off; rich. 8. one's money's worth. full value for the money one has paid for something. 9. put money on. to place a bet on. —Related adj.: pecuniary. [C13: from OF moneie, from L monēta; see MINT²]

moneybags ('mʌnɪ,bægz) n. (functioning as sing.) Inf. a very rich person.

moneychanger ('mʌnɪ,tʃeɪndʒə) n. 1. a person engaged in the business of exchanging currencies or money. 2. Chiefly U.S. a machine for dispensing coins.

moneyed or **monied** ('mʌnɪd) adj. 1. having a great deal of money; rich. 2. arising from or characterized by money.

money-grubbing adj. Inf. seeking greedily to obtain money. —'money-,grubber n.

moneylender ('mʌnɪ,lɛndə) n. a person who lends money at interest as a living. —'money,lending adj., n.

moneymaker ('mʌnɪ,meɪkə) n. 1. a person who is intent on accumulating money. 2. a person or thing that is or might be profitable. —'money,making adj., n.

money of account n. another name (esp. U.S. and Canad.) for unit of account.

money-spinner n. Inf. an enterprise, idea, person, or thing that is a source of wealth.

monger ('mʌŋgə) n. 1. (in combination except in archaic use) a trader or dealer: ironmonger. 2. (in combination) a promoter of something: warmonger. [OE mangere, ult. from L mangō dealer] —'mongering n., adj.

mongol ('mɒŋgəl) n. (not in technical use) a person affected by Down's syndrome.

Mongol ('mɒŋgɒl, -gəl) n. another word for **Mongolian**.

Mongolia (mɒŋ'gəʊlɪə) n. a vast region of central Asia, inhabited chiefly by Mongols: now divided into the Mongolian People's Republic, the Inner Mongolian Autonomous Region of China, and the Tuva ASSR of the Soviet Union; at its height during the 13th century under Genghis Khan.

mongolian (mɒŋ'gəʊlɪən) adj. (not in technical use) of, relating to, or affected by Down's syndrome.

Mongolian (mɒŋ'gəʊlɪən) adj. 1. of or relating to Mongolia, its people, or their language. ~n. 2. a native or inhabitant of Mongolia. 3. the language of Mongolia.

Mongolian People's Republic n. a republic in E central Asia: made a Chinese province in 1691; became autonomous in 1911 and a republic in 1924. It consists chiefly of a high plateau, with the Gobi Desert in the south, a large lake district in the northwest, and the Altai and Khangai Mountains in the west. Language: Khalkha. Currency: tugrik. Capital: Ulan Bator. Pop.: 1 965 300 (1987). Area: 1 565 000 sq. km (604 095 sq. miles). Former name (until 1924): **Outer Mongolia.**

Mongolic (mɒŋ'gɒlɪk) n. 1. a branch or subfamily of the Altaic family of languages, including Mongolian and Kalmuck. 2. another word for **Mongoloid.**

mongolism ('mɒŋgə,lɪzəm) n. Pathol. a former name (not in technical use) for **Down's syndrome.** [C20: the condition produces facial features similar to those of the Mongoloid peoples]

mongoloid ('mɒŋgə,lɔɪd) adj. (not in technical use) 1. relating to or characterized by Down's syndrome. ~n. 2. a person affected by Down's syndrome.

Mongoloid ('mɒŋgə,lɔɪd) adj. 1. of or relating to a major racial group of mankind, characterized by yellowish complexion, straight black hair, slanting eyes, short nose, and scanty facial hair, including most of the peoples of Asia, the Eskimos, and the North American Indians. ~n. 2. a member of this group.

mongoose ('mɒŋ,gu:s) n., pl. -gooses. any of various small predatory mammals occurring in Africa and from S Europe to SE Asia, typically having a long tail and brindled coat. [C17: from Marathi (a language of India) mangūs]

mongrel ('mʌŋgrəl) n. 1. a plant or animal, esp. a dog, of mixed or unknown breeding. 2. Derog. a person of mixed race. ~adj. 3. of mixed origin, breeding, character, etc. [C15: from obs. mong mixture] —'mongrelism n. —'mongre,lize or -ise vb. —,mongreli'zation or -i'sation n. —'mongrelly adj.

'mongst (mʌŋst) prep. Poetic. short for **amongst.**

monied ('mʌnɪd) adj. a less common spelling of **moneyed.**

monies ('mʌnɪz) n. Law, arch. a plural of **money.**

moniker or **monicker** ('mɒnɪkə) n. Sl. a person's name or nickname. [C19: from Shelta munnik, altered from Irish Gaelic ainm name]

monism ('mɒnɪzəm) n. 1. Philosophy. the doctrine that reality consists of only one basic substance or element, such as mind or matter. Cf. **dualism, pluralism.** 2. the attempt to explain anything in terms of one principle only. —'monist n., adj. —mo'nistic adj.

monition (məʊ'nɪʃən) n. 1. a warning or caution; admonition. 2. Christianity. a formal notice from a bishop or ecclesiastical court requiring a person to refrain from committing a specific offence. [C14: via OF from L monitiō, from monēre to warn]

monitor ('mɒnɪtə) n. 1. a person or piece of equipment that warns, checks, controls, or keeps a continuous record of something. 2. Education. a. a senior pupil with various supervisory duties, etc. b. a pupil assisting a teacher in classroom organization, etc. 3. a television set used in a studio for viewing or checking a programme being transmitted. 4. a. a loudspeaker used in a recording studio to determine quality or balance. b. a loudspeaker used on stage to enable musicians to hear themselves. 5. any of various large predatory lizards inhabiting warm regions of Africa, Asia, and Australia. 6. (formerly) a small heavily armoured warship used for coastal assault. ~vb. 7. to act as a monitor of. 8. (tr.) to observe or record (the activity or performance of) (an engine or other device). 9. (tr.) to check (the technical quality of) (a radio or television broadcast). [C16: from L, from monēre to advise] —monitorial (,mɒnɪ'tɔ:rɪəl) adj. —'monitorship n. —'monitress fem. n.

monitory ('mɒnɪtərɪ, -trɪ) adj. also **monitorial.** 1. warning or admonishing. ~n., pl. -ries. 2. Rare. a letter containing a monition.

monk (mʌŋk) n. a male member of a religious community bound by vows of poverty, chastity, and obedience. Related adj.: **monastic.** [OE munuc, from LL monachus, from LGk: solitary (man), from Gk monos alone] —'monkish adj.

Monk (mʌŋk) n. 1. **Thelonious (Sphere)** (θəˈləʊnɪəs) 1920–82, U.S. jazz pianist and composer. 2. a variant spelling of **Monck.**

monkey ('mʌŋkɪ) n. 1. any of numerous long-tailed primates excluding lemurs, tarsiers, etc.: see **Old World monkey, New World monkey.** 2. any primate except man. 3. a naughty or mischievous person, esp. a child. 4. the head of a pile-driver (**monkey engine**) or of some similar mechanical device. 5. U.S. & Canad. sl. an addict's dependence on a drug (esp. in **have a monkey on one's back**). 6. Sl. a butt of derision; someone made to look a fool (esp. in **make a monkey of**). 7. Sl. (esp. in bookmaking) $500. 8. U.S. & Canad. sl. $500. ~vb. 9. (intr.; usually foll. by around, with, etc.) to meddle, fool, or tinker. 10. (tr.) Rare. to imitate; ape. [C16: ?from Low G; cf. MLow G Moneke, name of the ape's son in the tale of Reynard the Fox]

monkey business n. Inf. mischievous, suspect, or dishonest behaviour or acts.

monkey flower n. any of various plants of the genus Mimulus, cultivated for their yellow or red flowers.

monkey jacket n. a short close-fitting jacket, esp. a waist-length jacket similar to a mess jacket.

monkey nut *n. Brit.* another name for a **peanut.**

monkey puzzle *n.* a South American coniferous tree having branches shaped like a candelabrum and stiff sharp leaves. Also called: **Chile pine.**

monkey's wedding *n. S. African inf.* a combination of rain and sunshine. [from ?]

monkey tricks *or U.S.* **monkey shines** *pl. n. Inf.* mischievous behaviour or acts.

monkey wrench *n.* a wrench with adjustable jaws.

monkfish ('mʌŋk,fɪʃ) *n., pl.* **-fish** *or* **-fishes. 1.** any of various angler fishes. **2.** another name for **angelfish** (sense 3).

monk's cloth *n.* a heavy cotton fabric of basket weave, used mainly for bedspreads.

monkshood ('mʌŋkshʊd) *n.* any of several poisonous N temperate plants that have hooded blue-purple flowers.

Monmouth[1] ('mɒnməθ) *n.* a market town in E Wales, in Gwent: Norman castle, where Henry V was born in 1387. Pop.: 7509 (1981).

Monmouth[2] ('mɒnməθ) *n.* **James Scott,** Duke of Monmouth. 1649–85, the illegitimate son of Charles II of England, he led a rebellion against James II in support of his own claim to the Crown; captured and beheaded.

Monmouthshire ('mɒnməθˌʃɪə, -ʃə) *n.* (until 1974) a county of E Wales, now corresponding roughly to the county of Gwent: administratively part of England for three centuries (until 1830).

Monnet (*French* mɔnɛ) *n.* **Jean** (ʒɑ̃). 1888–1979, French economist and public servant, regarded as founding father of the European Economic Community. He was first president (1952–55) of the European Coal and Steel Community.

mono ('mɒnəʊ) *adj.* **1.** short for **monophonic.** ~*n.* **2.** monophonic sound.

mono- *or before a vowel* **mon-** *combining form.* **1.** one; single: *monorail.* **2.** indicating that a chemical compound contains a single specified atom or group: *monoxide.* [from Gk *monos*]

monoacid (ˌmɒnəʊˈæsɪd), **monacid, monoacidic** (ˌmɒnəʊəˈsɪdɪk), *or* **monacidic** *adj. Chem.* (of a base) capable of reacting with only one molecule of a monobasic acid; having only one hydroxide ion per molecule.

monobasic (ˌmɒnəʊˈbeɪsɪk) *adj. Chem.* (of an acid, such as hydrogen chloride) having only one replaceable hydrogen atom per molecule.

monocarpic (ˌmɒnəʊˈkɑːpɪk) *or* **monocarpous** *adj.* (of some flowering plants) producing fruit only once before dying.

monochromatic (ˌmɒnəʊkrəʊˈmætɪk) *or* **monochroic** (ˌmɒnəʊˈkrəʊɪk) *adj.* (of light or other electromagnetic radiation) having only one wavelength.

monochrome ('mɒnəˌkrəʊm) *n.* **1.** a black-and-white photograph or transparency. **2.** *Photog.* black-and-white. **3. a.** a painting, drawing, etc., done in a range of tones of a single colour. **b.** the technique or art of this. **4.** (*modifier*) executed in or resembling monochrome: *a monochrome print.* ~Also called (for senses 3, 4): **monotint.** [C17: via Med. L from Gk *monokhrōmos* of one colour] —ˌmono'chromic *adj.* —ˈmono,chromist *n.*

monocle ('mɒnək³l) *n.* a lens for correcting defective vision of one eye, held in position by the facial muscles. [C19: from F, from LL, from MONO- + *oculus* eye] —'**monocled** *adj.*

monocline ('mɒnəʊˌklaɪn) *n.* a fold in stratified rocks in which the strata are inclined in the same direction from the horizontal. [C19: from MONO- + Gk *klīnein* to lean] —ˌmono'**clinal** *adj., n.*

monoclinic (ˌmɒnəʊˈklɪnɪk) *adj. Crystallog.* relating to or belonging to the crystal system characterized by three unequal axes, one pair of which are not at right angles to each other. [C19: from MONO- + Gk *klīnein* to lean]

monoclinous (ˌmɒnəʊˈklaɪnəs, ˈmɒnəʊˌklaɪnəs) *adj.* (of flowering plants) having the male and female reproductive organs on the same flower. Cf. **diclinous.** [C19: from MONO- Gk *klīne* bed] —'**mono,clinism** *n.*

monoclonal antibody (ˌmɒnəʊˈkləʊn³l) *n.* an antibody, produced by a single clone of cells grown in culture, that is both pure and specific and capable of proliferating indefinitely: used in diagnosis, therapy, and biotechnology.

monocotyledon (ˌmɒnəʊˌkɒtɪˈliːd³n) *n.* any of various flowering plants having a single embryonic seed leaf, leaves with parallel veins, and flowers with parts in

threes: includes grasses, lilies, palms, and orchids. Cf. **dicotyledon.** —ˌmono,coty'**ledonous** *adj.*

monocracy (mɒˈnɒkrəsɪ) *n., pl.* **-cies.** government by one person. —**monocrat** ('mɒnə,kræt) *n.* —,**mono'cratic** *adj.*

monocular (mɒˈnɒkjʊlə) *adj.* having or intended for the use of only one eye. [C17: from LL *monoculus* one-eyed] —**mo'nocularly** *adv.*

monoculture ('mɒnəʊ,kʌltʃə) *n.* the continuous growing of one type of crop.

monocycle ('mɒnə,saɪk³l) *n.* another name for **unicycle.**

monocyte ('mɒnəʊ,saɪt) *n.* the largest type of white blood cell that acts as part of the immune system by engulfing particles, such as invading microorganisms.

monody ('mɒnədɪ) *n., pl.* **-dies. 1.** (in Greek tragedy) an ode sung by a single actor. **2.** any poem of lament for someone's death. **3.** *Music.* a style of composition consisting of a single vocal part, usually with accompaniment. [C17: via LL from Gk *monōidia,* from MONO- + *aeidein* to sing] —**monodic** (mɒ'nɒdɪk) *adj.* —'**monodist** *n.*

monoecious (mɒ'niːʃəs) *adj.* **1.** (of some flowering plants) having the male and female reproductive organs in separate flowers on the same plant. **2.** (of some animals and lower plants) hermaphrodite. [C18: from NL *monoecia,* from MONO- + Gk *oikos* house]

monofilament (ˌmɒnəˈfɪləmənt) *or* **monofil** ('mɒnəfɪl) *n.* synthetic thread or yarn composed of a single strand rather than twisted fibres.

monogamy (mɒ'nɒgəmɪ) *n.* **1.** the state or practice of having only one husband or wife over a period of time. **2.** *Zool.* the practice of having only one mate. [C17: via F from LL *monogamia,* from Gk; see MONO- + -GAMY] —**mo'nogamist** *n.* —**mo'nogamous** *adj.*

monogenesis (ˌmɒnəʊˈdʒɛnɪsɪs) *or* **monogeny** (mɒ'nɒdʒɪnɪ) *n.* **1.** the hypothetical descent of all organisms from a single cell. **2.** asexual reproduction in animals. **3.** the direct development of an ovum into an organism resembling the adult. **4.** the hypothetical descent of all human beings from a single pair of ancestors.

monogram ('mɒnə,græm) *n.* a design of one or more letters, esp. initials, on clothing, stationery, etc. [C17: from LL *monogramma,* from Gk; see MONO-, -GRAM] —**monogrammatic** (ˌmɒnəgrəˈmætɪk) *adj.*

monograph ('mɒnə,grɑːf) *n.* **1.** a paper, book, or other work concerned with a single subject or aspect of a subject. ~*vb.* (*tr.*) **2.** to write a monograph on. —**monographer** (mɒ'nɒgrəfə) *or* **mo'nographist** *n.* —,**mono'graphic** *adj.*

monogyny (mɒ'nɒdʒɪnɪ) *n.* the custom of having only one female sexual partner over a period of time. —**mo'nogynous** *adj.*

monohull ('mɒnəʊ,hʌl) *n.* a sailing vessel with a single hull.

monokini ('mɒnəʊ,kiːnɪ) *n.* a woman's one-piece bathing garment usually equivalent to the bottom half of a bikini. [C20: from MONO- + BIKINI (as if *bikini* were from BI-)]

monolayer ('mɒnəʊ,leɪə) *n.* a single layer of atoms or molecules adsorbed on a surface. Also called: **molecular film.**

monolingual (ˌmɒnəʊˈlɪŋwəl) *adj.* knowing or expressed in only one language.

monolith ('mɒnəlɪθ) *n.* **1.** a large block of stone or anything that resembles one in appearance, intractability, etc. **2.** a statue, obelisk, column, etc., cut from one block of stone. **3.** a large hollow foundation piece sunk as a caisson and filled with concrete. [C19: via F from Gk *monolithos* made from a single stone] —,**mono'lithic** *adj.*

monologue ('mɒnə,lɒg) *n.* **1.** a long speech made by one actor in a play, film, etc., esp. when alone. **2.** a dramatic piece for a single performer. **3.** any long speech by one person, esp. when interfering with conversation. [C17: via F from Gk *monologos* speaking alone] —**monologic** (ˌmɒnəˈlɒdʒɪk) *or* ,**mono'logical** *adj.* —**monologist** ('mɒnə,lɒgɪst) *n.* —**monologize** *or* **-ise** (mɒ'nɒlədʒaɪz) *vb.*

monomania (ˌmɒnəʊˈmeɪnɪə) *n.* an excessive mental preoccupation with one thing, idea, etc. —,**mono'mani,ac** *n., adj.* —**monomaniacal** (ˌmɒnəʊməˈnaɪək³l) *adj.*

monomark ('mɒnəmɑːk) *n. Brit.* a series of letters or figures to identify goods, personal articles, etc.

monomer ('mɒnəmə) n. Chem. a compound whose molecules can join together to form a polymer. —**monomeric** (ˌmɒnə'mɛrɪk) adj.

monometallism (ˌmɒnəʊ'mɛtəˌlɪzəm) n. **1.** the use of one metal, esp. gold or silver, as the sole standard of value and currency. **2.** the economic policies supporting a monometallic standard. —**monometallic** (ˌmɒnəʊmɪ-'tælɪk) adj. —ˌmono'metallist n.

monomial (mɒ'nəʊmɪəl) n. **1.** Maths. an expression consisting of a single term, such as 5ax. ~adj. **2.** consisting of a single algebraic term. [C18: MONO- + (BIN)OMIAL]

monomorphic (ˌmɒnəʊ'mɔ:fɪk) or **monomorphous** adj. **1.** (of an individual organism) showing little or no change in structure during the entire life history. **2.** (of a species) existing or having parts that exist in only one form. **3.** (of a chemical compound) having only one crystalline form.

Monongahela (məˌnɒŋgə'hi:lə) n. a river in the northeastern U.S., flowing generally north to the Allegheny River at Pittsburgh, Pennsylvania, forming the Ohio River. Length: 206 km (128 miles).

mononucleosis (ˌmɒnəʊˌnju:klɪ'əʊsɪs) n. **1.** Pathol. the presence of a large number of monocytes in the blood. **2.** See **infectious mononucleosis**.

monophonic (ˌmɒnəʊ'fɒnɪk) adj. **1.** Also: **monaural**. (of a system of broadcasting, recording, or reproducing sound) using only one channel between source and loudspeaker. Sometimes shortened to **mono**. Cf. **stereophonic**. **2.** Music. of or relating to a style of musical composition consisting of a single melodic line.

monophthong ('mɒnəf,θɒŋ) n. a simple or pure vowel. [C17: from Gk monophthongos, from MONO- + thongos sound]

Monophysite (mɒ'nɒfɪ,saɪt) n. Christianity. a person who holds that there is only one nature in the person of Christ, which is primarily divine with human attributes. [C17: via Church L from LGk, from MONO- + phusis nature] —**Monophysitic** (ˌmɒnəʊfɪ'sɪtɪk) adj.

monoplane ('mɒnəʊ,pleɪn) n. an aeroplane with only one pair of wings. Cf. **biplane**.

monopolize or **-lise** (mə'nɒpə,laɪz) vb. (tr.) **1.** to have, control, or make use of fully, excluding others. **2.** to obtain, maintain, or exploit a monopoly of (a market, commodity, etc.). —**mo,nopoli'zation** or **-li'sation** n. —**mo'nopo,lizer** or **-,liser** n.

monopoly (mə'nɒpəlɪ) n., pl. **-lies**. **1.** exclusive control of the market supply of a product or service. **2. a.** an enterprise exercising this control. **b.** the product or service so controlled. **3.** Law. the exclusive right granted to a person, company, etc., by the state to purchase, manufacture, use, or sell some commodity or to trade in a specified area. **4.** exclusive control, possession, or use of something. [C16: from LL, from Gk monopōlion, from MONO- + pōlein to sell] —**mo'nopolist** n. —**mo,nopo'listic** adj.

Monopoly (mə'nɒpəlɪ) n. Trademark. a board game for two to six players who throw dice to advance their tokens, the object being to acquire the property on which their tokens land.

monorail ('mɒnəʊ,reɪl) n. a single-rail railway, often elevated and with suspended cars.

monosaccharide (ˌmɒnəʊ'sækə,raɪd) n. a simple sugar, such as glucose or fructose, that does not hydrolyse to yield other sugars.

monosodium glutamate (ˌmɒnəʊ'səʊdɪəm 'glu:tə,meɪt) n. a white crystalline substance that has little flavour itself but enhances protein flavours: used as a food additive.

monosyllabic (ˌmɒnəsɪ'læbɪk) adj. **1.** (of a word) containing only one syllable. **2.** characterized by monosyllables; curt. —**monosyl'labically** adv.

monosyllable ('mɒnə,sɪləbᵊl) n. a word of one syllable, esp. one used as a sentence.

monotheism ('mɒnəʊθɪˌɪzəm) n. the belief or doctrine that there is only one God. —'**mono,theist** n., adj. —ˌmonothe'istic adj. —ˌmonothe'istically adv.

monotint ('mɒnə,tɪnt) n. another word for **monochrome** (senses 3, 4).

monotone ('mɒnə,təʊn) n. **1.** a single unvaried pitch level in speech, sound, etc. **2.** utterance, etc., without change of pitch. **3.** lack of variety in style, expression, etc. ~adj. **4.** unvarying.

monotonous (mə'nɒtənəs) adj. **1.** tedious, esp. because of repetition. **2.** in unvarying tone. —**mo'notonously** adv. —**mo'notonousness** n.

monotony (mə'nɒtənɪ) n., pl. **-nies**. **1.** wearisome routine; dullness. **2.** lack of variety in pitch or cadence.

monotreme ('mɒnəʊ,tri:m) n. any mammal of a primitive order of Australia and New Guinea, having a single opening (cloaca) for the passage of eggs or sperm, faeces, and urine. The group contains only the echidnas and the platypus. [C19: via NL from MONO- + Gk trēma hole] —**monotrematous** (ˌmɒnəʊ'tri:mətəs) adj.

monotype ('mɒnə,taɪp) n. **1.** a single print made from a metal or glass plate on which a picture has been painted. **2.** Biol. a monotypic genus or species.

Monotype ('mɒnə,taɪp) n. **1.** Trademark. any of various typesetting systems, esp. originally one in which each character was cast individually from hot metal. **2.** type produced by such a system.

monotypic (ˌmɒnəʊ'tɪpɪk) adj. **1.** (of a genus or species) consisting of only one type of animal or plant. **2.** of or relating to a monotype.

monovalent (ˌmɒnəʊ'veɪlənt) adj. Chem. **a.** having a valency of one. **b.** having only one valency. ~Also: **univalent**. —ˌmono'valence or ˌmono'valency n.

monoxide (mɒ'nɒksaɪd) n. an oxide that contains one oxygen atom per molecule.

Monroe (mən'rəʊ) n. **1. James.** 1758–1831, U.S. statesman; fifth president of the U.S. (1817–25). He promulgated the Monroe Doctrine (1823). **2. Marilyn,** real name Norma Jean Baker or Mortenson. 1926–62, U.S. film actress. Her films include Niagara (1952), Gentlemen Prefer Blondes (1953), and Some Like It Hot (1959).

Monrovia (mɒn'rəʊvɪə) n. the capital and chief port of Liberia, on the Atlantic: founded in 1822 as a home for freed American slaves; University of Liberia (1862). Pop.: 500 000 (1985).

Mons (French mõs) n. a town in SW Belgium, capital of Hainaut province: scene of the first battle (1914) of the British Expeditionary Force during World War I. Pop.: 89 697 (1987 est.). Flemish name: **Bergen**.

Monseigneur French. (mõsɛɲœr) n., pl. **Messeigneurs** (mesɛɲœr). a title given to French bishops, prelates, and princes. [lit.: my lord]

monsieur (məs'jɜ:) n., pl. **messieurs**. a French title of address equivalent to sir when used alone or Mr before a name. [lit.: my lord]

Monsignor (mɒn'si:njə) n., pl. **Monsignors** or **Monsignori** (Italian monsiɲ'ɲo:ri). R.C. Church. an ecclesiastical title attached to certain offices. [C17: from It., from F MONSEIGNEUR]

monsoon (mɒn'su:n) n. **1.** a seasonal wind of S Asia from the southwest in summer and from the northeast in winter. **2.** the rainy season when the SW monsoon blows, from about April to October. **3.** any wind that changes direction with the seasons. [C16: from obs. Du. monssoen, from Port., from Ar. mawsim season] —**mon'soonal** adj.

mons pubis ('mɒnz 'pju:bɪs) n., pl. **montes pubis** ('mɒnti:z). the fatty flesh in human males over the junction of the pubic bones. Compare **mons veneris**. [C17: NL: hill of the pubes]

monster ('mɒnstə) n. **1.** an imaginary beast, usually made up of various animal or human parts. **2.** a person, animal, or plant with a marked deformity. **3.** a cruel, wicked, or inhuman person. **4. a.** a very large person, animal, or thing. **b.** (as modifier): a monster cake. [C13: from OF monstre, from L monstrum portent, from monēre to warn]

monstera (mɒn'stɪərə) n. any of various tropical evergreen climbing plants. [from ?]

monstrance ('mɒnstrəns) n. R.C. Church. a receptacle in which the consecrated Host is exposed for adoration. [C16: from Med. L mōnstrantia, from L mōnstrāre to show]

monstrosity (mɒn'strɒsɪtɪ) n., pl. **-ties**. **1.** an outrageous or ugly person or thing; monster. **2.** the state or quality of being monstrous.

monstrous ('mɒnstrəs) adj. **1.** abnormal, hideous, or unnatural in size, character, etc. **2.** (of plants and animals) abnormal in structure. **3.** outrageous, atrocious, or shocking. **4.** huge. **5.** of, relating to, or resembling a monster. —'**monstrously** adv. —'**monstrousness** n.

mons veneris ('mɒnz 'vɛnərɪs) n., pl. **montes veneris** ('mɒntiːz). the fatty flesh in human females over the junction of the pubic bones. Compare **mons pubis**. [C17: NL: hill of Venus]

montage (mɒn'tɑːʒ) n. **1.** the art or process of composing pictures of miscellaneous elements, such as other pictures or photographs. **2.** such a composition. **3.** a method of film editing by juxtaposition or partial superimposition of several shots to form a single image. **4.** a film sequence of this kind. [C20: from F, from *monter* to MOUNT[1]]

Montagu ('mɒntə,gjuː) n. **1. Charles.** See (Earl of) **Halifax. 2.** Lady **Mary Wortley.** 1689–1762, English writer, noted for her *Letters from the East* (1763).

Montaigne (*French* mɔ̃tɛɲ) n. **Michel Eyquem de** (miʃɛl ikɛm də). 1533–92, French writer. His life's work, the *Essays* (begun in 1571), established the essay as a literary genre and record the evolution of his moral ideas.

Montale (*Italian* mon'taːle) n. **Eugenio** (eu'dʒɛːnjo). 1896–1981, Italian poet: Nobel prize for literature 1975.

Montana (mɒn'tænə) n. a state of the western U.S.: consists of the Great Plains in the east and the Rocky Mountains in the west. Capital: Helena. Pop.: 819 000 (1986 est.). Area: 377 070 sq. km (145 587 sq. miles). Abbrevs.: **Mont.** or (with zip code) **MT** —**Mon'tanan** *adj., n.*

montane ('mɒnteɪn) *adj.* of or inhabiting mountainous regions. [C19: from L *montānus*, from *mons* MOUNTAIN]

Montauban (*French* mɔ̃tobā) n. a city in SW France: a Huguenot stronghold in the 16th and 17th centuries, taken by Richelieu in 1629. Pop.: 47 432 (1983 est.).

Montbéliard (*French* mɔ̃beljar) n. an industrial town in E France: former capital of the duchy of Burgundy. Pop.: 33 362 (1982).

Mont Blanc (*French* mɔ̃ blā) n. a massif in SW Europe, mainly between France and Italy: the highest mountain in the Alps; beneath it is **Mont Blanc Tunnel,** 12 km (7.5 miles) long. Highest peak (in France): 4807 m (15 771 ft.). Italian name: **Monte Bianco** ('monte 'bjaŋko).

montbretia (mɒn'briːʃə) n. any plant of an African genus related to the iris with ornamental orange or yellow flowers. [C19: NL, after A. F. E. Coquebert de *Montbret* (1780–1801), F botanist]

Montcalm (mɒnt'kɑːm; *French* mɔ̃kalm) n. **Louis Joseph** (lwi ʒozɛf), Marquis de Montcalm de Saint-Véran. 1712–59, French general in Canada (1756); killed in Quebec by British forces under General Wolfe.

Mont Cenis (*French* mɔ̃səni) n. See (Mont) **Cenis.**

Mont Cervin (mɔ̃ sɛrvɛ̃) n. the French name for the **Matterhorn.**

monte ('mɒntɪ) n. a gambling card game of Spanish origin. [C19: from Sp.: mountain, hence pile of cards]

Monte Carlo ('mɒntɪ 'kɑːləʊ; *French* mɔ̃te karlo) n. a town and resort forming part of the principality of Monaco, on the Riviera: famous casino and the destination of an annual car rally (the **Monte Carlo Rally**). Pop.: 12 000 (1985).

Monte Cassino ('mɒntɪ kə'siːnəʊ; *Italian* 'monte kas'siːno) n. a hill above Cassino in central Italy: site of Benedictine monastery (530 A.D.); in 1944 mistaken for German observation post and destroyed by the Allies.

Monte Corno (*Italian* 'monte 'korno) n. See (Monte) **Corno.**

Montefiore (,mɒntɪfɪ'ɔːrɪ) n. **Hugh (William).** born 1920, English Anglican prelate; suffragan bishop of Kingstonupon-Thames (1970–77) and bishop of Birmingham (1977–87).

Montego Bay (mɒn'tiːgəʊ) n. a port and resort in NW Jamaica: the second largest town on the island. Pop.: 59 614 (1982).

Montenegro (,mɒntɪ'niːgrəʊ) n. a constituent republic of Yugoslavia, bordering on the Adriatic: declared a kingdom in 1910 and united with Serbia, Croatia, and other territories in 1918 to form Yugoslavia. Capital: Titograd. Pop.: 610 000 (1985). Area: 13 812 sq. km (5387 sq. miles). —,**Monte'negrin** *adj., n.*

Monterey (,mɒntə'reɪ) n. a city in W California: capital of Spain's Pacific empire from 1774 to 1825; taken by the U.S. (1846). Pop.: 27 558 (1980).

Monterrey (,mɒntə'reɪ; *Spanish* mɔntɛ'rreɪ) n. a city in NE Mexico, capital of Nuevo Léon state: the third largest city in Mexico; a major industrial centre, esp. for metals. Pop.: 1 916 472 (1980).

Montespan (*French* mɔ̃tɛspā) n. **Marquise de,** title of *Françoise Athénaïs de Rochechouart.* 1641–1707, French noblewoman; mistress of Louis XIV of France.

Montesquieu (*French* mɔ̃tɛskjo) n. **Baron de la Brède et de** (barɔ̃ də la brɛd e də), title of *Charles Louis de Secondat.* 1689–1755, French political philosopher. His chief works are the satirical *Lettres persanes* (1721) and *L'Esprit des lois* (1748), a comparative analysis of various forms of government, which had a profound influence on political thought in Europe and the U.S.

Montessori (,mɒntɪ'sɔːrɪ; *Italian* montes'sɔːri) n. **Maria** (ma'riːa). 1870–1952, Italian educational reformer, who evolved the Montessori method of teaching children.

Montessori method n. a method of nursery education in which children are provided with generous facilities for practical play and allowed to develop at their own pace.

Monteux (*French* mɔ̃to) n. **Pierre** (pjɛr). 1875–1964, U.S. conductor, born in France.

Monteverdi (,mɒntɪ'vɛədɪ) n. **Claudio** ('klaʊdɪ,əʊ). ?1567–1643, Italian composer, noted esp. for his innovations in opera and for his expressive use of dissonance. His operas include *Orfeo* (1607) and *L'Incoronazione di Poppea* (1642) and he also wrote many motets and madrigals.

Montevideo (,mɒntɪvɪ'deɪəʊ; *Spanish* mɔnteβi'ðeo) n. the capital and chief port of Uruguay, in the south on the Río de la Plata estuary: the largest city in the country: University of the Republic (1849); resort. Pop.: 1 246 000 (1985 est.).

Montezuma II (,mɒntɪ'zuːmə) n. 1466–1520, Aztec emperor of Mexico (?1502–20). He was overthrown and killed by the Spanish conquistador Cortés.

Montfort ('mɒntfət) n. **Simon de,** Earl of Leicester. ?1208–65, English soldier, born in Normandy. He led the baronial rebellion against Henry III and ruled England from 1264 to 1265; he was killed at Evesham.

Montgolfier (*French* mɔ̃gɔlfje) n. **Jacques Étienne** (ʒak etjɛn), 1745–99, and his brother **Joseph Michel** (ʒozɛf miʃɛl), 1740–1810, French inventors, who built (1782) and ascended in (1783) the first practical hot-air balloon.

Montgomery[1] (mənt'gʌmərɪ) n. a city in central Alabama, on the Alabama River: state capital; capital of the Confederacy (1861–65). Pop.: 194 290 (1986 est.).

Montgomery[2] (mənt'gʌmərɪ) n. **Bernard Law,** 1st Viscount Montgomery of Alamein, nicknamed *Monty.* 1887–1976, British field marshal. As commander of the 8th Army in North Africa, he launched the offensive, beginning with the victory at El Alamein (1942), that drove Rommel's forces back to Tunis. He also commanded the ground forces in the invasion of Normandy (1944) and accepted Germany's surrender at Lüneburg Heath (May 7, 1945).

Montgomeryshire (mənt'gʌmərɪ,ʃɪə, -ʃə) n. (until 1974) a county of central Wales, now part of Powys.

month (mʌnθ) n. **1.** one of the twelve divisions (**calendar months**) of the calendar year. **2.** a period of time extending from one date to a corresponding date in the next calendar month. **3.** a period of four weeks or of 30 days. **4.** the period of time (**solar month**) taken by the moon to return to the same longitude after one complete revolution around the earth; 27.321 58 days (approximately 27 days, 7 hours, 43 minutes, 4.5 seconds). **5.** the period of time (**sidereal month**) taken by the moon to make one complete revolution around the earth, measured between two successive conjunctions with a particular star; 27.321 66 days (approximately 27 days, 7 hours, 43 minutes, 11 seconds). **6.** Also called: **lunation.** the period of time (**lunar or synodic month**) taken by the moon to make one complete revolution around the earth, measured between two successive new moons; 29.530 59 days (approximately 29 days, 12 hours, 44 minutes, 3 seconds). [OE *mōnath*]

Montherlant (*French* mɔ̃tɛrlā) n. **Henri (Millon)** de (āri də). 1896–1972, French novelist and dramatist: his novels include *Les Jeunes Filles* (1935–39) and *Le Chaos et la nuit* (1963).

monthly ('mʌnθlɪ) *adj.* **1.** occurring, done, appearing, payable, etc., once every month. **2.** lasting or valid for a month. ~*adv.* **3.** once a month. ~*n., pl.* **-lies. 4.** a book, periodical, magazine, etc., published once a month. **5.** *Inf.* a menstrual period.

Montluçon (*French* mɔ̃lysɔ̃) n. an industrial city in central France, on the Cher River. Pop.: 56 434 (1983 est.).

Montmartre (*French* mɔ̃martrə) *n.* a district of N Paris, on a hill above the Seine: the highest point in the city; famous for its associations with many artists.

Montparnasse (*French* mɔ̃parnas) *n.* a district of S Paris, on the left bank of the Seine: noted for its cafés, frequented by artists, writers, and students.

Montpelier (mɒnt'piːljə) *n.* a city in N central Vermont, on the Winooski River: the state capital. Pop.: 8241 (1980).

Montpellier (*French* mɔ̃pəlje) *n.* a city in S France, the chief town of Languedoc: its university was founded by Pope Nicholas IV in 1289; wine trade. Pop.: 189 213 (1983 est.).

Montreal (ˌmɒntrɪ'ɔːl) *n.* a port in central Canada, in S Quebec on **Montreal Island** at the junction of the Ottawa and St Lawrence Rivers: the country's largest city and a major port. Pop.: 980 354 (1981), with a conurbation of 1 015 420 (1986). French name: **Montréal** (mɔ̃real).

Montreuil (*French* mɔ̃trœj) *n.* an E suburb of Paris: formerly famous for peaches, but now increasingly industrialized. Pop.: 96 520 (1983 est.).

Montreux (*French* mɔ̃trø) *n.* a town and resort in W Switzerland, in Vaud canton on Lake Geneva: annual television festival. Pop.: 19 292 (1983 est.).

Montrose (mɒn'trəʊz) *n.* **James Graham,** 1st Marquess and 5th Earl of Montrose. 1612–50, Scottish general, noted for his victories in Scotland for Charles I in the Civil War. He was later captured and hanged.

Mont-Saint-Michel (*French* mɔ̃sɛ̃miʃɛl) *n.* a rocky islet off the coast of NW France, accessible at low tide by a causeway, in the **Bay of St Michel** (an inlet of the Gulf of St Malo): Benedictine abbey (966), used as a prison from the Revolution until 1863; reoccupied by Benedictine monks since 1966. Area: 1 hectare (3 acres).

Montserrat *n.* **1.** (ˌmɒntsə'ræt). a volcanic island in the Caribbean, in the Leeward Islands of the West Indies: a British crown colony. Capital: Plymouth. Pop.: 11 852 (1985). Area: 103 sq. km (40 sq. miles). **2.** (*Spanish* mɔnsɛ'rrat). a mountain in NE Spain, northwest of Barcelona: famous Benedictine monastery. Height: 1235 m (4054 ft.). Ancient name: **Mons Serratus** (mɒnz sə'rætəs).

monument ('mɒnjumənt) *n.* **1.** an obelisk, statue, building, etc., erected in commemoration of a person or event. **2.** a notable building or site, esp. one preserved as public property. **3.** a tomb or tombstone. **4.** a literary or artistic work regarded as commemorative of its creator or a particular period. **5.** *U.S.* a boundary marker. **6.** an exceptional example: *his lecture was a monument of tedium.* [C13: from L *monumentum,* from *monēre* to remind]

Monument ('mɒnjumənt) *n.* **the.** a tall columnar building designed (1671) by Sir Christopher Wren to commemorate the Fire of London (1666), which destroyed a large part of the medieval city.

monumental (ˌmɒnju'mɛntᵊl) *adj.* **1.** like a monument, esp. in large size, endurance, or importance. **2.** of, relating to, or being a monument. **3.** *Inf.* (intensifier): *monumental stupidity.* —ˌmonu'mentally *adv.*

Monza (*Italian* 'montsa) *n.* a city in N Italy, northeast of Milan: the ancient capital of Lombardy; scene of the assassination of King Umberto I in 1900; motor-racing circuit. Pop.: 122 064 (1986).

moo (muː) *vb.* **1.** (*intr.*) (of a cow, bull, etc.) to make a characteristic deep long sound; low. ~*interj.* **2.** an instance or imitation of this sound.

mooch (muːtʃ) *vb. Sl.* **1.** (*intr.*; often with *around*) to loiter or walk aimlessly. **2.** (*intr.*) to lurk; skulk. **3.** (*tr.*) to cadge. **4.** (*tr.*) *Chiefly U.S. & Canad.* to steal. [C17: ?from OF *muchier* to skulk] —'**moocher** *n.*

mood[1] (muːd) *n.* **1.** a temporary state of mind or temper: *a cheerful mood.* **2.** a sullen or gloomy state of mind, esp. when temporary: *she's in a mood.* **3.** a prevailing atmosphere or feeling. **4. in the mood.** in a favourable state of mind. [OE *mōd* mind, feeling]

mood[2] (muːd) *n.* **1.** *Grammar.* a category of the verb or verbal inflections that expresses semantic and grammatical differences, including such forms as the indicative, subjunctive, and imperative. **2.** *Logic.* one of the possible arrangements of the syllogism, classified by whether the component propositions are universal or particular and affirmative or negative. ~Also called: **mode.** [C16: from MOOD[1], infl. in meaning by MODE]

moody ('muːdɪ) *adj.* **moodier, moodiest. 1.** sullen, sulky, or gloomy. **2.** temperamental or changeable. —'**moodily** *adv.* —'**moodiness** *n.*

Moody ('muːdɪ) *n.* **Dwight Lyman.** 1837–99, U.S. evangelist and hymnodist, noted for his revivalist campaigns in Britain and the U.S. with I. D. Sankey.

Moog (muːg, məʊg) *n. Music, trademark.* a type of synthesizer. [C20: after Robert *Moog* (born 1934), U.S. engineer]

mooi (mɔɪ) *adj. S. African sl.* pleasing; nice. [from Afrik.]

mooli ('muːlɪ) *n.* a type of large white radish. [E African native name]

moolvie *or* **moolvi** ('muːlvɪ) *n.* (esp. in India) a Muslim doctor of the law, teacher, or learned man: also used as a title of respect. [C17: from Urdu, from Ar. *mawlawīy;* cf. MULLAH]

Moomba ('muːmbə) *n.* an annual carnival that takes place in Melbourne, Australia, in March. [from Abor. *moom* buttocks, anus; *moomba* orig. thought to be Abor. word meaning "Let's get together and have fun"]

moon (muːn) *n.* **1.** the natural satellite of the earth. **2.** the face of the moon as it is seen during its revolution around the earth, esp. at one of its phases: *new moon; full moon.* **3.** any natural satellite of a planet. **4.** moonlight. **5.** something resembling a moon. **6.** a month, esp. a lunar one. **7. over the moon.** *Inf.* extremely happy; ecstatic. ~*vb.* **8.** (when *tr.,* often foll. by *away;* when *intr.,* often foll. by *around*) to be idle in a listless way, as if in love, or to idle (time) away. **9.** (*intr.*) *Sl.* to expose one's buttocks to passers-by. [OE *mōna*] —'**moonless** *adj.*

Moon (muːn) *n.* **William.** 1818–94, British inventor of the Moon writing system in 1847, who, himself blind, taught blind children in Brighton and printed mainly religious works from stereotyped plates of his own designing.

moonbeam ('muːnˌbiːm) *n.* a ray of moonlight.

mooncalf ('muːnˌkɑːf) *n., pl.* **-calves** (-ˌkɑːvz). **1.** a born fool; dolt. **2.** a person who idles time away.

moon-faced *adj.* having a round face.

moonlight ('muːnˌlaɪt) *n.* **1.** light from the sun received on earth after reflection by the moon. **2.** (*modifier*) illuminated by the moon: *a moonlight walk.* ~*vb.* **-lighting, -lighted. 3.** (*intr.*) *Inf.* to work at a secondary job, esp. at night and illegally. —'**moonˌlighter** *n.*

moonlight flit *n. Brit. inf.* a hurried departure at night, esp. from rented accommodation to avoid payments of rent owed.

moonlit ('muːnlɪt) *adj.* illuminated by the moon.

moonquake ('muːnˌkweɪk) *n.* a light tremor of the moon, detected on the moon's surface.

moonscape ('muːnˌskeɪp) *n.* the general surface of the moon or a representation of it.

moonshine ('muːnˌʃaɪn) *n.* **1.** another word for **moonlight** (sense 1). **2.** *U.S. & Canad.* illegally distilled or smuggled whisky. **3.** foolish talk or thought.

moonshot ('muːnˌʃɒt) *n.* the launching of a spacecraft, rocket, etc., to the moon.

moonstone ('muːnˌstəʊn) *n.* a gem variety of orthoclase or albite that is white and translucent.

moonstruck ('muːnˌstrʌk) *or* **moonstricken** ('muːnˌstrɪkən) *adj.* deranged or mad.

moony ('muːnɪ) *adj.* **moonier, mooniest. 1.** *Inf.* dreamy or listless. **2.** of or like the moon.

moor[1] (mʊə, mɔː) *n.* a tract of unenclosed ground, usually covered with heather, coarse grass, bracken, and moss. [OE *mōr*]

moor[2] (mʊə, mɔː) *vb.* to secure (a ship, boat, etc.) with cables, ropes, or anchors, or (of a ship, boat, etc.) to be secured in this way. [C15: of Gmc origin; rel. to OE *mærelsrǣp* rope for mooring] —**moorage** ('mʊərɪdʒ) *n.*

Moor (mʊə, mɔː) *n.* a member of a Muslim people of North Africa, of mixed Arab and Berber descent. [C14: via OF from L *Maurus,* from Gk *Mauros,* ?from Berber] —'**Moorish** *adj.*

moorcock ('mʊəˌkɒk, 'mɔː-) *n.* the male of the red grouse.

Moore (mʊə, mɔː) *n.* **1. Bobby,** full name *Robert Frederick Moore.* born 1941, English footballer: captain of England team that won the World Cup in 1966. **2. George.** 1852–1933, Irish novelist. His works include *Esther Waters* (1894) and *The Brook Kerith* (1916). **3. G(eorge) E(dward).** 1873–1958, English philosopher, noted esp. for his *Principia Ethica* (1903). **4. Gerald.** 1899–1987, English pianist, noted as an accompanist esp. to *Lieder* singers. **5. Henry.** 1898–1986, English sculptor. His works are characterized by monumental organic forms and include the *Madonna and Child* (1943) at St Matthew's Church, Northampton. **6.** Sir **John.** 1761–1809, British general; commander of the British army (1808–09) in the Peninsular War: killed at Corunna. **7. Marianne.** 1887–1972, U.S. poet. **8. Thomas.** 1779–1852, Irish poet, best known for *Irish Melodies* (1807–34).

moorhen ('muə,hɛn, 'mɔː-) *n.* **1.** a bird of the rail family, inhabiting ponds, lakes, etc., having a black plumage, red bill, and a red shield above the bill. **2.** the female of the red grouse.

mooring ('muərɪŋ, 'mɔː-) *n.* **1.** a place for anchoring a vessel. **2.** a permanent anchor with a floating buoy, to which vessels can moor.

moorings ('muərɪŋz, 'mɔː-) *pl. n.* **1.** *Naut.* the ropes, anchors, etc., used in mooring a vessel. **2.** (*sometimes sing.*) something that provides security or stability.

Moorish idol *n.* a tropical marine spiny-finned fish that is common around coral reefs. It has a deeply compressed body with yellow and black stripes.

moorland ('muələnd) *n. Brit.* an area of moor.

moose (muːs) *n., pl.* **moose.** a large North American deer having large flattened palmate antlers: also occurs in Europe and Asia where it is called an elk. [C17: of Amerind origin]

Moose Jaw *n.* a city in W Canada, in S Saskatchewan. Pop.: 35 073 (1986).

moot (muːt) *adj.* **1.** subject or open to debate: *a moot point.* ~*vb.* **2.** (*tr.*) to suggest or bring up for debate. **3.** (*intr.*) to plead or argue hypothetical cases, as an academic exercise or as training for law students. ~*n.* **4.** a discussion or debate of a hypothetical case or point, held as an academic activity. **5.** (in Anglo-Saxon England) an assembly dealing with local legal and administrative affairs. [OE *gemōt*]

moot court *n.* a mock court trying hypothetical legal cases.

mop (mɒp) *n.* **1.** an implement with a wooden handle and a head made of twists of cotton or a piece of synthetic sponge, used for polishing or washing floors, or washing dishes. **2.** something resembling this, such as a tangle of hair. ~*vb.* **mopping, mopped.** (*tr.*) **3.** (often foll. by *up*) to clean or soak up as with a mop. ~See also **mop up.** [C15 *mappe*, ult. from L *mappa* napkin]

mope (məup) *vb.* (*intr.*) **1.** to be gloomy or apathetic. **2.** to move or act in an aimless way. ~*n.* **3.** a gloomy person. [C16: ?from obs. *mope* fool & rel. to *mop* grimace] —'**moper** *n.* —'**mopy** *adj.*

moped ('məupɛd) *n. Brit.* a light motorcycle not over 50cc. [C20: from MOTOR + PEDAL¹]

mopes (məups) *pl. n.* **the.** low spirits.

mopoke ('məu,pəuk) *n.* **1.** a small spotted owl of Australia and New Zealand. **2.** (in Australia) a frogmouth (bird) with reddish-brown or grey plumage. **3.** *Austral. & N.Z. sl.* a slow or lugubrious person. ~Also called: **morepork.** [C19: imit. of the bird's cry]

moppet ('mɒpɪt) *n.* a less common word for **poppet** (sense 1). [C17: from obs. *mop* rag doll; from ?]

mop up *vb.* (*tr., adv.*) **1.** to clean with a mop. **2.** *Inf.* to complete (a task, etc.). **3.** *Mil.* to clear (remaining enemy forces) after a battle, as by killing, taking prisoner, etc.

moquette (mɒ'kɛt) *n.* a thick velvety fabric used for carpets, upholstery, etc. [C18: from F; from ?]

MOR *abbrev. for* middle-of-the-road: used esp. in radio programming.

Mor. *abbrev. for* Morocco.

mora *or* **morra** ('mɔːrə) *n.* a guessing game played with the fingers, esp. in Italy and China. [C18: from It. *mora*]

Moradabad (,mɒrədə'bæd) *n.* a city in N India, in N Uttar Pradesh. Pop.: 332 663 (1981).

moraine (mɒ'reɪn) *n.* a mass of debris, carried by glaciers and forming ridges and mounds when deposited. [C18: from F, from Savoy dialect *morena*, from ?] —mo'**rainal** *or* mo'**rainic** *adj.*

moral ('mɒrəl) *adj.* **1.** concerned with or relating to human behaviour, esp. the distinction between good and bad or right and wrong behaviour: *moral sense.* **2.** adhering to conventionally accepted standards of conduct. **3.** based on a sense of right and wrong according to conscience: *moral courage; moral law.* **4.** having psychological rather than tangible effects: *moral support.* **5.** having the effects but not the appearance of (victory or defeat): *a moral victory.* **6.** having a strong probability: *a moral certainty.* ~*n.* **7.** the lesson to be obtained from a fable or event. **8.** a concise truth; maxim. **9.** (*pl.*) principles of behaviour in accordance with standards of right and wrong. **10.** *Austral. sl.* a certainty: *a moral to win.* [C14: from L *mōrālis* relating to morals or customs, from *mōs* custom] —'**morally** *adv.*

morale (mɒ'rɑːl) *n.* the degree of mental or moral confidence of a person or group. [C18: morals, from F, n. use of MORAL (adj.)]

moralist ('mɒrəlɪst) *n.* **1.** a person who seeks to regulate the morals of others. **2.** a person who lives in accordance with moral principles. —,**moral'istic** *adj.* —,**moral'isti-cally** *adv.*

morality (mə'rælɪtɪ) *n., pl.* **-ties. 1.** the quality of being moral. **2.** conformity, or degree of conformity, to conventional standards of moral conduct. **3.** a system of moral principles. **4.** an instruction or lesson in morals. **5.** short for **morality play.**

morality play *n.* a type of drama between the 14th and 16th centuries concerned with the conflict between personified virtues and vices.

moralize *or* **-lise** ('mɒrə,laɪz) *vb.* **1.** (*intr.*) to make moral pronouncements. **2.** (*tr.*) to interpret or explain in a moral sense. **3.** (*tr.*) to improve the morals of. —,**morali'zation** *or* **-li'sation** *n.* —'**mora,lizer** *or* -,**liser** *n.*

moral majority *n.* a presumed majority of people believed to be in favour of a stricter code of public morals. [C20: after *Moral Majority*, a right-wing U.S. religious organization, based on SILENT MAJORITY]

moral philosophy *n.* the branch of philosophy dealing with ethics.

Moral Rearmament *n.* a worldwide movement for moral and spiritual renewal founded by Frank Buchman in 1938. Also called: **Buchmanism.** Former name: **Oxford Group.**

moral theology *n.* the branch of theology dealing with ethics.

Morar ('mɔːrə) *n. Loch.* a lake in W Scotland, in the SW Highlands: the deepest in Scotland. Length: 18 km (11 miles). Depth: 296 m (987 ft.).

morass (mə'ræs) *n.* **1.** a tract of swampy low-lying land. **2.** a disordered or muddled situation or circumstance, esp. one that impedes progress. [C17: from Du. *moeras*, ult. from OF *marais* MARSH]

moratorium (,mɒrə'tɔːrɪəm) *n., pl.* **-ria** (-rɪə) *or* **-riums. 1.** a legally authorized postponement of the fulfilment of an obligation. **2.** an agreed suspension of activity. [C19: NL, from LL *morātōrius* dilatory, from *mora* delay]

Morava (mɒ'rɑːvə) *n.* **1.** a river in Czechoslovakia, rising in the Sudeten Mountains and flowing south to the Danube: forms part of the border between Czechoslovakia and Austria. Length: 370 km (230 miles). German name: **March. 2.** a river in E Yugoslavia, formed by the confluence of the Southern Morava and the Western Morava near Stalac: flows north to the Danube. Length: 209 km (130 miles). **3.** ('mɒrava). the Czech name for **Moravia.**

Moravia¹ (mə'reɪvɪə, mɒ-) *n.* a region of central Czechoslovakia, around the Morava River, bounded by the Bohemian-Moravian Highlands, the Sudeten Mountains, and the W Carpathians: became a separate Austrian crownland in 1848; made part of Czechoslovakia in 1918; valuable mineral resources. Czech name: **Morava.** German name: **Mähren.**

Moravia² (*Italian* mo'rɑːvja) *n.* **Alberto** (al'bɛrto), pen name of *Alberto Pincherle.* born 1907, Italian novelist and short-story writer: his works include *The Time of Indifference* (1929), *The Woman of Rome* (1949), *The Lie* (1966), and *Erotic Tales* (1985).

Moravian (mə'reɪvɪən, mɒ-) *adj.* **1.** of or relating to Moravia, its people, or their dialect of Czech. **2.** of or relating to the Moravian Church. ~*n.* **3.** the Moravian dialect. **4.** a native or inhabitant of Moravia. **5.** a member of the Moravian Church. —**Mo'ravianism** *n.*

moray (mɒ'reɪ) *n., pl.* **-rays.** a voracious marine coastal eel marked with brilliant colours. [C17: from Port. *moréia*, from L *mūrēna*, from Gk *muraina*]

Moray Firth *n.* an inlet of the North Sea on the NE coast of Scotland. Length: about 56 km (35 miles).

Morayshire ('mʌrɪ,ʃɪə, -ʃə) *n.* (until 1975) a county of NE Scotland, now part of Grampian region. Former name: **Elgin.**

morbid ('mɔːbɪd) *adj.* **1.** having an unusual interest in death or unpleasant events. **2.** gruesome. **3.** relating to or characterized by disease. [C17: from L *morbidus* sickly, from *morbus* illness] — **mor'bidity** *n.* — '**morbidly** *adv.* — '**morbidness** *n.*

morbid anatomy *n.* the branch of medical science concerned with the study of the structure of diseased organs and tissues.

morbific (mɔː'bɪfɪk) *adj.* causing disease.

Morbihan (*French* mɔrbiã) *n.* a department of NW France, in S Brittany. Capital: Vannes. Pop.: 590 889 (1982). Area: 7092 sq. km (2766 sq. miles).

mordant ('mɔːdᵊnt) *adj.* **1.** sarcastic or caustic. **2.** having the properties of a mordant. **3.** pungent. ~*n.* **4.** a substance used before the application of a dye, possessing the ability to fix colours. **5.** an acid or other corrosive fluid used to etch lines on a printing plate. [C15: from OF: biting, from *mordre* to bite, from L *mordēre*] — '**mordancy** *n.* — '**mordantly** *adv.*

Mordecai (ˌmɔːdə'kaɪ, 'mɔːdəˌkaɪ) *n. Old Testament.* the cousin of Esther who averted a threatened massacre of the Jews (Esther 2–9).

mordent ('mɔːdᵊnt) *n. Music.* a melodic ornament consisting of the rapid alternation of a note with a note one degree lower than it. [C19: from G, from It. *mordente*, from *mordere* to bite]

Mordvinian Autonomous Soviet Socialist Republic (mɔː'dvɪnɪən) *n.* an administrative division of the W central Soviet Union, in the middle Volga basin. Capital: Saransk. Pop.: 964 000 (1986). Area: 26 200 sq. km (10 110 sq. miles). Also called: **Mordovian Autonomous Soviet Socialist Republic** (mɔː'dəʊvɪən).

more (mɔː) *determiner.* **1. a.** the comparative of **much** or **many**: *more joy than you know; more sausages.* **b.** (*as pron.; functioning as sing. or pl.*): *he has more than she has; even more are dying.* **2. a.** additional; further: *no more bananas.* **b.** (*as pron.; functioning as sing. or pl.*): *I can't take any more; more than expected.* **3. more of.** to a greater extent or degree: *we see more of Sue; more of a nuisance.* ~*adv.* **4.** used to form the comparative of some adjectives and adverbs: *a more believable story; more quickly.* **5.** the comparative of **much**: *people listen to the radio more now.* **6. more or less. a.** as an estimate; approximately. **b.** to an unspecified extent or degree: *the party was ruined, more or less.* [OE *māra*]
▷ **Usage.** See at **most.**

More (mɔː) *n.* **1. Hannah.** 1745–1833, English writer, noted for her religious tracts, esp. *The Shepherd of Salisbury Plain.* **2. Sir Thomas.** 1478–1535, English statesman, humanist, and Roman Catholic Saint; lord chancellor to Henry VIII (1529–32). His opposition to the annulment of Henry's marriage to Catherine of Aragon and his refusal to recognize the Act of Supremacy resulted in his execution on a charge of treason. In *Utopia* (1516), he set forth his concept of the ideal state. Feast day: June 22.

Morea (mɔː'rɪə) *n.* the medieval name for the **Peloponnese.**

Moreau (*French* mɔro) *n.* **1. Gustave** (gystav) 1826–98, French symbolist painter. **2. Jeanne** (ʒan). born 1928, French stage and film actress. Her films include *Jules et Jim* (1961) and *Viva Maria* (1965). **3. Jean Victor** (ʒã viktɔr). 1763–1813, French general in the Revolutionary and Napoleonic Wars.

Morecambe ('mɔːkəm) *n.* a port and resort in NW England, in NW Lancashire on **Morecambe Bay** (an inlet of the Irish Sea). Pop. (with Heysham): 43 000 (1982 est.).

moreish *or* **morish** ('mɔːrɪʃ) *adj. Inf.* (of food) causing a desire for more.

morel (mɒ'rɛl) *n.* an edible fungus in which the mushroom has a pitted cap. [C17: from F *morille*, prob. of Gmc origin]

Morelia (*Spanish* mo'relia) *n.* a city in central Mexico, capital of Michoacán state: a cultural centre during colonial times; two universities. Pop.: 353 055 (1980). Former name (until 1828): **Valladolid.**

morello (mə'reləʊ) *n., pl.* **-los.** a variety of small very dark sour cherry. [C17: ?from Med. L *amārellum*, dim. of L *amārus* bitter, but also infl. by It. *morello* blackish]

Morelos (*Spanish* mo'relɔs) *n.* an inland state of S central Mexico, on the S slope of the great plateau. Capital: Cuernavaca. Pop.: 931 675 (1980). Area: 4988 sq. km (1926 sq. miles).

morendo (mɒr'ɛndəʊ) *adv. Music.* gradually dying away. [It.: dying]

moreover (mɔː'rəʊvə) *sentence connector.* in addition to what has already been said.

morepork ('mɔːˌpɔːk) *n.* another name, esp. in New Zealand, for **mopoke.**

mores ('mɔːreɪz) *pl. n.* the customs and conventions embodying the fundamental values of a group or society. [C20: from L, pl. of *mōs* custom]

Morgan ('mɔːgən) *n.* **1. Sir Henry.** 1635–88, Welsh buccaneer, who raided Spanish colonies in the West Indies for the English. **2. John Pierpont.** 1837–1913, U.S. financier, philanthropist, and art collector. **3. Thomas Hunt.** 1866–1945, U.S. biologist. He formulated the chromosome theory of heredity. Nobel prize for physiology or medicine 1933.

morganatic (ˌmɔːgə'nætɪk) *adj.* of or designating a marriage between a person of high rank and a person of low rank, by which the latter is not elevated to the higher rank and any issue have no rights to the succession of the higher party's titles, property, etc. [C18: from Med. L *mātrimōnium ad morganāticum* marriage based on the morning-gift (a token present after consummation representing the husband's only liability); *morganātica*, ult. from OHG *morgan* morning] — ˌ**morga'natically** *adv.*

morgen ('mɔːgən) *n.* **1.** a South African unit of area, equal to about two acres or 0.8 hectare. **2.** a unit of area, formerly used in Prussia and Scandinavia, equal to about two thirds of an acre. [C17: from Du.: morning, a morning's ploughing]

morgue (mɔːg) *n.* **1.** another word for **mortuary. 2.** *Inf.* a room or file containing clippings, etc., used for reference in a newspaper. [C19: from F *le Morgue*, a Paris mortuary]

moribund ('mɒrɪˌbʌnd) *adj.* **1.** near death. **2.** without force or vitality. [C18: from L, from *morī* to die] — ˌ**mori'bundity** *n.* — '**moriˌbundly** *adv.*

Mörike (*German* 'møːrɪkə) *n.* **Eduard** ('eːduart). 1804–75, German poet, noted for his lyrics, such as *On a Winter's Morning before Sunrise* and *At Midnight.*

Morisco (mə'rɪskəʊ) *or* **Moresco** (mə'rɛskəʊ) *n., pl.* **-cos** *or* **-coes. 1.** a Spanish Moor. **2.** a morris dance. ~*adj.* **3.** another word for **Moorish**; see **Moor.** [C16: from Sp., from *Moro* MOOR]

morish ('mɔːrɪʃ) *adj.* a variant spelling of **moreish.**

Morley[1] ('mɔːlɪ) *n.* an industrial town in N England, in West Yorkshire near Leeds. Pop.: 44 134 (1981).

Morley[2] ('mɔːlɪ) *n.* **1. Edward Williams.** 1838–1923, U.S. chemist who collaborated with A. A. Michelson in the Michelson-Morley experiment. **2. John,** Viscount Morley of Blackburn. 1838–1923, British Liberal statesman and writer; secretary of state for India (1905–10). **3. Robert.** born 1908, British actor. His films include *Major Barbara* (1940), *Oscar Wilde* (1960), and *The Blue Bird* (1976). **4. Thomas.** ?1557–?1603, English composer and organist, noted for his madrigals and his textbook on music, *A Plaine and Easie Introduction to Practicall Musicke* (1597).

Mormon ('mɔːmən) *n.* **1.** a member of the Church of Jesus Christ of Latter-day Saints, founded in 1830 in New York by Joseph Smith. **2.** a prophet whose supposed revelations were recorded by Joseph Smith in the Book of Mormon. ~*adj.* **3.** of or relating to the Mormons, their Church, or their beliefs. — '**Mormonism** *n.*

morn (mɔːn) *n.* a poetic word for **morning.** [OE *morgen*]

mornay ('mɔːneɪ) *adj.* (*often immediately postpositive*) denoting a cheese sauce: *eggs mornay.* [? after Philippe de MORNAY]

Mornay (*French* mɔrnɛ) *n.* **Philippe de** (filip də), Seigneur du Plessis-Marly. 1549–1623, French Huguenot leader. Also called: **Duplessis-Mornay.**

morning ('mɔːnɪŋ) *n.* **1.** the first part of the day, ending at noon. **2.** sunrise; daybreak; dawn. **3.** the beginning or early period. **4. the morning after.** *Inf.* the aftereffects of excess, esp. a hangover. **5.** (*modifier*) of, used in, or occurring in the morning: *morning coffee.* [C13 *morwening*, from MORN, on the model of EVENING]

morning-after pill *n.* an oral contraceptive that is effective if taken some hours after intercourse.

morning dress *n.* formal day dress for men, comprising a cutaway frock coat (**morning coat**), usually with grey trousers and top hat.

morning-glory *n., pl.* **-ries.** any of various mainly tropical plants of the convolvulus family, with trumpet-shaped blue, pink, or white flowers, which close in late afternoon.

mornings ('mɔːnɪŋz) *adv. Inf.* in the morning, esp. regularly, or during every morning.

morning sickness n. nausea occurring shortly after rising: a symptom of pregnancy.

morning star n. a planet, usually Venus, seen just before sunrise. Also called: **daystar**.

Moro[1] ('mɔːrəʊ) n. **1.** (pl. **-ros** or **-ro**) a member of a group of predominantly Muslim peoples of the S Philippines. **2.** the language of these peoples. [C19: via Sp. from L *Maurus* MOOR]

Moro[2] (Italian 'mɔːro) n. **Aldo** ('aldo). 1916–78, Italian Christian Democrat statesman; prime minister of Italy (1963–68; 1974–76) and minister of foreign affairs (1965–66; 1969–72; 1973–74). He negotiated the entry of the Italian Communist Party into coalition government before being kidnapped by the Red Brigades in 1978 and murdered.

morocco (mə'rɒkəʊ) n. a fine soft leather made from goatskins, used for bookbinding, shoes, etc. [C17: after MOROCCO, where it was orig. made]

Morocco (mə'rɒkəʊ) n. a kingdom in NW Africa, on the Mediterranean and the Atlantic: conquered by the Arabs in about 683, who introduced Islam; at its height under Berber dynasties (11th–13th centuries); became a French protectorate in 1912 and gained independence in 1956. It is mostly mountainous, with the Atlas Mountains in the centre and the Rif range along the Mediterranean coast, with the Sahara in the south and southeast; an important exporter of phosphates. Languages: Arabic, Berber, and French. Religion: mostly Sunni Muslim. Currency: dirham. Capital: Rabat. Pop.: 23 000 000 (1987 UN est.). Area: 500 000 sq. km (166 000 sq. miles). French name: **Maroc**. —**Moroccan** (mə'rɒkən) adj., n.

moron ('mɔːrɒn) n. **1.** a foolish or stupid person. **2.** a person having an intelligence quotient of between 50 and 70. [C20: from Gk *mōros* foolish] —**moronic** (mə'rɒnɪk) adj. —**mo'ronically** adv. —**'moronism** or **mo'ronity** n.

Moroni (mə'rəʊnɪ; French mɔrɔni) n. the capital of Comoros, on the island of Njazídja (Grande Comore). Pop.: 20 112 (1980 est.).

morose (mə'rəʊs) adj. ill-tempered or gloomy. [C16: from L *mōrōsus* peevish, from *mōs* custom, will] —**mo'rosely** adv. —**mo'roseness** n.

-morph n. combining form. indicating shape, form, or structure of a specified kind: *ectomorph*. [from Gk *-morphos*, from *morphē* shape] —**-morphic** or **-morphous** adj. combining form. —**-morphy** n. combining form.

morpheme ('mɔːfiːm) n. Linguistics. a speech element having a meaning or grammatical function that cannot be subdivided into further such elements. [C20: from F, from Gk *morphē* form, on the model of PHONEME] —**mor'phemic** adj. —**mor'phemically** adv.

Morpheus ('mɔːfɪəs, -fjuːs) n. Greek myth. the god of sleep and dreams. —**'Morphean** adj.

morphine ('mɔːfiːn) or **morphia** ('mɔːfɪə) n. an alkaloid extracted from opium: used in medicine as an anaesthetic and sedative. [C19: from F, from MORPHEUS]

morphogenesis (,mɔːfəʊ'dʒɛnɪsɪs) n. **1.** the development of form in an organism during its growth. **2.** the evolutionary development of form in an organism or part of an organism. —**morphogenetic** (,mɔːfəʊdʒɪ'nɛtɪk) adj.

morphology (mɔː'fɒlədʒɪ) n. **1.** the branch of biology concerned with the form and structure of organisms. **2.** the form and structure of words in a language. **3.** the form and structure of anything. —**morphologic** (,mɔːfə'lɒdʒɪk) or **,morpho'logical** adj. —**,morpho'logically** adv. —**mor'phologist** n.

Morphy ('mɔːfɪ) n. **Paul.** 1837–84, U.S. chess player, widely considered to have been the world's greatest player.

Morris ('mɒrɪs) n. **William.** 1834–96, English poet, Pre-Raphaelite painter, craftsman, and socialist writer. He founded the Kelmscott Press (1890).

Morris chair n. an armchair with an adjustable back. [C19: after William MORRIS]

morris dance n. any of various old English folk dances usually performed by men (**morris men**) adorned with bells and often representing characters from folk tales. Often shortened to **morris**. [C15 *moreys daunce* Moorish dance] —**morris dancing** n.

Morrison ('mɒrɪsˀn) n. **1. Herbert Stanley,** Baron Morrison of Lambeth. 1888–1965, British Labour statesman, Home Secretary and Minister for Home Security in

Churchill's War Cabinet (1942–45). **2. Jim,** full name *James Douglas Morrison*. 1943–71, U.S. rock singer and songwriter, lead vocalist with the Doors; noted for his Freudian imagery and moody performances.

morro ('mɒrəʊ) n., pl. **-ros** (-rəʊz). a rounded hill or promontory. [from Sp.]

morrow ('mɒrəʊ) n. (usually preceded by the) Arch. or poetic. **1.** the next day. **2.** the period following a specified event. **3.** the morning. [C13 *morwe*, from OE *morgen* morning]

Mors (mɔːz) n. the Roman god of death. Greek counterpart: **Thanatos**.

Morse (mɔːs) n. **Samuel Finley Breese** ('fɪnlɪ briːz). 1791–1872, U.S. inventor and painter. He invented the first electric telegraph and the Morse code.

Morse code n. a telegraph code used internationally for transmitting messages. Letters, numbers, etc., are represented by groups of shorter dots and longer dashes, or by groups of the corresponding sounds. [C19: after Samuel MORSE]

morsel ('mɔːsˀl) n. **1.** a small slice or mouthful of food. **2.** a small piece; bit. [C13: from OF, from *mors* a bite, from L *morsus*, from *mordēre* to bite]

mortal ('mɔːtˀl) adj. **1.** (of living beings, esp. human beings) subject to death. **2.** of or involving life or the world. **3.** ending in or causing death; fatal: *a mortal blow*. **4.** deadly or unrelenting: *a mortal enemy*. **5.** of or like the fear of death: *mortal terror*. **6.** great or very intense: *mortal pain*. **7.** conceivable or possible: *there was no mortal reason to go*. **8.** Sl. long and tedious: *for three mortal hours*. ~n. **9.** a mortal being. **10.** Inf. a person: *a mean mortal*. [C14: from L *mortālis*, from *mors* death] —**'mortally** adv.

mortality (mɔː'tælɪtɪ) n., pl. **-ties**. **1.** the condition of being mortal. **2.** great loss of life, as in war or disaster. **3.** the number of deaths in a given period. **4.** mankind; humanity.

mortal sin n. Christianity. a sin regarded as involving total loss of grace.

mortar ('mɔːtə) n. **1.** a mixture of cement or lime or both with sand and water, used as a bond between bricks or stones or as a covering on a wall. **2.** a cannon having a short barrel and relatively wide bore that fires low-velocity shells in high trajectories. **3.** a vessel, usually bowl-shaped, in which substances are pulverized with a pestle. ~vb. (tr.) **4.** to join (bricks or stones) or cover (a wall) with mortar. **5.** to fire on with mortars. [C13: from L *mortārium* basin in which mortar is mixed; in some senses, via OF *mortier* substance mixed inside such a vessel]

mortarboard ('mɔːtə,bɔːd) n. **1.** a black tasselled academic cap with a flat square top. **2.** a small square board with a handle on the underside for carrying mortar.

mortgage ('mɔːgɪdʒ) n. **1.** a conditional conveyance of property, esp. real property, as security for the repayment of a loan. **2.** the deed effecting such a transaction. **3.** the loan itself. ~vb. (tr.) **4.** to convey (property) by mortgage. **5.** Inf. to pledge. [C14: from OF, lit.: dead pledge] —**'mortgageable** adj.

mortgagee (,mɔːgɪ'dʒiː) n. Law. the party to a mortgage who makes the loan.

mortgagor (,mɔːgɪ'dʒɔː) or **mortgager** n. Property law. a person who borrows money by mortgaging his property to the lender as security.

mortician (mɔː'tɪʃən) n. Chiefly U.S. another word for **undertaker**. [C19: from MORTUARY + -ician, as in physician]

mortification (,mɔːtɪfɪ'keɪʃən) n. **1.** a feeling of humiliation. **2.** something causing this. **3.** Christianity. the practice of mortifying the senses. **4.** another word for **gangrene**.

mortify ('mɔːtɪ,faɪ) vb. **-fying, -fied. 1.** (tr.) to humiliate or cause to feel shame. **2.** (tr.) Christianity. to subdue and bring under control by self-denial, disciplinary exercises, etc. **3.** (intr.) to undergo tissue death or become gangrenous. [C14: via OF from Church L *mortificāre* to put to death, from L *mors* death + *facere* to do] —**'mortifier** n. —**'mortifying** adj.

Mortimer ('mɔːtɪmə) n. **1. John** (**Clifford**). born 1923, British barrister and playwright. His plays include *The Dock Brief* (1958) and he wrote the television series featuring the barrister Horace Rumpole. **2. Roger de,** 8th Baron of Wigmore and 1st Earl of March. 1287–1330, lover of Isabella, the wife of Edward II of England: they invaded England in 1326 and compelled the king to abdicate in favour of his son, Edward III; executed.

mortise *or* **mortice** ('mɔːtɪs) *n.* **1.** a slot or recess cut into a piece of wood, stone, etc., to receive a matching projection (tenon) of another piece, or a mortise lock. ~*vb.* (*tr.*) **2.** to cut a slot or recess in (a piece of wood, stone, etc.). **3.** to join (two pieces of wood, stone, etc.) by means of a mortise and tenon. [C14: from OF *mortoise*, ?from Ar. *murtazza* fastened in position]

mortise lock *n.* a lock set into a mortise in a door so that the mechanism of the lock is enclosed by the door.

mortmain ('mɔːt,meɪn) *n. Law.* the state or condition of lands, buildings, etc., held inalienably, as by an ecclesiastical or other corporation. [C15: from OF *mortemain*, from Med. L *mortua manus* dead hand, inalienable ownership]

Morton ('mɔːt^ən) *n.* **Jelly Roll,** real name *Ferdinand Joseph La Menthe Morton.* 1885–1941, U.S. jazz pianist, singer, and songwriter; one of the creators of New Orleans jazz.

mortuary ('mɔːtʃʊərɪ) *n.*, *pl.* **-aries. 1.** Also called: **morgue.** a building where dead bodies are kept before cremation or burial. ~*adj.* **2.** of or relating to death or burial. [C14 (as n., a funeral gift to a parish priest): via Med. L *mortuārium* (n.) from L *mortuārius* of the dead]

morwong ('mɔː,wɒŋ) *n.* a food fish of Australasian coastal waters. [from Abor.]

mosaic (mə'zeɪɪk) *n.* **1.** a design or decoration made up of small pieces of coloured glass, stone, etc. **2.** the process of making a mosaic. **3. a.** a mottled yellowing that occurs in the leaves of plants affected with any of various virus diseases. **b.** Also called: **mosaic disease.** any of the diseases, such as **tobacco mosaic,** that produce this discoloration. **4.** a light-sensitive surface on a television camera tube, consisting of a large number of granules of photoemissive material. [C16: via F & It. from Med. L, from LGk: mosaic work, from Gk: of the Muses, from *mousa* MUSE] —**mosaicist** (mə'zeɪɪsɪst) *n.*

Mosaic (məʊ'zeɪɪk) *adj.* of or relating to Moses or the laws and traditions ascribed to him.

Mosaic law *n. Bible.* the laws ascribed to Moses and contained in the Pentateuch.

moschatel (,mɒskə'tɛl) *n.* a small N temperate plant with greenish-white musk-scented flowers. Also called: **townhall clock, five-faced bishop.** [C18: via F from It. *moscatella,* dim. of *moscato* MUSK]

Moscow ('mɒskəʊ) *n.* the capital of the Soviet Union and of the RSFSR, on the Moskva River: dates from the 11th century; capital of the grand duchy of Russia from 1547 to 1712; made capital of the Soviet Union in 1918; centres on the medieval Kremlin; chief political, cultural, and industrial centre of the Soviet Union, with two universities. Pop.: 8 815 000 (1987). Russian name: **Moskva.**

Moseley ('məʊzlɪ) *n.* **Henry Gwyn-Jeffreys.** 1887–1915, English physicist. He showed that the wavelengths of x-rays emitted from the elements are related to their atomic numbers.

Moselle (məʊ'zɛl) *n.* **1.** a department of NE France, in Lorraine region. Capital: Metz. Pop.: 1 007 189 (1982). Area: 6253 sq. km (2439 sq. miles). **2.** a river in W Europe, rising in NE France and flowing northwest, forming part of the border between Luxembourg and West Germany, then northeast to the Rhine: many vineyards along its lower course. Length: 547 km (340 miles). German name: **Mosel** ('moːzəl). **3.** (*sometimes not cap.*) a German white wine from the Moselle valley.

Moses ('məʊzɪz) *n.* **1.** *Old Testament.* the Hebrew prophet who led the Israelites out of Egypt to the Promised Land and gave them divinely revealed laws. **2. Ed.** born 1956, U.S. hurdler; winner of the 400 m hurdles in the 1976 and 1984 Olympic Games. **3. Grandma,** real name *Anna Mary Robertson Moses.* 1860–1961, U.S. painter of primitives, who began to paint at the age of 75.

mosey ('məʊzɪ) *vb.* (*intr.*) *Inf.* (often foll. by *along* or *on*) to amble. [C19: from ?]

Moshesh (mɒ'ʃɛʃ) *or* **Moshoeshoe** (mɒ'ʃuʃu) *n.* died 1870, African chief, who founded the Basotho nation, now Lesotho.

Moskva (*Russian* mas'kva) *n.* **1.** transliteration of the Russian name for **Moscow. 2.** a river in the W central Soviet Union, rising in the Smolensk-Moscow upland, and flowing southeast through Moscow to the Oka River:

linked with the River Volga by the Moscow Canal. Length: about 500 km (310 miles).

Moslem ('mɒzləm) *n.*, *pl.* **-lems** *or* **-lem,** *adj.* a variant of **Muslim.** —**Moslemic** (mɒz'lɛmɪk) *adj.* —'**Moslemism** *n.*

Mosley ('məʊzlɪ) *n.* **Sir Oswald Ernald.** 1896–1980, British politician; founder of the British Union of Fascists (1932).

mosque (mɒsk) *n.* a Muslim place of worship. [C14: earlier *mosquee,* from OF via It. *moschea,* ult. from Ar. *masjid* temple]

mosquito (mə'skiːtəʊ) *n.*, *pl.* **-toes** *or* **-tos.** any dipterous insect of the family Culicidae: the females have a long proboscis adapted for piercing the skin of man and animals to suck their blood. See also **aedes, anopheles, culex.** [C16: from Sp., dim. of *mosca* fly, from L *musca*]

mosquito net *or* **netting** *n.* a fine curtain or net to keep mosquitoes out.

moss (mɒs) *n.* **1.** any of a class of plants, typically growing in dense mats on trees, rocks, moist ground, etc. **2.** a clump or growth of any of these plants. **3.** any of various similar but unrelated plants, such as Spanish moss and reindeer moss. **4.** *Scot. & N English.* a peat bog or marsh. [OE *mos* swamp] —'**moss,like** *adj.* —'**mossy** *adj.* —'**mossiness** *n.*

Moss (mɒs) *n.* **Stirling.** born 1929, English racing driver.

moss agate *n.* a variety of chalcedony with dark greenish mossy markings.

mossie ('mɒsɪ) *n.* another name for the **cape sparrow.** [from ?]

mosso ('mɒsəʊ) *adv. Music.* to be performed with rapidity. [It., p.p. of *muovere* to MOVE]

moss rose *n.* a variety of rose that has a mossy stem and calyx and fragrant pink flowers.

moss stitch *n.* a knitting stitch made up of alternate plain and purl stitches.

mosstrooper ('mɒs,truːpə) *n.* a raider in the Borders of England and Scotland in the mid-17th century. [C17 *moss,* in dialect sense: bog]

most (məʊst) *determiner.* **1. a.** a great majority of; nearly all: *most people like eggs.* **b.** (*as pron.*): *functioning as sing. or pl.*): *most of them don't know; most of it is finished.* **2. the most. a.** the superlative of **many** and **much:** *you have the most money; the most apples.* **b.** (*as pron.*): *the most he can afford is two pounds.* **3. at (the) most.** at the maximum: *that girl is four at the most.* **4. make the most of.** to use to the best advantage: *she makes the most of her accent.* ~*adv.* **5. the most.** used to form the superlative of some adjectives and adverbs: *the most beautiful daughter of all.* **6.** the superlative of **much:** *people welcome a drink most after work.* **7.** (intensifier): *a most absurd story.* [OE *māst* or *mǣst,* whence ME *most, mēst*]

▷ **Usage.** The meanings of *most* and *mostly* should not be confused. In *she was most affected by the news, most* is equivalent to *very* and is generally acceptable. In *she was mostly affected by the news,* the implication is that there was something else, in addition to the news, which affected her, although less so. *More* and *most* should also be distinguished when used in comparisons. *More* applies to cases involving two persons, objects, etc., *most* to cases involving three or more: *John is the more intelligent of the two; he is the most intelligent of the students.*

-most *suffix. forming the superlative degree of some adjectives and adverbs: hindmost; uppermost.* [OE *-mǣst, -mest,* orig. a sup. suffix, later mistakenly taken as from *mǣst* (adv.) most]

mostly ('məʊstlɪ) *adv.* **1.** almost entirely; chiefly. **2.** on many or most occasions; usually.

Most Reverend *n.* (in Britain) a courtesy title applied to Anglican and Roman Catholic archbishops.

Mosul ('məʊsəl) *n.* a city in N Iraq, on the River Tigris opposite the ruins of Nineveh: an important commercial centre with nearby Ayn Zalah oilfield; university. Pop.: 570 926 (1985 est.).

mot (məʊ) *n.* short for **bon mot.** [C16: via F from Vulgar L *mottum* (unattested) utterance, from L *muttum,* from *muttīre* to mutter]

MOT (in Britain and New Zealand) *abbrev. for:* **1.** Ministry of Transport (*Brit.,* now Transport Industries). **2.** *Brit.* the MOT test or test certificate.

mote (məʊt) n. a tiny speck. [OE *mot*]

motel (məʊˈtɛl) n. a roadside hotel for motorists. [C20: from *motor* + *hotel*]

motet (məʊˈtɛt) n. a polyphonic choral composition as an anthem in the Roman Catholic service. [C14: from OF, dim. of *mot* word; see MOT]

moth (mɒθ) n. any of numerous insects that typically have stout bodies with antennae of various shapes (but not clubbed), including large brightly coloured species, such as hawk moths, and small inconspicuous types, such as the clothes moths. Cf. **butterfly** (sense 1). [OE *moththe*]

mothball (ˈmɒθˌbɔːl) n. **1.** a small ball of camphor or naphthalene used to repel clothes moths in stored clothing, etc. **2. put in mothballs.** to postpone work on (a project, activity, etc.). ~vb. (tr.) **3.** to prepare (a ship) for a long period of storage by sealing with plastic. **4.** to take (a factory, etc.) out of operation but maintain it for future use. **5.** to postpone work on (a project, activity, etc.).

moth-eaten adj. **1.** decayed, decrepit, or outdated. **2.** eaten away by or as if by moths.

mother[1] (ˈmʌðə) n. **1. a.** a female who has given birth to offspring. **b.** (as modifier): a mother bird. **2.** (often cap.) esp. as a term of address) a person's own mother. **3.** a female substituting in the function of a mother. **4.** (often cap.) Chiefly arch. a term of address for an old woman. **5. a.** motherly qualities, such as maternal affection: it appealed to the mother in her. **b.** (as modifier): mother love. **c.** (in combination): mothercraft. **6. a.** a female or thing that creates, nurtures, protects, etc., something. **b.** (as modifier): mother church; mother earth. **7.** a title given to certain members of female religious orders. **8.** (modifier) native or innate: mother wit. ~vb. (tr.) **9.** to give birth to or produce. **10.** to nurture, protect, etc. as a mother. [OE *mōdor*] —**motherless** adj.

mother[2] (ˈmʌðə) n. a stringy slime containing various bacteria that forms on the surface of liquids undergoing fermentation. Also called: **mother of vinegar.** [C16: ?from MOTHER[1], but cf. Sp. *madre* scum, Du. *modder* dregs, MLow G *modder* decaying object, *mudde* sludge]

Mother Carey's chicken (ˈkɛərɪz) n. another name for **storm petrel.** [from ?]

mother country n. **1.** the original country of colonists or settlers. **2.** a person's native country.

Mother Goose n. the imaginary author of a collection of nursery rhymes. [C18: translated from F *Contes de ma mère l'Oye* (1697), a collection of tales by Charles PERRAULT]

motherhood (ˈmʌðəˌhʊd) n. **1.** the state of being a mother. **2.** the qualities characteristic of a mother.

Mothering Sunday (ˈmʌðərɪŋ) n. Brit. the fourth Sunday in Lent, when mothers traditionally receive presents from their children. Also called: **Mother's Day.**

mother-in-law n., pl. **mothers-in-law.** the mother of one's wife or husband.

motherland (ˈmʌðəˌlænd) n. a person's native country.

mother lode n. Mining. the principal lode in a system.

motherly (ˈmʌðəlɪ) adj. of or resembling a mother, esp. in warmth or protectiveness. —**motherliness** n.

mother-of-pearl n. a hard iridescent substance that forms the inner layer of the shells of certain molluscs, such as the oyster. It is used to make buttons, etc. Also called: **nacre.**

Mother's Day n. **1.** U.S. & Canad. the second Sunday in May, observed as a day in honour of mothers. **2.** See **Mothering Sunday.**

mother ship n. a ship providing facilities and supplies for a number of small vessels.

mother superior n., pl. **mother superiors** or **mothers superior.** the head of a community of nuns.

mother tongue n. **1.** the language first learned by a child. **2.** a language from which another has evolved.

Motherwell and Wishaw (ˈmʌðəwəl; ˈwɪʃɔː) n. a town in S central Scotland, in Strathclyde region on the River Clyde: formed by the union of the two towns in 1920; industrial centre. Pop.: 148 016 (1986).

mother wit n. native practical intelligence; common sense.

mothproof (ˈmɒθˌpruːf) adj. **1.** (esp. of clothes) chemically treated so as to repel clothes moths. ~vb. **2.** (tr.) to make (clothes, etc.) mothproof.

mothy (ˈmɒθɪ) adj. **mothier, mothiest. 1.** moth-eaten. **2.** containing moths; full of moths.

motif (məʊˈtiːf) n. **1.** a distinctive idea, esp. a theme elaborated on in a piece of music, literature, etc. **2.** Also called: **motive.** a recurring shape in a design. **3.** a single decoration, such as a symbol or name on a jumper, sweatshirt, etc. [C19: from F; see MOTIVE]

motile (ˈməʊtaɪl) adj. capable of moving spontaneously and independently. [C19: from L *mōtus* moved, from *movēre* to move] —**motility** (məʊˈtɪlɪtɪ) n.

motion (ˈməʊʃən) n. **1.** the process of continual change in the physical position of an object; movement. **2.** a movement or action, esp. of part of the human body; a gesture. **3. a.** the capacity for movement. **b.** a manner of movement, esp. walking; gait. **4.** a mental impulse. **5.** a formal proposal to be discussed and voted on in a debate, meeting, etc. **6.** Law. an application made to a judge or court for an order or ruling necessary to the conduct of legal proceedings. **7.** Brit. **a.** the evacuation of the bowels. **b.** excrement. **8. a.** part of a moving mechanism. **b.** the action of such a part. **9. go through the motions. a.** to act or perform the task (of doing something) mechanically or without sincerity. **b.** to mimic the action (of something) by gesture. **10. in motion.** operational or functioning (often in **set in motion, set the wheels in motion**). ~vb. **11.** (when tr., may take a clause as object or an infinitive) to signal or direct (a person) by a movement or gesture. [C15: from L *mōtiō* a moving, from *movēre* to move] —**motionless** adj.

motion picture n. a U.S. and Canad. term for **film** (sense 1).

motivate (ˈməʊtɪˌveɪt) vb. (tr.) to give incentive to. —**moti'vation** n.

motivational research (ˌməʊtɪˈveɪʃənəl) n. the application of psychology to the study of consumer behaviour, esp. the planning of advertising and sales campaigns. Also called: **motivation research.**

motive (ˈməʊtɪv) n. **1.** the reason for a certain course of action, whether conscious or unconscious. **2.** a variant of **motif** (sense 2). ~adj. **3.** of or causing motion: a motive force. **4.** of or acting as a motive; motivating. ~vb. (tr.) **5.** to motivate. [C14: from OF *motif*, from LL *mōtivus* (adj.) moving, from L *mōtus*, p.p. of *movēre* to move] —**'motiveless** adj.

motive power n. **1.** any source of energy used to produce motion. **2.** the means of supplying power to an engine, vehicle, etc.

mot juste French. (mo ʒyst) n., pl. **mots justes** (mo ʒyst). the appropriate word or expression.

motley (ˈmɒtlɪ) adj. **1.** made up of elements of varying type, quality, etc. **2.** multicoloured. ~n. **3.** a motley collection. **4.** the particoloured attire of a jester. [C14: ?from *mot* speck]

moto (ˈməʊtəʊ) n. Music. movement. [It.]

motocross (ˈməʊtəˌkrɒs) n. **1.** a motorcycle race across rough ground. **2.** another name for **rallycross.** [C20: from MOTO(R) + CROSS(-COUNTRY)]

motor (ˈməʊtə) n. **1. a.** the engine, esp. an internal-combustion engine, of a vehicle. **b.** (as modifier): a motor scooter. **2.** Also called: **electric motor.** a machine that converts electrical energy into mechanical energy. **3.** any device that converts another form of energy into mechanical energy to produce motion. **4. a.** Chiefly Brit. a car. **b.** (as modifier): motor spares. **5.** producing or causing motion. **6.** Physiol. **a.** of or relating to nerves or neurons that carry impulses that cause muscles to contract. **b.** of or relating to movement or to muscles that induce movement. ~vb. **7.** (intr.) to travel by car. **8.** (tr.) Brit. to transport by car. **9.** (intr.) Inf. to move fast; make good progress. [C16: from L *mōtor* a mover, from *movēre* to move]

motorbicycle (ˈməʊtəˌbaɪsɪkəl) n. **1.** a motorcycle. **2.** a moped.

motorbike (ˈməʊtəˌbaɪk) n. a less formal name for **motorcycle.**

motorboat (ˈməʊtəˌbəʊt) n. any boat powered by a motor.

motorbus (ˈməʊtəˌbʌs) n. a bus driven by an internal-combustion engine.

motorcade (ˈməʊtəˌkeɪd) n. a parade of cars. [C20: from MOTOR + CAVALCADE]

motorcar (ˈməʊtəˌkɑː) n. **1.** a more formal word for **car.** **2.** a self-propelled electric railway car.

motorcycle (ˈməʊtəˌsaɪkəl) n. **1.** Also called: **motorbike.** a two-wheeled vehicle that is driven by a petrol engine. ~vb. (intr.) **2.** to ride on a motorcycle. —**'motor,cyclist** n.

motorist ('məutərɪst) *n.* a driver of a car.
motorize *or* **-ise** ('məutə,raɪz) *vb.* (*tr.*) **1.** to equip with a motor. **2.** to provide (military units) with motor vehicles. —,motori'zation *or* -i'sation *n.*
motorman ('məutəmən) *n., pl.* -men. **1.** the driver of an electric train. **2.** the operator of a motor.
motormouth ('məutə,mauθ) *n. Sl.* a garrulous person.
motor scooter *n.* a light motorcycle with small wheels and an enclosed engine. Often shortened to **scooter.**
motor vehicle *n.* a road vehicle driven esp. by an internal-combustion engine.
motorway ('məutə,weɪ) *n. Brit.* a main road for fast-moving traffic, having separate carriageways for vehicles travelling in opposite directions.
Motown ('məu,taun) *n.* music combining rhythm and blues and pop, or gospel rhythms and modern ballad harmony. [C20: from *Mo(tor) Town,* nickname for Detroit, Michigan, where it originated]
motte (mɒt) *n. History.* a mound on which a castle was erected. [C14: see MOAT]
MOT test *n.* (in Britain) a compulsory annual test of the roadworthiness of motor vehicles over a certain age.
mottle ('mɒtªl) *vb.* **1.** (*tr.*) to colour with streaks or blotches of different shades. ~*n.* **2.** a mottled appearance, as of the surface of marble. [C17: back formation from MOTLEY]
motto ('mɒtəu) *n., pl.* -toes *or* -tos. **1.** a short saying expressing the guiding maxim or ideal of a family, organization, etc., esp. when part of a coat of arms. **2.** a verse or maxim contained in a paper cracker. **3.** a quotation prefacing a book or chapter of a book. [C16: via It. from L *muttum* utterance]
moue *French.* (mu) *n.* a pouting look.
moufflon ('mu:flɒn) *n.* a wild short-fleeced mountain sheep of Corsica and Sardinia. [C18: via F from Romance *mufrone,* from LL *mufrō*]
mouillé ('mwi:eɪ) *adj. Phonetics.* palatalized, as in the sounds represented by Spanish *ll* or *ñ,* (pronounced as (ʎ) and (ɲ)), or French *ll* (representing a (j) sound). [C19: from F, p.p. of *mouiller* to moisten, from L *mollis* soft]
moujik ('mu:ʒɪk) *n.* a variant spelling of **muzhik.**
mould[1] *or U.S.* **mold** (məuld) *n.* **1.** a shaped cavity used to give a definite form to fluid or plastic material. **2.** a frame on which something may be constructed. **3.** something shaped in or made on a mould. **4.** shape, form, design, or pattern. **5.** specific nature, character, or type. ~*vb.* (*tr.*) **6.** to make in a mould. **7.** to shape or form, as by using a mould. **8.** to influence or direct: *to mould opinion.* **9.** to cling to: *the skirt moulds her figure.* **10.** *Metallurgy.* to make (a material) into a mould used in casting. [C13 (n.): from OF *modle,* from L *modulus* a small measure] —'mouldable *or U.S.* 'moldable *adj.* —'moulder *or U.S.* 'molder *n.*
mould[2] *or U.S.* **mold** (məuld) *n.* **1.** a coating or discoloration caused by various fungi that develop in a damp atmosphere on the surface of food, fabrics, etc. **2.** any of the fungi that cause this growth. ~*vb.* **3.** to become or cause to become covered with this growth. ~Also called: **mildew.** [C15: dialect (N English) *mowlde* mouldy, from p.p. of *moulen* to become mouldy, prob. from ON]
mould[3] *or U.S.* **mold** (məuld) *n.* loose soil, esp. when rich in organic matter. [OE *molde*]
mouldboard *or U.S.* **moldboard** ('məuld,bɔ:d) *n.* the curved blade of a plough, which turns over the furrow.
moulder *or U.S.* **molder** ('məuldə) *vb.* (often foll. by *away*) to crumble or cause to crumble, as through decay. [C16: verbal use of MOULD[3]]
moulding *or U.S.* **molding** ('məuldɪŋ) *n.* **1.** *Archit.* **a.** a shaped outline, esp. one used on cornices, etc. **b.** a shaped strip made of wood, stone, etc. **2.** something moulded.
mouldy *or U.S.* **moldy** ('məuldɪ) *adj.* -dier, -diest. **1.** covered with mould. **2.** stale or musty, esp. from age or lack of use. **3.** *Sl.* boring; dull. —'mouldiness *or U.S.* 'moldiness *n.*
Moulins (*French* mulɛ̃) *n.* a market town in central France, on the Allier River. Pop.: 25 548 (1982).
Moulmein *or* **Maulmain** (maulˈmeɪn) *n.* a port in S Burma, near the mouth of the Salween River: exports teak and rice. Pop.: 202 967 (1983).
moult *or U.S.* **molt** (məult) *vb.* **1.** (of birds, mammals, arthropods, etc.) to shed (feathers, hair, or cuticle). ~*n.* **2.** the periodic process of moulting. [C14 *mouten,* from

OE *mūtian,* as in *bimūtian* to exchange for, from L *mūtāre* to change] —'moulter *or U.S.* 'molter *n.*
mound (maund) *n.* **1.** a raised mass of earth, debris, etc. **2.** any heap or pile. **3.** a small natural hill. **4.** an artificial ridge of earth, stone, etc., as used for defence. ~*vb.* **5.** (often foll. by *up*) to gather into a mound; heap. **6.** (*tr.*) to cover or surround with a mound: *to mound a grave.* [C16: earthwork, ?from OE *mund* hand, hence defence]
mound-builder *n.* another name for **megapode.**
Mound Builder *n.* a member of a group of prehistoric inhabitants of the Mississippi region of the U.S., who built altar mounds, tumuli, etc.
mount[1] (maunt) *vb.* **1.** to go up (a hill, stairs, etc.); climb. **2.** to get up on (a horse, a platform, etc.). **3.** (*intr.;* often foll. by *up*) to increase; accumulate: *excitement mounted.* **4.** (*tr.*) to fix onto a backing, setting, or support: *to mount a photograph; to mount a slide.* **5.** (*tr.*) to provide with a horse for riding, or to place on a horse. **6.** (of male animals) to climb onto (a female animal) for copulation. **7.** (*tr.*) to prepare (a play, etc.) for production. **8.** (*tr.*) to plan and organize (a campaign, etc.). **9.** (*tr.*) to prepare (a skeleton, etc.) for exhibition as a specimen. **10.** (*tr.*) to place or carry (weapons) in such a position that they can be fired. **11. mount guard.** See **guard.** ~*n.* **12.** a backing, setting, or support onto which something is fixed. **13.** the act or manner of mounting. **14.** a horse for riding. **15.** a slide used in microscopy. [C16: from OF *munter,* from Vulgar L *montāre* (unattested) from L *mons* MOUNT[2]] —'mountable *adj.* —'mounter *n.*
mount[2] (maunt) *n.* a mountain or hill: used in literature and (when cap.) in proper names: *Mount Everest.* [OE *munt,* from L *mons* mountain, but infl. in ME by OF *mont*]
mountain ('mauntɪn) *n.* **1. a.** a natural upward projection of the earth's surface, higher and steeper than a hill. **b.** (*as modifier*): *mountain scenery.* **c.** (*in combination*): *a mountaintop.* **2.** a huge heap or mass: *a mountain of papers.* **3.** anything of great quantity or size. **4.** a surplus of a commodity, esp. in the European Economic Community: *a butter mountain.* [C13: from OF *montaigne,* ult. from L *montānus,* from *mons* mountain]
mountain ash *n.* **1.** any of various trees, such as the European mountain ash or rowan, having clusters of small white flowers and bright red berries. **2.** any of several Australian eucalyptus trees, such as *Eucalyptus regnans.*
mountain avens *n.* See **avens** (sense 2).
mountain bike *n.* a type of sturdy bicycle with up to 15 gears, straight handlebars, and heavy-duty tyres.
mountain cat *n.* any of various wild feline mammals, such as the bobcat, lynx, or puma.
mountaineer (,mauntɪˈnɪə) *n.* **1.** a person who climbs mountains. **2.** a person living in a mountainous area. ~*vb.* **3.** (*intr.*) to climb mountains. —,mountain'eering *n.*
mountain goat *n.* any wild goat inhabiting mountainous regions.
mountain laurel *n.* any of various ericaceous shrubs or trees of E North America having leathery poisonous leaves and clusters of pink or white flowers. Also called: **calico bush.**
mountain lion *n.* another name for **puma.**
mountainous ('mauntɪnəs) *adj.* **1.** of or relating to mountains: *a mountainous region.* **2.** like a mountain, esp. in size or impressiveness.
mountain sickness *n.* nausea, headache, and shortness of breath caused by climbing to high altitudes. Also called: **altitude sickness.**
Mountbatten (maunt'bæt³n) *n.* **Louis (Francis Albert Victor Nicholas),** 1st Earl Mountbatten of Burma. (1900 – 79), British naval commander; great-grandson of Queen Victoria. During World War II he was supreme allied commander in SE Asia (1943 – 46). He was the last viceroy of India (1947) and governor general (1947 – 48); killed by an IRA bomb.
Mount Desert Island *n.* an island off the coast of Maine: lakes and granite peaks. Area: 279 sq. km (108 sq. miles).
mountebank ('mauntɪ,bæŋk) *n.* **1.** (formerly) a person who sold quack medicines in public places. **2.** a charlatan; fake. ~*vb.* **3.** (*intr.*) to play the mountebank. [C16: from It. *montambanco* a climber on a bench, from *montare* to MOUNT[1] + *banco* BENCH] —,mounte'bankery *n.*
mounted ('mauntɪd) *adj.* **1.** riding horses: *mounted police.* **2.** provided with a support, backing, etc.

Mountie or **Mounty** ('maʊntɪ) n., pl. **Mounties.** Inf. a member of the Royal Canadian Mounted Police. [from MOUNTED]

mounting ('maʊntɪŋ) n. another word for **mount**¹(sense 12).

mounting-block n. a block of stone formerly used to aid a person when mounting a horse.

Mount Isa ('aɪzə) n. a city in NE Australia in NW Queensland: mining of copper and other minerals. Pop.: 24 190 (1986 est.).

Mountjoy ('maʊnt,dʒɔɪ) n. **Doug.** born 1942, Welsh snooker player.

mourn (mɔːn) vb. **1.** to feel or express sadness for the death or loss of (someone or something). **2.** (intr.) to observe the customs of mourning, as by wearing black. [OE murnan] — 'mourner n.

mournful ('mɔːnfʊl) adj. **1.** evoking grief; sorrowful. **2.** gloomy; sad. — 'mournfully adv. — 'mournfulness n.

mourning ('mɔːnɪŋ) n. **1.** the act or feelings of one who mourns; grief. **2.** the conventional symbols of grief, such as the wearing of black. **3.** the period of time during which a death is officially mourned. ~adj. **4.** of or relating to mourning. — 'mourningly adv.

mourning band n. a piece of black material, esp. an armband, worn to indicate mourning.

mourning dove n. a brown North American dove with a plaintive song.

mouse n. (maʊs), pl. **mice** (maɪs). **1.** any of numerous small long-tailed rodents that are similar to but smaller than rats. See also **fieldmouse, harvest mouse, house mouse. 2.** any of various related rodents, such as the jumping mouse. **3.** a quiet, timid, or cowardly person. **4.** Computers. a hand-held device used to control cursor movements and computing functions without keying. **5.** Sl. a black eye. ~vb. (maʊz). **6.** to stalk and catch (mice, etc.). **7.** (intr.) to go about stealthily. [OE mūs] — 'mouse,like adj.

mouser ('maʊzə, 'maʊsə) n. a cat or other animal that is used to catch mice.

mousetrap ('maʊs,træp) n. **1.** any trap for catching mice, esp. one with a spring-loaded metal bar that is released by the taking of the bait. **2.** Brit. inf. cheese of indifferent quality.

moussaka or **mousaka** (muː'sɑːkə) n. a dish originating in the Balkan States, consisting of meat, aubergines, and tomatoes, topped with cheese sauce. [C20: from Mod. Gk]

mousse (muːs) n. **1.** a light creamy dessert made with eggs, cream, fruit, etc., set with gelatin. **2.** a similar dish made from fish or meat. **3.** short for **styling mousse**. [C19: from F: froth]

mousseline (French muslin) n. **1.** a fine fabric made of rayon or silk. **2.** a type of fine glass. [C17: F: MUSLIN]

Moussorgsky (muː'sɔːgskɪ; Russian 'musərkskij) n. a variant spelling of (Modest Petrovich) **Mussorgsky**.

moustache or U.S. **mustache** (mə'stɑːʃ) n. **1.** the unshaved growth of hair on the upper lip. **2.** a similar growth of hair or bristles (in animals). **3.** a mark like a moustache. [C16: via F from It. mostaccio, ult. from Doric Gk mustax upper lip] — **mous'tached** or U.S. **mus'tached** adj.

moustache cup n. a cup with a partial cover to protect a drinker's moustache.

Mousterian (muː'stɪərɪən) n. **1.** a culture characterized by flint flake tools and associated with Neanderthal man, dating from before 70 000–32 000 B.C. ~adj. **2.** of or relating to this culture. [C20: from F moustérien, from archaeological finds of the same period in the cave of Le Moustier, Dordogne, France]

mousy or **mousey** ('maʊsɪ) adj. **mousier, mousiest. 1.** resembling a mouse, esp. in hair colour. **2.** shy or ineffectual. **3.** infested with mice. — 'mousily adv. — 'mousiness n.

mouth n. (maʊθ), pl. **mouths** (maʊðz). **1.** the opening through which many animals take in food and issue vocal sounds. **2.** the system of organs surrounding this opening, including the lips, tongue, teeth, etc. **3.** the visible part of the lips on the face. **4.** a person regarded as a consumer of food: four mouths to feed. **5.** a particular manner of speaking: a foul mouth. **6.** Inf. boastful, rude, or excessive talk: he is all mouth. **7.** the point where a river issues into a sea or lake. **8.** the opening of a container, such as a jar. **9.** the opening of a cave, tunnel, volcano, etc. **10.** that part of the inner lip of a horse on

which the bit acts. **11.** a pout; grimace. **12. down in** or **at the mouth.** in low spirits. ~vb. (maʊð). **13.** to speak or say (something) insincerely, esp. in public. **14.** (tr.) to form (words) with movements of the lips but without speaking. **15.** (tr.) to take (something) into the mouth or to move (something) around inside the mouth. **16.** (intr.; usually foll. by at) to make a grimace. [OE mūth] — 'mouther ('maʊðə) n.

mouthful ('maʊθ,fʊl) n., pl. **-fuls. 1.** as much as is held in the mouth at one time. **2.** a small quantity, as of food. **3.** a long word or phrase that is difficult to say. **4.** Brit. inf. an abusive response.

mouth organ n. another name for **harmonica**.

mouthpart ('maʊθ,pɑːt) n. any of the paired appendages in arthropods that surround the mouth and are specialized for feeding.

mouthpiece ('maʊθ,piːs) n. **1.** the part of a wind instrument into which the player blows. **2.** the part of a telephone receiver into which a person speaks. **3.** the part of a container forming its mouth. **4.** a person who acts as a spokesman, as for an organization. **5.** a publication expressing the official views of an organization.

mouthwash ('maʊθ,wɒʃ) n. a medicated solution for gargling and cleansing the mouth.

mouthy ('maʊðɪ) adj. **mouthier, mouthiest.** bombastic; excessively talkative.

mouton ('muːtɒn) n. sheepskin processed to resemble the fur of another animal, esp. beaver or seal. [from F: sheep]

movable or **moveable** ('muːvəbᵊl) adj. **1.** able to be moved; not fixed. **2.** (esp. of Easter) varying in date from year to year. **3.** (usually spelt **moveable**) Law. denoting or relating to personal property as opposed to realty. ~n. **4.** (often pl.) a movable article, esp. a piece of furniture. — ,mova'bility or 'movableness n. — 'movably adv.

move (muːv) vb. **1.** to go or take from one place to another; change in position. **2.** (usually intr.) to change (one's dwelling, place of business, etc.). **3.** to be or cause to be in motion; stir. **4.** (intr.) (of machines, etc.) to work or operate. **5.** (tr.) to cause (to do something); prompt. **6.** (intr.) to begin to act: move soon or we'll lose the order. **7.** (intr.) to associate oneself with a specified social circle: to move in exalted spheres. **8.** (intr.) to make progress. **9.** (tr.) to arouse affection, pity, or compassion in; touch. **10.** (in board games) to change the position of (a piece) or (of a piece) to change position. **11.** (intr.) (of merchandise) to be disposed of by being bought. **12.** (when tr., often takes a clause as object; when intr., often foll. by for) to suggest (a proposal) formally, as in debating or parliamentary procedure. **13.** (intr.; usually foll. by on or along) to go away or to another place; leave. **14.** to cause (the bowels) to evacuate or (of the bowels) to be evacuated. ~n. **15.** the act of moving; movement. **16.** one of a sequence of actions, usually part of a plan; manoeuvre. **17.** the act of moving one's residence, place of business, etc. **18.** (in board games) **a.** a player's turn to move his piece. **b.** a manoeuvre of a piece. **19. get a move on.** Inf. **a.** to get started. **b.** to hurry up. **20. on the move. a.** travelling from place to place. **b.** advancing; succeeding. **c.** very active; busy. [C13: from Anglo-F mover, from L movēre]

move in vb. (mainly adv.) **1.** (also prep.) Also (when prep.): **move into.** to occupy or take possession of (a new residence, place of business, etc.). **2.** (intr.; often foll. by on) Inf. to creep close (to), as in preparing to capture. **3.** (intr.; often foll. by on) Inf. to try to gain power or influence (over).

movement ('muːvmənt) n. **1. a.** the act, process, or result of moving. **b.** an instance of moving. **2.** the manner of moving. **3. a.** a group of people with a common ideology. **b.** the organized action of such a group. **4.** a trend or tendency. **5.** the driving and regulating mechanism of a watch or clock. **6.** (often pl.) a person's location and activities during a specific time. **7. a.** the evacuation of the bowels. **b.** the matter evacuated. **8.** Music. a principal self-contained section of a symphony, sonata, etc. **9.** tempo or pace, as in music or literature. **10.** Fine arts. the appearance of motion in painting, sculpture, etc. **11.** Prosody. the rhythmical structure of verse. **12.** a positional change by one or a number of military units. **13.** a change in the market price of a security or commodity.

mover ('muːvə) n. **1.** Inf. a person, business, idea, etc., that is advancing or progressing. **2.** a person or thing that moves. **3.** a person who moves a proposal, as in a debate.

4. *U.S. & Canad.* a removal firm or a person who works for one.

movie ('muːvɪ) *n.* **a.** an informal word for **film** (sense 1). **b.** (*as modifier*): *movie ticket.*

moving ('muːvɪŋ) *adj.* **1.** arousing or touching the emotions. **2.** changing or capable of changing position. **3.** causing motion. —'**movingly** *adv.*

moving staircase *or* **stairway** *n.* less common terms for **escalator** (sense 1).

mow (maʊ) *vb.* **mowing, mowed, mowed** *or* **mown. 1.** to cut down (grass, crops, etc.), with a hand implement or machine. **2.** (*tr.*) to cut the growing vegetation of (a field, lawn, etc.). [OE *māwan*] —'**mower** *n.*

mow down *vb.* (*tr., adv.*) to kill in large numbers, esp. by gunfire.

mown (maʊn) *vb.* the past participle of **mow.**

Mozambique (,maʊzəm'biːk) *n.* a republic in SE Africa: colonized by the Portuguese from 1505 onwards and a slave-trade centre until 1878; made an overseas province of Portugal in 1951; became an independent republic in 1975. Currency: escudo. Capital: Maputo. Pop.: 14 543 000 (1987 est.). Area: 771 124 sq. km (297 846 sq. miles). Portuguese name: **Moçambique.** Also called (until 1975): **Portuguese East Africa.**

Mozambique Channel *n.* a strait between Mozambique and Madagascar. Length: about 1600 km (1000 miles). Width: 400 km (250 miles).

Mozart ('maʊtsɑːt) *n.* **Wolfgang Amadeus** ('vɔlfgaŋ ama'deːʊs). 1756–91, Austrian composer. A child prodigy and prolific genius, his works include operas, such as *The Marriage of Figaro* (1786), *Don Giovanni* (1787), and *The Magic Flute* (1791), symphonies, concertos for piano, violin, clarinet, and French horn, string quartets and quintets, sonatas, songs, and Masses, such as the unfinished *Requiem* (1791). —**Mo'zartean** *or* **Mo'zartian** *adj.*

mozzarella (,mɒtsə'rɛlə) *n.* a moist white Italian curd cheese made originally from buffalo milk. [from It., dim. of *mozza* a type of cheese, from *mozzare* to cut off]

mp 1. *abbrev. for* melting point. **2.** *Music. symbol for* mezzo piano. [It.: moderately soft]

MP *abbrev. for:* **1.** (in Britain, Canada, etc.) Member of Parliament. **2.** (in Britain) Metropolitan Police. **3.** Military Police. **4.** Mounted Police.

mpg *abbrev. for* miles per gallon.

mph *abbrev. for* miles per hour.

MPhil *or* **MPh** *abbrev. for* Master of Philosophy.

MPP (in Canada) *abbrev. for* Member of Provincial Parliament.

Mr ('mɪstə) *n., pl.* **Messrs.** a title used before a man's name or before some office that he holds: *Mr Jones; Mr President.* [C17: abbrev. of MISTER]

MR *abbrev. for:* **1.** (in Britain) Master of the Rolls. **2.** motivation(al) research.

MRC (in Britain) *abbrev. for* Medical Research Council.

m-RNA *abbrev. for* messenger RNA.

Mrs ('mɪsɪz) *n., pl.* **Mrs** *or* **Mesdames.** a title used before the name or names of a married woman. [C17: orig. abbrev. of MISTRESS]

Ms (mɪz, məz) *n.* a title substituted for **Mrs** or **Miss** to avoid making a distinction between married and unmarried women.

▷**Usage.** *Ms* as a form of address, while not universally liked, has gained wide acceptance in recent years particularly in written English. It fulfils the need for a title corresponding to *Mr* in contexts where it is thought desirable to avoid differentiating between married and unmarried women or where such distinction is irrelevant. It may also be used as a form of address on letters if it is not known whether the recipient is *Miss* or *Mrs.*

MS *abbrev. for:* **1.** Master of Surgery. **2.** (on gravestones, etc.) memoriae sacrum. [L: sacred to the memory of] **3.** multiple sclerosis.

MS. *or* **ms.** *pl.* **MSS.** *or* **mss.** *abbrev. for* manuscript.

MSc *abbrev. for* Master of Science.

MSC (in Britain) *abbrev. for* Manpower Services Commission.

MSG *abbrev. for* monosodium glutamate.

Msgr *abbrev. for* Monsignor.

MST *abbrev. for* Mountain Standard Time.

Mt *or* **mt** *abbrev. for:* **1.** mount: *Mt Everest.* **2.** Also: **mtn.** mountain.

MTech *abbrev. for* Master of Technology.

mtg *abbrev. for:* **1.** meeting. **2.** Also: **mtge.** mortgage.

mu (mjuː) *n.* the 12th letter in the Greek alphabet (M, μ).

Mubarak (mʊ'bɑːrək) *n.* (**Muhammad**) **Hosni** ('hʊsnɪ). born 1929, Egyptian statesman; president of Egypt from 1981.

much (mʌtʃ) *determiner.* **1. a.** (*usually used with a negative*) a great quantity or degree of: *there isn't much honey left.* **b.** (*as pron.*): *much has been learned from this.* **2. a bit much.** *Inf.* rather excessive. **3. make much of. a.** (*used with a negative*) to make sense of: *he couldn't make much of her babble.* **b.** to give importance to: *she made much of this fact.* **c.** to pay flattering attention to: *the reporters made much of the film star.* **4. not much of.** not to any appreciable degree or extent: *he's not much of an actor really.* **5. not up to much.** *Inf.* of a low standard: *this beer is not up to much.* ~*adv.* **6.** considerably: *they're much better now.* **7.** practically; nearly (esp. in **much the same**). **8.** (*usually used with a negative*) often; a great deal: *it doesn't happen much in this country.* **9. (as) much as.** even though; although: *much as I'd like to, I can't come.* ~See also **more, most.** [OE *mycel*]

muchness ('mʌtʃnɪs) *n.* **1.** *Arch. or inf.* magnitude. **2. much of a muchness.** *Brit.* very similar.

mucilage ('mjuːsɪlɪdʒ) *n.* **1.** a sticky preparation, such as gum or glue, used as an adhesive. **2.** a complex glutinous carbohydrate secreted by certain plants. [C14: via OLD from LL *mūcilāgo* mouldy juice, from L, from *mucēre* to be mouldy] —**mucilaginous** (,mjuːsɪ'lædʒɪnəs) *adj.*

muck (mʌk) *n.* **1.** farmyard dung or decaying vegetable matter. **2.** an organic soil rich in humus and used as a fertilizer. **3.** dirt or filth. **4.** *Sl., chiefly Brit.* rubbish. **5. make a muck of.** *Sl., chiefly Brit.* to ruin or spoil. ~*vb.* (*tr.*) **6.** to spread manure upon (fields, etc.). **7.** to soil or pollute. **8.** (usually foll. by *up*) *Brit. sl.* to ruin or spoil. **9.** (often foll. by *out*) to clear muck from. [C13: prob. from ON] —'**mucky** *adj.*

muck about *vb. Brit. sl.* **1.** (*intr.*) to waste time; misbehave. **2.** (when *intr.*, foll. by *with*) to interfere (with), annoy, or waste the time (of).

mucker ('mʌkə) *n. Brit. sl.* **a.** a friend; mate. **b.** a coarse person. —'**muckerish** *adj.*

muck in *vb.* (*intr., adv.*) *Brit. sl.* to share duties, work, etc. (with other people).

muckrake ('mʌk,reɪk) *vb.* (*intr.*) to seek out and expose scandal, esp. concerning public figures. —'**muck,raker** *n.* —'**muck,raking** *n.*

mucksweat ('mʌk,swɛt) *n. Brit. inf.* profuse sweat or a state of profuse sweating.

mucous ('mjuːkəs) *adj.* of, resembling, or secreting mucus. [C17: from L *mūcōsus* slimy, from MUCUS] —**mucosity** (mjuːˈkɒsɪtɪ) *n.*

mucous membrane *n.* a mucus-secreting membrane that lines body cavities or passages that are open to the external environment.

mucus ('mjuːkəs) *n.* the slimy protective secretion of the mucous membranes. [C17: from L: nasal secretions; cf. *mungere* to blow the nose]

mud (mʌd) *n.* **1.** a fine-grained soft wet deposit that occurs on the ground after rain, at the bottom of ponds, etc. **2.** *Inf.* slander or defamation. **3. clear as mud.** *Inf.* not at all clear. **4. here's mud in your eye.** *Inf.* a humorous drinking toast. **5. (someone's) name is mud.** *Inf.* (someone) is disgraced. **6. throw** (*or* **sling**) **mud at.** *Inf.* slander; vilify. ~*vb.* **mudding, mudded. 7.** (*tr.*) to soil or cover with mud. [C14: prob. from MLow G *mudde*]

mud bath *n.* **1.** a medicinal bath in heated mud. **2.** a dirty or muddy occasion, state, etc.

mudbrick ('mʌd,brɪk) *n.* a brick made with mud.

muddle ('mʌd'l) *vb.* (*tr.*) **1.** (often foll. by *up*) to mix up (objects, items, etc.). **2.** to confuse. **3.** *U.S.* to mix or stir (alcoholic drinks, etc.). ~*n.* **4.** a state of physical or mental confusion. [C16: ?from MDu. *moddelen* to make muddy] —'**muddled** *adj.* —'**muddler** *n.* —'**muddling** *adj., n.*

muddleheaded (,mʌd'l'hɛdɪd) *adj.* mentally confused or vague. —,**muddle'headedness** *n.*

muddle through *vb.* (*intr., adv.*) *Chiefly Brit.* to succeed in spite of lack of organization.

muddy ('mʌdɪ) *adj.* **-dier, -diest. 1.** covered or filled with mud. **2.** not clear or bright: *muddy colours.* **3.** cloudy: *a muddy liquid.* **4.** (esp. of thoughts) confused or vague. ~*vb.* **-dying, -died. 5.** to become or cause to become muddy. —'**muddily** *adv.* —'**muddiness** *n.*

mudfish ('mʌd,fɪʃ) *n., pl.* **-fish** *or* **-fishes.** any of various fishes, such as the bowfin, that live at the muddy bottoms of rivers, lakes, etc.

mud flat *n.* a tract of low muddy land that is covered at high tide and exposed at low tide.

mudguard ('mʌd,gɑːd) *n.* a curved part of a motorcycle, bicycle, etc., attached above the wheels to reduce the amount of water or mud thrown up by them. U.S. and Canad. name: **fender.**

mud hen *n.* any of various birds that frequent marshes, esp. the coots, rails, etc.

mudlark ('mʌd,lɑːk) *n.* **1.** (formerly) a person who made a living by picking up odds and ends in the mud of tidal rivers. **2.** *Sl., now rare.* a street urchin. **3.** *Austral. sl.* a racehorse that runs well on a wet or muddy course.

mud map *n. Austral.* **1.** a rough map drawn on the ground with a stick. **2.** any rough sketch map.

mudpack ('mʌd,pæk) *n.* a cosmetic astringent paste containing fuller's earth.

mud puppy *n.* an aquatic North American salamander having persistent larval features.

mudskipper ('mʌd,skɪpə) *n.* any of various gobies that occur in tropical coastal regions of Africa and Asia and can move on land by means of their strong pectoral fins.

mudslinging ('mʌd,slɪŋɪŋ) *n.* casting malicious slurs on an opponent, esp. in politics. —'**mud,slinger** *n.*

mudstone ('mʌd,stəʊn) *n.* a dark grey clay rock similar to shale.

mud turtle *n.* any of various small turtles that inhabit muddy rivers in North and Central America.

muesli ('mjuːzlɪ) *n.* a mixture of rolled oats, nuts, fruit, etc., eaten with milk. [Swiss G, from G *Mus* mush, purée + -*li*, dim. suffix]

muezzin (muːˈɛzɪn) *n. Islam.* the official of a mosque who calls the faithful to prayer from the minaret. [C16: from Ar. *mu'adhdhin*]

muff[1] (mʌf) *n.* an open-ended cylinder of fur or cloth into which the hands are placed for warmth. [C16: prob. from Du. *mof*, ult. from F *mouffle* MUFFLE[1]]

muff[2] (mʌf) *vb.* **1.** to perform (an action) awkwardly. **2.** (*tr.*) to bungle (a shot, catch, etc.). ~*n.* **3.** any unskilful play, esp. a dropped catch. **4.** any bungled action. **5.** a bungler. [C19: from ?]

muffin ('mʌfɪn) *n.* **1.** *Brit.* a thick round baked yeast roll, usually toasted and served with butter. **2.** *U.S. & Canad.* a small cup-shaped sweet bread roll, usually eaten hot with butter. [C18: ?from Low G *muffen* cakes]

muffin man *n. Brit.* (formerly) an itinerant seller of muffins.

muffle[1] ('mʌfⁱl) *vb.* (*tr.*) **1.** (often foll. by *up*) to wrap up (the head) in a scarf, cloak, etc., esp. for warmth. **2.** to deaden (a sound or noise), esp. by wrapping. **3.** to prevent (the expression of something) by (someone). ~*n.* **4.** something that muffles. **5.** a kiln with an inner chamber for firing porcelain, enamel, etc. [C15: prob. from OF; cf. OF *moufle* mitten, *emmoufle* wrapped up]

muffle[2] ('mʌfⁱl) *n.* the fleshy hairless part of the upper lip and nose in ruminants and some rodents. [C17: from F *mufle*, from ?]

muffler ('mʌflə) *n.* **1.** a thick scarf, collar, etc. **2.** the U.S. and Canad. name for **silencer** (sense 1).

mufti ('mʌftɪ) *n.* civilian dress, esp. as worn by a person who normally wears a military uniform. [C19: ?from MUFTI]

Mufti ('mʌftɪ) *n., pl.* **-tis.** a Muslim legal expert and adviser on the law of the Koran. [C16: from Ar. *muftī*, from *aftā* to give a (legal) decision]

Mufulira (,muːfuːˈlɪərə) *n.* a mining town in the Copper Belt of Zambia. Pop.: 187 000 (1980 est.).

mug[1] (mʌg) *n.* **1.** a drinking vessel with a handle, usually cylindrical and made of earthenware. **2.** Also called: **mugful.** the quantity held by a mug or its contents. [C16: prob. of Scand. origin]

mug[2] (mʌg) *n.* **1.** *Sl.* a person's face or mouth. **2.** *Sl.* a gullible person, esp. one who is swindled easily. **3.** a **mug's game.** a worthless activity. ~*vb.* **mugging, mugged. 4.** (*tr.*) *Inf.* to attack or rob (someone) violently. [C18: ?from MUG[1], since drinking vessels were sometimes modelled into the likeness of a face] —'**mugger** *n.*

Mugabe (muˈgɑːbɪ) *n.* **Robert.** born 1925, Zimbabwean politician; leader of one wing of the Patriotic Front and the Zanu party; prime minister (1980–87); president from 1987.

muggins ('mʌgɪnz) *n.* (*functioning as sing.*) **1.** *Brit. sl.* **a.** a simpleton. **b.** a title used humorously to refer to oneself. **2.** a card game. [C19: prob. from the surname *Muggins*]

muggy ('mʌgɪ) *adj.* **-gier, -giest.** (of weather, air, etc.) unpleasantly warm and humid. [C18: dialect *mug* drizzle, prob. of Scand. origin] —'**mugginess** *n.*

mug shot *n. Inf.* a photograph of a person's face, esp. one resembling a police-file picture.

mug up *vb.* (*adv.*) *Brit. sl.* to study (a subject) hard, esp. for an exam. [C19: from ?]

Muhammad (muˈhæməd) *n.* a variant of **Mohammed.**

Muhammad Ali *or* **Mohammad Ali** ('ɑːlɪ, ɑːˈliː, 'ælɪ) *n.* original name *Cassius* (*Marcellus*) *Clay.* born 1942, U.S. boxer, who was world heavyweight champion three times (1964–67; 1974–78; 1978).

Muhammadan *or* **Muhammedan** (muˈhæmədⁿn) *n., adj.* another word (not in Muslim use) for **Muslim.**

Mühlhausen (myːlˈhauzən) *n.* the German name for **Mulhouse.**

Muir (mjʊə) *n.* **Edwin.** 1887–1959, Scottish novelist, poet, and critic.

Muir Glacier *n.* a glacier in SE Alaska, in the St. Elias Mountains, flowing southeast from Mount Fairweather. Area: about 900 sq. km (350 sq. miles).

mujaheddin *or* **mujahedeen** (,muːdʒəhəˈdiːn) *pl. n.* (preceded by *the; sometimes cap.*) (in Afghanistan and Iran) fundamentalist Muslim guerrillas. [C20: from Ar. *mujāhidīn* fighters, ult. from JIHAD]

Mukden ('mʊkdən) *n.* a former name of **Shenyang.**

mukluk ('mʌklʌk) *n.* a soft boot, usually of sealskin, worn by Eskimos. [from Eskimo *muklok* large seal]

mulatto (mjuːˈlætəʊ) *n., pl.* **-tos** *or* **-toes. 1.** a person having one Negro and one White parent. ~*adj.* **2.** of a light brown colour; tawny. [C16: from Sp. *mulato* young mule, var. of *mulo* MULE[1]]

mulberry ('mʌlbərɪ, -brɪ) *n., pl.* **-ries. 1.** a tree having edible blackberry-like fruit, such as the white mulberry, the leaves of which are used to feed silkworms. **2.** the fruit of any of these trees. **3.** any of several similar or related trees. **4. a.** a dark purple colour. **b.** (*as adj.*): *a mulberry dress.* [C14: from L *mōrum*, from Gk *moron*; rel. to OE *mōrberie*]

mulch (mʌltʃ) *n.* **1.** half-rotten vegetable matter, peat, etc., used to prevent soil erosion or enrich the soil. ~*vb.* **2.** (*tr.*) to cover (the surface of land) with mulch. [C17: from obs. *mulch* soft; rel. to OE *mylisc* mellow]

Mulciber ('mʌlsɪbə) *n.* another name for **Vulcan**[1].

mulct (mʌlkt) *vb.* (*tr.*) **1.** to cheat or defraud. **2.** to fine (a person). ~*n.* **3.** a fine or penalty. [C15: via F from L *multa* a fine]

Muldoon (mʌlˈduːn) *n.* **Robert David.** born 1921, New Zealand statesman; prime minister of New Zealand (1975–84).

mule[1] (mjuːl) *n.* **1.** the sterile offspring of a male donkey and a female horse, used as a beast of burden. **2.** any hybrid animal: *a mule canary.* **3.** Also called: **spinning mule.** a machine that spins cotton into yarn and winds the yarn on spindles. **4.** *Inf.* an obstinate or stubborn person. [C13: from OF *mul*, from L *mūlus* ass, mule]

mule[2] (mjuːl) *n.* a backless shoe or slipper. [C16: from OF from L *mulleus* a magistrate's shoe]

muleta (mjuːˈlɛtə) *n.* the small cape attached to a stick used by the matador during a bullfight. [Sp.: small mule, crutch, from *mula* MULE[1]]

muleteer (,mjuːlɪˈtɪə) *n.* a person who drives mules.

mulga ('mʌlgə) *n. Austral.* **1.** any of various Australian acacia shrubs. **2.** scrub comprised of a dense growth of acacia. **3.** *Inf.* the outback; bush. [from Abor.]

Mulhacén (*Spanish* mulaˈθen) *n.* a mountain in S Spain, in the Sierra Nevada: the highest peak in Spain. Height: 3478 m (11 410 ft.).

Mülheim an der Ruhr (*German* 'myːlhaim an der 'ruːr) *or* **Mülheim** *n.* an industrial city in W West Germany, in North Rhine-Westphalia on the River Ruhr: river port. Pop.: 171 000 (1986).

Mulhouse (*French* mylyz) *n.* a city in E France, on the Rhône–Rhine canal: under German rule (1871–1918);

textiles. Pop.: 116 517 (1983 est.). German name: **Mühlhausen.**

muliebrity (ˌmjuːlɪˈɛbrɪtɪ) n. **1.** the condition of being a woman. **2.** femininity. [C16: via LL from L *muliēbris* womanly, from *mulier* woman]

mulish (ˈmjuːlɪʃ) adj. stubborn; obstinate. —ˈ**mulishly** adv. —ˈ**mulishness** n.

mull¹ (mʌl) vb. (tr.) (often foll. by *over*) to study or ponder. [C19: prob. from MUDDLE]

mull² (mʌl) vb. (tr.) to heat (wine, ale, etc.) with sugar and spices. [C17: from ?] —**mulled** adj.

mull³ (mʌl) n. a light muslin fabric of soft texture. [C18: earlier *mulmull*, from Hindi *malmal*]

mull⁴ (mʌl) n. Scot. a promontory. [C14: rel. to Gaelic *maol*, Icelandic *múli*]

Mull (mʌl) n. a mountainous island off the west coast of Scotland, in the Inner Hebrides, separated from the mainland by the **Sound of Mull.** Chief town: Tobermory. Pop.: 2605 (1981). Area: 909 sq. km (351 sq. miles).

mullah or **mulla** (ˈmʌlə, ˈmʊlə) n. (formerly) a Muslim scholar, teacher, or religious leader: also used as a title of respect. [C17: from Turkish *molla*, Persian & Hindi *mulla*, from Ar. *mawlā* master]

mullein (ˈmʌlɪn) n. any of various Mediterranean herbaceous plants such as the common mullein or Aaron's rod, typically having tall spikes of yellow flowers and broad hairy leaves. [C15: from OF *moleine*, prob. from OF *mol* soft, from L *mollis*]

muller (ˈmʌlə) n. a flat heavy implement of stone or iron used to grind material against a slab of stone, etc. [C15: prob. from *mullen* to grind to powder]

Muller (ˈmʌlə) n. **Hermann Joseph.** 1890–1967, U.S. geneticist, noted for his work on the transmutation of genes by x-rays: Nobel prize for physiology or medicine 1946.

Müller (German ˈmylər) n. **1. Friedrich Max** (ˈfriːdrɪç maks). 1823–1900, British Sanskrit scholar born in Germany. **2. Johann** (joˈhan). See **Regiomontanus. 3. Johannes Peter** (joˈhanəs ˈpeːtər). 1801–58, German physiologist, anatomist, and experimental psychologist. **4. Paul Hermann** (paul ˈhɛrman). 1899–1965, Swiss chemist. He synthesized DDT (1939) and discovered its use as an insecticide: Nobel prize for physiology or medicine 1948.

mullet (ˈmʌlɪt) n. any of various teleost food fishes such as the grey mullet or red mullet. [C15: via OF from L *mullus*, from Gk *mullos*]

mulligatawny (ˌmʌlɪɡəˈtɔːnɪ) n. a curry-flavoured soup of Anglo-Indian origin, made with meat stock. [C18: from Tamil *milakutanni*, from *milaku* pepper + *tanni* water]

Mulliken (ˈmʌlɪkən) n. **Robert Sanderson.** 1896–1986, U.S. physicist and chemist, who won the Nobel prize for chemistry (1966) for his work on chemical bonding and the electronic structure of molecules.

mullion (ˈmʌlɪən) n. **1.** a vertical member between the casements or panes of a window. ~vb. **2.** (tr.) to furnish (a window, screen, etc.) with mullions. [C16: var. of ME *munial*, from OF *moinel*, from ?]

mullock (ˈmʌlək) n. Austral. **1.** waste material from a mine. **2. poke mullock at.** Inf. to ridicule. [C14: rel. to OE *myl* dust, ON *mylja* to crush]

mulloway (ˈmʌləˌweɪ) n. a large Australian marine food fish. [C19: from ?]

Mulroney (mʌlˈrəʊnɪ) n. **Brian.** born 1939, Canadian statesman; Conservative prime minister from 1984.

Multan (ˌmʊlˈtɑːn) n. a city in central Pakistan, near the Chenab River. Pop.: 730 000 (1981).

multangular (mʌlˈtæŋɡjʊlə) or **multiangular** adj. having many angles.

multi- combining form. **1.** many or much: *multimillion*. **2.** more than one: *multistorey*. [from L *multus* much, many]

multifactorial (ˌmʌltɪfækˈtɔːrɪəl) adj. having many separate factors, causes, components, etc.: *multifactorial disease; multifactorial inheritance.*

multifarious (ˌmʌltɪˈfɛərɪəs) adj. having many parts of great variety. [C16: from LL *multifārius* manifold, from L *multifāriam* on many sides] —ˌ**multiˈfariously** adv. —ˌ**multiˈfariousness** n.

multiflora rose (ˌmʌltɪˈflɔːrə) n. an Asian climbing shrubby rose having clusters of small fragrant flowers.

multiform (ˈmʌltɪˌfɔːm) adj. having many forms. —ˌ**multiˈformity** n.

multigym (ˈmʌltɪˌdʒɪm) n. an exercise apparatus incorporating a variety of weights, used for toning the muscles.

multilateral (ˌmʌltɪˈlætərəl, -ˈlætrəl) adj. **1.** of or involving more than two nations or parties: *a multilateral pact.* **2.** having many sides. —ˌ**multiˈlaterally** adv.

multilingual (ˌmʌltɪˈlɪŋɡwəl) adj. **1.** able to speak more than two languages. **2.** written or expressed in more than two languages.

multimedia (ˌmʌltɪˈmiːdɪə) pl. n. the combined use of media such as television, slides, etc.

multimillionaire (ˌmʌltɪˌmɪljəˈnɛə) n. a person with a fortune of several million pounds, dollars, etc.

multinational (ˌmʌltɪˈnæʃənˀl) adj. **1.** (of a large business company) operating in several countries. ~n. **2.** such a company.

multiparous (mʌlˈtɪpərəs) adj. (of certain species of mammal) producing many offspring at one birth. [C17: from NL *multiparus*]

multipartite (ˌmʌltɪˈpɑːtaɪt) adj. **1.** divided into many parts or sections. **2.** Government. a less common word for **multilateral.**

multiple (ˈmʌltɪpˀl) adj. **1.** having or involving more than one part, individual, etc. **2.** Electronics, U.S. & Canad. (of a circuit) having a number of conductors in parallel. ~n. **3.** the product of a given number or polynomial and any other one: *6 is a multiple of 2.* **4.** short for **multiple store.** [C17: via F from LL *multiplus*, from L MULTIPLEX] —ˈ**multiply** adv.

multiple-choice adj. having a number of possible given answers out of which the correct one must be chosen.

multiple personality n. Psychiatry. a mental disorder in which an individual's personality appears to have become separated into two or more distinct personalities. Nontechnical name: **split personality.**

multiple sclerosis n. a chronic progressive disease of the central nervous system, resulting in speech and visual disorders, tremor, muscular incoordination, partial paralysis, etc.

multiple store n. one of several retail enterprises under the same ownership and management. Also called: **multiple shop.**

multiplex (ˈmʌltɪˌplɛks) n. **1.** Telecomm. **a.** the use of a common communications channel for sending two or more messages or signals. **b.** (as modifier): *a multiplex transmitter.* ~adj. **2.** a less common word for **multiple.** ~vb. **3.** to send (messages or signals) or (of messages and signals) to be sent by multiplex. [C16: from L: having many folds, from MULTI- + *plicāre* to fold]

multiplicand (ˌmʌltɪplɪˈkænd) n. a number to be multiplied by another number, the **multiplier.** [C16: from L *multiplicandus*, gerund of *multiplicāre* to MULTIPLY]

multiplication (ˌmʌltɪplɪˈkeɪʃən) n. **1.** a mathematical operation, the inverse of division, in which the product of two or more numbers or quantities is calculated. Usually written $a \times b$, $a.b$, ab. **2.** the act of multiplying or state of being multiplied. **3.** the act or process in animals, plants, or people, of reproducing or breeding.

multiplication sign n. the symbol $\times$, placed between numbers to be multiplied.

multiplication table n. one of a group of tables giving the results of multiplying two numbers together.

multiplicity (ˌmʌltɪˈplɪsɪtɪ) n., pl. **-ties. 1.** a large number or great variety. **2.** the state of being multiple.

multiplier (ˈmʌltɪˌplaɪə) n. **1.** a person or thing that multiplies. **2.** the number by which another number, the **multiplicand,** is multiplied. **3.** Physics. any instrument, such as a photomultiplier, for increasing an effect. **4.** Econ. the ratio of the total change in income (resulting from successive rounds of spending) to an initial autonomous change in expenditure.

multiply (ˈmʌltɪˌplaɪ) vb. **-plying, -plied. 1.** to increase or cause to increase in number, quantity, or degree. **2.** (tr.) to combine (two numbers or quantities) by multiplication. **3.** (intr.) to increase in number by reproduction.

,**multi'axial** adj.
,**multi'cellular** adj.
'**multi,coloured** adj.

,**multi'cultural** adj.
,**multidi'mensional** adj.

,**multidi'rectional** adj.
,**multi'faceted** adj.

,**multi'foliate** adj.
'**multi,hull** n.

[C13: from OF *multiplier*, from L *multiplicāre* to multiply, from *multus* much, many + *plicāre* to fold] — **'multi,pliable** *or* **multiplicable** ('mʌltɪ,plɪkəb³l) *adj.*

multistage ('mʌltɪ,steɪdʒ) *adj.* **1.** (of a rocket or missile) having several stages, each of which can be jettisoned after it has burnt out. **2.** (of a turbine, compressor, or supercharger) having more than one rotor. **3.** (of any process or device) having more than one stage.

multistorey (,mʌltɪ'stɔːrɪ) *adj.* **1.** (of a building) having many storeys. ~*n.* **2.** a multistorey car park.

multitrack ('mʌltɪ,træk) *adj.* (in sound recording) using tape containing two or more tracks, usually four to twenty-four.

multitude ('mʌltɪ,tjuːd) *n.* **1.** a large gathering of people. **2. the.** the common people. **3.** a large number. **4.** the state or quality of being numerous. [C14: via OF from L *multitūdō*]

multitudinous (,mʌltɪ'tjuːdɪnəs) *adj.* **1.** very numerous. **2.** *Rare.* great in extent, variety, etc. **3.** *Poetic.* crowded. — ,**multi'tudinously** *adv.* — ,**multi'tudinousness** *n.*

multi-user *adj.* (of a computer) capable of being used by several people at once.

multivalent (,mʌltɪ'veɪlənt) *adj.* another word for **polyvalent.** — ,**multi'valency** *n.*

mum[1] (mʌm) *n.* **1.** *Chiefly Brit.* an informal word for **mother. 2.** *Austral. & N.Z.* an informal word for **wife** (sense 1). [C19: a child's word]

mum[2] (mʌm) *adj.* **1.** keeping information, etc., to oneself; silent. ~*n.* **2. mum's the word.** (*interj.*) silence or secrecy is to be observed. [C14: suggestive of closed lips]

mum[3] (mʌm) *vb.* **mumming, mummed.** (*intr.*) to act in a mummer's play. [C16: verbal use of MUM[2]]

mumble ('mʌmb³l) *vb.* **1.** to utter indistinctly, as with the mouth partly closed. **2.** *Rare.* to chew (food) ineffectually. ~*n.* **3.** an indistinct or low utterance or sound. [C14 *momelen*, from MUM[2]] — **'mumbler** *n.* — **'mumbling** *adj.* — **'mumblingly** *adv.*

mumbo jumbo ('mʌmbəʊ) *n., pl.* **mumbo jumbos. 1.** foolish religious reverence, ritual, or incantation. **2.** meaningless or unnecessarily complicated language. **3.** an object of superstitious awe or reverence. [C18: prob. from W African *mama dyumbo*, name of a tribal god]

mu meson (mjuː) *n.* a former name for **muon.**

Mumford ('mʌmfəd) *n.* **Lewis.** born 1895, U.S. sociologist, whose works are chiefly concerned with the relationship between man and his environment. They include *The City in History* (1962) and *Roots of Contemporary Architecture* (1972).

mummer ('mʌmə) *n.* **1.** one of a group of masked performers in a folk play or mime. **2.** *Humorous or derog.* an actor. [C15: from OF *momeur*, from *momer* to mime]

mummery ('mʌmərɪ) *n., pl.* **-meries. 1.** a performance by mummers. **2.** hypocritical or ostentatious ceremony.

mummify ('mʌmɪ,faɪ) *vb.* **-fying, -fied. 1.** (*tr.*) to preserve (a body) as a mummy. **2.** (*intr.*) to dry up; shrivel. — ,**mummifi'cation** *n.*

mummy[1] ('mʌmɪ) *n., pl.* **-mies. 1.** an embalmed or preserved body, esp. as prepared for burial in ancient Egypt. **2.** a mass of pulp. **3.** a dark brown pigment. [C14: from OF *momie*, from Med. L, from Ar.: asphalt, from Persian *mūm* wax]

mummy[2] ('mʌmɪ) *n., pl.* **-mies.** *Chiefly Brit.* a child's word for **mother.** [C19: var. of MUM[1]]

mumps (mʌmps) *n.* (*functioning as sing. or pl.*) **1.** an acute contagious viral disease of the parotid salivary glands, characterized by swelling of the affected parts, fever, and pain beneath the ear. **2.** sulks. [C16: from *mump* to grimace] — **'mumpish** *adj.*

mumsy ('mʌmzɪ) *adj.* **-sier, -siest.** homely or drab. — **'mumsiness** *n.*

mun. *abbrev. for* municipal.

munch (mʌntʃ) *vb.* to chew (food) steadily, esp. with a crunching noise. [C14 *monche*, imit.]

Munch (mʊŋk) *n.* **Edvard** ('ɛdvard). 1863–1944, Norwegian painter and engraver, whose works, often on the theme of death, include *The Cry* (1893); a major influence on the expressionists, esp. on *die Brücke*.

München ('mʏnçən) *n.* the German name for **Munich.**

München-Gladbach (mʏnçən'glatbax) *n.* the former name of **Mönchen-Gladbach.**

mundane (mʌn'deɪn, 'mʌndeɪn) *adj.* **1.** everyday, ordinary, or banal. **2.** relating to the world or worldly matters. [C15: from F *mondain*, via LL, from L *mundus* world] — **mun'danely** *adv.* — **mun'daneness** *n.*

mung bean (mʌŋ) *n.* **1.** an E Asian bean plant grown for forage and as the source of bean sprouts for cookery. **2.** the seed of this plant.

Munich ('mjuːnɪk) *n.* a city in SW West Germany, capital of the state of Bavaria, on the Isar River: the third largest city in West Germany; became capital of Bavaria in 1508; headquarters of the Nazi movement in the 1920s; a major financial, commercial, and manufacturing centre. Pop.: 1 269 400 (1986). German name: **München.**

municipal (mjuː'nɪsɪp³l) *adj.* of or relating to a town, city, or borough or its local government. [C16: from L *mūnicipium* a free town, from *mūniceps* citizen, from *mūnia* responsibilities + *capere* to take] — **mu'nicipally** *adv.*

municipality (mjuː,nɪsɪ'pælɪtɪ) *n., pl.* **-ties. 1.** a city, town, or district enjoying local self-government. **2.** the governing body of such a unit.

municipalize *or* **-ise** (mjuː'nɪsɪpə,laɪz) *vb.* (*tr.*) **1.** to bring under municipal ownership or control. **2.** to make a municipality of. — **mu,nicipali'zation** *or* **-i'sation** *n.*

munificent (mjuː'nɪfɪsənt) *adj.* **1.** (of a person) generous; bountiful. **2.** (of a gift) liberal. [C16: back formation from L *mūnificentia* liberality, from *mūnificus*, from *mūnus* gift + *facere* to make] — **mu'nificence** *n.* — **mu'nificently** *adv.*

muniments ('mjuːnɪmənts) *pl. n. Law.* the title deeds and other documentary evidence relating to the title to land. [C15: via OF from L *munire* to defend]

munition (mjuː'nɪʃən) *vb.* (*tr.*) to supply with munitions. [C16: via F from L *mūnītiō* fortification, from *mūnīre* to fortify]

munitions (mjuː'nɪʃənz) *pl. n.* (*sometimes sing.*) military equipment and stores, esp. ammunition.

Munro[1] (mʌn'rəʊ) *n., pl.* **Munros.** *Mountaineering.* any separate mountain peak over 3000 feet high: originally used of Scotland only but now sometimes extended to other parts of the British Isles. [C20: after Hugh Thomas *Munro* (1856–1919), who listed these in 1891]

Munro[2] (mʌn'rəʊ) *n.* **H(ector) H(ugh)**, pen name **Saki.** 1870–1916, Scottish author, born in Burma, noted for his collections of satirical short stories, such as *Reginald* (1904) and *Beasts and Superbeasts* (1914).

Munster ('mʌnstə) *n.* a province of SW Ireland: the largest of the four provinces and historically a kingdom; consists of the counties of Clare, Cork, Kerry, Limerick, Tipperary, and Waterford. Capital: Cork. Pop.: 1 019 694 (1986). Area: 24 125 sq. km (9315 sq. miles).

Münster (*German* 'mʏnstər) *n.* a city in NW West Germany, capital of North Rhine-Westphalia state on the Dortmund – Ems Canal: scene of the signing of the Treaty of Westphalia (1648); became capital of Prussian Westphalia in 1815. Pop.: 268 900 (1986).

Münsterberg ('mʊnstə,bɜːg) *n.* **Hugo.** 1863–1916, German psychologist, in the U.S. from 1897, noted for his pioneering work in applied psychology.

muntjac *or* **muntjak** ('mʌnt,dʒæk) *n.* any small Asian deer typically having a chestnut-brown coat and small antlers. [C18: prob. from Javanese *mindjangan* deer]

muon ('mjuːɒn) *n.* a positive or negative elementary particle with a mass 207 times that of an electron. It was originally called the **mu meson.** [C20: short for MU MESON]

mural ('mjʊərəl) *n.* **1.** a large painting on a wall. ~*adj.* **2.** of or relating to a wall. [C15: from L *mūrālis*, from *mūrus* wall] — **'muralist** *n.*

Murasaki Shikibu (,mjʊərə'saːkɪ 'ʃiːkiː,buː) *n.* 11th-century Japanese court lady, author of *The Tale of Genji*, perhaps the world's first novel.

Murat (*French* myra) *n.* **Joachim** (ʒɔaʃɛ̃). 1767?–1815, French marshal, during the Napoleonic Wars; king of Naples (1808–15).

Murchison ('mɜːtʃɪsən) *n.* Sir **Roderick Impey.** 1792–1871, Scottish geologist: played a major role in establishing parts of the geological time scale, esp. the Silurian, Permian, and Devonian periods.

Murcia (*Spanish* 'murθja) *n.* **1.** a region and ancient kingdom of SE Spain, on the Mediterranean: taken by the

---

,**multi'polar** *adj.*   ,**multi'purpose** *adj.*   ,**multi'racial** *adj.*

Moors in the 8th century; an independent Muslim kingdom in the 11th and 12th centuries. **2.** a city in SE Spain, capital of Murcia province: trading centre for a rich agricultural region; silk industry; university (1915). Pop.: 284 585 (1981).

murder ('mɜːdə) n. **1.** the unlawful premeditated killing of one human being by another. Cf. **manslaughter. 2.** Inf. something dangerous, difficult, or unpleasant: driving around London is murder. **3. cry blue murder.** Inf. to make an outcry. **4. get away with murder.** Inf. to escape censure; do as one pleases. ~vb. (mainly tr.) **5.** (also intr.) to kill (someone) unlawfully with premeditation or during the commission of a crime. **6.** to kill brutally. **7.** Inf. to destroy; ruin. **8.** Inf. to defeat completely; beat decisively: the home team murdered their opponents. [OE morthor] —'murderer n. —'murderess fem. n.

murderous ('mɜːdərəs) adj. **1.** intending, capable of, or guilty of murder. **2.** Inf. very dangerous or difficult: a murderous road. —'murderously adv. —'murderousness n.

Murdoch ('mɜːdɒk) n. Dame **Iris.** born 1919, British novelist and philosopher. Her novels include The Bell (1958), A Severed Head (1961; play 1963), The Red and the Green (1965), A Word Child (1975), The Sea, The Sea (1978), The Philosopher's Pupil (1983), and The Book and the Brotherhood (1987).

Mureş ('muarɛʃ) n. a river in SE central Europe, rising in central Romania in the Carpathian Mountains and flowing west to the Tisza River at Szeged, Hungary. Length: 885 km (550 miles). Hungarian name: **Maros.**

murex ('mjuərɛks) n., pl. **murices** ('mjuərɪˌsiːz). any of a genus of spiny-shelled marine gastropods: formerly used as a source of the dye Tyrian purple. [C16: from L mūrex purple fish]

muriatic acid (ˌmjuərɪ'ætɪk) n. a former name for **hydrochloric acid.** [C17: from L muriāticus pickled, from muria brine]

Murillo (mjuə'rɪləu; Spanish mu'riʎo) n. **Bartolomé Esteban** (bartolo'me es'teβan). 1618–82, Spanish painter, esp. of religious subjects and beggar children.

murk or **mirk** (mɜːk) n. **1.** gloomy darkness. ~adj. **2.** an archaic variant of **murky.** [C13: prob. from ON myrkr darkness]

murky or **mirky** ('mɜːkɪ) adj. **murkier, murkiest** or **mirkier, mirkiest. 1.** gloomy or dark. **2.** cloudy or impenetrable as with smoke or fog. —'murkily or 'mirkily adv. —'murkiness or 'mirkiness n.

Murman Coast ('muəmən) or **Murmansk Coast** n. a coastal region of the NW Soviet Union, in the north of the Kola Peninsula: within the Arctic Circle, but ice-free.

Murmansk (Russian 'murmənsk) n. a port in the NW Soviet Union, on the Kola Inlet of the Barents Sea: founded in 1915; the world's largest town north of the Arctic Circle, with a large fishing fleet. Pop.: 432 000 (1987).

murmur ('mɜːmə) n. **1.** a continuous low indistinct sound, as of distant voices. **2.** an indistinct utterance: a murmur of satisfaction. **3.** a complaint; grumble: he made no murmur at my suggestion. **4.** Med. any abnormal soft blowing sound heard usually over the chest (**heart murmur**). ~vb. **5.** to utter (something) in a murmur. **6.** (intr.) to complain. [C14: as n., from L murmur; vb. via OF murmurer from L murmurāre to rumble] —'murmurer n. —'murmuring n., adj. —'murmuringly adv. —'murmurous adj.

murphy ('mɜːfɪ) n., pl. **-phies.** a dialect or informal word for **potato.** [C19: from the common Irish surname Murphy]

Murphy ('mɜːfɪ) n. **William Parry.** born 1892, U.S. physician: with G. R. Minot, he discovered the liver treatment for anaemia and they shared, with G. H. Whipple, the Nobel prize for physiology or medicine in 1934.

murrain ('mʌrɪn) n. **1.** any plaguelike disease in cattle. **2.** Arch. a plague. [C14: from OF morine, from morir to die, from L mori]

Murray ('mʌrɪ) n. a river in SE Australia, rising in New South Wales and flowing northwest into SE South Australia, then south into the sea at Encounter Bay: the main river of Australia, important for irrigation and power. Length: 2590 km (1609 miles).

Murray ('mʌrɪ) n. **1.** Sir **(George) Gilbert (Aimé).** 1866–1957, British classical scholar, born in Australia: noted for his verse translations of Greek dramatists, esp.

Euripides. **2.** Sir **James Augustus Henry.** 1837–1915, Scottish lexicographer; one of the original editors (1879–1915) of what became the Oxford English Dictionary. **3. Lionel,** known as **Len.** born 1922, English trades union leader; general secretary of the Trades Union Congress (1973–84).

Murray cod n. a large greenish Australian freshwater food fish. [after MURRAY River]

Murrumbidgee (ˌmʌrəm'bɪdʒɪ) n. a river in SE Australia, rising in S New South Wales and flowing north and west to the Murray River: important for irrigation. Length: 1690 km (1050 miles).

murther ('mɜːðə) n., vb. an archaic word for **murder.** —'murtherer n.

mus. abbrev. for: **1.** museum. **2.** music. **3.** musical.

MusB or **MusBac** abbrev. for Bachelor of Music.

muscadine ('mʌskədɪn, -ˌdaɪn) n. **1.** a woody climbing plant of the southeastern U.S. **2.** the musk-scented purple grape produced by this plant: used to make wine. [C16: from MUSCATEL]

muscae volitantes ('mʌsiː vɒlɪ'tæntiːz) pl. n. Pathol. moving black specks or threads seen before the eyes, caused by opaque fragments floating in the vitreous humour or a defect in the lens. [C18: NL: flying flies]

muscat ('mʌskət, -kæt) n. **1.** any of various grapevines that produce sweet white grapes used for making wine or raisins. **2.** another name for **muscatel** (sense 1). [C16: via OF from Provençal, from musc MUSK]

Muscat ('mʌskət, -kæt) n. the capital of the Sultanate of Oman, a port on the Gulf of Oman: a Portuguese port from the early 16th century; controlled by Persia (1650–1741). Pop.: 80 000 (1982). Arabic name: **Masqat.**

Muscat and Oman n. the former name (until 1970) of (the Sultanate of) **Oman.**

muscatel (ˌmʌskə'tɛl) or **muscadel** n. **1.** Also called: **muscat.** a rich sweet wine made from muscat grapes. **2.** the grape or raisin from a muscat vine. [C14: from OF muscadel, from OProvençal, from moscadel, from muscat musky]

muscle ('mʌsəl) n. **1.** a tissue composed of bundles of elongated cells capable of contraction and relaxation to produce movement in an organ or part. **2.** an organ composed of muscle tissue. **3.** strength or force. ~vb. **4.** (intr.; often foll. by in, on, etc.) Inf. to force one's way (in). [C16: from Medical L musculus little mouse, from the imagined resemblance of some muscles to mice] —'muscly adj.

muscle-bound adj. **1.** having overdeveloped and inelastic muscles. **2.** lacking flexibility.

muscleman ('mʌsəlˌmæn) n., pl. **-men. 1.** a man with highly developed muscles. **2.** a henchman employed by a gangster to intimidate or use violence upon victims.

Muscovite ('mʌskəˌvaɪt) n. **1.** a native or inhabitant of Moscow. ~adj. **2.** an archaic word for **Russian.**

Muscovy ('mʌskəvɪ) n. **1.** a Russian principality (13th to 16th centuries), of which Moscow was the capital. **2.** an archaic name for **Russia** and **Moscow.**

Muscovy duck or **musk duck** n. a large crested widely domesticated South American duck, having a greenish-black plumage with white markings and a large red caruncle on the bill. [C17: orig. musk duck, a name later mistakenly associated with MUSCOVY]

muscular ('mʌskjʊlə) adj. **1.** having well-developed muscles; brawny. **2.** of, relating to, or consisting of muscle. [C17: from NL muscularis, from musculus MUSCLE] —**muscularity** (ˌmʌskjʊ'lærɪtɪ) n. —'muscularly adv.

muscular dystrophy n. a genetic disease characterized by progressive deterioration and wasting of muscle fibres.

musculature ('mʌskjʊlətʃə) n. **1.** the arrangement of muscles in an organ or part. **2.** the total muscular system of an organism.

MusD or **MusDoc** abbrev. for Doctor of Music.

muse (mjuːz) vb. **1.** (when intr., often foll. by on or about) to reflect (about) or ponder (on), usually in silence. **2.** (intr.) to gaze thoughtfully. ~n. **3.** a state of abstraction. [C14: from OF muser, ?from mus snout, from Med. L mūsus]

muse (mjuːz) n. (often preceded by the) a goddess that inspires a creative artist, esp. a poet. [C14: from OF, from L Mūsa, from Gk Mousa a Muse]

Muse (mjuːz) n. Greek myth. any of nine sister goddesses, each of whom was regarded as the protectress of a different art or science.

musette (mjuː'zɛt) n. 1. a type of bagpipe popular in France during the 17th and 18th centuries. 2. a dance, originally accompanied by a musette. [C14: from OF, dim. of *muse* bagpipe]

museum (mjuː'zɪəm) n. a building where objects of historical, artistic, or scientific interest are exhibited and preserved. [C17: via L from Gk *Mouseion* home of the Muses, from *Mousa* MUSE]

museum piece n. 1. an object of sufficient age or interest to be kept in a museum. 2. *Inf.* a person or thing regarded as antiquated.

Museveni (musə'veɪnɪ) n. **Yoweri**. born 1944, Ugandan politician; president of Uganda from 1986.

mush[1] (mʌʃ) n. 1. a soft pulpy mass or consistency. 2. *U.S.* a thick porridge made from corn meal. 3. *Inf.* cloying sentimentality. [C17: from obs. *moose* porridge; prob. rel. to MASH]

mush[2] (mʌʃ) *Canad.* ~*interj.* 1. an order to dogs in a sled team to start up or go faster. ~*vb.* 2. to travel by or drive a dogsled. ~*n.* 3. a journey with a dogsled. [C19: ?from imperative of F *marcher* to advance]

mushroom ('mʌʃruːm, -rum) n. 1. a. the fleshy spore-producing body of any of various fungi, typically consisting of a cap at the end of a stem. Some species, such as the field mushroom, are edible. Cf. **toadstool**. b. (*as modifier*): *mushroom soup*. 2. a. something resembling a mushroom in shape or rapid growth. b. (*as modifier*): *mushroom expansion*. ~*vb.* (*intr.*) 3. to grow rapidly: *demand mushroomed overnight*. 4. to assume a mushroom-like shape. [C15: from OF *mousseron*, from LL *mussiriō*, from ?]

mushroom cloud n. the large mushroom-shaped cloud produced by a nuclear explosion.

mushy ('mʌʃɪ) adj. **mushier, mushiest.** 1. soft and pulpy. 2. *Inf.* excessively sentimental or emotional. —'**mushily** adv. —'**mushiness** n.

music ('mjuːzɪk) n. 1. an art form consisting of sequences of sounds in time, esp. tones of definite pitch organized melodically, harmonically and rhythmically. 2. the sounds so produced, esp. by singing or musical instruments. 3. written or printed music, such as a score or set of parts. 4. any sequence of sounds perceived as pleasing or harmonious. 5. **face the music.** *Inf.* to confront the consequences of one's actions. [C13: via OF from L *mūsica*, from Gk *mousikē* (*tekhnē*) (art) belonging to the Muses, from *Mousa* MUSE]

musical ('mjuːzɪkᵊl) adj. 1. of, relating to, or used in music. 2. harmonious; melodious: *musical laughter*. 3. talented in or fond of music. 4. involving or set to music. ~*n.* 5. Also called: **musical comedy.** a light romantic play or film having dialogue interspersed with songs and dances. —,**musi'cality** n. —'**musically** adv.

musical box or **music box** n. a mechanical instrument that plays tunes by means of pins on a revolving cylinder striking the tuned teeth of a comblike metal plate, contained in a box.

musical chairs n. (*functioning as sing.*) 1. a party game in which players walk around chairs while music is played, there being one more player than chairs. Whenever the music stops, the player who fails to find a chair is eliminated. 2. any situation involving several people in a series of interrelated changes.

musicassette ('mjuːzɪkə,sɛt) n. an audio cassette of prerecorded music.

music centre n. a single hi-fi unit containing a turntable, amplifier, radio and cassette player.

music drama n. 1. an opera in which the musical and dramatic elements are of equal importance and strongly interfused. 2. the genre of such operas. [C19: from G *Musikdrama*, coined by Wagner to describe his later operas]

music hall n. *Chiefly Brit.* 1. a variety entertainment consisting of songs, comic turns, etc. U.S. and Canad. name: **vaudeville.** 2. a theatre at which such entertainments are staged.

musician (mjuː'zɪʃən) n. a person who plays or composes music, esp. as a profession. —**mu'sicianly** adj. —**mu'sicianship** n.

musicology (,mjuːzɪ'kɒlədʒɪ) n. the scholarly study of music. —**musicological** (,mjuːzɪkə'lɒdʒɪkᵊl) adj. —,**musi'cologist** n.

music paper n. paper ruled or printed with a stave for writing music.

Musil (*German* 'muːzɪl) n. **Robert** ('roːbɛrt). 1880–1942, Austrian novelist, whose novel *The Man Without Qualities* (1930–42) is an ironic examination of contemporary ills.

musique concrète *French.* (myzik kɔ̃krɛt) n. another term for **concrete music.**

musk (mʌsk) n. 1. a strong-smelling glandular secretion of the male musk deer, used in perfumery. 2. a similar substance produced by certain other animals, such as the civet and otter, or manufactured synthetically. 3. a North American plant which has yellow flowers and was formerly cultivated for its musky scent. 4. the smell of musk or a similar heady smell. 5. (*modifier*) containing or resembling musk: *musk oil*. [C14: from LL *muscus*, from Gk, from Persian, prob. from Sansk. *mushkā* scrotum (from the appearance of the musk deer's musk bag), dim. of *mūsh* MOUSE]

musk deer n. a small central Asian mountain deer. The male secretes musk.

musk duck n. 1. another name for **Muscovy duck.** 2. a duck inhabiting swamps, lakes, and streams in Australia. The male emits a musky odour.

muskeg ('mʌs,kɛg) n. *Chiefly Canad.* 1. undrained boggy land 2. a bog or swamp of this nature. [C19: of Amerind origin: grassy swamp]

muskellunge ('mʌskə,lʌndʒ) or **maskinonge** ('mæskɪ,nɒndʒ) n., pl. **-lunges, -nonges** or **-lunge, -nonge.** a large North American freshwater game fish, related to the pike. Often shortened (informally) to **musky** or **muskie.** [C18 *maskinunga*, of Amerind origin]

musket ('mʌskɪt) n. a long-barrelled muzzle-loading shoulder gun used between the 16th and 18th centuries by infantry soldiers. [C16: from F *mousquet*, from It. *moschetto* arrow, earlier: sparrow hawk, from *moscha* a fly, from L *musca*]

musketeer (,mʌskɪ'tɪə) n. (formerly) a soldier armed with a musket.

musketry ('mʌskɪtrɪ) n. 1. muskets or musketeers collectively. 2. the technique of using small arms.

Muskie ('mʌskɪ) n. **Edmund (Sixtus).** born 1914, U.S. Democratic politician: Governor of Maine (1955–59): senator for Maine from 1958: Secretary of State (1980–81).

muskmelon ('mʌsk,mɛlən) n. 1. any of several varieties of the melon, such as the cantaloupe and honeydew. 2. the fruit of any of these melons, having ribbed or warty rind and sweet yellow, white, orange, or green flesh with a musky aroma.

musk ox n. a large bovid mammal, which has a dark shaggy coat, short legs, and widely spaced downward-curving horns, and emits a musky smell: now confined to the tundras of Canada and Greenland.

muskrat ('mʌsk,ræt) n., pl. **-rats** or **-rat.** 1. a North American beaver-like amphibious rodent, closely related to but larger than the voles. 2. the brown fur of this animal. ~Also called: **musquash.**

musk rose n. a Mediterranean rose, cultivated for its white musk-scented flowers.

musky ('mʌskɪ) adj. **muskier, muskiest.** resembling the smell of musk; having a heady or pungent sweet aroma. —'**muskiness** n.

Muslim ('muzlɪm, 'mʌz-) or **Moslem** n., pl. **-lims** or **-lim.** 1. a follower of the religion of Islam. ~*adj.* 2. of or relating to Islam, its doctrines, culture, etc. ~Also (but not in Muslim use): **Mohammedan, Muhammadan.** [C17: from Ar., lit.: one who surrenders] —'**Muslimism** or '**Moslemism** n.

muslin ('mʌzlɪn) n. a fine plain-weave cotton fabric. [C17: from F *mousseline*, from It., from Ar. *mawṣilīy* of Mosul (Iraq), where it was first produced]

musquash ('mʌskwɒʃ) n. another name for **muskrat,** esp. the fur. [C17: of Amerind origin]

muss (mʌs) *U.S. & Canad. inf.* ~*vb.* 1. (*tr.*; often foll. by *up*) to make untidy; rumple. ~*n.* 2. a state of disorder; muddle. [C19: prob. a blend of MESS + FUSS] —'**mussy** adj.

mussel ('mʌsᵊl) n. 1. any of various marine bivalves, esp. the edible mussel, having a dark slightly elongated shell and living attached to rocks, etc. 2. any of various freshwater bivalves, attached to rocks, sand, etc., having a flattened oval shell (a source of mother-of-pearl). [OE *muscle*, from Vulgar L *muscula* (unattested), from L *musculus*, dim. of *mūs* mouse]

Musset (*French* mysɛ) *n.* **Alfred de** (alfrɛd də). 1810–57, French romantic poet and dramatist: his works include the play *Lorenzaccio* (1834) and the lyrics *Les Nuits* (1835–37), tracing his love affair with George Sand.

Mussolini (ˌmʊsə'liːni; *Italian* musso'liːni) *n.* **Benito** (be'niːto) known as *il Duce*. 1883–1945, Italian Fascist dictator. After the Fascist march on Rome, he was appointed prime minister by King Victor Emmanuel III (1922) and assumed dictatorial powers. He annexed Abyssinia and allied Italy with Germany (1936), entering World War II in 1940. He was forced to resign following the Allied invasion of Sicily (1943) and was eventually shot by Italian partisans.

Mussorgsky *or* **Moussorgsky** (mu'sɔːɡskɪ; *Russian* 'musərkskij) *n.* **Modest Petrovich** (ma'dɛst pɪ'trɔvɪtʃ). 1839–81, Russian composer. He translated inflections of speech into melody in such works as the song cycle *Songs and Dances of Death* (1875–77) and the opera *Boris Godunov* (1874). His other works include *Pictures at an Exhibition* (1874) for piano.

Mussulman ('mʌsəlmən) *n. pl.* **-mans.** an archaic word for **Muslim.** [C16: from Persian *Musulmān* (pl.) from Ar. *Muslimīn*, pl. of MUSLIM]

must[1] (mʌst; *unstressed* məst, məs) *vb.* (takes an infinitive without *to* or an implied infinitive) used as an auxiliary: **1.** to express obligation or compulsion: *you must pay your dues*. In this sense, *must* does not form a negative. If used with a negative infinitive it indicates obligatory prohibition. **2.** to indicate necessity: *I must go to the bank tomorrow*. **3.** to indicate the probable correctness of a statement: *he must be there by now*. **4.** to indicate inevitability: *all good things must come to an end*. **5.** to express resolution: **a.** on the part of the speaker: *I must finish this*. **b.** on the part of another or others: *let him get drunk if he must*. **6.** (used emphatically) to express conviction or certainty on the part of the speaker: *you must be joking*. **7.** (foll. by *away*) used with an implied verb of motion to express compelling haste: *I must away*. ~*n.* **8.** an essential or necessary thing: *strong shoes are a must for hill walking*. [OE *mōste*, p.t. of *mōtan* to be allowed, be obliged to]

must[2] (mʌst) *n.* the pressed juice of grapes or other fruit ready for fermentation. [OE, from L *mustum* new wine, from *mustus* newborn]

must[3] (mʌst) *n.* mustiness or mould. [C17: back formation from MUSTY]

mustache (mə'staːʃ) *n.* the U.S. spelling of **moustache.** —**mus'tached** *adj.*

mustachio (mə'staːʃɪˌəʊ) *n., pl.* **-chios.** (*often pl.*) *Often humorous.* a moustache, esp. when bushy or elaborately shaped. [C16: from Sp. *mostacho* & It. *mostaccio*] —**mus'tachioed** *adj.*

Mustafa Kemal ('mʊstəfə kə'maːl) *n.* See (Kemal) **Atatürk.**

mustang ('mʌstæŋ) *n.* a small breed of horse, often wild or half wild, found in the southwestern U.S. [C19: from Mexican Sp. *mestengo*, from *mesta* a group of stray animals]

mustard ('mʌstəd) *n.* **1.** any of several Eurasian plants, esp. black mustard and white mustard, having yellow flowers and slender pods: cultivated for their pungent seeds. **2.** a paste made from the powdered seeds of any of these plants and used as a condiment. **3. a.** a brownish-yellow colour. **b.** (*as adj.*): *a mustard carpet*. **4.** *Sl., chiefly U.S.* zest or enthusiasm. [C13: from OF *moustarde*, from L *mustum* MUST[2], since the original was made by adding must]

mustard and cress *n.* seedlings of white mustard and garden cress, used in salads, etc.

mustard gas *n.* an oily liquid vesicant compound used in chemical warfare. Its vapour causes blindness and burns.

mustard plaster *n. Med.* a mixture of powdered black mustard seeds applied to the skin for its counterirritant effects.

musteline ('mʌstɪˌlaɪn, -lɪn) *adj.* of or belonging to a family of typically predatory mammals, including weasels, ferrets, badgers, skunks, and otters. [C17: from L *mustēlīnus*, from *mustēla* weasel]

muster ('mʌstə) *vb.* **1.** to call together (numbers of men) for duty, inspection, etc., or (of men) to assemble in this way. **2. muster in** *or* **out.** *U.S.* to enlist into or discharge from military service. **3.** (*tr.; sometimes foll. by *up*) to summon or gather: *to muster one's arguments; to muster*

up courage. **4.** (*tr.*) *Austral. & N.Z.* to round up (stock). ~*n.* **5.** an assembly of military personnel for duty, etc. **6.** a collection, assembly, or gathering. **7.** *Austral. & N.Z.* the act of rounding up stock. **8. pass muster.** to be acceptable. [C14: from OF *moustrer*, from L *monstrāre* to show, from *monstrum* portent]

musth *or* **must** (mʌst) *n.* (often preceded by *in*) a state of frenzied sexual excitement in the males of certain large mammals, esp. elephants. [C19: from Urdu *mast*, from Persian: drunk]

musty ('mʌstɪ) *adj.* **-tier, -tiest. 1.** smelling or tasting old, stale, or mouldy. **2.** old-fashioned, dull, or hackneyed: *musty ideas*. [C16: ? var. of obs. *moisty*] —**'mustily** *adv.* —**'mustiness** *n.*

mutable ('mjuːtəb*ə*l) *adj.* able to or tending to change. [C14: from L *mūtābilis* fickle, from *mūtāre* to change] —**ˌmuta'bility** *or* (*less commonly*) **'mutableness** *n.* —**'mutably** *adv.*

mutagen ('mjuːtədʒən) *n.* a substance that can induce genetic mutation. [C20: from MUTATION + -GEN] —**mutagenic** (ˌmjuːtə'dʒɛnɪk) *adj.*

mutant ('mjuːt*ə*nt) *n.* **1.** Also called: **mutation.** an animal, organism, or gene that has undergone mutation. ~*adj.* **2.** of, undergoing, or resulting from mutation. [C20: from L *mutāre* to change]

Mutare (mu:'taːrɪ) *n.* a city in E Zimbabwe, near the Mozambique border: rail and trade centre in a mining and tobacco-growing region. Pop.: 70 000 (1982 est.). Former name (until 1982): **Umtali.**

mutate (mjuː'teɪt) *vb.* to undergo or cause to undergo mutation. [C19: from L *mūtātus*, p.p. of *mūtāre* to change]

mutation (mjuː'teɪʃən) *n.* **1.** the act or process of mutating; change; alteration. **2.** a change or alteration. **3.** a change in the chromosomes or genes of a cell which may affect the structure and development of the resultant offspring. **4.** another word for **mutant** (sense 1). **5.** a physical characteristic of an individual resulting from this type of chromosomal change. **6.** *Phonetics.* **a.** (in Germanic languages) another name for **umlaut.** **b.** (in Celtic languages) a phonetic change in certain initial consonants caused by a preceding word. —**mu'tational** *adj.* —**mu'tationally** *adv.*

mutatis mutandis *Latin.* (mu:'taːtɪs mu:'tændɪs) (the necessary changes having been made.

mutch (mʌtʃ) *n.* a close-fitting linen cap formerly worn by women and children in Scotland. [C15: from MDu. *mutse* cap, from Med. L *almucia* AMICE]

mute (mjuːt) *adj.* **1.** not giving out sound or speech; silent. **2.** unable to speak; dumb. **3.** unspoken or unexpressed. **4.** *Law.* (of a person arraigned on indictment) refusing to answer a charge. **5.** *Phonetics.* another word for **plosive. 6.** (of a letter in a word) silent. ~*n.* **7.** a person who is unable to speak. **8.** *Law.* a person who refuses to plead. **9.** any of various devices used to soften the tone of stringed or brass instruments. **10.** *Phonetics.* a plosive consonant. **11.** a silent letter. **12.** an actor in a dumb show. **13.** a hired mourner. ~*vb.* (*tr.*) **14.** to reduce the volume of (a musical instrument) by means of a mute, soft pedal, etc. **15.** to subdue the strength of (a colour, tone, lighting, etc.). [C14 *muwet* from OF *mu*, from L *mūtus* silent] —**'mutely** *adv.* —**'muteness** *n.*

mute swan *n.* a Eurasian swan with a pure white plumage and an orange-red bill.

muti ('muːtɪ) *n. S. African.* medicine, esp. herbal. [from Zulu *umuthi* tree, shrub]

mutilate ('mjuːtɪˌleɪt) *vb.* (*tr.*) **1.** to deprive of a limb, essential part, etc.; maim. **2.** to expurgate, damage, etc. (a text, book, etc.). [C16: from L *mutilāre* to cut off; rel. to *mutilus* maimed] —**ˌmuti'lation** *n.* —**'mutiˌlative** *adj.* —**'mutiˌlator** *n.*

mutineer (ˌmjuːtɪ'nɪə) *n.* a person who mutinies.

mutinous ('mjuːtɪnəs) *adj.* **1.** openly rebellious. **2.** characteristic or indicative of mutiny. —**'mutinously** *adv.* —**'mutinousness** *n.*

mutiny ('mjuːtɪnɪ) *n., pl.* **-nies. 1.** open rebellion against constituted authority, esp. by seamen or soldiers against their officers. ~*vb.* **-nying, -nied. 2.** (*intr.*) to engage in mutiny. [C16: from obs. *mutine*, from OF *mutin* rebellious, from *meute* mutiny, ult. from L *movēre* to move]

mutism ('mjuːtɪzəm) *n.* **1.** the state of being mute. **2.** *Psychiatry.* **a.** a refusal to speak. **b.** the lack of development of speech.

mutt (mʌt) *n. Sl.* **1.** an inept, ignorant, or stupid person. **2.** a mongrel dog; cur. [C20: from MUTTONHEAD]

mutter ('mʌtə) *vb.* **1.** to utter (something) in a low and indistinct tone. **2.** (*intr.*) to grumble or complain. **3.** (*intr.*) to make a low continuous murmuring sound. ~*n.* **4.** a muttered sound or complaint. [C14 *moteren*] —'**muttering** *n., adj.*

mutton ('mʌt⁽ə⁾n) *n.* **1.** the flesh of sheep, esp. of mature sheep, used as food. **2. mutton dressed (up) as lamb.** an older person, thing, or idea dressed up to look young or new. [C13 *moton* sheep, from OF, from Med. L *multō*, of Celtic origin] —'**muttony** *adj.*

mutton bird *n.* any of several shearwaters, having a dark plumage with greyish underparts. In New Zealand, applied to one collected for food, esp. by Maoris. [C19: from the taste of its flesh]

mutton chop *n.* a piece of mutton from the loin.

muttonchops ('mʌt⁽ə⁾n,tʃɒps) *pl. n.* side whiskers trimmed in the shape of chops.

muttonhead ('mʌt⁽ə⁾n,hɛd) *n. Sl.* a stupid or ignorant person; fool. —'**mutton,headed** *adj.*

Muttra ('mʌtrə) *n.* the former name of **Mathura.**

mutual ('mjuːtʃʊəl) *adj.* **1.** experienced or expressed by each of two or more people about the other; reciprocal: *mutual distrust.* **2.** *Inf.* common to or shared by both: *a mutual friend.* **3.** denoting an insurance company, etc., in which the policyholders share the profits and expenses and there are no shareholders. [C15: from OF *mutuel*, from L *mūtuus* reciprocal (orig.: borrowed); rel. to *mūtāre* to change] —**mutuality** (,mjuːtʃʊ'ælɪtɪ) *n.* —'**mutually** *adv.*

▷ **Usage.** *Mutual* was originally used when only two people, or groups of people, were concerned, but is nowadays often extended to cover more than two and to mean "common" rather than "reciprocal": *several of the group felt that this course would be in their mutual interest.* It is used especially in instances where "common" might be ambiguous: *he sent an emissary who was a mutual friend to ask me to reconsider my decision.*

mutual induction *n.* the production of an electromotive force in a circuit by a current change in a second circuit magnetically linked to the first.

mutual insurance *n.* a system of insurance by which all policyholders become company members under contract to pay premiums into a common fund out of which claims are paid. See also **mutual** (sense 3).

mutuel ('mjuːtʃʊəl) *n.* short for **pari-mutuel.**

muu-muu ('muː,muː) *n.* a loose brightly coloured dress worn by women in Hawaii. [from Hawaiian]

Muzak ('mjuːzæk) *n. Trademark.* recorded light music played in shops, restaurants, factories, etc.

muzhik *or* **moujik** ('muːʒɪk) *n.* a Russian peasant, esp. under the tsars. [C16: from Russian: peasant]

Muzorewa (,muzə'reɪwə) *n.* **Abel (Tendekayi)** ('eɪb⁽ə⁾l). born 1925, Zimbabwean Methodist bishop and politician; president of the African National Council from 1971. He was one of the negotiators of an internal settlement (1978); prime minister of Rhodesia (1979–80).

muzzle ('mʌz⁽ə⁾l) *n.* **1.** the projecting part of the face, usually the jaws and nose, of animals such as the dog and horse. **2.** a guard or strap fitted over an animal's nose and jaws to prevent it biting or eating. **3.** the front end of a gun barrel. ~*vb.* (*tr.*) **4.** to prevent from being heard or noticed. **5.** to put a muzzle on (an animal). [C15 *mosel*, from OF *musel*, dim. of *muse* snout, from Med. L *mūsus*, from ?] —'**muzzler** *n.*

muzzle-loader *n.* a firearm receiving its ammunition through the muzzle. —'**muzzle-,loading** *adj.*

muzzle velocity *n.* the velocity of a projectile as it leaves a firearm's muzzle.

muzzy ('mʌzɪ) *adj.* **-zier, -ziest.** **1.** blurred or hazy. **2.** confused or befuddled. [C18: from ?] —'**muzzily** *adv.* —'**muzziness** *n.*

MVO (in Britain) *abbrev. for* Member of the Royal Victorian Order.

MW **1.** *symbol for* megawatt. **2.** *Radio. abbrev. for* medium wave.

Mweru ('mwɛəruː) *n.* a lake in central Africa, on the border between Zambia and Zaïre. Area: 4196 sq. km (1620 sq. miles).

Mx *Physics. symbol for* maxwell.

my (maɪ) *determiner.* **1.** of, belonging to, or associated with the speaker or writer (me): *my own ideas.* **2.** used in various forms of address: *my lord.* ~*interj.* **3.** an exclamation of surprise, awe, etc.: *my, how you've grown!* [C12 *mi*, var. of OE *mīn* when preceding a word beginning with a consonant]

myalgia (maɪ'ældʒɪə) *n.* pain in a muscle or a group of muscles. [C19: from MYO- + -ALGIA]

myalgic encephalomyelitis (maɪ'ældʒɪk ɛn,sɛfələʊ-,maɪɪ'laɪtɪs) *n.* a condition involving painful muscles and general weakness, sometimes persisting long after a viral illness. Also called: **postviral syndrome.** Usually abbreviated to: **ME.**

myalism ('maɪə,lɪzəm) *n.* a kind of witchcraft practised esp. in the West Indies. [C19: from *myal*, prob. West African]

myall ('maɪəl) *n.* **1.** any of several Australian acacias having hard scented wood. **2.** an Australian Aborigine living independently of society. [C19: Abor. name]

mycelium (maɪ'siːlɪəm) *n., pl.* **-lia** (-lɪə). the vegetative body of fungi: a mass of branching filaments (hyphae). [C19 (lit.: nail of fungus): from MYCO- + Gk *hēlos* nail] —my'**celial** *adj.*

Mycenae (maɪ'siːniː) *n.* an ancient Greek city in the NE Peloponnesus on the plain of Argos.

Mycenaean (,maɪsɪ'niːən) *adj.* **1.** of or relating to ancient Mycenae, or its inhabitants. **2.** of or relating to the Aegean civilization of Mycenae (1400 to 1100 B.C.).

-mycete *n. combining form.* indicating a member of a class of fungi: *myxomycete.* [from NL *-mycetes*, from Gk *mukētes*, pl. of *mukēs* fungus]

myco- *or before a vowel* **myc-** *combining form.* indicating fungus: *mycology.* [from Gk *mukēs* fungus]

mycology (maɪ'kɒlədʒɪ) *n.* the branch of botany concerned with the study of fungi. —**mycological** (,maɪkə'lɒdʒɪk⁽ə⁾l) *or* ,**myco'logic** *adj.* —my'**cologist** *n.*

mycosis (maɪ'kəʊsɪs) *n.* any infection or disease caused by fungus. —**mycotic** (maɪ'kɒtɪk) *adj.*

mycotoxin (,maɪkə'tɒksɪn) *n.* any of various toxic substances produced by fungi, some of which may affect food. —,**mycotox'ology** *n.*

myelin ('maɪɪlɪn) *or* **myeline** ('maɪɪ,liːn) *n.* a white tissue forming an insulating sheath (**myelin sheath**) around certain nerve fibres. Damage to the myelin sheath causes neurological disease, as in multiple sclerosis.

myelitis (,maɪɪ'laɪtɪs) *n.* inflammation of the spinal cord or of the bone marrow.

myeloma (,maɪə'ləʊmə) *n., pl.* **-mas** *or* **-mata** (-mətə). a usually malignant tumour of the bone marrow.

My Lai ('maɪ 'laɪ, 'miː) *n.* a village in S Vietnam where in 1968 U.S. troops massacred over 100 civilians.

myna, mynah, *or* **mina** ('maɪnə) *n.* any of various tropical Asian starlings, some of which can mimic human speech. [C18: from Hindi *mainā*, from Sansk. *madana*]

Mynheer (mə'nɪə) *n.* a Dutch title of address equivalent to *Sir* when used alone or to *Mr* before a name. [C17: from Du. *mijnheer* my lord]

myo- *or before a vowel* **my-** *combining form.* muscle: *myocardium.* [from Gk *mus* MUSCLE]

myocardium (,maɪəʊ'kɑːdɪəm) *n., pl.* **-dia** (-dɪə). the muscular tissue of the heart. [C19: *myo-* + *cardium*, from Gk *kardia* heart] —,**myo'cardial** *adj.*

myology (maɪ'ɒlədʒɪ) *n.* the branch of medical science concerned with muscles.

myope ('maɪəʊp) *n.* any person afflicted with myopia. [C18: via F from Gk *muōps*; see MYOPIA]

myopia (maɪ'əʊpɪə) *n.* inability to see distant objects clearly because the images are focused in front of the retina; short-sightedness. [C18: via NL from Gk *muōps* short-sighted, from *mūein* to close (the eyes), + *ōps* eye] —**myopic** (maɪ'ɒpɪk) *adj.* —my'**opically** *adv.*

myosin ('maɪəsɪn) *n.* the chief protein of muscle. [C19: from MYO- + -OSE² + -IN]

myosotis (,maɪə'səʊtɪs) *n.* any plant of the genus *Myosotis.* See **forget-me-not.** [C18: NL from Gk *muosōtis* mouse-ear (referring to its furry leaves), from *mus* mouse + *ous* ear]

myriad ('mɪrɪəd) *adj.* **1.** innumerable. ~*n.* (*also used in pl.*) **2.** a large indefinite number. **3.** *Arch.* ten thousand. [C16: via LL from Gk *murias* ten thousand]

myriapod ('mɪrɪə,pɒd) *n.* **1.** any of a group of terrestrial arthropods having a long segmented body and many walking limbs, such as the centipedes and millipedes. ~*adj.* **2.** of, relating to, or belonging to this group. [C19: from NL *Myriapoda.* See MYRIAD, -POD]

Myrmidon ('mɜːmɪˌdɒn, -dᵊn) n. **1.** *Greek myth.* one of a race of people who were led against Troy by Achilles. **2.** (*often not cap.*) a follower or henchman.

myrobalan (maɪˈrɒbələn, mɪ-) n. **1.** the dried plumlike fruit of various tropical trees used in dyeing, tanning, ink, and medicine. **2.** a dye extracted from this fruit. [C16: via L from Gk *murobalanos*, from *muron* ointment + *balanos* acorn]

Myron ('maɪərən) n. 5th century B.C., Greek sculptor. He worked mainly in bronze and introduced a greater variety of pose into Greek sculpture, as in his *Discobolus*.

myrrh (mɜː) n. **1.** any of several trees and shrubs of Africa and S Asia that exude an aromatic resin. **2.** the resin obtained from such a plant, used in perfume, incense, and medicine. [OE *myrre*, via L from Gk *murrha*, ult. from Akkadian *murrū*]

myrtle ('mɜːtᵊl) n. an evergreen shrub or tree, esp. a S European shrub with pink or white flowers and aromatic blue-black berries. [C16: from Med. L *myrtilla*, from L *myrtus*, from Gk *murtos*]

myself (maɪˈsɛlf) pron. **1. a.** the reflexive form of *I* or *me*. **b.** (intensifier): *I myself know of no answer.* **2.** (*preceded by a copula*) my usual self: *I'm not myself today.* **3.** *Not standard.* used instead of *I* or *me* in compound noun phrases: *John and myself are voting together.*

▷ **Usage.** The use of *myself* for *I* or *me* is often the result of an attempt to be elegant or correct. However, careful users of English only employ *myself* when it follows *I* or *me* in the same clause: *I cut myself*, but *he gave it to me* (not *myself*). The same is true of the other reflexives. This rule does permit constructions such as *he wrote it himself* (unassisted) and *he himself wrote it* (without an intermediary), but these are only to be used to reinforce a previous reference to the same individual.

Mysia ('mɪsɪə) n. an ancient region in the NW corner of Asia Minor. —'**Mysian** adj., n.

Mysore (maɪˈsɔː) n. **1.** a city in S India, in S Karnataka state: former capital of the state of Mysore; manufacturing and trading centre; university (1916). Pop.: 439 185 (1981). **2.** the former name (until 1973) of **Karnataka.**

mysterious (mɪˈstɪərɪəs) adj. **1.** characterized by or indicative of mystery. **2.** puzzling, curious. —**mys'teriously** adv. —**mys'teriousness** n.

mystery[1] ('mɪstərɪ, -trɪ) n., pl. **-teries. 1.** an unexplained or inexplicable event, phenomenon, etc. **2.** a person or thing that arouses curiosity or suspense because of an unknown, obscure, or enigmatic quality. **3.** the state or quality of being obscure, inexplicable, or enigmatic. **4.** a story, film, etc., which arouses suspense and curiosity because of facts concealed. **5.** *Christianity.* any truth that is divinely revealed but otherwise unknowable. **6.** *Christianity.* a sacramental rite, such as the Eucharist, or (*when pl.*) the consecrated elements of the Eucharist. **7.** (*often pl.*) any rites of certain ancient Mediterranean religions. **8.** short for **mystery play.** [C14: via L from Gk *mustērion* secret rites]

mystery[2] ('mɪstərɪ) n., pl. **-teries.** *Arch.* **1.** a trade, occupation, or craft. **2.** a guild of craftsmen. [C14: from Med. L *mistērium*, from L *ministerium* occupation, from *minister* official]

mystery play n. (in the Middle Ages) a type of drama based on the life of Christ. Cf. **miracle play.**

mystery tour n. an excursion to an unspecified destination.

mystic ('mɪstɪk) n. **1.** a person who achieves mystical experience or an apprehension of divine mysteries ~adj. **2.** another word for **mystical.** [C14: via L from Gk *mustikos*, from *mustēs* mystery initiate; rel. to *muein* to initiate into sacred rites]

mystical ('mɪstɪkᵊl) adj. **1.** relating to or characteristic of mysticism. **2.** *Christianity.* having a divine or sacred significance that surpasses human apprehension. **3.** having occult or metaphysical significance. —'**mystically** adv.

mysticism ('mɪstɪˌsɪzəm) n. **1.** belief in or experience of a reality surpassing normal human understanding or experience. **2.** a system of contemplative prayer and spirituality aimed at achieving direct intuitive experience of the divine. **3.** obscure or confused belief or thought.

mystify ('mɪstɪˌfaɪ) vb. **-fying, -fied.** (*tr.*) **1.** to confuse, bewilder, or puzzle. **2.** to make obscure. [C19: from F *mystifier*, from *mystère* MYSTERY[1] or *mystique* MYSTIC] —ˌmystifi'**cation** n. —'**mysti**ˌ**fying** adj.

mystique (mɪˈstiːk) n. an aura of mystery, power, and awe that surrounds a person or thing. [C20: from F (adj.): MYSTIC]

myth (mɪθ) n. **1. a.** a story about superhuman beings of an earlier age, usually of how natural phenomena, social customs, etc., came into existence. **b.** another word for **mythology** (senses 1, 3). **2.** a person or thing whose existence is fictional or unproven. [C19: via LL from Gk *muthos* fable]

myth. *abbrev. for:* **1.** mythological. **2.** mythology.

mythical ('mɪθɪkᵊl) or **mythic** adj. **1.** of or relating to myth. **2.** imaginary or fictitious. —'**mythically** adv.

mythicize or **-cise** ('mɪθɪˌsaɪz) vb. (*tr.*) to make into or treat as a myth. —'**mythicist** n.

mytho- *combining form.* myth: *mythopoeia.*

mythologize or **-gise** (mɪˈθɒləˌdʒaɪz) vb. **1.** to tell, study, or explain (myths). **2.** (*intr.*) to create or make up myths. **3.** (*tr.*) to convert into a myth. —my'**tholo**ˌ**gizer** or -ˌ**giser** n.

mythology (mɪˈθɒlədʒɪ) n., pl. **-gies. 1.** a body of myths, esp. one associated with a particular culture, person, etc. **2.** a body of stories about a person, institution, etc. **3.** myths collectively. **4.** the study of myths. —**mythological** (ˌmɪθəˈlɒdʒɪkᵊl) adj.

mythomania (ˌmɪθəʊˈmeɪnɪə) n. *Psychiatry.* the tendency to lie or exaggerate, occurring in some mental disorders. —ˌmytho'**mani**ˌac n., adj.

mythopoeia (ˌmɪθəʊˈpiːə) n. the composition or making of myths. [C19: from Gk, ult. from *muthos* myth + *poiein* to make] —ˌmytho'**poeic** adj.

mythos ('maɪθɒs, 'mɪθɒs) n., pl. **-thoi** (-θɔɪ). **1.** the complex of beliefs, values, attitudes, etc., characteristic of a specific group or society. **2.** another word for **myth** or **mythology.**

Mytilene (ˌmɪtɪˈliːnɪ) n. **1.** a port on the Greek island of Lesbos: Roman remains; Byzantine fortress. Pop.: 24 937 (1981). Modern Greek name: **Mitilíni. 2.** a former name for **Lesbos.**

myxo ('mɪksəʊ) n. *Austral. sl.* myxomatosis.

myxo- or before a vowel **myx-** *combining form.* mucus or slime: *myxomatosis.* [from Gk *muxa*]

myxoedema or *U.S.* **myxedema** (ˌmɪksɪˈdiːmə) n. a disease resulting from underactivity of the thyroid gland characterized by puffy eyes, face, and hands and mental sluggishness. See also **cretinism.**

myxoma (mɪkˈsəʊmə) n., pl. **-mas** or **-mata** (-mətə). a tumour composed of mucous connective tissue, usually situated in subcutaneous tissue. —**myxomatous** (mɪkˈsɒmətəs) adj.

myxomatosis (ˌmɪksəməˈtəʊsɪs) n. an infectious and usually fatal viral disease of rabbits characterized by swelling of the mucous membranes and formation of skin tumours.

myxomycete (ˌmɪksəʊmaɪˈsiːt) n. any of a group of organisms having a naked mass of protoplasm and characteristics of both plants and animals: usually classified as fungi.

myxovirus ('mɪksəʊˌvaɪrəs) n. any of a group of viruses that cause influenza, mumps, etc.

N

n *or* **N** (ɛn) *n., pl.* **n's, N's,** *or* **Ns. 1.** the 14th letter of the English alphabet. **2.** a speech sound represented by this letter.

n¹ *symbol for:* **1.** neutron. **2.** *Optics.* index of refraction. **3.** nano-.

n² (ɛn) *determiner.* an indefinite number (of): *there are n objects in a box.*

N *symbol for:* **1.** Also: **kt.** *Chess.* knight. **2.** newton(s). **3.** *Chem.* nitrogen. **4.** North. **5.** noun. **6.** (*in combination*) nuclear: *N-power; N-plant.*

n. *abbrev. for:* **1.** neuter. **2.** new. **3.** nominative. **4.** noon. **5.** note. **6.** noun. **7.** number.

N. *abbrev. for:* **1.** National(ist). **2.** Navy. **3.** New. **4.** Norse.

Na *the chemical symbol for* sodium. [L *natrium*]

NA *abbrev. for* North America.

NAAFI *or* **Naafi** ('næfɪ) *n.* **1.** *acronym for* Navy, Army, and Air Force Institutes: an organization providing canteens, shops, etc., for British military personnel at home or overseas. **2.** a canteen, shop, etc., run by this organization.

naartjie ('nɑːtʃɪ) *n. S. African.* a tangerine. [from Afrik., from Tamil]

nab (næb) *vb.* **nabbing, nabbed.** (*tr.*) *Inf.* **1.** to arrest (a criminal, etc.). **2.** to seize suddenly; snatch. [C17: ? of Scand. origin]

Nablus ('nɑːbləs) *n.* a town west of the River Jordan: near the site of ancient Shechem. Pop.: 80 000 (1984 est.).

nabob ('neɪbɒb) *n.* **1.** *Inf.* a rich or important man. **2.** (formerly) a European who made a fortune in India. **3.** another name for a **nawab.** [C17: from Port. *nababo*, from Hindi *nawwāb*; see NAWAB]

Nabokov (nə'bɒkɒf, 'næbə,kɒf) *n.* **Vladimir Vladimirovich** (vla'dimir vla'dimirəvitʃ). 1899–1977, U.S. novelist, born in Russia. His works include *Lolita* (1955), *Pnin* (1957), *Pale Fire* (1962), and *Ada* (1969). —**Nabokovian** (,næbə'kəʊvɪən) *adj.*

Nabonidus (,næbə'naɪdəs) *n. Old Testament.* the father of Belshazzar; last king of Babylon before it was captured by Cyrus in 539 B.C.

Naboth ('neɪbɒθ) *n. Old Testament.* an inhabitant of Jezreel, murdered by King Ahab at the instigation of his wife Jezebel for refusing to sell his vineyard (I Kings 21).

NAC *abbrev. for* National Advisory Council.

nacelle (nə'sɛl) *n.* a streamlined enclosure on an aircraft, not part of the fuselage, to accommodate an engine, passengers, crew, etc. [C20: from F: small boat, from LL *navicella*, a dim. of L *navis* ship]

Nachtmusik ('nɑːxtmuː,ziːk) *n.* a piece of music of a serenade-like character. [G: lit., night music]

NACODS ('neɪkɒdz) *n.* (in Britain) *acronym for* National Association of Colliery Overmen, Deputies, and Shotfirers.

nacre ('neɪkə) *n.* the technical name for **mother-of-pearl.** [C16: via F from OIt. *naccara*, from Ar. *naqqārah* shell, drum] —**'nacred** *adj.*

nacreous ('neɪkrɪəs) *adj.* relating to, consisting of, or having the lustre of mother-of-pearl.

NACRO *or* **Nacro** ('nækrəʊ) *n.* (in Britain) *acronym for* National Association for the Care and Resettlement of Offenders.

nadir ('neɪdɪə, 'næ-) *n.* **1.** the point on the celestial sphere directly below an observer and diametrically opposite the zenith. **2.** the lowest point; depths. [C14: from OF, from Ar. *nazir as-samt,* lit.: opposite the zenith]

nae (neɪ) *or* **na** (nɑː) a Scot. word for **no**² or **not.**

naevus *or U.S.* **nevus** ('niːvəs) *n., pl.* **-vi** (-vaɪ). any pigmented blemish on the skin; birthmark or mole. [C19: from L; rel. to (*g*)*natus* born, produced by nature] —**'naevoid** *or U.S.* **'nevoid** *adj.*

naff (næf) *adj. Brit. sl.* inferior or useless. [C19: ?from back slang on *fan,* short for FANNY]

naff off *sentence substitute. Brit sl.* a forceful expression of dismissal or contempt.

nag¹ (næg) *vb.* **nagging, nagged. 1.** to scold or annoy constantly. **2.** (when *intr.,* often foll. by *at*) to be a constant source of discomfort or worry (to). ~*n.* **3.** a person, esp. a woman, who nags. [C19: of Scand. origin] — '**nagger** *n.*

nag² (næg) *n.* **1.** *Often derog.* a horse. **2.** a small riding horse. [C14: of Gmc origin]

Nagaland ('nɑːgə,lænd) *n.* a state of NE India: formed in 1962 from parts of Assam and the North-East Frontier Agency; inhabited chiefly by Naga tribes; consists of almost inaccessible forested hills and mountains (the **Naga Hills**); shifting cultivation predominates. Capital: Kohima. Pop.: 773 281 (1981). Area: 16 488 sq. km (6366 sq. miles).

nagana (nə'gɑːnə) *n.* a disease of hoofed animals of central and southern Africa, transmitted by tsetse flies. [from Zulu *u-nakane*]

Nagano (nə'gɑːnəʊ) *n.* a city in central Japan, on central Honshu: Buddhist shrine; two universities. Pop.: 324 360 (1980).

Nagasaki (,nɑːgə'sɑːkɪ) *n.* a port in SW Japan, on W Kyushu: almost completely destroyed in 1945 by the second atomic bomb dropped on Japan by the U.S.; shipbuilding industry. Pop.: 449 000 (1985).

Nagorno-Karabakh Autonomous Region (nə'gɔːnəʊ-kərʌ'baːk) *n.* an administrative division of the S Soviet Union, in the S Azerbaijan SSR: acquired by Russia in 1813. In 1988 Armenian claims to the Region caused considerable unrest. Capital: Stepanakert. Pop.: 177 000 (1986). Area: 4400 sq. km (1700 sq. miles).

Nagoya ('nɑːgəʊjə) *n.* a city in central Japan, on S Honshu on Ise Bay: a major industrial centre. Pop.: 2 138 000 (1987).

Nagpur (næg'pʊə) *n.* a city in central India, in NE Maharashtra state: became capital of the kingdom of Nagpur (1743); capital of the Central Provinces (later Madhya Pradesh) from 1861 to 1956. Pop.: 1 215 425 (1981).

Nagy (*Hungarian* nɒdj) *n.* **Imre** ('imrɛ). 1896–1958, Hungarian statesman; prime minister (1953–55; 1956). He was removed from office and later executed when Soviet forces suppressed the revolution of 1956.

Nagyszeben ('nɒdjsɛː,bɛn) *n.* the Hungarian name for **Sibiu.**

Nagyvárad ('nɒdjvaːrɒd) *n.* the Hungarian name for **Oradea.**

Nah. *Bible. abbrev. for* Nahum.

Naha ('nɑːhə) *n.* a port in S Japan, on the SW coast of Okinawa Island: chief city of the Ryukyu Islands. Pop.: 304 000 (1985).

Nahuatl ('nɑːwɑːt³l, nɑː'wɑːt³l) *n.* **1.** (*pl.* **-tl** *or* **-tls**) a member of one of a group of Central American and Mexican Indian peoples including the Aztecs. **2.** the language of these peoples.

Nahum ('neɪhəm) *n. Old Testament.* **1.** a Hebrew prophet of the 7th century B.C. **2.** the book containing his oracles.

naiad ('naɪæd) *n., pl.* **-ads** *or* **-ades** (-ə,diːz). **1.** *Greek myth.* a nymph dwelling in a lake, river, or spring. **2.** the aquatic larva of the dragonfly, mayfly, and related insects. **3.** Also called: **water nymph.** a submerged aquatic plant, having narrow leaves and small flowers. [C17: via L from Gk *nāias* water nymph; rel. to *náein* to flow]

naïf (nɑː'iːf) *adj., n.* a less common word for **naive.**

nail (neɪl) *n.* **1.** a fastening device, usually made of metal, having a point at one end and a head at the other. **2.** anything resembling such a device in function or shape. **3.** the horny plate covering part of the dorsal surface of the fingers or toes. Related adj.: **ungual. 4.** the claw of a mammal, bird, or reptile. **5.** a unit of length, formerly used for measuring cloth, equal to two and a quarter inches. **6. hit the nail on the head.** to do or say something correct or telling. **7. on the nail.** (of payments) at once. ~*vb.* (*tr.*) **8.** to attach with or as if with nails. **9.** *Inf.* to arrest, catch, or seize. **10.** *Inf.* to hit or bring down, as with a shot. **11.** *Inf.* to expose or detect (a lie or liar). **12.** to fix (one's eyes, attention, etc.) on. **13.** to stud with nails. [OE *nægl*] — '**nailer** *n.*

nail-biting n. **1.** the act or habit of biting one's finger-nails. **2. a.** anxiety or tension. **b.** (as modifier): nail-biting suspense.

nail bomb n. an explosive device containing nails, used by terrorists to cause serious injuries in crowded situations.

nailbrush ('neɪl,brʌʃ) n. a small stiff-bristled brush for cleaning the fingernails.

nailfile ('neɪl,faɪl) n. a small file of metal or of board coated with emery, used to trim the nails.

nail polish or **varnish** or esp. U.S. **enamel** n. a quick-drying cosmetic lacquer applied to colour the nails or make them shiny or esp. both.

nail set n. a punch for driving the head of a nail below or flush with the surrounding surface.

nainsook ('neɪnsʊk, 'næn-) n. a light soft plain-weave cotton fabric. [C19: from Hindi, from nain eye + sukh delight]

Naipaul (naɪ'pɔːl) n. **V(idiadhar) S(urajprasad).** born 1932, Trinidadian novelist, living in Britain. His novels include A House for Mr Biswas (1961), Mr Stone and the Knights Companion (1963), In a Free State (1971), which won the Booker Prize, and A Bend in the River (1979).

naira ('naɪrə) n. the standard monetary unit of Nigeria. [C20: altered from Nigeria]

Nairnshire ('nɛən,ʃɪə, -ʃə) n. (until 1975) a county of NE Scotland, now part of the Highland region.

Nairobi (naɪ'rəʊbɪ) n. the capital of Kenya, in the southwest at an altitude of 1650 m (5500 ft.): founded in 1899; became capital in 1905; commercial and industrial centre; the **Nairobi National Park** (a game reserve) is nearby. Pop.: 827 800 (1985 est.).

naive, naïve (nɑː'iːv, naɪ'iːv), or **naïf** adj. **1.** having or expressing innocence and credulity; ingenuous. **2.** lacking developed powers of reasoning or criticism: a naive argument. [C17: from F fem. of naif, from OF: native, spontaneous, from L nātīvus NATIVE] —**na'ively, na'ively,** or **na'ifly** adv. —**na'iveness, na'iveness,** or **na'ifness** n.

naivety (naɪ'iːvtɪ), **naiveté,** or **naïveté** (,nɑːiːv'teɪ) n., pl. **-ties** or **-tés. 1.** the state or quality of being naive. **2.** a naive act or statement.

naked ('neɪkɪd) adj. **1.** having the body unclothed; undressed. **2.** having no covering; exposed: a naked flame. **3.** with no qualification or concealment: the naked facts. **4.** unaided by any optical instrument (esp. in **the naked eye**). **5.** with no protection or shield. **6.** (usually foll. by of) destitute: naked of weapons. **7.** (of animals) lacking hair, feathers, scales, etc. **8.** Law. **a.** unsupported by authority: a naked contract. **b.** lacking some essential condition to render valid; incomplete. [OE nacod] —**'nakedly** adv. —**'nakedness** n.

naked ladies n. (functioning as sing.) another name for **autumn crocus.**

naked lady n. a pink orchid found in Australia and New Zealand.

naked singularity n. Astron. a hypothetical location at which there would be a discontinuity in the space-time continuum as a result of the gravitational collapse of a spherical mass. See also **black hole.**

Nakhichevan (Russian nəxitʃɪ'vanj) n. a city in the SW Soviet Union, capital of the Nakhichevan ASSR: an ancient trading town; ceded to Russia in 1828. Pop.: 37 000 (1986 est.). Ancient name: **Naxuana** (,næk'swɑːnə).

Nakhichevan Autonomous Soviet Socialist Republic (nə,kɪtʃɛ'vɑːn) n. an administrative division of the S Soviet Union: belongs to the Azerbaijan SSR, from which it is separated by part of the Armenian SSR; annexed by Russia in 1828. Capital: Nakhichevan. Pop.: 272 000 (1986). Area: 5500 sq. km (2120 sq. miles).

Nakuru (nɑ'kuːruː) n. a town in W Kenya, on Lake Nakuru: commercial centre of an agricultural region. Pop.: 101 700 (1984 est.).

Nalchik (Russian 'naljtʃik) n. a city in the SW Soviet Union, capital of the Kabardino-Balkar ASSR, in a valley of the Greater Caucasus: health resort. Pop.: 213 000 (1981 est.).

NALGO ('nælgəʊ) n. (in Britain) acronym for National and Local Government Officers' Association.

Namangan (Russian nəman'gan) n. a city in the S central Soviet Union, in the E Uzbek SSR. Pop.: 241 000 (1981 est.).

Namaqualand (nə'mɑːkwə,lænd) n. a semiarid coastal region of South West Africa, extending from near Windhoek into Cape Province, South Africa: divided by the Orange River into **Little Namaqualand** in South Africa, and **Great Namaqualand** in Namibia; rich mineral resources. Area: 47 961 sq. km (18 518 sq. miles). Also called: **Namaland** ('nɑːmə,lænd).

namby-pamby (,næmbɪ'pæmbɪ) adj. **1.** sentimental or prim in a weak insipid way. **2.** clinging, feeble, or spineless. ~n., pl. **-bies. 3.** a person who is namby-pamby. [C18: a nickname of Ambrose Phillips (died 1749), whose pastoral verse was ridiculed for being insipid]

Nam Co ('nɑːm 'kɔː) or **Nam Tso** n. a salt lake in SW China, in SE Tibet at an altitude of 4629 m (15 186 ft.). Area: about 1800 sq. km (700 sq. miles). Also called: **Tengri Nor.**

name (neɪm) n. **1.** a word or term by which a person or thing is commonly and distinctively known. **2.** mere outward appearance as opposed to fact: he was ruler in name only. **3.** a word or phrase descriptive of character, usually abusive: to call a person names. **4.** reputation, esp., if unspecified, good reputation: he's made quite a name for himself. **5. a.** a famous person or thing: a name in the advertising world. **b.** Chiefly U.S. & Canad. (as modifier): a name product. **6. in the name of. a.** for the sake of. **b.** by the authority of. **7. name of the game. a.** anything that is significant or important. **b.** normal conditions, circumstances, etc.: in gambling, losing money's the name of the game. **8. to one's name.** belonging to one: I haven't a penny to my name. ~vb. (tr.) **9.** to give a name to. **10.** to refer to by name; cite: he named three French poets. **11.** to fix or specify: they have named a date for the meeting. **12.** to appoint or nominate: he was named Journalist of the Year. **13.** (tr.) to ban (an MP) from the House of Commons by mentioning him formally by name as being guilty of disorderly conduct. **14. name names.** to cite people, esp. in order to blame or accuse them. **15. name the day.** to choose the day for one's wedding. [OE nama, rel. to L nomen, Gk noma] —**'namable** or **'nameable** adj.

name-calling n. verbal abuse, esp. as a crude form of argument.

name day n. **1.** R.C. Church. the feast day of a saint whose name one bears. **2.** another name for **ticket day.**

name-dropping n. Inf. the practice of referring frequently to famous people, esp. as though they were intimate friends, in order to impress others. —**'name-,dropper** n.

nameless ('neɪmlɪs) adj. **1.** without a name. **2.** indescribable: a nameless horror seized him. **3.** too unpleasant or disturbing to be mentioned: nameless atrocities. —**'namelessness** n.

namely ('neɪmlɪ) adv. that is to say.

Namen ('nɑːmə) n. the Flemish name for **Namur.**

nameplate ('neɪm,pleɪt) n. a small panel on or next to the door of a room or building, bearing the occupant's name and profession.

namesake ('neɪm,seɪk) n. a person or thing named after another, or with the same name as another. [C17: prob. describing people connected for the name's sake]

nametape ('neɪm,teɪp) n. a tape attached to clothing, etc., bearing the owner's name.

Namhoi ('nɑːm'hɔɪ) n. another name for **Foshan.**

Namibia (nɑː'mɪbɪə, nə-) n. a disputed territory in southern Africa bordering on South Africa: annexed by Germany in 1884 and mandated by the League of Nations to South Africa in 1920. The mandate was terminated by the UN in 1966 but this was ignored by South Africa, as was the 1971 ruling by the International Court of Justice that the territory be surrendered. Official languages: Afrikaans and English. Religion: mostly animist, with some Christians. Currency: rand. Capital: Windhoek. Pop.: 1 184 000 (1986 est.). Area: 823 328 sq. km (317 887 sq. miles). Also called: **South West Africa.** Former name (1885–1919): **German Southwest Africa.** —**Na'mibian** adj., n.

Nam Tso ('nɑːm 'tsɔː) n. a variant transliteration of the Chinese name for **Nam Co.**

Namur (næ'mʊə; French namyr) n. **1.** a province of S Belgium. Capital: Namur. Pop.: 408 134 (1981 est.). Area: 3660 sq. km (1413 sq. miles). **2.** a town in S Belgium, capital of Namur province: strategically situated on a promontory between the Sambre and Meuse Rivers, besieged and captured many times. Pop.: 102 670 (1987 est.). Flemish name: **Namen.**

nan (næn), **nana**, or **nanna** ('nænə) n. a child's word for **grandmother.**

nana ('nɑːnə) n. Austral. sl. **1.** the head. **2. do one's nana.** to become very angry. **3. off one's nana.** mad; insane. [C19: prob. from BANANA]

Nanak ('nɑːnək) n. 1469–1538, Indian religious leader; founder of Sikhism.

nan bread or **naan** (nɑːn) n. (in Indian cookery) a slightly leavened bread in a large flat loaf shape. [from Hindi]

Nanchang or **Nan-ch'ang** ('næn'tʃæŋ) n. a walled city in SE China, capital of Jiangxi province, on the Kan River: largest city in the Poyang basin. Pop.: 1 120 000 (1986).

Nan-ching ('næn'tʃɪŋ) n. a variant spelling of **Nanjing.**

nancy ('nænsɪ) n., pl. **-cies.** an effeminate or homosexual boy or man. Also called: **nance, nancy boy.** [C20: from the girl's name Nancy]

Nancy ('nænsɪ; French nɑ̃si) n. a city in NE France: became the capital of the dukes of Lorraine in the 12th century, becoming French in 1766; administrative and financial centre. Pop.: 107 439 (1982 est.).

Nanda Devi ('nʌndə 'diːvɪ) n. a mountain in N India, in N Uttar Pradesh in the Himalayas. Height: 7817 m (25 645 ft.).

NAND circuit or **gate** (nænd) n. Electronics. a computer logic circuit having two or more input wires and one output wire that has an output signal if one or more of the input signals are at a low voltage. Cf. **OR circuit.** [C20: from not + AND; see NOT CIRCUIT, AND CIRCUIT]

Nanga Parbat ('nʌŋgə 'pɑːbʌt) n. a mountain in N India, in NW Kashmir in the W Himalayas. Height: 8126 m (26 660 ft.).

Nanhai ('nɑːn'haɪ) n. the Chinese name for the **South China Sea.**

Nanjing ('næn'dʒɪŋ), **Nanking** ('næn'kɪŋ) or **Nan-ching** n. a port in E central China, capital of Jiangsu province, on the Yangtze River: capital of the Chinese empire and a literary centre from the 14th to 17th centuries; capital of Nationalist China (1928–37); university (1928). Pop.: 2 250 000 (1986).

nankeen (næn'kiːn) or **nankin** ('nænkɪn) n. **1.** a hard-wearing buff-coloured cotton fabric. **2. a.** a pale greyish-yellow colour. **b.** (as adj.): a nankeen carpet. [C18: after Nanking, China, where it originated]

Nanning or **Nan-ning** ('næn'nɪŋ) n. a port in S China, capital of Guanxi Zhuang AR, on the Xiang River: rail links with North Vietnam. Pop.: 564 900 (1985 est.).

nanny ('nænɪ) n., pl. **-nies. 1.** a nurse or nursemaid for children. **2.** a child's word for **grandmother.** [C19: child's name for a nurse]

nannygai ('nænɪˌgaɪ) n., pl. **-gais.** an edible red Australian sea fish. [from Abor.]

nanny goat n. a female goat.

nano- combining form. denoting 10⁻⁹: nanosecond. Symbol: n [from L nānus dwarf, from Gk nanos]

nanometre ('nænəʊˌmiːtə) n. one thousand-millionth of a metre. Symbol: nm

nanosecond ('nænəʊˌsɛkənd) n. one thousand-millionth of a second. Symbol: ns

Nansen ('nænsən) n. **Fridtjof** ('fridjɔf). 1861–1930, Norwegian arctic explorer, statesman, and scientist. He crossed Greenland (1888–89) and attempted to reach the North Pole (1893–96), attaining a record 86° 14′ N (1895). He was the League of Nations' high commissioner for refugees (1920–22): Nobel peace prize 1922.

Nansen bottle n. an instrument used by oceanographers for obtaining samples of sea water from a desired depth. [C19: after F. NANSEN]

Nan Shan ('næn 'ʃæn) pl. n. a mountain range in N central China, mainly in Qinghai province, with peaks over 6000 m (20 000 ft.).

Nanterre (French nɑ̃tɛr) n. a town in N France, on the Seine: an industrial suburb of Paris. Pop.: 96 185 (1983 est.).

Nantes (French nɑ̃t) n. a port in W France, at the head of the Loire estuary: scene of the signing of the Edict of Nantes and of the Noyades (drownings) during the French Revolution; extensive shipyards, and large metallurgical and food processing industries. Pop.: 254 634 (1983 est.).

Nantong or **Nantung** ('næn'tʌŋ) n. a city in E China, in Jiangsu province on the Yangtze estuary. Pop.: 507 000 (1980 est.).

Nantucket (næn'tʌkɪt) n. an island off SE Massachusetts: formerly a centre of the whaling industry; now a resort. Length: nearly 24 km (15 miles). Width: 5 km (3 miles).

Naoise ('niːʃə) n. Irish myth. the husband of Deirdre, killed by his uncle Conchobar. See also **Deirdre.**

Naomi ('neɪəmɪ) n. Old Testament. the mother-in-law of Ruth (Ruth 1:2). Douay spelling: **Noemi.**

nap¹ (næp) vb. **napping, napped.** (intr.) **1.** to sleep for a short while; doze. **2.** to be inattentive or off guard (esp. in **catch someone napping**). ~n. **3.** a short light sleep; doze. [OE hnappian]

nap² (næp) n. **1. a.** the raised fibres of velvet or similar cloth. **b.** the direction in which these fibres lie. **2.** any similar downy coating. **3.** Austral. inf. blankets; bedding. ~vb. **napping, napped. 4.** (tr.) to raise the nap of (velvet, etc.) by brushing. [C15: prob. from MDu. noppe]

nap³ (næp) n. **1.** Also called: **napoleon.** a card game similar to whist, usually played for stakes. **2.** a call in this game, undertaking to win all five tricks. **3.** Horse racing. a tipster's choice for a certain winner. **4. nap hand.** a position in which there is a very good chance of success if a risk is taken. ~vb. **napping, napped.** (tr.) **5.** Horse racing. to name (a horse) as likely to win a race. [C19: from NAPOLEON, the card game]

napalm ('neɪpɑːm, 'næ-) n. **1.** a thick and highly incendiary liquid, usually consisting of petrol gelled with aluminium soaps, used in firebombs, flame-throwers, etc. ~vb. **2.** (tr.) to attack with napalm. [C20: from NA(PHTHENE) + palm(itate) salt of PALMITIC ACID]

nape (neɪp) n. the back of the neck. [C13: from ?]

napery ('neɪpərɪ) n. Rare. household linen, esp. table linen. [C14: from OF naperie, from nape tablecloth, from L mappa]

Naphtali ('næftəˌlaɪ) n. Old Testament. **1.** Jacob's sixth son, whose mother was Rachel's handmaid (Genesis 30:7–8). **2.** the tribe descended from him. **3.** the territory of this tribe, between the Sea of Galilee and the mountains of central Galilee. Douay spelling: **Nephtali.**

naphtha ('næfθə, 'næp-) n. a distillation product from coal tar or petroleum: used as a solvent and in petrol. [C16: via L from Gk, from Iranian]

naphthalene ('næfθəˌliːn, 'næp-) n. a white crystalline hydrocarbon with a characteristic penetrating odour, used in mothballs and in dyes, explosives, etc. Formula: $C_{10}H_8$. [C19: from NAPHTHA + ALCOHOL + -ENE] —**naphthalic** (næf'θælɪk, næp-) adj.

naphthene ('næfθiːn, 'næp-) n. any of various cyclic methylene hydrocarbons found in petroleum. [C20: from NAPHTHA + -ENE]

naphthol ('næfθɒl, 'næp-) n. a white crystalline solid having two isomeric forms, used in dyes and as an antioxidant. Formula: $C_{10}H_7OH$. [C19: from NAPHTHA + -OL¹]

Napier¹ ('neɪpɪə) n. a port in New Zealand, on N North Island on Hawke Bay: wool trade centre. Pop.: 52 300 (1983).

Napier² ('neɪpɪə) n. **1.** Sir **Charles James.** 1782–1853, British general and colonial administrator: conquered Sind (1843): governor of Sind (1843–47). **2. John.** 1550–1617, Scottish mathematician: invented logarithms and pioneered the decimal notation used today.

Napierian logarithm (nə'pɪərɪən, neɪ-) n. another name for **natural logarithm.**

Napier's bones pl. n. a set of graduated rods formerly used for multiplication and division. [C17: based on a method invented by John NAPIER]

napkin ('næpkɪn) n. **1.** Also called: **table napkin.** a usually square piece of cloth or paper used while eating to protect the clothes, wipe the mouth, etc.; serviette. **2.** Rare. a small piece of cloth. **3.** a more formal name for **nappy¹. 4.** a less common term for **sanitary towel.** [C15: from OF, from nape tablecloth, from L mappa cloth]

Naples ('neɪpəlz) n. a port in SW Italy, capital of Campania region, on the Bay of Naples: the third largest city in the country; founded by Greeks in the 6th century B.C.; incorporated into the Kingdom of the Two Sicilies in 1140 and its capital (1282–1503); university (1224). Pop.: 1 204 211 (1986). Ancient name: **Ne'apolis.** Italian name: **Napoli.** Related adj.: **Neapolitan. 2. Bay of.** an inlet of the Tyrrhenian Sea in the SW coast of Italy.

napoleon (nə'pəʊliən) *n.* **1.** a former French gold coin worth 20 francs. **2.** *Cards.* the full name for **nap**³ (sense 1). [C19: from F *napoléon*, after NAPOLEON I]

Napoleon I (nə'pəʊliən) *n.* full name *Napoleon Bonaparte.* 1769–1821, Emperor of the French (1804–15). He came to power as the result of a coup in 1799 and established an extensive European empire. A brilliant general, he defeated every European coalition against him until, irreparably weakened by the Peninsular War and the Russian campaign (1812), his armies were defeated at Leipzig (1813). He went into exile but escaped and ruled as emperor during the Hundred Days. He was finally defeated at Waterloo (1815). As an administrator, his achievements were of lasting significance and include the *Code Napoléon*, which remains the basis of French law. —**Na,po'le'onic** *adj.*

Napoleon II *n.* Duke of Reichstadt. 1811–32, son of Napoleon Bonaparte and Marie Louise. He was known as the *King of Rome* during the first French empire and was entitled Napoleon II by Bonapartists after Napoleon I's death (1821).

Napoleon III *n.* full name *Charles Louis Napoleon Bonaparte,* known as *Louis-Napoleon.* 1808–73, Emperor of the French (1852–70); nephew of Napoleon I. He led two abortive Bonapartist risings (1836; 1840) and was elected president of the Second Republic (1848), establishing the Second Empire in 1852. Originally successful in foreign affairs, he was deposed after the disastrous Franco-Prussian War.

Napoli ('na:poli) *n.* the Italian name for **Naples**.

nappe (næp) *n.* **1.** a large sheet or mass of rock, originally a recumbent fold, that has been thrust from its original position by earth movements. **2.** the sheet of water that flows over a dam or weir. **3.** *Geom.* either of the two parts into which a cone is divided by the vertex. [C20: from F: tablecloth]

nappy¹ ('næpɪ) *n., pl.* **-pies.** *Brit.* a piece of soft towelling or other absorbent material wrapped around a baby in order to absorb its excrement. Also called: **napkin**. U.S. and Canad. name: **diaper**. [C20: changed from NAPKIN]

nappy² ('næpɪ) *adj.* **-pier, -piest. 1.** having a nap; downy; fuzzy. **2.** (of beer) **a.** having a head; frothy. **b.** strong or heady.

Nara ('nɑ:rə) *n.* a city in central Japan, on S Honshu: the first permanent capital of Japan (710–784). Pop.: 328 000 (1985).

Narayan (nə'raɪjən) *n.* **R(asipuram) K(rishnaswamy).** born 1906, Indian novelist writing in English. His books include *Swami and Friends* (1938), *The Man-Eater of Malgudi* (1961), and *Under the Banyan Tree* (1985).

Narayanganj (nə'rɑːjən,gʌndʒ) *n.* a city in central Bangladesh, on the Ganges delta just southeast of Dhaka. Pop.: 196 139 (1981 est.).

Narbada (nə'bʌdə) *n.* another name for the **Narmada**.

Narbonne (*French* narbɔn) *n.* a city in S France: capital of the Roman province of **Gallia Narbonensis**; harbour silted up in the 14th century. Pop.: 39 246 (1983 est.).

narcissism ('nɑ:sɪ,sɪzəm) *or* **narcism** ('nɑ:sɪzəm) *n.* **1.** an exceptional interest in or admiration for oneself, esp. one's physical appearance. **2.** sexual satisfaction derived from contemplation of one's own physical endowments. [C19: after NARCISSUS] —**narcissist** *n.* —**narcis'sistic** *adj.*

narcissus (nɑ:'sɪsəs) *n., pl.* **-cissuses** *or* **-cissi** (-'sɪsaɪ). a plant of a Eurasian genus whose yellow, orange, or white flowers have a crown surrounded by spreading segments. [C16: via L from Gk *nárkissos*, ?from *narkē* numbness, because of narcotic properties attributed to the plant]

Narcissus (nɑ:'sɪsəs) *n. Greek myth.* a beautiful youth who fell in love with his reflection in a pool and pined away, becoming the flower that bears his name.

narco- *or sometimes before a vowel* **narc-** *combining form.* **1.** indicating numbness or torpor: *narcolepsy.* **2.** connected with or derived from illicit drug production: *narcoeconomies.* [from Gk *narkē* numbness]

narcoanalysis (,nɑ:kəʊə'nælɪsɪs) *n.* psychoanalysis of a patient in a trance induced by a narcotic drug.

narcolepsy ('nɑ:kə,lɛpsɪ) *n. Pathol.* a rare condition characterized by sudden episodes of deep sleep. —**,nar'co'leptic** *adj.*

narcosis (nɑ:'kəʊsɪs) *n.* unconsciousness induced by narcotics or general anaesthetics.

narcosynthesis (,nɑ:kəʊ'sɪnθɪsɪs) *n.* a method of treating severe personality disorders by working with the patient while he is under the influence of a barbiturate drug.

narcotic (nɑ:'kɒtɪk) *n.* **1.** any of a group of drugs, such as opium and morphine, that produce numbness and stupor. **2.** anything that relieves pain or induces sleep, mental numbness, etc. ~*adj.* **3.** of or relating to narcotics or narcotics addicts. **4.** of or relating to narcosis. [C14: via Med. L from Gk *narkōtikós*, from *narkoūn* to numb, from *narkē* numbness] —**nar'cotically** *adv.*

narcotism ('nɑ:kə,tɪzəm) *n.* stupor or addiction induced by narcotic drugs.

narcotize *or* **-tise** ('nɑ:kə,taɪz) *vb.* (*tr.*) to place under the influence of a narcotic drug. —**,narcoti'zation** *or* **-ti'sation** *n.*

nard (nɑ:d) *n.* **1.** another name for **spikenard. 2.** any of several plants whose aromatic roots were formerly used in medicine. [C14: via L from Gk *nárdos*, ? ult. from Sansk. *nalada* Indian spikenard]

nardoo ('nɑ:du:) *n.* (in Australia) **1.** any of certain cloverlike ferns that grow in swampy areas. **2.** the spores of such a plant, used as food. [C19: from Abor.]

nares ('nɛəri:z) *pl. n., sing.* **naris** ('nɛərɪs). *Anat.* the nostrils. [C17: from L; rel. to OE *nasu*, L *nāsus* nose] —**'narial** *adj.*

narghile, nargile, *or* **nargileh** ('nɑ:gɪlɪ, -,leɪ) *n.* another name for **hookah**. [C19: from F *narguilé*, from Persian *nārgīleh* a pipe having a bowl made of coconut shell, from *nārgīl* coconut]

nark (nɑ:k) *Sl.* ~*n.* **1.** *Brit., Austral., & N.Z.* an informer or spy: *copper's nark.* **2.** *Brit.* someone who complains in an irritating or whining manner. ~*vb.* **3.** *Brit., Austral., & N.Z.* to annoy, upset, or irritate. **4.** (*intr.*) *Brit., Austral., & N.Z.* to inform or spy, esp. for the police. **5.** (*intr.*) *Brit.* to complain irritatingly. [C19: prob. from Romany *nāk* nose]

narky ('nɑ:kɪ) *adj.* **narkier, narkiest.** *Sl.* irritable, complaining, or sarcastic.

Narmada (nə'mʌdə) *or* **Narbada** *n.* a river in central India, rising in Madhya Pradesh and flowing generally west to the Gulf of Cambay in a wide estuary: the second most sacred river in India. Length: 1290 km (801 miles).

Narraganset (,nærə'gænsɪt) *n.* **1.** (*pl.* **-set** *or* **-sets**) a member of a North American Indian people formerly living in Rhode Island. **2.** the language of this people, belonging to the Algonquian family.

Narragansett Bay *n.* an inlet of the Atlantic in SE Rhode Island: contains several islands, including Rhode Island, Prudence Island, and Conanicut Island.

narrate (nə'reɪt) *vb.* **1.** to tell (a story); relate. **2.** to speak in accompaniment of (a film, etc.). [C17: from L *narrāre* to recount, from *gnārus* knowing] —**nar'ratable** *adj.* —**nar'rator** *n.*

narration (nə'reɪʃən) *n.* **1.** the act or process of narrating. **2.** a narrated account or story.

narrative ('nærətɪv) *n.* **1.** an account or story, as of events, experiences, etc. **2.** the part of a literary work, etc., that relates events. **3.** the process or technique of narrating. ~*adj.* **4.** telling a story: *a narrative poem.* **5.** of or relating to narration: *narrative art.*

narrow ('nærəʊ) *adj.* **1.** small in breadth, esp. in comparison to length. **2.** limited in range or extent. **3.** limited in outlook. **4.** limited in means or resources. **5.** barely adequate or successful (esp. in **a narrow escape**). **6.** painstakingly thorough: *a narrow scrutiny.* **7.** *Finance.* denoting an assessment of liquidity as including notes and coin in circulation with the public, banks' till money, and banks' balances: *narrow money.* Cf. **broad** (sense 12). **8.** *Phonetics.* another word for **tense**¹ (sense 4). ~*vb.* **9.** to make or become narrow; limit; restrict. ~*n.* **10.** a narrow place, esp. a pass or strait. ~See also **narrows.** [OE *nearu*] —**'narrowly** *adv.* —**'narrowness** *n.*

narrow boat *n.* a long bargelike boat with a beam of 2.1 metres (7 feet), used on canals.

narrow gauge *n.* **1.** a railway track with a smaller distance between the lines than the standard gauge of 56½ inches. ~*adj.* **narrow-gauge. 2.** of or denoting a railway with a narrow gauge.

narrow-minded *adj.* having a biased or illiberal viewpoint; bigoted, intolerant, or prejudiced. —**,narrow-'mindedness** *n.*

narrows ('nærəʊz) *pl. n.* a narrow part of a strait, river, current, etc.

narthex ('nɑːθɛks) n. **1.** a portico at the west end of a church, esp. one at right angles to the nave. **2.** a rectangular entrance hall between the porch and nave of a church. [C17: via L from Med. Gk: enclosed porch (earlier: box), from Gk narthēx giant fennel, the stems of which were used to make boxes]

Narva (Russian 'narvə) n. a port in the W Soviet Union, in the Estonian SSR on the Narva River near the Gulf of Finland: developed around a Danish fortress in the 13th century; textile centre. Pop.: 78 000 (1983 est.).

Narvik ('nɑːvɪk; Norwegian 'narvik) n. a port in N Norway: scene of two naval battles in 1940; exports iron ore from Kiruna and Gällivare (Sweden). Pop.: 19 080 (1983 est.).

narwhal, narwal ('nɑːwəl), or **narwhale** ('nɑːˌweɪl) n. an arctic toothed whale having a black-spotted whitish skin and, in the male, a long spiral tusk. [C17: of Scand. origin; cf. Danish, Norwegian narhval, from ON nāhvalr, from nār corpse + hvalr whale]

nary ('nɛərɪ) adv. Dialect or inf. not; never: nary a man was left. [C19: var. of ne'er a never a]

NASA ('næsə) n. (in the U.S.) acronym for National Aeronautics and Space Administration.

nasal ('neɪzəl) adj. **1.** of the nose. **2.** Phonetics. pronounced with the soft palate lowered allowing air to escape via the nasal cavity. ~n. **3.** a nasal speech sound, such as English m, n, or ng. [C17: from F from LL nāsālis, from L nāsus nose] —**nasality** (neɪˈzælɪtɪ) n. —'**nasally** adv.

nasalize or -**lise** ('neɪzə‚laɪz) vb. (tr.) to pronounce nasally. —‚**nasali'zation** or -**li'sation** n.

nascent ('næsənt, 'neɪ-) adj. starting to grow or develop; being born. [C17: from L nascēns, present participle of nāscī to be born] —'**nascency** n.

nascent hydrogen n. Chem. hydrogen produced in a reactive form within the reaction mixture.

Nash (næʃ) n. **1. John.** 1752–1835, English town planner and architect. He designed Regent's Park, Regent Street, and the Marble Arch in London. **2. Ogden.** 1902–71, U.S. humorous poet. **3. Paul.** 1889–1946, English painter, noted esp. as a war artist in both World Wars and for his landscapes. **4. Richard,** known as Beau Nash. 1674–1762, English dandy. **5.** See (Thomas) **Nashe. 6.** Sir **Walter.** 1882–1968, New Zealand statesman, born in England: prime minister of New Zealand (1957–60).

Nashe or **Nash** (næʃ) n. **Thomas.** 1567–1601, English pamphleteer, satirist, and novelist, author of the first picaresque novel in English, The Unfortunate Traveller, or the Life of Jack Wilton (1594).

Nashville ('næʃvɪl) n. a city in central Tennessee, the state capital, on the Cumberland River: an industrial and commercial centre, noted for its recording industry. Pop.: 473 670 (1986 est.).

naso- combining form. nose: nasopharynx. [from L nāsus nose]

Nassau n. **1.** (German 'nasau). a region of central West Germany: formerly a duchy (1816–66), from which a branch of the House of Orange arose (represented by the present rulers of the Netherlands and Luxembourg); annexed to the Prussian province of Hesse-Nassau in 1866; corresponds to present-day W Hesse and NE Rhineland-Palatinate states. **2.** ('næsɔː). the capital and chief port of the Bahamas, on the NE coast of New Providence Island: resort. Pop.: 135 000 (1982 est.).

Nasser ('nɑːsə, 'næsə) n. **Gamal Abdel** (gəˈmɑːl 'æbdɛl). 1918–70, Egyptian soldier and statesman; president of Egypt (1956–70). He was one of the leaders of the coup that deposed King Farouk (1952) and became premier (1954). His nationalization of the Suez Canal (1956) led to an international crisis, and during his presidency Egypt was twice defeated by Israel (1956; 1967).

nastic movement ('næstɪk) n. a response of plant parts that is independent of the direction of the external stimulus, such as the opening of buds caused by an alteration in light intensity. [C19 nastic, from Gk nastos close-packed, from nassein to press down]

nasturtium (nəˈstɜːʃəm) n. a plant having round leaves and yellow, red, or orange trumpet-shaped spurred flowers. [C17: from L: kind of cress, from nāsus nose + tortus twisted; because the pungent smell causes one to wrinkle one's nose]

nasty ('nɑːstɪ) adj. **-tier, -tiest. 1.** unpleasant or repugnant. **2.** dangerous or painful: a nasty wound. **3.** spiteful

or ill-natured. **4.** obscene or indecent. ~n., pl. -**ties. 5.** an offensive or unpleasant person or thing: a video nasty. [C14: from ?; prob. rel. to Swedish dialect nasket & Du. nestig dirty] —'**nastily** adv. —'**nastiness** n.

NAS/UWT (in Britain) abbrev. for National Association of Schoolmasters/Union of Women Teachers.

nat. abbrev. for. **1.** national. **2.** native. **3.** natural.

natal ('neɪtəl) adj. of or relating to birth. [C14: from L nātālis of one's birth, from nātus, from nascī to be born]

Natal n. **1.** (nə'tæl). a province of E South Africa, between the Drakensberg and the Indian Ocean: set up as a republic by the Boers in 1838; became a British colony in 1843; joined South Africa in 1910. Capital: Pietermaritzburg. Pop.: 2 145 018 (1985). Area: 86 967 sq. km (33 578 sq. miles). **2.** (Portuguese na'tal). a port in NE Brazil, capital of Rio Grande do Norte state, near the mouth of the Potengi River. Pop.: 512 241 (1985).

natant ('neɪtənt) adj. floating or swimming. [C18: from L natāns, present participle of natāre to swim]

natation (nə'teɪʃən) n. a literary word for **swimming.** [C16: from L natātiō a swimming, from natāre to swim]

natatory (nə'teɪtərɪ) or **natatorial** (‚nætə'tɔːrɪəl) adj. of or relating to swimming. [C18: from LL natātōrius, from L natāre to swim]

natch (nætʃ) sentence substitute. Inf. short for **naturally.**

nates ('neɪtiːz) pl. n., sing. -**tis** (-tɪs). a technical word for the **buttocks.** [C17: from L]

NATFHE (in Britain) abbrev. for National Association of Teachers in Further and Higher Education.

Nathan ('neɪθən) n. Old Testament. a prophet at David's court (II Samuel 7:1–17; 12:1–15).

Nathanael (nə'θænjəl) n. New Testament. a Galilean who is perhaps to be identified with Bartholomew among the apostles (John 1:45–51; 21:1).

natheless ('neɪθlɪs) or **nathless** ('næθlɪs) Arch. sentence connector. nonetheless. [OE nāthylæs, from nā never + thý for that + læs less]

nation ('neɪʃən) n. **1.** an aggregation of people or peoples of one or more cultures, races, etc., organized into a single state: the Australian nation. **2.** a community of persons not constituting a state but bound by common descent, language, history, etc.: the French-Canadian nation. [C13: via OF from L nātiō birth, tribe, from nascī to be born] —'**nation,hood** n.

national ('næʃənəl) adj. **1.** of or relating to a nation as a whole. **2.** characteristic of a particular nation: the national dress of Poland. ~n. **3.** a citizen or subject. **4.** a national newspaper. —'**nationally** adv.

national anthem n. a patriotic song adopted by a nation for use on public occasions.

national assistance n. the former name for **supplementary benefit.**

national bank n. **1.** (in the U.S.) a commercial bank incorporated under a Federal charter and legally required to be a member of the Federal Reserve System. **2.** a bank operated by a government.

National Country Party n. an Australian political party drawing its main support from rural areas. Often shortened to: **National Party.**

national debt n. the total outstanding borrowings of a nation's central government.

National Economic Development Council n. an advisory body on economic policy in Britain, composed of representatives of government, management, and trade unions. Abbrevs.: **NEDC,** (inf.) **Neddy.**

National Enterprise Board n. a public corporation established in 1975 to help the economy of the UK, develop its industrial efficiency, and support its productive employment. Abbrev.: **NEB.**

National Football n. (in Australia) another name for **Australian Rules.**

National Front n. an extreme right-wing British political party founded in 1967.

National Gallery n. a major art gallery in London, in Trafalgar Square. It contains the largest collection of paintings in Britain.

national grid n. Brit. **1.** a network of high-voltage electric power lines linking major electric power stations. **2.** the metric coordinate system used in ordnance survey maps.

National Guard n. **1.** (sometimes not cap.) the armed force that was established in France in 1789 and existed intermittently until 1871. **2.** (in the U.S.) a state military force that can be called into federal service by the president.

National Health Service *n.* (in Britain) the system of national medical services since 1948, financed mainly by taxation. Abbrev: **NHS.**

national income *n. Econ.* the total of all incomes accruing over a specified period to residents of a country.

national insurance *n.* (in Britain) state insurance based on weekly contributions from employees and employers and providing payments to the unemployed, the sick, the retired, etc., as well as medical services.

nationalism ('næʃənə,lɪzəm) *n.* **1.** a sentiment based on common cultural characteristics that binds a population and often produces a policy of national independence. **2.** loyalty to one's country; patriotism. **3.** exaggerated or fanatical devotion to a national community. —'**nationalist** *n., adj.* —,**national'istic** *adj.*

Nationalist China *n.* an unofficial name for (the Republic of) **China.**

Nationalist Party *n.* (in South Africa) the largest political party in Parliament: composed mainly of centre to right-wing Afrikaners.

nationality (,næʃə'nælɪtɪ) *n., pl.* **-ties. 1.** the fact of being a citizen of a particular nation. **2.** a body of people sharing common descent, history, language, etc.; a nation. **3.** a national group: *30 different nationalities are found in this city.* **4.** national character. **5.** the fact of being a nation; national status.

nationalize *or* **-lise** ('næʃənə,laɪz) *vb.* (*tr.*) **1.** to put (an industry, resources, etc.) under state control. **2.** to make national in character or status. **3.** a less common word for **naturalize.** —,**nationali'zation** *or* **-li'sation** *n.*

national park *n.* an area of countryside designated by a national government as being of notable scenic, environmental, or historical importance.

National Park *n. N.Z.* a mountainous volcanic region in the North Island.

National Party *n.* **1.** (in New Zealand) the more conservative of the two main political parties. **2.** (in Australia) another name for **National Country Party.**

National Savings Bank *n.* (in Britain) a government savings bank, run through the Post Office.

national service *n. Chiefly Brit.* compulsory military service.

National Socialism *n. German history.* the doctrines and practices of the Nazis, involving the supremacy of Hitler as Führer, anti-Semitism, state control of the economy, and national expansion. —**National Socialist** *n., adj.*

national superannuation *n. N.Z.* a government pension given on the attainment of a specified age; old age pension.

National Theatre *n.* the former name of the **Royal National Theatre.**

National Trust *n.* (in Britain) an organization concerned with the preservation of historic buildings and areas of the countryside of great beauty.

nationwide ('neɪʃən,waɪd) *adj.* covering or available to the whole of a nation; national.

native ('neɪtɪv) *adj.* **1.** relating or belonging to a person by virtue of conditions existing at birth: *a native language.* **2.** natural or innate: *native wit.* **3.** born in a specified place: *a native Indian.* **4.** (when *postpositive*, foll. by *to*) originating in: *kangaroos are native to Australia.* **5.** relating to the indigenous inhabitants of a country: *the native art of the New Guinea Highlands.* **6.** (of metals) found naturally in the elemental form; not chemically combined as in an ore. **7.** unadulterated by civilization, artifice, or adornment; natural. **8.** *Arch.* related by birth or race. **9. go native.** (of a settler) to adopt the lifestyle of the local population, esp. when it appears less civilized. ~*n.* **10.** (usually foll. by *of*) a person born in a particular place: *a native of Geneva.* **11.** (usually foll. by *of*) a species of animal or plant originating in a particular place. **12.** a member of an indigenous people of a country, esp. a non-White people, as opposed to colonial immigrants. [C14: from L *nātīvus* innate, natural, from *nasci* to be born] —'**natively** *adv.* —'**nativeness** *n.*

native bear *n.* an Australian name for **koala.**

native-born *adj.* born in the country or area indicated.

native companion *n.* (in Australia) another name for **brolga.**

native dog *n. Austral.* a dingo.

Native States *pl. n.* the former 562 semi-independent states of India, ruled by Indians but subject to varying degrees of British authority: merged with provinces by 1948; largest states were Hyderabad, Gwalior, Baroda, Mysore, Cochin, Jammu and Kashmir, Travancore, Sikkim, and Indore. Also called: **Indian States and Agencies.**

nativity (nə'tɪvɪtɪ) *n., pl.* **-ties.** birth or origin. [C14: from LL *nātīvitas* birth; see NATIVE]

Nativity (nə'tɪvɪtɪ) *n.* **1.** the birth of Christ. **2.** the feast of Christmas as a commemoration of this. **3. a.** an artistic representation of the circumstances of the birth of Christ. **b.** (*as modifier*): *a Nativity play.*

NATO *or* **Nato** ('neɪtəʊ) *n. acronym for* North Atlantic Treaty Organization: an international organization established (1949) for purposes of collective security.

natron ('neɪtrən) *n.* a whitish or yellow mineral that consists of hydrated sodium carbonate and occurs in saline deposits and salt lakes. [C17: via F & Sp. from Ar. *natrūn,* from Gk *nitron* NITRE]

NATSOPA (næt'səʊpə) *n.* (in Britain) *acronym for* National Society of Operative Printers, Graphical and Media Personnel.

natter ('nætə) *Chiefly Brit. inf.* ~*vb.* **1.** (*intr.*) to talk idly and at length; chatter. ~*n.* **2.** prolonged idle chatter. [C19: from *gnatter* to grumble, imit.]

natterjack ('nætə,dʒæk) *n.* a European toad having a greyish-brown body marked with reddish warty processes. [C18: from ?]

natty ('nætɪ) *adj.* **-tier, -tiest.** *Inf.* smart; spruce; dapper. [C18: from obs. *netty,* from *net* NEAT[1]] —'**nattily** *adv.* —'**nattiness** *n.*

natural ('nætʃrəl) *adj.* **1.** of, existing in, or produced by nature: *natural science; natural cliffs.* **2.** in accordance with human nature. **3.** as is normal or to be expected: *the natural course of events.* **4.** not acquired; innate: *a natural gift for sport.* **5.** being so through innate qualities: *a natural leader.* **6.** not supernatural or strange: *natural phenomena.* **7.** genuine or spontaneous. **8.** lifelike: *she looked more natural without make-up.* **9.** not affected by man; wild: *in the natural state this animal is not ferocious.* **10.** being or made from organic material; not synthetic: *a natural fibre like cotton.* **11.** born out of wedlock. **12.** not adopted but rather related by blood: *her natural parents.* **13.** *Music.* **a.** not sharp or flat. **b.** (*postpositive*) denoting a note that is neither sharp nor flat. **c.** (of a key or scale) containing no sharps or flats. **14.** based on the principles and findings of human reason rather than on revelation: *natural religion.* ~*n.* **15.** *Inf.* a person or thing regarded as certain to qualify for success, selection, etc.: *the horse was a natural for first place.* **16.** *Music.* **a.** Also called (U.S.): **cancel.** an accidental cancelling a previous sharp or flat. Usual symbol: ♮ **b.** a note affected by this accidental. **17.** *Obs.* an imbecile; idiot. —'**naturalness** *n.*

natural childbirth *n.* a method of childbirth characterized by the absence of anaesthetics, in which the expectant mother is given special breathing and relaxing exercises.

natural gas *n.* a gaseous mixture, consisting mainly of methane, trapped below ground; used extensively as a fuel.

natural history *n.* **1.** the study of animals and plants in the wild state. **2.** the sum of these phenomena in a given place or at a given time. —**natural historian** *n.*

naturalism ('nætʃrə,lɪzəm) *n.* **1.** a movement, esp. in art and literature, advocating detailed realistic and factual description. **2.** the belief that all religious truth is based not on revelation but rather on the study of natural causes and processes. **3.** *Philosophy.* a scientific account of the world in terms of causes and natural forces. **4.** action or thought caused by natural instincts.

naturalist ('nætʃrəlɪst) *n.* **1.** a person who is versed in or interested in botany or zoology. **2.** a person who advocates or practises naturalism.

naturalistic (,nætʃrə'lɪstɪk) *adj.* **1.** of or reproducing nature in effect or characteristics. **2.** of or characteristic of naturalism. **3.** of naturalists. —,**natural'istically** *adv.*

naturalize *or* **-lise** ('nætʃrə,laɪz) *vb.* **1.** (*tr.*) to give citizenship to (a person of foreign birth). **2.** to be or cause to be adopted in another place, as a word, custom, etc. **3.** (*tr.*) to introduce (a plant or animal from another region) and cause it to adapt to local conditions. **4.** (*intr.*) (of a plant or animal) to adapt successfully to a foreign environment. **5.** (*tr.*) to make natural or more lifelike. —,naturali'zation *or* -li'sation *n.*

natural language *n.* a language that has evolved naturally as a means of communication among people, as opposed to an invented language or a code.

natural logarithm *n.* a logarithm to the base e. Usually written log$_e$ or ln. Also called: **Napierian logarithm.**

naturally ('nætʃrəlɪ) *adv.* **1.** in a natural way. **2.** instinctively. ~*adv., sentence substitute.* **3.** of course; surely.

natural number *n.* any of the positive integers 1, 2, 3, 4, . . .

natural philosophy *n.* physical science, esp. physics. —**natural philosopher** *n.*

natural resources *pl. n.* naturally occurring materials such as coal, fertile land, etc.

natural science *n.* the sciences that are involved in the study of the physical world and its phenomena, including biology, physics, chemistry, and geology.

natural selection *n.* a process resulting in the survival of those individuals from a population of animals or plants that are best adapted to the prevailing environmental conditions.

natural theology *n.* the attempt to derive theological truth, and esp. the existence of God, from empirical facts by reasoned argument. Cf. **revealed religion.**

natural wastage *n.* the loss of employees, etc., through not replacing those who retire or resign rather than dismissal or redundancy.

nature ('neitʃə) *n.* **1.** fundamental qualities; identity or essential character. **2.** (*often cap.*) the whole system of the existence, forces, and events of all physical life that are not controlled by man. **3.** plant and animal life, as distinct from man. **4.** a wild primitive state untouched by man. **5.** natural unspoilt countryside. **6.** disposition or temperament. **7.** desires or instincts governing behaviour. **8.** the normal biological needs of the body. **9.** sort; character. **10. against nature.** unnatural or immoral. **11. by nature.** essentially or innately. **12. call of nature.** *Inf.* the need to urinate or defecate. **13. from nature.** using natural models in drawing, painting, etc. **14. in** (*or* **of**) **the nature of.** essentially the same as; by way of. [C13: via OF from L *nātūra*, from *nātus*, p.p. of *nascī* to be born]

nature reserve *n.* an area of land that is protected and managed in order to preserve its flora and fauna.

nature strip *n. Austral. inf.* a grass strip running along in front of a house or beside a road or between carriageways.

nature study *n.* the study of the natural world, esp. animals and plants, by direct observation at an elementary level.

nature trail *n.* a path through countryside designed and usually signposted to draw attention to natural features of interest.

naturism ('neitʃə,rizəm) *n.* another name for **nudism.** —'**naturist** *n., adj.*

naturopathy (,nætʃə'rɒpæθɪ) *n.* the treatment of illness by stimulating natural healing, esp. by herbal remedies, manipulation, etc.—'**naturo,path** *n.* —,naturo'pathic *adj.*

Naucratis ('nɔːkrətɪs) *n.* an ancient Greek city in N Egypt, in the Nile delta: founded in the 7th century B.C.

naught (nɔːt) *n.* **1.** *Arch. or literary.* nothing; ruin or failure. **2.** a variant spelling (esp. U.S.) of **nought. 3. set at naught.** to disregard or scorn; disdain. ~*adv.* **4.** *Arch. or literary.* not at all: *it matters naught.* ~*adj.* **5.** *Obs.* worthless, ruined, or wicked. [OE *nāwiht*, from *nā* NO[1] + *wiht* thing, person]

naughty ('nɔːtɪ) *adj.* **-tier, -tiest. 1.** (esp. of children) mischievous or disobedient. **2.** mildly indecent; titillating. [C14: (orig.: needy, poor): from NAUGHT] —'**naughtily** *adv.* —'**naughtiness** *n.*

nauplius ('nɔːplɪəs) *n., pl.* **-plii** (-plɪ,aɪ). the larva of many crustaceans, having a rounded unsegmented body with three pairs of limbs. [C19: from L: type of shellfish, from Gk *Nauplios*, one of the sons of the Greek god Poseidon]

Nauru (nɑː'uːruː) *n.* an island republic in the SW Pacific, west of Kiribati: administered jointly by Australia, New Zealand, and Britain as a UN trust territory before becoming an independent member of the Commonwealth in 1968. The economy is based on export of phosphates. Languages: Nauruan (a Malayo-Polynesian language) and

English. Religion: Christian. Currency: Australian dollar. Pop.: 8100 (1987). Area: 2130 hectares (5263 acres). Former name: **Pleasant Island.** —**Na'uruan** *adj., n.*

nausea ('nɔːzɪə, -sɪə) *n.* **1.** the sensation that precedes vomiting. **2.** a feeling of revulsion. [C16: via L from Gk: seasickness, from *naus* ship]

nauseate ('nɔːzɪ,eɪt, -sɪ-) *vb.* **1.** (*tr.*) to arouse feelings of disgust or revulsion in. **2.** to feel or cause to feel sick. —'**nause,ating** *adj.*

nauseous ('nɔːzɪəs, -sɪəs) *adj.* **1.** causing nausea. **2.** distasteful; repulsive. —'**nauseously** *adv.* —'**nauseousness** *n.*

Nausicaä (nɔː'sɪkɪə) *n. Greek myth.* a daughter of Alcinous, king of the Phaeacians, who assisted the shipwrecked Odysseus after discovering him on a beach.

nautch *or* **nauch** (nɔːtʃ) *n.* an intricate traditional Indian dance performed by professional dancing girls. [C18: from Hindi *nāc*, from Sansk., from *nrtyati* he acts or dances]

nautical ('nɔːtɪkəl) *adj.* of or involving ships, navigation, or seamen. [C16: from L *nauticus*, from Gk *nautikos*, from *naus* ship] —'**nautically** *adv.*

nautical mile *n.* a unit of length, used esp. in navigation, equal to 1852 metres (6076.103 feet). Also called: **international nautical mile, air mile.**

nautilus ('nɔːtɪləs) *n., pl.* **-luses** *or* **-li** (-,laɪ). **1.** any of a genus of cephalopod molluscs, esp. the pearly nautilus. **2.** short for **paper nautilus.** [C17: via L from Gk *nautilos* sailor, from *naus* ship]

Navaho *or* **Navajo** ('nævə,həʊ) *n.* **1.** (*pl.* **-ho, -hos, -hoes** *or* **-jo, -jos, -joes**) a member of a North American Indian people of Arizona, New Mexico, and Utah. **2.** the language of this people. [C18: from Sp. *Navajó* pueblo, from Tena *Navahu* large planted field]

naval ('neivəl) *adj.* **1.** of, characteristic of, or having a navy. **2.** of or relating to ships; nautical. [C16: from L *nāvālis*, from *nāvis* ship]

naval architecture *n.* the designing of ships. —**naval architect** *n.*

navarin ('nævərɪn) *n.* a stew of mutton or lamb with root vegetables. [from F]

Navarino (nava'riːno) *n.* the Italian name for **Pylos.**

Navarre (nə'vɑː) *n.* a former kingdom of SW Europe: established in the 9th century by the Basques; the parts south of the Pyrenees joined Spain in 1515 and the N parts passed to France in 1589. Capital: Pamplona. Spanish name: **Navarra** (na'βarra).

nave[1] (neɪv) *n.* the central space in a church, extending from the narthex to the chancel and often flanked by aisles. [C17: via Med. L from L *nāvis* ship, from the similarity of shape]

nave[2] (neɪv) *n.* the central block or hub of a wheel. [OE *nafu, nafa*]

navel ('neivəl) *n.* **1.** the scar in the centre of the abdomen, usually forming a slight depression, where the umbilical cord was attached. Technical name: **umbilicus.** Related adj.: **umbilical. 2.** a central part or point. [OE *nafela*]

navel orange *n.* a sweet orange that has at its apex a navel-like depression enclosing an underdeveloped secondary fruit.

navelwort ('neivəl,wɜːt) *n.* another name for **pennywort** (sense 1).

navicular (nə'vɪkjʊlə) *Anat.* ~*adj.* **1.** shaped like a boat. ~*n.* **2.** a small boat-shaped bone of the wrist or foot. [C16: from LL *nāviculāris*, from L *nāvicula*, dim. of *nāvis* ship]

navigable ('nævɪgəbəl) *adj.* **1.** wide, deep, or safe enough to be sailed through: *a navigable channel.* **2.** capable of being steered: *a navigable raft.* —,naviga'bility *n.* —'**navigably** *adv.*

navigate ('nævɪ,geɪt) *vb.* **1.** to direct or plot the path or position of (a ship, an aircraft, etc.). **2.** (*tr.*) to travel over, through, or on in a boat, aircraft, etc. **3.** *Inf.* to direct (oneself) carefully or safely: *he navigated his way to the bar.* **4.** (*intr.*) (of a passenger in a motor vehicle) to give directions to the driver; point out the route. [C16: from L *nāvigāre* to sail, from *nāvis* ship + *agere* to drive]

navigation (,nævɪ'geɪʃən) *n.* **1.** the skill or process of plotting a route and directing a ship, aircraft, etc., along it. **2.** the act or practice of navigating: *dredging made navigation of the river possible.* —,navi'gational *adj.*

navigator ('nævɪ,geɪtə) *n.* **1.** a person who performs navigation. **2.** (esp. formerly) a person who explores by ship.

3. an instrument for assisting a pilot to navigate an aircraft.

Návpaktos (*Greek* 'nafpaktos) *n.* a port in W Greece, between the Gulfs of Corinth and Patras: scene of a naval battle (1571) in which Ottoman sea power was broken by the defeat of the Turkish fleets by those of Spain, Venice, and the Vatican. Pop.: 8170 (1971). Italian name: **Lepanto.**

Navratilova (næ,vrætɪ'louvə) *n.* **Martina.** born 1956, U.S. tennis player, born in Czechoslovakia: Wimbledon champion 1978, 1979, and 1982–87; world champion 1980 and 1984.

navvy ('nævɪ) *n., pl.* **-vies.** *Brit. inf.* a labourer on a building site, etc. [C19: from *navigator* builder of a *navigation* (in the sense canal)]

navy ('neɪvɪ) *n., pl.* **-vies.** **1.** the warships and auxiliary vessels of a nation or ruler. **2.** (*often cap.*) the branch of a country's armed services comprising such ships, their crews, and all their supporting services. **3.** short for **navy blue. 4.** *Arch. or literary.* a fleet of ships. [C14: via OF from Vulgar L *nāvia* (unattested) ship, from L *nāvis* ship]

navy blue *n.* **a.** a dark greyish-blue colour. **b.** (*as adj.*): *a navy-blue suit.* [C19: from the colour of the British naval uniform]

Navy List *n.* (in Britain) an official list of all commissioned officers of the Royal Navy.

navy yard *n.* a naval shipyard, esp. in the U.S.

nawab (nə'wɑːb) *n.* (formerly) a Muslim ruling prince or powerful landowner in India. [C18: from Hindi *nawwāb*, from Ar. *nuwwāb*, pl. of *na'ib* viceroy]

Naxos ('næksɒs) *n.* a Greek island in the S Aegean, the largest of the Cyclades: ancient centre of the worship of Dionysius. Pop.: 14 037 (1981). Area: 438 sq. km (169 sq. miles).

nay (neɪ) *sentence substitute.* **1.** a word for **no**[1]: archaic or dialectal except in voting by voice. ~*n.* **2.** a person who votes in the negative. ~*adv.* **3.** (*sentence modifier*) *Arch.* an emphatic form of **no**[1]. [C12: from ON *nei*, from *ne* not + *ei* ever]

Nayarit (*Spanish* naja'rit) *n.* a state of W Mexico, on the Pacific: includes the offshore Tres Marías Islands. Capital: Tepic. Pop.: 730 024 (1980). Area: 27 621 sq. km (10 772 sq. miles).

Nazarene (,næzə'riːn) *n.* **1.** an early name for a **Christian** (Acts 24:5) or (when preceded by *the*) for **Jesus Christ. 2.** a member of one of several groups of Jewish-Christians found principally in Syria. ~*adj.* **3.** of Nazareth in N Israel, or the Nazarenes.

Nazareth ('næzərɪθ) *n.* a town in N Israel, in Lower Galilee: the home of Jesus in his youth. Pop.: 44 900 (1982 est.).

Nazarite ('næzə,raɪt) *or* **Nazirite** *n.* a religious ascetic of ancient Israel. [C16: from L *Nazaraeus*, from Heb. *nāzar* to consecrate + -ITE[1]]

Naze (neɪz) *n.* **the. 1.** a flat marshy headland in SE England, in Essex on the North Sea coast. **2.** another name for **Lindesnes.**

Nazi ('nɑːtsɪ) *n., pl.* **-zis. 1.** a member of the fascist National Socialist German Workers' Party, which seized political control in Germany in 1933 under Adolf Hitler. ~*adj.* **2.** characteristic of or relating to the Nazis. [C20: from G, phonetic spelling of the first two syllables of *Nationalsozialist* National Socialist] —**Nazism** ('nɑːtsɪzəm) *or* **Naziism** ('nɑːtsɪ,ɪzəm) *n.*

Nb *the chemical symbol for* niobium.

NB *abbrev. for* New Brunswick.

NB, N.B., nb, *or* **n.b.** *abbrev. for* nota bene. [L: note well]

NCB (in Britain) *abbrev. for* National Coal Board: now **British Coal.**

NCO *abbrev. for* noncommissioned officer.

NCP (in Australia) *abbrev. for* National Country Party.

NCU (in Britain) *abbrev. for* National Communications Union.

nd *abbrev. for* no date.

Nd *the chemical symbol for* neodymium.

Ndjamena *or* **N'djamena** (ᵊndʒaː'meɪnə) *n.* the capital of Chad, in the southwest, at the confluence of the Shari and Logone Rivers: trading centre for livestock. Pop.: 511 700 (1985). Former name (until 1973): **Fort Lamy.**

Ndola (ᵊn'dəulə) *n.* a city in N Zambia: copper, cobalt, and sugar refineries. Pop.: 323 000 (1980 est.).

NDP (in Canada) *abbrev. for* New Democratic Party.

NDT (in Canada) *abbrev. for* Newfoundland Daylight Time.

Ne *the chemical symbol for* neon.

NE[1] *symbol for* northeast(ern).

NE[2] *or* **N.E.** *abbrev. for* New England.

ne- *combining form.* a variant of **neo-**, esp. before a vowel: *Nearctic.*

Neagh (neɪ) *n.* **Lough.** a lake in Northern Ireland, in SW Co. Antrim: the largest lake in the British Isles. Area: 388 sq. km (150 sq. miles).

Neanderthal man (nɪ'ændə,tɑːl) *n.* a type of primitive man occurring throughout much of Europe in late Palaeolithic times. [C19: from the anthropological findings (1857) in the Neandertal, a valley near Düsseldorf, Germany]

neap (niːp) *adj.* **1.** of, relating to, or constituting a neap tide. ~*n.* **2.** short for **neap tide.** [OE, as in *nēpflōd* neap tide, from ?]

Neapolitan (,nɪə'pɒlɪt²n) *n.* **1.** a native or inhabitant of Naples. ~*adj.* **2.** of or relating to Naples. [C15: from L *Neāpolītānus*, ult. from Gk *Neapolis* new town]

Neapolitan ice cream *n.* ice cream with several layers of different colours and flavours.

neap tide *n.* either of the tides that occur at the first or last quarter of the moon when the tide-generating forces of the sun and moon oppose each other and produce the smallest rise and fall in tidal level. Cf. **spring tide** (sense 1).

near (nɪə) *prep.* **1.** at or to a place or time not far away from; close to. ~*adv.* **2.** at or to a place or time not far away; close by. **3.** short for **nearly**: *I was damn near killed.* ~*adj.* **4.** (*postpositive*) at or in a place not far away. **5.** (*prenominal*) only just successful or only just failing: *a near escape.* **6.** (*postpositive*) *Inf.* miserly, mean. **7.** (*prenominal*) closely connected or intimate: *a near relation.* ~*vb.* **8.** to come or draw close (to). ~*n.* **9.** Also called: **nearside. a.** the left side of a horse, vehicle, etc. **b.** (*as modifier*): *the near foreleg.* [OE *nēar* (adv.), comp. of *nēah* close] —**'nearness** *n.*

nearby *adj.* ('nɪə,baɪ), *adv.* (,nɪə'baɪ). not far away; close at hand.

Nearctic (nɪ'ɑːktɪk) *adj.* of a zoogeographical region consisting of North America, north of the tropic of Cancer, and Greenland.

Near East *n.* **1.** another term for the **Middle East. 2.** (formerly) the Balkan States and the area of the Ottoman Empire.

near gale *n. Meteorol.* a wind of force seven on the Beaufort scale or from 32-38 mph.

nearly ('nɪəlɪ) *adv.* **1.** almost. **2. not nearly.** nowhere near: *not nearly enough.* **3.** closely: *the person most nearly concerned.*

near miss *n.* **1.** a bomb, shell, etc., that does not exactly hit the target. **2.** any attempt or shot that just fails to be successful. **3.** an incident in which two aircraft, etc., narrowly avoid collision.

nearside ('nɪə,saɪd) *n.* **1.** (usually preceded by *the*) *Chiefly Brit.* **a.** the side of a vehicle, etc., nearer the kerb. **b.** (*as modifier*): *the nearside door.* **2. a.** the left side of an animal, etc. **b.** (*as modifier*): *the nearside flank.*

near-sighted (,nɪə'saɪtɪd) *adj.* relating to or suffering from myopia. —**,near-'sightedly** *adv.*

near thing *n. Inf.* an event or action whose outcome is nearly a failure, success, disaster, etc.

neat[1] (niːt) *adj.* **1.** clean, tidy, and orderly. **2.** liking or insisting on order and cleanliness. **3.** smoothly or competently done; efficient: *a neat job.* **4.** pat or slick: *his excuse was suspiciously neat.* **5.** (of alcoholic drinks, etc.) undiluted. **6.** (of language) concise and well-phrased. **7.** *Sl., chiefly U.S. & Canad.* pleasing; admirable; excellent. [C16: from OF *net*, from L *nitidus* clean, from *nitēre* to shine] —**'neatly** *adv.* —**'neatness** *n.*

neat[2] (niːt) *n., pl.* **neat.** *Arch. or dialect.* a domestic bovine animal. [OE *neat*]

neaten ('niːt²n) *vb.* (*tr.*) to make neat; tidy.

neath *or* **'neath** (niːθ) *prep. Arch.* short for **beneath.**

neat's-foot oil *n.* a yellow oil obtained by boiling the feet and shinbones of cattle.

neb (nɛb) *n. Arch. or dialect.* **1.** the peak of a cap. **2.** the beak of a bird or the nose or snout of an animal. **3.** the projecting end of anything. [OE *nebb*]

NEB *abbrev. for:* **1.** New English Bible. **2.** National Enterprise Board.

Nebo ('ni:bəʊ) n. Mount. a mountain in Jordan, northeast of the Dead Sea: the highest point of a ridge known as Pisgah, from which Moses viewed the Promised Land just before his death (Deuteronomy 34:1). Height: 802 m (2631 ft.).

Nebraska (nɪ'bræskə) n. a state of the western U.S.: consists of an undulating plain. Capital: Lincoln. Pop.: 1 605 574 (1985 est.). Area: 197 974 sq. km (76 483 sq. miles). Abbrevs.: **Nebr.** or (with zip code) **NB** — **Ne'braskan** adj., n.

Nebuchadnezzar (ˌnɛbjʊkəd'nɛzə) or **Nebuchadrezzar** n. Old Testament. a king of Babylon, 605–562 B.C., who conquered and destroyed Jerusalem and exiled the Jews to Babylon (II Kings 24–25).

nebula ('nɛbjʊlə) n., pl. -lae (-,li:) or -las. 1. Astron. a diffuse cloud of particles and gases visible either as a hazy patch of light or an irregular dark region. 2. Pathol. opacity of the cornea. [C17: from L: mist, cloud] — 'nebular adj.

nebular hypothesis n. the theory that the solar system evolved from nebular matter.

nebulosity (ˌnɛbjʊ'lɒsɪtɪ) n., pl. -ties. 1. the state of being nebulous. 2. Astron. a nebula.

nebulous ('nɛbjʊləs) adj. 1. lacking definite form, shape, or content; vague or amorphous. 2. of a nebula. 3. Rare. misty or hazy. — 'nebulousness n.

NEC abbrev. for National Executive Committee.

necessaries ('nɛsɪsərɪz) pl. n. (sometimes sing.) what is needed; essential items: the necessaries of life.

necessarily ('nɛsɪsərɪlɪ, ˌnɛsɪ'sɛrɪlɪ) adv. 1. as an inevitable or natural consequence. 2. as a certainty: he won't necessarily come.

necessary ('nɛsɪsərɪ) adj. 1. needed to achieve a certain desired result; required. 2. inevitable: the necessary consequences of your action. 3. Logic. a. (of a statement, formula, etc.) true under all interpretations. b. (of a proposition) determined to be true by its meaning, so that its denial would be self-contradictory. Cf. **sufficient** (sense 2). 4. Rare. compelled, as by necessity or law; not free. ~n. 5. Inf. (preceded by the) the money required for a particular purpose. 6. **do the necessary.** Inf. to do something that is necessary in a particular situation. ~See also **necessaries.** [C14: from L necessārius indispensable, from necesse unavoidable]

necessitarianism (nɪˌsɛsɪ'tɛərɪəˌnɪzəm) n. Philosophy. the belief that human actions and choices are causally determined and cannot be willed. — **ne,cessi'tarian** n., adj.

necessitate (nɪ'sɛsɪˌteɪt) vb. (tr.) 1. to cause as an unavoidable result. 2. (usually passive) to compel or require (someone to do something).

necessitous (nɪ'sɛsɪtəs) adj. very needy; destitute; poverty-stricken.

necessity (nɪ'sɛsɪtɪ) n., pl. -ties. 1. (sometimes pl.) something needed; prerequisite: necessities of life. 2. a condition or set of circumstances that inevitably requires a certain result: it is a matter of necessity to wear formal clothes when meeting the Queen. 3. the state or quality of being obligatory or unavoidable. 4. urgent requirement, as in an emergency. 5. poverty or want. 6. Rare. compulsion through laws of nature; fate. 7. Logic. the property of being necessary. 8. **of necessity.** inevitably.

neck (nɛk) n. 1. the part of an organism connecting the head with the body. 2. the part of a garment around the neck. 3. something resembling a neck in shape or position: the neck of a bottle. 4. Anat. a constricted portion of an organ or part. 5. a narrow strip of land; peninsula or isthmus. 6. a strait or channel. 7. the part of a violin, cello, etc., that extends from the body to the tuning pegs and supports the fingerboard. 8. a solid block of lava from an extinct volcano, exposed after erosion of the surrounding rock. 9. the length of a horse's head and neck taken as an approximate distance by which one horse beats another in a race: to win by a neck. 10. Archit. the narrow band at the top of the shaft of a column. 11. Inf. impudence or cheek. 12. **get it in the neck.** Inf. to be reprimanded or punished severely. 13. **neck and neck.** absolutely level in a race or competition. 14. **neck of the woods.** Inf. a particular area: what brings you to this neck of the woods? 15. **neck or nothing.** at any cost. 16. **save one's** or **someone's neck.** Inf. to escape from or help someone else to escape from a difficult or dangerous situation. 17. **stick one's neck out.** Inf. to risk criticism, ridicule, etc., by speaking one's mind. ~vb. 18.

(intr.) Inf. to kiss or fondle someone or one another passionately. [OE hnecca]

Neckar ('nɛkɑː) n. a river in SW West Germany, rising in the Black Forest and flowing generally north into the Rhine at Mannheim. Length: 394 km (245 miles).

neckband ('nɛk,bænd) n. a band around the neck of a garment as finishing, decoration, or a base for a collar.

neckcloth ('nɛk,klɒθ) n. a large ornamental usually white cravat worn formerly by men.

Necker ('nɛkə; French nɛkɛr) n. **Jacques** (ʒak). 1732–1804, French financier and statesman, born in Switzerland; finance minister of France (1777–81; 1788–90). He attempted to reform the fiscal system and in 1789 he recommended summoning the States General. His subsequent dismissal was one of the causes of the storming of the Bastille (1789).

neckerchief ('nɛkətʃɪf, -ˌtʃiːf) n. a piece of ornamental cloth, often square, worn round the neck. [C14: from NECK + KERCHIEF]

necking ('nɛkɪŋ) n. Inf. the activity of kissing and embracing lovingly.

necklace ('nɛklɪs) n. 1. a chain, band, or cord, often bearing beads, pearls, jewels, etc., worn around the neck as an ornament, esp. by women. 2. (in South Africa) a. a tyre soaked in petrol, placed round a person's neck, and set on fire in order to burn the person to death. b. (as modifier): necklace victims. ~vb. (tr.) 3. (in South Africa) to kill a person by means of a necklace.

neckline ('nɛk,laɪn) n. the shape or position of the upper edge of a dress, blouse, etc.

necktie ('nɛk,taɪ) n. the U.S. name for **tie** (sense 10).

neckwear ('nɛk,wɛə) n. articles of clothing, such as ties, scarves, etc., worn round the neck.

necro- or before a vowel **necr-** combining form. indicating death, a dead body, or dead tissue: necrosis. [from Gk nekros corpse]

necrobiosis (ˌnɛkrəʊbaɪ'əʊsɪs) n. Physiol. the normal degeneration and death of cells.

necrolatry (nɛ'krɒlətrɪ) n. the worship of the dead.

necrology (nɛ'krɒlədʒɪ) n., pl. -gies. 1. a list of people recently dead. 2. a less common word for **obituary.** — **necrological** (ˌnɛkrə'lɒdʒɪkᵊl) adj.

necromancy ('nɛkrəʊˌmænsɪ) n. 1. the art of supposedly conjuring up the dead, esp. in order to obtain from them knowledge of the future. 2. black magic; sorcery. [C13: (sense 1) ult. from Gk nekromanteia, from nekros corpse; (sense 2) from Med. L nigromantia, from L niger black, which replaced necro- through folk etymology] — 'necro,mancer n. — ,necro'mantic adj.

necrophilia (ˌnɛkrəʊ'fɪlɪə) n. sexual attraction for or sexual intercourse with dead bodies. Also called: **necromania, necrophilism.** — **necrophile** ('nɛkrəʊ,faɪl) n. — ,necro'philic adj.

necropolis (nɛ'krɒpəlɪs) n., pl. -lises or -leis (-,leɪs). a burial site or cemetery. [C19: from Gk, from nekros dead + polis city]

necropsy ('nɛkrɒpsɪ) or **necroscopy** (nɛ'krɒskəpɪ) n., pl. -sies or -pies. another name for **autopsy.** [C19: from Gk nekros dead body + opsis sight]

necrosis (nɛ'krəʊsɪs) n. 1. the death of one or more cells in the body, usually within a localized area, as from an interruption of the blood supply. 2. death of plant tissue due to disease, frost, etc. [C17: NL, from Gk nekrōsis, from nekroun to kill, from nekros corpse] — **necrotic** (nɛ'krɒtɪk) adj.

nectar ('nɛktə) n. 1. a sugary fluid produced in the nectaries of flowers and collected by bees. 2. Classical myth. the drink of the gods. Cf. **ambrosia** (sense 1). 3. any delicious drink. [C16: via L from Gk néktar] — 'nectarous adj.

nectarine ('nɛktərɪn) n. 1. a variety of peach tree. 2. the fruit of this tree, which has a smooth skin. [C17: apparently from NECTAR]

nectary ('nɛktərɪ) n., pl. -ries. any of various structures secreting nectar that occur in the flowers, leaves, stipules, etc., of a plant. [C18: from NL nectarium, from NECTAR]

ned (nɛd) n. Sl. a hooligan. [from ?]

NEDC abbrev. for National Economic Development Council. Also (inf.): **Neddy** ('nɛdɪ).

neddy ('nɛdɪ) n., pl. -dies. a child's word for a **donkey.** [C18: from Ned, pet form of Edward]

Nederland ('ne:dərlɑnt) n. the Dutch name for the **Netherlands.**

née *or* **nee** (neɪ) *adj.* indicating the maiden name of a married woman: *Mrs Bloggs née Blandish.* [C19: from F: p.p. (fem.) of *naître* to be born, from L *nascī*]

need (niːd) *vb.* **1.** (*tr.*) to be in want of: *to need money.* **2.** (*tr.*) to be obliged: *to need to do more work.* **3.** (takes an infinitive without *to*) used as an auxiliary to express necessity or obligation and does not add *-s* when used with *he, she, it,* and singular nouns: *need he go?* **4.** (*intr.*) *Arch.* to be essential to: *there needs no reason for this.* ~*n.* **5.** the fact or an instance of feeling the lack of something: *he has need of a new coat.* **6.** a requirement: *the need for vengeance.* **7.** necessity or obligation: *no need to be frightened.* **8.** distress: *a friend in need.* **9.** poverty or destitution. ~See also **needs.** [OE *nēad, nied*]

needful ('niːdfʊl) *adj.* **1.** necessary; required. **2.** *Arch.* poverty-stricken. ~*n.* **3. the needful.** *Inf.* what is necessary, esp. money. — **'needfulness** *n.*

needle ('niːdəl) *n.* **1.** a pointed slender piece of metal with a hole in it through which thread is passed for sewing. **2.** a somewhat larger rod with a point at one end, used in knitting. **3.** a similar instrument with a hook at one end for crocheting. **4. a.** another name for **stylus** (sense 3). **b.** a small thin pointed device used to transmit the vibrations from a gramophone record to the pick-up. **5.** *Med.* the long hollow pointed part of a hypodermic syringe, which is inserted into the body. **6.** *Surgery.* a pointed instrument, often curved, for suturing, puncturing, or ligating. **7.** a long narrow stiff leaf in which water loss is greatly reduced: *pine needles.* **8.** any slender sharp spine. **9.** a pointer on the scale of a measuring instrument. **10.** short for **magnetic needle. 11.** a sharp pointed instrument used in engraving. **12.** anything long and pointed, such as an obelisk. **13.** *Inf.* **a.** anger or intense rivalry, esp. in a sporting encounter. **b.** (*as modifier*): *a needle match.* **14. have** *or* **get the needle.** *Brit. inf.* to feel dislike, nervousness, or annoyance: *she got the needle after he had refused her invitation.* ~*vb.* (*tr.*) **15.** *Inf.* to goad or provoke, as by constant criticism. **16.** to sew, embroider, or prick (fabric) with a needle. [OE *nǣdl*]

needlecord ('niːdəl,kɔːd) *n.* a corduroy fabric with narrow ribs.

needlepoint ('niːdəl,pɔɪnt) *n.* **1.** embroidery done on canvas with various stitches so as to resemble tapestry. **2.** another name for **point lace.**

needless ('niːdlɪs) *adj.* not required; unnecessary. — **'needlessly** *adv.* — **'needlessness** *n.*

needle time *n.* the limited time allocated by a radio channel to the broadcasting of music from records.

needlewoman ('niːdəl,wʊmən) *n., pl.* **-women.** a woman who does needlework; seamstress.

needlework ('niːdəl,wɜːk) *n.* sewing and embroidery.

needs (niːdz) *adv.* **1.** (preceded by or foll. by *must*) of necessity: *we must needs go.* ~*pl. n.* **2.** what is required; necessities: *his needs are modest.*

needy ('niːdɪ) *adj.* **needier, neediest. a.** in need of practical or emotional support; distressed. **b.** (*as collective n.; preceded by the*): *the needy.*

Néel (neɛl) *n.* **Louis** (lwi). born 1904, French physicist, noted for his research on magnetism; shared the Nobel prize for physics in 1970.

ne'er (nɛə) *adv.* a poetic contraction of **never.**

ne'er-do-well *n.* **1.** an improvident, irresponsible, or lazy person. ~*adj.* **2.** useless; worthless: *your ne'er-do-well schemes.*

nefarious (nɪ'fɛərɪəs) *adj.* evil; wicked; sinful. [C17: from L *nefārius,* from *nefās* unlawful deed, from *nē* not + *fās* divine law] — **ne'fariously** *adv.* — **ne'fariousness** *n.*

Nefertiti (,nɛfə'tiːtɪ) *or* **Nofretete** *n.* 14th century B.C., Egyptian queen; wife of Akhenaton.

neg. *abbrev. for* negative(ly).

negate (nɪ'geɪt) *vb.* (*tr.*) **1.** to nullify; invalidate. **2.** to contradict. [C17: from L *negāre,* from *neg-,* var. of *nec* not + *aio* I say] — **ne'gator** *or* **ne'gater** *n.*

negation (nɪ'geɪʃən) *n.* **1.** the opposite or absence of something. **2.** a negative thing or condition. **3.** the act of negating. **4.** *Logic.* a proposition that is the denial of another proposition and is true only if the original proposition is false.

negative ('nɛgətɪv) *adj.* **1.** expressing a refusal or denial: *a negative answer.* **2.** lacking positive qualities, such as enthusiasm or optimism. **3.** showing opposition or resistance. **4.** measured in a direction opposite to that regarded as positive. **5.** *Biol.* indicating movement or

growth away from a stimulus: *negative geotropism.* **6.** *Med.* indicating absence of the disease or condition for which a test was made. **7.** another word for **minus** (senses 3b, 4). **8.** *Physics.* **a.** (of an electric charge) having the same polarity as the charge of an electron. **b.** (of a body, system, ion, etc.) having a negative electric charge; having an excess of electrons. **9.** short for **electronegative. 10.** of or relating to a photographic negative. **11.** *Logic.* (of a categorical proposition) denying the satisfaction by the subject of the predicate, as in *some men are irrational; no pigs have wings.* ~*n.* **12.** a statement or act of denial or refusal. **13.** a negative thing. **14.** *Photog.* a piece of photographic film or a plate, previously exposed and developed, showing an image that, in black-and-white photography, has a reversal of tones. **15.** *Physics.* a negative object, such as a terminal or a plate in a voltaic cell. **16.** a sentence or other linguistic element with a negative meaning, as the English word *not.* **17.** a quantity less than zero. **18.** *Logic.* a negative proposition. **19. in the negative.** indicating denial or refusal. ~*vb.* (*tr.*) **20.** to deny; negate. **21.** to show to be false; disprove. **22.** to refuse consent to or approval of: *the proposal was negatived.* — **'negatively** *adv.* — **'negativeness** *or* **,nega'tivity** *n.*

negative feedback *n.* See **feedback.**

negative resistance *n.* a characteristic of certain electronic components in which an increase in the applied voltage increases the resistance, producing a proportional decrease in current.

negative sign *n.* the symbol (−) used to indicate a negative quantity or a subtraction.

negativism ('nɛgətɪv,ɪzəm) *n.* **1.** a tendency to be unconstructively critical. **2.** any sceptical or derisive system of thought. — **'negativist** *n., adj.*

Negev ('nɛgɛv) *or* **Negeb** ('nɛgɛb) *n.* the S part of Israel, on the Gulf of Aqaba: a triangular-shaped semidesert region, with large areas under irrigation; scene of fighting between Israeli and Egyptian forces in 1948. Chief town: Beersheba. Area: 12 820 sq. km (4950 sq. miles).

neglect (nɪ'glɛkt) *vb.* (*tr.*) **1.** to fail to give due care, attention, or time to: *to neglect a child.* **2.** to fail (to do something) through carelessness: *he neglected to tell her.* **3.** to disregard. ~*n.* **4.** lack of due care or attention; negligence: *the child starved through neglect.* **5.** the act or an instance of neglecting or the state of being neglected. [C16: from L *neglegere,* from *nec* not + *legere* to select]

neglectful (nɪ'glɛktfʊl) *adj.* (when *postpositive,* foll. by *of*) careless; heedless.

negligee, negligée, *or* **negligé** ('nɛglɪ,ʒeɪ) *n.* **1.** a woman's light dressing gown, esp. one that is lace-trimmed. **2.** any informal attire. [C18: from F *négligée,* p.p. (fem.) of *négliger* to NEGLECT]

negligence ('nɛglɪdʒəns) *n.* **1.** the state of being negligent. **2.** a negligent act. **3.** *Law.* a civil wrong whereby the defendant is in breach of a legal duty of care, resulting in injury to the plaintiff.

negligent ('nɛglɪdʒənt) *adj.* **1.** lacking attention, care, or concern; neglectful. **2.** careless or nonchalant. — **'negligently** *adv.*

negligible ('nɛglɪdʒəbəl) *adj.* so small, unimportant, etc., as to be not worth considering. — **'negligibly** *adv.*

negotiable (nɪ'gəʊʃəbəl) *adj.* **1.** able to be negotiated. **2.** (of a bill of exchange, promissory note, etc.) legally transferable in title from one party to another. — **ne,gotia'bility** *n.*

negotiate (nɪ'gəʊʃɪ,eɪt) *vb.* **1.** to talk (with others) to achieve (an agreement, etc.). **2.** (*tr.*) to succeed in passing round or over. **3.** (*tr.*) *Finance.* **a.** to transfer (a negotiable commercial paper) to another in return for value received. **b.** to sell (financial assets). **c.** to arrange for (a loan). [C16: from L *negōtiārī* to do business, from *negōtium* business, from *nec* not + *ōtium* leisure] — **ne,go-ti'ation** *n.* — **ne'goti,ator** *n.*

Negress ('niːgrɪs) *n.* a female Negro.

Negrillo (nɪ'grɪləʊ) *n., pl.* **-los** *or* **-loes.** a member of a dwarfish Negro race of central and southern Africa. [C19: from Sp., dim. of *negro* black]

Negri Sembilan ('nɛgrɪ sɛm'biːlən) *n.* a state of S Peninsular Malaysia: mostly mountainous, with large areas under paddy and rubber. Capital: Seremban. Pop.: 647 159 (1985 est.). Area: 6643 sq. km (2565 sq. miles).

Negrito (nɪˈgriːtəʊ) *n., pl.* **-tos** *or* **-toes**. a member of any of various dwarfish Negroid peoples of SE Asia and Melanesia. [C19: from Sp., dim. of *negro* black]

negritude (ˈniːgrɪˌtjuːd, ˈnɛg-) *n.* **1.** the fact of being a Negro. **2.** awareness and cultivation of the Negro heritage, values, and culture. [C20: from F, from *nègre* NEGRO]

Negro[1] (ˈniːgrəʊ) *n., pl.* **-groes**. **1.** a member of any of the dark-skinned indigenous peoples of Africa and their descendants elsewhere. ~*adj.* **2.** relating to or characteristic of Negroes. [C16: from Sp. or Port.: black, from L *niger*] —'**Negro,ism** *n.*

Negro[2] (ˈneɪgrəʊ, ˈnɛg-) *n.* **Río. 1.** a river in NW South America, rising in E Colombia (as the Guainía) and flowing east, then south as part of the border between Colombia and Venezuela, entering Brazil and continuing southeast to join the Amazon at Manáus. Length: about 2250 km (1400 miles). **2.** a river in S central Argentina, formed by the confluence of the Neuquén and Limay Rivers and flowing east and southeast to the Atlantic. Length: about 1014 km (630 miles). **3.** a river in central Uruguay, rising in S Brazil and flowing southwest into the Uruguay River. Length: about 467 km (290 miles).

Negroid (ˈniːgrɔɪd) *adj.* **1.** denoting, relating to, or belonging to one of the major racial groups of mankind, characterized by brown-black skin, crisp or woolly hair, a broad flat nose, and full lips. ~*n.* **2.** a member of this racial group.

Negropont (ˈnegrəʊˌpɒnt) *n.* **1.** the former English name for **Euboea. 2.** the medieval English name for **Chalcis.**

Negros (ˈneɪgrəʊs; *Spanish* ˈneɣrɒs) *n.* an island of the central Philippines, one of the Visayan Islands. Capital: Bacolod. Pop.: 2 749 700 (1980). Area: 13 670 sq. km (5278 sq. miles).

negus (ˈniːgəs) *n., pl.* **-guses.** a hot drink of port and lemon juice, usually spiced and sweetened. [C18: after Col. Francis *Negus* (died 1732), its E inventor]

Negus (ˈniːgəs) *n., pl.* **-guses.** a title of the emperor of Ethiopia. [from Amharic: king]

Neh. *Bible. abbrev. for* Nehemiah.

Nehemiah (ˌniːɪˈmaɪə) *n. Old Testament.* **1.** a Jewish official at the court of Artaxerxes, king of Persia, who in 444 B.C. became a leader in the rebuilding of Jerusalem after the Babylonian captivity. **2.** the book recounting the acts of Nehemiah.

Nehru (ˈneəruː) *n.* **1. Jawaharlal** (dʒəwəhəˈlɑːl). 1889–1964, Indian statesman and nationalist leader. He spent several periods in prison for his nationalist activities and practised a policy of noncooperation with Britain during World War II. He was the first prime minister of the republic of India (1947–64). **2.** his father, **Motilal** (məʊtɪˈlɑːl), known as *Pandit Nehru.* 1861–1931, Indian nationalist, lawyer, and journalist; first president of the reconstructed Indian National Congress.

neigh (neɪ) *n.* **1.** the high-pitched cry of a horse. ~*vb.* **2.** to make a neigh or utter with a sound like a neigh. [OE *hnǣgan*]

neighbour *or U.S.* **neighbor** (ˈneɪbə) *n.* **1.** a person who lives near or next to another. **2. a.** a person or thing near or next to another. **b.** (*as modifier*): *neighbour states.* ~*vb.* **3.** (when *intr.*, often foll. by *on*) to be or live close to. [OE *nēahbūr*, from *nēah* NIGH + *būr, gebūr* dweller; see BOOR] —'**neighbouring** *or U.S.* '**neighboring** *adj.*

neighbourhood *or U.S.* **neighborhood** (ˈneɪbəˌhʊd) *n.* **1.** the immediate environment; surroundings. **2.** a district where people live. **3.** the people in a particular area. **4.** *Maths.* the set of all points whose distance from a given point is less than a specified value. **5.** (*modifier*) living or situated in and serving the needs of a local area: *a neighbourhood community worker.* **6. in the neighbourhood of.** approximately.

neighbourhood watch *n.* a scheme under which members of a community agree together to take responsibility for keeping an eye on each other's property, as a way of preventing crime.

neighbourly *or U.S.* **neighborly** (ˈneɪbəlɪ) *adj.* kind, friendly, or sociable, as befits a neighbour. —'**neighbourliness** *or U.S.* '**neighborliness** *n.*

Neisse (ˈnaɪsə) *n.* **1.** Also called: **Glatzer Neisse** (ˈglɑːtsə). Polish name: **Nysa.** a river in SW Poland, rising on the Czechoslovakian border and flowing northwest to join the Oder near Brzeg. Length: about 193 km (120 miles). **2.** Also called: **Lusatian Neisse.** a river in E Europe, rising near Liberec, Czechoslovakia, and flowing

north to join the Oder: forms part of the German-Polish border. Length: 225 km (140 miles).

neither (ˈnaɪðə, ˈniːðə) *determiner.* **1. a.** not one nor the other (of two). **b.** (*as pronoun*): *neither can win.* ~*conj.* **2.** (*coordinating*) **a.** (used preceding alternatives joined by *nor*) not: *neither John nor Mary nor Joe went.* **b.** another word for **nor** (sense 2). ~*adv.* (*sentence modifier*) **3.** *Not standard.* another word for **either** (sense 4). [C13 (lit.: *ne either* not either): changed from OE *nāwther*, from *nāhwæther*, from *nā* not + *hwæther* which of two]

▷ **Usage.** A verb following a compound subject that uses *neither* . . . (*nor*) should be in the singular if both subjects are in the singular: *neither Jack nor John has done the work.* Where the subjects are different in number, the verb usually agrees with the subject nearest to it: *neither they nor Jack was able to come.* It may be considered preferable to rephrase the sentence in order to avoid this construction.

Nejd (nɛʒd, neɪd) *n.* a region of central Saudi Arabia: formerly an independent sultanate of Arabia; united with Hejaz to form the kingdom of Saudi Arabia (1932); now forms the Central Province. Capital: Riyadh. Pop.: 3 632 092 (1985 est.). Area: about 1 087 800 sq. km (420 000 sq. miles).

Nekrasov (*Russian* nɪˈkrasəf) *n.* **Nikolai Alekseyevich** (nikaˈlaj alɪkˈsjejɪvɪtʃ). 1821–77, Russian poet, who wrote chiefly about the sufferings of the peasantry.

nekton (ˈnɛktɒn) *n.* the population of free-swimming animals that inhabits the middle depths of a sea or lake. [C19: via G from Gk *nēkton* a swimming thing, from *nēkhein* to swim]

nelly (ˈnɛlɪ) *n.* **not on your nelly.** (*sentence substitute*). *Brit. sl.* certainly not.

nelson (ˈnɛlsən) *n.* any wrestling hold in which a wrestler places his arm or arms under his opponent's arm or arms from behind and exerts pressure with his palms on the back of his opponent's neck. [C19: from a proper name]

Nelson[1] (ˈnɛlsən) *n.* **1.** a town in NW England, in E Lancashire: textile industry. Pop.: 30 435 (1981). **2.** a port in New Zealand, on N South Island on Tasman Bay. Pop.: 44 900 (1987). **3. River.** a river in central Canada, in N central Manitoba, flowing from Lake Winnipeg northeast to Hudson Bay. Length: about 650 km (400 miles).

Nelson[2] (ˈnɛlsən) *n.* **1. Horatio,** Viscount Nelson. 1758–1805, British naval commander during the Revolutionary and Napoleonic Wars. He became rear admiral in 1797 after the battle of Cape St Vincent and in 1798 almost destroyed the French fleet at the battle of the Nile. He was killed at Trafalgar (1805) after defeating Villeneuve's fleet. **2. Willie.** born 1933, U.S. country singer and songwriter.

Neman *or* **Nyeman** (*Russian* ˈnjɛmən) *n.* a river in the W Soviet Union, rising in the Byelorussian SSSR and flowing generally northwest through the Lithuanian SSR to the Baltic. Length: 937 km (582 miles). Polish name: **Niemen.**

nematic (nɪˈmætɪk) *adj. Chem.* (of a substance) existing in or having a mesomorphic state in which a linear orientation of the molecules causes anisotropic properties. [C20: NEMAT(O)- (referring to the threadlike chains of molecules in liquid) + -IC]

nemato- *or before a vowel* **nemat-** *combining form.* indicating a threadlike form: *nematocyst.* [from Gk *nēma* thread]

nematocyst (ˈnɛmətəˌsɪst, nɪˈmætə-) *n.* a structure in coelenterates, such as jellyfish, consisting of a capsule containing a hollow coiled thread that can sting or paralyse.

nematode (ˈnɛməˌtəʊd) *n.* any of a class of unsegmented worms having a tough outer cuticle, including the hookworm and filaria. Also called: **nematode worm, roundworm.**

Nembutal (ˈnɛmbjuːˌtɑːl) *n.* a trademark for **pentobarbitone sodium.**

Nemea (nɪˈmiːə) *n.* (in ancient Greece) a valley in N Argolis in the NE Peloponnesus; site of the **Nemean Games,** a Panhellenic festival and athletic competition held every other year. —**Ne'mean** *adj.*

Nemean lion *n. Greek myth.* an enormous lion that was strangled by Hercules as his first labour.

nemertean (nɪˈmɜːtɪən) *or* **nemertine** (ˈnɛməˌtaɪn) *n.* **1.** any of a class of soft flattened ribbon-like marine worms having an eversible threadlike proboscis. ~*adj.* **2.** of or belonging to the *Nemertea.* [C19: via NL from Gk *Nēmertēs* a NEREID]

nemesia (nɪ'miːʒə) *n.* any plant of a southern African genus cultivated for their brightly coloured flowers. [C19: NL, from Gk *nemesion*, name of a plant resembling this]

Nemesis ('nɛmɪsɪs) *n.*, *pl.* **-ses** (-,siːz). **1.** *Greek myth.* the goddess of retribution and vengeance. **2.** (*sometimes not cap.*) any agency of retribution and vengeance. [C16: via L from Gk: righteous wrath, from *némein* to distribute what is due]

nemophila (nɛ'mɒfɪlə) *n.* an annual trailing plant with blue flowers. [from Gk *nemos* grove + *philos* loving]

neo- *or sometimes before a vowel* **ne-** *combining form.* **1.** (*sometimes cap.*) new, recent, or a modern form: *neoclassicism.* **2.** (*usually cap.*) the most recent subdivision of a geological period: *Neogene.* [from Gk *neos* new]

neoclassicism (,niːəʊ'klæsɪ,sɪzəm) *n.* **1.** a late 18th-and early 19th-century style in architecture and art, based on classical models. **2.** *Music.* a movement of the 1920s that sought to avoid the emotionalism of late romantic music. —**neoclassical** (,niːəʊ'klæsɪkᵊl) *or* ,neo'classic *adj.*

neocolonialism (,niːəʊkə'ləʊnɪə,lɪzəm) *n.* political control by an outside power of a country that is in theory independent, esp. through the domination of its economy. — ,neoco'lonialist *n.*, *adj.*

Neo-Darwinism (,niːəʊ'dɑːwɪn,ɪzəm) *n.* a modern theory of evolution that relates Darwinism to the occurrence of inheritable variation by genetic mutation.

neodymium (,niːəʊ'dɪmɪəm) *n.* a toxic silvery-white metallic element of the lanthanide series. Symbol: Nd; atomic no.: 60; atomic wt.: 144.24. [C19: NL; see NEO- + DIDYMIUM]

Neolithic (,niːə'lɪθɪk) *n.* **1.** the cultural period that was characterized by primitive farming and the use of polished stone and flint tools and weapons. ~*adj.* **2.** relating to this period.

neologism (nɪ'ɒlə,dʒɪzəm) *or* **neology** *n.*, *pl.* **-gisms** *or* **-gies.** **1.** a newly coined word, or a phrase or familiar word used in a new sense. **2.** the practice of using or introducing neologisms. [C18: via F from NEO- + *-logism*, from Gk *logos* word] —**ne'ologist** *n.*

neologize *or* **-gise** (nɪ'ɒlə,dʒaɪz) *vb.* (*intr.*) to invent or use neologisms.

neomycin (,niːəʊ'maɪsɪn) *n.* an antibiotic obtained from the bacterium *Streptomyces fradiae*, administered in the treatment of skin and eye infections. [C20: from NEO- + Gk *mukēs* fungus + -IN]

neon ('niːɒn) *n.* **1.** a colourless odourless rare gaseous element occurring in trace amounts in the atmosphere: used in illuminated signs and lights. Symbol: Ne; atomic no.: 10; atomic wt.: 20.179. **2.** (*modifier*) of or illuminated by neon: *neon sign.* [C19: via NL from Gk *neon* new]

neonatal (,niːəʊ'neɪtᵊl) *adj.* occurring in or relating to the first few weeks of life in human babies. — 'neo,nate *n.*

neon lamp *n.* a glass bulb or tube containing neon at low pressure that gives a pink or red glow when a voltage is applied.

neophyte ('niːəʊ,faɪt) *n.* **1.** a person newly converted to a religious faith. **2.** a novice in a religious order. **3.** a beginner. [C16: via Church L from New Testament Gk *neophutos* recently planted, from *néos* new + *phuton* a plant]

neoplasm ('niːəʊ,plæzəm) *n. Pathol.* any abnormal new growth of tissue; tumour.

Neo-Platonism (,niːəʊ'pleɪtə,nɪzəm) *n.* a philosophical system which was developed in the 3rd century A.D. as a synthesis of Platonic, Pythagorean, and Aristotelian elements. —**Neo-Platonic** (,niːəʊplə'tɒnɪk) *adj.* — ,Neo-'Platonist *n.*

neoprene ('niːəʊ,priːn) *n.* a synthetic rubber obtained by the polymerization of chloroprene, a colourless liquid derivative of butadiene, resistant to oil and ageing and used in waterproof products. [C20: from NEO- + PR(OPYL) + -ENE]

Neoptolemus (,niːɒp'tɒləməs) *n. Greek myth.* a son of Achilles and slayer of King Priam of Troy. Also called: **Pyrrhus.**

neoteny (nɪ'ɒtənɪ) *n.* the persistence of larval features in the adult form of an animal. [C19: from NL *neotenia*, from Gk NEO- + *teinein* to stretch]

neoteric (,niːəʊ'tɛrɪk) *Rare.* ~*adj.* **1.** belonging to a new fashion or trend; modern. ~*n.* **2.** a new writer or philosopher. [C16: via LL from Gk *neōterikos* young, fresh, from *neoteros* younger, more recent, from *neos* new, recent]

Nepal (nɪ'pɔːl) *n.* a kingdom in S Asia: the world's only Hindu kingdom; united in 1768 by the Gurkhas; consists of swampy jungle in the south and great massifs, valleys, and gorges of the Himalayas over the rest of the country, with many peaks over 8000 m (26 000 ft.) (notably Everest and Kangchenjunga). Official language: Nepali. Religion: Hindu and Mahayana Buddhist. Currency: rupee. Capital: Katmandu. Pop.: 17 567 000 (1987). Area: 147 797 sq. km (54 362 sq. miles). —**Nepalese** (,nɛpə'liːz) *adj.*, *n.*

Nepali (nɪ'pɔːlɪ) *n.* **1.** the official language of Nepal, also spoken in Sikkim and parts of India. **2.** (*pl.* **-pali** *or* **-palis**) a native or inhabitant of Nepal; a Nepalese. ~*adj.* **3.** of or relating to Nepal, its inhabitants, or their language; Nepalese.

nepenthe (nɪ'pɛnθɪ) *or* **nepenthes** (nɪ'pɛnθiːz) *n.* a drug that ancient writers referred to as a means of forgetting grief or trouble. [C16: via L from Gk *nēpenthes* sedative made from a herb, from *nē-* not + *penthos* grief]

nepeta ('nɛpɪtə, nə'pɛtə) *n.* any of a genus of plants found in N temperate regions. It includes catmint. [from L]

nephew ('nɛvjuː, 'nɛf-) *n.* a son of one's sister or brother. [C13: from OF *neveu*, from L *nepos*]

nephology (nɪ'fɒlədʒɪ) *n.* the study of clouds. [C19: from Gk *nephos* cloud + -LOGY]

nephridium (nɪ'frɪdɪəm) *n.*, *pl.* **-ia** (-ɪə). a simple excretory organ of many invertebrates, consisting of a tube through which waste products pass to the exterior. [C19: NL: little kidney]

nephrite ('nɛfraɪt) *n.* a tough fibrous mineral: a variety of jade. [C18: via G from Gk *nephros* kidney; it was thought to be beneficial in kidney disorders]

nephritic (nɪ'frɪtɪk) *adj.* **1.** of or relating to the kidneys. **2.** relating to or affected with nephritis.

nephritis (nɪ'fraɪtɪs) *n.* inflammation of a kidney.

nephro- *or before a vowel* **nephr-** *combining form.* kidney or kidneys: *nephritis.* [from Gk *nephros*]

nephrology (nɪ'frɒlədʒɪ) *n.* the branch of medicine concerned with diseases of the kidney.—**ne'phrologist** *n.*

nephron ('nɛfrɒn) *n.* one of the units of the kidney that secretes urine, via ducts, into the ureter.

ne plus ultra *Latin.* ('neɪ 'plʊs 'ʊltrɑː) *n.* the extreme or perfect point or state. [lit.: not more beyond (that is, go no further), allegedly a warning to sailors inscribed on the Pillars of Hercules at Gibraltar]

Nepos ('niːpɒs) *n.* **Cornelius.** ?100–?25 B.C., Roman historian and biographer; author of *De Viris illustribus.*

nepotism ('nɛpə,tɪzəm) *n.* favouritism shown to relatives or close friends by those with power. [C17: from It. *nepotismo*, from *nepote* NEPHEW, from the former papal practice of granting favours to nephews or other relatives] —'nepotist *n.*

Neptune¹ ('nɛptjuːn) *n.* the Roman god of the sea. Greek counterpart: **Poseidon.**

Neptune² ('nɛptjuːn) *n.* the eighth planet from the sun, having two satellites, Triton and Nereid.

neptunium (nɛp'tjuːnɪəm) *n.* a silvery metallic element synthesized in the production of plutonium and occurring in trace amounts in uranium ores. Symbol: Np; atomic no.: 93; half-life of most stable isotope, ^{237}Np: 2.14 × 10⁶ years. [C20: from NEPTUNE², the planet beyond Uranus, because neptunium is the element beyond uranium in the periodic table]

NERC *abbrev. for* Natural Environment Research Council.

Nereid ('nɪərɪɪd) *n.*, *pl.* **Nereides** (nə'riːədiːz). *Greek myth.* any of 50 sea nymphs who were the daughters of the sea god Nereus. [C17: via L from Gk]

Nereus ('nɪərɪ,uːs) *n. Greek myth.* a sea god who lived in the depths of the sea with his wife Doris and their daughters the Nereides.

Neri ('nɪərɪ) *n.* Saint **Philip.** Italian name *Filippo de' Neri.* 1515–95, Italian priest; founder of the Congregation of the Oratory (1564). Feast day: May 26.

nerine (niː'raɪnɪ) *n.* any of a genus of bulbous plants native to South Africa and grown elsewhere as greenhouse plants for their pink, red, or orange flowers: includes the Guernsey lily. [after the water nymph *Nerine* in Roman myth]

Nernst (*German* nɛrnst) *n.* **Walther Hermann** ('valtər 'hɛrman). 1864–1941, German physical chemist who formulated the third law of thermodynamics; Nobel prize for chemistry 1920.

Nero ('nɪərəʊ) *n.* full name *Nero Claudius Caesar Drusus Germanicus;* original name *Lucius Domitius Ahenobarbus.* 37–68 A.D., Roman emperor (54–68). He became notorious for his despotism and cruelty, and was alleged to have started the fire (64) that destroyed a large part of Rome.

neroli oil *or* **neroli** ('nɪərəlɪ) *n.* a brown oil distilled from the flowers of various orange trees: used in perfumery. [C17: after Anne Marie de la Tremoïlle of *Neroli,* French-born It. princess believed to have discovered it]

Neruda (*Spanish* ne'ruða) *n.* **Pablo** ('paβlo), real name *Neftali Ricardo Reyes.* 1904–73, Chilean poet. His works include *Veinte poemas de amor y una canción desesperada* (1924) and *Canto general* (1950), an epic history of the Americas: Nobel prize for literature 1971.

Nerva ('nɜːvə) *n.* full name *Marcus Cocceius Nerva.* ?30–98 A.D., Roman emperor (96–98), who introduced some degree of freedom after the repressive reign of Domitian. He adopted Trajan as his son and successor.

Nerval (*French* nɛrval) *n.* **Gérard de** (ʒerar də), real name *Gérard Labrunie.* 1808–55, French poet, noted esp. for the sonnets of mysticism, myth, and private passion in *Les Chimères* (1854).

nervate ('nɜːveɪt) *adj.* (of leaves) having veins.

nervation (nɜː'veɪʃən) *or* **nervature** ('nɜːvətʃə) *n.* a less common word for **venation.**

nerve (nɜːv) *n.* **1.** any of the cordlike bundles of fibres that conduct impulses between the brain or spinal cord and another part of the body. **2.** bravery or steadfastness. **3. lose one's nerve.** to become timid, esp. failing to perform some audacious act. **4.** *Inf.* effrontery; impudence. **5.** muscle or sinew (often in **strain every nerve**). **6.** a vein in a leaf or an insect's wing. ~*vb.* (*tr.*) **7.** to give courage to (oneself); steel (oneself). **8.** to provide with nerve or nerves. ~See also **nerves.** [C16: from L *nervus;* rel. to Gk *neuron*]

nerve cell *n.* another name for **neuron.**

nerve centre *n.* **1.** a group of nerve cells associated with a specific function. **2.** a principal source of control over any complex activity.

nerve fibre *n.* a threadlike extension of a nerve cell; axon.

nerve gas *n.* any of various poisonous gases that have a paralysing effect on the central nervous system that can be fatal.

nerve impulse *n.* the electrical wave transmitted along a nerve fibre, usually following stimulation of the nerve-cell body.

nerveless ('nɜːvlɪs) *adj.* **1.** calm and collected. **2.** listless or feeble. —'**nervelessly** *adv.*

nerve-racking *or* **nerve-wracking** *adj.* very distressing, exhausting, or harrowing.

nerves (nɜːvz) *pl. n. Inf.* **1.** the imagined source of emotional control: *my nerves won't stand it.* **2.** anxiety, tension, or imbalance: *she's all nerves.* **3. get on one's nerves.** to irritate or upset one.

Nervi (*Italian* 'nɛrvi) *n.* **Pier Luigi** (pjɛːr lu'iːdʒi). 1891–1979, Italian engineer and architect; noted for his pioneering use of reinforced concrete as a decorative material. He codesigned the UNESCO building in Paris (1953).

nervine ('nɜːviːn) *adj.* **1.** having a soothing effect upon the nerves. ~*n.* **2.** a nervine agent. [C17: from NL *nervīnus,* from L *nervus* NERVE]

nervous ('nɜːvəs) *adj.* **1.** very excitable or sensitive; highly strung. **2.** (often foll. by *of*) apprehensive or worried. **3.** of or containing nerves: *nervous tissue.* **4.** affecting the nerves or nervous tissue: *a nervous disease.* **5.** *Arch.* vigorous or forceful. —'**nervously** *adv.* —'**nervousness** *n.*

nervous breakdown *n.* any mental illness not primarily of organic origin, in which the patient ceases to function properly, often accompanied by severely impaired concentration, anxiety, insomnia, and lack of self-esteem.

nervous system *n.* the sensory and control apparatus of animals, consisting of a network of nerve cells (see **neuron**).

nervure ('nɜːvjʊə) *n.* **1.** *Entomol.* any of the chitinous rods that form the framework of an insect's wing; vein. **2.** *Bot.* any of the veins of a leaf. [C19: from F; see NERVE, -URE]

nervy ('nɜːvɪ) *adj.* **nervier, nerviest. 1.** *Brit. inf.* tense or apprehensive. **2.** having or needing bravery or endurance. **3.** *U.S. & Canad. inf.* brash or cheeky. **4.** *Arch.* muscular; sinewy.

nescience ('nɛsɪəns) *n.* a formal or literary word for **ignorance.** [C17: from LL *nescientia,* from L *nescīre* to be ignorant of, from *ne* not + *scīre* to know] —'**nescient** *adj.*

ness (nɛs) *n. Arch.* a promontory or headland. [OE *næs* headland]

Ness (nɛs) *n.* **Loch.** a lake in NW Scotland, in the Great Glen: said to be inhabited by a legendary aquatic monster. Length: 36 km (22.5 miles). Depth: 229 m (754 ft.).

-ness *suffix forming nouns chiefly from adjectives and participles.* indicating state, condition, or quality: *greatness; selfishness.* [OE *-nes,* of Gmc origin]

Nesselrode ('nɛsᵊl,rəʊd; *Russian* nɪsɪl'rɔdə) *n.* Count **Karl Robert.** 1780–1862, Russian diplomat: as foreign minister (1822–56), he negotiated the Treaty of Paris after the Crimean War (1856).

Nessus ('nɛsəs) *n. Greek myth.* a centaur that killed Hercules. A garment dipped in its blood fatally poisoned Hercules, who had been given it by Deianira who thought it was a love charm.

nest (nɛst) *n.* **1.** a place or structure in which birds, fishes, etc., lay eggs or give birth to young. **2.** a number of animals of the same species occupying a common habitat: *an ants' nest.* **3.** a place fostering something undesirable: *a nest of thievery.* **4.** a cosy or secluded place. **5.** a set of things, usually of graduated sizes, designed to fit together: *a nest of tables.* ~*vb.* **6.** (*intr.*) to make or inhabit a nest. **7.** (*intr.*) to hunt for birds' nests. **8.** (*tr.*) to place in a nest. **9.** *Computers.* to position data within other data at different ranks or levels so that the different levels of data can be used or accessed recursively. [OE]

nest egg *n.* **1.** a fund of money kept in reserve; savings. **2.** a natural or artificial egg left in a nest to induce hens to lay their eggs in it.

nestle ('nɛsᵊl) *vb.* **1.** (*intr.;* often foll. by *up* or *down*) to snuggle, settle, or cuddle closely. **2.** (*intr.*) to be in a sheltered position; lie snugly. **3.** (*tr.*) to shelter or place snugly or partly concealed, as in a nest. [OE *nestlian*]

nestling ('nɛstlɪŋ, 'nɛslɪŋ) *n.* **a.** a young bird not yet fledged. **b.** (*as modifier*): *a nestling thrush.* [C14: from NEST + -LING[1]]

Nestor ('nɛstɔː) *n. Greek myth.* the oldest and wisest of the Greeks in the Trojan War.

Nestorius (nɛ'stɔːrɪəs) *n.* died ?451 A.D., Syrian churchman; patriarch of Constantinople (428–431); deposed for heresy by the Council of Ephesus.

net[1] (nɛt) *n.* **1.** an openwork fabric of string, wire, etc.; mesh. **2.** a device made of net, used to protect or enclose things or to trap animals. **3.** a thin light mesh fabric used for curtains, etc. **4.** a plan, strategy, etc., intended to trap or ensnare: *the murderer slipped through the police net.* **5.** *Tennis, badminton, etc.* **a.** a strip of net that divides the playing area into two equal parts. **b.** a shot that hits the net. **6.** the goal in soccer, hockey, etc. **7.** (*often pl.*) *Cricket.* **a.** a pitch surrounded by netting, used for practice. **b.** a practice session in a net. **8.** another word for **network** (sense 2). ~*vb.* **netting, netted. 9.** (*tr.*) to ensnare. **10.** (*tr.*) to shelter or surround with a net. **11.** (*intr.*) *Tennis, badminton, etc.* to hit a shot into the net. **12.** to make a net out of (rope, string, etc.). [OE *net;* rel. to Gothic *nati,* Du. *net*]

net[2] *or* **nett** (nɛt) *adj.* **1.** remaining after all deductions, as for taxes, expenses, losses, etc.: *net profit.* Cf. **gross** (sense 2). **2.** (of weight) after deducting tare. **3.** final; conclusive (esp. in **net result**). ~*n.* **4.** net income, profits, weight, etc. ~*vb.* **netting, netted. 5.** (*tr.*) to yield or earn as clear profit. [C14: clean, neat, from F *net* NEAT[1]]

Netaji ('neɪtɑːdʒɪ) *n.* the title for (Subhash Chandra) **Bose.** [Hindi, from *neta* leader -JI]

netball ('nɛt,bɔːl) *n.* a game for two teams of seven players (usually women) played on a hard court. Points are scored by shooting the ball through a net hanging from a ring at the top of a pole.

Net Book Agreement *n.* an agreement between U.K. publishers and booksellers that prohibits booksellers from undercutting the price of books sold in bookshops.

net domestic product *n. Econ.* the gross domestic product minus an allowance for the depreciation of capital goods.

nether ('nɛðə) *adj.* below, beneath, or underground: *nether regions.* [OE *niothera, nithera,* lit.: further down, from *nither* down]

Netherlands ('nɛðələndz) n. (functioning as sing. or pl.) **the. 1.** Also called: **Holland.** a kingdom in NW Europe, on the North Sea: declared independence from Spain in 1581 as the United Provinces; became a major maritime and commercial power in the 17th century, gaining many overseas possessions; a member of the Common Market. It is mostly flat and low-lying, with about 40 per cent of the land being below sea level, much of it on polders protected by dykes. Language: Dutch. Religion: Christian majority, with both Protestant and Roman Catholic Churches. Currency: guilder. Capital: Amsterdam, with the seat of government at The Hague. Pop.: 14 615 125 (1987). Area: 40 883 sq. km (15 785 sq. miles). Dutch name: **Nederland. 2.** the kingdom of the Netherlands together with the Flemish-speaking part of Belgium, esp. as ruled by Spain and Austria before 1581; the Low Countries. —**Netherlander** ('nɛðə,lændə) n.

Netherlands Antilles pl. n. **the.** two groups of islands in the Caribbean, in the Lesser Antilles: overseas division of the Netherlands, consisting of the S group of Curaçao, Aruba, and Bonaire, and the N group of St Eustatius, Saba, and the S part of St Martin; economy based on refining oil from Venezuela. Capital: Willemstad (on Curaçao). Pop.: 176 000 (1987). Area: 996 sq. km (390 sq. miles). Former names: **Curaçao** (until 1949), **Dutch West Indies, Netherlands West Indies.**

Netherlands East Indies pl. n. **the.** a former name (1798–1945) for **Indonesia.**

Netherlands Guiana n. a former name for **Surinam.**

Netherlands West Indies pl. n. **the.** a former name for the **Netherlands Antilles.**

nethermost ('nɛðə,məʊst) adj. **the.** farthest down; lowest.

nether world n. **1.** the underworld. **2.** hell. ~Also called: **nether regions.**

net national product n. gross national product minus an allowance for the depreciation of capital goods.

net profit n. gross profit minus all operating costs not included in the calculation of gross profit, esp. wages, overheads, and depreciation.

net statutory income n. (in Britain) the total taxable income of a person for the tax assessment year, after the deduction of personal allowances.

netsuke ('nɛtsʊkɪ) n. (in Japan) a carved toggle, esp. of wood or ivory, originally used to tether a medicine box, purse, etc., worn dangling from the waist. [C19: from Japanese]

nett (nɛt) adj., n., vb. a variant spelling of **net².**

netting ('nɛtɪŋ) n. any netted fabric or structure.

nettle ('nɛtᵊl) n. **1.** a plant having serrated leaves with stinging hairs and greenish flowers. **2.** any of various other plants with stinging hairs or spines. **3.** any of various plants that resemble nettles, such as the dead-nettle. **4. grasp the nettle.** to attempt something with boldness and courage. ~vb. (tr.) **5.** to bother; irritate. **6.** to sting as a nettle does. [OE netele]

nettle rash n. a nontechnical name for **urticaria.**

network ('nɛt,wɜːk) n. **1.** an interconnected group or system: a network of shops. **2.** a system of intersecting lines, roads, veins, etc. **3.** another name for **net¹** (sense 1) or **netting. 4.** Radio & TV. a group of broadcasting stations that all transmit the same programme simultaneously. **5.** Electronics, computers. a system of interconnected components or circuits. ~vb. **6.** Radio & TV. to broadcast over a network. **7.** (of computers, terminals, etc.) to connect or be connected. **8.** (intr.) to form business contacts through informal social meetings.

Neubrandenburg (German nɔy'brandənbʊrk) n. a city in N East Germany: 14th-century city walls. Pop.: 52 998 (1972 est.).

Neuchâtel (French nøʃatɛl) n. **1.** a canton in the Jura Mountains of NW Switzerland. Capital: Neuchâtel. Pop.: 158 368 (1980). Area: 798 sq. km (308 sq. miles). **2.** a town in W Switzerland, capital of Neuchâtel canton, on Lake Neuchâtel: until 1848 the seat of the last hereditary rulers in Switzerland. Pop.: 31 800 (1984 est.). **3. Lake.** a lake in W Switzerland: the largest lake wholly in Switzerland. Area: 216 sq. km (83 sq. miles). ~German name (for senses 1, 2): **Neuenburg** ('nɔyənbʊrk).

Neuilly-sur-Seine (French nœjisyrsɛn) n. a town in N France, on the Seine: a suburb of NW Paris. Pop.: 65 961 (1983 est.).

Neumann n. **1.** (German 'nɔyman). **Johann Balthasar** (jo'han 'baltazar). 1687–1753, German rococo architect. His masterpiece is the church of Vierzehnheiligen in Bavaria. **2.** ('njuːmən). See (John) **von Neumann.**

neume or **neum** (njuːm) n. Music. one of a series of notational symbols used before the 14th century. [C15: from Med. L neuma group of notes sung on one breath, from Gk pneuma breath]

Neumünster (German nɔy'mynstər) n. a town in N West Germany, in Schleswig-Holstein: manufacturing of textiles and machinery. Pop.: 86 100 (1970).

neural ('njʊərəl) adj. of or relating to a nerve or the nervous system. —**'neurally** adv.

neuralgia (njʊ'rældʒə) n. severe spasmodic pain along the course of one or more nerves. —**neu'ralgic** adj.

neurasthenia (,njʊərəs'θiːnɪə) n. (no longer in technical use) a neurosis characterized by extreme lassitude and inability to cope with any but the most trivial tasks.

neuritis (njʊ'raɪtɪs) n. inflammation of a nerve or nerves, often accompanied by pain and loss of function in the affected part. —**neuritic** (njʊ'rɪtɪk) adj.

neuro- or before a vowel **neur-** combining form. indicating a nerve or the nervous system: neurology. [from Gk neuron nerve; rel. to L nervus]

neuroglia (njʊ'rɒglɪə) n. the delicate web of connective tissue that surrounds and supports nerve cells. [C19: from NEURO-+ LGk glia glue]

neurolemma (,njʊərəʊ'lɛmə) n. the thin membrane that forms a sheath around nerve fibres. [C19: NL, from NEURO- + Gk eilēma covering]

neurology (njʊ'rɒlədʒɪ) n. the study of the anatomy, physiology, and diseases of the nervous system. —**neurological** (,nʊərə'lɒdʒɪkᵊl) adj.

neuromuscular (,njʊərəʊ'mʌskjʊlə) adj. of, relating to, or affecting nerves and muscles.

neuron ('njʊərɒn) or **neurone** ('njʊərəʊn) n. a cell specialized to conduct nerve impulses: consists of a cell body, axon, and dendrites. Also called: **nerve cell.** —**neuronic** (njʊ'rɒnɪk) adj.

neuropathology (,njʊərəʊpə'θɒlədʒɪ) n. the study of diseases of the nervous system.

neuropathy (njʊ'rɒpəθɪ) n. any disease of the nervous system. —**neuropathic** (,njʊərəʊ'pæθɪk) adj. —**,neuro'pathically** adv.

neurophysiology (,njʊərəʊ,fɪzɪ'ɒlədʒɪ) n. the study of the functions of the nervous system. —**neurophysiological** (,njʊərəʊ,fɪzɪə'lɒdʒɪkᵊl) adj.

neuropterous (njʊ'rɒptərəs) or **neuropteran** adj. of or belonging to an order of insects having two pairs of large much-veined wings and biting mouthparts. [C18: from NL Neuroptera, from NEURO-+ Gk pteron wing]

neuroscience ('njʊərəʊsaɪəns) n. the study of the anatomy, physiology, and biochemistry of the nervous system.

neurosis (njʊ'rəʊsɪs) n., pl. **-ses** (-siːz). a relatively mild mental disorder, characterized by hysteria, anxiety, depression, or obsessive behaviour.

neurosurgery (,njʊərəʊ'sɜːdʒərɪ) n. the branch of surgery concerned with the nervous system. —**,neuro'surgical** adj.

neurotic (njʊ'rɒtɪk) adj. **1.** of or afflicted by neurosis. ~n. **2.** a person who is afflicted with a neurosis or who tends to be emotionally unstable. —**neu'rotically** adv. —**neu'roti,cism** n.

neurotomy (njʊ'rɒtəmɪ) n., pl. **-mies.** the surgical cutting of a nerve.

neurotransmitter (,njʊərəʊtrænz'mɪtə) n. a chemical by which a nerve cell communicates with another nerve cell or with a muscle.

neurovascular (,nʊərəʊ'væskjʊlə) adj. of or affecting both the nerves and the blood vessels.

Neusatz ('nɔyzats) n. the German name for **Novi Sad.**

Neuss (German nɔys) n. an industrial city in W West Germany, in North Rhine-Westphalia west of Düsseldorf: founded as a Roman fortress in the 1st century A.D. Pop.: 143 500 (1986). Latin name: **No'vaesium.**

Neustria ('njuːstrɪə) n. the western part of the kingdom of the Merovingian Franks formed in 561 A.D. in what is now N France. —**'Neustrian** adj.

neuter ('njuːtə) adj. **1.** Grammar. **a.** denoting or belonging to a gender of nouns which do not specify the sex of their referents. **b.** (as n.): German "Mädchen" (meaning *"girl") is a neuter.* **2.** (of animals and plants) having non-functional, underdeveloped, or absent reproductive organs. **3.** giving no indication of sex. ~*n.* **4.** a sexually underdeveloped female insect, such as a worker bee. **5.** a castrated animal. ~*vb.* **6.** (*tr.*) to castrate (an animal). [C14: from L, from *ne* not + *uter* either (of two)]

neutral ('nju:trəl) *adj.* **1.** not siding with any party to a war or dispute. **2.** of or belonging to a neutral party, country, etc. **3.** of no distinctive quality or type. **4.** (of a colour) **a.** having no hue; achromatic. **b.** dull, but harmonizing with most other colours. **5.** a less common term for **neuter** (sense 2). **6.** *Chem.* neither acidic nor alkaline. **7.** *Physics.* having zero charge or potential. **8.** *Phonetics.* (of a vowel) articulated with the tongue relaxed in mid-central position: *"about" begins with a neutral vowel.* ~*n.* **9.** a neutral person, nation, etc. **10.** a citizen of a neutral state. **11.** the position of the controls of a gearbox that leaves the transmission disengaged. [C16: from L *neutrālis;* see NEUTER] —'**neutrally** *adv.*

neutralism ('nju:trə,lɪzəm) *n.* (in international affairs) the policy of noninvolvement or nonalignment with power blocs. —'**neutralist** *n.*

neutrality (nju:'trælɪtɪ) *n.* **1.** the state of being neutral. **2.** the condition of being chemically or electrically neutral.

neutralize *or* **-ise** ('nju:trə,laɪz) *vb.* (*mainly tr.*) **1.** (*also intr.*) to render or become neutral by counteracting, mixing, etc. **2.** (*also intr.*) to make or become electrically or chemically neutral. **3.** to exclude (a country) from warfare or alliances by international agreement: *the great powers neutralized Belgium in the 19th century.* —,**neutrali'zation** *or* **-i'sation** *n.* —'**neutral,izer** *or* **-,iser** *n.*

neutretto (nju:'trɛtəʊ) *n., pl.* **-tos.** *Physics.* **1.** the neutrino associated with the muon. **2.** (formerly) any of various hypothetical neutral particles. [C20: from NEUTR(INO) + diminutive suffix *-etto*]

neutrino (nju:'tri:nəʊ) *n., pl.* **-nos.** *Physics.* a stable elementary particle with zero rest mass and spin $\frac{1}{2}$, that travels at the speed of light. [C20: from It., dim. of *neutrone* NEUTRON]

neutron ('nju:trɒn) *n. Physics.* a neutral elementary particle with approximately the same mass as a proton. In the nucleus of an atom it is stable but when free it decays. [C20: from NEUTRAL, on the model of ELECTRON]

neutron bomb *n.* a type of nuclear weapon designed to cause little blast or long-lived radioactive contamination. The neutrons destroy all life in the target area. Technical name: **enhanced radiation weapon.**

neutron number *n.* the number of neutrons in the nucleus of an atom. Symbol: *N*

neutron star *n.* a star, composed solely of neutrons, that has collapsed under its own gravity.

Neva ('ni:və; *Russian* nɪ'va) *n.* a river in the NW Soviet Union, flowing west to the Gulf of Finland by the delta on which Leningrad stands. Length: 74 km (46 miles).

Nevada (nɪ'vɑ:də) *n.* a state of the western U.S.: lies almost wholly within the Great Basin, a vast desert plateau; noted for production of gold and copper. Capital: Carson City. Pop.: 1 007 850 (1986 est.). Area: 284 612 sq. km (109 889 sq. miles). Abbrevs.: **Nev.** or (with zip code) **NV**

névé ('nɛveɪ) *n.* a mass of porous ice, formed from snow, that has not yet become frozen into glacier ice. [C19: from Swiss F *névé* glacier, from LL *nivātus* snow-cooled, from *nix* snow]

never ('nɛvə) *adv., sentence substitute.* **1.** at no time; not ever. **2.** certainly not; by no means; in no case. ~*sentence substitute.* **3.** Also: **well I never!** surely not! [OE *næfre,* from *ne* not + *æfre* EVER]

▷ **Usage.** In good usage, *never* is not used with simple past tenses to mean *not* (*I was asleep at midnight, so I did not see* (not *never saw*) *her go*).

nevermore (,nɛvə'mɔ:) *adv. Literary.* never again.

never-never *Inf.* ~*n.* **1.** *Brit.* the hire-purchase system of buying. **2.** *Austral.* remote desert country. ~*adj.* **3.** imaginary; idyllic (esp. in **never-never land**).

Nevers (*French* nəvɛr) *n.* a city in central France: capital of the former duchy of Nivernais; engineering industry. Pop.: 45 348 (1983 est.).

nevertheless (,nɛvəðə'lɛs) *sentence connector.* in spite of that; however; yet.

Nevis *n.* **1.** ('ni:vɪs, 'nɛvɪs). an island in the West Indies, in the Leeward Islands: part of St Kitts-Nevis; the volcanic

cone of **Nevis Peak,** which rises to 1002 m (3287 ft.), lies in the centre of the island. Capital: Charlestown. Pop.: 9300 (1980 est.). Area: 129 sq. km (50 sq. miles). **2.** ('nɛvɪs). See **Ben Nevis.**

Nevski ('nɛfskɪ; *Russian* 'njɛfskij) *n.* See **Alexander Nevski.**

new (nju:) *adj.* **1. a.** recently made or brought into being. **b.** (*as collective n.; preceded by the*)*: the new.* **2.** of a kind never before existing; novel: *a new concept in marketing.* **3.** recently discovered: *a new comet.* **4.** markedly different from what was before: *the new liberalism.* **5.** (often foll. by *to* or *at*) recently introduced (to); inexperienced (in) or unaccustomed (to): *new to this neighbourhood.* **6.** (*cap. in names or titles*) more or most recent of things with the same name: *the New Testament.* **7.** (*prenominal*) fresh; additional: *send some new troops.* **8.** (often foll. by *to*) unknown: *this is new to me.* **9.** (of a cycle) beginning or occurring again: *a new year.* **10.** (*prenominal*) (of crops) harvested early. **11.** changed, esp. for the better: *she returned a new woman.* **12.** up-to-date; fashionable. ~*adv.* (*usually in combination*) **13.** recently, freshly: *new-laid eggs.* **14.** anew; again. ~See also **news.** [OE *nīowe*] —'**newness** *n.*

New Age music *or* **New Age** *n.* a type of gentle melodic popular music originating in the U.S. in the late 1980s, which takes in elements of jazz, folk, and classical music and is played largely on synthesizers and acoustic instruments.

New Amsterdam *n.* the Dutch settlement established on Manhattan (1624–26); capital of New Netherlands; captured by the English and renamed New York in 1664.

Newark ('nju:ək) *n.* **1.** a town in N central England, in Nottinghamshire. Pop.: 24 100 (1985 est.). Official name: **Newark-on-Trent.** **2.** a port in NE New Jersey, just west of New York City, on Newark Bay and the Passaic River: the largest city in the state; founded in 1666 by Puritans from Connecticut; industrial and commercial centre. Pop.: 316 300 (1986).

New Australia *n.* the colony on socialist principles founded by William Lane in Paraguay in 1893.

New Australian *n.* an Australian name for a recent immigrant, esp. one from Europe.

New Bedford *n.* a port and resort in SE Massachusetts, near Buzzards Bay: settled by Plymouth colonists in 1652; a leading whaling port (18th–19th centuries). Pop.: 98 478 (1980).

newborn ('nju:,bɔ:n) *adj.* **1.** recently or just born. **2.** (of hope, faith, etc.) reborn.

New Britain *n.* an island in the S Pacific, northeast of New Guinea: the largest island of the Bismarck Archipelago; part of Papua New Guinea; mountainous, with several active volcanoes. Capital: Rabaul. Pop.: 268 400 (1987 est.). Area: 36 519 sq. km (14 100 sq. miles).

New Brunswick *n.* a province of SE Canada on the Gulf of St Lawrence and the Bay of Fundy: extensively forested. Capital: Fredericton. Pop.: 709 442 (1986). Area: 72 092 sq. km (27 835 sq. miles). Abbrev.: **NB.** —**New Brunswicker** ('brʌnzwɪkə) *n.*

Newbury ('nju:bərɪ) *n.* a market town in S England, in Berkshire: scene of a Parliamentarian victory (1643) and a Royalist victory (1644) during the Civil War; racecourse. Pop.: 26 396 (1981).

New Caledonia *n.* an island in the SW Pacific, east of Australia: forms, with its dependencies, an overseas territory of France; discovered by Captain Cook in 1774; rich mineral resources. Capital: Nouméa. Pop.: 153 500 (1987 est.). Area: 19 103 sq. km (7374 miles). French name: **Nouvelle-Calédonie.**

New Canadian *n. Canad.* a recent immigrant to Canada.

New Castile *n.* a region and former province of central Spain. Chief town: Toledo.

Newcastle[1] ('nju:,kɑ:sᵊl) *n.* a port in SE Australia, in E New South Wales near the mouth of the Hunter River: important industrial centre, with extensive steel, metalworking, engineering, shipbuilding, and chemical industries. Pop.: 300 000 (1985).

Newcastle[2] ('nju:,kɑ:sᵊl) *n.* **Duke of,** the title of *Thomas Pelham Holles.* 1693–1768, English Whig prime minister (1754–56; 1757–62).

Newcastle-under-Lyme *n.* a town in W central England, in Staffordshire. Pop.: 72 853 (1981). Often shortened to **Newcastle.**

Newcastle-upon-Tyne *n.* a port in NE England, administrative centre of Tyne and Wear, near the mouth of the River Tyne opposite Gateshead: Roman remains; engineering and shipbuilding industries; university (1937). Pop.: 192 454 (1981). Often shortened to **Newcastle.**

new chum *n.* **1.** *Austral. & N.Z. inf.* a recent British immigrant. **2.** *Austral.* a novice in any activity.

Newcomen ('nju:,kʌmən) *n.* **Thomas.** 1663–1729, English engineer who invented a steam engine, which James Watt later modified and developed.

newcomer ('nju:,kʌmə) *n.* a person who has recently arrived or started to participate in something.

New Delhi *n.* See **Delhi.**

newel ('nju:əl) *n.* **1.** the central pillar of a winding staircase, esp. one that is made of stone. **2.** Also called: **newel post.** the post at the top or bottom of a flight of stairs that supports the handrail. [C14: from OF *nouel* knob, from Med. L *nōdellus*, dim. of *nōdus* NODE]

New England *n.* **1.** the NE part of the U.S., consisting of the states of Maine, New Hampshire, Vermont, Massachusetts, Rhode Island, and Connecticut: settled originally chiefly by Puritans in the mid-17th century. **2.** a district in SE Australia, in the northern tablelands of New South Wales. — **New Englander** *n.*

New England Range *n.* a mountain range in SE Australia, in NE New South Wales: part of the Great Dividing Range. Highest peak: Ben Lomond, 1520 m (4986 ft.).

New English Bible *n.* a new translation of the Bible made between 1962 and 1970.

newfangled ('nju:'fæŋgəld) *adj.* newly come into existence or fashion, esp. excessively modern. [C14 *newefangel* liking new things, from *new* + *-fangel*, from OE *fōn* to take]

New Forest *n.* a region of woodland and heath in S England, in SW Hampshire: a hunting ground of the West Saxon kings; tourist area, noted for its ponies. Area: 336 sq. km (130 sq. miles).

Newfoundland ('nju:fəndlənd, -fənlənd, -,lænd; nju:'faundlənd) *n.* **1.** an island of E Canada, separated from the mainland by the Strait of Belle Isle: with the Coast of Labrador forms the province of Newfoundland; consists of a rugged plateau with the Long Range Mountains in the west. Area: 110 681 sq. km (42 734 sq. miles). **2.** a province of E Canada, consisting of the island of Newfoundland and the Coast of Labrador. Capital: St John's. Pop.: 568 349 (1986). Area: 404 519 sq. km (156 185 sq. miles). Abbrevs.: **Nfld** *or* **NF.** — **Newfoundlander** (nju:-'faundləndə) *n.*

New France *n.* the former French colonies and possessions in North America, most of which were lost to England and Spain by 1763: often restricted to the French possessions in Canada.

Newgate ('nju:gɪt, -,geɪt) *n.* a famous London prison, in use from the Middle Ages: demolished in 1902.

New Georgia *n.* **1.** a group of islands in the SW Pacific, in the Solomon Islands. **2.** the largest island in this group. Area: about 1300 sq. km (500 sq. miles).

New Granada *n.* **1.** a former Spanish presidency and later viceroyalty in South America. At its greatest extent it consisted of present-day Panama, Colombia, Venezuela, and Ecuador. **2.** the name of Colombia when it formed, with Panama, part of Great Colombia (1819–30).

New Guinea *n.* **1.** an island in the W Pacific, north of Australia: divided politically into Irian Jaya (a province of Indonesia) in the west and Papua New Guinea in the east. There is a central chain of mountains and a lowland area of swamps in the south and along the Sepik River in the north. Area: 775 213 sq. km (299 310 sq. miles). **2. Trust Territory of.** (until 1975) an administrative division of the former Territory of Papua and New Guinea, consisting of the NE part of the island of New Guinea together with the Bismarck Archipelago; now part of Papua New Guinea.

Newham ('nju:əm) *n.* a borough of E Greater London, on the River Thames: established in 1965. Pop.: 205 200 (1986 est.).

New Hampshire *n.* a state of the northeastern U.S.: generally hilly. Capital: Concord. Pop.: 998 000 (1985 est.). Area: 23 379 sq. km (9027 sq. miles). Abbrevs.: **N.H.** or (with zip code) **NH**

New Harmony *n.* a village in SW Indiana, on the Wabash River: scene of two experimental cooperative communities, the first founded in 1815 by George Rapp, a German religious leader, and the second by Robert Owen in 1825.

Newhaven ('nju:,heɪvᵊn) *n.* a ferry port and resort on the S coast of England, in East Sussex. Pop.: 9857 (1981).

New Haven *n.* an industrial city and port in S Connecticut, on Long Island Sound: settled in 1638 by English Puritans, who established it as a colony in 1643; seat of Yale University (1701). Pop.: 126 109 (1980).

New Hebrides *pl. n.* the former name (until 1980) of **Vanuatu.**

Ne Win ('neɪ 'wɪn) *n.* born 1911, Burmese statesman; prime minister (1958–60) and president (1974–82).

New Ireland *n.* an island in the S Pacific, in the Bismarck Archipelago, separated from New Britain by St George's Channel: part of Papua New Guinea. Chief town and port: Kavieng. Pop.: 78 900 (1987 est.). Area (including adjacent islands): 9850 sq. km (3800 sq. miles).

newish ('nju:ɪʃ) *adj.* fairly new.

New Jersey *n.* a state of the eastern U.S., on the Atlantic and Delaware Bay: mostly low-lying, with a heavy industrial area in the northeast and many coastal resorts. Capital: Trenton. Pop.: 7 562 000 (1985 est.). Area: 19 479 sq. km (7521 sq. miles). Abbrevs.: **N.J.** or (with zip code) **NJ**

New Jerusalem *n. Christianity.* heaven.

New Latin *n.* the form of Latin used since the Renaissance, esp. for scientific nomenclature.

New Look *n.* **the.** a fashion in women's clothes introduced in 1947, characterized by long full skirts.

newly ('nju:lɪ) *adv.* **1.** recently. **2.** again; anew: *newly raised hopes.* **3.** in a new manner; differently: *a newly arranged hairdo.*

newlywed ('nju:lɪ,wɛd) *n.* (*often pl.*) a recently married person.

Newman ('nju:mən) *n.* **1. John Henry.** 1801–90, English theologian. Originally an Anglican minister, he was a prominent figure in the Oxford Movement. He became a Roman Catholic (1845) and a priest (1847) and was made a cardinal (1879). His writings include the spiritual autobiography, *Apologia pro vita sua* (1864), a treatise on the nature of belief, *The Grammar of Assent* (1870), and many hymns. **2. Paul.** born 1925, U.S. film actor, whose films include *Hud* (1963), *Butch Cassidy and the Sundance Kid* (1969), *The Sting* (1973), *The Verdict* (1982), and *The Color of Money* (1986).

New Man *n.* **the.** a type of modern man who allows the caring side of his nature to show by being supportive and by sharing child care and housework.

Newmarket ('nju:,mɑːkɪt) *n.* a town in SE England, in W Suffolk: a famous horse-racing centre since the reign of James I. Pop.: 16 235 (1981).

new maths *n.* (*functioning as sing.*) *Brit.* an approach to mathematics in which the basic principles of set theory are introduced at an elementary level.

New Mexico *n.* a state of the southwestern U.S.: consists of high semiarid plateaus and mountains, crossed by the Rio Grande and the Pecos River; large Spanish-American and Indian populations; contains over two thirds of U.S. uranium reserves. Capital: Santa Fé. Pop.: 1 500 000 (1987 est.). Area: 314 451 sq. km (121 412 sq. miles). Abbrevs.: **N. Mex, N.M.,** or (with zip code) **NM** — **New Mexican** *adj., n.*

new moon *n.* the moon when it appears as a narrow waxing crescent.

New Netherland ('nɛðələnd) *n.* a Dutch North American colony of the early 17th century, centred on the Hudson valley. Captured by the English in 1664, it was divided into New York and New Jersey.

New Orleans ('ɔːliːənz, -lənz; ɔː'liːnz) *n.* a port in SE Louisiana, on the Mississippi River about 172 km (107 miles) from the sea: the largest city in the state and the second most important port in the U.S.; founded by the French in 1718; belonged to Spain (1763–1803). It is largely below sea level, built around the Vieux Carré (French quarter); famous for its annual Mardi Gras festival and for its part in the history of jazz; a major commercial, industrial, and transportation centre. Pop.: 554 500 (1986).

New Plymouth *n.* a port in New Zealand, on W North Island: founded in 1841. Pop.: 47 400 (1987).

Newport ('nju:,pɔːt) *n.* **1.** a port in SE Wales on the River Usk: steel industry. Pop.: 130 200 (1983). **2.** a port in SE

Rhode Island: founded in 1639, it became one of the richest towns of colonial America; centre of a large number of U.S. naval establishments. Pop.: 29 259 (1980). **3.** a town in S England, administrative centre of the Isle of Wight. Pop.: 23 570 (1981).

Newport News n. (functioning as sing.) a port in SE Virginia, at the mouth of the James River: an industrial centre, with one of the world's largest shipyards. Pop.: 144 903 (1980).

New Providence n. an island in the Atlantic, in the Bahamas. Chief town: Nassau. Pop.: 133 437 (1980). Area: 150 sq. km (58 sq. miles).

New Quebec n. a region of E Canada, formerly the Ungava district of Northwest Territories (1895–1912), extending from the line of the Eastmain and Hamilton Rivers north between Hudson Bay and Labrador: absorbed by Quebec in 1912: contains extensive iron deposits. Area: about 777 000 sq. km (300 000 sq. miles).

New Romney n. a market town in SE England, in Kent on Romney Marsh: of early importance as one of the Cinque Ports, but is now over 1.6 km (1 mile) inland. Pop.: 4563 (1981). Former name (until 1563): **Romney.**

news (njuːz) n. (functioning as sing.) **1.** important or interesting recent happenings. **2.** information about such events, as in the mass media. **3. the news.** a presentation, such as a radio broadcast, of information of this type. **4.** interesting or important information not previously known. **5.** a person, fashion, etc., widely reported in the mass media: she is news in the film world. [C15: from ME newes, pl. of newe new (adj.), a model of OF noveles or Med. L nova new things] — **'newsless** adj.

news agency n. an organization that collects news reports for newspapers, etc. Also called: **press agency.**

newsagent ('njuːz,eɪdʒənt) or U.S. **newsdealer** n. a shopkeeper who sells newspapers, stationery, etc.

newscast ('njuːz,kɑːst) n. a radio or television broadcast of the news. [C20: from NEWS + (BROAD)CAST] — **'news-,caster** n.

news conference n. another term for **press conference.**

newsflash ('njuːz,flæʃ) n. a brief item of important news, often interrupting a radio or television programme.

New Siberian Islands pl. n. an archipelago in the Arctic Ocean, off the N mainland of the Soviet Union, in the Yakut ASSR. Area: about 37 555 sq. km (14 500 sq. miles).

newsletter ('njuːz,letə) n. **1.** Also called: **news-sheet.** a printed periodical bulletin circulated to members of a group. **2.** History. a written or printed account of the news.

newsmonger ('njuːz,mʌŋgə) n. Old-fashioned. a gossip.

New South Wales n. a state of SE Australia: originally contained over half the continent, but was reduced by the formation of other states (1825–1911); consists of a narrow coastal plain, separated from extensive inland plains by the Great Dividing Range; the most populous state; mineral resources. Capital: Sydney. Pop.: 5 401 881 (1986). Area: 801 428 sq. km (309 433 sq. miles).

New Spain n. a Spanish viceroyalty of the 16th to 19th centuries, composed of Mexico, Central America north of Panama, the Spanish West Indies, the southwestern U.S., and the Philippines.

newspaper ('njuːz,peɪpə) n. a weekly or daily publication consisting of folded sheets and containing articles on the news, features, reviews, and advertisements. Often shortened to **paper.**

newspaperman ('njuːz,peɪpə,mæn) n., pl. **-men. 1.** a person who works for a newspaper as a reporter or editor. **2.** the owner or proprietor of a newspaper. **3.** a person who sells newspapers in the street.

newspeak ('njuː,spiːk) n. the language of bureaucrats and politicians, regarded as deliberately ambiguous and misleading. [C20: from 1984, a novel by George Orwell]

newsprint ('njuːz,prɪnt) n. an inexpensive wood-pulp paper used for newspapers.

newsreader ('njuːz,riːdə) n. a news announcer on radio or television.

newsreel ('njuːz,riːl) n. a short film with a commentary presenting current events.

newsroom ('njuːz,ruːm, -,rʊm) n. a room in a newspaper office, television station, etc., where news is received and prepared for publication or broadcasting.

newsstand ('njuːz,stænd) n. a portable stand or stall from which newspapers are sold.

New Style n. the present method of reckoning dates using the Gregorian calendar.

news vendor n. a person who sells newspapers.

newsworthy ('njuːz,wɜːðɪ) adj. sufficiently interesting to be reported in a news bulletin, etc.

newsy ('njuːzɪ) adj. **newsier, newsiest.** full of news, esp. gossipy or personal news.

newt (njuːt) n. any of various small semiaquatic amphibians having a long slender body and tail and short feeble legs. [C15: from a newt, a mistaken division of an ewt; ewt, from OE eveta EFT]

New Testament n. a collection of writings composed soon after Christ's death and added to the Jewish writings of the Old Testament to make up the Christian Bible.

newton ('njuːtʰn) n. the derived SI unit of force that imparts an acceleration of 1 metre per second per second to a mass of 1 kilogram. Symbol: N [C20: after Sir Isaac NEWTON]

Newton ('njuːtʰn) n. Sir **Isaac.** 1642–1727, English mathematician, physicist, astronomer, and philosopher, noted particularly for his law of gravitation, his three laws of motion, his theory that light is composed of corpuscles, and his development of calculus independently of Leibnitz. His works include Principia Mathematica (1687) and Opticks (1704). — **Newtonian** (njuː'təʊnɪən) adj.

Newtonian telescope n. a type of astronomical reflecting telescope in which light is reflected from a large concave mirror onto a plane mirror, and through a hole in the side of the body of the telescope to form an image.

Newton's law of gravitation n. the principle that two particles attract each other with forces directly proportional to the product of their masses divided by the square of the distance between them.

Newton's laws of motion pl. n. three laws of mechanics describing the motion of a body. **The first law** states that a body remains at rest or in uniform motion unless acted upon by a force. **The second law** states that a body's rate of change of momentum is proportional to the force causing it. **The third law** states that when a force acts on a body an equal and opposite force acts simultaneously on another body.

new town n. (in Britain) a town planned as a complete unit and built with government sponsorship, esp. to accommodate overspill population.

Newtown (,njuːtaʊn) n. a new town in central Wales, in Powys. Pop.: 8660 (1981).

Newtownabbey (,njuːtʰn'æbɪ) n. a town in Northern Ireland, in Co. Antrim on Belfast Lough: the third largest town in Northern Ireland, formed in 1958 by the amalgamation of seven villages; light industrial centre, esp. for textiles. Pop.: 56 149 (1981).

Newtown St Boswells ('njuːtaʊn sənt 'bɒzwəlz) n. a village in SE Scotland, administrative centre of Borders region: agricultural centre. Pop.: 1086 (1981).

new wave n. a movement in art, politics, etc., that consciously breaks with traditional ideas, esp. **the New Wave,** a movement in the French cinema of the 1960s, characterized by a fluid use of the camera.

New Windsor n. the official name of **Windsor**[1] (sense 1).

New World n. **the.** the Americas; the western hemisphere.

New World monkey n. any of a family of monkeys of Central and South America, many of which are arboreal and have a prehensile tail.

New Year n. the first day or days of the year in various calendars, usually a holiday.

New Year's Day n. January 1, celebrated as a holiday in many countries. Often shortened to (U.S. and Canad. inf.) **New Year's.**

New Year's Eve n. the evening of Dec. 31. See also **Hogmanay.**

New York n. **1.** Also called: **New York City.** a city in SE New York State, at the mouth of the Hudson River: the largest city and chief port of the U.S.; settled by the Dutch as New Amsterdam in 1624 and captured by the British in 1664, when it was named New York; consists of five boroughs (Manhattan, the Bronx, Queens, Brooklyn, and Richmond) and many islands, with its commercial and financial centre in Manhattan; the country's leading commercial and industrial city. Pop.: 7 262 700 (1986). Abbrevs.: **N.Y.C., NYC. 2.** a state of the northeastern U.S.: consists chiefly of a plateau with the Finger Lakes in the centre, the Adirondack Mountains in the northeast, the Catskill Mountains in the southeast, and Niagara Falls in the west. Capital: Albany. Pop.: 17 783 000 (1985 est.). Area: 123 882 sq. km (47 831 sq. miles). Abbrevs.: **N.Y.** or (with zip code) **NY** — **New Yorker** n.

New York Bay n. an inlet of the Atlantic at the mouth of the Hudson River: forms the harbour of the port of New York.

New York State Barge Canal n. a system of inland waterways in New York State, connecting the Hudson River with Lakes Erie and Ontario and, via Lake Champlain, with the St Lawrence. Length: 845 km (525 miles).

New Zealand ('zi:lənd) n. an independent dominion within the Commonwealth, occupying two main islands (North Island and South Island), Stewart Island, the Chatham Islands, and a number of minor islands in the SE Pacific: original Maori inhabitants surrendered sovereignty in 1840 and were finally subdued by 1870; became a dominion in 1907; a major world exporter of dairy products, wool, and meat. Official language: English. Religion: Christian majority. Currency: New Zealand dollar. Capital: Wellington. Pop.: 3 300 000 (1987 est.). Area: 268 867 sq. km (103 736 sq. miles). — **New Zealander** n.

Nexo (Danish 'negsoː) n. **Martin Andersen** ('marten). 1869–1954, Danish novelist. His chief works are the novels *Pelle the Conqueror* (1906–10), which deals with the labour movement, and *Ditte, Daughter of Man* (1917–21).

next (nɛkst) adj. **1.** immediately following: *the next patient to be examined*. **2.** immediately adjoining: *the next room*. **3.** closest to in degree: *the next-best thing*. **4. the next (Sunday) but one.** the (Sunday) after the next. ~adv. **5.** at a time immediately to follow: *the patient to be examined next*. **6.** next to. **a.** adjacent to: *the house next to ours*. **b.** following in degree: *next to your mother, who do you love most?* **c.** almost: *next to impossible*. ~prep. **7.** Arch. next to. [OE *nēhst*, sup. of *nēah* NIGH]

next door adj. (**next-door** when prenominal), adv. at or to the adjacent house, flat, etc.

next of kin n. a person's closest relative.

nexus ('nɛksəs) n., pl. **nexus. 1.** a means of connection; link; bond. **2.** a connected group or series. [C17: from L, from *nectere* to bind]

Ney (neɪ; French nɛ) n. **Michel** (miʃɛl), Duc d'Elchingen. 1769–1815, French marshal, who earned the epithet *Bravest of the Brave* at the battle of Borodino (1812) in the Napoleonic Wars. He rallied to Napoleon on his return from Elba and was executed for treason (1815).

Nez Percé ('nɛz 'pɜːs) n. **1.** (pl. **Nez Percés** ('pɜːsɪz) or **Nez Percé**) a member of a North American Indian people of the Pacific coast. **2.** the language of this people. [F, lit. pierced nose]

NF (in Britain) abbrev. for National Front.

Nfld. or **NF.** abbrev. for Newfoundland.

NFU (in Britain) abbrev. for National Farmers' Union.

NG abbrev. for: **1.** (in the U.S.) National Guard. **2.** New Guinea. **3.** Also: **ng.** no good.

NGA (in Britain) abbrev. for National Graphical Association.

ngaio ('naɪəʊ) n., pl. **ngaios.** a small evergreen New Zealand tree. [from Maori]

Ngaliema Mountain (ᵊŋgɑːˈljeɪmə) n. the Zaïrese name for (Mount) **Stanley.**

ngati ('nɑːti) n., pl. **ngati.** N.Z. a tribe or clan. [from Maori]

Nha Trang ('njɑː 'træŋ) n. a port in SE Vietnam, on the South China Sea: nearby temples of the Cham civilization; fishing industry. Pop.: 172 663 (1979).

NHI (in Britain) abbrev. for National Health Insurance.

NHS (in Britain) abbrev. for National Health Service.

Ni the chemical symbol for nickel.

NI abbrev. for: **1.** (in Britain) National Insurance. **2.** Northern Ireland. **3.** (in New Zealand) North Island.

niacin ('naɪəsɪn) n. another name for **nicotinic acid.** [C20: from NI(COTINIC) AC(ID) + -IN]

Niagara (naɪˈægrə, -ˈægərə) n. a river in NE North America, on the border between W New York State and Ontario, Canada, flowing from Lake Erie to Lake Ontario. Length: 45 km (28 miles).

Niagara Falls n. **1.** (functioning as pl.) the falls of the Niagara River, on the border between the U.S. and Canada: divided by Goat Island into the American Falls, 50 m (167 ft.) high, and the Horseshoe or Canadian Falls, 47 m (158 ft.) high. **2.** (functioning as sing.) a city in W New

York State, situated at the falls of the Niagara River. Pop.: 71 384 (1980). **3.** (functioning as sing.) a city in S Canada, in SE Ontario on the Niagara River just below the falls: linked to the city of Niagara Falls in the U.S. by three bridges. Pop.: 72 107 (1986).

Niamey (njaːˈmeɪ) n. the capital of Niger, in the southwest on the River Niger: became capital in 1926; airport and land route centre. Pop.: 399 100 (1983).

Niarchos (nɪˈɑːkɒs) n. **Stavros Spyro** ('stævrɒs 'spɪərəʊ). born 1909, Greek shipowner. He pioneered the use of supertankers in the 1950s.

nib (nɪb) n. **1.** the writing point of a pen, esp. an insertable tapered metal part. **2.** a point, tip, or beak. **3.** (pl.) crushed cocoa beans. ~vb. **nibbing, nibbed.** (tr.) **4.** to provide with a nib. **5.** to sharpen the nib of. [C16 (in the sense: beak): from ?]

nibble ('nɪbᵊl) vb. (when intr., often foll. by at) **1.** (esp. of animals) to take small repeated bites (of). **2.** to take dainty or tentative bites: *to nibble at a cake.* **3.** to bite (at) gently. ~n. **4.** a small mouthful. **5.** an instance of nibbling. [C15: rel. to Low G *nibbelen*] — '**nibbler** n.

Nibelung ('niːbəˌlʊŋ) n., pl. **-lungs** or **-lungen** (-ˌlʊŋən). German myth. **1.** any of the race of dwarfs who possessed a treasure hoard stolen by Siegfried. **2.** one of Siegfried's companions or followers. **3.** (in the *Nibelungenlied*) a member of the family of Gunther, king of Burgundy.

niblick ('nɪblɪk) n. Golf. (formerly) a club giving a great deal of lift. [C19: from ?]

nibs (nɪbz) n. **his nibs.** Sl. a mock title used of someone in authority. [C19: from ?]

Nicaea (naɪˈsiːə) n. an ancient city in NW Asia Minor, in Bithynia: site of the **first council of Nicaea** (325 A.D.), which composed the Nicene Creed. Modern Turkish name: **Iznik.** — **Nicene** ('naɪsiːn) or **Ni'caean** adj.

Nicaragua (ˌnɪkəˈrægjʊə, -gwə; Spanish nikaˈraywa) n. **1.** a republic in Central America, on the Caribbean and the Pacific: colonized by the Spanish from the 1520s; gained independence in 1821 and was annexed by Mexico, then coming a republic in 1838. Language: Spanish. Religion: Roman Catholic. Currency: córdoba. Capital: Managua. Pop.: 3 500 000 (1987 est.). Area: about 148 000 sq. km (57 140 sq. miles). **2. Lake.** a lake in SW Nicaragua, separated from the Pacific by an isthmus 19 km (12 miles) wide: the largest lake in Central America. Area: 8264 sq. km (3191 sq. miles). — ˌNica'raguan adj., n.

nice (naɪs) adj. **1.** pleasant: *a nice day.* **2.** kind or friendly: *a nice gesture of help.* **3.** good or satisfactory: *they made a nice job of it.* **4.** subtle or discriminating: *a nice point in the argument.* **5.** precise; skilful: *a nice fit.* **6.** Now rare. fastidious; respectable: *he was not too nice about his methods.* **7.** Obs. **a.** foolish or ignorant. **b.** delicate. **c.** shy; modest. **d.** wanton. [C13 (orig.: foolish): from OF *nice* simple, silly, from L *nescius*, from *nescire* to be ignorant] — '**nicely** adv. — '**niceness** n. — '**nicish** adj.

Nice (French nis) n. a city in SE France, on the Mediterranean: a leading resort of the French Riviera; founded by Phocaeans from Marseille in about the 3rd century B.C. Pop.: 342 489 (1983 est.).

nice-looking adj. Inf. attractive in appearance; pretty or handsome.

nicety ('naɪsɪtɪ) n., pl. **-ties. 1.** a subtle point: *a nicety of etiquette.* **2.** (usually pl.) a refinement or delicacy: *the niceties of first-class travel.* **3.** subtlety, delicacy, or precision. **4. to a nicety.** with precision.

niche (nɪtʃ, niːʃ) n. **1.** a recess in a wall, esp. one that contains a statue, etc. **2.** a position particularly suitable for the person occupying it: *he found his niche in politics.* **3.** Ecology. the status of a plant or animal within its community, which determines its activities, relationships with other organisms, etc. ~vb. **4.** (tr.) to place (a statue) in a niche; ensconce (oneself). [C17: from F, from OF *nichier* to nest, from Vulgar L *nīdicāre* (unattested), from L *nīdus* NEST]

Nicholas ('nɪkələs) n. **Saint.** 4th-century A.D. bishop of Myra, in Asia Minor; patron saint of Russia and of children, sailors, merchants, and pawnbrokers. Feast day: Dec. 6. See also **Santa Claus.**

Nicholas I n. **1. Saint,** called the Great. died 867 A.D., Italian ecclesiastic; pope (858–867). He championed papal supremacy. Feast day: Nov. 13. **2.** 1796–1855, tsar of

Russia (1825–55). He gained notoriety for his autocracy and his emphasis on military discipline and bureaucracy.

Nicholas II *n.* 1868–1918, tsar of Russia (1894–1917). After the disastrous Russo-Japanese War (1904–05), he was forced to summon a representative assembly, but his continued autocracy and incompetence precipitated the Russian Revolution (1917): he abdicated and was shot.

Nicholas V *n.* original name *Tommaso Parentucelli.* 1397–1455, Italian ecclesiastic; pope (1447–55). He helped to found the Vatican Library.

Nicholas of Cusa ('kju:zə) *n.* 1401–64, German cardinal, philosopher, and mathematician: anticipated Copernicus in asserting that the earth revolves around the sun.

Nicholson ('nɪkəlsən) *n.* **1. Ben.** 1894–1982, English painter, noted for his abstract still lifes. **2. Jack.** born 1937, U.S. film actor. His films include *Easy Rider* (1969), *One Flew Over the Cuckoo's Nest* (1974), and *Terms of Endearment* (1983). **3. John.** 1821–57, British general and administrator, born in Ireland: deputy commissioner in the Punjab (1851–56), where he became the object of hero-worship among the natives and kept the Punjab loyal during the Indian Mutiny: played a major role in the capture of Delhi.

Nichrome ('naɪ,krəʊm) *n. Trademark.* any of various alloys containing nickel, iron, and chromium, used in electrical heating elements, furnaces, etc.

Nicias ('nɪsɪəs) *n.* died 414 B.C., Athenian statesman and general. He ended the first part of the Peloponnesian War by making peace with Sparta (421).

nick (nɪk) *n.* **1.** a small notch or indentation. **2.** *Brit. sl.* a prison or police station. **3. in good nick.** *Inf.* in good condition. **4. in the nick of time.** just in time. ~*vb.* **5.** (*tr.*) to chip or cut. **6.** *Sl., chiefly Brit.* **a.** to steal. **b.** to arrest. **7.** (*intr.; often foll. by off*) *Inf.* to depart rapidly. **8. nick** (**someone**) **for.** *U.S. & Canad. sl.* to defraud (someone) to the extent of. **9.** to divide and reset (the tail muscles of a horse) to give the tail a high carriage. **10.** (*tr.*) to guess, catch, etc., exactly. [C15: ? changed from C14 *nocke* NOCK]

nickel ('nɪkəl) *n.* **1.** a malleable silvery-white metallic element that is corrosion-resistant: used in alloys, in electroplating, and as a catalyst in organic synthesis. Symbol: Ni; atomic no.: 28; atomic wt.: 58.71. **2.** a U.S. or Canadian coin worth five cents. ~*vb.* **-elling, -elled** *or U.S.* **-eling, -eled. 3.** (*tr.*) to plate with nickel. [C18: from G *Kupfernickel* niccolite, lit.: copper demon; it was mistakenly thought to contain copper]

nickelodeon (,nɪkə'ləʊdɪən) *n. U.S.* **1.** an early form of jukebox. **2.** (formerly) a Pianola, esp. one operated by inserting a five-cent piece. [C20: from NICKEL + (MEL)O-DEON]

nickel plate *n.* a thin layer of nickel deposited on a surface, usually by electrolysis.

nickel silver *n.* any of various white alloys containing copper, zinc, and nickel: used in making tableware, etc. Also called: **German silver.**

nicker[1] ('nɪkə) *vb.* (*intr.*) **1.** (of a horse) to neigh softly. **2.** to snigger. [C18: ?from NEIGH]

nicker[2] ('nɪkə) *n., pl.* **-er.** *Brit. sl.* a pound sterling. [C20: from ?]

Nicklaus ('nɪklaʊs) *n.* **Jack.** born 1940, U.S. professional golfer: won the British Open Championship (1966; 1970; 1978) and the U.S. Open Championship (1967; 1972; 1980).

nick-nack ('nɪk,næk) *n.* a variant spelling of **knick-knack.**

nickname ('nɪk,neɪm) *n.* **1.** a familiar, pet, or derisory name given to a person, animal, or place. **2.** a shortened or familiar form of a person's name: *Joe is a nickname for Joseph.* ~*vb.* **3.** (*tr.*) to call by a nickname. [C15 *a nekename,* mistaken division of *an ekename* an additional name]

Nicobar Islands ('nɪkə,bɑ:) *pl. n.* a group of 19 islands in the Indian Ocean, south of the Andaman Islands, with which they form a territory of India. Area: 1645 sq. km (635 sq. miles).

Nicodemus (,nɪkə'di:məs) *n. New Testament.* a Pharisee and a member of the Sanhedrin, who supported Jesus against the other Pharisees (John 8:50–52).

Nicolai (*German* niko'laɪ) *n.* **Carl Otto Ehrenfried** (karl 'ɔto 'e:rənfri:t). 1810–49, German composer: noted for his opera *The Merry Wives of Windsor* (1849).

Nicol prism ('nɪkəl) *n.* a device composed of two prisms of Iceland spar or calcite cut at specified angles and cemented together. It is used for producing plane-polarized light. [C19: after William *Nicol* (?1768–1851), Scot. physicist, its inventor]

Nicolson ('nɪkəlsən) *n.* Sir **Harold (George).** 1886–1968, English diplomat and author.

Nicosia (,nɪkə'si:ə, -'sɪə) *n.* the capital of Cyprus, in the central part on the Pedieos River: capital since the 10th century. Pop.: 163 700 (1986 est.).

nicotiana (nɪ,kəʊʃɪ'ɑ:nə) *n.* a plant of an American and Australian genus, having white, yellow, or purple fragrant flowers. Also called: **tobacco plant.** [C19: see NICOTINE]

nicotinamide (,nɪkə'tɪnə,maɪd) *n.* the amide of nicotinic acid: a component of the vitamin B complex. Formula: $C_6H_6ON_2$.

nicotine ('nɪkə,ti:n) *n.* a colourless oily acrid toxic liquid that turns yellowish-brown in air and light: the principal alkaloid in tobacco. [C19: from F, from NL *herba nicotiana* Nicot's plant, after J. *Nicot* (1530-1600), F diplomat who introduced tobacco into France] —'**nico,tined** *adj.* —**nicotinic** (,nɪkə'tɪnɪk) *adj.*

nicotinic acid *n.* a vitamin of the B complex that occurs in milk, liver, yeast, etc. Lack of it in the diet leads to the disease pellagra.

nicotinism ('nɪkəti:,nɪzəm) *n. Pathol.* a toxic condition of the body caused by nicotine.

Nictheroy (*Portuguese* nite'rɔɪ) *n.* another name for **Niterói.**

nictitate ('nɪktɪ,teɪt) *or* **nictate** ('nɪkteɪt) *vb.* a technical word for **blink.** [C19: from Med. L *nictitāre* to wink repeatedly, from L *nictāre* to blink] —,**nicti'tation** *or* **nic'tation** *n.*

nictitating membrane *n.* (in reptiles, birds, and some mammals) a thin fold of skin beneath the eyelid that can be drawn across the eye.

Nidaros (*Norwegian* 'ni:daro:s) *n.* the former name (1930–31) of **Trondheim.**

nidicolous (nɪ'dɪkələs) *adj.* (of young birds) remaining in the nest some time after hatching. [C19: from L *nidus* nest + *colere* to inhabit]

nidifugous (nɪ'dɪfjʊgəs) *adj.* (of young birds) leaving the nest very soon after hatching. [C19: from L *nidus* nest + *fugere* to flee]

nidify ('nɪdɪ,faɪ) *or* **nidificate** ('nɪdɪfɪ,keɪt) *vb.* **-fying, -fied.** (*intr.*) (of birds) to make or build a nest. [C17: from L *nidificāre,* from *nidus* a nest + *facere* to make] —,**nid-ifi'cation** *n.*

Niebuhr ('ni:bʊə) *n.* **1. Barthold Georg** ('bartɔlt 'geːɔrk). 1776–1831, German historian, noted for his critical approach to sources, esp. in *History of Rome* (1811–32). **2. Reinhold** ('raɪn,həʊld). 1892–1971, U.S. Protestant theologian. His works include *Moral Man and Immoral Society* (1932) and *The Nature and Destiny of Man* (1941–43).

niece (ni:s) *n.* a daughter of one's sister or brother. [C13: from OF: niece, granddaughter, ult. from L *neptis* granddaughter]

Niederösterreich ('ni:dərɔ:stəraɪç) *n.* the German name for **Lower Austria.**

Niedersachsen ('ni:dərzaksən) *n.* the German name for **Lower Saxony.**

niello (nɪ'ɛləʊ) *n., pl.* **-li** (-lɪ) *or* **-los. 1.** a black compound of sulphur and silver, lead, or copper used to incise a design on a metal surface. **2.** this process. **3.** an object decorated with niello. [C19: from It. from L *nigellus* blackish, from *niger* black]

Nielsen ('ni:lsən; *Danish* 'nelsən) *n.* **Carl (August)** (karl). 1865–1931, Danish composer. His works include six symphonies and the opera *Masquerade* (1906).

Niemen ('njɛmɛn) *n.* the Polish name for the **Neman.**

Niemeyer ('ni:,maɪə) *n.* **Oscar.** born 1907, Brazilian architect. His work includes many buildings in Brasília, esp. the president's palace (1959) and the cathedral (1964).

Niemöller (*German* 'ni:mœlər) *n.* **Martin** ('marti:n). 1892–1984, German Protestant theologian, who was imprisoned (1938–45) for his opposition to Hitler.

Nietzsche ('ni:tʃə) *n.* **Friedrich Wilhelm** ('fri:drɪç 'vɪlhɛlm). 1844–1900, German philosopher, poet, and critic, noted esp. for his concept of the superman and his rejection of traditional Christian values. His chief works are *The Birth of Tragedy* (1872), *Thus Spake Zarathustra*

(1883–91), and *Beyond Good and Evil* (1886). —**Nietzschean** ('niːtʃɪən) *n., adj.* — '**Nietzsche,ism** *or* '**Nietzschean,ism** *n.*

Nièvre (*French* njɛvrə) *n.* a department of central France, in Burgundy region. Capital: Nevers. Pop.: 239 635 (1982). Area: 6888 sq. km (2686 sq. miles).

niff (nɪf) *Brit. sl.* ~*n.* **1.** a bad smell. ~*vb.* (*intr.*) **2.** to stink. [C20: ?from SNIFF] — '**niffy** *adj.*

Niflheim ('nɪvᵊl,heɪm) *n. Norse myth.* the abode of the dead. [ON, lit.: mist home]

nifty ('nɪftɪ) *adj.* -**tier, -tiest.** *Inf.* **1.** pleasing, apt, or stylish. **2.** quick; agile. [C19: from ?] — '**niftily** *adv.* — '**niftiness** *n.*

nigella (naɪ'dʒɛlə) *n.* another name for **love-in-a-mist.**

Niger ('naɪdʒə) *n.* **1.** a landlocked republic in West Africa: important since earliest times for its trans-Saharan trade routes; made a French colony in 1922 and became fully independent in 1960; exports peanuts and livestock. Official language: French. Religion: mostly Muslim. Currency: franc. Capital: Niamey. Pop.: 6 608 000 (1987 est.). Area: 1 315 640 sq. km (507 969 sq. miles). **2.** a river in West Africa, rising in S Guinea and flowing in a great northward curve through Mali, then southwest through Niger and Nigeria to the Gulf of Guinea: the third longest river in Africa, with the largest delta, covering an area of 36 260 sq. km (14 000 sq. miles). Length: 4184 km (2600 miles). **3.** a state of W central Nigeria, formed in 1976 from part of North-Western State. Capital: Minna. Pop.: 1 961 800 (1984). Area: 65 037 sq. km (25 105 sq. miles).

Nigeria (naɪ'dʒɪərɪə) *n.* a republic in West Africa, on the Gulf of Guinea: Lagos annexed by the British in 1861; protectorates of Northern and Southern Nigeria formed in 1900 and united as a colony in 1914; gained independence as a member of the Commonwealth in 1960; Eastern Region seceded as the Republic of Biafra for the duration of the severe civil war (1967–70). It consists of a belt of tropical rain forest in the south, with semidesert in the extreme north and highlands in the east; the main export is petroleum. Official language: English; Hausa, Ibo, and Yoruba are the chief regional languages. Religion: animist, Muslim, and Christian. Currency: naira. Capital: Abuja. Pop.: 105 000 000 (1988 est.). Area: 923 773 sq. km (356 669 sq. miles). —**Ni'gerian** *adj., n.*

niggard ('nɪgəd) *n.* **1.** a stingy person. ~*adj.* **2.** *Arch.* miserly. [C14: ?from ON]

niggardly ('nɪgədlɪ) *adj.* **1.** stingy. **2.** meagre: *a niggardly salary.* ~*adv.* **3.** stingily; grudgingly. — '**niggardliness** *n.*

nigger ('nɪgə) *Derog.* ~*n.* **1.** another name for a Negro. **2.** a member of any dark-skinned race. **3. nigger in the woodpile.** a hidden snag. [C18: from C16 dialect *neeger*, from F *nègre*, from Sp. NEGRO]

niggle ('nɪgᵊl) *vb.* **1.** (*intr.*) to find fault continually. **2.** (*intr.*) to be preoccupied with details; fuss. **3.** (*tr.*) to irritate; worry. ~*n.* **4.** a trivial objection or complaint. **5.** a slight feeling as of misgiving, uncertainty, etc. [C16: from Scand.] — '**niggler** *n.* — '**niggly** *adj.*

niggling ('nɪglɪŋ) *adj.* **1.** petty. **2.** fussy. **3.** irritating. **4.** requiring painstaking work. **5.** persistently troubling.

nigh (naɪ) *adj., adv., prep.* an archaic, poetic, or dialect word for **near.** [OE *nēah, nēh*]

night (naɪt) *n.* **1.** the period of darkness that occurs each 24 hours, as distinct from day. **2.** (*modifier*) of, occurring, working, etc., at night: *a night nurse.* **3.** this period considered as a unit: *four nights later they left.* **4.** the period between sunset and retiring to bed; evening. **5.** the time between bedtime and morning. **6.** the weather at night: *a clear night.* **7.** the activity or experience of a person during a night. **8.** (*sometimes cap.*) any evening designated for a special observance or function. **9.** nightfall or dusk. **10.** a state or period of gloom, ignorance, etc. **11. make a night of it.** to celebrate for most of the night. ~Related adj.: **nocturnal.** ~See also **nights.** [OE *niht*]

night blindness *n. Pathol.* a nontechnical term for **nyctalopia.** — '**night-,blind** *adj.*

nightcap ('naɪt,kæp) *n.* **1.** a bedtime drink. **2.** a soft cap formerly worn in bed.

nightclothes ('naɪt,kləʊðz) *pl. n.* clothes worn in bed.

nightclub ('naɪt,klʌb) *n.* a place of entertainment open until late at night, usually offering food, drink, a floor show, dancing, etc.

nightdress ('naɪt,drɛs) *n. Brit.* a loose dress worn in bed by women. Also called: **nightgown, nightie.**

nightfall ('naɪt,fɔːl) *n.* the approach of darkness; dusk.

night fighter *n.* an interceptor aircraft used for operations at night.

nightgown ('naɪt,gaʊn) *n.* **1.** another name for **nightdress. 2.** a man's nightshirt.

nighthawk ('naɪt,hɔːk) *n.* **1.** any of various nocturnal American birds. **2.** *Inf.* another name for **night owl.**

nightie *or* **nighty** ('naɪtɪ) *n., pl.* **nighties.** *Inf.* short for **nightdress.**

nightingale ('naɪtɪŋ,geɪl) *n.* a brownish European songbird with a broad reddish-brown tail: well known for its musical song, usually heard at night. [OE *nihtegale*, from NIGHT + *galan* to sing]

Nightingale ('naɪtɪŋ,geɪl) *n.* **Florence,** known as *the Lady with the Lamp.* 1820–1910, English nurse, famous for her work during the Crimean War. She helped to raise the status and quality of the nursing profession and founded a training school for nurses in London (1860).

nightjar ('naɪt,dʒɑː) *n.* any of a family of nocturnal birds which have large eyes and feed on insects. [C17: NIGHT + JAR², so called from its discordant cry]

night latch *n.* a door lock operated by means of a knob on the inside and a key on the outside.

nightlife ('naɪt,laɪf) *n.* social life or entertainment taking place at night.

night-light *n.* a dim light burning at night, esp. for children.

nightlong ('naɪt,lɒŋ) *adj., adv.* throughout the night.

nightly ('naɪtlɪ) *adj.* **1.** happening or relating to each night. **2.** happening at night. ~*adv.* **3.** at night or each night.

nightmare ('naɪt,mɛə) *n.* **1.** a terrifying or deeply distressing dream. **2. a.** an event or condition resembling a terrifying dream. **b.** (*as modifier*): *a nightmare drive.* **3.** a thing that is feared. **4.** (formerly) an evil spirit supposed to suffocate sleeping people. [C13 (meaning: incubus; C16: bad dream): from NIGHT + OE *mare, mære* evil spirit, from Gmc] — '**night,marish** *adj.*

night owl *or* **nighthawk** *n. Inf.* a person who is or prefers to be up and about late at night.

nights (naɪts) *adv. Inf.* at night, esp. regularly: *he works nights.*

night safe *n.* a safe built into the outside wall of a bank, in which customers can deposit money at times when the bank is closed.

night school *n.* an educational institution that holds classes in the evening.

nightshade ('naɪt,ʃeɪd) *n.* any of various solanaceous plants, such as deadly nightshade and black nightshade. [OE *nihtscada*, apparently NIGHT + SHADE, referring to the poisonous or soporific qualities of these plants]

night shift *n.* **1.** a group of workers who work a shift during the night. **2.** the period worked.

nightshirt ('naɪt,ʃɜːt) *n.* a loose knee-length or longer shirtlike garment worn in bed by men.

nightspot ('naɪt,spɒt) *n.* an informal word for **nightclub.**

night-time *n.* the time from sunset to sunrise; night as distinct from day.

night watch *n.* **1.** a watch or guard kept at night, esp. for security. **2.** the period of time the watch is kept. **3.** a night watchman.

night watchman *n.* **1.** Also called: **night watch.** a person who keeps guard at night on a factory, public building, etc. **2.** *Cricket.* a batsman sent in to bat to play out time when a wicket has fallen near the end of a day's play.

nightwear ('naɪt,wɛə) *n.* apparel worn in bed or before retiring to bed; pyjamas, etc.

nigrescent (naɪ'grɛsᵊnt) *adj.* blackish; dark. [C18: from L *nigrescere* to grow black, from *niger* black] — **ni'grescence** *n.*

nihilism ('naɪɪ,lɪzəm) *n.* **1.** a complete denial of all established authority and institutions. **2.** *Philosophy.* an extreme form of scepticism that systematically rejects all values, belief in existence, etc. **3.** a revolutionary doctrine of destruction for its own sake. **4.** the practice of terrorism. [C19: from L *nihil* nothing] — '**nihilist** *n., adj.* —,**nihil'istic** *adj.* — **nihility** (naɪ'hɪlɪtɪ) *n.*

nihil obstat ('naɪhɪl 'ɒbstæt) the phrase used by a Roman Catholic censor to declare publication inoffensive to faith or morals. [L, lit.: nothing hinders]

Nihon ('niː'hɒn) *n.* transliteration of a Japanese name for **Japan.**

Niigata ('niːɪˌgɑːtə) *n.* a port in central Japan, on NW Honshu at the mouth of the Shinano River: the chief port on the Sea of Japan. Pop.: 476 000 (1985).

Nijinsky (nɪ'dʒɪnskɪ) *n.* **Waslaw** *or* **Vaslaw** (vats'laf). 1890–1950, Russian ballet dancer and choreographer, who was associated with Diaghilev. His creations include settings of Stravinsky's *Petrushka* and *The Rite of Spring.*

Nijmegen ('naɪˌmeɪgən; *Dutch* 'nɛimeːxə) *n.* an industrial town in the E Netherlands, in Gelderland province on the Waal River: the oldest town in the country; scene of the signing (1678) of the peace treaty between Louis XIV, the Netherlands, Spain, and the Holy Roman Empire. Pop.: 146 639 (1987). Latin name: ˌNovio'magus. German name: **Nimwegen**.

-nik *suffix forming nouns.* denoting a person associated with a specified state or quality: *beatnik.* [C20: from Russian *-nik*, as in SPUTNIK, also infl. by Yiddish *-nik* (agent suffix)]

Nikaria (nɪ'kɛɔrɪə, naɪ-) *n.* another name for **Icaria**.

Nike ('naɪkiː) *n. Greek myth.* the winged goddess of victory. Roman counterpart: **Victoria**. [from Gk: victory]

Nikko ('niːkəʊ) *n.* a town in central Japan, on NE Honshu: a major pilgrimage centre, with a 4th-century Shinto shrine, a Buddhist temple (767), and the shrines and mausoleums of the Tokugawa shoguns. Pop.: 23 885 (1980).

Nikolainkaupunki (*Finnish* ˌnikəlaɪn'kaʊpʊŋki) *n.* the former name of **Vaasa**.

Nikolayev (*Russian* nika'lajɪf) *n.* a city in the SW Soviet Union, in the S Ukrainian SSR on the Southern Bug about 64 km (40 miles) from the Black Sea: founded as a naval base in 1788; one of the leading Soviet Black Sea ports. Pop.: 501 000 (1987). Former name: **Vernoleninsk**.

nil (nɪl) *n.* nothing: used esp. in the scoring of certain games. [C19: from L]

Nile (naɪl) *n.* a river in Africa, rising in S central Burundi in its remotest headstream, the **Luvironza**: flows into Lake Victoria and leaves the lake as the **Victoria Nile**, flowing to Lake Albert, which is drained by the **Albert Nile**, becoming the White Nile on the border between Uganda and the Sudan; joined by its chief tributary, the **Blue Nile** (which rises near Lake Tana, Ethiopia) at Khartoum, and flows north to its delta on the Mediterranean; the longest river in the world. Length: (from the source of the Luvironza to the Mediterranean) 6741 km (4187 miles).

Nile green *n.* **a.** a pale bluish-green colour. **b.** (*as adj.*): *a Nile-green dress.*

nilgai ('nɪlgaɪ) *or* **nilghau** ('nɪlgɔː) *n., pl.* **-gai, -gais** *or* **-ghau, -ghaus.** a large Indian antelope, the male of which has small horns. [C19: from Hindi *nīlgāw*, from Sansk. *nīla* blue + *go* bull]

Nilgiri Hills ('nɪlgɪrɪ) *or* **Nilgiris** *pl. n.* a plateau in S India, in Tamil Nadu. Average height: 2000 m (6500 ft.), reaching 2635 m (8647 ft.) in Doda Betta.

Nilotic (naɪ'lɒtɪk) *adj.* **1.** of the Nile. **2.** of or belonging to a Negroid pastoral people inhabiting the S Sudan, parts of Kenya and Uganda, and neighbouring countries. **3.** relating to the group of languages spoken by the Nilotic peoples. [C17: via L from Gk *Neilotikós*, from *Neilos* the NILE]

Nilsson (*Swedish* 'nilsɔn) *n.* **Birgit** ('birgit). born 1918, Swedish operatic soprano.

nimble ('nɪmbᵊl) *adj.* **1.** agile, quick, and neat in movement. **2.** alert; acute. [OE *nǣmel* quick to grasp, & *numol* quick at seizing, both from *niman* to take] —**'nimbleness** *n.* —**'nimbly** *adv.*

nimbostratus (ˌnɪmbəʊ'streɪtəs, -'strɑːtəs) *n., pl.* **-ti** (-taɪ). a dark rain-bearing stratus cloud.

nimbus ('nɪmbəs) *n., pl.* **-bi** (-baɪ) *or* **-buses. 1. a.** a dark grey rain-bearing cloud. **b.** (*in combination*): *cumulonimbus clouds.* **2. a.** an emanation of light surrounding a saint or deity. **b.** a representation of this emanation. **3.** a surrounding aura. [C17: from L: cloud]

Nimby ('nɪmbɪ) *n. acronym for* not in my back yard.

Nîmes (*French* nim) *n.* a city in S France: Roman remains including an amphitheatre and the Pont du Gard aqueduct. Pop.: 126 374 (1983 est.).

Nimitz ('nɪmɪts) *n.* **Chester William.** 1885–1966, U.S. admiral; commander in chief of the U.S. Pacific fleet in World War II (1941–45).

Nimrod ('nɪmrɒd) *n.* **1.** a hunter famous for his prowess (Genesis 10:8–9). **2.** a person dedicated to or skilled in hunting.

Nimrud (nɪm'ruːd) *n.* an ancient city in Assyria, near the present-day city of Mosul (Iraq): founded in about 1250 B.C. and destroyed by the Medes in 612 B.C.; excavated by Sir Austen Henry Layard.

Nimwegen ('nɪmveːgən) *n.* the German name for **Nijmegen**.

Nimzowitsch ('nɪmzəˌvɪtʃ) *n.* **Aaron Isayevich** (ɪ'zaɪjevɪtʃ) 1886–1935, Latvian chess player and theorist; influential in enunciating the principles of the hypermodern school, of which he was the main instigator.

nincompoop ('nɪnkəmˌpuːp, 'nɪŋ-) *n.* a stupid person; fool; idiot. [C17: from ?]

nine (naɪn) *n.* **1.** the cardinal number that is the sum of one and eight. **2.** a numeral, 9, IX, etc., representing this number. **3.** something representing, represented by, or consisting of nine units, such as a playing card with nine symbols on it. **4.** Also: **nine o'clock.** nine hours after noon or midnight: *the play starts at nine.* **5.** dressed **(up) to the nines.** *Inf.* elaborately dressed. **6. 999** (in Britain) the telephone number of the emergency services. **7. nine to five.** normal office hours: *a nine-to-five job.* ~*determiner.* **8. a.** amounting to nine: *nine days.* **b.** (*as pronoun*): *nine are ready.* [OE *nigon*]

nine-days wonder *n.* something that arouses great interest but only for a short period.

ninefold ('naɪnˌfəʊld) *adj.* **1.** equal to or having nine times as many or as much. **2.** composed of nine parts. ~*adv.* **3.** by nine times as much.

ninepins ('naɪnˌpɪnz) *n.* **1.** (*functioning as sing.*) another name for **skittles**. **2.** (*sing.*) one of the pins used in this game.

nineteen ('naɪn'tiːn) *n.* **1.** the cardinal number that is the sum of ten and nine. **2.** a numeral, 19, XIX, etc., representing this number. **3.** something represented by, representing, or consisting of 19 units. **4. talk nineteen to the dozen.** to talk incessantly. ~*determiner.* **5. a.** amounting to nineteen: *nineteen pictures.* **b.** (*as pronoun*): *only nineteen left.* [OE *nigontīne*]

nineteenth (ˌnaɪn'tiːnθ) *adj.* **1.** (*usually prenominal*) **a.** coming after the eighteenth in numbering, position, etc.; being the ordinal number of *nineteen.* Often written: 19th. **b.** (*as n.*): *the nineteenth was rainy.* ~*n.* **2. a.** one of 19 equal parts of something. **b.** (*as modifier*): *a nineteenth part.* **3.** the fraction equal to one divided by 19 (1/19).

nineteenth hole *n. Golf, sl.* the bar in a golf clubhouse. [C20: from its being the next objective after a standard 18-hole round]

ninetieth ('naɪntɪɪθ) *adj.* **1.** (*usually prenominal*) **a.** being the ordinal number of *ninety* in numbering, position, etc. Often written: 90th. **b.** (*as n.*): *ninetieth in succession.* ~*n.* **2. a.** one of 90 equal parts of something. **b.** (*as modifier*): *a ninetieth part.* **3.** the fraction one divided by 90 (1/90).

ninety ('naɪntɪ) *n., pl.* **-ties. 1.** the cardinal number that is the product of ten and nine. **2.** a numeral, 90, XC, etc., representing this number. **3.** something represented by, representing, or consisting of 90 units. ~*determiner.* **4. a.** amounting to ninety: *ninety times.* **b.** (*as pronoun*): *at least ninety are missing.* [OE *nigontig*] —**'ninetieth** *adj., n.*

Nineveh ('nɪnɪvə) *n.* the ancient capital of Assyria, on the River Tigris opposite the present-day city of Mosul (N Iraq): at its height in the 8th and 7th centuries B.C.; destroyed in 612 B.C. by the Medes and Babylonians. —**'Ninevite** *n.*

Ningbo *or* **Ningpo** ('nɪŋ'pəʊ) *n.* a port in E China, in NE Zhejiang, on the Yung River, about 20 km (12 miles) from its mouth at Hangzhou Bay: one of the first sites of European settlement in China. Pop.: 1 020 000 (1986).

Ningsia *or* **Ninghsia** ('nɪŋ'ʃjɑː) *n.* **1.** a former province of NW China: mostly included in the Inner Mongolian AR in 1956, with the smaller part constituted as the Ningxia Hui AR in 1958. **2.** the former name of **Yinchuan**.

Ningxia Hui Autonomous Region ('nɪŋ'ʃjɑː 'huːɪ) *n.* an administrative division of NW China, south of the Inner Mongolian AR. Capital: Yinchuan. Pop.: 3 895 578 (1982). Area: 66 400 sq. km (25 896 sq. miles).

Ninian ('nɪnjən) *n.* **Saint.** ?360–?432 A.D., the first known apostle of Scotland; built a stone church (*candida casa*) at Whithorn on his native Solway; preached to the Picts.

ninny ('nɪnɪ) *n., pl.* **-nies.** a dull-witted person. [C16: ?from *an innocent* simpleton]

ninth (naɪnθ) *adj.* **1.** (*usually prenominal*) **a.** coming after the eighth in order, position, etc.; being the ordinal number of *nine*. Often written: 9th. **b.** (*as n.*): *ninth in line.* ~*n.* **2. a.** one of nine equal parts. **b.** (*as modifier*): *a ninth part.* **3.** the fraction one divided by nine (1/9). **4.** *Music.* an interval of one octave plus a second. ~*adv.* **5.** Also: **ninthly.** after the eighth person, position, event, etc. [OE *nigotha*]

Ninus ('naɪnəs) *n.* a king of Assyria and the legendary founder of Nineveh, husband of Semiramis.

Niobe ('naɪəbɪ) *n. Greek myth.* a daughter of Tantalus, whose children were slain after she boasted of them: although turned into stone, she continued to weep. —**Niobean** (naɪ'əʊbɪən) *adj.*

niobium (naɪ'əʊbɪəm) *n.* a ductile white superconductive metallic element that occurs principally in the black mineral columbite and tantalite. Symbol: Nb; atomic no.: 41; atomic wt.: 92.906. Former name: **columbium.** [C19: from NL, from NIOBE; because it occurred in TANTALITE]

Niort (*French* njɔr) *n.* a market town in W France. Pop.: 61 535 (1983 est.).

nip[1] (nɪp) *vb.* **nipping, nipped.** (*mainly tr.*) **1.** to compress, as between a finger and the thumb; pinch. **2.** (often foll. by *off*) to remove by clipping, biting, etc. **3.** (when *intr.*, often foll. by *at*) to give a small sharp bite (to): *the dog nipped at his heels.* **4.** (esp. of the cold) to affect with a stinging sensation. **5.** to harm through cold: *the frost nipped the young plants.* **6.** to check or destroy the growth of (esp. in **nip in the bud**). **7.** (*intr.*; foll. by *along, up, out,* etc.) *Brit. inf.* to hurry; dart. **8.** *Sl., chiefly U.S. & Canad.* to snatch. ~*n.* **9.** a pinch, snip, etc. **10.** severe frost or cold: *the first nip of winter.* **11. put the nips in.** *Austral. & N.Z. sl.* to exert pressure on someone, esp. in order to extort money. **12.** *Arch.* a taunting remark. **13. nip and tuck.** *U.S. & Canad.* neck and neck. [C14: from ON]

nip[2] (nɪp) *n.* **1.** a small drink of spirits; dram. ~*vb.* **nipping, nipped.** **2.** to drink spirits, esp. habitually in small amounts. [C18: from *nipperkin* a vessel holding a half-pint or less, from ?]

Nipigon ('nɪpəgɒn) *n. Lake.* a lake in central Canada, in NW Ontario, draining into Lake Superior via the **Nipigon River.** Area: 4843 sq. km (1870 sq. miles).

Nipissing ('nɪpɪsɪŋ) *n. Lake.* a lake in central Canada, in E Ontario between the Ottawa River and Georgian Bay. Area: 855 sq. km (330 sq. miles).

nipper ('nɪpə) *n.* **1.** a person or thing that nips. **2.** the large pincer-like claw of a lobster, crab, etc. **3.** *Inf., chiefly Brit.* a small child.

nippers ('nɪpəz) *pl. n.* an instrument or tool, such as a pair of pliers, for snipping or squeezing.

nipple ('nɪp²l) *n.* **1.** the small conical projection in the centre of each breast, which in women contains the outlet of the milk ducts. **2.** something resembling a nipple in shape or function. **3.** Also called: **grease nipple.** a small drilled bush, usually screwed into a bearing, through which grease is introduced. [C16: from earlier *neble, nible,* ?from NEB, NIB]

nipplewort ('nɪp²l,wɜːt) *n.* an annual Eurasian plant with pointed oval leaves and small yellow flower heads.

Nippon ('nɪpɒn) *n.* transliteration of a Japanese name for Japan. —**Nipponese** (,nɪpə'niːz) *adj., n.*

Nippur (nɪ'pʊə) *n.* an ancient Sumerian and Babylonian city, the excavated site of which is in SE Iraq: an important religious centre, abandoned in the 12th or 13th century.

nippy ('nɪpɪ) *adj.* **-pier, -piest.** **1.** (of weather) frosty or chilly. **2.** *Brit. inf.* **a.** quick; nimble; active. **b.** (of a motor vehicle) small and relatively powerful. **3.** (of dogs) inclined to bite. —**'nippily** *adv.*

NIREX ('naɪrɛks) *n.* acronym *for* Nuclear Industry Radioactive Waste Executive.

nirvana (nɪə'vɑːnə, nɜː-) *n. Buddhism, Hinduism.* final release from the cycle of reincarnation attained by extinction of all desires and individual existence, culminating (in Buddhism) in absolute blessedness, or (in Hinduism) in absorption into Brahman. [C19: from Sansk.: extinction, from *nir-* out + *vāti* it blows]

Niš or **Nish** (niːʃ) *n.* an industrial town in E Yugoslavia, in SE Serbia: situated on routes between central Europe and the Aegean. Pop.: 230 711 (1981).

Nishapur (,niːʃɑː'pʊə) *n.* a town in NE Iran, at an altitude of 1195 m (3920 ft.): birthplace and burial place of Omar Khayyam. Pop.: 59 101 (1976).

Nishinomiya (,niːʃɪ'nɒmɪjə) *n.* an industrial city in central Japan, on S Honshu, northwest of Osaka. Pop.: 421 000 (1985).

nisi ('naɪsaɪ) *adj.* (*postpositive*) *Law.* (of a court order) coming into effect on a specified date unless cause is shown why it should not: *a decree nisi.* [C19: from: unless, if not]

Nissen hut ('nɪs²n) *n.* a military shelter of semicircular cross section, made of corrugated steel sheet. [C20: after Lt Col. Peter *Nissen* (1871–1930), British mining engineer, its inventor]

nit[1] (nɪt) *n.* **1.** the egg of a louse, esp. adhering to human hair. **2.** the larva of a louse. [OE *hnitu*]

nit[2] (nɪt) *n.* a unit of luminance equal to 1 candela per square metre. [C20: from L *nitor* brightness]

nit[3] (nɪt) *n. Inf., chiefly Brit.* short for **nitwit.**

nit[4] (nɪt) *n.* a unit of information equal to 1.44 bits. Also called: **nepit.** [C20: from N(*apierian dig*)*it*]

nit[5] (nɪt) *n.* **keep nit.** *Austral. inf.* to keep watch, esp. during illegal activity. [C19: from *nix!* a shout of warning] —'**nit-,keeper** *n.*

Niterói (*Portuguese* nite'rɔi) *n.* a port in SE Brazil, on Guanabara Bay opposite Rio de Janeiro: contains Brazil's chief shipyards. Pop.: 442 706 (1985). Also called: **Nictheroy.**

nit-picking *Inf.* ~*n.* **1.** a concern with insignificant details, esp. with the intention of finding fault. ~*adj.* **2.** showing such a concern; fussy. [C20: from NIT[1] + PICK[1]] —'**nit-,picker** *n.*

nitrate ('naɪtreɪt) *n.* **1.** any salt or ester of nitric acid. **2.** a fertilizer containing nitrate salts. ~*vb.* **3.** (*tr.*) to treat with nitric acid or a nitrate. **4.** to convert or be converted into a nitrate. —**ni'tration** *n.*

nitre or *U.S.* **niter** ('naɪtə) *n.* another name for **potassium nitrate** or **sodium nitrate.** [C14: via OF from L *nitrum,* prob. from Gk *nitron*]

nitric ('naɪtrɪk) *adj.* of or containing nitrogen.

nitric acid *n.* a colourless corrosive liquid important in the manufacture of fertilizers, explosives, and many other chemicals. Formula: HNO_3. Former name: **aqua fortis.**

nitric oxide *n.* a colourless reactive gas. Formula: NO. Systematic name: **nitrogen monoxide.**

nitride ('naɪtraɪd) *n.* a compound of nitrogen with a more electropositive element.

nitrification (,naɪtrɪfɪ'keɪʃən) *n.* **1.** the oxidation of the ammonium compounds in dead organic material into nitrites and nitrates by soil nitrobacteria, making nitrogen available to plants. **2.** the addition of a nitro group to an organic compound.

nitrify ('naɪtrɪ,faɪ) *vb.* **-fying, -fied.** (*tr.*) **1.** to treat or cause to react with nitrogen. **2.** to treat (soil) with nitrates. **3.** (of nitrobacteria) to convert (ammonium compounds) into nitrates by oxidation. —'**nitri,fiable** *adj.*

nitrite ('naɪtraɪt) *n.* any salt or ester of nitrous acid.

nitro- or *before a vowel* **nitr-** *combining form.* **1.** indicating that a chemical compound contains a nitro group, $-NO_2$: *nitrobenzene.* **2.** indicating that a chemical compound is a nitrate ester: *nitrocellulose.* [from Gk *nitron* NATRON]

nitrobacteria (,naɪtrəʊbæk'tɪərɪə) *pl. n., sing.* **-terium** (-'tɪərɪəm). soil bacteria that are involved in nitrification.

nitrobenzene (,naɪtrəʊ'bɛnziːn) *n.* a yellow oily liquid compound, used as a solvent and in the manufacture of aniline. Formula: $C_6H_5NO_2$.

nitrocellulose (,naɪtrəʊ'sɛljʊ,ləʊs) *n.* another name (not in chemical usage) for **cellulose nitrate.**

nitrogen ('naɪtrədʒən) *n.* a colourless odourless relatively unreactive gaseous element that forms 78 per cent of the air and is an essential constituent of proteins and nucleic acids. Symbol: N; atomic no.: 7; atomic wt.: 14.0067.

nitrogen cycle *n.* the natural circulation of nitrogen by living organisms. Nitrates in the soil, derived from dead organic matter by bacterial action, are absorbed and synthesized into complex organic compounds by plants and reduced to nitrates again when the plants and the animals feeding on them die and decay.

nitrogen dioxide *n.* a red-brown poisonous gas that is an intermediate in the manufacture of nitric acid, a nitrating agent, and an oxidizer for rocket fuels. Formula: NO_2.

nitrogen fixation *n.* **1.** the conversion of atmospheric nitrogen into nitrogen compounds by soil bacteria in the root nodules of legumes, and by certain algae. **2.** a process in which atmospheric nitrogen is converted into a nitrogen compound, used esp. for fertilizer.

nitrogenize *or* **-ise** (ˈnaɪˈtrɒdʒɪ,naɪz) *vb.* to combine or treat with nitrogen or a nitrogen compound. **—ni,trogeni'zation** *or* **-i'sation** *n.*

nitrogen monoxide *n.* the systematic name for **nitric oxide.**

nitrogen mustard *n.* any of a class of organic compounds resembling mustard gas in their molecular structure: important in the treatment of cancer.

nitrogenous (naɪˈtrɒdʒɪnəs) *adj.* containing nitrogen or a nitrogen compound.

nitroglycerin (,naɪtrəʊˈglɪsərɪn) *or* **nitroglycerine** (,naɪtrəʊˈglɪsə,riːn) *n.* a pale yellow viscous explosive liquid made from glycerol and nitric and sulphuric acids. Formula: $CH_2NO_3CHNO_3CH_2NO_3$. Also called: **trinitroglycerin.**

nitromethane (,naɪtrəʊˈmiːθeɪn) *n.* an oily colourless liquid obtained from methane and used as a solvent and rocket fuel.

nitrous (ˈnaɪtrəs) *adj.* of, derived from, or containing nitrogen, esp. in a low valency state. [C17: from L *nitrōsus* full of natron]

nitrous acid *n.* a weak monobasic acid known only in solution and in the form of nitrite salts. Formula: HNO_2. Systematic name: **dioxonitric(III) acid.**

nitrous oxide *n.* a colourless gas with a sweet smell: used as an anaesthetic in dentistry. Formula: N_2O. Also called: **laughing gas.** Systematic name: **dinitrogen oxide.**

nitty (ˈnɪtɪ) *adj.* **-tier, -tiest.** infested with nits.

nitty-gritty (ˈnɪtɪˈgrɪtɪ) *n.* **the.** *Inf.* the basic facts of a matter, situation, etc.; the core. [C20: ? rhyming compound from GRIT]

nitwit (ˈnɪt,wɪt) *n. Inf.* a foolish or dull person. [C20: ?from NIT¹ + WIT¹]

Niue (ˈnjuːeɪ) *n.* an island in the S Pacific, between Tonga and the Cook Islands: annexed by New Zealand (1901); achieved full internal self-government in 1974. Chief town and port: Alofi. Pop.: 2442 (1987). Area: 260 sq. km (100 sq. miles). Also called: **Savage Island. —Niuean** (njuːˈɪən) *n., adj.*

Niven (ˈnɪvən) *n.* **David.** 1909–83, British film actor and author. His films include *The Prisoner of Zenda* (1937), *Around the World in 80 Days* (1956), *Casino Royale* (1967), and *Paper Tiger* (1975). He wrote the autobiographical *The Moon's a Balloon* (1972) and *Bring on the Empty Horses* (1975).

Nivernais (*French* nivɛrnɛ) *n.* a former province of central France, around Nevers.

nix¹ (nɪks) *Inf.* ~*sentence substitute.* **1.** another word for **no¹. ~***n.* **2.** a refusal. **3.** nothing. [C18: from G, inf. form of *nichts* nothing]

nix² (nɪks) *or (fem.)* **nixie** (ˈnɪksɪ) *n. Germanic myth.* a water sprite, usually unfriendly to humans. [C19: from G *Nixe,* from OHG *nihhus*]

Nixon (ˈnɪksən) *n.* **Richard M(ilhous).** born 1913, U.S. politician; 37th president from 1969 until he resigned in 1974.

Nizam (nɪˈzɑːm) *n.* the title of the ruler of Hyderabad, India, from 1724 to 1948.

Nizhni Novgorod (*Russian* ˈniʒnij ˈnɔvgərət) *n.* the former name (until 1932) of **Gorki¹.**

Nizhni Tagil (*Russian* ˈniʒnij taˈgil) *n.* a city in the central Soviet Union, on the E slopes of the Ural Mountains: a major metallurgical centre. Pop.: 427 000 (1987).

Njord (njɔːd) *or* **Njorth** (njɔːθ) *n. Norse myth.* the god of the sea, fishing, and prosperity.

Nkomo (əŋˈkəʊməʊ) *n.* **Joshua.** born 1917, Zimbabwean politician; coleader, with Robert Mugabe, of the Patriotic Front (1976–80); minister (1980–82) and from 1988.

Nkrumah (əŋˈkruːmə) *n.* **Kwame** (ˈkwɑːmɪ). 1909–72, Ghanaian statesman, prime minister (1957-60) and president (1960-66). He led demands for self-government in the 1950s, achieving Ghanaian independence in 1957. He was overthrown by a military coup (1966).

NMR *abbrev. for* nuclear magnetic resonance.

NNE *symbol for* north-northeast.

NNW *symbol for* north-northwest.

no¹ (nəʊ) *sentence substitute.* **1.** used to express denial, disagreement, refusal, etc. ~*n., pl.* **noes** *or* **nos.** **2.** an

answer or vote of *no.* **3. not take no for an answer.** to continue in a course of action, etc., despite refusals. **4.** (*often pl.*) a person who votes in the negative. **5. the noes have it.** there is a majority of votes in the negative. [OE *nā,* from *ne* not, no + *ā* ever]

no² (nəʊ) *determiner.* **1.** not any, not a, or not one: *there's no money left; no card in the file.* **2.** not at all: *she's no youngster.* **3.** (foll. by comparative adjectives and adverbs) not: *no less than forty; no taller than a child.* [OE *nā,* from *nān* NONE]

No¹ *or* **Noh** (nəʊ) *n., pl.* **No** *or* **Noh.** the stylized classic drama of Japan, developed in the 15th century or earlier, using music, dancing, and themes from religious stories or myths. [from Japanese *nō* talent, from Chinese *neng*]

No² *the chemical symbol for* nobelium.

No³ (nəʊ) *n.* **Lake.** a lake in the S central Sudan, where the Bahr el Jebel (White Nile) is joined by the Bahr el Ghazal. Area: about 103 sq. km (40 sq. miles).

No. *abbrev. for:* **1.** north(ern). **2.** Also: **no.** (*pl.* **Nos.** *or* **nos.**) number. [from F *numéro*]

n.o. *Cricket. abbrev. for* not out.

no-account *U.S. dialect.* ~*adj.* **1.** worthless; good-for-nothing. ~*n.* **2.** a worthless person.

Noah (ˈnəʊə) *n. Old Testament.* a Hebrew patriarch, who saved himself, his family, and a pair of each species of animal and bird from the Flood by building a ship (**Noah's Ark**) in which they all survived (Genesis 6–8). **—Noachian** (nəʊˈeɪkɪən) *or* **Noachic** (nəʊˈækɪk, -ˈeɪkɪk) *adj.*

nob¹ (nɒb) *n. Cribbage.* **1.** the jack of the suit turned up. **2. one for his nob.** the call made with this jack, scoring one point. [C19: from ?]

nob² (nɒb) *n. Sl., chiefly Brit.* a person of wealth or social distinction. [C19: from ?]

no-ball *n.* **1.** *Cricket.* an illegal ball, as for overstepping the crease, for which the batting side scores a run unless the batsman hits the ball, in which case he can only be out by being run out. **2.** *Rounders.* an illegal ball, esp. one bowled too high or too low. ~*interj.* **3.** *Cricket, rounders.* a call by the umpire indicating a no-ball.

nobble (ˈnɒbᵊl) *vb.* (*tr.*) *Brit. sl.* **1.** to disable (a racehorse), esp. with drugs. **2.** to win over or outwit (a person) by underhand means. **3.** to suborn (a person, esp. a juror) by threats, bribery, etc. **4.** to steal. **5.** to grab. **6.** to kidnap. [C19: from *nobbler,* from a false division of *an hobbler* (one who hobbles horses) as *a nobbler*]

Nobel (nəʊˈbɛl) *n.* **Alfred Bernhard** (ˈalfreːd ˈbæːrnhard). 1833–96, Swedish chemist, engineer, and philanthropist, noted for his invention of dynamite (1866) and for his bequest for the foundation of the Nobel prizes.

nobelium (nəʊˈbiːlɪəm) *n.* a transuranic element produced artificially from curium. Symbol: No; atomic no.: 102; half-life of most stable isotope, ^{255}No: 180 seconds (approx.). [C20: NL, after *Nobel* Institute, Stockholm, where it was discovered]

Nobel prize *n.* a prize for outstanding contributions to chemistry, physics, physiology or medicine, literature, economics, and peace that may be awarded annually; established 1901. [C20: after Alfred NOBEL]

Nobile (*Italian* nobile) *n.* **Umberto.** 1885–1978, Italian aeronautical engineer and aviator. He flew his *Norge* airship over the North Pole (1926) with Amundsen and his *Italia* airship over the Pole in 1928, crashing on the return.

nobility (nəʊˈbɪlɪtɪ) *n., pl.* **-ties.** **1.** a privileged class whose titles are conferred by descent or royal decree. **2.** the quality of being good; dignity: *nobility of mind.* **3.** (in the British Isles) the class of people holding the title of dukes, marquesses, earls, viscounts, or barons and their feminine equivalents; peerage.

nobilmente (,nəʊbɪlˈmɛnteɪ) *adj, adv. Music.* to be performed in a noble manner. [It.]

noble (ˈnəʊbᵊl) *adj.* **1.** of or relating to a hereditary class with special status, often derived from a feudal period. **2.** of or characterized by high moral qualities; magnanimous: *a noble deed.* **3.** having dignity or eminence; illustrious. **4.** imposing; magnificent: *a noble avenue of trees.* **5.** superior; excellent: *a noble strain of horses.* **6.** *Chem.* **a.** (of certain elements) chemically unreactive. **b.** (of certain metals, esp. copper, silver, and gold) resisting oxidation. ~*n.* **7.** a person belonging to a privileged class whose status is usually indicated by a title. **8.** (in the British Isles) a person holding the title of duke, marquess, earl, viscount, or baron, or a feminine equivalent. **9.** a former

British gold coin having the value of one third of a pound. [C13: via OF from L *nōbilis*, orig., capable of being known, hence well-known, from *noscere* to know] —'**nobleness** *n.* —'**nobly** *adv.*

nobleman ('nəʊbªlmən) *or (fem.)* **noblewoman** *n., pl.* -**men** *or* -**women.** a person of noble rank, title, or status; peer; aristocrat.

noble savage *n.* (in romanticism) an idealized view of primitive man.

noblesse oblige (nəʊ'blɛs əʊ'bliːʒ) *n. Often ironic.* the supposed obligation of nobility to be honourable and generous. [F, lit.: nobility obliges]

nobody ('nəʊbədɪ) *pron.* **1.** no person; no-one. ~*n., pl.* -**bodies. 2.** an insignificant person.

▷ **Usage.** See at **everyone.**

nock (nɒk) *n.* **1.** a notch on an arrow that fits on the bowstring. **2.** either of the grooves at each end of a bow that hold the bowstring. ~*vb.* (*tr.*) **3.** to fit (an arrow) on a bowstring. [C14: rel. to Swedish *nock* tip]

no-claim bonus *n.* a reduction on an insurance premium, esp. one covering a motor vehicle, if no claims have been made within a specified period. Also called: **no-claims bonus.**

noctambulism (nɒk'tæmbjʊˌlɪzəm) *or* **noctambulation** *n.* another word for **somnambulism.** [C19: from L *nox* night + *ambulāre* to walk]

noctilucent (ˌnɒktɪ'luːsªnt) *adj.* shining at night, as certain high-altitude clouds, believed to consist of meteor dust that reflects sunlight. [from L, from *nox* night + *lūcēre* to shine]

noctuid ('nɒktjʊɪd) *n.* any of a large family of nocturnal moths that includes the underwings. [C19: via NL from L *noctua* night owl, from *nox* night]

noctule ('nɒktjuːl) *n.* any of several large Old World insectivorous bats. [C18: prob. from LL *noctula* small owl, from L *noctua* night owl]

nocturnal (nɒk'tɜːnªl) *adj.* **1.** of, used during, occurring in, or relating to the night. **2.** (of animals) active at night. **3.** (of plants) having flowers that open at night and close by day. [C15: from LL *nocturnālis*, from L *nox* night] —ˌ**noctur'nality** *n.* —**noc'turnally** *adv.*

nocturne ('nɒktɜːn) *n.* **1.** a short, lyrical piece of music, esp. one for the piano. **2.** a painting of a night scene.

nod (nɒd) *vb.* **nodding, nodded. 1.** to lower and raise (the head) briefly, as to indicate agreement, etc. **2.** (*tr.*) to express by nodding: *she nodded approval.* **3.** (*intr.*) (of flowers, trees, etc.) to sway or bend forwards and back. **4.** (*intr.*) to let the head fall forwards through drowsiness; be almost asleep. **5.** (*intr.*) to be momentarily careless: *even Homer sometimes nods.* ~*n.* **6.** a quick down-and-up movement of the head, as in assent, command, etc. **7. nodding acquaintance.** a slight, casual, or superficial knowledge (of a subject or person). **8. on the nod.** *Inf.* agreed, as in committee, without formal procedure. **9.** See **land of Nod.** ~See also **nod off.** [C14 *nodde*, from ?] —'**nodding** *adj., n.*

noddle[1] ('nɒdªl) *n. Inf., chiefly Brit.* the head or brains: *use your noddle!* [C15: from ?]

noddle[2] ('nɒdªl) *vb. Inf., chiefly Brit.* to nod (the head), as through drowsiness. [C18: from NOD]

noddy ('nɒdɪ) *n., pl.* -**dies. 1.** any of several tropical terns, typically having a dark plumage. **2.** a fool or dunce. [C16: ? n. use of obs. *noddy* foolish, drowsy, ?from NOD (vb.); the bird is so called because it allows itself to be caught by hand]

node (nəʊd) *n.* **1.** a knot, swelling, or knob. **2.** the point on a plant stem from which the leaves or lateral branches grow. **3.** *Physics.* a point at which the amplitude of one of the two kinds of displacement in a standing wave has zero or minimum value. **4.** Also called: **crunode.** *Maths.* a point at which two branches of a curve intersect. **5.** *Maths., linguistics.* one of the objects of which a graph or a tree consists. **6.** *Astron.* either of the two points at which the orbit of a body intersects the plane of the ecliptic. **7.** *Anat.* any natural bulge or swelling, such as those along the course of a lymphatic vessel (**lymph node**). [C16: from L *nōdus* knot] —'**nodal** *adj.*

nod off *vb.* (*intr., adv.*) *Inf.* to fall asleep.

nodule ('nɒdjuːl) *n.* **1.** a small knot, lump, or node. **2.** any of the knoblike outgrowths on the roots of clover and other legumes that contain bacteria involved in nitrogen fixation. **3.** a small rounded lump of rock or mineral substance, esp. in a matrix of different rock material. [C17:

from L *nōdulus*, from *nōdus* knot] —'**nodular**, '**nodulose**, *or* '**nodulous** *adj.*

Noel *or* **Noël** (nəʊ'ɛl) *n.* (in carols, etc.) another word for **Christmas.** [C19: from F, from L *nātālis* a birthday]

noetic (nəʊ'ɛtɪk) *adj.* of or relating to the mind. [C17: from Gk *noētikos*, from *noein* to think]

Nofretete (ˌnɒfreˈtiːtɪ) *n.* a variant of **Nefertiti.**

nog *or* **nogg** (nɒg) *n.* **1.** Also called: **flip.** a drink, esp. an alcoholic one, containing beaten egg. **2.** *East Anglian dialect.* strong local beer. [C17 (orig.: a strong beer): from ?]

noggin ('nɒgɪn) *n.* **1.** a small quantity of spirits. **2.** a small mug. **3.** *Inf.* the head. [C17: from ?]

no-go area *n.* a district in a town that is barricaded off, usually by a paramilitary organization, which the police, army, etc., can only enter by force.

Noguchi (nɔː'guːtʃɪ) *n.* **Hideyo** ('hiːdɛˌjɔː). 1876–1928, Japanese bacteriologist, active in the U.S. He made important discoveries in the treatment of syphilis.

Noh (nəʊ) *n.* a variant spelling of **No**[1].

noir (nwɑː) *adj.* (of a film) showing characteristics of a *film noir*, in plot or style. [C20: from French, lit.: black]

noise (nɔɪz) *n.* **1.** a sound, esp. one that is loud or disturbing. **2.** loud shouting; clamour; din. **3.** any undesired electrical disturbance in a circuit, etc. **4.** (*pl.*) conventional comments or sounds conveying a reaction: *sympathetic noises.* **5. make a noise.** to talk a great deal or complain (about). ~*vb.* **6.** (*tr.*; usually foll. by *abroad* or *about*) to spread (news, gossip, etc.). [C13: from OF, from L: NAUSEA]

noiseless ('nɔɪzlɪs) *adj.* making little or no sound. —'**noiselessly** *adv.* —'**noiselessness** *n.*

noisette (nwɑː'zɛt) *adj.* **1.** flavoured with hazelnuts. **2.** nutbrown, as butter browned over heat. ~*n.* **3.** a small round or oval piece of meat. **4.** a hazelnut chocolate. [from F: hazelnut]

noisome ('nɔɪsəm) *adj.* **1.** (esp. of smells) offensive. **2.** harmful or noxious. [C14: from obs. *noy*, var. of ANNOY + -SOME[1]] —'**noisomeness** *n.*

noisy ('nɔɪzɪ) *adj.* **noisier, noisiest. 1.** making a loud or constant noise. **2.** full of or characterized by noise. —'**noisily** *adv.* —'**noisiness** *n.*

Nolan ('nəʊlən) *n.* **Sir Sidney.** born 1917, Australian painter, whose works explore themes in Australian folklore.

Nolde (German 'nɔldə) *n.* **Emil** ('eːmiːl). 1867–1956, German painter and engraver, noted particularly for his violent use of colour and the primitive masklike quality of his figures.

nolens volens Latin. ('nəʊlɛnz 'vəʊlɛnz) *adv.* whether willing or unwilling.

nolle prosequi ('nɒlɪ 'prɒsɪˌkwaɪ) *n. Law.* an entry made on the court record when the plaintiff or prosecutor undertakes not to continue the action or prosecution. [L: do not pursue]

nomad ('nəʊmæd) *n.* **1.** a member of a people or tribe who move from place to place to find pasture and food. **2.** a wanderer. [C16: via F from L *nomas* wandering shepherd, from Gk] —**no'madic** *adj.* —**no'madism** *n.*

no-man's-land *n.* **1.** land between boundaries, esp. an unoccupied zone between opposing forces. **2.** an unowned or unclaimed piece of land. **3.** an ambiguous area of activity.

nom de guerre ('nɒm də 'gɛə) *n., pl.* **noms de guerre** ('nɒm də 'gɛə). an assumed name. [F, lit.: war name]

nom de plume ('nɒm də 'pluːm) *n., pl.* **noms de plume** ('nɒm də 'pluːm). another term for **pen name.** [F]

nomenclature (nəʊ'menklətʃə; *U.S.* 'nəʊmənˌkleɪtʃər) *n.* the terminology used in a particular science, art, activity, etc. [C17: from L *nōmen-clātūra* list of names]

nominal ('nɒmɪnªl) *adj.* **1.** in name only; theoretical: *the nominal leader.* **2.** minimal in comparison with real worth; token: *a nominal fee.* **3.** of, constituting, or giving a name. **4.** *Grammar.* of or relating to a noun or noun phrase. ~*n.* **5.** *Grammar.* a noun, noun phrase, or syntactically similar structure. [C15: from L *nōminālis*, from *nōmen* name] —'**nominally** *adv.*

nominalism ('nɒmɪnªˌlɪzəm) *n.* the philosophical theory that a general word, such as *dog*, is merely a name and does not denote a real object, the general idea "dog". —'**nominalist** *n.*

nominal value *n.* another name for **par value.**

nominate ('nɒmɪˌneɪt) *vb. (mainly tr.)* **1.** to propose as a candidate, esp. for an elective office. **2.** to appoint to an office or position. **3.** (*intr.*) *Austral.* to stand as a candidate in an election. [C16: from L *nōmināre* to call by name, from *nōmen* name] —,**nomi'nation** *n.* —'**nomi,nator** *n.*

nominative ('nɒmɪnətɪv) *adj.* **1.** *Grammar.* denoting a case of nouns and pronouns in inflected languages that is used esp. to identify the subject of a finite verb. **2.** appointed rather than elected to a position, office, etc. ~*n.* **3.** *Grammar.* **a.** the nominative case. **b.** a word or speech element in the nominative case. [C14: from L *nōminātivus* belonging to naming, from *nōmen* name] —**nominatival** (,nɒmɪnə'taɪvəl) *adj.*

nominee (,nɒmɪ'niː) *n.* a person who is nominated to an office or as a candidate. [C17: from NOMINATE + -EE]

nomogram ('nɒmə,græm, 'nəʊmə-) *or* **nomograph** *n.* an arrangement of two linear or logarithmic scales such that an intersecting straight line enables intermediate values or values on a third scale to be read off. [C20: from Gk *nomos* law + -GRAM]

-nomy *n. combining form.* indicating a science or the laws governing a certain field of knowledge: *agronomy; economy.* [from Gk -*nomia* law] —-**nomic** *adj. combining form.*

non- *prefix.* **1.** indicating negation: *nonexistent.* **2.** indicating refusal or failure: *noncooperation.* **3.** indicating exclusion from a specified class: *nonfiction.* **4.** indicating lack or absence: *nonobjective; nonevent.* [from L *nōn* not]

nonage ('nəʊnɪdʒ) *n.* **1.** *Law.* the state of being under any of various ages at which a person may legally enter into certain transactions, such as marrying, etc. **2.** any period of immaturity.

nonagenarian (,nəʊnədʒɪ'nɛərɪən) *n.* **1.** a person who is from 90 to 99 years old. ~*adj.* **2.** of, relating to, or denoting a nonagenarian. [C19: from L *nōnāgēnārius*, from *nōnāginta* ninety]

nonaggression (,nɒnə'grɛʃən) *n.* **a.** restraint of aggression, esp. between states. **b.** (*as modifier*): *a nonaggression pact.*

nonagon ('nɒnə,gɒn) *n.* a polygon having nine sides. —**nonagonal** (nɒn'ægənəl) *adj.*

nonaligned (,nɒnə'laɪnd) *adj.* (of states, etc.) not part of a major alliance or power bloc. —,**nona'lignment** *n.*

nonce (nɒns) *n.* the present time or occasion (now only in **for the nonce**). [C12: from *for the nonce*, a mistaken division of *for then anes*, from *then* dative singular of *the* + *anes* ONCE]

nonce word *n.* a word coined for a single occasion.

nonchalant ('nɒnʃələnt) *adj.* casually unconcerned or indifferent; uninvolved. [C18: from F, from *nonchaloir* to lack warmth, from NON- + *chaloir* from L *calēre* to be warm] —'**nonchalance** *n.*

non-com ('nɒn,kɒm) *n.* short for **noncommissioned officer.**

noncombatant (nɒn'kɒmbətənt) *n.* **1.** a civilian in time of war. **2.** a member of the armed forces whose duties do not include fighting, such as a chaplain or surgeon.

noncommissioned officer (,nɒnkə'mɪʃənd) *n.* (in the armed forces) a person, such as a sergeant or corporal, who is appointed from the ranks as a subordinate officer.

noncommittal (,nɒnkə'mɪtəl) *adj.* not involving or revealing commitment to any particular opinion or course of action.

non compos mentis *Latin.* ('nɒn 'kɒmpɒs 'mɛntɪs) *adj.* mentally incapable of managing one's own affairs; of unsound mind. [L: not in control of one's mind]

nonconformist (,nɒnkən'fɔːmɪst) *n.* **1.** a person who does not conform to generally accepted patterns of behaviour or thought. ~*adj.* **2.** of or characterized by behaviour that does not conform to accepted patterns. —,**noncon'formity** *or* ,**noncon'formism** *n.*

Nonconformist (,nɒnkən'fɔːmɪst) *n.* **1.** a member of a Protestant denomination that dissents from an Established Church, esp. the Church of England. ~*adj.* **2.** of, relating to, or denoting Nonconformists. —,**Noncon'formity** *or* ,**Noncon'formism** *n.*

noncontributory (,nɒnkən'trɪbjʊtərɪ) *adj.* **1.** denoting an insurance or pension scheme for employees, the premiums of which are paid entirely by the employer. **2.** (of a state benefit) not dependent on national insurance contributions.

nondescript ('nɒndɪ,skrɪpt) *adj.* **1.** having no outstanding features. ~*n.* **2.** a nondescript person or thing. [C17: from NON- + L *dēscriptus*, p.p. of *dēscrībere* to copy]

none[1] (nʌn) *pron.* (*functioning as sing. or pl.*) **1.** not any of a particular class: *none of my letters has arrived.* **2.** no-one; nobody: *there were none to tell the tale.* **3.** not any (of): *none of it looks edible.* **4. none other.** no other person: *none other than the Queen herself.* **5. none the.** (*foll. by a comparative adj.*) in no degree: *she was none the worse for her ordeal.* **6. none too.** not very: *he was none too pleased.* [OE *nān*, lit.: not one]

▷ *Usage.* See at **everyone.**

none[2] (nəʊn) *n.* another word for **nones.**

nonentity (nɒn'ɛntɪtɪ) *n., pl.* -**ties. 1.** an insignificant person or thing. **2.** a nonexistent thing. **3.** the state of not existing; nonexistence.

nones (nəʊnz) *n.* (*functioning as sing. or pl.*) **1.** (in the Roman calendar) the ninth day before the ides of each month: the seventh day of March, May, July, and October, and the fifth of each other month. **2.** *Chiefly R.C. Church.* the fifth of the seven canonical hours of the divine office, originally fixed at the ninth hour of the day, about 3 p.m. [OE *nōn*, from L *nōna hora* ninth hour, from *nōnus* ninth]

nonesuch *or* **nonsuch** ('nʌn,sʌtʃ) *n. Arch.* a matchless person or thing; nonpareil.

nonet (nəʊ'nɛt) *n.* **1.** a piece of music for nine instruments or nine voices. **2.** a group of nine singers or instrumentalists.

nonetheless (,nʌnðə'lɛs) *sentence connector.* despite that; however; nevertheless.

non-Euclidean geometry *n.* the branch of modern geometry in which certain axioms of Euclidean geometry are denied.

nonevent (,nɒnɪ'vɛnt) *n.* a disappointing or insignificant occurrence, esp. one predicted to be important.

nonexecutive director (,nɒnɪg'zɛkjʊtɪv) *n.* a director of a commercial company who is not a full-time employee of the company.

,**nonaca'demic** *adj.*	,**noncom'bining** *adj.*	,**noncon'ventional** *adj.*	,**nondi'visible** *adj.*
,**nonac'ceptance** *n.*	,**noncom'mercial** *adj.*	,**noncon'vertible** *adj.*	,**nondoc'trinal** *adj.*
,**nonad'dictive** *adj.*	,**noncom'missioned** *adj.*	,**nonco,oper'ation** *n.*	,**nondog'matic** *adj.*
,**nonalco'holic** *adj.*	,**noncom'municant** *n.*	,**noncor'roborative** *adj.*	**non'drinker** *n.*
,**nonap'pearance** *n.*	,**noncom'municative** *adj.*	,**noncor'roding** *adj.*	**non'drip** *adj.*
,**nonat'tendance** *n.*	**non'communist** *n., adj.*	,**noncre'ative** *adj.*	**non'driver** *n.*
,**nonat'tributable** *adj.*	,**noncom'petitive** *adj.*	**non'criminal** *adj.*	**non'earning** *adj.*
non'basic *adj.*	,**noncom'pliance** *n.*	**non'critical** *adj.*	,**noneco'nomic** *adj.*
,**nonbel'ligerent** *adj.*	,**noncon'ciliatory** *adj.*	**non'culti,vated** *adj.*	,**nonef'fective** *adj.*
,**nonbio'logical** *adj.*	,**noncon'clusive** *adj.*	,**nonde'ciduous** *adj.*	,**none'lastic** *adj.*
non'breakable *adj.*	,**noncon'ductive** *adj.*	,**nonde'livery** *n.*	,**none'quivalent** *adj.*
non'carbo,nated *adj.*	,**noncon'ductor** *n.*	,**nondemo'cratic** *adj.*	,**nones'sential** *adj., n.*
non-'Catholic *adj., n.*	,**nonconfi'dential** *adj.*	,**nonde'monstrable** *adj.*	**non'ethical** *adj.*
non'cerebral *adj.*	,**noncon'flicting** *adj.*	,**nonde,nomi'national** *adj.*	,**nonex'changeable** *adj.*
non-'Christian *adj., n.*	,**noncon'secutive** *adj.*	,**nondepart'mental** *adj.*	**non'ex'istence** *n.*
non'classic *or* **non'classical** *adj.*	,**noncon'senting** *adj.*	,**nonde'pendence** *n.*	,**nonex'istent** *adj.*
	,**noncon'structive** *adj.*	,**nonde'tachable** *adj.*	,**nonex'plosive** *adj.*
non'classi,fied *adj.*	,**noncon'tagious** *adj.*	**non'deto,nating** *adj.*	**non'factual** *adj.*
non'clerical *adj.*	,**noncon'tributing** *adj.*	**non'disci,plinary** *adj.*	**non'fatal** *adj.*
non'clinical *adj.*	,**noncontro'versial** *adj.*	,**nondis'crimi,nating** *adj.*	**non'fattening** *adj.*
,**noncol'legiate** *adj.*			

nonfeasance (nɒn'fiːzᵊns) n. Law. 'a failure to act when under an obligation to do so. Cf. **malfeasance, misfeasance**. [C16: from NON- + *feasance* (obs.) doing, from F *faisance*, from *faire* to do, L *facere*]

nonferrous (nɒn'fɛrəs) adj. **1.** denoting any metal other than iron. **2.** not containing iron.

nonflammable (nɒn'flæməbᵊl) adj. incapable of burning or not easily set on fire.

nong (nɒŋ) n. Austral. sl. a stupid or incompetent person. [C19: ?from obs. E dialect *nigmenog* silly fellow, from ?]

nonillion (nəʊ'nɪljən) n. **1.** (in Britain, France, and Germany) the number represented as one followed by 54 zeros (10^{54}). **2.** (in the U.S. and Canada) the number represented as one followed by 30 zeros (10^{30}). Brit. word: **quintillion**. [C17: from F, from L *nōnus* ninth, on the model of MILLION]

nonintervention (ˌnɒnɪntə'vɛnʃən) n. refusal to intervene, esp. the abstention by a state from intervening in the affairs of other states or in its own internal disputes.

nonjudgmental (ˌnɒndʒʌdʒ'mɛntᵊl) adj. avoiding moral judgments, esp. relating to the conduct of others.

nonjuror (nɒn'dʒʊərə) n. a person who refuses to take an oath, as of allegiance.

Nonjuror (nɒn'dʒʊərə) n. any of a group of clergy in England and Scotland who declined to take the oath of allegiance to William and Mary in 1689.

nonmetal (nɒn'mɛtᵊl) n. any of a number of chemical elements that have acidic oxides and are poor conductors of heat and electricity. —**,nonme'tallic** adj.

nonmoral (nɒn'mɒrəl) adj. not involving morality or ethics; neither moral nor immoral.

Nono (Italian 'nɔːno) n. **Luigi** (lu'iːdʒi). born 1924, Italian composer of 12-tone music.

nonobjective (ˌnɒnəb'dʒɛktɪv) adj. of or designating an art movement in which things are depicted in an abstract or purely formalized way.

no-nonsense (ˌnəʊ'nɒnsəns) adj. sensible, practical, and straightforward: *a severe no-nonsense look.*

nonpareil ('nɒnpərəl, ˌnɒnpə'reɪl) n. a person or thing that is unsurpassed; peerless example. [C15: from F, from NON- + *pareil* similar]

nonplus (nɒn'plʌs) vb. **-plussing, -plussed** or U.S. **-plusing, -plused. 1.** (tr.) to put at a loss; confound. ~n., pl. **-pluses. 2.** a state of utter perplexity prohibiting action or speech. [C16: from L *nōn plus* no further]

non-profit-making adj. not yielding a profit, esp. because organized or established for some other reason: *a non-profit-making organization.*

nonproliferation (ˌnɒnprəˌlɪfər'eɪʃən) n. **a.** limitation of the production or spread of something, esp. nuclear or chemical weapons. **b.** (as modifier): *a nonproliferation treaty.*

non-pros (ˌnɒn'prɒs) n. **1.** short for **non prosequitur.** ~vb. **-prossing, -prossed. 2.** (tr.) to enter a judgment of non prosequitur against (a plaintiff).

non prosequitur ('nɒn prəʊ'sɛkwɪtə) n. Law. (formerly) a judgment in favour of a defendant when the plaintiff failed to take the necessary steps in an action within the time allowed. [L, lit.: he does not prosecute]

nonrepresentational (ˌnɒnrɛprɪzɛn'teɪʃənᵊl) adj. Art. another word for **abstract**.

nonresistant (ˌnɒnrɪ'zɪstənt) adj. **1.** incapable of resisting something, such as a disease; susceptible. **2.** History. (esp. in 17th-century England) practising passive obedience to royal authority even when its commands were unjust.

nonrestrictive (ˌnɒnrɪ'strɪktɪv) adj. **1.** not limiting. **2.** Grammar. denoting a relative clause that is not restrictive. Cf. **restrictive** (sense 2).

nonsense ('nɒnsəns) n. **1.** something that has or makes no sense; unintelligible language; drivel. **2.** conduct or action that is absurd. **3.** foolish behaviour: *she'll stand no nonsense.* **4.** things of little or no value; trash. ~interj. **5.** an exclamation of disagreement. —**nonsensical** (nɒn'sɛnsɪkᵊl) adj. —**non'sensically** adv. —**non'sensicalness** or **non,sensi'cality** n.

nonsense verse n. verse in which the sense is nonexistent or absurd.

non sequitur ('nɒn 'sɛkwɪtə) n. **1.** a statement having little or no relevance to what preceded it. **2.** Logic. a conclusion that does not follow from the premises. [L, lit.: it does not follow]

nonsmoker (nɒn'sməʊkə) n. **1.** a person who does not smoke. **2.** a train compartment in which smoking is forbidden. —**non'smoking** adj.

nonspecific urethritis n. inflammation of the urethra as a result of a venereal infection that cannot be traced to a specific cause. Abbrev.: **NSU.**

nonstandard (nɒn'stændəd) adj. **1.** denoting or characterized by idiom, vocabulary, etc., that is not regarded as correct and acceptable by educated native speakers of a language; not standard. **2.** deviating from a given standard.

nonstarter (nɒn'stɑːtə) n. **1.** a horse that fails to run in a race for which it has been entered. **2.** a person or thing that has little chance of success.

nonstick ('nɒn'stɪk) adj. (of saucepans, etc.) coated with a substance that prevents food sticking to them.

nonstop (nɒn'stɒp) adj., adv. without making a stop: *a nonstop flight.*

nonsuch ('nʌn,sʌtʃ) n. a variant spelling of **nonesuch.**

nonsuit (nɒn'suːt) Law. ~n. **1.** an order of a judge dismissing a suit when the plaintiff fails to show he has a good cause of action or fails to produce any evidence. ~vb. **2.** (tr.) to order the dismissal of the suit of (a person).

non troppo ('nɒn 'trɒpəʊ) adv. Music. (preceded by a direction, esp. a tempo marking) not to be observed too strictly (esp. in **allegro ma non troppo, adagio ma non troppo**). [It.]

non'finite adj.	non'maritime adj.	non'physical adj.	non'secular adj.
non'flexible adj.	non'member n.	non'playing adj.	non'segre,gated adj.
non'fluid adj.	non'membership n.	non'poisonous adj.	,nonse'lective adj.
non'freezing adj.	non'metric adj.	non'porous adj.	non'sexist adj.
,nonful'filment n.	non'migratory adj.	non'practising adj.	non'sexual adj.
non'functional adj.	non'militant adj.	non'predatory adj.	non'skilled adj.
non'fusible adj.	,nonminis'terial adj.	,nonpre'scriptive adj.	non'slip adj.
non'gaseous adj.	non'navigable adj.	,nonpro'fessional adj.	non'social adj.
,nongovern'mental adj.	,non-ne'gotiable adj.	non'racial adj.	non'soluble adj.
,nonhar'monic adj.	non-'nuclear adj.	non'radical adj.	non'speaking adj.
non'human adj.	,nonob'servance n.	,nonradio'active adj.	non'specialist n.
,nonin'fectious adj.	,nonoc'currence n.	non'reader n.	,nonspe'cific adj.
,nonin'flammable adj.	,nonoper'ational adj.	,nonrecog'nition n.	non'spiritual adj.
,nonin'flected adj.	non'operative adj.	,nonre'coverable adj.	non'staining adj.
,nonin'heritable adj.	,nonor'ganic adj.	non'registered adj.	,nonsta'tistical adj.
,nonin'tellectual adj.	non'paral,lel adj.	,nonre'ligious adj.	non'structural adj.
,noninter'secting adj.	,nonpa'rental adj.	,nonre'newable adj.	,nonsub'scriber n.
,nonin'toxi,cating adj.	,nonparlia'mentary adj.	,nonrepre'sentative adj.	non'surgical adj.
non'iron adj.	,nonpa'rochial adj.	non'resident n., adj.	non'swimmer n.
non'irritant adj., n.	,nonpar'tici,pating adj.	,nonresi'dential adj.	non'taxable adj.
non'lethal adj.	,nonparti'san or ,nonparti'zan adj.	non're'stricted adj.	non'teaching adj.
non'linear adj.		,nonre'turnable adj.	non'technical adj.
non'literary adj.	non'party adj.	non'rigid adj.	,nonterri'torial adj.
non'logical adj.	non'paying adj.	non'scheduled adj.	non'toxic adj.
non'luminous adj.	non'payment n.	,nonscien'tific adj.	,nontrans'ferable adj.
,nonmag'netic adj.	non'permanent adj.	non'seasonal adj.	non'tropical adj.
,nonma'lignant adj.	non'permeable adj.	,nonsec'tarian adj.	

non-U (nɒn'juː) *adj. Brit. inf.* (esp. of language) not characteristic of or used by the upper class.

nonunion (nɒn'juːnjən) *adj.* **1.** not belonging or related to a trade union: *nonunion workers.* **2.** not favouring or employing union labour: *a nonunion shop.* **3.** not produced by union labour.

nonvoter (nɒn'vəʊtə) *n.* **1.** a person who does not vote. **2.** a person not eligible to vote.

nonvoting (nɒn'vəʊtɪŋ) *adj.* **1.** of or relating to a nonvoter. **2.** *Finance.* (of shares, etc.) not entitling the holder to vote at company meetings.

noodle[1] ('nuːd^əl) *n.* (*often pl.*) a ribbon-like strip of pasta. [C18; from G *Nudel* from ?]

noodle[2] ('nuːd^əl) *n.* **1.** *U.S. & Canad. sl.* the head. **2.** a simpleton. [C18: ? a blend of NODDLE[1] & NOODLE[1]]

nook (nʊk) *n.* **1.** a corner or narrow recess. **2.** a secluded or sheltered place. [C13: from ?]

nooky *or* **nookie** ('nʊkɪ) *n. Sl.* lovemaking.

noon (nuːn) *n.* **1.** the middle of the day; 12 o'clock. **2.** *Poetic.* the most important part; culmination. [OE *nōn*, from L *nōna* (*hōra*) ninth hour (orig. 3 p.m., the ninth hour from sunrise)]

noonday ('nuːn,deɪ) *n.* the middle of the day; noon.

no-one *or* **no one** *pron.* no person; nobody.
▷ *Usage.* See at **everyone**.

noontime ('nuːn,taɪm) *or* **noontide** *n.* the middle of the day; noon.

Noordbrabant (noːrd'braːbant) *n.* the Dutch name for **North Brabant**.

Noordholland (noːrt'hɔlant) *n.* the Dutch name for **North Holland**.

noose (nuːs) *n.* **1.** a loop in the end of a rope, such as a lasso or hangman's halter, usually tied with a slipknot. **2.** something that restrains or traps. **3. put one's head in a noose.** to bring about one's own downfall. ~*vb.* (*tr.*) **4.** to secure as in a noose. **5.** to make a noose of or in. [C15: ?from Provençal *nous*, from L *nōdus* NODE]

no-par *adj.* (of securities) without a par value.

nor (nɔː; *unstressed* nə) *conj.* (*coordinating*) **1.** (used to join alternatives, the first of which is preceded by *neither*) and not: *neither measles nor mumps.* **2.** (foll. by a verb) (and) not ... either: *they weren't talented—nor were they particularly funny.* **3.** *Poetic.* neither— *nor wind nor rain.* [C13: contraction of OE *nōther*, from *nāhwæther* NEITHER]

Nor. *abbrev. for:* **1.** Norman. **2.** north. **3.** Norway. **4.** Norwegian.

noradrenaline (,nɔːrə'drɛnəlɪn, -liːn) *or* **noradrenalin** *n.* a hormone secreted by the adrenal medulla, increasing blood pressure and heart rate. U.S. name: **norepinephrine.**

NOR circuit *or* **gate** (nɔː) *n. Computers.* a logic circuit having two or more input wires and one output wire that has a high-voltage output signal only if all input signals are at a low voltage. Cf. **AND circuit.** [C20: from NOR; the action performed is similar to the operation of the conjunction *nor* in logic]

Nord (*French* nɔr) *n.* a department of N France, in Nord-Pas-de-Calais region. Capital: Lille. Pop.: 2 520 526 (1982). Area: 5774 sq. km (2252 sq. miles).

Nordau (*German* 'nɔrdau) *n.* **Max Simon** (maks 'ziːmɔn), original name *Max Simon Südfeld.* 1849–1923, German author, born in Hungary; a leader of the Zionist movement.

Nordenskjöld (*Swedish* 'nuːrdənfœld) *n.* Baron **Nils Adolf Erik** (nils 'aːdɔlf 'eːrik). 1832–1901, Swedish Arctic explorer and geologist, born in Finland. He was the first to navigate the Northeast Passage (1878–79).

Nordenskjöld Sea *n.* the former name of the **Laptev Sea.** [named after N. A. E. NORDENSKJÖLD]

nordic ('nɔːdɪk) *adj. Skiing.* of competitions in cross-country racing and ski-jumping. Cf. **alpine** (sense 4).

Nordic ('nɔːdɪk) *adj.* of or belonging to a subdivision of the Caucasoid race typified by the tall blond blue-eyed long-headed inhabitants of Scandinavia. [C19: from F *nordique*, from *nord* NORTH]

Nordkyn Cape (*Norwegian* 'nuːrçyn) *n.* a cape in N Norway: the northernmost point of the European mainland.

Nord–Pas-de-Calais (*French* nɔrpadəkalɛ) *n.* a region of N France, on the Straits of Dover (the **Pas de Calais**): coal-mining, textile, and metallurgical industries.

Nordrhein-Westfalen ('nɔrtrainvɛst'faːlən) *n.* the German name for **North Rhine-Westphalia.**

norepinephrine (,nɔːrɛpɪ'nɛfrɪn, -riːn) *n.* the U.S. name for **noradrenaline.**

Norfolk ('nɔːfək) *n.* **1.** a county of E England, on the North Sea and the Wash: low-lying, with large areas of fens in the west and the Broads in the east; rich agriculturally. Administrative centre: Norwich. Pop.: 727 800 (1986 est.). Area: 5368 sq. km (2072 sq. miles). **2.** a port in SE Virginia, on the Elizabeth River and Hampton Roads: headquarters of the U.S. Atlantic fleet; shipbuilding. Pop.: 274 800 (1986).

Norfolk Island *n.* an island in the S Pacific, between New Caledonia and N New Zealand: an Australian external territory; discovered by Captain Cook in 1774; a penal settlement in early years. Pop.: 1977 (1986). Area: 36 sq. km (14 sq. miles).

Norfolk jacket *n.* a man's single-breasted belted jacket with one or two chest pockets and a box pleat down the back. [C19: worn in NORFOLK for duck shooting]

Norge ('nɔrgə) *n.* the Norwegian name for **Norway.**

noria ('nɔːrɪə) *n.* a water wheel with buckets attached to its rim for raising water from a stream into irrigation canals, etc. [C18: via Sp. from Ar. *nā'ūra*, from *na'ara* to creak]

Noricum ('nɒrɪkəm) *n.* an Alpine kingdom of the Celts, south of the Danube: comprises present-day central Austria and parts of Bavaria; a Roman province from about 16 B.C.

nork (nɔːk) *n.* (*usually pl.*) *Austral. taboo sl.* a female breast. [C20: from ?]

norm (nɔːm) *n.* **1.** an average level of achievement or performance, as of a group. **2.** a standard of achievement or behaviour that is required, desired, or designated as normal. [C19: from L *norma* carpenter's square]

normal ('nɔːm^əl) *adj.* **1.** usual; regular; common; typical: *the normal level.* **2.** constituting a standard: *if we take this as normal.* **3.** *Psychol.* **a.** being within certain limits of intelligence, ability, etc. **b.** conforming to the conventions of one's group. **4.** (of laboratory animals) maintained in a natural state for purposes of comparison with animals treated with drugs, etc. **5.** *Chem.* (of a solution) containing a number of grams equal to the equivalent weight of the solute in each litre of solvent. **6.** *Geom.* another word for **perpendicular** (sense 1). ~*n.* **7.** the usual, average, or typical state, degree, form, etc. **8.** anything that is normal. **9.** *Geom.* a perpendicular line or plane. [C16: from L *normālis* conforming to the carpenter's square, from *norma* NORM] —**normality** (nɔː'mælɪtɪ) *or esp. U.S.* '**normalcy** *n.*

normal curve *n. Statistics.* a symmetrical bell-shaped curve representing the probability density function of a normal distribution.

normal distribution *n. Statistics.* a continuous distribution of a random variable with its mean, median, and mode equal.

normalize *or* **-ise** ('nɔːmə,laɪz) *vb.* (*tr.*) **1.** to bring or make into the normal state. **2.** to bring into conformity with a standard. **3.** to heat (steel) above a critical temperature and allow it to cool in air to relieve internal stresses; anneal. —,**normali'zation** *or* **-i'sation** *n.*

normally ('nɔːməlɪ) *adv.* **1.** as a rule; usually; ordinarily. **2.** in a normal manner.

Norman ('nɔːmən) *n.* **1.** (in the Middle Ages) a member of the people of Normandy in N France, descended from the 10th-century Scandinavian conquerors of the country and the native French. **2.** a native or inhabitant of Normandy. **3.** another name for **Norman French.** ~*adj.* **4.** of or characteristic of the Normans or their dialect of French. **5.** of or characteristic of Normandy. **6.** denoting or having the style of Romanesque architecture used in Britain from the Norman Conquest until the 12th century, characterized by the rounded arch, massive masonry walls, etc.

Norman Conquest *n.* the invasion and settlement of England by the Normans, following the Battle of Hastings (1066).

---

non'venomous *adj.* **non'vintage** *adj.* **non'violent** *adj.* **non'vocal** *adj.*
non'verbal *adj.*

Normandy ('nɔ:məndɪ) *n.* a former province of N France, on the English Channel: settled by Vikings under Rollo in the 10th century; scene of the Allied landings in 1944. Chief town: Rouen. French name: **Normandie** (nɔrmãdi).

Norman French *n.* the medieval Norman and English dialect of Old French.

normative ('nɔ:mətɪv) *adj.* **1.** implying, creating, or prescribing a norm or standard, as in language: *normative grammar*. **2.** expressing value judgments as contrasted with stating facts.

Norn[1] (nɔ:n) *n. Norse myth.* any of the three virgin goddesses of fate. [C18: ON]

Norn[2] (nɔ:n) *n.* the medieval Norse language of the Orkneys, Shetlands, and parts of N Scotland. [C17: from ON *norrǿna* Norwegian, from *northr* north]

Norodom Sihanouk (,nɒrə'dɒm 'si:ənʊk) *n.* See (Norodom) **Sihanouk.**

Norrköping (*Swedish* 'nɔrtçø:pin) *n.* a port in SE Sweden, near the Baltic. Pop.: 118 801 (1986).

Norse (nɔ:s) *adj.* **1.** of ancient and medieval Scandinavia or its inhabitants. **2.** of or characteristic of Norway. ~*n.* **3. a.** the N group of Germanic languages, spoken in Scandinavia. **b.** any one of these languages, esp. in their ancient or medieval forms. **4. the Norse.** (*functioning as pl.*) **a.** the Norwegians. **b.** the Vikings.

Norseman ('nɔ:smən) *n., pl.* -**men.** another name for a **Viking.**

north (nɔ:θ) *n.* **1.** one of the four cardinal points of the compass, at 0° or 360°, that is 90° from east and west and 180° from south. **2.** the direction along a meridian towards the North Pole. **3.** the direction in which a compass needle points; magnetic north. **4. the north.** (*often cap.*) any area lying in or towards the north. **5.** (*usually cap.*) *Cards.* the player or position at the table corresponding to north on the compass. ~*adj.* **6.** in, towards, or facing the north. **7.** (esp. of the wind) from the north. ~*adv.* **8.** in, to, or towards the north. [OE]

North[1] (nɔ:θ) *n.* **the. 1.** the northern area of England, generally regarded as reaching the southern boundaries of Yorkshire, Derbyshire, and Cheshire. **2.** (in the U.S.) the states north of the Mason-Dixon Line that were known as the Free States during the Civil War. **3.** the northern part of North America, esp. Alaska, the Yukon and the Northwest Territories. **4.** the countries of the world that are economically and technically advanced. ~*adj.* **5.** of or denoting the northern part of a specified country, area, etc.

North[2] (nɔ:θ) *n.* **1. Frederick,** 2nd Earl of Guildford, called *Lord North.* 1732–92, British statesman; prime minister (1770–82), dominated by George III. He was held responsible for the loss of the American colonies. **2.** Sir **Thomas.** ?1535–?1601, English translator of Plutarch's *Lives* (1579), which was the chief source of Shakespeare's Roman plays.

North Africa *n.* the part of Africa between the Mediterranean and the Sahara: consists chiefly of Morocco, Algeria, Tunisia, Libya, and N Egypt. — **North African** *adj., n.*

Northallerton (nɔ:'θælət³n) *n.* a market town in N England, administrative centre of North Yorkshire. Pop.: 13 800 (1985).

North America *n.* the third largest continent, linked with South America by the Isthmus of Panama and bordering on the Arctic Ocean, the N Atlantic, the Gulf of Mexico, and the Caribbean. It consists generally of a great mountain system (the Western Cordillera) extending along the entire W coast, actively volcanic in the extreme north and south, with the Great Plains to the east and the Appalachians still further east, separated from the Canadian Shield by an arc of large lakes (Great Bear, Great Slave, Winnipeg, Superior, Michigan, Huron, Erie, Ontario); reaches its greatest height of 6194 m (20 320 ft.) in Mount McKinley, Alaska, and its lowest point of 85 m (280 ft.) below sea level in Death Valley, California, and ranges from snowfields, tundra, and taiga in the north to deserts in the southwest and tropical forests in the extreme south. Pop.: 345 000 000 (1981 est.). Area: over 24 000 000 sq. km (9 500 000 sq. miles). — **North American** *adj., n.*

Northampton (nɔ:'θæmptən, nɔ:θ'hæmp-) *n.* **1.** a town in central England, administrative centre of Northamptonshire, on the River Nene: footwear and engineering industries. Pop.: 163 000 (1984 est.). **2.** short for **Northamptonshire.**

Northamptonshire (nɔ:'θæmptən,ʃɪə, -ʃə, nɔ:θ'hæmp-) *n.* a county of central England: agriculture, iron and steel, engineering, and footwear industries. Administrative centre: Northampton. Pop.: 554 400 (1986 est.). Area: 2367 sq. km (914 sq. miles). Abbrev.: **Northants.**

Northants (nɔ:'θænts) *abbrev. for* Northamptonshire.

North Atlantic Drift *or* **Current** *n.* the warm ocean current flowing northeast, under the influence of prevailing winds, from the Gulf of Mexico towards NW Europe and warming its climate. Also called: **Gulf Stream.**

North Borneo *n.* the former name (until 1963) of **Sabah.**

northbound ('nɔ:θ,baʊnd) *adj.* going or leading towards the north.

North Brabant *n.* a province of the S Netherlands: formed part of the medieval duchy of Brabant. Capital: 's Hertogenbosch. Pop.: 2 139 626 (1987 est.). Area: 4965 sq. km (1917 sq. miles). Dutch name: **Noordbrabant.**

north by east *n.* one point on the compass east of north.

north by west *n.* one point on the compass west of north.

North Cape *n.* **1.** a cape on N Mageroy Island, in the Arctic Ocean off the N coast of Norway. **2.** a cape on N North Island, New Zealand.

North Carolina *n.* a state of the southeastern U.S., on the Atlantic: consists of a coastal plain rising to the Piedmont Plateau and the Appalachian Mountains in the west. Capital: Raleigh. Pop.: 6 331 000 (1986 est.). Area: 126 387 sq. km (48 798 sq. miles). Abbrevs.: **N.C.** or (with zip code) **NC** —**North Carolinian** *adj., n.*

North Channel *n.* a strait between NE Ireland and SW Scotland, linking the North Atlantic with the Irish Sea.

Northcliffe ('nɔ:θklɪf) *n.* title of *Alfred Charles William Harmsworth.* 1865–1922, British newspaper proprietor. With his brother, 1st Viscount Rothermere, he built up a vast chain of newspapers. He founded the *Daily Mail* (1896), the *Daily Mirror* (1903), and acquired *The Times* (1908).

North Country *n.* (usually preceded by *the*) another name for **North** (sense 1).

Northd *abbrev. for* Northumberland.

North Dakota *n.* a state of the western U.S.: mostly undulating prairies and plains, rising from the Red River valley in the east to the Missouri plateau in the west, with the infertile Bad Lands in the extreme west. Capital: Bismarck. Pop.: 679 000 (1986 est.). Area: 183 019 sq. km (70 664 sq. miles). Abbrevs.: **N.Dak., N.D.,** or (with zip code) **ND** —**North Dakotan** *adj., n.*

northeast (,nɔ:θ'i:st; *Naut.* ,nɔ:r'i:st) *n.* **1.** the point of the compass or direction midway between north and east. **2.** (*often cap.;* usually preceded by *the*) any area lying in or towards this direction. ~*adj. also* **northeastern. 3.** (*sometimes cap.*) of or denoting the northeastern part of a specified country, area, etc.: *northeast Lincolnshire.* **4.** in, towards, or facing the northeast. **5.** (esp. of the wind) from the northeast. ~*adv.* **6.** in, to, or towards the northeast. — ,**north'easternmost** *adj.*

Northeast (,nɔ:θ'i:st) *n.* (usually preceded by *the*) the northeastern part of England, esp. Northumberland and Durham.

northeast by east *n.* one point on the compass east of northeast.

northeast by north *n.* one point on the compass north of northeast.

northeaster (,nɔ:θ'i:stə; *Naut.* ,nɔ:r'i:stə) *n.* a strong wind or storm from the northeast.

northeasterly (,nɔ:θ'i:stəlɪ; *Naut.* ,nɔ:r'i:stəlɪ) *adj., adv.* **1.** in, towards, or (esp. of a wind) from the northeast. ~*n., pl.* -**lies. 2.** a wind or storm from the northeast.

North East Frontier Agency *n.* the former name (until 1972) of **Arunachal Pradesh.**

Northeast Passage *n.* a shipping route along the Arctic coasts of Europe and Asia, between the Atlantic and Pacific: first navigated by Nordenskjöld (1878–79).

northeastward (,nɔ:θ'i:stwəd; *Naut.* ,nɔ:r'i:stwəd) *adj.* **1.** towards or (esp. of a wind) from the northeast. ~*n.* **2.** a direction towards or area in the northeast. — ,**north'eastwardly** *adj., adv.*

norther ('nɔ:ðə) *n. Chiefly southern U.S.* a wind or storm from the north.

northerly ('nɔ:ðəlɪ) *adj.* **1.** of or situated in the north. ~*adv., adj.* **2.** towards the north. **3.** from the north: *a northerly wind.* ~*n., pl.* -**lies. 4.** a wind from the north. — '**northerliness** *n.*

northern ('nɔːðən) *adj.* **1.** in or towards the north. **2.** (esp. of winds) proceeding from the north. **3.** (*sometimes cap.*) of or characteristic of the north or North.

Northern Dvina *n.* See **Dvina** (sense 1).

Northerner ('nɔːðənə) *n.* (*sometimes not cap.*) a native or inhabitant of the north of any specified region, esp. England, the U.S., or the far north of Canada.

northern hemisphere *n.* (*often caps.*) that half of the globe lying north of the equator.

Northern Ireland *n.* that part of the United Kingdom occupying the NE part of Ireland: separated from the rest of Ireland, which became independent in 1920, remaining part of the United Kingdom, with a separate Parliament (Stormont) and limited self-government: scene of severe conflict between Catholics and Protestants, including terrorist bombing from 1969: direct administration from Westminster from 1972. Capital: Belfast. Pop.: 1 488 077 (1981). Area: 14 121 sq. km (5452 sq. miles).

Northern Isles *pl. n.* the Orkneys and Shetland.

northern lights *pl. n.* another name for **aurora borealis**.

northernmost ('nɔːðən‚məʊst) *adj.* situated or occurring farthest north.

Northern Rhodesia *n.* the former name (until 1964) of **Zambia**.

Northern Territories *pl. n.* a former British protectorate in W Africa, established in 1897; attached to the Gold Coast in 1901; now constitutes the Northern Region of Ghana (since 1957).

Northern Territory *n.* an administrative division of N central Australia, on the Timor and Arafura Seas: includes Ashmore and Cartier Islands; the Arunta Desert lies in the east, the Macdonnell Ranges in the south, and Arnhem Land in the north (containing Australia's largest Aboriginal reservation). Capital: Darwin. Pop.: 154 000 (1986). Area: 1 347 525 sq. km (520 280 sq. miles).

North Holland *n.* a province of the NW Netherlands, on the peninsula between the North Sea and IJsselmeer: includes the West Frisian Island of Texel. Capital: Haarlem. Pop.: 2 334 209 (1987 est.). Area: 2663 sq. km (1029 sq. miles). Dutch name: **Noordholland**.

northing ('nɔːθɪŋ, -ðɪŋ) *n.* **1.** *Navigation.* movement or distance covered in a northerly direction, esp. as expressed in the resulting difference in latitude. **2.** *Astron.* a north or positive declination.

North Island *n.* (usually preceded by *the*) the northernmost of the two main islands of New Zealand. Pop.: 2 438 249 (1986). Area: 114 729 sq. km (44 297 sq. miles).

North Korea *n.* a republic in NE Asia, on the Sea of Japan and the Yellow Sea: established in 1948 as a people's republic; mostly rugged and mountainous, with fertile lowlands in the west. Language: Korean. Currency: won. Capital: Pyongyang. Pop.: 18 802 000 (1983 est.). Area: 122 313 sq. km (47 225 sq. miles). Official name: **Democratic People's Republic of Korea**. Korean name: **Chosŏn**. — **North Korean** *adj.*, *n.*

Northland ('nɔːθlənd) *n.* **1.** the peninsula containing Norway and Sweden. **2.** (in Canada) the far north. — '**Northlander** *n.*

Northman ('nɔːθmən) *n.*, *pl.* -**men.** another name for a **Viking.**

north-northeast *n.* **1.** the point on the compass or the direction midway between north and northeast. ~*adj.*, *adv.* **2.** in, from, or towards this direction.

north-northwest *n.* **1.** the point on the compass or the direction midway between northwest and north. ~*adj.*, *adv.* **2.** in, from, or towards this direction.

North Ossetian Autonomous Soviet Socialist Republic (ə'siːʃən) *n.* an administrative division of the S Soviet Union, on the N slopes of the central Caucasus Mountains. Capital: Ordzhonikidze. Pop.: 616 000 (1986). Area: about 8000 sq. km (3088 sq. miles).

North Pole *n.* **1.** the northernmost point on the earth's axis, at a latitude of 90°N, characterized by very low temperatures. **2.** Also called: **north celestial pole.** *Astron.* the point of intersection of the earth's extended axis and the northern half of the celestial sphere. **3.** (*usually not cap.*) the pole of a freely suspended magnet, which is attracted to the earth's magnetic North Pole.

North Rhine-Westphalia *n.* a state of W West Germany: formed in 1946 by the amalgamation of the Prussian province of Westphalia with the N part of the Prussian Rhine province and later with the state of Lippe; highly industrialized. Capital: Düsseldorf. Pop.: 16 665 300 (1986). Area:

34 039 sq. km (13 142 sq. miles). German name: **Nordrhein-Westfalen.**

North Riding *n.* (until 1974) an administrative division of Yorkshire, now constituting most of North Yorkshire.

North Saskatchewan *n.* a river in W Canada, rising in W Alberta and flowing northeast, east, and southeast to join the South Saskatchewan River and form the Saskatchewan River. Length: 1223 km (760 miles).

North Sea *n.* an arm of the Atlantic between Great Britain and the N European mainland. Area: about 569 800 sq. km (220 000 sq. miles). Former name: **German Ocean.**

North-Sea gas *n.* (in Britain) natural gas obtained from deposits below the North Sea.

North Star *n.* **the.** another name for **Polaris.**

Northumberland (nɔː'θʌmbələnd) *n.* the northernmost county of England, on the North Sea: hilly in the north (the Cheviots) and west (the Pennines), with many Roman remains, notably Hadrian's Wall; shipbuilding, coalmining. Administrative centre: Newcastle. Pop.: 301 000 (1986 est.). Area: 5032 sq. km (1943 sq. miles). Also called: **Northumbria.** Abbrev.: **Northd**

Northumbria (nɔː'θʌmbrɪə) *n.* **1.** (in Anglo-Saxon Britain) a region that stretched from the Humber to the Firth of Forth: formed in the 7th century A.D., it became an important intellectual centre; a separate kingdom until 876 A.D. **2.** another name for **Northumberland.** —**Nor'thumbrian** *adj.*

North Vietnam *n.* a region of N Vietnam, on the Gulf of Tonkin: an independent Communist state from 1954 until 1976. Area: 164 061 sq. km (63 344 sq. miles).

northward ('nɔːθwəd; *Naut.* 'nɔːðəd) *adj.* **1.** moving, facing, or situated towards the north. ~*n.* **2.** the northward part, direction, etc. ~*adv. also* **northwards. 3.** towards the north.

northwest (‚nɔːθ'wɛst; *Naut.* ‚nɔː'wɛst) *n.* **1.** the point of the compass or direction midway between north and west. **2.** (*often cap.*; usually preceded by *the*) any area lying in or towards this direction. ~*adj. also* **northwestern. 3.** (*sometimes cap.*) of or denoting the northwestern part of a specified country, area, etc.: *northwest Greenland.* ~*adj.*, *adv.* **4.** in, to, or towards the northwest. —‚**north'westernmost** *adj.*

Northwest (‚nɔːθ'wɛst) *n.* (usually preceded by *the*) the northwestern part of England, esp. Lancashire and the Lake District.

northwest by north *n.* one point on the compass north of northwest.

northwest by west *n.* one point on the compass south of northwest.

northwester (‚nɔːθ'wɛstə; *Naut.* ‚nɔː'wɛstə) *n.* a strong wind or storm from the northwest.

northwesterly (‚nɔːθ'wɛstəlɪ; *Naut.* ‚nɔː'wɛstəlɪ) *adj.*, *adv.* **1.** in, towards, or (esp. of a wind) from the northwest. ~*n.*, *pl.* -**lies. 2.** a wind or storm from the northwest.

North-West Frontier Province *n.* a province in N Pakistan between Afghanistan and Jammu and Kashmir: part of British India from 1901 until 1947; of strategic importance, esp. for the Khyber Pass. Capital: Peshawar. Pop.: 11 061 000 (1981). Area: 74 522 sq. km (28 773 sq. miles).

Northwest Passage *n.* the passage by sea from the Atlantic to the Pacific along the N coast of America: attempted for over 300 years by Europeans seeking a short route to the Far East, before being successfully navigated by Amundsen (1903–06).

Northwest Territories *pl. n.* the part of Canada north of the provinces and east of the Yukon Territory, including the islands of the Arctic, Hudson Bay, James Bay, and Ungava Bay; comprises over a third of Canada's total area; rich mineral resources. Pop.: 51 384 (1986). Area: 3 246 404 sq. km (1 253 438 sq. miles). Abbrev.: **NWT.**

Northwest Territory *n.* See **Old Northwest.**

northwestward (‚nɔːθ'wɛstwəd; *Naut.* ‚nɔː'wɛstwəd) *adj.* **1.** towards or (esp. of a wind) from the northwest. ~*n.* **2.** a direction towards or area in the northwest. —‚**north'westwardly** *adj.*, *adv.*

Northwich ('nɔːθwɪtʃ) *n.* a town in NW England, in Cheshire: salt and chemical industries. Pop.: 17 126 (1981).

North Yemen *n.* another name for **Yemen** (sense 1).

North Yorkshire *n.* a county in N England, formed in 1974 from most of the North Riding of Yorkshire and parts of the East and West Ridings. Administrative centre

Northallerton. Pop.: 699 800 (1986 est.). Area: 8309 sq. km (3207 sq. miles).

Norw. *abbrev. for:* **1.** Norway. **2.** Norwegian.

Norway ('nɔ:,weɪ) *n.* a kingdom in NW Europe, occupying the W part of the Scandinavian peninsula: first united in the Viking age (800–1050); under the rule of Denmark (1523–1814) and Sweden (1814–1905); became an independent monarchy in 1905. Its coastline is deeply indented by fjords and fringed with islands, rising inland to plateaus and mountains. Norway has a large fishing fleet and its merchant navy is among the world's largest. Language: Norwegian. Religion: mostly Lutheran. Currency: krone. Capital: Oslo. Pop.: 4 174 005 (1987). Area: 324 218 sq. km (125 181 sq. miles). Norwegian name: **Norge.**

Norway lobster *n.* a European lobster fished for food.

Norway rat *n.* another name for **brown rat.**

Norway spruce *n.* a European spruce tree having drooping branches and dark green needle-like leaves.

Norwegian (nɔ:'wi:dʒən) *adj.* **1.** of or characteristic of Norway, its language, or its people. ~*n.* **2.** any of the various North Germanic languages of Norway. **3.** a native or inhabitant of Norway.

Norwegian Sea *n.* part of the Arctic Ocean between Greenland and Norway.

Norwich ('nɒrɪdʒ) *n.* a city in E England, administrative centre of Norfolk: cathedral (founded 1096); University of East Anglia (1963); footwear industry. Pop.: 122 270 (1981).

Nos. *or* **nos.** *abbrev. for* numbers.

nose (nəʊz) *n.* **1.** the organ of smell and entrance to the respiratory tract, consisting of a prominent structure divided into two hair-lined air passages. Related adj.: **nasal.** **2.** the sense of smell itself: in animals, the ability to follow trails by scent (esp. in **a good nose**). **3.** the scent, aroma, bouquet of something, esp. wine. **4.** instinctive skill in discovering things (sometimes in **follow one's nose**): *he had a nose for good news stories.* **5.** any part resembling a nose in form or function, such as a nozzle or spout. **6.** the forward part of a vehicle, aircraft, etc. **7.** narrow margin of victory (in (**win**) **by a nose**). **8. cut off one's nose to spite one's face.** to carry out a vengeful action that hurts oneself more than another. **9. get up** (**someone's**) **nose.** *Inf.* to annoy or irritate (someone). **10. keep one's nose clean.** to stay out of trouble. **11. lead by the nose.** to make (someone) do unquestioningly all one wishes; dominate. **12. look down one's nose at.** *Inf.* to be disdainful of. **13. on the nose.** *Sl.* **a.** (in horserace betting) to win only: *I bet twenty pounds on the nose on that horse.* **b.** *Chiefly U.S. & Canad.* precisely; exactly. **c.** *Austral.* bad or bad-smelling. **14. pay through the nose.** *Inf.* to pay an exorbitant price. **15. put someone's nose out of joint.** *Inf.* to thwart or offend someone. **16. rub someone's nose in it.** *Inf.* to remind someone unkindly of a failing or error. **17. turn up one's nose** (**at**). *Inf.* to behave disdainfully (towards). **18. with one's nose in the air.** haughtily. ~*vb.* **19.** (*tr.*) (esp. of horses, dogs, etc.) to rub, touch, or sniff with the nose; nuzzle. **20.** to smell or sniff. **21.** (*intr.; usually foll. by after or for*) to search (for) by or as if by scent. **22.** to move or cause to move forwards slowly and carefully: *we nosed the car into the garage.* **23.** (*intr.;* foll. by *into, around, about,* etc.) to pry or snoop (into) or meddle (in). [OE *nosu*] —**'noseless** *adj.* —**'nose,like** *adj.*

nosebag ('nəʊz,bæg) *n.* a bag, fastened around the head of a horse and covering the nose, in which feed is placed.

noseband ('nəʊz,bænd) *n.* the detachable part of a horse's bridle that goes around the nose.

nosebleed ('nəʊz,bli:d) *n.* bleeding from the nose as the result of injury, etc.

nose cone *n.* the conical forward section of a missile, spacecraft, etc., designed to withstand high temperatures, esp. during re-entry into the earth's atmosphere.

nose dive *n.* **1.** a sudden plunge with the nose or front pointing downwards, esp. of an aircraft. **2.** *Inf.* a sudden drop or sharp decline: *prices took a nose dive.* ~*vb.* **nose-dive.** (*intr.*) **3.** to perform a nose dive.

nose flute *n.* (esp. in the South Sea Islands) a type of flute blown through the nose.

nosegay ('nəʊz,geɪ) *n.* a small bunch of flowers; posy. [C15: from NOSE + *gay* (arch.) toy]

nose job *n.* *Sl.* a surgical remodelling of the nose for cosmetic reasons.

nosepiece ('nəʊz,pi:s) *n.* **1.** a piece of armour to protect the nose. **2.** the connecting part of a pair of spectacles that rests on the nose; bridge. **3.** the part of a microscope to which one or more objective lenses are attached. **4.** a less common word for **noseband.**

nose rag *n.* *Sl.* a handkerchief.

nose ring *n.* a ring fixed through the nose, as for leading a bull.

nose wheel *n.* a wheel fitted to the forward end of a vehicle, esp. the landing wheel under the nose of an aircraft.

nosey ('nəʊzɪ) *adj.* a variant spelling of **nosy.**

nosh (nɒʃ) *Sl.* ~*n.* **1.** food or a meal. ~*vb.* **2.** to eat. [C20: from Yiddish; cf. G *naschen* to nibble]

nosh-up *n.* *Brit. sl.* a large and satisfying meal.

no-show *n.* a person who fails to take up a reserved seat, place, etc., without having cancelled it.

no-side *n.* *Rugby.* the end of a match, signalled by the referee's whistle.

nosocomial (,nɒsə'kəʊmɪəl) *adj.* of or denoting an infection that originates in a hospital. [C19: from Gk *nosokomos* one that tends the sick, from *nosos* disease + *komein* to tend]

nosology (nɒ'sɒlədʒɪ) *n.* the branch of medicine concerned with the classification of diseases. [C18: from Gk *nosos* disease] —**nosological** (,nɒsə'lɒdʒɪkᵊl) *adj.*

nostalgia (nɒ'stældʒə, -dʒɪə) *n.* **1.** a yearning for past circumstances, events, etc. **2.** the evocation of this emotion, as in a book, film, etc. **3.** homesickness. [C18: NL, from Gk *nostos* a return home + -ALGIA] —**nos'talgic** *adj.* —**nos'talgically** *adv.*

nostoc ('nɒstɒk) *n.* a blue-green gelatinous alga occurring in moist places. [C17: NL, coined by Paracelsus (1493–1541) Swiss physician]

Nostradamus (,nɒstrə'dɑ:məs) *n.* Latinized name of *Michel de Notredame.* 1503–66, French physician and astrologer; author of a book of prophecies in rhymed quatrains, *Centuries* (1555).

nostril ('nɒstrɪl) *n.* either of the two external openings of the nose. [OE *nosthyrl,* from *nosu* NOSE + *thyrel* hole]

nostrum ('nɒstrəm) *n.* **1.** a patent or quack medicine. **2.** a favourite remedy. [C17: from L: our own (make), from *noster* our]

nosy *or* **nosey** ('nəʊzɪ) *adj.* **nosier, nosiest.** *Inf.* prying or inquisitive. —**'nosily** *adv.* —**'nosiness** *n.*

nosy parker *n.* *Inf., chiefly Brit.* a prying person. [C20: arbitrary use of surname *Parker*]

not (nɒt) *adv.* **1. a.** used to negate the sentence, phrase, or word that it modifies: *I will not stand for it.* **b.** (in combination): *they cannot go.* **2. not that.** (*conj.*) Also (*arch.*): **not but what.** which is not to say or suppose that: *I expect to lose the game—not that I mind.* ~*sentence substitute.* **3.** used to indicate denial or refusal: *certainly not.* [C14 *not,* var. of *nought* nothing, from OE *nāwiht,* from *nā* no + *wiht* creature, thing]

nota bene *Latin.* ('nəʊtə 'bi:nɪ) note well; take note. Abbrevs.: **NB, N.B., nb, n.b.**

notability (,nəʊtə'bɪlɪtɪ) *n., pl.* **-ties. 1.** the quality of being notable. **2.** a distinguished person.

notable ('nəʊtəbᵊl) *adj.* **1.** worthy of being noted or remembered; remarkable. ~*n.* **2.** a notable person. [C14: via OF from L *notābilis,* from *notāre* to NOTE] —**'notably** *adv.*

notarize *or* **-rise** ('nəʊtə,raɪz) *vb.* (*tr.*) *U.S.* to attest to (a document, etc.), as a notary.

notary ('nəʊtərɪ) *n., pl.* **-ries. 1.** a notary public. **2.** (formerly) a clerk licensed to prepare legal documents. **3.** *Arch.* a clerk or secretary. [C14: from L *notārius* clerk, from *nota* a mark, note] —**notarial** (nəʊ'tɛərɪəl) *adj.* —**'notaryship** *n.*

notary public *n., pl.* **notaries public.** a public official, usually a solicitor, who is legally authorized to administer oaths, attest and certify certain documents, etc.

notation (nəʊ'teɪʃən) *n.* **1.** any series of signs or symbols used to represent quantities or elements in a specialized system, such as music or mathematics. **2.** the act or process of notating. **3.** a note or record. [C16: from L *notātiō,* from *notāre* to NOTE] —**no'tational** *adj.*

notch (nɒtʃ) *n.* **1.** a V-shaped cut or indentation; nick. **2.** a nick made in a tally stick. **3.** *U.S. & Canad.* a narrow gorge. **4.** *Inf.* a step or level (esp. in **a notch above**). ~*vb.* (*tr.*) **5.** to cut or make a notch in. **6.** to record with or as if with a notch. **7.** (usually foll. by *up*) *Inf.* to score or achieve: *the team notched up its fourth win.* [C16:

from incorrect division of *an otch* (as *a notch*), from OF *oche* notch, from L *obscāre*, from *secāre* to cut]

NOT circuit *or* **gate** (nɒt) *n. Computers.* a logic circuit that has a high-voltage output signal if the input signal is low, and vice versa: used extensively in computers. Also called: **inverter, negator.** [C20: the action performed on electrical signals is similar to the operation of *not* in logical constructions]

note (nəʊt) *n.* **1.** a brief record in writing, esp. a jotting for future reference. **2.** a brief informal letter. **3.** a formal written communication, esp. from one government to another. **4.** a short written statement giving any kind of information. **5.** a critical comment, explanatory statement, or reference in a book. **6.** short for **banknote. 7.** a characteristic atmosphere: *a note of sarcasm.* **8.** a distinctive vocal sound, as of a species of bird or animal. **9.** any of a series of graphic signs representing the pitch and duration of a musical sound. **10.** Also called (esp. U.S. and Canad.): **tone.** *Chiefly Brit.* a musical sound of definite fundamental frequency or pitch. **11.** *Chiefly Brit.* a key on a piano, organ, etc. **12.** a sound used as a signal or warning: *the note to retreat was sounded.* **13.** short for **promissory note. 14.** *Arch. or poetic.* a melody. **15. of note. a.** distinguished or famous. **b.** important: *nothing of note.* **16. strike the right (***or* **a false) note.** to behave appropriately (or inappropriately). **17. take note.** (often foll. by *of*) to pay attention (to). *~vb.* (*tr.; may take a clause as object*) **18.** to notice; perceive. **19.** to pay close attention to: *they noted every movement.* **20.** to make a written note of: *she noted the date in her diary.* **21.** to remark upon: *I note that you do not wear shoes.* **22.** to write down (music, a melody, etc.) in notes. **23.** a less common word for **annotate.** [C13: via OF from L *nota* sign] —**'noteless** *adj.*

notebook ('nəʊt,bʊk) *n.* a book for recording notes or memoranda.

notecase ('nəʊt,keɪs) *n.* a less common word for **wallet** (sense 1).

noted ('nəʊtɪd) *adj.* **1.** celebrated; famous. **2.** of special significance; noticeable. —**'notedly** *adv.*

notelet ('nəʊtlɪt) *n.* a folded card with a printed design on the front, for writing a short letter.

notepaper ('nəʊt,peɪpə) *n.* paper for writing letters; writing paper.

noteworthy ('nəʊt,wɜːðɪ) *adj.* worthy of notice; notable. —**'note,worthiness** *n.*

nothing ('nʌθɪŋ) *pron.* **1.** (*indefinite*) no thing; not anything: *I can give you nothing.* **2.** no part or share: *to have nothing to do with this crime.* **3.** a matter of no importance: *it doesn't matter, it's nothing.* **4.** indicating the absence of anything perceptible; nothingness. **5.** indicating the absence of meaning, value, worth, etc.: *to amount to nothing.* **6.** zero quantity; nought. **7. be nothing to. a.** not to concern or be significant to (someone). **b.** to be not nearly as good, etc., as. **8. have** *or* **be nothing to do with.** to have no connection with. **9. nothing but.** no more than; only. **10. nothing doing.** *Inf.* an expression of dismissal, refusal, etc. **11. nothing if not.** at the very least; certainly. **12. nothing less than** *or* **nothing short of.** downright; truly. **13. there's nothing to it.** it is very simple, easy, etc. **14. think nothing of. a.** to regard as easy or natural. **b.** to have no compunction about. **c.** to have a very low opinion of. *~adv.* **15.** in no way; not at all: *he looked nothing like his brother. ~n.* **16.** *Inf.* a person or thing of no importance or significance. **17. sweet nothings.** words of endearment or affection. [OE *nāthing, nān thing,* from *nān* NONE[1] + THING]

▷ **Usage.** *Nothing* always takes a singular verb in careful usage, although a plural verb is often heard in informal speech in sentences such as *nothing but books were on the shelf.*

nothingness ('nʌθɪŋnɪs) *n.* **1.** the state of being nothing; nonexistence. **2.** absence of consciousness or life. **3.** complete insignificance. **4.** something that is worthless.

notice ('nəʊtɪs) *n.* **1.** observation; attention: *to escape notice.* **2. take notice.** to pay attention. **3. take no notice of.** to ignore or disregard. **4.** a warning; announcement. **5.** a displayed placard or announcement giving information. **6.** advance notification of intention to end an arrangement, contract, etc., as of employment (esp. in **give notice**). **7. at short notice.** with notification only a little in advance. **8.** *Chiefly Brit.* dismissal from employment.

9. favourable, interested, or polite attention: *she was beneath his notice.* **10.** a theatrical or literary review: *the play received very good notices. ~vb.* **11.** to become aware (of); perceive; note. **12.** (*tr.*) to point out or remark upon. **13.** (*tr.*) to pay polite or interested attention to. **14.** (*tr.*) to acknowledge (an acquaintance, etc.). [C15: via OF from L *notitia* fame, from *nōtus* known]

noticeable ('nəʊtɪsəbəl) *adj.* easily seen or detected; perceptible. —**'noticeably** *adv.*

notice board *n. Brit.* a board on which notices, advertisements, bulletins, etc., are displayed. U.S. and Canad. name: **bulletin board.**

notifiable ('nəʊtɪ,faɪəbəl) *adj.* denoting certain infectious diseases, outbreaks of which must be reported to the public health authorities.

notification (,nəʊtɪfɪ'keɪʃən) *n.* **1.** the act of notifying. **2.** a formal announcement. **3.** something that notifies; a notice.

notify ('nəʊtɪ,faɪ) *vb.* **-fying, -fied.** (*tr.*) **1.** to tell. **2.** *Chiefly Brit.* to make known; announce. [C14: from OF *notifier,* from L *notificāre,* from *nōtus* known + *facere* to make] —**'noti,fier** *n.*

notion ('nəʊʃən) *n.* **1.** a vague idea; impression. **2.** an idea, concept, or opinion. **3.** an inclination or whim. *~See also* **notions.** [C16: from L *nōtiō* a becoming acquainted (with), examination (of), from *noscere* to know]

notional ('nəʊʃənəl) *adj.* **1.** expressing or consisting of ideas. **2.** not evident in reality; hypothetical or imaginary: *a notional tax credit.* **3.** characteristic of a notion, esp. in being speculative or abstract. **4.** *Grammar.* **a.** (of a word) having lexical meaning. **b.** another word for **semantic.** —**'notionally** *adv.*

notions ('nəʊʃənz) *pl. n. Chiefly U.S. & Canad.* pins, cotton, ribbon, etc., used for sewing; haberdashery.

notochord ('nəʊtə,kɔːd) *n.* a fibrous longitudinal rod in all embryo and some adult chordate animals, immediately above the gut, that supports the body. [C19: from Gk *nōton* the back + CHORD[1]]

notorious (nəʊ'tɔːrɪəs) *adj.* **1.** well-known for some bad or unfavourable quality, deed, etc.; infamous. **2.** *Rare.* generally known or widely acknowledged. [C16: from Med. L *notōrius* well-known, from *nōtus* known] —**notoriety** (,nəʊtə'raɪɪtɪ) *n.* —**no'toriously** *adv.*

notornis (nəʊ'tɔːnɪs) *n.* a rare flightless rail of New Zealand. [C19: NL, from Gk *notos* south + *ornis* bird]

not proven ('prəʊvən) *adj.* (*postpositive*) a third verdict available to Scottish courts, returned when there is insufficient evidence against the accused to convict.

Notre Dame ('nəʊtrə 'dɑːm, 'nɒtrə; *French* nɔtrədam) *n.* the early Gothic cathedral of Paris, on the Île de la Cité: built between 1163 and 1257.

no-trump *Cards. ~n.* also **no-trumps. 1.** a bid or contract to play without trumps. *~adj.* also **no-trumper. 2.** (of a hand) suitable for playing without trumps.

Nottingham ('nɒtɪŋəm) *n.* a city in N central England, administrative centre of Nottinghamshire, on the River Trent: scene of the outbreak of the Civil War (1642); famous for its associations with the Robin Hood legend; university (1881). Pop.: 271 080 (1981).

Nottinghamshire ('nɒtɪŋəm,ʃɪə, -ʃə) *n.* an inland county of central England: generally low-lying, with part of the S Pennines and the remnant of Sherwood Forest in the east. Administrative centre: Nottingham. Pop.: 1 006 400 (1986 est.). Area: 2164 sq. km (835 sq. miles). Abbrev.: **Notts.**

Notts (nɒts) *abbrev. for* Nottinghamshire.

Notus ('nəʊtəs) *n. Classical myth.* a personification of the south or southwest wind.

notwithstanding (,nɒtwɪθ'stændɪŋ) *prep.* **1.** (*often immediately postpositive*) in spite of; despite. *~conj.* **2.** (*subordinating*) although. *~sentence connector.* **3.** nevertheless.

Nouakchott (*French* nwakʃɔt) *n.* the capital of Mauritania, near the Atlantic coast: replaced St Louis as capital in 1957; situated on important caravan routes. Pop.: 500 000 (1985 est.).

nougat ('nuːgɑː) *n.* a hard chewy pink or white sweet containing chopped nuts, cherries, etc. [C19: via F from Provençal *nogat,* from *noga* nut, from L *nux* nut]

nought (nɔːt) *n.* also **naught, ought, aught. 1.** another name for **zero:** used esp. in numbering. *~n., adj., adv.* **2.** a variant spelling of **naught.** [OE *nōwiht,* from *ne* not, no + *ōwiht* something]

noughts and crosses n. (functioning as sing.) a game in which two players, one using a nought, "O", the other a cross, "X", alternately mark squares formed by two pairs of crossed lines, the winner being the first to get three of his symbols in a row. U.S. and Canad. term: **tick-tack-toe,** (U.S.) **crisscross.**

Nouméa (,nu:'meɪə; French numea) n. the capital and chief port of the French Overseas Territory of New Caledonia. Pop.: 60 112 (1983).

noun (naʊn) n. **a.** a word or group of words that refers to a person, place, or thing. **b.** (as modifier): a noun phrase. Abbrev.: **N, n.** [C14: via Anglo-F from L nōmen NAME] —'**nounal** adj. Related adj.: **nominal.**

nourish ('nʌrɪʃ) vb. (tr.) **1.** to provide with the materials necessary for life and growth. **2.** to encourage (an idea, etc.); foster: to nourish resentment. [C14: from OF norir, from L nūtrīre to feed] —'**nourisher** n. —'**nourishing** adj.

nourishment ('nʌrɪʃmənt) n. **1.** the act or state of nourishing. **2.** a substance that nourishes; food.

nous (naʊs) n. **1.** Metaphysics. mind or reason, esp. regarded as the principle governing all things. **2.** Brit. sl. common sense. [C17: from Gk: mind]

nouveau riche (,nu:vəʊ 'ri:ʃ) n., pl. **nouveaux riches** (,nu:vəʊ 'ri:ʃ). (often preceded by the) a person who has acquired wealth recently and is regarded as vulgarly ostentatious or lacking in social graces. [C19: from F lit.: new rich]

Nouvelle-Calédonie (nuvɛlkaledɔni) n. the French name for **New Caledonia.**

nouvelle cuisine ('nu:vɛl kwi:'zi:n) n. a style of preparing food, often raw or only lightly cooked, with unusual combinations of flavours. [C20: F, lit.: new cookery]

Nov. abbrev. for November.

nova ('nəʊvə) n., pl. **-vae** (-vi:) or **-vas.** a faint variable star that undergoes an explosion and fast increase of luminosity, decreasing to its original luminosity in months or years. [C19: NL nova (stella) new (star), from L novus new]

Novalis (German no'va:lɪs) n. real name Friedrich von Hardenberg. 1772–1801, German romantic poet. His works include the mystical Hymnen an die Nacht (1797; published 1800) and Geistliche Lieder (1799).

Nova Lisboa (Portuguese 'nɔvə liʒ'βoə) n. the former name (1928–73) of **Huambo.**

Novara (Italian no'va:ra) n. a city in NW Italy, in NE Piedmont: scene of the Austrian defeat of the Piedmontese in 1849. Pop.: 102 742 (1986).

Nova Scotia ('nəʊvə 'skəʊʃə) n. **1.** a peninsula in E Canada between the Gulf of St Lawrence and the Bay of Fundy. **2.** a province of E Canada, consisting of the Nova Scotia peninsula and Cape Breton Island: first settled by the French as Acadia. Capital: Halifax. Pop.: 873 199 (1986). Area: 52 841 sq. km (20 402 sq. miles). Abbrev.: **NS.** —'**Nova 'Scotian** n., adj.

Novaya Zemlya (Russian 'nɔvəjə zɪm'lja) n. an archipelago in the Arctic Ocean, off the NE coast of the Soviet Union: consists of two large islands and many islets. Area: about 81 279 sq. km (31 382 sq. miles).

novel[1] ('nɒvəl) n. **1.** an extended fictional work in prose dealing with character, action, thought, etc., esp. in the form of a story. **2. the novel.** the literary genre represented by novels. [C15: from OF novelle, from L novella (narrātiō) new (story); see NOVEL[2]]

novel[2] ('nɒvəl) adj. of a kind not seen before; fresh; new; original: a novel suggestion. [C15: from L novellus, dim. of novus new]

novelette (,nɒvə'lɛt) n. **1.** an extended prose narrative or short novel. **2.** a novel that is regarded as slight, trivial, or sentimental. **3.** a short piece of lyrical music, esp. for piano.

novelettish (,nɒvə'lɛtɪʃ) adj. characteristic of a novelette; trite or sentimental.

novelist ('nɒvəlɪst) n. a writer of novels.

novelistic (,nɒvə'lɪstɪk) adj. of or characteristic of novels, esp. in style or method of treatment.

novella (nəʊ'vɛlə) n., pl. **-las** or **-le** (-leɪ). **1.** a short narrative tale, esp. one having a satirical point, such as those in Boccaccio's Decameron. **2.** a short novel. [C20: from It.; see NOVEL[1]]

Novello (nə'vɛləʊ) n. Ivor, real name Ivor Novello Davies. 1893–1951, Welsh actor, composer, songwriter, and dramatist.

novelty ('nɒvəltɪ) n., pl. **-ties. 1. a.** the quality of being new and interesting. **b.** (as modifier): novelty value. **2.** a new or unusual experience. **3.** (often pl.) a small usually cheap new ornament or trinket. [C14: from OF novelté; see NOVEL[2]]

November (nəʊ'vɛmbə) n. the eleventh month of the year, consisting of 30 days. [C13: via OF from L: ninth month, from novem nine]

novena (nəʊ'vi:nə) n., pl. **-nae** (-ni:). R.C. Church. a devotion consisting of prayers or services on nine consecutive days. [C19: from Med. L, from L novem nine]

Novgorod (Russian 'nɔvgərət) n. a city in the NW Soviet Union, on the Volkhov River; became a principality in 862 under Rurik, an event regarded as the founding of the Russian state; a major trading centre in the Middle Ages; destroyed by Ivan the Terrible in 1570. Pop.: 228 000 (1987).

novice ('nɒvɪs) n. **1.** a person who is new to or inexperienced in a certain task, situation, etc.; beginner; tyro. **2.** a probationer in a religious order. **3.** a racehorse that has not won a specified number of races. [C14: via OF from L novīcius, from novus new]

Novi Sad (Serbo-Croatian 'nɔvi: 'sa:d) n. a port in NE Yugoslavia, on the River Danube: founded in 1690 as the seat of the Serbian patriarch; university (1960). Pop.: 257 685 (1981). German name: **Neusatz.**

novitiate or **noviciate** (nəʊ'vɪʃɪɪt, -,eɪt) n. **1.** the state of being a novice, esp. in a religious order, or the period for which this lasts. **2.** the part of a religious house where the novices live. [C17: from F noviciat, from L novīcius NOVICE]

Novocaine ('nəʊvə,keɪn) n. a trademark for **procaine hydrochloride.** See **procaine.**

Novokuznetsk (Russian nɔvəkuz'njetsk) n. a city in the S central Soviet Union: iron and steel works. Pop.: 581 000 (1981 est.). Former name (1932–61): **Stalinsk.**

Novosibirsk (Russian nəvəsi'birsk) n. a city in the central Soviet Union, on the River Ob: the largest town in Siberia; developed with the coming of the Trans-Siberian railway in 1893. Pop.: 1 423 000 (1987).

now (naʊ) adv. **1.** at or for the present time. **2.** immediately. **3.** in these times; nowadays. **4.** given the present circumstances: now we'll have to stay to the end. **5.** (preceded by just) very recently: he left just now. **6.** (often preceded by just) very soon: he is leaving just now. **7. (every) now and again** or **then.** occasionally; on and off. **8. now now!** an exclamation used to rebuke or pacify someone. ~conj. **9.** (subordinating; often foll. by that) seeing that: now you're in charge, things will be better. ~sentence connector. **10. a.** used as a hesitation word: now, I can't really say. **b.** used for emphasis: now listen to this. **c.** used at the end of a command: run along, now. ~n. **11.** the present time: now is the time to go. ~adj. **12.** Inf. of the moment; fashionable: the now look. [OE nū]

nowadays ('naʊə,deɪz) adv. in these times. [C14: from NOW + adays from OE a on + daeges genitive of DAY]

noway ('nəʊ,weɪ) adv. **1.** not at all. ~sentence substitute. **no way. 2.** used to make an emphatic refusal, denial, etc.

Nowel or **Nowell** (nəʊ'ɛl) n. archaic spellings of **Noel.**

nowhere ('nəʊwɛə) adv. **1.** in, at, or to no place; not anywhere. **2. get nowhere (fast).** Inf. to fail completely to make any progress. **3. nowhere near.** far from; not nearly. ~n. **4.** a nonexistent or insignificant place. **5. middle of nowhere.** a completely isolated place.

nowise ('nəʊ,waɪz) adv. in no manner; not at all.

nowt (naʊt) n. N English. a dialect word for **nothing.** [from NAUGHT]

Nox (nɒks) n. the Roman goddess of the night. Greek counterpart: **Nyx.**

noxious ('nɒkʃəs) adj. poisonous or harmful. [C17: from L noxius harmful, from noxa injury] —'**noxiously** adv. —'**noxiousness** n.

Noyon (French nwajɔ̃) n. a town in N France: scene of the coronations of Charlemagne (768) and Hugh Capet (987); birthplace of John Calvin. Pop.: 13 949 (1982).

nozzle ('nɒzəl) n. a projecting pipe or spout from which fluid is discharged. [C17 nosle, nosel, dim. of NOSE]

Np *the chemical symbol for* neptunium.
NP *or* **np.** *abbrev. for* Notary Public.
NPA *abbrev. for* Newspaper Publishers' Association.
NPL *abbrev. for* National Physical Laboratory.
NS *abbrev. for:* **1.** New Style (method of reckoning dates). **2.** Nova Scotia. **3.** Nuclear Ship.
NSB (in Britain) *abbrev. for* National Savings Bank.
NSC (in Britain) *abbrev. for* National Safety Council.
NSPCC (in Britain) *abbrev. for* National Society for the Prevention of Cruelty to Children.
NST (in Canada) *abbrev. for* Newfoundland Standard Time.
NSU *abbrev. for* nonspecific urethritis.
NSW *abbrev. for* New South Wales.
NT *abbrev. for:* **1.** (in Britain) National Trust. **2.** New Testament. **3.** Northern Territory. **4.** no-trump.
-n't *contraction of* not: used as an enclitic after *be* and *have* when they function as main verbs and after auxiliary verbs or verbs operating syntactically as auxiliaries: *can't; don't; isn't.*
nth (ɛnθ) *adj.* **1.** *Maths.* of or representing an unspecified ordinal number, usually the greatest in a series: *the nth power.* **2.** *Inf.* being the last or most extreme of a long series: *for the nth time.* **3. to the nth degree.** *Inf.* to the utmost extreme.
NTP *abbrev. for* normal temperature and pressure. Also: **STP.**
nt. wt. *or* **nt wt** *abbrev. for* net weight.
n-type *adj.* **1.** (of a semiconductor) having more conduction electrons than mobile holes. **2.** associated with or resulting from the movement of electrons in a semiconductor.
nu (njuː) *n.* the 13th letter in the Greek alphabet (N, ν), a consonant. [from Gk, of Semitic origin]
nuance (njuːˈɑːns, ˈnjuːɑːns) *n.* a subtle difference in colour, meaning, tone, etc. [C18: from F, from *nuer* to show light and shade, ult. from L *nūbēs* a cloud]
nub (nʌb) *n.* **1.** a small lump or protuberance. **2.** a small piece or chunk. **3.** the point or gist: *the nub of a story.* [C16: var. of *knub*, from MLow G *knubbe* KNOB] — **'nubbly** *or* **'nubby** *adj.*
nubble (ˈnʌbᵊl) *n.* a small lump. [C19: dim. of NUB]
Nubia (ˈnjuːbɪə) *n.* an ancient region of NE Africa, on the Nile, extending from Aswan to Khartoum. — **'Nubian** *n., adj.*
Nubian Desert *n.* a desert in the NE Sudan, between the Nile valley and the Red Sea: mainly a sandstone plateau.
nubile (ˈnjuːbaɪl) *adj.* (of a girl) **1.** ready or suitable for marriage by virtue of age or maturity. **2.** sexually attractive. [C17: from L *nūbilis*, from *nūbere* to marry] — **nubility** (njuːˈbɪlɪtɪ) *n.*
nucha (ˈnjuːkə) *n., pl.* **-chae** (-kiː). *Zool., anat.* the back or nape of the neck. [C14: from Med. L, from Ar.: spinal marrow] — **'nuchal** *adj.*
nuclear (ˈnjuːklɪə) *adj.* **1.** of or involving the nucleus of an atom: *nuclear fission.* **2.** *Biol.* of, relating to, or contained within the nucleus of a cell: *a nuclear membrane.* **3.** of, forming, or resembling any other kind of nucleus. **4.** of or operated by energy from fission or fusion of atomic nuclei: *a nuclear weapon.* **5.** involving or possessing nuclear weapons: *nuclear war.*
nuclear bomb *n.* a bomb whose force is due to uncontrolled nuclear fusion or nuclear fission.
nuclear energy *n.* energy released during a nuclear reaction as a result of fission or fusion. Also called: **atomic energy.**
nuclear family *n. Sociol., anthropol.* a primary social unit consisting of parents and their offspring.
nuclear fission *n.* the splitting of an atomic nucleus into approximately equal parts, either spontaneously or as a result of the impact of a particle usually with an associated release of energy. Sometimes shortened to **fission.**
nuclear fuel *n.* a fuel that provides nuclear energy, used in nuclear submarines, etc.
nuclear fusion *n.* a reaction in which two nuclei combine to form a nucleus with the release of energy. Sometimes shortened to **fusion.**
nuclear magnetic resonance *n.* a technique for determining the magnetic moments of nuclei by subjecting a substance to high-frequency radiation and a large magnetic field. It is used for determining structure, esp. in body scanning.

nuclear physics *n.* (*functioning as sing.*) the branch of physics concerned with the structure and behaviour of the nucleus and the particles of which it consists.
nuclear power *n.* power, esp. electrical or motive, produced by a nuclear reactor. Also called: **atomic power.**
nuclear reaction *n.* a process in which the structure and energy content of an atomic nucleus is changed by interaction with another nucleus or particle.
nuclear reactor *n.* a device in which a nuclear reaction is maintained and controlled for the production of nuclear energy. Sometimes shortened to **reactor.**
nuclear waste *n.* another name for **radioactive waste.**
nuclear winter *n.* a period of low temperatures and little light that has been suggested would occur after a nuclear war.
nuclease (ˈnjuːklɪˌeɪz) *n.* any of a group of enzymes that hydrolyse nucleic acids to simple nucleotides.
nucleate *adj.* (ˈnjuːklɪɪt, -ˌeɪt). **1.** having a nucleus. ~*vb.* (ˈnjuːklɪˌeɪt). (*intr.*) **2.** to form a nucleus.
nuclei (ˈnjuːklɪˌaɪ) *n.* a plural of **nucleus.**
nucleic acid (njuːˈkliːɪk, -ˈkleɪ-) *n. Biochem.* any of a group of complex compounds with a high molecular weight that are vital constituents of all living cells. See also **RNA, DNA.**
nucleo- *or before a vowel* **nucle-** *combining form.* **1.** nucleus or nuclear. **2.** nucleic acid. [from Latin *nucleus* kernel, from *nux* nut]
nucleolus (ˌnjuːklɪˈəʊləs) *n., pl.* **-li** (-laɪ). a small rounded body within a resting cell nucleus that contains RNA and proteins and is involved in protein synthesis. Also called: **nucleole.** [C19: from L, dim. of NUCLEUS] — **ˌnucleˈolar** *adj.*
nucleon (ˈnjuːklɪˌɒn) *n.* a proton or neutron, esp. one present in an atomic nucleus.
nucleonics (ˌnjuːklɪˈɒnɪks) *n.* (*functioning as sing.*) the branch of physics concerned with the applications of nuclear energy. — **ˌnucleˈonic** *adj.* — **ˌnucleˈonically** *adv.*
nucleon number *n.* the number of nucleons in an atomic nucleus; mass number.
nucleophile (ˈnjuːklɪəˌfaɪl) *n.* a molecule or ion that can donate electrons.— **nucleophilic** (ˌnjuːklɪəˈfɪlɪk) *adj.*
nucleoside (ˈnjuːklɪəˌsaɪd) *n. Biochem.* a compound containing a purine or pyrimidine base linked to a sugar (usually ribose or deoxyribose).
nucleotide (ˈnjuːklɪəˌtaɪd) *n. Biochem.* a compound consisting of a nucleoside linked to phosphoric acid.
nucleus (ˈnjuːklɪəs) *n., pl.* **-clei** *or* **-cleuses. 1.** a central or fundamental thing around which others are grouped; core. **2.** a centre of growth or development; basis: *the nucleus of an idea.* **3.** *Biol.* the spherical or ovoid compartment of a cell that contains the chromosomes and associated molecules that control the characteristics and growth of the cell. **4.** *Astron.* the central portion in the head of a comet, consisting of small solid particles of ice and frozen gases. **5.** *Physics.* the positively charged dense region at the centre of an atom, composed of protons and neutrons, about which electrons orbit. **6.** *Chem.* a fundamental group of atoms in a molecule serving as the base structure for related compounds. [C18: from L: kernel, from *nux* nut]
nuclide (ˈnjuːklaɪd) *n.* a species of atom characterized by its atomic number and its mass number. [C20: from NUCLEO-+ -ide, from Gk *eidos* shape]
nude (njuːd) *adj.* **1.** completely undressed. **2.** having no covering; bare; exposed. **3.** *Law.* **a.** lacking some essential legal requirement. **b.** (of a contract, etc.) made without consideration and void unless under seal. ~*n.* **4.** the state of being naked (esp. in **in the nude**). **5.** a naked figure, esp. in painting, sculpture, etc. [C16: from L *nūdus*] — **'nudely** *adv.*
nudge (nʌdʒ) *vb.* (*tr.*) **1.** to push (someone) gently, esp. with the elbow, to get attention; jog. **2.** to push slowly or lightly: *as I drove out, I just nudged the gatepost.* ~*n.* **3.** a gentle poke or push. [C17: ?from Scand.] — **'nudger** *n.*
nudibranch (ˈnjuːdɪˌbræŋk) *n.* a marine gastropod of an order characterized by a shell-less, often beautifully coloured, body bearing external gills. Also called: **sea slug.** [C19: from L *nudus* naked + *branche*, from L *branchia* gills]
nudism (ˈnjuːdɪzəm) *n.* the practice of nudity, esp. for reasons of health, etc. — **'nudist** *n., adj.*
nudity (ˈnjuːdɪtɪ) *n., pl.* **-ties.** the state or fact of being nude; nakedness.

Nuevo Laredo (*Spanish* 'nweβo la'reðo) *n.* a city and port of entry in NE Mexico, in Tamaulipas state on the Rio Grande opposite Laredo, Texas: oil industries. Pop.: 203 286 (1980).

Nuevo León ('nweɪvəʊ leɪ'əʊn, nuː'eɪ-; *Spanish* 'nweβo le'ɔn) *n.* a state of NE Mexico: the first centre of heavy industry in Latin America. Capital: Monterrey. Pop.: 2 463 298 (1980). Area: 64 555 sq. km (24 925 sq. miles).

Nuffield ('nʌfiːld) *n.* **William Richard Morris,** 1st Viscount Nuffield. 1877–1963, English motorcar manufacturer and philanthropist. He endowed Nuffield College at Oxford (1937) and the Nuffield Foundation (1943), a charitable trust for the furtherance of medicine and education.

nugatory ('njuːgətərɪ, -trɪ) *adj.* **1.** of little value; trifling. **2.** not valid: *a nugatory law.* [C17: from L *nūgātōrius,* from *nūgārī* to jest, from *nūgae* trifles]

nugget ('nʌgɪt) *n.* **1.** a small piece or lump, esp. of gold in its natural state. **2.** something small but valuable or excellent. [C19: from ?]

nuggety ('nʌgɪtɪ) *adj.* **1.** of or resembling a nugget. **2.** *Austral. & N.Z. inf.* (of a person) thickset; stocky.

nuisance ('njuːsəns) *n.* **1.** a person or thing that causes annoyance or bother. **2.** *Law.* something unauthorized that is obnoxious or injurious to the community at large or to an individual, esp. in relation to his ownership of property. **3. nuisance value.** the usefulness of a person's or thing's capacity to cause difficulties or irritation. [C15: via OF from *nuire* to injure, from L *nocēre*]

NUJ (in Britain) *abbrev. for* National Union of Journalists.

Nu Jiang ('nuː 'dʒjæŋ) *n.* the Chinese name for the **Salween.**

nuke (njuːk) *Sl., chiefly U.S. ~vb.* (*tr.*) **1.** to attack or destroy with nuclear weapons. *~n.* **2.** a nuclear bomb.

Nuku'alofa (ˌnuːkuːə'lɔːfə) *n.* the capital of Tonga, a port on the N coast of Tongatapu Island. Pop.: 28 899 (1986).

Nukus (*Russian* nu'kus) *n.* a city in the S Soviet Union, capital of the Kara-Kalpak ASSR, on the Amu Darya River. Pop.: 146 000 (1986).

null (nʌl) *adj.* **1.** without legal force; invalid; (esp. in **null and void**). **2.** without value or consequence; useless. **3.** lacking distinction; characterless. **4.** nonexistent; amounting to nothing. **5.** *Maths.* **a.** quantitatively zero. **b.** relating to zero. **c.** (of a set) having no members. **6.** *Physics.* involving measurement in which conditions are adjusted so that an instrument has a zero reading, as with a Wheatstone bridge. [C16: from L *nullus* none, from *ne* not + *ullus* any]

nullah ('nʌlə) *n.* (in India) a stream or drain. [C18: from Hindi *nālā*]

nulla-nulla (ˌnʌlə'nʌlə) *n. Austral.* a wooden club used as a weapon by Aborigines. Also called: **nulla.** [from Abor.]

Nullarbor Plain ('nʌləˌbɔː) *n.* a vast low plateau of S Australia: extends north from the Great Australian Bight to the Great Victoria Desert; has no surface water or trees. Area: 260 000 sq. km (100 000 sq. miles).

null hypothesis *n. Statistics.* the residual hypothesis if the alternative hypothesis tested against it fails to achieve a predetermined significance level.

nullify ('nʌlɪˌfaɪ) *vb.* **-fying, -fied.** (*tr.*) **1.** to render legally void or of no effect. **2.** to render ineffective or useless; cancel out. [C16: from LL *nullificāre* to despise, from L *nullus* of no account + *facere* to make] —ˌnullifi'ca-tion *n.*

nullity ('nʌlɪtɪ) *n., pl.* **-ties. 1.** the state of being null. **2.** a null or legally invalid act or instrument. **3.** something null, ineffective, characterless, etc. [C16: from Med. L *nullitās,* from L *nullus* no, not any]

NUM (in Britain) *abbrev. for* National Union of Mineworkers.

num. *abbrev. for:* **1.** number. **2.** numeral.

Num. *Bible. abbrev. for* Numbers.

Numantia (njuː'mæntɪə) *n.* an ancient city in N Spain: a centre of Celtic resistance to Rome in N Spain: captured by Scipio the Younger in 133 B.C. —**Nu'mantian** *adj., n.*

Numa Pompilius ('njuːmə pɒm'pɪlɪəs) *n.* the legendary second king of Rome (?715–?673 B.C.), said to have instituted religious rites.

numb (nʌm) *adj.* **1.** deprived of feeling through cold, shock, etc. **2.** unable to move; paralysed. *~vb.* **3.** (*tr.*) to make numb; deaden, shock, or paralyse. [C15 *nomen,* lit.: taken (with paralysis), from OE *niman* to take] —'numbly *adv.* —'numbness *n.*

numbat ('nʌmˌbæt) *n.* a small Australian marsupial having a long snout and tongue and strong claws for hunting and feeding on termites. [C20: from Abor.]

number ('nʌmbə) *n.* **1.** a concept of quantity that is or can be derived from a single unit, the sum of a collection of units, or zero. Every number occupies a unique position in a sequence, enabling it to be used in counting. See also **cardinal number, ordinal number. 2.** the symbol used to represent a number; numeral. **3.** a numeral or string of numerals used to identify a person or thing: *a telephone number.* **4.** the person or thing so identified or designated: *she was number seven in the race.* **5.** sum or quantity: *a large number of people.* **6.** one of a series, as of a magazine; issue. **7. a.** a self-contained piece of pop or jazz music. **b.** a self-contained part of an opera or other musical score. **8.** a group of people, esp. an exclusive group: *he was not one of our number.* **9.** *Sl.* a person, esp. a sexually attractive girl: *who's that nice little number?* **10.** *Inf.* an admired article: *that little number is by Dior.* **11.** a grammatical category for the variation in form of nouns, pronouns, and any words agreeing with them, depending on how many persons or things are referred to. **12. any number of.** several or many. **13. by numbers.** *Mil.* (of a drill procedure, etc.) performed step by step, each move being made on the call of a number. **14. get** *or* **have someone's number.** *Inf.* to discover a person's true character or intentions. **15. one's number is up.** *Brit. inf.* one is finished; one is ruined or about to die. **16. without** *or* **beyond number.** innumerable. *~vb.* (*mainly tr.*) **17.** to assign a number to. **18.** to add up to; total. **19.** (*also intr.*) to list (items) one by one; enumerate. **20.** (*also intr.*) to put or be put into a group, category, etc.: *they were numbered among the worst hit.* **21.** to limit the number of: *his days were numbered.* [C13: from OF *nombre,* from L *numerus*]

number crunching *n. Computers.* the large-scale processing of numerical data.

numberless ('nʌmbəlɪs) *adj.* **1.** too many to be counted; countless. **2.** not containing numbers.

number one *n.* **1.** the first in a series or sequence. **2.** an informal phrase for **oneself, myself,** etc.: *to look after number one.* **3.** *Inf.* the most important person; chief: *he's number one in the organization.* **4.** *Inf.* the best-selling pop record in any one week. *~adj.* **5.** first in importance, urgency, quality, etc.: *number one priority.*

numberplate ('nʌmbəˌpleɪt) *n.* a plate mounted on the front and back of a motor vehicle bearing the registration number. Usual U.S. term: **license plate,** (Canad.) **licence plate.**

Number Ten *n.* 10 Downing Street, the British prime minister's official London residence.

number theory *n.* the study of integers, their properties, and the relationship between integers.

numbfish ('nʌmˌfɪʃ) *n., pl.* **-fish** *or* **-fishes.** any of several electric rays. [C18: so called because it numbs its victims]

numbles ('nʌmb³lz) *pl. n. Arch.* the heart, lungs, liver, etc., of a deer or other animal. [C14: from OF *nombles,* pl. of *nomble* thigh muscle of a deer, changed from L *lumbulus,* dim. of *lumbus* loin]

numbskull ('nʌmˌskʌl) *n.* a variant spelling of **numskull.**

numen ('njuːmen) *n., pl.* **-mina** (-mɪnə). **1.** (esp. in ancient Roman religion) a deity or spirit presiding over a thing or place. **2.** a guiding principle, force, or spirit. [C17: from L: a nod (indicating a command), divine power]

numerable ('njuːmərəb³l) *adj.* able to be numbered or counted. —'numerably *adv.*

numeral ('njuːmərəl) *n.* **1.** a symbol or group of symbols used to express a number: for example, *6* (*Arabic*), *VI* (*Roman*), *110* (*binary*). *~adj.* **2.** of, consisting of, or denoting a number. [C16: from LL *numerālis* belonging to number, from L *numerus*]

numerate *adj.* ('njuːmərɪt). **1.** able to use numbers, esp. in arithmetical operations. *~vb.* ('njuːməˌreɪt). (*tr.*) **2.** to read (a numerical expression). **3.** a less common word for **enumerate.** [C18 (vb.): from L *numerus* number -ATE[1], by analogy with *literate*] —**numeracy** ('njuːmərəsɪ) *n.*

numeration (ˌnjuːmə'reɪʃən) *n.* **1.** the act or process of writing, reading, or naming numbers. **2.** a system of numbering. —'numerative *adj.*

numerator ('nju:mə,reɪtə) n. **1.** *Maths.* the dividend of a fraction: the numerator of 7/8 is 7. Cf. **denominator. 2.** a person or thing that numbers; enumerator.

numerical (nju:'mɛrɪkᵊl) *or* **numeric** *adj.* **1.** of, relating to, or denoting a number or numbers. **2.** measured or expressed in numbers: *numerical value.* —**nu'merically** *adv.*

numerology (,nju:mə'rɒlədʒɪ) n. the study of numbers, such as the figures in a birth date, and of their supposed influence on human affairs. —**numerological** (,nju:mərə'lɒdʒɪkᵊl) *adj.*

numerous ('nju:mərəs) *adj.* **1.** being many. **2.** consisting of many parts: *a numerous collection.* —**'numerously** *adv.* —**'numerousness** n.

Numidia (nju:'mɪdɪə) n. an ancient country of N Africa, corresponding roughly to present-day Algeria: flourished until its invasion by Vandals in 429; chief towns were Cirta and Hippo Regius. —**Nu'midian** n., *adj.*

numinous ('nju:mɪnəs) *adj.* **1.** denoting, being, or relating to a numen; divine. **2.** arousing spiritual or religious emotions. **3.** mysterious or awe-inspiring. [C17: from L *numin-,* NUMEN + -OUS]

numismatics (,nju:mɪz'mætɪks) n. (*functioning as sing.*) the study or collection of coins, medals, etc. Also called: ,**numisma'tology.** [C18: from F *numismatique,* from L *nomisma,* from Gk: piece of currency, from *nomizein* to have in use, from *nómos* use] —,**numis'matic** *adj.* —,**numis'matically** *adv.*

nummulite ('nʌmju,laɪt) n. any of a family of large fossil protozoans common in Tertiary times. [C19: from NL, from L *nummulus,* from *nummus* coin]

numskull *or* **numbskull** ('nʌm,skʌl) n. a stupid person; dolt; blockhead.

nun (nʌn) n. a female member of a religious order. [OE *nunne,* from Church L *nonna,* from LL: form of address used for an elderly woman] —**'nunhood** n. —**'nunlike** *adj.*

nun buoy n. *Naut.* a red buoy, conical at the top, marking the right side of a channel leading into a harbour. [C18: from obs. *nun* child's spinning top + BUOY]

Nunc Dimittis ('nʌŋk dɪ'mɪtɪs, 'nʊŋk) n. **1.** the Latin name for the Canticle of Simeon (Luke 2:29–32). **2.** a musical setting of this. [from the opening words (Vulgate): now let depart]

nunciature ('nʌnsɪətʃə) n. the office or term of office of a nuncio. [C17: from It. *nunziatura*]

nuncio ('nʌnʃɪ,əʊ, -sɪ-) n., *pl.* -**cios.** *R.C. Church.* a diplomatic representative of the Holy See. [C16: via It. from L *nuntius* messenger]

Nuneaton (nʌn'i:tᵊn) n. a town in central England, in Warwickshire. Pop.: 72 000 (1984 est.).

nunnery ('nʌnərɪ) n., *pl.* -**neries.** the convent or religious house of a community of nuns.

NUPE ('nju:pɪ) n. (in Britain) *acronym for* National Union of Public Employees.

nuptial ('nʌpʃəl, -tʃəl) *adj.* **1.** relating to marriage; conjugal: *nuptial vows.* **2.** *Zool.* of or relating to mating: *the nuptial flight of a queen bee.* [C15: from L *nuptiālis,* from *nuptiae* marriage, from *nubere* to marry] —**'nuptially** *adv.*

nuptials ('nʌpʃəlz, -tʃəlz) *pl. n.* (*sometimes sing.*) a marriage ceremony; wedding.

NUR (in Britain) *abbrev. for* National Union of Railwaymen.

nurd (nɜ:d) n. *Sl.* a stupid and feeble person. —**'nurdish** *adj.*

Nuremberg ('njʊərəm,bɜ:g) n. a city in SE West Germany, in N Bavaria: scene of annual Nazi rallies (1933–38), the anti-Semitic Nuremberg decrees (1935), and the trials of Nazi leaders for their war crimes (1945–46); important metalworking and electrical industries. Pop.: 466 500 (1986). German name: **Nürnberg.**

Nureyev ('njʊərɪef, nju'reɪ-) n. **Rudolf.** born 1939, Austrian ballet dancer, born in the Soviet Union: in England from 1961. He became an Austrian citizen in 1982.

Nuristan (,nʊərɪ'stɑ:n) n. a region of E Afghanistan: consists mainly of high mountains (including part of the Hindu Kush), steep narrow valleys, and forests. Area: about 13 000 sq. km (5000 sq. miles). Former name: **Kafiristan.**

Nurmi ('nɜ:mɪ; *Finnish* 'nurmi) n. **Paavo** ('pɑ:vɔ), known as *The Flying Finn.* 1897–1973, Finnish runner, winner of

the 1500, 5000, and 10 000 metres' races at the 1924 Olympic Games in Paris.

Nürnberg ('nyrnbɛrk) n. the German name for **Nuremberg.**

nurse (nɜ:s) n. **1.** a person, often a woman, who is trained to tend the sick and infirm, assist doctors, etc. **2.** short for **nursemaid. 3.** a woman employed to breast-feed another woman's child; wet nurse. **4.** a worker in a colony of social insects that takes care of the larvae. ~*vb.* (*mainly tr.*) **5.** (*also intr.*) to tend (the sick). **6.** (*also intr.*) to feed (a baby) at the breast. **7.** to try to cure (an ailment). **8.** to clasp fondly: *she nursed the child in her arms.* **9.** to look after (a child) as one's employment. **10.** to harbour; preserve: *to nurse a grudge.* **11.** to give special attention to, esp. in order to promote goodwill: *to nurse a difficult constituency.* **12.** *Billiards.* to keep (the balls) together for a series of cannons. [C16: from earlier *norice,* OF *nourice,* from LL *nūtrīcia,* from L *nūtrīcius* nourishing, from *nūtrīre* to nourish] —**'nursing** n., *adj.*

nursemaid ('nɜ:s,meɪd) *or* **nurserymaid** n. a woman employed to look after someone else's children. Often shortened to **nurse.**

nursery ('nɜ:srɪ) n., *pl.* -**ries. 1.** a room in a house set apart for children. **2.** a place where plants, young trees, etc., are grown commercially. **3.** an establishment providing daycare for babies and young children; crèche. **4.** anywhere serving to foster or nourish new ideas, etc. **5.** Also called: **nursery cannon.** *Billiards.* **a.** a series of cannons with the three balls adjacent to a cushion, esp. near a corner pocket. **b.** a cannon in such a series.

nurseryman ('nɜ:srɪmən) n., *pl.* -**men.** a person who owns or works in a nursery in which plants are grown.

nursery rhyme n. a short traditional verse or song for children, such as *Little Jack Horner.*

nursery school n. a school for young children, usually from three to five years old.

nursery slopes *pl. n.* gentle slopes used by beginners in skiing.

nursery stakes *pl. n.* a race for two-year-old horses.

nurse shark n. any of various sharks having an external groove on each side of the head between the mouth and nostril. [C15 *nusse fisshe* (later infl. in spelling by NURSE), ?from a division of obs. *an huss* shark, dogfish (from ?) as *a nuss*]

nursing home n. a private hospital or residence for aged or infirm persons.

nursing officer n. (in Britain) the official name for **matron** (sense 4).

nursling *or* **nurseling** ('nɜ:slɪŋ) n. a child or young animal that is being suckled, nursed, or fostered.

nurture ('nɜ:tʃə) n. **1.** the act or process of promoting the development, etc., of a child. **2.** something that nourishes. ~*vb.* (*tr.*) **3.** to feed or support. **4.** to educate or train. [C14: from OF *norriture,* from L *nūtrīre* to nourish] —**'nurtural** *adj.* —**'nurturer** n.

NUS (in Britain) *abbrev. for:* **1.** National Union of Seamen. **2.** National Union of Students.

Nusa Tenggara ('nu:sə tɛŋ'gɑ:rə) n. an island chain forming a province of Indonesia, east of Java: the main islands are Bali, Lombok, Sumbawa, Sumba, Flores, Alor, and Timor. Pop.: 6 156 600 (1986 est.). Area: 73 144 sq. km (28 241 sq. miles). Former name: **Lesser Sunda Islands.**

nut (nʌt) n. **1.** a dry one-seeded indehiscent fruit that usually possesses a woody wall. **2.** (*not in technical use*) any similar fruit, such as the walnut, having a hard shell and an edible kernel. **3.** the edible kernel of such a fruit. **4.** *Sl.* an eccentric or mad person. **5.** *Sl.* the head. **6. do one's nut.** *Brit. sl.* to be extremely angry. **7. off one's nut.** *Sl.* mad or foolish. **8.** a person or thing that presents difficulties (esp. in **a tough nut to crack**). **9.** the female component of a screwed assembly, having an internal spiral thread, esp. a small metallic block, usually hexagonal or square, that fits onto a bolt. **10.** Also called (U.S. and Canad.): **frog.** *Music.* **a.** the ridge at the upper end of the fingerboard of a violin, cello, etc., over which the strings pass to the tuning pegs. **b.** the end of a violin bow that is held by the player. **11.** a small usually gingery biscuit. **12.** *Brit.* a small piece of coal. ~*vb.* **nutting, nutted. 13.** (*intr.*) to gather nuts. ~See also **nuts.** [OE *hnutu*]

NUT (in Britain) *abbrev. for* National Union of Teachers.

nutant ('nju:tᵊnt) *adj. Bot.* having the apex hanging down. [C18: from L *nūtāre* to nod]

nutation (nju:'teɪʃən) n. **1.** *Astron.* a periodic variation in the precession of the earth's axis causing the earth's poles to oscillate about their mean position. **2.** the spiral growth of a shoot or similar plant organ, caused by variation in the growth rate in different parts. **3.** the act of nodding. [C17: from L *nutātiō*, from *nūtāre* to nod]

nutbrown ('nʌt'braʊn) *adj.* reddish-brown.

nutcase ('nʌt,keɪs) n. *Sl.* an insane or very foolish person.

nutcracker ('nʌt,krækə) n. **1.** (*often pl.*) a device for cracking the shells of nuts. **2.** either an Old World bird or a North American bird (**Clark's nutcracker**) having speckled plumage and feeding on nuts, seeds, etc.

nutgall ('nʌt,gɔːl) n. a nut-shaped gall caused by gall wasps on the oak and other trees.

nuthatch ('nʌt,hætʃ) n. a songbird having strong feet and bill, and feeding on insects, seeds, and nuts. [C14 *notehache*, from *note* nut + *hache* hatchet, from its habit of splitting nuts]

nuthouse ('nʌt,haʊs) n. *Sl.* a mental hospital.

nutmeg ('nʌt,mɛg) n. **1.** an East Indian evergreen tree cultivated in the tropics for its hard aromatic seed. See also **mace**[2]. **2.** the seed of this tree, used as a spice. [C13: from OF *nois muguede*, from OProvençal *noz muscada* musk-scented nut, from L *nux* NUT + *muscus* MUSK]

nutria ('nju:trɪə) n. another name for **coypu**, esp. the fur. [C19: from Sp., var. of *lutria*, ult. from L *lūtra* otter]

nutrient ('nju:trɪənt) n. **1.** any of the mineral substances that are absorbed by the roots of plants. **2.** any substance that nourishes an animal. ~*adj.* **3.** providing or contributing to nourishment. [C17: from L *nūtrīre* to nourish]

nutriment ('nju:trɪmənt) n. any material providing nourishment. [C16: from L *nūtrīmentum*, from *nūtrīre* to nourish] —**nutrimental** (,nju:trɪ'mɛntəl) adj.

nutrition (nju:'trɪʃən) n. **1.** a process in animals and plants involving the intake and assimilation of nutrient materials. **2.** the act or process of nourishing. **3.** the study of nutrition, esp. in humans. [C16: from LL *nūtrītiō*, from *nūtrīre* to nourish] —**nu'tritional** adj. —**nu'tritionist** n.

nutritious (nju:'trɪʃəs) adj. nourishing. [C17: from L *nūtricius*, from *nūtrix* NURSE] —**nu'tritiously** adv. —**nu'tritiousness** n.

nutritive ('nju:trɪtɪv) adj. **1.** providing nourishment. **2.** of, concerning, or promoting nutrition. ~n. **3.** a nutritious food.

nuts (nʌts) adj. **1.** a slang word for **insane**. **2.** (foll. by *about* or *on*) *Sl.* extremely fond (of) or enthusiastic (about). ~*interj.* **3.** *Sl.* an expression of contempt, refusal, or defiance.

nuts and bolts pl. n. *Inf.* the essential or practical details.

nutshell ('nʌt,ʃɛl) n. **1.** the shell around the kernel of a nut. **2. in a nutshell.** in essence; briefly.

nutter ('nʌtə) n. *Brit. sl.* a mad or eccentric person.

nutty ('nʌtɪ) adj. **-tier, -tiest. 1.** containing nuts. **2.** resembling nuts. **3.** a slang word for **insane**. **4.** (foll. by *over* or *about*) *Inf.* extremely enthusiastic (about). —**'nuttiness** n.

nux vomica ('nʌks 'vɒmɪkə) n. **1.** an Indian tree with orange-red berries containing poisonous seeds. **2.** any of the seeds of this tree, which contain strychnine and other poisonous alkaloids. **3.** a medicine manufactured from the seeds of this tree, formerly used as a heart stimulant. [C16: from Med. L: vomiting nut]

nuzzle ('nʌzəl) vb. **1.** to push or rub gently with the nose or snout. **2.** (*intr.*) to nestle; lie close. **3.** (*tr.*) to dig out with the snout. [C15 *nosele*, from NOSE (n.)]

NW *symbol for* northwest(ern).

NWMP (in Canada) *abbrev. for* North West Mounted Police.

NWT *abbrev. for* Northwest Territories (of Canada).

NY or **N.Y.** *abbrev. for* New York (city or state).

nyala ('njɑːlə) n., pl. **-la** or **-las. 1.** a spiral-horned southern African antelope with a fringe of white hairs along the length of the back and neck. **2. mountain nyala.** a similar Ethiopian animal lacking the white crest. [from Zulu]

Nyasa or **Nyassa** (nɪ'æsə, naɪ'æsə) n. **Lake.** a lake in central Africa at the S end of the Great Rift Valley: the third largest lake in Africa, drained by the Shiré River into the Zambezi. Area: about 28 500 sq. km (11 000 sq. miles). Malawi name: **Lake Malawi.**

Nyasaland (nɪ'æsə,lænd, naɪ'æsə-) n. the former name (until 1964) of **Malawi.**

NYC *abbrev. for* New York City.

nyctalopia (,nɪktə'ləʊpɪə) n. inability to see normally in dim light. Nontechnical name: **night blindness.** [C17: via LL from Gk *nuktálōps*, from *nux* night + *alaos* blind + *ōps* eye]

nyctitropism (nɪk'tɪtrə,pɪzəm) n. a tendency of some plant parts to assume positions at night that are different from their daytime positions. [C19: *nyct-*, from Gk *nukt-*, *nux* night + -TROPISM]

nye (naɪ) n. a flock of pheasants. Also called: **nide, eye.** [C15: from OF *ni*, from L *nīdus* nest]

Nyeman (*Russian* 'njɛmən) n. a variant spelling of **Neman.**

Nyerere (njə'rɛrɪ, nɪ-) n. **Julius Kambarage** (kæm'bɑːrɑːgə). born 1922, Tanzanian statesman; president (1964–85). He became prime minister of Tanganyika (1961) and president (1962), negotiating the union of Tanganyika and Zanzibar to form Tanzania (1964).

Nyíregyháza (*Hungarian* 'nji:rɛtjhɑːzɒ) n. a market town in NE Hungary. Pop.: 109 436 (1980 est.).

Nykøping (*Danish* 'nykøːbeŋ) n. a port in Denmark, on the W coast of Falster Island. Pop.: 64 199 (1986).

nylon ('naɪlɒn) n. **1.** a class of synthetic polyamide materials of which monofilaments are used for bristles, etc., and fibres can be spun into yarn. **2.** yarn or cloth made of nylon, used for clothing, stockings, etc. [C20: orig. a trademark]

nylons ('naɪlɒnz) pl. n. stockings made of nylon.

nymph (nɪmf) n. **1.** *Myth.* a spirit of nature envisaged as a beautiful maiden. **2.** *Chiefly poetic.* a beautiful young woman. **3.** the larva of insects such as the dragonfly. It resembles the adult, apart from having underdeveloped wings, and develops without a pupal stage. [C14: via OF from L, from Gk *numphē*] —**'nymphal** or **nymphean** ('nɪmfɪən) adj. —**'nymphlike** adj.

nympha ('nɪmfə) n., pl. **-phae** (-fiː). *Anat.* either one of the labia minora. [C17: from L: bride]

nymphet ('nɪmfɪt) n. a young girl who is sexually precocious and desirable. [C17 (meaning: a young nymph): dim. of NYMPH]

nympho ('nɪmfəʊ) n., pl. **-phos.** *Inf.* short for **nymphomaniac.**

nympholepsy ('nɪmfə,lɛpsɪ) n., pl. **-sies.** a state of violent emotion, esp. when associated with a desire for something that one cannot have. [C18: from Gk *numpholēptos* caught by nymphs, from *numphē* nymph + *lambanein* to seize] —**'nympho,lept** n. —,**nympho'leptic** adj.

nymphomania (,nɪmfə'meɪnɪə) n. a neurotic compulsion in women to have sexual intercourse with many men without being able to have lasting relationships with them. [C18: NL, from Gk *numphē* nymph + -MANIA] —,**nympho'maniac** n., adj.

Nysa ('naɪsə) n. the Polish name for the **Neisse** (sense 1).

nystagmus (nɪ'stægməs) n. involuntary movement of the eye comprising a smooth drift followed by a flick back. [C19: NL, from Gk *nustagmos*] —**nys'tagmic** adj.

Nyx (nɪks) n. *Greek myth.* the goddess of the night, daughter of Chaos. Roman counterpart: **Nox.**

N.Z., NZ, or **N. Zeal.** *abbrev. for* New Zealand.

NZBC (formerly) *abbrev. for* New Zealand Broadcasting Commission.

NZEF (in New Zealand) *abbrev. for* New Zealand Expeditionary Force, the New Zealand army that served 1914-18. **2NZEF** is used to refer to the Second New Zealand Expeditionary Force, in World War II.

O

o *or* **O** (əʊ) *n.*, *pl.* **o's, O's,** *or* **Os.** **1.** the 15th letter and fourth vowel of the English alphabet. **2.** any of several speech sounds represented by this letter, as in *code, pot, cow,* or *form.* **3.** another name for **nought.**

O¹ *symbol for:* **1.** *Chem.* oxygen. **2.** a human blood type of the ABO group. **3.** Old.

O² (əʊ) *interj.* **1.** a variant of **oh. 2.** an exclamation introducing an invocation, entreaty, wish, etc.: *O God! O for the wings of a dove!*

o. *abbrev. for:* **1.** octavo. **2.** old. **3.** only. **4.** order. **5.** *Pharmacol.* pint. [from L *octarius*]

O. *abbrev. for:* **1.** Ocean. **2.** octavo. **3.** old.

o' (ə) *prep. Inf. or arch.* shortened form of **of:** *a cup o' tea.*

O'- *prefix.* (in surnames of Irish Gaelic origin) descendant of: *O'Corrigan.* [from Irish Gaelic *ó, ua* descendant]

-o *suffix forming nouns.* indicating a diminutive or slang abbreviation: *wino.*

oaf (əʊf) *n.* a stupid or loutish person. [C17: var. of OE *œlf* ELF] —**'oafish** *adj.* —**'oafishness** *n.*

Oahu (əʊ'ɑːhuː) *n.* an island in central Hawaii: the third largest of the Hawaiian Islands. Chief town: Honolulu. Pop.: 816 700 (1986 est.). Area: 1574 sq. km (608 sq. miles).

oak (əʊk) *n.* **1.** any deciduous or evergreen tree or shrub having acorns as fruits and lobed leaves. **2. a.** the wood of any of these trees, used esp. as building timber and for making furniture. **b.** (*as modifier*): *an oak table.* **3.** any of various trees that resemble the oak, such as the poison oak. **4.** anything made of oak, esp. a heavy outer door to a set of rooms in an Oxford college. **5.** the leaves of an oak tree, worn as a garland. [OE *āc*]

oak apple *or* **gall** *n.* any of various brownish round galls on oak trees, containing the larvae of certain wasps.

oaken ('əʊkən) *adj.* made of the wood of the oak.

Oakham ('əʊkəm) *n.* a market town in E central England, in Leicestershire, formerly county own of Rutland. Pop.: 7996 (1981).

Oakland ('əʊklənd) *n.* a port and industrial centre in W California, on San Francisco Bay. Pop.: 356 960 (1986).

Oakley ('əʊklɪ) *n.* **Annie,** real name *Phoebe Anne Oakley Mozee.* 1860–1926, U.S. markswoman.

Oaks (əʊks) *n.* (*functioning as sing.*) **the.** a horse race for fillies held annually at Epsom since 1779: one of the classics of English flat racing. [named after an estate near Epsom]

oakum ('əʊkəm) *n.* loose fibre obtained by unravelling old rope, used esp. for caulking seams in wooden ships. [OE *ācuma,* var. of *ācumba,* lit.: off-combings, from *ā-* off + *-cumba,* from *cemban* to COMB]

Oakville ('əʊkvɪl) *n.* a city in SE Canada, in SE Ontario on Lake Ontario southwest of Toronto: motor-vehicle industry. Pop.: 75 773 (1981).

O & M *abbrev. for* organization and method (in studies of working methods).

OAP (in Britain) *abbrev. for* old age pension *or* pensioner.

oar (ɔː) *n.* **1.** a long shaft of wood for propelling a boat by rowing, having a broad blade that is dipped into and pulled against the water. **2.** short for **oarsman. 3. put one's oar in.** to interfere or interrupt. ~*vb.* **4.** to row or propel with or as if with oars. [OE *ār,* of Gmc origin] —**'oarless** *adj.* —**'oar,like** *adj.*

oarfish ('ɔː,fɪʃ) *n.*, *pl.* **-fish** *or* **-fishes.** a very long ribbonfish with long slender ventral fins. [C19: referring to the flattened oarlike body]

oarlock ('ɔː,lɒk) *n.* the usual U.S. and Canad. word for **rowlock.**

oarsman ('ɔːzmən) *n.*, *pl.* **-men.** a man who rows, esp. one who rows in a racing boat. —**'oarsmanship** *n.*

OAS *abbrev. for:* **1.** *Organisation de l'Armée Secrète;* an organization which opposed Algerian independence by acts of terrorism. **2.** Organization of American States.

oasis (əʊ'eɪsɪs) *n.*, *pl.* **-ses** (-siːz). **1.** a fertile patch in a desert occurring where the water table approaches or reaches the ground surface. **2.** a place of peace, safety, or happiness. [C17: via L from Gk, prob. from Egyptian]

oast (əʊst) *n. Chiefly Brit.* **1.** a kiln for drying hops. **2.** Also called: **oast house.** a building containing such kilns, usually having a conical or pyramidal roof. [OE *āst*]

oat (əʊt) *n.* **1.** an erect annual grass grown in temperate regions for its edible seed. **2.** (*usually pl.*) the seeds or fruits of this grass. **3.** any of various other grasses such as the wild oat. **4.** *Poetic.* a flute made from an oat straw. **5. feel one's oats.** *U.S. & Canad. inf.* **a.** to feel exuberant. **b.** to feel self-important. **6. sow one's (wild) oats.** to indulge in adventure or promiscuity during youth. [OE *āte,* from ?]

oatcake ('əʊt,keɪk) *n.* a crisp brittle unleavened biscuit made of oatmeal.

oaten ('əʊtⁿn) *adj.* made of oats or oat straw.

Oates (əʊts) *n.* **1.** Captain **Lawrence Edward Grace.** 1880–1912, English explorer. He died on Scott's second Antarctic expedition. **2. Titus** ('taɪtəs). 1649–1705, English conspirator. He fabricated the Popish Plot (1678), a supposed Catholic conspiracy to kill Charles II, burn London, and massacre Protestants. His perjury caused the execution of many innocent Catholics.

oath (əʊθ) *n.*, *pl.* **oaths** (əʊðz). **1.** a solemn pronouncement to affirm the truth of a statement or to pledge a person to some course of action. **2.** the form of such a pronouncement. **3.** an irreverent or blasphemous expression, esp. one involving the name of a deity; curse. **4. my oath.** *Austral. sl.* certainly; yes indeed. **5. on, upon,** *or* **under oath. a.** under the obligation of an oath. **b.** *Law.* having sworn to tell the truth, usually with one's hand on the Bible. **6. take an oath.** to declare formally with a pledge, esp. before giving evidence. [OE *āth*]

oatmeal ('əʊt,miːl) *n.* **1.** meal ground from oats, used for making porridge, oatcakes, etc. **2. a.** a greyish-yellow colour. **b.** (*as adj.*): *an oatmeal coat.*

OAU *abbrev. for* Organization of African Unity.

Oaxaca (wə'hɑːkə; *Spanish* oa'xaka) *n.* **1.** a state of S Mexico, on the Pacific: includes most of the Isthmus of Tehuantepec; inhabited chiefly by Indians. Capital: Oaxaca de Juárez. Pop.: 2 518 157 (1980). Area: 95 363 sq. km (36 820 sq. miles). **2.** a city in S Mexico, capital of Oaxaca state: founded in 1486 by the Aztecs and conquered by Spain in 1521. Pop.: 157 284 (1980). Official name: **Oaxaca de Juárez.**

Ob (*Russian* ɔpj) *n.* a river in the N central Soviet Union, formed at Bisk by the confluence of the Biya and Katun Rivers and flowing generally north to the **Gulf of Ob** (an inlet of the Arctic Ocean): one of the largest rivers in the world, with a drainage basin of about 2 930 000 sq. km (1 131 000 sq. miles). Length: 3682 km (2287 miles).

OB *Brit. abbrev. for:* **1.** Old Boy. **2.** outside broadcast.

ob. *abbrev. for:* **1.** (on tombstones, etc.) obiit. [L: he (or she) died] **2.** obiter. [L: incidentally; in passing] **3.** oboe.

ob- *prefix.* inverse or inversely: *obovate.* [from OF, from L *ob.* In compound words from L, *ob-* (and *oc-, of-, op-*) indicates: to, towards (*object*); against (*oppose*); away from (*obsolete*); before (*obstetric*); and is used as an intensifier (*oblong*)]

Obad. *Bible. abbrev. for* Obadiah.

Obadiah (,əʊbə'daɪə) *n. Old Testament.* **1.** a Hebrew prophet. **2.** the book containing his oracles, chiefly directed against Edom. Douay spelling: **Abdias** (æb'daɪəs).

Oban ('əʊbⁿn) *n.* a small port and resort in W Scotland, in NW Strathclyde on the Firth of Lorn. Pop.: 8134 (1981).

obbligato *or* **obligato** (,ɒblɪ'gɑːtəʊ) *Music.* ~*adj.*, *n.* **1.** not to be omitted in performance ~*n.*, *pl.* **-tos** *or* **-ti** (-tiː). **2.** an essential part in a score: *with oboe obbligato.* [C18: from It., from *obbligare* to OBLIGE]

obconic (ɒb'kɒnɪk) *adj. Bot.* (of a fruit) shaped like a cone and attached at the pointed end.

obcordate (ɒb'kɔːdeɪt) *adj. Bot.* heart-shaped and attached at the pointed end: *obcordate leaves.*

obdurate ('ɒbdjʊrɪt) *adj.* **1.** not easily moved by feelings or supplication; hardhearted. **2.** impervious to persuasion. [C15: from L *obdūrāre* to make hard, from *ob-* (intensive) + *dūrus* hard] —**'obduracy** *or* **'obdurateness** *n.* —**'obdurately** *adv.*

OBE *abbrev. for* Officer of the Order of the British Empire (a Brit. title).

obeah ('əʊbɪə) *n.* **1.** a kind of witchcraft practised by the Negroes of the West Indies. **2.** a charm used in this. [of W African origin]

obedience (ə'biːdɪəns) *n.* **1.** the condition or quality of being obedient. **2.** the act or an instance of obeying; dutiful or submissive behaviour. **3.** the authority vested in a Church or similar body. **4.** the collective group of persons submitting to this authority.

obedient (ə'biːdɪənt) *adj.* obeying or willing to obey. [C13: from OF, from L *oboediens*, present participle of *oboedīre* to OBEY] —**o'bediently** *adv.*

obeisance (əʊ'beɪsəns) *n.* **1.** an attitude of deference or homage. **2.** a gesture expressing obeisance. [C14: from OF *obéissant*, present participle of *obéir* to OBEY] —**o'beisant** *adj.*

obelisk ('ɒbɪlɪsk) *n.* **1.** a stone pillar having a square or rectangular cross section and sides that taper towards a pyramidal top. **2.** *Printing.* another name for **dagger** (sense 2). [C16: via L from Gk *obeliskos* a little spit, from *obelos* spit] —**obe'liscal** *adj.* —**obe'liskoid** *adj.*

obelus ('ɒbɪləs) *n., pl.* **-li** (-ˌlaɪ). **1.** a mark (— or ÷) used in editions of ancient documents to indicate spurious words or passages. **2.** another name for **dagger** (sense 2). [C14: via LL from Gk *obelos* spit]

Oberammergau (*German* ˈoːbərˈamərɡaʊ) *n.* a village in S West Germany, in Bavaria in the foothills of the Alps: famous for its Passion Play, performed by the villagers every ten years (except during the World Wars) since 1634, in thanksgiving for the end of the Black Death. Pop.: 4900 (1980 est.).

Oberhausen (*German* ˈoːbərhaʊzən) *n.* an industrial city in W West Germany, in North Rhine-Westphalia on the Rhine-Herne Canal: site of the first ironworks in the Ruhr. Pop.: 222 100 (1986).

Oberland ('əʊbəˌlænd) *n.* the lower parts of the Bernese Alps in central Switzerland, mostly in S Bern canton.

Oberon ('əʊbəˌrɒn) *n.* (in medieval folklore) the king of the fairies, husband of Titania.

Oberösterreich ('oːbərˌøːstəraɪç) *n.* the German name for **Upper Austria**.

obese (əʊ'biːs) *adj.* excessively fat or fleshy; corpulent. [C17: from L *obēsus*, from *ob-* (intensive) + *edere* to eat] —**o'besity** *or* **o'beseness** *n.*

obey (ə'beɪ) *vb.* **1.** to carry out (instructions or orders); comply with (demands). **2.** to behave or act in accordance with (one's feelings, whims, etc.). [C13: from OF *obéir*, from L *oboedīre*, from *ob-* towards + *audīre* to hear] —**o'beyer** *n.*

obfuscate ('ɒbfʌsˌkeɪt) *vb.* (*tr.*) **1.** to obscure or darken. **2.** to perplex or bewilder. [C16: from L *ob-* (intensive) + *fuscāre* to blacken, from *fuscus* dark] —**obfus'cation** *n.* —**'obfusˌcatory** *adj.*

obi ('əʊbɪ) *n., pl.* **obis** *or* **obi.** a broad sash tied in a large flat bow at the back, worn as part of the Japanese national costume. [C19: from Japanese]

obit ('ɒbɪt, 'əʊbɪt) *n. Inf.* **1.** short for **obituary.** **2.** a memorial service.

obiter dictum ('ɒbɪtə 'dɪktəm, 'əʊ-) *n., pl.* **obiter dicta** ('dɪktə). **1.** *Law.* an observation by a judge on some point of law not directly in issue in the case before him. **2.** any comment or remark made in passing. [L: something said in passing]

obituary (ə'bɪtjʊərɪ) *n., pl.* **-aries.** a published announcement of a death, often accompanied by a short biography of the dead person. [C18: from Med. L *obituārius*, from L *obīre* to fall] —**o'bituarist** *n.*

obj. *abbrev. for:* **1.** objection. **2.** *Grammar.* object(ive).

object¹ ('ɒbdʒɪkt) *n.* **1.** a tangible and visible thing. **2.** a person or thing seen as a focus for feelings, thought, etc. **3.** an aim or objective. **4.** *Inf.* a ridiculous or pitiable person, spectacle, etc. **5.** *Philosophy.* that towards which cognition is directed as contrasted with the thinking subject. **6.** *Grammar.* a noun, pronoun, or noun phrase whose referent is the recipient of the action of a verb. See also **direct object, indirect object. 7.** *Grammar.* a noun, pronoun, or noun phrase that is governed by a preposition. **8. no object.** not a hindrance or obstacle: *money is no object.* [C14: from LL *objectus* something thrown before (the mind), from L *obicere*; see OBJECT²]

object² (əb'dʒɛkt) *vb.* **1.** (*tr.; takes a clause as object*) to state as an objection. **2.** (*intr.; often foll. by to*) to raise

or state an objection (to); present an argument (against). [C15: from L *obicere*, from *ob-* against + *jacere* to throw] —**ob'jector** *n.*

object glass *n. Optics.* another name for **objective** (sense 10).

objectify (əb'dʒɛktɪˌfaɪ) *vb.* **-fying, -fied.** (*tr.*) to represent concretely; present as an object. —**obˌjectifi'cation** *n.*

objection (əb'dʒɛkʃən) *n.* **1.** an expression or feeling of opposition or dislike. **2.** a cause for such an expression or feeling. **3.** the act of objecting.

objectionable (əb'dʒɛkʃənəbəl) *adj.* unpleasant, offensive, or repugnant. —**obˌjectiona'bility** *or* **ob'jectionableness** *n.* —**ob'jectionably** *adv.*

objective (əb'dʒɛktɪv) *adj.* **1.** existing independently of perception or an individual's conceptions. **2.** undistorted by emotion or personal bias. **3.** of or relating to actual and external phenomena as opposed to thoughts, feelings, etc. **4.** *Med.* (of disease symptoms) perceptible to persons other than the individual affected. **5.** *Grammar.* denoting a case of nouns and pronouns, esp. in languages having only two cases, that is used to identify the direct object of a finite verb or preposition. See also **accusative. 6.** of or relating to a goal or aim. ~*n.* **7.** the object of one's endeavours; goal; aim. **8.** an actual phenomenon; reality. **9.** *Grammar.* the objective case. **10.** Also called: **object glass.** *Optics.* the lens or combination of lenses nearest to the object in an optical instrument. ~Abbrev.: **obj.** Cf. **subjective.** —**objectival** (ˌɒbdʒɛk'taɪvəl) *adj.* —**ob'jectively** *adv.* —**ˌobjec'tivity** *or* (*less commonly*) **ob'jectiveness** *n.*

objectivism (əb'dʒɛktɪˌvɪzəm) *n.* **1.** the tendency to stress what is objective. **2.** the philosophical doctrine that reality is objective, and that sense data correspond with it. —**ob'jectivist** *n., adj.* —**obˌjectiv'istic** *adj.*

object language *n.* a language described by another language. Cf. **metalanguage.**

object lesson *n.* a convincing demonstration of some principle or ideal.

object program *n.* a computer program transcribed from the equivalent source program into machine language by the compiler or assembler.

objet d'art *French.* (ɔbʒɛ dar) *n., pl.* **objets d'art** (ɔbʒɛ dar). a small object considered to be of artistic worth. [F: object of art]

objurgate ('ɒbdʒəˌgeɪt) *vb.* (*tr.*) to scold or reprimand. [C17: from L *objurgāre*, from *ob-* against + *jurgāre* to scold] —**ˌobjur'gation** *n.* —**'objurˌgator** *n.* —**objurgatory** (ɒb'dʒɜːgətərɪ, -trɪ) *adj.*

obl. *abbrev. for:* **1.** oblique. **2.** oblong.

oblate¹ ('ɒbleɪt) *adj.* having an equatorial diameter of greater length than the polar diameter: *the earth is an oblate sphere.* Cf. **prolate.** [C18: from NL *oblātus* lengthened, from L *ob-* towards + *lātus*, p.p. of *ferre* to bring]

oblate² ('ɒbleɪt) *n.* a person dedicated to a monastic or religious life. [C19: from F *oblat*, from Med. L *oblātus*, from L *offerre* to OFFER]

oblation (ɒ'bleɪʃən) *n.* **1.** *Christianity.* the offering of the Eucharist to God. **2.** any offering made for religious or charitable purposes. [C15: from Church L *oblātiō*; see OBLATE²] —**oblatory** ('ɒblətərɪ, -trɪ) *or* **ob'lational** *adj.*

obligate ('ɒblɪˌgeɪt) *vb.* **1.** to compel, constrain, or oblige morally or legally. **2.** (in the U.S.) to bind (property, funds, etc.) as security. ~*adj.* **3.** compelled, bound, or restricted. **4.** *Biol.* able to exist under only one set of environmental conditions. [C16: from L *obligāre* to OBLIGE] —**'obligable** *adj.* —**ob'ligative** *adj.* —**'obliˌgator** *n.*

obligation (ˌɒblɪ'geɪʃən) *n.* **1.** a moral or legal requirement; duty. **2.** the act of obligating or the state of being obligated. **3.** *Law.* **a.** a written contract containing a penalty. **b.** an instrument acknowledging indebtedness to secure the repayment of money borrowed. **4.** a person or thing to which one is bound morally or legally. **5.** a service or favour for which one is indebted.

obligato (ˌɒblɪ'ɡɑːtəʊ) *adj., n. Music.* a variant spelling of **obbligato.**

obligatory (ɒ'blɪgətərɪ, -trɪ) *adj.* **1.** required to be done, obtained, possessed, etc. **2.** of the nature of or constituting an obligation. —**ob'ligatorily** *adv.*

oblige (ə'blaɪdʒ) *vb.* **1.** (*tr.; often passive*) to bind or constrain (someone to do something) by legal, moral, or physical means. **2.** (*tr.; usually passive*) to make indebted or grateful (to someone) by doing a favour. **3.** to do a service or favour to (someone): *she obliged the guests with a song.* [C13: from OF *obliger*, from L *obligāre*, from *ob-* towards + *ligāre* to bind] —**o'bliger** *n.*

obligee (ˌɒblɪ'dʒiː) *n.* a person in whose favour an obligation, contract, or bond is created; creditor.

obliging (ə'blaɪdʒɪŋ) *adj.* ready to do favours; agreeable; kindly. —**o'bligingly** *adv.* —**o'bligingness** *n.*

obligor (ˌɒblɪ'gɔː) *n.* a person who binds himself by contract to perform some obligation; debtor.

oblique (ə'bliːk) *adj.* **1.** at an angle; slanting; sloping. **2.** *Geom.* **a.** (of lines, planes, etc.) neither perpendicular nor parallel to one another or to another line, plane, etc. **b.** not related to or containing a right angle. **3.** indirect or evasive. **4.** *Grammar.* denoting any case of nouns, pronouns, etc., other than the nominative and vocative. **5.** *Biol.* having asymmetrical sides or planes: *an oblique leaf.* ~*n.* **6.** something oblique, esp. a line. **7.** another name for **solidus** (sense 1). ~*vb.* (*intr.*) **8.** to take or have an oblique direction. **9.** (of a military formation) to move forward at an angle. [C15: from OF, from L *oblīquus*, from ?] —**o'bliquely** *adv.* —**o'bliqueness** *n.* —**obliquity** (ə'blɪkwɪtɪ) *n.*

oblique angle *n.* an angle that is not a right angle or any multiple of a right angle.

obliterate (ə'blɪtəˌreɪt) *vb.* (*tr.*) to destroy every trace of; wipe out completely. [C16: from L *oblitterāre* to erase, from *ob-* out + *littera* letter] —**o,blite'ration** *n.* —**o'bliterative** *adj.* —**o'bliter,ator** *n.*

oblivion (ə'blɪvɪən) *n.* **1.** the condition of being forgotten or disregarded. **2.** *Law.* amnesty; pardon. [C14: via OF from L *oblīviō* forgetfulness, from *oblīviscī* to forget]

oblivious (ə'blɪvɪəs) *adj.* (usually foll. by *of*) unaware or forgetful. —**ob'liviously** *adv.* —**ob'liviousness** *n.*

oblong ('ɒbˌlɒŋ) *adj.* **1.** having an elongated, esp. rectangular, shape. ~*n.* **2.** a figure or object having this shape. [C15: from L *oblongus*, from *ob-* (intensive) + *longus* LONG[1]]

obloquy ('ɒbləkwɪ) *n.*, *pl.* **-quies. 1.** defamatory or censorious statements, esp. when directed against one person. **2.** disgrace brought about by public abuse. [C15: from L *obloquium* contradiction, from *ob-* against + *loquī* to speak]

obnoxious (əb'nɒkʃəs) *adj.* **1.** extremely unpleasant. **2.** *Obs.* exposed to harm, injury, etc. [C16: from L *obnoxius*, from *ob-* to + *noxa* injury, from *nocēre* to harm] —**ob'noxiously** *adv.* —**ob'noxiousness** *n.*

oboe ('əʊbəʊ) *n.* **1.** a woodwind instrument consisting of a conical tube fitted with a mouthpiece having a double reed. It has a penetrating nasal tone. **2.** a person who plays this instrument in an orchestra. ~*Arch. form:* **hautboy.** [C18: via It. *oboe*, phonetic approximation to F *haut bois*, lit.: high wood (referring to its pitch)] —**'oboist** *n.*

oboe d'amore (dɑː'mɔːreɪ) *n.* a type of oboe pitched a minor third lower than the oboe itself: used chiefly in baroque music.

Obote (ɒ'bəʊteɪ, -tɪ) *n.* (**Apollo**) **Milton.** born 1924, Ugandan politician; prime minister of Uganda (1962–66) and president (1966–71; 1980–85). He was deposed by Amin in 1971 and remained in exile until 1980; deposed again in 1985 by the Acholi army.

O'Brien (ə'braɪən) *n.* **Edna.** born 1936, Irish novelist. Her books include *Country Girls* (1960) and *The High Road* (1988). She has also written plays, film scripts, and short stories.

obs. *abbrev. for:* **1.** observation. **2.** obsolete.

obscene (əb'siːn) *adj.* **1.** offensive or outrageous to accepted standards of decency or modesty. **2.** *Law.* (of publications, etc.) having a tendency to deprave or corrupt. **3.** disgusting; repellent. [C16: from L *obscēnus* inauspicious] —**ob'scenely** *adv.*

obscenity (əb'sɛnɪtɪ) *n.*, *pl.* **-ties. 1.** the state or quality of being obscene. **2.** an obscene act, statement, work, etc.

obscurant (əb'skjʊərənt) *n.* an opposer of reform and enlightenment. —**obscurantism** (ˌɒbskjʊə'ræn,tɪzəm) *n.* —,**obscu'rantist** *n.*, *adj.*

obscure (əb'skjʊə) *adj.* **1.** unclear. **2.** indistinct, vague, or indefinite. **3.** inconspicuous or unimportant. **4.** hidden, secret, or remote. **5.** (of a vowel) reduced to a neutral vowel (ə). **6.** gloomy, dark, clouded, or dim. ~*vb.* (*tr.*) **7.** to make unclear, vague, or hidden. **8.** to cover or cloud over. **9.** *Phonetics.* to pronounce (a vowel) so that

it becomes a neutral sound represented by (ə). [C14: via OF from L *obscūrus* dark] —**obscuration** (ˌɒbskjʊ-'reɪʃən) *n.* —**ob'scurely** *adv.* —**ob'scureness** *n.*

obscurity (əb'skjʊərɪtɪ) *n.*, *pl.* **-ties. 1.** the state or quality of being obscure. **2.** an obscure person or thing.

obsequies ('ɒbsɪkwɪz) *pl. n.*, *sing.* **-quy.** funeral rites. [C14: via Anglo-Norman from Med. L *obsequiae* (infl. by L *exsequiae*), from *obsequium* compliance]

obsequious (əb'siːkwɪəs) *adj.* **1.** obedient or attentive in an ingratiating or servile manner. **2.** *Now rare.* submissive or compliant. [C15: from L *obsequiōsus* compliant, from *obsequi* to follow] —**ob'sequiously** *adv.* —**ob'sequiousness** *n.*

observance (əb'zɜːvəns) *n.* **1.** recognition of or compliance with a law, custom, practice, etc. **2.** a ritual, ceremony, or practice, esp. of a religion. **3.** observation or attention. **4.** the degree of strictness of a religious order in following its rule. **5.** *Arch.* respectful or deferential attention.

observant (əb'zɜːvənt) *adj.* **1.** paying close attention to detail; watchful or heedful. **2.** adhering strictly to rituals, ceremonies, laws, etc. —**ob'servantly** *adv.*

observation (ˌɒbzə'veɪʃən) *n.* **1.** the act of observing or the state of being observed. **2.** a comment or remark. **3.** detailed examination of phenomena prior to analysis, diagnosis, or interpretation: *the patient was under observation.* **4.** the facts learned from observing. **5.** *Navigation.* **a.** a sight taken with an instrument to determine the position of an observer relative to that of a given heavenly body. **b.** the data so taken. —,**obser'vational** *adj.* —,**obser'vationally** *adv.*

observatory (əb'zɜːvətərɪ, -trɪ) *n.*, *pl.* **-ries. 1.** an institution or building specially designed and equipped for observing meteorological and astronomical phenomena. **2.** any building or structure providing an extensive view of its surroundings.

observe (əb'zɜːv) *vb.* **1.** (*tr.*; *may take a clause as object*) to see; perceive; notice: *we have observed that you steal.* **2.** (when *tr.*, *may take a clause as object*) to watch (something) carefully; pay attention to (something). **3.** to make observations of (something), esp. scientific ones. **4.** (when *intr.*, usually foll. by *on* or *upon*; when *tr.*, *may take a clause as object*) to make a comment or remark: *the speaker observed that times had changed.* **5.** (*tr.*) to abide by, keep, or follow (a custom, tradition, etc.). [C14: via OF from L *observāre*, from *ob-* to + *servāre* to watch] —**ob'servable** *adj.* —**ob'server** *n.*

obsess (əb'sɛs) *vb.* (*tr.*; when passive, foll. by *with* or *by*) to preoccupy completely; haunt. [C16: from L *obsessus* besieged, p.p. of *obsidēre*, from *ob-* in front of + *sedēre* to sit] —**ob'sessive** *adj.* —**ob'sessively** *adv.* —**ob'sessiveness** *n.*

obsession (əb'sɛʃən) *n.* **1.** *Psychiatry.* a persistent idea or impulse, often associated with anxiety and mental illness. **2.** a persistent preoccupation, idea, or feeling. **3.** the act of obsessing or the state of being obsessed. —**ob'sessional** *adj.* —**ob'sessionally** *adv.*

obsidian (ɒb'sɪdɪən) *n.* a dark glassy volcanic rock formed by very rapid solidification of lava. [C17: from L *obsidiānus*, erroneous transcription of *obsiānus* (*lapis*) (stone of) *Obsius*, (in Pliny) the discoverer of a stone resembling obsidian]

obsolesce (ˌɒbsə'lɛs) *vb.* (*intr.*) to become obsolete.

obsolescent (ˌɒbsə'lɛsənt) *adj.* becoming obsolete or out of date. [C18: from L *obsolescere*; see OBSOLETE] —,**obso'lescence** *n.*

obsolete ('ɒbsəˌliːt, ˌɒbsə'liːt) *adj.* **1.** out of use or practice; not current. **2.** out of date; unfashionable or outmoded. **3.** *Biol.* (of parts, organs, etc.) vestigial; rudimentary. [C16: from L *obsolētus* worn out, p.p. of *obsolēre* (unattested), from *ob-* opposite to + *solēre* to be used] —'**obso,letely** *adv.* —'**obso,leteness** *n.*

obstacle ('ɒbstək[ə]l) *n.* **1.** a person or thing that opposes or hinders something. **2.** *Brit.* a fence or hedge used in showjumping. [C14: via OF from L *obstāculum*, from *ob-* against + *stāre* to stand]

obstacle race *n.* a race in which competitors have to negotiate various obstacles.

obstetric (ɒb'stɛtrɪk) *or* **obstetrical** *adj.* of or relating to childbirth or obstetrics. [C18: via NL from L *obstetrīcius*, from *obstetrix* a midwife, lit.: woman who stands opposite, from *obstāre* to stand in front of; see OBSTACLE] —**ob'stetrically** *adv.*

obstetrician (ˌɒbstɛˈtrɪʃən) *n.* a physician who specializes in obstetrics.

obstetrics (ɒbˈstɛtrɪks) *n.* (*functioning as sing.*) the branch of medicine concerned with childbirth and the treatment of women before and after childbirth.

obstinacy (ˈɒbstɪnəsɪ) *n., pl.* **-cies.** **1.** the state or quality of being obstinate. **2.** an obstinate act, attitude, etc.

obstinate (ˈɒbstɪnɪt) *adj.* **1.** adhering fixedly to a particular opinion, attitude, course of action, etc. **2.** self-willed or headstrong. **3.** difficult to subdue or alleviate; persistent: *an obstinate fever.* [C14: from L *obstinātus*, p.p. of *obstināre* to persist in, from *ob-* (intensive) + *stin-*, var. of *stare* to stand] —**ˈobstinately** *adv.*

obstreperous (əbˈstrɛpərəs) *adj.* noisy or rough, esp. in resisting restraint or control. [C16: from L, from *ob-strepere*, from *ob-* against + *strepere* to roar] —**obˈstreperously** *adv.* —**obˈstreperousness** *n.*

obstruct (əbˈstrʌkt) *vb.* (*tr.*) **1.** to block (a road, passageway, etc.) with an obstacle. **2.** to make (progress or activity) difficult. **3.** to impede or block a clear view of. [C17: from L: built against, p.p. of *obstruere*, from *ob-* against + *struere* to build] —**obˈstructive** *adj., n.* —**obˈstructively** *adv.* —**obˈstructiveness** *n.* —**obˈstructor** *n.*

obstruction (əbˈstrʌkʃən) *n.* **1.** a person or thing that obstructs. **2.** the act or an instance of obstructing. **3.** delay of business, esp. in a legislature by means of procedural devices. **4.** *Sport.* the act of unfairly impeding an opposing player. —**obˈstructional** *adj.*

obstructionist (əbˈstrʌkʃənɪst) *n.* a person who deliberately obstructs business, etc., esp. in a legislature. —**obˈstructionism** *n.*

obtain (əbˈteɪn) *vb.* **1.** (*tr.*) to gain possession of; acquire; get. **2.** (*intr.*) to be customary, valid, or accepted: *a new law obtains in this case.* [C15: via OF from L *obtinēre* to take hold of] —**obˈtainable** *adj.* —**ob,tainaˈbility** *n.* —**obˈtainer** *n.* —**obˈtainment** *n.*

obtrude (əbˈtruːd) *vb.* **1.** to push (oneself, one's opinions, etc.) on others in an unwelcome way. **2.** (*tr.*) to push out or forward. [C16: from L *obtrūdere*, from *ob-*against + *trūdere* to push forward] —**obˈtruder** *n.* —**obtrusion** (əbˈtruːʒən) *n.*

obtrusive (əbˈtruːsɪv) *adj.* **1.** obtruding or tending to obtrude. **2.** sticking out; protruding; noticeable. —**obˈtrusively** *adv.* —**obˈtrusiveness** *n.*

obtuse (əbˈtjuːs) *adj.* **1.** mentally slow or emotionally insensitive. **2.** *Maths.* (of an angle) lying between 90° and 180°. **3.** not sharp or pointed. **4.** indistinctly felt, heard, etc.; dull: *obtuse pain.* **5.** (of a leaf or similar flat part) having a rounded or blunt tip. [C16: from L *obtūsus* dulled, p.p. of *obtundere* to beat down] —**obˈtusely** *adv.* —**obˈtuseness** *n.*

obverse (ˈɒbvɜːs) *adj.* **1.** facing or turned towards the observer. **2.** forming or serving as a counterpart. **3.** (of leaves) narrower at the base than at the top. ~*n.* **4.** a counterpart or complement. **5.** *Logic.* a proposition derived from another by replacing the original predicate by its negation and changing the proposition from affirmative to negative or vice versa, as *no sum is correct* from *every sum is incorrect.* **6.** the side of a coin that bears the main design or device. [C16: from L *obversus* turned towards, p.p. of *obvertere*] —**obˈversely** *adv.*

obvert (ɒbˈvɜːt) *vb.* (*tr.*) **1.** *Logic.* to deduce the obverse of (a proposition). **2.** *Rare.* to turn so as to show the main or other side. [C17: from L *obvertere* to turn towards] —**obˈversion** *n.*

obviate (ˈɒbvɪˌeɪt) *vb.* (*tr.*) to do away with. [C16: from LL *obviātus* prevented, p.p. of *obviāre*; see OBVIOUS] —**obˈviˈation** *n.*

obvious (ˈɒbvɪəs) *adj.* **1.** easy to see or understand; evident. **2.** exhibiting motives, feelings, intentions, etc., clearly or without subtlety. **3.** naive or unsubtle: *the play was rather obvious.* [C16: from L *obvius*, from *obviam* in the way] —**ˈobviously** *adv.* —**ˈobviousness** *n.*

OC *abbrev. for* Officer Commanding.

Oc. *abbrev. for* Ocean.

o/c *abbrev. for* overcharge.

ocarina (ˌɒkəˈriːnə) *n.* an egg-shaped wind instrument with a protruding mouthpiece and six to eight finger holes, producing an almost pure tone. [C19: from It.: little goose, from *oca* goose, ult. from L *avis* bird]

Occam (ˈɒkəm) *n.* a variant spelling of (William of) Ockham.

Occam's razor *n.* a variant spelling of **Ockham's razor.**

occas. *abbrev. for* occasional(ly).

occasion (əˈkeɪʒən) *n.* **1.** (sometimes foll. by *of*) the time of a particular happening or event. **2.** (sometimes foll. by *for*) a reason or cause (to do or be something); grounds: *there was no occasion to complain.* **3.** an opportunity (to do something); chance. **4.** a special event, time, or celebration: *the party was quite an occasion.* **5. on occasion.** every so often. **6. rise to the occasion.** to have the courage, wit, etc., to meet the special demands of a situation. **7. take occasion.** to avail oneself of an opportunity (to do something). ~*vb.* **8.** (*tr.*) to bring about, esp. incidentally or by chance. [C14: from L *occāsiō* a falling down, from *occidere*]

occasional (əˈkeɪʒənəl) *adj.* **1.** taking place from time to time; not frequent or regular. **2.** of, for, or happening on special occasions. **3.** serving as an occasion (for something). —**ocˈcasionally** *adv.*

occasional table *n.* a small table with no regular use.

occident (ˈɒksɪdənt) *n.* a literary or formal word for **west.** Cf. **orient.** [C14: via OF from L *occidere* to fall (with reference to the setting sun)] —**ˌocciˈdental** *adj.*

Occident (ˈɒksɪdənt) *n.* (usually preceded by *the*) **1.** the countries of Europe and America. **2.** the western hemisphere. —**ˌOcciˈdental** *adj., n.*

occipital (ɒkˈsɪpɪtəl) *adj.* **1.** of or relating to the back of the head or skull. ~*n.* **2.** short for **occipital bone.** [See OCCIPUT]

occipital bone *n.* the bone that forms the back part of the skull and part of its base.

occipital lobe *n.* the posterior portion of each cerebral hemisphere, concerned with the interpretation of visual sensory impulses.

occiput (ˈɒksɪˌpʌt) *n., pl.* **occiputs** or **occipita** (ɒkˈsɪpɪtə). the back part of the head or skull. [C14: from L, from *ob-* at the back of + *caput* head]

occlude (əˈkluːd) *vb.* **1.** (*tr.*) to block or stop up (a passage or opening); obstruct. **2.** (*tr.*) to prevent the passage of. **3.** (*tr.*) *Chem.* (of a solid) to incorporate (a substance) by absorption or adsorption. **4.** *Meteorol.* to form or cause to form an occluded front. **5.** *Dentistry.* to produce or cause to produce occlusion, as in chewing. [C16: from L *occlūdere*, from *ob-* (intensive) + *claudere* to close] —**ocˈcludent** *adj.*

occluded front *n.* *Meteorol.* the line or plane occurring where the cold front of a depression has overtaken the warm front, raising the warm sector from ground level. Also called: **occlusion.**

occlusion (əˈkluːʒən) *n.* **1.** the act of occluding or the state of being occluded. **2.** *Meteorol.* another term for **occluded front.** **3.** *Dentistry.* the normal position of the teeth when the jaws are closed. —**ocˈclusive** *adj.*

occult *adj.* (ɒˈkʌlt, ˈɒkʌlt). **1. a.** of or characteristic of mystical or supernatural phenomena or influences. **b.** (*as n.*): *the occult.* **2.** beyond ordinary human understanding. **3.** secret or esoteric. ~*vb.* (ɒˈkʌlt). **4.** *Astron.* (of a celestial body) to hide (another celestial body) from view by occultation or (of a celestial body) to become hidden by occultation. **5.** to hide or become hidden or shut off from view. **6.** (*intr.*) (of lights, esp. in lighthouses) to shut off at regular intervals. [C16: from L *occultus*, p.p. of *occulere*, from *ob-* over, up + *-culere*, rel. to *celāre* to conceal] —**ˈoccul,tism** *n.* —**ˈoccultist** *n.* —**ocˈcultness** *n.*

occultation (ˌɒkʌlˈteɪʃən) *n.* the temporary disappearance of one celestial body as it moves out of sight behind another body.

occupancy (ˈɒkjʊpənsɪ) *n., pl.* **-cies.** **1.** the act of occupying; possession of a property. **2.** *Law.* the possession and use of property by or without agreement and without any claim to ownership. **3.** *Law.* the act of taking possession of unowned property, esp. land, with the intent of thus acquiring ownership. **4.** the condition or fact of being an occupant, esp. a tenant. **5.** the period of time during which one is an occupant, esp. of property.

occupant (ˈɒkjʊpənt) *n.* **1.** a person, thing, etc., holding a position or place. **2.** *Law.* a person who has possession of something, esp. an estate, house, etc.; tenant. **3.** *Law.* a person who acquires by occupancy the title to something previously without an owner.

occupation (ˌɒkjʊˈpeɪʃən) *n.* **1.** a person's regular work or profession; job. **2.** any activity on which time is spent by a person. **3.** the act of occupying or the state of being occupied. **4.** the control of a country by a foreign military power. **5.** the period of time that a nation, place, or position is occupied. **6.** (*modifier*) for the use of the occupier of a particular property: *occupation road.* —,occu'pa**tional** *adj.*

occupational psychology *n.* the scientific study of mental or emotional problems associated with the working environment.

occupational therapy *n. Med.* creative activity, such as a craft or hobby to help a patient recover from a physical or mental illness.

occupier ('ɒkjuˌpaɪə) *n.* **1.** *Brit.* a person who is in possession or occupation of a house or land. **2.** a person or thing that occupies.

occupy ('ɒkjuˌpaɪ) *vb.* **-pying, -pied.** (*tr.*) **1.** to live or be established in (a house, flat, office, etc.). **2.** (*often passive*) to keep (a person) busy or engrossed. **3.** (*often passive*) to take up (time or space). **4.** to take and hold possession of, esp. as a demonstration: *students occupied the college buildings.* **5.** to fill or hold (a position or rank). [C14: from OF *occuper*, from L *occupāre* to seize hold of]

occur (ə'kɜː) *vb.* **-curring, -curred.** (*intr.*) **1.** to happen; take place; come about. **2.** to be found or be present; exist. **3.** (foll. by *to*) to be realized or thought of (by); suggest itself (to). [C16: from L *occurrere* to run up to]
▷ **Usage.** In careful English, *occur* and *happen* are not used of prearranged events: *the wedding took place* (not *occurred* or *happened*) *in the afternoon.*

occurrence (ə'kʌrəns) *n.* **1.** something that occurs; a happening; event. **2.** the act or an instance of occurring: *a crime of frequent occurrence.* —oc'current *adj.*

ocean ('əʊʃən) *n.* **1.** a very large stretch of sea, esp. one of the five oceans of the world, the Atlantic, Pacific, Indian, Arctic, and Antarctic. **2.** the body of salt water covering approximately 70 per cent of the earth's surface. **3.** a huge quantity or expanse: *an ocean of replies.* **4.** *Literary.* the sea. [C13: via OF from L *ōceanus*, from OCEANUS]

oceanarium (ˌəʊʃə'nɛərɪəm) *n., pl.* **-iums** or **-ia** (-ɪə). a large saltwater aquarium for marine life.

ocean-going *adj.* (of a ship, boat, etc.) suited for travel on the open ocean.

Oceania (ˌəʊʃɪ'ɑːnɪə) *n.* the islands of the central and S Pacific, including Melanesia, Micronesia, and Polynesia: sometimes also including Australasia and the Malay Archipelago. —,Oce'anian *adj., n.*

oceanic (ˌəʊʃɪ'ænɪk) *adj.* **1.** of or relating to the ocean. **2.** living in the depths of the ocean beyond the continental shelf at a depth exceeding 200 metres: *oceanic fauna.* **3.** huge or overwhelming.

Oceanid (əʊ'sɪənɪd) *n., pl.* **Oceanids** or **Oceanides** (ˌəʊsɪ'ænɪˌdiːz). *Greek myth.* an ocean nymph.

oceanography (ˌəʊʃə'nɒɡrəfɪ, ˌəʊʃɪə-) *n.* the branch of science dealing with the physical, chemical, geological, and biological features of the oceans. —,ocean'ographer *n.* —oceanographic (ˌəʊʃənə'ɡræfɪk, ˌəʊʃɪə-) or ,ocean**o'graphical** *adj.*

oceanology (ˌəʊʃə'nɒlədʒɪ, ˌəʊʃɪə-) *n.* the study of the sea, esp. of its economic geography.

Oceanus (əʊ'sɪənəs) *n. Greek myth.* a Titan, divinity of the stream believed to flow around the earth.

ocellus (ɒ'sɛləs) *n., pl.* **-li** (-laɪ). **1.** the simple eye of insects and some other invertebrates, consisting basically of light-sensitive cells. **2.** any eyelike marking in animals, such as the eyespot on the tail feather of a peacock. [C19: via NL from L small: eye, from *oculus* eye] —o'cellar *adj.* —ocellate ('ɒsɪˌleɪt) or 'ocel,lated *adj.* —,ocel'lation *n.*

ocelot ('ɒsɪˌlɒt, 'əʊ-) *n.* a feline mammal inhabiting Central and South America and having a dark-spotted buff-brown coat. [C18: via F from Nahuatl *ocelotl* jaguar]

och (ɒx) *interj. Scot. & Irish.* an expression of surprise, contempt, disagreement, etc.

oche ('ɒkɪ) *n. Darts.* the mark or ridge on the floor behind which a player must stand to throw. [from ?]

ochlocracy (ɒk'lɒkrəsɪ) *n., pl.* **-cies.** rule by the mob; mobocracy. [C16: via F, from Gk *okhlokratia*, from *okhlos* mob + *kratos* power] —ochlocrat ('ɒkləˌkræt) *n.* —,ochlo'cratic *adj.*

ochone (ɒ'xəʊn) *interj. Scot. & Irish.* an expression of sorrow or regret. [from Gaelic *ochóin*]

ochre or *U.S.* **ocher** ('əʊkə) *n.* **1.** any of various natural earths containing ferric oxide, silica, and alumina: used as yellow or red pigments. **2. a.** a moderate yellow-orange to orange colour. **b.** (*as adj.*): *an ochre dress.* ~*vb.* **ochreing, ochred** or *U.S.* **ochering** or **ochring, ochered** or **ochred. 3.** (*tr.*) to colour with ochre. [C15: from OF *ocre*, from L *ōchra*, from Gk *ōkhros* pale yellow] —**ochreous** ('əʊkrɪəs, 'əʊkərəs), **ochrous** ('əʊkrəs), **ochry** ('əʊkərɪ, 'əʊkrɪ) or *U.S.* **'ocherous, 'ochery** *adj.*

-ock *suffix forming nouns.* indicating smallness: *hillock.* [OE *-oc, -uc*]

Ockeghem or **Okeghem** ('ɒkəˌɡɛm; *Dutch* 'ɔkəxəm) *n.* **Johannes** (joː'hɑnəs), **Jean d'** (ʒɑ̃ d), or **Jan van** (jɑn vɑn). ?1430–?95, Flemish composer. Also: **Ockenheim** ('ɒkənˌhaɪm).

ocker ('ɒkə) *Austral. sl.* ~*n.* **1.** (*often cap.*) an uncultivated or boorish Australian. ~*adj.* **2.** typical of such a person. [C20: after an Australian TV character]

Ockham or **Occam** ('ɒkəm) *n.* **William of.** died ?1349, English nominalist philosopher, who contested the temporal power of the papacy and ended the conflict between nominalism and realism. See **Ockham's razor.**

Ockham's razor or **Occam's razor** *n.* a maxim, attributed to William of Ockham, stating that in explaining something assumptions must not be needlessly multiplied. Also called: **the principle of economy.**

o'clock (ə'klɒk) *adv.* **1.** used after a number from one to twelve to indicate the hour of the day or night. **2.** used after a number to indicate direction or position relative to the observer, twelve o'clock being directly ahead and other positions being obtained by comparisons with a clock face. [C18: abbrev. for *of the clock*]

OCR *abbrev. for* optical character reader *or* recognition.

oct. *abbrev. for* octavo.

Oct. *abbrev. for* October.

oct- *combining form.* a variant of **octo-** before a vowel.

octa- *combining form.* a variant of **octo-.**

octad ('ɒktæd) *n.* **1.** a group or series of eight. **2.** *Chem.* an element with a valency of eight. [C19: from Gk *oktās*, from *oktō* eight] —oc'tadic *adj.*

octagon ('ɒktəˌɡən) *n.* a polygon having eight sides. [C17: via L from Gk *oktagōnos* having eight angles] —octagonal (ɒk'tæɡənəl) *adj.*

octahedron (ˌɒktə'hiːdrən) *n., pl.* **-drons** or **-dra** (-drə). a solid figure having eight plane faces.

octal notation or **octal** ('ɒktəl) *n. Computers.* a number system having a base 8, one octal digit being equivalent to a group of three bits.

octane ('ɒkteɪn) *n.* a liquid hydrocarbon found in petroleum. Formula: C_8H_{18}.

octane number or **rating** *n.* a measure of the antiknock quality of a petrol expressed as a percentage.

octant ('ɒktənt) *n.* **1.** *Maths.* **a.** any of the eight parts into which the three planes containing the Cartesian coordinate axes divide space. **b.** an eighth part of a circle. **2.** *Astron.* the position of a celestial body when it is at an angular distance of 45° from another body. **3.** an instrument used for measuring angles, similar to a sextant but having a graduated arc of 45°. [C17: from L *octans* half quadrant, from *octo* eight]

octavalent (ˌɒktə'veɪlənt) *adj. Chem.* having a valency of eight.

octave ('ɒktɪv) *n.* **1. a.** the interval between two musical notes one of which has twice the pitch of the other and lies eight notes away from it counting inclusively along the diatonic scale. **b.** one of these two notes, esp. the one of higher pitch. **c.** (*as modifier*): *an octave leap.* **2.** *Prosody.* a rhythmic group of eight lines of verse. **3.** ('ɒkteɪv). **a.** a feast day and the seven days following. **b.** the final day of this period. **4.** the eighth of eight basic positions in fencing. **5.** any set or series of eight. ~*adj.* **6.** consisting of eight parts. [C14: (orig.: eighth day) via OF from Med. L *octāva diēs* eighth day (after a festival), from L *octo* eight]

Octavia (ɒk'teɪvɪə) *n.* died 11 B.C., wife of Mark Antony; sister of Augustus.

Octavian (ɒk'teɪvɪən) *n.* the name of **Augustus** before he became emperor (27 B.C.).

octavo (ɒk'teɪvəʊ) *n., pl.* **-vos. 1.** a book size resulting from folding a sheet of paper of a specified size to form eight leaves: *demi-octavo.* Often written: **8vo, 8°. 2.** a book of this size. [C16: from NL *in octavo* in an eighth (of a sheet)]

octennial (ɒk'tɛnɪəl) *adj.* **1.** occurring every eight years. **2.** lasting for eight years. [C17: from L *octennium*, from *octo* eight + *annus* year] —oc'tennially *adv.*

octet (ɒk'tɛt) *n.* **1.** any group of eight, esp. singers or musicians. **2.** a piece of music composed for such a group. **3.** *Prosody.* another word for **octave** (sense 2). **4.** *Chem.* a stable group of eight electrons. ~Also (for senses 1, 2, 3): **octette**. [C19: from L *octo* eight, on the model of DUET]

octillion (ɒk'tɪljən) *n.* **1.** (in Britain and Germany) the number represented as one followed by 48 zeros (10^{48}). **2.** (in the U.S., Canada, and France) the number represented as one followed by 27 zeros (10^{27}). [C17: from F, on the model of MILLION] —**oc'tillionth** *adj., n.*

octo-, **octa-**, *or before a vowel* **oct-** *combining form.* eight: *octosyllabic*; *octagon*. [from L *octo*, Gk *oktō*]

October (ɒk'təʊbə) *n.* the tenth month of the year, consisting of 31 days. [OE, from L, from *octo* eight, since it was the eighth month in Roman reckoning]

Octobrist (ɒk'təʊbrɪst) *n.* a member of a Russian political party favouring the constitutional reforms granted in a manifesto issued by Nicholas II in Oct. 1905.

octocentenary (,ɒktəʊsɛn'tiːnərɪ) *n., pl.* **-naries.** an 800th anniversary.

octogenarian (,ɒktəʊdʒɪ'nɛərɪən) *n.* **1.** a person who is from 80 to 89 years old. ~*adj.* **2.** of or relating to an octogenarian. [C19: from L *octōgēnārius* containing eighty, from *octōgēnī* eighty each]

octopus ('ɒktəpəs) *n., pl.* **-puses.** **1.** a cephalopod mollusc having a soft oval body with eight long suckered tentacles and occurring at the sea bottom. **2.** a powerful influential organization, etc., with far-reaching effects, esp. harmful ones. [C18: via NL from Gk *oktōpous* having eight feet]

octoroon *or* **octaroon** (,ɒktə'ruːn) *n.* a person having one quadroon and one White parent and therefore having one-eighth Negro blood. Cf. **quadroon.** [C19: OCTO- + -*roon* as in QUADROON]

octosyllable ('ɒktə,sɪləb°l) *n.* **1.** a line of verse composed of eight syllables. **2.** a word of eight syllables. —**octosyllabic** (,ɒktəʊsɪ'læbɪk) *adj.*

octroi ('ɒktrwɑː) *n.* **1.** a duty on goods brought into certain towns. **2.** the place where it is collected. **3.** the officers responsible for its collection. [C17: from F *octroyer* to concede, from Med. L *auctorizāre* to AUTHORIZE]

octuple ('ɒktjʊp°l) *n.* **1.** a quantity or number eight times as great as another. ~*adj.* **2.** eight times as much or as many. **3.** consisting of eight parts. ~*vb.* **4.** (*tr.*) to multiply by eight. [C17: from L *octuplus*, from *octo* eight + -*plus* as in *duplus* double]

ocular ('ɒkjʊlə) *adj.* **1.** of or relating to the eye. ~*n.* **2.** another name for **eyepiece.** [C16: from L *oculāris* from *oculus* eye] —**'ocularly** *adv.*

ocularist ('ɒkjʊlərɪst) *n.* a person who makes artificial eyes.

oculist ('ɒkjʊlɪst) *n. Med.* a former term for **ophthalmologist.** [C17: via F from L *oculus* eye]

od (ɒd, əʊd), **odyl**, *or* **odyle** ('ɒdɪl) *n. Arch.* a hypothetical force formerly thought to be responsible for many natural phenomena, such as magnetism, light, and hypnotism. [C19: coined by Baron Karl von Reichenbach (1788–1869), G scientist] —**'odic** *adj.*

OD[1] (,əʊ'diː) *Inf.* ~*n.* **1.** an overdose of a drug. ~*vb.* (*intr.*) **OD'ing, OD'd. 2.** to take an overdose of a drug. [C20: from *o(ver)d(ose)*]

OD[2] *abbrev. for:* **1.** Officer of the Day. **2.** Also: **o.d.** *Mil.* olive drab. **3.** Also: **O/D** *Banking.* **a.** on demand. **b.** overdrawn. **4.** ordnance datum. **5.** outside diameter.

odalisque *or* **odalisk** ('əʊdəlɪsk) *n.* a female slave or concubine. [C17: via F, changed from Turkish *ōdalik*, from *ōdah* room + -*lik*, n. suffix]

odd (ɒd) *adj.* **1.** unusual or peculiar in appearance, character, etc. **2.** occasional, incidental, or random: *odd jobs.* **3.** leftover or additional: *odd bits of wool.* **4. a.** not divisible by two. **b.** represented or indicated by a number that is not divisible by two: *graphs are on odd pages.* Cf. **even**[1] (sense 7). **5.** being part of a matched pair or set when the other or others are missing: *an odd sock.* **6.** (*in combination*) used to designate an indefinite quantity more than the quantity specified in round numbers: *fifty-odd pounds.* **7.** out of the way. **8. odd man out.** a person or thing excluded from others forming a group, unit, etc. ~*n.* **9.** *Golf.* **a.** one stroke more than the score of one's opponent. **b.** a handicap of one stroke. **10.** a thing or person that is odd in sequence or number. ~See also **odds.** [from ON *oddi* triangle, point] —**'oddly** *adv.* —**'oddness** *n.*

oddball ('ɒd,bɔːl) *Inf.* ~*n.* **1.** Also: **odd bod, odd fish.** a strange or eccentric person or thing. ~*adj.* **2.** strange or peculiar.

Oddfellow ('ɒd,fɛləʊ) *n.* a member of a secret benevolent and fraternal association founded in England in the 18th century.

oddity ('ɒdɪtɪ) *n., pl.* **-ties. 1.** an odd person or thing. **2.** an odd quality or characteristic. **3.** the condition of being odd.

odd-jobman *or* **odd-jobber** *n.* a person who does casual work, esp. domestic repairs.

oddment ('ɒdmənt) *n.* **1.** (*often pl.*) an odd piece or thing; leftover. **2.** *Printing.* **a.** pages that do not make a complete signature. **b.** any individual part of a book excluding the main text.

odd pricing *n.* pricing goods in such a way as to imply that a bargain is being offered, as £5.99 instead of £6.

odds (ɒdz) *pl. n.* **1.** (foll. by *on* or *against*) the probability, expressed as a ratio, that a certain event will take place: *the odds against the outsider are a hundred to one.* **2.** the amount, expressed as a ratio, by which the wager of one better is greater than that of another: *he was offering odds of five to one.* **3.** the likelihood that a certain state of affairs will be so: *the odds are that he is drunk.* **4.** an equalizing allowance, esp. one given to a weaker side in a contest. **5.** the advantage that one contender is judged to have over another. **6.** *Brit.* a significant difference (esp. in **it makes no odds**). **7. at odds.** on bad terms. **8. give** *or* **lay odds.** to offer a bet with favourable odds. **9. over the odds. a.** more than is expected, necessary, etc. **b.** unfair or excessive. **10. take odds.** to accept a bet with favourable odds. **11. what's the odds?** *Brit. inf.* what difference does it make?

odds and ends *pl. n.* miscellaneous items or articles.

odds-on *adj.* **1.** (of a horse, etc.) rated at even money or less to win. **2.** regarded as more or most likely to win, succeed, happen, etc.

ode (əʊd) *n.* **1.** a lyric poem, typically addressed to a particular subject, with lines of varying lengths and complex rhythms. **2.** (formerly) a poem meant to be sung. [C16: via F from LL *ōda*, from Gk *ōidē*, from *aeidein* to sing]

-ode[1] *n. combining form.* denoting resemblance: *nematode.* [from Gk -*ōdēs*, from *eidos* shape]

-ode[2] *n. combining form.* denoting a path or way: *electrode.* [from Gk -*odos*, from *hodos* a way]

Odense (*Danish* 'oːðənsə) *n.* a port in S Denmark, on Fyn Island: cathedral founded by King Canute in the 11th century. Pop.: 173 331 (1987).

Oder ('əʊdə) *n.* a river in central Europe, rising in N Czechoslovakia and flowing north and west, forming part of the border between East Germany and Poland to the Baltic. Length: 913 km (567 miles). Czech and Polish name: **Odra.**

Oder-Neisse Line ('əʊdə'naɪsə) *n.* the present-day boundary between Germany and Poland along the Rivers Oder and Neisse. Established in 1945, it originally separated the Soviet Zone of Germany from the regions of Germany under Polish administration.

Odessa (əʊ'dɛsə; *Russian* a'djɛsə) *n.* a port in the SW Soviet Union, in the S Ukrainian SSR on the Black Sea: the chief Russian grain port in the 19th century; university (1865); industrial centre and one of the largest ports in the Soviet Union. Pop.: 1 141 000 (1987).

odeum ('əʊdɪəm) *n., pl.* **odea** ('əʊdɪə). (esp. in ancient Greece and Rome) a building for musical performances. Also called: **odeon.** [C17: from L, from Gk *ōideion*, from *ōidē* ODE]

Odin ('əʊdɪn) *or* **Othin** *n. Norse myth.* the supreme creator god; the divinity of wisdom, culture, war, and the dead. Germanic counterpart: **Wotan, Woden.**

odious ('əʊdɪəs) *adj.* offensive; repugnant. [C17: from L; see ODIUM] —**'odiousness** *n.*

odium ('əʊdɪəm) *n.* **1.** the dislike accorded to a hated person or thing. **2.** hatred; repugnance. [C17: from L; rel. to *ōdī* I hate, *ōdussasthai* to be angry]

Odoacer (,ɒdə'eɪsə) *or* **Odovacar** (,əʊdə'vɑːkə) *n.* ?434–493 A.D., barbarian ruler of Italy (476–493); assassinated by Theodoric.

odometer (ɒ'dɒmɪtə, əʊ-) *n.* the usual U.S. and Canad. name for **mileometer.** [C18 *hodometer*, from Gk *hodos* way + -METER] —**o'dometry** *n.*

-odont *adj. and n. combining form.* -toothed: *acrodont.* [from Gk *odōn* tooth]

odonto- *or before a vowel* **odont-** *combining form.* indicating a tooth or teeth: *odontology.* [from Gk *odōn* tooth]

odontoglossum (ɒ,dɒntə'glɒsəm) *n.* a tropical American epiphytic orchid having clusters of brightly coloured flowers.

odontology (,ɒdɒn'tɒlədʒɪ) *n.* the branch of science concerned with the anatomy, development, and diseases of teeth. —**odontological** (ɒ,dɒntə'lɒdʒɪk^əl) *adj.* —,**odon-**'**tologist** *n.*

odoriferous (,əʊdə'rɪfərəs) *adj.* having or emitting an odour, esp. a fragrant one. —,**odor**'**iferously** *adv.* —,**odor**'**iferousness** *n.*

odorous ('əʊdərəs) *adj.* having or emitting a characteristic smell or odour. —'**odorously** *adv.* —'**odorousness** *n.*

odour *or U.S.* **odor** ('əʊdə) *n.* **1.** the property of a substance that gives it a characteristic scent or smell. **2.** a pervasive quality about something: *an odour of dishonesty.* **3.** repute or regard (in **in good odour, in bad odour**). **4.** *Arch.* a sweet-smelling fragrance. [C13: from OF *odur,* from L *odor*] —'**odourless** *or U.S.* '**odorless** *adj.*

Odovacar (,əʊdə'vɑːkə) *n.* a variant of **Odoacer.**

Odra ('ɔdra) *n.* the Czech and Polish name for the **Oder.**

Odysseus (ə'diːsɪəs) *n. Greek myth.* one of the foremost of the Greek heroes at the siege of Troy, noted for his courage and ingenuity. His return to his kingdom of Ithaca was fraught with adventures in which he lost all his companions and he was acknowledged by his wife Penelope only after killing her suitors. Roman name: **Ulysses.**

Odyssey ('ɒdɪsɪ) *n.* **1.** a Greek epic poem, attributed to Homer, describing the ten-year homeward wanderings of Odysseus after the fall of Troy. **2.** *(often not cap.)* any long eventful journey. —**Odyssean** (,ɒdɪ'siːən) *adj.*

Oe *symbol for* oersted.

OE *abbrev. for* Old English (language).

OECD *abbrev. for* Organization for Economic Cooperation and Development.

OED *abbrev. for* Oxford English Dictionary.

oedema *or* **edema** (ɪ'diːmə) *n., pl.* **-mata** (-mətə). **1.** *Pathol.* an excessive accumulation of serous fluid in the intercellular spaces of tissue. **2.** *Bot.* an abnormal swelling in a plant caused by parenchyma or an accumulation of water in the tissues. [C16: via NL from Gk *oidēma,* from *oidein* to swell] —**oedematous, edematous** (ɪ'dɛmətəs) *or* **oe'dema,tose, e'dema,tose** *adj.*

Oedipus ('iːdɪpəs) *n. Greek myth.* the son of Laius and Jocasta, the king and queen of Thebes, who killed his father, being unaware of his identity, and unwittingly married his mother, by whom he had four children. When the truth was revealed, he put out his eyes and Jocasta killed herself.

Oedipus complex *n. Psychoanal.* the usually unconscious desire of a child, esp. a male child, to possess sexually the parent of the opposite sex while excluding the parent of the same sex. —'**oedipal** *or* ,**oedi'pean** *adj.*

OEEC *abbrev. for* Organization for European Economic Cooperation. It was superseded by the OECD in 1961.

Oehlenschläger *or* **Öhlenschläger** (*Danish* 'øːlenslɛːgər) *n.* **Adam Gottlob** ('adam 'gɔtlɔp). 1779–1850, Danish romantic poet and dramatist.

oenology *or* **enology** (iː'nɒlədʒɪ) *n.* the study of wine. [C19: from Gk *oinos* wine + -LOGY] —**oenological** *or* **enological** (,iːnə'lɒdʒɪk^əl) *adj.* —**oe'nologist** *or* **e'nologist** *n.*

Oenone (iː'nəʊnɪ) *n. Greek myth.* a nymph of Mount Ida, whose lover Paris left her for Helen.

oenothera (iː'nɒθərə) *n.* any of various hardy biennial or herbaceous perennial plants having yellow flowers. Also called: **evening primrose.** [from Gk *oinothēras,* ?from *onothēras* a plant whose roots smell of wine]

o'er (ɔː, əʊə) *prep., adv.* a poetic contraction of **over.**

oersted ('ɜːstɛd) *n.* the cgs unit of magnetic field strength; the field strength that would cause a unit magnetic pole to experience a force of 1 dyne in free space. It is equivalent to 79.58 amperes per metre. Symbol: Oe [C20: after H. C. *Oersted* (1777–1851), Danish physicist who discovered electromagnetism]

oesophagus *or U.S.* **esophagus** (iː'sɒfəgəs) *n., pl.* **-gi** (-,ɡaɪ). the part of the alimentary canal between the pharynx and the stomach; gullet. [C16: via NL from Gk *oisophagos,* from *oisein,* future infinitive of *pherein* to

carry + *-phagos,* from *phagein* to eat] —**oesophageal** *or U.S.* **esophageal** (iː,sɒfə'dʒiːəl) *adj.*

oestradiol (,iːstrə'daɪɒl, ,ɛstrə-) *or U.S.* **estradiol** *n.* the most potent oestrogenic hormone secreted by the mammalian ovary: synthesized and used to treat oestrogen deficiency and cancer of the breast. [C20: from NL, from OESTRIN + DI-¹ + -OL¹]

oestrin ('iːstrɪn) *n.* an obsolete term for **oestrogen.** [C20: from OESTR(US) + -IN]

oestrogen ('iːstrədʒən, 'ɛstrə-) *or U.S.* **estrogen** *n.* any of several hormones that induce oestrus, stimulate changes in the female reproductive organs, and promote development of female secondary sexual characteristics. [C20: from OESTRUS + -GEN] —**oestrogenic** (,iːstrə'dʒɛnɪk, ,ɛstrə-) *or U.S.* **estrogenic** (,ɛstrə'dʒɛnɪk, ,iːstrə-) *adj.* —,**oestro'genically** *or U.S.* ,**estro'genically** *adv.*

oestrous cycle ('iːstrəs) *n.* a hormonally controlled cycle of activity of the reproductive organs in many female mammals.

oestrus ('iːstrəs, 'ɛstrəs) *or U.S.* **estrus** *n.* a regularly occurring period of sexual receptivity in most female mammals, except humans, during which ovulation occurs and copulation can take place; heat. [C17: from L *oestrus* gadfly, hence frenzy, from Gk *oistros*] —'**oestrous** *or U.S.* '**estrous** *adj.*

oeuvre *French.* (œvrə) *n.* **1.** a work of art, literature, music, etc. **2.** the total output of a writer, painter, etc. [ult. from L *opera,* pl. of *opus* work]

of (ɒv; *unstressed* əv) *prep.* **1.** used with a verbal noun or gerund to link it with a following noun that is either the subject or the object of the verb embedded in the gerund: *the breathing of a fine swimmer* (subject); *the breathing of clean air* (object). **2.** used to indicate possession, origin, or association: *the house of my sister; to die of hunger.* **3.** used after words or phrases expressing quantities: *a pint of milk.* **4.** constituted by, containing, or characterized by: *a family of idiots; a rod of iron; a man of some depth.* **5.** used to indicate separation, as in time or space: *within a mile of the town; within ten minutes of the beginning of the concert.* **6.** used to mark apposition: *the city of Naples; a speech on the subject of archaeology.* **7.** about; concerning: *speak to me of love.* **8.** used in passive constructions to indicate the agent: *he was beloved of all.* **9.** *Inf.* used to indicate a day or part of a period of time when some activity habitually occurs: *I go to the pub of an evening.* **10.** *U.S.* before the hour of: *a quarter of nine.* [OE (as prep. & adv.); rel. to L *ab*]

▷ **Usage.** See at **off.**

OF *abbrev. for* Old French (language).

off (ɒf) *prep.* **1.** used to indicate actions in which contact is absent, as between an object and a surface: *to lift a cup off the table.* **2.** used to indicate the removal of something that is appended to or in association with something else: *to take the tax off potatoes.* **3.** out of alignment with: *we are off course.* **4.** situated near to or leading away from: *just off the High Street.* **5.** not inclined towards: *I've gone off you.* ~*adv.* **6.** *(particle)* so as to deactivate or disengage: *turn off the radio.* **7.** *(particle)* **a.** so as to get rid of: *sleep off a hangover.* **b.** so as to be removed from, esp. as a reduction: *he took ten per cent off.* **8.** spent away from work or other duties: *take the afternoon off.* **9. a.** on a trip, journey, or race: *I saw her off at the station.* **b.** *(particle)* so as to be completely absent, used up, or exhausted: *this stuff kills off all vermin.* **10.** out from the shore or land: *the ship stood off.* **11. a.** out of contact; at a distance: *the ship was 10 miles off.* **b.** out of the present location: *the girl ran off.* **12.** away in the future: *August is less than a week off.* **13.** *(particle)* so as to be no longer taking place: *the match has been rained off.* **14.** *(particle)* removed from contact with something, as clothing from the body: *the girl took all her clothes off.* **15. off and on.** intermittently; from time to time: *he comes here off and on.* **16. off with.** *(interj.)* a command or an exhortation to remove or cut off (something specified): *off with his head; off with that coat.* ~*adj.* **17.** not on; no longer operative: *the off position on the dial.* **18.** *(postpositive)* not taking place; cancelled or postponed: *the meeting is off.* **19.** in a specified condition regarding money, provisions, etc.: *well off; how are you off for bread?* **20.** unsatisfactory or disappointing: *his performance was rather off; an off year for good tennis.* **21.** *(postpositive)* in a condition as specified: *I'd be better off*

without this job. **22.** (*postpositive*) no longer on the menu: *haddock is off.* **23.** (*postpositive*) (of food or drink) having gone bad, sour, etc.: *this milk is off.* ~*n.* **24.** *Cricket.* **a.** the part of the field on that side of the pitch to which the batsman presents his bat when taking strike. **b.** (*in combination*) a fielding position in this part of the field: *mid-off.* **c.** (*as modifier*): *the off stump.* [orig. var. of OF; fully distinguished from it in the 17th cent.]
▷ **Usage.** In educated usage, *off* is not followed by *from* or *of: he stepped off* (not *off of*) *the platform.* Careful writers also avoid using the word in the place of *from: they bought apples from* (rather than *off*) *the man.*

off. *abbrev. for:* **1.** offer. **2.** office. **3.** officer. **4.** official.

Offa ('ɒfə) *n.* died 796 A.D., king of Mercia (757–796), who constructed an earthwork (**Offa's Dyke**) between Wales and Mercia.

offal ('ɒfl) *n.* **1.** the edible internal parts of an animal, such as the heart, liver, and tongue. **2.** dead or decomposing organic matter. **3.** refuse; rubbish. [C14: from OFF + FALL, referring to parts fallen or cut off]

Offaly ('ɒfəlɪ) *n.* an inland county of E central Ireland, in Leinster province: formerly an ancient kingdom, which also included parts of Tipperary, Leix, and Kildare. County town: Tullamore. Pop.: 59 806 (1986). Area: 2000 sq. km (770 sq. miles).

offbeat ('ɒf,biːt) *n.* **1.** *Music.* any of the normally unaccented beats in a bar, such as the second and fourth beats in a bar of four-four time. ~*adj.* **2. a.** unusual, unconventional, or eccentric. **b.** (*as n.*): *he liked the offbeat in fashion.*

off-Broadway *adj.* **1.** designating the kind of experimental, low-budget, or noncommercial productions associated with theatre outside the Broadway area in New York. **2.** (of theatres) not located in Broadway.

off colour *adj.* (**off-colour** *when prenominal*). **1.** *Chiefly Brit.* slightly ill; unwell. **2.** indecent or indelicate; risqué.

offcut ('ɒf,kʌt) *n.* a piece of paper, wood, fabric, etc., remaining after the main pieces have been cut; remnant.

Offenbach[1] (*German* 'ɔfənbax) *n.* a city in S central West Germany, on the River Main in Hesse opposite Frankfurt am Main: leather-goods industry. Pop.: 107 200 (1986).

Offenbach[2] ('ɒfən,bɑːk; *French* ɔfɛnbak) *n.* **Jacques** (ʒak). 1819–80, German-born French composer of many operettas, including *Orpheus in the Underworld* (1858), and of the opera *The Tales of Hoffmann* (1881).

offence *or U.S.* **offense** (ə'fɛns) *n.* **1.** a violation or breach of a law, rule, etc. **2.** any public wrong or crime. **3.** annoyance, displeasure, or resentment. **4. give offence (to).** to cause annoyance or displeasure (to). **5. take offence.** to feel injured, humiliated, or offended. **6.** a source of annoyance, displeasure, or anger. **7.** attack; assault. **8.** *Arch.* injury or harm.

offend (ə'fɛnd) *vb.* **1.** to hurt the feelings, sense of dignity, etc., of (a person, etc.). **2.** (*tr.*) to be disagreeable to; disgust: *the smell offended him.* **3.** (*intr. except in archaic uses*) to break (a law). [C14: via OF *offendre* to strike against, from L *offendere*] —**of'fender** *n.* —**of'fending** *adj.*

offensive (ə'fɛnsɪv) *adj.* **1.** unpleasant or disgusting, as to the senses. **2.** causing anger or annoyance; insulting. **3.** for the purpose of attack rather than defence. ~*n.* **4.** (usually preceded by *the*) an attitude or position of aggression. **5.** an assault, attack, or military initiative, esp. a strategic one. —**of'fensively** *adv.* —**of'fensiveness** *n.*

offer ('ɒfə) *vb.* **1.** to present (something, someone, oneself, etc.) for acceptance or rejection. **2.** (*tr.*) to present as part of a requirement: *she offered English as a second subject.* **3.** (*tr.*) to provide or make accessible: *this stream offers the best fishing.* **4.** (*intr.*) to present itself: *if an opportunity should offer.* **5.** (*tr.*) to show or express willingness or the intention (to do something). **6.** (*tr.*) to put forward (a proposal, opinion, etc.) for consideration. **7.** (*tr.*) to present for sale. **8.** (*tr.*) to propose as payment; bid or tender. **9.** (when *tr.*, often foll. by *up*) to present (a prayer, sacrifice, etc.) as or during an act of worship. **10.** (*tr.*) to show readiness for: *to offer battle.* **11.** (*intr.*) *Arch.* to make a proposal of marriage. ~*n.* **12.** something, such as a proposal or bid, that is offered. **13.** the act of offering or the condition of being offered. **14.** a proposal of marriage. **15. on offer.** for sale at a reduced price. [OE, from L *offerre* to present, from *ob-* to + *ferre* to bring]

offering ('ɒfərɪŋ) *n.* **1.** something that is offered. **2.** a contribution to the funds of a religious organization. **3.** a sacrifice, as of an animal, to a deity.

offertory ('ɒfətərɪ) *n., pl.* **-tories.** *Christianity.* **1.** the oblation of the bread and wine at the Eucharist. **2.** the offerings of the worshippers at this service. **3.** the prayers said or sung while the worshippers' offerings are being brought to the altar during the **offertory procession.** [C14: from Church L *offertōrium* place appointed for offerings, from L *offerre* to OFFER]

offhand (,ɒf'hænd) *adj. also* **offhanded,** *adv.* **1.** without care, thought, attention, or consideration; sometimes, brusque or ungracious: *an offhand manner.* **2.** without preparation or warning; impromptu. —,**off'handedly** *adv.* —,**off'handedness** *n.*

office ('ɒfɪs) *n.* **1. a.** a room or rooms in which business, professional duties, clerical work, etc., are carried out. **b.** (*as modifier*): *office furniture; an office boy.* **2.** (*often pl.*) the building or buildings in which the work of an organization, such as a business, is carried on. **3.** a commercial or professional business: *the architect's office approved the plans.* **4.** the group of persons working in an office: *it was a happy office until she came.* **5.** (*cap. when part of a name*) (in Britain) a department of the national government: *the Home Office.* **6.** (*cap. when part of a name*) (in the U.S.) **a.** a governmental agency, esp. of the Federal government. **b.** a subdivision of such an agency: *Office of Science and Technology.* **7. a.** a position of trust, responsibility, or duty, esp. in a government or organization: *to seek office.* **b.** (*in combination*): *an office-holder.* **8.** duty or function: *the office of an administrator.* **9.** (*often pl.*) a minor task or service: *domestic offices.* **10.** (*often pl.*) an action performed for another, usually a beneficial action: *through his good offices.* **11.** a place where tickets, information, etc., can be obtained: *a ticket office.* **12.** *Christianity.* **a.** (*often pl.*) a ceremony or service, prescribed by ecclesiastical authorities, esp. one for the dead. **b.** *R.C. Church.* the official daily service. **c.** short for **divine office.** **13.** (*pl.*) the parts of a house or estate where work is done, goods are stored, etc. **14.** (*usually pl.*) *Brit., euphemistic.* a lavatory (esp. in **usual offices**). **15. in** (*or* **out of**) **office.** (of a government) in (*or* out of) power. **16. the office.** a hint or signal. [C13: via OF from L *officium* service, duty, from *opus* work, service + *facere* to do]

office block *n.* a large building designed to provide office accommodation.

office boy *n.* a boy employed in an office for running errands and other minor jobs.

officer ('ɒfɪsə) *n.* **1.** a person in the armed services who holds a position of responsibility, authority, and duty. **2.** See **police officer.** **3.** (on a non-naval ship) any person, including the captain and mate, who holds a position of authority and responsibility: *radio officer, engineer officer.* **4.** a person appointed or elected to a position of responsibility or authority in a government, society, etc. **5.** a government official: *a customs officer.* **6.** (in the Order of the British Empire) a member of the grade below commander. ~*vb.* (*tr.*) **7.** to furnish with officers. **8.** to act as an officer over (some section, group, organization, etc.).

officer of the day *n.* a military officer whose duty is to take charge of the security of the unit or camp for a day. Also called: **orderly officer.**

official (ə'fɪʃəl) *adj.* **1.** of or relating to an office, its administration, or its duration. **2.** sanctioned by, recognized by, or derived from authority: *an official statement.* **3.** having a formal ceremonial character: *an official dinner.* ~*n.* **4.** a person who holds a position in an organization, government department, etc., esp. a subordinate position. —**of'ficially** *adv.*

officialdom (ə'fɪʃəldəm) *n.* **1.** the outlook or behaviour of officials, esp. those rigidly adhering to regulations; bureaucracy. **2.** officials or bureaucrats collectively.

officialese (ə,fɪʃə'liːz) *n.* language characteristic of official documents, esp. when verbose or pedantic.

Official Receiver *n.* an officer appointed by the Department of Trade and Industry to receive the income and manage the estate of a bankrupt. See also **receiver** (sense 2).

officiant (ə'fɪʃɪənt) *n.* a person who presides and officiates at a religious ceremony.

officiate (ə'fɪʃɪ,eɪt) vb. (intr.) **1.** to hold the position, responsibility, or function of an official. **2.** to conduct a religious or other ceremony. [C17: from Med. L officiāre, from L officium; see OFFICE] —of,fici'ation n. —of'fici,ator n.

officious (ə'fɪʃəs) adj. **1.** unnecessarily or obtrusively ready to offer advice or services. **2.** Diplomacy. informal or unofficial. [C16: from L officiōsus kindly, from officium service; see OFFICE] —of'ficiously adv. —of'ficiousness n.

offing ('ɒfɪŋ) n. **1.** the part of the sea that can be seen from the shore. **2. in the offing.** likely to occur soon.

offish ('ɒfɪʃ) adj. Inf. aloof or distant in manner. —'offishly adv. —'offishness n.

off key adj. (**off-key** when prenominal), adv. **1.** Music. **a.** not in the correct key. **b.** out of tune. **2.** out of keeping; discordant.

off-licence n. Brit. **1.** a shop or a counter in a pub or hotel where alcoholic drinks are sold for consumption elsewhere. U.S. equivalents: **package store, liquor store.** **2.** a licence permitting such sales.

off limits adj. (**off-limits** when prenominal). **1.** U.S., chiefly mil. not to be entered; out of bounds. ~adv. **2.** in or into an area forbidden by regulations.

off line adj. (**off-line** when prenominal). **1.** of or concerned with a part of a computer system not connected to the central processing unit but controlled by a computer storage device. Cf. **on line.** **2.** disconnected from a computer; switched off.

off-load vb. (tr.) to get rid of (something unpleasant), as by delegation to another.

off-peak adj. of or relating to services as used outside periods of intensive use.

off-piste adj. of or relating to skiing on virgin snow off the regular runs.

off-putting adj. Brit. inf. arousing reluctance or aversion.

off-sales pl. n. Brit. sales of alcoholic drink for consumption off the premises by a pub or an off-licence attached to a pub.

off season adj. (**off-season** when prenominal). **1.** denoting or occurring during a period of little activity in a trade or business. ~n. **2.** such a period. ~adv. **3.** in an off-season period.

offset n. ('ɒf,sɛt). **1.** something that counterbalances or compensates for something else. **2. a.** a printing method in which the impression is made onto an intermediate surface, such as a rubber blanket, which transfers it to the paper. **b.** (modifier) relating to, involving, or printed by offset: offset letterpress. **3.** another name for **setoff. 4.** Bot. a short runner in certain plants that produces roots and shoots at the tip. **5.** a ridge projecting from a range of hills or mountains. **6.** a narrow horizontal or sloping surface formed where a wall is reduced in thickness towards the top. **7.** Surveying. a measurement of distance to a point at right angles to a survey line. ~vb. (,ɒf'sɛt), **-setting, -set. 8.** (tr.) to counterbalance or compensate for. **9.** (tr.) to print (text, etc.) using the offset process. **10.** (tr.) to construct an offset in (a wall). **11.** (intr.) to project or develop as an offset.

offshoot ('ɒf,ʃuːt) n. **1.** a shoot or branch growing from the main stem of a plant. **2.** something that develops or derives from a principal source or origin.

offshore (,ɒf'ʃɔː) adj., adv. **1.** from, away from, or at some distance from the shore. ~adj. **2.** sited or conducted at sea: offshore industries. **3.** based or operating abroad: offshore funds.

offside adj., adv. (,ɒf'saɪd). **1.** Sport. (in football, etc.) in a position illegally ahead of the ball when it is played. Cf. **onside.** ~n. ('ɒf,saɪd). **2.** (usually preceded by the) Chiefly Brit. **a.** the side of a vehicle, etc., nearest the centre of the road. **b.** (as modifier): the offside passenger door.

off-sider n. Austral. & N.Z. a partner or assistant.

offspring ('ɒf,sprɪŋ) n. **1.** the immediate descendant or descendants of a person, animal, etc.; progeny. **2.** a product, outcome, or result.

offstage ('ɒf'steɪdʒ) adj., adv. out of the view of the audience; off the stage.

off-the-peg adj. (of clothing) ready to wear; not produced especially for the person buying.

off-the-wall adj. (**off the wall** when postpositive). Sl. new or unexpected in an unconventional or eccentric

way. [C20: ?from the use of the phrase in handball and squash to describe a shot that is unexpected]

off-white n. **1.** a colour consisting of white with a tinge of grey or yellow. ~adj. **2.** of such a colour: an off-white coat.

oft (ɒft) adv. short for **often** (archaic or poetic except in combinations such as **oft-repeated** and **oft-recurring**). [OE oft; rel. to OHG ofto]

OFT (in Britain) abbrev. for Office of Fair Trading.

Oftel ('ɒf,tɛl) n. (in Britain) acronym for Office of Telecommunications: a Government body that monitors British Telecom.

often ('ɒfən) adv. **1.** frequently or repeatedly; much of the time. Arch. equivalents: 'often,times, 'oft,times. **2. as often as not.** quite frequently. **3. every so often.** at intervals. **4. more often than not.** in more than half the instances. ~adj. **5.** Arch. repeated; frequent. [C14: var. of OFT before vowels and h]

Ogaden (,ɒgɑ'dɛn) n. **the.** a region of SE Ethiopia, bordering on Somalia: consists of a desert plateau, inhabited by Somali nomads; a secessionist movement, supported by Somalia, has existed within the region since the early 1960s and led to bitter fighting between Ethiopia and Somalia (1977–78).

Ogasawara Gunto (,ɒgɑsɑ'wɑːrə 'ɡʌntəʊ) n. transliteration of the Japanese name for the **Bonin Islands.**

Ogbomosho (,ɒɡbə'məʊʃəʊ) n. a city in SW Nigeria: the third largest town in Nigeria; trading centre for an agricultural region. Pop.: 527 400 (1983).

Ogden ('ɒɡdən) n. **C(harles) K(ay).** 1889–1957, English linguist, who, with I. A. Richards, devised Basic English.

ogee ('əʊdʒiː) n. Archit. **1.** Also called: **talon.** a moulding having a cross section in the form of a letter S. **2.** short for **ogee arch.** [C15: prob. var. of OGIVE]

ogee arch n. Archit. a pointed arch having an S-shaped curve on both sides. Sometimes shortened to **ogee.**

Ogen melon ('əʊɡɛn) n. a variety of small melon with sweet pale orange flesh. [C20: after a kibbutz in Israel where it was first developed]

ogham or **ogam** ('ɒɡəm) n. an ancient alphabetical writing system used by the Celts in Britain, consisting of straight lines drawn or carved perpendicular to or at an angle to another long straight line. [C17: from Olrish ogom, from ?, but associated with the name Ogma, legendary inventor of this alphabet]

ogive ('əʊdʒaɪv, əʊ'dʒaɪv) n. **1.** a diagonal rib or groin of a Gothic vault. **2.** another name for **lancet arch.** [C17: from OF, from ?] —o'gival adj.

ogle ('əʊɡ'l) vb. **1.** to look at (someone, esp. a woman) amorously. **2.** (tr.) to stare or gape at. ~n. **3.** a flirtatious or lewd look. [C17: prob. from Low G oegeln, from oegen to look at] —'ogler n.

Oglethorpe ('əʊɡ'l,θɔːp) n. **James Edward.** 1696–1785, English general and colonial administrator; founder of the colony of Georgia (1733).

Ogooué or **Ogowe** (ɒ'ɡəʊweɪ) n. a river in W central Africa, rising in the SW Congo Republic and flowing generally northwest and north through Gabon to the Atlantic. Length: about 970 km (683 miles).

O grade n. (in Scotland). **1. a.** the basic level of the Scottish Certificate of Education. **b.** (as modifier): O-grade history. **2.** a pass in a subject at O grade: she has ten O grades.

ogre ('əʊɡə) n. **1.** (in folklore) a giant, usually given to eating human flesh. **2.** any monstrous or cruel person. [C18: from F, ?from L Orcus, god of the infernal regions] —'ogreish adj. —'ogress fem. n.

Ogun (əʊ'ɡun) n. a state of SW Nigeria, formed in 1976 from part of Western State. Capital: Abeokuta. Pop.: 2 596 000 (1984). Area: 13 600 sq. km (5250 sq. miles).

oh (əʊ) interj. an exclamation expressive of surprise, pain, pleasure, etc.

OHG abbrev. for Old High German.

Ohio (əʊ'haɪəʊ) n. **1.** a state of the central U.S., in the Midwest on Lake Erie: consists of prairies in the west and the Allegheny plateau in the east, the Ohio River forming the S and most of the E borders. Capital: Columbus. Pop.: 10 744 000 (1985 est.). Area: 107 044 sq. km (41 330 sq. miles). Abbrev. (with zip code): **OH 2.** a river in the eastern U.S., formed by the confluence of the Allegheny and Monongahela Rivers at Pittsburgh: flows generally west and southwest to join the Mississippi at Cairo, Illinois, as its chief E tributary. Length: 1570 km (975 miles).

Öhlenschläger *Danish.* ('ø:lənslɛ:γər) *n.* a variant spelling of **Oehlenschläger.**

ohm (əʊm) *n.* the derived SI unit of electric resistance; the resistance between two points on a conductor when a constant potential difference of 1 volt between them produces a current of 1 ampere. Symbol: Ω [C19: after Georg Simon OHM] —'**ohmage** *n.*

Ohm (əʊm) *n.* **Georg Simon** ('ge:ɔrk 'zi:mɔn). 1787–1854, German physicist, who formulated the law named after him.

ohmmeter ('əʊm,mi:tə) *n.* an instrument for measuring electrical resistance.

OHMS (in Britain and the Commonwealth) *abbrev. for* On Her (*or* His) Majesty's Service.

Ohm's law *n.* the principle that the electric current passing through a conductor is directly proportional to the potential difference across it, provided that the temperature remains constant. The constant of proportionality is the resistance of the conductor.

oho (əʊ'həʊ) *interj.* an exclamation expressing surprise, exultation, or derision.

-oid *suffix forming adjectives and associated nouns.* indicating likeness, resemblance, or similarity: *anthropoid.* [from Gk *-oeidēs* resembling, from *eidos* form]

-oidea *suffix forming plural proper nouns.* forming the names of zoological classes or superfamilies: *Canoidea.* [from NL, from L *-oīdēs* -OID]

oil (ɔɪl) *n.* **1.** any of a number of viscous liquids with a smooth sticky feel. They are usually flammable, insoluble in water, soluble in organic solvents, and are obtained from plants and animals, from mineral deposits, and by synthesis. See also **essential oil. 2. a.** another name for **petroleum. b.** (*as modifier*): *an oil engine; an oil rig.* **3. a.** any of a number of substances usually derived from petroleum and used for lubrication. **b.** (*in combination*): *an oilcan.* **c.** (*as modifier*): *an oil pump.* **4.** Also called: **fuel oil.** a fraction of petroleum used as a fuel in domestic heating, marine engines, etc. **5.** *Brit.* **a.** paraffin, esp. when used as a domestic fuel. **b.** (*as modifier*): *an oil lamp.* **6.** any substance of a consistency resembling that of oil: *oil of vitriol.* **7.** the solvent, usually linseed oil, with which pigments are mixed to make artists' paints. **8. a.** (*often pl.*) oil colour or paint. **b.** (*as modifier*): *an oil painting.* **9.** an oil painting. **10.** *Austral. & N.Z. sl.* facts or news. **11. strike oil. a.** to discover petroleum while drilling for it. **b.** *Inf.* to become very rich or successful. ~*vb.* (*tr.*) **12.** to lubricate, smear, polish, etc., with oil or an oily substance. **13. oil one's tongue.** *Inf.* to speak flatteringly or glibly. **14. oil someone's palm.** *Inf.* to bribe someone. **15. oil the wheels.** to make things run smoothly. [C12: from OF *oile*, from L *oleum* (olive) oil, from *olea* olive tree, from Gk *elaia* OLIVE] —'**oiler** *n.* —'**oil-,like** *adj.*

oil cake *n.* stock feed consisting of compressed cubes made from the residue of the crushed seeds of oil-bearing crops such as linseed.

oilcan ('ɔɪl,kæn) *n.* a container with a long nozzle for applying lubricating oil to machinery.

oilcloth ('ɔɪl,klɒθ) *n.* **1.** waterproof material made by treating one side of a cotton fabric with a drying oil or a synthetic resin. **2.** another name for **linoleum.**

oil drum *n.* a metal drum used to contain or transport oil.

oilfield ('ɔɪl,fi:ld) *n.* an area containing reserves of petroleum, esp. one that is already being exploited.

oilfired ('ɔɪl,faɪəd) *adj.* (of central heating, etc.) using oil as fuel.

oilman ('ɔɪlmən) *n., pl.* **-men. 1.** a person who owns or operates oil wells. **2.** a person who sells oil.

oil minister *n.* a government official in charge of representing the interests of an oil-producing country.

oil of vitriol *n.* another name for **sulphuric acid.**

oil paint *n.* paint made of pigment ground in oil, usually linseed oil.

oil painting *n.* **1.** a picture painted with oil paints. **2.** the art or process of painting with oil paints. **3. he's** *or* **she's no oil painting.** *Inf.* he or she is not regarded as good-looking.

oil palm *n.* a tropical African palm tree, the fruits of which yield palm oil.

oil rig *n.* See **rig** (sense 6).

Oil Rivers *pl. n.* the delta of the Niger River in S Nigeria.

oil sand *n.* a sandstone impregnated with hydrocarbons, esp. such deposits in Alberta, Canada.

oil shale *n.* a carbonaceous rock from which oil can be extracted.

oilskin ('ɔɪl,skɪn) *n.* **1. a.** a cotton fabric treated with oil and pigment to make it waterproof. **b.** (*as modifier*): *an oilskin hat.* **2.** (*often pl.*) a protective outer garment of this fabric.

oil slick *n.* a mass of floating oil covering an area of water.

oilstone ('ɔɪl,stəʊn) *n.* a stone with a fine grain lubricated with oil and used for sharpening cutting tools. See also **whetstone.**

oil well *n.* a boring into the earth or sea bed for the extraction of petroleum.

oily ('ɔɪlɪ) *adj.* **oilier, oiliest. 1.** soaked in or smeared with oil or grease. **2.** consisting of, containing, or resembling oil. **3.** flatteringly servile or obsequious. —'**oilily** *adv.* —'**oiliness** *n.*

oink (ɔɪŋk) *interj.* an imitation or representation of the grunt of a pig or the cry of a goose.

ointment ('ɔɪntmənt) *n.* **1.** a fatty or oily medicated preparation applied to the skin to heal or protect. **2.** a similar substance used as a cosmetic. [C14: from OF *oignement*, from L *unguentum* UNGUENT]

Oireachtas ('ɛrəkθəs) *n.* the parliament of the Republic of Ireland. [Irish Gaelic: assembly, from OIrish *airech* nobleman]

Oise (*French* waz) *n.* **1.** a department of N France, in Picardy region. Capital: Beauvais. Pop.: 661 781 (1982). Area: 5887 sq. km (2296 sq. miles). **2.** a river in N France, rising in Belgium, in the Ardennes, and flowing southwest to join the Seine at Conflans. Length: 302 km (188 miles).

Oistrakh ('ɔɪstra:k; *Russian* 'ɔjstrəx) *n.* **1. David** (da'vit). 1908–74, Soviet violinist. **2.** his son, **Igor** ('igərj). born 1931, Soviet violinist.

Oita ('ɔɪtə) *n.* an industrial city in SW Japan, on NE Kyushu: dominated most of Kyushu in the 16th century. Pop.: 390 000 (1985).

Ojibwa (əʊ'dʒɪbwə) *n.* **1.** (*pl.* **-was** *or* **-wa**) a member of a North American Indian people living west of Lake Superior. **2.** the language of this people.

O.K. (,əʊ'keɪ) *Inf.* ~*sentence substitute.* **1.** an expression of approval or agreement. ~*adj.* (*usually postpositive*), *adv.* **2.** in good or satisfactory condition. ~*vb.* **O.K.ing** (,əʊ'keɪɪŋ), **O.K.ed** (,əʊ'keɪd). **3.** (*tr.*) to approve or endorse. ~*n., pl.* **O.K.s. 4.** approval or agreement. ~Also: **okay.** [C19: ?from *o(ll) k(orrect)*, jocular alteration of *all correct*]

Okanagan (,əʊkə'na:gən) *n.* Also (U.S.): ,**Oka'nogan.** a river in North America that flows south from Okanagan Lake in Canada into the Columbia River in NE Washington, U.S. Length: about 483 km (300 miles).

Okanagan Lake *n.* a lake in SW Canada, in S British Columbia: drained by the Okanagan River into the Columbia River. Length: about 111 km (69 miles). Width: from 3.2–6.4 km (2–4 miles).

okapi (əʊ'ka:pɪ) *n., pl.* **-pis** *or* **-pi.** a ruminant mammal of the forests of central Africa, having a reddish-brown coat with horizontal white stripes on the legs, and small horns. [C20: from a Central African word]

Okavango *or* **Okovango** (,əʊkə'va:ŋgəʊ) *n.* a river in SW central Africa, rising in central Angola and flowing southeast, then east as part of the border between Angola and Namibia, then southeast across the Caprivi Strip to form a great marsh known as the **Okavango Basin.** Length: about 1600 km (1000 miles).

okay (,əʊ'keɪ) *sentence substitute, adj., adv., vb., n.* a variant spelling of **O.K.**

Okayama (,əʊkə'ja:mə) *n.* a city in SW Japan, on W Honshu on the Inland Sea. Pop.: 572 000 (1985).

Okeechobee (,əʊkɪ'tʃəʊbɪ) *n.* **Lake.** a lake in S Florida, in the Everglades: second largest freshwater lake wholly within the U.S. Area: 1813 sq. km (700 sq. miles).

Okefenokee Swamp (,əʊkəfɪ'nəʊkɪ) *n.* a swamp in SE Georgia and N Florida: protected flora and fauna. Area: 1554 sq. km (600 sq. miles).

Okeghem ('ɒkə,gɛm; *Dutch* 'ɔkəxəm) *n.* a variant spelling of **Ockeghem.**

Okhotsk ('əʊkɒtsk; *Russian* a'xɔtsk) *n.* **Sea of.** part of the NW Pacific, surrounded by the Kamchatka Peninsula, the Kurile Islands, Sakhalin Island, and the E coast of Siberia. Area: 1 589 840 sq. km (613 838 sq. miles).

Okinawa (,əʊkɪ'na:wə) *n.* a coral island of SW Japan, the largest of the Ryukyu Islands in the N Pacific: scene of heavy fighting in World War II; administered by the U.S.

(1945–72); agricultural. Chief town: Naha City. Pop.: 1 190 000 (1986 est.). Area: 1176 sq. km (454 sq. miles).

Oklahoma (ˌəʊkləˈhəʊmə) n. a state in the S central U.S.: consists of plains in the west, rising to mountains in the southwest and east; important for oil. Capital: Oklahoma City. Pop.: 3 305 000 (1986 est.). Area: 181 185 sq. km (69 956 sq. miles). Abbrevs.: **Okla.** or (with zip code) **OK** —ˌOkla'homan adj., n.

Oklahoma City n. a city in central Oklahoma: the state capital and a major agricultural and industrial centre. Pop.: 445 300 (1986 est.).

Okovango (ˌəʊkəˈvɑːŋgəʊ) n. a variant spelling of **Okavango.**

okra (ˈəʊkrə) n. **1.** an annual plant of the Old World tropics, with yellow-and-red flowers and edible oblong sticky green pods. **2.** the pod of this plant, eaten in soups, stews, etc. See also **gumbo** (sense 1). [C18: of West African origin]

-ol[1] suffix forming nouns. denoting a chemical compound containing a hydroxyl group, esp. alcohols and phenols: ethanol; quinol. [from ALCOHOL]

-ol[2] n. combining form. (not used systematically) a variant of **-ole**[1].

Olaf I (ˈəʊlɑf) or **Olav I** (ˈəʊlɑv) n. known as Olaf Tryggvesson. ?965–?1000 A.D., king of Norway (995–?1000). He began the conversion of Norway to Christianity.

Olaf II or **Olav II** n. Saint. 995–1030 A.D., king of Norway (1015–28), who worked to complete the conversion of Norway to Christianity; deposed by Canute; patron saint of Norway. Feast day: July 29.

Olaf V or **Olav V** n. born 1903, king of Norway from 1957; son of Haakon VII.

Öland (Swedish ˈøːland) n. an island in the Baltic Sea, separated from the mainland of SE Sweden by Kalmar Sound: the second largest Swedish island. Chief town: Borgholm. Pop.: 23 874 (1984 est.). Area: 1347 sq. km (520 sq. miles).

old (əʊld) adj. **1.** having lived or existed for a relatively long time: an old man; an old tradition; an old house. **2. a.** of or relating to advanced years or a long life: old age. **b.** (as collective n.; preceded by the): the old. **c. old and young.** people of all ages. **3.** decrepit or senile. **4.** worn with age or use: old clothes; an old car. **5. a.** (postpositive) having lived or existed for a specified period: a child who is six years old. **b.** (in combination): a six-year-old child. **c.** (as n. in combination): a six-year-old. **6.** (cap. when part of a name or title) earlier or earliest of two or more things with the same name: the old edition; the Old Testament. **7.** (cap. when part of a name) designating the form of a language in which the earliest known records are written: Old English. **8.** (prenominal) familiar through long acquaintance or repetition: an old friend; an old excuse. **9.** practised; hardened: old in cunning. **10.** (prenominal; often preceded by good) cherished; dear: used as a term of affection or familiarity: good old George. **11.** Inf. (with any of several nouns) used as a familiar form of address to a person: old thing; old bean; old stick. **12.** skilled through long experience (esp. in **an old hand**). **13.** out of date; unfashionable. **14.** remote or distant in origin or time of origin: an old culture. **15.** (prenominal) former; previous: my old house was small. **16. a.** (prenominal) established for a relatively long time: an old member. **b.** (in combination): old-established. **17.** sensible, wise, or mature: old beyond one's years. **18.** (intensifier) (esp. in **a high old time, any old thing, any old how,** etc.). **19. good old days.** an earlier period of time regarded as better than the present. **20. little old.** Inf. indicating affection, esp. humorous affection. **21. the old one** (or **gentleman**). Inf. a jocular name for **Satan.** ~n. **22.** an earlier or past time: in days of old. [OE eald] —'oldish adj. —'oldness n.

old age pension n. a former name for **retirement pension.** —**old age pensioner** n.

Old Bailey (ˈbeɪlɪ) n. the Central Criminal Court of England.

Old Bill (bɪl) n. (functioning as pl.; preceded by the) Brit. sl. policemen collectively. [C20: ?from the World War I cartoon of a soldier with a drooping moustache]

old boy n. **1.** (sometimes caps.) Brit. a male ex-pupil of a school. **2.** Inf., chiefly Brit. **a.** a familiar name used to refer to a man. **b.** an old man.

old boy network n. Brit. inf. the appointment to power of former pupils of the same small group of public schools or universities.

Old Castile n. a region of N Spain, on the Bay of Biscay: formerly a province. Spanish name: **Castilla la Vieja.**

Oldcastle (ˈəʊldˌkɑːsˀl) n. Sir **John,** Baron Cobham. ?1378–1417, Lollard leader. In 1411 he led an English army in France but in 1413 he was condemned as a heretic and later hanged and burnt. He is thought to have been a model for Shakespeare's character Falstaff in Henry IV.

Old Contemptibles pl. n. the British expeditionary force to France in 1914. [from the Kaiser's alleged reference to them as a "contemptible little army"]

old country n. the country of origin of an immigrant or an immigrant's ancestors.

Old Dart n. the. Austral. sl. Britain, esp. England. [C19: from ?]

Old Delhi n. See **Delhi.**

olden (ˈəʊldˀn) adj. an archaic or poetic word for **old** (often in **in olden days** and **in olden times**).

Oldenburg[1] (ˈəʊldˀnˌbɜːg; German ˈɔldənburk) n. **1.** a city in NW West Germany, in Lower Saxony: former capital of Oldenburg state. Pop.: 138 900 (1986). **2.** a former state of NW Germany: became part of Lower Saxony in 1946.

Oldenburg[2] (ˈəʊldˀnˌbɜːg) n. **Claes** (klɑːs). born 1929, U.S. pop sculptor and artist, born in Sweden.

Old English n. **1.** Also called: **Anglo-Saxon.** the English language from the time of the earliest Saxon settlements in the fifth century A.D. to about 1100. Abbrev.: **OE. 2.** Printing. a Gothic typeface commonly used in England up to the 18th century.

Old English sheepdog n. a breed of large bobtailed sheepdog with a profuse shaggy coat.

older (ˈəʊldə) adj. **1.** the comparative of **old. 2.** Also (of people): **elder.** of greater age.

old-fashioned adj. **1.** belonging to, characteristic of, or favoured by former times; outdated: old-fashioned ideas. **2.** favouring or adopting the dress, manners, fashions, etc., of a former time. **3.** Scot. & N English dialect. old for one's age: an old-fashioned child. ~n. **4.** a cocktail containing spirit, bitters, fruit, etc.

Oldfield (ˈəʊldˌfiːld) n. **Bruce.** born 1950, British fashion designer.

Old French n. the French language in its earliest forms, from about the 9th century up to about 1400. Abbrev.: **OF.**

old girl n. **1.** (sometimes caps.) Brit. a female ex-pupil of a school. **2.** Inf., chiefly Brit. **a.** a familiar name used to refer to a woman. **b.** an old woman.

Old Glory n. a nickname for the flag of the United States of America.

old gold n. **a.** a dark yellow colour, sometimes with a brownish tinge. **b.** (as adj.): an old-gold carpet.

old guard n. **1.** a group that works for a long-established or old-fashioned cause or principle. **2.** the conservative element in a political party or other group. [C19: after Napoleon's imperial guard]

Oldham (ˈəʊldəm) n. a town in NW England, in Greater Manchester. Pop.: 95 467 (1981).

old hat adj. (postpositive) old-fashioned or trite.

Old High German n. a group of West Germanic dialects that eventually developed into modern German; High German up to about 1200. Abbrev.: **OHG.**

oldie (ˈəʊldɪ) n. Inf. an old joke, song, film, person, etc.

Old Irish n. the Celtic language of Ireland up to about 900 A.D.

old lady n. an informal term for **mother** or **wife.**

Old Latin n. the Latin language before the classical period, up to about 100 B.C.

Old Low German n. the Saxon and Low Franconian dialects of German up to about 1200; the old form of modern Low German and Dutch. Abbrev.: **OLG.**

old maid n. **1.** a woman regarded as unlikely ever to marry; spinster. **2.** Inf. a prim, fastidious, or excessively cautious person. **3.** a card game in which players try to avoid holding the unpaired card at the end of the game. —ˌold-'maidish adj.

old man n. **1.** an informal term for **father** or **husband.** **2.** (sometimes caps.) Inf. a man in command, such as an employer, or captain of a ship. **3.** Sometimes facetious. an affectionate term used in addressing a man. **4.** Also called: **southernwood.** an aromatic shrubby wormwood of S Europe, having drooping yellow flowers.

5. *Christianity.* the unregenerate aspect of human nature.

old man's beard *n.* any of various plants having long trailing parts, esp. traveller's joy and Spanish moss.

old master *n.* **1.** one of the great European painters of the period 1500 to 1800. **2.** a painting by one of these.

old moon *n.* a phase of the moon lying between last quarter and new moon, when it appears as a waning crescent.

Old Nick *n. Inf.* a jocular name for **Satan.**

Old Norse *n.* the language or group of dialects of medieval Scandinavia and Iceland from about 700 to about 1350. Abbrev.: **ON.**

Old Northwest *n.* (in the early U.S.) the land between the Great Lakes, the Mississippi, and the Ohio River. Awarded to the U.S. in 1783, it was organized into the **Northwest Territory** in 1787 and now forms the states of Ohio, Indiana, Illinois, Wisconsin, Michigan, and part of Minnesota.

Old Pretender *n.* See (James Francis Edward) **Stuart.**

Old Prussian *n.* the former language of the non-German Prussians, belonging to the Baltic branch of the Indo-European family: extinct by 1700.

old rose *n.* **a.** a greyish-pink colour. **b.** (*as adj.*): *old-rose gloves.*

Old Saxon *n.* the Saxon dialect of Low German up to about 1200, from which modern Low German is derived. Abbrev.: **OS.**

old school *n.* **1.** *Chiefly Brit.* one's former school. **2.** a group of people favouring traditional ideas or conservative practices.

old school tie *n.* **1.** *Brit.* a distinctive tie that indicates which school the wearer attended. **2.** the attitudes, loyalties, values, etc., associated with British public schools.

Old South *n.* the American South before the Civil War.

oldster ('əʊldstə) *n. Inf.* an older person.

old style *n. Printing.* a type style reviving the characteristics of **old face,** a type style that originated in the 18th century and was characterized by having little contrast between thick and thin strokes.

Old Style *n.* the former method of reckoning dates using the Julian calendar. Cf. **New Style.**

Old Testament *n.* the collection of books comprising the sacred Scriptures of the Hebrews; the first part of the Christian Bible.

old-time *adj.* (*prenominal*) of or relating to a former time; old-fashioned: *old-time dancing.*

old-timer *n.* **1.** a person who has been in a certain place, occupation, etc. for a long time. **2.** *U.S.* an old man.

Olduvai Gorge ('ɒldʊˌvaɪ) *n.* a gorge in N Tanzania, north of the Ngorongoro Crater: fossil evidence of early man and other closely related species, together with artefacts.

old wives' tale *n.* a belief, usually superstitious or erroneous, passed on by word of mouth as a piece of traditional wisdom.

old woman *n.* **1.** an informal term for **mother** or **wife. 2.** a timid, fussy, or cautious person. —,**old-'womanish** *adj.*

old-world *adj.* of or characteristic of former times, esp., in Europe, quaint or traditional.

Old World *n.* that part of the world that was known before the discovery of the Americas; the eastern hemisphere.

Old World monkey *n.* any monkey such as a macaque, baboon, or mandrill, which has nostrils that are close together and a nonprehensile tail.

-ole[1] *or* **-ol** *n. combining form.* **1.** denoting an organic unsaturated compound containing a 5-membered ring: *thiazole.* **2.** denoting an aromatic organic ether: *anisole.* [from L *oleum* oil, from Gk *elaion,* from *elaia* olive]

-ole[2] *suffix of nouns.* indicating something small: *arteriole.* [from L *-olus,* dim. suffix]

oleaceous (ˌəʊlɪ'eɪʃəs) *adj.* of, relating to, or belonging to a family of trees and shrubs which includes the ash, jasmine, privet, lilac, and olive. [C19: via NL from L *olea* OLIVE; see also OIL]

oleaginous (ˌəʊlɪ'ædʒɪnəs) *adj.* **1.** resembling or having the properties of oil. **2.** containing or producing oil. [C17: from L *oleāginus,* from *olea* OLIVE; see also OIL]

oleander (ˌəʊlɪ'ændə) *n.* a poisonous evergreen Mediterranean shrub or tree with fragrant white, pink, or purple flowers. Also called: **rosebay.** [C16: from Med. L, var. of *arodandrum,* ?from L RHODODENDRON]

oleate ('əʊlɪˌeɪt) *n.* any salt or ester of oleic acid.

oleic acid (əʊ'liːɪk) *n.* a colourless oily liquid unsaturated acid occurring, as the glyceride, in almost all natural fats; used in making soaps, ointments, cosmetics, and lubricating oils. Formula: $CH_3(CH_2)_7CH:CH(CH_2)_7COOH.$ Systematic name: **cis-octadec-9-enoic acid.** [C19 *oleic,* from L *oleum* oil + -IC]

olein ('əʊlɪɪn) *n.* another name for **triolein.** [C19: from F *oléine,* from L *oleum* oil + -IN]

oleo- *combining form.* oil: *oleomargarine.* [from L *oleum* OIL]

oleomargarine (ˌəʊlɪəʊˌmɑːdʒə'riːn) *or* **oleomargarin** (ˌəʊlɪəʊ'mɑːdʒərɪn) *n.* another name (esp. U.S.) for **margarine.**

oleoresin (ˌəʊlɪəʊ'rɛzɪn) *n.* **1.** a semisolid mixture of a resin and essential oil, obtained from certain plants. **2.** *Pharmacol.* a liquid preparation of resins and oils, obtained by extraction from plants. —,**oleo'resinous** *adj.*

oleum ('əʊlɪəm) *n., pl.* **olea** ('əʊlɪə) *or* **oleums.** another name for **fuming sulphuric acid.** [from L: oil, referring to its oily consistency]

O level *n. Brit.* **1. a.** the former basic level of the General Certificate of Education. **b.** (*as modifier*): *O-level maths.* **2.** a pass in a particular subject at O level: *he has eight O levels.*

olfaction (ɒl'fækʃən) *n.* **1.** the sense of smell. **2.** the act or function of smelling.

olfactory (ɒl'fæktərɪ, -trɪ) *adj.* **1.** of or relating to the sense of smell. ~*n., pl.* **-ries. 2.** (*usually pl.*) an organ or nerve concerned with the sense of smell. [C17: from L *olfactus,* p.p. of *olfacere,* from *olere* to smell + *facere* to make]

OLG *abbrev. for* Old Low German.

oligarch ('ɒlɪˌgɑːk) *n.* a member of an oligarchy.

oligarchy ('ɒlɪˌgɑːkɪ) *n., pl.* **-chies. 1.** government by a small group of people. **2.** a state or organization so governed. **3.** a small body of individuals ruling such a state. **4.** *Chiefly U.S.* a small clique of private citizens who exert a strong influence on government. [C16: via Med. L from Gk *oligarkhia,* from *oligos* few + -ARCHY] —,**oli'garchic** *or* ,**oli'garchical** *adj.*

oligo- *or before a vowel* **olig-** *combining form.* indicating a few or little: *oligopoly.* [from Gk *oligos* little, few]

Oligocene ('ɒlɪgəʊˌsiːn, ɒ'lɪg-) *adj.* **1.** of, denoting, or formed in the third epoch of the Tertiary period. ~*n.* **2. the.** the Oligocene epoch or rock series. [C19: OLIGO- + -CENE]

oligochaete ('ɒlɪgəʊˌkiːt) *n.* **1.** any freshwater or terrestrial annelid worm having bristles borne singly along the length of the body: includes the earthworms. ~*adj.* **2.** of or relating to this type of worm. [C19: from NL from OLIGO- + Gk *khaitē* long hair]

oligopoly (ˌɒlɪ'gɒpəlɪ) *n., pl.* **-lies.** *Econ.* a market situation in which control over the supply of a commodity is held by a small number of producers. [C20: from OLIGO- + Gk *pōlein* to sell] —,**oli'go'listic** *adj.*

oligotrophic (ˌɒlɪgəʊ'trɒfɪk) *adj.* (of lakes and similar habitats) poor in nutrients and plant life and rich in oxygen. [C20: from OLIGO- + Gk *trophein* to nourish + -IC] —**oligotrophy** (ˌɒlɪ'gɒtrəfɪ) *n.*

Ólimbos ('ɔlɪmbɔs) *n.* transliteration of the Modern Greek name for (Mount) **Olympus** (sense 1).

olio ('əʊlɪˌəʊ) *n., pl.* **olios. 1.** a dish of many different ingredients. **2.** a miscellany or potpourri. [C17: from Sp. *olla* stew, from L: jar]

Oliphant ('ɒlɪfənt) *n.* Sir **Marcus Laurence Elwin.** born 1901, British nuclear physicist, born in Australia.

olivaceous (ˌɒlɪ'veɪʃəs) *adj.* of an olive colour.

olive ('ɒlɪv) *n.* **1.** an evergreen oleaceous tree of the Mediterranean region having white fragrant flowers and edible fruits that are black when ripe. **2.** the fruit of this plant, eaten as a relish and used as a source of olive oil. **3.** the wood of the olive tree, used for ornamental work. **4. a.** a yellow-green colour like that of an unripe olive. (*as adj.*): *an olive coat.* ~*adj.* **5.** of, relating to, or made of the olive tree, its wood, or its fruit. [C13: via OF from L *oliva,* rel. to Gk *elaia* olive tree]

olive branch *n.* **1.** a branch of an olive tree used to symbolize peace. **2.** any offering of peace or conciliation.

olive crown *n.* (esp. in ancient Greece and Rome) a garland of olive leaves awarded as a token of victory.

olive drab *n. U.S.* **1. a.** a dull but fairly strong greyish-olive colour. **b.** (*as adj.*): *an olive-drab jacket.* **2.** cloth or clothes in this colour, esp. the uniform of the U.S. Army.

olive green *n.* **a.** a colour that is greener, stronger, and brighter than olive; deep yellowish-green. **b.** (*as adj.*): *an olive-green coat.*

olive oil *n.* a pale yellow oil pressed from ripe olive fruits and used in cooking, medicines, etc.

Oliver ('ɒlɪvə) *n.* **1.** one of Charlemagne's 12 paladins. See also **Roland. 2. Joseph,** known as *King Oliver.* 1885–1938, U.S. pioneer jazz cornetist.

Olives ('ɒlɪvz) *n.* **Mount of.** a hill to the east of Jerusalem: in New Testament times the village Bethany (Mark 11:11) was on its eastern slope and Gethsemane on its western one.

Olivier (ə'lɪvɪ,eɪ) *n.* **Laurence (Kerr),** Baron Olivier of Brighton. born 1907, English stage, film, and television actor and director.

olivine ('ɒlɪ,viːn, ,ɒlɪ'viːn) *n.* any of a group of hard glassy olive-green minerals consisting of magnesium iron silicate in crystalline form. [C18: from G, after its colour]

olla ('ɒlə) *n.* **1.** a cooking pot. **2.** short for **olla podrida.** [Sp., from L *olla,* var. of *aulla* pot]

olla podrida ('ɒlə pɒ'driːdə) *n.* **1.** a Spanish dish, consisting of a stew with beans, sausages, etc. **2.** an assortment; miscellany. [Sp., lit.: rotten pot]

Olmütz ('ɔlmyts) *n.* the German name for **Olomouc.**

ology ('ɒlədʒɪ) *n., pl.* **-gies.** *Inf.* a science or other branch of knowledge. [C19: abstracted from words such as *theology, biology,* etc.; see -LOGY]

-ology *n. combining form.* See **-logy.**

Olomouc (*Czech* 'ɔlɔmɔuts) *n.* a city in Czechoslovakia, in North Moravia on the Morava River: capital of Moravia until 1640; university (1576). Pop.: 106 000 (1986). German name: **Olmütz.**

oloroso (,ɒlə'rəusəu) *n., pl.* **-sos.** a full-bodied golden-coloured sweet sherry. [Sp.: fragrant]

Olsztyn (*Polish* 'ɔlʃtin) *n.* a town in NE Poland: founded in 1334 by the Teutonic Knights; communications centre. Pop.: 147 000 (1985).

Olympia (ə'lɪmpɪə) *n.* **1.** a plain in Greece, in the NW Peloponnese: in ancient times a major sanctuary of Zeus and site of the original Olympic Games. **2.** a port in W Washington, the state capital, on Puget Sound. Pop.: 27 447 (1980).

Olympiad (ə'lɪmpɪ,æd) *n.* **1.** a staging of the modern Olympic Games. **2.** the four-year period between consecutive celebrations of the Olympic Games; a unit of ancient Greek chronology dating back to 776 B.C. **3.** an international contest in chess, bridge, etc.

Olympian (ə'lɪmpɪən) *adj.* **1.** of or relating to Mount Olympus or to the classical Greek gods. **2.** majestic or godlike in manner or bearing. **3.** of or relating to ancient Olympia, a plain in Greece, or its inhabitants. ~*n.* **4.** a god of Mount Olympus. **5.** an inhabitant of ancient Olympia. **6.** *Chiefly U.S.* a competitor in the Olympic Games.

Olympic (ə'lɪmpɪk) *adj.* **1.** of or relating to the Olympic Games. **2.** of or relating to ancient Olympia.

Olympic Games *n.* (*functioning as sing. or pl.*) **1.** the greatest Panhellenic festival, held every fourth year in honour of Zeus at ancient Olympia, consisting of games and festivities. **2.** Also called: **the Olympics.** the modern revival of these games, consisting of international athletic and sporting contests held every four years in a selected country.

Olympic Mountains *pl. n.* a mountain range in NW Washington: part of the Coast Range. Highest peak: Mount Olympus, 2427 m (7965 ft.).

Olympic Peninsula *n.* a large peninsula of W Washington.

Olympus (əu'lɪmpəs) *n.* **1. Mount.** a mountain in NE Greece, on the border between Thessaly and Macedonia: the highest mountain in Greece, believed in Greek mythology to be the dwelling place of the greater gods. Height: 2911 m (9550 ft.). Modern Greek name: **Ólimbos. 2. Mount.** a mountain in NW Washington: highest peak of the Olympic Mountains. Height: 2427 m (7965 ft.).

Olynthus (əu'lɪnθəs) *n.* an ancient city in N Greece: the centre of Chalcidice.

OM *abbrev. for* Order of Merit (a Brit. title).

-oma *n. combining form.* indicating a tumour: *carcinoma.* [from Gk *-ōma*]

Omagh (əu'maː, 'əumə) *n.* a market town in Northern Ireland, county town of Co. Tyrone. Pop.: 14 627 (1981).

Omaha ('əumə,haː) *n.* a city in E Nebraska, on the Missouri River opposite Council Bluffs, Iowa: the largest city in the state; the country's largest livestock market and meat-packing centre. Pop.: 314 255 (1980).

Oman (əu'maːn) *n.* a sultanate in SE Arabia, on the **Gulf of Oman** and the Arabian Sea: the most powerful state in Arabia in the 19th century, ruling Zanzibar, much of the Persian coast, and part of Pakistan. Language: Arabic. Religion: Muslim. Currency: rial. Capital: Muscat. Pop.: 1 200 000 (1987 est.). Area: about 212 400 sq. km (82 000 sq. miles). Former name (until 1970): **Muscat and Oman.** —**O'mani** *adj., n.*

Omar Khayyám ('əuma: kaɪ'aːm) *n.* ?1050–?1123, Persian poet, mathematician, and astronomer, noted for the *Rubaiyat,* a collection of quatrains, popularized in the West by Edward Fitzgerald's version (1859).

omasum (əu'meɪsəm) *n., pl.* **-sa** (-sə). another name for **psalterium.** [C18: from L: bullock's tripe]

Omayyad *or* **Ommiad** (əu'maɪæd) *n., pl.* **-yads, -yades** (-ə,diːz) *or* **-ads, -ades** (-ə,diːz). **1.** a caliph of the dynasty ruling (661–750 A.D.) from its capital at Damascus. **2.** an emir (756–929 A.D.) or caliph (929–1031 A.D.) of the Omayyad dynasty in Spain.

ombre *or U.S.* **omber** ('ɒmbə) *n.* an 18th-century card game. [C17: from Sp. *hombre* man, referring to the player who attempts to win the stakes]

ombudsman ('ɒmbudzmən) *n., pl.* **-men.** an official who investigates citizens' complaints against the government or its servants. Also called (Brit.): **Parliamentary Commissioner.** [C20: from Swedish: commissioner]

Omdurman (,ɒmdɜː'maːn) *n.* a city in the central Sudan, on the White Nile, opposite Khartoum: the largest town in the Sudan; scene of the **Battle of Omdurman** (1898), in which the Mahdi's successor was defeated by Lord Kitchener's forces. Pop.: 526 287 (1983).

-ome *n. combining form.* denoting a mass or part of a specified kind: *rhizome.* [var. of -OMA]

omega ('əumɪgə) *n.* **1.** the 24th and last letter of the Greek alphabet (Ω, ω). **2.** the ending or last of a series. [C16: from Gk *ō mega* big o]

omega minus *n.* an unstable negatively charged elementary particle, classified as a baryon, that has a mass 3276 times that of the electron.

omelette *or esp. U.S.* **omelet** ('ɒmlɪt) *n.* a savoury or sweet dish of beaten eggs cooked in fat. [C17: from F *omelette,* changed from *alumette,* from *alumelle* sword blade, changed by mistaken division from *la lemelle,* from L (see LAMELLA); apparently from the flat shape of the omelette]

omen ('əumən) *n.* **1.** a phenomenon or occurrence regarded as a sign of future happiness or disaster. **2.** prophetic significance. ~*vb.* **3.** (*tr.*) to portend. [C16: from L]

omentum (əu'mɛntəm) *n., pl.* **-ta** (-tə). *Anat.* a double fold of peritoneum connecting the stomach with other abdominal organs. [C16: from L: membrane, esp. a caul, from ?]

omertà *Italian.* (omer'ta) *n.* a conspiracy of silence.

omicron (əu'maɪkrɒn, 'ɒmɪkrɒn) *n.* the 15th letter in the Greek alphabet (O, o). [from Gk *ō mikron* small o]

ominous ('ɒmɪnəs) *adj.* **1.** foreboding evil. **2.** serving as or having significance as an omen. [C16: from L *ōmi-nōsus,* from OMEN] —**'ominously** *adv.* —**'ominousness** *n.*

omission (əu'mɪʃən) *n.* **1.** something that has been omitted or neglected. **2.** the act of omitting or the state of having been omitted. [C14: from L *omissiō,* from *omittere* to OMIT] —**o'missive** *adj.*

omit (əu'mɪt) *vb.* **omitting, omitted.** (*tr.*) **1.** to neglect to do or include. **2.** to fail (to do something). [C15: from L *omittere,* from *ob-* away + *mittere* to send] —**omissible** (əu'mɪsɪb³l) *adj.* —**o'mitter** *n.*

omni- *combining form.* all or everywhere: *omnipresent.* [from L *omnis* all]

omnibus ('ɒmnɪ,bʌs, -bəs) *n., pl.* **-buses. 1.** a formal word for **bus** (sense 1). **2.** Also called: **omnibus volume.** a collection of works by one author or several works on a similar topic, reprinted in one volume. ~*adj.* **3.** (*prenominal*) of, dealing with, or providing for many different things or cases. [C19: from L, lit.: for all, dative pl. of *omnis* all]

omnicompetent (,ɒmnɪ'kɒmpɪtənt) *adj.* able to judge or deal with all matters. —,**omni'competence** *n.*

omnidirectional (ˌɒmnɪdɪˈrɛkʃənʃl, -daɪ-) *adj.* (of an antenna) capable of transmitting and receiving radio signals equally in any direction of the horizontal plane.

omnifarious (ˌɒmnɪˈfɛərɪəs) *adj.* of many or all varieties or forms. [C17: from LL *omnifārius*, from L *omnis* all + *-farius* doing] —ˌomni'fariously *adv.* —ˌomni'fariousness *n.*

omnific (ɒmˈnɪfɪk) *or* **omnificent** (ɒmˈnɪfɪsənt) *adj. Rare.* creating all things. [C17: via Med. L from L *omni-* + *-ficus*, from *facere* to do] —om'nificence *n.*

omnipotent (ɒmˈnɪpətənt) *adj.* **1.** having very great or unlimited power. ~*n.* **2. the Omnipotent.** an epithet for God. [C14: via OF from L *omnipotens* all-powerful, from OMNI- + *potens*, from *posse* to be able] —om'nipotence *n.* —om'nipotently *adv.*

omnipresent (ˌɒmnɪˈprɛzʔnt) *adj.* (esp. of a deity) present in all places at the same time. —ˌomni'presence *n.*

omniscient (ɒmˈnɪsɪənt) *adj.* **1.** having infinite knowledge or understanding. **2.** having very great or seemingly unlimited knowledge. [C17: from Med. L *omnisciens*, from L OMNI- + *scīre* to know] —om'niscience *n.* —om'nisciently *adv.*

omnium-gatherum (ˈɒmnɪəmˈgæðərəm) *n. Often facetious.* a miscellaneous collection. [C16: from L *omnium* of all, + Latinized form of E *gather*]

omnivorous (ɒmˈnɪvərəs) *adj.* **1.** eating any type of food indiscriminately. **2.** taking in or assimilating everything, esp. with the mind. [C17: from L *omnivorus* all-devouring, from OMNI- + *vorāre* to eat greedily] —'omni,vore *n.* —om'nivorously *adv.* —om'nivorousness *n.*

Omphale (ˈɒmfəˌliː) *n. Greek myth.* a queen of Lydia, whom Hercules was required to serve as a slave to atone for the murder of Iphitus.

omphalos (ˈɒmfəˌlɒs) *n.* **1.** (in the ancient world) a sacred conical object, esp. a stone. The famous omphalos at Delphi was assumed to mark the centre of the earth. **2.** the central point. **3.** *Literary.* another word for **navel**. [Gk: navel]

Omsk (ɒmsk) *n.* a city in the central Soviet Union, at the confluence of the Irtysh and Om Rivers: a major industrial centre, with pipelines from the second Baku oilfield. Pop.: 1 134 000 (1987).

Omuta (ˈəʊmuːˌtɑː) *n.* a city in SW Japan, on W Kyushu on Ariake Bay: coal-mining centre. Pop.: 163 007 (1980).

on (ɒn) *prep.* **1.** in contact or connection with the surface of; at the upper surface of: *an apple on the ground; a mark on the tablecloth.* **2.** attached to: *a puppet on a string.* **3.** carried with: *I've no money on me.* **4.** in the immediate vicinity of; close to or along the side of: *a house on the sea.* **5.** within the time limits of (a day or date): *he arrived on Thursday.* **6.** being performed upon or relayed through the medium of: *what's on the television?* **7.** at the occasion of: *on his retirement.* **8.** used to indicate support, subsistence, contingency, etc.: *he lives on bread.* **9. a.** regularly taking (a drug): *she's on the pill.* **b.** addicted to: *he's on heroin.* **10.** by means of (something considered as a mode of transport) (esp. in **on foot, on horseback,** etc.). **11.** in the process or course of: *on a journey; on strike.* **12.** concerned with or relating to: *a programme on archaeology.* **13.** used to indicate the basis or grounds, as of a statement or action: *I have it on good authority.* **14.** against: used to indicate opposition: *they marched on the city at dawn.* **15.** used to indicate a meeting or encounter: *he crept up on her.* **16.** (used with an adj. preceded by *the*) indicating the manner or way in which an action is carried out: *on the sly; on the cheap.* ~*adv.* (*often used as a particle*) **17.** in the position or state required for the commencement or sustained continuation, as of a mechanical operation: *the radio's been on all night.* **18. a.** attached to, surrounding, or placed in contact with something: *the girl had nothing on.* **b.** taking place: *what's on tonight?* **19.** in a manner indicating continuity, persistence, etc.: *don't keep on about it; the play went on all afternoon.* **20.** in a direction towards something, esp. forwards: *we drove on towards London; march on!* **21. on and off.** intermittently; from time to time. **22. on and on.** without ceasing; continually. ~*adj.* **23.** functioning; operating: *the on position on a radio.* **24.** (*postpositive*) *Inf.* **a.** staked or wagered as a bet: *ten pounds on that horse.* **b.** performing, as on stage, etc.: *I'm on in five minutes.* **c.** definitely taking place: *the match is on for Friday.* **d.** charged to: *the drinks are on me.* **e.** tolerable or practicable, acceptable, etc.: *your plan just isn't on.* **25.** *Cricket.* (of a bowler) bowling. **26. on at.** *Inf.* nagging: *she was always on at her husband.* ~*n.* **27.** *Cricket.* **a.** (*modifier*) relating to or denoting the leg side of a cricket field or pitch: *an on drive.* **b.** (*in combination*) used to designate certain fielding positions on the leg side: *mid-on.* [OE *an, on*]

On (ɒn) *n.* the ancient Egyptian and biblical name for **Heliopolis.**

ON *abbrev. for* Old Norse.

-on *suffix forming nouns.* **1.** indicating a chemical substance: *interferon.* **2.** (in physics) indicating an elementary particle or quantum: *electron; photon.* **3.** (in chemistry) indicating an inert gas: *neon; radon.* [from ION]

onager (ˈɒnədʒə) *n., pl.* **-gri** (-ˌgraɪ) *or* **-gers.** **1.** a Persian variety of the wild ass. **2.** an ancient war engine for hurling stones, etc. [C14: from L: military engine for stone throwing, from L: wild ass, from Gk *onagros*, from *onos* ass + *agros* field]

onanism (ˈəʊnəˌnɪzəm) *n.* **1.** the withdrawal of the penis from the vagina before ejaculation. **2.** masturbation. [C18: after *Onan*, son of Judah; see Genesis 38:9] —'onanist *n., adj.* —ˌonan'istic *adj.*

Onassis (əʊˈnæsɪs) *n.* **Aristotle (Socrates).** 1906–75, Argentinian (formerly Greek) shipowner, born in Turkey. In 1968 he married **Jacqueline,** born 1929, the widow of U.S. President John F. Kennedy.

ONC (in Britain) *abbrev. for* Ordinary National Certificate.

once (wʌns) *adv.* **1.** one time; on one occasion or in one case. **2.** at some past time: *I could speak French once.* **3.** by one step or degree (of relationship): *a cousin once removed.* **4.** (in conditional clauses, negatives, etc.) ever; at all: *if you once forget it.* **5.** multiplied by one. **6. once and away. a.** conclusively. **b.** occasionally. **7. once and for all.** conclusively; for the last time. **8. once in a while.** occasionally; now and then. **9. once or twice** *or* **once and again.** a few times. **10. once upon a time.** used to begin fairy tales and children's stories. ~*conj.* **11.** (*subordinating*) as soon as; if ever: *once you begin, you'll enjoy it.* ~*n.* **12.** one occasion or case: *you may do it, this once.* **13. all at once. a.** suddenly. **b.** simultaneously. **14. at once. a.** immediately. **b.** simultaneously. **15. for once.** this time, if (or but) at no other time. [C12 *ones, anes,* adverbial genitive of *on,* an ONE]

once-over *n. Inf.* **1.** a quick examination or appraisal. **2.** a quick but comprehensive piece of work. **3.** a violent beating or thrashing. ~Esp. in **give (a person** or **thing) the** (or **a**) **once-over.**

oncer (ˈwʌnsə) *n.* **1.** *Brit. sl.* a one-pound note. **2.** *Austral. sl.* a person elected to Parliament who can only expect to serve one term. **3.** *Austral. & N.Z.* something which happens only once. [C20: from ONCE]

oncogene (ˈɒŋkəʊˌdʒiːn) *n.* any of several genes, present in all cells, that when abnormally activated can cause cancer. [C20: from Gk *onkos* mass, tumour + GENE] —oncogenic (ˌɒŋkəʊˈdʒɛnɪk) *adj.*

oncoming (ˈɒnˌkʌmɪŋ) *adj.* **1.** coming nearer in space or time; approaching. ~*n.* **2.** the approach or onset: *the oncoming of winter.*

oncost (ˈɒnˌkɒst) *n. Brit.* **1.** another word for **overhead** (sense 5). **2.** (*sometimes pl.*) another word for **overheads.**

OND (in Britain) *abbrev. for* Ordinary National Diploma.

on dit *French* (ɔ̃ di) *n., pl.* **on dits** (ɔ̃ di). a rumour; piece of gossip. [lit.: it is said; they say]

Ondo (ˈɒndəʊ) *n.* a state of SW Nigeria, on the Bight of Benin: formed in 1976 from part of Western State. Capital: Akure. Pop.: 4 617 200 (1984). Area: 14 400 sq. km (5559 sq. miles).

one (wʌn) *determiner.* **1. a.** single; lone; not two or more. **b.** (*as pron.*): *one is enough for now; one at a time.* **c.** (*in combination*): *one-eyed.* **2. a.** distinct from all others; only; unique: *one girl in a million.* **b.** (*as pron.*): *one of a kind.* **3. a.** a specified (person, item, etc.) as distinct from another or others of its kind: *raise one hand and then the other.* **b.** (*as pron.*): *which one is correct?* **4.** a certain; indefinite, or unspecified (time); some: *one day you'll be sorry.* **5.** *Inf.* an emphatic word for **a** or **an**[1]: *it was one hell of a fight.* **6.** a certain (person): *one Miss Jones was named.* **7. (all) in one.** combined; united. **8. all one. a.** all the same. **b.** of no consequence: *it's all one to me.* **9. at one.** (often foll. by *with*) in a state of agreement or harmony. **10. be made one.** to become married. **11. many a one.** many people. **12. neither one thing nor**

the other. indefinite, undecided, or mixed. **13. never a one.** none. **14. one and all.** everyone, without exception. **15. one by one.** one at a time; individually. **16. one or two.** a few. **17. one way and another.** on balance. **18. one with another.** on average. ~*pron.* **19.** an indefinite person regarded as typical of every person: *one can't say any more than that.* **20.** any indefinite person: used as the subject of a sentence to form an alternative grammatical construction to that of the passive voice: *one can catch fine trout in this stream.* **21.** *Arch.* an unspecified person: *one came to him.* ~*n.* **22.** the smallest natural number and the first cardinal number; unity. **23.** a numeral (1, I, i, etc.) representing this number. **24.** *Inf.* a joke or story (esp. in **the one about**). **25.** something representing, represented by, or consisting of one unit. **26.** Also **one o'clock.** one hour after noon or midnight. **27.** a blow or setback (esp. in **one in the eye for**). **28.** the **Evil one.** Satan. **29. the Holy One** *or* **the One above.** God. ~Related prefixes: **mono-, uni-.** [OE *ān*]

▷ **Usage.** Where the pronoun *one* is repeated, as in *one might think one would be unwise to say that,* he is sometimes substituted: *one might think he would be unwise to say that.* Careful writers avoid *one* like *he,* however, because of possible ambiguity: *he* in this case could refer either to the same person as *one* or to some other person.

-one *suffix forming nouns.* indicating that a chemical compound is a ketone: *acetone.* [arbitrarily from Gk *-ōnē,* fem. patronymic suffix, but ? infl. by *-one* in OZONE]

one another *pron.* the reflexive form of plural pronouns when the action, attribution, etc., is reciprocal: *they kissed one another; knowing one another.* Also: **each other.**

one-armed bandit *n. Inf.* a fruit machine operated by pulling down a lever at one side.

Onega (*Russian* a'njɛgə) *n.* a lake in the NW Soviet Union, mostly in the Karelian ASSR: the second largest lake in Europe and fourth largest in the Soviet Union. Area: 9891 sq. km (3819 sq. miles).

one-horse *adj.* **1.** drawn by or using one horse. **2.** (*prenominal*) *Inf.* small or obscure: *a one-horse town.*

Oneida (əʊ'naɪdə) *n., pl.* **-das** *or* **-da. Lake.** a lake in central New York State: part of the New York State Barge Canal system. Length: about 35 km (22 miles). Greatest width: 9 km (6 miles).

one-liner *n. Inf.* a short joke or witty remark.

one-man *adj.* consisting of or done by or for one man: *a one-man band; a one-man show.*

oneness ('wʌnɪs) *n.* **1.** the state or quality of being one; singleness. **2.** the state of being united; agreement. **3.** uniqueness. **4.** sameness.

one-night stand *n.* **1.** a performance given only once at any one place. **2.** *Inf.* a sexual encounter lasting only one evening or night.

one-off *n. Brit.* **a.** something that is carried out or made only once. **b.** (*as modifier*): *a one-off job.*

one-on-one *adj.* the U.S. term for **one-to-one** (sense 2).

one-parent family *n.* a household consisting of at least one dependent child and the mother or father, the other parent being dead or permanently absent. Also called: **single-parent family.**

one-piece *adj.* (of a garment, esp. a bathing costume) made in one piece.

onerous ('ɒnrəs, 'əʊ-) *adj.* **1.** laborious or oppressive. **2.** *Law.* (of a contract, etc.) having or involving burdens or obligations. [C14: from L *onerōsus* burdensome, from *onus* load] — **'onerously** *adv.* — **'onerousness** *n.*

oneself (wʌn'sɛlf) *pron.* **1. a.** the reflexive form of *one.* **b.** (intensifier): *one doesn't do that oneself.* **2.** (preceded by a copula) one's normal or usual self: *one doesn't feel oneself after such an experience.*

one-sided *adj.* **1.** considering or favouring only one side of a matter, problem, etc. **2.** having all the advantage on one side. **3.** larger or more developed on one side. **4.** having, existing on, or occurring on one side only. — **one-'sidedly** *adv.* — **one-'sidedness** *n.*

one-step *n.* an early 20th-century ballroom dance with long quick steps, the precursor of the foxtrot.

one-stop *adj.* having or providing a range of related services or goods in one place: *a one-stop shop.*

One Thousand Guineas *n.* See **Thousand Guineas.**

one-time *adj.* (prenominal) at some time in the past; former.

one-to-one *adj.* **1.** (of two or more things) corresponding exactly. **2.** denoting a relationship or encounter in which someone is involved with only one other person: *one-to-one tuition.* **3.** *Maths.* involving the pairing of each member of one set with only one member of another set, without remainder.

one-track *adj.* **1.** *Inf.* obsessed with one idea, subject, etc. **2.** having or consisting of a single track.

one-up *adj. Inf.* having an advantage or lead over someone or something. — **one-'upmanship** *n.*

one-way *adj.* **1.** moving or allowing travel in one direction only: *one-way traffic.* **2.** entailing no reciprocal obligation, action, etc.: *a one-way agreement.*

ongoing ('ɒn,gəʊɪŋ) *adj.* **1.** actually in progress: *ongoing projects.* **2.** continually moving forward; developing. **3.** remaining in existence; continuing.

onion ('ʌnjən) *n.* **1.** an alliaceous plant having greenish-white flowers: cultivated for its rounded edible bulb. **2.** the bulb of this plant, consisting of concentric layers of white succulent leaf bases with a pungent odour and taste. **3. know one's onions.** *Brit. sl.* to be fully acquainted with a subject. [C14: via Anglo-Norman from OF *oignon,* from L *unio* onion] — **'oniony** *adj.*

Onions ('ʌnjənz) *n.* **Charles Talbut.** 1873–1965, English lexicographer, an editor of the *Oxford English Dictionary.*

onionskin ('ʌnjən,skɪn) *n.* a glazed translucent paper.

Onitsha (ə'nɪtʃə) *n.* a port in S Nigeria, in Anambra State on the Niger River: industrial centre. Pop.: 268 700 (1973).

on line *adj.* (**on-line** when prenominal). of or concerned with a peripheral device that is directly connected to and controlled by the central processing unit of a computer. Cf. **off line.**

onlooker ('ɒn,lʊkə) *n.* a person who observes without taking part. — **'on,looking** *adj.*

only ('əʊnlɪ) *adj.* (prenominal) **1. the.** being single or very few in number: *the only men left in town were too old to bear arms.* **2.** (of a child) having no siblings. **3.** unique by virtue of being superior to anything else; peerless. **4. one and only. a.** (adj.) incomparable; unique. **b.** (as n.) the object of all one's love: *you are my one and only.* ~*adv.* **5.** without anyone or anything else being included; alone: *you have one choice only; only a genius can do that.* **6.** merely or just: *it's only Henry.* **7.** no more or no greater than: *we met only an hour ago.* **8.** used in conditional clauses introduced by *if* to emphasize the impossibility of the condition ever being fulfilled: *if I had only known, this would never have happened.* **9.** not earlier than; not ... until: *I only found out yesterday.* **10. if only** *or* **if ... only.** an expression used to introduce a wish, esp. one felt to be unrealizable. **11. only if.** never ... except when. **12. only too. a.** (intensifier): *he was only too pleased to help.* **b.** most regrettably (esp. in **only too true**). ~*sentence connector.* **13.** but; however: used to introduce an exception or condition: *play outside; only don't go into the street.* [OE *ānlic,* from *ān* ONE + *-lic* -LY[1]]

▷ **Usage.** In informal English, *only* is often used as a sentence connector: *it would have been possible, only he was not present at the time.* This use is avoided in careful usage, esp. in formal contexts: *it would have been possible had he been present.* In formal speech and writing, *only* is placed directly before the word or words that it modifies: *she could interview only three applicants in the morning.* In all but the most formal contexts, however, it is generally regarded as acceptable to put *only* before the verb: *she could only interview three applicants in the morning.*

o.n.o. *abbrev. for* or near(est) offer.

onomastics (,ɒnə'mæstɪks) *n.* (functioning as sing.) the study of proper names, esp. of their origins. [from Gk *onomastikos,* from *onomazein* to name, from *onoma* NAME]

onomatopoeia (,ɒnə,mætə'piːə) *n.* **1.** the formation of words whose sound is imitative of the sound of the noise or action designated, such as *hiss.* **2.** the use of such words for poetic or rhetorical effect. [C16: via LL from Gk *onoma* name + *poiein* to make] — **,ono,mato'poeic** *or* **onomatopoetic** (,ɒnə,mætəpəʊ'ɛtɪk) *adj.* — **,on-o,mato'poeically** *or* **,ono,matopo'etically** *adv.*

Onondaga (,ɒnən'dɑːgə) *n.* **Lake.** a salt lake in central New York State. Area: about 13 sq. km (5 sq. miles).

onrush ('ɒn,rʌʃ) n. a forceful forward rush or flow.

onset ('ɒn,sɛt) n. **1.** an attack; assault. **2.** a start; beginning.

onshore ('ɒn'ʃɔ:) adj., adv. **1.** towards the land: an onshore gale. **2.** on land; not at sea.

onside (,ɒn'saɪd) adj., adv. Football, etc. (of a player) in a legal position, as when behind the ball or with a required number of opponents between oneself and the opposing team's goal line. Cf. **offside**.

onslaught ('ɒn,slɔ:t) n. a violent attack. [C17: from MDu. aenslag, from aan ON + slag a blow]

Ont. abbrev. for Ontario.

Ontario (ɒn'tɛərɪəʊ) n. **1.** a province of central Canada: lies mostly on the Canadian Shield and contains the fertile plain of the lower Great Lakes and the St Lawrence River, one of the world's leading industrial areas; the second largest and the most populous province. Capital: Toronto. Pop.: 9 100 000 (1985 est.). Area: 891 198 sq. km (344 092 sq. miles). Abbrevs.: **Ont.** or **ON.** **2. Lake.** a lake between the U.S. and Canada, bordering on New York State and Ontario province: the smallest of the Great Lakes; linked with Lake Erie by the Niagara River and Welland Canal; drained by the St Lawrence. Area: 19 684 sq. km (7600 sq. miles). —**On'tarian** or **Ontarioan** (ɒn'tɛərɪ,əʊən) n., adj.

onto or **on to** ('ɒntʊ; unstressed 'ɒntə) prep. **1.** to a position that is on: step onto the train. **2.** having become aware of (something illicit or secret): the police are onto us. **3.** into contact with: get onto the factory.

▷ **Usage.** Onto is generally accepted as a word in its own right. On to is still used, however, where on is considered to be part of the verb: he moved on to the next platform as contrasted with he jumped onto the next platform.

onto- combining form. existence or being: ontogeny; ontology. [from LGk, from ōn (stem ont-) being, present participle of einai to be]

ontogeny (ɒn'tɒdʒənɪ) or **ontogenesis** (,ɒntə'dʒɛnɪsɪs) n. the entire sequence of events involved in the development of an individual organism. Cf. **phylogeny**. —**ontogenic** (,ɒntə'dʒɛnɪk) or **ontogenetic** (,ɒntədʒɪ'nɛtɪk) adj. —,**onto'genically** or **,ontoge'netically** adv.

ontology (ɒn'tɒlədʒɪ) n. **1.** Philosophy. the branch of metaphysics that deals with the nature of being. **2.** Logic. the set of entities presupposed by a theory. —,**onto'logical** adj. —,**onto'logically** adv.

onus ('əʊnəs) n., pl. **onuses.** a responsibility, task, or burden. [C17: L: burden]

onward ('ɒnwəd) adj. **1.** directed or moving forwards, onwards, etc. ~adv. **2.** a variant of **onwards**.

onwards ('ɒnwədz) or **onward** adv. at or towards a point or position ahead, in advance, etc.

onychophoran (,ɒnɪ'kɒfərən) n. a wormlike invertebrate having a segmented body and short unjointed limbs, and breathing by means of tracheae. [from NL Onychophora, from Gk onukh- claw + -PHORE]

-onym n. combining form. indicating a name or word: pseudonym. [from Gk -onumon, from var. of onoma name]

onyx ('ɒnɪks) n. **1.** a variety of chalcedony with alternating black-and-white parallel bands, used as a gemstone. **2.** a variety of calcite used as an ornamental stone; onyx marble. [C13: from L, from Gk: fingernail (so called from its veined appearance)]

oo- or **oö-** combining form. egg or ovum: oosperm. [from Gk ōion EGG]

oocyte ('əʊə,saɪt) n. an immature female germ cell that gives rise to an ovum after two meiotic divisions.

oodles ('u:d³lz) pl. n. Inf. great quantities: oodles of money. [C20: from ?]

oogamy (əʊ'ɒgəmɪ) n. sexual reproduction involving a small motile male gamete and a large much less motile female gamete. —o'ogamous adj.

Ookpik ('u:kpɪk) n. Canad. trademark. a sealskin doll resembling an owl, first made in 1963 by an Inuit and taken abroad as a symbol of Canadian handicrafts. [from Eskimo ukpik a snowy owl]

oolite ('əʊə,laɪt) n. any sedimentary rock, esp. limestone, consisting of tiny spherical concentric grains within a fine matrix. [C18: from F, from NL oolites, lit.: egg stone; prob. a translation of G Rogenstein roe stone] —**oolitic** (,əʊə'lɪtɪk) adj.

oology (əʊ'ɒlədʒɪ) n. the branch of ornithology concerned with the study of birds' eggs. —**oological** (,əʊə'lɒdʒɪk³l) adj. —o'ologist n.

oolong ('u:,lɒŋ) n. a kind of dark tea, grown in China, that is partly fermented before being dried. [C19: from Chinese wu lung, from wu black + lung dragon]

oomiak or **oomiac** ('u:mɪ,æk) n. a variant of **umiak.**

oompah ('u:m,pɑ:) n. a representation of the sound made by a deep brass instrument, esp. in military band music.

oomph (umf) n. Inf. **1.** enthusiasm, vigour, or energy. **2.** sex appeal. [C20: from ?]

oops (ups, u:ps) interj. an exclamation of surprise or of apology when someone drops something or makes a mistake.

Oostende (o:st'ɛndə) n. the Flemish name for **Ostend.**

ooze[1] (u:z) vb. **1.** (intr.) to flow or leak out slowly, as through pores or small holes. **2.** to exude or emit (moisture, etc.). **3.** (tr.) to overflow with: to ooze charm. **4.** (intr.; often foll. by away) to disappear or escape gradually. ~n. **5.** a slow flowing or leaking. **6.** an infusion of vegetable matter, such as oak bark, used in tanning. [OE wōs juice]

ooze[2] (u:z) n. **1.** a soft thin mud found at the bottom of lakes and rivers. **2.** a fine-grained marine deposit consisting of the hard parts of planktonic organisms. **3.** muddy ground, esp. of bogs. [OE wāse mud]

oozy[1] ('u:zɪ) adj. **oozier, ooziest.** moist or dripping.

oozy[2] ('u:zɪ) adj. **oozier, ooziest.** of, resembling, or containing mud; slimy. —'**ooziness** n.

OP abbrev. for Ordo Praedicatorum (the Dominicans). [L: Order of Preachers]

op. abbrev. for: **1.** opera. **2.** operation. **3.** operator. **4.** optical. **5.** opposite. **6.** opus.

o.p. or **O.P.** abbrev. for out of print.

opacity (əʊ'pæsɪtɪ) n., pl. **-ties. 1.** the state or quality of being opaque. **2.** the degree to which something is opaque. **3.** an opaque object or substance. **4.** obscurity of meaning; unintelligibility.

opah ('əʊpə) n. a large soft-finned deep-sea teleost fish having a deep, brilliantly coloured body. Also called: **moonfish, kingfish.** [C18: of West African origin]

opal ('əʊp³l) n. an amorphous form of hydrated silicon dioxide that can be of almost any colour. It is used as a gemstone. [C16: from L opalus, from Gk opallios, from Sansk. upala precious stone] —'**opal,like** adj.

opalescent (,əʊpə'lɛs³nt) adj. having or emitting an iridescence like that of an opal. —,**opa'lesce** vb. (intr.) —,**opal'escence** n.

opaline ('əʊpə,laɪn) adj. **1.** opalescent. ~n. **2.** an opaque or semiopaque whitish glass.

opaque (əʊ'peɪk) adj. **1.** not transmitting light; not transparent or translucent. **2.** not reflecting light; lacking lustre or shine; dull. **3.** hard to understand; unintelligible. **4.** unintelligent; dense. ~n. **5.** Photog. an opaque pigment used to block out areas on a negative. ~vb. **opaquing, opaqued.** (tr.) **6.** to make opaque. **7.** Photog. to block out areas on (a negative), using an opaque. [C15: from L opācus shady] —o'**paquely** adv. —o'**paqueness** n.

op. cit. (in textual annotations) abbrev. for opere citato. [L: in the work cited]

ope ('əʊp) vb., adj. an archaic or poetic word for **open.**

OPEC ('əʊpɛk) n. acronym for Organization of Petroleum-Exporting Countries.

open ('əʊp³n) adj. **1.** not closed or barred. **2.** affording free passage, access, view, etc.; not blocked or obstructed. **3.** not sealed, fastened, or wrapped. **4.** having the interior part accessible: an open drawer. **5.** extended, expanded, or unfolded: an open flower. **6.** ready for business. **7.** able to be obtained; available: the position is no longer open. **8.** unobstructed by buildings, trees, etc.: open countryside. **9.** free to all to join, enter, use, visit, etc.: an open competition. **10.** unengaged or unoccupied: the doctor has an hour open for you to call. **11.** (of a season or period) not restricted for purposes of hunting game or quarry of various kinds. **12.** not decided or finalized: an open question. **13.** ready to entertain new ideas; not biased or prejudiced. **14.** unreserved or candid. **15.** liberal or generous: an open hand. **16.** extended or eager to receive (esp. in **with open arms**). **17.** exposed to view; blatant: open disregard of the law. **18.** liable or susceptible: you will leave yourself open to attack. **19.** (of climate or seasons) free from frost; mild. **20.** free from navigational hazards, such as ice, sunken ships, etc. **21.** having large or numerous spacing or apertures: *open ranks.* **22.** full of small openings or gaps; porous: *an open texture.* **23.** *Music.* **a.** (of a string) not stopped with the finger. **b.** (of a pipe, such as an organ pipe) not closed at either end. **c.** (of a note) played on such a string or pipe. **24.** *Commerce.* in operation; active: *an open account.* **25.** (of a cheque) not crossed. **26.** (of a return ticket) not specifying a date for travel. **27.** *Sport.* (of a goal, court, etc.) unguarded or relatively unprotected. **28.** (of a wound) exposed to the air. **29.** (esp. of the large intestine) free from obstruction. **30.** undefended and of no military significance: *an open city.* **31.** *Phonetics.* **a.** denoting a vowel pronounced with the lips relatively wide apart. **b.** denoting a syllable that does not end in a consonant, as in *pa.* **32.** *Maths.* (of a set) containing points whose neighbourhood consists of other points of the same set. ~*vb.* **33.** to move from a closed or fastened position: *to open a window.* **34.** (when *intr.*, foll. by *on* or *onto*) to render, be, or become accessible or unobstructed: *to open a road; to open a parcel.* **35.** (*intr.*) to come into or appear in view: *the lake opened before us.* **36.** to extend or unfold or cause to extend or unfold: *to open a newspaper.* **37.** to disclose or uncover or be disclosed or uncovered: *to open one's heart.* **38.** to cause (the mind) to become receptive or (of the mind) to become receptive. **39.** to operate or cause to operate: *to open a shop.* **40.** (when *intr.*, sometimes foll. by *out*) to make or become less compact or dense in structure: *to open ranks.* **41.** to set or be set in action; start: *to open the batting.* **42.** (*tr.*) to arrange for (a bank account, etc.), usually by making an initial deposit. **43.** to turn to a specified point in (a book, etc.): *open at page one.* **44.** *Law.* to make the opening statement in (a case before a court of law). **45.** (*intr.*) *Cards.* to bet, bid, or lead first on a hand. ~*n.* **46.** (often after *the*) any wide or unobstructed space or expanse, esp. of land or water. **47.** See **open air. 48.** *Sport.* a competition which all may enter. **49. bring** (or **come**) **into the open.** to make (or become) evident or public. ~See also **open up.** [OE] — **'openable** *adj.* — **'opener** *n.* — **'openly** *adv.* — **'openness** *n.*

open air *n.* **a.** the place or space where the air is unenclosed; the outdoors. **b.** (*as modifier*): *an open-air concert.*

open-and-shut *adj.* easily decided or solved; obvious: *an open-and-shut case.*

opencast mining ('əʊp³n,kɑːst) *n. Brit.* mining by excavating from the surface. Also called (esp. U.S.): **strip mining,** (Austral. and N.Z.) **open cut mining.** [C18: from OPEN + arch. *cast* ditch, cutting]

open chain *n.* a chain of atoms in a molecule that is not joined at its ends into the form of a ring.

open cheque *n.* an uncrossed cheque that can be cashed at the drawee bank.

open circuit *n.* an incomplete electrical circuit in which no current flows.

Open College *n.* **the.** (in Britain) a college of art founded in 1987 for mature students studying foundation courses in arts and crafts by television programmes, written material, and tutorials.

open day *n.* an occasion on which an institution, such as a school, is open for inspection by the public.

open door *n.* **1.** a policy or practice by which a nation grants opportunities for trade to all other nations equally. **2.** free and unrestricted admission. ~*adj.* **open-door. 3.** open to all; accessible.

open-ended *adj.* without definite limits, as of duration or amount: *an open-ended contract.*

open-eyed *adj.* **1.** with the eyes wide open, as in amazement. **2.** watchful; alert.

open-faced *adj.* **1.** having an ingenuous expression. **2.** (of a watch) having no lid or cover other than the glass.

open-handed *adj.* generous. — **,open-'handedly** *adv.* — **,open-'handedness** *n.*

open-hearted *adj.* **1.** kindly and warm. **2.** disclosing intentions and thoughts clearly; candid. — **,open-'heartedness** *n.*

open-hearth furnace *n.* (esp. formerly) a steel-making reverberatory furnace in which pig iron and scrap are contained in a shallow hearth and heated by producer gas.

open-heart surgery *n.* surgical repair of the heart during which the blood circulation is often maintained mechanically.

open house *n.* **1.** a U.S. and Canad. name for **at-home. 2. keep open house.** to be always ready to receive guests.

opening ('əʊpənɪŋ) *n.* **1.** the act of making or becoming open. **2.** a vacant or unobstructed space, esp. one that will serve as a passageway; gap. **3.** *Chiefly U.S.* a tract in a forest in which trees are scattered or absent. **4.** the first part or stage of something. **5. a.** the first performance of something, esp. a theatrical production. **b.** (*as modifier*): *the opening night.* **6.** a specific or formal sequence of moves at the start of any of certain games, esp. chess or draughts. **7.** an opportunity or chance. **8.** *Law.* the preliminary statement made by counsel to the court or jury.

opening batsman *n. Cricket.* one of the two batsmen beginning an innings.

opening time *n. Brit.* the time at which pubs can legally start selling alcoholic drinks.

open letter *n.* a letter, esp. one of protest, addressed to a person but also made public, as through the press.

open market *n.* a market in which prices are determined by supply and demand, there are no barriers to entry, and trading is not restricted to a specific area.

open marriage *n.* a marriage in which the partners are free to pursue their own social and sexual lives.

open-minded *adj.* having a mind receptive to new ideas, arguments, etc.; unprejudiced. — **,open-'mindedness** *n.*

open-mouthed *adj.* **1.** having an open mouth, esp. in surprise. **2.** greedy or ravenous. **3.** clamorous or vociferous.

open-plan *adj.* having no or few dividing walls between areas: *an open-plan office floor.*

open prison *n.* a penal establishment in which the prisoners are trusted to serve their sentences and so do not need to be locked up.

open punctuation *n.* punctuation which has relatively few semicolons, commas, etc. Cf. **close punctuation.**

open-reel *adj.* another term for **reel-to-reel.**

open secret *n.* something that is supposed to be secret but is widely known.

open sesame *n.* a very successful means of achieving a result. [from the magical words used in the *Arabian Nights' Entertainment* to open the robbers' den]

open shop *n.* an establishment in which persons are employed irrespective of their membership of a trade union.

open slather *n.* See **slather.**

Open University *n.* **the.** (in Britain) a university founded in 1969 for mature students studying by television and radio lectures, correspondence courses, local counselling, and summer schools.

open up *vb.* (*adv.*) **1.** (*intr.*) to start firing a gun or guns. **2.** (*intr.*) to speak freely or without restraint. **3.** (*intr.*) *Inf.* (of a motor vehicle) to accelerate. **4.** (*tr.*) to render accessible: *the motorway opened up the remoter areas.* **5.** (*intr.*) to make or become more exciting or lively: *the game opened up after half-time.*

open verdict *n.* a finding by a coroner's jury of death without stating the cause.

openwork ('əʊp³n,wɜːk) *n.* ornamental work, as of metal or embroidery, having a pattern of openings or holes.

opera[1] ('ɒpərə, 'ɒprə) *n.* **1.** an extended dramatic work in which music constitutes a dominating feature. **2.** the branch of music or drama represented by such works. **3.** the score, libretto, etc., of an opera. **4.** a theatre where opera is performed. [C17: via It. from L: work, a work, pl. of *opus* work]

opera[2] ('ɒpərə) *n.* a plural of **opus.**

operable ('ɒpərəb³l, 'ɒprə-) *adj.* **1.** capable of being treated by a surgical operation. **2.** capable of being operated. **3.** capable of being put into practice. — **,oper-a'bility** *n.* — **'operably** *adv.*

opéra bouffe ('ɒprə 'buːf) *n., pl.* **opéras bouffes** ('ɒprə 'buːf). a type of light or satirical opera common in France during the 19th century. [F: comic opera]

opera buffa ('buːfə) *n., pl.* **opera buffas.** comic opera, esp. that originating in Italy during the 18th century. [It.: comic opera]

opéra comique (kɒ'miːk) *n., pl.* **opéras comiques** ('ɒprə kɒ'miːk). a type of opera current in France during the 19th century and characterized by spoken dialogue. [F: comic opera: it originated in satirical parodies of grand opera]

opera glasses *pl. n.* small low-powered binoculars used by audiences in theatres, etc.

opera hat n. a collapsible top hat operated by a spring.

opera house n. a theatre designed for opera.

operand ('ɒpə,rænd) n. a quantity or function upon which a mathematical operation is performed. [C19: from L *operandum* (something) to be worked upon, from *operāri* to work]

operant ('ɒpərənt) adj. **1.** producing effects; operating. ~n. **2.** a person or thing that operates.

opera seria ('sɪərɪə) n., pl. **opera serias.** a type of opera current in 18th-century Italy based on a serious plot, esp. a mythological tale. [It.: serious opera]

operate ('ɒpə,reɪt) vb. **1.** to function or cause to function. **2.** (tr.) to control the functioning of. **3.** to manage, direct, run, or pursue (a business, system, etc.). **4.** (intr.) to perform a surgical operation (upon a person or animal). **5.** (intr.) to produce a desired effect. **6.** (tr.; usually foll. by *on*) to treat or process in a particular or specific way. **7.** (intr.) to conduct military or naval operations. **8.** (intr.) to deal in securities on a stock exchange. [C17: from L *operāri* to work]

operatic (,ɒpə'rætɪk) adj. **1.** of or relating to opera. **2.** histrionic or exaggerated. —,oper'atically adv.

operating cycle n. the time taken by a firm to convert its raw materials into finished goods and thereafter sell them and collect payment.

operating system n. the software controlling a computer.

operating theatre n. a room in which surgical operations are performed.

operation (,ɒpə'reɪʃən) n. **1.** the act, process, or manner of operating. **2.** the state of being in effect, in action, or operative (esp. in **in** or **into operation**). **3.** a process, method, or series of acts, esp. of a practical or mechanical nature. **4.** *Surgery.* any manipulation of the body or one of its organs or parts to repair damage, arrest the progress of a disease, remove foreign matter, etc. **5. a.** a military or naval action, such as a campaign, manoeuvre, etc. **b.** (*cap. and prenominal when part of a name*): *Operation Crossbow.* **6.** *Maths.* any procedure, such as addition, in which one or more numbers or quantities are operated upon according to specific rules. **7.** a commercial or financial transaction.

operational (,ɒpə'reɪʃən³l) adj. **1.** of or relating to an operation. **2.** in working order and ready for use. **3.** *Mil.* capable of, needed in, or actually involved in operations. —,oper'ationally adv.

operationalism (,ɒpə'reɪʃənə,lɪzəm) or **operationism** (,ɒpə'reɪʃə,nɪzəm) n. *Philosophy.* the theory that scientific terms are derived by the experimental operations which determine their applicability. —,oper,ational'istic adj.

operations research n. the analysis of problems in business and industry involving quantitative techniques. Also called: **operational research.**

operative ('ɒpərətɪv) adj. **1.** in force, effect, or operation. **2.** exerting force or influence. **3.** producing a desired effect; significant: *the operative word.* **4.** of or relating to a surgical procedure. ~n. **5.** a worker, esp. one with a special skill. **6.** *U.S.* a private detective. —'operatively adv. —'operativeness or ,opera'tivity n.

operator ('ɒpə,reɪtə) n. **1.** a person who operates a machine, instrument, etc., esp. a telephone switchboard. **2.** a person who owns or operates an industrial or commercial establishment. **3.** a speculator, esp. one who operates on currency or stock markets. **4.** *Inf.* a person who manipulates affairs and other people. **5.** *Maths.* any symbol, term, letter, etc., used to indicate or express a specific operation or process, such as ʃ (the integral operator).

operculum (əʊ'pɜːkjʊləm) n., pl. **-la** (-lə) or **-lums. 1.** *Zool.* **a.** the hard bony flap covering the gill slits in fishes. **b.** the bony plate in certain gastropods covering the opening of the shell when the body is withdrawn. **2.** *Biol. & Bot.* any other covering or lid in various organisms. [C18: via NL from L: lid, from *operīre* to cover] —o'percular or **operculate** (əʊ'pɜːkjʊlɪt, -,leɪt) adj.

operetta (,ɒpə'rɛtə) n. a type of comic or light-hearted opera. [C18: from It.: a small OPERA¹] —,oper'ettist n.

ophicleide ('ɒfɪ,klaɪd) n. *Music.* an obsolete keyed wind instrument of bass pitch. [C19: from F *ophicléide*, from Gk *ophis* snake + *kleis* key]

ophidian (əʊ'fɪdɪən) adj. **1.** snakelike. **2.** of, relating to, or belonging to the suborder of reptiles that comprises the snakes. ~n. **3.** any reptile of this suborder; a snake.

[C19: from NL *Ophidia*, name of suborder, from Gk *ophidion*, from *ophis* snake]

Ophir ('əʊfə) n. *Bible.* a region, probably situated on the SW coast of Arabia on the Red Sea, renowned, esp. in King Solomon's reign, for its gold and precious stones (I Kings 9:28; 10:10).

ophthalmia (ɒf'θælmɪə) n. inflammation of the eye, often including the conjunctiva. [C16: via LL from Gk, from *ophthalmos* eye; see OPTIC]

ophthalmic (ɒf'θælmɪk) adj. of or relating to the eye.

ophthalmic optician n. See **optician.**

ophthalmo- or before a vowel **ophthalm-** combining form. indicating the eye or the eyeball. [from Gk *ophthalmos* EYE]

ophthalmology (,ɒfθæl'mɒlədʒɪ) n. the branch of medicine concerned with the eye and its diseases. —**ophthalmological** (ɒf,θælmə'lɒdʒɪk³l) adj. —,ophthal'mologist n.

ophthalmoscope (ɒf'θælmə,skəʊp) n. an instrument for examining the interior of the eye. —**ophthalmoscopic** (ɒf,θælmə'skɒpɪk) adj.

Ophüls ('ɔːfʊls; German 'ɔphyls) n. **Max** (maks). 1902– 57, German film director, whose films include *Liebelei* (1932), *La Signora di tutti* (1934), *La Ronde* (1950), *Le Plaisir* (1952), and *Lola Montes* (1955).

-opia n. combining form. indicating a visual defect or condition: *myopia*. [from Gk, from *ōps* eye] —**-opic** adj. combining form.

opiate n. ('əʊpɪɪt). **1.** any of various narcotic drugs containing opium. **2.** any other narcotic or sedative drug. **3.** something that soothes, deadens, or induces sleep. ~adj. ('əʊpɪɪt). **4.** containing or consisting of opium. **5.** inducing relaxation; soporific. ~vb. ('əʊpɪ,eɪt). (tr.) Rare. **6.** to treat with an opiate. **7.** to dull or deaden. [C16: from Med. L *opiātus*, from L *opium* OPIUM]

opine (əʊ'paɪn) vb. (when tr., *usually takes a clause as object*) to hold or express an opinion: *he opined that it was a mistake.* [C16: from L *opinārī*]

opinion (ə'pɪnjən) n. **1.** judgment or belief not founded on certainty or proof. **2.** the prevailing or popular feeling or view: *public opinion.* **3.** evaluation, impression, or estimation of the value or worth of a person or thing. **4.** an evaluation or judgment given by an expert: *a medical opinion.* **5.** the advice given by counsel on a case submitted to him for his view on the legal points involved. **6. a matter of opinion.** a point open to question. **7. be of the opinion (that).** to believe (that). [C13: via OF from L *opiniō* belief, from *opinārī* to think]

opinionated (ə'pɪnjə,neɪtɪd) adj. holding obstinately and unreasonably to one's own opinions; dogmatic. —o'pinion,atedly adv. —o'pinion,atedness n.

opinionative (ə'pɪnjənətɪv) adj. Rare. **1.** of or relating to opinion. **2.** another word for **opinionated.** —o'piniona-tively adv. —o'pinionativeness n.

opinion poll n. another term for a **poll** (sense 3).

opium ('əʊpɪəm) n. **1.** an addictive narcotic drug extracted from the seed capsules of the opium poppy: used in medicine as an analgesic and hypnotic. **2.** something having a tranquillizing or stupefying effect. [C14: from L: poppy juice, from Gk *opion*, dim. of *opos*, juice of a plant]

opium poppy n. a poppy of SW Asia, with greyish-green leaves and typically white or reddish flowers: widely cultivated as a source of opium.

Oporto (ə'pɔːtəʊ) n. a port in NW Portugal, near the mouth of the Douro River: the second largest city in Portugal, famous for port wine (begun in 1678). Pop.: 344 500 (1985). Portuguese name: **Pôrto.**

opossum (ə'pɒsəm) n., pl. **-sums** or **-sum. 1.** a thick-furred marsupial, esp. the **common opossum** of North and South America, having an elongated snout and a hairless prehensile tail. **2.** Austral. & N.Z. any of various similar animals, esp. a phalanger. ~Often shortened to **possum.** [C17: from Algonquian *aposoum*]

opp. abbrev. for: **1.** opposed. **2.** opposite.

Oppenheimer ('ɒpən,haɪmə) n. **J(ulius) Robert.** 1904– 67, U.S. nuclear physicist. He was director of the Los Alamos laboratory (1943–45), which produced the first atomic bomb. He opposed the development of the hydrogen bomb (1949) and in 1953 was alleged to be a security risk. He was later exonerated.

opponent (ə'pəʊnənt) n. **1.** a person who opposes another in a contest, battle, etc. **2.** Anat. an opponent muscle. ~adj. **3.** opposite, as in position. **4.** Anat. (of a muscle) bringing two parts into opposition. **5.** opposing; contrary. [C16: from L *oppōnere* to oppose] —**op'ponency** *n.*

opportune ('ɒpə,tjuːn) *adj.* **1.** occurring at a time that is suitable or advantageous. **2.** fit or suitable for a particular purpose or occurrence. [C15: via OF from L *opportūnus*, from *ob-* to + *portus* harbour (orig.: coming to the harbour, obtaining timely protection)] —**'oppor,tunely** *adv.* —**'opportuneness** *n.*

opportunist (,ɒpə'tjuːnɪst) *n.* **1.** a person who adapts his actions, responses, etc., to take advantage of opportunities, circumstances, etc. ~*adj.* **2.** taking advantage of opportunities and circumstances in this way. —,**oppor'tunism** *n.*

opportunistic (,ɒpətjʊ'nɪstɪk) *adj.* **1.** of or characterized by opportunism. **2.** *Med.* (of an infection) caused by any microorganism that is harmless to a healthy person but debilitates a person whose immune system has been weakened.

opportunity (,ɒpə'tjuːnɪtɪ) *n.*, *pl.* **-ties. 1.** a favourable, appropriate, or advantageous combination of circumstances. **2.** a chance or prospect.

opportunity shop *n. Austral. & N.Z.* a shop selling used goods for charitable funds.

opposable (ə'pəʊzəbʰl) *adj.* **1.** capable of being opposed. **2.** Also: **apposable.** (of the thumb of primates, esp. man) capable of being moved into a position facing the other digits so as to be able to touch the ends of each. **3.** capable of being placed opposite something else. —**op,posa'bility** *n.* —**op'posably** *adv.*

oppose (ə'pəʊz) *vb.* **1.** (*tr.*) to fight against, counter, or resist strongly. **2.** (*tr.*) to be hostile or antagonistic to; be against. **3.** (*tr.*) to place or set in opposition; contrast or counterbalance. **4.** (*tr.*) to place opposite or facing. **5.** (*intr.*) to be or act in opposition. [C14: via OF from L *oppōnere*, from *ob-* against + *pōnere* to place] —**op'poser** *n.* —**op'posing** *adj.* —**oppositive** (ə'pɒzɪtɪv) *adj.*

opposite ('ɒpəzɪt, -sɪt) *adj.* **1.** situated or being on the other side or at each side of something between. **2.** facing or going in contrary directions: *opposite ways.* **3.** diametrically different in character, tendency, belief, etc. **4.** *Bot.* **a.** (of leaves) arranged in pairs on either side of the stem. **b.** (of parts of a flower) arranged opposite the middle of another part. **5.** *Maths.* (of a side in a triangle) facing a specified angle. Abbrev.: **opp.** ~*n.* **6.** a person or thing that is opposite; antithesis. ~*prep.* **7.** Also: **opposite to.** facing; corresponding to (something on the other side of a division). **8.** as a co-star with: *she played opposite Olivier.* ~*adv.* **9.** on opposite sides: *she lives opposite.* —**'oppositely** *adv.* —**'oppositeness** *n.*

opposite number *n.* a person holding an equivalent and corresponding position on another side or situation.

opposition (,ɒpə'zɪʃən) *n.* **1.** the act of opposing or the state of being opposed. **2.** hostility, unfriendliness, or antagonism. **3.** a person or group antagonistic or opposite in aims to another. **4. a.** (usually preceded by *the*) a political party or group opposed to the ruling party or government. **b.** (*cap. as part of a name, esp. in Britain and Commonwealth countries*): *Her Majesty's Loyal Opposition.* **c. in opposition.** (of a political party) opposing the government. **5.** a position facing or opposite another. **6.** something that acts as an obstacle to some course or progress. **7.** *Astron.* the position of an outer planet or the moon when it is in line with the earth as seen from the sun and is approximately at its nearest to the earth. **8.** *Astrol.* an exact aspect of 180° between two planets, etc., an orb of 8° being allowed. **9.** *Logic.* the relation between propositions having the same subject and predicate but differing in quality, quantity, or both, as with *all men are wicked; no men are wicked; some men are not wicked.* —,**oppo'sitional** *adj.* —,**oppo'sitionist** *n.* —,**oppo'sitionless** *adj.*

oppress (ə'prɛs) *vb.* (*tr.*) **1.** to subjugate by cruelty, force, etc. **2.** to afflict or torment. **3.** to lie heavy on (the mind, etc.). [C14: via OF from Med. L *oppressāre*, from L *opprimere*, from *ob-* against + *premere* to press] —**op'pressing** *adj.* —**op'pression** *n.* —**op'pressor** *n.*

oppressive (ə'prɛsɪv) *adj.* **1.** cruel, harsh, or tyrannical. **2.** heavy, constricting, or depressing. —**op'pressively** *adv.* —**op'pressiveness** *n.*

opprobrious (ə'prəʊbrɪəs) *adj.* **1.** expressing scorn, disgrace, or contempt. **2.** shameful or infamous. —**op'probriously** *adv.* —**op'probriousness** *n.*

opprobrium (ə'prəʊbrɪəm) *n.* **1.** the state of being abused or scornfully criticized. **2.** reproach or censure. **3.** a cause of disgrace or ignominy. [C17: from L *ob-* against + *probrum* a shameful act]

oppugn (ə'pjuːn) *vb.* (*tr.*) to call into question; dispute. [C15: from L *oppugnāre*, from *ob-* against + *pugnāre* to fight, from *pugnus* clenched fist] —**op'pugner** *n.*

Ops (ɒps) *n.* the Roman goddess of abundance and fertility, wife of Saturn. Greek counterpart: **Rhea.**

opsin ('ɒpsɪn) *n.* the protein that together with retinene makes up the purple visual pigment rhodopsin. [C20: back formation from RHODOPSIN]

-opsis *n. combining form.* indicating a specified appearance or resemblance: *meconopsis.* [from Gk *opsis* sight]

opsit-bank ('ɒpsɪt-) *n. S. African.* a bench for two people, formerly used for courting couples. [from Afrik., from Du.]

opsonin ('ɒpsənɪn) *n.* a constituent of blood serum that renders bacteria more susceptible to ingestion by phagocytes. [C20: from Gk *opsōnion* victuals] —**opsonic** (ɒp'sɒnɪk) *adj.*

opt (ɒpt) *vb.* (when *intr.*, foll. by *for*) to show preference (for) or choose (to do something). See also **opt in, opt out.** [C19: from L *optāre* to choose]

opt. *abbrev. for:* **1.** Grammar. optative. **2.** optical. **3.** optician. **4.** optimum. **5.** optional.

optative ('ɒptətɪv) *adj.* **1.** indicating or expressing choice or wish. **2.** Grammar. denoting a mood of verbs in Greek and Sanskrit expressing a wish. ~*n.* **3.** Grammar. **a.** the optative mood. **b.** a verb in this mood. [C16: via F *optatif*, from LL *optātīvus*, from L *optāre* to desire]

optic ('ɒptɪk) *adj.* **1.** of or relating to the eye or vision. **2.** a less common word for **optical.** ~*n.* **3.** an informal word for **eye**[1]. **4.** *Brit., trademark.* a device attached to an inverted bottle for dispensing measured quantities of liquid. [C16: from Med. L *opticus*, from Gk *optikos*, from *optos* visible; rel. to *ōps* eye]

optical ('ɒptɪkʰl) *adj.* **1.** of, relating to, producing, or involving light. **2.** of or relating to the eye or to the sense of sight; optic. **3.** (esp. of a lens) aiding vision or correcting a visual disorder. —**'optically** *adv.*

optical activity *n.* the ability of substances that are optical isomers to rotate the plane of polarization of a transmitted beam of plane-polarized light.

optical character reader *n.* a computer peripheral device enabling letters, numbers, or other characters usually printed on paper to be optically scanned and input to a storage device, such as magnetic tape. The device uses the process of **optical character recognition.** Abbrev. (for both *reader* and *recognition*): **OCR.**

optical crown *n.* an optical glass of low dispersion and relatively low refractive index.

optical disc *n.* a small computer disc that can store a very large amount of visual data in digital form: used esp. for long-term storage, as of archive material.

optical fibre *n.* a communications cable consisting of a thin glass fibre in a protective sheath. Light transmitted along the fibre may be modulated with vision, sound, or data signals. See also **fibre optics.**

optical flint *n.* an optical glass of high dispersion and high refractive index containing lead oxide, used in the manufacture of lenses, artificial gems, and cut glass.

optical glass *n.* any of several types of clear homogeneous glass of known refractive index used in the construction of lenses, etc.

optical isomerism *n.* isomerism of chemical compounds in which the two isomers differ only in that their molecules are mirror images of each other. —**optical isomer** *n.*

optician (ɒp'tɪʃən) *n.* a general name used to refer to: **a.** an **ophthalmic optician.** one qualified to examine the eyes and prescribe and supply spectacles and contact lenses. **b.** a **dispensing optician.** one who supplies and fits spectacle frames and lenses, but is not qualified to prescribe lenses.

optics ('ɒptɪks) *n.* (*functioning as sing.*) the branch of science concerned with vision and the generation, nature, propagation, and behaviour of electromagnetic light.

optimal ('ɒptɪməl) *adj.* another word for **optimum** (sense 2).

optimism ('ɒptɪ,mɪzəm) *n.* **1.** the tendency to expect the best in all things. **2.** hopefulness; confidence. **3.** the doctrine of the ultimate triumph of good over evil. **4.** the philosophical doctrine that this is the best of all possible worlds. ~Cf. **pessimism**. [C18: from F *optimisme*, from L *optimus* best, sup. of *bonus* good] —'**optimist** *n.* —,**opti'mistic** *adj.* —,**opti'mistically** *adv.*

optimize *or* **-mise** ('ɒptɪ,maɪz) *vb.* **1.** (*tr.*) to take the full advantage of. **2.** (*tr.*) to plan or carry out (an economic activity) with maximum efficiency. **3.** (*intr.*) to be optimistic. **4.** (*tr.*) to write or modify (a computer program) to achieve maximum efficiency. —,**optimi'zation** *or* **-mi'sation** *n.*

optimum ('ɒptɪməm) *n., pl.* **-ma** (-mə) *or* **-mums**. **1.** a condition, degree, amount, or compromise that produces the best possible result. ~*adj.* **2.** most favourable or advantageous; best: *optimum conditions*. [C19: from L: the best (thing), from *optimus* best; see OPTIMISM]

opt *vb.* (*intr., adv.*) to choose to be involved in or part of a scheme, etc.

option ('ɒpʃən) *n.* **1.** the act or an instance of choosing or deciding. **2.** the power or liberty to choose. **3.** an exclusive opportunity, usually for a limited period, to buy something at a future date: *a six-month option on the Canadian rights to this book*. **4.** *Stock Exchange.* the right, purchased from a dealer, to buy or sell shares at a fixed price at some time in the future. **5.** See **local option**. **6.** something chosen; choice. **7. keep** (*or* **leave**) **one's options open**. not to commit oneself. **8. soft option**. an easy alternative. [C17: from L *optiō* free choice, from *optāre* to choose]

optional ('ɒpʃənᵊl) *adj.* possible but not compulsory; left to personal choice. —'**optionally** *adv.*

optometrist (ɒp'tɒmɪtrɪst) *n.* a person who is qualified to examine the eyes and prescribe and supply spectacles and contact lenses. Also called (esp. Brit.): **ophthalmic optician.**

optometry (ɒp'tɒmɪtrɪ) *n.* the science or practice of testing visual acuity and prescribing corrective lenses. —**optometric** (,ɒptə'mɛtrɪk) *adj.*

opt out *vb.* (*intr., adv.; often foll. by of*) to choose not to be involved (in) or part (of).

opulent ('ɒpjʊlənt) *adj.* **1.** having or indicating wealth. **2.** abundant or plentiful. [C17: from L *opulens*, from *opēs* (pl.) wealth] —'**opulence** *or* (*less commonly*) '**opulency** *n.* —'**opulently** *adv.*

opuntia (ɒ'pʌnʃɪə) *n.* a cactus, esp. the prickly pear, having fleshy branched stems and green, red, or yellow flowers. [C17: NL, from L *Opuntia* (*herba*) the Opuntian (plant), from *Opus*, ancient town of Locris, Greece]

opus ('əʊpəs) *n., pl.* **opuses** *or* **opera**. **1.** an artistic composition, esp. a musical work. **2.** (*often cap.*) (usually followed by a number) a musical composition by a particular composer, generally catalogued in order of publication: *Beethoven's opus 61*. Abbrev.: **op**. [C18: from L: a work]

or[1] (ɔː; *unstressed* ə) *conj.* (*coordinating*) **1.** used to join alternatives. **2.** used to join rephrasings of the same thing: *twelve, or a dozen*. **3.** used to join two alternatives when the first is preceded by *either* or *whether*: *either yes or no*. **4. one or two, four or five**, etc. a few. **5.** a poetic word for *either* or *whether*, as the first element in correlatives, with *or* also preceding the second alternative. [C13: contraction of *other*, changed (through infl. of EITHER) from OE *oththe*]

▷ **Usage.** See at **either** and **neither.**

or[2] (ɔː) *adj.* (*usually postpositive*) *Heraldry.* of the metal gold. [C16: via F from L *aurum* gold]

OR *abbrev. for:* **1.** operational research. **2.** *Mil.* other ranks.

-or[1] *suffix forming nouns from verbs.* a person or thing that does what is expressed by the verb: *actor; conductor; generator; sailor*. [via OF *-eur, -eor*, from L *-or* or *-ātor*]

-or[2] *suffix forming nouns.* **1.** indicating state, condition, or activity: *terror; error*. **2.** the U.S. spelling of **-our.**

ora ('ɔːrə) *n.* the plural of **os**[2].

orache *or esp. U.S.* **orach** ('ɒrɪtʃ) *n.* any of several herbaceous plants or small shrubs of the goosefoot family, esp. **garden orache**, which is cultivated as a vegetable. They have typically greyish-green lobed leaves and inconspicuous flowers. [C15: from OF *arache*, from L *atriplex*, from Gk *atraphaxus*, from ?]

oracle ('ɒrəkᵊl) *n.* **1.** a prophecy revealed through the medium of a priest or priestess at the shrine of a god. **2.** a shrine at which an oracular god is consulted. **3.** an agency through which a prophecy is transmitted. **4.** any

person or thing believed to indicate future action with infallible authority. [C14: via OF from L *ōrāculum*, from *ōrāre* to request]

Oracle ('ɒrəkᵊl) *n. Trademark. acronym for* Optional Reception of Announcements by Coded Line Electronics: the teletext service of Independent Television.

oracular (ɒ'rækjʊlə) *adj.* **1.** of or relating to an oracle. **2.** wise and prophetic. **3.** mysterious or ambiguous. —o'**racularly** *adv.*

oracy ('ɔːrəsɪ) *n.* the capacity to express oneself in and understand speech. [C20: from L *or-, os* mouth, by analogy with *literacy*]

Oradea (*Romanian* o'radea) *n.* an industrial city in NW Romania, in Transylvania: ceded by Hungary (1919). Pop.: 208 507 (1985). German name: **Grosswardein**. Hungarian name: **Nagyvárad.**

oral ('ɔːrəl, 'ɒrəl) *adj.* **1.** spoken or verbal. **2.** relating to, affecting, or for use in the mouth: *an oral thermometer*. **3.** denoting a drug to be taken by mouth: *an oral contraceptive*. **4.** of, relating to, or using spoken words. **5.** *Psychoanal.* relating to a stage of psychosexual development during which the child's interest is concentrated on the mouth. ~*n.* **6.** an examination in which the questions and answers are spoken rather than written. [C17: from LL *ōrālis*, from L *ōs* face] —'**orally** *adv.*

oral history *n.* the memories of living people about events or social conditions in their earlier lives taped and preserved as historical evidence.

oral hygienist *n.* an assistant to a dentist who instructs patients in cleaning the teeth and periodontal care. Also called: **dental hygienist.**— **oral hygiene** *n.*

oral society *n.* a society that has not developed literacy.

Oran (ə'ræn, ə'rɑːn; *French* ɔrɑ̃) *n.* a port in NW Algeria: the second largest city in the country; scene of the destruction by the British of most of the French fleet in the harbour in 1940 to prevent its capture by the Germans. Pop.: 500 000 (1987).

orange ('ɒrɪndʒ) *n.* **1.** any of several citrus trees, esp. **sweet orange** and the Seville orange, cultivated in warm regions for their round edible fruit. **2. a.** the fruit of any of these trees, having a yellowish-red bitter rind and segmented juicy flesh. **b.** (*as modifier*): *orange peel*. **3.** the hard wood of any of these trees. **4.** any of a group of colours, such as that of the skin of an orange, that lie between red and yellow in the visible spectrum. **5.** a dye or pigment producing these colours. **6.** orange cloth or clothing: *dressed in orange*. **7.** any of several trees or herbaceous plants that resemble the orange, such as mock orange. ~*adj.* **8.** of the colour orange. [C14: via OF *auranja*, from Ar. *nāranj*, from Persian, from Sansk. *nāranga*]

Orange[1] *n.* **1.** ('ɒrɪndʒ) a river in S Africa, rising in NE Lesotho and flowing generally west across the South African plateau to the Atlantic: the longest river in South Africa. Length: 2093 km (1300 miles). **2.** (*French* ɔrɑ̃ʒ). a town in SE France: a small principality in the Middle Ages, the descendants of which formed the House of Orange. Pop.: 27 502 (1982). Ancient name: **Arausio** (ə'rausɪəʊ).

Orange[2] ('ɒrɪndʒ) *n.* **1.** a princely family of Europe. Its possessions, originally centred in S France, passed in 1544 to the count of Nassau, who became William I of Orange and helped to found the United Provinces of the Netherlands. Since 1815 it has been the name of the reigning house of the Netherlands. **2.** (*modifier*) of or relating to the Orangemen. **3.** (*modifier*) of or relating to the royal dynasty of Orange.

orangeade (,ɒrɪndʒ'eɪd) *n.* an effervescent or still orange-flavoured drink.

orange blossom *n.* the flowers of the orange tree, traditionally worn by brides.

Orange Free State *n.* a province of central South Africa, between the Orange and Vaal rivers: settled by Boers in 1836 after the Great Trek; annexed by Britain in 1848; became a province of South Africa in 1910; economy based on agriculture and mineral resources (esp. gold and uranium). Capital: Bloemfontein. Pop.: 1 863 327 (1987). Area: 29 152 sq. km (49 866 sq. miles).

Orangeman ('ɒrɪndʒmən) *n., pl.* **-men**. a member of a society founded as a secret order in Ireland (1795) to uphold Protestantism. [C18: after William, prince of *Orange*, later William III]

Orangeman's Day n. the 12th of July, celebrated by Protestants in Northern Ireland and elsewhere, to commemorate the anniversary of the Battle of the Boyne (1690).

orange pekoe n. a superior grade of black tea growing in India and Sri Lanka.

orangery ('ɒrɪndʒərɪ, -dʒrɪ) n., pl. **-eries.** a building, such as a greenhouse, in which orange trees are grown.

orange stick n. a small stick used to clean the fingernails and cuticles.

orangewood ('ɒrɪndʒ,wud) n. **a.** the hard fine-grained yellowish wood of the orange tree. **b.** (as modifier): an orangewood table.

orang-utan (ɔː,ræŋuː'tæn, ,ɔːræŋ'uːtæn) or **orang-outang** (ɔː,ræŋuː'tæŋ, ,ɔːræŋ'uːtæŋ) n. a large anthropoid ape of the forests of Sumatra and Borneo, with shaggy reddish-brown hair and strong arms. Sometimes shortened to **orang.** [C17: from Malay orang hutan, from ōrang man + hūtan forest]

orate (ɔː'reɪt) vb. (intr.) **1.** to make or give an oration. **2.** to speak pompously and lengthily.

oration (ɔː'reɪʃən) n. **1.** a formal public declaration or speech. **2.** any rhetorical, lengthy, or pompous speech. [C14: from L ōrātiō speech, harangue, from ōrāre to plead, pray]

orator ('ɒrətə) n. **1.** a public speaker, esp. one versed in rhetoric. **2.** a person given to lengthy or pompous speeches. **3.** Obs. the plaintiff in a cause of action in chancery.

oratorio (,ɒrə'tɔːrɪəu) n., pl. **-rios.** a dramatic but unstaged musical composition for soloists, chorus, and orchestra, based on a religious theme. [C18: from It., lit.: ORATORY[2], referring to the Church of the Oratory at Rome where musical services were held]

oratory[1] ('ɒrətərɪ, -trɪ) n. **1.** the art of public speaking. **2.** rhetorical skill or style. [C16: from L (ars) ōrātōria (the art of) public speaking] —,ora'torical adj. —,ora'torically adv.

oratory[2] ('ɒrətərɪ, -trɪ) n., pl. **-ries.** a small room or secluded place, set apart for private prayer. [C14: from Anglo-Norman, from Church L ōrātōrium place of prayer, from ōrāre to plead, pray]

orb (ɔːb) n. **1.** (in regalia) an ornamental sphere surmounted by a cross. **2.** a sphere; globe. **3.** Poetic. another word for eye[1]. **4.** Obs. or poetic. **a.** a celestial body, esp. the earth or sun. **b.** the orbit of a celestial body. ~vb. **5.** to make or become circular or spherical. **6.** (tr.) an archaic word for encircle. [C16: from L orbis circle, disc]

orbicular (ɔː'bɪkjulə), **orbiculate,** or **orbiculated** adj. **1.** circular or spherical. **2.** (of a leaf or similar flat part) circular or nearly circular. —**orbicularity** (ɔː,bɪkju'lærɪtɪ) n. —**or'bicularly** adv.

orbit ('ɔːbɪt) n. **1.** Astron. the curved path followed by a planet, satellite, etc., in its motion around another celestial body. **2.** a range or field of action or influence; sphere. **3.** the bony cavity containing the eyeball; eye socket. **4.** Zool. **a.** the skin surrounding the eye of a bird. **b.** the hollow in which lies the eye or eyestalk of an insect. **5.** Physics. the path of an electron around the nucleus of an atom. **6. go into orbit.** Inf. to reach an extreme and often uncontrolled state: when he realized the price he nearly went into orbit. ~vb. **7.** to move around (a body) in a curved path. **8.** (tr.) to send (a satellite, spacecraft, etc.) into orbit. **9.** (intr.) to move in or as if in an orbit. [C16: from L orbita course, from orbis circle]— '**orbitally** adv.

orbital ('ɔːbɪtəl) adj. **1.** of or denoting an orbit. **2.** n. the region around an atomic nucleus, or around two nuclei in a molecule, within which an electron moves.

orbital velocity n. the velocity required by a spacecraft to enter and maintain a given orbit.

orc (ɔːk) n. **1.** any of various whales, such as the killer and grampus. **2.** a mythical monster. [C16: via L orca, ?from Gk orux whale]

Orcadian (ɔː'keɪdɪən) n. **1.** a native or inhabitant of the Orkneys. ~adj. **2.** of or relating to the Orkneys. [from L Orcades the Orkney Islands]

orchard ('ɔːtʃəd) n. **1.** an area of land devoted to the cultivation of fruit trees. **2.** a collection of fruit trees especially cultivated. [OE orceard, ortigeard, from ort-, from L hortus garden + geard YARD[2]]

orchestra ('ɔːkɪstrə) n. **1.** a large group of musicians, esp. one whose members play a variety of different instruments. **2.** a group of musicians, each playing the same

type of instrument. **3.** Also called: **orchestra pit.** the space reserved for musicians in a theatre, immediately in front of or under the stage. **4.** Chiefly U.S. & Canad. the stalls in a theatre. **5.** (in ancient Greek theatre) the semicircular space in front of the stage. [C17: via L from Gk: the space in the theatre for the chorus, from orkheisthai to dance] —**orchestral** (ɔː'kɛstrəl) adj. —**or'chestrally** adv.

orchestrate ('ɔːkɪ,streɪt) vb. (tr.) **1.** to score or arrange (a piece of music) for orchestra. **2.** to arrange, organize, or build up for special or maximum effect. —**,orches'tration** n. —'**orches,trator** n.

orchid ('ɔːkɪd) n. a terrestrial or epiphytic plant having flowers of unusual shapes and beautiful colours, usually with one petal larger than the other two. The flowers are specialized for pollination by certain insects. [C19: from NL Orchideae; see ORCHIS]

orchil ('ɔːkɪl, -tʃɪl) or **archil** n. **1.** a purplish dye obtained by treating various lichens with aqueous ammonia. **2.** the lichens yielding this dye. [C15: from OF orcheil, from ?]

orchis ('ɔːkɪs) n. **1.** a N temperate terrestrial orchid having fleshy tubers and spikes of typically pink flowers. **2.** any of various temperate or tropical orchids such as the fringed orchis. [C16: via L from Gk orkhis testicle; so called from the shape of its roots]

OR circuit or **gate** (ɔː) n. Computers. a logic circuit having two or more input wires and one output wire that gives a high-voltage output signal if one or more input signals are at a high voltage: used extensively as a basic circuit in computers. [C20: from its similarity to the function of or in logical constructions]

Orcus ('ɔːkəs) n. another name for **Dis** (sense 1).

Orczy ('ɔːtsɪ) n. Baroness **Emmuska** ('ɛmuʃkə). 1865–1947, British novelist, born in Hungary; author of The Scarlet Pimpernel (1905).

Ord (ɔːd) n. a river in NE Western Australia, rising on the Kimberley Plateau and flowing generally north to the Timor Sea: subject of a major irrigation scheme. Length: about 500 km (300 miles).

ord. abbrev. for: **1.** order. **2.** ordinal. **3.** ordinance. **4.** ordinary.

ordain (ɔː'deɪn) vb. (tr.) **1.** to consecrate (someone) as a priest; confer holy orders upon. **2.** (may take a clause as object) to decree, appoint, or predestine irrevocably. **3.** (may take a clause as object) to order, establish, or enact with authority. [C13: from Anglo-Norman ordeiner, from LL ordināre, from L ordo ORDER] —**or'dainer** n. —**or'dainment** n.

ordeal (ɔː'diːl) n. **1.** a severe or trying experience. **2.** History. a method of trial in which the innocence of an accused person was determined by subjecting him to physical danger, esp. by fire or water. [OE ordāl, ordēl verdict]

order ('ɔːdə) n. **1.** a state in which all components or elements are arranged logically, comprehensibly, or naturally. **2.** an arrangement or disposition of things in succession; sequence: alphabetical order. **3.** an established or customary method or state, esp. of society. **4.** a peaceful or harmonious condition of society: order reigned in the streets. **5.** (often pl.) a class, rank, or hierarchy: the lower orders. **6.** Biol. any of the taxonomic groups into which a class is divided and which contains one or more families. **7.** an instruction that must be obeyed; command. **8. a.** a commission or instruction to produce or supply something in return for payment. **b.** the commodity produced or supplied. **c.** (as modifier): order form. **9.** a procedure followed by an assembly, meeting, etc. **10.** (cap. when part of a name) a body of people united in a particular aim or purpose. **11.** (usually cap.) Also called: **religious order.** a group of persons who bind themselves by vows in order to devote themselves to the pursuit of religious aims. **12.** (often pl.) another name for **holy orders, major orders,** or **minor orders. 13.** History. a society of knights constituted as a fraternity, such as the Knights Templars. **14. a.** a group of people holding a specific honour for service or merit, conferred on them by a sovereign or state. **b.** the insignia of such a group. **15. a.** any of the five major classical styles of architecture classified by the style of columns and entablatures used. **b.** any style of architecture. **16.** Christianity. **a.** the sacrament by which bishops, priests, etc., have their offices conferred upon them. **b.** any of the degrees into which the ministry is divided. **c.** the office of an ordained Christian minister. **17.** *Maths.* **a.** the number of times a function must be differentiated to obtain a given derivative. **b.** the order of the highest derivative in a differential equation. **c.** the number of rows or columns in a determinant or square matrix. **d.** the number of members of a finite group. **18.** *Mil.* (often preceded by *the*) the dress, equipment, or formation directed for a particular purpose or undertaking: *battle order.* **19. a tall order.** something difficult, demanding, or exacting. **20. in order. a.** in sequence. **b.** properly arranged. **c.** appropriate or fitting. **21. in order that.** (*conj.*) with the purpose that; so that. **22. in order to.** (*prep.*; foll. by an infinitive) so that it is possible to: *to eat in order to live.* **23. keep order.** to maintain or enforce order. **24. of** or **in the order of.** having an approximately specified size or quantity. **25. on order.** having been ordered but not having been delivered. **26. out of order. a.** not in sequence. **b.** not working. **c.** not following the rules or customary procedure. **27. to order. a.** according to a buyer's specifications. **b.** on request or demand. ~*vb.* **28.** (*tr.*) to give a command to (a person or animal to do or be something). **29.** to request (something) to be supplied or made, esp. in return for payment. **30.** (*tr.*) to instruct or command to move, go, etc. (to a specified place): *they ordered her into the house.* **31.** (*tr.; may take a clause as object*) to authorize; prescribe: *the doctor ordered a strict diet.* **32.** (*tr.*) to arrange, regulate, or dispose (articles, etc.) in their proper places. **33.** (*tr.*) (of fate) to will; ordain. ~*interj.* **34.** an exclamation demanding that orderly behaviour be restored. [C13: from OF *ordre*, from L *ordō*] —'**orderer** *n.*

order in council *n.* (in Britain) a decree of the Cabinet, usually made under the authority of a statute: in theory a decree of the sovereign and Privy Council.

orderly ('ɔːdəlɪ) *adj.* **1.** in order, properly arranged, or tidy. **2.** obeying or appreciating method, system, and arrangement. **3.** *Mil.* of or relating to orders: *an orderly book.* ~*n., pl.* **-lies. 4.** *Med.* a male hospital attendant. **5.** *Mil.* a junior rank detailed to carry orders or perform minor tasks for a more senior officer. —'**orderliness** *n.*

orderly room *n. Mil.* a room in the barracks of a battalion or company used for general administrative purposes.

order of magnitude *n.* a numerical value expressed to the nearest power of ten.

Order of Merit *n. Brit.* an order conferred on civilians and servicemen for eminence in any field.

order of the day *n.* **1.** the general directive of a commander in chief or the specific instructions of a commanding officer. **2.** *Inf.* the prescribed or only thing offered or available. **3.** (in Parliament) any item of public business ordered to be considered on a specific day. **4.** an agenda or programme.

Order of the Garter *n.* See **Garter.**

order paper *n.* a list indicating the order in which business is to be conducted, esp. in Parliament.

ordinal ('ɔːdɪnᵊl) *adj.* **1.** denoting a certain position in a sequence of numbers. **2.** of, relating to, or characteristic of an order in biological classification. ~*n.* **3.** short for **ordinal number. 4.** a book containing the forms of services for the ordination of ministers. **5.** *R.C. Church.* a service book.

ordinal number *n.* a number denoting relative position in a sequence, such as *first, second, third.* Sometimes shortened to **ordinal.**

ordinance ('ɔːdɪnəns) *n.* an authoritative regulation, decree, law, or practice. [C14: from OF *ordenance*, from L *ordināre* to set in order]

ordinarily ('ɔːdᵊnrɪlɪ) *adv.* in ordinary, normal, or usual practice; usually; normally.

ordinary ('ɔːdᵊnrɪ) *adj.* **1.** of common or established type or occurrence. **2.** familiar, everyday, or unexceptional. **3.** uninteresting or commonplace. **4.** having regular or ex officio jurisdiction: *an ordinary judge.* **5.** *Maths.* (of a differential equation) containing two variables only and derivatives of one of the variables with respect to the other. ~*n., pl.* **-naries. 6.** a common or average situation, amount, or degree (esp. in **out of the ordinary**). **7.** a normal or commonplace person or thing. **8.** *Civil law.* a judge who exercises jurisdiction in his own right. **9.** (*usually cap.*) an ecclesiastic, esp. a bishop, holding an office to which certain jurisdictional powers are attached. **10.** *R.C. Church.* **a.** the parts of the Mass that do not vary

from day to day. **b.** a prescribed form of divine service, esp. the Mass. **11.** the U.S. name for **penny-farthing. 12.** *Heraldry.* any of several conventional figures, such as the bend, and the cross, commonly charged upon shields. **13.** *History.* a clergyman who visited condemned prisoners. **14.** *Brit. obs.* **a.** a meal provided regularly at a fixed price. **b.** the inn, etc., providing such meals. **15. in ordinary.** *Brit.* (used esp. in titles) in regular service or attendance: *physician in ordinary to the sovereign.* [C16 (adj.) & C13 (some n. senses): ult. from L *ordinārius* orderly, from *ordō* order]

Ordinary level *n.* a formal name for **O level.**

ordinary rating *n.* a rank in the Royal Navy comparable to that of a private in the army.

ordinary seaman *n.* a seaman of the lowest rank, being insufficiently experienced to be an able-bodied seaman.

ordinary shares *pl. n.* shares representing part of the capital issued by a company and entitling their holders to a variable dividend according to the profitability of the company and to a claim on net assets. U.S. equivalent: **common stock.** Cf. **preference shares.**

ordinate ('ɔːdɪnɪt) *n.* the vertical or *y*-coordinate of a point in a two-dimensional system of Cartesian coordinates. Cf. **abscissa.** [C16: from NL (*linea*) *ordināte* (*applicāta*) (line applied) in an orderly manner from *ordināre* to arrange in order]

ordination (ˌɔːdɪ'neɪʃən) *n.* **1. a.** the act of conferring holy orders. **b.** the reception of holy orders. **2.** the condition of being ordained or regulated. **3.** an arrangement or order.

ordnance ('ɔːdnəns) *n.* **1.** cannon or artillery. **2.** military supplies; munitions. **3. the.** a department of an army or government dealing with military supplies. [C14: var. of ORDINANCE]

ordnance datum *n.* mean sea level calculated from observation taken at Newlyn, Cornwall, and used as the official basis for height calculation on British maps. Abbrev.: **OD.**

Ordnance Survey *n.* the official map-making body of the British or Irish government.

Ordovician (ˌɔːdəʊ'vɪʃɪən) *adj.* **1.** of, denoting, or formed in the second period of the Palaeozoic era, between the Cambrian and Silurian periods. ~*n.* **2. the.** the Ordovician period or rock system. [C19: from L *Ordovices*, ancient Celtic tribe in N Wales]

ordure ('ɔːdjʊə) *n.* excrement; dung. [C14: via OF, from *ord* dirty, from L *horridus* shaggy]

Ordzhonikidze *or* **Orjonikidze** (*Russian* ardʒəni'kidzɪ) *n.* a city in the S Soviet Union, capital of the North Ossetian ASSR on the N slopes of the Caucasus. Pop.: 313 000 (1987). Former names: **Vladikavkaz** (until 1944); **Dzaudzhikau** (1944–54).

ore (ɔː) *n.* any naturally occurring mineral or aggregate of minerals from which economically important constituents, esp. metals, can be extracted. [OE *ār, ōra*]

öre ('ɔːrə) *n., pl.* **öre.** a Scandinavian monetary unit worth one hundredth of a Swedish krona and (**øre**) one hundredth of a Danish or Norwegian krone.

oread ('ɔːrɪˌæd) *n. Greek myth.* a mountain nymph. [C16: via L from Gk *Oreias*, from *oros* mountain]

Örebro (*Swedish* œːrə'bruː) *n.* a town in S Sweden: one of Sweden's oldest towns; scene of the election of Jean Bernadotte as heir to the throne in 1810. Pop.: 118 443 (1986).

oregano (ˌɒrɪ'gɑːnəʊ) *n.* **1.** a Mediterranean variety of wild marjoram (*Origanum vulgare*), with pungent leaves. **2.** the dried powdered leaves of this plant, used to season food. [C18: American Sp., from Sp., from L *orīganum*, from Gk *origanon* an aromatic herb, ? marjoram]

Oregon ('ɒrɪgən) *n.* a state of the northwestern U.S., on the Pacific: consists of the Coast and Cascade Ranges in the west and a plateau in the east; important timber production. Capital: Salem. Pop.: 2 698 000 (1986 est.). Area: 251 418 sq. km (97 073 sq. miles). Abbrevs.: **Oreg.** or (with zip code) **OR**

Oregon trail *n.* an early pioneering route across the central U.S., from Independence, W Missouri, to the Columbia River country of N Oregon: used chiefly between 1804 and 1860. Length: about 3220 km (2000 miles).

Orel *or* **Oryol** (*Russian* a'rjɔl) *n.* a city in the central Soviet Union. Pop.: 335 000 (1987).

Ore Mountains (ɔː) *pl. n.* another name for the **Erzgebirge.**

Orenburg ('ɒrən,bɜːg; *Russian* arın'burk) *n.* a city in the E Soviet Union, on the Ural River. Pop.: 537 000 (1987). Former name (1938–57): **Chkalov.**

Orense (*Spanish* o'rense) *n.* a city in NW Spain, in Galicia on the Miño River: warm springs. Pop.: 94 346 (1981).

Orestes (ɒ'rɛstiːz) *n. Greek myth.* the son of Agamemnon and Clytemnestra, who killed his mother and her lover Aegisthus in revenge for their murder of his father.

Øresund (œːrə'sund) *n.* the Swedish and Danish name for the **Sound.**

orfe (ɔːf) *n.* a small slender European cyprinoid fish, occurring in two colour varieties, namely the **silver orfe** and the **golden orfe,** popular aquarium fishes. [C17: from G; rel. to L *orphus,* Gk *orphos* the sea perch]

Orff (ɔːf) *n.* **Carl** (karl). 1895–1982, German composer. His works include the secular oratorio *Carmina Burana* (1937) and the opera *Antigone* (1949).

organ ('ɔːgən) *n.* **1. a.** Also called: **pipe organ.** a large complex musical keyboard instrument in which sound is produced by means of a number of pipes arranged in sets or stops, supplied with air from a bellows. **b.** (*as modifier*): *organ stop; organ loft.* **2.** any instrument, such as a harmonium, in which sound is produced in this way. **3.** a fully differentiated structural and functional unit, such as a kidney or a root, in an animal or plant. **4.** an agency or medium of communication, esp. a periodical issued by a specialist group or party. **5.** an instrument with which something is done or accomplished. **6.** a euphemistic word for **penis.** [C13: from OF *organe,* from L *organum* implement, from Gk *organon* tool]

organdie *or esp. U.S.* **organdy** ('ɔːgəndɪ) *n., pl.* **-dies.** a fine and slightly stiff cotton fabric used for dresses, etc. [C19: from F *organdi,* from ?]

organelle (,ɔːgə'nɛl) *n.* a structural and functional unit in a cell or unicellular organism. [C20: from NL *organella,* from L *organum;* see ORGAN]

organ-grinder *n.* a street musician playing a hand organ for money.

organic (ɔː'gænɪk) *adj.* **1.** of, relating to, or derived from living plants and animals. **2.** of or relating to animal or plant constituents or products having a carbon basis. **3.** of or relating to one or more organs of an animal or plant. **4.** of, relating to, or belonging to the class of chemical compounds that are formed from carbon: *an organic compound.* **5.** constitutional in the structure of something; fundamental; integral. **6.** of or characterized by the coordination of integral parts; organized. **7.** of or relating to the essential constitutional laws regulating the government of a state: *organic law.* **8.** of, relating to, or grown with the use of fertilizers or pesticides deriving from animal or vegetable matter. ~*n.* **9.** any substance, such as a fertilizer or pesticide, that is derived from animal or vegetable matter. —**or'ganically** *adv.*

organic chemistry *n.* the branch of chemistry concerned with the compounds of carbon.

organism ('ɔːgə,nɪzəm) *n.* **1.** any living animal or plant, including any bacterium or virus. **2.** anything resembling a living creature in structure, behaviour, etc. —,**organ'ismal** *or* ,**organ'ismic** *adj.* —,**organ'ismically** *adv.*

organist ('ɔːgənɪst) *n.* a person who plays the organ.

organization *or* **-isation** (,ɔːgənaɪ'zeɪʃən) *n.* **1.** the act of organizing or the state of being organized. **2.** an organized structure or whole. **3.** a business or administrative concern united and constructed for a particular end. **4.** a body of administrative officials, as of a government department, etc. **5.** order, tidiness, or system; method. —,**organi'zational** *or* **-i'sational** *adj.*

organize *or* **-ise** ('ɔːgə,naɪz) *vb.* **1.** to form (parts or elements of something) into a structured whole; coordinate. **2.** (*tr.*) to arrange methodically or in order. **3.** (*tr.*) to provide with an organic structure. **4.** (*tr.*) to enlist (the workers) (of a factory, etc.) in a trade union. **5.** (*intr.*) to join or form an organization or trade union. **6.** (*tr.*) *Inf.* to put (oneself) in an alert and responsible frame of mind. [C15: from Med. L *organizare,* from L *organum* ORGAN] —'**organ,izer** *or* **-,iser** *n.*

organometallic (ɔː,gænəumɪ'tælɪk) *adj.* of, concerned with, or being an organic compound with one or more metal atoms in its molecules.

organon ('ɔːgə,nɒn) *or* **organum** *n., pl.* **-na** (-nə), **-nons** *or* **-na,** **-nums.** **1.** *Epistemology.* a system of logical or

scientific rules, esp. that of Aristotle. **2.** *Arch.* a sense organ, regarded as an instrument for acquiring knowledge. [C16: from Gk: implement; see ORGAN]

organotin (ɔː,gænəu'tɪn) *adj.* of, concerned with, or being an organic compound with one or more tin atoms in its molecules: used as a pesticide, hitherto considered to decompose safely, now found to be toxic in the food chain.

organza (ɔː'gænzə) *n.* a thin stiff fabric of silk, cotton, nylon, rayon, etc. [C20: from ?]

orgasm ('ɔːgæzəm) *n.* **1.** the most intense point during sexual excitement. **2.** *Rare.* intense or violent excitement. [C17: from NL *orgasmus,* from Gk *orgasmos,* from *organ* to mature, swell] —**or'gasmic** *or* **or'gastic** *adj.*

orgeat ('ɔːʒɑː) *n.* a drink made from barley or almonds, and orangeflower water. [C18: via F, from *orge* barley, from L *hordeum*]

orgy ('ɔːdʒɪ) *n., pl.* **-gies.** **1.** a wild gathering marked by promiscuous sexual activity, excessive drinking, etc. **2.** an act of immoderate or frenzied indulgence. **3.** (*often pl.*) secret religious rites of Dionysus, Bacchus, etc., marked by drinking, dancing, and songs. [C16: from F *orgies,* from L *orgia,* from Gk: nocturnal festival] —,**or-gi'astic** *adj.*

oribi ('ɒrɪbɪ) *n., pl.* **-bi** *or* **-bis.** a small African antelope of the grasslands and bush south of the Sahara, with fawn-coloured coat and, in the male, ridged spikelike horns. [C18: from Afrik., prob. from Hottentot *arab*]

oriel ('ɔːrɪəl) *n.* a bay window, esp. one that is supported by one or more brackets or corbels. Also called: **oriel window.** [C14: from OF *oriol* gallery, ?from Med. L *auleolum* niche]

orient *n.* ('ɔːrɪənt). **1.** *Poetic.* another word for **east.** Cf. **occident. 2.** *Arch.* the eastern sky or the dawn. **3. a.** the iridescent lustre of a pearl. **b.** (*as modifier*): *orient pearls.* **4.** a pearl of high quality. ~*adj.* ('ɔːrɪənt). **5.** *Now chiefly poetic.* oriental. **6.** *Arch.* (of the sun, stars, etc.) rising. ~*vb.* ('ɔːrɪ,ent). **7.** to adjust or align (oneself or something else) according to surroundings or circumstances. **8.** (*tr.*) to position or set (a map, etc.) with reference to the compass or other specific directions. **9.** (*tr.*) to build (a church) with the chancel end facing in an easterly direction. [C18: via F from L *oriēns* rising (sun), from *orīrī* to rise]

▷ **Usage.** See at **orientate.**

Orient ('ɔːrɪənt) *n.* (usually preceded by *the*) **1.** the countries east of the Mediterranean. **2.** the eastern hemisphere.

oriental (,ɔːrɪ'ɛntªl) *adj.* another word for **eastern.**

Oriental (,ɔːrɪ'ɛntªl) *adj.* **1.** (*sometimes not cap.*) of or relating to the Orient. **2.** of or denoting a region consisting of southeastern Asia from India to Borneo, Java, and the Philippines. ~*n.* **3.** (*sometimes not cap.*) an inhabitant, esp. a native, of the Orient.

Orientalism (,ɔːrɪ'ɛntə,lɪzəm) *n.* **1.** knowledge of or devotion to the Orient. **2.** an Oriental quality, style, or trait. —,**Ori'entalist** *n.* —,**Ori,ental'istic** *adj.*

orientate (,ɔːrɪɛn,teɪt) *vb.* another word for **orient** (senses 7, 8, 9).

▷ **Usage.** Careful users avoid *orientate* as an unnecessary back formation from *orientation,* since *orient* has the same range of meanings. Nevertheless, there can be little doubt that either form is acceptable. The excessive use of *orientate* and *orientation* in such phrases as *orientation course* (preparatory course), *profits-orientated systems* (those designed to produce high profits), and *student-orientated lectures* (lectures written with students in mind) is frowned on in careful usage as jargon.

orientation (,ɔːrɪɛn'teɪʃən) *n.* **1.** the act or process of orienting or the state of being oriented. **2.** positioning with relation to the compass or other specific directions. **3.** the adjustment or alignment of oneself or one's ideas to surroundings or circumstances. **4.** Also called: **orientation course.** *Chiefly U.S. & Canad.* **a.** a course, lecture, etc., introducing a new situation or environment. **b.** (*as modifier*): *an orientation talk.* **5.** *Psychol.* the knowledge of one's own temporal, social, and practical circumstances. **6.** the siting of a church on an east-west axis. —,**orien'tational** *adj.*

-oriented *suffix forming adjectives.* geared or directed towards: *sports-oriented.*

orienteer (,ɔːrɪən'tɪə) *vb.* (*intr.*) **1.** to take part in orienteering. ~*n.* **2.** a person who takes part in orienteering.

orienteering (ˌɔːrɪɛn'tɪərɪŋ) n. a sport in which contestants race on foot over a course consisting of checkpoints found with the aid of a map and a compass. [C20: from Swedish orientering]

orifice ('ɒrɪfɪs) n. Chiefly technical. an opening or mouth into a cavity; vent; aperture. [C16: via F from LL ōrificium, from L ōs mouth + facere to make]

oriflamme ('ɒrɪˌflæm) n. a scarlet flag adopted as the national banner of France in the Middle Ages. [C15: via OF, from L aurum gold + flamma flame]

orig. abbrev. for: 1. origin. 2. original(ly).

origami (ˌɒrɪ'gɑːmɪ) n. the art or process, originally Japanese, of paper folding. [from Japanese, from ori a fold + kami paper]

origan ('ɒrɪgən) n. another name for **marjoram** (sense 2). [C16: from L orīganum, from Gk origanon an aromatic herb]

origanum (ˌɒrɪ'gɑːnəm) n. See **oregano**.

Origen ('ɒrɪˌdʒɛn) n. ?185–?254 A.D., Christian theologian, born in Alexandria. His writings include Hexapla, a synopsis of the Old Testament, Contra Celsum, a defence of Christianity, and De principiis, a statement of Christian theology.

origin ('ɒrɪdʒɪn) n. 1. a primary source; derivation. 2. the beginning of something; first part. 3. (often pl.) ancestry or parentage; birth; extraction. 4. Anat. a. the end of a muscle, opposite its point of insertion. b. the beginning of a nerve or blood vessel or the site where it first starts to branch out. 5. Maths. a. the point of intersection of coordinate axes or planes. b. the point whose coordinates are all zero. [C16: from F origine, from L origō beginning, from oriri to spring from]

original (ə'rɪdʒɪnᵊl) adj. 1. of or relating to an origin or beginning. 2. fresh and unusual; novel. 3. able to think of or carry out new ideas or concepts. 4. being that from which a copy, translation, etc., is made. ~n. 5. the first and genuine form of something, from which others are derived. 6. a person or thing used as a model in art or literature. 7. a person whose way of thinking is unusual or creative. 8. the first form or occurrence of something. —o'riginally adv.

originality (əˌrɪdʒɪ'nælɪtɪ) n., pl. -ties. 1. the quality or condition of being original. 2. the ability to create or innovate.

original sin n. a state of sin held to be innate in mankind as the descendants of Adam.

originate (ə'rɪdʒɪˌneɪt) vb. 1. to come or bring into being. 2. (intr.) U.S. & Canad. (of a bus, train, etc.) to begin its journey at a specified point. —o,rigi'nation n. —o'rig.i,nator n.

Orinoco (ˌɒrɪ'nəʊkəʊ) n. a river in N South America, rising in S Venezuela and flowing west, then north as part of the border between Colombia and Venezuela, then east to the Atlantic by a great delta: the third largest river system in South America, draining an area of 945 000 sq. km (365 000 sq. miles); reaches a width of 22 km (14 miles) during the rainy season. Length: about 2575 km (1600 miles).

oriole ('ɔːrɪˌəʊl) n. 1. a tropical Old World songbird, such as the **golden oriole**, having a long pointed bill and a mostly yellow-and-black plumage. 2. an American songbird, esp. the Baltimore oriole, with a typical male plumage of black with either orange or yellow. [C18: from Med. L oryolus, from L aureolus, dim. of aureus, from aurum gold]

Orion[1] (ə'raɪən) n. Greek myth. a Boeotian giant famed as a great hunter, who figures in several tales.

Orion[2] (ə'raɪən) n. a constellation containing two first-magnitude stars (Betelgeuse and Rigel) and a distant low-density emission nebula (the **Orion Nebula**).

orison ('ɒrɪzᵊn) n. Literary. another word for **prayer**[1]. [C12: from OF oreison, from LL ōrātiō, from L: speech, from ōrāre to speak]

Orissa (ɒ'rɪsə) n. a state of E India, on the Bay of Bengal: part of the province of Bihar and Orissa (1912–36); enlarged by the addition of 25 native states in 1949. Capital: Bhubaneswar. Pop.: 26 272 054 (1981). Area: 155 825 sq. km (60 164 sq. miles).

Oriya (ɒ'riːə) n. 1. (pl. -ya) a member of a people of India living chiefly in Orissa. 2. the state language of Orissa, belonging to the Indo-European family.

Orizaba (ˌɒrɪ'zɑːbə; Spanish ori'θaβa) n. 1. a city and resort in SE Mexico, in Veracruz state. Pop.: 114 848 (1980). 2. **Pico de.** the Spanish name for **Citlaltépetl**.

Orjoníkidze (Russian ardʒɒni'kidzɪ) n. a variant spelling of **Ordzhonikidze**.

Orkneys ('ɔːknɪz), **Orkney** ('ɔːknɪ), or **Orkney Islands** pl. n. a group of over 70 islands off the NE coast of Scotland, separated from the mainland by the Pentland Firth: constitutes an island authority of Scotland; low-lying and treeless; prehistoric remains. Administrative centre: Kirkwall. Pop.: 19 266 (1986 est.). Area: 974 sq. km (376 sq. miles). —**Orkneyman** n.

Orléanais (French ɔrleanɛ) n. a former province of N central France, centred on Orléans.

Orléans[1] (ɔː'lɪənz; French ɔrleɑ̃) n. a city in N central France, on the River Loire: famous for its deliverance by Joan of Arc from the long English siege in 1429; university (1305); an important rail and road junction. Pop.: 105 530 (1983 est.).

Orléans[2] (French ɔrleɑ̃) n. **Louis Philippe Joseph** (lwi filip ʒozɛf), Duc d'Orléans, known as Philippe Egalité (after 1792). 1747–93, French nobleman, who supported the French Revolution and voted for the death of the king, his cousin, but was executed after his son fled to Austria.

Orlon ('ɔːlɒn) n. Trademark. a crease-resistant acrylic fibre or fabric used for clothing, etc.

orlop or **orlop deck** ('ɔːlɒp) n. Naut. (in a vessel with four or more decks) the lowest deck. [C15: from Du. overloopen to spill]

Orly ('ɔːliː; French ɔrli) n. a suburb of SE Paris, France, with an international airport.

Ormandy ('ɔːməndɪ) n. **Eugene.** 1899–1985, U.S. conductor, born in Hungary.

ormer ('ɔːmə) n. 1. Also called: **sea-ear.** an edible marine gastropod mollusc that has an ear-shaped shell perforated with holes and occurs near the Channel Islands. 2. any other abalone. [C17: from F, apparently from L auris ear + mare sea]

ormolu ('ɔːməˌluː) n. 1. a. a gold-coloured alloy of copper, tin, or zinc used to decorate furniture, etc. b. (as modifier): an ormolu clock. 2. gold prepared for gilding. [C18: from F or moulu ground gold]

Ormuz ('ɔːmʌz) n. a variant spelling of **Hormuz**.

ornament n. ('ɔːnəmənt). 1. anything that enhances the appearance of a person or thing. 2. decorations collectively: she was totally without ornament. 3. a small decorative object. 4. something regarded as a source of pride or beauty. 5. Music. any of several decorations, such as the trill, etc. ~vb. ('ɔːnəˌmɛnt). (tr.) 6. to decorate with or as if with ornaments. 7. to serve as an ornament to. [C14: from L ornāmentum, from ornāre to adorn] —ˌornamen'tation n.

ornamental (ˌɔːnə'mɛntᵊl) adj. 1. of value as an ornament; decorative. 2. (of a plant) used to decorate houses, gardens, etc. ~n. 3. a plant cultivated for show or decoration. —ˌorna'mentally adv.

ornate (ɔː'neɪt) adj. 1. heavily or elaborately decorated. 2. (of style in writing, etc.) over-embellished; flowery. [C15: from L ornāre to decorate] —or'nately adv. —or'nateness n.

Orne (French ɔrn) n. a department of NW France, in Basse-Normandie. Capital: Alençon. Pop.: 295 472 (1982). Area: 6144 sq. km (2396 sq. miles).

ornery ('ɔːnərɪ) adj. U.S. & Canad. dialect or inf. 1. stubborn or vile-tempered. 2. low; treacherous: an ornery trick. 3. ordinary. [C19: alteration of ORDINARY] —'orneriness n.

ornitho- or before a vowel **ornith-** combining form. bird or birds. [from Gk ornis, ornith- bird]

ornithology (ˌɔːnɪ'θɒlədʒɪ) n. the study of birds. —ornithological (ˌɔːnɪθə'lɒdʒɪkᵊl) adj. —ˌornitho'logically adv. —ˌorni'thologist n.

ornithorhynchus (ˌɔːnɪθəʊ'rɪŋkəs) n. the technical name for **duck-billed platypus**. [C19: NL, from ORNITHO- + Gk rhunkhos bill]

oro-[1] combining form. mountain: orogeny. [from Gk oros]

oro-[2] combining form. oral; mouth: oromaxillary. [from L, from ōs]

orogeny (ɒ'rɒdʒɪnɪ) or **orogenesis** (ˌɒrəʊ'dʒɛnɪsɪs) n. the formation of mountain ranges. —**orogenic** (ˌɒrəʊ'dʒɛnɪk) or **orogenetic** (ˌɒrəʊdʒɪ'nɛtɪk) adj.

Orontes (ɒ'rɒntiːz) n. a river in SW Asia, rising in Lebanon and flowing north through Syria into Turkey, where it turns west to the Mediterranean. Length: 571 km (355 miles). Arabic name: **'Asi.**

orotund ('ɒrəʊˌtʌnd) *adj.* **1.** (of the voice) resonant; booming. **2.** (of speech or writing) bombastic; pompous. [C18: from L *ore rotundo* with rounded mouth]

Orozco (*Spanish* oˈrɒθko) *n.* **José Clemente** (xoˈse kleˈmente). 1883–1949, Mexican painter, noted for his monumental humanistic murals.

orphan ('ɔːfən) *n.* **1. a.** a child, one or both of whose parents are dead. **b.** (*as modifier*): *an orphan child.* ~*vb.* **2.** (*tr.*) to deprive of one or both parents. [C15: from LL *orphanus*, from Gk *orphanos*]

orphanage ('ɔːfənɪdʒ) *n.* **1.** an institution for orphans and abandoned children. **2.** the state of being an orphan.

Orphean ('ɔːfɪən) *adj.* **1.** of or relating to Orpheus. **2.** melodious or enchanting.

Orpheus ('ɔːfɪəs, -fjuːs) *n. Greek myth.* a poet and lyre-player credited with the authorship of the poems forming the basis of Orphism. He married Eurydice and sought her in Hades after her death. He failed to win her back and was killed by a band of bacchantes.

Orphic ('ɔːfɪk) *adj.* **1.** of or relating to Orpheus or Orphism, a mystery religion of ancient Greece. **2.** (*sometimes not cap.*) mystical or occult. —**'Orphically** *adv.*

orpine ('ɔːpaɪn) *or* **orpin** ('ɔːpɪn) *n.* a succulent perennial N temperate plant with toothed leaves and heads of small purplish-white flowers. [C14: from OF, apparently from *orpiment*, a yellow mineral (? referring to the yellow flowers of a related species)]

Orpington ('ɔːpɪŋtən) *n.* a district of SE London, part of the Greater London borough of Bromley from 1965.

orrery ('ɒrərɪ) *n., pl.* **-ries.** a mechanical model of the solar system in which the planets can be moved at the correct relative velocities around the sun. [C18: orig. made for Charles Boyle, Earl of *Orrery*]

orris *or* **orrice** ('ɒrɪs) *n.* **1.** any of various irises that have fragrant rhizomes. **2.** Also: **orrisroot.** the rhizome of such a plant, prepared and used as perfume. [C16: var. of IRIS]

Orsini (*Italian* orˈsiːni) *n.* an Italian aristocratic family that was prominent in Rome from the 12th to the 18th century.

Orsk (*Russian* ɔrsk) *n.* a city in the S central Soviet Union, on the Ural River: a major railway and industrial centre, with an oil refinery linked by pipeline with the Emba field (on the Caspian). Pop.: 273 000 (1987).

Ortega (ɔːˈteɪgə) *n.* **Daniel**, full surname *Ortega Saavedra*. born 1945, Nicaraguan politician and former resistance leader; president of Nicaragua from 1985.

Ortegal (*Spanish* ɔrteˈyal) *n.* **Cape.** a cape in NW Spain, projecting into the Bay of Biscay.

Ortega y Gasset (*Spanish* ɔrˈteya i gaˈsɛt) *n.* **José** (xoˈse). 1883–1955, Spanish essayist and philosopher. His best-known work is *The Revolt of the Masses* (1930).

orthicon ('ɔːθɪˌkɒn) *n.* a television camera tube in which an optical image produces a corresponding electrical charge pattern on a mosaic surface that is scanned from behind by an electron beam. The resulting discharge of the mosaic provides the output signal current. See also **image orthicon.** [C20: from ORTHO- + ICON(OSCOPE)]

ortho- *or before a vowel* **orth-** *combining form.* **1.** straight or upright: *orthorhombic.* **2.** perpendicular or at right angles: *orthogonal.* **3.** correct or right: *orthodontics.* **4.** (*often in italics*) denoting an organic compound containing a benzene ring with substituents attached to adjacent carbon atoms (the 1,2- positions). **5.** denoting an oxyacid regarded as the highest hydrated form of such an anhydride or a salt of such an acid: *orthophosphoric acid.* **6.** denoting a diatomic substance in which the spins of the two atoms are parallel: *orthohydrogen.* [from Gk *orthos* straight, upright]

orthochromatic (ˌɔːθəʊkrəʊˈmætɪk) *adj. Photog.* of or relating to an emulsion giving a rendering of relative light intensities of different colours that corresponds approximately to the colour sensitivity of the eye, esp. one that is insensitive to red light. Sometimes shortened to **ortho.** —**orthochromatism** (ˌɔːθəʊˈkrəʊməˌtɪzəm) *n.*

orthoclase ('ɔːθəʊˌkleɪs, -ˌkleɪz) *n.* a white or coloured feldspar mineral consisting of an aluminium silicate of potassium in monoclinic crystalline form.

orthodontics (ˌɔːθəʊˈdɒntɪks) *or* **orthodontia** (ˌɔːθəʊˈdɒntɪə) *n.* (*functioning as sing.*) the branch of

dentistry concerned with preventing or correcting irregularities of the teeth. —**ˌortho'dontic** *adj.* —**ˌortho'dontist** *n.*

orthodox ('ɔːθəˌdɒks) *adj.* **1.** conforming with established standards, as in religion, behaviour, or attitudes. **2.** conforming to the Christian faith as established by the early Church. [C16: via Church L from Gk *orthodoxos*, from *orthos* correct + *doxa* belief] —**'ortho,doxy** *n.*

Orthodox ('ɔːθəˌdɒks) *adj.* **1.** of or relating to the Orthodox Church of the East. **2.** (*sometimes not cap.*) of or relating to Orthodox Judaism.

Orthodox Church *n.* **1.** the collective body of those Eastern Churches that were separated from the western Church in the 11th century and are in communion with the Greek patriarch of Constantinople. **2.** any of these Churches.

Orthodox Judaism *n.* a form of Judaism characterized by traditional interpretation and strict observance of the Mosaic Law.

orthoepy ('ɔːθəʊˌɛpɪ) *n.* the study of correct or standard pronunciation. [C17: from Gk *orthoepeia*, from ORTHO- straight + *epos* word] —**orthoepic** (ˌɔːθəʊˈɛpɪk) *adj.* —**ˌortho'epically** *adv.*

orthogenesis (ˌɔːθəʊˈdʒɛnɪsɪs) *n.* **1.** *Biol.* **a.** evolution of a group of organisms in a particular direction, which is generally predetermined. **b.** the theory that proposes such a development. **2.** the theory that there is a series of stages through which all cultures pass in the same order. —**orthogenetic** (ˌɔːθəʊdʒɪˈnɛtɪk) *adj.* —**ˌorthoge'netically** *adv.*

orthogonal (ɔːˈθɒgənᵊl) *adj.* relating to, consisting of, or involving right angles; perpendicular. —**or'thogonally** *adv.*

orthographic (ˌɔːθəˈgræfɪk) *or* **orthographical** *adj.* of or relating to spelling. —**ˌortho'graphically** *adv.*

orthography (ɔːˈθɒgrəfɪ) *n., pl.* **-phies.** **1.** a writing system. **2. a.** spelling considered to be correct. **b.** the principles underlying spelling. **3.** the study of spelling. —**or'thographer** *or* **or'thographist** *n.*

orthopaedics *or U.S.* **orthopedics** (ˌɔːθəʊˈpiːdɪks) *n.* (*functioning as sing.*) **1.** the branch of surgery concerned with disorders of the spine and joints and the repair of deformities of these parts. **2.** dental orthopaedics. another name for **orthodontics.** —**ˌortho'paedic** *or U.S.* **ˌortho'pedic** *adj.* —**ˌortho'paedist** *or U.S.* **ˌortho'pedist** *n.*

orthopteran (ɔːˈθɒptərən) *n.* **1.** Also: **orthopteron** (*pl.* **-tera** (-tərə)) any orthopterous insect. ~*adj.* **2.** another word for **orthopterous.**

orthopterous (ɔːˈθɒptərəs) *adj.* of, relating to, or belonging to a large order of insects, including crickets, locusts, and grasshoppers, having leathery forewings and membranous hind wings.

orthoptic (ɔːˈθɒptɪk) *adj.* relating to normal binocular vision.

orthoptics (ɔːˈθɒptɪks) *n.* (*functioning as sing.*) the science or practice of correcting defective vision, as by exercises to strengthen weak eye muscles. —**or'thoptist** *n.*

orthorhombic (ˌɔːθəʊˈrɒmbɪk) *adj. Crystallog.* relating to the crystal system characterized by three mutually perpendicular unequal axes.

Ortles (*Italian* 'ɔːtles) *pl. n.* a range of the Alps in N Italy. Highest peak: 3899 m (12 792 ft.). Also called: **Ortler** ('ɔːtlə).

ortolan ('ɔːtələn) *n.* **1.** a brownish Old World bunting regarded as a delicacy. **2.** any of various other small birds eaten as delicacies, esp. the bobolink. [C17: via F from L *hortulānus*, from *hortulus*, dim. of *hortus* garden]

Orton ('ɔːtən) *n.* **Joe.** 1933–67, British dramatist, noted for his black comedies: these include *Entertaining Mr Sloane* (1964), *Loot* (1965), and *What the Butler Saw* (1969).

Oruro (*Spanish* oˈruro) *n.* a city in W Bolivia: a former silver-mining centre; university (1892); tin, copper, and tungsten. Pop.: 178 393 (1985).

Orvieto (*Italian* orˈvjɛːto) *n.* a market town in central Italy, in Umbria: Etruscan remains. Pop.: 23 559 (1981 est.). Latin name: **Urbs Vetus** (ʊəbz 'viːtəs).

Orwell ('ɔːwəl, -wɛl) *n.* **George**, real name *Eric Arthur Blair*. 1903–50, English novelist and essayist, born in India. He is notable for his social criticism, as in *The Road to Wigan Pier* (1932); his account of his experiences of the Spanish Civil War *Homage to Catalonia* (1938); and his satirical novels *Animal Farm* (1945), an allegory on the Russian Revolution, and *1984* (1949), in which he depicts an authoritarian state of the future. —**Orwellian** (ɔ:'wɛliən) *adj.*

-ory[1] *suffix forming nouns.* **1.** indicating a place for: *observatory.* **2.** something having a specified use: *directory.* [via OF *-orie*, from L *-ōrium*, *-ōria*]

-ory[2] *suffix forming adjectives.* of or relating to; characterized by; having the effect of: *contributory.* [via OF *-orie*, from L *-ōrius*]

Oryol (*Russian* a'rjɔl) *n.* a variant spelling of **Orel**.

oryx ('ɒrɪks) *n., pl.* **-yxes** *or* **-yx.** any large African antelope of the genus *Oryx*, typically having long straight nearly upright horns. [C14: via L from Gk *orux* stonemason's axe, used also of the pointed horns of an antelope]

os[1] (ɒs) *n., pl.* **ossa** ('ɒsə). *Anat.* the technical name for **bone.** [C16: from L: bone]

os[2] (ɒs) *n., pl.* **ora.** *Anat., zool.* a mouth or mouthlike part or opening. [C18: from L]

Os *the chemical symbol for* osmium.

OS *abbrev. for:* **1.** Old Saxon (language). **2.** Old Style. **3.** Ordinary Seaman. **4.** (in Britain) Ordnance Survey. **5.** outsize.

Osage orange (əu'seɪdʒ) *n.* **1.** a North American thorny tree, grown for hedges and ornament. **2.** the warty orange-like fruit of this plant. [from *Osage* Amerind tribe]

Osaka (əu'sɑːkə) *n.* a port in S Japan, on S Honshu on **Osaka Bay** (an inlet of the Pacific): the third largest city in Japan (the chief commercial city during feudal times); university (1931); an industrial and commercial centre. Pop.: 2 636 000 (1985).

Osborne ('ɒzbən, -,bɔ:n) *n.* **John (James).** born 1929, English dramatist. His plays include *Look Back in Anger* (1956), containing the prototype of the angry young man, Jimmy Porter, *The Entertainer* (1957), and *Inadmissible Evidence* (1965).

Oscar ('ɒskə) *n.* any of several small gold statuettes awarded annually in the United States for outstanding achievements in films. Official name: **Academy Award.** [C20: said to have been named after a remark made by an official that it reminded him of his uncle Oscar]

Oscar II *n.* 1829–1907, king of Sweden (1872–1907) and of Norway (1872–1905).

oscillate ('ɒsɪ,leɪt) *vb.* **1.** (*intr.*) to move or swing from side to side regularly. **2.** (*intr.*) to waver between opinions, courses of action, etc. **3.** *Physics.* to undergo or produce or cause to undergo or produce oscillation. [C18: from L *oscillāre* to swing]

oscillating universe theory *n.* the theory that the universe is oscillating between periods of expansion and contraction.

oscillation (,ɒsɪ'leɪʃən) *n.* **1.** *Statistics, physics.* **a.** regular fluctuation in value, position, or state about a mean value, such as the variation in an alternating current. **b.** a single cycle of such a fluctuation. **2.** the act or process of oscillating. —**oscillatory** ('ɒsɪlətərɪ, -trɪ) *adj.*

oscillator ('ɒsɪ,leɪtə) *n.* **1.** a circuit or instrument for producing an alternating current or voltage of a required frequency. **2.** any instrument for producing oscillations. **3.** a person or thing that oscillates.

oscillogram (ɒ'sɪlə,græm) *n.* the recording obtained from an oscillograph or the trace on an oscilloscope screen.

oscillograph (ɒ'sɪlə,grɑːf) *n.* a device for producing a graphical record of the variation of an oscillating quantity, such as an electric current. —**oscillographic** (ɒ,sɪlə'græfɪk) *adj.* —**oscillography** (,ɒsɪ'lɒgrəfɪ) *n.*

oscilloscope (ɒ'sɪlə,skəup) *n.* an instrument for producing a representation of a rapidly changing quantity on the screen of a cathode-ray tube.

oscine ('ɒsaɪn, 'ɒsɪn) *adj.* of, relating to, or belonging to the suborder of passerine birds that includes most of the songbirds. [C17: via NL from L *oscen* singing bird]

oscitancy ('ɒsɪtənsɪ) *or* **oscitance** *n., pl.* **-tancies** *or* **-tances.** **1.** the state of being drowsy, lazy, or inattentive. **2.** the act of yawning. ~Also called: **oscitation.** [C17: from L *oscitāre* to yawn] —**'oscitant** *adj.*

oscular ('ɒskjulə) *adj.* **1.** *Zool.* of or relating to a mouthlike aperture, esp. of a sponge. **2.** of or relating to the mouth or to kissing.

osculate ('ɒskju,leɪt) *vb.* **1.** *Usually humorous.* to kiss. **2.** (*intr.*) (of an organism) to be intermediate between

two taxonomic groups. **3.** *Geom.* to touch in osculation. [C17: from L *ōsculārī* to kiss]

osculation (,ɒskju'leɪʃən) *n.* **1.** *Maths.* a point at which two branches of a curve have a common tangent, each branch extending in both directions of the tangent. **2.** *Rare.* the act of kissing. —**osculatory** ('ɒskjulətərɪ, -trɪ) *adj.*

-ose[1] *suffix forming adjectives.* possessing; resembling: *grandiose.* [from L *-ōsus;* see -OUS]

-ose[2] *suffix forming nouns.* **1.** indicating a carbohydrate, esp. a sugar: *lactose.* **2.** indicating a decomposition product of protein: *albumose.* [from GLUCOSE]

Oshawa ('ɒʃəwə) *n.* a city in central Canada, in SE Ontario on Lake Ontario: motor-vehicle industry. Pop.: 123 651 (1986).

Oshogbo (ə'ʃɒgbəu) *n.* a city in SW Nigeria: trade centre. Pop.: 405 000 (1986).

osier ('əuzɪə) *n.* **1.** any of various willow trees, whose flexible branches or twigs are used for making baskets, etc. **2.** a twig or branch from such a tree. **3.** any of several North American dogwoods, esp. the red osier. [C14: from OF, prob. from Med. L *ausēria, ?* of Gaulish origin]

Osijek (*Serbo-Croatian* 'ɒsijɛk) *n.* a town in N Yugoslavia, in E Croatia on the Drava River: under Turkish rule from 1526 to 1687. Pop.: 158 790 (1981). Ancient name: **Mursa** ('muəsə).

Osiris (əu'saɪrɪs) *n.* an ancient Egyptian god, ruler of the underworld and judge of the dead. —**O'sirian** *adj.*

-osis *suffix forming nouns.* **1.** indicating a process or state: *metamorphosis.* **2.** indicating a diseased condition: *tuberculosis.* **3.** indicating the formation or development of something: *fibrosis.* [from Gk, suffix used to form nouns from verbs with infinitives in *-oein* or *-oun*]

Oslo ('ɒzləu; *Norwegian* 'uslu) *n.* the capital and chief port of Norway, in the southeast at the head of **Oslo Fjord** (an inlet of the Skagerrak): founded in about 1050; university (1811); a major commercial and industrial centre, producing about a quarter of Norway's total output. Pop.: 451 099 (1987). Former names: **Christiania** (1624–1877), **Kristi'ania** (1877–1924).

Osman I ('ɒzmən, ɒz'mɑːn) *or* **Othman I** *n.* 1259–1326, Turkish sultan; founder of the Ottoman Empire.

Osmanli (ɒz'mænlɪ) *adj.* **1.** of or relating to the Ottoman Empire. ~*n.* **2.** (formerly) a subject of the Ottoman Empire. [C19: from Turkish, from OSMAN I]

osmiridium (,ɒzmɪ'rɪdɪəm) *n.* a very hard corrosion-resistant white or grey natural alloy of osmium and iridium: used in pen nibs, etc. [C19: from OSM(IUM) + IRIDIUM]

osmium ('ɒzmɪəm) *n.* a very hard brittle bluish-white metal, the heaviest known element, occurring with platinum and alloyed with iridium in osmiridium. Symbol: Os; atomic no.: 76; atomic wt.: 190.2. [C19: from Gk *osmē* smell, from its penetrating odour]

osmose ('ɒzməus, -məuz, 'ɒs-) *vb.* to undergo or cause to undergo osmosis. [C19 (n.): abstracted from the earlier terms *endosmose* and *exosmose;* rel. to Gk *ōsmos* push]

osmosis (ɒz'məusɪs, ɒs-) *n.* **1.** the tendency of the solvent of a less concentrated solution of dissolved molecules to pass through a semipermeable membrane into a more concentrated solution until both solutions are of the same concentration. **2.** diffusion through any membrane or porous barrier, as in dialysis. [C19: Latinized form from OSMOSE, from Gk *ōsmos* push] —**osmotic** (ɒz'mɒtɪk, ɒs-) *adj.* —**os'motically** *adv.*

osmotic pressure *n.* the pressure necessary to prevent osmosis into a given solution when the solution is separated from the pure solvent by a semipermeable membrane.

osmunda (ɒz'mʌndə) *or* **osmund** ('ɒzmənd) *n.* any of a genus of ferns having large spreading fronds. [C13: from OF *osmonde,* from ?]

Osnabrück (*German* ɔsna'bryk) *n.* an industrial city in N West Germany, in Lower Saxony: a member of the Hanseatic League in the Middle Ages. Pop.: 153 200 (1986).

osprey ('ɒsprɪ, -preɪ) *n.* **1.** a large broad-winged fish-eating diurnal bird of prey, with a dark back and whitish head and underparts. Often called (U.S. and Canad.): **fish hawk.** **2.** any of the feathers of various other birds, used esp. as trimming for hats. [C15: from OF *ospres,* apparently from L *ossifraga,* lit.: bone-breaker, from *os* bone + *frangere* to break]

Ossa ('ɒsə) *n.* a mountain in NE Greece, in E Thessaly: famous in mythology for the attempt of the twin giants,

Otus and Ephialtes, to reach heaven by piling Ossa on Olympus and Pelion on Ossa. Height: 1978 m (6489 ft.).

ossein ('ɒsɪɪn) *n.* a protein that forms the organic matrix of bone. [C19: from L *osseus* bony, from *os* bone]

osseous ('ɒsɪəs) *adj.* consisting of or containing bone, bony. [C17: from L *osseus*, from *os* bone] —'**osseously** *adv.*

Ossetia (ɒ'si:ʃə) *n.* a region of the SW Soviet Union, in the Caucasus: consists administratively of the North Ossetian ASSR of the RSFSR and the South Ossetian AR of the Georgian SSR. —**Os'setic** *or* **Os'setian** *adj.*

Ossian ('ɒsɪən) *n.* a legendary Irish hero and bard of the 3rd century A.D. See also (James) **Macpherson.** —,**Ossi'anic** *adj.*

Ossietzky (,ɒsɪ'ɛtskɪ) *n.* **Carl von** (karl fɔn). 1889–1938, German pacifist leader. He was imprisoned for revealing Germany's secret rearmament (1931–32) and again under Hitler (1933–36): Nobel peace prize 1935.

ossify ('ɒsɪ,faɪ) *vb.* **-fying, -fied.** **1.** to convert or be converted into bone. **2.** (*intr.*) (of habits, attitudes, etc.) to become inflexible. [C18: from F *ossifier*, from L *os* bone + *facere* to make] —,**ossifi'cation** *n.* —'**ossi,fier** *n.*

ossuary ('ɒsjuərɪ) *n., pl.* **-aries.** any container for the burial of human bones, such as an urn or vault. [C17: from LL *ossuārium*, from L *os* bone]

osteal ('ɒstɪəl) *adj.* **1.** of or relating to bone or to the skeleton. **2.** composed of bone; osseous. [C19: from Gk *osteon* bone]

osteitis (,ɒstɪ'aɪtɪs) *n.* inflammation of a bone. —**osteitic** (,ɒstɪ'ɪtɪk) *adj.*

Ostend (ɒs'tɛnd) *n.* a port and resort in NW Belgium, in West Flanders on the North Sea. Pop.: 68 318 (1987 est.). French name: **Ostende** (ɔstãd). Flemish name: **Oostende.**

ostensible (ɒ'stɛnsɪbᵊl) *adj.* **1.** apparent; seeming. **2.** pretended. [C18: via F from Med. L *ostensibilis*, from L *ostendere* to show, from *ob-* before + *tendere* to extend] —**os,tensi'bility** *n.* —**os'tensibly** *adv.*

ostensive (ɒ'stɛnsɪv) *adj.* **1.** obviously or manifestly demonstrative. **2.** (of a definition) giving examples of objects to which a word or phrase is properly applied. **3.** a less common word for **ostensible.** [C17: from LL *ostentīvus*, from L *ostendere* to show; see OSTENSIBLE] —**os'tensively** *adv.*

ostentation (,ɒstɛn'teɪʃən) *n.* pretentious, showy, or vulgar display. —,**osten'tatious** *adj.* —,**osten'tatiously** *adv.* —,**osten'tatiousness** *n.*

osteo- *or before a vowel* **oste-** *combining form.* indicating bone or bones. [from Gk *osteon*]

osteoarthritis (,ɒstɪəʊɑː'θraɪtɪs) *n.* chronic inflammation of the joints, esp. those that bear weight, with pain and stiffness. —**osteoarthritic** (,ɒstɪəʊɑː'θrɪtɪk) *adj., n.*

osteology (,ɒstɪ'ɒlədʒɪ) *n.* the study of the structure and function of bones. —**osteological** (,ɒstɪə'lɒdʒɪkᵊl) *adj.* —,**osteo'logically** *adv.* —,**oste'ologist** *n.*

osteoma (,ɒstɪ'əʊmə) *n., pl.* **-mata** (-mətə) *or* **-mas.** a benign tumour composed of bone or bonelike tissue.

osteomalacia (,ɒstɪəʊmə'leɪʃɪə) *n.* a disease characterized by softening of the bones, resulting from a deficiency of vitamin D and of calcium and phosphorus. [C19: from NL, from OSTEO- + Gk *malakia* softness] —,**osteoma'lacial** *or* **osteomalacic** (,ɒstɪəʊmə'læsɪk) *adj.*

osteomyelitis (,ɒstɪəʊ,maɪ'laɪtɪs) *n.* inflammation of bone marrow, caused by infection.

osteopathy (,ɒstɪ'ɒpəθɪ) *n.* a system of healing based on the manipulation of bones or other parts of the body. —'**osteo,path** *n.* —**osteopathic** (,ɒstɪə'pæθɪk) *adj.* —,**osteo'pathically** *adv.*

osteoplasty ('ɒstɪə,plæstɪ) *n., pl.* **-ties.** the branch of surgery concerned with bone repair or bone grafting.

osteoporosis (,ɒstɪəʊpɔː'rəʊsɪs) *n.* porosity and brittleness of the bones caused by lack of calcium in the bone matrix. [C19: from OSTEO- + PORE² + -OSIS] —**osteoporotic** (,ɒstɪəʊpɔː'rɒtɪk) *adj.*

Österreich ('ø:stəraɪç) *n.* the German name for **Austria.**

Ostia ('ɒstɪə) *n.* an ancient town in W central Italy, originally at the mouth of the Tiber but now about 6 km (4 miles) inland: served as the port of ancient Rome; harbours built by Claudius and Trajan; ruins excavated since 1854.

ostinato (,ɒstɪ'nɑːtəʊ) *n., pl.* **-tos. a.** a continuously reiterated musical phrase. **b.** (*as modifier*): *an ostinato passage.* [It.: from L *obstinātus* OBSTINATE]

ostler *or* **hostler** ('ɒslə) *n. Arch.* a stableman, esp. one at an inn. [C15: var. of *hostler*, from HOSTEL]

ostmark ('ɒstmɑːk) *n.* the standard monetary unit of East Germany, divided into 100 pfennigs. [lit.: east mark]

Ostpreussen ('ɒstprɔɪsən) *n.* the German name for **East Prussia.**

ostracize *or* **-ise** ('ɒstrə,saɪz) *vb.* (*tr.*) **1.** to exclude or banish (a person) from a particular group, society, etc. **2.** (in ancient Greece) to punish by temporary exile. [C17: from Gk *ostrakizein* to select someone for banishment by voting on potsherds, from *ostrakon* potsherd] —'**ostracism** *n.* —'**ostra,cizable** *or* **-isable** *adj.* —'**ostra,cizer** *or* **-iser** *n.*

Ostrava (*Czech* 'ɒstrava) *n.* an industrial city in N Czechoslovakia, on the River Oder: the chief coal-mining area in Czechoslovakia, in Upper Silesia. Pop.: 328 000 (1986).

ostrich ('ɒstrɪtʃ) *n., pl.* **-triches** *or* **-trich.** **1.** a fast-running flightless African bird that is the largest living bird with stout two-toed feet and dark feathers, except on the naked head, neck, and legs. **2. American ostrich.** another name for **rhea. 3.** a person who refuses to recognize the truth, reality, etc. [C13: from OF *ostrice*, from L *avis* bird + LL *struthio* ostrich, from Gk *strouthion*]

Ostwald (*German* 'ɔstvalt) *n.* **Wilhelm** ('vɪlhɛlm). 1853–1932, German chemist, noted for his pioneering work in catalysis. He also invented a process for making nitric acid from ammonia and developed a new theory of colour: Nobel prize for chemistry 1909.

Oświęcim (*Polish* ɔʃ'fjɛntʃim) *n.* the Polish name for **Auschwitz.**

OT *abbrev. for:* **1.** occupational therapy. **2.** Old Testament. **3.** overtime.

Otago (ɒ'tɑːgəʊ) *n.* an administrative district of New Zealand, formerly a province, founded by Scottish settlers in the south of South Island. The University of Otago (1869) in Dunedin is the oldest university in New Zealand. Chief town: Dunedin. Pop. (urban area): 105 600 (1983 est.).

otalgia (əʊ'tældʒɪə, -dʒə) *n.* the technical name for **earache.**

OTC (in Britain) *abbrev. for:* **1.** Officers' Training Corps. **2.** *Stock Exchange.* over the counter: denoting dealings between brokers in areas for which no official market prices are quoted.

OTE *abbrev. for* on target earnings: referring to the salary a salesman should be able to achieve.

other ('ʌðə) *determiner.* **1. a.** (when used before a singular noun, usually preceded by *the*) the remaining (one or ones in a group of which one or some have been specified): *I'll read the other sections of the paper later.* **b. the other.** (*as pron.; functioning as sing.*): *one walks while the other rides.* **2.** (a) different (one or ones from that or those already specified or understood): *no other man but you.* **3.** additional; further: *there are no other possibilities.* **4.** (preceded by *every*) alternate; two: *it buzzes every other minute.* **5. other than.** apart from; besides: *a lady other than his wife.* **b.** different from: *he couldn't be other than what he is.* Archaic form: **other from. 6. no other.** *Arch.* nothing else: *I can do no other.* **7. or other.** (preceded by a phrase or word with *some*) used to add vagueness to the preceding pronoun, noun, or noun phrase: *he's somewhere or other.* **8. other things being equal.** conditions being the same or unchanged. **9. the other day, night,** etc. a few days, nights, etc., ago. **10. the other thing.** an unexpressed alternative. ~*pron.* **11.** another: *show me one other.* **12.** (*pl.*) additional or further ones. **13.** (*pl.*) other people or things. **14. the others.** the remaining ones (of a group). ~*adv.* **15.** (usually used with a negative and foll. by *than*) otherwise; differently: *they couldn't behave other than they do.* [OE *ōther*] —'**otherness** *n.*

other-directed *adj.* guided by values derived from external influences.

other ranks *pl. n.* (*rarely sing.*) *Chiefly Brit.* (in the armed forces) all those who do not hold a commissioned rank.

otherwise ('ʌðə,waɪz) *sentence connector.* **1.** or else; if not, then: *go home — otherwise your mother will worry.* ~*adv.* **2.** differently: *I wouldn't have thought otherwise.* **3.** in other respects: *an otherwise hopeless situation.* ~*adj.* **4.** (*predicative*) of an unexpected nature; different: *the facts are otherwise.* ~*pron.* **5.** something different in outcome: *success or otherwise.* [C14: from OE *on ōthre wisan* in other manner]

other world *n.* the spirit world or afterlife.
otherworldly (ˌʌðə'wɜːldlɪ) *adj.* **1.** of or relating to the spiritual or imaginative world. **2.** impractical or unworldly. — ˌother'worldliness *n.*
Othin ('əʊðɪn) *n.* a variant of **Odin.**
Othman ('ɒθmən, ɒθ'mɑːn) *adj.*, *n.* a variant of **Ottoman.**
Othman I *n.* a variant of **Osman I.**
Otho I ('əʊθəʊ) *n.* a variant of **Otto I.**
otic ('əʊtɪk, 'ɒtɪk) *adj.* of or relating to the ear. [C17: from Gk ōtikos, from ous ear]
-otic *suffix forming adjectives.* **1.** relating to or affected by: *sclerotic.* **2.** causing: *narcotic.* [from Gk -ōtikos]
otiose ('əʊtɪˌəʊs, -ˌəʊz) *adj.* **1.** serving no useful purpose: *otiose language.* **2.** *Rare.* indolent; lazy. [C18: from L ōtiōsus leisured, from ōtium leisure] — **otiosity** (ˌəʊtɪ'ɒsɪtɪ) *or* 'oti,oseness *n.*
otitis (əʊ'taɪtɪs) *n.* inflammation of the ear.
oto- *or before a vowel* **ot-** *combining form.* indicating the ear. [from Gk ous, ōt- ear]
otolaryngology (ˌəʊtəʊˌlærɪŋ'gɒlədʒɪ) *n.* another name for **otorhinolaryngology.** — **otolaryngological** (ˌəʊtəʊləˌrɪŋgə'lɒdʒɪkəl) *adj.* — ˌoto,laryn'gologist *n.*
otolith ('əʊtəʊˌlɪθ) *n.* any of the granules of calcium carbonate in the inner ear of vertebrates. Movement of otoliths, caused by a change in the animal's position, stimulates sensory hair cells, which convey information to the brain. — ˌoto'lithic *adj.*
otology (əʊ'tɒlədʒɪ) *n.* the branch of medicine concerned with the ear. — **otological** (ˌəʊtə'lɒdʒɪkəl) *adj.* — **o'tologist** *n.*
otorhinolaryngology (ˌəʊtəʊˌraɪnəʊˌlærɪŋ'gɒlədʒɪ) *n.* the branch of medicine concerned with the ear, nose, and throat. Sometimes called **otolaryngology.**
otoscope ('əʊtəʊˌskəʊp) *n.* a medical instrument for examining the external ear. — **otoscopic** (ˌəʊtəʊ'skɒpɪk) *adj.*
Otranto (*Italian* 'ɔːtranto) *n.* a small port in SE Italy, in Apulia on the **Strait of Otranto:** the most easterly town in Italy; dates back to Greek times and was an important Roman port; its ruined castle was the setting of Horace Walpole's *Castle of Otranto.* Pop.: 4811 (1981 est.).
OTT *Sl. abbrev. for* over the top.
ottava rima (əʊ'tɑːvə 'riːmə) *n. Prosody.* a stanza form consisting of eight iambic pentameter lines, rhyming a b a b a b c c. [It.: eighth rhyme]
Ottawa ('ɒtəwə) *n.* **1.** the capital of Canada, in E Ontario on the Ottawa River: name changed from Bytown to Ottawa in 1854. Pop.: 300 763 (1986). **2.** a river in central Canada, rising in W Quebec and flowing west, then southeast to join the St Lawrence River as its chief tributary at Montreal; forms the border between Quebec and Ontario for most of its length. Length: 1120 km (696 miles).
otter ('ɒtə) *n.*, *pl.* **-ters** *or* **-ter.** **1.** a freshwater carnivorous mammal, esp. the **Eurasian otter,** typically having smooth fur, a streamlined body, and webbed feet. **2.** the fur of this animal. **3.** a type of fishing tackle consisting of a weighted board to which hooked and baited lines are attached. [OE otor]
otter hound *n.* a large rough-coated dog of a breed formerly used for otter hunting.
Otto (*German* 'ɒto) *n.* **Rudolf** ('ruːdɒlf). 1869–1937, German theologian: his best-known work is *The Idea of the Holy* (1923).
Otto I ('ɒtəʊ) *or* **Otho I** *n.* called *the Great.* 912–73 A.D., king of Germany (936–73); Holy Roman Emperor (962–73).
ottoman ('ɒtəmən) *n.*, *pl.* **-mans.** **1. a.** a low padded seat, usually armless, sometimes in the form of a chest. **b.** a cushioned footstool. **2.** a corded fabric. [C17: from F ottomane, fem. of OTTOMAN]
Ottoman ('ɒtəmən) *or* **Othman** ('ɒθmən) *adj.* **1.** *History.* of or relating to the Ottomans or the Ottoman Empire. **2.** denoting or relating to the Turkish language. ~*n.*, *pl.* **-mans.** **3.** a member of a Turkish people who invaded the Near East in the late 13th century. [C17: from F, via Med. L, from Ar. Othmāni Turkish, from Turkish Othman OSMAN I]
Ottoman Empire *n.* the former Turkish empire in Europe, Asia, and Africa, which lasted from the late 13th century until the end of World War I.
Otway ('ɒtweɪ) *n.* **Thomas.** 1652–85, English dramatist, noted for *The Orphan* (1680) and *Venice Preserv'd* (1682).

ou (əʊ) *n. S. African. sl.* a man. [from Afrik., ?from Du.]
OU *abbrev. for:* **1.** the Open University. **2.** Oxford University.
Ouachita *or* **Washita** ('wɒʃɪˌtɔː) *n.* a river in the S central U.S., rising in the **Ouachita Mountains** and flowing east, south, and southeast into the Red River in E Louisiana. Length: 974 km (605 miles).
Ouagadougou (ˌwɑːgə'duːguː) *n.* the capital of Burkina-Faso, on the central plateau: terminus of the railway from Abidjan (Côte d'Ivoire). Pop.: 375 000 (1985).
ouananiche (ˌwɑːnə'niːʃ) *n.* a landlocked variety of the Atlantic salmon found in lakes in SE Canada. [from Canad. F, of Amerind origin, from wananish, dim. of wanans salmon]
oubaas ('əʊˌbɑːs) *n. S. African.* a man in authority. [from Afrik., from Du. oud old + baas boss]
Oubangui (uː'bɑːŋgiː, juː'bæŋgɪ) *n.* the French name for **Ubangi.**
oubliette (ˌuːblɪ'ɛt) *n.* a dungeon, the only entrance to which is through the top. [C19: from F, from oublier to forget]
ouch (aʊtʃ) *interj.* an exclamation of sharp sudden pain.
Oudh (aʊd) *n.* a region of N India, in central Uttar Pradesh: annexed by Britain in 1856 and a centre of the Indian Mutiny (1857–58); joined with Agra in 1877, becoming the United Provinces of Agra and Oudh in 1902, which were renamed Uttar Pradesh in 1950.
Ouessant (wesɑ̃) *n.* the French name for **Ushant.**
ought[1] (ɔːt) *vb.* (foll. by *to; takes an infinitive or implied infinitive*) used as an auxiliary: **1.** to indicate duty or obligation: *you ought to pay.* **2.** to express prudent expediency: *you ought to see him.* **3.** (usually with reference to future time) to express probability or expectation: *you ought to finish this by Friday.* **4.** to express a desire or wish on the part of the speaker: *you ought to come next week.* [OE āhte, p.t. of āgan to OWE]
▷**Usage.** In careful English, *ought* is not used with *did* or *had. I ought not to do it,* not *I didn't ought to do it; I ought not to have done it,* not *I hadn't ought to have done it.*
ought[2] (ɔːt) *pron.*, *adv.* a variant spelling of **aught.**
ought[3] (ɔːt) *n.* a less common word for **nought** (zero). [C19: mistaken division of a nought as an ought; see NOUGHT]
Ouija ('wiːdʒə) *n. Trademark.* a board on which are marked the letters of the alphabet. Answers to questions are spelt out by a pointer and are supposedly formed by spirits. [C19: from F oui yes + G ja yes]
Oujda (uːdʒ'dɑː) *n.* a city in NE Morocco, near the border with Algeria: frontier post. Pop.: 260 082 (1982).
Oulu ('ɔːuluː) *n.* an industrial city and port in W Finland, on the Gulf of Bothnia: university (1959). Pop.: 97 869 (1986). Swedish name: **Uleåborg.**
ouma ('əʊmɑː) *n.* (in South Africa) **1.** grandmother, esp. in titular use with her surname. **2.** *Sl.* any elderly woman. [from Afrik., from Du. oma grandmother]
ounce[1] (aʊns) *n.* **1.** a unit of weight equal to one sixteenth of a pound (avoirdupois). Abbrev.: **oz.** **2.** a unit of weight equal to one twelfth of a Troy or Apothecaries' pound; 1 ounce is equal to 480 grains. **3.** short for **fluid ounce. 4.** a small portion or amount. [C14: from OF unce, from L uncia a twelfth]
ounce[2] (aʊns) *n.* another name for **snow leopard.** [C18: from OF once, by mistaken division of lonce as if l'once, from L LYNX]
oupa ('əʊpɑː) *n. S. African.* **1.** grandfather, esp. in titular use with surname. **2.** *Sl.* any elderly man. [Afrik.]
our ('aʊə) *determiner.* **1.** of, belonging to, or associated in some way with us: *our best vodka; our parents are good to us.* **2.** belonging to or associated with all people or people in general: *our nearest planet is Venus.* **3.** a formal word for *my* used by editors or other writers, and monarchs. [OE ūre (genitive pl.), from US]
-our *suffix forming nouns.* indicating state, condition, or activity: *behaviour; labour.* [in OF -eur, from L -or, n. suffix]
Our Father *n.* another name for the **Lord's Prayer,** taken from its opening words.
ours ('aʊəz) *pron.* **1.** something or someone belonging to or associated with us: *ours have blue tags.* **2. of ours.** belonging to or associated with us.
ourself (aʊə'sɛlf) *pron. Arch.* a variant of **myself,** formerly used by monarchs or editors.

ourselves (auə'sɛlvz) *pron.* **1. a.** the reflexive form of *we* or *us.* **b.** (intensifier): *we ourselves will finish it.* **2.** (*preceded by a copula*) our usual selves: *we are ourselves when we're together.* **3.** *Not standard.* used instead of *we* or *us* in compound noun phrases: *other people and ourselves.*

▷ **Usage.** See at **myself.**

-ous *suffix forming adjectives.* **1.** having or full of: *dangerous; spacious.* **2.** (in chemistry) indicating that an element is chemically combined in the lower of two possible valency states: *ferrous.* Cf. **-ic** (sense 2). [from OF, from L *-ōsus* or *-us*, Gk *-os*, adj. suffixes]

Ouse (uːz) *n.* **1.** Also called: **Great Ouse.** a river in E England, rising in Northamptonshire and flowing northeast to the Wash near King's Lynn; for the last 56 km (35 miles) follows mainly artificial channels. Length: 257 km (160 miles). **2.** a river in NE England, in Yorkshire, formed by the confluence of the Swale and Ure Rivers: flows southeast to the Humber. Length: 92 km (57 miles). **3.** a river in S England, rising in Sussex and flowing south to the English Channel. Length: 48 km (30 miles).

ousel ('uːzəl) *n.* a variant spelling of **ouzel.**

oust (aʊst) *vb.* (*tr.*) **1.** to force out of a position or place; supplant or expel. **2.** *Property law.* to deprive (a person) of the possession of land, etc. [C16: from Anglo-Norman *ouster*, from L *obstāre* to withstand]

ouster ('aʊstə) *n. Property law.* the act of dispossessing of freehold property; eviction.

out (aʊt) *adv.* (*when predicative, can in some senses be regarded as adj.*) **1.** (*often used as a particle*) at or to a point beyond the limits of some location; outside: *get out at once.* **2.** (*particle*) used to indicate exhaustion or extinction: *the sugar's run out; put the light out.* **3.** not in a particular place, esp., not at home. **4.** public; revealed: *the secret is out.* **5.** on sale or on view to the public: *the book is being brought out next May.* **6.** (of the sun, stars, etc.) visible. **7.** in flower: *the roses are out now.* **8.** not in fashion, favour, or current usage: *that plan is out.* **9.** not or not any longer worth considering: *that plan is out.* **10.** not allowed: *smoking on duty is out.* **11.** (of a fire or light) no longer burning or providing illumination. **12.** not working: *the radio's out.* **13.** Also: **out on strike.** on strike. **14.** (of a jury) withdrawn to consider a verdict in private. **15.** (*particle*) out of consciousness: *she passed out.* **16.** (*particle*) used to indicate a burst of activity as indicated by the verb: *fever broke out.* **17.** (*particle*) used to indicate obliteration of an object: *the graffiti was painted out.* **18.** (*particle*) used to indicate an approximate drawing or description: *chalk out.* **19.** at or to the fullest length or extent: *spread out.* **20.** loudly; clearly: *calling out.* **21.** desirous of or intent on (something or doing something): *I'm out for as much money as I can get.* **22.** (*particle*) used to indicate a goal or object achieved at the end of the action specified by the verb: *he worked it out.* **23.** (*preceded by a superlative*) existing: *the friendliest dog out.* **24.** an expression in signalling, radio, etc., to indicate the end of a transmission. **25.** used up; exhausted: *our supplies are completely out.* **26.** worn into holes: *out at the elbows.* **27.** inaccurate, deficient, or discrepant: *out by six pence.* **28.** not in office or authority. **29.** completed or concluded, as of time: *before the year is out.* **30.** *Obs.* (of a young woman) in or into society: *Lucinda had a large party when she came out.* **31.** *Sport.* denoting the state in which a player is caused to discontinue active participation, esp. in some specified role. **32. out of. a.** at or to a point outside: *out of his reach.* **b.** away from; not in: *stepping out of line; out of focus.* **c.** because of; motivated by: *out of jealousy.* **d.** from (a material or source): *made out of plastic.* **e.** not or no longer having any of (a substance, material, etc.): *we're out of sugar.* **f.** no longer in a specified state or condition: *out of work; out of practice.* **g.** (of a horse) born of. ~*adj.* **33.** directed or indicating direction outwards: *the out tray.* **34.** (of an island) remote from the mainland. ~*prep.* **35.** *Nonstandard or U.S.* out of; out through: *he ran out the door.* ~*interj.* **36. a.** an exclamation of dismissal, reproach, etc. **b.** (in wireless telegraphy) an expression used to signal that the speaker is signing off. **37. out with it.** a command to make something known immediately, without missing any details. ~*n.* **38.** *Chiefly U.S.* a method of escape from a place, difficult situation, etc. **39.** *Baseball.* an instance of causing a batter to be out by fielding. ~*vb.* **40.** (*tr.*) to put or throw out. **41.** (*intr.*) to be made known or effective despite efforts to the contrary (esp. in **the truth will out**). [OE *ūt*]

out- *prefix.* **1.** excelling or surpassing in a particular action: *outlast; outlive.* **2.** indicating an external location or situation away from the centre: *outpost; outpatient.* **3.** indicating emergence, an issuing forth, etc.: *outcrop; outgrowth.* **4.** indicating the result of an action: *outcome.*

outage ('aʊtɪdʒ) *n.* **1.** a quantity of goods missing or lost after storage or shipment. **2.** a period of power failure, machine stoppage, etc.

out and away *adv.* by far.

out-and-out *adj.* (*prenominal*) thoroughgoing; complete.

outback ('aʊt,bæk) *n.* **a.** the remote bush country of Australia. **b.** (*as modifier*): *outback life.*

outbalance (,aʊt'bæləns) *vb.* another word for **outweigh.**

outboard ('aʊt,bɔːd) *adj.* **1.** (of a boat's engine) portable, with its own propeller, and designed to be attached externally to the stern. **2.** in a position away from, or further away from, the centre line of a vessel or aircraft, esp. outside the hull or fuselage. ~*adv.* **3.** away from the centre line of a vessel or aircraft, esp. outside the hull or fuselage. ~*n.* **4.** an outboard motor.

outbound ('aʊt,baʊnd) *adj.* going out; outward bound.

outbrave (aʊt'breɪv) *vb.* (*tr.*) **1.** to surpass in bravery. **2.** to confront defiantly.

outbreak ('aʊt,breɪk) *n.* a sudden, violent, or spontaneous occurrence, esp. of disease or strife.

outbuilding ('aʊt,bɪldɪŋ) *n.* a building separate from a main building; outhouse.

outburst ('aʊt,bɜːst) *n.* **1.** a sudden and violent expression of emotion. **2.** an explosion or eruption.

outcast ('aʊt,kɑːst) *n.* **1.** a person who is rejected or excluded from a social group. **2.** a vagabond or wanderer. **3.** anything thrown out or rejected. ~*adj.* **4.** rejected, abandoned, or discarded; cast out.

outcaste ('aʊt,kɑːst) *n.* **1.** a person who has been expelled from a caste. **2.** a person having no caste. ~*vb.* **3.** (*tr.*) to cause (someone) to lose his caste.

outclass (,aʊt'klɑːs) *vb.* (*tr.*) **1.** to surpass in class, quality, etc. **2.** to defeat easily.

outcome ('aʊt,kʌm) *n.* something that follows from an action or situation; result; consequence.

outcrop *n.* ('aʊt,krɒp). **1.** part of a rock formation or mineral vein that appears at the surface of the earth. **2.** an emergence; appearance. ~*vb.* (,aʊt'krɒp), **-cropping, -cropped. 3.** (*intr.*) (of rock strata, mineral veins, etc.) to protrude through the surface of the earth.

outcry *n.* ('aʊt,kraɪ), *pl.* **-cries. 1.** a widespread or vehement protest. **2.** clamour; uproar. ~*vb.* (,aʊt'kraɪ), **-crying, -cried. 3.** (*tr.*) to cry louder or make more noise than (someone or something).

outdated (,aʊt'deɪtɪd) *adj.* old-fashioned or obsolete.

outdo (,aʊt'duː) *vb.* **-doing, -did, -done.** (*tr.*) to surpass or exceed in performance.

outdoor ('aʊt,dɔː) *adj.* (*prenominal*) taking place, existing, or intended for use in the open air: *outdoor games; outdoor clothes.* Also: **out-of-door.**

outdoors (,aʊt'dɔːz) *adv.* **1.** Also: **out-of-doors.** in the open air; outside. ~*n.* **2.** the world outside or far away from human habitation.

outer ('aʊtə) *adj.* (*prenominal*) **1.** being or located on the outside; external. **2.** further from the middle or central part. ~*n.* **3.** *Archery.* **a.** the white outermost ring on a target. **b.** a shot that hits this ring. **4.** *Austral. & N.Z.* the unsheltered part of the spectator area at a sports ground. **5. on the outer.** *Austral. & N.Z.* excluded or neglected.

outer bar *n.* (in England) a collective name for junior barristers who plead from outside the bar of the court.

Outer Hebrides *pl. n.* See **Hebrides.**

Outer Mongolia *n.* the former name (until 1924) of the **Mongolian People's Republic.**

outermost ('aʊtə,məʊst) *adj.* furthest from the centre or middle; outmost.

outer space *n.* any region of space beyond the atmosphere of the earth.

,**out'act** *vb.*
,**out'bargain** *vb.*

,**out'bid** *vb.*
,**out'box** *vb.*

,**out'dance** *vb.*
,**out'dare** *vb.*

,**out'distance** *vb.*
,**out'drink** *vb.*

outfall ('aʊt,fɔːl) n. the end of a river, sewer, drain, etc., from which it discharges.

outfield ('aʊt,fiːld) n. **1.** *Cricket.* the area of the field relatively far from the pitch; the deep. Cf. **infield** (sense 1). **2.** *Baseball.* **a.** the area of the playing field beyond the lines connecting first, second, and third bases. **b.** the positions of the left fielder, centre fielder, and right fielder taken collectively. **3.** *Agriculture.* farmland most distant from the farmstead. — '**out,fielder** n.

outfit ('aʊt,fɪt) n. **1.** a set of articles or equipment for a particular task, etc. **2.** a set of clothes, esp. a carefully selected one. **3.** *Inf.* any group or association regarded as a cohesive unit, such as a military company, etc. ~vb. **-fitting, -fitted. 4.** to furnish or be furnished with an outfit, equipment, etc. — '**out,fitter** n.

outflank (,aʊt'flæŋk) vb. (tr.) **1.** to go around the flank of (an opposing army, etc.). **2.** to get the better of.

outflow ('aʊt,fləʊ) n. **1.** anything that flows out, such as liquid, money, etc. **2.** the amount that flows out. **3.** the act or process of flowing out.

outfox (,aʊt'fɒks) vb. (tr.) to surpass in guile or cunning.

outgeneral (,aʊt'dʒɛnərəl) vb. **-alling, -alled** or *U.S.* **-aling, -aled.** (tr.) to surpass in generalship.

outgo vb. (,aʊt'gəʊ), **-going, -went, -gone. 1.** (tr.) to exceed or outstrip. ~n. ('aʊt,gəʊ). **2.** cost; outgoings; outlay. **3.** something that goes out; outflow.

outgoing ('aʊt,gəʊɪŋ) adj. **1.** departing; leaving. **2.** retiring from office. **3.** friendly and sociable. ~n. **4.** the act of going out.

outgoings ('aʊt,gəʊɪŋz) pl.n. expenditure.

outgrow (,aʊt'grəʊ) vb. **-growing, -grew, -grown.** (tr.) **1.** to grow too large for (clothes, shoes, etc.). **2.** to lose (a habit, idea, reputation, etc.) in the course of development or time. **3.** to grow larger or faster than.

outgrowth ('aʊt,grəʊθ) n. **1.** a thing growing out of a main body. **2.** a development, result, or consequence. **3.** the act of growing out.

outgun (,aʊt'gʌn) vb. **-gunning, -gunned.** (tr.) **1.** to surpass in fire power. **2.** to surpass in shooting. **3.** *Inf.* to surpass or excel.

outhouse ('aʊt,haʊs) n. a building near to, but separate from, a main building; outbuilding.

outing ('aʊtɪŋ) n. a short outward and return journey; trip; excursion.

outjockey (,aʊt'dʒɒkɪ) vb. (tr.) to outwit by deception.

outlandish (aʊt'lændɪʃ) adj. **1.** grotesquely unconventional in appearance, habits, etc. **2.** *Arch.* foreign. — **out'landishly** adv. — **out'landishness** n.

outlaw ('aʊt,lɔː) n. **1.** (formerly) a person excluded from the law and deprived of its protection. **2.** any fugitive from the law, esp. a habitual transgressor. ~vb. (tr.) **3.** to put (a person) outside the law and deprive of its protection. **4.** to ban. — '**out,lawry** n.

outlay n. ('aʊt,leɪ). **1.** an expenditure of money, effort, etc. ~vb. (,aʊt'leɪ), **-laying, -laid. 2.** (tr.) to spend (money, etc.).

outlet ('aʊtlɛt, -lɪt) n. **1.** an opening or vent permitting escape or release. **2. a.** a market for a product or service. **b.** a commercial establishment retailing the goods of a particular producer or wholesaler. **3.** a channel that drains a body of water. **4.** a point in a wiring system from which current can be taken to supply electrical devices.

outlier ('aʊt,laɪə) n. **1.** an outcrop of rocks that is entirely surrounded by older rocks. **2.** a person, thing, or part situated away from a main or related body. **3.** a person who lives away from his place of work, duty, etc.

outline ('aʊt,laɪn) n. **1.** a preliminary or schematic plan, draft, etc. **2.** (usually pl.) the important features of a theory, work, etc. **3.** the line by which an object or figure is or appears to be bounded. **4. a.** a drawing or manner of drawing consisting only of external lines. **b.** (as modifier): an outline map. ~vb. (tr.) **5.** to draw or display the outline of. **6.** to give the main features or general idea of.

outlive (,aʊt'lɪv) vb. (tr.) **1.** to live longer than (someone). **2.** to live beyond (a date or period): he outlived the century. **3.** to live through (an experience).

outlook ('aʊt,lʊk) n. **1.** a mental attitude or point of view. **2.** the probable or expected condition or outcome of

something: the weather outlook. **3.** the view from a place. **4.** view or prospect. **5.** the act or state of looking out.

outlying ('aʊt,laɪɪŋ) adj. distant or remote from the main body or centre, as of a town or region.

outmanoeuvre or *U.S.* **outmaneuver** (,aʊtmə'nuːvə) vb. (tr.) to secure a strategic advantage over by skilful manoeuvre.

outmoded (,aʊt'məʊdɪd) adj. no longer fashionable or widely accepted. — ,**out'modedly** adv. — ,**out'modedness** n.

outmost ('aʊt,məʊst) adj. another word for **outermost.**

out of bounds adj. (postpositive), adv. **1.** (often foll. by to) not to be entered (by); barred (to). **2.** outside specified or prescribed limits.

out of date adj. (out-of-date when prenominal), adv. no longer valid, current, or fashionable; outmoded.

out-of-door adj. (prenominal) another term for **outdoor.**

out-of-doors adv., adj. (postpositive) in the open air; outside. Also: **outdoors.**

out of pocket adj. (out-of-pocket when prenominal). **1.** (postpositive) having lost money, as in a commercial enterprise. **2.** without money to spend. **3.** (prenominal) (of expenses) unbudgeted and paid for in cash.

out of the way adj. (out-of-the-way when prenominal). **1.** distant from more populous areas. **2.** uncommon or unusual.

outpatient ('aʊt,peɪʃənt) n. a nonresident hospital patient. Cf. **inpatient.**

outpoint (,aʊt'pɔɪnt) vb. (tr.) to score more points than.

outport ('aʊt,pɔːt) n. **1.** *Chiefly Brit.* a subsidiary port built in deeper water than the original port. **2.** *Canad.* a small fishing village of Newfoundland.

outpost ('aʊt,pəʊst) n. **1.** *Mil.* **a.** a position stationed at a distance from the area occupied by a major formation. **b.** the troops assigned to such a position. **2.** an outlying settlement or position.

outpour n. ('aʊt,pɔː). **1.** the act of flowing or pouring out. **2.** something that pours out. ~vb. (,aʊt'pɔː). **3.** to pour or cause to pour out freely or rapidly.

outpouring ('aʊt,pɔːrɪŋ) n. **1.** a passionate or exaggerated outburst; effusion. **2.** another word for **outpour** (senses 1, 2).

output ('aʊt,pʊt) n. **1.** the act of production or manufacture. **2.** the amount produced, as in a given period: a weekly output. **3.** the material produced, manufactured, etc. **4.** *Electronics.* **a.** the power, voltage, or current delivered by a circuit or component. **b.** the point at which the signal is delivered. **5.** the power, energy, or work produced by an engine or a system. **6.** *Computers.* **a.** the information produced by a computer. **b.** the operations and devices involved in producing this information. **7.** (modifier) of or relating to electronic or computer output: output signal. ~vb. **8.** (tr.) *Computers.* to cause (data) to be emitted as output.

outrage ('aʊt,reɪdʒ) n. **1.** a wantonly vicious or cruel act. **2.** a gross violation of decency, morality, honour, etc. **3.** profound indignation, anger, or hurt, caused by such an act. ~vb. (tr.) **4.** to cause profound indignation, anger, or resentment in. **5.** to offend grossly. **6.** to commit an act of wanton viciousness, cruelty, or indecency on. **7.** a euphemistic word for **rape**[1]. [C13 (meaning: excess): via F from outré beyond, from L ultrā]

outrageous (aʊt'reɪdʒəs) adj. **1.** being or having the nature of an outrage. **2.** grossly offensive to decency, authority, etc. **3.** violent or unrestrained in behaviour or temperament. **4.** extravagant or immoderate. — **out'rageously** adv. — **out'rageousness** n.

outrank (,aʊt'ræŋk) vb. (tr.) **1.** to be of higher rank than. **2.** to take priority over.

outré ('uːtreɪ) adj. deviating from what is usual or proper. [C18: from F, p.p. of outrer to pass beyond]

outride (,aʊt'raɪd) vb. **-riding, -rode, -ridden.** (tr.) **1.** to outdo by riding faster, farther, or better than. **2.** (of a vessel) to ride out (a storm).

outrider ('aʊt,raɪdə) n. **1.** a person who goes in advance to investigate, discover a way, etc.; scout. **2.** a person

,**out'face** vb.	,**out'hit** vb.	,**out'number** vb.	,**out'race** vb.
,**out'fight** vb.	,**out'jump** vb.	,**out'pace** vb.	,**out'range** vb.
,**out'fly** vb.	,**out'last** vb.	,**outper'form** vb.	,**out'reach** vb.
,**out'guess** vb.	,**out'match** vb.	,**out'play** vb.	

who rides in front of or beside a carriage, esp. as an attendant or guard. **3.** *U.S.* a mounted herdsman.

outrigger ('aʊt,rɪgə) *n.* **1.** a framework for supporting a pontoon outside and parallel to the hull of a boat to provide stability. **2.** a boat equipped with such a framework, esp. one of the canoes of the South Pacific. **3.** any projecting framework attached to a boat, aircraft, building, etc., to act as a support. **4.** *Rowing.* another name for **rigger** (sense 2). [C18: from OUT- + RIG + -ER¹]

outright *adj.* ('aʊt,raɪt). (*prenominal*) **1.** without qualifications or limitations: *outright ownership.* **2.** complete; total. **3.** straightforward; direct. ~*adv.* (,aʊt'raɪt). **4.** without restrictions. **5.** without reservation or concealment: *ask outright.* **6.** instantly: *he was killed outright.*

outrush (,aʊt'rʌʃ) *n.* a flowing or rushing out.

outset ('aʊt,sɛt) *n.* a start; beginning (esp. in **from** (*or* at) **the outset**).

outside *prep.* (,aʊt'saɪd). **1.** (sometimes foll. by *of*) on or to the exterior of: *outside the house.* **2.** beyond the limits of. **3.** apart from; other than: *no-one knows outside you.* ~*adj.* ('aʊt,saɪd). **4.** (*prenominal*) situated on the exterior: *an outside lavatory.* **5.** remote; unlikely. **6.** not a member of. **7.** the greatest possible or probable (prices, odds, etc.). ~*adv.* (,aʊt'saɪd). **8.** outside a specified thing or place; out of doors. **9.** *Sl.* not in prison. ~*n.* ('aʊt'saɪd). **10.** the external side or surface. **11.** the external appearance or aspect. **12.** (of a pavement, etc.) the side nearest the road or away from a wall. **13.** *Sport.* an outside player, as in football. **14.** (*pl.*) the outer sheets of a ream of paper. **15.** *Canad.* (in the north) the settled parts of Canada. **16. at the outside.** *Inf.* at the most or at the greatest extent: *two days at the outside.*

▷ **Usage.** In careful usage, *outside* and *inside* are preferred to *outside of* and *inside of*: *she waits outside* (not *outside of*) *the school.*

outside broadcast *n. Radio, television.* a broadcast not made from a studio.

outsider (,aʊt'saɪdə) *n.* **1.** a person or thing excluded from or not a member of a set, group, etc. **2.** a contestant, esp. a horse, thought unlikely to win in a race. **3.** *Canad.* a person who does not live in the Arctic regions.

outsize ('aʊt,saɪz) *adj.* **1.** Also: **outsized.** very large or larger than normal. ~*n.* **2.** something outsize, such as a garment or person. **3.** (*modifier*) relating to or dealing in outsize clothes: *an outsize shop.*

outskirts ('aʊt,skɜːts) *pl. n.* (*sometimes sing.*) outlying or bordering areas, districts, etc., as of a city.

outsmart (,aʊt'smɑːt) *vb.* (*tr.*) *Inf.* to get the better of; outwit.

outspan *S. African.* ~*n.* ('aʊt,spæn). **1.** an area on a farm kept available for travellers to rest and refresh animals, etc. **2.** the act of unharnessing or unyoking. ~*vb.* (,aʊt'spæn), **-spanning, -spanned. 3.** to unharness or unyoke (animals). [C19: partial translation of Afrik. *uitspan,* from *uit* out + *spannen* to stretch]

outspoken (,aʊt'spəʊkən) *adj.* **1.** candid or bold in speech. **2.** said or expressed with candour or boldness.

outspread *vb.* (,aʊt'sprɛd), **-spreading, -spread. 1.** to spread out. ~*adj.* ('aʊt'sprɛd). **2.** spread or stretched out. **3.** scattered or diffused widely. ~*n.* ('aʊt,sprɛd). **4.** a spreading out.

outstanding (,aʊt'stændɪŋ) *adj.* **1.** superior; excellent. **2.** prominent, remarkable, or striking. **3.** unsettled, unpaid, or unresolved. **4.** (of shares, bonds, etc.) issued and sold. **5.** projecting or jutting upwards or outwards. —,**out'standingly** *adv.*

outstation ('aʊt,steɪʃən) *n.* a station or post at a distance from the base station or in a remote region.

outstay (,aʊt'steɪ) *vb.* (*tr.*) **1.** to stay longer than. **2.** to stay beyond (a limit). **3. outstay one's welcome.** See **overstay** (sense 2).

outstretch (,aʊt'strɛtʃ) *vb.* (*tr.*) **1.** to extend or expand; stretch out. **2.** to stretch or extend beyond.

outstrip (,aʊt'strɪp) *vb.* **-stripping, -stripped.** (*tr.*) **1.** to surpass in a sphere of activity, competition, etc. **2.** to be or grow greater than. **3.** to go faster than and leave behind.

outtake ('aʊt,teɪk) *n.* an unreleased take from a recording session, film, or television programme.

out tray *n.* (in an office, etc.) a tray for outgoing correspondence, documents, etc.

outturn ('aʊt,tɜːn) *n.* another word for **output** (sense 2).

outvote (,aʊt'vəʊt) *vb.* (*tr.*) to defeat by a majority of votes.

outward ('aʊtwəd) *adj.* **1.** of or relating to what is apparent or superficial. **2.** of or relating to the outside of the body. **3.** belonging or relating to the external, as opposed to the mental, spiritual, or inherent. **4.** of, relating to, or directed towards the outside or exterior. **5. the outward man. a.** *Theol.* the body as opposed to the soul. **b.** *Facetious.* clothing. ~*adv.* **6.** (of a ship) away from port. **7.** a variant of **outwards.** ~*n.* **8.** the outward part; exterior. —'**outwardness** *n.*

Outward Bound movement *n.* (in Britain) a scheme to provide adventure training for young people.

outwardly ('aʊtwədlɪ) *adv.* **1.** in outward appearance. **2.** with reference to the outside or outer surface; externally.

outwards ('aʊtwədz) *or* **outward** *adv.* towards the outside; out.

outwear (,aʊt'wɛə) *vb.* **-wearing, -wore, -worn.** (*tr.*) **1.** to use up or destroy by wearing. **2.** to last or wear longer than. **3.** to outlive, outgrow, or develop beyond. **4.** to deplete or exhaust in strength, determination, etc.

outweigh (,aʊt'weɪ) *vb.* (*tr.*) **1.** to prevail over; overcome. **2.** to be more important or significant than. **3.** to be heavier than.

outwit (,aʊt'wɪt) *vb.* **-witting, -witted.** (*tr.*) to get the better of by cunning or ingenuity.

outwith (,aʊt'wɪθ) *prep. Scot.* outside; beyond.

outwork *n.* ('aʊt,wɜːk). **1.** (*often pl.*) defences which lie outside main defensive works. **2.** work done away from the factory, etc., by which it has been commissioned. ~*vb.* (,aʊt'wɜːk), **-working, -worked** *or* **-wrought.** (*tr.*) **3.** to work better, harder, etc., than. **4.** to work out to completion. —'**out,worker** *n.*

ouzel *or* **ousel** ('uːzəl) *n.* **1.** short for **water ouzel.** See **dipper** (sense 2). **2.** an archaic name for the (European) **blackbird.** [OE *ōsle*]

ouzo ('uːzəʊ) *n., pl.* **ouzos.** a strong aniseed-flavoured spirit from Greece. [Mod. Gk *ouzon,* from ?]

ova ('əʊvə) *n.* the plural of **ovum.**

oval ('əʊvəl) *adj.* **1.** having the shape of an ellipse or ellipsoid. ~*n.* **2.** anything that is oval in shape, such as a sports ground. **3.** *Austral.* **a.** an Australian Rules ground. **b.** any sports field. [C16: from Med. L *ōvālis,* from L *ōvum* egg] —'**ovally** *adv.* —'**ovalness** *or* **ovality** (əʊ'vælɪtɪ) *n.*

Oval ('əʊvəl) *n.* **the.** a cricket ground in central London, in the borough of Lambeth.

ovariectomy (əʊ,vɛərɪ'ɛktəmɪ) *n., pl.* **-mies.** *Surgery.* surgical removal of an ovary or ovarian tumour.

ovary ('əʊvərɪ) *n., pl.* **-ries. 1.** either of the two female reproductive organs, which produce ova and secrete oestrogen hormones. **2.** the corresponding organ in some brate and invertebrate animals. **3.** *Bot.* the hollow basal region of a carpel containing one or more ovules. [C17: from NL *ōvārium,* from L *ōvum* egg] —**ovarian** (əʊ-'vɛərɪən) *adj.*

ovate ('əʊveɪt) *adj.* **1.** shaped like an egg. **2.** (esp. of a leaf) shaped like the longitudinal section of an egg, with the broader end at the base. [C18: from L *ōvātus* egg-shaped] —'**ovately** *adv.*

ovation (əʊ'veɪʃən) *n.* **1.** an enthusiastic reception, esp. one of prolonged applause. **2.** a victory procession less glorious than a triumph awarded to a Roman general. [C16: from L *ovātiō* rejoicing, from *ovāre* to exult] —**o'vational** *adj.*

oven ('ʌvən) *n.* **1.** an enclosed heated compartment or receptacle for baking or roasting food. **2.** a similar device, usually lined with a refractory material, used for drying substances, firing ceramics, heat-treating, etc. [OE *ofen*] —'**oven-,like** *adj.*

ovenbird ('ʌvən,bɜːd) *n.* **1.** any of numerous small brownish South American passerine birds that build oven-shaped clay nests. **2.** a common North American warbler that has an olive-brown striped plumage with an orange crown and builds a cup-shaped nest on the ground.

oven-ready adj. (of various foods) bought already prepared so that they are ready to be cooked in the oven.

ovenware ('ʌv°n,wɛə) n. heat-resistant dishes in which food can be both cooked and served.

over ('əuvə) prep. **1.** directly above; on the top of; via the top or upper surface of: over one's head. **2.** on or to the other side of: over the river. **3.** during; through or throughout (a period of time). **4.** in or throughout all parts of: to travel over England. **5.** throughout the whole extent of: over the racecourse. **6.** above; in preference to. **7.** by the agency of (an instrument of telecommunication): over the radio. **8.** more than: over a century ago. **9.** on the subject of; about: an argument over nothing. **10.** while occupied in: discussing business over golf. **11.** having recovered from the effects of. **12. over and above.** added to; in addition to. ~adv. **13.** in a state, condition, situation, or position that is placed or put over something: to climb over. **14.** (particle) so as to cause to fall: knocking over a policeman. **15.** at or to a point across intervening space, water, etc. **16.** throughout a whole area: the world over. **17.** (particle) from beginning to end, usually cursorily: to read a document over. **18.** throughout a period of time: stay over for this week. **19.** (esp. in signalling and radio) it is now your turn to speak, act, etc. **20.** more than is expected or usual: not over well. **21. over again.** once more. **22. over against. a.** opposite to. **b.** contrasting with. **23. over and over.** (often foll. by again) repeatedly. ~adj. **24.** (postpositive) finished; no longer in progress. ~adv., adj. **25.** remaining; surplus (often in **left over**). ~n. **26.** Cricket. **a.** a series of six balls bowled by a bowler from the same end of the pitch. **b.** the play during this. [OE ofer]

over- prefix. **1.** excessive or excessively; beyond an agreed or desirable limit: overcharge; overdue. **2.** indicating superior rank: overseer. **3.** indicating location or movement above: overhang. **4.** indicating movement downwards: overthrow.

overage (,əuvər'eɪdʒ) adj. beyond a specified age.

overall adj. (prenominal) **1.** from one end to the other. **2.** including or covering everything: the overall cost. ~adv. (,əuvər'ɔːl). **3.** in general; on the whole. ~n. ('əuvər,ɔːl). **4.** Brit. a protective work garment usually worn over ordinary clothes. **5.** (pl.) hard-wearing work trousers with a bib and shoulder straps or jacket attached.

overarch (,əuvər'ɑːtʃ) vb. (tr.) to form an arch over.

overarm ('əuvər,ɑːm) adj. **1.** Sport, esp. cricket. bowled, thrown, or performed with the arm raised above the shoulder. ~adv. **2.** with the arm raised above the shoulder.

overawe (,əuvər'ɔː) vb. (tr.) to subdue, restrain, or overcome by affecting with a feeling of awe.

overbalance vb. (,əuvə'bæləns). **1.** to lose or cause to lose balance. **2.** (tr.) another word for **outweigh**. ~n. ('əuvə,bæləns). **3.** excess of weight, value, etc.

overbear (,əuvə'bɛə) vb. **-bearing, -bore, -borne. 1.** (tr.) to dominate or overcome. **2.** (tr.) to press or bear down with weight or physical force. **3.** to produce (fruit, etc.) excessively.

overbearing (,əuvə'bɛərɪŋ) adj. **1.** domineering or dictatorial in manner or action. **2.** of particular or overriding importance or significance. — ,over'bearingly adv.

overblown (,əuvə'bləun) adj. **1.** overdone or excessive. **2.** bombastic; turgid: overblown prose. **3.** (of flowers) past the stage of full bloom.

overboard ('əuvə,bɔːd) adv. **1.** from on board a vessel into the water. **2. go overboard.** Inf. **a.** to be extremely enthusiastic. **b.** to go to extremes. **3. throw overboard.** to reject or abandon.

overbuild (,əuvə'bɪld) vb. **-building, -built.** (tr.) **1.** to build over or on top of. **2.** to erect too many buildings in (an area). **3.** to build too large or elaborately.

overburden vb. (,əuvə'bɜːd°n). **1.** (tr.) to load with excessive weight, work, etc. ~n. ('əuvə,bɜːd°n). **2.** an excessive burden or load. **3.** Geol. the sedimentary rock material that covers coal seams, mineral veins, etc. —,over'burdensome adj.

overcast adj. ('əuvə,kɑːst). **1.** covered over or obscured, esp. by clouds. **2.** Meteorol. (of the sky) cloud-covered. **3.** gloomy or melancholy. **4.** sewn over by overcasting. ~vb. (,əuvə'kɑːst). **5.** to sew (an edge, as of a hem) with long stitches passing successively over the edge. ~n. ('əuvə,kɑːst). **6.** Meteorol. the state of the sky when it is cloud-covered.

overcharge vb. (,əuvə'tʃɑːdʒ). **1.** to charge too much. **2.** (tr.) to fill or load beyond capacity. **3.** Literary. another word for **exaggerate**. ~n. ('əuvə,tʃɑːdʒ). **4.** an excessive price or charge. **5.** an excessive load.

overcloud (,əuvə'klaud) vb. **1.** to make or become covered with clouds. **2.** to make or become dark or dim.

overcoat ('əuvə,kəut) n. a warm heavy coat worn over the outer clothes in cold weather.

overcome (,əuvə'kʌm) vb. **-coming, -came, -come. 1.** (tr.) to get the better of in a conflict. **2.** (tr.; often passive) to render incapable or powerless by laughter, sorrow, exhaustion, etc. **3.** (tr.) to surmount obstacles, objections, etc. **4.** (intr.) to be victorious.

overcrop (,əuvə'krɒp) vb. **-cropping, -cropped.** (tr.) to exhaust (land) by excessive cultivation.

overdo (,əuvə'duː) vb. **-doing, -did, -done.** (tr.) **1.** to take or carry too far; do to excess. **2.** to exaggerate, overelaborate, or overplay. **3.** to cook or bake too long. **4. overdo it** or **things.** to overtax one's strength, capacity, etc.

overdose n. ('əuvə,dəus). **1.** (esp. of drugs) an excessive dose. ~vb. (,əuvə'dəus). **2.** to take an excessive dose or give an excessive dose to. —,over'dosage n.

overdraft ('əuvə,drɑːft) n. **1.** a withdrawal of money in excess of the credit balance on a bank account. **2.** the amount of money withdrawn thus.

overdraw (,əuvə'drɔː) vb. **-drawing, -drew, -drawn. 1.** to draw on (a bank account) in excess of the credit balance. **2.** (tr.) to exaggerate in describing or telling.

overdress vb. (,əuvə'drɛs). **1.** to dress (oneself or another) too elaborately or finely. ~n. ('əuvə,drɛs). **2.** a dress that may be worn over a jumper, blouse, etc.

overdrive n. ('əuvə,draɪv). **1.** a very high gear in a motor vehicle used at high speeds to reduce wear. ~vb. (,əuvə'draɪv). **-driving, -drove, -driven. 2.** (tr.) to drive too hard or too far; overwork or overuse.

overdub (in multitrack recording) ~vb. (,əuvə'dʌb), **-dubbing, -dubbed. 1.** to add (new sound) on a spare track or tracks. ~n. ('əuvə,dʌb). **2.** the blending of various layers of sound in one recording by this method.

overdue (,əuvə'djuː) adj. past the time specified, required, or preferred for arrival, occurrence, payment, etc.

,overa'bundance n.	'over,bid n.	,over,consci'entious adj.	,overdi'lute vb.
,overac'centu,ate vb.	,over'bold adj.	,overcon'servative adj.	,over'distant adj.
,over'act vb.	,over'book vb.	,overcon'siderate adj.	,overdi'versi,fy vb.
,over'active adj.	,over'busy adj.	,overcon'sumption n.	,over'drama,tize or -ise vb.
,overaf'fect vb.	,over'buy vb.	,over'cook vb.	,over'drink vb.
,overag'gressive adj.	,overca'pacity n.	,over'costly adj.	,over'eager adj.
,overam'bitious adj.	,over'careful adj.	,over'critical adj.	,over'eat vb.
,over'ana,lyse vb.	,over'cautious adj.	,over'crowd vb.	,over'edu,cate vb.
,over,ani'mation n.	,over'civil adj.	,over'curious adj.	,overef'fusive adj.
,over'anxious adj.	,over'common adj.	,over'deco,rate vb.	,overe'laborate adj., vb.
,overap'preciative adj.	,over'compen,sate vb.	,over'delicate adj.	,overem'bellish vb.
,over,appre'hensive adj.	,overcom'petitive adj.	,overde'pendence n.	,overe'motional adj.
,overas'sert vb.	,overcom'placency n.	,overde'pendent adj.	,over'emphasis n.
,overas'sertive adj.	,over'complex adj.	,over'detailed adj.	,over'empha,size or -ise vb.
,overas'sessment n.	,over'compli,cate vb.	,overde'velop vb.	,overen'thusiasm n.
,overat'tentive adj.	,overcon'cern n.	,over'diligent adj.	,overen,thusi'astic adj.
,over'bid vb.	,over'confident adj.		

overestimate vb. (ˌəʊvərˈɛstɪˌmeɪt). **1.** (tr.) to estimate too highly. ~n. (ˌəʊvərˈɛstɪmɪt). **2.** an estimate that is too high. —**over**ˌ**esti**ˈ**mation** n.

overexpose (ˌəʊvərɪksˈpəʊz) vb. (tr.) **1.** to expose too much or for too long. **2.** Photog. to expose (a film, etc.) for too long or with too bright a light.

overflow vb. (ˌəʊvəˈfləʊ), **-flowing, -flowed, -flown. 1.** to flow or run over (a limit, brim, etc.). **2.** to fill or be filled beyond capacity so as to spill or run over. **3.** (intr.; usually foll. by with) to be filled with happiness, tears, etc. **4.** (tr.) to spread or cover over; flood or inundate. ~n. (ˈəʊvəˌfləʊ). **5.** overflowing matter, esp. liquid. **6.** any outlet that enables surplus liquid to be discharged or drained off. **7.** the amount by which a limit, capacity, etc., is exceeded.

overfold (ˈəʊvəˌfəʊld) n. Geol. a fold in the form of an anticline in which one limb is more steeply inclined than the other.

overgrow (ˌəʊvəˈgrəʊ) vb. **-growing, -grew, -grown. 1.** (tr.) to grow over or across (an area, path, etc.). **2.** (tr.) to choke or supplant by a stronger growth. **3.** (tr.) to grow too large for. **4.** (intr.) to grow beyond normal size. —**ˈover**ˌ**growth** n.

overhand (ˈəʊvəˌhænd) adj. **1.** thrown or performed with the hand raised above the shoulder. **2.** sewn with thread passing over two edges in one direction. ~adv. **3.** with the hand above the shoulder; overarm. **4.** with shallow stitches passing over two edges. ~vb. **5.** to sew (two edges) overhand.

overhang vb. (ˌəʊvəˈhæŋ), **-hanging, -hung. 1.** to project or extend beyond (a surface, building, etc.). **2.** (tr.) to hang or be suspended over. **3.** (tr.) to menace, threaten, or dominate. ~n. (ˈəʊvəˌhæŋ). **4.** a formation, object, etc., that extends beyond or hangs over something, such as an outcrop of rock overhanging a mountain face. **5.** the amount or extent of projection.

overhaul vb. (ˌəʊvəˈhɔːl). (tr.) **1.** to examine carefully for faults, necessary repairs, etc. **2.** to make repairs or adjustments to (a car, machine, etc.). **3.** to overtake. ~n. (ˈəʊvəˌhɔːl). **4.** a thorough examination and repair.

overhead adj. (ˈəʊvəˌhɛd). **1.** situated or operating above head height or some other reference level. **2.** (prenominal) inclusive: the overhead price included meals. ~adv. (ˌəʊvəˈhɛd). **3.** over or above head height, esp. in the sky. ~n. (ˈəʊvəˌhɛd). **4. a.** a stroke in racket games played from above head height. **b.** (as modifier): an overhead smash. **5.** (modifier) of, concerned with, or resulting from overheads: overhead costs.

overhead camshaft n. a type of camshaft situated above the cylinder head in an internal-combustion engine.

overhead projector n. a projector that throws an enlarged image of a transparency onto a surface above and behind the person using it.

overheads (ˈəʊvəˌhɛdz) pl. n. business expenses, such as rent, that are not directly attributable to any department or product and can therefore be assigned only arbitrarily.

overhead-valve engine n. a type of internal-combustion engine in which the inlet and exhaust valves are in the cylinder head above the pistons. U.S. name: **valve-in-head engine.**

overhear (ˌəʊvəˈhɪə) vb. **-hearing, -heard.** (tr.) to hear (a person, remark, etc.) without the knowledge of the speaker.

overheat (ˌəʊvəˈhiːt) vb. **1.** to make or become excessively hot. **2.** (tr.; often passive) to make very agitated, irritated, etc. **3.** (tr.) to stimulate excessively: overheat the economy. ~n. **4.** the condition of being overheated.

Overijssel (Dutch oːvərˈɛisəl) n. a province of the E Netherlands: generally low-lying. Capital: Zwolle. Pop.: 1 003 915 (1987 est.). Area: 3929 sq. km (1517 sq. miles).

overjoy (ˌəʊvəˈdʒɔɪ) vb. (tr.) to give great delight to. —ˌover**ˈjoyed** adj.

overkill (ˈəʊvəˌkɪl) n. **1.** the capability to deploy more weapons, esp. nuclear weapons, than is necessary to ensure military advantage. **2.** any capacity or treatment that is greater than that required or appropriate.

overland (ˈəʊvəˌlænd) adj. (prenominal), adv. **1.** over or across land. ~vb. **2.** Austral. to drive (cattle or sheep) overland. —**ˈover**ˌ**lander** n.

overlap vb. (ˌəʊvəˈlæp), **-lapping, -lapped. 1.** (of two things) to extend or lie partly over (each other). **2.** to cover and extend beyond (something). **3.** (intr.) to coincide partly in time, subject, etc. ~n. (ˈəʊvəˌlæp). **4.** a part that overlaps or is overlapped. **5.** the amount, length, etc., overlapping. **6.** Geol. the horizontal extension of the lower beds in a series of rock strata beyond the upper beds.

overlay vb. (ˌəʊvəˈleɪ), **-laying, -laid.** (tr.) **1.** to lay or place over or upon (something else). **2.** (often foll. by with) to cover, overspread, or conceal (with). **3.** (foll. by with) to cover (a surface) with an applied decoration: ebony overlaid with silver. **4.** to achieve the correct printing pressure all over (a forme or plate) by adding to the appropriate areas of the packing. ~n. (ˈəʊvəˌleɪ). **5.** something that is laid over something else; covering. **6.** an applied decoration or layer, as of gold leaf. **7.** a transparent sheet giving extra details to a map or diagram over which it is designed to be placed. **8.** Printing. material, such as paper, used to overlay a forme or plate.

overleaf (ˌəʊvəˈliːf) adv. on the other side of the page.

overlie (ˌəʊvəˈlaɪ) vb. **-lying, -lay, -lain.** (tr.) **1.** to lie or rest upon. Cf. **overlay. 2.** to kill (a baby or newborn animal) by lying upon it.

overlong (ˌəʊvəˈlɒŋ) adj., adv. too or excessively long.

overlook vb. (ˌəʊvəˈlʊk). (tr.) **1.** to fail to notice or take into account. **2.** to disregard deliberately or indulgently. **3.** to afford a view of from above: the house overlooks the bay. **4.** to rise above. **5.** to look at carefully. **6.** to cast the evil eye over (someone). ~n. (ˈəʊvəˌlʊk). U.S. **7.** a high place affording a view. **8.** an act of overlooking.

overlord (ˈəʊvəˌlɔːd) n. a supreme lord or master. —**ˈover**ˌ**lordship** n.

overly (ˈəʊvəlɪ) adv. too; excessively.

overman vb. (ˌəʊvəˈmæn), **-manning, -manned. 1.** (tr.) to supply with an excessive number of men. ~n. (ˈəʊvəˌmæn), pl. **-men. 2.** a man who oversees others. **3.** a superman.

overmaster (ˌəʊvəˈmɑːstə) vb. (tr.) to overpower.

overmatch Chiefly U.S. ~vb. (ˌəʊvəˈmætʃ). (tr.) **1.** to be more than a match for. **2.** to match with a superior opponent. ~n. (ˈəʊvəˌmætʃ). **3.** a person superior in ability. **4.** a match in which one contestant is superior.

overmuch (ˌəʊvəˈmʌtʃ) adv., adj. **1.** too much; very much. ~n. **2.** an excessive amount.

overnice (ˌəʊvəˈnaɪs) adj. too fastidious, precise, etc.

overnight adv. (ˌəʊvəˈnaɪt). **1.** for the duration of the night. **2.** in or as if in the course of one night; suddenly: the situation changed overnight. ~adj. (ˈəʊvəˌnaɪt). (usually prenominal) **3.** done in, occurring in, or lasting the night: an overnight stay. **4.** staying for one night. **5.** for use during a single night. **6.** occurring in or as if in the course of one night; sudden: an overnight victory.

overpass n. (ˈəʊvəˌpɑːs). **1.** another name for **flyover** (sense 1). ~vb. (ˌəʊvəˈpɑːs). **-passing, -passed, -past.** (tr.) Now rare. **2.** to pass over, through, or across. **3.** to exceed. **4.** to ignore.

ˌover**ˈcitable** adj.	ˌover**ˈfeed** vb.	ˌoveri**ˈdeal**ˌ**ize** or -ˌ**ise** vb.	ˌover**ˈissue** vb., n.
ˌover**ˈexer**ˌ**cise** vb.	ˌover**ˈfill** vb.	ˌover**ˈim**ˈaginative** adj.	ˌover**ˈladen** adj.
ˌover**ˈex**ˈert** vb.	ˌover**ˈfish** vb.	ˌoverim**ˈpress** vb.	ˌover**ˈlarge** adj.
ˌover**ex**ˈpand** vb.	ˌover**ˈfly** vb.	ˌoverin**ˈcline** vb.	ˌover**ˈlavish** adj.
ˌover**ex**ˈpansion** n.	ˌover**ˈfond** adj.	ˌoverin**ˈdulge** vb.	ˌover**ˈleap** vb.
ˌover**ex**ˈpenditure** n.	ˌover**ˈfull** adj.	ˌoverin**ˈdulgence** n.	ˌover**ˈload** vb.
ˌover**ex**ˈplicit** adj.	ˈover**ˌgarment** n.	ˌoverin**ˈflate** vb.	ˈover**ˌload** n.
ˌover**ex**ˈpressive** adj.	ˌover**ˌgenerali**ˈzation** or	ˌoverin**ˈfluence** vb.	ˌover**ˈmany** adj.
ˌover**ex**ˈtend** vb.	-i**ˈsation** n.	ˌoverin**ˈsistent** adj.	ˌover**ˈmeasure** n.
ˌover**fa**ˈmiliar** adj.	ˌover**ˈgenerous** adj.	ˌoverin**ˈsure** vb.	ˌover**ˈmodest** adj.
ˌover**ˈfanciful** adj.	ˌover**ˈhastily** adv.	ˌoverin**ˈtense** adj.	ˌover**ˈmodi**ˌ**fy** vb.
ˌover**ˈfar** adj., adv.	ˌover**ˈhasty** adj.	ˌoverin**ˈterest** n.	ˌover**ˌopti**ˈmistic** adj.
ˌover**fas**ˈtidious** adj.	ˌover**ˌideal**ˈistic** adj.	ˌoverin**ˈvest** vb.	ˌover**ˌparˈticular** adj.

overplay (ˌəʊvə'pleɪ) *vb.* **1.** (*tr.*) to exaggerate the importance of. **2.** to act or behave in an exaggerated manner. **3. overplay one's hand.** to overestimate the worth or strength of one's position.

overpower (ˌəʊvə'paʊə) *vb.* (*tr.*) **1.** to conquer or subdue by superior force. **2.** to have such a strong effect on as to make helpless or ineffective. **3.** to supply with more power than necessary. —**over'powering** *adj.*

overprint *vb.* (ˌəʊvə'prɪnt). **1.** (*tr.*) to print (additional matter or another colour) on a sheet of paper. ~*n.* ('əʊvəˌprɪnt). **2.** additional matter or another colour printed onto a previously printed sheet. **3.** additional matter applied to a finished postage stamp by printing, stamping, etc.

overqualified (ˌəʊvə'kwɒlɪfaɪd) *adj.* having more managerial experience or academic qualifications than required for a particular job.

overrate (ˌəʊvə'reɪt) *vb.* (*tr.*) to assess too highly.

overreach (ˌəʊvə'riːtʃ) *vb.* **1.** to defeat or thwart (oneself) by attempting to do or gain too much. **2.** (*tr.*) to aim for but miss by going too far. **3.** to get the better of (a person) by trickery. **4.** (*tr.*) to reach beyond or over. **5.** (*intr.*) to reach or go too far. **6.** (*intr.*) (of a horse) to strike the back of a forefoot with the edge of the opposite hind foot.

overreact (ˌəʊvərɪ'ækt) *vb.* (*intr.*) to react excessively to something. —**overre'action** *n.*

override *vb.* (ˌəʊvə'raɪd), **-riding, -rode, -ridden.** (*tr.*) **1.** to set aside or disregard with superior authority or power. **2.** to supersede or annul. **3.** to dominate or vanquish by or as if by trampling down. **4.** to take manual control of (a system that is usually under automatic control). **5.** to extend or pass over, esp. to overlap. **6.** to ride (a horse, etc.) too hard. **7.** to ride over. ~*n.* ('əʊvəˌraɪd). **8.** a device that can override an automatic control.

overrider ('əʊvəˌraɪdə) *n.* either of two attachments fitted to the bumper of a motor vehicle to prevent it interlocking with that of another vehicle.

overriding (ˌəʊvə'raɪdɪŋ) *adj.* taking precedence.

overrule (ˌəʊvə'ruːl) *vb.* (*tr.*) **1.** to disallow the arguments of (a person) by the use of authority. **2.** to rule or decide against (an argument, decision, etc.). **3.** to prevail over, dominate, or influence. **4.** to exercise rule over.

overrun *vb.* (ˌəʊvə'rʌn), **-running, -ran, -run. 1.** (*tr.*) to swarm or spread over rapidly. **2.** to run over (something); overflow. **3.** to extend or run beyond a limit. **4.** (*intr.*) (of an engine) to run with a closed throttle at a speed dictated by that of the vehicle it drives. **5.** (*tr.*) to print (a book, journal, etc.) in a greater quantity than ordered. **6.** (*tr.*) *Printing.* to transfer (set type) from one column, line, or page, to another. **7.** (*tr.*) *Arch.* to run faster than. ~*n.* ('əʊvəˌrʌn). **8.** the act or an instance of overrunning. **9.** the amount or extent of overrunning. **10.** the number of copies of a publication in excess of the quantity ordered.

overseas *adv.* (ˌəʊvə'siːz). **1.** beyond the sea; abroad. ~*adj.* ('əʊvə'siːz). **2.** of, to, in, from, or situated in countries beyond the sea. **3.** Also: **oversea.** of or relating to passage over the sea. ~*n.* (ˌəʊvə'siːz). **4.** (*functioning as sing.*) *Inf.* a foreign country or foreign countries collectively.

oversee (ˌəʊvə'siː) *vb.* **-seeing, -saw, -seen.** (*tr.*) **1.** to watch over and direct; supervise. **2.** to watch secretly or accidentally. **3.** *Arch.* to scrutinize; inspect.

overseer ('əʊvəˌsiːə) *n.* **1.** a person who oversees others, esp. workmen. **2.** *Brit. history.* a minor official of a parish attached to the poorhouse.

oversell (ˌəʊvə'sɛl) *vb.* **-selling, -sold. 1.** (*tr.*) to sell more of (a commodity, etc.) than can be supplied. **2.** to use excessively aggressive methods in selling (commodities). **3.** (*tr.*) to exaggerate the merits of.

overset (ˌəʊvə'sɛt) *vb.* **-setting, -set.** (*tr.*) **1.** to disturb or upset. **2.** *Printing.* to set (type or copy) in excess of the space available.

oversew ('əʊvəˌsəʊ, ˌəʊvə'səʊ) *vb.* **-sewing, -sewed, -sewn.** to sew (two edges) with close stitches that pass over them both.

oversexed (ˌəʊvə'sɛkst) *adj.* having an excessive preoccupation with sexual activity.

overshadow (ˌəʊvə'ʃædəʊ) *vb.* (*tr.*) **1.** to render insignificant or less important in comparison. **2.** to cast a shadow or gloom over.

overshoe ('əʊvəˌʃuː) *n.* a protective shoe worn over an ordinary shoe.

overshoot *vb.* (ˌəʊvə'ʃuːt), **-shooting, -shot. 1.** to shoot or go beyond (a mark or target). **2.** (of an aircraft) to fly or taxi too far along a runway. **3.** (*tr.*) to pass swiftly over or down over, as water over a wheel. ~*n.* ('əʊvəˌʃuːt). **4.** an act or instance of overshooting. **5.** the extent of such overshooting.

overshot ('əʊvəˌʃɒt) *adj.* **1.** having or designating an upper jaw that projects beyond the lower jaw. **2.** (of a water wheel) driven by a flow of water that passes over the wheel.

oversight ('əʊvəˌsaɪt) *n.* **1.** an omission or mistake, esp. one made through failure to notice something. **2.** supervision.

oversize *adj.* (ˌəʊvə'saɪz). **1.** Also: **oversized.** larger than the usual size. ~*n.* ('əʊvəˌsaɪz). **2.** a size larger than the usual or proper size. **3.** something that is oversize.

overskirt ('əʊvəˌskɜːt) *n.* an outer skirt, esp. one that reveals a decorative underskirt.

overspend *vb.* (ˌəʊvə'spɛnd), **-spending, -spent. 1.** to spend in excess of (one's desires or what one can afford or is allocated). **2.** (*tr.; usually passive*) to wear out; exhaust. ~*n.* ('əʊvəˌspɛnd). **3.** the amount by which someone or something is overspent.

overspill *n.* ('əʊvəˌspɪl). **1. a.** something that spills over or is in excess. **b.** (*as modifier*): *overspill population.* ~*vb.* (ˌəʊvə'spɪl), **-spilling, -spilt** *or* **-spilled. 2.** (*intr.*) to overflow.

overstate (ˌəʊvə'steɪt) *vb.* (*tr.*) to state too strongly; exaggerate or overemphasize. —**over'statement** *n.*

overstay (ˌəʊvə'steɪ) *vb.* (*tr.*) **1.** to stay beyond the time, limit, or duration of. **2. overstay** *or* **outstay one's welcome.** to stay (at a party, etc.), longer than pleases the host or hostess.

overstep (ˌəʊvə'stɛp) *vb.* **-stepping, -stepped.** (*tr.*) to go beyond (a certain or proper limit).

overstrung (ˌəʊvə'strʌŋ) *adj.* **1.** too highly strung; tense. **2.** (of a piano) having two sets of strings crossing each other at an oblique angle.

overstuff (ˌəʊvə'stʌf) *vb.* (*tr.*) **1.** to force too much into. **2.** to cover (furniture, etc.) entirely with upholstery.

oversubscribe (ˌəʊvəsəb'skraɪb) *vb.* (*tr.; often passive*) to subscribe or apply for in excess of available supply.

overt ('əʊvɜːt, əʊ'vɜːt) *adj.* **1.** open to view; observable. **2.** *Law.* open; deliberate. [C14: via OF, from *ovrir* to open, from L *aperire*] —**'overtly** *adv.*

overtake (ˌəʊvə'teɪk) *vb.* **-taking, -took, -taken. 1.** *Chiefly Brit.* to move past (another vehicle or person) travelling in the same direction. **2.** (*tr.*) to pass or do better than, after catching up with. **3.** (*tr.*) to come upon suddenly or unexpectedly: *night overtook him.* **4.** (*tr.*) to catch up with; draw level with.

overtax (ˌəʊvə'tæks) *vb.* (*tr.*) **1.** to tax too heavily. **2.** to impose too great a strain on.

overthrow *vb.* (ˌəʊvə'θrəʊ), **-throwing, -threw, -thrown. 1.** (*tr.*) to effect the downfall or destruction of (a ruler, institution, etc.), esp. by force. **2.** (*tr.*) to throw or turn over. **3.** to throw (something, esp. a ball) too far. ~*n.* ('əʊvəˌθrəʊ). **4.** downfall; destruction. **5.** *Cricket.* **a.** a ball thrown back too far by a fielder. **b.** a run scored because of this.

overthrust ('əʊvə,θrʌst) *n. Geol.* a reverse fault in which the rocks on the upper surface of a fault plane have moved over the rocks on the lower surface.

overtime *n.* ('əʊvə,taɪm). **1. a.** work at a regular job done in addition to regular working hours. **b.** (*as modifier*): *overtime pay.* **2.** the rate of pay established for such work. **3.** time in excess of a set period. **4.** *Sport, U.S. & Canad.* extra time. ~*adv.* ('əʊvə,taɪm). **5.** beyond the regular or stipulated time. ~*vb.* (,əʊvə'taɪm). **6.** (*tr.*) to exceed the required time for (a photographic exposure, etc.).

overtone ('əʊvə,təʊn) *n.* **1.** (*often pl.*) additional meaning or nuance: *overtones of despair.* **2.** *Music, acoustics.* any of the tones, with the exception of the fundamental, that constitute a musical sound and contribute to its quality.

overture ('əʊvə,tjʊə) *n.* **1.** *Music.* **a.** a piece of orchestral music that is played at the beginning of an opera or oratorio, often containing the main musical themes of the work. **b.** a one-movement orchestral piece, usually having a descriptive or evocative title. **2.** (*often pl.*) a proposal, act, or gesture initiating a relationship, negotiation, etc. **3.** something that introduces what follows. ~*vb.* (*tr.*) **4.** to make or present an overture to. **5.** to introduce with an overture. [C14: via OF from LL *apertūra* opening, from L *aperire* to open]

overturn *vb.* (,əʊvə'tɜːn). **1.** to turn or cause to turn from an upright or normal position. **2.** (*tr.*) to overthrow or destroy. **3.** (*tr.*) to invalidate; reverse. ~*n.* ('əʊvə,tɜːn). **4.** the act of overturning or the state of being overturned.

overview ('əʊvə,vjuː) *n.* a general survey.

overweening (,əʊvə'wiːnɪŋ) *adj.* **1.** (of a person) excessively arrogant or presumptuous. **2.** (of opinions, appetites, etc.) excessive; immoderate. [C14: from OVER + *weening* from OE *wēnan* WEEN] —,**over'weeningness** *n.*

overweight *adj.* (,əʊvə'weɪt). **1.** weighing more than is usual, allowed, or healthy. ~*n.* ('əʊvə,weɪt). **2.** extra or excess weight. ~*vb.* (,əʊvə'weɪt). (*tr.*) **3.** to give too much emphasis or consideration to. **4.** to add too much weight to. **5.** to weigh down.

overwhelm (,əʊvə'wɛlm) *vb.* (*tr.*) **1.** to overpower the thoughts, emotions, or senses of. **2.** to overcome with irresistible force. **3.** to cover over or bury completely. **4.** to weigh or rest upon overpoweringly. —,**over'whelming** *adj.*

overwind (,əʊvə'waɪnd) *vb.* **-winding, -wound.** (*tr.*) to wind (a watch, etc.) beyond the proper limit.

overwork *vb.* (,əʊvə'wɜːk). **1.** (*mainly tr.*) **1.** (*also intr.*) to work too hard or too long. **2.** to use too much: *to overwork an excuse.* **3.** to decorate the surface of. ~*n.* ('əʊvə,wɜːk). **4.** excessive or excessively tiring work.

overwrite (,əʊvə'raɪt) *vb.* **-writing, -wrote, -written. 1.** to write (something) in an excessively ornate style. **2.** to write too much about (someone or something). **3.** to write on top of (other writing). **4.** to record on a storage medium, such as a magnetic disk, thus destroying what was originally recorded there.

overwrought (,əʊvə'rɔːt) *adj.* **1.** full of nervous tension; agitated. **2.** too elaborate; fussy: *an overwrought style.* **3.** (*often postpositive* and foll. by *with*) with the surface decorated or adorned.

Ovett ('ɒvɛt) *n.* **Steve.** born 1955, British runner.

ovi- or **ovo-** *combining form.* egg or ovum: *oviform; oviviparous.* [from L *ōvum*]

Ovid ('ɒvɪd) *n.* Latin name *Publius Ovidius Naso.* 43 B.C.–?17 A.D., Roman poet. His verse includes poems on love, *Ars Amatoria,* on myths, *Metamorphoses,* and on his sufferings in exile, *Tristia.* —**Ovidian** (ɒ'vɪdɪən) *adj.*

oviduct ('ɒvɪ,dʌkt, 'əʊ-) *n.* the tube through which ova are conveyed from an ovary. Also called (in mammals): **Fallopian tube.** —**oviducal** (,ɒvɪ'djuːkəl, ,əʊ-) or ,**ovi'ductal** *adj.*

Oviedo (*Spanish* o'βjeðo) *n.* a city in NW Spain: capital of Asturias from 810 until 1002; centre of a coal and iron mining area. Pop.: 184 473 (1981).

oviform ('əʊvɪ,fɔːm) *adj. Biol.* shaped like an egg.

ovine ('əʊvaɪn) *adj.* of, relating to, or resembling a sheep. [C19: from LL *ovinus,* from L *ovis* sheep]

oviparous (əʊ'vɪpərəs) *adj.* (of fishes, reptiles, birds, etc.) producing eggs that hatch outside the body of the mother. Cf. **ovoviviparous, viviparous** (sense 1). —**oviparity** (,əʊvɪ'pærɪtɪ) *n.* —**o'viparously** *adv.*

ovipositor (,əʊvɪ'pɒzɪtə) *n.* **1.** the egg-laying organ of most female insects, consisting of a pair of specialized appendages at the end of the abdomen. **2.** a similar organ in certain female fishes, formed by an extension of the edges of the genital opening. [C19:from OVI- + L *positor,* from *ponere* to place] —,**ovi'posit** *vb.* (*intr.*)

ovoid ('əʊvɔɪd) *adj.* **1.** egg-shaped. ~*n.* **2.** something that is ovoid.

ovoviviparous (,əʊvəʊvaɪ'vɪpərəs) *adj.* (of certain reptiles, fishes, etc.) producing eggs that hatch within the body of the mother. Cf. **oviparous, viviparous** (sense 1). —**ovoviviparity** (,əʊvəʊ,vaɪvɪ'pærɪtɪ) *n.*

ovulate ('ɒvjʊ,leɪt) *vb.* (*intr.*) to produce or discharge eggs from an ovary. [C19: via OVULE] —,**ovu'lation** *n.*

ovule ('ɒvjuːl) *n.* **1.** a small body in seed-bearing plants that contains the egg cell and develops into the seed after fertilization. **2.** *Zool.* an immature ovum. [C19: via F from Med. L *ōvulum* a little egg, from L *ōvum* egg] —'**ovular** *adj.*

ovum ('əʊvəm) *n., pl.* **ova.** an unfertilized female gamete; egg cell. [from L: egg]

ow (aʊ) *interj.* an exclamation of pain.

owe (əʊ) *vb.* (*mainly tr.*) **1.** to be under an obligation to pay (someone) the amount of. **2.** (*intr.*) to be in debt: *he still owes for his house.* **3.** (often foll. by *to*) to have as a result (of). **4.** to feel the need or obligation to do, give, etc. **5.** to hold or maintain in the mind or heart (esp. in **owe a grudge**). [OE *āgan* to have (C12: to have to)]

Owen ('əʊɪn) *n.* **1. David (Anthony Llewellyn).** born 1938, British Social Democrat politician: entered parliament as a member of the Labour Party; foreign secretary (1977–79); cofounder of the Social Democratic Party (1981) and its leader from 1983. **2.** Sir **Richard.** 1804–92, English comparative anatomist and palaeontologist. **3. Robert.** 1771–1858, Welsh industrialist and social reformer. He formed a model industrial community at New Lanark, Scotland, and pioneered co-operative societies. His books include *New View of Society* (1813). **4. Wilfred.** 1893–1918, English poet of World War I, who was killed in action.

Owen gun *n.* a type of simple, recoil-operated sub-machine-gun first used by Australian forces in World War II. [after E. E. *Owen* (1915–49), its Australian inventor]

Owens ('əʊɪnz) *n.* **Jesse,** real name *John Cleveland.* 1913–80, U.S. athlete.

Owen Stanley Range *n.* a mountain range in SE New Guinea. Highest peak: Mount Victoria, 4073 m (13 363 ft.).

Owerri (ə'wɛrɪ) *n.* a market town in S Nigeria, capital of Imo state. Pop.: 35 010 (1983 est.).

owing ('əʊɪŋ) *adj.* **1.** (*postpositive*) owed; due. **2. owing to.** because of or on account of.
▷**Usage.** See at **due.**

owl (aʊl) *n.* **1.** a nocturnal bird of prey having large front-facing eyes, a small hooked bill, soft feathers, and a short neck. **2.** any of various breeds of owl-like fancy domestic pigeon. **3.** a person who looks or behaves like an owl, esp. in having a solemn manner. [OE *ūle*] —'**owlish** *adj.* —'**owl-,like** *adj.*

owlet ('aʊlɪt) *n.* a young or nestling owl.

own (əʊn) *determiner.* (*preceded by a possessive*) **1. a.** (intensifier): *John's own idea.* **b.** (*as pron.*): *I'll use my own.* **2.** on behalf of oneself or in relation to oneself: *he is his own worst enemy.* **3. come into one's own. a.** to fulfil one's potential. **b.** to receive what is due to one. **4. hold one's own.** to maintain one's situation or position, esp. in spite of opposition or difficulty. **5. on one's own. a.** without help. **b.** by oneself; alone. ~*vb.* **6.** (*tr.*) to have as one's possession. **7.** (when *intr.,* often foll. by *up, to,* or *up to*) to confess or admit; acknowledge. **8.** (*tr.; takes a clause as object*) *Now rare.* to concede: *I own that you are right.* [OE *āgen,* orig. p.p. of *āgan* to have. See OWE] —'**owner** *n.* —'**ownership** *n.*

,**over'tire** *vb.* | ,**over'train** *vb.* | ,**over'value** *vb.* | ,**over'willing** *adj.*
,**over'top** *vb.* | ,**over'trump** *vb.* | ,**over'water** *vb.* | ,**over'zealous** *adj.*
,**over'trade** *vb.* | ,**over'use** *vb., n.* | ,**over'weigh** *vb.*

own brand *n.* a product which displays the name of the retailer rather than the producer.

owner-occupier *n.* someone who has bought or is buying the house in which he lives.

own goal *n.* **1.** *Soccer.* a goal scored by a player accidentally kicking the ball into his own team's net. **2.** *Inf.* any action that results in disadvantage to the person who took it or to his associates.

ox (ɒks) *n., pl.* **oxen**. **1.** an adult castrated male of any domesticated species of cattle used for draught work and meat. **2.** any bovine mammal, esp. any of the domestic cattle. [OE *oxa*]

oxalic acid (ɒk'sælɪk) *n.* a colourless poisonous crystalline acid found in many plants: used as a bleach and a cleansing agent for metals. Formula: $(COOH)_2$. Recommended name: **ethanedioic acid**. [C18: from F *oxalique*, from L *oxalis* garden sorrel; see OXALIS]

oxalis ('ɒksəlɪs, ɒk'sælɪs) *n.* a plant having clover-like leaves which contain oxalic acid and white, pink, red, or yellow flowers. See also **wood sorrel**. [C18: via L from Gk: sorrel, sour wine, from *oxus* acid, sharp]

oxblood ('ɒks,blʌd) *or* **oxblood red** *adj.* of a dark reddish-brown colour.

oxbow ('ɒks,bəʊ) *n.* **1.** a U-shaped piece of wood fitted under and around the neck of a harnessed ox and attached to the yoke. **2.** also called: **oxbow lake**. a small curved lake lying on the flood plain of a river and constituting the remnant of a former meander.

Oxbridge ('ɒks,brɪdʒ) *n.* **a.** the British universities of Oxford and Cambridge, esp. considered as ancient and prestigious academic institutions, bastions of privilege and superiority, etc. **b.** (*as modifier*): *Oxbridge arrogance*.

oxen ('ɒksən) *n.* the plural of **ox**.

Oxenstierna *or* **Oxenstjerna** (*Swedish* 'uksənʃæːrna) *n.* **Count Axel** ('aksəl). 1583–1654, Swedish statesman. He was chancellor (1612–54) and successfully directed Swedish foreign policy for most of the Thirty Years' War.

oxeye ('ɒks,aɪ) *n.* **1.** a Eurasian composite plant having daisy-like flower heads with yellow rays and dark centres. **2.** any of various North American plants having daisy-like flowers. **3.** **oxeye daisy**. a type of hardy perennial chrysanthemum.

ox-eyed *adj.* having large round eyes, like those of an ox.

Oxfam ('ɒks,fæm) *n.* *acronym for* Oxford Committee for Famine Relief.

Oxford[1] ('ɒksfəd) *n.* **1.** a city in S England, administrative centre of Oxfordshire, at the confluence of the Rivers Thames and Cherwell: Royalist headquarters during the Civil War; university, consisting of 40 separate colleges, the oldest being University College (1249); motor-vehicle industry. Pop.: 116 000 (1983 est.). **2.** a type of stout laced shoe with a low heel. **3.** a lightweight fabric of plain or twill weave used esp. for men's shirts.

Oxford[2] ('ɒksfəd) *n.* **1st Earl of**. title of (Robert) **Harley**.

Oxford bags *pl. n.* trousers with very wide baggy legs.

Oxford blue *n.* **1. a.** a dark blue colour. **b.** (*as adj.*): *an Oxford-blue scarf.* **2.** a person who has been awarded a blue from Oxford University.

Oxford Movement *n.* a movement within the Church of England that began at Oxford in 1833. It affirmed the continuity of the Church with early Christianity and strove to restore the High-Church ideals of the 17th century. Also called: **Tractarianism**.

Oxfordshire ('ɒksfəd,ʃɪə, -ʃə) *n.* an inland county of S central England: situated mostly in the basin of the Upper Thames, with the Cotswolds in the west and the Chilterns in the southeast. Administrative centre: Oxford. Pop.: 574 700 (1986 est.). Area: 2608 sq. km (1007 sq. miles). Abbrev.: **Oxon**.

oxidant ('ɒksɪdənt) *n.* a substance that acts or is used as an oxidizing agent. Also called (esp. in rocketry): **oxidizer**.

oxidation (,ɒksɪ'deɪʃən) *n.* **a.** the act or process of oxidizing. **b.** (*as modifier*): *an oxidation state.* —'**oxi,date** *vb.* —,**oxi'dational** *adj.* —'**oxi,dative** *adj.*

oxidation-reduction *n.* **a.** a reversible chemical process usually involving the transfer of electrons, in which one reaction is an oxidation and the reverse reaction is a reduction. **b.** (*as modifier*): *an oxidation-reduction reaction.* ~Also: **redox**.

oxide ('ɒksaɪd) *n.* **1.** any compound of oxygen with another element. **2.** any organic compound in which an oxygen atom is bound to two alkyl groups; an ether. [C18: from F, from *ox(ygène)* + *(ac)ide*]

oxidize *or* **-ise** ('ɒksɪ,daɪz) *vb.* **1.** to undergo or cause to undergo a chemical reaction with oxygen, as in formation of an oxide. **2.** to form or cause to form a layer of metal oxide, as in rusting. **3.** to lose or cause to lose hydrogen atoms. **4.** to undergo or cause to undergo a decrease in the number of electrons. —,**oxidi'zation** *or* **-i'sation** *n.*

oxidizing agent *n.* *Chem.* a substance that oxidizes another substance, being itself reduced in the process.

oxlip ('ɒks,lɪp) *n.* **1.** a Eurasian woodland plant, with small drooping pale yellow flowers. **2.** a similar and related plant that is a natural hybrid between the cowslip and primrose. [OE *oxanslyppe*, lit.: ox's slippery dropping; see SLIP[3]]

oxo acid ('ɒksəʊ) *n.* another name for **oxy acid**.

Oxon *abbrev. for* Oxfordshire. [from L *Oxonia*]

Oxon. *abbrev. for* (in degree titles, etc.) of Oxford. [from L *Oxoniensis*]

Oxonian (ɒk'səʊnɪən) *adj.* **1.** of or relating to Oxford or Oxford University. ~*n.* **2.** a member of Oxford University. **3.** an inhabitant or native of Oxford.

oxpecker ('ɒks,pɛkə) *n.* either of two African starlings, having flattened bills with which they obtain food from the hides of cattle. Also called: **tick-bird**.

oxtail ('ɒks,teɪl) *n.* the skinned tail of an ox, used esp. in soups and stews.

oxter ('ɒukstə) *n.* *Scot., Irish, & N English dialect.* the armpit. [C16: from OE *oxta*]

oxtongue ('ɒks,tʌŋ) *n.* **1.** any of various Eurasian composite plants having oblong bristly leaves and clusters of dandelion-like flowers. **2.** any of various other plants having bristly tongue-shaped leaves. **3.** the tongue of an ox, braised or cooked as food.

Oxus ('ɒksəs) *n.* the ancient name for the **Amu Darya**.

oxy-[1] *combining form.* denoting something sharp; acute: *oxytone*. [from Gk, from *oxus*]

oxy-[2] *combining form.* containing or using oxygen: *oxyacetylene*.

oxyacetylene (,ɒksɪə'sɛtɪ,liːn) *n.* **a.** a mixture of oxygen and acetylene; used in a blowpipe for cutting or welding metals at high temperatures. **b.** (*as modifier*): *an oxyacetylene burner*.

oxyacid (,ɒksɪ'æsɪd) *n.* any acid that contains oxygen with the acidic hydrogen atoms bound to oxygen atoms. Also called: **oxo acid**.

oxygen ('ɒksɪdʒən) *n.* **a.** a colourless odourless highly reactive gaseous element: the most abundant element in the earth's crust. Symbol: O; atomic no.: 8; atomic wt.: 15.9994. **b.** (*as modifier*): *an oxygen mask*. —**oxygenic** (,ɒksɪ'dʒɛnɪk) *or* **oxygenous** (ɒk'sɪdʒɪnəs) *adj.*

oxygenate ('ɒksɪdʒɪ,neɪt) *or* **oxygenize** *or* **-ise** *vb.* to enrich or be enriched with oxygen: *to oxygenate blood*. —,**oxygen'ation** *n.* —'**oxygen,izer** *or* **-iser** *n.*

oxygen tent *n.* *Med.* a transparent enclosure covering a bedridden patient, into which oxygen is released to help maintain respiration.

oxyhaemoglobin (,ɒksɪ,hiːməʊ'gləʊbɪn) *n.* *Biochem.* the bright red product formed when oxygen from the lungs combines with haemoglobin in the blood.

oxyhydrogen (,ɒksɪ'haɪdrɪdʒən) *n.* **a.** a mixture of hydrogen and oxygen used to provide an intense flame for welding. **b.** (*as modifier*): *an oxyhydrogen blowpipe*.

oxymoron (,ɒksɪ'mɔːrɒn) *n., pl.* **-mora** (-'mɔːrə). *Rhetoric.* an epigrammatic effect, by which contradictory terms are used in conjunction: *beautiful tyrant*. [C17: via NL from Gk *oxumōron*, from *oxus* sharp + *mōros* stupid]

oyer and terminer ('ɔɪə; 'tɜːmɪnə) *n.* **1.** *English law.* (formerly) a commission issued to judges to try cases on assize. **2.** the court in which such a hearing was held. [C15: from Anglo-Norman, from *oyer* to hear + *terminer* to judge]

oyez *or* **oyes** ('əʊ'jɛs, -'jɛz) *sentence substitute.* **1.** a cry, usually uttered three times, by a public crier or court official for silence and attention before making a proclamation. ~*n.* **2.** such a cry. [C15: via Anglo-Norman from OF *oiez*! hear!]

Oyo ('əʊjəʊ) *n.* a state of SW Nigeria, formed in 1976 from part of Western State. Capital: Ibadan. Pop.: 8 372 300 (1984). Area: 17 600 sq. km (6794 sq. miles).

oyster ('ɔɪstə) *n.* **1. a.** an edible marine bivalve mollusc having a rough irregularly shaped shell and occurring on the sea bed, mostly in coastal waters. **b.** (*as modifier*): *oyster farm; oyster knife.* **2.** any of various similar and related molluscs, such as the pearl oyster and the saddle oyster. **3.** the oyster-shaped piece of dark meat in the hollow of the pelvic bone of a fowl. **4.** something from which advantage, delight, profit, etc., may be derived: *the world is his oyster.* **5.** *Inf.* a very uncommunicative person. ~*vb.* **6.** (*intr.*) to dredge for, gather, or raise oysters. [C14 *oistre,* from OF *uistre,* from L *ostrea,* from Gk *ostreon;* rel. to Gk *osteon* bone, *ostrakon* shell]

oyster bed *n.* a place, esp. on the sea bed, where oysters breed and grow naturally or are cultivated for food or pearls. Also called: **oyster bank, oyster park.**

oystercatcher ('ɔɪstə,kætʃə) *n.* a shore bird having a black or black-and-white plumage and a long stout laterally compressed red bill.

oyster crab *n.* any of several small soft-bodied crabs that live as commensals in the mantles of oysters.

oyster plant *n.* **1.** another name for **salsify** (sense 1). **2.** Also called: **sea lungwort.** a prostrate coastal plant with clusters of blue flowers.

oz *or* **oz.** *abbrev. for* ounce. [from It. *onza*]

Oz (ɒz) *n. Austral. sl.* Australia.

Ozalid ('ɒzəlɪd) *n.* **1.** *Trademark.* a method of duplicating type matter, illustrations, etc., when printed on translucent paper. **2.** a reproduction produced by this method.

Ozark Plateau ('əʊzɑːk) *n.,* **Ozark Mountains,** *or* **Ozarks** *pl. n.* an eroded plateau in S Missouri, N Arkansas, and NE Oklahoma. Area: about 130 000 sq. km (50 000 sq. miles).

ozocerite *or* **ozokerite** (əʊ'zəʊkə,raɪt) *n.* a brown or greyish wax that occurs associated with petroleum and is used for making candles and waxed paper. [C19: from G *Ozokerit,* from Gk *ozein* odour + *kēros* beeswax]

ozone ('əʊzəʊn, əʊ'zəʊn) *n.* **1.** a colourless gas with a chlorine-like odour, formed by an electric discharge in oxygen: a strong oxidizing agent, used in bleaching, sterilizing water, purifying air, etc. Formula: O_3. **2.** *Inf.* clean bracing air, as found at the seaside. [C19: from G *Ozon,* from Gk: smell] —**ozonic** (əʊ'zɒnɪk) *or* **'ozonous** *adj.*

ozonize *or* **-ise** ('əʊzəʊ,naɪz) *vb.* (*tr.*) **1.** to convert (oxygen) into ozone. **2.** to treat (a substance) with ozone. —**,ozoni'zation** *or* **-i'sation** *n.* — **'ozon'izer** *or* **-,iser** *n.*

ozonosphere (əʊ'zəʊnə,sfɪə, -'zɒnə-) *or* **ozone layer** *n.* a region of ozone concentration in the stratosphere that absorbs high-energy solar ultraviolet rays.

P

p *or* **P** (piː) *n.*, *pl.* **p's, P's,** or **Ps.** **1.** the 16th letter of the English alphabet. **2.** a speech sound represented by this letter. **3. mind one's p's and q's.** to be careful to behave correctly and use polite or suitable language.

p *symbol for:* **1.** (in Britain) penny *or* pence. **2.** *Music.* piano: an instruction to play quietly. **3.** *Physics.* pico-. **4.** *Physics.* **a.** momentum. **b.** proton. **c.** pressure.

P *symbol for:* **1.** *Chem.* phosphorus. **2.** *Physics.* **a.** parity. **b.** poise. **c.** power. **d.** pressure. **3.** (on road signs) parking. **4.** *Chess.* pawn. **5.** *Currency.* **a.** peseta. **b.** peso. **6.** (of a medicine or drug) available only from a chemist's shop, but not requiring a prescription to obtain it.

p. *abbrev. for:* **1.** (*pl.* **pp.**) page. **2.** part. **3.** participle. **4.** past. **5.** per. **6.** pint. **7.** pipe. **8.** population. **9.** post. [L: after] **10.** pro. [L: in favour of; for]

pa (paː) *n.* an informal word for **father.**

Pa *the chemical symbol for* protactinium.

PA *abbrev. for:* **1.** personal assistant. **2.** *Mil.* Post Adjutant. **3.** power of attorney. **4.** press agent. **5.** Press Association. **6.** private account. **7.** public-address system. **8.** publicity agent. **9.** Publishers Association. **10.** purchasing agent.

p.a. *abbrev. for* per annum. [L: yearly]

Pabst (*German* paːpst) *n.* **G(eorge) W(ilhelm)**. 1885–1967, German film director, whose films include *Joyless Street* (1925), *Pandora's Box* (1929), and *The Last Act* (1954).

pabulum ('pæbjʊləm) *n.* *Rare.* **1.** food. **2.** food for thought. [C17: from L, from *pascere* to feed]

PABX (in Britain) *abbrev. for* private automatic branch exchange. See also **PBX.**

paca ('paːkə, 'pækə) *n.* a large burrowing rodent of Central and South America, having white-spotted brown fur. [C17: from Sp., from Amerind]

pace[1] (peɪs) *n.* **1. a.** a single step in walking. **b.** the distance covered by a step. **2.** a measure of length equal to the average length of a stride, approximately 3 feet. **3.** speed of movement, esp. of walking or running. **4.** rate or style of proceeding at some activity: *to live at a fast pace.* **5.** manner or action of stepping, walking, etc.; gait. **6.** any of the manners in which a horse or other quadruped walks or runs. **7.** a manner of moving, sometimes developed in the horse, in which the two legs on the same side are moved at the same time. **8. keep pace with.** to proceed at the same speed as. **9. put (someone) through his paces.** to test the ability of (someone). **10. set the pace.** to determine the rate at which a group runs or walks or proceeds at some other activity. ~*vb.* **11.** (*tr.*) to set or determine the pace for, as in a race. **12.** (often foll. by *about, up and down,* etc.) to walk with regular slow or fast paces, as in boredom, agitation, etc.: *to pace the room.* **13.** (*tr.*; often foll. by *out*) to measure by paces: *to pace out the distance.* **14.** (*intr.*) to walk with slow regular strides. **15.** (*intr.*) (of a horse) to move at the pace (the specially developed gait). [C13: via OF from L *passūs* step, from *pandere* to extend (the legs as in walking)]

pace[2] ('peɪsɪ; *Latin* 'paːke) *prep.* with due deference to: used to acknowledge politely someone who disagrees. [C19: from L, from *pāx* peace]

pacemaker ('peɪsˌmeɪkə) *n.* **1.** a person, horse, vehicle, etc., used in a race or speed trial to set the pace. **2.** a person, organization, etc., regarded as being the leader in a particular activity. **3.** Also called: **cardiac pacemaker.** a small area of specialized tissue within the wall of the heart whose spontaneous electrical activity initiates and controls the heartbeat. **4.** Also called: **artificial pacemaker.** an electronic device to assume the functions of the natural cardiac pacemaker.

pacer ('peɪsə) *n.* **1.** a horse trained to move at a special gait. **2.** another word for **pacemaker** (sense 1).

pacesetter ('peɪsˌsɛtə) *n.* another word for **pacemaker** (senses 1, 2).

paceway ('peɪsˌweɪ) *n.* *Austral.* a racecourse for trotting and pacing.

pachisi (pə'tʃiːzɪ) *n.* an Indian game somewhat resembling backgammon, played on a cruciform board using six cowries as dice. [C18: from Hindi, from *pacīs* twenty-five (the highest throw)]

Pachuca (*Spanish* pa'tʃuka) *n.* a city in central Mexico, capital of Hidalgo state, in the Sierra Madre Oriental: silver mines; university (1961). Pop.: 135 248 (1980).

pachyderm ('pækɪˌdɜːm) *n.* any very large thick-skinned mammal, such as an elephant, rhinoceros, or hippopotamus. [C19: from F *pachyderme,* from Gk *pakhudermos,* from *pakhus* thick + *derma* skin] — ˌpachy'dermatous *adj.*

pacific (pə'sɪfɪk) *adj.* **1.** tending or conducive to peace; conciliatory. **2.** not aggressive. **3.** free from conflict; peaceful. [C16: from OF, from L *pācificus,* from *pāx* peace + *facere* to make] —pa'cifically *adv.*

Pacific (pə'sɪfɪk) *n.* **1. the.** short for **Pacific Ocean.** ~*adj.* **2.** of or relating to the Pacific Ocean or its islands.

Pacific Islands *pl. n.* a former Trust Territory; an island group in the W Pacific Ocean, mandated to Japan after World War I and assigned to the U.S. by the United Nations in 1947: comprised 2141 islands (96 inhabited) of the Caroline, Marshall, and Mariana groups (excluding Guam). In 1978 the Northern Marianas became a commonwealth in union with the U.S. The three remaining entities consisting of the Marshall Islands, the Republic of Belau (formerly Palau), and the Federated States of Micronesia became self-governing during the period 1979–80. In 1982 they signed agreements of free association with the U.S. Administrative centre: Saipan (Mariana Islands). Land area: about 1800 sq. km (700 sq. miles), scattered over about 7 500 000 sq. km (3 000 000 sq. miles) of ocean.

Pacific Northwest *n.* the region of North America lying north of the Columbia River and west of the Rockies.

Pacific Ocean *n.* the world's largest and deepest ocean, lying between Asia and Australia and North and South America. Area: about 165 760 000 sq. km (64 000 000 sq. miles). Average depth: 4215 m (14 050 ft.). Greatest depth: Challenger Deep (in the Marianas Trench), 11 033 m (37 073 ft.). Greatest width: (between Panama and Mindanao, Philippines) 17 066 km (10 600 miles).

pacifier ('pæsɪˌfaɪə) *n.* **1.** a person or thing that pacifies. **2.** *U.S. & Canad.* a baby's dummy or teething ring.

pacifism ('pæsɪˌfɪzəm) *n.* **1.** the belief that violence of any kind is unjustifiable and that one should not participate in war, etc. **2.** the belief that international disputes can be settled by arbitration rather than war. — 'pacifist *n.*, *adj.*

pacify ('pæsɪˌfaɪ) *vb.* **-fying, -fied.** (*tr.*) **1.** to calm the anger or agitation of; mollify. **2.** to restore to peace or order. [C15: from OF *pacifier;* see PACIFIC] —'paci,fiable *adj.* —**pacification** (ˌpæsɪfɪ'keɪʃən) *n.*

pack[1] (pæk) *n.* **1. a.** a bundle or load, esp. one carried on the back. **b.** (*as modifier*): *a pack animal.* **2.** a collected amount of anything. **3.** a complete set of similar things, esp. a set of 52 playing cards. **4.** a group of animals of the same kind, esp. hunting animals: *a pack of hounds.* **5.** any group or band that associates together, esp. for criminal purposes. **6.** any group or set regarded dismissively: *a pack of fools; a pack of lies.* **7.** *Rugby.* the forwards of a team. **8.** the basic organizational unit of Cub Scouts and Brownie Guides. **9.** a small package, carton, or container, used to retail commodities, esp. foodstuffs, cigarettes, etc. **10.** short for **pack ice. 11.** the quantity of something, such as food, packaged for preservation. **12.** *Med.* a sheet or blanket, either damp or dry, for wrapping about the body, esp. for its soothing effect. **13.** another name for **rucksack** or **backpack. 14.** Also called: **face pack.** a cream treatment that cleanses and tones the skin. **15.** a parachute folded and ready for use. **16. go to the pack.** *Austral. & N.Z. inf.* to fall into a worse state or condition. **17.** *Computers.* another name for **deck** (sense 5). ~*vb.* **18.** to place or arrange (articles) in (a container), such as clothes in a suitcase. **19.** (*tr.*) to roll up into a bundle.

20. (when *passive*, often foll. by *out*) to press tightly together; cram: *the audience packed into the foyer; the hall was packed out.* **21.** to form (snow, ice, etc.) into a hard compact mass or (of snow, etc.) to become compacted. **22.** (*tr.*) to press in or cover tightly. **23.** (*tr.*) to load (a horse, donkey, etc.) with a burden. **24.** (often foll. by *off* or *away*) to send away or go away, esp. hastily. **25.** (*tr.*) to seal (a joint) by inserting a layer of compressible material between the faces. **26.** (*tr.*) *Med.* to treat with a pack. **27.** (*tr.*) *Sl.* to be capable of inflicting (a blow, etc.): *he packs a mean punch.* **28.** (*tr.*) *U.S. inf.* to carry or wear habitually: *he packs a gun.* **29.** (*tr.*; often foll. by *in, into, to,* etc.) *U.S., Canad., & N.Z.* to carry (goods, etc.), esp. on the back. **30. send packing.** *Inf.* to dismiss peremptorily. ~See also **pack in, pack up.** [C13: from ?] —'**packable** *adj.*

pack² (pæk) *vb.* (*tr.*) to fill (a legislative body, committee, etc.) with one's own supporters: *to pack a jury.* [C16: ? changed from PACT]

package ('pækɪdʒ) *n.* **1.** any wrapped or boxed object or group of objects. **2. a.** a proposition, offer, or thing for sale in which separate items are offered together as a unit. **b.** (*as modifier*): *a package holiday; a package deal.* **3.** the act or process of packing or packaging. **4.** *Computers.* a set of programs designed for a specific type of problem. **5.** the usual U.S. and Canad. word for **packet** (sense 1). ~*vb.* (*tr.*) **6.** to wrap in or put into a package. **7.** to design and produce a package for (retail goods). **8.** to group (separate items) together as a single unit. **9.** to compile (complete books) for a publisher to market. —'**packager** *n.*

packaging ('pækɪdʒɪŋ) *n.* **1.** the box or wrapping in which a product is offered for sale. **2.** the presentation of a person, product, etc., to the public in a way designed to build up a favourable image.

pack drill *n.* a military punishment of marching about carrying a full pack of equipment.

packer ('pækə) *n.* **1.** a person or company whose business is to pack goods, esp. food: *a meat packer.* **2.** a person or machine that packs.

packet ('pækɪt) *n.* **1.** a small or medium-sized container of cardboard, paper, etc., often together with its contents: *a packet of biscuits.* Usual U.S. and Canad. word: **package.** **2.** a small package; parcel. **3.** Also called: **packet boat.** a boat that transports mail, passengers, goods, etc., on a fixed short route. **4.** *Sl.* a large sum of money: *to cost a packet.* ~*vb.* **5.** (*tr.*) to wrap up in a packet or as a packet. [C16: from OF *pacquet,* from *pacquer* to pack, from ODu. *pak* a pack]

packhorse ('pæk,hɔːs) *n.* a horse used to transport goods, equipment, etc.

pack ice *n.* a large area of floating ice, consisting of pieces that have become massed together.

pack in *vb.* (*tr., adv.*) *Brit. & N.Z. inf.* to stop doing (something) (esp. in **pack it in**).

packing ('pækɪŋ) *n.* **1. a.** material used to cushion packed goods. **b.** (*as modifier*): *a packing needle.* **2.** the packaging of foodstuffs. **3.** any substance or material used to make joints watertight or gastight.

pack rat *n.* a rat of W North America, having a long tail that is furry in some species.

packsaddle ('pæk,sæd²l) *n.* a saddle hung with packs, equipment, etc., used on a pack animal.

packthread ('pæk,θrɛd) *n.* a strong twine for sewing or tying up packages.

pack up *vb.* (*adv.*) **1.** to put (things) away in a proper or suitable place. **2.** *Inf.* to give up (an attempt) or stop doing (something). **3.** (*intr.*) (of an engine, etc.) to fail to operate; break down.

pact (pækt) *n.* an agreement or compact between two or more parties, nations, etc. [C15: from OF *pacte,* from L *pactum,* from *pacisci* to agree]

pad¹ (pæd) *n.* **1.** a thick piece of soft material used to make something comfortable, give it shape, or protect it. **2.** Also called: **stamp pad, ink pad.** a block of firm absorbent material soaked with ink for transferring to a rubber stamp. **3.** Also called: **notepad, writing pad.** a number of sheets of paper fastened together along one edge. **4.** a flat piece of stiff material used to back a piece of blotting paper. **5. a.** the fleshy cushion-like underpart of the foot of a cat, dog, etc. **b.** any of the parts constituting such a structure. **6.** any of various level surfaces or flat-topped

structures, such as a launch pad. **7.** the large flat floating leaf of the water lily. **8.** *Sl.* a person's residence. ~*vb.* **padding, padded.** (*tr.*) **9.** to line, stuff, or fill out with soft material, esp. in order to protect or shape. **10.** (often foll. by *out*) to inflate with irrelevant or false information: *to pad out a story.* [C16: from ?]

pad² (pæd) *vb.* **padding, padded.** **1.** (*intr.*; often foll. by *along, up,* etc.) to walk with a soft or muffled tread. **2.** (when *intr.*, often foll. by *around*) to travel (a route, etc.) on foot, esp. at a slow pace; tramp: *to pad around the country.* ~*n.* **3.** a dull soft sound, esp. of footsteps. [C16: ?from MDu. *paden,* from *pad* PATH]

Padang ('pɑːdæŋ) *n.* a port in W Indonesia, in W Sumatra at the foot of the **Padang Highlands** on the Indian Ocean. Pop.: 480 000 (1980).

padded cell *n.* a room, esp. one in a mental hospital, with padded surfaces in which violent inmates are placed.

padding ('pædɪŋ) *n.* **1.** any soft material used to pad clothes, etc. **2.** superfluous material put into a speech or written work to pad it out; waffle. **3.** inflated or false entries in a financial account, esp. an expense account.

paddle¹ ('pæd²l) *n.* **1.** a short light oar with a flat blade at one or both ends, used without a rowlock. **2.** Also called: **float.** a blade of a water wheel or paddle wheel. **3.** a period of paddling: *to go for a paddle upstream.* **4. a.** a paddle wheel used to propel a boat. **b.** (*as modifier*): *a paddle steamer.* **5.** any of various instruments shaped like a paddle and used for beating, mixing, etc. **6.** a table-tennis bat. **7.** the flattened limb of a seal, turtle, etc., specialized for swimming. ~*vb.* **8.** to propel (a canoe, etc.) with a paddle. **9. paddle one's own canoe. a.** to be self-sufficient. **b.** to mind one's own business. **10.** (*tr.*) to stir or mix with or as if with a paddle. **11.** to row (a boat) steadily, but not at full pressure. **12.** (*intr.*) to swim with short rapid strokes, like a dog. **13.** (*tr.*) *U.S. & Canad. inf.* to spank. [C15: from ?] —'**paddler** *n.*

paddle² ('pæd²l) *vb.* (*mainly intr.*) **1.** to walk or play barefoot in shallow water, mud, etc. **2.** to dabble the fingers, hands, or feet in water. **3.** to walk unsteadily, like a baby. **4.** (*tr.*) *Arch.* to fondle with the fingers. ~*n.* **5.** the act of paddling in water. [C16: from ?] —'**paddler** *n.*

paddle wheel *n.* a large wheel fitted with paddles, turned by an engine to propel a vessel.

paddock ('pædək) *n.* **1.** a small enclosed field, usually near a house or stable. **2.** (in horse racing) the enclosure in which horses are paraded and mounted before a race. **3.** *Austral. & N.Z.* any area of fenced land. [C17: var. of dialect *parrock,* from OE *pearruc* enclosure, of Gmc origin. See PARK]

paddy¹ ('pædɪ) *n., pl.* **-dies.** **1.** Also called: **paddy field.** a field planted with rice. **2.** rice as a growing crop or when harvested but not yet milled. [from Malay *pādi*]

paddy² ('pædɪ) *n., pl.* **-dies.** *Brit. inf.* a fit of temper. [C19: from *Paddy* inf. name for an Irishman]

pademelon or **paddymelon** ('pædɪ,mɛlən) *n.* a small wallaby of coastal scrubby regions of Australia. [C19: of Abor. origin]

Paderborn (German paːdər'bɔrn) *n.* a market town in NW West Germany, in North Rhine-Westphalia: scene of the meeting between Charlemagne and Pope Leo III (799 A.D.) that led to the foundation of the Holy Roman Empire. Pop.: 110 155 (1980 est.).

Paderewski (*Polish* padɛ'rɛfski) *n.* **Ignace Jan** (iɲas jan). 1860–1941, Polish pianist, composer, and statesman; prime minister (1919).

padlock ('pæd,lɒk) *n.* **1.** a detachable lock having a hinged or sliding shackle, which can be used to secure a door, lid, etc., by passing the shackle through rings or staples. ~*vb.* **2.** (*tr.*) to fasten as with a padlock. [C15 *pad,* from ?]

Padova ('paːdova) *n.* the Italian name for **Padua.**

padre ('paːdrɪ) *n. Inf.* (*sometimes cap.*) **1.** father: used to address or refer to a priest. **2.** a chaplain to the armed forces. [via Sp. or It. from L *pater* father]

padsaw ('pæd,sɔː) *n.* a small narrow saw used for cutting curves. [C19: from PAD¹ (in the sense: a handle that can be fitted to various tools) + SAW¹]

Padua ('pædʒʊə, 'pædjʊə) *n.* a city in NE Italy, in Veneto: important in Roman and Renaissance times; university (1222); botanical garden (1545). Pop.: 225 760 (1986). Latin name: **Patavium** (pə'teɪvɪəm). Italian name: **Padova.**

Padus ('peɪdəs) *n.* the Latin name for the **Po**[2].

paean *or U.S. (sometimes)* **pean** ('piːən) *n.* **1.** a hymn sung in ancient Greece in thanksgiving to a deity. **2.** any song of praise. **3.** enthusiastic praise: *the film received a paean from the critics.* [C16: via L from Gk *paiān* hymn to Apollo, from his title *Paiān*, the physician of the gods]

paediatrician *or U.S.* **pediatrician** (ˌpiːdɪəˈtrɪʃən) *n.* a medical practitioner who specializes in paediatrics.

paediatrics *or U.S.* **pediatrics** (ˌpiːdɪˈætrɪks) *n. (functioning as sing.)* the branch of medical science concerned with children and their diseases. —ˌpaediˈatric *or U.S.* ˌpediˈatric *adj.*

paedo-, *before a vowel* **paed-**, *or esp. U.S.* **pedo-, ped-** *combining form.* indicating a child or children: *paedophilia.* [from Gk *pais, paid-* child]

paedomorphosis (ˌpiːdəˈmɔːfəsɪs) *n.* the resemblance of adult animals to the young of their ancestors.

paedophilia *or esp. U.S.* **pedophilia** (ˌpiːdəʊˈfɪlɪə) *n.* the condition of being sexually attracted to children. —**paedophile** *or esp. U.S.* **pedophile** ('piːdəʊˌfaɪl) *or* ˌpaedoˈphiliˌac *or esp. U.S.* ˌpedoˈphiliˌac *n., adj.*

paella (paɪˈɛlə) *n., pl.* **-las** (-ləz). **1.** a Spanish dish made from rice, shellfish, chicken, and vegetables. **2.** the pan in which a paella is cooked. [from Catalan, from OF *paelle*, from L *patella* small pan]

paeony ('piːənɪ) *n., pl.* **-nies.** a variant spelling of **peony**.

Paestum ('pɛstəm) *n.* an ancient Greek colony on the coast of Lucania in S Italy.

pagan ('peɪgən) *n.* **1.** a member of a group professing any religion other than Christianity, Judaism, or Islam. **2.** a person without any religion; heathen. —*adj.* **3.** of or relating to pagans. **4.** heathen; irreligious. [C14: from Church L *pāgānus* civilian (hence, not a soldier of Christ), from L: villager, from *pāgus* village] —ˈ**pagandom** *n.* —ˈ**paganˌish** *adj.* —ˈ**paganism** *n.*

Paganini (*Italian* pagaˈniːni) *n.* **Niccolò** (nikkoˈlɔ). 1782–1840, Italian violinist and composer.

paganize *or* **-ise** ('peɪgəˌnaɪz) *vb.* to become pagan or convert to paganism.

page[1] (peɪdʒ) *n.* **1.** one side of one of the leaves of a book, newspaper, etc., or the written or printed matter it bears. **2.** such a leaf considered as a unit. **3.** an episode, phase, or period: *a glorious page in the revolution.* ~*vb.* **4.** another word for **paginate**. [C15: via OF from L *pāgina*]

page[2] (peɪdʒ) *n.* **1.** a boy employed to run errands, carry messages, etc., for the guests in a hotel, club, etc. **2.** a youth in attendance at official functions or ceremonies, esp. weddings. **3.** *Medieval history.* **a.** a boy in training for knighthood in personal attendance on a knight. **b.** a youth in the personal service of a person of rank. ~*vb.* (*tr.*) **4.** to call out the name of (a person), esp. by a loudspeaker system, so as to give him a message. **5.** to call (a person) by an electronic device, such as a bleep. **6.** to act as a page to or attend as a page. [C13: via OF from It. *paggio*, prob. from Gk *paidion* boy, from *pais* child]

Page (peɪdʒ) *n.* **1.** Sir **Earle** (**Christmas Grafton**). 1880–1961, Australian statesman; co-leader, with S. M. Bruce, of the federal government of Australia (1923–29). **2.** Sir **Frederick Handley**. 1885–1962, English pioneer in the design and manufacture of aircraft.

pageant ('pædʒənt) *n.* **1.** an elaborate colourful display portraying scenes from history, etc. **2.** any magnificent or showy display, procession, etc. [C14: from Med. L *pāgina* scene of a play, from L: PAGE[1]]

pageantry ('pædʒəntrɪ) *n., pl.* **-ries.** **1.** spectacular display or ceremony. **2.** *Arch.* pageants collectively.

pageboy ('peɪdʒˌbɔɪ) *n.* **1.** a smooth medium-length hairstyle with the ends of the hair curled under. **2.** a less common word for **page**[2].

pager ('peɪdʒə) *n.* an electronic device used to call a person.

page-three *modifier. Brit.* denoting a scantily dressed attractive girl, as photographed on page three of some tabloid newspapers.

paginate ('pædʒɪˌneɪt) *vb. (tr.)* to number the pages of (a book, manuscript, etc.) in sequence. Cf. **foliate**. —ˌpagiˈnation *n.*

pagoda (pəˈgəʊdə) *n.* an Indian or Far Eastern temple, esp. a tower, usually pyramidal and having many storeys. [C17: from Port. *pagode*, ult. from Sansk. *bhagavatī* divine]

pagoda tree *n.* a Chinese leguminous tree with ornamental white flowers.

Pago Pago ('pɑːŋɡəʊ 'pɑːŋɡəʊ) *n.* a port in American Samoa, on SE Tutuila Island. Pop.: 3400 (1985 est.). Former name: **Pango Pango**.

Pahang (pəˈhʌŋ) *n.* a state of Peninsular Malaysia, on the South China Sea: the largest Malayan state; mountainous and heavily forested. Capital: Kuala Lipis. Pop.: 921 360 (1985 est.). Area: 35 964 sq. km (13 886 sq. miles).

Pahlavi ('pɑːləvɪ) *n.* **1. Mohammed Reza** ('rɪzə). 1919–80, shah of Iran (1941–79); forced into exile (1979) during civil unrest following which an Islamic republic was established led by the Ayatollah Khomeini. **2.** his father, **Reza**. 1877–1944, shah of Iran (1925–41). Originally an army officer, he gained power by a coup d'état (1921) and was chosen shah by the National Assembly. He reorganized the army and did much to modernize Iran.

Pahsien ('pɑːʃjɛn) *n.* another name for Chongqing.

paid (peɪd) *vb.* **1.** the past tense and past participle of **pay**[1]. **2. put paid to.** *Chiefly Brit. & N.Z.* to end or destroy: *breaking his leg put paid to his hopes of running in the Olympics.*

Paignton ('peɪntən) *n.* a town and resort in SW England, in Devon: administratively part of Torbay since 1968.

pail (peɪl) *n.* **1.** a bucket, esp. one made of wood or metal. **2.** Also called: **pailful.** the quantity that fills a pail. [OE *pægel*]

paillasse ('pælɪˌæs, ˌpælɪˈæs) *n.* a variant spelling (esp. U.S.) of **palliasse**.

pain (peɪn) *n.* **1.** the sensation of acute physical hurt or discomfort caused by injury, illness, etc. **2.** emotional suffering or mental distress. **3. on pain of.** subject to the penalty of. **4.** Also called: **pain in the neck.** *Inf.* a person or thing that is a nuisance. ~*vb.* (*tr.*) **5.** to cause (a person) hurt, grief, anxiety, etc. **6.** *Inf.* to annoy; irritate. ~See also **pains**. [C13: from OF *peine*, from L *poena* punishment, grief, from Gk *poinē* penalty] —ˈ**painless** *adj.*

Paine (peɪn) *n.* **Thomas.** 1737–1809, American political pamphleteer, born in England. His works include the pamphlets *Common Sense* (1776) and *Crisis* (1776–83), supporting the American colonists' fight for independence; *The Rights of Man* (1791–92), a justification of the French Revolution; and *The Age of Reason* (1794–96), a defence of deism.

pained (peɪnd) *adj.* having or expressing pain or distress, esp. mental or emotional distress.

painful ('peɪnful) *adj.* **1.** causing pain; distressing: *a painful duty.* **2.** affected with pain. **3.** tedious or difficult. **4.** *Inf.* extremely bad. —ˈ**painfully** *adv.* —ˈ**painfulness** *n.*

painkiller ('peɪnˌkɪlə) *n.* **1.** an analgesic drug or agent. **2.** anything that relieves pain.

pains (peɪnz) *pl. n.* **1.** care or trouble (esp. in **take pains, be at pains to**). **2.** painful sensations experienced during contractions in childbirth; labour pains.

painstaking ('peɪnzˌteɪkɪŋ) *adj.* extremely careful, esp. as to fine detail. —ˈ**painsˌtakingly** *adv.* —ˈ**painsˌtakingness** *n.*

paint (peɪnt) *n.* **1.** a substance used for decorating or protecting a surface, esp. a mixture consisting of a solid pigment suspended in a liquid that dries to form a hard coating. **2.** a dry film of paint on a surface. **3.** *Inf.* face make-up, such as rouge. **4.** short for **greasepaint**. ~*vb.* **5.** to make (a picture) of (a figure, landscape, etc.) with paint applied to a surface such as canvas. **6.** to coat (a surface, etc.) with paint, as in decorating. **7.** (*tr.*) to apply (liquid, etc.) onto (a surface): *she painted the cut with antiseptic.* **8.** (*tr.*) to apply make-up onto (the face, lips, etc.). **9.** (*tr.*) to describe vividly in words. **10. paint the town red.** *Inf.* to celebrate uninhibitedly. [C13: from OF *peint* painted, from *peindre* to paint, from L *pingere* to paint] —ˈ**painty** *adj.*

paintbox ('peɪntˌbɒks) *n.* a box containing a tray of dry watercolour paints.

paintbrush ('peɪntˌbrʌʃ) *n.* a brush used to apply paint.

Painted Desert *n.* a section of the high plateau country of N central Arizona, along the N side of the Little Colorado River Valley: brilliant-coloured rocks; occupied largely by Navaho and Hopi Indians. Area: about 20 000 sq. km (7500 sq. miles).

painted lady *n.* a migratory butterfly with pale brownish-red mottled wings.

painter[1] ('peɪntə) n. **1.** a person who paints surfaces as a trade. **2.** an artist who paints pictures. —'**painterly** adj.

painter[2] ('peɪntə) n. a line attached to the bow of a boat for tying it up. [C15: prob. from OF penteur strong rope]

painting ('peɪntɪŋ) n. **1.** the art of applying paints to canvas, etc. **2.** a picture made in this way. **3.** the act of applying paint to a surface.

paintwork ('peɪnt,wɜːk) n. a surface, such as wood or a car body, that is painted.

pair (peə) n., pl. **pairs** or (functioning as sing. or pl.) **pair. 1.** two identical or similar things matched for use together: a pair of socks. **2.** two persons, animals, things, etc., used or grouped together: a pair of horses; a pair of scoundrels. **3.** an object considered to be two identical or similar things joined together: a pair of trousers. **4.** two people joined in love or marriage. **5.** a male and a female animal of the same species kept for breeding purposes. **6.** Parliament. **a.** two opposed members who both agree not to vote on a specified motion. **b.** the agreement so made. **7.** two playing cards of the same rank or denomination. **8.** one member of a matching pair: I can't find the pair to this glove. ~vb. **9.** (often foll. by off) to arrange or fall into groups of twos. **10.** to group or be grouped in matching pairs. **11.** to join or be joined in marriage; mate or couple. **12.** (when tr., usually passive) Parliament. to form or cause to form a pair. [C13: from OF paire, from L paria equal (things), from pār equal]
▷**Usage.** Like other collective nouns, pair takes a singular or a plural verb according to whether it is seen as a unit or as a collection of two things: the pair of cuff links was gratefully received; that pair (the two of them) are on very good terms.

paisley ('peɪzlɪ) n. **1.** a pattern of small curving shapes with intricate detailing. **2.** a soft fine wool fabric traditionally printed with this pattern. **3.** a shawl made of this fabric, popular in the late 19th century. **4.** (modifier) of or decorated with this pattern: a paisley scarf. [C19: after PAISLEY[1]]

Paisley[1] ('peɪzlɪ) n. an industrial town in SW Scotland, in central Strathclyde region: one of the world's chief centres for the manufacture of thread, linen, and gauze in the 19th century. Pop.: 84 789 (1981).

Paisley[2] ('peɪzlɪ) n. Rev. **Ian (Richard Kyle)**. born 1926, Northern Ireland politician; Protestant and Loyalist.

pajamas (pə'dʒɑːməz) pl. n. the U.S. spelling of **pyjamas**.

pakeha ('pɑːkɪ,hɑː) n. N.Z. a European, as distinct from a Maori: Maori and pakeha. [from Maori]

Paki ('pækɪ) Brit. sl. derog. ~n., pl. **Pakis. 1.** a Pakistani or person of Pakistani descent. ~adj. **2.** Pakistani or of Pakistani descent.

Pakistan (,pɑːkɪ'stɑːn) n. **1.** a republic in S Asia, on the Arabian Sea: formerly West Pakistan until East Pakistan gained independence as Bangladesh in 1971; contains the fertile plains of the Indus valley rising to mountains in the north and west. Official language: Urdu. Religion: mostly Muslim. Currency: rupee. Capital: Islamabad. Pop.: 102 200 000 (1987 est.). Area: 801 508 sq. km (309 463 sq. miles). **2.** a former republic in S Asia consisting of the provinces of West Pakistan and East Pakistan (now Bangladesh), 1500 km (900 miles) apart: formed in 1947 from the predominantly Muslim parts of India. —,**Paki'stani** n., adj.

pakora (pə'kɔːrə) n. an Indian dish consisting of pieces of vegetable, chicken, etc., dipped in spiced batter and deep-fried. [C20: from Hindi]

pal (pæl) Inf. ~n. **1.** a close friend; comrade. ~vb. **palling, palled. 2.** (intr.; usually foll. by with) to associate as friends. [C17: from E Gypsy: brother, ult. from Sansk. bhrātar BROTHER]

PAL (pæl) n. acronym for phase alternation line: a colour-television broadcasting system used generally in Europe.

palace ('pælɪs) n. (cap. when part of a name) **1.** the official residence of a reigning monarch. **2.** the official residence of various high-ranking people, as of an archbishop. **3.** a large and richly furnished building resembling a royal palace. [C13: from OF palais, from L Palātium PALATINE]

Palacio Valdés (Spanish pa'laθjo bal'des) n. **Armando** (ar'mando). 1853–1938, Spanish novelist and critic.

paladin ('pælədɪn) n. **1.** one of the legendary twelve peers of Charlemagne's court. **2.** a knightly champion. [C16: via F from It. paladino, from L palātīnus imperial official]

palaeo-, before a vowel **palae-** or esp. U.S. **paleo-, pale-** combining form. old, ancient, or prehistoric: palaeography. [from Gk palaios old]

palaeobotany or U.S. **paleobotany** (,pælɪəʊ'bɒtənɪ) n. the study of fossil plants. —,**palaeo'botanist** or U.S. ,**paleo'botanist** n.

Palaeocene or U.S. **Paleocene** ('pælɪəʊ,siːn) adj. **1.** of, denoting, or formed in the first epoch of the Tertiary period. ~n. **2.** the. the Palaeocene epoch or rock series. [C19: from F, from paléo PALAEO- + Gk kainos new]

palaeoclimatology or U.S. **paleoclimatology** (,pælɪəʊ,klaɪmə'tɒlədʒɪ) n. the study of climates of the geological past.

palaeography or U.S. **paleography** (,pælɪ'ɒgrəfɪ) n. **1.** the study of the handwritings of the past, and often the manuscripts, etc., so that they may be dated, read, etc. **2.** a handwriting of the past. —,**palae'ographer** or U.S. ,**pale'ographer** n. —**palaeographic** (,pælɪəʊ'græfɪk), ,**palaeo'graphical** or U.S. ,**paleo'graphic**, ,**paleo'graphical** adj.

Palaeolithic or U.S. **Paleolithic** (,pælɪəʊ'lɪθɪk) n. **1.** the period of the emergence of primitive man and the manufacture of unpolished chipped stone tools, about 2.5 million to 3 million years ago. ~adj. **2.** (sometimes not cap.) of or relating to this period.

palaeomagnetism or U.S. **paleomagnetism** (,pælɪəʊ'mægnɪtɪzəm) n. the study of the fossil magnetism in rocks, used to determine the past configuration of the earth's constituents.

palaeontology or U.S. **paleontology** (,pælɪɒn'tɒlədʒɪ) n. the study of fossils to determine the structure and evolution of extinct animals and plants and the age and conditions of deposition of the rock strata in which they are found. [C19: from PALAEO- + ONTO- + -LOGY] —**palaeontological** or U.S. **paleontological** (,pælɪ,ɒntə'lɒdʒɪkəl) adj. —,**palaeon'tologist** or U.S. ,**paleon'tologist** n.

Palaeozoic (,pælɪəʊ'zəʊɪk) adj. **1.** of, denoting, or relating to an era of geological time that began 600 million years ago with the Cambrian period and lasted about 375 million years until the end of the Permian period. ~n. **2.** the. the Palaeozoic era. [C19: from PALAEO- + Gk zóē life + -IC]

palanquin or **palankeen** (,pælən'kiːn) n. a covered litter, formerly used in the Orient, carried on the shoulders of four men. [C16: from Port. palanquim, from Prakrit pallanka, from Sansk. paryanka couch]

palatable ('pælətəb[o]l) adj. **1.** pleasant to taste. **2.** acceptable or satisfactory. —,**palata'bility** or '**palatableness** n. —'**palatably** adv.

palatal ('pælət[o]l) adj. **1.** Also: **palatine.** of or relating to the palate. **2.** Phonetics. of, relating to, or denoting a speech sound articulated with the blade of the tongue touching the hard palate. ~n. **3.** Also called: **palatine.** the bony plate that forms the palate. **4.** Phonetics. a palatal speech sound, such as (j). —'**palatally** adv.

palatalize or **-lise** ('pælətə,laɪz) vb. (tr.) to pronounce (a speech sound) with the blade of the tongue touching the palate. —,**palatali'zation** or **-li'sation** n.

palate ('pælɪt) n. **1.** the roof of the mouth, separating the oral and nasal cavities. See **hard palate, soft palate. 2.** the sense of taste: she had no palate for the wine. **3.** relish or enjoyment. [C14: from L palātum, ? of Etruscan origin]

palatial (pə'leɪʃəl) adj. of, resembling, or suitable for a palace; sumptuous. —**pa'latially** adv.

palatinate (pə'lætɪnɪt) n. a territory ruled by a palatine prince or noble or count palatine.

Palatinate (pə'lætɪnɪt) n. **1.** the. either of two territories in SW Germany, once ruled by the counts palatine. **Upper Palatinate** is now in Bavaria; **Lower** or **Rhine Palatinate** is now in Rhineland-Palatinate, Baden-Württemberg, and Hesse. German name: **Pfalz. 2.** a native or inhabitant of the Palatinate. —'**Pala,tine** adj., n.

palatine[1] ('pælə,taɪn) adj. **1.** (of an individual) possessing royal prerogatives in a territory. **2.** of or relating to a count palatine, county palatine, palatinate, or palatine. **3.** of or relating to a palace. ~n. **4.** Feudal history. the lord of a palatinate. **5.** any of various important officials at the late Roman, Merovingian, or Carolingian courts. [C15: via F from L palātīnus belonging to the palace, from palātium; see PALACE]

palatine² ('pælə,taɪn) *adj.* **1.** of the palate. ~*n.* **2.** either of two bones forming the hard palate. [C17: from F *palatin*, from L *palátum* palate]

Palatine ('pælə,taɪn) *n.* **1.** one of the Seven Hills of Rome: traditionally the site of the first settlement of Rome. ~*adj.* **2.** of, relating to, or designating this hill.

Palau Islands (pɑːˈlaʊ) *pl. n.* a former name (until 1981) of the (Republic of) **Belau.**

palaver (pəˈlɑːvə) *n.* **1.** tedious or time-consuming business, esp. when of a formal nature: *all the palaver of filling in forms.* **2.** confused talk and activity; hubbub. **3.** (often used humorously) a conference. ~*vb.* **5.** (*intr.*) (often used humorously) to have a conference. **6.** (*intr.*) to talk confusedly. **7.** (*tr.*) to flatter or cajole. [C18: from Port. *palavra* talk, from L *parabola* PARABLE]

Palawan (*Spanish* paˈlavan) *n.* an island of the SW Philippines between the South China Sea and the Sulu Sea: the westernmost island in the country; mountainous and forested. Capital: Puerto Princesa. Pop.: 311 548 (1980). Area: 11 785 sq. km (4550 sq. miles).

pale¹ (peɪl) *adj.* **1.** lacking brightness or colour: *pale morning light.* **2.** (of a colour) whitish. **3.** dim or wan: *the pale stars.* **4.** feeble: *a pale effort.* ~*vb.* **5.** to make or become pale or paler; blanch. **6.** (*intr.*; often foll. by *before*) to lose superiority (in comparison to): *her beauty paled before that of her hostess.* [C13: from OF *palle*, from L *pallidus*, from *pallēre* to look wan] — **'palely** *adv.* — **'paleness** *n.* — **'palish** *adj.*

pale² (peɪl) *n.* **1.** a wooden post or strip used as an upright member in a fence. **2.** an enclosing barrier, esp. a fence made of pales. **3.** an area enclosed by a pale. **4.** *Heraldry.* a vertical stripe, usually in the centre of a shield. **5. beyond the pale.** outside the limits of social convention. [C14: from OF *pal*, from L *pālus* stake]

paleface ('peɪl,feɪs) *n.* a derogatory term for a White person, said to have been used by North American Indians.

Palembang (pɑːˈlɛmbɑːŋ) *n.* a port in W Indonesia, in S Sumatra; oil refineries; university (1955). Pop.: 786 000 (1980 est.).

Palencia (*Spanish* paˈlenθia) *n.* a city in N central Spain: earliest university in Spain (1208); seat of Castilian kings (12th–13th centuries); communications centre. Pop.: 71 716 (1981).

Palenque (*Spanish* paˈleŋke) *n.* the site of an ancient Mayan city in S Mexico famous for its architectural ruins.

paleo- *or before a vowel* **pale-** *combining form.* variants (esp. U.S.) of **palaeo-.**

Palermo (pəˈlɛəməʊ, -ˈlɜː-; *Italian* paˈlɛrmo) *n.* the capital of Sicily, on the NW coast: founded by the Phoenicians in the 8th century B.C. Pop.: 723 732 (1986).

Palestine ('pælɪˌstaɪn) *n.* **1.** Also called: the **Holy Land, Canaan.** the area between the Jordan River and the Mediterranean Sea in which most of the biblical narrative is located. **2.** the province of the Roman Empire in this region. **3.** the former British mandatory territory created by the League of Nations in 1922 (but effective from 1920), and including all of the present territories of Israel and Jordan between which it was partitioned by the UN in 1948.

Palestine Liberation Organization *n.* an organization founded in 1964 with the aim of creating a state for Palestinian Arabs and removing the state of Israel. Abbrev.: **PLO.**

Palestinian (ˌpælɪˈstɪnɪən) *adj.* **1.** of or relating to Palestine.~*n.* **2.** a native or inhabitant of the former British mandate, or their descendants, esp. such Arabs now living in Jordan, Lebanon, or Israel, or as refugees from Israeli-occupied territory.

Palestrina (ˌpæleˈstriːnə) *n.* **Giovanni Pierluigi da** (dʒ oˈvanni pierˈluiːdʒi da). ?1525–94, Italian composer and master of counterpoint. His works, nearly all for unaccompanied choir and religious in nature, include the *Missa Papae Marcelli* (1555).

palette ('pælɪt) *n.* **1.** Also: **pallet.** a flat piece of wood, plastic, etc., used by artists as a surface on which to mix their paints. **2.** the range of colours characteristic of a particular artist, painting, or school of painting: *a restricted palette.* [C17: from F, dim. of *pale* shovel, from L *pala* spade]

palette *or* **pallet knife** *n.* a spatula with a thin flexible blade used in painting and cookery.

Paley ('peɪlɪ) *n.* **William.** 1743–1805, English theologian and utilitarian philosopher. His chief works are *The Principles of Moral and Political Philosophy* (1785), *Horae Paulinae* (1790), *A View of the Evidences of Christianity* (1794), and *Natural Theology* (1802).

palfrey ('pɔːlfrɪ) *n. Arch.* a light saddle horse, esp. ridden by women. [C12: from OF *palefrei*, from Med. L, from LL *paraverēdus*, from Gk *para* beside + L *verēdus* light fleet horse, of Celtic origin]

Pali ('pɑːlɪ) *n.* an ancient language of India derived from Sanskrit; the language of the Buddhist scriptures. [C19: from Sansk. *pāli-bhāsa*, from *pāli* canon + *bhāsa* language, of Dravidian origin]

palimony ('pælɪmənɪ) *n. U.S.* alimony awarded to a nonmarried partner after the break-up of a long-term relationship. [C20: from PAL + ALIMONY]

palimpsest ('pælɪmp,sɛst) *n.* **1.** a manuscript on which two or more texts have been written, each one being erased to make room for the next. ~*adj.* **2.** (of a text) written on a palimpsest. **3.** (of a document, etc.) used as a palimpsest. [C17: from L *palimpsestus*, from Gk *palimpsēstos*, from *palin* again + *psēstos* rubbed smooth]

palindrome ('pælɪn,drəʊm) *n.* a word or phrase the letters of which, when taken in reverse order, read the same: *able was I ere I saw Elba.* [C17: from Gk *palindromos* running back again] — **palindromic** (ˌpælɪnˈdrɒmɪk) *adj.*

paling ('peɪlɪŋ) *n.* **1.** a fence made of pales. **2.** pales collectively. **3.** a single pale. **4.** the act of erecting pales.

palisade (ˌpælɪˈseɪd) *n.* **1.** a strong fence made of stakes driven into the ground, esp. for defence. **2.** one of the stakes used in such a fence. ~*vb.* **3.** (*tr.*) to enclose with a palisade. [C17: via F from OProvençal *palissada*, ult. from L *pālus* stake]

Palk Strait (pɔːk, pɔːlk) *n.* a channel between SE India and N Ceylon. Width: about 64 km (40 miles).

pall¹ (pɔːl) *n.* **1.** a cloth covering, usually black, spread over a coffin or tomb. **2.** a coffin, esp. during the funeral ceremony. **3.** a dark heavy covering; shroud: *the clouds formed a pall over the sky.* **4.** a depressing or oppressive atmosphere: *her bereavement cast a pall on the party.* **5.** *Heraldry.* a Y-shaped bearing. **6.** *Christianity.* a small square linen cloth with which the chalice is covered at the Eucharist. ~*vb.* **7.** (*tr.*) to cover or depress with a pall. [OE *pæll,* from L *pallium* cloak]

pall² (pɔːl) *vb.* **1.** (*intr.*; often foll. by *on*) to become boring, insipid, or tiresome (to): *history classes palled on me.* **2.** to cloy or satiate, or become cloyed or satiated. [C14: var. of APPAL]

Palladian (pəˈleɪdɪən) *adj.* denoting, relating to, or having the style of architecture created by Andrea Palladio. [C18: after Andrea PALLADIO] — **Pal'ladian,ism** *n.*

Palladio (*Italian* palˈlaːdio) *n.* **Andrea** (anˈdrɛːa). 1508–80, Italian architect who revived and developed classical architecture, esp. the ancient Roman ideals of symmetrical planning and harmonic proportions. His treatise *Four Books on Architecture* (1570) and his designs for villas and palaces profoundly influenced 18th-century domestic architecture in England and the U.S.

palladium¹ (pəˈleɪdɪəm) *n.* a ductile malleable silvery-white element of the platinum metal group: used as a catalyst and, alloyed with gold, in jewellery; etc. Symbol: Pd; atomic no.: 46; atomic wt.: 106.4. [C19: after the asteroid *Pallas,* at the time (1803) a recent discovery]

palladium² (pəˈleɪdɪəm) *n.* something believed to ensure protection; safeguard. [C17: after the *Palladium*, a statue of Pallas Athena, Gk goddess of wisdom]

Pallas Athena *or* **Pallas** *n.* another name for **Athena.**

pallbearer ('pɔːl,bɛərə) *n.* a person who carries or escorts the coffin at a funeral.

pallet¹ ('pælɪt) *n.* a straw-filled mattress or bed. [C14: from Anglo-Norman *paillet*, from OF *paille* straw, from L *palea* straw]

pallet² ('pælɪt) *n.* **1.** an instrument with a handle and a flat, sometimes flexible, blade used by potters for shaping. **2.** a portable platform for storing and moving goods. **3.** *Horology.* the locking lever that engages and disengages to give impulses to the balance. **4.** a variant spelling of **palette** (sense 1). **5.** *Music.* a flap valve that opens to admit air to the wind chest of an organ. [C16: from OF *palette* a little shovel, from L *pala* spade]

palletize *or* **-ise** ('pælətaɪz) *vb.* (*tr.*) to store or transport (goods) on pallets. — **,palleti'zation** *or* **-i'sation** *n.*

palliasse *or esp. U.S.* **paillasse** ('pælɪˌæs, ˌpælɪ'æs) *n.* a straw-filled mattress; pallet. [C18: from F *paillasse*, from It. *pagliaccio*, ult. from L *palea* PALLET[1]]

palliate ('pælɪˌeɪt) *vb.* (*tr.*) **1.** to lessen the severity of (pain, disease, etc.) without curing; alleviate. **2.** to cause (an offence, etc.) to seem less serious; extenuate. [C16: from LL *palliāre* to cover up, from L *pallium* a cloak] —ˌpalli'ation *n.*

palliative ('pælɪətɪv) *adj.* **1.** relieving without curing. ~*n.* **2.** something that palliates, such as a sedative drug. —'palliatively *adv.*

pallid ('pælɪd) *adj.* lacking colour, brightness, or vigour: *a pallid complexion; a pallid performance.* [C17: from L *pallidus*, from *pallēre* to be PALE[1]] —'pallidly *adv.* —'pallidness *or* pal'lidity *n.*

pall-mall ('pæl'mæl) *n. Obs.* **1.** a game in which a ball is driven by a mallet along an alley and through an iron ring. **2.** the alley itself. [C17: from obs. F, from It. *pallamaglio*, from *palla* ball + *maglio* mallet]

Pall Mall ('pæl 'mæl) *n.* a street in London, noted for its many clubs.

pallor ('pælə) *n.* a pale condition, esp. when unnatural: *fear gave his face a deathly pallor.* [C17: from L: whiteness (of the skin), from *pallēre* to be PALE[1]]

pally ('pælɪ) *adj.* **-lier, -liest.** *Inf.* on friendly terms.

palm[1] (pɑːm) *n.* **1.** the inner part of the hand from the wrist to the base of the fingers. **2.** a linear measure based on the breadth or length of a hand, equal to three to four inches (7.5 to 10 centimetres) or seven to ten inches (17.5 to 25 centimetres) respectively. **3.** the part of a glove that covers the palm. **4. a.** one side of the blade of an oar. **b.** the face of the fluke of an anchor. **5.** a flattened part of the antlers of certain deer. **6. in the palm of one's hand.** at one's mercy or command. ~*vb.* (*tr.*) **7.** to conceal in or about the hand, as in sleight-of-hand tricks, etc. ~See also **palm off.** [C14 *paume*, via OF from L *palma*] —**palmar** ('pælmə) *adj.*

palm[2] (pɑːm) *n.* **1.** any treelike plant of a tropical and subtropical family having a straight unbranched trunk crowned with large pinnate or palmate leaves. **2.** a leaf or branch of any of these trees, a symbol of victory, success, etc. **3.** merit or victory. [OE, from L *palma*, from the likeness of its spreading fronds to a hand; see PALM[1]] —**palmaceous** (pæl'meɪ[j]əs) *adj.*

Palma (*Spanish* 'palma) *n.* the capital of the Balearic Islands, on the SW coast of Majorca: a tourist centre. Pop.: 295 351 (1986 est.). Official name: **Palma de Mallorca.**

palmate ('pælmeɪt, -mɪt) *or* **palmated** *adj.* **1.** shaped like an open hand: *palmate antlers.* **2.** *Bot.* having five lobes that spread out from a common point: *palmate leaves.* **3.** (of most water birds) having three toes connected by a web.

Palm Beach *n.* a town in SE Florida, on an island between Lake Worth (a lagoon) and the Atlantic: major resort and tourist centre. Pop.: 9729 (1980).

palmer ('pɑːmə) *n.* (in medieval Europe) **1.** a pilgrim bearing a palm branch as a sign of his visit to the Holy Land. **2.** any pilgrim. [C13: from OF *palmier*, from Med. L, from L *palma* PALM[2]]

Palmer ('pɑːmə) *n.* **1. Arnold.** born 1929, U.S. professional golfer: won the U.S. Open Championship (1960) and the British Open Championship (1961; 1962). **2. Samuel.** 1805–81, English painter of visionary landscapes, influenced by William Blake.

Palmer Archipelago *n.* a group of islands between South America and Antarctica: part of the British colony of Falkland Islands and Dependencies. Former name: **Antarctic Archipelago.**

Palmer Land *n.* the S part of the Antarctic Peninsula.

Palmer Peninsula *n.* the former name (until 1964) for the **Antarctic Peninsula.**

Palmerston[1] ('pɑːməstən) *n.* the former name (1869–1911) of **Darwin**[1].

Palmerston[2] ('pɑːməstən) *n.* **Henry John Temple**, 3rd Viscount Palmerston. 1784–1865, British statesman; foreign secretary (1830–34; 1835–41; 1846–51); prime minister (1855–58; 1859–65). His talent was for foreign affairs, in which he earned a reputation as a British nationalist and for high-handedness and gunboat diplomacy.

Palmerston North *n.* a city in New Zealand, in the S North Island on the Manawatu River. Pop. (urban area): 93 700 (1987).

palmetto (pæl'mɛtəʊ) *n., pl.* **-tos** *or* **-toes.** any of several small chiefly tropical palms with fan-shaped leaves. [C16: from Sp. *palmito* a little PALM[2]]

Palmira (*Spanish* pal'mira) *n.* a city in W Colombia: agricultural trading centre. Pop.: 140 481 (1973).

palmistry ('pɑːmɪstrɪ) *n.* the process or art of telling fortunes, etc., by the configuration of lines and bumps on a person's hand. Also called: **chiromancy.** [C15 *pawmestry*, from *paume* PALM[1]; the second element is unexplained] —'palmist *n.*

palmitic acid (pæl'mɪtɪk) *n.* a white crystalline solid that is a saturated fatty acid: used in the manufacture of soap and candles. Formula: $C_{15}H_{31}COOH$. Systematic name: **hexadecanoic acid.** [C19: from F]

palm off *vb.* (*tr., adv.; often foll. by on*) **1.** to offer, sell, or spend fraudulently: *to palm off a counterfeit coin.* **2.** to divert in order to be rid of: *I palmed the unwelcome visitor off on John.*

palm oil *n.* an oil obtained from the fruit of certain palms, used as an edible fat and in soap, etc.

Palm Sunday *n.* the Sunday before Easter commemorating Christ's triumphal entry into Jerusalem.

palmy ('pɑːmɪ) *adj.* **palmier, palmiest. 1.** prosperous, flourishing, or luxurious: *a palmy life.* **2.** covered with, relating to, or resembling palms.

palmyra (pæl'maɪrə) *n.* a tall tropical Asian palm with large fan-shaped leaves used for thatching and weaving. [C17: from Port. *palmeira* palm tree; ? infl. by PALMYRA city in Syria]

Palmyra (pæl'maɪrə) *n.* **1.** an ancient city in central Syria: said to have been built by Solomon. Biblical name: **Tadmor. 2.** an island in the central Pacific, in the Line Islands: under U.S. administration.

Palo Alto *n.* **1.** ('pæləʊ 'æltəʊ). a city in W California, southeast of San Francisco: founded in 1891 as the seat of Stanford University. Pop.: 55 225 (1980). **2.** (*Spanish* 'palo 'alto). a battlefield in E Mexico, northwest of Monterrey, where the first battle (1846) of the Mexican War took place, in which the Mexicans under General Mariano Arista were defeated by the Americans under General Zachary Taylor.

Palomar ('pæləˌmɑː) *n.* **Mount.** a mountain in S California, northeast of San Diego: site of **Mount Palomar Observatory,** which has a large (200-inch) reflecting telescope. Height: 1871 m (6140 ft.).

palomino (ˌpæləˈmiːnəʊ) *n., pl.* **-nos.** a golden horse with a white mane and tail. [American Sp., from Sp.: dovelike, from L, from *palumbēs* ring dove]

Palos (*Spanish* 'palɒs) *n.* a village and former port in SW Spain: starting point of Columbus' voyage of discovery to America (1492).

palp (pælp) *or* **palpus** ('pælpəs) *n., pl.* **palps** *or* **palpi** ('pælpaɪ). either of a pair of sensory appendages that arise from the mouthparts of crustaceans and insects. [C19: from F, from L *palpus* a touching]

palpable ('pælpəb[ə]l) *adj.* **1.** (*usually prenominal*) easily perceived by the senses or the mind; obvious: *a palpable lie.* **2.** capable of being touched; tangible. [C14: from LL *palpābilis* that may be touched, from L *palpāre* to touch] —ˌpalpa'bility *n.* —'palpably *adv.*

palpate ('pælpeɪt) *vb.* (*tr.*) *Med.* to examine (an area of the body) by the sense of touch. [C19: from L *palpāre* to stroke] —**pal'pation** *n.*

palpebral ('pælpɪbrəl) *adj.* of or relating to the eyelid. [C19: from LL, from L *palpebra* eyelid]

palpitate ('pælpɪˌteɪt) *vb.* (*intr.*) **1.** (of the heart) to beat rapidly. **2.** to flutter or tremble. [C17: from L *palpitāre* to throb, from *palpāre* to stroke] —'palpitant *adj.* —ˌpalpi'tation *n.*

palsy ('pɔːlzɪ) *Pathol.* ~*n., pl.* **-sies. 1.** paralysis, esp. of a specified type: *cerebral palsy.* ~*vb.* **-sying, -sied.** (*tr.*) **2.** to paralyse. [C13 *palesi*, from OF *paralisie*, from L PARALYSIS] —'palsied *adj.*

palter ('pɔːltə) *vb.* (*intr.*) **1.** to act or talk insincerely. **2.** to haggle. [C16: from ?]

paltry ('pɔːltrɪ) *adj.* **-trier, -triest. 1.** insignificant; meagre. **2.** worthless or petty. [C16: from Low Gmc *palter*, *paltrig* ragged] —'paltrily *adv.* —'paltriness *n.*

paludal (pə'ljuːd[ə]l) *adj. Rare.* **1.** of or relating to marshes. **2.** malarial. [C19: from L *palus* marsh]

paludism ('pæljʊˌdɪzəm) *n.* a less common word for **malaria.** [C19: from L *palus* marsh]

palynology (ˌpælɪˈnɒlədʒɪ) *n.* the study of living and fossil pollen grains and plant spores. [C20: from Gk *palunein* to scatter + -LOGY] —**palynological** (ˌpælɪnəˈlɒdʒɪkəl) *adj.* —ˌpalyˈnologist *n.*

Pamirs (pəˈmɪəz) *pl. n.* **the.** a mountainous area of central Asia, mainly in the Tadzhik SSR of the Soviet Union and partly in the Kirghiz SSR, extending into China and Afghanistan: consists of a complex of high ranges, from which the Tian Shan projects to the north, the Kunlun and Karakoram to the east, and the Hindu Kush to the west. Highest peak: Kongur Shan, 7719 m (25 326 ft.). Also called: **Paˈmir**.

Pamlico Sound (ˈpæmlɪkəʊ) *n.* an inlet of the Atlantic between the E coast of North Carolina and its chain of offshore islands. Length: 130 km (80 miles).

pampas (ˈpæmpəz) *n.* (*functioning as sing. or more often pl.*) **a.** the extensive grassy plains of temperate South America, esp. in Argentina. **b.** (*as modifier*): *pampas dwellers.* [C18: from American Sp. *pampa* (sing.), from Amerind *bamba* plain] —**pampean** (ˈpæmpɪən, pæmˈpiːən) *adj.*

pampas grass (ˈpæmpəs, -pəz) *n.* any of various large South American grasses, widely cultivated for their large feathery silver-coloured flower branches.

Pampeluna (ˌpæmpəˈluːnə) *n.* the former name of **Pamplona**.

pamper (ˈpæmpə) *vb.* (*tr.*) **1.** to treat with affectionate and usually excessive indulgence; coddle; spoil. **2.** *Arch.* to feed to excess. [C14: of Gmc origin] —**ˈpamperer** *n.*

pamphlet (ˈpæmflɪt) *n.* **1.** a brief publication generally having a paper cover; booklet. **2.** a brief treatise, often on a subject of current interest, in pamphlet form. [C14 *pamflet*, from Med. L *Pamphilus* title of a 12th-century amatory poem from Gk *Pamphilos* proper name]

pamphleteer (ˌpæmflɪˈtɪə) *n.* **1.** a person who writes or issues pamphlets. ~*vb.* **2.** (*intr.*) to write or issue pamphlets.

Pamphylia (pæmˈfɪlɪə) *n.* an area on the S coast of ancient Asia Minor.

Pamplona (pæmˈpləʊnə; *Spanish* pamˈplona) *n.* a city in N Spain in the foothills of the Pyrenees: capital of the kingdom of Navarre from the 11th century until 1841. Pop.: 184 340 (1986 est.). Former name: **Pampeluna**.

pan[1] (pæn) *n.* **1. a.** a wide metal vessel used in cooking. **b.** (*in combination*): *saucepan.* **2.** Also called: **panful.** the amount such a vessel will hold. **3.** any of various similar vessels used in industry, etc. **4.** a dish used esp. by gold prospectors for separating gold from gravel by washing and agitating. **5.** either of the two dishlike receptacles on a balance. **6.** Also called: **lavatory pan.** *Brit.* the bowl of a lavatory. **7. a.** a natural or artificial depression in the ground where salt can be obtained by the evaporation of brine. **b.** a natural depression containing water or mud. **8.** See **hardpan, brainpan.** **9.** a small cavity containing priming powder in the locks of old guns. **10.** a hard substratum of soil. ~*vb.* **panning, panned.** **11.** (when *tr.,* often foll. by *off* or *out*) to wash (gravel) in a pan to separate particles of (valuable minerals) from it. **12.** (*intr.;* often foll. by *out*) (of gravel, etc.) to yield valuable minerals by this process. **13.** (*tr.*) *Inf.* to criticize harshly: *the critics panned his new play.* ~See also **pan out.** [OE *panne*]

pan[2] (pæn) *vb.* **panning, panned. 1.** to move (a film camera) or (of a film camera) to be moved so as to follow a moving object or obtain a panoramic effect. ~*n.* **2.** the act of panning. [C20: shortened from PANORAMIC]

Pan (pæn) *n. Greek myth.* the god of fields, woods, shepherds, and flocks, represented as a man with a goat's legs, horns, and ears. Related adjs.: **Pandean, Panic.**

pan- *combining form.* **1.** all or every: *panchromatic.* **2.** including or relating to all parts or members: *Pan-American; pantheistic.* [from Gk *pan,* neuter of *pas* all]

panacea (ˌpænəˈsɪə) *n.* a remedy for all diseases or ills. [C16: via L from Gk *panakeia,* from *pan* all + *akēs* remedy] —ˌpanaˈcean *adj.*

panache (pəˈnæʃ, -ˈnɑːʃ) *n.* **1.** a dashing manner; swagger: *he rides with panache.* **2.** a plume on a helmet. [C16: via F from OIt. *pennacchio,* from LL *pinnāculum* feather, from L *pinna* feather]

panada (pəˈnɑːdə) *n.* a mixture of flour, water, etc., or of breadcrumbs soaked in milk, used as a thickening. [C16: from Sp., from *pan* bread, from L *pānis*]

Panaji (pɑːˈnɑːdʒiː) *n.* a variant of **Panjim.**

Panama (ˌpænəˈmɑː, ˈpænəˌmɑː) *n.* **1.** a republic in Central America, occupying the Isthmus of Panama: gained independence from Spain in 1821 and joined Greater Colombia; became independent in 1903, with the immediate area around the canal forming the Canal Zone under U.S. jurisdiction; in 1979 Panama assumed sovereignty over the Canal Zone. Languages: Spanish and English. Religion: chiefly Roman Catholic. Currency: balboa. Capital: Panama City. Pop.: 2 277 000 (1987 est.). Area: 75 650 sq. km (29 201 sq. miles). **2. Isthmus of.** an isthmus linking North and South America, between the Pacific and the Caribbean. Length: 676 km (420 miles). Width (at its narrowest point): 50 km (31 miles). Former name: (Isthmus of) **Darien. 3. Gulf of.** a wide inlet of the Pacific in Panama. —**Panamanian** (ˌpænəˈmeɪnɪən) *adj., n.*

Panama Canal *n.* a canal across the Isthmus of Panama, linking the Atlantic and Pacific Oceans: extends from Colón on the Caribbean Sea southeast to Balboa on the Gulf of Panama; built by the U.S. (1904–14), after an unsuccessful previous attempt (1881–89) by the French under de Lesseps. Length: 64 km (40 miles).

Panama Canal Zone *n.* See **Canal Zone.**

Panama City *n.* the capital of Panama, near the Pacific entrance of the Panama Canal: developed rapidly with the building of the Panama Canal; seat of the University of Panama (1935). Pop.: 439 996 (1987).

Panama hat *n.* (*sometimes not cap.*) a hat made of the plaited leaves of a palmlike plant of Central and South America. Often shortened to **panama** or **Panama.**

Pan-American *adj.* of, relating to, or concerning North, South, and Central America collectively or the advocacy of political or economic unity among American countries. —**ˈPan-Aˈmericanˌism** *n.*

panatella (ˌpænəˈtɛlə) *n.* a long slender cigar. [American Sp. *panetela* long slim biscuit, from It. *panatella* small loaf, from *pane* bread, from L *pānis*]

Panay (pɑːˈnaɪ) *n.* an island in the central Philippines, the westernmost of the Visayan Islands. Pop.: 2 595 314 (1980). Area: 12 300 sq. km (4750 sq. miles).

pancake (ˈpænˌkeɪk) *n.* **1.** a thin flat cake made from batter and fried on both sides. **2.** a stick or flat cake of compressed make-up. **3.** Also called: **pancake landing.** an aircraft landing made by levelling out a few feet from the ground and then dropping onto it. ~*vb.* **4.** to cause (an aircraft) to make a pancake landing or (of an aircraft) to make a pancake landing.

Pancake Day *n.* another name for **Shrove Tuesday.** See **Shrovetide.**

panchromatic (ˌpænkrəʊˈmætɪk) *adj. Photog.* (of an emulsion or film) made sensitive to all colours. —**panchromatism** (pænˈkrəʊməˌtɪzəm) *n.*

pancreas (ˈpæŋkrɪəs) *n.* a large elongated glandular organ, situated behind the stomach, that secretes insulin and pancreatic juice. [C16: via NL from Gk *pankreas,* from *pan-* + *kreas* flesh] —**pancreatic** (ˌpæŋkrɪˈætɪk) *adj.*

pancreatic juice *n.* the clear alkaline secretion of the pancreas that is released into the duodenum and contains digestive enzymes.

pancreatin (ˈpæŋkrɪətɪn) *n.* the powdered extract of the pancreas of certain animals, used in medicine as an aid to the digestion.

panda (ˈpændə) *n.* **1.** Also called: **giant panda.** a large black-and-white herbivorous bearlike mammal, related to the raccoons and inhabiting the bamboo forests of China. **2. lesser** *or* **red panda.** a closely related smaller animal resembling a raccoon, of the mountain forests of S Asia, having a reddish-brown coat and ringed tail. [C19: via F from a native Nepalese word]

panda car *n. Brit.* a police patrol car.

pandanus (pænˈdeɪnəs) *n., pl.* -**nuses.** any of various Old World tropical palmlike plants having leaves and roots yielding a fibre used for making mats, etc. [C19: via NL from Malay *pandan*]

Pandarus (ˈpændərəs) *n.* **1.** *Greek myth.* the leader of the Lycians, allies of the Trojans in their war with the Greeks. He broke the truce by shooting Menelaus with an arrow and was killed in the ensuing battle by Diomedes. **2.** (in medieval legend) the procurer of Cressida on behalf of Troilus.

Pandean (pæn'di:ən) *adj.* of or relating to the god Pan.
pandect ('pændɛkt) *n.* **1.** a treatise covering all aspects of a particular subject. **2.** (*often pl.*) the complete body of laws of a country; legal code, esp. the digest of Roman civil law made in the 6th century by order of Justinian. [C16: via LL from Gk *pandektēs* containing everything, from PAN- + *dektēs* receiver]
pandemic (pæn'dɛmɪk) *adj.* **1.** (of a disease) affecting persons over a wide geographical area; extensively epidemic. ~*n.* **2.** a pandemic disease. [C17: from LL *pandēmus*, from Gk *pandēmos* general, from PAN- + *demos* the people]
pandemonium (,pændɪ'məunɪəm) *n.* **1.** wild confusion; uproar. **2.** a place of uproar and chaos. [C17: coined by Milton for the capital of hell in *Paradise Lost*, from PAN- + Gk *daimōn* DEMON]
pander ('pændə) *vb.* **1.** (*intr.*; foll. by *to*) to give gratification (to weaknesses or desires). **2.** (*arch.* when tr.) to act as a go-between in a sexual intrigue (for). ~*n. also* **panderer**. **3.** a person who caters for vulgar desires. **4.** a person who procures a sexual partner for another; pimp. [C16 (*n.*): from *Pandare* Pandarus, in legend, the procurer of Cressida for Troilus]
pandit ('pʌndɪt; *spelling pron.* 'pændɪt) *n. Hinduism.* a variant of **pundit** (sense 3).
P & L *abbrev. for* profit and loss.
P & O *abbrev. for* Peninsular and Oriental (Steamship Company).
Pandora (pæn'dɔ:rə) *or* **Pandore** (pæn'dɔ:, 'pændɔ:) *n. Greek myth.* the first woman, made out of earth as the gods' revenge on man for obtaining fire from Prometheus. Given a box (**Pandora's box**) that she was forbidden to open, she disobeyed out of curiosity and released from it all the ills that beset man, leaving only hope within. [from Gk, lit.: all-gifted]
p & p *Brit. abbrev. for* postage and packing.
pane (peɪn) *n.* **1.** a sheet of glass in a window or door. **2.** a panel of a window, door, wall, etc. **3.** a flat section or face, as of a cut diamond. [C13: from OF *pan* portion, from L *pannus* rag]
panegyric (,pænɪ'dʒɪrɪk) *n.* a formal public commendation; eulogy. [C17: via F & L from Gk, from *panēguris* public gathering] —,**pane'gyrical** *adj.* —,**pane'gyrically** *adv.* —,**pane'gyrist** *n.* —**panegyrize** *or* **-rise** ('pænɪdʒɪ,raɪz) *vb.*
panel ('pænᵊl) *n.* **1.** a flat section of a wall, door, etc. **2.** any distinct section of something formed from a sheet of material, esp. of a car body. **3.** a piece of material inserted in a skirt, etc. **4. a.** a group of persons selected to act as a team in a quiz, to discuss a topic before an audience, etc. **b.** (*as modifier*): *a panel game*. **5.** *Law.* **a.** a list of persons summoned for jury service. **b.** the persons on a jury. **6.** *Scots Law.* a person accused of a crime. **7. a.** a thin board used as a surface or backing for an oil painting. **b.** a painting done on such a surface. **8.** any picture with a length much greater than its breadth. **9.** See **instrument panel**. **10.** *Brit.* (formerly) **a.** a list of patients insured under the National Health Insurance Scheme. **b.** a list of medical practitioners available for consultation by these patients. ~*vb.* **-elling, -elled** *or U.S.* **-eling, -eled**. (*tr.*) **11.** to furnish or decorate with panels. **12.** *Law.* **a.** to empanel (a jury). **b.** (in Scotland) to bring (a person) to trial; indict. [C13: from OF: portion, from *pan* piece of cloth, from L *pannus*]
panel beater *n.* a person who beats out the bodywork of motor vehicles, etc.
panelling *or U.S.* **paneling** ('pænᵊlɪŋ) *n.* **1.** panels collectively, as on a wall or ceiling. **2.** material used for making panels.
panellist *or U.S.* **panelist** ('pænᵊlɪst) *n.* a member of a panel, esp. on radio or television.
panel pin *n.* a slender nail with a narrow head.
panel saw *n.* a saw with a long narrow blade for cutting thin wood.
panel van *n. Austral. & N.Z.* a small van.
pang (pæŋ) *n.* a sudden brief sharp feeling, as of loneliness, physical pain, or hunger. [C16: var. of earlier *prange*, of Gmc origin]
panga ('pæŋgə) *n.* a broad heavy knife of E Africa. [from a native E African word]
Pangaea *or* **Pangea** (pæn'dʒi:ə) *n.* the ancient supercontinent, comprising all the present continents joined together, which began to break up about 200 million years

ago. See also **Laurasia, Gondwanaland**. [C20: from Gk, lit.: all-earth]
Pang-fou ('pæŋ'fu:) *n.* a variant transliteration of the Chinese name for **Bengbu**.
pangolin (pæŋ'gəulɪn) *n.* a mammal of tropical Africa, S Asia, and Indonesia, having a scaly body and a long snout for feeding on ants and termites. Also called: **scaly anteater**. [C18: from Malay *peng-gōling*, from *gōling* to roll over; from its ability to roll into a ball]
Pango Pango ('pɑːŋgəu 'pɑːŋgəu) *n.* the former name of **Pago Pago**.
panhandle[1] ('pæn,hændᵊl) *n.* (*sometimes cap.*) (in the U.S.) a narrow strip of land that projects from one state into another.
panhandle[2] ('pæn,hændᵊl) *vb. U.S. inf.* to beg from (passers-by). [C19: prob. a back formation from *panhandler* a person who begs with a pan] —'**pan,handler** *n.*
Panhellenic (,pænhɛ'lɛnɪk) *adj.* of or relating to all the Greeks or all Greece.
panic ('pænɪk) *n.* **1.** a sudden overwhelming feeling of terror or anxiety, esp. one affecting a whole group of people. **2.** (*modifier*) of or resulting from such terror: *panic measures*. **3.** (*modifier*) for use in an emergency: *panic stations; panic button*. ~*vb.* **-icking, -icked. 4.** to feel or cause to feel panic. [C17: from F *panique*, from NL, from Gk *panikos* emanating from PAN, considered as the source of irrational fear] —'**panicky** *adj.*
Panic ('pænɪk) *adj.* of or relating to the god Pan.
panic button *n.* a button or switch that operates a safety device, for use in an emergency.
panic grass *n.* any of various grasses, such as millet, grown in warm and tropical regions for fodder and grain. [C15 *panic*, from L *pānicum*, prob. a back formation from *pānicula* PANICLE]
panicle ('pænɪkᵊl) *n.* a compound raceme, as in the oat. [C16: from L *pānicula* tuft, dim. of *panus* thread, ult. from Gk *penos* web] —'**panicled** *adj.* —**paniculate** (pə'nɪkj-ʊ,leɪt, -lɪt) *adj.*
panic-stricken *or* **panic-struck** *adj.* affected by panic.
panjandrum (pæn'dʒændrəm) *n.* a pompous self-important official or person of rank. [C18: after a character in a nonsense work (1755) by S. Foote, E playwright]
Panjim ('pɑːn,ʒɪm) *or* **Panaji** *n.* the capital of the Indian union territory of Goa, Daman, and Diu: a port on the Arabian Sea on the coast of Goa. Pop.: 43 165 (1981).
Pankhurst ('pæŋkhɜ:st) *n.* **1.** Dame **Christabel**. 1880–1958, English suffragette. **2.** her mother, **Emmeline**. 1858–1928, English suffragette leader, who founded the militant Women's Social and Political Union (1903). **3. Sylvia**, daughter of Emmeline Pankhurst. 1882–1960, English suffragette and pacifist.
pan loaf *n. Scot.* a loaf of bread with a light crust all the way round. Often shortened to **pan**.
Panmunjom ('pɑːn'mun'dʒɒm) *n.* a village in the demilitarized zone of Korea: site of truce talks leading to the end of the Korean War (1950–53).
pannage ('pænɪdʒ) *n. Arch.* **1.** the right to pasture pigs in a forest. **2.** payment for this. **3.** acorns, beech mast, etc., on which pigs feed. [C13: from OF *pasnage*, ult. from L *pastion-, pastiō* feeding, from *pascere* to feed]
pannier ('pænɪə) *n.* **1.** a large basket, esp. one of a pair slung over a beast of burden. **2.** one of a pair of bags slung either side of the back wheel of a motorcycle, etc. **3.** (esp. in the 18th century) **a.** a hooped framework to distend a woman's skirt. **b.** one of two puffed-out loops of material worn drawn back onto the hips. [C13: from OF *panier*, from L *pānārium* basket for bread, from *pānis* bread]
pannikin ('pænɪkɪn) *n. Chiefly Brit.* a small metal cup or pan. [C19: from PAN[1] + -KIN]
pannikin boss *n. Austral. sl.* a minor overseer.
Pannonia (pə'nəunɪə) *n.* a region of the ancient world south and west of the Danube: made a Roman province in 6 A.D.
panoply ('pænəplɪ) *n., pl.* **-plies. 1.** a complete or magnificent array. **2.** the entire equipment of a warrior. [C17: via F from Gk, from PAN- + *hopla* armour] —'**panoplied** *adj.*
panoptic (pæn'ɒptɪk) *adj.* taking in all parts, aspects, etc., in a single view; all-embracing. [C19: from Gk *panoptēs* seeing everything]
panorama (,pænə'rɑːmə) *n.* **1.** an extensive unbroken view in all directions. **2.** a wide or comprehensive survey

of a subject. **3.** a large extended picture of a scene, un-rolled before spectators a part at a time so as to appear continuous. **4.** another name for **cyclorama.** [C18: from PAN- + Gk *horama* view] —**panoramic** (ˌpænəˈræmɪk) *adj.* —ˌpanoˈramically *adv.*

pan out *vb.* (*intr., adv.*) *Inf.* to work out; result.

panpipes (ˈpænˌpaɪps) *pl. n.* (*often sing.; often cap.*) a number of reeds or whistles of graduated lengths bound together to form a musical wind instrument. Also called: **pipes of Pan, syrinx.**

pansy (ˈpænzɪ) *n., pl.* **-sies. 1.** a garden plant having flowers with rounded velvety petals, white, yellow, or purple in colour. See also **wild pansy. 2.** *Sl.* an effeminate or homosexual man or boy. [C15: from OF *pensée* thought, from *penser* to think, from L *pensāre*]

pant (pænt) *vb.* **1.** to breathe with noisy deep gasps, as when out of breath from exertion. **2.** to say (something) while breathing thus. **3.** (*intr.*; often foll. *by for*) to have a frantic desire (for). **4.** (*intr.*) to throb rapidly. ~*n.* **5.** the act or an instance of panting. **6.** a short deep gasping noise. [C15: from OF *pantaisier*, from Gk *phantasioun* to have visions, from *phantasia* FANTASY]

pantalets *or* **pantalettes** (ˌpæntəˈlɛts) *pl. n.* **1.** long drawers extending below the skirts: worn during the 19th century. **2.** ruffles for the ends of such drawers. [C19: dim. of PANTALOONS]

pantaloon (ˌpæntəˈluːn) *n.* **1.** (in pantomime) an absurd old man, the butt of the clown's tricks. **2.** (*usually cap.*) (in commedia dell'arte) a lecherous old merchant dressed in pantaloons. [C16: from F *Pantalon*, from It. *Pantalone*, prob. from *San Pantaleone*, a fourth-century Venetian saint]

pantaloons (ˌpæntəˈluːnz) *pl. n.* **1.** *History.* **a.** men's tight-fitting trousers fastened below the calf or under the shoe. **b.** children's trousers resembling these. **2.** *Inf.* any trousers, esp. baggy ones.

pantechnicon (pænˈtɛknɪkən) *n. Brit.* **1.** a large van, esp. one used for furniture removals. **2.** a warehouse where furniture is stored. [C19: from PAN- + Gk *tekhnikon* relating to the arts, from *tekhnē* art; orig. a London bazaar, later used as a furniture warehouse]

Pantelleria (*Italian* pantelleˈriːa) *n.* an Italian island in the Mediterranean, between Sicily and Tunisia: of volcanic origin; used by the Romans as a place of banishment. Pop.: 7860 (1981 est.). Area: 83 sq. km (32 sq. miles). Ancient name: **Cossyra** (kəˈsaɪrə).

pantheism (ˈpænθɪˌɪzəm) *n.* **1.** the doctrine that regards God as identical with the material universe or the forces of nature. **2.** readiness to worship all gods. —ˈpantheist *n.* —ˌpantheˈistic *or* ˌpantheˈistical *adj.* —ˌpantheˈistically *adv.*

pantheon (ˈpænθɪən) *n.* **1.** (esp. in ancient Greece or Rome) a temple to all the gods. **2.** all the gods of a religion. **3.** a building commemorating a nation's dead heroes. [C14: via L from Gk *Pantheion*, from PAN- + *-theios* divine, from *theos* god]

Pantheon (pænˈθiːən, ˈpænθɪən) *n.* a circular temple in Rome dedicated to all the gods, built by Agrippa in 27 B.C., rebuilt by Hadrian 120–24 A.D., and used since 609 A.D. as a Christian church.

panther (ˈpænθə) *n., pl.* **-thers** *or* **-ther. 1.** another name for **leopard** (sense 1), esp. the black variety (**black panther**). **2.** *U.S. & Canad.* any of various related animals, esp. the puma. [C14: from OF *pantère*, from L *panthēra*, from Gk *panthēr*]

panties (ˈpæntɪz) *pl. n.* a pair of women's or children's underpants.

pantihose (ˈpæntɪˌhəʊz) *pl. n.* See **panty hose.**

pantile (ˈpænˌtaɪl) *n.* a roofing tile, with an S-shaped cross section, so that the downward curve of one tile overlaps the upward curve of the next.

pantisocracy (ˌpæntɪˈsɒkrəsɪ) *n., pl.* **-cies.** a community, social group, etc., in which all have rule and everyone is equal. [C18: (coined by Robert SOUTHEY) from Gk, from PANTO-+ *isos* equal + -CRACY]

panto (ˈpæntəʊ) *n., pl.* **-tos.** *Brit. inf.* short for **pantomime** (sense 1).

panto- *or before a vowel* **pant-** *combining form.* all: *pantisocracy; pantograph; pantomime.* [from Gk *pant-, pas*]

pantograph (ˈpæntəˌgrɑːf) *n.* **1.** an instrument consisting of pivoted levers for copying drawings, maps, etc., to any scale. **2.** a sliding type of current collector, esp. a diamond-shaped frame mounted on a train roof in contact

with an overhead wire. **3.** a device used to suspend a studio lamp so that its height can be adjusted. —**pantographic** (ˌpæntəˈgræfɪk) *adj.*

pantomime (ˈpæntəˌmaɪm) *n.* **1.** (in Britain) a kind of play performed at Christmas time characterized by farce, music, lavish sets, stock roles, and topical jokes. **2.** a theatrical entertainment in which words are replaced by gestures and bodily actions. **3.** action without words as a means of expression. **4.** *Inf., chiefly Brit.* a confused or farcical situation. ~*vb.* **5.** another word for **mime.** [C17: via L from Gk *pantomīmos*] —**pantomimic** (ˌpæntəˈmɪmɪk) *adj.* —**pantomimist** (ˈpæntəˌmaɪmɪst) *n.*

pantothenic acid (ˌpæntəˈθɛnɪk) *n.* an oily acid that is a vitamin of the B complex: occurs widely in animal and vegetable foods. [C20: from Gk *pantothen* from every side]

pantry (ˈpæntrɪ) *n., pl.* **-tries.** a small room in which provisions, cooking utensils, etc., are kept; larder. [C13: via Anglo-Norman from OF *paneterie* store for bread, ult. from L *pānis* bread]

pants (pænts) *pl. n.* **1.** *Brit.* an undergarment covering the body from the waist to the thighs or knees. **2.** the usual U.S. and Canad. name for **trousers. 3. bore, scare,** etc., **the pants off.** *Inf.* to bore, scare, etc., extremely. [C19: shortened from *pantaloons*]

panty girdle (ˈpæntɪ) *n.* a foundation garment with a crotch, often of lighter material than a girdle.

panty hose *pl. n.* the U.S. name for **tights** (sense 1). Also (Canad. and N.Z.) **pantyhose,** (Austral.) **pantihose.**

panzer (ˈpænzə; *German* ˈpantsər) *n.* **1.** (*modifier*) of or relating to the fast mechanized armoured units employed by the German army in World War II: *a panzer attack.* **2.** a vehicle belonging to a panzer unit, esp. a tank. **3.** (*pl.*) armoured troops. [C20: from G, from MHG, from OF *panciere* coat of mail, from L *pantex* PAUNCH]

Pão de Açúcar (pəʊn di aˈsukar) *n.* the Portuguese name for the **Sugar Loaf Mountain.**

Paoting *or* **Pao-ting** (ˈpaʊˈtɪŋ) *n.* a variant transliteration of the Chinese name for **Baoding.**

Paotow (ˈpaʊˈtaʊ) *n.* a variant transliteration of the Chinese name for **Baotou.**

pap[1] (pæp) *n.* **1.** any soft or semiliquid food, esp. for babies or invalids; mash. **2.** worthless or oversimplified ideas, etc.; drivel. **3.** *S. African.* maize porridge. [C15: from MLow G *pappe*, via Med. L from L *pappāre* to eat]

pap[2] (pæp) *n.* **1.** *Arch.* or *Scot. & N English dialect.* a nipple or teat. **2.** something resembling a breast, such as one of a pair of rounded hilltops. [C12: from ON, imit. of a sucking sound]

papa (pəˈpɑː) *n. Old-fashioned.* an informal word for **father.** [C17: from F, a children's word for father]

papacy (ˈpeɪpəsɪ) *n., pl.* **-cies. 1.** the office or term of office of a pope. **2.** the system of government in the Roman Catholic Church that has the pope as its head. [C14: from Med. L *pāpātia,* from *pāpa* POPE]

Papadopoulos (ˌpæpəˈdɒpələs; *Greek* papaˈðɔpulɔs) *n.* **George.** born 1919, Greek army officer and statesman; prime minister (1967–73) and president (1973) in Greece's military government.

papain (pəˈpeɪɪn, -ˈpaɪɪn) *n.* an enzyme occurring in the unripe fruit of the papaya tree: used as a meat tenderizer and in medicine as an aid to protein digestion. [C19: from PAPAYA]

papal (ˈpeɪpəl) *adj.* of or relating to the pope or the papacy. —ˈpapally *adv.*

Papal States *pl. n.* the temporal domain of the popes in central Italy from 756 A.D. until the unification of Italy in 1870. Also called: **States of the Church.**

Papandreou (ˌpæpənˈdreɪuː; *Greek* papanˈðreu) *n.* **Andreas (George)** (anˈdreas). born 1919, Greek economist and socialist politician; prime minister from 1981.

paparazzo (ˌpæpəˈrætsəʊ) *n., pl.* **-razzi** (-ˈrætsiː). a free-lance photographer who specializes in candid camera shots of famous people. [C20: from It.]

papaver (pæˈpɑːvə) *n.* any of a genus of hardy annual or perennial plants with showy flowers; poppy. [L: poppy]

papaveraceous (pəˌpeɪvəˈreɪʃəs) *adj.* of or relating to a family of plants having large showy flowers and a cylindrical seed capsule with pores beneath the lid: includes the poppies and greater celandine. [C19: from NL, from L *papāver* poppy]

papaverine (pə'peɪvə,riːn, -rɪn) *n.* a white crystalline alkaloid found in opium and used to treat coronary spasms and certain types of colic. [C19: from L *papāver* poppy]

papaw (pə'pɔː) *or* **pawpaw** *n.* **1.** Also called: **custard apple. a.** a bush or small tree of Central North America, having small fleshy edible fruit. **b.** the fruit of this tree. **2.** another name for **papaya**. [C16: from Sp. PAPAYA]

papaya (pə'paɪə) *n.* **1.** a West Indian evergreen tree with a crown of large dissected leaves and large green hanging fruit. **2.** the fruit of this tree, having a yellow sweet edible pulp and small black seeds. ~Also called: **papaw, pawpaw.** [C15 *papaye*, from Sp. *papaya*, of Amerind origin]

Papeete (,pɑːpɪ'iːtɪ) *n.* the capital of French Polynesia, on the NW coast of Tahiti: one of the largest towns in the S Pacific. Pop.: 62 735 (1983).

Papen (*German* 'paːpən) *n.* **Franz von** (frants fɔn) 1879–1969, German statesman; chancellor (1932) and vice chancellor (1933–34) under Hitler, whom he was instrumental in bringing to power.

paper ('peɪpə) *n.* **1.** a substance made from cellulose fibres derived from rags, wood, etc., and formed into flat thin sheets suitable for writing on, decorating walls, wrapping, etc. **2.** a single piece of such material, esp. if written or printed on. **3.** (*usually pl.*) documents for establishing the identity of the bearer. **4.** (*pl.*) Also called: **ship's papers.** official documents relating to a ship. **5.** (*pl.*) collected diaries, letters, etc. **6.** See **newspaper, wallpaper. 7.** *Government.* See **white paper, green paper. 8.** a lecture or treatise on a specific subject. **9.** a short essay. **10. a.** a set of examination questions. **b.** the student's answers. **11.** *Commerce.* See **commercial paper. 12.** *Theatre sl.* a free ticket. **13. on paper.** in theory, as opposed to fact. ~*adj.* **14.** made of paper: *paper cups do not last long.* **15.** thin like paper: *paper walls.* **16.** (*prenominal*) existing only as recorded on paper but not yet in practice: *paper expenditure.* **17.** taking place in writing: *paper battles.* ~*vb.* **18.** to cover (walls) with wallpaper. **19.** (*tr.*) to cover or furnish with paper. **20.** (*tr.*) *Theatre sl.* to fill (a performance, etc.) by giving away free tickets (esp. in **paper the house**). ~See also **paper over.** [C14: from L PAPYRUS] —'**paperer** *n.* —'**papery** *adj.*

paperback ('peɪpə,bæk) *n.* **1.** a book or edition with covers made of flexible card. ~*adj.* **2.** of or denoting a paperback or publication of paperbacks. ~*vb.* **3.** (*tr.*) to publish a paperback edition of a book.

paperbark ('peɪpə,bɑːk) *n.* any of several Australian trees of swampy regions, having papery bark that can be peeled off in thin layers.

paperboy ('peɪpə,bɔɪ) *n.* a boy employed to deliver newspapers, etc. —'**paper,girl** *fem. n.*

paper chase *n.* a cross-country run in which a runner lays a trail of paper for others to follow.

paperclip ('peɪpə,klɪp) *n.* a clip for holding sheets of paper together, esp. one of bent wire.

paper-cutter *n.* a machine for cutting paper, usually a blade mounted over a table.

paperhanger ('peɪpə,hæŋə) *n.* a person who hangs wallpaper as an occupation.

paperknife ('peɪpə,naɪf) *n., pl.* **-knives.** a knife with a comparatively blunt blade for opening sealed envelopes, etc.

paper money *n.* paper currency issued by the government or the central bank as legal tender and which circulates as a substitute for specie.

paper mulberry *n.* a small E Asian tree, the inner bark of which was formerly used for making paper in Japan. See also **tapa.**

paper nautilus *n.* a cephalopod mollusc of warm and tropical seas, having a papery external spiral shell. Also called: **argonaut.**

paper over *vb.* (*tr., adv.*) to conceal (something controversial or unpleasant).

paper tape *n.* a strip of paper used in computers, telex machines, etc., for recording information in the form of punched holes.

paper tiger *n.* a nation, institution, etc., that appears powerful but is in fact weak or insignificant. [C20: translation of a Chinese phrase first applied to the U.S.]

paperweight ('peɪpə,weɪt) *n.* a small heavy object to prevent loose papers from scattering.

paperwork ('peɪpə,wɜːk) *n.* clerical work, such as the writing of reports or letters.

Paphian ('peɪfɪən) *adj.* **1.** of or relating to Paphos. **2.** of or relating to Aphrodite. **3.** *Literary.* of sexual love.

Paphlagonia (,pæflə'gəʊnɪə) *n.* an ancient country and Roman province in N Asia Minor, on the Black Sea.

Paphos[1] ('peɪfɒs) *n.* a village in SW Cyprus, near the sites of two ancient cities: famous as the centre of Aphrodite worship and traditionally the place at which she landed after her birth among the waves.

Paphos[2] ('peɪfɒs) *or* **Paphus** ('peɪfəs) *n. Greek myth.* the son of Pygmalion and Galatea, who succeeded his father on the throne of Cyprus.

papier-mâché (,pæpjeɪ'mæʃeɪ) *n.* **1.** a hard strong substance made of paper pulp or layers of paper mixed with paste, size, etc., and moulded when moist. ~*adj.* **2.** made of papier-mâché. [C18: from F, lit.: chewed paper]

papilionaceous (pə,pɪlɪə'neɪʃəs) *adj.* of, relating to, or belonging to a family of leguminous plants having irregular flowers: includes peas, beans, clover, alfalfa, gorse, and broom. [C17: from NL, from L *pāpiliō* butterfly]

papilla (pə'pɪlə) *n., pl.* **-lae** (-liː). **1.** the small projection of tissue at the base of a hair, tooth, or feather. **2.** any similar protuberance. [C18: from L: nipple] —**pa'pillary** *or* '**papillate** *adj.*

papilloma (,pæpɪ'ləʊmə) *n., pl.* **-mata** (-mətə) *or* **-mas.** *Pathol.* a benign tumour forming a rounded mass. [C19: from PAPILLA + -OMA]

papillon ('pæpɪ,lɒn) *n.* a breed of toy dog with large ears. [F: butterfly, from L *pāpiliō*]

papillote ('pæpɪ,ləʊt) *n.* **1.** a paper frill around cutlets, etc. **2. en papillote** (ã papijɔt). (of food) cooked in oiled greaseproof paper or foil. [C18: from F PAPILLON]

papist ('peɪpɪst) *n., adj.* (*often cap.*) *Usually disparaging.* another term for **Roman Catholic.** [C16: from F *papiste*, from Church L *pāpa* POPE] —**pa'pistical** *or* **pa'pistic** *adj.* —'**papistry** *n.*

papoose (pə'puːs) *n.* an American Indian baby. [C17: from Algonquian *papoos*]

pappus ('pæpəs) *n., pl.* **pappi** ('pæpaɪ). a ring of fine feathery hairs surrounding the fruit in composite plants, such as the thistle. [C18: via NL from Gk *pappos* old man, old man's beard, hence: pappus, down] —'**pappose** *or* '**pappous** *adj.*

paprika ('pæprɪkə, pæ'priː-) *n.* **1.** a mild powdered seasoning made from a sweet variety of red pepper. **2.** the fruit or plant from which this seasoning is obtained. [C19: via Hungarian from Serbian, from *papar* PEPPER]

Pap test *or* **smear** (pæp) *n. Med.* an examination of stained cells in a smear taken of bodily secretions, esp. from the uterus, for detection of cancer. [C20: after George *Papanicolaou* (1883–1962), U.S. anatomist, who devised it]

Papua ('pæpjʊə) *n.* **1. Territory of.** a former territory of Australia, consisting of SE New Guinea and adjacent islands: now part of Papua New Guinea. Former name (1888–1906): **British New Guinea. 2. Gulf of.** an inlet of the Coral Sea in the SE coast of New Guinea. —'**Papuan** *adj., n.*

Papua New Guinea *n.* a country in the SW Pacific; consists of the E half of New Guinea, the Bismarck Archipelago, the W Solomon Islands, Trobriand Islands, D'Entrecasteaux Islands, Woodlark Island, and the Louisiade Archipelago; administered by Australia from 1949 until 1975, when it became an independent member of the Commonwealth. Currency: kina. Capital: Port Moresby. Pop.: 3 006 799 (1980). Area: 461 693 sq. km (178 260 sq. miles).

papule ('pæpjuːl) *or* **papula** ('pæpjʊlə) *n., pl.* **-ules** *or* **-ulae** (-jʊ,liː). *Pathol.* a small solid usually round elevation of the skin. [C19: from L *papula* pustule] —'**papular** *adj.*

papyrology (,pæpɪ'rɒlədʒɪ) *n.* the study of ancient papyri. —,**papy'rologist** *n.*

papyrus (pə'paɪrəs) *n., pl.* **-ri** (-raɪ) *or* **-ruses. 1.** a tall aquatic plant of S Europe and N and central Africa. **2.** a kind of paper made from the stem pith of this plant, used by the ancient Egyptians, Greeks, and Romans. **3.** an ancient document written on this paper. [C14: via L from Gk *papūros* reed used in making paper]

par (pɑː) *n.* **1.** an accepted standard, such as an average (esp. in **up to par**). **2.** a state of equality (esp. in **on a par with**). **3.** *Finance.* the established value of the unit of one national currency in terms of the unit of another. **4.** *Commerce.* **a.** See **par value. b.** equality between the current market value of a share, bond, etc., and its face value, indicated by **at par**; **above** (*or* **below**) **par** indicates that the market value is above (or below) face value. **5.** *Golf.* a standard score for a hole or course that a good player should make: *par for the course was 72.* ~*adj.* **6.** average or normal. **7.** (*usually prenominal*) of or relating to par: *par value.* [C17: from L *pār* equal]

par. *abbrev. for:* **1.** paragraph. **2.** parallel. **3.** parenthesis. **4.** parish.

para ('pærə) *n. Inf.* **1. a.** a soldier in an airborne unit. **b.** an airborne unit. **2.** a paragraph.

Pará (*Portuguese* pa'ra) *n.* **1.** a state of N Brazil, on the Atlantic: mostly dense tropical rainforest. Capital: Belém. Pop.: 3 410 088 (1980). Area: 1 248 042 sq. km (474 896 sq. miles). **2.** another name for **Belém. 3.** an estuary in N Brazil into which flow the Tocantins River and a branch of the Amazon. Length: about 320 km (200 miles).

para-¹ *or before a vowel* **par-** *prefix.* **1.** beside; near: *parameter.* **2.** beyond: *parapsychology.* **3.** resembling: *paratyphoid fever.* **4.** defective; abnormal: *paranoia.* **5.** (*usually in italics*) denoting that an organic compound contains a benzene ring with substituents attached to atoms that are directly opposite (the 1,4- positions): *paracresol.* **6.** denoting an isomer, polymer, or compound related to a specified compound: *paraldehyde.* **7.** denoting the form of a diatomic substance in which the spins of the two constituent atoms are antiparallel: *parahydrogen.* [from Gk *para* (prep.) alongside, beyond]

para-² *combining form.* indicating an object that acts as a protection against something: *parachute*; *parasol.* [via F from It. *para-*, from *parare* to defend, ult. from L *parāre* to prepare]

para-aminobenzoic acid (ə,maɪnəʊbɛn'zəʊɪk, -,miː-) *n. Biochem.* an acid present in yeast and liver: used in the manufacture of dyes and pharmaceuticals.

parabasis (pə'ræbəsɪs) *n., pl.* **-ses** (-,siːz). (in classical Greek comedy) an address by the chorus. [C19: from Gk, from *parabanein* to step forward]

parabiosis (,pærəbaɪ'əʊsɪs) *n.* **1.** the natural union of two individuals, such as Siamese twins. **2.** a similar union induced for experimental or therapeutic purposes. [C20: from PARA-¹ + Gk *biōsis* manner of life, from *bios* life] —**parabiotic** (,pærəbaɪ'ɒtɪk) *adj.*

parable ('pærəbᵊl) *n.* **1.** a short story that uses familiar events to illustrate a religious or ethical situation. **2.** any of the stories of this kind told by Jesus Christ. [C14: from OF *parabole*, from L *parabola* comparison, from Gk *parabolē* analogy, from *paraballein* to throw alongside]

parabola (pə'ræbələ) *n.* a conic section formed by the intersection of a cone by a plane parallel to its side. [C16: via NL from Gk *parabolē* a setting alongside; see PARABLE]

parabolic¹ (,pærə'bɒlɪk) *adj.* **1.** of, relating to, or shaped like a parabola. **2.** shaped like a paraboloid: *a parabolic mirror.*

parabolic² (,pærə'bɒlɪk) *or* **parabolical** *adj.* of or like a parable. —,**para'bolically** *adv.*

parabolic aerial *n.* a formal name for **dish aerial.**

paraboloid (pə'ræbə,lɔɪd) *n.* a geometric surface whose sections parallel to two coordinate planes are parabolic and whose sections parallel to the third plane are either elliptical or hyperbolic. —**pa,rabo'loidal** *adj.*

Paracelsus (,pærə'sɛlsəs) *n.* **Philippus Aureolus** ('fɪlɪpəs ,ɔːrɪ'əʊləs), real name *Theophrastus Bombastus von Hohenheim.* 1493–1541, Swiss physician and alchemist, who pioneered the use of specific treatment, based on observation and experience, to remedy particular diseases.

paracetamol (,pærə'siːtə,mɒl, -'sɛtə-) *n.* a mild analgesic drug. [C20: from *para-acetamidophenol*]

parachronism (pə'rækrə,nɪzəm) *n.* an error in dating, esp. by giving too late a date. [C17: from PARA-¹ + *-chronism*, as in ANACHRONISM]

parachute ('pærə,ʃuːt) *n.* **1.** a device used to retard the fall of a person or package from an aircraft, consisting of a large fabric canopy connected to a harness. ~*vb.* **2.** (of troops, supplies, etc.) to land or cause to land by parachute from an aircraft. [C18: from F, from PARA-² + *chute* fall] —'**para,chutist** *n.*

Paraclete ('pærə,kliːt) *n. Christianity.* the Holy Ghost as comforter or advocate. [C15: via OF from Church L *Paraclētus*, from LGk *Paraklētos* advocate, from Gk *parakalein* to summon help]

parade (pə'reɪd) *n.* **1.** an ordered, esp. ceremonial, march or procession, as of troops being reviewed. **2.** Also called: **parade ground.** a place where military formations regularly assemble. **3.** a visible show or display: *to make a parade of one's grief.* **4.** a public promenade or street of shops. **5.** a successive display of things or people. **6. on parade. a.** on display. **b.** showing oneself off. ~*vb.* **7.** (when *intr.*, often foll. by *through* or *along*) to walk or march, esp. in a procession. **8.** (*tr.*) to exhibit or flaunt: *he was parading his medals.* **9.** (*tr.*) to cause to assemble in formation, as for a military parade. **10.** (*intr.*) to walk about in a public place. [C17: from F: a making ready, a boasting display] —**pa'rader** *n.*

paradigm ('pærə,daɪm) *n.* **1.** the set of all the inflected forms of a word. **2.** a pattern or model. **3.** (in the philosophy of science) a general conception of the nature of scientific endeavour within which a given enquiry is undertaken. [C15: via F & L from Gk *paradeigma* pattern, from *paradeiknunai* to compare] —**paradigmatic** (,pærədɪg'mætɪk) *adj.*

paradise ('pærə,daɪs) *n.* **1.** heaven as the ultimate abode or state of the righteous. **2.** *Islam.* the sensual garden of delights that the Koran promises the faithful after death. **3.** Also called: **limbo.** (according to some theologians) the intermediate abode or state of the just prior to the Resurrection of Jesus. **4.** the Garden of Eden. **5.** any place or condition that fulfils all one's desires or aspirations. **6.** a park in which foreign animals are kept. [OE, from Church L *paradīsus*, from Gk *paradeisos* garden, of Persian origin] —**paradisiacal** (,pærədɪ'saɪəkᵊl), **paradisiac** (,pærə'dɪsɪ,æk), *or* **paradisaical** (,pærədɪ'seɪkᵊl) *adj.*

paradise duck *n.* a New Zealand duck with bright plumage.

paradox ('pærə,dɒks) *n.* **1.** a seemingly absurd or self-contradictory statement that is or may be true: *religious truths are often expressed in paradox.* **2.** a self-contradictory proposition, such as *I always tell lies.* **3.** a person or thing exhibiting apparently contradictory characteristics. **4.** an opinion that conflicts with common belief. [C16: from LL *paradoxum*, from Gk *paradoxos* opposed to existing notions] —,**para'doxical** *adj.* —,**para'doxically** *adv.*

paradoxical sleep *n. Physiol.* sleep that appears to be deep but that is characterized by rapid eye movements, heavier breathing, and increased electrical activity of the brain.

paraffin ('pærəfɪn) *n.* **1.** Also called: **paraffin oil**, (esp. U.S. and Canad.) **kerosene.** a liquid mixture consisting mainly of alkane hydrocarbons, used as an aircraft fuel, in domestic heaters, and as a solvent. **2.** another name for **alkane. 3.** See **paraffin wax. 4.** See **liquid paraffin.** ~*vb.* (*tr.*) **5.** to treat with paraffin. [C19: from G, from L *parum* too little + *affinis* adjacent; so called from its chemical inertia]

paraffin wax *n.* a white insoluble odourless waxlike solid consisting mainly of alkane hydrocarbons, used in candles, waterproof paper, and as a sealing agent. Also called: **paraffin.**

paragliding ('pærə,glaɪdɪŋ) *n.* the sport of cross-country gliding using a specially designed parachute shaped like flexible wings. The parachutist glides from an aeroplane to a predetermined landing area.

paragon ('pærəgən) *n.* a model of excellence; pattern: *a paragon of virtue.* [C16: via F from OIt. *paragone* comparison, from Med. Gk *parakonē*, from PARA-¹ + *akonē* whetstone]

paragraph ('pærə,grɑːf) *n.* **1.** (in a piece of writing) one of a series of subsections each usually devoted to one idea and each marked by the beginning of a new line, indention, etc. **2.** *Printing.* the character ¶, used to indicate the beginning of a new paragraph. **3.** a short article, etc., in a newspaper. ~*vb.* (*tr.*) **4.** to form into paragraphs. **5.** to express or report in a paragraph. [C16: from Med. L *paragraphus*, from Gk *paragraphos* line drawing attention to part of a text, from *paragraphein* to write beside] —**paragraphic** (,pærə'græfɪk) *adj.*

paragraphia (,pærə'grɑːfɪə) *n. Psychiatry.* the habitual writing of a different word or letter from the one intended, often the result of a mental disorder. [C20: from NL; see PARA-¹, -GRAPH]

Paraguay ('pærə,gwaɪ) *n.* **1.** an inland republic in South America: colonized by the Spanish from 1537, gaining independence in 1811; lost 142 500 sq. km (55 000 sq.

miles) of territory and over half its population after its defeat in the war against Argentina, Brazil, and Uruguay (1865–70). It is divided by the Paraguay River into a sparsely inhabited semiarid region (Chaco) in the west, and a central region of wooded hills, tropical forests, and rich grasslands, rising to the Paraná plateau in the east. Official languages: Spanish and Guarani. Religion: Roman Catholic. Currency: guarani. Capital: Asunción. Pop.: 3 897 000 (1987). Area: 406 750 sq. km (157 047 sq. miles). **2.** a river in South America flowing south through Brazil and Paraguay to the Paraná River. Length: about 2400 km (1500 miles). —**Para'guayan** *adj., n.*

Paraguay tea *n.* another name for **maté.**

parahydrogen (ˌpærəˈhaɪdrədʒən) *n. Chem.* the form of molecular hydrogen in which the nuclei of the two atoms in each molecule spin in opposite directions.

Paraíba (*Portuguese* paraˈiba) *n.* **1.** a state of NE Brazil, on the Atlantic: consists of a coastal strip, with hills and plains inland; irrigated agriculture. Capital: João Pessoa. Pop.: 2 769 521 (1980). Area: 56 371 sq. km (21 765 sq. miles). **2.** Also called: **Paraíba do Sul** ('duː sul). a river in SE Brazil, flowing southwest and then northeast to the Atlantic near Campos. Length: 1060 km (660 miles). **3.** Also called: **Paraíba do Norte** ('duː 'nɔrtə). a river in NE Brazil, in Paraíba state, flowing northeast and east to the Atlantic. Length: 386 km (240 miles). **4.** the former name (until 1930) of **João Pessoa.**

parakeet *or* **parrakeet** ('pærəˌkiːt) *n.* any of numerous small long-tailed parrots. [C16: from Sp. *periquito* & OF *paroquet* parrot, from ?]

paraldehyde (pəˈrældɪˌhaɪd) *n.* a colourless liquid substance that is a cyclic trimer of acetaldehyde: used as a hypnotic.

paralipsis (ˌpaerəˈlɪpsɪs) *or* **paraleipsis** (ˌpærəˈlaɪpsɪs) *n., pl.* **-ses** (-siːz). a rhetorical device in which an idea is emphasized by the pretence that it is too obvious to discuss, as in *there are many practical drawbacks, not to mention the cost.* [C16: via LL from Gk: neglect, from *paraleipein* to leave aside]

parallax ('pærəˌlæks) *n.* **1.** an apparent change in the position of an object resulting from a change in position of the observer. **2.** *Astron.* the angle subtended at a celestial body, esp. a star, by the radius of the earth's orbit. [C17: via F from NL *parallaxis,* from Gk: change, from *parallassein* to change] —**parallactic** (ˌpærəˈlæktɪk) *adj.*

parallel ('pærəˌlɛl) *adj.* (when *postpositive,* usually foll. by *to*) **1.** separated by an equal distance at every point; never touching or intersecting: *parallel walls.* **2.** corresponding; similar: *parallel situations.* **3.** *Music.* Also: **consecutive.** (of two or more parts or melodies) moving in similar motion but keeping the same interval apart throughout: *parallel fifths.* **4.** *Grammar.* denoting syntactic constructions in which the constituents of one construction correspond to those of the other. **5.** *Computers.* operating on several items of information, instructions, etc., simultaneously. ~*n.* **6.** *Maths.* one of a set of parallel lines, planes, etc. **7.** an exact likeness. **8.** a comparison. **9.** Also called: **parallel of latitude.** any of the imaginary lines around the earth parallel to the equator, designated by degrees of latitude. **10. a.** a configuration of two or more electrical components connected between two points in a circuit so that the same voltage is applied to each (esp. in **in parallel**). Cf. **series** (sense 6). **b.** (*as modifier*): *a parallel circuit.* **11.** *Printing.* the character (‖) used as a reference mark. ~*vb.* **-leling,** **-leled.** (*tr.*) **12.** to make parallel. **13.** to supply a parallel to. **14.** to be a parallel to or correspond with: *your experience parallels mine.* [C16: via F & L from Gk *parallēlos* alongside one another]

parallel bars *pl. n. Gymnastics.* a pair of wooden bars on uprights used for various exercises.

parallelepiped (ˌpærəˌlɛlɪˈpaɪpɛd) *or* **parallelepipedon** (ˌpærəˌlɛlɪˈpaɪpɪdən) *n.* a geometric solid whose six faces are parallelograms. [C16: from Gk, from *parallēlos* PARALLEL + *epipedon* plane surface, from EPI- + *pedon* ground]

parallelism ('pærəˌlɛlɪzəm) *n.* **1.** the state of being parallel. **2.** *Grammar.* the repetition of a syntactic construction in successive sentences for rhetorical effect. **3.** *Philosophy.* the doctrine that mental and physical processes are regularly correlated but are not casually connected, so that, for example, pain always accompanies, but is not caused by, a pinprick.

parallelogram (ˌpærəˈlɛləˌgræm) *n.* a quadrilateral whose opposite sides are parallel and equal in length. [C16: via F from LL, from Gk *parallēlogrammon,* from *parallēlos* PARALLEL + *grammē* line]

parallelogram rule *n. Maths, physics.* a rule for finding the resultant of two vectors by constructing a parallelogram with two adjacent sides representing the magnitudes and directions of the vectors, the diagonal through the point of intersection of the vectors representing their resultant.

paralogism (pəˈræləˌdʒɪzəm) *n.* **1.** *Logic, obs.* an argument that is unintentionally invalid. Cf. **sophism. 2.** any invalid argument or conclusion. [C16: via LL from Gk *paralogismos,* from *paralogizesthai* to argue fallaciously, from PARA-¹ + *-logizesthai,* ult. from *logos* word] —**pa'ralogist** *n.*

paralyse *or U.S.* **-lyze** ('pærəˌlaɪz) *vb.* (*tr.*) **1.** *Pathol.* to affect with paralysis. **2.** *Med.* to render (a part of the body) insensitive to pain, touch, etc. **3.** to make immobile; transfix. [C19: from F *paralyser,* from *paralysie* PARALYSIS] —**ˌparaly'sation** *or U.S.* **-ly'zation** *n.* —**'para,lyser** *or U.S.* **-,lyzer** *n.*

paralysis (pəˈrælɪsɪs) *n., pl.* **-ses** (-ˌsiːz). **1.** *Pathol.* **a.** impairment or loss of voluntary muscle function or of sensation (**sensory paralysis**) in a part or area of the body. **b.** a disease characterized by such impairment or loss; palsy. **2.** cessation or impairment of activity: *paralysis of industry by strikes.* [C16: via L from Gk *paralusis;* see PARA-¹, -LYSIS]

paralytic (ˌpærəˈlɪtɪk) *adj.* **1.** of, relating to, or of the nature of paralysis. **2.** afflicted with or subject to paralysis. **3.** *Brit. inf.* very drunk. ~*n.* **4.** a person afflicted with paralysis.

paramagnetism (ˌpærəˈmægnɪˌtɪzəm) *n. Physics.* a weakly magnetic condition of substances with a relative permeability just greater than unity: used in some low temperature techniques. —**paramagnetic** (ˌpærəməgˈnɛtɪk) *adj.*

Paramaribo (ˌpærəˈmærɪˌbəʊ; *Dutch* paːraːˈmaːriːboː) *n.* the capital and chief port of Surinam, 27 km (17 miles) from the Atlantic on the Surinam River: the only large town in the country. Pop.: 77 558 (1986 est.).

paramatta *or* **parramatta** (ˌpærəˈmætə) *n.* a lightweight twill-weave dress fabric of wool with silk or cotton, now used esp. for rubber-proofed garments. [C19: after *Parramatta,* New South Wales, Australia, where orig. produced]

paramecium (ˌpærəˈmiːsɪəm) *n., pl.* **-cia** (-sɪə). any of a genus of freshwater protozoa having an oval body covered with cilia and a ventral groove for feeding. [C18: NL, from Gk *paramēkēs* elongated, from PARA-¹ + *mēkos* length]

paramedic (ˌpærəˈmɛdɪk) *or* **paramedical** *n.* **1.** a person, such as a laboratory technician, who supplements the work of the medical profession. ~*adj.* **2.** of or designating such a person.

parameter (pəˈræmɪtə) *n.* **1.** an arbitrary constant that determines the specific form of a mathematical expression, such as *a* and *b* in $y = ax^2 + b$. **2.** a characteristic constant of a statistical population, such as its variance or mean. **3.** *Inf.* any constant or limiting factor: *a designer must work within the parameters of budget and practicality.* [C17: from NL; see PARA-¹, -METER] —**parametric** (ˌpærəˈmɛtrɪk) *adj.*

parametric amplifier *n.* a type of high-frequency amplifier in which energy is transferred to the input signal through a circuit with a varying reactance.

paramilitary (ˌpærəˈmɪlɪtərɪ, -trɪ) *adj.* **1.** denoting or relating to a group of personnel with military structure functioning either as a civil force or in support of military forces. **2.** denoting or relating to a force with military structure conducting armed operations against a ruling power.

paramount ('pærəˌmaʊnt) *adj.* of the greatest importance or significance. [C16: via Anglo-Norman from OF *paramont,* from *par* by + *-amont* above, from L *ad montem* to the mountain] —**'para,mountcy** *n.* —**'para,mountly** *adv.*

paramour ('pærəˌmʊə) *n.* **1.** *Now usually derog.* a lover, esp. adulterous. **2.** an archaic word for **beloved.** [C13: from OF, lit.: through love]

Paraná *n.* **1.** (parəˈna) a state of S Brazil, on the Atlantic: consists of a coastal plain and a large rolling plateau with extensive forests. Capital: Curitiba. Pop.: 7 629 405 (1980). Area: 199 555 sq. km (77 048 sq. miles). **2.** (para'na). a city in E Argentina, on the Paraná River opposite Santa Fe: capital of Argentina (1853–1862). Pop.: 160 000 (1980). **3.** (*Portuguese* parə'na; *Spanish* para'na). a river in central South America, formed in S Brazil by the confluence of the Rio Grande and the Paranaíba River and flowing generally south to the Atlantic through the Río de la Plata estuary. Length: 2900 km (1800 miles).

parang ('pɑːræŋ) *n.* a Malay short stout straight-edged knife used in Borneo. [C19: from Malay]

paranoia (,pærə'nɔɪə) *n.* **1.** a mental disorder characterized by any of several types of delusions, as of grandeur or persecution. **2.** *Inf.* intense fear or suspicion, esp. when unfounded. [C19: via NL from Gk: frenzy, from *paranoos* distraught, from PARA-[1] + *noos* mind] —**'para,noid, paranoiac** (,pærə'nɔɪɪk) *or* **paranoic** (,pærə'nɔʊɪk) *adj., n.*

paranormal (,pærə'nɔːməl) *adj.* **1.** beyond normal explanation. ~*n.* **2. the.** paranormal happenings generally.

parapet ('pærəpɪt, -,pɛt) *n.* **1.** a low wall or railing along the edge of a balcony, roof, etc. **2.** *Mil.* a rampart, mound of sandbags, etc., in front of a trench giving protection from fire. [C16: from It. *parapetto*, lit.: chest-high wall, from L *pectus* breast]

paraph ('pærəf) *n.* a flourish after a signature, originally to prevent forgery. [C14: via F from Med. L *paraphus*, var. of *paragraphus* PARAGRAPH]

paraphernalia (,pærəfə'neɪlɪə) *pl. n.* (*sometimes functioning as sing.*) **1.** miscellaneous articles or equipment. **2.** *Law.* (formerly) articles of personal property given to a married woman by her husband and regarded in law as her possessions. [C17: via Med. L from L *parapherna* personal property of a married woman, apart from her dowry, from Gk, from PARA-[1] + *phernē* dowry, from *pherein* to carry]

paraphrase ('pærə,freɪz) *n.* **1.** an expression of a statement or text in other words. ~*vb.* **2.** to put into other words; restate. [C16: via F from L *paraphrasis*, from Gk, from *paraphrazein* to recount] —**paraphrastic** (,pærə'fræstɪk) *adj.*

paraplegia (,pærə'pliːdʒə) *n. Pathol.* paralysis of the lower half of the body, usually as the result of disease or injury of the spine. [C17: via NL from Gk: a blow on one side, from PARA-[1] + *plēssein* to strike] —**para'plegic** *adj., n.*

parapraxis (,pærə'præksɪs) *n., pl.* **-praxes** (-'præksiːz) *Psychoanal.* a minor error in action, such as a slip of the tongue. [C20: from PARA-[1] + Gk *praxis* a deed]

parapsychology (,pærəsaɪ'kɒlədʒɪ) *n.* the study of mental phenomena, such as telepathy, which are beyond the scope of normal physical explanation. —**,parapsy'chologist** *n.*

Paraquat ('pærə,kwɒt) *n. Trademark.* a yellow extremely poisonous weedkiller.

parascending ('pærə,sɛndɪŋ) *n.* a sport in which a parachutist, starting from ground level, is towed by a vehicle until he is airborne and then descends in the normal way.

paraselene (,pærəsɪ'liːnɪ) *n., pl.* **-nae** (-niː). a bright image of the moon on a lunar halo. Also called: **mock moon**. [C17: NL, from PARA-[1] + Gk *selēnē* moon]

parasite ('pærə,saɪt) *n.* **1.** an animal or plant that lives in or on another (the host) from which it obtains nourishment. **2.** a person who habitually lives at the expense of others; sponger. [C16: via L from Gk *parasitos* one who lives at another's expense, from PARA-[1] + *sitos* grain] —**parasitic** (,pærə'sɪtɪk) *or* **,para'sitical** *adj.* —**,para'sitically** *adv.* —**'parasi,tism** *n.*

parasitize *or* **-tise** ('pærəsɪ,taɪz) *vb.* (*tr.*) **1.** to infest with parasites. **2.** to live on (another organism) as a parasite. —**,parasiti'zation** *or* **-ti'sation** *n.*

parasitology (,pærəsaɪ'tɒlədʒɪ) *n.* the branch of biology that is concerned with the study of parasites. —**,parasit'ologist** *n.*

parasol ('pærə,sɒl) *n.* an umbrella used for protection against the sun; sunshade. [C17: via F from It. *parasole*, from PARA-[2] + *sole* sun, from L *sōl*]

parasuicide (,pærə'suːɪsaɪd) *n.* an attempt to inflict an injury on oneself, not motivated by a desire to die.

parasympathetic (,pærə,sɪmpə'θɛtɪk) *adj.* *Anat., Physiol.* of or relating to the division of the autonomic nervous system that acts by slowing the heartbeat, constricting the bronchi of the lungs, stimulating the smooth

muscles of the digestive tract, etc. Cf. **sympathetic** (sense 4).

parasynthesis (,pærə'sɪnθɪsɪs) *n.* formation of words by compounding a phrase and adding an affix, as *light-headed*, *light + head* with the affix *-ed*. —**parasynthetic** (,pærəsɪn'θɛtɪk) *adj.*

parataxis (,pærə'tæksɪs) *n.* the juxtaposition of clauses without the use of a conjunction, as *None of my friends stayed—they all left early*. [C19: NL from Gk, from *paratassein*, lit.: to arrange side by side] —**paratactic** (,pærə'tæktɪk) *adj.*

parathion (,pærə'θaɪɒn) *n.* a toxic oil used as an insecticide. [from PARA-[1] + Gk *theion* sulphur]

parathyroid gland (,pærə'θaɪrɔɪd) *n.* any one of the small egg-shaped endocrine glands situated near or embedded within the thyroid gland.

paratroops ('pærə,truːps) *pl. n.* troops trained and equipped to be dropped by parachute into a battle area. Also called: **paratroopers**.

paratyphoid fever (,pærə'taɪfɔɪd) *n.* a disease resembling but less severe than typhoid fever, caused by bacteria of the genus *Salmonella*.

paravane ('pærə,veɪn) *n.* a torpedo-shaped device towed from the bow of a vessel so that the cables will cut the anchors of any moored mines. [C20: from PARA-[2] + VANE]

par avion *French.* (par avjɔ̃) *adv.* by aeroplane: used in labelling mail sent by air.

parazoan (,pærə'zəʊən) *n., pl.* **-zoa** (-'zəʊə). any multicellular invertebrate of a division of the animal kingdom, the sponges. [C19: from *parazoa*, on the model of *protozoa* & *metazoa*, from PARA-[1] + Gk *zōon* animal]

parboil ('pɑː,bɔɪl) *vb.* (*tr.*) **1.** to boil until partially cooked. **2.** to subject to uncomfortable heat. [C15: from OF *parboillir*, from LL *perbullīre* to boil thoroughly (see PER-, BOIL[1]); modern meaning due to confusion of *par-* with *part*]

parbuckle ('pɑː,bʌk³l) *n.* **1.** a rope sling for lifting or lowering a heavy cylindrical object, such as a cask. ~*vb.* **2.** (*tr.*) to raise or lower (an object) with such a sling. [C17 *parbunkel*: from ?]

Parcae ('pɑːsiː) *pl. n., sing.* **Parca** ('pɑːkə). **the.** the Roman goddesses of fate. Greek counterparts: The **Moirai**.

parcel ('pɑːs³l) *n.* **1.** something wrapped up; package. **2.** a group of people or things having some common characteristic. **3.** a quantity of some commodity offered for sale; lot. **4.** a distinct portion of land. ~*vb.* **-celling, -celled** *or U.S.* **-celing, -celed.** (*tr.*) **5.** (often foll. by *up*) to make a parcel of; wrap up. **6.** (often foll. by *out*) to divide (up) into portions. [C14: from OF *parcelle*, from L *particula* PARTICLE]

parch (pɑːtʃ) *vb.* **1.** to deprive or be deprived of water; dry up: *the sun parches the fields.* **2.** (*tr.; usually passive*) to make very thirsty. **3.** (*tr.*) to roast (corn, etc.) lightly. [C14: from ?]

Parcheesi (pɑː'tʃiːzɪ) *n. Trademark.* a board game derived from the ancient game of pachisi.

parchment ('pɑːtʃmənt) *n.* **1.** the skin of certain animals, such as sheep, treated to form a durable material, as for manuscripts. **2.** a manuscript, etc., made of this material. **3.** a type of stiff yellowish paper resembling parchment. [C13: from OF *parchemin*, via L from Gk *pergamēnē*, from *Pergamēnos* of Pergamum (where parchment was made); OF *parchemin* was infl. by *parche* leather, from L *Parthica* (*pellis*) Parthian (leather)]

pard (pɑːd) *n. Arch.* a leopard or panther. [C13: via OF from L *pardus*, from Gk *pardos*]

pardon ('pɑːd³n) *vb.* (*tr.*) **1.** to excuse or forgive (a person) for (an offence, mistake, etc.): *to pardon someone; to pardon a fault.* ~*n.* **2.** forgiveness. **3. a.** release from punishment for an offence. **b.** the warrant granting such release. **4.** a Roman Catholic indulgence. ~*sentence substitute.* **5.** Also: **pardon me; I beg your pardon. a.** sorry; excuse me. **b.** what did you say? [C13: from OF, from Med. L *perdōnum*, from *perdōnāre* to forgive freely, from L *per* (intensive) + *dōnāre* to grant] —**'pardonable** *adj.* —**'pardonably** *adv.*

pardoner ('pɑːd³nə) *n.* (before the Reformation) a person licensed to sell ecclesiastical indulgences.

Pardubice (*Czech* 'pardubitsɛ) *n.* a city in NW Czechoslovakia, on the Elbe River: 13th-century cathedral; oil refinery. Pop.: 94 000 (1986).

pare (pɛə) *vb.* (*tr.*) **1.** to peel (the outer layer) from (something). **2.** to cut the edges from (the nails). **3.** to decrease bit by bit. [C13: from OF *parer* to adorn, from L *parāre* to make ready] — **'parer** *n.*

Paré (*French* pare) *n.* **Ambroise** (ābrwaz). ?1517–90, French surgeon. He reintroduced ligature of arteries following amputation instead of cauterization.

paregoric (ˌpærə'gɒrɪk) *n.* a medicine consisting of opium, benzoic acid, and camphor, formerly widely used to relieve diarrhoea and coughing. [C17 (meaning: relieving pain): via LL from Gk *parēgoros* relating to soothing speech, from PARA-[1] (beside) + *agora* assembly]

pareira (pə'rɛərə) *n.* the root of a South American climbing plant, used as a diuretic, tonic, and as a source of curare. [C18: from Port. *pareira brava*, lit.: wild vine]

parenchyma (pə'rɛŋkɪmə) *n.* **1.** a soft plant tissue consisting of simple thin-walled cells: constitutes the greater part of fruits, stems, roots, etc. **2.** animal tissue that constitutes the essential part of an organ as distinct from the blood vessels, connective tissue, etc. [C17: via NL from Gk *parenkhuma* something poured in beside, from PARA-[1] + *enkhuma* infusion] — **parenchymatous** (ˌpærɛŋ'kɪmətəs) *adj.*

parent ('pɛərənt) *n.* **1.** a father or mother. **2.** a person acting as a father or mother; guardian. **3.** *Rare.* an ancestor. **4.** a source or cause. **5.** an organism or organization that has produced one or more organisms similar to itself. **6.** *Physics, chem.* a precursor, such as a nucleus or compound, of a derived entity. [C15: via OF from L *parens* parent, from *parere* to bring forth] — **pa'rental** *adj.* — **'parenthood** *n.*

parentage ('pɛərəntɪdʒ) *n.* **1.** ancestry. **2.** derivation from a particular origin. **3.** a less common word for **parenthood**.

parent company *n.* a company that owns a number of subsidiary companies.

parenteral (pæ'rɛntərəl) *adj. Med.* **1.** (esp. of the route by which a drug is administered) by means other than through the digestive tract, esp. by injection. **2.** designating a drug to be injected. [C20: from PARA-[1] + ENTERO- + -AL[1]]

parenthesis (pə'rɛnθɪsɪs) *n., pl.* **-ses** (-ˌsiːz). **1.** a phrase, often explanatory or qualifying, inserted into a passage with which it is not grammatically connected, and marked off by brackets, dashes, etc. **2.** Also called: **bracket.** either of a pair of characters, (), used to enclose such a phrase or as a sign of aggregation in mathematical or logical expressions. **3.** an interlude; interval. **4. in parenthesis.** inserted as a parenthesis. [C16: via LL from Gk: something placed in besides, from *parentithenai*, from PARA-[1] + EN-[2] + *tithenai* to put] — **parenthetic** (ˌpærən'θɛtɪk) *or* **ˌparen'thetical** *adj.* — **ˌparen'thetically** *adv.*

parenthesize *or* **-sise** (pə'rɛnθɪˌsaɪz) *vb.* (*tr.*) **1.** to place in parentheses. **2.** to insert as a parenthesis. **3.** to intersperse (a speech, writing, etc.) with parentheses.

parenting ('pɛərəntɪŋ) *n.* all the skills and experience of bringing up children.

parent teacher association *n.* a social group of the parents of children at a school and their teachers formed in order to foster better understanding between them and to organize fund-raising activities on behalf of the school.

parergon (pə'rɛəgɒn) *n., pl.* **-ga** (-gə). work that is not one's main employment. [C17: from L, from Gk, from PARA-[1] + *ergon* work]

paresis (pə'riːsɪs, 'pærɪsɪs) *n., pl.* **-ses** (-ˌsiːz). *Pathol.* incomplete or slight paralysis of motor functions. [C17: via NL from Gk: a relaxation, from *parienai* to let go] — **pa'retic** (pə'rɛtɪk) *adj.*

Pareto (*Italian* pa'rɛːto) *n.* **Vilfredo** (vil'freːdo). 1848–1923, Italian sociologist and economist. He anticipated Fascist principles of government in his *Mind and Society* (1916).

par excellence *French.* (par ɛksɛlɑ̃s; *English* pɑːr 'ɛksələns) *adv.* to a degree of excellence; beyond comparison. [F, lit.: by (way of) excellence]

parfait (pɑː'feɪ) *n.* a rich frozen dessert made from eggs and cream, fruit, etc. [from F: PERFECT]

parget ('pɑːdʒɪt) *n.* **1.** Also called: **pargeting. a.** plaster, mortar, etc., used to line chimney flues or cover walls. **b.** plasterwork that has incised ornamental patterns. ~*vb.* (*tr.*). **2.** to cover or decorate with parget. [C14: from OF *pargeter* to throw over, from *par* PER- + *geter* to throw]

parhelic circle *n. Meteorol.* a luminous band at the same altitude as the sun, parallel to the horizon, caused by reflection of the sun's rays by ice crystals in the atmosphere.

parhelion (pɑː'hiːlɪən) *n., pl.* **-lia** (-lɪə). one of several bright spots on the parhelic circle or solar halo, caused by the diffraction of light by ice crystals in the atmosphere. Also called: **mock sun.** [C17: via L from Gk *parēlion*, from PARA-[1](beside) + *hēlios* sun] — **par'helic** *or* **parheliacal** (ˌpɑːhɪ'laɪək³l) *adj.*

pariah (pə'raɪə, 'pærɪə) *n.* **1.** a social outcast. **2.** (formerly) a member of a low caste in South India. [C17: from Tamil *paraiyan* drummer, from *parai* drum: members were drummers at festivals]

pariah dog *n.* another term for **pye-dog.**

Paricutín (*Spanish* pariku'tin) *n.* a volcano in W central Mexico, in Michoacán state, formed in 1943 after a week of earth tremors; grew to a height of 2500 m (8200 ft.) in a year and buried the village of Paricutín.

parietal (pə'raɪɪt³l) *adj.* **1.** *Anat., biol.* of or forming the walls of a bodily cavity: *the parietal bones of the skull.* **2.** of or relating to the side of the skull. **3.** (of plant ovaries) having ovules attached to the walls. **4.** *U.S.* living or having authority within a college. ~*n.* **5.** a parietal bone. [C16: from LL *parietālis*, from L *pariēs* wall]

parietal lobe *n.* the portion of each cerebral hemisphere concerned with the perception of sensations of touch, temperature, and taste and with muscular movements.

pari-mutuel (ˌpærɪ'mjuːtʃʊəl) *n., pl.* **pari-mutuels** *or* **paris-mutuels** (ˌpærɪ'mjuːtʃʊəlz). a system of betting in which those who have bet on the winners of a race share in the total amount wagered less a percentage for the management. [C19: from F, lit.: mutual wager]

paring ('pɛərɪŋ) *n.* (*often pl.*) something pared or cut off.

pari passu *Latin.* (ˌpærɪ 'pæsuː, 'pɑːrɪ) *adv. Usually legal.* with equal speed or progress.

Paris[1] ('pærɪs; *French* pari) *n.* the capital of France, in the north on the River Seine: constitutes a department; dates from the 3rd century B.C., becoming capital of France in 987; centre of the French Revolution; centres around its original site on an island in the Seine, the **Île de la Cité**, containing Notre Dame; university (1150). Pop.: 2 292 024 (1983 est.). Ancient name: **Lutetia.** [via F and OF, from LL (*Lūtētia*) *Parisiōrum* (marshes) of the *Parisii*, a tribe of Celtic Gaul] — **Parisian** (pə'rɪzɪən) *n., adj.*

Paris[2] ('pærɪs) *n.* **1.** *Greek myth.* a prince of Troy, whose abduction of Helen from her husband Menelaus started the Trojan War. **2.** *Matthew.* ?1200–59, English chronicler, whose principal work is the *Chronica Majora.*

Paris Commune *n. French history.* the council established in Paris in the spring of 1871 in opposition to the National Assembly and esp. to the peace negotiated with Prussia following the Franco-Prussian War.

Paris green *n.* an emerald-green poisonous substance used as a pigment and insecticide.

parish ('pærɪʃ) *n.* **1.** a subdivision of a diocese, having its own church and a clergyman. **2.** the churchgoers of such a subdivision. **3.** (in England and, formerly, Wales) the smallest unit of local government. **4.** (in Louisiana) a county. **5.** (in Quebec and New Brunswick, Canada) a subdivision of a county. **6.** the people living in a parish. **7. on the parish.** *History.* receiving parochial relief. [C13: from OF *paroisse*, from Church L, from LGk, from *paroikos* Christian, sojourner, from Gk: neighbour, from PARA-[1] (beside) + *oikos* house]

parish clerk *n.* a person designated to assist in various church duties.

parish council *n.* (in England and, formerly, Wales) the administrative body of a parish. See **parish** (sense 3).

parishioner (pə'rɪʃənə) *n.* a member of a particular parish.

parish pump *adj.* of only local interest; parochial.

parish register *n.* a book in which the births, baptisms, marriages, and deaths in a parish are recorded.

parity[1] ('pærɪtɪ) *n., pl.* **-ties. 1.** equality of rank, pay, etc. **2.** close or exact analogy or equivalence. **3.** *Finance.* the amount of a foreign currency equivalent to a specific sum of domestic currency. **4.** equality between prices of commodities or securities in two separate markets. **5.** *Physics.* **a.** a property of a physical system characterized by the behaviour of the sign of its wave function when reflected in space. The wave function either remains unchanged (**even parity**) or changes in sign (**odd parity**).

b. a quantum number describing this property, equal to +1 for even parity systems and −1 for odd parity systems. Symbol: *P* **6.** *Maths.* a relationship between two integers. If both are odd or both even they have the same parity; if one is odd and one even they have different parity. [C16: from LL *pāritās*; see PAR]

parity check *n.* a check made of computer data to ensure that the total number of bits of value 1 (or 0) in each unit of information remains odd or even after transfer between a peripheral device and the memory or vice versa.

park (pɑːk) *n.* **1.** a large area of land preserved in a natural state for recreational use by the public. **2.** a piece of open land in a town with public amenities. **3.** a large area of land forming a private estate. **4.** an area designed to accommodate a number of related enterprises: *a business park.* **5.** *U.S. & Canad.* a playing field or sports stadium. **6. the park.** *Brit. inf.* a soccer pitch. **7.** a gear selector position on the automatic transmission of a motor vehicle that acts as a parking brake. **8.** the area in which the equipment and supplies of a military formation are assembled. ~*vb.* **9.** to stop and leave (a vehicle) temporarily. **10.** to manoeuvre (a motor vehicle) into a space for it to be left: *try to park without hitting the kerb.* **11.** (*tr.*) *Inf.* to leave or put somewhere: *park yourself in front of the fire.* **12.** (*intr.*) *Mil.* to arrange equipment in a park. **13.** (*tr.*) to enclose in or as a park. [C13: from OF *parc*, from Med. L *parricus* enclosure, from Gmc]

Park (pɑːk) *n.* **1. Mungo** (ˈmʌŋgəʊ). 1771–1806, Scottish explorer. He led two expeditions (1795–97; 1805–06) to trace the course of the Niger in Africa. He was drowned during the second expedition. **2. Chung Hee** (ˈtʃʊŋ ˈhiː). 1917–79, South Korean politician; president of the Republic of Korea (1963–79); assassinated.

parka (ˈpɑːkə) *n.* a warm weatherproof coat with a hood, originally worn by Eskimos. [C19: from Aleutian: skin]

Parker (ˈpɑːkə) *n.* **1. Charlie.** nickname *Bird* or *Yardbird.* 1920–55, U.S. jazz alto saxophonist and composer; the leading exponent of early bop. **2. Dorothy (Rothschild).** 1893–1967, U.S. writer, noted esp. for the ironical humour of her short stories. **3. Matthew.** 1504–75, English prelate. As archbishop of Canterbury (1559–75), he supervised Elizabeth I's religious settlement.

Parkes (pɑːks) *n.* Sir **Henry.** 1815–96, Australian journalist and politician born in England, five times premier of New South Wales, advocate of free trade and Federation, and a founder of the public education system.

parkin (ˈpɑːkɪn) *n. Brit.* moist spicy ginger cake usually containing oatmeal. [C19: from ?]

parking lot *n.* the U.S. and Canad. term for **car park.**

parking meter *n.* a timing device, usually coin-operated, that indicates how long a vehicle may be left parked.

parking orbit *n.* an orbit around the earth or moon in which a spacecraft can be placed temporarily in order to prepare for the next step in its programme.

parking ticket *n.* a summons served for a parking offence.

Parkinson's disease (ˈpɑːkɪnsənz) *n.* a progressive chronic disorder of the central nervous system characterized by impaired muscular coordination and tremor. Often shortened to **Parkinson's. Also called: parkinsonism.** [C19: after James *Parkinson* (1755–1824), E surgeon, who first described it]

Parkinson's law *n.* the notion, expressed facetiously as a law of economics, that work expands to fill the time available for its completion. [C20: after C. N. *Parkinson* (born 1909), E economist, who formulated it]

park keeper *n.* (in Britain) an official who patrols and supervises a public park.

parkland (ˈpɑːkˌlænd) *n.* grassland with scattered trees.

parky (ˈpɑːkɪ) *adj.* **parkier, parkiest.** (*usually postpositive*) *Brit. inf.* (of the weather) chilly; cold. [C19: ?from PERKY]

Parl. *abbrev. for:* **1.** Parliament. **2.** Also: **parl.** parliamentary.

parlance (ˈpɑːləns) *n.* a particular manner of speaking, esp. when specialized; idiom: *political parlance.* [C16: from OF, from *parler* to talk, via Med. L from LL *parabola* speech]

parlando (pɑːˈlændəʊ) *adj., adv. Music.* to be performed as though speaking. [It.: speaking]

parley (ˈpɑːlɪ) *n.* **1.** a discussion, esp. between enemies under a truce to decide terms of surrender, etc. ~*vb.* **2.** (*intr.*) to discuss, esp. with an enemy. [C16: from F, from

parler to talk, from Med. L *parabolāre*, from LL *parabola* speech]

parliament (ˈpɑːləmənt) *n.* **1.** an assembly of the representatives of a political nation or people, often the supreme legislative authority. **2.** any legislative or deliberative assembly, conference, etc. [C13: from Anglo-L *parliamentum*, from OF *parlement*, from *parler* to speak; see PARLEY]

Parliament (ˈpɑːləmənt) *n.* **1.** the highest legislative authority in Britain, consisting of the House of Commons, which exercises effective power, the House of Lords, and the sovereign. **2.** a similar legislature in another country or state. **3.** any of the assemblies of such a body created by a general election and royal summons and dissolved before the next election.

parliamentarian (ˌpɑːləmənˈtɛərɪən) *n.* **1.** an expert in parliamentary procedures. ~*adj.* **2.** of or relating to a parliament.

parliamentary (ˌpɑːləˈmɛntərɪ) *adj.* (*sometimes cap.*) **1.** of or proceeding from a parliament or Parliament: *a parliamentary decree.* **2.** conforming to the procedures of a parliament or Parliament: *parliamentary conduct.* **3.** having a parliament or Parliament.

Parliamentary Commissioner *or in full* **Parliamentary Commissioner for Administration** *n.* (in Britain) the official name for **ombudsman** (sense 2).

parliamentary private secretary *n.* (in Britain) a backbencher in Parliament who assists a minister. Abbrev.: **PPS.**

parliamentary secretary *n.* a member of Parliament appointed to assist a minister of the Crown with his departmental responsibilities.

parlour *or U.S.* **parlor** (ˈpɑːlə) *n.* **1.** *Old-fashioned.* a living room, esp. one kept tidy for the reception of visitors. **2.** a small room for guests away from the public rooms in an inn, club, etc. **3.** *Chiefly U.S., Canad., & N.Z.* a room or shop equipped as a place of business: *a billiard parlor.* **4.** a building equipped for milking cows in. [C13: from Anglo-Norman *parlur*, from OF *parleur* room in convent for receiving guests, from *parler* to speak; see PARLEY]

parlous (ˈpɑːləs) *Arch. or humorous.* ~*adj.* **1.** dangerous or difficult. **2.** cunning. ~*adv.* **3.** extremely. [C14 *perlous*, var. of PERILOUS] —**'parlously** *adv.*

Parma *n.* **1.** (*Italian* ˈparma). a city in N Italy, in Emilia-Romagna: capital of the duchy of Parma and Piacenza from 1545 until it became part of Italy in 1860; important food industry (esp. Parmesan cheese). Pop.: 175 842 (1986). **2.** (ˈpɑːmə). a city in NE Ohio, south of Cleveland. Pop.: 92 548 (1980). —**Parmesan** (ˌpɑːmɪˈzæn, ˈpɑːmɪˌzæn) *adj., n.*

Parmenides (pɑːˈmɛnɪˌdiːz) *n.* 5th century B.C., Greek philosopher, born in Italy. He held that the universe is single and unchanging and denied the existence of change and motion. His doctrines are expounded in his poem *On Nature,* of which only fragments are extant.

Parmesan cheese *n.* a hard dry cheese used grated, esp. on pasta dishes and soups.

Parmigianino (*Italian* parmidʒaˈnino) *n.* real name *Girolamo Francesco Maria Mazzola.* 1503–40, Italian painter; one of the originators of mannerism. Also called: **Parmigiano** (parmiˈdʒano).

Parnaíba *or* **Parnahiba** (*Portuguese* parnaˈiba) *n.* a river in NE Brazil, rising in the Serra das Mangabeiras and flowing generally northeast, to the Atlantic. Length: about 1450 km (900 miles).

Parnassus (pɑːˈnæsəs) *n.* **1. Mount.** a mountain in central Greece: in ancient times sacred to Apollo and the Muses. **2. a.** the world of poetry. **b.** a centre of poetic or other creative activity. —**Par'nassian** *adj.*

Parnell (ˈpɑːnəl, pɑːˈnɛl) *n.* **Charles Stewart.** 1846–91, Irish nationalist, who led the Irish Home Rule movement in Parliament (1880–90) with a calculated policy of obstruction. Although Gladstone was converted to Home Rule (1886), Parnell's career was ruined by the scandal over his adultery with Mrs. O'Shea. —**'Parnel,lism** *n.* —**'Parnellite** *n., adj.*

parochial (pəˈrəʊkɪəl) *adj.* **1.** narrow in outlook or scope; provincial. **2.** of or relating to a parish. [C14: via OF from Church L *parochiālis;* see PARISH] —**pa'rochial,ism** *n.* —**pa'rochially** *adv.*

parody (ˈpærədɪ) *n., pl.* **-dies. 1.** a musical, literary, or other composition that mimics the style of another composer, author, etc., in a humorous or satirical way. **2.**

something so badly done as to seem an intentional mockery; travesty. ~vb. **-dying, -died. 3.** (tr.) to make a parody of. [C16: via L from Gk *paroidiā* satirical poem, from PARA-[1] + *ōidē* song] —**parodic** (pə'rɒdɪk) or **pa'rodical** adj. —'**parodist** n.

parol ('pærəl, pə'rəʊl) Law. ~n. **1.** an oral statement; word of mouth (now only in **by parol**). ~adj. **2. a.** (of a contract, lease, etc.) made orally or in writing but not under seal. **b.** expressed or given by word of mouth: *parol evidence*. [C15: from OF *parole* speech; see PAROLE]

parole (pə'rəʊl) n. **1. a.** the freeing of a prisoner before his sentence has expired, on the condition that he is of good behaviour. **b.** the duration of such conditional release. **2.** a promise given by a prisoner, as to be of good behaviour if granted liberty or partial liberty. **3.** *Linguistics.* language as manifested in the individual speech acts of particular speakers. **4. on parole.** conditionally released from detention. ~vb. (tr.) **5.** to place (a person) on parole. [C17: from OF, from *parole d'honneur* word of honour; *parole* from LL *parabola* speech] —**parolee** (pə,rəʊ'liː) n.

paronomasia (,pærənəʊ'meɪzɪə) n. *Rhetoric.* a play on words, esp. a pun. [C16: via L from Gk, from *paronomazein* to make a change in naming, from PARA-[1] (besides) + *onomazein* to name, from *onoma* a name]

Páros ('pærɒs) n. a Greek island in the S Aegean Sea, in the Cyclades: site of the discovery (1627) of the Parian Chronicle, a marble tablet outlining Greek history from before 1000 B.C. to about 354 B.C. (now at Oxford University). Pop.: 7881 (1981 est.). Area: 166 sq. km (64 sq. miles). —'**Parian** adj., n.

parotid (pə'rɒtɪd) adj. **1.** relating to or situated near the parotid gland. ~n. **2.** See **parotid gland.** [C17: via F, via L from Gk *parōtis*, from PARA-[1] (near) + *-ōtis*, from *ous* ear]

parotid gland n. a large salivary gland, in man situated in front of and below each ear.

parotitis (,pærə'taɪtɪs) n. inflammation of the parotid gland. See also **mumps.**

-parous adj. combining form. giving birth to: *oviparous.* [from L *-parus*, from *parere* to bring forth]

paroxysm ('pærək,sɪzəm) n. **1.** an uncontrollable outburst: *a paroxysm of giggling.* **2.** *Pathol.* **a.** a sudden attack or recurrence of a disease. **b.** any fit or convulsion. [C17: via F from Med. L *paroxysmus* annoyance, from Gk, from *paroxunein* to goad, from PARA-[1] (intensifier) + *oxunein* to sharpen, from *oxus* sharp] —,**parox'ysmal** adj.

parquet ('pɑːkeɪ, -kɪ) n. **1.** a floor covering of pieces of hardwood fitted in a decorative pattern; parquetry. **2.** Also called: **parquet floor.** a floor so covered. **3.** *U.S.* the stalls of a theatre. ~vb. (tr.) **4.** to cover a floor with parquet. [C19: from OF: small enclosure, from *parc* enclosure; see PARK]

parquetry ('pɑːkɪtrɪ) n. a geometric pattern of inlaid pieces of wood, esp. as used to cover a floor.

parr (pɑː) n., pl. **parrs** or **parr.** a salmon up to two years of age. [C18: from ?]

Parr (pɑː) n. **Catherine.** 1512–48, sixth wife of Henry VIII of England.

parrakeet ('pærə,kiːt) n. a variant spelling of **parakeet.**

parramatta (,pærə'mætə) n. a variant spelling of **paramatta.**

parricide ('pærɪ,saɪd) n. **1.** the act of killing either of one's parents. **2.** a person who kills his or her parent. [C16: from L *parricīdium* murder of a parent or relative, & from *parricīda* one who murders a relative, from *parri-* (rel. to Gk *pēos* kinsman) + -CIDE] —,**parri'cidal** adj.

parrot ('pærət) n. **1.** any of several related tropical and subtropical birds having a short hooked bill, bright plumage, and an ability to mimic sounds. **2.** a person who repeats or imitates the words or actions of another. ~vb. **3.** (tr.) to repeat or imitate without understanding. [C16: prob. from F *paroquet*, from ?]

parrot-fashion adv. *Inf.* without regard for meaning; by rote: *she learned it parrot-fashion.*

parrot fever or **disease** n. another name for **psittacosis.**

parrotfish ('pærət,fɪʃ) n., pl. **-fish** or **-fishes.** a brightly coloured tropical marine percoid fish having parrot-like jaws.

Parrott ('pærət) n. **John.** born 1964, British snooker player.

parry ('pærɪ) vb. **-rying, -ried. 1.** to ward off (an attack, etc.) by blocking or deflecting, as in fencing. **2.** (tr.) to evade (questions, etc.), esp. adroitly. ~n., pl. **-ries. 3.** an act of parrying. **4.** a skilful evasion, as of a question. [C17: from F *parer* to ward off, from L *parāre* to prepare]

Parry ('pærɪ) n. **1.** Sir (**Charles**) **Hubert** (**Hastings**). 1848–1918, English composer, noted esp. for his choral works. **2.** Sir **William Edward.** 1790–1855, English arctic explorer, who searched for the Northwest Passage (1819–25) and attempted to reach the North Pole (1827).

parse (pɑːz) vb. *Grammar.* to assign constituent structure to (a sentence or the words in a sentence). [C16: from L *pars* (*orātiōnis*) part (of speech)]

parsec ('pɑː,sɛk) n. a unit of astronomical distance equivalent to 3.0857 × 10[16] metres or 3.262 light years. [C20: from PARALLAX + SECOND[2]]

Parsee or **Parsi** (,pɑː'siː, 'pɑː,siː) n. an adherent of a Zoroastrian religion, the practitioners of which were driven out of Persia by the Muslims in the eighth century A.D. It is now found chiefly in western India. [C17: from Persian *Pārsī* a Persian, from OPersian *Pārsa* PERSIA] —'**Parsee,ism** or '**Parsi,ism** n.

parser ('pɑːzə) n. *Computers.* a program that interprets ordinary language typed into a computer by recognizing key words or analysing sentence structure and then translating it into the appropriate machine language.

Parsifal ('pɑːsɪf°l, -,fɑːl) n. a variant of **Parzival.**

parsimony ('pɑːsɪmənɪ) n. extreme care in spending; niggardliness. [C15: from L *parcimōnia*, from *parcere* to spare] —**parsimonious** (,pɑːsɪ'məʊnɪəs) adj. —,**parsi'moniously** adv.

parsley ('pɑːslɪ) n. **1.** a S European umbelliferous plant, widely cultivated for its curled aromatic leaves, which are used in cooking. **2.** any of various similar and related plants, such as fool's-parsley and cow parsley. [C14 *persely*, from OE *petersilie* + OF *persil, peresil,* both ult. from L *petroselinum* rock parsley, from Gk, from *petra* rock + *selinon* parsley]

parsnip ('pɑːsnɪp) n. **1.** an umbelliferous plant cultivated for its long whitish root. **2.** the root of this plant, eaten as a vegetable. [C14: from OF *pasnaie*, from L *pastināca*, from *pastināre* to dig, from *pastinum* two-pronged tool for digging]

parson ('pɑːs°n) n. **1.** a parish priest in the Church of England. **2.** any clergyman. [C13: from Med. L *persōna* parish priest, from L: personage; see PERSON]

parsonage ('pɑːs°nɪdʒ) n. the residence of a parson, as provided by the parish.

parson bird n. another name for **tui.**

Parsons ('pɑːsənz) n. Sir **Charles Algernon.** 1854–1931, English engineer, who developed the steam turbine.

parson's nose n. the fatty extreme end portion of the tail of a fowl when cooked.

part (pɑːt) n. **1.** a piece or portion of a whole. **2.** an integral constituent of something: *dancing is part of what we teach.* **3.** an amount less than the whole; bit: *they only recovered part of the money.* **4.** one of several equal divisions: *mix two parts flour to one part water.* **5.** an actor's role in a play. **6.** a person's proper role or duty: *everyone must do his part.* **7.** (*often pl.*) region; area: *you're well known in these parts.* **8.** *Anat.* any portion of a larger structure. **9.** a component that can be replaced in a machine, etc. **10.** the U.S. and Canad. word for **parting** (sense 1). **11.** *Music.* one of a number of separate melodic lines which is assigned to one or more instrumentalists or singers. **12. for one's part.** as far as one is concerned. **13. for the most part.** generally. **14. in part.** to some degree; partly. **15. of many parts.** having many different abilities. **16. on the part of.** on behalf of. **17. part and parcel.** an essential ingredient. **18. play a part. a.** to pretend to be what one is not. **b.** to have something to do with; be instrumental. **19. take in good part.** to respond to (teasing, etc.) with good humour. **20. take part in.** to participate in. **21. take someone's part.** to support one person in an argument, etc. ~vb. **22.** to divide or separate from one another; take or come apart: *to part the curtains; the seams parted when I washed the dress.* **23.** to go away or cause to go away from one another: *the couple parted amicably.* **24.** (*intr.;* foll. by *from*) to leave; say goodbye to. **25.** (*intr.;* foll. by *with*) to relinquish, esp. reluctantly: *I couldn't part with my teddy bear.* **26.** (tr.; foll. by *from*) to cause to relinquish, esp. reluctantly: *he's not easily parted from his*

cash. **27.** (*intr.*) to split; separate: *the path parts here.*
28. (*tr.*) to arrange (the hair) in such a way that a line of scalp is left showing. **29.** (*intr.*) *Euphemistic.* to die. **30.** (*intr.*) *Arch.* to depart. ~*adv.* **31.** to some extent; partly. ~See also **parts.** [C13: via OF from L *partīre* to divide, from *pars* a part]
part. *abbrev. for:* **1.** participle. **2.** particular.
partake (pɑːˈteɪk) *vb.* **-taking, -took, -taken.** (*mainly intr.*) **1.** (foll. by *in*) to have a share; participate. **2.** (foll. by *of*) to take or receive a portion, esp. of food or drink. **3.** (foll. by *of*) to suggest or have some of the quality (of): *music partaking of sadness.* [C16: back formation from *partaker*, earlier *part taker*, based on L *particeps* partici-pant] —**par'taker** *n.*
parterre (pɑːˈtɛə) *n.* **1.** a formally patterned flower gar-den. **2.** the pit of a theatre. [C17: from F, from *par* along + *terre* ground]
parthenogenesis (ˌpɑːθɪnəʊˈdʒɛnɪsɪs) *n.* a type of repro-duction, occurring in some insects and flowers, in which the unfertilized ovum develops directly into a new individ-ual. [C19: from Gk *parthenos* virgin + *genesis* birth] —**parthenogenetic** (ˌpɑːθɪˌnəʊdʒɪˈnɛtɪk) *adj.*
Parthenon (ˈpɑːθəˌnɒn, -nən) *n.* the temple on the Acrop-olis in Athens built in the 5th century B.C. and regarded as the finest example of the Greek Doric order.
Parthenopaeus (ˌpɑːθənəʊˈpiːəs) *n. Greek myth.* one of the Seven against Thebes, son of Atalanta.
Parthenope (pɑːˈθɛnəpɪ) *n. Greek myth.* a siren, who drowned herself when Odysseus evaded the lure of the sirens' singing. Her body was said to have been cast ashore at what became Naples.
Parthia (ˈpɑːθɪə) *n.* a country in ancient Asia, southeast of the Caspian Sea, that expanded into a great empire domi-nating SW Asia in the 2nd century B.C. It was destroyed by the Seleucids in the 3rd century A.D. —**'Parthian** *n., adj.*
Parthian shot *n.* a hostile remark or gesture delivered while departing. [alluding to the custom of Parthian arch-ers who shot their arrows backwards while retreating]
partial (ˈpɑːʃəl) *adj.* **1.** relating to only a part; not general or complete: *a partial eclipse.* **2.** biased: *a partial judge.* **3.** (*postpositive;* foll. by *to*) having a particular liking (for). **4.** *Maths.* designating or relating to an operation in which only one of a set of independent variables is con-sidered at a time. ~*n.* **5.** Also called: **partial tone.** *Mu-sic, acoustics.* any of the component tones of a single musical sound. **6.** *Maths.* a partial derivative. [C15: from OF *parcial*, from LL *partiālis* incomplete, from L *pars* part] —**'partially** *adv.* —**'partialness** *n.*
▷ **Usage.** In strict usage, a difference is sometimes made be-tween the meanings of *partially* "not fully or completely", and *partly* "concerning only a part" or "in part". The dis-tinction can be helpful in a sentence such as *the book, which was written partly in English and partly in French, was only partially completed when he died.* In practice, however, the two words are used interchangea-bly.
partial derivative *n.* the derivative of a function of two or more variables with respect to one of the variables, the other or others being considered constant. Written *∂f/∂x.*
partiality (ˌpɑːʃɪˈælɪtɪ) *n., pl.* **-ties. 1.** favourable bias. **2.** (usually foll. by *for*) liking or fondness. **3.** the state of being partial.
partible (ˈpɑːtəbªl) *adj.* (esp. of property or an inheri-tance) divisible; separable. [C16: from LL *partibilis*, from *part-, pars* part]
participate (pɑːˈtɪsɪˌpeɪt) *vb.* (*intr.;* often foll. by *in*) to take part, be or become actively involved, or share (in). [C16: from L *participāre*, from *pars* part + *capere* to take] —**par'ticipant** *adj., n.* —**par,tici'pation** *n.* —**par'tici,pator** *n.* —**par'ticipatory** *adj.*
participle (ˈpɑːtɪsɪpªl) *n.* a nonfinite form of verbs, in Eng-lish and other languages, used adjectivally and in the for-mation of certain compound tenses. See also **present participle, past participle.** [C14: via OF from L *par-ticipium*, from *particeps*, from *pars* part + *capere* to take] —**participial** (ˌpɑːtɪˈsɪpɪəl) *adj.* —**,parti'cipially** *adv.*
particle (ˈpɑːtɪkªl) *n.* **1.** an extremely small piece of mat-ter; speck. **2.** a very tiny amount; iota: *it doesn't make a particle of difference.* **3.** a function word, esp. (in certain languages) a word belonging to an uninflected class hav-ing grammatical function: *"up"* is sometimes regarded as an adverbial particle. **4.** a common affix, such as *re-,*

un-, or *-ness.* **5.** *Physics.* a body with finite mass that can be treated as having negligible size, and internal structure. **6.** See **elementary particle.** [C14: from L *particula* a small part, from *pars* part]
particle accelerator *n.* a machine for accelerating charged elementary particles to very high energies, used in nuclear physics.
parti-coloured (ˈpɑːtɪˌkʌləd) *adj.* having different colours in different parts; variegated. [C16 *parti*, from (obs.) *party* of more than one colour, from OF: striped, from L *partīre* to divide]
particular (pəˈtɪkjʊlə) *adj.* **1.** (*prenominal*) of or belong-ing to a single or specific person, thing, category, etc.; spe-cific; special: *the particular demands of the job.* **2.** (*prenominal*) exceptional or marked: *a matter of partic-ular importance.* **3.** (*prenominal*) relating to or provid-ing specific details or circumstances: *a particular account.* **4.** exacting or difficult to please, esp. in details; fussy. **5.** (of the solution of a differential equation) ob-tained by giving specific values to the arbitrary constants in a general equation. **6.** *Logic.* (of a proposition) af-firming or denying something about only some members of a class of objects, as in *some men are not wicked.* Cf. **universal** (sense 9). ~*n.* **7.** a separate distinct item that helps to form a generalization: *opposed to general.* **8.** (*often pl.*) an item of information; detail: *complete in ev-ery particular.* **9. in particular.** especially or exactly. [C14: from OF *particuler*, from LL *particulāris* concern-ing a part, from L *particula* PARTICLE] —**par'ticularly** *adv.*
particularism (pəˈtɪkjʊləˌrɪzəm) *n.* **1.** exclusive attach-ment to the interests of one group, class, sect, etc. **2.** the principle of permitting each state in a federation the right to further its own interests. **3.** *Christian theol.* the doc-trine that divine grace is restricted to the elect. —**par'tic-ularist** *n., adj.*
particularity (pəˌtɪkjʊˈlærɪtɪ) *n., pl.* **-ties. 1.** (*often pl.*) a specific circumstance: *the particularities of the affair.* **2.** great attentiveness to detail; fastidiousness. **3.** the quality of being precise: *a description of great particular-ity.* **4.** the state or quality of being particular as opposed to general; individuality.
particularize *or* **-ise** (pəˈtɪkjʊləˌraɪz) *vb.* **1.** to treat in detail; give details (about). **2.** (*intr.*) to go into detail. —**par,ticulari'zation** *or* **-i'sation** *n.*
particulate (pɑːˈtɪkjʊlɪt, -ˌleɪt) *n.* **1.** a substance consist-ing of separate particles. ~*adj.* **2.** of or made up of sepa-rate particles.
parting (ˈpɑːtɪŋ) *n.* **1.** *Brit.* the line of scalp showing when sections of hair are combed in opposite directions. U.S. and Canad. equivalent: **part. 2.** the act of separating or the state of being separated. **3. a.** a departure or leave-taking, esp. one causing a final separation. **b.** (*as modi-fier*): *a parting embrace.* **4.** a place or line of separation or division. **5.** a euphemism for **death.** ~*adj.* (*pre-nominal*) **6.** *Literary.* departing: *the parting day.* **7.** serving to divide or separate.
partisan *or* **partizan** (ˌpɑːtɪˈzæn, ˈpɑːtɪˌzæn) *n.* **1.** an ad-herent or devotee of a cause, party, etc. **2.** a member of an armed resistance group within occupied territory. ~*adj.* **3.** of, relating to, or characteristic of a partisan. **4.** excessively devoted to one party, faction, etc.; one-sided. [C16: via F from OIt. *partigiano*, from *parte* faction, from L *pars* part] —**,parti'sanship** *or* **,parti'zanship** *n.*
partita (pɑːˈtiːtə) *n., pl.* **-te** (-teɪ) *or* **-tas** *Music.* a type of suite. [It.: divided (piece), from L *partīre* to divide]
partite (ˈpɑːtaɪt) *adj.* **1.** (*in combination*) composed of or divided into a specified number of parts: *bipartite.* **2.** (esp. of plant leaves) divided almost to the base to form two or more parts. [C16: from L *partīre* to divide]
partition (pɑːˈtɪʃən) *n.* **1.** a division into parts; separa-tion. **2.** something that separates, such as a large screen dividing a room in two. **3.** a part or share. **4.** *Property law.* a division of property, esp. realty, among joint own-ers. ~*vb.* (*tr.*) **5.** (often foll. by *off*) to separate or appor-tion into sections: *to partition a room off with a large screen.* **6.** *Property law.* to divide (property, esp. realty) among joint owners. [C15: via OF from L *partītiō*, from *partīre* to divide] —**par'titioner** *or* **par'titionist** *n.*
partitive (ˈpɑːtɪtɪv) *adj.* **1.** *Grammar.* indicating that a noun involved in a construction refers only to a part of what it otherwise refers to. The phrase *some of the butter*

is a partitive construction. **2.** serving to separate or divide into parts. ~*n.* **3.** *Grammar.* a partitive linguistic element or feature. [C16: from Med. L *partitīvus* serving to divide, from L *partīre* to divide] — '**partitively** *adv.*

partly ('pɑːtlɪ) *adv.* not completely.

▷ **Usage.** See at **partial.**

partner ('pɑːtnə) *n.* **1.** an ally or companion: *a partner in crime.* **2.** a member of a partnership. **3.** one of a pair of dancers or players on the same side in a game: *my bridge partner.* **4.** either member of a couple in a relationship. ~*vb.* **5.** to be or cause to be a partner (of). [C14: var. (infl. by PART) of *parcener* one who shares equally with another, from OF *parçonier*, ult. from L *partīre* to divide]

partnership ('pɑːtnəʃɪp) *n.* **1. a.** a contractual relationship between two or more persons carrying on a joint business venture. **b.** the deed creating such a relationship. **c.** the persons associated in such a relationship. **2.** the state or condition of being a partner.

part of speech *n.* a class of words sharing important syntactic or semantic features; a group of words in a language that may occur in similar positions or fulfil similar functions in a sentence. The chief parts of speech in English are noun, pronoun, adjective, determiner, adverb, verb, preposition, conjunction, and interjection.

parton ('pɑːˌtɒn) *n. Physics.* a hypothetical elementary particle postulated as a constituent of neutrons and protons. [from PART + -ON]

Parton ('pɑːtən) *n.* **Dolly.** born 1946, U.S. country and pop singer and songwriter.

partook (pɑːˈtʊk) *vb.* the past tense of **partake.**

partridge ('pɑːtrɪdʒ) *n., pl.* **-tridges** *or* **-tridge.** any of various small Old World game birds of the pheasant family, esp. the common or European partridge. [C13: from OF *perdriz*, from L *perdix*, from Gk]

parts (pɑːts) *pl. n.* **1.** personal abilities or talents: *a man of many parts.* **2.** short for **private parts.**

Parts of Holland *n.* See **Holland**[1] (sense 3).

Parts of Kesteven *n.* See (Parts of) **Kesteven.**

Parts of Lindsey *n.* See (Parts of) **Lindsey.**

part song *n.* **1.** a song composed in harmonized parts. **2.** (*in more technical usage*) a piece of homophonic choral music in which the topmost part carries the melody.

part-time *adj.* **1.** for less than the entire time appropriate to an activity: *a part-time job.* ~*adv.* **part time. 2.** on a part-time basis: *he works part time.* ~Cf. **full-time.** — ˌ**part-'timer** *n.*

parturient (pɑːˈtjʊərɪənt) *adj.* **1.** of or relating to childbirth. **2.** giving birth. **3.** producing a new idea, etc. [C16: via L *parturīre*, from *parere* to bring forth] — **par'turiency** *n.*

parturition (ˌpɑːtjʊˈrɪʃən) *n.* the act or process of giving birth. [C17: from LL *parturītiō*, from *parturīre* to be in labour]

part work *n. Brit.* a series of magazines issued weekly or monthly, which are designed to be bound together to form a complete book.

party ('pɑːtɪ) *n., pl.* **-ties. 1. a.** a social gathering for pleasure, often held as a celebration. **b.** (*as modifier*): *party spirit.* **c.** (*in combination*): *partygoer.* **2.** a group of people associated in some activity: *a rescue party.* **3. a.** (*often cap.*) a group of people organized together to further a common political aim, etc. **b.** (*as modifier*): *party politics.* **4.** a person, esp. one entering into a contract. **5.** the person or persons taking part in legal proceedings: *a party to the action.* **6.** *Inf., humorous.* a person. ~*vb.* **-ties, -tying, -tied.** (*intr.*) **7.** *Inf.* to celebrate; revel. ~*adj.* **7.** *Heraldry.* (of a shield) divided vertically into two colours, metals, or furs. [C13: from OF *partie* part, from L *partīre* to divide; see PART]

party line *n.* **1.** a telephone line serving two or more subscribers. **2.** the policies or dogma of a political party, etc.

party wall *n. Property law.* a wall separating two properties or pieces of land and over which each of the adjoining owners has certain rights.

par value *n.* the value imprinted on the face of a share certificate or bond and used to assess dividend, capital ownership, or interest.

parvenu *or* (*fem.*) **parvenue** ('pɑːvəˌnjuː) *n.* **1.** a person who, having risen socially or economically, is considered to be an upstart. ~*adj.* **2.** of or characteristic of a parvenu. [C19: from F, from *parvenir* to attain, from L *pervenīre*, from *per* through + *venīre* to come]

parvovirus ('pɑːvəʊˌvaɪrəs) *n.* any of a group of viruses characterized by their very small size, each of which is specific to a particular species, as for example canine parvovirus. [C20: NL, from L *parvus* little + VIRUS]

Parzival (*German* 'partsifal) *or* **Parsifal** *n. German myth.* the hero of a medieval cycle of legends about the Holy Grail. English equivalent: **Percival.**

pas (pɑː) *n., pl.* **pas.** a dance step or movement, esp. in ballet. [C18: from F, lit.: step]

Pasadena (ˌpæsəˈdiːnə) *n.* a city in SW California, east of Los Angeles. Pop.: 129 900 (1986 est.).

Pasargadae (pæˈsɑːgəˌdiː) *n.* an ancient city in Persia, northeast of Persepolis in present-day Iran: built by Cyrus the Great.

Pasay ('pɑːsaɪ) *n.* a city in the Philippines, on central Luzon just south of Manila, on Manila Bay. Pop.: 287 770 (1980). Also called: **Rizal.**

pascal ('pæskəl) *n.* the derived SI unit of pressure; the pressure exerted on an area of 1 square metre by a force of 1 newton; equivalent to 10 dynes per square centimetre or 1.45×10^{-4} pound per square inch. Symbol: Pa [C20: after B. PASCAL]

Pascal (*French* paskal) *n.* **Blaise** (blɛz). 1623–62, French philosopher, mathematician, and physicist. As a scientist, he made important contributions to hydraulics and the study of atmospheric pressure and, with Fermat, developed the theory of probability. His chief philosophical works are *Lettres provinciales* (1656–57), written in defence of Jansenism and against the Jesuits, and *Pensées* (1670), fragments of a Christian apologia.

PASCAL ('pæsˌkæl) *n.* a high-level computer-programming language developed as a teaching language.

Pascal's triangle *n.* a triangular figure consisting of rows of numbers, each number being obtained by adding together the two numbers on either side of it in the row above. [C17: after B. PASCAL]

paschal ('pæskəl) *adj.* **1.** of or relating to **Passover** (sense 1). **2.** of or relating to **Easter.** [C15: from OF *pascal*, via Church L from Heb. *pesakh* Passover]

Paschal Lamb *n.* **1.** (*sometimes not caps.*) *Old Testament.* the lamb killed and eaten on the first day of the Passover. **2.** Christ regarded as this sacrifice.

pas de basque (ˌpɑː də ˈbɑː) *n., pl.* **pas de basque.** a dance step performed usually on the spot and used esp. in reels and jigs. [from F, lit.: Basque step]

Pas-de-Calais (*French* padkalɛ) *n.* a department of N France, in Nord-Pas-de-Calais region, on the Straits of Dover (the **Pas de Calais**): the part of France closest to the British Isles. Capital: Arras. Pop.: 1 412 413 (1982). Area: 6752 sq. km (2633 sq. miles).

pas de deux (*French* paddø) *n., pl.* **pas de deux.** *Ballet.* a sequence for two dancers. [F: step for two]

pash (pæʃ) *n. Sl.* infatuation. [C20: from PASSION]

pasha *or* **pacha** ('pɑːʃə, 'pæʃə) *n.* (formerly) a high official of the Ottoman Empire or the modern Egyptian kingdom: placed after a name when used as a title. [C17: from Turkish *paşa*]

pashm ('pæʃəm) *n.* the underfur of various Tibetan animals, esp. goats, used for Cashmere shawls. [from Persian, lit.: wool]

Pashto, Pushto ('pʌʃtəʊ), *or* **Pushtu** *n.* **1.** a language of Afghanistan and NW Pakistan. **2.** (*pl.* **-to** *or* **-tos, -tu** *or* **-tus**) a speaker of the Pashto language; a Pathan. ~*adj.* **3.** denoting or relating to this language or a speaker of it.

Pasionaria (*Spanish* pasjoˈnarja) *n.* **La** (la), real name *Dolores Ibarruri.* born 1895, Spanish Communist leader, who lived in exile in the Soviet Union (1939–75).

Pasiphaë (pəˈsɪfiɪ) *n. Greek myth.* the wife of Minos and mother (by a bull) of the Minotaur.

Pasmore ('pæsˌmɔː) *n.* **Victor.** born 1908, British artist. Originally influenced by cubism, he has devoted himself to abstract paintings and reliefs since 1947.

paso doble ('pæsəʊ 'dəʊbleɪ) *n., pl.* **paso dobles** *or* **pasos dobles.** **1.** a modern ballroom dance in fast duple time. **2.** a piece of music composed for or in the rhythm of this dance. [Sp.: double step]

Pasolini (*Italian* pazoˈlini) *n.* **Pier Paolo** (pjɛr 'paːolo). 1922–75, Italian film director. His films include *The Gospel according to St. Matthew* (1964), *Oedipus Rex* (1967), *Theorem* (1968), *Pigsty* (1969), and *Decameron* (1970).

pas op ('pɑːs ˌɒp) *interj. S. African.* beware. [Afrik.]

pasqueflower ('pɑːskˌflaʊə) *n.* **1.** a small purple-flowered plant of N and Central Europe and W Asia. **2.** any of several related North American plants. [C16: from F *passefleur*, from *passer* to excel + *fleur* flower; changed to *pasqueflower* Easter flower, because it blooms at Easter]

pasquinade (ˌpæskwɪˈneɪd) *n.* an abusive lampoon or satire, esp. one posted in a public place. [C17: from It. *Pasquino* name given to an ancient Roman statue disinterred in 1501, which was annually posted with satirical verses]

pass (pɑːs) *vb.* **1.** to go onwards or move by or past (a person, thing, etc.). **2.** to run, extend, or lead through, over, or across (a place): *the route passes through the city.* **3.** to go through or cause to go through (an obstacle or barrier): *to pass a needle through cloth.* **4.** to move or cause to move onwards or over: *he passed his hand over her face.* **5.** (*tr.*) to go beyond or exceed: *this victory passes all expectation.* **6.** to gain or cause to gain an adequate mark or grade in (an examination, course, etc.). **7.** (often foll. by *away* or *by*) to elapse or allow to elapse: *we passed the time talking.* **8.** (*intr.*) to take place or happen: *what passed at the meeting?* **9.** to speak or exchange or be spoken or exchanged: *angry words passed between them.* **10.** to spread or cause to spread: *we passed the news round the class.* **11.** to transfer or exchange or be transferred or exchanged: *the bomb passed from hand to hand.* **12.** (*intr.*) to undergo change or transition: *to pass from joy to despair.* **13.** (when *tr.*, often foll. by *down*) to transfer or be transferred by inheritance: *the house passed to the younger son.* **14.** to agree to or be agreed to by a legislative body, etc.: *the assembly passed 10 resolutions.* **15.** (*tr.*) (of a legislative measure) to undergo (a procedural stage) and be agreed: *the bill passed the committee stage.* **16.** (when *tr.*, often foll. by *on* or *upon*) to pronounce (judgment, findings, etc.): *the court passed sentence.* **17.** to go or allow to go without comment or censure: *the insult passed unnoticed.* **18.** (*intr.*) to opt not to exercise a right, as by not answering a question or not making a bid or a play in card games. **19.** to discharge (urine, etc.) from the body. **20.** (*intr.*) to come to an end or disappear: *his anger soon passed.* **21.** (*intr.; usually foll. by for* or *as*) to be likely to be mistaken for (someone or something else): *you could easily pass for your sister.* **22.** (*intr.; foll. by away, on,* or *over*) *Euphemistic.* to die. **23.** *Sport.* to hit, kick, or throw (the ball, etc.) to another player. **24. bring to pass.** *Arch.* to cause to happen. **25. come to pass.** *Arch.* to happen. ~*n.* **26.** the act of passing. **27.** a route through a range of mountains where there is a gap between peaks. **28.** a permit, licence, or authorization to do something without restriction. **29. a.** a document allowing entry to and exit from a military installation. **b.** a document authorizing leave of absence. **30.** *Brit.* **a.** the passing of a college or university examination to a satisfactory standard but not as high as honours. **b.** (*as modifier*): *a pass degree.* **31.** a dive, sweep, or bombing or landing run by an aircraft. **32.** a motion of the hand or of a wand as part of a conjuring trick. **33.** *Inf.* an attempt to invite sexual intimacy. **34.** a state of affairs, esp. a bad one (esp. in **a pretty pass**). **35.** *Sport.* the transfer of a ball, etc., from one player to another. **36.** *Fencing.* a thrust or lunge. **37.** *Bridge, etc.* the act of passing (making no bid). ~*sentence substitute* **38.** *Bridge, etc.* a call indicating that a player has no bid to make. ~See also **pass off, pass out,** etc. [C13: from OF *passer* to pass, surpass, from L *passūs* step]

pass. *abbrev. for:* **1.** passive. **2.** passenger. **3.** passage.

passable ('pɑːsəbᵊl) *adj.* **1.** adequate, fair, or acceptable. **2.** (of an obstacle) capable of being crossed. **3.** (of currency) valid for circulation. **4.** (of a proposed law) able to be enacted. —'**passableness** *n.* —'**passably** *adv.*

passacaglia (ˌpæsəˈkɑːljə) *n.* **1.** an old Spanish dance in slow triple time. **2.** a slow instrumental piece characterized by a series of variations on a particular theme played over a repeated bass part. [C17: earlier *passacalle*, from Sp. *pasacalle* street dance, from *paso* step + *calle* street]

passage ('pæsɪdʒ) *n.* **1.** a channel, opening, etc., through or by which a person may pass. **2.** *Music.* a section or division of a piece, movement, etc. **3.** a way, as in a hall or lobby. **4.** a section of a written work, speech, etc. **5.** a journey, esp. by ship. **6.** the act or process of passing from one place, condition, etc., to another: *passage of a gas through a liquid.* **7.** the permission, right, or freedom to pass: *to be denied passage through a country.* **8.** the

enactment of a law by a legislative body. **9.** *Rare.* an exchange, as of blows, words, etc. [C13: from OF from *passer* to PASS]

passageway ('pæsɪdʒˌweɪ) *n.* a way, esp. one in or between buildings; passage.

Passamaquoddy Bay (ˌpæsəməˈkwɒdɪ) *n.* an inlet of the Bay of Fundy between New Brunswick (Canada) and Maine (U.S.) at the mouth of the St Croix River.

pass band *n.* the band of frequencies that is transmitted with maximum efficiency through a circuit, filter, etc.

passbook ('pɑːsˌbʊk) *n.* **1.** a book for keeping a record of withdrawals from and payments into a building society. **2.** another name for **bankbook**. **3.** *S. African.* an official document to identify the bearer, his race, residence, and employment.

passé ('pɑːseɪ, 'pæseɪ) *adj.* **1.** out-of-date: *passé ideas.* **2.** past the prime; faded: *a passé society beauty.* [C18: from F, p.p. of *passer* to PASS]

passenger ('pæsɪndʒə) *n.* **1. a.** a person travelling in a car, train, boat, etc., not driven by him. **b.** (*as modifier*): *a passenger seat.* **2.** *Chiefly Brit.* a member of a group or team who is not participating fully in the work. [C14: from OF *passager* passing, from PASSAGE]

passenger pigeon *n.* a gregarious North American pigeon, now extinct.

passe-partout (ˌpæspɑːˈtuː) *n.* **1.** a mounting for a picture in which strips of gummed paper bind together the glass, picture, and backing. **2.** the gummed paper used for this. **3.** a mat on which a photograph, etc., is mounted. **4.** something that secures entry everywhere, esp. a master key. [C17: from F, lit.: pass everywhere]

passepied (pɑːsˈpjeɪ) *n., pl.* **-pieds** (-ˈpjeɪ). **1.** a lively minuet in triple time, popular in the 17th century. **2.** a piece of music composed for or in the rhythm of this dance. [C17: from F: pass foot]

passer-by *n., pl.* **passers-by.** a person that is passing or going by, esp. on foot.

passerine ('pæsəˌraɪn, -ˌriːn) *adj.* **1.** of, relating to, or belonging to an order of birds characterized by the perching habit: includes the larks, finches, starlings, etc. ~*n.* **2.** any bird belonging to this order. [C18: from L *passer* sparrow]

passim Latin. ('pæsɪm) *adv.* here and there; throughout: used to indicate that what is referred to occurs frequently in the work cited.

passing ('pɑːsɪŋ) *adj.* **1.** transitory or momentary: *a passing fancy.* **2.** cursory or casual in action or manner: *a passing reference.* ~*adv., adj.* **3.** *Arch.* to an extreme degree: *the events were passing strange.* ~*n.* **4.** a place where or means by which one may pass, cross, ford, etc. **5.** a euphemistic word for **death. 6. in passing.** by the way; incidentally.

passing bell *n.* a bell rung to announce a death or a funeral. Also called: **death knell.**

passing note *or U.S.* **passing tone** *n.* a nonharmonic note through which a melody passes from one harmonic note to the next.

passion ('pæʃən) *n.* **1.** ardent love or affection. **2.** intense sexual love. **3.** a strong affection or enthusiasm for an object, concept, etc.: *a passion for poetry.* **4.** any strongly felt emotion, such as love, hate, envy, etc. **5.** an outburst of anger: *he flew into a passion.* **6.** the object of an intense desire, ardent affection, or enthusiasm. **7.** an outburst expressing intense emotion: *he burst into a passion of sobs.* **8.** the sufferings and death of a Christian martyr. [C12: via F from Church L *passiō* suffering, from L *pati* to suffer] —'**passional** *adj.* —'**passionless** *adj.*

Passion ('pæʃən) *n.* **1.** the sufferings of Christ from the Last Supper to his death on the cross. **2.** any of the four Gospel accounts of this. **3.** a musical setting of this: *the St Matthew Passion.*

passionate ('pæʃənɪt) *adj.* **1.** manifesting or exhibiting intense sexual feeling or desire. **2.** capable of, revealing, or characterized by intense emotion. **3.** easily roused to anger; quick-tempered. —'**passionately** *adv.*

passionflower ('pæʃənˌflaʊə) *n.* any plant of a tropical American genus cultivated for their red, yellow, greenish, or purple showy flowers: some species have edible fruit. [C17: from alleged resemblance betweeen parts of the flower and the instruments of the Crucifixion]

passion fruit *n.* the edible fruit of any of various passionflowers, esp. granadilla.

Passion play *n.* a play depicting the Passion of Christ.

passive ('pæsɪv) *adj.* **1.** not active or not participating perceptibly in an activity, organization, etc. **2.** unresisting and receptive to external forces; submissive. **3.** affected or acted upon by an external object or force. **4.** *Grammar.* denoting a voice of verbs in sentences in which the grammatical subject is the recipient of the action described by the verb, as *was broken* in the sentence *The glass was broken by a boy.* **5.** *Chem.* (of a substance, esp. a metal) apparently chemically unreactive. **6.** *Electronics, telecomm.* **a.** capable only of attenuating a signal: *a passive network.* **b.** not capable of amplifying a signal or controlling a function: *a passive communications satellite.* **7.** *Finance.* (of a bond, share, debt, etc.) yielding no interest. ~*n.* **8.** *Grammar.* **a.** the passive voice. **b.** a passive verb. [C14: from L *passivus* susceptible of suffering, from *patī* to undergo] —'**passively** *adv.* —**pas'sivity** *or* '**passiveness** *n.*

passive resistance *n.* resistance to a government, law, etc., without violence, as by fasting, demonstrating, or refusing to cooperate.

passive smoking *n.* the inhalation of smoke from other people's cigarettes by a nonsmoker.

passkey ('pɑːsˌkiː) *n.* **1.** any of various keys, esp. a latchkey. **2.** another term for **master key** or **skeleton key**.

pass law *n.* (in South Africa) a law restricting the movement of Black Africans.

pass off *vb.* (*adv.*) **1.** to be or cause to be accepted in a false character: *he passed the fake diamonds off as real.* **2.** (*intr.*) to come to a gradual end; disappear: *eventually the pain passed off.* **3.** (*intr.*) to take place: *the meeting passed off without disturbance.* **4.** (*tr.*) to set aside or disregard: *I managed to pass off his insult.*

pass out *vb.* (*adv.*) **1.** (*intr.*) *Inf.* to become unconscious; faint. **2.** (*intr.*) *Brit.* (esp. of an officer cadet) to qualify for a military commission, etc. **3.** (*tr.*) to distribute.

pass over *vb.* **1.** (*tr., adv.*) to take no notice of; disregard: *they passed me over in the last round of promotions.* **2.** (*intr., prep.*) to disregard (something bad or embarrassing).

Passover ('pɑːsˌəʊvə) *n.* **1.** an eight-day Jewish festival celebrated in commemoration of the passing over or sparing of the Israelites in Egypt (Exodus 12). **2.** another term for the **Paschal Lamb.** [C16: from *pass over*, translation of Heb. *pesah*, from *pāsah* to pass over]

passport ('pɑːspɔːt) *n.* **1.** an official document issued by a government, identifying an individual, granting him permission to travel abroad, and requesting the protection of other governments for him. **2.** a quality, asset, etc., that gains a person admission or acceptance. [C15: from F *passeport*, from *passer* to PASS + PORT[1]]

pass up *vb.* (*tr., adv.*) *Inf.* to let go by; ignore: *I won't pass up this opportunity.*

password ('pɑːsˌwɜːd) *n.* **1.** a secret word, phrase, etc., that ensures admission by proving identity, membership, etc. **2.** an action, quality, etc., that gains admission or acceptance.

past (pɑːst) *adj.* **1.** completed, finished, and no longer in existence: *past happiness.* **2.** denoting or belonging to the time that has elapsed at the present moment: *the past history of the world.* **3.** denoting a specific unit of time that immediately precedes the present one: *the past month.* **4.** (*prenominal*) denoting a person who has held an office or position; former: *a past president.* **5.** *Grammar.* denoting any of various tenses of verbs that are used in describing actions, events, or states that have been begun or completed at the time of utterance. ~*n.* **6. the past.** the period of time that has elapsed: *forget the past.* **7.** the history, experience, or background of a nation, person, etc. **8.** an earlier period of someone's life, esp. one regarded as disreputable. **9.** *Grammar.* **a.** a past tense. **b.** a verb in a past tense. ~*adv.* **10.** at a time before the present; ago: *three years past.* **11.** on or onwards: *I greeted him but he just walked past.* ~*prep.* **12.** beyond in time: *it's past midnight.* **13.** beyond in place or position: *the library is past the church.* **14.** moving beyond: *he walked past me.* **15.** beyond or above the reach, limit, or scope of: *his foolishness is past comprehension.* **16. past it.** *Inf.* unable to perform the tasks one could do when one was younger. **17. not put it past someone.** to

consider someone capable of (the action specified). [C14: from *passed,* p.p. of PASS]

pasta ('pæstə) *n.* any of several variously shaped edible preparations made from a flour and water dough, such as spaghetti. [It., from LL: PASTE]

paste (peɪst) *n.* **1.** a mixture of a soft or malleable consistency, such as toothpaste. **2.** an adhesive made from water and flour or starch, used for joining pieces of paper, etc. **3.** a preparation of food, such as meat, that has been pounded to a creamy mass, for spreading on bread, etc. **4.** any of various sweet doughy confections: *almond paste.* **5.** dough, esp. for making pastry. **6. a.** a hard shiny glass used for making imitation gems. **b.** an imitation gem made of this glass. **7.** the combined ingredients of porcelain. See also **hard paste, soft paste.** ~*vb.* (*tr.*) **8.** (often foll. by *on* or *onto*) to attach as by using paste: *he pasted posters onto the wall.* **9.** (usually foll. by *with*) to cover (a surface) with paper, etc.: *he pasted the wall with posters.* **10.** *Sl.* to thrash or beat; defeat. [C14: via OF from LL *pasta* dough, from Gk *pastē* barley porridge, from *passein* to sprinkle]

pasteboard ('peɪstˌbɔːd) *n.* **1.** a stiff board formed from layers of paper or pulp pasted together. ~*adj.* **2.** flimsy or fake.

pastel ('pæstəl, pæ'stɛl) *n.* **1. a.** a substance made of ground pigment bound with gum. **b.** a crayon of this. **c.** a drawing done in such crayons. **2.** the medium or technique of pastel drawing. **3.** a pale delicate colour. ~*adj.* **4.** (of a colour) pale; delicate: *pastel blue.* [C17: via F from It. *pastello,* from LL *pastellus* woad, dim. of *pasta* PASTE] —'**pastelist** *or* '**pastellist** *n.*

pastern ('pæstən) *n.* the part of a horse's foot between the fetlock and the hoof. [C14: from OF *pasturon,* from *pasture* a hobble, from L *pāstōrius* of a shepherd, from PASTOR]

Pasternak ('pæstəˌnæk; *Russian* pəstɪr'nak) *n.* **Boris Leonidovich** (ba'ris lɪə'nidəvitʃ). 1890–1960, Soviet lyric poet, novelist, and translator, noted particularly for his novel of the Russian Revolution, *Dr. Zhivago* (1957). He was awarded the Nobel prize for literature in 1958, but was forced to decline it.

paste-up *n. Printing.* a sheet of paper or board on which are pasted artwork, proofs, etc., for photographing prior to making a plate.

Pasteur (*French* pastœr) *n.* **Louis** (lwi). 1822–95, French chemist and bacteriologist. His discovery that the fermentation of milk and alcohol was caused by microorganisms resulted in the process of pasteurization. He also devised methods of immunization against anthrax and rabies and pioneered stereochemistry.

pasteurism ('pæstəˌrɪzəm, -stjə-, 'pɑː-) *n. Med.* a method of securing immunity from rabies or of treating patients with other viral infections by the serial injection of progressively more virulent suspensions of the causative virus. Also called: **Pasteur treatment.**

pasteurization *or* **-isation** (ˌpæstəraɪ'zeɪʃən, -stjə-, ˌpɑː-) *n.* the process of heating beverages, such as milk, beer, wine, or cider, or solid foods, such as cheese or crab meat, to destroy harmful microorganisms.

pasteurize *or* **-ise** ('pæstəˌraɪz, -stjə-, 'pɑː-) *vb.* (*tr.*) to subject (milk, beer, etc.) to pasteurization. —'**pasteuˌr izer** *or* **-iser** *n.*

pastiche (pæ'stiːʃ) *or* **pasticcio** (pæ'stɪtʃəʊ) *n., pl.* **-tiches** *or* **-ticcios.** **1.** a work of art that mixes styles, materials, etc. **2.** a work of art in the style of another artist. [C19: F *pastiche,* It. *pasticcio,* lit.: piecrust (hence, something blended) from LL *pasta* PASTE]

pastille *or* **pastil** ('pæstɪl) *n.* **1.** a small flavoured or medicated lozenge. **2.** an aromatic substance burnt to fumigate the air. [C17: via F from L *pastillus* small loaf, from *pānis* bread]

pastime ('pɑːsˌtaɪm) *n.* an activity or entertainment which makes time pass pleasantly.

past master *n.* **1.** a person with talent for, or experience in, a particular activity. **2.** a person who has held the office of master in a guild, etc.

Pasto (*Spanish* 'pasto) *n.* a city in SE Colombia, at an altitude of 2590 m (8500 ft.). Pop.: 252 115 (1985).

pastor ('pɑːstə) *n.* **1.** a clergyman or priest in charge of a congregation. **2.** a person who exercises spiritual guidance over a number of people. **3.** a S Asian starling having a black head and wings and a pale pink body. [C14: from L: shepherd, from *pascere* to feed] —'**pastorship** *n.*

pastoral ('pɑːstərəl) *adj.* **1.** of, characterized by, or depicting rural life, scenery, etc. **2.** (of a literary work) dealing with an idealized form of rural existence. **3.** (of land) used for pasture. **4.** of or relating to a clergyman or priest in charge of a congregation or his duties as such. **5.** of or relating to shepherds, their work, etc. ~*n.* **6.** a literary work or picture portraying rural life, esp. in an idealizing way. **7.** *Music.* a variant spelling of **pastorale**. **8. a.** a letter from a clergyman to the people under his charge. **b.** the letter of a bishop to the clergy or people of his diocese. **c.** Also called: **pastoral staff.** the crosier carried by a bishop. [C15: from L, from PASTOR] —**'pastoralism** *n.* —**'pastorally** *adv.*

pastorale (ˌpæstəˈrɑːl) *n., pl.* **-rales.** *Music.* **1.** a composition evocative of rural life, sometimes with a droning accompaniment. **2.** a musical play based on a rustic story. [C18: It., from L: PASTORAL]

pastoralist ('pɑːstərəlɪst) *n. Austral.* a grazier raising sheep, cattle, etc., on a large scale.

pastorate ('pɑːstərɪt) *n.* **1.** the office or term of office of a pastor. **2.** a body of pastors.

pastourelle (ˌpɑːstuːˈrɛl) *n. Music.* **1.** a pastoral piece of music. **2.** one of the figures in a quadrille. [C19: from F: little shepherdess]

past participle *n.* a participial form of verbs used to modify a noun that is logically the object of a verb, also used in certain compound tenses and passive forms of the verb.

past perfect *Grammar.* ~*adj.* **1.** denoting a tense of verbs used in relating past events where the action had already occurred at the time of the action of a main verb that is itself in a past tense. In English this is a compound tense formed with *had* plus the past participle. ~*n.* **2. a.** the past perfect tense. **b.** a verb in this tense.

pastrami (pəˈstrɑːmɪ) *n.* highly seasoned smoked beef. [from Yiddish, from Romanian *pastramă*, from *păstra* to preserve]

pastry ('peɪstrɪ) *n., pl.* **-tries.** **1.** a dough of flour, water, and fat. **2.** baked foods, such as tarts, made with this dough. **3.** an individual cake or pastry pie. [C16: from PASTE]

pasturage ('pɑːstʃərɪdʒ) *n.* **1.** the business of grazing cattle. **2.** another word for **pasture.**

pasture ('pɑːstʃə) *n.* **1.** land covered with grass or herbage and grazed by or suitable for grazing by livestock. **2.** the grass or herbage growing on it. ~*vb.* **3.** (*tr.*) to cause (livestock) to graze or (of livestock) to graze (a pasture). [C13: via OF from LL *pāstūra*, from *pascere* to feed]

pasty¹ ('peɪstɪ) *adj.* **pastier, pastiest.** **1.** of or like the colour, texture, etc., of paste. **2.** (esp. of the complexion) pale or unhealthy-looking. —**'pastily** *adv.* —**'pastiness** *n.*

pasty² ('pæstɪ) *n., pl.* **pasties.** a round of pastry folded over a filling of meat, vegetables, etc. [C13: from OF *pastée*, from LL *pasta* dough]

PA system *n.* See **public-address system.**

pat¹ (pæt) *vb.* **patting, patted.** **1.** to hit (something) lightly with the palm of the hand or some other flat surface: *to pat a ball.* **2.** to slap (a person or animal) gently, esp. on the back, as an expression of affection, congratulation, etc. **3.** (*tr.*) to shape, smooth, etc., with a flat instrument or the palm. **4.** (*intr.*) to walk or run with light footsteps. **5. pat (someone) on the back.** *Inf.* to congratulate. ~*n.* **6.** a light blow with something flat. **7.** a gentle slap. **8.** a small mass of something: *a pat of butter.* **9.** the sound of patting. **10. pat on the back.** *Inf.* a gesture or word indicating approval. [C14: ? imit.]

pat² (pæt) *adv.* **1.** Also: **off pat.** exactly or fluently memorized: *he recited it pat.* **2.** opportunely or aptly. **3. stand pat. a.** *Chiefly U.S. & Canad.* to refuse to abandon a belief, decision, etc. **b.** (in poker, etc.) to play without adding new cards to the hand dealt. ~*adj.* **4.** exactly right; apt: *a pat reply.* **5.** too exactly fitting; glib: *a pat answer to a difficult problem.* **6.** exactly right: *a pat hand in poker.* [C17: ? adv. use of "with a light stroke") of PAT¹]

pat³ (pæt) *n.* **on one's pat.** *Austral. inf.* alone. [C20: rhyming slang, from *Pat* Malone]

pat. *abbrev. for* patent(ed).

patagium (pəˈteɪdʒɪəm) *n., pl.* **-gia** (-dʒɪə). **1.** a web of skin in bats and gliding mammals that functions as a wing. **2.** a membranous fold of skin connecting a bird's wing to the shoulder. [C19: from NL, from L, from Gk *patageion* gold border on a tunic]

Patagonia (ˌpætəˈgəʊnɪə) *n.* **1.** the southernmost region of South America, in Argentina and Chile extending from the Andes to the Atlantic. **2.** an arid tableland in the southernmost part of Argentina, rising towards the Andes in the west. —ˌPata'gonian *adj.*

patch (pætʃ) *n.* **1.** a piece of material used to mend a garment, etc., or to make patchwork, a sewn-on pocket, etc. **2. a.** a small plot of land. **b.** its produce: *a patch of cabbages.* **3.** *Med.* **a.** a protective covering for an injured eye. **b.** any protective dressing. **4.** an imitation beauty spot made of black silk, etc., worn esp. in the 18th century. **5.** an identifying piece of fabric worn on the shoulder of a uniform. **6.** a small contrasting section: *a patch of cloud in the blue sky.* **7.** a scrap; remnant. **8. not a patch on.** not nearly as good as. **9. strike** *or* **hit a bad patch.** to have a difficult time. ~*vb.* (*tr.*) **10.** to mend or supply (a garment, etc.) with a patch or patches. **11.** to put together or produce with patches. **12.** (of material) to serve as a patch to. **13.** (often foll. by *up*) to mend hurriedly or in a makeshift way. **14.** (often foll. by *up*) to make (up) or settle (a quarrel, etc.). **15.** to connect (electric circuits) together temporarily by means of a patch board. [C16 *pacche*, ?from F *pieche* PIECE] —**'patcher** *n.*

patch board *or* **panel** *n.* a device with a large number of sockets into which electrical plugs can be inserted to form many different temporary circuits: used in telephone exchanges, computer systems, etc. Also called: **plugboard.**

patchouli *or* **patchouly** ('pætʃʊlɪ, pəˈtʃuːlɪ) *n., pl.* **-lis** *or* **-lies.** **1.** any of several Asiatic trees, the leaves of which yield a heavy fragrant oil. **2.** the perfume made from this oil. [C19: from Tamil *paccilai*, from *paccu* green + *ilai* leaf]

patch pocket *n.* a pocket on the outside of a garment.

patch test *n. Med.* a test to detect an allergic reaction by applying small amounts of a suspected substance to the skin.

patchwork ('pætʃˌwɜːk) *n.* **1.** needlework done by sewing pieces of different materials together. **2.** something made up of various parts.

patchy ('pætʃɪ) *adj.* **patchier, patchiest.** **1.** irregular in quality, occurrence, intensity, etc.: *a patchy essay.* **2.** having or forming patches. —**'patchily** *adv.* —**'patchiness** *n.*

pate (peɪt) *n.* the head, esp. with reference to baldness or (in facetious use) intelligence. [C14: from ?]

pâté ('pæteɪ) *n.* **1.** a spread of finely minced liver, poultry, etc., served usually as an hors d'oeuvre. **2.** a savoury pie. [C18: from F: PASTE]

pâté de foie gras (pɑte də fwa grɑ) *n., pl.* **pâtés de foie gras** (pɑte). a smooth rich paste made from the liver of a specially fattened goose. [F: pâté of fat liver]

patella (pəˈtɛlə) *n., pl.* **-lae** (-liː). *Anat.* a small flat triangular bone in front of and protecting the knee joint. Nontechnical name: **kneecap.** [C17: from L, from *patina* shallow pan] —**pa'tellar** *adj.*

paten ('pætⁿn) *n.* a plate, usually made of silver or gold, esp. for the bread in the Eucharist. [C13: from OF *patene*, from Med. L, from L *patina* pan]

patency ('peɪtⁿnsɪ) *n.* the condition of being obvious.

patent ('peɪtⁿnt, 'pætⁿnt) *n.* **1. a.** a government grant to an inventor assuring him the sole right to make, use, and sell his invention for a limited period. **b.** a document conveying such a grant. **2.** an invention, privilege, etc., protected by a patent. **3. a.** an official document granting a right. **b.** any right granted by such a document. ~*adj.* **4.** open or available for inspection (esp. in **letters patent, patent writ**). **5.** ('peɪtⁿnt). obvious: *their scorn was patent to everyone.* **6.** concerning protection, appointment, etc., of or by a patent or patents. **7.** proprietary. **8.** (esp. of a bodily passage or duct) being open or unobstructed. ~*vb.* (*tr.*) **9.** to obtain a patent for. **10.** to grant by a patent. [C14: via OF from L *patēre* to lie open; n. use, short for *letters patent*, from Med. L *litterae patentes* letters lying open (to public inspection)] —**'patentable** *adj.* —ˌpaten'tee *n.* —ˌpaten'tor *n.*

▷ *Usage.* The pronunciation "'pætⁿnt" is heard in *letters patent* and *Patent Office* and is the usual U.S. pronunciation for all senses. In Britain "'pætⁿnt" is sometimes heard for senses 1, 2, and 3, but "peɪtⁿnt" is commoner and is regularly used in collocations like *patent leather.*

patent leather ('peɪtⁿnt) *n.* leather processed with lacquer to give a hard glossy surface.

patently ('peɪt³ntlɪ) *adv.* obviously.
patent medicine ('peɪt³nt) *n.* a medicine with a patent, available without a prescription.
Patent Office ('pæt³nt) *n.* a government department that issues patents.
Patent Rolls ('pæt³nt) *pl. n.* (in Britain) the register of patents issued.
pater ('peɪtə) *n. Brit. sl.* another word for **father:** now chiefly used facetiously. [from L]
Pater ('peɪtə) *n.* **Walter (Horatio).** 1839–94, English essayist and critic, noted for his prose style and his advocation of the "love of art for its own sake". His works include the philosophical romance *Marius the Epicurean* (1885), *Studies in the History of the Renaissance* (1873), and *Imaginary Portraits* (1887).
paterfamilias (,peɪtəfə'mɪlɪˌæs) *n., pl.* **patresfamilias** (,pɑːtreɪzfə'mɪlɪˌæs). the male head of a household. [L: father of the family]
paternal (pə'tɜːn³l) *adj.* **1.** relating to or characteristic of a father; fatherly. **2.** (*prenominal*) related through the father: *his paternal grandfather.* **3.** inherited or derived from the male parent. [C17: from LL *paternālis,* from L *pater* father] —**pa'ternally** *adv.*
paternalism (pə'tɜːnə,lɪzəm) *n.* the attitude or policy of a government or other authority that manages the affairs of a country, company, etc., in the manner of a father, esp. in usurping individual responsibility. —**pa'ternalist** *n., adj.* —**pa,ternal'istic** *adj.* —**pa,ternal'istically** *adv.*
paternity (pə'tɜːnɪtɪ) *n.* **1. a.** the fact or state of being a father. **b.** (*as modifier*): *a paternity suit was filed against the man.* **2.** descent or derivation from a father. **3.** authorship or origin. [C15: from LL *paternitās,* from L *pater* father]
paternoster (,pætə'nɒstə) *n.* **1.** *R.C. Church.* the beads at the ends of each decade of the rosary at which the Paternoster is recited. **2.** a type of fishing tackle in which short lines and hooks are attached at intervals to the main line. **3.** a type of lift in which platforms are attached to continuous chains: passengers enter while it is moving. [L, lit.: our father (from the opening of the Lord's Prayer)]
Paternoster (,pætə'nɒstə) *n.* (*sometimes not cap.*) *R.C. Church.* **1.** the Lord's Prayer, esp. in Latin. **2.** the recital of this as an act of devotion.
Paterson[1] ('pætəs³n) *n.* a city in NE New Jersey: settled by the Dutch in the late 17th century. Pop.: 139 160 (1986 est.).
Paterson[2] ('pætəs³n) *n.* **Andrew Barton,** known as *Banjo Paterson.* 1864–1941, Australian poet. His works include "Waltzing Matilda" and "The Man from Snowy River".
Paterson's curse *n.* an Australian name for **viper's bugloss.**
path (pɑːθ) *n., pl.* **paths** (pɑːðz). **1.** a road or way, esp. a narrow trodden track. **2.** a surfaced walk, as through a garden. **3.** the course or direction in which something moves: *the path of a whirlwind.* **4.** a course of conduct: *the path of virtue.* [OE *pœth*] —**'pathless** *adj.*
-path *n. combining form.* **1.** denoting a person suffering from a specified disease or disorder: *neuropath.* **2.** denoting a practitioner of a particular method of treatment: *osteopath.* [back formation from -PATHY]
path. *abbrev. for:* **1.** pathological. **2.** pathology.
Pathan (pə'tɑːn) *n.* a member of the Pashto-speaking people of Afghanistan, NW Pakistan, and elsewhere. [C17: from Hindi]
pathetic (pə'θetɪk) *adj.* **1.** evoking or expressing pity, sympathy, etc. **2.** distressingly inadequate: *the old man sat huddled before a pathetic fire.* **3.** *Brit. sl.* ludicrously or contemptibly uninteresting or worthless. **4.** *Obs.* of or affecting the feelings. [C16: from F *pathétique,* via LL from Gk *pathetikos* sensitive, from *pathos* suffering] —**pa'thetically** *adv.*
pathetic fallacy *n.* (in literature) the presentation of inanimate objects in nature as possessing human feelings.
pathfinder ('pɑːθ,faɪndə) *n.* **1.** a person who makes or finds a way, esp. through unexplored areas or fields of knowledge. **2.** an aircraft or parachutist that indicates a target area by dropping flares, etc. **3.** a radar device used for navigation or homing onto a target.
patho- *or before a vowel* **path-** *combining form.* disease: *pathology.* [from Gk *pathos* suffering]
pathogen ('pæθə,dʒen) *n.* any agent that can cause disease. —**,patho'genic** *adj.*

pathogenesis (,pæθə'dʒenɪsɪs) *or* **pathogeny** (pə'θɒdʒɪnɪ) *n.* the development of a disease. —**pathogenetic** (,pæθədʒɪ'netɪk) *adj.*
pathological (,pæθə'lɒdʒɪk³l) *or* (*less commonly*) **pathologic** *adj.* **1.** of or relating to pathology. **2.** relating to, involving, or caused by disease. **3.** *Inf.* compulsively motivated: *a pathological liar.* —**,patho'logically** *adv.*
pathology (pə'θɒlədʒɪ) *n., pl.* **-gies.** **1.** the branch of medicine concerned with the cause, origin, and nature of disease, including the changes occurring as a result of disease. **2.** the manifestations of disease, esp. changes occurring in tissues or organs. —**pa'thologist** *n.*
pathos ('peɪθɒs) *n.* **1.** the quality or power, esp. in literature or speech, of arousing feelings of pity, sorrow, etc. **2.** a feeling of sympathy or pity. [C17: from Gk: suffering]
pathway ('pɑːθ,weɪ) *n.* **1.** a path. **2.** *Biochem.* a chain of reactions associated with a particular metabolic process.
-pathy *n. combining form.* **1.** indicating feeling or perception: *telepathy.* **2.** indicating disease: *psychopathy.* **3.** indicating a method of treating disease: *osteopathy.* [from Gk *patheia* suffering; see PATHOS] —**-pathic** *adj. combining form.*
Patiala (,pʌtɪ'ɑːlə) *n.* a city in N India, in E Punjab: seat of the Punjabi University (1962). Pop.: 205 141 (1981).
patience ('peɪʃəns) *n.* **1.** tolerant and even-tempered perseverance. **2.** the capacity for calmly enduring pain, trying situations, etc. **3.** *Brit.* any of various card games for one player only. U.S. word: **solitaire.** [C13: via OF from L *patientia* endurance, from *patī* to suffer]
patient ('peɪʃənt) *adj.* **1.** enduring trying circumstances with even temper. **2.** tolerant; understanding. **3.** capable of accepting delay with equanimity. **4.** persevering or diligent: *a patient worker.* ~*n.* **5.** a person who is receiving medical care. [C14: see PATIENCE] —**'patiently** *adv.*
patina[1] ('pætɪnə) *n., pl.* **-nas.** **1.** a film formed on the surface of a metal, esp. the green oxidation of bronze or copper. **2.** any fine layer on a surface: *a patina of frost.* **3.** the sheen on a surface caused by long handling. [C18: from It.: coating, from L: PATINA[2]]
patina[2] ('pætɪnə) *n., pl.* **-nae** (-,niː). a broad shallow dish used in ancient Rome. [from L, from Gk *patanē* platter]
patio ('pætɪ,əʊ) *n., pl.* **-tios.** **1.** an open inner courtyard, esp. one in a Spanish or Spanish-American house. **2.** an area adjoining a house, esp. one that is paved. [C19: from Sp.: courtyard]
patisserie (pə'tiːsərɪ) *n.* **1.** a shop where fancy pastries are sold. **2.** such pastries. [C18: F, from *pâtissier* pastry cook, ult. from LL *pasta* PASTE]
Patmore ('pætmɔː) *n.* **Coventry (Kersey Dighton).** 1823–96, English poet. His works, celebrating both conjugal and divine love, include *The Angel in the House* (1854–62) and *The Unknown Eros* (1877).
Patmos ('pætmɒs) *n.* a Greek island in the Aegean, in the NW Dodecanese: St. John's place of exile (about 95 A.D.), where he wrote the Apocalypse. Pop.: 2534 (1981). Area: 34 sq. km (13 sq. miles).
Patna ('pætnə) *n.* a city in NE India, capital of Bihar state, on the River Ganges: founded in the 5th century B.C.; university (1917); centre of a rice-growing region. Pop.: 773 720 (1981).
Patna rice *n.* a variety of long-grain rice, used for savoury dishes.
patois ('pætwɑː) *n., pl.* **patois** ('pætwɑːz). **1.** a regional dialect of a language, usually considered substandard. **2.** the jargon of a particular group. [C17: from OF: rustic speech, ?from *patoier* to handle awkwardly, from *patte* paw]
Paton ('peɪt³n) *n.* **Alan (Stewart).** 1903–88, South African writer, noted esp. for his novel dealing with the racial problem in South Africa, *Cry, the Beloved Country* (1965).
pat. pend. *abbrev. for* patent pending.
Patras (pə'træs, 'pætrəs) *n.* a port in W Greece, in the NW Peloponnese on the **Gulf of Patras** (an inlet of the Ionian Sea): one of the richest cities in Greece until the 3rd century B.C.; under Turkish rule from 1458 to 1687 and from 1715 until the War of Greek Independence, which began here in 1821. Pop.: 140 878 (1981). Modern Greek name: **Pátrai** ('patre).
patri- *combining form.* father: *patricide; patriarch.* [from L *pater,* Gk *patēr* father]
patrial ('peɪtrɪəl) *n.* (in Britain, formerly) a person having by statute the right of abode in the United Kingdom. [C20: from L *patria* native land]

patriarch ('peɪtrɪ,ɑːk) n. 1. the male head of a tribe or family. 2. a very old or venerable man. 3. *Bible.* a. any of a number of persons regarded as the fathers of the human race. b. any of the three ancestors of the Hebrew people: Abraham, Isaac, or Jacob. c. any of Jacob's twelve sons, regarded as the ancestors of the twelve tribes of Israel. 4. *Early Christian Church.* the bishop of one of several principal sees, esp. those of Rome, Antioch, and Alexandria. 5. *Eastern Orthodox Church.* the bishops of the four ancient principal sees of Constantinople, Antioch, Alexandria, and Jerusalem, and also of Russia, Rumania, and Serbia. 6. *R.C. Church.* a. a title given to the pope. b. a title given to a number of bishops, esp. of the Uniat Churches, indicating their rank as immediately below that of the pope. 7. the oldest or most venerable member of a group, community, etc. 8. a person regarded as the founder of a community, tradition, etc. [C12: via OF from Church L *patriarcha*] —,**patri'archal** *adj.*

patriarchate ('peɪtrɪ,ɑːkɪt) n. the office, jurisdiction, province, or residence of a patriarch.

patriarchy ('peɪtrɪ,ɑːkɪ) n., pl. -chies. 1. a form of social organization in which a male is the head of the family and descent, kinship, and title are traced through the male line. 2. any society governed by such a system.

patrician (pə'trɪʃən) n. 1. a member of the hereditary aristocracy of ancient Rome. 2. (in medieval Europe) a member of the upper class in numerous Italian republics and German free cities. 3. an aristocrat. 4. a person of refined conduct, tastes, etc. ~adj. 5. (esp. in ancient Rome) of, relating to, or composed of patricians. 6. aristocratic. [C15: from OF *patricien*, from L *patricius* noble, from *pater* father]

patricide ('pætrɪ,saɪd) n. 1. the act of killing one's father. 2. a person who kills his father. —,**patri'cidal** *adj.*

Patrick ('pætrɪk) n. Saint. 5th century A.D., British missionary in Ireland; patron saint of Ireland. Feast day: March 17.

patrilineal (,pætrɪ'lɪnɪəl) *adj.* tracing descent, kinship, or title through the male line.

patrimony ('pætrɪmənɪ) n., pl. -nies. 1. an inheritance from one's father or other ancestor. 2. the endowment of a church. [C14 *patrimoyne*, from OF, from L *patrimonium* paternal inheritance] —**patrimonial** (,pætrɪ'məunɪəl) *adj.*

patriot ('peɪtrɪət, 'pæt-) n. a person who vigorously supports his country and its way of life. [C16: via F from LL *patriōta*, from Gk *patriōtēs*, from *patris* native land; rel. to Gk *pater* father; cf. L *pater* father, *patria* fatherland] —**patriotic** (,pætrɪ'ɒtɪk) *adj.* —,**patri'otically** *adv.*

patriotism ('pætrɪə,tɪzəm) n. devotion to one's own country and concern for its defence.

patristic (pə'trɪstɪk) or **patristical** *adj.* of or relating to the Fathers of the Church, their writings, or the study of these. —**pa'tristics** η. (*functioning as sing.*)

Patroclus (pə'trɒkləs) n. *Greek myth.* a friend of Achilles, killed in the Trojan War by Hector. His death made Achilles return to the fight after his quarrel with Agamemnon.

patrol (pə'trəʊl) n. 1. the action of going round a town, etc., at regular intervals for purposes of security or observation. 2. a person or group that carries out such an action. 3. a military detachment with the mission of security or combat with enemy forces. 4. a division of a troop of Scouts or Guides. ~vb. -trolling, -trolled. 5. to engage in a patrol of (a place). [C17: from F *patrouiller*, from *patouiller* to flounder in mud, from *patte* paw] —**pa'troller** n.

patrol car n. a police car used for patrolling streets and motorways.

patrology (pə'trɒlədʒɪ) n. 1. the study of the writings of the Fathers of the Church. 2. a collection of such writings. [C17: from Gk *patr-*, *patēr* father + -LOGY] —**pa'trologist** n.

patrol wagon n. the usual U.S., Austral., and N.Z. term for **Black Maria.**

patron[1] ('peɪtrən) n. 1. a person who sponsors or aids artists, charities, etc.; protector or benefactor. 2. a customer of a shop, hotel, etc., esp. a regular one. 3. See **patron saint.** [C14: via OF from L *patrōnus* protector, from *pater* father] —**'patroness** *fem. n.*

patron[2] (patrɔ̃) n. the owner of a restaurant, hotel. etc., esp. of a French one. [F]

patronage ('pætrənɪdʒ) n. 1. a. the support given or custom brought by a patron. b. the position of a patron. 2.

(in politics) a. the practice of making appointments to office, granting contracts, etc. b. the favours, etc., so distributed. 3. a. a condescending manner. b. any kindness done in a condescending way.

patronize or **-ise** ('pætrə,naɪz) vb. 1. to behave or treat in a condescending way. 2. (tr.) to act as a patron by sponsoring or bringing trade to. —'**patron,izer** or -,**iser** n. —'**patron,izing** or -,**ising** adj. —'**patron,izingly** or -,**isingly** adv.

patron saint n. a saint regarded as the particular guardian of a country, person, etc.

patronymic (,pætrə'nɪmɪk) *adj.* 1. (of a name) derived from the name of its bearer's father or ancestor. ~n. 2. a patronymic name. [C17: via LL from Gk *patronumikos*, from *pater* father + *onoma* NAME]

patroon (pə'truːn) n. U.S. a Dutch land holder in New Netherland and New York with manorial rights in the colonial era. [C18: from Du.: PATRON[1]]

patsy ('pætsɪ) n., pl. -sies. Sl., chiefly U.S. & Canad. a person who is easily cheated, victimized, etc. [C20: from ?]

patten ('pæt³n) n. a wooden clog or sandal on a raised wooden platform or metal ring. [C14: from OF *patin*, prob. from *patte* paw]

patter[1] ('pætə) vb. 1. (intr.) to walk or move with quick soft steps. 2. to strike with or make a quick succession of light tapping sounds. ~n. 3. a quick succession of light tapping sounds, as of feet: *the patter of mice.* [C17: from PAT[1]]

patter[2] ('pætə) n. 1. the glib rapid speech of comedians, etc. 2. quick idle talk; chatter. 3. the jargon of a particular group, etc.; lingo. ~vb. 4. (intr.) to speak glibly and rapidly. 5. to repeat (prayers, etc.) in a mechanical or perfunctory manner. [C14: from L *pater* in *Pater Noster* Our Father]

pattern ('pæt³n) n. 1. an arrangement of repeated or corresponding parts, decorative motifs, etc. 2. a decorative design: *a paisley pattern.* 3. a style: *various patterns of cutlery.* 4. a plan or diagram used as a guide in making something: *a paper pattern for a dress.* 5. a standard way of moving, acting, etc.: *traffic patterns.* 6. a model worthy of imitation: *a pattern of kindness.* 7. a representative sample. 8. a wooden or metal shape or model used in a foundry to make a mould. ~vb. (tr.) 9. (often foll. by *after* or *on*) to model. 10. to arrange as or decorate with a pattern. [C14 *patron*, from Med. L *patrōnus* example, from PATRON[1]]

Patti ('pætɪ) n. **Adelina** (ade'liːna). 1843–1919, Italian operatic coloratura soprano, born in Spain.

Patton ('pæt³n) n. **George Smith.** 1885–1945, U.S. general, who successfully developed tank warfare as an extension of cavalry tactics in World War II: captured Palermo, Sicily (1942) and much of France (1944).

patty ('pætɪ) n., pl. -ties. 1. a small cake of minced food. 2. a small pie. [C18: from F PÂTÉ]

patu ('pɑːtuː) n., pl. **patus.** N.Z. a short Maori club, now ceremonial only. [from Maori]

patulous ('pætjʊləs) *adj. Bot.* spreading widely or expanded: *patulous branches.* [C17: from L *patulus* open, from *patēre* to lie open]

Pau (French po) n. a city in SW France: residence of the French kings of Navarre; tourist centre for the Pyrenees. Pop.: 81 904 (1983 est.).

paua ('pɑːuɑ) n. an edible abalone of New Zealand, having an iridescent shell used for jewellery, etc. [from Maori]

paucity ('pɔːsɪtɪ) n. 1. insufficiency; dearth. 2. smallness of number; fewness. [C15: from L *paucitās* scarcity, from *paucus* few]

Paul (pɔːl) n. 1. Saint. Also called: **Paul the Apostle, Saul of Tarsus.** original name *Saul.* died ?67 A.D., one of the first Christian missionaries to the Gentiles, who died a martyr in Rome. Until his revelatory conversion he had assisted in persecuting the Christians. He wrote many of the Epistles in the New Testament. Feast day: June 29. 2. **Jean.** See **Jean Paul.** 3. **Les,** real name *Lester Polfuss.* born 1915, U.S. guitarist: creator of the solid-body electric guitar and pioneer in multitrack recording.

Paul III n. original name *Alessandro Farnese.* 1468–1549, Italian ecclesiastic; pope (1534–49). He excommunicated Henry VIII of England (1538) and inaugurated the Counter-Reformation by approving the establishment of the Jesuits (1540), instituting the Inquisition in Italy, and convening the Council of Trent (1545).

Paul VI *n.* original name *Giovanni Battista Montini.* 1897–1978, Italian ecclesiastic; pope (1963–1978).

Pauli ('pɔːlɪ, 'paʊlɪ) *n.* **Wolfgang** ('vɒlf,gæŋ). 1900–58, U.S. physicist, born in Austria. He formulated the exclusion principle (1924) and postulated the existence of the neutrino (1931), later confirmed by Fermi: Nobel prize for physics 1945.

Pauli exclusion principle *n. Physics.* the principle that two identical fermions cannot occupy the same quantum state in a body such as an atom; sometimes shortened to **exclusion principle.**

Pauline ('pɔːlaɪn) *adj.* relating to Saint Paul or his doctrines.

Pauling ('pɔːlɪŋ) *n.* **Linus Carl** ('laɪnəs). born 1901, U.S. chemist, noted particularly for his work on the nature of the chemical bond and his opposition to nuclear tests: Nobel prize for chemistry 1954; Nobel peace prize 1962.

Paulinus (pɔː'laɪnəs) *n.* **Saint.** died 644 A.D., Roman missionary to England; first bishop of York and archbishop of Rochester. Feast day: Oct. 10.

Paul Jones *n.* an old-time dance in which partners are exchanged. [C19: named after John Paul JONES]

paulownia (pɔː'ləʊnɪə) *n.* a tree of a Japanese genus, esp. one having large heart-shaped leaves and clusters of purplish or white flowers. [C19: NL, after Anna *Paulovna,* daughter of Paul I of Russia]

Paumotu Archipelago (paʊ'məʊtuː) *n.* another name for the **Tuamotu Archipelago.**

paunch (pɔːntʃ) *n.* **1.** the belly or abdomen, esp. when protruding. **2.** another name for **rumen.** ~*vb.* (*tr.*) **3.** to stab in the stomach; disembowel. [C14: from Anglo-Norman *paunche,* from OF *pance,* from L *panticēs* (pl.) bowels] —'**paunchy** *adj.* —'**paunchiness** *n.*

pauper ('pɔːpə) *n.* **1.** a person who is extremely poor. **2.** (formerly) a person supported by public charity. [C16: from L: poor] —'**pauper,ism** *n.*

pauperize *or* **-ise** ('pɔːpə,raɪz) *vb.* (*tr.*) to make a pauper of; impoverish.

Pausanias (pɔː'seɪnɪəs) *n.* 2nd-century A.D. Greek geographer and historian. His *Description of Greece* gives a valuable account of the topography of ancient Greece.

pause (pɔːz) *vb.* (*intr.*) **1.** to cease an action temporarily. **2.** to hesitate; delay: *she replied without pausing.* ~*n.* **3.** a temporary stop or rest, esp. in speech or action; short break. **4.** *Prosody.* another word for **caesura. 5.** Also called: **fermata.** *Music.* a continuation of a note or rest beyond its normal length. Usual symbol: ⌢ **6. give pause to.** to cause to hesitate. [C15: from L *pausa* pause, from Gk *pausis,* from *pauein* to halt]

pav (pæv) *n. Austral.. & N.Z. inf.* short for **pavlova.**

pavane *or* **pavan** (pə'vɑːn, 'pævᵊn) *n.* **1.** a slow and stately dance of the 16th and 17th centuries. **2.** a piece of music composed for or in the rhythm of this dance. [C16 *pavan,* via F from Sp. *pavana,* from OIt. *padovana* Paduan (dance), from *Padova* Padua]

Pavarotti (*Italian* pava'rɔti) *n.* **Luciano.** born 1935, Italian operatic tenor.

pave (peɪv) *vb.* (*tr.*) **1.** to cover (a road, etc.) with a firm surface suitable for travel, as with paving stones or concrete. **2.** to serve as the material for a pavement or other hard layer: *bricks paved the causeway.* **3.** (often foll. by *with*) to cover with a hard layer (of): *shelves paved with marble.* **4.** to prepare or make easier (esp. in **pave the way**). [C14: from OF *paver,* from L *pavīre* to ram down] —'**paver** *n.*

pavement ('peɪvmənt) *n.* **1.** a hard-surfaced path for pedestrians alongside and a little higher than a road. U.S. and Canad. word: **sidewalk. 2.** the material used in paving. [C13: from L *pavīmentum* hard floor, from *pavīre* to beat hard]

Pavese (*Italian* pa've:se) *n.* **Cesare** ('tʃeːzare). 1908–50, Italian writer and translator. His works include collections of poems, such as *Verrà la morte e avra i tuoi occhi* (1953), short stories, such as the collection *Notte di festa* (1953), and the novel *La Luna e i falò* (1950).

pavilion (pə'vɪljən) *n.* **1.** *Brit.* a building at a sports ground, esp. a cricket pitch, in which players change, etc. **2.** a summerhouse or other decorative shelter. **3.** a building or temporary structure, esp. one that is open and ornamental, for housing exhibitions, etc. **4.** a large ornate tent, esp. one with a peaked top, as used by medieval armies. **5.** one of a set of buildings that together form a hospital or other large institution. ~*vb.* (*tr.*) *Literary.* **6.**

to place as in a pavilion: *pavilioned in splendour.* **7.** to provide with a pavilion or pavilions. [C13: from OF *pavillon* canopied structure, from L *pāpiliō* butterfly, tent]

paving ('peɪvɪŋ) *n.* **1.** a paved surface; pavement. **2.** material used for a pavement.

Pavlodar (*Russian* pəvla'dar) *n.* a port in the S Soviet Union, in the NE Kazakh SSR on the Irtysh River: major industrial centre with an oil refinery. Pop.: 331 000 (1987).

Pavlov ('pævlɒv; *Russian* 'pavləf) *n.* **Ivan Petrovich** (i'van pɪ'trɔvitʃ). 1849–1936, Soviet physiologist. His study of conditioned reflexes in dogs influenced behaviourism. He also made important contributions to the study of digestion: Nobel prize for physiology or medicine 1904. —**Pav'lovian** *adj.*

Pavlova[1] (pæv'ləʊvə) *n.* a meringue cake topped with whipped cream and fruit. [C20: after Anna PAVLOVA]

Pavlova[2] (pæv'ləʊvə; *Russian* 'pavləvə) *n.* **Anna** ('annə). 1885–1931, Russian ballerina.

paw (pɔː) *n.* **1.** any of the feet of a four-legged mammal, bearing claws or nails. **2.** *Inf.* a hand, esp. one that is large, clumsy, etc. ~*vb.* **3.** to scrape or contaminate with the paws or feet. **4.** (*tr.*) *Inf.* to touch or caress in a clumsy, rough, or overfamiliar manner. [C13: via OF from Gmc]

pawky ('pɔːkɪ) *adj.* **pawkier, pawkiest.** *Dialect or Scot.* having a dry wit. [C17: from Scot. *pawk* trick, from ?] —'**pawkily** *adv.* —'**pawkiness** *n.*

pawl (pɔːl) *n.* a pivoted lever shaped to engage with a ratchet wheel to prevent motion in a particular direction. [C17: ?from Du. *pal* pawl]

pawn[1] (pɔːn) *vb.* (*tr.*) **1.** to deposit (an article) as security for the repayment of a loan, esp. from a pawnbroker. **2.** to stake: *to pawn one's honour.* ~*n.* **3.** an article deposited as security. **4.** the condition of being so deposited (esp. in **in pawn**). **5.** a person or thing that is held as a security. **6.** the act of pawning. [C15: from OF *pan* security, from L *pannus* cloth, apparently because clothing was often left as a surety] —'**pawnage** *n.*

pawn[2] (pɔːn) *n.* **1.** a chess man of the lowest theoretical value. **2.** a person, group, etc., manipulated by another. [C14: from Anglo-Norman *poun,* from OF, from Med. L *pedō* infantryman, from L *pēs* foot]

pawnbroker ('pɔːn,brəʊkə) *n.* a dealer licensed to lend money at a specified rate of interest on the security of movable personal property, which can be sold if the loan is not repaid within a specified period. —'**pawn,broking** *n.*

pawnshop ('pɔːn,ʃɒp) *n.* the premises of a pawnbroker.

pawn ticket *n.* a receipt for goods pawned.

pawpaw ('pɔː,pɔː) *n.* another name for **papaw** or **papaya.**

pax (pæks) *n.* **1.** *Chiefly R.C. Church.* **a.** the kiss of peace. **b.** a small metal or ivory plate, formerly used to convey the kiss of peace from the celebrant at Mass to those attending it. ~*interj.* **2.** *Brit. school sl.* a call signalling an end to hostilities or claiming immunity from the rules of a game. [L: peace]

Pax (pæks) *n.* the Roman goddess of peace. Greek counterpart: **Irene.** [L: peace]

PAX (pæks) *abbrev. for* private automatic exchange.

Paxton ('pækstən) *n.* Sir **Joseph.** 1801–65, English architect, who designed Crystal Palace (1851), the first large structure of prefabricated glass and iron parts.

pay[1] (peɪ) *vb.* **paying, paid. 1.** to discharge (a debt, obligation, etc.) by giving or doing something: *he paid his creditors.* **2.** (when *intr.,* often foll. by *for*) to give (money, etc.) to (a person) in return for goods or services: *they pay their workers well; they pay by the hour.* **3.** to give or afford (a person, etc.) a profit or benefit: *it pays one to be honest.* **4.** (*tr.*) to give or bestow (a compliment, regards, attention, etc.). **5.** (*tr.*) to make (a visit or call). **6.** (*intr.;* often foll. by *for*) to give compensation or make amends. **7.** (*tr.*) to yield a return of: *the shares pay 15 per cent.* **8.** *Austral. inf.* to acknowledge or accept (something) as true, just, etc. **9. pay one's way. a.** to contribute one's share of expenses. **b.** to remain solvent without outside help. ~*n.* **10. a.** money given in return for work or services; a salary or wage. **b.** (*as modifier*): *a pay slip; a pay claim.* **11.** paid employment (esp. in **in the pay of**). **12.** (*modifier*) requiring the insertion of money before or during use: *a pay phone.* **13.** (*modifier*) rich enough in minerals to be profitably worked: *pay gravel.* ~See also **pay back, pay for,** etc. [C12: from OF *payer,*

from L *pācāre* to appease (a creditor), from *pāx* peace]
—'**payer** *n.*

pay[2] (peɪ) *vb.* **paying, payed.** (*tr.*) *Naut.* to caulk (the seams of a wooden vessel) with pitch or tar. [C17: from OF *peier*, from L *picāre*, from *pix* pitch]

payable ('peɪəbəl) *adj.* **1.** (often foll. by *on*) to be paid: *payable on the third of each month.* **2.** that is capable of being paid. **3.** capable of being profitable. **4.** (of a debt, etc.) imposing an obligation on the debtor to pay, esp. at once.

pay back *vb.* (*tr., adv.*) **1.** to retaliate against: *to pay someone back for an insult.* **2.** to give or do (something equivalent) in return for a favour, insult, etc. **3.** to repay (a loan, etc.).

pay bed *n.* an informal name for **private pay bed.**

payday ('peɪˌdeɪ) *n.* the day on which wages or salaries are paid.

pay dirt *n. Chiefly U.S.* **1.** soil, gravel, ore, etc. that contains sufficient minerals to make it worthwhile mining. **2.** *Inf.* **hit** (*or* **strike**) **pay dirt.** to become wealthy, successful, etc.

PAYE (in Britain and New Zealand) *abbrev. for* pay as you earn; a system by which income tax levied on wage and salary earners is paid by employers directly to the government.

payee (peɪ'iː) *n.* the person to whom a cheque, money order, etc., is made out.

pay for *vb.* (*prep.*) **1.** to make payment for. **2.** (*intr.*) to suffer or be punished, as for a mistake, wrong decision, etc.

paying guest *n.* a euphemism for **lodger.**

payload ('peɪˌləʊd) *n.* **1.** that part of a cargo earning revenue. **2. a.** the passengers, cargo, or bombs carried by an aircraft. **b.** the equipment carried by a rocket, satellite, or spacecraft. **3.** the explosive power of a warhead, bomb, etc., carried by a missile or aircraft.

paymaster ('peɪˌmɑːstə) *n.* an official of a government, business, etc., responsible for the payment of wages and salaries.

payment ('peɪmənt) *n.* **1.** the act of paying. **2.** a sum of money paid. **3.** something given in return; punishment or reward.

paynim ('peɪnɪm) *n. Arch.* **1.** a heathen or pagan. **2.** a Muslim. [C13: from OF *paienime*, from LL *pāgānismus* paganism, from *pāgānus* PAGAN]

pay off *vb.* **1.** (*tr., adv.*) to pay all that is due in wages, etc., and discharge from employment. **2.** (*tr., adv.*) to pay the complete amount of (a debt, bill, etc.). **3.** (*intr., adv.*) to turn out to be profitable, effective, etc.: *the gamble paid off.* **4.** (*tr., adv. or intr., prep.*) to take revenge on (a person) or for (a wrong done): *to pay someone off for an insult.* **5.** (*tr., adv.*) *Inf.* to give a bribe to. ~*n.* **payoff. 6.** the final settlement, esp. in retribution. **7.** *Inf.* the climax, consequence, or outcome of events, a story, etc. **8.** the final payment of a debt, salary, etc. **9.** the time of such a payment. **10.** *Inf.* a bribe.

payola (peɪ'əʊlə) *n. Inf.* **1.** a bribe given to secure special treatment, esp. to a disc jockey to promote a commercial product. **2.** the practice of paying or receiving such bribes. [C20: from PAY[1] + *-ola*, as in PIANOLA]

pay out *vb.* (*adv.*) **1.** to distribute (money, etc.); disburse. **2.** (*tr.*) to release (a rope) gradually, hand over hand.

payphone ('peɪˌfəʊn) *n.* a coin-operated telephone.

payroll ('peɪˌrəʊl) *n.* **1.** a list of employees, specifying the salary or wage of each. **2.** the total of these amounts or the actual money equivalent.

Paysandú (*Spanish* paisan'du) *n.* a port in W Uruguay, on the Uruguay River: the third largest city in the country. Pop.: 75 200 (1985).

Pays de la Loire (*French* pei də la lwar) *n.* a region of W France, on the Bay of Biscay: generally low-lying, drained by the River Loire and its tributaries; agricultural.

payt *abbrev. for* payment.

pay up *vb.* (*adv.*) to pay (money) promptly, in full, or on demand.

Pb *the chemical symbol for* lead. [from NL *plumbum*]

PB *Athletics. abbrev. for* personal best.

PBX (in Britain) *abbrev. for* private branch exchange; a telephone system that handles the internal and external calls of a building, firm, etc.

pc *abbrev. for* **1.** per cent. **2.** personal computer. **3.** postcard. **4.** (in prescriptions) post cibum. [L: after meals]

PC *abbrev. for* **1.** Parish Council(lor). **2.** (in Britain) Police Constable. **3.** (in Britain) Privy Council(lor). **4.** (in Canada) Progressive Conservative.

pc. *abbrev. for* **1.** (*pl.* **pcs.**) piece. **2.** price.

PCB *abbrev. for* polychlorinated biphenyl; any of a group of compounds in which chlorine atoms replace the hydrogen atoms in biphenyl: used in electrical insulators and in the manufacture of plastics; a toxic pollutant.

PCP *n. Trademark.* phencyclidine; a depressant drug used illegally as a hallucinogen.

pd *abbrev. for* **1.** paid. **2.** Also: **PD.** per diem. **3.** potential difference.

Pd *the chemical symbol for* palladium.

PDSA (in Britain) *abbrev. for* People's Dispensary for Sick Animals.

PDT (in the U.S. and Canada) *abbrev. for* Pacific Daylight Time.

PE *abbrev. for* **1.** physical education. **2.** potential energy. **3.** Presiding Elder. **4.** Also: **p.e.** printer's error. **5.** *Statistics.* probable error. **6.** Protestant Episcopal.

pea (piː) *n.* **1.** an annual climbing plant with small white flowers and long green pods containing edible green seeds: cultivated in temperate regions. **2.** the seed of this plant, eaten as a vegetable. **3.** any of several other leguminous plants, such as the sweet pea. [C17: from PEASE (incorrectly assumed to be a pl.)]

Peabody ('piːˌbɒdɪ) *n.* **George.** 1795–1869, U.S. merchant, banker, and philanthropist in the U.S. and England.

peace (piːs) *n.* **1. a.** the state existing during the absence of war. **b.** (*as modifier*): *peace negotiations.* **2.** (*often cap.*) a treaty marking the end of a war. **3.** a state of harmony between people or groups. **4.** law and order within a state: *a breach of the peace.* **5.** absence of mental anxiety (often in **peace of mind**). **6.** a state of stillness, silence, or serenity. **7. at peace. a.** in a state of harmony or friendship. **b.** in a state of serenity. **c.** dead: *the old lady is at peace now.* **8. hold** *or* **keep one's peace.** to keep silent. **9. keep the peace.** to maintain law and order. ~*vb.* **10.** (*intr.*) *Obs. except as an imperative.* to be or become silent or still. ~*modifier.* **11.** denoting a person or thing symbolizing support for international peace: *peace women.* [C12: from OF *pais*, from L *pāx*]

peaceable ('piːsəbəl) *adj.* **1.** inclined towards peace. **2.** tranquil; calm. —'**peaceableness** *n.* —'**peaceably** *adv.*

Peace Corps *n.* an agency of the U.S. government that sends volunteers to developing countries to work on educational projects, etc.

peaceful ('piːsfʊl) *adj.* **1.** not in a state of war or disagreement. **2.** calm; tranquil. **3.** of, relating to, or in accord with a time of peace. **4.** inclined towards peace. —'**peacefully** *adv.* —'**peacefulness** *n.*

peacekeeping ('piːsˌkiːpɪŋ) *n.* **a.** the maintenance of peace, esp. the prevention of further fighting between hostile forces. **b.** (*as modifier*): *a UN peacekeeping force.*

peacemaker ('piːsˌmeɪkə) *n.* a person who establishes peace, esp. between others. —'**peace,making** *n.*

peace offering *n.* **1.** something given to an adversary in the hope of procuring or maintaining peace. **2.** *Judaism.* a sacrificial meal shared between the offerer and Jehovah.

peace pipe *n.* a long decorated pipe smoked by North American Indians, esp. as a token of peace. Also called: **calumet.**

Peace River *n.* a river in W Canada, rising in British Columbia as the Finlay River and flowing northeast into the Slave River. Length: 1715 km (1065 miles).

peace sign *n.* a gesture made with the palm of the hand outwards and the index and middle fingers raised in a V.

peacetime ('piːsˌtaɪm) *n.* **a.** a period without war; time of peace. **b.** (*as modifier*): *a peacetime agreement.*

peach[1] (piːtʃ) *n.* **1.** a small tree with pink flowers and rounded edible fruit: cultivated in temperate regions. **2.** the soft juicy fruit of this tree, which has a downy reddish-yellow skin, yellowish-orange sweet flesh, and a single stone. **3. a.** a pinkish-yellow to orange colour. **b.** (*as adj.*): *a peach dress.* **4.** *Inf.* a person or thing that is especially pleasing. [C14 *peche*, from OF, from Med. L *persica*, from L *Persicum mālum* Persian apple]

peach[2] (piːtʃ) *vb.* (*intr.*) *Sl.* to inform against an accomplice. [C15: var. of earlier *apeche*, from F, from LL *impedicāre* to entangle; see IMPEACH]

peach brandy *n.* (esp. in S. Africa) a coarse brandy made from fermented peaches.

peach melba *n.* a dessert made of halved peaches, vanilla ice cream, and raspberries.

peachy ('pi:tʃɪ) *adj.* **peachier, peachiest. 1.** of or like a peach, esp. in colour or texture. **2.** *Inf.* excellent; fine. — **'peachiness** *n.*

peacock ('pi:,kɒk) *n.*, *pl.* **-cocks** *or* **-cock. 1.** a male peafowl, having a crested head and a very large fanlike tail marked with blue and green eyelike spots. **2.** another name for **peafowl. 3.** a vain strutting person. ~*vb.* **4.** to display (oneself) proudly. [C14 *pecok, pe-* from OE *pāwa* (from L *pāvō* peacock) + COCK[1]] — **'pea,cockish** *adj.* — **'pea,hen** *fem. n.*

Peacock ('pi:,kɒk) *n.* **Thomas Love.** 1785–1866, English novelist and poet, noted for his satirical romances, including *Headlong Hall* (1816) and *Nightmare Abbey* (1818).

peacock blue *n.* **a.** a greenish-blue colour. **b.** (*as adj.*): *a peacock-blue car.*

peafowl ('pi:,faʊl) *n.*, *pl.* **-fowls** *or* **-fowl.** either of two large pheasants of India and Ceylon and of SE Asia. The males (see **peacock** (sense 1)) have a characteristic bright plumage.

pea green *n.* **a.** a yellowish-green colour. **b.** (*as adj.*): *a pea-green teapot.*

pea jacket *or* **peacoat** ('pi:,kəʊt) *n.* a sailor's short heavy woollen overcoat. [C18: from Du. *pijjekker*, from *pij* coat of coarse cloth + *jekker* jacket]

peak[1] (pi:k) *n.* **1.** a pointed end, edge, or projection: *the peak of a roof.* **2.** the pointed summit of a mountain. **3.** a mountain with a pointed summit. **4.** the point of greatest development, strength, etc.: *the peak of his career.* **5. a.** a sharp increase followed by a sharp decrease: *a voltage peak.* **b.** the maximum value of this quantity. **c.** (*as modifier*): *peak voltage.* **6.** Also called: **visor.** a projecting piece on the front of some caps. **7.** *Naut.* **a.** the extreme forward (**forepeak**) or aft (**afterpeak**) part of the hull. **b.** (of a fore-and-aft quadrilateral sail) the after uppermost corner. **c.** the after end of a gaff. ~*vb.* **8.** to form or reach or cause to form or reach a peak. **9.** (*tr.*) *Naut.* to set (a gaff) or tilt (oars) vertically. ~*adj.* **10.** of or relating to a period of greatest use or demand: *peak viewing hours.* [C16: ?from PIKE[2], infl. by BEAK[1]]

peak[2] (pi:k) *vb.* (*intr.*) to become wan, emaciated, or sickly. [C16: from ?] — **'peaky** *or* **'peakish** *adj.*

Peak District *n.* a region of N central England, in N Derbyshire at the S end of the Pennines: consists of moors in the north and a central limestone plateau; many caves. Highest point: 727 m (2088 ft.).

Peake (pi:k) *n.* **Mervyn.** 1911–68, English novelist, poet, and illustrator. In his trilogy *Gormenghast* (1946–59), he creates, with vivid imagination, a grotesque Gothic world.

peaked (pi:kt) *adj.* having a peak; pointed.

peak load *n.* the maximum load on an electrical power-supply system.

peal (pi:l) *n.* **1.** a loud prolonged usually reverberating sound, as of bells, thunder, or laughter. **2.** *Bell-ringing.* a series of changes rung in accordance with specific rules. **3.** (*not in technical usage*) the set of bells in a belfry. ~*vb.* **4.** (*intr.*) to sound with a peal or peals. **5.** (*tr.*) to give forth loudly and sonorously. **6.** (*tr.*) to ring (bells) in peals. [C14 *pele*, var. of *apele* APPEAL]

peanut ('pi:,nʌt) *n.* **a.** a leguminous plant widely cultivated for its edible seeds. **b.** the edible nutlike seed of this plant, used for food and as a source of oil. Also called: **groundnut, monkey nut.** ~See also **peanuts.**

peanut butter *n.* a brownish oily paste made from peanuts.

peanuts ('pi:,nʌts) *n.* *Sl.* a trifling amount of money.

pear (pɛə) *n.* **1.** a widely cultivated tree, having white flowers and edible fruits. **2.** the sweet gritty-textured juicy fruit of this tree, which has a globular base and tapers towards the apex. **3.** the wood of this tree, used for making furniture. [OE *pere*, ult. from L *pirum*]

pearl[1] (pɜːl) *n.* **1.** a hard smooth lustrous typically rounded structure occurring on the inner surface of the shell of a clam or oyster around an invading particle such as a sand grain; much valued as a gem. **2.** any artificial gem resembling this. **3.** See **mother-of-pearl. 4.** a person or thing that is like a pearl, esp. in beauty or value. **5.** a pale greyish-white colour, often with a bluish tinge. ~*adj.* **6.** of, made of, or set with pearl or mother-of-pearl. **7.** having the shape or colour of a pearl. ~*vb.* **8.** (*tr.*) to set with or as if with pearls. **9.** to shape into or assume a pearl-like form or colour. **10.** (*intr.*) to dive or search for

pearls. [C14: from OF, from Vulgar L *pernula* (unattested), from L *perna* sea mussel]

pearl[2] (pɜːl) *n.*, *vb.* a variant spelling of **purl**[1](senses 2, 3, 5).

pearl ash *n.* the granular crystalline form of potassium carbonate.

pearl barley *n.* barley ground into small round grains, used esp. in soups and stews.

Pearl Harbor *n.* an almost landlocked inlet of the Pacific on the S coast of the island of Oahu, Hawaii: site of a U.S. naval base attacked by the Japanese in 1941, resulting in the U.S. entry into World War II.

Pearl River *n.* **1.** a river in central Mississippi, flowing southwest and south to the Gulf of Mexico. Length: 789 km (490 miles). **2.** the English name for the **Zhu Jiang.**

pearly ('pɜːlɪ) *adj.* **pearlier, pearliest. 1.** resembling a pearl, esp. in lustre. **2.** decorated with pearls or mother-of-pearl. ~*n.*, *pl.* **pearlies.** *Brit.* **3.** a London costermonger or his wife who wear on ceremonial occasions a traditional dress of dark clothes covered with pearl buttons. **4.** (*pl.*) the clothes or the buttons themselves. — **'pearliness** *n.*

Pearly Gates *pl. n.* *Inf.* the entrance to heaven.

pearly king *or* (*fem.*) **pearly queen** *n.* the London costermonger whose ceremonial clothes display the most lavish collection of pearl buttons.

pearly nautilus *n.* any of several cephalopod molluscs of warm and tropical seas, having a partitioned pale pearly external shell with brown stripes. Also called: **chambered nautilus.**

pearmain ('pɛə,meɪn) *n.* any of several varieties of apple having a red skin. [C15: from OF *permain* a type of pear, ?from L *Parmēnsis* of Parma]

Pears (pɪəz) *n.* Sir **Peter.** 1910–86, English operatic tenor.

peart (pɪət) *adj.* *Dialect.* lively; spirited; brisk. [C15: var. of PERT] — **'peartly** *adv.*

Peary ('pɪərɪ) *n.* **Robert Edwin.** 1856–1920, U.S. arctic explorer, generally regarded as the first man to reach the North Pole (1909).

peasant ('pɛzᵊnt) *n.* **1.** a member of a class of low social status that depends on either cottage industry or agricultural labour as a means of subsistence. **2.** *Inf.* a person who lives in the country; rustic. **3.** *Inf.* an uncouth or uncultured person. [C15: from Anglo-F, from OF *paisant*, from *pais* country, from L *pāgus* rural area]

peasantry ('pɛzᵊntrɪ) *n.* peasants as a class.

pease (pi:z) *n.*, *pl.* **pease.** *Arch.* or *dialect.* another word for **pea.** [OE *peose*, via LL from L *pisa* peas, pl. of *pisum*, from Gk *pison*]

peasecod *or* **peascod** ('pi:z,kɒd) *n.* *Arch.* the pod of a pea plant. [C14: from PEASE + COD[2]]

pease pudding *n.* (esp. in Britain) a dish of split peas that have been soaked and boiled.

peashooter ('pi:,ʃu:tə) *n.* a tube through which dried peas are blown, used as a toy weapon.

peasouper (,pi:'su:pə) *n.* **1.** *Inf.*, *chiefly Brit.* dense dirty yellowish fog. **2.** *Canad.* a disparaging name for a **French Canadian.**

peat (pi:t) *n.* **a.** a compact brownish deposit of partially decomposed vegetable matter saturated with water: found in uplands and bogs and used as a fuel (when dried) and as a fertilizer. **b.** (*as modifier*): *peat bog.* [C14: from Anglo-L *peta*, ?from Celtic] — **'peaty** *adj.*

peat moss *n.* any of various mosses, esp. sphagnum, that grow in wet places and decay to form peat. See also **sphagnum.**

pebble ('pɛbᵊl) *n.* **1.** a small smooth rounded stone, esp. one worn by the action of water. **2. a.** a transparent colourless variety of rock crystal, used for making certain lenses. **b.** such a lens. **3.** (*modifier*) *Inf.* (of a lens or of spectacles) thick, with a high degree of magnification or distortion. **4. a.** a grainy irregular surface, esp. on leather. **b.** leather having such a surface. ~*vb.* (*tr.*) **5.** to cover with pebbles. **6.** to impart a grainy surface to (leather). [OE *papolstān*, from *papol-* (? imit.) + *stān* stone] — **'pebbly** *adj.*

pebble dash *n.* *Brit.* a finish for external walls consisting of small stones embedded in plaster.

pecan (pɪ'kæn, 'pi:kən) *n.* **1.** a hickory tree of the southern U.S. having deeply furrowed bark and edible nuts. **2.** the smooth oval nut of this tree, which has a sweet oily kernel. [C18: from Algonquian *paccan*]

peccable ('pɛkəbᵊl) *adj.* liable to sin. [C17: via F from Med. L *peccābilis*, from L *peccāre* to sin]

peccadillo (,pɛkə'dɪləʊ) *n.*, *pl.* **-los** *or* **-loes.** a petty sin or fault. [C16: from Sp., from *pecado* sin, from L *peccātum*, from *peccāre* to transgress]

peccant ('pɛkənt) *adj. Rare.* **1.** guilty of an offence; corrupt. **2.** violating or disregarding a rule; faulty. **3.** producing disease; morbid. [C17: from L *peccans*, from *peccāre* to sin] —**'peccancy** *n.*

peccary ('pɛkərɪ) *n.*, *pl.* **-ries** *or* **-ry.** either of two piglike mammals of forests of southern North America, Central and South America. [C17: from Carib]

Pechora (*Russian* pɪ'tʃɔrə) *n.* a river in the NW Soviet Union, rising in the Ural Mountains and flowing north in a great arc to the **Pechora Sea** (the SE part of the Barents Sea). Length: 1814 km (1127 miles).

peck¹ (pɛk) *n.* **1.** a unit of dry measure equal to 8 quarts or one quarter of a bushel. **2.** a container used for measuring this quantity. **3.** a large quantity or number. [C13: from Anglo-Norman, from ?]

peck² (pɛk) *vb.* **1.** (when *intr.*, sometimes foll. by *at*) to strike with the beak or with a pointed instrument. **2.** (*tr.*; sometimes foll. by *out*) to dig (a hole, etc.) by pecking. **3.** (*tr.*) (of birds) to pick up (corn, worms, etc.) by pecking. **4.** (*intr.*; often foll. by *at*) to nibble or pick (at one's food). **5.** *Inf.* to kiss (a person) quickly and lightly. **6.** (*intr.*) foll. by *at*) to nag. ~*n.* **7.** a quick light blow, esp. from a bird's beak. **8.** a mark made by such a blow. **9.** *Inf.* a quick light kiss. [C14: from ?]

pecker ('pɛkə) *n. Brit. sl.* spirits (esp. in **keep one's pecker up**).

pecking order *n.* **1.** Also called: **peck order.** a natural hierarchy in a group of gregarious birds, such as domestic fowl. **2.** any hierarchical order, as among people in a particular group.

Peckinpah ('pɛkɪn,pɑː) *n.* **Sam(uel David).** 1926–84, U.S. film director, esp. of Westerns, such as *The Wild Bunch* (1969). Among his other films are *Straw Dogs* (1971), *Bring me the Head of Alfredo Garcia* (1974), and *Cross of Iron* (1977).

peckish ('pɛkɪʃ) *adj. Inf., chiefly Brit.* feeling slightly hungry. [C18: from PECK²]

Pecos ('peɪkəs; *Spanish* 'pekɔs) *n.* a river in the southwestern U.S., rising in N central New Mexico and flowing southeast to the Rio Grande. Length: about 1180 km (735 miles).

Pécs (*Hungarian* peːtʃ) *n.* an industrial city in SW Hungary: university (1367). Pop.: 179 000 (1985).

pecten ('pɛktɪn) *n.*, *pl.* **-tens** *or* **-tines** (-tɪ,niːz). **1.** a comblike structure in the eye of birds and reptiles, consisting of a network of blood vessels projecting inwards from the retina. **2.** any other comblike part or organ. [C18: from L: a comb, from *pectere* to comb]

pectin ('pɛktɪn) *n. Biochem.* any of the acidic polysaccharides that occur in ripe fruit and vegetables: used in the manufacture of jams because of their ability to solidify to a gel. [C19: from Gk *pēktos* congealed, from *pegnuein* to set] —**'pectic** *or* **'pectinous** *adj.*

pectoral ('pɛktərəl) *adj.* **1.** of or relating to the chest, breast, or thorax: *pectoral fins*. **2.** worn on the breast or chest: *a pectoral medallion*. ~*n.* **3.** a pectoral organ or part, esp. a muscle or fin. **4.** a medicine for disorders of the chest or lungs. **5.** anything worn on the chest or breast for decoration or protection. [C15: from L *pectorālis*, from *pectus* breast] —**'pectorally** *adv.*

pectoral fin *n.* either of a pair of fins, situated just behind the head in fishes, that help to control the direction of movement during locomotion.

pectoral muscle *n.* either of two large chest muscles (**pectoralis major** and **pectoralis minor**), that assist in movements of the shoulder and upper arm.

peculate ('pɛkjʊ,leɪt) *vb.* to appropriate or embezzle (public money, etc.). [C18: from L *peculārī*, from *peculium* private property (orig., cattle); see PECULIAR] —**,pecu'lation** *n.* —**'pecu,lator** *n.*

peculiar (pɪ'kjuːlɪə) *adj.* **1.** strange or unusual; odd: *a peculiar idea*. **2.** distinct from others; special. **3.** (*postpositive*; foll. by *to*) belonging characteristically or exclusively (to): *peculiar to North America.* [C15: from L *peculiāris* concerning private property, from *peculium*, lit.: property in cattle, from *pecus* cattle] —**pe'culiarly** *adv.*

peculiarity (pɪ,kjuːlɪ'ærɪtɪ) *n.*, *pl.* **-ties.** **1.** a strange or unusual habit or characteristic. **2.** a distinguishing trait, etc., that is characteristic of a particular person; idiosyncrasy. **3.** the state or quality of being peculiar.

pecuniary (pɪ'kjuːnɪərɪ) *adj.* **1.** of or relating to money. **2.** *Law.* (of an offence) involving a monetary penalty. [C16: from L *pecūniāris*, from *pecūnia* money] —**pe'cuniarily** *adv.*

pecuniary advantage *n. Law.* financial advantage that is dishonestly obtained by deception and that constitutes a criminal offence.

-ped *or* **-pede** *n. combining form.* foot or feet: *quadruped; centipede.* [from L *pēs, ped-* foot]

pedagogue *or U.S.* (*sometimes*) **pedagog** ('pɛdə,gɒg) *n.* **1.** a teacher or educator. **2.** a pedantic or dogmatic teacher. [C14: from L *paedagōgus*, from Gk *paidagōgos* slave who looked after his master's son, from *pais* boy + *agōgos* leader] —**,peda'gogic** *or* **,peda'gogical** *adj.* —**,peda'gogically** *adv.*

pedagogy ('pɛdə,gɒgɪ, -,gɒdʒɪ, -,gəʊdʒɪ) *n.* the principles, practice, or profession of teaching.

pedal¹ ('pɛdᵊl) *n.* **1. a.** any foot-operated lever, esp. one of the two levers that drive the chainwheel of a bicycle, the foot brake, clutch control, or accelerator of a car, one of the levers on an organ controlling deep bass notes, or one of the levers on a piano used to mute or sustain tone. **b.** (*as modifier*): *a pedal cycle.* ~*vb.* **-alling, -alled** *or U.S.* **-aling, -aled. 2.** to propel (a bicycle, etc.) by operating the pedals. **3.** (*intr.*) to operate the pedals of an organ, piano, etc. **4.** to work (pedals of any kind). [C17: from L *pedālis*; see PEDAL²]

pedal² ('piːdᵊl) *adj.* of or relating to the foot or feet. [C17: from L *pedālis*, from *pēs* foot]

pedal point ('pɛdᵊl) *n. Music.* a sustained bass note, over which the other parts move bringing changing harmonies. Often shortened to **pedal.**

pedant ('pɛdᵊnt) *n.* **1.** a person who relies too much on academic learning or who is concerned chiefly with insignificant detail. **2.** *Arch.* a schoolmaster or teacher. [C16: via OF from It. *pedante* teacher] —**pedantic** (pɪ'dæntɪk) *adj.* —**pe'dantically** *adv.*

pedantry ('pɛdᵊntrɪ) *n.*, *pl.* **-ries.** the habit or an instance of being a pedant, esp. in the display of useless knowledge or minute observance of petty rules or details.

pedate ('pɛdeɪt) *adj.* **1.** (of a plant leaf) deeply divided into several lobes. **2.** *Zool.* having or resembling a foot: *a pedate appendage.* [C18: from L *pedātus* equipped with feet, from *pēs* foot]

peddle ('pɛdᵊl) *vb.* **1.** to go from place to place selling (goods, esp. small articles). **2.** (*tr.*) to sell (illegal drugs, esp. narcotics). **3.** (*tr.*) to advocate (ideas, etc.) persistently: *to peddle a new philosophy.* [C16: back formation from PEDLAR]

peddler ('pɛdlə) *n.* **1.** a person who sells illegal drugs, esp. narcotics. **2.** the usual U.S. spelling of **pedlar.**

pederasty *or* **paederasty** ('pɛdə,ræstɪ) *n.* homosexual relations between men and boys. [C17: from NL *paederastia*, from Gk, from *pais* boy + *erastēs* lover, from *eran* to love] —**peder,ast** *or* **paeder,ast** *n.* —**,peder'astic** *or* **,paeder'astic** *adj.*

pedestal ('pɛdɪstᵊl) *n.* **1.** a base that supports a column, statue, etc. **2.** a position of eminence or supposed superiority (esp. in **place, put,** *or* **set on a pedestal**). [C16: from F *piédestal*, from OIt. *piedestallo*, from *pie* foot + *di* of + *stallo* a stall]

pedestrian (pɪ'dɛstrɪən) *n.* **1. a.** a person travelling on foot; walker. **b.** (*as modifier*): *a pedestrian precinct.* ~*adj.* **2.** dull; commonplace: *a pedestrian style of writing.* [C18: from L *pedester*, from *pēs* foot]

pedestrian crossing *n. Brit.* a path across a road marked as a crossing for pedestrians.

pedestrianize *or* **-ise** (pɪ'dɛstrɪə,naɪz) *vb.* (*tr.*) to convert (a street, etc.) into an area for the use of pedestrians only. —**pe,destriani'zation** *or* **-i'sation** *n.*

pedi- *combining form.* indicating the foot: *pedicure.* [from L *pēs, ped-* foot]

pedicab ('pɛdɪ,kæb) *n.* a pedal-operated tricycle, available for hire in some Asian countries, with an attached seat for one or two passengers.

pedicel ('pɛdɪ,sɛl) *n.* **1.** the stalk bearing a single flower of an inflorescence. **2.** Also called: **peduncle.** *Biol.* any short stalk bearing an organ or organism. ~Also called:

pedicle. [C17: from NL *pedicellus*, from L *pedĭculus*, from *pēs* foot]

pediculosis (pɪ,dɪkjʊ'ləʊsɪs) *n. Pathol.* the state of being infested with lice. [C19: via NL from L *pedĭculus* louse] —**pediculous** (pɪ'dɪkjʊləs) *adj.*

pedicure ('pɛdɪ,kjʊə) *n.* treatment of the feet, either by a medical expert or a cosmetician. [C19: via F from L *pēs* foot + *curāre* to care for]

pedigree ('pɛdɪ,griː) *n.* **1. a.** the line of descent of a pure-bred animal. **b.** (*as modifier*): *a pedigree bull.* **2.** a document recording this. **3.** a genealogical table, esp. one indicating pure ancestry. [C15: from OF *pie de grue* crane's foot, alluding to the spreading lines used in a genealogical chart] —**'pedi,greed** *adj.*

pediment ('pɛdɪmənt) *n.* a low-pitched gable, esp. one that is triangular as used in classical architecture. [C16: from obs. *periment*, ? workman's corruption of PYRAMID] —**pedi'mental** *adj.*

pedipalp ('pɛdɪ,pælp) *n.* either member of the second pair of head appendages of arachnids: specialized for feeding, locomotion, etc. [C19: from NL *pedipalpi*, from L *pēs* foot + *palpus* palp]

pedlar *or esp. U.S.* **peddler** ('pɛdlə) *n.* a person who peddles; hawker. [C14: changed from *peder*, from *ped*, *pedde* basket, from ?]

pedo- *or before a vowel* **ped-** a variant (esp. U.S.) of **paedo-**.

pedology (pɪ'dɒlədʒɪ) *n.* the study of soils. [C20: from Gk *pedon* ground, earth + -OLOGY]

pedometer (pɪ'dɒmɪtə) *n.* a device that records the number of steps taken in walking and hence the distance travelled.

peduncle (pɪ'dʌŋkªl) *n.* **1.** the stalk of a plant bearing an inflorescence or solitary flower. **2.** *Anat., pathol.* any stalklike structure. **3.** *Biol.* another name for **pedicel** (sense 2). [C18: from NL *pedunculus*, from L *pedĭculus* little foot] —**peduncular** (pɪ'dʌŋkjʊlə) *or* **pedunculate** (pɪ'dʌŋkjʊlɪt, -,leɪt) *adj.*

pee (piː) *Inf.* ~*vb.* **peeing, peed. 1.** (*intr.*) to urinate. ~*n.* **2.** urine. **3.** the act of urinating. [C18: euphemistic for PISS, based on the initial letter]

Peebles ('piːbªlz) *n.* a town in SE Scotland, in Borders region. Pop.: 6705 (1981).

Peeblesshire ('piːbªlz,ʃɪə, -ʃə) *n.* (until 1975) a county of SE Scotland, now part of the Borders region. Also called: **Tweeddale.**

peek (piːk) *vb.* **1.** (*intr.*) to glance quickly or furtively. ~*n.* **2.** such a glance. [C14 *pike*, rel. to M Du *kiken* to peek]

peekaboo ('piːkə,buː) *n.* **1.** a game for young children, in which one person hides his face and suddenly reveals it and cries "peekaboo". ~*adj.* **2.** (of a garment) made of fabric that is sheer or patterned with small holes. [C16: from PEEK + BOO]

peel[1] (piːl) *vb.* **1.** (*tr.*) to remove (the skin, rind, etc.) of (a fruit, egg, etc.). **2.** (*intr.*) (of paint, etc.) to be removed from a surface, esp. by weathering. **3.** (*intr.*) (of a surface) to lose its outer covering of paint, etc., esp. by weathering. **4.** (*intr.*) (of a person or part of the body) to shed skin in flakes or (of skin) to be shed in flakes, esp. as a result of sunburn. ~*n.* **5.** the skin or rind of a fruit, etc. ~See also **peel off.** [OE *pilian* to strip off the outer layer, from L *pilāre* to make bald, from *pilus* a hair] —**'peeler** *n.*

peel[2] (piːl) *n.* a long-handled shovel used by bakers for moving bread in an oven. [C14 *pele*, from OF, from L *pāla* spade, from *pangere* to drive in]

peel[3] (piːl) *n. Brit.* a fortified tower of the 16th century on the borders of Scotland. [C14 (fence made of stakes): from OF *piel* stake, from L *pālus*]

Peel (piːl) *n.* Sir **Robert.** 1788–1850, British statesman; Conservative prime minister (1834–35; 1841–46). As Home Secretary (1828–30) he founded the Metropolitan Police and in his second ministry carried through a series of free-trade budgets culminating in the repeal of the Corn Laws (1846), which split the Tory party. —**'Peelite** *n.*

Peele (piːl) *n.* **George.** ?1556–?96, English dramatist and poet. His works include the pastoral drama *The Arraignment of Paris* (1584) and the comedy *The Old Wives' Tale* (1595).

peeler ('piːlə) *n. Irish & obs. Brit. sl.* another word for **policeman.** [C19: from the founder of the police force, Sir Robert PEEL]

peeling ('piːlɪŋ) *n.* a strip of skin, rind, bark, etc., that has been peeled off: *a potato peeling.*

peel off *vb.* (*adv.*) **1.** to remove or be removed by peeling. **2.** (*intr.*) *Sl.* to undress. **3.** (*intr.*) (of an aircraft) to turn away as by banking, and leave a formation.

peen (piːn) *n.* **1.** the end of a hammer head opposite the striking face, often rounded or wedge-shaped. ~*vb.* **2.** (*tr.*) to strike with the peen of a hammer or a stream of metal shot. [C17: var. of *pane*, ?from F *panne*, ult. from L *pinna* point]

peep[1] (piːp) *vb.* (*intr.*) **1.** to look furtively or secretly, as through a small aperture or from a hidden place. **2.** to appear partially or briefly: *the sun peeped through the clouds.* ~*n.* **3.** a quick or furtive look. **4.** the first appearance: *the peep of dawn.* [C15: var. of PEEK]

peep[2] (piːp) *vb.* (*intr.*) **1.** (esp. of young birds) to utter shrill small noises. **2.** to speak in a weak voice. ~*n.* **3.** a peeping sound. [C15: imit.]

peeper ('piːpə) *n.* **1.** a person who peeps. **2.** (*often pl.*) a slang word for **eye**[1] (sense 1).

peephole ('piːp,həʊl) *n.* a small aperture, as in a door for observing callers before opening.

Peeping Tom *n.* a man who furtively observes women undressing; voyeur. [C19: after the tailor who, according to legend, peeped at Lady Godiva when she rode naked through Coventry]

peepshow ('piːp,ʃəʊ) *n.* a box with a peephole through which a series of pictures can be seen.

peepul ('piːpªl) *or* **pipal** *n.* an Indian tree resembling the banyan: regarded as sacred by Buddhists. Also called: **bo tree.** [C18: from Hindi *pīpal*, from Sansk. *pippala*]

peer[1] (pɪə) *n.* **1.** a member of a nobility; nobleman. **2.** a person who holds any of the five grades of the British nobility: duke, marquess, earl, viscount, and baron. See also **life peer. 3.** a person who is an equal in social standing, rank, age, etc.: *to be tried by one's peers.* [C14 (in sense 3): from OF *per*, from L *pār* equal]

peer[2] (pɪə) *vb.* (*intr.*) **1.** to look intently with or as if with difficulty: *to peer into the distance.* **2.** to appear partially or dimly: *the sun peered through the fog.* [C16: from Flemish *pieren* to look with narrowed eyes]

peerage ('pɪərɪdʒ) *n.* **1.** the whole body of peers; aristocracy. **2.** the position, rank, or title of a peer. **3.** (esp. in the British Isles) a book listing the peers and giving their genealogy.

peeress ('pɪərɪs) *n.* **1.** the wife or widow of a peer. **2.** a woman holding the rank of a peer in her own right.

peer group *n.* a social group composed of individuals of approximately the same age.

peerless ('pɪəlɪs) *adj.* having no equals; matchless.

peeve (piːv) *Inf.* ~*vb.* **1.** (*tr.*) to irritate; vex; annoy. ~*n.* **2.** something that irritates; vexation. [C20: back formation from PEEVISH] —**peeved** *adj.*

peevish ('piːvɪʃ) *adj.* fretful or irritable. [C14: from ?] —**'peevishly** *adv.* —**'peevishness** *n.*

peewee ('piːwiː) *n.* a small black-and-white Australian bird with long thin legs. [imit.]

peewit *or* **pewit** ('piːwɪt) *n.* another name for **lapwing.** [C16: imit. of its call]

peg (pɛg) *n.* **1.** a small cylindrical pin or dowel used to join two parts together. **2.** a pin pushed or driven into a surface: used to mark scores, define limits, support coats, etc. **3.** any of several pins on a violin, etc., which can be turned so as to tune strings wound around them. **4.** Also called: **clothes peg.** *Brit.* a split or hinged pin for fastening wet clothes to a line to dry. U.S. and Canad. equivalent: **clothespin. 5.** *Brit.* a small drink of wine or spirits. **6.** an opportunity or pretext for doing something: *a peg on which to hang a theory.* **7.** *Inf.* a level of self-esteem, importance, etc. (esp. in **bring** *or* **take down a peg). 8.** *Inf.* See **peg leg. 9. off the peg.** *Chiefly Brit.* (of clothes) ready-to-wear, as opposed to tailor-made. ~*vb.* **pegging, pegged. 10.** (*tr.*) to knock or insert a peg into. **11.** (*tr.*) to secure with pegs: *to peg a tent.* **12.** (*tr.*) to mark (a score) with pegs, as in some card games. **13.** (*tr.*) *Inf.* to throw (stones, etc.) at a target. **14.** (*intr.*; foll. by *away, along,* etc.) *Chiefly Brit.* to work steadily: *he pegged away at his job for years.* **15.** (*tr.*) to stabilize (the price of a commodity, an exchange rate, etc.). [C15: from Low Gmc *pegge*]

Pegasus ('pɛgəsəs) *n. Greek myth.* an immortal winged horse, which sprang from the blood of the slain Medusa and enabled Bellerophon to achieve many great deeds as his rider.

pegboard ('pɛg,bɔːd) n. **1.** a board having a pattern of holes into which small pegs can be fitted, used for playing certain games or keeping a score. **2.** another name for **solitaire** (sense 1). **3.** hardboard perforated by a pattern of holes in which articles may be hung, as for display.

peg leg n. Inf. **1.** an artificial leg, esp. one made of wood. **2.** a person with an artificial leg.

pegmatite ('pɛgmə,taɪt) n. any of a class of coarse-grained intrusive igneous rocks consisting chiefly of quartz and feldspar. [C19: from Gk *pegma* something joined together]

peg out vb. (adv.) **1.** (intr.) Inf. to collapse or die. **2.** (intr.) Cribbage. to score the point that wins the game. **3.** (tr.) to mark or secure with pegs: *to peg out one's claims to a piece of land.*

peg top n. a child's spinning top, usually made of wood with a metal centre pin.

peg-top adj. (of skirts, trousers, etc.) wide at the hips then tapering off towards the ankle.

Pegu (pɛ'guː) n. a city in S Burma: capital of a united Burma (16th century). Pop.: 150 447 (1983).

PEI abbrev. for Prince Edward Island.

peignoir ('peɪnwɑː) n. a woman's dressing gown. [C19: from F, from *peigner* to comb, since the garment was worn while the hair was combed]

Peipus ('paɪpəs) n. a lake in the W Soviet Union, on the boundary between the RSFSR and Estonia: drains into the Gulf of Finland. Area: 3512 sq. km (1356 sq. miles). Russian name: **Chudskoye Ozero.**

Peiraeus (paɪ'riːəs, pɪ'reɪ-) n. a variant spelling of **Piraeus.**

Peirce (pɪəs) n. **Charles Sanders.** 1839–1914, U.S. logician, philosopher, and mathematician; pioneer of pragmatism.

pejoration (,piːdʒə'reɪʃən) n. **1.** semantic change whereby a word acquires unfavourable connotations. **2.** the process of worsening.

pejorative (pɪ'dʒɒrətɪv, 'piːdʒər-) adj. **1.** (of words, expressions, etc.) having an unpleasant or disparaging connotation. ~n. **2.** a pejorative word, etc. [C19: from F *péjoratif*, from LL *pējōrātus*, p.p. of *pējōrāre* to make worse, from L *pēior* worse] —**pe'joratively** adv.

pekan ('pɛkən) n. another name for **fisher** (the animal). [C18: from Canad. F *pékan*, from Amerind]

peke (piːk) n. Inf. a Pekingese dog.

Peking ('piː'kɪŋ) n. the capital of the People's Republic of China, in the northeast in central Hebei province: dates back to the 12th century B.C.; consists of two central walled cities, the Outer City (containing the commercial quarter) and the Inner City, which contains the Imperial City, within which is the Purple or Forbidden City; three universities. Pop.: 5 860 000 (1986). Chinese name: **Beijing.**

Pekingese (,piːkɪŋ'iːz) or **Pekinese** (,piːkə'niːz) n. **1.** (pl. **-ese**) a small breed of pet dog with a profuse straight coat, curled plumed tail, and short wrinkled muzzle. **2.** the dialect of Mandarin Chinese spoken in Peking. **3.** (pl. **-ese**) a native or inhabitant of Peking. ~adj. **4.** of Peking or its inhabitants.

Peking man n. an early type of man, of the Lower Palaeolithic age, remains of which were found in a cave near Peking.

pekoe ('piːkəʊ) n. a high-quality tea made from the downy tips of the young buds of the tea plant. [C18: from Chinese *peh ho*, from *peh* white + *ho* down]

pelage ('pɛlɪdʒ) n. the coat of a mammal, consisting of hair, wool, fur, etc. [C19: via F from OF *pel* animal's coat, from L *pilus* hair]

Pelagian Islands (pɛ'leɪdʒɪən) pl. n. a group of Italian islands (Lampedusa, Linosa, and Lampione) in the Mediterranean, between Tunisia and Malta. Pop.: 4620 (1968 est.). Area: about 27 sq. km (11 sq. miles). Italian name: **Isole Pelagie** ('iːzole pe'ladʒe)

Pelagianism (pɛ'leɪdʒɪə,nɪzəm) n. Christianity. a heretical doctrine, first formulated by Pelagius, that rejected the concept of original sin. —**Pe'lagian** n., adj.

pelagic (pɛ'lædʒɪk) adj. **1.** of or relating to the open sea: *pelagic whaling.* **2.** (of marine life) occurring in the upper waters of open sea. [C17: from L *pelagicus*, from *pelagus*, from Gk *pelagos* sea]

Pelagius (pɛ'leɪdʒɪəs) n. ?360–?420 A.D., British monk, who originated the body of doctrines known as Pelagianism and was condemned for heresy (417).

pelargonium (,pɛlə'gəʊnɪəm) n. any plant of a chiefly southern African genus having circular or lobed leaves and red, pink, or white aromatic flowers: includes many cultivated geraniums. [C19: via NL from Gk *pelargos* stork, on the model of GERANIUM; from the likeness of the seed vessels to a stork's bill]

Pelé ('pɛleɪ) n. real name *Edson Arantes do Nascimento.* born 1940, Brazilian footballer.

Pelée (pə'leɪ) n. **Mount.** a volcano in the West Indies, in N Martinique: erupted in 1902, killing every person but one in the town of St. Pierre. Height: 1463 m (4800 ft.).

Peleus ('pɛlɪəs, 'piːljəs) n. Greek myth. a king of the Myrmidons; father of Achilles.

Pelew Islands (pɪ'luː) pl. n. a former name of (the Republic of) **Belau.**

pelf (pɛlf) n. Contemptuous. money or wealth; lucre. [C14: from OF *pelfre* booty]

pelham ('pɛləm) n. a horse's bit for a double bridle, less severe than a curb but more severe than a snaffle. [prob. from the name *Pelham*]

Pelias ('piːlɪ,æs) n. Greek myth. a son of Poseidon and Tyro. He feared his nephew Jason and sent him to recover the Golden Fleece, hoping he would not return.

pelican ('pɛlɪkən) n. any aquatic bird of a tropical and warm water family. They have a long straight flattened bill, with a distensible pouch for engulfing fish. [OE *pellican*, from LL *pelicānus*, from Gk *pelekān*]

pelican crossing n. a type of road crossing with a pedestrian-operated traffic-light system. [C20: from *pe(destrian) li(ght) con(trolled) crossing*, with -con adapted to -can of *pelican*]

Pelion ('piːlɪən) n. a mountain in NE Greece, in E Thessaly. In Greek mythology it was the home of the centaurs. Height: 1548 m (5079 ft.). Modern Greek name: **Pilion.**

pelisse (pɛ'liːs) n. **1.** a fur-trimmed cloak. **2.** a loose coat, usually fur-trimmed, worn esp. by women in the early 19th century. [C18: via OF from Med. L *pellicia* cloak, from L *pellis* skin]

Pella ('pɛlə) n. an ancient city in N Greece: the capital of Macedonia under Philip II.

pellagra (pə'leɪgrə, -'læ-) n. Pathol. a disease caused by a dietary deficiency of nicotinic acid, characterized by scaling of the skin, inflammation of the mouth, diarrhoea, mental impairment, etc. [C19: via It. from *pelle* skin + -agra, from Gk *agra* paroxysm] —**pel'lagrous** adj.

pellet ('pɛlɪt) n. **1.** a small round ball, esp. of compressed matter. **2. a.** an imitation bullet used in toy guns. **b.** a piece of small shot. **3.** a stone ball formerly used in a catapult. **4.** Ornithol. a mass of undigested food that is regurgitated by birds of prey. **5.** a small pill. ~vb. (tr.) **6.** to strike with pellets. **7.** to make or form into pellets. [C14: from OF *pelote*, from Vulgar L *pilota* (unattested), from L *pila* ball]

Pelletier (French pɛltje) n. **Pierre Joseph** (pjɛr ʒozɛf). 1788–1842, French chemist, who isolated quinine, chlorophyll, and other chemical substances.

pellitory ('pɛlɪtərɪ, -trɪ) n., pl. **-ries. 1.** any of various plants of a S and W European genus, esp. wall pellitory, that grow in crevices and have long narrow leaves and small pink flowers. **2. pellitory of Spain.** a small Mediterranean plant, the root of which contains an oil formerly used to relieve toothache. [C16 *peletre*, from OF *piretre*, from L, from Gk *purethron*, from *pur* fire, from the hot pungent taste of the root]

pell-mell ('pɛl'mɛl) adv. **1.** in a confused headlong rush: *the hounds ran pell-mell into the yard.* **2.** in a disorderly manner: *the things were piled pell-mell in the room.* ~adj. **3.** disordered; tumultuous: *a pell-mell rush for the exit.* ~n. **4.** disorder; confusion. [C16: from OF *pesle-mesle*, jingle based on *mesler* to MEDDLE]

pellucid (pɛ'luːsɪd) adj. **1.** transparent or translucent. **2.** extremely clear in style and meaning. [C17: from L *pellūcidus*, var. of *perlūcidus*, from *perlūcēre* to shine through] —**,pellu'cidity** or **pel'lucidness** n. —**pel'lucidly** adv.

pelmet ('pɛlmɪt) n. an ornamental drapery or board fixed above a window to conceal the curtain rail. [C19: prob. from F *palmette* palm-leaf decoration on cornice moulding]

Peloponnese (ˌpɛləpə'niːs) n. **the.** the S peninsula of Greece, joined to central Greece by the Isthmus of Corinth: chief cities in ancient times were Sparta and Corinth, now Patras. Pop.: 1 012 528 (1981). Area: 21 439 sq. km (8361 sq. miles). Medieval name: **Morea.** Modern Greek name: **Peloponnesos.** Also called: **Peloponnesus.** —**Peloponnesian** (ˌpɛləpə'niːʃən) adj.

Pelops ('piːlɒps) n. Greek myth. the son of Tantalus, who as a child was killed by his father and served up as a meal for the gods.

pelota (pə'lɒtə) n. any of various games played in Spain, Spanish America, SW France, etc., by two players who use a basket strapped to their wrists or a wooden racket to propel a ball against a specially marked wall. [C19: from Sp.: ball, from OF pelote; see PELLET]

Pelotas (Portuguese pe'lɔtɐʃ) n. a port in S Brazil, in Rio Grande do Sul on the Canal de São Gonçalo. Pop.: 197 092 (1980).

pelt[1] (pɛlt) vb. **1.** (tr.) to throw (missiles, etc.) at (a person, etc.). **2.** (tr.) to hurl (insults, etc.) at (a person, etc.). **3.** (intr.; foll. by along, etc.) to hurry. **4.** (intr.) to rain heavily. ~n. **5.** a blow. **6.** speed (esp. in **at full pelt**). [C15: from ?]

pelt[2] (pɛlt) n. **1.** the skin of a fur-bearing animal, esp. when it has been removed from the carcass. **2.** the hide of an animal, stripped of hair. [C15: ? back formation from PELTRY]

peltate ('pɛlteɪt) adj. (of leaves) having the stalk attached to the centre of the lower surface. [C18: from L peltātus equipped with a pelta small shield]

peltry ('pɛltrɪ) n., pl. **-ries.** the pelts of animals collectively. [C15: from OF peleterie collection of pelts, from L pilus hair]

pelvic fin n. either of a pair of fins attached to the pelvic girdle of fishes that help to control the direction of movement during locomotion.

pelvic inflammatory disease n. inflammation of a woman's womb, Fallopian tubes, or ovaries as a result of infection with one of a group of bacteria.

pelvis ('pɛlvɪs) n., pl. **-vises** or **-ves** (-viːz). **1.** the large funnel-shaped structure at the lower end of the trunk of most vertebrates. **2.** Also called: **pelvic girdle.** the bones that form this structure. **3.** any anatomical cavity or structure shaped like a funnel or cup. [C17: from L: basin] —'**pelvic** adj.

Pemba ('pɛmbə) n. an island in the Indian Ocean, off the E coast of Africa north of Zanzibar: part of Tanzania; produces most of the world's cloves. Chief town: Chake Chake. Pop.: 256 950 (1985 est.). Area: 984 sq. km (380 sq. miles).

Pembroke ('pɛmbruk) n. a town in SW Wales, in Dyfed on Milford Haven: 11th-century castle where Henry VII was born. Pop.: 15 618 (1981).

Pembrokeshire ('pɛmbrukˌʃɪə, -ʃə) n. (until 1974) a county of SW Wales, now part of Dyfed.

pemmican or **pemican** ('pɛmɪkən) n. a small pressed cake of shredded dried meat, pounded into paste, used originally by American Indians and now chiefly for emergency rations. [C19: from Amerind pimikân, from pimii grease]

pemphigus ('pɛmfɪgəs, pɛm'faɪ-) n. Pathol. any of a group of blistering skin diseases. [C18: via NL from Gk pemphix bubble]

pen[1] (pɛn) n. **1.** an implement for writing or drawing using ink, formerly consisting of a sharpened and split quill, and now of a metal nib attached to a holder. See also **ballpoint, fountain pen. 2.** the writing end of such an implement; nib. **3.** style of writing. **4. the pen.** writing as an occupation. ~vb. **penning, penned. 5.** (tr.) to write or compose. [OE pinne, from LL penna (quill) pen, from L: feather]

pen[2] (pɛn) n. **1.** an enclosure in which domestic animals are kept. **2.** any place of confinement. **3.** a dock for servicing submarines, esp. having a bombproof roof. ~vb. **penning, penned** or **pent. 4.** (tr.) to enclose in a pen. [OE penn]

pen[3] (pɛn) n. U.S. & Canad. inf. short for **penitentiary** (sense 1).

pen[4] (pɛn) n. a female swan. [C16: from ?]

PEN (pɛn) n. acronym for International Association of Poets, Playwrights, Editors, Essayists, and Novelists.

Pen. abbrev. for Peninsula.

penal ('piːnᵊl) adj. **1.** of, relating to, constituting, or prescribing punishment. **2.** used or designated as a place of punishment: a penal institution. [C15: from LL poenālis concerning punishment, from L poena penalty] —'**penally** adv.

penal code n. the codified body of the laws that relate to crime and its punishment.

penalize or **-ise** ('piːnəˌlaɪz) vb. (tr.) **1.** to impose a penalty on (someone), as for breaking a law or rule. **2.** to inflict a disadvantage on. **3.** Sport. to award a free stroke, point, or penalty against (a player or team). **4.** to declare (an act) legally punishable. —ˌpenali'zation or -i'sation n.

penalty ('pɛnᵊltɪ) n., pl. **-ties. 1.** a legal or official punishment, such as a term of imprisonment. **2.** some other form of punishment, such as a fine or forfeit for not fulfilling a contract. **3.** loss, suffering, or other unfortunate result of one's own action, error, etc. **4.** Sport, games, etc. a handicap awarded against a player or team for illegal play, such as a free shot at goal by the opposing team. [C16: from Med. L poenālitās penalty; see PENAL]

penalty area n. another name for **penalty box** (sense 1).

penalty box n. **1.** Soccer. a rectangular area in front of the goal, within which a penalty is awarded for a foul by the defending team. **2.** Ice hockey. a bench for players serving time penalties.

penalty rates pl. n. Austral. & N.Z. rates of pay for employees working outside normal hours.

penance ('pɛnəns) n. **1.** voluntary self-punishment to atone for a sin, crime, etc. **2.** a feeling of regret for one's wrongdoings. **3.** Christianity. a punishment usually consisting of prayer, fasting, etc., imposed by church authority as a condition of absolution. **4.** R.C. Church. a sacrament in which repentant sinners are absolved on condition of confession of their sins to a priest and of performing a penance. ~vb. **5.** (tr.) (of ecclesiastical authorities) to impose a penance upon (a sinner). [C13: via OF from L paenitentia repentance]

Penang (pɪ'næŋ) n. **1.** a state of Peninsular Malaysia: consists of the island of Penang and the province Wellesley on the mainland, which first united administratively in 1798 as a British colony. Capital: George Town. Pop.: 1 049 282 (1985 est.). Area: 1031 sq. km (398 sq. miles). **2.** a forested island off the NW coast of Malaya, in the Strait of Malacca. Area: 293 sq. km (113 sq. miles). Former name (until about 1867): **Prince of Wales Island. 3.** another name for **George Town.**

penates (pə'nɑːtiːz) pl. n. See **lares and penates.**

pence (pɛns) n. a plural of **penny.**

▷Usage. Since the decimalization of British currency and the introduction of the abbreviation **p,** as in 10p, 85p, etc., the abbreviation has tended to replace pence in speech, as in 4p (ˌfɔː'piː), etc.

penchant ('pɒnʃɒn) n. strong inclination or liking; bent or taste. [C17: from F, from pencher to incline, from L pendēre to be suspended]

Penchi ('pɛn'tʃiː) n. a variant transliteration of the Chinese name for **Benxi.**

pencil ('pɛnsᵊl) n. **1.** a thin cylindrical instrument used for writing, drawing, etc., consisting of a rod of graphite or other marking substance usually encased in wood and sharpened. **2.** something similar in shape or function: a styptic pencil. **3.** a narrow set of lines or rays, such as light rays, diverging from or converging to a point. **4.** Rare. an artist's individual style. **5.** a type of artist's brush. ~vb. **-cilling, -cilled** or U.S. **-ciling, -ciled. 6.** to draw, colour, or write with a pencil. **7.** to mark with a pencil. [C14: from OF pincel, from L pēnicillus painter's brush, from pēniculus a little tail] —'**penciller** or U.S. '**penciler** n.

pend (pɛnd) vb. (intr.) to await judgment or settlement. [C15: from L pendēre to hang]

pendant ('pɛndənt) n. **1. a.** an ornament that hangs from a piece of jewellery. **b.** a necklace with such an ornament. **2.** a hanging light, esp. a chandelier. **3.** a carved ornament that is suspended from a ceiling or roof. ~adj. **4.** a variant spelling of **pendent.** [C14: from OF, from pendre to hang, from L pendēre to hang down]

pendent ('pɛndənt) adj. **1.** dangling. **2.** jutting. **3.** (of a grammatical construction) incomplete. **4.** a less common word for **pending.** ~n. **5.** a variant spelling of **pendant.**

[C15: from OF *pendant*, from *pendre* to hang; see PEN-DANT] —'**pendency** *n.*

pendentive (pɛn'dɛntɪv) *n.* any of four triangular sections of vaulting with concave sides, positioned at a corner of a rectangular space to support a dome. [C18: from F *pendentif*, from L *pendens* hanging, from *pendere* to hang]

Penderecki (*Polish* pɛndɛ'rɛtski) *n.* **Krzystof** ('kʃiʃtɔf). born 1933, Polish composer, noted for his highly individual orchestration. His works include *Threnody for the Victims of Hiroshima* for strings (1960), *Stabat Mater* (1962), and the *Polish Requiem* (1980–84).

pending ('pɛndɪŋ) *prep.* **1.** while waiting for. ~*adj.* (*postpositive*) **2.** not yet decided, confirmed, or finished. **3.** imminent: *these developments have been pending for some time.*

pendragon (pɛn'drægən) *n.* a supreme war chief or leader of the ancient Britons. [Welsh, lit.: head dragon]

pendulous ('pɛndjʊləs) *adj.* hanging downwards, esp. so as to swing from side to side. [C17: from L *pendulus*, from *pendere* to hang down] —'**pendulously** *adv.* —'**pendulousness** *n.*

pendulum ('pɛndjʊləm) *n.* **1.** a body mounted so that it can swing freely under the influence of gravity. **2.** such a device used to regulate a clock mechanism. **3.** something that changes fairly regularly: *the pendulum of public opinion.* [C17: from L *pendulus* PENDULOUS]

Penelope (pə'nɛləpɪ) *n. Greek myth.* the wife of Odysseus, who remained true to him during his long absence despite the importunities of many suitors.

peneplain *or* **peneplane** ('pi:nɪ,pleɪn) *n.* a relatively flat land surface produced by erosion. [C19: from L *paene* almost + PLAIN[1]]

penetrant ('pɛnɪtrənt) *adj.* **1.** sharp; penetrating. ~*n.* **2.** *Chem.* a substance that lowers the surface tension of a liquid and thus causes it to penetrate or be absorbed more easily. **3.** a person or thing that penetrates.

penetrate ('pɛnɪ,treɪt) *vb.* **1.** to find or force a way into or through (something); pierce; enter. **2.** to diffuse through (a substance, etc.); permeate. **3.** (*tr.*) to see through: *their eyes could not penetrate the fog.* **4.** (*tr.*) (of a man) to insert the penis into the vagina of (a woman). **5.** (*tr.*) to grasp the meaning of (a principle, etc.). **6.** (*intr.*) to be understood: *his face lit up as the new idea penetrated.* [C16: from L *penetrāre*] —'**penetrable** *adj.* —,**penetra'bility** *n.* —'**pene,trator** *n.*

penetrating ('pɛnɪ,treɪtɪŋ) *adj.* tending to or able to penetrate: *a penetrating mind; a penetrating voice.* —'**pene,tratingly** *adv.*

penetration (,pɛnɪ'treɪʃən) *n.* **1.** the act or an instance of penetrating. **2.** the ability or power to penetrate. **3.** keen insight or perception. **4.** *Mil.* an offensive manoeuvre that breaks through an enemy's defensive position.

Peneus (pɪ'ni:əs) *n.* the ancient name for the **Salambria.**

pen friend *n.* a person with whom one exchanges letters, often a person in another country whom one has not met. Also called: **pen pal.**

Penghu *or* **P'eng-hu** ('pɛŋ'hu:) *n.* transliteration of the Chinese name for the **Pescadores.**

Pengpu ('pɛŋ'pu:) *n.* a variant transliteration of the Chinese name for **Bengbu.**

penguin ('pɛŋgwɪn) *n.* a flightless marine bird of cool southern, esp. Antarctic, regions: they have wings modified as flippers, webbed feet, and feathers lacking barbs. [C16: ?from Welsh *pen gwyn*, from *pen* head + *gwyn* white]

penicillin (,pɛnɪ'sɪlɪn) *n.* any of a group of antibiotics with powerful action against bacteria: obtained from the fungus *Penicillium.* [C20: from PENICILLIUM]

penicillium (,pɛnɪ'sɪlɪəm) *n., pl.* **-cilliums** *or* **-cillia** (-'sɪlɪə). any saprophytic fungus of the genus *Penicillium*, which commonly grow as a green or blue mould on stale food. [C19: NL, from L *pēnicillus* tuft of hairs; from the appearance of the sporangia of this fungus]

penillion *or* **pennillion** (pɪ'nɪlɪən) *pl. n., sing.* **penill** (pɪ'nɪl). the Welsh art or practice of singing poetry in counterpoint to a traditional melody played on the harp. [from Welsh: verses]

peninsula (pɪ'nɪnsjʊlə) *n.* a narrow strip of land projecting into a sea or lake from the mainland. [C16: from L, lit.: almost an island, from *paene* almost + *insula* island] —**pen'insular** *adj.*

Peninsula *n.* **the.** short for the **Iberian Peninsula.**

penis ('pi:nɪs) *n., pl.* **-nises** *or* **-nes** (-ni:z). the male organ of copulation in higher vertebrates, also used for urine excretion in many mammals. [C17: from L: penis] —**penile** ('pi:naɪl) *adj.*

penitent ('pɛnɪtənt) *adj.* **1.** feeling regret for one's sins; repentant. ~*n.* **2.** a person who is penitent. **3.** *Christianity.* **a.** a person who repents his sins and seeks forgiveness for them. **b.** *R.C. Church.* a person who confesses his sins and submits to a penance. [C14: from Church L *paenitēns* regretting, from *paenitēre* to repent, from ?] —'**penitence** *n.* —'**penitently** *adv.*

penitential (,pɛnɪ'tɛnʃəl) *adj.* **1.** of, showing, or constituting penance. ~*n.* **2.** *Chiefly R.C. Church.* a book or compilation of instructions for confessors. **3.** a less common word for **penitent** (senses 2, 3). —,**peni'tentially** *adv.*

penitentiary (,pɛnɪ'tɛnʃərɪ) *n., pl.* **-ries. 1.** (in the U.S. and Canada) a state or federal prison. **2.** *R.C. Church.* **a.** a cardinal who presides over a tribunal that decides all matters affecting the sacrament of penance. **b.** this tribunal itself. ~*adj.* **3.** another word for **penitential** (sense 1). **4.** *U.S. & Canad.* (of an offence) punishable by imprisonment in a penitentiary. [C15 (meaning also: an officer dealing with penances): from Med. L *poenitēntiārius*, from L *paenitēns* PENITENT]

Penki ('pɛn'tʃi:) *n.* a variant transliteration of the Chinese name for **Benxi.**

penknife ('pɛn,naɪf) *n., pl.* **-knives.** a small knife with one or more blades that fold into the handle; pocketknife.

penman ('pɛnmən) *n., pl.* **-men. 1.** a person skilled in handwriting. **2.** a person who writes by hand in a specified way: *a bad penman.* **3.** an author. **4.** *Rare.* a scribe.

penmanship ('pɛnmənʃɪp) *n.* style or technique of writing by hand.

Penn (pɛn) *n.* **1. Arthur.** born 1922, U.S. film director: films include *Bonnie and Clyde* (1967), *Alice's Restaurant* (1969), *Little Big Man* (1970), *The Missouri Breaks* (1976), and *Four Friends* (1981). **2. William.** 1644–1718, English Quaker and founder of Pennsylvania.

penna ('pɛnə) *n., pl.* **-nae** (-ni:). *Ornithol.* any large feather that has a vane and forms part of the main plumage of a bird. [L: feather]

pen name *n.* an author's pseudonym. Also called: **nom de plume.**

pennant ('pɛnənt) *n.* **1.** a type of pennon, esp. one flown from vessels as identification or for signalling. **2.** *Chiefly U.S., Canad., & Austral.* **a.** a flag serving as an emblem of championship in certain sports. **b.** (*as modifier*): *pennant cricket.* [C17: prob. a blend of PENDANT & PENNON]

pennate ('pɛneɪt) *adj. Biol.* **1.** having feathers, wings, or winglike structures. **2.** another word for **pinnate.** [C19: from L *pennātus*, from *penna* wing]

Penney ('pɛnɪ) *n.* **William George, Baron of East Hendred.** born 1909, British mathematician. He worked on the first atom bomb and became chairman of the UK Atomic Energy Authority (1964–67).

penni ('pɛnɪ) *n., pl.* **-nia** (-nɪə) *or* **-nis.** a Finnish monetary unit worth one hundredth of a markka. [Finnish, from Low G *pennig* PENNY]

penniless ('pɛnɪlɪs) *adj.* very poor; almost totally without money. —'**pennilessly** *adv.* —'**pennilessness** *n.*

Pennine Alps ('pɛnaɪn) *pl. n.* a range of the Alps between Switzerland and Italy. Highest peak: Monte Rosa, 4634 m (15 204 ft.).

Pennines ('pɛnaɪnz) *pl. n.* a system of hills in England, extending from the Cheviot Hills in the north to the River Trent in the south: forms the watershed for the main rivers of N England. Highest peak: Cross Fell, 893 m (2930 ft.). Also called: (the) **Pennine Chain.**

Pennine Way *n.* a long-distance footpath extending from Edale, Derbyshire, for 402 km (250 miles) to Kirk Yetholm, Roxburghshire.

pennon ('pɛnən) *n.* **1.** a long flag, often tapering and divided at the end, originally a knight's personal flag. **2.** a small tapering or triangular flag borne on a ship or boat. **3.** a poetic word for **wing.** [C14: via OF ult. from L *penna* feather]

Pennsylvania (,pɛnsɪl'veɪnɪə) *n.* a state of the northeastern U.S.: almost wholly in the Appalachians, with the Allegheny Plateau to the west and a plain in the southeast; the second most important U.S. state for manufacturing. Capital: Harrisburg. Pop.: 11 889 000 (1986 est.). Area: 116 462 sq. km (44 956 sq. miles). Abbrevs.: **Pa., Penn., Penna.,** or (with zip code) **PA**

Pennsylvania Dutch n. **1.** a dialect of German spoken in E Pennsylvania. **2.** (preceded by *the; functioning as pl.*) a group of German-speaking people in E Pennsylvania, descended from 18th-century settlers from SW Germany and Switzerland. settlers from SW Germany and Switzerland.

Pennsylvanian (ˌpɛnsɪlˈveɪnɪən) adj. **1.** of the state of Pennsylvania. **2.** (in North America) of, denoting, or formed in the upper of two divisions of the Carboniferous period. ~n. **3.** an inhabitant or native of the state of Pennsylvania. **4.** (preceded by *the*) the Pennsylvanian period or rock system.

penny (ˈpɛnɪ) n., pl. **pennies** or **pence** (pɛns). **1.** Also called: **new penny.** *Brit.* a bronze coin having a value equal to one hundredth of a pound. Abbrev.: **p. 2.** *Brit.* (before 1971) a bronze or copper coin having a value equal to one twelfth of a shilling. Abbrev.: **d. 3.** (pl. **pennies**). *U.S. & Canad.* a cent. **4.** a coin of similar value, as used in several other countries. **5.** (*used with a negative*) *Inf., chiefly Brit.* the least amount of money: *I don't have a penny.* **6. a pretty penny.** *Inf.* a considerable sum of money. **7. spend a penny.** *Brit. inf.* to urinate. **8. the penny dropped.** *Inf., chiefly Brit.* the explanation of something was finally realized. [OE *penig, pening*]

penny arcade n. *Chiefly U.S.* a public place with various coin-operated machines for entertainment.

Penny Black n. the first adhesive postage stamp, issued in Britain in 1840.

penny-dreadful n., pl. **-fuls.** *Brit. inf.* a cheap, often lurid book or magazine.

penny-farthing n. *Brit.* an early type of bicycle with a large front wheel and a small rear wheel, the pedals being on the front wheel.

penny-pinching adj. **1.** excessively careful with money; miserly. ~n. **2.** miserliness. —**'penny-ˌpincher** n.

pennyroyal (ˌpɛnɪˈrɔɪəl) n. **1.** a Eurasian plant with hairy leaves and small mauve flowers, yielding an aromatic oil used in medicine. **2.** a similar and related plant of E North America. [C16: var. of Anglo-Norman *puliol real*, from OF *pouliol* (from L *pūleium* pennyroyal) + *real* ROYAL]

pennyweight (ˈpɛnɪˌweɪt) n. a unit of weight equal to 24 grains or one twentieth of an ounce (Troy).

penny whistle n. a type of flageolet with six finger holes, esp. a cheap metal one. Also called: **tin whistle.**

penny-wise adj. **1.** greatly concerned with saving small sums of money. **2. penny-wise and pound-foolish.** careful about trifles but wasteful in large ventures.

pennywort (ˈpɛnɪˌwɜːt) n. **1.** a Eurasian rock plant with whitish-green tubular flowers and rounded leaves. **2.** a marsh plant of Europe and North Africa, having circular leaves and greenish-pink flowers. **3.** any of various other plants with rounded penny-like leaves.

pennyworth (ˈpɛnɪˌwɜːθ) n. **1.** the amount that can be bought for a penny. **2.** a small amount: *he hasn't got a pennyworth of sense.*

penology (piːˈnɒlədʒɪ) n. **1.** the branch of the social sciences concerned with the punishment of crime. **2.** the science of prison management. [C19: from Gk *poinē* punishment] —**penological** (ˌpiːnəˈlɒdʒɪkəl) adj. —**peˈnologist** n.

pen pal n. another name for **pen friend.**

penpusher (ˈpɛnˌpʊʃə) n. a person who writes a lot, esp. a clerk involved with boring paperwork. —**'penˌpushing** adj., n.

Penrith (pɛnˈrɪθ) n. a market town in NW England, in Cumbria. Pop.: 12 205 (1981).

pension[1] (ˈpɛnʃən) n. **1.** a regular payment made by the state to people over a certain age to enable them to subsist without having to work. **2.** a regular payment made by an employer to former employees after they retire. **3.** any regular payment made by way of patronage, or in recognition of merit, service, etc.: *a pension paid to a disabled soldier.* ~vb. **4.** (tr.) to grant a pension to. [C14: via OF from L *pēnsiō* a payment, from *pendere* to pay] —**'pensionable** adj. —**'pensionary** adj. —**'pensioner** n.

pension[2] *French.* (pɑ̃sjɔ̃) n. (in France and some other countries) a relatively cheap boarding house. [C17: from F; extended meaning of *pension* grant; see PENSION[1]]

pension off vb. (tr., adv.) **1.** to cause to retire from a job and pay a pension to. **2.** to discard, because of age: *to pension off submarines.*

pensive (ˈpɛnsɪv) adj. **1.** deeply or seriously thoughtful, often with a tinge of sadness. **2.** expressing or suggesting pensiveness. [C14: from OF *pensif*, from *penser* to think, from L *pensāre* to consider] —**'pensively** adv. —**'pensiveness** n.

penstemon (pɛnˈstiːmən) n. a variant (esp. U.S.) of **pentstemon.**

penstock (ˈpɛnˌstɒk) n. **1.** a conduit that supplies water to a hydroelectric power plant. **2.** a channel bringing water from the head gates to a water wheel. **3.** a sluice for controlling water flow. [C17: from PEN[2] + STOCK]

pent (pɛnt) vb. a past tense and past participle of **pen**[2].

penta- combining form. five: *pentagon; pentameter.* [from Gk *pente*]

pentacle (ˈpɛntəkəl) n. **1.** another name for **pentagram.** [C16: from It. *pentacolo* something having five corners]

pentad (ˈpɛntæd) n. **1.** a group or series of five. **2.** the number or sum of five. **3.** a period of five years. **4.** *Chem.* a pentavalent element, atom, or radical. [C17: from Gk *pentas* group of five]

pentadactyl (ˌpɛntəˈdæktɪl) adj. (of the limbs of amphibians, reptiles, birds, and mammals) having a hand or foot bearing five digits.

pentagon (ˈpɛntəˌgɒn) n. a polygon having five sides. —**pentagonal** (pɛnˈtægənəl) adj.

Pentagon (ˈpɛntəˌgɒn) n. **1.** the five-sided building in Arlington, Virginia, that houses the headquarters of the U.S. Department of Defense. **2.** the military leadership of the U.S.

pentagram (ˈpɛntəˌgræm) n. **1.** a star-shaped figure with five points. **2.** such a figure used by the Pythagoreans, Black magicians, etc. ~Also called: **pentacle, pentangle.**

pentahedron (ˌpɛntəˈhiːdrən) n., pl. **-drons** or **-dra** (-drə). a solid figure having five plane faces. —**pentaˈhedral** adj.

pentamerous (pɛnˈtæmərəs) adj. consisting of five parts, esp. (of flowers) having the petals, sepals, and other parts arranged in groups of five.

pentameter (pɛnˈtæmɪtə) n. **1.** a verse line consisting of five metrical feet. **2.** (in classical prosody) a verse line consisting of two dactyls, one stressed syllable, two dactyls, and a final stressed syllable. ~adj. **3.** designating a verse line consisting of five metrical feet.

pentane (ˈpɛnteɪn) n. an alkane hydrocarbon having three isomers, esp. the isomer with a straight chain of carbon atoms (n-pentane) which is a colourless flammable liquid used as a solvent.

pentangle (ˈpɛnˌtæŋgəl) n. another name for **pentagram.**

pentanoic acid (ˌpɛntəˈnəʊɪk) n. a colourless liquid carboxylic acid used in making perfumes, flavourings, and pharmaceuticals. Formula: $CH_3(CH_2)_3COOH$. Former name: **valeric acid.**

Pentateuch (ˈpɛntəˌtjuːk) n. the first five books of the Old Testament. [C16: from Church L *pentateuchus*, from Gk PENTA- + *teukhos* tool (in LGk: scroll)] —**Pentaˈteuchal** adj.

pentathlon (pɛnˈtæθlən) n. an athletic contest consisting of five different events. [C18: from Gk *pentathlon*, from PENTA- + *athlon* contest]

pentatomic (ˌpɛntəˈtɒmɪk) adj. *Chem.* having five atoms in the molecule.

pentatonic scale (ˌpɛntəˈtɒnɪk) n. *Music.* any of several scales consisting of five notes.

pentavalent (ˌpɛntəˈveɪlənt) adj. *Chem.* having a valency of five. Also: **quinquevalent.**

Pentecost (ˈpɛntɪˌkɒst) n. **1.** a Christian festival occurring on Whit Sunday commemorating the descent of the Holy Ghost on the apostles. **2.** *Judaism.* the harvest festival, celebrated on the fiftieth day after the second day of Passover. [OE, from Church L, from Gk *pentēkostē* fiftieth (day after the Resurrection)]

Pentecostal (ˌpɛntɪˈkɒstəl) adj. **1.** (*usually prenominal*) of or relating to any of various Christian groups that emphasize the charismatic aspects of Christianity and adopt a fundamental attitude to the Bible. **2.** of or relating to Pentecost or the influence of the Holy Spirit. ~n. **3.** a member of a Pentecostal Church. —**ˌPenteˈcostalist** n., adj.

Pentelikon (pɛn'tɛlɪkɒn) n. a mountain in SE Greece, near Athens: famous for its white marble, worked regularly from the 6th century B.C., from which the chief buildings and sculptures in Athens are made. Height: 1109 m (3638 ft.). Latin name: **Pen'telicus**.

Penthesileia or **Penthesilea** (,pɛnθəsɪ'leɪə) n. Greek myth. the daughter of Ares and queen of the Amazons, whom she led to the aid of Troy. She was slain by Achilles.

Pentheus ('pɛnθɪəs) n. Greek myth. the grandson of Cadmus and his successor as king of Thebes, who resisted the introduction of the cult of Dionysus. In revenge the god drove him mad and he was torn to pieces by a group of bacchantes, one of whom was his mother.

penthouse ('pɛnt,haʊs) n. **1.** a flat or maisonette built onto the top floor or roof of a block of flats. **2.** a construction on the roof of a building, esp. one used to house machinery, etc. **3.** a shed built against a building, esp. one that has a sloping roof. [C14 pentis (later penthouse), from OF apentis, from LL appendicium appendage, from L appendere to hang from; see APPEND]

Pentland Firth ('pɛntlənd) n. a channel between the mainland of N Scotland and the Orkney Islands: notorious for rough seas. Length: 32 km (20 miles). Width: up to 13 km (8 miles).

pentobarbitone sodium (,pɛntə'bɑːbɪ,təʊn) n. a barbiturate drug used in medicine as a sedative and hypnotic.

pentode ('pɛntəʊd) n. **1.** an electronic valve having five electrodes: a cathode, anode, and three grids. **2.** (modifier) (of a transistor) having three terminals at the base or gate. [C20: from PENTA- + Gk hodos way]

Pentothal sodium ('pɛntə,θæl) n. a trademark for **thiopentone sodium**.

pentstemon (pɛnt'stiːmən) or esp. U.S. **penstemon** n. any plant of a North American genus having white, pink, red, blue, or purple flowers with five stamens, one of which is sterile. [C18: NL, from PENTA- + Gk stēmōn thread (here: stamen)]

pent-up adj. not released; repressed: pent-up emotions.

pentyl acetate ('pɛntaɪl, -tɪl) n. a colourless combustible liquid used as a solvent for paints, in the extraction of penicillin, in photographic film, and as a flavouring. Formula: $C_2H_5OOCCH_3$. Also called: **amyl acetate**.

penult ('pɛnʌlt, pɪ'nʌlt) n. the last syllable but one in a word. [C16: L paenultima syllaba, from paene ultima almost the last]

penultimate (pɪ'nʌltɪmɪt) adj. **1.** next to the last. ~n. **2.** anything next to last, esp. a penult.

penumbra (pɪ'nʌmbrə) n., pl. **-brae** (-briː) or **-bras**. **1.** a fringe region of half shadow resulting from the partial obstruction of light by an opaque object. **2.** Astron. the lighter and outer region of a sunspot. **3.** Painting. the area in which light and shade blend. [C17: via NL from L paene almost + umbra shadow] —**pe'numbral** adj.

penurious (pɪ'njʊərɪəs) adj. **1.** niggardly with money. **2.** lacking money or means. **3.** scanty. —**pe'nuriously** adv. —**pe'nuriousness** n.

penury ('pɛnjʊrɪ) n. **1.** extreme poverty. **2.** extreme scarcity. [C15: from L pēnūria dearth, from ?]

Penza (Russian 'pjɛnzə) n. a city in the W Soviet Union: manufacturing centre. Pop.: 540 000 (1987).

Penzance (pɛn'zæns) n. a town in SW England, in SW Cornwall: the westernmost town in England; resort and fishing port. Pop.: 19 521 (1981).

peon[1] ('piːən, 'piːɒn) n. **1.** a Spanish-American farm labourer or unskilled worker. **2.** (formerly, in Spanish America) a debtor compelled to work off his debts. **3.** any very poor person. [C19: from Sp. peón peasant, from Med. L pedō man who goes on foot, from L pēs foot] —**'peonage** n.

peon[2] (pjuːn, 'piːən, 'piːɒn) n. (in India, Sri Lanka, etc., esp. formerly) **1.** a messenger or attendant, esp. in an office. **2.** a native policeman. **3.** a foot soldier. [C17: from Port. peão orderly; see PEON[1]]

peony or **paeony** ('piːənɪ) n., pl. **-nies. 1.** any of a genus of shrubs and plants of Eurasia and North America, having large pink, red, white, or yellow flowers. **2.** the flower of any of these plants. [OE peonie, from L paeōnia, from Gk paiōnia; rel. to paiōnios healing, from paiōn physician]

people ('piːpᵊl) n. (usually functioning as pl.) **1.** persons collectively or in general. **2.** a group of persons considered together: blind people. **3.** (pl. **peoples**) the

persons living in a country and sharing the same nationality: the French people. **4.** one's family: he took her home to meet his people. **5.** persons loyal to someone powerful: the king's people accompanied him in exile. **6.** the **people. a.** the mass of persons without special distinction, privileges, etc. **b.** the body of persons in a country, etc., esp. those entitled to vote. ~vb. **7.** (tr.) to provide with or as if with people or inhabitants. [C13: from OF pople, from L populus]

▷ **Usage.** See at **person**.

people's democracy n. (in Communist ideology) a country or government in transition from bourgeois democracy to socialism.

people's front n. a less common term for **popular front**.

Peoria (piː'ɔːrɪə) n. a port in N central Illinois, on the Illinois River. Pop.: 110 290 (1986 est.).

pep (pɛp) n. **1.** high spirits, energy, or vitality. ~vb. **pepping, pepped. 2.** (tr.; usually foll. by up) to liven by imbuing with new vigour. [C20: short for PEPPER]

PEP abbrev. for political and economic planning.

peperomia (,pɛpər'əʊmɪə) n. any of a genus of tropical plants cultivated for their ornamental foliage. [C19: NL from Gk peperi pepper + omoros similar]

Pepin the Short ('pɛpɪn) n. died 768 A.D., king of the Franks (751–768); son of Charles Martel and father of Charlemagne. He deposed the Merovingian king (751) and founded the Carolingian dynasty.

peplum ('pɛpləm) n., pl. **-lums** or **-la** (-lə). a flared ruffle attached to the waist of a jacket, bodice, etc. [C17: from L: full upper garment, from Gk peplos shawl]

pepo ('piːpəʊ) n., pl. **-pos**. the fruit of any of various plants, such as the melon, cucumber, and pumpkin, having a firm rind, fleshy watery pulp, and numerous seeds. [C19: from L: pumpkin, from Gk pepōn edible gourd, from peptein to ripen]

pepper ('pɛpə) n. **1.** a woody climbing plant, Piper nigrum, of the East Indies, having small black berry-like fruits. **2.** the dried fruit of this plant, which is ground to produce a sharp hot condiment. See also **black pepper, white pepper. 3.** any of various other plants of the genus Piper. **4.** Also called: **capsicum**. any of various tropical plants, the fruits of which are used as a vegetable and a condiment. See also **sweet pepper, red pepper, cayenne pepper. 5.** the fruit of any of these capsicums, which has a mild or pungent taste. **6.** the condiment made from the fruits of any of these plants. ~vb. (tr.) **7.** to season with pepper. **8.** to sprinkle liberally; dot: his prose was peppered with alliteration. **9.** to pelt with small missiles. [OE piper, from L, from Gk peperi]

pepper-and-salt adj. **1.** (of cloth, etc.) marked with a fine mixture of black and white. **2.** (of hair) streaked with grey.

peppercorn ('pɛpə,kɔːn) n. **1.** the small dried berry of the pepper plant. **2.** something trifling.

peppercorn rent n. a rent that is very low or nominal.

pepper mill n. a small hand mill used to grind peppercorns.

peppermint ('pɛpə,mɪnt) n. **1.** a temperate mint plant with purple or white flowers and downy leaves, which yield a pungent oil. **2.** the oil from this plant, which is used as a flavouring. **3.** a sweet flavoured with peppermint.

pepper pot n. **1.** a small container with perforations in the top for sprinkling pepper. **2.** a West Indian stew of meat, etc., highly seasoned with an extract of bitter cassava.

pepper tree n. any of several evergreen trees of a chiefly South American genus having yellowish-white flowers and bright red ornamental fruits.

peppery ('pɛpərɪ) adj. **1.** flavoured with or tasting of pepper. **2.** quick-tempered; irritable. **3.** full of bite and sharpness: a peppery speech. —**'pepperiness** n.

pep pill n. Inf. a tablet containing a stimulant drug.

peppy ('pɛpɪ) adj. **-pier, -piest.** Inf. full of vitality; bouncy or energetic. —**'peppily** adv. —**'peppiness** n.

pepsin ('pɛpsɪn) n. an enzyme produced in the stomach, which, when activated by acid, splits proteins into peptones. [C19: via G from Gk pepsis, from peptein to digest]

pep talk n. Inf. an enthusiastic talk designed to increase confidence, production, cooperation, etc.

peptic ('pɛptɪk) adj. **1.** of, relating to, or promoting digestion. **2.** of, relating to, or caused by pepsin or the action of the digestive juices. [C17: from Gk *peptikos* capable of digesting, from *peptein* to digest]

peptic ulcer *n. Pathol.* an ulcer of the mucous membrane lining those parts of the alimentary tract exposed to digestive juices, including the oesophagus, the stomach, and the duodenum.

peptide ('pɛptaɪd) *n.* any of a group of compounds consisting of two or more amino acids linked by chemical bonding between their respective carboxyl and amino groups.

peptide bond *n. Biochem.* a chemical amide linkage, =CHCONHCH=, formed by the condensation of the amino group of one amino acid with the carboxyl group of another.

peptone ('pɛptəʊn) *n. Biochem.* any of a group of compounds that form an intermediary group in the digestion of proteins to amino acids. [C19: from G *Pepton*, from Gk *pepton* something digested, from *peptein* to digest] —**peptonic** (pɛp'tɒnɪk) *adj.*

Pepys (piːps) *n.* **Samuel.** 1633–1703, English diarist and naval administrator. His diary, which covers the period 1660–69, is a vivid account of London life through such disasters as the Great Plague, the Fire of London, and the intrusion of the Dutch fleet up the Thames.

per (pɜː; *unstressed* pə) *determiner.* **1.** for every: *three pence per pound.* ~*prep.* **2.** (esp. in some Latin phrases) by; through. **3. as per.** according to: *as per specifications.* **4. as per usual.** *Inf.* as usual. [C15: from L: by, for each]

per. *abbrev. for:* **1.** period. **2.** person.

per- *prefix.* **1.** indicating that a chemical compound contains a high proportion of a specified element: *peroxide.* **2.** indicating that a chemical element is in a higher than usual state of oxidation: *permanganate.* [from L *per* through. In compound words borrowed from L, *per-* indicates: through (*pervade*); throughout (*permanent*); away (*perfidy*); and is used as an intensifier (*permutation*)]

Pera ('pɪərə) *n.* the former name of Beyoğlu.

peracid (pɜː'ræsɪd) *n.* an acid, such as perchloric acid (HClO₄), in which the element forming the acid radical exhibits its highest valency.

peradventure (pərəd'vɛntʃə, ,pɜːr-) *Arch.* ~*adv.* **1.** by chance; perhaps. ~*n.* **2.** chance or doubt. [C13: from OF *par aventure* by chance]

Peraea *or* **Perea** (pə'riːə) *n.* a region of ancient Palestine, east of the River Jordan and the Dead Sea.

Perak ('pɛərə, 'pɪərə, pɪ'ræk) *n.* a state of NW Peninsular Malaysia, on the Strait of Malacca: tin mining. Capital: Ipoh. Pop.: 2 020 135 (1985 est.). Area: 20 680 sq. km (8030 sq. miles).

perambulate (pə'ræmbjʊ,leɪt) *vb.* **1.** to walk about (a place). **2.** (*tr.*) to walk round in order to inspect. [C16: from L *perambulāre* to traverse, from *per-* through + *ambulāre* to walk] —**per,ambu'lation** *n.* —**perambulatory** (pə'ræmbjʊlətərɪ, -trɪ) *adj.*

perambulator (pə'ræmbjʊ,leɪtə) *n.* a formal word for **pram**[1].

per annum (pər 'ænəm) *adv.* every year or by the year. [L]

P-E ratio *abbrev. for* price-earnings ratio.

percale (pə'keɪl, -'kɑːl) *n.* a close-textured woven cotton fabric, used esp. for sheets. [C17: via F from Persian *pargālah* piece of cloth]

per capita (pə 'kæpɪtə) *adj., adv.* of or for each person. [L, lit.: according to heads]

perceive (pə'siːv) *vb.* **1.** to become aware of (something) through the senses; recognize or observe. **2.** (*tr.; may take a clause as object*) to come to comprehend; grasp. [C13: from OF *perçoivre*, from L *percipere* to seize entirely] —**per'ceivable** *adj.* —**per'ceivably** *adv.*

per cent (pə 'sɛnt) *adv.* **1.** Also: **per centum.** in or for every hundred. ~*n. also* **percent. 2.** a percentage or proportion. **3.** (*often pl.*) securities yielding a rate of interest as specified: *he bought three percents.* [C16: from Med. L *per centum* out of every hundred]

percentage (pə'sɛntɪdʒ) *n.* **1.** proportion or rate per hundred parts. **2.** *Commerce.* the interest, tax, commission, or allowance on a hundred items. **3.** any proportion in relation to the whole. **4.** *Inf.* profit or advantage.

percentile (pə'sɛntaɪl) *n.* one of 99 actual or notional values of a variable dividing its distribution into 100 groups with equal frequencies. Also called: **centile.**

percept ('pɜːsɛpt) *n.* **1.** a concept that depends on recognition by the senses, such as sight, of some external object or phenomenon. **2.** an object or phenomenon that is perceived. [C19: from L *perceptum*, from *percipere* to PERCEIVE]

perceptible (pə'sɛptəbəl) *adj.* able to be perceived; noticeable or recognizable. —**per,cepti'bility** *n.* —**per'ceptibly** *adv.*

perception (pə'sɛpʃən) *n.* **1.** the act or the effect of perceiving. **2.** insight or intuition gained by perceiving. **3.** the ability or capacity to perceive. **4.** way of perceiving; view. **5.** the process by which an organism detects and interprets information from the external world by means of the sensory receptors. [C15: from L *perceptiō* comprehension; see PERCEIVE] —**per'ceptional** *adj.* —**perceptual** (pə'sɛptjʊəl) *adj.*

perceptive (pə'sɛptɪv) *adj.* **1.** quick at perceiving; observant. **2.** perceptual. **3.** able to perceive. —**per'ceptively** *adv.* —,**percep'tivity** *or* **per'ceptiveness** *n.*

Perceval ('pɜːsɪvəl) *n.* **Spencer.** 1762–1812, British statesman; prime minister (1809–12); assassinated.

perch[1] (pɜːtʃ) *n.* **1.** a pole, branch, or other resting place above ground on which a bird roosts. **2.** a similar resting place for a person or thing. **3.** another name for **rod** (sense 7). ~*vb.* **4.** (usually foll. by *on*) to alight, rest, or cause to rest on or as if on a perch: *the bird perched on the branch; the cap was perched on his head.* [C13 *perche* stake, from OF, from L *pertica* long staff]

perch[2] (pɜːtʃ) *n., pl.* **perch** *or* **perches.** **1.** any of a family of freshwater spiny-finned teleost fishes of Europe and North America: valued as food and game fishes. **2.** any of various similar or related fishes. [C13: from OF *perche*, from L *perca*, from Gk *perkē*]

perchance (pə'tʃɑːns) *adv. Arch. or poetic.* **1.** perhaps; possibly. **2.** by chance; accidentally. [C14: from Anglo-F *par chance*]

Percheron ('pɜːʃə,rɒn) *n.* a compact heavy breed of carthorse. [C19: from F, from *le Perche*, region of NW France, where the breed originated]

perchloric acid (pə'klɔːrɪk) *n.* a colourless syrupy oxyacid of chlorine containing a greater proportion of oxygen than chloric acid. It is a powerful oxidizing agent. Formula: HClO₄. Systematic name: **chloric(VII) acid.**

percipient (pə'sɪpɪənt) *adj.* **1.** able to perceive. **2.** perceptive. ~*n.* **3.** a person who perceives. [C17: from L *percipiens* observing, from *percipere* to grasp] —**per'cipience** *n.* —**per'cipiently** *adv.*

Percival *or* **Perceval** ('pɜːsɪvəl) *n.* (in Arthurian legend) a knight in King Arthur's court. German equivalent: **Parzival.**

percolate *vb.* ('pɜːkə,leɪt). **1.** to cause (a liquid) to pass through a fine mesh, porous substance, etc., or (of a liquid) to pass through a fine mesh, etc.; trickle: *rain percolated through the roof.* **2.** to permeate; penetrate gradually: *water percolated the road.* **3.** to make (coffee) or (of coffee) to be made in a percolator. ~*n.* ('pɜːkəlɪt, -,leɪt). **4.** a product of percolation. [C17: from L *percolāre*, from PER- + *cōlāre* to strain, from *cōlum* a strainer; see COLANDER] —**percolable** ('pɜːkələbəl) *adj.* —,**perco'lation** *n.*

percolator ('pɜːkə,leɪtə) *n.* a kind of coffeepot in which boiling water is forced up through a tube and filters down through the coffee grounds into a container.

per contra (pə 'kɒntrə) *adv.* on the contrary. [from L]

percuss (pə'kʌs) *vb.* (*tr.*) **1.** to strike sharply, rapidly, or suddenly. **2.** *Med.* to tap on (a body surface) with the fingertips or a special hammer to aid diagnosis. [C16: from L *percutere*, from *per-* through + *quatere* to shake] —**per'cussor** *n.*

percussion (pə'kʌʃən) *n.* **1.** the act, an instance, or an effect of percussing. **2.** *Music.* the family of instruments in which sound arises from the striking of materials with sticks or hammers. **3.** *Music.* instruments of this family constituting a section of an orchestra, etc. **4.** *Med.* the act of percussing a body surface. **5.** the act of exploding a percussion cap. [C16: from L *percussiō*, from *percutere* to hit; see PERCUSS] —**per'cussive** *adj.* —**per'cussively** *adv.* —**per'cussiveness** *n.*

percussion cap *n.* a detonator consisting of a paper or thin metal cap containing material that explodes when struck.

percussion instrument *n.* any of various musical instruments that produce a sound when their resonating surfaces are struck directly, as with a stick or mallet, or by leverage action.

percussionist (pə'kʌʃənɪst) *n. Music.* a person who plays any of several percussion instruments.

percutaneous (,pɜːkjʊ'teɪnɪəs) *adj. Med.* effected through the skin, as in the absorption of an ointment.

Percy ('pɜːsɪ) *n.* **1.** Sir **Henry**, known as *Harry Hotspur.* 1364–1403, English rebel, who was killed leading an army against Henry IV. **2. Thomas.** 1729–1811, English bishop and antiquary. His *Reliques of Ancient English Poetry* (1765) stimulated the interest of Romantic writers in old English and Scottish ballads.

Perdido (*Spanish* pɛr'ðiðo) *n.* **Monte** ('mɔnte). a mountain in NE Spain, in the central Pyrenees. Height: 3352 m (10 997 ft.). French name: (Mont) **Perdu.**

per diem ('pɜː 'daɪɛm, 'diːɛm) *adv.* **1.** every day or by the day. ~*n.* **2.** an allowance for daily expenses. [from L]

perdition (pə'dɪʃən) *n.* **1.** *Christianity.* **a.** final and irrevocable spiritual ruin. **b.** this state as one that the wicked are said to be destined to endure forever. **2.** another word for **hell. 3.** *Arch.* utter ruin or destruction. [C14: from LL *perditiō* ruin, from L *perdere* to lose, from PER- (away) + *dāre* to give]

Perdu (pɛrdy) *n.* **Mont.** the French name for (Monte) **Perdido.**

perdurable (pə'djʊərəbəl) *adj. Rare.* extremely durable. [C13: from LL *perdūrābilis,* from L *per-* (intensive) + *dūrābilis* long-lasting, from *dūrus* hard]

père *French.* (pɛr; *English* pɛə) *n.* an addition to a French surname to specify the father rather than the son of the same name: *Dumas père.*

Perea (pə'riːə) *n.* a variant spelling of **Peraea.**

Père David's deer *n.* a large grey deer, surviving only in captivity. [C20: after Father A. *David* (died 1900), F missionary]

peregrinate ('pɛrɪgrɪ,neɪt) *vb.* **1.** (*intr.*) to travel or wander about from place to place; voyage. **2.** (*tr.*) to travel through (a place). [C16: from L, from *peregrīnārī* to travel; see PEREGRINE] —,**peregri'nation** *n.* —'**peregri,nator** *n.*

peregrine ('pɛrɪgrɪn) *adj. Arch.* **1.** coming from abroad. **2.** travelling. [C14: from L *peregrīnus* foreign, from *per-eger* being abroad, from *per* through + *ager* land (that is, beyond one's own land)]

peregrine falcon *n.* a falcon occurring in most parts of the world, having a dark plumage on the back and wings and lighter underparts.

Pereira (*Spanish* pe'rɛira) *n.* a town in W central Colombia: cattle trading and coffee processing. Pop.: 301 715 (1985).

Perelman ('pɛrəlmən, 'pɜːl-) *n.* **S(idney) J(oseph).** 1904–79, U.S. humorous writer. After scriptwriting for the Marx Brothers, he published many collections of articles, including *Crazy Like a Fox* (1944) and *Eastward, Hi!* (1977).

peremptory (pə'rɛmptərɪ) *adj.* **1.** urgent or commanding: *a peremptory ring on the bell.* **2.** not able to be remitted or debated; decisive. **3.** dogmatic. **4.** *Law.* **a.** admitting of no denial or contradiction; precluding debate. **b.** obligatory rather than permissive. [C16: from Anglo-Norman *peremptorie,* from L *peremptōrius* decisive, from *perimere* to take away completely] —**per'empto-rily** *adv.* —**per'emptoriness** *n.*

perennial (pə'rɛnɪəl) *adj.* **1.** lasting throughout the year or through many years. **2.** everlasting; perpetual. ~*n.* **3.** a woody or herbaceous plant that continues its growth for at least three years. [C17: from L *perennis* continual, from *per* through + *annus* year] —**per'ennially** *adv.*

Peres ('pɛrɛs) *n.* **Shimon** (ʃiː'məʊn). born 1923, Israeli statesman, born in Poland: prime minister (1984–86).

perestroika (pɛrə'strɔɪkə) *n.* the policy of restructuring the Soviet economy, etc., under the leadership of Mikhail Gorbachov. [C20: Russian, lit.: reconstruction]

Pérez de Cuéllar ('pɛrɛs də 'kweɪja:) *n.* **Javier** ('jævɪeɪ) born 1920, Peruvian diplomat and UN secretary-general from 1982.

perfect *adj.* ('pɜːfɪkt). **1.** having all essential elements. **2.** unblemished; faultless: *a perfect gemstone.* **3.** correct or precise: *perfect timing.* **4.** utter or absolute: *a perfect stranger.* **5.** excellent in all respects: *a perfect day.* **6.** *Maths.* exactly divisible into equal integral or polynomial roots: *36 is a perfect square.* **7.** *Bot.* **a.** (of flowers) having functional stamens and pistils. **b.** (of plants) having all parts present. **8.** *Grammar.* denoting a tense of verbs used in describing an action that has been completed. In English this is formed with *have* or *has* plus the past participle. **9.** *Music.* **a.** of or relating to the intervals of the unison, fourth, fifth, and octave. **b.** (of a cadence) ending on the tonic chord, giving a feeling of conclusion. Also: **final.** ~*n.* ('pɜːfɪkt). **10.** *Grammar.* **a.** the perfect tense. **b.** a verb in this tense. ~*vb.* (pə'fɛkt). (*tr.*) **11.** to make perfect; improve to one's satisfaction: *he is in Paris to perfect his French.* **12.** to make fully accomplished. [C13: from L *perfectus,* from *perficere* to perform, from *per-* through + *facere* to do]

▷ **Usage.** See at **unique.**

perfect gas *n.* another name for **ideal gas.**

perfectible (pə'fɛktəbəl) *adj.* capable of becoming or being made perfect. —**per,fecti'bility** *n.*

perfection (pə'fɛkʃən) *n.* **1.** the act of perfecting or the state or quality of being perfect. **2.** the highest quality of a quality, etc. **3.** an embodiment of perfection. [C13: from L *perfectiō* a completing, from *perficere* to finish]

perfectionism (pə'fɛkʃə,nɪzəm) *n.* **1.** *Philosophy.* the doctrine that man can attain perfection in this life. **2.** the demand for the highest standard of excellence. —**per'fectionist** *n., adj.*

perfective (pə'fɛktɪv) *adj.* **1.** tending to perfect. **2.** *Grammar.* denoting an aspect of verbs used to express that the action or event described by the verb is or was completed: *I lived in London for ten years* is perfective; *I have lived in London for ten years* is imperfective, since the implication is that I still live in London.

perfectly ('pɜːfɪktlɪ) *adv.* **1.** completely, utterly, or absolutely. **2.** in a perfect way.

perfect number *n.* an integer, such as 28, that is equal to the sum of all its possible factors, excluding itself.

perfect participle *n.* another name for **past participle.**

perfect pitch *n.* another name (not in technical usage) for **absolute pitch** (sense 1).

perfervid (pɜː'fɜːvɪd) *adj. Literary.* extremely ardent or zealous. [C19: from NL *perfervidus*]

perfidious (pə'fɪdɪəs) *adj.* guilty, treacherous, or faithless; deceitful. [C18: from L, from *perfidus* faithless] —**per'fidiously** *adv.* —**per'fidiousness** *n.* —'**perfidy** *n.*

perfoliate (pə'fəʊlɪɪt, -,eɪt) *adj.* (of a leaf) having a base that completely encloses the stem, so that the stem appears to pass through it. [C17: from NL *perfoliātus,* from L *per-* through + *folium* leaf] —**per,foli'ation** *n.*

perforate *vb.* ('pɜːfə,reɪt). **1.** to make a hole or holes in (something). **2.** (*tr.*) to punch rows of holes between (stamps, etc.) for ease of separation. ~*adj.* ('pɜːfərɪt). **3.** *Biol.* pierced by small holes: *perforate shells.* **4.** *Philately.* another word for **perforated.** [C16: from L *perforāre,* from *per-* through + *forāre* to pierce] —**perforable** ('pɜːfərəbəl) *adj.* —'**perfo,rator** *n.*

perforated ('pɜːfə,reɪtɪd) *adj.* **1.** pierced with holes. **2.** (esp. of stamps) having perforations.

perforation (,pɜːfə'reɪʃən) *n.* **1.** the act of perforating or the state of being perforated. **2.** a hole or holes made in something. **3. a.** a method of making individual stamps, etc. easily separable by punching holes along their margins. **b.** the holes punched in this way. Abbrev.: **perf.**

perforce (pə'fɔːs) *adv.* by necessity; unavoidably. [C14: from OF *par force*]

perform (pə'fɔːm) *vb.* **1.** to carry out (an action). **2.** (*tr.*) to fulfil: *to perform someone's request.* **3.** to present or enact (a play, concert, etc.): *the group performed Hamlet.* [C14: from Anglo-Norman *parfourner* (infl. by *forme* FORM), from OF *parfournir,* from *par-* PER- + *fournir* to provide] —**per'formable** *adj.* —**per'former** *n.*

performance (pə'fɔːməns) *n.* **1.** the act, process, or art of performing. **2.** an artistic or dramatic production: *last night's performance was terrible.* **3.** manner or quality of functioning: *a machine's performance.* **4.** *Inf.* mode of conduct or behaviour, esp. when distasteful: *what did you mean by that performance at the restaurant?* **5.** *Inf.* any tiresome procedure: *the performance of preparing to go out in the snow.*

performance art *n.* a theatrical presentation that incorporates various art forms, such as dance, sculpture, etc.

performative (pə'fɔːmətɪv) *adj. Linguistics, philosophy.* **1. a.** denoting an utterance that itself constitutes the act described by the verb. For example, the sentence *I con-fess that I was there* is itself a confession. **b.** (*as n.*): *that sentence is a performative.* **2. a.** denoting a verb that may be used as the main verb in such an utterance. **b.** (*as n.*): *"promise" is a performative.*

performing arts the arts, such as a music and drama, that require a public performance.

perfume *n.* ('pɜːfjuːm). **1.** a mixture of alcohol and fragrant essential oils extracted from flowers, etc., or made synthetically. **2.** a scent or odour, esp. a fragrant one. *~vb.* (pə'fjuːm). **3.** (*tr.*) to impart a perfume to. [C16: from F *parfum*, prob. from OProvençal *perfum*, from *perfumar* to make scented, from *per* through (from L) + *fumar* to smoke, from L *fumāre* to smoke]

perfumer (pə'fjuːmə) *n.* a person who makes or sells perfume.

perfumery (pə'fjuːmərɪ) *n.*, *pl.* **-eries.** **1.** a place where perfumes are sold. **2.** a factory where perfumes are made. **3.** the process of making perfumes. **4.** perfumes in general.

perfunctory (pə'fʌŋktərɪ) *adj.* **1.** done superficially, only as a matter of routine. **2.** dull or indifferent. [C16: from LL *perfunctōrius* negligent, from *perfunctus* dispatched, from *perfungī* to fulfil] —**per'functorily** *adv.* —**per'functoriness** *n.*

perfuse (pə'fjuːz) *vb.* (*tr.*) to suffuse or permeate (a liquid, colour, etc.) through or over (something). [C16: from L *perfūsus* wetted, from *perfundere* to pour over]

Pergamum ('pɜːgəməm) *n.* **1.** an ancient city in NW Asia Minor, in Mysia: capital of a major Hellenistic monarchy of the same name that later became a Roman province. **2.** the ancient name for **Bergama.**

pergola ('pɜːgələ) *n.* a horizontal trellis or framework, supported on posts, that carries climbing plants. [C17: via It. from L *pergula* projection from a roof, from *pergere* to go forward]

Pergolesi (*Italian* pergo'leːsi) *n.* **Giovanni Battista** (dʒo-'vanni bat'tista). 1710–36, Italian composer: his works include the operetta *La Serva padrona* (1733) and the *Stabat Mater* (1736) for women's voices.

perhaps (pə'hæps; *informal* præps) *adv.* **1. a.** possibly; maybe. **b.** (*as sentence modifier*): *he'll arrive tomorrow, perhaps. ~sentence substitute.* **2.** it may happen, be so, etc.; maybe. [C16 *perhappes*, from *per* by + *happes* chance]

peri ('pɪərɪ) *n.*, *pl.* **-ris. 1.** (in Persian folklore) one of a race of beautiful supernatural beings. **2.** any beautiful fairy-like creature. [C18: from Persian: fairy, from Avestan *pairikā* witch]

peri- *prefix.* **1.** enclosing, encircling, or around: *pericardium; pericarp.* **2.** near or adjacent: *perihelion.* [from Gk *peri* around]

perianth ('pɛrɪˌænθ) *n.* the outer part of a flower, consisting of the calyx and corolla. [C18: from F *périanthe*, from NL, from PERI- + Gk *anthos* flower]

periapt ('pɛrɪˌæpt) *n. Rare.* a charm or amulet. [C16: via F from Gk *periapton*, from PERI- + *haptos* clasped, from *haptein* to fasten]

pericarditis (ˌpɛrɪkɑː'daɪtɪs) *n.* inflammation of the pericardium.

pericardium (ˌpɛrɪ'kɑːdɪəm) *n.*, *pl.* **-dia** (-dɪə). the membranous sac enclosing the heart. [C16: via NL from Gk *perikardion*, from PERI- + *kardia* heart] —**peri'cardial** *or* ˌperi'cardiˌac *adj.*

pericarp ('pɛrɪˌkɑːp) *n.* the part of a fruit enclosing the seeds that develops from the wall of the ovary. [C18: via F from NL *pericarpium*] —ˌperi'carpial *adj.*

perichondrium (ˌpɛrɪ'kɒndrɪəm) *n.*, *pl.* **-dria** (-drɪə). the fibrous membrane that covers the cartilage. [C18: NL, from PERI-+ Gk *chondros* cartilage]

periclase ('pɛrɪˌkleɪs) *n.* a mineral consisting of magnesium oxide. [C19: from NL *periclasia*, from Gk *peri* very + *klasis* a breaking, referring to its perfect cleavage]

Pericles ('pɛrɪˌkliːz) *n.* ?495–429 B.C., Athenian statesman and leader of the popular party, who contributed greatly to Athens' political and cultural supremacy in Greece. In power from about 460 B.C., he was responsible for the construction of the Parthenon. He conducted the Peloponnesian War (431–404B.C.) successfully until his death. —ˌPeri'clean *adj.*

pericline ('pɛrɪˌklaɪn) *n.* **1.** a white translucent variety of albite in the form of elongated crystals. **2.** Also called: **dome.** a dome-shaped formation of stratified rock with its

slopes following the direction of folding. [C19: from Gk *periklinēs* sloping on all sides] — ˌperi'clinal *adj.*

pericranium (ˌpɛrɪ'kreɪnɪəm) *n.*, *pl.* **-nia** (-nɪə). the fibrous membrane covering the external surface of the skull. [C16: NL, from Gk *perikranion*]

peridot ('pɛrɪˌdɒt) *n.* a pale green transparent variety of the olivine chrysolite, used as a gemstone. [C14: from OF *peritot*, from ?]

perigee ('pɛrɪˌdʒiː) *n.* the point in its orbit around the earth when the moon or a satellite is nearest the earth. [C16: via F from Gk *perigeion*, from PERI- + *gea* earth] —ˌperi'gean *adj.*

periglacial (ˌpɛrɪ'gleɪʃəl) *adj.* relating to a region bordering a glacier: *periglacial climate.*

perihelion (ˌpɛrɪ'hiːlɪən) *n.*, *pl.* **-lia** (-lɪə). the point in its orbit when a planet or comet is nearest the sun. [C17: from NL *perihēlium*, from PERI- + Gk *hēlios* sun]

peril ('pɛrɪl) *n.* exposure to risk or harm; danger or jeopardy. [C13: via OF from L *periculum*]

perilous ('pɛrɪləs) *adj.* very hazardous or dangerous: *a perilous journey.* —**perilously** *adv.* —**perilousness** *n.*

perilune ('pɛrɪˌluːn) *n.* the point in a lunar orbit when a spacecraft is nearest the moon. [C20: from PERI- + -*lune,* from L *lūna* moon]

perimeter (pə'rɪmɪtə) *n.* **1.** *Maths.* **a.** the curve or line enclosing a plane area. **b.** the length of this curve or line. **2. a.** any boundary around something. **b.** (*as modifier*): *a perimeter fence.* **3.** a medical instrument for measuring the field of vision. [C16: from F *périmètre,* from L *perimetros*] —**perimetric** (ˌpɛrɪ'mɛtrɪk) *adj.*

perinatal (ˌpɛrɪ'neɪtəl) *adj.* of or occurring in the period from about three months before to one month after birth.

perineum (ˌpɛrɪ'niːəm) *n.*, *pl.* **-nea** (-'niːə). **1.** the region of the body between the anus and the genital organs. **2.** the surface of the human trunk between the thighs. [C17: from NL, from Gk *perinaion,* from PERI- + *inein* to empty] —ˌperi'neal *adj.*

period ('pɪərɪəd) *n.* **1.** a portion of time of indefinable length: *he spent a period away from home.* **2. a.** a portion of time specified in some way: *Picasso's blue period.* **b.** (*as modifier*): *period costume.* **3.** a nontechnical name for an occurence of menstruation. **4.** *Geol.* a unit of geological time during which a system of rocks is formed: *the Jurassic period.* **5.** a division of time, esp. of the academic day. **6.** *Physics, maths.* the time taken to complete one cycle of a regularly recurring phenomenon; the reciprocal of frequency. Symbol: *T* **7.** *Astron.* **a.** the time required by a body to make one complete rotation on its axis. **b.** the time interval between two successive maxima or minima of light variation of a variable star. **8.** *Chem.* one of the horizontal rows of elements in the periodic table. Each period starts with an alkali metal and ends with a rare gas. **9.** another term (esp. U.S. and Canad.) for **full stop. 10.** a complete sentence, esp. one with several clauses. **11.** a completion or end. [C14 *peryod,* from L *periodus,* from Gk *periodos* circuit, from PERI- + *hodos* way]

periodic (ˌpɪərɪ'ɒdɪk) *adj.* **1.** happening or recurring at intervals; intermittent. **2.** of, relating to, or resembling a period. **3.** having or occurring in repeated periods or cycles. —ˌperi'odically *adv.* —**periodicity** (ˌpɪərɪə'dɪsɪtɪ) *n.*

periodical (ˌpɪərɪ'ɒdɪkəl) *n.* **1.** a publication issued at regular intervals, usually monthly or weekly. *~adj.* **2.** of or relating to such publications. **3.** published at regular intervals. **4.** periodic or occasional.

periodic function *n. Maths.* a function whose value is repeated at constant intervals.

periodic law *n.* the principle that the chemical properties of the elements are periodic functions of their atomic weights or, more accurately, of their atomic numbers.

periodic sentence *n. Rhetoric.* a sentence in which the completion of the main clause is left to the end, thus creating an effect of suspense.

periodic table *n.* a table of the elements, arranged in order of increasing atomic number, based on the periodic law.

periodontal ('pɛrɪə'dɒntəl) *adj.* of, denoting, or affecting the gums and other tissues surrounding the teeth: *periodontal disease.*

periodontics (ˌpɛrɪə'dɒntɪks) *n.* (*functioning as sing.*) the branch of dentistry concerned with diseases affecting the tissues and structures that surround teeth. Also called:

periodontology. [C19: from PERI- + -odontics, from Gk *odŏn* tooth] — ,**perio'dontical** *adj.*

periosteum (,pɛrɪ'ɒstɪəm) *n.*, *pl.* **-tea** (-tɪə). a thick fibrous two-layered membrane covering the surface of bones. [C16: NL, from Gk *periosteon*, from PERI- + *osteon* bone] — ,**peri'osteal** *adj.*

peripatetic (,pɛrɪpə'tɛtɪk) *adj.* **1.** itinerant. **2.** *Brit.* employed in two or more educational establishments and travelling from one to another: *a peripatetic football coach.* ~*n.* **3.** a peripatetic person. [C16: from L *peripatēticus*, from Gk, from *peripatein* to pace to and fro] — ,**peripa'tetically** *adv.*

Peripatetic (,pɛrɪpə'tɛtɪk) *adj.* **1.** of or relating to the teachings of Aristotle, who used to teach philosophy while walking about the Lyceum in ancient Athens. ~*n.* **2.** a student of Aristotelianism.

peripeteia (,pɛrɪpɪ'taɪə, -'tɪə) *n.* (esp. in drama) an abrupt turn of events or reversal of circumstances. [C16: from Gk, from PERI- + *piptein* to fall (to change suddenly, lit.: to fall around)]

peripheral (pə'rɪfərəl) *adj.* **1.** not relating to the most important part of something; incidental. **2.** of or relating to a periphery. **3.** *Anat.* of, relating to, or situated near the surface of the body: *a peripheral nerve.* — **pe'ripherally** *adv.*

peripheral device *or* **unit** *n.* *Computers.* any device, such as a card punch, line printer, etc., concerned with input/output, storage, etc. Often shortened to **peripheral.**

periphery (pə'rɪfəri) *n.*, *pl.* **-eries. 1.** the outermost boundary of an area. **2.** the outside surface of something. [C16: from LL *peripheria*, from Gk, from PERI- + *pherein* to bear]

periphrasis (pə'rɪfrəsɪs) *n.*, *pl.* **-rases** (-rə,siːz). **1.** a roundabout way of expressing something; circumlocution. **2.** an expression of this kind. [C16: via L from Gk, from PERI- + *phrazein* to declare]

periphrastic (,pɛrɪ'fræstɪk) *adj.* **1.** employing or involving periphrasis. **2.** expressed in two or more words rather than by an inflected form of one: used esp. of a tense of a verb where the alternative word is an auxiliary verb, as in *He does go.* — ,**peri'phrastically** *adv.*

perisarc ('pɛrɪ,sɑːk) *n.* the outer chitinous layer secreted by colonial hydrozoan coelenterates. [C19: from PERI- + -sarc, from Gk *sarx* flesh]

periscope ('pɛrɪ,skəʊp) *n.* any of a number of optical instruments that enable the user to view objects that are not in the direct line of vision, such as one in a submarine for looking above the surface of the water. They have a system of mirrors or prisms to reflect the light. [C19: from Gk *periskopein* to look around] — **periscopic** (,pɛrɪ'skɒpɪk) *adj.*

perish ('pɛrɪʃ) *vb.* **1.** (*intr.*) to be destroyed or die, esp. in an untimely way. **2.** (*tr.* sometimes foll. by *with* or *from*) to cause to suffer: *we were perished with cold.* **3.** to rot or cause to rot: *leather perishes if exposed to bad weather.* ~*n.* **4. do a perish.** *Austral. inf.* to die or come near to dying of thirst or starvation. [C13: from OF *périr*, from L *perire* to pass away entirely]

perishable ('pɛrɪʃəbəl) *adj.* **1.** liable to rot. ~*n.* **2.** (*often pl.*) a perishable article, esp. food. — ,**perisha'bility** *or* '**perishableness** *n.*

perishing ('pɛrɪʃɪŋ) *adj.* **1.** *Inf.* (of weather, etc.) extremely cold. **2.** *Sl.* (intensifier qualifying something undesirable): *it's a perishing nuisance!* — '**perishingly** *adv.*

perisperm ('pɛrɪ,spɜːm) *n.* the nutritive tissue surrounding the embryo in certain seeds.

perissodactyl (pə,rɪsəʊ'dæktɪl) *n.* **1.** any of an order of placental mammals having hooves with an odd number of toes: includes horses, tapirs, and rhinoceroses. ~*adj.* **2.** of, relating to, or belonging to this order. [C19: from NL *perissodactylus*, from Gk *perissos* uneven + *daktulos* digit]

peristalsis (,pɛrɪ'stælsɪs) *n.*, *pl.* **-ses** (-siːz). *Physiol.* the succession of waves of involuntary muscular contraction of various bodily tubes, esp. of the alimentary tract, where it effects transport of food and waste products. [C19: from NL, from PERI- + Gk *stalsis* compression, from *stellein* to press together] — ,**peri'staltic** *adj.*

peristome ('pɛrɪ,stəʊm) *n.* **1.** a fringe of pointed teeth surrounding the opening of a moss capsule. **2.** any of various parts surrounding the mouth of invertebrates such as

echinoderms, earthworms, and protozoans. [C18: from NL *peristoma*, from PERI- + Gk *stoma* mouth]

peristyle ('pɛrɪ,staɪl) *n.* **1.** a colonnade round a court or building. **2.** an area bounded by a colonnade. [C17: via F from L *peristylum*, from Gk *peristulon*, from PERI- + *stulos* column]

peritoneum (,pɛrɪtə'niːəm) *n.*, *pl.* **-nea** (-'niːə) *or* **-neums.** a serous sac that lines the walls of the abdominal cavity and covers the viscera. [C16: via LL from Gk *peritonaion*, from *peritonos* stretched around] — ,**peri-to'neal** *adj.*

peritonitis (,pɛrɪtə'naɪtɪs) *n.* inflammation of the peritoneum.

periwig ('pɛrɪ,wɪg) *n.* a wig, such as a peruke. [C16 *perwyke*, changed from F *perruque* wig, PERUKE]

periwinkle[1] ('pɛrɪ,wɪŋkəl) *n.* any of various edible marine gastropods having a spirally coiled shell. Often shortened to **winkle.** [C16: from ?]

periwinkle[2] ('pɛrɪ,wɪŋkəl) *n.* any of several Eurasian evergreen plants having trailing stems and blue flowers. [C14 *pervenke*, from OE *perwince*, from LL *pervinca*]

perjure ('pɜːdʒə) *vb.* (*tr.*) *Criminal law.* to render (oneself) guilty of perjury. [C15: from OF *parjurer*, from L *perjūrāre*, from PER- + *jūrāre* to make an oath, from *jūs* law] — '**perjurer** *n.*

perjured ('pɜːdʒəd) *adj.* *Criminal law.* **1. a.** having sworn falsely. **b.** having committed perjury. **2.** involving or characterized by perjury: *perjured evidence.*

perjury ('pɜːdʒəri) *n.*, *pl.* **-juries.** *Criminal law.* the offence committed by a witness in judicial proceedings who, having been lawfully sworn, wilfully gives false evidence. [C14: from Anglo-F *parjurie*, from L *perjūrium* a false oath; see PERJURE] — **perjurious** (pɜː'dʒʊərɪəs) *or* '**perjurous** *adj.*

perk[1] (pɜːk) *adj.* **1.** pert; brisk; lively. ~*vb.* **2.** See **perk up.** [C16: see PERK UP]

perk[2] (pɜːk) *vb. Inf.* short for **percolate** (sense 3).

perk[3] (pɜːk) *n. Brit. inf.* short for **perquisite.**

perk up *vb.* (*adv.*) **1.** to make or become more cheerful, hopeful, or lively. **2.** to rise or cause to rise briskly: *the dog's ears perked up.* **3.** (*tr.*) to make smarter in appearance: *she perked up her outfit with a bright scarf.* [C14 *perk*, ?from Norman F *perquer;* see PERCH[1]]

perky ('pɜːkɪ) *adj.* **perkier, perkiest. 1.** jaunty; lively. **2.** confident; spirited. — '**perkily** *adv.* — '**perkiness** *n.*

Perlis ('pɛəlɪs, 'pɜː-) *n.* a state of NW Peninsular Malaysia, on the Andaman Sea: a dependency of Thailand until 1909. Capital: Kangar. Pop.: 166 948 (1985 est.). Area: 803 sq. km (310 sq. miles).

perlite ('pɜːlaɪt) *n.* a variety of obsidian consisting of masses of globules. [C19: from F, from *perle* PEARL[1]]

perm[1] (pɜːm) *n.* **1.** a hairstyle produced by treatment with heat, chemicals, etc. which gives long-lasting waves or curls. Also called (esp. formerly): **permanent wave.** ~*vb.* (*tr.*) **2.** to give a perm to (hair).

perm[2] (pɜːm) *n. Inf.* short for **permutate, permutation** (sense 4).

Perm (*Russian* pjermj) *n.* a port in the central Soviet Union, on the Kama River: oil refinery; university (1916). Pop.: 1 075 000 (1987). Former name (1940–62): **Molotov.**

permafrost ('pɜːmə,frɒst) *n.* ground that is permanently frozen. [C20: from PERMA(NENT) + FROST]

permalloy (pɜːm'ælɔɪ) *n.* any of various alloys containing iron and nickel and sometimes smaller amounts of chromium and molybdenum.

permanence ('pɜːmənəns) *n.* the state or quality of being permanent.

permanency ('pɜːmənənsɪ) *n.*, *pl.* **-cies. 1.** a person or thing that is permanent. **2.** another word for **permanence.**

permanent ('pɜːmənənt) *adj.* **1.** existing or intended to exist for an indefinite period: *a permanent structure.* **2.** not expected to change; not temporary: *a permanent condition.* [C15: from L *permanens* continuing, from *permanēre* to stay to the end] — '**permanently** *adv.*

permanent magnet *n.* a magnet, often of steel, that retains its magnetization after the magnetic field producing it has been removed.

permanent press *n.* a chemical treatment for clothing that makes the fabric crease-resistant and sometimes provides a garment with a permanent crease or pleats.

permanent wave *n.* another name (esp. formerly) for **perm**[1] (sense 1).

permanent way *n. Chiefly Brit.* the track of a railway, including the sleepers, rails, etc.

permanganate (pə'mæŋgə,neɪt, -nɪt) *n.* a salt of permanganic acid.

permanganic acid (,pɜ:mæn'gænɪk) *n.* a monobasic acid known only in solution and in the form of permanganate salts. Formula: $HMnO_4$. Systematic name: **manganic(VII) acid.**

permeability (,pɜ:mɪə'bɪlɪtɪ) *n.* **1.** the state or quality of being permeable. **2.** a measure of the ability of a medium to modify a magnetic field, expressed as the ratio of the magnetic flux density in the medium to the field strength; measured in henries per metre. Symbol: μ.

permeable ('pɜ:mɪəb³l) *adj.* capable of being permeated, esp. by liquids. [C15: from LL *permeābilis*, from L *permeāre* to pervade; see PERMEATE] —**'permeably** *adv.*

permeance ('pɜ:mɪəns) *n.* **1.** the act of permeating. **2.** the reciprocal of the reluctance of a magnetic circuit. —**'permeant** *adj., n.*

permeate ('pɜ:mɪ,eɪt) *vb.* **1.** to penetrate or pervade (a substance, area, etc.): *a lovely smell permeated the room.* **2.** to pass through or cause to pass through by osmosis or diffusion: *to permeate a membrane.* [C17: from L *permeāre*, from *per*-through + *meāre* to pass] —,**perme'ation** *n.* —**'permeative** *adj.*

Permian ('pɜ:mɪən) *adj.* **1.** of, denoting, or formed in the last period of the Palaeozoic era, between the Carboniferous and Triassic periods. ~*n.* **2. the.** the Permian period or rock system. [C19: after PERM, Russia]

permissible (pə'mɪsəb³l) *adj.* permitted; allowable. —**per,missi'bility** *n.* —**per'missibly** *adv.*

permission (pə'mɪʃən) *n.* authorization to do something.

permissive (pə'mɪsɪv) *adj.* **1.** tolerant; lenient: *permissive parents.* **2.** indulgent in matters of sex: *a permissive society.* **3.** granting permission. —**per'missively** *adv.* —**per'missiveness** *n.*

permit *vb.* (pə'mɪt), **-mitting, -mitted. 1.** (*tr.*) to grant permission to do something: *you are permitted to smoke.* **2.** (*tr.*) to consent to or tolerate: *she will not permit him to come.* **3.** (when *intr.*, often foll. by *of*; when *tr.*, often foll. by an infinitive) to allow the possibility (of): *the passage permits of two interpretations; his work permits him to relax nowadays.* ~*n.* ('pɜ:mɪt). **4.** an official document granting authorization; licence. **5.** permission. [C15: from L *permittere*, from *per*- through + *mittere* to send] —**per'mitter** *n.*

permittivity (,pɜ:mɪ'tɪvɪtɪ) *n., pl.* **-ties.** a measure of the ability of a substance to transmit an electric field.

permutate ('pɜ:mju,teɪt) *vb.* to alter the sequence or arrangement (of): *endlessly permutating three basic designs.*

permutation (,pɜ:mjʊ'teɪʃən) *n.* **1.** *Maths.* **a.** an ordered arrangement of the numbers, terms, etc., of a set into specified groups: *the permutations of a, b, and c, taken two at a time, are ab, ba, ac, ca, bc, cb.* **b.** a group formed in this way. **2.** a combination of items, etc., made by reordering. **3.** an alteration; transformation. **4.** a fixed combination for selections of results on football pools. Usually shortened to **perm.** [C14: from L *permūtātiō*, from *permūtāre* to change thoroughly] —,**permu'tational** *adj.*

permute (pə'mju:t) *vb.* (*tr.*) **1.** to change the sequence of. **2.** *Maths.* to subject to permutation. [C14: from L *permūtāre*, from PER- + *mūtāre* to change]

Pernambuco (,pɜ:nəm'bju:kəʊ; *Portuguese* pernəm'buku) *n.* **1.** a state of NE Brazil, on the Atlantic: consists of a humid coastal plain rising to a high inland plateau. Capital: Recife. Pop.: 6 147 080 (1980). Area: 98 280 sq. km (37 946 sq. miles). **2.** the former name of **Recife.**

pernicious (pə'nɪʃəs) *adj.* **1.** wicked or malicious: *pernicious lies.* **2.** causing grave harm; deadly. [C16: from L *perniciōsus*, from *perniciēs* ruin, from PER- (intensive) + *nex* death] —**per'niciously** *adv.* —**per'niciousness** *n.*

pernicious anaemia *n.* a form of anaemia characterized by lesions of the spinal cord, weakness, sore tongue, diarrhoea, etc.: associated with inadequate absorption of vitamin B_{12}.

pernickety (pə'nɪkɪtɪ) *adj. Inf.* **1.** excessively precise; fussy. **2.** (of a task) requiring close attention. [C19: orig. Scot. from ?]

Pernik (*Bulgarian* 'pɛrnik) *n.* an industrial town in W Bulgaria, on the Struma River. Pop.: 94 845 (1985). Former name (1949–62): **Dimitrovo.**

Perón (*Spanish* pe'rɔn) *n.* **1. Juan Domingo** (xwan do'mɪŋgo). 1895–1974, Argentine soldier and statesman; dictator (1946–55). He was deposed in 1955, remaining in exile until 1973, when he was elected president (1973–74). **2.** his third wife, **María Estella** (ma'ria es'teʎa), known as *Isabel.* born 1930, president of Argentina (1974–76); deposed. **3. (María) Eva (Duarte) de Perón** ('eβa), known as *Evita.* Second wife of Juan Domingo Perón. 1919–52, Argentine film actress: active in politics and social welfare (1946–52). —**Pe'ronist** *n., adj.*

peroneal (,pɛrə'ni:əl) *adj. Anat.* of or relating to the fibula. [C19: from NL *peronē*, from Gk: fibula]

perorate ('pɛrə,reɪt) *vb.* (*intr.*) **1.** to speak at length, esp. in a formal manner. **2.** to conclude a speech or sum up.

peroration (,pɛrə'reɪʃən) *n.* the conclusion of a speech or discourse, in which points made previously are summed up. [C15: from L *perōrātiō*, from PER- (thoroughly) + *ōrāre* to speak]

perovskite (pe'rɒvskaɪt) *n.* a yellow, brown, or greyish-black mineral. [C19: after *Perovski*, Russian mineralogist]

peroxide (pə'rɒksaɪd) *n.* **1.** short for **hydrogen peroxide**, esp. when used for bleaching hair. **2.** any of a class of metallic oxides, such as sodium peroxide, Na_2O_2. **3.** (*not in technical usage*) any of certain dioxides, such as manganese(VI) oxide, MnO_2, that resemble peroxides in their formula. **4.** any of a class of organic compounds whose molecules contain two oxygen atoms bound together. **5.** (*modifier*) of, relating to, bleached with, or resembling peroxide: *a peroxide blonde.* ~*vb.* **6.** (*tr.*) to bleach (the hair) with peroxide.

perpendicular (,pɜ:pən'dɪkjʊlə) *adj.* **1.** at right angles. **2.** denoting, relating to, or having the style of Gothic architecture used in England during the 14th and 15th centuries, characterized by tracery having vertical lines. **3.** upright; vertical. ~*n.* **4.** *Geom.* a line or plane perpendicular to another. **5.** any instrument used for indicating the vertical line through a given point. [C14: from L *perpendiculāris*, from *perpendiculum* a plumb line, from *per*- through + *pendēre* to hang] —**perpendicularity** (,pɜ:pən,dɪkjʊ'lærɪtɪ) *n.* —,**perpen'dicularly** *adv.*

perpetrate ('pɜ:pɪ,treɪt) *vb.* (*tr.*) to perform or be responsible for (a deception, crime, etc.). [C16: from L *perpetrāre*, from *per*- (thoroughly) + *patrāre* to perform] —,**perpe'tration** *n.* —**'perpe,trator** *n.*

perpetual (pə'pɛtjʊəl) *adj.* **1.** (*usually prenominal*) eternal; permanent. **2.** (*usually prenominal*) seemingly ceaseless because often repeated: *your perpetual complaints.* [C14: via OF from L *perpetuālis* universal, from *perpes* continuous, from *per*- (thoroughly) + *petere* to go towards] —**per'petually** *adv.*

perpetual motion *n.* motion of a hypothetical mechanism that continues indefinitely without any external source of energy. It is impossible in practice because of friction.

perpetuate (pə'pɛtjʊ,eɪt) *vb.* (*tr.*) to cause to continue: *to perpetuate misconceptions.* [C16: from L *perpetuāre* to continue without interruption, from *perpetuus* PERPETUAL] —**per,petu'ation** *n.*

perpetuity (,pɜ:pɪ'tju:ɪtɪ) *n., pl.* **-ties. 1.** eternity. **2.** the state of being perpetual. **3.** *Property law.* a limitation preventing the absolute disposal of an estate for longer than the period allowed by law. **4.** an annuity that is payable indefinitely. **5. in perpetuity.** for ever. [C15: from OF *perpetuite*, from L *perpetuitās* continuity; see PERPETUAL]

Perpignan (*French* pɛrpiɲɑ̃) *n.* a town in S France: historic capital of Roussillon. Pop.: 113 646 (1982).

perplex (pə'plɛks) *vb.* (*tr.*) **1.** to puzzle; bewilder; confuse. **2.** to complicate: *to perplex an issue.* [C15: from obs. *perplex* (adj.) intricate, from L *perplexus* entangled, from *per*- (thoroughly) + *plectere* to entwine] —**perplexedly** (pə'plɛksɪdlɪ, -'plɛkstlɪ) *adv.* —**per'plexingly** *adv.*

perplexity (pə'plɛksɪtɪ) *n., pl.* **-ties. 1.** the state of being perplexed. **2.** the state of being intricate or complicated. **3.** something that perplexes.

per pro ('pɜ: 'prəʊ) *prep.* by delegation to: through the agency of: used when signing documents on behalf of someone else. [L: abbrev. of *per prōcūrātiōnem*]

▷ **Usage.** In formal correspondence, when Brenda Smith is

signing on behalf of Peter Jones, she should write *Peter Jones per pro* (or *pp*) *Brenda Smith*, not the other way about.

perquisite ('pɜːkwɪzɪt) *n.* **1.** an incidental benefit gained from a certain type of employment, such as the use of a company car. **2.** a customary benefit received in addition to a regular income. **3.** a customary tip. **4.** something expected or regarded as an exclusive right. ~Often shortened (informal) to **perk.** [C15: from Med. L *perquīsītum*, from L *perquīrere* to seek earnestly for something]

Perrault (*French* pɛro) *n.* **Charles** (ʃarl). 1628–1703, French author, noted for his *Contes de ma mère l'oye* (1697), which contains the fairy tales *Little Red Riding Hood, Cinderella,* and *The Sleeping Beauty.*

Perrier water *or* **Perrier** ('pɛrɪeɪ) *n. Trademark.* a sparkling mineral water from the south of France. [C20: after a spring, *Source Perrier,* at Vergèze, France]

Perrin (*French* pɛrɛ̃) *n.* **Jean Baptiste** (ʒɑ̃ batist). 1870–1942, French physicist. His researches on the distribution and diffusion of particles in colloids (1911) gave evidence for the physical reality of molecules, confirmed the explanation of Brownian movement in terms of kinetic theory, and determined the magnitude of the Avogadro constant. He also studied cathode rays: Nobel prize for physics 1926.

perron ('pɛrən) *n.* an external flight of steps, esp. one at the front entrance of a building. [C14: from OF, from *pierre* stone, from L *petra*]

perry ('pɛrɪ) *n., pl.* **-ries.** wine made of pears, similar in taste to cider. [C14 *pereye,* from OF *peré,* ult. from L *pirum* pear]

Perry ('pɛrɪ) *n.* **1. Fred**(**erick John**). born 1909, English tennis and table-tennis player; world singles table-tennis champion (1929); Wimbledon singles champion (1934–36). **2. Matthew Calbraith.** 1794–1858, U.S. naval officer, who led a naval expedition to Japan that obtained a treaty (1854) opening up Japan to western trade. **3.** his brother, **Oliver Hazard.** 1785–1819, U.S. naval officer. His defeat of a British squadron on Lake Erie (1813) was the turning point in the War of 1812, leading to the recapture of Detroit.

pers. *abbrev. for:* **1.** person. **2.** personal.

Pers. *abbrev. for* Persia(n).

perse (pɜːs) *n.* **a.** a dark greyish-blue colour. **b.** (*as adj.*): *perse cloth.* [C14: from OF, from Med. L *persus,* ? changed from L *Persicus* Persian]

per se ('pɜː 'seɪ) *adv.* by or in itself; intrinsically. [L]

persecute ('pɜːsɪˌkjuːt) *vb.* (*tr.*) **1.** to oppress, harass, or maltreat, esp. because of race, religion, etc. **2.** to bother persistently. [C15: from OF, from *persecuteur,* from LL *persecūtor* pursuer, from *persequī* to take vengeance upon] —,**perse'cution** *n.* —'**perse,cutive** *adj.* —'**perse,cutor** *n.*

persecution complex *n. Psychol.* an acute irrational fear that other people are plotting one's downfall.

Persephone (pəˈsɛfənɪ) *n. Greek myth.* a daughter of Zeus and Demeter, abducted by Hades and made his wife and queen of the underworld, but allowed part of each year to leave it. Roman counterpart: **Proserpina.**

Persepolis (pəˈsɛpəlɪs) *n.* the capital of ancient Persia in the Persian Empire and under the Seleucids: founded by Darius; sacked by Alexander the Great in 330 B.C.

Perseus ('pɜːsɪəs) *n. Greek myth.* a son of Zeus and Danaë, who with Athena's help slew the Gorgon Medusa and rescued Andromeda from a sea monster.

perseverance (ˌpɜːsɪˈvɪərəns) *n.* **1.** continued steady belief or efforts; persistence. **2.** *Christian theol.* continuance in a state of grace.

perseveration (pɜːˌsɛvəˈreɪʃən) *n. Psychol.* the tendency for an impression, idea, or feeling to dissipate only slowly and to recur during subsequent experiences.

persevere (ˌpɜːsɪˈvɪə) *vb.* (*intr.; often foll. by in*) to show perseverance. [C14: from OF *perseverer,* from L, from *perseverus* very strict; see SEVERE]

Pershing ('pɜːʃɪŋ) *n.* **John Joseph,** nickname *Black Jack.* 1860–1948, U.S. general. He was commander in chief of the American Expeditionary Force in Europe (1917–19).

Persia ('pɜːʃə) *n.* **1.** the former name (until 1935) of **Iran. 2.** another name for **Persian Empire.**

Persian ('pɜːʃən) *adj.* **1.** of or relating to ancient Persia or modern Iran, their inhabitants, or their languages. ~*n.*

2. a native, citizen, or inhabitant of modern Iran; an Iranian. **3.** the language of Iran or Persia in any of its ancient or modern forms.

Persian carpet *or* **rug** *n.* a carpet or rug made in Persia or the Near East by knotting silk or wool yarn by hand onto a woven backing in rich colours and flowing or geometric designs.

Persian cat *n.* a long-haired variety of domestic cat.

Persian Empire *n.* the S Asian empire established by Cyrus the Great in the 6th century B.C. and overthrown by Alexander the Great in the 4th century B.C. At its height it extended from India to Europe.

Persian Gulf *n.* a shallow arm of the Arabian Sea between SW Iran and Arabia: linked with the Arabian Sea by the Strait of Hormus and the Gulf of Oman; important for the oilfields on its shores. Area: 233 000 sq. km (90 000 sq. miles).

Persian lamb *n.* **1.** a black loosely curled fur from the karakul lamb. **2.** a karakul lamb.

persiennes (ˌpɜːsɪˈɛnz) *pl. n.* outside window shutters having louvres. [C19: from F, from *persien* Persian]

persiflage ('pɜːsɪˌflɑːʒ) *n.* light frivolous conversation, style, or treatment; friendly teasing. [C18: via F from *persifler* to tease, from *per-* (intensive) + *siffler* to whistle, from L *sībilāre* to whistle]

persimmon (pɜːˈsɪmən) *n.* **1.** any of several tropical trees, typically having hard wood and large orange-red fruit. **2.** the sweet fruit of any of these trees, which is edible when completely ripe. [C17: from Amerind]

Persis ('pɜːsɪs) *n.* an ancient region of SW Iran: homeland of the Achaemenid dynasty.

persist (pəˈsɪst) *vb.* (*intr.*) **1.** (often foll. by *in*) to continue steadfastly or obstinately despite opposition. **2.** to continue without interruption: *the rain persisted throughout the night.* [C16: from L *persistere,* from *per-* (intensive) + *sistere* to stand steadfast] —**per'sister** *n.*

persistence (pəˈsɪstəns) *or* **persistency** *n.* **1.** the quality of persisting; tenacity. **2.** the act of persisting; continued effort or existence.

persistent (pəˈsɪstənt) *adj.* **1.** showing persistence. **2.** incessantly repeated; unrelenting: *your persistent questioning.* **3.** (of plant parts) remaining attached to the plant after the normal time of withering. **4.** *Zool.* (of parts normally present only in young stages) present in the adult. **5.** (of a chemical, esp. when used as a insecticide) slow to break down. —**per'sistently** *adv.*

person ('pɜːsən) *n., pl.* **persons. 1.** an individual human being. **2.** the body of a human being: *guns hidden on his person.* **3.** a grammatical category into which pronouns and forms of verbs are subdivided depending on whether they refer to the speaker, the person addressed, or some other individual, thing, etc. **4.** a human being or a corporation recognized in law as having certain rights and obligations. **5. in person.** actually present: *the author will be there in person.* [C13: from OF *persone,* from L *persōna* mask, ?from Etruscan *phersu* mask]

▷ **Usage.** *People* is the word usually used to refer to more than one individual: *there were a hundred people at the reception. Persons* is rarely used, except in official English: *several persons were interviewed.*

-person *n. combining form.* sometimes used instead of *-man* and *-woman* or *-lady: chairperson.*

▷ **Usage.** See at **-man.**

persona (pɜːˈsəʊnə) *n., pl.* **-nae** (-niː). **1.** (*often pl.*) a character in a play, novel, etc. **2.** (in Jungian psychology) the mechanism that conceals a person's true thoughts and feelings, esp. in adaptation to the outside world. [L: mask]

personable ('pɜːsənəbᵊl) *adj.* pleasant in appearance and personality. —'**personableness** *n.* —'**personably** *adv.*

personage ('pɜːsənɪdʒ) *n.* **1.** an important or distinguished person. **2.** another word for **person** (sense 1). **3.** *Rare.* a figure in literature, history, etc.

persona grata *Latin.* (pɜːˈsəʊnə ˈɡrɑːtə) *n., pl.* **personae gratae** (pɜːˈsəʊniː ˈɡrɑːtiː). an acceptable person, esp. a diplomat.

personal ('pɜːsənᵊl) *adj.* **1.** of or relating to the private aspects of a person's life: *personal letters.* **2.** (*prenominal*) of or relating to a person's body, its care, or its appearance: *personal hygiene.* **3.** (*prenominal*) belonging to or intended for a particular person and no-one else: *for your personal use.* **4.** (*prenominal*) undertaken by an individual: *a personal appearance by a celebrity.* **5.** referring to or involving a person's individual personality, intimate affairs, etc., esp. in an offensive way: *personal remarks; don't be so personal.* **6.** having the attributes of an individual conscious being: *a personal God.* **7.** of, relating to, or denoting grammatical person. **8.** *Law.* of or relating to movable property, as money, etc.

▷ **Usage.** *Personal* is sometimes used unnecessarily for emphasis: *my personal opinion is that he will not.* In formal contexts it is preferable to restrict it to instances where a distinction is made between private and official views, policies, etc.: *the prime minister gave me her personal opinion, which was not that of the cabinet.*

personal column *n.* a newspaper column containing personal messages and advertisements.

personal computer *n.* a small inexpensive computer used in word processing, computer games, etc.

personality (ˌpɜːsəˈnælɪtɪ) *n., pl.* **-ties. 1.** *Psychol.* the sum total of all the behavioural and mental characteristics by means of which an individual is recognized as being unique. **2.** the distinctive character of a person that makes him socially attractive: *a salesman needs a lot of personality.* **3.** a well-known person in a certain field, such as entertainment. **4.** a remarkable person. **5.** (*often pl.*) a personal remark.

personalize *or* **-ise** (ˈpɜːsənəˌlaɪz) *vb.* (*tr.*) **1.** to endow with personal or individual qualities. **2.** to mark (stationery, clothing, etc.) with a person's initials, name, etc. **3.** to take (a remark, etc.) personally. **4.** another word for **personify.** —**ˌpersonaliˈzation** *or* **-iˈsation** *n.*

personally (ˈpɜːsənəlɪ) *adv.* **1.** without the help or intervention of others: *I'll attend to it personally.* **2.** (*sentence modifier*) in one's own opinion or as regards oneself: *personally, I hate onions.* **3.** as if referring to oneself: *to take the insults personally.* **4.** as a person: *we like him personally, but professionally he's incompetent.*

personal pronoun *n.* a pronoun having a definite person or thing as an antecedent and functioning grammatically in the same way as the noun that it replaces. The personal pronouns include *I, you, he, she, it, we,* and *they.*

personal property *n. Law.* movable property, such as furniture or money. Also called: **personalty.** Cf. **real property.**

personal stereo *n.* a small audio cassette player worn attached to a belt and used with lightweight headphones.

persona non grata *Latin.* (pɜːˈsəʊnə nɒn ˈɡrɑːtə) *n., pl.* **personae non gratae** (pɜːˈsəʊniː nɒn ˈɡrɑːtiː). **1.** an unacceptable or unwelcome person. **2.** a diplomat who is not acceptable to the government to whom he is accredited.

personate (ˈpɜːsəˌneɪt) *vb.* (*tr.*) **1.** to act the part of (a character in a play); portray. **2.** *Criminal law.* to assume the identity of (another person) with intent to deceive. —ˌ**personˈation** *n.* —ˈ**personative** *adj.* —ˈ**personˌator** *n.*

personification (pɜːˌsɒnɪfɪˈkeɪʃən) *n.* **1.** the attribution of human characteristics to things, abstract ideas, etc. **2.** the representation of an abstract quality or idea in the form of a person, creature, etc., as in art and literature. **3.** a person or thing that personifies. **4.** a person or thing regarded as an embodiment of a quality: *he is the personification of optimism.*

personify (pɜːˈsɒnɪˌfaɪ) *vb.* **-fying, -fied.** (*tr.*) **1.** to attribute human characteristics to (a thing or abstraction). **2.** to represent (an abstract quality) in human or animal form. **3.** (of a person or thing) to represent (an abstract quality), as in art. **4.** to be the embodiment of. —per'soniˌfier *n.*

personnel (ˌpɜːsəˈnɛl) *n.* **1.** the people employed in an organization or for a service. **2. a.** the department that interviews, appoints, or keeps records of employees. **b.** (*as modifier*): *a personnel officer.* [C19: from F, ult. from LL *persōnālis* personal (adj.); see PERSON]

perspective (pəˈspɛktɪv) *n.* **1.** a way of regarding situations, facts, etc., and judging their relative importance. **2.** the proper or accurate point of view or the ability to see it; objectivity: *try to get some perspective on your troubles.* **3.** a view over some distance in space or time; prospect. **4.** the theory or art of suggesting three dimensions on a two-dimensional surface, in order to recreate the appearance and spatial relationships that objects or a scene in recession present to the eye. **5.** the appearance of objects, buildings, etc., relative to each other, as determined by their distance from the viewer, or the effects of this

distance on their appearance. [C14: from Med. L *perspectiva ars* the science of optics, from L *perspicere* to inspect carefully] —per'spectively *adv.*

Perspex (ˈpɜːspɛks) *n. Trademark.* any of various clear acrylic resins.

perspicacious (ˌpɜːspɪˈkeɪʃəs) *adj.* acutely perceptive or discerning. [C17: from L *perspicax,* from *perspicere* to look at closely] —ˌperspiˈcaciously *adv.* —**perspicacity** (ˌpɜːspɪˈkæsɪtɪ) *or* ˌperspiˈcaciousness *n.*

perspicuous (pəˈspɪkjʊəs) *adj.* (of speech or writing) easily understood; lucid. [C15: from L *perspicuus* transparent, from *perspicere* to explore thoroughly] —per'spicuously *adv.* —per'spicuousness *or* perspicuity (ˌpɜːspɪˈkjuːɪtɪ) *n.*

perspiration (ˌpɜːspəˈreɪʃən) *n.* **1.** the salty fluid secreted by the sweat glands of the skin. **2.** the act of secreting this fluid. —**perspiratory** (pəˈspaɪərətərɪ) *adj.*

perspire (pəˈspaɪə) *vb.* to secrete or exude (perspiration) through the pores of the skin. [C17: from L *perspīrāre* to blow, from *per-* (through) + *spīrāre* to breathe] —per'spiringly *adv.*

persuade (pəˈsweɪd) *vb.* (*tr.; may take a clause as object or an infinitive*) **1.** to induce, urge, or prevail upon successfully: *he finally persuaded them to buy it.* **2.** to cause to believe; convince: *even with the evidence, the police were not persuaded.* [C16: from L *persuādēre,* from *per-* (intensive) + *suādēre* to urge, advise] —per'suadable *or* per'suasible *adj.* —per,suada'bility *or* per,suasi'bility *n.* —per'suader *n.*

persuasion (pəˈsweɪʒən) *n.* **1.** the act of persuading or of trying to persuade. **2.** the power to persuade. **3.** a strong belief. **4.** an established creed or belief, esp. a religious one. **5.** a sect, party, or faction. [C14: from L *persuāsiō*]

persuasive (pəˈsweɪsɪv) *adj.* having the power or tending to persuade: *a persuasive salesman.* —per'suasively *adv.* —per'suasiveness *n.*

pert (pɜːt) *adj.* **1.** saucy, impudent, or forward. **2.** jaunty: *a pert little hat.* **3.** *Obs.* clever or brisk. [C13: var. of earlier *apert,* from L *apertus* open, from *aperīre* to open] —'pertly *adv.* —'pertness *n.*

pert. *abbrev. for* pertaining.

pertain (pəˈteɪn) *vb.* (*intr.; often foll. by to*) **1.** to have reference or relevance. **2.** to be appropriate. **3.** to belong (to) or be a part (of). [C14: from L *pertinēre,* from *per-* (intensive) + *tenēre* to hold]

Perth (pɜːθ) *n.* **1.** a city in central Scotland, in Tayside region on the River Tay: capital of Scotland from the 12th century until the assassination of James I there in 1437. Pop.: 41 654 (1984 est.). **2.** a city in SW Australia, capital of Western Australia, on the Swan River: major industrial centre; University of Western Australia (1911). Pop.: 1 025 340 (1986).

Perthshire (ˈpɜːθˌʃɪə, -ʃə) *n.* (until 1975) a county of central Scotland, now part of Central and Tayside regions.

pertinacious (ˌpɜːtɪˈneɪʃəs) *adj.* **1.** doggedly resolute in purpose or belief; unyielding. **2.** stubbornly persistent. [C17: from L *pertināx,* from *per-* (intensive) + *tenāx* clinging, from *tenēre* to hold] —ˌperti'naciously *adv.* —**pertinacity** (ˌpɜːtɪˈnæsɪtɪ) *or* ˌperti'naciousness *n.*

pertinent (ˈpɜːtɪnənt) *adj.* relating to the matter at hand; relevant. [C14: from L *pertinēns,* from *pertinēre* to PERTAIN] —'pertinence *or* 'pertinency *n.* —'pertinently *adv.*

perturb (pəˈtɜːb) *vb.* (*tr.; often passive*) **1.** to disturb the composure of; trouble. **2.** to throw into disorder. **3.** *Physics, astron.* to cause (a planet, electron, etc.) to undergo a perturbation. [C14: from OF *pertourber,* from L *perturbāre* to confuse, from *per-* (intensive) + *turbāre* to agitate] —per'turbable *adj.* —per'turbing *adj.*

perturbation (ˌpɜːtəˈbeɪʃən) *n.* **1.** the act of perturbing or the state of being perturbed. **2.** a cause of disturbance. **3.** *Physics.* a secondary influence on a system that modifies simple behaviour, such as the effect of the other electrons on one electron in an atom. **4.** *Astron.* a small continuous deviation in the orbit of a planet or comet, due to the attraction of neighbouring planets.

pertussis (pəˈtʌsɪs) *n.* the technical name for **whooping cough.** [C18: NL, from L *per-* (intensive) + *tussis* cough] —per'tussal *adj.*

Peru (pəˈruː) *n.* a republic in W South America, on the Pacific: the centre of the great Inca Empire when conquered by the Spanish in 1532; gained independence in 1824 by defeating Spanish forces with armies led by San Martín and Bolívar; consists of a coastal desert, rising to the Andes; an important exporter of minerals and a major fishing nation. Official languages: Spanish and Quechua. Religion: Roman Catholic. Currency: inti. Capital: Lima. Pop.: 17 031 221 (1981). Area: 1 285 215 sq. km (496 222 sq. miles). —**Peruvian** (pə'ruːvɪən) *adj., n.*

Peru Current *n.* a cold ocean current flowing northwards off the Pacific coast of South America. Also called: **Humboldt Current.**

Perugia (pə'ruːdʒə; *Italian* pe'ruːdʒa) *n.* **1.** a city in central Italy, in Umbria: centre of the Umbrian school of painting (15th century); university (1308); Etruscan and Roman remains. Pop.: 146 713 (1986). Ancient name: **Pe'rusia. 2. Lake.** another name for (Lake) **Trasimene.**

Perugino (*Italian* peru'dʒino) *n.* **Il** (il), real name *Pietro Vannucci.* 1446–1523, Italian painter; master of Raphael. His works include the fresco *Christ giving the Keys to Peter* in the Sistine Chapel, Rome.

peruke (pə'ruːk) *n.* a wig for men in the 17th and 18th centuries. Also called: **periwig.** [C16: from F *perruque*, from It. *perrucca* wig, from ?]

peruse (pə'ruːz) *vb. (tr.)* **1.** to read or examine with care; study. **2.** to browse or read in a leisurely way. [C15 (meaning: to use up): from PER- (intensive) + USE] —**pe'rusal** *n.* —**pe'ruser** *n.*

Perutz (pə'ruts) *n.* **Max Ferdinand.** born 1914, British biochemist, born in Austria. With J. C. Kendrew, he worked on the structure of haemoglobin and shared the Nobel prize for chemistry 1962.

Peruzzi (*Italian* pe'ruttsi) *n.* **Baldassare Tommaso** (baldas'saːre tom'maːzo). 1481–1536, Italian architect and painter of the High Renaissance. The design of the Palazzo Massimo, Rome, is attributed to him.

perv (pɜːv) *Sl.* ~*n.* **1.** a pervert. **2.** *Austral.* a lascivious look. ~*vb. also* **perve.** (*intr.*) **3.** *Austral.* to behave like a voyeur.

pervade (pɜː'veɪd) *vb. (tr.)* to spread through or throughout, esp. subtly or gradually; permeate. [C17: from L *pervādere,* from *per-* through + *vādere* to go] —**pervasion** (pɜː'veɪʒən) *n.* —**pervasive** (pɜː'veɪsɪv) *adj.* —**per'vasively** *adv.* —**per'vasiveness** *n.*

perverse (pə'vɜːs) *adj.* **1.** deliberately deviating from what is regarded as normal, good, or proper. **2.** persistently holding to what is wrong. **3.** wayward or contrary; obstinate. [C14: from OF *pervers,* from L *perversus* turned the wrong way] —**per'versely** *adv.* —**per'verseness** *or* **per'versity** *n.*

perversion (pə'vɜːʃən) *n.* **1.** any abnormal means of obtaining sexual satisfaction. **2.** the act of perverting or the state of being perverted. **3.** a perverted form or usage.

pervert *vb.* (pə'vɜːt). (*tr.*) **1.** to use wrongly or badly. **2.** to interpret wrongly or badly; distort. **3.** to lead into deviant or perverted beliefs or behaviour; corrupt. **4.** to debase. ~*n.* ('pɜːvɜːt). **5.** a person who practises sexual perversion. [C14: from OF *pervertir,* from L *pervertere* to turn the wrong way] —**per'verted** *adj.* —**per'verter** *n.* —**per'vertible** *adj.* —**per'versive** *adj.*

pervious ('pɜːvɪəs) *adj.* **1.** able to be penetrated; permeable. **2.** receptive to new ideas, etc.; open-minded. [C17: from L *pervius,* from *per-* (through) + *via* a way] —**'perviously** *adv.* —**'perviousness** *n.*

pes (peɪz, piːz) *n., pl.* **pedes** ('pɛdiːz). the technical name for the human **foot.** [C19: NL: foot]

Pesaro (*Italian* 'peːzaro) *n.* a port and resort in E central Italy, in the Marches on the Adriatic. Pop.: 90 579 (1983 est.). Ancient name: **Pisaurum** (pɪ'saʊrəm).

Pescadores (,pɛskə'dɔːriz) *pl. n.* a group of 64 islands in Formosa Strait, separated from Taiwan (to which it belongs) by the **Pescadores Channel.** Pop.: 100 927 (1987 est.). Area: 127 sq. km (49 sq. miles). Chinese names: **Penghu, P'eng-hu.**

Pescara (*Italian* pes'kaːra) *n.* a city and resort in E central Italy, on the Adriatic. Pop.: 131 027 (1986).

peseta (pə'seɪtə; *Spanish* pe'seta) *n.* the standard monetary unit of Spain, divided into 100 céntimos. [C19: from Sp., dim. of PESO]

Peshawar (pə'fɔːə) *n.* a city in N Pakistan, at the E end of the Khyber Pass: one of the oldest cities in Pakistan and capital of the ancient kingdom of Gandhara; university (1950). Pop.: 555 000 (1981 est.).

pesky ('pɛskɪ) *adj.* **peskier, peskiest.** *U.S. & Canad. inf.* troublesome. [C19: prob. changed from *pesty;* see PEST] —**'peskily** *adv.* —**'peskiness** *n.*

peso ('peɪsəʊ; *Spanish* 'peso) *n., pl.* **-sos** (-səʊz; *Spanish* -sos). the standard monetary unit of Argentina, Bolivia, Colombia, Cuba, the Dominican Republic, Mexico, the Philippines, and Uruguay. [C16: from Sp.: weight, from L *pēnsum* something weighed out, from *pendere* to weigh]

pessary ('pɛsərɪ) *n., pl.* **-ries.** *Med.* **1.** a device for inserting into the vagina, either as a support for the uterus or (**diaphragm pessary**) as a contraceptive. **2.** a vaginal suppository. [C14: from LL *pessārium,* from L *pessum,* from Gk *pessos* plug]

pessimism ('pɛsɪ,mɪzəm) *n.* **1.** the tendency to expect the worst in all things. **2.** the doctrine of the ultimate triumph of evil over good. **3.** the doctrine that this world is corrupt and that man's sojourn in it is a preparation for some other existence. [C18: from L *pessimus* worst, sup. of *malus* bad] —**'pessimist** *n.* —**,pessi'mistic** *adj.* —**,pessi'mistically** *adv.*

pest (pɛst) *n.* **1.** a person or thing that annoys, esp. by imposing itself when it is not wanted; nuisance. **2.** any organism that damages crops, or injures or irritates livestock or man. **3.** *Rare.* an epidemic disease. [C16: from L *pestis* plague, from ?]

Pestalozzi (,pɛstə'lɒtsɪ) *n.* **Johann Heinrich** (jo'han 'hainrɪç). 1746–1827, Swiss educational reformer. His emphasis on learning by observation exerted a wide influence on elementary education.

pester ('pɛstə) *vb. (tr.)* to annoy or nag continually. [C16: from OF *empestrer* to hobble (a horse), from Vulgar L *impāstōriāre* (unattested) to use a hobble, ult. from L *pastor* herdsman]

pesticide ('pɛstɪ,saɪd) *n.* a chemical used for killing pests, esp. insects. —**,pesti'cidal** *adj.*

pestiferous (pɛ'stɪfərəs) *adj.* **1.** *Inf.* troublesome; irritating. **2.** breeding, carrying, or spreading infectious disease. **3.** corrupting; pernicious. [C16: from L *pestifer,* from *pestis* contagion + *ferre* to bring]

pestilence ('pɛstɪləns) *n.* **1. a.** any epidemic of a deadly infectious disease, such as the plague. **b.** such a disease. **2.** an evil influence.

pestilent ('pɛstɪlənt) *adj.* **1.** annoying; irritating. **2.** highly destructive morally or physically; pernicious. **3.** likely to cause epidemic or infectious disease. [C14: from L *pestilens* unwholesome, from *pestis* plague] —**'pestilently** *adv.* —**pestilential** (,pɛstɪ'lɛnʃəl) *adj.* —**,pesti'lentially** *adv.*

pestle ('pɛsᵊl) *n.* **1.** a club-shaped instrument for mixing or grinding substances in a mortar. **2.** a tool for pounding or stamping. ~*vb.* **3.** to pound (a substance or object) with or as if with a pestle. [C14: from OF *pestel,* from L *pistillum*]

pesto ('pɛstəʊ) *n.* a sauce for pasta, consisting of basil leaves, nuts, garlic, oil, and Parmesan cheese, all crushed together. [It., shortened form of *pestato,* p.p. of *pestare* to pound, crush]

pet[1] (pɛt) *n.* **1.** a tame animal kept for companionship, amusement, etc. **2.** a person who is fondly indulged; favourite: *teacher's pet.* ~*adj.* **3.** kept as a pet: *a pet dog.* **4.** of or for pet animals: *pet food.* **5.** particularly cherished: *a pet hatred.* **6.** familiar or affectionate: *a pet name.* ~*vb.* **petting, petted. 7.** (*tr.*) to treat (a person, animal, etc.) as a pet; pamper. **8.** (*tr.*) to pat or fondle (an animal, child, etc.). **9.** (*intr.*) *Inf.* (of two people) to caress each other in an erotic manner. [C16: from ?] —**'petter** *n.*

pet[2] (pɛt) *n.* a fit of sulkiness, esp. at what is felt to be a slight; pique. [C16: from ?]

Pet. *Bible. abbrev. for* Peter.

peta- *prefix.* denoting 10^{15}: *petametres.* Symbol: P [C20: so named because it is the SI prefix after TERA-; on the model of PENTA-, the prefix after TETRA-]

Pétain (*French* petɛ̃) *n.* **Henri Philippe Omer** (ɑ̃ri filip ɔmɛr). 1856–1951, French marshal, noted for his victory at Verdun (1916) in World War I and his leadership of the pro-Nazi government of unoccupied France at Vichy (1940–44); imprisoned for treason (1945).

petal ('pɛtᵊl) *n.* any of the separate parts of the corolla of a flower: often brightly coloured. [C18: from NL *petalum,* from Gk *petalon* leaf] —**'petaline** *adj.* —**'petalled** *adj.* —**'petal-,like** *adj.*

-petal *adj. combining form.* seeking: *centripetal.* [from NL *-petus*, from L *petere* to seek]

petard (pɪ'tɑːd) *n.* **1.** (formerly) a device containing explosives used to breach a wall, doors, etc. **2. hoist with one's own petard.** being the victim of one's own schemes, etc. [C16: from F: firework, from *péter* to break wind, from L *pēdere*]

petaurist (pət'ɔːrɪst) *n.* another name for **flying phalanger.** [C19: from L, from Gk *petauristēs* performer on the springboard]

petcock ('pɛt,kɒk) *n.* a small valve for checking the water content of a steam boiler or draining waste from the cylinder of a steam engine. [C19: from PET[1] or ? F *pet*, from *péter* to break wind + COCK[1]]

petechia (pɪ'tiːkɪə) *n., pl.* **-chiae** (-kɪ,iː). a minute discoloured spot on the surface of the skin. [C18: via NL from It. *petecchia* freckle, from ?] —**pe'techial** *adj.*

peter[1] ('piːtə) *vb. (intr.)* foll. by *out* or *away*) to fall (off) in volume, intensity, etc., and finally cease. [C19: from ?]

peter[2] ('piːtə) *n. Sl.* **1.** a safe, till, or cashbox. **2.** a prison cell. [C17 (meaning a case): from the name *Peter*]

Peter ('piːtə) *n. New Testament.* **Saint.** Also called: **Simon Peter.** died ?67 A.D., a fisherman of Bethsaida, who became leader of the apostles and is regarded by Roman Catholics as the first pope; probably martyred at Rome.

Peter I *n.* known as *Peter the Great.* 1672–1725, tsar of Russia (1682–1725), who assumed sole power in 1689. He introduced many reforms in government, technology, and the western European ideas. He also acquired new territories for Russia in the Baltic and founded the new capital of St Petersburg (1703).

Peter III *n.* 1728–62, grandson of Peter I and tsar of Russia (1762): deposed in a coup d'état led by his wife (later Catherine II); assassinated.

Peterborough ('piːtəbrə, -brə) *n.* **1.** a city in central England, in N Cambridgeshire on the River Nene: industrial centre; under development as a new town since 1968. Pop.: 138 500 (1985 est.). **2. Soke of.** a former administrative county of Northamptonshire: part of Northamptonshire since 1965. **3.** a city in SE Canada, in SE Ontario: manufacturing centre. Pop.: 60 620 (1981).

Peterlee ('piːtə,liː) *n.* a new town in Co. Durham, founded in 1948. Pop.: 22 756 (1981).

peterman ('piːtəmən) *n., pl.* **-men.** *Sl.* a burglar skilled in safe-breaking. [C19: from PETER[2]]

Petermann Peak ('piːtəmən) *n.* a mountain in E Greenland. Height: 2932 m (9645 ft.).

Peter Pan *n.* a youthful, boyish, or immature man. [C20: after the main character in *Peter Pan* (1904), a play by J. M. BARRIE]

Peter Principle *n.* **the.** the theory, usually taken facetiously, that all members in a hierarchy rise to their own level of incompetence. [C20: from the book *The Peter Principle* (1969) by Dr Lawrence J. *Peter* and Raymond Hull]

Petersburg ('piːtəz,bɜːg) *n.* a city in SE Virginia, on the Appomattox River: scene of prolonged fighting (1864–65) during the final months of the American Civil War. Pop.: 41 055 (1980).

petersham ('piːtəʃəm) *n.* **1.** a thick corded ribbon used to stiffen belts, etc. **2.** a heavy woollen fabric used for coats, etc. **3.** a kind of overcoat made of such fabric. [C19: after Viscount *Petersham* (died 1851), E army officer]

Peterson ('piːtəsⁿn) *n.* **Oscar (Emmanuel).** born 1925, Canadian jazz pianist and singer, who led his own trio from the early 1950s.

Peter's pence *or* **Peter pence** *n.* **1.** an annual tax, originally of one penny, formerly levied for the maintenance of the Papal See: abolished by Henry VIII in 1534. **2.** a voluntary contribution made by Roman Catholics in many countries for the same purpose. [C13: referring to St PETER, considered as the first pope]

Peters' projection *n.* a form of modified Mercator's map projection that gives prominence to Third World countries. [C20: after Arno *Peters*, G historian]

Peter the Hermit *n.* ?1050–1115, French monk and preacher of the First Crusade.

pethidine ('pɛθɪ,diːn) *n.* a white crystalline water-soluble drug used as an analgesic. [C20: ? a blend of PIPERIDINE + ETHYL]

petiole ('pɛtɪ,əʊl) *n.* **1.** the stalk by which a leaf is attached to the plant. **2.** *Zool.* a slender stalk or stem, as

between the thorax and abdomen of ants. [C18: via F from L *petiolus* little foot, from *pēs* foot] —**petiolate** ('pɛtɪə,leɪt) *adj.*

petit ('pɛtɪ) *adj. (prenominal) Chiefly law.* of lesser importance; small. [C14: from OF: little, from ?]

petit bourgeois ('buəʒwɑː) *n., pl.* **petits bourgeois** ('buəʒwɑːz). **1.** Also called: **petite bourgeoisie, petty bourgeoisie.** the section of the middle class with the lowest social status, as shopkeepers, lower clerical staff, etc. **2.** a member of this stratum. ~*adj.* **3.** of, relating to, or characteristic of the petit bourgeois, esp. indicating a sense of self-righteousness and conformity to established standards of behaviour.

petite (pə'tiːt) *adj.* (of a woman) small, delicate, and dainty. [C18: from F, fem. of *petit* small]

petit four (fɔː) *n., pl.* **petits fours** (fɔːz). any of various very small fancy cakes and biscuits. [F, lit.: little oven]

petition (pɪ'tɪʃən) *n.* **1.** a written document signed by a large number of people demanding some form of action from a government or other authority. **2.** any formal request to a higher authority; entreaty. **3.** *Law.* a formal application in writing made to a court asking for some specific judicial action: *a petition for divorce.* **4.** the action of petitioning. ~*vb.* **5.** (*tr.*) to address or present a petition to (a person in authority, government, etc.): *to petition Parliament.* **6.** (*intr.;* foll. by *for*) to seek by petition: *to petition for a change in the law.* [C14: from L *petitiō*, from *petere* to seek] —**pe'titionary** *adj.*

petitioner (pɪ'tɪʃənə) *n.* **1.** a person who presents a petition. **2.** *Chiefly Brit.* the plaintiff in a divorce suit.

petitio principii (pɪ'tɪʃɪ,əʊ prɪn'kɪpɪ,aɪ) *n. Logic.* a form of fallacious reasoning in which the conclusion has been assumed in the premises; begging the question. [C16: L, translation of Gk *to en arkhei aiteisthai* an assumption at the beginning]

petit jury *n.* a jury of 12 persons empanelled to determine the facts of a case and decide the issue pursuant to the direction of the court on points of law. Also called: **petty jury.** —**petit juror** *n.*

petit larceny *n.* (formerly, in England) the stealing of property valued at 12 pence or under. Abolished 1827. Also called: **petty larceny.**

petit mal (mæl) *n.* a mild form of epilepsy characterized by periods of impairment or loss of consciousness for up to 30 seconds. Cf. **grand mal.** [C19: F: little illness]

petit point ('pɛtɪ 'pɔɪnt; *French* pəti pwɛ̃) *n.* **1.** a small diagonal needlepoint stitch used for fine detail. **2.** work done with such stitches. [F: small point]

Petőfi (*Hungarian* 'pɛtøːfi) *n.* **Sándor** ('ʃɑːndor). 1823–49, Hungarian lyric poet and patriot.

Petra ('pɛtrə, 'piːtrə) *n.* an ancient city in the south of present-day Jordan; capital of the Nabataean kingdom.

Petrarch ('pɛtrɑːk) *n.* Italian name *Francesco Petrarca.* 1304–74, Italian lyric poet and scholar, who greatly influenced the values of the Renaissance. His collection of poems *Canzoniere,* inspired by his ideal love for Laura, was written in the Tuscan dialect. He also wrote much in Latin, esp. the epic poem *Africa* (1341) and the *Secretum* (1342), a spiritual self-analysis. —**Pe'trarchan** *adj.*

Petrarchan sonnet *n.* a sonnet form associated with the poet Petrarch, having an octave rhyming a b b a a b b a and a sestet rhyming either c d e c d e or c d c d c d.

petrel ('pɛtrəl) *n.* any of a family of oceanic birds having a hooked bill and tubular nostrils: includes albatrosses, storm petrels, and shearwaters. [C17: var. of earlier *pitteral,* associated by folk etymology with St *Peter,* because the bird appears to walk on water]

Petri dish ('piːtrɪ) *n.* a shallow dish, often with a cover, used in laboratories, esp. for producing cultures of microorganisms. [C19: after J. R. *Petri* (1852–1921), G bacteriologist]

Petrie ('pɛtrɪ) *n.* Sir (**William Matthew**) **Flinders.** 1853–1942, English Egyptologist and archaeologist.

petrifaction (,pɛtrɪ'fækʃən) *or* **petrification** (,pɛtrɪfɪ'keɪʃən) *n.* **1.** the act or process of forming petrified organic material. **2.** the state of being petrified.

Petrified Forest *n.* a national park in E Arizona, containing petrified coniferous trees about 170 000 000 years old.

petrify ('pɛtrɪ,faɪ) *vb.* **-fying, -fied. 1.** (*tr.; often passive*) to convert (organic material) into a fossilized form by impregnation with dissolved minerals so that the original appearance is preserved. **2.** to make or become dull, unresponsive, etc.; deaden. **3.** (*tr.; often passive*) to stun or daze with horror, fear, etc. [C16: from F *pétrifier*, ult. from Gk *petra* stone] —'**petri,fier** *n.*

petro- *or before a vowel* **petr-** *combining form.* **1.** indicating stone or rock: *petrology.* **2.** indicating petroleum, its products, etc.: *petrochemical.* [from Gk *petra* rock or *petros* stone]

petrochemical (,pɛtrəʊ'kɛmɪkəl) *n.* **1.** any substance, such as acetone or ethanol, obtained from petroleum. ~*adj.* **2.** of, concerned with, or obtained from petrochemicals or related to petrochemistry. —,**petro'chemistry** *n.*

petrodollar ('pɛtrəʊ,dɒlə) *n.* money earned by a country by the exporting of petroleum.

petroglyph ('pɛtrə,glɪf) *n.* a drawing or carving on rock, esp. a prehistoric one. [C19: via F from Gk *petra* stone + *gluphē* carving]

Petrograd ('pɛtrəʊ,græd; *Russian* pɪtra'grat) *n.* a former name (1914–24) of **Leningrad**.

petrography (pɛ'trɒgrəfɪ) *n.* the branch of petrology concerned with the description and classification of rocks. —pe'**trographer** *n.* —**petrographic** (,pɛtrə'græfɪk) *or* ,**petro'graphical** *adj.*

petrol ('pɛtrəl) *n.* any one of various volatile flammable liquid mixtures of hydrocarbons, obtained from petroleum and used as a solvent and a fuel for internal-combustion engines. U.S. and Canad. name: **gasoline.** [C16: via F from Med. L PETROLEUM]

petrolatum (,pɛtrə'leɪtəm) *n.* a translucent gelatinous substance obtained from petroleum; used as a lubricant and in medicine as an ointment base. Also called: **petroleum jelly.**

petrol bomb *n.* **1.** a device filled with petrol that bursts into flames on impact. ~*vb.* **petrol-bomb.** (*tr.*) **2.** to attack with petrol bombs.

petroleum (pə'trəʊlɪəm) *n.* a dark-coloured thick flammable crude oil occurring in sedimentary rocks, consisting mainly of hydrocarbons. Fractional distillation separates the crude oil into petrol, paraffin, diesel oil, lubricating oil, etc. Fuel oil, paraffin wax, asphalt, and carbon black are extracted from the residue. [C16: from Med. L, from L *petra* stone + *oleum* oil]

petroleum jelly *n.* another name for **petrolatum.**

petrology (pɛ'trɒlədʒɪ) *n., pl.* -**gies.** the study of the composition, origin, structure, and formation of rocks. —**petrological** (,pɛtrə'lɒdʒɪkəl) *adj.* —pe'**trologist** *n.*

petrol station *n. Brit.* another term for **filling station.**

Petronius (pɪ'trəʊnɪəs) *n.* **Gaius** ('gaɪəs), known as *Petronius Arbiter.* died 66 A.D., Roman satirist, supposed author of the *Satyricon*, a picaresque account of the licentiousness of contemporary society.

Petropavlovsk (*Russian* pɪtra'pavləfsk) *n.* a city in the S Soviet Union, in the N Kazakh SSR on the Ishim River. Pop.: 252 000 (1987).

Petrópolis (*Portuguese* pe'trɔpulis) *n.* a city in SE Brazil, north of Rio de Janeiro: resort. Pop.: 149 427 (1980).

Petrosian (pɪ'trəʊʒən) *n.* **Tigran** (tig'ran). 1929–84, Soviet chess player; world champion (1963–69).

petrous ('pɛtrəs, 'piː-) *adj. Anat.* denoting the dense part of the temporal bone that surrounds the inner ear. [C16: from L *petrōsus* full of rocks] —**petrosal** (pɛ'trəʊsəl) *adj.*

Petrovsk (*Russian* pɪ'trɔfsk) *n.* the former name (until 1921) of **Makhachkala.**

Petrozavodsk (*Russian* pɪtrəza'vɔtsk) *n.* a city in the NW Soviet Union, capital of the Karelian ASSR, on Lake Onega: developed around ironworks established by Peter the Great in 1703; university (1940). Pop.: 264 000 (1987).

Petsamo (*Finnish* 'pɛtsamɔ) *n.* a former territory of N Finland ceded by the Soviet Union to Finland in 1920 and taken back in 1940; now part of the northwest RSFSR.

petticoat ('pɛtɪ,kəʊt) *n.* **1.** a woman's underskirt. **2.** *Inf.* **a.** a humorous or mildly disparaging name for a woman. **b.** (*as modifier*): *petticoat politics.* [C15: see PETTY, COAT]

pettifogger ('pɛtɪ,fɒgə) *n.* **1.** a lawyer who conducts unimportant cases, esp. one who resorts to trickery. **2.** any person who quibbles. [C16: from PETTY + *fogger*, from ?, perhaps from *Fugger*, a family (C15–16) of G financiers] —'**petti,foggery** *n.* —'**petti,fog** *vb.* -**fogging**, -**fogged.** (*intr.*) —'**petti,fogging** *adj.*

pettish ('pɛtɪʃ) *adj.* peevish; petulant. [C16: from PET[2]] —'**pettishly** *adv.* —'**pettishness** *n.*

petty ('pɛtɪ) *adj.* -**tier**, -**tiest.** **1.** trivial; trifling: *petty details.* **2.** narrow-minded, mean: *petty spite.* **3.** minor or subordinate in rank: *petty officialdom.* **4.** *Law.* a variant

of **petit.** [C14: from OF PETIT] —'**pettily** *adv.* —'**pettiness** *n.*

petty cash *n.* a small cash fund for minor incidental expenses.

petty jury *n.* a variant of **petit jury.**

petty larceny *n.* a variant of **petit larceny.**

petty officer *n.* a noncommissioned officer in a naval service comparable in rank to a sergeant in an army or marine corps.

petty sessions *n.* (*functioning as sing. or pl.*) another term for **magistrates' court.**

petulant ('pɛtjʊlənt) *adj.* irritable, impatient, or sullen in a peevish or capricious way. [C16: via OF from L *petulāns* bold, from *petulāre* (unattested) to attack playfully, from *petere* to assail] —'**petulance** *or* '**petulancy** *n.* —'**petulantly** *adv.*

petunia (pɪ'tjuːnɪə) *n.* any plant of a tropical American genus cultivated for their colourful funnel-shaped flowers. [C19: via NL from obs. F *petun* variety of tobacco, from Tupi *petyn*]

petuntse (pɪ'tʌntsɪ, -'tʊn-) *n.* a fusible mineral used in hard-paste porcelain. [C18: from Chinese, from *pe* white + *tun* heap + *tzu* offspring]

Pevsner ('pɛvznə) *n.* **1. Antoine** (ɑ̃twan). 1886–1962, French constructivist sculptor and painter, born in Russia; brother of Naum Gabo. **2.** Sir **Nikolaus** ('nɪkəlaʊs). 1902–83, British architectural historian, born in Germany: his monumental series *Buildings of England* (1951–74) describes every structure of account in the country.

pew (pjuː) *n.* **1.** (in a church) **a.** one of several long benchlike seats with backs, used by the congregation. **b.** an enclosed compartment reserved for the use of a family or other small group. **2.** *Brit. inf.* a seat (esp. in **take a pew**). [C14 *pywe*, from OF, from L *podium* a balcony, from Gk *podion* supporting structure, from *pous* foot]

pewit *or* **peewit** ('piːwɪt) *n.* other names for **lapwing.** [C13: imit. of the bird's cry]

pewter ('pjuːtə) *n.* **1. a.** any of various alloys containing tin, lead, and sometimes copper and antimony. **b.** (*as modifier*): *pewter ware; a pewter tankard.* **2.** plate or kitchen utensils made from pewter. [C14: from OF *peaultre*, from ?] —'**pewterer** *n.*

peyote (peɪ'əʊtɪ, pɪ-) *n.* another name for **mescal** (the plant). [Mexican Sp., from Nahuatl *peyotl*]

pF *abbrev. for* picofarad.

pf. *abbrev for:* **1.** perfect. **2.** Also: **pfg.** pfennig. **3.** preferred.

Pfalz (pfalts) *n.* the German name for the **Palatinate.**

pfennig ('fɛnɪg; *German* 'pfɛnɪç) *n., pl.* -**nigs** *or* -**nige** (*German* -nɪgə). a German monetary unit worth one hundredth of a mark. [G: PENNY]

Pforzheim (*German* 'pfɔrtshaim) *n.* a city in West Germany, in W Baden-Württemberg: centre of the German watch and jewellery industry. Pop.: 104 452 (1987).

PG *symbol for* a film certified for viewing by anyone, but which contains scenes that may be unsuitable for children, for whom parental guidance is necessary. [C20: from abbrev. of *parental guidance*]

pg. *abbrev. for* page.

Pg. *abbrev. for:* **1.** Portugal. **2.** Portuguese.

pH *n.* potential of hydrogen; a measure of the acidity or alkalinity of a solution. Pure water has a pH of 7, acid solutions have a pH less than 7, and alkaline solutions a pH greater than 7.

phacelia (fæ'siːlɪə) *n.* any of a genus of N American plants having clusters of blue flowers. [NL from Gk *phakelos* a cluster]

Phaeacian (fiː'eɪʃən) *n. Greek myth.* one of a race of people inhabiting the island of Scheria visited by Odysseus on his way home from the Trojan War.

Phaedra ('fiːdrə) *n. Greek myth.* the wife of Theseus, who falsely accused her stepson Hippolytus of raping her because he spurned her amorous advances.

Phaedrus ('fiːdrəs) *n.* ?15 B.C.–?50 A.D., Roman author of five books of Latin verse fables, based chiefly on Aesop.

Phaëthon ('feɪəθən) *n. Greek myth.* the son of Helios (the sun god) who borrowed his father's chariot and nearly set the earth on fire by approaching too close to it. Zeus averted the catastrophe by striking him down with a thunderbolt.

phaeton ('feɪtən) *n.* a light four-wheeled horse-drawn carriage with or without a top. [C18: from F, from L, from Gk PHAËTHON]

-phage n. combining form. indicating something that eats or consumes something specified: bacteriophage. [from Gk -phagos; see PHAGO-] —**phagous** adj. combining form.

phago- or before a vowel **phag-** combining form. eating, consuming, or destroying: phagocyte. [from Gk phagein to consume]

phagocyte ('fægə,saɪt) n. a cell or protozoan that engulfs particles, such as microorganisms. —**phagocytic** (,fægə'sɪtɪk) adj.

phagocytosis (,fægəsaɪ'təʊsɪs) n. the process by which a cell, such as a white blood cell, ingests microorganisms, other cells, etc.

-phagy or **-phagia** n. combining form. indicating an eating or devouring: anthropophagy. [from Gk -phagia; see PHAGO-]

phalange ('fælændʒ) n., pl. **phalanges** (fæ'lændʒiːz). Anat. another name for **phalanx** (sense 4). [C16: via F, ult. from Gk PHALANX]

phalangeal (fə'lændʒɪəl) adj. Anat. of or relating to a phalanx or phalanges.

phalanger (fə'lændʒə) n. any of various Australasian arboreal marsupials having dense fur and a long tail. Also called (Austral.): **possum**. See also **flying phalanger**. [C18: via NL from Gk phalaggion spider's web, referring to its webbed hind toes]

phalanx ('fælæŋks) n., pl. **phalanxes** or **phalanges** (fæ'lændʒiːz). **1.** an ancient Greek and Macedonian battle formation of hoplites presenting long spears from behind a wall of overlapping shields. **2.** any closely ranked unit or mass of people: the police formed a phalanx to protect the embassy. **3.** a number of people united for a common purpose. **4.** Anat. any of the bones of the fingers or toes. **5.** Bot. a bundle of stamens. [C16: via L from Gk: infantry formation in close ranks, bone of finger or toe]

phalarope ('fælə,rəʊp) n. any of a family of aquatic shore birds of northern oceans and lakes, having a long slender bill and lobed toes. [C18: via F from NL Phalaropus, from Gk phalaris coot + pous foot]

phallic ('fælɪk) adj. **1.** of, relating to, or resembling a phallus: a phallic symbol. **2.** Psychoanal. relating to a stage of psychosexual development during which a male child's interest is concentrated on the genital organs. **3.** of or relating to phallicism.

phallicism ('fælɪ,sɪzəm) or **phallism** n. the worship or veneration of the phallus.

phallus ('fæləs) n., pl. **-li** (-laɪ) or **-luses**. **1.** another word for **penis**. **2.** an image of the male sexual organ, esp. as a symbol of reproductive power. [C17: via LL from Gk phallos]

-phane n. combining form. indicating something resembling a specified substance: cellophane. [from Gk phainein to shine, appear]

phanerogam ('fænərəʊ,gæm) n. any plant of a former major division which included all seed-bearing plants; a former name for **spermatophyte**. [C19: from NL phanerogamus, from Gk phaneros visible + gamos marriage] —**phanerogamic** or **phanerogamous** (,fænə'rɒgəməs) adj.

phantasm ('fæntæzəm) n. **1.** a phantom. **2.** an illusory perception of an object, person, etc. [C13: from OF fantasme, from L phantasma, from Gk] —**phantasmal** or **phantasmic** adj.

phantasmagoria (,fæntæzmə'gɔːrɪə) or **phantasmagory** (fæn'tæzməgərɪ) n. **1.** Psychol. a shifting medley of real or imagined figures, as in a dream. **2.** Films. a sequence of pictures made to vary in size rapidly. **3.** a shifting scene composed of different elements. [C19: prob. from F, from PHANTASM + -agorie, ?from Gk ageirein to gather together] —**phantasmagoric** (,fæntæzmə'gɒrɪk) or **phantasma'gorical** adj.

phantasy ('fæntəsɪ) n., pl. **-sies**. an archaic spelling of **fantasy**.

phantom ('fæntəm) n. **1. a.** an apparition or spectre. **b.** (as modifier): a phantom army marching through the sky. **2.** the visible representation of something abstract, esp. as in a dream or hallucination: phantoms of evil haunted his sleep. **3.** something apparently unpleasant or horrific that has no material form. [C13: from OF fantosme, from L phantasma]

phantom limb n. the illusion that a limb still exists following its amputation, sometimes with the sensation of pain (**phantom limb pain**).

-phany n. combining form. indicating a manifestation: theophany. [from Gk -phania, from phainein to show] —**-phanous** adj. combining form.

phar., Phar., pharm., or **Pharm.** abbrev. for: **1.** pharmaceutical. **2.** pharmacist. **3.** pharmacopoeia. **4.** pharmacy.

Pharaoh ('fɛərəʊ) n. the title of the ancient Egyptian kings. [OE Pharaon, via L, Gk, & Heb., ult. from Egyptian pr-'o great house] —**Pharaonic** (fɛə'rɒnɪk) adj.

Pharisaic (,færɪ'seɪɪk) or **Pharisaical** adj. **1.** Judaism. of, relating to, or characteristic of the Pharisees or Pharisaism. **2.** (often not cap.) righteously hypocritical. —**Phari'saically** adv.

Pharisaism ('færɪseɪ,ɪzəm) or **Phariseeism** ('færɪsiː,ɪzəm) n. **1.** Judaism. the tenets and customs of the Pharisees. **2.** (often not cap.) observance of the external forms of religion without genuine belief; hypocrisy.

Pharisee ('færɪ,siː) n. **1.** a member of an ancient Jewish sect teaching strict observance of Jewish traditions. **2.** (often not cap.) a self-righteous or hypocritical person. [OE Farīsēus, ult. from Aramaic perīshāiyā, pl. of perish separated]

pharmaceutical (,fɑːmə'sjuːtɪkəl) or (less commonly) **pharmaceutic** adj. of or relating to drugs or pharmacy. [C17: from LL pharmaceuticus, from Gk pharmakeus purveyor of drugs; see PHARMACY] —**pharma'ceutically** adv.

pharmaceutics (,fɑːmə'sjuːtɪks) n. **1.** (functioning as sing.) another term for **pharmacy** (sense 1). **2.** pharmaceutical remedies.

pharmacist ('fɑːməsɪst) n. a person qualified to prepare and dispense drugs.

pharmaco- combining form. indicating drugs: pharmacology. [from Gk pharmakon drug]

pharmacognosy (,fɑːmə'kɒgnəsɪ) n. the study of crude drugs of plant and animal origin. [C19: from PHARMACO- + gnosy, from Gk gnosis knowledge] —**pharma'cognosist** n.

pharmacology (,fɑːmə'kɒlədʒɪ) n. the science or study of drugs, including their characteristics, action, and uses. —**pharmacological** (,fɑːməkə'lɒdʒɪkəl) adj. —**pharmaco'logically** adv. —**pharma'cologist** n.

pharmacopoeia or U.S. (sometimes) **pharmacopeia** (,fɑːməkə'piːə) n. an authoritative book containing a list of medicinal drugs with their uses, preparation, dosages, formulas, etc. [C17: via NL from Gk pharmakopoiia art of preparing drugs, from PHARMACO- + -poiia, from poiein to make] —**pharmaco'poeial** adj.

pharmacy ('fɑːməsɪ) n., pl. **-cies**. **1.** Also: **pharmaceutics**. the practice or art of preparing and dispensing drugs. **2.** a dispensary. [C14: from Med. L pharmacia, from Gk pharmakeia making of drugs, from pharmakon drug]

pharos ('fɛərɒs) n. any marine lighthouse or beacon. [C16: after a large Hellenistic lighthouse on an island off Alexandria in Egypt]

Pharsalus (fɑː'seɪləs) n. an ancient town in Thessaly in N Greece. Several major battles were fought nearby, including Caesar's victory over Pompey (48 B.C.).

pharyngeal (,færɪn'dʒiːəl) or **pharyngal** (fə'rɪŋgəl) adj. **1.** of, relating to, or situated in or near the pharynx. **2.** Phonetics. pronounced with an articulation in or constriction of the pharynx. [C19: from NL pharyngeus; see PHARYNX]

pharyngitis (,færɪn'dʒaɪtɪs) n. inflammation of the pharynx.

pharynx ('færɪŋks) n., pl. **pharynges** (fæ'rɪndʒiːz) or **pharynxes**. the part of the alimentary canal between the mouth and the oesophagus. [C17: via NL from Gk pharunx throat]

phase (feɪz) n. **1.** any distinct or characteristic period or stage in a sequence of events: there were two phases to the resolution. **2.** Astron. one of the recurring shapes of the portion of the moon or an inferior planet illuminated by the sun. **3.** Physics. the fraction of a cycle of a periodic quantity that has been completed at a specific reference time, expressed as an angle. **4.** Physics. a particular stage in a periodic process or phenomenon. **5. in phase**. (of two waveforms) reaching corresponding phases at the same time. **6. out of phase**. (of two waveforms) not in phase. **7.** Chem. a distinct state of matter characterized by homogeneous composition and properties and the possession of a clearly defined boundary. **8.** *Zool.* a variation in the normal form of an animal, esp. a colour variation, brought about by seasonal or geographical change. ~*vb.* (*tr.*) **9.** (*often passive*) to execute, arrange, or introduce gradually or in stages: *the withdrawal was phased over several months.* **10.** (sometimes foll. by *with*) to cause (a part, process, etc.) to function or coincide with (another part, etc.): *he tried to phase the intake and output of the machine; he phased the intake with the output.* **11.** *Chiefly U.S.* to arrange (processes, goods, etc.) to be supplied or executed when required. [C19: from NL *phases*, pl. of *phasis*, from Gk: aspect] —**'phasic** *adj.*

phase in *vb.* (*tr., adv.*) to introduce in a gradual or cautious manner: *the legislation was phased in over two years.*

phase modulation *n.* a type of modulation in which the phase of a radio carrier wave is varied by an amount proportional to the instantaneous amplitude of the modulating signal.

phase out *vb.* (*tr., adv.*) **1.** to discontinue or withdraw gradually. ~*n.* **phase-out. 2.** *Chiefly U.S.* the action or an instance of phasing out: *a phase-out of conventional forces.*

phase rule *n.* the principle that in any system in equilibrium the number of degrees of freedom is equal to the number of components less the number of phases plus two.

-phasia *n. combining form.* indicating speech disorder of a specified kind: *aphasia.* [from Gk, from *phanai* to speak] —**-phasic** *adj. and n. combining form.*

phatic ('fætɪk) *adj.* (of speech) used to establish social contact and to express sociability rather than specific meaning. [C20: from Gk *phat(os)* spoken + -IC]

PhD *abbrev. for* Doctor of Philosophy. Also: **DPhil.**

pheasant ('fezᵊnt) *n.* **1.** any of various long-tailed gallinaceous birds, having a brightly-coloured plumage in the male: native to Asia but introduced elsewhere. **2.** any of various other related birds, including the quails and partridges. **3.** *U.S. & Canad.* any of several other gallinaceous birds, esp. the ruffed grouse. [C13: from OF *fesan*, from L *phāsiānus*, from Gk *phasianos ornis* Phasian bird, after the River *Phasis*, in Colchis]

Phebe ('fiːbɪ) *n.* a variant spelling of **Phoebe.**

Pheidippides *or* **Phidippides** (faɪ'dɪpɪˌdiːz) *n.* Athenian athlete, who ran to Sparta to seek help against the Persians before the Battle of Marathon (490 B.C.).

phellem ('fɛləm) *n. Bot.* the technical name for **cork** (sense 4). [C20: from Gk *phellos* cork + PHLOEM]

phenacetin (fɪ'næsɪtɪn) *n.* a white crystalline solid used in medicine to relieve pain and fever. Also called: **acetophenetidin.** [C19: from PHENO- + ACETYL + -IN]

pheno- *or before a vowel* **phen-** *combining form.* **1.** showing or manifesting: *phenotype.* **2.** indicating that a molecule contains benzene rings: *phenobarbitone.* [from Gk *phaino-* shining, from *phainein* to show; its use in a chemical sense is exemplified in *phenol*, so called because orig. prepared from illuminating gas]

phenobarbitone (ˌfiːnəʊ'bɑːbɪˌtəʊn) *or* **phenobarbital** (ˌfiːnəʊ'bɑːbɪtᵊl) *n.* a white crystalline derivative of barbituric acid used as a sedative for treating insomnia and epilepsy.

phenocryst ('fiːnəˌkrɪst, 'fɛn-) *n.* any of several large crystals in igneous rocks such as porphyry. [C19: from PHENO-(shining) + CRYSTAL]

phenol ('fiːnɒl) *n.* **1.** Also called: **carbolic acid.** a white crystalline derivative of benzene, used as an antiseptic and disinfectant and in the manufacture of resins, explosives, and pharmaceuticals. Formula: C_6H_5OH. **2.** *Chem.* any of a class of organic compounds whose molecules contain one or more hydroxyl groups bound directly to a carbon atom in an aromatic ring. —**phe'nolic** *adj.*

phenolic resin *n.* any one of a class of resins derived from phenol, used in paints, adhesives, and as thermosetting plastics.

phenology (fɪ'nɒlədʒɪ) *n.* the study of recurring phenomena, such as animal migration, esp. as influenced by climatic conditions. [C19: from PHENO(MENON) + -LOGY] —**phenological** (ˌfiːnə'lɒdʒɪkᵊl) *adj.* —**phe'nologist** *n.*

phenolphthalein (ˌfiːnɒl'θeɪliːn, -lɪɪn, -'θæl-) *n.* a colourless crystalline compound used in medicine as a laxative and in chemistry as an indicator. [from PHENO- + *phthal-*, short form of NAPHTHALENE + -IN]

phenomena (fɪ'nɒmɪnə) *n.* a plural of **phenomenon.**

phenomenal (fɪ'nɒmɪnᵊl) *adj.* **1.** of or relating to a phenomenon. **2.** extraordinary; outstanding; remarkable: *a phenomenal achievement.* **3.** *Philosophy.* known or perceived by the senses rather than the mind. —**phe'nomenally** *adv.*

phenomenalism (fɪ'nɒmɪnəˌlɪzəm) *n. Philosophy.* the doctrine that statements about physical objects and the external world can be analysed in terms of possible or actual experiences, and that entities, such as physical objects, are only mental constructions out of phenomenal appearances. —**phe'nomenalist** *n., adj.*

phenomenology (fɪˌnɒmɪ'nɒlədʒɪ) *n. Philosophy.* **1.** the movement that concentrates on the detailed description of conscious experience. **2.** the science of phenomena as opposed to the science of being. —**phenomenological** (fɪˌnɒmɪnə'lɒdʒɪkᵊl) *adj.*

phenomenon (fɪ'nɒmɪnən) *n., pl.* **-ena** (-ɪnə) *or* **-enons. 1.** anything that can be perceived as an occurrence or fact by the senses. **2.** any remarkable occurrence or person. **3.** *Philosophy.* **a.** the object of perception, experience, etc. **b.** (in the writings of Kant) a thing as it appears, as distinguished from its real nature as a thing-in-itself. [C16: via LL from Gk *phainomenon*, from *phainesthai* to appear, from *phainein* to show]

▷ **Usage.** Although *phenomena* is often treated as if it were singular, correct usage is to employ *phenomenon* with a singular construction and *phenomena* with a plural: *that is an interesting phenomenon* (not *phenomena*); *several new phenomena were recorded in his notes.*

phenotype ('fiːnəʊˌtaɪp) *n.* the physical constitution of an organism as determined by the interaction of its genetic constitution and the environment. —**phenotypic** (ˌfiːnəʊ'tɪpɪk) *or* ˌpheno'typical *adj.* —ˌpheno'typically *adv.*

phenyl ('fiːnaɪl, 'fɛnɪl) *n.* (*modifier*) of, containing, or consisting of the monovalent group C_6H_5, derived from benzene: *a phenyl group.*

phenylalanine (ˌfiːnaɪl'æləˌniːn) *n.* an essential amino acid; a component of proteins.

phenylketonuria (ˌfiːnaɪlˌkiːtə'njʊərɪə) *n.* a congenital metabolic disorder characterized by the abnormal accumulation of phenylalanine in the body fluids, resulting in mental deficiency. [C20: NL; see PHENYL, KETONE, -URIA]

pheromone ('fɛrəˌməʊn) *n.* a chemical substance, secreted externally by certain animals, such as insects, affecting the behaviour of other animals of the same species. [C20 *phero-*, from Gk *pherein* to bear + (HOR)MONE]

phew (fjuː) *interj.* an exclamation of relief, surprise, disbelief, weariness, etc.

phi (faɪ) *n., pl.* **phis.** the 21st letter in the Greek alphabet, Φ, φ.

phial ('faɪəl) *n.* a small bottle for liquids, etc.; vial. [C14: from OF *fiole*, from L *phiola* saucer, from Gk *phialē* wide shallow vessel]

Phi Beta Kappa ('faɪ 'beɪtə 'kæpə, 'biːtə) *n.* (in the U.S.) **1.** a national honorary society, founded in 1776, membership of which is based on high academic ability. **2.** a member of this society. [from the initial of the Gk motto *philosophia biou kubernētēs* philosophy the guide of life]

Phidias ('fɪdɪˌæs) *n.* 5th century B.C., Greek sculptor, regarded as one of the greatest of sculptors. He executed the sculptures of the Parthenon and the colossal statue of Zeus at Olympia, one of the Seven Wonders of the World: neither survives in the original. —**'Phidian** *adj.*

Phidippides (faɪ'dɪpɪˌdiːz) *n.* a variant spelling of **Pheidippides.**

phil. *abbrev. for:* **1.** philharmonic. **2.** philosophy.

Phil. *abbrev. for:* **1.** Philadelphia. **2.** *Bible.* Philippians. **3.** Philippines.

Philadelphia (ˌfɪlə'dɛlfɪə) *n.* a city and port in SE Pennsylvania, at the confluence of the Delaware and Schuylkill Rivers: the fourth largest city in the U.S.; founded by Quakers in 1682; cultural and financial centre of the American colonies and the federal capital (1790–1800); scene of the Continental Congresses (1774–83) and the signing of the Declaration of Independence (1776). Pop.: 1 642 900 (1986).

philadelphus (ˌfɪlə'dɛlfəs) *n.* any of a N temperate genus of shrubs cultivated for their strongly scented showy flowers. See also **mock orange** (sense 1). [C19: NL, from Gk *philadelphon* mock orange, lit.: loving one's brother]

Philae ('faɪliː) n. an island in Upper Egypt, in the Nile north of the Aswan Dam: of religious importance in ancient times; almost submerged since the raising of the level of the dam.

philander (fɪ'lændə) vb. (intr.; often foll. by with) (of a man) to flirt with women. [C17: from Gk philandros fond of men, used as a name for a lover in literary works] —**phi'landerer** n.

philanthropic (ˌfɪlən'θrɒpɪk) or **philanthropical** adj. showing concern for humanity, esp. by performing charitable actions, donating money, etc. —ˌphilan'thropically adv.

philanthropy (fɪ'lænθrəpɪ) n., pl. -pies. 1. the practice of performing charitable or benevolent actions. 2. love of mankind in general. [C17: from LL philanthrōpia, from Gk: love of mankind, from philos loving + anthrōpos man] —**phi'lanthropist** or **philanthrope** ('fɪlənˌθrəʊp) n.

philately (fɪ'lætəlɪ) n. the collection and study of postage stamps. [C19: from F philatélie, from PHILO- + Gk ateleia exemption from charges (here referring to stamps)] —**philatelic** (ˌfɪlə'tɛlɪk) adj. —ˌphila'telically adv. —**phi'latelist** n.

Philby ('fɪlbɪ) n. **Harold**, known as Kim. 1912–88, English double agent; defected to the Soviet Union (1963).

-phile or **-phil** n. combining form. indicating a person or thing having a fondness for something specified: bibliophile. [from Gk philos loving]

Philem. Bible. abbrev. for Philemon.

Philemon[1] (faɪ'liːmɒn) n. New Testament. 1. a Christian of Colossae whose escaped slave came to meet Paul. 2. the book (in full **The Epistle of Paul the Apostle to Philemon**), asking Philemon to forgive the slave for escaping.

Philemon[2] (faɪ'liːmɒn) n. Greek myth. a poor Phrygian, who with his wife Baucis offered hospitality to the disguised Zeus and Hermes.

philharmonic (ˌfɪlhɑː'mɒnɪk, ˌfɪlə-) adj. 1. fond of music. 2. (cap. when part of a name) denoting an orchestra, choir, society, etc., devoted to music. ~n. 3. (cap. when part of a name) a specific philharmonic choir, orchestra, or society. [C18: from F philharmonique, from It. filarmonico music-loving]

philhellene (fɪl'hɛliːn) n. 1. a lover of Greece and Greek culture. 2. European history. a supporter of the cause of Greek national independence. —**philhellenic** (ˌfɪlhɛ'liːnɪk) adj.

-philia n. combining form. 1. indicating a tendency towards: haemophilia. 2. indicating an abnormal liking for: necrophilia. [from Gk philos loving] —**-philiac** n. combining form. —**-philous** or **-philic** adj. combining form.

philibeg ('fɪlɪˌbɛg) n. a variant spelling of **filibeg**.

Philip ('fɪlɪp) n. 1. New Testament. **a.** an apostle from Bethsaida (John 1:43–51; 6:5–7; 12:21; 14:8). **b.** Also called: **Philip the Evangelist.** one of the seven deacons appointed by the early Church. **c.** Also called: **Philip the Tetrarch.** one of the sons of Herod the Great, who was ruler of part of former Judaea (4 B.C.–34 A.D.) (Luke 3:1). 2. **King**, American Indian name Metacomet. died 1676, American Indian chief, the son of Massasoit. He waged King Philip's War against the colonists of New England (1675–76) and was killed in battle. 3. **Prince.** another name for the (Duke of) **Edinburgh**.

Philip II n. 1. 382–336 B.C., king of Macedonia (359–336); the father of Alexander the Great. 2. known as Philip Augustus. 1165–1223, Capetian king of France (1180–1223); set out on the Third Crusade with Richard I of England (1190). 3. 1527–98, king of Spain (1556–98) and king of Portugal (1580–98) as Philip I; the husband of Mary I of England (1554–58). He championed the Counter-Reformation, sending the Armada against England (1588).

Philip IV n. known as Philip the Fair. 1268–1314, king of France (1285–1314): he challenged the power of the papacy, obtaining the elevation of Clement V as pope residing at Avignon (the beginning of the Babylonian captivity of the papacy).

Philip V n. 1683–1746, king of Spain (1700–46) and founder of the Bourbon dynasty in Spain. His accession began the War of Spanish Succession (1701–13).

Philip VI n. 1293–1350, first Valois king of France (1328–50). Edward III of England claimed his throne, which with other disputes led to the beginning of the Hundred Years' War (1337).

Philippeville ('fɪlɪpˌvɪl) n. the former name of **Skikda**.

Philippi (fɪ'lɪpaɪ, 'fɪlɪ-) n. an ancient city in NE Macedonia: scene of the victory of Antony and Octavian over Brutus and Cassius (42 B.C.). —**Phi'lippian** adj.

philippic (fɪ'lɪpɪk) n. a bitter or impassioned speech of denunciation; invective. [C16: after the orations of Demosthenes, against PHILIP of Macedon]

Philippine ('fɪlɪˌpiːn) n., adj. another word for **Filipino**.

Philippines ('fɪlɪˌpiːnz, ˌfɪlɪ'piːnz) n. (functioning as sing.) **Republic of the.** a republic in SE Asia, occupying an archipelago of about 7100 islands (including Luzon, Mindanao, Samar, and Negros): became a Spanish colony in 1571 but ceded to the U.S. in 1898 after the Spanish-American War; gained independence in 1946. The islands are generally mountainous and volcanic. Languages: chiefly Pilipino, based on Tagalog, and English. Religion: chiefly Roman Catholic. Currency: peso. Capital: Manila. 57 360 000 (1987 est.). Area: 299 765 sq. km (115 740 sq. miles).

Philippine Sea n. part of the NW Pacific Ocean, east and north of the Philippines.

Philippopolis (ˌfɪlɪ'pɒpəlɪs) n. transliteration of the Greek name for **Plovdiv**.

Philips ('fɪlɪps) n. **Ambrose**. 1674–1749, English pastoral poet and dramatist.

Philip the Good n. 1396–1467, duke of Burgundy (1419–67), under whose rule Burgundy was one of the most powerful states in Europe.

Philistia (fɪ'lɪstɪə) n. an ancient country on the coast of SW Palestine. —**Phi'listian** adj.

Philistine ('fɪlɪˌstaɪn) n. 1. a person who is hostile towards culture, the arts, etc.; a smug boorish person. 2. a member of the non-Semitic people who inhabited ancient Philistia. ~adj. 3. (sometimes not cap.) boorishly uncultured. 4. of or relating to the ancient Philistines. —**Philistinism** ('fɪlɪstɪˌnɪzəm) n.

Phillip ('fɪlɪp) n. **Arthur**. 1738–1814, English naval commander; captain general of the First Fleet, which carried convicts from Portsmouth to Sydney Cove, Australia, where he founded New South Wales.

Phillips ('fɪlɪps) n. Captain **Mark**. born 1948, English three-day-event horseman; husband of Anne, The Princess Royal.

phillumenist (fɪ'ljuːməˌnɪst, -'luː-) n. a person who collects matchbox labels. [C20: from PHILO- + L lumen light + -IST]

philo- or before a vowel **phil-** combining form. indicating a love of: philology; philanthropic. [from Gk philos loving]

Philoctetes (ˌfɪlɒk'tiːtiːz, fɪ'lɒktɪˌtiːz) n. Greek myth. a hero of the Trojan War, in which he killed Paris with the bow and poisoned arrows given to him by Hercules.

philodendron (ˌfɪlə'dɛndrən) n., pl. -drons or -dra (-drə). an evergreen climbing plant of a tropical American genus: cultivated as a house plant. [C19: NL from Gk: lover of trees]

philogyny (fɪ'lɒdʒɪnɪ) n. Rare. fondness for women. [C17: from Gk philogunia, from PHILO- + gunē woman] —**phi'logynist** n.

Philo Judaeus ('faɪləʊ dʒuː'diːəs) n. ?20 B.C.–?54 A.D., Jewish philosopher, born in Alexandria. He sought to reconcile Judaism with Greek philosophy.

philology (fɪ'lɒlədʒɪ) n. (no longer in scholarly use) 1. comparative and historical linguistics. 2. the scientific analysis of written records and literary texts. 3. the study of literature. [C17: from L philologia, from Gk: love of language] —**philological** (ˌfɪlə'lɒdʒɪkəl) adj. —ˌphilo'logically adv. —**phi'lologist** or (less commonly) **phi'lologer** n.

philomel ('fɪləˌmɛl) or **philomela** (ˌfɪləʊ'miːlə) n. poetic names for a **nightingale**. [C14 philomene, via Med. L from L philomēla, from Gk]

Philomela (ˌfɪləʊ'miːlə) n. Greek myth. an Athenian princess, who was raped and had her tongue cut out by her brother-in-law Tereus, and subsequently was transformed into a nightingale. See **Procne**.

philoprogenitive (ˌfɪləʊprəʊ'dʒɛnɪtɪv) adj. Rare. 1. fond of children. 2. producing many offspring.

philos. *abbrev. for:* **1.** philosopher. **2.** philosophical.

philosopher (fɪ'lɒsəfə) *n.* **1.** a student, teacher, or devotee of philosophy. **2.** a person of philosophical temperament, esp. one who is patient, wise, and stoical. **3.** (formerly) an alchemist or devotee of occult science.

philosopher's stone *n.* a stone or substance thought by alchemists to be capable of transmuting base metals into gold.

philosophical (ˌfɪlə'sɒfɪkəl) *or* **philosophic** *adj.* **1.** of or relating to philosophy or philosophers. **2.** reasonable, wise, or learned. **3.** calm and stoical, esp. in the face of difficulties or disappointments. — ˌphilo'sophically *adv.*

philosophical analysis *n.* a philosophical method in which language and experience are analysed in an attempt to provide new insights into various philosophical problems.

philosophize *or* **-phise** (fɪ'lɒsəˌfaɪz) *vb.* **1.** (*intr.*) to make philosophical pronouncements and speculations. **2.** (*tr.*) to explain philosophically. — **phi'loso,phizer** *or* -ˌphiser *n.*

philosophy (fɪ'lɒsəfɪ) *n., pl.* **-phies. 1.** the academic discipline concerned with making explicit the nature and significance of ordinary and scientific beliefs and investigating the intelligibility of concepts by means of rational argument concerning their presuppositions, implications, and interrelationships. **2.** the particular doctrines relating to these issues of a specific individual or school: *the philosophy of Descartes.* **3.** the basic principles of a discipline: *the philosophy of law.* **4.** any system of belief, values, or tenets. **5.** a personal outlook or viewpoint. **6.** serenity of temper. [C13: from OF *filosofie*, from L *philosophia*, from Gk, from *philosophos* lover of wisdom]

-philous *or* **-philic** *adj. combining form.* indicating love of or fondness for: *heliophilous.* [from L *-philus*, from Gk *-philos*]

philtre *or U.S.* **philter** ('fɪltə) *n.* a drink supposed to arouse desire. [C16: from L *philtrum*, from Gk *philtron* love potion, from *philos* loving]

phimosis (faɪ'məʊsɪs) *n.* abnormal tightness of the foreskin, preventing its being retracted. [C17: via NL from Gk: a muzzling]

phiz (fɪz) *n. Sl., chiefly Brit.* the face or a facial expression. Also called: **phizog** (fɪ'zɒg). [C17: colloquial shortening of PHYSIOGNOMY]

Phiz (fɪz) *n.* real name *Hablot Knight Browne.* 1815–82, English painter, noted for his illustrations for Dickens' novels.

phlebitis (flɪ'baɪtɪs) *n.* inflammation of a vein. [C19: via NL from Gk] — **phlebitic** (flɪ'bɪtɪk) *adj.*

phlebo- *or before a vowel* **phleb-** *combining form.* indicating a vein: *phlebotomy.* [from Gk *phleps, phleb-* vein]

phlebotomy (flɪ'bɒtəmɪ) *n., pl.* **-mies.** surgical incision into a vein. [C14: from OF *flebothomie*, from LL *phlebotomia*, from Gk]

Phlegethon ('flɛgɪˌθɒn) *n. Greek myth.* a river of fire in Hades. [C14: from Gk, lit.: blazing, from *phlegethein* to flame, blaze]

phlegm (flɛm) *n.* **1.** the viscid mucus secreted by the walls of the respiratory tract. **2.** *Arch.* one of the four bodily humours. **3.** apathy; stolidity. **4.** imperturbability; coolness. [C14: from OF *fleume*, from LL *phlegma*, from Gk: inflammation, from *phlegein* to burn] — 'phlegmy *adj.*

phlegmatic (flɛg'mætɪk) *or* **phlegmatical** *adj.* **1.** having a stolid or unemotional disposition. **2.** not easily excited. — **phleg'matically** *adv.*

phloem ('fləʊɛm) *n.* tissue in higher plants that conducts synthesized food substances to all parts of the plant. [C19: via G from Gk *phloos* bark]

phlogiston (flɒ'dʒɪstɒn, -tən) *n. Chem.* a hypothetical substance formerly thought to be present in all combustible materials. [C18: via NL from Gk, from *phlogizein* to set alight]

phlox (flɒks) *n., pl.* **phlox** *or* **phloxes.** any of a chiefly North American genus of plants cultivated for their clusters of white, red, or purple flowers. [C18: via L from Gk: a plant of glowing colour, lit.: flame]

phlyctena (flɪk'tiːnə) *n., pl.* **-nae** (-niː). *Pathol.* a small blister, vesicle, or pustule. [C17: via NL from Gk *phluktaina*, from *phluzein* to swell]

Phnom Penh *or* **Pnom Penh** (nɒm pɛn) *n.* the capital of Kampuchea, a port in the south at the confluence of the Mekong and Tonle Sap Rivers: capital of the country since 1865; university (1960). Pop.: 500 000 (1983 est.).

-phobe *n. combining form.* indicating one that fears or hates: *xenophobe.* [from Gk *-phobos* fearing] — -**phobic** *adj. combining form.*

phobia ('fəʊbɪə) *n. Psychiatry.* an abnormal intense and irrational fear of a given situation, organism, or object. [C19: from Gk *phobos* fear] — 'phobic *adj., n.*

-phobia *n. combining form.* indicating an extreme abnormal fear of or aversion to: *acrophobia; claustrophobia.* [via L from Gk, from *phobos* fear] — -**phobic** *adj. combining form.*

Phocaea (fəʊ'siːə) *n.* an ancient port in Asia Minor, the northernmost of Ionian cities on the W coast of Asia Minor: an important maritime state (about 1000–600 B.C.).

Phocis ('fəʊsɪs) *n.* an ancient district of central Greece, on the Gulf of Corinth: site of the Delphic oracle.

phocomelia (ˌfəʊkəʊ'miːlɪə) *n.* a congenital deformity characterized esp. by short stubby hands or feet attached close to the body. [C19: via NL from Gk *phōkē* a seal + *melos* a limb]

phoebe ('fiːbɪ) *n.* any of several greyish-brown North American flycatchers. [C19: imit.]

Phoebe *or* **Phebe** ('fiːbɪ) *n.* **1.** *Classical myth.* a Titaness, who later became identified with Artemis (Diana) as goddess of the moon. **2.** *Poetic.* a personification of the moon.

Phoebus ('fiːbəs) *n.* **1.** Also called: **Phoebus Apollo.** *Greek myth.* Apollo as the sun god. **2.** *Poetic.* a personification of the sun. [C14: via L from Gk *Phoibos* bright; related to *phaos* light]

Phoenicia (fə'nɪʃɪə, -'niː-) *n.* an ancient maritime country extending from the Mediterranean Sea to the Lebanon Mountains, now occupied by the coastal regions of Lebanon and parts of Syria and Israel: consisted of a group of city-states, at their height between about 1200 and 1000 B.C., that were leading traders of the ancient world.

Phoenician (fə'nɪʃɪən, -'niːʃən) *n.* **1.** a member of an ancient Semitic people of NW Syria. **2.** the extinct language of this people. ~*adj.* **3.** of Phoenicia, the Phoenicians, or their language.

phoenix *or U.S.* **phenix** ('fiːnɪks) *n.* **1.** a legendary Arabian bird said to set fire to itself and rise anew from the ashes every 500 years. **2.** a person or thing of surpassing beauty or quality. [OE *fenix*, via L from Gk *phoinix*]

Phoenix ('fiːnɪks) *n.* a city in central Arizona, capital city of the state, on the Salt River. Pop.: 881 640 (1986 est.).

Phoenix Islands *pl. n.* a group of eight coral islands in the central Pacific: administratively part of Kiribati. Area: 28 sq. km (11 sq. miles).

Phomvihane ('pɒmvɪhɑːn) *n.* **Kaysone** ('kaɪsɒn). born 1920, Laotian Communist statesman; prime minister of Laos from 1975.

phon (fɒn) *n.* a unit of loudness that measures the intensity of a sound by the number of decibels it is above a reference tone. [C20: via G from Gk *phōnē* sound]

phonate (fəʊ'neɪt) *vb.* (*intr.*) to articulate speech sounds, esp. voiced speech sounds. [C19: from Gk *phōnē* voice] — pho'nation *n.*

phone[1] (fəʊn) *n., vb.* short for **telephone.**

phone[2] (fəʊn) *n. Phonetics.* a single speech sound. [C19: from Gk *phōnē* sound, voice]

-phone *combining form.* **1.** (*forming nouns*) indicating a device giving off sound: *telephone.* **2.** (*forming nouns and adjectives*) (a person) speaking a particular language: *Francophone.* [from Gk *phōnē* voice, sound] — -**phonic** *adj. combining form.*

phonecard ('fəʊnˌkɑːd) *n.* **1.** a public telephone that is operated by a special card instead of coins. **2.** the card used.

phone-in *n.* **a.** a radio or television programme in which listeners' or viewers' questions, comments, etc., are telephoned to the studio and broadcast live as part of a discussion. **b.** (*as modifier*): *a phone-in programme.*

phoneme ('fəʊniːm) *n. Linguistics.* one of the set of speech sounds in any given language that serve to distinguish one word from another. [C20: via F from Gk *phōnēma* sound, speech] — **phonemic** (fə'niːmɪk) *adj.*

phonemics (fə'niːmɪks) *n.* (*functioning as sing.*) that aspect of linguistics concerned with the classification and analysis of the phonemes of a language. — **pho'nemicist** *n.*

phonetic (fə'nɛtɪk) *adj.* **1.** of or relating to phonetics. **2.** denoting any perceptible distinction between one speech sound and another. **3.** conforming to pronunciation: *phonetic spelling.* [C19: from NL *phōnēticus*, from Gk, from *phōnein* to make sounds, speak] —**pho'netically** *adv.*

phonetics (fə'nɛtɪks) *n.* (*functioning as sing.*) the science concerned with the study of speech processes, including the production, perception, and analysis of speech sounds. —**phonetician** (,fəʊnɪ'tɪʃən) *or* **phonetist** ('fəʊnɪtɪst) *n.*

phoney *or esp. U.S.* **phony** ('fəʊnɪ) *Inf.* ~*adj.* **-nier, -niest. 1.** not genuine; fake. **2.** (of a person) insincere or pretentious. ~*n., pl.* **-neys** *or esp. U.S.* **-nies. 3.** an insincere or pretentious person. **4.** something that is not genuine; a fake. [C20: from ?] —**'phoneyness** *or esp. U.S.* **'phoniness** *n.*

phonics ('fonɪks) *n.* (*functioning as sing.*) **1.** an obsolete name for **acoustics** (sense 1). **2.** a method of teaching people to read by training them to associate letters with their phonetic values. —**'phonic** *adj.* —**'phonically** *adv.*

phono- *or before a vowel* **phon-** *combining form.* indicating a sound or voice: *phonograph; phonology.* [from Gk *phōnē* sound, voice]

phonogram ('fəʊnə,græm) *n.* any written symbol standing for a sound, syllable, morpheme, or word. —,**phono'gramic** *or* ,**phono'grammic** *adj.*

phonograph ('fəʊnə,grɑːf) *n.* **1.** an early form of gramophone capable of recording and reproducing sound on wax cylinders. **2.** another U.S. and Canad. word for **gramophone** or **record player.**

phonography (fəʊ'nɒɡrəfɪ) *n.* **1.** a writing system that represents sounds by individual symbols. **2.** the employment of such a writing system. —**phonographic** (,fəʊnə'græfɪk) *adj.*

phonology (fə'nɒlədʒɪ) *n., pl.* **-gies. 1.** the study of the sound system of a language or of languages in general. **2.** such a sound system. —**phonological** (,fəʊnə'lɒdʒɪkəl, ,fɒn-) *adj.* —,**phono'logically** *adv.* —**pho'nologist** *n.*

phonon ('fəʊnɒn) *n. Physics.* a quantum of vibrational energy in the acoustic vibrations of a crystal lattice. [C20: from PHONO- + -ON]

-phony *n. combining form.* indicating a specified type of sound: *cacophony; euphony.* [from Gk *-phōnia,* from *phōnē* sound] —*-phonic adj. combining form.*

phooey ('fuːɪ) *interj. Inf.* an exclamation of scorn, contempt, etc. [C20: prob. var. of PHEW]

-phore *n. combining form.* indicating one that bears or produces: *semaphore.* [from NL *-phorus,* from Gk *-phoros* bearing, from *pherein* to bear] —**-phorous** *adj. combining form.*

-phoresis *n. combining form.* indicating a transmission: *electrophoresis.* [from Gk *phorēsis* being carried, from *pherein* to bear]

phormium ('fɔːmɪəm) *n.* any of a genus of plants of the lily family with tough leathery evergreen leaves. Also called: **New Zealand flax, flax lily.** [C19: NL from Gk *phormos* basket]

phosgene ('fozdʒiːn) *n.* a colourless poisonous gas: used in chemical warfare and in the manufacture of pesticides, dyes, and polyurethane resins. [C19: from Gk *phos* light + *-gene,* var. of -GEN]

phosphate ('fosfeɪt) *n.* **1.** any salt or ester of any phosphoric acid. **2.** (*often pl.*) any of several chemical fertilizers containing phosphorous compounds. [C18: from F *phosphat;* see PHOSPHORUS, -ATE[1]] —**phosphatic** (fos'fætɪk) *adj.*

phosphatide ('fosfə,taɪd) *n.* another name for **phospholipid.**

phosphene ('fosfiːn) *n.* the sensation of light caused by pressure on the eyelid of a closed eye. [C19: from Gk *phos* light + *phainein* to show]

phosphide ('fosfaɪd) *n.* any compound of phosphorus with another element, esp. a more electropositive element.

phosphine ('fosfiːn) *n.* a colourless inflammable gas that is slightly soluble in water and has a strong fishy odour: used as a pesticide. Formula: PH_3.

phosphite ('fosfaɪt) *n.* any salt or ester of phosphorous acid.

phospho- *or before a vowel* **phosph-** *combining form.* containing phosphorus: *phosphoric.* [from F, from *phosphore* PHOSPHORUS]

phospholipid (,fosfə'lɪpɪd) *n.* any of a group of fatty compounds: important constituents of all membranes. Also called: **phosphatide.**

phosphonic acid (fos'fonɪk) *n.* the systematic name for **phosphorous acid.**

phosphor ('fosfə) *n.* a substance capable of emitting light when irradiated with particles of electromagnetic radiation. [C17: from F, ult. from Gk *phósphoros* PHOSPHORUS]

phosphorate ('fosfə,reɪt) *vb.* to treat or combine with phosphorus.

phosphor bronze *n.* any of various hard corrosion-resistant alloys containing phosphorus: used in gears, bearings, cylinder casings, etc.

phosphoresce (,fosfə'rɛs) *vb.* (*intr.*) to exhibit phosphorescence.

phosphorescence (,fosfə'rɛsəns) *n.* **1.** *Physics.* a fluorescence that persists after the bombarding radiation producing it has stopped. **2.** the light emitted in phosphorescence. **3.** the emission of light in which insufficient heat is evolved to cause fluorescence. Cf. **fluorescence.** —,**phospho'rescent** *adj.*

phosphoric (fos'forɪk) *adj.* of or containing phosphorus in the pentavalent state.

phosphoric acid *n.* **1.** a colourless solid tribasic acid used in the manufacture of fertilizers and soap. Formula: H_3PO_4. Systematic name: **phosphoric(V) acid.** Also called: **orthophosphoric acid. 2.** any oxyacid of phosphorus produced by reaction between phosphorus pentoxide and water.

phosphorous ('fosfərəs) *adj.* of or containing phosphorus in the trivalent state.

phosphorous acid *n.* **1.** a white or yellowish hygroscopic crystalline dibasic acid. Formula: H_3PO_3. Systematic name: **phosphonic acid.** Also called: **orthophosphorous acid. 2.** any oxyacid of phosphorus containing less oxygen than the corresponding phosphoric acid.

phosphorus ('fosfərəs) *n.* **1.** an allotropic nonmetallic element occurring in phosphates and living matter. Ordinary phosphorus is a toxic flammable phosphorescent white solid; the red form is less reactive and nontoxic: used in matches, pesticides, and alloys. The radioisotope **phosphorus-32** (**radiophosphorus**), with a half-life of 14.3 days, is used in radiotherapy and as a tracer. Symbol: P; atomic no.: 15; atomic wt.: 30.974. **2.** a less common name for a **phosphor.** [C17: via L from Gk *phósphoros* light-bringing, from *phós* light + *pherein* to bring]

Phosphorus ('fosfərəs) *n.* a morning star, esp. Venus.

phossy jaw ('fosɪ) *n.* a gangrenous condition of the lower jawbone caused by prolonged exposure to phosphorus fumes. [C19: *phossy,* colloquial shortening of PHOSPHORUS]

phot (fot, fəʊt) *n.* a unit of illumination equal to one lumen per square centimetre. 1 phot is equal to 10 000 lux. [C20: from Gk *phós* light]

phot. *abbrev. for:* **1.** photograph. **2.** photographic. **3.** photography.

photic ('fəʊtɪk) *adj.* **1.** of or concerned with light. **2.** designating the zone of the sea where photosynthesis takes place.

photo ('fəʊtəʊ) *n., pl.* **-tos.** short for **photograph.**

photo- *combining form.* **1.** of, relating to, or produced by light: *photosynthesis.* **2.** indicating a photographic process: *photolithography.* [from Gk *phós, phót-* light]

photo call *n.* a time arranged for photographers, esp. press photographers, to take pictures of a celebrity.

photocell ('fəʊtəʊ,sɛl) *n.* a device in which the photoelectric or photovoltaic effect or photoconductivity is used to produce a current or voltage when exposed to light or other electromagnetic radiation. They are used in exposure meters, burglar alarms, etc. Also called: **photoelectric cell, electric eye.**

photochemistry (,fəʊtəʊ'kɛmɪstrɪ) *n.* the branch of chemistry concerned with the chemical effects of light and other electromagnetic radiations. —**photochemical** (,fəʊtəʊ'kɛmɪkəl) *adj.*

photocomposition (,fəʊtəʊ,kɒmpə'zɪʃən) *n.* another name (esp. U.S. and Canad.) for **filmsetting.**

photoconductivity (,fəʊtəʊ,kɒndʌk'tɪvɪtɪ) *n.* the change in the electrical conductivity of certain substances, such as selenium, as a result of the absorption of electromagnetic radiation. —**photoconductive** (,fəʊtəʊkən'dʌktɪv) *adj.* —,**photocon'ductor** *n.*

photocopier ('fəʊtəʊ,kɒpɪə) *n.* an instrument using light-sensitive photographic materials to reproduce written, printed, or graphic work.

photocopy ('fəʊtəʊ,kɒpɪ) *n., pl.* **-copies. 1.** a photographic reproduction of written, printed, or graphic work. ~*vb.* **-copying, -copied. 2.** to reproduce (written, printed, or graphic work) on photographic material.

photoelectric (,fəʊtəʊɪ'lɛktrɪk) *adj.* of or concerned with electric or electronic effects caused by light or other electromagnetic radiation. —**photoelectricity** (,fəʊtəʊɪlɛk'trɪsɪtɪ) *n.*

photoelectric cell *n.* another name for **photocell.**

photoelectric effect *n.* **1.** the ejection of electrons from a solid by an incident beam of sufficiently energetic electromagnetic radiation. **2.** any phenomenon involving electricity and electromagnetic radiation, such as photoemission.

photoelectron (,fəʊtəʊɪ'lɛktrɒn) *n.* an electron ejected from an atom, molecule, or solid by an incident photon.

photoemission (,fəʊtəʊɪ'mɪʃən) *n.* the emission of electrons due to the impact of electromagnetic radiation.

photoengraving (,fəʊtəʊɪn'greɪvɪŋ) *n.* **1.** a photomechanical process for producing letterpress printing plates. **2.** a plate made by this process. **3.** a print made from such a plate. — ,**photoen'grave** *vb.* (*tr.*)

photo finish *n.* **1.** a finish of a race in which contestants are so close that a photograph is needed to decide the result. **2.** any race or competition in which the winners are separated by a very small margin.

Photofit ('fəʊtəʊ,fɪt) *n. Trademark.* **a.** a method of combining photographs of facial features, hair, etc., into a composite picture of a face: used by the police to trace suspects, criminals, etc. **b.** (*as modifier*): *a Photofit picture.*

photoflash ('fəʊtəʊ,flæʃ) *n.* another name for **flashbulb.**

photoflood ('fəʊtəʊ,flʌd) *n.* a highly incandescent tungsten lamp used for indoor photography, television, etc.

photog. *abbrev. for:* **1.** photograph. **2.** photographer. **3.** photographic. **4.** photography.

photogenic (,fəʊtə'dʒɛnɪk) *adj.* **1.** (esp. of a person) having a general facial appearance that looks attractive in photographs. **2.** *Biol.* producing or emitting light. — ,**photo'genically** *adv.*

photogram ('fəʊtə,græm) *n.* **1.** a picture, usually abstract, produced on a photographic material without the use of a camera. **2.** *Obs.* a photograph.

photogrammetry (,fəʊtəʊ'græmɪtrɪ) *n.* the process of making measurements from photographs, used esp. in the construction of maps from aerial photographs.

photograph ('fəʊtə,grɑːf) *n.* **1.** an image of an object, person, scene, etc., in the form of a print or slide recorded by a camera. Often shortened to **photo.** ~*vb.* **2.** to take a photograph of (an object, person, scene, etc.).

photographic (,fəʊtə'græfɪk) *adj.* **1.** of or relating to photography. **2.** like a photograph in accuracy or detail. **3.** (of a person's memory) able to retain facts, appearances, etc., in precise detail. — ,**photo'graphically** *adv.*

photography (fə'tɒɡrəfɪ) *n.* **1.** the process of recording images on sensitized material by the action of light, x-rays, etc. **2.** the art, practice, or occupation of taking photographs. —**pho'tographer** *n.*

photogravure (,fəʊtəʊɡrə'vjʊə) *n.* **1.** any of various methods in which an intaglio plate for printing is produced by the use of photography. **2.** matter printed from such a plate. [C19: from PHOTO- + F *gravure* engraving]

photojournalism (,fəʊtəʊ'dʒɜːnᵊ,lɪzəm) *n.* journalism in which photographs are the predominant feature. — ,**photo'journalist** *n.*

photokinesis (,fəʊtəʊkɪ'niːsɪs, -kaɪ-) *n. Biol.* the movement of an organism in response to the stimulus of light.

photolithography (,fəʊtəʊlɪ'θɒɡrəfɪ) *n.* **1.** a lithographic printing process using photographically made plates. Often shortened to **photolitho. 2.** *Electronics.* a process used in the manufacture of semiconductor devices and printed circuits in which a particular pattern is transferred from a photograph onto a substrate. — ,**photoli'thographer** *n.*

photoluminescence (,fəʊtəʊ,luːmɪ'nɛsəns) *n.* luminescence resulting from the absorption of light or infrared or ultraviolet radiation.

photolysis (fəʊ'tɒlɪsɪs) *n.* chemical decomposition caused by light or other electromagnetic radiation. —**photolytic** (,fəʊtəʊ'lɪtɪk) *adj.*

photomechanical (,fəʊtəʊmɪ'kænɪkᵊl) *adj.* of or relating to any of various methods by which printing plates are made using photography. — ,**photome'chanically** *adv.*

photometer (fəʊ'tɒmɪtə) *n.* an instrument used in photometry, usually one that compares the illumination produced by a particular light source with that produced by a standard source.

photometry (fəʊ'tɒmɪtrɪ) *n.* **1.** the measurement of the intensity of light. **2.** the branch of physics concerned with such measurements. —**pho'tometrist** *n.*

photomicrograph (,fəʊtəʊ'maɪkrə,grɑːf) *n.* a photograph of a microscope image. — **photomicrography** (,fəʊtəʊmaɪ'krɒɡrəfɪ) *n.*

photomontage (,fəʊtəʊmɒn'tɑːʒ) *n.* **1.** the technique of producing a composite picture by combining several photographs. **2.** the composite picture so produced.

photomultiplier (,fəʊtəʊ'mʌltɪ,plaɪə) *n.* a device sensitive to electromagnetic radiation which produces a detectable pulse of current.

photon ('fəʊtɒn) *n.* a quantum of electromagnetic radiation with energy equal to the product of the frequency of the radiation and the Planck constant.

photo-offset *n. Printing.* an offset process in which the plates are produced photomechanically.

photoperiodism (,fəʊtəʊ'pɪərɪə,dɪzəm) *n.* the response of plants and animals by behaviour, growth, etc., to the period of daylight in every 24 hours (**photoperiod**). — ,**photo,peri'odic** *adj.*

photophobia (,fəʊtəʊ'fəʊbɪə) *n.* **1.** *Pathol.* abnormal sensitivity of the eyes to light. **2.** *Psychiatry.* abnormal fear of sunlight or well-lit places. — ,**photo'phobic** *adj.*

photopolymer (,fəʊtəʊ'pɒlɪmə) *n.* a polymeric material that is sensitive to light: used in printing plates, microfilms, etc.

photoreceptor (,fəʊtəʊrɪ'sɛptə) *n. Zool., physiol.* a light-sensitive cell or organ that conveys impulses through the sensory neuron connected to it.

photosensitive (,fəʊtəʊ'sɛnsɪtɪv) *adj.* sensitive to electromagnetic radiation, esp. light. — ,**photo,sensi'tivity** *n.* — ,**photo'sensitize** *or* **-tise** *vb.* (*tr.*)

photoset ('fəʊtəʊ,sɛt) *vb.* **-setting, -set.** another word for **filmset.** — ,**photo,setter** *n.*

photosphere ('fəʊtəʊ,sfɪə) *n.* the visible surface of the sun. —**photospheric** (,fəʊtəʊ'sfɛrɪk) *adj.*

Photostat ('fəʊtəʊ,stæt) *n.* **1.** *Trademark.* a machine or process used to make photographic copies of written, printed, or graphic matter. **2.** any copy made by such a machine. ~*vb.* **-statting** *or* **-stating, -statted** *or* **-stated. 3.** to make a Photostat copy (of). — ,**photo'static** *adj.*

photosynthesis (,fəʊtəʊ'sɪnθɪsɪs) *n.* (in plants) the synthesis of organic compounds from carbon dioxide and water using light energy absorbed by chlorophyll. — ,**photo'synthesize** *or* **-sise** *vb.* —**photosynthetic** (,fəʊtəʊsɪn'θɛtɪk) *adj.* — ,**photosyn'thetically** *adv.*

phototaxis (,fəʊtəʊ'tæksɪs) *n.* the movement of an entire organism in response to light.

phototropism (,fəʊtəʊ'trəʊpɪzəm) *n.* the growth response of plant parts to the stimulus of light, producing a bending towards the light source. — ,**photo'tropic** *adj.*

photovoltaic effect (,fəʊtəʊvɒl'teɪɪk) *n.* the effect when electromagnetic radiation falls on a thin film of one solid deposited on the surface of a dissimilar solid producing a difference in potential between the two materials.

phrasal verb *n.* a phrase that consists of a verb plus an adverbial or prepositional particle, esp. one the meaning of which cannot be deduced from the constituents: *"take in" meaning "deceive" is a phrasal verb.*

phrase (freɪz) *n.* **1.** a group of words forming a syntactic constituent of a sentence. Cf. **clause** (sense 1). **2.** an idiomatic or original expression. **3.** manner or style of speech or expression. **4.** *Music.* a small group of notes forming a coherent unit of melody. ~*vb.* (*tr.*) **5.** *Music.* to divide (a melodic line, part, etc.) into musical phrases, esp. in performance. **6.** to express orally or in a phrase. [C16: from L *phrasis,* from Gk: speech, from *phrazein* to tell] — '**phrasal** *adj.*

phrase book *n.* a book containing frequently used expressions and their equivalents in a foreign language.

phrase marker *n. Linguistics.* a representation, esp. a tree diagram, of the constituent structure of a sentence.

phraseogram ('freɪzɪə,græm) *n.* a symbol representing a phrase, as in shorthand.

phraseology (ˌfreɪzɪ'ɒlədʒɪ) n., pl. **-gies. 1.** the manner in which words or phrases are used. **2.** a set of phrases used by a particular group of people. —**phraseological** (ˌfreɪzɪə'lɒdʒɪk°l) adj.

phrasing ('freɪzɪŋ) n. **1.** the way in which something is expressed, esp. in writing; wording. **2.** Music. the division of a melodic line, part, etc., into musical phrases.

phrenetic (frɪ'nɛtɪk) adj. an obsolete spelling of **frenetic.** —**phre'netically** adv.

phrenic ('frɛnɪk) adj. **1. a.** of or relating to the diaphragm. **b.** (as n.): the phrenic. **2.** Obs. of or relating to the mind. [C18: from NL phrenicus, from Gk phrēn mind, diaphragm]

phrenology (frɪ'nɒlədʒɪ) n. (formerly) the branch of science concerned with determination of the strength of the faculties by the shape and size of the skull overlying the parts of the brain thought to be responsible for them. —**phrenological** (ˌfrɛnə'lɒdʒɪk°l) adj. —**phre'nologist** n.

phrensy ('frɛnzɪ) n., pl. **-sies** an obsolete spelling of **frenzy.**

Phrixus ('frɪksəs) n. Greek myth. the son of Athamas and Nephele who escaped the wrath of his father's mistress, Ino, by flying to Colchis on a winged ram with a golden fleece. See also **Helle, Golden Fleece.**

Phrygia ('frɪdʒɪə) n. an ancient country of W central Asia Minor.

Phrygian ('frɪdʒɪən) adj. **1.** of or relating to ancient Phrygia, its inhabitants, or their extinct language. **2.** Music. of or relating to an authentic mode represented by the natural diatonic scale from E to E. ~n. **3.** a native or inhabitant of ancient Phrygia. **4.** an ancient language of Phrygia.

Phrygian cap n. a conical cap of soft material worn during ancient times, that became a symbol of liberty during the French Revolution.

phthisis ('θaɪsɪs, 'fθaɪ-, 'taɪ-) n. any disease that causes wasting of the body, esp. pulmonary tuberculosis. [C16: via L from Gk, from phthinein to waste away]

phut (fʌt) Inf. ~n. **1.** a representation of a muffled explosive sound. ~adv. **2. go phut.** to break down or collapse. [C19: imit.]

phycomycete (ˌfaɪkəʊ'maɪsiːt) n. any of a class of filamentous fungi: includes certain mildews and moulds. [from Gk phukos seaweed + -MYCETE]

Phyfe (faɪf) n. **Duncan.** ?1768–1854, U.S. cabinet-maker, born in Scotland.

phyla ('faɪlə) n. the plural of **phylum.**

phylactery (fɪ'læktərɪ) n., pl. **-teries. 1.** Judaism. either of the pair of blackened square cases containing parchments inscribed with biblical passages, bound by leather thongs to the head and left arm, and worn by Jewish men during weekday morning prayers. **2.** a reminder. **3.** Arch. an amulet or charm. [C14: from LL phylactērium, from Gk phulaktērion outpost, from phulax a guard]

phyletic (faɪ'lɛtɪk) adj. of or relating to the evolutionary development of organisms. [C19: from Gk phuletikos tribal]

-phyll or **-phyl** n. combining form. leaf: chlorophyll. [from Gk phullon]

phyllo- or before a vowel **phyll-** combining form. leaf: phyllopod. [from Gk phullon leaf]

phyllode ('fɪləʊd) n. a flattened leafstalk that resembles and functions as a leaf. [C19: from NL phyllodium, from Gk phullōdēs leaflike]

phylloquinone (ˌfɪləʊkwɪ'nəʊn) n. a viscous fat-soluble liquid occurring in plants: essential for the production of prothrombin, required in blood clotting. Also called: **vitamin K₁.**

phyllotaxis (ˌfɪlə'tæksɪs) or **phyllotaxy** n., pl. **-taxes** (-'tæksiːz) or **-taxies. 1.** the arrangement of the leaves on a stem. **2.** the study of this arrangement. —**phyllo-'tactic** adj.

-phyllous adj. combining form. having leaves of a specified number or type: monophyllous. [from Gk -phullos of a leaf]

phylloxera (ˌfɪlɒk'sɪərə, fɪ'lɒksərə) n., pl. **-rae** (-riː) or **-ras.** any of a genus of homopterous insects, such as vine phylloxera, typically feeding on plant juices. [C19: NL, from PHYLLO- + xēros dry]

phylo- or before a vowel **phyl-** combining form. tribe; race; phylum: phylogeny. [from Gk phulon race]

phylogeny (faɪ'lɒdʒɪnɪ) or **phylogenesis** (ˌfaɪləʊ'dʒɛnɪsɪs) n., pl. **-nies** or **-geneses** (-'dʒɛnɪ,siːz). Biol. the sequence of events involved in the evolution of a species, genus, etc. Cf. **ontogeny.** [C19: from PHYLO- + -GENY] —**phylogenic** (ˌfaɪləʊ'dʒɛnɪk) or **phylogenetic** (ˌfaɪləʊdʒɪ'nɛtɪk) adj.

phylum ('faɪləm) n., pl. **-la. 1.** a major taxonomic division of the animals and plants that contain one or more classes. **2.** a group of related language families or linguistic stocks. [C19: NL, from Gk phulon race]

phys. abbrev. for: **1.** physical. **2.** physician. **3.** physics. **4.** physiological. **5.** physiology.

physalis (faɪ'seɪlɪs) n. any of a genus of plants producing inflated orange seed vessels. See **Chinese lantern.** [NL from Gk physallis bladder]

physic ('fɪzɪk) n. **1.** Rare. a medicine, esp. a cathartic. **2.** Arch. the art or skill of healing. ~vb. **-icking, -icked.** (tr.) **3.** Arch. to treat (a patient) with medicine. [C13: from OF fisique, via L from Gk phusikē, from phusis nature]

physical ('fɪzɪk°l) adj. **1.** of or relating to the body, as distinguished from the mind or spirit. **2.** of, relating to, or resembling material things or nature: the physical universe. **3.** of or concerned with matter and energy. **4.** of or relating to physics. —'**physically** adv.

physical anthropology n. the branch of anthropology dealing with the genetic aspect of human development and its physical variations.

physical chemistry n. the branch of chemistry concerned with the way in which the physical properties of substances depend on their chemical structure, properties, and reactions.

physical education n. training and practice in sports, gymnastics, etc. Abbrev.: **PE.**

physical geography n. the branch of geography that deals with the natural features of the earth's surface.

physical jerks pl. n. Brit. inf. See **jerk¹** (sense 6).

physical science n. any of the sciences concerned with nonliving matter, such as physics, chemistry, astronomy, and geology.

physical therapy n. another term for **physiotherapy.**

physician (fɪ'zɪʃən) n. **1.** a person legally qualified to practise medicine, esp. other than surgery; doctor of medicine. **2.** Arch. any person who treats diseases; healer. [C13: from OF fisicien, from fisique PHYSIC]

physicist ('fɪzɪsɪst) n. a person versed in or studying physics.

physics ('fɪzɪks) n. (functioning as sing.) **1.** the branch of science concerned with the properties of matter and energy and the relationships between them. It is based on mathematics and traditionally includes mechanics, optics, electricity and magnetism, acoustics, and heat. Modern physics, based on quantum theory, includes atomic, nuclear, particle, and solid-state studies. **2.** physical properties of behaviour: the physics of the electron. **3.** Arch. natural science. [C16: from L physica, translation of Gk ta phusika natural things, from phusis nature]

physio- or before a vowel **phys-** combining form. **1.** of or relating to nature or natural functions: physiology. **2.** physical: physiotherapy. [from Gk phusio, ult. from phuein to make grow]

physiocrat ('fɪzɪəʊ,kræt) n. a believer in the 18th-century French economic theory that the inherent natural order governing society was based on land and its natural products as the only true form of wealth. [C18: from F physiocrate; see PHYSIO-, -CRAT] —**physiocracy** (ˌfɪzɪ'ɒkrəsɪ) n.

physiognomy (ˌfɪzɪ'ɒnəmɪ) n. **1.** a person's features considered as an indication of personality. **2.** the art or practice of judging character from facial features. **3.** the outward appearance of something. [C14: from OF phisonomie, via Med. L, from LGk phusiognōmia, from phusis nature + gnōmōn judge] —**physiognomic** (ˌfɪzɪə'nɒmɪk) or **physiog'nomical** adj. —**physiog'nomically** adv. —**physi'ognomist** n.

physiography (ˌfɪzɪ'ɒgrəfɪ) n. another name for **geomorphology** or **physical geography.** —**physi'ographer** n. —**physiographic** (ˌfɪzɪə'græfɪk) or **physio'graphical** adj.

physiol. abbrev. for: **1.** physiological. **2.** physiology.

physiology (ˌfɪzɪ'ɒlədʒɪ) n. **1.** the branch of science concerned with the functioning of organisms. **2.** the processes and functions of all or part of an organism. [C16: from L physiologia, from Gk] —**physi'ologist** n.

—**physiological** (ˌfɪzɪə'lɒdʒɪk²l) *adj.* — ˌphysio'logi-cally *adv.*

physiotherapy (ˌfɪzɪəʊ'θɛrəpɪ) *n.* the treatment of disease, injury, etc., by physical means, such as massage or exercises, rather than by drugs. —ˌphysio'therapist *n.*

physique (fɪ'ziːk) *n.* the general appearance of the body with regard to size, shape, muscular development, etc. [C19: via F from *physique* (adj.) natural, from L *physicus* physical]

-phyte *n. combining form.* indicating a plant of a specified type or habitat: *lithophyte*. [from Gk *phuton* plant] —**-phytic** *adj. combining form.*

phyto- *or before a vowel* **phyt-** *combining form.* indicating a plant or vegetation: *phytogenesis*. [from Gk *phuton* plant, from *phuein* to make grow]

phytogenesis (ˌfaɪtəʊ'dʒɛnɪsɪs) *or* **phytogeny** (faɪ'tɒdʒənɪ) *n.* the branch of botany concerned with the origin and evolution of plants.

phyton ('faɪtɒn) *n.* a unit of plant structure, usually considered as the smallest part of the plant that is capable of growth when detached from the parent plant. [C20: from Gk; see -PHYTE]

phytopathology (ˌfaɪtəʊpə'θɒlədʒɪ) *n.* the branch of botany concerned with diseases of plants.

phytoplankton (ˌfaɪtə'plæŋktən) *n.* the plant constituent of plankton, mainly unicellular algae.

phytotoxin (ˌfaɪtə'tɒksɪn) *n.* a toxin, such as strychnine, that is produced by a plant.

pi¹ (paɪ) *n., pl.* **pis.** 1. the 16th letter in the Greek alphabet (Π, π). 2. *Maths.* a transcendental number, fundamental to mathematics, that is the ratio of the circumference of a circle to its diameter. Approximate value: 3.141 592 . . . ; symbol: π [C18 (mathematical use): representing the first letter of Gk *periphereia* PERIPHERY]

pi² *or* **pie** (paɪ) *n., pl.* **pies.** 1. a jumbled pile of printer's type. 2. a jumbled mixture. ~*vb.* **piing, pied** *or* **pieing, pied.** (*tr.*) 3. to spill and mix (set type) indiscriminately. 4. to mix up. [C17: from ?]

pi³ (paɪ) *adj. Brit. sl.* See **pious** (senses 2, 3).

Piacenza (*Italian* pja'tʃɛntsa) *n.* a town in N Italy, in Emilia-Romagna on the River Po. Pop.: 105 626 (1986). Latin name: **Placentia** (plə'sɛntʃɪə).

piacevole (piːætʃ'eɪvəʊleɪ) *adv. Music.* in an agreeable, pleasant manner. [It.]

piacular (paɪ'ækjʊlə) *adj.* 1. making expiation. 2. requiring expiation. [C17: from L *piāculum* propitiatory sacrifice, from *piāre* to appease]

Piaf (*French* pjaf) *n.* **Edith** (edit), real name *Edith Giovanna Gassion*, known as *the Little Sparrow*, 1915–63, French singer.

piaffe (pɪ'æf) *n. Dressage.* a slow trot done on the spot. [C18: from F, from *piaffer* to strut]

Piaget (*French* pjaʒɛ) *n.* **Jean** (ʒɑ̃). 1896–1980, Swiss psychologist, noted for his work on the development of the cognitive functions in children.

pia mater ('paɪə 'meɪtə) *n.* the innermost of the three membranes (see **meninges**) that cover the brain and spinal cord. [C16: from Med. L, lit.: pious mother]

pianism ('piːə,nɪzəm) *n.* technique, skill, or artistry in playing the piano. —**pia'nistic** *adj.*

pianissimo (pɪə'nɪsɪ,məʊ) *adj., adv. Music.* to be performed very quietly. Symbol: *pp* [C18: from It., sup. of *piano* soft]

pianist ('pɪənɪst) *n.* a person who plays the piano.

piano¹ (pɪ'ænəʊ) *n., pl.* **-anos.** a musical stringed instrument played by depressing keys that cause hammers to strike the strings and produce audible vibrations. [C19: short for PIANOFORTE]

piano² ('pjɑːnəʊ) *adj., adv. Music.* to be performed softly. [C17: from It., from L *plānus* flat]

piano accordion (pɪ'ænəʊ) *n.* an accordion in which the right hand plays a piano-like keyboard. See **accordion.** —**piano accordionist** *n.*

pianoforte (pɪ,ænəʊ'fɔːtɪ) *n.* the full name for **piano¹.** [C18: from It., orig. (*gravecembalo col*) *piano e forte* (harpsichord with) soft & loud; see PIANO², FORTE²]

Pianola (pɪə'nəʊlə) *n. Trademark.* a type of mechanical piano in which the keys are depressed by air pressure, this air flow being regulated by perforations in a paper roll.

piano roll (pɪ'ænəʊ) *n.* a perforated roll of paper for a Pianola.

piastre *or* **piaster** (pɪ'æstə) *n.* 1. the standard monetary unit of the former republic of South Vietnam. 2. **a.** a fractional monetary unit of Egypt, Lebanon, Sudan, and Syria worth one hundredth of a pound. **b.** Also called: **kurus.** a Turkish monetary unit worth one hundredth of a lira. **c.** a Libyan monetary unit worth one hundredth of a dinar. [C17: from F *piastre*, from It. *piastra d'argento* silver plate]

Piauí (*Portuguese* pja'ui) *n.* a state of NE Brazil, on the Atlantic: rises to a semiarid plateau, with the more humid Paranaíba valley in the west. Capital: Teresina. Pop.: 2 138 790 (1980). Area: 250 934 sq. km (96 886 sq. miles).

Piave (*Italian* 'pjaːve) *n.* a river in NE Italy, rising near the border with Austria and flowing south and southeast to the Adriatic: the main line of Italian defence during World War I. Length: 220 km (137 miles).

piazza (pɪ'ætsə; *Italian* 'pjattsa) *n.* 1. a large open square in an Italian town. 2. *Chiefly Brit.* a covered passageway or gallery. [C16: from It.: marketplace, from L *platēa* courtyard, from Gk *plateia*; see PLACE]

pibroch ('piːbrɒk; *Gaelic* 'piːbrɒx) *n.* a form of music for Scottish bagpipes, consisting of a theme and variations. [C18: from Gaelic *piobaireachd*, from *piobair* piper]

pic (pɪk) *n., pl.* **pics** *or* **pix.** *Inf.* a photograph or illustration. [C20: shortened from PICTURE]

pica¹ ('paɪkə) *n.* 1. another word for **em.** 2. (formerly) a size of printer's type equal to 12 point. 3. a typewriter type size having 10 characters to the inch. [C15: from Anglo-L *pica* list of ecclesiastical regulations, apparently from L *pica* magpie, with reference to its habit of collecting things; the connection between the orig. sense & the typography meanings is obscure]

pica² ('paɪkə) *n. Pathol.* an abnormal craving to ingest substances such as clay, dirt, or hair. [C16: from Medical L, from L: magpie, an allusion to its omnivorous feeding habits]

picador ('pɪkə,dɔː) *n. Bullfighting.* a horseman who pricks the bull with a lance to weaken it. [C18: from Sp., lit.: pricker, from *picar* to prick]

Picard (*French* pikar) *n.* **Jean** (ʒɑ̃). 1620–82, French astronomer. He was the first to make a precise measurement of a longitude line, enabling him to estimate the earth's radius.

Picardy ('pɪkədɪ) *n.* a region of N France: mostly lowlying; scene of heavy fighting in World War I. French name: **Picardie** (pikardi).

picaresque (ˌpɪkə'rɛsk) *adj.* of or relating to a type of fiction in which the hero, a rogue, goes through a series of episodic adventures. [C19: via F from Sp. *picaresco*, from *pícaro* a rogue]

picaroon (ˌpɪkə'ruːn) *n. Arch.* an adventurer or rogue. [C17: from Sp. *picarón*, from *pícaro*]

Picasso (pɪ'kæsəʊ) *n.* **Pablo** ('pæbləʊ). 1881–1973, Spanish painter and sculptor, resident in France: a highly influential figure in 20th-century art and a founder, with Braque, of cubism. A prolific artist, his works include *The Dwarf Dancer* (1901), belonging to his blue period; the first cubist painting *Les Demoiselles d'Avignon* (1907); *Three Dancers* (1925), which appeared in the first surrealist exhibition; and *Guernica* (1937), inspired by an event in the Spanish Civil War.

picayune (ˌpɪkə'juːn) *adj. also* **picayunish.** *U.S. & Canad. inf.* 1. of small value or importance. 2. mean; petty. ~*n.* 3. any coin of little value, esp. a five-cent piece. 4. an unimportant person or thing. [C19: from F *picaillon* coin from Piedmont, from Provençal *picaioun*, from ?]

Piccadilly (ˌpɪkə'dɪlɪ) *n.* one of the main streets of London, running from Piccadilly Circus to Hyde Park Corner.

piccalilli ('pɪkə,lɪlɪ) *n.* a pickle of mixed vegetables in a mustard sauce. [C18 *piccalillo*, ? based on PICKLE]

piccanin ('pɪkə,nɪn) *n. S. African inf.* a Black African child. [var. of PICCANINNY]

piccaninny *or esp. U.S.* **pickaninny** (ˌpɪkə'nɪnɪ) *n., pl.* **-nies.** a small Negro or Aboriginal child. [C17: ?from Port. *pequenino* tiny one, from *pequeno* small]

Piccard (*French* pikar) *n.* 1. **Auguste** (ogyst). 1884–1962, Swiss physicist, whose study of cosmic rays led to his pioneer balloon ascents in the stratosphere (1931–32). 2. his twin brother, **Jean Félix** (ʒɑ̃ feliks). 1884–1963, U.S. chemist and aeronautical engineer, born in

Switzerland, noted for his balloon ascent into the stratosphere (1934).

piccolo ('pɪkə,ləʊ) *n.*, *pl.* **-los.** a woodwind instrument an octave higher than the flute. [C19: from It.: small]

pick[1] (pɪk) *vb.* **1.** to choose (something) deliberately or carefully, as from a number; select. **2.** to pluck or gather (fruit, berries, or crops) from (a tree, bush, field, etc.). **3.** (*tr.*) to remove loose particles from (the teeth, the nose, etc.). **4.** (esp. of birds) to nibble or gather (corn, etc.). **5.** (*tr.*) to pierce, dig, or break up (a hard surface) with a pick. **6.** (*tr.*) to form (a hole, etc.) in this way. **7.** (when *intr.*, foll. by *at*) to nibble (at) fussily or without appetite. **8.** to separate (strands, fibres, etc.), as in weaving. **9.** (*tr.*) to provoke (an argument, fight, etc.) deliberately. **10.** (*tr.*) to steal (money or valuables) from (a person's pocket). **11.** (*tr.*) to open (a lock) with an instrument other than a key. **12.** to pluck the strings of (a guitar, banjo, etc.). **13.** (*tr.*) to make (one's way) carefully on foot: *they picked their way through the rubble.* **14. pick and choose.** to select fastidiously, fussily, etc. **15. pick someone's brains.** to obtain information or ideas from someone. *~n.* **16.** freedom or right of selection (esp. in **take one's pick**). **17.** a person, thing, etc., that is chosen first or preferred: *the pick of the bunch.* **18.** the act of picking. **19.** the amount of a crop picked at one period or from one area. *~See also* **pick at, pick off,** etc. [C15: from earlier *piken* to pick, infl. by F *piquer* to pierce] **—'picker** *n.*

pick[2] (pɪk) *n.* **1.** a tool with a handle carrying a long steel head curved and tapering to a point at one or both ends, used for loosening soil, breaking rocks, etc. **2.** any of various tools used for picking, such as an ice pick or toothpick. **3.** a plectrum. [C14: ? a var. of PIKE[2]]

pickaback ('pɪkə,bæk) *n.*, *adv.* another word for **piggyback.**

pick at *vb.* (*intr.*, *prep.*) to make criticisms of in a niggling or petty manner.

pickaxe *or U.S.* **pickax** ('pɪk,æks) *n.* **1.** a large pick or mattock. *~vb.* **2.** to use a pickaxe on (earth, rocks, etc.). [C15: from earlier *pikois* (but infl. also by AXE), from OF, from *pic* PICK[2]]

pickerel ('pɪkərəl, 'pɪkrəl) *n.*, *pl.* **-el** *or* **-els.** **1.** a small pike. **2.** any of several North American freshwater game fishes of the pike family. [C14: dim. of PIKE[1]]

Pickering ('pɪkərɪŋ) *n.* **1. Edward Charles.** 1846–1919, U.S. astronomer, who invented the meridian photometer. **2.** his brother, **William Henry.** 1858–1938, U.S. astronomer, who discovered Phoebe, the ninth satellite of Saturn, and predicted (1919) the existence and position of Pluto.

picket ('pɪkɪt) *n.* **1.** a pointed stake that is driven into the ground to support a fence, etc. **2.** an individual or group standing outside an establishment to make a protest, to dissuade or prevent employees or clients from entering, etc. **3.** a small detachment of troops positioned to give early warning of attack. *~vb.* **4.** to post or serve as pickets at (a factory, embassy, etc.). **5.** to guard (a main body or place) by using or acting as a picket. **6.** (*tr.*) to fasten (a horse or other animal) to a picket. **7.** (*tr.*) to fence (an area, etc.) with pickets. [C18: from F *piquet*, from OF *piquer* to prick; see PIKE[2]] **—'picketer** *n.*

picket fence *n.* a fence consisting of pickets driven into the ground.

picket line *n.* a line of people acting as pickets.

Pickford ('pɪkfəd) *n.* **Mary,** real name *Gladys Mary Smith.* 1893–1983, U.S. actress in silent films, born in Canada.

pickings ('pɪkɪŋz) *pl. n.* (*sometimes sing.*) money, profits, etc., acquired easily; spoils.

pickle ('pɪk^əl) *n.* **1.** (*often pl.*) vegetables, such as onions, etc., preserved in vinegar, brine, etc. **2.** any food preserved in this way. **3.** a liquid or marinade, such as spiced vinegar, for preserving vegetables, meat, fish, etc. **4.** *Chiefly U.S. & Canad.* a cucumber that has been preserved and flavoured in a pickling solution, as brine or vinegar. **5.** *Inf.* an awkward or difficult situation: *to be in a pickle.* **6.** *Brit. inf.* a mischievous child. *~vb.* (*tr.*) **7.** to preserve in a pickling liquid. **8.** to immerse (a metallic object) in a liquid, such as an acid, to remove surface scale. [C14: ?from MDu. *pekel*] **—'pickler** *n.*

pickled ('pɪk^əld) *adj.* **1.** preserved in a pickling liquid. **2.** *Inf.* intoxicated; drunk.

picklock ('pɪk,lɒk) *n.* **1.** a person who picks locks. **2.** an instrument for picking locks.

pick-me-up *n. Inf.* a tonic or restorative, esp. a special drink taken as a stimulant.

pick off *vb.* (*tr.*, *adv.*) to aim at and shoot one by one.

pick on *vb.* (*intr.*, *prep.*) to select for something unpleasant, esp. in order to bully or blame.

pick out *vb.* (*tr.*, *adv.*) **1.** to select for use or special consideration, etc., as from a group. **2.** to distinguish (an object from its surroundings), as in painting: *she picked out the woodwork in white.* **3.** to recognize (a person or thing): *we picked out his face among the crowd.* **4.** *to* distinguish (sense or meaning) as from a mass of detail or complication. **5.** to play (a tune) tentatively, as by ear.

pickpocket ('pɪk,pɒkɪt) *n.* a person who steals from the pockets of others in public places.

pick-up *n.* **1.** the light balanced arm of a record player that carries the wires from the cartridge to the preamplifier. **2.** an electromagnetic transducer that converts vibrations into electric signals. **3.** another name for **cartridge** (sense 2). **4.** a small truck with an open body used for light deliveries. **5.** *Inf., chiefly U.S.* an ability to accelerate rapidly: *this car has good pick-up.* **6.** *Inf.* a casual acquaintance, usually one made with sexual intentions. **7.** *Inf.* **a.** a stop to collect passengers, goods, etc. **b.** the people or things collected. **8.** *Inf.* an improvement. **9.** *Sl.* a pick-me-up. *~vb.* **pick up.** (*adv.*) **10.** (*tr.*) to gather up in the hand or hands. **11.** (*reflexive*) to raise (oneself) after a fall or setback. **12.** (*tr.*) to obtain casually, incidentally, etc. **13.** (*intr.*) to improve in health, condition, activity, etc.: *the market began to pick up.* **14.** (*tr.*) to learn gradually or as one goes along. **15.** to resume; return to. **16.** (*tr.*) to accept the responsibility for paying (a bill). **17.** (*tr.*) to collect or give a lift to (passengers, goods, etc.). **18.** (*tr.*) *Inf.* to become acquainted with, esp. with a view to having sexual relations. **19.** (*tr.*) *Inf.* to arrest. **20.** to increase (speed). **21.** (*tr.*) to receive (electrical signals, a radio signal, sounds, etc.).

Pickwickian (pɪk'wɪkɪən) *adj.* **1.** of, relating to, or resembling Mr Pickwick in Charles Dickens' *The Pickwick Papers,* esp. in being naive or benevolent. **2.** (of the use or meaning of a word, etc.) odd or unusual.

picky ('pɪkɪ) *adj.* **pickier, pickiest.** *Inf.* fussy; finicky. **—'pickily** *adv.* **—'pickiness** *n.*

picnic ('pɪknɪk) *n.* **1.** a trip or excursion on which people bring food to be eaten in the open air. **2. a.** any informal meal eaten outside. **b.** (*as modifier*): *a picnic lunch.* **3.** *Inf.* an easy or agreeable task. *~vb.* **-nicking, -nicked.** **4.** (*intr.*) to eat or take part in a picnic. [C18: from F *piquenique*, from ?] **—'picnicker** *n.*

picnic races *pl. n. Austral.* horse races for amateur riders held in rural areas.

pico- *prefix.* denoting 10⁻¹²: *picofarad.* Symbol: p [from Sp. *pico* small quantity, odd number, peak]

Pico de Aneto (*Spanish* 'piko de a'neto) *n.* See **Aneto.**

Pico della Mirandola (*Italian* 'piːko ˌdɛlla mi'randola) *n.* Count **Giovanni** (dʒo'vanni). 1463–94, Italian Platonist philosopher. His attempt to reconcile the ideas of classical, Christian, and Arabic writers in a collection of 900 theses, prefaced by his *Oration on the Dignity of Man* (1486), was condemned by the pope.

Pico de Teide (*Spanish* 'piko de 'teiðe) *n.* See **Teide.**

picot ('piːkəʊ) *n.* any of a pattern of small loops, as on lace. [C19: from F: small point, from *pic* point]

picotee (ˌpɪkə'tiː) *n.* a type of carnation having pale petals edged with a darker colour. [C18: from F *picoté* marked with points, from *picot* PICOT]

picric acid ('pɪkrɪk) *n.* a toxic sparingly soluble crystalline yellow acid. Formula: $C_6H_3(NO_2)_3$. Systematic name: **2,4,6-trinitrophenol.** Used as a dye, antiseptic, and explosive. [C19: from Gk *pikros* bitter + -IC]

Pict (pɪkt) *n.* a member of any of the peoples who lived in N Britain in the first to the fourth centuries A.D. [OE *Peohtas*; later forms from LL *Pictī* painted men, from *pingere* to paint] **—'Pictish** *adj.*

pictograph ('pɪktə,grɑːf) *n.* **1.** a picture or symbol standing for a word or group of words, as in written Chinese. **2.** a chart on which symbols are used to represent values. *~Also called:* **pictogram.** [C19: from L *pictus*, from *pingere* to paint] **—pictographic** (ˌpɪktə'græfɪk) *adj.* **—pictography** (pɪk'tɒgrəfɪ) *n.*

pictorial (pɪk'tɔːrɪəl) *adj.* **1.** relating to, consisting of, or expressed by pictures. **2.** (of language, style, etc.) suggesting a picture; vivid; graphic. *~n.* **3.** a magazine, newspaper, etc., containing many pictures. [C17: from LL

pictōrius, from L *pictor* painter, from *pingere* to paint]
—**pic'torially** *adv.*

picture ('pɪktʃə) *n.* **1. a.** a visual representation of something, such as a person or scene, produced on a surface, as in a photograph, painting, etc. **b.** (*as modifier*): *picture gallery; picture postcard.* **2.** a mental image: *a clear picture of events.* **3.** a verbal description, esp. one that is vivid. **4.** a situation considered as an observable scene: *the political picture.* **5.** a person or thing resembling another: *he was the picture of his father.* **6.** a person, scene, etc., typifying a particular state: *the picture of despair.* **7.** the image on a television screen. **8.** a motion picture; film. **9. the pictures.** *Chiefly Brit.* a cinema or film show. **10.** another name for **tableau vivant. 11. in the picture.** informed about a situation. ~*vb.* (*tr.*) **12.** to visualize or imagine. **13.** to describe or depict, esp. vividly. **14.** (*often passive*) to put in a picture or make a picture of: *they were pictured sitting on the rocks.* [C15: from L *pictūra* painting, from *pingere* to paint]

picture card *n.* another name for **court card.**

picture hat *n.* a hat with a very wide brim.

picture moulding *n.* **1.** the edge around a framed picture. **2.** Also called: **picture rail.** the moulding or rail near the top of a wall from which pictures are hung.

picture palace *or* **house** *n. Brit., old-fashioned.* another name for **cinema.**

picturesque (,pɪktʃə'rɛsk) *adj.* **1.** visually pleasing, esp. in being striking or quaint: *a picturesque view.* **2.** (of language) graphic; vivid. [C18: from F *pittoresque* (but also infl. by PICTURE), from It., from *pittore* painter, from L *pictor*] —,pictur'esquely *adv.* —,pictur'esqueness *n.*

picture tube *n.* another name for **television tube.**

picture window *n.* a large window having a single pane of glass, usually facing a view.

picture writing *n.* **1.** any writing system that uses pictographs. **2.** a system of artistic expression and communication using pictures.

piddle ('pɪdªl) *vb.* **1.** (*intr.*) *Inf.* to urinate. **2.** (when *tr.*, often foll. by *away*) to spend (one's time) aimlessly; fritter. [C16: from ?] —'piddler *n.*

piddling ('pɪdlɪŋ) *adj. Inf.* petty; trifling; trivial.

piddock ('pɪdək) *n.* a marine bivalve boring into rock, clay, or wood by means of sawlike shell valves. [C19: from ?]

pidgin ('pɪdʒɪn) *n.* a language made up of elements of two or more other languages and used for contacts, esp. trading contacts, between the speakers of other languages. [C19: ?from Chinese pronunciation of E *business*]

pidgin English *n.* a pidgin in which one of the languages involved is English.

pie[1] (paɪ) *n.* **1.** a baked sweet or savoury filling in a pastry-lined dish, often covered with a pastry crust. **2. pie in the sky.** illusory hope or promise of some future good. [C14: from ?]

pie[2] (paɪ) *n.* an archaic or dialect name for **magpie.** [C13: via OF from L *pica* magpie]

pie[3] (paɪ) *n., vb. Printing.* a variant spelling of **pi**[2].

piebald ('paɪ,bɔːld) *adj.* **1.** marked in two colours, esp. black and white. ~*n.* **2.** a black-and-white horse. [C16: PIE[2] + BALD; see also PIED]

pie cart *n. N.Z.* a mobile van selling warmed-up food and drinks.

piece (piːs) *n.* **1.** an amount or portion forming a separate mass or structure; bit: *a piece of wood.* **2.** a small part, item, or amount forming part of a whole, esp. when broken off or separated: *a piece of bread.* **3.** a length by which a commodity is sold, esp. cloth, wallpaper, etc. **4.** an instance or occurrence: *a piece of luck.* **5.** an example or specimen of a style or type: *a beautiful piece of Dresden.* **6.** *Inf.* an opinion or point of view: *to state one's piece.* **7.** a literary, musical, or artistic composition. **8.** a coin: *a fifty-pence piece.* **9.** a small object used in playing certain games: *chess pieces.* **10.** a firearm or cannon. **11.** any chessman other than a pawn. **12.** *Brit. dialect.* a packed lunch taken to work. **13.** *N.Z.* fragments of fleece wool. **14. go to pieces. a.** (of a person) to lose control of oneself; have a breakdown. **b.** (of a building, organization, etc.) to disintegrate. **15. nasty piece of work.** *Brit. inf.* a cruel or mean person. **16. of a piece.** of the same kind; alike. ~*vb.* (*tr.*) **17.** (often foll. by *together*) to fit or assemble piece by piece. **18.** (often foll. by *up*) to patch or make up (a garment, etc.) by adding pieces. [C13 from OF, of Gaulish origin]

pièce de résistance *French.* (pjɛs də rezistãs) *n.* **1.** the principal or most outstanding item in a series. **2.** the main dish of a meal.

piece goods *pl. n.* goods, esp. fabrics, made in standard widths and lengths.

piecemeal ('piːs,miːl) *adv.* **1.** by degrees; bit by bit; gradually. **2.** in or into pieces. ~*adj.* **3.** fragmentary or unsystematic: *a piecemeal approach.* [C13 *pecemele*, from PIECE + *-mele*, from OE *mǣlum* quantity taken at one time]

piece of eight *n., pl.* **pieces of eight.** a former Spanish coin worth eight reals; peso.

piecework ('piːs,wɜːk) *n.* work paid for according to the quantity produced.

pie chart *n.* a circular graph divided into sectors proportional to the magnitudes of the quantities represented.

piecrust table ('paɪ,krʌst) *n.* a round table, edged with moulding suggestive of a pie crust.

pied (paɪd) *adj.* having markings of two or more colours. [C14: from PIE[2]; an allusion to the magpie's colouring]

pied-à-terre (,pjeɪtɑː'tɛə) *n., pl.* **pieds-à-terre** ('pjeɪtɑː'tɛə). a flat or other lodging for occasional use. [from F, lit.: foot on (the) ground]

piedmont ('piːdmɒnt) *adj.* (*prenominal*) (of glaciers, plains, etc.) formed or situated at the foot of a mountain. [via F from It. *piémonte*, from *pié*, var. of *piede* foot + *mont* mountain]

Piedmont ('piːdmɒnt) *n.* **1.** a region of NW Italy: consists of the upper Po Valley; mainly agricultural. Chief town: Turin. Pop.: 4 389 430 (1985 est.). Area: 25 399 sq. km (9807 sq. miles). Italian name: **Piemonte. 2.** a low plateau of the eastern U.S., between the coastal plain and the Appalachian Mountains.

pied wagtail *n.* a British songbird with a black throat and back, long black tail, and white underparts and face.

pie-eyed *adj. Sl.* drunk.

Piemonte (*Italian* pje'monte) *n.* the Italian name for **Piedmont** (sense 1).

pier (pɪə) *n.* **1.** a structure with a deck that is built out over water, and used as a landing place, promenade, etc. **2.** a pillar that bears heavy loads. **3.** the part of a wall between two adjacent openings. **4.** another name for **buttress** (sense 1). [C12 *per*, from Anglo-L *pera* pier supporting a bridge]

pierce (pɪəs) *vb.* (*mainly tr.*) **1.** to form or cut (a hole) in (something) as with a sharp instrument. **2.** to thrust into sharply or violently: *the thorn pierced his heel.* **3.** to force (a way, route, etc.) through (something). **4.** (of light, etc.) to shine through or penetrate (darkness). **5.** (*also intr.*) to discover or realize (something) suddenly or (of an idea, etc.) to become suddenly apparent. **6.** (of sounds or cries) to sound sharply through (the silence, etc.). **7.** to move or affect deeply or sharply: *the cold pierced their bones.* **8.** (*intr.*) to penetrate: *piercing cold.* [C13 *percen*, from OF *percer*, ult. from L *pertundere*, from *per* through + *tundere* to strike] —'piercing *adj.* —'piercingly *adv.*

Pierce (pɪəs) *n.* **Franklin.** 1804–69, U.S. statesman; 14th president of the U.S. (1853–57).

pier glass *n.* a tall narrow mirror, designed to hang on the wall between windows.

Pieria (paɪ'ɪərɪə) *n.* a region of ancient Macedonia, west of the Gulf of Salonika: site of the Pierian Spring.

Pierian Spring (paɪ'ɪərɪən) *n.* a sacred fountain in Pieria, in Greece, fabled to inspire those who drank from it.

Pierides (paɪ'ɪrɪ,diːz) *pl. n. Greek myth.* **1.** another name for the Muses (see **Muse**). **2.** nine maidens of Thessaly, who were defeated in a singing contest by the Muses and turned into magpies for their effrontery.

pieris ('paɪrɪs) *n.* an evergreen shrub with white flowers like lily of the valley in spring. [from L, from Gk PIERIA the haunt of the Muses]

Piero della Francesca (*Italian* 'pjɛːro ,dɛlla fran'tʃeska) *n.* ?1420–92, Italian painter, noted particularly for his frescoes of the *Legend of the True Cross* in San Francesco, Arezzo.

Piero di Cosimo (*Italian* 'pjɛːro di 'kɔːzimo) *n.* 1462–1521, Italian painter, noted for his mythological works.

Pierre (pɪə) *n.* a city in central South Dakota, capital of the state, on the Missouri River: the smallest state capital of the U.S. Pop.: 11 973 (1980).

Pierrot ('pɪərəʊ; *French* pjɛro) *n.* **1.** a male character from French pantomime with a whitened face, white costume, and pointed hat. **2.** (*usually not cap.*) a clown so made up.

pier table *n.* a side table designed to stand against a wall between windows.

pietà (pɪɛ'tɑː) *n.* a sculpture, painting, or drawing of the dead Christ, supported by the Virgin Mary. [It.: pity, from L *pietās* PIETY]

Pietermaritzburg (,piːtə'mærɪts,bɜːg) *n.* a city in E South Africa, capital of Natal province: founded in 1839 by the Boers: gateway to Natal's mountain resorts. Pop.: 133 809 (1986).

pietism ('paɪɪ,tɪzəm) *n.* exaggerated or affected piety. — 'pietist *n.* — pie'tistic *or* ,pie'tistical *adj.*

piet-my-vrou ('pɪt,meɪ'frəʊ) *n. S. African.* a red-breasted cuckoo. [imit.]

piety ('paɪɪtɪ) *n., pl.* -ties. **1.** dutiful devotion to God and observance of religious principles. **2.** the quality of being pious. **3.** a pious action, saying, etc. **4.** *Now rare.* devotion and obedience to parents or superiors. [C13 *piete,* from OF, from L *pietās* piety, dutifulness, from *pius* pious]

piezoelectric effect (paɪ,iːzəʊɪ'lɛktrɪk) *or* **piezoelectricity** (paɪ,iːzəʊɪlɛk'trɪsɪtɪ) *n. Physics.* **a.** the production of electricity or electric polarity by applying a mechanical stress to certain crystals. **b.** the converse effect in which stress is produced in a crystal as a result of an applied potential difference. [C19: from Gk *piezein* to press] — pi,ezoe'lectrically *adv.*

piffle ('pɪfˀl) *Inf.* ~*n.* **1.** nonsense. ~*vb.* **2.** (*intr.*) to talk or behave feebly. [C19: from ?]

piffling ('pɪflɪŋ) *adj. Inf.* worthless; trivial.

pig (pɪg) *n.* **1.** any artiodactyl mammal of an African and Eurasian family, esp. the domestic pig, typically having a long head with a movable snout and a thick bristle-covered skin. Related adj.: **porcine.** **2.** *Inf.* a dirty, greedy, or bad-mannered person. **3.** the meat of swine; pork. **4.** *Derog.* a slang word for **policeman.** **5. a.** a mass of metal cast into a simple shape. **b.** the mould used. **6.** *Brit. inf.* something that is difficult or unpleasant. **7. a pig in a poke.** something bought or received without prior sight or knowledge. **8. make a pig of oneself.** *Inf.* to overindulge oneself. ~*vb.* **pigging, pigged. 9.** (*intr.*) (of a sow) to give birth. **10.** (*intr.*) Also: **pig it.** *Inf.* to live in squalor. **11.** (*tr.*) *Inf.* to devour (food) greedily. [C13 *pigge,* from ?]

pigeon¹ ('pɪdʒɪn) *n.* **1.** any of numerous related birds having a heavy body, small head, short legs, and long pointed wings. **2.** *Sl.* a victim or dupe. [C14: from OF *pijon* young dove, from LL *pīpiō* young bird, from *pīpīre* to chirp]

pigeon² ('pɪdʒɪn) *Brit. inf.* concern or responsibility (often in **it's his, her,** etc., **pigeon**). [C19: altered from PIDGIN]

pigeon breast *n.* a deformity of the chest characterized by an abnormal protrusion of the breastbone, caused by rickets.

pigeonhole ('pɪdʒɪn,həʊl) *n.* **1.** a small compartment for papers, letters, etc., as in a bureau. **2.** a hole or recess in a dovecote for pigeons to nest in. ~*vb.* (*tr.*) **3.** to put aside or defer. **4.** to classify or categorize.

pigeon-toed *adj.* having the toes turned inwards.

pigface ('pɪg,feɪs) *n. Austral.* a creeping succulent plant having bright-coloured flowers and red fruits and often grown for ornament.

piggery ('pɪgərɪ) *n., pl.* -geries. **1.** a place where pigs are kept. **2.** great greediness.

piggish ('pɪgɪʃ) *adj.* **1.** like a pig, esp. in appetite or manners. **2.** *Inf., chiefly Brit.* obstinate or mean. — 'piggishly *adv.* — 'piggishness *n.*

Piggott ('pɪgət) *n.* **Lester (Keith).** born 1935, English flat-racing jockey: by 1983 he had won the Derby nine times.

piggy ('pɪgɪ) *n., pl.* -gies. **1.** a child's word for a **pig. 2.** a child's word for a **toe.** ~*adj.* -gier, -giest. **3.** another word for **piggish.**

piggyback ('pɪgɪ,bæk) *or* **pickaback** *n.* **1.** a ride on the back and shoulders of another person. **2.** a system whereby a vehicle, aircraft, etc., is transported for part of its journey on another vehicle. ~*adv.* **3.** on the back and shoulders of another person. **4.** on or as an addition. ~*adj.* **5.** of or for a piggyback: *a piggyback ride; piggyback lorry trains.* **6.** of or relating to a type of heart transplant in which the transplanted heart functions in conjunction with the patient's own heart.

piggy bank *n.* a child's coin bank shaped like a pig with a slot for coins.

pig-headed *adj.* stupidly stubborn. — ,pig-'headedly *adv.* — ,pig-'headedness *n.*

pig iron *n.* crude iron produced in a blast furnace and poured into moulds.

Pig Island *n. N.Z. inf.* New Zealand. — **Pig Islander** *n.*

piglet ('pɪglɪt) *n.* a young pig.

pigmeat ('pɪg,miːt) *n.* a less common name for pork, ham, or bacon.

pigment ('pɪgmənt) *n.* **1.** a substance occurring in plant or animal tissue and producing a characteristic colour. **2.** any substance used to impart colour. **3.** a powder that is mixed with a liquid to give a paint, ink, etc. [C14: from L *pigmentum,* from *pingere* to paint] — 'pigmentary *adj.*

pigmentation (,pɪgmən'teɪʃən) *n.* **1.** coloration in plants, animals, or man caused by the presence of pigments. **2.** the deposition of pigment in animals, plants, or man.

Pigmy ('pɪgmɪ) *n., pl.* -mies. a variant spelling of **Pygmy.**

pignut ('pɪg,nʌt) *n.* **1.** Also called: **hognut. a.** the bitter nut of any of several North American hickory trees. **b.** any of the trees bearing such a nut. **2.** another name for **earthnut.**

pig-root *vb.* (*intr.*) *Austral. & N.Z. sl.* (of a horse) to buck slightly.

Pigs (pɪgz) *n.* **Bay of.** See **Bay of Pigs.**

pigskin ('pɪg,skɪn) *n.* **1.** the skin of the domestic pig. **2.** leather made of this skin. **3.** *U.S. & Canad. inf.* a football. ~*adj.* **4.** made of pigskin.

pigsticking ('pɪg,stɪkɪŋ) *n.* the sport of hunting wild boar. — 'pig,sticker *n.*

pigsty ('pɪg,staɪ) *or U.S. & Canad.* **pigpen** *n., pl.* -sties. **1.** a pen for pigs; sty. **2.** *Brit.* an untidy place.

pigswill ('pɪg,swɪl) *n.* waste food or other edible matter fed to pigs. Also called: **pig's wash.**

pigtail ('pɪg,teɪl) *n.* **1.** a plait of hair or one of two plaits on either side of the face. **2.** a twisted roll of tobacco.

pika ('paɪkə) *n.* a burrowing mammal of mountainous regions of North America and Asia, having short rounded ears, a rounded body, and rudimentary tail. [C19: from E Siberian *piika*]

pikau ('piːkaʊ) *n. N.Z.* a pack, knapsack, or rucksack. [Maori]

pike¹ (paɪk) *n., pl.* **pike** *or* **pikes. 1.** any of several large predatory freshwater teleost fishes having a broad flat snout, strong teeth, and an elongated body covered with small scales. **2.** any of various similar fishes. [C14: short for *pikefish,* from OE *pīc* point, with reference to the shape of its jaw.]

pike² (paɪk) *n.* **1.** a medieval weapon consisting of a metal spearhead joined to a long pole. **2.** a point or spike. ~*vb.* **3.** (*tr.*) to pierce using a pike. [OE *pīc* point, from ?] — 'pikeman *n.*

pike³ (paɪk) *n.* short for **turnpike** (senses 1, 2).

pike⁴ (paɪk) *n. Northern English dialect.* a pointed or conical hill. [OE *pīc*]

pike⁵ (paɪk) *or* **piked** (paɪkt) *adj.* (of the body position of a diver) bent at the hips but with the legs straight.

pike⁶ (paɪk) *vb.* (*intr.*; foll. by *out*) *Austral. sl.* to shirk. [from PIKER]

pikeperch ('paɪk,pɜːtʃ) *n., pl.* -perch *or* -perches. any of various pikelike freshwater teleost fishes of the perch family of Europe.

piker ('paɪkə) *n. U.S., Austral., & N.Z. sl.* **1.** a lazy person; shirker. **2.** a mean person. [C19: from *Pike* county, Missouri, U.S.A.]

Pikes Peak *n.* a mountain in central Colorado, in the Rockies. Height: 4300 m (14 109 ft.).

pikestaff ('paɪk,stɑːf) *n.* the wooden handle of a pike.

pilaster (pɪ'læstə) *n.* a shallow rectangular column attached to the face of a wall. [C16: from F *pilastre,* from L *pīla* pillar] — pi'lastered *adj.*

Pilate ('paɪlət) *n.* **Pontius** ('pɒnʃəs, 'pɒntɪəs). Roman procurator of Judaea (?26–?36 A.D.), who ordered the crucifixion of Jesus, allegedly reluctantly against his better judgment.

Pilatus (*German* pi'laːtʊs) *n.* a mountain in central Switzerland, in Unterwalden canton: derives its name from the legend that the body of Pontius Pilate lay in a former lake on the mountain. Height: 2122 m (6962 ft.).

pilau (pɪ'laʊ), **pilaf, pilaff** ('pɪlæf), *or* **pilaw** (pɪ'lɔː) *n.* a dish originating from the East, consisting of rice flavoured with spices and cooked in stock, to which meat, poultry, or fish may be added. [C17: from Turkish *pilāw*, from Persian]

pilchard ('pɪltʃəd) *n.* a European food fish of the herring family, with a rounded body covered with large scales. [C16 *pylcher*, from ?]

Pilcomayo (*Spanish* pilko'majo) *n.* a river in S central South America, rising in W central Bolivia and flowing southeast, forming the border between Argentina and Paraguay, to the Paraguay River at Asunción. Length: about 1600 km (1000 miles).

pile¹ (paɪl) *n.* **1.** a collection of objects laid on top of one another; heap; mound. **2.** *Inf.* a large amount of money (esp. in **make a pile**). **3.** (*often pl.*) *Inf.* a large amount: *a pile of work.* **4.** a less common word for **pyre**. **5.** a large building or group of buildings. **6.** *Physics.* a structure of uranium and a moderator used for producing atomic energy; nuclear reactor. ~*vb.* **7.** (often foll. by *up*) to collect or be collected into or as if into a pile: *snow piled up in the drive.* **8.** (*intr.*; foll. by *in, into, off, out,* etc.) to move in a group, esp. in a hurried or disorganized manner: *to pile off the bus.* **9. pile it on.** *Inf.* to exaggerate. ~See also **pile up.** [C15: via OF from L *pīla* stone pier]

pile² (paɪl) *n.* **1.** a long column of timber, concrete, or steel, driven into the ground as a foundation for a structure. ~*vb.* (*tr.*) **2.** to drive (piles) into the ground. **3.** to support (a structure) with piles. [OE *pīl,* from L *pīlum*]

pile³ (paɪl) *n.* **1.** the yarns in a fabric that stand up or out from the weave, as in carpeting, velvet, etc. **2.** soft fine hair, fur, wool, etc. [C15: from Anglo-Norman *pyle,* from L *pilus* hair]

pileate ('paɪlɪt, -,eɪt, 'pɪl-) *or* **pileated** ('paɪlɪ,eɪtɪd, 'pɪl-) *adj.* **1.** (of birds) having a crest. **2.** *Bot.* having a pileus. [C18: from L *pileātus* wearing a felt cap, from PILEUS]

pile-driver *n.* a machine that drives piles into the ground.

pileous ('paɪlɪəs, 'pɪl-) *adj. Biol.* **1.** hairy. **2.** of or relating to hair. [C19: ult. from L *pilus* a hair]

piles (paɪlz) *pl. n.* a nontechnical name for **haemorrhoids.** [C15: from L *pilae* balls (referring to the external piles)]

pileum ('paɪlɪəm, 'pɪl-) *n.,* pl. **-lea** (-lɪə). the top of a bird's head from the base of the bill to the occiput. [C19: NL, from L PILEUS]

pile up *vb.* (*adv.*) **1.** to gather or be gathered in a pile. **2.** *Inf.* to crash or cause to crash. ~*n.* **pile-up. 3.** *Inf.* a multiple collision of vehicles.

pileus ('paɪlɪəs) *n.,* pl. **-lei** (-lɪ,aɪ). the upper cap-shaped part of a mushroom. [C18: (botanical use): NL, from L: felt cap]

pilewort ('paɪl,wɜːt) *n.* any of several plants, such as lesser celandine, thought to be effective in treating piles.

pilfer ('pɪlfə) *vb.* to steal (minor items), esp. in small quantities. [C14 *pylfre* (n.) from OF *pelfre* booty] — **'pilferage** *n.* — **'pilferer** *n.*

pilgrim ('pɪlgrɪm) *n.* **1.** a person who undertakes a journey to a sacred place. **2.** any wayfarer. [C12: from Provençal *pelegrin,* from L *peregrīnus* foreign, from *per* through + *ager* land]

pilgrimage ('pɪlgrɪmɪdʒ) *n.* **1.** a journey to a shrine or other sacred place. **2.** a journey or long search made for exalted or sentimental reasons. ~*vb.* **3.** (*intr.*) to make a pilgrimage.

Pilgrim Fathers *or* **Pilgrims** *pl. n.* **the.** the English Puritans who sailed on the Mayflower to New England, where they founded Plymouth Colony in SE Massachusetts (1620).

piliferous (paɪ'lɪfərəs) *adj.* (esp. of plants) bearing or ending in a hair or hairs. [C19: from L *pilus* hair + -FEROUS] — **'pili,form** *adj.*

piling ('paɪlɪŋ) *n.* **1.** the act of driving piles. **2.** a number of piles. **3.** a structure formed of piles.

Pilion ('pɪljɔn) *n.* transliteration of the Modern Greek name for **Pelion.**

pill¹ (pɪl) *n.* **1.** a small spherical or ovoid mass of a medicinal substance, intended to be swallowed whole. **2. the pill.** (*sometimes cap.*) *Inf.* an oral contraceptive. **3.** something unpleasant that must be endured (esp. in **bitter pill to swallow**). **4.** *Sl.* a ball or disc. **5.** *Sl.* an unpleasant or boring person. ~*vb.* **6.** (*tr.*) to give pills to. [C15: from MFlemish *pille,* from L *pilula* a little ball, from *pila* ball]

pill² (pɪl) *vb.* **1.** *Arch. or dialect.* to peel or skin (something). **2.** *Arch.* to pillage or plunder (a place, etc.). [OE *pilian,* from L *pilāre* to strip]

pillage ('pɪlɪdʒ) *vb.* **1.** to rob (a town, village, etc.) of (booty or spoils). ~*n.* **2.** the act of pillaging. **3.** something obtained by pillaging; booty. [C14: via OF from *piller* to despoil, prob. from *peille* rag, from L *pīleus* felt cap] — **'pillager** *n.*

pillar ('pɪlə) *n.* **1.** an upright structure of stone, brick, metal, etc. that supports a superstructure. **2.** something resembling this in shape or function: *a pillar of smoke.* **3.** a prominent supporter: *a pillar of the Church.* **4. from pillar to post.** from one place to another. [C13: from OF *pilier,* from L *pīla*]

pillar box *n.* (in Britain) a red pillar-shaped public letter box situated on a pavement.

Pillars of Hercules *pl. n.* the two promontories at the E end of the Strait of Gibraltar: the Rock of Gibraltar on the European side and the Jebel Musa on the African side; according to legend, formed by Hercules.

pillbox ('pɪl,bɒks) *n.* **1.** a box for pills. **2.** a small enclosed fortified emplacement, made of reinforced concrete. **3.** a small round hat.

pillion ('pɪljən) *n.* **1.** a seat or place behind the rider of a motorcycle, scooter, horse, etc. ~*adv.* **2.** on a pillion: *to ride pillion.* [C16: from Gaelic; cf. Scot. *pillean,* Irish *pillín* couch]

pilliwinks ('pɪlɪ,wɪŋks) *pl. n.* a medieval instrument of torture for the fingers. [C14: from ?]

pillory ('pɪlərɪ) *n.,* pl. **-ries. 1.** a wooden framework into which offenders were formerly locked by the neck and wrists and exposed to public abuse and ridicule. **2.** exposure to public scorn or abuse. ~*vb.* **-rying, -ried.** (*tr.*) **3.** to expose to public scorn or ridicule. **4.** to punish by putting in a pillory. [C13: from Anglo-L *pillorium,* from OF *pilori,* from ?]

pillow ('pɪləʊ) *n.* **1.** a cloth case stuffed with feathers, foam rubber, etc., used to support the head, esp. during sleep. **2.** Also called: **cushion.** a padded cushion or board on which pillow lace is made. **3.** anything like a pillow in shape or function. ~*vb.* (*tr.*) **4.** to rest (one's head) on or as if on a pillow. **5.** to serve as a pillow for. [OE *pylwe,* from L *pulvīnus* cushion]

pillowcase ('pɪləʊ,keɪs) *or* **pillowslip** ('pɪləʊ,slɪp) *n.* a removable washable cover of cotton, linen, nylon, etc., for a pillow.

pillow fight *n.* a mock fight in which participants thump each other with pillows.

pillow lace *n.* lace made by winding thread around bobbins on a padded cushion or board. Cf. **point lace.**

pillow talk *n.* confidential talk between sexual partners in bed.

Pílos ('pilɔs) *n.* transliteration of the Modern Greek name for **Pylos.**

pilose ('paɪləʊz) *adj. Biol.* covered with fine soft hairs: *pilose leaves.* [C18: from L *pilōsus,* from *pilus* hair] — **pilosity** (paɪ'lɒsɪtɪ) *n.*

pilot ('paɪlət) *n.* **1.** a person who is qualified to operate an aircraft or spacecraft in flight. **2. a.** a person who is qualified to steer or guide a ship into or out of a port, river mouth, etc. **b.** (*as modifier*): *a pilot ship.* **3.** a person who steers a ship. **4.** a person who acts as a leader or guide. **5.** *Machinery.* a guide used to assist in joining two mating parts together. **6.** an experimental programme on radio or television. **7.** (*modifier*) serving as a test or trial: *a pilot project.* **8.** (*modifier*) serving as a guide: *a pilot beacon.* ~*vb.* (*tr.*) **9.** to act as pilot of. **10.** to control the course of. **11.** to guide or lead (a project, people, etc.). [C16: from F *pilote,* from Med. L *pilotus,* ult. from Gk *pēdon* oar]

pilotage ('paɪlətɪdʒ) *n.* **1.** the act of piloting an aircraft or ship. **2.** a pilot's fee.

pilot balloon *n.* a meteorological balloon used to observe air currents.

pilot fish *n.* a small fish of tropical and subtropical seas, marked with dark vertical bands: often accompanies sharks.

pilot house *n. Naut.* an enclosed structure on the bridge of a vessel from which it can be navigated; a wheelhouse.

pilot lamp *n.* a small light in an electric circuit or device that lights when the current is on.

pilot light *n.* **1.** a small auxiliary flame that ignites the main burner of a gas appliance. **2.** a small electric light used as an indicator.

pilot officer *n.* the most junior commissioned rank in the British Royal Air Force and in certain other air forces.

pilot study *n.* a small-scale experiment undertaken to decide whether and how to launch a full-scale project.

Pils (pɪlz, pɪls) *n.* a type of lager-like beer. [C20: abbrev. of PILSNER]

Pilsen ('pɪlzən) *n.* the German name for **Plzeň**.

Pilsner ('pɪlznə) *or* **Pilsener** *n.* a type of pale beer with a strong flavour of hops. [after PILSEN, where it was orig. brewed]

Pilsudski (*Polish* piw'sutski) *n.* **Józef** ('juzɛf). 1867–1935, Polish nationalist leader and statesman; president (1918–21) and premier (1926–28; 1930).

pilule ('pɪljuːl) *n.* a small pill. [C16: via F from L *pilula* little ball, from *pila* ball] —'**pilular** *adj.*

pimento (pɪ'mɛntəʊ) *n.*, *pl.* **-tos.** another name for **allspice** or **pimiento**. [C17: from Sp. *pimiento* pepper plant, from Med. L *pigmenta* spiced drink, from L *pigmentum* PIGMENT]

pi meson *n.* another name for **pion**.

pimiento (pɪ'mjɛntəʊ, -'mɛn-) *n.*, *pl.* **-tos.** a Spanish pepper with a red fruit used as a vegetable. Also called: **pimento**. [var. of PIMENTO]

pimp[1] (pɪmp) *n.* **1.** a man who solicits for a prostitute or brothel. **2.** a man who procures sexual gratification for another; procurer; pander. ~*vb.* **3.** (*intr.*) to act as a pimp. [C17: from ?]

pimp[2] (pɪmp) *Sl., chiefly Austral. & N.Z.* ~*n.* **1.** a spy or informer. ~*vb.* **2.** (*intr.;* often foll. by *on*) to inform (on). [from ?]

pimpernel ('pɪmpə,nɛl, -nǝl) *n.* any of several plants, such as the scarlet pimpernel, typically having small star-shaped flowers. [C15: from OF *pimpernelle*, ult. from L *piper* PEPPER]

pimple ('pɪmp²l) *n.* a small round usually inflamed swelling of the skin. [C14: rel. to OE *pipilian* to break out in spots] —'**pimpled** *adj.* —'**pimply** *adj.* —'**pimpliness** *n.*

pin (pɪn) *n.* **1.** a short stiff straight piece of wire pointed at one end and either rounded or having a flattened head at the other: used mainly for fastening pieces of cloth, paper, etc. **2.** short for **cotter pin, hairpin, panel pin, rolling pin,** or **safety pin. 3.** an ornamental brooch, esp. a narrow one. **4.** a badge worn fastened to the clothing by a pin. **5.** something of little or no importance (esp. in **not care** *or* **give a pin (for)**). **6.** a peg or dowel. **7.** anything resembling a pin in shape, function, etc. **8.** (in various bowling games) a usually club-shaped wooden object set up in groups as a target. **9.** Also called: **safety pin.** a clip on a hand grenade that prevents its detonation until removed or released. **10.** *Naut.* **a.** See **belaying pin. b.** the sliding closure for a shackle. **11.** *Music.* a metal tuning peg on a piano. **12.** *Surgery.* a metal rod, esp. of stainless steel, for holding together adjacent ends of fractured bones during healing. **13.** *Chess.* a position in which a piece is pinned against a more valuable piece or the king. **14.** *Golf.* the flagpole marking the hole on a green. **15.** (*usually pl.*) *Inf.* a leg. ~*vb.* **pinning, pinned.** (*tr.*) **16.** to attach, hold, or fasten with or as if with a pin or pins. **17.** to transfix with a pin, spear, etc. **18.** (foll. by *on*) *Inf.* to place (the blame for something): *he pinned the charge on his accomplice.* **19.** *Chess.* to cause (an enemy piece) to be effectively immobilized since moving it would reveal a check or expose a more valuable piece to capture. ~See also **pin down.** [OE *pinn*]

pinaceous (paɪ'neɪʃəs) *adj.* of, relating to, or belonging to a family of conifers with needle-like leaves: includes pine, spruce, fir, larch, and cedar. [C19: via NL from L *pīnus* a pine]

pinafore ('pɪnə,fɔː) *n.* **1.** *Chiefly Brit.* an apron, esp. one with a bib. **2.** Also called: **pinafore dress.** a dress with a sleeveless bodice or bib top, worn over a jumper or blouse. [C18: from PIN + AFORE]

Pinar del Río (*Spanish* pi'nar ðɛl 'rrio) *n.* a city in W Cuba: tobacco industry. Pop.: 95 476 (1981).

pinaster (paɪ'næstə) *n.* a Mediterranean pine tree with paired needles and prickly cones. Also called: **maritime** (*or* **cluster**) **pinaster.** [C16: from L: wild pine, from *pīnus* pine]

pinball ('pɪn,bɔːl) *n.* **a.** a game in which the player shoots a small ball through several hazards on a table, electrically operated machine, etc. **b.** (*as modifier*): *a pinball machine.*

pince-nez ('pæns,neɪ, 'pɪns-; *French* pɛ̃sne) *n.*, *pl.* **pince-nez.** eyeglasses that are held in place only by means of a clip over the bridge of the nose. [C19: F, lit.: pinch-nose]

pincers ('pɪnsəz) *pl. n.* **1.** Also called: **pair of pincers.** a gripping tool consisting of two hinged arms with handles at one end and, at the other, curved bevelled jaws that close on the workpiece. **2.** the pair or pairs of jointed grasping appendages in lobsters and certain other arthropods. [C14: from OF *pinceour*, from OF *pincier* to pinch]

pinch (pɪntʃ) *vb.* **1.** to press (something, esp. flesh) tightly between two surfaces, esp. between a finger and thumb. **2.** to confine, squeeze, or painfully press (toes, fingers, etc.) because of lack of space: *these shoes pinch.* **3.** (*tr.*) to cause stinging pain to: *the cold pinched his face.* **4.** (*tr.*) to make thin or drawn-looking, as from grief, lack of food, etc. **5.** (usually foll. by *on*) to provide (oneself or another person) with meagre allowances, amounts, etc. **6. pinch pennies.** to live frugally because of meanness or to economize. **7.** (usually foll. by *off, out,* or *back*) to remove the tips of (buds, shoots, etc.) to correct or encourage growth. **8.** (*tr.*) *Inf.* to steal or take without asking. **9.** (*tr.*) *Inf.* to arrest. ~*n.* **10.** a squeeze or sustained nip. **11.** the quantity of a substance, such as salt, that can be taken between a thumb and finger. **12.** a very small quantity. **13.** (usually preceded by *the*) sharp, painful, or extreme stress, need, etc.: *feeling the pinch of poverty.* **14.** *Sl.* a robbery. **15.** *Sl.* a police raid or arrest. **16. at a pinch.** if absolutely necessary. [C16: prob. from OF *pinchier* (unattested)]

pinchbeck ('pɪntʃ,bɛk) *n.* **1.** an alloy of copper and zinc, used as imitation gold. **2.** a spurious or cheap imitation. ~*adj.* **3.** made of pinchbeck. **4.** sham or cheap. [C18 (the alloy), C19 (something spurious): after C. *Pinchbeck* (?1670–1732), E watchmaker who invented it]

pinchpenny ('pɪntʃ,pɛnɪ) *adj.* **1.** niggardly; miserly. ~*n.*, *pl.* **-nies. 2.** a miserly person.

Pinckney ('pɪŋknɪ) *n.* **1. Charles Cotesworth.** 1746–1825, U.S. statesman, who was a member of the convention that framed the U.S. Constitution (1787). **2.** his brother, **Thomas.** 1750–1828, U.S. soldier and politician. He was U.S. minister to Britain (1792–96) and special envoy to Spain (1795–96).

pincushion ('pɪn,kuʃən) *n.* a small well-padded cushion in which pins are stuck ready for use.

Pindar ('pɪndə) *n.* ?518–?438 B.C., Greek lyric poet, noted for his *Epinikia*, odes commemorating victories in the Greek games. —**Pindaric** (pɪn'dærɪk) *adj.*

pin down *vb.* (*tr., adv.*) **1.** to force (someone) to make a decision or carry out a promise. **2.** to define clearly: *he had a vague suspicion that he couldn't quite pin down.* **3.** to confine to a place.

Pindus ('pɪndəs) *n.* a mountain range in central Greece between Epirus and Thessaly. Highest peak: Mount Smólikas, 2633 m (8639 ft.). Modern Greek name: **Píndhos** ('pinðos).

pine[1] (paɪn) *n.* **1.** any of a genus of evergreen resinous coniferous trees of the N hemisphere, with long needle-shaped leaves (**pine needles**) and brown cones. **2.** the wood of any of these trees. [OE *pin*, from L *pīnus* pine]

pine[2] (paɪn) *vb.* **1.** (*intr.;* often foll. by *for* or an infinitive) to feel great longing or desire; yearn. **2.** (*intr.;* often foll. by *away*) to become ill or thin through worry, longing, etc. [OE *pīnian* to torture, from *pīn* pain, from Med. L *pēna*, from L *poena* PAIN]

pineal eye ('pɪnɪəl) *n.* an outgrowth of the pineal gland that forms an eyelike structure on the top of the head in certain cold-blooded vertebrates. [C19: from F, from L *pīnea* pine cone]

pineal gland *or* **body** *n.* a pea-sized organ situated at the base of the brain that secretes a hormone, melatonin, into the bloodstream. Technical names: **epiphysis, epiphysis cerebri.**

pineapple ('paɪn,æp²l) *n.* **1.** a tropical American plant cultivated for its large fleshy edible fruit. **2.** the fruit of this plant, consisting of an inflorescence clustered around a fleshy axis and surmounted by a tuft of leaves. **3.** *Mil. sl.* a hand grenade. [C14 *pinappel* pine cone; C17: applied to the fruit because of its appearance]

pine cone *n.* the seed-producing structure of a pine tree. See **cone** (sense 3a).

pine marten *n.* a marten of N European and Asian coniferous woods, having dark brown fur with a creamy-yellow patch on the throat.

pinene ('paɪniːn) *n.* either of two isomeric terpenes, found in many essential oils and constituting the main part of oil of turpentine. [C20: from PINE¹ + -ENE]

Pinero (pɪ'nɪərəʊ) *n.* Sir **Arthur Wing**. 1855–1934, English dramatist. His works include the farce *Dandy Dick* (1887) and the problem play *The Second Mrs Tanqueray* (1893).

Pines (paɪnz) *n.* **Isle of.** the former name of the (Isle of) **Youth**.

pine tar *n.* a brown or black semisolid or viscous substance, produced by the destructive distillation of pine wood, used in roofing compositions, paints, medicines, etc.

pinfeather ('pɪn,fɛðə) *n. Ornithol.* a feather emerging from the skin and still enclosed in its horny sheath.

pinfold ('pɪn,fəʊld) *n.* **1.** a pound for stray cattle. ~*vb.* **2.** (*tr.*) to gather or confine in or as if in a pinfold. [OE *pundfald*]

ping (pɪŋ) *n.* **1.** a short high-pitched resonant sound, as of a bullet striking metal or a sonar echo. ~*vb.* **2.** (*intr.*) to make such a noise. [C19: imit.]

pinger ('pɪŋə) *n.* a device that makes a pinging sound, esp. one that can be preset to ring at a particular time.

Ping-Pong ('pɪŋ,pɒŋ) *n. Trademark.* another name for **table tennis**. Also: **ping pong**.

pinhead ('pɪn,hɛd) *n.* **1.** the head of a pin. **2.** something very small. **3.** *Inf.* a stupid person. —'**pin,headed** *adj.* —'**pin,headedness** *n.*

pinhole ('pɪn,həʊl) *n.* a small hole made with or as if with a pin.

pinion¹ ('pɪnjən) *n.* **1.** *Chiefly poetic.* a bird's wing. **2.** the part of a bird's wing including the flight feathers. ~*vb.* (*tr.*) **3.** to hold or bind (the arms) of (a person) so as to restrain or immobilize him. **4.** to confine or shackle. **5.** to make (a bird) incapable of flight by removing the flight feathers. [C15: from OF *pignon* wing, from L *pinna* wing]

pinion² ('pɪnjən) *n.* a cogwheel that engages with a larger wheel or rack. [C17: from F *pignon* cogwheel, from OF *peigne* comb, from L *pecten*]

Piniós (pi'njɒs) *n.* transliteration of the Modern Greek name for the **Salambria**.

pink¹ (pɪŋk) *n.* **1.** a pale reddish colour. **2.** pink cloth or clothing: *dressed in pink*. **3.** any of various Old World plants, such as the garden pink, cultivated for their fragrant flowers. See also **carnation** (sense 1). **4.** the flower of any of these plants. **5.** the highest or best degree, condition, etc. (esp. in **in the pink**). **6. a.** a huntsman's scarlet coat. **b.** a huntsman who wears a scarlet coat. ~*adj.* **7.** of the colour pink. **8.** *Brit. inf.* left-wing. **9.** (of a huntsman's coat) scarlet or red. ~*vb.* **10.** (*intr.*) another word for **knock** (sense 7). [C16 (the flower), C18 (the colour): ? short for PINKEYE] —'**pinkish** *or* '**pinky** *adj.* —'**pinkness** *n.*

pink² (pɪŋk) *vb.* (*tr.*) **1.** to prick lightly with a sword, etc. **2.** to decorate (leather, etc.) with a perforated or punched pattern. **3.** to cut with pinking shears. [C14: ? of Low G origin]

pink³ (pɪŋk) *n.* a sailing vessel with a narrow overhanging transom. [C15: from MDu. *pinke*, from ?]

Pinkerton ('pɪŋkətən) *n.* **Allan**. 1819–84, U.S. private detective, born in Scotland. He founded the first detective agency in the U.S. (1850) and organized an intelligence system in the Federal States of America (1861).

pinkeye ('pɪŋk,aɪ) *n.* **1.** Also called: **acute conjunctivitis**. an acute contagious inflammation of the conjunctiva of the eye, characterized by redness, discharge, etc. **2.** Also called: **infectious keratitis**. a similar condition affecting the cornea of horses and cattle. [C16: partial translation of obs. Du. *pinck oogen* small eyes]

pinkie *or* **pinky** ('pɪŋkɪ) *n., pl.* **-ies**. *Scot., U.S., & Canad.* the little finger. [C19: from Du. *pinkje*]

pinking shears *pl. n.* scissors with a serrated edge on one or both blades, producing a wavy edge to material cut, thus preventing fraying.

pink salmon *n.* **1.** any salmon having pale pink flesh. **2.** the flesh of such a fish.

pin money *n.* **1.** an allowance by a husband to his wife for personal expenditure. **2.** money saved or earned for incidental expenses.

pinna ('pɪnə) *n., pl.* **-nae** (-niː) *or* **-nas**. **1.** any leaflet of a pinnate compound leaf. **2.** *Zool.* a feather, wing, fin, etc. **3.** another name for **auricle** (sense 2). [C18: via NL from L: wing]

pinnace ('pɪnɪs) *n.* any of various kinds of ship's tender. [C16: from F *pinace*, ?from OSp. *pinaza*, lit.: something made of pine, ult. from L *pinus* pine]

pinnacle ('pɪnəkəl) *n.* **1.** the highest point, esp. of fame, success, etc. **2.** a towering peak, as of a mountain. **3.** a slender upright structure in the form of a spire on the top of a buttress, gable, or tower. ~*vb.* (*tr.*) **4.** to set as on a pinnacle. **5.** to furnish with a pinnacle or pinnacles. **6.** to crown with a pinnacle. [C14: via OF from LL *pinnāculum* a peak, from L *pinna* wing]

pinnate ('pɪneɪt, 'pɪnɪt) *adj.* **1.** like a feather in appearance. **2.** (of compound leaves) having the leaflets growing opposite each other in pairs on either side of the stem. [C18: from L *pinnātus*, from *pinna* feather] —'**pinnately** *adv.* —**pin'nation** *n.*

pinniped ('pɪnɪ,pɛd) *adj.* **1.** of, relating to, or belonging to an order of aquatic placental mammals having a streamlined body and limbs specialized as flippers: includes seals, sea lions, and the walrus. ~*n.* **2.** any pinniped animal. [C19: from NL *pinnipēs*, from L *pinna* fin + *pēs* foot]

pinnule ('pɪnjuːl) *n.* **1.** any of the lobes of a leaflet of a pinnate compound leaf, which is itself pinnately divided. **2.** *Zool.* any feather-like part, such as any of the arms of a sea lily. [C16: from L *pinnula*, dim. of *pinna* feather] —'**pinnular** *adj.*

pinny ('pɪnɪ) *n., pl.* **-nies**. a child's or informal name for **pinafore** (sense 1).

Pinochet (Ugarte) ('piːnə,ʃeɪ) *n.* **Augusto** (au'gusto). born 1915, Chilean general and statesman; president of Chile from 1974, following his overthrow of Allende (1973).

pinochle *or* **pinocle** ('piːnʌkəl) *n.* **1.** a card game for two to four players similar to bezique. **2.** the combination of queen of spades and jack of diamonds in this game. [C19: from ?]

pinpoint ('pɪn,pɔɪnt) *vb.* (*tr.*) **1.** to locate or identify exactly: *to pinpoint a problem; to pinpoint a place on a map*. ~*n.* **2.** an insignificant or trifling thing. **3.** the point of a pin. **4.** (*modifier*) exact: *a pinpoint aim*.

pinprick ('pɪn,prɪk) *n.* **1.** a slight puncture made by or as if by a pin. **2.** a small irritation. ~*vb.* **3.** (*tr.*) to puncture with or as if with a pin.

pins and needles *n.* (*functioning as sing.*) *Inf.* **1.** a tingling sensation in the fingers, toes, legs, etc., caused by the return of normal blood circulation after its temporary impairment. **2. on pins and needles**. in a state of anxious suspense.

Pinsk (*Russian* pinsk) *n.* a city in the W Soviet Union, in the SW Byelorussian SSR: capital of a principality (13th–14th centuries). Pop.: 113 000 (1986 est.).

pinstripe ('pɪn,straɪp) *n.* (in textiles) a very narrow stripe in fabric or the fabric itself.

pint (paɪnt) *n.* **1.** a unit of liquid measure of capacity equal to one eighth of a gallon. 1 Brit. pint is equal to 0.568 litre, 1 U.S. pint to 0.473 litre. **2.** a unit of dry measure of capacity equal to one half of a quart. 1 U.S. dry pint is equal to one sixty-fourth of a U.S. bushel or 0.5506 litre. **3.** a measure having such a capacity. **4.** *Brit. inf.* **a.** a pint of beer. **b.** a drink of beer: *he's gone out for a pint*. [C14: from OF *pinte*, from ?; ?from Med. L *pincta* marks used in measuring liquids, ult. from L *pingere* to paint]

pinta ('paɪntə) *n. Inf.* a pint of milk. [C20: phonetic by Columbus on his first voyage to America (1492).

pintail ('pɪn,teɪl) *n., pl.* **-tails** *or* **-tail**. a greyish-brown duck with a pointed tail.

Pinter ('pɪntə) *n.* **Harold**. born 1930, English dramatist. His plays, such as *The Caretaker* (1960), *The Homecoming* (1965), *Landscape* (1968), and *Mountain Language* (1988), are noted for their equivocal and halting dialogue.

pintle ('pɪntəl) *n.* **1.** a pin or bolt forming the pivot of a hinge. **2.** the link bolt, hook, or pin on a vehicle's towing bracket. **3.** the needle or plunger of the injection valve of an oil engine. [OE *pintel* penis]

pinto ('pɪntəʊ) *U.S. & Canad.* ~*adj.* **1.** marked with patches of white; piebald. ~*n., pl.* **-tos**. **2.** a pinto horse.

[C19: from American Sp. (orig.: painted, spotted), ult. from L *pingere* to paint]

pint-size or **pint-sized** adj. Inf. very small.

pin tuck n. a narrow, ornamental fold, esp. used on shirt fronts and dress bodices.

Pinturicchio (*Italian* pintu'rikkjo) or **Pintoricchio** (*Italian* pinto'rikkjo) n. real name *Bernardino di Betto*. ?1454–1513, Italian painter of the Umbrian school.

pin-up n. 1. Inf. a. a picture of a sexually attractive person, esp. when partially or totally undressed. b. (as modifier): a pin-up magazine. 2. Sl. a person who has appeared in such a picture. 3. a photograph of a famous personality.

pinus radiata ('paɪnəs ,reɪdɪ'ɑːtə) n. a pine tree grown in New Zealand and Australia to produce building timber.

pinwheel ('pɪn,wiːl) n. another name for a **Catherine wheel** (sense 1).

pinworm ('pɪn,wɜːm) n. a parasitic nematode worm, infecting the colon, rectum, and anus of humans. Also called: **threadworm**.

piny ('paɪnɪ) adj. **pinier, piniest.** of, resembling, or covered with pine trees.

Pinyin ('pɪn'jɪn) n. a system of spelling used to transliterate Chinese characters into the Roman alphabet.

Pinzón (*Spanish* pin'θɔn) n. 1. **Martín Alonzo** (mar'tin a'lɒnθo). ?1440–93, Spanish navigator, who commanded the *Pinta* on Columbus' first expedition (1492–93), which he abandoned in a vain attempt to be the first to arrive back in Spain. 2. his brother, **Vicente Yáñez** (bi'θente 'janeθ). ?1460–?1524, Spanish navigator, who commanded the *Niña* on Columbus' first expedition (1492–93).

pion ('paɪɒn) or **pi meson** n. Physics. a meson having a positive or negative charge and a rest mass 273 times that of the electron, or no charge and a rest mass 264 times that of the electron.

pioneer (,paɪə'nɪə) n. 1. a. a colonist, explorer, or settler of a new land, region, etc. b. (as modifier): a pioneer wagon. 2. an innovator or developer of something new. 3. Mil. a member of an infantry group that digs entrenchments, makes roads, etc. ~vb. 4. to be a pioneer (in or of). 5. (tr.) to initiate, prepare, or open up: to pioneer a medical programme. [C16: from OF paonier infantryman, from paon PAWN²]

pious ('paɪəs) adj. 1. having or expressing reverence for a god or gods; religious; devout. 2. marked by reverence. 3. marked by false reverence; sanctimonious. 4. sacred; not secular. [C17: from L pius] —'**piously** adv. —'**piousness** n.

Piozzi ('pjɔːtsɪ) n. **Hester Lynch.** See (Hester Lynch) **Thrale.**

pip¹ (pɪp) n. 1. the seed of a fleshy fruit, such as an apple or pear. 2. any of the segments marking the surface of a pineapple. [C18: short for PIPPIN]

pip² (pɪp) n. 1. a short high-pitched sound, a sequence of which can act as a time signal, esp. on radio. 2. a radar blip. 3. a. a device, such as a spade, diamond, heart, or club on a playing card. b. any of the spots on dice or dominoes. 4. Inf. the emblem worn on the shoulder by junior officers in the British Army, indicating their rank. ~vb. **pipping, pipped.** 5. (of a young bird) a. (intr.) to chirp; peep. b. to pierce (the shell of its egg) while hatching. 6. (intr.) to make a short high-pitched sound. [C16 (in the sense: spot); C17 (vb.); C20 (in the sense: short high-pitched sound): ? imit.]

pip³ (pɪp) n. 1. a contagious disease of poultry characterized by the secretion of thick mucus in the mouth and throat. 2. Facetious sl. a minor human ailment. 3. Brit. sl. a bad temper or depression (esp. in **give** (someone) **the pip**). ~vb. **pipping, pipped.** 4. Brit. sl. to cause to be annoyed or depressed. [C15: from MDu. pippe, ult. from L pituita phlegm]

pip⁴ (pɪp) vb. **pipping, pipped.** (tr.) Brit. sl. 1. to wound, esp. with a gun. 2. to defeat (a person), esp. when his success seems certain (often in **pip at the post**). 3. to blackball or ostracize. [C19 (orig. in the sense: to blackball): prob. from PIP²]

pipal ('piːpəl) n. a variant of **peepul.**

pipe¹ (paɪp) n. 1. a long tube of metal, plastic, etc., used to convey water, oil, gas, etc. 2. a long tube or case. 3. an object made in various shapes and sizes, consisting of a small bowl with an attached tubular stem, in which tobacco or other substances are smoked. 4. Also called:

pipeful. the amount of tobacco that fills the bowl of a pipe. 5. **put that in your pipe and smoke it.** Inf. accept that fact if you can. 6. Zool., bot. any of various hollow organs, such as the respiratory passage of certain animals. 7. a. any musical instrument whose sound production results from the vibration of an air column in a simple tube. b. any of the tubular devices on an organ. 8. **the pipes.** See **bagpipes.** 9. a shrill voice or sound, as of a bird. 10. a. a boatswain's pipe. b. the sound it makes. 11. (pl.) Inf. the respiratory tract or vocal cords. 12. Metallurgy. a conical hole in the head of an ingot. 13. a cylindrical vein of rich ore. 14. Also called: **volcanic pipe.** a vertical cylindrical passage in a volcano through which molten lava is forced during eruption. ~vb. 15. to play (music) on a pipe. 16. (tr.) to summon or lead by a pipe: to pipe the dancers. 17. to utter (something) shrilly. 18. a. to signal orders to (the crew) by a boatswain's pipe. b. (tr.) to signal the arrival or departure of: to pipe the admiral aboard. 19. (tr.) to convey (water, gas, etc.) by a pipe or pipes. 20. (tr.) to provide with pipes. 21. (tr.) to trim (an article, esp. of clothing) with piping. 22. to force cream or icing, etc., through a shaped nozzle to decorate food. ~See also **pipe down, pipe up.** [OE pīpe (n.), pīpian (vb.), ult. from L pīpāre to chirp]

pipe² (paɪp) n. 1. a large cask for wine, oil, etc. 2. a measure of capacity for wine equal to four barrels or 105 Brit. gallons. 3. a cask holding this quantity with its contents. [C14: via OF (in the sense: tube), ult. from L pīpāre to chirp]

pipeclay ('paɪp,kleɪ) n. 1. a fine white pure clay, used in the manufacture of tobacco pipes and pottery and for whitening leather and similar materials. ~vb. 2. (tr.) to whiten with pipeclay.

pipe cleaner n. a short length of thin wires twisted so as to hold tiny tufts of yarn: used to clean the stem of a tobacco pipe.

piped music n. light popular music prerecorded and played through amplifiers in a shop, restaurant, factory, etc., as background music.

pipe down vb. (intr., adv.) Inf. to stop talking, making noise, etc.

pipe dream n. a fanciful or impossible plan or hope. [alluding to dreams produced by smoking an opium pipe]

pipefish ('paɪp,fɪʃ) n., pl. **-fish** or **-fishes.** any of various teleost fishes having a long tubelike snout and an elongated body covered with bony plates. Also called: **needlefish.**

pipefitting ('paɪp,fɪtɪŋ) n. a. the act or process of bending and joining pipes. b. the branch of plumbing involving this. —'**pipe,fitter** n.

pipeline ('paɪp,laɪn) n. 1. a long pipe used to transport oil, natural gas, etc. 2. a medium of communication, esp. a private one. 3. **in the pipeline.** in the process of being completed, delivered, or produced. ~vb. (tr.) 4. to convey by pipeline. 5. to supply with a pipeline.

pipe major n. the noncommissioned officer responsible for the training of a pipe band.

pipe organ n. another name for **organ** (the musical instrument).

piper ('paɪpə) n. 1. a person who plays a pipe or bagpipes. 2. **pay the piper and call the tune.** to bear the cost of an undertaking and control it.

Piper ('paɪpə) n. **John.** born 1903, British artist. An official war artist in World War II, he is known also for his stained glass in Coventry Cathedral and his sets for Benjamin Britten's Opera Death in Venice (1973).

piperidine (pɪ'perɪ,diːn) n. a liquid compound with a peppery ammoniacal odour: used in making rubbers and curing epoxy resins.

piperine ('pɪpə,raɪn) n. an alkaloid that is the active ingredient of pepper, used as a flavouring and as an insecticide. [C19: from L piper PEPPER]

piperonal ('pɪpərəʊ,næl) n. a white fragrant aldehyde used in flavourings, perfumery, and suntan lotions.

pipette (pɪ'pet) n. a slender glass tube for transferring or measuring out known volumes of liquid. [C19: via F: little pipe]

pipe up vb. (intr., adv.) 1. to commence singing or playing a musical instrument: the band piped up. 2. to speak up, esp. in a shrill voice.

pipi ('pɪpi) n., pl. **pipi** or **pipis. 1.** an edible shellfish of New Zealand. 2. an Australian mollusc of sandy beaches, widely used as bait. [from Maori]

piping ('paɪpɪŋ) n. 1. pipes collectively, as in the plumbing of a house. 2. a cord of icing, whipped cream, etc., often used to decorate desserts and cakes. 3. a thin strip of covered cord or material, used to edge hems, etc. 4. the sound of a pipe or bagpipes. 5. the art or technique of playing a pipe or bagpipes. 6. a shrill voice or sound, esp. a whistling sound. ~adj. 7. making a shrill sound. 8. **piping hot.** extremely hot.

pipistrelle (,pɪpɪ'strɛl) n. any of a genus of numerous small brownish insectivorous bats, occurring in most parts of the world. [C18: via F from It. *pipistrello*, from L *vespertiliō* a bat, from *vesper* evening, because of its nocturnal habits]

pipit ('pɪpɪt) n. any of various songbirds, esp. the **meadow pipit**, having brownish speckled plumage and a long tail. [C18: prob. imit.]

pipkin ('pɪpkɪn) n. a small earthenware vessel. [C16: ? dim. of PIPE[2]; see -KIN]

pippin ('pɪpɪn) n. any of several varieties of eating apple. [C13: from OF *pepin*, from ?]

pipsissewa (pɪp'sɪsəwə) n. any of several ericaceous plants of an Asian and American genus, having jagged evergreen leaves and white or pinkish flowers. Also called: **wintergreen.** [C19: from Algonquian *pipisisikweu*, lit.: it breaks it into pieces, so called because believed to be efficacious in treating bladder stones]

pipsqueak ('pɪp,skwiːk) n. *Inf.* a person or thing that is insignificant or contemptible.

piquant ('piːkənt, -kɑːnt) adj. 1. having an agreeably pungent or tart taste. 2. lively or stimulating to the mind. [C16: from F (lit.: prickling), from *piquer* to prick, goad] —'**piquancy** n. —'**piquantly** adv.

pique (piːk) n. 1. a feeling of resentment or irritation, as from having one's pride wounded. ~vb. **piquing, piqued.** (tr.) 2. to cause to feel resentment or irritation. 3. to excite or arouse. 4. (foll. by *on* or *upon*) to pride or congratulate (oneself). [C16: from F, from *piquer* to prick]

piqué ('piːkeɪ) n. a close-textured fabric of cotton, silk, or spun rayon woven with lengthwise ribs. [C19: from F *piqué* pricked, from *piquer* to prick]

piquet (pɪ'kɛt, -'keɪ) n. a card game for two people played with a reduced pack. [C17: from F, from ?]

piracy ('paɪrəsɪ) n., pl. **-cies.** 1. *Brit.* robbery on the seas. 2. a felony, such as robbery or hijacking, committed aboard a ship or aircraft. 3. the unauthorized use or appropriation of patented or copyrighted material, ideas, etc. [C16: from Anglo-L *pirātia*, from LGk *peirāteia*; see PIRATE]

Piraeus *or* **Peiraeus** (paɪ'riːəs, pɪ'reɪ-) n. a port in SE Greece, adjoining Athens: the country's chief port; founded in the 5th century B.C. as the port of Athens. Pop.: 196 389 (1981). Modern Greek name: **Piraiévs** (,pɪrɛ'ɛfs).

Pirandello (*Italian* piran'dɛllo) n. **Luigi** (lu'iːdʒi). 1867–1936, Italian short-story writer, novelist, and dramatist. His plays include *Right you are (If you think so)* (1917), *Six Characters in Search of an Author* (1921), and *Henry IV* (1922): Nobel prize for literature 1934.

Piranesi (*Italian* pira'neːsi) n. **Giambattista** (dʒambat'tista). 1720–78, Italian etcher and architect: etchings include *Imaginary Prisons* and *Views of Rome.*

piranha *or* **piraña** (pɪ'rɑːnjə) n. any of various small freshwater voracious fishes of tropical America, having strong jaws and sharp teeth. [C19: via Port. from Tupi: fish with teeth, from *pirá* fish + *sainha* tooth]

pirate ('paɪrɪt) n. 1. a person who commits piracy. 2. **a.** a vessel used by pirates. **b.** (*as modifier*): *a pirate ship.* 3. a person who illicitly uses or appropriates someone else's literary, artistic, or other work. 4. **a.** a person or group of people who broadcast illegally. **b.** (*as modifier*): *a pirate radio station.* ~vb. 5. (tr.) to use, appropriate, or reproduce (artistic work, ideas, etc.) illicitly. [C15: from L *pirāta*, from Gk *peirātēs* one who attacks, from *peira* an attack] —**piratic** (paɪ'rætɪk) *or* **pi'ratical** adj. —**pi'ratically** adv.

Pirithoüs (paɪ'rɪθəʊəs) n. *Greek myth.* a prince of the Lapiths, who accomplished many great deeds with his friend Theseus.

pirogue (pɪ'rəʊg) *or* **piragua** (pɪ'rɑːgwə, -'ræg-) n. any of various kinds of dugout canoes. [C17: via F from Sp., of Amerind origin]

pirouette (,pɪrʊ'ɛt) n. 1. a body spin, esp. in dancing, on the toes or the ball of the foot. ~vb. 2. (intr.) to perform a pirouette. [C18: from F, from OF *pirouet* spinning top]

Pisa ('piːzə; *Italian* 'piːsa) n. a city in Tuscany, NW Italy, near the mouth of the River Arno: flourishing maritime republic (11th–12th centuries), contains a university (1343), a cathedral (1063), and the Leaning Tower (begun in 1174 and about 5 m (17 ft.) from perpendicular); tourism. Pop.: 104 384 (1986).

Pisanello (*Italian* pisa'nɛllo) n. **Antonio** (an'tɔːnjo). ?1395–?1455, Italian painter and medallist; a major exponent of the International Gothic style. He is best known for his portrait medals and drawings of animals.

Pisano (*Italian* pi'saːno) n. 1. **Giovanni** (dʒo'vanni). ?1250–?1320, Italian sculptor, who successfully integrated classical and Gothic elements in his sculptures, esp. in his pulpit in St Andrea, Pistoia. 2. his father, **Nicola** (ni'kɔːla). ?1220–?84, Italian sculptor, who pioneered the classical style and is often regarded as a precursor of the Italian Renaissance: noted esp. for his pulpit in the baptistry of Pisa Cathedral.

piscatorial (,pɪskə'tɔːrɪəl) *or* **piscatory** ('pɪskətərɪ, -trɪ) adj. 1. of or relating to fish, fishing, or fishermen. 2. devoted to fishing. [C19: from L *piscātōrius*, from *piscātor* fisherman] —,**pisca'torially** adv.

Pisces ('paɪsiːz, 'pɪ-) n., *Latin genitive* **Piscium** ('paɪsɪəm). 1. *Astron.* a faint extensive zodiacal constellation lying between Aquarius and Aries on the ecliptic. 2. *Astrol.* Also called: the **Fishes.** the twelfth sign of the zodiac. The sun is in this sign between about Feb. 19 and March 20. 3. **a.** a taxonomic group that comprises all fishes. See **fish** (sense 1). **b.** a taxonomic group that comprises the bony fishes only. See **teleost.** [C14: L: the fish (pl.)]

pisci- *combining form.* fish: *pisciculture.* [from L *piscis*]

pisciculture ('pɪsɪ,kʌltʃə) n. the rearing and breeding of fish under controlled conditions. —,**pisci'cultural** adj. —,**pisci'culturist** n., adj.

piscina (pɪ'siːnə) n., pl. **-nae** (-niː) *or* **-nas.** *R.C. Church.* a stone basin, with a drain, in a church or sacristy where water used at Mass is poured away. [C16: from L: fish pond, from *piscis* a fish]

piscine ('pɪsaɪn) adj. of, relating to, or resembling a fish.

piscivorous (pɪ'sɪvərəs) adj. feeding on fish.

Pisgah ('pɪzgə) n. **Mount.** *Old Testament.* the mountain slopes to the northeast of the Dead Sea, from one of which, Mount Nebo, Moses viewed Canaan.

pish (pʃ, pɪʃ) interj. 1. an exclamation of impatience or contempt. ~vb. 2. to make this exclamation at (someone or something).

Pishpek (pɪʃ'pɛk) n. the former name (until 1926) of **Frunze.**

pisiform ('pɪsɪ,fɔːm) adj. 1. *Zool., bot.* resembling a pea. ~n. 2. a small pealike bone on the ulnar side of the carpus. [C18: via NL from L *pīsum* pea + *forma* shape]

Pisistratus (paɪ'sɪstrətəs) n. ?600–527 B.C., tyrant of Athens: he established himself in firm control of the city following his defeat of his aristocratic rivals at Pallene (546).

pismire ('pɪs,maɪə) n. an archaic or dialect word for an **ant.** [C14 (lit.: urinating ant, from the odour of formic acid): from PISS + obs. *mire* ant, from ON]

piss (pɪs) *Taboo sl.* ~vb. 1. (intr.) to urinate. 2. (tr.) to discharge as or in one's urine: *to piss blood.* ~n. 3. an act of urinating. 4. urine. [C13: from OF *pisser*, prob. imit.]

Pissarro (pɪ'saːrəʊ; *French* pisaro) n. **Camille** (kamij). 1830–1903, French impressionist painter, esp. of landscapes.

piss artist n. *Sl.* 1. a boastful but shallow person. 2. a heavy drinker.

pissed (pɪst) adj. *Brit. taboo sl.* drunk.

piss off vb. (adv.) *Taboo sl.* 1. (tr.; *often passive*) to annoy, irritate, or disappoint. 2. (intr.) *Chiefly Brit.* to go away; depart: often used to dismiss a person.

piss-up n. *Sl.* a party involving a considerable amount of drinking.

pistachio (pɪ'staːʃɪ,əʊ) n., pl. **-chios.** 1. a tree of the Mediterranean region and W Asia, with small hard-shelled nuts. 2. Also called: **pistachio nut.** the nut of this tree, having an edible green kernel. 3. the sweet flavour of the pistachio nut, used in ice creams, etc. ~adj. 4. of a yellowish-green colour. [C16: via It. & L from Gk *pistakion* pistachio nut, from *pistakē* pistachio tree, from Persian *pistah*]

piste (piːst) n. a slope or course for skiing. [C18: via OF from OIt. *pista*, from *pistare* to tread down]

pistil ('pɪstɪl) *n.* the female reproductive part of a flower, consisting of one or more separate or fused carpels. [C18: from L *pistillum* pestle]

pistillate ('pɪstɪlɪt, -,leɪt) *adj.* (of plants) **1.** having pistils but no anthers. **2.** having or producing pistils.

Pistoia (*Italian* pis'to:ja) *n.* a city in N Italy, in N Tuscany: scene of the defeat and death of Catiline in 62 B.C. Pop.: 91 993 (1983 est.).

pistol ('pɪstᵊl) *n.* **1.** a short-barrelled handgun. **2. hold a pistol to a person's head.** to threaten a person in order to force him to do what one wants. ~*vb.* **-tolling, -tolled** *or U.S.* **-toling, -toled. 3.** (*tr.*) to shoot with a pistol. [C16: from F *pistole*, from G, from Czech *pišt'ala* pistol, pipe]

pistole (pɪs'təʊl) *n.* any of various gold coins of varying value, formerly used in Europe. [C16: from OF, shortened from *pistolet*, lit.: little PISTOL]

pistol grip *n.* **a.** a handle shaped like the butt of a pistol. **b.** (*as modifier*): *a pistol-grip camera.*

pistol-whip *vb.* **-whipping, -whipped.** (*tr.*) *U.S.* to beat or strike with a pistol barrel.

piston ('pɪstən) *n.* a disc or cylindrical part that slides to and fro in a hollow cylinder. In an internal-combustion engine it is attached by a pivoted connecting rod to a crankshaft or flywheel, thus converting reciprocating motion into rotation. [C18: via F from OIt. *pistone*, from *pistare* to grind, from L *pinsere* to beat]

piston ring *n.* a split ring that fits into a groove on the rim of a piston to provide a spring-loaded seal against the cylinder wall.

piston rod *n.* **1.** the rod that connects the piston of a reciprocating steam engine to the crosshead. **2.** a less common name for a **connecting rod.**

pit[1] (pɪt) *n.* **1.** a large, usually deep opening in the ground. **2. a.** a mine or excavation, esp. for coal. **b.** the shaft in a mine. **c.** (*as modifier*): *pit pony; pit prop.* **3.** a concealed danger or difficulty. **4. the pit.** hell. **5.** Also called: **orchestra pit.** the area that is occupied by the orchestra in a theatre, located in front of the stage. **6.** an enclosure for fighting animals or birds. **7.** *Anat.* **a.** a small natural depression on the surface of a body, organ, or part. **b.** the floor of any natural bodily cavity: *the pit of the stomach.* **8.** *Pathol.* a small indented scar at the site of a former pustule; pockmark. **9.** a working area at the side of a motor-racing track for servicing or refuelling vehicles. **10.** *U.S.* a section on the floor of a commodity exchange devoted to a special line of trading. **11.** the ground floor of the auditorium of a theatre. **12.** another word for **pitfall** (sense 2). ~*vb.* **pitting, pitted. 13.** (*tr.; often foll. by against*) to match in opposition, esp. as antagonists. **14.** to mark or become marked with pits. **15.** (*tr.*) to place or bury in a pit. [OE *pytt*, from L *puteus*]

pit[2] (pɪt) *Chiefly U.S. & Canad.* ~*n.* **1.** the stone of a cherry, etc. ~*vb.* **pitting, pitted.** (*tr.*) **2.** to extract the stone from (a fruit). [C19: from Du.: kernel]

pitapat ('pɪtə,pæt) *adv.* **1.** with quick light taps. ~*vb.* **-patting, -patted. 2.** (*intr.*) to make quick light taps. ~*n.* **3.** such taps. [C16: imit.]

pit bull terrier *n.* a dog resembling the Staffordshire bull terrier but somewhat larger: originally developed for dogfighting.

Pitcairn Island (pɪt'kɛən, 'pɪtkɛən) *n.* an island in the S Pacific: forms with other islands a British colony; uninhabited until the landing in 1790 of the mutineers of H.M.S. *Bounty* and their Tahitian companions. Pop.: 57 (1986). Area: 4.6 sq. km (1.75 sq. miles).

pitch[1] (pɪtʃ) *vb.* **1.** to hurl or throw (something); cast; fling. **2.** (*usually tr.*) to set up (a camp, tent, etc.). **3.** (*tr.*) to set the level, character, or slope of. **4.** (*intr.*) to slope downwards. **5.** (*intr.*) to fall forwards or downwards. **6.** (*intr.*) (of a vessel) to dip and raise its bow and stern alternately. **7.** (*tr.*; foll. by *up*) *Cricket.* to bowl (a ball) so that it bounces near the batsman. **8.** (*intr.*) (of a missile, aircraft, etc.) to deviate from a stable flight attitude by movement of the longitudinal axis about the lateral axis. **9.** (*tr.*) (in golf, etc.) to hit (a ball) steeply into the air. **10.** (*tr.*) *Music.* **a.** to sing or play accurately (a note, interval, etc.). **b.** (*usually passive*) (of a wind instrument) to specify or indicate its basic key or harmonic series by its size, manufacture, etc. **11.** *Baseball.* **a.** (*tr.*) to throw (a baseball) to a batter. **b.** (*intr.*) to act as a

pitcher in a baseball game. ~*n.* **12.** the degree of elevation or depression. **13. a.** the angle of descent of a downward slope. **b.** such a slope. **14.** the extreme height or depth. **15.** *Mountaineering.* a section of a route between two belay points. **16.** the degree of slope of a roof. **17.** the distance between corresponding points on adjacent members of a body of regular form, esp. the distance between teeth on a gearwheel or between threads on a screw thread. **18.** the pitching motion of a ship, missile, etc. **19.** *Music.* **a.** the auditory property of a note that is conditioned by its frequency relative to other notes: *high pitch; low pitch.* **b.** an absolute frequency assigned to a specific note, fixing the relative frequencies of all other notes. **20.** *Cricket.* the rectangular area between the stumps, 22 yards long and 10 feet wide; the wicket. **21.** the act or manner of pitching a ball, as in cricket, etc. **22.** *Chiefly Brit.* a vendor's station, esp. on a pavement. **23.** *Sl.* a persuasive sales talk, esp. one routinely repeated. **24.** *Chiefly Brit.* (in many sports) the field of play. **25.** *Golf.* Also called: **pitch shot.** an approach shot in which the ball is struck in a high arc. **26. queer someone's pitch.** *Brit. inf.* to upset someone's plans. ~See also **pitch in, pitch into.** [C13 *picchen*]

pitch[2] (pɪtʃ) *n.* **1.** any of various heavy dark viscid substances obtained as a residue from the distillation of tars. **2.** any of various similar substances, such as asphalt, occurring as natural deposits. **3.** crude turpentine obtained as sap from pine trees. ~*vb.* **4.** (*tr.*) to apply pitch to (something). [OE *pic*, from L *pix*]

pitch-black *adj.* **1.** extremely dark; unlit: *the room was pitch-black.* **2.** of a deep black colour.

pitchblende ('pɪtʃ,blɛnd) *n.* a blackish mineral that occurs in veins, frequently associated with silver: the principal source of uranium and radium. [C18: partial translation of G *Pechblende*, from *Pech* PITCH[2] (from its black colour) + BLENDE]

pitch-dark *adj.* extremely or completely dark.

pitched battle *n.* **1.** a battle ensuing from the deliberate choice of time and place. **2.** any fierce encounter, esp. one with large numbers.

pitcher[1] ('pɪtʃə) *n.* a large jug, usually rounded with a narrow neck and often of earthenware, used mainly for holding water. [C13: from OF *pichier*, from Med. L *picārium*, var. of *bicārium* BEAKER]

pitcher[2] ('pɪtʃə) *n. Baseball.* the player on the fielding team who throws the ball to the batter.

pitcher plant *n.* any of various insectivorous plants, having leaves modified to form pitcher-like organs that attract and trap insects, which are then digested.

pitchfork ('pɪtʃ,fɔːk) *n.* **1.** a long-handled fork with two or three long curved tines for tossing hay. ~*vb.* (*tr.*) **2.** to use a pitchfork on (something). **3.** to thrust (someone) unwillingly into a position.

pitch in *vb.* (*intr., adv.*) **1.** to cooperate or contribute. **2.** to begin energetically.

pitch into *vb.* (*intr., prep.*) *Inf.* **1.** to assail physically or verbally. **2.** to get on with doing (something).

pitch pine *n.* **1.** any of various coniferous trees of North America: valued as a source of turpentine and pitch. **2.** the wood of any of these trees.

pitch pipe *n.* a small pipe that sounds a note or notes of standard frequency. It is used for establishing the correct starting note for unaccompanied singing.

pitchy ('pɪtʃɪ) *adj.* **pitchier, pitchiest. 1.** full of or covered with pitch. **2.** resembling pitch. —'**pitchiness** *n.*

piteous ('pɪtɪəs) *adj.* exciting or deserving pity. —'**piteously** *adv.* —'**piteousness** *n.*

pitfall ('pɪt,fɔːl) *n.* **1.** an unsuspected difficulty or danger. **2.** a trap in the form of a concealed pit, designed to catch men or wild animals. [OE *pytt* PIT[1] + *fealle* trap]

pith (pɪθ) *n.* **1.** the soft fibrous tissue lining the inside of the rind in fruits such as the orange. **2.** the essential or important part, point, etc. **3.** weight; substance. **4.** *Bot.* the central core of unspecialized cells surrounded by conducting tissue in stems. **5.** the soft central part of a bone, feather, etc. ~*vb.* (*tr.*) **6.** to kill (animals) by severing the spinal cord. **7.** to remove the pith from (a plant). [OE *pitha*]

pithead ('pɪt,hɛd) *n.* the top of a mine shaft and the buildings, hoisting gear, etc., around it.

pithecanthropus (ˌpɪθɪkæn'θrəʊpəs) *n.*, *pl.* **-pi** (-ˌpaɪ). any primitive apelike man of the former genus *Pithecanthropus*, now included in the genus *Homo.* See **Java man.** [C19: NL, from Gk *pithēkos* ape + *anthrōpos* man]

pith helmet *n.* a lightweight hat made of the pith of the sola, an E Indian swamp plant, that protects the wearer from the sun. Also called: **topee, topi.**

pithos ('pɪθɒs, 'paɪ-) *n.*, *pl.* **-thoi** (-θɔɪ). a large ceramic container for oil or grain. [from Gk]

pithy ('pɪθɪ) *adj.* **pithier, pithiest.** **1.** terse and full of meaning or substance. **2.** of, resembling, or full of pith. —'**pithily** *adv.* —'**pithiness** *n.*

pitiable ('pɪtɪəb³l) *adj.* exciting or deserving pity or contempt. —'**pitiableness** *n.* —'**pitiably** *adv.*

pitiful ('pɪtɪfʊl) *adj.* **1.** arousing or deserving pity. **2.** arousing or deserving contempt. **3.** *Arch.* full of pity or compassion. —'**pitifully** *adv.* —'**pitifulness** *n.*

pitiless ('pɪtɪlɪs) *adj.* having or showing little or no pity or mercy. —'**pitilessly** *adv.* —'**pitilessness** *n.*

pitman ('pɪtmən) *n.*, *pl.* **-men.** *Chiefly Scot. & N English.* a person who works in a pit, esp. a coal miner.

Pitman ('pɪtmən) *n.* Sir **Isaac.** 1813–97, English inventor of a system of phonetic shorthand (1837).

piton ('piːtɒn) *n. Mountaineering.* a metal spike that may be driven into a crevice and used to secure a rope, etc. [C20: from F: ringbolt]

pits (pɪts) *pl. n.* **the.** *Sl.* the worst possible person, place, or thing. [C20: from ? *armpits*]

Pitt (pɪt) *n.* **1. William,** known as *Pitt the Elder*, 1st Earl of Chatham. 1708–78, British statesman. He was first minister (1756–57; 1757–61; 1766–68) and achieved British victory in the Seven Years' War (1756–63). **2.** his son **William,** known as *Pitt the Younger*. 1759–1806, British statesman. As prime minister (1783–1801; 1804–06), he carried through important fiscal and tariff reforms. From 1793, his attention was focused on the wars with revolutionary and Napoleonic France.

pitta bread *or* **pitta** ('pɪtə) *n.* a flat rounded slightly leavened bread, originally from the Middle East. [from Mod. Gk: a cake]

pittance ('pɪt³ns) *n.* a small amount or portion, esp. a meagre allowance of money. [C16: from OF *pietance* ration, ult. from L *pietās* duty]

pitter-patter ('pɪtəˌpætə) *n.* **1.** the sound of light rapid taps or pats, as of raindrops. ~*vb.* **2.** (*intr.*) to make such a sound. ~*adv.* **3.** with such a sound.

Pittsburgh ('pɪtsbɜːg) *n.* a port in SW Pennsylvania, at the confluence of the Allegheny and Monongahela Rivers, which form the Ohio River: settled around Fort Pitt in 1758; developed rapidly with the discovery of iron deposits and one of the world's richest coalfields; the largest river port in the U.S. and an important industrial centre, with large steel mills. Pop.: 387 490 (1986).

pituitary (pɪ'tjuːɪtərɪ) *n.*, *pl.* **-taries.** **1.** See **pituitary gland.** ~*adj.* **2.** of or relating to the pituitary gland. [C17: from LL *pītuītārius* slimy, from *pītuīta* phlegm]

pituitary gland *or* **body** *n.* the master endocrine gland, attached by a stalk to the base of the brain. Its two lobes secrete hormones affecting skeletal growth, development of the sex glands, and the functioning of the other endocrine glands.

pit viper *n.* any venomous snake of a New World family, having a heat-sensitive organ in a pit on each side of the head: includes the rattlesnakes.

pity ('pɪtɪ) *n.*, *pl.* **pities.** **1.** sympathy or sorrow felt for the sufferings of another. **2. have** (*or* **take**) **pity on.** to have sympathy or show mercy for. **3.** something that causes regret. **4.** an unfortunate chance: *what a pity you can't come.* ~*vb.* **pitying, pitied.** (*tr.*) **5.** to feel pity for. [C13: from OF *pité*, from L *pietās* duty] —'**pitying** *adj.* —'**pityingly** *adv.*

pityriasis (ˌpɪtə'raɪəsɪs) *n.* any of a group of skin diseases characterized by the shedding of dry flakes of skin. [C17: via NL from Gk *pituriasis* scurfiness, from *pituron* bran]

più (pju:) *adv.* (*in combination*) *Music.* more (quickly, etc.): *più allegro.* [It., from L *plus* more]

piupiu ('piːuːˌpiːuː) *n.* a skirt made from leaves of the New Zealand flax, worn by Maoris on ceremonial occasions. [from Maori]

Piura (*Spanish* 'pjura) *n.* a city in NW Peru: the oldest colonial city in Peru, founded by Pizarro in 1532; commercial centre of an agricultural district. Pop.: 186 354 (1981).

Pius II ('paɪəs) *n.* pen name *Aeneas Silvius*, original name *Enea Silvio de' Piccolomini.* 1405–64, Italian ecclesiastic, humanist, poet, and historian; pope (1458–64).

Pius IV *n.* original name *Giovanni Angelo de' Medici.* 1499–1565, pope (1559–65). He reconvened the Council of Trent (1562), confirming its final decrees.

Pius V *n.* **Saint.** original name *Michele Ghislieri.* 1504–72, pope (1566–72). He attempted to enforce the reforms decreed by the Council of Trent, excommunicated Elizabeth I of England (1570), and organized the alliance that defeated the Turks at Lepanto (1571). Feast day: Apr. 30.

Pius VII *n.* original name *Luigi Barnaba Chiaramonti.* 1740–1823, Italian ecclesiastic; pope (1800–23). He concluded a concordat with Napoleon (1801) and consecrated him as emperor of France (1804), but resisted his annexation of the Papal States (1809).

Pius IX *n.* original name *Giovanni Maria Mastai-Ferretti.* 1792–1878, Italian ecclesiastic; pope (1846–78). He refused to recognize the incorporation of Rome and the Papal States in the kingdom of Italy, confining himself to the Vatican after 1870. He decreed the dogma of the Immaculate Conception (1854) and convened the Vatican Council, which laid down the doctrine of papal infallibility (1870).

Pius X *n.* **Saint.** original name *Giuseppe Sarto.* 1835–1914, Italian ecclesiastic; pope (1903–14). He condemned Modernism (1907) and initiated a new codification of canon law. Feast day: Aug. 21.

Pius XI *n.* original name *Achille Ratti.* 1857–1939, Italian ecclesiastic; pope (1922–39). He signed the Lateran Treaty (1929), by which the Vatican City was recognized as an independent state. His encyclicals condemned Nazism and Communism.

Pius XII *n.* original name *Eugenio Pacelli.* 1876–1958, Italian ecclesiastic; pope (1939–58): his attitude towards Nazi German anti-Semitism has been a matter of controversy.

pivot ('pɪvət) *n.* **1.** a short shaft or pin supporting something that turns; fulcrum. **2.** the end of a shaft or arbor that terminates in a bearing. **3.** a person or thing upon which progress, success, etc., depends. **4.** the person or position from which a military formation takes its reference when altering position, etc. ~*vb.* **5.** (*tr.*) to mount on or provide with a pivot or pivots. **6.** (*intr.*) to turn on or as if on a pivot. [C17: from OF]

pivotal ('pɪvət³l) *adj.* **1.** of, involving, or acting as a pivot. **2.** of crucial importance.

pix[1] (pɪks) *n.* a plural of **pic.**

pix[2] (pɪks) *n.* a less common spelling of **pyx.**

pixel ('pɪksɛl) *n.* any of a number of very small picture elements that make up a picture, as on a visual display unit. [C20: from *pix* pictures + *el(ement)*]

pixie *or* **pixy** ('pɪksɪ) *n.*, *pl.* **pixies.** (in folklore) a fairy or elf. [C17: from ?]

pixilated *or* **pixillated** ('pɪksɪˌleɪtɪd) *adj. Chiefly U.S.* **1.** eccentric or whimsical. **2.** *Sl.* drunk. [C20: from PIXIE + *-lated*, as in *stimulated, titillated,* etc.]

Pizarro (pɪ'zɑːrəʊ; *Spanish* pi'θarrɔ) *n.* **Francisco** (fran'θisko). ?1475–1541, Spanish conqueror of Peru. He landed in Peru (1532), murdered the Inca King Atahualpa (1533), and founded Lima as the new capital of Peru (1535). He was murdered by his own followers.

pizza ('piːtsə) *n.* a dish of Italian origin consisting of a baked disc of dough covered with cheese and tomatoes, etc. [C20: from It., ?from Vulgar L *picea* (unattested), ? rel. to Med. Gk *pitta* cake]

pizzazz *or* **pizazz** (pə'zæz) *n. Inf.* an attractive combination of energy and style; sparkle. Also: **bezazz.**

pizzeria (ˌpiːtsə'riːə) *n.* a place where pizzas are made, sold, or eaten.

pizzicato (ˌpɪtsɪ'kɑːtəʊ) *Music.* ~*adj., adv.* **1.** (in music for the violin family) to be plucked with the finger. ~*n.* **2.** this style or technique of playing. [C19: from It.: pinched, from *pizzicare* to twist]

pizzle ('pɪz³l) *n. Arch. or dialect.* the penis of an animal, esp. a bull. [C16: of Gmc origin]

pk *pl.* **pks** *abbrev. for:* **1.** pack. **2.** park. **3.** peak.
pkg. *pl.* **pkgs.** *abbrev. for* package.
pl *abbrev. for:* **1.** place. **2.** plate. **3.** plural.
Pl. (in street names) *abbrev. for* Place.
PLA *abbrev. for* Port of London Authority.
plaas (plɑːs) *n. S. African.* a farm. [from Afrik., from Du.]
placable ('plækəbəl) *adj.* easily placated or appeased. [C15: via OF from L *plăcābilis*, from *plăcāre* to appease] —,placa'bility *n.*
placard ('plækɑːd) *n.* **1.** a notice for public display; poster. **2.** a small plaque or card. ~*vb.* (*tr.*) **3.** to post placards on or in. **4.** to advertise by placards. **5.** to display as a placard. [C15: from OF *plaquart*, from *plaquier* to plate, lay flat; see PLAQUE]
placate (plə'keɪt) *vb.* (*tr.*) to pacify or appease. [C17: from L *plăcāre*] —pla'cation *n.* —pla'catory *adj.*
place (pleɪs) *n.* **1.** a particular point or part of space or of a surface, esp. that occupied by a person or thing. **2.** a geographical point, such as a town, city, etc. **3.** a position or rank in a sequence or order. **4.** an open square lined with houses in a city or town. **5.** space or room. **6.** a house or living quarters. **7.** a country house with grounds. **8.** any building or area set aside for a specific purpose. **9.** a passage in a book, play, film, etc.: *to lose one's place*. **10.** proper, right, or customary surroundings (esp. in **out of place, in place**). **11.** right, prerogative, or duty: *it is your place to give a speech*. **12.** appointment, position, or job: *a place at college*. **13.** position, condition, or state: *if I were in your place*. **14. a.** a space or seat, as at a dining table. **b.** (*as modifier*): *place mat*. **15.** *Maths.* the relative position of a digit in a number. **16.** any of the best times in a race. **17.** *Horse racing.* **a.** *Brit.* the first, second, or third position at the finish. **b.** *U.S. & Canad.* the first or usually the second position at the finish. **c.** (*as modifier*): *a place bet*. **18. all over the place.** in disorder or disarray. **19. give place (to).** to make room (for) or be superseded (by). **20. go places.** *Inf.* **a.** to travel. **b.** to become successful. **21. in place of. a.** instead of; in lieu of: *go in place of my sister*. **b.** in exchange for: *he gave her it in place of her ring*. **22. know one's place.** to be aware of one's inferior position. **23. put someone in his** (*or* **her**) **place.** to humble someone who is arrogant, conceited, forward, etc. **24. take one's place.** to take up one's usual or specified position. **25. take place.** to happen or occur. **26. take the place of.** to be a substitute for. ~*vb.* (*mainly tr.*) **27.** to put or set in a particular or appropriate place. **28.** to find or indicate the place of. **29.** to identify or classify by linking with an appropriate context: *to place a face*. **30.** to regard or view as being: *to place prosperity above sincerity*. **31.** to make (an order, bet, etc.). **32.** to find a home or job for (someone). **33.** to appoint to an office or position. **34.** (often foll. by *with*) to put under the care (of). **35.** to direct or aim carefully. **36.** (*passive*) *Brit.* to cause (a racehorse, greyhound, athlete, etc.) to arrive in first, second, third, or sometimes fourth place. **37.** (*intr.*) *U.S. & Canad.* (of a racehorse, greyhound, etc.) to finish among the first three in a contest, esp. in second position. **38.** to invest (funds). **39.** (*tr.*) to insert (an advertisement) in a newspaper, journal, etc. [C13: via OF from L *platēa* courtyard, from Gk *plateia*, from *platus* broad]
placebo (plə'siːbəʊ) *n., pl.* **-bos** *or* **-boes.** **1.** *Med.* an inactive substance administered to a patient usually to compare its effects with those of a real drug but sometimes for the psychological benefit to the patient through his believing he is receiving treatment. **2.** something said or done to please or humour another. **3.** *R.C. Church.* a traditional name for the vespers of the office for the dead. [C13 (in the ecclesiastical sense): from L *Placebo Domino* I shall please the Lord; C19 (in the medical sense)]
placebo effect *n. Med.* a positive therapeutic effect claimed by a patient after receiving a placebo believed by him to be an active drug.
place card *n.* a card placed on a dinner table before a seat, indicating who is to sit there.
place kick *Football, etc.* ~*n.* **1.** a kick in which the ball is placed in position before it is kicked. ~*vb.* **place-kick.** **2.** to kick (a ball) in this way.
placement ('pleɪsmənt) *n.* **1.** the act of placing or the state of being placed. **2.** arrangement or position. **3.** the process of finding employment.
placenta (plə'sentə) *n., pl.* **-tas** *or* **-tae** (-tiː). **1.** the vascular organ formed in the uterus of most mammals during

pregnancy, consisting of both maternal and embryonic tissues and providing oxygen and nutrients for the fetus. **2.** *Bot.* the part of the ovary of flowering plants to which the ovules are attached. [C17: via L from Gk *plakoeis* flat cake, from *plax* flat] —pla'cental *adj.*
placer ('plæsə) *n.* **a.** surface sediment containing particles of gold or some other valuable mineral. **b.** (*in combination*): *placer-mining*. [C19: from American Sp.: deposit, from Sp. *plaza* PLACE]
place setting *n.* the cutlery, crockery, and glassware laid for one person at a dining table.
placet ('pleɪsɛt) *n.* a vote or expression of assent by saying *placet*. [C16: from L, lit.: it pleases]
placid ('plæsɪd) *adj.* having a calm appearance or nature. [C17: from L *placidus* peaceful] —**placidity** (plə'sɪdɪtɪ) *or* '**placidness** *n.* —'**placidly** *adv.*
placing ('pleɪsɪŋ) *n. Stock Exchange.* a method of issuing securities to the public using an intermediary, such as a stockbroking firm.
placket ('plækɪt) *n. Dressmaking.* **1.** a piece of cloth sewn in under a closure with buttons, zips, etc. **2.** the closure itself. [C16: ?from MDu. *plackaet* breastplate, from Med. L *placca* metal plate]
placoid ('plækɔɪd) *adj.* **1.** platelike or flattened. **2.** (of the scales of sharks) toothlike; composed of dentine with an enamel tip and basal pulp cavity. [C19: from Gk *plac-, plax* flat]
plafond (plə'fɒn; *French* plafɔ̃) *n.* a ceiling, esp. one having ornamentation. [C17: from F, from *plat* flat + *fond* bottom, from L *fundus*]
plagal ('pleɪɡəl) *adj.* **1.** (of a cadence) progressing from the subdominant to the tonic chord, as in the *Amen* of a hymn. **2.** (of a mode) commencing upon the dominant of an authentic mode, but sharing the same final as the authentic mode. ~Cf. **authentic** (sense 4). [C16: from Med. L *plagālis*, from *plaga*, ?from Gk *plagos* side]
plage (plɑːʒ) *n.* another name for **flocculus** (sense 1). [F, lit.: beach]
plagiarism ('pleɪdʒə,rɪzəm) *n.* **1.** the act of plagiarizing. **2.** something plagiarized. [C17: from L *plagiārus* plunderer, from *plagium* kidnapping] —'**plagiarist** *n.* —,**pla-gia'ristic** *adj.*
plagiarize *or* **-ise** ('pleɪdʒə,raɪz) *vb.* to appropriate (ideas, passages, etc.) from (another work or author). —'**plagi-a,rizer** *or* **-iser** *n.*
plagioclase ('pleɪdʒɪəʊ,kleɪz) *n.* a series of feldspar minerals consisting of a mixture of sodium and calcium aluminium silicates in triclinic crystalline form. [C19: from Gk, from *plagos* side + -CLASE] —**plagioclastic** (,pleɪdʒɪəʊ'klæstɪk) *adj.*
plague (pleɪɡ) *n.* **1.** any widespread and usually highly contagious disease with a high fatality rate. **2.** an infectious disease of rodents, esp. rats, transmitted to man by the bite of the rat flea. **3.** See **bubonic plague.** **4.** something that afflicts or harasses. **5.** *Inf.* an annoyance or nuisance. **6.** a pestilence, affliction, or calamity on a large scale, esp. when regarded as sent by God. ~*vb.* **plaguing, plagued.** (*tr.*) **7.** to afflict or harass. **8.** to bring down a plague upon. **9.** *Inf.* to annoy. [C14: from LL *plăga* pestilence, from L: a blow]
plaguy *or* **plaguey** ('pleɪɡɪ) *Arch., inf.* ~*adj.* **1.** disagreeable or vexing. ~*adv.* **2.** disagreeably or annoyingly. —'**plaguily** *adv.*
plaice (pleɪs) *n., pl.* **plaice** *or* **plaices.** **1.** a European flatfish having an oval brown body marked with red or orange spots and valued as a food fish. **2.** *U.S. & Canad.* any of various other related fishes. [C13: from OF *plaiz*, from LL *platessa* flatfish, from Gk *platus* flat]
plaid (plæd, pleɪd) *n.* **1.** a long piece of cloth of a tartan pattern, worn over the shoulder as part of Highland costume. **2. a.** a crisscross weave or cloth. **b.** (*as modifier*): *a plaid scarf*. [C16: from Scot. Gaelic *plaide*, from ?]
Plaid Cymru (,plaɪd 'kʌmrɪ) *n.* the Welsh nationalist party. [Welsh]
plain¹ (pleɪn) *adj.* **1.** flat or smooth; level. **2.** not complicated; clear: *the plain truth*. **3.** not difficult; simple or easy: *a plain task*. **4.** honest or straightforward. **5.** lowly, esp. in social rank or education. **6.** without adornment or show: *a plain coat*. **7.** (of fabric) without pattern or of simple untwilled weave. **8.** not attractive. **9.** not mixed; simple: *plain vodka*. **10.** *Knitting.* of or done in plain. ~*n.* **11.** a level or almost level tract of country. **12.** a simple stitch in knitting made by passing the wool

round the front of the needle. ~*adv.* **13.** (intensifier): *just plain tired.* [C13: from OF: simple, from L *plānus* level, clear] —'**plainly** *adv.* —'**plainness** *n.*

plain² (pleɪn) *vb.* a dialect or poetic word for **complain**. [C14 *pleignen*, from OF *plaindre* to lament, from L *plangere* to beat]

plainchant ('pleɪn,tʃɑːnt) *n.* another name for **plainsong**. [C18: from F, for Med. L *cantus plānus*]

plain chocolate *n.* chocolate with a slightly bitter flavour and dark colour.

plain clothes *pl. n.* **a.** ordinary clothes, as distinguished from uniform, as worn by a police detective on duty. **b.** (*as modifier*): *a plain-clothes policeman.*

plain flour *n.* flour to which no raising agent has been added.

plain sailing *n.* **1.** *Inf.* smooth or easy progress. **2.** *Naut.* sailing in a body of water that is unobstructed; clear sailing.

plainsman ('pleɪnzmən) *n., pl.* -**men.** a person who lives in a plains region, esp. in the Great Plains of North America.

plainsong ('pleɪn,sɒŋ) *n.* the style of unison unaccompanied vocal music used in the medieval Church, esp. in Gregorian chant. [C16: translation of Med. L *cantus plānus*]

plain-spoken *adj.* candid; frank; blunt.

plaint (pleɪnt) *n.* **1.** *Arch.* a complaint or lamentation. **2.** *Law.* a statement in writing of grounds of complaint made to a court of law. [C13: from OF *plainte*, from L *planctus* lamentation, from *plangere* to beat]

plaintiff ('pleɪntɪf) *n.* a person who brings a civil action in a court of law. [C14: from legal F *plaintif*, from OF *plaintif* (adj.) complaining, from *plainte* PLAINT]

plaintive ('pleɪntɪv) *adj.* expressing melancholy; mournful. [C14: from OF *plaintif* grieving, from PLAINT] —'**plaintively** *adv.* —'**plaintiveness** *n.*

plait (plæt) *n.* **1.** a length of hair, etc., that has been plaited. **2.** a rare spelling of **pleat.** ~*vb.* **3.** (*tr.*) to intertwine (strands or strips) in a pattern. [C15 *pleyt*, from OF *pleit*, from L *plicāre* to fold]

plan (plæn) *n.* **1.** a detailed scheme, method, etc., for attaining an objective. **2.** (*sometimes pl.*) a proposed, usually tentative idea for doing something. **3.** a drawing to scale of a horizontal section through a building taken at a given level. **4.** an outline, sketch, etc. ~*vb.* **planning, planned. 5.** to form a plan (for) or make plans (for). **6.** (*tr.*) to make a plan of (a building). **7.** (*tr.; takes a clause as object or an infinitive*) to have in mind as a purpose; intend. [C18: via F from L *plānus* flat]

planar ('pleɪnə) *adj.* **1.** of or relating to a plane. **2.** lying in one plane; flat. [C19: from LL *plānāris* on level ground, from L *plānus* flat]

planarian (plə'nɛərɪən) *n.* any of various free-living mostly aquatic flatworms, having a three-branched intestine. [C19: from NL *Plānāria* type genus, from LL *plānārius* flat; see PLANE¹]

planar process *n.* a method of producing diffused junctions in semiconductor devices. A pattern of holes is etched into an oxide layer formed on a silicon substrate, into which impurities are diffused through the holes.

planchet ('plɑːntʃɪt) *n.* a piece of metal ready to be stamped as a coin, medal, etc.; flan. [C17: from F: little board, from *planche* PLANK]

planchette (plɑːn'ʃɛt) *n.* a heart-shaped board on wheels with a pencil attached that writes messages under supposed spirit guidance. [C19: from F: little board, from *planche* PLANK]

Planck (plæŋk; *German* plaŋk) *n.* **Max (Karl Ernst Ludwig)** (maks). 1858–1947, German physicist who first formulated the quantum theory (1900): Nobel prize for physics 1918.

Planck constant *or* **Planck's constant** *n.* a fundamental constant equal to the energy of any quantum of radiation divided by its frequency.

plane¹ (pleɪn) *n.* **1.** *Maths.* a flat surface in which a straight line joining any two of its points lies entirely on that surface. **2.** a level surface. **3.** a level of existence, attainment, etc. **4. a.** short for **aeroplane. b.** a wing or supporting surface of an aircraft. ~*adj.* **5.** level or flat. **6.** *Maths.* lying entirely in one plane. ~*vb.* (*intr.*) **7.** to glide. **8.** (of a boat) to rise partly and skim over the water when moving at a certain speed. [C17: from L *plānum* level surface]

plane² (pleɪn) *n.* **1.** a tool with a steel blade set obliquely in a wooden or iron body, for smoothing timber surfaces, cutting grooves, etc. **2.** a flat tool, usually metal, for smoothing the surface of clay or plaster in a mould. ~*vb.* (*tr.*) **3.** to smooth or cut (timber, etc.) using a plane. **4.** (often foll. by *off*) to remove using a plane. [C14: via OF from LL *plāna* plane, from *plānāre* to level]

plane³ (pleɪn) *n.* See **plane tree.**

plane geometry *n.* the study of the properties of plane curves, figures, etc.

plane polarization *n.* a type of polarization in which waves of light or other radiation are restricted to vibration in a single plane.

planet ('plænɪt) *n.* **1.** Also called: **major planet.** any of the nine celestial bodies, Mercury, Venus, earth, Mars, Jupiter, Saturn, Uranus, Neptune, or Pluto, that revolve around the sun in elliptical orbits. **2.** any celestial body revolving around a star. **3.** *Astrol.* any of the planets of the solar system, excluding the earth but including the sun and moon, each thought to rule one or sometimes two signs of the zodiac. [C12: via OF from LL *planēta*, from Gk *planētēs* wanderer, from *planaein* to wander]

plane table *n.* a surveying instrument consisting of a drawing board mounted on adjustable legs.

planetarium (,plænɪ'tɛərɪəm) *n., pl.* -**iums** *or* -**ia** (-ɪə). **1.** an instrument for simulating the apparent motions of the sun, moon, and planets by projecting images of these bodies onto a domed ceiling. **2.** a building in which such an instrument is housed. **3.** a model of the solar system.

planetary ('plænɪtərɪ, -trɪ) *adj.* **1.** of a planet. **2.** mundane; terrestrial. **3.** wandering or erratic. **4.** *Astrol.* under the influence of one of the planets. **5.** (of a gear) having an axis that rotates around that of another gear.

planetesimal hypothesis (,plænɪ'tɛsɪməl) *n.* the discredited theory that the close passage of a star to the sun caused many small bodies (**planetesimals**) to be drawn from the sun, eventually coalescing to form the planets. [C20: *planetesimal*, from PLANET + INFINITESIMAL]

planetoid ('plænɪ,tɔɪd) *n.* another name for **asteroid** (sense 1). —,**plane'toidal** *adj.*

plane tree *or* **plane** *n.* a tree with ball-shaped heads of fruit and leaves with pointed lobes. [C14 *plane*, from OF, from L *platanus*, from Gk, from *platos* wide, referring to the leaves]

plangent ('plændʒənt) *adj.* **1.** having a loud deep sound. **2.** resonant and mournful. [C19: from L *plangere* to beat (esp. the breast, in grief)]

planimeter (plæ'nɪmɪtə) *n.* a mechanical instrument for measuring the area of an irregular plane figure by moving a point attached to an arm. —**pla'nimetry** *n.*

planish ('plænɪʃ) *vb.* (*tr.*) to give a final finish to (metal, etc.) by hammering or rolling. [C16: from OF *planir* to smooth out, from L *plānus* flat]

planisphere ('plænɪ,sfɪə) *n.* a projection or representation of all or part of a sphere on a plane surface. [C14: from Med. L *plānisphaerium*, from L *plānus* flat + Gk *sphaira* globe]

plank (plæŋk) *n.* **1.** a stout length of sawn timber. **2.** something that supports or sustains. **3.** one of the policies in a political party's programme. **4. walk the plank.** to be forced by pirates, etc., to walk to one's death off the end of a plank jutting out from the side of a ship. ~*vb.* **5.** (*tr.*) to cover or provide with planks. [C13: from OF *planke*, from LL *planca* board, from *plancus* flat-footed]

planking ('plæŋkɪŋ) *n.* a number of planks.

plankton ('plæŋktən) *n.* the organisms inhabiting the surface layer of a sea or lake, consisting of small drifting plants and animals. [C19: via G from Gk *planktos* wandering, from *plazesthai* to roam]

planning permission *n.* (in Britain) formal permission granted by a local authority for the development or changed use of land or buildings.

plano- *or sometimes before a vowel* **plan-** *combining form.* indicating flatness or planeness: *plano-concave.* [from L *plānus* flat]

plano-concave (,pleɪnəʊ'kɒnkeɪv) *adj.* (of a lens) having one side concave and the other plane.

plano-convex (,pleɪnəʊ'kɒnvɛks) *adj.* (of a lens) having one side convex and the other plane.

plant¹ (plɑːnt) *n.* **1.** any living organism that typically synthesizes its food from inorganic substances, lacks specialized sense organs, and has no powers of locomotion. **2.** such an organism that is smaller than a shrub or tree; a herb. **3.** a cutting, seedling, or similar structure, esp. when ready for transplantation. **4.** *Inf.* a thing positioned secretly for discovery by another, esp. in order to incriminate an innocent person. ~*vb.* (*tr.*) **5.** (often foll. by *out*) to set (seeds, crops, etc.) into (ground) to grow. **6.** to place firmly in position. **7.** to establish; found. **8.** (foll. by *with*) to stock or furnish. **9.** to implant in the mind. **10.** *Sl.* to deliver (a blow). **11.** *Inf.* to position or hide, esp. in order to deceive or observe. **12.** *Inf.* to hide or secrete, esp. for some illegal purpose or in order to incriminate someone. [OE, from *planta* a shoot] —'**plantable** *adj.*

plant[2] (plɑːnt) *n.* **1.** the land, buildings, and equipment used in carrying on an industry or business. **2.** a factory or workshop. **3.** mobile mechanical equipment for construction, road-making, etc. [C20: special use of PLANT[1]]

Plantagenet (plæn'tædʒɪnɪt) *n.* a line of English kings, ruling from the ascent of Henry II (1154) to the death of Richard III (1485). [C12: from OF, lit.: sprig of broom, with reference to the crest of the Angevin kings, from L *planta* sprig + *genista* broom]

plantain[1] ('plæntɪn) *n.* any of various N temperate plants, esp. the great plantain, which has a rosette of broad leaves and a slender spike of small greenish flowers. See also **ribwort**. [C14 *plauntein*, from OF, from L *plantāgō*, from *planta* sole of the foot]

plantain[2] ('plæntɪn) *n.* a large tropical plant with a green-skinned banana-like fruit which is eaten as a staple food in many tropical regions. [C16: Sp. *platano* plantain, PLANE TREE]

plantain lily *n.* any of several Asian plants of the genus *Hosta*, having broad ribbed leaves.

plantar ('plæntə) *adj.* of or on the sole of the foot. [C18: from L *plantāris*, from *planta* sole of the foot]

plantation (plæn'teɪʃən) *n.* **1.** an estate, esp. in tropical countries, where cash crops such as rubber, oil palm, etc., are grown on a large scale. **2.** a group of cultivated trees or plants. **3.** (formerly) a colony or group of settlers.

planter ('plɑːntə) *n.* **1.** the owner or manager of a plantation. **2.** a machine designed for rapid and efficient planting of seeds. **3.** a colonizer or settler. **4.** a decorative pot for house plants.

plantigrade ('plæntɪˌɡreɪd) *adj.* **1.** walking with the entire sole of the foot touching the ground, as man and bears. ~*n.* **2.** a plantigrade animal. [C19: via F from NL *plantigradus*, from L *planta* sole of the foot + *gradus* a step]

plant louse *n.* another name for an **aphid**.

plaque (plæk, plɑːk) *n.* **1.** an ornamental or commemorative inscribed tablet. **2.** a small flat brooch or badge. **3.** *Pathol.* any small abnormal patch on or within the body. **4.** short for **dental plaque**. [C19: from F, from *plaquier* to plate, from MDu. *placken* to beat into a thin plate]

plash (plæʃ) *vb., n.* a less common word for **splash**. [OE *plæsc*, prob. imit.] —'**plashy** *adj.*

-plasia or **-plasy** *n. combining form.* indicating growth, development, or change. [from NL, from Gk *plasis* a moulding, from *plassein* to mould] —**-plastic** *adj. combining form.*

plasm ('plæzəm) *n.* **1.** protoplasm of a specified type: *germ plasm*. **2.** a variant of **plasma**.

-plasm *n. combining form.* (in biology) indicating the material forming cells: *protoplasm*. [from Gk *plasma* something moulded; see PLASMA] —**-plasmic** *adj. combining form.*

plasma ('plæzmə) or **plasm** *n.* **1.** the clear yellowish fluid portion of blood or lymph in which the corpuscles and cells are suspended. **2.** Also called: **blood plasma**. a sterilized preparation of such fluid, taken from the blood, for use in transfusions. **3.** a former name for **protoplasm** or **cytoplasm**. **4.** *Physics.* a hot ionized gas containing positive ions and electrons. **5.** a green variety of chalcedony. [C18: from LL: something moulded, from Gk, from *plassein* to mould] —**plasmatic** (plæz'mætɪk) or '**plasmic** *adj.*

plasma torch *n.* an electrical device for converting a gas into a plasma, used for melting metal, etc.

plasmid ('plæzmɪd) *n.* a small circle of bacterial DNA that is independent of the main bacterial chromosome. Plasmids often contain genes for drug resistances and can be transmitted between bacteria of the same and different species: used in genetic engineering. [C20: from PLASM + -ID[1]]

plasmodium (plæz'məʊdɪəm) *n., pl.* **-dia** (-dɪə). **1.** an amoeboid mass of protoplasm, containing many nuclei: a stage in the life cycle of certain organisms. **2.** a parasitic protozoan which causes malaria. [C19: NL; see PLASMA, -ODE[1]] —**plas'modial** *adj.*

plasmolysis (plæz'mɒlɪsɪs) *n.* the shrinkage of protoplasm away from cell walls that occurs as a result of excessive water loss, esp. in plant cells.

Plassey ('plæsɪ) *n.* a village in NE India, in W Bengal: scene of Clive's victory (1757) over Siraj-ud-daula, which established British supremacy over India.

-plast *n. combining form.* indicating a living cell or particle of living matter: *protoplast*. [from Gk *plastos* formed, from *plassein* to form]

plaster ('plɑːstə) *n.* **1.** a mixture of lime, sand, and water that is applied to a wall or ceiling as a soft paste that hardens when dry. **2.** *Brit.* an adhesive strip of material for dressing a cut, wound, etc. **3.** short for **mustard plaster** or **plaster of Paris**. ~*vb.* **4.** to coat (a wall, ceiling, etc.) with plaster. **5.** (*tr.*) to apply like plaster: *she plastered make-up on her face*. **6.** (*tr.*) to cause to lie flat or to adhere. **7.** (*tr.*) to apply a plaster cast to. **8.** (*tr.*) *Sl.* to strike or defeat with great force. [OE, from Med. L *plastrum* medicinal salve, building plaster, via L from Gk *emplastron* curative dressing] —'**plasterer** *n.*

plasterboard ('plɑːstəˌbɔːd) *n.* a thin rigid board, in the form of a layer of plaster compressed between two layers of fibreboard, used to form or cover walls, etc.

plastered ('plɑːstəd) *adj. Sl.* intoxicated; drunk.

plaster of Paris *n.* **1.** a white powder that sets to a hard solid when mixed with water, used for making sculptures and casts, as an additive for lime plasters, and for making casts for setting broken limbs. **2.** the hard plaster produced when this powder is mixed with water. [C15: from Med. L *plastrum parisiense*, orig. made from the gypsum of *Paris*]

plastic ('plæstɪk) *n.* **1.** any one of a large number of synthetic materials that have a polymeric structure and can be moulded when soft and then set. Plastics are used in the manufacture of many articles and in coatings, artificial fibres, etc. ~*adj.* **2.** made of plastic. **3.** easily influenced; impressionable. **4.** capable of being moulded or formed. **5. a.** of moulding or modelling: *the plastic arts*. **b.** produced or apparently produced by moulding: *the plastic draperies of Giotto's figures*. **6.** having the power to form or influence: *the plastic forces of the imagination*. **7.** *Biol.* able to change, develop, or grow: *plastic tissues*. **8.** *Sl.* superficially attractive yet unoriginal or artificial: *plastic food*. [C17: from L *plasticus* relating to moulding, from Gk *plastikos*, from *plassein* to form] —'**plastically** *adv.* —**plasticity** (plæ'stɪsɪtɪ) *n.*

-plastic *adj. combining form.* growing or forming. [from Gk *plastikos*; see PLASTIC]

plastic bomb *n.* a bomb consisting of plastic explosive fitted around a detonator.

plastic bullet *n.* a bullet consisting of a cylinder of plastic about four inches long, generally causing less severe injuries than an ordinary bullet, and used esp. for riot control. Also called: **baton round**.

plastic explosive *n.* an adhesive jelly-like explosive substance.

Plasticine ('plæstɪˌsiːn) *n. Trademark.* a soft coloured material used, esp. by children, for modelling.

plasticize or **-cise** ('plæstɪˌsaɪz) *vb.* to make or become plastic, as by the addition of a plasticizer. —ˌ**plastici'zation** or **-ci'sation** *n.*

plasticizer or **-ciser** ('plæstɪˌsaɪzə) *n.* any of a number of substances added to materials. Their uses include softening and improving the flexibility of plastics and preventing dried paint coatings from becoming too brittle.

plastic money *n.* credit cards as opposed to cash.

plastic surgery *n.* the branch of surgery concerned with therapeutic or cosmetic repair or re-formation of missing, injured, or malformed tissues or parts. —**plastic surgeon** *n.*

plastid ('plæstɪd) *n.* any of various small particles in the cells of plants and some animals which contain starch, oil, protein, etc. [C19: via G from Gk *plastēs* sculptor, from *plassein* to form]

plastron ('plæstrən) *n.* the bony plate forming the ventral part of the shell of a tortoise or turtle. [C16: via F from It. *piastrone*, from *piastra* breastplate, from L *emplastrum* PLASTER] —'**plastral** *adj.*

-plasty n. *combining form.* indicating plastic surgery: *rhinoplasty.* [from Gk *-plastia;* see -PLAST]

plat[1] (plæt) n. a small area of ground; plot. [C16 (also in ME place names): orig. a var. of PLOT[2]]

plat[2] (plæt) vb. **platting, platted,** n. a dialect variant spelling of **plait.** [C16]

Plata (*Spanish* 'plata) n. **Río de la** ('rio de la). an estuary on the SE coast of South America, between Argentina and Uruguay, formed by the Uruguay and Paraná Rivers. Length: 275 km (171 miles). Width: (at its mouth) 225 km (140 miles). Also called: **La Plata.** English name: (River) **Plate.**

Plataea (plə'ti:ə) n. an ancient city in S Boeotia, traditionally an ally of Athens: scene of the defeat of a great Persian army by the Greeks in 479 B.C.

platan ('plætən) n. another name for **plane tree.** [C14: see PLANE TREE]

plat du jour ('pla: də 'ʒʊə; *French* pla dy zur) n., pl. **plats du jour** ('pla:z də 'ʒʊə; *French* pla dy zur). the specially prepared or recommended dish of the day on a restaurant's menu. [F, lit.: dish of the day]

plate (pleɪt) n. **1. a.** a shallow usually circular dish made of porcelain, earthenware, glass, etc., on which food is served. **b.** (*as modifier*): *a plate rack.* **2. a.** Also called: **plateful.** the contents of a plate. **b.** *Austral. & N.Z.* a plate of cakes, sandwiches, etc., brought by a guest to a party: *everyone was asked to bring a plate.* **3.** an entire course of a meal: *a cold plate.* **4.** any shallow receptacle, esp. for receiving a collection in church. **5.** flat metal of uniform thickness obtained by rolling, usually having a thickness greater than about three millimetres. **6.** a thin coating of metal usually on another metal, as produced by electrodeposition. **7.** metal or metalware that has been coated in this way: *Sheffield plate.* **8.** dishes, cutlery, etc., made of gold or silver. **9.** a sheet of metal, plastic, rubber, etc., having a printing surface produced by a process such as stereotyping. **10.** a print taken from such a sheet or from a woodcut. **11.** a thin flat sheet of a substance, such as metal or glass. **12.** a small piece of metal, plastic, etc., designed to bear an inscription and to be fixed to another surface. **13.** armour made of overlapping or articulated pieces of thin metal. **14.** *Photog.* a sheet of glass, or sometimes metal, coated with photographic emulsion on which an image can be formed by exposure to light. **15.** a device for straightening teeth. **16.** an informal word for **denture** (sense 1). **17.** *Anat.* any flat platelike structure. **18. a.** a cup awarded to the winner of a sporting contest, esp. a horse race. **b.** a race or contest for such a prize. **19.** any of the rigid layers of the earth's lithosphere. **20.** *Electronics, chiefly U.S.* the anode in an electronic valve. **21.** a horizontal timber joist that supports rafters. **22.** a light horseshoe for flat racing. **23.** *R.C. Church.* Also called: **Communion plate.** a flat plate held under the chin of a communicant in order to catch any fragments of the consecrated Host. **24. on a plate.** acquired without trouble: *he was handed the job on a plate.* **25. on one's plate.** waiting to be done or dealt with. ~vb. (tr.) **26.** to coat (a surface, usually metal) with a thin layer of other metal by electrolysis, etc. **27.** to cover with metal plates, as for protection. **28.** *Printing.* to make a stereotype or electrotype from (type or another plate). **29.** to form (metal) into plate, esp. by rolling. [C13: from OF: thin metal sheet, something flat, from Vulgar L *plattus* (unattested)]

Plate (pleɪt) n. **River.** the English name for the (Río de la) **Plata.**

plateau ('plætəʊ) n., pl. **-eaus** or **-eaux** (-əʊz). **1.** a wide mainly level area of elevated land. **2.** a relatively long period of stability; levelling off: *the rising prices reached a plateau.* [C18: from F, from OF *platel* something flat, from *plat* flat]

Plateau ('plætəʊ) n. a state of central Nigeria, formed in 1976 from part of Benue-Plateau State: tin mining. Capital: Jos. Pop.: 3 313 600 (1983 est.). Area: 31 350 sq. km (12 102 sq. miles).

plated ('pleɪtɪd) adj. **a.** coated with a layer of metal. **b.** (*in combination*): *gold-plated.*

plate glass n. glass formed into a thin sheet by rolling, used for windows, etc.

platelayer ('pleɪt,leɪə) n. *Brit.* a workman who lays and maintains railway track. U.S. equivalent: **trackman.**

platelet ('pleɪtlɪt) n. a minute particle occurring in the blood of vertebrates and involved in the clotting of the blood. [C19: a small PLATE]

platen ('plætən) n. **1.** a flat plate in a printing press that presses the paper against the type. **2.** the roller on a typewriter, against which the keys strike. [C15: from OF *platine,* from *plat* flat]

plater ('pleɪtə) n. **1.** a person or thing that plates. **2.** *Horse racing.* a mediocre horse entered chiefly for minor races.

plate tectonics n. (*functioning as sing.*) *Geol.* the study of the earth's crust with reference to the theory that the lithosphere is divided into rigid blocks (plates) that float on semimolten rock and are thus able to interact with each other at their boundaries.

platform ('plætfɔ:m) n. **1.** a raised floor or other horizontal surface. **2.** a raised area at a railway station, from which passengers have access to the trains. **3.** See **drilling platform. 4.** the declared principles, aims, etc., of a political party, etc. **5. a.** the thick raised sole of some shoes. **b.** (*as modifier*): *platform shoes.* **6.** a vehicle or level place on which weapons are mounted and fired. [C16: from F *plateforme,* from *plat* flat + *forme* layout]

platform ticket n. a ticket for admission to railway platforms but not for travel.

Plath (plæθ) n. **Sylvia.** 1932–63, U.S. poet living in England. She wrote two volumes of verse, *The Colossus* (1960) and *Ariel* (1965), and a novel, *The Bell Jar* (1963).

plating ('pleɪtɪŋ) n. **1.** a coating or layer of material, esp. metal. **2.** a layer or covering of metal plates.

platiniridium (,plætɪnɪ'rɪdɪəm) n. any alloy of platinum and iridium.

platinize or **-nise** ('plætɪ,naɪz) vb. (tr.) to coat with platinum. —,platini'zation or **-ni'sation** n.

platinum ('plætɪnəm) n. a ductile malleable silvery-white metallic element, very resistant to heat and chemicals: used in jewellery, laboratory apparatus, electrical contacts, dentistry, electroplating, and as a catalyst. Symbol: Pt; atomic no.: 78; atomic wt.: 195.09. [C19: NL, from Sp. *platina* silvery element, from *plata* silver, from Provençal: silver plate + the suffix *-um*]

platinum black n. *Chem.* a black powder consisting of very finely divided platinum metal.

platinum-blond or (*fem.*) **platinum-blonde** adj. **1.** (of hair) of a pale silver-blond colour. **2. a.** having hair of this colour. **b.** (*as n.*): *she was a platinum blonde.*

platinum metal n. any of the group of precious metallic elements consisting of ruthenium, rhodium, palladium, osmium, iridium, and platinum.

platitude ('plætɪ,tju:d) n. **1.** a trite, dull, or obvious remark. **2.** staleness or insipidity of thought or language; triteness. [C19: from F, lit.: flatness, from *plat* flat] —,plati'tudinous adj.

platitudinize or **-ise** (,plætɪ'tju:dɪ,naɪz) vb. (intr.) to speak or write in platitudes.

Plato ('pleɪtəʊ) n. ?427–?347 B.C., Greek philosopher: with his teacher Socrates and his pupil Aristotle, he is regarded as the initiator of western philosophy. His influential theory of ideas, which makes a distinction between objects of sense perception and the universal ideas or forms of which they are an expression, is formulated in such dialogues as *Phaedo, Symposium,* and *The Republic.* Other works include *The Apology* and *Laws.*

Platonic (plə'tɒnɪk) adj. **1.** of or relating to Plato or his teachings. **2.** (*often not cap.*) free from physical desire: *Platonic love.* —**Pla'tonically** adv.

Platonic solid n. any of the five possible regular polyhedrons: cube, tetrahedron, octahedron, icosahedron, and dodecahedron.

Platonism ('pleɪtə,nɪzəm) n. the teachings of Plato and his followers; esp. the philosophical theory that the meanings of general words are real entities (forms) and that particular objects have properties in common by virtue of their relationship with these forms. —'Platonist n.

platoon (plə'tu:n) n. **1.** *Mil.* a subunit of a company, usually comprising three sections of ten to twelve men. **2.** a group of people sharing a common activity, etc. [C17: from F *peloton* little ball, group of men, from *pelote* ball; see PELLET]

Plattdeutsch (*German* 'platdɔytʃ) n. another name for **Low German.** [lit.: flat German]

Platte (plæt) n. a river system of the central U.S., formed by the confluence of the **North Platte** and **South Platte**

at North Platte, Nebraska: flows generally east to the Missouri River. Length: 499 km (310 miles).

platteland ('platə,lant) n. **the.** (in South Africa) the area outside the cities and chief towns. [C20: from Afrik., from Du *plat* flat + *land* country]

platter ('plætə) n. a large shallow usually oval dish or plate. [C14: from Anglo-Norman *plater*, from *plat* dish, from OF *plat* flat; see PLATE]

platy- *combining form.* indicating something flat, as **platyhelminth,** the flatworm. [from Gk *platus* flat]

platypus ('plætɪpəs) n., pl. **-puses.** See **duck-billed platypus.** [C18: NL, from PLATY- + *-pus*, from Gk *pous* foot]

platyrrhine ('plætɪ,raɪn) or **platyrrhinian** (,plætɪ'rɪnɪən) adj. **1.** (esp. of New World monkeys) having widely separated nostrils opening to the side of the face. **2.** (of a human) having an unusually short wide nose. [C19: from NL *platyrrhinus*, from PLATY- + *-rrhinus*, from Gk *rhis* nose]

plaudit ('plɔːdɪt) n. (*usually pl.*) **1.** an expression of enthusiastic approval. **2.** a round of applause. [C17: from earlier *plaudite*, from L: applaud!, from *plaudere* to APPLAUD]

Plauen (*German* 'plauən) n. a city in S central East Germany: textile centre. Pop.: 78 800 (1981).

plausible ('plɔːzɪbᵊl) adj. **1.** apparently reasonable, valid, truthful, etc.: *a plausible excuse.* **2.** apparently trustworthy or believable: *a plausible speaker.* [C16: from L *plausibilis* worthy of applause, from *plaudere* to APPLAUD] —,**plausi'bility** or **'plausibleness** n. —**'plausibly** adv.

Plautus ('plɔːtəs) n. **Titus Maccius** ('taɪtəs 'mæksɪəs). ?254–?184 B.C., Roman comic dramatist. His 21 extant works, adapted from Greek plays, esp. those by Menander, include *Menaechmi* (the basis of Shakespeare's *The Comedy of Errors*), *Miles Gloriosus*, *Rudens*, and *Captivi*.

play (pleɪ) vb. **1.** to occupy oneself in (a sport or diversion). **2.** (*tr.*) to contend against (an opponent) in a sport or game: *Ed played Tony at chess and lost.* **3.** to fulfil or cause to fulfil (a particular role) in a team game: *he plays in the defence.* **4.** (*intr.;* often foll. by *about* or *around*) to behave carelessly, esp. in a way that is unconsciously cruel or hurtful: *to play about with a young girl's affections.* **5.** (when *intr.*, often foll. by *at*) to perform or act the part (of) in or as in a dramatic production. **6.** to perform (a dramatic production). **7. a.** to have the ability to perform on (a musical instrument): *David plays the harp.* **b.** to perform as specified: *he plays out of tune.* **8.** (*tr.*) **a.** to reproduce (a piece of music, note, etc.) on an instrument. **b.** to perform works by: *to play Brahms.* **9.** to discharge or cause to discharge: *he played the water from the hose onto the garden.* **10.** to cause (a radio, etc.) to emit sound. **11.** to move freely, quickly, or irregularly: *lights played on the scenery.* **12.** (*tr.*) *Stock Exchange.* to speculate or operate aggressively for gain in (a market). **13.** (*tr.*) *Angling.* to attempt to tire (a hooked fish) by alternately letting out and reeling in line. **14.** to put (a card, counter, piece, etc.) into play. **15.** to gamble. **16. play fair** (*or* **false**). (often foll. by *with*) to prove oneself fair (*or* unfair) in one's dealings. **17. play for time.** to delay the outcome of some activity so as to gain time to one's own advantage. **18. play into the hands of.** to act directly to the advantage of (an opponent). ~n. **19.** a dramatic composition written for performance by actors on a stage, etc.; drama. **20.** the performance of a dramatic composition. **21. a.** games, exercise, or other activity undertaken for pleasure, esp. by children. **b.** (*in combination*): *playroom.* **22.** conduct: *fair play.* **23.** the playing of a game or the period during which a game is in progress: *rain stopped play.* **24.** *U.S.* a manoeuvre in a game: *a brilliant play.* **25.** the situation of a ball, etc., that is within the defined area and being played according to the rules (in **in play, out of play**). **26.** gambling. **27.** activity or operation: *the play of the imagination.* **28.** freedom of movement: *too much play in the rope.* **29.** light, free, or rapidly shifting motion: *the play of light on the water.* **30.** fun, jest, or joking: *I only did it in play.* **31. call into play.** to bring into operation. **32. make a play for.** *Inf.* to make an obvious attempt to gain. ~See also **play along, playback,** etc. [OE *plega* (n.), *plegan* (vb.)] —**'playable** adj.

play-act vb. **1.** (*intr.*) to pretend or make believe. **2.** (*intr.*) to behave in an overdramatic or affected manner.

3. to act in or as in (a play). —**'play-,acting** n. —**'play-,actor** n.

play along vb. (*adv.*) **1.** (*intr.;* usually foll. by *with*) to cooperate (with), esp. as a temporary measure. **2.** (*tr.*) to manipulate as if in a game, esp. for one's own advantage: *he played the widow along until she gave him her money.*

playback ('pleɪ,bæk) n. **1.** the act or process of reproducing a recording, esp. on magnetic tape. **2.** the part of a tape recorder serving to reproduce or used for reproducing recorded material. ~vb. **play back.** (*adv.*) **3.** to reproduce (recorded material) on (a magnetic tape) by means of a tape recorder.

playbill ('pleɪ,bɪl) n. **1.** a poster or bill advertising a play. **2.** the programme of a play.

playboy ('pleɪ,bɔɪ) n. a man, esp. one of private means, who devotes himself to the pleasures of nightclubs, female company, etc.

play down vb. (*tr., adv.*) to make little or light of; minimize the importance of.

player ('pleɪə) n. **1.** a person who participates in or is skilled at some game or sport. **2.** a person who plays a game or sport professionally. **3.** a person who plays a musical instrument. **4.** an actor.

Player ('pleɪə) n. **Gary** ('gærɪ). born 1935, South African professional golfer: won the British Open Championship (1959; 1968; 1974) and the U.S. Open Championship (1965).

player piano n. a mechanical piano; Pianola.

playful ('pleɪful) adj. **1.** full of high spirits and fun: *a playful kitten.* **2.** good-natured and humorous: *a playful remark.* —**'playfully** adv.

playgoer ('pleɪ,gəuə) n. a person who goes to theatre performances, esp. frequently.

playground ('pleɪ,graund) n. **1.** an outdoor area for children's play, esp. one having swings, slides, etc., or adjoining a school. **2.** a place popular as a sports or holiday resort.

playgroup ('pleɪ,gruːp) n. a regular meeting of small children for supervised creative play.

playhouse ('pleɪ,haus) n. **1.** a theatre. **2.** *U.S.* a small house for children to play in.

playing card n. one of a pack of 52 rectangular pieces of stiff card, used for playing a wide variety of games, each card having one or more symbols of the same kind on the face, but an identical design on the reverse.

playing field n. *Chiefly Brit.* a field or open space used for sport.

playlet ('pleɪlɪt) n. a short play.

playlist ('pleɪ,lɪst) n. a list of records chosen for playing, as on a radio station.

playmate ('pleɪ,meɪt) or **playfellow** n. a friend or partner in play or recreation.

play off vb. (*adv.*) **1.** (*tr.;* usually foll. by *against*) to manipulate as if in playing a game: *to play one person off against another.* **2.** (*intr.*) to take part in a play-off. ~n. **play-off. 3.** *Sport.* an extra contest to decide the winner when competitors are tied. **4.** *Chiefly U.S. & Canad.* a contest or series of games to determine a championship.

play on vb. (*intr.*) **1.** (*adv.*) to continue to play. **2.** (*prep.*) Also: **play upon.** to exploit or impose upon (the feelings or weakness of another).

play on words n. another term for **pun**[1].

playpen ('pleɪ,pen) n. a small enclosure, usually portable, in which a young child can be left to play in safety.

playschool ('pleɪ,skuːl) n. an informal nursery group for preschool children.

plaything ('pleɪ,θɪŋ) n. **1.** a toy. **2.** a person regarded or treated as a toy.

playtime ('pleɪ,taɪm) n. a time for play or recreation, esp. the school break.

play up vb. (*adv.*) **1.** (*tr.*) to highlight: *to play up one's best features.* **2.** *Brit. inf.* to behave irritatingly (towards). **3.** (*intr.*) *Brit. inf.* (of a machine, etc.) to function erratically: *the car is playing up again.* **4.** to hurt; give (one) trouble: *my back's playing up again.* **5. play up to. a.** to support (another actor) in a performance. **b.** to try to gain favour with by flattery.

playwright ('pleɪ,raɪt) n. a person who writes plays.

plaza ('plɑːzə) n. **1.** an open space or square, esp. in Spain. **2.** *Chiefly U.S. & Canad.* a modern complex of shops, buildings, and parking areas. [C17: from Sp., from L *platēa* courtyard; see PLACE]

plc *or* **PLC** *abbrev. for* public limited company.

plea (pliː) *n.* **1.** an earnest entreaty or request. **2. a.** *Law.* something alleged by or on behalf of a party to legal proceedings in support of his claim or defence. **b.** *Criminal law.* the answer made by an accused to the charge: *a plea of guilty.* **c.** (in Scotland and formerly in England) a suit or action at law. [C13: from Anglo-Norman *plai,* from OF *plaid* lawsuit, from Med. L *placitum* court order (lit.: what is pleasing), from L *placēre* to please]

plead (pliːd) *vb.* **pleading, pleaded, plead** (plɛd), *or esp. Scot. & U.S.* **pled. 1.** (when *intr.,* often foll. by *with*) to appeal earnestly or humbly (to). **2.** (*tr.; may take a clause as object*) to give as an excuse: *to plead ignorance.* **3.** *Law.* to declare oneself to be (guilty or not guilty) in answer to the charge. **4.** *Law.* to advocate (a case) in a court of law. **5.** (*intr.*) *Law.* **a.** to file pleadings. **b.** to address a court as an advocate. [C13: from OF *plaidier,* from Med. L *placitāre* to have a lawsuit, from L *placēre* to please] — **'pleadable** *adj.* — **'pleader** *n.*

pleadings ('pliːdɪŋz) *pl. n. Law.* the formal written statements presented alternately by the plaintiff and defendant in a lawsuit.

pleasance ('plɛzəns) *n.* **1.** a secluded part of a garden laid out with trees, walks, etc. **2.** *Arch.* enjoyment or pleasure. [C14 *plesaunce,* from OF *plaisance,* ult. from *plaisir* to PLEASE]

pleasant ('plɛzᵊnt) *adj.* **1.** giving or affording pleasure; enjoyable. **2.** having pleasing or agreeable manners, appearance, habits, etc. **3.** *Obs.* merry and lively. [C14: from OF *plaisant,* from *plaisir* to PLEASE] — **'pleasantly** *adv.*

Pleasant Island *n.* the former name of **Nauru.**

pleasantry ('plɛzᵊntrɪ) *n., pl.* **-ries. 1.** (*often pl.*) an agreeable or amusing remark, etc., often one made in order to be polite: *they exchanged pleasantries.* **2.** an agreeably humorous manner or style. [C17: from F *plaisanterie,* from *plaisant* PLEASANT]

please (pliːz) *vb.* **1.** to give satisfaction, pleasure, or contentment to (a person). **2.** to be the will of or have the will (to): *if it pleases you; the court pleases.* **3. if you please.** if you will or wish, sometimes used in ironic exclamation. **4. pleased with.** happy because of. **5. please oneself.** to do as one likes. ~*adv.* **6.** (*sentence modifier*) used in making polite requests, pleading, etc. **7. yes please.** a polite formula for accepting an offer, invitation, etc. [C14 *plese,* from OF *plaisir,* from L *placēre*] — **pleased** *adj.* — **pleasedly** ('pliːzɪdlɪ) *adv.*

Pleasence ('plɛzəns) *n. Donald.* born 1919, British actor. His films include *Dr Crippen* (1962) and *Cul de Sac* (1966).

pleasing ('pliːzɪŋ) *adj.* giving pleasure; likable or gratifying. — **'pleasingly** *adv.*

pleasurable ('plɛʒərəbᵊl) *adj.* enjoyable, agreeable, or gratifying. — **'pleasurably** *adv.*

pleasure ('plɛʒə) *n.* **1.** an agreeable or enjoyable sensation or emotion: *the pleasure of hearing good music.* **2.** something that gives enjoyment: *his garden was his only pleasure.* **3. a.** amusement, recreation, or enjoyment. **b.** (*as modifier*): *a pleasure ground.* **4.** *Euphemistic.* sexual gratification: *he took his pleasure of her.* **5.** a person's preference. ~*vb.* **6.** (when *intr.,* often foll. by *in*) *Arch.* to give pleasure to or take pleasure (in). [C14 *plesir,* from OF]

pleat (pliːt) *n.* **1.** any of various types of fold formed by doubling back fabric, etc., and pressing, stitching, or steaming into place. ~*vb.* **2.** (*tr.*) to arrange (material, part of a garment, etc.) in pleats. [C16: var. of PLAIT]

pleb (plɛb) *n.* **1.** short for **plebeian. 2.** *Brit. inf., often derog.* a common vulgar person.

plebeian (plə'biːən) *adj.* **1.** of or characteristic of the common people, esp. those of ancient Rome. **2.** lacking refinement; philistine or vulgar: *plebeian tastes.* ~*n.* **3.** one of the common people, esp. one of the Roman plebs. **4.** a person who is coarse, vulgar, etc. [C16: from L *plēbēius* of the people, from *plēbs* the common people of ancient Rome] — **ple'beian,ism** *n.*

plebiscite ('plɛbɪ,saɪt, -sɪt) *n.* **1.** a direct vote by the electorate of a state, region, etc., on some question, usually of national importance. **2.** any expression of public opinion on some matter. ~See also **referendum.** [C16: from OF *plébiscite,* from L *plēbiscitum* decree of the people, from *plēbs* the populace + *scīscere* to decree, from *scīre* to know] — **plebiscitary** (plə'bɪsɪtərɪ, -trɪ) *adj.*

plectrum ('plɛktrəm) *or* **plectron** ('plɛktrən) *n., pl.* **-tra** (-trə), **-trums** *or* **-tra, -trons.** any implement for plucking a string, such as a small piece of plastic, wood, etc., used to strum a guitar. [C17: from L, from Gk *plektron,* from *plessein* to strike]

pled (plɛd) *vb. U.S. or* (*esp. in legal usage*) *Scot.* a past tense and past participle of **plead.**

pledge (plɛdʒ) *n.* **1.** a formal or solemn promise or agreement. **2. a.** collateral for the payment of a debt or the performance of an obligation. **b.** the condition of being collateral (esp. in **in pledge**). **3.** a token: *the gift is a pledge of their sincerity.* **4.** an assurance of support or goodwill, conveyed by drinking a toast: *we drank a pledge to their success.* **5.** a person who binds himself, as by becoming bail or surety for another. **6. take** *or* **sign the pledge.** to make a vow to abstain from alcoholic drink. ~*vb.* **7.** to promise formally or solemnly. **8.** (*tr.*) to bind by or as if by a pledge: *they were pledged to secrecy.* **9.** to give or offer (one's word, freedom, property, etc.) as a guarantee, as for the repayment of a loan. **10.** to drink a toast to (a person, cause, etc.). [C14: from OF *plege,* from LL *plebium* security, from *plebīre* to pledge, of Gmc origin] — **'pledgable** *adj.* — **'pledger** *or* **'pledgor** *n.*

pledgee (plɛdʒ'iː) *n.* **1.** a person to whom a pledge is given. **2.** a person to whom property is delivered as a pledge.

pledget ('plɛdʒɪt) *n.* a small flattened pad of wool, cotton, etc., esp. for use as a pressure bandage to be applied to wounds. [C16: from ?]

-plegia *n. combining form.* indicating a specified type of paralysis: *paraplegia.* [from Gk, from *plēgē* stroke, from *plessein* to strike] — **-plegic** *adj. and n. combining form.*

pleiad ('plaɪəd) *n.* a brilliant or talented group, esp. one with seven members. [C16: orig. F *Pléiade,* name given by Ronsard to himself and six other poets, ult. after the PLEIADES]

Pleiades ('plaɪə,diːz) *pl. n. Greek myth.* the seven daughters of Atlas, placed as stars in the sky either to save them from the pursuit of Orion or, in another account, after they had killed themselves for grief over the death of their half-sisters the Hyades.

Pleiocene ('plaɪəu,siːn) *adj., n.* a variant spelling of **Pliocene.**

Pleistocene ('plaɪstə,siːn) *adj.* **1.** of, denoting, or formed in the first epoch of the Quaternary period. It was characterized by extensive glaciations of the N hemisphere and the evolutionary development of man. ~*n.* **2. the.** the Pleistocene epoch or rock series. [C19: from Gk *pleistos* most + *kainos* recent]

plenary ('pliːnərɪ, 'plɛn-) *adj.* **1.** full, unqualified, or complete: *plenary powers; plenary indulgence.* **2.** (of assemblies, councils, etc.) attended by all the members. [C15: from LL *plēnārius,* from L *plēnus* full] — **'plenarily** *adv.*

plenipotentiary (,plɛnɪpə'tɛnʃərɪ) *adj.* **1.** (esp. of a diplomatic envoy) invested with or possessing full authority. **2.** conferring full authority. **3.** (of power or authority) full; absolute. ~*n., pl.* **-aries. 4.** a person invested with full authority to transact business, esp. a diplomat authorized to represent a country. See also **envoy**[1] (sense 1). [C17: from Med. L *plēnipotentiārius,* from L *plēnus* full + *potentia* POWER]

plenitude ('plɛnɪ,tjuːd) *n.* **1.** abundance. **2.** the condition of being full or complete. [C15: via OF from L *plēnitūdō,* from *plēnus* full]

plenteous ('plɛntɪəs) *adj.* **1.** ample; abundant: *a plenteous supply of food.* **2.** producing or yielding abundantly: *a plenteous grape harvest.* [C13 *plenteus,* from OF, from *plentif,* from *plenté* PLENTY] — **'plenteously** *adv.* — **'plenteousness** *n.*

plentiful ('plɛntɪful) *adj.* **1.** ample; abundant. **2.** having or yielding an abundance: *a plentiful year.* — **'plentifully** *adv.* — **'plentifulness** *n.*

plenty ('plɛntɪ) *n., pl.* **-ties. 1.** (often foll. by *of*) a great number, amount, or quantity; lots: *plenty of time; there are plenty of cars on display here.* **2.** ample supplies or resources: *the age of plenty.* **3. in plenty.** existing in abundance: *food in plenty.* ~*determiner.* **4. a.** very many; ample: *plenty of people believe in ghosts.* **b.** (*as pron.*): *that's plenty, thanks.* ~*adv.* **5.** *Inf.* fully or abundantly: *the coat was plenty big enough.* [C13: from OF *plenté,* from LL *plēnitās* fullness, from L *plēnus* full]

Plenty ('plɛntɪ) *n.* **Bay of.** a large bay of the Pacific on the NE coast of the North Island, New Zealand.

plenum ('pli:nəm) n., pl. **-nums** or **-na** (-nə). **1.** an enclosure containing gas at a higher pressure than the surrounding environment. **2.** a fully attended meeting. **3.** (esp. in the philosophy of the Stoics) space regarded as filled with matter. [C17: from L: space filled with matter, from *plēnus* full]

pleochroism (plɪ'ɒkrəʊˌɪzəm) n. a property of certain crystals of absorbing light waves selectively and therefore of showing different colours when looked at from different directions. [C19: from Gk *pleiōn* more, from *polus* many + *-chroism* from *khrōs* skin colour] —**pleochroic** (ˌpliːə'krəʊɪk) adj.

pleomorphism (ˌpliːə'mɔːfɪzəm) or **pleomorphy** ('pliːəˌmɔːfɪ) n. **1.** the occurrence of more than one different form in the life cycle of a plant or animal. **2.** another word for **polymorphism** (sense 2). —ˌpleo'morphic adj.

pleonasm ('pliːəˌnæzəm) n. Rhetoric. **1.** the use of more words than necessary or an instance of this, such as *a tiny little child*. **2.** a word or phrase that is superfluous. [C16: from L *pleonasmus*, from Gk *pleonasmos* excess, from *pleonazein* to be redundant] —ˌpleo'nastic adj.

plesiosaur ('pliːsɪəˌsɔː) n. any of various marine reptiles of Jurassic and Cretaceous times, having a long neck, short tail, and paddle-like limbs. [C19: from NL *plēsiosaurus*, from Gk *plēsios* near + *sauros* a lizard]

plethora ('plɛθərə) n. **1.** superfluity or excess; overabundance. **2.** Pathol., obs. a condition caused by dilation of superficial blood vessels, characterized esp. by a reddish face. [C16: via Med. L from Gk *plēthōrē* fullness, from *plēthein* to grow full] —**plethoric** (plɛ'θɒrɪk) adj.

pleura ('plʊərə) n., pl. **pleurae** ('plʊəriː). the thin transparent membrane enveloping the lungs and lining the walls of the thoracic cavity. [C17: via Med. L from Gk: side, rib] —'pleural adj.

pleurisy ('plʊərɪsɪ) n. inflammation of the pleura, characterized by pain that is aggravated by deep breathing or coughing. [C14: from OF *pleurisie*, from LL, from Gk *pleuritis*, from *pleura* side] —**pleuritic** (plʊ'rɪtɪk) adj., n.

pleuro- or before a vowel **pleur-** combining form. **1.** of or relating to the side. **2.** indicating the pleura. [from Gk *pleura* side]

pleuropneumonia (ˌplʊərəʊnjuː'məʊnɪə) n. the combined disorder of pleurisy and pneumonia.

Pleven (Bulgarian 'plɛvɛn) or **Plevna** (Bulgarian 'plɛvna) n. a town in N Bulgaria: taken by Russia from the Turks in 1877 after a siege of 143 days. Pop.: 129 782 (1985).

Plexiglas ('plɛksɪˌglɑːs) n. U.S. trademark. a transparent plastic, polymethyl methacrylate, used for combs, plastic sheeting, etc.

plexor ('plɛksə) or **plessor** n. Med. a small hammer with a rubber head for use in percussion of the chest and testing reflexes. [C19: from Gk *plēxis* a stroke, from *plēssein* to strike]

plexus ('plɛksəs) n., pl. **-uses** or **-us.** **1.** any complex network of nerves, blood vessels, or lymphatic vessels. **2.** an intricate network or arrangement. [C17: NL, from L *plectere* to braid]

pliable ('plaɪəb°l) adj. easily moulded, bent, influenced, or altered. —ˌplia'bility or 'pliableness n. —'pliably adv.

pliant ('plaɪənt) adj. **1.** easily bent; supple: *a pliant young tree*. **2.** adaptable; yielding readily to influence; compliant. [C14: from OF, from *plier* to fold; see PLY²] —'pliancy n. —'pliantly adv.

plicate ('plaɪkeɪt) or **plicated** adj. having or arranged in parallel folds or ridges; pleated: *a plicate leaf; plicate rock strata.* [C18: from L *plicātus* folded, from *plicāre* to fold] —pli'cation n.

plié ('pliːeɪ) n. a classic ballet practice posture with back erect and knees bent. [F: bent]

plier ('plaɪə) n. a person who plies a trade.

pliers ('plaɪəz) pl. n. a gripping tool consisting of two hinged arms usually with serrated jaws. [C16: from PLY¹]

plight¹ (plaɪt) n. a condition of extreme hardship, danger, etc. [C14 *plit*, from OF *pleit* fold; prob. infl. by OE *pliht* PLIGHT²]

plight² (plaɪt) vb. (tr.) **1.** to promise formally or pledge (allegiance, support, etc.). **2. plight one's troth.** to make a promise, esp. of marriage. ~n. **3.** Arch. or dialect. a solemn promise, esp. of engagement; pledge. [OE *pliht* peril] —'plighter n.

plimsoll or **plimsole** ('plɪmsəl) n. Brit. a light rubber-soled canvas shoe worn for various sports. Also called: **gym shoe.** [C20: from the resemblance of the sole to a Plimsoll line]

Plimsoll line ('plɪmsəl) n. another name for **load line.** [C19: after Samuel *Plimsoll* (1824–98), English MP, who advocated its adoption]

plinth (plɪnθ) n. **1.** the rectangular slab or block that forms the lowest part of the base of a column, pedestal, or pier. **2.** Also called: **plinth course.** the lowest part of the wall of a building, esp. one that is formed of a course of stone or brick. **3.** a flat block on either side of a door-frame, where the architrave meets the skirting. [C17: from L *plinthus*, from Gk *plinthos* brick]

Pliny ('plɪnɪ) n. **1.** known as *Pliny the Elder*. Latin name *Gaius Plinius Secundus*. 23–79 A.D., Roman writer, the author of the encyclopedic *Natural History* (77). **2.** his nephew, known as *Pliny the Younger*. Latin name *Gaius Plinius Caecilius Secundus*. ?62–?113 A.D., Roman writer and administrator, noted for his letters.

Pliocene or **Pleiocene** ('plaɪəʊˌsiːn) adj. **1.** of, denoting, or formed in the last epoch of the Tertiary period, during which many modern mammals appeared. ~n. **2. the.** the Pliocene epoch or rock series. [C19: from Gk *pleiōn* more, from *polus* many + *-cene* from *kainos* recent]

plissé ('pliːseɪ, 'plɪs-) n. **1.** fabric with a wrinkled finish, achieved by treatment involving caustic soda: *cotton plissé.* **2.** such a finish on a fabric. [F: pleated]

PLO abbrev. for Palestine Liberation Organization.

plod (plɒd) vb. **plodding, plodded.** **1.** to make (one's way) or walk along (a path, etc.) with heavy usually slow steps. **2.** (intr.) to work slowly and perseveringly. ~n. **3.** the act of plodding. [C16: imit.] —'plodder n. —'plodding adj. —'ploddingly adv.

Ploeşti (Romanian plo'jeʃtj) n. a city in SE central Romania: centre of the Romanian petroleum industry. Pop.: 234 021 (1985).

-ploid adj. and n. combining form. indicating a specific multiple of a single set of chromosomes: *diploid*. [from Gk *-pl(oos)* -fold + -OID] —'ploidy n. combining form.

plonk¹ (plɒŋk) vb. **1.** (often foll. by *down*) to drop or be dropped heavily: *he plonked the money on the table.* ~n. **2.** the act or sound of plonking. [var. of PLUNK]

plonk² (plɒŋk) n. Inf. alcoholic drink, usually wine, esp. of inferior quality. [C20: ?from F *blanc* white, as in *vin blanc* white wine]

plonker ('plɒŋkə) n. Sl. a stupid person. [C20: from PLONK¹]

plop (plɒp) n. **1.** the characteristic sound made by an object dropping into water without a splash. ~vb. **plopping, plopped.** **2.** to fall or cause to fall with the sound of a plop: *the stone plopped into the water.* ~interj. **3.** an exclamation imitative of this sound: *to go plop.* [C19: imit.]

plosion ('pləʊʒən) n. Phonetics. the sound of an abrupt break or closure, esp. the audible release of a stop. Also called: **explosion.**

plosive ('pləʊsɪv) Phonetics. ~adj. **1.** accompanied by plosion. ~n. **2.** a plosive consonant; stop. [C20: from F, from *explosif* EXPLOSIVE]

plot¹ (plɒt) n. **1.** a secret plan to achieve some purpose, esp. one that is illegal or underhand. **2.** the story or plan of a play, novel, etc. **3.** Mil. a graphic representation of an individual or tactical setting that pinpoints an artillery target. **4.** Chiefly U.S. a diagram or chart. ~vb. **plotting, plotted.** **5.** to plan secretly (something illegal, revolutionary, etc.); conspire. **6.** (tr.) to mark (a course, as of a ship or aircraft) on a map. **7.** (tr.) to make a plan or map of. **8. a.** to locate and mark (points) on a graph by means of coordinates. **b.** to draw (a curve) through these points. **9.** (tr.) to construct the plot of (a literary work, etc.). [C16: from PLOT²; infl. by obs. *complot* conspiracy, from OF, from ?] —'plotter n.

plot² (plɒt) n. a small piece of land: *a vegetable plot.* [OE]

Plotinus (pləʊ'taɪnəs) n. ?205–?270 A.D., Roman Neo-Platonist philosopher, born in Egypt.

plough or esp. U.S. **plow** (plaʊ) n. **1.** an agricultural implement with sharp blades for cutting or turning over the earth. **2.** any of various similar implements, such as a device for clearing snow. **3.** ploughed land. **4. put one's hand to the plough.** to begin or undertake a task. ~vb. **5.** to till (the soil, etc.) with a plough. **6.** to make (furrows or grooves) in (something) with or as if with a plough. **7.** (when intr., usually foll. by *through*) to move (through something) in the manner of a plough. **8.** (*intr.*; foll. by *through*) to work at slowly or perseveringly. **9.** (*intr.*; foll. by *into* or *through*) (of a vehicle) to run uncontrollably into something in its path. **10.** (*intr.*) *Brit. sl.* to fail an examination. [OE *plōg* plough land] —**'plougher** or *esp. U.S.* **'plower** *n.*

Plough (plaʊ) *n.* **the.** the group of the seven brightest stars in the constellation Ursa Major. Also called: **Charles's Wain.** Usual U.S. name: the **Big Dipper.**

plough back *vb.* (*tr.*, *adv.*) to reinvest (the profits of a business) in the same business.

ploughman or *esp. U.S.* **plowman** ('plaʊmən) *n.*, *pl.* **-men.** a man who ploughs, esp. using horses.

ploughman's lunch *n.* a snack lunch, served esp. in a pub, consisting of bread and cheese with pickle.

ploughshare or *esp. U.S.* **plowshare** ('plaʊˌʃɛə) *n.* the horizontal pointed cutting blade of a mouldboard plough.

Plovdiv (*Bulgarian* 'plɔvdif) *n.* a city in S Bulgaria on the Maritsa River: the second largest town in Bulgaria; conquered by Philip II of Macedonia in 341 B.C.; capital of Roman Thracia; commercial centre of a rich agricultural region. Pop.: 342 201 (1985). Greek name: **Philippopolis.**

plover ('plʌvə) *n.* **1.** any of a family of shore birds, typically having a round head, straight bill, and large pointed wings. **2. green plover.** another name for **lapwing.** [C14: from OF *plovier* rainbird, from L *pluvia* rain]

plow (plaʊ) *n.*, *vb.* the usual U.S. spelling of **plough.**

Plowright ('plaʊˌraɪt) *n.* **Joan.** born 1929, British actress, married to Lord Olivier.

ploy (plɔɪ) *n.* **1.** a manoeuvre or tactic in a game, conversation, etc. **2.** any business, job, hobby, etc., with which one is occupied: *angling is his latest ploy.* **3.** *Chiefly Brit.* a frolic, escapade, or practical joke. [C18: orig. Scot. & N English, obs. n. sense of EMPLOY meaning an occupation]

PLP (in Britain) *abbrev. for* Parliamentary Labour Party.

PLR *abbrev. for* Public Lending Right.

pluck (plʌk) *vb.* **1.** (*tr.*) to pull off (feathers, fruit, etc.) from (a fowl, tree, etc.). **2.** (when *intr.*, foll. by *at*) to pull or tug. **3.** (*tr.*; foll. by *off*, *away*, etc.) *Arch.* to pull (something) forcibly or violently (from something or someone). **4.** (*tr.*) to sound the strings) of (a musical instrument) with the fingers, a plectrum, etc. **5.** (*tr.*) *Sl.* to fleece or swindle. ~*n.* **6.** courage, usually in the face of difficulties or hardship. **7.** a sudden pull or tug. **8.** the heart, liver, and lungs, esp. of an animal used for food. [OE *pluccian*, *plyccan*] —**'plucker** *n.*

pluck up *vb.* (*tr.*, *adv.*) **1.** to pull out; uproot. **2.** to muster (courage, one's spirits, etc.).

plucky ('plʌkɪ) *adj.* **pluckier, pluckiest.** having or showing courage in the face of difficulties, danger, etc. —**'pluckily** *adv.* —**'pluckiness** *n.*

plug (plʌg) *n.* **1.** a piece of wood, cork, or other material, used to stop up holes or waste pipes or as a wedge for taking a screw or nail. **2.** a device having one or more pins to which an electric cable is attached: used to make an electrical connection when inserted into a socket. **3.** Also called: **volcanic plug.** a mass of solidified magma filling the neck of an extinct volcano. **4.** See **sparking plug. 5. a.** a cake of pressed or twisted tobacco, esp. for chewing. **b.** a small piece of such a cake. **6.** *Inf.* a favourable mention of a product, show, etc., as on television. ~*vb.* **plugging, plugged. 7.** (*tr.*) to stop up or secure (a hole, gap, etc.) with or as if with a plug. **8.** (*tr.*) to insert or use (something) as a plug: *to plug a finger into one's ear.* **9.** (*tr.*) *Inf.* to make favourable and often-repeated mentions of (a song, product, show, etc.), as on television. **10.** (*tr.*) *Sl.* to shoot: *he plugged six rabbits.* **11.** (*tr.*) *Sl.* to punch. **12.** (*intr.*; foll. by *along*, *away*, etc.) *Inf.* to work steadily or persistently. [C17: from MDu. *plugge*] —**'plugger** *n.*

plughole ('plʌɡˌhəʊl) *n.* a hole in a sink, etc., through which waste water drains and which can be closed with a plug.

plug in *vb.* (*tr.*, *adv.*) to connect (an electrical appliance, etc.) with a power source by means of an electrical plug.

plug-ugly *adj.* **1.** *Inf.* extremely ugly. ~*n.*, *pl.* **-uglies. 2.** *U.S. sl.* a city tough; ruffian. [C19: from ?]

plum (plʌm) *n.* **1.** a small rosaceous tree with an edible oval fruit that is purple, yellow, or green and contains an oval stone. **2.** the fruit of this tree. **3.** a raisin, as used in a cake or pudding. **4. a.** a dark reddish-purple colour. **b.**

(*as adj.*): *a plum carpet.* **5.** *Inf.* **a.** something of a superior or desirable kind, such as a financial bonus. **b.** (*as modifier*): *a plum job.* [OE *plūme*]

plumage ('plu:mɪdʒ) *n.* the layer of feathers covering the body of a bird. [C15: from OF, from *plume* feather, from L *plūma* down]

plumate ('plu:meɪt, -mɪt) or **plumose** *adj. Zool., bot.* **1.** of or possessing feathers or plumes. **2.** covered with small hairs: *a plumate seed.* [C19: from L *plumātus* covered with feathers; see PLUME]

plumb (plʌm) *n.* **1.** a weight, usually of lead, suspended at the end of a line and used to determine water depth or verticality. **2.** the perpendicular position of a freely suspended plumb line (esp. in *out of plumb, off plumb*). ~*adv. also* **plumb. 3.** vertical or perpendicular. **4.** *Inf., chiefly U.S.* (intensifier): *plumb stupid.* **5.** *Inf.* exactly; precisely. ~*vb.* **6.** (*tr.*; often foll. by *up*) to test the alignment of or adjust to the vertical with a plumb line. **7.** (*tr.*) to experience (the worst extremes of): *to plumb the depths of despair.* **8.** (*tr.*) to understand or master (something obscure): *to plumb a mystery.* **9.** to connect or join (a device such as a tap) to a water pipe or drainage system. [C13: from OF *plomb* (unattested) lead line, from *plon* lead, from L *plumbum*] —**'plumbable** *adj.*

plumbago (plʌm'beɪɡəʊ) *n.*, *pl.* **-gos. 1.** a plant of warm regions, having clusters of blue, white, or red flowers. **2.** another name for **graphite.** [C17: from L: lead ore, translation of Gk *polubdaina*, from *polubdos* lead]

plumber ('plʌmə) *n.* a person who installs and repairs pipes, fixtures, etc., for water, drainage, and gas. [C14: from OF *plommier* worker in lead, from LL *plumbārius*, from L *plumbum* lead]

plumbing ('plʌmɪŋ) *n.* **1.** the trade or work of a plumber. **2.** the pipes, fixtures, etc., used in a water, drainage, or gas installation. **3.** the act or process of using a plumb.

plumbism ('plʌmˌbɪzəm) *n.* chronic lead poisoning. [C19: from L *plumbum* lead]

plumb line *n.* a string with a metal weight, or **plumb bob,** at one end that, when suspended, points directly towards the earth's centre of gravity and so is used to determine verticality, depth, etc.

plumb rule *n.* a plumb line attached to a narrow board, used by builders, surveyors, etc.

plume (plu:m) *n.* **1.** a feather, esp. one that is large or ornamental. **2.** a feather or cluster of feathers worn esp. formerly as a badge or ornament in a headband, hat, etc. **3.** *Biol.* any feathery part. **4.** something that resembles a plume: *a plume of smoke.* **5.** a token or decoration of honour; prize. ~*vb.* (*tr.*) **6.** to adorn with feathers or plumes. **7.** (of a bird) to clean or preen (itself or its feathers). **8.** (foll. by *on* or *upon*) to pride or congratulate (oneself). [C14: from OF, from L *plūma* downy feather]

plummet ('plʌmɪt) *vb.* **1.** (*intr.*) to drop down; plunge. ~*n.* **2.** the weight on a plumb line; plumb bob. **3.** a lead plumb used by anglers. [C14: from OF *plommet* ball of lead, from *plomb* lead, from L *plumbum* lead]

plummy ('plʌmɪ) *adj.* **-mier, -miest. 1.** of, full of, or resembling plums. **2.** *Brit. inf.* (of speech) deep, refined, and somewhat drawling. **3.** *Brit. inf.* choice; desirable.

plumose ('plu:məʊs, -məʊz) *adj.* another word for **plumate.** [C17: from L *plūmōsus* feathery]

plump[1] (plʌmp) *adj.* **1.** well filled out or rounded; chubby: *a plump turkey.* **2.** bulging; full: *a plump wallet.* ~*vb.* **3.** (often foll. by *up* or *out*) to make or become plump: *to plump up a pillow.* [C15 (meaning: dull, rude), C16 (in current senses): ?from MDu. *plomp* blunt] —**'plumply** *adv.* —**'plumpness** *n.*

plump[2] (plʌmp) *vb.* **1.** (often foll. by *down, into,* etc.) to drop or fall suddenly and heavily. **2.** (*intr.*; foll. by *for*) to give support (to) or make a choice (of) one out of a group or number. ~*n.* **3.** a heavy abrupt fall or the sound of this. ~*adv.* **4.** suddenly or heavily. **5.** straight down; directly: *the helicopter landed plump in the middle of the field.* ~*adj., adv.* **6.** in a blunt, direct, or decisive manner. [C14: prob. imit.]

plum pudding *n. Brit.* a boiled or steamed pudding made with flour, suet, sugar, and dried fruit.

plumule ('plu:mju:l) *n.* **1.** the embryonic shoot of seed-bearing plants. **2.** a down feather of young birds. [C18: from LL *plūmula* a little feather]

plumy ('plu:mɪ) *adj.* **plumier, plumiest. 1.** plumelike; feathery. **2.** consisting of, covered with, or adorned with feathers.

plunder ('plʌndə) vb. 1. to steal (valuables, goods, sacred items, etc.) from (a town, church, etc.) by force, esp. in time of war; loot. 2. (tr.) to rob or steal (choice or desirable things) from (a place): to plunder an orchard. ~n. 3. anything taken by plundering; booty. 4. the act of plundering; pillage. [C17: prob. from Du. plunderen (orig.: to plunder household goods)] —'**plunderer** n.

plunge (plʌndʒ) vb. 1. (usually foll. by into) to thrust or throw (something, oneself, etc.): they plunged into the sea. 2. to throw or be thrown into a certain condition: the room was plunged into darkness. 3. (usually foll. by into) to involve or become involved deeply (in). 4. (intr.) to move or dash violently or with great speed or impetuosity. 5. (intr.) to descend very suddenly or steeply: the ship plunged in heavy seas; a plunging neckline. 6. (intr.) Inf. to speculate or gamble recklessly, for high stakes, etc. ~n. 7. a leap or dive. 8. Inf. a swim; dip. 9. a pitching or tossing motion. 10. **take the plunge.** Inf. to resolve to do something dangerous or irrevocable. [C14: from OF plongier, from Vulgar L plumbicāre (unattested) to sound with a plummet, from L plumbum lead]

plunger ('plʌndʒə) n. 1. a rubber suction cup used to clear blocked drains, etc. 2. a device or part of a machine that has a plunging or thrusting motion; piston. 3. Inf. a reckless gambler.

plunk (plʌŋk) vb. 1. to pluck (the strings) of (a banjo, etc.) or (of such an instrument) to give forth a sound when plucked. 2. (often foll. by down) to drop or be dropped, esp. heavily or suddenly. ~n. 3. the act or sound of plunking. [C20: imit.]

pluperfect (plu:'pɜ:fɪkt) adj., n. Grammar. another term for **past perfect.** [C16: from L plūs quam perfectum more than perfect]

plural ('pluərəl) adj. 1. containing, involving, or composed of more than one. 2. denoting a word indicating that more than one referent is being referred to or described. ~n. 3. Grammar. **a.** the plural number. **b.** a plural form. [C14: from OF plurel, from LL plūrālis concerning many, from L plūs more] —'**plurally** adv.

pluralism ('pluərə,lɪzəm) n. 1. the holding by a single person of more than one ecclesiastical benefice or office; plurality. 2. Sociol. a theory of society as several autonomous but interdependent groups. 3. the existence in a society of groups having distinctive ethnic origin, cultural forms, religions, etc. 4. Philosophy. **a.** the metaphysical doctrine that reality consists of more than two basic types of substance. Cf. **monism, dualism. b.** the metaphysical doctrine that reality consists of independent entities rather than one unchanging whole. —'**pluralist** n., adj. —,**plural'istic** adj.

plurality (pluə'rælɪt) n., pl. **-ties.** 1. the state of being plural. 2. Maths. a number greater than one. 3. the U.S. term for **relative majority.** 4. a large number. 5. the greater number; majority. 6. another word for **pluralism** (sense 1).

pluralize or **-ise** ('pluərə,laɪz) vb. 1. (intr.) to hold more than one ecclesiastical benefice or office at the same time. 2. to make or become plural.

pluri- combining form. denoting several. [from L plur-, plus more, plures several]

plus (plʌs) prep. 1. increased by the addition of: four plus two. 2. with or with the addition of: a good job, plus a new car. ~adj. 3. (prenominal) indicating or involving addition: a plus sign. 4. another word for **positive** (senses 7, 8). 5. on the positive part of a scale or coordinate axis: a value of +x. 6. indicating the positive side of an electrical circuit. 7. involving advantage: a plus factor. 8. (postpositive) Inf. having a value above that which is stated: she had charm plus. 9. (postpositive) slightly above a specified standard: he received a B+ grade for his essay. ~n. 10. short for **plus sign.** 11. a positive quantity. 12. Inf. something positive or to the good. 13. a gain, surplus, or advantage. ~Mathematical symbol: + [C17: from L: more]
▷ Usage. Plus, together with, and along with do not create compound subjects in the way that and does: the number of the verb depends on that of the subject to which plus, together with, or along with is added: this task, plus all the others, was (not were) undertaken by the government.

plus fours pl. n. men's baggy knickerbockers reaching below the knee, now only worn for golf, etc. [C20: because

made with four inches of material to hang over at the knee]

plush (plʌʃ) n. 1. a fabric with a cut pile that is longer and softer than velvet. ~adj. 2. Also: **plushy.** Inf. lavishly appointed; rich; costly. [C16: from F pluche, from OF peluchier to pluck, ult. from L pilus a hair] —'**plushly** adv.

plus sign n. the symbol +, indicating addition or positive quantity.

Plutarch ('plu:tɑ:k) n. ?46–?120 A.D., Greek biographer and philosopher, noted for his Parallel Lives of distinguished Greeks and Romans.

Pluto[1] ('plu:təu) n. Gk myth. the god of the underworld; Hades. —**Plu'tonian** adj.

Pluto[2] ('plu:təu) n. the smallest planet and the farthest known from the sun. [L, from Gk Ploutōn, lit.: the rich one]

plutocracy (plu:'tɒkrəsɪ) n., pl. **-cies.** 1. the rule of society by the wealthy. 2. a state or government characterized by the rule of the wealthy. 3. a class that exercises power by virtue of its wealth. [C17: from Gk ploutokratia, from ploutos wealth + -kratia rule] —**plutocratic** (,plu:tə'krætɪk) adj. —,**pluto'cratically** adv.

plutocrat ('plu:tə,kræt) n. a member of a plutocracy.

pluton ('plu:tɒn) n. any mass of igneous rock that has solidified below the surface of the earth. [C20: back formation from PLUTONIC]

plutonic (plu:'tɒnɪk) adj. (of igneous rocks) derived from magma that has cooled and solidified below the surface of the earth. [C20: after PLUTO[1]]

plutonium (plu:'təunɪəm) n. a highly toxic metallic transuranic element. It occurs in trace amounts in uranium ores and is produced in a nuclear reactor by neutron bombardment of uranium-238. The most stable isotope, **plutonium-239,** readily undergoes fission and is used as a reactor fuel. Symbol: Pu; atomic no.: 94; half-life of ^{239}Pu: 24 360 years. [C20: after PLUTO[2] because Pluto lies beyond Neptune and plutonium was discovered soon after NEPTUNIUM]

Plutus ('plu:təs) n. the Greek god of wealth. [from Gk ploutos wealth]

pluvial ('plu:vɪəl) adj. 1. of, characterized by, or due to the action of rain; rainy. ~n. 2. Geol. a period of persistent heavy rainfall. [C17: from L pluviālis rainy, from pluvia rain]

pluviometer (,plu:vɪ'ɒmɪtə) n. another name for **rain gauge.** —**pluviometric** (,plu:vɪə'metrɪk) adj. —,**pluvi-o'metrically** adv.

ply[1] (plaɪ) vb. **plying, plied.** (mainly tr.) 1. to carry on, pursue, or work at (a job, trade, etc.). 2. to manipulate or wield (a tool, etc.). 3. to sell (goods, wares, etc.), esp. at a regular place. 4. (usually foll. by with) to provide (with) or subject (to) repeatedly or persistently: he plied us with drink; he plied the speaker with questions. 5. (intr.) to work steadily or diligently. 6. (also intr.) (esp. of a ship, etc.) to travel regularly along (a route) or in (an area): to ply the trade routes. [C14 plye, short for aplye to APPLY]

ply[2] (plaɪ) n., pl. **plies.** 1. **a.** a layer, fold, or thickness, as of yarn. **b.** (in combination): four-ply. 2. a thin sheet of wood glued to other similar sheets to form plywood. 3. one of the strands twisted together to make rope, yarn, etc. [C15: from OF pli fold, from plier to fold, from L plicāre]

Plymouth ('plɪməθ) n. 1. a port in SW England, in SW Devon on **Plymouth Sound** (an inlet of the English Channel): Britain's chief port in Elizabethan times; the last port visited by the Pilgrim Fathers in the Mayflower before sailing to America; naval base. Pop.: 243 895 (1981). 2. a city in SE Massachusetts, on **Plymouth Bay:** the first permanent European settlement in New England; founded by the Pilgrim Fathers. Pop.: 35 913 (1980).

Plymouth Brethren pl. n. a religious sect founded about 1827, strongly Puritanical in outlook and having no organized ministry.

plywood ('plaɪ,wud) n. a structural board consisting of thin layers of wood glued together under pressure, with the grain of one layer at right angles to the grain of the adjoining layer.

Plzeň (Czech 'plzɛnj) n. an industrial city in W Czechoslovakia. Pop.: 175 000 (1986). German name: **Pilsen.**

pm *abbrev. for* premium.

Pm *the chemical symbol for* promethium.

PM *abbrev. for:* **1.** Past Master (of a fraternity). **2.** Paymaster. **3.** Postmaster. **4.** Prime Minister. **5.** *Mil.* Provost Marshal.

p.m., P.M., pm, *or* **PM** *abbrev. for:* **1.** (indicating the time from midday to midnight) post meridiem. [L: after noon] **2.** post-mortem (examination).

PMG *abbrev. for:* **1.** Paymaster General. **2.** Postmaster General.

PMS *abbrev. for* premenstrual syndrome.

PMT *abbrev. for* premenstrual tension.

PNdB *abbrev. for* perceived noise decibel.

pneumatic (njʊˈmætɪk) *adj.* **1.** of or concerned with air, gases, or wind. **2.** (of a machine or device) operated by compressed air or by a vacuum. **3.** containing compressed air: *a pneumatic tyre.* **4.** (of the bones of birds) containing air spaces which reduce their weight as an adaptation to flying. ~*n.* **5.** a pneumatic tyre. [C17: from LL *pneumaticus* of air or wind, from Gk, from *pneuma* breath, wind] —**pneuˈmatically** *adv.*

pneumatics (njʊˈmætɪks) *n.* (*functioning as sing.*) the branch of physics concerned with the mechanical properties of gases, esp. air.

pneumatology (ˌnjuːməˈtɒlədʒɪ) *n.* **1.** the branch of theology concerned with the Holy Ghost and other spiritual beings. **2.** an obsolete name for **psychology** (the science).

pneumatophore (njuːˈmætəʊˌfɔː) *n.* **1.** a specialized root of certain swamp plants, such as the mangrove, that branches upwards and undergoes gaseous exchange with the atmosphere. **2.** a polyp such as the Portuguese man-of-war, that is specialized as a float.

pneumococcus (ˌnjuːməʊˈkɒkəs) *n., pl.* **-cocci** (-ˈkɒksaɪ). a bacterium that causes pneumonia.

pneumoconiosis (ˌnjuːməʊˌkəʊnɪˈəʊsɪs) *or* **pneumonoconiosis** (ˌnjuːmənəʊˌkəʊnɪˈəʊsɪs) *n.* any disease of the lungs or bronchi caused by the inhalation of metallic or mineral particles. [C19: shortened from *pneumonoconiosis*, from Gk *pneumōn* lung + *-coniosis*, from *konis* dust]

pneumoencephalogram (ˌnjuːməʊɛnˈsɛfələˌɡræm) *n.* See **encephalogram.**

pneumogastric (ˌnjuːməʊˈɡæstrɪk) *adj. Anat.* **1.** of or relating to the lungs and stomach. **2.** a former term for **vagus.**

pneumonectomy (ˌnjuːməʊˈnɛktəmɪ) *or* **pneumectomy** *n., pl.* **-mies.** the surgical removal of a lung or part of a lung. [C20: from Gk *pneumōn* lung + -ECTOMY]

pneumonia (njuːˈməʊnɪə) *n.* inflammation of one or both lungs, in which the air sacs (alveoli) become filled with liquid. [C17: NL from Gk from *pneumōn* lung] —**pneumonic** (njuːˈmɒnɪk) *adj.*

pneumothorax (ˌnjuːməʊˈθɔːræks) *n.* the abnormal presence of air between the lung and the wall of the chest (pleural cavity), resulting in collapse of the lung.

p-n junction *n. Electronics.* a boundary between a p-type and n-type semiconductor that functions as a rectifier and is used in diodes and junction transistors.

Pnom Penh (ˈnɒm ˈpɛn) *n.* a variant spelling of **Phnom Penh.**

po (pəʊ) *n., pl.* **pos.** *Brit.* an informal word for **chamber pot.** [C19: from POT¹]

Po¹ *the chemical symbol for* polonium.

Po² (pəʊ) *n.* a river in N Italy, rising in the Cottian Alps and flowing northeast to Turin, then east to the Adriatic: the longest river in Italy. Length: 652 km (405 miles). Latin name: **Padus.**

PO *abbrev. for:* **1.** Personnel Officer. **2.** petty officer. **3.** Pilot Officer. **4.** Also: **p.o.** postal order. **5.** Post Office.

poach¹ (pəʊtʃ) *vb.* **1.** to catch (game, fish, etc.) illegally by trespassing on private property. **2.** to encroach on or usurp (another person's rights, duties, etc.) or steal (an idea, employee, etc.). **3.** *Tennis, badminton, etc.* to take or play (shots that should belong to one's partner). **4.** to break up (land) into wet muddy patches, as by riding over it. [C17: from OF *pocher*, of Gmc origin] —**ˈpoacher** *n.*

poach² (pəʊtʃ) *vb.* to simmer (eggs, fish, etc.) very gently in water, milk, stock, etc. [C15: from OF *pochier* to enclose in a bag (as the yolks are enclosed by the whites)] —**ˈpoacher** *n.*

Pocahontas (ˌpɒkəˈhɒntəs) *n.* original name *Matoaka;* married name *Rebecca Rolfe.* ?1595–1617, American Indian, who allegedly saved the colonist Captain John Smith from being killed.

pochard (ˈpəʊtʃəd) *n., pl.* **-chards** *or* **-chard.** any of various diving ducks, esp. a European variety, the male of which has a grey-and-black body and a reddish head. [C16: from ?]

pock (pɒk) *n.* **1.** any pustule resulting from an eruptive disease, esp. from smallpox. **2.** another word for **pockmark** (sense 1). [OE *pocc*] —**ˈpocky** *adj.*

pocket (ˈpɒkɪt) *n.* **1.** a small bag or pouch in a garment for carrying small articles, money, etc. **2.** any bag or pouch or anything resembling this. **3.** *S. African.* a bag or sack of vegetables or fruit. **4.** a cavity in the earth, etc., such as one containing ore. **5.** a small enclosed or isolated area: *a pocket of resistance.* **6.** any of the six holes with pouches or nets let into the corners and sides of a billiard table. **7. in one's pocket.** under one's control. **8. in** *or* **out of pocket.** having made a profit or loss. **9. line one's pockets.** to make money, esp. by dishonesty when in a position of trust. **10.** (*modifier*) small: *a pocket edition.* ~*vb.* (*tr.*) **11.** to put into one's pocket. **12.** to take surreptitiously or unlawfully; steal. **13.** (*usually passive*) to confine in or as if in a pocket. **14.** to conceal or keep back: *he pocketed his pride and asked for help.* **15.** *Billiards, etc.* to drive (a ball) into a pocket. [C15: from Anglo-Norman *poket* a little bag, from *poque* bag, from MDu. *poke* bag] —**ˈpocketless** *adj.*

pocket battleship *n.* a small heavily armed battle cruiser specially built to conform with treaty limitations on tonnage and armament.

pocket billiards *n.* (*functioning as sing.*) *Billiards.* **1.** another name for **pool²** (sense 5). **2.** any game played on a table in which the object is to pocket the balls, esp. snooker and pool.

pocketbook (ˈpɒkɪtˌbʊk) *n. Chiefly U.S.* a small bag or case for money, papers, etc.

pocket borough *n.* (before the Reform Act of 1832) an English borough constituency controlled by one person or family who owned the land.

pocketful (ˈpɒkɪtfʊl) *n., pl.* **-fuls.** as much as a pocket will hold.

pocketknife (ˈpɒkɪtˌnaɪf) *n., pl.* **-knives.** a small knife with one or more blades that fold into the handle; penknife.

pocket money *n.* **1.** *Brit.* a small weekly sum of money given to children by parents as an allowance. **2.** money for day-to-day spending, incidental expenses, etc.

pockmark (ˈpɒkˌmɑːk) *n.* **1.** Also called: **pock.** a pitted scar left on the skin after the healing of a smallpox or similar pustule. **2.** any pitting of a surface that resembles or suggests such scars. ~*vb.* **3.** (*tr.*) to scar or pit with pockmarks.

poco (ˈpəʊkəʊ; *Italian* ˈpɔːko) *or* **un poco** *adj., adv.* (*in combination*) *Music.* a little; to a small degree. [from It.: little, from L *paucus* few]

poco a poco *adv.* (*in combination*) *Music.* little by little: *poco a poco rall.* [It.]

pod (pɒd) *n.* **1. a.** the fruit of any leguminous plant, consisting of a long two-valved case that contains seeds. **b.** the seedcase as distinct from the seeds. **2.** any similar fruit. **3.** a streamlined structure attached to an aircraft and used to house a jet engine, fuel tank, armament, etc. ~*vb.* **podding, podded. 4.** (*tr.*) to remove the pod from. [C17: ? back formation from earlier *podware* bagged vegetables]

-pod *or* **-pode** *n. combining form.* indicating a certain type or number of feet: *arthropod; tripod.* [from Gk *-podos* footed, from *pous* foot]

podagra (pəˈdæɡrə) *n.* gout of the foot or big toe. [C15: via L from Gk, from *pous* foot + *agra* a trap]

poddy (ˈpɒdɪ) *n., pl.* **-dies.** *Austral.* a handfed calf or lamb. [?from *poddy* (adj.) fat]

Podgorica *or* **Podgoritsa** (*Russian* ˈpɔdɡɔˌriːtsa) *n.* the former name (until 1946) of **Titograd.**

podgy (ˈpɒdʒɪ) *adj.* **podgier, podgiest. 1.** short and fat; chubby. **2.** (of the face, arms, etc.) unpleasantly chubby and pasty-looking. [C19: from *podge* a short plump person] —**ˈpodgily** *adv.* —**ˈpodginess** *n.*

podium (ˈpəʊdɪəm) *n., pl.* **-diums** *or* **-dia** (-dɪə). **1.** a small raised platform used by lecturers, conductors, etc. **2.** a plinth that supports a colonnade or wall. **3.** a low

wall surrounding the arena of an ancient amphitheatre.
4. *Zool.* any footlike organ, such as the tube foot of a star-fish. [C18: from L: platform, from Gk *podion* little foot, from *pous* foot]

-podium *n. combining form.* a part resembling a foot: *pseudopodium.* [from NL: footlike; see PODIUM]

Podolsk (*Russian* pa'dɔljsk) *n.* an industrial city in the W central Soviet Union, near Moscow. Pop.: 209 000 (1987).

podophyllin (ˌpɒdəʊ'fɪlɪn) *n.* a bitter yellow resin obtained from the dried underground stems of the May apple and mandrake: used as a cathartic. [C19: from NL *Podophyllum*, genus of herbs, from *podo-*, from Gk *pous* foot + *phullon* leaf]

-podous *adj. combining form.* having feet of a certain kind or number: *cephalopodous.*

podzol ('pɒdzɒl) *or* **podsol** ('pɒdsɒl) *n.* a type of soil characteristic of coniferous forest regions having a greyish-white colour in its upper layers from which certain minerals have leached. [C20: from Russian: ash ground]

Poe (pəʊ) *n.* **Edgar Allan.** 1809–49, U.S. short-story writer, poet, and critic. Most of his short stories, such as *The Fall of the House of Usher* (1839) and the *Tales of the Grotesque and Arabesque* (1840), are about death, decay, and madness. *The Murders in the Rue Morgue* (1841) is regarded as the first modern detective story.

poem ('pəʊɪm) *n.* **1.** a composition in verse, usually characterized by words chosen for their sound and suggestive power as well as for their sense, and using such techniques as metre, rhyme, and alliteration. **2.** a literary composition that is not in verse but exhibits the intensity of imagination and language common to it: *a prose poem.* **3.** anything resembling a poem in beauty, effect, etc. [C16: from L *poēma*, from Gk, var. of *poiēma* something created, from *poiein* to make]

poesy ('pəʊɪzɪ) *n., pl.* **-sies. 1.** an archaic word for **poetry. 2.** *Poetic.* the art of writing poetry. [C14: via OF from L *poēsis*, from Gk, from *poiēsis* poetic art, from *poiein* to make]

poet ('pəʊɪt) *or (sometimes when fem.)* **poetess** *n.* **1.** a person who writes poetry. **2.** a person with great imagination and creativity. [C13: from L *poēta*, from Gk *poiētēs* maker, poet]

poetaster (ˌpəʊɪ'tæstə, -'teɪ-) *n.* a writer of inferior verse. [C16: from Med. L; see POET, -ASTER]

poetic (pəʊ'ɛtɪk) *or* **poetical** *adj.* **1.** of poetry. **2.** characteristic of poetry, as in being elevated, sublime, etc. **3.** characteristic of a poet. **4.** recounted in verse. —**po'etically** *adv.*

poeticize (pəʊ'ɛtɪˌsaɪz), **poetize** ('pəʊɪˌtaɪz) *or* **poeticise, poetise** *vb.* **1.** (*tr.*) to put into poetry or make poetic. **2.** (*intr.*) to speak or write poetically.

poetic justice *n.* fitting retribution.

poetic licence *n.* justifiable departure from conventional rules of form, fact, etc., as in poetry.

poetics (pəʊ'ɛtɪks) *n.* (*usually functioning as sing.*) **1.** the principles and forms of poetry or the study of these. **2.** a treatise on poetry.

poet laureate *n., pl.* **poets laureate.** *Brit.* the poet appointed as court poet of Britain who is given a lifetime post in the Royal Household.

poetry ('pəʊɪtrɪ) *n.* **1.** literature in metrical verse. **2.** the art or craft of writing verse. **3.** poetic qualities, spirit, or feeling in anything. **4.** anything resembling poetry in rhythm, beauty, etc. [C14: from Med. L *poētria*, from L *poēta* POET]

po-faced *adj.* wearing a disapproving stern expression. [C20: changed from *poor-faced*]

pogo stick ('pəʊgəʊ) *n.* a stout pole with a handle at the top, steps for the feet and a spring at the bottom, so that the user can spring up, down, and along on it. [C20: from ?]

pogrom ('pɒgrəm) *n.* an organized persecution or extermination of an ethnic group, esp. of Jews. [C20: via Yiddish from Russian: destruction, from *po-* like + *grom* thunder]

Pohai (ˌpəʊ'haɪ) *n.* a variant transliteration of the Chinese name for **Bohai.**

pohutukawa (pəˌhuːtuː'kaːwə) *n.* a New Zealand tree which grows on the coast and produces red flowers in the summer. Also called: **Christmas tree.**

poi (pɔɪ) *n. N.Z.* a ball of woven New Zealand flax swung rhythmically by Maori women while performing poi dances.

poi dance *n. N.Z.* a women's formation dance that involves singing and manipulating a poi.

-poiesis *n. combining form.* indicating the act of making or producing something specified. [from Gk, from *poiēsis* a making; see POESY] —**poietic** *adj. combining form.*

poignant ('pɔɪnjənt, -nənt) *adj.* **1.** sharply distressing or painful to the feelings. **2.** to the point; cutting or piercing: *poignant wit.* **3.** keen or pertinent in mental appeal: *a poignant subject.* **4.** pungent in smell. [C14: from OF, from L *pungens* pricking, from *pungere* to sting] —'**poignancy** *or* '**poignance** *n.* —'**poignantly** *adv.*

poikilothermic (ˌpɔɪkɪləʊ'θɜːmɪk) *or* **poikilothermal** (ˌpɔɪkɪləʊ'θɜːməl) *adj.* (of all animals except birds and mammals) having a body temperature that varies with the temperature of the surroundings. [C19: from Gk *poikilos* various + THERMAL] —ˌpoikilo'thermy *n.*

Poincaré (*French* pwɛ̃kare) *n.* **1. Jules Henri** (ʒyl ɑ̃ri). 1854–1912, French mathematician, physicist, and philosopher. He made important contributions to the theory of functions and to astronomy and electromagnetic theory. **2.** his cousin, **Raymond** (rɛmɔ̃). 1860–1934, French statesman; premier of France (1912–13; 1922–24; 1926–29); president (1913–20).

poinciana (ˌpɔɪnsɪ'ɑːnə) *n.* a tree of a tropical genus having large orange or red flowers. [C17: NL, after M. de *Poinci,* 17th-cent. governor of the French Antilles]

poind (pɔɪnd) *vb.* (*tr.*) *Scots Law.* **1.** to take (property of a debtor, etc.) in execution of distress; distrain. **2.** to impound (stray cattle, etc.). [C15: from Scot., var. of OE *pyndan* to impound]

poinsettia (pɔɪn'sɛtɪə) *n.* a shrub of Mexico and Central America, widely cultivated for its showy scarlet bracts, which resemble petals. [C19: NL, after J. P. *Poinsett* (1799–1851), U.S. Minister to Mexico]

point (pɔɪnt) *n.* **1.** a dot or tiny mark. **2.** a location, spot, or position. **3.** any dot used in writing or printing, such as a decimal point or a full stop. **4.** the sharp tapered end of a pin, knife, etc. **5.** *Maths.* **a.** a geometric element having no dimensions whose position is located by means of its coordinates. **b.** a location: *point of inflection.* **6.** a small promontory. **7.** a specific condition or degree. **8.** a moment: *at that point he left the room.* **9.** a reason, aim, etc.: *the point of this exercise is to train new teachers.* **10.** an essential element in an argument: *I take your point.* **11.** a suggestion or tip. **12.** a detail or item. **13.** a characteristic, physical attribute, etc.: *he has his good points.* **14.** a distinctive characteristic or quality of an animal, esp. one used as a standard in judging livestock. **15.** (*often pl.*) any of the extremities, such as the tail, ears, or feet, of a domestic animal. **16.** (*often pl.*) *Ballet.* the tip of the toes. **17.** a single unit for measuring or counting, as in the scoring of a game. **18.** *Printing.* a unit of measurement equal to one twelfth of a pica. There are approximately 72 points to the inch. **19.** *Finance.* a unit of value used to quote security and commodity prices and their fluctuations. **20.** *Navigation.* **a.** one of the 32 marks on the compass indicating direction. **b.** the angle of 11°15′ between two adjacent marks. **21.** *Cricket.* a fielding position at right angles to the batsman on the off side and relatively near the pitch. **22.** either of the two electrical contacts that make or break the current flow in the distributor of an internal-combustion engine. **23.** *Brit.* (*often pl.*) a junction of railway tracks in which a pair of rails can be moved so that a train can be directed onto either of two lines. U.S. and Canad. equivalent: **switch. 24.** (*often pl.*) a piece of ribbon, cord, etc., with metal tags at the end: used during the 16th and 17th centuries to fasten clothing. **25.** *Brit.* short for **power point. 26.** the position of the body of a pointer or setter when it discovers game. **27.** *Boxing.* a mark awarded for a scoring blow, knockdown, etc. **28.** any diacritic used in a writing system, esp. in a phonetic transcription, to indicate modifications of vowels or consonants. **29.** *Jewellery.* a unit of weight equal to 0.01 carat. **30.** the act of pointing. **31. at** (*or on*) **the point of.** at the moment immediately before: *on the point of leaving the room.* **32. beside the point.** irrelevant. **33. case in point.** a specific or relevant instance. **34. make a point of. a.** to make (something) one's regular habit. **b.** to do (something) because one thinks it important. **35. not to put too fine a point on it.** to speak plainly and bluntly. **36. score points off.** to gain an advantage at someone else's expense. **37. to the point.** relevant. **38. up to a point.** not completely. ~*vb.* **39.** (usually foll. by *at* or *to*) to indicate the location or direction of by or as by extending (a finger or other pointed object) towards it: *he pointed to the front door; don't point that gun at me.* **40.** (*intr.;* usually foll. by *at* or *to*) to indicate or identify a specific person or thing among several: *all evidence pointed to Donald as the murderer.* **41.** (*tr.*) to direct or face in a specific direction: *point me in the right direction.* **42.** (*tr.*) to sharpen or taper. **43.** (*intr.*) (of gun dogs) to indicate the place where game is lying by standing rigidly with the muzzle turned in its direction. **44.** (*tr.*) to finish or repair the joints of (brickwork, masonry, etc.) with mortar or cement. **45.** (*tr.*) *Music.* to mark (a psalm text) with vertical lines to indicate the points at which the music changes during chanting. **46.** (*tr.*) *Phonetics.* to provide (a letter or letters) with diacritics. **47.** (*tr.*) to provide (a Hebrew or similar text) with vowel points. ~See also **point off, point out, point up.** [C13: from OF: spot, from L *punctum* a point, from *pungere* to pierce]

point-blank *adj.* **1. a.** aimed or fired at a target so close that it is unnecessary to make allowance for the drop in the course of the projectile. **b.** permitting such aim or fire without loss of accuracy: *at point-blank range.* **2.** aimed or fired at nearly zero range. **3.** plain or blunt: *a point-blank question.* ~*adv.* **4.** directly or straight. **5.** plainly or bluntly. [C16: from POINT + BLANK (in the sense: centre spot of an archery target)]

Point de Galle (pɔɪnt də 'ɡɑːlə) *n.* a former name of **Galle.**

point duty *n.* the stationing of a policeman or traffic warden at a road junction to control and direct traffic.

pointe (pɔɪnt) *n. Ballet.* the tip of the toe (esp. in **on pointes**). [from F: point]

Pointe-à-Pitre (*French* pwɛ̃tapitrə) *n.* the chief port of Guadeloupe, on SW Grande Terre Island in the Caribbean. Pop.: 25 310 (1982).

pointed ('pɔɪntɪd) *adj.* **1.** having a point. **2.** cutting or incisive: *a pointed wit.* **3.** obviously directed at a particular person or aspect: *pointed criticism.* **4.** emphasized or made conspicuous: *pointed ignorance.* **5.** (of an arch or style of architecture) Gothic. **6.** *Music.* (of a psalm text) marked to show changes in chanting. **7.** (of Hebrew text) with vowel points marked. — 'pointedly *adv.*

Pointe-Noire (*French* pwɛ̃tnwar) *n.* a port in the S Congo Republic, on the Atlantic: the country's chief port and former capital (1950–58). Pop.: 297 392 (1984).

pointer ('pɔɪntə) *n.* **1.** a person or thing that points. **2.** an indicator on a measuring instrument. **3.** a long rod or cane used by a lecturer to point to parts of a map, blackboard, etc. **4.** one of a breed of large smooth-coated gun dogs, usually white with black, liver, or lemon markings. **5.** a helpful piece of information.

pointillism ('pwæntɪˌlɪzəm) *n.* the technique of painting elaborated from impressionism, in which dots of unmixed colour are juxtaposed on a white ground so that from a distance they fuse in the viewer's eye into appropriate intermediate tones. [C19: from F, from *pointiller* to mark with tiny dots, from *pointille* little point, from It., from *punto* POINT] — 'pointillist *n.*, *adj.*

pointing ('pɔɪntɪŋ) *n.* the act or process of repairing or finishing joints in brickwork, masonry, etc., with mortar.

point lace *n.* lace made by a needle with buttonhole stitch on a paper pattern. Also called: **needlepoint.** Cf. **pillow lace.**

pointless ('pɔɪntlɪs) *adj.* **1.** without a point. **2.** without meaning, relevance, or force. **3.** *Sport.* without a point scored. — 'pointlessly *adv.*

point off *vb.* (*tr., adv.*) to mark off from the right-hand side (a number of decimal places) in a whole number to create a mixed decimal: *point off three decimal places in 12345 and you get 12.345.*

point of honour *n., pl.* **points of honour.** a circumstance, event, etc., that involves the defence of one's principles, social honour, etc.

point of no return *n.* **1.** a point at which an irreversible commitment must be made to an action, progression, etc. **2.** a point in a journey at which, if one continues, supplies will be insufficient for a return to the starting place.

point of order *n., pl.* **points of order.** a question raised in a meeting as to whether the rules governing procedures are being breached.

point of sale *n.* (in retail distribution) **a.** the place and time when a sale is made. **b.** (*as modifier*): *a point-of-sale display.*

point of view *n., pl.* **points of view.** **1.** a position from which someone or something is observed. **2.** a mental viewpoint or attitude.

point out *vb.* (*tr., adv.*) to indicate or specify.

pointsman ('pɔɪntsˌmæn, -mən) *n., pl.* **-men.** **1.** a person who operates railway points. **2.** a policeman or traffic warden on point duty.

point source *n. Optics.* a source of light or other radiation that can be considered to have negligible dimensions.

point-to-point *n. Brit.* a steeplechase organized by a recognized hunt or other body, usually restricted to amateurs riding horses that have been regularly used in hunting.

point up *vb.* (*tr., adv.*) to emphasize, esp. by identifying: *he pointed up the difficulties.*

poise[1] (pɔɪz) *n.* **1.** composure or dignity of manner. **2.** physical balance. **3.** equilibrium; stability. **4.** the position of hovering. ~*vb.* **5.** to be or cause to be balanced or suspended. **6.** (*tr.*) to hold, as in readiness: *to poise a lance.* [C16: from OF *pois* weight, from L *pēnsum*, from *pendere* to weigh]

poise[2] (pwɑːz, pɔɪz) *n.* the cgs unit of viscosity; the viscosity of a fluid in which a tangential force of 1 dyne per square centimetre maintains a difference in velocity of 1 centimetre per second between two parallel planes 1 centimetre apart. Symbol: P [C20: after Jean Louis Marie *Poiseuille* (1799–1869), F physician]

poised (pɔɪzd) *adj.* **1.** self-possessed; dignified. **2.** balanced and prepared for action.

poison ('pɔɪzən) *n.* **1.** any substance that can impair function or otherwise injure the body. **2.** something that destroys, corrupts, etc. **3.** a substance that retards a chemical reaction or the activity of a catalyst. **4.** a substance that absorbs neutrons in a nuclear reactor and thus slows down the reaction. ~*vb.* (*tr.*) **5.** to give poison to (a person or animal), esp. with intent to kill. **6.** to add poison to. **7.** to taint or infect with or as if with poison. **8.** (foll. by *against*) to turn (a person's mind) against: *he poisoned her mind against me.* **9.** to retard or stop (a chemical or nuclear reaction) by the action of a poison. [C13: from OF *puison* potion, from L *pōtiō* a drink, esp. a poisonous one, from *pōtāre* to drink] — 'poisoner *n.*

poison ivy *n.* any of several North American shrubs or climbing plants that cause an itching rash on contact.

poisonous ('pɔɪzənəs) *adj.* **1.** having the effects or qualities of a poison. **2.** capable of killing or inflicting injury. **3.** corruptive or malicious. — 'poisonously *adv.* — 'poisonousness *n.*

poison-pen letter *n.* a letter written in malice, usually anonymously, and intended to abuse, frighten, or insult the recipient.

poison sumach *n.* a swamp shrub of the southeastern U.S. that causes an itching rash on the skin.

Poisson distribution ('pwɑːsɔ̃n) *n. Statistics.* a distribution that represents the number of events occurring randomly in a fixed time at an average rate λ. [C19: after S. D. *Poisson* (1781–1840), F mathematician]

Poitiers (*French* pwatje) *n.* a city in S central France: capital of the former province of Poitou until 1790; scene of the battle (1356) in which the English under the Black Prince defeated the French; university (1432). Pop.: 79 725 (1983 est.).

Poitou (*French* pwatu) *n.* a former province of W central France, on the Atlantic. Chief town: Poitiers.

Poitou-Charentes (*French* pwatuʃarɑ̃t) *n.* a region of W central France, on the Bay of Biscay: mainly low-lying.

poke[1] (pəʊk) *vb.* **1.** (*tr.*) to jab or prod, as with the elbow, a stick, etc. **2.** (*tr.*) to make (a hole) or as by poking. **3.** (when *intr.*, often foll. by *at*) to thrust (at). **4.** (*tr.*) *Inf.* to hit with the fist; punch. **5.** (usually foll. by *in, through,* etc.) to protrude or cause to protrude: *don't poke your arm out of the window.* **6.** (*tr.*) to stir (a fire, etc.) by poking. **7.** (*intr.*) to meddle or intrude. **8.** (*intr.;* often foll. by *about* or *around*) to search or pry. **9. poke one's nose into.** to interfere with or meddle in. ~*n.* **10.** a jab or prod. **11.** *Inf.* a blow with one's fist; punch. [C14: from Low G & MDu. *poken* to prod]

poke[2] (pəʊk) *n.* **1.** *Dialect.* a pocket or bag. **2. a pig in a poke.** See **pig.** [C13: from OF *poque*, of Gmc origin]

poke[3] (pəʊk) *n.* **1.** Also called: **poke bonnet.** a bonnet with a brim that projects at the front, popular in the 18th and 19th centuries. **2.** the brim itself. [C18: from POKE[1] (in the sense: to project)]

poker[1] ('pəʊkə) *n.* a metal rod, usually with a handle, for stirring a fire.

poker[2] ('pəʊkə) *n.* a card game of bluff and skill in which bets are made on the hands dealt, the highest-ranking hand winning the pool. [C19: prob. from F *poque* similar card game]

poker face *n. Inf.* a face without expression, as that of a poker player attempting to conceal the value of his cards. — **'poker-,faced** *adj.*

poker machine *n. Austral. & N.Z.* a fruit machine.

pokerwork ('pəʊkə,wɜːk) *n.* the art of producing pictures or designs on wood by charring it with a heated tool.

pokeweed ('pəʊk,wiːd), **pokeberry,** *or* **pokeroot** *n.* a tall North American plant that has a poisonous purple root used medicinally. [C18 *poke*, from Algonquian *puccoon* plant used in dyeing, from *pak* blooɑ]

pokie ('pəʊki) *n. Austral. inf.* short for **poker machine.**

poky *or* **pokey** ('pəʊki) *adj.* **pokier, pokiest.** **1.** (esp. of rooms) small and cramped. **2.** *Inf., chiefly U.S.* without speed or energy; slow. [C19: from POKE[1] (in sl. sense: to confine)] — **'pokily** *adv.* — **'pokiness** *n.*

pol. *abbrev. for:* **1.** political. **2.** politics.

Pol. *abbrev. for:* **1.** Poland. **2.** Polish.

Pola ('pɔːla) *n.* the Italian name for **Pula.**

Poland ('pəʊlənd) *n.* a republic in central Europe, on the Baltic: first united in the 10th century; dissolved after the third partition effected by Austria, Russia, and Prussia in 1795; re-established independence in 1918; invaded by Germany in 1939; ruled by a Communist government since 1947. It consists chiefly of a low undulating plain in the north, rising to a low plateau in the south, with the Sudeten and Carpathian Mountains along the S border. Language: Polish. Currency: zloty. Capital: Warsaw. Pop.: 37 572 000 (1987). Area: 311 730 sq. km (120 359 sq. miles). Polish name: **Polska.**

Polanski (pə'lænski) *n.* **Roman.** born 1933, Polish film director with a taste for the macabre, as in *Repulsion* (1965) and *Rosemary's Baby* (1968).

polar ('pəʊlə) *adj.* **1.** at, near, or relating to either of the earth's poles or the area inside the Arctic or Antarctic Circles: *polar regions.* **2.** having or relating to a pole or poles. **3.** pivotal or guiding in the manner of the Pole Star. **4.** directly opposite, as in tendency or character. **5.** *Chem.* (of a molecule) having an uneven distribution of electrons and thus a permanent dipole moment: *water has polar molecules.*

polar bear *n.* a white carnivorous bear of coastal regions of the North Pole.

polar circle *n.* a term for either the **Arctic Circle** or **Antarctic Circle.**

polar coordinates *pl. n.* a pair of coordinates for locating a point in a plane by means of the length of a radius vector, r, which pivots about the origin to establish the angle, θ, that the position of the point makes with a fixed line. Usually written (r, θ).

polar distance *n.* the angular distance of a star, planet, etc., from the celestial pole; the complement of the declination.

polar front *n. Meteorol.* a front dividing cold polar air from warmer temperate or tropical air.

Polari (pə'lɑːri) *n.* an English slang derived from the Lingua Franca of Mediterranean ports; brought to England by sailors from the 16th century onwards. [C19: from It. *parlare* to speak]

polarimeter (,pəʊlə'rɪmɪtə) *n.* an instrument for measuring the polarization of light. — **polarimetric** (,pəʊləri'metrik) *adj.*

Polaris (pə'lɑːrɪs) *n.* **1.** Also called: the **Pole Star, North Star.** the brightest star in the constellation Ursa Minor, situated slightly less than 1° from the north celestial pole. **2.** a type of U.S. two-stage intermediate-range ballistic missile, usually fired by a submerged submarine. [from Med. L *stella polāris* polar star]

polariscope (pəʊ'læri,skəʊp) *n.* an instrument for detecting polarized light or for observing objects under polarized light, esp. for detecting strain in transparent materials.

polarity (pəʊ'læriti) *n., pl.* **-ties.** **1.** the condition of having poles. **2.** the condition of a body or system in which it has opposing physical properties, esp. magnetic poles or electric charge. **3.** the particular state of a part that has polarity: *an electrode with positive polarity.* **4.** the state of having or expressing two directly opposite tendencies, opinions, etc.

polarization *or* **-isation** (,pəʊləraɪ'zeɪʃən) *n.* **1.** the condition of having or giving polarity. **2.** *Physics.* the phenomenon in which waves of light or other radiation are restricted to certain directions of vibration.

polarize *or* **-ise** ('pəʊlə,raɪz) *vb.* **1.** to acquire or cause to acquire polarity or polarization. **2.** *(tr.)* to cause (people) to adopt extreme opposing positions: *to polarize opinion.* — **'polar,izer** *or* **-,iser** *n.*

polar lights *pl. n.* the aurora borealis in the N hemisphere or the aurora australis in the S hemisphere.

polarography (,pəʊlə'rɒgrəfi) *n.* a technique for analysing and studying ions in solution by using an electrolytic cell with a very small cathode and obtaining a graph (**polarogram**) of the current against the potential to determine the concentration and nature of the ions.

Polaroid ('pəʊlə,rɔɪd) *n. Trademark.* **1.** a type of plastic sheet that can polarize a transmitted beam of normal light because it is composed of long parallel molecules. It only transmits plane-polarized light if these molecules are parallel to the plane of polarization. **2. Polaroid Land Camera.** any of several types of camera yielding a finished print by means of a special developing and processing technique that occurs inside the camera and takes only a few seconds.

polder ('pəʊldə, 'pɒl-) *n.* a stretch of land reclaimed from the sea or a lake, esp. in the Netherlands. [C17: from MDu. *polre*]

pole[1] (pəʊl) *n.* **1.** a long slender usually round piece of wood, metal, or other material. **2.** the piece of timber on each side of which a pair of carriage horses are hitched. **3.** another name for **rod** (sense 7). **4. up the pole.** *Brit., Austral., & N.Z. inf.* **a.** slightly mad. **b.** mistaken; on the wrong track. ~*vb.* **5.** *(tr.)* to strike or push with a pole. **6.** *(tr.)* **a.** to set out (an area of land or garden) with poles. **b.** to support (a crop, such as hops) on poles. **7.** to punt (a boat). [OE *pāl*, from L *pālus* a stake]

pole[2] (pəʊl) *n.* **1.** either of the two antipodal points where the earth's axis of rotation meets the earth's surface. See also **North Pole, South Pole.** **2.** *Physics.* **a.** either of the two regions at the extremities of a magnet to which the lines of force converge. **b.** either of two points at which there are opposite electric charges, as at the terminals of a battery. **3.** *Biol.* either end of the axis of a cell, spore, ovum, or similar body. **4.** either of two mutually exclusive or opposite actions, opinions, etc. **5. poles apart** (*or* **asunder**). having widely divergent opinions, tastes, etc. [C14: from L *polus* end of an axis, from Gk *polos* pivot]

Pole[1] (pəʊl) *n.* a native, inhabitant, or citizen of Poland or a speaker of Polish.

Pole[2] (pəʊl) *n.* **Reginald.** 1500–58, English cardinal; last Roman Catholic archbishop of Canterbury (1556–58).

poleaxe *or U.S.* **poleax** ('pəʊl,æks) *n.* **1.** another term for a battle-axe or a butcher's axe. ~*vb.* **2.** *(tr.)* to hit or fell with or as if with a poleaxe. [C14 *pollax* battle-axe, from POLL + AXE]

polecat ('pəʊl,kæt) *n., pl.* **-cats** *or* **-cat.** **1.** a dark brown musteline mammal of Europe, Asia, and N Africa, that is closely related to but larger than the weasel and gives off an unpleasant smell. **2.** *U.S.* a nontechnical name for **skunk** (sense 1). [C14 *polcat*, ?from OF *pol* cock, from L *pullus*, + CAT; from its preying on poultry]

polemic (pə'lemik) *adj. also* **polemical.** **1.** of or involving dispute or controversy. ~*n.* **2.** an argument or controversy, esp. over a doctrine, belief, etc. **3.** a person engaged in such controversy. [C17: from Med. L *polemicus*, from Gk *polemikos* relating to war, from *polemos* war] — **po'lemically** *adv.* — **polemicist** (pə'lemisist) *n.*

polemics (pə'lemiks) *n. (functioning as sing.)* the art or practice of dispute or argument, as in attacking or defending a doctrine or belief.

pole position *n.* **1.** (in motor racing) the starting position on the inside of the front row, generally considered the best one. **2.** an advantageous starting position.

pole star *n.* a guiding principle, rule, etc.

Pole Star *n.* **the.** the star closest to the N celestial pole at any particular time. At present this is Polaris, but it will eventually be replaced owing to precession of the earth's axis.

pole vault *n.* **1. the.** a field event in which competitors attempt to clear a high bar with the aid of an extremely flexible long pole. ~*vb.* **pole-vault. 2.** (*intr.*) to perform a pole vault or compete in the pole vault. —'**pole-** **,vaulter** *n.*

poley ('pəʊlɪ) *adj. Austral.* (of cattle) hornless or polled.

police (pə'liːs) *n.* **1.** (often preceded by *the*) the organized civil force of a state, concerned with maintenance of law and order. **2.** (*functioning as pl.*) the members of such a force collectively. **3.** any organized body with a similar function: *security police.* ~*vb.* (*tr.*) **4.** to regulate, control, or keep in order by means of a police or similar force. **5.** to observe or record the activity or enforcement of: *a committee was set up to police the new agreement on picketing.* [C16: via F from L *polītīa* administration; see POLITY]

police dog *n.* a dog, often an Alsatian, trained to help the police, as in tracking.

policeman (pə'liːsmən) *or* (*fem.*) **policewoman** *n., pl.* **-men** *or* **-women.** a member of a police force, esp. one holding the rank of constable.

police officer *n.* a member of a police force, esp. a constable; policeman.

police state *n.* a state or country in which a repressive government maintains control through the police.

police station *n.* the office or headquarters of the police force of a district.

policing (pə'liːsɪŋ) *n.* the policies, techniques, and practice of a police force in keeping order, preventing crime, etc.

policy[1] ('pɒlɪsɪ) *n., pl.* **-cies. 1.** a plan of action adopted or pursued by an individual, government, party, business, etc. **2.** wisdom, shrewdness, or sagacity. **3.** (*often pl.*) *Scot.* the improved grounds surrounding a country house. [C14: from OF *policie*, from L *polītīa* administration, POLITY]

policy[2] ('pɒlɪsɪ) *n., pl.* **-cies.** a document containing a contract of insurance. [C16: from OF *police* certificate, from Olt. from L *apodixis* proof, from Gk *apodeixis*] —'**poli-** **cy,holder** *n.*

polio ('pəʊlɪəʊ) *n.* short for **poliomyelitis.**

poliomyelitis (,pəʊlɪəʊ,maɪə'laɪtɪs) *n.* an acute infectious viral disease, esp. affecting children. In its paralytic form the brain and spinal cord are involved, causing paralysis and wasting of muscle. Also called: **infantile paralysis.** [C19: NL, from Gk *polios* grey + *muelos* marrow]

polish ('pɒlɪʃ) *vb.* **1.** to make or become smooth and shiny by rubbing, esp. with wax or an abrasive. **2.** (*tr.*) to make perfect or complete. **3.** to make or become elegant or refined. ~*n.* **4.** a finish or gloss. **5.** the act of polishing. **6.** a substance used to produce a shiny, often protective surface. **7.** elegance or refinement, esp. in style, manner, etc. [C13 *polis*, from OF *polir*, from L *polīre* to polish] —'**polisher** *n.*

Polish ('pəʊlɪʃ) *adj.* **1.** of, relating to, or characteristic of Poland, its people, or their language. ~*n.* **2.** the official language of Poland.

Polish Corridor *n.* the strip of land through E Pomerania providing Poland with access to the sea (1919–39), given to her in 1919 in the Treaty of Versailles, and separating East Prussia from the rest of Germany. It is now part of Poland.

polished ('pɒlɪʃt) *adj.* **1.** accomplished: *a polished actor.* **2.** impeccably or professionally done: *a polished performance.* **3.** (of rice) having had the outer husk removed by milling.

polish off *vb.* (*tr., adv.*) *Inf.* **1.** to finish or process completely. **2.** to dispose of or kill.

polish up *vb.* (*adv.*) **1.** to make or become smooth and shiny by polishing. **2.** (when *intr.*, foll. by *on*) to study or practise until adept (at); improve: *he's polishing up on his German.*

Politburo ('pɒlɪt,bjʊərəʊ) *n.* **1.** the executive and policy-making committee of a Communist Party. **2.** the supreme policy-making authority in most Communist countries. [C20: from Russian: contraction of *Politicheskoe Buro* political bureau]

polite (pə'laɪt) *adj.* **1.** showing a great regard for others, as in manners, speech, etc.; courteous. **2.** cultivated or refined: *polite society.* **3.** elegant or polished: *polite letters.* [C15: from L *polītus* polished] —**po'litely** *adv.* —**po'liteness** *n.*

politesse (,pɒlɪ'tɛs) *n.* formal or genteel politeness. [C18: via F from It. *politezza*, ult. from L *polīre* to polish]

Politian (pəʊ'lɪʃən, pɒ-) *n.* Italian name *Angelo Polliziano;* original name *Angelo Ambrogini.* 1454–94, Florentine humanist and poet.

politic ('pɒlɪtɪk) *adj.* **1.** artful or shrewd; ingenious. **2.** crafty or unscrupulous; cunning. **3.** wise or prudent, esp. in statesmanship: *a politic choice.* **4.** an archaic word for **political.** ~ See also **body politic.** [C15: from OF *politique*, from L *polīticus* concerning civil administration, from Gk, from *polītēs* citizen, from *polis* city] —'**politicly** *adv.*

political (pə'lɪtɪk²l) *adj.* **1.** of or relating to the state, government, public administration, etc. **2. a.** of or relating to government policy-making as distinguished from administration or law. **b.** of or relating to the civil aspects of government as distinguished from the military. **3.** of, dealing with, or relating to politics: *a political person.* **4.** of or relating to the parties and the partisan aspects of politics. **5.** organized with respect to government: *a political unit.* —**po'litically** *adv.*

political economy *n.* the former name for **economics** (sense 1).

political prisoner *n.* a person imprisoned for holding or expressing particular political beliefs.

political science *n.* the study of the state, government, and politics: one of the social sciences. —**political scientist** *n.*

politician (,pɒlɪ'tɪʃən) *n.* **1.** a person actively engaged in politics, esp. a full-time professional member of a deliberative assembly. **2.** a person who is experienced or skilled in government or administration; statesman. **3.** *Disparaging, chiefly U.S.* a person who engages in politics out of a wish for personal gain.

politicize *or* **-ise** (pə'lɪtɪ,saɪz) *vb.* **1.** (*tr.*) to render political in tone, interest, or awareness. **2.** (*intr.*) to participate in political discussion or activity. —**po,litici'zation** *or* **-i'sation** *n.*

politicking ('pɒlɪtɪkɪŋ) *n.* political activity, esp. seeking votes.

politico (pə'lɪtɪ,kəʊ) *n., pl.* **-cos.** *Chiefly U.S.* an informal word for a **politician** (senses 1, 3). [C17: from It. or Sp.]

politics ('pɒlɪtɪks) *n.* **1.** (*functioning as sing.*) the art and science of directing and administrating states and other political units; government. **2.** (*functioning as sing.*) the complex or aggregate of relationships of people in society, esp. those relationships involving authority or power. **3.** (*functioning as pl.*) political activities or affairs: *party politics.* **4.** (*functioning as sing.*) the business or profession of politics. **5.** (*functioning as sing. or pl.*) any activity concerned with the acquisition of power, etc.: *company politics are frequently vicious.* **6.** manoeuvres or factors leading up to or influencing (something): *the politics of the decision.* **7.** (*functioning as pl.*) opinions, sympathies, etc., with respect to politics: *his conservative politics.*

polity ('pɒlɪtɪ) *n., pl.* **-ties. 1.** a form of government or organization of a society, etc.; constitution. **2.** a politically organized society, etc. **3.** the management of public affairs. **4.** political organization. [C16: from L *polītīa*, from Gk *politeia* citizenship, civil administration, from *polītēs* citizen, from *polis* city]

Polk (pəʊk) *n.* **James Knox.** 1795–1849, U.S. statesman; 11th president of the U.S. (1845–49). During his administration, Texas and territory now included in New Mexico, Colorado, Utah, Nevada, Arizona, Oregon, and California were added to the Union.

polka ('pɒlkə) *n.* **1.** a 19th-century Bohemian dance with three steps and a hop, in fast duple time. **2.** a piece of music composed for or in the rhythm of this dance. ~*vb.* **-kaing, -kaed. 3.** (*intr.*) to dance a polka. [C19: via F from Czech *pulka* half-step]

polka dot *n.* one of a pattern of small circular regularly spaced spots on a fabric.

poll (pəʊl) *n.* **1.** the casting, recording, or counting of votes in an election; a voting. **2.** the result of such a voting: *a heavy poll.* **3.** Also called: **opinion poll. a.** a canvassing of a representative sample of people on some question in order to determine the general opinion. **b.** the results of such a canvassing. **4.** any counting or enumeration, esp. for taxation or voting purposes. **5.** the back part of the head of an animal. ~*vb.* (*mainly tr.*) **6.** to receive (a vote or quantity of votes): *he polled 10 000 votes.* **7.** to receive, take, or record the votes of: *he polled the whole town.* **8.** to canvass (a person, group, area, etc.) as part of a survey of opinion. **9.** (*sometimes intr.*) to cast (a vote) in an election. **10.** to clip or shear. **11.** to remove or cut short the horns (of cattle). [C13 (in the sense: a human head) & C17 (in the sense: votes): from MLow G *polle* hair of the head, head, top of a tree]

pollack *or* **pollock** ('pɒlək) *n.*, *pl.* **-lacks, -lack** *or* **-locks, -lock.** a gadoid food fish that has a projecting lower jaw and occurs in northern seas. [C17: from earlier Scot. *podlok*, from ?]

Pollack ('pɒlək) *n.* **Sydney.** born 1934, U.S. film director. His films include *Tootsie* (1982) and *Out of Africa* (1986).

Pollaiuolo (*Italian* pollaj'wɔːlo) *n.* **1. Antonio** (an'tɔːnjo), ?1432–98, Florentine painter, sculptor, goldsmith, and engraver: his paintings include the *Martyrdom of St Sebastian.* **2.** his brother **Piero** ('pjɛːro). ?1443–96, Florentine painter and sculptor.

pollan ('pɒlən) *n.* any of several varieties of whitefish that occur in lakes in Northern Ireland. [C18: prob. from Irish *poll* lake]

pollard ('pɒləd) *n.* **1.** an animal, such as a sheep or deer, that has either shed its horns or antlers or has had them removed. **2.** a tree that has had its branches cut back to encourage a more bushy growth. ~*vb.* **3.** (*tr.*) to convert into a pollard; poll. [C16: hornless animal; see POLL]

pollen ('pɒlən) *n.* a substance produced by the anthers of seed-bearing plants, consisting of numerous fine grains containing the male gametes. [C16: from L: powder] —**pollinic** (pə'lɪnɪk) *adj.*

Pollen ('pɒlən) *n.* **Daniel.** 1813–96, New Zealand statesman, born in Ireland: prime minister of New Zealand (1876).

pollen analysis *n.* another name for **palynology.**

pollen count *n.* a measure of the pollen present in the air over a 24-hour period, often published to enable sufferers from hay fever to predict the severity of their attacks.

pollex ('pɒlɛks) *n.*, *pl.* **-lices** (-lɪˌsiːz). the first digit of the forelimb of amphibians, reptiles, birds, and mammals, such as the thumb of man. [C19: from L: thumb, big toe] —**pollical** ('pɒlɪkᵊl) *adj.*

pollinate ('pɒlɪˌneɪt) *vb.* (*tr.*) to transfer pollen from the anthers to the stigma of (a flower). —**polli'nation** *n.* —**'polli,nator** *n.*

polling booth *n.* a semienclosed space in which a voter stands to mark a ballot paper during an election.

polling station *n.* a building, such as a school, designated as the place to which voters go during an election in order to cast their votes.

polliwog *or* **pollywog** ('pɒlɪˌwɒg) *n. Dialect, U.S., & Canad.* a tadpole. [C15 *polwygle*]

Pollock ('pɒlək) *n.* **1.** Sir **Frederick.** 1845–1937, English legal scholar: with Maitland, he wrote *History of English Law before the Time of Edward I* (1895). **2. Jackson.** 1912–56, U.S. abstract expressionist painter; chief exponent of action painting in the U.S.

pollster ('pəʊlstə) *n.* a person who conducts opinion polls.

poll tax *n.* a tax levied per head of adult population.

pollutant (pə'luːtᵊnt) *n.* a substance that pollutes, esp. a chemical produced as a waste product of an industrial process.

pollute (pə'luːt) *vb.* (*tr.*) **1.** to contaminate, as with poisonous or harmful substances. **2.** to make morally corrupt. **3.** to desecrate. [C14 *polute*, from L *polluere* to defile] —**pol'luter** *n.* —**pol'lution** *n.*

Pollux ('pɒləks) *n. Classical myth.* See **Castor and Pollux.**

Pollyanna (ˌpɒlɪ'ænə) *n.* a person who is optimistic. [C20: after the chief character in *Pollyanna* (1913), a novel by Eleanor Porter (1868–1920), U.S. writer]

polo ('pəʊləʊ) *n.* **1.** a game similar to hockey played on horseback using long-handled mallets (**polo sticks**) and a wooden ball. **2.** short for **water polo. 3.** Also called: **polo neck. a.** a collar on a garment, worn rolled over to fit closely round the neck. **b.** a garment, esp. a sweater, with such a collar. [C19: from Balti (dialect of Kashmir): ball, from Tibetan *pulu*]

Polo ('pəʊləʊ) *n.* **Marco** ('mɑːkəʊ). 1254–1324, Venetian merchant, famous for his account of his travels in Asia. After travelling overland to China (1271–75), he spent 17 years serving Kublai Khan before returning to Venice by sea (1292–95).

polonaise (ˌpɒlə'neɪz) *n.* **1.** a ceremonial marchlike dance in three-four time from Poland. **2.** a piece of music composed for or in the rhythm of this dance. **3.** a woman's costume with a tight bodice and an overskirt drawn back to show a decorative underskirt. [C18: from F *danse polonaise* Polish dance]

polonium (pə'ləʊnɪəm) *n.* a very rare radioactive element that occurs in trace amounts in uranium ores. Symbol: Po; atomic no.: 84; half-life of most stable isotope, ^{209}Po: 103 years. [C19: NL, from Med. L *Polōnia* Poland; in honour of the nationality of its discoverer, Marie Curie]

polony (pə'ləʊnɪ) *n.*, *pl.* **-nies.** *Brit.* another name for **Bologna sausage.**

Pol Pot ('pɒl 'pɒt) *n.*, original name *Kompong Thom.* born 1925, Kampuchean Communist statesman; prime minister of Kampuchea (1976; 1977–79); overthrown by Vietnamese forces.

Polska ('pɒlska) *n.* the Polish name for **Poland.**

Poltava (*Russian* pal'tava) *n.* a city in the SW Soviet Union, in the E Ukrainian SSR: scene of the victory (1709) of the Russians under Peter the Great over the Swedes under Charles XII. Pop.: 309 000 (1987).

poltergeist ('pɒltəˌgaɪst) *n.* a spirit believed to manifest its presence by noises and acts of mischief, such as throwing furniture about. [C19: from G, from *poltern* to be noisy + *Geist* GHOST]

poltroon (pɒl'truːn) *n.* an abject or contemptible coward. [C16: from OF *poultron*, from OIt. *poltrone* lazy good-for-nothing, apparently from *poltrīre* to lie indolently in bed]

poly ('pɒlɪ) *n.*, *pl.* **polys.** *Inf.* short for **polytechnic.**

poly- *combining form.* **1.** more than one; many or much: *polyhedron.* **2.** having an excessive or abnormal number or amount: *polyphagia.* [from Gk *polus* much, many]

polyamide (ˌpɒlɪ'æmaɪd, -mɪd) *n.* any of a class of synthetic polymeric materials, including nylon.

polyandry ('pɒlɪˌændrɪ) *n.* **1.** the practice or condition of being married to more than one husband at the same time. **2.** the practice in animals of a female mating with more than one male during one breeding season. **3.** the condition in flowers of having a large indefinite number of stamens. [C18: from Gk *poluandria*, from POLY- + *-andria* from *anēr* man] —**poly'androus** *adj.*

polyanthus (ˌpɒlɪ'ænθəs) *n.*, *pl.* **-thuses.** any of several hybrid garden primroses with brightly coloured flowers. [C18: NL, from Gk: having many flowers]

polyatomic (ˌpɒlɪə'tɒmɪk) *adj.* (of a molecule) containing more than two atoms.

poly bag ('pɒlɪ) *n. Brit. inf.* a polythene bag, esp. one used to store or protect food or household articles.

polybasic (ˌpɒlɪ'beɪsɪk) *adj.* (of an acid) having two or more replaceable hydrogen atoms per molecule.

Polybius (pə'lɪbɪəs) *n.* ?205–?123 B.C., Greek historian. Under the patronage of Scipio the Younger, he wrote in 40 books a history of Rome from 264 B.C. to 146 B.C.

Polycarp ('pɒlɪˌkɑːp) *n.* **Saint.** ?69–?155 A.D., Christian martyr and bishop of Smyrna, noted for his letter to the church at Philippi. Feast day: Feb. 23.

polycarpic (ˌpɒlɪ'kɑːpɪk) *or* **polycarpous** *adj.* (of a plant) able to produce flowers and fruit several times in succession. —'**poly,carpy** *n.*

polycentrism (ˌpɒlɪ'sɛntrɪzəm) *n.* the fact or advocacy of the existence of more than one predominant ideological or political centre in a political system, alliance, etc., in the Communist world.

polychaete ('pɒlɪˌkiːt) *n.* **1.** a marine annelid worm having a distinct head and paired fleshy appendages (parapodia) that bear bristles and are used in swimming. ~*adj.* also **polychaetous. 2.** of or denoting such a creature. [C19: from NL, from Gk *polukhaitēs* having much hair]

polychromatic (ˌpɒlɪkrəʊ'mætɪk), **polychromic** (ˌpɒlɪ'krəʊmɪk), *or* **polychromous** *adj.* **1.** having various or changing colours. **2.** (of light or other radiation) containing radiation with more than one wavelength. —**polychromatism** (ˌpɒlɪ'krəʊməˌtɪzəm) *n.*

polyclinic (ˌpɒlɪ'klɪnɪk) *n.* a hospital or clinic able to treat a wide variety of diseases.

Polyclitus, Polycleitus (ˌpɒlɪ'klaɪtəs), or **Polycletus** (ˌpɒlɪ'kliːtəs) n. 5th-century B.C. Greek sculptor, noted particularly for his idealized bronze sculptures of the male nude, such as the *Doryphoros*.

polycotyledon (ˌpɒlɪˌkɒtɪ'liːd°n) n. any of various plants, esp. gymnosperms, that have or appear to have more than two cotyledons. —**ˌpolyˌcoty'ledonous** *adj.*

Polycrates (pə'lɪkrəˌtiːz) n. died ?522 B.C., Greek tyrant of Samos, who was crucified by a Persian satrap.

polycyclic (ˌpɒlɪ'saɪklɪk) *adj.* **1.** (of a molecule or compound) having molecules that contain two or more closed rings of atoms. **2.** *Biol.* having two or more rings or whorls: *polycyclic shells.* ~*n.* **3.** a polycyclic compound.

polydactyl (ˌpɒlɪ'dæktɪl) *adj. also* **polydactylous. 1.** (of man and other vertebrates) having more than the normal number of digits. ~*n.* **2.** a human or other vertebrate having more than the normal number of digits.

Polydeuces (ˌpɒlɪ'djuːsiːz) n. the Greek name of **Pollux.** See **Castor and Pollux.**

polyester (ˌpɒlɪ'estə) n. any of a large class of synthetic materials that are polymers containing recurring -COO- groups: used as plastics, textile fibres, and adhesives.

polyethene (ˌpɒlɪ'εθiːn) n. the systematic name for **polythene.**

polyethylene (ˌpɒlɪ'εθɪˌliːn) n. another name for **polythene.**

polygamy (pə'lɪɡəmɪ) n. **1.** the practice of having more than one wife or husband at the same time. **2.** the condition of having male, female, and hermaphrodite flowers on the same plant or on separate plants of the same species. **3.** the practice in male animals of having more than one mate during one breeding season. [C16: via F from Gk *polugamia*] —**po'lygamist** n. —**po'lygamous** *adj.* —**po'lygamously** *adv.*

polygene ('pɒlɪˌdʒiːn) n. any of a group of genes that each produce a small quantitative effect on a particular characteristic, such as height.

polygenesis (ˌpɒlɪ'dʒɛnɪsɪs) n. **1.** *Biol.* evolution of organisms from different ancestral groups. **2.** the hypothetical descent of different races from different ultimate ancestors. —**polygenetic** (ˌpɒlɪdʒɪ'nɛtɪk) *adj.*

polyglot ('pɒlɪˌɡlɒt) *adj.* **1.** having a command of many languages. **2.** written in or containing many languages. ~*n.* **3.** a person with a command of many languages. **4.** a book, esp. a Bible, containing several versions of the same text written in various languages. **5.** a mixture of languages. [C17: from Gk *poluglōttos*, lit.: many-tongued]

Polygnotus (ˌpɒlɪɡ'nəʊtəs) n. 5th century B.C., Greek painter: associated with Cimon in rebuilding Athens.

polygon ('pɒlɪˌɡɒn) n. a closed plane figure bounded by three or more straight sides that meet in pairs in the same number of vertices and do not intersect other than at these vertices. Specific polygons are named according to the number of sides, such as triangle, pentagon, etc. [C16: via L from Gk *polugōnon* figure with many angles] —**polygonal** (pə'lɪɡən°l) *adj.* —**po'lygonally** *adv.*

polygonum (pə'lɪɡənəm) n. a plant having stems with knotlike joints and spikes of small white, green, or pink flowers. [C18: NL, from Gk *polugonon* knotgrass, from *polu-* POLY- + *-gonon*, from *gonu* knee]

polygraph ('pɒlɪˌɡrɑːf) n. **1.** an instrument for the simultaneous recording of several involuntary physiological activities, including pulse rate and perspiration, used esp. as a lie detector. **2.** a device for producing copies of written matter. [C18: from Gk *polugraphos* writing copiously]

polygyny (pə'lɪdʒɪnɪ) n. **1.** the practice or condition of being married to more than one wife at the same time. **2.** the practice in animals of a male mating with more than one female during one breeding season. **3.** the condition in flowers of having many styles. [C18: from POLY- + *-gyny*, from Gk *gunē* a woman] —**po'lygynous** *adj.*

polyhedron (ˌpɒlɪ'hiːdrən) n., pl. **-drons** or **-dra** (-drə). a solid figure consisting of four or more plane faces (all polygons), pairs of which meet along an edge, three or more edges meeting at a vertex. Specific polyhedrons are named according to the number of faces, such as tetrahedron, icosahedron, etc. [C16: from *poluedron*, from POLY- + *hedron* side] —**poly'hedral** *adj.*

Polyhymnia (ˌpɒlɪ'hɪmnɪə) n. *Greek myth.* the Muse of singing, mime, and sacred dance. [L, from Gk *Polumnia* full of songs]

polymath ('pɒlɪˌmæθ) n. a person of great and varied learning. [C17: from Gk *polumathēs* having much knowledge] —**polymathy** (pə'lɪməθɪ) n.

polymer ('pɒlɪmə) n. a naturally occurring or synthetic compound, such as starch or Perspex, that has large molecules made up of many relatively simple repeated units. —**polymerism** (pə'lɪməˌrɪzəm, 'pɒlɪmə-) n.

polymeric (ˌpɒlɪ'mɛrɪk) *adj.* of, concerned with, or being a polymer: *a polymeric compound.* [C19: from Gk *polumerēs* having many parts]

polymerization or **-isation** (pəˌlɪməraɪ'zeɪʃən, ˌpɒlɪməraɪ-) n. the act or process of forming a polymer or copolymer.

polymerize or **-ise** ('pɒlɪməˌraɪz, pə'lɪmə-) vb. to react or cause to react to form a polymer.

polymerous (pə'lɪmərəs) *adj. Biol.* having or being composed of many parts.

polymorph ('pɒlɪˌmɔːf) n. a species of animal or plant, or a crystalline form of a chemical compound, that exhibits polymorphism. [C19: from Gk *polumorphos* having many forms]

polymorphism (ˌpɒlɪ'mɔːfɪzəm) n. **1.** the occurrence of more than one form of individual in a single species within an interbreeding population. **2.** the existence or formation of different types of crystal of the same chemical compound.

polymorphous (ˌpɒlɪ'mɔːfəs) or **polymorphic** *adj.* **1.** having, taking, or passing through many different forms or stages. **2.** exhibiting or undergoing polymorphism.

Polynesia (ˌpɒlɪ'niːʒə, -ʒɪə) n. one of the three divisions of islands in the Pacific, the others being Melanesia and Micronesia: includes Samoa, Society, Marquesas, Mangareva, Tuamotu, Cook, and Tubuai Islands, and Tonga. [C18: via F from POLY- + Gk *nēsos* island]

Polynesian (ˌpɒlɪ'niːʒən, -ʒɪən) *adj.* **1.** of or relating to Polynesia, its people, or any of their languages. ~*n.* **2.** a member of the people that inhabit Polynesia, generally of Caucasoid features with light skin and wavy hair. **3.** a branch of the Malayo-Polynesian family of languages, including Maori and Hawaiian.

polyneuritis (ˌpɒlɪnjʊ'raɪtɪs) n. inflammation of many nerves at the same time.

Polynices (ˌpɒlɪ'naɪsiːz) n. *Greek myth.* a son of Oedipus and Jocasta, for whom the Seven Against Thebes sought to regain Thebes. He and his brother Eteocles killed each other in single combat before its walls.

polynomial (ˌpɒlɪ'nəʊmɪəl) *adj.* **1.** of, consisting of, or referring to two or more names or terms. ~*n.* **2. a.** a mathematical expression consisting of a sum of terms each of which is the product of a constant and one or more variables raised to a positive or zero integral power. **b.** Also called: **multinomial.** any mathematical expression consisting of the sum of a number of terms. **3.** *Biol.* a taxonomic name consisting of more than two terms, such as *Parus major minor* in which *minor* designates the subspecies.

polynucleotide (ˌpɒlɪ'njuːklɪəˌtaɪd) n. *Biochem.* a molecular chain of nucleotides chemically bonded by a series of ester linkages between the phosphoryl group of one nucleotide and the hydroxyl group of the sugar in the adjacent nucleotide.

polynya ('pɒlənˌjɑː) n. a stretch of open water surrounded by ice, esp. near the mouths of large rivers, in arctic seas. [C19: from Russian, from *poly* open]

polyp ('pɒlɪp) n. **1.** *Zool.* one of the two forms of individual that occur in coelenterates. It usually has a hollow cylindrical body with a ring of tentacles around the mouth. **2.** Also called: **polypus.** *Pathol.* a small growth arising from the surface of a mucous membrane. [C16 *polip*, from F *polype* nasal polyp, from L *pōlypus*, from Gk *polupous* having many feet] —'**polypous** or '**polypoid** *adj.*

polypeptide (ˌpɒlɪ'peptaɪd) n. any of a group of natural or synthetic polymers made up of amino acids chemically linked together; includes the proteins.

polypetalous (ˌpɒlɪ'petələs) *adj.* (of flowers) having many distinct or separate petals.

polyphagia (ˌpɒlɪ'feɪdʒə) n. **1.** an abnormal desire to consume excessive amounts of food. **2.** the habit or condition, in certain animals, esp. certain insects, of feeding on many different types of food. [C17: NL, from Gk, from *poluphagos* eating much] —**polyphagous** (pə'lɪfəɡəs) *adj.*

polyphase ('pɒlɪˌfeɪz) *adj.* **1.** (of an electrical system, circuit, or device) having or using alternating voltages of the same frequency, the phases of which are cyclically displaced by fractions of a period. **2.** having more than one phase.

Polyphemus (ˌpɒlɪˈfiːməs) n. Greek myth. a cyclops who imprisoned Odysseus and his companions in his cave. To effect his escape, Odysseus blinded him.

polyphone (ˈpɒlɪˌfəʊn) n. a letter or character having more than one phonetic value, such as c in English.

polyphonic (ˌpɒlɪˈfɒnɪk) adj. **1.** Music. composed of relatively independent parts; contrapuntal. **2.** many-voiced. **3.** Phonetics. denoting a polyphone. —**poly'phonically** adv.

polyphony (pəˈlɪfənɪ) n., pl. **-nies. 1.** polyphonic style of composition or a piece of music utilizing it. **2.** the use of polyphones in a writing system. [C19: from Gk poluphōnia diversity of tones] —**po'lyphonous** adj. —**po'lyphonously** adv.

polyploid (ˈpɒlɪˌplɔɪd) adj. (of cells, organisms, etc.) having more than twice the basic (haploid) number of chromosomes. —**poly'ploidal** adj. —**'poly,ploidy** n.

polypod (ˈpɒlɪˌpɒd) adj. **1.** (esp. of insect larvae) having many legs or similar appendages. ~n. **2.** an animal of this type.

polypody (ˈpɒlɪˌpəʊdɪ) n., pl. **-dies.** any of various ferns having deeply divided leaves and round naked sporangia. [C15: from L polypodium, from Gk, from POLY- + pous foot]

polypropylene (ˌpɒlɪˈprəʊpɪˌliːn) n. any of various tough flexible synthetic thermoplastic materials made by polymerizing propylene. Systematic name: **polypropene** (ˌpɒlɪˈprəʊpiːn).

polypus (ˈpɒlɪpəs) n., pl. **-pi** (-paɪ). Pathol. another word for **polyp** (sense 2). [C16: via L from Gk: POLYP]

polysaccharide (ˌpɒlɪˈsækəˌraɪd, -rɪd) or **polysaccharose** (ˌpɒlɪˈsækəˌrəʊz, -ˌrəʊs) n. any one of a class of carbohydrates whose molecules contain linked monosaccharide units: includes starch, inulin, and cellulose.

polysemy (ˌpɒlɪˈsiːmɪ, pəˈlɪsəmɪ) n. the existence of several meanings in a single word. [C20: from NL polysēmia, from Gk polusēmos having many meanings] —**poly'semous** adj.

polysomic (ˌpɒlɪˈsəʊmɪk) adj. of, relating to, or designating a basically diploid chromosome complement, in which some but not all the chromosomes are represented more than twice.

polystyrene (ˌpɒlɪˈstaɪriːn) n. a synthetic thermoplastic material obtained by polymerizing styrene; used as a white rigid foam (**expanded polystyrene**) for insulating and packing and as a glasslike material in light fittings.

polysyllable (ˈpɒlɪˌsɪləbªl) n. a word consisting of more than two syllables. —**polysyllabic** (ˌpɒlɪsɪˈlæbɪk) adj. —**,polysyl'labically** adv.

polysyndeton (ˌpɒlɪˈsɪndɪtən) n. Rhetoric. the use of several conjunctions in close succession, esp. where some might be omitted, as in he ran and jumped and laughed for joy. [C16: POLY- + -syndeton, from Gk sundetos bound together]

polytechnic (ˌpɒlɪˈtɛknɪk) n. **1.** Brit. a college offering advanced courses in many fields at and below degree standard. ~adj. **2.** of or relating to technical instruction and training. [C19: via F from Gk polutekhnos skilled in many arts]

polytetrafluoroethylene (ˌpɒlɪˌtɛtrəˌfluərəʊˈɛθɪˌliːn) n. a white thermoplastic material with a waxy texture, made by polymerizing tetrafluoroethylene. It is used for making gaskets, hoses, insulators, bearings, and for coating metal surfaces. Abbrev.: **PTFE.** Also called (trademark): **Teflon.**

polytheism (ˈpɒlɪθiːˌɪzəm, ˌpɒlɪˈθiːɪzəm) n. the worship of or belief in more than one god. —**polythe'istic** adj. —**polythe'istically** adv.

polythene (ˈpɒlɪˌθiːn) n. any one of various light thermoplastic materials made from ethylene with properties depending on the molecular weight of the polymer. Systematic name: **polyethene.** Also called: **polyethylene.**

polytonality (ˌpɒlɪtəʊˈnælɪtɪ) or **polytonalism** n. Music. the simultaneous use of more than two different keys or tonalities. —**poly'tonal** adj. —**poly'tonally** adv.

polyunsaturated (ˌpɒlɪʌnˈsætʃəˌreɪtɪd) adj. of or relating to a class of animal and vegetable fats, the molecules of which consist of long carbon chains with many double

bonds. Polyunsaturated compounds do not contain cholesterol.

polyurethane (ˌpɒlɪˈjuərəˌθeɪn) n. a class of synthetic materials commonly used as a foam for insulation and packing.

polyvalent (ˌpɒlɪˈveɪlənt, pəˈlɪvələnt) adj. **1.** Chem. having more than one valency. **2.** (of a vaccine) effective against several strains of the same disease-producing microorganism, antigen, or toxin. —**,poly'valency** n.

polyvinyl (ˌpɒlɪˈvaɪnɪl, -ˈvaɪnªl) n. (modifier) designating a plastic or resin formed by polymerization of a vinyl derivative.

polyvinyl acetate n. a colourless odourless tasteless resin used in emulsion paints and adhesives and for sealing porous surfaces.

polyvinyl chloride n. the full name of **PVC.**

polyvinyl resin n. any of a class of thermoplastic resins made by polymerizing a vinyl compound. The commonest type is PVC.

Polyxena (pɒˈlɪksɪnə) n. Greek myth. a daughter of King Priam of Troy, who was sacrificed on the command of Achilles' ghost.

polyzoan (ˌpɒlɪˈzəʊən) n., adj. another word for **bryozoan.** [C19: from NL, Polyzoa class name, from POLY- + -zoan, from Gk zoion an animal]

pom (pɒm) n. Austral. & N.Z. sl. short for **pommy.**

POM abbrev. for prescription only medicine (or medication).

pomace (ˈpʌmɪs) n. **1.** the pulpy residue of apples or similar fruit after crushing and pressing, as in cider-making. **2.** any pulpy substance left after crushing, mashing, etc. [C16: from Med. L pōmācium cider, from L pōmum apple]

pomaceous (pɒˈmeɪʃəs) adj. of, relating to, or bearing pomes, such as the apple and quince trees. [C18: from NL pōmāceus, from L pōmum apple]

pomade (pəˈmɑːd) n. **1.** a perfumed oil or ointment put on the hair, as to make it smooth and shiny. ~vb. **2.** (tr.) to put pomade on. ~Also: **pomatum.** [C16: from F pommade, from It. pomato (orig. made partly from apples), from L pōmum apple]

pomander (pəʊˈmændə) n. **1.** a mixture of aromatic substances in a sachet or an orange, formerly carried as scent or as a protection against disease. **2.** a container for such a mixture. [C15: from OF pome d'ambre, from Med. L pōmum ambrae apple of amber]

Pombal (Portuguese pomˈbal) n. **Marquês de** (mərkeʃ ˈdə). title of Sebastião José de Carvalho e Mello. 1699–1782, Portuguese statesman, who dominated Portuguese government from 1750 to 1777 and instituted many administrative and economic reforms.

pome (pəʊm) n. the fleshy fruit of the apple and related plants, consisting of an enlarged receptacle enclosing the ovary and seeds. [C15: from OF, from LL pōma, pl. of L pōmum apple]

pomegranate (ˈpɒmɪˌgrænɪt, ˈpɒmˌgrænɪt) n. **1.** an Asian shrub or small tree cultivated in semitropical regions for its edible fruit. **2.** the many-chambered globular fruit of this tree, which has tough reddish rind, juicy red pulp, and many seeds. [C14: from OF pome grenate, from L pōmum apple + grenate, from grānātus full of seeds]

pomelo (ˈpɒmɪˌləʊ) n., pl. **-los. 1.** Also called: **shaddock.** the edible yellow fruit, resembling a grapefruit, of a tropical tree widely grown in oriental regions. **2.** U.S. another name for **grapefruit.** [C19: from Du. pompelmoes]

Pomerania (ˌpɒməˈreɪnɪə) n. a region of N central Europe, extending along the S coast of the Baltic Sea from Stralsund to the Vistula River: now chiefly in Poland, with a small area in NE East Germany. German name: **Pommern.** Polish name: **Pomorze.**

Pomeranian (ˌpɒməˈreɪnɪən) adj. **1.** of or relating to Pomerania. ~n. **2.** a breed of toy dog of the spitz type with a long thick straight coat.

pomfret (ˈpʌmfrɪt, ˈpɒm-) or **pomfret-cake** n. a small black rounded confection of liquorice. Also called: **Pontefract cake.** [C19: from Pomfret, earlier form of PONTEFRACT, where orig. made]

pomiculture (ˈpɒmɪˌkʌltʃə) n. the cultivation of fruit. [C19: from L pōmum fruit + CULTURE]

pommel (ˈpʌməl, ˈpɒm-) n. **1.** the raised part on the front of a saddle. **2.** a knob at the top of a sword or similar weapon. ~vb. **-melling, -melled** or U.S. **-meling, -meled. 3.** a less common word for **pummel.** [C14: from OF pomel knob, from Vulgar L *pōmellum* (unattested) little apple, from L *pōmum* apple]

Pommern ('pɔmərn) *n.* the German name for **Pomerania.**

pommy ('pɒmɪ) *n.*, *pl.* **-mies.** (*sometimes cap.*) *Sl.* a mildly offensive word used by Australians and New Zealanders for a British person. Sometimes shortened to **pom.** [C20: from ?, ? a blend of IMMIGRANT & POMEGRANATE (alluding to the red cheeks of British immigrants)]

pomology (pɒ'mɒlədʒɪ) *n.* the branch of horticulture concerned with the study and cultivation of fruit. [C19: from NL *pōmologia*, from L *pōmum* fruit] —**pomological** (,pɒmə'lɒdʒɪkᵊl) *adj.*

Pomona[1] (pə'məunə) *n.* another name for **Mainland** (in the Orkneys).

Pomona[2] (pə'məunə) *n.* the Roman goddess of fruit trees.

Pomorze (pɔ'mɔʒɛ) *n.* the Polish name for **Pomerania.**

pomp (pɒmp) *n.* **1.** stately or magnificent display; ceremonial splendour. **2.** vain display, esp. of dignity or importance. **3.** *Obs.* a procession or pageant. [C14: from OF *pompe*, from L *pompa* procession, from Gk *pompē*]

pompadour ('pɒmpə,duə) *n.* an early 18th-century hairstyle for women, having the front hair arranged over a pad to give it greater height and bulk. [C18: after the Marquise de POMPADOUR, who originated it]

Pompadour (*French* pɔ̃padur) *n.* **Marquise de,** title of *Jeanne Antoinette Poisson.* 1721–64, mistress of Louis XV of France (1745–64), whom she greatly influenced.

pompano ('pɒmpə,nəu) *n.*, *pl.* **-no** *or* **-nos.** **1.** any of several food fishes of American coastal regions of the Atlantic. **2.** a spiny-finned food fish of North American coastal regions of the Pacific. [C19: from Sp. *pámpano*, from ?]

Pompeii (pɒm'peiɪ) *n.* an ancient city in Italy, southeast of Naples: buried by an eruption of Vesuvius (79 A.D.); excavation of the site, which is extremely well preserved, began in 1748. —**Pompeiian** (pɒm'peɪən, -'piː-) *adj.*, *n.*

Pompey[1] ('pɒmpɪ) *n.* an informal name for **Portsmouth.**

Pompey[2] ('pɒmpɪ) *n.* called *Pompey the Great;* Latin name *Gnaeus Pompeius Magnus.* 106–48 B.C., Roman general and statesman; a member with Caesar and Crassus of the first triumvirate (60). He later quarrelled with Caesar, who defeated him at Pharsalus (48). He fled to Egypt and was murdered.

Pompidou (*French* pɔ̃pidu) *n.* **Georges** (ʒɔrʒ). 1911–74, French statesman; president of France (1969–74).

pom-pom ('pɒmpɒm) *n.* an automatic rapid-firing small-calibre cannon, esp. a type of anti-aircraft cannon used in World War II. Also called: **pompom.** [C19: imit.]

pompon ('pɒmpɒn) *or* **pompom** *n.* **1.** a ball of tufted silk, wool, feathers, etc., worn on a hat for decoration. **2. a.** the small globelike flower head of certain varieties of dahlia and chrysanthemum. **b.** (*as modifier*): *pompon dahlia.* [C18: from F, from OF *pompe* knot of ribbons, from ?]

pomposo (pɒm'pəusəu) *adv. Music.* in a pompous manner. [It.]

pompous ('pɒmpəs) *adj.* **1.** exaggeratedly or ostentatiously dignified or self-important. **2.** ostentatiously lofty in style: *a pompous speech.* **3.** *Rare.* characterized by ceremonial pomp or splendour. —**pomposity** (pɒm'pɒsɪtɪ) *or* **pompousness** *n.* —**pompously** *adv.*

'pon (pɒn) *Poetic or arch. contraction of* upon.

ponce (pɒns) *Derog. sl., chiefly Brit.* ~*n.* **1.** a man given to ostentatious or effeminate display. **2.** another word for **pimp**[1]. ~*vb.* **3.** (*intr.; often foll. by* around *or* about) to act like a ponce. [C19: from Polari, from Sp. *pu(n)to* male prostitute or F *pront* prostitute]

Ponce (*Spanish* 'pɒnθe) *n.* a port in S Puerto Rico, on the Caribbean: the second largest town on the island; settled in the 16th century. Pop.: 190 000 (1984 est.).

Ponce de León ('pɒns də 'liːən; *Spanish* 'pɒnθe ðe le'ɔn) *n.* **Juan** (xwan). ?1460–1521, Spanish explorer. He settled (1509) and governed (1510–12) Puerto Rico and discovered (1513) Florida.

poncho ('pɒntʃəu) *n.*, *pl.* **-chos.** a cloak of a kind originally worn in South America, made of a rectangular or circular piece of cloth with a hole in the middle for the head. [C18: from American Sp., of Amerind origin, from *pantho* woollen material]

pond (pɒnd) *n.* a pool of still water, often artificially created. [C13 *ponde* enclosure]

ponder ('pɒndə) *vb.* (when *intr.*, sometimes foll. by *on* or *over*) to give thorough or deep consideration (to); meditate (upon). [C14: from OF *ponderer*, from L *ponderāre* to weigh, consider, from *pondus* weight] —**'ponderable** *adj.*

ponderous ('pɒndərəs) *adj.* **1.** heavy; huge. **2.** (esp. of movement) lacking ease or lightness; lumbering or graceless. **3.** dull or laborious: *a ponderous oration.* [C14: from L *ponderōsus* of great weight, from *pondus* weight] —**'ponderously** *adv.* —**'ponderousness** *or* **ponderosity** (,pɒndə'rɒsɪtɪ) *n.*

Pondicherry (,pɒndɪ'tʃɛrɪ) *n.* **1.** a Union Territory of SE India: transferred from French to Indian administration in 1954 and made a Union Territory in 1962. Capital: Pondicherry. Pop.: 604 136 (1981). Area: 479 sq. km (185 sq. miles). **2.** a port in SE India, capital of the Union Territory of Pondicherry, on the Coromandel Coast. Pop.: 251 000 (1981).

pond lily *n.* another name for **water lily.**

pondok ('pɒndɒk) *or* **pondokie** *n. Derog.* (in southern Africa) a crudely made house built of tin sheet, reeds, etc. [C20: from Malay *pondók* leaf house]

Pondoland ('pɒndəu,lænd) *n.* part of the Transkei, South Africa: inhabited chiefly by the Pondo people.

pond scum *n.* a greenish layer floating on the surface of stagnant waters, consisting of algae.

pondweed ('pɒnd,wiːd) *n.* **1.** any of various water plants of the genus *Potamogeton*, which grow in ponds and slow streams. **2.** Also called: **waterweed.** *Brit.* any of various water plants, such as mare's-tail, that have thin or much-divided leaves.

pone[1] (pəun, 'pəunɪ) *n. Cards.* the player to the right of the dealer, or the nondealer in two-handed games. [C19: from L: put!, that is, play, from *ponere* to put]

pone[2] (pəun) *n. Southern U.S.* bread made of maize. Also called: **pone bread, corn pone.** [C17: of Amerind origin]

pong (pɒŋ) *Brit. inf.* ~*n.* **1.** a disagreeable or offensive smell; stink. ~*vb.* **2.** (*intr.*) to stink. [C20: ?from Romany *pan* to stink] —**'pongy** *adj.*

ponga ('pʊŋə) *n.* a tall New Zealand tree fern with large leathery leaves.

pongee (pɒn'dʒiː, 'pɒndʒiː) *n.* **1.** a thin plain-weave silk fabric from China or India, left in its natural colour. **2.** a cotton or rayon fabric similar to this. [C18: from Mandarin Chinese (Peking) *pen-chī* woven at home, from *pen* own + *chi* loom]

pongid ('pɒŋgɪd, 'pɒndʒɪd) *n.* **1.** any primate of the family Pongidae, which includes the gibbons and the great apes. ~*adj.* **2.** of this family. [from NL *Pongo* type genus, from Congolese *mpongo* ape]

pongo ('pɒŋgəu) *n.*, *pl.* **-gos.** an anthropoid ape, esp. an orang-utan or (formerly) a gorilla. [C17: from Congolese *mpongo*]

poniard ('pɒnjəd) *n.* **1.** a small dagger with a slender blade. ~*vb.* **2.** (*tr.*) to stab with a poniard. [C16: from OF *poignard*, from *poing* fist, from L *pugnus*]

pons Varolii (pɒnz və'rəulɪ,aɪ) *n.*, *pl.* **pontes Varolii** ('pɒntiːz). a broad white band of connecting nerve fibres that bridges the hemispheres of the cerebellum in mammals. Sometimes shortened to **pons.** [C18: NL, lit.: bridge of Varoli, after Costanzo *Varoli* (?1543–75), It. anatomist]

Ponta Delgada (*Portuguese* 'pɒntə ðɛl'gaðə) *n.* a port in the E Azores, on S São Miguel Island: chief commercial centre of the archipelago. Pop.: 22 200 (1981).

Pontchartrain ('pɒntʃə,treɪn) *n.* **Lake.** a shallow lagoon in SE Louisiana, linked with the Gulf of Mexico by a narrow channel, the **Rigolets:** resort and fishing centre. Area: 1620 sq. km (625 sq. miles).

Pontefract ('pɒntɪ,frækt) *n.* an industrial town in N England, in West Yorkshire: castle (1069), in which Richard II was imprisoned and murdered (1400). Pop.: 32 836 (1981).

Pontevedra (*Spanish* pɒnte'βeðra) *n.* a port in NW Spain: takes its name from a 12-arched Roman bridge, the Pons Vetus. Pop.: 64 184 (1981).

Pontiac ('pɒntɪ,æk) *n.* died 1769, chief of the Ottawa Indians, who led a rebellion against the British (1763–66).

Pontianak (,pɒntɪ'ɑːnæk) *n.* a port in Indonesia, on W coast of Borneo almost exactly on the equator. Pop.: 304 000 (1981 est.).

Pontic ('pɒntɪk) *adj.* denoting or relating to the Black Sea. [C15: from L *Ponticus*, from Gk, from *Pontos* PONTUS]

pontifex ('pɒntɪˌfɛks) *n.*, *pl.* **pontifices** (pɒn'tɪfɪˌsiːz). (in ancient Rome) any of the senior members of the Pontifical College, presided over by the **Pontifex Maximus**. [C16: from L, ?from Etruscan but infl. by folk etymology as if meaning lit.: bridge-maker]

pontiff ('pɒntɪf) *n.* a former title of the pagan high priest at Rome, later used of popes and occasionally of other bishops, and now confined to the pope. [C17: from F *pontife*, from L PONTIFEX]

pontifical (pɒn'tɪfɪk³l) *adj.* **1.** of, relating to, or characteristic of a pontiff. **2.** having an excessively authoritative manner; pompous. ~*n.* **3.** *R.C. Church, Church of England.* a book containing the prayers and ritual instructions for ceremonies restricted to a bishop. —**pon'tifically** *adv.*

pontificals (pɒn'tɪfɪk³lz) *pl. n. Chiefly R.C. Church.* the insignia and special vestments worn by a bishop, esp. when celebrating High Mass.

pontificate *vb.* (pɒn'tɪfɪˌkeɪt). (*intr.*) **1.** to speak or behave in a pompous or dogmatic manner. **2.** to serve or officiate at a Pontifical Mass. ~*n.* (pɒn'tɪfɪkɪt). **3.** the office or term of office of a pope.

Pontine Marshes ('pɒntaɪn) *pl. n.* an area of W Italy, southeast of Rome: formerly malarial swamps, drained in 1932–34 after numerous attempts since 160 B.C. had failed. Italian name: **Agro Pontino** ('aːgro pon'tiːno)

Pontius Pilate ('pɒnʃəs, 'pɒntɪəs 'paɪlət) *n.* See **Pilate**.

pontoon[1] (pɒn'tuːn) *n.* **a.** a watertight float or vessel used where buoyancy is required in water, as in supporting a bridge, in salvage work, or where a temporary or mobile structure is required in military operations. **b.** (*as modifier*): *a pontoon bridge*. [C17: from F *ponton*, from L *pontō* punt, from *pōns* bridge]

pontoon[2] (pɒn'tuːn) *n.* a gambling game in which players try to obtain card combinations better than the banker's but never worth more than 21 points. Also called: **twenty-one** (esp. U.S.), **vingt-et-un**. [C20: prob. an alteration of F *vingt-et-un*, lit.: twenty-one]

Pontormo (*Italian* pon'tormo) *n.* **Jacopo da** ('jaːkopo da). original name *Jacopo Carrucci*. 1494–1556, Italian mannerist painter.

Pontus ('pɒntəs) *n.* an ancient region of NE Asia Minor, on the Black Sea: became a kingdom in the 4th century B.C.; at its height under Mithridates VI (about 115–63 B.C.), when it controlled all Asia Minor; defeated by the Romans in the mid-1st century B.C.

Pontus Euxinus (juːk'saɪnəs) *n.* the Latin name of the **Black Sea**.

Pontypool (ˌpɒntɪ'puːl) *n.* an industrial town in E Wales, in Gwent: famous for lacquered ironware in the 18th century. Pop.: 36 761 (1981).

Pontypridd (ˌpɒntɪ'priːð) *n.* an industrial town in S Wales, in SE Mid Glamorgan. Pop.: 32 992 (1981).

pony ('pəʊnɪ) *n.*, *pl.* **-nies. 1.** any of various breeds of small horse, usually under 14.2 hands. **2.** a small drinking glass, esp. for liqueurs. **3.** anything small of its kind. **4.** *Brit. sl.* a sum of £25, esp. in bookmaking. **5.** Also called: **trot.** *U.S. sl.* a translation used by students, often illicitly; crib. [C17: from Scot. *powney*, ?from obs. F *poulenet* a little colt, from L *pullus* young animal, foal]

ponytail ('pəʊnɪˌteɪl) *n.* a hairstyle for girls and women in which the hair is gathered together tightly by a band at the back of the head into a loose-hanging fall.

pony trekking *n.* the act of riding ponies cross-country, esp. as a pastime.

pooch (puːtʃ) *n. Chiefly U.S. & Canad.* a slang word for **dog**. [from ?]

poodle ('puːd³l) *n.* **1.** a breed of dog with curly hair, which is generally clipped from ribs to tail. **2.** a servile person; lackey. [C19: from G *Pudel*, short for *Pudelhund*, from *pudeln* to splash + *Hund* dog; formerly trained as water dogs]

poof (pʊf, puːf), **poove** (puːv), or **poofter** ('puːftə) *n. Brit. derog. sl.* a male homosexual. [C20: from F *pouffe* puff]

pooh (puː) *interj.* an exclamation of disdain, contempt, or disgust.

Pooh-Bah ('puː'bɑː) *n.* a pompous self-important official holding several offices at once and fulfilling none of them. [C19: after the character, the Lord-High-Everything-Else, in *The Mikado* (1885), by Gilbert & Sullivan]

pooh-pooh ('puː'puː) *vb.* (*tr.*) to express disdain or scorn for; dismiss or belittle.

pool[1] (puːl) *n.* **1.** a small body of still water, usually fresh; small pond. **2.** a small isolated collection of spilt liquid; puddle: *a pool of blood.* **3.** a deep part of a stream or river where the water runs very slowly. **4.** an underground accumulation of oil or gas. **5.** See **swimming pool**. [OE *pōl*]

pool[2] (puːl) *n.* **1.** any communal combination of resources, funds, etc.: *a typing pool.* **2.** the combined stakes of the betters in many gambling games; kitty. **3.** *Commerce.* a group of producers who agree to establish and maintain output levels and high prices, each member of the group being allocated a maximum quota. **4.** *Finance, chiefly U.S.* a joint fund organized by security-holders for speculative or manipulative purposes on financial markets. **5.** any of various billiard games in which the object is to pot all the balls with the cue ball, esp. that played with 15 coloured and numbered balls, popular in the U.S.; pocket billiards. ~*vb.* (*tr.*) **6.** to combine (investments, money, interests, etc.) into a common fund, as for a joint enterprise. **7.** *Commerce.* to organize a pool of (enterprises). [C17: from F *poule*, lit.: hen used to signify stakes in a card game, from Med. L *pulla* hen, from L *pullus* young animal]

Poole (puːl) *n.* a port and resort in S England, in Dorset on **Poole Harbour**. Pop.: 123 000 (1984 est.).

Pool Malebo ('puːl mə'liːbəʊ) *n.* the Zaïrese name for **Stanley Pool**.

pools (puːlz) *pl. n.* **the** *Brit.* an organized nationwide principally postal gambling pool betting on the result of football matches. Also called: **football pools**.

Poona *or* **Pune** ('puːnə) *n.* a city in W India, in W Maharashtra: under British rule served as the seasonal capital of the Bombay Presidency. Pop.: 1 202 848 (1981).

poop[1] (puːp) *Naut.* ~*n.* **1.** a raised structure at the stern of a vessel, esp. a sailing ship. **2.** Also called: **poop deck.** a raised deck at the stern of a ship. ~*vb.* **3.** (*tr.*) (of a wave or sea) to break over the stern of (a vessel). **4.** (*intr.*) (of a vessel) to ship a wave or sea over the stern, esp. repeatedly. [C15: from OF *pupe*, from L *puppis*]

poop[2] (puːp) *vb. U.S. & Canad. sl.* **1.** (*tr.*; usually passive) to cause to become exhausted; tire: *he was pooped after the race.* **2.** (*intr.*; usually foll. by *out*) to give up or fail: *he pooped out of the race.* [C14 *poupen* to blow, ? imit.]

Poopó (*Spanish* poo'po) *n.* **Lake.** a lake in SW Bolivia, at an altitude of 3688 m (12 100 ft.): fed by the Desaguadero River. Area: 2540 sq. km (980 sq. miles).

poor (pʊə, pɔː) *adj.* **1.** lacking financial or other means of subsistence; needy. **2.** characterized by or indicating poverty: *the country had a poor economy.* **3.** scanty or inadequate: *a poor salary.* **4.** (when *postpositive*, usually foll. by *in*) badly supplied (with resources, etc.): *a region poor in wild flowers.* **5.** inferior. **6.** contemptible or despicable. **7.** disappointing or disagreeable: *a poor play.* **8.** (*prenominal*) deserving of pity; unlucky: *poor John is ill again.* [C13: from OF *povre*, from L *pauper*] —'**poorness** *n.*

poor box *n.* a box, esp. one in a church, used for the collection of alms or money for the poor.

poorhouse ('pʊəˌhaʊs, 'pɔː-) *n.* another name for **workhouse** (sense 1).

poor law *n. English history.* a law providing for the relief or support of the poor from parish funds.

poorly ('pʊəlɪ, 'pɔː-) *adv.* **1.** badly. ~*adj.* **2.** (*usually postpositive*) *Inf.* in poor health; rather ill.

poort (pʊət) *n.* (in South Africa) a steep narrow mountain pass, usually following a river or stream. [C19: from Afrik., from Du.: gateway]

poor White *n. Often offens.* **a.** a poverty-stricken and underprivileged White person, esp. in the southern U.S. and South Africa. **b.** (*as modifier*): *poor White trash.*

pop[1] (pɒp) *vb.* **popping, popped. 1.** to make or cause to make a light sharp explosive sound. **2.** to burst open with such a sound. **3.** (*intr.*; often foll. by *in, out,* etc.) *Inf.* to come (to) or go (from) rapidly or suddenly. **4.** (*intr.*) (esp. of the eyes) to protrude: *her eyes popped with amazement.* **5.** to shoot at (a target) with a firearm. **6.** (*tr.*) to place with a sudden movement: *she popped some tablets into her mouth.* **7.** (*tr.*) *Inf.* to pawn: *he popped his watch yesterday.* **8.** (*tr.*) *Sl.* to take (a drug) in pill form or as an injection. **9. pop the question.** *Inf.* to propose marriage. ~*n.* **10.** a light sharp explosive sound;

crack. **11.** *Inf.* a flavoured nonalcoholic carbonated beverage. ~*adv.* **12.** with a popping sound. ~See also **pop off.** [C14: imit.]

pop² (pɒp) *n.* **1. a.** music of general appeal, esp. among young people, that originated as a distinctive genre in the 1950s. It is generally characterized by a heavy rhythmic element and the use of electrical amplification. **b.** *(as modifier): a pop group.* **2.** *Inf.* a piece of popular or light classical music. ~*adj.* **3.** *Inf.* short for **popular.**

pop³ (pɒp) *n.* **1.** an informal word for **father. 2.** *Inf.* a name used in addressing an old man.

POP *abbrev. for* Post Office Preferred (size of envelopes, etc.).

pop. *abbrev. for:* **1.** popular(ly). **2.** population.

pop art *n.* a movement in modern art that imitates the methods, styles, and themes of popular culture and mass media, such as comic strips, advertising, and science fiction.

popcorn ('pɒp,kɔːn) *n.* **1.** a variety of maize having hard pointed kernels that puff up and burst when heated. **2.** the puffed edible kernels of this plant.

pope (pəʊp) *n.* **1.** *(often cap.)* the bishop of Rome as head of the Roman Catholic Church. **2.** *Eastern Orthodox Churches.* a title sometimes given to a parish priest or to the Greek Orthodox patriarch of Alexandria. [OE *papa*, from Church L: bishop, esp. of Rome, from LGk *papas* father-in-God, from Gk *pappas* father] —'**popedom** *n.*

Pope (pəʊp) *n.* **Alexander.** 1688–1744, English poet, regarded as the most brilliant satirist of the Augustan period, esp. with his *Imitations of Horace* (1733–38). His technical virtuosity is most evident in *The Rape of the Lock* (1712–14). Other works include *The Dunciad* (1728; 1742), the *Moral Essays* (1731–35), and *An Essay on Man* (1733–34).

popery ('pəʊpərɪ) *n.* a derogatory name for **Roman Catholicism.**

popeyed ('pɒp,aɪd) *adj.* **1.** having bulging prominent eyes. **2.** staring in astonishment.

popgun ('pɒp,gʌn) *n.* a toy gun that fires a pellet or cork by means of compressed air.

popinjay ('pɒpɪn,dʒeɪ) *n.* **1.** a conceited, foppish, or excessively talkative person. **2.** an archaic word for **parrot. 3.** the figure of a parrot used as a target. [C13 *papeniai*, from OF *papegay* a parrot, from Sp., from Ar. *babaghā*]

popish ('pəʊpɪʃ) *adj. Derog.* belonging to or characteristic of Roman Catholicism.

poplar ('pɒplə) *n.* **1.** a tree of N temperate regions, having triangular leaves, flowers borne in catkins, and light soft wood. **2.** *U.S.* the tulip tree. [C14: from OF *poplier*, from L *pōpulus*]

poplin ('pɒplɪn) *n.* a strong fabric, usually of cotton, in plain weave with fine ribbing. [C18: from F *papeline*, ?from *Poperinge*, a centre of textile manufacture in Flanders]

popliteal (pɒp'lɪtɪəl, ,pɒplɪ'tiːəl) *adj.* of, relating to, or near the part of the leg behind the knee. [C18: from NL *popliteus* the muscle behind the knee joint, from L *poples* the ham of the knee]

Popocatépetl (,pɒpə'kætəpetəl, -,kætə'petəl; *Spanish* popoka'tepetl) *n.* a volcano in SE central Mexico, southeast of Mexico City. Height: 5452 m (17 887 ft.).

pop off *vb. (intr., adv.) Inf.* **1.** to depart suddenly or unexpectedly. **2.** to die, esp. suddenly.

Popov (*Russian* pa'pɔf) *n.* **Alexander Stepanovich** (alɪk'sandᵊr stɪ'panəvitʃ). 1859–1906, Russian physicist, the first to use an aerial in experiments with radio waves.

poppadom *or* **poppadum** ('pɒpədəm) *n.* a thin round crisp Indian bread, fried or roasted and served with curry, etc. [from Hindi]

popper ('pɒpə) *n.* **1.** a person or thing that pops. **2.** *Brit.* an informal name for **press stud. 3.** *Chiefly U.S. & Canad.* a container for cooking popcorn in. **4.** *Sl.* an amyl nitrite capsule, crushed and inhaled by drug users.

Popper ('pɒpə) *n.* **Sir Karl.** born 1902, British philosopher, born in Vienna. In *The Logic of Scientific Discovery* (1934), he proposes that knowledge cannot be absolutely confirmed, but rather that science progresses by the experimental refutation of the current theory and its consequent replacement by a new theory, equally provisional but covering more of the known data. *The Open Society and its Enemies* (1945) is a critique of dogmatic political philosophies, such as Marxism. Other works are *The Poverty of Historicism* (1957), *Conjectures and Refutations* (1963), and *Objective Knowledge* (1972). —**Popperian** (pɒ'pɪərɪən) *n., adj.*

poppet ('pɒpɪt) *n.* **1.** a term of affection for a small child or sweetheart. **2.** Also called: **poppet valve.** a mushroom-shaped valve that is lifted from its seating by applying an axial force to its stem. **3.** *Naut.* a temporary supporting brace for a vessel hauled on land. [C14: early var. of PUPPET]

popping crease *n. Cricket.* a line four feet in front of and parallel with the bowling crease, at or behind which the batsman stands. [C18: from POP¹ (in the obs. sense: to hit) + CREASE]

popple ('pɒpᵊl) *vb. (intr.)* **1.** (of boiling water or a choppy sea) to heave or toss; bubble. **2.** (often foll. by *along*) (of a stream or river) to move with an irregular tumbling motion. [C14: imit.]

poppy ('pɒpɪ) *n., pl.* **-pies. 1.** any of numerous papaveraceous plants having red, orange, or white flowers and a milky sap. **2.** any of several similar or related plants, such as the California poppy and Welsh poppy. **3.** any of the drugs, such as opium, that are obtained from these plants. **4. a.** a strong red to reddish-orange colour. **b.** *(as adj.): a poppy dress.* **5.** an artificial red poppy flower worn to mark Remembrance Sunday. [OE *popæg*, ult. from L *papāver*]

poppycock ('pɒpɪ,kɒk) *n. Inf.* nonsense. [C19: from Du. dialect *pappekak*, lit.: soft excrement]

Poppy Day *n.* an informal name for **Remembrance Sunday.**

poppyhead ('pɒpɪ,hɛd) *n.* **1.** the hard dry seed-containing capsule of a poppy. **2.** a carved ornament, esp. one used on the top of the end of a pew or bench in Gothic church architecture.

poppy seed *n.* the small grey seeds of one type of poppy flower, used esp. on loaves.

pop socks *pl. n.* knee-length nylon stockings.

popsy ('pɒpsɪ) *n., pl.* **-sies.** *Old-fashioned Brit. sl.* an attractive young woman. [C19: dim. from *pop*, shortened from POPPET; orig. a nursery term]

populace ('pɒpjʊləs) *n. (sometimes functioning as pl.)* **1.** local inhabitants. **2.** the common people; masses. [C16: via F from It. *popolaccio* the common herd, from *popolo* people, from L *populus*]

popular ('pɒpjʊlə) *adj.* **1.** widely favoured or admired. **2.** favoured by an individual or limited group: *I'm not very popular with her.* **3.** prevailing among the general public; common: *popular discontent.* **4.** appealing to or comprehensible to the layman: *a popular lecture on physics.* ~*n.* **5.** *(usually pl.)* a cheap newspaper with a mass circulation. [C15: from L *populāris* of the people, democratic] —**popularity** (,pɒpjʊ'lærɪtɪ) *n.* —'**popularly** *adv.*

popular front *n. (often cap.)* any of the left-wing groups or parties that were organized from 1935 onwards to oppose the spread of fascism.

popularize *or* **-ise** ('pɒpjʊlə,raɪz) *vb. (tr.)* **1.** to make popular. **2.** to make or cause to become easily understandable or acceptable. —,**populari'zation** *or* **-i'sation** *n.* —'**popular,izer** *or* **-,iser** *n.*

populate ('pɒpjʊ,leɪt) *vb. (tr.)* **1.** *(often passive)* to live in; inhabit. **2.** to provide a population for; colonize or people. [C16: from Med. L *populāre*, from L *populus* people]

population (,pɒpjʊ'leɪʃən) *n.* **1.** *(sometimes functioning as pl.)* all the persons inhabiting a specified place. **2.** the number of such inhabitants. **3.** *(sometimes functioning as pl.)* all the people of a particular class in a specific area: *the Chinese population of San Francisco.* **4.** the act or process of providing a place with inhabitants; colonization. **5.** *Ecology.* a group of individuals of the same species inhabiting a given area. **6.** *Astron.* either of two main groups of stars classified according to age and location. **7.** *Statistics.* the entire aggregate of individuals or items from which samples are drawn.

population explosion *n.* a rapid increase in the size of a population caused by such factors as a sudden decline in infant mortality or an increase in life expectancy.

Populist ('pɒpjʊlɪst) *n.* **1.** *U.S. history.* a member of the People's Party, formed largely by agrarian interests to contest the 1892 presidential election. **2.** *(often not cap.)* a politician or other person who claims to support the interests of the ordinary people. ~*adj.* **3.** of or relating to the People's Party or any individual or movement with similar aims. — '**Populism** n.

populous ('pɒpjʊləs) adj. containing many inhabitants. [C15: from LL populōsus] —'**populously** adv. —'**populousness** n.

porangi ('pɔːræŋɪ) adj. N.Z. inf. crazy; mad. [from Maori]

porbeagle ('pɔː,biːgɜl) n. any of several voracious sharks of northern seas. Also called: **mackerel shark**. [C18: from Cornish porgh-bugel, from ?]

porcelain ('pɔːslɪn) n. **1.** a more or less translucent ceramic material, the principal ingredients being kaolin and petuntse (hard paste) or other clays, bone ash, etc. **2.** an object made of this or such objects collectively. **3.** (modifier) of, relating to, or made from this material: a porcelain cup. [C16: from F porcelaine, from It. porcellana cowrie shell, lit.: relating to a sow, from porcella little sow, from porca sow, from L; see PORK] —**porcellaneous** (,pɔːsə'leɪnɪəs) adj.

porch (pɔːtʃ) n. **1.** a low structure projecting from the doorway of a house and forming a covered entrance. **2.** U.S. & Canad. a veranda. [C13: from F porche, from L porticus portico]

porcine ('pɔːsaɪn) adj. of or characteristic of pigs. [C17: from L porcinus, from porcus a pig]

porcupine ('pɔːkjʊ,paɪn) n. any of various large rodents that have a body covering of protective spines or quills. [C14 porc despyne pig with spines, from OF porc espin; see PORK, SPINE] —'**porcu,pinish** adj. —'**porcu,piny** adj.

porcupine fish n. any of various fishes of temperate and tropical seas having a body that is covered with sharp spines and can be inflated into a globe. Also called: **globefish**.

porcupine grass n. Austral. another name for **spinifex**.

pore[1] (pɔː) vb. (intr.) **1.** (foll. by over) to make a close intent examination or study (of): he pored over the documents for several hours. **2.** (foll. by over, on, or upon) to think deeply (about). **3.** (foll. by over, on, or upon) Rare. to gaze fixedly (upon). [C13 pouren]

pore[2] (pɔː) n. **1.** any small opening in the skin or outer surface of an animal. **2.** any other small hole, such as a space in a rock, etc. [C14: from LL porus, from Gk poros passage, pore]

porgy ('pɔːgɪ) n., pl. **-gy** or **-gies.** any of various perchlike fishes, many of which occur in American Atlantic waters. [C18: from Sp. pargo, from L phager, from Gk phagros sea bream]

Pori (Finnish 'pɒrɪ) n. a port in SW Finland, on the Gulf of Bothnia. Pop.: 77 805 (1986). Swedish name: **Björneborg**.

poriferan (pɔː'rɪfərən) n. any invertebrate of the phylum Porifera, which comprises the sponges. [C19: from NL porifer bearing pores]

Porirua (,pɒrɪ'ruːə) n. a city in New Zealand, on the North Island just north of Wellington. Pop.: 40 800 (1981).

pork (pɔːk) n. the flesh of pigs used as food. [C13: from OF porc, from L porcus pig]

porker ('pɔːkə) n. a pig, esp. a young one, fattened to provide meat.

pork pie n. a pie filled with minced seasoned pork.

porkpie hat ('pɔːk,paɪ) n. a hat with a round flat crown and a brim that can be turned up or down.

porky ('pɔːkɪ) adj. **porkier, porkiest. 1.** characteristic of pork. **2.** Inf. fat; obese.

porn (pɔːn) or **porno** ('pɔːnəʊ) n., adj. Inf. short for **pornography** or **pornographic**.

pornography (pɔː'nɒgrəfɪ) n. **1.** writings, pictures, films, etc., designed to stimulate sexual excitement. **2.** the production of such material. ~Sometimes (informal) shortened to **porn** or **porno**. [C19: from Gk pornographos writing of harlots] —**por'nographer** n. —**pornographic** (,pɔːnə'græfɪk) adj. —,**porno'graphically** adv.

poromeric (,pɔːrə'mɛrɪk) adj. **1.** (of a plastic) permeable to water vapour. ~n. **2.** a substance having this characteristic, esp. one used in place of leather in making shoe uppers. [C20: from PORO(SITY) + (POLY)MER + -IC]

porous ('pɔːrəs) adj. **1.** able to absorb water, air, or other fluids. **2.** Biol. & geol. having pores. [C14: from Med. L porōsus, from LL porus PORE[2]] —'**porously** adv. —**porosity** (pɔː'rɒsɪtɪ) or '**porousness** n.

porphyria (pɔː'fɪrɪə) n. a hereditary disease of body metabolism, producing abdominal pain, mental confusion, etc. [C19: from NL, from porphyrin a purple substance excreted by patients suffering from this condition, from Gk porphura purple]

porphyry ('pɔːfɪrɪ) n., pl. **-ries. 1.** a reddish-purple rock consisting of large crystals of feldspar in a finer groundmass of feldspar, hornblende, etc. **2.** any igneous rock with large crystals embedded in a finer groundmass of minerals. [C14 porfurie, from LL, from Gk porphuritēs (lithos) purple (stone), from porphuros purple] —,**porphy'ritic** adj.

porpoise ('pɔːpəs) n., pl. **-poise** or **-poises.** any of various small cetacean mammals having a blunt snout and many teeth. [C14: from F pourpois, from Med. L porcopiscus, from L porcus pig + piscis fish]

porridge ('pɒrɪdʒ) n. **1.** a dish made from oatmeal or another cereal, cooked in water or milk to a thick consistency. **2.** Sl. a term of imprisonment. [C16: var. (infl. by ME porray pottage) of POTTAGE]

porringer ('pɒrɪndʒə) n. a small dish, often with a handle, for soup, porridge, etc. [C16: changed from ME potinger, poteger, from OF, from potage soup; see POTTAGE]

Porsena ('pɔːsɪnə) or **Porsenna** (pɔː'sɛnə) n. **Lars** (lɑːz). 6th century B.C., a legendary Etruscan king, alleged to have besieged Rome in a vain attempt to reinstate Tarquinius Superbus on the throne.

Porson ('pɔːsªn) n. **Richard.** 1759–1808, English classical scholar, noted for his editions of Aeschylus and Euripides.

port[1] (pɔːt) n. **1.** a town or place alongside navigable water with facilities for the loading and unloading of ships. **2.** See **port of entry**. [OE, from L portus]

port[2] (pɔːt) n. **1.** Also called (formerly): **larboard.** the left side of an aircraft or vessel when facing the nose or bow. Cf. **starboard** (sense 1). ~vb. **2.** to turn or be turned towards the port. [C17: from ?]

port[3] (pɔːt) n. a sweet fortified dessert wine. [C17: after Oporto, Portugal, from where it came orig.]

port[4] (pɔːt) n. **1.** Naut. **a.** an opening in the side of a ship, fitted with a watertight door, for access to the holds. **b.** See **porthole** (sense 1). **2.** a small opening in a wall, armoured vehicle, etc., for firing through. **3.** an aperture by which fluid enters or leaves the cylinder head of an engine, compressor, etc. **4.** Electronics. a logical circuit for the input and ouput of data. **5.** Chiefly Scot. a gate in a town or fortress. [OE, from L porta gate]

port[5] (pɔːt) vb. (tr.) Mil. to carry (a rifle, etc.) in a position diagonally across the body with the muzzle near the left shoulder. [C14: from OF, from porter to carry, from L portāre]

port[6] (pɔːt) n. Austral. a travelling bag, such as a suitcase. [C20: shortened from PORTMANTEAU]

Port. abbrev. for: **1.** Portugal. **2.** Portuguese.

portable ('pɔːtəbªl) adj. **1.** able to be carried or moved easily, esp. by hand. ~n. **2.** an article designed to be readily carried by hand, such as a television, typewriter, etc. [C14: from LL portābilis, from L portāre to carry] —,**porta'bility** n. —'**portably** adv.

Port Adelaide n. the chief port of South Australia, near Adelaide on St Vincent Gulf. Pop.: 37 000 (1985).

Portadown (,pɔːtə'daʊn) n. a town in S Northern Ireland, in the district of Armagh. Pop.: 21 333 (1981).

portage ('pɔːtɪdʒ) n. **1.** the act of carrying; transport. **2.** the cost of carrying or transporting. **3.** the transporting of boats, supplies, etc., overland between navigable waterways. **4.** the route used for such transport. ~vb. **5.** to transport (boats, supplies, etc.) thus. [C15: from F, from OF porter to carry]

Portakabin ('pɔːtə,kæbɪn) n. Trademark. a portable building quickly set up for use as a temporary office, etc.

portal ('pɔːtªl) n. an entrance, gateway, or doorway, esp. one that is large and impressive. [C14: via OF from Med. L portāle, from L porta gate]

portal vein n. any vein connecting two capillary networks, esp. in the liver.

portamento (,pɔːtə'mɛntəʊ) n., pl. **-ti** (-tɪ). Music. a smooth slide from one note to another in which intervening notes are not separately discernible. [C18: from It.: a carrying, from L portāre to carry]

Port Arthur n. **1.** a former penal settlement (1833–70) in Australia, on the S coast of the Tasman Peninsula, Tasmania. **2.** the former name of **Lüshun**.

portative ('pɔːtətɪv) adj. **1.** a less common word for **portable. 2.** concerned with the act of carrying. [C14: from F, from L portāre to carry]

Port-au-Prince ('pɔːtəʊ'prɪns; French pɔrtoprɛ̃s) n. the capital and chief port of Haiti, in the south on the Gulf of

Gonaïves: founded in 1749 by the French; university (1944). Pop.: 472 895 (1987 est.).

Port Blair (blɛə) *n.* the capital of the Indian Union Territory of the Andaman and Nicobar Islands, a port on the SE coast of South Andaman Island: a former penal colony. Pop.: 49 634 (1981).

portcullis (pɔːt'kʌlɪs) *n.* an iron or wooden grating suspended vertically in grooves in the gateway of a castle or town and able to be lowered so as to bar the entrance. [C14 *port colice*, from OF *porte coleïce* sliding gate, from *porte* door + *coleïce*, from *couler* to slide, from LL *cōlāre* to filter]

Porte (pɔːt) *n.* short for Sublime Porte; the court or government of the Ottoman Empire. [C17: shortened from F *Sublime Porte* High Gate, rendering the Turkish title *Babi Ali*, the imperial gate, regarded as the seat of government]

porte-cochere (ˌpɔːtkɒ'ʃɛə) *n.* **1.** a large covered entrance for vehicles leading into a courtyard. **2.** a large roof projecting over a drive to shelter travellers entering or leaving vehicles. [C17: from F: carriage entrance]

Port Elizabeth *n.* a port in South Africa, in SE Cape Province on Algoa Bay: motor-vehicle manufacture; resort. Pop.: 277 844 (1985).

portend (pɔː'tɛnd) *vb.* (*tr.*) to give warning of; foreshadow. [C15: from L *portendere* to indicate]

portent ('pɔːtɛnt) *n.* **1.** a sign of a future event; omen. **2.** momentous or ominous significance: *a cry of dire portent.* **3.** a marvel. [C16: from L *portentum* sign, from *portendere* to portend]

portentous (pɔː'tɛntəs) *adj.* **1.** of momentous or ominous significance. **2.** miraculous, amazing, or awe-inspiring. **3.** self-important or pompous.

porter[1] ('pɔːtə) *n.* **1.** a man employed to carry luggage, parcels, supplies, etc., at a railway station or hotel. **2.** *U.S. & Canad.* a railway employee who waits on passengers, esp. in a sleeper. [C14: from OF *portour*, from LL *portātōr*, from L *portāre* to carry] — **'porterage** *n.*

porter[2] ('pɔːtə) *n.* **1.** *Chiefly Brit.* a person in charge of a gate or door; doorman or gatekeeper. **2.** a person employed as a caretaker and doorkeeper who also answers inquiries. **3.** a person in charge of the maintenance of a building, esp. a block of flats. [C13: from OF *portier*, from LL *portārius*, from L *porta* door]

porter[3] ('pɔːtə) *n. Brit.* a dark sweet ale brewed from black malt. [C18: from *porter's ale*, apparently because it was a favourite beverage of porters]

Porter ('pɔːtə) *n.* **1. Cole.** 1893–1964, U.S. composer and lyricist of musical comedies. His most popular songs include *Night and Day* and *Let's do It.* **2. Sir George.** born 1920, British chemist, who shared a Nobel prize for chemistry in 1967 for his work on flash photolysis. **3. Katherine Anne.** 1894–1980, U.S. short-story writer and novelist. Her best-known collections of stories are *Flowering Judas* (1930) and *Pale Horse, Pale Rider* (1939). **4. Peter.** born 1929, Australian poet, living in Britain. **5. William Sidney.** original name of **O. Henry.**

porterhouse ('pɔːtəˌhaʊs) *n.* **1.** Also called: **porterhouse steak.** a thick choice steak of beef cut from the middle ribs or sirloin. **2.** (formerly) a place in which porter, beer, etc., and sometimes chops and steaks, were served. [C19 (sense 1): said to be after a porterhouse in New York]

portfire ('pɔːtˌfaɪə) *n.* a slow-burning fuse used for firing rockets and fireworks and, in mining, for igniting explosives. [C17: from F *porte-feu*, from *porter* to carry + *feu* fire]

portfolio (pɔːt'fəʊlɪəʊ) *n., pl.* **-os. 1.** a flat case, esp. of leather, used for carrying maps, drawings, etc. **2.** the contents of such a case, such as drawings or photographs, that demonstrate recent work. **3.** such a case used for carrying ministerial or state papers. **4.** the responsibilities or role of the head of a government department: *the portfolio for foreign affairs.* **5. Minister without portfolio.** a cabinet minister who is not responsible for any government department. **6.** the complete investments held by an individual investor or a financial organization. [C18: from It. *portafoglio*, from *portāre* to carry + *foglio* leaf, from L *folium*]

portfolio management *n.* the service provided by an investment adviser who manages a financial portfolio on behalf of the investor.

Port-Gentil (*French* pɔrʒɑ̃ti) *n.* the chief port of Gabon, in the west near the mouth of the Ogooué River: oil refinery. Pop.: 124 400 (1985 est.).

Port Harcourt ('hɑːkət, -kɔːt) *n.* a port in S Nigeria, capital of Rivers state on the Niger delta: the nation's second largest port; industrial centre. Pop.: 296 200 (1983).

porthole ('pɔːtˌhəʊl) *n.* **1.** a small aperture in the side of a vessel to admit light and air, fitted with a watertight cover. Sometimes shortened to **port. 2.** an opening in a wall or parapet through which a gun can be fired.

portico ('pɔːtɪkəʊ) *n., pl.* **-coes** or **-cos. 1.** a covered entrance to a building; porch. **2.** a covered walkway in the form of a roof supported by columns or pillars, esp. one built on to the exterior of a building. [C17: via It. from L *porticus*]

portière (ˌpɔːtɪ'ɛə; *French* pɔrtjɛr) *n.* a curtain hung in a doorway. [C19: via F from Med. L *portāria*, from L *porta* door] — **ˌporti'èred** *adj.*

Porţile de Fier (pɔr'tsiːlɛ dɛ 'fjɛr) *n.* the Romanian name for the **Iron Gate.**

portion ('pɔːʃən) *n.* **1.** a part of a whole. **2.** a part allotted or belonging to a person or group. **3.** an amount of food served to one person; helping. **4.** *Law.* **a.** a share of property, esp. one coming to a child from the estate of his parents. **b.** a dowry. **5.** a person's lot or destiny. ~*vb.* (*tr.*) **6.** to divide up; share out. **7.** to give a share to (a person). [C13: via OF from L *portiō*] — **'portionless** *adj.*

Port Jackson *n.* an inlet of the Pacific on the coast of SE Australia, forming a fine natural harbour: site of the city of Sydney, spanned by Sydney Harbour Bridge.

Portland ('pɔːtlənd) *n.* **1. Isle of.** a rugged limestone peninsula in SW England, in Dorset, connected to the mainland by a narrow isthmus and by Chesil Bank: the lighthouse of **Portland Bill** lies at the S tip; famous for the quarrying of **Portland stone,** a fine building material. Pop.: 10 915 (1981). **2.** an inland port in NW Oregon, on the Willamette River: the largest city in the state; shipbuilding and chemical industries. Pop.: 387 870 (1986). **3.** a port in SW Maine, on Casco Bay: the largest city in the state; settled by Englishmen in 1632, destroyed successively by French, Indian, and British attacks, and rebuilt; capital of Maine (1820–32). Pop.: 61 572 (1980).

Portland cement *n.* a cement that hardens under water and is made by heating clay and crushed chalk or limestone. [C19: after the Isle of PORTLAND, because its colour resembles that of the stone quarried there]

Portlaoise (ˌpɔːt'liːʃə) *n.* a town in central Ireland, county town of Co. Laoighis: site of a top-security prison. Pop.: 8500 (1985).

Port Louis ('luːɪs, 'luːiː) *n.* the capital and chief port of Mauritius, on the NW coast on the Indian Ocean. Pop.: 138 482 (1986).

portly ('pɔːtlɪ) *adj.* **-lier, -liest. 1.** stout or corpulent. **2.** *Arch.* stately; impressive. [C16: from PORT[5](in the sense: deportment)] — **'portliness** *n.*

Port Lyautey (ljəʊ'teɪ) *n.* the former name (1932–56) of **Mina Hassan Tani.**

portmanteau (pɔːt'mæntəʊ) *n., pl.* **-teaus** or **-teaux** (-təʊz). **1.** (formerly) a large travelling case made of stiff leather, esp. one hinged at the back so as to open out into two compartments. **2.** (*modifier*) embodying several uses or qualities: *the heroine is a portmanteau figure of all the virtues.* [C16: from F: cloak carrier]

portmanteau word *n.* another name for **blend** (sense 7). [C19: from the idea that two meanings are packed into one word]

Port Moresby ('mɔːzbɪ) *n.* the capital and chief port of Papua New Guinea, on the SE coast on the Gulf of Papua: important Allied base in World War II. Pop.: 152 100 (1987 est.).

Port Nicholson *n.* the former name for Wellington Harbour.

Pôrto ('portu) *n.* the Portuguese name for **Oporto.**

Pôrto Alegre (*Portuguese* 'portu a'lɛgri) *n.* a port in S Brazil, capital of the Rio Grande do Sul state: the country's chief inland port; the chief commercial centre of S Brazil, with two universities (1936 and 1948). Pop.: 1 275 483 (1985).

Portobello (ˌpɔːtəʊ'bɛləʊ) *n.* a small port in Panama, on the Caribbean northeast of Colón: the most important port in South America in colonial times; declined with the opening of the Panama Canal. Pop.: 2657 (1980 est.).

port of call n. **1.** a port where a ship stops. **2.** any place visited on a traveller's itinerary.

port of entry n. Law. an airport, harbour, etc., where customs officials are stationed to supervise the entry into and exit from a country of persons and merchandise.

Port of Spain n. the capital and chief port of Trinidad and Tobago, on the W coast of Trinidad. Pop.: 57 400 (1986 est.).

Porto Novo ('pɔːtəʊ 'nəʊvəʊ) n. the capital of Benin, in the southwest on a coastal lagoon: formerly a centre of Portuguese settlement and the slave trade. Pop.: 208 258 (1982).

Porto Rico ('pɔːtə 'riːkəʊ) n. the former name (until 1932) of **Puerto Rico.** —**Porto Rican** adj., n.

Pôrto Velho (Portuguese 'portu 'vɛʌu) n. a city in W Brazil, capital of the federal territory of Rondônia on the Madeira River. Pop.: 101 644 (1980).

Port Phillip Bay or **Port Phillip** n. a bay in SE Australia, which forms the harbour of Melbourne.

portrait ('pɔːtrɪt, -treɪt) n. **1.** a painting or other likeness of an individual, esp. of the face. **2.** a verbal description, esp. of a person's character. [C16: from F, from portraire to PORTRAY] —**'portraitist** n.

portraiture ('pɔːtrɪtʃə) n. **1.** the practice or art of making portraits. **2. a.** a portrait. **b.** portraits collectively. **3.** a verbal description.

portray (pɔː'treɪ) vb. (tr.) **1.** to make a portrait of. **2.** to depict in words. **3.** to play the part of (a character) in a play or film. [C14: from OF portraire to depict, from L prōtrahere to drag forth] —**por'trayal** n. —**por'trayer** n.

Port Royal n. **1.** a fortified town in SE Jamaica, at the entrance to Kingston harbour: capital of Jamaica in colonial times. **2.** the former name (until 1710) of **Annapolis Royal.**

Port Said ('sɑːiːd, saɪd) n. a port in NE Egypt, at the N end of the Suez Canal: founded in 1859 when the Suez Canal was begun; became the largest coaling station in the world and later an oil-bunkering port; damaged in the Arab–Israeli wars of 1967 and 1973. Pop.: 374 000 (1985).

Port-Salut ('pɔː sə'luː; French pɔrsaly) n. a mild semihard whole-milk cheese of a round flat shape. Also called: **Port du Salut.** [C19: named after the Trappist monastery at Port du Salut in NW France where it was first made]

Portsmouth ('pɔːtsməθ) n. **1.** a port in S England, in Hampshire on the English Channel: Britain's chief naval base. Pop.: 179 419 (1981). Informal name: **Pompey. 2.** a port in SE Virginia, on the Elizabeth River: naval base; shipyards. Pop.: 111 000 (1986 est.).

Port Sudan n. the chief port of the Sudan, in the NE on the Red Sea. Pop.: 206 727 (1983).

Port Talbot ('tɔːlbət, 'tæl-) n. a port in SE Wales, in West Glamorgan on Swansea Bay: established as a coal port in the mid-19th century; large steelworks; ore terminal. Pop.: 47 313 (1981).

Portugal ('pɔːtjʊgəl) n. a republic in SW Europe, on the Atlantic: became an independent monarchy in 1139 and expelled the Moors in 1249 after more than four centuries of Muslim rule; became a republic in 1910; under the dictatorship of Salazar from 1932 until 1968, when he was succeeded by Dr Caetano, who was overthrown by a junta in 1974. Language: Portuguese. Religion: Roman Catholic. Currency: escudo. Capital: Lisbon. Pop.: 10 312 000 (1987). Area: 91 530 sq. km (35 340 sq. miles).

Portuguese (,pɔːtjʊ'giːz) n. **1.** the official language of Portugal and Brazil; it belongs to the Romance group of the Indo-European family. **2.** (pl. **-guese**) a native, citizen, or inhabitant of Portugal. ~adj. **3.** of Portugal, its inhabitants, or their language.

Portuguese East Africa n. a former name (until 1975) of **Mozambique.**

Portuguese Guinea n. the former name (until 1974) of **Guinea-Bissau.** —**Portuguese Guinean** adj., n.

Portuguese India n. a former Portuguese overseas province on the W coast of India, consisting of Goa, Daman, and Diu: established between 1505 and 1510; annexed by India in 1961.

Portuguese man-of-war n. any of several large hydrozoans having an aerial float and long stinging tentacles. Sometimes shortened to **man-of-war.**

Portuguese Timor n. a former Portuguese overseas province in the Malay Archipelago, consisting of the east of the island of Timor, an enclave on the NW coast, and the islands of Ataúro and Jaco: annexed by Indonesia (1975).

Portuguese West Africa n. a former name (until 1975) of **Angola.**

portulaca (,pɔːtjʊ'lækə, -'leɪkə) n. any of a genus of plants of tropical and subtropical America, having yellow, red, or purple showy flowers. [C16: from L: PURSLANE]

POSB (in New Zealand and formerly in Britain) abbrev. for Post Office Savings Bank.

pose¹ (pəʊz) vb. **1.** to assume or cause to assume a physical attitude, as for a photograph or painting. **2.** (intr.; often foll. by as) to present oneself (as something one is not). **3.** (intr.) to affect an attitude in order to impress others. **4.** (tr.) to put forward or ask: to pose a question. **5.** (intr.) Sl. to adopt a particular style of appearance and stand or strut around, esp. in bars, discotheques, etc., in order to attract attention. ~n. **6.** a physical attitude, esp. one deliberately adopted for an artist or photographer. **7.** a mode of behaviour that is adopted for effect. [C14: from OF poser to set in place, from LL pausāre to cease, put down (infl. by L pōnere to place)]

pose² (pəʊz) vb. (tr.) Rare. to puzzle or baffle. [C16: from obs. appose, from L appōnere to put to]

Poseidon (pɒ'saɪdⁿn) n. Greek myth. the god of the sea and of earthquakes; brother of Zeus, Hades, and Hera. He is generally depicted in art wielding a trident. Roman counterpart: **Neptune.**

Posen ('pɔːzən) n. the German name for **Poznań.**

poser¹ ('pəʊzə) n. **1.** a person who poses. **2.** Inf. a person who likes to be seen in trendsetting clothes in fashionable bars, discos, etc.

poser² ('pəʊzə) n. a baffling or insoluble question.

poseur (pəʊ'zɜː) n. a person who strikes an attitude or assumes a pose in order to impress others. [C19: from F, from poser to POSE¹]

posh (pɒʃ) adj. Inf., chiefly Brit. **1.** smart, elegant, or fashionable. **2.** upper-class or genteel. [C19: often said to be an acronym of port out, starboard home, the most desirable location for a cabin in British ships sailing to & from the East, being the shaded side; but more likely from obs. sl. posh (n.) a dandy]

posit ('pɒzɪt) vb. (tr.) **1.** to assume or put forward as fact or the factual basis for an argument; postulate. **2.** to put in position. [C17: from L pōnere to place]

position (pə'zɪʃən) n. **1.** place, situation, or location: he took up a position to the rear. **2.** the appropriate or customary location: the telescope is in position for use. **3.** the manner in which a person or thing is placed; arrangement. **4.** Mil. an area or point occupied for tactical reasons. **5.** point of view; stand: what's your position on this issue? **6.** social status, esp. high social standing. **7.** a post of employment; job. **8.** the act of positing a fact or viewpoint. **9.** something posited, such as an idea. **10.** Sport. the part of a field or playing area where a player is placed or where he generally operates. **11.** Music. the vertical spacing or layout of the written notes in a chord. **12.** (in classical prosody) the situation in which a short vowel may be regarded as long, that is, when it occurs before two or more consonants. **13.** Finance. the market commitment of an investor in securities or a trader in commodities: a short position. **14. in a position.** (foll. by an infinitive) able (to). ~vb. (tr.) **15.** to put in the proper or appropriate place; locate. **16.** Sport. to place (oneself or another player) in a particular part of the field or playing area. [C15: from LL positiō a positioning, affirmation, from pōnere to place] —**po'sitional** adj.

positional notation n. the method of denoting numbers by the use of a finite number of digits, each digit having its value multiplied by its place value, as in $936 = (9 \times 100) + (3 \times 10) + 6$.

positive ('pɒzɪtɪv) adj. **1.** expressing certainty or affirmation: a positive answer. **2.** possessing actual or specific qualities; real: a positive benefit. **3.** tending to emphasize what is good or laudable; constructive: he takes a very positive attitude when correcting pupils' mistakes. **4.** tending towards progress or improvement. **5.** Philosophy. constructive rather than sceptical. **6.** (prenominal) Inf. (intensifier): a positive delight. **7.** Maths. having a value greater than zero: a positive number. **8.** Maths. **a.** measured in a direction opposite to that regarded as negative. **b.** having the same magnitude as but opposite sense to an equivalent negative quantity. **9.** Grammar. denoting the usual form of an adjective as opposed to its comparative or superlative form. **10.** *Physics.* **a.** (of an electric charge) having an opposite polarity to the charge of an electron and the same polarity as the charge of a proton. **b.** (of a body, system, ion, etc.) having a positive electric charge. **11.** short for **electropositive**. **12.** *Med.* (of the results of an examination or test) indicating the presence of a suspected disorder or organism. ~*n.* **13.** something that is positive. **14.** *Maths.* a quantity greater than zero. **15.** *Photog.* a print or slide showing a photographic image whose colours or tones correspond to those of the original subject. **16.** *Grammar.* the positive degree of an adjective or adverb. **17.** a positive object, such as a terminal or plate in a voltaic cell. [C13: from LL *positīvus*, from *pōnere* to place] — **'positiveness** *n.*

positive discrimination *n.* the provision of special opportunities for a disadvantaged group.

positive feedback *n.* See **feedback** (sense 1).

positively ('pɒzɪtɪvlɪ) *adv.* **1.** in a positive manner. **2.** (intensifier): *he disliked her; in fact, he positively hated her.*

positive vetting *n.* the checking of a person's background, to assess his suitability for a position that may involve national security.

positivism ('pɒzɪtɪ,vɪzəm) *n.* **1.** a form of empiricism, esp. as established by Auguste Comte, that rejects metaphysics and theology and holds that experimental investigation and observation are the only sources of substantial knowledge. See also **logical positivism**. **2.** the quality of being definite, certain, etc. — **'positivist** *n., adj.*

positron ('pɒzɪ,trɒn) *n. Physics.* the antiparticle of the electron, having the same mass but an equal and opposite charge. [C20: from *posi(tive* + *elec)tron*]

positronium (,pɒzɪ'trəʊnɪəm) *n. Physics.* a short-lived entity consisting of a positron and an electron bound together.

posology (pə'sɒlədʒɪ) *n.* the branch of medicine concerned with the determination of appropriate doses of drugs or agents. [C19: from F *posologie*, from Gk *posos* how much]

poss. *abbrev. for:* **1.** possession. **2.** possessive. **3.** possible. **4.** possibly.

posse ('pɒsɪ) *n.* **1.** *U.S.* short for **posse comitatus**, the able-bodied men of a district forming a group upon whom the sheriff may call for assistance in maintaining law and order. **2.** (in W Canada), a troop of trained horses and riders who perform at stampedes. **3.** *Law.* possibility (esp. in **in posse**). [C16: from Med. L (n.): power, from L (vb.): to be able]

posse comitatus (,kɒmɪ'tɑːtəs) *n.* the formal legal term for **posse** (sense 1). [Med. L: strength (manpower) of the county]

possess (pə'zɛs) *vb.* (*tr.*) **1.** to have as one's property; own. **2.** to have as a quality, characteristic, etc.: *to possess good eyesight.* **3.** to have knowledge of: *to possess a little French.* **4.** to gain control over or dominate: *whatever possessed you to act so foolishly?* **5.** (foll. by *of*) to cause to be the owner or possessor: *I am possessed of the necessary information.* **6.** to have sexual intercourse with. **7.** *Now rare.* to maintain (oneself or one's feelings) in a certain state or condition: *possess yourself in patience until I tell you the news.* [C15: from OF *possesser*, from L *possidēre*] — **pos'sessor** *n.* — **pos'sessory** *adj.*

possessed (pə'zɛst) *adj.* **1.** (foll. by *of*) owning or having. **2.** (*usually postpositive*) under the influence of a powerful force, such as a spirit or strong emotion. **3.** a less common term for **self-possessed.**

possession (pə'zɛʃən) *n.* **1.** the act of possessing or state of being possessed: *in possession of the crown.* **2.** anything that is owned or possessed. **3.** (*pl.*) wealth or property. **4.** the state of being controlled by or as if by evil spirits. **5.** the occupancy of land, property, etc., whether or not accompanied by ownership: *to take possession of a house.* **6.** a territory subject to a foreign state: *colonial possessions.* **7.** *Sport.* control of the ball, puck, etc., as exercised by a player or team: *he got possession in his own half.*

possessive (pə'zɛsɪv) *adj.* **1.** of or relating to possession. **2.** having or showing an excessive desire to possess or dominate: *a possessive husband.* **3.** *Grammar.* **a.** another word for **genitive**. **b.** denoting an inflected form of a noun or pronoun used to convey the idea of possession, association, etc., as *my* or *Harry's.* ~*n.* **4.** *Grammar.* **a.**

the possessive case. **b.** a word or speech element in the possessive case. — **pos'sessively** *adv.* — **pos'sessiveness** *n.*

posset ('pɒsɪt) *n.* a drink of hot milk curdled with ale, beer, etc., flavoured with spices, formerly used as a remedy for colds. [C15 *poshoote*, from ?]

possibility (,pɒsɪ'bɪlɪtɪ) *n., pl.* **-ties.** **1.** the state or condition of being possible. **2.** anything that is possible. **3.** a competitor, candidate, etc., who has a moderately good chance of winning, being chosen, etc. **4.** (*often pl.*) a future prospect or potential: *my new house has great possibilities.*

possible ('pɒsɪb³l) *adj.* **1.** capable of existing, taking place, or proving true without contravention of any natural law. **2.** capable of being achieved: *it is not possible to finish in three weeks.* **3.** having potential: *the idea is a possible money-spinner.* **4.** feasible but less than probable: *it is possible that man will live on Mars.* **5.** *Logic.* (of a statement, formula, etc.) capable of being true under some interpretation or in some circumstances. ~*n.* **6.** another word for **possibility** (sense 3). [C14: from L *possibilis* that may be, from *posse* to be able]

possibly ('pɒsɪblɪ) *sentence substitute, adv.* **1. a.** perhaps or maybe. **b.** (*as sentence modifier*): *possibly he'll come.* ~*adv.* **2.** by any chance; at all: *he can't possibly come.*

possum ('pɒsəm) *n.* **1.** an informal name for **opossum**. **2.** an Australian and New Zealand name for **phalanger**. **3. play possum.** to pretend to be dead, ignorant, asleep, etc., in order to deceive an opponent. **4. stir the possum** *Austral. sl.* to cause trouble.

post[1] (pəʊst) *n.* **1.** a length of wood, metal, etc., fixed upright to serve as a support, marker, point of attachment, etc. **2.** *Horse racing.* **a.** either of two upright poles marking the beginning (**starting post**) and end (**winning post**) of a racecourse. **b.** the finish of a horse race. ~*vb.* (*tr.*) **3.** (sometimes foll. by *up*) to fasten or put up (a notice) in a public place. **4.** to announce by or as if by means of a poster: *to post banns.* **5.** to publish (a name) on a list. **6.** to denounce publicly; brand. [OE, from L *postis*]

post[2] (pəʊst) *n.* **1.** a position to which a person is appointed or elected; appointment; job. **2.** a position to which a person, such as a sentry, is assigned for duty. **3.** a permanent military establishment. **4.** *Brit.* either of two military bugle calls (**first post** and **last post**) giving notice of the time to retire for the night. **5.** See **trading post**. ~*vb.* **6.** (*tr.*) to assign to or station at a particular place or position. **7.** *Chiefly Brit.* to transfer to a different unit or ship on taking up a new appointment, etc. [C16: from F *poste*, from It. *posto*, ult. from L *pōnere* to place]

post[3] (pəʊst) *n.* **1.** *Chiefly Brit.* letters, packages, etc., that are transported and delivered by the Post Office; mail. **2.** *Chiefly Brit.* a single collection or delivery of mail. **3.** *Brit.* an official system of mail delivery. **4.** (formerly) any of a series of stations furnishing relays of men and horses to deliver mail over a fixed route. **5.** a rider who carried mail between such stations. **6.** *Brit.* a postbox or post office: *take this to the post.* **7.** any of various book sizes, esp. 5¼ by 8¼ inches (**post octavo**). **8. by return of post.** *Brit.* by the next mail in the opposite direction. ~*vb.* **9.** (*tr.*) *Chiefly Brit.* to send by post. *U.S. and Canad. word:* **mail. 10.** (*tr.*) *Book-keeping.* **a.** to enter (an item) in a ledger. **b.** (often foll. by *up*) to compile or enter all paper items in (a ledger). **11.** (*tr.*) to inform of the latest news. **12.** (*intr.*) (formerly) to travel with relays of post horses. **13.** *Arch.* to travel or dispatch with speed; hasten. ~*adv.* **14.** with speed; rapidly. **15.** (formerly) by means of post horses. [C16: via F from It. *poste*, from L *posita* something placed, from *pōnere* to put]

post- *prefix.* **1.** after in time or sequence; following; subsequent: *postgraduate.* **2.** behind; posterior to: *postorbital.* [from L, from *post* after, behind]

postage ('pəʊstɪdʒ) *n.* the charge for delivering a piece of mail.

postage meter *n. Chiefly U.S. & Canad.* a postal franking machine. Also called: **postal meter.**

postage stamp *n.* **1.** a printed paper label with a gummed back for attaching to mail as an official indication that the required postage has been paid. **2.** a mark printed on an envelope, etc., serving the same function.

postal ('pəʊstᵊl) *adj.* of or relating to a Post Office or to the mail-delivery service. —'**postally** *adv.*

postal note *n. Austral. & N.Z.* the usual name for **postal order.**

postal order *n.* a written order for the payment of a sum of money, to a named payee, obtainable and payable at a post office.

postbag ('pəʊst,bæg) *n.* **1.** *Chiefly Brit.* another name for **mailbag. 2.** the mail received by a magazine, radio programme, public figure, etc.

postbox ('pəʊst,bɒks) *n.* another name for **letter box** (sense 2).

postcard ('pəʊst,kɑːd) *n.* a card, often bearing a photograph, picture, etc., on one side (**picture postcard**), for sending a message by post without an envelope. Also called (U.S.): **postal card.**

post chaise *n.* a closed four-wheeled horse-drawn coach used as a rapid means for transporting mail and passengers in the 18th and 19th centuries. [C18: from POST³ + CHAISE]

postcode ('pəʊst,kəʊd) *n.* a code of letters and digits used as part of a postal address to aid the sorting of mail. Also called: **postal code.** U.S. name: **zip code.**

postdate (pəʊst'deɪt) *vb.* (*tr.*) **1.** to write a future date on (a document, etc.), as on a cheque to prevent it being paid until then. **2.** to assign a date to (an event, period, etc.) that is later than its previously assigned date of occurrence. **3.** to be or occur at a later date than.

postdoctoral (pəʊst'dɒktərəl) *adj.* of, relating to, or designating studies, research, or professional work above the level of a doctorate.

poster ('pəʊstə) *n.* **1.** a placard or bill posted in a public place as an advertisement. **2.** a person who posts bills.

poste restante ('pəʊst rɪ'stænt) *n.* **1.** an address on mail indicating that it should be kept at a specified post office until collected by the addressee. **2.** the mail-delivery service or post-office department that handles mail having this address. ~U.S. and Canad. equivalent: **general delivery.** [F, lit.: mail remaining]

posterior (pɒ'stɪərɪə) *adj.* **1.** situated at the back of or behind something. **2.** coming after or following another in a series. **3.** coming after in time. ~*n.* **4.** the buttocks; rump. [C16: from L: latter, from *posterus* coming next, from *post* after] —**pos'teriorly** *adv.*

posterity (pɒ'stɛrɪtɪ) *n.* **1.** future or succeeding generations. **2.** all of one's descendants. [C14: from F *postérité*, from L *posteritās*, from *posterus* coming after, from *post* after]

postern ('pɒstən) *n.* a back door or gate, esp. one that is for private use. [C13: from OF *posterne*, from LL *posterula* (*jānua*) a back (entrance), from *posterus* coming behind]

poster paint *or* **colour** *n.* a gum-based opaque watercolour paint used for writing posters, etc.

post-free *adv., adj.* **1.** *Brit.* with the postage prepaid; post-paid. **2.** free of postal charge.

postglacial (pəʊst'gleɪsɪəl, -ʃəl) *adj.* formed or occurring after a glacial period.

postgraduate (pəʊst'grædjʊɪt) *n.* a student who has obtained a degree from a university, etc., and is pursuing studies for a more advanced qualification. Also (U.S. and Canad.): **graduate.**

posthaste ('pəʊst'heɪst) *adv.* **1.** with great haste. ~*n.* **2.** *Arch.* great haste.

post horn *n.* a simple valveless natural horn consisting of a long tube of brass or copper.

post horse *n.* (formerly) a horse kept at an inn or post house for use by postriders or for hire to travellers.

post house *n.* (formerly) a house or inn where horses were kept for postriders or for hire to travellers.

posthumous ('pɒstjʊməs) *adj.* **1.** happening or continuing after one's death. **2.** (of a book, etc.) published after the author's death. **3.** (of a child) born after the father's death. [C17: from L *postumus* the last, but modified as though from L *post* after + *humus* earth, that is, after the burial] —'**posthumously** *adv.*

posthypnotic suggestion (,pəʊsthɪp'nɒtɪk) *n.* a suggestion made to the subject while he is in a hypnotic trance, to be acted upon at some time after emerging from the trance.

postiche (pɒ'stiːʃ) *adj.* **1.** (of architectural ornament) inappropriately applied; sham. **2.** false or artificial; spurious. ~*n.* **3.** another term for **hairpiece** (sense 2). **4.** anything that is false; sham or pretence. [C19: from F, from It. *apposticcio* (n.), from LL *appositīcius* (adj.); see APPOSITE]

postilion *or* **postillion** (pɒ'stɪljən) *n.* a person who rides the near horse of the leaders in order to guide a team of horses drawing a coach. [C16: from F *postillon*, from It. *postiglione*, from *posta* POST³]

postimpressionism (,pəʊstɪm'prɛʃə,nɪzəm) *n.* a movement in painting in France at the end of the 19th century which rejected the naturalism and momentary effects of impressionism but adapted its use of pure colour to paint subjects with greater subjective emotion. —,**postim-'pressionist** *n., adj.*

posting ('pəʊstɪŋ) *n.* an appointment to a position or post.

postliminy (pəʊst'lɪmɪnɪ) *or* **postliminium** (,pəʊstlɪ-'mɪnɪəm) *n., pl.* -**nies** *or* -**ia** (-ɪə). *International law.* the right by which persons and property seized in war are restored to their former status on recovery. [C17: from L *post* behind + *limen, liminis* threshold]

postlude ('pəʊstluːd) *n. Music.* a final or concluding piece or movement. [C19: from POST- + -*lude*, from L *lūdus* game; cf. PRELUDE]

postman ('pəʊstmən) *or* (*fem.*) **postwoman** *n., pl.* -**men** *or* -**women.** a person who carries and delivers mail as a profession.

postman's knock *n.* a children's party game in which a kiss is exchanged for a pretend letter.

postmark ('pəʊst,mɑːk) *n.* **1.** any mark stamped on mail by postal officials, usually showing the date and place of posting. ~*vb.* **2.** (*tr.*) to put such a mark on (mail).

postmaster ('pəʊst,mɑːstə) *or* (*fem.*) **postmistress** *n.* an official in charge of a local post office.

postmaster general *n., pl.* **postmasters general.** the executive head of the postal service in certain countries.

postmeridian (,pəʊstmə'rɪdɪən) *adj.* after noon; in the afternoon or evening. [C17: from L *postmerīdiānus* in the afternoon]

post meridiem ('pəʊst mə'rɪdɪəm) the full form of **p.m.** [C17: L: after noon]

post mill *n.* a windmill built around a central post on which the whole mill can be turned so that the sails catch the wind.

postmillennialism (,pəʊstmɪ'lɛnɪə,lɪzəm) *n. Christian theol.* the doctrine or belief that the Second Coming of Christ will be preceded by the millennium. —,**post-mil'lennialist** *n.*

postmodernism (pəʊst'mɒdə,nɪzəm) *n.* (in the arts, architecture, etc.) a rejection of all the hitherto accepted certainties that underpinned modern style and content. —**post'modernist** *n., adj.*

postmortem (pəʊst'mɔːtəm) *adj.* **1.** (*prenominal*) occurring after death. ~*n.* **2.** analysis or study of a recent event: *a postmortem on a game of chess.* **3.** See **postmortem examination.** [C18: from L, lit.: after death]

postmortem examination *n.* dissection and examination of a dead body to determine the cause of death. Also called: **autopsy, necropsy.**

post-obit (pəʊst'əʊbɪt, -'ɒbɪt) *Chiefly law.* ~*n.* **1.** a bond given by a borrower, payable after the death of a specified person, esp. one given to a moneylender by an expectant heir promising to repay when his interest falls into possession. ~*adj.* **2.** taking effect after death. [C18: from L *post obitum* after death]

post office *n.* a building or room where postage stamps are sold and other postal business is conducted.

Post Office *n.* a government department or authority in many countries responsible for postal services and often telecommunications.

post office box *n.* a private numbered place in a post office, in which letters are kept until called for.

postoperative (pəʊst'ɒpərətɪv) *adj.* of or occurring in the period following a surgical operation.

post-paid *adv., adj.* with the postage prepaid.

---

post'classical *adj.*	,post-Dar'winian *adj.*	,poste'lection *adj.*	post'natal *adj.*
post'coital *adj.*	,postde,velop'mental *adj.*	post-'Marxian *adj.*	post'nuptial *adj.*
,postconso'nantal *adj.*	,postdiag'nostic *adj.*	,postmeno'pausal *adj.*	,postpi'tuitary *adj.*
,postconva'lescent *adj.*	,postdi'gestive *adj.*	post'nasal *adj.*	

postpone 1009 potent

postpone (pəʊst'pəʊn, pə'spəʊn) *vb.* (*tr.*) **1.** to put off or delay until a future time. **2.** to put behind in order of importance; defer. [C16: from L *postpōnere* to put after] —**post'ponement** *n.*

postpositive (pəʊst'pɒzɪtɪv) *adj.* **1.** (of an adjective or other modifier) placed after the word modified, either immediately after, as in *two men abreast*, or as part of a complement, as in *those men are bad.* ~*n.* **2.** a postpositive modifier.

postprandial (pəʊst'prændɪəl) *adj. usually humorous.* after a meal.

postrider ('pəʊst,raɪdə) *n.* (formerly) a person who delivered post on horseback.

postscript ('pəʊs,skrɪpt, 'pəʊst-) *n.* **1.** a message added at the end of a letter, after the signature. **2.** any supplement, as to a document or book. [C16: from LL *postscribere* to write after]

postulant ('pɒstjʊlənt) *n.* a person who makes a request or application, esp. a candidate for admission to a religious order. [C18: from L *postulāns* asking, from *postulāre* to ask]

postulate *vb.* ('pɒstjʊ,leɪt). (*tr.; may take a clause as object*) **1.** to assume to be true or existent; take for granted. **2.** to ask, demand, or claim. **3.** to nominate (a person) to a post or office subject to approval by a higher authority. ~*n.* ('pɒstjʊlɪt). **4.** something taken as self-evident or assumed as the basis of an argument. **5.** a prerequisite. **6.** a fundamental principle. **7.** *Logic, maths.* an unproved statement that should be taken for granted: used as an initial premise in a process of reasoning. [C16: from L *postulāre* to ask for] —**,postu'lation** *n.*

postulator ('pɒstjʊ,leɪtə) *n. R.C. Church.* a person who presents a plea for the beatification or canonization of some deceased person.

posture ('pɒstʃə) *n.* **1.** a position or attitude of the limbs or body. **2.** a characteristic manner of bearing the body: *good posture.* **3.** the disposition of the parts of a visible object. **4.** a mental attitude. **5.** a state or condition. **6.** a false or affected attitude; pose. ~*vb.* **7.** to assume or cause to assume a bodily attitude. **8.** (*intr.*) to assume an affected posture; pose. [C17: via F from It. *postura*, from L *positūra*, from *pōnere* to place] —**'postural** *adj.* —**'posturer** *n.*

postviral syndrome (,pəʊst'vaɪrəl) *n.* a condition that sometimes occurs after a viral infection in which the sufferer may experience extreme muscular fatigue or various other symptoms over a long period. Abbrev.: **PVS.**

posy ('pəʊzɪ) *n., pl.* **-sies. 1.** a small bunch of flowers. **2.** *Arch.* a brief motto or inscription, esp. one on a trinket or a ring. [C16: var. of POESY]

pot[1] (pɒt) *n.* **1.** a container, usually round and deep and often having a handle and lid, used for cooking and other domestic purposes. **2.** the amount that a pot will hold; potful. **3.** a large mug or tankard. **4.** *Austral.* any of various measures used for serving beer. **5.** the money or stakes in the pool in gambling games. **6.** a wicker trap for catching fish, esp. crustaceans: *a lobster pot.* **7.** *Billiards, etc.* a shot by which a ball is pocketed. **8.** a chamber pot, esp. a small one designed for a baby or toddler. **9.** (*often pl.*) *Inf.* a large amount (esp. of money). **10.** *Inf.* a prize or trophy. **11.** *Chiefly Brit.* short for **chimneypot. 12.** short for **flowerpot, teapot. 13.** See **potbelly. 14. go to pot.** to go to ruin. ~*vb.* **potting, potted.** (*mainly tr.*) **15.** to put or preserve (meat, etc.) in a pot. **16.** to plant (a cutting, seedling, etc.) in soil in a flowerpot. **17.** to cause (a baby or toddler) to use or sit on a pot. **18.** to shoot (game) for food rather than for sport. **19.** (*also intr.*) to shoot casually or without careful aim. **20.** (*also intr.*) to shape clay as a potter. **21.** *Billiards, etc.* to pocket (a ball). **22.** *Inf.* to capture or win. [LOE *pott*, from Med. L *pottus* (unattested), ?from L *pōtus* a drink]

pot[2] (pɒt) *n. Sl.* cannabis used as a drug in any form. [C20: ? shortened from Mexican Indian *potiguaya*]

potable ('pəʊtəb²l) *adj.* drinkable. [C16: from LL *pōtābilis* drinkable, from L *pōtāre* to drink] —**,pota'bility** *n.*

potae ('pɒtaɪ) *n. N.Z.* a hat. [Maori]

potage *French.* (pɔtaʒ; *English* pəʊ'tɑːʒ) *n.* any thick soup. [C16: from OF; see POTTAGE]

potamic (pə'tæmɪk) *adj.* of or relating to rivers. [C19: from Gk *potamos* river]

potash ('pɒt,æʃ) *n.* **1.** another name for **potassium carbonate** or **potassium hydroxide. 2.** potassium chemically combined in certain compounds: *chloride of potash.* [C17 *pot ashes*, translation of obs. Du. *potaschen*; because orig. obtained by evaporating the lye of wood ashes in pots]

potassium (pə'tæsɪəm) *n.* a light silvery element of the alkali metal group that is highly reactive and rapidly oxidizes in air. Symbol: K; atomic no.: 19; atomic wt.: 39.102. [C19: NL *potassa* potash] —**po'tassic** *adj.*

potassium-argon dating *n.* a technique for determining the age of minerals based on the occurrence in natural potassium of a small fixed amount of radioisotope ^{40}K that decays to the stable argon isotope ^{40}Ar with a half-life of 1.28 × 10^9 years. Measurement of the ratio of these isotopes thus gives the age of the mineral.

potassium bromide *n.* a white crystalline soluble substance with a bitter saline taste used in making photographic papers and plates and in medicine as a sedative. Formula: KBr.

potassium carbonate *n.* a white odourless substance used in making glass and soft soap and as an alkaline cleansing agent. Formula: K_2CO_3.

potassium chlorate *n.* a white crystalline soluble substance used in explosives and as a disinfectant and bleaching agent. Formula: $KClO_3$.

potassium cyanide *n.* a white poisonous granular soluble solid substance used in photography. Formula: KCN.

potassium hydrogen tartrate *n.* a white soluble crystalline salt used in baking powders, soldering fluxes, and laxatives. Formula: $KHC_4H_4O_6$. Also called: **cream of tartar.**

potassium hydroxide *n.* a white deliquescent alkaline solid used in the manufacture of soap, liquid shampoos, and detergents. Formula: KOH.

potassium nitrate *n.* a colourless or white crystalline compound used in gunpowders, pyrotechnics, fertilizers, and as a preservative for foods (**E 252**). Formula: KNO_3. Also called: **saltpetre, nitre.**

potassium permanganate *n.* a dark purple poisonous odourless soluble crystalline solid, used as a bleach, disinfectant, and antiseptic. Formula: $KMnO_4$. Systematic name: **potassium manganate(V).**

potation (pəʊ'teɪʃən) *n.* **1.** the act of drinking. **2.** a drink or draught, esp. of alcoholic drink. [C15: from L *pōtātiō*, from *pōtāre* to drink]

potato (pə'teɪtəʊ) *n., pl.* **-toes. 1. a.** a plant of South America widely cultivated for its edible tubers. **b.** the starchy oval tuber of this plant, which has a brown or red skin and is cooked and eaten as a vegetable. **2.** any of various similar plants, esp. the sweet potato. [C16: from Sp. *patata* white potato, from Taino *batata* sweet potato]

potato beetle *n.* another name for the **Colorado beetle.**

potato chip *n.* (*usually pl.*) **1.** another name for **chip** (sense 4). **2.** the U.S. and Canad. term for **crisp** (sense 10).

potato crisp *n.* (*usually pl.*) another name for **crisp** (sense 10).

potbelly ('pɒt,belɪ) *n., pl.* **-lies. 1.** a protruding or distended belly. **2.** a person having such a belly. —**'pot,bellied** *adj.*

potboiler ('pɒt,bɔɪlə) *n. Inf.* an artistic work of little merit produced quickly to make money.

pot-bound *adj.* (of a pot plant) having grown to fill all the available root space and therefore lacking room for continued growth.

potboy ('pɒt,bɔɪ) *or* **potman** ('pɒtmən) *n., pl.* **-boys** *or* **-men.** *Chiefly Brit.* (esp. formerly) a man employed at a public house to serve beer, etc.

potch (pɒtʃ) *n. Chiefly Austral., sl.* inferior quality opal. [C20: from ?]

poteen (pɒ'tiːn) *or* **poitín** (pɒ'tʃiːn) *n.* (in Ireland) illicit spirit, often distilled from potatoes. [C19: from Irish *poitín* little pot, from *pota* pot]

Potemkin *or* **Potyomkin** (pɒ'tɛmkɪn; *Russian* pa'tjomkin) *n.* **Grigori Aleksandrovich** (gri'gorij alık'sandrəvitʃ). 1739–91, Russian soldier and statesman; lover of Catherine II, whose favourite he remained until his death.

potent[1] ('pəʊt²nt) *adj.* **1.** possessing great strength; powerful. **2.** (of arguments, etc.) persuasive or forceful. **3.**

influential or authoritative. **4.** tending to produce violent physical or chemical effects: *a potent poison.* **5.** (of a male) capable of having sexual intercourse. [C15: from L *potēns* able, from *posse* to be able] —'**potency** *or* 'po-tence *n.* —'**potently** *adv.*

potent[2] (ˈpəʊtənt) *adj. Heraldry.* (of a cross) having flat bars across the ends of the arms. [C17: from obs. *potent* a crutch, from L *potentia* power]

potentate (ˈpəʊtənˌteɪt) *n.* a ruler or monarch. [C14: from LL *potentātus*, from L: rule, from *potens* powerful, from *posse* to be able]

potential (pəˈtɛnʃəl) *adj.* **1. a.** possible but not yet actual. **b.** (*prenominal*) capable of being or becoming; latent. **2.** *Grammar.* (of a verb) expressing possibility, as English *may* and *might.* ~*n.* **3.** latent but unrealized ability: *Jones has great potential as a sales manager.* **4.** *Grammar.* a potential verb or verb form. **5.** short for **electric potential.** [C14: from OF *potencial*, from LL *potentiālis*, from L *potentia* power] —po'**tentially** *adv.*

potential difference *n.* the difference in electric potential between two points in an electric field; the work that has to be done in transferring unit positive charge from one point to the other, measured in volts. Abbrev.: **pd.**

potential energy *n.* the energy of a body or system as a result of its position in an electric, magnetic, or gravitational field. Abbrev.: **PE.**

potentiality (pəˌtɛnʃɪˈælɪtɪ) *n., pl.* -ties. **1.** latent or inherent capacity for growth, fulfilment, etc. **2.** a person or thing that possesses this.

potentiate (pəˈtɛnʃɪˌeɪt) *vb.* (*tr.*) **1.** to cause to be potent. **2.** *Med.* to increase (the individual action or effectiveness) of two drugs by administering them in combination.

potentilla (ˌpəʊtənˈtɪlə) *n.* any rosaceous plant or shrub of the N temperate genus *Potentilla*, having five-petalled flowers. [C16: NL, from Med. L: garden valerian, from L *potēns* powerful]

potentiometer (pəˌtɛnʃɪˈɒmɪtə) *n.* **1.** an instrument for determining a potential difference of electromotive force. **2.** a device used in electronic circuits, esp. as a volume control. Sometimes shortened to **pot.** — po,**tenti'ometry** *n.*

potful (ˈpɒtful) *n.* the amount held by a pot.

pother (ˈpɒðə) *n.* **1.** a commotion, fuss, or disturbance. **2.** a choking cloud of smoke, dust, etc. ~*vb.* **3.** to make or be troubled or upset. [C16: from ?]

potherb (ˈpɒtˌhɜːb) *n.* any plant having leaves, flowers, stems, etc., that are used in cooking.

pothole (ˈpɒtˌhəʊl) *n.* **1.** *Geog.* **a.** a deep hole in limestone areas resulting from action by running water. **b.** a circular hole in the bed of a river produced by abrasion. **2.** a deep hole produced in a road surface by wear or weathering.

potholing (ˈpɒtˌhəʊlɪŋ) *n. Brit.* a sport in which participants explore underground caves. —'**pot,holer** *n.*

pothook (ˈpɒtˌhʊk) *n.* **1.** a curved or S-shaped hook used for suspending a pot over a fire. **2.** a long hook used for lifting hot pots, lids, etc. **3.** an S-shaped mark, often made by children when learning to write.

pothouse (ˈpɒtˌhaʊs) *n. Brit.* (formerly) a small tavern or pub.

pothunter (ˈpɒtˌhʌntə) *n.* **1.** a person who hunts for profit without regard to the rules of sport. **2.** *Inf.* a person who enters competitions for the sole purpose of winning prizes.

potion (ˈpəʊʃən) *n.* a drink, esp. of medicine, poison, or some supposedly magic beverage. [C13: via OF from L *pō-tiō* a drink, esp. a poisonous one, from *pōtāre* to drink]

Potiphar (ˈpɒtɪfə) *n. Old Testament.* one of Pharaoh's officers, who bought Joseph as a slave (Genesis 37:36).

potlatch (ˈpɒtˌlætʃ) *n. Anthropol.* a competitive ceremonial activity among certain North American Indians, involving a lavish distribution of gifts to emphasize the wealth and status of the chief or clan. [C19: of Amerind origin, from *patshatl* a present]

potluck (ˈpɒtˈlʌk) *n. Inf.* **1.** whatever food happens to be available without special preparation. **2.** whatever is available (esp. in **take potluck**).

pot marigold *n.* a Central European and Mediterranean plant grown for its rayed orange-and-yellow showy flowers.

Potomac (pəˈtəʊmək) *n.* a river in the E central U.S., rising in the Appalachian Mountains of West Virginia: flows northeast, then generally southeast to Chesapeake Bay.

Length (from the confluence of headstreams): 462 km (287 miles).

potoroo (ˌpɒtəˈruː) *n.* another name for **kangaroo rat.** [from Abor.]

Potosí (*Spanish* potoˈsi) *n.* a city in S Bolivia, at an altitude of 4066 m (13 340 ft.): one of the highest cities in the world; developed with the discovery of local silver in 1545; tin mining; university (1571). Pop.: 109 876 (1984).

potpourri (ˌpəʊˈpʊərɪ) *n., pl.* -ris. **1.** a collection of mixed flower petals dried and preserved in a pot to scent the air. **2.** a collection of unrelated items; miscellany. **3.** a medley of popular tunes. [C18: from F, lit.: rotten pot, translation of Sp. *olla podrida* miscellany]

pot roast *n.* meat cooked slowly in a covered pot with very little water.

Potsdam (ˈpɒtsdæm; *German* ˈpɔtsdam) *n.* a city in central East Germany, on the Havel River: residence of Prussian kings and German emperors and scene of the **Potsdam Conference** of 1945. Pop.: 140 198 (1986).

potsherd (ˈpɒtˌʃɜːd) *or* **potshard** (ˈpɒtˌʃɑːd) *n.* a broken fragment of pottery. [C14: from POT[1] + *schoord* piece of broken crockery; see SHARD]

pot shot *n.* **1.** a chance shot taken casually, hastily, or without careful aim. **2.** a shot fired to kill game in disregard of the rules of sport. **3.** a shot fired at quarry within easy range.

pot still *n.* a type of still in which heat is applied directly to the pot in which the wash is contained: used in distilling whisky.

pottage (ˈpɒtɪdʒ) *n.* a thick soup. [C13: from OF *potage* contents of a pot, from *pot* POT[1]]

potted (ˈpɒtɪd) *adj.* **1.** placed or grown in a pot. **2.** cooked or preserved in a pot: *potted shrimps.* **3.** *Inf.* abridged: *a potted version of a novel.*

potter[1] (ˈpɒtə) *n.* a person who makes pottery.

potter[2] (ˈpɒtə) *or esp. U.S. & Canad.* **putter** *vb.* **1.** (*intr.*; often foll. by *about* or *around*) to busy oneself in a desultory though agreeable manner. **2.** (*intr.*; often foll. by *along* or *about*) to move with little energy or direction: *to potter about town.* **3.** (*tr.*; usually foll. by *away*) to waste (time): *to potter the day away.* [C16 (in the sense: to poke repeatedly): from OE *potian* to thrust] —'**potterer** *or esp. U.S.* '**putterer** *n.*

Potter (ˈpɒtə) *n.* **1.** Beatrix. 1866–1943, English author and illustrator of children's animal stories, such as *The Tale of Peter Rabbit* (1902). **2.** Dennis (Christopher George). born 1935, British playwright. His TV successes include *Pennies from Heaven* (1978) and *The Singing Detective* (1986). **3.** Paulus. 1625–54, Dutch painter, esp. of animals.

Potteries (ˈpɒtərɪz) *pl. n.* the. (*sometimes functioning as sing.*) a region of W central England, in Staffordshire, in which the china industries are concentrated.

potter's field *n.* **1.** *New Testament.* the land bought by the Sanhedrin with the money paid for the betrayal of Jesus, to be used as a burial place for strangers (Acts 1:19; Matthew 27:7). **2.** *U.S.* a cemetery where the poor or unidentified are buried at the public's expense.

potter's wheel *n.* a device with a horizontal rotating disc, on which clay is moulded by hand.

pottery (ˈpɒtərɪ) *n., pl.* -teries. **1.** articles made from earthenware and baked in a kiln. **2.** a place where such articles are made. **3.** the craft or business of making such articles. [C15: from OF *poterie*, from *potier* potter, from *pot* POT[1]]

potting shed *n.* a building in which plants are set in flowerpots and in which empty pots, potting compost, etc., are stored.

pottle (ˈpɒtəl) *n. Arch.* a liquid measure equal to half a gallon. [C14 *potel*, from OF: a small pot]

potto (ˈpɒtəʊ) *n., pl.* -tos. a short-tailed prosimian primate having vertebral spines protruding through the skin in the neck region. Also called: **kinkajou.** [C18: of W African origin]

Pott's disease (pɒts) *n.* a disease of the spine, characterized by weakening and gradual disintegration of the vertebrae. [C18: after Percivall *Pott* (1714–88), E surgeon]

Pott's fracture *n.* a fracture of the lower part of the fibula, usually with the dislocation of the ankle. [C18: see POTT'S DISEASE]

potty[1] (ˈpɒtɪ) *adj.* -tier, -tiest. *Brit. inf.* **1.** foolish or slightly crazy. **2.** trivial or insignificant. **3.** (foll. by *about*) very keen (on). [C19: ?from POT[1]] —'**pottiness** *n.*

potty[2] ('pɒtɪ) *n.*, *pl.* **-ties.** a child's word for **chamber pot.**
Potyomkin (*Russian* pa'tjɔmkɪn) *n.* a variant spelling of **Potemkin.**
pouch (paʊtʃ) *n.* **1.** a small flexible baglike container: *a tobacco pouch.* **2.** a saclike structure in any of various animals, such as the cheek fold in rodents. **3.** *Anat.* any sac, pocket, or pouchlike cavity. **4.** a Scot. word for **pocket.** ~*vb.* **5.** (*tr.*) to place in or as if in a pouch. **6.** to arrange or become arranged in a pouchlike form. **7.** (*tr.*) (of certain birds and fishes) to swallow. [C14: from OF *pouche*, from OF *poche* bag] —'**pouchy** *adj.*
pouf *or* **pouffe** (puːf) *n.* **1.** a large solid cushion used as a seat. **2. a.** a woman's hairstyle, fashionable esp. in the 18th century, in which the hair is piled up in rolled puffs. **b.** a pad set in the hair to make such puffs. **3.** (*also* puf). *Brit. derog. sl.* less common spellings of **poof.** [C19: from F]
poulard *or* **poularde** ('puːlɑːd) *n.* a hen that has been spayed for fattening. Cf. **capon.** [C18: from OF *pollarde*, from *polle* hen]
Poulenc (*French* pulɛ̃ːk) *n.* **Francis.** 1899–1963, French composer; a member of Les Six. His works include the operas *Les Mamelles de Tirésias* (1947) and *Dialogues des Carmélites* (1957), and the ballet *Les Biches* (1924).
poult (pəʊlt) *n.* the young of a gallinaceous bird, esp. of domestic fowl. [C15: var. of *poulet* PULLET]
poulterer ('pəʊltərə) *n. Brit.* another word for a **poultryman.** [C17: from obs. *poulter*, from OF *pouletier*, from *poulet* PULLET]
poultice ('pəʊltɪs) *n. Med.* a local moist and often heated application for the skin used to improve the circulation, treat inflamed areas, etc. [C16: from earlier *pultes*, from L *puls* a thick porridge]
poultry ('pəʊltrɪ) *n.* domestic fowls collectively. [C14: from OF *pouletrie*, from *pouletier* poultry dealer]
poultryman ('pəʊltrɪmən) *or* **poulterer** *n.*, *pl.* **-trymen** *or* **-terers.** **1.** Also called: **chicken farmer.** a person who rears domestic fowls for their eggs or meat. **2.** a dealer in poultry.
pounce[1] (paʊns) *vb.* **1.** (*intr.*; often foll. by *on* or *upon*) to spring or swoop, as in capturing prey. ~*n.* **2.** the act of pouncing; a spring or swoop. **3.** the claw of a bird of prey. [C17: apparently from ME *punson* pointed tool] —'**pouncer** *n.*
pounce[2] (paʊns) *n.* **1.** a very fine resinous powder, esp. of cuttlefish bone, formerly used to dry ink. **2.** a fine powder, esp. of charcoal, that is tapped through perforations in paper in order to transfer the design to another surface. ~*vb.* (*tr.*) **3.** to dust (paper) with pounce. **4.** to transfer (a design) by means of pounce. [C18: from OF *ponce*, from L *pūmex* pumice]
pouncet box ('paʊnsɪt) *n.* a box with a perforated top used for perfume. [C16 *pouncet*, ? alteration of *pounced* perforated]
pound[1] (paʊnd) *vb.* **1.** (when *intr.*, often foll. by *on* or *at*) to strike heavily and often. **2.** (*tr.*) to beat to a pulp; pulverize. **3.** (*tr.*; foll. by *out*) to produce, as by typing heavily. **4.** to walk or move with heavy steps or thuds. **5.** (*intr.*) to throb heavily. ~*n.* **6.** the act of pounding. [OE *pūnian*] —'**pounder** *n.*
pound[2] (paʊnd) *n.* **1.** an avoirdupois unit of weight that is divided into 16 ounces and is equal to 0.453 592 kilograms. Abbrev.: **lb.** **2.** a troy unit of weight divided into 12 ounces equal to 0.373 242 kilograms. **3. a.** the standard monetary unit of the United Kingdom, divided into 100 pence. Official name: **pound sterling.** **b.** (*as modifier*): *a pound note.* **4.** the standard monetary unit of various other countries, including Cyprus, Egypt, Israel, and Malta. **5.** Also called: **pound Scots.** a former Scottish monetary unit originally worth an English pound but later declining in value to 1 shilling 8 pence. [OE *pund*, from L *pondō*]
pound[3] (paʊnd) *n.* **1.** an enclosure for keeping officially removed vehicles or distrained goods or animals, esp. stray dogs. **2.** a place where people are confined. **3.** a trap for animals. ~*vb.* **4.** (*tr.*) to confine in or as if in a pound; impound, imprison, or restrain. [C14: from LOE *pund-*, as in *pundfeald* PINFOLD]
Pound (paʊnd) *n.* **Ezra** (**Loomis**). 1885–1972, U.S. poet, translator, and critic, living in Europe. Indicted for treason by the U.S. government (1945) for pro-Fascist broadcasts during World War II, he was committed to a mental

hospital until 1958. He was a founder of imagism and championed the early work of such writers as T. S. Eliot, Joyce, and Hemingway. His life work, the *Cantos* (1925–70), is an unfinished sequence of poems, which incorporates mythological and historical materials in several languages as well as political, economic, and autobiographical elements.
poundage ('paʊndɪdʒ) *n.* **1.** a charge of so much per pound of weight. **2.** a charge of so much per pound sterling. **3.** a weight expressed in pounds.
poundal ('paʊnd³l) *n.* the fps unit of force; the force that imparts an acceleration of 1 foot per second per second to a mass of 1 pound. Abbrev.: **pdl.** [C19: from POUND[2] + QUINTAL]
-pounder ('paʊndə) *n.* (*in combination*) **1.** something weighing a specified number of pounds: *a 200-pounder.* **2.** something worth a specified number of pounds: *a ten-pounder.* **3.** a gun that discharges a shell weighing a specified number of pounds: *a two-pounder.*
pound sterling *n.* See **pound**[2] (sense 3).
pour (pɔː) *vb.* **1.** to flow or cause to flow in a stream. **2.** (*tr.*) to emit in a profuse way. **3.** (*intr.*; often foll. by *down*) Also: **pour with rain.** to rain heavily. **4.** (*intr.*) to move together in large numbers; swarm. **5.** (*intr.*) to serve tea, coffee, etc.: *shall I pour?* **6. it never rains but it pours.** events, esp. unfortunate ones, come in rapid succession. **7. pour oil on troubled waters.** to calm a quarrel, etc. ~*n.* **8.** a pouring, downpour, etc. [C13: from ?] —'**pourer** *n.*
pourboire *French.* (purbwar) *n.* a tip; gratuity. [lit.: for drinking]
poussin (*French* pusɛ̃) *n.* a young chicken reared for eating. [from F]
Poussin (*French* pusɛ̃) *n.* **Nicolas** (nikɔlɑ). 1594–1665, French painter, regarded as a leader of French classical painting. He is best known for the austere historical and biblical paintings and landscapes of his later years.
pout[1] (paʊt) *vb.* **1.** to thrust out (the lips), as when sullen or (of the lips) to be thrust out. **2.** (*intr.*) to swell out; protrude. **3.** (*tr.*) to utter with a pout. ~*n.* **4.** Also: **the pouts.** a fit of sullenness. **5.** the act or state of pouting. [C14: from ?] —'**poutingly** *adv.*
pout[2] (paʊt) *n.*, *pl.* **pout** *or* **pouts.** **1.** short for **eelpout.** **2.** Also called: **horned pout.** a N American catfish with barbels round the mouth. **3.** any of various gadoid food fishes. [OE *-pūte*, as in *ælepūte* eelpout]
pouter ('paʊtə) *n.* **1.** a person or thing that pouts. **2.** a breed of domestic pigeon with a large crop capable of being greatly puffed out.
poverty ('pɒvətɪ) *n.* **1.** the condition of being without adequate food, money, etc. **2.** scarcity: *a poverty of wit.* **3.** a lack of elements conducive to fertility in soil. [C12: from OF *poverté*, from L *paupertās* restricted means, from *pauper* poor]
poverty-stricken *adj.* suffering from extreme poverty.
poverty trap *n.* the situation of being unable to raise one's living standard because one is dependent on state benefits which are reduced if one gains any extra income.
pow (paʊ) *interj.* an exclamation imitative of a collision, explosion, etc.
POW *abbrev. for* prisoner of war.
powan ('paʊən) *n.* a freshwater whitefish occurring in some Scottish lakes. [C17: Scot. var. of POLLAN]
powder ('paʊdə) *n.* **1.** a substance in the form of tiny loose particles. **2.** any of various preparations in this form, such as gunpowder, face powder, or soap powder. ~*vb.* **3.** to turn into powder; pulverize. **4.** (*tr.*) to cover or sprinkle with or as if with powder. [C13: from OF *poldre*, from L *pulvis* dust] —'**powderer** *n.* —'**powdery** *adj.*
powder blue *n.* a dusty pale blue colour.
powder burn *n.* a superficial burn of the skin caused by a momentary intense explosion.
powder flask *n.* a small flask or case formerly used to carry gunpowder.
powder horn *n.* a powder flask consisting of the hollow horn of an animal.
powder keg *n.* **1.** a small barrel to hold gunpowder. **2.** a potential source of violence, disaster, etc.
powder metallurgy *n.* the science and technology of producing solid metal components from metal powder by compaction and sintering.

powder monkey *n.* (formerly) a boy who carried powder from the magazine to the guns on warships.

powder puff *n.* a soft pad of fluffy material used for applying cosmetic powder to the skin.

powder room *n.* a ladies' cloakroom.

powdery mildew *n.* a plant disease characterized by a white powdery growth on stems and leaves, caused by parasitic fungi.

Powell ('pauǝl) *n.* **1.** ('pǝuǝl). **Anthony Dymoke** ('dɪmǝk). born 1905, English novelist, best known for his sequence of novels under the general title *A Dance to the Music of Time* (1951–75). **2. Cecil Frank.** 1903–69, English physicist, who was awarded the Nobel prize for physics in 1950 for his discovery of the pi-meson. **3. Earl,** known as *Bud Powell.* 1924–1966, U.S. modern-jazz pianist. **4.** (**John**) **Enoch.** born 1912, British politician. An outspoken opponent of Commonwealth immigration into Britain and of British membership of the Common Market, in 1974 he resigned from the Conservative Party, returning to Parliament as a United Ulster Unionist Council member (1974–87).

power ('pauǝ) *n.* **1.** ability to do something. **2.** (*often pl.*) a specific ability, capacity, or faculty. **3.** political, financial, social, etc., force or influence. **4.** control or dominion or a position of control, dominion, or authority. **5.** a state or other political entity with political, industrial, or military strength. **6.** a person or group that exercises control, influence, or authority: *he's a power in the state.* **7.** a prerogative, privilege, or liberty. **8.** legal authority to act for another. **9. a.** a military force. **b.** military potential. **10.** *Maths.* **a.** the value of a number or quantity raised to some exponent. **b.** another name for **exponent** (sense 4). **11.** *Physics, engineering.* a measure of the rate of doing work expressed as the work done per unit time. It is measured in watts, horsepower, etc. **12. a.** the rate at which electrical energy is fed into or taken from a device or system. It is measured in watts. **b.** (*as modifier*): *a power amplifier.* **13.** the ability to perform work. **14. a.** mechanical energy as opposed to manual labour. **b.** (*as modifier*): *a power tool.* **15.** a particular form of energy: *nuclear power.* **16. a.** a measure of the ability of a lens or optical system to magnify an object. **b.** another word for **magnification.** **17.** *Inf.* a large amount: *a power of good.* **18. in one's power.** (*often foll. by an infinitive*) able or allowed (to). **19. in** (**someone's**) **power.** under the control of (someone). **20. the powers that be.** established authority. ~*vb.* **21.** (*tr.*) to give or provide power to. **22.** (*tr.*) to fit (a machine) with a motor or engine. **23.** *Inf.* to move or cause to move by the exercise of physical power. [C13: from Anglo-Norman *poer,* from Vulgar L *potēre* (unattested), from L *posse* to be able]

powerboat ('pauǝ,bǝut) *n.* a boat, esp. a fast one, propelled by an inboard or outboard motor.

powerboating ('pauǝ,bǝutɪŋ) *n.* the sport of driving powerboats in racing competitions.

power cut *n.* a temporary interruption or reduction in the supply of electrical power.

power dive *n.* **1.** a steep dive by an aircraft with its engines at high power. ~*vb.* **power-dive. 2.** to cause (an aircraft) to perform a power dive or (of an aircraft) to perform a power dive.

powerful ('pauǝful) *adj.* **1.** having great power. **2.** extremely effective or efficient: *a powerful drug.* ~*adv.* **3.** *Dialect.* very: *he ran powerful fast.* —'**powerfully** *adv.* —'**powerfulness** *n.*

powerhouse ('pauǝ,haus) *n.* **1.** an electrical generating station or plant. **2.** *Inf.* a forceful or powerful person or thing.

powerless ('pauǝlɪs) *adj.* without power or authority. —'**powerlessly** *adv.* —'**powerlessness** *n.*

power of attorney *n.* **1.** legal authority to act for another person in certain specified matters. **2.** the document conferring such authority.

power pack *n.* a device for converting the current from a supply into direct or alternating current at the voltage required by a particular electrical or electronic device.

power plant *n.* **1.** the complex, including machinery, associated equipment, and the structure housing it, that is used in the generation of power, esp. electrical power. **2.** the equipment supplying power to a particular machine.

power point *n.* an electrical socket mounted on or recessed into a wall.

power station *n.* an electrical generating station.

power steering *n.* a form of steering used on vehicles, where the torque applied to the steering wheel is augmented by engine power. Also called: **power-assisted steering.**

power structure *n.* the structure or distribution of power and authority in a community.

Powhatan (,pauhǝ'tæn, pau'hæt°n) *n.* American Indian name *Wahunsonacock.* died 1618, American Indian chief of a confederacy of tribes; father of Pocahontas.

powwow ('pau,wau) *n.* **1.** a talk, conference, or meeting. **2.** a magical ceremony of certain North American Indians. **3.** (among certain North American Indians) a medicine man. **4.** a meeting of North American Indians. ~*vb.* **5.** (*intr.*) to hold a powwow. [C17: of Amerind origin]

Powys[1] ('pauɪs) *n.* a county in E Wales, formed in 1974 from most of Breconshire, Montgomeryshire, and Radnorshire. Administrative centre: Llandrindod Wells. Pop.: 112 400 (1986 est.). Area: 5077 sq. km (1960 sq. miles).

Powys[2] ('pǝuɪs) *n.* **John Cowper** ('ku:pǝ). 1872–1963, English novelist, essayist, and poet, who spent much of his life in the U.S. His novels include *Wolf Solent* (1929), *A Glastonbury Romance* (1932), and *Owen Glendower* (1940).

pox (poks) *n.* **1.** any disease characterized by the formation of pustules on the skin that often leave pockmarks when healed. **2.** (usually preceded by *the*) an informal name for **syphilis. 3. a pox on** (**someone** *or* **something**). (*interj.*) *Arch.* an expression of intense disgust or aversion. [C15: changed from *pocks,* pl. of POCK]

Poyang *or* **P'o-yang** ('pɔ:'jæŋ) *n.* a lake in E China, in N Jiangxi province, connected by canal with the Yangtze River: the second largest lake in China. Area (at its greatest): 2780 sq. km (1073 sq. miles).

Poznań (*Polish* 'poz_najn) *n.* a city in W Poland, on the Warta River: the centre of Polish resistance to German rule (1815–1918, 1939–45). Pop.: 553 000 (1985). German name: **Posen.**

Pozsony ('pozonj) *n.* the Hungarian name for **Bratislava.**

pozzuolana (,potswǝ'lɑ:nǝ) *or* **pozzolana** (,potsǝ'lɑ:nǝ) *n.* **1.** a type of porous volcanic ash used in making hydraulic cements. **2.** any of various artificial substitutes for this ash used in cements. [C18: from It.: of POZZUOLI]

Pozzuoli (*Italian* pot'tswɔ:li) *n.* a port in SW Italy, in Campania on the **Gulf of Pozzuoli** (an inlet of the Bay of Naples): in a region of great volcanic activity; founded in the 6th century B.C. by the Greeks. Pop.: 71 664 (1981 est.).

pp *abbrev. for:* **1.** past particple. **2.** per procurationem. See **per pro.** ~ **3.** *Music. symbol for* pianissimo.

pp *or* **PP** *abbrev. for:* **1.** parcel post. **2.** post-paid. **3.** (in prescriptions) post prandium. [L: after a meal] **4.** prepaid.

PP *abbrev. for:* **1.** Parish Priest. **2.** past President.

pp. *abbrev. for* pages.

ppd *abbrev. for:* **1.** post-paid. **2.** prepaid.

PPE *abbrev. for* philosophy, politics, and economics: a university course.

ppm *Chem. abbrev. for* parts per million.

ppr *or* **p.pr.** *abbrev. for* present participle.

PPS *abbrev. for:* **1.** parliamentary private secretary. **2.** Also: **pps** post postscriptum. [L: after postscript; additional postscript]

PQ *abbrev. for:* **1.** (in Canada) Parti Québecois. **2.** Province of Quebec.

pr *abbrev. for:* **1.** (*pl.* **prs**) pair. **2.** power. **3.** power.

Pr *the chemical symbol for* praseodymium.

PR *abbrev. for:* **1.** proportional representation. **2.** public relations. **3.** Puerto Rico.

pr. *abbrev. for:* **1.** price. **2.** pronoun.

practicable ('præktɪkǝb°l) *adj.* **1.** capable of being done; feasible. **2.** usable. [C17: from F *praticable,* from *pratiquer* to practise; see PRACTICAL] —,**practica'bility** *or* '**practicableness** *n.* —'**practicably** *adv.*
▷ **Usage.** See at **practical.**

practical ('præktɪk°l) *adj.* **1.** of, involving, or concerned with experience or actual use; not theoretical. **2.** of or concerned with ordinary affairs, work, etc. **3.** adapted or adaptable for use. **4.** of, involving, or trained by practice. **5.** being such for all general purposes; virtual. ~*n.* **6.** an examination or lesson in a practical subject. [C17: from earlier *practic*, from F *pratique*, via LL from Gk *prak-tikos*, from *prassein* to experience] —,**practi'cality** or **'practicalness** n.

▷ **Usage**. In careful usage, a distinction is made between *practical* and *practicable*. *Practical* refers to a person, idea, project, etc., as being more concerned with or relevant to practice than theory: *he is a very practical person; the idea had no practical application*. *Practicable* refers to a project or idea as being capable of being done or put into effect: *the plan was expensive, yet practicable*.

practical joke n. a prank or trick usually intended to make the victim appear foolish. —**practical joker** n.

practically ('præktɪkəlɪ, -klɪ) adv. **1.** virtually; almost: *it rained practically every day*. **2.** in actuality rather than in theory: *what can we do practically to help?*

practice ('præktɪs) n. **1.** a usual or customary action: *it was his practice to rise at six*. **2.** repetition of an activity in order to achieve mastery and fluency. **3.** the condition of having mastery of a skill or activity through repetition (esp. in **in practice, out of practice**). **4.** the exercise of a profession: *he set up practice as a lawyer*. **5.** the act of doing something: *he put his plans into practice*. **6.** the established method of conducting proceedings in a court of law. ~*vb.* **7.** the U.S. spelling of **practise**. [C16: from Med. L *practicāre* to practise, from Gk *praktikē* practical work, from *prattein* to do]

practise or U.S. **practice** ('præktɪs) vb. **1.** to do or cause to do repeatedly in order to gain skill. **2.** (*tr.*) to do (something) habitually or frequently: *they practise ritual murder*. **3.** to observe or pursue (something): *to practise Christianity*. **4.** to work at (a profession, etc.): *he practises medicine*. **5.** (foll. by *on* or *upon*) to take advantage of (someone, someone's credulity, etc.). [C15: see PRACTICE]

practised or U.S. **practiced** ('præktɪst) adj. **1.** expert; skilled; proficient. **2.** acquired or perfected by practice.

practitioner (præk'tɪʃənə) n. **1.** a person who practises a profession or art. **2.** Christian Science. a person authorized to practise spiritual healing. [C16: from *practician*, from OF, from *pratiquer* to PRACTISE]

Prado ('prɑːdəʊ) n. an art gallery in Madrid housing an important collection of Spanish paintings.

prae- *prefix*. an archaic variant of **pre-**.

praedial or **predial** ('priːdɪəl) adj. **1.** of or relating to land, farming, etc. **2.** attached to or occupying land. [C16: from Med. L *praediālis*, from L *praedium* farm, estate]

praesidium (prɪ'sɪdɪəm) n. a variant of **presidium**.

praetor or esp. U.S. **pretor** ('priːtə, -tɔː) n. (in ancient Rome) any of several senior magistrates ranking just below the consuls. [C15: from L: one who leads the way, prob. from *praeīre*, from *prae-* before + *īre* to go] —**prae'torian** or **pre'torian** adj., n. —**'praetorship** or **'pretorship** n.

Praetorius (German prɛ'toːriʊs) n. **Michael** ('mɪçaeːl). 1571–1621, German composer and musicologist, noted esp. for his description of contemporary musical practices and instruments, *Syntagma musicum* (1615–19).

pragmatic (præg'mætɪk) adj. **1.** advocating behaviour that is dictated more by practical consequences than by theory. **2.** Philosophy. of pragmatism. **3.** involving everyday or practical business. **4.** of or concerned with the affairs of a state or community. **5.** Rare. meddlesome; officious. Also for senses 3, 5): **pragmatical**. [C17: from LL *prāgmaticus*, from Gk *prāgmatikos* from *pragma* act, from *prattein* to do] —**prag,mati'cality** n. —**prag'matically** adv.

pragmatic sanction n. an edict, decree, or ordinance issued with the force of fundamental law by a sovereign.

pragmatism ('prægmə,tɪzəm) n. **1.** action or policy dictated by consideration of the practical consequences rather than by theory. **2.** Philosophy. the doctrine that the content of a concept consists only in its practical applicability. —**'pragmatist** n., adj.

Prague (prɑːg) n. the capital and largest city of Czechoslovakia, on the Vltava River: a rich commercial centre during the Middle Ages; site of Charles University (1348) and a technical university (1707); scene of defenestrations (1419 and 1618) that contributed to the outbreak of the Hussite Wars and the Thirty Years' War respectively. Pop.: 1 194 000 (1986). Czech name: **Praha**.

Praha ('praha) n. the Czech name for **Prague**.

prairie ('prɛərɪ) n. (*often pl.*) a treeless grassy plain of the central U.S. and S Canada. [C18: from F, from OF *praierie*, from L *prātum* meadow]

prairie chicken, fowl, grouse, or **hen** n. either of two mottled brown-and-white grouse of North America.

prairie dog n. any of several rodents that live in large complex burrows in the prairies of North America. Also called: **prairie marmot**.

prairie oyster n. a drink consisting of raw unbeaten egg, vinegar or Worcester sauce, salt, and pepper: a supposed cure for a hangover.

Prairie Provinces pl. n. the Canadian provinces of Manitoba, Saskatchewan, and Alberta, which lie in the N Great Plains region of North America: the chief wheat and petroleum producing area of Canada.

prairie schooner n. Chiefly U.S. a horse-drawn covered wagon used in the 19th century to cross the prairies of North America.

prairie wolf n. another name for **coyote**.

praise (preɪz) n. **1.** the act of expressing commendation, admiration, etc. **2.** the rendering of homage and gratitude to a deity. **3. sing someone's praises.** to commend someone highly. ~*vb.* (*tr.*) **4.** to express commendation, admiration, etc., for. **5.** to proclaim the glorious attributes of (a deity) with homage and thanksgiving. [C13: from OF *preisier*, from LL *pretiāre* to esteem highly, from L *pretium* prize]

praiseworthy ('preɪz,wɜːðɪ) adj. deserving of praise; commendable. —**'praise,worthily** adv. —**'praise,worthiness** n.

Prakrit ('prɑːkrɪt) n. any of the vernacular Indic languages as distinguished from Sanskrit: spoken from about 300 B.C. to the Middle Ages. [C18: from Sansk. *prākrta* original] —**Pra'kritic** adj.

praline ('prɑːliːn) n. **1.** a confection of nuts with caramelized sugar. **2.** Also called: **sugared almond.** a sweet consisting of an almond encased in sugar. [C18: from F, after César de Choiseul, comte de Plessis-*Praslin* (1598–1675), F field marshal whose chef first concocted it]

pralltriller ('prɑːl,trɪlə) n. an ornament used in 18th-century music consisting of an inverted mordent with an added initial upper note. [G: bouncing trill]

pram[1] (præm) n. Brit. a cotlike four-wheeled carriage for a baby. U.S. term: **baby carriage**. [C19: shortened & altered from PERAMBULATOR]

pram[2] (prɑːm) n. Naut. a light tender with a flat bottom and a bow formed from the ends of the side and bottom planks meeting in a small raised transom. [C16: from MDu. *prame*]

prance (prɑːns) vb. **1.** (*intr.*) to swagger or strut. **2.** (*intr.*) to caper, gambol, or dance about. **3.** (*intr.*) (of a horse) to move with high lively springing steps. **4.** (*tr.*) to cause to prance. ~n. **5.** the act or an instance of prancing. [C14 *prauncen*, from ?] —**'prancer** n. —**'prancing** adj.

prandial ('prændɪəl) adj. Facetious. of or relating to a meal. [C19: from L *prandium* meal, luncheon]

prang (præŋ) Chiefly Brit. sl. ~n. **1.** an accident or crash in an aircraft, car, etc. **2.** an aircraft bombing raid. ~vb. **3.** to crash or damage (an aircraft, car, etc.). **4.** to damage (a town, etc.) by bombing. [C20: ? imit.]

prank[1] (præŋk) n. a mischievous trick or joke. [C16: from ?] —**'prankish** adj. —**'prankster** n.

prank[2] (præŋk) vb. **1.** (*tr.*) to dress or decorate showily or gaudily. **2.** (*intr.*) to make an ostentatious display. [C16: from MDu. *pronken*]

prase (preɪz) n. a light green translucent variety of chalcedony. [C14: from F, from L *prasius* a leek-green stone, from Gk *prasios*, from *prason* a leek]

praseodymium (,preɪzɪəʊ'dɪmɪəm) n. a malleable ductile silvery-white element of the lanthanide series of metals. Symbol: Pr; atomic no.: 59; atomic wt.: 140.91. [C20: NL, from Gk *prasios* of a leek-green colour + DIDYMIUM]

prate (preɪt) vb. **1.** (*intr.*) to talk idly and at length; chatter. **2.** (*tr.*) to utter in an idle or empty way. ~n. **3.** idle or trivial talk; chatter. [C15: of Gmc origin] —**'prater** n. —**'prating** adj.

pratfall ('præt,fɔːl) n. U.S. & Canad. sl. a fall upon one's buttocks. [C20: from C16 *prat* buttocks (from ?) + FALL]

pratincole ('prætɪŋ,kəʊl, 'preɪ-) n. any of various swallow-like shore birds of the Old World, having long pointed wings, short legs, and a short bill. [C18: from NL *pratincola* field-dwelling, from L *prātum* meadow + *incola* inhabitant]

Prato (*Italian* 'pra:to) *n.* a walled city in central Italy, in Tuscany: woollen industry. Pop.: 164 595 (1986). Official name: **Prato in Toscana** (in tos'ka:na).

prattle ('præt³l) *vb.* **1.** (*intr.*) to talk in a foolish or childish way; babble. **2.** (*tr.*) to utter in a foolish or childish way. ~*n.* **3.** foolish or childish talk. [C16: from MLow G *pratelen* to chatter] —'**prattler** *n.* —'**prattling** *adj.*

prau (prau) *n.* a variant of **proa**.

prawn (prɔːn) *n.* **1.** any of various small edible marine decapod crustaceans having a slender flattened body with a long tail and two pairs of pincers. **2. come the raw prawn with**. *Austral. inf.* to attempt to deceive. [C15: from ?]

praxis ('præksɪs) *n., pl.* **praxes** ('præksiːz) *or* **praxises**. **1.** the practice of a field of study, as opposed to the theory. **2.** a practical exercise. **3.** accepted practice or custom. [C16: via Med. L from Gk: deed, action, from *prassein* to do]

Praxiteles (præk'sɪtɪˌliːz) *n.* 4th-century B.C. Greek sculptor: his works include statues of Hermes at Olympia, which survives, and of Aphrodite at Cnidus.

pray (preɪ) *vb.* **1.** (when *intr.*, often foll. by *for;* when *tr.*, usually takes a clause as object) to utter prayers (to God or other object of worship). **2.** (when *tr.*, usually takes a clause as object or an *infinitive*) to beg or implore: *she prayed to be allowed to go.* ~*sentence substitute.* **3.** *Arch.* I beg you; please: *pray, leave us alone.* [C13: from OF *preier*, from L *precārī* to implore, from *prex* an entreaty]

prayer[1] (prɛə) *n.* **1.** a personal communication or petition addressed to a deity, esp. in the form of supplication, adoration, praise, contrition, or thanksgiving. **2.** a similar personal communication that does not involve adoration, addressed to beings closely associated with a deity, such as saints. **3.** the practice of praying: *prayer is our solution to human problems.* **4.** (*often pl.*) a form of devotion spent mainly or wholly praying: *morning prayers.* **5.** (*cap. when part of a recognized name*) a form of words used in praying: *the Lord's Prayer.* **6.** an object or benefit prayed for. **7.** an earnest request or entreaty. [C13 *preiere*, from OF, from Med. L, from L *precārius* obtained by begging, from *prex* prayer] —'**prayerful** *adj.*

prayer[2] ('preɪə) *n.* a person who prays.

prayer book (prɛə) *n.* a book containing the prayers used at church services or recommended for private devotions.

prayer rug (prɛə) *n.* the small carpet on which a Muslim kneels and prostrates himself while saying his prayers. Also called: **prayer mat.**

prayer wheel (prɛə) *n. Buddhism.* (esp. in Tibet) a wheel or cylinder inscribed with or containing prayers, each revolution of which is counted as an uttered prayer, so that such prayers can be repeated by turning it.

praying mantis *or* **mantid** *n.* another name for **mantis**.

PRB *abbrev. for* Pre-Raphaelite Brotherhood.

pre- *prefix.* before in time, position, etc.: *predate; pre-eminent.* [from L *prae* before]

preach (priːtʃ) *vb.* **1.** to make known (religious truth) or give religious or moral instruction or exhortation in (sermons). **2.** to advocate (a virtue, action, etc.), esp. in a moralizing way. [C13: from OF *prechier*, from Church L *praedicāre*, from L: to proclaim in public; see PREDICATE]

preacher ('priːtʃə) *n.* a person who preaches, esp. a Protestant clergyman.

preachify ('priːtʃɪˌfaɪ) *vb.* **-fying, -fied.** (*intr.*) *Inf.* to preach or moralize in a tedious manner. —,**preachifi'cation** *n.*

preachment ('priːtʃmənt) *n.* **1.** the act of preaching. **2.** a tedious or pompous sermon.

preachy ('priːtʃɪ) *adj.* **preachier, preachiest.** *Inf.* inclined to or marked by preaching.

preamble (priː'æmb³l) *n.* **1.** a preliminary or introductory statement, esp. attached to a statute setting forth its

purpose. **2.** a preliminary event, fact, etc. [C14: from OF *préambule*, from LL *praeambulum*, from L *prae-* before + *ambulāre* to walk]

preamplifier (priː'æmplɪˌfaɪə) *n.* an electronic amplifier used to improve the signal-to-noise ratio of an electronic device. It boosts a low-level signal to an intermediate level before it is transmitted to the main amplifier.

prebend ('prɛbənd) *n.* **1.** the stipend assigned by a cathedral or collegiate church to a canon or member of the chapter. **2.** the land, tithe, or other source of such a stipend. **3.** a less common word for **prebendary. 4.** *Church of England.* the office of a prebendary. [C15: from OF *prébende*, from Med. L *praebenda* stipend, from L *praebēre* to offer, from *prae* forth + *habēre* to have] —**prebendal** (prɪ'bɛnd³l) *adj.*

prebendary ('prɛbəndərɪ, -drɪ) *n., pl.* **-daries. 1.** a canon or member of the chapter of a cathedral or collegiate church who holds a prebend. **2.** *Church of England.* an honorary canon with the title of prebendary.

Precambrian *or* **Pre-Cambrian** (priː'kæmbrɪən) *adj.* **1.** of, denoting, or formed in the earliest geological era, which lasted for about 4 000 000 000 years before the Cambrian period. ~*n.* **2. the.** the Precambrian era.

precancel (priː'kæns³l) *vb.* **-celling, -celled** *or U.S.* **-celing, -celed.** (*tr.*) to cancel (postage stamps) before placing them on mail.

precarious (prɪ'kɛərɪəs) *adj.* **1.** liable to failure or catastrophe; insecure; perilous. **2.** *Arch.* dependent on another's will. [C17: from L *precārius* obtained by begging, from *prex* PRAYER[1]] —**pre'cariously** *adv.* —**pre'cariousness** *n.*

precast ('priː,kɑːst) *adj.* (esp. of concrete when employed as a structural element in building) cast in a particular form before being used.

precaution (prɪ'kɔːʃən) *n.* **1.** an action taken to avoid a dangerous or undesirable event. **2.** caution practised beforehand; circumspection. [C17: from F, from LL *praecautiō*, from L, from *prae* before + *cavēre* to beware] —**pre'cautionary** *adj.*

precede (prɪ'siːd) *vb.* **1.** to go or be before (someone or something) in time, place, rank, etc. **2.** (*tr.*) to preface or introduce. [C14: via OF from L *praecēdere* to go before]

precedence ('prɛsɪdəns) *or* **precedency** *n.* **1.** the act of preceding or the condition of being precedent. **2.** the ceremonial order or priority to be observed on formal occasions: *the officers were seated according to precedence.* **3.** a right to preferential treatment: *I take precedence over you.*

precedent *n.* ('prɛsɪdənt). **1.** *Law.* a judicial decision that serves as an authority for deciding a later case. **2.** an example or instance used to justify later similar occurrences. ~*adj.* (prɪ'siːd³nt, 'prɛsɪdənt). **3.** preceding.

precedented ('prɛsɪˌdɛntɪd) *adj.* (of a decision, etc.) supported by having a precedent.

precedential (ˌprɛsɪ'dɛnʃəl) *adj.* **1.** of or serving as a precedent. **2.** having precedence.

preceding (prɪ'siːdɪŋ) *adj.* (*prenominal*) going or coming before; former.

precentor (prɪ'sɛntə) *n.* **1.** a cleric who directs the choral services in a cathedral. **2.** a person who leads a congregation or choir in the sung parts of church services. [C17: from LL *praecentor*, from *prae* before + *canere* to sing] —**precentorial** (ˌpriːsɛn'tɔːrɪəl) *adj.* —**pre'centor,ship** *n.*

precept ('priːsɛpt) *n.* **1.** a rule or principle for action. **2.** a guide or rule for morals; maxim. **3.** a direction, esp. for a technical operation. **4.** *Law.* **a.** a writ or warrant. **b.** (in England) an order to collect money under a rate. [C14: from L *praeceptum* injunction, from *praecipere* to admonish, from *prae* before + *capere* to take] —**pre'ceptive** *adj.*

preceptor (prɪ'sɛptə) *n. Rare.* a tutor or instructor. —**preceptorial** (ˌpriːsɛp'tɔːrɪəl) *or* **pre'ceptoral** *adj.* —**pre'ceptress** *fem. n.*

,**preab'sorb** *vb.*	,**preado'lescent** *n., adj.*	**pre'arm** *vb.*	,**preas'sumption** *n.*
,**preac'cept** *vb.*	**pre'adver,tise** *vb.*	,**prear'range** *vb.*	,**preas'surance** *n.*
,**preac'custom** *vb.*	,**preal'lot** *vb.*	,**prear'ranged** *adj.*	**pre'boil** *vb.*
,**preac'quaint** *vb.*	,**prean'nounce** *vb.*	,**prear'rangement** *n.*	,**pre-Byz'an,tine** *adj.*
,**prea'dapt** *vb.*	,**preap'pearance** *n.*	,**preascer'tain** *vb.*	**pre'cancerous** *adj.*
,**pread'dress** *vb.*	,**preappli'cation** *n.*	,**preas'semble** *vb.*	**pre-'Celtic** *adj.*
,**pread'just** *vb.*	,**preap'point** *vb.*	,**preas'sign** *vb.*	**pre'censor** *vb.*

precession (prɪˈsɛʃən) *n.* **1.** the act of preceding. **2.** See **precession of the equinoxes. 3.** the motion of a spinning body, such as a top, gyroscope, or planet, in which it wobbles so that the axis of rotation sweeps out a cone. [C16: from LL *praecessiō*, from L *praecēdere* to precede] —**pre'cessional** *adj.* —**pre'cessionally** *adv.*

precession of the equinoxes *n.* the slightly earlier occurrence of the equinoxes each year due to the slow continuous westward shift of the equinoctial points along the ecliptic.

precinct ('priːsɪŋkt) *n.* **1. a.** an enclosed area or building marked by a fixed boundary such as a wall. **b.** such a boundary. **2.** an area in a town, often closed to traffic, that is designed or reserved for a particular activity: *a shopping precinct.* **3.** *U.S.* **a.** a district of a city for administrative or police purposes. **b.** a polling district. [C15: from Med. L *praecinctum* (something) surrounded, from L *praecingere* to gird around]

precincts ('priːsɪŋkts) *pl. n.* the surrounding region or area.

preciosity (ˌprɛʃɪˈɒsɪtɪ) *n., pl.* **-ties.** fastidiousness or affectation.

precious ('prɛʃəs) *adj.* **1.** beloved; dear; cherished. **2.** very costly or valuable. **3.** very fastidious or affected, as in speech, manners, etc. **4.** *Inf.* worthless: *you and your precious ideas!* ~*adv.* **5.** *Inf.* (intensifier): *there's precious little left.* [C13: from OF *precios*, from L *pretiōsus* valuable, from *pretium* price] —'**preciously** *adv.* —'**preciousness** *n.*

precious metal *n.* gold, silver, or platinum.

precious stone *n.* any of certain rare minerals, such as diamond, ruby, or opal, that are highly valued as gemstones.

precipice ('prɛsɪpɪs) *n.* **1.** the steep sheer face of a cliff or crag. **2.** the cliff or crag itself. [C16: from L *praecipitium* steep place, from *praeceps* headlong] —'**precipiced** *adj.*

precipitant (prɪˈsɪpɪtənt) *adj.* **1.** hasty or impulsive; rash. **2.** rushing or falling rapidly or without heed. **3.** abrupt or sudden. ~*n.* **4.** *Chem.* a substance that causes a precipitate to form. —**pre'cipitance** *or* **pre'cipitancy** *n.*

precipitate *vb.* (prɪˈsɪpɪˌteɪt). **1.** (*tr.*) to cause to happen too soon; bring on. **2.** to throw or fall from or as from a height. **3.** to cause (moisture) to condense and fall as snow, rain, etc., or (of moisture, rain, etc.) to condense and fall thus. **4.** *Chem.* to undergo or cause to undergo a process in which a dissolved substance separates from solution as a fine suspension of solid particles. ~*adj.* (prɪˈsɪpɪtɪt). **5.** rushing ahead. **6.** done rashly or with undue haste. **7.** sudden and brief. ~*n.* (prɪˈsɪpɪtɪt). **8.** *Chem.* a precipitated solid. [C16: from L *praecipitāre* to throw down headlong, from *praeceps* steep, from *prae* before + *caput* head] —**pre'cipitable** *adj.* —**pre,cipita'bility** *n.* —**pre'cipitately** *adv.* —**pre'cipi,tator** *n.*

precipitation (prɪˌsɪpɪˈteɪʃən) *n.* **1.** *Meteorol.* **a.** rain, snow, sleet, dew, etc., formed by condensation of water vapour in the atmosphere. **b.** the deposition of these on the earth's surface. **2.** the formation of a chemical precipitate. **3.** the act of precipitating or the state of being precipitated. **4.** rash or undue haste.

precipitous (prɪˈsɪpɪtəs) *adj.* **1.** resembling a precipice. **2.** very steep. **3.** hasty or precipitate. —**pre'cipitously** *adv.* —**pre'cipitousness** *n.*

precis *or* **précis** ('preɪsiː) *n., pl.* **precis** *or* **précis** ('preɪsiːz). **1.** a summary of a text; abstract. ~*vb.* **2.** (*tr.*) to make a precis of. [C18: from F: PRECISE]

precise (prɪˈsaɪs) *adj.* **1.** strictly correct in amount or value: *a precise sum.* **2.** particular: *this precise location.* **3.** using or operating with total accuracy: *precise instruments.* **4.** strict in observance of rules, standards, etc.: *a precise mind.* [C16: from F *précis*, from L *praecīdere* to curtail, from *prae* before + *caedere* to cut] —**pre'cisely** *adv.* —**pre'ciseness** *n.*

precision (prɪˈsɪʒən) *n.* **1.** the quality of being precise; accuracy. **2.** (*modifier*) characterized by a high degree of exactness: *precision grinding.* [C17: from L *praecīsiō* a cutting off; see PRECISE] —**pre'cisionism** *n.* —**pre'cisionist** *n.*

preclude (prɪˈkluːd) *vb.* (*tr.*) **1.** to exclude or debar. **2.** to make impossible, esp. beforehand. [C17: from L *praeclūdere* to shut up, from *prae* before + *claudere* to close] —**preclusion** (prɪˈkluːʒən) *n.* —**preclusive** (prɪˈkluːsɪv) *adj.*

precocial (prɪˈkəʊʃəl) *adj.* **1.** denoting birds whose young, after hatching, are covered with down and capable of leaving the nest within a few days. ~*n.* **2.** a precocial bird. ~Cf. **altricial.**

precocious (prɪˈkəʊʃəs) *adj.* **1.** ahead in development, such as the mental development of a child. **2.** *Bot.* flowering or ripening early. [C17: from L *praecox*, from *prae* early + *coquere* to ripen] —**pre'cociously** *adv.* —**pre'cociousness** *or* **precocity** (prɪˈkɒsɪtɪ) *n.*

precognition (ˌpriːkɒɡˈnɪʃən) *n. Psychol.* the alleged ability to foresee future events. [C17: from LL *praecognitiō* foreknowledge, from *praecognoscere* to foresee] —**precognitive** (priːˈkɒɡnɪtɪv) *adj.*

preconceive (ˌpriːkənˈsiːv) *vb.* (*tr.*) to form an idea of beforehand. —**preconception** (ˌpriːkənˈsɛpʃən) *n.*

precondition (ˌpriːkənˈdɪʃən) *n.* **1.** a necessary or required condition; prerequisite. ~*vb.* **2.** (*tr.*) *Psychol.* to present successively two stimuli to (an organism) without reinforcement so that they become associated; if a response is then conditioned to the second stimulus on its own, the same response will be evoked by the first stimulus.

preconize *or* **-ise** ('priːkəˌnaɪz) *vb.* (*tr.*) **1.** to announce or commend publicly. **2.** to summon publicly. **3.** (of the pope) to approve the appointment of (a nominee) to one of the higher dignities in the Roman Catholic Church. [C15: from Med. L *praecōnizāre* to make an announcement, from L *praecō* herald] —**,preconi'zation** *or* **-i'sation** *n.*

precursor (prɪˈkɜːsə) *n.* **1.** a person or thing that precedes and announces someone or something to come. **2.** a predecessor. **3.** a substance that gives rise to another more important substance. [C16: from L *praecursor* one who runs in front, from *praecurrere*, from *prae* in front + *currere* to run]

precursory (prɪˈkɜːsərɪ) *or* **precursive** *adj.* **1.** serving as a precursor. **2.** preliminary.

pred. *abbrev. for* predicate.

predacious *or* **predaceous** (prɪˈdeɪʃəs) *adj.* (of animals) habitually hunting and killing other animals for food. [C18: from L *praeda* plunder] —**pre'daciousness, pre'daceousness,** *or* **predacity** (prɪˈdæsɪtɪ) *n.*

predate (priːˈdeɪt) *vb.* (*tr.*) **1.** to affix a date to (a document, paper, etc.) that is earlier than the actual date. **2.** to assign a date to (an event, period, etc.) that is earlier than the actual or previously assigned date of occurrence. **3.** to be or occur at an earlier date than; precede in time.

predation (prɪˈdeɪʃən) *n.* a relationship between two species of animal in a community, in which one hunts, kills, and eats the other.

predator ('prɛdətə) *n.* **1.** any carnivorous animal. **2.** a predatory person or thing.

predatory ('prɛdətərɪ) *adj.* **1.** *Zool.* another word for **predacious. 2.** of or characterized by plundering, robbing, etc. [C16: from L *praedātōrius* rapacious, from *praedārī* to pillage, from *praeda* booty] —**'predatorily** *adv.* —**'predatoriness** *n.*

predecease (ˌpriːdɪˈsiːs) *vb.* to die before (some other person).

predecessor ('priːdɪˌsɛsə) *n.* **1.** a person who precedes another, as in an office. **2.** something that precedes something else. **3.** an ancestor. [C14: via OF from LL *praedēcessor*, from *prae* before + *dēcēdere* to go away]

predella (prɪˈdɛlə) *n., pl.* **-le** (-liː). **1.** a painting or a series of small paintings in a long strip forming the lower edge of an altarpiece or the face of an altar step. **2.** a platform in a church upon which the altar stands. [C19: from It.: step, prob. from OHG *bret* board]

predestinarian (ˌpriːdɛstɪˈnɛərɪən) *n.* **1.** a person who believes in divine predestination. ~*adj.* **2.** of or relating to predestination or those who believe in it.

predestinate *vb.* (priːˈdɛstɪˌneɪt). **1.** another word for **predestine.** ~*adj.* (priːˈdɛstɪnɪt, -ˌneɪt). **2.** predestined.

---

predestination (priːˌdɛstɪˈneɪʃən) n. **1.** Christian theol. **a.** the act of God foreordaining every event from eternity. **b.** the doctrine or belief, esp. associated with Calvin, that the final salvation of some of mankind is foreordained from eternity by God. **2.** the act of predestining or the state of being predestined.

predestine (priːˈdɛstɪn) or **predestinate** vb. (tr.) **1.** to determine beforehand. **2.** Christian theol. (of God) to decree from eternity (any event, esp. the final salvation of individuals). [C14: from L praedestināre to resolve beforehand]

predetermine (ˌpriːdɪˈtɜːmɪn) vb. (tr.) **1.** to determine beforehand. **2.** to influence or bias. —ˌprede'terminable adj. —ˌprede'terminate adj. —ˌprede,termi'nation n.

predicable ('prɛdɪkəbəl) adj. **1.** capable of being predicated or asserted. ~n. **2.** a quality that can be predicated. **3.** Logic, obs. any of the five Aristotelian classes of predicates, namely genus, species, difference, property, and relation. [C16: from L praedicābilis, from praedicāre to assert publicly; see PREDICATE] —ˌpredica'bility n.

predicament **1.** (prɪˈdɪkəmənt). n. a perplexing, embarrassing, or difficult situation. **2.** ('prɛdɪkəmənt). Logic. a logical category. [C14: from LL praedicāmentum what is predicated, from praedicāre to announce; see PREDICATE]

predicant ('prɛdɪkənt) adj. **1.** of or relating to preaching. ~n. **2.** a member of a religious order founded for preaching, esp. a Dominican. [C17: from L praedicāns preaching, from praedicāre to say publicly; see PREDICATE]

predicate vb. ('prɛdɪˌkeɪt). (mainly tr.) **1.** (also intr.; when tr., may take a clause as object) to declare or affirm. **2.** to imply or connote. **3.** (foll. by on or upon) Chiefly U.S. to base (a proposition, argument, etc.). **4.** Logic. to assert (a property or condition) of the subject of a proposition. ~n. ('prɛdɪkɪt). **5.** Grammar. the part of a sentence in which something is asserted or denied of the subject of a sentence. **6.** Logic. a term, property, or condition that is affirmed or denied concerning the subject of a proposition. ~adj. ('prɛdɪkɪt). **7.** of or relating to something that has been predicated. [C16: from L praedicāre to assert publicly, from prae in front + dīcere to say] —ˌpredi'cation n.

predicate calculus n. the system of symbolic logic concerned not only with relations between propositions as wholes but also with the representation by symbols of individuals and predicates in propositions. See also **propositional calculus**.

predicative (prɪˈdɪkətɪv) adj. Grammar. relating to or occurring within the predicate of a sentence: a predicative adjective. Cf. **attributive.** —pre'dicatively adv.

predict (prɪˈdɪkt) vb. (tr.; may take a clause as object) to state or make a declaration about in advance; foretell. [C17: from L praedīcere to mention beforehand] —pre'dictable adj. —pre,dicta'bility n. —pre'dictably adv. —pre'dictor n.

prediction (prɪˈdɪkʃən) n. **1.** the act of predicting. **2.** something predicted; a forecast.

predigest (ˌpriːdaɪˈdʒɛst, -dɪ-) vb. (tr.) to treat (food) artificially to aid subsequent digestion in the body. —ˌpredi'gestion n.

predikant (ˌprɛdɪˈkænt) n. a minister in the Dutch Reformed Church, esp. in South Africa. [from Du., from OF predicant, from LL, from praedicāre to PREACH]

predilection (ˌpriːdɪˈlɛkʃən) n. a predisposition, preference, or bias. [C18: from F prédilection, from Med. L praedīligere to prefer, from L prae before + dīligere to love]

predispose (ˌpriːdɪˈspəʊz) vb. (tr.) (often foll. by to or towards) to incline or make (someone) susceptible to something beforehand. —ˌpredis'posal n. —ˌpredis-po'sition n.

predominant (prɪˈdɒmɪnənt) adj. **1.** superior in power, influence, etc., over others. **2.** prevailing. —pre'dominance n. —pre'dominantly adv.

predominate vb. (prɪˈdɒmɪˌneɪt). (intr.) **1.** (often foll. by over) to have power, influence, or control. **2.** to prevail or preponderate. ~adj. (prɪˈdɒmɪnɪt). **3.** another word for **predominant.** [C16: from Med. L praedominārī, from L

prae before + dominārī to bear rule] —pre'dominately adv. —pre,domi'nation n.

pre-eclampsia (ˌpriːɪˈklæmpsɪə) n. a serious condition that can occur late in pregnancy. If not treated it can lead to eclampsia.

pre-eminent (prɪˈɛmɪnənt) adj. extremely eminent or distinguished; outstanding. —pre'eminence n. —pre-'eminently adv.

pre-empt (prɪˈɛmpt) vb. **1.** (tr.) to acquire in advance of or to the exclusion of others; appropriate. **2.** (tr.) Chiefly U.S. to occupy (public land) in order to acquire a prior right to purchase. **3.** (intr.) Bridge. to make a high opening bid, often on a weak hand, to shut out opposition bidding. —pre-'emptor n.

pre-emption (prɪˈɛmpʃən) n. **1.** Law. the purchase of or right to purchase property in preference to others. **2.** International law. the right of a government to intercept and seize property of the subjects of another state while in transit, esp. in time of war. [C16: from Med. L praeemptiō, from praeemere to buy beforehand]

pre-emptive (prɪˈɛmptɪv) adj. **1.** of, involving, or capable of pre-emption. **2.** Bridge. (of a high bid) made to shut out opposition bidding. **3.** Mil. designed to reduce or destroy an enemy's attacking strength before it can use it: a pre-emptive strike.

preen (priːn) vb. **1.** (of birds) to maintain (feathers) in a healthy condition by arrangement, cleaning, and other contact with the bill. **2.** to dress or array (oneself) carefully; primp. **3.** (usually foll. by on) to pride or congratulate (oneself). [C14 preinen, prob. from prunen, infl. by prenen to prick; suggestive of the pricking movement of the bird's beak] —'preener n.

pref. abbrev. for: **1.** preface. **2.** prefatory. **3.** preference. **4.** preferred. **5.** prefix.

prefab ('priːˌfæb) n. a building that is prefabricated, esp. a small house.

prefabricate (priːˈfæbrɪˌkeɪt) vb. (tr.) to manufacture sections of (a building) so that they can be easily transported to and rapidly assembled on a building site. —ˌpre,fabri'cation n.

preface ('prɛfɪs) n. **1.** a statement written as an introduction to a literary or other work, typically explaining its scope, intention, method, etc.; foreword. **2.** anything introductory. ~vb. (tr.) **3.** to furnish with a preface. **4.** to serve as a preface to. [C14: from Med. L praefātia, from L praefātiō a saying beforehand, from praefārī to utter in advance] —'prefacer n.

prefatory ('prɛfətərɪ, -trɪ) or **prefatorial** (ˌprɛfəˈtɔːrɪəl) adj. of or serving as a preface; introductory. [C17: from L praefārī to say in advance]

prefect ('priːfɛkt) n. **1.** (in France, Italy, etc.) the chief administrative officer in a department. **2.** (in France, etc.) the head of a police force. **3.** Brit. a schoolchild appointed to a position of limited power over his fellows. **4.** (in ancient Rome) any of several magistrates or military commanders. **5.** R.C. Church. one of two senior masters in a Jesuit school or college. [C14: from L praefectus one put in charge, from praeficere to place in authority over, from prae before + facere to do] —**prefectorial** (ˌpriːfɛkˈtɔːrɪəl) adj.

prefecture ('priːfɛkˌtjʊə) n. **1.** the office, position, or area of authority of a prefect. **2.** the official residence of a prefect in France, etc.

prefer (prɪˈfɜː) vb. **-ferring, -ferred. 1.** (when tr., may take a clause as object or an infinitive) to like better or value more highly: I prefer to stand. **2.** Law. (esp. of the police) to put (charges) before a court, magistrate, etc., for consideration and judgment. **3.** (tr.; often passive) to advance in rank over another or others; promote. [C14: from L praeferre to carry in front, prefer]

preferable ('prɛfərəbəl) adj. preferred or more desirable. —'preferably adv.

preference ('prɛfərəns, 'prɛfrəns) n. **1.** the act of preferring. **2.** something or someone preferred. **3.** International trade. the granting of favour or precedence to particular foreign countries, as by levying differential tariffs.

preference shares *pl. n. Brit.* fixed-interest shares issued by a company and giving their holders a prior right over ordinary shareholders to payment of dividend and to repayment of capital if the company is liquidated. U.S. name: **preferred stock.** Cf. **ordinary shares.**

preferential (ˌprɛfəˈrɛnʃəl) *adj.* **1.** showing or resulting from preference. **2.** giving, receiving, or originating from preference in international trade. —ˌpreferˈentially *adv.*

preferment (prɪˈfɜːmənt) *n.* **1.** the act of promoting to a higher position, office, etc. **2.** the state of being preferred for promotion or social advancement. **3.** the act of preferring.

prefigure (priːˈfɪɡə) *vb.* (*tr.*) **1.** to represent or suggest in advance. **2.** to imagine beforehand. —ˌprefiguˈration *n.* —preˈfigurement *n.*

prefix *n.* (ˈpriːfɪks). **1.** *Grammar.* an affix that precedes the stem to which it is attached, as for example *un-* in *unhappy.* Cf. **suffix** (sense 1). **2.** something coming or placed before. ~*vb.* (priːˈfɪks, ˈpriːfɪks). (*tr.*) **3.** to put or place before. **4.** *Grammar.* to add (a morpheme) as a prefix to the beginning of a word. —**prefixion** (priːˈfɪkʃən) *n.*

prefrontal (priːˈfrʌntəl) *adj.* in or relating to the foremost part of the frontal lobe of the brain.

preglacial (priːˈɡleɪsɪəl, -ʃəl) *adj.* formed or occurring before a glacial period, esp. before the Pleistocene epoch.

pregnable (ˈprɛɡnəbəl) *adj.* capable of being assailed or captured. [C15 *prenable,* from OF *prendre* to take, from L *prehendere* to catch]

pregnant (ˈprɛɡnənt) *adj.* **1.** carrying a fetus or fetuses within the womb. **2.** full of meaning or significance. **3.** inventive or imaginative. **4.** prolific or fruitful. [C16: from L *praegnāns* with child, from *prae* before + (*g*)*nascī* to be born] —**pregnancy** *n.* —**pregnantly** *adv.*

prehensile (prɪˈhɛnsaɪl) *adj.* adapted for grasping, esp. by wrapping around a support: *a prehensile tail.* [C18: from F *préhensile,* from L *prehendere* to grasp] —**prehensility** (ˌpriːhɛnˈsɪlɪtɪ) *n.*

prehension (prɪˈhɛnʃən) *n.* **1.** the act of grasping. **2.** apprehension by the mind.

prehistoric (ˌpriːhɪˈstɒrɪk) *or* **prehistorical** *adj.* of or relating to man's development before the appearance of the written word. —**prehisˈtorically** *adv.* —preˈhistory *n.*

pre-ignition (ˌpriːɪɡˈnɪʃən) *n.* ignition of all or part of the explosive charge in an internal-combustion engine before the exact instant necessary for correct operation.

prejudge (priːˈdʒʌdʒ) *vb.* (*tr.*) to judge beforehand, esp. without sufficient evidence.

prejudice (ˈprɛdʒʊdɪs) *n.* **1.** an opinion formed beforehand, esp. an unfavourable one based on inadequate facts. **2.** the act or condition of holding such opinions. **3.** intolerance of or dislike for people of a specific race, religion, etc. **4.** disadvantage or injury resulting from prejudice. **5. in** (*or* **to**) **the prejudice of.** to the detriment of. **6. without prejudice.** *Law.* without dismissing or detracting from an existing right or claim. ~*vb.* (*tr.*) **7.** to cause to be prejudiced. **8.** to disadvantage or injure by prejudice. [C13: from OF *préjudice,* from L *praejūdicium,* from *prae* before + *jūdicium* sentence, from *jūdex* a judge]

prejudicial (ˌprɛdʒʊˈdɪʃəl) *adj.* causing prejudice; damaging. —ˌprejuˈdicially *adv.*

prelacy (ˈprɛləsɪ) *n., pl.* **-cies. 1.** Also called: **prelature. a.** the office or status of a prelate. **b.** prelates collectively. **2.** *Often derog.* government of the Church by prelates.

prelapsarian (ˌpriːlæpˈsɛərɪən) *adj.* of or relating to the human state before the Fall: *prelapsarian innocence.*

prelate (ˈprɛlɪt) *n.* a Church dignitary of high rank, such as a cardinal, bishop, or abbot. [C13: from OF *prélat,* from Church L *praelātus,* from *praeferre* to hold in special esteem] —**prelatic** (prɪˈlætɪk) *or* **preˈlatical** *adj.*

preliminaries (prɪˈlɪmɪnərɪz) *pl. n.* the full word for **prelims.**

preliminary (prɪˈlɪmɪnərɪ) *adj.* **1.** (*usually prenominal*) occurring before or in preparation; introductory. ~*n., pl.* **-naries. 2.** a preliminary event or occurrence. **3.** an eliminating contest held before the main competition.

[C17: from NL *praelīmināris,* from L *prae* before + *līmen* threshold] —**preˈliminarily** *adv.*

prelims (ˈpriːlɪmz, prəˈlɪmz) *pl. n.* **1.** Also called: **front matter.** the pages of a book, such as the title page and contents, before the main text. **2.** the first public examinations taken for the bachelor's degree in some universities. **3.** (in Scotland) the school examinations taken before public examinations. [C19: a contraction of PRELIMINARIES]

prelude (ˈprɛljuːd) *n.* **1. a.** a piece of music that precedes a fugue, or forms the first movement of a suite, or an introduction to an act in an opera, etc. **b.** (esp. for piano) a self-contained piece of music. **2.** an introduction or preceding event, occurrence, etc. **3.** to serve as a prelude to (something). **4.** (*tr.*) to introduce by a prelude. [C16: from Med. L *praelūdium,* from *prae* before + L *lūdere* to play] —**preludial** (prɪˈljuːdɪəl) *adj.*

premarital (priːˈmærɪtəl) *adj.* (esp. of sexual relations) occurring before marriage.

premature (ˌprɛməˈtjʊə, ˈprɛməˌtjʊə) *adj.* **1.** occurring or existing before the normal or expected time. **2.** impulsive or hasty: *a premature judgment.* **3.** (of an infant) born before the end of the full period of gestation. [C16: from L *praemātūrus* very early from *prae* in advance + *mātūrus* ripe] —ˌprema'turely *adv.*

premedical (priːˈmɛdɪkəl) *adj.* **1.** of or relating to a course of study prerequisite for entering medical school. **2.** of or relating to a person engaged in such a course of study.

premedication (ˌpriːmɛdɪˈkeɪʃən) *n. Surgery.* any drugs administered to sedate and otherwise prepare a patient for general anaesthesia.

premeditate (prɪˈmɛdɪˌteɪt) *vb.* to plan or consider (something, such as a violent crime) beforehand. —preˈmediˌtator *n.*

premeditation (prɪˌmɛdɪˈteɪʃən) *n.* **1.** *Law.* prior resolve to do some act or to commit a crime. **2.** the act of premeditating.

premenstrual tension *or* **syndrome** *n.* symptoms, esp. nervous tension, that may be experienced because of hormonal changes in the days before a menstrual period starts. Abbrev.: **PMT.**

premier (ˈprɛmjə) *n.* **1.** another name for **prime minister. 2.** any of the heads of government of the Canadian provinces and the Australian states. **3.** *Austral.* a team that wins a premiership. ~*adj.* (*prenominal*) **4.** first in importance, rank, etc. **5.** first in occurrence; earliest. [C15: from OF: first, from L *prīmārius* principal, from *prīmus* first]

premiere (ˈprɛmɪˌɛə, ˈprɛmɪə) *n.* **1.** the first public performance of a film, play, opera, etc. **2.** the leading lady in a theatre company. ~*vb.* **3.** (*tr.*) to give a premiere of: *the show will be premiered on Broadway.* [C19: from F, fem. of *premier* first]

premiership (ˈprɛmjəˌʃɪp) *n.* **1.** the office of premier. **2.** *Austral.* **a.** a championship competition held among a number of sporting clubs. **b.** a victory in such a championship.

premillennialism (ˌpriːmɪˈlɛnɪəˌlɪzəm) *n.* the doctrine or belief that the millennium will be preceded by the Second Coming of Christ. —ˌpremilˈlennialist *n.* —ˌpremilˈlenarian *n., adj.*

premise *n. also* **premiss.** (ˈprɛmɪs). **1.** *Logic.* a statement that is assumed to be true for the purpose of an argument from which a conclusion is drawn. ~*vb.* (prɪˈmɪz, ˈprɛmɪs). **2.** (when *tr., may take a clause as object*) to state or assume (a proposition) as a premise in an argument, etc. [C14: from OF *prémisse,* from Med. L *praemissa* sent on before, from L *praemittere* to dispatch in advance]

premises (ˈprɛmɪsɪz) *pl. n.* **1.** a piece of land together with its buildings, esp. considered as a place of business. **2.** *Law.* (in a deed, etc.) the matters referred to previously; the aforesaid.

premium (ˈpriːmɪəm) *n.* **1.** an amount paid in addition to a standard rate, price, wage, etc.; bonus. **2.** the amount paid or payable, usually in regular instalments, for an insurance policy. **3.** the amount above nominal or par

---

ˈpreˈflight *adj.*	ˈpreˈfreeze *vb.*	preˈheat *vb.*	ˌpreinˈform *vb.*
preˈform *vb.*	ˌpre-Gerˈmanic *adj.*	ˌpre-Hoˈmeric *adj.*	ˌpreinˈstruct *vb.*
ˌpreforˈmation *n.*	pre-ˈGreek *adj.*	preˈindiˌcate *vb.*	pre-ˈMarxian *adj.*
preˈfranked *adj.*	preˈharden *vb.*	ˌpreinˈdustrial *adj.*	preˈmenstrual *adj.*

value at which something sells. **4.** an offer of something free or at a reduced price as an inducement to buy a commodity or service. **5.** a prize given to the winner of a competition. **6.** *U.S.* an amount sometimes charged for a loan of money in addition to the interest. **7.** great value or regard: *to put a premium on someone's services.* **8. at a premium. a.** in great demand, usually because of scarcity. **b.** above par. [C17: from L *praemium* prize]

Premium Savings Bonds *pl. n.* (in Britain) bonds issued by the Treasury since 1956 for purchase by the public. No interest is paid but there is a monthly draw for cash prizes of various sums. Also called: **premium bonds.**

premolar (priːˈməʊlə) *adj.* **1.** situated before a molar tooth. ~*n.* **2.** any one of eight bicuspid teeth in the human adult, two on each side of both jaws between the first molar and the canine.

premonition (ˌprɛməˈnɪʃən) *n.* **1.** an intuition of a future, usually unwelcome, occurrence; foreboding. **2.** an early warning of a future event. [C16: from LL *praemonitiō*, from L *praemonēre* to admonish beforehand, from *prae* before + *monēre* to warn] —**premonitory** (prɪˈmɒnɪtərɪ, -trɪ) *adj.*

Premonstratensian (ˌpriːmɒnstrəˈtɛnsɪən) *adj.* **1.** of or denoting an order of regular canons founded in 1119 at Prémontré, in France. ~*n.* **2.** a member of this order.

prenatal (priːˈneɪtᵊl) *adj.* **1.** occurring or present before birth; during pregnancy. ~*n.* **2.** *Inf.* a prenatal examination. ~Also: **antenatal.**

prenominal (priːˈnɒmɪnᵊl) *adj.* placed before a noun, esp. (of an adjective or sense of an adjective) used only before a noun.

prentice (ˈprɛntɪs) *n.* an archaic word for **apprentice.**

preoccupation (priːˌɒkjʊˈpeɪʃən) *n.* **1.** the state of being preoccupied, esp. mentally. **2.** something that preoccupies the mind.

preoccupied (priːˈɒkjʊˌpaɪd) *adj.* **1.** engrossed or absorbed in something, esp. one's own thoughts. **2.** already occupied or used.

preoccupy (priːˈɒkjʊˌpaɪ) *vb.* **-pying, -pied.** (*tr.*) **1.** to engross the thoughts or mind of. **2.** to occupy before or in advance of another. [C16: from L *praeoccupāre* to capture in advance]

preordain (ˌpriːɔːˈdeɪn) *vb.* (*tr.*) to ordain, decree, or appoint beforehand.

prep (prɛp) *n. Inf.* short for **preparation** (sense 5) or (chiefly U.S.) **preparatory school.**

prep. *abbrev. for:* **1.** preparation. **2.** preparatory. **3.** preposition.

preparation (ˌprɛpəˈreɪʃən) *n.* **1.** the act or process of preparing. **2.** the state of being prepared; readiness. **3.** (*often pl.*) a measure done in order to prepare for something; provision: *to make preparations for something.* **4.** something that is prepared, esp. a medicine. **5.** (esp. in a boarding school) **a.** homework. **b.** the period reserved for this. Usually shortened to **prep. 6.** *Music.* **a.** the anticipation of a dissonance so that the note producing it in one chord is first heard in the preceding chord as a consonance. **b.** a note so employed.

preparative (prɪˈpærətɪv) *adj.* **1.** preparatory. ~*n.* **2.** something that prepares. —**preˈparatively** *adv.*

preparatory (prɪˈpærətərɪ, -trɪ) *adj.* **1.** serving to prepare. **2.** introductory. **3.** occupied in preparation. **4. preparatory to.** before: *a drink preparatory to eating.* —**preˈparatorily** *adv.*

preparatory school *n.* **1.** (in Britain) a private school, usually single-sex and for children between the ages of 6 and 13, generally preparing pupils for public school. **2.** (in the U.S.) a private secondary school preparing pupils for college. ~Often shortened to **prep school.**

prepare (prɪˈpɛə) *vb.* **1.** to make ready or suitable in advance for some use, event, etc.: *to prepare a meal; to prepare to go.* **2.** to put together using parts or ingredients; construct. **3.** (*tr.*) to equip or outfit, as for an expedition. **4.** (*tr.*) *Music.* to soften the impact of (a dissonant note) by the use of preparation. **5. be prepared.** (foll. by an *infinitive*) to be willing and able: *I'm not prepared to reveal these figures.* [C15: from L *praeparāre*, from *prae* before + *parāre* to make ready] —**preˈparer** *n.*

preparedness (prɪˈpɛərɪdnɪs) *n.* the state of being prepared, esp. militarily ready for war.

prepay (priːˈpeɪ) *vb.* **-paying, -paid.** (*tr.*) to pay for in advance. —**preˈpayable** *adj.*

prepense (prɪˈpɛns) *adj.* (*postpositive*) (usually in legal contexts) premeditated (esp. in **malice prepense**). [C18: from Anglo-Norman *purpensé*, from OF *purpenser* to consider in advance, from L *pēnsāre* to consider]

preponderant (prɪˈpɒndərənt) *adj.* greater in weight, force, influence, etc. —**preˈponderance** *n.* —**preˈponderantly** *adv.*

preponderate (prɪˈpɒndəˌreɪt) *vb.* (*intr.*) **1.** (often foll. by *over*) to be more powerful, important, numerous, etc. (than). **2.** to be of greater weight than something else. [C17: from LL *praeponderāre* to be of greater weight, from *pondus* weight] —**preˌponderˈation** *n.*

preposition (ˌprɛpəˈzɪʃən) *n.* a word or group of words used before a noun or pronoun to relate it grammatically or semantically to some other constituent of a sentence. [C14: from L *praepositiō* a putting before, from *pōnere* to place] —**ˌprepoˈsitional** *adj.* —**ˌprepoˈsitionally** *adv.*

▷**Usage.** The practice of ending a sentence with a preposition (*they are the people I hate talking to*) has been much condemned, but careful users avoid it only where it would be stylistically clumsy.

prepossess (ˌpriːpəˈzɛs) *vb.* (*tr.*) **1.** to preoccupy or engross mentally. **2.** to influence in advance, esp. to make a favourable impression on beforehand. —**ˌprepos'session** *n.*

prepossessing (ˌpriːpəˈzɛsɪŋ) *adj.* creating a favourable impression; attractive.

preposterous (prɪˈpɒstərəs) *adj.* contrary to nature, reason, or sense; absurd; ridiculous. [C16: from L *praeposterus* reversed, from *prae* in front + *posterus* following] —**preˈposterously** *adv.* —**preˈposterousness** *n.*

prepotency (prɪˈpəʊtᵊnsɪ) *n.* **1.** the quality of possessing greater power or influence. **2.** *Genetics.* the ability of one parent to transmit more characteristics to its offspring than the other parent. **3.** *Bot.* the ability of pollen from one source to bring about fertilization more readily than that from other sources. —**preˈpotent** *adj.*

preppy (ˈprɛpɪ) *Inf.* ~*adj.* **1.** of or denoting a style of neat, understated, and often expensive clothes; young but classic. ~*n., pl.* **-pies. 2.** a person exhibiting such style. [C20: orig. U.S., from *preppy* a person who attends a PRE-PARATORY SCHOOL]

prep school *n. Inf.* See **preparatory school.**

prepuce (ˈpriːpjuːs) *n.* **1.** the retractable fold of skin covering the tip of the penis. Nontechnical name: **foreskin. 2.** a similar fold of skin covering the tip of the clitoris. [C14: from L *praepūtium*]

prequel (ˈpriːkwəl) *n.* a film that is made about an earlier stage of a story or character's life because the later part of it has already made a successful film. [C20: from PRE- + (se)quel]

Pre-Raphaelite (ˌpriːˈræfəlaɪt) *n.* **1.** a member of the **Pre-Raphaelite Brotherhood,** an association of painters and writers founded in 1848 to revive the fidelity to nature and the vivid realistic colour considered typical of Italian painting before Raphael. ~*adj.* **2.** of, in the manner of, or relating to Pre-Raphaelite painting and painters. —**ˌPre-ˈRaphaelitˌism** *n.*

prerequisite (priːˈrɛkwɪzɪt) *adj.* **1.** required as a prior condition. ~*n.* **2.** something required as a prior condition.

prerogative (prɪˈrɒgətɪv) *n.* **1.** an exclusive privilege or right exercised by a person or group of people holding a particular office or hereditary rank. **2.** any privilege or right. **3.** a power, privilege, or immunity restricted to a sovereign or sovereign government. ~*adj.* **4.** having or able to exercise a prerogative. [C14: from L *praerogātīva* privilege, earlier: group with the right to vote first, from *prae* before + *rogāre* to ask]

pres. *abbrev. for:* **1.** present (time). **2.** presidential.

Pres. *abbrev. for* President.

presage *n.* (ˈprɛsɪdʒ). **1.** an intimation or warning of something about to happen; portent; omen. **2.** a sense of what is about to happen; foreboding. ~*vb.* (ˈprɛsɪdʒ, prɪ'seɪdʒ). (*tr.*) **3.** to have a presentiment of. **4.** to give a forewarning of; portend. [C14: from L *praesāgium*, from *praesāgīre* to perceive beforehand] —**pre'sageful** *adj.* —**pre'sager** *n.*

presale ('priː,seɪl) *n.* the practice of arranging the sale of a product before it is available. —**pre'sell** *vb.* (*tr.*)

presbyopia (,prɛzbɪ'əʊpɪə) *n.* a progressively diminishing ability of the eye to focus, noticeable from middle to old age, caused by loss of elasticity of the crystalline lens. [C18: NL, from Gk *presbus* old man + *ōps* eye] —**presbyopic** (,prɛzbɪ'ɒpɪk) *adj.*

presbyter ('prɛzbɪtə) *n.* **1. a.** an elder of a congregation in the early Christian Church. **b.** (in some Churches having episcopal politics) an official who is subordinate to a bishop and has administrative and sacerdotal functions. **2.** (in some hierarchical Churches) another name for **priest.** **3.** (in the Presbyterian Church) an elder. [C16: from LL, from Gk *presbuteros* an older man, from *presbus* old man] —,**presby'terial** *adj.*

presbyterian (,prɛzbɪ'tɪərɪən) *adj.* **1.** of or designating Church government by presbyters or lay elders. ~*n.* **2.** an upholder of this type of Church government. —,**presby'terianism** *n.*

Presbyterian (,prɛzbɪ'tɪərɪən) *adj.* **1.** of or relating to any of various Protestant Churches governed by presbyters or lay elders and adhering to various modified forms of Calvinism. ~*n.* **2.** a member of a Presbyterian Church. —,**Presby'terianism** *n.*

presbytery ('prɛzbɪtərɪ) *n.*, *pl.* **-teries. 1.** *Presbyterian Church.* **a.** a local Church court. **b.** the congregations within the jurisdiction of any such court. **2.** the part of a church east of the choir, in which the main altar is situated; a sanctuary. **3.** presbyters or elders collectively. **4.** *R.C. Church.* the residence of a parish priest. [C15: from OF *presbiterie*, from Church L, from Gk *presbyterion*; see PRESBYTER]

prescience ('prɛsɪəns) *n.* knowledge of events before they take place; foreknowledge. [C14: from L *praescīre* to foreknow] —'**prescient** *adj.*

Prescott ('prɛskət) *n.* **William Hickling** ('hɪklɪŋ). 1796– 1858, U.S. historian, noted for his work on the history of Spain and her colonies.

prescribe (prɪ'skraɪb) *vb.* **1.** (*tr.*) to lay down as a rule or directive. **2.** *Med.* to recommend or order the use of (a drug or other remedy). [C16: from L *praescrībere* to write previously] —**pre'scriber** *n.*

prescript ('priːskrɪpt) *n.* something laid down or prescribed. [C16: from L *praescrīptum* something written down beforehand, from *praescrībere* to PRESCRIBE]

prescription (prɪ'skrɪpʃən) *n.* **1. a.** written instructions from a physician to a pharmacist stating the form, dosage, strength, etc., of a drug to be issued to a specific patient. **b.** the drug or remedy prescribed. **2.** written instructions for an optician on the proper grinding of lenses for spectacles. **3.** the act of prescribing. **4.** something that is prescribed. **5.** a long-established custom or a claim based on one. **6.** *Law.* **a.** the uninterrupted possession of property over a stated time, after which a right or title is acquired (**positive prescription**). **b.** the barring of adverse claims to property, etc., after a specified time has elapsed, allowing the possessor to acquire title (**negative prescription**). [C14: from legal L *praescriptiō* an order; see PRESCRIBE]

prescriptive (prɪ'skrɪptɪv) *adj.* **1.** making or giving directions, rules, or injunctions. **2.** sanctioned by long-standing custom. **3.** based upon legal prescription: *a prescriptive title.* —**pre'scriptively** *adv.* —**pre'scriptiveness** *n.*

presence ('prɛzəns) *n.* **1.** the state or fact of being present. **2.** immediate proximity. **3.** personal appearance or bearing, esp. of a dignified nature. **4.** an imposing or dignified personality. **5.** an invisible spirit felt to be nearby. **6.** *Electronics.* a recording control that boosts mid-range frequencies. **7.** *Obs.* assembly or company. [C14: via OF from L *praesentia* a being before, from *praeesse* to be before]

presence chamber *n.* the room in which a great person, such as a monarch, receives guests, assemblies, etc.

presence of mind *n.* the ability to remain calm and act constructively during times of crisis.

present[1] ('prɛzᵊnt) *adj.* **1.** (*prenominal*) in existence at the time at which something is spoken or written. **2.** (*postpositive*) being in a specified place, thing, etc.: *the murderer is present in this room.* **3.** (*prenominal*) now being dealt with or under discussion: *the present author.* **4.** *Grammar.* denoting a tense of verbs used when the action or event described is occurring at the time of utterance or when the speaker does not wish to make any explicit temporal reference. **5.** *Arch.* instant: *present help is at hand.* ~*n.* **6.** *Grammar.* **a.** the present tense. **b.** a verb in this tense. **7. at present.** now. **8. for the present.** for the time being; temporarily. **9. the present.** the time being; now. ~See also **presents.** [C13: from L *praesens*, from *praeesse* to be in front of]

present[2] *vb.* (prɪ'zɛnt). (*mainly tr.*) **1.** to introduce (a person) to another, esp. to someone of higher rank. **2.** to introduce to the public: *to present a play.* **3.** to introduce and compere (a radio or television show). **4.** to show; exhibit: *he presented a brave face to the world.* **5.** to bring or suggest to the mind: *to present a problem.* **6.** to put forward; submit: *she presented a proposal for a new book.* **7.** to award: *to present a prize; to present a university with a foundation scholarship.* **8.** to offer formally: *to present one's compliments.* **9.** to hand over for action or settlement: *to present a bill.* **10.** to depict in a particular manner: *the actor presented Hamlet as a very young man.* **11.** to salute someone with (one's weapon) (usually in **present arms**). **12.** to aim (a weapon). **13.** to nominate (a clergyman) to a bishop for institution to a benefice in his diocese. **14.** to lay (a charge, etc.) before a court, magistrate, etc., for consideration or trial. **15.** to bring a formal charge or accusation against (a person); indict. **16.** (*intr.*) *Med.* to seek treatment for a particular problem: *she presented with postnatal depression.* **17.** (*intr.*) *Inf.* to produce a specified impression: *she presents well in public.* **18. present oneself.** to appear, esp. at a specific time and place. ~*n.* ('prɛzᵊnt). **19.** a gift. [C13: from OF *presenter*, from L *praesentāre* to exhibit, from *praesens* PRESENT[1]]

presentable (prɪ'zɛntəbᵊl) *adj.* **1.** fit to be presented or introduced to other people. **2.** fit to be displayed or offered. —**pre'sentableness** *or* **pre,senta'bility** *n.* —**pre'sentably** *adv.*

presentation (,prɛzən'teɪʃən) *n.* **1.** the act of presenting or state of being presented. **2.** the manner of presenting; delivery or overall impression. **3.** a verbal report, often with illustrative material: *a presentation on the company results.* **4. a.** an offering, as of a gift. **b.** (*as modifier*): *a presentation copy of a book.* **5.** a performance or representation, as of a play. **6.** the formal introduction of a person, as at court; debut. **7.** the act or right of nominating a clergyman to a benefice. —,**presen'tational** *adj.*

presentationism (,prɛzən'teɪʃə,nɪzəm) *n.* *Philosophy.* the theory that objects are identical with our perceptions of them. Cf. **representationalism.** —,**presen'tationist** *n.*, *adj.*

presentative (prɪ'zɛntətɪv) *adj.* **1.** *Philosophy.* able to be known or perceived immediately. **2.** conferring the right of ecclesiastical presentation.

present-day *n.* (*modifier*) of the modern day; current: *I don't like present-day fashions.*

presenter (prɪ'zɛntə) *n.* **1.** a person who presents something or someone. **2.** *Radio, television.* a person who introduces a show, links items, etc.

presentient (prɪ'sɛnʃənt) *adj.* characterized by or experiencing a presentiment. [C19: from L *praesentiens*, from *praesentire*, from *prae-* PRE- + *sentire* to feel]

presentiment (prɪ'zɛntɪmənt) *n.* a sense of something about to happen; premonition. [C18: from obs. F, from *pressentir* to sense beforehand]

presently ('prɛzəntlɪ) *adv.* **1.** in a short while; soon. **2.** *Chiefly Scot., U.S., & Canad.* at the moment. **3.** an archaic word for **immediately.**

presentment (prɪ'zɛntmənt) *n.* **1.** the act of presenting or state of being presented; presentation. **2.** something presented, such as a picture, play, etc. **3.** *Law.* a statement on oath by a jury of something within their own knowledge or observation. **4.** *Commerce.* the presenting of a bill of exchange, promissory note, etc.

present participle ('prɛzᵊnt) *n.* a participial form of verbs used adjectivally when the action it describes is contemporaneous with that of the main verb of a sentence and also used in the formation of certain compound tenses. In English this form ends in *-ing*.

present perfect ('prɛzˀnt) *adj.*, *n. Grammar.* another term for **perfect** (senses 8, 10).

presents ('prɛzənts) *pl. n. Law.* used in a deed or document to refer to itself: *know all men by these presents.*

preservative (prɪ'zɜːvətɪv) *n.* **1.** something that preserves, esp. a chemical added to foods. ~*adj.* **2.** tending or intended to preserve.

preserve (prɪ'zɜːv) *vb. (mainly tr.)* **1.** to keep safe from danger or harm; protect. **2.** to protect from decay or dissolution; maintain: *to preserve old buildings.* **3.** to maintain possession of; keep up: *to preserve a façade of indifference.* **4.** to prevent from decomposition or chemical change. **5.** to prepare (food), as by salting, so that it will resist decomposition. **6.** to make preserves of (fruit, etc.). **7.** to rear and protect (game) in restricted places for hunting or fishing. **8.** (*intr.*) to maintain protection for game in preserves. ~*n.* **9.** something that preserves or is preserved. **10.** a special domain: *archaeology is the preserve of specialists.* **11.** (*usually pl.*) fruit, etc., prepared by cooking with sugar. **12.** areas where game is reared for private hunting or fishing. [C14: via OF, from LL *praeserváre*, lit.: to keep safe in advance, from L *prae* before + *serváre* to keep safe] —**pre'servable** *adj.* —**preservation** (ˌprɛzə'veɪʃən) *n.* —**pre'server** *n.*

preshrunk (priː'ʃrʌŋk) *adj.* (of fabrics) having undergone shrinking during manufacture so that further shrinkage will not occur.

preside (prɪ'zaɪd) *vb. (intr.)* **1.** to sit in or hold a position of authority, as over a meeting. **2.** to exercise authority; control. [C17: via F from L *praesidére* to superintend, from *prae* before + *sedére* to sit]

presidency ('prɛzɪdənsɪ) *n.*, *pl.* **-cies.** **1.** the office, dignity, or term of a president. **2.** (*often cap.*) the office of president of a republic, esp. of the President of the U.S.

president ('prɛzɪdənt) *n.* **1.** (*often cap.*) the head of state of a republic, esp. of the U.S. **2.** (in the U.S.) the chief executive officer of a company, corporation, etc. **3.** a person who presides over an assembly, meeting, etc. **4.** the chief executive officer of certain establishments of higher education. [C14: via OF from LL *praesidens* ruler; see PRESIDE] —**presidential** (ˌprɛzɪ'dɛnʃəl) *adj.* —ˌpresi'dentially *adv.* —'presidentship *n.*

presidium or **praesidium** (prɪ'sɪdɪəm) *n.* **1.** (*often cap.*) (in Communist countries) a permanent committee of a larger body, such as a legislature, that acts for it when it is in recess. **2.** a collective presidency. [C20: from Russian *prezidium*, from L *praesidium*, from *praesidére* to superintend; see PRESIDE]

Presley ('prɛzlɪ) *n.* **Elvis (Aaron** or **Aron).** 1935–77, U.S. rock and roll singer. His recordings include "That's all Right (Mama)" (1954), "Heartbreak Hotel" (1956), "Hound Dog" (1956), numbers from the films *Loving You* and *Jailhouse Rock* (both 1957), and *Elvis is back* (1960).

press[1] (prɛs) *vb.* **1.** to apply or exert weight, force, or steady pressure (on): *he pressed the button on the camera.* **2.** (*tr.*) to squeeze or compress so as to alter in shape. **3.** to apply heat or pressure to (clothing) so as to smooth out creases. **4.** to make (objects) from soft material by pressing with a mould, etc., esp. to make gramophone records from plastic. **5.** (*tr.*) to clasp; embrace. **6.** (*tr.*) to extract or force out (juice) by pressure (from). **7.** (*tr.*) to force or compel. **8.** to importune (a person) insistently: *they pressed for an answer.* **9.** to harass or cause harassment. **10.** (*tr.*) to plead or put forward strongly: *to press a claim.* **11.** (*intr.*) to be urgent. **12.** (*tr.*; *usually passive*) to have little of: *we're hard pressed for time.* **13.** (when *intr.*, often foll. by *on* or *forward*) to hasten or advance or cause to hasten or advance in a forceful manner. **14.** (*intr.*) to crowd; push. **15.** (*tr.*) *Arch.* to trouble or oppress. ~*n.* **16.** any machine that exerts pressure to form, shape, or cut materials or to extract liquids, compress solids, or hold components together while an adhesive joint is formed. **17.** See **printing press. 18.** the art or process of printing. **19.** **to (the) press**, to be printed: *when is this book going to press?* **20. a. the press**, news media collectively, esp. newspapers. **b.** (*as modifier*): *press relations.* **21.** the opinions and reviews in the

newspapers, etc.: *the play received a poor press.* **22.** the act of pressing or state of being pressed. **23.** the act of crowding or pushing together. **24.** a closely packed throng; crowd. **25.** a cupboard, esp. a large one used for storing clothes or linen. **26.** a wood or metal clamp to prevent tennis rackets, etc., from warping when not in use. [C14 *pressen*, from OF *presser*, from L, from *premere* to press]

press[2] (prɛs) *vb.* (*tr.*) **1.** to recruit (men) by forcible measures for military service. **2.** to use for a purpose other than intended (esp. in **press into service**). ~*n.* **3.** recruitment into military service by forcible measures, as by a press gang. [C16: back formation from *prest* to recruit soldiers; also infl. by PRESS[1]]

press agent *n.* a person employed to obtain favourable publicity, such as notices in newspapers, for an organization, actor, etc.

press box *n.* an area reserved for reporters, as in a sports stadium.

Pressburg ('prɛsbʊrk) *n.* the German name for **Bratislava.**

press conference *n.* an interview for press reporters given by a politician, film star, etc.

press gallery *n.* an area for newspaper reporters, esp. in a legislative assembly.

press gang *n.* **1.** (formerly) a detachment of men used to press civilians for service in the navy or army. ~*vb.* **press-gang.** (*tr.*) **2.** to force (a person) to join the navy or army by a press gang. **3.** to induce (a person) to perform a duty by forceful persuasion.

pressing ('prɛsɪŋ) *adj.* **1.** demanding immediate attention. **2.** persistent or importunate. ~*n.* **3.** a large specified number of gramophone records produced at one time from a master record. —'**pressingly** *adv.*

pressman ('prɛsmən, -ˌmæn) *n.*, *pl.* **-men.** **1.** a journalist. **2.** a person who operates a printing press.

press of sail *n. Naut.* the most sail a vessel can carry under given conditions. Also called: **press of canvas.**

press release *n.* an official announcement or account of a news item circulated to the press.

pressroom ('prɛsˌruːm, -ˌrʊm) *n.* the room in a printing establishment that houses the printing presses.

press stud *n.* a fastening device consisting of one part with a projecting knob that snaps into a hole on another like part, used esp. on clothing. Canad. equivalent: **dome fastener.**

press-up *n.* an exercise in which the body is alternately raised from and lowered to the floor by the arms only, the trunk being kept straight. Also called (U.S. and Canad.): **push-up.**

pressure ('prɛʃə) *n.* **1.** the state of pressing or being pressed. **2.** the exertion of force by one body on the surface of another. **3.** a moral force that compels: *to bring pressure to bear.* **4.** urgent claims or demands: *to work under pressure.* **5.** a burdensome condition that is hard to bear: *the pressure of grief.* **6.** the force applied to a unit area of a surface, usually measured in pascals, millibars, torrs, or atmospheres. **7.** short for **atmospheric pressure** or **blood pressure.** ~*vb.* (*tr.*) **8.** to constrain or compel, as by moral force. **9.** another word for **pressurize.** [C14: from LL *pressúra* a pressing, from L *premere* to press]

pressure cooker *n.* a strong hermetically sealed pot in which food may be cooked quickly under pressure at a temperature above the normal boiling point of water. —'**pressure-ˌcook** *vb.*

pressure group *n.* a group of people who seek to exert pressure on legislators, public opinion, etc., in order to promote their own ideas or welfare.

pressure point *n.* any of several points on the body above an artery that, when firmly pressed, will control bleeding from the artery at a point farther away from the heart.

pressure suit *n.* an inflatable suit worn by a person flying at high altitudes or in space, to provide protection from low pressure.

pressurize or **-ise** ('prɛʃəˌraɪz) *vb.* (*tr.*) **1.** to increase the pressure in (an enclosure, such as an aircraft cabin) in order to maintain approximately atmospheric pressure

---

pre'set *vb.*
pre'shape *vb.*

pre'shrink *vb.*

pre'soak *vb.*

ˌpre-So'cratic *adj.*

when the external pressure is low. **2.** to increase pressure on (a fluid). **3.** to make insistent demands of (someone); coerce. — ˌpressuriˈzation *or* -iˈsation *n.*

pressurized-water reactor *n.* a type of nuclear reactor that uses water under pressure as both coolant and moderator.

presswork ('presˌwɜːk) *n.* the operation of, or matter printed by, a printing press.

Prestel ('prestel) *n. Trademark.* (in Britain) the Post Office public viewdata service.

Prester John ('prestə) *n.* a legendary Christian priest and king, believed in the Middle Ages to have ruled in the Far East, but identified in the 14th century with the king of Ethiopia. [C14 *Prestre Johan*, from Med. L *presbyter Iohannes* Priest John]

prestidigitation (ˌprestɪˌdɪdʒɪ'teɪʃən) *n.* another name for **sleight of hand.** [C19: from F: quick-fingeredness, from L *praestigiae* tricks, prob. infl. by F *preste* nimble, & L *digitus* finger] — ˌpresti'digiˌtator *n.*

prestige (pre'stiːʒ) *n.* **1.** high status or reputation achieved through success, influence, wealth, etc.; renown. **2. a.** the power to impress; glamour. **b.** (*modifier*): *a prestige car.* [C17: via F from L *praestigiae* tricks] — **prestigious** (pre'stɪdʒəs) *adj.*

prestissimo (pre'stɪsɪˌməʊ) *Music.* ~*adj., adv.* **1.** to be played as fast as possible. ~*n., pl.* -**mos. 2.** a piece to be played in this way. [C18: from It.: very quickly, from *presto* fast]

presto ('prestəʊ) *adj., adv.* **1.** *Music.* to be played very fast. ~*adv.* **2.** immediately (esp. in **hey presto**). ~*n., pl.* -**tos. 3.** *Music.* a passage directed to be played very quickly. [C16: from It.: fast, from LL *praestus* (adj.) ready to hand, L *praestō* (adv.) present]

Preston ('prestən) *n.* a town in NW England, administrative centre of Lancashire, on the River Ribble: developed as a weaving centre (17th–18th centuries). Pop.: 125 000 (1983 est.).

Prestonpans (ˌprestən'pænz) *n.* a small town and resort in SE Scotland, in Lothian region on the Firth of Forth: scene of the battle (1745) in which the Jacobite army of Prince Charles Edward defeated government forces under Sir John Cope. Pop.: 7620 (1981).

prestressed concrete (ˌpriː'strest) *n.* concrete that contains steel wires that are stretched to counteract the stresses that will occur under load.

Prestwich ('prestwɪtʃ) *n.* a town in NW England, in Greater Manchester. Pop.: 31 198 (1981).

presumably (prɪ'zjuːməblɪ) *adv.* (*sentence modifier*) one supposes that: *presumably he won't see you, if you're leaving tomorrow.*

presume (prɪ'zjuːm) *vb.* **1.** (when *tr.*, *often takes a clause as object*) to take (something) for granted; assume. **2.** (when *tr.*, *often foll. by an infinitive*) to dare (to do something): *do you presume to copy my work?* **3.** (*intr.*; foll. by *on or upon*) to rely on or depend: *don't presume on his agreement.* **4.** (*intr.*; foll. by *on or upon*) to take advantage (of): *don't presume upon his good nature too far.* **5.** (*tr.*) *Law.* to take as proved until contrary evidence is produced. [C14: via OF from L *praesūmere* to take in advance, from *prae* before + *sūmere* to take] — **presumedly** (prɪ'zjuːmɪdlɪ) *adv.* — **pre'suming** *adj.*

presumption (prɪ'zʌmpʃən) *n.* **1.** the act of presuming. **2.** bold or insolent behaviour. **3.** a belief or assumption based on reasonable evidence. **4.** a basis on which to presume. **5.** *Law.* an inference of the truth of a fact from other facts proved. [C13: via OF from L *praesumptiō* anticipation, from *praesūmere* to take beforehand; see PRESUME]

presumptive (prɪ'zʌmptɪv) *adj.* **1.** based on presumption or probability. **2.** affording reasonable ground for belief. — **pre'sumptively** *adv.*

presumptuous (prɪ'zʌmptjʊəs) *adj.* characterized by presumption or tending to presume; bold; forward. — **pre'sumptuously** *adv.* — **pre'sumptuousness** *n.*

presuppose (ˌpriːsə'pəʊz) *vb.* (*tr.*) **1.** to take for granted. **2.** to require as a necessary prior condition. — **presupposition** (ˌpriːsʌpə'zɪʃən) *n.*

pretence *or U.S.* **pretense** (prɪ'tens) *n.* **1.** the act of pretending. **2.** a false display; affectation. **3.** a claim, esp. a false one, to a right, title, or distinction. **4.** make-believe. **5.** a pretext.

pretend (prɪ'tend) *vb.* **1.** (when *tr.*, *usually takes a clause as object or an infinitive*) to claim or allege (something untrue). **2.** (*tr.; may take a clause as object or an infinitive*) to make believe, as in a play: *you pretend to be Ophelia.* **3.** (*intr.*; foll. by *to*) to present a claim, esp. a dubious one: *to pretend to the throne.* **4.** (*intr.*; foll. by *to*) *Obs.* to aspire as a candidate or suitor (for). ~*adj.* **5.** make-believe; imaginary. [C14: from L *praetendere* to stretch forth, feign]

pretender (prɪ'tendə) *n.* **1.** a person who pretends or makes false allegations. **2.** a person who mounts a claim, as to a throne or title.

pretension (prɪ'tenʃən) *n.* **1.** (*often pl.*) a false claim, esp. to merit, worth, or importance. **2.** a specious or unfounded allegation; pretext. **3.** the quality of being pretentious.

pretentious (prɪ'tenʃəs) *adj.* **1.** making claim to distinction or importance, esp. undeservedly. **2.** ostentatious. — **pre'tentiously** *adv.* — **pre'tentiousness** *n.*

preterite *or esp. U.S.* **preterit** ('preterɪt) *Grammar.* ~*n.* **1.** a tense of verbs used to relate past action, formed in English by inflection of the verb, as *jumped, swam.* **2.** a verb in this tense. ~*adj.* **3.** denoting this tense. [C14: from LL *praeteritum* (*tempus*) past (time), from L *praeterīre* to go by, from *preter-* beyond + *īre* to go]

pretermit (ˌpriːtə'mɪt) *vb.* -**mitting,** -**mitted.** (*tr.*) *Rare.* **1.** to disregard. **2.** to fail to do; neglect; omit. [C16: from L *praetermittere* to let pass, from *preter-* beyond + *mittere* to send]

preternatural (ˌpriːtə'nætʃrəl) *adj.* **1.** beyond what is ordinarily found in nature; abnormal. **2.** another word for **supernatural.** [C16: from Med. L *praeternātūrālis*, from L *praeter natūram* beyond the scope of nature] — ˌpreter'naturally *adv.*

pretext ('priːtekst) *n.* **1.** a fictitious reason given in order to conceal the real one. **2.** a pretence. [C16: from L *praetextum* disguise, from *praetexere* to weave in front, disguise]

pretor ('priːtə, -tɔː) *n.* a variant (esp. U.S.) spelling of **praetor.**

Pretoria (prɪ'tɔːrɪə) *n.* the administrative capital of South Africa and capital of Transvaal province: two universities (1873, 1930); large steelworks. Pop.: 741 300 (1985).

Pretorius (prɪ'tɔːrɪəs) *n.* **1. Andries Wilhelmus Jacobus** ('ɑndriːs wɪl'helmys jaː'koːbys). 1799–1853, a Boer leader in the Great Trek (1838) to escape British sovereignty; he also led an expedition to the Transvaal (1848). The town Pretoria was named after him. **2.** his son, **Marthinus Wessels** (mar'tiːnys 'wesəls). 1819–1901, first president of the South African Republic (1857–71) and of the Orange Free State (1859–63).

prettify ('prɪtɪˌfaɪ) *vb.* -**fying,** -**fied.** (*tr.*) to make pretty, esp. in a trivial fashion; embellish. — ˌprettifi'cation *n.* — 'pretti fier *n.*

pretty ('prɪtɪ) *adj.* -**tier,** -**tiest. 1.** pleasing or appealing in a delicate or graceful way. **2.** dainty, neat, or charming. **3.** *Inf., often ironical.* excellent, grand, or fine: *here's a pretty mess!* **4.** commendable; good of its kind: *he replied with a pretty wit.* **5.** *Inf.* effeminate; foppish. **6.** *Arch. or Scot.* vigorous or brave. **7. sitting pretty.** *Inf.* in a favourable or satisfactory state. ~*n., pl.* -**ties. 8.** a pretty person or thing. ~*adv. Inf.* **9.** fairly; somewhat. **10.** very. ~*vb.* -**tying,** -**tied. 11.** (*tr.*; often foll. by *up*) to make pretty; adorn. [OE *prættig* clever] — 'prettily *adv.* — 'prettiness *n.*

▷ **Usage.** The use of *pretty* as an adverb meaning *fairly* or *quite* is accepted informal usage but is avoided in formal contexts by careful writers of English: *the profit was fairly* (not *pretty*) *large that year.*

pretty-pretty *adj. Inf.* excessively or ostentatiously pretty.

pretzel ('pretsəl) *n.* a brittle savoury biscuit, in the form of a knot or stick, eaten esp. in Germany and the U.S. [C19: from G, from OHG *brezitella*]

Preussen ('prɔʏsən) *n.* the German name for **Prussia.**

prevail (prɪ'veɪl) *vb.* (*intr.*) **1.** (often foll. by *over* or *against*) to prove superior; gain mastery: *skill will prevail.* **2.** to be the most important feature; be prevalent. **3.** to exist widely; be in force. **4.** (often foll. by *on* or *upon*) to succeed in persuading or inducing. [C14: from L *praevalēre* to be superior in strength] — **pre'vailer** *n.*

---

pre'surgical *adj.*   **pre'test** *vb.*

prevailing (prɪ'veɪlɪŋ) *adj.* **1.** generally accepted; widespread: *the prevailing opinion.* **2.** most frequent; predominant: *the prevailing wind is from the north.* —**pre'vailingly** *adv.*

prevalent ('prɛvələnt) *adj.* **1.** widespread or current. **2.** superior in force or power; predominant. —**'prevalence** *n.* —**'prevalently** *adv.*

prevaricate (prɪ'værɪ,keɪt) *vb.* (*intr.*) to speak or act falsely or evasively with intent to deceive. [C16: from L *praevāricārī* to walk crookedly, from *prae* beyond + *vāricāre* to straddle the legs] —**pre,vari'cation** *n.* —**pre'vari,cator** *n.*

prevent (prɪ'vɛnt) *vb.* **1.** (*tr.*) to keep from happening, esp. by taking precautionary action. **2.** (*tr.; often foll. by from*) to keep (someone from doing something). **3.** (*intr.*) to interpose or act as a hindrance. **4.** (*tr.*) *Arch.* to anticipate or precede. [C15: from L *praevenīre*, from *prae* before + *venīre* to come] —**pre'ventable** *or* **pre'ventible** *adj.* —**pre'ventably** *or* **pre'ventibly** *adv.*

▷ **Usage.** *Prevent* in the sense of definition 2, above, is in strict usage followed either by *from* or by the possessive case: *there is nothing to prevent Mary from going* or *there is nothing to prevent Mary's going.* The use of prevent in a construction such as *there is nothing to prevent Mary going* is regarded by careful writers and speakers of English as less acceptable and should be restricted to informal contexts.

prevention (prɪ'vɛnʃən) *n.* **1.** the act of preventing. **2.** a hindrance or impediment.

preventive (prɪ'vɛntɪv) *adj.* **1.** tending or intended to prevent or hinder. **2.** *Med.* tending to prevent disease; prophylactic. **3.** (in Britain) of, relating to, or belonging to the customs and excise service or the coastguard. ~*n.* **4.** something that serves to prevent or hinder. **5.** *Med.* any drug or agent that tends to prevent disease. Also (for senses 1, 2, 4, 5): **preventative.** —**pre'ventively** *or* **pre'ventatively** *adv.*

Prévert (*French* prevɛr) *n.* **Jacques** (ʒak). 1900–77, Parisian poet, satirist, and writer of film scripts, noted esp. for his song poems. He was a member of the surrealist group from 1925 to 1929.

preview ('priː,vjuː) *n.* **1.** an advance view or sight. **2.** an advance showing before public presentation of a film, art exhibition, etc., usually before an invited audience. ~*vb.* **3.** (*tr.*) to view in advance.

Previn ('prɛvɪn) *n.* **André** ('ɒndreɪ). born 1929, U.S. orchestral conductor, born in Germany; living in Britain.

previous ('priːvɪəs) *adj.* **1.** (*prenominal*) existing or coming before something else. **2.** (*postpositive*) *Inf.* taking place or done too soon; premature. **3. previous to.** before. [C17: from L *praevius* leading the way, from *prae* before + *via* way] —**'previously** *adv.* —**'previousness** *n.*

previous question *n.* **1.** (in the House of Commons) a motion to drop the present topic under debate, put in order to prevent a vote. **2.** (in the House of Lords and U.S. legislative bodies) a motion to vote on a bill without delay.

previse (prɪ'vaɪz) *vb.* (*tr.*) *Rare.* **1.** to predict or foresee. **2.** to notify in advance. [C16: from L *praevidēre* to foresee] —**prevision** (prɪ'vɪʒən) *n.*

Prévost d'Exiles (*French* prevo dɛgzil) *n.* **Antoine François** (ɑ̃twan frɑ̃swa), known as *Abbé Prévost.* 1697–1763, French novelist, noted for his romance *Manon Lescaut* (1731), which served as the basis for operas by Puccini and Massenet.

prey (preɪ) *n.* **1.** an animal hunted or captured by another for food. **2.** a person or thing that becomes the victim of a hostile person, influence, etc. **3. bird** *or* **beast of prey.** a bird or animal that preys on others for food. **4.** an archaic word for **booty.** ~*vb.* (*intr.; often foll. by on or upon*) **5.** to hunt food by killing other animals. **6.** to make a victim (of others), as by profiting at their expense. **7.** to exert a depressing or obsessive effect (on the mind, spirits, etc.). [C13: from OF *preie*, from L *praeda* booty] —**'preyer** *n.*

Priam ('praɪəm) *n. Greek myth.* the last king of Troy, killed at its fall. He was father by Hecuba of Hector, Paris, and Cassandra.

priapic (praɪ'æpɪk, -'eɪ-) *or* **priapean** (,praɪə'piːən) *adj.* **1.** (*sometimes cap.*) of or relating to Priapus. **2.** a less common word for **phallic.**

priapism ('praɪə,pɪzəm) *n. Pathol.* prolonged painful erection of the penis, caused by neurological disorders, etc. [C17: from LL *priāpismus*, ult. from Gk PRIAPUS]

Priapus (praɪ'eɪpəs) *n.* **1.** (in classical antiquity) the god of the male procreative power and of gardens and vineyards. **2.** (*often not cap.*) a representation of the penis.

Pribilof Islands ('prɪbɪlɒf) *pl. n.* a group of islands in the Bering Sea, off SW Alaska, belonging to the U.S.: the breeding ground of the northern fur seal. Area: about 168 sq. km (65 sq. miles). Also called: **Fur Seal Islands.**

price (praɪs) *n.* **1.** the sum in money or goods for which anything is or may be bought or sold. **2.** the cost at which anything is obtained. **3.** the cost of bribing a person. **4.** a sum of money offered as a reward for a capture or killing. **5.** value or worth, esp. high worth. **6.** *Gambling.* another word for **odds.** **7. at any price.** whatever the price or cost. **8. at a price.** at a high price. **9. what price (something)?** what are the chances of (something) happening now? ~*vb.* (*tr.*) **10.** to fix the price of. **11.** to discover the price of. **12. price out of the market.** to charge so highly for as to prevent the sale, hire, etc., of. [C13 *pris*, from OF, from L *pretium*] —**'pricer** *n.*

price control *n.* the establishment and maintenance of maximum price levels for basic goods and services by a government.

price-earnings ratio *n.* the ratio of the price of a share on the stock exchange to the earnings per share, used as a measure of a company's future profitability. Abbrev.: **P-E ratio.**

price-fixing *n.* **1.** the setting of prices by agreement among producers and distributors. **2.** another name for **price control** or **resale price maintenance.**

priceless ('praɪslɪs) *adj.* **1.** of inestimable worth; invaluable. **2.** *Inf.* extremely amusing or ridiculous. —**'pricelessly** *adv.* —**'pricelessness** *n.*

price ring *n.* a group of traders formed to maintain the prices of their goods.

pricey *or* **pricy** ('praɪsɪ) *adj.* **pricier, priciest.** an informal word for **expensive.**

prick (prɪk) *vb.* (*mainly tr.*) **1. a.** to make (a small hole) in (something) by piercing lightly with a sharp point. **b.** to wound in this manner. **2.** (*intr.*) to cause or have a piercing or stinging sensation. **3.** to cause to feel a sharp emotional pain: *knowledge of such poverty pricked his conscience.* **4.** to puncture. **5.** to outline by dots or punctures. **6.** (*also intr.; usually foll. by up*) to rise or raise erect: *the dog pricked his ears up.* **7.** (*usually foll. by out or off*) to transplant (seedlings) into a larger container. **8.** *Arch.* to urge on, esp. to spur a horse on. **9. prick up one's ears.** to start to listen attentively; become interested. ~*n.* **10.** the act of pricking or the sensation of being pricked. **11.** a mark made by a sharp point; puncture. **12.** a sharp emotional pain: *a prick of conscience.* **13.** a taboo slang word for **penis.** **14.** *Sl., derog.* an obnoxious or despicable person. **15.** an instrument or weapon with a sharp point. **16.** the track of an animal, esp. a hare. **17. kick against the pricks.** to hurt oneself by struggling against something in vain. [OE *prica* point, puncture] —**'pricker** *n.*

pricket ('prɪkɪt) *n.* **1.** a male deer in the second year of life having unbranched antlers. **2.** a sharp metal spike on which to stick a candle. [C14 *priket*, from *prik* PRICK]

prickle ('prɪkəl) *n.* **1.** *Bot.* a pointed process arising from the outer layer of a stem, leaf, etc., and containing no woody tissue. Cf. **thorn.** **2.** a pricking or stinging sensation. ~*vb.* **3.** to feel or cause to feel a stinging sensation. **4.** (*tr.*) to prick, as with a thorn. [OE *pricel*]

prickly ('prɪklɪ) *adj.* **-lier, -liest.** **1.** having or covered with prickles. **2.** stinging. **3.** irritable. **4.** full of difficulties: *a prickly problem.* —**'prickliness** *n.*

prickly heat *n.* a nontechnical name for **miliaria.**

prickly pear *n.* **1.** any of various tropical cactuses having flattened or cylindrical spiny joints and oval fruit that is edible in some species. **2.** the fruit of any of these plants.

pride (praɪd) *n.* **1.** a feeling of honour and self-respect; a sense of personal worth. **2.** excessive self-esteem; conceit. **3.** a source of pride. **4.** satisfaction or pleasure in one's own or another's success, achievements, etc. (esp.

in **take** (**a**) **pride in**). **5.** the better or superior part of something. **6.** the most flourishing time. **7.** a group (of lions). **8.** courage; spirit. **9.** *Arch.* pomp or splendour. **10. pride of place.** the most important position. ~*vb.* **11.** (*tr.*; foll. by *on* or *upon*) to take pride in (oneself) for. [OE *prȳda*] —'**prideful** *adj.* —'**pridefully** *adv.*

Pride (praɪd) *n.* **Thomas.** died 1658, English soldier on the Parliamentary side during the Civil War. He expelled members of the Long Parliament hostile to the army (**Pride's Purge,** 1648) and signed Charles I's death warrant.

prie-dieu (priːˈdjɜː) *n.* a piece of furniture consisting of a low surface for kneeling upon and a narrow front surmounted by a rest, for use when praying. [C18: from F, from *prier* to pray + *Dieu* God]

prier *or* **pryer** ('praɪə) *n.* a person who pries.

priest (priːst) *n.* **1.** a person ordained to act as a mediator between God and man in administering the sacraments, preaching, etc. **2.** (in episcopal Churches) a minister in the second grade of the hierarchy of holy orders, ranking below a bishop but above a deacon. **3.** a minister of any religion. **4.** an official who offers sacrifice on behalf of the people and performs other religious ceremonies. ~*vb.* **5.** (*tr.*) to make a priest; ordain. [OE *prēost,* apparently from PRESBYTER] —'**priestess** *fem. n.* —'**priest,hood** *n.* —'**priest,like** *adj.* —'**priestly** *adj.*

priestcraft ('priːst,krɑːft) *n.* **1.** the art and skills involved in the work of a priest. **2.** *Derog.* the influence of priests upon politics.

priest-hole *or* **priest's hole** *n.* a secret chamber in certain houses in England, built as a hiding place for Roman Catholic priests when they were proscribed in the 16th and 17th centuries.

Priestley ('priːstlɪ) *n.* **1. J(ohn) B(oynton).** 1894–1984, English author. His works include the novels *The Good Companions* (1929) and *Angel Pavement* (1930) and the comedy *Laburnum Grove* (1933). **2. Joseph.** 1733–1804, English chemist, political theorist, and clergyman, in the U.S. from 1794. He discovered oxygen (1774) independently of Scheele and isolated and described many other gases.

prig[1] (prɪg) *n.* a person who is smugly self-righteous and narrow-minded. [C18: from ?] —'**priggery** *or* '**priggishness** *n.* —'**priggish** *adj.* —'**priggishly** *adv.*

prig[2] (prɪg) *Brit. sl.* ~*vb.* **prigging, prigged. 1.** another word for **steal.** ~*n.* **2.** another word for **thief.** [C16: from ?]

prim (prɪm) *adj.* **primmer, primmest. 1.** affectedly proper, precise, or formal. ~*vb.* **primming, primmed. 2.** (*tr.*) to make prim. **3.** to purse (the mouth) primly or (of the mouth) to be so pursed. [C18: from ?] —'**primly** *adv.* —'**primness** *n.*

prima ballerina ('priːmə) *n.* a leading female ballet dancer. [from It., lit.: first ballerina]

primacy ('praɪməsɪ) *n., pl.* -**cies. 1.** the state of being first in rank, grade, etc. **2.** *Christianity.* the office, rank, or jurisdiction of a primate, senior bishop, or pope. [C19: from It.: first lady]

prima donna ('priːmə 'dɒnə) *n., pl.* **prima donnas. 1.** a leading female operatic star. **2.** *Inf.* a temperamental person. [C19: from It.: first lady]

prima facie ('praɪmə 'feɪʃɪ) *adv.* at first sight; as it seems at first. [C15: from L, from *prīmus* first + *faciēs* FACE]

prima-facie evidence *n. Law.* evidence that is sufficient to establish a fact or to raise a presumption of the truth unless controverted.

primal ('praɪməl) *adj.* **1.** first or original. **2.** chief or most important. [C17: from Med. L *primālis,* from L *prīmus* first]

primaquine ('praɪmə,kwiːn) *n.* a synthetic drug used in the treatment of malaria. [C20: from *prima-,* from L *prīmus* first + QUIN(OLIN)E]

primarily ('praɪmərəlɪ) *adv.* **1.** principally; chiefly; mainly. **2.** at first; originally.

primary ('praɪmərɪ) *adj.* **1.** first in importance, degree, rank, etc. **2.** first in position or time, as in a series. **3.** fundamental; basic. **4.** being the first stage; elementary. **5.** (*prenominal*) of or relating to the education of children up to the age of 11. **6.** (of the flight feathers of a bird's wing) growing from the manus. **7. a.** being the part of an electric circuit, such as a transformer, in which a changing current induces a current in a neighbouring circuit: *a primary coil.* **b.** (of a current) flowing in such a circuit. **8. a.** (of a product) consisting of a natural raw material;

unmanufactured. **b.** (of production or industry) involving the extraction or winning of such products. **9.** (of Latin, Greek, or Sanskrit tenses) referring to present or future time. **10.** *Geol., obs.* relating to the Palaeozoic or earlier eras. ~*n., pl.* -**ries. 11.** a person or thing that is first in rank, occurrence, etc. **12.** (in the U.S.) a preliminary election in which the voters of a state or region choose a party's convention delegates, nominees for office, etc. Full name: **primary election. 13.** short for **primary colour** or **primary school. 14.** any of the flight feathers growing from the manus of a bird's wing. **15.** a primary coil, winding, inductance, or current in an electric circuit. **16.** *Astron.* a celestial body around which one or more specified secondary bodies orbit: *the sun is the primary of the earth.* [C15: from L *primārius* principal, from *prīmus* first]

primary accent *or* **stress** *n. Linguistics.* the strongest accent in a word or breath group, as that on the first syllable of *agriculture.*

primary cell *n.* an electric cell that generates an electromotive force by the direct and usually irreversible conversion of chemical energy into electrical energy. Also called: **voltaic cell.**

primary colour *n.* **1.** any of three colours (usually red, green, and blue) that can be mixed to match any other colour, including white light but excluding black. **2.** any one of the colours cyan, magenta, or yellow. An equal mixture of the three produces a black pigment. **3.** any one of the colours red, yellow, green, or blue. All other colours look like a mixture of two or more of these colours.

primary school *n.* **1.** (in England and Wales) a school for children below the age of 11. It is usually divided into an infant and a junior section. **2.** (in Scotland) a school for children below the age of 12. **3.** (in the U.S. and Canad.) a school equivalent to the first three or four grades of elementary school.

primate[1] ('praɪmeɪt) *n.* **1.** any placental mammal of the order *Primates,* typically having flexible hands, good eyesight, and, in the higher apes, a highly developed brain: includes lemurs, apes, and man. ~*adj.* **2.** of, relating to, or belonging to the order *Primates.* [C18: from NL *primates,* pl. of *primās* principal, from *prīmus* first] —**primatial** (praɪˈmeɪʃəl) *adj.*

primate[2] ('praɪmeɪt) *n.* **1.** another name for an **archbishop. 2. Primate of all England.** the Archbishop of Canterbury. **3. Primate of England.** the Archbishop of York. [C13: from OF, from L *primās* principal, from *prīmus* first]

prime (praɪm) *adj.* **1.** (*prenominal*) first in quality or value; first-rate. **2.** (*prenominal*) fundamental; original. **3.** (*prenominal*) first in importance; chief. **4.** *Maths.* **a.** having no factors except itself or one: $x^2 + x + 3$ *is a prime polynomial.* **b.** (foll. by *to*) having no common factors (with): *20 is prime to 21.* **5.** *Finance.* having the best credit rating: *prime investments.* ~*n.* **6.** the time when a thing is at its best. **7.** a period of power, vigour, etc. (esp. in **the prime of life**). **8.** *Maths.* short for **prime number. 9.** *Chiefly R.C. Church.* the second of the seven canonical hours of the divine office, originally fixed for the first hour of the day, at sunrise. **10.** the first of eight basic positions from which a parry or attack can be made in fencing. ~*vb.* **11.** to prepare (something). **12.** (*tr.*) to apply a primer, such as paint or size, to (a surface). **13.** (*tr.*) to fill (a pump) with its working fluid before starting, in order to expel air from it before starting. **14. prime the pump. a.** see **pump priming. b.** to make an initial input in order to set a process going. **15.** (*tr.*) to increase the quantity of fuel in the float chamber of (a carburettor) in order to facilitate the starting of an engine. **16.** (*tr.*) to insert a primer into (a gun, mine, etc.) preparatory to detonation or firing. **17.** (*tr.*) to provide with facts beforehand; brief. [(adj.) C14: from L *prīmus* first; (n.) C13: from L *prīma (hora)* the first (hour); (vb.) C16: from ?] —'**primeness** *n.*

prime cost *n.* the portion of the cost of a commodity that varies directly with the amount of it produced, principally comprising materials and labour. Also called: **variable cost.**

prime meridian *n.* the 0° meridian from which the other meridians are calculated, usually taken to pass through Greenwich.

prime minister *n.* **1.** the head of a parliamentary government. **2.** the chief minister of a sovereign or a state.

prime mover *n.* **1.** the original force behind an idea, enterprise, etc. **2. a.** the source of power, such as fuel, wind, electricity, etc., for a machine. **b.** the means of extracting power from such a source, such as a steam engine.

prime number *n.* an integer that cannot be factorized into other integers but is only divisible by itself or 1, such as 2, 3, 7, and 11.

primer[1] ('praɪmə) *n.* an introductory text, such as a school textbook. [C14: via Anglo-Norman, from Med. L *prīmārius* (*liber*) a first (book), from L *prīmārius* PRIMARY]

primer[2] ('praɪmə) *n.* **1.** a person or thing that primes. **2.** a device, such as a tube containing explosive, for detonating the main charge in a gun, mine, etc. **3.** a substance, such as paint, applied to a surface as a base, sealer, etc. [C15: see PRIME (vb.)]

prime rate *n.* the lowest commercial interest rate charged by a bank at a particular time.

primers ('praɪməz) *n.* (*functioning as sing.*) *N.Z. inf.* the youngest classes in a primary school: *in the primers.*

prime time *n.* the peak viewing time on television, for which advertising rates are the highest.

primeval *or* **primaeval** (praɪ'miːvəl) *adj.* of or belonging to the first ages of the world. [C17: from L *prīmaevus* youthful, from *prīmus* first + *aevum* age] —**pri'mevally** *or* **pri'maevally** *adv.*

priming ('praɪmɪŋ) *n.* **1.** something used to prime. **2.** a substance used to ignite an explosive charge.

primitive ('prɪmɪtɪv) *adj.* **1.** of or belonging to the beginning; original. **2.** characteristic of an early state, esp. in being crude or uncivilized: *a primitive dwelling.* **3.** *Anthropol.* denoting a preliterate and nonindustrial social system. **4.** *Biol.* of, relating to, or resembling an early stage in development: *primitive amphibians.* **5.** showing the characteristics of primitive painters; untrained, childlike, or naive. **6.** *Geol.* of or denoting rocks formed in or before the Palaeozoic era. **7.** denoting a word from which another word is derived, as for example *hope*, from which *hopeless* is derived. **8.** *Protestant theol.* of or associated with a group that breaks away from a sect, denomination, or Church in order to return to what is regarded as the original simplicity of the Gospels. ~*n.* **9.** a primitive person or thing. **10. a.** an artist whose work does not conform to traditional standards of Western painting, such as a painter from an African civilization. **b.** a painter of the pre-Renaissance era in European painting. **c.** a painter of any era whose work appears childlike or untrained. **11.** a work by such an artist. **12.** a word from which another word is derived. **13.** *Maths.* a curve or other form from which another is derived. [C14: from L *prīmitīvus* earliest of its kind from *prīmus* first] —**'primitively** *adv.* —**'primitiveness** *n.*

primitivism ('prɪmɪtɪˌvɪzəm) *n.* **1.** the condition of being primitive. **2.** the belief that the value of primitive cultures is superior to that of the modern world. —**'primitivist** *n.*, *adj.*

primo ('priːməʊ) *n.*, *pl.* **-mos** *or* **-mi** (-miː). *Music.* **1.** the upper or right-hand part of a piano duet. **2.** *tempo primo.* at the same speed as at the beginning of the piece. [It.: first, from L *prīmus*]

Primo de Rivera (*Spanish* 'primo de ri'βera) *n.* **1.** José **Antonio** (xo'se an'tonjo). 1903–36, Spanish politician; founded Falangism, a Fascist movement founded in 1933. **2.** his father, **Miguel** (mi'γεl). 1870–1930, Spanish general; dictator of Spain (1923–30).

primogenitor (ˌpraɪməʊ'dʒɛnɪtə) *n.* **1.** a forefather; ancestor. **2.** an earliest parent or ancestor, as of a race. [C17: alteration of PROGENITOR after PRIMOGENITURE]

primogeniture (ˌpraɪməʊ'dʒɛnɪtʃə) *n.* **1.** the state of being a first-born. **2.** *Law.* the right of an eldest son to succeed to the estate of his ancestor to the exclusion of all others. [C17: from Med. L *prīmōgenitūra* birth of a first child, from L *prīmō* at first + LL *genitūra* a birth] —**primogenitary** (ˌpraɪməʊ'dʒɛnɪtərɪ, -trɪ) *adj.*

primordial (praɪ'mɔːdɪəl) *adj.* **1.** existing at or from the beginning; primeval. **2.** constituting an origin; fundamental. **3.** *Biol.* relating to an early stage of development. [C14: from LL *prīmōrdiālis* original, from L *prīmus* first + *ōrdīrī* to begin] —**pri'mordiality** *n.* —**pri'mordially** *adv.*

primp (prɪmp) *vb.* to dress (oneself), esp. in fine clothes; prink. [C19: prob. from PRIM]

primrose ('prɪmˌrəʊz) *n.* **1.** any of various temperate plants of the genus *Primula*, esp. a European variety which has pale yellow flowers. **2.** short for **evening primrose**. **3.** Also called: **primrose yellow**. a light yellow, sometimes with a greenish tinge. ~*adj.* **4.** of or abounding in primroses. **5.** of the colour primrose. [C15: from OF *primerose*, from Med. L *prīma rosa* first rose]

primrose path *n.* (often preceded by *the*) a pleasurable way of life.

primula ('prɪmjʊlə) *n.* any plant of the N temperate genus *Primula*, having white, yellow, pink, or purple funnel-shaped flowers with five spreading petals: includes the primrose, oxlip, cowslip, and polyanthus. [C18: NL, from Med. L *prīmula* (*vēris*) little first one (of the spring)]

primum mobile *Latin.* ('praɪmʊm 'məʊbɪlɪ) *n.* **1.** a prime mover. **2.** *Astron.* the outermost empty sphere in the Ptolemaic system that was thought to revolve around the earth from east to west in 24 hours carrying with it the inner spheres of the planets, sun, moon, and fixed stars. [C15: from Med. L: first moving (thing)]

Primus ('praɪməs) *n. Trademark.* a portable paraffin cooking stove, used esp. by campers. Also called: **Primus stove.**

prince (prɪns) *n.* **1.** (in Britain) a son of the sovereign or of one of the sovereign's sons. **2.** a nonreigning male member of a sovereign family. **3.** the monarch of a small territory that was at some time subordinate to an emperor or king. **4.** any monarch. **5.** a nobleman in various countries, such as Italy and Germany. **6.** an outstanding member of a specified group: *a merchant prince*. [C13: via OF from L *princeps* first man, ruler] —**'princedom** *n.* —**'prince,like** *adj.*

prince consort *n.* the husband of a female sovereign, who is himself a prince.

Prince Edward Island *n.* an island in the Gulf of St Lawrence that constitutes the smallest Canadian province. Capital: Charlottetown. Pop.: 126 646 (1986). Area: 5656 sq. km (2184 sq. miles). Abbrev.: **PE.** —**Prince Edward Islander** *n.*

princeling ('prɪnslɪŋ) *n.* **1.** a young prince. **2.** Also called: **princelet.** the ruler of an insignificant territory.

princely ('prɪnslɪ) *adj.* **-lier, -liest.** **1.** generous or lavish. **2.** of or characteristic of a prince. ~*adv.* **3.** in a princely manner. —**'princeliness** *n.*

Prince of Darkness *n.* another name for **Satan.**

Prince of Peace *n. Bible.* the future Messiah (Isaiah 9:6): held by Christians to be Christ.

Prince of Wales[1] *n.* the eldest son and heir apparent of the British sovereign.

Prince of Wales[2] *n.* **Cape.** a cape in W Alaska, on the Bering Strait opposite the coast of the extreme NE Soviet Union: the westernmost point of North America.

Prince of Wales Island *n.* **1.** an island in N Canada, in the Northwest Territories. Area: about 36 000 sq. km (14 000 sq. miles). **2.** an island in SE Alaska, the largest island in the Alexander Archipelago. Area: about 4000 sq. km (1500 sq. miles). **3.** an island in NE Australia, in N Queensland in the Torres Strait. **4.** the former name (until about 1867) of the island of **Penang.**

prince regent *n.* a prince who acts as regent during the minority, disability, or absence of the legal sovereign.

Prince Regent *n.* George IV as regent of Great Britain and Ireland during the insanity of his father (1811–20).

Prince Rupert *n.* a port in W Canada, on the coast of British Columbia: one of the W termini of the Canadian National transcontinental railway. Pop.: 15 755 (1986).

prince's-feather *n.* **1.** a garden plant with spikes of bristly brownish-red flowers. **2.** a tall tropical plant with hanging spikes of pink flowers.

princess (prɪn'sɛs) *n.* **1.** (in Britain) a daughter of the sovereign or of one of the sovereign's sons. **2.** a nonreigning female member of a sovereign family. **3.** the wife and consort of a prince. **4.** *Arch.* a female sovereign. **5.** Also: **princess dress.** a style of dress having a fitted bodice and A-line skirt without a seam at the waistline.

princess royal *n.* **1.** the eldest daughter of a British or (formerly) a Prussian sovereign. **2.** *Caps.* the title of Princess Anne.

Princeton ('prɪnstən) *n.* a town in central New Jersey: settled by Quakers in 1696; an important educational centre, seat of Princeton University (founded at Elizabeth in 1747 and moved here in 1756); scene of the battle (1777) during the War of American Independence in which Washington's troops defeated the British on the university campus. Pop.: 12 035 (1983).

principal ('prɪnsɪp³l) *adj.* (*prenominal*) **1.** first in importance, rank, value, etc. **2.** denoting capital or property as opposed to interest, etc. ~*n.* **3.** a person who is first in importance or directs some event, organization, etc. **4.** *Law.* **a.** a person who engages another to act as his agent. **b.** an active participant in a crime. **c.** the person primarily liable to fulfil an obligation. **5.** the head of a school or other educational institution. **6.** (in Britain) a civil servant of an executive grade who is in charge of a section. **7.** *Finance.* **a.** capital or property, as contrasted with income. **b.** the original amount of a debt on which interest is calculated. **8.** a main roof truss or rafter. **9.** *Music.* either of two types of open diapason organ stops. [C13: via OF from L *principālis* chief, from *princeps* chief man] —'**principally** *adv.* —'**principalship** *n.*

principal boy *n.* the leading male role in a pantomime, played by a woman.

principality (,prɪnsɪ'pælɪtɪ) *n., pl.* **-ties. 1.** a territory ruled by a prince or from which a prince draws his title. **2.** the authority of a prince.

principal nursing officer *n.* a grade of nurse concerned with administration in the British National Health Service.

principal parts *pl. n. Grammar.* the main inflected forms of a verb, from which all other inflections may be deduced.

principate ('prɪnsɪ,peɪt) *n.* **1.** a state ruled by a prince. **2.** a form of rule in the early Roman Empire in which some republican forms survived.

Principe ('prɪnsɪpɪ; *Portuguese* 'prĩsipə) *n.* an island in the Gulf of Guinea, off the W coast of Africa: part of São Tomé and Principe. Area: 150 sq. km (58 sq. miles).

principle ('prɪnsɪp³l) *n.* **1.** a standard or rule of personal conduct: *he'd stoop to anything - he has no principles.* **2.** a set of such moral rules: *a man of principle.* **3.** a fundamental or general truth. **4.** the essence of something. **5.** a source; origin. **6.** a law concerning a natural phenomenon or the behaviour of a system: *the principle of the conservation of mass.* **7.** *Chem.* a constituent of a substance that gives the substance its characteristics. **8. in principle.** in theory. **9. on principle.** because of or in demonstration of a principle. [C14: from L *principium* beginning, basic tenet]

principled ('prɪnsɪp³ld) *adj.* **a.** having high moral principles. **b.** (*in combination*): *high-principled.*

prink (prɪŋk) *vb.* **1.** to dress (oneself, etc.) finely; deck out. **2.** (*intr.*) to preen oneself. [C16: prob. changed from PRANK² (to adorn)]

print (prɪnt) *vb.* **1.** to reproduce (text, pictures, etc.), esp. in large numbers, by applying ink to paper or other material. **2.** to produce or reproduce (a manuscript, data, etc.) in print, as for publication. **3.** to write (letters, etc.) in the style of printed matter. **4.** to mark or indent (a surface) by pressing (something) onto it. **5.** to produce a photographic print from (a negative). **6.** (*tr.*) to fix in the mind or memory. **7.** (*tr.*) to make (a mark) by applying pressure. ~*n.* **8.** printed matter such as newsprint. **9.** a printed publication such as a book. **10. in print. a.** in printed or published form. **b.** (of a book, etc.) offered for sale by the publisher. **11. out of print.** no longer available from a publisher. **12.** a design or picture printed from an engraved plate, wood block, or other medium. **13.** printed text, esp. with regard to the typeface: *small print.* **14.** a positive photographic image produced from a negative image on film. **15. a.** a fabric with a printed design. **b.** (*as modifier*): *a print dress.* **16. a.** a mark made by pressing something onto a surface. **b.** a stamp, die, etc., that makes such an impression. **17.** See **fingerprint.** ~See also **print out.** [C13 *priente,* from OF: something printed, from *preindre* to make an impression, from L *premere* to press] —'**printable** *adj.*

printed circuit *n.* an electronic circuit in which certain components and the connections between them are formed by etching a metallic coating on or by electrodeposition on one or both sides of a thin insulating board.

printer ('prɪntə) *n.* **1.** a person or business engaged in printing. **2.** a machine or device that prints. **3.** *Computers.* an output device for printing results on paper.

printer's devil *n.* an apprentice or errand boy in a printing establishment.

printing ('prɪntɪŋ) *n.* **1.** the business or art of producing printed matter. **2.** printed text. **3.** Also called: **impression.** all the copies of a book, etc., printed at one time. **4.** a form of writing in which letters resemble printed letters.

printing press *n.* any of various machines used for printing.

printmaker ('prɪnt,meɪkə) *n.* a person who makes print or prints, esp. a craftsman or artist.

print out *vb.* (*tr., adv.*) **1.** (of a computer output device) to produce (printed information). ~*n.* **print-out. 2.** such printed information.

print shop *n.* a place in which printing is carried out.

prior¹ ('praɪə) *adj.* **1.** (*prenominal*) previous. **2. prior to.** before; until. [C18: from L: previous]

prior² ('praɪə) *n.* **1.** the superior of a community in certain religious orders. **2.** the deputy head of a monastery or abbey, immediately below the abbot. [C11: from LL: head, from L (adj.): previous, from OL *pri* before] —'**priorate** *n.* —'**prioress** *fem. n.*

Prior ('praɪə) *n.* **Matthew.** 1664–1721, English poet and diplomat, noted for his epigrammatic occasional verse.

priority (praɪ'ɒrɪtɪ) *n., pl.* **-ties. 1.** the condition of being prior; antecedence; precedence. **2.** the right of precedence over others. **3.** something given specified attention: *my first priority.*

priory ('praɪərɪ) *n., pl.* **-ories.** a religious house governed by a prior or prioress, sometimes being subordinate to an abbey. [C13: from Med. L *prīōria*]

Pripet ('priːpɪt) *n.* a river in the W Soviet Union, rising in the NW Ukrainian SSR and flowing northeast into the Byelorussian SSR across the **Pripet Marshes** (the largest swamp in Europe), then east into the Dnieper River. Length: about 800 km (500 miles). Russian name: **Pripyat** ('prɪpjɑtj).

Priscian ('prɪʃɪən) *n.* Latin name *Priscianus Caesariensis.* 6th century A.D., Latin grammarian.

prise *or* **prize** (praɪz) *vb.* (*tr.*) **1.** to force open by levering. **2.** to extract or obtain with difficulty: *they had to prise the news out of him.* [C17: from OF *prise* a taking, from *prendre* to take, from L *prehendere;* see PRIZE¹]

prism ('prɪzəm) *n.* **1.** a transparent polygonal solid, often having triangular ends and rectangular sides, for dispersing light into a spectrum or for reflecting light: used in binoculars, periscopes, etc. **2.** *Maths.* a polyhedron having parallel bases and sides that are parallelograms. [C16: from Med. L *prisma,* from Gk: something shaped by sawing, from *prizein* to saw]

prismatic (prɪz'mætɪk) *adj.* **1.** of or produced by a prism. **2.** exhibiting bright spectral colours: *prismatic light.* **3.** *Crystallog.* another word for **orthorhombic.** — **pris'matically** *adv.*

prison ('prɪz³n) *n.* **1.** a public building used to house convicted criminals and accused persons awaiting trial. **2.** any place of confinement. [C12: from OF *prisun,* from L *prēnsiō* a capturing, from *prehendere* to lay hold of]

prisoner ('prɪzənə) *n.* **1.** a person kept in custody as a punishment for a crime, while awaiting trial, or for some other reason. **2.** a person confined by any of various restraints: *we are all prisoners of time.* **3. take (someone) prisoner.** to capture and hold (someone) as a prisoner.

prisoner of war *n.* a person, esp. a serviceman, captured by an enemy in time of war. Abbrev.: **POW.**

prisoner's base *n.* a children's game involving two teams, members of which chase and capture each other.

prissy ('prɪsɪ) *adj.* **-sier, -siest.** fussy and prim, esp. in a prudish way. [C20: prob. from PRIM + SISSY] —'**prissily** *adv.* —'**prissiness** *n.*

Priština (*Serbo-Croatian* 'priːʃtina) *n.* a city in S Yugoslavia, capital of the Kosovo-Metohija autonomous region: under Turkish control until 1912; nearby is the 14th-century Gračanica monastery. Pop.: 216 040 (1981).

pristine ('prɪstaɪn, -tiːn) *adj.* **1.** of or involving the earliest period, state, etc.; original. **2.** pure; uncorrupted. [C15: from L *pristinus* primitive]

prithee ('prɪðɪ) *interj. Arch.* pray thee; please. [C16: shortened from *I pray thee*]

privacy ('praɪvəsɪ, 'prɪvəsɪ) *n.* **1.** the condition of being private. **2.** secrecy.

private ('praɪvɪt) *adj.* **1.** not widely or publicly known: *they had private reasons for the decision.* **2.** confidential; secret: *a private conversation.* **3.** not for general or public use: *a private bathroom.* **4.** of or provided by a private individual or organization rather than by the state.

5. (*prenominal*) individual; special: *my own private recipe*. **6.** (*prenominal*) having no public office, rank, etc.: *a private man*. **7.** (*prenominal*) denoting a soldier of the lowest military rank. **8.** (of a place) retired; not overlooked. ~*n.* **9.** a soldier of the lowest rank in many armies and marine corps. **10. in private.** in secret. [C14: from L *privātus* belonging to one individual, withdrawn from public life, from *privāre* to deprive] —'**privately** *adv.*

private bill *n.* a bill presented to Parliament or Congress on behalf of a private individual, corporation, etc.

private company *n.* a limited company that does not issue shares for public subscription and whose owners do not enjoy an unrestricted right to transfer their shareholdings. Cf. **public company.**

private detective *n.* an individual privately employed to investigate a crime or make other inquiries. Also called: **private investigator.**

private enterprise *n.* economic activity undertaken by private individuals or organizations under private ownership.

privateer (ˌpraɪvə'tɪə) *n.* **1.** an armed privately owned vessel commissioned for war service by a government. **2.** Also called: **privateersman.** a member of the crew of a privateer. ~*vb.* **3.** (*intr.*) to serve as a privateer.

private eye *n. Inf.* a private detective.

private hotel *n.* **1.** a hotel in which the proprietor has the right to refuse to accept a person as a guest. **2.** *Austral. & N.Z.* a hotel not having a licence to sell alcoholic liquor.

private income *n.* an income from sources other than employment, such as investment. Also called: **private means.**

private life *n.* the social life or personal relationships of an individual, esp. of a celebrity.

private member *n.* a member of a legislative assembly not having an appointment in the government.

private member's bill *n.* a parliamentary bill sponsored by a Member of Parliament who is not a government minister.

private parts *or* **privates** *pl. n.* euphemistic terms for **genitals.**

private patient *n. Brit.* a patient receiving medical treatment not paid for by the National Health Service.

private pay bed *n.* (in Britain) a hospital bed reserved for private patients who are charged by the health service for use of hospital facilities.

private practice *n. Brit.* medical practice that is not part of the National Health Service.

private school *n.* a school under the financial and managerial control of a private body, accepting mostly fee-paying pupils.

private secretary *n.* **1.** a secretary entrusted with the personal and confidential matters of a business executive. **2.** a civil servant who acts as aide to a minister or senior government official.

private sector *n.* the part of a country's economy that consists of privately owned enterprises.

privation (praɪ'veɪʃən) *n.* **1.** loss or lack of the necessities of life, such as food and shelter. **2.** hardship resulting from this. **3.** the state of being deprived. [C14: from L *privātiō* deprivation]

privative ('prɪvətɪv) *adj.* **1.** causing privation. **2.** expressing lack or negation, as for example the English suffix *-less* and prefix *un-*. [C16: from L *privātīvus* indicating loss] —'**privatively** *adv.*

privatize *or* **-ise** ('praɪvɪˌtaɪz) *vb.* (*tr.*) to take into, or return to, private ownership, a company or concern that has previously been owned by the state. —'**privati**,**zation** *or* **-i**,**sation** *n.*

privet ('prɪvɪt) *n.* **a.** any of a genus of shrubs, esp. one having oval dark green leaves, white flowers, and purplish-black berries. **b.** (*as modifier*): *a privet hedge*. [C16: from ?]

privilege ('prɪvɪlɪdʒ) *n.* **1.** a benefit, immunity, etc., granted under certain conditions. **2.** the advantages and immunities enjoyed by a small usually powerful group or class, esp. to the disadvantage of others: *one of the obstacles to social harmony is privilege*. **3.** *U.S. Stock Exchange.* a speculative contract permitting its purchaser to make optional purchases or sales of securities at a specified time over a limited period. ~*vb.* (*tr.*) **4.** to bestow a privilege or privileges upon. **5.** (foll. by *from*) to free or exempt. [C12: from OF *privilège*, from L *privilēgium* law relevant to rights of an individual, from *prīvus* an individual + *lēx* law]

privileged ('prɪvɪlɪdʒd) *adj.* **1.** enjoying or granted as a privilege or privileges. **2.** *Law.* **a.** not actionable as a libel or slander. **b.** (of a communication, document, etc.) that a witness cannot be compelled to divulge.

privity ('prɪvɪtɪ) *n., pl.* **-ties.** **1.** a legally recognized relationship existing between two parties, such as that between the parties to a contract: *privity of contract*. **2.** secret knowledge that is shared. [C13: from OF *priveté*]

privy ('prɪvɪ) *adj.* **privier, priviest.** **1.** (*postpositive*; foll. by *to*) participating in the knowledge of something secret. **2.** *Arch.* secret, hidden, etc. ~*n., pl.* **privies.** **3.** a lavatory, esp. an outside one. **4.** *Law.* a person in privity with another. See **privity.** [C13: from OF *privé* something private, from L *privātus* PRIVATE] —'**privily** *adv.*

privy council *n.* **1.** the council of state of a monarch, esp. formerly. **2.** *Arch.* a secret council.

Privy Council *n.* **1.** the private council of the British sovereign, consisting of all current and former ministers of the Crown and other distinguished subjects, all of whom are appointed for life. **2.** (in Canada), a ceremonial body of advisers of the governor general, the chief of them being the Federal cabinet ministers. —**Privy Councillor** *n.*

privy purse *n.* (*often cap.*) **1.** an allowance voted by Parliament for the private expenses of the monarch. **2.** an official of the royal household responsible for dealing with the monarch's private expenses. Full name: **Keeper of the Privy Purse.**

privy seal *n.* (*often cap.*) (in Britain) a seal affixed to certain documents issued by royal authority: of less importance than the great seal.

prize¹ (praɪz) *n.* **1. a.** a reward or honour for having won a contest, competition, etc. **b.** (*as modifier*): *prize jockey; prize essay*. **2.** something given to the winner of any game of chance, lottery, etc. **3.** something striven for. **4.** any valuable property captured in time of war, esp. a vessel. [C14: from OF *prise* a capture, from L *prehendere* to seize; infl. by ME *prise* reward]

prize² (praɪz) *vb.* (*tr.*) to esteem greatly; value highly. [C15 *prise*, from OF *preisier* to PRAISE]

prize court *n. Law.* a court having jurisdiction to determine how property captured at sea in wartime is to be distributed.

prizefight ('praɪzˌfaɪt) *n.* a boxing match for a prize or purse. —'**prize**,**fighter** *n.* —'**prize**,**fighting** *n.*

prize ring *n.* **1.** the enclosed area or ring used by prizefighters. **2. the prize ring.** the sport of prizefighting.

pro¹ (prəʊ) *adv.* **1.** in favour of a motion, issue, course of action, etc. ~*prep.* **2.** in favour of. ~*n., pl.* **pros.** **3.** (*usually pl.*) an argument or vote in favour of a proposal or motion. See also **pros and cons.** [from L *prō* (prep.) in favour of]

pro² (prəʊ) *n., pl.* **pros,** *adj. Inf.* **1.** short for **professional.** **2.** a prostitute. [C19]

PRO *abbrev. for:* **1.** Public Records Office. **2.** public relations officer.

pro-¹ *prefix.* **1.** in favour of; supporting: *pro-Chinese*. **2.** acting as a substitute for: *proconsul; pronoun*. [from L *prō* (adv. & prep.). In compound words borrowed from L, *prō-* indicates: forward, out (*project*); away from (*prodigal*); onward (*proceed*); in front of (*provide, protect*); on behalf of (*procure*); substitute for (*pronominal*); and sometimes intensive force (*promiscuous*)]

pro-² *prefix.* before in time or position; anterior; forward: *prognathous*. [from Gk *pro* (prep.) before (in time, position, etc.)]

proa ('prəʊə) *or* **prau** *n.* any of several kinds of canoe-like boats used in the South Pacific, esp. one equipped with an outrigger and sails. [C16: from Malay *parāhū* a boat]

pro-am ('prəʊ'æm) *adj.* (of a golf tournament, etc.) involving both professional and amateur players.

probability (ˌprɒbə'bɪlɪtɪ) *n., pl.* **-ties.** **1.** the condition of being probable. **2.** an event or other thing that is probable. **3.** *Statistics.* a measure of the degree of confidence

,**proa'mendment** *adj.*　　　　　,**proannex'ation** *adj.*　　　　　,**proarbi'tration** *adj.*　　　　　,**proauto'mation** *adj.*
,**pro-A'merican** *adj., n.*　　　　　,**proap'proval** *adj.*

one may have in the occurrence of an event, measured on a scale from zero (impossibility) to one (certainty).

probable ('prɒbəb°l) *adj.* **1.** likely to be or to happen but not necessarily so. **2.** most likely: *the probable cause of the accident.* ~*n.* **3.** a person who is probably to be chosen for a team, event, etc. [C14: via OF from L *probābilis* that may be proved, from *probāre* to prove]

probably ('prɒbəblɪ) *adv.* **1.** (*sentence modifier*) in all likelihood or probability: *I'll probably see you tomorrow.* ~*sentence substitute.* **2.** I believe such a thing may be the case.

probang ('prəʊbæŋ) *n. Surgery.* a long flexible rod, often with a small sponge at one end, for inserting into the oesophagus, as to apply medication. [C17: var., apparently by association with PROBE, of *provang*, coined by W. Rumsey (1584–1660), Welsh judge, its inventor; from ?]

probate ('prəʊbɪt, -beɪt) *n.* **1.** the process of officially proving the validity of a will. **2.** the official certificate stating a will to be genuine and conferring on the executors power to administer the estate. **3.** (*modifier*) relating to probate: *a probate court.* ~*vb.* **4.** (*tr.*) *Chiefly U.S.* to establish officially the validity of (a will). [C15: from L *probāre* to inspect]

probation (prə'beɪʃən) *n.* **1.** a system of dealing with offenders by placing them under the supervision of a probation officer. **2. on probation. a.** under the supervision of a probation officer. **b.** undergoing a test period. **3.** a trial period, as for a teacher. —**pro'bational** *or* **pro'bationary** *adj.*

probationer (prə'beɪʃənə) *n.* a person on probation.

probation officer *n.* an officer of a court who supervises offenders placed on probation and assists and befriends them.

probe (prəʊb) *vb.* **1.** (*tr.*) to search into closely. **2.** to examine (something) with or as if with a probe. ~*n.* **3.** something that probes or tests. **4.** *Surgery.* a slender instrument for exploring a wound, sinus, etc. **5.** a thorough inquiry, such as one by a newspaper into corrupt practices. **6.** *Electronics.* a lead connecting to or containing a monitoring circuit used for testing. **7.** anything which provides or acts as a coupling, esp. a flexible tube extended from an aircraft to link it with another so that it can refuel. **8.** See **space probe.** [C16: from Med. L *proba* investigation, from L *probāre* to test] —'**probeable** *adj.* —'**prober** *n.*

probity ('prəʊbɪtɪ) *n.* confirmed integrity. [C16: from L *probitās* honesty, from *probus* virtuous]

problem ('prɒbləm) *n.* **1. a.** any thing, matter, person, etc., that is difficult to deal with. **b.** (*as modifier*): *a problem child.* **2.** a puzzle, question, etc., set for solution. **3.** *Maths.* a statement requiring a solution usually by means of several operations or constructions. **4.** (*modifier*) designating a literary work that deals with difficult moral questions: *a problem play.* [C14: from LL *problēma*, from Gk: something put forward]

problematic (,prɒblə'mætɪk) *or* **problematical** *adj.* **1.** having the nature of a problem; uncertain; questionable. **2.** *Logic, obs.* (of a proposition) asserting that a property may or may not hold. —,**problem'atically** *adv.*

pro bono publico *Latin.* ('prəʊ 'bəʊnəʊ 'pʊblɪkəʊ) for the public good.

proboscidean *or* **proboscidian** (,prəʊbɒ'sɪdɪən) *adj.* **1.** of or belonging to an order of massive herbivorous placental mammals having tusks and a long trunk: contains the elephants. ~*n.* **2.** any proboscidean animal.

proboscis (prəʊ'bɒsɪs) *n., pl.* **-cises** *or* **-cides** (-sɪ,diːz). **1.** a long flexible prehensile trunk or snout, as of an elephant. **2.** the elongated mouthpart of certain insects. **3.** any similar organ. **4.** *Inf., facetious.* a person's nose. [C17: via L from Gk *proboskis* trunk of an elephant, from *boskein* to feed]

procaine ('prəʊkeɪn, prəʊ'keɪn) *n.* a colourless or white crystalline water-soluble substance used, as the hydrochloride, as a local anaesthetic. [C20: from PRO-¹ + (CO)CAINE]

procathedral (,prəʊkə'θiːdrəl) *n.* a church serving as a cathedral.

procedure (prə'siːdʒə) *n.* **1.** a way of acting or progressing, esp. an established method. **2.** the established form

of conducting the business of a legislature, the enforcement of a legal right, etc. **3.** *Computers.* another name for **subroutine.** —**pro'cedural** *adj.* —**pro'cedurally** *adv.*

proceed (prə'siːd) *vb.* (*intr.*) **1.** (often foll. by *to*) to advance or carry on, esp. after stopping. **2.** (often foll. by *with*) to continue: *he proceeded with his reading.* **3.** (often foll. by *against*) to institute or carry on a legal action. **4.** to originate; arise: *evil proceeds from the heart.* [C14: from L *prōcēdere* to advance] —**pro'ceeder** *n.*

proceeding (prə'siːdɪŋ) *n.* **1.** an act or course of action. **2. a.** a legal action. **b.** any step taken in a legal action. **3.** (*pl.*) the minutes of the meetings of a society, etc. **4.** (*pl.*) legal action; litigation. **5.** (*pl.*) the events of an occasion.

proceeds ('prəʊsiːdz) *pl. n.* **1.** the profit or return derived from a commercial transaction, investment, etc. **2.** the result, esp. the total sum, accruing from some undertaking.

process¹ ('prəʊsɛs) *n.* **1.** a series of actions which produce a change or development: *the process of digestion.* **2.** a method of doing or producing something. **3.** progress or course of time. **4. in the process of.** during or in the course of. **5. a.** a summons commanding a person to appear in court. **b.** the whole proceedings in an action at law. **6.** a natural outgrowth or projection of a part or organism. **7.** (*modifier*) relating to the general preparation of a printing forme or plate by the use, at some stage, of photography. ~*vb.* (*tr.*) **8.** to subject to a routine procedure; handle. **9.** to treat or prepare by a special method, esp. to treat (food) in order to preserve it: *to process cheese.* **10. a.** to institute legal proceedings against. **b.** to serve a process on. **11.** *Photog.* **a.** to develop, rinse, fix, wash, and dry (exposed film, etc.). **b.** to produce final prints or slides from (undeveloped film). **12.** *Computers.* to perform operations on (data) according to programmed instructions in order to obtain the required information. [C14: from OF *procès*, from L *prōcessus* an advancing, from *prōcēdere* to proceed]

process² (prə'sɛs) *vb.* (*intr.*) to proceed in a procession. [C19: back formation from PROCESSION]

process industry *n.* a manufacturing industry, such as oil refining, which converts bulk raw materials into a workable form.

procession (prə'sɛʃən) *n.* **1.** the act of proceeding in a regular formation. **2.** a group of people or things moving forwards in an orderly, regular, or ceremonial manner. **3.** *Christianity.* the emanation of the Holy Spirit. ~*vb.* **4.** (*intr.*) *Rare.* to go in procession. [C12: via OF from L *prōcessiō* a marching forwards]

processional (prə'sɛʃənəl) *adj.* **1.** of or suitable for a procession. ~*n.* **2.** *Christianity.* **a.** a book containing the prayers, hymns, etc., prescribed for processions. **b.** a hymn, etc., used in a procession.

processor ('prəʊsɛsə) *n.* **1.** *Computers.* another name for **central processing unit.** **2.** a person or thing that carries out a process.

process-server *n.* a sheriff's officer who serves legal documents such as writs for appearance in court.

procès-verbal *French.* (prɔsɛvɛrbal) *n., pl.* **-baux** (-bo). a written record of an official proceeding; minutes. [C17: from F: see PROCESS, VERBAL]

prochronism ('prəʊkrə,nɪzəm) *n.* an error in dating that places an event earlier than it actually occurred. [C17: from PRO-² + Gk *khronos* time + -ISM, by analogy with ANACHRONISM]

proclaim (prə'kleɪm) *vb.* (*tr.*) **1.** (*may take a clause as object*) to announce publicly. **2.** (*may take a clause as object*) to indicate plainly. **3.** to praise or extol. [C14: from L *prōclāmāre* to shout aloud] —**proclamation** (,prɒklə'meɪʃən) *n.* —**pro'claimer** *n.* —**proclamatory** (prə'klæmətərɪ, -trɪ) *adj.*

proclitic (prəʊ'klɪtɪk) *adj.* **1. a.** denoting a monosyllabic word or form having no stress and pronounced as a prefix of the following word, as in English *'t* for *it* in *'twas.* **b.** (in classical Greek) denoting a word that throws its accent onto the following word. ~*n.* **2.** a proclitic word or form. [C19: from NL *proclīticus*, from Gk *proklinein* to lean forwards; on the model of ENCLITIC]

---

pro'biblical *adj.*	pro'business *adj.*	,procentrali'zation	*or* pro'church *adj.*
pro-'Bolshevik *adj., n.*	pro'capitalist *adj.*	-i'sation *adj.*	pro'clerical *adj.*
pro-'British *adj.*	pro-'Catholic *adj., n.*		

proclivity (prəˈklɪvɪtɪ) n., pl. **-ties.** a tendency or inclination. [C16: from L *prōclīvitās*, from *prōclīvis* steep, from *clīvus* a slope]

Proclus (ˈprəʊkləs, ˈprɒk-) n. ?410–485 A.D., Greek Neo-Platonist philosopher.

Procne (ˈprɒknɪ) n. *Greek myth.* a princess of Athens, who punished her husband for raping her sister Philomela by feeding him the flesh of their son. She was changed at her death into a swallow. See **Philomela.**

proconsul (prəʊˈkɒnsᵊl) n. **1.** a governor of a colony or other dependency. **2.** (in ancient Rome) the governor of a senatorial province. —**proconsular** (prəʊˈkɒnsjʊlə) adj.

Procopius (prəʊˈkəʊpɪəs) n. ?490–?562 A.D., Byzantine historian, noted for his account of the wars of Justinian I against the Persians, Vandals, and Ostrogoths.

procrastinate (prəʊˈkræstɪˌneɪt, prə-) vb. (*usually intr.*) to put off (an action) until later; delay. [C16: from L *prōcrāstināre* to postpone until tomorrow, from PRO-[1] + *crās* tomorrow] —**proˌcrastiˈnation** n. —**proˈcrasti,nator** n.

procreate (ˈprəʊkrɪˌeɪt) vb. **1.** to beget or engender (offspring). **2.** (tr.) to bring into being. [C16: from L *prōcreāre*, from PRO-[1] + *creāre* to create] —**ˈprocreant** or **ˈprocreˌative** adj. —**ˌprocreˈation** n. —**ˈprocreˌator** n.

Procrustean (prəʊˈkrʌstɪən) adj. tending or designed to produce conformity by violent or ruthless methods.

Procrustes (prəʊˈkrʌstiːz) n. *Greek myth.* a robber, who put travellers in his bed, stretching or lopping off their limbs so that they fitted it. [C16: from Gk *Prokroustēs* the stretcher, from *prokrouein* to extend by hammering out]

proctology (prɒkˈtɒlədʒɪ) n. the branch of medical science concerned with the rectum. [from Gk *prōktos* rectum + -OLOGY]

proctor (ˈprɒktə) n. **1.** a member of the staff of certain universities having duties including the enforcement of discipline. **2.** (formerly) an agent, esp. one engaged to conduct another's case in a court. **3.** *Church of England.* one of the elected representatives of the clergy in Convocation. [C14: syncopated var. of PROCURATOR] —**proctorial** (prɒkˈtɔːrɪəl) adj.

procumbent (prəʊˈkʌmbənt) adj. **1.** (of stems) trailing loosely along the ground. **2.** leaning forwards or lying on the face. [C17: from L *prōcumbere* to fall forwards]

procurator (ˈprɒkjʊˌreɪtə) n. **1.** (in ancient Rome) a civil official of the emperor's administration, often employed as the governor of a minor province. **2.** *Rare.* a person engaged by another to manage his affairs. [C13: from L: a manager, from *prōcūrāre* to attend to] —**procuracy** (ˈprɒkjʊrəsɪ) or **ˈprocuˌratorship** n. —**procuratorial** (ˌprɒkjʊərəˈtɔːrɪəl) adj.

procurator fiscal n. (in Scotland) a legal officer who performs the functions of public prosecutor and coroner.

procure (prəˈkjʊə) vb. **1.** (tr.) to obtain or acquire; secure. **2.** to obtain (women or girls) to act as prostitutes. [C13: from L *prōcūrāre* to look after] —**proˈcurable** adj. —**proˈcurement, proˈcural,** or **procuration** (ˌprɒkjʊˈreɪʃən) n.

procurer (prəˈkjʊərə) n. a person who procures, esp. one who procures women as prostitutes.

prod (prɒd) vb. **prodding, prodded. 1.** to poke or jab with or as if with a pointed object. **2.** (tr.) to rouse to action. ~n. **3.** the act or an instance of prodding. **4.** a sharp object. **5.** a stimulus or reminder. [C16: from ?] —**ˈprodder** n.

prod. abbrev. for: **1.** produce. **2.** produced. **3.** product.

prodigal (ˈprɒdɪgᵊl) adj. **1.** recklessly wasteful or extravagant, as in disposing of goods or money. **2.** lavish: *prodigal of compliments.* ~n. **3.** a person who spends lavishly or squanders money. [C16: from Med. L *prōdigālis* wasteful, from L, from *prōdigere* to squander, from *agere* to drive] —**ˌprodiˈgality** n. —**ˈprodigally** adv.

prodigious (prəˈdɪdʒəs) adj. **1.** vast in size, extent, power, etc. **2.** wonderful or amazing. [C16: from L *prōdigiōsus* marvellous, from *prōdigium;* see PRODIGY] —**proˈdigiously** adv. —**proˈdigiousness** n.

prodigy (ˈprɒdɪdʒɪ) n., pl. **-gies. 1.** a person, esp. a child, of unusual or marvellous talents. **2.** anything that is a

cause of wonder. **3.** something monstrous or abnormal. [C16: from L *prōdigium* an unnatural happening]

produce vb. (prəˈdjuːs). **1.** to bring (something) into existence; yield. **2.** (tr.) to make: *she produced a delicious dinner.* **3.** (tr.) to give birth to. **4.** (tr.) to present to view: *to produce evidence.* **5.** (tr.) to bring before the public: *he produced a film last year.* **6.** (tr.) to act as producer of. **7.** (tr.) *Geom.* to extend (a line). ~n. (ˈprɒdjuːs). **8.** anything produced; a product. **9.** agricultural products collectively: *farm produce.* [C15: from L *prōdūcere* to bring forward] —**proˈducible** adj. —**proˌduciˈbility** n.

producer (prəˈdjuːsə) n. **1.** a person or thing that produces. **2.** *Brit.* a person responsible for the artistic direction of a play. **3.** *U.S. & Canad.* a person who organizes the stage production of a play, including the finance, management, etc. **4.** the person who takes overall administrative responsibility for a film or television programme. Cf. **director** (sense 4). **5.** *Econ.* a person or business enterprise that generates goods or services for sale. Cf. **consumer** (sense 1). **6.** *Chem.* an apparatus or plant for making producer gas.

producer gas n. a mixture of carbon monoxide and nitrogen produced by passing air over hot coke, used mainly as a fuel.

product (ˈprɒdʌkt) n. **1.** something produced by effort, or some mechanical or industrial process. **2.** the result of some natural process. **3.** a result or consequence. **4.** *Maths.* the result of the multiplication of two or more numbers, quantities, etc. [C15: from L *prōductum* (something) produced, from *prōdūcere* to bring forth]

production (prəˈdʌkʃən) n. **1.** the act of producing. **2.** anything that is produced; a product. **3.** the amount produced or the rate at which it is produced. **4.** *Econ.* the creation or manufacture of goods and services with exchange value. **5.** any work created as a result of literary or artistic effort. **6.** the presentation of a play, opera, etc. **7.** *Brit.* the artistic direction of a play. **8.** (*modifier*) manufactured by mass production: *a production model of a car.* —**proˈductional** adj.

production line n. a factory system in which parts or components of the end product are transported by a conveyor through a number of different sites at each of which a manual or machine operation is performed on them.

productive (prəˈdʌktɪv) adj. **1.** producing or having the power to produce; fertile. **2.** yielding favourable results. **3.** *Econ.* **a.** producing goods and services that have exchange value: *productive assets.* **b.** relating to such production: *the productive processes of an industry.* **4.** (*postpositive;* foll. by *of*) resulting in: *productive of good results.* —**proˈductively** adv. —**proˈductiveness** n.

productivity (ˌprɒdʌkˈtɪvɪtɪ) n. **1.** the output of an industrial concern in relation to the materials, labour, etc., it employs. **2.** the state of being productive.

proem (ˈprəʊɛm) n. an introduction or preface, such as to a work of literature. [C14: from L *prooemium* introduction, from Gk *prooimion,* from PRO-[2] + *hoimē* song] —**proemial** (prəʊˈiːmɪəl) adj.

proenzyme (prəʊˈɛnzaɪm) n. the inactive form of an enzyme; zymogen.

Prof. abbrev. for Professor.

profane (prəˈfeɪn) adj. **1.** having or indicating contempt, irreverence, or disrespect for a divinity or something sacred. **2.** not designed for religious purposes; secular. **3.** not initiated into the inner mysteries or sacred rites. **4.** coarse or blasphemous: *profane language.* ~vb. (tr.) **5.** to treat (something sacred) with irreverence. **6.** to put to an unworthy use. [C15: from L *profānus* outside the temple] —**profanation** (ˌprɒfəˈneɪʃən) n. —**proˈfanely** adv. —**proˈfaneness** n. —**proˈfaner** n.

profanity (prəˈfænɪtɪ) n., pl. **-ties. 1.** the state or quality of being profane. **2.** vulgar or irreverent action, speech, etc.

profess (prəˈfɛs) vb. **1.** (tr.) to affirm or acknowledge: *to profess ignorance; to profess a belief in God.* **2.** (tr.) to claim (something), often insincerely or falsely: *to profess to be a skilled driver.* **3.** to receive or be received into a religious order, as by taking vows. [C14: from L *profitērī* to confess openly]

---

pro-ˈCommunist adj., n.
ˌprocoˈnscription adj.
ˌproconserˈvation adj.

ˌpro-ˈDarˈwinian adj., n.
ˌprodemoˈcratic adj.
ˌprodisˈarmament adj.

ˌprodissoˈlution adj.
ˌproenˈforcement adj.
ˌpro-Euroˈpean adj., n.

ˌprodisˈfascist adj., n.
proˈfeminist adj., n.

professed (prə'fɛst) *adj.* (*prenominal*) **1.** avowed or acknowledged. **2.** alleged or pretended. **3.** professing to be qualified as: *a professed philosopher.* **4.** having taken vows of a religious order. —**professedly** (prə'fɛsɪdlɪ) *adv.*

profession (prə'fɛʃən) *n.* **1.** an occupation requiring special training in the liberal arts or sciences, esp. one of the three learned professions, law, theology, or medicine. **2.** the body of people in such an occupation. **3.** an avowal; declaration. **4.** Also called: **profession of faith.** a declaration of faith in a religion, esp. as made on entering the Church or an order belonging to it. [C13: from Med. L *professiō* the taking of vows upon entering a religious order, from L: public acknowledgment; see PROFESS]

professional (prə'fɛʃənᵊl) *adj.* **1.** of, suitable for, or engaged in as a profession. **2.** engaging in an activity as a means of livelihood. **3. a.** extremely competent in a job, etc. **b.** (of a piece of work or anything performed) produced with competence or skill. **4.** undertaken or performed by people who are paid. ~*n.* **5.** a person who belongs to one of the professions. **6.** a person who engages for his livelihood in some activity also pursued by amateurs. **7.** a person who engages in an activity with great competence. **8.** an expert player of a game who gives instruction, esp. to members of a club by whom he is hired. —**pro'fessiona,lism** *n.* —**pro'fessionally** *adv.*

professional foul *n. Football.* a deliberate foul committed as a last-ditch tactic to prevent an opponent from scoring.

professor (prə'fɛsə) *n.* **1.** the principal teacher in a field of learning at a university or college; a holder of a university chair. **2.** *Chiefly U.S. & Canad.* any teacher in a university or college. **3.** a person who professes his opinions, beliefs, etc. [C14: from Med. L: one who has made his profession in a religious order, from L: a public teacher; see PROFESS] —**professorial** (,prɒfɪ'sɔ:rɪəl) *adj.* —,**profes'sorially** *adv.* —,**profes'soriate** *or* **pro'fessorship** *n.*

proffer ('prɒfə) *vb.* **1.** (*tr.*) to offer for acceptance. ~*n.* **2.** the act of proffering. [C13: from OF *proffrir*, from PRO-¹ + *offrir* to offer]

proficient (prə'fɪʃənt) *adj.* **1.** having great facility (in an art, occupation, etc.); skilled. ~*n.* **2.** an expert. [C16: from L *prōficere* to make progress] —**pro'ficiency** *n.* —**pro'ficiently** *adv.*

profile ('prəʊfaɪl) *n.* **1.** a side view or outline of an object, esp. of a human head. **2.** a short biographical sketch. **3.** a graph, table, etc., representing the extent to which a person, field, or object exhibits various tested characteristics: *a population profile.* **4.** a vertical section of soil or rock showing the different layers. **5.** the outline of the shape of a river valley either from source to mouth (**long profile**) or at right angles to the flow of the river (**cross profile**). ~*vb.* **6.** (*tr.*) to draw, write, or make a profile of. [C17: from It. *profilo*, from *profilare* to sketch lightly, from L *filum* thread] — **'profiler** *or* **profilist** ('prəʊfɪlɪst) *n.*

profit ('prɒfɪt) *n.* **1.** (*often pl.*) excess of revenues over outlays and expenses in a business enterprise. **2.** the monetary gain derived from a transaction. **3.** income derived from property or an investment, as contrasted with capital gains. **4.** *Econ.* the income accruing to a successful entrepreneur and held to be the motivating factor of a capitalist economy. **5.** a gain, benefit, or advantage. ~*vb.* **6.** to gain or cause to gain profit. [C14: from L *prōfectus* advance, from *prōficere* to make progress] — **'profitless** *adj.*

profitable ('prɒfɪtəbᵊl) *adj.* affording gain or profit. — ,**profita'bility** *n.* — **'profitably** *adv.*

profit and loss *n. Book-keeping.* an account compiled at the end of a financial year showing that year's revenue and expense items and indicating gross and net profit or loss.

profit centre *n.* a section of a commercial organization which is allocated financial targets in its own right.

profiteer (,prɒfɪ'tɪə) *n.* **1.** a person who makes excessive profits, esp. by charging exorbitant prices for goods in short supply. ~*vb.* **2.** (*intr.*) to make excessive profits.

profiterole ('prɒfɪtə,rəʊl, prə'fɪtə,rəʊl) *n.* a small case of choux pastry with a sweet or savoury filling. [C16: from F, lit.: a small profit]

profit-sharing *n.* a system in which a portion of the net profit of a business is distributed to its employees, usually in proportion to their wages or their length of service.

profligate ('prɒflɪgɪt) *adj.* **1.** shamelessly immoral or debauched. **2.** wildly extravagant or wasteful. ~*n.* **3.** a profligate person. [C16: from L *prōflīgātus* corrupt, from *prōflīgāre* to overthrow, from PRO-¹ + *flīgere* to beat] —**profligacy** ('prɒflɪgəsɪ) *n.* — **'profligately** *adv.*

pro forma ('prəʊ 'fɔ:mə) *adj.* **1.** prescribing a set form or procedure. ~*adv.* **2.** performed in a set manner. [L: for form's sake]

profound (prə'faʊnd) *adj.* **1.** penetrating deeply into subjects or ideas: *a profound mind.* **2.** showing or requiring great knowledge or understanding: *a profound treatise.* **3.** situated at or extending to a great depth. **4.** stemming from the depths of one's nature: *profound regret.* **5.** intense or absolute: *profound silence.* **6.** thoroughgoing; extensive: *profound changes.* ~*n.* **7.** *Arch. or literary.* a great depth; abyss. [C14: from OF *profund*, from L *profundus* deep, from *fundus* bottom] — **pro'foundly** *adv.* —**profundity** (prə'fʌndɪtɪ) *n.*

profuse (prə'fju:s) *adj.* **1.** plentiful or abundant: *profuse compliments.* **2.** (often foll. by *in*) free or generous in the giving (of): *profuse in thanks.* [C15: from L *profundere* to pour lavishly] —**pro'fusely** *adv.* —**pro'fuseness** *or* **pro'fusion** *n.*

progenitive (prəʊ'dʒɛnɪtɪv) *adj.* capable of bearing offspring. — **pro'genitiveness** *n.*

progenitor (prəʊ'dʒɛnɪtə) *n.* **1.** a direct ancestor. **2.** an originator or founder. [C14: from L: ancestor, from *gignere* to beget]

progeny ('prɒdʒɪnɪ) *n., pl.* -**nies.** **1.** the immediate descendant or descendants of a person, animal, etc. **2.** a result or outcome. [C13: from L *prōgeniēs* lineage; see PROGENITOR]

progesterone (prəʊ'dʒɛstə,rəʊn) *n.* a steroid hormone, secreted mainly by the corpus luteum in the ovary, that prepares and maintains the uterus for pregnancy. [C20: from PRO-¹ + GE(STATION) + STER(OL) + -ONE]

progestogen (prəʊ'dʒɛstədʒən) *n.* any of a group of steroid hormones with progesterone-like activity, used in oral contraceptives and in treating gynaecological disorders.

prognathous (prɒg'neɪθəs) *or* **prognathic** (prɒg'næθɪk) *adj.* having a projecting lower jaw. [C19: from PRO-² + Gk *gnathos* jaw]

prognosis (prɒg'nəʊsɪs) *n., pl.* -**noses** (-'nəʊsi:z). **1.** *Med.* a prediction of the course or outcome of a disease. **2.** any prediction. [C17: via L from Gk: knowledge beforehand]

prognostic (prɒg'nɒstɪk) *adj.* **1.** of or serving as a prognosis. **2.** predicting. ~*n.* **3.** *Med.* any symptom or sign used in making a prognosis. **4.** a sign of some future occurrence. [C15: from OF *pronostique*, from L *prognōsticum*, from Gk, from *progignōskein* to know in advance]

prognosticate (prɒg'nɒstɪ,keɪt) *vb.* **1.** to foretell (future events); prophesy. **2.** (*tr.*) to foreshadow or portend. [C16: from Med. L *prognōsticāre* to predict] —**prog,nosti'cation** *n.* —**prog'nosticative** *adj.* —**prog'nosti,cator** *n.*

program *or* (*sometimes*) **programme** ('prəʊgræm) *n.* **1.** a sequence of coded instructions fed into a computer, enabling it to perform specified logical and arithmetical operations on data. ~*vb.* -**gramming,** -**grammed. 2.** (*tr.*) to feed a program into (a computer). **3.** (*tr.*) to arrange (data) in a suitable form so that it can be processed by a computer. **4.** (*intr.*) to write a program. — **'programmer** *n.*

programmable *or* **programable** (prəʊ'græməbəl) *adj.* capable of being programmed for automatic operation or computer processing.

programme *or U.S.* **program** ('prəʊgræm) *n.* **1.** a written or printed list of the events, performers, etc., in a public performance. **2.** a performance presented at a scheduled time, esp. on radio or television. **3.** a specially arranged selection of things to be done: *what's the programme for this afternoon?* **4.** a plan, schedule, or procedure. **5.** a syllabus or curriculum. ~*vb.* -**gramming,** -**grammed** *or U.S.* -**graming,** -**gramed. 6.** to design or schedule (something) as a programme. ~*n., vb.* **7.** *Computers.* a variant spelling of **program.** [C17: from LL *programma*, from Gk: written public notice, from PRO-² + *graphein* to write] —**program'matic** *adj.*

programmed learning *n.* a teaching method in which the material to be learnt is broken down into easily understandable parts on which the pupil is able to test himself.

programme music *n.* music that is intended to depict or evoke a scene or idea.

programming language *n.* a language system by which instructions to a computer are coded, using a set of characters that is mutually comprehensible to user and computer.

progress *n.* ('prəʊgres). **1.** movement forwards, esp. towards a place or objective. **2.** satisfactory development or advance. **3.** advance towards completion or perfection. **4.** (*modifier*) of or relating to progress: *a progress report.* **5.** (formerly) a stately royal journey. **6. in progress.** taking place. ~*vb.* (prə'gres). **7.** (*intr.*) to move forwards or onwards. **8.** (*intr.*) to move towards completion or perfection. **9.** (*tr.*) to be responsible for the satisfactory progress of (a project, etc.) to completion. [C15: from L *prógressus*, from *prógredi* to advance, from *gradī* to step]

progression (prə'greʃən) *n.* **1.** the act of progressing; advancement. **2.** the act or an instance of moving from one thing in a sequence to the next. **3.** *Maths.* a sequence of numbers in which each term differs from the succeeding term by a constant relation. See also **arithmetic progression, geometric progression, harmonic progression. 4.** *Music.* movement from one note or chord to the next. —**pro'gressional** *adj.*

progressive (prə'gresɪv) *adj.* **1.** of or relating to progress. **2.** progressing by steps or degrees. **3.** (*often cap.*) favouring or promoting political or social reform: *a progressive policy.* **4.** denoting an educational system that allows flexibility in learning procedures, based on activities determined by the needs and capacities of the individual child. **5.** (esp. of a disease) advancing in severity, complexity, or extent. **6.** (of a dance, card game, etc.) involving a regular change of partners. **7.** denoting an aspect of verbs in some languages, including English, used to express continuous activity: *a progressive aspect of the verb "to walk" is "is walking".* ~*n.* **8.** a person who advocates progress, as in education, politics, etc. **9. a.** the progressive aspect of a verb. **b.** a verb in this aspect. —**pro'gressively** *adv.* —**pro'gressiveness** *n.* —**pro'gressivism** *n.* —**pro'gressivist** *n.*

prohibit (prə'hɪbɪt) *vb.* (*tr.*) **1.** to forbid by law or other authority. **2.** to hinder or prevent. [C15: from L *prohibēre* to prevent, from PRO-¹ + *habēre* to hold] —**pro'hibiter** or **pro'hibitor** *n.*

prohibition (ˌprəʊɪ'bɪʃən) *n.* **1.** the act of prohibiting or state of being prohibited. **2.** an order or decree that prohibits. **3.** (*sometimes cap.*) (esp. in the U.S.) a policy of legally forbidding the manufacture, sale, or consumption of alcoholic beverages. **4.** *Law.* an order of a superior court forbidding an inferior court to determine a matter outside its jurisdiction. —ˌ**prohi'bitionary** *adj.* —ˌ**prohi'bitionist** *n.*

Prohibition (ˌprəʊɪ'bɪʃən) *n.* the period (1920–33) when the manufacture, sale, and transportation of intoxicating liquors were banned in the U.S. —ˌ**Prohi'bitionist** *n.*

prohibitive (prə'hɪbɪtɪv) or (*less commonly*) **prohibitory** (prə'hɪbɪtərɪ, -trɪ) *adj.* **1.** prohibiting or tending to prohibit. **2.** (esp. of prices) tending or designed to discourage sale or purchase. —**pro'hibitively** *adv.* —**pro'hibitiveness** *n.*

project *n.* ('prɒdʒekt). **1.** a proposal, scheme, or design. **2. a.** a task requiring considerable or concerted effort, such as one by students. **b.** the subject of such a task. ~*vb.* (prə'dʒekt). **3.** (*tr.*) to propose or plan. **4.** (*tr.*) to throw forwards. **5.** to jut or cause to jut out. **6.** (*tr.*) to make a prediction based on known data and observations. **7.** (*tr.*) to transport in the imagination: *to project oneself into the future.* **8.** (*tr.*) to cause (an image) to appear on a surface. **9.** to cause (one's voice) to be heard clearly at a distance. **10.** *Psychol.* **a.** (*intr.*) (esp. of a child) to believe that others share one's subjective mental life. **b.** to impute to others (one's hidden desires). **11.** (*tr.*) *Geom.*

to draw a projection of. **12.** (*intr.*) to communicate effectively, esp. to a large gathering. [C14: from L *prōicere* to throw down]

projectile (prə'dʒektaɪl) *n.* **1.** an object thrown forwards. **2.** any self-propelling missile, esp. a rocket. **3.** any object that can be fired from a gun, such as a shell. ~*adj.* **4.** designed to be hurled forwards. **5.** projecting forwards. **6.** *Zool.* another word for **protrusile.** [C17: from NL *prōjectilis* jutting forwards]

projection (prə'dʒekʃən) *n.* **1.** the act of projecting or the state of being projected. **2.** a part that juts out. **3.** See **map projection. 4.** the representation of a line, figure, or solid on a given plane as it would be seen from a particular direction or in accordance with an accepted set of rules. **5.** a scheme or plan. **6.** a prediction based on known evidence and observations. **7. a.** the process of showing film on a screen. **b.** the images shown. **8.** *Psychol.* **a.** the belief that others share one's subjective mental life. **b.** the process of projecting one's own hidden desires and impulses. —**pro'jectional** *adj.* —**pro'jective** *adj.*

projectionist (prə'dʒekʃənɪst) *n.* a person responsible for the operation of film projection machines.

projective geometry *n.* the branch of geometry concerned with the properties of solids that are invariant under projection and section.

projector (prə'dʒektə) *n.* **1.** an optical instrument that projects an enlarged image of individual slides. Full name: **slide projector. 2.** an optical instrument in which a film is wound past a lens so that the frames can be viewed as a continuously moving sequence. Full name: **film** or **cine projector. 3.** a device for projecting a light beam. **4.** a person who devises projects.

prokaryote or **procaryote** (prəʊ'kærɪəʊt) *n.* an organism having cells in which the genetic material is in a single filament of DNA, not enclosed in a nucleus. Cf. **eukaryote.** [from PRO- + KARYO- + -*ote* as in *zygote*]

Prokofiev (prə'kɒfɪˌef; *Russian* pra'kɔfjɪf) *n.* **Sergei Sergeyevich** (sɪr'gjej sɪr'gjejɪvɪtʃ). 1891–1953, Soviet composer. His compositions include the orchestral fairy tale *Peter and the Wolf* (1936), the opera *The Love for Three Oranges* (1921), and seven symphonies.

Prokopyevsk (*Russian* pra'kɔpjɪfsk) *n.* a city in the S Soviet Union, in Kemerovo Region: the chief coal-mining centre of the Kuznetsk Basin. Pop.: 278 000 (1987).

prolapse ('prəʊlæps, prəʊ'læps) *Pathol.* ~*n.* **1.** Also: **prolapsus** (prəʊ'læpsəs). the sinking or falling down of an organ or part. ~*vb.* (*intr.*) **2.** (of an organ, etc.) to sink from its normal position. [C17: from L *prōlābī* to slide along]

prolate ('prəʊleɪt) *adj.* having a polar diameter of greater length than the equatorial diameter. Cf. **oblate¹.** [C17: from L *prōferre* to enlarge] —'**prolately** *adv.*

prole (prəʊl) *n., adj. Derog. sl., chiefly Brit.* short for **proletarian.**

prolegomenon (ˌprəʊlɛ'gɒmɪnən) *n., pl.* **-na** (-nə). (*often pl.*) a preliminary discussion, esp. a formal critical introduction to a lengthy text. [C17: from Gk, from *prolegein*, from PRO-² + *legein* to say] —'**prole'gomenal** *adj.*

prolepsis (prəʊ'lepsɪs) *n., pl.* **-ses** (-siːz). **1.** a rhetorical device by which objections are anticipated and answered in advance. **2.** use of a word after a verb in anticipation of its becoming applicable through the action of the verb, as *flat* in *hammer it flat.* [C16: via LL from Gk: anticipation, from *prolambanein* to anticipate, from PRO-² + *lambanein* to take] —**pro'leptic** *adj.*

proletarian (ˌprəʊlɪ'tɛərɪən) *adj.* **1.** of or belonging to the proletariat. ~*n.* **2.** a member of the proletariat. [C17: from L *prōlētārius* one whose only contribution to the state was his offspring, from *prōlēs* offspring] —ˌ**prole'tarianism** *n.*

proletariat (ˌprəʊlɪ'tɛərɪət) *n.* **1.** all wage-earners collectively. **2.** the lower or working class. **3.** (in Marxist theory) the class of wage-earners, esp. industrial workers, in a capitalist society, whose only possession of significant material value is their labour. **4.** (in ancient Rome) the lowest class of citizens, who had no property. [C19: via F from L *prōlētārius* PROLETARIAN]

ˌ**proimmi'gration** *adj.*   ˌ**prointe'gration** *adj.*   ˌ**proin'vestment** *adj.*

pro'industry *adj.*   ˌ**prointer'vention** *adj.*   **pro'labour** *adj.*

proliferate (prə'lɪfə,reɪt) vb. **1.** to grow or reproduce (new parts, cells, etc.) rapidly. **2.** to grow or increase rapidly. [C19: from Med. L *prōlifer* having offspring, from L *prōlēs* offspring + *ferre* to bear] —**pro,lifer'ation** n. —**pro'liferative** adj.

prolific (prə'lɪfɪk) adj. **1.** producing fruit, offspring, etc., in abundance. **2.** producing constant or successful results. **3.** (often foll. by *in* or *of*) rich or fruitful. [C17: from Med. L *prōlificus*, from L *prōlēs* offspring] —**pro'lifically** adv. —**pro'lificness** or **pro'lificacy** n.

prolix ('prəʊlɪks, prəʊ'lɪks) adj. **1.** (of a speech, book, etc.) so long as to be boring. **2.** long-winded. [C15: from L *prōlixus* stretched out widely, from *līquī* to flow] —**pro'lixity** n. —**pro'lixly** adv.

prolocutor (prəʊ'lɒkjʊtə) n. a chairman, esp. of the lower house of clergy in a convocation of the Anglican Church. [C15: from L: advocate, from *loquī* to speak] —**pro'locutorship** n.

prologue or U.S. (often) **prolog** ('prəʊlɒg) n. **1.** the prefatory lines introducing a play or speech. **2.** a preliminary act or event. **3.** (in early opera) **a.** an introductory scene in which a narrator summarizes the main action of the work. **b.** a brief independent play preceding the opera, esp. in honour of a patron. ~vb. **-loguing, -logued** or U.S. **-loging, -loged. 4.** (tr.) to introduce with a prologue. [C13: from L *prologus*, from Gk, from PRO-² + *logos* discourse]

prolong (prə'lɒŋ) vb. (tr.) to lengthen; extend. [C15: from LL *prōlongāre* to extend, from L PRO-¹ + *longus* long] —**prolongation** (,prəʊlɒŋ'geɪʃən) n.

prolusion (prə'lu:ʒən) n. **1.** a preliminary written exercise. **2.** an introductory essay. [C17: from L *prōlūsiō*, from *prōlūdere* to practise beforehand, from PRO-¹ + *lūdere* to play] —**prolusory** (prə'lu:zərɪ) adj.

prom (prɒm) n. **1.** Brit. short for **promenade** (sense 1) or **promenade concert. 2.** U.S. & Canad. inf. a formal dance held at a high school or college.

PROM (prɒm) n. Computers. acronym for Programmable Read Only Memory.

promenade (,prɒmə'nɑ:d) n. **1.** Chiefly Brit. a public walk, esp. at a seaside resort. **2.** a leisurely walk, esp. one in a public place for pleasure or display. **3.** a marchlike step in dancing. **4.** a marching sequence in a square or country dance. ~vb. **5.** to take a promenade in or through (a place). **6.** (intr.) Dancing. to perform a promenade. **7.** (tr.) to display or exhibit (someone or oneself) on or as if on a promenade. [C16: from F, from *promener* to lead out for a walk, from LL *prōmināre* to drive (cattle) along, from *mināre* to drive, prob. from *minārī* to threaten] —**,prome'nader** n.

promenade concert n. a concert at which some of the audience stand rather than sit.

promenade deck n. an upper covered deck of a passenger ship for the use of the passengers.

promethazine (prəʊ'mɛθə,zi:n) n. an antihistamine drug used to treat allergies and to prevent vomiting. [C20: from PRO(PYL) + (DI-¹) + METH(YL + AMINE) + AZINE]

Prometheus (prə'mi:θɪəs) n. Greek myth. a Titan, who stole fire from Olympus to give to mankind and in punishment was chained to a rock, where an eagle tore at his liver until Hercules freed him. —**Pro'methean** adj., n.

promethium (prə'mi:θɪəm) n. a radioactive element of the lanthanide series artificially produced by the fission of uranium. Symbol: Pm; atomic no.: 61; half-life of most stable isotope, ¹⁴⁵Pm: 17.7 years. [C20: NL from PROMETHEUS]

prominence ('prɒmɪnəns) n. **1.** the state of being prominent. **2.** something that is prominent, such as a protuberance. **3.** relative importance. **4.** Astron. an eruption of incandescent gas from the sun's surface, visible during a total eclipse.

prominent ('prɒmɪnənt) adj. **1.** jutting or projecting outwards. **2.** standing out from its surroundings; noticeable. **3.** widely known; eminent. [C16: from L *prōmināre* to jut out, from PRO-¹ + *ēminēre* to project] —**'prominently** adv.

promiscuous (prə'mɪskjʊəs) adj. **1.** indulging in casual and indiscriminate sexual relationships. **2.** consisting of a number of dissimilar parts or elements mingled indiscriminately. **3.** indiscriminate in selection. **4.** casual or heedless. [C17: from L *prōmiscuus* indiscriminate, from

PRO-¹ + *miscēre* to mix] —**pro'miscuously** adv. —**promiscuity** (,prɒmɪ'skju:ɪtɪ) or **pro'miscuousness** n.

promise ('prɒmɪs) vb. **1.** (often foll. by *to*; when tr., may take a clause as object or an infinitive) to give an assurance of (something to someone): *I promise that I will come.* **2.** (tr.) to undertake to give (something to someone): *he promised me a car for my birthday.* **3.** (when tr., takes an infinitive) to cause people to expect that one is likely (to be or do something): *she promises to be a fine soprano.* **4.** (tr.; usually passive) Obs. to betroth: *I'm promised to Bill.* **5.** (tr.) to assure (someone) of the authenticity or inevitability of something: *there'll be trouble, I promise you.* ~n. **6.** an assurance given by one person to another agreeing or guaranteeing to do or not to do something. **7.** indication of forthcoming excellence: *a writer showing considerable promise.* **8.** the thing of which an assurance is given. [C14: from L *prōmissum* a promise, from *prōmittere* to send forth] —**,promi'see** n. —**'promiser** or (Law) **'promisor** n.

Promised Land n. **1.** Old Testament. the land of Canaan, promised by God to Abraham and his descendants as their heritage (Genesis 12:7). **2.** Christianity. heaven. **3.** any longed-for place where one expects to find greater happiness.

promising ('prɒmɪsɪŋ) adj. showing promise of future success. —**'promisingly** adv.

promissory ('prɒmɪsərɪ) adj. **1.** containing, relating to, or having the nature of a promise. **2.** Insurance. stipulating how the provisions of an insurance contract will be fulfilled.

promissory note n. Commerce. a document containing a signed promise to pay a stated sum of money to a specified person at a designated date or on demand. Also called: **note, note of hand.**

promo ('prəʊməʊ) n., pl. **-mos.** Inf. something used to promote a product, esp. a videotape film used to promote a pop record. [C20: shortened from *promotion*]

promontory ('prɒməntərɪ, -trɪ) n., pl. **-ries. 1.** a high point of land, esp. of rocky coast, that juts out into the sea. **2.** Anat. any of various projecting structures. [C16: from L *prōmunturium* headland]

promote (prə'məʊt) vb. (tr.) **1.** to encourage the progress or existence of. **2.** to raise to a higher rank, status, etc. **3.** to advance (a pupil or student) to a higher course, class, etc. **4.** to work for: *to promote reform.* **5.** to encourage the sale of (a product) by advertising or securing financial support. [C14: from L *prōmovēre* to push onwards] —**pro'motion** n. —**pro'motional** adj.

promoter (prə'məʊtə) n. **1.** a person or thing that promotes. **2.** a person who helps to organize, develop, or finance an undertaking. **3.** a person who organizes and finances a sporting event, esp. a boxing match.

prompt (prɒmpt) adj. **1.** performed or executed without delay. **2.** quick or ready to act or respond. ~adv. **3.** Inf. punctually. ~vb. **4.** (tr.) to urge (someone to do something). **5.** to remind (an actor, singer, etc.) of lines forgotten during a performance. **6.** (tr.) to refresh the memory of. **7.** (tr.) to give rise to by suggestion: *his affairs will prompt discussion.* ~n. **8.** Commerce. **a.** the time limit allowed for payment of the debt incurred by purchasing on credit. **b.** Also called: **prompt note.** a memorandum sent to a purchaser to remind him of the time limit and the sum due. **9.** anything that serves to remind. [C15: from L *promptus* evident, from *prōmere* to produce, from *emere* to buy] —**'promptly** adv. —**'promptness** n.

prompter ('prɒmptə) n. **1.** a person offstage who reminds the actors of forgotten lines or cues. **2.** a person, thing, etc., that prompts.

promptitude ('prɒmptɪ,tju:d) n. the quality of being prompt; punctuality.

prompt side n. Theatre. the side of the stage where the prompter is, usually to the actor's left in Britain and to his right in the United States.

promulgate ('prɒməl,geɪt) vb. (tr.) **1.** to put into effect (a law, decree, etc.), esp. by formal proclamation. **2.** to announce officially. **3.** to make widespread. [C16: from L *prōmulgāre* to bring to public knowledge] —**,promul'gation** n. —**'promul,gator** n.

pron. abbrev. for: **1.** pronominal. **2.** pronoun. **3.** pronounced. **4.** pronunciation.

---

pro'military adj.　　　**,promi'nority** adj.　　　**pro'modern** adj.　　　**pro'monarchist** adj., n.

pronate (prəʊ'neɪt) *vb.* (*tr.*) to turn (the forearm or hand) so that the palmar surface is directed downwards. [C19: from LL *prōnāre* to bow] —**pro'nation** *n.* —**pro'nator** *n.*

prone (prəʊn) *adj.* **1.** lying flat or face downwards; prostrate. **2.** sloping or tending downwards. **3.** having an inclination to do something. [C14: from L *prōnus* bent forward, from PRO-[1]] —**'pronely** *adv.* —**'proneness** *n.*

-prone *adj. combining form.* liable or disposed to suffer: *accident-prone.*

prong (prɒŋ) *n.* **1.** a sharply pointed end of an instrument, such as on a fork. **2.** any pointed projecting part. ~*vb.* **3.** (*tr.*) to prick or spear with or as if with a prong. [C15] —**pronged** *adj.*

pronghorn ('prɒŋ,hɔːn) *n.* a ruminant mammal inhabiting rocky deserts of North America and having small branched horns. Also called: **American antelope.**

pronominal (prəʊ'nɒmɪn³l) *adj.* relating to or playing the part of a pronoun. [C17: from LL *prōnōminālis*, from *prōnōmen* a PRONOUN] —**pro'nominally** *adv.*

pronoun ('prəʊ,naʊn) *n.* one of a class of words that serves to replace a noun or noun phrase that has already been or is about to be mentioned in the sentence or context. Abbrev.: **pron.** [C16: from L *prōnōmen*, from PRO-[1] + *nōmen* noun]

pronounce (prə'naʊns) *vb.* **1.** to utter or articulate (a sound or sounds). **2.** (*tr.*) to utter (words) in the correct way. **3.** (*tr.; may take a clause as object*) to proclaim officially: *I now pronounce you man and wife.* **4.** (when *tr.*, *may take a clause as object*) to declare as one's judgment: *to pronounce the death sentence upon someone.* [C14: from L *prōnuntiāre* to announce] —**pro'nounceable** *adj.* —**pro'nouncer** *n.*

pronounced (prə'naʊnst) *adj.* **1.** strongly marked or indicated. **2.** (of a sound) articulated with vibration of the vocal cords; voiced. —**pronouncedly** (prə'naʊnsɪdlɪ) *adv.*

pronouncement (prə'naʊnsmənt) *n.* **1.** an official or authoritative announcement. **2.** the act of declaring or uttering formally.

pronto ('prɒntəʊ) *adv. Inf.* at once. [C20: from Sp.: quick, from L *promptus* PROMPT]

pronunciation (prə,nʌnsɪ'eɪʃən) *n.* **1.** the act, instance, or manner of pronouncing sounds. **2.** the supposedly correct manner of pronouncing sounds in a given language. **3.** a phonetic transcription of a word.

proof (pruːf) *n.* **1.** any evidence that establishes or helps to establish the truth, validity, quality, etc., of something. **2.** *Law.* the whole body of evidence upon which the verdict of a court is based. **3.** *Maths, logic.* a sequence of steps or statements that establishes the truth of a proposition. **4.** the act of testing the truth of something (esp. in **put to the proof**). **5.** *Scots Law.* trial before a judge without a jury. **6.** *Printing.* a trial impression made from composed type for the correction of errors. **7.** (in engraving, etc.) a print made by an artist or under his supervision for his own satisfaction before he hands the plate over to a professional printer. **8.** *Photog.* a trial print from a negative. **9. a.** the alcoholic strength of proof spirit. **b.** the strength of a liquor as measured on a scale in which the strength of proof spirit is 100 degrees. ~*adj.* **10.** (*usually postpositive;* foll. by *against*) impervious (to): *the roof is proof against rain.* **11.** having the alcoholic strength of proof spirit. **12.** of proved impenetrability: *proof armour.* ~*vb.* **13.** (*tr.*) to take a proof from (type matter, a plate, etc.). **14.** to proofread (text) or inspect (a print, etc.), as for approval. **15.** to render (something) proof, esp. to waterproof. [C13: from OF *preuve* a test, from LL *proba*, from L *probāre* to test]

-proof *adj., vb. combining form.* (to make) impervious to; secure against (damage by): *waterproof.* [from PROOF (adj.)]

proofread ('pruːf,riːd) *vb.* **-reading, -read** (-,rɛd). to read (copy or printer's proofs) and mark errors to be corrected. —**'proof,reader** *n.*

proof spirit *n.* (in Britain) a mixture of alcohol and water or an alcoholic beverage that contains 49.28 per cent of alcohol by weight, 57.1 per cent by volume at 51°F: used until 1980 as a standard of alcoholic liquids.

prop[1] (prɒp) *vb.* **propping, propped.** (*tr.; often foll. by up*) **1.** to support with a rigid object, such as a stick. **2.** (usually also foll. by *against*) to place or lean on. **3.** to sustain or support. ~*n.* **4.** something that gives rigid support, such as a stick. **5.** short for **clothes prop. 6.** a person or thing giving support, as of a moral nature. **7.** *Rugby.* either of the forwards at either end of the front row of a scrum. [C15]

prop[2] (prɒp) *n.* short for **property** (sense 8).

prop[3] (prɒp) *n.* an informal word for **propeller.**

prop. *abbrev. for:* **1.** proper(ly). **2.** property. **3.** proposition. **4.** proprietor.

propaedeutic (,prəʊpɪ'djuːtɪk) *n.* **1.** (*often pl.*) preparatory instruction basic to further study of an art or science. ~*adj. also* **propaedeutical. 2.** of, relating to, or providing such instruction. [C19: from Gk *propaideuein* to teach in advance, from PRO-[2] + *paideuein* to rear]

propaganda (,prɒpə'gændə) *n.* **1.** the organized dissemination of information, allegations, etc., to assist or damage the cause of a government, movement, etc. **2.** such information, allegations, etc. [C18: from It., use of *propaganda* in the NL title *Sacra Congregatio de Propaganda Fide* Sacred Congregation for Propagating the Faith] —,**propa'gandism** *n.* —,**propa'gandist** *n., adj.*

Propaganda (,prɒpə'gændə) *n. R.C. Church.* a congregation responsible for directing the work of the foreign missions.

propagandize *or* **-ise** (,prɒpə'gændaɪz) *vb.* **1.** (*tr.*) to spread by, or subject to, propaganda. **2.** (*intr.*) to spread or organize propaganda.

propagate ('prɒpə,geɪt) *vb.* **1.** *Biol.* to reproduce or cause to reproduce; breed. **2.** (*tr.*) *Horticulture.* to produce (plants) by layering, grafting, cuttings, etc. **3.** (*tr.*) to promulgate. **4.** *Physics.* to transmit, esp. in the form of a wave: *to propagate sound.* **5.** (*tr.*) to transmit (characteristics) from one generation to the next. [C16: from L *propāgāre* to increase (plants) by cuttings, from *propāgēs* a cutting, from *pangere* to fasten] —,**propa'gation** *n.* —,**propagative** *adj.* —**'prop-a,gator** *n.*

propane ('prəʊpeɪn) *n.* a flammable gaseous alkane found in petroleum and used as a fuel. Formula: $CH_3CH_2CH_3$. [C19: from PROPIONIC (ACID) + -ANE]

propanoic acid (,prəʊpə'nəʊɪk) *n.* a colourless liquid carboxylic acid used in inhibiting the growth of moulds in bread. Formula: CH_3CH_2COOH. Former name: **propionic acid.** [C20: from PROPANE + -OIC]

pro patria *Latin.* ('prəʊ 'pætrɪ,ɑː) for one's country.

propel (prə'pɛl) *vb.* **-pelling, -pelled.** (*tr.*) to impel, drive, or cause to move forwards. [C15: from L *prōpellere*] —**pro'pellant** *or* **pro'pellent** *n.*

propeller (prə'pɛlə) *n.* **1.** a device having blades radiating from a central hub that is rotated to produce thrust to propel a ship, aircraft, etc. **2.** a person or thing that propels.

propelling pencil *n.* a pencil consisting of a metal or plastic case containing a replaceable lead. As the point is worn away the lead can be extended, usually by turning part of the case.

propene ('prəʊpiːn) *n.* a colourless gaseous alkene obtained by cracking petroleum. Formula: $CH_3CH:CH_2$. Also called: **propylene.**

propensity (prə'pɛnsɪtɪ) *n., pl.* **-ties. 1.** a natural tendency. **2.** *Obs.* partiality. [C16: from L *prōpensus* inclined to, from *prōpendēre* to hang forwards]

proper ('prɒpə) *adj.* **1.** (*usually prenominal*) appropriate or usual: *in its proper place.* **2.** suited to a particular purpose: *use the proper knife to cut the bread.* **3.** correct in behaviour. **4.** vigorously or excessively moral. **5.** up to a required or regular standard. **6.** (*immediately postpositive*) (of an object, quality, etc.) referred to so as to exclude anything not directly connected with it: *his claim is connected with the deed proper.* **7.** (*postpositive;* foll. by *to*) belonging to or characteristic of a person or thing. **8.** (*prenominal*) *Brit. inf.* (intensifier) *I felt a proper fool.* **9.** (*usually postpositive*) (of heraldic colours) considered correct for the natural colour of the object depicted: *three martlets proper.* **10.** *Arch.* pleasant or good. **11. good and proper.** *Inf.* thoroughly. ~*n.* **12.** the parts of the Mass that vary according to the particular day or feast on which the Mass is celebrated. [C13: via OF from L *prōprius* special] —**'properly** *adv.* —**'properness** *n.*

---

pro'nationalist *adj., n.*

proper fraction *n.* a fraction in which the numerator has a lower absolute value than the denominator, as $\frac{1}{2}$ or $x/(3 + x^2)$.

proper motion *n.* the very small continuous change in the direction of motion of a star relative to the sun.

proper noun *or* **name** *n.* the name of a person, place, or object, as for example *Iceland, Patrick,* or *Uranus.* Cf. **common noun.**

propertied ('prɒpətɪd) *adj.* owning land or property.

Propertius (prə'pɜːʃɪəs, -ʃəs) *n.* **Sextus** ('sɛkstəs). ?50– ?15 B.C., Roman elegiac poet.

property ('prɒpətɪ) *n., pl.* **-ties.** **1.** something of value, either tangible, such as land, or intangible, such as copyrights. **2.** *Law.* the right to possess, use, and dispose of anything. **3.** possessions collectively. **4. a.** land or real estate. **b.** *(as modifier):* **property rights.** **5.** *Chiefly Austral.* a ranch or station. **6.** a quality or characteristic attribute, such as the density or strength of a material. **7.** *Logic, obs.* Also called: **proprium** ('prəʊpɪəm). an attribute that is not essential to a species but is common and peculiar to it. **8.** any movable object used on the set of a stage play or film. Usually shortened to **prop.** [C13: from OF *propriété,* from L *proprietās* something personal, from *proprius* one's own]

property centre *n.* a service for buying and selling property, including conveyancing, provided by a group of local solicitors. In full: **solicitors' property centre.**

property man *n.* a member of the stage crew in charge of the stage properties. Usually shortened to **propman.**

prophecy ('prɒfɪsɪ) *n., pl.* **-cies. 1. a.** a message of divine truth revealing God's will. **b.** the act of uttering such a message. **2.** a prediction or guess. **3.** the charismatic endowment of a prophet. [C13: ult. from Gk *prophētēs* PROPHET]

prophesy ('prɒfɪˌsaɪ) *vb.* **-sying, -sied. 1.** to foretell (something) by or as if by divine inspiration. **2.** *(intr.) Arch.* to give instructions in religious subjects. [C14 *prophecien,* from PROPHECY] —'**prophe,siable** *adj.* —'**prophe,sier** *n.*

prophet ('prɒfɪt) *n.* **1.** a person who supposedly speaks by divine inspiration, esp. one through whom a divinity expresses his will. **2.** a person who predicts the future: *a prophet of doom.* **3.** a spokesman for a movement, doctrine, etc. [C13: from OF *prophète,* from L, from Gk *prophētēs* one who declares the divine will, from PRO-² + *phanai* to speak] —'**prophetess** *fem. n.*

Prophet ('prɒfɪt) *n.* **the. 1.** the principal designation of Mohammed as the founder of Islam. **2.** a name for Joseph Smith as the founder of the Mormon Church.

prophetic (prə'fɛtɪk) *adj.* **1.** of or relating to a prophet or prophecy. **2.** of the nature of a prophecy; predictive. —**pro'phetically** *adv.*

prophylactic (ˌprɒfɪ'læktɪk) *adj.* **1.** protecting from or preventing disease. **2.** protective or preventive. ~*n.* **3.** a prophylactic drug or device. **4.** *Chiefly U.S.* another name for **condom.** [C16: via F from Gk *prophulaktikos,* from *prophulassein* to guard by taking advance measures, from PRO-² + *phulax* a guard]

prophylaxis (ˌprɒfɪ'læksɪs) *n.* the prevention of disease or control of its possible spread.

propinquity (prə'pɪŋkwɪtɪ) *n.* **1.** nearness in place or time. **2.** nearness in relationship. [C14: from L *propinquitās,* from *propinquus* near, from *prope* nearby]

propionic acid (ˌprəʊpɪ'ɒnɪk) *n.* the former name for **propanoic acid.** [C19: from Gk *pro-* first + *pionic,* from *piōn* fat, because it is first in order of the fatty acids]

propitiate (prə'pɪʃɪˌeɪt) *vb. (tr.)* to appease or make well disposed; conciliate. [C17: from L *propitiāre,* from *propitius* gracious] —**pro'pitiable** *adj.* —**pro,piti'ation** *n.* —**pro'pitiative** *adj.* —**pro'piti,ator** *n.* —**pro'pitiatory** *adj.*

propitious (prə'pɪʃəs) *adj.* **1.** favourable or auspicious. **2.** gracious or favourably inclined. [C15: from L *propitius* well disposed, from *prope* close to] —**pro'pitiously** *adv.* —**pro'pitiousness** *n.*

propjet ('prɒpˌdʒɛt) *n.* another name for **turboprop.**

propolis ('prɒpəlɪs) *n.* a greenish-brown resinous aromatic substance collected by bees from the buds of trees for use in the construction of hives. Also called: **bee glue, hive dross.** [C17: via L from Gk: suburb, bee glue, from *pro-* before + *polis* city]

proponent (prə'pəʊnənt) *n.* a person who argues in favour of something or puts forward a proposal, etc. [C16: from L *prōpōnere* to PROPOSE]

Propontis (prə'pɒntɪs) *n.* the ancient name for (the Sea of) **Marmara.**

proportion (prə'pɔːʃən) *n.* **1.** relative magnitude or extent; ratio. **2.** correct or desirable relationship between parts; symmetry. **3.** a part considered with respect to the whole. **4.** *(pl.)* dimensions or size: *a building of vast proportions.* **5.** a share or quota. **6.** a relationship that maintains a constant ratio between two variable quantities: *prices increase in proportion to manufacturing costs.* **7.** *Maths.* a relationship between four numbers or quantities in which the ratio of the first pair equals the ratio of the second pair. ~*vb. (tr.)* **8.** to adjust in relative amount, size, etc. **9.** to cause to be harmonious in relationship of parts. [C14: from L *prōportiō,* from *prō portione,* lit.: for (its, one's) PORTION] —**pro'portionable** *adj.* —**pro'portionment** *n.*

proportional (prə'pɔːʃənˀl) *adj.* **1.** of, involving, or being in proportion. ~*n.* **2.** *Maths.* an unknown term in a proportion: *in a/b = c/x, x is the fourth proportional.* —**pro,portion'ality** *n.* —**pro'portionally** *adv.*

proportional representation *n.* representation of parties in an elective body in proportion to the votes they win. Abbrev.: **PR.**

proportionate *adj.* (prə'pɔːʃənɪt). **1.** being in proper proportion. ~*vb.* (prə'pɔːʃəˌneɪt). **2.** *(tr.)* to make proportionate. —**pro'portionately** *adv.*

proposal (prə'pəʊzˀl) *n.* **1.** the act of proposing. **2.** something proposed, as a plan. **3.** an offer, esp. of marriage.

propose (prə'pəʊz) *vb.* **1.** (when *tr., may take a clause as object)* to put forward (a plan, etc.) for consideration. **2.** *(tr.)* to nominate, as for a position. **3.** *(tr.)* to intend (to do something): *I propose to leave town now.* **4.** *(tr.)* to announce the drinking of (a toast). **5.** *(intr.; often foll. by to)* to make an offer of marriage. [C14: from OF *proposer,* from L *prōpōnere* to display, from PRO-¹ + *pōnere* to place] —**pro'posable** *adj.* —**pro'poser** *n.*

proposition (ˌprɒpə'zɪʃən) *n.* **1.** a proposal for consideration. **2.** *Logic.* the content of a sentence that affirms or denies something and is capable of being true or false. **3.** *Maths.* a statement or theorem, usually containing its proof. **4.** *Inf.* a person or matter to be dealt with: *he's a difficult proposition.* **5.** *Inf.* an invitation to engage in sexual intercourse. ~*vb.* **6.** *(tr.)* to propose a plan, deal, etc., to, esp. to engage in sexual intercourse. [C14 *proposicioun,* from L *prōpositiō* a setting forth; see PROPOSE] —,**propo'sitional** *adj.*

propositional calculus *n.* the system of symbolic logic concerned only with the relations between propositions as wholes, taking no account of their internal structure. Cf. **predicate calculus.**

propound (prə'paʊnd) *vb. (tr.)* **1.** to put forward for consideration. **2.** *English law.* to produce (a will or similar instrument) to the proper court or authority for its validity to be established. [C16 *propone,* from L *prōpōnere* to set forth, from PRO-¹ + *pōnere* to place] —**pro'pounder** *n.*

propranolol (prəʊ'prænəˌlɒl) *n.* a drug used in the treatment of heart disease.

proprietary (prə'praɪɪtərɪ, -trɪ) *adj.* **1.** of or belonging to property or proprietors. **2.** privately owned and controlled. **3.** *Med.* denoting a drug manufactured and distributed under a trade name. ~*n., pl.* **-taries. 4.** *Med.* a proprietary drug. **5.** a proprietor or proprietors collectively. **6. a.** right to property. **b.** property owned. **7.** (in Colonial America) an owner of a **proprietary colony,** a colony which was granted by the Crown to a particular person or group. [C15: from LL *proprietārius* an owner, from *proprius* one's own] —**pro'prietarily** *adv.*

proprietary name *n.* a name which is restricted in use by virtue of being a trade name.

proprietor (prə'praɪətə) *n.* **1.** an owner of a business. **2.** a person enjoying exclusive right of ownership to some property. —**proprietorial** (prəˌpraɪə'tɔːrɪəl) *adj.* —**pro'prietress** *or* **pro'prietrix** *fem. n.*

propriety (prə'praɪɪtɪ) *n., pl.* **-ties. 1.** the quality or state of being appropriate or fitting. **2.** conformity to the prevailing standard of behaviour, speech, etc. **3. the proprieties.** the standards of behaviour considered correct by polite society. [C15: from OF *propriété*, from L *proprietās* a peculiarity, from *proprius* one's own]

proprioceptor (ˌprəʊprɪəˈsɛptə) *n. Physiol.* any receptor, as in the inner ear, muscles, etc., that supplies information about the state of the body. [C20: from *proprio-*, from L *proprius* one's own + RECEPTOR] —ˌproprio'ceptive *adj.*

proptosis (prɒpˈtəʊsɪs) *n., pl.* **-ses** (-siːz). *Pathol.* the forward displacement of an organ or part, such as the eyeball. [C17: via LL from Gk, from *propiptein* to fall forwards]

propulsion (prəˈpʌlʃən) *n.* **1.** the act of propelling or the state of being propelled. **2.** a propelling force. [C15: from L *prōpellere* to propel] —**propulsive** (prəˈpʌlsɪv) *or* **pro'pulsory** *adj.*

propyl ('prəʊpɪl) *n.* (*modifier*) of or containing the monovalent group of atoms C_3H_7 -. [C19: from PROP(IONIC ACID) + -YL]

propylaeum (ˌprɒpɪˈliːəm) *or* **propylon** ('prɒpɪˌlɒn) *n., pl.* **-laea** (-'liːə) *or* **-lons, -la** (-lə). a portico, esp. one that forms the entrance to a temple. [C18: via L from Gk *propulaion* before the gate, from PRO-[2] + *pulē* gate]

propylene ('prəʊpɪˌliːn) *n.* another name for **propene**. [C19]

propylene glycol *n.* a colourless viscous compound used as an antifreeze and brake fluid. Formula: $CH_3CH(OH)CH_2OH$. Systematic name: **1,2-dihydroxypropane**.

pro rata ('prəʊ 'rɑːtə) in proportion. [Med. L]

prorate (prəʊˈreɪt, 'prəʊreɪt) *vb. Chiefly U.S. & Canad.* to divide, assess, or distribute proportionately. [C19: from PRO RATA] —**pro'ratable** *adj.* —**pro'ration** *n.*

prorogue (prəˈrəʊg) *vb.* to discontinue the meetings of (a legislative body) without dissolving it. [C15: from L *prorogāre*, lit.: to ask publicly] —**prorogation** (ˌprəʊrəˈgeɪʃən) *n.*

prosaic (prəʊˈzeɪɪk) *adj.* **1.** lacking imagination. **2.** having the characteristics of prose. [C16: from LL *prōsaicus*, from L *prōsa* PROSE] —**pro'saically** *adv.*

pros and cons *pl. n.* the various arguments in favour of and against a motion, course of action, etc. [C16: from L *prō* for + *con*, from *contrā* against]

proscenium (prəˈsiːnɪəm) *n., pl.* **-nia** (-nɪə) *or* **-niums**. **1.** the arch or opening separating the stage from the auditorium together with the area immediately in front of the arch. **2.** (in ancient theatres) the stage itself. [C17: via L from Gk *proskēnion*, from *pro-* before + *skēnē* scene]

prosciutto (prəʊˈʃuːtəʊ; *Italian* proˈʃutto) *n.* cured ham from Italy: usually served as an hors d'oeuvre. [It., lit.: dried beforehand]

proscribe (prəʊˈskraɪb) *vb.* (*tr.*) **1.** to condemn or prohibit. **2.** to outlaw; banish; exile. [C16: from L *prōscrībere* to put up a public notice, from *prō-* in public + *scrībere* to write] —**pro'scriber** *n.* —**proscription** (prəʊˈskrɪpʃən) *n.*

prose (prəʊz) *n.* **1.** spoken or written language distinguished from poetry by its lack of a marked metrical structure. **2.** a passage set for translation into a foreign language. **3.** commonplace or dull discourse, expression, etc. **4.** (*modifier*) written in prose. **5.** (*modifier*) matter-of-fact. ~*vb.* **6.** to write (something) in prose. **7.** (*intr.*) to speak or write in a tedious style. [C14: via OF from L *prōsa ōrātiō* straightforward speech, from *prorsus* prosaic, from *prōvertere* to turn forwards] —**'prose,like** *adj.*

prosecute ('prɒsɪˌkjuːt) *vb.* **1.** (*tr.*) to bring a criminal action against (a person). **2.** (*intr.*) **a.** to seek redress by legal proceedings. **b.** to institute or conduct a prosecution. **3.** (*tr.*) to practise (a profession or trade). **4.** (*tr.*) to continue to do (a task, etc.). [C15: from L *prōsequī* to follow] —**'prose,cutable** *adj.* —**'prose,cutor** *n.*

prosecution (ˌprɒsɪˈkjuːʃən) *n.* **1.** the act of prosecuting or the state of being prosecuted. **2. a.** the institution and conduct of legal proceedings against a person. **b.** the proceedings brought in the name of the Crown to put an accused on trial. **3.** the lawyers acting for the Crown to put the case against a person. **4.** the following up or carrying on of something begun.

proselyte ('prɒsɪˌlaɪt) *n.* **1.** a person newly converted to a religious faith, esp. a Gentile converted to Judaism. ~*vb.*

2. a less common word for **proselytize**. [C14: from Church L *prosēlytus*, from Gk *prosēlutos* recent arrival, convert, from *proserchesthai* to draw near] —**proselytism** ('prɒsɪlɪˌtɪzəm) *n.* —**proselytic** (ˌprɒsɪˈlɪtɪk) *adj.*

proselytize *or* **-ise** ('prɒsɪlɪˌtaɪz) *vb.* to convert (someone) from one religious faith to another. —**'proselyt,izer** *or* -,**iser** *n.*

prosencephalon (ˌprɒsɛnˈsɛfəlɒn) *n., pl.* **-la** (-lə). the part of the brain that develops from the anterior portion of the neural tube. Nontechnical name: **forebrain**. [C19: from NL, from Gk *prosō* forward + *enkephalos* brain]

prosenchyma (prɒsˈɛŋkɪmə) *n.* a plant tissue consisting of long narrow cells with pointed ends: occurs in conducting tissue. [C19: from NL, from Gk *pros-* towards + *enkhuma* infusion]

Proserpina (prəʊˈsɜːpɪnə) *n.* the Roman goddess of the underworld. Greek counterpart: **Persephone**.

prosimian (prəʊˈsɪmɪən) *n.* **1.** any of a primitive suborder of primates, including lemurs, lorises, and tarsiers. ~*adj.* **2.** of or belonging to this suborder. [C19: via NL from L *sīmia* ape]

prosit *German.* ('prɔːzɪt) *sentence substitute.* good health! cheers! [G, from L, lit.: may it prove beneficial]

prosody ('prɒsədɪ) *n.* **1.** the study of poetic metre and of the art of versification. **2.** a system of versification. **3.** the patterns of stress and intonation in a language. [C15: from L *prosōdia* accent of a syllable, from Gk *prosōidia* song set to music, from *pros* towards + *ōidē*, from *aoidē* song; see ODE] —**prosodic** (prəˈsɒdɪk) *adj.* —**'prosodist** *n.*

prosopopoeia *or* **prosopopeia** (ˌprɒsəpəˈpiːə) *n.* **1.** *Rhetoric.* another word for **personification**. **2.** a figure of speech that represents an imaginary, absent, or dead person speaking or acting. [C16: via L from Gk *prosōpopoiia* dramatization, from *prosōpon* face + *poiein* to make]

prospect *n.* ('prɒspɛkt). **1.** (*sometimes pl.*) a probability of future success. **2.** a view or scene. **3.** a mental outlook. **4.** expectation, or what one expects. **5.** a prospective buyer, project, etc. **6.** a survey or observation. **7.** *Mining.* **a.** a known or likely deposit of ore. **b.** the location of a deposit of ore. **c.** the yield of mineral obtained from a sample of ore. ~*vb.* (prəˈspɛkt). **8.** (when *intr.*, often foll. by *for*) to explore (a region) for gold or other valuable minerals. **9.** (*tr.*) to work (a mine) to discover its profitability. **10.** (*intr.*; often foll. by *for*) to search (for). [C15: from L *prōspectus* distant view, from *prōspicere* to look into the distance]

prospective (prəˈspɛktɪv) *adj.* **1.** looking towards the future. **2.** (*prenominal*) expected or likely. —**pro'spectively** *adv.*

prospector (prəˈspɛktə) *n.* a person who searches for gold, petroleum, etc.

prospectus (prəˈspɛktəs) *n., pl.* **-tuses. 1.** a formal statement giving details of a forthcoming event, such as the issue of shares. **2.** a brochure giving details of courses, as at a school.

prosper ('prɒspə) *vb.* (*usually intr.*) to thrive, succeed, etc., or cause to thrive, etc., in a healthy way. [C15: from L *prosperāre* to succeed, from *prosperus* fortunate, from PRO-[1] + *spēs* hope]

prosperity (prɒˈspɛrɪtɪ) *n.* the condition of prospering; success or wealth.

prosperous ('prɒspərəs) *adj.* **1.** flourishing; prospering. **2.** wealthy. —**'prosperously** *adv.*

prostaglandin (ˌprɒstəˈglændɪn) *n.* any of a group of hormone-like compounds found in all mammalian tissues, which stimulate the muscles and affect the nervous system. [C20: from *prosta(te) gland* + -IN; orig. believed to be secreted by the prostate gland]

prostate ('prɒsteɪt) *n.* **1.** Also called: **prostate gland.** a gland in male mammals that surrounds the neck of the bladder and secretes a liquid constituent of the semen. ~*adj.* **2.** Also: **prostatic** (prɒˈstætɪk). of the prostate gland. [C17: via Med. L from Gk *prostatēs* something standing in front (of the bladder), from *pro-* in front + *histanai* to cause to stand]

prosthesis ('prɒsθɪsɪs) *n., pl.* **-ses** (-ˌsiːz). **1.** *Surgery.* **a.** the replacement of a missing bodily part with an artificial substitute. **b.** an artificial part such as a limb, eye, or

---

tooth. **2.** *Linguistics.* another word for **prothesis.** [C16: via LL from Gk: an addition, from *prostithenai* to add, from *pros-* towards + *tithenai* to place] —**prosthetic** (prɒs'θɛtɪk) *adj.* —**pros'thetically** *adv.*

prosthetics (prɒs'θɛtɪks) *n.* (*functioning as sing.*) the branch of surgery concerned with prosthesis.

prostitute ('prɒstɪ,tjuːt) *n.* **1.** a woman who engages in sexual intercourse for money. **2.** a man who engages in such activity, esp. in homosexual practices. **3.** a person who offers his talent for unworthy purposes. ~*vb.* (*tr.*) **4.** to offer (oneself or another) in sexual intercourse for money. **5.** to offer for unworthy purposes. [C16: from L *prōstituere* to expose to prostitution, from *prō-* in public + *statuere* to cause to stand] —,**prosti'tution** *n.* —'**prosti,tutor** *n.*

prostrate *adj.* ('prɒstreɪt). **1.** lying face downwards, as in submission. **2.** exhausted physically or emotionally. **3.** helpless or defenceless. **4.** (of a plant) growing closely along the ground. ~*vb.* (prɒ'streɪt). (*tr.*) **5.** to cast (oneself) down, as in submission. **6.** to lay or throw down flat. **7.** to make helpless. **8.** to make exhausted. [C14: from L *prōsternere* to throw to the ground, from *prō-* before + *sternere* to lay low] —**pros'tration** *n.*

prostyle ('prəʊstaɪl) *adj.* **1.** (of a building) having a row of columns in front, esp. as in the portico of a Greek temple. ~*n.* **2.** a prostyle building, portico, etc. [C17: from L *prostȳlos*, from Gk: with pillars in front, from PRO-² + *stulos* pillar]

prosy ('prəʊzɪ) *adj.* **prosier, prosiest. 1.** of the nature of or similar to prose. **2.** dull, tedious, or long-winded. —'**prosily** *adv.* —'**prosiness** *n.*

Prot. *abbrev. for:* **1.** Protectorate. **2.** Protestant.

protactinium (,prəʊtæk'tɪnɪəm) *n.* a toxic radioactive element that occurs in uranium ores and is produced by neutron irradiation of thorium. Symbol: Pa; atomic no.: 91; half-life of most stable isotope, ²³¹Pa: 32 500 years.

protagonist (prəʊ'tæɡənɪst) *n.* **1.** the principal character in a play, story, etc. **2.** a supporter, esp. when important or respected, of a cause, party, etc. [C17: from Gk *prōtagōnistēs*, from *prōtos* first + *agōnistēs* actor] —**pro'tagonism** *n.*

▷ **Usage.** The use of *protagonist* as in definition 2 is regarded as unacceptable by some people on the grounds that the word derives from the Greek *prōtos* first, higher ranking, not from Latin *pro* in favour of. While the second sense has undoubtedly developed as a result of confusion over the etymology it is now well established in English; careful writers and speakers may, however, prefer to avoid this use and employ an alternative word such as *proponent, champion,* or *advocate.* In either of its uses, the word has the sense of *chief* and so does not need to be qualified by this or any similar adjective: *a protagonist of the movement* not *a leading protagonist of the movement.*

Protagoras (prəʊ'tæɡə,ræs) *n.* ?485–?411 B.C., Greek philosopher and sophist, famous for his dictum "Man is the measure of all things."

protasis ('prɒtəsɪs) *n., pl.* **-ses** (-siːz). **1.** *Logic, grammar.* the antecedent of a conditional statement, such as *it rains* in *if it rains the game will be cancelled.* **2.** (in classical drama) the introductory part of a play. [C17: via L from Gk: a proposal, from *pro-* before + *teinein* to extend]

protea ('prəʊtɪə) *n.* a shrub of tropical and southern Africa, having flowers with coloured bracts arranged in showy heads. [C20: from NL, from PROTEUS]

protean (prəʊ'tiːən, 'prəʊtɪən) *adj.* readily taking on various shapes or forms; variable. [C16: from PROTEUS]

protease ('prəʊtɪ,eɪs) *n.* any enzyme involved in proteolysis. [C20: from PROTEIN + -ASE]

protect (prə'tɛkt) *vb.* (*tr.*) **1.** to defend from trouble, harm, etc. **2.** *Econ.* to assist (domestic industries) by the imposition of protective tariffs on imports. **3.** *Commerce.* to provide funds in advance to guarantee payment of (a note, etc.). [C16: from L *prōtegere* to cover before]

protection (prə'tɛkʃən) *n.* **1.** the act of protecting or the condition of being protected. **2.** something that protects. **3. a.** the imposition of duties on imports, for the protection of domestic industries against overseas competition, etc. **b.** Also called: **protectionism.** the system or theory

of such restrictions. **4.** *Inf.* **a.** Also called: **protection money.** money demanded by gangsters for freedom from molestation. **b.** freedom from molestation purchased in this way. —**pro'tection,ism** *n.* —**pro'tectionist** *n., adj.*

protective (prə'tɛktɪv) *adj.* **1.** giving or capable of giving protection. **2.** *Econ.* of or intended for protection of domestic industries. ~*n.* **3.** something that protects. **4.** a condom. —**pro'tectively** *adv.* —**pro'tectiveness** *n.*

protective coloration *n.* the coloration of an animal that enables it to blend with its surroundings and therefore escape the attention of predators.

protector (prə'tɛktə) *n.* **1.** a person or thing that protects. **2.** *History.* a person who exercised royal authority during the minority, absence, or incapacity of the monarch. —**pro'tectress** *fem. n.*

Protector (prə'tɛktə) *n.* short for **Lord Protector,** the title borne by Oliver Cromwell (1653–58) and by Richard Cromwell (1658–59) as heads of state during the period known as the Protectorate.

protectorate (prə'tɛktərɪt) *n.* **1. a.** a territory largely controlled by but not annexed to a stronger state. **b.** the relation of a protecting state to its protected territory. **2.** the office or period of office of a protector.

protégé *or* (*fem.*) **protégée** ('prəʊtɪ,ʒeɪ) *n.* a person who is protected and aided by the patronage of another. [C18: from F *protéger* to PROTECT]

protein ('prəʊtiːn) *n.* any of a large group of nitrogenous compounds of high molecular weight that are essential constituents of all living organisms. [C19: via G from Gk *prōteios* primary, from *protos* first + -IN] —,**protein'aceous, pro'teinic,** *or* **pro'teinous** *adj.*

pro tempore Latin. ('prəʊ 'tɛmpərɪ) *adv., adj.* for the time being. Often shortened to **pro tem** (prəʊ 'tɛm).

proteolysis (,prəʊtɪ'ɒlɪsɪs) *n.* the hydrolysis of proteins into simpler compounds by the action of enzymes. [C19: from NL, from *proteo-* (from PROTEIN) + -LYSIS] —**proteolytic** (,prəʊtɪə'lɪtɪk) *adj.*

protest *n.* ('prəʊtɛst). **1. a.** public, often organized, manifestation of dissent. **b.** (*as modifier*): *a protest march.* **2.** a formal or solemn objection. **3.** a formal notarial statement drawn up on behalf of a creditor and declaring that the debtor has dishonoured a bill of exchange, etc. **4.** the act of protesting. ~*vb.* (prə'tɛst). **5.** (when *intr.*, foll. by *against, at, about,* etc.; when *tr.,* may take a clause as object) to make a strong objection (to something, esp. a supposed injustice or offence). **6.** (when *tr.,* may take a clause as object) to disagree; object: *"I'm O.K." she protested.* **7.** (when *tr.,* may take a clause as object) to assert in a formal or solemn manner. **8.** (*tr.*) *Chiefly U.S.* to object forcefully to: *leaflets protesting Dr King's murder.* [C14: from L *prōtestārī* to make a formal declaration, from *prō-* before + *testārī* to assert] —**pro'testant** *adj., n.* —**pro'tester** *or* **pro'testor** *n.* —**pro'testingly** *adv.*

Protestant ('prɒtɪstənt) *n.* **a.** an adherent of Protestantism. **b.** (*as modifier*): *the Protestant Church.*

Protestantism ('prɒtɪstən,tɪzəm) *n.* the religion of any of the Churches of Western Christendom that are separated from the Roman Catholic Church and adhere substantially to principles established during the Reformation.

protestation (,prəʊtɛs'teɪʃən) *n.* **1.** the act of protesting. **2.** a strong declaration.

Proteus ('prəʊtiəs) *n.* Greek myth. a prophetic sea god capable of changing his shape at will.

prothalamion (,prəʊθə'leɪmɪən) *or* **prothalamium** *n., pl.* **-mia** (-mɪə). a song or poem in celebration of a marriage. [C16: from Gk *pro-* before + *thalamos* marriage]

prothallus (prəʊ'θæləs) *or* **prothallium** (prəʊ'θælɪəm) *n., pl.* **-li** (-laɪ) *or* **-lia** (-lɪə). *Bot.* the small flat green disc of tissue that bears the reproductive organs of pteridophytes. [C19: from NL, from *pro-* before + Gk *thallus* a young shoot]

prothesis ('prɒθɪsɪs) *n., pl.* **-ses** (-siːz). **1.** a development of a language by which a syllable is prefixed to a word to facilitate pronunciation: *Latin "scala" gives Spanish "escala" by prothesis.* **2.** *Eastern Orthodox Church.* the solemn preparation of the Eucharistic elements before consecration. [C16: via LL from Gk: a setting out in public, from *pro-* forth + *thesis* a placing] —**prothetic** (prə'θɛtɪk) *adj.* —**pro'thetically** *adv.*

pro'syndicalism *n.*

prothrombin (prəʊ'θrɒmbɪn) n. Biochemistry. a zymogen found in blood that gives rise to thrombin on activation.

protist ('prəʊtɪst) n. any organism belonging to a large group, including bacteria, protozoans, and fungi, regarded as distinct from plants and animals. [C19: from NL Protista most primitive organisms, from Gk prōtistos the very first, from prōtos first]

protium ('prəʊtɪəm) n. the most common isotope of hydrogen, having a mass number of 1. [C20: NL, from PROTO- + -IUM]

proto- or sometimes before a vowel **prot-** combining form. 1. first: protomartyr. 2. primitive or original: prototype. 3. first in a series of chemical compounds: protoxide. [from Gk prōtos first, from pro before]

protocol ('prəʊtə,kɒl) n. 1. the formal etiquette and procedure for state and diplomatic ceremonies. 2. a record of an agreement, esp. in international negotiations, etc. 3. a. an amendment to a treaty or convention. b. an annexe appended to a treaty to deal with subsidiary matters. 4. Chiefly U.S. a record of data or observations on a particular experiment or proceeding. [C16: from Med. L prōtocollum, from LGk prōtokollon sheet glued to the front of a manuscript, from PROTO- + kolla glue]

protohuman (,prəʊtəʊ'hjuːmən) n. 1. any of various prehistoric primates that resembled modern man. ~adj. 2. of these primates.

Proto-Indo-European n. the prehistoric unrecorded language that was the ancestor of all Indo-European languages.

protomartyr (,prəʊtəʊ'mɑːtə) n. 1. St Stephen as the first Christian martyr. 2. the first martyr to lay down his life in any cause.

proton ('prəʊtɒn) n. a stable, positively charged elementary particle, found in atomic nuclei in numbers equal to the atomic number of the element. [C20: from Gk prōtos first]

protoplasm ('prəʊtə,plæzəm) n. Biol. the living contents of a cell: a complex translucent colourless colloidal substance. [C19: from NL, from PROTO- + Gk plasma form] —,proto'plasmic, ,proto'plasmal, or ,protoplas'matic adj.

prototype ('prəʊtə,taɪp) n. 1. one of the first units manufactured of a product, which is tested so that the design can be changed if necessary before the product is manufactured commercially. 2. a person or thing that serves as an example of a type. 3. Biol. the ancestral or primitive form of a species. —,proto'typal, **prototypic** (,prəʊtə'tɪpɪk), or ,proto'typical adj.

protozoan (,prəʊtə'zəʊən) n., pl. -zoa (-'zəʊə). 1. Also **protozoon**. any minute invertebrate of a phylum including amoebas and foraminifers. ~adj. also **protozoic**. 2. of or belonging to this group. [C19: via NL from Gk PROTO- + zoion animal]

protract (prə'trækt) vb. (tr.) 1. to lengthen or extend (a speech, etc.). 2. (of a muscle) to draw, thrust, or extend (a part, etc.) forwards. 3. to plot using a protractor and scale. [C16: from L prōtrahere to prolong, from PRO-¹ + trahere to drag] —pro'tracted adj. —protractedly adv. —pro'traction n.

protractile (prə'træktaɪl) adj. able to be extended: protractile muscle.

protractor (prə'træktə) n. 1. an instrument for measuring or drawing angles on paper, usually a flat semicircular transparent plastic sheet graduated in degrees. 2. Anat. a former term for **extensor**.

protrude (prə'truːd) vb. 1. to thrust forwards or outwards. 2. to project or cause to project. [C17: from L, from PRO-² + trudere to thrust] —pro'trusion n. —pro'trusive adj.

protrusile (prə'truːsaɪl) adj. Zool. capable of being thrust forwards: protrusile jaws.

protuberant (prə'tjuːbərənt) adj. swelling out; bulging. [C17: from LL prōtūberāre to swell, from PRO-¹ + tūber swelling] —pro'tuberance or pro'tuberancy n. —pro'tuberantly adv.

proud (praʊd) adj. 1. (foll. by of, an infinitive, or a clause) pleased or satisfied, as with oneself, one's possessions, achievements, etc. 2. feeling honoured or gratified by some distinction. 3. having an inordinately high opinion of oneself; haughty. 4. characterized by or proceeding from a sense of pride: a proud moment. 5. having a proper sense of self-respect. 6. stately or distinguished. 7. bold or fearless. 8. (of a surface, edge, etc.) projecting or protruding. 9. (of animals) restive or excited, esp. sexually. ~adv. 10. do (someone) proud. a. to entertain (someone) on a grand scale: they did us proud at the hotel. b. to honour (someone): his honesty did him proud. [LOE prūd, from OF prud, prod brave, from LL prōde useful, from L prōdesse to be of value] —'proudly adv. —'proudness n.

proud flesh n. a mass of tissue formed around a healing wound.

Proudhon (French prudɔ̃) n. **Pierre Joseph** (pjɛr ʒɔzɛf). 1809–65, French socialist, whose pamphlet What is Property? (1840) declared that property is theft.

Proust (French prust) n. 1. **Joseph Louis** (ʒozɛf lwi). 1754–1826, French chemist, who formulated the law of constant proportions. 2. **Marcel** (marsɛl). 1871–1922, French novelist whose long novel À la recherche du temps perdu (1913–27) deals with the relationship of the narrator to themes such as art, time, memory, and society.

Prout (praʊt) n. 1. **Ebenezer**. 1835–1909, English musicologist and composer, noted for his editions of works by Handel and J. S. Bach. 2. **William**. 1785–1850, English chemist, noted for his modification of the atomic theory.

Prov. abbrev. for: 1. Provençal. 2. Bible. Proverbs. 3. Province. 4. Provost.

prove (pruːv) vb. **proving, proved; proved** or **proven**. (mainly tr.) 1. (may take a clause as object or an infinitive) to demonstrate the truth or validity of, esp. by using an established sequence of procedures. 2. to establish the quality of, esp. by experiment. 3. Law. to establish the genuineness of (a will). 4. to show (oneself) able or courageous. 5. (copula) to be found (to be): this has proved useless. 6. (intr.) (of dough) to rise in a warm place before baking. [C12: from OF prover, from L probāre to test, from probus honest] —'provable adj. —'provably adv. —,prova'bility n.

proven ('pruːvⁿ, 'prəʊ-) vb. 1. a past participle of **prove**. 2. See **not proven**. ~adj. 3. tried; tested: a proven method.

provenance ('prɒvɪnəns) n. a place of origin, as of a work of art. [C19: from F, from provenir, from L prōvenīre to originate, from venīre to come]

Provençal (,prɒvɒn'sɑːl; French prɔvɑ̃sal) adj. 1. denoting or characteristic of Provence, its inhabitants, their dialect of French, or their Romance language. ~n. 2. a language of Provence, closely related to French and Italian, belonging to the Romance group of the Indo-European family. 3. a native or inhabitant of Provence.

Provence (French prɔvɑ̃s) n. a former province of SE France, on the Mediterranean, and the River Rhône: forms part of the administrative region of Provence-Alpes-Côte d'Azur.

provender ('prɒvɪndə) n. 1. fodder for livestock. 2. food in general. [C14: from OF provendre, from LL praebenda grant, from L praebēre to proffer]

proverb ('prɒvɜːb) n. 1. a short memorable saying embodying some commonplace fact. 2. a person or thing exemplary of a characteristic: Antarctica is a proverb for extreme cold. 3. Bible. a wise saying providing guidance. [C14: from OF from L prōverbium, from verbum word]

proverbial (prə'vɜːbɪəl) adj. 1. (prenominal) commonly or traditionally referred to as an example of some peculiarity, characteristic, etc. 2. of, embodied in, or resembling a proverb. —pro'verbially adv.

provide (prə'vaɪd) vb. (mainly tr.) 1. to furnish or supply. 2. to afford; yield: this meeting provides an opportunity to talk. 3. (intr.; often foll. by for or against) to take careful precautions: he provided against financial ruin by wise investment. 4. (intr.; foll. by for) to supply means of support (to): he provides for his family. 5. (of a person, law, etc.) to state as a condition; stipulate. 6. to confer and induct into ecclesiastical offices. [C15: from L prōvidēre to provide for, from prō- beforehand + vidēre to see] —pro'vider n.

providence ('prɒvɪdəns) n. 1. a. Christianity. God's foreseeing protection and care of his creatures. b. such protection and care as manifest by some other force. 2. a supposed manifestation of such care and guidance. **3.** the foresight or care exercised by a person in the management of his affairs.

Providence¹ ('prɒvɪdəns) *n. Christianity.* God, esp. as showing foreseeing care of his creatures.

Providence² ('prɒvɪdəns) *n.* a port in NE Rhode Island, capital of the state, at the head of Narragansett Bay: founded by Roger Williams in 1636. Pop.: 157 200 (1986 est.).

provident ('prɒvɪdənt) *adj.* **1.** providing for future needs. **2.** exercising foresight in the management of one's affairs. **3.** characterized by foresight. [C15: from L *prōvidens* foreseeing, from *prōvidēre* to PROVIDE] —**'providently** *adv.*

providential (,prɒvɪ'dɛnʃəl) *adj.* characteristic of or presumed to proceed from or as if from divine providence. —,**provi'dentially** *adv.*

provident society *n.* a mutual insurance society catering esp. for those on a low income, providing sickness, death, and pension benefits.

providing (prə'vaɪdɪŋ) *or* **provided** *conj.* (*subordinating;* sometimes foll. by *that*) on the condition or understanding (that): *I'll play, providing you pay me.*

province ('prɒvɪns) *n.* **1.** a territory governed as a unit of a country or empire. **2.** (*pl.;* usually preceded by *the*) those parts of a country lying outside the capital and other large cities and regarded as outside the mainstream of sophisticated culture. **3.** an area of learning, activity, etc. **4.** the extent of a person's activities or office. **5.** an ecclesiastical territory, having an archbishop or metropolitan at its head. **6.** an administrative and territorial subdivision of a religious order. **7.** *History.* a region of the Roman Empire outside Italy ruled by a governor from Rome. [C14: from OF, from L *prōvincia* conquered territory]

Provincetown ('prɒvɪns,taʊn) *n.* a village in SE Massachusetts, at the tip of Cape Cod: scene of the first landing place of the Pilgrims (1620) and of the signing of the Mayflower Compact (1620). Pop.: 3536 (1980).

provincewide ('prɒvɪns,waɪd) *Canad.* ~*adj.* **1.** covering or available to the whole of a province: *a provincewide referendum.* ~*adv.* **2.** throughout a province: *an advertising campaign to go provincewide.*

provincial (prə'vɪnʃəl) *adj.* **1.** of or connected with a province. **2.** characteristic of or connected with the provinces. **3.** having attitudes and opinions supposedly common to people living in the provinces; unsophisticated; limited. **4.** *N.Z.* denoting a football team representing a province, one of the historical administrative areas of New Zealand. ~*n.* **5.** a person lacking the sophistications of city life; rustic or narrow-minded individual. **6.** a person coming from or resident in a province or the provinces. **7.** the head of an ecclesiastical province. **8.** the head of a territorial subdivision of a religious order. —**provinciality** (prə,vɪnʃɪ'ælɪtɪ) *n.* —**pro'vincially** *adv.*

provincialism (prə'vɪnʃə,lɪzəm) *n.* **1.** narrowness of mind; lack of sophistication. **2.** a word or attitude characteristic of a provincial. **3.** attention to the affairs of one's local area rather than the whole nation. **4.** the state or quality of being provincial.

provirus ('prəʊ,vaɪrəs) *n.* the inactive form of a virus in a host cell.

provision (prə'vɪʒən) *n.* **1.** the act of supplying food, etc. **2.** something that is supplied. **3.** preparations (esp. in **make provision for**). **4.** (*pl.*) food and other necessities, as for an expedition. **5.** a condition or stipulation incorporated in a document; proviso. **6.** the conferring of and induction into ecclesiastical offices. ~*vb.* **7.** (*tr.*) to supply with provisions. [C14: from L *prōvīsiō* a providing; see PROVIDE] —**pro'visioner** *n.*

provisional (prə'vɪʒənəl) *adj.* subject to later alteration; temporary or conditional: *a provisional decision.* —**pro'visionally** *adv.*

Provisional (prə'vɪʒənəl) *adj.* **1.** designating one of the two factions of the IRA and Sinn Féin that have existed since a split in late 1969. The Provisional movement advocates terrorism to achieve Irish unity. ~*n.* **2.** Also called: **Provo.** a member of the Provisional IRA or Sinn Féin.

proviso (prə'vaɪzəʊ) *n., pl.* **-sos** *or* **-soes. 1.** a clause in a document or contract that embodies a condition or stipulation. **2.** a condition or stipulation. [C15: from Med. L

prōvīsō quod it being provided that, from L *prōvīsus* provided]

provisory (prə'vaɪzərɪ) *adj.* **1.** containing a proviso; conditional. **2.** provisional. **3.** making provision. —**pro'visorily** *adv.*

Provo ('prəʊvəʊ) *n., pl.* **-vos.** another name for a **Provisional** (sense 2).

provocation (,prɒvə'keɪʃən) *n.* **1.** the act of provoking or inciting. **2.** something that causes indignation, anger, etc.

provocative (prə'vɒkətɪv) *adj.* serving or intended to provoke or incite, esp. to anger or sexual desire: *a provocative look; a provocative remark.* —**pro'vocatively** *adv.*

provoke (prə'vəʊk) *vb.* (*tr.*) **1.** to anger or infuriate. **2.** to incite or stimulate. **3.** to promote (anger, indignation, etc.) in a person. **4.** to cause; bring about: *the accident provoked an inquiry.* [C15: from L *prōvocāre* to call forth] —**pro'voking** *adj.* —**pro'vokingly** *adv.*

provost ('prɒvəst) *n.* **1.** the head of certain university colleges or schools. **2.** (formerly) the principal magistrate of a Scottish burgh; now only a courtesy title. **3.** *Church of England.* the senior dignitary of one of the more recent cathedral foundations. **4.** *R.C. Church.* **a.** the head of a cathedral chapter. **b.** (formerly) the member of a monastic community second in authority under the abbot. **5.** (in medieval times) an overseer, steward, or bailiff. [OE *profost,* from Med. L *prōpositus* placed at the head (of), from L *praepōnere* to place first]

provost marshal (prə'vəʊ) *n.* the officer in charge of military police in a camp or city.

prow (praʊ) *n.* the bow of a vessel. [C16: from OF *proue,* from L *prora,* from Gk *prōra*]

prowess ('praʊɪs) *n.* **1.** outstanding or superior skill or ability. **2.** bravery or fearlessness, esp. in battle. [C13: from OF *proesce,* from *prou* good]

prowl (praʊl) *vb.* **1.** (when *intr.,* often foll. by *around* or *about*) to move stealthily around (a place) as if in search of prey or plunder. ~*n.* **2.** the act of prowling. **3. on the prowl. a.** moving around stealthily. **b.** pursuing members of the opposite sex. [C14 *prollen,* from ?] —**'prowler** *n.*

prox. *abbrev. for* proximo (next month).

proximal ('prɒksɪməl) *adj. Anat.* situated close to the centre, median line, or point of attachment or origin. —**'proximally** *adv.*

proximate ('prɒksɪmɪt) *adj.* **1.** next or nearest in space or time. **2.** very near; close. **3.** immediately preceding or following in a series. **4.** a less common word for **approximate.** [C16: from LL *proximāre* to draw near, from L *proximus* next, from *prope* near] —**'proximately** *adv.*

proximity (prɒk'sɪmɪtɪ) *n.* **1.** nearness in space or time. **2.** nearness or closeness in a series. [C15: from L *proximitās* closeness; see PROXIMATE]

proximo ('prɒksɪməʊ) *adv. Now rare except when abbreviated in formal correspondence.* in or during the next or coming month: *a letter of the seventh proximo.* Abbrev.: **prox.** Cf. **instant, ultimo.** [C19: from L: in or on the next]

proxy ('prɒksɪ) *n., pl.* **proxies. 1.** a person authorized to act on behalf of someone else; agent: *to vote by proxy.* **2.** the authority, esp. in the form of a document, given to a person to act on behalf of someone else. [C15 *prokesye,* from *procuracy,* from L *prōcūrātiō* procuration; see PRO-CURE]

prude (pru:d) *n.* a person who affects or shows an excessively modest, prim, or proper attitude, esp. regarding sex. [C18: from F, from *prudefemme,* from OF *prode femme* respectable woman; see PROUD] —**'prudery** *n.* —**'prudish** *adj.* —**'prudishly** *adv.*

prudence ('pru:dəns) *n.* **1.** caution in practical affairs; discretion. **2.** care taken in the management of one's resources. **3.** consideration for one's own interests. **4.** the quality of being prudent.

prudent ('pru:dənt) *adj.* **1.** discreet or cautious in managing one's activities; circumspect. **2.** practical and careful in providing for the future. **3.** exercising good judgment. [C14: from L *prūdēns* far-sighted, from *prōvidens* acting with foresight; see PROVIDENT] —**'prudently** *adv.*

prudential (pru:'dɛnʃəl) *adj.* **1.** characterized by or resulting from prudence. **2.** exercising sound judgment. —**pru'dentially** *adv.*

Prudentius (pru:'dɛnʃəs) *n.* **Aurelius Clemens** (ɔː'ri:lɪəs 'klɛmɛnz). 348–410 A.D., Latin Christian poet,

'pro'war *adj.*

born in Spain. His works include the allegory *Psychomachia.*

Prud'hon (*French* pryd5) *n.* **Pierre Paul** (pjɛr pɔl). 1758–1823, French painter, noted for the romantic and mysterious aura of his portraits.

pruinose ('pruːɪˌnəʊs, -ˌnəʊz) *adj. Bot.* coated with a powdery or waxy bloom. [C19: from L *pruinōsus* frost-covered, from *pruīna* hoarfrost]

prune[1] (pruːn) *n.* **1.** a purplish-black partially dried fruit of any of several varieties of plum tree. **2.** *Sl.*, *chiefly Brit.* a dull or foolish person. **3. prunes and prisms.** denoting an affected and mincing way of speaking. [C14: from OF *prune*, from L *prūnum* plum, from Gk *prounon*]

prune[2] (pruːn) *vb.* **1.** to remove (dead or superfluous twigs, branches, etc.) from a (tree, shrub, etc.), esp. by cutting off. **2.** to remove (anything undesirable or superfluous) from (a book, etc.). [C15: from OF *proignier* to clip, prob. from *provigner* to prune vines, ult. from L *propāgo* a cutting] —'**prunable** *adj.* —'**pruner** *n.*

prunella (pruːˈnɛlə) *n.* a strong fabric, esp. a twill-weave worsted, formerly used for academic gowns and the uppers of some shoes. [C17: ?from *prunelle*, a green French liqueur, with reference to the colour of the cloth]

pruning hook *n.* a tool with a curved steel blade terminating in a hook, used for pruning.

prurient ('prʊərɪənt) *adj.* **1.** unusually or morbidly interested in sexual thoughts or practices. **2.** exciting lustfulness. [C17: from L *prūrīre* to lust after, itch] —'**prurience** *n.* —'**pruriently** *adv.*

prurigo (prʊəˈraɪgəʊ) *n.* a chronic inflammatory disease of the skin characterized by intense itching. [C19: from L: an itch] —**pruriginous** (prʊəˈrɪdʒɪnəs) *adj.*

pruritus (prʊəˈraɪtəs) *n. Pathol.* any intense sensation of itching. [C17: from L: an itching; see PRURIENT] —**pruritic** (prʊəˈrɪtɪk) *adj.*

Prussia ('prʌʃə) *n.* a former German state in N and central Germany, extending from France and the Low Countries to the Baltic Sea and Poland: developed as the chief military power of the Continent, leading the North German Confederation from 1867–71, when the German Empire was established; dissolved in 1947 and divided between East and West Germany, Poland, and the Soviet Union. Area: (in 1939) 294 081 sq. km (113 545 sq. miles). German name: **Preussen.**

Prussian ('prʌʃən) *adj.* **1.** of Prussia, or its people, esp. of the Junkers and their formal military tradition. ~*n.* **2.** a native or inhabitant of Prussia. **3. Old Prussian.** the extinct Baltic language of the non-German inhabitants of Prussia.

Prussian blue *n.* **1.** a dark blue insoluble crystalline compound of iron, ferric ferrocyanide, used as a pigment in paints. **2. a.** the blue or deep greenish-blue colour of this. **b.** (*as adj.*): *a Prussian-blue carpet.*

prussic acid ('prʌsɪk) *n.* the extremely poisonous aqueous solution of hydrogen cyanide. [C18: from F *acide prussique* Prussian acid, because obtained from Prussian blue]

Prut (*Russian* prut) *n.* a river in E Europe, rising in the SW Ukrainian SSR and flowing generally southeast, forming part of the border between Romania and the Soviet Union, to join the River Danube. Length: 853 km (530 miles).

pry[1] (praɪ) *vb.* **prying, pried. 1.** (*intr.; often foll. by into*) to make an impertinent or uninvited inquiry (about a private matter, topic, etc.). ~*n., pl.* **pries. 2.** the act of prying. **3.** a person who pries. [C14: from ?]

pry[2] (praɪ) *vb.* **prying, pried.** the U.S. and Canad. word for **prise.** [C14: from ?]

pryer ('praɪə) *n.* a variant spelling of **prier.**

Prynne (prɪn) *n.* **William.** 1600–69, English Puritan leader and pamphleteer, whose ears were cut off in punishment for his attacks on Laud.

Przemyśl (*Polish* 'pʃɛmɪʃl) *n.* a city in SE Poland, near the border with the Soviet Union on the San River: a fortress in the early Middle Ages; belonged to Austria (1722–1918). Pop.: 64 100 (1983).

Przewalski's horse (ˌpɜːʒəˈvælskɪz) *n.* a rare wild horse of W Mongolia, having an erect mane and no forelock. [C19: after the Russian explorer Nikolai *Przewalski* (1839–88), who discovered it]

PS *abbrev. for:* **1.** Passenger Steamer. **2.** Police Sergeant. **3.** Also: **ps.** postscript. **4.** private secretary. **5.** prompt side.

Ps. *or* **Psa.** *Bible. abbrev. for* Psalm(s).

psalm (sɑːm) *n.* **1.** (*often cap.*) any of the sacred songs that constitute a book (Psalms) of the Old Testament. **2.** a musical setting of one of these. **3.** any sacred song. [OE, from LL *psalmus*, from Gk *psalmos* song accompanied on the harp, from *psallein* to play (the harp)] —**psalmic** ('sɑːmɪk, 'sæl-) *adj.*

psalmist ('sɑːmɪst) *n.* the composer of a psalm or psalms, esp. (when *cap.* and preceded by *the*) David, traditionally regarded as the author of the Book of Psalms.

psalmody ('sɑːmədɪ, 'sæl-) *n., pl.* -**dies. 1.** the act of singing psalms or hymns. **2.** the art of setting psalms to music. [C14: via LL from Gk *psalmōdia* singing accompanied by a harp, from *psalmos* (see PSALM) + *ōidē* ODE] —'**psalmodist** *n.* —**psalmodic** (sæl'mɒdɪk) *adj.*

Psalter ('sɔːltə) *n.* **1.** another name for the Book of Psalms, esp. in the version in the Book of Common Prayer. **2.** a translation, musical, or metrical version of the Psalms. **3.** a book containing a version of Psalms. [OE *psaltere*, from LL *psaltērium*, from Gk *psaltērion* stringed instrument, from *psallein* to play a stringed instrument]

psalterium (sɔːlˈtɪərɪəm) *n., pl.* -**teria** (-ˈtɪərɪə). the third compartment of the stomach of ruminants. Also called: **omasum.** [C19: from L *psaltērium* PSALTER; from the similarity of its folds to the pages of a book]

psaltery ('sɔːltərɪ) *n., pl.* -**teries.** *Music.* an ancient stringed instrument similar to the lyre, but having a trapezoidal sounding board over which the strings are stretched.

p's and q's *pl. n.* behaviour; manners (esp. in **mind one's p's and q's**). [altered from *p(lea)se and (than)k yous*]

PSBR (in Britain) *abbrev. for* public sector borrowing requirement; the money required by the public sector of the economy for expenditure on items that are not financed from income.

psephology (sɛ'fɒlədʒɪ) *n.* the statistical and sociological study of elections. [C20: from Gk *psephos* pebble, vote + -LOGY, from the ancient Greeks' custom of voting with pebbles] —**psephological** (ˌsɛfə'lɒdʒɪkᵊl) *adj.* —ˌ**psepho'logically** *adv.* —**pse'phologist** *n.*

pseud (sjuːd) *n.* **1.** *Inf.* a false or pretentious person. ~*adj.* **2.** another word for **pseudo.**

Pseudepigrapha (ˌsjuːdɪ'pɪgrəfə) *pl. n.* various Jewish writings from the first century B.C. to the first century A.D. that claim to have been divinely revealed but which have been excluded from the Greek canon of the Old Testament. [C17: from Gk *pseudepigraphos* falsely entitled, from PSEUDO- + *epigraphein* to inscribe] —**Pseudepigraphic** (ˌsjuːdɛpɪ'græfɪk) *or* ,**Pseudepi'graphical** *adj.*

pseudo ('sjuːdəʊ) *adj. Inf.* not genuine.

pseudo- *or sometimes before a vowel* **pseud-** *combining form.* **1.** false, pretending, or unauthentic: *pseudo-intellectual.* **2.** having a close resemblance to: *pseudopodium.* [from Gk *pseudēs* false, from *pseudein* to lie]

pseudocarp ('sjuːdəʊˌkɑːp) *n.* a fruit, such as the apple, that includes parts other than the ripened ovary. —ˌ**pseudo'carpous** *adj.*

pseudomorph ('sjuːdəʊˌmɔːf) *n.* a mineral that has an uncharacteristic crystalline form as a result of assuming the shape of another mineral that it has replaced. —ˌ**pseudo'morphic** *or* ,**pseudo'morphous** *adj.* —ˌ**pseudo'morphism** *n.*

pseudonym ('sjuːdəˌnɪm) *n.* a fictitious name adopted esp. by an author. [C19: via F from Gk *pseudōnumon*] —ˌ**pseudo'nymity** *n.* —**pseudonymous** (sjuː'dɒnɪməs) *adj.*

,pseudoan'tique *adj.*	,pseudo'classic *or*	,pseudo-E,liza'bethan *adj.*	,pseudo'literary *adj.*
,pseudoar'chaic *adj.*	,pseudo'classical *adj.*	,pseudo-'Georgian *adj.*	,pseudo,medi'eval *adj.*
,pseudo,aristo'cratic *adj.*	,pseudo'classi,cism *n.*	,pseudo-'Gothic *adj.*	,pseudo'modern *adj.*
,pseudoar'tistic *adj.*	,pseudo'culti,vated *adj.*	,pseudo-'Grecian *adj.*	,pseudo'mythical *adj.*
,pseudo-Bo'hemian *adj.*	,pseudo,demo'cratic *adj.*	,pseudohis'torical *adj.*	,pseudo,ori'ental *adj.*

pseudopodium (ˌsjuːdəʊ'pəʊdɪəm) *n.*, *pl.* **-dia** (-dɪə). a temporary projection from the cell of a protozoan, etc., used for feeding and locomotion.

psf *abbrev. for* pounds per square foot.

pshaw (pʃɔː) *interj. Becoming rare.* an exclamation of disgust, impatience, disbelief, etc.

psi[1] (psaɪ) *n.* **1.** the 23rd letter of the Greek alphabet (Ψ, ψ), a composite consonant, transliterated as *ps.* **2.** paranormal or psychic phenomena collectively.

psi[2] *abbrev. for* pounds per square inch.

psilocybin (ˌsɪlə'saɪbɪn, ˌsaɪlə-) *n.* a crystalline phosphate ester that is the active principle of the hallucinogenic fungus *Psilocybe mexicana.* Formula: $C_{12}H_{17}N_2O_4P$. [C20: from NL *Psilocybe* (from Gk *psilos* bare + *kubē* head) + -IN]

psi particle *n.* a type of elementary particle thought to be formed from charmed quarks. See **charm** (sense 7).

psittacine ('sɪtəˌsaɪn, -sɪn) *adj.* of, relating to, or resembling a parrot. [C19: from LL *psittacīnus,* from L *psittacus* a parrot]

psittacosis (ˌsɪtə'kəʊsɪs) *n.* a viral disease of parrots and other birds that can be transmitted to man, in whom it produces pneumonia. Also called: **parrot fever.** [C19: from NL, from L *psittacus* a parrot, from Gk *psittakos;* see -OSIS]

Pskov (*Russian* pskɔf) *n.* **1.** a city in the W Soviet Union, on the Velikaya River: one of the oldest Russian cities, at its height in the 13th and 14th centuries. Pop.: 202 000 (1987). **2. Lake.** the S part of Lake Peipus in the W Soviet Union, linked to the main part by a channel 24 km (15 miles) long. Area: about 1000 sq. km (400 sq. miles).

psoas ('səʊəs) *n.* either of two muscles of the loins that aid in flexing and rotating the thigh. [C17: from NL, from Gk *psoai* (pl.)]

psoriasis (sə'raɪəsɪs) *n.* a skin disease characterized by the formation of reddish spots and patches covered with silvery scales. [C17: via NL from Gk: itching disease, from *psōra* itch] —**psoriatic** (ˌsɔːrɪ'ætɪk) *adj.*

psst (pst) *interj.* an exclamation of beckoning, esp. one made surreptitiously.

PST (in the U.S. and Canada) *abbrev. for* Pacific Standard Time.

PSV *abbrev. for* public service vehicle.

psych *or* **psyche** (saɪk) *vb.* (*tr.*) *Inf.* to psychoanalyse. See also **psych out, psych up.** [C20: shortened from PSYCHOANALYSE]

psyche ('saɪkɪ) *n.* the human mind or soul. [C17: from L, from Gk *psukhē* breath, soul]

Psyche ('saɪkɪ) *n. Greek myth.* a beautiful girl loved by Eros (Cupid), who became the personification of the soul.

psychedelic (ˌsaɪkɪ'dɛlɪk) *adj.* **1.** relating to or denoting new or altered perceptions or sensory experiences, as through the use of hallucinogenic drugs. **2.** denoting any of the drugs, esp. LSD, that produce these effects. **3.** *Inf.* (of painting, etc.) having the vivid colours and complex patterns popularly associated with the visual effects of psychedelic states. [C20: from PSYCHE + Gk *delos* visible] —**psyche'delically** *adv.*

psychiatry (saɪ'kaɪətrɪ) *n.* the branch of medicine concerned with the diagnosis and treatment of mental disorders. —**psychiatric** (ˌsaɪkɪ'ætrɪk) *or* **psychi'atrical** *adj.* —**psychi'atrically** *adv.* —**psy'chiatrist** *n.*

psychic ('saɪkɪk) *adj.* **1. a.** outside the possibilities defined by natural laws, as mental telepathy. **b.** (of a person) sensitive to forces not recognized by natural laws. **2.** mental as opposed to physical. *~n.* **3.** a person who is sensitive to parapsychological forces or influences. —**'psychical** *adj.* —**'psychically** *adv.*

psycho ('saɪkəʊ) *n.*, *pl.* **-chos,** *adj.* an informal word for **psychopath** or **psychopathic.**

psycho- *or sometimes before a vowel* **psych-** *combining form.* indicating the mind or psychological or mental processes: *psychology; psychosomatic.* [from Gk *psukhē* spirit, breath]

psychoactive (ˌsaɪkəʊ'æktɪv) *adj.* (of drugs such as LSD and barbiturates) capable of affecting mental activity. Also: **psychotropic.**

psychoanalyse *or esp. U.S.* **-lyze** (ˌsaɪkəʊ'ænəˌlaɪz) *vb.* (*tr.*) to examine or treat (a person) by psychoanalysis.

psychoanalysis (ˌsaɪkəʊə'nælɪsɪs) *n.* a method of studying the mind and treating mental and emotional disorders based on revealing and investigating the role of the unconscious mind. —**psychoanalyst** (ˌsaɪkəʊ'ænəlɪst) *n.* —**psychoanalytic** (ˌsaɪkəʊˌænə'lɪtɪk) *or* **psycho,ana'lytical** *adj.* —**psycho,ana'lytically** *adv.*

psychobiology (ˌsaɪkəʊbaɪ'ɒlədʒɪ) *n. Psychol.* the attempt to understand the psychology of organisms in terms of their biological functions and structures. —**psychobiological** (ˌsaɪkəʊˌbaɪə'lɒdʒɪk°l) *adj.* —**psychobi'ologist** *n.*

psychochemical (ˌsaɪkəʊ'kɛmɪk°l) *n.* **1.** any of various chemical compounds whose primary effect is the alteration of the normal state of consciousness. *~adj.* **2.** of such compounds.

psychodrama ('saɪkəʊˌdrɑːmə) *n. Psychiatry.* a form of group therapy in which individuals act out situations from their past.

psychodynamics (ˌsaɪkəʊdaɪ'næmɪks) *n.* (*functioning as sing.*) *Psychol.* the study of interacting motives and emotions. —**psychody'namic** *adj.*

psychogenic (ˌsaɪkəʊ'dʒɛnɪk) *adj. Psychol.* (esp. of disorders or symptoms) of mental, rather than organic, origin. —**psycho'genically** *adv.*

psychokinesis (ˌsaɪkəʊkɪ'niːsɪs, -kaɪ-) *n.* (in parapsychology) alteration of the state of an object supposedly by mental influence alone. [C20: from PSYCHO- + Gk *kinēsis* motion]

psycholinguistics (ˌsaɪkəʊlɪŋ'gwɪstɪks) *n.* (*functioning as sing.*) the psychology of language, including language acquisition by children, language disorders, etc. —**psycho'linguist** *n.*

psychological (ˌsaɪkə'lɒdʒɪk°l) *adj.* **1.** of or relating to psychology. **2.** of or relating to the mind or mental activity. **3.** having no real or objective basis; arising in the mind: *his backaches are all psychological.* **4.** affecting the mind. —**psycho'logically** *adv.*

psychological moment *n.* the most appropriate time for producing a desired effect.

psychological warfare *n.* the military application of psychology, esp. to attempts to influence morale in time of war.

psychologize *or U.S.* **-gise** (saɪ'kɒləˌdʒaɪz) *vb.* (*intr.*) **1.** to make interpretations of mental processes. **2.** to carry out investigation in psychology.

psychology (saɪ'kɒlədʒɪ) *n.*, *pl.* **-gies. 1.** the scientific study of all forms of human and animal behaviour. **2.** *Inf.* the mental make-up of an individual that causes him to think or act in the way he does. —**psy'chologist** *n.*

psychometrics (ˌsaɪkəʊ'mɛtrɪks) *n.* (*functioning as sing.*) **1.** the branch of psychology concerned with the design and use of psychological tests. **2.** the application of statistical techniques to psychological testing.

psychometry (saɪ'kɒmɪtrɪ) *n. Psychol.* **1.** measurement and testing of mental states and processes. **2.** (in parapsychology) the supposed ability to deduce facts about events by touching objects related to them. —**psychometric** (ˌsaɪkəʊ'mɛtrɪk) *or* **psycho'metrical** *adj.* —**psycho'metrically** *adv.*

psychomotor (ˌsaɪkəʊ'məʊtə) *adj.* of, relating to, or characterizing movements of the body associated with mental activity.

psychoneurosis (ˌsaɪkəʊnjʊ'rəʊsɪs) *n.*, *pl.* **-roses** (-'rəʊsiːz). another word for **neurosis.**

psychopath ('saɪkəʊˌpæθ) *n.* a person afflicted with a personality disorder characterized by a tendency to commit antisocial and sometimes violent acts and a failure to feel guilt for such acts. —**psycho'pathic** *adj.* —**psycho'pathically** *adv.*

psychopathology (ˌsaɪkəʊpə'θɒlədʒɪ) *n.* the scientific study of mental disorders. —**psychopathological** (ˌsaɪkəʊˌpæθə'lɒdʒɪk°l) *adj.*

psychopathy (saɪ'kɒpəθɪ) *n.* any mental disorder or disease.

psychopharmacology (ˌsaɪkəʊˌfɑːmə'kɒlədʒɪ) *n.* the study of drugs that affect the mind.

ˌpseudoˌphilo'sophical *adj.*	ˌpseudoˌpsycho'logical *adj.*
ˌpseudopro'fessional *adj.*	

ˌpseudo'scholarly *adj.*	ˌpseudoˌscien'tific *adj.*
ˌpseudo'science *n.*	ˌpseudo-Vic'torian *adj.*

psychophysics (ˌsaɪkəʊ'fɪzɪks) *n.* (*functioning as sing.*) the branch of psychology concerned with the relationship between physical stimuli and their effects on the organism. — ˌpsycho'physical *adj.*

psychophysiology (ˌsaɪkəʊˌfɪzɪ'ɒlədʒɪ) *n.* the branch of psychology concerned with the physiological basis of mental processes. —**psychophysiological** (ˌsaɪkəʊˌfɪzɪə'lɒdʒɪkᵊl) *adj.*

psychosexual (ˌsaɪkəʊ'sɛksjʊəl) *adj.* of or relating to the mental aspects of sex, such as sexual fantasies. — ˌpsycho'sexually *adv.*

psychosis (saɪ'kəʊsɪs) *n.*, *pl.* **-choses** (-'kəʊsiːz). any form of severe mental disorder in which the individual's contact with reality becomes highly distorted. [C19: NL, from PSYCHO- + -OSIS]

psychosocial (ˌsaɪkəʊ'səʊʃəl) *adj.* of or relating to processes or factors that are both social and psychological in origin.

psychosomatic (ˌsaɪkəʊsə'mætɪk) *adj.* of disorders, such as stomach ulcers, thought to be caused or aggravated by psychological factors such as stress.

psychosurgery (ˌsaɪkəʊ'sɜːdʒərɪ) *n.* any surgical procedure on the brain, such as a frontal lobotomy, to relieve serious mental disorders. —**psychosurgical** (ˌsaɪkəʊ'sɜːdʒɪkᵊl) *adj.*

psychotherapy (ˌsaɪkəʊ'θɛrəpɪ) *n.* the treatment of nervous disorders by psychological methods. —**psycho,thera'peutic** *adj.* — ˌpsycho,thera'peutically *adv.* — ˌpsycho'therapist *n.*

psychotic (saɪ'kɒtɪk) *Psychiatry.* ~*adj.* **1.** of or characterized by psychosis. ~*n.* **2.** a person suffering from psychosis. —**psy'chotically** *adv.*

psychotomimetic (saɪˌkɒtəʊmɪ'mɛtɪk) *adj.* (of drugs such as LSD and mescaline) capable of inducing psychotic symptoms.

psych out *vb.* (*mainly tr., adv.*) *Inf.* **1.** to guess correctly the intentions of (another). **2.** to analyse (a problem, etc.) psychologically. **3.** to intimidate or frighten.

psychrometer (saɪ'krɒmɪtə) *n.* a type of hygrometer consisting of two thermometers, one of which has a dry bulb and the other a bulb that is kept moist and ventilated.

psych up *vb.* (*tr., adv.*) *Inf.* to get (oneself or another) into a state of psychological readiness for an action, performance, etc.

pt *abbrev. for:* **1.** part. **2.** patient. **3.** payment. **4.** point. **5.** port. **6.** pro tempore.

Pt *abbrev. for:* (in place names): **1.** Point. **2.** Port. ~ **3.** *the chemical symbol for* platinum.

PT *abbrev. for:* **1.** physical therapy. **2.** physical training. **3.** postal telegraph.

pt. *abbrev. for:* **1.** pint. **2.** preterite.

PTA *abbrev. for:* **1.** Parent-Teacher Association. **2.** (in Britain) Passenger Transport Authority.

Ptah (ptɑː, tɑː) *n.* (in ancient Egypt) a major god worshipped as the creative power, esp. at Memphis.

ptarmigan ('tɑːmɪgən) *n.*, *pl.* **-gans** *or* **-gan.** any of several arctic and subarctic grouse, esp. one which has a white winter plumage. [C16: changed (? infl. by Gk *pteron* wing) from Scot. Gaelic *tarmachan*, from ?]

Pte *Mil. abbrev. for* private.

pteridology (ˌtɛrɪ'dɒlədʒɪ) *n.* the branch of botany concerned with the study of ferns. [C19: from *pterido-*, from Gk *pteris* fern + -LOGY] —**pteridological** (ˌtɛrɪdəʊ'lɒdʒɪkᵊl) *adj.*

pteridophyte ('tɛrɪdəʊˌfaɪt) *n.* a plant, such as a fern, reproducing by spores and having vascular tissue, roots, stems, and leaves. [C19: from *pterido-*, from Gk *pteris* fern + -PHYTE]

ptero- *combining form.* a wing, or a part resembling a wing: *pterodactyl.* [from Gk *pteron*]

pterodactyl (ˌtɛrə'dæktɪl) *n.* an extinct flying reptile having membranous wings supported on an elongated fourth digit.

pteropod ('tɛrəˌpɒd) *n.* a small marine gastropod mollusc in which the foot is expanded into two winglike lobes for swimming. Also called: **sea butterfly.**

pterosaur ('tɛrəˌsɔː) *n.* any of an order of extinct flying reptiles of Jurassic and Cretaceous times: included the pterodactyls.

-pterous *or* **-pteran** *adj. combining form.* indicating a specified number or type of wings: *dipterous.* [from Gk *-pteros*, from *pteron* wing]

pterygoid process ('tɛrɪˌgɔɪd) *n. Anat.* either of two long bony plates extending downwards from each side of the sphenoid bone within the skull. [C18 *pterygoid*, from Gk *pterugoeidēs*, from *pterux* wing; see -OID]

PTO *or* **pto** *abbrev. for* please turn over.

Ptolemaic (ˌtɒlɪ'meɪɪk) *adj.* **1.** of or relating to the ancient astronomer Ptolemy or to his conception of the universe. **2.** of or relating to the Macedonian dynasty that ruled Egypt from the death of Alexander the Great (323 B.C.) to the death of Cleopatra (30 B.C.).

Ptolemaic system *n.* the theory of planetary motion developed by Ptolemy from the hypotheses of earlier philosophers, stating that the earth lay at the centre of the universe with the sun, the moon, and the known planets revolving around it in complicated orbits. Beyond the largest of these orbits lay a sphere of fixed stars.

Ptolemy ('tɒlɪmɪ) *n.* Latin name *Claudius Ptolemaeus.* 2nd-century A.D. Greek astronomer, mathematician, and geographer. His *Geography* was the standard geographical textbook until the discoveries of the 15th century. His system of astronomy (see **Ptolemaic system**), as expounded in the *Almagest*, remained undisputed until the Copernican system was evolved.

Ptolemy I *n.* called *Ptolemy Soter.* ?367–283 B.C., king of Egypt (323–285 B.C.), a general of Alexander the Great, who obtained Egypt on Alexander's death and founded the Ptolemaic dynasty: his capital Alexandria became the centre of Greek culture.

Ptolemy II *n.* called *Philadelphus.* 309–246 B.C., the son of Ptolemy I; king of Egypt (285–246). Under his rule the power, prosperity, and culture of Egypt was at its height.

ptomaine *or* **ptomain** ('təʊmeɪn) *n.* any of a group of amines formed by decaying organic matter. [C19: from It. *ptomaina*, from Gk *ptoma* corpse, from *piptein* to fall]

ptomaine poisoning *n.* a popular term for **food poisoning.** Ptomaines were once erroneously thought to be a cause of food poisoning.

ptosis ('təʊsɪs) *n.*, *pl.* **ptoses** ('təʊsiːz). prolapse or drooping of a part, esp. the eyelid. [C18: from Gk: a falling] —**ptotic** ('tɒtɪk) *adj.*

pty *Austral., N.Z., & S. African. abbrev. for* proprietary.

ptyalin ('taɪəlɪn) *n. Biochemistry.* an amylase secreted in the saliva of man and other animals. [C19: from Gk *ptualon* saliva, from *ptuein* to spit]

p-type *adj.* **1.** (of a semiconductor) having a density of mobile holes in excess of that of conduction electrons. **2.** associated with or resulting from the movement of holes in a semiconductor: *p-type conductivity.*

Pu *the chemical symbol for* plutonium.

pub (pʌb) *n.* **1.** *Chiefly Brit.* a building with a bar and one or more public rooms licensed for the sale and consumption of alcoholic drink, often also providing light meals. Formal name: **public house. 2.** *Austral. & N.Z.* a hotel. ~*vb.* **pubbing, pubbed. 3.** (*intr.*) *Inf.* to visit a pub or pubs (esp. in **go pubbing**).

pub. *abbrev. for:* **1.** public. **2.** publication. **3.** published. **4.** publisher. **5.** publishing.

pub-crawl *Inf., chiefly Brit.* ~*n.* **1.** a drinking tour of a number of pubs or bars. ~*vb.* **2.** (*intr.*) to make such a tour.

puberty ('pjuːbətɪ) *n.* the period at the beginning of adolescence when the sex glands become functional. Also called: **pubescence.** [C14: from L *pūbertās* maturity, from *pūber* adult] — 'pubertal *adj.*

pubes ('pjuːbiːz) *n.*, *pl.* **pubes. 1.** the region above the external genital organs, covered with hair from the time of puberty. **2.** pubic hair. **3.** the pubic bones. **4.** the plural of **pubis.** [from L]

pubescent (pjuː'bɛsᵊnt) *adj.* **1.** arriving or arrived at puberty. **2.** (of certain plants and animals or their parts) covered with a layer of fine short hairs or down. [C17: from L *pūbēscere* to reach manhood, from *pūber* adult] —**pu'bescence** *n.*

pubic ('pjuːbɪk) *adj.* of or relating to the pubes or pubis: *pubic hair.*

pubis ('pjuːbɪs) *n.*, *pl.* **-bes.** one of the three sections of the hipbone that forms part of the pelvis. [C16: shortened from NL *os pūbis* bone of the PUBES]

public ('pʌblɪk) *adj.* **1.** of or concerning the people as a whole. **2.** open to all: *public gardens.* **3.** performed or made openly: *public proclamation.* **4.** (*prenominal*) well-known: *a public figure.* **5.** (*usually prenominal*) maintained at the expense of, serving, or for the use of a community: *a public library.* **6.** open, acknowledged, or notorious: *a public scandal.* **7. go public.** (of a private company) to issue shares for subscription by the public. *~n.* **8.** the community or people in general. **9.** a section of the community grouped because of a common interest, activity, etc.: *the racing public.* [C15: from L *pūblicus,* changed from *pōplicus* of the people, from *populus* people] —**'publicly** *adv.*

public-address system *n.* a system of microphones, amplifiers, and loudspeakers for increasing the sound level, used in auditoriums, public gatherings, etc. Sometimes shortened to **PA system.**

publican ('pʌblɪkən) *n.* **1.** (in Britain) a person who keeps a public house. **2.** (in ancient Rome) a public contractor, esp. one who farmed the taxes of a province. [C12: from OF *publicain,* from L *pūblicānus* tax gatherer, from *pūblicum* state revenues]

publication (,pʌblɪ'keɪʃən) *n.* **1.** the act or process of publishing a printed work. **2.** any printed work offered for sale or distribution. **3.** the act or an instance of making information public. [C14: via OF from L *pūblicātiō* confiscation of property, from *pūblicāre* to seize for public use]

public bar *n. Brit.* a bar in a public house usually serving drinks at a cheaper price than in the lounge bar.

public company *n.* a limited company whose shares may be purchased by the public and traded freely on the open market and whose share capital is not less than a statutory minimum; public limited company. Cf. **private company.**

public convenience *n.* a public lavatory.

public corporation *n.* (in Britain) an organization established to run a nationalized industry or state-owned enterprise. The chairman and board members are appointed by a government minister, and the government has overall control.

public domain *n.* **1.** the status of a published work upon which the copyright has expired or which has not been subject to copyright. **2. in the public domain.** generally known or accessible.

public enemy *n.* a notorious person, such as a criminal, who is regarded as a menace to the public.

public house *n.* **1.** *Brit.* the formal name for a **pub. 2.** *U.S. & Canad.* an inn, tavern, or small hotel.

publicist ('pʌblɪsɪst) *n.* **1.** a person who publicizes something, esp. a press or publicity agent. **2.** a journalist. **3.** *Rare.* a person learned in public or international law.

publicity (pʌ'blɪsɪtɪ) *n.* **1. a.** the technique or process of attracting public attention to people, products, etc., as by the use of the mass media. **b.** (*as modifier*): *a publicity agent.* **2.** public interest aroused by such a technique or process. **3.** information used to draw public attention to people, products, etc. **4.** the state of being public. [C18: via F from Med. L *pūblicitās;* see PUBLIC]

publicize *or* **-ise** ('pʌblɪ,saɪz) *vb.* (*tr.*) to bring to public notice; advertise.

public lending right *n.* the right of authors to receive payment when their books are borrowed from public libraries.

public limited company *n.* another name for **public company.** Abbrev.: **plc** *or* **PLC.**

public nuisance *n.* **1.** *Law.* an illegal act causing harm to members of a community rather than to any individual. **2.** *Inf.* a person generally considered objectionable.

public opinion *n.* the attitude of the public, esp. as a factor in determining action, policy, etc.

public prosecutor *n. Law.* an official in charge of prosecuting important cases.

Public Record Office *n.* an institution in which official records are stored and kept available for inspection by the public.

public relations *n.* (*functioning as sing. or pl.*) **1. a.** the practice of creating, promoting, or maintaining goodwill and a favourable image among the public towards an institution, public body, etc. **b.** the professional staff employed for this purpose. Abbrev.: **PR. c.** the techniques employed. **d.** (*as modifier*): *the public-relations industry.* **2.** the relationship between an organization and the public.

public school *n.* **1.** (in England and Wales) a private independent fee-paying secondary school. **2.** in certain Canadian provinces, a public elementary school as

distinguished from a separate school. **3.** any school that is part of a free local educational system.

public sector *n.* the part of an economy which consists of state-owned institutions, including nationalized industries and services provided by local authorities.

public servant *n.* **1.** an elected or appointed holder of a public office. **2.** the Austral. and N.Z. equivalent of **civil servant.**

public service *n.* the Austral. and N.Z. equivalent of the **civil service.**

public-spirited *adj.* having or showing active interest in the good of the community.

public utility *n.* an enterprise concerned with the provision to the public of essentials, such as electricity or water. Also called (in the U.S.): **public-service corporation.**

public works *pl. n.* engineering projects and other constructions, financed and undertaken by a government for the community.

publish ('pʌblɪʃ) *vb.* **1.** to produce and issue (printed matter) for distribution and sale. **2.** (*intr.*) to have one's written work issued for publication. **3.** (*tr.*) to announce formally or in public. **4.** (*tr.*) to communicate (defamatory matter) to someone other than the person defamed: *to publish a libel.* [C14: from OF *puplier,* from L *pūblicāre* to make PUBLIC] —**'publishable** *adj.*

publisher ('pʌblɪʃə) *n.* **1.** a company or person engaged in publishing periodicals, books, music, etc. **2.** *U.S. & Canad.* the proprietor of a newspaper.

Puccini (pʊ'tʃiːnɪ) *n.* **Giacomo** ('dʒaːkomo). 1858–1924, Italian operatic composer, noted for the dramatic realism of his operas, which include *Manon Lescaut* (1893), *La Bohème* (1896), *Tosca* (1900), and *Madame Butterfly* (1904).

puce (pjuːs) *n., adj.* (of) a colour varying from deep red to dark purplish brown. [C18: shortened from F *couleur puce* flea colour, from L *pūlex* flea]

puck[1] (pʌk) *n.* a small disc of hard rubber used in ice hockey. [C19: from ?]

puck[2] (pʌk) *n.* a mischievous or evil spirit. [OE *pūca,* from ?] —**'puckish** *adj.*

pucka ('pʌkə) *adj.* a less common spelling of **pukka.**

pucker ('pʌkə) *vb.* **1.** to gather (a soft surface such as the skin) into wrinkles, or (of such a surface) to be so gathered. *~n.* **2.** a wrinkle, crease, or irregular fold. [C16: ? rel. to POKE[2], from the baglike wrinkles]

pudding ('pʊdɪŋ) *n.* **1.** a sweetened usually cooked dessert made in many forms and of various ingredients. **2.** a savoury dish, usually consisting partially of pastry or batter: *steak-and-kidney pudding.* **3.** the dessert course in a meal. **4.** a sausage-like mass of meat, oatmeal, etc., stuffed into a prepared skin or bag and boiled. [C13 *poding*] —**'puddingy** *adj.*

pudding stone *n.* a conglomerate rock in which there is a difference in colour and composition between the pebbles and the matrix.

puddle ('pʌdºl) *n.* **1.** a small pool of water, esp. of rain. **2.** a small pool of any liquid. **3.** a worked mixture of wet clay and sand that is impervious to water and is used to line a pond or canal. *~vb.* (*tr.*) **4.** to make (clay, etc.) into puddle. **5.** to subject (iron) to puddling. [C14 *podel,* dim. of OE *pudd* ditch, from ?] —**'puddler** *n.* —**'puddly** *adj.*

puddling ('pʌdlɪŋ) *n.* a process for converting pig iron into wrought iron by heating it with ferric oxide in a furnace and stirring it to oxidize the carbon.

pudency ('pjuːdºnsɪ) *n.* modesty or prudishness. [C17: from LL *pudentia,* from L *pudēre* to feel shame]

pudendum (pjuː'dɛndəm) *n., pl.* **-da** (-də). (*often pl.*) the human external genital organs collectively, esp. of a female. [C17: from LL, from L *pudenda* the shameful (parts), from *pudēre* to be ashamed] —**pu'dendal** *or* **pudic** ('pjuːdɪk) *adj.*

pudgy ('pʌdʒɪ) *adj.* **pudgier, pudgiest.** a variant spelling (esp. U.S.) of **podgy.** [C19: from ?] —**'pudgily** *adv.* —**'pudginess** *n.*

Pudsey ('pʊdzɪ) *n.* a town in N England, in West Yorkshire between Leeds and Bradford. Pop.: 38 977 (1981).

Puebla (*Spanish* 'pweβla) *n.* **1.** an inland state of S central Mexico, situated on the Anáhuac Plateau. Capital: Puebla. Pop.: 3 279 960 (1980). Area: 33 919 sq. km (13 096 sq. miles). **2.** a city in S Mexico, capital of Puebla state: founded in 1532; university (1537). Pop.: 835 759 (1980). Full name: **Puebla de Zaragoza** (de θara'ɣoθa).

pueblo ('pwɛbləʊ; *Spanish* 'pweβlo) *n., pl.* **-los** (-ləʊz; *Spanish* -los). **1.** a communal village, built by certain Indians of the southwestern U.S. and parts of Latin America, consisting of one or more flat-roofed houses. **2.** (in Spanish America) a village or town. [C19: from Sp.: people, from L *populus*]

Pueblo ('pwɛbləʊ) *n., pl.* **-lo** *or* **-los.** a member of any of the North American Indian peoples who live in pueblos.

puerile ('pjʊəraɪl) *adj.* **1.** exhibiting silliness; immature; trivial. **2.** of or characteristic of a child. [C17: from L *puerīlis* childish, from *puer* a boy] —'**puerilely** *adv.* —**puerility** (pjʊə'rɪlɪtɪ) *n.*

puerperal (pjuː'ɜːpərəl) *adj.* of or occurring during the period following childbirth. [C18: from NL *puerperālis*, from L *puerperium* childbirth, ult. from *puer* boy + *parere* to bear]

puerperal fever *n.* a serious, formerly widespread, form of blood poisoning caused by infection contracted during childbirth.

puerperal psychosis *n.* a mental disorder sometimes occurring in women after childbirth, characterized by deep depression.

Puerto Rico ('pwɜːtəʊ 'riːkəʊ, 'pwɛə-) *n.* an autonomous commonwealth (in association with the U.S.) occupying the smallest and easternmost of the Greater Antilles in the Caribbean: one of the most densely populated areas in the world; ceded by Spain to the U.S. in 1899. Capital: San Juan. Pop.: 3 300 000 (1987). Area: 8674 sq. km (3349 sq. miles). Former name (until 1932): **Porto Rico.** Abbrev.: **PR.** —**Puerto Rican** *adj., n.*

puff (pʌf) *n.* **1.** a short quick gust or emission, as of wind, smoke, etc. **2.** the amount of wind, smoke, etc., released in a puff. **3.** the sound made by a puff. **4.** an instance of inhaling and expelling the breath as in smoking. **5.** a light aerated pastry usually filled with cream, jam, etc. **6.** a powder puff. **7.** exaggerated praise, as of a book, product, etc., esp. through an advertisement. **8.** a piece of clothing fabric gathered up so as to bulge in the centre while being held together at the edges. **9.** a cylindrical roll of hair pinned in place in a coiffure. **10.** *U.S.* a quilted bed cover. **11.** one's breath (esp. in **out of puff**). **12.** *Derog. sl.* a male homosexual. ~*vb.* **13.** to blow or breathe or cause to blow or breathe in short quick draughts. **14.** (*tr.*; often foll. by *out; usually passive*) to cause to be out of breath. **15.** to take draws at (a cigarette, etc.). **16.** (*intr.*) to move with or by the emission of puffs: *the steam train puffed up the incline.* **17.** (often foll. by *up, out,* etc.) to swell, as with air, pride, etc. **18.** (*tr.*) to praise with exaggerated empty words, often in advertising. **19.** (*tr.*) to apply (powder, dust, etc.) to (something). [OE *pyffan*] —'**puffy** *adj.*

puff adder *n.* **1.** a large venomous African viper that inflates its body when alarmed. **2.** another name for **hognose snake.**

puffball ('pʌf,bɔːl) *n.* **1.** any of various fungi having a round fruiting body that discharges a cloud of brown spores when mature. **2.** short for **puffball skirt.**

puffball skirt *n.* a skirt or a dress with a skirt that puffs out wide and is nipped into a narrow hem.

puffer ('pʌfə) *n.* **1.** a person or thing that puffs. **2.** Also called: **globefish.** a marine fish with an elongated spiny body that can be inflated to form a globe.

puffin ('pʌfɪn) *n.* any of various northern diving birds, having a black-and-white plumage and a brightly coloured vertically flattened bill. [C14: ? of Cornish origin]

puff pastry *or U.S.* **puff paste** *n.* a dough used for making a rich flaky pastry.

puff-puff *n. Brit.* a children's name for a steam locomotive or railway train.

pug[1] (pʌg) *n.* a small compact breed of dog with a smooth coat, lightly curled tail, and a short wrinkled nose. [C16: from ?] —'**puggish** *adj.*

pug[2] (pʌg) *vb.* **pugging, pugged.** (*tr.*) **1.** to mix (clay) with water to form a malleable mass or paste, often in a **pug mill.** **2.** to fill or stop with clay or a similar substance. [C19: from ?]

pug[3] (pʌg) *n.* a slang name for **boxer** (sense 1). [C20: shortened from PUGILIST]

Puget Sound ('pjuːdʒɪt) *n.* an inlet of the Pacific in NW Washington. Length: about 130 km (80 miles).

pugging ('pʌgɪŋ) *n.* material such as clay, sawdust, etc., inserted between wooden flooring and ceiling to deaden sound. Also called: **pug.**

puggree, pugree ('pʌgrɪ) *or* **puggaree, pugaree** ('pʌgərɪ) *n.* **1.** the usual Indian word for **turban.** **2.** a scarf, usually pleated, around the crown of some hats, esp. sun helmets. [C17: from Hindi *pagrī*, from Sansk. *parikara*]

pugilism ('pjuːdʒɪ,lɪzəm) *n.* the art, practice, or profession of fighting with the fists; boxing. [C18: from L *pugil* a boxer] —'**pugilist** *n.* —,**pugi'listic** *adj.* —,**pugi'listically** *adv.*

Pugin ('pjuːdʒɪn) *n.* **Augustus** (**Welby Northmore**). 1812–52, English architect; a leader of the English Gothic revival. He collaborated with Sir Charles Barry on the Palace of Westminster (begun 1836).

Puglia ('puʎʎa) *n.* the Italian name for **Apulia.**

pugnacious (pʌg'neɪʃəs) *adj.* readily disposed to fight; belligerent. [C17: from L *pugnāx*] —**pug'naciously** *adv.* —**pugnacity** (pʌg'næsɪtɪ) *n.*

pug nose *n.* a short stubby upturned nose. [C18: from PUG[1]] —'**pug-,nosed** *adj.*

puisne ('pjuːnɪ) *adj.* (esp. of a subordinate judge) of lower rank. [C16: from Anglo-F, from OF *puisné* born later, from L *posteā* afterwards + *nascī* to be born]

puissance ('pjuːɪsᵊns, 'pwiːsɑːns) *n.* **1.** a competition in showjumping that tests a horse's ability to jump large obstacles. **2.** *Arch. or poetic.* power. [C15: from OF; see PUISSANT]

puissant ('pjuːɪsᵊnt) *adj. Arch. or poetic.* powerful. [C15: from OF, ult. from L *potēns* mighty, from *posse* to have power] —'**puissantly** *adv.*

puke (pjuːk) *Sl.* ~*vb.* **1.** to vomit. ~*n.* **2.** the act of vomiting. **3.** the matter vomited. [C16: prob. imit.]

pukeko ('pʊkəkəʊ) *n., pl.* **-kos.** a New Zealand wading bird with bright plumage. [from Maori]

pukka *or* **pucka** ('pʌkə) *adj. Anglo-Indian.* properly or perfectly done, constructed, etc.; good; genuine. [C17: from Hindi *pakkā* firm, from Sansk. *pakva*]

Pula (*Serbo-Croatian* 'puːla) *n.* a port in NW Yugoslavia, in NW Croatia at the S tip of the Istrian Peninsula: made a Roman military base in 178 B.C.; became the main Austro-Hungarian naval station and passed to Italy in 1919, then to Yugoslavia in 1947. Pop.: 77 278 (1981 est.). Latin name: **Pietas Julia** (paɪ'ɛtæs 'juːlɪə). Italian name: **Pola.**

pulchritude ('pʌlkrɪ,tjuːd) *n. Formal or literary.* physical beauty. [C15: from L *pulchritūdō*, from *pulcher* beautiful] —,**pulchri'tudinous** *adj.*

pule (pjuːl) *vb.* (*intr.*) to cry plaintively; whimper. [C16: ? imit.] —'**puler** *n.*

Pulitzer ('pʊlɪtsə) *n.* **Joseph.** 1847–1911, U.S. newspaper publisher, born in Hungary. He established the Pulitzer prizes.

Pulitzer prize *n.* one of a group of prizes established by Joseph Pulitzer and awarded yearly since 1917 for excellence in American journalism, literature, and music.

pull (pʊl) *vb.* (*mainly tr.*) **1.** (*also intr.*) to exert force on (an object) so as to draw it towards the source of the force. **2.** to remove; extract: *to pull a tooth.* **3.** to strip of feathers, hair, etc.; pluck. **4.** to draw the entrails from (a fowl). **5.** to rend or tear. **6.** to strain (a muscle or tendon). **7.** (usually foll. by *off*) *Inf.* to bring about: *to pull off a million-pound deal.* **8.** (often foll. by *on*) *Inf.* to draw out (a weapon) for use: *he pulled a knife on his attacker.* **9.** *Inf.* to attract: *the pop group pulled a crowd.* **10.** (*intr.*; usually foll. by *on* or *at*) to drink or inhale deeply: *to pull at one's pipe.* **11.** to make (a grimace): *to pull a face.* **12.** (*also intr.*; foll. by *away, out, over,* etc.) to move (a vehicle) or (of a vehicle) to be moved in a specified manner. **13.** (*intr.*) to possess or exercise the power to move: *this car doesn't pull well on hills.* **14.** *Printing.* to take (a proof) from type. **15.** *Golf, baseball, etc.* to hit (a ball) so that it veers away from the direction in which the player intended to hit it. **16.** *Cricket.* to hit (a ball pitched straight or on the off side) to the leg side. **17.** (*also intr.*) to row (a boat) or take a stroke of (an oar) in rowing. **18.** (of a rider) to restrain (a horse), esp. to prevent it from winning a race. **19. pull a fast one.** *Sl.* to play a sly trick. **20. pull apart** *or* **to pieces.** to criticize harshly. **21. pull (one's) punches. a.** *Inf.* to restrain the force of one's criticisms or actions. **b.** *Boxing.* to restrain the force of one's blows. ~*n.* **22.** an act or an instance of pulling or being pulled. **23.** the force or effort used in pulling: *the pull of the moon affects the tides.* **24.** the act or an instance of taking in drink or smoke. **25.** *Printing.* a proof taken from type: *the first pull was smudged.* **26.**

something used for pulling, such as a handle. **27.** *Inf.* special advantage or influence: *his uncle is chairman of the company, so he has quite a lot of pull.* **28.** *Inf.* the power to attract attention or support. **29.** a period of rowing. **30.** a single stroke of an oar in rowing. **31.** the act of pulling the ball in golf, cricket, etc. **32.** the act of reining in a horse. ~See also **pull down, pull in,** etc. [OE *pullian*] —'**puller** *n.*

pull down *vb.* (*tr., adv.*) to destroy or demolish: *the old houses were pulled down.*

pullet ('pʊlɪt) *n.* a young hen of the domestic fowl, less than one year old. [C14: from OF *poulet* chicken, from L *pullus* a young animal or bird]

pulley ('pʊlɪ) *n.* **1.** a wheel with a grooved rim in which a rope can run in order to change the direction of a force applied to the rope, etc. **2.** a number of such wheels pivoted in parallel in a block, used to raise heavy loads. **3.** a wheel with a flat, convex, or grooved rim mounted on a shaft and driven by or driving a belt passing around it. [C14 *poley,* from OF *polie,* from Vulgar L *polidium* (unattested), apparently from LGk *polidion* (unattested) a little pole, from Gk *polos* axis]

pull in *vb.* (*adv.*) **1.** (*intr.; often foll. by to*) to reach a destination: *the train pulled in at the station.* **2.** (*intr.*) Also: **pull over.** (of a motor vehicle) **a.** to draw in to the side of the road. **b.** to stop (at a café, lay-by, etc.). **3.** (*tr.*) to attract: *his appearance will pull in the crowds.* **4.** (*tr.*) *Brit. sl.* to arrest. **5.** (*tr.*) to earn or gain (money). ~*n.* **pull-in. 6.** *Brit.* a roadside café, esp. for lorry drivers.

Pullman ('pʊlmən) *n., pl.* **-mans.** a luxurious railway coach. Also called: **Pullman car.** [C19: after G. M. *Pullman* (1831–97), its U.S. inventor]

pull off *vb.* (*tr.*) **1.** to remove (clothing) forcefully. **2.** (*adv.*) to succeed in performing (a difficult feat).

pull out *vb.* (*adv.*) **1.** (*tr.*) to extract. **2.** (*intr.*) to depart: *the train pulled out of the station.* **3.** *Mil.* to withdraw or be withdrawn: *the troops were pulled out of the ruined city.* **4.** (*intr.*) (of a motor vehicle) **a.** to draw away from the side of the road. **b.** to draw out from behind another vehicle to overtake. **5.** (*intr.*) to abandon a position or situation. **6.** (foll. by *of*) to level out (from a dive). ~*n.* **pull-out. 7.** an extra leaf of a book that folds out. **8.** a removable section of a magazine, etc.

pullover ('pʊl,əʊvə) *n.* a garment, esp. a sweater, that is pulled on over the head.

pull through *vb.* to survive or recover or cause to survive or recover, esp. after a serious illness or crisis. Also: **pull round.**

pull together *vb.* **1.** (*intr., adv.*) to cooperate, or work harmoniously. **2. pull oneself together.** *Inf.* to regain one's self-control or composure.

pullulate ('pʌljʊ,leɪt) *vb.* (*intr.*) **1.** (of animals, etc.) to breed abundantly. **2.** (of plants) to sprout, bud, or germinate. [C17: from L *pullulāre* to sprout, from *pullulus* a baby animal, from *pullus* young animal] —,**pullu'lation** *n.*

pull up *vb.* (*adv.*) **1.** (*tr.*) to remove by the roots. **2.** (often foll. by *with* or *on*) to move level (with) or ahead (of), esp. in a race. **3.** to stop: *the car pulled up suddenly.* **4.** (*tr.*) to rebuke. ~*n.* **pull-up. 5.** *Brit.* a roadside café; pull-in.

pulmonary ('pʌlmənərɪ, 'pʊl-) *adj.* **1.** of or affecting the lungs. **2.** having lungs or lunglike organs. [C18: from L *pulmōnārius,* from *pulmō* a lung]

pulmonary artery *n.* either of the two arteries that convey oxygen-depleted blood from the heart to the lungs.

pulmonary vein *n.* any one of the four veins that convey oxygen-rich blood from the lungs to the heart.

pulp (pʌlp) *n.* **1.** soft or fleshy plant tissue, such as the succulent part of a fleshy fruit. **2.** a moist mixture of cellulose fibres, as obtained from wood, from which paper is made. **3. a.** a magazine or book containing trite or sensational material, and usually printed on cheap rough paper. **b.** (*as modifier*): *a pulp novel.* **4.** *Dentistry.* the soft innermost part of a tooth, containing nerves and blood vessels. **5.** any soft soggy mass. **6.** *Mining.* pulverized ore. ~*vb.* **7.** to reduce (a material) to pulp or (of a material) to be reduced to pulp. **8.** (*tr.*) to remove the pulp from (fruit, etc.). [C16: from L *pulpa*] —'**pulpy** *adj.*

pulpit ('pʊlpɪt) *n.* **1.** a raised platform, usually surrounded by a barrier, set up in churches as the appointed place for preaching, etc. **2.** a medium for expressing an

opinion, such as a newspaper column. **3.** (usually preceded by *the*) **a.** the preaching of the Christian message. **b.** the clergy or their influence. [C14: from L *pulpitum* a platform]

pulpwood ('pʌlp,wʊd) *n.* pine, spruce, or any other soft wood used to make paper.

pulque ('pʊlkɪ) *n.* a light alcoholic drink from Mexico made from the juice of various agave plants. [C17: from Mexican Sp., apparently from Nahuatl, from *puliuhqui* decomposed, since it will only keep for a day]

pulsar ('pʌl,sɑː) *n.* any of a number of very small stars first discovered in 1967, which rotate fast, emitting regular pulses of polarized radiation. [C20: from PULS(ATING) ST)AR, on the model of QUASAR]

pulsate (pʌl'seɪt) *vb.* (*intr.*) **1.** to expand and contract with a rhythmical beat; throb. **2.** *Physics.* to vary in intensity, magnitude, etc. **3.** to quiver or vibrate. [C18: from L *pulsāre* to push] —**pulsative** ('pʌlsətɪv) *adj.* —**pul'sation** *n.* —**pul'sator** *n.* —**pulsatory** ('pʌlsətərɪ, -trɪ) *adj.*

pulsatilla (,pʌlsə'tɪlə) *n.* any of a genus of plants related to the anemone, with feathery or hairy foliage. [C16: from Med. L, from *pulsāta* beaten (by the wind)]

pulsating star *n.* a type of variable star, the variation in brightness resulting from expansion and subsequent contraction of the star.

pulse¹ (pʌls) *n.* **1.** *Physiol.* **a.** the rhythmical contraction and expansion of an artery at each beat of the heart. **b.** a single such pulsation. **2.** *Physics, electronics.* **a.** a transient sharp change in some quantity normally constant in a system. **b.** one of a series of such transient disturbances, usually recurring at regular intervals. **3. a.** a recurrent rhythmical series of beats, vibrations, etc. **b.** any single beat, wave, etc., in such a series. **4.** an inaudible electronic "ping" to operate a slide projector. **5.** bustle, vitality, or excitement: *the pulse of a city.* **6. keep one's finger on the pulse.** to be well informed about current events, opinions, etc. ~*vb.* **7.** (*intr.*) to beat, throb, or vibrate. **8.** (*tr.*) to provide an electronic pulse to operate (a slide projector). [C14 *pous,* from L *pulsus* a beating, from *pellere* to beat] —'**pulseless** *adj.*

pulse² (pʌls) *n.* **1.** the edible seeds of any of several leguminous plants, such as peas, beans, and lentils. **2.** the plant producing any of these. [C13 *pols,* from OF, from L *puls* pottage of pulse]

pulsejet ('pʌls,dʒɛt) *n.* a type of ramjet engine in which air is admitted through movable vanes that are closed by the pressure resulting from each intermittent explosion of the fuel in the combustion chamber, thus causing a pulsating thrust. Also called: **pulsejet engine, pulsojet.**

pulse modulation *n. Electronics.* a type of modulation in which a train of pulses is used as the carrier wave, one or more of its parameters, such as amplitude, being modulated or modified in order to carry information.

pulsimeter (pʌl'sɪmɪtə) *n. Med.* an instrument for measuring the rate of pulse.

pulverize *or* **-ise** ('pʌlvə,raɪz) *vb.* **1.** to reduce (a substance) to fine particles, as by grinding, or (of a substance) to be so reduced. **2.** (*tr.*) to destroy completely. [C16: from LL *pulverizare,* from L *pulvis* dust] —'**pulver,izable** *or* **-,isable** *adj.* —,**pulveri'zation** *or* **-i'sation** *n.* —'**pulver,izer** *or* **-,iser** *n.*

pulverulent (pʌl'vɛrʊlənt) *adj.* consisting of, covered with, or crumbling to dust or fine particles. [C17: from L *pulverulentus,* from *pulvis* dust]

puma ('pjuːmə) *n.* a large American feline mammal that resembles a lion, having a plain greyish-brown coat and long tail. Also called: **cougar, mountain lion.** [C18: via Sp. from Quechua]

pumice ('pʌmɪs) *n.* **1.** Also called: **pumice stone.** a light porous volcanic rock used for scouring and, in powdered form, as an abrasive and for polishing. ~*vb.* **2.** (*tr.*) to rub or polish with pumice. [C15 *pomys,* from OF *pomis,* from L *pūmex*] —**pumiceous** (pjuː'mɪʃəs) *adj.*

pummel ('pʌməl) *vb.* **-melling, -melled** *or U.S.* **-meling, -meled.** (*tr.*) to strike repeatedly with or as if with the fists. Also (less commonly): **pommel.** [C16: see POMMEL]

pump¹ (pʌmp) *n.* **1.** any device for compressing, driving, raising, or reducing the pressure of a fluid, esp. by means of a piston or set of rotating impellers. ~*vb.* **2.** (when *tr.,* usually foll. by *from, out,* etc.) to raise or drive (air, liquid, etc., esp. into or from something) with a pump. **3.** (*tr.;* usually foll. by *in* or *into*) to supply in large amounts: *to pump capital into a project.* **4.** (*tr.*) to deliver (bullets, etc.) repeatedly. **5.** to operate (something, esp. a handle) in the manner of a pump or (of something) to work in this way: *to pump the pedals of a bicycle*. **6.** (*tr.*) to obtain (information) from (a person) by persistent questioning. **7.** (*intr.; usually foll. by from or out of*) (of liquids) to flow freely in large spurts: *oil pumped from the fissure*. **8. pump iron.** *Sl.* to exercise with weights; do body-building exercises. [C15: from MDu. *pumpe* pipe, prob. from Sp. *bomba*, imit.]

pump² (pʌmp) *n.* **1.** a low-cut low-heeled shoe without fastenings, worn esp. for dancing. **2.** a type of shoe with a rubber sole, used in games such as tennis; plimsoll. [C16: from ?]

pumpernickel ('pʌmpə,nɪkªl) *n.* a slightly sour black bread, originating in Germany, made of coarse rye flour. [C18: from G, from ?]

pumpkin ('pʌmpkɪn) *n.* **1.** any of several creeping plants of the genus *Cucurbita*. **2.** the large round fruit of any of these plants, which has a thick orange rind, pulpy flesh, and numerous seeds. [C17: from earlier *pumpion*, from OF, from L *pepo*, from Gk, from *peptein* to ripen]

pump priming *n.* **1.** the process of introducing fluid into a pump to improve starting and to expel air from it. **2.** government expenditure designed to stimulate economic activity in stagnant or depressed areas. **3.** another term for **deficit financing.**

pun¹ (pʌn) *n.* **1.** the use of words to exploit ambiguities and innuendoes for humorous effect; a play on words. An example is: *"Ben Battle was a soldier bold, And used to war's alarms: But a cannonball took off his legs, So he laid down his arms."* (Thomas Hood). ~*vb.* **punning, punned. 2.** (*intr.*) to make puns. [C17: ?from It. *puntiglio* wordplay; see PUNCTILIO]

pun² (pʌn) *vb.* **punning, punned.** (*tr.*) *Brit.* to pack (earth, rubble, etc.) by pounding. [C16: var. of POUND¹]

puna *Spanish.* ('puna) *n.* **1.** a high cold dry plateau. **2.** another name for **mountain sickness.** [C17: from American Sp., of Amerind origin]

Punakha *or* **Punaka** ('puːnəkə) *n.* a town in W central Bhutan: a former capital of the country.

punch¹ (pʌntʃ) *vb.* **1.** to strike at, esp. with a clenched fist. **2.** (*tr.*) *Western U.S.* to herd or drive (cattle), esp. for a living. **3.** (*tr.*) to poke with a stick, etc. ~*n.* **4.** a blow with the fist. **5.** *Inf.* point or vigour: *his arguments lacked punch.* [C15: ? var. of *pounce*, from OF *poinçonner* to stamp] —'**puncher** *n.*

punch² (pʌntʃ) *n.* **1.** a tool or machine for piercing holes in a material. **2.** a tool or machine used for stamping a design on something or shaping it by impact. **3.** the solid die of a punching machine. **4.** *Computers.* a device for making holes in a card or paper tape. ~*vb.* **5.** (*tr.*) to pierce, cut, stamp, shape, or drive with a punch. [C14: shortened from *puncheon*, from OF *ponçon*; see PUNCHEON²]

punch³ (pʌntʃ) *n.* any mixed drink containing fruit juice and, usually, alcoholic liquor, generally hot and spiced. [C17: ?from Hindi *pānch*, from Sansk. *pañca* five; it orig. had five ingredients]

Punch (pʌntʃ) *n.* the main character in the traditional children's puppet show **Punch and Judy.**

punchball ('pʌntʃ,bɔːl) *n.* **1.** Also called (U.S. and Canad.): **punching bag.** a stuffed or inflated ball or bag, either suspended or supported by a flexible rod, that is punched for exercise, esp. boxing training. **2.** *U.S.* a game resembling baseball.

punchbowl ('pʌntʃ,bəʊl) *n.* **1.** a large bowl for serving punch, often having small drinking glasses hooked around the rim. **2.** *Brit.* a bowl-shaped depression in the land.

punch-drunk *adj.* **1.** demonstrating or characteristic of the behaviour of a person who has suffered repeated blows to the head, esp. a professional boxer. **2.** dazed; stupefied.

punched card *or esp. U.S.* **punch card** *n.* a card on which data can be coded in the form of punched holes. In computing, there are usually 80 columns and 12 rows, each column containing a pattern of holes representing one character.

punched tape *or U.S.* (*sometimes*) **perforated tape** *n.* other terms for **paper tape.**

puncheon¹ ('pʌntʃən) *n.* a large cask of variable capacity, usually between 70 and 120 gallons. [C15 *poncion*, from OF *ponchon*, from ?]

puncheon² ('pʌntʃən) *n.* **1.** a short wooden post used as a vertical strut. **2.** a less common name for **punch²** (sense 1). [C14 *ponson*, from OF *ponçon*, from L *punctiō* a puncture, from *pungere* to prick]

Punchinello (,pʌntʃɪ'nɛləʊ) *n.*, *pl.* **-los** *or* **-loes. 1.** a clown from Italian puppet show, the prototype of Punch. **2.** (*sometimes not cap.*) any grotesque or absurd character. [C17: from earlier *Polichinello*, from It. *Polecenella*, from *pulcino* chicken, ult. from L *pullus* young animal]

punch line *n.* the culminating part of a joke, funny story, etc., that gives it its point.

punch-up *n. Brit. inf.* a fight or brawl.

punchy ('pʌntʃɪ) *adj.* **punchier, punchiest. 1.** an informal word for **punch-drunk. 2.** *Inf.* incisive or forceful. —'**punchily** *adv.* —'**punchiness** *n.*

punctate ('pʌŋkteɪt) *adj.* having or marked with minute spots or depressions. [C18: from NL *punctātus*, from L *punctum* a point] —**punc'tation** *n.*

punctilio (pʌŋk'tɪlɪ,əʊ) *n.*, *pl.* **-tilios. 1.** strict attention to minute points of etiquette. **2.** a petty formality or fine point of etiquette. [C16: from It. *puntiglio* small point, from L *punctum* point]

punctilious (pʌŋk'tɪlɪəs) *adj.* **1.** paying scrupulous attention to correctness in etiquette. **2.** attentive to detail. —**punc'tiliously** *adv.* —**punc'tiliousness** *n.*

punctual ('pʌŋktjʊəl) *adj.* **1.** arriving or taking place at an arranged time. **2.** (of a person) having the characteristic of always keeping to arranged times. **3.** *Obs.* precise; exact. **4.** *Maths.* consisting of or confined to a point. [C14: from Med. L *punctuālis* concerning detail, from L *punctum* point] —,**punctu'ality** *n.* —'**punctually** *adv.*

punctuate ('pʌŋktjʊ,eɪt) *vb.* (*mainly tr.*) **1.** (*also intr.*) to insert punctuation marks into (a written text). **2.** to interrupt or insert at frequent intervals: *a meeting punctuated by heckling.* **3.** to give emphasis to. [C17: from Med. L *punctuāre* to prick, from L, from *pungere* to puncture]

punctuation (,pʌŋktjʊ'eɪʃən) *n.* **1.** the use of symbols not belonging to the alphabet of a writing system to indicate aspects of the intonation and meaning not otherwise conveyed in the written language. **2.** the symbols used for this purpose.

punctuation mark *n.* any of the signs used in punctuation, such as a comma.

puncture ('pʌŋktʃə) *n.* **1.** a small hole made by a sharp object. **2.** a perforation and loss of pressure in a pneumatic tyre. **3.** the act of puncturing or perforating. ~*vb.* **4.** (*tr.*) to pierce a hole in (something) with a sharp object. **5.** to cause (something pressurized, esp. a tyre) to lose pressure by piercing, or (of a tyre, etc.) to collapse in this way. **6.** (*tr.*) to depreciate (a person's self-esteem, pomposity, etc.). [C14: from L *punctūra*, from *pungere* to prick]

pundit ('pʌndɪt) *n.* **1.** a self-appointed expert. **2.** (formerly) a learned person. **3.** Also: **pandit.** a Brahman learned in Sanskrit and, esp. in Hindu religion, philosophy or law. [C17: from Hindi *pandit*, from Sansk. *pandita* learned man]

Pune ('puːnə) *n.* another name for **Poona.**

punga ('pʌŋə) *n.* a variant spelling of **ponga.**

pungent ('pʌndʒənt) *adj.* **1.** having an acrid smell or sharp bitter flavour. **2.** (of wit, satire, etc.) biting; caustic. **3.** *Biol.* ending in a sharp point. [C16: from L *pungens* piercing, from *pungere* to prick] —'**pungency** *n.* —'**pungently** *adv.*

Punic ('pjuːnɪk) *adj.* **1.** of or relating to ancient Carthage or the Carthaginians. **2.** treacherous; faithless. ~*n.* **3.** the language of the Carthaginians; a late form of Phoenician. [C15: from L *Pūnicus*, var. of *Poenicus* Carthaginian, from Gk *Phoinix*]

punish ('pʌnɪʃ) *vb.* **1.** to force (someone) to undergo a penalty for some crime or misdemeanour. **2.** (*tr.*) to inflict punishment for (some crime, etc.). **3.** (*tr.*) to treat harshly, esp. as by overexertion: *to punish a horse.* **4.** (*tr.*) *Inf.* to consume in large quantities: *to punish the bottle.* [C14 *punisse*, from OF *punir*, from L *pūnīre* to punish, from *poena* penalty] —'**punishable** *adj.* —'**punisher** *n.* —'**punishing** *adj.*

punishment ('pʌnɪʃmənt) *n.* **1.** a penalty for a crime or offence. **2.** the act of punishing or state of being punished. **3.** *Inf.* rough treatment.

punitive ('pjuːnɪtɪv) *adj.* relating to, involving, or with the intention of inflicting punishment: *a punitive expedition.*

[C17: from Med. L *pūnītīvus* concerning punishment, from L *pūnīre* to punish] —'**punitively** *adv.*

Punjab (pʌn'dʒɑːb, 'pʌndʒɑːb) *n.* **1.** (formerly) a province in NW British India: divided between India and Pakistan in 1947. **2.** a state of NW India: reorganized in 1966 as a Punjabi-speaking state, a large part forming the new state of Haryana; mainly agricultural. Capital: Chandigarh. Pop.: 16 669 755 (1981). Area: 50 255 sq. km (19 403 sq. miles).

Punjabi (pʌn'dʒɑːbɪ) *n.* **1.** (*pl.* **-bis**) a member of the chief people of the Punjab. **2.** the language of the Punjab, belonging to the Indic branch of the Indo-European family. ~*adj.* **3.** of the Punjab, its people, or their language.

Punjab States *pl. n.* (formerly) a group of states in NW India, amalgamated in 1956 with Punjab state.

punk[1] (pʌŋk) *n.* **1.** an inferior or worthless person or thing. **2. a.** a youth movement of the late 1970s, characterized by anti-Establishment slogans and the wearing of worthless articles such as safety pins for decoration. **b.** (*as modifier*): *a punk record.* **3.** worthless articles collectively. **4.** short for **punk rock. 5.** *Obs.* a young male homosexual; catamite. **6.** *Obs.* a prostitute. ~*adj.* **7.** rotten or worthless. [C16: from ?]

punk[2] (pʌŋk) *n.* dried decayed wood or other substance that smoulders when ignited: used as tinder. [C18: from ?]

punka *or* **punkah** ('pʌŋkə) *n.* **1.** a fan made of a palm leaf or leaves. **2.** a large fan made of palm leaves, etc., worked mechanically to cool a room. [C17: from Hindi *pankhā*, from Sansk. *paksaka* fan, from *paksa* wing]

punk rock *n.* rock music in a style of the late 1970s, characterized by offensive or aggressive lyrics and performance. —**punk rocker** *n.*

punnet ('pʌnɪt) *n. Chiefly Brit.* a small basket for fruit. [C19: ? dim. of dialect *pun* POUND[2]]

punster ('pʌnstə) *n.* a person who is fond of making puns, esp. one who makes a tedious habit of this.

punt[1] (pʌnt) *n.* **1.** an open flat-bottomed boat with square ends, propelled by a pole. ~*vb.* **2.** to propel (a boat, esp. a punt) by pushing with a pole on the bottom of a river, etc. [OE *punt* shallow boat, from L *pontō* punt]

punt[2] (pʌnt) *n.* **1.** a kick in certain sports, such as rugby, in which the ball is released and kicked before it hits the ground. ~*vb.* **2.** to kick (a ball, etc.) using a punt. [C19: ? var. of dialect *bunt* to push]

punt[3] (pʌnt) *Chiefly Brit.* ~*vb.* **1.** (*intr.*) to gamble; bet. ~*n.* **2.** a gamble or bet, esp. against the bank, as in roulette, or on horses. **3.** Also called: **punter.** a person who bets. **4. take a punt at.** *Austral. & N.Z. inf.* to make an attempt at. [C18: from F *ponter* to punt, from *ponte* bet laid against the banker, from Sp. *punto* point, from L *punctum*]

punt[4] (punt) *n.* the Irish pound. [Irish Gaelic: pound]

Punta Arenas (*Spanish* 'punta a'renas) *n.* a port in S Chile, on the Strait of Magellan: the southernmost city in the world. Pop.: 67 600 (1983 est.). Former name: **Magallanes.**

punter[1] ('pʌntə) *n.* a person who punts a boat.

punter[2] ('pʌntə) *n.* a person who kicks a ball.

punter[3] ('pʌntə) *n.* **1.** one who gambles or bets. **2.** *Sl.* any client or customer, esp. a prostitute's client. **3.** *Sl.* a victim of a con man.

puny ('pjuːnɪ) *adj.* **-nier, -niest. 1.** small and weakly. **2.** paltry; insignificant. [C16: from OF *puisne* PUISNE] —'**puniness** *n.*

pup (pʌp) *n.* **1. a.** a young dog; puppy. **b.** the young of various other animals, such as the seal. **2. in pup.** (of a bitch) pregnant. **3.** *Inf., chiefly Brit.* a conceited young man (esp. in **young pup**). **4. sell (someone) a pup.** to swindle (someone) by selling him something worthless. ~*vb.* **pupping, pupped. 5.** (of dogs, seals, etc.) to give birth to (young). [C18: back formation from PUPPY]

pupa ('pjuːpə)`*n., pl.* **-pae** (-piː) *or* **-pas.** an insect at the immobile nonfeeding stage of development between larva and adult, when many internal changes occur. [C19: via NL, from L: a doll] —'**pupal** *adj.*

pupate (pjuː'peɪt) *vb.* (*intr.*) (of an insect larva) to develop into a pupa. —**pu'pation** *n.*

pupil[1] ('pjuːpᵊl) *n.* **1.** a student who is taught by a teacher. **2.** *Civil & Scots Law.* a boy under 14 or a girl under 12 who is in the care of a guardian. [C14: from L *pupillus* an orphan, from *pūpus* a child] —'**pupillage** *or U.S.* '**pupilage** *n.* —'**pupillary** *or* '**pupilary** *adj.*

pupil[2] ('pjuːpᵊl) *n.* the dark circular aperture at the centre of the iris of the eye, through which light enters. [C16: from L *pūpilla*, dim. of *pūpa* doll; from the tiny reflections in the eye] —'**pupillary** *or* '**pupilary** *adj.*

pupiparous (pjuː'pɪpərəs) *adj.* (of certain dipterous flies) producing young that have already reached the pupa stage at the time of hatching. [C19: from NL *pupiparus*, from PUPA + *parere* to bring forth]

puppet ('pʌpɪt) *n.* **1. a.** a small doll or figure moved by strings attached to its limbs or by the hand inserted in its cloth body. **b.** (*as modifier*): *a puppet theatre.* **2. a.** a person, state, etc., that appears independent but is controlled by another. **b.** (*as modifier*): *a puppet government.* [C16 *popet*, ?from OF *poupette* little doll, ult. from L *pūpa* doll]

puppeteer (ˌpʌpɪ'tɪə) *n.* a person who manipulates puppets.

puppetry ('pʌpɪtrɪ) *n.* **1.** the art of making and manipulating puppets and presenting puppet shows. **2.** unconvincing or specious presentation.

puppy ('pʌpɪ) *n., pl.* **-pies. 1.** a young dog; pup. **2.** *Inf., contemptuous.* a brash or conceited young man; pup. [C15 *popi*, from OF *popée* doll] —'**puppyhood** *n.* —'**puppyish** *adj.*

puppy fat *n.* fatty tissue that develops in childhood or adolesence and usually disappears with maturity.

puppy love *n.* another term for **calf love.**

Purana (pʊ'rɑːnə) *n.* any of a class of Sanskrit writings not included in the Vedas, characteristically recounting the birth and deeds of Hindu gods and the creation of the universe. [C17: from Sansk.: ancient, from *purā* formerly]

Purbeck marble *or* **stone** ('pɜːbɛk) *n.* a fossil-rich limestone that takes a high polish. [C15: after *Purbeck*, Dorset, where quarried]

purblind ('pɜːˌblaɪnd) *adj.* **1.** partly or nearly blind. **2.** lacking in insight or understanding; obtuse. [C13: see PURE, BLIND]

Purcell ('pɜːsᵊl) *n.* **1. Edward Mills.** born 1912, U.S. physicist, noted for his work on the magnetic moments of atomic nuclei: shared the Nobel prize for physics (1952). **2. Henry.** ?1659–95, English composer, noted chiefly for his rhythmic and harmonic subtlety in setting words. His works include the opera *Dido and Aeneas* (1689), music for the theatrical pieces *King Arthur* (1691) and *The Fairy Queen* (1692), several choral odes, fantasias, sonatas, and church music.

purchase ('pɜːtʃɪs) *vb.* (*tr.*) **1.** to obtain (goods, etc.) by payment. **2.** to obtain by effort, sacrifice, etc.: *to purchase one's freedom.* **3.** to draw or lift (a load) with mechanical apparatus. ~*n.* **4.** something that is purchased. **5.** the act of buying. **6.** acquisition of an estate by any lawful means other than inheritance. **7.** the mechanical advantage achieved by a lever. **8.** a firm foothold, grasp, etc., as for climbing something. [C13: from OF *porchacier* to strive to obtain; see CHASE[1]] —'**purchasable** *adj.* —'**purchaser** *n.*

purchase tax *n.* (in Britain, formerly) a tax levied on nonessential consumer goods and added to selling prices by retailers.

purdah ('pɜːdə) *n.* **1.** the custom in some Muslim and Hindu communities of keeping women in seclusion, with clothing that conceals them completely when they go out. **2.** a screen in a Hindu house used to keep the women out of view. [C19: from Hindi *parda* veil, from Persian *pardah*]

pure (pjʊə) *adj.* **1.** not mixed with any extraneous or dissimilar materials, elements, etc. **2.** free from tainting or polluting matter: *pure water.* **3.** free from moral taint or defilement: *pure love.* **4.** (*prenominal*) (intensifier): *a pure coincidence.* **5.** (of a subject, etc.) studied in its theoretical aspects rather than for its practical applications: *pure mathematics.* **6.** (of a vowel) pronounced with more or less unvarying quality without any glide. **7.** (of a consonant) not accompanied by another consonant. **8.** of unmixed descent. **9.** *Genetics, biol.* breeding true; homozygous. [C13: from OF *pur*, from L *pūrus* unstained] —'**purely** *adv.* —'**pureness** *n.*

purebred *adj.* ('pjʊə'brɛd). **1.** denoting a pure strain obtained through many generations of controlled breeding. ~*n.* ('pjʊə,brɛd). **2.** a purebred animal.

purée ('pjʊəreɪ) *n.* **1.** a smooth thick pulp of sieved fruit, vegetables, meat, or fish. ~*vb.* **-réeing, -réed. 2.** (*tr.*) to make (cooked foods) into a purée. [C19: from F *purer* to PURIFY]

purfle ('pɜːfᵊl) *n. also* **purfling**. **1.** a ruffled or curved ornamental band, as on clothing, furniture, etc. ~*vb.* **2.** (*tr.*) to decorate with such a band. [C14: from OF *purfiler* to decorate with a border, from *fil* thread, from L *fīlum*]

purgation (pɜː'geɪʃən) *n.* the act of purging or state of being purged; purification.

purgative ('pɜːgətɪv) *Med.* ~*n.* **1.** a drug or agent for purging the bowels. ~*adj.* **2.** causing evacuation of the bowels. — **'purgatively** *adv.*

purgatory ('pɜːgətərɪ, -trɪ) *n.* **1.** *Chiefly R.C. Church.* a state or place in which the souls of those who have died in a state of grace are believed to undergo a limited amount of suffering to expiate their venial sins. **2.** a place or condition of suffering or torment, esp. one that is temporary. [C13: from OF *purgatoire*, from Med. L *pūrgātōrium*, lit.: place of cleansing, from L *pūrgāre* to purge] — **,purga'torial** *adj.*

purge (pɜːdʒ) *vb.* **1.** (*tr.*) to rid (something) of (impure elements). **2.** (*tr.*) to rid (a state, political party, etc.) of (dissident people). **3.** (*tr.*) **a.** to empty (the bowels) by evacuation of faeces. **b.** to cause (a person) to evacuate his bowels. **4. a.** to clear (a person) of a charge. **b.** to free (oneself) of guilt, as by atonement. **5.** (*intr.*) to be purified. ~*n.* **6.** the act or process of purging. **7.** the elimination of opponents or dissidents from a state, political party, etc. **8.** a purgative drug or agent. [C14: from OF *purger*, from L *pūrgāre* to purify]

Puri ('puəriː, puə'riː) *n.* a port in E India, in Orissa on the Bay of Bengal: 12th-century temple of Jagannath. Pop.: 100 942 (1981).

purificator ('pjuərɪfɪ,keɪtə) *n. Christianity.* a small white linen cloth used to wipe the chalice and paten at the Eucharist.

purify ('pjuərɪ,faɪ) *vb.* **-fying, -fied. 1.** to free (something) of contaminating or debasing matter. **2.** (*tr.*) to free (a person, etc.) from sin or guilt. **3.** (*tr.*) to make clean, as in a ritual. [C14: from OF *purifier*, from LL *pūrificāre* to cleanse, from *pūrus* pure + *facere* to make] — **,purifi'cation** *n.* — **purificatory** ('pjuərɪfɪ,keɪtərɪ, -trɪ) *adj.* — **'puri,fier** *n.*

Purim ('puərɪm; *Hebrew* puː'riːm) *n.* a Jewish holiday in February or March to commemorate the deliverance of the Jews from the massacre planned by Haman (Esther 9). [Heb. *pūrīm*, pl. of *pūr* lot; from the casting of lots by Haman]

purine ('pjuəriːn) *or* **purin** ('pjuərɪn) *n.* **1.** a colourless crystalline solid that can be prepared from uric acid. Formula: $C_5H_5N_4$. **2.** any of a number of nitrogenous bases that are derivatives of purine. [C19: from G *Purin*]

puriri (puː'riːriː) *n.* a New Zealand tree with hard timber and red berries. [from Maori]

purism ('pjuə,rɪzəm) *n.* insistence on traditional canons of correctness of form or purity of style or content. — **'purist** *adj., n.* — **pu'ristic** *adj.*

puritan ('pjuərɪtᵊn) *n.* **1.** a person who adheres to strict moral or religious principles, esp. one opposed to luxury and sensual enjoyment. ~*adj.* **2.** characteristic of a puritan. [C16: from LL *pūritās* purity] — **'puritan,ism** *n.*

Puritan ('pjuərɪtᵊn) (in the late 16th and 17th centuries) ~*n.* **1.** any of the extreme English Protestants who wished to purify the Church of England of most of its ceremony and other aspects that they deemed to be Catholic. ~*adj.* **2.** of or relating to the Puritans. — **'Puritan,ism** *n.*

puritanical (,pjuərɪ'tænɪkᵊl) *adj. Usually disparaging.* strict in moral or religious outlook, esp. in shunning sensual pleasures. **2.** (*sometimes cap.*) of or relating to a puritan or the Puritans. — **,puri'tanically** *adv.*

purity ('pjuərɪtɪ) *n.* the state or quality of being pure.

purl[1] (pɜːl) *n.* **1.** a knitting stitch made by doing a plain stitch backwards. **2.** a decorative border, as of lace. **3.** gold or silver wire thread. ~*vb.* **4.** to knit in purl stitch. **5.** to edge (something) with a purl. ~Also (for senses 2, 3, 5): **pearl.** [C16: from dialect *pirl* to twist into a cord]

purl[2] (pɜːl) *vb.* **1.** (*intr.*) (of a stream, etc.) to flow with a gentle swirling or rippling movement and a murmuring sound. ~*n.* **2.** a swirling movement of water; eddy. **3.** a murmuring sound, as of a shallow stream. [C16: rel. to Norwegian *purla* to bubble]

purler ('pɜːlə) *n. Inf.* a headlong or spectacular fall (esp. in **come a purler**).

purlieu ('pɜːljuː) *n.* **1.** *English history.* land on the edge of a forest once included within the bounds of the royal forest but later separated although still subject to some of the forest laws. **2.** (*usually pl.*) a neighbouring area; outskirts. **3.** (*often pl.*) a place one frequents; haunt. [C15 *purlewe*, from Anglo-F *puralé* a going through (infl. also by OF *lieu* place), from OF *puraler*, from *pur* through + *aler* to go]

purlin *or* **purline** ('pɜːlɪn) *n.* a horizontal beam that provides intermediate support for the common rafters of a roof construction. [C15: from ?]

purloin (pɜː'lɔɪn) *vb.* to steal. [C15: from OF *porloigner* to put at a distance, from *por-* for + *loin* distant, from L *longus* long] — **pur'loiner** *n.*

purple ('pɜːpᵊl) *n.* **1.** a colour between red and blue. **2.** a dye or pigment producing such a colour. **3.** cloth of this colour, often used to symbolize royalty or nobility. **4.** (usually preceded by *the*) high rank; nobility. **5. a.** the official robe of a cardinal. **b.** the rank of a cardinal as signified by this. ~*adj.* **6.** of the colour purple. **7.** (of writing) excessively elaborate or full of imagery: *purple prose.* [OE, from L *purpura* purple dye, from Gk *porphura* the purple fish (murex)] — **'purpleness** *n.* — **'purplish** *or* **'purply** *adj.*

purple heart *n.* **1.** any of several tropical American trees. **2.** *Inf., chiefly Brit.* a heart-shaped purple tablet consisting mainly of amphetamine.

Purple Heart *n.* a decoration awarded to members of the U.S. Armed Forces for a wound received in action.

purple patch *n.* **1.** Also called: **purple passage.** a section in a piece of writing characterized by fanciful or ornate language. **2.** *Austral. sl.* a period of good fortune.

purport *vb.* (pɜː'pɔːt). (*tr.*) **1.** to claim to be (true, official, etc.) by manner or appearance, esp. falsely. **2.** (esp. of speech or writing) to signify or imply. ~*n.* ('pɜːpɔːt). **3.** meaning; significance. **4.** object; intention. [C15: from Anglo-F: contents, from OF *porporter* to convey, from L *portāre*]

purpose ('pɜːpəs) *n.* **1.** the reason for which anything is done, created, or exists. **2.** a fixed design or idea that is the object of an action or other effort. **3.** determination: *a man of purpose.* **4.** practical advantage or use: *to work to good purpose.* **5.** that which is relevant (esp. in **to** *or* **from the purpose**). **6.** *Arch.* purport. **7. on purpose.** intentionally. ~*vb.* **8.** (*tr.*) to intend or determine to do (something). [C13: from OF *porpos*, from *porposer* to plan, from L *prōpōnere* to PROPOSE] — **'purposeless** *adj.*

purpose-built *adj.* made to serve a specific purpose.

purposeful ('pɜːpəsfʊl) *adj.* **1.** having a definite purpose in view. **2.** determined. — **'purposefully** *adv.* — **'purposefulness** *n.*

purposely ('pɜːpəslɪ) *adv.* on purpose.

purposive ('pɜːpəsɪv) *adj.* **1.** having or indicating conscious intention. **2.** serving a purpose; useful. — **'purposively** *adv.* — **'purposiveness** *n.*

purpura ('pɜːpjʊrə) *n. Pathol.* any of several blood diseases marked by purplish spots caused by subcutaneous bleeding. [C18: via L from Gk *porphura* a shellfish yielding purple dye]

purr (pɜː) *vb.* **1.** (*intr.*) (esp. of cats) to make a low vibrant sound, usually considered as expressing pleasure, etc. **2.** (*tr.*) to express (pleasure, etc.) by this sound or by a sound suggestive of purring. ~*n.* **3.** a purring sound. [C17: imit.]

purse (pɜːs) *n.* **1.** a small bag or pouch for carrying money, esp. coins. **2.** *U.S. & Canad.* a woman's handbag. **3.** anything resembling a small bag or pouch in form or function. **4.** wealth; funds; resources. **5.** a sum of money that is offered, esp. as a prize. ~*vb.* **6.** (*tr.*) to contract (the mouth, lips, etc.) into a small rounded shape. [OE *purs*, prob. from LL *bursa* bag, ult. from Gk: leather]

purser ('pɜːsə) *n.* an officer aboard a ship or aircraft who keeps the accounts and attends to the welfare of the passengers.

purse seine *n.* a large net that encloses fish and is then closed at the bottom by means of a line resembling the string formerly used to draw shut the neck of a money pouch.

purse strings *pl. n.* control of expenditure (esp. in **hold** *or* **control the purse strings**).

purslane ('pɜːslɪn) *n.* a plant with fleshy leaves used (esp. formerly) in salads and as a potherb. [C14 *purcelane*, from OF *porcelaine*, from LL, from L *porcillāca*, var. of *portulāca*]

pursuance (pə'sjuːəns) *n.* the carrying out or pursuing of an action, plan, etc.

pursuant (pə'sjuːənt) *adj.* **1.** (*usually postpositive; often foll. by* to) *Chiefly law.* in agreement or conformity. **2.** *Arch.* pursuing. [C17: rel. to ME *poursuivant* following after, from OF; see PURSUE] —**pur'suantly** *adv.*

pursue (pə'sjuː) *vb.* **-suing, -sued.** (*mainly tr.*) **1.** (*also intr.*) to follow (a fugitive, etc.) in order to capture or overtake. **2.** to follow closely or accompany: *ill health pursued her.* **3.** to seek or strive to attain (some desire, etc.). **4.** to follow the precepts of (a plan, policy, etc.). **5.** to apply oneself to (studies, interests, etc.). **6.** to follow persistently or seek to become acquainted with. **7.** to continue to discuss or argue (a point, subject, etc.). [C13: from Anglo-Norman *pursiwer*, from OF *poursivre*, from L *prōsequi* to follow after] —**pur'suer** *n.*

pursuit (pə'sjuːt) *n.* **1. a.** the act of pursuing. **b.** (*as modifier*): *a pursuit plane.* **2.** an occupation or pastime. **3.** (in cycling) a race in which the riders set off at intervals along the track and attempt to overtake each other. [C14: from OF *poursieute*, from *poursivre* to PURSUE]

pursuivant ('pɜːsɪvənt) *n.* **1.** the lowest rank of heraldic officer. **2.** *History.* a state or royal messenger. **3.** *History.* a follower or attendant. [C14: from OF, from *poursivre* to PURSUE]

purulent ('pjʊərʊlənt) *adj.* of, relating to, or containing pus. [C16: from L *pūrulentus*, from *pūs*] —'**purulence** *n.* —'**purulently** *adv.*

Purus (*Spanish, Portuguese* pu'rus) *n.* a river in NW central South America, rising in SE Peru and flowing northeast to the Amazon. Length: about 3200 km (2000 miles).

purvey (pə'veɪ) *vb.* (*tr.*) **1.** to sell or provide (commodities, esp. foodstuffs) on a large scale. **2.** to publish (lies, scandal, etc.). [C13: from OF *porveeir*, from L *prōvidēre* to PROVIDE] —**pur'veyor** *n.*

purveyance (pə'veɪəns) *n.* **1.** *History.* the collection or requisition of provisions for a sovereign. **2.** *Rare.* the act of purveying.

purview ('pɜːvjuː) *n.* **1.** scope of operation. **2.** breadth or range of outlook. **3.** *Law.* the body of a statute, containing the enacting clauses. [C15: from Anglo-Norman *purveu*, from *porveeir* to furnish; see PURVEY]

pus (pʌs) *n.* the yellow or greenish fluid product of inflammation. [C16: from L *pūs*]

Pusan ('puː'sæn) *n.* a port in SE South Korea, on the Korean Strait: the second largest city and chief port of the country; industrial centre; two universities. Pop.: 3 516 768 (1985).

Pusey ('pjuːzɪ) *n.* **Edward Bouverie** ('buːvərɪ). 1800–82, English ecclesiastic; a leader with Keble and Newman of the Oxford Movement.

push (pʊʃ) *vb.* **1.** (when *tr.*, often foll. by *off, away,* etc.) to apply steady force to in order to move. **2.** to thrust (one's way) through something, such as a crowd. **3.** (*tr.*) to encourage or urge (a person) to some action, decision, etc. **4.** (when *intr.*, often foll. by *for*) to be an advocate or promoter (of): *to push for acceptance of one's theories.* **5.** (*tr.*) to use one's influence to help (a person): *to push one's own candidate.* **6.** to bear upon (oneself or another person) in order to achieve better results, etc. **7.** (*tr.*) to rely too much on: *to push one's luck.* **8.** *Cricket, etc.* to hit (a ball) with a stiff pushing stroke. **9.** (*tr.*) *Inf.* to sell (narcotic drugs) illegally. **10.** (*intr.*; foll. by *out, into,* etc.) to extend: *the cliffs pushed out to the sea.* ~*n.* **11.** the act of pushing; thrust. **12.** a part or device that is pressed to operate some mechanism. **13.** *Inf.* drive, energy, etc. **14.** *Inf.* a special effort or attempt to advance, as of an army: *to make a push.* **15.** *Austral. sl.* a group, gang, or clique. **16.** *Cricket, etc.* a stiff pushing stroke. **17. at a push.** *Inf.* with difficulty; only just. **18. the push.** *Inf., chiefly Brit.* dismissal, esp. from employment. ~See also **push off, push in,** etc. [C13: from OF *pousser,* from L *pulsāre,* from *pellere* to drive]

push-bike *n. Brit.* an informal name for **bicycle.**

push button *n.* **1.** an electrical switch operated by pressing a button, which closes or opens a circuit. ~*modifier.* **push button. 2. a.** operated by a push button: *a push-button radio.* **b.** initiated as simply as by pressing a button: *push-button warfare.*

pushcart ('pʊʃˌkɑːt) *n.* another name (esp. U.S. and Canad.) for **barrow**[1] (sense 3).

pushchair ('pʊʃˌtʃɛə) *n. Brit.* a chair-shaped carriage for a small child. U.S. and Canad. word: **stroller.** Austral. words: **pusher, stroller.**

pushed (pʊʃt) *adj.* (often foll. by *for*) *Inf.* short (of) or in need (of time, money, etc.).

pusher ('pʊʃə) *n.* **1.** *Inf.* a person who sells illegal drugs, esp. narcotics such as heroin. **2.** *Inf.* an aggressively ambitious person. **3.** a person or thing that pushes. **4.** *Austral.* the usual name for **pushchair.**

push in *vb.* (*intr., adv.*) to force one's way into a group of people, queue, etc.

pushing ('pʊʃɪŋ) *adj.* **1.** enterprising or aggressively ambitious. **2.** impertinently self-assertive. ~*adv.* **3.** almost or nearly (a certain age, speed, etc.): *pushing fifty.* —'**pushingly** *adv.*

Pushkin ('pʊʃkɪn) *n.* **Aleksander Sergeyevich** (alɪk'sandr sɪr'gjeɪvɪtʃ). 1799–1837, Russian poet, novelist, and dramatist. His works include the romantic verse tale *The Prisoner of the Caucasus* (1822), the verse novel *Eugene Onegin* (1833), the tragedy *Boris Godunov* (1825), and the novel *The Captain's Daughter* (1836).

push off *vb.* (*adv.*) **1.** Also: **push out.** to move into open water, as by being cast off from a mooring. **2.** (*intr.*) *Inf.* to go away; leave.

pushover ('pʊʃˌəʊvə) *n. Inf.* **1.** something that is easily achieved. **2.** a person, team, etc., that is easily taken advantage of or defeated.

push-pull *n.* (*modifier*) using two similar electronic devices made to operate out of phase with each other to produce a signal that replicates the input waveform: *a push-pull amplifier.*

push-start *vb.* (*tr.*) **1.** to start (a motor vehicle) by pushing it while it is in gear, thus turning the engine. ~*n.* **2.** this process.

push through *vb.* (*tr.*) to compel to accept: *the bill was pushed through Parliament.*

Pushto ('pʌʃtəʊ) or **Pushtu** ('pʌʃtuː) *n., adj.* variant spellings of **Pashto.**

push-up *n.* the U.S. and Canad. term for **press-up.**

pushy ('pʊʃɪ) *adj.* **pushier, pushiest.** *Inf.* **1.** offensively assertive. **2.** aggressively or ruthlessly ambitious. —'**pushily** *adv.* —'**pushiness** *n.*

pusillanimous (ˌpjuːsɪ'lænɪməs) *adj.* characterized by a lack of courage or determination. [C16: from LL *pusillanimis* from L *pusillus* weak + *animus* courage] —**pusillanimity** (ˌpjuːsɪlə'nɪmɪtɪ) *n.* —ˌpusil'lanimously *adv.*

puss (pʊs) *n.* **1.** an informal name for a **cat. 2.** *Sl.* a girl or woman. **3.** an informal name for a **hare.** [C16: rel. to MLow G *pūs*]

pussy[1] ('pʊsɪ) *n., pl.* **pussies. 1.** Also called: **puss, pussycat.** an informal name for a **cat. 2.** a furry catkin. **3.** *Taboo sl.* the female pudenda. [C18: from PUSS]

pussy[2] ('pʊsɪ) *adj.* **-sier, -siest.** containing or full of pus.

pussyfoot ('pʊsɪˌfʊt) *vb.* (*intr.*) *Inf.* **1.** to move about stealthily or warily like a cat. **2.** to avoid committing oneself.

pussy willow ('pʊsɪ) *n.* a willow tree with silvery silky catkins.

pustulant ('pʌstjʊlənt) *adj.* **1.** causing the formation of pustules. ~*n.* **2.** an agent causing such formation.

pustulate *vb.* ('pʌstjʊˌleɪt). **1.** to form or cause to form into pustules. ~*adj.* ('pʌstjʊlɪt). **2.** covered with pustules. —ˌpustu'lation *n.*

pustule ('pʌstjuːl) *n.* **1.** a small inflamed elevated area of skin containing pus. **2.** any spot resembling a pimple. [C14: from L *pustula* a blister, var. of *pūsula*] —**pustular** ('pʌstjʊlə) *adj.*

put (pʊt) *vb.* **putting, put.** (*mainly tr.*) **1.** to cause to be (in a position or place): *to put a book on the table.* **2.** to cause to be (in a state, relation, etc.): *to put one's things in order.* **3.** (foll. by *to*) to cause (a person) to experience or suffer: *to put to death.* **4.** to set or commit (to an action, task, or duty), esp. by force: *he put him to work.* **5.** to render or translate: *to put into English.* **6.** to set (words) in a musical form (esp. in **put to music**). **7.** (foll. by *at*) to estimate: *he put the distance at fifty miles.* **8.** (foll. by *to*) to utilize: *he put his knowledge to use.* **9.** (foll. by *to*) to couple (a female animal) with a male for breeding: *the farmer put his heifer to the bull.* **10.** to express: *to put it bluntly.* **11.** to make (an end or limit): *to put an end to the proceedings.* **12.** to present for consideration; propose: *he put the question to the committee.*

13. to invest (money) in or expend (time, energy, etc.) on: *he put five thousand pounds into the project.* **14.** to impart: *to put zest into a party.* **15.** to throw or cast. **16. not know where to put oneself.** to feel embarrassed. **17. stay put.** to remain in one place; remain stationary. ~*n.* **18.** a throw, esp. in putting the shot. **19.** Also called: **put option.** *Stock Exchange.* an option to sell a stated number of securities at a specified price during a limited period. ~See also **put about, put across,** etc. [C12 *puten* to push]

put about *vb.* (*adv.*) **1.** *Naut.* to change course. **2.** (*tr.*) to make widely known: *he put about the news of the air disaster.* **3.** (*tr.; usually passive*) to disconcert or disturb.

put across *vb.* (*tr.*) **1.** (*adv.*) to communicate in a comprehensible way: *he couldn't put things across very well.* **2. put one across.** *Inf.* to get (someone) to believe a claim, excuse, etc., by deception: *they put one across their teacher.*

put aside *vb.* (*tr., adv.*) **1.** to move (an object, etc.) to one side, esp. in rejection. **2.** to save: *to put money aside for a rainy day.* **3.** to disregard: *let us put aside our differences.*

putative ('pju:tətɪv) *adj.* (*prenominal*) **1.** commonly regarded as being: *the putative father.* **2.** considered to exist or have existed; inferred. [C15: from LL *putātīvus* supposed, from L *putāre* to consider] —**'putatively** *adv.*

put away *vb.* (*tr., adv.*) **1.** to return (something) to the proper place. **2.** to save: *to put away money for the future.* **3.** to lock up in a prison, mental institution, etc.: *they put him away for twenty years.* **4.** to eat or drink, esp. in large amounts.

put back *vb.* (*tr., adv.*) **1.** to return to its former place. **2.** to move to a later time: *the wedding was put back a fortnight.* **3.** to impede the progress of: *the strike put back production.*

put by *vb.* (*tr., adv.*) to set aside for the future; save.

put down *vb.* (*tr., adv.*) **1.** to make a written record of. **2.** to repress: *to put down a rebellion.* **3.** to consider: *they put him down for an ignoramus.* **4.** to attribute: *I put the mistake down to inexperience.* **5.** to put (an animal) to death, because of old age or illness. **6.** to table on the agenda: *the MPs put down a motion on the increase in crime.* **7.** *Sl.* to reject or humiliate. ~*n.* **put-down. 8.** a cruelly crushing remark.

put forth *vb.* (*tr., adv.*) *Formal.* **1.** to propose. **2.** (of a plant) to produce or bear (leaves, etc.).

put forward *vb.* (*tr., adv.*) **1.** to propose; suggest. **2.** to offer the name of; nominate.

put in *vb.* (*adv.*) **1.** (*intr.*) *Naut.* to bring a vessel into port. **2.** (often foll. by *for*) to apply (for a job, etc.). **3.** (*tr.*) to submit: *he put in his claims form.* **4.** to intervene with (a remark) during a conversation. **5.** (*tr.*) to devote (time, effort, etc.): *he put in three hours overtime last night.* **6.** (*tr.*) to establish or appoint: *he put in a manager.* **7.** (*tr.*) *Cricket.* to cause to bat: *England won the toss and put the visitors in to bat.*

Putnam ('pʌtnəm) *n.* **1. Israel.** 1718–90, American general in the War of Independence. **2.** his cousin **Rufus.** 1738–1824, American soldier in the War of Independence; surveyor general of the U.S. (1796–1803).

put off *vb.* (*tr.*) **1.** (*adv.*) to postpone: *they have put off the dance until tomorrow.* **2.** (*adv.*) to evade (a person) by postponement or delay: *they tried to put him off, but he came anyway.* **3.** (*adv.*) to cause aversion: *he was put off by her appearance.* **4.** (*prep.*) to cause to lose interest in: *the accident put him off driving.*

put on *vb.* (*tr., mainly adv.*) **1.** to clothe oneself in. **2.** (*usually passive*) to adopt (an attitude or feeling) insincerely: *his misery was just put on.* **3.** to present (a play, show, etc.). **4.** to add: *she put on weight.* **5.** to cause (an electrical device) to function. **6.** (*also prep.*) to wager (money) on a horse race, game, etc. **7.** (*also prep.*) to impose: *to put a tax on cars.* **8.** *Cricket.* to cause (a bowler) to bowl.

put out *vb.* (*tr., adv.*) **1.** (*often passive*) **a.** to annoy; anger. **b.** to disturb; confuse. **2.** to extinguish (a fire, light, etc.). **3.** to poke forward: *to put out one's tongue.* **4.** to be a source of inconvenience to: *I hope I'm not putting you out.* **5.** to publish; broadcast: *the authorities put out a leaflet.* **6.** to render unconscious. **7.** to dislocate: *he put out his shoulder in the accident.* **8.** to give out (work

to be done) at different premises. **9.** to lend (money) at interest. **10.** *Cricket, etc.* to dismiss (a player or team).

put over *vb.* (*tr., adv.*) **1.** *Inf.* to communicate (facts, information, etc.). **2.** *Chiefly U.S.* to postpone. **3. put (a fast) one over on.** *Inf.* to get (someone) to believe a claim, excuse, etc., by deception: *he put one over on his boss.*

put-put ('pʌt,pʌt) *Inf.* ~*n.* **1.** a light chugging or popping sound, as made by a petrol engine. ~*vb.* **-putting, -putted.** **2.** (*intr.*) to make such a sound.

putrefy ('pju:trɪ,faɪ) *vb.* **-fying, -fied.** (of organic matter) to decompose or rot with an offensive smell. [C15: from OF *putrefier* + L *putrefacere,* from *puter* rotten + *facere* to make] —**putrefaction** (,pju:trɪ'fækʃən) *n.* —,**putre'factive** or **putre'facient** (,pju:trɪ'feɪʃənt) *adj.*

putrescent (pju:'trɛsənt) *adj.* **1.** becoming putrid; rotting. **2.** characterized by or undergoing putrefaction. [C18: from L *putrescere* to become rotten] —**pu'trescence** *n.*

putrid ('pju:trɪd) *adj.* **1.** (of organic matter) in a state of decomposition: *putrid meat.* **2.** morally corrupt. **3.** sickening; foul: *a putrid smell.* **4.** *Inf.* deficient in quality or value: *a putrid film.* [C16: from L *putridus,* from *putrēre* to be rotten] —**pu'tridity** or **'putridness** *n.* —**'putridly** *adv.*

Putsch (pʊtʃ) *n.* a violent and sudden uprising; political revolt. [C20: from G: from Swiss G: a push, imit.]

putt (pʌt) *Golf.* ~*n.* **1.** a stroke on the green with a putter to roll the ball into or near the hole. ~*vb.* **2.** to strike (the ball) in this way. [C16: of Scot. origin]

puttee or **putty** ('pʌtɪ) *n., pl.* **-tees** or **-ties.** (*often pl.*) a strip of cloth worn wound around the leg from the ankle to the knee, esp. as part of a uniform in World War I. [C19: from Hindi *pattī,* from Sansk. *pattikā,* from *patta* cloth]

putter[1] ('pʌtə) *n. Golf.* **1.** a club with a short shaft for putting, usually having a solid metal head. **2.** a golfer who putts: *he is a good putter.*

putter[2] ('pʌtə) *vb.* the usual U.S. and Canad. word for **potter**[2]. —**'putterer** *n.*

putter[3] ('pʊtə) *n.* **1.** a person who puts: *the putter of a question.* **2.** a person who puts the shot.

put through *vb.* (*tr., mainly adv.*) **1.** to carry out to a conclusion: *he put through his plan.* **2.** (*also prep.*) to organize the processing of: *she put through his application to join the organization.* **3.** to connect by telephone. **4.** to make (a telephone call).

putting green ('pʌtɪŋ) *n.* **1.** (on a golf course) the area of closely mown grass at the end of a fairway where the hole is. **2.** an area of smooth grass with several holes for putting games.

Puttnam ('pʌtnəm) *n.* **David.** British film producer. Films include *Chariots of Fire* (1981) and *The Killing Fields* (1984).

putto ('pʊtəʊ) *n., pl.* **-ti** (-tiː). a representation of a small boy, a cherub or cupid, esp. in baroque painting or sculpture. [from It., from L *putus* boy]

putty ('pʌtɪ) *n., pl.* **-ties.** **1.** a stiff paste made of whiting and linseed oil that is used to fix glass into frames and to fill cracks in woodwork, etc. **2.** any substance with a similar function or appearance. **3.** a mixture of lime and water with sand or plaster of Paris used on plaster as a finishing coat. **4.** (*as modifier*): *a putty knife.* **5.** a person who is easily influenced: *he's putty in her hands.* **6. a.** a colour varying from greyish yellow to greyish brown. **b.** (*as adj.*): *putty wool.* ~*vb.* **-tying, -tied.** **7.** (*tr.*) to fix, fill, or coat with putty. [C17: from F *potée* a potful]

Putumayo (*Spanish* putu'majo) *n.* a river in NW South America, rising in S Colombia and flowing southeast as most of the border between Colombia and Peru, entering the Amazon in Brazil: scene of the Putumayo rubber scandal (1910–11) during the rubber boom, in which many Indians were enslaved and killed by rubber exploiters. Length: 1578 km (980 miles). Brazilian name: **Içá.**

put up *vb.* (*adv., mainly tr.*) **1.** to build; erect: *to put up a statue.* **2.** to accommodate or be accommodated at: *can you put me up for tonight?* **3.** to increase (prices). **4.** to submit (a plan, case, etc.). **5.** to offer: *to put a house up for sale.* **6.** to give: *to put up a good fight.* **7.** to provide (money) for: *they put up five thousand for the new project.* **8.** to preserve or can (jam, etc.). **9.** to pile up (long hair) on the head in any of several styles. **10.** (*also intr.*) to nominate or be nominated as a candidate: *he put up for president.* **11.** *Arch.* to return (a weapon) to its holder:

put up your sword!　**12. put up to. a.** to inform or instruct (a person) about (tasks, duties, etc.).　**b.** to incite to.　**13. put up with.** *Inf.* to endure; tolerate. ~*adj.* **put-up.**　**14.** dishonestly or craftily prearranged (esp. in **put-up job**).

put upon *vb.* (*intr., prep.; usually passive*)　**1.** to presume on (a person's generosity, good nature, etc.): *he's always being put upon.*　**2.** to impose hardship on: *he was sorely put upon.*

Puvis de Chavannes (*French* pyvis də ʃavan) *n.* **Pierre Cécile** (pjɛr sesil). 1824–98, French mural painter.

Puy de Dôme (pwi də dom) *n.* **1.** a department of central France in Auvergne region. Capital: Clermont-Ferrand. Pop.: 594 365 (1982). Area: 8016 sq. km (3126 sq. miles).　**2.** a mountain in central France, in the Auvergne Mountains: a volcanic plug. Height: 1485 m (4872 ft.).

Puy de Sancy (*French* pwi də sãsi) *n.* a mountain in S central France: highest peak of the Monts Dore. Height: 1886 m (6188 ft.).

Pu-yi ('puːˈjiː) *n.* **Henry.** 1906–67, last emperor of China as Xuan-Tong (1908–12); emperor of the Japanese puppet state of Manchukuo as Kang-de (1934–45).

puzzle ('pʌzªl) *vb.* **1.** to perplex or be perplexed.　**2.** (*intr.; foll. by over*) to ponder about the cause of: *he puzzled over her absence.*　**3.** (*tr.; usually foll. by out*) to solve by mental effort: *he puzzled out the meaning.* ~*n.* **4.** a person or thing that puzzles.　**5.** a problem that cannot be easily solved.　**6.** the state of being puzzled.　**7.** a toy, game, or question presenting a problem that requires skill or ingenuity for its solution. [C16: from ?] —'**puzzlement** *n.* —'**puzzler** *n.* —'**puzzling** *adj.* —'**puzzlingly** *adv.*

PVC *abbrev. for* polyvinyl chloride; a synthetic thermoplastic material made by polymerizing vinyl chloride. The flexible forms are used in insulation, shoes, etc. Rigid PVC is used for moulded articles.

PVS *abbrev. for* postviral syndrome.

Pvt. *Mil. abbrev. for* private.

PW *abbrev. for* policewoman.

PWR *abbrev. for* pressurized-water reactor.

pyaemia *or* **pyemia** (paɪˈiːmɪə) *n.* blood poisoning characterized by pus-forming microorganisms in the blood. [C19: from NL, from Gk *puon* pus + *haima* blood] —py'**aemic** *or* py'**emic** *adj.*

Pydna ('pɪdnə) *n.* a town in ancient Macedonia: site of a major Roman victory over the Macedonians, resulting in the downfall of their kingdom (168 B.C.).

pye-dog, pie-dog, *or* **pi-dog** ('paɪˌdɒg) *n.* an ownerless half-wild Asian dog. [C19: Anglo-Indian, from Hindi *pāhī* outsider]

pyelitis (ˌpaɪəˈlaɪtɪs) *n.* inflammation of the pelvis of the kidney. [C19: NL, from Gk *puelos* trough] —**pyelitic** (ˌpaɪəˈlɪtɪk) *adj.*

Pygmalion (pɪgˈmeɪlɪən) *n. Greek myth.* a king of Cyprus, who fell in love with the statue of a woman he had sculpted and which his prayers brought to life as Galatea.

pygmy *or* **pigmy** ('pɪgmɪ) *n., pl.* -**mies. 1.** an abnormally undersized person.　**2.** something that is a very small example of its type.　**3.** a person of little importance or significance.　**4.** (*modifier*) very small. [C14 *pigmeis* the Pygmies, from L *Pygmaeus* a Pygmy, from Gk *pugmaios* undersized, from *pugmē* fist] —**pygmaean** *or* **pygmean** (pɪgˈmiːən) *adj.*

Pygmy *or* **Pigmy** ('pɪgmɪ) *n., pl.* -**mies.** a member of one of the dwarf peoples of Equatorial Africa, noted for their hunting and forest culture.

Pyjama cricket *n. Austral. inf.* one-day cricket, esp. when played at night in coloured uniforms.

pyjamas *or U.S.* **pajamas** (pəˈdʒɑːməz) *pl. n.* **1.** loose-fitting nightclothes comprising a jacket or top and trousers.　**2.** full loose-fitting ankle-length trousers worn by either sex in various Eastern countries. [C19: from Hindi, from Persian *pai* leg + *jāma* garment]

pyknic ('pɪknɪk) *adj.* characterized by a broad squat fleshy physique with a large chest and abdomen. [C20: from Gk *puknos* thick]

pylon ('paɪlən) *n.* **1.** a large vertical steel tower-like structure supporting high-tension electrical cables.　**2.** a post or tower for guiding pilots or marking a turning point in a race.　**3.** a streamlined aircraft structure for attaching an engine pod, etc., to the main body of the aircraft.　**4.** a monumental gateway, such as one at the entrance to an ancient Egyptian temple. [C19: from Gk *pulōn* a gateway]

pylorus (paɪˈlɔːrəs) *n., pl.* -**ri** (-raɪ). the small circular opening at the base of the stomach through which partially digested food passes to the duodenum. [C17: via LL from Gk *pulórus* gatekeeper, from *pulē* gate + *ouros* guardian]

Pylos ('paɪlɒs) *n.* a port in SW Greece, in the SW Peloponnese; scene of a defeat of the Spartans by the Athenians (425 B.C.) during the Peloponnesian War and of the Battle of Navarino (see **Navarino**). Italian name: **Navarino.** Modern Greek name: **Pílos.**

Pym (pɪm) *n.* **John.** ?1584–1643, leading English parliamentarian during the events leading to the Civil War. He took a prominent part in the impeachment of Buckingham (1626) and of Strafford and Laud (1640).

pyo- *or before a vowel* **py-** *combining form.* denoting pus: *pyosis.* [from Gk *puon*]

Pyongyang *or* **P'yŏng-yang** ('pjɒŋˈjæŋ) *n.* the capital of North Korea, in the southwest on the Taedong River: industrial centre; university (1946). Pop.: 1 280 000 (1981).

pyorrhoea *or esp. U.S.* **pyorrhea** (ˌpaɪəˈrɪə) *n.* inflammation of the gums characterized by the discharge of pus and loosening of the teeth; periodontal disease.

pyracantha (ˌpaɪrəˈkænθə) *n.* any of a genus of shrubs with yellow, orange, or scarlet berries, widely cultivated for ornament. [C17: from Gk *purakantha*, from PYRO- + *akantha* thorn]

pyramid ('pɪrəmɪd) *n.* **1.** a huge masonry construction that has a square base and, as in the case of the ancient Egyptian royal tombs, four sloping triangular sides.　**2.** an object or structure resembling such a construction.　**3.** *Maths.* a solid having a polygonal base and triangular sides that meet in a common vertex.　**4.** *Crystallography.* a crystal form in which three planes intersect all three axes of the crystal.　**5.** *Finance.* a group of enterprises containing a series of holding companies structured so that the top holding company controls the entire group with a relatively small proportion of the total capital invested.　**6.** (*pl.*) a game similar to billiards. ~*vb.* **7.** to build up or be arranged in the form of a pyramid.　**8.** *Finance.* to form (companies) into a pyramid. [C16 (earlier *pyramis*): from L *pyramis*, from Gk *puramis*, prob. from Egyptian] —**pyramidal** (pɪˈræmɪdªl), ,**pyra'midical,** *or* ,**pyra'midic** *adj.* —**py'ramidally** *or* ,**pyra'midically** *adv.*

pyramid selling *n.* a practice adopted by some manufacturers of advertising for distributors and selling them batches of goods. The first distributors then advertise for more distributors who are sold subdivisions of the original batches at an increased price. This process continues until the final distributors are left with a stock that is unsaleable except at a loss.

Pyramus and Thisbe ('pɪrəməs; 'θɪzbɪ) *n.* (in Greek legend) two lovers of Babylon: Pyramus, wrongly supposing Thisbe to be dead, killed himself and she, encountering him in his death throes, did the same.

pyre ('paɪə) *n.* a pile of wood or other combustible material, esp. one for cremating a corpse. [C17: from L *pyra*, from Gk *pura* hearth, from *pur* fire]

Pyrenees (ˌpɪrəˈniːz) *pl. n.* a mountain range between France and Spain, extending from the Bay of Biscay to the Mediterranean. Highest peak: Pico de Aneto, 3404 m (11 168 ft.). —**Pyre'nean** *adj.*

Pyrénées *or* **Pyrénées-Atlantiques** (*French* pirenez-atlātik) *n.* a department of SW France in Aquitaine region. Capital: Pau. Pop.: 555 696 (1982). Area: 7712 sq. km (3008 sq. miles). Former name: **Basses-Pyrénées.**

Pyrénées-Orientales (*French* pirenezɔrjātal) *n.* a department of S France, in Languedoc-Roussillon region. Capital: Perpignan. Pop.: 334 557 (1982). Area: 4144 sq. km (1616 sq. miles).

pyrethrin (paɪˈriːθrɪn) *n.* either of two oily compounds found in pyrethrum and used as insecticides. [C19: from PYRETHRUM + -IN]

pyrethrum (paɪˈriːθrəm) *n.* **1.** any of several cultivated Eurasian chrysanthemums with white, pink, red, or purple flowers.　**2.** any insecticide prepared from the dried flowers of any of these plants. [C16: via L from Gk *purethron* feverfew, prob. from *puretos* fever; see PYRETIC]

pyretic (paɪˈrɛtɪk) *adj. Pathology.* of, relating to, or characterized by fever. [C18: from NL *pyreticus*, from Gk *puretos* fever, from *pur* fire]

Pyrex ('paɪrɛks) *n. Trademark.* **a.** any of a variety of glasses that have low coefficients of expansion, making them suitable for heat-resistant glassware used in cookery and chemical apparatus. **b.** (*as modifier*): *a Pyrex dish.*

pyrexia (paɪˈrɛksɪə) *n.* a technical name for **fever.** [C18: from NL, from Gk *pyrexis*, from *puressein* to be feverish, from *pur* fire] —**py'rexial** *or* **py'rexic** *adj.*

pyridine ('pɪrɪˌdiːn) *n.* a colourless hygroscopic liquid heterocyclic compound with a characteristic odour: used as a solvent and in preparing other organic chemicals. Formula: C_5H_5N. [C19: from PYRO- + -ID^2 + -INE^2]

pyridoxine (ˌpɪrɪˈdɒksiːn) *n. Biochemistry.* a derivative of pyridine that is a precursor of the compounds pyridoxal and pyridoxamine. Also called: **vitamin B$_6$.**

pyrimidine (paɪˈrɪmɪˌdiːn) *n.* **1.** a liquid or crystalline organic compound with a penetrating odour. Formula: $C_4H_4N_2$. **2.** any of a number of similar compounds having a basic structure that is derived from pyrimidine, and which are constituents of nucleic acids. [C20: var. of PYRIDINE]

pyrite ('paɪraɪt) *n.* a yellow mineral consisting of iron sulphide in cubic crystalline form. It occurs in igneous and metamorphic rocks and in veins, associated with various metals, and is used mainly in the manufacture of sulphuric acid and paper. Formula: FeS$_2$. Also called: **iron pyrites, pyrites.** [C16: from L *pyrites* flint, from Gk *puritēs* (*lithos*) fire(stone), from *pur* fire] —**pyritic** (paɪˈrɪtɪk) *adj.*

pyrites (paɪˈraɪtiːz; *in combination* 'paɪraɪts) *n., pl.* -**tes.** **1.** another name for **pyrite. 2.** any of a number of other disulphides of metals, esp. of copper and tin.

pyro- *or before a vowel* **pyr-** *combining form.* **1.** denoting fire or heat: *pyromania; pyrometer.* **2.** *Chem.* denoting a new substance obtained by heating another: *pyroboric acid is obtained by heating boric acid.* **3.** *Mineralogy.* **a.** having a property that changes upon the application of heat. **b.** having a flame-coloured appearance: *pyroxylin.* [from Gk *pur* fire]

pyroelectricity (ˌpaɪrəʊɪlɛkˈtrɪsɪtɪ) *n.* the development of opposite charges at the ends of the axis of certain crystals as a result of a change in temperature.

pyrogallol (ˌpaɪrəʊˈgælɒl) *n.* a crystalline soluble phenol with weakly acidic properties: used as a photographic developer and for absorbing oxygen in gas analysis. Formula: $C_6H_3(OH)_3$. [C20: from PYRO- + GALL(IC ACID) + -OL^1]

pyrogenic (ˌpaɪrəʊˈdʒɛnɪk) *or* **pyrogenous** (paɪˈrɒdʒɪnəs) *adj.* **1.** produced by or producing heat. **2.** *Pathology.* causing or resulting from fever. **3.** *Geol.* less common words for **igneous.**

pyrography (paɪˈrɒɡrəfɪ) *n.* another name for **pokerwork.**

pyroligneous (ˌpaɪrəʊˈlɪɡnɪəs) *or* **pyrolignic** *adj.* (of a substance) produced by the action of heat on wood, esp. by destructive distillation.

pyrolysis (paɪˈrɒlɪsɪs) *n.* **1.** the application of heat to chemical compounds in order to cause decomposition. **2.** such chemical decomposition. —**pyrolytic** (ˌpaɪrəʊˈlɪtɪk) *adj.*

pyromania (ˌpaɪrəʊˈmeɪnɪə) *n. Psychiatry.* the uncontrollable impulse and practice of setting things on fire. —ˌpyro'mani,ac *n.*

pyrometer (paɪˈrɒmɪtə) *n.* an instrument for measuring high temperatures, esp. by measuring the brightness or total quantity of the radiation produced. —**pyrometric** (ˌpaɪrəʊˈmɛtrɪk) *or* ˌpyro'metrical *adj.* —ˌpyro'metrically *adv.* —py'rometry *n.*

pyrope ('paɪrəʊp) *n.* a deep yellowish-red garnet that consists of magnesium aluminium silicate and is used as a gemstone. [C14 (used loosely of a red gem; modern sense C19): from OF *pirope*, from L *pyrōpus* bronze, from Gk *purōpus* fiery-eyed]

pyrophoric (ˌpaɪrəʊˈfɒrɪk) *adj.* **1.** (of a chemical) igniting spontaneously on contact with air. **2.** (of an alloy) producing sparks when struck or scraped: *lighter flints are made of pyrophoric alloy.* [C19: from NL *pyrophorus*, from Gk *purophoros* fire-bearing, from *pur* fire + *pherein* to bear]

pyrosis (paɪˈrəʊsɪs) *n. Pathology.* a technical name for **heartburn.** [C18: from NL, from Gk: a burning, from *puroun* to burn, from *pur* fire]

pyrostat ('paɪrəʊˌstæt) *n.* **1.** a device that activates an alarm or extinguisher in the event of a fire. **2.** a thermostat for use at high temperatures. —ˌpyro'static *adj.*

pyrotechnics (ˌpaɪrəʊˈtɛknɪks) *n.* **1.** (*functioning as sing.*) the art of making fireworks. **2.** (*functioning as*

sing. or pl.) a firework display. **3.** (*functioning as sing. or pl.*) brilliance of display, as in the performance of music. —ˌpyro'technic *or* ˌpyro'technical *adj.*

pyroxene (paɪˈrɒksiːn) *n.* any of a large group of minerals consisting of the silicates of magnesium, iron, and calcium. They occur in basic igneous rocks. [C19: PYRO- + -xene from Gk *xenos* foreign, because mistakenly thought to have originated elsewhere when found in igneous rocks]

pyroxylin (paɪˈrɒksɪlɪn) *n.* a yellow substance obtained by nitrating cellulose with a mixture of nitric and sulphuric acids; guncotton: used to make collodion, plastics, lacquers, and adhesives.

Pyrrha ('pɪrə) *n. Greek myth.* the wife of Deucalion, saved with him from the flood loosed upon mankind by Zeus.

pyrrhic ('pɪrɪk) *Prosody.* ~*n.* **1.** a metrical foot of two short or unstressed syllables. ~*adj.* **2.** of or composed in pyrrhics. [C16: via L, from Gk *purrhikhē*, said to be after its inventor *Purrhikhos*]

Pyrrhic victory *n.* a victory in which the victor's losses are as great as those of the defeated. Also called: **Cadmean victory.** [after PYRRHUS, who defeated the Romans at Asculum in 279 B.C. but suffered heavy losses]

Pyrrho ('pɪrəʊ) *n.* ?365–?275 B.C., Greek philosopher; founder of scepticism. He maintained that true wisdom and happiness lie in suspension of judgment, since certain knowledge is impossible to attain. —'Pyrrhonism *n.* —'Pyrrhonist *n.*, *adj.*

Pyrrhus ('pɪrəs) *n.* **1.** 319–272 B.C., king of Epirus (306–272). He invaded Italy but was ultimately defeated by the Romans (275 B.C.). **2.** another name for **Neoptolemus.** —'Pyrrhic *adj.*

pyruvic acid (paɪˈruːvɪk) *n.* a liquid formed during the metabolism of proteins and carbohydrates, helping to release energy to the body. [C19: from PYRO- + L *uva* grape]

Pythagoras (paɪˈθæɡərəs) *n.* ?580–?500 B.C., Greek philosopher and mathematician. He founded a religious brotherhood, which followed a life of strict asceticism and greatly influenced the development of mathematics and its application to music and astronomy.

Pythagoras' theorem *n.* the theorem that in a right-angled triangle the square of the length of the hypotenuse equals the sum of the squares of the other two sides.

Pythagorean (paɪˌθæɡəˈriːən) *adj.* **1.** of or relating to Pythagoras. ~*n.* **2.** a follower of Pythagoras.

Pytheas ('pɪθɪəs) *n.* 4th century B.C., Greek navigator. He was the first Greek to visit and describe the coasts of Spain, France, and the British Isles and may have reached Iceland.

Pythia ('pɪθɪə) *n. Greek myth.* the priestess of Apollo at Delphi, who transmitted the oracles.

Pythian ('pɪθɪən) *adj. also* **Pythic. 1.** of or relating to Delphi or its oracle. ~*n.* **2.** the priestess of Apollo at the oracle of Delphi. [C16: via L *Pȳthius* from Gk *Puthios* of Delphi]

Pythias ('pɪθɪˌæs) *n.* See **Damon and Pythias.**

python ('paɪθən) *n.* any of a family of large nonvenomous snakes of Africa, S Asia, and Australia. They reach a length of more than 20 feet and kill their prey by constriction. [C16: NL, after PYTHON] —**pythonic** (paɪˈθɒnɪk) *adj.*

Python ('paɪθən) *n. Greek myth.* a dragon, killed by Apollo at Delphi.

pythoness ('paɪθənɛs) *n.* a woman, such as Apollo's priestess at Delphi, believed to be possessed by an oracular spirit. [C14 *phitonesse*, ult. from Gk *Puthōn* PYTHON]

pyuria (paɪˈjʊərɪə) *n. Pathol.* any condition characterized by the presence of pus in the urine. [C19: from NL, from Gk *puon* pus + *ouron* urine]

pyx (pɪks) *n.* **1.** Also called: **pyx chest.** the chest in which coins from the British mint are placed to be tested for weight, etc. **2.** *Christianity.* any receptacle in which the Eucharistic Host is kept. [C14: from L *pyxis* small box, from Gk *puxos* box tree]

pyxidium (pɪkˈsɪdɪəm) *or* **pyxis** ('pɪksɪs) *n., pl.* -**ia** (-ɪə) *or* **pyxides** ('pɪksɪˌdiːz). the dry fruit of such plants as the plantain: a capsule whose upper part falls off when mature so that the seeds are released. [C19: via NL from Gk *puxidion* a little box, from *puxis* box]

pyxis ('pɪksɪs) *n., pl.* **pyxides** ('pɪksɪˌdiːz). **1.** a small box used by the ancient Greeks and Romans to hold medicines, etc. **2.** another name for **pyxidium.** [C14: via L from Gk: box]

Q

q *or* **Q** (kju:) *n.*, *pl.* **q's, Q's,** *or* **Qs. 1.** the 17th letter of the English alphabet. **2.** a speech sound represented by this letter.

q *symbol for* quintal.

Q *symbol for:* **1.** *Physics.* heat. **2.** *Chess.* queen. **3.** question.

q. *abbrev. for:* **1.** quart. **2.** quarter. **3.** quarterly. **4.** query. **5.** question. **6.** quire.

Q. *abbrev. for:* **1.** quartermaster. **2.** (*pl.* **Qq., qq.**) Also: **q.** quarto. **3.** Quebec. **4.** Queen. **5.** question. **6.** *Electronics.* Q factor.

Qaboos bin Said (kə'bu:s bɪn 'saɪd) *n.* born 1940, sultan of Oman from 1970.

Qaddafi (gə'dɑ:fɪ) *n.* **Moamar al** ('məʊə,mɑ: ,æl). See (Moamar al) **Gaddafi.**

Qaddish ('kædɪʃ) *n.*, *pl.* **Qaddishim.** a variant spelling of **Kaddish.**

Qairwan (kaɪə'wɑːn) *n.* a variant of **Kairouan.**

QANTAS ('kwɒntəs) *n.* the national airline of Australia. [C20: from *Q(ueensland) a(nd) N(orthern) T(erritory) A(erial) S(ervices Ltd.)*]

QARANC *abbrev. for* Queen Alexandra's Royal Army Nursing Corps.

Qatar *or* **Katar** (kæ'tɑ:) *n.* a state in E Arabia, occupying a peninsula in the Persian Gulf: under Persian rule until the 19th century; became a British protectorate in 1916; declared independence in 1971; exports petroleum and natural gas. Language: Arabic. Religion: Sunni Muslim. Currency: riyal. Capital: Doha. Pop.: 371 863 (1987). Area: about 11 000 sq. km (4250 sq. miles). —**Qa'tari** *or* **Ka'tari** *adj.*, *n.*

Qattara Depression (kə'tɑːrə) *n.* an arid basin in the Sahara, in NW Egypt, impassable to vehicles. Area: about 18 000 sq. km (7000 sq. miles). Lowest point: 133 m (435 ft.) below sea level.

QB *abbrev. for* Queen's Bench.

QC *abbrev. for* Queen's Counsel.

QED *abbrev. for* quod erat demonstrandum. [L: which was to be shown or proved]

Qeshm ('kɛʃəm) *or* **Qishm** *n.* **1.** the largest island in the Persian Gulf: part of Iran. Area: 1336 sq. km (516 sq. miles). **2.** the chief town of this island.

Q factor *n.* **1.** a measure of the relationship between stored energy and rate of energy dissipation in certain electrical components, devices, etc. **2.** Also called: **Q value.** the heat released in a nuclear reaction. ~Symbol: Q [C20: short for *quality factor*]

Q fever *n.* an acute disease characterized by fever and pneumonia, transmitted to man by a rickettsia. [C20: from *q(uery) fever* (the cause being orig. unknown)]

Qingdao ('tʃɪŋ'daʊ), **Tsingtao,** *or* **Chingtao** *n.* a port in E China, in E Shandong province on Jiazhou Bay, developed as a naval base and fort in 1891. Shandong university (1926). Pop.: 1 250 000 (1984).

Qinghai, Tsinghai, *or* **Chinghai** ('tʃɪŋ'haɪ) *n.* **1.** a province of NW China: consists largely of mountains and high plateaus. Capital: Xining. Pop.: 4 020 000 (1985). Area: 721 000 sq. km (278 400 sq. miles). **2.** the Pinyin transliteration of the Chinese name for **Koko Nor.**

Qiqihar, Chichihaerh, *or* **Ch'i-ch'i-haerh** ('tʃiː,tʃiːˈhɑː) *n.* a city in NE China, in Heilongjiang province on the Nonni River. Pop.: 1 260 000 (1986).

Qishm ('kɪʃəm) *n.* a variant of **Qeshm.**

Qld *abbrev. for* Queensland.

QM *abbrev. for* Quartermaster.

QMG *abbrev. for* Quartermaster General.

Qom (kɒm), **Qum,** *or* **Kum** *n.* a city in NW central Iran: a place of pilgrimage for Shiite Muslims. Pop.: 550 630 (1986).

qr. *pl.* **qrs.** *abbrev. for:* **1.** quarter. **2.** quarterly. **3.** quire.

Q-ship *n.* a merchant ship with concealed guns, used to decoy enemy ships. [C20: from *Q* short for QUERY]

QSM (in New Zealand) *abbrev. for* Queen's Service Medal.

QSO *abbrev. for:* **1.** quasi-stellar object. **2.** (in New Zealand) Queen's Service Order.

qt *pl.* **qt** *or* **qts** *abbrev. for* quart.

q.t. *Inf.* **1.** *abbrev. for* quiet. **2. on the q.t.** secretly.

qua (kweɪ, kwɑ:) *prep.* in the capacity of; by virtue of being. [C17: from L, ablative sing. (fem.) of *qui* who]

quack[1] (kwæk) *vb.* (*intr.*) **1.** (of a duck) to utter a harsh guttural sound. **2.** to make a noise like a duck. ~*n.* **3.** the sound made by a duck. [C17: imit.]

quack[2] (kwæk) *n.* **1. a.** an unqualified person who claims medical knowledge or other skills. **b.** (*as modifier*): *a quack doctor.* **2.** *Brit., Austral., & N.Z. inf.* a doctor; physician or surgeon. ~*vb.* **3.** (*intr.*) to act in the manner of a quack. [C17: short for QUACKSALVER] —**'quackish** *adj.*

quackery ('kwækərɪ) *n.*, *pl.* **-eries.** the activities or methods of a quack.

quack grass *n.* another name for **couch grass.**

quacksalver ('kwæk,sælvə) *n.* an archaic word for **quack**[2]. [C16: from Du., from *quack,* apparently: to hawk + *salf* SALVE]

quad[1] (kwɒd) *n.* short for **quadrangle.**

quad[2] (kwɒd) *n. Printing.* a block of type metal used for spacing. [C19: shortened from QUADRAT]

quad[3] (kwɒd) *n.* short for **quadruplet.**

quad[4] (kwɒd) *adj., n. Inf.* short for **quadraphonic** *or* **quadraphonics.**

Quadragesima (,kwɒdrə'dʒɛsɪmə) *n.* the first Sunday in Lent. Also called: **Quadragesima Sunday.** [C16: from Med. L *quadrāgēsima dies* the fortieth day]

Quadragesimal (,kwɒdrə'dʒɛsɪməl) *adj.* of, relating to, or characteristic of Lent.

quadrangle ('kwɒd,ræŋgəl) *n.* **1.** *Geom.* a plane figure consisting of four points connected by four lines. **2.** a rectangular courtyard, esp. one having buildings on all four sides. **3.** the building surrounding such a courtyard. [C15: from LL *quadrangulum* figure having four corners] —**quadrangular** (kwɒ'dræŋgjʊlə) *adj.*

quadrant ('kwɒdrənt) *n.* **1.** *Geom.* **a.** a quarter of the circumference of a circle. **b.** the area enclosed by two perpendicular radii of a circle. **c.** any of the four sections into which a plane is divided by two coordinate axes. **2.** a piece of a mechanism in the form of a quarter circle. **3.** an instrument formerly used in astronomy and navigation for measuring the altitudes of stars. [C14: from L *quadrāns* a quarter] —**quadrantal** (kwɒ'dræntəl) *adj.*

quadraphonics *or* **quadrophonics** (,kwɒdrə'fɒnɪks) *n.* (*functioning as sing.*) a system of sound recording and reproduction that uses four independent loudspeakers to give directional sources of sound. —**,quadra'phonic** *or* **,quadro'phonic** *adj.*

quadrat ('kwɒdrət) *n.* **1.** *Ecology.* an area of vegetation selected at random for study. **2.** *Printing.* an archaic name for **quad**[2]. [C14 (meaning "a square"): var. of QUADRATE]

quadrate *n.* ('kwɒdrɪt, -reɪt). **1.** a cube, square, or a square or cubelike object. **2.** one of a pair of bones of the upper jaw of fishes, amphibians, reptiles, and birds. ~*adj.* ('kwɒdrɪt, -reɪt). **3.** of or relating to this bone. **4.** square or rectangular. ~*vb.* ('kwɒdreɪt). **5.** (*tr.*) to make square or rectangular. **6.** (often foll. by *with*) to conform or cause to conform. [C14: from L *quadrāre* to make square]

quadratic (kwɒ'drætɪk) *Maths.* ~*n.* **1.** Also called: **quadratic equation.** an equation containing one or more terms in which the variable is raised to the power of two, but no terms in which it is raised to a higher power. ~*adj.* **2.** of or relating to the second power.

quadrature ('kwɒdrətʃə) *n.* **1.** *Maths.* the process of determining a square having an area equal to that of a given figure or surface. **2.** the process of making square or dividing into squares. **3.** *Astron.* a configuration in which two celestial bodies form an angle of 90° with a third body. **4.** *Electronics.* the relationship between two waves that are 90° out of phase.

quadrella (kwɒ'drɛlə) *n. Austral.* a form of betting in which the punter must select the winner of four specified races.

quadrennial (kwɒ'drɛnɪəl) *adj.* **1.** occurring every four years. **2.** lasting four years. ~*n.* **3.** a period of four years. —**quad'rennially** *adv.*

quadrennium (kwɒ'drɛnɪəm) *n., pl.* **-niums** *or* **-nia** (-nɪə). a period of four years. [C17: from L *quadriennium*, from QUADRI- + *annus* year]

quadri- *or before a vowel* **quadr-** *combining form.* four: *quadrilateral.* [from L; cf. *quattuor* four]

quadric ('kwɒdrɪk) *Maths.* ~*adj.* **1.** having or characterized by an equation of the second degree. **2.** of the second degree. ~*n.* **3.** a quadric curve, surface, or function.

quadriceps ('kwɒdrɪˌsɛps) *n., pl.* **-cepses** (-ˌsɛpsɪz) *or* **-ceps.** *Anat.* a large four-part muscle of the front of the thigh, which extends the leg. [C19: NL, from QUADRI- + *-ceps* as in BICEPS]

quadrifid ('kwɒdrɪfɪd) *adj. Bot.* divided into four lobes or other parts: *quadrifid leaves.*

quadrilateral (ˌkwɒdrɪ'lætərəl) *adj.* **1.** having or formed by four sides. ~*n.* **2.** Also called: **tetragon.** a polygon having four sides.

quadrille[1] (kwɒ'drɪl) *n.* **1.** a square dance for four couples. **2.** a piece of music for such a dance. [C18: via F from Sp. *cuadrilla,* dim. of *cuadro* square, from L *quadra*]

quadrille[2] (kwɒ'drɪl, kwə-) *n.* an old card game for four players. [C18: from F, from Sp. *cuartillo,* from *cuarto* fourth, from L *quartus,* infl. by QUADRILLE[1]]

quadrillion (kwɒ'drɪljən) *n.* **1.** (in Britain, France, and Germany) the number represented as one followed by 24 zeros (10²⁴). U.S. and Canad. word: **septillion.** **2.** (in the U.S. and Canada) the number represented as one followed by 15 zeros (10¹⁵). ~*determiner.* **3.** amounting to this number: *a quadrillion atoms.* [C17: from F *quadrillon,* from QUADRI- + *-illion,* on the model of *million*] —**quad'rillionth** *adj.*

quadrinomial (ˌkwɒdrɪ'nəʊmɪəl) *n.* an algebraic expression containing four terms.

quadriplegia (ˌkwɒdrɪ'pliːdʒɪə) *n.* paralysis of all four limbs. Also called: **tetraplegia.** [C20: from QUADRI- + Gk *plēssein* to strike] —**quadriplegic** (ˌkwɒdrɪ'pliːdʒɪk) *adj.*

quadrivalent (ˌkwɒdrɪ'veɪlənt) *adj. Chem.* another word for **tetravalent.** —ˌquadri'valency *or* ˌquadri'valence *n.*

quadrivium (kwɒ'drɪvɪəm) *n., pl.* **-ia** (-ɪə). (in medieval learning) a course consisting of arithmetic, geometry, astronomy, and music. [from Med. L, from L: crossroads, from QUADRI- + *via* way]

quadroon (kwɒ'druːn) *n.* a person who is one-quarter Negro. [C18: from Sp. *cuarterón,* from *cuarto* quarter, from L *quartus*]

quadrumanous (kwɒ'druːmənəs) *adj.* (of monkeys and apes) having all four feet specialized for use as hands. [C18: from NL *quadrumanus,* from QUADRI- + L *manus* hand]

quadruped ('kwɒdrʊˌpɛd) *n.* **1.** an animal, esp. a mammal, that has all four limbs specialized for walking. ~*adj.* **2.** having four feet. [C17: from L *quadrupēs,* from *quadru-* (see QUADRI-) + *pēs* foot] —**quadrupedal** (kwɒ'druːpɪd°l) *adj.*

quadruple ('kwɒdrʊp°l, kwɒ'druːp°l) *vb.* **1.** to multiply by four or increase fourfold. ~*adj.* **2.** four times as much or as many; fourfold. **3.** consisting of four parts. **4.** *Music.* having four beats in each bar. ~*n.* **5.** a quantity or number four times as great as another. [C16: via OF from L *quadruplus,* from *quadru-* (see QUADRI-) + *-plus* -fold] —**'quadruply** *adv.*

quadruplet ('kwɒdrʊplɪt, kwɒ'druːplɪt) *n.* **1.** one of four offspring born at one birth. **2.** a group of four similar things. **3.** *Music.* a group of four notes to be played in a time value of three.

quadruplicate *adj.* (kwɒ'druːplɪkɪt). **1.** fourfold or quadruple. ~*vb.* (kwɒ'druːplɪˌkeɪt). **2.** to multiply or be multiplied by four. ~*n.* (kwɒ'druːplɪkɪt). **3.** a group or set of four things. [C17: from L *quadruplicāre* to increase fourfold]

quaestor ('kwiːstə) *or U.S. (sometimes)* **questor** ('kwɛstə) *n.* any of several magistrates of ancient Rome, usually a financial administrator. [C14: from L, from *quaerere* to inquire] —**quaestorial** (kwɛ'stɔːrɪəl) *adj.*

quaff (kwɒf) *vb.* to drink heartily or in one draught. [C16: ? imit.; cf. MLow G *quassen* to eat or drink excessively] —**'quaffer** *n.*

quag (kwæg) *n.* a quagmire. [C16: ? rel. to QUAKE]

quagga ('kwægə) *n., pl.* **-gas** *or* **-ga.** a recently extinct member of the horse family of southern Africa: it had zebra-like stripes on the head and shoulders. [C18: from obs. Afrik., from Hottentot *qùagga*]

quaggy ('kwægɪ) *adj.* **-gier, -giest. 1.** resembling a quagmire; boggy. **2.** soft or flabby.

quagmire ('kwæg,maɪə) *n.* **1.** a soft wet area of land that gives way under the feet; bog. **2.** an awkward, complex, or embarrassing situation. [C16: from QUAG + MIRE]

quahog ('kwɑː,hɒg) *n.* an edible clam native to the Atlantic coast of North America, having a large heavy rounded shell. [C18: from Amerind, short for *poquauhock,* from *pohkeni* dark + *hogki* shell]

quaich *or* **quaigh** (kweɪx) *n. Scot.* a small shallow drinking cup, usually with two handles. [from Gaelic *cuach* cup]

Quai d'Orsay (*French* ke dɔrsɛ) *n.* the quay along the south bank of the Seine, Paris, where the French foreign office is situated.

quail[1] (kweɪl) *n., pl.* **quails** *or* **quail.** any of various small Old World game birds having rounded bodies and small tails. [C14: from OF *quaille,* from Med. L *quaccula,* prob. imit.]

quail[2] (kweɪl) *vb.* (*intr.*) to shrink back with fear; cower. [C15: ?from OF *quailler,* from L *coāgulāre* to curdle]

quaint (kweɪnt) *adj.* **1.** attractively unusual, esp. in an old-fashioned style. **2.** odd or inappropriate. [C13 (in the sense: clever): from OF *cointe,* from L *cognitus* known, from *cognoscere* to ascertain] —**'quaintly** *adv.* —**'quaintness** *n.*

quair (kwɛə) *n. Scot.* a book. [var. of QUIRE[1]]

quake (kweɪk) *vb.* (*intr.*) **1.** to shake or tremble with or as with fear. **2.** to convulse or quiver, as from instability. ~*n.* **3.** a quaking. **4.** *Inf.* an earthquake. [OE *cwacian*]

Quaker ('kweɪkə) *n.* **1.** a member of the Society of Friends, a Christian sect founded by George Fox about 1650. Quakers reject sacraments, ritual, and formal ministry, and have promoted many causes for social reform. ~*adj.* **2.** of the Society of Friends or its beliefs or practices. [C17: orig. a derog. nickname] —**'Quakeress** *fem. n.* —**'Quakerish** *adj.* —**'Quakerism** *n.*

quaking ('kweɪkɪŋ) *adj.* unstable or unsafe to walk on, as a bog or quicksand.

quaking grass *n.* any of various grasses having delicate branches that shake in the wind.

quaky ('kweɪkɪ) *adj.* **quakier, quakiest.** inclined to quake; shaky. —**'quakiness** *n.*

qualification (ˌkwɒlɪfɪ'keɪʃən) *n.* **1.** an ability, quality, or attribute, esp. one that fits a person to perform a particular job or task. **2.** a condition that modifies or limits; restriction. **3.** a qualifying or being qualified.

qualified ('kwɒlɪˌfaɪd) *adj.* **1.** having the abilities, qualities, attributes, etc., necessary to perform a particular job or task. **2.** limited, modified, or restricted; not absolute.

qualify ('kwɒlɪˌfaɪ) *vb.* **-fying, -fied. 1.** to provide or be provided with the abilities or attributes necessary for a task, office, duty, etc.: *his degree qualifies him for the job.* **2.** (*tr.*) to make less strong, harsh, or violent; moderate or restrict. **3.** (*tr.*) to modify or change the strength or flavour of. **4.** (*tr.*) *Grammar.* another word for **modify. 5.** (*tr.*) to attribute a quality to; characterize. **6.** (*intr.*) to progress to the final stages of a competition, as by winning preliminary contests. [C16: from OF *qualifier,* from Med. L *qualificāre* to characterize, from L *quālis* of what kind + *facere* to make] —**'quali,fiable** *adj.* —**'quali,fier** *n.*

qualitative ('kwɒlɪtətɪv) *adj.* involving or relating to distinctions based on quality or qualities. —**'qualitatively** *adv.*

qualitative analysis *n.* See **analysis** (sense 4).

quality ('kwɒlɪtɪ) *n., pl.* **-ties. 1.** a distinguishing characteristic or attribute. **2.** the basic character or nature of something. **3.** a feature of personality. **4.** degree or standard of excellence, esp. a high standard. **5.** (formerly) high social status or the distinction associated with it. **6.** musical tone colour; timbre. **7.** *Logic.* the characteristic of a proposition that makes it affirmative or negative. **8.** *Phonetics.* the distinctive character of a vowel, determined by the configuration of the mouth, tongue, etc. **9.** (*modifier*) having or showing excellence or superiority: *a quality product.* [C13: from OF *qualité,* from L *quālitās* state, from *quālis* of what sort]

quality control *n.* control of the relative quality of a manufactured product, usually by statistical sampling techniques.

qualm (kwɑːm) *n.* **1.** a sudden feeling of sickness or nausea. **2.** a pang of doubt, esp. concerning moral conduct; scruple. **3.** a sudden sensation of misgiving. [OE *cwealm* death or plague] —'**qualmish** *adj.*

quandary ('kwɒndrɪ) *n., pl.* **-ries.** a difficult situation; predicament; dilemma. [C16: from ?; ? rel. to L *quandō* when]

quandong, quandang ('kwɒn,dɒŋ), *or* **quantong** ('kwɒn,tɒŋ) *n.* **1.** Also called: **native peach. a.** a small Australian tree. **b.** the edible fruit or nut of this tree. **2. silver quandong. a.** an Australian tree. **b.** its timber. [from Abor.]

quango ('kwæŋgəʊ) *n., pl.* **-gos.** *acronym for* quasi-autonomous nongovernmental organization.

quant (kwɒnt) *n.* **1.** a long pole for propelling a boat, esp. a punt. ~*vb.* **2.** to propel (a boat) with a quant. [C15: prob. from L *contus* pole, from Gk *kontos*]

Quant (kwɒnt) *n.* **Mary.** born 1934, English fashion designer, whose Chelsea Look of miniskirts and geometrically patterned fabrics dominated London fashion in the 1960s.

quanta ('kwɒntə) *n.* the plural of **quantum.**

quantic ('kwɒntɪk) *n.* a homogeneous function of two or more variables in a rational and integral form. [C19: from L *quantus* how great]

quantifier ('kwɒntɪ,faɪə) *n.* **1.** *Logic.* a symbol indicating the quantity of a term: *the existential quantifier corresponds to the words "there is something, such that".* **2.** *Grammar.* a word or phrase, such as *some, all,* or *no,* expressing quantity.

quantify ('kwɒntɪ,faɪ) *vb.* **-fying, -fied.** (*tr.*) **1.** to discover or express the quantity of. **2.** *Logic.* to specify the quantity of (a term) by using a quantifier, such as *all, some,* or *no.* [C19: from Med. L *quantificāre,* from L *quantus* how much + *facere* to make] —'**quantifiable** *adj.* —,**quantifi**'**cation** *n.*

quantitative ('kwɒntɪtətɪv) *or* **quantitive** *adj.* **1.** involving or relating to considerations of amount or size. **2.** capable of being measured. **3.** *Prosody.* of a metrical system that is based on the length of syllables. —'**quantitatively** *or* '**quantitively** *adv.*

quantitative analysis *n.* See **analysis** (sense 4).

quantity ('kwɒntɪtɪ) *n., pl.* **-ties. 1. a.** a specified or definite amount, number, etc. **b.** (*as modifier*): *a quantity estimate.* **2.** the aspect of anything that can be measured, weighed, counted, etc. **3. unknown quantity.** a person or thing whose action, effort, etc., is unknown or unpredictable. **4.** a large amount. **5.** *Maths.* an entity having a magnitude that may be denoted by a numerical expression. **6.** *Physics.* a specified magnitude or amount. **7.** *Logic.* the characteristic of a proposition that makes it universal or particular. **8.** *Prosody.* the relative duration of a syllable or the vowel in it. [C14: from OF *quantité,* from L *quantitās* amount, from *quantus* how much]

quantity surveyor *n.* a person who estimates the cost of the materials and labour necessary for a construction job.

quantize *or* **-ise** ('kwɒntaɪz) *vb.* (*tr.*) **1.** *Physics.* to restrict (a physical quantity) to one of a set of fixed values. **2.** *Maths.* to limit to values that are multiples of a basic unit. —,**quanti**'**zation** *or* **-i**'**sation** *n.*

quantum ('kwɒntəm) *n., pl.* **-ta. 1.** *Physics.* **a.** the smallest quantity of some physical property that a system can possess according to the quantum theory. **b.** a particle with such a unit of energy. **2.** amount or quantity, esp. a specific amount. ~*adj.* **3.** of or designating a major breakthrough or sudden advance: *a quantum leap forward.* [C17: from L *quantus* (adj.) how much]

quantum electrodynamics *n.* *Physics.* the study of electromagnetic radiation and its interaction with charged particles in terms of quantum theory.

quantum mechanics *n.* (*functioning as sing.*) the branch of mechanics, based on the quantum theory, used for interpreting the behaviour of elementary particles and atoms, which do not obey Newtonian mechanics.

quantum meruit *Latin.* ('mɛruːɪt) as much as he has earned.

quantum number *n.* *Physics.* one of a set of integers or half-integers characterizing the energy states of a particle or system of particles.

quantum theory *n.* a theory concerning the behaviour of physical systems based on the idea that they can only possess certain properties, such as energy and angular momentum, in discrete amounts (quanta).

quaquaversal (,kwɑːkwə'vɜːsəl) *adj.* *Geol.* directed outwards in all directions from a common centre. [C18: from L *quāquā* in every direction + *versus* towards]

quarantine ('kwɒrən,tiːn) *n.* **1.** a period of isolation or detention, esp. of persons or animals arriving from abroad, to prevent the spread of disease. **2.** the place where such detention is enforced. **3.** any period or state of enforced isolation. ~*vb.* **4.** (*tr.*) to isolate in or as if in quarantine. [C17: from It. *quarantina* period of forty days, from *quaranta* forty, from L *quadrāgintā*]

quarantine flag *n.* *Naut.* the yellow signal flag for the letter Q, flown alone from a vessel to indicate that there is no disease aboard or, with a second signal flag, to indicate that there is disease aboard. Also called: **yellow jack.**

quark[1] (kwɑːk) *n.* *Physics.* any of a number of hypothetical elementary particles with electric charge $+2/3$ or $-1/3$ of the electron charge, postulated to be fundamental units of all baryons and mesons. [C20: coined by James JOYCE in the novel *Finnegans Wake,* and given special application in physics]

quark[2] (kwɑːk) *n.* a type of low-fat soft cheese. [from G]

Quarles (kwɔːlz, kwɑːlz) *n.* **Francis.** 1592–1644, English poet.

quarrel[1] ('kwɒrəl) *n.* **1.** an angry disagreement; argument. **2.** a cause of dispute; grievance. ~*vb.* **-relling, -relled** *or* U.S. **-reling, -reled.** (*intr.*; often foll. by *with*) **3.** to engage in a disagreement or dispute; argue. **4.** to find fault; complain. [C14: from OF *querele,* from L *querēlla* complaint, from *querī* to complain] —'**quarreller** *or* U.S. '**quarreler** *n.*

quarrel[2] ('kwɒrəl) *n.* **1.** an arrow having a four-edged head, fired from a crossbow. **2.** a small square or diamond-shaped pane of glass. [C13: from OF *quarrel* pane, from Med. L *quadrellus,* dim. of L *quadrus* square]

quarrelsome ('kwɒrəlsəm) *adj.* inclined to quarrel or disagree; belligerent.

quarrian *or* **quarrion** ('kwɒrɪən) *n.* a cockatiel of inland Australia that feeds on seeds and grasses. [C20: prob. from Abor.]

quarry[1] ('kwɒrɪ) *n., pl.* **-ries. 1.** an open surface excavation for the extraction of building stone, slate, marble, etc. **2.** a copious source, esp. of information. ~*vb.* **-rying, -ried. 3.** to extract (stone, slate, etc.) from or as if from a quarry. **4.** (*tr.*) to excavate a quarry in. **5.** to obtain (something) diligently and laboriously. [C15: from OF *quarriere,* from *quarre* (unattested) square-shaped stone, from L *quadrāre* to make square]

quarry[2] ('kwɒrɪ) *n., pl.* **-ries. 1.** an animal, etc., that is hunted, esp. by other animals; prey. **2.** anything pursued. [C14 *quirre* entrails offered to the hounds, from OF *cuirée* what is placed on the hide, from *cuir* hide, from L *corium* leather; prob. also infl. by OF *coree* entrails, from L *cor* heart]

quarryman ('kwɒrɪmən) *n., pl.* **-men.** a man who works in or manages a quarry.

quarry tile *n.* an unglazed floor tile.

quart (kwɔːt) *n.* **1.** a unit of liquid measure equal to a quarter of a gallon or two pints. 1 U.S. quart (0.946 litre) is equal to 0.8326 U.K. quart. 1 U.K. quart (1.136 litres) is equal to 1.2009 U.S. quarts. **2.** a unit of dry measure equal to 2 pints or one eighth of a peck. [C14: from OF *quarte,* from L *quartus* fourth]

quartan ('kwɔːt³n) *adj.* (of a fever) occurring every third day. [C13: from L *febris quartāna* fever occurring every fourth day, reckoned inclusively]

quarte (kɑːt) *n.* the fourth of eight basic positions from which a parry or attack can be made in fencing. [C18: F from OF *quarte,* from L *quartus* fourth]

quarter ('kwɔːtə) *n.* **1.** one of four equal parts of an object, quantity, etc. **2.** the fraction equal to one divided by four ($\frac{1}{4}$). **3.** U.S., Canad., etc. a 25-cent piece. **4.** a unit of weight equal to a quarter of a hundredweight. 1 U.S. quarter is equal to 25 pounds; 1 Brit. quarter is equal to 28 pounds. **5.** short for **quarter-hour. 6.** a fourth part of a year; three months. **7.** *Astron.* **a.** one fourth of the moon's period of revolution around the earth. **b.** either of two phases of the moon when half of the lighted surface is visible. **8.** *Inf.* a unit of weight equal to a quarter of a pound or 4 ounces. **9.** *Brit.* a unit of capacity for grain, etc., usually equal to 8 U.K. bushels. **10.** *Sport.* one of the four periods into which certain games are divided. **11.** *Naut.* the part of a vessel's side towards the stern. **12.** a region or district of a town or city: *the Spanish quarter.* **13.** a region, direction, or point of the compass. **14.** (*sometimes pl.*) an unspecified person or group of people: *to get word from the highest quarter.* **15.** mercy or pity, as shown to a defeated opponent (esp. in **ask for** or **give quarter**). **16.** any of the four limbs, including the adjacent parts, of a quadruped or bird. **17.** *Heraldry.* one of four quadrants into which a shield may be divided. ~*vb.* **18.** (*tr.*) to divide into four equal parts. **19.** (*tr.*) to divide into any number of parts. **20.** (*tr.*) (esp. formerly) to dismember (a human body). **21.** to billet or be billeted in lodgings, esp. (of military personnel) in civilian lodgings. **22.** (*intr.*) (of hounds) to range over an area of ground in search of game or the scent of quarry. **23.** (*intr.*) *Naut.* (of the wind) to blow onto a vessel's quarter. **24.** (*tr.*) *Heraldry.* **a.** to divide (a shield) into four separate bearings. **b.** to place (one set of arms) in diagonally opposite quarters to another. ~*adj.* **25.** being or consisting of one of four equal parts. ~See also **quarters.** [C13: from OF *quartier*, from L *quartārius* a fourth part, from *quartus* fourth]

quarterback ('kwɔːtə,bæk) *n.* a player in American football who directs attacking play.

quarter-bound *adj.* (of a book) having a binding consisting of two types of material, the better type being used on the spine.

quarter day *n.* any of four days in the year when certain payments become due. In England, Wales, and Ireland these are Lady Day, Midsummer Day, Michaelmas, and Christmas. In Scotland they are Candlemas, Whit Sunday, Lammas, and Martinmas.

quarterdeck ('kwɔːtə,dɛk) *n. Naut.* the after part of the weather deck of a ship, traditionally the deck for official or ceremonial use.

quartered ('kwɔːtəd) *adj.* **1.** *Heraldry.* (of a shield) divided into four sections, each having contrasting arms or having two sets of arms, each repeated in diagonally opposite corners. **2.** (of a log) sawn into four equal parts along two diameters at right angles to each other.

quarterfinal (,kwɔːtə'faɪnªl) *n.* the round before the semifinal in a competition.

quarter-hour *n.* **1.** a period of 15 minutes. **2.** either of the points on a timepiece that mark 15 minutes before or after the hour.

quartering ('kwɔːtərɪŋ) *n.* **1.** *Mil.* the allocation of accommodation to service personnel. **2.** *Heraldry.* **a.** the marshalling of several coats of arms on one shield, usually representing intermarriages. **b.** any coat of arms marshalled in this way.

quarterlight ('kwɔːtə,laɪt) *n. Brit.* a small pivoted window in the door of a car for ventilation.

quarterly ('kwɔːtəlɪ) *adj.* **1.** occurring, done, paid, etc., at intervals of three months. **2.** of, relating to, or consisting of a quarter. ~*n., pl.* **-lies. 3.** a periodical issued every three months. ~*adv.* **4.** once every three months.

quartermaster ('kwɔːtə,mɑːstə) *n.* **1.** an officer responsible for accommodation, food, and equipment in a military unit. **2.** a rating in the navy, usually a petty officer, with particular responsibility for navigational duties.

quarter-miler *n.* an athlete who specializes in running the quarter mile.

quartern ('kwɔːtən) *n.* **1.** a fourth part of certain weights or measures. **2.** Also called: **quartern loaf.** *Brit.* **a.** a type of loaf 4 inches square. **b.** any loaf weighing 1600 g. [C13: from OF *quarteron*, from *quart* a quarter]

quarter note *n.* the usual U.S. and Canad. name for **crotchet** (sense 1).

quarter plate *n.* a photographic plate measuring 8.3 × 10.8 cm.

quarters ('kwɔːtəz) *pl. n.* **1.** accommodation, esp. as provided for military personnel. **2.** the stations assigned to crew members of a warship: *general quarters.*

quarter sessions *n.* (*functioning as sing. or pl.*) (formerly) any of various courts held four times a year before justices of the peace or a recorder.

quarterstaff ('kwɔːtə,stɑːf) *n., pl.* **-staves** (-,steɪvz). a stout iron-tipped wooden staff about 6ft. long, formerly used as a weapon. [C16: from ?]

quarter tone *n. Music.* a quarter of a whole tone.

quartet or **quartette** (kwɔː'tɛt) *n.* **1.** a group of four singers or instrumentalists or a piece of music composed for such a group. **2.** any group of four. [C18: from It. *quartetto*, dim. of *quarto* fourth]

quartic ('kwɔːtɪk) *adj., n.* another word for **biquadratic.** [C19: from L *quartus* fourth]

quartile ('kwɔːtaɪl) *n.* **1.** *Statistics.* one of three values of a variable dividing its distribution into four groups with equal frequencies. ~*adj.* **2.** *Statistics.* of a quartile. **3.** *Astrol.* denoting an aspect of two heavenly bodies when their longitudes differ by 90°. [C16: from Med. L *quartīlis*, from L *quartus* fourth]

quarto ('kwɔːtəʊ) *n., pl.* **-tos.** a book size resulting from folding a sheet of paper into four leaves or eight pages. [C16: from NL *in quartō* in quarter]

quartz (kwɔːts) *n.* a hard glossy mineral consisting of silicon dioxide in crystalline form. It occurs as colourless rock crystal and as several impure coloured varieties including agate, chalcedony, flint, and amethyst. Formula: SiO_2. [C18: from G *Quarz*, of Slavic origin]

quartz clock or **watch** *n.* a clock or watch that is operated by a vibrating quartz crystal.

quartz crystal *n.* a thin plate or rod cut from a piece of piezoelectric quartz and ground so that it vibrates at a particular frequency.

quartz glass *n.* a colourless glass composed of almost pure silica, resistant to very high temperatures.

quartz-iodine lamp or **quartz lamp** *n.* an electric light bulb consisting of a quartz envelope enclosing an inert gas containing iodine vapour and a tungsten filament: used for car headlights, cine projectors, etc.

quartzite ('kwɔːtsaɪt) *n.* **1.** a sandstone composed of quartz. **2.** a very hard rock consisting of intergrown quartz crystals.

quasar ('kweɪzɑː, -sɑː) *n.* any of a class of quasi-stellar objects that are powerful sources of radio waves and other forms of energy. Many have large red shifts, which imply distances of several thousand million light years. [C20: from *quas*(*i-stell*)*ar* (*radio source*)]

quash (kwɒʃ) *vb.* (*tr.*) **1.** to subdue forcefully and completely. **2.** to annul or make void (a law, etc.). **3.** to reject (an indictment, etc.) as invalid. [C14: from OF *quasser*, from L *quassāre* to shake]

quasi- *combining form.* **1.** almost but not really; seemingly: *a quasi-religious cult.* **2.** resembling but not actually being; so-called: *a quasi-scholar.* [from L, lit.: as if]

Quasimodo (*Italian* kwa'zi:modo) *n.* **Salvatore** (sal-va'to:re). 1901–68, Italian poet, whose early work expresses symbolist ideas and techniques. His later work is more concerned with political and social issues: Nobel prize for literature 1959.

quasi-stellar object ('kwɑːzɪ, 'kweɪsɑː) *n.* a member of any of several classes of astronomical bodies, including **quasars** and **quasi-stellar galaxies,** both of which have exceptionally large red shifts. Abbrev.: **QSO.**

quassia ('kwɒʃə) *n.* **1.** any of a genus of tropical American trees having bitter bark and wood. **2.** the wood of this tree or a bitter compound extracted from it, formerly used as a tonic and vermifuge, now used in insecticides. [C18: from NL, after Graman *Quassi*, a slave who discovered (1730) the medicinal value of the root]

quatercentenary (,kwætəsən'ti:nərɪ) *n., pl.* **-naries.** a 400th anniversary. [C19: from L *quater* four times + CENTENARY] —,**quatercen'tennial** (,kwætəsɛn'tɛnɪəl) *adj., n.*

quaternary (kwə'tɜːnərɪ) *adj.* **1.** consisting of fours or by fours. **2.** fourth in a series. **3.** *Chem.* containing or being an atom bound to four other atoms or groups. ~*n., pl.* **-naries. 4.** the number four or a set of four. [C15: from L *quaternārius* each containing four, from *quaternī* by fours, from *quattuor* four]

Quaternary (kwə'tɜːnərɪ) *adj.* **1.** of or denoting the most recent period of geological time, which succeeded the Tertiary period one million years ago. ~*n.* **2. the.** the Quaternary period or rock system.

quaternion (kwə'tɜːnɪən) *n.* **1.** *Maths.* a generalized complex number consisting of four components, of the form $x = x_0 + x_1\mathbf{i} + x_2\mathbf{j} + x_3\mathbf{k}$, where $x, x_0 \ldots x_3$ are real numbers and $\mathbf{i}^2 = \mathbf{j}^2 = \mathbf{k}^2 = -1$, $\mathbf{ij} = -\mathbf{ji} = \mathbf{k}$, etc. **2.** a set of four. [C14: from LL, from L *quaternī* four at a time]

Quathlamba (kwa:t'lɑːmbɑː) *n.* the Sotho name for the **Drakensberg.**

quatrain ('kwɒtreɪn) *n.* a stanza or poem of four lines. [C16: from F, from *quatre* four, from L *quattuor*]

Quatre Bras (*French* katrə bra) *n.* a village in Belgium near Brussels; site of a battle in June 1815 where Wellington defeated the French under Marshal Ney, immediately preceding the battle of Waterloo.

quatrefoil ('kætrə,fɔɪl) *n.* **1.** a leaf composed of four leaflets. **2.** *Archit.* a carved ornament having four foils arranged about a common centre. [C15: from OF, from *quatre* four + *-foil* leaflet]

quattrocento (,kwætrəʊ'tʃɛntəʊ) *n.* the 15th century, esp. in reference to Renaissance Italian art and literature. [It., lit.: four hundred (short for fourteen hundred)]

quaver ('kweɪvə) *vb.* **1.** to say or sing (something) with a trembling voice. **2.** (*intr.*) (esp. of the voice) to quiver or tremble. **3.** (*intr.*) *Rare.* to sing or play trills. ~*n.* **4.** *Music.* a note having the time value of an eighth of a semibreve. Usual U.S. and Canad. name: **eighth note. 5.** a tremulous sound or note. [C15 (in the sense: to vibrate): from *quaven* to tremble, of Gmc origin] —'**quavering** *adj.* —'**quaveringly** *adv.*

quay (ki:) *n.* a wharf, typically one built parallel to the shoreline. [C14 *keye*, from OF *kai*, of Celtic origin]

quayage ('ki:ɪdʒ) *n.* **1.** a system of quays. **2.** a charge for the use of a quay.

Quayle (kweɪl) *n.* **James Danforth**, known as *Dan.* born 1947, U.S. Republican politician; vice president of the U.S. from 1989.

quayside ('ki:,saɪd) *n.* the edge of a quay along the water.

Que. *abbrev. for* Quebec.

quean (kwi:n) *n.* **1.** *Arch.* **a.** a boisterous impudent woman. **b.** a prostitute. **2.** *Scot.* an unmarried girl. [OE *cwene*]

queasy ('kwi:zɪ) *adj.* **-sier, -siest. 1.** having the feeling that one is about to vomit; nauseous. **2.** feeling or causing uneasiness. [C15: from ?] —'**queasily** *adv.* —'**queasiness** *n.*

Quebec (kwɪ'bɛk, kə-, kɛ-) *n.* **1.** a province of E Canada: the largest Canadian province; a French colony from 1608 to 1763, when it passed to Britain; lying mostly on the Canadian Shield, it has vast areas of forest and extensive tundra and is populated mostly in the plain around the St Lawrence River. Capital: Quebec. Pop.: 6 572 300 (1985 est.). Area: 1 540 680 sq. km (594 860 sq. miles). Abbrev.: **PQ. 2.** a port in E Canada, capital of the province of Quebec, situated on the St Lawrence River: founded in 1608 by Champlain; scene of the battle of the Plains of Abraham (1759), by which the British won Canada from the French. Pop.: 164 580 (1986). —**Que'becker** *or* **Que'becer** *n.*

Québecois (*French* kebɛkwa) *n., pl.* **-cois** (-kwa). a native or inhabitant of the province of Quebec, esp. a French-speaking one.

quebracho (keɪ'brɑ:tʃəʊ) *n., pl.* **-chos** (-tʃəʊz). **1.** either of two South American trees having a tannin-rich hard wood used in tanning and dyeing. **2.** a South American tree, whose bark yields alkaloids used in medicine and tanning. **3.** the wood or bark of any of these trees. [C19: from American Sp., from *quiebracha*, from *quebrar* to break (from L *crepāre* to rattle) + *hacha* axe (from F)]

Quechua ('kɛtʃwə) *n.* **1.** (*pl.* **-uas** or **-ua**) a member of any of a group of South American Indian peoples of the Andes, including the Incas. **2.** the language or family of languages spoken by these peoples. —'**Quechuan** *adj., n.*

queen (kwi:n) *n.* **1.** a female sovereign who is the official ruler or head of state. **2.** the wife of a king. **3.** a woman or a thing personified as a woman considered the best or most important of her kind: *the queen of ocean liners.* **4.** *Sl.* an effeminate male homosexual. **5.** the only fertile female in a colony of bees, ants, etc. **6.** an adult female cat. **7.** a playing card bearing the picture of a queen. **8.** the most powerful chess piece, able to move in a straight line in any direction or diagonally. ~*vb.* **9.** *Chess.* to promote (a pawn) to a queen when it reaches the eighth rank. **10.** (*tr.*) to crown as queen. **11.** (*intr.*) to reign as queen. **12. queen it.** (often foll. by *over*) *Inf.* to behave in an overbearing manner. [OE *cwēn*]

Queen-Anne *n.* **1.** a style of furniture popular in England about 1700–20 and in America about 1720–70, characterized by the use of curves, walnut veneer, and the cabriole leg. ~*adj.* **2.** in or of this style. **3.** of a style of architecture popular in early 18th-century England, characterized by red-brick construction with classical ornamentation.

Queen Anne's lace *n.* another name for the **wild carrot.**

queen bee *n.* **1.** the fertile female bee in a hive. **2.** *Inf.* a woman in a position of dominance over her associates.

Queenborough in Sheppey ('kwi:nbərə; 'ʃɛpɪ) *n.* a town in SE England, in Kent: formed in 1968 by the amalgamation of Queenborough, Sheerness, and Sheppey. Pop.: 33 362 (1981).

Queen Charlotte Islands *pl. n.* a group of about 150 islands off the W coast of Canada: part of British Columbia. Pop.: 5884 (1981). Area: 9596 sq. km (3705 sq. miles).

queen consort *n.* the wife of a reigning king.

queen dowager *n.* the widow of a king.

Queen Elizabeth Islands *pl. n.* a group of islands off the N coast of Canada: the northernmost islands of the Canadian Arctic archipelago, lying N of latitude 74°N; part of the Northwest Territories. Area: about 390 000 sq. km (150 000 sq. miles).

queenly ('kwi:nlɪ) *adj.* **-lier, -liest. 1.** resembling or appropriate to a queen. ~*adv.* **2.** in a manner appropriate to a queen.

Queen Mab (mæb) *n.* (in British folklore) a bewitching fairy who rules over men's dreams.

Queen Maud Land (mɔ:d) *n.* the large section of Antarctica between Coats Land and Enderby Land: claimed by Norway in 1939.

Queen Maud Range *n.* a mountain range in Antarctica, in S Ross Dependency, extending for about 800 km (500 miles).

queen mother *n.* the widow of a former king who is also the mother of the reigning sovereign.

queen olive *n.* a variety of olive having large fleshy fruit suitable for pickling.

queen post *n.* one of a pair of vertical posts that connect the tie beam of a truss to the principal rafters. Cf. **king post.**

Queens (kwi:nz) *n.* a borough of E New York City, on Long Island. Pop.: 1 891 325 (1980).

Queen's Award for Industry *n.* (in Britain) an award given to firms that have outstanding export records or have made technological advances.

Queen's Bench *n.* (in England when the sovereign is female) one of the divisions of the High Court of Justice.

Queensberry rules ('kwi:nzbərɪ) *pl. n.* **1.** the code of rules followed in modern boxing. **2.** *Inf.* gentlemanly conduct, esp. in a dispute. [C19: after the ninth Marquess of *Queensberry*, who originated the rules in 1869]

Queen's Counsel *n.* **1.** (in England when the sovereign is female) a barrister appointed Counsel to the Crown on the recommendation of the Lord Chancellor. **2.** (in Canada) an honorary title which may be bestowed by the government on lawyers with long experience.

Queen's County *n.* the former name of **Laoighis.**

Queen's English *n.* (when the British sovereign is female) standard Southern British English.

queen's evidence *n. English law.* evidence given for the Crown against his former associates in crime by an accomplice (esp. in **turn queen's evidence**). U.S. equivalent: **state's evidence.**

Queen's Guide *n.* (in Britain and the Commonwealth when the sovereign is female) a Guide who has passed the highest tests of proficiency.

queen's highway *n.* **1.** (in Britain when the sovereign is female) any public road or right of way. **2.** (in Canada) a main road maintained by the provincial government.

Queensland ('kwi:nz,lænd, -lənd) *n.* a state of NE Australia: fringed on the Pacific side by the Great Barrier Reef; the Great Dividing Range lies in the east, separating the coastal lowlands from the dry Great Artesian Basin in the south. Capital: Brisbane. Pop.: 2 587 315 (1986). Area: 1 727 500 sq. km (667 000 sq. miles). —'**Queens,lander** *n.*

Queensland nut *n.* another name for **macadamia.**

Queen's Scout *n.* (in Britain and the Commonwealth when the sovereign is female) a Scout who has passed the highest tests of proficiency. U.S. equivalent: **Eagle Scout.**

Queenstown ('kwi:nz,taʊn) *n.* the former name (1849–1922) of **Cóbh.**

queer (kwɪə) *adj.* **1.** differing from the normal or usual; odd or strange. **2.** dubious; shady. **3.** faint, giddy, or queasy. **4.** *Inf., derog.* homosexual. **5.** *Inf.* eccentric or slightly mad. **6.** *Sl.* worthless or counterfeit. ~*n.* **7.** *Inf., derog.* a homosexual. ~*vb.* (*tr.*) *Inf.* **8.** to spoil or thwart (esp. in **queer someone's pitch**). **9.** to put in a difficult position. [C16: ?from G *quer* oblique, ult. from OHG *twērh*] —'**queerly** *adv.* —'**queerness** *n.*

queer fish *n. Brit. inf.* an odd person.

queer street *n.* (*sometimes cap.*) *Inf.* a difficult situation, such as debt or bankruptcy (in **in queer street**).

quell (kwɛl) *vb.* (*tr.*) **1.** to suppress (rebellion, etc.); subdue. **2.** to overcome or allay. [OE *cwellan* to kill] —'**queller** *n.*

Quelpart ('kwɛl,pɑːt) *n.* another name for **Cheju.**

Quemoy (kɛ'mɔɪ) *n.* an island in Formosa Strait, off the SE coast of China: administratively part of Taiwan. Pop. (with associated islets): 57 847 (1982). Area: 130 sq. km (50 sq. miles).

quench (kwɛntʃ) *vb.* (*tr.*) **1.** to satisfy (one's thirst, desires, etc.); slake. **2.** to put out (a fire, etc.); extinguish. **3.** to put down; suppress; subdue. **4.** to cool (hot metal) by plunging it into cold water. [OE *ācwencan* to extinguish] —'**quenchable** *adj.* —'**quencher** *n.*

Queneau (*French* kəno) *n.* **Raymond** (rɛmɔ̃) 1903–76. French writer, influenced in the 1920s by surrealism. His novels include *Zazie dans le métro* (1959).

quenelle (kə'nɛl) *n.* a ball of finely sieved meat or fish. [C19: from F, from G *Knödel* dumpling, from OHG *knodo* knot]

Querétaro (*Spanish* ke'retaro) *n.* **1.** an inland state of central Mexico: economy based on agriculture and mining. Capital: Querétaro. Pop.: 837 003 (1983 est.). Area: 11 769 sq. km (4544 sq. miles). **2.** a city in central Mexico, capital of Querétaro state: scene of the signing (1848) of the treaty ending the U.S.-Mexican War and of the execution of Emperor Maximilian (1867). Pop.: 293 586 (1980).

querist ('kwɪərɪst) *n.* a person who makes inquiries or queries; questioner.

quern (kwɜːn) *n.* a stone hand mill for grinding corn. [OE *cweorn*]

querulous ('kwɛrʊləs, 'kwɛrjʊ-) *adj.* **1.** inclined to make whining or peevish complaints. **2.** characterized by or proceeding from a complaining fretful attitude or disposition. [C15: from L *querulus*, from *querī* to complain] —'**querulously** *adv.* —'**querulousness** *n.*

query ('kwɪərɪ) *n., pl.* **-ries. 1.** a question, esp. one expressing doubt. **2.** a question mark. ~*vb.* **-rying, -ried.** (*tr.*) **3.** to express uncertainty, doubt, or an objection concerning (something). **4.** to express as a query. **5.** *U.S.* to put a question to (a person); ask. [C17: from earlier *quere*, from L *quaere* ask!, from *quaerere* to seek]

Quesnay (*French* kɛnɛ) *n.* **François** (frɑ̃swa). 1694–1774, French political economist, encyclopedist, and physician. He propounded the theory championed by the physiocrats in his *Tableau économique* (1758).

quest (kwɛst) *n.* **1.** a looking for or seeking; search. **2.** (in medieval romance) an expedition by a knight or knights to accomplish some task, such as finding the Holy Grail. **3.** the object of a search; a goal or target. ~*vb.* (*mainly intr.*) **4.** (foll. by *for* or *after*) to go in search (of). **5.** (of dogs, etc.) to search for game. **6.** (*also tr.*) *Arch.* to seek or pursue. [C14: from OF *queste*, from L *quaesita* sought, from *quaerere* to seek] —'**quester** *n.* —'**questing** *adj.* —'**questingly** *adv.*

question ('kwɛstʃən) *n.* **1.** a form of words addressed to a person in order to elicit information or evoke a response; interrogative sentence. **2.** a point at issue: *it's only a question of time until she dies.* **3.** a difficulty or uncertainty. **4. a.** an act of asking. **b.** an investigation into some problem. **5.** a motion presented for debate. **6. put the question.** to require members of a deliberative assembly to vote on a motion presented. **7.** *Law.* a matter submitted to a court or other tribunal. **8. beyond (all) question.** beyond (any) dispute or doubt. **9. call in** or **into question. a.** to make (something) the subject of disagreement. **b.** to cast doubt upon the validity, truth, etc., of (something). **10. in question.** under discussion: *this is the man in question.* **11. out of the question.** beyond consideration; unthinkable or impossible. **12. put to the question.** (formerly) to interrogate by torture. ~*vb.* (*mainly tr.*) **13.** to put a question or questions to (a person); interrogate. **14.** to make (something) the subject of dispute. **15.** to express uncertainty about the validity, truth, etc., of (something); doubt. [C13: via OF from L *quaestiō*, from *quaerere* to seek] —'**questioner** *n.*

questionable ('kwɛstʃənəbəl) *adj.* **1.** (esp. of a person's morality or honesty) admitting of some doubt; dubious.

2. of disputable value or authority. —'**questionableness** *n.* —'**questionably** *adv.*

questioning ('kwɛstʃənɪŋ) *adj.* **1.** proceeding from or characterized by a feeling of doubt or uncertainty. **2.** intellectually stimulated. —'**questioningly** *adv.*

questionless ('kwɛstʃənlɪs) *adj.* **1.** blindly adhering; unquestioning. **2.** a less common word for **unquestionable.** —'**questionlessly** *adv.*

question mark *n.* **1.** the punctuation mark ?, used at the end of questions and in other contexts where doubt or ignorance is implied. **2.** this mark used for any other purpose, as to draw attention to a possible mistake.

question master *n. Brit.* the chairman of a quiz or panel game.

questionnaire (,kwɛstʃə'nɛə, ,kɛs-) *n.* a set of questions on a form, submitted to a number of people in order to collect statistical information.

question time *n.* (in parliamentary bodies of the British type) the time set aside each day for questions to government ministers.

Quetta ('kwɛtə) *n.* a city in W central Pakistan, at an altitude of 1650 m (5500 ft.): a summer resort, military station, and trading centre. Pop.: 285 000 (1981).

quetzal ('kɛtsəl) *n., pl.* **-zals** *or* **-zales** (-'sɑːlɛs). **1.** a crested bird of Central and N South America, which has a brilliant green, red, and white plumage and, in the male, long tail feathers. **2.** the standard monetary unit of Guatemala. [via American Sp. from Nahuatl *quetzalli* brightly coloured tail feather]

Quetzalcoatl (,kɛtsəlkəʊ'ætᵊl) *n.* a god of the Aztecs and Toltecs, represented as a feathered serpent.

queue (kjuː) *Chiefly Brit.* ~*n.* **1.** a line of people, vehicles, etc., waiting for something. **2.** a pigtail. ~*vb.* **queueing** *or* **queuing, queued. 3.** (*intr.*, often foll. by *up*) to form or remain in a line while waiting. Usual U.S. word: **line.** [C16 (in the sense: tail); C18 (in the sense: pigtail): via F from L *cauda* tail]

queue-jump *vb.* (*intr.*) **1.** to take a place in a queue ahead of those already queueing; push in. **2.** to obtain some advantage out of turn or unfairly. —'**queue-jumper** *n.*

Quezon City ('keɪzɒn) *n.* a city in the Philippines, on central Luzon adjoining Manila: capital of the Philippines from 1948 to 1976; seat of the University of the Philippines (1908). Pop.: 1 326 000 (1984).

Quezon y Molina ('keɪzɒn iː mɒ'liːnə; *Spanish* ke'θɒn i mo'lina) *n.* **Manuel Luis** (ma'nwɛl lwis). 1878–1944, Philippine statesman: first president of the Philippines (from 1935) and head of the government in exile after the Japanese conquest of the islands in World War II.

quibble ('kwɪbᵊl) *vb.* (*intr.*) **1.** to make trivial objections. **2.** *Arch.* to play on words; pun. ~*n.* **3.** a trivial objection or equivocation, esp. one used to avoid an issue. **4.** *Arch.* a pun. [C17: prob. from obs. *quib*, ?from L *quibus* (from *quī* who, which), as used in legal documents, with reference to their obscure phraseology] —'**quibbler** *n.* —'**quibbling** *adj.*

Quiberon (*French* kibrɔ̃) *n.* a peninsula of NW France, on the S coast of Brittany: a naval battle was fought off its coast in 1759 during the Seven Years' War, in which the English defeated the French.

quiche (kiːʃ) *n.* an open savoury tart with an egg custard filling to which bacon, onion, cheese, etc., are added. [F, from G *Kuchen* cake]

quick (kwɪk) *adj.* **1.** performed or occurring during a comparatively short time: *a quick move.* **2.** lasting a short time; brief. **3.** accomplishing something in a time that is shorter than normal: *a quick worker.* **4.** characterized by rapidity of movement; fast. **5.** immediate or prompt. **6.** (*postpositive*) eager or ready to perform (an action): *quick to criticize.* **7.** responsive to stimulation; alert; lively. **8.** eager or enthusiastic for learning. **9.** easily excited or aroused. **10.** nimble in one's movements or actions: *quick fingers.* **11.** *Arch.* alive; living. **b.** (*as n.*) living people (esp. in **the quick and the dead**). **12. quick with child.** *Arch.* pregnant. ~*n.* **13.** any area of sensitive flesh, esp. that under a toenail or fingernail. **14.** the most important part (of a thing). **15. cut (someone) to the quick.** to hurt (someone's) feelings deeply. ~*adv. Inf.* **16.** in a rapid manner; swiftly. **17.** *Inf.* soon: *I hope he comes quick.* ~*sentence substitute.* **18.** a command to perform an action immediately. [OE *cwicu* living] —'**quickly** *adv.* —'**quickness** *n.*

quick-change artist *n.* an actor or entertainer who undertakes several rapid changes of costume during his performance.

quicken ('kwɪkən) *vb.* **1.** to make or become faster; accelerate. **2.** to impart to or receive vigour, enthusiasm, etc.: *science quickens man's imagination.* **3.** to make or become alive; revive. **4. a.** (of an unborn fetus) to begin to show signs of life. **b.** (of a pregnant woman) to reach the stage of pregnancy at which movements of the fetus can be felt.

quick-freeze *vb.* **-freezing, -froze, -frozen.** (*tr.*) to preserve (food) by subjecting it to rapid refrigeration at temperatures of 0°C or lower.

quickie ('kwɪkɪ) *n. Inf.* **1.** Also called (esp. Brit.): **quick one.** a speedily consumed alcoholic drink. **2.** anything made or done rapidly.

quicklime ('kwɪk,laɪm) *n.* another name for **calcium oxide.**

quick march *n.* **1.** a march at quick time or the order to proceed at such a pace. ~*sentence substitute.* **2.** a command to commence such a march.

quicksand ('kwɪk,sænd) *n.* a deep mass of loose wet sand that sucks anything on top of it inextricably into it.

quickset ('kwɪk,sɛt) *Chiefly Brit.* ~*n.* **1. a.** a plant or cutting, esp. of hawthorn, set so as to form a hedge. **b.** such plants or cuttings collectively. **2.** a hedge composed of such plants. ~*adj.* **3.** composed of such plants.

quicksilver ('kwɪk,sɪlvə) *n.* **1.** another name for **mercury** (sense 1). ~*adj.* **2.** rapid or unpredictable in movement or change.

quickstep ('kwɪk,stɛp) *n.* **1.** a modern ballroom dance in rapid quadruple time. **2.** a piece of music composed for or in the rhythm of this dance. ~*vb.* **-stepping, -stepped. 3.** (*intr.*) to perform this dance.

quick-tempered *adj.* readily roused to anger; irascible.

quickthorn ('kwɪk,θɔːn) *n.* hawthorn, esp. when planted as a hedge. [C17: prob. from *quick* in the sense "fast-growing": cf. QUICKSET]

quick time *n. Mil.* the normal marching rate of 120 paces to the minute.

quick-witted *adj.* having a keenly alert mind, esp. as used to avert danger, make effective reply, etc. — ,quick-'wittedly *adv.* — ,quick-'wittedness *n.*

quid¹ (kwɪd) *n.* a piece of tobacco, suitable for chewing. [OE *cwidu* chewing resin]

quid² (kwɪd) *n.*, *pl.* **quid.** *Brit. sl.* **1.** a pound (sterling). **2. (be) quids in.** (to be) in a very favourable or advantageous position. [C17: from ?]

quiddity ('kwɪdɪtɪ) *n.*, *pl.* **-ties. 1.** the essential nature of something. **2.** a petty or trifling distinction; quibble. [C16: from Med. L *quidditās*, from L *quid* what]

quidnunc ('kwɪd,nʌŋk) *n.* a person eager to learn news and scandal; gossipmonger. [C18: from L, lit.: what now]

quid pro quo ('kwɪd prəʊ 'kwəʊ) *n.*, *pl.* **quid pro quos. 1.** a reciprocal exchange. **2.** something given in compensation, esp. an advantage or object given in exchange for another. [C16: from L: something for something]

quiescent (kwɪ'ɛs⁽ə⁾nt) *adj.* quiet, inactive, or dormant. [C17: from L *quiescere* to rest] — qui'escence *or* qui'escency *n.* — qui'escently *adv.*

quiet ('kwaɪət) *adj.* **1.** characterized by an absence of noise. **2.** calm or tranquil: *the sea is quiet tonight.* **3.** free from activities, distractions, etc.; untroubled: *a quiet life.* **4.** short of work, orders, etc.; not busy: *business is quiet today.* **5.** private; not public; secret: *a quiet word with someone.* **6.** free from anger, impatience, or other extreme emotion. **7.** free from pretentiousness; modest or reserved: *quiet humour.* **8.** *Astron.* (of the sun) exhibiting a very low number of sunspots, solar flares, etc.; inactive. ~*n.* **9.** the state of being silent, peaceful, or untroubled. **10. on the quiet.** without other people knowing. ~*vb.* **11.** a less common word for **quieten.** [C14: from L *quiētus*, p.p. of *quiēscere* to rest, from *quiēs* repose] — 'quietness *n.*

quieten ('kwaɪət⁽ə⁾n) *vb. Chiefly Brit.* **1.** (often foll. by *down*) to make or become calm, silent, etc. **2.** (*tr.*) to allay (fear, doubts, etc.).

quietism ('kwaɪə,tɪzəm) *n.* **1.** a form of religious mysticism originating in Spain in the late 17th century, requiring complete passivity to God's will. **2.** passivity and calmness of mind towards external events. — 'quietist *n.*, *adj.*

quietly ('kwaɪətlɪ) *adv.* **1.** in a quiet manner. **2. just quietly.** *Austral.* confidentially.

quietude ('kwaɪə,tjuːd) *n.* the state or condition of being quiet, peaceful, calm, or tranquil.

quietus (kwaɪ'iːtəs, -'eɪtəs) *n.*, *pl.* **-tuses. 1.** anything that serves to quash, eliminate, or kill. **2.** a release from life; death. **3.** the discharge or settlement of debts, duties, etc. [C16: from L *quiētus est*, lit.: he is at rest]

quiff (kwɪf) *n. Brit.* a tuft of hair brushed up above the forehead. [C19: from ?]

quill (kwɪl) *n.* **1. a.** any of the large stiff feathers of the wing or tail of a bird. **b.** the long hollow part of a feather; calamus. **2.** Also called: **quill pen.** a feather made into a pen for writing. **3.** any of the stiff hollow spines of a porcupine or hedgehog. **4.** a device, formerly made from a crow quill, for plucking a harpsichord string. **5.** a small roll of bark, esp. one of dried cinnamon. **6.** a bobbin or spindle. **7.** a fluted fold, as in a ruff. ~*vb.* (*tr.*) **8.** to wind (thread, etc.) onto a spool or bobbin. **9.** to make or press fluted folds in (a ruff, etc.). [C15 (in the sense: hollow reed or pipe): from ?; cf. MLow G *quiele* quill]

Quilmes (*Spanish* 'kilmes) *n.* a city in E Argentina: a resort and suburb of Buenos Aires. Pop.: 441 780 (1980).

quilt (kwɪlt) *n.* **1.** a cover for a bed, consisting of a soft filling sewn between two layers of material, usually with crisscross seams. **2.** short for **continental quilt. 3.** a bedspread. **4.** anything resembling a quilt. ~*vb.* (*tr.*) **5.** to stitch together (two pieces of fabric) with (a thick padding or lining) between them. **6.** to create (a garment, etc.) in this way. **7.** to pad with material. [C13: from OF *coilte* mattress, from L *culcita* stuffed item of bedding] — 'quilted *adj.* — 'quilter *n.*

quilting ('kwɪltɪŋ) *n.* **1.** material for quilts. **2.** the act of making a quilt. **3.** quilted work.

Quimper (*French* kɛ̃pɛr) *n.* a city in NW France: capital of Finistère department. Pop.: 54 597 (1983 est.).

quin (kwɪn) *n. Brit.* short for **quintuplet** (sense 1). U.S. and Canad. word: **quint.**

quinary ('kwaɪnərɪ) *adj.* **1.** of or by fives. **2.** fifth in a series. **3.** (of a number system) having a base of five. [C17: from L *quīnārius* containing five, from *quīnī* five each]

quince (kwɪns) *n.* **1.** a small widely cultivated Asian tree with edible pear-shaped fruits. **2.** the fruit of this tree, much used in preserves. [C14 *quince* pl. of *quyn*, from OF *coin*, from L *cotōneum*, from Gk *kudōnion* quince]

quincentenary (,kwɪnsɛn'tiːnərɪ) *n.*, *pl.* **-naries.** a 500th anniversary. [C19: irregularly from L *quinque* five + CENTENARY] — **quincentennial** (,kwɪnsɛn'tɛnɪəl) *adj.*, *n.*

quincunx ('kwɪnkʌŋks) *n.* a group of five objects arranged in the shape of a rectangle with one at each of the four corners and the fifth in the centre. [C17: from L: five twelfths, from *quinque* five + *uncia* twelfth; in ancient Rome, this was a coin worth five twelfths of an AS² and marked with five spots] — **quincuncial** (kwɪn'kʌnʃəl) *adj.*

Quine (kwaɪn) *n.* **Willard van Orman.** born 1908, U.S. philosopher. His works include *Word and Object* (1960), *Philosophy of Logic* (1970), and *The Roots of Reference* (1973).

quinella (kwɪ'nɛlə) *n. Austral.* a form of betting in which the punter must select the first and second place-winners, in any order. [from American Sp. *quiniela*]

Qui Nhon ('kwiː 'njʊŋ) *n.* a port in SE Vietnam, on the South China Sea. Pop.: 130 534 (1979).

quinidine ('kwɪnɪ,diːn) *n.* a crystalline alkaloid drug used to treat heart arrhythmias.

quinine (kwɪ'niːn; *U.S.* 'kwaɪnaɪn) *n.* a bitter crystalline alkaloid extracted from cinchona bark, the salts of which are used as a tonic, analgesic, etc., and in malaria therapy. [C19: from Sp. *quina* cinchona bark, from Quechua *kina* bark]

Quinn (kwɪn) *n.* **Anthony.** born 1915, U.S. film actor, born in Mexico: noted esp. for his performances in *La Strada* (1954) and *Zorba the Greek* (1964).

quinol ('kwɪnɒl) *n.* another name for **hydroquinone.**

quinoline ('kwɪnə,liːn, -lɪn) *n.* an oily colourless insoluble compound synthesized by heating aniline, nitrobenzene, glycerol, and sulphuric acid: used as a food preservative and in the manufacture of dyes and antiseptics. Formula: C_9H_7N.

quinquagenarian (,kwɪŋkwədʒɪ'nɛərɪən) *n.* **1.** a person between 50 and 59 years old. ~*adj.* **2.** being between 50 and 59 years old. **3.** of a quinquagenarian. [C16: from L *quinquāgēnārius* containing fifty, from *quinquāgēnī* fifty each]

Quinquagesima (ˌkwɪŋkwə'dʒɛsɪmə) *n.* the Sunday preceding Lent. Also called: **Quinquagesima Sunday.** [C14: via Med. L from L *quinquāgēsima diēs* fiftieth day]

quinquecentenary (ˌkwɪŋkwɪsɛn'tiːnərɪ) *n., pl.* **-naries.** another name for **quincentenary.**

quinquennial (kwɪn'kwɛnɪəl) *adj.* **1.** occurring once every five years or over a period of five years. ~*n.* **2.** a fifth anniversary. —**quin'quennially** *adv.*

quinquennium (kwɪn'kwɛnɪəm) *n., pl.* **-nia** (-nɪə). a period or cycle of five years. [C17: from L *quinque* five + *annus* year]

quinquereme (ˌkwɪŋkwɪ'riːm) *n.* an ancient Roman galley with five banks of oars. [C16: from L *quinquerēmis,* from *quinque-*five + *rēmus* oar]

quinquevalent (ˌkwɪŋkwɪ'veɪlənt) *adj. Chem.* another word for **pentavalent.** —ˌquinque'valency *or* ˌquinque'valence *n.*

quinsy ('kwɪnzɪ) *n.* inflammation of the tonsils and surrounding tissues with the formation of abscesses. [C14: via OF & Med. L from Gk *kunankhē,* from *kuōn* dog + *ankhein* to strangle]

quint[1] *n.* **1.** (kwɪnt). an organ stop sounding a note a fifth higher. **2.** (kɪnt). *Piquet.* a sequence of five cards in the same suit. [C17: from F *quinte,* from L *quintus* fifth]

quint[2] (kwɪnt) *n.* the U.S. and Canad. word for **quin.**

quintain ('kwɪntɪn) *n.* (esp. in medieval Europe) a post or target set up for tilting exercises for mounted knights or foot soldiers. [C14: from OF *quintaine,* from L: street in a Roman camp between the fifth & sixth maniples (the maniple was a unit of 120–200 soldiers in ancient Rome), from *quintus* fifth]

quintal ('kwɪntᵊl) *n.* **1.** a unit of weight equal to (esp. in Britain) 112 pounds or (esp. in U.S.) 100 pounds. **2.** a unit of weight equal to 100 kilograms. [C15: via OF from Ar. *qintār,* possibly from L *centēnārius* consisting of a hundred]

quintan ('kwɪntən) *adj.* (of a fever) occurring every fourth day. [C17: from L *febris quintāna* fever occurring every fifth day, reckoned inclusively]

Quintana Roo (*Spanish* kin'tana 'rɔo) *n.* a state of SE Mexico, on the E Yucatán Peninsula: hot, humid, forested, and inhabited chiefly by Maya Indians. Capital: Chetumal. Pop.: 290 242 (1983 est.). Area: 50 350 sq. km (16 228 sq. miles).

quinte (kænt) *n.* the fifth of eight basic positions from which a parry or attack can be made in fencing. [C18: F from L *quintus* fifth]

quintessence (kwɪn'tɛsəns) *n.* **1.** the most typical representation of a quality, state, etc. **2.** an extract of a substance containing its principle in its most concentrated form. **3.** (in ancient philosophy) ether, the fifth essence or element, which was thought to be the constituent matter of the heavenly bodies and latent in all things. [C15: via F from Med. L *quinta essentia* the fifth essence, translation of Gk] —**quintessential** (ˌkwɪntɪ'sɛnʃəl) *adj.* —ˌquintes'sentially *adv.*

quintet *or* **quintette** (kwɪn'tɛt) *n.* **1.** a group of five singers or instrumentalists or a piece of music composed for such a group. **2.** any group of five. [C19: from It. *quintetto,* from *quinto* fifth]

Quintilian (kwɪn'tɪljən) *n.* Latin name *Marcus Fabius Quintilianus.* ?35–?96 A.D., Roman rhetorician and teacher.

quintillion (kwɪn'tɪljən) *n., pl.* **-lions** *or* **-lion. 1.** (in Britain, France, and Germany) the number represented as one followed by 30 zeros (10^{30}). U.S. and Canad. word: **nonillion. 2.** (in the U.S. and Canada) the number represented as one followed by 18 zeros (10^{18}). Brit. word: **trillion.** [C17: from L *quintus* fifth + *-illion,* as in MILLION] —**quin'tillionth** *adj.*

quintuple ('kwɪntjʊpᵊl, kwɪn'tjuːpᵊl) *vb.* **1.** to multiply by five. ~*adj.* **2.** five times as much or as many; fivefold. **3.** consisting of five parts. ~*n.* **4.** a quantity or number five times as great as another. [C16: from F, from L *quintus,* on the model of QUADRUPLE]

quintuplet ('kwɪntjʊplɪt, kwɪn'tjuːplɪt) *n.* **1.** one of five offspring born at one birth. **2.** a group of five similar things. **3.** *Music.* a group of five notes to be played in a time value of three or four.

quintuplicate *adj.* (kwɪn'tjuːplɪkɪt). **1.** fivefold or quintuple. ~*vb.* (kwɪn'tjuːplɪˌkeɪt). **2.** to multiply or be multiplied by five. ~*n.* (kwɪn'tjuːplɪkɪt). **3.** a group or set of five things.

quip (kwɪp) *n.* **1.** a sarcastic remark. **2.** a witty saying. **3.** *Arch.* another word for **quibble.** ~*vb.* **quipping, quipped. 4.** (*intr.*) to make a quip. [C16: from earlier *quippy,* prob. from L *quippe* indeed, to be sure] —'quip-**ster** *n.*

quire[1] ('kwaɪə) *n.* **1.** a set of 24 or 25 sheets of paper. **2.** four sheets of paper folded to form 16 pages. **3.** a set of all the sheets in a book. [C15 *quayer,* from OF *quaier,* from L *quaternī* four at a time, from *quater* four times]

quire[2] ('kwaɪə) *n.* an obsolete spelling of **choir.**

Quirinal ('kwɪrɪnᵊl) *n.* one of the seven hills on which ancient Rome was built.

Quirinus (kwɪ'raɪnəs) *n. Roman myth.* a god of war, who came to be identified with the deified Romulus.

quirk (kwɜːk) *n.* **1.** a peculiarity of character; mannerism or foible. **2.** an unexpected twist or turn: *a quirk of fate.* **3.** a continuous groove in an architectural moulding. **4.** a flourish, as in handwriting. [C16: from ?] —'quirkiness *n.* —'quirky *adj.*

quirt (kwɜːt) *U.S.* ~*n.* **1.** a whip with a leather thong at one end. ~*vb.* (*tr.*) **2.** to strike with a quirt. [C19: from Sp. *cuerda* CORD]

quisling ('kwɪzlɪŋ) *n.* a traitor who aids an occupying enemy force; collaborator. [C20: after Major Vidkun *Quisling* (1887–1945), Norwegian collaborator with the Nazis]

quit (kwɪt) *vb.* **quitting, quitted,** *or* (*chiefly U.S.*) **quit. 1.** (*tr.*) to depart from; leave. **2.** to resign; give up (a job). **3.** (*intr.*) (of a tenant) to give up occupancy of premises and leave them. **4.** to desist or cease from (something or doing something). **5.** (*tr.*) to pay off (a debt). **6.** (*tr.*) *Arch.* to conduct or acquit (oneself); comport (oneself). ~*adj.* **7.** (*usually predicative;* foll. by *of*) free (from); released (from). [C13: from OF *quitter,* from L *quiētus* QUIET]

▷ **Usage.** Some users of English have felt that *quit* in the sense of *leave* is informal, but this use is quite standard at all levels of language. Careful users do not use *quit* to mean *cease* (*he never quit moaning*) because this is felt to be an Americanism.

quitch grass (kwɪtʃ) *n.* another name for **couch grass.** Sometimes shortened to **quitch.** [OE *cwice;* ? rel. to *cwicu* living, QUICK (with the implication that the grass cannot be killed)]

quitclaim ('kwɪtˌkleɪm) *Law.* ~*n.* **1.** a renunciation of a claim or right. ~*vb.* **2.** (*tr.*) to renounce (a claim). [C14: from Anglo-F *quiteclame,* from *quite* QUIT + *clamer* to declare (from L *clamāre* to shout)]

quite (kwaɪt) *adv.* **1.** completely or absolutely: *you're quite right.* **2.** (*not used with a negative*) somewhat: *she's quite pretty.* **3.** in actuality; truly. **4. quite a** *or* **an.** (*not used with a negative*) of an exceptional, considerable, or noticeable kind: *quite a girl.* **5. quite something.** a remarkable or noteworthy thing or person. ~*sentence substitute.* **6.** Also: **quite so.** an expression used to indicate agreement. [C14: adverbial use of *quite* (adj.) QUIT]

▷ **Usage.** See at **very.**

Quito ('kiːtəʊ; *Spanish* 'kito) *n.* the capital of Ecuador, in the north at an altitude of 2850 m (9350 ft.), just south of the equator: the oldest capital in South America, existing many centuries before the Incan conquest in 1487; a cultural centre since the beginning of Spanish rule (1534); two universities. Pop.: 1 110 248 (1982).

quitrent ('kwɪtˌrɛnt) *n.* (formerly) a rent payable by a freeholder or copyholder to his lord in lieu of services.

quits (kwɪts) *adj.* (*postpositive*) *Inf.* **1.** on an equal footing; even. **2. call it quits.** to agree to end a dispute, contest, etc., agreeing that honours are even.

quittance ('kwɪtᵊns) *n.* **1.** release from debt or other obligation. **2.** a receipt or other document certifying this. [C13: from OF, from *quitter* to release from obligation; see QUIT]

quitter ('kwɪtə) *n.* a person who gives up easily.

quiver[1] ('kwɪvə) *vb.* **1.** (*intr.*) to shake with a tremulous movement; tremble. ~*n.* **2.** the state, process, or noise of shaking or trembling. [C15: from obs. *cwiver* quick, nimble] —'quivering *adj.* —'quivery *adj.*

quiver[2] ('kwɪvə) *n.* a case for arrows. [C13: from OF *cuivre*]

qui vive (ˌkiː ˈviːv) n. **on the qui vive.** on the alert; attentive. [C18: from F, lit.: long live who?, sentry's challenge (equivalent to "Whose side are you on?")]

Quixote ('kwɪksət; *Spanish* kiˈxote) n. See **Don Quixote.**

quixotic (kwɪk'sɒtɪk) adj. preoccupied with an unrealistically optimistic or chivalrous approach to life; impractically idealistic. [C18: after DON QUIXOTE] —**quix'otically** adv.

quiz (kwɪz) n., pl. **quizzes. 1. a.** an entertainment in which the knowledge of the players is tested by a series of questions. **b.** (*as modifier*): *a quiz programme.* **2.** any set of quick questions designed to test knowledge. **3.** an investigation by close questioning. **4.** Obs. a practical joke. **5.** Obs. a puzzling individual. **6.** Obs. a person who habitually looks quizzically at others. ~vb. **quizzing, quizzed.** (tr.) **7.** to investigate by close questioning; interrogate. **8.** U.S. & Canad. inf. to test the knowledge of (a student or class). **9.** (tr.) Obs. to look quizzically at, esp. through a small monocle. [C18: from ?] — **'quizzer** n.

quizzical ('kwɪzɪkəl) adj. questioning and mocking or supercilious. —'**quizzically** adv.

Qum (kʊm) n. a variant of **Qom.**

Qumran ('kʊmrɑːn) n. See **Khirbet Qumran.**

Qungur ('kʊŋʊə) n. a variant transliteration of the Chinese name for **Kongur Shan.**

quod (kwɒd) n. Chiefly Brit. a slang word for **jail.** [C18: from ?]

quod erat demonstrandum Latin. ('kwɒd 'ɛræt ˌdɛmənˈstrændʊm) (at the conclusion of a proof, esp. of a theorem in Euclidean geometry) which was to be proved. Abbrev.: **QED.**

quodlibet ('kwɒdlɪˌbɛt) n. **1.** a light piece of music. **2.** a subtle argument, esp. one prepared as an exercise on a theological topic. [C14: from L, from *quod* what + *libet* pleases, that is, whatever you like]

quoin (kwɔɪn, kɔɪn) n. **1.** an external corner of a wall. **2.** a stone forming the external corner of a wall. **3.** another name for **keystone** (sense 1). **4.** Printing. a wedge or an expanding device used to lock type up in a chase. **5.** a wedge used for any of various other purposes. [C16: var. of *coin* (in former sense of corner)]

quoit (kɔɪt) n. a ring of iron, plastic, etc., used in the game of quoits. [C15: from ?]

quoits (kɔɪts) pl. n. (*usually functioning as sing.*) a game in which quoits are tossed at a stake in the ground in attempts to encircle it.

quokka ('kwɒkə) n. a small wallaby of Western Australia, now rare. [of Abor. origin]

quondam ('kwɒndæm) adj. (*prenominal*) of an earlier time; former. [C16: from L]

quorate ('kwɔːˌreɪt) adj. Brit. consisting of or being a quorum: *the meeting was quorate.*

quorum ('kwɔːrəm) n. a minimum number of members in an assembly, etc., required to be present before any business can be transacted. [C15: from L, lit.: of whom, occurring in L commissions in the formula *quorum vos . . . duos* (etc.) *volumus* of whom we wish that you be . . . two (etc.)]

quota ('kwəʊtə) n. **1.** the proportional share or part that is due from, due to, or allocated to a person or group. **2.** a

prescribed number or quantity, as of items to be imported or students admitted to a college, etc. [C17: from L *quota pars* how big a share?, from *quotus* of what number]

quotable ('kwəʊtəbəl) adj. apt or suitable for quotation. —ˌquota'bility n.

quotation (kwəʊ'teɪʃən) n. **1.** a phrase or passage from a book, etc., remembered and spoken, esp. to support a point. **2.** the act or habit of quoting. **3.** Commerce. a statement of the current market price of a commodity. **4.** an estimate of costs submitted by a contractor to a prospective client. **5.** Printing. a quadrat used to fill up spaces.

quotation mark n. either of the punctuation marks used to begin or end a quotation, respectively " and " or ' and '. Also called: **inverted comma.**

quote (kwəʊt) vb. **1.** to recite a quotation. **2.** (tr.) to put quotation marks round (a phrase, etc.). **3.** Stock Exchange. to state (a current market price) of (a security or commodity). ~n. **4.** an informal word for **quotation. 5.** (*often pl.*) an informal word for **quotation mark.** ~interj. **6.** an expression used to indicate that the words that follow it form a quotation. [C14: from Med. L *quotāre* to assign reference numbers to passages, from L *quot* how many]

quoted company n. a company whose shares are quoted on the stock exchange.

quote-unquote interj. an expression used before or part before and part after a quotation to identify it as such, and sometimes to dissociate the writer or speaker from it.

quoth (kwəʊθ) vb. Arch. (used with all pronouns except *thou* and *you*, and with nouns) said. [OE *cwæth*, third person sing. of *cwethan* to say]

quotha ('kwəʊθə) interj. Arch. an expression of mild sarcasm, used in picking up a word or phrase used by someone else. [C16: from *quoth a* quoth he]

quotidian (kwəʊ'tɪdɪən) adj. **1.** (esp. of fever) recurring daily. **2.** commonplace. ~n. **3.** a fever characterized by attacks that recur daily. [C14: from L *quotīdiānus*, var. of *cottīdiānus* daily]

quotient ('kwəʊʃənt) n. **1. a.** the result of the division of one number or quantity by another. **b.** the integral part of the result of division. **2.** a ratio of two numbers or quantities to be divided. [C15: from L *quotiens* how often]

quo vadis ('kwəʊ 'vɑːdɪs) whither goest thou? [L from the Vulgate version of John 16:5]

quo warranto ('kwəʊ wɒ'ræntəʊ) n. Law. a proceeding initiated to determine or (formerly) a writ demanding by what authority a person claims an office, franchise, or privilege. [from Med. L: by what warrant]

Qur'an (kʊ'rɑːn, -'ræn) n. a variant spelling of **Koran.**

q.v. (denoting a cross-reference) abbrev. for quod vide. [NL: which (word, item, etc.) see]

Qwaqwa ('kwɑːkwə) n. a Bantustan in South Africa, in the Orange Free State; the only Bantustan without exclaves. Also called: **Basotho-Qwaqwa.** Former name (until 1972): **Basotho-Ba-Borwa.**

qwerty or **QWERTY keyboard** ('kwɜːtɪ) n. the standard English language typewriter keyboard layout with the characters q, w, e, r, t, and y at the top left of the keyboard.

R

r *or* **R** (ɑ:) *n.*, *pl.* **r's**, **R's**, *or* **Rs. 1.** the 18th letter of the English alphabet. **2.** a speech sound represented by this letter. **3.** See **three Rs, the.**

R *symbol for:* **1.** *Chem.* gas constant. **2.** *Chem.* radical. **3.** *Currency.* **a.** rand. **b.** rupee. **4.** Réaumur (scale). **5.** *Physics, electronics.* resistance. **6.** roentgen *or* röntgen. **7.** *Chess.* rook. **8.** Royal.

r. *abbrev. for:* **1.** rare. **2.** recto. **3.** Also: **r** rod (unit of length). **4.** ruled. **5.** *Cricket.* run(s).

R. *abbrev. for:* **1.** rabbi. **2.** rector. **3.** Regiment. **4.** Regina. [L: Queen] **5.** Republican. **6.** Rex. [L: King] **7.** River. **8.** Royal.

R. *or* **r.** *abbrev. for:* **1.** radius. **2.** railway. **3.** registered (trademark). **4.** right. **5.** river. **6.** road. **7.** rouble.

Ra[1] *the chemical symbol for* radium.

Ra[2] (rɑ:) *or* **Re** *n.* the ancient Egyptian sun god, depicted as a man with a hawk's head surmounted by a solar disc and serpent.

RA *abbrev. for:* **1.** rear admiral. **2.** *Astron.* right ascension. **3.** (in Britain) Royal Academician *or* Academy. **4.** (in Britain) Royal Artillery.

RAAF *abbrev. for* Royal Australian Air Force.

Rabat (rə'bɑ:t) *n.* the capital of Morocco, in the northwest on the Atlantic coast: became a fortified military centre in the 12th century and a Corsair republic in the 17th century. Pop.: 556 000 (1984).

Rabaul (rɑ:'baul) *n.* a port in Papua New Guinea, on NE New Britain Island, in the Bismarck Archipelago: capital of the Territory of New Guinea until 1941; almost surrounded by volcanoes. Pop.: 14 954 (1980).

Rabbath Ammon ('ræbəθ 'æmən) *n. Old Testament.* the ancient royal city of the Ammonites, on the site of modern Amman.

rabbet ('ræbɪt) *or* **rebate** *n.* **1.** a recess, groove, or step, usually of rectangular section, cut into a piece of timber to receive a mating piece. ~*vb.* (*tr.*) **2.** to cut a rabbet in (timber). **3.** to join (pieces of timber) using a rabbet. [C15: from OF *rabattre* to beat down]

rabbi ('ræbaɪ) *n.*, *pl.* **-bis. 1.** the spiritual leader of a Jewish congregation; the chief religious minister of a synagogue. **2.** a scholar learned in Jewish Law, esp. one authorized to teach it. [Heb., from *rabh* master + *-ī* my]

rabbinate ('ræbɪnɪt) *n.* **1.** the position, function, or tenure of office of a rabbi. **2.** rabbis collectively.

rabbinic (rə'bɪnɪk) *or* **rabbinical** (rə'bɪnɪkᵊl) *adj.* of or relating to the rabbis, their teachings, writings, views, language, etc. —**rab'binically** *adv.*

Rabbinic (rə'bɪnɪk) *n.* the form of the Hebrew language used by the rabbis of the Middle Ages.

rabbit ('ræbɪt) *n.*, *pl.* **-bits** *or* **-bit. 1.** any of various common gregarious burrowing mammals of Europe and North Africa. They are closely related and similar to hares but are smaller and have shorter ears. **2.** the fur of such an animal. **3.** *Brit. inf.* a poor performer at a game or sport. ~*vb.* (*intr.*) **4.** to hunt or shoot rabbits. **5.** (often foll. by *on* or *away*) *Brit. inf.* to talk inconsequentially; chatter. [C14: ?from Walloon *robett*, dim. of Flemish *robbe* rabbit, from ?]

rabbit fever *n. Pathol.* another name for **tularaemia.**

rabbit punch *n.* a short sharp blow to the back of the neck that can cause loss of consciousness or even death. Austral. name: **rabbit killer.**

rabble ('ræbᵊl) *n.* **1.** a disorderly crowd; mob. **2. the rabble.** *Contemptuous.* the common people. [C14 (in the sense: a pack of animals): from ?]

rabble-rouser *n.* a person who manipulates the **passions of the mob; demagogue.** —**'rabble-,rousing** *adj.*, *n.*

Rabelais ('ræbə,leɪ; *French* rablɛ) *n.* **François** (frɑ̃swa). ?1494–1553, French writer. His written works, esp. *Gargantua and Pantagruel* (1534), contain a lively mixture of earthy wit, common sense, and satire.

Rabelaisian (,ræbə'leɪzɪən, -ʒən) *adj.* **1.** of, relating to, or resembling the work of Rabelais, esp. by broad, often bawdy humour and sharp satire. ~*n.* **2.** a student or admirer of Rabelais. —**,Rabe'laisianism** *n.*

rabid ('ræbɪd, 'reɪ-) *adj.* **1.** relating to or having rabies. **2.** zealous; fanatical; violent; raging. [C17: from L *rabidus* frenzied, from *rabere* to be mad] —**rabidity** (rə'bɪdɪtɪ) *or* **'rabidness** *n.* —**'rabidly** *adv.*

rabies ('reɪbiːz) *n. Pathol.* an acute infectious viral disease of the nervous system transmitted by the saliva of infected animals, esp. dogs. [C17: from L: madness, from *rabere* to rave] —**rabic** ('ræbɪk) *or* **rabietic** (,reɪbɪ'ɛtɪk) *adj.*

RAC *abbrev. for:* **1.** Royal Armoured Corps. **2.** Royal Automobile Club.

raccoon *or* **racoon** (rə'kuːn) *n.*, *pl.* **-coons** *or* **-coon. 1.** an omnivorous mammal, esp. the **North American raccoon,** inhabiting forests of North and Central America. Raccoons have a pointed muzzle, long tail, and greyish-black fur with black bands around the tail and across the face. **2.** the fur of the raccoon. [C17: from Algonquian *ärähkun*, from *ärähkunēm* he scratches with his hands]

race[1] (reɪs) *n.* **1.** a contest of speed, as in running, etc. **2.** any competition or rivalry. **3.** rapid or constant onward movement: *the race of time.* **4.** a rapid current of water, esp. one through a narrow channel that has a tidal range greater at one end than the other. **5.** a channel of a stream, esp. one for conducting water to or from a water wheel for energy: *a mill race.* **6. a.** a channel or groove that contains ball bearings or roller bearings. **b.** the inner or outer cylindrical ring in a ball bearing or roller bearing. **7.** *Austral. & N.Z.* a narrow passage or enclosure in a sheep yard through which sheep pass individually, as to a sheep dip. **8.** *Austral.* a wire tunnel through which footballers pass from the changing room onto a football field. **9.** *Arch.* the span or course of life. ~*vb.* **10.** to engage in a contest of speed with (another). **11.** to engage in a race, esp. as a profession: *to race pigeons.* **12.** to move or go as fast as possible. **13.** to run (an engine, propeller, etc.) or (of an engine, propeller, etc.) to run at high speed, esp. after reduction of the load or resistance. ~See also **races.** [C13: from ON *rās* running]

race[2] (reɪs) *n.* **1.** a group of people of common ancestry, distinguished from others by physical characteristics, such as hair type, colour of skin, stature, etc. **2. the human race.** human beings collectively. **3.** a group of animals or plants having common characteristics that distinguish them from other members of the same species, usually forming a geographically isolated group; subspecies. **4.** a group of people sharing the same interests, characteristics, etc.: *the race of authors.* [C16: from F, from It. *razza*, from ?]

Race (reɪs) *n.* **Cape.** a cape at the SE extremity of Newfoundland, Canada.

racecard ('reɪs,kɑːd) *n.* a card at a race meeting with the races and runners, etc., printed on it.

racecourse ('reɪs,kɔːs) *n.* a long broad track, over which horses are raced. Also called (esp. U.S. and Canad.): **racetrack.**

racehorse ('reɪs,hɔːs) *n.* a horse specially bred for racing.

raceme (rə'siːm) *n.* an inflorescence in which the flowers are borne along the main stem. [C18: from L *racēmus* bunch of grapes] —**'race,mose** *adj.*

race meeting *n.* a prearranged fixture for racing horses (or greyhounds) over a set course.

racemic (rə'siːmɪk, -'sɛm-) *adj. Chem.* of, concerned with, or being a mixture of dextrorotatory and laevorotatory isomers in such proportions that the mixture has no optical activity. [C19: from RACEME + -IC] —**racemism** ('ræsɪ,mɪzəm) *n.*

racer ('reɪsə) *n.* **1.** a person, animal, or machine that races. **2.** a turntable used to traverse a heavy gun. **3.** any of several slender nonvenomous North American snakes, such as the **striped racer.**

race relations *n.* **1.** (*functioning as pl.*) the relations between members of two or more human races, esp. within a single community. **2.** (*functioning as sing.*) the branch of sociology concerned with such relations.

race riot *n.* a riot among members of different races in the same community.

races ('reɪsɪz) *pl. n.* **the races.** a series of contests of speed between horses (or greyhounds) over a set course.

racetrack ('reɪs,træk) *n.* **1.** a circuit or course, esp. an oval one, used for motor racing, etc. **2.** the usual U.S. and Canad. word for **racecourse.**

raceway ('reɪs,weɪ) *n.* **1.** another word for **race**[1] (senses 5, 6). **2.** *Chiefly U.S.* a racetrack.

Rachel ('reɪtʃəl) *n. Old Testament.* the second and best-loved wife of Jacob; mother of Joseph and Benjamin (Genesis 29–35).

rachis *or* **rhachis** ('reɪkɪs) *n., pl.* **rachises, rhachises** *or* **rachides, rhachides** ('ræki,di:z, 'reɪ-). **1.** *Bot.* the main axis or stem of an inflorescence or compound leaf. **2.** *Ornithol.* the shaft of a feather, esp. the part that carries the barbs. **3.** another name for **spinal column.** [C17: via NL from Gk *rhakhis* ridge] —**rachial, rhachial** ('reɪkɪəl) *or* **rachidial, rhachidial** (rə'kɪdɪəl) *adj.*

rachitis (rə'kaɪtɪs) *n. Pathol.* another name for **rickets.** —**rachitic** (rə'kɪtɪk) *adj.*

Rachmaninoff *or* **Rachmaninov** (ræk'mænɪ,nɒf; *Russian* rax'maninəf) *n.* **Sergei Vassilievich** (sɪr'gjeɪ va'siljivitʃ). 1873–1943, Russian piano virtuoso and composer.

Rachmanism ('rækmə,nɪzəm) *n.* extortion or exploitation by a landlord of tenants of slum property. [C20: after Perec *Rachman* (1920–62), British property-owner]

racial ('reɪʃəl) *adj.* **1.** denoting or relating to the division of the human species into races on grounds of physical characteristics. **2.** characteristic of any such group. —**racially** *adv.*

racialism ('reɪʃə,lɪzəm) *or* **racism** *n.* **1.** the belief that races have distinctive cultural characteristics determined by hereditary factors and that this endows some races with an intrinsic superiority. **2.** abusive or aggressive behaviour towards members of another race on the basis of such a belief. —**racialist** *or* **racist** *n., adj.*

Racine (*French* rasin) *n.* **Jean Baptiste** (ʒɑ batist). 1639–99, French tragic poet and dramatist. His plays include *Andromaque* (1667), *Bérénice* (1670), and *Phèdre* (1677).

rack[1] (ræk) *n.* **1.** a framework for holding, carrying, or displaying a specific load or object. **2.** a toothed bar designed to engage a pinion to form a mechanism that will adjust the position of something. **3.** (preceded by *the*) an instrument of torture that stretched the body of the victim. **4.** a cause or state of mental or bodily stress, suffering, etc. (esp. in **on the rack**). **5.** *U.S. & Canad.* (in pool, snooker, etc.) **a.** the triangular frame used to arrange the balls for the opening shot. **b.** the balls so grouped. Brit. equivalent: **frame.** ~*vb.* (*tr.*) **6.** to torture on the rack. **7.** to cause great suffering to: *guilt racked his conscience.* **8.** to strain or shake (something) violently: *the storm racked the town.* **9.** to place or arrange in or on a rack. **10.** to move (parts of machinery or a mechanism) using a toothed rack. **11.** to raise (rents) exorbitantly. **12. rack one's brains.** to strain in mental effort. [C14 *rekke*, prob. from MDu. *rec* framework] —**racker** *n.*

rack[2] (ræk) *n.* destruction; wreck (obs. except in **go to rack and ruin**). [C16: var. of WRACK[1]]

rack[3] (ræk) *n.* another word for **single-foot.** [C16: ? based on ROCK[2]]

rack[4] (ræk) *n.* **1.** a group of broken clouds moving in the wind. ~*vb.* **2.** (*intr.*) (of clouds) to be blown along by the wind. [OE *wræc* what is driven]

rack[5] (ræk) *vb.* (*tr.*) to clear (wine, beer, etc.) as by siphoning it off from the dregs. [C15: from OProvençal *arraca*, from *raca* dregs of grapes after pressing]

rack-and-pinion *n.* **1.** a device for converting rotary into linear motion and vice versa, in which a gearwheel (the pinion) engages with a flat toothed bar (the rack). ~*adj.* **2.** of a type of steering gear in motor vehicles) having a track rod with a rack along part of its length that engages with a pinion attached to the steering column.

racket[1] ('rækɪt) *n.* **1.** a noisy disturbance or loud commotion; clamour; din. **2.** an illegal enterprise carried on for profit, such as extortion, fraud, etc. **3.** *Sl.* a business or occupation: *what's your racket?* **4.** *Music.* a medieval woodwind instrument of deep bass pitch. ~*vb.* **5.** (*intr.*; often foll. by *about*) *Now rare.* to go about gaily or noisily, in search of pleasure, etc. [C16: prob. imit.] —**rackety** *adj.*

racket[2] *or* **racquet** ('rækɪt) *n.* **1.** a bat consisting of an open network of strings stretched in an oval frame with a

handle, used to strike a tennis ball, etc. **2.** a snowshoe shaped like a tennis racket. ~*vb.* **3.** (*tr.*) to strike (a ball, etc.) with a racket. ~See also **rackets.** [C16: from F *raquette*, from Ar. *rāhat* palm of the hand]

racketeer (,rækɪ'tɪə) *n.* **1.** a person engaged in illegal enterprises for profit. ~*vb.* **2.** (*intr.*) to operate an illegal enterprise. —**,racket'eering** *n.*

racket press *n.* a device consisting of a frame closed by a spring mechanism, for keeping taut the strings of a tennis racket, squash racket, etc.

rackets ('rækɪts) *n.* (*functioning as sing.*) **a.** a game similar to squash played in a four-walled court by two or four players using rackets and a small hard ball. **b.** (*as modifier*): *a rackets court.*

Rackham ('rækəm) *n.* **Arthur.** 1867–1939, English artist, noted for his book illustrations, esp. of fairy tales.

rack railway *n.* a steep mountain railway having a middle rail fitted with a rack that engages a pinion on the locomotive to provide traction. Also called: **cog railway.**

rack-rent *n.* **1.** a high rent that annually equals the value of the property upon which it is charged. **2.** any extortionate rent. ~*vb.* **3.** to charge an extortionate rent for. —**'rack-,renter** *n.*

racon ('reɪkɒn) *n.* another name for **radar beacon.** [C20: from RA(DAR) + (BEA)CON]

raconteur (,rækɒn'tɜ:) *n.* a person skilled in telling stories. [C19: F, from *raconter* to tell]

racoon (rə'ku:n) *n., pl.* **-coons** *or* **-coon.** a variant spelling of **raccoon.**

racquet ('rækɪt) *n.* a variant spelling of **racket**[2].

racy ('reɪsɪ) *adj.* **racier, raciest. 1.** (of a person's manner, literary style, etc.) having a distinctively lively and spirited quality. **2.** having a characteristic or distinctive flavour: *a racy wine.* **3.** suggestive; slightly indecent; risqué. —**'racily** *adv.* —**'raciness** *n.*

rad[1] (ræd) *n.* a unit of absorbed ionizing radiation dose equivalent to an energy absorption per unit mass of 0.01 joule per kilogram of irradiated material. [C20: from RADI-ATION]

rad[2] *symbol for* radian.

rad. *abbrev. for:* **1.** radical. **2.** radius.

RADA ('rɑ:də) *n.* (in Britain) *acronym for* Royal Academy of Dramatic Art.

radar ('reɪdɑ:) *n.* **1.** a method for detecting the position and velocity of a distant object. A narrow beam of extremely high-frequency radio pulses is transmitted and reflected by the object back to the transmitter. The direction of the reflected beam and the time between transmission and reception of a pulse determine the position of the object. **2.** the equipment used in such detection. [C20: ra(dio) d(etecting) a(nd) r(anging)]

radar beacon *n.* a device for transmitting a coded radar signal in response to a signal from an aircraft or ship. The coded signal is then used by the navigator to determine his position. Also called: **racon.**

radarscope ('reɪdɑ:,skəʊp) *n.* a cathode-ray oscilloscope on which radar signals can be viewed.

radar trap *n.* a device using radar to detect motorists who exceed the speed limit.

Radcliffe ('rædklɪf) *n.* **Ann.** 1764–1823, English novelist, noted for her Gothic romance *The Mysteries of Udolpho* (1794).

raddle ('ræd°l) *vb.* **1.** (*tr.*) *Chiefly Brit.* to paint (the face) with rouge. ~*n., vb.* **2.** another word for **ruddle.** [C16: var. of RUDDLE]

raddled ('ræd°ld) *adj.* (esp. of a person) unkempt or run-down in appearance.

Radetzky (*German* ra'dɛtski) *n.* Count **Joseph** ('jo:zɛf). 1766–1858, Austrian field marshal: served in the war against Sardinia (1848–9), winning brilliant victories in Custozza (1848) and Novara (1849): governor of Lombardy-Venetia in N Italy (1849-57).

radial ('reɪdɪəl) *adj.* **1.** (of lines, etc.) emanating from a common central point; arranged like the radii of a circle. **2.** of, like, or relating to a radius or ray. **3.** short for **radial-ply. 4.** *Anat.* of or relating to the radius or forearm. **5.** *Astron.* (of velocity) in a direction along the line of sight of a celestial object and measured by means of the red shift (or blue shift) of the spectral lines of the object. ~*n.* **6.** a radial part or section. [C16: from Med. L *radiālis*, from RADIUS] —**radially** *adv.*

radial engine *n.* an internal-combustion engine having a number of cylinders arranged about a central crankcase.

radial-ply *adj.* (of a motor tyre) having the fabric cords in the outer casing running radially to enable the sidewalls to be flexible.

radial symmetry *n.* a type of structure of an organism in which a vertical cut through the axis in any of two or more planes produces two halves that are mirror images of each other. Cf. **bilateral symmetry.**

radian ('reɪdɪən) *n.* an SI unit of plane angle; the angle between two radii of a circle that cut off on the circumference an arc equal in length to the radius. 1 radian is equivalent to 57.296 degrees. Symbol: rad. [C19: from RADIUS]

radiance ('reɪdɪəns) *or* **radiancy** *n., pl.* **-ances** *or* **-ancies. 1.** the quality or state of being radiant. **2.** a measure of the amount of electromagnetic radiation leaving or arriving at a point on a surface.

radiant ('reɪdɪənt) *adj.* **1.** sending out rays of light; bright; shining. **2.** characterized by health, happiness, etc.: *a radiant smile.* **3.** emitted or propagated by or as radiation; radiated: *radiant heat.* **4.** sending out heat by radiation: *a radiant heater.* **5.** *Physics.* (of a physical quantity in photometry) evaluated by absolute energy measurements: *radiant flux.* ~*n.* **6.** a point or object that emits radiation, esp. the part of a heater that gives out heat. **7.** *Astron.* the point in the sky from which a meteor shower appears to emanate. [C15: from L *radiāre* to shine, from *radius* ray of light] — **'radiancy** *n.* — **'radiantly** *adv.*

radiant energy *n.* energy that is emitted or propagated in the form of particles or electromagnetic radiation.

radiant heat *n.* heat transferred in the form of electromagnetic radiation rather than by conduction or convection; infrared radiation.

radiata pine (‚reɪdɪ'ɑːtə) *n.* a pine tree grown in Australia and New Zealand to produce building timber. Often shortened to **radiata.** [from NL]

radiate *vb.* ('reɪdɪ‚eɪt). **1.** Also: **eradiate.** to emit (heat, light, or other forms of radiation) or (of heat, light, etc.) to be emitted as radiation. **2.** (*intr.*) (of lines, beams, etc.) to spread out from a centre or be arranged in a radial pattern. **3.** (*tr.*) (of a person) to show (happiness, etc.) to a great degree. ~*adj.* ('reɪdɪɪt, -‚eɪt). **4.** having rays; radiating. **5.** (of a capitulum) consisting of ray flowers. **6.** (of animals) showing radial symmetry. [C17: from L *radiāre* to emit rays] — **'radiative** *adj.*

radiation (‚reɪdɪ'eɪʃən) *n.* **1.** *Physics.* **a.** the emission or transfer of radiant energy as particles, electromagnetic waves, sound, etc. **b.** the particles, etc., emitted, esp. the particles and gamma rays emitted in nuclear decay. **2.** Also called: **radiation therapy.** *Med.* treatment using a radioactive substance. **3.** the act, state, or process of radiating or being radiated. — ‚**radi'ational** *adj.*

radiation sickness *n.* *Pathol.* illness caused by overexposure of the body to ionizing radiations from radioactive material or x-rays.

radiator ('reɪdɪ‚eɪtə) *n.* **1.** a device for heating a room, building, etc., consisting of a series of pipes through which hot water or steam passes. **2.** a device for cooling an internal-combustion engine, consisting of thin-walled tubes through which water passes. **3.** *Electronics.* the part of an aerial or transmission line that radiates electromagnetic waves.

radical ('rædɪkəl) *adj.* **1.** of, relating to, or characteristic of the basic or inherent constitution of a person or thing; fundamental: *a radical fault.* **2.** concerned with or tending to concentrate on fundamental aspects of a matter; searching or thoroughgoing: *radical thought.* **3.** favouring or tending to produce extreme or fundamental changes in political, economic, or social conditions, institutions, etc.: *a radical party.* **4.** of or arising from the root or the base of the stem of a plant: *radical leaves.* **5.** *Maths.* of, relating to, or containing roots of numbers or quantities. **6.** *Linguistics.* of or relating to the root of a word. ~*n.* **7.** a person who favours extreme or fundamental change in existing institutions or in political, social, or economic conditions. **8.** *Maths.* a root of a number or quantity, such as $^3\sqrt{5}$, $\sqrt{x}$. **9.** *Chem.* **a.** short for **free radical. b.** another name for **group** (sense 9). **10.** *Linguistics.* another word for **root**[1] (sense 8). [C14: from LL *rādicālis* having roots, from L *rādix* a root] — **'radicalness** *n.*

radicalism ('rædɪkə‚lɪzəm) *n.* **1.** the principles, desires, or practices of political radicals. **2.** a radical movement, esp. in politics. — ‚**radical'istic** *adj.* — ‚**radical'istically** *adv.*

radically ('rædɪkəlɪ) *adv.* thoroughly; completely; fundamentally: *to alter radically.*

radical sign *n.* the symbol $\sqrt{}$ placed before a number or quantity to indicate the extraction of a root, esp. a square root. The value of a higher root is indicated by a raised digit in front of the symbol, as in $^3\sqrt{}$.

radicand ('rædɪ‚kænd, ‚rædɪ'kænd) *n.* a number or quantity from which a root is to be extracted, usually preceded by a radical sign: 3 *is the radicand of* $\sqrt{3}$. [C20: from L *rādicandum*, lit.: that which is to be rooted, from *rādicāre*, from *rādix* root]

radicchio (ræ'diːkɪəʊ) *n., pl.* **-chios.** an Italian variety of chicory, having purple leaves streaked with white that are eaten raw in salads.

radices ('reɪdɪ‚siːz) *n.* a plural of **radix.**

radicle ('rædɪkəl) *n.* **1.** *Bot.* **a.** the part of the embryo of seed-bearing plants that develops into the main root. **b.** a very small root or rootlike part. **2.** *Anat.* any bodily structure resembling a rootlet, esp. one of the smallest branches of a vein or nerve. **3.** *Chem.* a variant spelling of **radical** (sense 9). [C18: from L *rādicula*, from *rādix* root]

Radiguet (*French* radigɛ) *n.* **Raymond** (rɛmɔ̃). 1903–23, French novelist; the author of *The Devil in the Flesh* (1923) and *Count d'Orgel* (1924).

radii ('reɪdɪ‚aɪ) *n.* a plural of **radius.**

radio ('reɪdɪəʊ) *n., pl.* **-dios. 1.** the use of electromagnetic waves, lying in the radio-frequency range, for broadcasting, two-way communications, etc. **2.** an electronic device designed to receive, demodulate, and amplify radio signals from sound broadcasting stations, etc. **3.** the broadcasting, content, etc., of radio programmes: *he thinks radio is poor these days.* **4.** the occupation or profession concerned with any aspect of the broadcasting of radio programmes. **5.** short for **radiotelegraph, radiotelegraphy,** *or* **radiotelephone. 6.** (*modifier*) **a.** of, relating to, or sent by radio signals: *a radio station.* **b.** of, concerned with, using, or operated by radio frequencies: *radio spectrum.* **c.** relating to or produced for radio: *radio drama.* ~*vb.* **-dioing, -dioed. 7.** to transmit (a message, etc.) to (a person, etc.) by means of radio waves. ~Also called (esp. Brit.): **wireless.** [C20: short for *radiotelegraphy*]

radio- *combining form.* **1.** denoting radio, broadcasting, or radio frequency: *radiogram.* **2.** indicating radioactivity or radiation: *radiocarbon; radiochemistry.* [from F, from L *radius* ray]

radioactive (‚reɪdɪəʊ'æktɪv) *adj.* exhibiting, using, or concerned with radioactivity. — ‚**radio'actively** *adv.*

radioactive dating *n.* another term for **radiometric dating.**

radioactive decay *n.* disintegration of a nucleus that occurs spontaneously or as a result of electron capture. Also called: **disintegration.**

radioactive series *n.* *Physics.* a series of nuclides each of which undergoes radioactive decay into the next member of the series, ending with a stable element, usually lead.

radioactive waste *n.* any waste material containing radionuclides. Also called: **nuclear waste.**

radioactivity (‚reɪdɪəʊæk'tɪvɪtɪ) *n.* the spontaneous emission of radiation from atomic nuclei. The radiation can consist of alpha, beta, or gamma radiation.

radio astronomy *n.* a branch of astronomy in which the radio telescope is used to detect and analyse radio signals received on earth from radio sources in space.

radio beacon *n.* a fixed radio transmitting station that broadcasts a characteristic signal by means of which a vessel or aircraft can determine its bearing or position.

radiobiology (‚reɪdɪəʊbaɪ'ɒlədʒɪ) *n.* the branch of biology concerned with the effects of radiation on living organisms and the study of biological processes using radioactive substances as tracers. —**radiobiological** (‚reɪdɪəʊ‚baɪə'lɒdʒɪkəl) *adj.* — ‚**radio‚bio'logically** *adv.* — ‚**radiobi'ologist** *n.*

radiocarbon (‚reɪdɪəʊ'kɑːbən) *n.* a radioactive isotope of carbon, esp. carbon-14. See **carbon** (sense 1).

radiocarbon dating *n.* See **carbon dating.**

radiochemistry (‚reɪdɪəʊ'kɛmɪstrɪ) *n.* the chemistry of radioactive elements and their compounds. — ‚**radio'chemical** *adj.* — ‚**radio'chemist** *n.*

radio compass *n.* any navigational device that gives a bearing by determining the direction of incoming radio waves transmitted from a particular radio station or beacon. See also **goniometer** (sense 2).

radio control *n.* remote control by means of radio signals from a transmitter. —**'radio-con'trolled** *adj.*

radioelement (,reɪdɪəʊ'ɛlɪmənt) *n.* an element that is naturally radioactive.

radio frequency *n.* **1. a.** any frequency that lies in the range 10 kilohertz to 300 000 megahertz and can be used for broadcasting. Abbrevs.: **rf, RF. b.** (*as modifier*): *a radio-frequency amplifier.* **2.** the frequency transmitted by a particular radio station.

radiogram ('reɪdɪəʊ,græm) *n.* **1.** *Brit.* a unit comprising a radio and record player. **2.** a message transmitted by radiotelegraphy. **3.** another name for **radiograph.**

radiograph ('reɪdɪəʊ,grɑːf) *n.* an image produced on a specially sensitized photographic film or plate by radiation, usually by x-rays or gamma rays.

radiography (,reɪdɪ'ɒgrəfɪ) *n.* the production of radiographs of opaque objects for use in medicine, surgery, industry, etc. —**,radi'ographer** *n.* —**radiographic** (,reɪdɪəʊ'græfɪk) *adj.* —**,radio'graphically** *adv.*

radio-immuno-assay ('reɪdɪəʊ,ɪmjʊnəʊ'æseɪ) *n.* a sensitive immunological assay, making use of radioactive labelling, of such things as hormone levels in the blood.

radioisotope (,reɪdɪəʊ'aɪsətəʊp) *n.* a radioactive isotope. —**radioisotopic** (,reɪdɪəʊ,aɪsə'tɒpɪk) *adj.*

radiolarian (,reɪdɪəʊ'lɛərɪən) *n.* any of various marine protozoans typically having a siliceous shell and stiff radiating pseudopodia. [C19: from NL *Radiolaria*, from LL *radiolus* little sunbeam, from L *radius* ray]

radiology (,reɪdɪ'ɒlədʒɪ) *n.* the use of x-rays and radioactive substances in the diagnosis and treatment of disease. —**,radi'ologist** *n.*

radiometer (,reɪdɪ'ɒmɪtə) *n.* any instrument for the detection or measurement of radiant energy. —**radiometric** (,reɪdɪəʊ'mɛtrɪk) *adj.* —**,radi'ometry** *n.*

radiometric dating *n.* any method of dating material based on the decay of its constituent radioactive atoms, such as potassium-argon dating or rubidium-strontium dating. Also called: **radioactive dating.**

radiopaging ('reɪdɪəʊ,peɪdʒɪŋ) *n.* a system whereby a person carrying a small radio receiver (**pager**) is alerted when it emits a sound or other signal in response to a call from a distant location.

radiopaque (,reɪdɪəʊ'peɪk) *or* **radio-opaque** *adj.* not permitting x-rays or other radiation to pass through. —**radiopacity** (,reɪdɪəʊ'pæsɪtɪ) *or* **,radio-o'pacity** *n.*

radioscopy (,reɪdɪ'ɒskəpɪ) *n.* another word for **fluoroscopy.** —**radioscopic** (,reɪdɪəʊ'skɒpɪk) *adj.* —**,radi-o'scopically** *adv.*

radiosonde ('reɪdɪəʊ,sɒnd) *n.* an airborne instrument to send meteorological information back to earth by radio. [C20: RADIO- + F *sonde* sounding line]

radio source *n.* a celestial object, such as a supernova remnant or quasar, that is a source of radio waves.

radio spectrum *n.* the range of electromagnetic frequencies used in radio transmission, between 10 kilohertz and 300 000 megahertz.

radio star *n.* a former name for **radio source.**

radiotelegraphy (,reɪdɪəʊtɪ'lɛgrəfɪ) *n.* a type of telegraphy in which messages (usually in Morse code) are transmitted by radio waves. —**,radio'tele,graph** *vb., n.* —**radiotelegraphic** (,reɪdɪəʊ,tɛlɪ'græfɪk) *adj.*

radiotelephone (,reɪdɪəʊ'tɛlɪ,fəʊn) *n.* **1.** a device for communications by means of radio waves rather than by transmitting along wires or cables. ~*vb.* **2.** to telephone (a person) by radiotelephone. —**radiotelephonic** (,reɪdɪəʊ,tɛlɪ'fɒnɪk) *adj.* —**radiotelephony** (,reɪdɪəʊtɪ-'lɛfənɪ) *n.*

radio telescope *n.* an instrument used in radio astronomy to pick up and analyse radio waves from space and also to transmit radio waves.

radioteletype (,reɪdɪəʊ'tɛlɪ,taɪp) *n.* **1.** a teleprinter that transmits or receives information by means of radio waves. **2.** a network of such devices widely used for communicating news, messages, etc. Abbrevs.: **RTT, RTTY.**

radiotherapy (,reɪdɪəʊ'θɛrəpɪ) *n.* the treatment of disease by means of alpha or beta particles emitted from an implanted or ingested radioisotope, or by means of a beam of high-energy radiation. —**radiotherapeutic** (,reɪdɪəʊ,θɛrə'pjuːtɪk) *adj.* —**,radio'therapist** *n.*

radio wave *n.* an electromagnetic wave of radio frequency.

radish ('rædɪʃ) *n.* **1.** any of a genus of plants of Europe and Asia, with petals arranged like a cross, cultivated for their edible roots. **2.** the root of this plant, which has a pungent taste and is eaten raw in salads. [OE *rǣdic*, from L *rādīx* root]

radium ('reɪdɪəm) *n.* **a.** a highly radioactive luminescent white element of the alkaline earth group of metals. It occurs in pitchblende and other uranium ores. Symbol: Ra; atomic no.: 88; half-life of most stable isotope, ^{226}Ra: 1620 years. **b.** (*as modifier*): *radium needle.* [C20: from L *radius* ray]

radium therapy *n.* treatment of disease, esp. cancer, by exposing affected tissues to radiation from radium.

radius ('reɪdɪəs) *n., pl.* **-dii** *or* **-diuses. 1.** a straight line joining the centre of a circle or sphere to any point on the circumference or surface. **2.** the length of this line, usually denoted by the symbol *r.* **3.** *Anat.* the outer, slightly shorter of the two bones of the human forearm, extending from the elbow to the wrist. **4.** a corresponding bone in other vertebrates. **5.** any of the veins of an insect's wing. **6.** a group of ray flowers, occurring in such plants as the daisy. **7. a.** any radial or radiating part, such as a spoke. **b.** (*as modifier*): *a radius arm.* **8.** a circular area of a size indicated by the length of its radius: *the police stopped every lorry within a radius of four miles.* **9.** the operational limit of a ship, aircraft, etc. [C16: from L: rod, ray, spoke]

radix ('reɪdɪks) *n., pl.* **-dices** *or* **-dixes. 1.** *Maths.* any number that is the base of a number system or of a system of logarithms: *10 is the radix of the decimal system.* **2.** *Biol.* the root or point of origin of a part or organ. **3.** *Linguistics.* a less common word for **root**[1] (sense 8). [C16: from L *rādīx* root]

radix point *n.* a point, such as the decimal point in the decimal system, separating the integral part of a number from the fractional part.

Radnorshire ('rædnə,ʃɪə, -ʃə) *or* **Radnor** *n.* (until 1974) a county of E Wales, now part of Powys.

Radom (*Polish* 'radɔm) *n.* a city in E Poland: under Austria from 1795 to 1815 and Russia from 1815 to 1918. Pop.: 214 000 (1985).

radome ('reɪdəʊm) *n.* a protective housing for a radar antenna made from a material that is transparent to radio waves. [C20: RA(DAR) + DOME]

radon ('reɪdɒn) *n.* a colourless radioactive element of the rare gas group, the most stable isotope of which, radon-222, is a decay product of radium. Symbol: Rn; atomic no.: 86; half-life of ^{222}Rn: 3.82 days. [C20: from RADIUM + -ON]

radula ('rædjʊlə) *n., pl.* **-lae** (-,liː). a horny tooth-bearing strip on the tongue of molluscs that is used for rasping food. [C19: from LL: a scraping iron, from L *rādere* to scrape] —**'radular** *adj.*

Raeburn ('reɪ,bɜːn) *n.* **Sir Henry.** 1756–1823, Scottish portrait painter.

RAF (*Not standard* ræf) *abbrev. for* Royal Air Force.

Rafferty ('ræfətɪ) *or* **Rafferty's rules** *pl. n. Austral. & N.Z. sl.* no rules at all. [C20: from ?]

raffia *or* **raphia** ('ræfɪə) *n.* **1.** a palm tree, native to Madagascar, that has large plumelike leaves, the stalks of which yield a useful fibre. **2.** the fibre obtained from this plant, used for weaving, etc. **3.** any of several related palms or the fibre obtained from them. [C19: from Malagasy]

raffish ('ræfɪʃ) *adj.* **1.** careless or unconventional in dress, manners, etc.; rakish. **2.** tawdry; flashy; vulgar. [C19: from *raff* rubbish, rabble] —**'raffishly** *adv.* —**'raffishness** *n.*

raffle ('ræf°l) *n.* **1. a.** a lottery in which the prizes are goods rather than money. **b.** (*as modifier*): *a raffle ticket.* ~*vb.* **2.** (*tr.; often foll. by off*) to dispose of (goods) in a raffle. [C14 (a dice game): from OF, from ?] —**'raffler** *n.*

Raffles ('ræf°lz) *n.* **Sir Thomas Stamford.** 1781–1826, British colonial administrator: founded Singapore (1819) as a station for the British East India Company.

rafflesia (ræ'fliːzɪə) *n.* any of various tropical Asian parasitic leafless plants, the flowers of which grow up to 45 cm (18 inches) across, smell of putrid meat, and are pollinated by carrion flies. [C19: NL, after Sir Stamford RAFFLES, who discovered it]

raft (rɑ:ft) *n.* **1.** a buoyant platform of logs, planks, etc., used as a vessel or moored platform. **2.** a thick slab of reinforced concrete laid over soft ground to provide a foundation for a building. ~*vb.* **3.** to convey on or travel by raft, or make a raft from. [C15: from ON *raptr* RAFTER]

rafter ('rɑ:ftə) *n.* any one of a set of parallel sloping beams that form the framework of a roof. [OE *ræfter*]

RAFVR *abbrev. for* Royal Air Force Volunteer Reserve.

rag[1] (ræg) *n.* **1. a.** a small piece of cloth, such as one torn from a discarded garment, or such pieces of cloth collectively. **b.** (*as modifier*): *a rag doll.* **2.** a fragmentary piece of any material; scrap; shred. **3.** *Inf.* a newspaper, esp. one considered as worthless, sensational, etc. **4.** *Inf.* an item of clothing. **5.** *Inf.* a handkerchief. **6.** *Brit. sl., esp. naval.* a flag or ensign. [C14: prob. back formation from RAGGED from OE *raggig*]

rag[2] (ræg) *vb.* **ragging, ragged.** (*tr.*) **1.** to draw attention facetiously and persistently to the shortcomings of (a person). **2.** *Brit.* to play rough practical jokes on. ~*n.* **3.** *Brit.* a boisterous practical joke. **4.** (in British universities, etc.) **a.** a period in which various events are organized to raise money for charity. **b.** (*as modifier*): *rag day.* [C18: from ?]

rag[3] (ræg) *Jazz.* ~*n.* **1.** a piece of ragtime music. ~*vb.* **ragging, ragged.** **2.** (*tr.*) to compose or perform in ragtime. [C20: from RAGTIME]

raga ('rɑ:gə) *n.* (in Indian music) **1.** any of several conventional patterns of melody and rhythm that form the basis for freely interpreted compositions. **2.** a composition based on one of these patterns. [C18: from Sansk. *rāga* tone, colour]

ragamuffin ('rægə,mʌfɪn) *n.* a ragged unkempt person, esp. a child. [C14 *Ragamoffyn*, a demon in the poem *Piers Plowman* (1393); prob. based on RAG[1]]

rag-and-bone man *n. Brit.* a man who buys and sells discarded clothing, etc. U.S. equivalent: **junkman**.

ragbag ('ræg,bæg) *n.* **1.** a bag for storing odd rags. **2.** a confused assortment; jumble.

ragbolt ('ræg,bəʊlt) *n.* a bolt that has angled projections on it to prevent it working loose.

rage (reɪdʒ) *n.* **1.** intense anger; fury. **2.** violent movement or action, esp. of the sea, wind, etc. **3.** great intensity of hunger or other feelings. **4.** a fashion or craze (esp. in **all the rage**). **5.** *Austral. & N.Z. inf.* a dance or party. ~*vb.* (*intr.*) **6.** to feel or exhibit intense anger. **7.** (esp. of storms, fires, etc.) to move or surge with great violence. **8.** (esp. of a disease) to spread rapidly and uncontrollably. [C13: via OF from L *rabiēs* madness]

ragged ('rægɪd) *adj.* **1.** (of clothes) worn to rags; tattered. **2.** (of a person) dressed in tattered clothes. **3.** having a neglected or unkempt appearance: *ragged weeds.* **4.** having a rough or uneven surface or edge; jagged. **5.** uneven or irregular: *a ragged beat; a ragged shout.* [C13: prob. from *ragge* RAG[1]] —'**raggedly** *adv.* —'**raggedness** *n.*

ragged robin *n.* a plant related to the carnation family and native to Europe and Asia, that has pink or white flowers with ragged petals. See also **catchfly**.

raggedy ('rægɪdɪ) *adj. Inf., chiefly U.S. & Canad.* somewhat ragged; tattered: *a raggedy doll.*

ragi, raggee, *or* **raggy** ('rægɪ) *n.* a cereal grass, cultivated in Africa and Asia for its edible grain. [C18: from Hindi]

raglan ('ræglən) *n.* **1.** a coat, jumper, etc., with sleeves that continue to the collar instead of having armhole seams. ~*adj.* **2.** cut in this design: *a raglan sleeve.* [C19: after Lord RAGLAN]

Raglan ('ræglən) *n.* **Fitzroy James Henry Somerset,** 1st Baron Raglan. 1788–1855, British field marshal, diplomatist, politician, and protégé of Wellington: commanded British troops (1854–55) in the Crimean War.

ragout (ræ'gu:) *n.* **1.** a richly seasoned stew of meat and vegetables. ~*vb.* **-gouting** (-'gu:ɪŋ), **-gouted** (-'gu:d). **2.** (*tr.*) to make into a ragout. [C17: from F, from *ragoûter* to stimulate the appetite again, from *ra-* RE- + *goûter* from L *gustāre* to taste]

ragtag ('ræg,tæg) *n. Derog.* the common people; rabble (esp. in **ragtag and bobtail**). [C19]

ragtime ('ræg,taɪm) *n.* a style of jazz piano music, developed by Scott Joplin around 1900, having a two-four rhythm base and a syncopated melody. [C20: prob. from RAGGED + TIME]

rag trade *n. Inf.* the clothing business.

Ragusa (*Italian* ra'guːza) *n.* **1.** an industrial town in SE Sicily. Pop.: 65 163 (1983 est.). **2.** the Italian name (until 1918) for **Dubrovnik**.

ragweed ('ræg,wiːd) *n.* a North American plant of the composite family such as the **common ragweed**. Its green tassel-like flowers produce large amounts of pollen, which causes hay fever. Also called: **ambrosia**.

ragworm ('ræg,wɜːm) *n.* any polychaete worm living chiefly in burrows in sand and having a flattened body with a row of fleshy lateral appendages along each side. U.S. name: **clamworm**.

ragwort ('ræg,wɜːt) *n.* any of several European plants of the composite family that have yellow daisy-like flowers. See also **groundsel**.

rah (rɑː) *interj. Inf., chiefly U.S.* short for **hurrah**.

raid (reɪd) *n.* **1.** a sudden surprise attack. **2.** an attempt by speculators to force down commodity prices by rapid selling. ~*vb.* **3.** to make a raid against (a person, thing, etc.). [C15: Scot. dialect, from OE *rād* military expedition] —'**raider** *n.*

rail[1] (reɪl) *n.* **1.** a horizontal bar of wood, etc., supported by vertical posts, functioning as a fence, barrier, etc. **2.** a horizontal bar fixed to a wall on which to hang things: *a picture rail.* **3.** a horizontal framing member in a door. Cf. **stile**[2]. **4.** short for **railing**. **5.** one of a pair of parallel bars laid on a track, roadway, etc., that serve as a guide and running surface for the wheels of a train, tramcar, etc. **6. a.** short for **railway**. **b.** (*as modifier*): *rail transport.* **7.** *Naut.* a trim for finishing the top of a bulwark. **8. off the rails. a.** into or in a state of disorder. **b.** eccentric or mad. ~*vb.* (*tr.*) **9.** to provide with a rail or railings. **10.** (usually foll. by *in* or *off*) to fence (an area) with rails. [C13: from OF *raille* rod, from L *rēgula* ruler]

rail[2] (reɪl) *vb.* (*intr.*; foll. by *at* or *against*) to complain bitterly or vehemently. [C15: from OF *railler* to mock, from OProvençal *ralhar* to chatter, from LL *ragere* to yell] —'**railer** *n.*

rail[3] (reɪl) *n.* any of various small cranelike wading marsh birds with short wings and neck, long legs, and dark plumage. [C15: from OF *raale*, ?from L *rādere* to scrape]

railcar ('reɪl,kɑː) *n.* a passenger-carrying railway vehicle consisting of a single coach with its own power unit.

railcard ('reɪl,kɑːd) *n. Brit.* an identity card issued to people, such as senior citizens or students, entitled to cheap rail fares.

railhead ('reɪl,hɛd) *n.* **1.** a terminal of a railway. **2.** the farthest point reached by completed track on an unfinished railway.

railing ('reɪlɪŋ) *n.* **1.** (*often pl.*) a fence, balustrade, or barrier that consists of rails supported by posts. **2.** rails collectively or material for making rails.

raillery ('reɪlərɪ) *n., pl.* **-leries. 1.** light-hearted satire or ridicule; banter. **2.** a bantering remark. [C17: from F, from *railler* to tease; see RAIL[2]]

railroad ('reɪl,rəʊd) *n.* **1.** the usual U.S. word for **railway**. ~*vb.* **2.** (*tr.*) *Inf.* to force (a person) into (an action) with haste or by unfair means.

railway ('reɪl,weɪ) *or U.S.* **railroad** *n.* **1.** a permanent track composed of a line of parallel metal rails fixed to sleepers, for transport of passengers and goods in trains. **2.** any track for the wheels of a vehicle to run on: *a cable railway.* **3.** the entire equipment, rolling stock, buildings, property, and system of tracks used in such a transport system. **4.** the organization responsible for operating a railway network. **5.** (*modifier*) of, relating to, or used on a railway: *a railway engine.*

raiment ('reɪmənt) *n. Arch. or poetic.* attire; clothing. [C15: from *arrayment*, from OF *areement*; see ARRAY]

rain (reɪn) *n.* **1. a.** precipitation from clouds in the form of drops of water, formed by the condensation of water vapour in the atmosphere. **b.** a fall of rain; shower. **c.** (*in combination*): *a raindrop.* **2.** a large quantity of anything falling rapidly or in quick succession: *a rain of abuse.* **3.** (**come**) **rain or** (**come**) **shine.** regardless of the weather or circumstances. **4. right as rain.** *Brit. inf.* perfectly all right. ~*vb.* **5.** (*intr.*; with *it* as subject) to be the case that rain is falling. **6.** (often with *it* as subject) to fall or cause to fall like rain. **7.** (*tr.*) to bestow in large measure: *to rain abuse on someone.* **8. rained off.** cancelled or postponed on account of rain. U.S. and Canad. term: **rained out.** ~See also **rains.** [OE *regn*] —'**rainless** *adj.*

rainbow ('reɪn,bəʊ) *n.* **1. a.** a bow-shaped display in the sky of the colours of the spectrum, caused by the refraction and reflection of the sun's rays through rain. **b.** (*as modifier*): *a rainbow pattern.* **2.** an illusory hope: *to chase rainbows.* **3.** (*modifier*) of or relating to a political grouping together by several minorities, esp. of different races: *the rainbow coalition.*

Rainbow Bridge *n.* a natural stone bridge over a creek in SE Utah. Height: 94 m (309 ft.). Span: 85 m (278 ft.).

rainbow trout *n.* a freshwater trout of North American origin, marked with many black spots and two longitudinal red stripes.

rain check *n. U.S. & Canad.* **1.** a ticket stub for a baseball game that allows readmission on a future date if the event is cancelled because of rain. **2.** the deferral of acceptance of an offer. **3. take a rain check.** *Inf.* to accept or request the postponement of an offer.

raincoat ('reɪn,kəʊt) *n.* a coat made of a waterproof material.

rainfall ('reɪn,fɔːl) *n.* **1.** precipitation in the form of raindrops. **2.** *Meteorol.* the amount of precipitation in a specified place and time.

rainforest ('reɪn,fɒrɪst) *n.* dense forest found in tropical areas of heavy rainfall.

rain gauge *n.* an instrument for measuring rainfall or snowfall, consisting of a cylinder covered by a funnel-like lid.

Rainier ('reɪnɪə; reɪ'nɪə, rə-) *n.* **Mount.** a mountain in W Washington State: the highest mountain in the state and in the Cascade Range. Height: 4392 m (14 410 ft.).

Rainier III ('reɪnɪ,eɪ; *French* rɛnje) *n.* full name *Rainier Louis Henri Maxence Bertrand de Grimaldi.* born 1923, ruling prince of Monaco from 1949. He married (1956) the U.S. actress Grace Kelly (1928–82).

rainproof ('reɪn,pruːf) *adj.* **1.** Also: **'rain,tight.** (of garments, materials, etc.) impermeable to rainwater. ~*vb.* **2.** (*tr.*) to make rainproof.

rains (reɪnz) *pl. n.* **the rains.** the season of heavy rainfall, esp. in the tropics.

rain shadow *n.* the relatively dry area on the leeward side of high ground in the path of rain-bearing winds.

rainstorm ('reɪn,stɔːm) *n.* a storm with heavy rain.

rainwater ('reɪn,wɔːtə) *n.* pure water from rain (as distinguished from spring water, tap water, etc., which may contain minerals and impurities).

rainwear ('reɪnweə) *n.* clothing designed to be worn in the rain, such as waterproof and water-resistant garments.

rainy ('reɪnɪ) *adj.* **rainier, rainiest. 1.** characterized by a large rainfall: *a rainy climate.* **2.** wet or showery; bearing rain. —'**rainily** *adv.* —'**raininess** *n.*

rainy day *n.* a future time of need, esp. financial.

raise (reɪz) *vb.* (*mainly tr.*) **1.** to move or elevate to a higher position or level; lift. **2.** to set or place in an upright position. **3.** to construct, build, or erect: *to raise a barn.* **4.** to increase in amount, size, value, etc.: *to raise prices.* **5.** to increase in degree, strength, intensity, etc.: *to raise one's voice.* **6.** to advance in rank or status; promote. **7.** to arouse or awaken from sleep or death. **8.** to stir up or incite; activate: *to raise a mutiny.* **9. raise Cain** (*or* **the devil, hell, the roof,** etc.). **a.** to create a disturbance, esp. by making a great noise. **b.** to protest vehemently. **10.** to give rise to; cause or provoke: *to raise a smile.* **11.** to put forward for consideration: *to raise a question.* **12.** to cause to assemble or gather together: *to raise an army.* **13.** to grow or cause to grow: *to raise a crop.* **14.** to bring up; rear: *to raise a family.* **15.** to cause to be heard or known; utter or express: *to raise a shout.* **16.** to bring to an end; remove: *to raise a siege.* **17.** to cause (bread, etc.) to rise, as by the addition of yeast. **18.** *Poker.* to bet more than (the previous player). **19.** *Bridge.* to bid (one's partner's suit) at a higher level. **20.** *Naut.* to cause (something) to seem to rise above the horizon by approaching: *we raised land after 20 days.* **21.** to establish radio communications with: *we raised Moscow last night.* **22.** to obtain (money, funds, etc.). **23.** to bring (a surface, a design, etc.) into relief; cause to project. **24.** to cause (a blister, etc.) to form on the skin. **25.** *Maths.* to multiply (a number) by itself a specified number of times: *8 is 2 raised to the power 3.* **26. raise one's glass (to).** to drink a toast (to). **27. raise one's hat.** *Old-fashioned.* to take one's hat briefly off one's head as a greeting or mark of respect. ~*n.* **28.** the act or

an instance of raising. **29.** *Chiefly U.S. & Canad.* an increase, esp. in salary, wages, etc.; rise. [C12: from ON *reisa*] —'**raisable** *or* '**raiseable** *adj.*

raised beach *n.* a wave-cut platform raised above the shoreline by a relative fall in the water level.

raisin ('reɪzⁿn) *n.* a dried grape. [C13: from OF: grape, ult. from L *racēmus* cluster of grapes] —'**raisiny** *adj.*

raison d'être *French.* (rɛzɔ̃ dɛtrə) *n.*, *pl.* **raisons d'être** (rɛzɔ̃ dɛtrə). reason or justification for existence.

raj (rɑːdʒ) *n.* **1.** (in India) government; rule. **2.** (cap. and preceded by *the*) the British government in India before 1947. [C19: from Hindi, from Sansk., from *rājati* he rules]

rajah *or* **raja** ('rɑːdʒə) *n.* **1.** (in India, formerly) a ruler: sometimes used as a title preceding a name. **2.** a Malayan or Javanese prince or chieftain. [C16: from Hindi, from Sansk. *rājan* king]

Rajasthan (,rɑːdʒə'stɑːn) *n.* a state of NW India, bordering on Pakistan: formed in 1958; contains the Thar Desert in the west. Capital: Jaipur. Pop.: 34 102 912 (1981). Area: 342 239 sq. km (132 111 sq. miles).

Rajkot ('rɑːdʒkəʊt) *n.* a city in W India, in S Gujarat. Pop.: 444 156 (1981).

Rajput *or* **Rajpoot** ('rɑːdʒpʊt) *n. Hinduism.* one of a Hindu military caste claiming descent from the Kshatriya, the original warrior caste. [C16: from Hindi, from Sansk. *rājan* king]

Rajputana (,rɑːdʒpʊ'tɑːnə) *n.* a former group of princely states in NW India: now mostly part of Rajasthan.

Rakata (rə'kɑːtə) *n.* another name for **Krakatoa.**

rake¹ (reɪk) *n.* **1.** a hand implement consisting of a row of teeth set in a headpiece attached to a long shaft and used for gathering hay, straw, etc., or for smoothing loose earth. **2.** any of several mechanical farm implements equipped with rows of teeth or rotating wheels mounted with tines and used to gather hay, straw, etc. **3.** any of various implements similar in shape or function. **4.** the act of raking. ~*vb.* **5.** to scrape, gather, or remove (leaves, refuse, etc.) with a rake. **6.** to level or prepare (a surface) with a rake. **7.** (*tr.; sometimes foll. by out*) to clear (ashes, etc.) from (a fire). **8.** (*tr.; foll. by up or together*) to gather (items or people) with difficulty, as from a scattered area or limited supply. **9.** (*tr.; often foll. by through, over,* etc.) to search or examine carefully. **10.** (when *intr.,* foll. by *against, along,* etc.) to scrape or graze: *the ship raked the side of the quay.* **11.** (*tr.*) to direct (gunfire) along the length of (a target): *machine-guns raked the column.* **12.** (*tr.*) to sweep (one's eyes) along the length of (something); scan. ~See also **rake in, rake-off,** etc. [OE *raca*] —'**raker** *n.*

rake² (reɪk) *n.* a dissolute man, esp. one in fashionable society; roué. [C17: short for *rakehell* a dissolute man]

rake³ (reɪk) *vb.* (*mainly intr.*) **1.** to incline from the vertical by a perceptible degree, esp. (of a ship's mast) towards the stern. **2.** (*tr.*) to construct with a backward slope. ~*n.* **3.** the degree to which an object, such as a ship's mast, inclines from the perpendicular, esp. towards the stern. **4.** *Theatre.* the slope of a stage from the back towards the footlights. **5.** the angle between the working face of a cutting tool and a plane perpendicular to the surface of the workpiece. [C17: from ?; ? rel. to G *ragen* to project, Swedish *raka*]

rake in *vb.* (*tr., adv.*) *Inf.* to acquire (money) in large amounts.

rake-off *Sl.* ~*n.* **1.** a share of profits, esp. one that is illegal or given as a bribe. ~*vb.* **rake off. 2.** (*tr., adv.*) to take or receive (such a share of profits).

rake up *vb.* (*tr., adv.*) to revive, discover, or bring to light (something forgotten): *to rake up an old quarrel.*

raki *or* **rakee** (rɑː'kiː, 'rækɪ) *n.* a strong spirit distilled in Turkey from grain, usually flavoured with aniseed or other aromatics. [C17: from Turkish *rāqi*]

rakish¹ ('reɪkɪʃ) *adj.* dissolute; profligate. [C18: from RAKE²] —'**rakishly** *adv.* —'**rakishness** *n.*

rakish² ('reɪkɪʃ) *adj.* **1.** dashing; jaunty: *a hat set at a rakish angle.* **2.** *Naut.* (of a ship or boat) having lines suggestive of speed. [C19: prob. from RAKE³]

rale *or* **râle** (rɑːl) *n. Med.* an abnormal crackling sound heard on auscultation of the chest, usually caused by the accumulation of fluid in the lungs. [C19: from F, from *râler* to breathe with a rattling sound]

Raleigh¹ ('rɔːlɪ, 'rɑː-) *n.* a city in E central North Carolina, capital of the state. Pop.: 180 430 (1986 est.).

Raleigh[2] or **Ralegh** ('rɔːlɪ, 'rɑː-) n. Sir **Walter**. ?1552–1618, English courtier, explorer, and writer; favourite of Elizabeth I. After unsuccessful attempts to colonize Virginia (1584–89), he led two expeditions to the Orinoco to search for gold (1595; 1616). He introduced tobacco and potatoes into England, and was imprisoned (1603–16) for conspiracy under James I. He was beheaded in 1618.

rallentando (,rælɛn'tændəʊ) adj., adv. Music. becoming slower. Also: **ritardando**. [C19: It., from *rallentare* to slow down]

rally[1] ('rælɪ) vb. **-lying, -lied. 1.** to bring (a group, unit, etc.) into order, as after dispersal, or (of such a group) to reform and come to order. **2.** (when intr., foll. by to) to organize (supporters, etc.) for a common cause or (of such people) to come together for a purpose. **3.** to summon up (one's strength, spirits, etc.) or (of a person's health, strength, or spirits) to revive or recover. **4.** (intr.) Stock Exchange. to increase sharply after a decline. **5.** (intr.) Tennis, squash, etc. to engage in a rally. ~n., pl. **-lies. 6.** a large gathering of people for a common purpose. **7.** a marked recovery of strength or spirits, as during illness. **8.** a return to order after dispersal or rout, as of troops, etc. **9.** Stock Exchange. a sharp increase in price or trading activity after a decline. **10.** Tennis, squash, etc. an exchange of several shots before one player wins the point. **11.** a type of motoring competition over public roads. [C16: from OF *rallier*, from RE- + *alier* to write] —'**rallier** n.

rally[2] ('rælɪ) vb. **-lying, -lied.** to mock or ridicule (someone) in a good-natured way; chaff; tease. [C17: from OF *railler* to tease; see RAIL[2]]

rallycross ('rælɪ,krɒs) n. a form of motor sport in which cars race over a one-mile circuit of rough grass with some hard-surfaced sections.

rally round vb. (intr.) to come to the aid of (someone); offer moral or practical support.

ram (ræm) n. **1.** an uncastrated adult male sheep. **2.** a piston or moving plate, esp. one driven hydraulically or pneumatically. **3.** the falling weight of a pile driver. **4.** short for **battering ram. 5.** a pointed projection in the stem of an ancient warship for puncturing the hull of enemy ships. **6.** a warship equipped with a ram. ~vb. **ramming, rammed. 7.** (tr.; usually foll. by into) to force or drive, as by heavy blows: *to ram a post into the ground*. **8.** (of a moving object) to crash with force (against another object) or (of two moving objects) to collide in this way. **9.** (tr.; often foll. by in or down) to stuff or cram (something into a hole, etc.). **10.** (tr.; foll. by onto, against, etc.) to thrust violently: *he rammed the books onto the desk*. **11.** (tr.) to present (an idea, argument, etc.) forcefully or aggressively (esp. in **ram (something) down someone's throat**). **12.** (tr.) to drive (a charge) into a firearm. [OE *ramm*] —'**rammer** n.

Ram (ræm) n. **the.** the constellation Aries, the first sign of the zodiac.

RAM[1] (ræm) n. Computers. acronym for random access memory: a temporary storage space which loses its contents when the computer is switched off.

RAM[2] abbrev. for Royal Academy of Music.

Ramadan or **Rhamadhan** (,ræmə'dɑːn) n. **1.** a period of 30 days in the ninth month of the Muslim year, during which strict fasting is observed from sunrise to sunset. **2.** the fast itself. [C16: from Ar., lit.: the hot month, from *ramad* dryness]

Ramakrishna (,rɑːmə'krɪʃnə) n. **Sri** (sriː). 1834–86, Hindu yogi and religious reformer. He preached the equal value of all religions as different paths to God.

Raman effect ('rɑːmən) n. the change in wavelength of light that is scattered by electrons within a material. The effect is used in **Raman spectroscopy** for studying the properties of molecules. [C20: after Sir Chandasekhara *Raman* (1888–1970), Indian physicist]

Ramat Gan (rɑː'mɑːt 'gɑːn) n. a city in Israel, E of Tel Aviv. Pop.: 115 500 (1986).

Rambert ('rɒmbɛə) n. Dame **Marie**. 1888–1982, British ballet dancer and teacher, born in Poland: founded the **Ballet Rambert** (1926).

ramble ('ræmbəl) vb. (intr.) **1.** to stroll about freely, as for relaxation, with no particular direction. **2.** (of paths, streams, etc.) to follow a winding course; meander. **3.** to grow or develop in a random fashion. **4.** (of speech, writing, etc.) to lack organization. ~n. **5.** a leisurely stroll, esp. in the countryside. [C17: prob. rel. to MDu. *rammelen* to ROAM (of animals)]

rambler ('ræmblə) n. **1.** a weak-stemmed plant that straggles over other vegetation. **2.** a person who rambles, esp. one who takes country walks. **3.** a person who lacks organization in his speech or writing.

rambling ('ræmblɪŋ) adj. **1.** straggling or sprawling haphazardly: *a rambling old house*. **2.** (of speech or writing) diffuse and disconnected. **3.** (of a plant, esp. a rose) climbing and straggling. **4.** nomadic; wandering.

Ramboesque (,ræmbəʊ'ɛsk) adj. looking or behaving like or characteristic of Rambo, a fictional film character noted for his mindless brutality and aggression. [C20: after *Rambo, First Blood II*, released in Britain 1985] —'**Rambo,ism** n.

rambunctious (ræm'bʌŋkʃəs) adj. Inf. boisterous; unruly. [C19: prob. from Icelandic *ram* (intensifying prefix) + *-bunctious*, from BUMPTIOUS] —**ram'bunctiousness** n.

rambutan (ræm'buːtʰn) n. **1.** a tree related to the soapberry, native to SE Asia, that has bright red edible fruit covered with hairs. **2.** the fruit of this tree. [C18: from Malay, from *rambut* hair]

RAMC abbrev. for Royal Army Medical Corps.

Rameau (French ramo) n. **Jean Philippe** (ʒɑ̃ filip). 1683–1764, French composer. His works include the opera *Castor et Pollux* (1737), chamber music, harpsichord pieces, church music, and cantatas. His *Traité de l'harmonie* (1722) was of fundamental importance in the development of modern harmony.

ramekin or **ramequin** ('ræmɪkɪn) n. **1.** a savoury dish made from a cheese mixture baked in a fireproof container. **2.** the container itself. [C18: F *ramequin*, of Gmc origin]

Rameses ('ræmɪ,siːz) n. a variant of **Ramses.**

ramification (,ræmɪfɪ'keɪʃən) n. **1.** the act or process of ramifying or branching out. **2.** an offshoot or subdivision. **3.** a structure of branching parts.

ramify ('ræmɪ,faɪ) vb. **-fying, -fied. 1.** to divide into branches or branchlike parts. **2.** (intr.) to develop complicating consequences. [C16: from F *ramifier*, from L *rāmus* branch + *facere* to make]

Ramillies ('ræmɪliːz; French ramiji) n. a village in central Belgium where the Duke of Marlborough defeated the French in 1706.

ramjet or **ramjet engine** ('ræm,dʒɛt) n. **a.** a type of jet engine in which fuel is burned in a duct using air compressed by the forward speed of the aircraft. **b.** an aircraft powered by such an engine.

ramose ('reɪməʊs, ræ'məʊs) or **ramous** ('reɪməs) adj. having branches. [C17: from L *rāmōsus*, from *rāmus* branch] —'**ramosely** or '**ramously** adv. —**ramosity** (ræ'mɒsɪtɪ) n.

ramp (ræmp) n. **1.** a sloping floor, path, etc., that joins two surfaces at different levels. **2.** a movable stairway by which passengers enter and leave an aircraft. **3.** the act of ramping. **4.** Brit. sl. a swindle, esp. one involving exorbitant prices. ~vb. (intr.) **5.** (often foll. by about or around) (esp. of animals) to rush around in a wild excited manner. **6.** to act in a violent or threatening manner (esp. in **ramp and rage**). [C18 (n.): from C13 *rampe*, from OF *ramper* to crawl or rear, prob. of Gmc origin]

rampage vb. (ræm'peɪdʒ). **1.** (intr.) to rush about in a violent or agitated fashion. ~n. ('ræmpeɪdʒ, ræm'peɪdʒ). **2.** angry or destructive behaviour. **3. on the rampage.** behaving violently or destructively. [C18: from Scot., from ?; ? based on RAMP] —**ram'pageous** adj. —**ram'pageously** adv. —**ram'pager** n.

rampant ('ræmpənt) adj. **1.** unrestrained or violent in behaviour, etc. **2.** growing or developing unchecked. **3.** (postpositive) Heraldry. (of a beast) standing on the hind legs, the right foreleg raised above the left. **4.** (of an arch) having one abutment higher than the other. [C14: from OF *ramper* to crawl, rear; see RAMP] —'**rampancy** n. —'**rampantly** adv.

rampart ('ræmpɑːt) n. **1.** the surrounding embankment of a fort, often including any walls, parapets, etc., that are built on the bank. **2.** any defence or bulwark. ~vb. **3.** (tr.) to provide with a rampart; fortify. [C16: from OF, from RE-+ *emparer* to take possession of, from OProvençal *antparar*, from L *ante* before + *parāre* to prepare]

rampike ('ræm,paɪk) n. Canad. a tall tree that has been burned or is bare of branches.

rampion ('ræmpɪən) n. a plant, native to Europe and Asia, that has clusters of bell-shaped bluish flowers and an edible white tuberous root used in salads. [C16: prob. from OF *raiponce*, from OIt. *raponzo*, from *rapa* turnip, from L *rāpum*]

Rampur ('ræmpʊə) n. a city in N India, in N Uttar Pradesh. Pop.: 204 610 (1981).

ramrod ('ræm,rod) n. **1.** a rod for cleaning the barrel of a rifle, etc. **2.** a rod for ramming in the charge of a muzzle-loading firearm.

Ramsay ('ræmzɪ) n. **1. Allan.** ?1686–1758, Scottish poet, editor, and bookseller, noted particularly for his pastoral comedy *The Gentle Shepherd* (1725): first person to introduce the circulating library in Scotland. **2.** his son, **Allan.** 1713–84, Scottish portrait painter. **3. James Andrew Broun.** See (1st Marquis and 10th Earl of) **Dalhousie. 3.** Sir **William.** 1852–1916, Scottish chemist. He discovered argon (1894) with Rayleigh, isolated helium (1895), and identified neon, krypton, and xenon: Nobel prize for chemistry 1904.

Ramses ('ræmsiːz) or **Rameses** n. any of 12 kings of ancient Egypt, who ruled from ?1315 to ?1090 B.C.

Ramses II or **Rameses II** n. died ?1225 B.C., king of ancient Egypt (?1292–?25). His reign was marked by war with the Hittites and the construction of many colossal monuments, esp. the rock temple at Abu Simbel.

Ramses III or **Rameses III** n. died ?1167 B.C., king of ancient Egypt (?1198–?67). His reign was marked by wars in Libya and Syria.

Ramsgate ('ræmz,geɪt) n. a port and resort in SE England, in E Kent on the North Sea coast. Pop.: 39 642 (1981).

ramshackle ('ræm,ʃækᵊl) adj. (esp. of buildings) rickety, shaky, or derelict. [C17 *ramshackled*, from obs. *ransackle* to RANSACK]

ramsons ('ræmzənz, -sənz) pl. n. (usually functioning as sing.) **1.** a broad-leaved garlic native to Europe and Asia. **2.** the bulbous root of this plant, eaten as a relish. [OE *hramesa*]

ran (ræn) vb. the past tense of **run.**

RAN abbrev. for Royal Australian Navy.

Rancagua (Spanish raŋ'kagwa) n. a city in central Chile. Pop.: 152 132 (1985 est.).

ranch (rɑːntʃ) n. **1.** a large tract of land, esp. one in North America, together with the necessary personnel, buildings, and equipment, for rearing livestock, esp. cattle. **2. a.** any large farm for the rearing of a particular kind of livestock or crop: *a mink ranch.* **b.** the buildings, land, etc., connected with it. ~vb. **3.** (intr.) to run a ranch. **4.** (tr.) to raise (animals) on or as if on a ranch. [C19: from Mexican Sp. *rancho* small farm] —'**rancher** n.

rancherie ('rɑːntʃərɪ) n. (in British Columbia, Canada) a settlement of North American Indians, esp. on a reserve. [from Sp. *rancheria*]

Ranchi ('ræntʃɪ) n. an industrial city in E India, in S Bihar between the coal and iron belts of the Chota Nagpur Plateau. Pop.: 487 485 (1981).

rancid ('rænsɪd) adj. **1.** (of food) having an unpleasant stale taste or smell as the result of decomposition. **2.** (of a taste or smell) rank or sour; stale. [C17: from L *rancidus*, from *rancēre* to stink] —'**rancidness** or **rancidity** (ræn'sɪdɪtɪ) n.

rancour or U.S. **rancor** ('ræŋkə) n. malicious resentfulness or hostility; spite. [C14: from OF, from LL *rancor* rankness] —'**rancorous** adj. —'**rancorously** adv.

rand[1] (rænd, rɒnt) n. the standard monetary unit of the Republic of South Africa, divided into 100 cents. [C20: from Afrik., from WITWATERSRAND, referring to the goldmining there; rel. to RAND[2]]

rand[2] (rænd) n. **1.** Shoemaking. a leather strip put in the heel of a shoe before the lifts are put on. **2.** Dialect. **a.** a strip or margin; border. **b.** a strip of cloth; selvage. [OE; rel. to OHG *rant* border, rim of a shield, ON *rönd* shield, rim]

Rand (rænd) n. **the.** short for **Witwatersrand.**

R & B abbrev. for rhythm and blues.

R & D abbrev. for research and development.

Randers (Danish 'ranərs) n. a port and industrial centre in Denmark, in E Jutland on **Randers Fjord** (an inlet of the Kattegat). Pop.: 62 134 (1982 est.).

Randolph ('rændɒlf, -dəlf) n. **1. Edmund Jennings,** 1753–1813, U.S. politician. He was a member of the convention that framed the U.S. constitution (1787), attorney general (1789–94), and secretary of state (1794–95). **2.**

John, called *Randolph of Roanoke.* 1773–1833, U.S. politician, noted for his eloquence: in 1820 he opposed the Missouri Compromise that outlawed slavery. **3.** Sir **Thomas;** 1st Earl of Moray. Died 1332, Scottish soldier: regent after the death of Robert the Bruce (1329).

random ('rændəm) adj. **1.** lacking any definite plan or prearranged order; haphazard: *a random selection.* **2.** Statistics. **a.** having a value which cannot be determined but only described in terms of probability: *a random variable.* **b.** chosen without regard to any characteristics of the individual members of the population so that each has an equal chance of being selected: *random sampling.* ~n. **3. at random.** not following any prearranged order. [C14: from OF *random*, from *randir* to gallop, of Gmc origin] —'**randomly** adv. —'**randomness** n.

random access n. another name for **direct access.**

randomize or **-ise** ('rændə,maɪz) vb. (tr.) to set up (a selection process, sample, etc.) in a deliberately random way in order to enhance the statistical validity of any results obtained. —,**randomi'zation** or **-i'sation** n. —'**random,izer** or -,**iser** n.

R and R U.S. mil. abbrev. for rest and recreation.

randy ('rændɪ) adj. **randier, randiest. 1.** Inf., chiefly Brit. sexually eager or lustful. **2.** Chiefly Scot. lacking any sense of propriety; reckless. ~n., pl. **randies. 3.** Chiefly Scot. a rude or reckless person. [C17: prob. from obs. *rand* to RANT] —'**randily** adv. —'**randiness** n.

ranee ('rɑːnɪ) n. a variant spelling of **rani.**

rang (ræŋ) vb. the past tense of **ring**[2].
▷ **Usage.** See at **ring**[2].

rangatira (,rʌŋgə'tɪərə) n. N.Z. a Maori chief of either sex. [from Maori]

range (reɪndʒ) n. **1.** the limits within which a person or thing can function effectively: *the range of vision.* **2.** the limits within which any fluctuation takes place: *a range of values.* **3.** the total products of a manufacturer, designer, or stockist: *the new spring range.* **4. a.** the maximum effective distance of a projectile fired from a weapon. **b.** the distance between a target and a weapon. **5.** an area set aside for shooting practice or rocket testing. **6.** the total range which a ship, aircraft, or land vehicle is capable of covering without taking on fresh fuel: *the range of this car is about 160 miles.* **7.** Maths. (of a function or variable) the set of values that a function or variable can take. **8.** U.S. & Canad. **a.** an extensive tract of open land on which livestock can graze. **b.** (as modifier): *range cattle.* **9.** the geographical region in which a species of plant or animal normally grows or lives. **10.** a rank, row, or series of items. **11.** a series or chain of mountains. **12.** a large stove with burners and one or more ovens, usually heated by solid fuel. **13.** the act or process of ranging. ~vb. **14.** to establish or be situated in a line, row, or series. **15.** (tr.; often reflexive, foll. by with) to put into a specific category; classify: *she ranges herself with the angels.* **16.** (foll. by on) to aim or point (a telescope, gun, etc.) or (of a gun, telescope, etc.) to be pointed or aimed. **17.** to establish the distance of (a target) from (a weapon). **18.** (intr.) (of a gun or missile) to have a specified range. **19.** (when intr., foll. by over) to wander about (in) an area; roam (over). **20.** (intr.; foll. by over) (of an animal or plant) to live or grow in its normal habitat. **21.** (tr.) to put (cattle) to graze on a range. **22.** (intr.) to fluctuate within specific limits. **23.** (intr.) to extend or run in a specific direction. **24.** (intr.) Naut. (of a vessel) to swing back and forth while at anchor. **25.** (tr.) to make (lines of printers' type) level or even at the margin. [C13: from OF: row, from *ranger* to position, from *renc* line]

rangefinder ('reɪndʒ,faɪndə) n. an instrument for determining the distance of an object from the observer, esp. in order to sight a gun or focus a camera.

ranger ('reɪndʒə) n. **1.** Brit. (sometimes cap.) an official in charge of a forest, park, nature reserve, etc. **2.** Orig. U.S. a person employed to patrol a State or national park. Brit. equivalent: **warden. 3.** U.S. one of a body of armed troops employed to police a State or district: *a Texas ranger.* **4.** (in the U.S.) a commando specially trained in making raids. **5.** a person who wanders about; a rover.

Ranger or **Ranger Guide** ('reɪndʒə) n. Brit. a member of the senior branch of the Guides.

rangiora (,ræŋgɪ'ɔːrə) n. a broad-leaved shrub of New Zealand. [from Maori]

Rangoon (ræŋ'guːn) *n.* the capital and chief port of Burma: an industrial city and transport centre; dominated by the gold-covered Shwe Dagon pagoda, 112 m (368 ft.) high. Pop.: 2 458 712 (1983).

rangy ('reɪndʒɪ) *adj.* **rangier, rangiest. 1.** having long slender limbs. **2.** adapted to wandering or roaming. **3.** allowing considerable freedom of movement; spacious. — **'rangily** *adv.* — **'ranginess** *n.*

rani *or* **ranee** ('rɑːnɪ) *n.* a queen or princess; the wife of a rajah. [C17: from Hindi: queen, from Sansk. *rājñī*]

Ranjit Singh ('rʌndʒɪt 'sɪŋ) *n.* called *the Lion of the Punjab.* 1780–1839; founder of the Sikh kingdom in the Punjab.

rank¹ (ræŋk) *n.* **1.** a position, esp. an official one, within a social organization: *the rank of captain.* **2.** high social or other standing; status. **3.** a line or row of people or things. **4.** the position of an item in any ordering or sequence. **5.** *Brit.* a place where taxis wait to be hired. **6.** a line of soldiers drawn up abreast of each other. **7.** any of the eight horizontal rows of squares on a chessboard. **8. close ranks.** to maintain discipline or solidarity. **9. pull rank.** to get one's own way by virtue of one's superior position or rank. **10. rank and file. a.** the ordinary soldiers, excluding the officers. **b.** the great mass or majority of any group, as opposed to the leadership. **c.** (*modifier*): *rank-and-file support.* ~*vb.* **11.** (*tr.*) to arrange (people or things) in rows or lines; range. **12.** to accord or be accorded a specific position in an organization or group. **13.** (*tr.*) to array a set of objects as a sequence: *to rank students by their test scores.* **14.** (*intr.*) to be important; rate: *money ranks low in her order of priorities.* **15.** *Chiefly U.S.* to take precedence or surpass in rank. [C16: from OF *ranc* row, rank, of Gmc origin]

rank² (ræŋk) *adj.* **1.** showing vigorous and profuse growth: *rank weeds.* **2.** highly offensive or disagreeable, esp. in smell or taste. **3.** (*prenominal*) complete or absolute; utter: *a rank outsider.* **4.** coarse or vulgar; gross: *his language was rank.* [OE *ranc* straight, noble] — **'rankly** *adv.* — **'rankness** *n.*

Rank (*German* raŋk) *n.* **Otto** ('ɔto). 1884–1939, Austrian psychoanalyst, noted for his theory that the trauma of birth may be reflected in certain forms of mental illness.

ranker ('ræŋkə) *n.* **1.** a soldier in the ranks. **2.** a commissioned officer who entered service as a noncommissioned recruit.

ranking ('ræŋkɪŋ) *adj.* **1.** *Chiefly U.S. & Canad.* prominent; high ranking. **2.** *Caribbean sl.* possessed of style; exciting. ~*n.* **3.** a position on a scale; rating: *a ranking in a tennis tournament.*

rankle ('ræŋkˀl) *vb.* (*intr.*) to cause severe and continuous irritation, anger, or bitterness; fester. [C14 *ranclen,* from OF *draoncle* ulcer, from L *dracunculus* dim. of *dracō* serpent]

ransack ('rænsæk) *vb.* (*tr.*) **1.** to search through every part of (a house, box, etc.); examine thoroughly. **2.** to plunder; pillage. [C13: from ON *rann* house + *saka* to search] — **'ransacker** *n.*

ransom ('rænsəm) *n.* **1.** the release of captured prisoners, property, etc., on payment of a stipulated price. **2.** the price demanded or stipulated for such a release. **3. hold to ransom. a.** to keep (prisoners, etc.) in confinement until payment for their release is received. **b.** to attempt to force (a person) to comply with one's demands. **4. a king's ransom.** a very large amount of money or valuables. ~*vb.* (*tr.*) **5.** to pay a stipulated price and so obtain the release of (prisoners, property, etc.). **6.** to set free (prisoners, property, etc.) upon receiving the payment demanded. **7.** to redeem; rescue: *Christ ransomed men from sin.* [C14: from OF *ransoun,* from L *redemptiō* a buying back] — **'ransomer** *n.*

Ransome ('rænsəm) *n.* **Arthur.** 1884–1967, English writer, best known for his books for children, including *Swallows and Amazons* (1930) and *Great Northern?* (1947).

rant (rænt) *vb.* **1.** to utter (something) in loud, violent, or bombastic tones. ~*n.* **2.** loud, declamatory, or extravagant speech; bombast. [C16: from Du. *ranten* to rave] — **'ranter** *n.* — **'ranting** *adj., n.* — **'rantingly** *adv.*

ranunculaceous (rə,nʌŋkjʊ'leɪʃəs) *adj.* of, relating to, or belonging to a N temperate family of flowering plants typically having flowers with five petals and numerous anthers and styles. The family includes the buttercup, clematis, and columbine.

ranunculus (rə'nʌŋkjʊləs) *n., pl.* **-luses** *or* **-li** (-,laɪ). any of a genus of ranunculaceous plants having finely divided leaves and typically yellow five-petalled flowers. The genus includes buttercup, crowfoot, and spearwort. [C16: from L: tadpole, from *rāna* frog]

RAOC *abbrev. for* Royal Army Ordnance Corps.

rap¹ (ræp) *vb.* **rapping, rapped. 1.** to strike (a fist, stick, etc.) against (something) with a sharp quick blow; knock. **2.** (*intr.*) to make a sharp loud sound, esp. by knocking. **3.** (*tr.*) to rebuke or criticize sharply. **4.** (*tr.*; foll. by *out*) to put (forth) in sharp rapid speech; utter in an abrupt fashion: *to rap out orders.* **5.** (*intr.*) *Sl.* to talk, esp. volubly. **6.** (*intr.*) to perform a rhythmic monologue with musical backing. **7. rap over the knuckles.** to reprimand. ~*n.* **8.** a sharp quick blow or the sound produced by such a blow. **9.** a sharp rebuke or criticism. **10.** *Sl.* voluble talk; chatter. **11. a.** a fast, rhythmic monologue over a musical backing. **b.** (*as modifier*): *rap music.* **12. beat the rap.** *U.S. & Canad. sl.* to escape punishment or be acquitted of a crime. **13. take the rap.** *Sl.* to suffer the punishment for a crime, whether guilty or not. [C14: prob. from ON; cf. Swedish *rappa* to beat]

rap² (ræp) *n.* (*used with a negative*) the least amount (esp. in **not care a rap**). [C18: prob. from *ropaire* counterfeit coin formerly current in Ireland]

rap³ (ræp) *vb., n. Austral. inf.* a variant spelling of **wrap** (senses 7, 12).

rapacious (rə'peɪʃəs) *adj.* **1.** practising pillage or rapine. **2.** greedy or grasping. **3.** (of animals, esp. birds) subsisting by catching living prey. [C17: from L *rapāx,* from *rapere* to seize] — **ra'paciously** *adv.* — **rapacity** (rə'pæsɪtɪ) *or* **ra'paciousness** *n.*

Rapacki (*Polish* ra'patski) *n.* **Adam** ('adam). 1909–70, Polish politician: foreign minister (1956–68): proposed (1957) the denuclearization of Poland, Czechoslovakia, East Germany, and West Germany (the **Rapacki Plan**): rejected by the West because of Soviet predominance in conventional weapons.

Rapallo (*Italian* ra'pallo) *n.* a port and resort in NW Italy, in Liguria on the **Gulf of Rapallo** (an inlet of the Ligurian Sea): scene of the signing of two treaties after World War I. Pop.: 28 318 (1981 est.).

Rapa Nui ('rɑːpɑ: 'nuːɪ) *n.* another name for **Easter Island.**

rape¹ (reɪp) *n.* **1.** the offence of forcing a person, esp. a woman, to submit to sexual intercourse against that person's will. **2.** the act of despoiling a country in warfare. **3.** any violation or abuse: *the rape of justice.* **4.** *Arch.* abduction: *the rape of the Sabine women.* ~*vb.* (*mainly tr.*) **5.** to commit rape upon (a person). **6.** *Arch.* to carry off by force; abduct. [C14: from L *rapere* to seize] — **'rapist** *n.*

rape² (reɪp) *n.* a Eurasian plant that is cultivated for its seeds, **rapeseed,** which yield a useful oil, **rape oil,** and as a fodder plant. Also called: **colza, cole.** [C14: from L *rāpum* turnip]

rape³ (reɪp) *n.* (*often pl.*) the skins and stalks of grapes left after wine-making: used in making vinegar. [C17: from F *râpe,* of Gmc origin]

Raphael ('ræfeɪəl) *n.* **1.** *Bible.* one of the archangels; the angel of healing and the guardian of Tobias (Tobit 3:17; 5-12). **2.** original name *Raffaello Santi or Sanzio.* 1483–1520, Italian painter and architect, regarded as one of the greatest artists of the High Renaissance. His many paintings include the *Sistine Madonna* (?1513) and the *Transfiguration* (unfinished, 1520). — ,**Raphael'esque** *adj.*

raphia ('ræfɪə) *n.* a variant spelling of **raffia.**

raphide ('reɪfaɪd) *or* **raphis** ('reɪfɪs) *n., pl.* **raphides** ('ræfɪ,diːz). needle-shaped crystals, usually of calcium oxalate, that occur in many plant cells. [C18: from F, from Gk *rhaphis* needle]

rapid ('ræpɪd) *adj.* **1.** (of an action) performed or occurring during a short interval of time; quick. **2.** acting or moving quickly; fast: *a rapid worker.* ~See also **rapids.** [C17: from L *rapidus* tearing away, from *rapere* to seize] — **'rapidly** *adv.* — **rapidity** (rə'pɪdɪtɪ) *or* **'rapidness** *n.*

rapid eye movement *n.* movement of the eyeballs during paradoxical sleep, while the sleeper is dreaming. Abbrev.: **REM.**

rapid fire *n.* **1.** a fast rate of gunfire. ~*adj.* **rapid-fire. 2.** firing shots rapidly. **3.** done, delivered, or occurring in rapid succession.

rapids ('ræpɪdz) pl. n. part of a river where the is very fast and turbulent.

rapier ('reɪpɪə) n. **1.** a long narrow two-edged sword with a guarded hilt, used as a thrusting weapon, popular in the 16th and 17th centuries. **2.** a smaller single-edged 18th-century sword used principally in France. [C16: from OF *espee rapiere*, lit.: rasping sword]

rapine ('ræpaɪn) n. the seizure of property by force; pillage. [C15: from L *rapīna* plundering, from *rapere* to snatch]

rappee (ræ'piː) n. a moist English snuff. [C18: from F *tabac râpé*, lit.: scraped tobacco]

rappel (ræ'pɛl) vb. **-pelling, -pelled,** n. **1.** another word for **abseil.** ~n. **2.** (formerly) a drumbeat to call soldiers to arms. [C19: from F, from *rappeler* to call back, from L *appellāre* to summon]

rapport (ræ'pɔː) n. (often foll. by *with*) a sympathetic relationship or understanding. See also **en rapport.** [C15: from F, from *rapporter* to bring back, from RE- + *aporter*, from L *apportāre*, from *ad* to + *portāre* to carry]

rapprochement French. (raprɔʃmā) n. a resumption of friendly relations, esp. between two countries. [C19: lit.: bringing closer]

rapscallion (ræp'skæljən) n. a disreputable person; rascal or rogue. [C17: from earlier *rascallion*; see RASCAL]

rapt[1] (ræpt) adj. **1.** totally absorbed; engrossed; spellbound, esp. through or as if through emotion: *rapt with wonder.* **2.** characterized by or proceeding from rapture: *a rapt smile.* [C14: from L *raptus* carried away, from *rapere* to seize] — **'raptly** adv.

rapt[2] (ræpt) adj. Austral. inf. a variant spelling of **wrapped** (sense 3).

raptor ('ræptə) n. another name for **bird of prey.** [C17: from L plunderer, from *rapere* to take by force]

raptorial (ræp'tɔːrɪəl) adj. Zool. **1.** (of the feet of birds) adapted for seizing prey. **2.** of or relating to birds of prey. [C19: from L *raptor* robber, from *rapere* to snatch]

rapture ('ræptʃə) n. **1.** the state of mind resulting from feelings of high emotion; joyous ecstasy. **2.** (*often pl.*) an expression of ecstatic joy. **3.** Arch. the act of transporting a person from one sphere of existence to another. ~vb. **4.** (tr.) Arch. or literary. to enrapture. [C17: from Med. L *raptūra*, from L *raptus* RAPT[1]] — **'rapturous** adj.

rara avis ('rɛərə 'eɪvɪs) n., pl. **rarae aves** ('rɛəriː 'eɪviːz). an unusual, uncommon, or exceptional person or thing. [L: rare bird]

rare[1] (rɛə) adj. **1.** not widely known; not frequently used or experienced; uncommon or unusual: *a rare word.* **2.** not widely distributed; not generally occurring: *a rare herb.* **3.** (of a gas, esp. the atmosphere at high altitudes) having a low density; thin; rarefied. **4.** uncommonly great; extreme: *kind to a rare degree.* **5.** exhibiting uncommon excellence: *rare skill.* [C14: from L *rārus* sparse] — **'rareness** n.

rare[2] (rɛə) adj. (of meat, esp. beef) undercooked. [OE *hrēr*; rel. to *hreaw* RAW]

rarebit ('rɛəbɪt) n. another term for **Welsh rabbit.** [C18: by folk etymology from (WELSH) RABBIT; see RARE[2], BIT[1]]

rare earth n. **1.** any oxide of a lanthanide. **2.** Also called: **rare-earth element.** any element of the lanthanide series.

raree show ('rɛəri) n. **1.** a street show or carnival. **2.** another name for **peepshow.** [C17: *raree* from RARE[1]]

rarefaction (,rɛərɪ'fækʃən) or **rarefication** (,rɛərɪfɪ'keɪʃən) n. the act or process of making less dense or the state of being less dense. — ,**rare'factive** adj.

rarefied ('rɛərɪ,faɪd) adj. **1.** exalted in nature or character; lofty: *a rarefied spiritual existence.* **2.** current within only a small group. **3.** thin: *air rarefied at altitude.*

rarefy ('rɛərɪ,faɪ) vb. **-fying, -fied.** to make or become rarer or less dense; thin out. [C14: from OF *raréfier*, from L *rārēfacere*, from *rārus* RARE[1] + *facere* to make] — **'rar e,fiable** adj. — **'rare,fier** n.

rare gas n. another name for **inert gas.**

rarely ('rɛəlɪ) adv. **1.** hardly ever; seldom. **2.** to an unusual degree; exceptionally. **3.** Dialect. uncommonly well; excellently: *he did rarely at market yesterday.*

raring ('rɛərɪŋ) adj. ready; willing; enthusiastic (esp. in **raring to go**). [C20: from *rare*, var. of REAR[2]]

rarity ('rɛərɪtɪ) n., pl. **-ties. 1.** a rare person or thing, esp. something valued because it is uncommon. **2.** the state of being rare.

Rarotonga (,rɛərə'tɒŋgə) n. an island in the S Pacific, in the SW Cook Islands: the chief island of the group. Chief settlement: Avarua. Pop.: 9530 (1981). Area: 67 sq. km (26 sq. miles).

rasbora (ræz'bɔːrə) n. any of the small cyprinid fishes of tropical Asia and East Africa. Many species are brightly coloured and are popular aquarium fishes. [from NL, from an East Indian language]

rascal ('rɑːskəl) n. **1.** a disreputable person; villain. **2.** a mischievous or impish rogue. **3.** an affectionate or mildly reproving term, esp. for a child: *you little rascal.* **4.** Obs. a person of lowly birth. ~adj. **5.** (prenominal) Obs. **a.** belonging to the rabble. **b.** dishonest; knavish. [C14: from OF *rascaille* rabble, ?from OF *rasque* mud]

rascality (rɑː'skælɪtɪ) n., pl. **-ties.** mischievous or disreputable character or action.

rascally ('rɑːskəlɪ) adj. **1.** dishonest or mean; base. ~adv. **2.** in a dishonest or mean fashion.

rase (reɪz) vb. a variant spelling of **raze.**

rash[1] (ræʃ) adj. **1.** acting without due thought; impetuous. **2.** resulting from excessive haste or impetuosity: *a rash word.* [C14: from OHG *rasc* hurried, clever] — **'rashly** adv. — **'rashness** n.

rash[2] (ræʃ) n. **1.** Pathol. any skin eruption. **2.** a series of unpleasant and unexpected occurrences: *a rash of forest fires.* [C18: from OF *rasche*, from *raschier* to scratch, from L *rādere* to scrape]

rasher ('ræʃə) n. a thin slice of bacon or ham. [C16: from ?]

Rasht (ræʃt) or **Resht** n. a city in NW Iran, near the Caspian Sea: agricultural and commercial centre in a rice-growing area. Pop.: 293 881 (1986).

Rask (Danish rasg) n. **Rasmus Christian** ('rasmus 'kresdjan). 1787–1832, Danish philologist. He pioneered comparative philology with his work on Old Norse (1818).

Rasmussen (Danish 'rasmusən) n. **Knud Johan Victor** (knuð jo'han 'viktɔr). 1879–1933, Danish arctic explorer and ethnologist. He led several expeditions through the Arctic in support of his theory that the North American Indians were originally migrants from Asia.

rasp (rɑːsp) n. **1.** a harsh grating noise. **2.** a coarse file with rows of raised teeth. ~vb. **3.** (tr.) to scrape or rub (something) roughly, esp. with a rasp; abrade. **4.** to utter with or make a harsh grating noise. **5.** to irritate (one's nerves); grate (upon). [C16: from OF *raspe*, of Gmc origin; cf. OHG *raspōn* to scrape] — **'rasper** n. — **'rasping** adj. — **'raspish** adj.

raspberry ('rɑːzbərɪ, -brɪ) n., pl. **-ries. 1.** a prickly rosaceous shrub of North America and Europe that has pinkish-white flowers and typically red berry-like fruits (drupelets). See also **bramble. 2. a.** the fruit of any such plant. **b.** (as modifier): *raspberry jelly.* **3. a.** a dark purplish-red colour. **b.** (as adj.): *a raspberry dress.* **4.** a spluttering noise made with the tongue and lips to express contempt (esp. in **blow a raspberry**). [C17: from earlier *raspis* raspberry, from ? + BERRY]

Rasputin (ræ'spjuːtɪn; Russian ras'putin) n. **Grigori Efimovich** (gri'gɔrij jɪ'fiməvitʃ). ?1871–1916, Siberian peasant monk, notorious for his debauchery, who wielded great influence over Tsarina Alexandra. He was assassinated by a group of Russian noblemen.

Ras Tafari (ræs tə'fɑːrɪ) n. See **Haile Selassie.**

Rastafarian (,ræstə'fɛərɪən) n. **1.** a member of a Jamaican cult that regards Ras Tafari, the former emperor of Ethiopia, Haile Selassie, as God. ~adj. **2.** of, characteristic of, or relating to the Rastafarians. ~Often shortened to **Rasta.**

raster ('ræstə) n. a pattern of horizontal scanning lines traced by an electron beam, esp. on a television screen. [C20: via G from L: rake, from *rādere* to scrape]

rat (ræt) n. **1.** any of numerous long-tailed Old World rodents, that are similar to but larger than mice and are now distributed all over the world. **2.** Inf. a person who deserts his friends or associates, esp. in time of trouble. **3.** Inf. a worker who works during a strike; blackleg; scab. **4.** Inf. a despicable person. **5. have** or **be rats.** Austral. sl. to be mad or eccentric. **6. smell a rat.** to detect something suspicious. ~vb. **ratting, ratted. 7.** (intr.; usually foll. by *on*) **a.** to divulge secret information (about); betray the trust (of). **b.** to default (on); abandon. **8.** to hunt and kill rats. [OE *rætt*]

rata ('rɑːtə) *n.* a New Zealand tree with red flowers. [from Maori]

ratable *or* **rateable** ('reɪtəbᵊl) *adj.* **1.** able to be rated or evaluated. **2.** *Brit.* (of property) liable to payment of rates. —,**rata'bility** *or* ,**ratea'bility** *n.* —'**ratably** *or* '**rateably** *adv.*

ratable value *or* **rateable value** *n. Brit.* a fixed value assigned to a property by a local authority, on the basis of which variable annual rates are charged.

ratafia (,rætə'fiə) *or* **ratafee** (,rætə'fiː) *n.* **1.** any liqueur made from fruit or from brandy with added fruit. **2.** a flavouring essence made from almonds. **3.** *Chiefly Brit.* Also called: **ratafia biscuit.** a small macaroon flavoured with almonds. [C17: from West Indian Creole F]

ratan (ræ'tæn) *n.* a variant spelling of **rattan.**

ratatat-tat ('rætə,tæt'tæt) *or* **ratatat** ('rætə'tæt) *n.* the sound of knocking on a door.

ratatouille (,rætə'twiː) *n.* a vegetable casserole made of tomatoes, aubergines, peppers, etc., fried in oil and stewed slowly. [C19: from F, from *touiller* to stir, from L, from *tudes* hammer]

ratbag ('ræt,bæg) *n. Sl.* an eccentric, stupid, or unreliable person.

rat-catcher *n.* a person whose job is to destroy or drive away vermin, esp. rats.

ratchet ('rætʃɪt) *n.* **1.** a device in which a toothed rack or wheel is engaged by a pawl to permit motion in one direction only. **2.** the toothed rack or wheel forming part of such a device. [C17: from F *rochet*, from OF *rocquet* blunt head of a lance, of Gmc origin]

rate[1] (reɪt) *n.* **1.** a quantity or amount considered in relation to or measured against another quantity or amount: *a rate of 70 miles an hour.* **2.** a price or charge with reference to a standard or scale: *rate of interest.* **3.** a charge made per unit for a commodity, service, etc. **4.** See **rates.** **5.** the relative speed of progress or change of something variable; pace: *the rate of production has doubled.* **6. a.** relative quality; class or grade. **b.** (*in combination*): *first-rate ideas.* **7. at any rate.** in any case; at all events; anyway. ~*vb.* (*mainly tr.*) **8.** (*also intr.*) to assign or receive a position on a scale of relative values; rank: *he is rated fifth in the world.* **9.** to estimate the value of; evaluate: *we rate your services highly.* **10.** to be worthy of; deserve: *this hotel does not rate four stars.* **11.** to consider; regard: *I rate him among my friends.* **12.** *Brit.* to assess the value of (property) for the purpose of local taxation. [C15: from OF, from Med. L *rata*, from L *prō ratā parte* according to a fixed proportion, from *ratus* fixed, from *rērī* to think, decide]

▷ **Usage.** The use of the verb *rate* alone with the sense of thinking highly of something is avoided in careful usage: *the clients do not think highly of* (not *do not rate*) *the new system.*

rate[2] (reɪt) *vb.* (*tr.*) to scold or criticize severely; rebuke harshly. [C14: ? rel. to Swedish *rata* to chide]

rateable ('reɪtəbᵊl) *adj.* a variant spelling of **ratable.**

rate-cap ('reɪt,kæp) *vb.* (*tr.*) **-capping, -capped.** (in Britain) to impose on (a local authority) an upper limit on the rate it may levy. — '**rate-,capping** *n.*

ratel ('reɪtᵊl) *n.* a carnivorous mammal related to the badger family, inhabiting wooded regions of Africa and S Asia. It has a massive body, strong claws, and a thick coat that is paler on the back. It feeds on honey and small animals. [C18: from Afrik.]

rate of exchange *n.* See **exchange rate.**

ratepayer ('reɪt,peɪə) *n. Brit.* a person who pays local rates, esp. a householder.

rates (reɪts) *pl. n. Brit.* a tax on property levied by a local authority.

rate support grant *n.* (in Britain) a government grant paid to a local authority to finance a proportion of its expenditure.

Rathenau (*German* 'rɑːtənau) *n.* **Walther** ('valtər). 1867–1922, German industrialist and statesman: he organized the German war industries during World War I, became minister of reconstruction (1921) and of foreign affairs (1922), and was largely responsible for the treaty of Rapallo with Russia. His assassination by right-wing extremists caused a furore.

rather ('rɑːðə) *adv.* (*in senses 1-4, not used with a negative*) **1.** relatively or fairly; somewhat: *it's rather dull.* **2.** to a significant or noticeable extent; quite: *she's rather pretty.* **3.** to a limited extent or degree: *I rather thought that was the case.* **4.** with better or more just cause: *this text is rather to be deleted than rewritten.* **5.** more readily or willingly; sooner: *I would rather not see you tomorrow.* ~*sentence connector.* **6.** on the contrary: *it's not cold. Rather, it's very hot.* ~*sentence substitute.* ('rɑː'ðɜː). **7.** an expression of strong affirmation: *Is it worth seeing? Rather!* [OE *hrathor* comp. of *hræth* READY, quick]

▷ **Usage.** Both *would* and *had* are used with *rather* in sentences such as *I would rather* (or *had rather*) *go to the film than to the play. Had rather* is less common and now widely regarded as slightly old-fashioned.

ratify ('rætɪ,faɪ) *vb.* **-fying, -fied.** (*tr.*) to give formal approval or consent to. [C14: via OF from L *ratus* fixed (see RATE[1]) + *facere* to make] — '**rati,fiable** *adj.* —,**ratifi'cation** *n.* — '**rati,fier** *n.*

rating[1] ('reɪtɪŋ) *n.* **1.** a classification according to order or grade; ranking. **2.** an ordinary seaman. **3.** *Sailing.* a handicap assigned to a racing boat based on its dimensions, draught, etc. **4.** the estimated financial or credit standing of a business enterprise or individual. **5.** *Radio, television, etc.* a figure based on statistical sampling indicating what proportion of the total audience tune in to a specific programme.

rating[2] ('reɪtɪŋ) *n.* a sharp scolding or rebuke.

ratio ('reɪʃɪəʊ) *n., pl.* **-tios. 1.** a measure of the relative size of two classes expressible as a proportion: *the ratio of boys to girls is 2 to 1.* **2.** *Maths.* a quotient of two numbers or quantities. See also **proportion** (sense 6). [C17: from L: a reckoning, from *rērī* to think]

ratiocinate (,rætɪ'ɒsɪ,neɪt) *vb.* (*intr.*) to think or argue logically and methodically; reason. [C17: from L *ratiōcinārī* to calculate, from *ratiō* REASON] —,**rati,oci'nation** *n.* —,**rati'oci,native** *adj.* —,**rati'oci,nator** *n.*

ration ('ræʃən) *n.* **1. a.** a fixed allowance of food, provisions, etc., esp. a statutory one for civilians in time of scarcity or soldiers in time of war. **b.** (*as modifier*): *a ration book.* **2.** a sufficient or adequate amount: *you've had your ration of television for today.* ~*vb.* (*tr.*) **3.** (often foll. by *out*) to distribute (provisions), esp. to an army. **4.** to restrict the distribution or consumption of (a commodity) by (people): *the government has rationed sugar.* ~See also **rations.** [C18: via F from L *ratiō* REASON]

rational ('ræʃənᵊl) *adj.* **1.** using reason or logic in thinking out a problem. **2.** in accordance with the principles of logic or reason; reasonable. **3.** of sound mind; sane: *the patient seemed quite rational.* **4.** endowed with the capacity to reason: *man is a rational being.* **5.** *Maths.* **a.** expressible as a ratio of two integers: *a rational number.* **b.** (of an expression, equation, etc.) containing no variable either in irreducible radical form or raised to a fractional power. ~*n.* **6.** a rational number. [C14: from L *ratiōnālis*, from *ratiō* REASON] —,**ratio'nality** *n.* —'**rationally** *adv.* —'**rationalness** *n.*

rationale (,ræʃə'nɑːl) *n.* a reasoned exposition, esp. one defining the fundamental reasons for an action, etc. [C17: from NL, from L *ratiōnālis*]

rationalism ('ræʃənə,lɪzəm) *n.* **1.** reliance on reason rather than intuition to justify one's beliefs or actions. **2.** *Philosophy.* the doctrine that knowledge is acquired by reason without regard to experience. **3.** the belief that knowledge and truth are ascertained by rational thought and not by divine or supernatural revelation. —'**rationalist** *n.* —,**rational'istic** *adj.* —,**rational'istically** *adv.*

rationalize *or* **-ise** ('ræʃənə,laɪz) *vb.* **1.** to justify (one's actions) with plausible reasons, esp. after the event. **2.** to apply logic or reason to (something). **3.** (*tr.*) to eliminate unnecessary equipment, etc., from (a factory, etc.), in order to make it more efficient. **4.** (*tr.*) *Maths.* to eliminate radicals without changing the value of (an expression) or the roots of (an equation). —,**rationali'zation** *or* **-i'sation** *n.* —'**rational,izer** *or* **-,iser** *n.*

rational number *n.* any real number of the form a/b, where a and b are integers and b is not zero, as 7 or 7/3.

rations ('ræʃənz) *pl. n.* (*sometimes sing.*) a fixed daily allowance of food, esp. to military personnel or when supplies are limited.

Ratisbon ('rætɪz,bɒn) *n.* the former English name for **Regensburg.**

ratite ('rætaɪt) *adj.* **1.** (of flightless birds) having a breast-bone that lacks a keel for the attachment of flight mus-cles. **2.** of or denoting the flightless birds, that have a flat breastbone, feathers lacking vanes, and reduced wings. ~*n.* **3.** a bird, such as an ostrich that belongs to this group; a flightless bird. [C19: from L *ratis* raft]

rat kangaroo *n.* any of several ratlike kangaroos that oc-cur in Australia and Tasmania.

ratline *or* **ratlin** ('rætlɪn) *n. Naut.* any of a series of light lines tied across the shrouds of a sailing vessel for climb-ing aloft. [C15: from ?]

ratoon *or* **rattoon** (ræ'tuːn) *n.* **1.** a new shoot that grows from near the root of crop plants, esp. the sugar cane, af-ter the old growth has been cut back. ~*vb.* **2.** to propa-gate by such a growth. [C18: from Sp. *retoño*, from RE- + *otoñar* to sprout in autumn, from *otoño* AUTUMN]

rat race *n.* a continual routine of hectic competitive activ-ity: *working in the City is a real rat race.*

ratsbane ('ræts,beɪn) *n.* rat poison, esp. arsenic oxide.

rat-tail *n.* **1. a.** a horse's tail that has no hairs. **b.** a horse having such a tail. **2.** a style of spoon in which the line of the handle is prolonged in a tapering moulding along the back of the bowl.

rattan *or* **ratan** (ræ'tæn) *n.* **1.** a climbing palm having tough stems used for wickerwork and canes. **2.** the stems of such a plant collectively. **3.** a stick made from one of these stems. [C17: from Malay *rōtan*]

ratter ('rætə) *n.* **1.** a dog or cat that catches and kills rats. **2.** another word for **rat** (sense 3).

Rattigan ('rætɪgən) *n.* **Sir Terence Mervyn.** 1911–77, English playwright. His plays include *The Winslow Boy* (1946), *Separate Tables* (1954), and *Ross* (1960).

rattle ('ræt³l) *vb.* **1.** to make a rapid succession of short sharp sounds, as of loose pellets colliding when shaken in a container. **2.** to shake with such a sound. **3.** to send, move, drive, etc., with such a sound: *the car rattled along the country road.* **4.** (*intr.;* foll. by *on*) to chatter idly: *he rattled on about his work.* **5.** (*tr.;* foll. by *off, out,* etc.) to recite perfunctorily or rapidly. **6.** (*tr.*) *Inf.* to disconcert; make frightened or anxious. ~*n.* **7.** a rapid succession of short sharp sounds. **8.** a baby's toy filled with small pel-lets that rattle when shaken. **9.** a series of loosely con-nected horny segments on the tail of a rattlesnake, vibrated to produce a rattling sound. **10.** any of various European scrophulariaceous plants having a capsule in which the seeds rattle, such as the **red rattle** and the **yel-low rattle**. **11.** idle chatter. **12.** *Med.* another name for **rale**. [C14: from MDu. *ratelen*, imit.] —'rattly *adj.*

Rattle ('ræt³l) *n.* **Simon.** born 1955, British conductor. Principal conductor of the City of Birmingham Symphony Orchestra from 1980.

rattlebrain ('ræt³l,breɪn), **rattlehead,** *or* **rattlepate** *n. Sl.* a light-minded person, full of idle talk.

rattler ('rætlə) *n.* **1.** a person or thing that rattles. **2.** *Inf.* a rattlesnake.

rattlesnake ('ræt³l,sneɪk) *n.* any of the venomous New World snakes such as the **black** or **timber rattlesnake** belonging to the family of pit vipers. They have a series of loose horny segments on the tail that are vibrated to pro-duce a buzzing or whirring sound.

rattletrap ('ræt³l,træp) *n. Inf.* a broken-down old vehicle, esp. an old car.

rattling ('rætlɪŋ) *adv. Inf.* (intensifier qualifying some-thing good, fine, etc.): *a rattling good lunch.*

ratty ('rætɪ) *adj.* **-tier, -tiest. 1.** *Brit. & N.Z. inf.* irrita-ble; annoyed. **2.** *Inf.* (of the hair) straggly, unkempt, or greasy. **3.** *U.S. & Canad. sl.* shabby; dilapidated. **4.** *Aus-tral. sl.* mad, eccentric, or odd. **5.** of, like, or full of rats. —'rattily *adv.* —'rattiness *n.*

raucous ('rɔːkəs) *adj.* (of voices, cries, etc.) harshly or hoarsely loud. [C18: from L *raucus* hoarse] —'raucously *adv.* —'raucousness *n.*

raunchy ('rɔːntʃɪ) *adj.* **-chier, -chiest.** *Sl.* **1. a.** lecherous or smutty. **b.** openly sexual; earthy. **2.** *Chiefly U.S.* slov-enly; dirty. [C20: from ?] —'raunchily *adv.* —'raunchi-ness *n.*

raupo ('raʊpəʊ) *n., pl.* **-pos.** a marsh reed common in New Zealand. [from Maori]

Rauschenberg ('raʊʃənbɜːg) *n.* **Robert.** born 1925, U.S. artist; one of the foremost exponents of pop art.

rauwolfia (rɔː'wʊlfɪə, raʊ-) *n.* **1.** a tropical flowering tree or shrub of SE Asia with latex in its stem. **2.** the pow-dered root of this plant: a source of various drugs, esp.

reserpine. [C19: NL, after Leonhard *Rauwolf* (died 1596), G botanist]

ravage ('rævɪdʒ) *vb.* **1.** to cause extensive damage to. ~*n.* **2.** (*often pl.*) destructive action: *the ravages of time.* [C17: from F, from OF *ravir* to snatch away, RAVISH] —'ravager *n.*

rave (reɪv) *vb.* **1.** to utter (something) in a wild or inco-herent manner, as when delirious. **2.** (*intr.*) to speak in an angry uncontrolled manner. **3.** (*intr.*) (of the sea, wind, etc.) to rage or roar. **4.** (*intr.;* foll. by *over* or *about*) *Inf.* to write or speak (about) with great enthusi-asm. **5.** (*intr.*) *Brit. sl.* to enjoy oneself wildly or uninhib-itedly. ~*n.* **6.** *Inf.* **a.** enthusiastic or extravagant praise. **b.** (*as modifier*): *a rave review.* **7.** Also called: **rave-up.** *Brit. sl.* a party. [C14 *raven*, apparently from OF *resver* to wander]

ravel ('ræv³l) *vb.* **-elling, -elled** *or U.S.* **-eling, -eled. 1.** to tangle (threads, fibres, etc.) or (of threads, etc.) to be-come entangled. **2.** (often foll. by *out*) to tease or draw out (the fibres of a fabric) or (of a fabric) to fray out in loose ends; unravel. **3.** (*tr.;* usually foll. by *out*) to disen-tangle or resolve: *to ravel out a complicated story.* ~*n.* **4.** a tangle or complication. [C16: from MDu. *ravelen*] —'raveller *n.* —'ravelly *adj.*

Ravel (*French* ravɛl) *n.* **Maurice (Joseph)** (mɔris). 1875–1937, French composer, noted for his use of unresolved dissonances and mastery of tone colour. His works in-clude *Gaspard de la Nuit* (1908) and *Le Tombeau de Couperin* (1917) for piano, *Boléro* (1928) for orchestra, and the ballet *Daphnis et Chloé* (1912).

raven[1] ('reɪv³n) *n.* **1.** a large passerine bird of the crow family, having a large straight bill, long wedge-shaped tail, and black plumage. **2. a.** a shiny black colour. **b.** (*as adj.*): *raven hair.* [OE *hræfn*]

raven[2] ('ræv³n) *vb.* **1.** to seize or seek (plunder, prey, etc.). **2.** to eat (something) voraciously or greedily. [C15: from OF *raviner* to attack impetuously; see RAVENOUS]

ravening ('rævənɪŋ) *adj.* (of animals) voracious; preda-tory. —'raveningly *adv.*

Ravenna (rə'vɛnə; *Italian* ra'venna) *n.* a city and port in NE Italy, in Emilia-Romagna: capital of the Western Ro-man Empire from 402 to 476, of the Ostrogoths from 493 to 526, and of the Byzantine exarchate from 584 to 751; famous for its ancient mosaics. Pop.: 136 016 (1986).

ravenous ('rævənəs) *adj.* **1.** famished; starving. **2.** rapa-cious; voracious. [C16: from OF *ravineux*, from L *rapina* plunder, from *rapere* to seize] —'ravenously *adv.* —'ravenousness *n.*

raver ('reɪvə) *n. Brit. sl.* a person who leads a wild or uninhibited social life.

ravine (rə'viːn) *n.* a deep narrow steep-sided valley. [C15: from OF: torrent, from L *rapīna* robbery, infl. by L *rapidus* RAPID, both from *rapere* to snatch]

raving ('reɪvɪŋ) *adj.* **1. a.** delirious; frenzied. **b.** (*as adv.*): *raving mad.* **2.** *Inf.* (intensifier): *a raving beauty.* ~*n.* **3.** (*usually pl.*) frenzied or wildly extravagant talk or utterances. —'ravingly *adv.*

ravioli (,rævɪ'əʊlɪ) *n.* small squares of pasta containing a savoury mixture of meat, cheese, etc. [C19: It. dialect, lit.: little turnips, from It. *rava* turnip, from L *rāpa*]

ravish ('rævɪʃ) *vb.* (*tr.*) **1.** (*often passive*) to enrapture. **2.** to rape. **3.** *Arch.* to carry off by force. [C13: from OF *ravir*, from L *rapere* to seize] —'ravisher *n.* —'ravish-ment *n.*

ravishing ('rævɪʃɪŋ) *adj.* delightful; lovely; entrancing. —'ravishingly *adv.*

raw (rɔː) *adj.* **1.** (of food) not cooked. **2.** (*prenominal*) in an unfinished, natural, or unrefined state; not treated by manufacturing or other processes: *raw materials.* **3.** (of the skin, a wound, etc.) having the surface exposed or ab-raded, esp. painfully. **4.** (of an edge of material) unhem-med; liable to fray. **5.** ignorant, inexperienced, or immature: *a raw recruit.* **6.** (*prenominal*) not selected or modified: *raw statistics.* **7.** frank or realistic: *a raw picture of a marriage.* **8.** (of spirits) undiluted. **9.** *Chiefly U.S.* coarse, vulgar, or obscene. **10.** (of the weather) harshly cold and damp. **11.** *Inf.* unfair; unjust (esp. in **a raw deal**). ~*n.* **12. in the raw. a.** *Inf.* without clothes; naked. **b.** in a natural or unmodified state. **13. the raw.** *Brit. inf.* a sensitive point: *his criticism touched me on the raw.* [OE *hreaw*] —'rawish *adj.* —'rawly *adv.* —'rawness *n.*

Rawalpindi (rɔːlˈpɪndɪ) *n.* an ancient city in N Pakistan: interim capital of Pakistan (1959–67) during the building of Islamabad. Pop.: 928 000 (1981).
rawboned (ˈrɔːˈbəʊnd) *adj.* having a lean bony physique.
rawhide (ˈrɔːˌhaɪd) *n.* **1.** untanned hide. **2.** a whip or rope made of strips cut from such a hide.
rawinsonde (ˈreɪwɪnˌsɒnd) *n.* a hydrogen balloon carrying meteorological instruments and a radar target, enabling the velocity of winds in the atmosphere to be measured. [C20: blend of *radar* + *wind* + *radiosonde*]
raw material *n.* **1.** material on which a particular manufacturing process is carried out. **2.** a person or thing regarded as suitable for some particular purpose: *raw material for the army.*
raw silk *n.* **1.** untreated silk fibres reeled from the cocoon. **2.** fabric woven from such fibres.
Rawsthorne (ˈrɔːsˌθɔːn) *n.* **Alan.** 1905–71, English composer, whose works include three symphonies, several concertos, and a set of *Symphonic Studies* (1939).
ray[1] (reɪ) *n.* **1.** a narrow beam of light; gleam. **2.** a slight indication: *a ray of solace.* **3.** *Maths.* a straight line extending from a point. **4.** a thin beam of electromagnetic radiation or particles. **5.** any of the bony or cartilaginous spines of the fin of a fish that form the support for the soft part of the fin. **6.** any of the arms or branches of a starfish. ~*vb.* **7.** (of an object) to emit (light) in rays or (of light) to issue in the form of rays. **8.** (*intr.*) (of lines, etc.) to extend in rays or on radiating paths. **9.** (*tr.*) to adorn (an ornament, etc.) with rays or radiating lines. [C14: from OF *rai*, from L *radius* spoke]
ray[2] (reɪ) *n.* any of various marine selachian fishes typically having a flattened body, greatly enlarged winglike pectoral fins, gills on the undersurface of the fins, and a long whiplike tail. [C14: from OF *raie*, from L *raia*]
ray[3] (reɪ) *n. Music.* (in tonic sol-fa) the second degree of any major scale; supertonic. [C14: see GAMUT]
Ray[1] (reɪ) *n.* **Cape.** a promontory in SW Newfoundland, Canada.
Ray[2] (reɪ) *n.* **1. John.** 1627–1705, English naturalist. He originated natural botanical classification and the division of flowering plants into monocotyledons and dicotyledons. **2. Man,** real name *Emmanuel Rudnitsky.* 1890–1976, U.S. surrealist photographer. **3. Satyajit** (ˈsætjədʒɪt). born 1921, Indian film director.
ray flower *or* **floret** *n.* any of the small strap-shaped flowers in the flower head of certain composite plants, such as the daisy.
ray gun *n.* (in science fiction) a gun that emits rays to paralyse, stun, or destroy.
Rayleigh (ˈreɪlɪ) *n.* **Lord,** title of *John William Strutt,* 1842–1919, English physicist. He discovered argon (1894) with Ramsay and made important contributions to the theory of sound: Nobel prize for physics 1904.
rayless (ˈreɪlɪs) *adj.* **1.** dark; gloomy. **2.** lacking rays: *a rayless flower.*
raylet (ˈreɪlɪt) *n.* a small ray.
rayon (ˈreɪɒn) *n.* **1.** any of a number of textile fibres made from wood pulp or other forms of cellulose. **2.** any fabric made from such a fibre. **3.** (*as modifier*): *a rayon shirt.* [C20: from F, from OF *rai* RAY[1]]
raze *or* **rase** (reɪz) *vb.* (*tr.*) **1.** to demolish (buildings, etc.) completely (esp. in **raze to the ground**). **2.** to delete; erase. **3.** *Arch.* to graze. [C16: from OF *raser*, from L *rādere* to scrape] —ˈ**razer** *or* ˈ**raser** *n.*
razoo (rɑːˈzuː) *n., pl.* **-zoos.** *Austral. & N.Z. inf.* an imaginary coin: *not a brass razoo; they took every last razoo.* [C20: from ?]
razor (ˈreɪzə) *n.* **1.** a sharp implement used esp. for shaving the face. **2. on a razor's edge** *or* **razor-edge.** in an acute dilemma. ~*vb.* **3.** (*tr.*) to cut or shave with a razor. [C13: from OF *raseor*, from *raser* to shave; see RAZE]
razorback (ˈreɪzəˌbæk) *n.* **1.** Also called: **finback.** another name for the **common rorqual** (see **rorqual**). **2.** a wild pig of the U.S., having a narrow body, long legs, and a ridged back.
razorbill (ˈreɪzəˌbɪl) *or* **razor-billed auk** *n.* a common auk of the North Atlantic, having a thick laterally compressed bill with white markings.
razor blade *n.* a small rectangular piece of metal sharpened on one or both long edges for use in a razor for shaving.
razor-shell *n.* any of various sand-burrowing bivalve molluscs which have a long tubular shell. U.S. name: **razor clam.**
razor wire *n.* strong wire with pieces of sharp metal set across it at close intervals.
razz (ræz) *U.S. & Canad. sl.* ~*vb.* **1.** (*tr.*) to make fun of; deride. ~*n.* **2.** short for **raspberry** (sense 4).
razzle-dazzle (ˈræzəlˈdæzəl) *or* **razzmatazz** (ˈræzməˈtæz) *n. Sl.* **1.** noisy or showy fuss or activity. **2.** a spree or frolic. [C19: rhyming compound from DAZZLE]
Rb *the chemical symbol for* rubidium.
RC *abbrev. for:* **1.** Red Cross. **2.** Roman Catholic.
RCA *abbrev. for:* **1.** Radio Corporation of America. **2.** Royal College of Art.
RCAF *abbrev. for* Royal Canadian Air Force.
RC CH *abbrev. for* Roman Catholic Church.
RCM *abbrev. for* Royal College of Music.
RCMP *abbrev. for* Royal Canadian Mounted Police.
RCN *abbrev. for:* **1.** Royal Canadian Navy. **2.** Royal College of Nursing.
RCP *abbrev. for* Royal College of Physicians.
RCS *abbrev. for:* **1.** Royal College of Science. **2.** Royal College of Surgeons. **3.** Royal Corps of Signals.
rd *abbrev. for:* **1.** road. **2.** rod (unit of length). **3.** round. **4.** *Physics.* rutherford.
Rd *abbrev. for* Road.
RDC (in Britain, formerly) *abbrev. for* Rural District Council.
re[1] (reɪ, riː) *n. Music.* a variant of **ray**[3].
re[2] (riː) *prep.* with reference to. [C18: from L *rē*, ablative case of *rēs* thing]
▷ **Usage.** *Re,* in contexts such as *re your letter, your remarks have been noted* or *he spoke to me re your complaint,* is common in business. In general English *with reference to* is preferable in the former case and *about* or *concerning* in the latter. The use of *re* is often restricted to the letter heading.
Re[1] (reɪ) *n.* another name for **Ra.**
Re[2] *the chemical symbol for* rhenium.
RE *abbrev. for:* **1.** Religious Education. **2.** Royal Engineers.
re- *prefix.* **1.** indicating return to a previous condition, withdrawal, etc.: *rebuild; renew.* **2.** indicating repetition of an action: *remarry.* [L]
▷ **Usage.** Verbs with *re-* indicate repetition or restoration. It is unnecessary to add an adverb such as *back* or *again: This must not occur again* (not *recur again*).
reach (riːtʃ) *vb.* **1.** (*tr.*) to arrive at or get to (a place, person, etc.) in the course of movement or action: *to reach the office.* **2.** to extend as far as (a point or place): *to reach the ceiling; can you reach?* **3.** (*tr.*) to come to (a certain condition or situation): *to reach the point of starvation.* **4.** (*intr.*) to extend in influence or operation: *the Roman conquest reached throughout England.* **5.** (*tr.*) *Inf.* to pass or give (something to a person) with the outstretched hand. **6.** (*intr.;* foll. by *out, for,* or *after*) to make a movement (towards), as if to grasp or touch. **7.** (*tr.*) to make contact or communication with (someone): *we tried to reach him all day.* **8.** (*tr.*) to strike, esp. in fencing or boxing. **9.** (*tr.*) to amount to (a certain sum): *to reach five million.* **10.** (*intr.*) *Naut.* to sail on a tack with the wind on or near abeam. ~*n.* **11.** the act of reaching. **12.** the extent or distance of reaching: *within reach.* **13.** the range of influence, power, etc. **14.** an open stretch of water, esp. on a river. **15.** *Naut.* the direction or distance sailed by a vessel on one tack. [OE *rǣcan*] —ˈ**reachable** *adj.* —ˈ**reacher** *n.*
reach-me-down *n.* **1. a.** (*often pl.*) a cheaply ready-made or second-hand garment. **b.** (*as modifier*): *reach-me-down finery.* **2.** (*modifier*) not original; derivative: *reach-me-down ideas.*
react (rɪˈækt) *vb.* **1.** (*intr.;* foll. by *to, upon,* etc.) (of a person or thing) to act in response to another person, a stimulus, etc. **2.** (*intr.;* foll. by *against*) to act in an opposing or contrary manner. **3.** (*intr.*) *Physics.* to exert an equal force in the opposite direction to an acting force. **4.**

ˌ**reabˈsorb** *vb.*
ˌ**reacˈcept** *vb.*
ˌ**reacˈceptance** *n.*
ˌ**reacˈclaim** *vb.*
ˌ**reacˈcredit** *vb.*
ˌ**reacˈcustom** *vb.*
ˌ**reaˈcidiˌfy** *vb.*
ˌ**reacˈquaint** *vb.*
ˌ**reacˈquaintance** *n.*
ˌ**reacˈquire** *vb.*
ˌ**reacquiˈsition** *n.*

Chem. to undergo or cause to undergo a chemical reaction. [C17: from LL *reagere*, from RE- + L *agere* to do] —**re'active** *adj.*

re-act (ri:'ækt) *vb.* (*tr.*) to act or perform again.

reactance (rɪ'æktəns) *n.* the opposition to the flow of alternating current by the capacitance or inductance of an electrical circuit.

reactant (rɪ'æktənt) *n.* a substance that participates in a chemical reaction.

reaction (rɪ'ækʃən) *n.* **1.** a response to some foregoing action or stimulus. **2.** the reciprocal action of two things acting together. **3.** opposition to change, esp. political change, or a desire to return to a former system. **4.** a response indicating a person's feelings or emotional attitude. **5.** *Med.* **a.** any effect produced by the action of a drug. **b.** any effect produced by a substance (allergen) to which a person is allergic. **6.** *Chem.* a process that involves changes in the structure and energy content of atoms, molecules, or ions. **7.** the equal and opposite force that acts on a body whenever it exerts a force on another body. —**re'actional** *adj.*

reactionary (rɪ'ækʃənərɪ, -ʃənrɪ) *or* **reactionist** *adj.* **1.** of, relating to, or characterized by reaction, esp. against radical political or social change. ~*n.*, *pl.* -**aries** *or* -**ists**. **2.** a person opposed to radical change. —**re'actionism** *n.*

reaction engine *or* **motor** *n.* an engine, such as a jet engine, that ejects gas at high velocity and develops its thrust from the ensuing reaction.

reaction turbine *n.* a turbine in which the working fluid is accelerated by expansion in both the static nozzles and the rotor blades.

reactivate (rɪ'æktɪˌveɪt) *vb.* (*tr.*) to make (something) active again. —**re,acti'vation** *n.*

reactor (rɪ'æktə) *n.* **1.** *Chem.* a substance, such as a reagent, that undergoes a reaction. **2.** short for **nuclear reactor**. **3.** a vessel in which a chemical reaction takes place. **4.** a coil of low resistance and high inductance that introduces reactance into a circuit. **5.** *Med.* a person sensitive to a particular drug or agent.

read[1] (ri:d) *vb.* **reading, read** (rɛd). **1.** to comprehend the meaning of (something written or printed) by looking at and interpreting the written or printed characters. **2.** (when *tr.*, often foll. by *out*) to look at, interpret, and speak aloud (something written or printed). **3.** (*tr.*) to interpret the significance or meaning of through scrutiny and recognition: *to read a map.* **4.** (*tr.*) to interpret or understand the meaning of (signs, characters, etc.) other than by visual means: *to read Braille.* **5.** (*tr.*) to have sufficient knowledge of (a language) to understand the written or printed word. **6.** (*tr.*) to discover or make out the true nature or mood of: *to read someone's mind.* **7.** to interpret or understand (something read) in a specified way: *I read this speech as satire.* **8.** (*tr.*) to adopt as a reading in a particular passage: *for "boon" read "bone".* **9.** (*intr.*) to have or contain a certain form or wording: *the sentence reads as follows.* **10.** to undertake a course of study in (a subject): *to read history.* **11.** to gain knowledge by reading: *he read about the war.* **12.** (*tr.*) to register, indicate, or show: *the meter reads 100.* **13.** (*tr.*) to put into a specified condition by reading: *to read a child to sleep.* **14.** (*tr.*) to hear and understand, esp. when using a two-way radio: *we are reading you loud and clear.* **15.** *Computers.* to obtain (data) from a storage device, such as magnetic tape. **16. read a lesson** (*or* **lecture**). *Inf.* to censure or reprimand. ~*n.* **17.** matter suitable for reading: *this book is a very good read.* **18.** the act or a spell of reading. ~See also **read into, read out**, etc. [OE *rǣdan* to advise, explain]

read[2] (rɛd) *vb.* **1.** the past tense and past participle of **read**[1]. ~*adj.* **2.** having knowledge gained from books (esp. in **widely read** and **well-read**). **3. take (something) as read.** to take (something) for granted as a fact; understand or presume.

readable ('ri:dəb²l) *adj.* **1.** (of handwriting, etc.) able to be read or deciphered; legible. **2.** (of style of writing) interesting, easy, or pleasant to read. —,**reada'bility** *or* '**readableness** *n.* —'**readably** *adv.*

Reade (ri:d) *n.* **Charles.** 1814–84, English novelist: author of *The Cloister and the Hearth* (1861), a historical romance.

reader ('ri:də) *n.* **1.** a person who reads. **2.** *Chiefly Brit.* a member of staff below a professor but above a senior lecturer at a university. **3. a.** a book that is part of a planned series for those learning to read. **b.** a standard textbook, esp. for foreign-language learning. **4.** a person who reads aloud in public. **5.** a person who reads and assesses the merit of manuscripts submitted to a publisher. **6.** a proofreader. **7.** short for **lay reader**.

readership ('ri:dəʃɪp) *n.* all the readers collectively of a particular publication or author: *a readership of five million.*

reading ('ri:dɪŋ) *n.* **1. a.** the act of a person who reads. **b.** (*as modifier*): *a reading room.* **2. a.** ability to read. **b.** (*as modifier*): *a child of reading age.* **3.** any matter that can be read; written or printed text. **4.** a public recital or rendering of a literary work. **5.** the form of a particular word or passage in a given text, esp. where more than one version exists. **6.** an interpretation, as of a piece of music, a situation, or something said or written. **7.** knowledge gained from books: *a person of little reading.* **8.** a measurement indicated by a gauge, dial, scientific instrument, etc. **9.** *Parliamentary procedure.* **a.** the formal recital of the body or title of a bill in a legislative assembly in order to begin one of the stages of its passage. **b.** one of the three stages in the passage of a bill through a legislative assembly. See **first reading, second reading, third reading**. **10.** the formal recital of something written, esp. a will.

Reading ('rɛdɪŋ) *n.* a town in S England, administrative centre of Berkshire, on the River Thames: university (1892). Pop.: 123 731 (1981).

read into (ri:d) *vb.* (*tr.*, *prep.*) to discern in or infer from a statement (meanings not intended by the speaker or writer).

read out (ri:d) *vb.* (*adv.*) **1.** (*tr.*) to read (something) aloud. **2.** (*tr.*) *U.S.* to expel (someone) from a political party or other society. **3.** to retrieve information from a computer memory or storage device. ~*n.* **read-out. 4. a.** the act of retrieving information from a computer memory or storage device. **b.** the information retrieved.

read up (ri:d) *vb.* (*adv.*; when *intr.*, often foll. by *on*) to acquire information about (a subject) by reading intensively.

read-write head ('ri:d'raɪt) *n.* *Computers.* an electromagnet that can both read and write information on a magnetic tape or disk.

ready ('rɛdɪ) *adj.* **readier, readiest. 1.** in a state of completion or preparedness, as for use or action. **2.** willing or eager: *ready helpers.* **3.** prompt or rapid: *a ready response.* **4.** (*prenominal*) quick in perceiving; intelligent: *a ready mind.* **5.** (*postpositive*) (foll. by *to*) on the point (of) or liable (to): *ready to collapse.* **6.** (*postpositive*) conveniently near (esp. in **ready to hand**). **7. make** *or* **get ready.** to prepare (oneself or something) for use or action. ~*n.* **8.** *Inf.* (*often preceded by* the) short for **ready money. 9. at** *or* **to the ready. a.** (of a rifle) in the position adopted prior to aiming and firing. **b.** poised for use or action: *with pen at the ready.* ~*vb.* **readying, readied.** (*tr.*) **10.** to put in a state of readiness; prepare. [OE (*ge*)*rǣde*] —'**readily** *adv.* —'**readiness** *n.*

ready-made *adj.* **1.** made for purchase and immediate use by any customer. **2.** extremely convenient or ideally suited: *a ready-made solution.* **3.** unoriginal or conventional: *ready-made phrases.* ~*n.* **4.** a ready-made article, esp. a garment.

ready-mix *n.* **1.** (*modifier*) consisting of ingredients blended in advance, esp. of food that is ready to cook or eat after addition of milk or water: *a ready-mix cake.* **2.** concrete that is mixed before or during delivery to a building site.

ready money *n.* funds for immediate use; cash. Also: **the ready, the readies.**

ready reckoner *n.* a table of numbers used to facilitate simple calculations, esp. one for working out interest, etc.

ready-to-wear *adj.* (**ready to wear** *when postpositive*). **1.** (of clothes) not tailored for the wearer; of a standard size. ~*n.* **2.** an article or suit of such clothes.

,**rea'dapt** *vb.*
,**read'dress** *vb.*

,**read'journ** *vb.*
,**read'journment** *n.*

,**rea'djust** *vb.*
,**read'mission** *n.*

,**read'mit** *vb.*
,**rea'dopt** *vb.*

reafforest (ˌriːəˈfɒrɪst) *or* **reforest** *vb.* (*tr.*) to replant (an area that was formerly forested). —ˌreafˌforestˈation *or* ˌreforestˈation *n.*

Reagan (ˈreɪɡən) *n.* **Ronald.** born 1911, U.S. film actor and Republican statesman: Governor of California (1966–74): president of the U.S. (1981–89).

reagent (riːˈeɪdʒənt) *n.* a substance for use in a chemical reaction, esp. for use in chemical synthesis and analysis.

real[1] (rɪəl) *adj.* **1.** existing or occurring in the physical world; not imaginary, fictitious, or theoretical; actual. **2.** (*prenominal*) true; actual; not false: *the real reason.* **3.** (*prenominal*) deserving the name; rightly so called: *a real friend.* **4.** not artificial or simulated; genuine: *real fur.* **5.** (of food, etc.) traditionally made and having a distinct flavour: *real ale; real cheese.* **6.** *Philosophy.* existent or relating to actual existence (as opposed to nonexistent, potential, contingent, or apparent). **7.** (*prenominal*) *Econ.* (of prices, incomes, etc.) considered in terms of purchasing power rather than nominal currency value. **8.** (*prenominal*) denoting or relating to immovable property such as land and tenements: *real estate.* **9.** *Maths.* involving or containing real numbers alone; having no imaginary part. **10.** *Inf.* (intensifier): *a real genius.* **11. the real thing.** the genuine article, not a substitute. ~*n.* **12. for real.** *Sl.* not as a test or trial; in earnest. **13. the real.** that which exists in fact; reality. [C15: from OF *réel*, from LL *reālis*, from L *rēs* thing] —ˈrealness *n.*

real[2] (reɪˈɑːl) *n.*, *pl.* **reals** *or* **reales** (*Spanish* reˈales). a former small Spanish or Spanish-American silver coin. [C17: from Sp., lit.: royal, from L *rēgālis; see* REGAL]

real ale *n.* any beer which is allowed to ferment in the barrel and which is pumped up from the keg without using carbon dioxide.

real estate *n.* another term, chiefly U.S. and Canad., for **real property.**

realgar (rɪˈælɡə) *n.* a rare orange-red soft mineral consisting of arsenic sulphide in monoclinic crystalline form. [C14: via Med. L from Ar. *rahj al-ghar* powder of the mine]

realism (ˈrɪəˌlɪzəm) *n.* **1.** awareness or acceptance of the physical universe, events, etc., as they are, as opposed to the abstract or ideal. **2.** a style of painting and sculpture that seeks to represent the familiar or typical in real life. **3.** any similar style in other arts, esp. literature. **4.** *Philosophy.* the thesis that general terms refer to entities that have a real existence separate from the individuals which fall under them. **5.** *Philosophy.* the theory that physical objects continue to exist whether they are perceived or not. —ˈrealist *n.*

realistic (ˌrɪəˈlɪstɪk) *adj.* **1.** showing awareness and acceptance of reality. **2.** practical or pragmatic rather than ideal or moral. **3.** (of a book, etc.) depicting what is real and actual. **4.** of or relating to philosophical realism. —ˌrealˈistically *adv.*

reality (rɪˈælɪtɪ) *n.*, *pl.* **-ties. 1.** the state of things as they are or appear to be, rather than as one might wish them to be. **2.** something that is real. **3.** the state of being real. **4.** *Philosophy.* **a.** that which exists, independent of human awareness. **b.** the totality of facts. **5. in reality.** actually; in fact.

realize *or* **-ise** (ˈrɪəˌlaɪz) *vb.* **1.** (when *tr.*, *may take a clause as object*) to become conscious or aware of (something). **2.** (*tr.*, *often passive*) to bring (a plan, ambition, etc.) to fruition. **3.** (*tr.*) to give (a drama or film) the appearance of reality. **4.** (*tr.*) (of goods, property, etc.) to sell for or make (a certain sum): *this table realized £800.* **5.** (*tr.*) to convert (property or goods) into cash. **6.** (*tr.*) (of a musicologist or performer) to reconstruct (a composition) from an incomplete set of parts. —ˈrealˌizable *or* -ˌisable *adj.* —ˈrealˌizably *or* -ˌisably *adv.* —ˌrealiˈzation *or* -iˈsation *n.* —ˈrealˌizer *or* -ˌiser *n.*

real life *n.* actual human life, as lived by real people, esp. contrasted with the lives of fictional characters: *miracles don't happen in real life.*

really (ˈrɪəlɪ) *adv.* **1.** in reality; in actuality; assuredly: *it's really quite harmless.* **2.** truly; genuinely: *really beautiful.* ~*interj.* **3.** an exclamation of dismay, disapproval, doubt, surprise, etc. **4. not really?** an exclamation of surprise or polite doubt.
▷ *Usage.* See at **very.**

realm (rɛlm) *n.* **1.** a royal domain; kingdom: *peer of the realm.* **2.** a field of interest, study, etc.: *the realm of the occult.* [C13: from OF *reialme,* from L *regimen* rule, infl. by OF *reial,* from L *rēgālis* REGAL]

real number *n.* any rational or irrational number. See **number.**

real presence *n.* the doctrine that the body of Christ is actually present in the Eucharist.

real property *n. Property law.* immoveable property, esp. freehold land. Cf. **personal property.**

real tennis *n.* an ancient form of tennis played in a four-walled indoor court.

real-time *adj.* denoting or relating to a data-processing system in which a computer is on-line to a source of data and processes the data as it is generated.

realtor (ˈrɪəltə, -ˌtɔː) *n.* a U.S. word for an **estate agent,** esp. an accredited one. [C20: from REALTY + -OR[1]]

realty (ˈrɪəltɪ) *n.* another term for **real property.**

ream[1] (riːm) *n.* **1.** a number of sheets of paper, formerly 480 sheets (**short ream**) now 500 sheets (**long ream**) or 516 sheets (**printer's ream** or **perfect ream**). One ream is equal to 20 quires. **2.** (*often pl.*) *Inf.* a large quantity, esp. of written matter: *he wrote reams.* [C14: from OF, from Sp., from Ar. *rizmah* bale]

ream[2] (riːm) *vb.* (*tr.*) **1.** to enlarge (a hole) by use of a reamer. **2.** *U.S.* to extract (juice) from (a citrus fruit) using a reamer. [C19: ?from C14 *remen* to open up, from OE *rȳman* to widen]

reamer (ˈriːmə) *n.* **1.** a steel tool with a cylindrical or tapered shank around which longitudinal teeth are ground, used for smoothing the bores of holes accurately to size. **2.** *U.S.* a utensil with a conical projection used for extracting juice from citrus fruits.

reap (riːp) *vb.* **1.** to cut or harvest (a crop) from (a field). **2.** (*tr.*) to gain or get (something) as a reward for or result of some action or enterprise. [OE *riopan*] —ˈreapable *adj.*

reaper (ˈriːpə) *n.* **1.** a person who reaps or a machine for reaping. **2. the grim reaper.** death.

rear[1] (rɪə) *n.* **1.** the back or hind part. **2.** the area or position that lies at the back: *a garden at the rear of the house.* **3.** the section of a military force farthest from the front. **4.** an informal word for **buttocks** (see **buttock**). **5. bring up the rear.** to be at the back in a procession, race, etc. **6. in the rear.** at the back. **7.** (*modifier*) of or in the rear: *the rear side.* [C17: prob. from REARWARD or REARGUARD]

rear[2] (rɪə) *vb.* **1.** (*tr.*) to care for and educate (children) until maturity; raise. **2.** (*tr.*) to breed (animals) or grow (plants). **3.** (*tr.*) to place or lift (a ladder, etc.) upright. **4.** (*tr.*) to erect (a monument, building, etc.). **5.** (*intr.*; *often* foll. by *up*) (esp. of horses) to lift the front legs in the air and stand nearly upright. **6.** (*intr.*; *often* foll. by *up* or *over*) (esp. of tall buildings) to rise high; tower. **7.** (*intr.*) to start with anger, resentment, etc. [OE *ræran*] —ˈrearer *n.*

rear admiral *n.* an officer holding flag rank in any of certain navies junior to a vice admiral.

Reardon (ˈrɪədən) *n.* **Ray.** born 1932, Welsh snooker player: world champion 1970, 1973–76, 1978.

rearguard (ˈrɪəˌɡɑːd) *n.* **1.** a detachment detailed to protect the rear of a military formation, esp. in retreat. **2.** an entrenched or conservative element, as in a political party. **3.** (*modifier*) of, relating to, or characteristic of a rearguard: *a rearguard action.* [C15: from OF *rereguarde,* from *rer,* from L *retro* back + *guarde* GUARD]

rear light *or* **lamp** *n.* a red light, usually one of a pair, attached to the rear of a motor vehicle. U.S. and Canad. names: **taillight, tail lamp.**

ˌreafˈfirm *vb.*	ˌrealˈlot *vb.*	ˌreaniˈmation *n.*	ˌreapˈpointment *n.*
ˌreaffirˈmation *n.*	reˈalter *vb.*	ˌreapˈpear *vb.*	ˌreapˈportion *vb.*
ˌreaˈlign *vb.*	ˌrealterˈation *n.*	ˌreapˈpearance *n.*	ˌreapˈpraisal *n.*
ˌreaˈlignment *n.*	reˈanaˌlyse *vb.*	ˌreappliˈcation *n.*	ˌreapˈpraise *vb.*
reˈalloˌcate *vb.*	ˌreaˈnalysis *n.*	ˌreapˈply *vb.*	reˈargue *vb.*
ˌrealloˈcation *n.*	reˈaniˌmate *vb.*	ˌreapˈpoint *vb.*	

rearm (riː'ɑːm) *vb.* **1.** to arm again. **2.** (*tr.*) to equip (an army, etc.) with better weapons. —**re'armament** *n.*

rearmost ('rɪə,məʊst) *adj.* nearest the rear; coming last.

rear-view mirror *n.* a mirror on a motor vehicle enabling the driver to see traffic behind him.

rearward ('rɪəwəd) *adj., adv.* **1.** Also (for adv. only): **rearwards.** towards or in the rear. ~*n.* **2.** a position in the rear, esp. the rear division of a military formation. [C14 (*as n.*: the part of an army behind the main body of troops): from Anglo-F *rerewarde*, var. of *reregarde*; see REARGUARD]

Rea Silvia ('rɪə 'sɪlvɪə) *n.* a variant spelling of **Rhea Silvia.**

reason ('riːzᵊn) *n.* **1.** the faculty of rational argument, deduction, judgment, etc. **2.** sound mind; sanity. **3.** a cause or motive, as for a belief, action, etc. **4.** an argument in favour or a justification for something. **5.** *Philosophy.* the intellect regarded as a source of knowledge, as contrasted with experience. **6.** *Logic.* a premise of an argument in favour of the given conclusion. **7. by reason of.** because of. **8. in or within reason.** within moderate or justifiable bounds. **9. it stands to reason.** it is logical or obvious. **10. listen to reason.** to be persuaded peaceably. **11. reasons of State.** political justifications for an immoral act. ~*vb.* **12.** (when *tr.*, *takes a clause as object*) to think logically or draw (logical conclusions) from facts or premises. **13.** (*intr.*; usually foll. by *with*) to seek to persuade by reasoning. **14.** (*tr.*; often foll. by *out*) to work out or resolve (a problem) by reasoning. [C13: from OF *reisun*, from L *ratiō* reckoning, from *rēri* to think] —'**reasoner** *n.*

▷ **Usage.** Careful users of English avoid the expression *the reason is because...* since *the reason is...* and *because* mean the same thing. *Because* should be replaced by *that: the reason is that...*

reasonable ('riːzənəbᵊl) *adj.* **1.** showing reason or sound judgment. **2.** having the ability to reason. **3.** having modest or moderate expectations. **4.** moderate in price. **5.** fair; average: *reasonable weather.* —'**reasonably** *adv.* —'**reasonableness** *n.*

reasoned ('riːzᵊnd) *adj.* well thought-out or well presented: *a reasoned explanation.*

reasoning ('riːzənɪŋ) *n.* **1.** the act or process of drawing conclusions from facts, evidence, etc. **2.** the arguments, proofs, etc., so adduced.

reassure (,riːə'ʃʊə) *vb.* (*tr.*) **1.** to relieve (someone) of anxieties; restore confidence to. **2.** to insure again. —,reas'surance *n.* —,reas'surer *n.* —,reas'suringly *adv.*

Réaumur ('reɪə,mjʊə) *adj.* indicating measurement on the Réaumur scale.

Réaumur scale *n.* a scale of temperature in which the freezing point of water is taken as 0° and the boiling point as 80°. [C18: after René de *Réaumur* (1683–1757), F physicist, who introduced it]

reave (riːv) *vb.* **reaving, reaved** *or* **reft.** *Arch.* **1.** to carry off (property, prisoners, etc.) by force. **2.** (*tr.*; foll. by *of*) to deprive; strip. See **reive.** [OE *rēafian*]

rebate[1] *n.* ('riːbeɪt). **1.** a refund of a fraction of the amount payable; discount. ~*vb.* (rɪ'beɪt). (*tr.*) **2.** to deduct (a part) of a payment from (the total). **3.** *Arch.* to reduce. [C15: from OF *rabattre* to beat down, hence reduce, from RE- + *abatre* to put down] —**re'batable** *or* **re'bateable** *adj.* —**re'bater** *n.*

rebate[2] ('riːbeɪt, 'ræbɪt) *n., vb.* another word for **rabbet.**

rebec *or* **rebeck** ('riːbɛk) *n.* a medieval stringed instrument resembling the violin but having a lute-shaped body. [C16: from OF *rebebe*, from Ar. *rebāb*; ? infl. by OF *bec* beak]

Rebecca (rɪ'bɛkə) *n. Old Testament.* the sister of Laban, who became the wife of Isaac and the mother of Esau and Jacob (Genesis 24–27). Douay spelling: **Rebekah.**

rebel *vb.* (rɪ'bɛl). **-belling, -belled.** (*intr.*; often foll. by *against*) **1.** to resist or rise up against a government or authority, esp. by force of arms. **2.** to dissent from an accepted moral code or convention of behaviour, etc. **3.** to show repugnance (towards). ~*n.* ('rɛbᵊl). **4. a.** a person who rebels. **b.** (*as modifier*): *a rebel soldier.* **5.** a person who dissents from some accepted moral code or convention of behaviour, etc. [C13: from OF *rebelle*, from L *rebellis* insurgent, from RE- + *bellum* war]

rebellion (rɪ'bɛljən) *n.* **1.** organized opposition to a government or other authority. **2.** dissent from an accepted moral code or convention of behaviour, etc. [C14: via OF from L *rebelliō* revolt (of those conquered); see REBEL]

rebellious (rɪ'bɛljəs) *adj.* **1.** showing a tendency towards rebellion. **2.** (of a problem, etc.) difficult to overcome; refractory. —**re'belliously** *adv.* —**re'belliousness** *n.*

rebirth (riː'bɜːθ) *n.* **1.** a revival or renaissance: *the rebirth of learning.* **2.** a second or new birth.

rebore *n.* ('riː,bɔː). **1.** the process of boring out the cylinders of a worn reciprocating engine and fitting oversize pistons. ~*vb.* (riː'bɔː). **2.** (*tr.*) to carry out this process.

rebound *vb.* (rɪ'baʊnd). (*intr.*) **1.** to spring back, as from a sudden impact. **2.** to misfire, esp. so as to hurt the perpetrator. ~*n.* ('riːbaʊnd). **3.** the act or an instance of rebounding. **4. on the rebound. a.** in the act of springing back. **b.** *Inf.* in a state of recovering from rejection, etc.: *he married her on the rebound from an unhappy love affair.* [C14: from OF *rebondir*, from RE- + *bondir* to BOUND[2]]

rebounder (rɪ'baʊndə) *n.* a type of small trampoline used for aerobic exercising.

rebozo (rɪ'bəʊzəʊ) *n., pl.* **-zos.** a long wool or linen scarf covering the shoulders and head, worn by Latin American women. [C19: from Sp., from *rebozar* to muffle]

rebuff (rɪ'bʌf) *vb.* (*tr.*) **1.** to snub, reject, or refuse (help, sympathy, etc.). **2.** to beat back (an attack); repel. ~*n.* **3.** a blunt refusal or rejection; snub. [C16: from OF *rebuffer*, from It., from *ribuffo* a reprimand, from *ri-* RE- + *buffo* puff, gust, apparently imit.]

rebuke (rɪ'bjuːk) *vb.* (*tr.*) to scold or reprimand (someone). ~*n.* **2.** a reprimand or scolding. [C14: from OF *rebuker*, from RE- + *buchier* to hack down, from *busche* log, of Gmc origin] —**re'bukable** *adj.* —**re'buker** *n.* —**re'bukingly** *adv.*

rebus ('riːbəs) *n., pl.* **-buses.** **1.** a puzzle consisting of pictures, symbols, etc., representing syllables and words; the word *hear* might be represented by H and a picture of an ear. **2.** a heraldic device that is a pictorial representation of the name of the bearer. [C17: from F *rébus*, from L *rēbus* by things from RES]

rebut (rɪ'bʌt) *vb.* **-butting, -butted.** (*tr.*) to refute or disprove, esp. by offering a contrary contention or argument. [C13: from OF *reboter*, from RE- + *boter* to thrust, BUTT[3]] —**re'buttable** *adj.* —**re'buttal** *n.*

rebutter (rɪ'bʌtə) *n.* **1.** *Law.* a defendant's pleading in reply to a plaintiff's surrejoinder. **2.** a person who rebuts.

rec. *abbrev. for:* **1.** receipt. **2.** recipe. **3.** record.

recalcitrant (rɪ'kælsɪtrənt) *adj.* **1.** not susceptible to control; refractory. ~*n.* **2.** a recalcitrant person. [C19: via F from L, from RE- + *calcitrāre* to kick, from *calx* heel] —**re'calcitrance** *n.*

recalescence (,riːkə'lɛsəns) *n.* a sudden spontaneous increase in the temperature of cooling iron. [C19: from L *recalēscere* to grow warm again, from RE- + *calēscere*, from *calēre* to be hot] —,recal'esce *vb.* (*intr.*) —,reca'lescent *adj.*

recall (rɪ'kɔːl) *vb.* (*tr.*) **1.** (*may take a clause as object*) to bring back to mind; recollect; remember. **2.** to order to return. **3.** to revoke or take back. **4.** to cause (one's thoughts, attention, etc.) to return from a reverie or digression. ~*n.* **5.** the act of recalling or state of being recalled. **6.** revocation or cancellation. **7.** the ability to remember things; recollection. **8.** *Mil.* (formerly) a signal to call back troops, etc. **9.** *U.S.* the process by which elected officials may be deprived of office by popular vote. —**re'callable** *adj.*

recant (rɪ'kænt) *vb.* to repudiate or withdraw (a former belief or statement), esp. formally in public. [C16: from L *recantāre*, from RE- + *cantāre* to sing] —**recantation** (ˌriːkænˈteɪʃən) *n.* —**re'canter** *n.*

recap *vb.* ('riːˌkæp, riːˈkæp), -**capping,** -**capped,** *n.* ('riːˌkæp). *Inf.* short for **recapitulate** or **recapitulation.** —**re'cappable** *adj.*

recapitulate (ˌriːkəˈpɪtjʊˌleɪt) *vb.* **1.** to restate the main points of (an argument, speech, etc.). **2.** (*tr.*) (of an animal) to repeat (stages of its evolutionary development) during the embryonic stages of its life. [C16: from LL *recapitulāre*, lit.: to put back under headings; see CAPITU-LATE] —ˌreca'pitulative *or* ˌreca'pitulatory *adj.*

recapitulation (ˌriːkəˌpɪtjʊˈleɪʃən) *n.* **1.** the act of recapitulating, esp. summing up, as at the end of a speech. **2.** Also called: **palingenesis.** *Biol.* the apparent repetition in the embryonic development of an animal of the changes that occurred during its evolutionary history. **3.** *Music.* the repeating of earlier themes, esp. in the final section of a movement in sonata form.

recapture (riːˈkæptʃə) *vb.* (*tr.*) **1.** to capture or take again. **2.** to recover, renew, or repeat (a lost or former ability, sensation, etc.). ~*n.* **3.** the act of recapturing or fact of being recaptured.

recce ('rɛkɪ) *n., vb.,* -**ceing,** -**ced** *or* -**ceed.** a slang word for **reconnaissance** or **reconnoitre.**

recd *or* **rec'd** *abbrev. for* received.

recede (rɪˈsiːd) *vb.* (*intr.*) **1.** to withdraw from a point or limit; go back: *the tide receded.* **2.** to become more distant: *hopes of rescue receded.* **3.** to slope backwards: *apes have receding foreheads.* **4. a.** (of a man's hair) to cease to grow at the temples and above the forehead. **b.** (of a man) to start to go bald in this way. **5.** to decline in value. **6.** (usually foll. by *from*) to draw back or retreat, as from a promise. [C15: from L *recēdere* to go back, from RE- + *cēdere* to yield]

re-cede (riːˈsiːd) *vb.* (*tr.*) to restore to a former owner.

receipt (rɪˈsiːt) *n.* **1.** a written acknowledgment by a receiver of money, goods, etc., that payment or delivery has been made. **2.** the act of receiving or fact of being received. **3.** (*usually pl.*) an amount or article received. **4.** *Obs.* another word for **recipe.** ~*vb.* **5.** (*tr.*) to acknowledge payment of (a bill), as by marking it. [C14: from OF *receite,* from Med. L *recepta,* from L *recipere* to RECEIVE]

receivable (rɪˈsiːvəbəl) *adj.* **1.** suitable for or capable of being received, esp. as payment or legal tender. **2.** (of a bill, etc.) awaiting payment: *accounts receivable.* ~*n.* **3.** (*usually pl.*) the part of the assets of a business represented by accounts due for payment.

receive (rɪˈsiːv) *vb.* (*mainly tr.*) **1.** to take (something offered) into one's hand or possession. **2.** to have (an honour, blessing, etc.) bestowed. **3.** to accept delivery or transmission of (a letter, etc.). **4.** to be informed of (news). **5.** to hear and consent to or acknowledge (a confession, etc.). **6.** (of a container) to take or hold (a substance, commodity, or certain amount). **7.** to support or sustain (the weight of something); bear. **8.** to apprehend or perceive (ideas, etc.). **9.** to experience, undergo, or meet with: *to receive a crack on the skull.* **10.** (*also intr.*) to be at home to (visitors). **11.** to greet or welcome (guests), esp. in formal style. **12.** to admit (a person) to a place, society, condition, etc.: *he was received into the priesthood.* **13.** to accept or acknowledge (a precept or principle) as true or valid. **14.** to convert (incoming radio signals) into sounds, pictures, etc., by means of a receiver. **15.** (*also intr.*) *Tennis, etc.* to play at the other end from the server. **16.** (*also intr.*) to partake of (the Christian Eucharist). **17.** (*intr.*) *Chiefly Brit.* to buy and sell stolen goods. [C13: from OF *receivre,* from L *recipere,* from RE- + *capere* to take]

received (rɪˈsiːvd) *adj.* generally accepted or believed: *received wisdom.*

Received Pronunciation *n.* the accent of standard Southern British English. Abbrev.: **RP.**

receiver (rɪˈsiːvə) *n.* **1.** a person who receives something; recipient. **2.** a person appointed by a court to manage property pending the outcome of litigation, during the infancy of the owner, or after the owner has been declared bankrupt or insane. **3.** *Chiefly Brit.* a person who receives stolen goods knowing that they have been stolen. **4.** the equipment in a telephone, radio, or television that receives incoming electrical signals or modulated radio

waves and converts them into the original audio or video signals. **5.** the detachable part of a telephone that is held to the ear. **6.** *Chem.* a vessel in which the distillate is collected during distillation. **7.** *U.S. sport.* a player whose function is to receive the ball.

receivership (rɪˈsiːvəʃɪp) *n. Law.* **1.** the office or function of a receiver. **2.** the condition of being administered by a receiver.

receiving order *n. Brit.* a court order appointing a receiver to manage the property of a debtor or bankrupt.

recension (rɪˈsɛnʃən) *n.* **1.** a critical revision of a literary work. **2.** a text revised in this way. [C17: from L *recēnsiō,* from *recēnsēre,* from RE- + *cēnsēre* to assess]

recent ('riːsᵊnt) *adj.* having appeared, happened, or been made not long ago; modern, fresh, or new. [C16: from L *recens* fresh; rel. to Gk *kainos* new] —'**recently** *adv.* —'**recentness** *or* '**recency** *n.*

Recent ('riːsᵊnt) *adj., n. Geol.* another word for **Holocene.**

receptacle (rɪˈsɛptəkᵊl) *n.* **1.** an object that holds something; container. **2.** *Bot.* **a.** the enlarged or modified tip of the flower stalk that bears the parts of the flower. **b.** the part of lower plants that bears the reproductive organs or spores. [C15: from L *receptāculum* store-place, from *receptāre,* from *recipere* to RECEIVE]

reception (rɪˈsɛpʃən) *n.* **1.** the act of receiving or state of being received. **2.** the manner in which something, such as a guest or a new idea, is received: *a cold reception.* **3.** a formal party for guests, such as after a wedding. **4.** an area in an office, hotel, etc., where visitors or guests are received and appointments or reservations dealt with. **5.** short for **reception room. 6.** the quality or fidelity of a received radio broadcast: *the reception was poor.* [C14: from L *receptiō,* from *recipere* to RECEIVE]

reception centre *n.* temporary accommodation provided in an emergency for homeless people.

receptionist (rɪˈsɛpʃənɪst) *n.* a person employed in an office, surgery, etc., to receive clients or guests, arrange appointments, etc.

reception room *n.* **1.** a room in a private house suitable for entertaining guests. **2.** a room in a hotel suitable for receptions, etc.

receptive (rɪˈsɛptɪv) *adj.* **1.** able to apprehend quickly. **2.** tending to receive new ideas or suggestions favourably. **3.** able to hold or receive. —**re'ceptively** *adv.* —**receptivity** (ˌriːsɛpˈtɪvɪtɪ) *or* **re'ceptiveness** *n.*

receptor (rɪˈsɛptə) *n.* **1.** *Physiol.* a sensory nerve ending that changes specific stimuli into nerve impulses. **2.** any of various devices that receive information, signals, etc.

recess *n.* (rɪˈsɛs, 'riːsɛs). **1.** a space, such as a niche or alcove, set back or indented. **2.** (*often pl.*) a secluded or secret place: *recesses of the mind.* **3.** a cessation of business, such as the closure of Parliament during a vacation. **4.** *Anat.* a small cavity or depression in a bodily organ. **5.** *U.S. & Canad.* a break between classes at a school. ~*vb.* (rɪˈsɛs). **6.** (*tr.*) to place or set (something) in a recess. **7.** (*tr.*) to build a recess in (a wall, etc.). [C16: from L *recessus* a retreat, from *recēdere* to RECEDE]

recession¹ (rɪˈsɛʃən) *n.* **1.** a temporary depression in economic activity or prosperity. **2.** the withdrawal of the clergy and choir in procession after a church service. **3.** the act of receding. **4.** a part of a building, wall, etc., that recedes. [C17: from L *recessiō;* see RECESS]

recession² (rɪˈsɛʃən) *n.* the act of restoring possession to a former owner. [C19: from RE- + CESSION]

recessional (rɪˈsɛʃənᵊl) *adj.* **1.** of or relating to recession. ~*n.* **2.** a hymn sung as the clergy and choir withdraw after a church service.

recessive (rɪˈsɛsɪv) *adj.* **1.** tending to recede or go back. **2.** *Genetics.* **a.** (of a gene) capable of producing its characteristic phenotype in the organism only when its allele is identical. **b.** (of a character) controlled by such a gene. Cf. **dominant** (sense 4). **3.** *Linguistics.* (of stress) tending to be placed on or near the initial syllable of a polysyllabic word. ~*n.* **4.** *Genetics.* a recessive gene or character. —**re'cessively** *adv.* —**re'cessiveness** *n.*

recharge (ˌriːˈtʃɑːdʒ) *vb.* (*tr.*) **1.** to cause (an accumulator, capacitor, etc.) to take up and store electricity again. **2.** to revive or renew (one's energies) (esp. in **recharge one's batteries**). —**re'chargeable** *adj.*

---

recherché (rə'ʃɛəʃeɪ) *adj.* **1.** known only to connoisseurs; choice or rare. **2.** studiedly refined or elegant. [C18: from F: p.p. of *rechercher* to make a thorough search for]

recidivism (rɪ'sɪdɪˌvɪzəm) *n.* habitual relapse into crime. [C19: from L *recidivus* falling back, from RE- + *cadere* to fall] —**re'cidivist** *n.*, *adj.* —**re**₁**cidi'vistic** *or* **re'cidivous** *adj.*

Recife (rɛ'siːfə) *n.* a port at the easternmost point of Brazil on the Atlantic: capital of Pernambuco state; built partly on an island, with many waterways and bridges. Pop.: 1 184 215 (1980). Former name: **Pernambuco**.

recipe ('rɛsɪpɪ) *n.* **1.** a list of ingredients and directions for making something, esp. when preparing food. **2.** *Med.* (formerly) a medical prescription. **3.** a method for achieving some desired objective: *a recipe for success.* [C14: from L, lit.: take (it)! from *recipere* to take]

recipient (rɪ'sɪpɪənt) *n.* **1.** a person who or thing that receives. ~*adj.* **2.** receptive. [C16: via F from L, from *recipere* to RECEIVE] —**re'cipience** *or* **re'cipiency** *n.*

reciprocal (rɪ'sɪprək³l) *adj.* **1.** of, relating to, or designating something given by each of two people, countries, etc., to the other; mutual: *reciprocal trade.* **2.** given or done in return: *a reciprocal favour.* **3.** (of a pronoun) indicating that action is given and received by each subject; for example, *each other* in *they started to shout at each other.* **4.** *Maths.* of or relating to a number or quantity divided into one. ~*n.* **5.** something that is reciprocal. **6.** Also called: **inverse.** *Maths.* a number or quantity that when multiplied by a given number or quantity gives a product of one: *the reciprocal of 2 is 0.5.* [C16: from L *reciprocus* alternating] —**re**₁**cipro'cality** *n.* —**re'ciprocally** *adv.*

reciprocate (rɪ'sɪprəˌkeɪt) *vb.* **1.** to give or feel in return. **2.** to move or cause to move backwards and forwards. **3.** (*intr.*) to be correspondent or equivalent. [C17: from L *reciprocāre*, from *reciprocus* RECIPROCAL] —**re**₁**cipro'cation** *n.* —**re'ciprocative** *or* **re'cipro**₁**catory** *adj.* —**re'cipro**₁**cator** *n.*

reciprocating engine *n.* an engine in which one or more pistons move backwards and forwards inside a cylinder or cylinders.

reciprocity (ˌrɛsɪ'prɒsɪtɪ) *n.* **1.** reciprocal action or relation. **2.** a mutual exchange of commercial or other privileges. [C18: via F from L *reciprocus* RECIPROCAL]

recision (rɪ'sɪʒən) *n.* the act of cancelling or rescinding; annulment: *the recision of a treaty.* [C17: from L *recisiō*, from *recīdere* to cut back]

recital (rɪ'saɪt³l) *n.* **1.** a musical performance by a soloist. **2.** the act of reciting or repeating something learned or prepared. **3.** an account, narration, or description. **4.** (*often pl.*) *Law.* the preliminary statement in a deed showing the reason for its existence and explaining the operative part. —**re'citalist** *n.*

recitation (ˌrɛsɪ'teɪʃən) *n.* **1.** the act of reciting from memory, esp. a formal reading of verse before an audience. **2.** something recited.

recitative¹ (ˌrɛsɪtə'tiːv) *n.* a passage in a musical composition, esp. the narrative parts in an oratorio, reflecting the natural rhythms of speech. [C17: from It. *recitativo*; see RECITE]

recitative² (rɪ'saɪtətɪv) *adj.* of or relating to recital.

recite (rɪ'saɪt) *vb.* **1.** to repeat (a poem, etc.) aloud from memory before an audience. **2.** (*tr.*) to give a detailed account of. **3.** (*tr.*) to enumerate (examples, etc.). [C15: from L *recitāre* to cite again, from RE- + *citāre* to summon] —**re'citable** *adj.* —**re'citer** *n.*

reck (rɛk) *vb. Arch.* (*used mainly with a negative*) **1.** to mind or care about (something): *to reck nought.* **2.** (*usually impersonal*) to concern or interest (someone). [OE *reccan*]

reckless ('rɛklɪs) *adj.* having or showing no regard for danger or consequences; heedless; rash: *a reckless driver.* [OE *recceleās*; see RECK, -LESS] —**'recklessly** *adv.* —**'recklessness** *n.*

Recklinghausen (*German* rɛklɪŋ'hauzən) *n.* an industrial city in NW West Germany, in North Rhine-Westphalia on the N edge of the Ruhr. Pop.: 117 600 (1986).

reckon ('rɛkən) *vb.* **1.** to calculate or ascertain by calculating; compute. **2.** (*tr.*) to include; count as part of a set or class. **3.** (*usually passive*) to consider or regard: *he is*

reckoned clever. **4.** (when *tr., takes a clause as object*) to think or suppose; be of the opinion: *I reckon you don't know.* **5.** (*intr.*; foll. by *with*) to settle accounts (with). **6.** (*intr.*; foll. by *with* or *without*) to take into account or fail to take into account: *they reckoned without John.* **7.** (*intr.*; foll. by *on* or *upon*) to rely or depend: *I reckon on your support.* **8.** (*tr.*) *Inf.* to have a high opinion of. **9. to be reckoned with.** of considerable importance or influence. [OE (*ge*)*recenian* recount]

▷ **Usage.** Some senses of *reckon* are considered informal. The usage *I reckon on your support* is avoided in formal contexts, while in the sentence *It will snow tonight, I reckon,* the words *believe, suppose, think,* or *imagine* are preferred.

reckoner ('rɛkənə) *n.* any of various devices or tables used to facilitate reckoning, esp. a ready reckoner.

reckoning ('rɛkənɪŋ) *n.* **1.** the act of counting or calculating. **2.** settlement of an account or bill. **3.** a bill or account. **4.** retribution for one's actions (esp. in **day of reckoning**). **5.** *Navigation.* short for **dead reckoning.**

reclaim (rɪ'kleɪm) *vb.* (*tr.*) **1.** to regain possession of. **2.** to convert (desert, marsh, etc.) into land suitable for growing crops. **3.** to recover (useful substances) from waste products. **4.** to convert (someone) from sin, folly, vice, etc. ~*n.* **5.** the act of reclaiming or state of being reclaimed. [C13: from OF *réclamer*, from L *reclāmāre* to cry out, from RE- + *clāmāre* to shout] —**re'claimable** *adj.* —**re'claimant** *or* **re'claimer** *n.*

reclamation (ˌrɛklə'meɪʃən) *n.* **1.** the conversion of desert, marsh, etc., into land suitable for cultivation. **2.** the recovery of useful substances from waste products. **3.** the act of reclaiming or state of being reclaimed.

réclame *French.* (reklam) *n.* **1.** public acclaim or attention; publicity. **2.** the capacity for attracting publicity.

reclinate ('rɛklɪˌneɪt) *adj. Bot.* naturally curved or bent backwards so that the upper part rests on the ground. [C18: from L *reclīnātus* bent back]

recline (rɪ'klaɪn) *vb.* to rest in a leaning position. [C15: from OF *recliner*, from L *reclīnāre*, from RE-+ *clīnāre* to LEAN¹] —**re'clinable** *adj.* —**reclination** (ˌrɛklɪ'neɪʃən) *n.*

recliner (rɪ'klaɪnə) *n.* a person or thing that reclines, esp. a type of armchair having a back that can be adjusted to slope at various angles.

recluse (rɪ'kluːs) *n.* **1.** a person who lives in seclusion, esp. to devote himself to prayer and religious meditation; a hermit. ~*adj.* **2.** solitary; retiring. [C13: from OF *reclus,* from LL *reclūdere* to shut away, from L RE- + *claudere* to close] —**reclusion** (rɪ'kluːʒən) *n.* —**re'clusive** *adj.*

recognition (ˌrɛkəg'nɪʃən) *n.* **1.** the act of recognizing or fact of being recognized. **2.** acceptance or acknowledgment of a claim, duty, etc. **3.** a token of thanks. **4.** formal acknowledgment of a government or of the independence of a country. [C15: from L *recognitiō*, from *recognoscere,* from RE-+ *cognoscere* to know] —**recognitive** (rɪ'kɒgnɪtɪv) *or* **re'cognitory** *adj.*

recognizance *or* **recognisance** (rɪ'kɒgnɪzəns) *n. Law.* **a.** a bond entered into before a court or magistrate by which a person binds himself to do a specified act, as to appear in court on a stated day, keep the peace, or pay a debt. **b.** a monetary sum pledged to the performance of such an act. [C14: from OF *reconoissance,* from *reconoistre* to RECOGNIZE] —**re'cognizant** *or* **re'cognisant** *adj.*

recognize *or* **-ise** ('rɛkəgˌnaɪz) *vb.* (*tr.*) **1.** to perceive (a person or thing) to be the same as or belong to the same class as something previously seen or known; know again. **2.** to accept or be aware of (a fact, problem, etc.): *to recognize necessity.* **3.** to give formal acknowledgment of the status or legality of (a government, a representative, etc.). **4.** *Chiefly U.S. & Canad.* to grant (a person) the right to speak in a deliberative body. **5.** to give a token of thanks for (a service rendered, etc.). **6.** to make formal acknowledgment of (a claim, etc.). **7.** to show approval or appreciation of (something good). **8.** to acknowledge or greet (a person). [C15: from L *recognoscere,* from RE- + *cognoscere* to know] —**'recog**₁**nizable** *or* **-isable** *adj.* —**recog**₁**niza'bility** *or* **-isa'bility** *n.* —**'recog**₁**nizably** *or* **-isably** *adv.* —**'recog**₁**nizer** *or* **-iser** *n.*

recoil *vb.* (rɪ'kɔɪl). (*intr.*) **1.** to jerk back, as from an impact or violent thrust. **2.** (often foll. by *from*) to draw back in fear, horror, or disgust. **3.** (foll. by *on* or *upon*) to go wrong, esp. so as to hurt the perpetrator. **4.** (of an atom, etc.) to change momentum as a result of the emission of a particle. ~*n.* (rɪˈkɔɪl, ˈriːkɔɪl). **5. a.** the backward movement of a gun when fired. **b.** the distance moved. **6.** the motion acquired by an atom, etc., as a result of its emission of a particle. **7.** the act of recoiling. [C13: from OF *reculer*, from RE- + *cul* rump, from L *cūlus*] —**re**ˈ**coiler** *n.*

recollect (ˌrɛkəˈlɛkt) *vb.* (when *tr.*, *often takes a clause as object*) to recall from memory; remember. [C16: from L *recolligere*, from RE- + *colligere* to COLLECT] —**ˌrecolˈlection** *n.* —**ˌrecolˈlective** *adj.* —**ˌrecolˈlectively** *adv.*

recombinant DNA (riːˈkɒmbɪnənt) *n.* DNA molecules that are extracted from different sources and chemically joined together.

recombination (ˌriːkɒmbɪˈneɪʃən) *n. Genetics.* any of several processes by which genetic material of different origins becomes combined.

recommend (ˌrɛkəˈmɛnd) *vb.* (*tr.*) **1.** (*may take a clause as object or an infinitive*) to advise as the best course or choice; counsel. **2.** to praise or commend: *to recommend a new book.* **3.** to make attractive or advisable: *the trip has little to recommend it.* **4.** *Arch.* to entrust (a person or thing) to someone else's care; commend. [C14: via Med. L from L RE-+ *commendāre* to COMMEND] —**ˌrecomˈmendable** *adj.* —**ˌrecomˈmendatory** *adj.* —**ˌrecomˈmender** *n.*

recommendation (ˌrɛkəmɛnˈdeɪʃən) *n.* **1.** the act of recommending. **2.** something that recommends, esp. a letter. **3.** something that is recommended, such as a course of action.

recommit (ˌriːkəˈmɪt) *vb.* **-mitting**, **-mitted.** (*tr.*) **1.** to send (a bill) back to a committee for further consideration. **2.** to commit again. —**ˌrecomˈmitment** *or* **ˌrecomˈmittal** *n.*

recompense (ˈrɛkəmˌpɛns) *vb.* (*tr.*) **1.** to pay or reward for service, work, etc. **2.** to compensate for loss, injury, etc. ~*n.* **3.** compensation for loss, injury, etc. **4.** reward, remuneration, or repayment. [C15: from OF *recompenser*, from L RE- + *compensāre* to balance in weighing] —**ˈrecomˌpensable** *adj.* —**ˈrecomˌpenser** *n.*

reconcile (ˈrɛkənˌsaɪl) *vb.* (*tr.*) **1.** (*often passive; usually foll. by to*) to make (oneself or another) no longer opposed; cause to acquiesce in something unpleasant: *she reconciled herself to poverty.* **2.** to become friendly with (someone) after estrangement or to re-establish friendly relations between (two or more people). **3.** to settle (a quarrel). **4.** to make (two apparently conflicting things) compatible or consistent with each other. **5.** to reconsecrate (a desecrated church, etc.). [C14: from L *reconciliāre*, from RE- + *conciliāre* to make friendly, CONCILIATE] —**ˈreconˌcilement** *n.* —**ˈreconˌciler** *n.* —**reconciliation** (ˌrɛkənˌsɪlɪˈeɪʃən) *n.* —**reconciliatory** (ˌrɛkənˈsɪlɪətərɪ, -trɪ) *adj.*

recondite (rɪˈkɒndaɪt, ˈrɛkənˌdaɪt) *adj.* **1.** requiring special knowledge; abstruse. **2.** dealing with abstruse or profound subjects. [C17: from L *reconditus* hidden away, from RE- + *condere* to conceal] —**reˈconditely** *adv.* —**reˈconditeness** *n.*

recondition (ˌriːkənˈdɪʃən) *vb.* (*tr.*) to restore to good condition or working order: *to recondition an engine.* —**reˈconditioned** *adj.*

reconnaissance (rɪˈkɒnɪsəns) *n.* **1.** the act of reconnoitring. **2.** the process of obtaining information about the position, etc., of an enemy. **3.** a preliminary inspection of an area of land. [C18: from F, from OF *reconoistre* to explore, RECOGNIZE]

reconnoitre *or U.S.* **reconnoiter** (ˌrɛkəˈnɔɪtə) *vb.* **1.** to survey or inspect (an enemy's position, region of land, etc.). ~*n.* **2.** the act or process of reconnoitring; a reconnaissance. [C18: from obs. F *reconnoître* to inspect, explore; see RECOGNIZE] —**ˌreconˈnoitrer** *or U.S.* **ˌreconˈnoiterer** *n.*

reconsider (ˌriːkənˈsɪdə) *vb.* to consider (something) again, with a view to changing one's policy or course of action. —**ˌreconˌsiderˈation** *n.*

reconstitute (riːˈkɒnstɪˌtjuːt) *vb.* (*tr.*) **1.** to restore (food, etc.) to its former or natural state, as by the addition of water to a concentrate. **2.** to reconstruct; form again. —**reconstituent** (ˌriːkənˈstɪtjʊənt) *adj.*, *n.* —**reconˈstitution** *n.*

reconstruct (ˌriːkənˈstrʌkt) *vb.* (*tr.*) **1.** to construct or form again; rebuild. **2.** to form a picture of (a crime, past event, etc.) by piecing together evidence. —**ˌreconˈstructible** *adj.* —**ˌreconˈstruction** *n.* —**ˌreconˈstructive** *or* **ˌreconˈstructional** *adj.* —**ˌreconˈstructor** *n.*

reconvert (ˌriːkənˈvɜːt) *vb.* (*tr.*) **1.** to change (something) back to a previous state or form. **2.** to bring (someone) back to his former religion. —**reconversion** (ˌriːkənˈvɜːʃən) *n.*

record *n.* (ˈrɛkɔːd). **1.** an account in permanent form, esp. in writing, preserving knowledge or information. **2.** a written account of some transaction that serves as legal evidence of the transaction. **3.** a written official report of the proceedings of a court of justice or legislative body. **4.** anything serving as evidence or as a memorial: *the First World War is a record of human folly.* **5.** (*often pl.*) information or data on a specific subject collected methodically over a long period: *weather records.* **6. a.** the best or most outstanding amount, rate, height, etc., ever attained, as in some field of sport: *a world record.* **b.** (*as modifier*): *a record time.* **7.** the sum of one's recognized achievements, career, or performance. **8.** a list of crimes of which an accused person has previously been convicted. **9. have a record.** to be a known criminal. **10.** Also called: **gramophone record, disc.** a thin disc of a plastic material upon which sound has been recorded. **11.** the markings made by a recording instrument such as a seismograph. **12.** *Computers.* a group of data or piece of information preserved as a unit in machine-readable form. **13. for the record.** for the sake of strict factual accuracy. **14. go on record.** to state one's views publicly. **15. off the record.** confidential or confidentially. **16. on record. a.** stated in a public document. **b.** publicly known. **17. set** *or* **put the record straight.** to correct an error. ~*vb.* (rɪˈkɔːd). (*mainly tr.*) **18.** to set down in some permanent form so as to preserve the true facts of: *to record the minutes of a meeting.* **19.** to contain or serve to relate (facts, information, etc.). **20.** to indicate, show, or register: *his face recorded his disappointment.* **21.** to remain as or afford evidence of: *these ruins record the life of the Romans in Britain.* **22.** (*also intr.*) to make a recording of (music, speech, etc.) for reproduction, esp. on a record player or tape recorder, or for later broadcasting. **23.** (*also intr.*) (of an instrument) to register or indicate (information) on a scale: *the barometer recorded a low pressure.* [C13: from OF *recorder*, from L *recordārī* to remember, from RE- + *cor* heart] —**reˈcordable** *adj.*

recorded delivery *n.* a Post Office service by which an official record of posting and delivery is obtained for a letter or package.

recorder (rɪˈkɔːdə) *n.* **1.** a person who records, such as an official or historian. **2.** something that records, esp. an apparatus that provides a permanent record of experiments, etc. **3.** short for **tape recorder. 4.** *Music.* a wind instrument of the flute family, blown through a fipple in the mouth end, having a reedlike quality of tone. **5.** (in England) a barrister or solicitor of at least ten years' standing appointed to sit as a part-time judge in the crown court. —**reˈcordership** *n.*

recording (rɪˈkɔːdɪŋ) *n.* **1. a.** the act or process of making a record, esp. of sound on a gramophone record or magnetic tape. **b.** (*as modifier*): *recording studio.* **2.** the record or tape so produced. **3.** something that has been recorded, esp. a radio or television programme.

Recording Angel *n.* an angel who supposedly keeps a record of every person's good and bad acts.

ˌrecoloniˈzation *or* **-ˌiˈsation** *n.*	**ˌrecomˈmencement** *n.*	**ˌreconˈsoliˌdate** *vb.*
reˈcoloˌnize *or* **-ˌnise** *vb.*	**ˌrecomˈpose** *vb.*	**ˌreconˌsoliˈdation** *n.*
reˈcolour *vb.*	**ˌreconˈfirm** *vb.*	**ˌreconˈvene** *vb.*
ˌrecomˈbine *vb.*	**ˌreconfirˈmation** *n.*	**ˌreconˈvey** *vb.*
ˌrecomˈmence *vb.*	**ˌreconˈnect** *vb.*	**ˌreconˈvict** *vb.*
	ˌreconˈnection *n.*	
reˈconquer *vb.*		
reˈconquest *n.*		
reˈconseˌcrate *vb.*		
ˌreconseˈcration *n.*		
ˌreconˈsign *vb.*		
ˌreconˈsignment *n.*		

record player *n.* a device for reproducing the sounds stored on a record. A stylus vibrates in accordance with the undulations of the walls of the groove in the record as it rotates.

recount (rɪˈkaʊnt) *vb.* (*tr.*) to tell the story or details of; narrate. [C15: from OF *reconter*, from RE- + *conter* to tell; see COUNT¹] —**reˈcountal** *n.*

re-count *vb.* (riːˈkaʊnt). **1.** to count (votes, etc.) again. ~*n.* (ˈriːˌkaʊnt). **2.** a second or further count, esp. of votes in an election.

recoup (rɪˈkuːp) *vb.* **1.** to regain or make good (a financial or other loss). **2.** (*tr.*) to reimburse or compensate (someone), as for a loss. **3.** *Law.* to keep back (something due), having rightful claim to do so. ~*n.* **4.** *Rare.* the act of recouping; recoupment. [C15: from OF *recouper* to cut back, from RE- + *couper*, from *coper* to behead] —**reˈcoupable** *adj.* —**reˈcoupment** *n.*

recourse (rɪˈkɔːs) *n.* **1.** the act of resorting to a person, course of action, etc., in difficulty (esp. in **have recourse to**). **2.** a person, organization, or course of action that is turned to for help, etc. **3.** the right to demand payment, esp. from the drawer or endorser of a bill of exchange or other negotiable instrument when the person accepting it fails to pay. **4. without recourse.** a qualified endorsement on such a negotiable instrument, by which the endorser protects himself from liability to subsequent holders. [C14: from OF *recours*, from LL *recursus* a running back, from RE- + L *currere* to run]

recover (rɪˈkʌvə) *vb.* **1.** (*tr.*) to find again or obtain the return of (something lost). **2.** to regain (loss of money, time, etc.). **3.** (of a person) to regain (health, spirits, composure, etc.). **4.** to regain (a former and better condition): *industry recovered after the war.* **5.** *Law.* **a.** (*tr.*) to gain (something) by the judgment of a court of law: *to recover damages.* **b.** (*intr.*) to succeed in a lawsuit. **6.** (*tr.*) to obtain (useful substances) from waste. **7.** (*intr.*) (in fencing, rowing, etc.) to make a recovery. [C14: from OF *recoverer*, from L *recuperāre* RECUPERATE] —**reˈcoverable** *adj.* —**reˌcoveraˈbility** *n.* —**reˈcoverer** *n.*

re-cover (riːˈkʌvə) *vb.* (*tr.*) **1.** to cover again. **2.** to provide (furniture, etc.) with a new cover.

recovery (rɪˈkʌvərɪ) *n.*, *pl.* **-eries. 1.** the act or process of recovering, esp. from sickness, a shock, or a setback. **2.** restoration to a former or better condition. **3.** the regaining of something lost. **4.** the extraction of useful substances from waste. **5.** the retrieval of a space capsule after a spaceflight. **6.** *Law.* the obtaining of a right, etc., by the judgment of a court. **7.** *Fencing.* a return to the position of guard after making an attack. **8.** *Swimming, rowing, etc.* the action of bringing the arm, an oar, etc., forward for another stroke. **9.** *Golf.* a stroke played from the rough or a bunker to the fairway or green.

recreant (ˈrɛkrɪənt) *Arch.* ~*adj.* **1.** cowardly; fainthearted. **2.** disloyal. ~*n.* **3.** a disloyal or cowardly person. [C14: from OF, from *recroire* to surrender, from RE- + L *crēdere* to believe] —**ˈrecreance** *or* **ˈrecreancy** *n.* —**ˈrecreantly** *adv.*

recreate (ˈrɛkrɪˌeɪt) *vb. Rare.* to amuse (oneself or someone else). [C15: from L *recreāre* to invigorate, renew, from RE- + *creāre* to CREATE] —**ˈrecreative** *adj.* —**ˈrecreaˌtively** *adv.* —**ˈrecreˌator** *n.*

re-create (ˌriːkrɪˈeɪt) *vb.* to create anew; reproduce. —**ˌre-creˈation** *n.* —**ˌre-creˈator** *n.*

recreation (ˌrɛkrɪˈeɪʃən) *n.* **1.** refreshment of health or spirits by relaxation and enjoyment. **2.** an activity that promotes this. **3. a.** restriction of free time between school lessons. **b.** (*as modifier*): *recreation period.* —**ˌrecreˈational** *adj.*

recriminate (rɪˈkrɪmɪˌneɪt) *vb.* (*intr.*) to return an accusation against someone or engage in mutual accusations. [C17: via Med. L, from L *crimināri* to accuse, from *crimen* accusation] —**reˌcrimiˈnation** *n.* —**reˈcriminative** *or* **reˈcriminatory** *adj.* —**reˈcrimiˌnator** *n.*

recrudesce (ˌriːkruːˈdɛs) *vb.* (*intr.*) (of a disease, trouble, etc.) to break out or appear again after a period of dormancy. [C19: from L *recrūdēscere*, from RE- + *crūdēscere* to grow worse, from *crūdus* bloody, raw] —**ˌrecruˈdescence** *n.*

recruit (rɪˈkruːt) *vb.* **1. a.** to enlist (men) for military service. **b.** to raise or strengthen (an army, etc.) by enlistment. **2.** (*tr.*) to enrol or obtain (members, support, etc.).

3. to furnish or be furnished with a fresh supply; renew. **4.** *Arch.* to recover (health, spirits, etc.). ~*n.* **5.** a newly joined member of a military service. **6.** any new member or supporter. [C17: from F *recrute* lit.: new growth, from *recroître*, from L, from RE- + *crēscere* to grow] —**reˈcruitable** *adj.* —**reˈcruiter** *n.* —**reˈcruitment** *n.*

recta (ˈrɛktə) *n.* a plural of **rectum.**

rectal (ˈrɛktəl) *adj.* of or relating to the rectum. —**ˈrectally** *adv.*

rectangle (ˈrɛkˌtæŋgəl) *n.* a parallelogram having four right angles. [C16: from Med. L *rectangulum*, from L *rectus* straight + *angulus* angle]

rectangular (rɛkˈtæŋgjʊlə) *adj.* **1.** shaped like a rectangle. **2.** having or relating to right angles. **3.** mutually perpendicular: *rectangular coordinates.* **4.** having a base or section shaped like a rectangle. —**recˌtanguˈlarity** *n.* —**recˈtangularly** *adv.*

rectangular coordinates *pl. n.* the Cartesian coordinates in a system of mutually perpendicular axes.

rectangular hyperbola *n.* a hyperbola with perpendicular asymptotes.

recti (ˈrɛktaɪ) *n.* the plural of **rectus.**

recti- *or before a vowel* **rect-** *combining form.* straight or right: *rectangle.* [from L *rectus*]

rectifier (ˈrɛktɪˌfaɪə) *n.* **1.** an electronic device that converts an alternating current to a direct current. **2.** *Chem.* an apparatus for condensing a hot vapour to a liquid in distillation; condenser. **3.** a thing or person that rectifies.

rectify (ˈrɛktɪˌfaɪ) *vb.* **-fying, -fied.** (*tr.*) **1.** to put right; correct; remedy. **2.** to separate (a substance) from a mixture or refine (a substance) by fractional distillation. **3.** to convert (alternating current) into direct current. **4.** *Maths.* to determine the length of (a curve). [C14: via OF from Med. L *rectificāre*, from L *rectus* straight + *facere* to make] —**ˈrectiˌfiable** *adj.* —**ˌrectifiˈcation** *n.*

rectilinear (ˌrɛktɪˈlɪnɪə) *or* **rectilineal** *adj.* **1.** in, moving in, or characterized by a straight line. **2.** consisting of, bounded by, or formed by a straight line. —**ˌrectiˈlinearly** *or* **ˌrectiˈlineally** *adv.*

rectitude (ˈrɛktɪˌtjuːd) *n.* **1.** moral or religious correctness. **2.** correctness of judgment. [C15: from LL *rectitūdō*, from L *rectus* right, from *regere* to rule]

recto (ˈrɛktəʊ) *n.*, *pl.* **-tos. 1.** the front of a sheet of printed paper. **2.** the right-hand pages of a book. Cf. **verso** (sense 1b). [C19: from L *rectō foliō* on the right-hand page]

rectocele (ˈrɛktəʊˌsiːl) *n. Pathol.* a protrusion or herniation of the rectum into the vagina.

rector (ˈrɛktə) *n.* **1.** *Church of England.* a clergyman in charge of a parish in which, as its incumbent, he would formerly have been entitled to the whole of the tithes. **2.** *R.C. Church.* a cleric in charge of a college, religious house, or congregation. **3.** *Protestant Episcopal Church.* a clergyman in charge of a parish. **4.** *Chiefly Brit.* the head of certain schools, colleges, or universities. **5.** (in Scotland) a high-ranking official in a university. **6.** (in South Africa) a principal of an Afrikaans university. [C14: from L: director, ruler, from *regere* to rule] —**ˈrectorate** *n.* —**rectorial** (rɛkˈtɔːrɪəl) *adj.* —**ˈrectorship** *n.*

rectory (ˈrɛktərɪ) *n.*, *pl.* **-ries. 1.** the official house of a rector. **2.** *Church of England.* the office and benefice of a rector.

rectrix (ˈrɛktrɪks) *n.*, *pl.* **rectrices** (ˈrɛktrɪˌsiːz, rɛkˈtraɪsiːz). any of the large stiff feathers of a bird's tail, used in controlling the direction of flight. [C17: from LL, fem. of L *rector* RECTOR]

rectum (ˈrɛktəm) *n.*, *pl.* **-tums** *or* **-ta.** the lower part of the alimentary canal, between the sigmoid flexure of the colon and the anus. [C16: from NL *rectum intestinum* the straight intestine]

rectus (ˈrɛktəs) *n.*, *pl.* **-ti.** *Anat.* a straight muscle. [C18: from NL *rectus musculus*]

recumbent (rɪˈkʌmbənt) *adj.* **1.** lying down; reclining. **2.** (of an organ) leaning or resting against another organ. [C17: from L *recumbere* to lie back, from RE- + *cumbere* to lie] —**reˈcumbence** *or* **reˈcumbency** *n.* —**reˈcumbently** *adv.*

recuperate (rɪˈkuːpəˌreɪt, -ˈkjuː-) *vb.* **1.** (*intr.*) to recover from illness or exhaustion. **2.** to recover (financial losses, etc.). [C16: from L *recuperāre* to recover, from RE-

+ *capere* to gain] —**re****cuper'ation** *n.* —**re'cuperative** *adj.*

recur (rɪ'kɜː) *vb.* -**curring**, -**curred**. (*intr.*) **1.** to happen again. **2.** (of a thought, etc.) to come back to the mind. **3.** (of a problem, etc.) to come up again. **4.** *Maths.* (of a digit or group of digits) to be repeated an infinite number of times at the end of a decimal fraction. [C15: from L *recurrere*, from RE- + *currere* to run] —**re'curring** *adj.*

recurrent (rɪ'kʌrənt) *adj.* **1.** tending to happen again or repeatedly. **2.** *Anat.* (of certain nerves, etc.) turning back, so as to run in the opposite direction. —**re'currence** *n.* —**re'currently** *adv.*

recurrent fever *n.* another name for **relapsing fever.**

recurring decimal *n.* a rational number that contains a pattern of digits repeated indefinitely after the decimal point.

recursion (rɪ'kɜːʃən) *n.* **1.** the act or process of returning or running back. **2.** *Maths, logic.* the application of a function to its own values to generate an infinite sequence of values. [C17: from L *recursio*, from *recurrere* RECUR] —**re'cursive** *adj.*

recurve (rɪ'kɜːv) *vb.* to curve or bend (something) back or down or (of something) to be so curved or bent. [C16: from L *recurvāre*, from RE- + *curvāre* to CURVE]

recusant ('rɛkjʊzənt) *n.* **1.** (in 16th to 18th century England) a Roman Catholic who did not attend the services of the Church of England. **2.** any person who refuses to submit to authority. ~*adj.* **3.** (formerly, of Catholics) refusing to attend services of the Church of England. **4.** refusing to submit to authority. [C16: from L *recūsāns* refusing, from *recūsāre*, from RE- + *causārī* to dispute, from *causa* a CAUSE] —'**recusance** *or* '**recusancy** *n.*

recycle (riː'saɪk³l) *vb.* (*tr.*) **1.** to pass (a substance) through a system again for further treatment or use. **2.** to reclaim for further use: *to recycle water.* ~*n.* **3.** the repetition of a fixed sequence of events.

red¹ (rɛd) *n.* **1.** any of a group of colours, such as that of a ripe tomato or fresh blood. **2.** a pigment or dye of or producing these colours. **3.** red cloth or clothing: *dressed in red.* **4.** a red ball in snooker, etc. **5.** (in roulette) one of two colours on which players may place even bets. **6.** short for **red wine. 7. in the red.** *Inf.* in debt. **8. see red.** *Inf.* to become very angry. ~*adj.* **redder**, **reddest**. **9.** of the colour red. **10.** reddish in colour or having parts or marks that are reddish: *red deer.* **11.** having the face temporarily suffused with blood, being a sign of anger, shame, etc. **12.** (of the complexion) rosy; florid. **13.** (of the eyes) bloodshot. **14.** (of the hands) stained with blood. **15.** bloody or violent: *red revolution.* ~*vb.* **redding, redded. 16.** another word for **redden**. [OE *rēad*] —'**reddish** *adj.* —'**redness** *n.*

red² (rɛd) *vb.* **redding, red** *or* **redded**. (*tr.*) a variant spelling of **redd**.

Red (rɛd) *Inf.* ~*adj.* **1.** Communist, Socialist, or Soviet. **2.** radical, leftist, or revolutionary. ~*n.* **3.** a member or supporter of a Communist or Socialist Party or a national of the Soviet Union. **4.** a radical, leftist, or revolutionary. [C19: from the colour chosen to symbolize revolutionary socialism]

redact (rɪ'dækt) *vb.* (*tr.*) to put (a literary work, etc.) into appropriate form for publication; edit. [C15: from L *redigere* to bring back, from *red-* RE- + *agere* to drive] —**re'daction** *n.* —**re'dactor** *n.*

red admiral *n.* a butterfly of temperate Europe and Asia, having black wings with red and white markings. See also **white admiral.**

red algae *pl. n.* the numerous algae which contain a red pigment in addition to chlorophyll. The group includes carrageen and dulse.

redback ('rɛd,bæk) *n. Austral.* a small, venomous spider, the female of which has a red stripe on its back. Also called: **redback spider.**

red bark *n.* a kind of cinchona containing a high proportion of alkaloids.

red biddy *n. Inf.* cheap red wine fortified with methylated spirits.

red blood cell *n.* another name for **erythrocyte.**

red-blooded *adj. Inf.* vigorous; virile. —,**red-'blooded-ness** *n.*

redbreast ('rɛd,brɛst) *n.* any of various birds having a red breast, esp. the Old World robin.

redbrick ('rɛd,brɪk) *n.* (*modifier*) denoting, relating to, or characteristic of a provincial British university of relatively recent foundation.

Redbridge ('rɛd,brɪdʒ) *n.* a borough of NE Greater London: includes part of Epping Forest. Pop.: 227 900 (1986 est.).

redcap ('rɛd,kæp) *n.* **1.** *Brit. inf.* a military policeman. **2.** *U.S. & Canad.* a porter at an airport or station.

red card *n. Soccer.* a card of a red colour displayed by a referee to indicate that a player has been sent off.

red carpet *n.* **1.** a strip of red carpeting laid for important dignitaries to walk on. **2. a.** deferential treatment accorded to a person of importance. **b.** (*as modifier*): *a red-carpet reception.*

red cedar *n.* **1.** any of several North American coniferous trees, esp. a juniper that has fragrant reddish wood. **2.** the wood of any of these trees. **3.** any of several Australian timber trees.

red cent *n.* (*used with a negative*) *Inf.*, chiefly *U.S.* a cent considered as a trivial amount of money (esp. in **not have a red cent**, etc.).

redcoat ('rɛd,kəʊt) *n.* **1.** (formerly) a British soldier. **2.** *Canad. inf.* another name for **Mountie.**

red coral *n.* any of several corals, the skeletons of which are pinkish red in colour and used to make ornaments, etc.

red corpuscle *n.* another name for **erythrocyte.**

Red Crescent *n.* the emblem of the Red Cross Society in a Muslim country.

Red Cross *n.* **1.** an international humanitarian organization (**Red Cross Society**) formally established by the Geneva Convention of 1864. **2.** the emblem of this organization, consisting of a red cross on a white background.

redcurrant (,rɛd'kʌrənt) *n.* **1.** a N temperate shrub having greenish flowers and small edible rounded red berries. **2. a.** the fruit of this shrub. **b.** (*as modifier*): *redcurrant jelly.*

redd *or* **red** (rɛd) *Scot. & N English dialect.* ~*vb.* **redding, redd** *or* **redded**. **1.** (*tr.*; often foll. by *up*) to bring order to; tidy (up). ~*n.* **2.** the act or an instance of redding. [C15: *redden* to clear, ? a variant of RID] —'**redder** *n.*

red deer *n.* a large deer formerly widely distributed in the woodlands of Europe and Asia. The coat is reddish brown in summer and the short tail is surrounded by a patch of light-coloured hair.

Red Deer *n.* **1.** a town in S Alberta on the Red Deer River: trade centre for mixed farming, dairying region, and natural gas processing. Pop: 54 309 (1986). **2.** a river in W Canada, in SW Alberta, flowing southeast into the South Saskatchewan River. Length: about 620 km (385 miles). **3.** a river in W Canada, flowing east through **Red Deer Lake** into Lake Winnipegosis. Length: about 225 km (140 miles).

redden ('rɛd³n) *vb.* **1.** to make or become red. **2.** (*intr.*) to flush with embarrassment, anger, etc.

Redding ('rɛdɪŋ) *n. Otis.* 1941–67, U.S. soul singer and songwriter. His recordings include "Respect" (1965), *Dictionary of Soul* (1966), and "(Sittin' on) The Dock of the Bay" (1968).

Redditch ('rɛdɪtʃ) *n.* a town in W central England, in Hereford and Worcester: designated a new town in the mid-1960s; metal-working industries. Pop.: 73 500 (1985 est.).

reddle ('rɛd³l) *n., vb.* a variant spelling of **ruddle.**

red duster *n. Brit.* an informal name for the **Red Ensign.**

red dwarf *n.* one of a class of stars of relatively small mass and low luminosity.

rede (riːd) *Arch.* ~*n.* **1.** advice or counsel. **2.** an explanation. ~*vb.* (*tr.*) **3.** to advise; counsel. **4.** to explain. [OE *rǣdan* to rule]

red earth *n.* a clayey zonal soil of tropical savanna lands, formed by extensive chemical weathering and coloured by iron compounds.

redeem (rɪ'diːm) *vb.* (*tr.*) **1.** to recover possession or ownership of by payment of a price or service; regain. **2.** to convert (bonds, shares, etc.) into cash. **3.** to pay off (a loan, etc.). **4.** to recover (something pledged, mortgaged, or pawned). **5.** to convert (paper money) into bullion or specie. **6.** to fulfil (a promise, pledge, etc.). **7.** to exchange (coupons, etc.) for goods. **8.** to reinstate in someone's estimation or good opinion: *he redeemed himself by his altruistic action.* **9.** to make amends for. **10.** to recover from captivity, esp. by a money payment. **11.** *Christianity.* (of Christ as Saviour) to free (humanity) from sin by death on the Cross. [C15: from OF *redimer*, from L *redimere*, from *red-* RE- + *emere* to buy] —re'deemable *or* re'demptible *adj.* —re'deemer *n.*

Redeemer (rɪ'diːmə) *n.* **the.** Jesus Christ as having brought redemption to mankind.

redeeming (rɪ'diːmɪŋ) *adj.* serving to compensate for faults or deficiencies.

redemption (rɪ'dɛmpʃən) *n.* **1.** the act or process of redeeming. **2.** the state of being redeemed. **3.** *Christianity.* **a.** deliverance from sin through the incarnation, sufferings, and death of Christ. **b.** atonement for guilt. [C14: via OF from L *redemptiō* a buying back; see REDEEM] —re'demptional, re'demptive, *or* re'demptory *adj.* —re'demptively *adv.*

Red Ensign *n.* the ensign of the British Merchant Navy, having the Union Jack on a red background at the upper corner of the vertical edge alongside the hoist. It was also the national flag of Canada until 1965.

redeploy (ˌriːdɪ'plɔɪ) *vb.* to assign new positions or tasks to (labour, troops, etc.). —ˌrede'ployment *n.*

redevelopment area (ˌriːdɪ'vɛləpmənt) *n.* an urban area in which all or most of the buildings are demolished and rebuilt.

redeye ('rɛdˌaɪ) *n.* **1.** *U.S. sl.* inferior whisky. **2.** another name for **rudd.**

red-faced *adj.* **1.** flushed with embarrassment or anger. **2.** having a florid complexion. —**red-facedly** (ˌrɛd'feɪsɪdlɪ, -'feɪstlɪ) *adv.*

redfin ('rɛd,fɪn) *n.* any of various small cyprinid fishes with reddish fins.

redfish ('rɛd,fɪʃ) *n., pl.* **-fish** *or* **-fishes. 1.** a male salmon that has recently spawned. Cf. **blackfish** (sense 2). **2.** *Canad.* another name for **kokanee.**

red flag *n.* **1.** a symbol of socialism, communism, or revolution. **2.** a warning of danger or a signal to stop.

Redford ('rɛdfəd) *n.* **Robert.** born 1936, U.S. film actor. His films include *The Chase* (1966), *Butch Cassidy and the Sundance Kid* (1969), *The Sting* (1973), *All the President's Men* (1976), and *Ordinary People* (1980), which he directed.

red fox *n.* the common European fox which has a reddish-brown coat.

red giant *n.* a giant star that emits red light.

Redgrave ('rɛd,greɪv) *n.* **1. Lynn.** born 1944, English stage and film actress. Her films include *Georgy Girl* (1966), *The Virgin Soldiers* (1969), *The National Health* (1973), and *The Happy Hooker* (1975). **2.** her father, Sir **Michael.** 1908–85, English stage and film actor. Among his films are *The Lady Vanishes* (1938), *The Dam Busters* (1955), *The Loneliness of the Long Distance Runner* (1963), and *The Go-Between* (1971). **3.** his elder daughter, **Vanessa.** born 1937, English stage and film actress, whose roles include performances in the films *Blow Up* (1966), *Isadora* (1968), *Mary, Queen of Scots* (1972), and *Julia* (1977): noted also for her left-wing politics.

red grouse *n.* a reddish-brown grouse of upland moors of Great Britain.

Red Guard *n.* a member of a Communist Chinese youth movement.

red-handed *adj.* (*postpositive*) in the act of committing a crime or doing something wrong or shameful (esp. in **catch red-handed**). [C19 (earlier, C15 *red hand*)] —ˌred-'handedly *adv.* —ˌred-'handedness *n.*

red hat *n.* the broad-brimmed crimson hat given to cardinals as the symbol of their rank.

redhead ('rɛd,hɛd) *n.* a person with red hair. —'red,headed *adj.*

red heat *n.* **1.** the temperature at which a substance is red-hot. **2.** the state or condition of being red-hot.

red herring *n.* **1.** anything that diverts attention from a topic or line of inquiry. **2.** a herring cured by salting and smoking.

red-hot *adj.* **1.** (esp. of metal) heated to the temperature at which it glows red. **2.** extremely hot. **3.** keen, excited, or eager. **4.** furious; violent: *red-hot anger.* **5.** very recent or topical: *red-hot information.* **6.** *Austral. sl.* extreme, unreasonable, or unfair.

red-hot poker *n.* a liliaceous plant: widely cultivated for its showy spikes of red or yellow flowers.

Red Indian *n., adj.* another name, now considered offensive, for **American Indian.** [see REDSKIN]

redingote ('rɛdɪŋ,ɡəʊt) *n.* **1.** a man's full-skirted outer coat of the 18th and 19th centuries. **2.** a woman's coat of the 18th century, with an open-fronted skirt, revealing a decorative underskirt. **3.** a woman's coat with a close-fitting top and a full skirt. [C19: from F, from E *riding coat*]

redintegrate (rɛ'dɪntɪ,ɡreɪt) *vb.* (*tr.*) to make whole or complete again; restore to a perfect state; renew. [C15: from L *redintegrāre* to renew, from *red-* RE- + *integer* complete] —re,dinte'gration *n.* —red'integrative *adj.*

redistribution (ˌriːdɪstrɪ'bjuːʃən) *n.* **1.** the act or an instance of distributing again. **2.** a revision of the number of seats in the Canadian House of Commons allocated to each province, made every ten years on the basis of a new census.

redivivus (ˌrɛdɪ'vaɪvəs) *adj. Rare.* returned to life; revived. [C17: from LL, from L *red-* RE- + *vīvus* alive]

red lead (lɛd) *n.* a bright-red poisonous insoluble oxide of lead.

red-letter day *n.* a memorably important or happy occasion. [C18: from the red letters used in ecclesiastical calendars to indicate saints' days and feasts]

red light *n.* **1.** a signal to stop, esp. a red traffic signal. **2.** a danger signal. **3. a.** a red lamp indicating that a house is a brothel. **b.** (*as modifier*): *a red-light district.*

redline ('rɛd,laɪn) *vb.* (*tr.*) (esp. of a bank or group of banks) to refuse to consider giving a loan to (a person or country) because of the presumed risks involved.

red meat *n.* any meat that is dark in colour, esp. beef and lamb. Cf. **white meat.**

Redmond ('rɛdmənd) *n.* **John Edward.** 1856–1918, Irish politician. He led the Parnellites from 1891 and helped to procure the Home Rule bill of 1912, but was considered too moderate by extreme nationalists.

red mullet *n.* a food fish of European waters with a pair of long barbels beneath the chin and a reddish coloration. U.S. name: **goatfish.**

redneck ('rɛd,nɛk) *n. Disparaging.* **1.** (in the southwestern U.S.) a poor uneducated White farm worker. **2.** a person or institution that is extremely reactionary. ~*adj.* **3.** reactionary and bigoted: *redneck laws.*

redo (riː'duː) *vb.* **-doing, -did, -done.** (*tr.*) **1.** to do over again. **2.** *Inf.* to redecorate, esp. thoroughly: *we redid the house last summer.*

red ochre *n.* any of various natural red earths containing ferric oxide: used as pigments.

redolent ('rɛdəʊlənt) *adj.* **1.** having a pleasant smell; fragrant. **2.** (*postpositive;* foll. by *of* or *with*) having the odour or smell (of): *a room redolent of flowers.* **3.** (*postpositive;* foll. by *of* or *with*) reminiscent or suggestive (of): *a picture redolent of the 18th century.* [C14: from L *redolens* smelling (of), from *redolēre* to give off an odour, from *red-* RE- + *olēre* to smell] —'redolence *or* 'redolency *n.* —'redolently *adv.*

Redon (*French* rədɔ̃) *n.* **Odilon** (ɔdilɔ̃). 1840–1916, French symbolist painter and etcher. He foreshadowed the surrealists in his paintings of fantastic dream images.

redouble (rɪ'dʌbəl) *vb.* **1.** to make or become much greater in intensity, number, etc.: *to redouble one's efforts.* **2.** to send back (sounds) or (of sounds) to be sent back. **3.** *Bridge.* to double (an opponent's double). ~*n.* **4.** the act of redoubling.

redoubt (rɪ'daʊt) *n.* **1.** an outwork or fieldwork defending a hilltop, pass, etc. **2.** a temporary defence work built inside a fortification as a last defensive position. [C17: via F from obs. It. *ridotta*, from Med. L *reductus* shelter, from L *redūcere*, from RE- + *dūcere* to lead]

redoubtable (rɪ'daʊtəbəl) *adj.* **1.** to be feared; formidable. **2.** worthy of respect. [C14: from OF, from *redouter* to

dread, from RE- + *douter* to be afraid, DOUBT]
—**re'doubtableness** *n.* —**re'doubtably** *adv.*

redound (rɪ'daʊnd) *vb.* **1.** (*intr.*; foll. by *to*) to have an advantageous or disadvantageous effect (on): *brave deeds redound to your credit.* **2.** (*intr.*; foll. by *on* or *upon*) to recoil or rebound. **3.** (*tr.*) *Arch.* to reflect; bring: *his actions redound dishonour upon him.* [C14: from OF *redonder*, from L *redundāre* to stream over, from *red-* RE- + *undāre* to rise in waves]

redox ('ri:dɒks) *n.* (*modifier*) another term for **oxidation-reduction.** [C20: from RED(UCTION) + OX(IDATION)]

red pepper *n.* **1.** any of several varieties of the pepper plant cultivated for their hot pungent red podlike fruits. **2.** the fruit of any of these plants. **3.** the ripe red fruit of the sweet pepper. **4.** another name for **cayenne pepper.**

Red Planet *n.* **the.** an informal name for **Mars**[2].

redpoll ('rɛd,pɒl) *n.* either of two widely distributed types of finches, having a greyish-brown plumage with a red crown and pink breast.

red rag *n.* a provocation; something that infuriates. [so called because red objects supposedly infuriate bulls]

redress (rɪ'drɛs) *vb.* (*tr.*) **1.** to put right (a wrong), esp. by compensation; make reparation for. **2.** to correct or adjust (esp. in **redress the balance**). **3.** to make compensation to (a person) for a wrong. ~*n.* **4.** the act or an instance of setting right a wrong; remedy or cure. **5.** compensation, amends, or reparation for a wrong, injury, etc. [C14: from OF *redrecier* to set up again, from RE- + *drecier* to straighten; see DRESS] —**re'dressable** *or* **re'dressible** *adj.* —**re'dresser** *or* **re'dressor** *n.*

re-dress (ri:'drɛs) *vb.* (*tr.*) to dress (something) again.

Red River *n.* **1.** Also called: **Red River of the South.** a river in the S central U.S., flowing east from N Texas through Arkansas into the Mississippi in Louisiana. Length: 1639 km (1018 miles). **2.** a river in the northern U.S., flowing north as the border between North Dakota and Minnesota and into Lake Winnipeg, Canada. Length: 515 km (320 miles). **3.** a river in SE Asia, rising in SW China in Yünnan province and flowing southeast across N Vietnam to the Gulf of Tongkin: the chief river of N Vietnam, with an extensive delta. Length: 500 km (310 miles). Vietnamese name: **Song Koi.**

Red River cart *n.* *Canad. history.* a strongly-built, two-wheeled, ox- or horse-drawn cart used in W Canada.

red rose *n.* *English history.* the emblem of the House of Lancaster.

red salmon *n.* any salmon having reddish flesh, esp. the sockeye salmon.

Red Sea *n.* a long narrow sea between Arabia and NE Africa, linked with the Mediterranean in the north by the Suez Canal and with the Indian Ocean in the south: occasionally reddish in appearance through algae. Area: 438 000 sq. km (169 000 sq. miles).

redshank ('rɛd,ʃæŋk) *n.* any of various large common European sandpipers, esp. the **spotted redshank**, having red legs.

red shift *n.* a shift in the spectral lines of a stellar spectrum towards the red end of the visible region relative to the wavelength of these lines in the terrestrial spectrum.

redskin ('rɛd,skɪn) *n.* an informal name, now considered offensive, for an **American Indian.** [so called because one now extinct tribe painted themselves with red ochre]

red snapper *n.* any of various marine percoid food fishes of the snapper family, having a reddish coloration, common in American coastal regions of the Atlantic.

red spider *n.* short for **red spider mite** (see **spider mite**).

Red Spot *n.* a reddish oval spot, about 48 000 kilometres long, seen to drift around the S hemisphere of Jupiter.

red squirrel *n.* a reddish-brown squirrel, inhabiting woodlands of Europe and parts of Asia.

redstart ('rɛd,stɑːt) *n.* **1.** a European songbird of the thrush family: the male has a black throat, orange-brown tail and breast, and grey back. **2.** a North American warbler. [OE *rēad* red + *steort* tail]

red tape *n.* obstructive official routine or procedure; time-consuming bureaucracy. [C18: from the red tape used to bind official government documents]

reduce (rɪ'djuːs) *vb.* (*mainly tr.*) **1.** (*also intr.*) to make or become smaller in size, number, etc. **2.** to bring into a certain state, condition, etc.: *to reduce a forest to ashes; he*

was reduced to tears. **3.** (*also intr.*) to make or become slimmer; lose or cause to lose excess weight. **4.** to impoverish (esp. in **in reduced circumstances**). **5.** to bring into a state of submission to one's authority; subjugate: *the whole country was reduced after three months.* **6.** to bring down the price of (a commodity). **7.** to lower the rank or status of; demote: *reduced to the ranks.* **8.** to set out systematically as an aid to understanding; simplify: *his theories are reduced in a treatise.* **9.** *Maths.* to modify or simplify the form of (an expression or equation), esp. by substitution of one term by another. **10.** to thin out (paint) by adding oil, turpentine, etc. **11.** (*also intr.*) *Chem.* **a.** to undergo or cause to undergo a chemical reaction with hydrogen. **b.** to lose or cause to lose oxygen atoms. **c.** to undergo or cause to undergo an increase in the number of electrons. **12.** *Photog.* to lessen the density of (a negative or print). **13.** *Surgery.* to manipulate or reposition (a broken or displaced bone, organ, or part) back to its normal site. [C14: from L *redūcere* to bring back, from RE- + *dūcere* to lead] —**re'ducible** *adj.* —**re,duci'bility** *n.* —**re'ducibly** *adv.*

reducer (rɪ'djuːsə) *n.* **1.** *Photog.* a chemical solution used to lessen the density of a negative or print by oxidizing some of the blackened silver to soluble silver compounds. **2.** a pipe fitting connecting two pipes of different diameters. **3.** a person or thing that reduces.

reducing agent *n.* *Chem.* a substance that reduces another substance in a chemical reaction, being itself oxidized in the process.

reducing glass *n.* a lens or curved mirror that produces an image smaller than the object observed.

reductase (rɪ'dʌkteɪz) *n.* any enzyme that catalyses a biochemical reduction reaction. [C20: from REDUCTION + -ASE]

reductio ad absurdum (rɪ'dʌktɪəʊ æd æb'sɜːdəm) *n.* **1.** a method of disproving a proposition by showing that its inevitable consequences would be absurd. **2.** a method of indirectly proving a proposition by assuming its negation to be true and showing that this leads to an absurdity. **3.** application of a principle or proposed principle to an instance in which it is absurd. [L, lit.: reduction to the absurd]

reduction (rɪ'dʌkʃən) *n.* **1.** the act or process or an instance of reducing. **2.** the state or condition of being reduced. **3.** the amount by which something is reduced. **4.** a form of an original resulting from a reducing process, such as a copy on a smaller scale. **5.** *Maths.* **a.** the process of converting a fraction into its decimal form. **b.** the process of dividing out the common factors in the numerator and denominator of a fraction. —**re'ductive** *adj.*

reduction formula *n.* *Maths.* a formula expressing the values of a trigonometric function of any angle greater than 90° in terms of a function of an acute angle.

reductionism (rɪ'dʌkʃə,nɪzəm) *n.* **1.** the analysis of complex things, data, etc., into less complex constituents. **2.** *Often disparaging.* any theory or method that holds that a complex idea, system, etc., can be completely understood in terms of its simpler parts or components. —**re'ductionist** *n.*, *adj.* —**re,duction'istic** *adj.*

redundancy (rɪ'dʌndənsɪ) *n.*, *pl.* **-cies. 1. a.** the state or condition of being redundant or superfluous, esp. superfluous in one's job. **b.** (*as modifier*): *a redundancy payment.* **2.** excessive proliferation or profusion, esp. of superfluity.

redundant (rɪ'dʌndənt) *adj.* **1.** surplus to requirements; unnecessary or superfluous. **2.** verbose or tautological. **3.** deprived of one's job because it is no longer necessary. [C17: from L *redundans* overflowing, from *redundāre* to stream over; see REDOUND] —**re'dundantly** *adv.*

red underwing *n.* a large noctuid moth having hind wings coloured red and black.

reduplicate *vb.* (rɪ'djuːplɪ,keɪt). **1.** to make or become double; repeat. **2.** to repeat (a sound or syllable) in a word or (of a sound or syllable) to be repeated. ~*adj.* (rɪ'djuːplɪkɪt). **3.** doubled or repeated. **4.** (of petals or sepals) having the margins curving outwards. —**re,du pli'cation** *n.* —**re'duplicative** *adj.*

red-water *n.* a disease of cattle which destroys the red blood cells, characterized by the passage of red or blackish urine.

---

red wine *n.* wine made from black grapes and coloured by their skins.

redwing ('rɛd,wɪŋ) *n.* a small European thrush having a speckled breast, reddish flanks, and brown back.

redwood ('rɛd,wʊd) *n.* a giant coniferous tree of coastal regions of California, having reddish fibrous bark and durable timber.

reebok ('riːbʌk, -bɒk) *n., pl.* **-boks** *or* **-bok.** a variant spelling of **rhebok.**

re-echo (riː'ɛkəʊ) *vb.* **-oing, -oed. 1.** to echo (a sound that is already an echo); resound. **2.** (*tr.*) to repeat like an echo.

reed (riːd) *n.* **1.** any of various widely distributed tall grasses that grow in swamps and shallow water and have jointed hollow stalks. **2.** the stalk, or stalks collectively, of any of these plants, esp. as used for thatching. **3.** *Music.* **a.** a thin piece of cane or metal inserted into the tubes of certain wind instruments, which sets in vibration the air column inside the tube. **b.** a wind instrument or organ pipe that sounds by means of a reed. **4.** one of the several vertical parallel wires on a loom that may be moved upwards to separate the warp threads. **5.** a small semicircular architectural moulding. **6.** an archaic word for **arrow. 7. broken reed.** a weak, unreliable, or ineffectual person. ~*vb.* (*tr.*) **8.** to fashion into or supply with reeds or reeding. **9.** to thatch using reeds. [OE *hreod*]

Reed (riːd) *n.* **1. Sir Carol.** 1906–76, English film director. His films include *The Third Man* (1949), *An Outcast of the Islands* (1951), and *Oliver!* (1968), for which he won an Oscar. **2. Lou.** born ?1942, U.S. rock singer, songwriter, and guitarist: member of the Velvet Underground (1965–70). His albums include *Transformer* (1972), *Berlin* (1973), and *Street Hassle* (1978). **3. Walter.** 1851–1902, U.S. physician, who proved that yellow fever is transmitted by mosquitoes (1900).

reedbuck ('riːd,bʌk) *n., pl.* **-bucks** *or* **-buck.** an antelope of Africa south of the Sahara, having a buff-coloured coat and inward-curving horns.

reed bunting *n.* a common European bunting that has a brown streaked plumage with, in the male, a black head.

reed grass *n.* a tall perennial grass of rivers and ponds of Europe, Asia, and Canada.

reeding ('riːdɪŋ) *n.* **1.** a set of small semicircular architectural mouldings. **2.** the milling on the edges of a coin.

reedling ('riːdlɪŋ) *n.* a titlike Eurasian songbird, common in reed beds, which belongs to the family of Old World flycatchers and has a tawny back and tail and, in the male, a grey-and-black head. Also called: **bearded tit.**

reed mace *n.* a tall reedlike marsh plant, with straplike leaves and flowers in long brown spikes. Also called: (popularly) **bulrush, cat's-tail.**

reed organ *n.* **1.** a wind instrument, such as the harmonium, accordion, or harmonica, in which the sound is produced by reeds, each reed producing one note only. **2.** a type of pipe organ in which all the pipes are fitted with reeds.

reed pipe *n.* **1.** a wind instrument, such as a clarinet, whose sound is produced by a vibrating reed. **2.** an organ pipe sounded by a vibrating reed.

reedsman ('riːdzmən) *or U.S.* **reedman** *n., pl.* **-men.** a jazz musician who plays any of a number of wind instruments with a reed, such as the saxophone or clarinet.

reed stop *n.* an organ stop controlling a rank of reed pipes.

reed warbler *n.* any of various common Old World warblers that inhabit marshy regions and have a brown plumage.

reedy ('riːdɪ) *adj.* **reedier, reediest. 1.** (of a place) abounding in reeds. **2.** of or like a reed. **3.** having a tone like a reed instrument; shrill or piping. — '**reedily** *adv.* — '**reediness** *n.*

reef[1] (riːf) *n.* **1.** a ridge of rock, sand, coral, etc., the top of which lies close to the surface of the sea. **2.** a vein of ore, esp. one of gold-bearing quartz. **3.** (*cap.*) **the. a.** the Great Barrier Reef in Australia. **b.** the Witwatersrand in

South Africa, a gold-bearing ridge. [C16: from MDu. *ref*, from ON *rif* RIB[1], REEF[2]]

reef[2] (riːf) *Naut.* ~*n.* **1.** the part gathered in when sail area is reduced, as in a high wind. ~*vb.* **2.** to reduce the area of (sail) by taking in a reef. **3.** (*tr.*) to shorten or bring inboard (a spar). [C14: from MDu. *rif*; rel. to ON *rif* reef, RIB[1]]

Reef (riːf) *n.* **the.** another name for the **Witwatersrand.**

reefer ('riːfə) *n.* **1.** *Naut.* a person who reefs, such as a midshipman. **2.** another name for **reefing jacket. 3.** *Sl.* a hand-rolled cigarette containing cannabis. [C19: from REEF[2]; applied to the cigarette from its resemblance to the rolled reef of a sail]

reefing jacket *n.* a man's short double-breasted jacket of sturdy wool.

reef knot *n.* a knot consisting of two overhand knots turned opposite ways. Also called: **square knot.**

reef point *n.* *Naut.* one of several short lengths of line stitched through a sail for tying a reef.

reek (riːk) *vb.* **1.** (*intr.*) to give off or emit a strong unpleasant odour; smell or stink. **2.** (*intr.; often foll. by of*) to be permeated (by): *the letter reeks of subservience.* **3.** (*tr.*) to treat with smoke; fumigate. **4.** (*tr.*) *Chiefly dialect.* to give off or emit (smoke, fumes, etc.). ~*n.* **5.** a strong offensive smell; stink. **6.** *Chiefly dialect.* smoke or steam; vapour. [OE *rēocan*] — '**reeky** *adj.*

reel[1] (riːl, rɪəl) *n.* **1.** any of various cylindrical objects or frames that turn on an axis and onto which film, tape, wire, etc., may be wound. U.S. equivalent: **spool. 2.** *Angling.* a device for winding, casting, etc., consisting of a revolving spool with a handle, attached to a fishing rod. ~*vb.* (*tr.*) **3.** to wind (cotton, thread, etc.) onto a reel. **4.** (foll. by *in, out,* etc.) to wind or draw with a reel: *to reel in a fish.* [OE *hrēol*] — '**reelable** *adj.* — '**reeler** *n.*

reel[2] (riːl, rɪəl) *vb.* (*mainly intr.*) **1.** to sway, esp. under the shock of a blow or through dizziness or drunkenness. **2.** to whirl about or have the feeling of whirling about: *his brain reeled.* ~*n.* **3.** a staggering or swaying motion or sensation. [C14 *relen*, prob. from REEL[1]]

reel[3] (riːl, rɪəl) *n.* **1.** any of various lively Scottish dances for a fixed number of couples who combine in square and circular formations. **2.** a piece of music composed for or in the rhythm of this dance. [C18: from REEL[2]]

reel-fed *adj.* *Printing.* involving or printing on a web of paper: *a reel-fed press.*

reelman ('riːlmən, 'rɪəl-) *n., pl.* **-men.** *Austral. & N.Z.* the member of a beach life-saving team who controls the reel on which the line is wound.

reel off *vb.* (*tr., adv.*) to recite or write fluently and without apparent effort.

reel-to-reel *adj.* **1.** (of magnetic tape) wound from one reel to another in use. **2.** (of a tape recorder) using magnetic tape wound from one reel to another, as opposed to cassettes.

re-entrant (riː'ɛntrənt) *adj.* **1.** (of an angle) pointing inwards. ~*n.* **2.** an angle or part that points inwards.

re-entry (riː'ɛntrɪ) *n., pl.* **-tries. 1.** the act of retaking possession of land, etc. **2.** the return of a spacecraft into the earth's atmosphere.

reeve[1] (riːv) *n.* **1.** *English history.* the local representative of the king in a shire until the early 11th century. **2.** (in medieval England) a manorial steward who supervised the daily affairs of the manor. **3.** *Canad. government.* (in some provinces) a president of a local council, esp. in a rural area. **4.** (formerly) a minor local official in England and the U.S. [OE *gerēva*]

reeve[2] (riːv) *vb.* **reeving, reeved** *or* **rove.** (*tr.*) *Naut.* **1.** to pass (a rope or cable) through an eye or other narrow opening. **2.** to fasten by passing through or around something. [C17: ?from Du. *rēven* REEF[2]]

reeve[3] (riːv) *n.* the female of the ruff (the bird). [C17: from ?]

re-export *vb.* (,riːɪk'spɔːt, ,riːˈɛkspɔːt). **1.** to export (imported goods, esp. after processing). ~*n.* (riː'ɛkspɔːt). **2.**

---

re-'edit *vb.*	,**re-e'mergence** *n.*	,**re-en'actment** *n.*	,**re-es'tablish** *vb.*
re-'edu,cate *vb.*	,**re-e'mergent** *adj.*	,**re-en'force** *vb.*	,**re-e'valu,ate** *vb.*
re-,edu'cation *n.*	**re-em'pha,size** *or* -,**sise** *vb.*	,**re-en'forcement** *n.*	,**re-e,valu'ation** *n.*
,**re-e'lect** *vb.*	,**re-em'ploy** *vb.*	**re-'enter** *vb.*	,**re-ex'amine** *vb.*
,**re-e'lection** *n.*	,**re-em'ployment** *n.*	,**re-e'quip** *vb.*	,**re-ex'hibit** *vb.*
re-'eligible *adj.*	,**re-en'act** *vb.*	**re-e'rect** *vb.*	,**re-ex'perience** *vb.*
,**re-e'merge** *vb.*			

the act of re-exporting. **3.** a re-exported commodity. —**,re-expor'tation** n. —**,re-ex'porter** n.

ref (rɛf) n. Inf. short for **referee**.

ref. abbrev. for: **1.** referee. **2.** reference. **3.** reformed.

refection (rɪ'fɛkʃən) n. refreshment with food and drink. [C14: from L refectiō a restoring, from reficere, from RE- + facere to make]

refectory (rɪ'fɛktərɪ, -trɪ) n., pl. **-ries.** a dining hall in a religious or academic institution. [C15: from LL refectōrium, from L refectus refreshed]

refectory table n. a long narrow dining table supported by two trestles.

refer (rɪ'fɜː) vb. **-ferring, -ferred.** (often foll. by to). **1.** (intr.) to make mention (of). **2.** (tr.) to direct the attention of (someone) for information, facts, etc.: the reader is referred to Chomsky, 1965. **3.** (intr.) to seek information (from): he referred to his notes. **4.** (intr.) to be relevant (to); pertain or relate (to). **5.** (tr.) to assign or attribute: Cromwell referred his victories to God. **6.** (tr.) to hand over for consideration, reconsideration, or decision: to refer a complaint to another department. **7.** (tr.) to hand back to the originator as unacceptable or unusable. **8.** (tr.) Brit. to fail (a student) in an examination. **9. refer to drawer.** a request by a bank that the payee consult the drawer concerning a cheque payable by that bank. **10.** (tr.) to direct (a patient, client, etc.) to another doctor, agency, etc. [C14: from L referre, from RE- + ferre to BEAR[1]] —**referable** ('rɛfərəb[ə]l) or **referrable** (rɪ'fɜːrəb[ə]l) adj. —**re'ferral** n. —**re'ferrer** n.

▷ **Usage.** The common practice of adding back to refer is tautologous, since this meaning is already contained in the re-of refer: this refers to (not back to) what has already been said. However, when refer is used in the sense of passing a document or question for further consideration to the person from whom it was received, it may be appropriate to say he referred the matter back.

referee (,rɛfə'riː) n. **1.** a person to whom reference is made, esp. for an opinion, information, or a decision. **2.** the umpire or judge in any of various sports, esp. football and boxing. **3.** a person who is willing to testify to the character or capabilities of someone. **4.** Law. a person appointed by a court to report on a matter. ~vb. **-eeing, -eed. 5.** to act as a referee (in); preside (over).

reference ('rɛfərəns, 'rɛfrəns) n. **1.** the act or an instance of referring. **2.** something referred, esp. proceedings submitted to a referee in law. **3.** a direction of the attention to a passage elsewhere or to another book, etc. **4.** a book or passage referred to. **5.** a mention or allusion: this book contains several references to the Civil War. **6.** the relation between a word or phrase and the object or idea to which it refers. **7. a.** a source of information or facts. **b.** (as modifier): a reference book; a reference library. **8.** a written testimonial regarding one's character or capabilities. **9.** a person referred to for such a testimonial. **10. a.** (foll. by to) relation or delimitation, esp. to or by membership of a specific group: without reference to sex or age. **b.** (as modifier): a reference group. **11. terms of reference.** the specific limits of responsibility that determine the activities of an investigating body, etc. ~vb. (tr.) **12.** to furnish or compile a list of references for (a publication, etc.). **13.** to make a reference to; refer to. ~prep. **14.** Business jargon. with reference to: reference your letter of the 9th inst. Abbrev.: **re.** —**referential** (,rɛfə'rɛnʃəl) adj.

referendum (,rɛfə'rɛndəm) n., pl. **-dums** or **-da** (-də). **1.** submission of an issue of public importance to the direct vote of the electorate. **2.** a vote on such a measure. ~See also **plebiscite.** [C19: from L: something to be carried back, from referre to REFER]

referent ('rɛfərənt) n. the object or idea to which a word or phrase refers. [C19: from L referens from referre to RE-FER]

referred pain n. Psychol. pain felt at some place other than its actual place of origin.

refill vb. (riː'fɪl) **1.** to fill (something) again. ~n. ('riː,fɪl). **2.** a replacement for a consumable substance in a permanent container. **3.** a second or subsequent filling. —**re'fillable** adj.

refine (rɪ'faɪn) vb. **1.** to make or become free from impurities or foreign matter; purify. **2.** (tr.) to separate (a mixture) into pure constituents, as in an oil refinery. **3.** to

make or become elegant or polished. **4.** (intr.; often foll. by on or upon) to enlarge or improve (upon) by making subtle or fine distinctions. **5.** (tr.) to make (language) more subtle or polished. [C16: from RE- + FINE[1]] —**re'finable** adj. —**re'finer** n.

refined (rɪ'faɪnd) adj. **1.** not coarse or vulgar; genteel, elegant, or polite. **2.** subtle; discriminating. **3.** freed from impurities; purified.

refinement (rɪ'faɪnmənt) n. **1.** the act of refining or the state of being refined. **2.** a fine or delicate point or distinction; a subtlety. **3.** fineness or precision of thought, expression, manners, etc. **4.** an improvement to a piece of equipment, etc.

refinery (rɪ'faɪnərɪ) n., pl. **-eries.** a factory for the purification of some crude material, such as sugar, oil, etc.

refit vb. (riː'fɪt), **-fitting, -fitted. 1.** to make or be made ready for use again by repairing, re-equipping, or resupplying. ~n. ('riː,fɪt). **2.** a repair or re-equipping, as of a ship, for further use. —**re'fitment** n.

refl. abbrev. for: **1.** reflection. **2.** reflective. **3.** reflex(ive).

reflate (riː'fleɪt) vb. to inflate or be inflated again. [C20: back formation from REFLATION]

reflation (riː'fleɪʃən) n. **1.** an increase in economic activity. **2.** an increase in the supply of money and credit designed to cause such economic activity. ~Cf. **inflation** (sense 2). [C20: from RE- + -flation, as in INFLATION]

reflect (rɪ'flɛkt) vb. **1.** to undergo or cause to undergo a process in which light, other electromagnetic radiation, sound, particles, etc., are thrown back after impinging on a surface. **2.** (of a mirror, etc.) to form an image of (something) by reflection. **3.** (tr.) to show or express: his tactics reflect his desire for power. **4.** (tr.) to bring as a consequence: their success reflected great credit on them. **5.** (intr.; foll. by on or upon) to cause to be regarded in a specified way: her behaviour reflects well on her. **6.** (intr.; often foll. by on or upon) to cast dishonour or honour, credit or discredit, etc. (on). **7.** (intr.; usually foll. by on) to think, meditate, or ponder. [C15: from L reflectere, from RE- + flectere to bend] —**re'flectingly** adv.

reflectance (rɪ'flɛktəns) or **reflection factor** n. a measure of the ability of a surface to reflect light or other electromagnetic radiation, equal to the ratio of the reflected flux to the incident flux.

reflecting telescope n. a type of telescope in which the initial image is formed by a concave mirror. Also called: **reflector.** Cf. **refracting telescope.**

reflection or **reflexion** (rɪ'flɛkʃən) n. **1.** the act of reflecting or the state of being reflected. **2.** something reflected or the image so produced, as by a mirror. **3.** careful or long consideration or thought. **4.** attribution of discredit or blame. **5.** Maths. a transformation in which the direction of one axis is reversed or changes the polarity of one of the variables. **6.** Anat. the bending back of a structure or part upon itself. —**re'flectional** or **re'flexional** adj.

reflection density n. Physics. a measure of the extent to which a surface reflects light or other electromagnetic radiation. Symbol: D

reflective (rɪ'flɛktɪv) adj. **1.** characterized by quiet thought or contemplation. **2.** capable of reflecting: a reflective surface. **3.** produced by reflection. —**re'flectively** adv.

reflectivity (,riːflɛk'tɪvɪtɪ) n. **1.** Physics. a measure of the ability of a surface to reflect radiation, equal to the reflectance of a layer of material sufficiently thick for the reflectance not to depend on the thickness. **2.** Also: **reflectiveness.** the quality or capability of being reflective.

reflector (rɪ'flɛktə) n. **1.** a person or thing that reflects. **2.** a surface or object that reflects light, sound, heat, etc. **3.** another name for **reflecting telescope.**

reflet (rə'fleɪ) n. an iridescent glow or lustre, as on ceramic ware. [C19: from F: a reflection, from It. riflesso, from L reflexus, from reflectere to reflect]

reflex n. ('riːflɛks). **1. a.** an immediate involuntary response, such as coughing, evoked by a given stimulus. **b.** (as modifier): a reflex action. See also **reflex arc. 2. a.** a mechanical response to a particular situation, involving no conscious decision. **b.** (as modifier): a reflex response. **3.** a reflection; an image produced by or as if by reflection. ~*adj.* ('riːflɛks). **4.** *Maths.* (of an angle) between 180° and 360°. **5.** (*prenominal*) turned, reflected, or bent backwards. ~*vb.* (rɪˈflɛks). **6.** (*tr.*) to bend, turn, or reflect backwards. [C16: from L *reflexus* bent back, from *reflectere* to reflect] —**reˈflexible** *adj.* —**reˌflexiˈbility** *n.*

reflex arc *n. Physiol.* the neural pathway over which impulses travel to produce a reflex action.

reflex camera *n.* a camera in which the image is composed and focused on a large ground-glass viewfinder screen.

reflexion (rɪˈflɛkʃən) *n. Brit.* a less common spelling of **reflection.** —**reˈflexional** *adj.*

reflexive (rɪˈflɛksɪv) *adj.* **1.** denoting a class of pronouns that refer back to the subject of a sentence or clause. Thus, in *that man thinks a great deal of himself*, the pronoun *himself* is reflexive. **2.** denoting a verb used transitively with the reflexive pronoun as its direct object, as in *to dress oneself*. **3.** *Physiol.* of or relating to a reflex. ~*n.* **4.** a reflexive pronoun or verb. —**reˈflexively** *adv.* —**reˈflexiveness** *or* **reflexivity** (ˌriːflɛkˈsɪvɪtɪ) *n.*

reflexology (ˌriːflɛkˈsɒlədʒɪ) *n.* a form of therapy in alternative medicine in which the soles of the feet are massaged: designed to stimulate the blood supply and nerves and thus relieve tension. —**ˌreflexˈologist** *n.*

reflux ('riːflʌks) *vb.* **1.** *Chem.* to boil or be boiled in a vessel attached to a condenser, so that the vapour condenses and flows back into the vessel. ~*n.* **2.** *Chem.* **a.** an act of refluxing. **b.** (*as modifier*): *a reflux condenser.* **3.** the act or an instance of flowing back; ebb. [C15: from Med. L *refluxus*, from L *refluere* to flow back]

reform (rɪˈfɔːm) *vb.* **1.** (*tr.*) to improve (an existing institution, law, etc.) by alteration or correction of abuses. **2.** to give up or cause to give up a reprehensible habit or immoral way of life. ~*n.* **3.** an improvement or change for the better, esp. as a result of correction of legal or political abuses or malpractices. **4.** a principle, campaign, or measure aimed at achieving such change. **5.** improvement of morals or behaviour. [C14: via OF from L *reformāre* to form again] —**reˈformable** *adj.* —**reˈformative** *adj.* —**reˈformer** *n.*

re-form (riːˈfɔːm) *vb.* to form anew. —ˌ**re-forˈmation** *n.*

reformation (ˌrɛfəˈmeɪʃən) *n.* **1.** the act or an instance of reforming or the state of being reformed. **2.** (*usually cap.*) a religious and political movement of 16th-century Europe that began as an attempt to reform the Roman Catholic Church and resulted in the establishment of the Protestant Churches. —ˌ**reforˈmational** *adj.*

reformatory (rɪˈfɔːmətərɪ, -trɪ) *n.*, *pl.* **-ries.** **1.** Also called: **reform school.** (formerly) a place of instruction where young offenders were sent for corrective training. ~*adj.* **2.** having the purpose or function of reforming.

Reformed (rɪˈfɔːmd) *adj.* **1.** of or designating a Protestant Church, esp. the Calvinist. **2.** of or designating Reform Judaism.

reformism (rɪˈfɔːmɪzəm) *n.* a doctrine advocating reform, esp. political or religious reform rather than abolition. —**reˈformist** *n.*

refract (rɪˈfrækt) *vb.* **1.** to cause to undergo refraction. **2.** (*tr.*) to measure the amount of refraction of (the eye, a lens, etc.). [C17: from L *refractus* broken up, from *refringere*, from RE- + *frangere* to break] —**reˈfractable** *adj.* —**reˈfractive** *adj.*

refracting telescope *n.* a type of telescope in which the image is formed by a set of lenses. Also called: **refractor.** Cf. **reflecting telescope.**

refraction (rɪˈfrækʃən) *n.* **1.** *Physics.* the change in direction of a propagating wave, such as light or sound, in passing from one medium to another in which it has a different velocity. **2.** the amount by which a wave is refracted. **3.** the ability of the eye to refract light. —**reˈfractional** *adj.*

refractive index *n. Physics.* a measure of the extent to which a medium refracts light; the ratio of the speed of light in free space to that in the medium.

refractometer (ˌriːfrækˈtɒmɪtə) *n.* any instrument for measuring the refractive index. —**refractometric** (rɪˌfræktəˈmɛtrɪk) *adj.* —ˌ**refracˈtometry** *n.*

refractor (rɪˈfræktə) *n.* **1.** an object or material that refracts. **2.** another name for **refracting telescope.**

refractory (rɪˈfræktərɪ) *adj.* **1.** unmanageable or obstinate. **2.** *Med.* not responding to treatment. **3.** *Physiol.* (of a nerve or muscle) incapable of responding to stimulation. **4.** (of a material) able to withstand high temperatures without fusion or decomposition. ~*n.*, *pl.* **-ries.** **5.** a material, such as fire clay, that is able to withstand high temperatures. —**reˈfractorily** *adv.* —**reˈfractoriness** *n.*

refrain[1] (rɪˈfreɪn) *vb.* (*intr.*; usually foll. by *from*) to abstain (from action); forbear. [C14: from L *refrēnāre* to check with a bridle, from RE- + *frēnum* a bridle] —**reˈfrainer** *n.* —**reˈfrainment** *n.*

refrain[2] (rɪˈfreɪn) *n.* **1.** a regularly recurring melody, such as the chorus of a song. **2.** a much repeated saying or idea. [C14: via OF, ult. from L *refringere* to break into pieces]

refrangible (rɪˈfrændʒɪbᵊl) *adj.* capable of being refracted. [C17: from L *refringere* to break up, from RE- + *frangere* to break] —**reˌfrangiˈbility** *or* **reˈfrangibleness** *n.*

refresh (rɪˈfrɛʃ) *vb.* **1.** (*usually tr. or reflexive*) to make or become fresh or vigorous, as through rest, drink, or food; revive or reinvigorate. **2.** (*tr.*) to enliven (something worn or faded), as by adding new decorations. **3.** to pour cold water over previously blanched and drained food. **4.** (*tr.*) to stimulate (the memory, etc.). **5.** (*tr.*) to replenish, as with new equipment or stores. [C14: from OF *refreschir*; see RE-, FRESH] —**reˈfresher** *n.* —**reˈfreshing** *adj.*

refresher course *n.* a short educational course for people to review their subject and developments in it.

refreshment (rɪˈfrɛʃmənt) *n.* **1.** the act of refreshing or the state of being refreshed. **2.** (*pl.*) snacks and drinks served as a light meal.

refrigerant (rɪˈfrɪdʒərənt) *n.* **1.** a fluid capable of changes of phase at low temperatures: used as the working fluid of a refrigerator. **2.** a cooling substance, such as ice or solid carbon dioxide. **3.** *Med.* an agent that provides a sensation of coolness or reduces fever. ~*adj.* **4.** causing cooling or freezing.

refrigerate (rɪˈfrɪdʒəˌreɪt) *vb.* to make or become frozen or cold, esp. for preservative purposes; chill or freeze. [C16: from L *refrīgerāre* to make cold, from RE- + *frīgus* cold] —**reˈfrigerˌation** *n.* —**reˈfrigerative** *adj.* —**reˈfrigeratory** *adj.*, *n.*

refrigerator (rɪˈfrɪdʒəˌreɪtə) *n.* a chamber in which food, drink, etc., are kept cool. Informal name: **fridge.**

refringent (rɪˈfrɪndʒənt) *adj. Physics.* of, concerned with, or causing refraction; refractive. [C18: from L *refringere*; see REFRACT] —**reˈfringency** *or* **reˈfringence** *n.*

reft (rɛft) *vb.* a past tense and past participle of **reave.**

refuel (riːˈfjuːəl) *vb.* **-elling, -elled** *or* U.S. **-eling, -eled.** to supply or be supplied with fresh fuel.

refuge ('rɛfjuːdʒ) *n.* **1.** shelter or protection, as from the weather or danger. **2.** any place, person, action, or thing that offers protection, help, or relief. [C14: via OF from L *refugium*, from *refugere*, from RE- + *fugere* to escape]

refugee (ˌrɛfjʊˈdʒiː) *n.* **a.** a person who has fled from some danger or problem, esp. political persecution. **b.** (*as modifier*): *a refugee camp.* —ˌ**refuˈgeeism** *n.*

refugium (rɪˈfjuːdʒɪəm) *n.*, *pl.* **-gia** (-dʒɪə). a geographical region that has remained unaltered by a climatic change affecting surrounding regions and that therefore forms a haven for relict fauna and flora. [C20: L: REFUGE]

refulgent (rɪˈfʌldʒənt) *adj. Literary.* shining, brilliant, or radiant. [C16: from L *refulgēre*, from RE- + *fulgēre* to shine] —**reˈfulgence** *or* **reˈfulgency** *n.* —**reˈfulgently** *adv.*

refund *vb.* (rɪˈfʌnd). (*tr.*) **1.** to give back (money, etc.), as when an article purchased is unsatisfactory. **2.** to reimburse (a person). ~*n.* ('riːˌfʌnd). **3.** return of money to a purchaser or the amount so returned. [C14: from L *refundere*, from RE- + *fundere* to pour] —**reˈfundable** *adj.* —**reˈfunder** *n.*

re-fund (riːˈfʌnd) *vb.* (*tr.*) *Finance.* to discharge (an old or matured debt) by new borrowing, as by a new bond issue. [C20: from RE- + FUND]

refurbish (riːˈfɜːbɪʃ) *vb.* (*tr.*) to renovate, re-equip, or restore. —**reˈfurbishment** *n.*

refusal (rɪˈfjuːzᵊl) *n.* **1.** the act or an instance of refusing. **2.** the opportunity to reject or accept; option.

---

reˈfloat *vb.*
reˈfocus *vb.*

reˈfold *vb.*
reˈforge *vb.*

reˈfreeze *vb.*

reˈfurnish *vb.*

refuse[1] (rɪˈfjuːz) *vb.* **1.** (*tr.*) to decline to accept (something offered): *to refuse promotion.* **2.** to decline to give or grant (something) to (a person, etc.). **3.** (when *tr.*, *takes an infinitive*) to express determination not (to do something); decline: *he refuses to talk about it.* **4.** (of a horse) to be unwilling to take (a jump). [C14: from OF *refuser*, from L *refundere* to pour back] —**reˈfusable** *adj.* —**reˈfuser** *n.*

refuse[2] (ˈrɛfjuːs) *n.* **a.** anything thrown away; waste; rubbish. **b.** (*as modifier*): *a refuse collection.* [C15: from OF *refuser* to REFUSE[1]]

refusenik *or* **refusnik** (rɪˈfjuːznɪk) *n.* a Jew in the Soviet Union who has been refused permission to emigrate. [C20: from REFUSE[1] + -NIK]

refute (rɪˈfjuːt) *vb.* (*tr.*) to prove (a statement, theory, charge, etc.) of (a person) to be false or incorrect; disprove. [C16: from L *refūtāre* to rebut] —**refutable** (ˈrɛfjʊtəbəl, rɪˈfjuː-) *adj.* —**ˈrefutably** *adv.* —ˌrefuˈtation *n.* —**reˈfuter** *n.*

▷ *Usage. Refute* is often used incorrectly as a synonym of *deny.* In careful usage, however, to *deny* something is to state that it is untrue; to *refute* something is to assemble evidence in order to prove it untrue: *all he could was deny the allegations since he was unable to refute them.*

reg. *abbrev. for:* **1.** regiment. **2.** register(ed). **3.** registrar. **4.** regular(ly). **5.** regulation.

regain (rɪˈɡeɪn) *vb.* (*tr.*) **1.** to take or get back; recover. **2.** to reach again. —**reˈgainer** *n.*

regal (ˈriːɡəl) *adj.* of, relating to, or befitting a king or queen; royal. [C14: from L *rēgālis*, from *rēx* king] —**reˈgality** *n.* —**ˈregally** *adv.*

regale (rɪˈɡeɪl) *vb.* (*tr.*; usually foll. by *with*) **1.** to give delight or amusement to: *he regaled them with stories.* **2.** to provide with choice or abundant food or drink. ~*n.* **3.** *Arch.* **a.** a feast. **b.** a delicacy of food or drink. [C17: from F *régaler*, from *gale* pleasure] —**reˈgalement** *n.*

regalia (rɪˈɡeɪlɪə) *n.* (*pl.*, *sometimes functioning as sing.*) **1.** the ceremonial emblems or robes of royalty, high office, an order, etc. **2.** any splendid or special clothes; finery. [C16: from Med. L: royal privileges, from L *rēgālis* REGAL]

regard (rɪˈɡɑːd) *vb.* **1.** to look closely or attentively at (something or someone); observe steadily. **2.** (*tr.*) to hold (a person or thing) in respect, admiration, or affection: *we regard your work very highly.* **3.** (*tr.*) to look upon or consider in a specified way: *she regarded her brother as her responsibility.* **4.** (*tr.*) to relate to; concern; have a bearing on. **5.** to take notice of or pay attention to (something); heed: *he has never regarded the conventions.* **6. as regards.** (*prep.*) in respect of; concerning. ~*n.* **7.** a gaze; look. **8.** attention; heed: *he spends without regard to his bank balance.* **9.** esteem, affection, or respect. **10.** reference, relation, or connection (esp. in **with regard to** *or* **in regard to**). **11.** (*pl.*) good wishes or greetings (esp. in **with kind regards,** used at the close of a letter). **12. in this regard.** on this point. [C14: from OF *regarder* to look at, care about, from RE- + *garder* to GUARD]

regardant (rɪˈɡɑːdənt) *adj.* (*usually postpositive*) *Heraldry.* (of a beast) shown looking backwards over its shoulder. [C15: from OF; see REGARD]

regardful (rɪˈɡɑːdfʊl) *adj.* **1.** (often foll. by *of*) showing regard (for); heedful (of). **2.** showing regard, respect, or consideration. —**reˈgardfully** *adv.*

regarding (rɪˈɡɑːdɪŋ) *prep.* in respect of; on the subject of.

regardless (rɪˈɡɑːdlɪs) *adj.* **1.** (usually foll. by *of*) taking no regard or heed; heedless. ~*adv.* **2.** in spite of everything; disregarding drawbacks. —**reˈgardlessly** *adv.* —**reˈgardlessness** *n.*

regatta (rɪˈɡætə) *n.* an organized series of races of yachts, rowing boats, etc. [C17: from obs. It. *rigatta* contest, from ?]

regd *abbrev. for* registered.

regelation (ˌriːdʒɪˈleɪʃən) *n.* the rejoining together of two pieces of ice as a result of melting under pressure at the interface between them and subsequent refreezing. —**ˈreˌgeˌlate** *vb.*

regency (ˈriːdʒənsɪ) *n.*, *pl.* -cies. **1.** government by a regent. **2.** the office of a regent. **3.** a territory under the

jurisdiction of a regent. [C15: from Med. L *regentia*, from L *regere* to rule]

Regency (ˈriːdʒənsɪ) *n.* (preceded by *the*) **1.** (in Britain) the period (1811–20) of the regency of the Prince of Wales (later George IV). **2.** (in France) the period (1715–23) of the regency of Philip, Duke of Orleans. ~*adj.* **3.** characteristic of or relating to the Regency periods or to the styles of architecture, art, etc., produced in them.

regenerate *vb.* (rɪˈdʒɛnəˌreɪt). **1.** to undergo or cause to undergo moral, spiritual, or physical renewal or invigoration. **2.** to form or be formed again; come or bring into existence once again. **3.** to replace (lost or damaged tissues or organs) by new growth, or to cause (such tissues) to be replaced. **4.** (*tr.*) *Electronics.* to use positive feedback to improve the demodulation and amplification of a signal. ~*adj.* (rɪˈdʒɛnərɪt). **5.** morally, spiritually, or physically renewed or reborn. —**reˈgeneracy** *n.* —**reˌgenerˈation** *n.* —**reˈgenerative** *adj.* —**reˈgeneratively** *adv.* —**reˈgeneˌrator** *n.*

Regensburg (*German* ˈreːɡənsburk) *n.* a city in SE West Germany, in Bavaria on the River Danube: a free Imperial city from 1245 and the leading commercial city of S Germany in the 12th and 13th centuries; the Imperial Diet was held in the town hall from 1663 to 1806. Pop.: 132 604 (1980 est.). Former English name: **Ratisbon.**

regent (ˈriːdʒənt) *n.* **1.** the ruler or administrator of a country during the minority, absence, or incapacity of its monarch. **2.** *U.S. & Canad.* a member of the governing board of certain schools and colleges. ~*adj.* **3.** (*usually postpositive*) acting or functioning as a regent: *a queen regent.* [C14: from L *regēns*, from *regere* to rule] —**ˈregental** *adj.* —**ˈregentship** *n.*

regent-bird *n.* *Austral.* a bowerbird, the male of which has showy yellow and velvety-black plumage. [after the PRINCE REGENT]

Reger (*German* ˈreːɡər) *n.* **Max** (maks). 1873–1916, German composer, noted esp. for his organ works.

reggae (ˈrɛɡeɪ) *n.* a type of West Indian popular music having four beats to the bar, the upbeat being strongly accented. [C20: of West Indian origin]

Reggio di Calabria (*Italian* ˈreddʒo di kaˈlaːbrja) *n.* a port in S Italy, in Calabria on the Strait of Messina: founded about 720 B.C. by Greek colonists. Pop.: 178 821 (1986).

Reggio nell'Emilia (*Italian* ˈreddʒo nɛlleˈmiːlja) *n.* a city in N central Italy, in Emilia-Romagna: founded in the 2nd century B.C. by Marcus Aemilius Lepidus; ruled by the Este family in the 15th–18th centuries. Pop.: 130 086 (1986).

regicide (ˈrɛdʒɪˌsaɪd) *n.* **1.** the killing of a king. **2.** a person who kills a king. [C16: from L *rēx* king + -CIDE] —ˌregiˈcidal *adj.*

regime *or* **régime** (reɪˈʒiːm) *n.* **1.** a system of government or a particular administration: *a fascist regime.* **2.** a social system or order. **3.** *Med.* another word for **regimen** (sense 1). [C18: from F, from L *regimen* guidance, from *regere* to rule]

regimen (ˈrɛdʒɪˌmɛn) *n.* **1.** Also called: **regime.** *Med.* a systematic course of therapy, often including a recommended diet. **2.** administration or rule. [C14: from L: guidance]

regiment *n.* (ˈrɛdʒɪmənt). **1.** a military formation varying in size from a battalion to a number of battalions. **2.** a large number in regular or organized groups. ~*vb.* (ˈrɛdʒɪˌmɛnt). (*tr.*) **3.** to force discipline or order on, esp. in a domineering manner. **4.** to organize into a regiment. **5.** to form into organized groups. [C14: via OF from LL *regimentum* government, from L *regere* to rule] —ˌregiˈmental *adj.* —ˌregiˈmentally *adv.* —ˌregimenˈtation *n.*

regimentals (ˌrɛdʒɪˈmɛntəlz) *pl. n.* **1.** the uniform and insignia of a regiment. **2.** military dress.

Regin (ˈreɪɡɪn) *n.* *Norse myth.* a dwarf smith, tutor of Sigurd, whom he encouraged to kill Fafnir for the gold he guarded.

Regina[1] (rɪˈdʒaɪnə) *n.* queen: now used chiefly in documents, inscriptions, etc. Cf. **Rex.**

Regina[2] (rɪˈdʒaɪnə) *n.* a city in W Canada, capital and largest city of Saskatchewan: founded in 1882 as Pile O'Bones. Pop.: 186 521 (1986).

---

reˈgalvaˌnize *or* -ˌnise *vb.*   reˈgermiˌnate *vb.*   ˌregermiˈnation *n.*   reˈgild *vb.*
reˈgather *vb.*

Regiomontanus (ˌriːdʒɪəʊmɒnˈteɪnəs, -ˈtɑː-, -ˈtæn-) n. original name *Johann Müller*. 1436–76, German mathematician and astronomer, who furthered the development of trigonometry.

region (ˈriːdʒən) n. **1.** any large, indefinite, and continuous part of a surface or space. **2.** an area considered as a unit for geographical, functional, social, or cultural reasons. **3.** an administrative division of a country, or a Canadian province. **4.** a realm or sphere of activity or interest. **5.** range, area, or scope: *in what region is the price likely to be?* **6.** a division or part of the body: *the lumbar region.* [C14: from L *regiō*, from *regere* to govern]

regional (ˈriːdʒənᵊl) adj. of, characteristic of, or limited to a region. —**ˈregionally** adv.

regionalism (ˈriːdʒənəˌlɪzəm) n. **1.** division of a country into administrative regions having partial autonomy. **2.** loyalty to one's home region; regional patriotism. —**ˈregionalist** n., adj.

régisseur French. (reʒisœr) n. an official in a dance company with varying duties, usually including directing productions. [F, from *régir* to manage]

register (ˈrɛdʒɪstə) n. **1.** an official or formal list recording names, events, or transactions. **2.** the book in which such a list is written. **3.** an entry in such a list. **4.** a recording device that accumulates data, totals sums of money, etc.: *a cash register.* **5.** a movable plate that controls the flow of air into a furnace, chimney, room, etc. **6.** Music. **a.** the timbre characteristic of a certain manner of voice production. **b.** any of the stops on an organ as classified in respect of its tonal quality: *the flute register.* **7.** Printing. the exact correspondence of lines of type, etc., on the two sides of a printed sheet of paper. **8.** a form of a language associated with a particular social situation or subject matter. **9.** the act or an instance of registering. ~vb. **10.** (tr.) to enter or cause someone to enter (an event, person's name, ownership, etc.) on a register. **11.** to show or be shown on a scale or other measuring instrument: *the current didn't register on the meter.* **12.** to show or be shown in a person's face, bearing, etc.: *his face registered surprise.* **13.** (intr.) Inf. to have an effect; make an impression: *the news of her uncle's death just did not register.* **14.** to send (a letter, package, etc.) by registered post. **15.** (tr.) Printing. to adjust (a printing press, forme, etc.) to ensure that the printed matter is in register. [C14: from Med. L *registrum*, from L *regerere* to transcribe, from RE- + *gerere* to bear] —**ˈregistrable** adj.

registered post n. **1.** a Post Office service by which compensation is paid for loss or damage to mail for which a registration fee has been paid. **2.** mail sent by this service.

Registered Trademark n. See **trademark** (sense 1).

register office n. Brit. a government office where civil marriages are performed and births, marriages, and deaths are recorded. Often called: **registry office.**

register ton n. the full name for **ton**[1] (sense 6).

registrar (ˌrɛdʒɪˈstrɑː, ˈrɛdʒɪˌstrɑː) n. **1.** a person who keeps official records. **2.** an administrative official responsible for student records, enrolment procedure, etc., in a school, college, or university. **3.** Brit. & N.Z. a hospital doctor senior to a houseman but junior to a consultant. **4.** Austral. the chief medical administrator of a large hospital. **5.** Chiefly U.S. a person employed by a company to maintain a register of its security issues. —**ˈregisˌtrarship** n.

registration (ˌrɛdʒɪˈstreɪʃən) n. **1. a.** the act of registering or state of being registered. **b.** (as modifier): *a registration number.* **2.** an entry in a register. **3.** a group of people, such as students, who register at a particular time. **4.** Austral. **a.** a tax payable by the owner of a motor vehicle. **b.** the period paid for.

registration document n. Brit. a document giving identification details of a motor vehicle, including its manufacturer, date of registration, and owner's name.

registration number n. a sequence of letters and numbers assigned to a motor vehicle when it is registered, usually indicating the year and place of registration, displayed on numberplates at the front and rear of the vehicle.

registration plate n. Austral. & N.Z. the numberplate of a vehicle.

registry (ˈrɛdʒɪstrɪ) n., pl. **-tries. 1.** a place where registers are kept. **2.** the registration of a ship's country of origin: *a ship of Liberian registry.* **3.** another word for **registration.**

registry office n. Brit. another term for **register office.**

Regius professor (ˈriːdʒɪəs) n. Brit. a person appointed by the Crown to a university chair founded by a royal patron. [C17: *regius*, from L: royal, from *rex* king]

reglet (ˈrɛglɪt) n. **1.** a flat narrow architectural moulding. **2.** Printing. a strip of oiled wood used for spacing between lines. [C16: from OF, lit.: a little rule, from *régle* rule, from L *régula*]

regmaker (ˈrɛxˌmɑːkə) n. S. African. a drink to relieve the symptoms of a hangover. [from Afrik., right maker]

regnal (ˈrɛgnəl) adj. **1.** of a sovereign or reign. **2.** designating a year of a sovereign's reign calculated from the date of accession. [C17: from Med. L *régnālis*, from L *régnum* sovereignty; see REIGN]

regnant (ˈrɛgnənt) adj. **1.** (postpositive) reigning. **2.** prevalent; current. [C17: from L *regnāre* to REIGN] —**ˈregnancy** n.

regorge (rɪˈgɔːdʒ) vb. **1.** (tr.) to vomit up; disgorge. **2.** (intr.) (esp. of water) to flow or run back. [C17: from F *regorger*; see GORGE]

regress vb. (rɪˈgrɛs). **1.** (intr.) to return or revert, as to a former place, condition, or mode of behaviour. **2.** (tr.) Statistics. to measure the extent to which a (dependent variable) is associated with one or more independent variables. ~n. (ˈriːgrɛs). **3.** movement in a backward direction; retrogression. [C14: from L *regressus*, from *regredī* to go back, from RE- + *gradī* to go] —**reˈgressive** adj. —**reˈgressor** n.

regression (rɪˈgrɛʃən) n. **1.** Psychol. the adoption by an adult of behaviour more appropriate to a child. **2.** Statistics. **a.** the measure of the association between one variable (the dependent variable) and other variables (the independent variables). **b.** (as modifier): *regression curve.* **3.** the act of regressing.

regret (rɪˈgrɛt) vb. **-gretting, -gretted.** (tr.) **1.** (may take a clause as object or an infinitive) to feel sorry, repentant, or upset about. **2.** to bemoan or grieve the death or loss of. ~n. **3.** a sense of repentance, guilt, or sorrow. **4.** a sense of loss or grief. **5.** (pl.) a polite expression of sadness, esp. in a formal refusal of an invitation. [C14: from OF *regreter*, from ON] —**reˈgretful** adj. —**reˈgretfully** adv. —**reˈgretfulness** n. —**reˈgrettable** adj. —**reˈgrettably** adv.

regroup (riːˈgruːp) vb. **1.** to reorganize (military forces), esp. after an attack or a defeat. **2.** (tr.) to rearrange into a new grouping.

Regt abbrev. for: **1.** Regent. **2.** Regiment.

regulable (ˈrɛgjʊləbᵊl) adj. able to be regulated.

regular (ˈrɛgjʊlə) adj. **1.** normal, customary, or usual. **2.** according to a uniform principle, arrangement, or order. **3.** occurring at fixed or prearranged intervals: *a regular call on a customer.* **4.** following a set rule or normal practice; methodical or orderly. **5.** symmetrical in appearance or form; even: *regular features.* **6.** (prenominal) organized, elected, conducted, etc., in a proper or officially prescribed manner. **7.** (prenominal) officially qualified or recognized: *he's not a regular doctor.* **8.** (prenominal) (intensifier): *a regular fool.* **9.** U.S. & Canad. inf. likable, dependable, or nice: *a regular guy.* **10.** denoting or relating to the personnel or units of the permanent military services: *a regular soldier.* **11.** (of flowers) having any of their parts, esp. petals, alike in size, etc.; symmetrical. **12.** Grammar. following the usual pattern of formation in a language. **13.** Maths. **a.** (of a polygon) equilateral and equiangular. **b.** (of a polyhedron) having identical regular polygons as faces. **c.** (of a prism) having regular polygons as bases. **d.** (of a pyramid) having a regular polygon as a base and the altitude passing through the centre of the base. **14.** Bot. (of a flower) having radial symmetry. **15.** (postpositive) subject to the rule of an established religious order or community: *canons regular.* ~n. **16.** a professional long-term serviceman in a military unit. **17.** Inf. a person who does something regularly, such as attending a theatre. **18.** a member of a religious order or congregation, as contrasted with a secular. [C14: from OF *reguler*, from L *régulāris* of a bar of wood or metal, from *régula* ruler,

model] —,**regu'larity** *n.* —'**regular,ize** *or* -,**ise** *vb.*
—'**regularly** *adv.*

regulate ('rɛgjʊ,leɪt) *vb.* (*tr.*) **1.** to adjust (the amount of heat, sound, etc.) as required; control. **2.** to adjust (an instrument or appliance) so that it operates correctly. **3.** to bring into conformity with a rule, principle, or usage. [C17: from LL *rēgulāre* to control, from L *rēgula* ruler] —'**regulative** *or* '**regulatory** *adj.* —'**regulatively** *adv.*

regulation (,rɛgjʊ'leɪʃən) *n.* **1.** the act or process of regulating. **2.** a rule, principle, or condition that governs procedure or behaviour. **3.** (*modifier*) as required by official rules: *regulation uniform.* **4.** (*modifier*) normal; usual; conforming to accepted standards: *a regulation haircut.*

regulator ('rɛgjʊ,leɪtə) *n.* **1.** a person or thing that regulates. **2.** the mechanism by which the speed of a time-piece is regulated. **3.** any of various mechanisms or devices, such as a governor valve, for controlling fluid flow, pressure, temperature, etc.

regulo ('rɛgjʊləʊ) *n.* any of a number of temperatures to which a gas oven may be set: *cook at regulo 4.* [C20: from *Regulo*, trademark for a type of thermostatic control on gas ovens]

regulus ('rɛgjʊləs) *n.*, *pl.* -**luses** *or* -**li** (-,laɪ). impure metal forming beneath the slag during the smelting of ores. [C16: from L: a petty king, from *rēx* king; formerly used for *antimony*, because it combines readily with gold, the king of metals] —'**reguline** *adj.*

Regulus ('rɛgjʊləs) *n.* **Marcus Atilius** ('mɑːkəs ə'tɪlɪəs). died ?250 B.C., Roman general; consul (267; 256). Captured by the Carthaginians in the First Punic War, he was sent to Rome on parole to deliver the enemy's peace terms, advised the Senate to refuse them, and was tortured to death on his return to Carthage.

regurgitate (rɪ'gɜːdʒɪ,teɪt) *vb.* **1.** to vomit forth (partially digested food). **2.** (of some birds and animals) to bring back to the mouth (undigested or partly digested food to feed the young). **3.** (*intr.*) to be cast up or out, esp. from the mouth. [C17: from Med. L *regurgitāre*, from RE- + *gurgitāre* to flood, from L *gurges* whirlpool] —**re'gurgitant** *n.*, *adj.* —**re,gurgi'tation** *n.*

rehabilitate (,riːə'bɪlɪ,teɪt) *vb.* (*tr.*) **1.** to help (a physically or mentally disabled person or an ex-prisoner) to readapt to society or a new job, as by vocational guidance, retraining, or therapy. **2.** to restore to a former position or rank. **3.** to restore the good reputation of. [C16: from Med. L *rehabilitāre* to restore, from RE- + L *habilitās* skill] —,**reha,bili'tation** *n.* —,**reha'bilitative** *adj.*

Rehabilitation Department *n.* NZ. a government department set up after World War II to assist ex-servicemen. Often shortened to **rehab.**

rehash (riː'hæʃ) *vb.* **1.** (*tr.*) to rework, reuse, or make over (old or already used material). ~*n.* **2.** something consisting of old, reworked, or reused material. [C19: from RE- + HASH¹ (to chop into pieces)]

rehearsal (rɪ'hɜːsəl) *n.* **1.** a session of practising a play, concert, etc., in preparation for public performance. **2. in rehearsal.** being prepared for public performance.

rehearse (rɪ'hɜːs) *vb.* **1.** to practise (a play, concert, etc.), in preparation for public performance. **2.** (*tr.*) to run through; recount; recite: *he rehearsed the grievances of the committee.* **3.** (*tr.*) to train or drill (a person) for public performance. [C16: from Anglo-Norman *rehearser*, from OF *rehercier* to harrow a second time, from RE- + *herce* harrow] —**re'hearser** *n.*

reheat *vb.* (riː'hiːt). **1.** to heat or be heated again: *to reheat yesterday's soup.* **2.** (*tr.*) to add fuel to (the exhaust gases of an aircraft jet engine) to produce additional heat and thrust. ~*n.* ('riː,hiːt), *also* **reheating.** **3.** a process in which additional fuel is ignited in the exhaust gases of a jet engine to produce additional thrust. —**re'heater** *n.*

rehoboam (,riːə'bəʊəm) *n.* a wine bottle holding the equivalent of six normal bottles. [after *Rehoboam*, a son of King Solomon, from Heb., lit.: the nation is enlarged]

Reich¹ (raɪk) *n.* **1.** the Holy Roman Empire (962–1806) (**First Reich**). **2.** the Hohenzollern empire in Germany from 1871 to 1918 (**Second Reich**). **3.** the Nazi dictatorship in Germany from 1933–45 (**Third Reich**). [G: kingdom]

Reich² (raɪk; *German* raɪç) *n.* **Wilhelm** ('vɪlhɛlm). 1897–1957, Austrian psychologist, lived in the U.S. An ardent socialist and advocate of sexual freedom, he proclaimed a cosmic unity of all energy and built a machine (the orgone accumulator) to concentrate this energy on human beings. His books include *The Function of the Orgasm* (1927).

Reichenberg ('raɪçənbɛrk) *n.* the German name for **Liberec.**

Reichsmark ('raɪks,mɑːk) *n.*, *pl.* -**marks** *or* -**mark.** the standard monetary unit of Germany between 1924 and 1948.

Reichstag ('raɪks,tɑːg) *n.* **1.** the legislative assembly of Germany (1867–1933). **2.** the building in Berlin in which this assembly met.

Reid (riːd) *n.* **1. Sir George Houston.** 1845–1918, Australian statesman, born in Scotland: premier of New South Wales (1894–99); prime minister of Australia (1904–05). **2. Thomas.** 1710–96, Scottish philosopher and founder of what came to be known as the philosophy of common sense.

reify ('riːɪ,faɪ) *vb.* -**fying**, -**fied.** (*tr.*) to consider or make (an abstract idea or concept) real or concrete. [C19: from L *rēs* thing] —,**reifi'cation** *n.* —,**reifi'catory** *adj.* —'**re-i,fier** *n.*

Reigate ('raɪgɪt, -geɪt) *n.* a town in S England, in Surrey at the foot of the North Downs. Pop.: 52 554 (1981).

reign (reɪn) *n.* **1.** the period during which a monarch is the official ruler of a country. **2.** a period during which a person or thing is dominant or powerful: *the reign of violence.* ~*vb.* (*intr.*) **3.** to exercise the power and authority of a sovereign. **4.** to be accorded the rank and title of a sovereign without having ruling authority. **5.** to predominate; prevail: *darkness reigns.* **6.** (*usually present participle*) to be the most recent winner of a contest, etc.: *the reigning champion.* [C13: from OF *reigne*, from L *rēgnum* kingdom, from *rēx* king]

reimburse (,riːɪm'bɜːs) *vb.* (*tr.*) to repay or compensate (someone) for (money already spent, losses, damages, etc.). [C17: from RE- + *imburse*, from Med. L *imbursāre* to put in a moneybag, from *bursa* PURSE] —,**reim'bursable** *adj.* —,**reim'bursement** *n.* —,**reim'burser** *n.*

reimport *vb.* (,riːɪm'pɔːt, riː'ɪmpɔːt). **1.** (*tr.*) to import (goods manufactured from exported raw materials). ~*n.* (riː'ɪmpɔːt). **2.** the act of reimporting. **3.** a reimported commodity. —,**reimpor'tation** *n.*

Reims *or* **Rheims** (riːmz; *French* rɛs) *n.* a city in NE France: scene of the coronation of most French monarchs. Pop.: 178 821 (1983).

rein (reɪn) *n.* **1.** (*often pl.*) one of a pair of long straps, usually connected together and made of leather, used to control a horse. **2.** a similar device used to control a very young child. **3.** any form or means of control: *to take up the reins of government.* **4.** the direction in which a rider turns (in **on a left rein**). **5.** something that restrains, controls, or guides. **6. give (a) free rein.** to allow considerable freedom; remove restraints. **7. keep a tight rein on.** to control carefully; limit: *we have to keep a tight rein on expenditure.* ~*vb.* **8.** (*tr.*) to check, restrain, hold back, or halt with or as if with reins. **9.** to control or guide (a horse) with a rein or reins: *they reined his*. ~See also **rein in.** [C13: from OF *resne*, from L *retinēre* to hold back, from RE- + *tenēre* to hold]

reincarnate *vb.* (riː'ɪnkɑː,neɪt). (*tr.*; *often passive*) **1.** to cause to undergo reincarnation; be born again. ~*adj.* (,riːɪn'kɑːnɪt). **2.** born again in a new body.

reincarnation (,riːɪnkɑː'neɪʃən) *n.* **1.** the belief that on the death of the body the soul transmigrates to or is born again in another body. **2.** the incarnation or embodiment of a soul in a new body after it has left the old one at physical death. **3.** embodiment again in a new form, as of a principle or idea. —,**reincar'nationist** *n.*, *adj.*

reindeer ('reɪn,dɪə) *n.*, *pl.* -**deer** *or* -**deers.** a large deer, having large branched antlers in the male and female and inhabiting the arctic regions. It also occurs in North America, where it is known as a caribou. [C14: from ON *hreindȳri*, from *hreinn* reindeer + *dȳr* animal]

---

re'hang *vb.*
re'harness *vb.*
re'hear *vb.*

re'heel *vb.*
re'hire *vb.*
re'house *vb.*

,reim'pose *vb.*
,reim'prison *vb.*
,reim'corpo,rate *vb.*

,rein,corpo'ration *n.*
,rein'cur *vb.*

Reindeer Lake n. a lake in W Canada, in Saskatchewan and Manitoba: drains into the Churchill River via the **Reindeer River.** Area: 6390 sq. km (2467 sq. miles).

reindeer moss n. any of various lichens which occur in arctic and subarctic regions, providing food for reindeer.

reinforce (,riːɪnˈfɔːs) vb. (tr.) **1.** to give added strength or support to. **2.** to give added emphasis to; stress or increase: his rudeness reinforced my determination. **3.** to give added support to (a military force) by providing more men, supplies, etc. [C17: from F renforcer] — ˌreinˈforcement n.

reinforced concrete n. concrete with steel bars, mesh, etc., embedded in it to enable it to withstand tensile and shear stresses.

Reinhardt (ˈraɪnˌhɑːt) n. **1. Django** (ˈdʒæŋɡəʊ), real name Jean Baptiste Reinhardt. 1910–53, Belgian jazz guitarist, whose work was greatly influenced by Gypsy music. With Stéphane Grappelli, he led the Quintet of the Hot Club of France between 1934 and 1939. **2. Max,** original name Max Goldmann. 1873–1943, Austrian theatre producer and director, in the U.S. after 1933.

rein in vb. (adv.) to stop (a horse) by pulling on the reins.

reins (reɪnz) pl. n. Arch. the kidneys or loins. [C14: from OF, from L rēnēs the kidneys]

reinstate (,riːɪnˈsteɪt) vb. (tr.) to restore to a former rank or condition. — ˌreinˈstatement n. — ˌreinˈstator n.

reinsurer (,riːɪnˈʃʊərə) n. an insurance company which will accept business from other insurance companies, thus enabling the risks to be spread. — ˌreinˈsurance n.

reiterate (riːˈɪtəˌreɪt) vb. (tr.; may take a clause as object) to say or do again or repeatedly. [C16: from L reiterāre, from RE- + iterāre to do again, from iterum again] — reˌiterˈation n. — reˈiterative adj. — reˈiteratively adv.

Reith (riːθ) n. **John (Charles Walsham),** 1st Baron. 1889–1971, British public servant: first general manager (1922–27) and first director general (1927–38) of the BBC. — ˈReithian or ˈReithean adj.

reive (riːv) vb. (intr.) Scot. & N English dialect. to go on a plundering raid; see REAVE. — ˈreiver n.

reject vb. (rɪˈdʒɛkt). (tr.) **1.** to refuse to accept, use, believe, etc. **2.** to throw out as useless or worthless; discard. **3.** to rebuff (a person). **4.** (of an organism) to fail to accept (a foreign tissue graft or organ transplant). ~n. (ˈriːdʒɛkt). **5.** something rejected as imperfect, unsatisfactory, or useless. [C15: from L reicere to throw back, from RE-+ jacere to hurl] — reˈjecter or reˈjector n. — reˈjection n. — reˈjective adj.

rejig (riːˈdʒɪɡ) vb. **-jigging, -jigged.** (tr.) **1.** to re-equip (a factory or plant). **2.** Inf. to rearrange, manipulate, etc., sometimes in an unscrupulous way. ~n. **3.** the act or process of rejigging. — reˈjigger n.

rejoice (rɪˈdʒɔɪs) vb. (when tr., takes a clause as object or an infinitive; when intr., often foll. by in) to feel or express great joy or happiness. [C14: from OF resjoir, from RE- + joir to be glad, from L gaudēre to rejoice] — reˈjoicer n.

rejoin[1] (riːˈdʒɔɪn) vb. **1.** to come again into company with (someone or something). **2.** (tr.) to put or join together again; reunite.

rejoin[2] (rɪˈdʒɔɪn) vb. (tr.) **1.** to answer or reply. **2.** Law. to answer (a plaintiff's reply). [C15: from OF rejoign-, stem of rejoindre; see RE-, JOIN]

rejoinder (rɪˈdʒɔɪndə) n. **1.** a reply or response to a question or remark. **2.** Law. (in pleading) the answer made by a defendant to the plaintiff's reply. [C15: from OF rejoindre to REJOIN[2]]

rejuvenate (rɪˈdʒuːvɪˌneɪt) vb. (tr.) **1.** to give new youth, restored vitality, or youthful appearance to. **2.** (usually passive) Geog. to cause (a river) to begin eroding more vigorously to a new lower base level. [C19: from RE- + L juvenis young] — reˌjuveˈnation n. — reˈjuveˌnator n.

rejuvenesce (rɪ,dʒuːvəˈnɛs) vb. **1.** to make or become youthful or restored to vitality. **2.** Biol. to convert (cells)

or (of cells) to be converted into a more active form. — reˌjuveˈnescence n. — reˌjuveˈnescent adj.

rel. abbrev. for: **1.** relating. **2.** relative(ly). **3.** released. **4.** religion. **5.** religious.

relapse (rɪˈlæps) vb. (intr.) **1.** to lapse back into a former state or condition, esp. one involving bad habits. **2.** to become ill again after apparent recovery. ~n. **3.** the act or an instance of relapsing. **4.** the return of ill health after an apparent or partial recovery. [C16: from L relabī, from RE- + labī to slip, slide] — reˈlapser n.

relapsing fever n. any of various infectious diseases characterized by recurring fever, caused by the bite of body lice or ticks. Also called: **recurrent fever.**

relate (rɪˈleɪt) vb. **1.** (tr.) to tell or narrate (a story, etc.). **2.** (often foll. by to) to establish association (between two or more things) or (of something) to have relation or reference (to something else). **3.** (intr.; often foll. by to) to form a sympathetic or understanding relationship (with other people, things, etc.). [C16: from L relātus brought back, from referre, from RE- + ferre to bear] — reˈlatable adj. — reˈlater n.

▷ **Usage.** Relate is frequently applied to personal relationships, as in sense 3, but this usage is vague and is avoided by careful speakers and writers.

related (rɪˈleɪtɪd) adj. **1.** connected; associated. **2.** connected by kinship or marriage. — reˈlatedness n.

relation (rɪˈleɪʃən) n. **1.** the state or condition of being related or the manner in which things are related. **2.** connection by blood or marriage; kinship. **3.** a person who is connected by blood or marriage; relative. **4.** reference or regard (esp. in **in** or **with relation to**). **5.** the position, association, connection, or status of one person or thing with regard to another. **6.** the act of relating or narrating. **7.** an account or narrative. **8.** Law. the statement of grounds of complaint made by a relator. **9.** Logic, maths. **a.** an association between ordered pairs of objects, numbers, etc., such as ... is greater than .... **b.** the set of ordered pairs whose members have such an association. ~See also **relations.** [C14: from L relātiō a narration, a relation (between philosophical concepts)]

relational (rɪˈleɪʃənᵊl) adj. **1.** Grammar. indicating or expressing syntactic relation, as for example the case endings in Latin. **2.** having relation or being related.

relations (rɪˈleɪʃənz) pl. n. **1.** social, political, or personal connections or dealings between or among individuals, groups, nations, etc. **2.** family or relatives. **3.** Euphemistic. sexual intercourse.

relationship (rɪˈleɪʃənʃɪp) n. **1.** the state of being connected or related. **2.** association by blood or marriage; kinship. **3.** the mutual dealings, connections, or feelings that exist between two countries, people, etc. **4.** an emotional or sexual affair or liaison.

relative (ˈrɛlətɪv) adj. **1.** having meaning or significance only in relation to something else; not absolute. **2.** (prenominal) (of a scientific quantity) being measured or stated relative to some other substance or measurement: relative density. **3.** (prenominal) comparative or respective: the relative qualities of speed and accuracy. **4.** (postpositive; foll. by to) in proportion (to); corresponding (to): earnings relative to production. **5.** having reference (to); pertinent (to). **6.** Grammar. denoting or belonging to a class of words that function as subordinating conjunctions introducing relative clauses such as who, which, and that. Cf. **demonstrative. 7.** Grammar. denoting or relating to a clause (**relative clause**) that modifies a noun or pronoun occurring earlier in the sentence. **8.** (of a musical key or scale) having the same key signature as another key or scale. ~n. **9.** a person who is related by blood or marriage; relation. **10.** a relative pronoun, clause, or grammatical construction. [C16: from LL relātivus referring] — ˈrelatively adv. — ˈrelativeness n.

relative aperture n. Photog. the ratio of the equivalent focal length of a lens to the effective aperture of the lens.

ˌreinˈduce vb.	ˌreinˈsert vb.	ˌreinteˈgration n.	ˌreinˈvasion n.
ˌreinˈduction n.	ˌreinˈsertion n.	ˌreinˈterpret vb.	ˌreinˈvestiˌgate vb.
ˌreinˈfect vb.	ˌreinˈspect vb.	ˌreinˌterpreˈtation n.	ˌreinˌvestiˈgation n.
ˌreinˈfection n.	ˌreinˈspection n.	ˌreinˈterroˌgate vb.	reˈjudge vb.
ˌreinˈfuse vb.	ˌreinˈstruct vb.	ˌreinˌterroˈgation n.	reˈkey vb.
ˌreinˈfusion n.	ˌreinˈstruction n.	ˌreintroˈduce vb.	reˈkindle vb.
ˌreinˈocuˌlate vb.	ˌreinˈsure vb.	ˌreintroˈduction n.	reˈlabel vb.
ˌreinˈocuˈlation n.	reˈinteˌgrate vb.	ˌreinˈvade vb.	

relative atomic mass *n.* another name for **atomic weight.**

relative density *n.* the ratio of the density of a substance to the density of a standard substance under specified conditions. For liquids and solids the standard is usually water at 4°C. For gases the standard is air or hydrogen at the same temperature and pressure as the substance. See also **specific gravity, vapour density.**

relative frequency *n. Statistics.* the ratio of the actual number of favourable events to the total possible number of events.

relative humidity *n.* the mass of water vapour present in the air expressed as a percentage of the mass present in an equal volume of saturated air at the same temperature.

relative majority *n. Brit.* the excess of votes or seats won by the winner of an election over the runner-up when no candidate or party has more than 50 per cent. Cf. **absolute majority.**

relative molecular mass *n.* another name for **molecular weight.**

relative permeability *n.* the ratio of the permeability of a medium to that of free space.

relative permittivity *n.* the ratio of the permittivity of a substance to that of free space.

relativism ('rɛlətɪˌvɪzəm) *n.* any theory holding that truth or moral or aesthetic value, etc., is not universal or absolute but may differ between individuals or cultures. —'**relativist** *n., adj.* —ˌrelativ'**istic** *adj.*

relativity (ˌrɛlə'tɪvɪtɪ) *n.* **1.** either of two theories developed by Albert Einstein, the **special theory of relativity,** which requires that the laws of physics shall be the same as seen by any two different observers in uniform relative motion, and the **general theory of relativity,** which considers observers with relative acceleration and leads to a theory of gravitation. **2.** the state or quality of being relative.

relator (rɪ'leɪtə) *n.* **1.** a person who relates a story; narrator. **2.** *English law.* a person who gives information upon which the attorney general brings an action.

relatum (rɪ'leɪtəm) *n., pl.* **-ta** (-tə). *Logic.* one of the objects between which a relation is said to hold.

relax (rɪ'læks) *vb.* **1.** to make (muscles, a grip, etc.) less tense or rigid or (of muscles, a grip, etc.) to become looser or less rigid. **2.** (*intr.*) to take rest, as from work or effort. **3.** to lessen the force of (effort, concentration) or (of effort) to become diminished. **4.** to make (rules or discipline) less rigid or strict or (of rules, etc.) to diminish in severity. **5.** (*intr.*) (of a person) to become less formal; unbend. [C15: from L *relaxāre* to loosen, from RE- + *laxāre*, from *laxus* loose] —re'**laxed** *adj.* —relaxedly (rɪ'læksɪdlɪ) *adv.* —re'**laxer** *n.*

relaxant (rɪ'læksˀnt) *n.* **1.** *Med.* a drug or agent that relaxes, esp. one that relaxes tense muscles. ~*adj.* **2.** of or tending to produce relaxation.

relaxation (ˌriːlæk'seɪʃən) *n.* **1.** rest or refreshment, as after work or effort; recreation. **2.** a form of rest or recreation: *his relaxation is cricket.* **3.** a partial lessening of a punishment, duty, etc. **4.** the act of relaxing or state of being relaxed. **5.** *Physics.* the return of a system to equilibrium after a displacement from this state.

relaxin (rɪ'læksɪn) *n.* **1.** a mammalian polypeptide hormone secreted during pregnancy, which relaxes the pelvic ligaments. **2.** a preparation of this hormone, used to facilitate childbirth. [C20: from RELAX + -IN]

relay *n.* ('riːleɪ). **1.** a person or team of people relieving others, as on a shift. **2.** a fresh team of horses, etc., posted along a route to relieve others. **3.** the act of relaying or process of being relayed. **4.** short for **relay race. 5.** an automatic device that controls a valve, switch, etc., by means of an electric motor, solenoid, or pneumatic mechanism. **6.** *Electronics.* an electrical device in which a small change in current or voltage controls the switching on or off of circuits. **7.** *Radio.* **a.** a combination of a receiver and transmitter designed to receive radio signals and retransmit them. **b.** (*as modifier*): *a relay station.* ~*vb.* (rɪ'leɪ). (*tr.*) **8.** to carry or spread (news or information) by relays. **9.** to supply or replace with relays. **10.** to retransmit (a signal) by means of a relay. **11.** *Brit.* to broadcast (a performance) by sending out signals through a transmitting station. [C15 *relaien,* from OF *relaier* to

leave behind, from RE- + *laier* to leave, ult. from L *laxāre* to loosen]

relay race *n.* a race between two or more teams of contestants in which each contestant covers a specified portion of the distance.

release (rɪ'liːs) *vb.* (*tr.*) **1.** to free (a person or animal) from captivity or imprisonment. **2.** to free (someone) from obligation or duty. **3.** to free (something) from (one's grip); let fall. **4.** to issue (a record, film, or book) for sale or circulation. **5.** to make (news or information) known or allow (news, etc.) to be made known. **6.** *Law.* to relinquish (a right, claim, or title) in favour of someone else. ~*n.* **7.** the act of freeing or state of being freed. **8.** the act of issuing for sale or publication. **9.** something issued for sale or public showing, esp. a film or a record: *a new release from Bob Dylan.* **10.** a news item, etc., made available for publication, broadcasting, etc. **11.** *Law.* the surrender of a claim, right, title, etc., in favour of someone else. **12.** a control mechanism for starting or stopping an engine. [C13: from OF *relesser,* from L *relaxāre* to slacken] —re'**leaser** *n.*

relegate ('rɛlɪˌgeɪt) *vb.* (*tr.*) **1.** to move to a position of less authority, importance, etc.; demote. **2.** (*usually passive*) *Chiefly Brit.* to demote (a football team, etc.) to a lower division. **3.** to assign or refer (a matter) to another. **4.** (foll. by *to*) to banish or exile. **5.** to assign (something) to a particular group or category. [C16: from L *relēgāre,* from RE- + *lēgāre* to send] —'**rele,gatable** *adj.* —ˌrele'**gation** *n.*

relent (rɪ'lɛnt) *vb.* (*intr.*) **1.** to change one's mind about some decision, esp. a harsh one; become more mild or amenable. **2.** (of the pace or intensity of something) to slacken. **3.** (of the weather) to become more mild. [C14: from RE- + L *lentāre* to bend, from *lentus* flexible]

relentless (rɪ'lɛntlɪs) *adj.* **1.** (of an enemy, etc.) implacable; inflexible; inexorable. **2.** (of pace or intensity) sustained; unremitting. —re'**lentlessly** *adv.* —re'**lentlessness** *n.*

relevant ('rɛlɪvənt) *adj.* having direct bearing on the matter in hand; pertinent. [C16: from Med. L *relevans,* from L *relevāre,* from RE- + *levāre* to raise, RELIEVE] —'**relevance** *or* '**relevancy** *n.* —'**relevantly** *adv.*

reliable (rɪ'laɪəbˀl) *adj.* able to be trusted; dependable. —reˌlia'**bility** *or* re'**liableness** *n.* —re'**liably** *adv.*

reliance (rɪ'laɪəns) *n.* **1.** dependence, confidence, or trust. **2.** something or someone upon which one relies. —re'**liant** *adj.* —re'**liantly** *adv.*

relic ('rɛlɪk) *n.* **1.** something that has survived from the past, such as an object or custom. **2.** something treasured for its past associations; keepsake. **3.** (*usually pl.*) a remaining part or fragment. **4.** *R.C. Church, Eastern Church.* part of the body of a saint or his belongings, venerated as holy. **5.** *Inf.* an old or old-fashioned person or thing. **6.** (*pl.*) *Arch.* the remains of a dead person; corpse. [C13: from OF *relique,* from L *reliquiae* remains, from *relinquere* to leave behind]

relict ('rɛlɪkt) *n.* **1.** *Ecology.* **a.** a group of animals or plants that exists as a remnant of a formerly widely distributed group. **b.** (*as modifier*): *a relict fauna.* **2.** *Geol.* a mountain, lake, glacier, etc., that is a remnant of a pre-existing formation after a destructive process has occurred. **3.** an archaic word for **widow. 4.** an archaic word for **relic.** [C16: from L *relictus* left behind, from *relinquere* to RELINQUISH]

relief (rɪ'liːf) *n.* **1.** a feeling of cheerfulness or optimism that follows the removal of anxiety, pain, or distress. **2.** deliverance from or alleviation of anxiety, pain, etc. **3. a.** help or assistance, as to the poor or needy. **b.** (*as modifier*): *relief work.* **4.** a diversion from monotony. **5.** a person who replaces another at some task or duty. **6.** a bus, plane, etc., that carries additional passengers when a scheduled service is full. **7.** a road (**relief road**) carrying traffic round an urban area; bypass. **8. a.** the act of freeing a beleaguered town, fortress, etc.: *the relief of Mafikeng.* **b.** (*as modifier*): *a relief column.* **9.** Also called: **relievo, rilievo.** *Sculpture, archit.* **a.** the projection of forms or figures from a flat ground, so that they are partly or wholly free of it. **b.** a piece of work of this kind. **10.** a printing process that employs raised surfaces from which ink is transferred to the paper. **11.** any vivid effect

---

re'learn *vb.*   **re'let** *vb.*

resulting from contrast: *comic relief.* **12.** variation in altitude in an area; difference between highest and lowest level. **13.** *Law.* redress of a grievance or hardship: *to seek relief through the courts.* **14. on relief.** *U.S. & Canad.* (of people) in receipt of government aid because of personal need. [C14: from OF, from *relever;* see RELIEVE]

relief map *n.* a map that shows the configuration and height of the land surface, usually by means of contours.

relieve (rɪˈliːv) *vb.* (*tr.*) **1.** to bring alleviation of (pain, distress, etc.) to (someone). **2.** to bring aid or assistance to (someone in need, etc.). **3.** to take over the duties or watch of (someone). **4.** to bring aid or a relieving force to (a besieged town, etc.). **5.** to free (someone) from an obligation. **6.** to make (something) less unpleasant, arduous, or monotonous. **7.** to bring into relief or prominence, as by contrast. **8.** (foll. by *of*) *Inf.* to take from: *the thief relieved him of his watch.* **9. relieve oneself.** to urinate or defecate. [C14: from OF *relever,* from L *relevāre* to lift up, relieve, from RE-+ *levāre* to lighten] —**reˈlievable** *adj.* —**reˈliever** *n.*

relieved (rɪˈliːvd) *adj.* (*postpositive; often foll. by* at, about, *etc.*) experiencing relief, esp. from worry or anxiety.

religieuse *French.* (rəliʒjøz) *n.* a nun. [C18: fem. of RELIGIEUX]

religieux *French.* (rəliʒjø) *n., pl.* **-gieux** (-ʒjø). a member of a monastic order or clerical body. [C17: from L *religiōsus* religious]

religion (rɪˈlɪdʒən) *n.* **1.** belief in, worship of, or obedience to a supernatural power or powers considered to be divine or to have control of human destiny. **2.** any formal or institutionalized expression of such belief: *the Christian religion.* **3.** the attitude and feeling of one who believes in a transcendent controlling power or powers. **4.** *Chiefly R.C. Church.* the way of life entered upon by monks and nuns: *to enter religion.* **5.** something of overwhelming importance to a person: *football is his religion.* [C12: via OF from L *religiō* fear of the supernatural, piety, prob. from *religāre,* from RE-+ *ligāre* to bind]

religionism (rɪˈlɪdʒəˌnɪzəm) *n.* extreme religious fervour. —**reˈligionist** *n., adj.*

religiose (rɪˈlɪdʒɪˌəʊs) *adj.* affectedly or extremely pious; sanctimoniously religious. —**reˈligiˌosely** *adv.* —**religiosity** (rɪˌlɪdʒɪˈɒsɪtɪ) *n.*

religious (rɪˈlɪdʒəs) *adj.* **1.** of, relating to, or concerned with religion. **2. a.** pious; devout; godly. **b.** (*as collective n.; preceded by* the): *the religious.* **3.** appropriate to or in accordance with the principles of a religion. **4.** scrupulous, exact, or conscientious. **5.** *Christianity.* of or relating to a way of life dedicated to religion and defined by a monastic rule. ~*n.* **6.** *Christianity.* a monk or nun. —**reˈligiously** *adv.* —**reˈligiousness** *n.*

relinquish (rɪˈlɪŋkwɪʃ) *vb.* (*tr.*) **1.** to give up (a task, struggle, etc.); abandon. **2.** to surrender or renounce (a claim, right, etc.). **3.** to release; let go. [C15: from F *relinquir,* from L *relinquere,* from RE-+ *linquere* to leave] —**reˈlinquisher** *n.* —**reˈlinquishment** *n.*

reliquary (ˈrɛlɪkwərɪ) *n., pl.* **-quaries.** a receptacle or repository for relics, esp. relics of saints. [C17: from OF *reliquaire,* from *relique* RELIC]

relique (rəˈliːk, ˈrɛlɪk) *n.* an archaic spelling of **relic.**

reliquiae (rɪˈlɪkwɪˌiː) *pl. n.* fossil remains of animals or plants. [C19: from L: remains]

relish (ˈrɛlɪʃ) *vb.* (*tr.*) **1.** to savour or enjoy (an experience) to the full. **2.** to anticipate eagerly; look forward to. **3.** to enjoy the taste or flavour of (food, etc.); savour. ~*n.* **4.** liking or enjoyment, as of something eaten or experienced (esp. in **with relish**). **5.** pleasurable anticipation: *he didn't have much relish for the idea.* **6.** an appetizing or spicy food added to a main dish to enhance its flavour. **7.** an appetizing taste or flavour. **8.** a zestful trace or touch: *there was a certain relish in all his writing.* [C16: from earlier *reles* aftertaste, from OF, from *relaisser* to leave behind; see RELEASE] —**ˈrelishable** *adj.*

relive (riːˈlɪv) *vb.* (*tr.*) to experience (a sensation, event, etc.) again, esp. in the imagination. —**reˈlivable** *adj.*

relocate (ˌriːləʊˈkeɪt) *vb.* to move or be moved to a new place, esp. (of an employee, a business, etc.) to a new area or place of employment. —**ˌreloˈcation** *n.*

reluctance (rɪˈlʌktəns) *or* **reluctancy** *n.* **1.** lack of eagerness or willingness; disinclination. **2.** *Physics.* a measure of the resistance of a closed magnetic circuit to a magnetic flux. [C16: from L *reluctārī* to resist, from RE-+ *luctārī* to struggle]

reluctant (rɪˈlʌktənt) *adj.* not eager; unwilling; disinclined. [C17: from L *reluctārī* to resist] —**reˈluctantly** *adv.*

reluctivity (ˌrɛlʌkˈtɪvɪtɪ) *n., pl.* **-ties.** *Physics.* a specific or relative reluctance of a magnetic material. [C19: from obs. *reluct* to struggle + *-ivity*]

rely (rɪˈlaɪ) *vb.* **-lying, -lied.** (*intr.;* foll. by on or *upon*) **1.** to be dependent (on): *he relies on his charm.* **2.** to have trust or confidence (in): *you can rely on us.* [C14: from OF *relier* to fasten together, from L *religāre,* from RE-+ *ligāre* to tie]

REM *abbrev. for* rapid eye movement.

remain (rɪˈmeɪn) *vb.* (*mainly intr.*) **1.** to stay behind or in the same place: *to remain at home.* **2.** (*copula*) to continue to be: *to remain cheerful.* **3.** to be left, as after use, the passage of time, etc. **4.** to be left to be done, said, etc.: *it remains to be pointed out.* [C14: from OF *remanoir,* from L *remanēre,* from RE-+ *manēre* to stay]

remainder (rɪˈmeɪndə) *n.* **1.** a part or portion that is left, as after use, subtraction, expenditure, the passage of time, etc.: *the remainder of the milk.* **2.** *Maths.* **a.** the amount left over when one quantity cannot be exactly divided by another: *for 10 ÷ 3, the remainder is 1.* **b.** another name for **difference** (sense 7). **3.** *Property law.* a future interest in property; an interest in a particular estate that will pass to one at some future date, as on the death of the current possessor. **4.** a number of copies of a book left unsold when demand ceases, which are sold at a reduced price. ~*vb.* **5.** (*tr.*) to sell (copies of a book) as a remainder.

remains (rɪˈmeɪnz) *pl. n.* **1.** any pieces, fragments, etc., that are left unused or still extant, as after use, consumption, the passage of time: *archaeological remains.* **2.** the body of a dead person; corpse. **3.** Also called: **literary remains.** the unpublished writings of an author at the time of his death.

remake *n.* (ˈriːˌmeɪk). **1.** something that is made again, esp. a new version of an old film. **2.** the act of making again. ~*vb.* (riːˈmeɪk), **-making, -made. 3.** (*tr.*) to make again or anew.

remand (rɪˈmɑːnd) *vb.* (*tr.*) **1.** *Law.* (of a court or magistrate) to send (a prisoner or accused person) back into custody. **2.** to send back. ~*n.* **3.** the sending of a prisoner or accused person back into custody to await trial. **4.** the act of remanding or state of being remanded. **5. on remand.** in custody or on bail awaiting trial. [C15: from Med. L *remandāre* to send back word, from L RE-+ *mandāre* to command]

remand centre *n.* (in England) an institution to which accused persons are sent for detention while awaiting appearance before a court.

remanence (ˈrɛmənəns) *n. Physics.* the ability of a material to retain magnetization after the removal of the magnetizing field. [C17: from L *remanēre* to stay behind]

remark (rɪˈmɑːk) *vb.* **1.** (when *intr.,* often foll. by on or *upon;* when *tr., may take a clause as object*) to pass a casual comment (about); reflect in informal speech or writing. **2.** (*tr.; may take a clause as object*) to perceive; observe; notice. ~*n.* **3.** a brief casually expressed thought or opinion. **4.** notice, comment, or observation: *the event passed without remark.* **5.** a variant of **remarque.** [C17: from OF *remarquer* to observe, from RE-+ *marquer* to note, MARK[1]] —**reˈmarker** *n.*

remarkable (rɪˈmɑːkəbəl) *adj.* **1.** worthy of note or attention: *a remarkable achievement.* **2.** unusual, striking, or extraordinary: *a remarkable sight.* —**reˈmarkableness** *n.* —**reˈmarkably** *adv.*

remarque (rɪˈmɑːk) *n.* a mark in the margin of an engraved plate to indicate the stage of production. [C19: from F; see REMARK]

Remarque (rɪˈmɑːk) *n.* **Erich Maria** (ˈeːrɪç maˈriːa). 1898–1970, U.S. novelist, born in Germany, noted for his novel of World War I, *All Quiet on the Western Front* (1929).

---

reˈlight *vb.*　　　**reˈload** *vb.*　　　**reˈmarriage** *n.*　　　**reˈmarry** *vb.*

remaster (riː'mɑːstə) vb. (tr.) to make a new master audio recording, now usually digital, from (an earlier original recording), in order to produce compact discs or stereo records with improved sound reproduction.

Rembrandt ('rɛmbrænt) n. full name *Rembrandt Harmensz* (or *Harmenszoon*) *van Rijn* (or *van Ryn*). 1606–69, Dutch painter, noted for his handling of shade and light, esp. in his portraits. —,**Rembrandt'esque** adj.

REME ('riːmɪ) n. acronym for Royal Electrical and Mechanical Engineers.

remedial (rɪ'miːdɪəl) adj. **1.** affording a remedy; curative. **2.** denoting or relating to special teaching for backward and slow learners: *remedial education.* —**re'medially** adv.

remedy ('rɛmɪdɪ) n., pl. **-dies. 1.** (usually foll. by *for* or *against*) any drug or agent that cures a disease or controls its symptoms. **2.** (usually foll. by *for* or *against*) anything that serves to cure defects, improve conditions, etc.: *a remedy for industrial disputes.* **3.** the legally permitted variation from the standard weight or quality of coins. ~vb. (tr.) **4.** to relieve or cure (a disease, etc.) by a remedy. **5.** to put to rights (a fault, error, etc.); correct. [C13: from Anglo-Norman *remedie*, from L *remedium* a cure, from *remederī*, from RE- + *medērī* to heal] —**remediable** (rɪ'miːdɪəbʰl) adj. —**re'mediably** adv. —'**remediless** adj.

remember (rɪ'mɛmbə) vb. **1.** to become aware of (something forgotten) again; bring back to one's consciousness. **2.** to retain (an idea, intention, etc.) in one's conscious mind: *remember to do one's shopping.* **3.** (tr.) to give money, etc., to (someone), as in a will or in tipping. **4.** (tr.; foll. by *to*) to mention (a person's name) to another person, as by way of greeting: *remember me to your mother.* **5.** (tr.) to mention (a person) favourably, as in prayer. **6.** (tr.) to commemorate (a person, event, etc.): *to remember the dead of the wars.* **7. remember oneself.** to recover one's good manners after a lapse. [C14: from OF *remembrer*, from LL *rememorārī* to recall to mind, from L RE- + *memor* mindful] —**re'memberer** n.

remembrance (rɪ'mɛmbrəns) n. **1.** the act of remembering or state of being remembered. **2.** something that is remembered; reminiscence. **3.** a memento or keepsake. **4.** the extent in time of one's power of recollection. **5.** the act of honouring some past event, person, etc.

Remembrance Day n. **1.** (in Britain) another name for **Remembrance Sunday. 2.** (in Canada) a statutory holiday observed on November 11 in memory of the dead of both World Wars.

remembrancer (rɪ'mɛmbrənsə) n. **1.** *Arch.* a reminder, memento, or keepsake. **2.** (*usually cap.*) (in Britain) any of several officials of the Exchequer, esp. one (**Queen's** *or* **King's Remembrancer**) whose duties include collecting debts due to the Crown. **3.** (*usually cap.*) an official (**City Remembrancer**) appointed by the Corporation of the City of London to represent its interests to Parliament.

Remembrance Sunday n. (in Britain) the Sunday closest to November 11, on which the dead of both World Wars are commemorated. Also called: **Remembrance Day.**

remex ('riːmɛks) n., pl. **remiges** ('rɛmɪˌdʒiːz). any of the large flight feathers of a bird's wing. [C18: from L: rower, from *rēmus* oar] —**remigial** (rɪ'mɪdʒɪəl) adj.

remind (rɪ'maɪnd) vb. (tr.; usually foll. by *of; may take a clause as object or an infinitive*) to cause (a person) to remember (something or to do something); put (a person) in mind (of something): *remind me to phone home; flowers remind me of holidays.* —**re'minder** n.

remindful (rɪ'maɪndfʊl) adj. **1.** serving to remind. **2.** (*postpositive*) mindful.

reminisce (ˌrɛmɪ'nɪs) vb. (intr.) to talk or write about old times, past experiences, etc.

reminiscence (ˌrɛmɪ'nɪsəns) n. **1.** the act of recalling or narrating past experiences. **2.** (*often pl.*) some past experience, event, etc., that is recalled. **3.** an event, phenomenon, or experience that reminds one of something else. **4.** *Philosophy.* the doctrine that the mind has seen the universal forms of all things in a previous disembodied existence.

reminiscent (ˌrɛmɪ'nɪsᵊnt) adj. **1.** (*postpositive; foll. by of*) stimulating memories (of) or comparisons (with). **2.** characterized by reminiscence. **3.** (of a person) given to reminiscing. [C18: from L *reminiscī* to call to mind, from RE- + *mēns* mind] —,**remi'niscently** adv.

remise (rɪ'maɪz) vb. **1.** (tr.) *Law.* to give up or relinquish (a right, claim, etc.). **2.** (intr.) *Fencing.* to make a remise. ~n. **3.** *Fencing.* a second thrust made on the same lunge after the first has missed. **4.** *Obs.* a coach house. [C17: from F *remettre* to put back, from L *remittere*, from RE- + *mittere* to send]

remiss (rɪ'mɪs) adj. (*postpositive*) **1.** lacking in care or attention to duty; negligent. **2.** lacking in energy. [C15: from L *remissus*, from *remittere*, from RE- + *mittere* to send] —**re'missly** adv. —**re'missness** n.

remissible (rɪ'mɪsɪbʰl) adj. able to be remitted. [C16: from L *remissibilis*; see REMIT] —**re,missi'bility** n.

remission (rɪ'mɪʃən) or (*less commonly*) **remittal** (rɪ'mɪtʰl) n. **1.** the act of remitting or state of being remitted. **2.** a reduction of the term of a sentence of imprisonment, as for good conduct. **3.** forgiveness for sin. **4.** discharge or release from penalty, obligation, etc. **5.** lessening of intensity; abatement, as in the symptoms of a disease. **6.** *Rare.* the act of sending a remittance. —**re'missive** adj. —**re'missively** adv.

remit vb. (rɪ'mɪt), **-mitting, -mitted.** (*mainly tr.*) **1.** (*also intr.*) to send (payment, etc.), as for goods or service, esp. by post. **2.** *Law.* (esp. of an appeal court) to send back (a case) to an inferior court for further consideration. **3.** to cancel or refrain from exacting (a penalty or punishment). **4.** (*also intr.*) to relax (pace, intensity, etc.) or (of pace) to slacken or abate. **5.** to postpone; defer. **6.** *Arch.* to pardon or forgive (crime, sins, etc.). ~n. ('riːmɪt, rɪ'mɪt). **7.** area of authority (of a committee, etc.). **8.** *Law.* the transfer of a case from one court or jurisdiction to another. **9.** the act of remitting. [C14: from L *remittere*, from RE- + *mittere* to send] —**re'mittable** adj. —**re'mitter** n.

remittance (rɪ'mɪtəns) n. **1.** payment for goods or services received or as an allowance, esp. when sent by post. **2.** the act of remitting.

remittance man n. a man living abroad on money sent from home, esp. in the days of the British Empire.

remittent (rɪ'mɪtᵊnt) adj. (of the symptoms of a disease) characterized by periods of diminished severity. —**re'mittence** n. —**re'mittently** adv.

remix vb. (riː'mɪks). **1.** to change the balance and separation of (a recording). ~n. ('riːmɪks). **2.** a remixed version of a recording.

remnant ('rɛmnənt) n. **1.** (*often pl.*) a part left over after use, processing, etc. **2.** a surviving trace or vestige: *a remnant of imperialism.* **3.** a piece of material from the end of a roll. ~adj. **4.** remaining; left over. [C14: from OF *remenant* remaining, from *remanoir* to REMAIN]

remonetize or **-ise** (riː'mʌnɪˌtaɪz) vb. (tr.) to reinstate as legal tender: *to remonetize silver.* —**re,moneti'zation** or **-i'sation** n.

remonstrance (rɪ'mɒnstrəns) n. **1.** the act of remonstrating. **2.** a protest or reproof, esp. a petition protesting against something.

remonstrant (rɪ'mɒnstrənt) n. **1.** a person who remonstrates, esp. one who signs a remonstrance. ~adj. **2.** *Rare.* remonstrating.

remonstrate ('rɛmənˌstreɪt) vb. (intr.) (usually foll. by *with, against,* etc.) to argue in protest or objection: *to remonstrate with the government.* [C16: from Med. L *remonstrāre* to point out (errors, etc.), from L RE- + *monstrāre* to show] —,**remon'stration** n. —**remonstrative** (rɪ'mɒnstrətɪv) adj. —'**remon,strator** n.

remontant (rɪ'mɒntənt) adj. **1.** (esp. of roses) flowering more than once in a single season. ~n. **2.** a rose having such a growth. [C19: from F: coming up again, from *remonter*]

remora ('rɛmərə) n. a marine spiny-finned fish which has a flattened elongated body and attaches itself to larger fish, rocks, etc., by a sucking disc on the top of the head. [C16: from L, from RE- + *mora* delay; from its alleged habit of delaying ships]

're,match n.
re'measure vb.
re'measurement n.

,remilitari'zation or -i'sation n.

re'milita,rize or -,rise vb.
re'model vb.

,remodifi'cation n.
re'modi,fy vb.

remorse (rɪ'mɔːs) n. **1.** a sense of deep regret and guilt for some misdeed. **2.** compunction; pity; compassion. [C14: from Med. L *remorsus* a gnawing, from L *remordēre*, from RE- + *mordēre* to bite] —re'**morseful** adj. —re'**morsefully** adv. —re'**morsefulness** n. —re'**morseless** adj.

remote (rɪ'məʊt) adj. **1.** located far away; distant. **2.** far from society or civilization; out-of-the-way. **3.** distant in time. **4.** distantly related or connected: a remote cousin. **5.** slight or faint (esp. in **not the remotest idea**). **6.** (of a person's manner) aloof or abstracted. **7.** operated from a distance; remote-controlled: a remote monitor. [C15: from L *remōtus* far removed, from *removēre*, from RE- + *movēre* to move] —re'**motely** adv. —re'**moteness** n.

remote control n. control of a system or activity from a distance, usually by radio, ultrasonic, or electrical signals. —re'**mote-con'trolled** adj.

remote sensor n. any instrument, such as a radar device or camera, that scans the earth or another planet from space in order to collect data about some aspect of it. —**remote sensing** adj., n.

rémoulade (ˌrɛmə'leɪd) n. a mayonnaise sauce flavoured with herbs, mustard, and capers, served with salads, cold meat, etc. [C19: from F, from dialect *ramolas* horseradish, from L *armoracea*]

remould vb. (ˌriː'məʊld). (tr.) **1.** to mould again. **2.** to bond a new tread onto the casing of (a worn pneumatic tyre). ~n. ('riːˌməʊld). **3.** a tyre made by this process.

remount vb. (riː'maʊnt). **1.** to get on (a horse, bicycle, etc.) again. **2.** (tr.) to mount (a picture, jewel, exhibit, etc.) again. ~n. ('riːˌmaʊnt). **3.** a fresh horse.

removal (rɪ'muːvəl) n. **1.** the act of removing or state of being removed. **2. a.** a change of residence. **b.** (as modifier): a removal company. **3.** dismissal from office.

removalist (rɪ'muːvəlɪst) n. Austral. a person or company that transports household effects to a new home.

remove (rɪ'muːv) vb. (mainly tr.) **1.** to take away and place elsewhere. **2.** to dismiss (someone) from office. **3.** to do away with; abolish; get rid of. **4.** Euphemistic. to assassinate; kill. **5.** (intr.) Formal. to change the location of one's home or place of business. ~n. **6.** the act of removing, esp. (formal) a removal of one's residence or place of work. **7.** the degree of difference: only one remove from madness. **8.** Brit. (in certain schools) a class or form. [C14: from OF *removoir*, from L *removēre*; see MOVE] —re'**movable** adj. —re,mova'**bility** n. —re'**mover** n.

removed (rɪ'muːvd) adj. **1.** separated by distance or abstract distinction. **2.** (postpositive) separated by a degree of descent or kinship: the child of a person's first cousin is his first cousin once removed.

Remscheid (German 'rɛmʃaɪt) n. an industrial city in W West Germany, in North Rhine-Westphalia. Pop.: 121 000 (1986).

remunerate (rɪ'mjuːnəˌreɪt) vb. (tr.) to reward or pay for work, service, etc. [C16: from L *remūnerārī* to reward, from RE- + *mūnerāre* to give, from *mūnus* a gift] —re,muner'**ation** n. —re'**munerable** adj. —re'**munerative** adj. —re'**muneratively** adv. —re'**muner,ator** n.

Remus ('riːməs) n. Roman myth. the brother of Romulus.

renaissance (rə'neɪsəns; U.S. also 'rɛnəˌsɒns) or **renascence** n. a revival or rebirth, esp. of culture and learning. [C19: from F, from L RE- + *nascī* to be born]

Renaissance (rə'neɪsəns; U.S. also 'rɛnəˌsɒns) n. **1.** the great revival of art, literature, and learning in Europe in the 14th, 15th, and 16th centuries. **2.** the spirit, culture, art, science, and thought of this period. ~adj. **3.** of, characteristic of, or relating to the Renaissance, its culture, etc.

renal ('riːnəl) adj. of, relating to, resembling, or situated near the kidney. [C17: from F, from LL *rēnālis*, from L *rēnēs* kidneys, from ?]

renal pelvis n. a small funnel-shaped cavity of the kidney into which urine is discharged before passing into the ureter.

renascent (rɪ'næsənt, -'neɪ-) adj. becoming active or vigorous again; reviving: renascent nationalism. [C18: from L *renascī* to be born again]

rencounter (rɛn'kaʊntə) Arch. ~n. also **rencontre** (rɛn'kɒntə). **1.** an unexpected meeting. **2.** a hostile clash, as of two armies, adversaries, etc.; skirmish. ~vb. **3.** to meet (someone) unexpectedly. [C16: from F *rencontre*, from *rencontrer*; see ENCOUNTER]

rend (rɛnd) vb. **rending, rent. 1.** to tear with violent force or to be torn in this way; rip. **2.** (tr.) to tear or pull (one's clothes, etc.), esp. as a manifestation of rage or grief. **3.** (tr.) (of a noise or cry) to disturb (the silence) with a shrill or piercing tone. [OE *rendan*] —'**rendible** adj.

render ('rɛndə) vb. (tr.) **1.** to present or submit (accounts, etc.) for payment, etc. **2.** to give or provide (aid, charity, a service, etc.). **3.** to show (obedience), as expected. **4.** to give or exchange, as by way of return or requital: to render blow for blow. **5.** to cause to become: grief had rendered him simple-minded. **6.** to deliver (a verdict or opinion) formally. **7.** to portray or depict (something), as in painting, music, or acting. **8.** to translate (something). **9.** (sometimes foll. by up) to yield or give: the tomb rendered up its secret. **10.** (often foll. by back) to return (something); give back. **11.** to cover the surface of (brickwork, etc.) with a coat of plaster. **12.** (often foll. by down) to extract (fat) from (meat) by melting. ~n. **13.** a first thin coat of plaster applied to a surface. **14.** one who or that which rends. [C14: from OF *rendre*, from L *reddere* to give back (infl. by L *prendere* to grasp), from RE- + *dare* to give] —'**renderable** adj. —'**renderer** n. —'**rendering** n.

rendezvous ('rɒndɪˌvuː) n., pl. -**vous** (-ˌvuːz). **1.** a meeting or appointment to meet at a specified time and place. **2.** a place where people meet. ~vb. (intr.) **3.** to meet at a specified time or place. [C16: from F, from *rendez-vous!* present yourselves! from *se rendre* to present oneself; see RENDER]

rendition (rɛn'dɪʃən) n. **1.** a performance of a musical composition, dramatic role, etc. **2.** a translation. **3.** the act of rendering. [C17: from obs. F, from LL *redditiō*; see RENDER]

renegade ('rɛnɪˌgeɪd) n. **1. a.** a person who deserts his cause or faith for another; traitor. **b.** (as modifier): a renegade priest. **2.** any outlaw or rebel. [C16: from Sp. *renegado*, ult. from L RE- + *negāre* to deny]

renege or **renegue** (rɪ'niːg, -'neɪg) vb. **1.** (intr.; often foll. by on) to go back (on one's promise, etc.). ~vb., n. **2.** Cards. other words for **revoke**. [C16 (in the sense: to deny, renounce): from Med. L *renegāre* to renounce] —re'**neger** or re'**neguer** n.

renew (rɪ'njuː) vb. (mainly tr.) **1.** to take up again. **2.** (also intr.) to begin (an activity) again; recommence. **3.** to restate or reaffirm (a promise, etc.). **4.** (also intr.) to make (a lease, etc.) valid for a further period. **5.** to regain or recover (vigour, strength, activity, etc.). **6.** to restore to a new or fresh condition. **7.** to replace (an old or worn-out part or piece). **8.** to replenish (a supply, etc.). —re'**newable** adj. —re'**newal** n. —re'**newer** n.

renewable energy n. another name for **alternative energy**.

Renfrew ('rɛnfruː) n. a shipbuilding town in W central Scotland, in Strathclyde region W of Glasgow. Pop.: 21 396 (1981).

Renfrewshire ('rɛnfruːʃɪə, -ʃə) n. (until 1975) a county of W central Scotland, on the Firth of Clyde: now part of Strathclyde region.

Reni (Italian 'rɛːni) n. **Guido** ('gwiːdo). 1575–1642, Italian baroque painter and engraver.

reni- combining form. kidney or kidneys: reniform. [from L *rēnēs*]

reniform ('rɛnɪˌfɔːm) adj. having the shape or profile of a kidney: a reniform leaf.

renin ('riːnɪn) n. a proteolytic enzyme secreted by the kidneys, which plays an important part in the maintenance of blood pressure. [C20: from RENI- + -IN]

Rennes (French rɛn) n. a city in NW France: the ancient capital of Brittany. Pop.: 195 785 (1983 est.).

rennet ('rɛnɪt) n. **1.** the membrane lining the fourth stomach of a young calf. **2.** a substance prepared esp. from the stomachs of calves and used for curdling milk in making cheese. [C15: rel. to OE *gerinnan* to curdle, RUN]

rennin ('rɛnɪn) n. an enzyme that occurs in gastric juice and is an active constituent of rennet. It coagulates milk. [C20: from RENNET + -IN]

---

re'**name** vb.　　　　ˌrene'**gotiable** adj.　　　　ˌrene'**goti,ate** vb.　　　　ˌrenegoti'**ation** n.

Reno ('ri:nəʊ) n. a city in W Nevada, at the foot of the Sierra Nevada: noted as a divorce, wedding, and gambling centre by reason of its liberal laws. Pop.: 115 210 (1986 est.).

Renoir ('rɛnwɑː; *French* rənwar) n. **1. Jean** (ʒɑ̃). 1894–1979, French film director: his films include *La grande illusion* (1937), *La règle du jeu* (1939), and *Diary of a Chambermaid* (1945). **2.** his father, **Pierre Auguste** (pjɛr ogyst). 1841–1919, French painter. One of the initiators of impressionism, he broke away from the movement with his later paintings, esp. his many nude studies, which are more formal compositions.

renounce (rɪ'naʊns) vb. **1.** (*tr.*) to give up formally (a claim or right): *to renounce a title.* **2.** (*tr.*) to repudiate: *to renounce Christianity.* **3.** (*tr.*) to give up (some habit, etc.) voluntarily: *to renounce one's old ways.* **4.** (*intr.*) *Cards.* to fail to follow suit because one has no more cards of the suit led. ~n. **5.** *Cards.* a failure to follow suit. [C14: from OF *renoncer*, from L *renuntiāre*, from RE- + *nuntiāre* to announce, from *nuntius* messenger] —re'nouncement n. —re'nouncer n.

renovate ('rɛnə,veɪt) vb. (*tr.*) **1.** to restore (something) to good condition. **2.** to revive or refresh (one's spirits, health, etc.). [C16: from L *renovāre*, from RE- + *novāre* to make new] —,reno'vation n. —'reno,vative adj. —'reno,vator n.

renown (rɪ'naʊn) n. widespread reputation, esp. of a good kind; fame. [C14: from Anglo-Norman *renoun*, from OF *renom*, from *renomer* to celebrate, from RE- + *nomer* to name, from L *nōmināre*] —re'nowned adj.

rent[1] (rɛnt) n. **1.** a payment made periodically by a tenant to a landlord or owner for the occupation or use of land, buildings, etc. **2.** *Econ.* the return derived from the cultivation of land in excess of production costs. **3. for rent.** *Chiefly U.S. & Canad.* available for use and occupation subject to the payment of rent. ~vb. **4.** (*tr.*) to grant (a person) the right to use one's property in return for periodic payments. **5.** (*tr.*) to occupy or use (property) in return for periodic payments. **6.** (*intr.*; often foll. by *at*) to be let or rented (for a specified rental). [C12: from OF *rente* revenue, from Vulgar L *rendere* (unattested) to yield; see RENDER] —'rentable adj. —'renter n.

rent[2] (rɛnt) n. **1.** a slit or opening made by tearing or rending. **2.** a breach or division. ~vb. **3.** the past tense and past participle of **rend.**

rental ('rɛntəl) n. **1. a.** the amount paid by a tenant as rent. **b.** an income derived from rents received. **2.** property available for renting. ~adj. **3.** of or relating to rent.

rent boy n. a young male prostitute.

rent control n. regulation by law of the rent a landlord can charge for domestic accommodation and of his right to evict tenants.

rent-free adj., adv. without payment of rent.

rentier *French.* (rɑ̃tje) n. a person whose income consists primarily of fixed unearned amounts, such as rent or interest. [from *rente*; see RENT[1]]

rent-roll n. **1.** a register of lands and buildings owned by a person, company, etc., showing the rent due from each tenant. **2.** the total income arising from rented property.

renunciation (rɪ,nʌnsɪ'eɪʃən) n. **1.** the act or an instance of renouncing. **2.** a formal declaration renouncing something. [C14: from L *renunciātiō* a declaration, from *renuntiāre* to report] —re'nunciative or re'nunciatory adj.

rep[1] or **repp** (rɛp) n. a silk, wool, rayon, or cotton fabric with a transversely corded surface. [C19: from F *reps*, ?from E *ribs*] —**repped** adj.

rep[2] (rɛp) n. *Theatre.* short for **repertory company.**

rep[3] (rɛp) n. **1.** short for **representative** (sense 2). **2.** *N.Z. inf.* a rugby player selected to represent his district.

rep[4] (rɛp) n. *U.S. inf.* short for **reputation.**

rep. abbrev. for: **1.** report. **2.** reporter. **3.** reprint.

Rep. abbrev. for: **1.** *U.S.* Representative. **2.** Republic. **3.** *U.S.* Republican.

repair[1] (rɪ'pɛə) vb. (*tr.*) **1.** to restore (something damaged or broken) to good working or working order. **2.** to heal (a breach or division) in (something): *to repair a broken*

marriage. **3.** to make amends for (a mistake, injury, etc.). ~n. **4.** the act, task, or process of repairing. **5.** a part that has been repaired. **6.** state or condition: *in good repair.* [C14: from OF *reparer*, from L *reparāre*, from RE- + *parāre* to make ready] —re'pairable adj. —re'pairer n.

repair[2] (rɪ'pɛə) vb. (*intr.*) **1.** (usually foll. by *to*) to go (to a place). **2.** (usually foll. by *to*) to have recourse (to) for help, etc.: *to repair to one's lawyer.* ~n. **3.** a haunt or resort. [C14: from OF *repairier*, from L *repatriāre* to return to one's native land, from L RE- + *patria* fatherland]

repairman (rɪ'pɛə,mæn) n., pl. -men. a man whose job it is to repair machines, etc.

repand (rɪ'pænd) adj. *Bot.* having a wavy margin: *a repand leaf.* [C18: from L *repandus* bent backwards, from RE- + *pandus* curved] —re'pandly adv.

reparable ('rɛpərəb³l, 'rɛprə-) adj. able to be repaired, recovered, or remedied. [C16: from L *reparābilis*, from *reparāre* to REPAIR[1]] —'reparably adv.

reparation (,rɛpə'reɪʃən) n. **1.** the act or process of making amends. **2.** (usually pl.) compensation exacted as an indemnity from a defeated nation by the victors. **3.** the act or process of repairing or state of having been repaired. [C14 *reparacioun*, ult. from L *reparāre* to REPAIR[1]] —reparative (rɪ'pærətɪv) or re'paratory adj.

repartee (,rɛpɑː'tiː) n. **1.** a sharp, witty, or aphoristic remark made as a reply. **2.** skill in making sharp witty replies. [C17: from F *repartie*, from *repartir* to retort, from RE- + *partir* to go away]

repast (rɪ'pɑːst) n. a meal or the food provided at a meal: *a light repast.* [C14: from OF, from *repaistre* to feed, from LL *repāscere*, from L RE- + *pāscere* to feed, pasture (of animals)]

repatriate vb. (riː'pætrɪ,eɪt). **1.** (*tr.*) to send back (a person) to the country of his birth or citizenship. ~n. (riː'pætrɪɪt). **2.** a person who has been repatriated. [C17: from LL *repatriāre*, from L RE- + *patria* fatherland] —re,patri'ation n.

repay (rɪ'peɪ) vb. -**paying,** -**paid. 1.** to pay back (money, etc.) to (a person); refund or reimburse. **2.** to make a return for (something): *to repay kindness.* —re'payable adj. —re'payment n.

repeal (rɪ'piːl) vb. (*tr.*) **1.** to annul or rescind officially; revoke: *these laws were repealed.* ~n. **2.** an instance or the process of repealing; annulment. [C14: from OF *repeler*, from RE- + *apeler* to call, APPEAL] —re'pealable adj. —re'pealer n.

repeat (rɪ'piːt) vb. **1.** (when *tr.*, *may take a clause as object*) to do or experience (something) again once or several times, esp. to say or write (something) again. **2.** (*intr.*) to occur more than once: *the last figure repeats.* **3.** (*tr.*; *may take a clause as object*) to reproduce (the words, sounds, etc.) uttered by someone else; echo. **4.** (*tr.*) to utter (a poem, etc.) from memory; recite. **5.** (*intr.*) (of food) to be tasted again after ingestion as the result of belching. **6.** (*tr.*; *may take a clause as object*) to tell to another person (the secrets imparted to one by someone else). **7.** (*intr.*) (of a clock) to strike the hour or quarter-hour just past. **8.** (*intr.*) *U.S.* to vote (illegally) more than once in a single election. **9. repeat oneself.** to say or do the same thing more than once, esp. so as to be tedious. ~n. **10. a.** the act or an instance of repeating. **b.** (*as modifier*): *a repeat performance.* **11.** a word, action, etc., that is repeated. **12.** an order made out for goods, etc., that duplicates a previous order. **13.** *Radio, television.* a broadcast of a programme which has been broadcast before. **14.** *Music.* a passage that is an exact restatement of the passage preceding it. [C14: from OF *repeter*, from L *repetere*, from RE- + *petere* to seek] —re'peatable adj.

repeated (rɪ'piːtɪd) adj. done, made, or said again and again; continual. —re'peatedly adv.

repeater (rɪ'piːtə) n. **1.** a person or thing that repeats. **2.** Also called: **repeating firearm.** a firearm capable of discharging several shots without reloading. **3.** a timepiece which strikes the hour or quarter-hour just past, when a spring is pressed. **4.** *Electrical engineering.* a device that

---

re'nomi,nate vb.	,reoccu'pation n.	,reorgani'zation or -i'sa-	,reorien'tation n.
,renomi'nation n.	re'occu,py vb.	tion n.	re'pack vb.
,renotifi'cation n.	,reoc'currence n.	re'organ,ize or -,ise vb.	re'package vb.
re'noti,fy vb.	re'open vb.	re'organ,izer or -,iser n.	re'paint vb.
re'number vb.	re'order vb., n.	re'ori,ent vb.	re'paper vb.

amplifies or augments incoming electrical signals and re-transmits them.

repeating decimal *n.* another name for **recurring decimal.**

repechage (,rɛpɪ'ʃɑ:ʒ) *n.* a heat of a competition, esp. in rowing or fencing, in which eliminated contestants have another chance to qualify for the next round or the final. [C19: from F *repêchage*, lit.: fishing out again, from RE- + *pêcher* to fish + -AGE]

repel (rɪ'pɛl) *vb.* **-pelling, -pelled.** (*mainly tr.*) **1.** to force or drive back (something or somebody). **2.** (*also intr.*) to produce a feeling of aversion or distaste in (someone or something); be disgusting (to). **3.** to be effective in keeping away, controlling, or resisting: *a spray that repels flies.* **4.** to have no affinity for; fail to mix with or absorb: *water and oil repel each other.* **5.** to disdain to accept (something); turn away from or spurn: *she repelled his advances.* [C15: from L *repellere*, from RE- + *pellere* to push] —**re'peller** *n.* —**re'pellingly** *adv.*

▷ **Usage.** See at **repulse.**

repellent (rɪ'pɛlənt) *adj.* **1.** distasteful or repulsive. **2.** driving or forcing away or back; repelling. ~*n. also* **repellant. 3.** something, esp. a chemical substance, that repels: *insect repellent.* **4.** a substance with which fabrics are treated to increase their resistance to water. —**re'pellence** *or* **re'pellency** *n.* —**re'pellently** *adv.*

repent[1] (rɪ'pɛnt) *vb.* to feel remorse (for); be contrite (about); show penitence (for). [C13: from OF *repentir*, from RE- + *pentir*, from L *paenitēre* to repent] —**re'penter** *n.*

repent[2] ('ri:pənt) *adj. Bot.* lying or creeping along the ground: *repent stems.* [C17: from L *rēpere* to creep]

repentance (rɪ'pɛntəns) *n.* **1.** remorse or contrition for one's past actions. **2.** an act or the process of being repentant; penitence. —**re'pentant** *adj.*

repercussion (,ri:pə'kʌʃən) *n.* **1.** (*often pl.*) a result or consequence of an action or event: *the repercussions of the war are still felt.* **2.** a recoil after impact; a rebound. **3.** a reflection, esp. of sound; echo or reverberation. [C16: from L *repercussiō*, from *repercutere* to strike back] —**,reper'cussive** *adj.*

repertoire ('rɛpə,twɑ:) *n.* **1.** all the works collectively that a company, actor, etc., is competent to perform. **2.** the entire stock of things available in a field or of a kind. **3. in repertoire.** denoting the performance of two or more plays, etc., by the same company in the same venue on different evenings over a period of time: *"Tosca" returns to Leeds next month in repertoire with "Wozzeck".* [C19: from F, from LL *repertōrium* inventory; see REPERTORY]

repertory ('rɛpətərɪ, -trɪ) *n., pl.* **-ries. 1.** the entire stock of things available in a field or of a kind; repertoire. **2.** a building or place where a stock of things is kept; repository. **3.** short for **repertory company.** [C16: from LL *repertōrium* storehouse, from L *reperīre* to obtain, from RE- + *parere* to bring forth] —**repertorial** (,rɛpə'tɔ:rɪəl) *adj.*

repertory company *n.* a theatrical company that performs plays from a repertoire. U.S. name: **stock company.**

repetend ('rɛpɪ,tɛnd) *n.* **1.** *Maths.* the digit in a recurring decimal that repeats itself. **2.** anything repeated. [C18: from L *repetendum* what is to be repeated, from *repetere* to REPEAT]

répétiteur *French.* (repetitœr) *n.* a member of an opera company who coaches the singers.

repetition (,rɛpɪ'tɪʃən) *n.* **1.** the act or an instance of repeating; reiteration. **2.** a thing, word, action, etc., that is repeated. **3.** a replica or copy. —**repetitive** (rɪ'pɛtɪtɪv) *adj.*

repetitious (,rɛpɪ'tɪʃəs) *adj.* characterized by unnecessary repetition. —**,repe'titiously** *adv.* —**,repe'titiousness** *n.*

repine (rɪ'paɪn) *vb.* (*intr.*) to be fretful or low-spirited through discontent. [C16: from RE- + PINE[2]]

replace (rɪ'pleɪs) *vb.* (*tr.*) **1.** to take the place of; supersede. **2.** to substitute a person or thing for (another); put in place of: *to replace an old pair of shoes.* **3.** to restore to its rightful place. —**re'placeable** *adj.* —**re'placer** *n.*

replacement (rɪ'pleɪsmənt) *n.* **1.** the act or process of replacing. **2.** a person or thing that replaces another.

replay *n.* ('ri:,pleɪ). **1.** Also called: **action replay.** a showing again of a sequence of action in slow motion immediately after it happens. **2.** a second match between a pair or group of contestants. ~*vb.* (ri:'pleɪ). **3.** to play again (a record, sporting contest, etc.).

replenish (rɪ'plɛnɪʃ) *vb.* (*tr.*) **1.** to make full or complete again by supplying what has been used up. **2.** to put fresh fuel on (a fire). [C14: from OF *replenir*, from RE- + *plenir*, from L *plēnus* full] —**re'plenisher** *n.* —**re'plenishment** *n.*

replete (rɪ'pli:t) *adj.* (*usually postpositive*) **1.** (often foll. by *with*) copiously supplied (with); abounding (in). **2.** having one's appetite completely or excessively satisfied; gorged; satiated. [C14: from L *replētus*, from *replēre*, from RE- + *plēre* to fill] —**re'pletely** *adv.* —**re'pleteness** *n.* —**re'pletion** *n.*

replevin (rɪ'plɛvɪn) *Law.* ~*n.* **1.** the recovery of goods unlawfully taken, made subject to establishing the validity of the recovery in a legal action and returning the goods if the decision is adverse. **2.** (formerly) a writ of replevin. ~*vb.* **3.** another word for **replevy.** [C15: from Anglo-F, from OF *replevir* to give security for, from RE- + *plevir* to PLEDGE]

replevy (rɪ'plɛvɪ) *Law.* ~*vb.* **-plevying, -plevied.** (*tr.*) **1.** to recover possession of (goods) by replevin. ~*n., pl.* **-plevies. 2.** another word for **replevin.** [C15: from OF *replevir; see* REPLEVIN] —**re'pleviable** *or* **re'plevisable** *adj.*

replica ('rɛplɪkə) *n.* an exact copy or reproduction, esp. on a smaller scale. [C19: from It., lit.: a reply, from *replicare*, from L: to bend back, repeat]

replicate *vb.* ('rɛplɪ,keɪt). (*mainly tr.*) **1.** (*also intr.*) to make or be a copy (of); reproduce. **2.** to fold (something) over on itself; bend back. ~*adj.* ('rɛplɪkɪt). **3.** folded back on itself: *a replicate leaf.* [C19: from L *replicātus* bent back; see REPLICA] —**,repli'cation** *n.* —**'replicative** *adj.*

reply (rɪ'plaɪ) *vb.* **-plying, -plied.** (*mainly intr.*) **1.** to make answer (to) in words or writing or by an action; respond. **2.** (*tr.; takes a clause as object*) to say (something) in answer: *he replied that he didn't want to come.* **3.** *Law.* to answer a defendant's plea. **4.** to return (a sound); echo. ~*n., pl.* **-plies. 5.** an answer; response. **6.** the answer made by a plaintiff or petitioner to a defendant's case. [C14: from OF *replier* to fold again, reply, from L *replicāre*, from RE- + *plicāre* to fold] —**re'plier** *n.*

repoint (,ri:'pɔɪnt) *vb.* (*tr.*) to repair the joints of (brickwork, masonry, etc.) with mortar or cement.

report (rɪ'pɔ:t) *n.* **1.** an account prepared after investigation and published or broadcast. **2.** a statement made widely known; rumour: *according to report, he is not dead.* **3.** an account of the deliberations of a committee, body, etc.: *a report of parliamentary proceedings.* **4.** *Brit.* a statement on the progress of each schoolchild. **5.** a written account of a case decided at law. **6.** comment on a person's character or actions; reputation: *he is of good report here.* **7.** a sharp loud noise, esp. one made by a gun. ~*vb.* (when *tr.*, *may take a clause as object;* when *intr.*, often foll. by *on*). **8.** to give an account of; describe. **9.** to give an account of the results of an investigation (into): *to report on housing conditions.* **10.** (of a committee, legislative body, etc.) to make a formal report on (a bill). **11.** (*tr.*) to complain about (a person), esp. to a superior. **12.** to present (oneself) or be present at an appointed place for a specific purpose: *report to the manager's office.* **13.** (*intr.*) to say or show that one is (in a certain state): *to report fit.* **14.** (*intr.; foll. by to*) to be responsible (to) and under the authority (of). **15.** (*intr.*) to act as a reporter. **16.** *Law.* to take down in writing details of (the proceedings of a court of law, etc.) as a record or for publication. [C14: from OF, from *reporter*, from L *reportāre*, from RE- + *portāre* to carry] —**re'portable** *adj.* —**re'portedly** *adv.*

reportage (rɪ'pɔ:tɪdʒ, ,rɛpɔ:'tɑ:ʒ) *n.* **1.** the act or process of reporting news or other events of general interest. **2.** a journalist's style of reporting.

---

reported speech n. another term for **indirect speech.**

reporter (rɪ'pɔːtə) n. **1.** a person who reports, esp. one employed to gather news for a newspaper or broadcasting organization. **2.** a person authorized to report the proceedings of a legislature.

report stage n. the stage preceding the third reading in the passage of a bill through Parliament.

repose¹ (rɪ'pəʊz) n. **1.** a state of quiet restfulness; peace or tranquillity. **2.** dignified calmness of manner; composure. ~vb. **3.** to lie or lay down at rest. **4.** (intr.) to lie when dead, as in the grave. **5.** (intr.; foll. by on, in, etc.) Formal. to be based (on): your plan reposes on a fallacy. [C15: from OF reposer, from LL repausāre, from RE- + pausāre to stop] —re'posal n. —re'poser n. —re'poseful adj. —re'posefully adv.

repose² (rɪ'pəʊz) vb. (tr.) **1.** to put (trust) in a person or thing. **2.** to place or put (an object) somewhere. [C15: from L repōnere to store up, from RE- + pōnere to put] —re'posal n.

repository (rɪ'pɒzɪtərɪ, -trɪ) n., pl. -ries. **1.** a place or container in which things can be stored for safety. **2.** a place where things are kept for exhibition; museum. **3.** a place of burial; sepulchre. **4.** a person to whom a secret is entrusted; confidant. [C15: from L repositōrium, from repōnere to place]

repossess (,riːpə'zɛs) vb. (tr.) to take back possession of (property), esp. for nonpayment of money due under a hire-purchase agreement. —**repossession** (,riːpə'zɛʃən) n. —**repos'sessor** n.

repoussé (rə'puːseɪ) adj. **1.** raised in relief, as a design on a thin piece of metal hammered through from the underside. ~n. **2.** a design or surface made in this way. [C19: from F, from repousser, from RE- + pousser to PUSH]

repp (rɛp) n. a variant spelling of **rep¹.**

reprehend (,rɛprɪ'hɛnd) vb. (tr.) to find fault with; criticize. [C14: from L reprehendere to hold fast, rebuke, from RE- + prendere to grasp] —,repre'hender n. —,repre'hension n.

reprehensible (,rɛprɪ'hɛnsɪb°l) adj. open to criticism or rebuke; blameworthy. [C14: from LL reprehensibilis, from L reprehendere; see REPREHEND] —,repre,hensi'bility n. —,repre'hensibly adv.

represent (,rɛprɪ'zɛnt) vb. (tr.) **1.** to stand as an equivalent of; correspond to. **2.** to act as a substitute or proxy (for). **3.** to act as or be the authorized delegate or agent for (a person, country, etc.): an MP represents his constituency. **4.** to serve or use as a means of expressing: letters represent the sounds of speech. **5.** to exhibit the characteristics of; exemplify; typify: romanticism in music is represented by Beethoven. **6.** to present an image of through the medium of a picture or sculpture; portray. **7.** to bring clearly before the mind. **8.** to set forth in words; state or explain. **9.** to describe as having a specified character or quality: he represented her as a saint. **10.** to act out the part of on stage; portray. [C14: from L repraesentāre to exhibit, from RE- + praesentāre to PRESENT²] —**repre'sentable** adj. —,repre,senta'bility n.

re-present (,riːprɪ'zɛnt) vb. (tr.) to present again. —**re-presentation** (,riː,prɛzɛn'teɪʃən) n.

representation (,rɛprɪzɛn'teɪʃən) n. **1.** the act or an instance of representing or the state of being represented. **2.** anything that represents, such as a verbal or pictorial portrait. **3.** anything that is represented, such as an image brought clearly to mind. **4.** the principle by which delegates act for a constituency. **5.** a body of representatives. **6.** an instance of acting for another in a particular capacity, such as executor. **7.** a dramatic production or performance. **8.** (often pl.) a statement of facts, true or alleged, esp. one set forth by way of remonstrance or expostulation.

representational (,rɛprɪzɛn'teɪʃən°l) adj. **1.** Art. depicting objects, scenes, etc., directly as seen; naturalistic. **2.** of or relating to representation.

representationalism (,rɛprɪzɛn'teɪʃənə,lɪzəm) or **representationism** n. **1.** Philosophy. the doctrine that in perceptions of objects what is before the mind is not the object but a representation of it. Cf. **presentationism. 2.** Art. the practice of depicting objects, scenes, etc., directly as seen. —,represen,tational'istic adj. —,represen'tationist n., adj.

representative (,rɛprɪ'zɛntətɪv) n. **1.** a person or thing that represents another. **2.** a person who represents and tries to sell the products or services of a firm. **3.** a typical example. **4.** a person representing a constituency in a deliberative, legislative, or executive body, esp. (cap.) a member of the **House of Representatives** (the lower house of Congress). ~adj. **5.** serving to represent; symbolic. **6. a.** exemplifying a class or kind; typical. **b.** containing or including examples of all the interests, types, etc., in a group. **7.** acting as deputy or proxy for another. **8.** representing a constituency or the whole people in the process of government: a representative council. **9.** of or relating to the political representation of the people: representative government. **10.** of or relating to a mental picture or representation. —,repre'sentatively adv. —,repre'sentativeness n.

repress (rɪ'prɛs) vb. (tr.) **1.** to keep (feelings, etc.) under control; suppress or restrain. **2.** to put into a state of subjugation: to repress a people. **3.** Psychol. to banish (unpleasant thoughts) from one's conscious mind. [C14: from L reprimere to press back, from RE- + premere to PRESS¹] —**re'pressed** adj. —**re'presser** or **re'pressor** n. —**re'pressible** adj. —**re'pression** n. —**re'pressive** adj.

re-press (riː'prɛs) vb. (tr.) **1.** to press again, esp. to reproduce more gramophone records by a second pressing.

reprieve (rɪ'priːv) vb. (tr.) **1.** to postpone or remit the punishment of (a person, esp. one condemned to death). **2.** to give temporary relief to (a person or thing), esp. from otherwise irrevocable harm. ~n. **3.** a postponement or remission of punishment. **4.** a warrant granting a postponement. **5.** a temporary relief from pain or harm; respite. [C16: from OF repris (something) taken back, from reprendre, from L reprehendere; ? also infl. by obs. E repreve to reprove] —**re'prievable** adj. —**re'priever** n.

reprimand ('rɛprɪ,mɑːnd) n. **1.** a reproof or formal admonition; rebuke. ~vb. **2.** (tr.) to admonish or rebuke, esp. formally. [C17: from F réprimande, from L reprimenda (things) to be repressed; see REPRESS] —,repri'manding adj.

reprint n. ('riː,prɪnt). **1.** a reproduction in print of any matter already published. **2.** a reissue of a printed work using the same type, plates, etc., as the original. ~vb. (riː'prɪnt). **3.** (tr.) to print again. —**re'printer** n.

reprisal (rɪ'praɪz°l) n. **1.** the act or an instance of retaliation in any form. **2.** (often pl.) retaliatory action against an enemy in wartime. **3.** (formerly) the forcible seizure of the property or subjects of one nation by another. [C15: from OF reprisaille, from OIt., from riprendere to recapture, from L reprehendere; see REPREHEND]

reprise (rɪ'priːz) Music. ~n. **1.** the repeating of an earlier theme. ~vb. **2.** to repeat (an earlier theme). [C14: from OF, from reprendre to take back, from L reprehendere; see REPREHEND]

repro ('riːprəʊ) n., pl. -pros. **1.** short for **reproduction** (sense 2): repro furniture. **2.** short for **reproduction proof.**

reproach (rɪ'prəʊtʃ) vb. (tr.) **1.** to impute blame to (a person) for an action or fault; rebuke. ~n. **2.** the act of reproaching. **3.** rebuke or censure; reproof. **4.** disgrace or shame: to bring reproach upon one's family. **5.** above or **beyond reproach.** perfect; beyond criticism. [C15: from OF reprochier, from L RE- + prope near] —**re'proachable** adj. —**re'proacher** n. —**re'proachingly** adv.

reproachful (rɪ'prəʊtʃfʊl) adj. full of or expressing reproach. —**re'proachfully** adv. —**re'proachfulness** n.

reprobate ('rɛprəʊ,beɪt) adj. **1.** morally unprincipled; depraved. **2.** Christianity. condemned to eternal punishment in hell. ~n. **3.** an unprincipled, depraved, or damned person. **4.** a disreputable or roguish person. ~vb. (tr.) **5.** to disapprove of; condemn. **6.** (of God) to condemn to eternal punishment in hell. [C16: from LL reprobātus held in disfavour, from L RE- + probāre to test, APPROVE] —**reprobacy** ('rɛprəbəsɪ) n. —'**repro,bater** n. —,repro'bation n.

reprocess (riː'prəʊsɛs) vb. (tr.) to treat again (something already made and used) in order to make it reusable in some form. —**re'processing** n., adj.

,repo'sition vb., n.   re'pot vb.   re'price vb.

reproduce (ˌriːprəˈdjuːs) vb. (mainly tr.) **1.** to make a copy, representation, or imitation of; duplicate. **2.** (also intr.) Biol. to undergo or cause to undergo a process of reproduction. **3.** to produce again; bring back into existence again; re-create. **4.** (intr.) to come out (well, badly, etc.) when copied. —ˌreproˈducer n. —ˌreproˈducible adj. —ˌreproˈducibly adv. —ˌreproˌduciˈbility n.

reproduction (ˌriːprəˈdʌkʃən) n. **1.** Biol. any of various processes, either sexual or asexual, by which an animal or plant produces one or more individuals similar to itself. **2. a.** an imitation or facsimile of a work of art. **b.** (as modifier): a reproduction portrait. **3.** the quality of sound from an audio system. **4.** the act or process of reproducing.

reproduction proof n. Printing. a proof of very good quality used for photographic reproduction to make a printing plate.

reproductive (ˌriːprəˈdʌktɪv) adj. of, relating to, characteristic of, or taking part in reproduction. —ˌreproˈductively adv. —ˌreproˈductiveness n.

reprography (rɪˈprɒɡrəfɪ) n. the art or process of copying, reprinting, or reproducing printed material. —ˈreprographic (ˌreprəˈɡræfɪk) adj. —ˌreproˈgraphically adv.

reproof (rɪˈpruːf) n. an act or expression of rebuke or censure. Also: **reproval** (rɪˈpruːvˀl). [C14 reproffe, from OF reprove, from LL reprobāre to disapprove of; see REPROBATE]

re-proof (riːˈpruːf) vb. (tr.) **1.** to treat (a coat, jacket, etc.) so as to renew its texture, waterproof qualities, etc. **2.** to provide a new proof of (a book, galley, etc.).

reprove (rɪˈpruːv) vb. (tr.) to rebuke or scold. [C14: from OF reprover, from LL reprobāre, from L RE- + probāre to examine] —reˈprovable adj. —reˈprover n. —reˈprovingly adv.

reptant (ˈreptənt) adj. Biol. creeping, crawling, or lying along the ground. [C17: from L reptāre to creep]

reptile (ˈreptaɪl) n. **1.** any of the cold-blooded vertebrates characterized by lungs, an outer covering of horny scales or plates, and young produced in eggs, such as the tortoises, turtles, snakes, lizards, and crocodiles. **2.** a grovelling insignificant person: you miserable little reptile! ~adj. **3.** creeping, crawling, or squirming. [C14: from LL reptilis creeping, from L repere to crawl] —**reptilian** (rɛpˈtɪlɪən) n., adj.

Repton (ˈreptˀn) n. Humphry. 1752–1818, English landscape gardener.

republic (rɪˈpʌblɪk) n. **1.** a form of government in which the people or their elected representatives possess the supreme power. **2.** a political or national unit possessing such a form of government. **3.** a constitutional form in which the head of state is an elected or nominated president. [C17: from F république, from L rēspublica, lit.: public thing, from rēs thing + publica PUBLIC]

republican (rɪˈpʌblɪkən) adj. **1.** of, resembling, or relating to a republic. **2.** supporting or advocating a republic. ~n. **3.** a supporter or advocate of a republic.

Republican (rɪˈpʌblɪkən) adj. **1.** of, belonging to, or relating to a Republican Party. **2.** of, belonging to, or relating to the Irish Republican Army. ~n. **3.** a member or supporter of a Republican Party. **4.** a member or supporter of the Irish Republican Army.

republicanism (rɪˈpʌblɪkəˌnɪzəm) n. **1.** the principles or theory of republican government. **2.** support for a republic. **3.** (often cap.) support for a Republican Party.

Republican Party n. **1.** one of the two major political parties in the U.S.: established around 1854. **2.** any of a number of political parties in other countries, usually so named to indicate their opposition to monarchy.

Republic of Ireland n. See Ireland[1] (sense 2).

repudiate (rɪˈpjuːdɪˌeɪt) vb. (tr.) **1.** to reject the authority or validity of; refuse to accept or ratify. **2.** to refuse to acknowledge or pay (a debt). **3.** to cast off or disown (a son, lover, etc.). [C16: from L repudiāre to put away, from repudium separation, divorce, from RE- + pudēre to be ashamed] —reˈpudiable adj. —reˌpudiˈation n. —reˈpudiative adj. —reˈpudiˌator n.

repugnant (rɪˈpʌɡnənt) adj. **1.** repellent to the senses; causing aversion. **2.** distasteful; offensive; disgusting. **3.** contradictory; inconsistent or incompatible. [C14: from L repugnāns resisting, from repugnāre, from RE- + pugnāre to fight] —reˈpugnance n. —reˈpugnantly adv.

repulse (rɪˈpʌls) vb. (tr.) **1.** to drive back or ward off (an attacking force); repel; rebuff. **2.** to reject with coldness or discourtesy: she repulsed his advances. ~n. **3.** the act or an instance of driving back or warding off; rebuff. **4.** a cold discourteous rejection or refusal. [C16: from L repellere to drive back] —reˈpulser n.

▷ **Usage.** The verbs repulse and repel share the meaning of physically driving back or away, but they can be carefully distinguished in other senses. Although the related adjective repulsive has the meaning of causing feelings of disgust, repulse does not mean to drive away by arousing disgust. Instead, repel is normally used in this sense, and repulse is used when the required meaning is to reject coldly or drive away with discourtesy.

repulsion (rɪˈpʌlʃən) n. **1.** a feeling of disgust or aversion. **2.** Physics. a force separating two objects, such as the force between two like electric charges.

repulsive (rɪˈpʌlsɪv) adj. **1.** causing or occasioning repugnance; loathsome; disgusting or distasteful. **2.** tending to repel, esp. by coldness and discourtesy. **3.** Physics. concerned with, producing, or being a repulsion. —reˈpulsively adv. —reˈpulsiveness n.

reputable (ˈrepjʊtəbˀl) adj. **1.** having a good reputation; honoured, trustworthy, or respectable. **2.** (of words) acceptable as good usage; standard. —ˈreputably adv.

reputation (ˌrepjʊˈteɪʃən) n. **1.** the estimation in which a person or thing is generally held; opinion. **2.** a high opinion generally held about a person or thing; esteem. **3.** notoriety or fame, esp. for some specified characteristic. [C14: from L reputātiō, from reputāre to calculate; see REPUTE]

repute (rɪˈpjuːt) vb. **1.** (tr.; usually passive) to consider (a person or thing) to be as specified: he is reputed to be rich. ~n. **2.** public estimation; reputation: a writer of little repute. [C15: from OF reputer, from L reputāre, from RE- + putāre to think]

reputed (rɪˈpjuːtɪd) adj. (prenominal) generally reckoned or considered; supposed: the reputed writer of two epic poems. —reˈputedly adv.

request (rɪˈkwest) vb. (tr.) **1.** to express a desire for, esp. politely; ask for or demand: to request a bottle of wine. ~n. **2.** the act or an instance of requesting, esp. in the form of a written statement, etc.; petition or solicitation. **3. by request.** in accordance with someone's desire. **4. in request.** in demand; popular: he is in request all over the world. **5. on request.** on the occasion of a demand or request: application forms are available on request. [C14: from OF requeste, from Vulgar L requaerere; see REQUIRE, QUEST] —reˈquester n.

request stop n. a point on a route at which a bus, etc., will stop only if signalled to do so. U.S. equivalent: **flag stop.**

Requiem (ˈrekwɪəm) n. **1.** R.C. Church. a Mass celebrated for the dead. **2.** a musical setting of this Mass. **3.** any piece of music composed or performed as a memorial to a dead person. [C14: from L requiēs rest, from the introit, Requiem aeternam dona eis Rest eternal grant unto them]

requiem shark n. any of a family of sharks occurring mostly in tropical seas and characterized by a nictitating membrane.

requiescat (ˌrekwɪˈeskæt) n. a prayer for the repose of the souls of the dead. [L, from requiescat in pace may he rest in peace]

require (rɪˈkwaɪə) vb. (mainly tr.; may take a clause as object or an infinitive) **1.** to have need of; depend upon; want. **2.** to impose as a necessity; make necessary: this work requires precision. **3.** (also intr.) to make formal request (for); insist upon. **4.** to call upon or oblige (a person) authoritatively; order or command: to require someone to account for his actions. [C14: from OF requerre, via Vulgar L from L requīrere to seek to know; also infl. by quaerere to seek] —reˈquirer n.

requirement (rɪˈkwaɪəmənt) n. **1.** something demanded or imposed as an obligation. **2.** a thing desired or needed. **3.** the act or an instance of requiring.

ˌreproˈgrammable or ˌreproˈgramable adj.

ˌrepubliˈcation n. reˈpublish vb.

reˈpurchase vb., n.

reˈpuriˌfy vb.

requisite ('rɛkwɪzɪt) *adj.* **1.** absolutely essential; indispensable. ~*n.* **2.** something indispensable; necessity. [C15: from L *requisītus* sought after, from *requīrere* to seek for] —**'requisitely** *adv.*

requisition (,rɛkwɪ'zɪʃən) *n.* **1.** a request or demand, esp. an authoritative or formal one. **2.** an official form on which such a demand is made. **3.** the act of taking something over, esp. temporarily for military or public use. ~*vb.* (*tr.*) **4.** to demand and take for use, esp. by military or public authority. **5.** (*may take an infinitive*) to require (someone) formally to do (something): *to requisition a soldier to drive an officer's car.* —,requi'sitionary *adj.* —,requi'sitionist *n.*

requite (rɪ'kwaɪt) *vb.* (*tr.*) to make return to (a person for a kindness or injury); repay with a similar action. [C16: RE- + obs. *quite* to discharge, repay; see QUIT] —**re'quitable** *adj.* —**re'quital** *n.* —**re'quitement** *n.* —**re'quiter** *n.*

reredos ('rɪədɒs) *n.* **1.** a screen or wall decoration at the back of an altar. **2.** another word for **fireback.** [C14: from OF *areredos*, from *arere* behind + *dos* back, from L *dorsum*]

rerun *vb.* (riː'rʌn), **-running, -ran.** (*tr.*) **1.** to broadcast or put on (a film, etc.) again. **2.** to run (a race, etc.) again. ~*n.* ('riː,rʌn). **3.** a film, etc., that is broadcast again; repeat. **4.** a race that is run again.

res (reɪs) *n., pl.* **res.** *Latin.* a thing, matter, or object.

res. *abbrev. for:* **1.** research. **2.** reserve. **3.** residence. **4.** resides. **5.** resigned. **6.** resolution.

resale price maintenance ('riːseɪl) *n.* the practice by which a manufacturer establishes a fixed or minimum price for the resale of a brand product by retailers or other distributors. U.S. equivalent: **fair trade.** Abbrev.: **rpm.**

rescind (rɪ'sɪnd) *vb.* (*tr.*) to annul or repeal. [C17: from L *rescindere* to cut off, from *re-* (intensive) + *scindere* to cut] —**re'scindable** *adj.* —**re'scinder** *n.* —**re'scindment** *n.*

rescission (rɪ'sɪʒən) *n.* the act of rescinding.

rescript ('riː,skrɪpt) *n.* **1.** (in ancient Rome) a reply by the emperor to a question on a point of law. **2.** any official announcement or edict; a decree. **3.** something rewritten. [C16: from L *rescriptum* reply, from *rescribere* to write back]

rescue ('rɛskjuː) *vb.* **-cuing, -cued.** (*tr.*) **1.** to bring (someone or something) out of danger, etc.; deliver or save. **2.** to free (a person) from legal custody by force. **3.** *Law.* to seize (goods) by force. ~*n.* **4. a.** the act or an instance of rescuing. **b.** (*as modifier*): *a rescue party.* **5.** the forcible removal of a person from legal custody. **6.** *Law.* the forcible seizure of goods or property. [C14 *rescowen*, from OF *rescourre*, from RE- + *escourre* to pull away, from L *excutere* to shake off, from *quatere* to shake] —**'rescuer** *n.*

research (rɪ'sɜːtʃ) *n.* **1.** systematic investigation to establish facts or collect information on a subject. ~*vb.* **2.** to carry out investigations into (a subject, etc.). [C16: from OF *recercher* to seek, search again, from RE- + *cercher* to SEARCH] —**re'searchable** *adj.* —**re'searcher** *n.*

research and development *n.* a commercial company's application of scientific research to develop new products. Abbrev.: **R & D.**

reseat (riː'siːt) *vb.* (*tr.*) **1.** to show (a person) to a new seat. **2.** to put a new seat on (a chair, etc.). **3.** to provide new seats for (a theatre, etc.). **4.** to re-form the seating of (a valve).

resect (rɪ'sɛkt) *vb.* (*tr.*) *Surgery.* to cut out part of (a bone, organ, or other structure or part). [C17: from L *resecāre*, from RE- + *secāre* to cut]

resection (rɪ'sɛkʃən) *n.* **1.** *Surgery.* excision of part of a bone, organ, or other part. **2.** *Surveying.* a method of fixing the position of a point by making angular observations to three fixed points. —**re'sectional** *adj.*

resemblance (rɪ'zɛmbləns) *n.* **1.** the state or quality of resembling; likeness or similarity. **2.** the degree or extent to which a likeness exists. **3.** semblance; likeness. —**re'semblant** *adj.*

resemble (rɪ'zɛmbᵊl) *vb.* (*tr.*) to possess some similarity to; be like. [C14: from OF *resembler*, from RE- + *sembler* to look like, from L *similis* like] —**re'sembler** *n.*

resent (rɪ'zɛnt) *vb.* (*tr.*) to feel bitter, indignant, or aggrieved at. [C17: from F *ressentir*, from RE- + *sentir* to feel, from L *sentīre* to perceive; see SENSE] —**re'sentful** *adj.* —**re'sentment** *n.*

reserpine ('rɛsəpɪn) *n.* an insoluble alkaloid, extracted from the roots of a rauwolfia, used medicinally to lower blood pressure and as a sedative and tranquillizer. [C20: from G *Reserpin*, prob. from the NL name of the plant]

reservation (,rɛzə'veɪʃən) *n.* **1.** the act or an instance of reserving. **2.** something reserved, esp. accommodation or a seat. **3.** (*often pl.*) a stated or unstated qualification of opinion that prevents one's wholehearted acceptance of a proposal, etc. **4.** an area of land set aside, esp. (in the U.S. and Canada) for American Indian peoples. **5.** *Brit.* the strip of land between the two carriageways of a dual carriageway. **6.** the act or process of keeping back, esp. for oneself; withholding. **7.** *Law.* a right or interest retained by the grantor in property dealings.

reserve (rɪ'zɜːv) *vb.* (*tr.*) **1.** to keep back or set aside, esp. for future use or contingency; retain: *I reserve the right to question these men later.* **2.** to keep for oneself or contingency; withhold. **3.** to obtain or secure by advance arrangement: *I have reserved two tickets for tonight's show.* **4.** to delay delivery of (a judgment). ~*n.* **5. a.** something kept back or set aside, esp. for future use or contingency. **b.** (*as modifier*): *a reserve stock.* **6.** the state or condition of being reserved: *I have plenty in reserve.* **7.** a tract of land set aside for a special purpose: *a nature reserve.* **8.** *Austral. & N.Z.* a public park. **9.** *Canad.* an Indian reservation. **10.** *Sport.* a substitute. **11.** (*often pl.*) **a.** a part of an army not committed to immediate action in a military engagement. **b.** that part of a nation's armed services not in active service. **12.** coolness or formality of manner; restraint, silence, or reticence. **13.** (*often pl.*) *Finance.* liquid assets or a portion of capital not invested or a portion of profits not distributed by a bank or business enterprise and held to meet future liabilities or contingencies. **14. without reserve.** without reservations; fully. [C14: from OF *reserver*, from L *reservāre*, from RE- + *servāre* to keep] —**re'servable** *adj.* —**re'server** *n.*

re-serve (riː'sɜːv) *vb.* (*tr.*) to serve again.

reserve bank *n.* one of the twelve banks forming part of the U.S. Federal Reserve System.

reserve currency *n.* foreign currency that is acceptable as a medium of international payments and is held in reserve by many countries.

reserved (rɪ'zɜːvd) *adj.* **1.** set aside for use by a particular person. **2.** cool or formal in manner; restrained or reticent. **3.** destined; fated: *a man reserved for greatness.* —**reservedly** (rɪ'zɜːvɪdlɪ) *adv.* —**re'servedness** *n.*

reserved list *n.* *Brit.* a list of retired naval, army, or air-force officers available for recall to active service in an emergency.

reserved occupation *n.* *Brit.* an occupation from which one will not be called up for military service in time of war.

reserve-grade *adj.* *Austral.* denoting a sporting team of the second rank in a club.

reserve price *n.* *Brit.* the minimum price acceptable to the owner of property being auctioned or sold. Also called (esp. Scot. and U.S.): **upset price.**

reservist (rɪ'zɜːvɪst) *n.* one who serves in the reserve formations of a nation's armed forces.

reservoir ('rɛzə,vwɑː) *n.* **1.** a natural or artificial lake or large tank used for collecting and storing water for community use. **2.** *Biol.* a cavity in an organism containing fluid. **3.** a place where a great stock of anything is accumulated. **4.** a large supply of something: *a reservoir of talent.* [C17: from F *réservoir*, from *réserver* to RESERVE]

reservoir rock *n.* porous and permeable rock containing producible oil or gas in its pore spaces.

reset[1] *vb.* (riː'sɛt), **-setting, -set.** (*tr.*) **1.** to set again (a broken bone, matter in type, a gemstone, etc.). **2.** to restore (a gauge, etc.) to zero. ~*n.* ('riː,sɛt). **3.** the act or an instance of setting again. **4.** a thing that is set again. —**re'setter** *n.*

reset[2] *Scot.* ~*vb.* (riː'sɛt), **-setting, -set.** **1.** to receive or handle (goods) knowing they have been stolen. ~*n.* ('riːsɛt). **2.** the receiving of stolen goods. [C14: from OF

---

re'read *vb.*   re'route *vb.*   re'schedule *vb.*   re'sealable *adj.*
,rere'cording *n.*   re'salable *or* re'saleable   re'seal *vb.*
re'roof *vb.*   *adj.*

receter, from L *receptāre,* from *recipere* to receive]
—**re'setter** *n.*

res gestae ('dʒɛstiː) *pl. n.* **1.** things done or accomplished; achievements. **2.** *Law.* incidental facts and circumstances that are admissible in evidence because they explain the matter at issue. [L]

Resht (rɛʃt) *n.* a variant of **Rasht.**

reside (rɪ'zaɪd) *vb.* (*intr.*) *Formal.* **1.** to live permanently (in a place); have one's home (in): *he resides in London.* **2.** (of things, qualities, etc.) to be inherently present (in); be vested (in): *political power resides in military strength.* [C15: from L *residēre* to sit back, from RE-+ *sedēre* to sit] —**re'sider** *n.*

residence ('rɛzɪdəns) *n.* **1.** the place in which one resides; abode or home. **2.** a large imposing house; mansion. **3.** the fact of residing in a place or a period of residing. **4. in residence. a.** actually resident: *the Queen is in residence.* **b.** designating a creative artist resident and active for a set period at a college, gallery, etc.: *writer in residence.*

residency ('rɛzɪdənsɪ) *n., pl.* **-cies. 1.** a variant of **residence. 2.** *U.S. & Canad.* the period, following internship, during which a physician undergoes specialized training. **3.** (in India, formerly) the official house of the governor general at the court of a native prince.

resident ('rɛzɪdənt) *n.* **1.** a person who resides in a place. **2.** (esp. formerly) a representative of the British government in a British protectorate. **3.** (in India, formerly) a representative of the British governor general at the court of a native prince. **4.** a bird or animal that does not migrate. **5.** *Brit. & N.Z.* a junior doctor who lives in the hospital where he works. **6.** *U.S. & Canad.* a physician who lives in the hospital while undergoing specialist training after completing his internship. *~adj.* **7.** living in a place; residing. **8.** living or staying at a place in order to discharge a duty, etc. **9.** (of qualities, etc.) existing or inherent (in). **10.** (of birds and animals) not in the habit of migrating. —**'residentship** *n.*

residential (,rɛzɪ'dɛnʃəl) *adj.* **1.** suitable for or allocated for residence: *a residential area.* **2.** relating to residence. —**,resi'dentially** *adv.*

residentiary (,rɛzɪ'dɛnʃərɪ) *adj.* **1.** residing in a place, esp. officially. **2.** obliged to reside in an official residence: *a residentiary benefice. ~n., pl.* **-tiaries. 3.** a clergyman obliged to reside in the place of his official appointment.

residual (rɪ'zɪdjʊəl) *adj.* **1.** of, relating to, or designating a residue or remainder; remaining; leftover. **2.** *U.S.* of or relating to the payment of residuals. *~n.* **3.** something left over as a residue; remainder. **4.** *Statistics.* **a.** the difference between the mean of a set of observations and one particular observation. **b.** the difference between the numerical value of one particular observation and the theoretical result. **5.** (*often pl.*) payment made to an actor, musician, etc., for subsequent use of film in which the person appears. —**re'sidually** *adv.*

residual unemployment *n.* the unemployment that remains in periods of full employment, as a result of those mentally, physically, or emotionally unfit to work.

residuary (rɪ'zɪdjʊərɪ) *adj.* **1.** of, relating to, or constituting a residue; residual. **2.** *Law.* entitled to the residue of an estate after payment of debts and distribution of specific gifts.

residue ('rɛzɪ,djuː) *n.* **1.** matter remaining after something has been removed. **2.** *Law.* what is left of an estate after the discharge of debts and distribution of specific gifts. [C14: from OF *residu,* from L *residuus* remaining over, from *residēre* to stay behind]

residuum (rɪ'zɪdjʊəm) *n., pl.* **-ua** (-jʊə). a more formal word for **residue.**

resign (rɪ'zaɪn) *vb.* **1.** (when *intr.,* often foll. by *from*) to give up tenure of (a job, office, etc.). **2.** (*tr.*) to reconcile (oneself) to; yield: *to resign oneself to death.* **3.** (*tr.*) to give up (a right, claim, etc.); relinquish. [C14: from OF *resigner,* from L *resignāre* to unseal, destroy, from RE- + *signāre* to seal] —**re'signer** *n.*

re-sign (riː'saɪn) *vb.* to sign again.

resignation (,rɛzɪg'neɪʃən) *n.* **1.** the act of resigning. **2.** a formal document stating one's intention to resign. **3.** a submissive unresisting attitude; passive acquiescence.

resigned (rɪ'zaɪnd) *adj.* characteristic of or proceeding from an attitude of resignation; acquiescent or submissive. —**resignedly** (rɪ'zaɪnɪdlɪ) *adv.* —**re'signedness** *n.*

resile (rɪ'zaɪl) *vb.* (*intr.*) to spring or shrink back; recoil or resume original shape. [C16: from OF *resilir,* from L *resilīre* to jump back, from RE- + *salīre* to jump] —**re'silement** *n.*

resilient (rɪ'zɪlɪənt) *adj.* **1.** (of an object) capable of regaining its original shape or position after bending, stretching, or other deformation; elastic. **2.** (of a person) recovering easily and quickly from illness, hardship, etc. —**re'silience** *or* **re'siliency** *n.* —**re'siliently** *adv.*

resin ('rɛzɪn) *n.* **1.** Also called: **rosin.** any of a group of solid or semisolid amorphous compounds that are obtained directly from certain plants as exudations. **2.** any of a large number of synthetic, usually organic, materials that have a polymeric structure, esp. such a substance in a raw state before it is moulded or treated with plasticizer, etc. *~vb.* **3.** (*tr.*) to treat or coat with resin. [C14: from OF *resine,* from L *rēsīna,* from Gk *rhētinē* resin from a pine] —**'resinous** *adj.* —**'resinously** *adv.* —**'resinousness** *n.*

resinate ('rɛzɪ,neɪt) *vb.* (*tr.*) to impregnate with resin.

resipiscence (,rɛsɪ'pɪsəns) *n. Literary.* acknowledgment that one has been mistaken. [C16: from LL *resipiscentia,* from *resipiscere* to recover one's senses, from L *sapere* to know] —**,resi'piscent** *adj.*

resist (rɪ'zɪst) *vb.* **1.** to stand firm (against); not yield (to); fight (against). **2.** (*tr.*) to withstand the deleterious action of; be proof against: *to resist corrosion.* **3.** (*tr.*) to oppose; refuse to accept or comply with: *to resist arrest.* **4.** (*tr.*) to refrain from, esp. in spite of temptation (esp. in **cannot resist (something)**). *~n.* **5.** a substance used to protect something, esp. a coating that prevents corrosion. [C14: from L *resistere,* from RE- + *sistere* to stand firm] —**re'sister** *n.* —**re'sistible** *adj.* —**re,sisti'bility** *n.* —**re'sistibly** *adv.* —**re'sistless** *adj.*

resistance (rɪ'zɪstəns) *n.* **1.** the act or an instance of resisting. **2.** the capacity to withstand something, esp. the body's natural capacity to withstand disease. **3. a.** the opposition to a flow of electric current through a circuit component, medium, or substance. It is measured in ohms. Symbol: R **b.** (*as modifier*): *a resistance thermometer.* **4.** any force that tends to retard or oppose motion: *air resistance; wind resistance.* **5.** *Physics.* the magnitude of the real part of the acoustic or mechanical impedance. **6. line of least resistance.** the easiest, but not necessarily the best or most honourable, course of action. **7.** See **passive resistance.** —**re'sistant** *adj., n.*

Resistance (rɪ'zɪstəns) *n.* **the.** an illegal organization fighting for national liberty in a country under enemy occupation.

resistance thermometer *n.* an accurate type of thermometer in which temperature is calculated from the resistance of a coil of wire or of a semiconductor placed at the point at which the temperature is to be measured.

Resistencia (*Spanish* rɛsis'tenθja) *n.* a city in NE Argentina, on the Paraná River. Pop.: 218 000 (1980).

resistivity (,riːzɪs'tɪvɪtɪ) *n.* **1.** the electrical property of a material that determines the resistance of a piece of given dimensions. It is measured in ohms. Former name: **specific resistance. 2.** the power or capacity to resist; resistance.

resistor (rɪ'zɪstə) *n.* an electrical component designed to introduce a known value of resistance into a circuit.

resit (riː'sɪt) *vb.* **-sitting, -sat.** (*tr.*) **1.** to sit (an examination) again. *~n.* **2.** an examination which one must sit again.

res judicata (,dʒuːdɪ'kɑːtə) *or* **res adjudicata** *n. Law.* a matter already adjudicated upon that cannot be raised again. [L]

Resnais (*French* rɛnɛ) *n.* **Alain** (alɛ̃). born 1922, French film director, whose films include *Hiroshima mon amour* (1959), *L'Année dernière à Marienbad* (1961), *La Vie est un roman* (1983), and *Melo* (1987).

resoluble (rɪ'zɒljʊbəl, 'rɛzəl-) *or* **resolvable** *adj.* able to be resolved or analysed. [C17: from LL *resolubilis,* from L *resolvere;* see RESOLVE] —**re,solu'bility, re,solva'bility** *or* **re'solubleness, re'solvableness** *n.*

re-soluble (riː'sɒljʊbᵊl) *adj.* capable of being dissolved again. —**re·'solubleness** *or* **re-,solu'bility** *n.* —**re·'solubly** *adv.*

resolute ('rɛzə,luːt) *adj.* **1.** firm in purpose or belief; steadfast. **2.** characterized by resolution; determined: *a resolute answer.* [C16: from L *resolutus*, from *resolvere* to RESOLVE] —**'reso,lutely** *adv.* —**'reso,luteness** *n.*

resolution (,rɛzə'luːʃən) *n.* **1.** the act or an instance of resolving. **2.** firmness or determination. **3.** something resolved or determined; decision. **4.** a formal expression of opinion by a meeting. **5.** a judicial decision on some matter; verdict; judgment. **6.** the act of separating something into its constituent parts or elements. **7.** *Med.* subsidence of the symptoms of a disease, esp. the disappearance of inflammation without pus. **8.** *Music.* the process in harmony whereby a dissonant note or chord is followed by a consonant one. **9.** the ability of a television or film image to reproduce fine detail. **10.** *Physics.* another word for **resolving power.** —**'reso'lutioner** *or* **,reso'lutionist** *n.*

resolve (rɪ'zɒlv) *vb.* (*mainly tr.*) **1.** (*takes a clause as object or an infinitive*) to decide or determine firmly. **2.** to express (an opinion) formally, esp. by a vote. **3.** (*also intr.*; usually foll. by *into*) to separate or cause to separate (into) (constituent parts). **4.** (*usually reflexive*) to change; alter: *the ghost resolved itself into a tree.* **5.** to make up the mind of; cause to decide: *the tempest resolved him to stay at home.* **6.** to find the answer or solution to. **7.** to explain away or dispel: *to resolve a doubt.* **8.** to bring to an end; conclude: *to resolve an argument.* **9.** *Med.* to cause (an inflammation) to subside, esp. without the formation of pus. **10.** *Music.* (*also intr.*) to follow (a dissonant note or chord) by one producing a consonance. **11.** *Physics.* to distinguish between (separate parts) of (an image) as in a microscope, telescope, or other optical instrument. ~*n.* **12.** something determined or decided; resolution: *he had made a resolve to work all day.* **13.** firmness of purpose; determination: *nothing can break his resolve.* [C14: from L *resolvere* to unfasten, reveal, from RE- + *solvere* to loosen] —**re'solvable** *adj.* —**re,solva'bility** *n.* —**re'solver** *n.*

resolved (rɪ'zɒlvd) *adj.* fixed in purpose or intention; determined. —**resolvedly** (rɪ'zɒlvɪdlɪ) *adv.* —**re'solvedness** *n.*

resolvent (rɪ'zɒlvənt) *adj.* **1.** serving to dissolve or separate something into its elements; resolving. ~*n.* **2.** a drug or agent able to reduce swelling or inflammation.

resolving power *n.* **1.** Also called: **resolution.** *Physics.* the ability of a microscope or telescope to produce separate images of closely placed objects. **2.** *Photog.* the ability of an emulsion to show up fine detail in an image.

resonance ('rɛzənəns) *n.* **1.** the condition or quality of being resonant. **2.** sound produced by a body vibrating in sympathy with a neighbouring source of sound. **3.** the condition of a body or system when it is subjected to a periodic disturbance of the same frequency as the natural frequency of the body or system. **4.** amplification of speech sounds by sympathetic vibration in the bone structure of the head and chest, resounding in the cavities of the nose, mouth, and pharynx. **5.** *Electronics.* the condition of an electrical circuit when the frequency is such that the capacitive and inductive reactances are equal in magnitude. **6.** *Med.* the sound heard when tapping a hollow bodily structure, esp. the chest or abdomen. **7.** *Chem.* the phenomenon in which the electronic structure of a molecule can be represented by two or more hypothetical structures involving single, double, and triple chemical bonds. **8.** *Physics.* the condition of a system in which there is a sharp maximum probability for the absorption of electromagnetic radiation or capture of particles. [C16: from L *resonāre* to RESOUND]

resonant ('rɛzənənt) *adj.* **1.** resounding or re-echoing. **2.** producing resonance: *resonant walls.* **3.** full of, or intensified by, resonance: *a resonant voice.* —**'resonantly** *adv.*

resonate ('rɛzə,neɪt) *vb.* **1.** to resound or cause to resound; reverberate. **2.** *Chem., electronics.* to exhibit or cause to exhibit resonance. [C19: from L *resonāre*] —**,reso'nation** *n.*

resonator ('rɛzə,neɪtə) *n.* any body or system that displays resonance, esp. a tuned electrical circuit or a conducting cavity in which microwaves are generated by a resonant current.

resorb (rɪ'sɔːb) *vb.* (*tr.*) to absorb again. [C17: from L *resorbēre*, from RE- + *sorbēre* to suck in] —**re'sorbent** *adj.* —**re'sorption** *n.* —**re'sorptive** *adj.*

resorcinol (rɪ'zɔːsɪ,nɒl) *n.* a colourless crystalline phenol, used in making dyes, drugs, resins, and adhesives. Formula: $C_6H_4(OH)_2$. [C19: NL, from RESIN + *orcinol*, a crystalline solid] —**re'sorcinal** *adj.*

resort (rɪ'zɔːt) *vb.* (*intr.*) **1.** (usually foll. by *to*) to have recourse (to) for help, use, etc.: *to resort to violence.* **2.** to go, esp. often or habitually: *to resort to the beach.* ~*n.* **3.** a place to which many people go for recreation, etc.: *a holiday resort.* **4.** the use of something as a means, help, or recourse. **5.** **last resort.** the last possible course of action open to one. [C14: from OF *resortir*, from RE- + *sortir* to emerge] —**re'sorter** *n.*

re-sort (riː'sɔːt) *vb.* (*tr.*) to sort again.

resound (rɪ'zaʊnd) *vb.* (*intr.*) **1.** to ring or echo with sound; reverberate. **2.** to make a prolonged echoing noise: *the trumpet resounded.* **3.** (of sounds) to echo or ring. **4.** to be widely famous: *his fame resounded throughout India.* [C14: from OF *resoner*, from L *resonāre* to sound again]

re-sound (riː'saʊnd) *vb.* to sound or cause to sound again.

resounding (rɪ'zaʊndɪŋ) *adj.* **1.** clear and emphatic: *a resounding vote of confidence.* **2.** resonant; reverberating. —**re'soundingly** *adv.*

resource (rɪ'zɔːs, -'sɔːs) *n.* **1.** capability, ingenuity, and initiative; quick-wittedness: *a man of resource.* **2.** (*often pl.*) a source of economic wealth, esp. of a country or business enterprise. **3.** a supply or source of aid or support; something resorted to in time of need. **4.** a means of doing something; expedient. [C17: from OF *ressourse* relief, from *resourdre*, from L *resurgere*, from RE- + *surgere* to rise] —**re'sourceless** *adj.*

resourceful (rɪ'zɔːsful, -'sɔːs-) *adj.* ingenious, capable, and full of initiative. —**re'sourcefully** *adv.* —**re'sourcefulness** *n.*

respect (rɪ'spɛkt) *n.* **1.** an attitude of deference, admiration, or esteem; regard. **2.** the state of being honoured or esteemed. **3.** a detail, point, or characteristic: *they differ in some respects.* **4.** reference or relation (esp. in **in respect of, with respect to**). **5.** polite or kind regard; consideration: *respect for people's feelings.* **6.** (*often pl.*) an expression of esteem or regard (esp. in **pay one's respects**). ~*vb.* (*tr.*) **7.** to have an attitude of esteem towards: *to respect one's elders.* **8.** to pay proper attention to; not violate: *to respect Swiss neutrality.* **9.** *Arch.* to concern or refer to. [C14: from L *rēspicere* to look back, pay attention to, from RE- + *specere* to look] —**re'specter** *n.*

respectable (rɪ'spɛktəbᵊl) *adj.* **1.** having or deserving the respect of other people; estimable; worthy. **2.** having good social standing or reputation. **3.** having socially or conventionally acceptable morals, etc.: *a respectable woman.* **4.** relatively or fairly good; considerable: *a respectable salary.* **5.** fit to be seen by other people; presentable. —**re,specta'bility** *n.* —**re'spectably** *adv.*

respectful (rɪ'spɛktful) *adj.* full of, showing, or giving respect. —**re'spectfully** *adv.* —**re'spectfulness** *n.*

respecting (rɪ'spɛktɪŋ) *prep.* concerning; regarding.

respective (rɪ'spɛktɪv) *adj.* belonging or relating separately to each of several people or things; several: *we took our respective ways home.* —**re'spectiveness** *n.*

respectively (rɪ'spɛktɪvlɪ) *adv.* (in listing a number of items or attributes that refer to another list) separately in the order given: *he gave Janet and John a cake and a chocolate respectively.*

Respighi (*Italian* res'piːgi) *n.* **Ottorino** (otto'riːno). 1879–1936, Italian composer, noted esp. for his suites *The Fountains of Rome* (1917) and *The Pines of Rome* (1924).

respirable ('rɛspɪrəbᵊl) *adj.* **1.** able to be breathed. **2.** suitable or fit for breathing. —**,respira'bility** *n.*

respiration (,rɛspɪ'reɪʃən) *n.* **1.** the process in living organisms of taking in oxygen from the surroundings and giving out carbon dioxide. **2.** the chemical breakdown of complex organic substances that takes place in the cells and tissues of animals and plants, during which energy is released and carbon dioxide produced. —**respiratory** ('rɛspɪrətərɪ, -trɪ) *or* ,**respi'rational** *adj.*

respirator ('rɛspɪ,reɪtə) *n.* **1.** an apparatus for providing long-term artificial respiration. **2.** a device worn over the mouth and nose to prevent inhalation of noxious fumes or to warm cold air before it is breathed.

respiratory quotient n. Biol. the ratio of the volume of carbon dioxide expired to the volume of oxygen consumed by an organism, tissue, or cell in a given time.

respire (rɪ'spaɪə) vb. **1.** to inhale and exhale (air); breathe. **2.** (intr.) to undergo the process of respiration. [C14: from L respīrāre to exhale, from RE- + spīrāre to breathe]

respite ('rɛspɪt, -paɪt) n. **1.** a pause from exertion; interval of rest. **2.** a temporary delay. **3.** a temporary stay of execution; reprieve. ~vb. **4.** (tr.) to grant a respite to; reprieve. [C13: from OF respit, from L respectus a looking back; see RESPECT]

resplendent (rɪ'splɛndənt) adj. having a brilliant or splendid appearance. [C15: from rēsplendēre, from RE- + splendēre to shine] —**re'splendence** or **re'splendency** n. —**re'splendently** adv.

respond (rɪ'spɒnd) vb. **1.** to state or utter (something) in reply. **2.** (intr.) to act in reply; react: to respond by issuing an invitation. **3.** (intr.; foll. by to) to react favourably: this patient will respond to treatment. **4.** an archaic word for **correspond.** ~n. **5.** Archit. a pilaster or an engaged column that supports an arch or a lintel. **6.** Christianity. a choral anthem chanted in response to a lesson read. [C14: from OF respondre, from L respondēre to return like for like, from RE- + spondēre to pledge] —**re'spondence** or **re'spondency** n. —**re'sponder** n.

respondent (rɪ'spɒndənt) n. **1.** Law. a person against whom a petition is brought. ~adj. **2.** a less common word for **responsive.**

response (rɪ'spɒns) n. **1.** the act of responding; reply or reaction. **2.** Bridge. a bid replying to a partner's bid or double. **3.** (usually pl.) Christianity. a short sentence or phrase recited or sung in reply to the officiant at a church service. **4.** Electronics. the ratio of the output to the input level of an electrical device. **5.** a glandular, muscular, or electrical reaction that arises from stimulation of the nervous system. [C14: from L respōnsum answer, from respondēre to RESPOND] —**re'sponseless** adj.

responser or **responsor** (rɪ'spɒnsə) n. a radio or radar receiver used to receive and display signals from a transponder.

responsibility (rɪ,spɒnsɪ'bɪlɪtɪ) n., pl. **-ties. 1.** the state or position of being responsible. **2.** a person or thing for which one is responsible.

responsible (rɪ'spɒnsɪbəl) adj. **1.** (postpositive; usually foll. by for) having control or authority (over). **2.** (postpositive; foll. by to) being accountable for one's actions and decisions (to): responsible to one's commanding officer. **3.** (of a position, duty, etc.) involving decision and accountability. **4.** (often foll. by for) being the agent or cause (of some action): responsible for a mistake. **5.** able to take rational decisions without supervision; accountable for one's own actions. **6.** able to meet financial obligations; of sound credit. [C16: from L respōnsus, from respondēre to RESPOND] —**re'sponsibleness** n. —**re'sponsibly** adv.

responsive (rɪ'spɒnsɪv) adj. **1.** reacting or replying quickly or favourably, as to a suggestion, initiative, etc. **2.** (of an organism) reacting to a stimulus. —**re'sponsively** adv. —**re'sponsiveness** n.

responsory (rɪ'spɒnsərɪ) n., pl. **-ries.** an anthem or chant recited or sung after a lesson in a church service. [C15: from LL respōnsōrium, from L respondēre to answer]

rest[1] (rɛst) n. **1. a.** relaxation from exertion or labour. **b.** (as modifier): a rest period. **2.** repose; sleep. **3.** any relief or refreshment, as from worry. **4.** calm; tranquillity. **5.** death regarded as repose: eternal rest. **6.** cessation from motion. **7. at rest. a.** not moving. **b.** calm. **c.** dead. **d.** asleep. **8.** a pause or interval. **9.** a mark in a musical score indicating a pause of specific duration. **10.** Prosody. a pause at the end of a line; caesura. **11.** a shelter or lodging: a seaman's rest. **12.** a thing or place on which to put something for support or to steady it. **13.** Billiards, snooker. any of various special poles sometimes used as supports for the cue. **14. come to rest.** to slow down and stop. **15. lay to rest.** to bury (a dead person). **16. set (someone's mind).** to reassure (someone) or settle (someone's mind). ~vb. **17.** to take or give rest, as by sleeping, lying down, etc. **18.** to place or position (oneself, etc.) for rest or relaxation. **19.** (tr.)

to place or position for support or steadying: to rest one's elbows on the table. **20.** (intr.) to be at ease; be calm. **21.** to cease or cause to cease from motion or exertion. **22.** (intr.) to remain without further attention or action: let the matter rest. **23.** to direct (one's eyes) or (of one's eyes) to be directed: her eyes rested on the child. **24.** to depend or cause to depend; base; rely: the whole argument rests on one crucial fact. **25.** (intr.; foll. by with, on, upon, etc.) to be a responsibility (of): it rests with us to apportion blame. **26.** Law. to finish the introduction of evidence in (a case). **27.** to put pastry in a cool place to allow the gluten to contract. **28. rest on one's oars.** to stop doing anything for a time. [OE ræst, reste, of Gmc origin] —**'rester** n.

rest[2] (rɛst) n. (usually preceded by the) **1.** something left or remaining; remainder. **2.** the others: the rest of the world. ~vb. **3.** (copula) to continue to be (as specified); remain: rest assured. [C15: from OF rester to remain, from L rēstāre, from RE- + stāre to stand]

rest area n. Austral. & N.Z. a motorists' stopping place, usually off a highway, equipped with tables, seats, etc.

restaurant ('rɛstə,rɒŋ, 'rɛstrɒŋ) n. a commercial establishment where meals are prepared and served to customers. [C19: from F, from restaurer to RESTORE]

restaurant car n. Brit. a railway coach in which meals are served. Also called: **dining car.**

restaurateur (,rɛstərə'tɜ:) n. a person who owns or runs a restaurant. [C18: via F from LL restaurātor, from L restaurāre to RESTORE]

rest-cure n. a rest taken as part of a course of medical treatment, so as to relieve stress, anxiety, etc. **2.** an easy time or assignment: usually used with a negative: it's no rest-cure, I assure you.

restful ('rɛstful) adj. **1.** giving or conducive to rest. **2.** being at rest; tranquil; calm. —**'restfully** adv. —**'restfulness** n.

restharrow ('rɛst,hærəʊ) n. any of a genus of Eurasian papilionaceous plants with tough woody stems and roots. [C16: from rest, var. of ARREST (to hinder, stop) + HARROW]

resting ('rɛstɪŋ) adj. **1.** not moving or working; at rest. **2.** Euphemistic. (of an actor) out of work. **3.** (esp. of plant spores) undergoing a period of dormancy before germination.

restitution (,rɛstɪ'tju:ʃən) n. **1.** the act of giving back something that has been lost or stolen. **2.** Law. compensating for loss or injury by reverting as far as possible to the original position. **3.** the return of an object or system to its original state, esp. after elastic deformation. [C13: from L restitūtiō, from restituere to rebuild, from RE- + statuere to set up] —**'resti,tutive** or **,resti'tutory** adj.

restive ('rɛstɪv) adj. **1.** restless, nervous, or uneasy. **2.** impatient of control or authority. [C16: from OF restif balky, from rester to remain] —**'restively** adv. —**'restiveness** n.

restless ('rɛstlɪs) adj. **1.** unable to stay still or quiet. **2.** ceaselessly active or moving: the restless wind. **3.** worried; anxious; uneasy. **4.** not restful; without repose: a restless night. —**'restlessly** adv. —**'restlessness** n.

rest mass n. the mass of an object that is at rest relative to an observer. It is the mass used in Newtonian mechanics.

restoration (,rɛstə'reɪʃən) n. **1.** the act of restoring to a former or original condition, place, etc. **2.** the giving back of something lost, stolen, etc. **3.** something restored, replaced, or reconstructed. **4.** a model or representation of an extinct animal, etc. **5.** (usually cap.) Brit. history. the re-establishment of the monarchy in 1660 or the reign of Charles II (1660–85).

restorative (rɪ'stɒrətɪv) adj. **1.** tending to revive or renew health, spirits, etc. ~n. **2.** anything that restores or revives, esp. a drug.

restore (rɪ'stɔ:) vb. (tr.) **1.** to return (something) to its original or former condition. **2.** to bring back to health, good spirits, etc. **3.** to return (something lost, stolen, etc.) to its owner. **4.** to reintroduce or re-enforce: to restore discipline. **5.** to reconstruct (an extinct animal, etc.). [C13: from OF, from L rēstaurāre to rebuild, from RE- + -staurāre, as in instaurāre to renew] —**re'storable** adj. —**re'storer** n.

restrain (rɪ'streɪn) vb. (tr.) **1.** to hold (someone) back from some action, esp. by force. **2.** to deprive (someone) of liberty, as by imprisonment. **3.** to limit or restrict. [C14 restreyne, from OF restreindre, from L rēstringere, from RE- + stringere to draw, bind] —re'strainable adj. —restrainedly (rɪ'streɪnɪdlɪ) adv. —re'strainer n.

restraint (rɪ'streɪnt) n. **1.** the ability to control or moderate one's impulses, passions, etc. **2.** the act of restraining or the state of being restrained. **3.** something that restrains; restriction. [C15: from OF restreinte, from restreindre to RESTRAIN]

restraint of trade n. action interfering with the freedom to compete in business.

restrict (rɪ'strɪkt) vb. (often foll. by to) to confine or keep within certain, often specified, limits or selected bounds. [C16: from L rēstrictus bound up, from rēstringere; see RESTRAIN]

restricted (rɪ'strɪktɪd) adj. **1.** limited or confined. **2.** not accessible to the general public or (esp. U.S.) out of bounds to military personnel. **3.** Brit. denoting a zone in which a speed limit or waiting restrictions for vehicles apply. —re'strictedly adv. —re'strictedness n.

restriction (rɪ'strɪkʃən) n. **1.** something that restricts; a restrictive measure, law, etc. **2.** the act of restricting or the state of being restricted. —re'strictionist n., adj.

restrictive (rɪ'strɪktɪv) adj. **1.** restricting or tending to restrict. **2.** Grammar. denoting a relative clause or phrase that restricts the number of possible referents of its antecedent. The relative clause in Americans who live in New York is restrictive; the relative clause in Americans, who are generally extrovert, is nonrestrictive. —re'strictively adv. —re'strictiveness n.

restrictive practice n. Brit. **1.** a trading agreement against the public interest. **2.** a practice of a union or other group tending to limit the freedom of other workers or employers.

rest room n. U.S. & Canad. a room in a public building with toilets, washbasins, and, sometimes, couches.

result (rɪ'zʌlt) n. **1.** something that ensues from an action, policy, etc.; outcome; consequence. **2.** a number, quantity, or value obtained by solving a mathematical problem. **3.** U.S. a decision of a legislative body. **4.** (often pl.) the final score or outcome of a sporting contest. **5.** Sport. a win. ~vb. (intr.) **6.** (often foll. by from) to be the outcome or consequence (of). **7.** (foll. by in) to issue or terminate (in a specified way, etc.); end: to result in tragedy. [C15: from L resultāre to rebound, spring from, from RE- + saltāre to leap]

resultant (rɪ'zʌltənt) adj. **1.** that results; resulting. ~n. **2.** Maths, physics. a single vector that is the vector sum of two or more other vectors.

resume (rɪ'zju:m) vb. **1.** to begin again or go on with (something interrupted). **2.** (tr.) to occupy again, take back, or recover: to resume one's seat; resume the presidency. **3.** Arch. to summarize; make a résumé of. [C15: from L resūmere, from RE- + sūmere to take up] —re'sumable adj. —re'sumer n.

résumé ('rɛzjʊˌmeɪ) n. **1.** a short descriptive summary, as of events, etc. **2.** U.S. another name for **curriculum vitae.** [C19: from F, from résumer to RESUME]

resumption (rɪ'zʌmpʃən) n. the act of resuming or beginning again. [C15: via OF from LL resumptiō, from L resūmere to RESUME] —re'sumptive adj. —re'sumptively adv.

resupinate (rɪ'sju:pɪnɪt) adj. Bot. (of plant parts) reversed or inverted in position, so as to appear to be upside down. [C18: from L resupīnātus bent back, from resupīnāre, from RE- + supīnāre to place on the back] —re,supi'nation n.

resurge (rɪ'sɜ:dʒ) vb. (intr.) Rare. to rise again as if from the dead. [C16: from L resurgere to rise again, reappear, from RE- + surgere to lift, arise]

resurgent (rɪ'sɜ:dʒənt) adj. rising again, as to new life, vigour, etc.: resurgent nationalism. —re'surgence n.

resurrect (,rɛzə'rɛkt) vb. **1.** to rise or raise from the dead; bring or be brought back to life. **2.** (tr.) to bring back into use or activity; revive. **3.** (tr.) Facetious. (formerly) to exhume and steal (a body) from its grave.

resurrection (,rɛzə'rɛkʃən) n. **1.** a supposed act or instance of a dead person coming back to life. **2.** belief in

the possibility of this as part of a religious or mystical system. **3.** the condition of those who have risen from the dead: we shall all live in the resurrection. **4.** (usually cap.) Christian theol. the rising again of Christ from the tomb three days after his death. **5.** (usually cap.) the rising again from the dead of all men at the Last Judgment. [C13: via OF from LL resurrectiō, from L resurgere to rise again] —,resur'rectional or ,resur'rectionary adj.

resurrectionism (,rɛzə'rɛkʃəˌnɪzəm) n. belief that men will rise again from the dead, esp. according to Christian doctrine.

resurrectionist (,rɛzə'rɛkʃənɪst) n. **1.** Facetious. (formerly) a body snatcher. **2.** a person who believes in the Resurrection.

resurrection plant n. any of several unrelated desert plants that form a tight ball when dry and unfold and bloom when moistened.

resuscitate (rɪ'sʌsɪˌteɪt) vb. (tr.) to restore to consciousness; revive. [C16: from L resuscitāre, from RE- + suscitāre to raise, from sub- up from below + citāre to rouse, from citus quick] —re,susci'tation n. —re'suscitative adj. —re'susci,tator n.

ret (rɛt) vb. **retting, retted.** (tr.) to moisten or soak (flax, hemp, etc.) in order to separate the fibres from the woody tissue by beating. [C15: of Gmc origin]

ret. abbrev. for: **1.** retain. **2.** retired. **3.** return(ed).

retable (rɪ'teɪbʰl) n. an ornamental screenlike structure above and behind an altar. [C19: from F, from Sp. retablo, from L retrō behind + tabula board]

retail ('ri:teɪl) n. **1.** the sale of goods individually or in small quantities to consumers. Cf. **wholesale.** ~adj. **2.** of, relating to, or engaged in such selling: retail prices. ~adv. **3.** in small amounts or at a retail price. ~vb. **4.** to sell or be sold in small quantities to consumers. **5.** (rɪ'teɪl). (tr.) to relate (gossip, scandal, etc.) in detail. [C14: from OF retaillier, from RE- + taillier to cut; see TAILOR] —'retailer n.

retail price index n. a measure of the changes in the average level of retail prices of selected goods, usually on a monthly basis. Abbrev.: **RPI.**

retain (rɪ'teɪn) vb. (tr.) **1.** to keep in one's possession. **2.** to be able to hold or contain: soil that retains water. **3.** (of a person) to be able to remember (information, etc.) without difficulty. **4.** to hold in position. **5.** to keep for one's future use, as by paying a retainer or nominal charge. **6.** Law. to engage the services of (a barrister) by payment of a preliminary fee. [C14: from OF retenir, from L retinēre to hold back, from RE- + tenēre to hold] —re'tainable adj. —re'tainment n.

retained object n. Grammar. a direct or indirect object of a passive verb. The phrase the drawings in she was given the drawings is a retained object.

retainer (rɪ'teɪnə) n. **1.** History. a supporter or dependant of a person of rank. **2.** a servant, esp. one who has been with a family for a long time. **3.** a clip, frame, or similar device that prevents a part of a machine, etc., from moving. **4.** a fee paid in advance to secure first option on the services of a barrister, jockey, etc. **5.** a reduced rent paid for a flat, etc., to reserve it for future use.

retaining wall n. a wall constructed to hold back earth, loose rock, etc. Also called: **revetment.**

retake vb. (ri:'teɪk), **-taking, -took, -taken.** (tr.) **1.** to take back or capture again: to retake a fortress. **2.** Films. to shoot (a scene) again. **3.** to tape (a recording) again. ~n. ('ri:,teɪk). **4.** Films. a rephotographed scene. **5.** a retaped recording. —re'taker n.

retaliate (rɪ'tælɪ,eɪt) vb. (intr.) **1.** to take retributory action, esp. by returning some injury or wrong in kind. **2.** to cast (accusations) back upon a person. [C17: from LL retāliāre, from L RE- + tālis of such kind] —re,tali'ation n. —re'taliative or re'taliatory adj.

retard (rɪ'ta:d) vb. (tr.) to delay or slow down (the progress or speed) of (something). [C15: from OF retarder, from L retardāre, from RE- + tardāre to make slow, from tardus sluggish]

retardant (rɪ'ta:dᵊnt) n. **1.** a substance that reduces the rate of a chemical reaction. ~adj. **2.** having a slowing effect.

retardation (,ri:ta:'deɪʃən) or **retardment** (rɪ'ta:dmənt) n. **1.** the act of retarding or the state of being retarded.

---

re'string vb.
re'structure vb.

re'style vb.

re'surface vb.

,resur'vey vb., n.

2. something that retards. —**re'tardative** *or* **re'tardatory** *adj.*

retarded (rɪ'tɑːdɪd) *adj.* underdeveloped, usually mentally and esp. having an IQ of 70 to 85.

retarder (rɪ'tɑːdə) *n.* **1.** a person or thing that retards. **2.** a substance added to slow down the rate of a chemical change, such as one added to cement to delay its setting.

retch (rɛtʃ, riːtʃ) *vb.* **1.** (*intr.*) to undergo an involuntary spasm of ineffectual vomiting. ~*n.* **2.** an involuntary spasm of ineffectual vomiting. [OE *hrǣcan*; rel. to ON *hrēkja* to spit]

retd *abbrev. for:* **1.** retired. **2.** retained. **3.** returned.

rete ('riːtɪ) *n.*, *pl.* **retia** ('riːʃɪə, -tɪə). *Anat.* any network of nerves or blood vessels; plexus. [C14 (referring to a metal network used with an astrolabe): from L *rēte* net] —**retial** ('riːʃɪəl) *adj.*

retention (rɪ'tɛnʃən) *n.* **1.** the act of retaining or state of being retained. **2.** the capacity to hold or retain liquid, etc. **3.** the capacity to remember. **4.** *Pathol.* the abnormal holding within the body of urine, faeces, etc. [C14: from L *retentiō*, from *retinēre* to RETAIN]

retentive (rɪ'tɛntɪv) *adj.* having the capacity to retain or remember. —**re'tentively** *adv.* —**re'tentiveness** *n.*

Réti ('reɪtɪ) *n.* **Richard.** 1889–1929, Hungarian chess player and theorist; influential in enunciating the theories of the hypermodern school.

retiarius (,riːtɪ'ɛərɪəs, ,riːʃɪ-) *n.*, *pl.* **-arii** (-'ɛərɪ,aɪ). (in ancient Rome) a gladiator armed with a net and trident. [L, from *rēte* net]

reticent ('rɛtɪsənt) *adj.* not communicative; not saying all that one knows; taciturn; reserved. [C19: from L *reticēre* to keep silent, from RE- + *tacēre* to be silent] —**'reticence** *n.* —**'reticently** *adv.*

reticle ('rɛtɪkᵊl) *or (less commonly)* **reticule** *n.* a network of fine lines, wires, etc., placed in the focal plane of an optical instrument. [C17: from L *rēticulum* a little net, from *rēte* net]

reticulate *adj.* (rɪ'tɪkjʊlɪt), *also* **reticular.** **1.** in the form of a network or having a network of parts: *a reticulate leaf.* ~*vb.* (rɪ'tɪkjʊ,leɪt). **2.** to form or be formed into a net. [C17: from LL *rēticulātus* made like a net] —**re'ticulately** *adv.* —**re,ticu'lation** *n.*

reticule ('rɛtɪ,kjuːl) *n.* **1.** (formerly) a woman's small bag or purse, usually with a drawstring and made of net, beading, brocade, etc. **2.** a less common variant of **reticle.** [C18: from F *réticule*, from L *rēticulum* RETICLE]

reticulum (rɪ'tɪkjʊləm) *n.*, *pl.* **-la** (-lə). **1.** any fine network, esp. one in the body composed of cells, fibres, etc. **2.** the second compartment of the stomach of ruminants. [C17: from L: little net, from *rēte* net]

retiform ('riːtɪ,fɔːm, 'rɛt-) *adj. Rare.* netlike; reticulate. [C17: from L *rēte* net + *forma* shape]

retina ('rɛtɪnə) *n.*, *pl.* **-nas** *or* **-nae** (-,niː). the light-sensitive membrane forming the inner lining of the posterior wall of the eyeball. [C14: from Med. L, ?from L *rēte* net] —**'retinal** *adj.*

retinene ('rɛtɪ,niːn) *n.* a yellow pigment, the aldehyde of vitamin A, that is involved in the formation of rhodopsin. [C20: from RETINA + -ENE]

retinitis (,rɛtɪ'naɪtɪs) *n.* inflammation of the retina. [C20: from NL, from RETINA + -ITIS]

retinoscopy (,rɛtɪ'nɒskəpɪ) *n. Ophthalmol.* a procedure for detecting errors of refraction in the eye by means of an instrument (**retinoscope**) that reflects a beam of light from a mirror into the eye. —**retinoscopic** (,rɛtɪnə'skɒpɪk) *adj.* —**,retino'scopically** *adv.* —**,reti'noscopist** *n.*

retinue ('rɛtɪ,njuː) *n.* a body of aides and retainers attending an important person. [C14: from OF *retenue*, from *retenir* to RETAIN]

retiral (rɪ'taɪərᵊl) *n.* *esp. Scot.* the act of retiring; retirement.

retire (rɪ'taɪə) *vb.* (*mainly intr.*) **1.** (*also tr.*) to give up or to cause (a person) to give up his work, esp. on reaching pensionable age. **2.** to go away, as into seclusion, for recuperation, etc. **3.** to go to bed. **4.** to recede or disappear: *the sun retired behind the clouds.* **5.** to withdraw from a sporting contest, esp. because of injury. **6.** (*also tr.*) to pull back (troops, etc.) from battle or (of troops, etc.) to fall back. **7.** (*tr.*) to remove (money, bonds,

shares, etc.) from circulation. [C16: from F *retirer*, from OF RE- + *tirer* to pull, draw] —**re'tired** *adj.* —**re'tirement** *n.* —**re'tirer** *n.*

retirement pension *n.* *Brit.* a weekly payment made by the government to a retired man over 65 or a woman over 60.

retiring (rɪ'taɪərɪŋ) *adj.* shunning contact with others; shy; reserved. —**re'tiringly** *adv.*

retool (riː'tuːl) *vb.* **1.** to replace, re-equip, or rearrange the tools in (a factory, etc.). **2.** (*tr.*) *Chiefly U.S. & Canad.* to revise or reorganize.

retort[1] (rɪ'tɔːt) *vb.* **1.** (when *tr.*, *takes a clause as object*) to utter (something) quickly, wittily, or angrily, in response. **2.** to use (an argument) against its originator. ~*n.* **3.** a sharp, angry, or witty reply. **4.** an argument used against its originator. [C16: from L *retorquēre*, from RE- + *torquēre* to twist, wrench] —**re'torter** *n.*

retort[2] (rɪ'tɔːt) *n.* **1.** a glass vessel with a long tapering neck that is bent down, used for distillation. **2.** a vessel used for heating ores in the production of metals or heating coal to produce gas. ~*vb.* **3.** (*tr.*) to heat in a retort. [C17: from F *retorte*, from Med. L *retorta*, from L *retorquēre* to twist back; see RETORT[1]]

retouch (riː'tʌtʃ) *vb.* **1.** to restore, correct, or improve (a painting, make-up, etc.) with new touches. **2.** *Photog.* to alter (a negative or print) by painting over blemishes or adding details. ~*n.* **3.** the art or practice of retouching. **4.** a detail that is the result of retouching. **5.** a photograph, painting, etc., that has been retouched. —**re'toucher** *n.*

retrace (rɪ'treɪs) *vb.* (*tr.*) **1.** to go back over (one's steps, a route, etc.) again. **2.** to go over (a past event) in the mind; recall. **3.** to go over (a story, account, etc.) from the beginning.

re-trace (riː'treɪs) *vb.* (*tr.*) to trace (a map, etc.) again.

retract (rɪ'trækt) *vb.* **1.** (*tr.*) to draw in (a part or appendage): *a snail can retract its horns; to retract the landing gear of an aircraft.* **2.** to withdraw (a statement, opinion, charge, etc.) as invalid or unjustified. **3.** to go back on (a promise or agreement). [C16: from L *retractāre* to withdraw, from *tractāre*, from *trahere* to drag] —**re'tractable** *or* **re'tractible** *adj.* —**re'traction** *n.* —**re'tractive** *adj.*

retractile (rɪ'træktaɪl) *adj.* capable of being drawn in: *the retractile claws of a cat.* —**retractility** (,riːtræk'tɪlɪtɪ) *n.*

retractor (rɪ'træktə) *n.* **1.** *Anat.* any of various muscles that retract an organ or part. **2.** *Surgery.* an instrument for holding back an organ or part. **3.** a person or thing that retracts.

retral ('riːtrəl, 'rɛtrəl) *adj. Rare.* at, near, or towards the back. [C19: from L *retrō* backwards] —**'retrally** *adv.*

retread *vb.* (riː'trɛd), **-treading, -treaded. 1.** (*tr.*) another word for **remould** (sense 2). ~*n.* ('riː,trɛd). **2.** another word for **remould** (sense 3). **3.** *N.Z. sl.* a pensioner who has resumed employment, esp. in the same profession as formerly.

re-tread (riː'trɛd) *vb.* **-treading, -trod, -trodden** *or* **-trod.** (*tr.*) to tread (one's steps, etc.) again.

retreat (rɪ'triːt) *vb.* (*mainly intr.*) **1.** *Mil.* to withdraw or retire in the face of or from action with an enemy. **2.** to retire or withdraw, as to seclusion or shelter. **3.** (of a person's features) to slope back; recede. **4.** (*tr.*) *Chess.* to move (a piece) back. ~*n.* **5.** the act of retreating or withdrawing. **6.** *Mil.* **a.** a withdrawal or retirement in the face of the enemy. **b.** a bugle call signifying withdrawal or retirement. **7.** retirement or seclusion. **8.** a place to which one may retire for religious contemplation. **9.** a period of seclusion, esp. for religious contemplation. **10.** an institution for the care and treatment of the mentally ill, infirm, elderly, etc. [C14: from OF *retret*, from *retraire* to withdraw, from L *retrahere* to pull back]

retrench (rɪ'trɛntʃ) *vb.* **1.** to reduce (costs); economize. **2.** (*tr.*) to shorten, delete, or abridge. [C17: from OF *retrenchier*, from RE- + *trenchier* to cut, from L *truncāre* to lop] —**re'trenchment** *n.*

retribution (,rɛtrɪ'bjuːʃən) *n.* **1.** the act of punishing or taking vengeance for wrongdoing, sin, or injury. **2.** punishment or vengeance. [C14: via OF from Church L *retribūtiō*, from L *retribuere*, from RE- + *tribuere* to pay] —**retributive** (rɪ'trɪbjʊtɪv) *adj.* —**re'tributively** *adv.*

---

re'testi,fy *vb.*   **'re,think** *n.*   **re'title** *vb.*   **,retrans'mission** *n.*
re'think *vb.*   **re'tie** *vb.*   **re'train** *vb.*   **re'trial** *n.*

retrieval (rɪ'triːvªl) n. **1.** the act or process of retrieving. **2.** the possibility of recovery, restoration, or rectification. **3.** a computer operation that recalls data from a file.

retrieve (rɪ'triːv) vb. (mainly tr.) **1.** to get or fetch back again; recover. **2.** to bring back to a more satisfactory state; revive. **3.** to rescue or save. **4.** to recover or make newly available (stored information) from a computer system. **5.** (also intr.) (of dogs) to find and fetch (shot game, etc.). **6.** Tennis, etc. to return successfully (a shot difficult to reach). **7.** to recall; remember. ~n. **8.** the act of retrieving. **9.** the chance of being retrieved. [C15: from OF retrover, from RE- + trouver to find, ?from Vulgar L tropāre (unattested) to compose] —**re'trievable** adj.

retriever (rɪ'triːvə) n. **1.** one of a breed of large dogs that can be trained to retrieve game. **2.** any dog used to retrieve shot game. **3.** a person or thing that retrieves.

retro ('rɛtrəʊ) n., pl. **-ros. 1.** short for **retrorocket.** ~adj. **2.** denoting something associated with or revived from the past: retro fashion.

retro- prefix. **1.** back or backwards: retroactive. **2.** located behind: retrochoir. [from L retrō behind, backwards]

retroact ('rɛtrəʊ,ækt) vb. (intr.) **1.** to act in opposition. **2.** to influence or have reference to past events. —**,retro'action** n.

retroactive (,rɛtrəʊ'æktɪv) adj. **1.** applying or referring to the past: retroactive legislation. **2.** effective from a date or for a period in the past. —**,retro'actively** adv. —**,retroac'tivity** n.

retrocede (,rɛtrəʊ'siːd) vb. **1.** (tr.) to give back; return. **2.** (intr.) to go back; recede. —**retrocession** (,rɛtrəʊ'sɛʃən) or **,retro'cedence** n. —**,retro'cessive** or **,retro'cedent** adj.

retrochoir ('rɛtrəʊ,kwaɪə) n. the space in a large church or cathedral behind the high altar.

retrofire ('rɛtrəʊ,faɪə) n. **1.** the act of firing a retrorocket. **2.** the moment at which it is fired.

retrofit ('rɛtrəʊ,fɪt) vb. **-fitting, -fitted.** (tr.) to equip (a car, aircraft, etc.) with new parts, safety devices, etc., after manufacture.

retroflex ('rɛtrəʊ,flɛks) or **retroflexed** adj. **1.** bent or curved backwards. **2.** Phonetics. of or involving retroflexion. [C18: from L retrōflexus, from retrōflectere, from RETRO- + flectere to bend]

retroflexion or **retroflection** (,rɛtrəʊ'flɛkʃən) n. **1.** the act or condition of bending or being bent backwards. **2.** the act of turning the tip of the tongue upwards and backwards in the articulation of a vowel or a consonant.

retrograde ('rɛtrəʊ,greɪd) adj. **1.** moving or bending backwards. **2.** (esp. of order) reverse or inverse. **3.** tending towards an earlier worse condition; declining or deteriorating. **4.** Astron. **a.** occurring or orbiting in a direction opposite to that of the earth's motion around the sun. Cf. **direct** (sense 18). **b.** occurring or orbiting in a direction around a planet opposite to the planet's rotational direction. **c.** appearing to move in a clockwise direction due to the rotational period exceeding the period of revolution around the sun: Venus has retrograde rotation. ~vb. (intr.) **5.** to move in a retrograde direction; retrogress. [C14: from L retrōgradī, from gradi to walk, go] —**,retrogra'dation** n. —**'retro,gradely** adv.

retrogress (,rɛtrəʊ'grɛs) vb. (intr.) **1.** to go back to an earlier, esp. worse, condition; degenerate or deteriorate. **2.** to move backwards; recede. [C19: from L retrōgressus having moved backwards; see RETROGRADE] —**,retro'gression** n. —**,retro'gressive** adj. —**,retro'gressively** adv.

retrorocket ('rɛtrəʊ,rɒkɪt) n. a small auxiliary rocket engine on a larger rocket, missile, or spacecraft, that produces thrust in the opposite direction to the direction of flight in order to decelerate. Often shortened to **retro.**

retrorse (rɪ'trɔːs) adj. (esp. of plant parts) pointing backwards. [C19: from L retrōrsus, from retrōversus turned back, from RETRO- + vertere to turn] —**re'trorsely** adv.

retrospect ('rɛtrəʊ,spɛkt) n. the act of surveying things past (often in **in retrospect**). [C17: from L retrōspicere to look back, from RETRO- + specere to look] —**,retro'spection** n.

retrospective (,rɛtrəʊ'spɛktɪv) adj. **1.** looking or directed backwards, esp. in time; characterized by retrospection. **2.** applying to the past; retroactive. ~n. **3.** an exhibition of an artist's life's work. —**,retro'spectively** adv.

retroussé (rə'truːseɪ) adj. (of a nose) turned up. [C19: from F retrousser to tuck up]

retroversion (,rɛtrəʊ'vɜːʃən) n. **1.** the act of turning or condition of being turned backwards. **2.** the condition of a part or organ, esp. the uterus, that is turned backwards. —**'retro,verted** adj.

Retrovir ('rɛtrəʊ,vɪə) n. Trademark. the brand name for AZT.

retrovirus ('rɛtrəʊ,vaɪrəs) n. any of several viruses that are able to reverse the normal flow of genetic information from DNA to RNA by transcribing RNA into DNA: many retroviruses are known to cause cancer in animals.

retsina (rɛt'siːnə) n. a Greek wine flavoured with resin. [Mod. Gk, from It. resina RESIN]

return (rɪ'tɜːn) vb. **1.** (intr.) to come back to a former place or state. **2.** (tr.) to give, take, or carry back; replace or restore. **3.** (tr.) to repay or recompense, esp. with something of equivalent value: return the compliment. **4.** (tr.) to earn or yield (profit or interest) as an income from an investment or venture. **5.** (intr.) to come back or revert in thought or speech: I'll return to that later. **6.** (intr.) to recur or reappear: the symptoms have returned. **7.** to answer or reply. **8.** (tr.) to vote into office; elect. **9.** (tr.) (of a jury) to deliver or render (a verdict). **10.** (tr.) to submit (a report, etc.) about (someone or something) to someone in authority. **11.** (tr.) Cards. to lead back (the suit led by one's partner). **12.** (tr.) Ball games. to hit, throw, or play (a ball) back. **13. return thanks.** (of Christians) to say grace before a meal. ~n. **14.** the act or an instance of coming back. **15.** something that is given or sent back, esp. unsatisfactory merchandise or a theatre ticket for resale. **16.** the act or an instance of putting, sending, or carrying back; replacement or restoration. **17.** (often pl.) the yield or profit from an investment or venture. **18.** the act or an instance of reciprocation or repayment (esp. in **in return for**). **19.** a recurrence or reappearance. **20.** an official report, esp. of the financial condition of a company. **21. a.** a form (a **tax return**) on which a statement of one's taxable income is made. **b.** the statement itself. **22.** (often pl.) a statement of the votes counted at an election. **23.** an answer or reply. **24.** Brit. short for **return ticket. 25.** Archit. a part of a building that forms an angle with the façade. **26.** Law. a report by a bailiff or other officer on the outcome of a formal document such as a writ, summons, etc. **27.** Cards. a lead of a card in the suit that one's partner has previously led. **28.** Ball games. the act of playing or throwing a ball, etc., back. **29. by return (of post).** Brit. by the next post back to the sender. **30. many happy returns (of the day).** a conventional birthday greeting. ~adj. **31.** of, relating to, or characterized by a return: a return visit. **32.** denoting a second, reciprocal occasion: a return match. [C14: from OF retorner; see RE-, TURN] —**re'turnable** adj. —**re'turner** n.

returned soldier n. Austral. & N.Z. a soldier who has served abroad. Also (Austral. and Canad.): **returned man.**

returning officer n. (in Britain, Canada, Australia, etc.) an official in charge of conducting an election in a constituency.

return ticket n. Brit. a ticket entitling a passenger to travel to his destination and back.

retuse (rɪ'tjuːs) adj. Bot. having a rounded apex and a central depression. [C18: from L retundere to make blunt, from RE- + tundere to pound]

Reuben ('ruːbɪn) n. Old Testament. **1.** the eldest son of Jacob and Leah: one of the 12 patriarchs of Israel (Genesis 29:30). **2.** the Israelite tribe descended from him. **3.** the territory of this tribe, lying to the northeast of the Dead Sea. Douay spelling: **Ruben.**

Reuchlin (German 'rɔʏçliːn) n. **Johann** (jo'han). 1455– 1522, German humanist, who promoted the study of Greek and Hebrew.

reunify (riː'juːnɪ,faɪ) vb. **-fying, -fied.** (tr.) to bring together again (something, esp. a country previously divided). —**,reunifi'cation** n.

reunion (riː'juːnjən) n. **1.** the act of coming together again. **2.** the state or condition of having been brought

---

re'try vb.   **re'turf** vb.   **re'type** vb.

together again. **3.** a gathering of relatives, friends, or former associates.

Réunion (riːˈjuːnjən; *French* reynjɔ̃) *n.* an island in the Indian Ocean, in the Mascarene Islands: an overseas region of France, having been in French possession since 1642. Capital: Saint-Denis. Pop.: 584 600 (1987 est.). Area: 2510 sq. km (970 sq. miles).

reunite (ˌriːjuːˈnaɪt) *vb.* to bring or come together again. —ˌreuˈnitable *adj.*

Reus (*Spanish* rɛus) *n.* a city in NE Spain, northwest of Tarragona: became commercially important after the establishment of an English colony (about 1750). Pop.: 80 710 (1981).

Reuter (ˈrɔɪtə) *n.* Baron **Paul Julius von** (paul ˈjuːliʊs fɔn). original name *Israel Beer Josaphat*. 1816–99, German telegrapher, who founded a news agency in London (1851).

Reutlingen (*German* ˈrɔytlɪŋən) *n.* a city in SW West Germany, in Baden-Württemberg: founded in the 11th century; an Imperial free city from 1240 until 1802; textile industry. Pop.: 96 046 (1983 est.).

rev (rɛv) *Inf.* ~*n.* **1.** revolution per minute. ~*vb.* **revving, revved. 2.** (often foll. by *up*) to increase the speed of revolution of (an engine).

rev. *abbrev. for:* **1.** revenue. **2.** reverse(d). **3.** review. **4.** revise(d). **5.** revision. **6.** revolution. **7.** revolving.

Rev. *abbrev. for:* **1.** *Bible.* Revelation (of Saint John the Divine). **2.** Reverend.

Reval (ˈreːval) *n.* the German name for **Tallinn.**

revalue (riːˈvæljuː) *or U.S.* **revaluate** *vb.* **1.** to adjust the exchange value of (a currency), esp. upwards. Cf. **devalue. 2.** (*tr.*) to make a fresh valuation of. —reˌvaluˈation *n.*

revamp (riːˈvæmp) *vb.* (*tr.*) **1.** to patch up or renovate; repair or restore. ~*n.* **2.** something that has been renovated or revamped. **3.** the act or process of revamping. [C19: from RE- + VAMP²]

revanchism (rɪˈvæntʃɪzəm) *n.* **1.** a foreign policy aimed at revenge or the regaining of lost territories. **2.** support for such a policy. [C20: from F *revanche* REVENGE] —reˈvanchist *n., adj.*

rev counter *n. Brit.* an informal name for **tachometer.**

Revd *abbrev. for* Reverend.

reveal (rɪˈviːl) *vb.* (*tr.*) **1.** (*may take a clause as object or an infinitive*) to disclose (a secret); divulge. **2.** to expose to view or show (something concealed). **3.** (of God) to disclose (divine truths). ~*n.* **4.** *Archit.* the vertical side of an opening in a wall, esp. the side of a window or door between the frame and the front of the wall. [C14: from OF *reveler*, from L *revēlāre* to unveil, from RE- + *vēlum* a VEIL] —reˈvealable *adj.* —reˈvealer *n.* —reˈvealment *n.*

revealed religion *n.* religion that is based on the revelation by God to man of ideas that he would not have arrived at by reason alone.

revealing (rɪˈviːlɪŋ) *adj.* **1.** of significance or import: *a very revealing experience.* **2.** showing more of the body than is usual: *a revealing costume.* —reˈvealingly *adv.*

reveille (rɪˈvælɪ) *n.* **1.** a signal, given by a bugle, drum, etc., to awaken soldiers or sailors in the morning. **2.** the hour at which this takes place. [C17: from F *réveillez!* awake! from RE- + OF *esveillier* to be wakeful, ult. from L *vigilāre* to keep watch]

revel (ˈrɛvəl) *vb.* **-elling, -elled** *or U.S.* **-eling, -eled.** (*intr.*) **1.** (foll. by *in*) to take pleasure or wallow: *to revel in success.* **2.** to take part in noisy festivities; make merry. ~*n.* **3.** (*often pl.*) an occasion of noisy merrymaking. [C14: from OF *reveler* to be merry, noisy, from L *rebellāre* to revolt] —ˈreveller *n.*

revelation (ˌrɛvəˈleɪʃən) *n.* **1.** the act or process of disclosing something previously secret or obscure, esp. something true. **2.** a fact disclosed or revealed, esp. in a dramatic or surprising way. **3.** *Christianity.* God's disclosure of his own nature and his purpose for mankind. [C14: from Church L *revēlātiō*, from L *revēlāre* to REVEAL] —ˌreveˈlational *adj.*

Revelation (ˌrɛvəˈleɪʃən) *n.* (*popularly, often pl.*) the last book of the New Testament, containing visionary descriptions of heaven, and of the end of the world. Also called:

the **Apocalypse,** the **Revelation of Saint John the Divine.**

revelationist (ˌrɛvəˈleɪʃənɪst) *n.* a person who believes that God has revealed certain truths to man.

revelry (ˈrɛvlrɪ) *n., pl.* **-ries.** noisy or unrestrained merrymaking.

revenant (ˈrɛvɪnənt) *n.* something, esp. a ghost, that returns. [C19: from F: ghost, from *revenir,* from L *revenīre,* from RE- + *venīre* to come]

revenge (rɪˈvɛndʒ) *n.* **1.** the act of retaliating for wrongs or injury received; vengeance. **2.** something done as a means of vengeance. **3.** the desire to take vengeance. **4.** a return match, regarded as a loser's opportunity to even the score. ~*vb.* (*tr.*) **5.** to inflict equivalent injury or damage for (injury received). **6.** to take vengeance for (oneself or another); avenge. [C14: from OF *revenger,* from LL *revindicāre,* from RE- + *vindicāre* to VINDICATE] —reˈvenger *n.* —reˈvenging *adj.* —reˈvengingly *adv.*

revengeful (rɪˈvɛndʒfʊl) *adj.* full of or characterized by desire for vengeance; vindictive. —reˈvengefully *adv.* —reˈvengefulness *n.*

revenue (ˈrɛvɪˌnjuː) *n.* **1.** the income accruing from taxation to a government. **2. a.** a government department responsible for the collection of government revenue. **b.** (*as modifier*): *revenue men.* **3.** the gross income from a business enterprise, investment, etc. **4.** a particular item of income. **5.** a source of income. [C16: from OF, from *revenir* to return, from L *revenīre;* see REVENANT]

revenue cutter *n.* a small lightly armed boat used to enforce customs regulations and catch smugglers.

reverb (rɪˈvɜːb) *n.* an electronic device that creates artificial acoustics.

reverberate (rɪˈvɜːbəˌreɪt) *vb.* **1.** (*intr.*) to resound or reecho. **2.** to reflect or be reflected many times. **3.** (*intr.*) to rebound or recoil. **4.** (*intr.*) (of the flame or heat in a reverberatory furnace) to be deflected onto the metal or ore on the hearth. **5.** (*tr.*) to heat, melt, or refine (a metal or ore) in a reverberatory furnace. [C16: from L *reverberāre,* from RE- + *verberāre* to beat, from *verber* a lash] —reˈverberantly *adv.* —reˌverberˈation *n.* —reˈverberative *adj.* —reˈverbeˌrator *n.* —reˈverberatory *adj.*

reverberation time *n.* a measure of the acoustic properties of a room, equal to the time taken for a sound to fall in intensity by 60 decibels. It is usually measured in seconds.

reverberatory furnace *n.* a metallurgical furnace having a curved roof that deflects heat onto the charge so that the fuel is not in direct contact with the ore.

revere (rɪˈvɪə) *vb.* (*tr.*) to be in awe of and respect deeply; venerate. [C17: from L *reverērī,* from RE- + *verērī* to fear, be in awe of]

Revere (rɪˈvɪə) *n.* **Paul.** 1735–1818, American patriot and silversmith, best known for his night ride on April 18, 1775, to warn the Massachusetts colonists of the coming of the British troops.

reverence (ˈrɛvərəns) *n.* **1.** a feeling or attitude of profound respect, usually reserved for the sacred or divine. **2.** an outward manifestation of this feeling, esp. a bow or act of obeisance. **3.** the state of being revered or commanding profound respect. ~*vb.* **4.** (*tr.*) to revere or venerate.

Reverence (ˈrɛvərəns) *n.* (preceded by *Your* or *His*) a title sometimes used to address or refer to a Roman Catholic priest.

reverend (ˈrɛvərənd) *adj.* **1.** worthy of reverence. **2.** relating to or designating a clergyman. ~*n.* **3.** *Inf.* a clergyman. [C15: from L *reverendus* fit to be revered]

Reverend (ˈrɛvərənd) *adj.* a title of respect for a clergyman. Abbrev.: **Rev., Revd.**

▷**Usage.** *Reverend* with a surname alone (*Reverend Smith*), as a term of address ("*Yes, Reverend*"), or in the salutation of a letter (*Dear Rev. Mr Smith*) are all considered to be wrong usage. Preferred are (the) *Reverend John Smith* or *Reverend Mr Smith* and *Dear Mr Smith.*

reverent (ˈrɛvərənt) *adj.* feeling, expressing, or characterized by reverence. [C14: from L *reverēns* respectful] —ˈreverently *adv.*

reverential (ˌrɛvəˈrɛnʃəl) *adj.* resulting from or showing reverence. —ˌreverˈentially *adv.*

ˌreupˈholster *vb.*   reˈusable *adj.*   reˈuse *vb., n.*   reˈvarnish *vb.*

reverie ('rɛvərɪ) *n.* **1.** an act or state of absent-minded daydreaming: *to fall into a reverie.* **2.** a piece of instrumental music suggestive of a daydream. **3.** *Arch.* a fanciful or visionary notion; daydream. [C14: from OF *resverie* wildness, from *resver* to behave wildly, from ?]

revers (rɪ'vɪə) *n., pl.* **-vers** (-'vɪəz). (*usually pl.*) the turned-back lining of part of a garment, esp. of a lapel or cuff. [C19: from F, lit.: REVERSE]

reversal (rɪ'vɜːsəl) *n.* **1.** the act or an instance of reversing. **2.** a change for the worse; reverse. **3.** the state of being reversed. **4.** the annulment of a judicial decision, esp. by an appeal court.

reverse (rɪ'vɜːs) *vb.* (*mainly tr.*) **1.** to turn or set in an opposite direction, order, or position. **2.** to change into something different or contrary; alter completely: *reverse one's policy.* **3.** (*also intr.*) to move or cause to move backwards or in an opposite direction: *to reverse a car.* **4.** to run (machinery, etc.) in the opposite direction to normal. **5.** to turn inside out. **6.** *Law.* to revoke or set aside (a judgment, decree, etc.); annul. **7. reverse the charge(s).** to make a telephone call at the recipient's expense. ~*n.* **8.** the opposite or contrary of something. **9.** the back or rear side of something. **10.** a change to an opposite position, state, or direction. **11.** a change for the worse; setback or defeat. **12. a.** the mechanism or gears by which machinery, a vehicle, etc., can be made to reverse its direction. **b.** (*as modifier*): *reverse gear.* **13.** the side of a coin bearing a secondary design. **14. a.** printed matter in which normally black or coloured areas, esp. lettering, appear white, and vice versa. **b.** (*as modifier*): *reverse plates.* **15. in reverse.** in an opposite or backward direction. **16. the reverse of.** emphatically not; not at all: *he was the reverse of polite when I called.* ~*adj.* **17.** opposite or contrary in direction, position, order, nature, etc.; turned backwards. **18.** back to front; inverted. **19.** operating or moving in a manner contrary to that which is usual. **20.** denoting or relating to a mirror image. [C14: from OF, from L *reversus*, from *revertere* to turn back] —**re'versely** *adv.* —**re'verser** *n.*

reverse-charge *adj.* (*prenominal*) (of a telephone call) made at the recipient's expense.

reverse transcriptase (træn'skrɪpteɪz) *n.* an enzyme present in retroviruses that copies RNA into DNA, thus reversing the usual flow of genetic information in which DNA is copied into RNA.

reverse video *n. Computers.* highlighting by reversing the colours of normal characters and background on a visual display unit.

reversible (rɪ'vɜːsɪbəl) *adj.* **1.** capable of being reversed: *a reversible decision.* **2.** capable of returning to an original condition. **3.** *Chem., physics.* capable of assuming or producing either of two possible states and changing from one to the other: *a reversible reaction.* **4.** (of a fabric or garment) woven, printed, or finished so that either side may be used as the outer side. ~*n.* **5.** a reversible garment, esp. a coat. —**re,versi'bility** *n.* —**re'versibly** *adv.*

reversing light *n.* a light on the rear of a motor vehicle to provide illumination when the vehicle is being reversed.

reversion (rɪ'vɜːʃən) *n.* **1.** a return to an earlier condition, practice, or belief; act of reverting. **2.** *Biol.* the return of individuals, organs, etc., to a more primitive condition or type. **3.** *Property law.* **a.** an interest in an estate that reverts to the grantor or his heirs at the end of a period, esp. at the end of the life of a grantee. **b.** an estate so reverting. **c.** the right to succeed to such an estate. **4.** the benefit payable on the death of a life-insurance policyholder. —**re'versionary** *or* **re'versional** *adj.*

revert (rɪ'vɜːt) *vb.* (*intr.;* foll. by *to*). **1.** to go back to a former practice, condition, belief, etc.: *he reverted to his old wicked ways.* **2.** to take up again or come back to a former topic. **3.** *Biol.* (of individuals, organs, etc.) to return to a more primitive, earlier, or simpler condition or type. **4.** *Property law.* (of an estate or interest in land) to return to its former owner or his heirs. **5. revert to type.** to resume characteristics that were thought to have disappeared. [C13: from L *revertere*, from RE- + *vertere* to turn] —**re'verter** *n.* —**re'vertible** *adj.*

revet (rɪ'vɛt) *vb.* **-vetting, -vetted.** to face (a wall or embankment) with stones. [C19: from F *revêt*, from OF *revestir* to reclothe; see REVETMENT]

revetment (rɪ'vɛtmənt) *n.* **1.** a facing of stones, sandbags, etc., to protect a wall, embankment, or earthworks. **2.** another name for **retaining wall.** [C18: from F *revêtement*, lit.: a reclothing, from *revêtir;* ult. from L RE- + *vestire* to clothe]

review (rɪ'vjuː) *vb.* (*mainly tr.*) **1.** to look at or examine again: *to review a situation.* **2.** to look back upon (a period of time, sequence of events, etc.); remember: *he reviewed his achievements with pride.* **3.** to inspect, esp. formally or officially: *the general reviewed his troops.* **4.** *Law.* to re-examine (a decision) judicially. **5.** to write a critical assessment of (a book, film, play, concert, etc.), esp. as a profession. ~*n.* **6.** Also called: **reviewal.** the act or an instance of reviewing. **7.** a general survey or report: *a review of the political situation.* **8.** a critical assessment of a book, film, play, concert, etc., esp. one printed in a newspaper or periodical. **9.** a publication containing such articles. **10.** a second consideration; re-examination. **11.** a retrospective survey. **12.** a formal or official inspection. **13.** a U.S. and Canad. word for **revision** (sense 2). **14.** *Law.* judicial re-examination of a case, esp. by a superior court. **15.** a less common spelling of **revue.** [C16: from F, from *revoir* to see again, from L RE- + *vidēre* to see] —**re'viewer** *n.*

revile (rɪ'vaɪl) *vb.* to use abusive or scornful language against (someone or something). [C14: from OF *reviler*, from RE- + *vil* VILE] —**re'vilement** *n.* —**re'viler** *n.*

revise (rɪ'vaɪz) *vb.* **1.** (*tr.*) to change or amend: *to revise one's opinion.* **2.** *Brit.* to reread (a subject or notes on it) so as to memorize it, esp. for an examination. **3.** (*tr.*) to prepare a new version or edition of (a previously printed work). ~*n.* **4.** the act, process, or result of revising; revision. [C16: from L *revisere*, from RE- + *vīsere* to inspect, from *vidēre* to see] —**re'visal** *n.* —**re'viser** *n.*

Revised Standard Version *n.* a revision by American scholars of the American Standard Version of the Bible. The New Testament was published in 1946 and the entire Bible in 1953.

Revised Version *n.* a revision of the Authorized Version of the Bible by two committees of British scholars, the New Testament being published in 1881 and the Old in 1885.

revision (rɪ'vɪʒən) *n.* **1.** the act or process of revising. **2.** *Brit.* the process of rereading a subject or notes on it, esp. for an examination. **3.** a corrected or new version of a book, article, etc. —**re'visionary** *adj.*

revisionism (rɪ'vɪʒə,nɪzəm) *n.* **1.** (*sometimes cap.*) **a.** a moderate, nonrevolutionary version of Marxism developed in Germany around 1900. **b.** (in Marxist-Leninist ideology) any dangerous departure from the true interpretation of Marx's teachings. **2.** the advocacy of revision of some political theory, etc. —**re'visionist** *n., adj.*

revisory (rɪ'vaɪzərɪ) *adj.* of, relating to, or having the power of revision.

revitalize *or* **-lise** (riː'vaɪtə,laɪz) *vb.* (*tr.*) to restore vitality or animation to.

revival (rɪ'vaɪvəl) *n.* **1.** the act or an instance of reviving or the state of being revived. **2.** an instance of returning to life or consciousness; restoration of vigour or vitality. **3.** a renewed use, acceptance of, or interest in (past customs, styles, etc.): *the Gothic revival.* **4.** a new production of a play that has not been recently performed. **5.** a reawakening of faith. **6.** an evangelistic meeting or meetings intended to effect such a reawakening in those present.

revivalism (rɪ'vaɪvə,lɪzəm) *n.* **1.** a movement that seeks to reawaken faith. **2.** the tendency or desire to revive former customs, styles, etc. —**re'vivalist** *n.* —**re,vival'istic** *adj.*

revive (rɪ'vaɪv) *vb.* **1.** to bring or be brought back to life, consciousness, or strength: *revived by a drop of whisky.* **2.** to give or assume new vitality; flourish again or cause to flourish again. **3.** to make or become operative or active again: *the youth movement was revived.* **4.** to bring or come back to mind. **5.** (*tr.*) *Theatre.* to mount a new production of (an old play). [C15: from OF *revivre* to live again, from L *revivere*, from RE- + *vīvere* to live] —**re'vivable** *adj.* —**re,viva'bility** *n.* —**re'viver** *n.* —**re'viving** *adj.*

revivify (rɪ'vɪvɪ,faɪ) *vb.* **-fying, -fied.** (*tr.*) to give new life or spirit to. —**re,vivifi'cation** *n.*

revocable ('rɛvəkəbᵊl) *or* **revokable** (rɪ'vəʊkəbᵊl) *adj.* capable of being revoked. —,**revoca'bility** *or* **re,voka'bility** *n.* —'**revocably** *or* **re'vokably** *adv.*

revocation (,rɛvə'keɪʃən) *n.* **1.** the act of revoking or state of being revoked. **2. a.** the cancellation or annulment of a legal instrument. **b.** the withdrawal of an offer, power of attorney, etc. —**revocatory** ('rɛvəkətərɪ, -trɪ) *adj.*

revoice (riː'vɔɪs) *vb.* (*tr.*) **1.** to utter again; echo. **2.** to adjust the design of (an organ pipe or wind instrument) as after disuse or to conform with modern pitch.

revoke (rɪ'vəʊk) *vb.* **1.** (*tr.*) to take back or withdraw; cancel; rescind. **2.** (*intr.*) *Cards.* to break a rule by failing to follow suit when able to do so. ~*n.* **3.** *Cards.* the act of revoking. [C14: from L *revocāre* to call back, withdraw, from RE- + *vocāre* to call] —**re'voker** *n.*

revolt (rɪ'vəʊlt) *n.* **1.** a rebellion or uprising against authority. **2. in revolt.** in the process or state of rebelling. ~*vb.* **3.** (*intr.*) to rise up in rebellion against authority. **4.** (*usually passive*) to feel or cause to feel revulsion, disgust, or abhorrence. [C16: from F *révolter*, from OIt. *rivoltare* to overturn, ult. from L *revolvere* to roll back]

revolting (rɪ'vəʊltɪŋ) *adj.* **1.** causing revulsion; nauseating, disgusting, or repulsive. **2.** *Inf.* unpleasant or nasty. —**re'voltingly** *adv.*

revolute ('rɛvə,luːt) *adj.* (esp. of the margins of a leaf) rolled backwards and downwards. [C18: from L *revolūtus* rolled back; see REVOLVE]

revolution (,rɛvə'luːʃən) *n.* **1.** the overthrow or repudiation of a regime or political system by the governed. **2.** (in Marxist theory) the inevitable, violent transition from one system of production in a society to the next. **3.** a far-reaching and drastic change, esp. in ideas, methods, etc. **4. a.** movement in or as if in a circle. **b.** one complete turn in such a circle: *33 revolutions per minute.* **5. a.** the orbital motion of one body, such as a planet, around another. **b.** one complete turn in such motion. **6.** a cycle of successive events or changes. [C14: via OF from LL *revolūtiō*, from L *revolvere* to REVOLVE]

revolutionary (,rɛvə'luːʃənərɪ) *n.*, *pl.* **-aries. 1.** a person who advocates or engages in revolution. ~*adj.* **2.** relating to or characteristic of a revolution. **3.** advocating or engaged in revolution. **4.** radically new or different: *a revolutionary method of making plastics.*

Revolutionary (,rɛvə'luːʃənərɪ) *adj.* **1.** *Chiefly U.S.* of or relating to the War of American Independence (1775–83). **2.** of or relating to any of various other Revolutions, esp. the **Russian Revolution** (1917) or the **French Revolution** (1789).

revolutionist (,rɛvə'luːʃənɪst) *n.* **1.** a less common word for a **revolutionary.** ~*adj.* **2.** of or relating to revolution or revolutionaries.

revolutionize *or* **-ise** (,rɛvə'luːʃə,naɪz) *vb.* (*tr.*) **1.** to bring about a radical change in: *science has revolutionized civilization.* **2.** to inspire or infect with revolutionary ideas: *they revolutionized the common soldiers.* **3.** to cause a revolution in (a country, etc.). —,**revo'lution,izer** *or* -,**iser** *n.*

revolve (rɪ'vɒlv) *vb.* **1.** to move or cause to move around a centre or axis; rotate. **2.** (*intr.*) to occur periodically or in cycles. **3.** to consider or be considered. **4.** (*intr.*; foll. by *around* or *about*) to be centred or focused (upon): *Juliet's thoughts revolved around Romeo.* ~*n.* **5.** *Theatre.* a circular section of a stage that can be rotated by electric power to provide a scene change. [C14: from L *revolvere*, from RE- + *volvere* to roll, wind] —**re'volvable** *adj.*

revolver (rɪ'vɒlvə) *n.* a pistol having a revolving multichambered cylinder that allows several shots to be discharged without reloading.

revolving (rɪ'vɒlvɪŋ) *adj.* denoting or relating to an engine, such as a radial aero engine, in which the cylinders revolve about a fixed shaft.

revolving credit *n.* a letter of credit for a fixed sum, specifying that the beneficiary may make repeated use of the credit provided that the fixed sum is never exceeded.

revolving door *n.* a door that rotates about a vertical axis, esp. one with four leaves at right angles to each other, thereby excluding draughts.

revue (rɪ'vjuː) *n.* a light entertainment consisting of topical sketches, songs, dancing, etc. [C20: from F; see RE-VIEW]

revulsion (rɪ'vʌlʃən) *n.* **1.** a sudden violent reaction in feeling, esp. one of extreme loathing. **2.** the act or an instance of drawing back or recoiling from something. **3.** the diversion of disease from one part of the body to another by cupping, counterirritants, etc. [C16: from L *revulsiō* a pulling away, from *revellere*, from RE- + *vellere* to pull, tear]

revulsive (rɪ'vʌlsɪv) *adj.* **1.** of or causing revulsion. ~*n.* **2.** *Med.* a counterirritant. —**re'vulsively** *adv.*

reward (rɪ'wɔːd) *n.* **1.** something given in return for a deed or service rendered. **2.** a sum of money offered, esp. for help in finding a criminal or for the return of lost or stolen property. **3.** profit or return. **4.** something received in return for good or evil; deserts. ~*vb.* **5.** (*tr.*) to give something to (someone), esp. in gratitude for (a service rendered); recompense. [C14: from OF *rewarder*, from RE- + *warder* to care for, guard, of Gmc origin] —**re'wardless** *adj.*

rewarding (rɪ'wɔːdɪŋ) *adj.* giving personal satisfaction; gratifying.

rewa-rewa ('reɪwə'reɪwə) *n.* a tall tree of New Zealand, yielding reddish timber. [C19: from Maori]

rewind *vb.* (riː'waɪnd), **-winding, -wound. 1.** (*tr.*) to wind back, esp. a film or tape onto the original reel. ~*n.* ('riː,waɪnd, riː'waɪnd). **2.** something rewound. **3.** the act of rewinding. —**re'winder** *n.*

rewire (riː'waɪə) *vb.* (*tr.*) to provide (a house, engine, etc.) with new wiring. —**re'wirable** *adj.*

reword (riː'wɜːd) *vb.* (*tr.*) to alter the wording of; express differently.

rework (riː'wɜːk) *vb.* (*tr.*) **1.** to use again in altered form. **2.** to rewrite or revise. **3.** to reprocess for use again.

rewrite *vb.* (riː'raɪt), **-writing, -wrote, -written.** (*tr.*) **1.** to write (material) again, esp. changing the words or form. ~*n.* ('riː,raɪt). **2.** something rewritten.

Rex (rɛks) *n.* king: part of the official title of a king, now used chiefly in documents, legal proceedings, on coins, etc. Cf. **Regina**[1]. [L]

Rexine ('rɛksiːn) *n. Trademark.* a form of artificial leather.

Reye's syndrome (raɪz, reɪz) *n.* a rare metabolic disease in children that can be fatal, involving damage to the brain, liver, and kidneys. [C20: after R.D.K. *Reye* (1912-78), Austral. paediatrician]

Reykjavik ('reɪkjə,viːk) *n.* the capital and chief port of Iceland, situated in the southwest: its buildings are heated by natural hot water. Pop.: 91 394 (1986).

Reynard *or* **Renard** ('rɛnəd, 'rɛnɑːd) *n.* a name for a fox, used in fables, etc.

Reynaud (*French* rɛno) *n.* **Paul** (pɔl). 1878–1966, French statesman: premier during the defeat of France by Germany (1940); later imprisoned by the Germans.

Reynolds ('rɛnəldz) *n.* **Sir Joshua.** 1723–92, English portrait painter. He was the first president of the Royal Academy (1768): the annual lectures he gave there, published as *Discourses*, are important contributions to art theory and criticism.

Reynosa (*Spanish* re'nosa) *n.* a city in E Mexico, in Tamaulipas state on the Rio Grande. Pop.: 211 412 (1980).

RF *abbrev. for* radio frequency.

RFC *abbrev. for:* **1.** Royal Flying Corps. **2.** Rugby Football Club.

RGS *abbrev. for* Royal Geographical Society.

rh *or* **RH** *abbrev. for* right hand.

Rh **1.** *the chemical symbol for* rhodium. ~ **2.** *abbrev. for* rhesus (esp. in **Rh factor**).

RHA *abbrev. for* Royal Horse Artillery.

rhabdomancy ('ræbdə,mænsɪ) *n.* divination for water or mineral ore by means of a rod or wand. [C17: via LL from LGk *rhabdomanteia*, from Gk *rhabdos* rod + *manteia* divination] —'**rhabdo,mantist** *or* '**rhabdo,mancer** *n.*

rhachis ('reɪkɪs) *n.*, *pl.* **rhachises** *or* **rhachides** ('ræki,diːz, 'reɪ-). a variant spelling of **rachis.**

Rhadamanthus *or* **Rhadamanthys** (,rædə'mænθəs) *n. Greek myth.* one of the judges of the dead in the underworld. —,**Rhada'manthine** *adj.*

---

re'wash *vb.*
re'weigh *vb.*

re'weld *vb.*

re'wrap *vb.*

re'zone *vb.*

Rhaetia ('riːʃɪə) *n.* an Alpine province of ancient Rome including parts of present-day Tyrol and E Switzerland. —**Rhaetian** ('riːʃən) *adj., n.*

Rhaetian Alps *pl. n.* a section of the central Alps along E Switzerland's borders with Austria and Italy. Highest peak: Piz Bernina, 4049 m (13 284 ft.).

rhapsodic (ræp'sɒdɪk) *adj.* **1.** of or like a rhapsody. **2.** lyrical or romantic.

rhapsodize *or* **-ise** ('ræpsə,daɪz) *vb.* **1.** to speak or write (something) with extravagant enthusiasm. **2.** (*intr.*) to recite or write rhapsodies. —**'rhapsodist** *n.*

rhapsody ('ræpsədɪ) *n., pl.* **-dies. 1.** *Music.* a composition free in structure and highly emotional in character. **2.** an expression of ecstatic enthusiasm. **3.** (in ancient Greece) an epic poem or part of an epic recited by a rhapsodist. **4.** a literary work composed in an intense or exalted style. **5.** rapturous delight or ecstasy. [C16: via L from Gk *rhapsōidia*, from *rhaptein* to sew together + *ōidē* song]

rhatany ('rætənɪ) *n., pl.* **-nies. 1.** either of two South American leguminous shrubs that have thick fleshy roots. **2.** the dried roots used as an astringent. ~Also called: **krameria.** [C19: from NL *rhatānia*, ult. from Quechua *ratánya*]

rhea (rɪə) *n.* either of two large fast-running flightless birds inhabiting the open plains of S South America. They are similar to but smaller than the ostrich. [C19: NL; arbitrarily after RHEA]

Rhea ('rɪə) *n. Greek myth.* a Titaness, wife of Cronus and mother of several of the gods, including Zeus: a fertility goddess. Roman counterpart: **Ops.**

Rhea Silvia *or* **Rea Silvia** ('sɪlvɪə) *n. Roman myth.* the mother of Romulus and Remus by Mars. See also **Ilia.**

rhebuck *or* **rhebok** ('riːbʌk) *n., pl.* **-boks** *or* **-bok.** an antelope of southern Africa, having woolly brownish-grey hair. [C18: Afrik., from Du. *reebok* ROEBUCK]

Rhee (riː) *n.* **Syngman** ('sɪŋmən). 1875–1965, Korean statesman, leader of the campaign for independence from Japan; first president of South Korea (1948–60). Popular unrest forced his resignation.

Rheims (riːmz; *French* rɛ̃s) *n.* a variant spelling of **Reims.**

Rhein (raɪn) *n.* the German name for the **Rhine.**

Rheinland ('raɪnlant) *n.* the German name for the **Rhineland.**

Rheinland-Pfalz ('raɪnlant'pfalts) *n.* the German name for **Rhineland-Palatinate.**

Rhenish ('rɛnɪʃ, 'riː-) *adj.* **1.** of or relating to the River Rhine or the lands adjacent to it. ~*n.* **2.** another word for **hock** (the wine).

rhenium ('riːnɪəm) *n.* a dense silvery-white metallic element that has a high melting point. Symbol: Re; atomic no.: 75; atomic wt.: 186.2. [C19: NL, from *Rhēnus* the Rhine]

rheo- *combining form.* indicating stream, flow, or current: *rheostat.* [from Gk *rheos* stream, anything flowing, from *rhein* to flow]

rheology (rɪ'ɒlədʒɪ) *n.* the branch of physics concerned with the flow and change of shape of matter, esp. the viscosity of liquids. —**rheological** (,riːə'lɒdʒɪkəl) *adj.* —**rhe'ologist** *n.*

rheostat ('rɪə,stæt) *n.* a variable resistance, usually a coil of wire with a terminal at one end and a sliding contact that moves along the coil to tap off the current. —**,rheo'static** *adj.*

Rhesus ('riːsəs) *n. Greek myth.* a king of Thrace, who arrived in the tenth year of the Trojan War to aid Troy. Odysseus and Diomedes stole his horses because an oracle had said that if these horses drank from the River Xanthus, Troy would not fall.

rhesus baby ('riːsəs) *n.* a baby suffering from haemolytic disease at birth as its red blood cells (which are Rh positive) have been attacked in the womb by antibodies from its Rh negative mother. [C20: see RH FACTOR]

rhesus factor *n.* See **Rh factor.**

rhesus monkey *n.* a macaque monkey of S Asia. [C19: NL, arbitrarily from Gk *Rhesos*, mythical Thracian king]

rhetoric ('rɛtərɪk) *n.* **1.** the study of the technique of using language effectively. **2.** the art of using speech to persuade, influence, or please; oratory. **3.** excessive ornamentation and contrivance in spoken or written discourse; bombast. **4.** speech or discourse that pretends to significance but lacks true meaning: *mere rhetoric.* [C14:

via L from Gk *rhētorikē* (*tekhnē*) (the art of) rhetoric, from *rhētōr* teacher of rhetoric, orator]

rhetorical (rɪ'tɒrɪkəl) *adj.* **1.** concerned with effect or style rather than content or meaning: bombastic. **2.** of or relating to rhetoric or oratory. —**rhe'torically** *adv.*

rhetorical question *n.* a question to which no answer is required: used esp. for dramatic effect. An example is *Who knows?* (with the implication *Nobody knows*).

rhetorician (,rɛtə'rɪʃən) *n.* **1.** a teacher of rhetoric. **2.** a stylish or eloquent writer or speaker. **3.** a pompous or extravagant speaker.

rheum (ruːm) *n.* a watery discharge from the eyes or nose. [C14: from OF *reume*, ult. from Gk *rheuma* bodily humour, stream, from *rhein* to flow] —**'rheumy** *adj.*

rheumatic (ruː'mætɪk) *adj.* **1.** of, relating to, or afflicted with rheumatism. ~*n.* **2.** a person afflicted with rheumatism. [C14: ult. from Gk *rheumatikos*, from *rheuma* a flow; see RHEUM] —**rheu'matically** *adv.*

rheumatic fever *n.* a disease characterized by inflammation and pain in the joints.

rheumatics (ruː'mætɪks) *n.* (*functioning as sing.*) *Inf.* rheumatism.

rheumatism ('ruːmə,tɪzəm) *n.* any painful disorder of joints, muscles, or connective tissue. [C17: from L *rheumatismus* catarrh, from Gk *rheumatismos;* see RHEUM]

rheumatoid ('ruːmə,tɔɪd) *adj.* (of symptoms) resembling rheumatism.

rheumatoid arthritis *n.* a chronic disease characterized by inflammation and swelling of joints (esp. in the hands, wrists, knees, and feet), muscle weakness, and fatigue.

rheumatology (,ruːmə'tɒlədʒɪ) *n.* the study of rheumatic diseases. —**rheumatological** (,ruːmətə'lɒdʒɪkəl) *adj.*

Rheydt (*German* raɪt) *n.* an industrial town in W West Germany, in North Rhine-Westphalia. Pop.: 100 939 (1974 est.).

Rh factor *n.* an antigen commonly found in human blood: the terms **Rh positive** and **Rh negative** are used to indicate its presence or absence. It may cause a haemolytic reaction, esp. during pregnancy or following transfusion of blood that does not contain this antigen. Full name: **rhesus factor.** [after the rhesus monkey, in which it was first discovered]

rhinal ('raɪnəl) *adj.* of or relating to the nose.

Rhine (raɪn) *n.* a river in central and W Europe, rising in SE Switzerland: flows through Lake Constance north through West Germany and west through the Netherlands to the North Sea. Length: about 1320 km (820 miles). Dutch name: **Rijn.** French name: **Rhin** (rɛ̃). German name: **Rhein.**

Rhineland ('raɪn,lænd, -lənd) *n.* the region of West Germany surrounding the Rhine. German name: **Rheinland.**

Rhineland-Palatinate *n.* a state of W West Germany: formed in 1946 from the S part of the Prussian Rhine province, the Palatinate, and parts of Rhine-Hesse and Hesse-Nassau; agriculture (with over two thirds of West Germany's vineyards) and tourism are important. Capital: Mainz. Pop.: 3 641 000 (1981 est.). Area: 19 832 sq. km (7657 sq. miles). German name: **Rheinland-Pfalz.**

Rhine Palatinate *n.* See **Palatinate.**

rhinestone ('raɪn,stəun) *n.* an imitation gem made of paste. [C19: translation of F *caillou du Rhin*, referring to Strasbourg, where such gems were made]

Rhine wine (raɪn) *n.* any wine produced along the Rhine, characteristically a white table wine.

rhinitis (raɪ'naɪtɪs) *n.* inflammation of the mucous membrane that lines the nose. —**rhinitic** (raɪ'nɪtɪk) *adj.*

rhino[1] ('raɪnəu) *n., pl.* **-nos** *or* **-no.** short for **rhinoceros.**

rhino[2] ('raɪnəu) *n. Brit.* a slang word for **money.** [C17: from ?]

rhino- *or before a vowel* **rhin-** *combining form.* the nose: *rhinology.* [from Gk *rhis, rhin*]

rhinoceros (raɪ'nɒsərɒs, -'nɒsrəs) *n., pl.* **-oses** *or* **-os.** any of several mammals constituting a family of SE Asia and Africa and having either one horn on the nose, like the **Indian rhinoceros,** or two horns, like the African **white rhinoceros.** They have a very thick skin and a massive body. [C13: via L from Gk *rhinokerōs*, from *rhis* nose + *keras* horn] —**rhinocerotic** (,raɪnəusɪ'rɒtɪk) *adj.*

rhinology (raɪ'nɒlədʒɪ) *n.* the branch of medical science concerned with the nose. —**rhinological** (,raɪnə'lɒdʒɪkəl) *adj.* —**rhi'nologist** *n.*

rhinoplasty ('raɪnəu,plæstɪ) *n.* plastic surgery of the nose. —**,rhino'plastic** *adj.*

rhinoscopy (raɪˈnɒskəpɪ) n. Med. examination of the nasal passages, esp. with a special instrument called a **rhinoscope** (ˈraɪnəʊˌskəʊp).

rhizo- or before a vowel **rhiz-** combining form. root: rhizocarpous. [from Gk rhiza]

rhizocarpous (ˌraɪzəʊˈkɑːpəs) adj. **1.** (of plants) producing subterranean flowers and fruit. **2.** (of plants) having perennial roots but stems and leaves that wither.

rhizoid (ˈraɪzɔɪd) n. any of various hairlike structures that function as roots in mosses, ferns, and fungi. — **rhiˈzoidal** adj.

rhizome (ˈraɪzəʊm) n. a thick horizontal underground stem whose buds develop into new plants. Also called: **rootstock**, **rootstalk**. [C19: from NL rhizoma, from Gk, from rhiza a root] —**rhizomatous** (raɪˈzɒmətəs, -ˈzəʊ-) adj.

rhizopod (ˈraɪzəʊˌpɒd) n. **1.** any of various protozoans characterized by naked protoplasmic processes (pseudopodia). ~adj. **2.** of, relating to, or belonging to rhizopods.

rho (rəʊ) n., pl. **rhos.** the 17th letter in the Greek alphabet (P, ρ).

rhodamine (ˈrəʊdəˌmiːn, -mɪn) n. any one of a group of synthetic red or pink basic dyestuffs used for wool and silk. [C20: from RHODO- + AMINE]

Rhode Island (rəʊd) n. a state of the northeastern U.S., bordering on the Atlantic: the smallest state in the U.S.; mainly low-lying and undulating, with an indented coastline in the east and uplands in the northwest. Capital: Providence. Pop.: 975 000 (1986 est.). Area: 2717 sq. km (1049 sq. miles). Abbrevs.: **R.I.** or (with zip code) **RI**

Rhode Island Red n. a breed of domestic fowl, originating in America, characterized by a dark reddish-brown plumage and the production of brown eggs.

Rhodes[1] (rəʊdz) n. **1.** a Greek island in the SE Aegean Sea, about 16 km (10 miles) off the Turkish coast: the largest of the Dodecanese and the most easterly island in the Aegean. Capital: Rhodes. Pop.: 40 392 (1981). Area: 1400 sq. km (540 sq. miles). **2.** a port on this island, in the NE: founded in 408 B.C.; of great commercial and political importance in the 3rd century B.C.; suffered several earthquakes, notably in 225, when the Colossus was destroyed. Pop.: 40 656 (1981). ~Ancient Greek name: **Rhodos.** Modern Greek name: **Ródhos.**

Rhodes[2] (rəʊdz) n. **Cecil John.** 1853–1902, British colonial financier and statesman in South Africa. He made a fortune in diamond and gold mining and, as prime minister of the Cape Colony (1890–96), he helped to extend British territory. He established the annual **Rhodes scholarships** to Oxford.

Rhodesia (rəʊˈdiːʃə, -zɪə) n. a former name (1964–78) for **Zimbabwe.** — **Rhoˈdesian** adj., n.

Rhodesia and Nyasaland n. **Federation of.** a federation consisting of Northern Rhodesia, Southern Rhodesia, and Nyasaland, which existed from 1953 to 1963.

Rhodesian man (rəʊˈdiːʃən) n. a type of early man, occurring in Africa in late Pleistocene times and resembling Neanderthal man.

Rhodes scholarship (rəʊdz) n. one of 72 scholarships founded by Cecil Rhodes, awarded annually to Commonwealth and U.S. students to study at Oxford University. — **Rhodes scholar** n.

Rhodian (ˈrəʊdɪən) adj. **1.** of or relating to the island of Rhodes. ~n. **2.** a native or inhabitant of Rhodes.

rhodium (ˈrəʊdɪəm) n. a hard silvery-white element of the platinum metal group. Used as an alloying agent to harden platinum and palladium. Symbol: Rh; atomic no.: 45; atomic wt.: 102.90. [C19: NL, from Gk rhodon rose, from the pink colour of its compounds]

rhodo- or before a vowel **rhod-** combining form. rose or rose-coloured: rhododendron; rhodolite. [from Gk rhodon rose]

rhodochrosite (ˌrəʊdəʊˈkrəʊsaɪt) n. a pink, grey, or brown mineral that consists of manganese carbonate in hexagonal crystalline form. Formula: MnCO₃. [C19: from Gk rhodokhrōs, from rhodon rose + khrōs colour]

rhododendron (ˌrəʊdəˈdɛndrən) n. any of various shrubs native to S Asia but widely cultivated in N temperate regions. They are mostly evergreen and have clusters of showy red, purple, pink, or white flowers. [C17: from L: oleander, from Gk, from rhodon rose + dendron tree]

rhodolite (ˈrəʊdəˌlaɪt) n. a pale violet or red variety of garnet, used as a gemstone.

rhodonite (ˈrəʊdəˌnaɪt) n. a brownish translucent mineral consisting of manganese silicate in crystalline form with calcium, iron, or magnesium sometimes replacing the manganese. It is used as an ornamental stone, glaze, and pigment. [C19: from G Rhodonit, from Gk rhodon rose + -ITE[1]]

Rhodope Mountains (ˈrɒdəpɪ, rɒˈdəʊ-) pl. n. a mountain range in SE Europe, in the Balkan Peninsula extending along the border between Bulgaria and Greece. Highest peak: Mount Musala (Bulgaria), 2925 m (9597 ft.).

rhodopsin (rəʊˈdɒpsɪn) n. a red pigment in the rods of the retina in vertebrates. Also called: **visual purple.** also **iodopsin.** [C20: from RHODO- + Gk opsis sight + -IN]

Rhodos (ˈrɒðɒs) n. the Ancient Greek name for **Rhodes.**

rhomb (rɒm) n. another name for **rhombus.**

rhombencephalon (ˌrɒmbɛnˈsɛfəˌlɒn) n. the part of the brain that develops from the posterior portion of the embryonic neural tube. Nontechnical name: **hindbrain.** [C20: from RHOMBUS + ENCEPHALON]

rhombic aerial n. a directional travelling-wave aerial, usually horizontal, consisting of two conductors forming a rhombus.

rhombohedral (ˌrɒmbəʊˈhiːdrəl) adj. **1.** of or relating to a rhombohedron. **2.** Crystallog. another term for **trigonal** (sense 2).

rhombohedron (ˌrɒmbəʊˈhiːdrən) n., pl. **-drons** or **-dra** (-drə). a six-sided prism whose sides are parallelograms. [C19: from RHOMBUS + -HEDRON]

rhomboid (ˈrɒmbɔɪd) n. **1.** a parallelogram having adjacent sides of unequal length. ~adj. also **rhomˈboidal. 2.** having such a shape. [C16: from LL, from Gk rhomboeidēs shaped like a RHOMBUS]

rhombus (ˈrɒmbəs) n., pl. **-buses** or **-bi** (-baɪ). an oblique-angled parallelogram having four equal sides. Also called: **rhomb.** [C16: from Gk rhombos something that spins; rel. to rhembein to whirl] — **ˈrhombic** adj.

rhonchus (ˈrɒŋkəs) n., pl. **-chi** (-kaɪ). a rattling or whistling respiratory sound resembling snoring, caused by secretions in the trachea or bronchi. [C19: from L, from Gk rhenkhos snoring]

Rhondda (ˈrɒnðə) n. a town in S Wales, in Mid Glamorgan on two branches of the **Rhondda Valley:** developed into a major coal-mining centre after 1807 and grew to a population of 167 900 in 1924. Pop.: 81 725 (1981).

Rhône (rəʊn) n. **1.** a river in W Europe, rising in S Switzerland in the **Rhône glacier** and flowing to Lake Geneva, then into France through gorges between the Alps and Jura and south to its delta on the Gulf of Lions: important esp. for hydroelectricity and for wine production along its valley. Length: 812 km (505 miles). **2.** a department of E central France, in the Rhône-Alpes region. Capital: Lyons. Pop.: 1 445 208 (1982). Area: 3233 sq. km (1261 sq. miles).

Rhône-Alpes (French ronalp) n. a region of E France: mainly mountainous, rising to the edge of the Massif Central in the west and the French Alps in the east; drained by the Rivers Rhône, Saône, and Isère.

RHS abbrev. for: **1.** Royal Historical Society. **2.** Royal Horticultural Society. **3.** Royal Humane Society.

rhubarb (ˈruːbɑːb) n. **1.** any of several temperate and subtropical plants, esp. **common garden rhubarb,** which has long green and red acid-tasting edible leafstalks, usually eaten sweetened and cooked. **2.** the leafstalks of this plant. **3.** a related plant of central Asia, having a bitter-tasting underground stem that can be dried and used as a laxative or astringent. **4.** U.S. & Canad. sl. a heated discussion or quarrel. ~interj., n., vb. **5.** the noise made by actors to simulate conversation, esp. by repeating the word rhubarb. [C14: from OF reubarbe, from Med. L reubarbum, prob. var. of rha barbarum, from rha rhubarb (from Gk, ?from Rha, ancient name of the Volga) + L barbarus barbarian]

rhumb (rʌm) n. short for **rhumb line.**

rhumba (ˈrʌmbə, ˈrʊm-) n., pl. **-bas.** a variant spelling of **rumba.**

rhumb line n. **1.** an imaginary line on the surface of a sphere that intersects all meridians at the same angle. **2.** the course navigated by a vessel or aircraft that maintains a uniform compass heading. [C16: from OSp. rumbo, apparently from MDu. ruum space, ship's hold, infl. by RHOMBUS]

rhyme or (Arch.) **rime** (raɪm) n. **1.** identity of the terminal sounds in lines of verse or in words. **2.** a word that is identical to another in its terminal sound: "while" is a *rhyme for "mile".* **3.** a piece of poetry, esp. having corresponding sounds at the ends of the lines. **4. rhyme or reason.** sense, logic, or meaning. ~*vb.* **5.** to use (a word) or (of a word) to be used so as to form a rhyme. **6.** to render (a subject) into rhyme. **7.** to compose (verse) in a metrical structure. ~*See also* **eye rhyme.** [C12: from OF *rime*, ult. from OHG *rīm* a number; spelling infl. by RHYTHM]

rhymester, rimester ('raɪmstə), **rhymer,** *or* **rimer** *n.* a poet, esp. one considered to be mediocre; poetaster or versifier.

rhyming slang *n.* slang in which a word is replaced by another word or phrase that rhymes with it; e.g. *apples and pears* meaning *stairs.*

rhyolite ('raɪə,laɪt) *n.* a fine-grained igneous rock consisting of quartz, feldspars, and mica or amphibole. [C19: *rhyo-*from Gk *rhuax* a stream of lava + -LITE] —**rhyolitic** (,raɪə'lɪtɪk) *adj.*

Rhys (riːs) *n.* **Jean (Ella Gwendolen Rees Williams).** ?1890–1979, Welsh novelist and short-story writer, born in Dominica. Her novels include *Voyage in the Dark* (1934), *Good Morning, Midnight* (1939), and *Wide Sargasso Sea* (1966).

rhythm ('rɪðəm) *n.* **1. a.** the arrangement of the durations of and accents on the notes of a melody, usually laid out into regular groups (**bars**) of beats. **b.** any specific arrangement of such groupings; time: *quadruple rhythm.* **2.** (in poetry) **a.** the arrangement of words into a sequence of stressed and unstressed or long and short syllables. **b.** any specific such arrangement; metre. **3.** (in painting, sculpture, etc.) a harmonious sequence or pattern of masses alternating with voids, of light alternating with shade, of alternating colours, etc. **4.** any sequence of regularly recurring functions or events, such as certain physiological functions of the body. [C16: from L *rhythmus,* from Gk *rhuthmos*; rel. to *rhein* to flow]

rhythm and blues *n.* (*functioning as sing.*) any of various kinds of popular music derived from or influenced by the blues. Abbrev.: **R & B.**

rhythmical ('rɪðmɪk°l) *or* **rhythmic** *adj.* of, relating to, or characterized by rhythm, as in movement or sound; metrical, periodic, or regularly recurring. —'**rhythmically** *adv.* —**rhythmicity** (rɪð'mɪsɪtɪ) *n.*

rhythm method *n.* a method of contraception by restricting sexual intercourse to those days in a woman's menstrual cycle when conception is considered least likely to occur.

rhythm section *n.* those instruments in a band or group (usually piano, double bass, and drums) whose prime function is to supply the rhythm.

RI *abbrev. for:* **1.** Regina et Imperatrix. [L: Queen and Empress] **2.** Rex et Imperator. [L: King and Emperor] **3.** Royal Institution.

ria (rɪə) *n.* a long narrow inlet of the seacoast, being a former valley that was submerged by the sea. [C19: from Sp., from *rio* river]

rialto (rɪ'æltəʊ) *n., pl.* **-tos.** a market or exchange. [C19: after the RIALTO]

Rialto (rɪ'æltəʊ) *n.* an island in Venice, Italy, linked with San Marco Island by the **Rialto Bridge** (1590) over the Grand Canal: the business centre of medieval and renaissance Venice.

riata *or* **reata** (rɪ'ɑːtə) *n.* *South & West U.S.* a lariat or lasso. [C19: from American Sp., from Sp. *reatar* to tie together again, from RE- + *atar* to tie, from L *aptāre* to fit]

rib[1] (rɪb) *n.* **1.** any of the 24 elastic arches of bone that together form the chest wall in man. All are attached behind to the thoracic part of the spinal column. **2.** the corresponding bone in other vertebrates. **3.** a cut of meat including one or more ribs. **4.** a part or element similar in function or appearance to a rib, esp. a structural member or a ridge. **5.** a structural member in a wing that extends from the leading edge to the trailing edge. **6.** a projecting moulding or band on the underside of a vault or ceiling. **7.** one of a series of raised rows in knitted fabric. **8.** a raised ornamental line on the spine of a book where the stitching runs across it. **9.** any of the transverse stiffening timbers or joists forming the frame of a ship's hull. **10.** any of the larger veins of a leaf. **11.** a vein of ore in rock. **12.** a projecting ridge of a mountain; spur. ~*vb.* **ribbing, ribbed.** (*tr.*) **13.** to furnish or support with a rib or ribs. **14.** to mark with or form into ribs or ridges. **15.** to knit plain and purl stitches alternately in order to make raised

rows in (knitting). [OE *ribb;* rel. to OHG *rippi,* ON *rif* REEF[1]] —'**ribless** *adj.*

rib[2] (rɪb) *vb.* **ribbing, ribbed.** (*tr.*) *Inf.* to tease or ridicule. [C20: short for *rib-tickle* (vb.)]

RIBA *abbrev. for* Royal Institute of British Architects.

ribald ('rɪb°ld) *adj.* **1.** coarse, obscene, or licentious, usually in a humorous or mocking way. ~*n.* **2.** a ribald person. [C13: from OF *ribauld,* from *riber* to live licentiously, of Gmc origin]

ribaldry ('rɪb°ldrɪ) *n.* ribald language or behaviour.

riband *or* **ribband** ('rɪbənd) *n.* a ribbon, esp. one awarded for some achievement. [C14: var. of RIBBON]

Ribbentrop (*German* 'rɪbəntrɔp) *n.* **Joachim von** ('joːaxɪm fɔn). 1893–1946, German Nazi politician: foreign minister under Hitler (1938–45). He was hanged after conviction as a war criminal at Nuremberg.

ribbing ('rɪbɪŋ) *n.* **1.** a framework or structure of ribs. **2.** a pattern of ribs in woven or knitted material. **3.** *Inf.* teasing.

Ribble ('rɪb°l) *n.* a river in NW England, flowing south and west through Lancashire to the Irish Sea. Length: 121 km (75 miles).

ribbon ('rɪb°n) *n.* **1.** a narrow strip of fine material, esp. silk, used for trimming, tying, etc. **2.** something resembling a ribbon; a long strip. **3.** a long thin flexible band of metal used as a graduated measure, spring, etc. **4.** a long narrow strip of ink-impregnated cloth for making the impression of type characters on paper in a typewriter, etc. **5.** (*pl.*) ragged strips or shreds (esp. in **torn to ribbons**). **6.** a small strip of coloured cloth signifying membership of an order or award of military decoration, prize, etc. ~*vb.* (*tr.*) **7.** to adorn with a ribbon or ribbons. **8.** to mark with narrow ribbon-like marks. [C14 *ryban,* from OF *riban,* apparently of Gmc origin]

ribbon development *n.* *Brit.* the building of houses in a continuous row along a main road.

ribbonfish ('rɪb°n,fɪʃ) *n., pl.* **-fish** *or* **-fishes.** any of various soft-finned deep-sea fishes that have an elongated compressed body.

ribbonwood ('rɪb°n,wʊd) *n.* a small evergreen malvaceous tree of New Zealand. Its wood is used in furniture-making. Also: **lacebark.**

ribcage ('rɪb,keɪdʒ) *n.* the bony structure of the ribs and their connective tissue that encloses the lungs, heart, etc.

Ribeirão Prêto (*Portuguese* riβai'rəu 'pretu) *n.* a city in SE Brazil, in São Paulo state. Pop.: 300 704 (1980).

Ribera (*Spanish* ri'βera) *n.* **José de** (xo'se de) also called *Jusepe de Ribera,* Italian nickname *Lo Spagnoletto* (The Little Spaniard). 1588–1652, Spanish artist, living in Italy. His religious pictures often dwell on horrible suffering, presented in realistic detail.

riboflavin *or* **riboflavine** (,raɪbəʊ'fleɪvɪn) *n.* a vitamin of the B complex that occurs in green vegetables, milk, fish, egg yolk, liver, and kidney: used as a yellow or orange food colouring (**E 101**). Also called: **vitamin B**$_2$. [C20: from RIBOSE + FLAVIN]

ribonuclease (,raɪbəʊ'njuːklɪ,eɪz) *n.* any of a group of enzymes that catalyse the hydrolysis of RNA. [C20: from RIBONUCLE(IC ACID) + -ASE]

ribonucleic acid (,raɪbəʊnju:'kliːɪk, -'kleɪ-) *n.* the full name of **RNA.** [C20: from RIBO(SE) + NUCLEIC ACID]

ribose ('raɪbəʊz, -bəʊs) *n.* a sugar that occurs in RNA and riboflavin. [C20: changed from *arabinose,* from (GUM) ARAB(IC) + -IN + -OSE[2]]

ribosomal RNA (,raɪbə'səʊməl) *n.* a type of RNA thought to form the component of ribosomes on which the translation of messenger RNA into protein chains is accomplished.

ribosome ('raɪbə,səʊm) *n.* any of numerous minute particles in the cytoplasm of cells that contain RNA and protein and are the site of protein synthesis. [C20: from RIBO(NUCLEIC ACID) + -SOME[3]] —**ribo'somal** *adj.*

rib-tickler *n.* a very amusing joke or story. —'**rib-,tickling** *adj.*

ribwort ('rɪb,wɜːt) *n.* a Eurasian plant that has lancelike ribbed leaves. Also called: **ribgrass.** See also **plantain**[1].

Ricardo (rɪ'kɑːdəʊ) *n.* **David.** 1772–1823, English economist. His main work is *Principles of Political Economy and Taxation* (1817). —**Ri'cardian** *adj., n.*

Riccio ('rɪtsɪəʊ) *n.* a variant of *Rizzio.*

rice (raɪs) *n.* **1.** an erect grass that grows in East Asia on wet ground and has yellow oblong edible grains that become white when polished. **2.** the grain of this plant.

~vb. **3.** (*tr.*) *U.S. & Canad.* to sieve (potatoes or other vegetables) to a coarse mashed consistency. [C13 *rys*, via F, It., & L from Gk *orūza*, of Oriental origin]

Rice (raɪs) *n.* **Elmer**, original name *Elmer Reizenstein.* 1892–1967, U.S. dramatist. His plays include *The Adding Machine* (1923) and *Street Scene* (1929), which was made into a musical by Kurt Weill in 1947.

rice bowl *n.* **1.** a small bowl used for eating rice. **2.** a fertile rice-producing region.

rice paper *n.* **1.** a thin edible paper made from the straw of rice, on which macaroons and similar cakes are baked. **2.** a thin delicate Chinese paper made from the **rice-paper plant**, the pith of which is pared and flattened into sheets.

rich (rɪtʃ) *adj.* **1. a.** well supplied with wealth, property, etc.; owning much. **b.** (*as collective n.; preceded by the*): *the rich.* **2.** (when *postpositive*, usually foll. by *in*) having an abundance of natural resources, minerals, etc.: *a land rich in metals.* **3.** producing abundantly; fertile: *rich soil.* **4.** (when *postpositive*, foll. by *in* or *with*) well supplied (with desirable qualities); abundant (in): *a country rich with cultural interest.* **5.** of great worth or quality: *a rich collection of antiques.* **6.** luxuriant or prolific: *a rich growth of weeds.* **7.** expensively elegant, elaborate, or fine; costly: *a rich display.* **8.** (of food) having a large proportion of flavoursome or fatty ingredients. **9.** having a full-bodied flavour: *a rich ruby port.* **10.** (of a smell) pungent or fragrant. **11.** (of colour) intense or vivid; deep: *a rich red.* **12.** (of sound or a voice) full, mellow, or resonant. **13.** (of a fuel-air mixture) containing a relatively high proportion of fuel. **14.** very amusing or ridiculous: *a rich joke.* *~n.* **15.** See **riches**. [OE *rice* (orig. of persons: great, mighty), of Gmc origin, ult. from Celtic] —**'richness** *n.*

Richard I ('rɪtʃəd) *n.* nicknamed *Coeur de Lion* or *the Lion-Heart.* 1157–99, king of England (1189–99); a leader of the third crusade (1191). On his way home, he was captured in Austria (1192) and held to ransom. After a brief return to England, where he was crowned again (1194), he spent the rest of his life in France.

Richard II *n.* 1367–1400, king of England (1377–99), whose reign was troubled by popular discontent and baronial opposition. He was forced to abdicate in favour of Henry Bolingbroke, who became Henry IV.

Richard III *n.* 1452–85, king of England (1483–85), notorious as the suspected murderer of his two young nephews in the Tower of London. He proved an able administrator until his brief reign was ended by his death at the hands of Henry Tudor (later Henry VII) at the battle of Bosworth.

Richard ('rɪtʃəd) *n.* **Cliff**, real name *Harry Rodger Webb.* born 1940, British pop singer. Film musicals include *The Young Ones* (1961) and *Summer Holiday* (1962).

Richards ('rɪtʃədz) *n.* **1. I(vor) A(rmstrong).** 1893–1979, English literary critic and linguist, who, with C. K. Ogden, wrote *The Meaning of Meaning* (1923) and devised Basic English. **2. Viv**, full name *Isaac Vivian Alexander Richards.* born 1952, West Indian cricketer; captained the West Indies from 1985.

Richardson ('rɪtʃədsən) *n.* **1. Henry Handel.** pen name of *Ethel Florence Lindesay Richardson*, 1870–1946, Australian novelist; author of the trilogy *The Fortunes of Richard Mahony* (1917–29). **2.** Sir **Owen Willans.** 1879–1959, English physicist; a pioneer in the study of atomic physics: Nobel prize for physics 1928. **3.** Sir **Ralph (David).** 1902–83, English stage and screen actor. **4. Samuel.** 1689–1761, English novelist whose psychological insight and use of the epistolary form exerted a great influence on the development of the novel. His chief novels are *Pamela* (1740) and *Clarissa* (1747).

Richelieu ('rɪʃə,ljɜː; *French* riʃəljø) *n.* **Armand Jean du Plessis** (armɑ̃ ʒɑ̃ dy plɛsi). 1585–1642, French statesman and cardinal, principal minister to Louis XIII and virtual ruler of France (1624–42). He destroyed the power of the Huguenots and strengthened the crown in France and the role of France in Europe.

Richelieu River *n.* a river in E Canada, in S Quebec, rising in Lake Champlain and flowing north to the St. Lawrence River. Length: 338 km (210 miles).

riches ('rɪtʃɪz) *pl. n.* wealth; an abundance of money, valuable possessions, or property.

Richler ('rɪʃlə) *n.* **Mordecai.** born 1931, Canadian novelist. His novels include *St Urbain's Horseman* (1971) and *Joshua Now and Then* (1981).

richly ('rɪtʃlɪ) *adv.* **1.** in a rich or elaborate manner: *a richly decorated carving.* **2.** fully and appropriately: *he was richly rewarded.*

Richmond ('rɪtʃmənd) *n.* **1.** a borough of Greater London, on the River Thames: formed in 1965 by the amalgamation of Barnes, Richmond, and Twickenham; site of Hampton Court Palace and the Royal Botanic Gardens at Kew. Pop.: 157 867 (1981). Official name: **Richmond-upon-Thames.** **2.** a town in N England, in North Yorkshire. Pop.: 7731 (1981). **3.** a port in E Virginia, the state capital, at the falls of the James River: developed after the establishment of a trading post (1637); scene of the Virginia Conventions of 1774 and 1775; Confederate capital in the American Civil War. Pop.: 217 700 (1986). **4.** a borough of SW New York City: consists of Staten Island and several smaller islands. Pop.: 219 214 (1970).

Richter *n.* **1.** (*German* 'rɪçtər). **Johann Friedrich** (jo'han 'friːdrɪç), wrote under the name *Jean Paul.* 1763–1825, German romantic novelist. His works include *Hesperus* (1795) and *Titan* (1800–03). **2.** (*Russian* 'rɪxtɪr). **Sviatoslav** (svɪtɑ'slaf). born 1914, Soviet concert pianist.

Richter scale ('rɪxtə) *n.* a scale for expressing the magnitude of an earthquake, ranging from 0 to over 8. [C20: after Charles *Richter* (1900–85), U.S. seismologist]

Richthofen (*German* 'rɪçthoːfən) *n.* Baron **Manfred von** ('manfreːt fɔn), nickname *the Red Baron.* 1892–1918, German aviator; commander during World War I of the 11th Chasing Squadron (**Richthofen's Flying Circus**). He was credited with 80 air victories before he was shot down.

rick[1] (rɪk) *n.* **1.** a large stack of hay, corn, etc., built in a regular-shaped pile, esp. with a thatched top. *~vb.* **2.** (*tr.*) to stack into ricks. [OE *hrēac*]

rick[2] (rɪk) *n.* **1.** a wrench or sprain, as of the back. *~vb.* **2.** (*tr.*) to wrench or sprain (a joint, a limb, the back, etc.). [C18: var. of *wrick*]

rickets ('rɪkɪts) *n.* (*functioning as sing. or pl.*) a disease mainly of children, characterized by softening of developing bone, and hence bow legs, caused by a deficiency of vitamin D. [C17: from ?]

rickettsia (rɪ'kɛtsɪə) *n., pl.* **-siae** (-sɪ,iː) *or* **-sias.** any of a group of parasitic microorganisms, that live in the tissues of ticks, mites, etc., and cause disease when transmitted to man. [C20: after Howard T. *Ricketts* (1871–1910), U.S. pathologist] —**rick'ettsial** *adj.*

rickettsial disease *n.* any of several acute infectious diseases, such as typhus, caused by ticks, mites, or body lice infected with rickettsiae.

rickety ('rɪkɪtɪ) *adj.* **1.** (of a structure, piece of furniture, etc.) likely to collapse or break. **2.** feeble. **3.** resembling or afflicted with rickets. [C17: from RICKETS] —**'ricketiness** *n.*

rickrack *or* **ricrac** ('rɪk,ræk) *n.* a zigzag braid used for trimming. [C20: reduplication of RACK[1]]

rickshaw ('rɪkʃɔː) *or* **ricksha** ('rɪkʃə) *n.* **1.** Also called: **jinrikisha.** a small two-wheeled passenger vehicle drawn by one or two men, used in parts of Asia. **2.** Also called: **trishaw.** a similar vehicle with three wheels, propelled by a man pedalling as on a tricycle. [C19: shortened from JINRIKISHA]

ricochet ('rɪkə,ʃeɪ, 'rɪkə,ʃɛt) *vb.* **-cheting** (-,ʃeɪɪŋ), **-cheted** (-,ʃeɪd) *or* **-chetting** (-,ʃɛtɪŋ), **-chetted** (-,ʃɛtɪd). **1.** (*intr.*) (esp. of a bullet) to rebound from a surface, usually with a whining or zipping sound. *~n.* **2.** the motion or sound of a rebounding object, esp. a bullet. **3.** an object that ricochets. [C18: from F, from ?]

ricotta (rɪ'kɒtə) *n.* a soft white unsalted cheese made from sheep's milk. [It., from L *recocta* recooked, from *recoquere*, from RE- + *coquere* to COOK]

RICS *abbrev. for* Royal Institution of Chartered Surveyors.

rictus ('rɪktəs) *n., pl.* **-tus** *or* **-tuses.** **1.** the gap or cleft of an open mouth or beak. **2.** a fixed or unnatural grin or grimace as in horror or death. [C18: from L, from *ringi* to gape] —**'rictal** *adj.*

rid (rɪd) *vb.* **ridding, rid** *or* **ridded.** (*tr.*) **1.** (foll. by *of*) to relieve from something disagreeable or undesirable; make free (of). **2. get rid of.** to relieve or free oneself of (something unpleasant or undesirable). [C13 (meaning: to clear land): from ON *rythja*]

riddance ('rɪd³ns) *n.* the act of getting rid of something; removal (esp. in **good riddance**).

ridden ('rɪdᵊn) vb. **1.** the past participle of **ride.** ~adj. **2.** (in combination) afflicted or dominated by something specified: disease-ridden.

riddle[1] ('rɪdᵊl) n. **1.** a question, puzzle, or verse so phrased that ingenuity is required for elucidation of the answer or meaning. **2.** a person or thing that puzzles, perplexes, or confuses. ~vb. **3.** to solve, explain, or interpret (a riddle). **4.** (intr.) to speak in riddles. [OE rædelle, rædelse, from ræd counsel] —'**riddler** n.

riddle[2] ('rɪdᵊl) vb. (tr.) **1.** (usually foll. by with) to pierce or perforate with numerous holes: riddled with bullets. **2.** to put through a sieve; sift. ~n. **3.** a sieve, esp. a coarse one used for sand, grain, etc. [OE hriddel a sieve] —'**riddler** n.

ride (raɪd) vb. **riding, rode, ridden. 1.** to sit on and control the movements of (a horse or other animal). **2.** (tr.) to sit on and propel (a bicycle or similar vehicle). **3.** (intr.; often foll. by on or in) to be carried along or travel on or in a vehicle: she rides to work on the bus. **4.** (tr.) to travel over or traverse: they rode the countryside in search of shelter. **5.** (tr.) to take part in by riding: to ride a race. **6.** to travel through or be carried across (sea, sky, etc.): the small boat rode the waves; the moon was riding high. **7.** (tr.) U.S. & Canad. to cause to be carried: to ride someone out of town. **8.** (intr.) to be supported as if floating: the candidate rode to victory on his new policies. **9.** (intr.) (of a vessel) to lie at anchor. **10.** (tr.) (of a vessel) to be attached to (an anchor). **11.** (tr.) (esp. of a male animal) to copulate with; mount. **12.** (tr.; usually passive) to tyrannize over or dominate: ridden by fear. **13.** (tr.) Inf. to persecute, esp. by constant or petty criticism: don't ride me so hard. **14.** (intr.) Inf. to continue undisturbed: let it ride. **15.** (tr.) to endure successfully; ride out. **16.** (tr.) to yield slightly to (a punch, etc.) to lessen its impact. **17.** (intr.; often foll. by on) (of a bet) to remain placed: let your winnings ride on the same number. **18. ride again.** Inf. to return to a former activity or scene. **19. ride for a fall.** to act in such a way as to invite disaster. **20. riding high.** confident, popular, and successful. ~n. **21.** a journey or outing on horseback or in a vehicle. **22.** a path specially made for riding on horseback. **23.** transport in a vehicle; lift: can you give me a ride to the station? **24.** a device or structure, such as a roller coaster at a fairground, in which people ride for pleasure or entertainment. **25. take for a ride.** Inf. **a.** to cheat, swindle, or deceive. **b.** to take (someone) away in a car and murder him. [OE rīdan] —'**ridable** or '**rideable** adj.

ride out vb. (tr., adv.) to endure successfully; survive (esp. in **ride out the storm**).

rider ('raɪdə) n. **1.** a person or thing that rides. **2.** an additional clause, amendment, or stipulation added to a document, esp. (in Britain) a legislative bill at its third reading. **3.** Brit. a statement made by a jury in addition to its verdict, such as a recommendation for mercy. **4.** any of various objects or devices resting on or strengthening something else. —'**riderless** adj.

ride up vb. (intr., adv.) to work away from the proper position: her new skirt rode up.

ridge (rɪdʒ) n. **1.** a long narrow raised land formation with sloping sides. **2.** any long narrow raised strip or elevation, as on a fabric or in a ploughed land. **3.** Anat. any elongated raised margin or border on a bone, tissue, etc. **4. a.** the top of a roof at the junction of two sloping sides. **b.** (as modifier): a ridge tile. **5.** Meteorol. an elongated area of high pressure, esp. an extension of an anticyclone. Cf. **trough** (sense 4). ~vb. **6.** to form into a ridge or ridges. [OE hrycg] —'**ridge,like** adj. —'**ridgy** adj.

ridgepole ('rɪdʒ,pəʊl) n. **1.** a timber along the ridge of a roof, to which the rafters are attached. **2.** the horizontal pole at the apex of a tent.

ridgeway ('rɪdʒ,weɪ) n. Brit. a road or track along a ridge, esp. one of great antiquity.

ridicule ('rɪdɪ,kjuːl) n. **1.** language or behaviour intended to humiliate or mock. ~vb. **2.** (tr.) to make fun of or mock. [C17: from F, from L rīdiculus, from rīdēre to laugh]

ridiculous (rɪ'dɪkjʊləs) adj. worthy of or exciting ridicule; absurd, preposterous, laughable, or contemptible. [C16: from L rīdiculōsus, from rīdēre to laugh] —**ri'diculousness** n.

riding[1] ('raɪdɪŋ) n. **1. a.** the art or practice of horsemanship. **b.** (as modifier): a riding school. **2.** a track for riding.

riding[2] ('raɪdɪŋ) n. (cap. when part of a name) any of the three former administrative divisions of Yorkshire: **North Riding, East Riding,** and **West Riding.** [from OE thriding, from ON thrithjungr a third]

riding crop n. a short whip with a handle at one end for opening gates.

riding lamp or **light** n. a light on a boat or ship showing that it is at anchor.

Ridley ('rɪdlɪ) n. **Nicholas.** ?1500–55, English bishop, who helped to revise the liturgy under Edward VI. He was burnt at the stake for refusing to disavow his Protestant beliefs when Mary I assumed the throne.

Riefenstahl (German 'riːfənʃtaːl) n. **Leni.** ('leːni). born 1902, German photographer and film director, best known for her Nazi propaganda films, such as Triumph of the Will (1934).

Riemann (German 'riːman) n. **Georg Friedrich Bernhard** ('geːork 'friːdrɪç 'bɛrnhart). 1826–66, German mathematician whose non-Euclidean geometry was used by Einstein as a basis for his general theory of relativity. —**Rie'mannian** adj.

riempie ('rɪmpɪ) n. S. African. a leather thong or lace used mainly to make chair seats. [C19: Afrik., dim. of riem, from Du.: RIM]

Rienzi (rɪ'ɛnzɪ; Italian 'rjɛntsi) or **Rienzo** (rɪ'ɛnzəʊ; Italian 'rjɛntso) n. **Cola di** ('kɔːla di). 1313–54, Italian radical political reformer in Rome.

riesling ('riːzlɪŋ, 'raɪz-) n. **1.** a dry white wine from the Rhine valley in Germany and from certain districts in other countries. **2.** the grape used to make this wine. [C19: from G, from earlier Rüssling, from ?]

rife (raɪf) adj. (postpositive) **1.** of widespread occurrence; current. **2.** very plentiful; abundant. **3.** (foll. by with) rich or abounding (in): a garden rife with flowers. [OE rīfe] —'**rifely** adv. —'**rifeness** n.

riff (rɪf) Jazz, rock. ~n. **1.** an ostinato played over changing harmonies. ~vb. **2.** (intr.) to play riffs. [C20: prob. altered from REFRAIN[2]]

riffle ('rɪfᵊl) vb. **1.** (when intr., often foll. by through) to flick rapidly through (pages of a book, etc.). **2.** to shuffle (cards) by halving the pack and flicking the corners together. **3.** to make or become a riffle. ~n. **4.** U.S. & Canad. **a.** a rapid in a stream. **b.** a rocky shoal causing a rapid. **c.** a ripple on water. **5.** Mining. a contrivance on the bottom of a sluice, containing grooves for trapping particles of gold. **6.** the act or an instance of riffling. [C18: prob. from RUFFLE[1], infl. by RIPPLE[1]]

riffraff ('rɪf,ræf) n. (sometimes functioning as pl.) worthless people, esp. collectively; rabble. [C15 rif and raf, from OF rif et raf; rel. to rifler to plunder, and rafle a sweeping up]

rifle[1] ('raɪfᵊl) n. **1. a.** a firearm having a long barrel with a spirally grooved interior, which imparts to the bullet spinning motion and thus greater accuracy over a longer range. **b.** (as modifier): rifle fire. **2.** (formerly) a large cannon with a rifled bore. **3.** one of the grooves in a rifled bore. **4.** (pl.) a unit of soldiers equipped with rifles. **5.** (cap. when part of a name): the King's Own Rifles. ~vb. (tr.) **5.** to make spiral grooves inside the barrel of (a gun). [C18: from OF rifler to scratch; rel. to Low G rifeln from riefe groove]

rifle[2] ('raɪfᵊl) vb. (tr.) **1.** to search (a house, safe, etc.) and steal from it; ransack. **2.** to steal and carry off: to rifle goods. [C14: from OF rifler to plunder, scratch, of Gmc origin] —'**rifler** n.

riflebird ('raɪfᵊl,bɜːd) n. any of various Australian birds of paradise whose plumage has a metallic sheen.

rifleman ('raɪfᵊlmən) n., pl. **-men. 1.** a person skilled in the use of a rifle, esp. a soldier. **2.** a wren of New Zealand.

rifle range n. an area used for target practice with rifles.

rifling ('raɪflɪŋ) n. **1.** the cutting of spiral grooves on the inside of a firearm's barrel. **2.** the series of grooves so cut.

rift (rɪft) n. **1.** a gap or space made by cleaving or splitting. **2.** Geol. a fault produced by tension on either side of the fault plane. **3.** a gap between two cloud masses; break or chink. **4.** a break in friendly relations between people, nations, etc. ~vb. **5.** to burst or cause to burst open; split. [C13: from ON]

rift valley *n.* a long narrow valley resulting from the subsidence of land between two faults.

rig (rɪg) *vb.* **rigging, rigged.** (*tr.*) **1.** *Naut.* to equip (a vessel, mast, etc.) with (sails, rigging, etc.). **2.** *Naut.* to set up or prepare ready for use. **3.** to put the components of (an aircraft, etc.) into their correct positions. **4.** to manipulate in a fraudulent manner, esp. for profit: *to rig prices.* ~*n.* **5.** *Naut.* the distinctive arrangement of the sails, masts, etc., of a vessel. **6.** the installation used in drilling for and exploiting natural gas and oil deposits: *an oil rig.* **7.** apparatus or equipment. **8.** *U.S. & Canad.* an articulated lorry. ~See also **rig out, rig up.** [C15: of Scand. origin; rel. to Norwegian *rigga* to wrap]

Riga ('riːgə) *n.* a port in the W Soviet Union, capital of the Latvian SSR, on the **Gulf of Riga** at the mouth of the Western Dvina: a major trading centre of the Baltic since Viking times. Pop.: 900 000 (1987).

rigadoon (ˌrɪgə'duːn) *n.* **1.** an old Provençal couple dance, light and graceful, in lively duple time. **2.** a piece of music composed for or in the rhythm of this dance. [C17: from F, allegedly after *Rigaud*, a dancing master at Marseilles]

rigamarole ('rɪgəməˌrəʊl) *n.* a variant of **rigmarole.**

-rigged *adj.* (*in combination*) (of a sailing vessel) having a rig of a certain kind: *ketch-rigged; schooner-rigged.*

rigger ('rɪgə) *n.* **1.** a workman who rigs vessels, etc. **2.** *Rowing.* a bracket on a boat to support a projecting rowlock. **3.** a person skilled in the use of pulleys, cranes, etc.

rigging ('rɪgɪŋ) *n.* **1.** the shrouds, stays, etc., of a vessel. **2.** the bracing wires, struts, and lines of a biplane, etc. **3.** any form of lifting gear.

right (raɪt) *adj.* **1.** in accordance with accepted standards of moral or legal behaviour, justice, etc.: *right conduct.* **2.** correct or true: *the right answer.* **3.** appropriate, suitable, or proper: *the right man for the job.* **4.** most favourable or convenient: *the right time to act.* **5.** in a satisfactory condition: *things are right again now.* **6.** indicating or designating the correct time: *the clock is right.* **7.** correct in opinion or judgment. **8.** sound in mind or body. **9.** (*usually prenominal*) of, designating, or located near the side of something or someone that faces east when the front is turned towards the north. **10.** (*usually prenominal*) worn on a right hand, foot, etc. **11.** (*sometimes cap.*) of, designating, belonging to, or relating to the political or intellectual right (see sense 36). **12.** (*sometimes cap.*) conservative: *the right wing of the party.* **13.** *Geom.* **a.** formed by or containing a line or plane perpendicular to another line or plane. **b.** having the axis perpendicular to the base: *a right circular cone.* **c.** straight: *a right line.* **14.** relating to or designating the side of cloth worn or facing outwards. **15. in one's right mind.** sane. **16. she'll be right.** *Austral. & N.Z. inf.* that's all right; not to worry. **17. the right side of. a.** in favour with: *you'd better stay on the right side of him.* **b.** younger than: *she's still on the right side of fifty.* **18. too right.** *Austral. & N.Z. inf.* an exclamation of agreement. ~*adv.* **19.** in accordance with correctness or truth: *to guess right.* **20.** in the appropriate manner: *do it right next time!* **21.** in a straight line: *right to the top.* **22.** in the direction of the east from the point of view of a person or thing facing north. **23.** absolutely or completely: *he went right through the floor.* **24.** all the way: *the bus goes right into town.* **25.** without delay: *I'll be right over.* **26.** exactly or precisely: *right here.* **27.** in a manner consistent with a legal or moral code: *do right by me.* **28.** in accordance with propriety; fittingly: *it serves you right.* **29.** to good or favourable advantage: *it all came out right in the end.* **30.** (esp. in religious titles) most or very: *right reverend.* **31. right, left, and centre.** on all sides. ~*n.* **32.** any claim, title, etc., that is morally just or legally granted as allowable or due to a person: *I know my rights.* **33.** anything that accords with the principles of legal or moral justice. **34.** the fact or state of being in accordance with reason, truth, or accepted standards (esp. in **in the right**). **35.** the right side, direction, position, area, or part: *the right of the army.* **36.** (*often cap.* and preceded by *the*) the supporters or advocates of social, political, or economic conservatism or reaction. **37.** *Boxing.* **a.** a punch with the right hand. **b.** the right hand. **38.** (*often pl.*) *Finance.* the privilege of a company's shareholders to subscribe for new issues of the company's shares on advantageous terms. **39. by right** (*or* **rights**). properly: *by rights you should be in bed.* **40. in**

one's own right. having a claim or title oneself rather than through marriage or other connection. **41. to rights.** consistent with justice or orderly arrangement: *he put the matter to rights.* ~*vb.* (*mainly tr.*) **42.** (*also intr.*) to restore to or attain a normal, esp. an upright, position: *the raft righted in a few seconds.* **43.** to make (something) accord with truth or facts. **44.** to restore to an orderly state or condition. **45.** to compensate for or redress (esp. in **right a wrong**). ~*interj.* **46.** an expression of agreement or compliance. [OE *riht, reoht*] —'**rightable** *adj.* —'**righter** *n.* —'**rightness** *n.*

right about *n.* **1.** a turn executed through 180°. ~*adj., adv.* **2.** in the opposite direction.

right angle *n.* **1.** the angle between radii of a circle that cut off on the circumference an arc equal in length to one quarter of the circumference; an angle of 90° or $\pi/2$ radians. **2. at right angles.** perpendicular or perpendicularly. —'**right-,angled** *adj.*

right-angled triangle *n.* a triangle one angle of which is a right angle. U.S. and Canad. name: **right triangle.**

right ascension *n.* *Astron.* the angular distance measured eastwards along the celestial equator from the vernal equinox to the point at which the celestial equator intersects a great circle passing through the celestial pole and the heavenly object in question.

right away *adv.* without delay.

righteous ('raɪtʃəs) *adj.* **1. a.** characterized by, proceeding from, or in accordance with accepted standards of morality, justice, or uprightness: *a righteous man.* **b.** (*as collective n.; preceded by the*): *the righteous.* **2.** morally justifiable or right: *righteous indignation.* [OE *rīhtwīs,* from RIGHT + WISE[2]] —'**righteously** *adv.* —'**righteousness** *n.*

rightful ('raɪtful) *adj.* **1.** in accordance with what is right. **2.** (*prenominal*) having a legally or morally just claim: *the rightful owner.* **3.** (*prenominal*) held by virtue of a legal or just claim: *my rightful property.* —'**rightfully** *adv.*

right-hand *adj.* (*prenominal*) **1.** of, located on, or moving towards the right: *a right-hand bend.* **2.** for use by the right hand. **3. right-hand man.** one's most valuable assistant.

right-handed *adj.* **1.** using the right hand with greater skill or ease than the left. **2.** performed with the right hand. **3.** made for use by the right hand. **4.** turning from left to right. —,**right-'handedness** *n.*

rightist ('raɪtɪst) *adj.* **1.** of, tending towards, or relating to the political right or its principles. ~*n.* **2.** a person who supports or belongs to the political right. —'**rightism** *n.*

rightly ('raɪtlɪ) *adv.* **1.** in accordance with the true facts. **2.** in accordance with principles of justice or morality. **3.** with good reason: *he was rightly annoyed with her.* **4.** properly or suitably. **5.** (*used with a negative*) *Inf.* with certainty (usually in **I don't rightly know**).

right-minded *adj.* holding opinions or principles that accord with what is right or with the opinions of the speaker.

righto *or* **right oh** ('raɪt'əʊ) *sentence substitute. Brit. inf.* an expression of agreement or compliance.

right off *adv.* immediately; right away.

right of way *n., pl.* **rights of way. 1.** the right of one vehicle or vessel to take precedence over another, as laid down by law or custom. **2. a.** the legal right of someone to pass over another's land, acquired by grant or by long usage. **b.** the path used by this right. **3.** *U.S.* the strip of land over which a power line, road, etc., extends.

right-on *adj. Inf.* modern, trendy, and socially aware or relevant: *a suitably right-on title like 'The workers control the means of production'.*

Right Reverend *adj.* (in Britain) a title of respect for an Anglican or Roman Catholic bishop.

rights issue *n. Stock Exchange.* an issue of new shares offered by a company to its existing shareholders on favourable terms.

right-thinking ('raɪt'θɪŋkɪŋ) *adj.* possessing reasonable and generally acceptable opinions.

rightward ('raɪtwəd) *adj.* **1.** situated on or directed towards the right. ~*adv.* **2.** a variant of **rightwards.**

rightwards ('raɪtwədz) *or* **rightward** *adv.* towards or on the right.

right whale *n.* a large whalebone whale which is grey or black, has a large head and no dorsal fin, and is hunted as a source of whalebone and oil. [C19: ? because it was *right* for hunting]

right wing *n.* **1.** (*often cap.*) the conservative faction of an assembly, party, etc. **2.** the part of an army or field of battle on the right from the point of view of one facing the enemy. **3. a.** the right-hand side of the field of play from the point of view of a team facing its opponent's goal. **b.** a player positioned in this area in any of various games. ~*adj.* **right-wing. 4.** of, belonging to, or relating to the right wing. — **'right-'winger** *n.*

Rigi ('ri:gɪ) *n.* a mountain in the Alps of N central Switzerland, between Lakes Lucerne, Zug, and Lauerz.

rigid ('rɪdʒɪd) *adj.* **1.** physically inflexible or stiff: *a rigid piece of plastic.* **2.** rigorously strict: *rigid rules.* [C16: from L *rigidus,* from *rigēre* to be stiff] —**ri'gidity** *n.* —**'rigidly** *adv.*

rigidify (rɪ'dʒɪdɪˌfaɪ) *vb.* **-fying, -fied.** to make or become rigid.

rigmarole ('rɪgməˌrəʊl) *or* **rigamarole** *n.* **1.** any long complicated procedure. **2.** a set of incoherent or pointless statements. [C18: from earlier *ragman roll* a list, prob. a roll used in a medieval game, wherein characters were described in verse, beginning with *Ragemon le bon Ragman the good*]

rigor ('raɪgɔ:, 'rɪgə) *n.* **1.** *Med.* a sudden feeling of chilliness, often accompanied by shivering: it sometimes precedes a fever. **2.** ('rɪgə). *Pathol.* rigidity of a muscle. **3.** a state of rigidity assumed in reaction to shock. [see RIGOUR]

rigor mortis ('rɪgə 'mɔ:tɪs) *n. Pathol.* the stiffness of joints and muscular rigidity of a dead body. [C19: L, lit.: rigidity of death]

rigorous ('rɪgərəs) *adj.* **1.** harsh, strict, or severe: *rigorous discipline.* **2.** severely accurate: *rigorous book-keeping.* **3.** (esp. of weather) extreme or harsh. **4.** *Maths, logic.* (of a proof) making the validity of each step explicit. — **'rigorously** *adv.*

rigour *or U.S.* **rigor** ('rɪgə) *n.* **1.** harsh but just treatment or action. **2.** a severe or cruel circumstance: *the rigours of famine.* **3.** strictness, harshness, or severity of character. **4.** strictness in judgment or conduct. [C14: from L *rigor*]

rig out *vb.* **1.** (*tr., adv.;* often foll. by *with*) to equip or fit out (with): *his car is rigged out with gadgets.* **2.** to dress or be dressed: *rigged out smartly.* ~*n.* **rigout. 3.** *Inf.* a person's clothing or costume, esp. a bizarre outfit.

rig up *vb.* (*tr., adv.*) to erect or construct, esp. as a temporary measure: *cameras were rigged up to televise the event.*

Rig-Veda (rɪg'veɪdə) *n.* a compilation of Hindu poems dating from 2000 B.C. or earlier. [C18: from Sansk. *rigveda,* from *ric* song of praise + VEDA]

Rijeka (rɪ'ɛkə; *Serbo-Croatian* ri'jɛka) *n.* a port in NW Yugoslavia, in Croatia: an ancient town, changing hands many times before passing to Yugoslavia in 1947. Pop.: 193 044 (1983). Italian name: **Fiume.**

Rijksmuseum ('raɪxsmjuːˌzɪəm) *n.* a museum in Amsterdam housing the national art collection of the Netherlands.

Rijn (rɛjn) *n.* the Dutch name for the **Rhine.**

Rijswijk ('raɪsvaɪk; *Dutch* 'rɛjswɛjk) *n.* a town in the SW Netherlands, in South Holland province on the SE outskirts of The Hague: scene of the signing (1697) of the **Treaty of Rijswijk,** ending the War of the Grand Alliance. Pop.: 51 378 (1982 est.). English name: **Ryswick.**

rile (raɪl) *vb.* (*tr.*) **1.** to annoy or anger. **2.** *U.S. & Canad.* to agitate (water, etc.). [C19: var. of ROIL]

Rilke ('rɪlkə) *n.* **Rainer Maria** ('raɪnər ma'riːa). 1875–1926, Austro-German poet, born in Prague. Author of intense visionary lyrics, notably in the *Duino Elegies* (1922) and *Sonnets to Orpheus* (1923).

rill (rɪl) *n.* **1.** a brook or stream. **2.** a small channel or gulley, such as one formed during soil erosion. **3.** Also: **rille.** one of many winding cracks on the moon. [C15: from Low G *rille*]

rim (rɪm) *n.* **1.** the raised edge of an object, esp. of something more or less circular such as a cup or crater. **2.** the peripheral part of a wheel, to which the tyre is attached. **3.** *Basketball.* the hoop from which the net is suspended. ~*vb.* **rimming, rimmed.** (*tr.*) **4.** to put a rim on (a pot, cup, wheel, etc.). [OE *rima*]

Rimbaud (*French* rɛ̃bo) *n.* **Arthur** (artyr). 1854–91, French poet, whose work, culminating in the prose poetry of *Illuminations* (published 1884), greatly influenced the

symbolists. *A Season in Hell* (1873) draws on his tempestuous homosexual affair with Verlaine, after which he abandoned writing (aged about 20) and spent the rest of his life travelling.

rime[1] (raɪm) *n.* **1.** frost formed by the freezing of water droplets in fog onto solid objects. ~*vb.* **2.** (*tr.*) to cover with rime or something resembling rime. [OE *hrīm*]

rime[2] (raɪm) *n., vb.* an archaic spelling of **rhyme.**

rim-fire *adj.* **1.** (of a cartridge) having the primer in the rim of the base. **2.** (of a firearm) adapted for such cartridges.

Rimini ('rɪmɪnɪ) *n.* a port and resort in NE Italy, in Emilia-Romagna on the N Adriatic coast. Pop.: 130 698 (1986). Ancient name: **Ariminum.**

rimose (raɪ'məʊs, -'məʊz) *adj.* (esp. of plant parts) having the surface marked by a network of cracks. [C18: from L *rīmōsus,* from *rīma* a split]

Rimsky-Korsakov ('rɪmskɪ'kɔːsəkɒf; *Russian* 'rimskij-'kɔrsəkəf) *n.* **Nikolai Andreyevich** (nika'laj an'drjejivitʃ). 1844–1908, Russian composer; noted for such works as the orchestral suite *Scheherazade* (1888) and the opera *Le Coq d'or* (first performed in 1910).

rimu ('riːmuː) *n.* a New Zealand tree. Also called: **red pine.** [from Maori]

rimy ('raɪmɪ) *adj.* **rimier, rimiest.** coated with rime.

rind (raɪnd) *n.* **1.** a hard outer layer or skin on bacon, cheese, etc. **2.** the outer layer of a fruit or of the spore-producing body of certain fungi. **3.** the outer layer of the bark of a tree. [OE *rinde*]

rinderpest ('rɪndəˌpɛst) *n.* an acute contagious viral disease of cattle, characterized by severe inflammation of the intestinal tract and diarrhoea. [C19: from G *Rinderpest* cattle pest]

ring[1] (rɪŋ) *n.* **1.** a circular band of a precious metal often set with gems and worn upon the finger as an adornment or as a token of engagement or marriage. **2.** any object or mark that is circular in shape. **3.** a circular path or course: *to run around in a ring.* **4.** a group of people or things standing or arranged so as to form a circle: *a ring of spectators.* **5.** an enclosed space, usually circular in shape, where circus acts are performed. **6.** a square raised platform, marked off by ropes, in which contestants box or wrestle. **7. the ring.** the sport of boxing. **8.** throw one's hat in the ring. to announce one's intention to be a candidate or contestant. **9.** a group of people, usually illegal, cooperating for the purpose of controlling the market in antiques, etc. **10.** (esp. at country fairs) an enclosure where horses, cattle, and other livestock are paraded and auctioned. **11.** an area reserved for betting at a racecourse. **12.** a circular strip of bark cut from a tree or branch. **13.** a single turn in a spiral. **14.** *Geom.* the area of space lying between two concentric circles. **15.** *Maths.* a set that is subject to two binary operations, addition and multiplication, such that the set is a commutative group under addition and is closed under multiplication, this latter operation being associative. **16.** *Bot.* short for **annual ring. 17.** *Chem.* a closed loop of atoms in a molecule. **18.** one of the systems of circular bands orbiting the planets Saturn and Uranus. **19. run rings around.** *Inf.* to outclass completely. ~*vb.* **ringing, ringed.** (*tr.*) **20.** to surround with, or as if with, or form a ring. **21.** to mark a bird with a ring or clip for subsequent identification. **22.** to fit a ring in the nose of (a bull, etc.) so that it can be led easily. **23.** to ringbark. [OE *hring*] —**ringed** *adj.*

ring[2] (rɪŋ) *vb.* **ringing, rang, rung. 1.** to emit or cause to emit a resonant sound, characteristic of certain metals when struck. **2.** to cause (a bell, etc.) to emit a ringing sound by striking it once or repeatedly or (of a bell) to emit such a sound. **3. a.** (*tr.*) to cause (a large bell) to emit a ringing sound by pulling on a rope attached to a wheel on which the bell swings back and forth, being sounded by a clapper inside it. **b.** (*intr.*) (of a bell) to sound by being swung in this way. **4.** (*intr.*) (of a building, place, etc.) to be filled with sound: *the church rang with singing.* **5.** (*intr.*; foll. by *for*) to call by means of a bell, etc.: *to ring for the butler.* **6.** Also: **ring up.** *Chiefly Brit.* to call (a person) by telephone. **7.** (*tr.*) to strike or tap (a coin) in order to assess its genuineness by the sound produced. **8.** (*intr.*) (of the ears) to have or give the sensation of humming or ringing. **9. ring a bell.** to bring something to the mind or memory: *that rings a bell.* **10. ring down the curtain. a.** to lower the curtain at the end of a theatrical performance. **b.** (foll. by *on*) to put an end (to). **11. ring false.** to give the impression of being false. **12. ring true.** to give the impression of being true. ~*n.* **13.** the act of or a sound made by ringing. **14.** a sound produced by or suggestive of a bell. **15.** any resonant or metallic sound: *the ring of trumpets.* **16.** *Inf.*, *chiefly Brit.* a telephone call. **17.** the complete set of bells in a tower or belfry: *a ring of eight bells.* **18.** an inherent quality or characteristic: *his explanation has the ring of sincerity.* ~See also **ring in, ring off,** etc. [OE *hringan*]

▷ *Usage. Rang* and *sang* are the correct forms of the past tenses of *ring* and *sing*, although *rung* and *sung* are still heard informally and dialectally: *he rung (rang) the bell.*

ringbark ('rıŋ,baːk) *vb.* (*tr.*) to kill (a tree) by cutting away a strip of bark from around the trunk.

ring binder *n.* a loose-leaf binder with metal rings that can be opened to insert perforated paper.

ringbolt ('rıŋ,bəʊlt) *n.* a bolt with a ring fitted through an eye attached to the bolt head.

ringdove ('rıŋ,dʌv) *n.* **1.** another name for **wood pigeon. 2.** an Old World turtledove, having a black band around the neck.

ringed plover *n.* a European shorebird with a greyish-brown back, white underparts, a black throat band, and orange legs.

ringer ('rıŋə) *n.* **1.** a person or thing that rings a bell, etc. **2.** Also called: **dead ringer.** *Sl.* a person or thing that is almost identical to another. **3.** *Chiefly U.S.* a contestant, esp. a horse, entered in a competition under false representations of identity, record, or ability. **4.** *Austral.* a stockman; station hand. **5.** *Austral.* the fastest shearer in a shed. **6.** *Austral. inf.* the fastest or best at anything. **7.** a quoit thrown so as to encircle a peg. **8.** such a throw.

ring finger *n.* the third finger, esp. of the left hand, on which a wedding ring is worn.

ringhals ('rıŋ,hæls) or **rinkhals** *n.*, *pl.* **-hals** or **-halses.** a venomous snake of southern Africa, which spits venom at its enemies from a distance. [Afrik., lit.: ring neck]

ring in *vb.* (*adv.*) **1.** (*intr.*) *Chiefly Brit.* to report to someone by telephone. **2.** (*tr.*) to accompany the arrival of with bells (esp. in **ring in the new year**). ~*n.* **ring-in. 3.** *Austral. & N.Z. sl.* a person or thing that is not normally a member of a particular group; outsider.

ringing tone *n. Brit.* a sequence of pairs of tones heard by the dialler on a telephone when the number dialled is ringing. Cf. **engaged tone, dialling tone.**

ringleader ('rıŋ,liːdə) *n.* a person who leads others in unlawful or mischievous activity.

ringlet ('rıŋlıt) *n.* **1.** a lock of hair hanging down in a spiral curl. **2.** a butterfly that occurs in S Europe and has dark brown wings marked with small black-and-white eyespots. —'**ringleted** *adj.*

ring main *n.* a domestic electrical supply in which outlet sockets are connected to the mains supply through a continuous closed circuit (**ring circuit**).

ringmaster ('rıŋ,maːstə) *n.* the master of ceremonies in a circus.

ring-necked *adj.* (of animals, esp. certain birds and snakes) having a band of distinctive colour around the neck.

ring-necked pheasant *n.* a common pheasant originating in Asia. The male has a bright plumage with a band of white around the neck and the female is mottled brown.

ring off *vb.* (*intr., adv.*) *Chiefly Brit.* to terminate a telephone conversation by replacing the receiver; hang up.

ring out *vb.* (*adv.*) **1.** (*tr.*) to accompany the departure of with bells (esp. in **ring out the old year**). **2.** (*intr.*) to send forth a loud resounding noise.

ring ouzel *n.* a European thrush common in rocky areas. The male has a blackish plumage and the female is brown.

ring road *n.* a main road that bypasses a town or town centre. U.S. names: **belt, beltway.**

ringside ('rıŋ,saıd) *n.* **1.** the row of seats nearest a boxing or wrestling ring. **2. a.** any place affording a close uninterrupted view. **b.** (*as modifier*): *a ringside seat.*

ringtail ('rıŋ,teıl) *n. Austral.* any of several tree-living phalangers having curling prehensile tails used to grasp branches while climbing.

ring up *vb.* (*adv.*) **1.** *Chiefly Brit.* to make a telephone call (to). **2.** (*tr.*) to record on a cash register. **3. ring up the curtain. a.** to begin a theatrical performance. **b.** (often foll. by *on*) to make a start (on).

ringworm ('rıŋ,wɜːm) *n.* any of various fungal infections of the skin or nails, often appearing as itching circular patches. Also called: **tinea.**

rink (rıŋk) *n.* **1.** an expanse of ice for skating on, esp. one that is artificially prepared and under cover. **2.** an area for roller-skating on. **3.** a building or enclosure for ice-skating or roller-skating. **4.** *Bowls.* a strip of the green on which a game is played. **5.** *Curling.* the strip of ice on which the game is played. **6.** (in bowls and curling) the players on one side in a game. [C14 (Scots): from OF *renc* row]

rinkhals ('rıŋk,hæls) *n.* a South African name for **ringhals.**

rink rat *n. Canad. sl.* a youth who helps with odd chores around an ice-hockey rink in return for free admission to games, etc.

rinse (rıns) *vb.* (*tr.*) **1.** to remove soap from (clothes, etc.) by applying clean water in the final stage in washing. **2.** to wash lightly, esp. without using soap. **3.** to give a light tint to (hair). ~*n.* **4.** the act or an instance of rinsing. **5.** *Hairdressing.* a liquid preparation put on the hair when wet to give a tint to it: *a blue rinse.* [C14: from OF *rincer*, from L *recens* fresh] —'**rinser** *n.*

Rio Branco (*Portuguese* 'riu 'brəŋku) *n.* **1.** a city in W Brazil, capital of Acre state. Pop.: 374 000 (1987). **2.** a river in Brazil, flowing south to the Rio Negro. Length: 644 km (400 miles).

Rio Bravo ('rio 'braβo) *n.* the Mexican name for the **Rio Grande.**

Rio de Janeiro ('riːəʊ də dʒə'nıərəʊ) or **Rio** *n.* **1.** a port in SE Brazil, on Guanabara Bay: the country's chief port and its capital from 1763 to 1960; backed by mountains, notably Sugar Loaf Mountain; founded by the French in 1555 and taken by the Portuguese in 1567. Pop.: 5 615 149 (1985). **2.** a state of E Brazil. Capital: Rio de Janeiro. Pop.: 13 021 000 (1986 est.). Area: 42 911 sq. km (16 568 sq. miles).

Río de la Plata ('riːəʊ də laː 'plaːtə) *n.* See **Plata.**

Rio de Oro (*Spanish* 'rio ðe 'oro) *n.* a former region of W Africa: comprised the S part of the Spanish Sahara (now Western Sahara).

Rio Grande *n.* **1.** ('riːəʊ 'grænd, 'grændı). a river in North America, rising in SW Colorado and flowing southeast to the Gulf of Mexico, forming the border between the U.S. and Mexico. Length: about 3030 km (1885 miles). Mexican name: **Río Bravo. 2.** (*Portuguese* 'riu 'grəndi). a port in SE Brazil, in SE Rio Grande do Sul state: serves as the port for Pôrto Alegre. Pop.: 124 706 (1980).

Rio Grande do Norte (*Portuguese* 'riu 'grəndi do 'nɔrti) *n.* a state of NE Brazil, on the Atlantic: much of it is semi-arid plateau. Capital: Natal. Pop.: 2 163 000 (1986 est.). Area: 53 014 sq. km (20 469 sq. miles).

Rio Grande do Sul (*Portuguese* 'riu 'grəndi du 'sul) *n.* a state of S Brazil, on the Atlantic. Capital: Pôrto Alegre. Pop.: 8 608 000 (1986). Area: 282 183 sq. km (108 951 sq. miles).

Río Muni (*Spanish* 'rio 'muni) *n.* one of the two provinces of Equatorial Guinea: comprises the mainland part of the country, with some offshore islands. Capital: Bata. Pop.: 203 000 (1968 est.). Area: 26 021 sq. km (10 047 sq. miles).

Río Negro ('riːəʊ 'neıgrəʊ, 'nɛg-; *Spanish* 'rio 'neɣro) *n.* See **Negro**[2].

riot ('raıət) *n.* **1. a.** a disturbance made by an unruly mob or (in law) three or more persons. **b.** (*as modifier*): *a riot shield.* **2.** unrestrained revelry. **3.** an occasion of boisterous merriment. **4.** *Sl.* a person who occasions boisterous merriment. **5.** a dazzling display: *a riot of colour.* **6.** *Hunting.* the indiscriminate following of any scent by hounds. **7.** *Arch.* wanton lasciviousness. **8. run riot. a.** to behave without restraint. **b.** (of plants) to grow profusely. ~*vb.* **9.** (*intr.*) to take part in a riot. **10.** (*intr.*) to indulge in unrestrained revelry. **11.** (*tr.*; foll. by *away*) to spend (time or money) in wanton or loose living. [C13: from OF *riote* dispute, from *ruihoter* to quarrel, prob. from *ruir* to make a commotion, from L *rugīre* to roar] —'**rioter** *n.*

Riot Act *n.* **1.** *Criminal law.* (formerly, in England) a statute of 1715 by which persons committing a riot had to disperse within an hour of the reading of the act by a magistrate. **2. read the riot act to.** to warn or reprimand severely.

riotous ('raɪətəs) *adj.* **1.** proceeding from or of the nature of riots or rioting. **2.** characterized by wanton revelry: *riotous living.* **3.** characterized by unrestrained merriment: *riotous laughter.* —'**riotously** *adv.* —'**riotousness** *n.*

riot shield *n.* (in Britain) a large oblong curved transparent shield used by police controlling crowds.

rip[1] (rɪp) *vb.* **ripping, ripped. 1.** to tear or be torn violently or roughly. **2.** (*tr.*; foll. by *off* or *out*) to remove hastily or roughly. **3.** (*intr.*) *Inf.* to move violently or precipitously. **4.** (*intr.*; foll. by *into*) *Inf.* to pour violent abuse (on). **5.** (*tr.*) to saw or split (wood) in the direction of the grain. **6. let rip.** to act or speak without restraint. ~*n.* **7.** a tear or split. **8.** short for **ripsaw.** ~See also **rip off.** [C15: ?from Flemish *rippen*]

rip[2] (rɪp) *n.* short for **riptide.** [C18: ?from RIP[1]]

rip[3] (rɪp) *n. Inf., arch.* **1.** a debauched person. **2.** an old worn-out horse. [C18: ?from *rep*, shortened from REPROBATE]

RIP *abbrev. for* requiescat *or* requiescant in pace. [L: may he, she, *or* they rest in peace]

riparian (raɪ'pɛərɪən) *adj.* **1.** of, inhabiting, or situated on the bank of a river. **2.** denoting or relating to the legal rights of the owner of land on a river bank, such as fishing. ~*n.* **3.** *Property law.* a person who owns land on a river bank. [C19: from L, from *rīpa* river bank]

ripcord ('rɪp,kɔːd) *n.* **1.** a cord that when pulled opens a parachute from its pack. **2.** a cord on the gas bag of a balloon that when pulled enables gas to escape and the balloon to descend.

ripe (raɪp) *adj.* **1.** (of fruit, grain, etc.) mature and ready to be eaten or used. **2.** mature enough to be eaten or used: *ripe cheese.* **3.** fully developed in mind or body. **4.** resembling ripe fruit, esp. in redness or fullness: *a ripe complexion.* **5.** (*postpositive;* foll. by *for*) ready or eager (to undertake or undergo an action). **6.** (*postpositive;* foll. by *for*) suitable: *the time is not yet ripe.* **7.** mature in judgment or knowledge. **8.** advanced but healthy (esp. in **a ripe old age**). **9.** *Sl.* **a.** complete; thorough. **b.** excessive; exorbitant. **10.** *Sl.* slightly indecent; risqué. [OE *rīpe*] —'**ripely** *adv.* —'**ripeness** *n.*

ripen ('raɪpᵊn) *vb.* to make or become ripe.

ripieno (,rɪpɪ'eɪnəʊ) *n., pl.* **-ni** (-niː) *or* **-nos.** *Music.* a supplementary instrument or player. [It.]

Ripley ('rɪplɪ) *n.* **George.** 1802–80, U.S. social reformer and transcendentalist: founder of the Brook Farm experiment in communal living in Massachusetts (1841).

rip off *vb.* (*tr.*) **1.** to tear roughly (from). **2.** (*adv.*) *Sl.* to steal from or cheat (someone). ~*n.* **rip-off. 3.** *Sl.* a grossly overpriced article. **4.** *Sl.* the act of stealing or cheating.

Ripon ('rɪpᵊn) *n.* a city in N England, in North Yorkshire: cathedral (12th–16th centuries). Pop.: 11 952 (1981).

riposte (rɪ'pɒst, rɪ'pəʊst) *n.* **1.** a swift sharp reply in speech or action. **2.** *Fencing.* a counterattack made immediately after a successful parry. ~*vb.* **3.** (*intr.*) to make a riposte. [C18: from F, from It., from *rispondere* to reply]

ripper ('rɪpə) *n.* **1.** a person or thing that rips. **2.** a murderer who dissects or mutilates his victim's body. **3.** *Sl., chiefly Austral. & N.Z.* a fine or excellent person or thing.

ripping ('rɪpɪŋ) *adj. Arch. Brit. sl.* excellent; splendid. —'**rippingly** *adv.*

ripple[1] ('rɪpᵊl) *n.* **1.** a slight wave or undulation on the surface of water. **2.** a small wave or undulation in fabric, hair, etc. **3.** a sound reminiscent of water flowing quietly in ripples: *a ripple of laughter.* **4.** *Electronics.* an oscillation of small amplitude superimposed on a steady value. **5.** *U.S. & Canad.* another word for **riffle** (sense 4). ~*vb.* **6.** (*intr.*) to form ripples or flow with an undulating motion. **7.** (*tr.*) to stir up (water) so as to form ripples. **8.** (*tr.*) to make ripple marks. **9.** (*intr.*) (of sounds) to rise and fall gently. [C17: ?from RIP[1]] —'**rippler** *n.* —'**rippling** *or* '**ripply** *adj.*

ripple[2] ('rɪpᵊl) *n.* **1.** a special kind of comb designed to separate the seed from the stalks in flax or hemp. ~*vb.* **2.** (*tr.*) to comb with this tool. [C14: of Gmc origin] —'**rippler** *n.*

ripple effect *n.* the repercussions of an event or situation experienced far beyond its immediate location.

ripple mark *n.* one of a series of small wavy ridges that is formed by waves on a beach, by a current in a sandy riverbed, or by wind on land.

rip-roaring *adj. Inf.* characterized by excitement, intensity, or boisterous behaviour.

ripsaw ('rɪp,sɔː) *n.* a handsaw for cutting along the grain of timber.

ripsnorter ('rɪp,snɔːtə) *n. Sl.* a person or thing noted for intensity or excellence. —'**rip,snorting** *adj.*

riptide ('rɪp,taɪd) *n.* **1.** Also called: **rip.** a stretch of turbulent water in the sea, caused by the meeting of currents. **2.** Also called: **rip current.** a strong current, esp. one flowing outwards from the shore.

rise (raɪz) *vb.* **rising, rose, risen** ('rɪzᵊn). (*mainly intr.*) **1.** to get up from a lying, sitting, kneeling, or prone position. **2.** to get out of bed, esp. to begin one's day: *he always rises early.* **3.** to move from a lower to a higher position or place. **4.** to ascend or appear above the horizon: *the sun is rising.* **5.** to increase in height or level: *the water rose above the normal level.* **6.** to attain higher rank, status, or reputation: *he will rise in the world.* **7.** to be built or erected: *those blocks of flats are rising fast.* **8.** to appear: *new troubles rose to afflict her.* **9.** to increase in strength, degree, etc.: *the wind is rising.* **10.** to increase in amount or value: *house prices are always rising.* **11.** to swell up: *dough rises.* **12.** to become erect, stiff, or rigid: *the hairs on his neck rose in fear.* **13.** (of one's stomach or gorge) to manifest nausea. **14.** to revolt: *the people rose against their oppressors.* **15.** to slope upwards: *the ground rises beyond the lake.* **16.** to be resurrected. **17.** to originate: *that river rises in the mountains.* **18.** (of a session of a court, legislative assembly, etc.) to come to an end. **19.** *Angling.* (of fish) to come to the surface of the water. **20.** (often foll. by *to*) *Inf.* to respond (to teasing, etc.). ~*n.* **21.** the act or an instance of rising. **22.** an increase in height. **23.** an increase in rank, status, or position. **24.** an increase in amount, cost, or value. **25.** an increase in degree or intensity. **26.** *Brit.* an increase in salary or wages. U.S. and Canad. word: **raise. 27.** the vertical height of a step or of a flight of stairs. **28.** the vertical height of a roof above the walls or columns. **29.** *Angling.* the act or instance of fish coming to the surface of the water to take flies, etc. **30.** the beginning, origin, or source. **31.** a piece of rising ground; incline. **32. get** *or* **take a rise out of.** *Sl.* to provoke an angry or petulant reaction from. **33. give rise to.** to cause the development of. [OE *rīsan*]

riser ('raɪzə) *n.* **1.** a person who rises, esp. from bed: *an early riser.* **2.** the vertical part of a stair. **3.** a vertical pipe, esp. one within a building.

rise to *vb.* (*intr., prep.*) to respond adequately to (the demands of something, esp. a testing challenge).

risibility (,rɪzɪ'bɪlɪtɪ) *n., pl.* **-ties. 1.** a tendency to laugh. **2.** hilarity; laughter.

risible ('rɪzɪbᵊl) *adj.* **1.** having a tendency to laugh. **2.** causing laughter; ridiculous. [C16: from LL *risibilis*, from L *rīdēre* to laugh] —'**risibly** *adv.*

rising ('raɪzɪŋ) *n.* **1.** a rebellion; revolt. **2.** the leaven used to make dough rise in baking. ~*adj.* (*prenominal*) **3.** increasing in rank, status, or reputation: *a rising young politician.* **4.** growing up to adulthood: *the rising generation.* ~*adv.* **5.** *Inf.* approaching: *he's rising 50.*

rising damp *n.* capillary movement of moisture from the ground into the walls of buildings, resulting in damage up to a level of 3 feet.

rising trot *n.* a horse's trot in which the rider rises from the saddle every second beat.

risk (rɪsk) *n.* **1.** the possibility of incurring misfortune or loss. **2.** *Insurance.* **a.** chance of a loss or other event on which a claim may be filed. **b.** the type of such an event, such as fire or theft. **c.** the amount of the claim should such an event occur. **d.** a person or thing considered with respect to the characteristics that may cause an insured event to occur. **3. at risk.** vulnerable. **4. take** *or* **run a risk.** to proceed in an action without regard to the possibility of danger involved. ~*vb.* (*tr.*) **5.** to expose to danger or loss. **6.** to act in spite of the possibility of (injury or loss): *to risk a fall in climbing.* [C17: from F, from It., from *rischiare* to be in peril, from Gk *rhiza* cliff (from the hazards of sailing along rocky coasts)]

risk capital *n. Chiefly Brit.* capital invested in an issue of ordinary shares, esp. of a speculative enterprise. Also called: **venture capital.**

risky ('rɪskɪ) *adj.* **riskier, riskiest.** involving danger. —'**riskily** *adv.* —'**riskiness** *n.*

risotto (rɪ'zɒtəʊ) n., pl. **-tos.** a dish of rice cooked in stock and served variously with tomatoes, cheese, chicken, etc. [C19: from It., from *riso* RICE]

risqué ('rɪskeɪ) adj. bordering on impropriety or indecency: *a risqué joke.* [C19: from F *risquer* to hazard, RISK]

rissole ('rɪsəʊl) n. a mixture of minced cooked meat coated in egg and breadcrumbs and fried. [C18: from F, prob. ult. from L *russus* red]

risus sardonicus ('riːsəs sɑː'dɒnɪkəs) n. *Pathol.* fixed contraction of the facial muscles resulting in a peculiar distorted grin, caused esp. by tetanus. Also called: **trismus cynicus** ('trɪzməs 'sɪnɪkəs). [C17: NL, lit.: sardonic laugh]

rit. *Music. abbrev. for:* **1.** ritardando. **2.** ritenuto.

ritardando (ˌrɪtɑː'dændəʊ) adj., adv. another term for **rallentando.** Abbrev.: **rit.** [C19: from It., from *ritardare* to slow down]

rite (raɪt) n. **1.** a formal act prescribed or customary in religious ceremonies: *the rite of baptism.* **2.** a particular body of such acts, esp. of a particular Christian Church: *the Latin rite.* **3.** a Christian Church: *the Greek rite.* [C14: from L *ritus* religious ceremony]

ritenuto (ˌrɪtə'nuːtəʊ) adj., adv. *Music.* **1.** held back momentarily. **2.** Abbrev.: **rit.** another term for **rallentando.** [C19: from It., from L *ritenēre* to hold back]

rite of passage n. a ceremony performed in some cultures at times when an individual changes his status, as at puberty and marriage.

ritornello (ˌrɪtə'nɛləʊ) n., pl. **-los** or **-li** (-liː). *Music.* a short piece of instrumental music interpolated in a song. [It., lit.: a little return]

ritual ('rɪtjʊəl) n. **1.** the prescribed or established form of a religious or other ceremony. **2.** such prescribed forms in general or collectively. **3.** stereotyped activity or behaviour. **4.** any formal act, institution, or procedure that is followed consistently: *the ritual of the law.* ~adj. **5.** of or characteristic of religious, social, or other rituals. [C16: from L *rituālis*, from *ritus* RITE] —**'ritually** adv.

ritualism ('rɪtjʊəˌlɪzəm) n. **1.** exaggerated emphasis on the importance of rites and ceremonies. **2.** the study of rites and ceremonies, esp. magical or religious ones. —**'ritualist** n. —**ˌritual'istic** adj. —**ˌritual'istically** adv.

ritualize or **-ise** ('rɪtjʊəˌlaɪz) vb. **1.** (intr.) to engage in ritualism or devise rituals. **2.** (tr.) to make (something) into a ritual.

ritzy ('rɪtsɪ) adj. **ritzier, ritziest.** *Sl.* luxurious or elegant. [C20: after the hotels established by César *Ritz* (1850–1918), Swiss hotelier] —**'ritzily** adv. —**'ritziness** n.

rival ('raɪvᵊl) n. **1. a.** a person, organization, team, etc., that competes with another for the same object or in the same field. **b.** (as modifier): *rival suitors.* **2.** a person or thing that is considered the equal of another: *she is without rival in the field of physics.* ~vb. **-valling, -valled** or U.S. **-valing, -valed.** (tr.) **3.** to be the equal or near equal of: *an empire that rivalled Rome.* **4.** to try to equal or surpass. [C16: from L *rivalis*, lit.: one who shares the same brook, from *rivus* a brook]

rivalry ('raɪvəlrɪ) n., pl. **-ries. 1.** the act of rivalling. **2.** the state of being a rival or rivals.

rive (raɪv) vb. **riving, rived, rived** or **riven** ('rɪvᵊn). (usually passive) **1.** to split asunder: *a tree riven by lightning.* **2.** to tear apart: *riven to shreds.* [C13: from ON *rífa*]

river ('rɪvə) n. **1. a.** a large natural stream of fresh water flowing along a definite course, usually into the sea, being fed by tributary streams. **b.** (as modifier): *river traffic.* **c.** (in combination): *riverside; riverbed.* Related adj.: **fluvial. 2.** any abundant stream or flow: *a river of blood.* [C13: from OF, from L *ripārius* of a river bank, from *ripa* bank] —**'riverless** adj.

Rivera (Spanish ri'βera) n. **Diego** ('djeɣo). 1886–1957, Mexican painter, noted for his monumental murals in public buildings, which are influenced by Aztec art and depict revolutionary themes.

riverine ('rɪvəˌraɪn) adj. **1.** of, like, relating to, or produced by a river. **2.** located or dwelling near a river; riparian.

Rivers ('rɪvəz) n. a state of S Nigeria, in the Niger River Delta on the Gulf of Guinea. Capital: Port Harcourt. Pop.: 2 883 300 (1984). Area: 17 941 sq. km (6929 sq. miles).

Riverside ('rɪvəˌsaɪd) n. a city in SW California. Pop.: 196 750 (1986 est.).

rivet ('rɪvɪt) n. **1.** a short metal pin for fastening two or more pieces together, having a head at one end, the other end being hammered flat after being passed through holes in the pieces. ~vb. (tr.) **2.** to join by riveting. **3.** to hammer in order to form into a head. **4.** (often passive) to cause to be fixed, as in fascinated attention, horror, etc.: *to be riveted to the spot.* [C14: from OF, from *river* to fasten, from ?] —**'riveter** n. —**'riveting** adj.

riviera (ˌrɪvɪ'ɛərə) n. a coastal region reminiscent of the Riviera.

Riviera (ˌrɪvɪ'ɛərə) n. the Mediterranean coastal region between Cannes, France, and La Spezia, Italy: contains some of Europe's most popular resorts. [C18: from It. lit.: shore, ult. from L *ripa* bank, shore]

rivière (ˌrɪvɪ'ɛə) n. a necklace the diamonds or other precious stones of which gradually increase in size up to a large centre stone. [C19: from F: brook, RIVER]

rivulet ('rɪvjʊlɪt) n. a small stream. [C16: from It. *rivoletto*, from L *rivulus*, from *rivus* stream]

Riyadh (rɪ'jɑːd) n. the joint capital (with Mecca) of Saudi Arabia, situated in a central oasis: the largest city in the country. Pop.: 1 000 000 (1984 est.).

riyal (rɪ'jɑːl) n. the standard monetary and currency unit of Saudi Arabia, Yemen, or Dubai. [from Ar. *riyāl*, from Sp. *real*]

Rizal[1] (Spanish ri'θal) n. another name for **Pasay.**

Rizal[2] (Spanish ri'θal) n. **Jose** (xo'se). 1861–96, Philippine nationalist, executed by the Spanish during the Philippine revolution of 1896.

Rizzio ('rɪtsɪəʊ) or **Riccio** n. **David.** ?1533–66, Italian musician and courtier who became the secretary and favourite of Mary, Queen of Scots. He was murdered at the instigation of a group of nobles, including Mary's husband, Darnley.

RL abbrev. for Rugby League.

rly abbrev. for railway.

rm abbrev. for: **1.** ream. **2.** room.

RM abbrev. for: **1.** Royal Mail. **2.** Royal Marines. **3.** (in Canada) Rural Municipality.

RMA abbrev. for Royal Military Academy (Sandhurst).

rms abbrev. for root mean square.

Rn the chemical symbol for radon.

RN abbrev. for: **1.** (in Canada) Registered Nurse. **2.** Royal Navy.

RNA n. *Biochem.* ribonucleic acid; any of a group of nucleic acids, present in all living cells, that play an essential role in the synthesis of proteins.

RNAS abbrev. for: **1.** Royal Naval Air Service(s). **2.** Royal Naval Air Station.

RNIB (in Britain) abbrev. for Royal National Institute for the Blind.

RNLI abbrev. for Royal National Lifeboat Institution.

RNZAF abbrev. for Royal New Zealand Air Force.

RNZN abbrev. for Royal New Zealand Navy.

roach[1] (rəʊtʃ) n., pl. **roaches** or **roach.** a European freshwater food fish having a deep compressed body and reddish ventral and tail fins. [C14: from OF *roche*, from ?]

roach[2] (rəʊtʃ) n. **1.** short for **cockroach. 2.** *Sl.* the butt of a cannabis cigarette.

roach[3] (rəʊtʃ) n. *Naut.* the curve at the foot of a square sail. [C18: from ?]

road (rəʊd) n. **1. a.** an open way, usually surfaced with tarmac or concrete, providing passage from one place to another. **b.** (as modifier): *road traffic; a road sign.* **c.** (in combination): *the roadside.* **2. a.** a street. **b.** (cap. when part of a name): *London Road.* **3.** *Brit.* one of the tracks of a railway. **4.** a way, path, or course: *the road to fame.* **5.** (often pl.) *Naut.* Also called: **roadstead.** a partly sheltered anchorage. **6.** a drift or tunnel in a mine, esp. a level one. **7. hit the road.** *Sl.* to start or resume travelling. **8. one for the road.** *Inf.* a last alcoholic drink before leaving. **9. on the road. a.** travelling about; on tour. **b.** leading a wandering life. **10. take (to) the road.** to begin a journey or tour. [OE *rād*; rel. to *ridan* to RIDE] —**'roadless** adj.

roadblock ('rəʊdˌblɒk) n. a barrier set up across a road by the police or military, in order to stop a fugitive, inspect traffic, etc.

road-fund licence n. *Brit.* a licence showing that the tax payable in respect of a motor vehicle has been paid. [C20: from the former *road fund* for the maintenance of public highways]

road hog *n. Inf.* a selfish or aggressive driver.

roadholding ('rəʊd,həʊldɪŋ) *n.* the extent to which a motor vehicle is stable and does not skid, esp. on sharp bends or wet roads.

roadhouse ('rəʊd,haʊs) *n.* a pub, restaurant, etc., that is situated at the side of a road.

road hump *n.* the official name for **sleeping policeman.**

roadie ('rəʊdɪ) *n. Inf.* a person who transports and sets up equipment for a band or group. [C20: shortened from *road manager*]

road metal *n.* crushed rock, broken stone, etc., used to construct a road.

road movie *n.* a genre of film in which the chief character is travelling or on the run, often as it were, in search of, or to escape from, himself.

roadroller ('rəʊd,rəʊlə) *n.* a motor vehicle with heavy rollers for compressing road surfaces during road-making.

road show *n.* **1.** *Radio.* **a.** a live programme, usually with some audience participation, transmitted from a radio van taking a particular show on the road. **b.** the personnel and equipment needed for such a show. **2.** a group of entertainers on tour. **3.** any occasion when an organization attracts publicity while touring or visiting: *the royal road show.*

roadstead ('rəʊd,stɛd) *n. Naut.* another word for **road** (sense 5).

roadster ('rəʊdstə) *n.* **1.** *Arch.* an open car, esp. one seating only two. **2.** a kind of bicycle.

road tax *n.* a tax paid, usually annually, on motor vehicles in use on the roads.

road test *n.* **1.** a test to ensure that a vehicle is roadworthy, esp. after repair or servicing, by driving it on roads. **2.** a test of something in actual use. ~*vb.* **road-test.** (*tr.*) **3.** to test (a vehicle, etc.) in this way.

road train *n. Austral.* a truck pulling one or more large trailers, esp. on western roads.

roadway ('rəʊd,weɪ) *n.* **1.** the surface of a road. **2.** the part of a road that is used by vehicles.

roadwork ('rəʊd,wɜːk) *n.* sports training by running along roads.

road works *pl. n.* repairs to a road or cable under a road, esp. when forming a hazard or obstruction to traffic.

roadworthy ('rəʊd,wɜːðɪ) *adj.* (of a motor vehicle) mechanically sound; fit for use on the roads. —'**road,worthiness** *n.*

roam (rəʊm) *vb.* **1.** to travel or walk about with no fixed purpose or direction. ~*n.* **2.** the act of roaming. [C13: from ?] —'**roamer** *n.*

roan (rəʊn) *adj.* **1.** (of a horse) having a bay (**red roan**), chestnut (**strawberry roan**), or black (**blue roan**) coat sprinkled with white hairs. ~*n.* **2.** a horse having such a coat. **3.** a soft sheepskin leather used in bookbinding, etc. [C16: from OF, from Sp. *roano*, prob. from Gothic *rauths* red]

Roanoke Island ('rəʊə,nəʊk) *n.* an island off the coast of North Carolina: site of the first attempted English settlement in America. Length: 19 km (12 miles). Average width: 5 km (3 miles).

roar (rɔː) *vb.* (*mainly intr.*) **1.** (of lions and other animals) to utter characteristic loud growling cries. **2.** (*also tr.*) (of people) to utter (something) with a loud deep cry, as in anger or triumph. **3.** to laugh in a loud hearty unrestrained manner. **4.** (of horses) to breathe with laboured rasping sounds. **5.** (of the wind, waves, etc.) to blow or break loudly and violently, as during a storm. **6.** (of a fire) to burn fiercely with a roaring sound. **7.** (*tr.*) to bring (oneself) into a certain condition by roaring: *to roar oneself hoarse.* ~*n.* **8.** a loud deep cry, uttered by a person or crowd, esp. in anger or triumph. **9.** a prolonged loud cry of certain animals, esp. lions. **10.** any similar noise made by a fire, the wind, an engine, etc. [OE *rārian*] —'**roarer** *n.*

roaring ('rɔːrɪŋ) *adj.* **1.** *Inf.* very brisk and profitable (esp. in a **roaring trade**). ~*adv.* **2.** noisily or boisterously (esp. in **roaring drunk**). ~*n.* **3.** a loud prolonged cry. —'**roaringly** *adv.*

roast (rəʊst) *vb.* (*mainly tr.*) **1.** to cook (meat or other food) by dry heat, usually with added fat and esp. in an oven. **2.** to brown or dry (coffee, etc.) by exposure to heat. **3.** *Metallurgy.* to heat (an ore) in order to produce a concentrate that is easier to smelt. **4.** to heat (oneself or something) to an extreme degree, as when sunbathing,

etc. **5.** (*intr.*) to be excessively and uncomfortably hot. **6.** (*tr.*) *Inf.* to criticize severely. ~*n.* **7.** something that has been roasted, esp. meat. [C13: from OF *rostir*, of Gmc origin] —'**roaster** *n.*

roasting ('rəʊstɪŋ) *Inf.* ~*adj.* **1.** extremely hot. ~*n.* **2.** severe criticism.

rob (rɒb) *vb.* **robbing, robbed.** **1.** to take something from (someone) illegally, as by force. **2.** (*tr.*) to plunder (a house, etc.). **3.** (*tr.*) to deprive unjustly: *to be robbed of an opportunity.* [C13: from OF *rober*, of Gmc origin] —'**robber** *n.*

Robbe-Grillet (*French* rɔbɡrijɛ) *n.* **Alain** (alɛ̃). born 1922, French novelist. Author of *The Voyeur* (1955) and *Jealousy* (1957), he is one of the leading practitioners of the antinovel.

Robben Island ('rɒbᵊn) *n.* a small island 11 km (7 miles) off the Cape Peninsula: used by the South African government to house political prisoners.

robbery ('rɒbərɪ) *n., pl.* **-beries.** **1.** *Criminal law.* the stealing of property from a person by using or threatening to use force. **2.** the act or an instance of robbing.

Robbia ('rəʊbɪə; *Italian* 'rɔbbja) *n.* **1. Andrea della** (an'drɛːa 'dɛlla). 1435–1525, Florentine sculptor, best known for his polychrome reliefs and his statues of infants in swaddling clothes. **2.** his uncle, **Luca della** ('luːka 'dɛlla). ?1400–82, Florentine sculptor, who perfected a technique of enamelling terra cotta for reliefs.

Robbins ('rɒbɪnz) *n.* **Jerome.** born 1918, U.S. ballet dancer and choreographer. He choreographed the musicals *The King and I* (1951) and *West Side Story* (1957).

robe (rəʊb) *n.* **1.** any loose flowing garment, esp. the official vestment of a peer, judge, or academic. **2.** a dressing gown or bathrobe. ~*vb.* **3.** to put a robe, etc., on (oneself or someone else). [C13: from OF; of Gmc origin]

Robert I ('rɒbət) *n.* known as *Robert the Bruce.* 1274–1329, king of Scotland (1306–29): he defeated the English army of Edward II at Bannockburn (1314) and gained recognition of Scotland's independence (1328).

Robert II *n.* 1316–90, king of Scotland (1371–90).

Robert III *n.* ?1337–1406, king of Scotland (1390–1406), son of Robert II.

Robeson ('rəʊbsən) *n.* **Paul.** 1898–1976, U.S. bass singer, actor, and leader in the Black civil rights movement.

Robespierre ('rəʊbzpjɛə; *French* rɔbzpjɛr) *n.* **Maximilien François Marie Isidore de** (maksimiljɛ̃ frɑ̃swa mari izidɔr də). 1758–94, French revolutionary and Jacobin leader: established the Reign of Terror as a member of the Committee of Public Safety (1793–94): executed in the coup d'état of Thermidor (1794).

robin ('rɒbɪn) *n.* **1.** Also called: **robin redbreast.** a small Old World songbird related to the thrushes. The male has a brown back, orange-red breast and face, and grey underparts. **2.** a North American thrush similar to but larger than the Old World robin. [C16: arbitrary use of given name]

Robin Hood *n.* a legendary English outlaw of the reign of Richard I, who lived in Sherwood Forest and robbed the rich to give to the poor.

robinia (rə'bɪnɪə) *n.* any tree of the leguminous genus *Robinia*, esp. the locust tree.

Robinson ('rɒbɪnsən) *n.* **1. Edward G.,** real name *Emanuel Goldenberg.* 1893–1973, U.S. film actor, born in Romania, famous esp. for gangster roles. His films include *Little Caesar* (1930), *Brother Orchid* (1940), *Double Indemnity* (1944), and *All My Sons* (1948). **2. Edwin Arlington.** 1869–1935, U.S. poet, author of narrative verse, often based on Arthurian legend. His works include *Collected Poems* (1922), *The Man Who Died Twice* (1924), and *Tristram* (1927). **3. Smokey,** real name *William Robinson.* born 1940, U.S. Motown singer, songwriter, and producer. His hits include "The Tears of a Clown" (1970) (with the Miracles) and "Being with you" (1981). **4. "Sugar" Ray,** real name *Walker Smith.* born 1920, U.S. boxer, winner of the world middleweight championship on five separate occasions.

roborant ('rəʊbərənt, 'rɒb-) *adj.* **1.** tending to fortify or increase strength. ~*n.* **2.** a drug or agent that increases strength. [C17: from L *roborāre* to strengthen, from *rōbur* an oak]

robot ('rəʊbɒt) *n.* **1.** any automated machine programmed to perform specific mechanical functions in the manner of a man. **2.** (*modifier*) automatic: *a robot pilot.* **3.** a person who works or behaves like a machine. **4.** *S. African.* a set of traffic lights. [C20: (used in *R.U.R.*, a play by Karel Capek) from Czech *robota* work] —**ro'botic** *adj.* —'**robot-,like** *adj.*

robot bomb *n.* another name for the **V-1.**

robot dancing *or* **robotic dancing** (rəʊ'bɒtɪk) *n.* a dance of the 1980s, characterized by jerky, mechanical movements. Also called: **robotics.**

robotics (rəʊ'bɒtɪks) *n.* (*functioning as sing.*) **1.** the science or technology of designing, building, and using robots. **2.** another name for **robot dancing.**

Rob Roy ('rɒb 'rɔɪ) *n.* real name *Robert Macgregor.* 1671–1734, Scottish outlaw.

Robson[1] ('rɒbsən) *n.* **Mount.** a mountain in SW Canada, in E British Columbia: the highest peak in the Canadian Rockies. Height: 3954 m (12 972 ft.).

Robson[2] ('rɒbsən) *n.* **Dame Flora.** 1902–84, English stage and film actress.

robust (rəʊ'bʌst, 'rəʊbʌst) *adj.* **1.** strong in constitution. **2.** sturdily built: *a robust shelter.* **3.** requiring or suited to physical strength: *a robust sport.* **4.** (esp. of wines) having a full-bodied flavour. **5.** rough or boisterous. **6.** (of thought, intellect, etc.) straightforward. [C16: from L *rōbustus,* from *rōbur* an oak, strength] —**ro'bustly** *adv.* —**ro'bustness** *n.*

robustious (rəʊ'bʌstʃəs) *adj. Arch.* **1.** rough; boisterous. **2.** strong, robust, or stout. —**ro'bustiously** *adv.* —**ro'bustiousness** *n.*

roc (rɒk) *n.* (in Arabian legend) a bird of enormous size and power. [C16: from Ar., from Persian *rukh*]

ROC *abbrev. for* Royal Observer Corps.

Roca ('rəʊkə) *n.* **Cape.** a cape in SW central Portugal, near Lisbon: the westernmost point of continental Europe.

rocaille (rɒ'kaɪ) *n.* decorative rock or shell work, esp. as ornamentation in a rococo fountain, grotto, or interior. [from F, from *roc* ROCK[1]]

rocambole ('rɒkəm,bəʊl) *n.* a variety of alliaceous plant whose garlic-like bulb is used for seasoning. [C17: from F, from G *Rockenbolle,* lit.: distaff bulb (with reference to its shape)]

Rocard (*French* rɔka:r) *n.* **Michel.** born 1930, French politician: prime minister of France from 1988.

Rochdale ('rɒtʃ,deɪl) *n.* a town in NW England, in Greater Manchester: textile industry. Pop.: 92 704 (1981).

Rochelle salt *n.* a white crystalline double salt used in Seidlitz powder. Formula: $KNaC_4H_4O_6.4H_2O$.

roche moutonnée (rəʊʃ ,mu:tə'neɪ) *n., pl.* **roches moutonnées** (rəʊʃ ,mu:tə'neɪz) a rounded mass of rock smoothed and striated by ice that has flowed over it. [C19: F, lit.: fleecy rock, from *mouton* sheep]

Rochester ('rɒtʃɪstə) *n.* **1.** a city in SE England, in Kent on the River Medway: with Chatham and Gillingham forms the conurbation of the Medway towns. Pop.: 52 505 (1981). **2.** a city in NW New York State, on Lake Ontario. Pop.: 235 970 (1986).

rochet ('rɒtʃɪt) *n.* a white surplice with tight sleeves, worn by bishops, abbots, and certain other Church dignitaries. [C14: from OF, from *roc* coat, of Gmc origin]

rock[1] (rɒk) *n.* **1.** *Geol.* any aggregate of minerals that makes up part of the earth's crust. It may be unconsolidated, such as a sand, clay, or mud, or consolidated, such as granite, limestone, or coal. **2.** any hard mass of consolidated mineral matter, such as a boulder. **3.** *U.S., Canad., & Austral.* a stone. **4.** a person or thing suggesting a rock, esp. in being dependable, unchanging, or providing firm foundation. **5.** *Brit.* a hard sweet, typically a long brightly coloured peppermint-flavoured stick, sold esp. in holiday resorts. **6.** *Sl.* a jewel, esp. a diamond. **7.** *Sl.* another name for **crack** (sense 28). **8.** **on the rocks. a.** in a state of ruin or destitution. **b.** (of drinks, esp. whisky) served with ice. [C14: from OF *roche,* from ?]

rock[2] (rɒk) *vb.* **1.** to move or cause to move from side to side or backwards and forwards. **2.** to reel or sway or cause (someone) to reel or sway, as with a violent shock or emotion. **3.** (*tr.*) to shake or move (something) violently. **4.** (*intr.*) to dance in the rock-and-roll style. ~*n.* **5.** a rocking motion. **6.** short for **rock and roll. 7.** Also called: **rock music.** any of various styles of pop music having a heavy beat, derived from rock and roll. [OE *roccian*]

Rock (rɒk) *n.* **the.** an informal name for **Gibraltar.**

rockabilly ('rɒkə,bɪlɪ) *n.* a fast, spare style of White rock music which originated in the mid-1950s in the U.S. South. [C20: from ROCK (AND ROLL) + (HILL)BILLY]

rock and roll *or* **rock'n'roll** *n.* **1. a.** a type of pop music originating in the 1950s as a blend of rhythm and blues and country and western. **b.** (*as modifier*): *the rock-and-roll era.* **2.** dancing performed to such music, with exaggerated body movements stressing the beat. ~*vb.* **3.** (*intr.*) to perform this dance. —**rock and roller** *or* **rock'n'roller** *n.*

rock bass (bæs) *n.* an eastern North American freshwater food fish, related to the sunfish family.

rock bottom *n.* **a.** the lowest possible level. **b.** (*as modifier*): *rock-bottom prices.*

rock-bound *adj.* hemmed in or encircled by rocks. Also (poetic): **rock-girt.**

rock cake *n.* a small cake containing dried fruit and spice, with a rough surface supposed to resemble a rock.

rock crystal *n.* a pure transparent colourless quartz, used in electronic and optical equipment.

rock dove *or* **pigeon** *n.* a common dove from which domestic and feral pigeons are descended.

Rockefeller ('rɒkə,felə) *n.* **1. John D**(avison). 1839–1937, U.S. industrialist and philanthropist. **2.** his son, **John D**(avison). 1874–1960, U.S. capitalist and philanthropist. **3.** his son, **Nelson** (**Aldrich**). 1908–79, U.S. politician; governor of New York State (1958–74); vice president (1974–76).

rocker ('rɒkə) *n.* **1.** any of various devices that transmit or operate with a rocking motion. See also **rocker arm. 2.** another word for **rocking chair. 3.** either of two curved supports on the legs of a chair on which it may rock. **4. a.** an ice skate with a curved blade. **b.** the curve itself. **5.** *Brit.* an adherent of a youth movement rooted in the 1950s, characterized by motorcycle trappings. **6. off one's rocker.** *Sl.* crazy.

rocker arm *n.* a lever that rocks about a central pivot, esp. one in an internal-combustion engine that transmits the motion of a pushrod or cam to a valve.

rockery ('rɒkərɪ) *n., pl.* **-eries.** a garden constructed with rocks, esp. one where alpine plants are grown.

rocket ('rɒkɪt) *n.* **1.** a self-propelling device, esp. a cylinder containing a mixture of solid explosives, used as a firework, distress signal, etc. **2. a.** any vehicle propelled by a rocket engine, esp. one used to carry a spacecraft, etc. **b.** (*as modifier*): *rocket launcher.* **3.** *Brit. & N.Z. inf.* a severe reprimand (esp. in **get a rocket**). ~*vb.* **4.** (*tr.*) to propel (a missile, spacecraft, etc.) by means of a rocket. **5.** (*intr.*; foll. by *off, away,* etc.) to move off at high speed. **6.** (*intr.*) to rise rapidly: *he rocketed to the top.* [C17: from OF, from It. *rochetto,* dim. of *rocca* distaff, of Gmc origin]

rocket engine *n.* a reaction engine in which a fuel and oxidizer are burnt in a combustion chamber, the products of combustion expanding through a nozzle and producing thrust.

rocketry ('rɒkɪtrɪ) *n.* the science and technology of the design, operation, maintenance, and launching of rockets.

rockfish ('rɒk,fɪʃ) *n., pl.* **-fish** *or* **-fishes. 1.** any of various fishes that live among rocks, such as the goby, bass, etc. **2.** *Brit.* any of several coarse fishes when used as food, esp. the dogfish or wolffish.

Rockford ('rɒkfəd) *n.* a city in N Illinois, on the Rock River. Pop.: 139 712 (1980).

rock garden *n.* a garden featuring rocks or rockeries.

Rockhampton (rɒk'hæmptən, -'hæmtən) *n.* a port in Australia, in E Queensland on the Fitzroy River. Pop.: 57 020 (1986 est.).

Rockies ('rɒkɪz) *pl. n.* another name for the **Rocky Mountains.**

rocking chair *n.* a chair set on curving supports so that the sitter may rock backwards and forwards.

Rockingham ('rɒkɪŋəm) *n.* **Marquess of,** title of *Charles Watson-Wentworth.* 1730–82, British statesman and leader of the Whig opposition, whose members were known as the **Rockingham Whigs**; prime minister (1765–66; 1782). He opposed the war with the American colonists.

rocking horse *n.* a toy horse mounted on a pair of rockers on which a child can rock to and fro in a seesaw movement.

rocking stone n. a boulder so delicately poised that it can be rocked.

rockling ('roklɪŋ) n., pl. **-lings** or **-ling.** a small gadoid fish which has an elongated body with barbels around the mouth and occurs mainly in the North Atlantic Ocean. [C17: from ROCK¹ + -LING¹]

rock lobster n. another name for the **spiny lobster.**

rock melon n. U.S., Austral., & N.Z. another name for **cantaloupe.**

rock pigeon n. another name for **rock dove.**

rock plant n. any plant that grows on rocks or in rocky ground.

rock rabbit n. S. African. another name for **dassie.** See **hyrax.**

rockrose ('rok,rəʊz) n. any of various shrubs or herbaceous plants cultivated for their yellow-white or reddish roselike flowers.

rock salmon n. Brit. a former term for **rockfish** (sense 2).

rock salt n. another name for **halite.**

rock snake or **python** n. any large Australasian python of the genus Liasis.

rock tripe n. Canad. any of various edible lichens that grow on rocks and are used in the North as a survival food.

Rockwell ('rok,wɛl, -wəl) n. **Norman.** 1894–1978, U.S. illustrator, noted esp. for magazine covers.

rock wool n. another name for **mineral wool.**

rocky¹ ('rokɪ) adj. **rockier, rockiest.** 1. consisting of or abounding in rocks: a rocky shore. 2. unyielding: rocky determination. 3. hard like rock: rocky muscles. —'rockiness n.

rocky² ('rokɪ) adj. **rockier, rockiest.** 1. weak or unstable. 2. Inf. (of a person) dizzy; nauseated. —'rockily adv. —'rockiness n.

Rocky Mountains or **Rockies** pl. n. the chief mountain system of W North America, extending from British Columbia to New Mexico: forms the Continental Divide. Highest peak: Mount Elbert, 4399 m (14 431 ft.). Mount McKinley (6194 m (20 320 ft.)), in the Alaska Range, is not strictly part of the Rocky Mountains.

Rocky Mountain spotted fever n. an acute rickettsial disease characterized by high fever, chills, pain in muscles and joints, etc. It is caused by the bite of an infected tick.

rococo (rə'kəʊkəʊ) n. (often cap.) 1. a style of architecture and decoration that originated in France in the early 18th century, characterized by elaborate but graceful ornamentation. 2. an 18th-century style of music characterized by prettiness and extreme use of ornamentation. 3. any florid or excessively ornamental style. ~adj. 4. denoting, being in, or relating to the rococo. 5. florid or excessively elaborate. [C19: from F, from ROCAILLE, from roc ROCK¹]

rod (rod) n. 1. a slim cylinder of metal, wood, etc. 2. a switch or bundle of switches used to administer corporal punishment. 3. any of various staffs of insignia or office. 4. power, esp. of a tyrannical kind: a dictator's iron rod. 5. a straight slender shoot, stem, or cane of a woody plant. 6. See **fishing rod.** 7. Also called: **pole, perch. a.** a unit of length equal to 5½ yards. **b.** a unit of square measure equal to 30½ square yards. 8. Surveying. another name (esp. U.S.) for **staff¹** (sense 8). 9. Also called: **retinal rod.** any of the elongated cylindrical cells in the retina of the eye, which are sensitive to dim light but not to colour. 10. any rod-shaped bacterium. 11. U.S. a slang name for **pistol.** 12. short for **hot rod.** [OE rodd] —'rod,like adj.

rode (rəʊd) vb. the past tense of **ride.**

rodent ('rəʊd²nt) n. **a.** any of the relatively small placental mammals having constantly growing incisor teeth specialized for gnawing. The group includes rats, mice, squirrels, etc. **b.** (as modifier): rodent characteristics. [C19: from L rōdere to gnaw] —'rodent-,like adj.

rodent ulcer n. a slow-growing malignant tumour on the face, usually occurring at the edge of the eyelids, lips, or nostrils.

rodeo ('rəʊdɪ,əʊ) n., pl. **-deos.** Chiefly U.S. & Canad. 1. a display of the skills of cowboys, including bareback riding. 2. the rounding up of cattle for branding, etc. 3. an enclosure for cattle that have been rounded up. [C19: from Sp., from rodear to go around, from rueda a wheel, from L rota]

Rodgers ('rodʒəz) n. **Richard.** 1902–79, U.S. composer of musical comedies. He collaborated with the librettist

Lorenz Hart on such musicals as A Connecticut Yankee (1927), On Your Toes (1936), and Pal Joey (1940). After Hart's death his librettist was Oscar Hammerstein II. Two of their musicals, Oklahoma! (1943) and South Pacific (1949), received the Pulitzer Prize.

Ródhos ('roðos) n. transliteration of the Modern Greek name for **Rhodes.**

Rodin (French rodɛ̃) n. **Auguste** (ogyst). 1840–1917, French sculptor, noted for his portrayal of the human form. His works include The Kiss (1886), The Burghers of Calais (1896), and The Thinker (1905).

Rodney ('rodnɪ) n. **George Brydges,** 1st Baron Rodney. 1719–92, English admiral: captured Martinique (1762): defeated the Spanish at Cape St Vincent (1780) and the French under Admiral de Grasse off Dominica (1782), restoring British superiority in the Caribbean.

rodomontade (,rodəmon'teɪd, -'tɑːd) Literary. ~n. 1. **a.** boastful words or behaviour. **b.** (as modifier): rodomontade behaviour. ~vb. 2. (intr.) to boast or rant. [C17: from F, from It. rodomonte a boaster, from Rodomonte, the name of a braggart king of Algiers in epic poems]

roe¹ (rəʊ) n. 1. Also called: **hard roe.** the ovary of a female fish filled with mature eggs. 2. Also called: **soft roe.** the testis of a male fish filled with mature sperm. [C15: from MDu. roge, from OHG roga]

roe² (rəʊ) n., pl. **roes** or **roe.** short for **roe deer.** [OE rā(ha)]

roebuck ('rəʊ,bʌk) n., pl. **-bucks** or **-buck.** the male of the roe deer.

roe deer n. a small graceful deer of woodlands of Europe and Asia. The antlers are small and the summer coat is reddish-brown.

roentgen or **röntgen** ('rontgən, -tjən, 'rɛnt-) n. a unit of dose of electromagnetic radiation equal to the dose that will produce in air a charge of 0.258×10^{-3} coulomb on all ions of one sign. [C19: after W. K. ROENTGEN]

Roentgen or **Röntgen** ('rontgən, -tjən, 'rɛnt-; German 'rœntgən) n. **Wilhelm Konrad** ('vɪlhɛlm 'kɔnraːt). 1845–1923, German physicist, who in 1895 discovered x-rays: Nobel prize for physics 1901.

roentgen ray n. a former name for **x-ray.**

Roeselare ('ruːsəlaːrə) n. the Flemish name for **Roulers.**

Roethke ('rɛtkə) n. **Theodore.** 1908–63, U.S. poet, whose books include Words for the Wind (1957) and The Far Field (1964).

rogation (rəʊ'geɪʃən) n. (usually pl.) Christianity. a solemn supplication, esp. in a form of ceremony prescribed by the Church. [C14: from L rogātiō, from rogāre to ask, make supplication]

Rogation Days pl. n. April 25 (the **Major Rogation**) and the Monday, Tuesday, and Wednesday before Ascension Day, observed by Christians as days of solemn supplication and marked by processions and special prayers.

roger ('rodʒə) interj. 1. (used in signalling, telecommunications, etc.) message received and understood. 2. an expression of agreement. 3. Taboo sl. (of a man) to copulate (with). [C20: from the name Roger, representing R for received]

Rogers ('rodʒəz) n. 1. **Ginger,** real name Virginia McMath. born 1911, U.S. dancer and film actress, who partnered Fred Astaire. 2. **Richard.** born 1933, British architect. His works include the Pompidou Centre in Paris (1971–77; with Renzo Piano) and the Lloyd's building in London (1986). 3. **William Penn Adair,** known as Will. 1879–1935, U.S. actor, newspaper columnist, and humorist in the homespun tradition.

Roget ('roʒeɪ) n. **Peter Mark.** 1779–1869, English physician, who on retirement devised a Thesaurus of English Words and Phrases (1852), a classified list of synonyms.

rogue (rəʊg) n. 1. a dishonest or unprincipled person, esp. a man. 2. Often jocular. a mischievous or wayward person, often a child. 3. any inferior or defective specimen, esp. a defective crop plant. 4. Arch. a vagrant. 5. **a.** an animal of vicious character that leads a solitary life. **b.** (as modifier): a rogue elephant. ~vb. 6. (tr.) to rid (a field or crop) of plants that are inferior, diseased, etc. [C16: from ?]

roguery ('rəʊgərɪ) n., pl. **-gueries.** 1. behaviour characteristic of a rogue. 2. a roguish or mischievous act.

rogues' gallery n. a collection of portraits of known criminals kept by the police for identification purposes.

roguish ('rəʊgɪʃ) adj. 1. dishonest or unprincipled. 2. mischievous. —'roguishly adv.

roil ('roɪl) vb. **1.** (tr.) to make (a liquid) cloudy or turbid by stirring up dregs or sediment. **2.** (intr.) (esp. of a liquid) to be agitated. **3.** (intr.) Dialect. to be noisy. **4.** (tr.) Now rare. another word for **rile** (sense 1). [C16: from ?]

roister ('rɔɪstə) vb. (intr.) **1.** to engage in noisy or unrestrained merrymaking. **2.** to brag, bluster, or swagger. [C16: from OF rustre lout, from ruste uncouth, from L rusticus rural] —'**roisterer** n. —'**roisterous** adj. —'**roisterously** adv.

Roland ('rəʊlənd) n. **1.** the greatest of the legendary 12 peers or paladins (of whom Oliver was another) in attendance on Charlemagne. **2. a Roland for an Oliver.** an effective retort or retaliation.

role or **rôle** (rəʊl) n. **1.** a part or character in a play, film, etc., to be played by an actor or actress. **2.** Psychol. the part played by a person in a particular social setting, influenced by his expectation of what is appropriate. **3.** usual function: what is his role in the organization? [C17: from F rôle ROLL, an actor's script]

role-playing n. Psychol. activity in which a person imitates, consciously or unconsciously, a role uncharacteristic of himself. See also **psychodrama**.

Rolf (rɒlf) or **Rolf the Ganger** n. other names for **Rollo**.

roll (rəʊl) vb. **1.** to move or cause to move along by turning over and over. **2.** to move or cause to move along on wheels or rollers. **3.** to flow or cause to flow onwards in an undulating movement. **4.** (intr.) (of animals, etc.) to turn onto the back and kick. **5.** (intr.) to extend in undulations: the hills roll down to the sea. **6.** (intr.; usually foll. by around) to move or occur in cycles. **7.** (intr.) (of a planet, the moon, etc.) to revolve in an orbit. **8.** (intr.; foll. by on, by, etc.) to pass or elapse: the years roll by. **9.** to rotate or cause to rotate wholly or partially: to roll one's eyes. **10.** to curl, cause to curl, or admit of being curled, so as to form a ball, tube, or cylinder. **11.** to make or form by shaping into a ball, tube, or cylinder: to roll a cigarette. **12.** (often foll. by out) to spread or cause to spread out flat or smooth under or as if under a roller: to roll pastry. **13.** to emit or utter with a deep prolonged reverberating sound: the thunder rolled continuously. **14.** to trill or cause to be trilled: to roll one's r's. **15.** (intr.) (of a vessel, aircraft, rocket, etc.) to turn from side to side around the longitudinal axis. **16.** to cause (an aircraft) to execute a roll or (of an aircraft) to execute a roll (sense 34). **17.** (intr.) to walk with a swaying gait, as when drunk. **18.** Chiefly U.S. to throw (dice). **19.** (intr.) to operate or begin to operate: the presses rolled. **20.** (intr.) Inf. to make progress: let the good times roll. **21.** (tr.) Inf., chiefly U.S. & N.Z. to rob (a helpless person). ~n. **22.** the act or an instance of rolling. **23.** anything rolled up in a cylindrical form: a roll of newspaper. **24.** an official list or register, esp. of names: an electoral roll. **25.** a rounded mass: rolls of flesh. **26.** a cylinder used to flatten something; roller. **27.** a small cake of bread for one person. **28.** a flat pastry or cake rolled up with a meat (**sausage roll**), jam (**jam roll**), or other filling. **29.** a swell or undulation on a surface: the roll of the hills. **30.** a swaying, rolling, or unsteady movement or gait. **31.** a deep prolonged reverberating sound: the roll of thunder. **32.** a trilling sound; trill. **33.** a very rapid beating of the sticks on a drum. **34.** a flight manoeuvre in which an aircraft makes one complete rotation about its longitudinal axis without loss of height or change in direction. **35.** Sl. an act of sexual intercourse or petting (esp. in **a roll in the hay**). **36.** U.S. sl. an amount of money, esp. a wad of paper money. **37. strike off the roll(s). a.** to expel from membership. **b.** to debar (a solicitor) from practising, usually because of dishonesty. ~See also **roll in, roll on,** etc. [C14 rollen, from OF roler, from L rotulus, dim. of rota a wheel]

Rolland (French rɔlɑ̃) n. **Romain** (rɔmɛ̃). 1866–1944, French novelist, dramatist, and essayist, best known for his cycle of novels about a musical genius, Jean-Christophe, (1904–12): Nobel prize for literature 1915.

rollbar ('rəʊl,bɑː) n. a bar that reinforces the frame of a car used for racing, rallying, etc., to protect the driver if the car should turn over.

roll call n. the reading aloud of an official list of names, those present responding when their names are read out.

rolled gold n. a metal, such as brass, coated with a thin layer of gold. Also (U.S.): **filled gold**.

rolled-steel joist n. a steel beam, esp. one with a cross section in the form of a letter H or I. Abbrev.: **RSJ**.

roller ('rəʊlə) n. **1.** a cylinder having an absorbent surface and a handle, used for spreading paint. **2.** Also called: **garden roller**. a heavy cast-iron cylinder on an axle to which a handle is attached; used for flattening lawns. **3.** a long heavy wave of the sea, advancing towards the shore. **4.** a hardened cylinder of precision-ground steel that forms one of the rolling components of a roller bearing or of a linked driving chain. **5.** a cylinder fitted on pivots, used to enable heavy objects to be easily moved. **6.** Printing. a cylinder, usually of hard rubber, used to ink a plate before impression. **7.** any of various other cylindrical devices that rotate about a cylinder, used for any of various purposes. **8.** a small cylinder onto which a woman's hair may be rolled to make it curl. **9.** Med. a bandage consisting of a long strip of muslin rolled tightly into a cylindrical form before application. **10.** any of various Old World birds, such as the **European roller**, that have a blue, green, and brown plumage, a slightly hooked bill, and an erratic flight. **11.** (often cap.) a variety of tumbler pigeon. **12.** a person or thing that rolls. **13.** short for **steamroller**.

rollerball ('rəʊlə,bɔːl) n. a pen having a small moving nylon, plastic, or metal ball as a writing point.

roller bearing n. a bearing in which a shaft runs on a number of hardened-steel rollers held within a cage.

roller coaster n. another term for **big dipper**.

roller derby n. a race on roller skates, esp. one involving aggressive tactics.

roller skate n. **1.** a device having straps for fastening to a shoe and four small wheels that enable the wearer to glide swiftly over a floor. ~vb. **roller-skate**. **2.** (intr.) to move on roller skates. —**roller skater** n.

roller towel n. **1.** a towel with the two ends sewn together, hung on a roller. **2.** a towel wound inside a roller enabling a clean section to be pulled out when needed.

rollick ('rɒlɪk) vb. **1.** (intr.) to behave in a carefree or boisterous manner. ~n. **2.** a boisterous or carefree escapade. [C19: Scot. dialect, prob. from ROMP + FROLIC]

rollicking[1] ('rɒlɪkɪŋ) adj. boisterously carefree. [C19: from ROLLICK]

rollicking[2] ('rɒlɪkɪŋ) n. Brit. inf. a very severe telling-off. [C20: from ROLLICK (vb.) (in former sense: to be angry, make a fuss); ? infl. by BOLLOCKING]

roll in vb. (mainly intr.) **1.** (adv.) to arrive in abundance or in large numbers. **2.** (adv.) to arrive at one's destination. **3. be rolling in.** (prep.) Sl. to abound or luxuriate in (wealth, money, etc.).

rolling ('rəʊlɪŋ) adj. **1.** having gentle rising and falling slopes: rolling country. **2.** progressing by stages or by occurrences in different places in succession: a rolling strike. **3.** subject to regular review and updating: a rolling plan for overseas development. **4.** reverberating: rolling thunder. **5.** Sl. extremely rich. **6.** that may be turned up or down: a rolling hat brim. ~adv. **7.** Sl. swaying or staggering (in **rolling drunk**).

rolling mill n. **1.** a mill or factory where ingots of heated metal are passed between rollers to produce sheets or bars of a required cross section and form. **2.** a machine having rollers that may be used for this purpose.

rolling pin n. a cylinder with handles at both ends used for rolling dough, pastry, etc., out flat.

rolling stock n. the wheeled vehicles collectively used on a railway, including the locomotives, passenger coaches, etc.

rolling stone n. a restless or wandering person.

Rolling Stones pl. n. **the**. British rock group (formed 1962): comprising Mick Jagger, Keith Richards (born 1943; guitar, vocals), Brian Jones (1942–69; guitar), Charlie Watts (born 1941; drums), Bill Wyman (born 1936; bass guitar), and subsequently Mick Taylor (born 1948; guitar; with the group 1969–74) and Ron Wood (born 1947; guitar; with the group from 1975). See also Michael Philip Jagger.

rollmop ('rəʊl,mɒp) n. a herring fillet rolled, usually around onion slices, and pickled in spiced vinegar. [C20: from G Rollmops, from rollen to ROLL + Mops pug dog]

rollneck ('rəʊl,nɛk) adj. **1.** (of a garment) having a high neck that may be rolled over. ~n. **2.** a rollneck sweater or other garment.

Rollo ('rɒləʊ) n. ?860–?930 A.D., Norse war leader who received from Charles the Simple a fief that formed the basis of the duchy of Normandy. Also called: **Rolf, Rolf the Ganger**.

roll of honour *n.* a list of those who have died in war for their country.

roll on *vb.* **1.** *Brit.* used to express the wish that an eagerly anticipated event or date will come quickly: *roll on Saturday.* ~*adj.* **roll-on.** **2.** (of a deodorant, etc.) dispensed by means of a revolving ball fitted into the neck of the container. ~*n.* **roll-on.** **3.** a woman's foundation garment, made of elasticated material and having no fastenings.

roll-on/roll-off *adj.* denoting a cargo ship or ferry designed so that vehicles can be driven straight on and straight off.

roll out *vb.* (*tr., adv.*) **1.** to cause (pastry) to become flatter and thinner by pressure with a rolling pin. **2.** to show (a new type of aircraft) to the public for the first time. **3.** to launch (a new film, product, etc.) in a series of successive waves, as over the whole country. ~*n.* **roll-out.** **4.** a presentation to the public of a new aircraft, product, etc.; a launch.

roll over *vb.* (*adv.*) **1.** (*intr.*) to overturn. **2.** (*intr.*) (of an animal, esp. a dog) to lie on its back while kicking its legs in the air. **3.** (*intr.*) to capitulate. **4.** (*tr.*) to continue (a loan, debt, etc.) in force for a further period. ~*n.* **roll-over.** **5.** an instance of such continuance of a loan, debt, etc.

roll-top desk *n.* a desk having a slatted wooden panel that can be pulled down over the writing surface when not in use.

roll up *vb.* (*adv.*) **1.** to form or cause to form a cylindrical shape. **2.** (*tr.*) to wrap (an object) round on itself or on an axis: *to roll up a map.* **3.** (*intr.*) *Inf.* to arrive, esp. in a vehicle. **4.** (*intr.*) *Austral.* to assemble; congregate. ~*n.* **roll-up.** **5.** *Brit. inf.* a cigarette made by hand from loose tobacco and cigarette papers. **6.** *Austral.* the number attending a meeting, etc.

roly-poly ('rəʊlɪ'pəʊlɪ) *adj.* **1.** plump, buxom, or rotund. ~*n., pl.* **-lies.** **2.** *Brit.* a strip of suet pastry spread with jam, fruit, or a savoury mixture, rolled up, and baked or steamed. [C17: apparently by reduplication from *roly,* from ROLL]

ROM (rɒm) *n. Computers. acronym for* read only memory: a storage device that holds data permanently and cannot be altered by the programmer.

rom. *Printing. abbrev. for* roman (type).

Rom. *abbrev. for:* **1.** Roman. **2.** Romance (languages). **3.** Romania(n). **4.** *Bible.* Romans.

Roma ('rɔːma) *n.* the Italian name for **Rome.**

Romagna (*Italian* ro'maɲɲa) *n.* an area of N Italy: part of the Papal States up to 1860.

Romaic (rəʊ'meɪɪk) *Obs.* ~*n.* **1.** the modern Greek vernacular. ~*adj.* **2.** of or relating to Greek. [C19: from Gk *Rhōmaikos* Roman, with reference to the Eastern Roman Empire]

Romains (*French* rɔmɛ̃) *n.* **Jules** (ʒyl). pseudonym of *Louis Farigoule.* 1885–1972, French poet, dramatist, and novelist. His works include the novel *Men of Good Will* (1932–46).

roman ('rəʊmən) *adj.* **1.** of, relating to, or denoting a vertical style of printing type: the usual form of type for most printed matter. Cf. **italic.** ~*n.* **2.** roman type. [C16: so called because the style of letters is that used in ancient Roman inscriptions]

Roman ('rəʊmən) *adj.* **1.** of or relating to Rome or its inhabitants in ancient or modern times. **2.** of or relating to Roman Catholicism or the Roman Catholic Church. ~*n.* **3.** a citizen or inhabitant of ancient or modern Rome.

roman à clef *French.* (rɔmã a kle) *n., pl.* **romans à clef** (rɔmã a kle). a novel in which real people are depicted under fictitious names. [lit.: novel with a key]

Roman alphabet *n.* the alphabet evolved by the ancient Romans for the writing of Latin, derived ultimately from the Phoenicians. The alphabet serves for writing most of the languages of W Europe.

Roman candle *n.* a firework that produces a continuous shower of sparks punctuated by coloured balls of fire. [C19: it originated in Italy]

Roman Catholic *adj.* **1.** of or relating to the Roman Catholic Church. ~*n.* **2.** a member of this Church. ~Often shortened to **Catholic. — Roman Catholicism** *n.*

Roman Catholic Church *n.* the Christian Church over which the pope presides, with administrative headquarters in the Vatican. Also called: **Catholic Church, Church of Rome.**

romance *n.* (rə'mæns, 'rəʊmæns). **1.** a love affair. **2.** love, esp. romantic love idealized for its purity or beauty. **3.** a spirit of or inclination for adventure or mystery. **4.** a mysterious, exciting, sentimental, or nostalgic quality, esp. one associated with a place. **5.** a narrative in verse or prose, written in a vernacular language in the Middle Ages, dealing with adventures of chivalrous heroes. **6.** any similar narrative work dealing with events and characters remote from ordinary life. **7.** a story, novel, film, etc., dealing with love, usually in an idealized or sentimental way. **8.** an extravagant, absurd, or fantastic account. **9.** a lyrical song or short instrumental composition having a simple melody. ~*vb.* (rə'mæns). **10.** (*intr.*) to tell, invent, or write extravagant or romantic fictions. **11.** (*intr.*) to tell extravagant or improbable lies. **12.** (*intr.*) to have romantic thoughts. **13.** (*intr.*) (of a couple) to indulge in romantic behaviour. **14.** (*tr.*) to be romantically involved with. [C13 *romauns,* from OF *romans,* ult. from L *Rōmānicus* Roman] —**ro'mancer** *n.*

Romance (rə'mæns, 'rəʊmæns) *adj.* **1.** denoting, relating to, or belonging to the languages derived from Latin, including Italian, Spanish, Portuguese, French, and Romanian. **2.** denoting a word borrowed from a Romance language. ~*n.* **3.** this group of languages.

Roman Empire *n.* **1.** the territories ruled by ancient Rome. At its height the Roman Empire included W and S Europe, N Africa, and SW Asia. In 395 A.D. it was divided into the **Eastern Roman Empire,** whose capital was Byzantium, and the **Western Roman Empire,** whose capital was Rome. **2.** the government of Rome and its dominions by the emperors from 27 B.C. **3.** the Byzantine Empire. **4.** the Holy Roman Empire.

Romanesque (,rəʊmə'nɛsk) *adj.* **1.** denoting or having the style of architecture used in W and S Europe from the 9th to the 12th century, characterized by the rounded arch and massive-masonry wall construction. **2.** denoting a corresponding style in painting, sculpture, etc. [C18: see ROMAN, -ESQUE]

Roman holiday *n.* entertainment or pleasure that depends on the suffering of others. [C19: from Byron's poem *Childe Harold* (IV, 141)]

Romania (rəʊ'meɪnɪə), **Rumania,** *or* **Roumania** *n.* a republic in SE Europe, bordering on the Black Sea: united in 1861; became independent in 1878; Communist government set up in 1945; became a socialist republic in 1965. It consists chiefly of a great central arc of the Carpathian Mountains and Transylvanian Alps, with the plains of Walachia, Moldavia, and Dobriya on the south and east and the Pannonian Plain in the west. Language: Romanian. Currency: leu. Capital: Bucharest. Pop.: 22 724 836 (1980 est.). Area: 237 500 sq. km (91 699 sq. miles).

Romanian (rəʊ'meɪnɪən), **Rumanian,** *or* **Roumanian** *n.* **1.** the official language of Romania. **2.** a native, citizen, or inhabitant of Romania. ~*adj.* **3.** relating to, denoting, or characteristic of Romania, its people, or their language.

Romanic (rəʊ'mænɪk) *adj.* another word for **Roman** or **Romance.**

Romanism ('rəʊmə,nɪzəm) *n.* Roman Catholicism, esp. when regarded as excessively or superstitiously ritualistic. —'**Romanist** *n.*

Romanize *or* **-nise** ('rəʊmə,naɪz) *vb.* **1.** (*tr.*) to impart a Roman Catholic character to (a ceremony, etc.). **2.** (*intr.*) to be converted to Roman Catholicism. **3.** (*tr.*) to transcribe (a language) into the Roman alphabet. —,**Romani'zation** *or* **-ni'sation** *n.*

Roman law *n.* the system of jurisprudence of ancient Rome, codified under Justinian and forming the basis of many modern legal systems.

Roman nose *n.* a nose having a high prominent bridge.

Roman numerals *pl. n.* the letters used by the Romans for the representation of cardinal numbers, still used occasionally today. The integers are represented by the following letters: I (= 1), V (= 5), X (= 10), L (= 50), C (= 100), D (= 500), and M (= 1000). VI = 6 (V + I) but IV = 4 (V – I).

Romano (*Italian* ro'ma:no) *n*. See **Giulio Romano**.

Romanov ('rəumənɒf; *Russian* ra'manəf) *n*. any of the Russian imperial dynasty that ruled from the crowning (1613) of Mikhail Fyodorovich to the abdication (1917) of Nicholas II during the February Revolution.

Romansch *or* **Romansh** (rəu'mænʃ) *n*. a group of Romance dialects spoken in the Swiss canton of Grisons; an official language of Switzerland since 1938. [C17: from Romansch, lit.: Romance language]

romantic (rəu'mæntɪk) *adj*. **1**. of, relating to, imbued with, or characterized by romance. **2**. evoking or given to thoughts and feelings of love, esp. idealized or sentimental love: *a romantic setting*. **3**. impractical, visionary, or idealistic: *a romantic scheme*. **4**. *Often euphemistic*. imaginary or fictitious: *a romantic account of one's war service*. **5**. (*often cap*.) of or relating to a movement in European art, music, and literature in the late 18th and early 19th centuries, characterized by an emphasis on feeling and content rather than order and form. ~*n*. **6**. a person who is romantic, as in being idealistic, amorous, or soulful. **7**. a person whose tastes in art, literature, etc., lie mainly in romanticism. **8**. (*often cap*.) a poet, composer, etc., of the romantic period or whose main inspiration is romanticism. [C17: from F, from obs. *romant* story, romance, from OF *romans* ROMANCE] —**ro'mantically** *adv*.

romanticism (rəu'mæntɪˌsɪzəm) *n*. **1**. (*often cap*.) the theory, practice, and style of the romantic art, music, and literature of the late 18th and early 19th centuries, usually opposed to classicism. **2**. romantic attitudes, ideals, or qualities. —**ro'manticist** *n*.

romanticize *or* **-cise** (rəu'mæntɪˌsaɪz) *vb*. **1**. (*intr*.) to think or act in a romantic way. **2**. (*tr*.) to interpret according to romantic precepts. **3**. to make or become romantic, as in style. —**ro,mantici'zation** *or* **-ci'sation** *n*.

Romany *or* **Romani** ('rɒmənɪ, 'rəu-) *n*. **1. a**. (*pl*. **-nies** *or* **-nis**) another name for a **Gypsy**. **b**. (*as modifier*): *Romany customs*. **2**. the language of the Gypsies, belonging to the Indic branch of the Indo-European family. [C19: from Romany *romani* (adj.) Gypsy, ult. from Sansk. *domba* man of a low caste of musicians, of Dravidian origin]

romanza (rəu'mænzə) *n*. a short instrumental piece of songlike character. [It.]

romaunt (rə'mɔ:nt) *n*. *Arch*. a verse romance. [C16: from OF; see ROMANTIC]

Romberg ('rɒmbɜ:g) *n*. **Sigmund**. 1887–1951, U.S. composer of operettas, born in Hungary. He wrote *The Student Prince* (1924) and *The Desert Song* (1926).

Rome (rəum) *n*. **1**. the capital of Italy, on the River Tiber: includes the independent state of the Vatican City; traditionally founded by Romulus on the Palatine Hill in 753 B.C., later spreading to six other hills east of the Tiber; capital of the Roman Empire; a great cultural and artistic centre, esp. during the Renaissance. Pop.: 2 815 457 (1986). Italian name: **Roma**. **2**. the Roman Empire. **3**. the Roman Catholic Church or Roman Catholicism.

Romeo ('rəumɪəu) *n*., *pl*. **Romeos**. an ardent male lover. [after the hero of Shakespeare's *Romeo and Juliet*]

Romish ('rəumɪʃ) *adj*. *Usually derog*. of or resembling Roman Catholic beliefs or practices.

Rommel (*German* 'rɒməl) *n*. **Erwin** ('ɛrviːn), nicknamed *the Desert Fox*. 1891–1944, German field marshal, noted for his brilliant generalship in N Africa in World War II. Later a commander in N France, he committed suicide after the officers' plot against Hitler.

Romney ('rɒmnɪ, 'rʌm-) *n*. **George**. 1734–1802, English painter, who painted more than 50 portraits of Lady Hamilton in various historical roles.

Romney Marsh ('rɒmnɪ, 'rʌm-) *n*. a marshy area of SE England, on the Kent coast between New Romney and Rye: includes Dungeness.

romp (rɒmp) *vb*. (*intr*.) **1**. to play or run about wildly, boisterously, or joyfully. **2**. **romp home** (*or* **in**). to win a race, etc., easily. ~*n*. **3**. a noisy or boisterous game or prank. **4**. *Arch*. a playful or boisterous child, esp. a girl. **5**. an easy victory. [C18: prob. var. of RAMP, from OF *ramper* to crawl, climb]

rompers ('rɒmpəz) *pl. n*. **1**. a one-piece baby garment consisting of trousers and a bib with straps. **2**. *N.Z.* a type of costume worn by schoolgirls for games and gymnastics.

Romulus ('rɒmjuləs) *n*. *Roman myth*. the founder of Rome, suckled with his twin brother Remus by a she-wolf

after they were abandoned in infancy. Their parents were Rhea Silvia and Mars. Romulus later killed Remus in an argument over the new city.

Roncesvalles ('rɒnsəˌvælz; *Spanish* rɔnθeθ'βaʎes) *n*. a village in N Spain, in the Pyrenees: a nearby pass was the scene of the defeat of Charlemagne and death of Roland in 778. French name: **Roncevaux** (rɔ̃svo).

rondavel (ˌrɒn'dɑːvəl) *n*. *S. African*. a circular building, often thatched. [from ?]

rondeau ('rɒndəu) *n*., *pl*. **-deaux** (-dəu, -dəuz). a poem consisting of 13 or 10 lines with two rhymes and having the opening words of the first line used as an unrhymed refrain. [C16: from OF, from *rondel* a little round, from *rond* ROUND]

rondel ('rɒndəl) *n*. a rondeau consisting of three stanzas of 13 or 14 lines with a two-line refrain appearing twice or three times. [C14: from OF, lit.: a little circle, from *rond* ROUND]

rondo ('rɒndəu) *n*., *pl*. **-dos**. a piece of music in which a refrain is repeated between episodes: often constitutes the form of the last movement of a sonata or concerto. [C18: from It., from F RONDEAU]

Rondônia (*Portuguese* rõ'donja) *n*. a state of W Brazil: consists chiefly of tropical rainforest; a centre of the Amazon rubber boom until about 1912. Capital: Pôrto Velho. Pop.: 776 000 (1986 est.). Area: 243 043 sq. km (93 839 sq. miles). Former name (until 1956): **Guaporé**.

rone (rəun) *or* **ronepipe** *n*. *Scot*. a drainpipe for carrying rainwater from a roof. [C19: from ?]

Ronsard (*French* rɔ̃sar) *n*. **Pierre de** (pjɛr də). 1524–85, French poet, foremost of the **Pléiade**.

röntgen ('rɒntgən, -tjən, 'rɛnt-) *n*. a variant spelling of **roentgen**.

Röntgen ('rɒntgən, -tjən, 'rɛnt-; *German* 'rœntgən) *n*. a variant spelling of (Wilhelm Konrad) **Roentgen**.

roo (ru:) *n*. *Austral. inf*. a kangaroo.

rood (ru:d) *n*. **1. a**. a crucifix, esp. one set on a beam or screen at the entrance to the chancel of a church. **b**. (*as modifier*): *rood screen*. **2**. the Cross on which Christ was crucified. **3**. a unit of area equal to one quarter of an acre or 0.10117 hectare. **4**. a unit of area equal to one square rod. [OE *rōd*]

Roodepoort-Maraisburg ('ruːdə,puət məˈreɪsbɜːg) *n*. an industrial city in NE South Africa, in S Transvaal on the Witwatersrand. Pop.: 141 764 (1986).

roof (ru:f) *n*., *pl*. **roofs** (ru:fs, ru:vz). **1. a**. a structure that covers or forms the top of a building. **b**. (*in combination*): *the rooftop*. **c**. (*as modifier*): *a roof garden*. **2**. the top covering of a vehicle, oven, or other structure: *the roof of a car*. **3**. *Anat*. any structure that covers an organ or part: *the roof of the mouth*. **4**. a highest or topmost point or part: *Mount Everest is the roof of the world*. **5**. a house or other shelter: *a poor man's roof*. **6**. **hit** (*or* **raise** *or* **go through**) **the roof**. *Inf*. to get extremely angry. ~*vb*. **7**. (*tr*.) to provide or cover with a roof or rooflike part. [OE *hrōf*] —'**roofer** *n*. —'**roofless** *adj*.

roof garden *n*. a garden on a flat roof of a building.

roofing ('ru:fɪŋ) *n*. **1**. material used to construct a roof. **2**. the act of constructing a roof.

roof rack *n*. a rack attached to the roof of a motor vehicle for carrying luggage, skis, etc.

rooftree ('ru:f,tri:) *n*. another name for **ridgepole**.

rooibos ('rɔɪ,bɒs, 'ruɪ,bɒs) *n*. any of various South African trees with red leaves. [from Afrik. *rooi* red + *bos* bush]

rooibos tea *n*. *S. African*. a tealike drink made from the leaves of the rooibos.

rooikat ('rɔɪ,kæt, 'ruɪ,kæt) *n*. a South African lynx. [from Afrik. *rooi* red + *kat* cat]

rooinek ('rɔɪ,nɛk, 'ruɪ,nɛk) *n*. *S. African*. a facetious name for an **Englishman**. [C19: Afrik., lit.: red neck]

rook[1] (ruk) *n*. **1**. a large Eurasian passerine bird, with a black plumage and a whitish base to its bill. **2**. *Sl*. a swindler or cheat, esp. one who cheats at cards. ~*vb*. **3**. (*tr*.) *Sl*. to overcharge, swindle, or cheat. [OE *hrōc*]

rook[2] (ruk) *n*. a chesspiece that may move any number of unoccupied squares in a straight line, horizontally or vertically. Also called: **castle**. [C14: from OF *rok*, ult. from Ar. *rukhkh*]

rookery ('rukərɪ) *n*., *pl*. **-eries**. **1**. a group of nesting rooks. **2**. a clump of trees containing rooks' nests. **3. a**. a breeding ground or communal living area of certain other birds or mammals, esp. penguins or seals. **b.** a colony of any such creatures. **4.** *Arch.* an overcrowded slum.

rookie ('rʊkɪ) *n. Inf.* a newcomer, esp. a raw recruit in the army. [C20: changed from RECRUIT]

room (ruːm, rʊm) *n.* **1.** space or extent, esp. unoccupied or unobstructed space for a particular purpose: *is there room to pass?* **2.** an area within a building enclosed by a floor, a ceiling, and walls or partitions. **3.** (*functioning as sing. or pl.*) the people present in a room: *the whole room was laughing.* **4.** (foll. by *for*) opportunity or scope: *room for manoeuvre.* **5.** (*pl.*) a part of a house, hotel, etc., that is rented out as separate accommodation: *living in dingy rooms in Dalry.* ~*vb.* **6.** (*intr.*) to occupy or share a room or lodging: *where does he room?* [OE *rūm*] — '**roomer** *n.*

roomful ('ruːm,fʊl, 'rʊm-) *n., pl.* -**fuls.** a number or quantity sufficient to fill a room: *a roomful of furniture.*

rooming house *n. U.S. & Canad.* a house having self-contained furnished rooms or flats for renting.

roommate ('ruːm,meɪt, 'rʊm-) *n.* a person with whom one shares a room or lodging.

room service *n.* service in a hotel providing meals, drinks, etc., in guests' rooms.

roomy ('ruːmɪ, 'rʊmɪ) *adj.* **roomier, roomiest.** spacious. — '**roomily** *adv.* — '**roominess** *n.*

Roosevelt ('rəʊzə,velt) *n.* **1.** (**Anna**) **Eleanor.** 1884– 1962, U.S. writer, diplomat, and advocate of liberal causes: delegate to the United Nations (1945–52). **2.** her husband, **Franklin Delano** ('delə,nəʊ), known as *FDR.* 1882–1945, 32nd president of the U.S. (1933–45); elected four times. He instituted major reforms (the **New Deal**) to counter the economic crisis of the 1930s and was a forceful leader during World War II. **3. Theodore.** 1858–1919, 26th president of the U.S. (1901–09). A proponent of extending military power, he won for the U.S. the right to build the Panama Canal (1903). He won the Nobel peace prize (1906), for mediating in the Russo-Japanese war.

roost (ruːst) *n.* **1.** a place, perch, branch, etc., where birds, esp. domestic fowl, rest or sleep. **2.** a temporary place to rest or stay. ~*vb.* **3.** (*intr.*) to rest or sleep on a roost. **4.** (*intr.*) to settle down or stay. **5. come home to roost.** to have unfavourable repercussions. [OE *hrōst*]

Roost (ruːst) *n.* **the.** a powerful current caused by conflicting tides around the Shetland and Orkney Islands. [C16: from ON *rōst*]

rooster ('ruːstə) *n. Chiefly U.S. & Canad.* the male of the domestic fowl; a cock.

root[1] (ruːt) *n.* **1. a.** the organ of a higher plant that anchors the rest of the plant in the ground and absorbs water and mineral salts from the soil. **b.** (loosely) any of the branches of such an organ. **2.** any plant part, such as a tuber, that is similar to a root in function or appearance. **3. a.** the essential part or nature of something: *your analysis strikes at the root of the problem.* **b.** (*as modifier*): *the root cause of the problem.* **4.** *Anat.* the embedded portion of a tooth, nail, hair, etc. **5.** origin or derivation. **6.** (*pl.*) a person's sense of belonging in a community, place, etc., esp. the one in which he was born or brought up. **7.** *Bible.* a descendant. **8.** *Linguistics.* the form of a word that remains after removal of all affixes. **9.** *Maths.* a quantity that when multiplied by itself a certain number of times equals a given quantity: *3 is a cube root of 27.* **10.** Also called: **solution.** *Maths.* a number that when substituted for the variable satisfies a given equation. **11.** *Music.* (in harmony) the note forming the foundation of a chord. **12.** *Austral. & N.Z. sl.* sexual intercourse. **13. root and branch.** (*adv.*) entirely; utterly. ~Related *adj.*: **radical.** ~*vb.* **14.** (*intr.*) Also: **take root.** to establish a root and begin to grow. **15.** (*intr.*) Also: **take root.** to become established, embedded, or effective. **16.** (*tr.*) to embed with or as if with a root or roots. **17.** *Austral. & N.Z. sl.* to have sexual intercourse (with). ~See also **root out, roots.** [OE *rōt*, from ON] — '**rooter** *n.* — '**root,like** *adj.* — '**rooty** *adj.* — '**rootiness** *n.*

root[2] (ruːt) *vb.* (*intr.*) **1.** (of a pig) to burrow in or dig up the earth in search of food, using the snout. **2.** (foll. by *about, around, in,* etc.) *Inf.* to search vigorously but unsystematically. [C16: changed (through infl. of ROOT[1]) from earlier *wroot,* from OE *wrōtan;* rel. to OE *wrōt* snout] — '**rooter** *n.*

root[3] (ruːt) *vb.* (*intr.; usually foll. by for*) *Inf.* to give support to (a contestant, team, etc.), as by cheering. [C19: ?

var. of Scot. *rout* to make a loud noise, from ON *rauta* to roar]

root beer *n. U.S. & Canad.* an effervescent drink made from extracts of various roots and herbs.

root canal *n.* the passage in the root of a tooth through which its nerves and blood vessels enter the pulp cavity.

root climber *n.* any of various climbing plants, such as the ivy, that adhere to a supporting structure by means of small roots growing from the side of the stem.

root crop *n.* a crop, as of turnips or beets, cultivated for the food value of its roots.

rooted ('ruːtɪd) *adj.* **1.** having roots. **2.** deeply felt: *rooted objections.*

root ginger *n.* the raw underground stem of the ginger plant used finely chopped or grated, esp. in Chinese dishes.

root hair *n.* any of the hollow hairlike outgrowths of the outer cells of a root, just behind the tip, that absorb water and salts from the soil.

rootle ('ruːtəl) *vb.* (*intr.*) *Brit.* another word for **root**[2].

rootless ('ruːtlɪs) *adj.* having no roots, esp. (of a person) having no ties with a particular place.

rootlet ('ruːtlɪt) *n.* a small root.

root mean square *n.* the square root of the average of the squares of a set of numbers or quantities: *the root mean square of 1, 2, and 4 is* $\sqrt{[(1^2 + 2^2 + 4^2)/3]} = \sqrt{7}$. Abbrev.: **rms.**

root nodule *n.* a swelling on the root of a leguminous plant, such as clover, that contains bacteria capable of nitrogen fixation.

root out *vb.* (*tr., adv.*) to remove or eliminate completely: *we must root out inefficiency.*

roots (ruːts) *adj.* (of popular music) going back to the origins of a style, esp. in being genuine and unpretentious: *roots rock.*

rootstock ('ruːt,stɒk) *n.* **1.** another name for **rhizome. 2.** another name for **stock** (sense 7). **3.** *Biol.* a basic structure from which offshoots have developed.

ropable *or* **ropeable** ('rəʊpəbəl) *adj.* **1.** capable of being roped. **2.** *Austral. & N.Z. inf.* **a.** angry. **b.** wild or intractable: *a ropable beast.*

rope (rəʊp) *n.* **1. a.** a fairly thick cord made of intertwined hemp or other fibres or of wire or other strong material. **b.** (*as modifier*): *a rope ladder.* **2.** a row of objects fastened to form a line: *a rope of pearls.* **3.** a quantity of material wound in the form of a cord. **4.** a filament or strand, esp. of something viscous or glutinous: *a rope of slime.* **5. give (someone) enough (or plenty of) rope to hang himself.** to allow (someone) to accomplish his own downfall by his own foolish acts. **6. know the ropes.** to have a thorough understanding of a particular sphere of activity. **7. on the ropes. a.** *Boxing.* driven against the ropes enclosing the ring by an opponent's attack. **b.** in a hopeless position. **8. the rope. a.** a rope halter used for hanging. **b.** death by hanging. ~*vb.* **9.** (*tr.*) to bind or fasten with or as if with a rope. **10.** (*tr.;* usually foll. by *off*) to enclose or divide by means of a rope. **11.** (when *intr.,* foll. by *up*) *Mountaineering.* to tie (climbers) together with a rope. [OE *rāp*]

rope in *vb.* (*tr., adv.*) **1.** *Brit.* to persuade to take part in some activity. **2.** *U.S. & Canad.* to trick or entice into some activity.

rope's end *n.* a short piece of rope, esp. as formerly used for flogging sailors.

ropewalk ('rəʊp,wɔːk) *n.* a long narrow usually covered path or shed where ropes are made.

ropy *or* **ropey** ('rəʊpɪ) *adj.* **ropier, ropiest. 1.** *Brit. inf.* **a.** inferior. **b.** slightly unwell. **2.** (of a viscous or sticky substance) forming strands. **3.** resembling a rope. — '**ropily** *adv.* — '**ropiness** *n.*

Roquefort ('rɒkfɔː) *n.* a blue-veined cheese with a strong flavour, made from ewe's and goat's milk. [C19: after *Roquefort,* village in S France]

roquet ('rəʊkɪ) *Croquet.* ~*vb.* -**queting** (-kɪɪŋ), -**queted** (-kɪd). **1.** to drive one's ball against (another person's ball) in order to be allowed to croquet. ~*n.* **2.** the act of roqueting. [C19: var. of CROQUET]

Roraima (*Portuguese* rɔ'raima) *n.* a federal territory of N Brazil: chiefly rainforest. Capital: Boa Vista. Area: 230 104 sq. km (89 740 sq. miles). Pop.: 79 407 (1980).

ro-ro ('rəʊrəʊ) *adj. acronym for* roll-on/roll-off.

rorqual ('rɔːkwəl) *n.* any of several whalebone whales that have a dorsal fin and a series of grooves along the throat and chest. Also called: **finback**. [C19: from F, from Norwegian *rörhval*, from ON *reytharhvalr*, from *reythr* (from *rauthr* red) + *hvalr* whale]

Rorschach test ('rɔːʃɑːk) *n. Psychol.* a personality test consisting of a number of unstructured inkblots presented for interpretation. [C20: after Hermann *Rorschach* (1884–1922), Swiss psychiatrist]

rort (rɔːt) *n. Austral. sl.* **1.** a rowdy party or celebration. **2.** a fraud; deception. [C20: back formation from E dialect *rorty* (in the sense: good, splendid)] —**'rorty** *adj.*

Rosa[1] ('rəʊzə; *Italian* 'rɔːza) *n.* **Monte** ('mɒntɪ; *Italian* 'monte). a mountain between Italy and Switzerland: the highest in the Pennine Alps. Height: 4634 m (15 204 ft.).

Rosa[2] (*Italian* 'rɔːza) *n.* **Salvator** ('salvatɔr). 1615–73, Italian artist, noted esp. for his romantic landscapes.

rosace ('rəʊzeɪs) *n.* **1.** another name for **rose window**. **2.** another name for **rosette**. [C19: from F, from L *rosāceus* ROSACEOUS]

rosaceous (rəʊ'zeɪʃəs) *adj.* **1.** of or belonging to the Rosaceae, a family of plants typically having white, yellow, pink, or red five-petalled flowers. The family includes the rose, strawberry, blackberry, and many fruit trees. **2.** like a rose, esp., rose-coloured. [C18: from L *rosāceus* composed of roses, from *rosa* ROSE[1]]

rosarian (rəʊ'zɛərɪən) *n.* a person who cultivates roses, esp. professionally.

Rosario (rəʊ'sɑːrɪəʊ; *Spanish* rɔ'sarjo) *n.* an inland port in E Argentina, on the Paraná River: the second largest city in the country; industrial centre. Pop.: 935 471 (1980).

rosarium (rəʊ'zɛərɪəm) *n., pl.* **-sariums** *or* **-saria** (-'zɛərɪə). a rose garden. [C19: NL]

rosary ('rəʊzərɪ) *n., pl.* **-saries.** **1.** *R.C. Church.* **a.** a series of prayers counted on a string of beads, usually five or 15 decades of Aves, each decade beginning with a Paternoster and ending with a Gloria. **b.** a string of 55 or 165 beads used to count these prayers as they are recited. **2.** (in other religions) a similar string of beads used in praying. **3.** an archaic word for a **garland** (of flowers, etc.). [C14: from L *rosārium* rose garden, from *rosārius* of roses, from *rosa* ROSE[1]]

Roscius ('rɒskɪəs, -sɪəs) *n.* **1.** full name *Quintus Roscius Gallus.* died 62 B.C., Roman actor. **2.** any actor. —**'Roscian** *adj.*

Roscommon (rɒs'kɒmən) *n.* an inland county of N central Ireland, in Connacht: economy based on cattle and sheep farming. County town: Roscommon. Pop.: 54 551 (1986). Area: 2463 sq. km (951 sq. miles).

rose[1] (rəʊz) *n.* **1. a.** a shrub or climbing plant having prickly stems, compound leaves, and fragrant flowers. **b.** (*in combination*): rosebush. **2.** the flower of any of these plants. **3.** any of various similar plants, such as the Christmas rose. **4. a.** a purplish-pink colour. **b.** (*as adj.*): *rose paint.* **5.** a rose, or a representation of one, as the national emblem of England. **6. a.** a cut for a gemstone, having a hemispherical faceted crown and a flat base. **b.** a gem so cut. **7.** a perforated cap fitted to a watering can or hose, causing the water to issue in a spray. **8.** a design or decoration shaped like a rose; rosette. **9.** *History.* See **red rose, white rose**. **10. bed of roses**. a situation of comfort or ease. **11. under the rose**. in secret; privately; sub rosa. ~*vb.* **12.** (*tr.*) to make rose-coloured; cause to blush or redden. [OE, from L *rosa*, prob. from Gk *rhodon* rose] —**'rose,like** *adj.*

rose[2] (rəʊz) *vb.* the past tense of **rise**.

rosé ('rəʊzeɪ) *n.* any pink wine, made either by removing the skins of red grapes after only a little colour has been extracted or by mixing red and white wines. [C19: from F, lit.: pink, from L *rosa* ROSE[1]]

roseate ('rəʊzɪ,eɪt) *adj.* **1.** of the colour rose or pink. **2.** excessively or idealistically optimistic.

rosebay ('rəʊz,beɪ) *n.* **1.** any of several rhododendrons. **2. rosebay willowherb.** a perennial plant that has spikes of deep pink flowers and is widespread in N temperate regions. **3.** another name for **oleander**.

Rosebery ('rəʊzbərɪ, -brɪ) *n.* **Earl of**, title of *Archibald Philip Primrose*. 1847–1929, British statesman; Liberal prime minister (1894–95).

rosebud ('rəʊz,bʌd) *n.* **1.** the bud of a rose. **2.** *Literary.* a pretty young woman.

rose campion *n.* a European plant widely cultivated for its pink flowers. Its stems and leaves are covered with white woolly down. Also called: **dusty miller**.

rose chafer *or* **beetle** *n.* a British beetle that has a greenish-golden body with a metallic lustre and feeds on plants.

rose-coloured *adj.* **1.** of the colour rose; rosy. **2.** excessively optimistic. **3. see through rose-coloured glasses** (*or* **spectacles**). to view in an excessively optimistic light.

rose-cut *adj.* (of a gemstone) cut with a hemispherical faceted crown and a flat base.

rosehip ('rəʊz,hɪp) *n.* the berry-like fruit of a rose plant.

rosella (rəʊ'zɛlə) *n.* any of various Australian parrots. [C19: prob. alteration of *Rose-hiller*, after Rose Hill, Parramatta, near Sydney]

rosemary ('rəʊzmərɪ) *n., pl.* **-maries.** an aromatic European shrub widely cultivated for its grey-green evergreen leaves, which are used in cookery and in the manufacture of perfumes. It is the traditional flower of remembrance. [C15: earlier *rosmarine*, from L *rōs* dew + *marīnus* marine; modern form infl. by folk etymology, as if ROSE[1] + *Mary*]

rose of Sharon ('ʃærən) *n.* a creeping shrub native to SE Europe but widely cultivated, having large yellow flowers. Also called: **Aaron's beard**.

roseola (rəʊ'ziːələ) *n. Pathol.* **1.** any red skin rash. **2.** another name for **rubeola**. [C19: from NL, dim. of L *roseus* rosy] —**ro'seolar** *adj.*

rosery ('rəʊzərɪ) *n., pl.* **-series.** a bed or garden of roses.

Rosetta (rəʊ'zɛtə) *n.* a town in N Egypt, in the Nile delta. Pop.: 36 711 (1966).

Rosetta stone *n.* a basalt slab discovered in 1799 at Rosetta, dating to the reign of Ptolemy V (196 B.C.) and carved with parallel inscriptions in hieroglyphics, Egyptian demotic, and Greek, which provided the key to the decipherment of ancient Egyptian texts.

rosette (rəʊ'zɛt) *n.* **1.** a decoration resembling a rose, esp. an arrangement of ribbons in a rose-shaped design worn as a badge or presented as a prize. **2.** another name for **rose window**. **3.** *Bot.* a circular cluster of leaves growing from the base of a stem. [C18: from OF: a little ROSE[1]]

Rosewall ('rəʊz,wɔːl) *n.* **Ken(neth)**. born 1934, Australian tennis player: Australian champion 1953, 1955, and 1971–72; U.S. champion 1956 and 1970.

rose-water *n.* **1.** scented water made by the distillation of rose petals or by impregnation with oil of roses. **2.** (*modifier*) elegant or delicate, esp. excessively so.

rose window *n.* a circular window, esp. one that has ornamental tracery radiating from the centre to form a symmetrical roselike pattern. Also called: **wheel window, rosette**.

rosewood ('rəʊz,wʊd) *n.* the hard dark wood of any of various tropical trees. It has a roselike scent and is used in cabinetwork.

Rosh Hashanah *or* **Rosh Hashana** ('rɒʃ həˈʃɑːnə; *Hebrew* 'rɒʃ haʃaˈna) *n.* the Jewish New Year festival, celebrated on the first and second of Tishri. [from Heb., lit.: beginning of the year, from *rōsh* head + *hash-shānāh* year]

Rosicrucian (,rəʊzɪ'kruːʃən) *n.* **1.** a member of a society professing esoteric religious doctrines, venerating the rose and Cross as symbols of Christ's Resurrection and Redemption, and claiming various occult powers. ~*adj.* **2.** of or designating the Rosicrucians or Rosicrucianism. [C17: from L *Rosae Crucis* Rose of the Cross, translation of the G name Christian *Rosenkreuz*, supposed founder of the society]

rosin ('rɒzɪn) *n.* **1.** Also called: **colophony**. a translucent brittle amber substance produced in the distillation of crude turpentine oleoresin and used esp. in making varnishes, printing inks, and sealing waxes and for treating the bows of stringed instruments. **2.** another name for **resin** (sense 1). ~*vb.* **3.** (*tr.*) to treat or coat with rosin. [C14: var. of RESIN] —**'rosiny** *adj.*

Roskilde (*Danish* 'rɔskilə) *n.* a city in Denmark, on NE Sjælland west of Copenhagen: capital of Denmark from the 10th century to 1443; scene of the signing (1658) of the **Peace of Roskilde** between Denmark and Sweden. Pop.: 48 756 (1985).

ROSPA ('rɒspə) *n.* (in Britain) *acronym for* Royal Society for the Prevention of Accidents.

Ross (rɒs) *n.* **1. Diana**. born 1944, U.S. singer: lead vocalist with Motown group the Supremes (1961–69), whose hits include "Baby Love" (1964). Her subsequent recordings include *Lady Sings the Blues* (film soundtrack,

1972). **2.** Sir **James Clark.** 1800–62, British naval officer; explorer of the Arctic and Antarctic. He located the north magnetic pole (1831) and discovered the Ross Sea during an Antarctic voyage (1839–43). **3.** his uncle, Sir **John.** 1777–1856, Scottish naval officer and Arctic explorer. **4.** Sir **Ronald.** 1857–1932, English bacteriologist, who discovered the transmission of malaria by mosquitoes: Nobel prize for physiology or medicine 1902.

Ross and Cromarty ('krɒmətɪ) n. (until 1975) a county of NW Scotland, including the island of Lewis and many islets: now part of the Highland region.

Ross Dependency n. a section of Antarctica administered by New Zealand: includes the coastal regions of Victoria Land and King Edward VII Land, the Ross Sea and islands, and the Ross Ice Shelf. Area: about 414 400 sq. km (160 000 sq. miles).

Rossellini (rɒsə'liːnɪ) n. **Roberto.** 1906–77, Italian film director. His films include *Rome, Open City* (1945), *Paisà* (1946), and *L'Amore* (1948).

Rossetti (rɒ'zɛtɪ) n. **1. Christina Georgina.** 1830–94, English poet. **2.** her brother, **Dante Gabriel.** 1828–82, English poet and painter: a leader of the Pre-Raphaelites.

Rossini (rɒ'siːnɪ) n. **Gioacchino Antonio** (dʒoak'kiːno an'tɔːnjo). 1792–1868, Italian composer, esp. of operas, such as *The Barber of Seville* (1816) and *William Tell* (1829).

Ross Island n. an island in the W Ross Sea: contains the active volcano Mount Erebus.

Rossiya (ra'siːjə) n. transliteration of the Russian name for **Russia.**

Ross Sea n. a large arm of the S Pacific in Antarctica, incorporating the Ross Ice Shelf and lying between Victoria Land and the Edward VII Peninsula.

Rostand (*French* rɔstɑ̃) n. **Edmond** (ɛdmɔ̃). 1868–1918, French playwright and poet in the romantic tradition; best known for his verse drama *Cyrano de Bergerac* (1897).

roster ('rɒstə) n. **1.** a list or register, esp. one showing the order of people enrolled for duty. ~vb. **2.** (tr.) to place on a roster. [C18: from Du. *rooster* grating or list (the lined paper looking like a grid)]

Rostock ('rɒstɒk) n. a port in N East Germany, on the Warnow estuary 13 km (8 miles) from the Baltic and its outport, Warnemünde: the chief port of East Germany; university (1419). Pop.: 245 606 (1986).

Rostov or **Rostov-on-Don** ('rɒstɒv) n. a port in the S Soviet Union, on the River Don 48 km (30 miles) from the Sea of Azov: industrial centre. Pop.: 957 000 (1981 est.).

Rostropovich (,rɒstrə'pəʊvɪtʃ; *Russian* rəstra'pɔvitʃ) n. **Mstislav Leopoldovich** ('mɪstɪslɑːv; *Russian* msti'slaf lea'pɔldavitʃ). born 1927, Soviet cellist, composer, and conductor; became a US citizen in 1978 after losing Soviet citizenship.

rostrum ('rɒstrəm) n., pl. **-trums** or **-tra** (-trə). **1.** any platform on which public speakers stand to address an audience. **2.** a platform in front of an orchestra on which the conductor stands. **3.** another word for **ram** (sense 5). **4.** the prow of an ancient Roman ship. **5.** *Biol., zool.* a beak or beaklike part. [C16: from L *rostrum* beak, ship's prow, from *rōdere* to nibble, gnaw; in pl., *rostra* orator's platform, because this platform in the Roman forum was adorned with the prows of captured ships] —'**rostral** adj.

rosy ('rəʊzɪ) adj. **rosier, rosiest. 1.** of the colour rose or pink. **2.** having a healthy pink complexion: *rosy cheeks.* **3.** optimistic, esp. excessively so: *a rosy view of social improvements.* **4.** resembling or abounding in roses. —'**rosily** adv. —'**rosiness** n.

rot (rɒt) vb. **rotting, rotted. 1.** to decay or cause to decay as a result of bacterial or fungal action. **2.** (intr.; usually foll. by *off* or *away*) to crumble (off) or break (away), as from decay or long use. **3.** (intr.) to become weak or depressed through inertia, confinement, etc.; languish: *rotting in prison.* **4.** to become or cause to become morally degenerate. ~n. **5.** the process of rotting or the state of being rotten. **6.** something decomposed. Related adj.: **putrid. 7.** short for **dry rot. 8.** *Pathol.* any putrefactive decomposition of tissues. **9.** a condition in plants characterized by decay of tissues, caused by bacteria, fungi, etc. **10.** *Vet. science.* a contagious fungal disease of sheep. **11.** (*also interj.*) nonsense; rubbish. [OE *rotian* (vb.); rel. to ON, *rotna*] C13 (n.), from ON]

rota ('rəʊtə) n. *Chiefly Brit.* a register of names showing the order in which people take their turn to perform certain duties. [C17: from L: a wheel]

Rota ('rəʊtə) n. *R.C. Church.* the supreme ecclesiastical tribunal.

rotary ('rəʊtərɪ) adj. **1.** operating by rotation. **2.** turning; revolving. ~n., pl. **-ries. 3.** a part of a machine that rotates about an axis. **4.** *U.S. & Canad.* another term for **roundabout** (sense 2). [C18: from Med. L *rotārius*, from L *rota* wheel]

Rotary Club n. any of the local clubs that form **Rotary International,** an international association of professional and business men founded in the U.S. in 1905 to promote community service. —**Rotarian** (rəʊ'tɛərɪən) n., adj.

rotary engine n. **1.** an internal-combustion engine having radial cylinders that rotate about a fixed crankshaft. **2.** an engine, such as a turbine or wankel engine, in which power is transmitted directly to rotating components.

rotary plough or **tiller** n. an implement with a series of blades mounted on a power-driven shaft which rotates so as to break up soil.

rotary press n. a machine for printing from a revolving cylindrical forme, usually onto a continuous strip of paper.

rotary table n. a chain or gear-driven unit, mounted in the derrick floor which rotates the drill pipe and bit.

rotate vb. (rəʊ'teɪt). **1.** to turn or cause to turn around an axis; revolve or spin. **2.** to follow or cause to follow a set sequence. **3.** to replace (one set of personnel) with another. ~adj. ('rəʊteɪt). **4.** *Bot.* designating a corolla the petals of which radiate like the spokes of a wheel. —'ro'tatable adj.

rotation (rəʊ'teɪʃən) n. **1.** the act of rotating; rotary motion. **2.** a regular cycle of events in a set order or sequence. **3.** a planned sequence of cropping according to which the crops grown in successive seasons on the same land are varied so as to make a balanced demand on its resources of fertility. **4.** the spinning motion of a body, such as a planet, about an internal axis. **5.** *Maths.* **a.** a circular motion of a configuration about a given point, without a change in shape. **b.** a transformation in which the coordinate axes are rotated by a fixed angle about the origin. —ro'tational adj.

rotator (rəʊ'teɪtə) n. **1.** a person, device, or part that rotates or causes rotation. **2.** *Anat.* any of various muscles that revolve a part on its axis.

rotatory ('rəʊtətərɪ, -trɪ) or (less commonly) **rotative** adj. of, possessing, or causing rotation. —'rotatorily adv.

rote (rəʊt) n. **1.** a habitual or mechanical routine or procedure. **2. by rote.** by repetition; by heart (often in **learn by rote**). [C14: from ?]

rotenone ('rəʊtɪ,nəʊn) n. a white odourless crystalline substance extracted from the roots of derris: a powerful insecticide. [C20: from Japanese *rōten* derris + -ONE]

rotgut ('rɒt,gʌt) n. *Facetious sl.* alcoholic drink, esp. spirits, of inferior quality.

Roth (rɒθ) n. **Philip.** born 1933, U.S. novelist. His works include *Goodbye, Columbus* (1959), *Pornoy's Complaint* (1969), *My Life as a Man* (1974), and *The Prague Orgy* (1985).

Rotherham ('rɒðərəm) n. an industrial town in N England, in South Yorkshire. Pop.: 81 988 (1981).

Rothermere ('rɒðə,mɪə) n. **Viscount.** title of *Harold Sidney Harmsworth.* 1868–1940, British newspaper magnate.

Rothesay ('rɒθsɪ) n. a town in SW Scotland, in Strathclyde region, on the E coast of Bute Island. Pop.: 5408 (1981).

Rothko ('rɒθkəʊ) n. **Mark.** 1903–70, U.S. abstract expressionist painter, born in Russia.

Rothschild ('rɒθtʃaɪld, 'rɒθs-) n. a powerful family of European Jewish bankers, prominent members of which were: **1.** Lionel Nathan, Baron de Rothschild. 1809–79, British banker and first Jewish member of Parliament. **2.** his grandfather **Meyer Amschel** ('maɪər 'amʃəl). 1743–1812, German financier and founder of the Rothschild banking firm. **3.** his son, **Nathan Meyer,** Baron de Rothschild. 1777–1836, British banker, born in Germany.

rotifer ('rəʊtɪfə) n. a minute aquatic multicellular invertebrate having a ciliated wheel-like organ used in feeding and locomotion: common constituents of freshwater plankton. Also called: **wheel animalcule.** [C18: from NL

Rotifera, from L *rota* wheel + *ferre* to bear] —**rotiferal** (rəʊˈtɪfərəl) *or* **roˈtiferous** *adj.*

rotisserie (rəʊˈtɪsərɪ) *n.* **1.** a rotating spit on which meat, poultry, etc., can be cooked. **2.** a shop or restaurant where meat is roasted to order. [C19: from F, from OF *rostir* to ROAST]

rotogravure (ˌrəʊtəʊɡrəˈvjʊə) *n.* **1.** a printing process using cylinders with many small holes, from which ink is transferred to a moving web of paper, etc., in a rotary press. **2.** printed material produced in this way, esp. magazines. [C20: from L *rota* wheel + GRAVURE]

rotor (ˈrəʊtə) *n.* **1.** the rotating member of a machine or device, such as the revolving arm of the distributor of an internal-combustion engine. **2.** a rotating device having radiating blades projecting from a hub which produces thrust to lift and propel a helicopter. [C20: shortened form of ROTATOR]

Rotorua (ˌrəʊtəˈruːə) *n.* a city in New Zealand, on N central North Island at the SW end of Lake Rotorua: centre of forestry; noted for volcanic activity. Pop.: 52 200 (1987).

Rotovator (ˈrəʊtəˌveɪtə) *n. Trademark.* a mechanical cultivator with rotary blades. [C20: *Rotavator* from ROTA(RY) + (CULTI)VATOR] —**ˈRotoˌvate** *vb.* (*tr.*)

rotten (ˈrɒtⁿn) *adj.* **1.** decomposing, decaying, or putrid. **2.** breaking up, esp. through age or hard use: *rotten ironwork.* **3.** morally corrupt. **4.** disloyal or treacherous. **5.** *Inf.* unpleasant: *rotten weather.* **6.** *Inf.* unsatisfactory or poor: *rotten workmanship.* **7.** *Inf.* miserably unwell. **8.** *Inf.* distressed and embarrassed: *I felt rotten breaking the bad news to him.* [C13: from ON *rottin*; rel. to OE *rotian* to ROT] —**ˈrottenly** *adv.* —**ˈrottenness** *n.*

rotten borough *n.* (before the Reform Act of 1832) any of certain English parliamentary constituencies with few or no electors.

rottenstone (ˈrɒtⁿnˌstəʊn) *n.* a much-weathered limestone, rich in silica: used in powdered form for polishing metal.

rotter (ˈrɒtə) *n. Sl., chiefly Brit.* a worthless, unpleasant, or despicable person.

Rotterdam (ˈrɒtəˌdæm) *n.* a port in the SW Netherlands, in South Holland province: the second largest city of the Netherlands and one of the world's largest ports; oil refineries, shipbuilding yards, etc. Pop.: 572 642 (1987).

rotund (rəʊˈtʌnd) *adj.* **1.** rounded or spherical in shape. **2.** plump. **3.** sonorous or grandiloquent. [C18: from L *rotundus* round, from *rota* wheel] —**roˈtundity** *n.* —**roˈtundly** *adv.*

rotunda (rəʊˈtʌndə) *n.* a circular building or room, esp. one that has a dome. [C17: from It. *rotonda*, from L *rotundus* round, from *rota* a wheel]

Rouault (ruːˈəʊ; *French* rwo) *n.* **Georges** (ʒɔrʒ). 1871–1958, French expressionist artist. His work is deeply religious; it includes much stained glass.

Roubaix (*French* rubɛ) *n.* a city in N France near the Belgian border: forms, with Tourcoing, a large industrial conurbation. Pop.: 109 490 (1983 est.).

Roubiliac *or* **Roubillac** (rubijak) *n.* **Louis-François** (lwifrɑ̃swa). ?1695–1762, French sculptor: lived chiefly in England: his sculptures include the statue of Handel in Vauxhall Gardens (1737).

rouble *or* **ruble** (ˈruːbⁿl) *n.* the standard monetary unit of the Soviet Union. [C16: from Russian *rubl* silver bar, from ORussian *rublĭ* bar, block of wood, from *rubiti* to cut up]

roué (ˈruːeɪ) *n.* a debauched or lecherous man; rake. [C19: from F, lit.: one broken on the wheel; with reference to the fate deserved by a debauchee]

Rouen (*French* rwɑ̃) *n.* a city in N France, on the River Seine: the chief river port of France; became capital of the duchy of Normandy in 912; scene of the burning of Joan of Arc (1431); university (1964). Pop.: 113 740 (1983 est.).

rouge (ruːʒ) *n.* **1.** a red powder or cream, used as a cosmetic for adding redness to the cheeks. **2.** short for **jeweller's rouge.** ~*vb.* **3.** (*tr.*) to apply rouge to. [C18: F: red, from L *rubeus*]

rouge et noir (ˈruːʒ eɪ ˈnwɑː) *n.* a card game in which the players put their stakes on any of two red and two black diamond-shaped spots marked on the table. [F, lit.: red and black]

Rouget de Lisle (*French* ruʒɛ də lil) *n.* **Claude Joseph** (klod ʒozɛf). 1760–1836, French army officer: composer of the *Marseillaise* (1792), the French national anthem.

rough (rʌf) *adj.* **1.** (of a surface) not smooth; uneven or irregular. **2.** (of ground) covered with scrub, boulders,

etc. **3.** denoting or taking place on uncultivated ground: *rough grazing.* **4.** shaggy or hairy. **5.** turbulent: *a rough sea.* **6.** (of performance or motion) uneven; irregular: *a rough engine.* **7.** (of behaviour or character) rude, coarse, or violent. **8.** harsh or sharp: *rough words.* **9.** *Inf.* severe or unpleasant: *a rough lesson.* **10.** (of work, etc.) requiring physical rather than mental effort. **11.** *Inf.* ill: *he felt rough after an evening of heavy drinking.* **12.** unfair: *rough luck.* **13.** harsh or grating to the ear. **14.** without refinement, luxury, etc. **15.** not perfected in any detail; rudimentary: *rough workmanship; rough justice.* **16.** not prepared or dressed: *rough gemstones.* **17.** (of a guess, etc.) approximate. **18.** having the sound of *h*; aspirated. **19. rough on.** *Inf., chiefly Brit.* **a.** severe towards. **b.** unfortunate for (a person). **20. the rough side of one's tongue.** harsh words; a rebuke. ~*n.* **21.** rough ground. **22.** a sketch or preliminary piece of artwork. **23.** unfinished or crude state (esp. in **in the rough**). **24. the rough.** *Golf.* the part of the course bordering the fairways where the grass is untrimmed. **25.** *Inf.* a violent person; thug. **26.** the unpleasant side of something (esp. in **take the rough with the smooth**). ~*adv.* **27.** roughly. **28. sleep rough.** to spend the night in the open; be without shelter. ~*vb.* (*tr.*) **29.** to make rough; roughen. **30.** (foll. by *out*, etc.) to prepare (a sketch, report, etc.) in preliminary form. **31. rough it.** *Inf.* to live without the usual comforts of life. ~See also **rough up.** [OE *rūh*] —**ˈroughly** *adv.* —**ˈroughness** *n.*

roughage (ˈrʌfɪdʒ) *n.* **1.** the coarse indigestible constituents of food, which provide bulk to the diet and aid digestion. **2.** any rough material.

rough-and-ready *adj.* **1.** crude, unpolished, or hastily prepared, but sufficient for the purpose. **2.** (of a person) without formality or refinement.

rough-and-tumble *n.* **1.** a fight or scuffle without rules. ~*adj.* **2.** characterized by disorderliness and disregard for rules.

rough breathing *n.* (in Greek) the sign (ʽ) placed over an initial vowel, indicating that (in ancient Greek) it was pronounced with an *h*.

roughcast (ˈrʌfˌkɑːst) *n.* **1.** a coarse plaster used to cover the surface of an external wall. **2.** any rough or preliminary form, model, etc. ~*adj.* **3.** covered with roughcast. ~*vb.* **-casting, -cast. 4.** to apply roughcast to (a wall, etc.). **5.** to prepare in rough. —**ˈroughˌcaster** *n.*

rough-cut *n.* a first basic edited version of a film with the scenes in sequence and the soundtrack synchronized.

rough diamond *n.* **1.** an unpolished diamond. **2.** an intrinsically trustworthy or good person with uncouth manners or dress.

rough-dry *adj.* **1.** (of clothes or linen) dried ready for pressing. ~*vb.* **-drying, -dried. 2.** (*tr.*) to dry (clothes, etc.) without ironing them.

roughen (ˈrʌfⁿn) *vb.* to make or become rough.

rough-hew *vb.* **-hewing, -hewed; -hewed** *or* **-hewn.** (*tr.*) to cut or shape roughly without finishing the surface.

roughhouse (ˈrʌfˌhaʊs) *n. Sl.* rough, disorderly, or noisy behaviour.

roughish (ˈrʌfɪʃ) *adj.* somewhat rough.

roughneck (ˈrʌfˌnɛk) *n. Sl.* **1.** a rough or violent person; thug. **2.** a worker in an oil-drilling operation.

rough puff pastry *n.* a rich flaky pastry.

roughrider (ˈrʌfˌraɪdə) *n.* a rider of wild or unbroken horses.

roughshod (ˈrʌfˌʃɒd) *adj.* **1.** (of a horse) shod with rough-bottomed shoes to prevent sliding. ~*adv.* **2. ride roughshod over.** to domineer over or act with complete disregard for.

rough stuff *n. Inf.* violence.

rough trade *n. Sl.* (in homosexual use) a tough or violent sexual partner, esp. one casually picked up.

rough up *vb.* (*tr., adv.*) **1.** *Inf.* to treat violently; beat up. **2.** to cause (feathers, hair, etc.) to stand up by rubbing against the grain.

roulade (ruːˈlɑːd) *n.* **1.** something cooked in the shape of a roll, esp. a slice of meat. **2.** an elaborate run in vocal music. [C18: from F, lit.: a rolling, from *rouler* to ROLL]

Roulers (ruːˈlɛəz; *French* rulɛr) *n.* a city in NW Belgium, in West Flanders province. Pop.: 51 866 (1982 est.). Flemish name: **Roeselare.**

roulette (ruːˈlɛt) *n.* **1.** a gambling game in which a ball is dropped onto a spinning horizontal wheel divided into numbered slots, with players betting on the slot into which the ball will fall. **2.** a toothed wheel for making a line of perforations. **3.** a curve generated by a point on one curve rolling on another. ~*vb.* (*tr.*) **4.** to use a roulette on (something), as in engraving, making stationery, etc. [C18: from F, from *rouelle*, dim. of *roue* a wheel, from L *rota*]

Roumania (ruː'meɪnɪə) *n.* a variant of **Romania**. —**Rou'manian** *adj.*, *n.*

round (raʊnd) *adj.* **1.** having a flat circular shape, as a hoop. **2.** having the shape of a ball. **3.** curved; not angular. **4.** involving or using circular motion. **5.** (*prenominal*) complete: *a round dozen.* **6.** *Maths.* **a.** forming or expressed by a whole number, with no fraction. **b.** expressed to the nearest ten, hundred, or thousand: *in round figures.* **7.** (of a sum of money) considerable. **8.** fully depicted or developed, as a character in a book. **9.** full and plump: *round cheeks.* **10.** (of sound) full and sonorous. **11.** (of pace) brisk; lively. **12.** (*prenominal*) (of speech) candid; unmodified: *a round assertion.* **13.** (of a vowel) pronounced with rounded lips. ~*n.* **14.** a round shape or object. **15. in the round. a.** in full detail. **b.** *Theatre.* with the audience all round the stage. **16.** a session, as of a negotiation: *a round of talks.* **17.** a series: *a giddy round of parties.* **18. the daily round.** the usual activities of one's day. **19.** a stage of a competition: *he was eliminated in the first round.* **20.** (*often pl.*) a series of calls: *a milkman's round.* **21.** a playing of all the holes on a golf course. **22.** a single turn of play by each player, as in a card game. **23.** one of a number of periods in a boxing, wrestling, or other match. **24.** a single discharge by a gun. **25.** a bullet or other charge of ammunition. **26.** a number of drinks bought at one time for a group of people. **27.** a single slice of bread. **28.** a general outburst of applause, etc. **29.** movement in a circle. **30.** *Music.* a part song in which the voices follow each other at equal intervals at the same pitch. **31.** a sequence of bells rung in order of treble to tenor. **32.** a cut of beef from the thigh. **33. go** *or* **make the rounds. a.** to go from place to place, as in making social calls. **b.** (of information, rumour, etc.) to be passed around, so as to be generally known. ~*prep.* **34.** surrounding, encircling, or enclosing: *a band round her head.* **35.** on all or most sides of: *to look round one.* **36.** on or outside the circumference or perimeter of. **37.** from place to place in: *driving round Ireland.* **38.** reached by making a partial circuit about: *the shop round the corner.* **39.** revolving round (a centre or axis): *the earth's motion round its axis.* ~*adv.* **40.** on all or most sides. **41.** on or outside the circumference or perimeter: *the racing track is two miles round.* **42.** to all members of a group: *pass the food round.* **43.** in rotation or revolution: *the wheels turn round.* **44.** by a circuitous route: *the road to the farm goes round by the pond.* **45.** to a specific place: *she came round to see me.* **46. all year round.** throughout the year. ~*vb.* **47.** to make or become round. **48.** (*tr.*) to encircle; surround. **49.** to move or cause to move with turning motion: *to round a bend.* **50.** (*tr.*) **a.** to pronounce (a speech sound) with rounded lips. **b.** to purse (the lips). ~See also **round down**, **round off**, etc. [C13: from OF *ront*, from L *rotundus* round, from *rota* a wheel] —**'roundish** *adj.* —**'roundness** *n.*

▷ **Usage.** See at **around**.

roundabout ('raʊndə,baʊt) *n.* **1.** *Brit.* a revolving circular platform provided with wooden animals, seats, etc., on which people ride for amusement; merry-go-round. **2.** a road junction in which traffic streams circulate around a central island. U.S. and Canad. name: **traffic circle.** ~*adj.* **3.** indirect; devious. ~*adv.*, *prep.* **round about. 4.** on all sides: *spectators standing round about.* **5.** approximately: *at round about 5 o'clock.*

round dance *n.* **1.** a dance in which the dancers form a circle. **2.** a ballroom dance, such as the waltz, in which couples revolve.

round down *vb.* (*tr.*, *adv.*) to lower (a number) to the nearest whole number or ten, hundred, or thousand below it.

rounded ('raʊndɪd) *adj.* **1.** round or curved. **2.** mature or complete. **3.** (of the lips) pursed. **4.** (of a speech sound) articulated with rounded lips.

roundel ('raʊnd³l) *n.* **1.** a form of rondeau consisting of three stanzas each of three lines with a refrain after the

first and the third. **2.** a circular identifying mark in national colours on military aircraft. **3.** a small circular window, medallion, etc. **4.** a round plate of armour used to protect the armpit. **5.** another word for **roundelay.** [C13: from OF *rondel;* see RONDEL]

roundelay ('raʊndɪ,leɪ) *n.* **1.** Also called: **roundel.** a slow medieval dance performed in a circle. **2.** a song in which a line or phrase is repeated as a refrain. [C16: from OF *rondelet* a little rondel, from *rondel;* also infl. by LAY⁴]

rounders ('raʊndəz) *n.* (*functioning as sing.*) *Brit.* a ball game in which players run between posts after hitting the ball, scoring a **rounder** if they run round all four before the ball is retrieved.

Roundhead ('raʊnd,hɛd) *n. English history.* a supporter of Parliament against Charles I during the Civil War. [referring to their short-cut hair]

roundhouse ('raʊnd,haʊs) *n.* **1.** *U.S.* a building in which railway locomotives are serviced, radial tracks being fed by a central turntable. **2.** *U.S. boxing sl.* a swinging punch or style of punching. **3.** an obsolete word for **jail.** **4.** *Obs.* a cabin on the quarterdeck of a sailing ship.

rounding ('raʊndɪŋ) *n. Computers.* a process in which a number is approximated as the closest number that can be expressed using the number of bits or digits available.

roundly ('raʊndlɪ) *adv.* **1.** frankly, bluntly, or thoroughly: *to be roundly criticized.* **2.** in a round manner or so as to be round.

round off *vb.* (*tr.*, *adv.*) **1.** (often foll. by *with*) to complete, esp. agreeably: *we rounded off the evening with a brandy.* **2.** to make less jagged.

round on *vb.* (*intr.*, *prep.*) to attack or reply to (someone) with sudden irritation or anger.

round robin *n.* **1.** a petition or protest having the signatures in a circle to disguise the order of signing. **2.** a tournament in which each player plays against every other player.

round-shouldered *adj.* denoting a faulty posture characterized by drooping shoulders and a slight forward bending of the back.

roundsman ('raʊndzmən) *n., pl.* **-men. 1.** *Brit.* a person who makes rounds, as for inspection or to deliver goods. **2.** *Austral. & N.Z.* a reporter covering a particular district or topic.

round table *n.* **a.** a meeting of parties or people on equal terms for discussion. **b.** (*as modifier*): *a round-table conference.*

Round Table *n.* **the. 1.** (in Arthurian legend) the table of King Arthur, shaped so that his knights could sit around it without any having precedence. **2.** Arthur and his knights collectively. **3.** one of an organization of clubs of young business and professional men who meet in order to further charitable work.

round-the-clock *adj.* (*or as adv.* **round the clock**) throughout the day and night.

round trip *n.* a trip to a place and back again, esp. returning by a different route.

round up *vb.* (*tr.*, *adv.*) **1.** to gather together: *to round ponies up.* **2.** to raise (a number) to the nearest whole number or ten, hundred, or thousand above it. ~*n.* **roundup. 3.** the act of gathering together livestock, esp. cattle, so that they may be branded, counted, or sold. **4.** any similar act of bringing together: *a roundup of today's news.*

roundworm ('raʊnd,wɜːm) *n.* a nematode worm that is a common intestinal parasite of man and pigs.

roup (raʊp) *Scot. & N English dialect.* ~*vb.* (*tr.*) **1.** to sell by auction. ~*n.* **2.** an auction. [C16 (orig.: to shout): of Scand. origin]

rouse (raʊz) *vb.* **1.** to bring (oneself or another person) out of sleep, etc., or (of a person) to come to consciousness in this way. **2.** (*tr.*) to provoke: *to rouse someone's anger.* **3. rouse oneself.** to become energetic. **4.** to start or cause to start from cover: *to rouse game birds.* **5.** (*intr.;* foll. by *on*) *Austral.* to scold or rebuke. [C15 in sense of hawks ruffling their feathers): from ?] —**'rouser** *n.*

rouseabout ('raʊzə,baʊt) *n.* **1.** *Austral. & N.Z.* an unskilled labourer in a shearing shed. **2.** a variant of **roustabout** (sense 1).

rousing ('raʊzɪŋ) *adj.* tending to excite; lively or vigorous: *a rousing chorus.* —**'rousingly** *adv.*

Rousseau (*French* ruso) *n.* **1. Henri** (ɑ̃ri), known as *le Douanier.* 1844–1910, French painter, who created bold dreamlike pictures, often of exotic landscapes in a naive style. Among his works are *Sleeping Gypsy* (1897) and *Jungle with a Lion* (1904–06). He also worked as a customs official. **2. Jean Jacques** (ʒɑ̃ ʒak). 1712–78, French philosopher and writer, born in Switzerland, who strongly influenced the theories of the French Revolution and the romantics. Many of his ideas spring from his belief in the natural goodness of man, whom he felt was warped by society. His works include *Du contrat social* (1762), *Emile* (1762), and his *Confessions* (1782). **3. Théodore** (teɔdɔr). 1812–67, French landscape painter: leader of the Barbizon school.

Roussillon (*French* rusijɔ̃) *n.* a former province of S France: united with Aragon in 1172; passed to the French crown in 1659; now forms part of the region of Languedoc-Roussillon.

roust (raʊst) *vb.* (*tr.; often foll. by* out) to rout or stir, as out of bed. [C17: ?from ROUSE]

roustabout (ˈraʊstəˌbaʊt) *n.* **1.** an unskilled labourer on an oil rig. **2.** *Austral. & N.Z.* a variant of **rouseabout** (sense 1).

rout[1] (raʊt) *n.* **1.** an overwhelming defeat. **2.** a disorderly retreat. **3.** a noisy rabble. **4.** *Law.* a group of three or more people proceeding to commit an illegal act. **5.** *Arch.* a large party or social gathering. ~*vb.* **6.** (*tr.*) to defeat and cause to flee in confusion. [C13: from Anglo-Norman *rute*, from OF: disorderly band, from L *ruptus*, from *rumpere* to burst]

rout[2] (raʊt) *vb.* **1.** to dig over or turn up (something), esp. (of an animal) with the snout; root. **2.** (*tr.; usually foll. by* out or up) to find by searching. **3.** (*tr.; usually foll. by* out) to drive out: *they routed him out of bed at midnight.* **4.** (*tr.; often foll. by* out) to hollow or gouge out. **5.** (*intr.*) to search, poke, or rummage. [C16: var. of ROOT[2]]

route (ruːt) *n.* **1.** the choice of roads taken to get to a place. **2.** a regular journey travelled. ~*vb.* (*tr.*) **3.** to plan the route of; send by a particular route. [C13: from OF *rute*, from Vulgar L *rupta via* (unattested), lit.: a broken (established) way, from L *ruptus*, from *rumpere* to break]
▷**Usage.** When forming the present participle or verbal noun from the verb *to route* it is preferable to retain the *e* in order to distinguish the word from *routing*, the present participle or verbal noun from *rout*[1], to defeat or *rout*[2], to dig, rummage: *the routeing of buses from the city centre to the suburbs.* The spelling *routing* in this sense is, however, sometimes encountered, esp. in American English.

routemarch (ˈruːtˌmɑːtʃ) *n.* **1.** *Mil.* a long training march. **2.** *Inf.* any long exhausting walk.

router (ˈraʊtə) *n.* any of various tools or machines for hollowing out, cutting grooves, etc.

routine (ruːˈtiːn) *n.* **1.** a usual or regular method of procedure, esp. one that is unvarying. **2.** *Computers.* a program or part of a program performing a specific function: *an input routine.* **3.** a set sequence of dance steps. **4.** *Inf.* a hackneyed or insincere speech. ~*adj.* **5.** relating to or characteristic of routine. [C17: from OF, from *route* a customary way, ROUTE] —**rouˈtinely** *adv.*

roux (ruː) *n.* a mixture of equal amounts of fat and flour, heated, blended, and used as a basis for sauces. [F: brownish, from L *russus* RUSSET]

rove[1] (rəʊv) *vb.* **1.** to wander about (a place) with no fixed direction; roam. **2.** (*intr.*) (of the eyes) to look around; wander. ~*n.* **3.** the act of roving. [C15 *roven* (in archery) to shoot at a target chosen at random (C16: to wander, stray), from ON]

rove[2] (rəʊv) *vb.* **1.** (*tr.*) to pull out and twist (fibres of wool, cotton, etc.) lightly, as before spinning. ~*n.* **2.** wool, cotton, etc., thus prepared. [C18: from ?]

rove[3] (rəʊv) *vb.* a past tense and past participle of **reeve**[2].

rover[1] (ˈrəʊvə) *n.* **1.** a person who roves. **2.** *Archery.* a mark selected at random for use as a target. **3.** *Australian Rules football.* a player without a fixed position who, with the ruckmen, forms the ruck. [C15: from ROVE[1]]

rover[2] (ˈrəʊvə) *n.* a pirate or pirate ship. [C14: prob. from MDu. or MLow G, from *roven* to rob]

Rover or **Rover Scout** (ˈrəʊvə) *n. Brit.* the former name for **Venture Scout.**

roving commission *n.* authority or power given in a general area, without precisely defined terms of reference.

row[1] (rəʊ) *n.* **1.** an arrangement of persons or things in a line: *a row of chairs.* **2.** *Chiefly Brit.* a street, esp. a narrow one lined with identical houses. **3.** a line of seats, as

in a cinema, theatre, etc. **4.** *Maths.* a horizontal linear arrangement of numbers, quantities, or terms. **5.** a horizontal rank of squares on a chessboard or draughtboard. **6. a hard row to hoe.** a difficult task or assignment. **7. in a row.** in succession; one after the other: *he won two gold medals in a row.* [OE *rāw, rǣw*]

row[2] (rəʊ) *vb.* **1.** to propel (a boat) by using oars. **2.** (*tr.*) to carry (people, goods, etc.) in a rowing boat. **3.** to be propelled by means of (oars or oarsmen). **4.** (*intr.*) to take part in the racing of rowing boats as a sport. **5.** (*tr.*) to race against in a boat propelled by oars: *Oxford row Cambridge every year.* ~*n.* **6.** an act, instance, period, or distance of rowing. **7.** an excursion in a rowing boat. [OE *rōwan*] —**ˈrower** *n.*

row[3] (raʊ) *n.* **1.** a noisy quarrel. **2.** a noisy disturbance: *we couldn't hear the music for the row next door.* **3.** a reprimand. ~*vb.* **4.** (*intr.; often foll. by* with) to quarrel noisily. **5.** (*tr.*) *Arch.* to reprimand. [C18: from ?]

rowan (ˈrəʊən, ˈraʊ-) *n.* another name for the (European) **mountain ash.** [C16: of Scand. origin]

rowdy (ˈraʊdɪ) *adj.* **-dier, -diest. 1.** tending to create noisy disturbances; rough, loud, or disorderly: *a rowdy gang of football supporters.* ~*n., pl.* **-dies.** a person who behaves in such a fashion. [C19: orig. U.S. sl., ? rel. to ROW[3]] —**ˈrowdily** *adv.* —**ˈrowdiness** or **ˈrowdyism** *n.*

Rowe (rəʊ) *n.* **Nicholas.** 1674–1718, English dramatist; poet laureate (1715–18). His plays include *Tamerlane* (1702), *The Fair Penitent* (1703), and *Jane Shore* (1714).

rowel (ˈraʊəl) *n.* **1.** a small spiked wheel attached to a spur. **2.** *Vet. science.* a piece of leather inserted under the skin of a horse to cause a discharge. ~*vb.* **-elling, -elled** or U.S. **-eling, -eled.** (*tr.*) **3.** to goad (a horse) using a rowel. **4.** *Vet. science.* to insert a rowel in (the skin of a horse) to cause a discharge. [C14: from OF *roel* a little wheel, from *roe* a wheel, from L *rota*]

rowing boat (ˈrəʊɪŋ) *n. Chiefly Brit.* a small pleasure boat propelled by one or more pairs of oars. Usual U.S. and Canad. word: **rowboat.**

rowing machine (ˈrəʊɪŋ) *n.* a device with oars and a sliding seat, resembling a sculling boat, used to provide exercise.

Rowlandson (ˈrəʊləndsən) *n.* **Thomas.** 1756–1827, English caricaturist, noted for the vigour of his attack on sordid aspects of contemporary society and on statesmen such as Napoleon.

rowlock (ˈrɒlək) *n.* a swivelling device attached to the gunwale of a boat that holds an oar in place. Usual U.S. and Canad. word: **oarlock.**

Roxas y Acuña (*Spanish* ˈroxas i aˈkuɲa) *n.* **Manuel** (maˈnwel). 1892–1948, Philippine statesman; first president of the Republic of the Philippines (1946–48).

Roxburghshire (ˈrɒksbərəˌʃɪə, ˌʃə) *n.* (until 1975) a county of SE Scotland, now part of the Borders region.

royal (ˈrɔɪəl) *adj.* **1.** of, relating to, or befitting a king, queen, or other monarch; regal. **2.** (*prenominal; often cap.*) established by, chartered by, under the patronage of, or in the service of royalty: *the Royal Society of St George.* **3.** being a member of a royal family. **4.** above the usual or normal in standing, size, quality, etc. **5.** *Inf.* unusually good or impressive; first-rate. **6.** *Naut.* just above the topgallant (in **royal mast**). ~*n.* **7.** (*sometimes cap.*) a member of a royal family. **8.** Also: **royal stag.** a stag with antlers having 12 or more branches. **9.** *Naut.* a sail set next above the topgallant, on a royal mast. **10.** a size of printing paper, 20 by 25 inches. [C14: from OF *roial*, from L *rēgālis* fit for a king, from *rēx* king; cf. REGAL] —**ˈroyally** *adv.*

Royal Academy *n.* a society founded by George III in 1768 to foster a national school of painting, sculpture, and design in England. Full name: **Royal Academy of Arts.**

Royal Air Force *n.* the air force of Great Britain. Abbrev.: **RAF.**

royal assent *n. Brit.* the formal signing of an act of Parliament by the sovereign, by which it becomes law.

royal blue *n.* **a.** a deep blue colour. **b.** (*as adj.*): *a royal-blue carpet.*

Royal Commission *n.* (in Britain) a body set up by the monarch on the recommendation of the prime minister to gather information about the operation of existing laws or to investigate any social, educational, or other matter.

royal fern *n.* a fern of damp regions, having large fronds up to 2 metres (7 feet) in height.

royal flush *n. Poker.* a hand made up of the five top honours of a suit.

royalist ('rɔɪəlɪst) *n.* **1.** a supporter of a monarch or monarchy, esp. during the English Civil War. **2.** *Inf.* an extreme reactionary: *an economic royalist.* ~*adj.* **3.** of or relating to royalists. —'**royalism** *n.*

royal jelly *n.* a substance secreted by the pharyngeal glands of worker bees and fed to all larvae when very young and to larvae destined to become queens throughout their development.

Royal Leamington Spa *n.* the official name of **Leamington Spa.**

Royal Marines *pl. n. Brit.* a corps of soldiers specially trained in amphibious warfare. Abbrev.: **RM.**

Royal National Theatre *n.* a theatre complex in London, on the S bank of the Thames (opened 1976). The prefix Royal was added in 1988. It houses the Royal National Theatre Company.

Royal Navy *n.* the navy of Great Britain. Abbrev.: **RN.**

royal palm *n.* any of several palm trees of tropical America, having a tall trunk with a tuft of feathery pinnate leaves.

royal standard *n.* a flag bearing the arms of the British sovereign, flown only when she or he is present.

royal tennis *n.* another name for **real tennis.**

royalty ('rɔɪəltɪ) *n., pl.* **-ties. 1.** the rank, power, or position of a king or queen. **2. a.** royal persons collectively. **b.** a person who belongs to a royal family. **3.** any quality characteristic of a monarch. **4.** a percentage of the revenue from the sale of a book, performance of a theatrical work, use of a patented invention or of land, etc., paid to the author, inventor, or proprietor.

royal warrant *n.* an authorization to a tradesman to supply goods to a royal household.

Royce (rɔɪs) *n.* **Josiah.** 1855–1916, U.S. philosopher of monistic idealism. In his ethical studies he emphasized the need for individual loyalty to the world community.

rozzer ('rɒzə) *n. Sl.* a policeman. [C19: from ?]

RPI (in Britain) *abbrev. for* retail price index.

rpm *abbrev. for:* **1.** resale price maintenance. **2.** revolutions per minute.

RR *abbrev. for:* **1.** Right Reverend. **2.** *Canad. & U.S.* rural route.

-rrhagia *n. combining form.* (in pathology) an abnormal discharge: *menorrhagia.* [from Gk *-rrhagia* a bursting forth, from *rhēgnunai* to burst]

-rrhoea *or esp. U.S.* **-rrhea** *n. combining form.* (in pathology) a flow: *diarrhoea.* [from NL, from Gk *-rrhoia,* from *rhein* to flow]

r-RNA *abbrev. for* ribosomal RNA.

Rs *symbol for* rupees.

RS (in Britain) *abbrev. for* Royal Society.

RSA *abbrev. for:* **1.** Republic of South Africa. **2.** (in New Zealand) Returned Services Association. **3.** Royal Scottish Academician. **4.** Royal Scottish Academy. **5.** Royal Society of Arts.

RSFSR *abbrev. for* Russian Soviet Federative Socialist Republic.

RSI *abbrev. for* repetitive strain injury.

RSL (in Australia) *abbrev. for* Returned Services League.

RSM *abbrev. for:* **1.** regimental sergeant major. **2.** Royal School of Music. **3.** Royal Society of Medicine.

RSNZ *abbrev. for* Royal Society of New Zealand.

RSPB (in Britain) *abbrev. for* Royal Society for the Protection of Birds.

RSPCA (in Britain) *abbrev. for* Royal Society for the Prevention of Cruelty to Animals.

RSV *abbrev. for* Revised Standard Version (of the Bible).

RSVP *abbrev. for* répondez s'il vous plaît. [F: please reply]

rt *abbrev. for* right.

RTE *abbrev. for* Radio Telefis Eireann. [Irish Gaelic: Irish Radio and Television]

Rt Hon. *abbrev. for* Right Honourable.

Ru *the chemical symbol for* ruthenium.

RU *abbrev. for* Rugby Union.

Ruanda-Urundi (ru'ændəu'rundɪ) *n.* a former territory of central Africa: part of German East Africa from 1890; a League of Nations mandate under Belgian administration from 1919; a United Nations trusteeship from 1946; divided into the independent states of Rwanda and Burundi in 1962.

rub (rʌb) *vb.* **rubbing, rubbed. 1.** to apply pressure and friction to (something) with a backward and forward motion. **2.** to move (something) with pressure along, over, or against (a surface). **3.** to chafe or fray. **4.** (*tr.*) to bring into a certain condition by rubbing: *rub it clean.* **5.** (*tr.*) to spread with pressure, esp. in order to cause to be absorbed: *she rubbed ointment into his back.* **6.** (*tr.*) to mix (fat) into flour with the fingertips, as in making pastry. **7.** (foll. by *off, out, away,* etc.) to remove or be removed by rubbing: *the mark would not rub off the chair.* **8.** (*intr.*) *Bowls.* (of a bowl) to be slowed or deflected by an uneven patch on the green. **9.** (*tr.; often* foll. by *together*) to move against each other with pressure and friction (esp. in **rub one's hands,** often a sign of glee, keen anticipation, or satisfaction, and **rub noses,** a greeting among Eskimos). **10. rub (up) the wrong way.** to arouse anger in; annoy. ~*n.* **11.** the act of rubbing. **12.** (preceded by an obstacle or difficulty (esp. in **there's the rub**). **13.** something that hurts the feelings or annoys; cut; rebuke. **14.** *Bowls.* an uneven patch in the green. ~See also **rub along, rub down,** etc. [C15: ?from Low G *rubben,* from ?]

Rub' al Khali ('rub æl 'kɑːlɪ) *n.* a desert in S Arabia, mainly in Saudi Arabia, extending southeast from Nejd to Hadramaut and northeast from Yemen to the United Arab Emirates. Area: about 777 000 sq. km (300 000 sq. miles). English names: **Great Sandy Desert, Empty Quarter.** Also called: **Ar Rimal, Dahna.**

rub along *vb.* (*intr., adv.*) *Brit.* **1.** to continue in spite of difficulties. **2.** to maintain an amicable relationship; not quarrel.

rubato (ru:'bɑːtəu) *Music.* ~*n., pl.* **-tos. 1.** flexibility of tempo in performance. ~*adj., adv.* **2.** to be played with a flexible tempo. [C19: from It. *tempo rubato,* lit.: stolen time, from *rubare* to ROB]

rubber[1] ('rʌbə) *n.* **1.** Also called: **India rubber, gum elastic, caoutchouc.** a cream to dark brown elastic material obtained by coagulating and drying the latex from certain plants, esp. the rubber tree. **2.** any of a large variety of elastomers produced from natural rubber or by synthetic means. **3.** *Chiefly Brit.* a piece of rubber used for erasing something written; eraser. **4.** a cloth, pad, etc., used for polishing. **5.** a person who rubs something in order to smooth, polish, or massage. **6.** (*often pl.*) *Chiefly U.S. & Canad.* a rubberized waterproof overshoe. **7.** *Sl.* a condom. **8.** (*modifier*) made of or producing rubber: *a rubber ball; a rubber factory.* [C17: from RUB + -ER[1]; the tree was so named because its product was used for rubbing out writing] —'**rubbery** *adj.*

rubber[2] ('rʌbə) *n.* **1.** *Bridge, whist, etc.* **a.** a match of three games. **b.** the deal that wins such a match. **2.** a series of matches or games in any of various sports. [C16: from ?]

rubber band *n.* a continuous loop of thin rubber, used to hold papers, etc., together. Also called: **elastic band.**

rubber cement *n.* any of a number of adhesives made by dissolving rubber in a solvent such as benzene.

rubberize *or* **-ise** ('rʌbə,raɪz) *vb.* (*tr.*) to coat or impregnate with rubber.

rubberneck ('rʌbə,nɛk) *Sl.* ~*n.* **1.** a person who stares or gapes inquisitively. **2.** a sightseer or tourist. ~*vb.* **3.** (*intr.*) to stare in a naive or foolish manner.

rubber plant *n.* **1.** a plant with glossy leathery leaves that grows as a tall tree in India and Malaya but is cultivated as a house plant in Europe and North America. **2.** any of several tropical trees, the sap of which yields crude rubber.

rubber stamp *n.* **1.** a device used for imprinting dates, etc., on forms, invoices, etc. **2.** automatic authorization of a payment, proposal, etc. **3.** a person who makes such automatic authorizations; a cipher or person of little account. ~*vb.* **rubber-stamp.** (*tr.*) **4.** to imprint (forms, invoices, etc.) with a rubber stamp. **5.** *Inf.* to approve automatically.

rubber tree *n.* a tropical American tree cultivated throughout the tropics, esp. in Malaya, for the latex of its stem, which is the major source of commercial rubber.

rubbing ('rʌbɪŋ) *n.* an impression taken of an incised or raised surface by laying paper over it and rubbing with wax, graphite, etc.

rubbish ('rʌbɪʃ) *n.* **1.** worthless, useless, or unwanted matter. **2.** discarded or waste matter; refuse. **3.** foolish words or speech; nonsense. ~*vb.* **4.** (*tr.*) *Inf.* to criticize; attack verbally. [C14 *robys*, from ?] —**'rubbishy** *adj.*

rubble ('rʌbᵊl) *n.* **1.** fragments of broken stones, bricks, etc. **2.** debris from ruined buildings. **3.** Also called: **rubblework.** masonry constructed of broken pieces of rock, stone, etc. [C14 *robyl*; ? rel. to RUBBISH, or to ME *rubben* to rub] —**'rubbly** *adj.*

Rubbra ('rʌbrə) *n.* (**Charles**) **Edmund.** 1901–86, English composer of works in a traditional idiom.

rub down *vb.* (*adv.*) **1.** to dry or clean (a horse, athlete, oneself, etc.) vigorously, esp. after exercise. **2.** to make or become smooth by rubbing. **3.** (*tr.*) to prepare (a surface) for painting by rubbing it with sandpaper. ~*n.* **rubdown.** **4.** the act of rubbing down.

rube (ruːb) *n.* *U.S. sl.* an unsophisticated countryman. [C20: prob. from the name *Reuben*]

rubella (ruː'bɛlə) *n.* a mild contagious viral disease, somewhat similar to measles, characterized by cough, sore throat, and skin rash. Also called: **German measles.** [C19: from NL, from L *rubellus* reddish, from *rubeus* red]

rubellite ('ruːbɪˌlaɪt, ruː'bɛl-) *n.* a red transparent variety of tourmaline, used as a gemstone. [C18: from L *rubellus* reddish]

Rubens ('ruːbɪnz) *n.* Sir **Peter Paul.** 1577–1640, Flemish painter, regarded as the greatest exponent of the Baroque: appointed (1609) painter to Archduke Albert of Austria, who gave him many commissions, artistic and diplomatic. He was knighted by Charles I of England in 1629. His prolific output includes the triptych in Antwerp Cathedral, *Descent from the Cross* (1611–14), *The Rape of the Sabines* (1635), and his *Self-Portrait* (?1639).

rubeola (ruː'biːələ) *n.* the technical name for **measles.** [C17: from NL, from L *rubeus* reddish]

Rubicon ('ruːbɪkən) *n.* **1.** a stream in N Italy: in ancient times the boundary between Italy and Cisalpine Gaul. By leading his army across it and marching on Rome in 49 B.C., Julius Caesar committed himself to civil war with the senatorial party. **2.** (*sometimes not cap.*) a point of no return. **3.** a penalty in piquet by which the score of a player who fails to reach 100 points in six hands is added to his opponent's. **4. cross** (*or* **pass**) **the Rubicon.** to commit oneself irrevocably to some course of action.

rubicund ('ruːbɪkənd) *adj.* of a reddish colour; ruddy; rosy. [C16: from L *rubicundus*, from *rubēre* to be ruddy, from *ruber* red] —**rubicundity** (ˌruːbɪ'kʌndɪtɪ) *n.*

rubidium (ruː'bɪdɪəm) *n.* a soft highly reactive radioactive element of the alkali metal group. It is used in electronic valves, photocells, and special glass. Symbol: Rb; atomic no.: 37; atomic wt.: 85.47; half-life of ⁸⁷Rb: 5 × 10¹¹ years. [C19: from NL, from L *rubidus* dark red, with reference to the two red lines in its spectrum] —**ru'bidic** *adj.*

rubidium-strontium dating *n.* a technique for determining the age of minerals based on the occurrence in natural rubidium of a fixed amount of the radioisotope ⁸⁷Rb which decays to the stable strontium isotope ⁸⁷Sr with a half-life of 5 × 10¹¹ years.

rubiginous (ruː'bɪdʒɪnəs) *adj.* rust-coloured. [C17: from L *rūbiginōsus*, from *rūbīgō* rust, from *ruber* red]

rub in *vb.* (*tr., adv.*) **1.** to spread with pressure, esp. in order to cause to be absorbed. **2. rub it in.** *Inf.* to harp on something distasteful to a person.

Rubinstein ('ruːbɪnˌstaɪn) *n.* **1. Anton Grigorevich** (an'tɔn grɪ'gɔrjɪvɪtʃ). 1829–94, Russian composer and pianist. **2. Artur** ('artur). 1886–1982, U.S. pianist, born in Poland.

ruble ('ruːbᵊl) *n.* a variant spelling of **rouble.**

rub off *vb.* **1.** to remove or be removed by rubbing. **2.** (*intr.; often foll. by on or onto*) to have an effect through close association or contact: *her crude manners have rubbed off on you.*

rub out *vb.* (*tr., adv.*) **1.** to remove or be removed with a rubber. **2.** *U.S. sl.* to murder.

rubric ('ruːbrɪk) *n.* **1.** a title, heading, or initial letter in a book, manuscript, or section of a legal code, esp. one printed or painted in red ink or in some similarly distinguishing manner. **2.** a set of rules of conduct or procedure. **3.** a set of directions for the conduct of Christian church services, often printed in red in a prayer book or missal. [C15 *rubrike* red ochre, red lettering, from L *rubrīca* (*terra*) red (earth), ruddle, from *ruber* red] —**'rubrical** *adj.* —**'rubrically** *adv.*

ruby ('ruːbɪ) *n., pl.* **-bies. 1.** a deep red transparent precious variety of corundum: used as a gemstone, in lasers,

and for bearings and rollers in watchmaking. **2. a.** the deep-red colour of a ruby. **b.** (*as adj.*): *ruby lips.* **3. a.** something resembling, made of, or containing a ruby. **b.** (*as modifier*): *a ruby necklace.* **4.** (*modifier*) denoting a fortieth anniversary: *our ruby wedding.* [C14: from OF *rubi*, from L *rubeus*, from *ruber* red]

RUC *abbrev. for* Royal Ulster Constabulary.

ruche (ruːʃ) *n.* a strip of pleated or frilled lawn, lace, etc., used to decorate blouses, dresses, etc. [C19: from F, lit.: beehive, from Med. L *rūsca* bark of a tree, of Celtic origin]

ruching ('ruːʃɪŋ) *n.* **1.** material used for a ruche. **2.** a ruche or ruches collectively.

ruck[1] (rʌk) *n.* **1.** a large number or quantity; mass, esp. of undistinguished people or things. **2.** (in a race) a group of competitors who are well behind the leaders. **3.** *Rugby.* a loose scrum that forms around the ball when it is on the ground. **4.** *Australian Rules football.* the three players who do not have fixed positions but follow the ball closely. ~*vb.* **5.** (*intr.*) *Rugby.* to try to win the ball by mauling and scrummaging. [C13 (meaning "heap of firewood"): ?from ON]

ruck[2] (rʌk) *n.* **1.** a wrinkle, crease, or fold. ~*vb.* **2.** (usually foll. by *up*) to become or make wrinkled, creased, or puckered. [C18: from Scand. origin; rel. to ON *hrukka*]

ruckman ('rʌkmən) *n., pl.* **-men.** *Australian Rules football.* either of two players who, with the rover, form the ruck.

ruck-rover *n.* *Australian Rules football.* a player playing a role midway between that of the rover and the ruckmen.

rucksack ('rʌkˌsæk) *n.* a large bag, usually having two straps, carried on the back and often used by climbers, campers, etc. Also called: **backpack.** [C19: from G, lit.: back sack]

ruction ('rʌkʃən) *n.* *Inf.* **1.** an uproar; noisy or quarrelsome disturbance. **2.** (*pl.*) an unpleasant row; trouble. [C19: ? changed from INSURRECTION]

rudaceous (ruː'deɪʃəs) *adj.* (of conglomerate, breccia, and similar rocks) composed of coarse-grained material. [C20: from L *rudis* coarse, rough + -ACEOUS]

rudbeckia (rʌd'bɛkɪə) *n.* any of a genus of North American plants of the composite family, cultivated for their showy flowers, which have golden-yellow rays and green or black conical centres. See also **black-eyed Susan.** [C18: NL, after Olaus *Rudbeck* (1630–1702), Swedish botanist]

rudd (rʌd) *n.* a European freshwater fish, having a compressed dark greenish body and reddish ventral and tail fins. [C17: prob. from dialect *rud* red colour, from OE *rudu* redness]

Rudd (rʌd) *n.* **Steele,** pen name of *Arthur Hoey Davis,* 1868–1935, Australian author. His works include *On Our Selection* (1899), *Our New Selection* (1902), and *Back at Our Selection* (1906), which featured the characters Dad and Dave.

rudder ('rʌdə) *n.* **1.** *Naut.* a pivoted vertical vane that projects into the water at the stern and can be used to steer a vessel. **2.** a vertical control surface attached to the rear of the fin used to steer an aircraft. **3.** anything that guides or directs. [OE *rōther*] —**'rudderless** *adj.*

rudderpost ('rʌdəˌpəʊst) *n.* *Naut.* **1.** a postlike member at the forward edge of a rudder. **2.** the part of the stern frame of a vessel to which a rudder is fitted.

ruddle ('rʌdᵊl), **raddle,** *or* **reddle** *n.* **1.** a red ochre, used esp. to mark sheep. ~*vb.* **2.** (*tr.*) to mark (sheep) with ruddle. [C16: dim. formed from OE *rudu* redness; see RUDD]

ruddy ('rʌdɪ) *adj.* **-dier, -diest. 1.** (of the complexion) having a healthy reddish colour. **2.** coloured red or pink: *a ruddy sky.* ~*adv., adj. Inf., chiefly Brit.* **3.** (intensifier) bloody; damned: *a ruddy fool.* [OE *rudig,* from *rudu* redness] —**'ruddily** *adv.* —**'ruddiness** *n.*

rude (ruːd) *adj.* **1.** insulting or uncivil; discourteous; impolite. **2.** lacking refinement; coarse or uncouth. **3.** vulgar or obscene: *a rude joke.* **4.** roughly or crudely made: *we made a rude shelter on the island.* **5.** rough or harsh in sound, appearance, or behaviour. **6.** humble or lowly. **7.** (*prenominal*) robust or sturdy: *in rude health.* **8.** (*prenominal*) approximate or imprecise: *a rude estimate.* [C14: via OF from L *rudis* coarse, unformed] —**'rudely** *adv.* —**'rudeness** *or* (*inf.*) **'rudery** *n.*

ruderal ('ruːdərəl) *n.* **1.** a plant that grows on waste ground. ~*adj.* **2.** growing in waste places. [C19: from NL *rūderālis,* from L *rūdus* rubble]

rudiment ('ru:dɪmənt) n. **1.** (often pl.) the first principles or elementary stages of a subject. **2.** (often pl.) a partially developed version of something. **3.** Biol. an organ or part in an embryonic or vestigial state. [C16: from L rudimentum a beginning, from rudis unformed]

rudimentary (,ru:dɪ'mɛntərɪ, -trɪ) or **rudimental** adj. **1.** basic; fundamental. **2.** incompletely developed; vestigial: rudimentary leaves. —,**rudi'mentarily** or (less commonly) ,rudi'mentally adv.

rudish ('ru:dɪʃ) adj. somewhat rude.

Rudolf ('ru:dɒlf) n. **Lake.** the former name (until 1979) of (Lake) **Turkana.**

Rudolf I or **Rudolph I** ('ru:dɒlf) n. 1218–91, king of Germany (1273–91): founder of the Hapsburg dynasty based on the duchies of Styria and Austria.

rue[1] (ru:) vb. rued, ruing. **1.** to feel sorrow, remorse, or regret for (one's own wrongdoing, past events, etc.). ~n. **2.** Arch. sorrow, pity, or regret. [OE hrēowan] —'**ruer** n.

rue[2] (ru:) n. an aromatic Eurasian shrub with small yellow flowers and evergreen leaves which yield an acrid volatile oil, formerly used medicinally as a narcotic and stimulant. Archaic name: **herb of grace.** [C14: from OF, from L rūta, from Gk rhutē]

rueful ('ru:fʊl) adj. **1.** feeling or expressing sorrow or regret: a rueful face. **2.** inspiring sorrow or pity. —'**ruefully** adv. —'**ruefulness** n.

ruff[1] (rʌf) n. **1.** a circular pleated or fluted collar of lawn, muslin, etc., worn by both men and women in the 16th and 17th centuries. **2.** a natural growth of long or coloured hair or feathers around the necks of certain animals or birds. **3.** an Old World shore bird of the sandpiper family, the male of which has a large erectile ruff of feathers in the breeding season. [C16: back formation from RUFFLE[1]] —'**ruff,like** adj.

ruff[2] (rʌf) Cards. ~n., vb. **1.** another word for **trump**[1]. ~n. **2.** an old card game similar to whist. [C16: from OF roffle; ? changed from It. trionfa TRUMP[1]]

ruffe or **ruff** (rʌf) n. a European freshwater teleost fish of the perch family, having a single spiny dorsal fin. [C15: ? alteration of ROUGH (referring to its scales)]

ruffian ('rʌfɪən) n. a violent or lawless person; hoodlum. [C16: from OF rufien, from It. ruffiano pander] —'**ruffianism** n. —'**ruffianly** adj.

ruffle[1] ('rʌfₗ) vb. **1.** to make, be, or become irregular or rumpled: a breeze ruffling the water. **2.** to annoy, irritate, or be annoyed or irritated. **3.** (tr.) to make into a ruffle; pleat. **4.** (of a bird) to erect (its feathers) in anger, display, etc. **5.** (tr.) to flick (cards, pages, etc.) rapidly. ~n. **6.** an irregular or disturbed surface. **7.** a strip of pleated material used as a trim. **8.** Zool. another name for **ruff**[1] (sense 2). **9.** annoyance or irritation. [C13: of Gmc origin; cf. MLow G ruffelen to crumple, ON hrufla to scratch]

ruffle[2] ('rʌfₗ) n. **1.** a low continuous drumbeat. ~vb. **2.** (tr.) to beat (a drum) with a low repetitive beat. [C18: from earlier ruff, imit.]

rufous ('ru:fəs) adj. reddish-brown. [C18: from L rūfus]

rug (rʌg) n. **1.** a floor covering, smaller than a carpet and made of thick wool or of other material, such as an animal skin. **2.** Chiefly Brit. a blanket, esp. one used for travellers. **3. pull the rug out from under.** to betray, expose, or leave defenceless. [C16: of Scand. origin]

ruga ('ru:gə) n., pl. **-gae** (-dʒi:). (usually pl.) Anat. a fold, wrinkle, or crease. [C18: L]

rugby or **rugby football** ('rʌgbɪ) n. a form of football played with an oval ball in which the handling and carrying of the ball is permitted. Also called: **rugger.** See also **rugby league, rugby union.** [after the public school at Rugby, where it was first played]

Rugby ('rʌgbɪ) n. a town in central England, in E Warwickshire: famous public school, founded in 1567. Pop.: 59 564 (1981). —'**Rugbeian** adj., n.

rugby league n. a form of rugby football played between teams of 13 players, professionalism being allowed.

rugby union n. a form of rugby football played only by amateurs, in teams of 15.

rugged ('rʌgɪd) adj. **1.** having an uneven or jagged surface. **2.** rocky or steep: rugged scenery. **3.** (of the face) strong-featured and furrowed. **4.** rough, severe, or stern in character. **5.** without refinement or culture; rude: rugged manners. **6.** involving hardship; harsh: he leads a rugged life in the mountains. **7.** difficult or hard: a rugged test. **8.** (of equipment, machines, etc.) designed to withstand rough treatment or use in rough conditions. **9.** Chiefly

U.S. & Canad. sturdy or strong; robust. [C14: from ON] —'**ruggedly** adv. —'**ruggedness** n.

rugger ('rʌgə) n. Chiefly Brit. an informal name for **rugby.**

rugose ('ru:gəʊs, -gəʊz) adj. wrinkled: rugose leaves. [C18: from L rūgōsus, from rūga wrinkle] —'**rugosely** adv. —**rugosity** (ru:'gɒsɪtɪ) n.

Ruhr (rʊə; German ru:r) n. the chief coalmining and industrial region of West Germany: in North Rhine-Westphalia around the valley of the **River Ruhr** (a tributary of the Rhine 235 km (146 miles) long). German name: **Ruhrgebiet** ('ru:rgə,bi:t).

ruin ('ru:ɪn) n. **1.** a destroyed or decayed building or town. **2.** the state of being destroyed or decayed. **3.** loss of wealth, position, etc., or something that causes such loss; downfall. **4.** something that is severely damaged: his life was a ruin. **5.** a person who has suffered a downfall, bankruptcy, etc. **6.** Arch. loss of her virginity by a woman outside marriage. ~vb. **7.** (tr.) to bring to ruin; destroy. **8.** (tr.) to injure or spoil: the town has been ruined with tower blocks. **9.** (intr.) Arch. or poetic. to fall into ruins; collapse. **10.** (tr.) Arch. to seduce and abandon (a woman). [C14: from OF ruine, from L ruīna a falling down, from ruere to fall violently]

ruination (,ru:ɪ'neɪʃən) n. **1.** the act of ruining or the state of being ruined. **2.** something that causes ruin.

ruinous ('ru:ɪnəs) adj. causing, tending to cause, or characterized by ruin or destruction. —'**ruinously** adv. —'**ruinousness** n.

Ruisdael or **Ruysdael** ('ri:zdɑ:l, -deɪl, 'raɪz-; Dutch 'rœiz-dɑ:l) n. **Jacob van** ('ja:kɔp van). ?1628–82, Dutch landscape painter.

rule (ru:l) n. **1.** an authoritative regulation or direction concerning method or procedure, as for a court of law, legislative body, game, or other activity: judges' rules; play according to the rules. **2.** the exercise of governmental authority or control: the rule of Caesar. **3.** the period of time in which a monarch or government has power: his rule lasted 100 days. **4.** a customary form or procedure: he made a morning swim his rule. **5.** (usually preceded by the) the common order of things: violence was the rule rather than the exception. **6.** a prescribed method or procedure for solving a mathematical problem. **7.** any of various devices with a straight edge for guiding or measuring; ruler: a carpenter's rule. **8.** Printing. **a.** a printed or drawn character in the form of a long thin line. **b.** another name for **dash**[1] (sense 12): en rule; em rule. **c.** a strip of metal used to print such a line. **9.** Christianity. a systematic body of prescriptions followed by members of a religious order. **10.** Law. an order by a court or judge. **11. as a rule.** normally or ordinarily. ~vb. **12.** to exercise governing or controlling authority over (a people, political unit, individual, etc.). **13.** (when tr., often takes a clause as object) to decide authoritatively; decree: the chairman ruled against the proposal. **14.** (tr.) to mark with straight parallel lines or one straight line. **15.** (tr.) to restrain or control. **16.** (intr.) to be customary or prevalent: chaos rules in this school. **17.** (intr.) to be pre-eminent or superior: football rules in the field of sport. **18. rule the roost** (or **roast**). to be pre-eminent; be in charge. [C13: from OF riule, from L rēgula a straight edge] —'**rulable** adj.

rule of three n. a mathematical rule asserting that the value of one unknown quantity in a proportion is found by multiplying the denominator of each ratio by the numerator of the other.

rule of thumb n. **a.** a rough and practical approach, based on experience, rather than theory. **b.** (as modifier): a rule-of-thumb decision.

rule out vb. (tr., adv.) **1.** to dismiss from consideration. **2.** to make impossible; preclude.

ruler ('ru:lə) n. **1.** a person who rules or commands. **2.** Also called: **rule.** a strip of wood, metal, or other material, having straight edges, used for measuring and drawing straight lines.

Rules (ru:lz) pl. n. **1.** short for **Australian Rules** (football). **2. the Rules.** English history. the neighbourhood around certain prisons in which trusted prisoners were allowed to live under specified restrictions.

ruling ('ru:lɪŋ) n. **1.** a decision of someone in authority, such as a judge. **2.** one or more parallel ruled lines. ~adj. **3.** controlling or exercising authority. **4.** predominant.

rum[1] (rʌm) *n.* spirit made from sugar cane. [C17: ? shortened from C16 *rumbullion*, from ?]

rum[2] (rʌm) *adj.* **rummer, rummest.** *Brit. sl.* strange; peculiar; odd. [C19: ?from Romany *rom* man] — **'rumly** *adv.* — **'rumness** *n.*

Rumania (ruːˈmeɪnɪə) *n.* a variant of **Romania.** — **Ru'manian** *adj.*, *n.*

rumba *or* **rhumba** (ˈrʌmbə, 'rʊm-) *n.* **1.** a rhythmic and syncopated Cuban dance in duple time. **2.** a ballroom dance derived from this. **3.** a piece of music composed for or in the rhythm of this dance. [C20: from Sp.: lavish display, from ?]

rumble (ˈrʌmbᵊl) *vb.* **1.** to make or cause to make a deep resonant sound: *thunder rumbled in the sky.* **2.** (*intr.*) to move with such a sound: *the train rumbled along.* **3.** (*tr.*) to utter with a rumbling sound: *he rumbled an order.* **4.** (*tr.*) *Brit. sl.* to find out about (someone or something): *the police rumbled their plans.* **5.** (*intr.*) *U.S. sl.* to be involved in a gang fight. ~*n.* **6.** a deep resonant sound. **7.** a widespread murmur of discontent. **8.** *U.S. & N.Z. sl.* a gang fight. [C14: ?from MDu. *rummelen*] — **'rumbler** *n.* — **'rumbling** *adj.*

rumble seat *n.* *U.S. & Canad.* a folding outside seat at the rear of some early cars; dicky.

rumbustious (rʌmˈbʌstʃəs) *adj.* boisterous or unruly. [C18: prob. var. of ROBUSTIOUS] — **rum'bustiously** *adv.* — **rum'bustiousness** *n.*

rumen (ˈruːmɛn) *n.*, *pl.* **-mens** *or* **-mina** (-mɪnə). the first compartment of the stomach of ruminants, in which food is partly digested before being regurgitated as cud. [C18: from L: gullet]

Rumford (ˈrʌmfəd) *n.* **Count.** See (Benjamin) **Thompson.**

ruminant (ˈruːmɪnənt) *n.* **1.** any of a suborder of artiodactyl mammals which chew the cud and have a stomach of four compartments. The suborder includes deer, antelopes, cattle, sheep, and goats. **2.** any other animal that chews the cud, such as a camel. ~*adj.* **3.** of, relating to, or belonging to this suborder. **4.** (of members of this suborder and related animals, such as camels) chewing the cud; ruminating. **5.** meditating or contemplating in a slow quiet way.

ruminate (ˈruːmɪˌneɪt) *vb.* **1.** (of ruminants) to chew (the cud). **2.** (when *intr.*, often foll. by *upon, on,* etc.) to meditate or ponder (upon). [C16: from L *rūmināre* to chew the cud, from RUMEN] — **,rumi'nation** *n.* — **'ruminative** *adj.* — **'ruminatively** *adv.* — **'rumi,nator** *n.*

rummage (ˈrʌmɪdʒ) *vb.* **1.** (when *intr.*, often foll. by *through*) to search (through) while looking for something, often causing disorder. ~*n.* **2.** an act of rummaging. **3.** a jumble of articles. [C14 (in the sense: to pack a cargo): from OF *arrumage*, from *arrumer* to stow in a ship's hold, prob. of Gmc origin] — **'rummager** *n.*

rummage sale *n.* **1.** the U.S. and Canad. term for **jumble sale.** **2.** a sale of unclaimed property.

rummer (ˈrʌmə) *n.* a drinking glass having an ovoid bowl on a short stem. [C17: from Du. *roemer* a glass for drinking toasts, from *roemen* to praise]

rummy (ˈrʌmɪ) *or* **rum** *n.* a card game based on collecting sets and sequences. [C20: ?from RUM[2]]

rumour *or* *U.S.* **rumor** (ˈruːmə) *n.* **1. a.** information, often a mixture of truth and untruth, passed around verbally. **b.** (*in combination*): *a rumourmonger.* **2.** gossip or hearsay. ~*vb.* **3.** (*tr.*; *usually passive*) to pass around or circulate in the form of a rumour: *it is rumoured that the Queen is coming.* [C14: via OF from L *rūmor* common talk]

rump (rʌmp) *n.* **1.** the hindquarters of a mammal, not including the legs. **2.** the rear part of a bird's back, nearest to the tail. **3.** a person's buttocks. **4.** Also called: **rump steak.** a cut of beef from behind the loin. **5.** an inferior remnant. [C15: from ON] — **'rumpless** *adj.*

rumple (ˈrʌmpᵊl) *vb.* **1.** to make or become crumpled or dishevelled. ~*n.* **2.** a wrinkle, fold, or crease. [C17: from MDu. *rompelen;* rel. to OE *gerumpen* wrinkled] — **'rumply** *adj.*

Rump Parliament *or* **the Rump** *n.* *English history.* the remainder of the Long Parliament after Pride's Purge. It sat from 1648–53.

rumpus (ˈrʌmpəs) *n.*, *pl.* **-puses.** a noisy, confused, or disruptive commotion. [C18: from ?]

rumpus room *n.* *U.S., Canad., & N.Z.* a room used for noisy activities, such as parties or children's games.

run (rʌn) *vb.* **running, ran, run.** **1.** (*intr.*) **a.** (of a two-legged creature) to move on foot at a rapid pace so that both feet are off the ground for part of each stride. **b.** (of a four-legged creature) to move at a rapid gait. **2.** (*tr.*) to pass over (a distance, route, etc.) in running: *to run a mile.* **3.** (*intr.*) to run in or finish a race as specified, esp. in a particular position: *John is running third.* **4.** (*tr.*) to perform as by running: *to run an errand.* **5.** (*intr.*) to flee; run away. **6.** (*tr.*) to bring into a specified state by running: *to run oneself to a standstill.* **7.** (*tr.*) to track down or hunt (an animal): *to run a fox to earth.* **8.** (*tr.*) to set (animals) loose on (a field or tract of land) so as to graze freely: *he ran stock on that pasture last year.* **9.** (*intr.*; often foll. by *over, round,* or *up*) to make a short trip or brief visit: *I'll run over this afternoon.* **10.** (*intr.*) to move quickly and easily on wheels by rolling, or in any of certain other ways: *a sledge running over snow.* **11.** to move or cause to move with a specified result: *to run a ship aground; run into a tree.* **12.** (often foll. by *over*) to move or pass or cause to move or pass quickly: *to run one's eyes over a page.* **13.** (*tr.*; foll. by *into, out of, through,* etc.) to force, thrust, or drive: *she ran a needle into her finger.* **14.** (*tr.*) to drive or maintain and operate (a vehicle). **15.** (*tr.*) to give a lift to (someone) in a vehicle: *he ran her to the station.* **16.** to ply or cause to ply between places on a route: *the bus runs from Piccadilly to Golders Green.* **17.** to function or cause to function: *the engine is running smoothly.* **18.** (*tr.*) to manage: *to run a company.* **19.** to extend or continue or cause to extend or continue in a particular direction, for a particular duration or distance, etc.: *the road runs north; the play ran for two years.* **20.** (*intr.*) *Law.* to have legal force or effect: *the lease runs for two more years.* **21.** (*tr.*) to be subjected to, be affected by, or incur: *to run a risk; run a temperature.* **22.** (*intr.*; often foll. by *to*) to be characterized (by); tend or incline: *to run to fat.* **23.** (*intr.*) to recur persistently or be inherent: *red hair runs in my family.* **24.** to cause or allow (liquids) to flow or (of liquids) to flow: *the well has run dry.* **25.** (*intr.*) to melt and flow: *the wax grew hot and began to run.* **26.** *Metallurgy.* **a.** to melt or fuse. **b.** (*tr.*) to cast (molten metal): *to run lead into ingots.* **27.** (*intr.*) (of waves, tides, rivers, etc.) to rise high, surge, or be at a specified height: *a high sea was running that night.* **28.** (*intr.*) to be diffused: *the colours in my dress ran when I washed it.* **29.** (*intr.*) (of stitches) to unravel or come undone or (of a garment) to have stitches unravel or come undone. **30.** (*intr.*) (of growing creepers, etc.) to trail, spread, or climb: *ivy running over a cottage wall.* **31.** (*intr.*) to spread or circulate quickly: *a rumour ran through the town.* **32.** (*intr.*) to be stated or reported: *his story runs as follows.* **33.** to publish or print or be published or printed in a newspaper, magazine, etc.: *they ran his story in the next issue.* **34.** (often foll. by *for*) *Chiefly U.S. & Canad.* to be a candidate or present as a candidate for political or other office: *Jones is running for president.* **35.** (*tr.*) to get past or through: *to run a blockade.* **36.** (*tr.*) to deal in (arms, etc.), esp. by importing illegally: *he runs guns for the rebels.* **37.** *Naut.* to sail (a vessel, esp. a sailing vessel) or (of such a vessel) to be sailed with the wind coming from astern. **38.** (*intr.*) (of fish) to migrate upstream from the sea, esp. in order to spawn. **39.** (*tr.*) *Cricket.* to score (a run or number of runs) by hitting the ball and running between the wickets. **40.** (*tr.*) *Billiards, etc.* to make (a number of successful shots) in sequence. **41.** (*tr.*) *Golf.* to hit (the ball) so that it rolls along the ground. **42.** (*tr.*) *Bridge.* to cash (all one's winning cards in a long suit) successively. ~*n.* **43.** an act, instance, or period of running. **44.** a gait, pace, or motion faster than a walk: *she went off at a run.* **45.** a distance covered by running or a period of running: *a run of ten miles.* **46.** an instance or period of travelling in a vehicle, esp. for pleasure: *to go for a run in the car.* **47.** free and unrestricted access: *we had the run of the house.* **48. a.** a period of time during which a machine, computer, etc., operates. **b.** the amount of work performed in such a period. **49.** a continuous or sustained period: *a run of good luck.* **50.** a continuous sequence of performances: *the play had a good run.* **51.** *Cards.* a sequence of winning cards in one suit: *a run of spades.* **52.** tendency or trend: *the run of the market.* **53.** type, class, or category: *the usual run of* *graduates.* **54.** (usually foll. by *on*) a continuous and urgent demand: *a run on the dollar.* **55.** a series of unravelled stitches, esp. in tights; ladder. **56.** the characteristic pattern or direction of something: *the run of the grain on wood.* **57. a.** a period during which water or other liquid flows. **b.** the amount of such a flow. **58.** a pipe, channel, etc., through which water or other liquid flows. **59.** *U.S.* a small stream. **60.** a steeply inclined course, esp. a snow-covered one used for skiing. **61.** an enclosure for domestic fowls or other animals: *a chicken run.* **62.** (esp. in Australia and New Zealand) a tract of land for grazing livestock. **63.** the migration of fish upstream in order to spawn. **64.** *Mil.* **a.** a mission in a warplane. **b.** Also called: **bombing run.** an approach by a bomber to a target. **65.** the movement of an aircraft along the ground during takeoff or landing. **66.** *Music.* a rapid scalelike passage of notes. **67.** *Cricket.* a score of one, normally achieved by both batsmen running from one end of the wicket to the other after one of them has hit the ball. **68.** *Baseball.* an instance of a batter touching all four bases safely, thereby scoring. **69.** *Golf.* the distance that a ball rolls after hitting the ground. **70. a run for (one's) money.** *Inf.* **a.** a close competition. **b.** pleasure derived from an activity. **71. in the long run.** as the eventual outcome of a series of events, etc. **72. in the short run.** as the immediate outcome of a series of events, etc. **73. on the run. a.** escaping from arrest; fugitive. **b.** in rapid flight; retreating: *the enemy is on the run.* **c.** hurrying from place to place. **74. the runs.** *Sl.* diarrhoea. ~See also **runaway, run across,** etc. [OE *runnen,* p.p. of (*ge*)*rinnan*]

runabout ('rʌnə,baʊt) *n.* **1.** a small light vehicle or aeroplane. ~*vb.* **run about. 2.** (*intr., adv.*) to move busily from place to place.

run across *vb.* (*intr., prep.*) to meet unexpectedly; encounter by chance.

run along *vb.* (*intr., adv.*) (often said patronizingly) to go away; leave.

run around *Inf.* ~*vb.* (*intr., adv.*) **1.** (often foll. by *with*) to associate habitually (with). **2.** to behave in a fickle or promiscuous manner. ~*n.* **run-around. 3.** deceitful or evasive treatment of a person (esp. in **give** *or* **get the run-around**).

run away *vb.* (*intr., adv.*) **1.** to take flight; escape. **2.** to go away; depart. **3.** (of a horse) to gallop away uncontrollably. **4. run away with. a.** to abscond or elope with: *he ran away with his boss's daughter.* **b.** to make off with; steal. **c.** to escape from the control of: *his enthusiasm ran away with him.* **d.** to win easily or be assured of victory in (a competition): *he ran away with the race.* ~*n.* **runaway. 5. a.** a person or animal that runs away. **b.** (*as modifier*): *a runaway horse.* **6.** the act or an instance of running away. **7.** (*modifier*) rising rapidly, as prices: *runaway inflation.* **8.** (*modifier*) (of a race, victory, etc.) easily won.

runcible spoon ('rʌnsɪbˀl) *n.* a forklike utensil with two broad prongs and one sharp curved prong. [*runcible* coined by Edward Lear, in a nonsense poem (1871)]

Runcie ('rʌnsɪ) *n.* **Robert (Alexander Kennedy).** born 1921, Archbishop of Canterbury from 1980.

Runcorn ('rʌŋ,kɔːn) *n.* a town in NW England, in N Cheshire on the Manchester Ship Canal; port and industrial centre; designated a new town in 1964. Pop.: 64 117 (1981).

run down *vb.* (*mainly adv.*) **1.** to allow (an engine, etc.) to lose power gradually and cease to function or (of an engine, etc.) to do this. **2.** to decline or reduce in number or size: *the firm ran down its sales force.* **3.** (*tr.; usually passive*) to tire, sap the strength of, or exhaust: *he was thoroughly run down.* **4.** (*tr.*) to criticize adversely; decry. **5.** (*tr.*) to hit and knock to the ground with a moving vehicle. **6.** (*tr.*) *Naut.* to collide with and cause to sink. **7.** (*tr.*) to pursue and find or capture: *to run down a fugitive.* **8.** (*tr.*) to read swiftly or perfunctorily: *he ran down their list of complaints.* ~*adj.* **run-down. 9.** tired; exhausted. **10.** worn-out, shabby, or dilapidated. ~*n.* **run-down. 11.** a brief review, résumé, or summary. **12.** the process of a mechanism coming gradually to a standstill after the power is removed. **13.** a reduction in number or size.

Rundstedt ('rʊndstɛt; *German* 'rʊntʃtɛt) *n.* **Karl Rudolf Gerd von** (karl 'ruːdɔlf gɛrt fɔn). 1875–1953, German field marshal; directed the conquest of Poland and France

in World War II; commander of the Western Front (1942–44); led the Ardennes counteroffensive (Dec. 1944).

rune (ruːn) *n.* **1.** any of the characters of an ancient Germanic alphabet, in use, esp. in Scandinavia, from the 3rd century A.D. to the end of the Middle Ages. **2.** any obscure piece of writing using mysterious symbols. **3.** a kind of Finnish poem or a stanza in such a poem. [OE *rūn,* from ON *rūn* secret] — **'runic** *adj.*

rung[1] (rʌŋ) *n.* **1.** one of the bars or rods that form the steps of a ladder. **2.** a crosspiece between the legs of a chair, etc. **3.** *Naut.* a spoke on a ship's wheel or a handle projecting from the periphery. [OE *hrung*] — **'rungless** *adj.*

rung[2] (rʌŋ) *vb.* the past participle of **ring**[2].
▷**Usage. See at ring**[2].

run in *vb.* (*adv.*) **1.** to run (an engine) gently, usually when it is new. **2.** (*tr.*) to insert or include. **3.** (*intr.*) (of an aircraft) to approach a point or target. **4.** (*tr.*) *Inf.* to take into custody; arrest. ~*n.* **run-in. 5.** *Inf.* an argument or quarrel. **6.** *Printing.* matter inserted in an existing paragraph.

run into *vb.* (*prep., mainly intr.*) **1.** (*also tr.*) to collide with or cause to collide with: *her car ran into a tree.* **2.** to encounter unexpectedly. **3.** (*also tr.*) to be beset by: *the project ran into financial difficulties.* **4.** to extend to; be of the order of: *debts running into thousands.*

runnel ('rʌnˀl) *n. Literary.* a small stream. [C16: from OE *rynele*; rel. to RUN]

runner ('rʌnə) *n.* **1.** a person who runs, esp. an athlete. **2.** a messenger for a bank, etc. **3.** a person engaged in the solicitation of business. **4.** a person on the run; fugitive. **5. a.** a person or vessel engaged in smuggling. **b.** (*in combination*): *a gunrunner.* **6.** a person who operates, manages, or controls something. **7. a.** either of the strips of metal or wood on which a sledge runs. **b.** the blade of an ice skate. **8.** a roller or guide for a sliding component. **9.** *Bot.* **a.** Also called: **stolon.** a slender horizontal stem, as of the strawberry, that grows along the surface of the soil and propagates by producing roots and shoots at the nodes or tip. **b.** a plant that propagates in this way. **10.** a strip of lace, linen, etc., placed across a table or dressing table for protection and decoration. **11.** another word for **rocker** (on a rocking chair).

runner bean *n.* another name for **scarlet runner.**

runner-up *n., pl.* **runners-up.** a contestant finishing a race or competition in second place.

running ('rʌnɪŋ) *adj.* **1.** maintained continuously; incessant: *running commentary.* **2.** (*postpositive*) without interruption; consecutive: *he lectured for two hours running.* **3.** denoting or relating to the scheduled operation of a public vehicle: *the running time of a train.* **4.** accomplished at a run: *a running jump.* **5.** moving or slipping easily, as a rope or a knot. **6.** (of a wound, etc.) discharging pus. **7.** prevalent; current: *running prices.* **8.** repeated or continuous: *a running design.* **9.** (of plants, plant stems, etc.) creeping along the ground. **10.** flowing: *running water.* **11.** (of handwriting) having the letters run together. ~*n.* **12.** management or organization: *the running of a company.* **13.** operation or maintenance: *the running of a machine.* **14.** competition or competitive situation (in **in the running, out of the running**). **15. make the running.** to set the pace in a competition or race.

running board *n.* a footboard along the side of a vehicle, esp. an early motorcar.

running head *or* **title** *n. Printing.* a heading printed at the top of every page of a book.

running light *n. Naut.* one of several lights displayed by vessels operating at night.

running mate *n.* **1.** *U.S.* a candidate for the subordinate of two linked positions, esp. a candidate for the vice-presidency. **2.** a horse that pairs another in a team.

running repairs *pl. n.* repairs that do not, or do not greatly, interrupt operations.

runny ('rʌnɪ) *adj.* **-nier, -niest. 1.** tending to flow; liquid. **2.** (of the nose) exuding mucus.

Runnymede ('rʌnɪ,miːd) *n.* a meadow on the S bank of the Thames near Windsor, where King John met his rebellious barons in 1215 and acceded to Magna Carta.

run off *vb.* (*adv.*) **1.** (*intr.*) to depart in haste. **2.** (*tr.*) to produce quickly, as copies on a duplicating machine. **3.** to drain (liquid) or (of liquid) to be drained. **4.** (*tr.*) to decide (a race) by a run-off. **5. run off with. a.** to steal;

purloin. **b.** to elope with. ~*n.* **run-off. 6.** an extra race, contest, election, etc., to decide the winner after a tie. **7.** *N. Z.* grazing land for store cattle. **8.** that portion of rainfall that runs into streams as surface water rather than being absorbed by the soil. **9.** the overflow of a liquid from a container.

run-of-the-mill *adj.* ordinary, average, or undistinguished in quality, character, or nature.

run on *vb.* (*adv.*) **1.** (*intr.*) to continue without interruption. **2.** to write with linked-up characters. **3.** *Printing.* to compose text matter without indentation or paragraphing. ~*n.* **run-on. 4.** *Printing.* **a.** text matter composed without indenting. **b.** an additional quantity required in excess of the originally stated amount, whilst the job is being produced. **5. a.** a word added at the end of a dictionary entry whose meaning can be easily inferred from the definition of the headword. **b.** (*as modifier*): *a run-on entry.*

run out *vb.* (*adv.*) **1.** (*intr.; often foll. by of*) to exhaust (a supply of something) or (of a supply) to become exhausted. **2. run out on.** *Inf.* to desert or abandon. **3.** (*tr.*) *Cricket.* to dismiss (a running batsman) by breaking the wicket with the ball, or with the ball in the hand, while he is out of his ground. ~*n.* **run-out. 4.** *Cricket.* dismissal of a batsman by running him out.

run over *vb.* **1.** (*tr., adv.*) to knock down (a person) with a moving vehicle. **2.** (*intr.*) to overflow the capacity of (a container). **3.** (*intr., prep.*) to examine hastily or make a rapid survey of. **4.** (*intr., prep.*) to exceed (a limit): *we've run over our time.*

runt (rʌnt) *n.* **1.** the smallest and weakest young animal in a litter, esp. the smallest piglet in a litter. **2.** *Derog.* an undersized or inferior person. **3.** a large pigeon, originally bred for eating. [C16: from ?] —'**runtish** *or* '**runty** *adj.* —'**runtiness** *n.*

run through *vb.* **1.** (*tr., adv.*) to transfix with a sword or other weapon. **2.** (*intr., prep.*) to exhaust (money) by wasteful spending. **3.** (*intr., prep.*) to practise or rehearse: *let's run through the plan.* **4.** (*intr., prep.*) to examine hastily. ~*n.* **run-through. 5.** a practice or rehearsal. **6.** a brief survey.

run to *vb.* (*intr., prep.*) to be sufficient for: *my income doesn't run to luxuries.*

run up *vb.* (*tr., adv.*) **1.** to amass; incur: *to run up debts.* **2.** to make by sewing together quickly. **3.** to hoist: *to run up a flag.* ~*n.* **run-up. 4.** an approach run by an athlete for the long jump, pole vault, etc. **5.** a preliminary or preparatory period: *the run-up to the election.*

runway ('rʌn,weɪ) *n.* **1.** a hard level roadway from which aircraft take off and on which they land. **2.** *Forestry, North American.* a chute for sliding logs down. **3.** a narrow ramp extending from the stage into the audience in a theatre, etc.

Runyon ('rʌnjən) *n.* (**Alfred**) **Damon.** 1884–1946, U.S. short-story writer, best known for his humorous tales about racy Broadway characters. His story collections include *Guys and Dolls* (1932), which became the basis of a musical (1950).

rupee (ruː'piː) *n.* the standard monetary unit of India, Pakistan, Sri Lanka, the Maldive Islands, Mauritius, the Seychelles, and Nepal. [C17: from Hindi *rupaīyā*, from Sansk. *rūpya* coined silver, from *rūpa* shape, beauty]

Rupert ('ruːpət) *n.* **Prince.** 1619–82, German-born nephew of Charles I: Royalist general during the Civil War (until 1646) and commander of the Royalist fleet (1648–50). After the Restoration he was an admiral of the English fleet in wars against the Dutch.

Rupert's Land *n.* (formerly, in Canada) the territories granted by Charles II to the Hudson's Bay Company in 1670 and ceded to the Canadian Government in 1870, comprising all the land watered by rivers flowing into Hudson Bay.

rupiah (ruː'piːə) *n., pl.* **-ah** *or* **-ahs.** the standard monetary unit of Indonesia. [from Hindi: RUPEE]

rupture ('rʌptʃə) *n.* **1.** the act of breaking or bursting or the state of being broken or burst. **2.** a breach of peaceful or friendly relations. **3.** *Pathol.* **a.** the breaking or tearing of a bodily structure or part. **b.** another word for **hernia.** ~*vb.* **4.** to break or burst. **5.** to affect or be affected with a rupture or hernia. **6.** to undergo or cause to undergo a breach in relations or friendship. [C15: from L *ruptūra*, from *rumpere* to burst forth] —'**rupturable** *adj.*

rural ('rʊərəl) *adj.* **1.** of, relating to, or characteristic of the country or country life. **2.** living in the country. **3.** of, relating to, or associated with farming. ~Cf. **urban.** [C15: via OF from L *rūrālis*, from *rūs* the country] —'**ruralism** *n.* —'**ruralist** *n.* —**ru'rality** *n.* —'**rurally** *adv.*

rural dean *n. Chiefly Brit.* a clergyman having authority over a group of parishes.

rural district *n.* (formerly) a rural division of a county.

ruralize *or* **-ise** ('rʊərə,laɪz) *vb.* **1.** (*tr.*) to make rural in character, appearance, etc. **2.** (*intr.*) to go into the country to live. —,**rurali'zation** *or* **-i'sation** *n.*

rural route *n. U.S. & Canad.* a mail service or route in a rural area, the mail being delivered by car or van.

Rurik *or* **Ryurik** ('rʊərɪk) *n.* died 879. Varangian (Scandinavian Viking) leader who founded the Russian monarchy. He gained control over Novgorod (?862) and his dynasty, the **Rurikids,** ruled until 1598.

Ruritania (,rʊərɪ'teɪnɪə, -njə) *n.* **1.** an imaginary kingdom of central Europe: setting of several novels by Anthony Hope, esp. *The Prisoner of Zenda* (1894). **2.** any setting of adventure, romance, and intrigue. —,**Ruri'tanian** *adj., n.*

rusbank ('rʊs,bæŋk) *n. S. African.* a wooden bench or settle without upholstery. [from Afrik., from Du. *rust* rest + *bank* bench]

ruse (ruːz) *n.* an action intended to mislead, deceive, or trick; stratagem. [C15: from OF: trick, esp. to evade capture, from *ruser* to retreat, from L *recūsāre* to refuse]

Ruse ('ruːseɪ) *n.* a city in NE Bulgaria, on the River Danube: the chief river port and one of the largest industrial centres in Bulgaria. Pop.: 183 746 (1985).

rush[1] (rʌʃ) *vb.* **1.** to hurry or cause to hurry; hasten. **2.** (*tr.*) to make a sudden attack upon (a fortress, position, person, etc.). **3.** (*when intr.,* often foll. by *at, in,* or *into*) to proceed or approach in a reckless manner. **4. rush one's fences.** to proceed with precipitate haste. **5.** (*intr.*) to come, flow, swell, etc., quickly or suddenly: *tears rushed to her eyes.* **6.** (*tr.*) *Sl.* to cheat, esp. by grossly overcharging. **7.** (*tr.*) *U.S. & Canad.* to make a concerted effort to secure the agreement, participation, etc., of (a person). **8.** (*tr.*) *Rugby.* (of a pack) to move (the ball) forwards by short kicks and runs. ~*n.* **9.** the act or condition of rushing. **10.** a sudden surge towards someone or something: *a gold rush.* **11.** a sudden surge of sensation, esp. from a drug. **12.** a sudden demand. **13.** (*usually pl.*) (in film-making) the initial prints of a scene before editing. ~*adj.* (*prenominal*) **14.** requiring speed or urgency: *a rush job.* **15.** characterized by much movement, business, etc.: *a rush period.* [C14 *ruschen,* from OF *ruser* to put to flight, from L *recūsāre* to refuse] —'**rusher** *n.*

rush[2] (rʌʃ) *n.* **1.** an annual or perennial plant growing in wet places and typically having grasslike cylindrical leaves and small green or brown flowers. **2.** something valueless; a trifle; straw: *not worth a rush.* **3.** short for **rush light.** [OE *risce, rysce*] —'**rush,like** *adj.* —'**rushy** *adj.*

Rushdie ('rʌʃdɪ) *n.* (**Ahmed**) **Salman** ('sælmən). born 1947, British writer, born in India. His novels include *Grimus* (1975), *Midnight's Children* (1981) which won the Booker McConnell prize, *Shame* (1983), and *The Satanic Verses* (1988).

rush hour *n.* a period at the beginning and end of the working day when large numbers of people are travelling to or from work.

rush light *or* **candle** *n.* a narrow candle, formerly in use, made from the pith of various types of rush dipped in tallow.

Rushmore ('rʌʃmɔː) *n.* **Mount.** a mountain in W South Dakota, in the Black Hills: a national memorial, with the faces of Washington, Lincoln, Jefferson, and Roosevelt carved into its side by Gutzon Borglum between 1927 and 1941. Height: 1841 m (6040 ft.).

rusk (rʌsk) *n.* a light bread dough, sweet or plain, baked twice until it is brown, hard, and crisp: often given to babies. [C16: from Sp. or Port. *rosca* screw, bread shaped in a twist, from ?]

Ruskin ('rʌskɪn) *n.* **John.** 1819–1900, English art critic and social reformer. He was a champion of the Gothic Revival and the Pre-Raphaelites and saw a close connection between art and morality. From about 1860 he argued vigorously for social and economic planning. His works include *Modern Painters* (1843–60), *The Stones of Venice*

(1851–53), *Unto this Last* (1862), *Time and Tide* (1867), and *Fors Clavigera* (1871–84).

Russ. *abbrev. for* Russia(n).

Russell ('rʌs³l) *n.* **1. Bertrand (Arthur William)**, 3rd Earl Russell. 1872–1970, English philosopher and mathematician. His books include *Principles of Mathematics* (1903), *Principia Mathematica* (1910–13) with A. N. Whitehead, *Introduction to Mathematical Philosophy* (1919), *The Problems of Philosophy* (1912), *The Analysis of Mind* (1921), and *An Enquiry into Meaning and Truth* (1940): Nobel prize for literature 1950. **2. George William,** pen name Æ. 1867–1935, Irish poet and journalist. **3. John,** 1st Earl Russell. 1792–1878, British statesman; prime minister (1846–52; 1865–66). He led the campaign to carry the 1832 Reform Act. **4. Ken.** born 1927, English film director. His films include *Women in Love* (1969), *The Music Lovers* (1970), *The Boy Friend* (1971), *Valentino* (1977), and *Gothic* (1986).

russet ('rʌsɪt) *n.* **1.** brown with a yellowish or reddish tinge. **2.** a rough homespun fabric, reddish-brown in colour, formerly in use for clothing. **3.** any of various apples with rough brownish-red skins. ~*adj.* **4.** *Arch.* simple; homely; rustic: *a russet life.* **5.** of the colour russet: *russet hair.* [C13: from Anglo-Norman, from OF *rosset*, from *rous*, from L *russus;* rel. to L *ruber* red] — **'russety** *adj.*

Russia ('rʌʃə) *n.* **1.** another name for the **Russian Empire. 2.** another name for the **Soviet Union. 3.** another name for the **Russian Soviet Federative Socialist Republic.** Russian name: **Rossiya.**

Russia leather *n.* a smooth dyed leather made from calfskin and scented with birch tar oil, originally produced in Russia.

Russian ('rʌʃən) *n.* **1.** the official language of the Soviet Union: an Indo-European language belonging to the East Slavonic branch. **2.** a native or inhabitant of Russia or the Soviet Union. ~*adj.* **3.** of, relating to, or characteristic of Russia or the Soviet Union, its people, or their language.

Russian Empire *n.* the tsarist empire in Asia and E Europe, overthrown by the Russian Revolution of 1917.

Russianize *or* **-ise** ('rʌʃənaɪz) *vb.* to make or become Russian in style, etc. — **,Russiani'zation** *or* **-i'sation** *n.*

Russian roulette *n.* **1.** an act of bravado in which each person in turn spins the cylinder of a revolver loaded with only one cartridge and presses the trigger with the barrel against his own head. **2.** any foolish or potentially suicidal undertaking.

Russian salad *n.* a salad of cold diced cooked vegetables mixed with mayonnaise and pickles.

Russian Soviet Federative Socialist Republic *n.* the largest administrative division of the Soviet Union (over 76 per cent of the total area and 55 per cent of the population), extending from the Baltic to the Pacific and from the Arctic Ocean to the Caspian Sea: ranges from arctic to subtropical in climate and includes tundra, forests, steppes, and rich arable land; contains 20 major nationality groups and produces about 70 per cent of the agricultural and industrial output of the Soviet Union. Capital: Moscow. Pop.: 145 311 000 (1987). Area: 17 074 984 sq. km (6 592 658 sq. miles). Abbrev.: **RSFSR.**

Russian Turkestan *n.* See **Turkestan.**

Russian Zone *n.* another name for the **Soviet Zone.**

Russo- ('rʌsəʊ) *combining form.* Russia or Russian: *Russo-Japanese.*

rust (rʌst) *n.* **1.** a reddish-brown oxide coating formed on iron or steel by the action of oxygen and moisture. **2.** Also called: **rust fungus.** *Plant pathol.* **a.** any of a group of fungi which are parasitic on cereal plants, conifers, etc. **b.** any of various plant diseases characterized by reddish-brown discoloration of the leaves and stem, esp. that caused by the rust fungi. **3. a.** a strong brown colour, sometimes with a reddish or yellowish tinge. **b.** (*as adj.*): *a rust carpet.* **4.** any corrosive or debilitating influence, esp. lack of use. ~*vb.* **5.** to become or cause to become coated with a layer of rust. **6.** to deteriorate or cause to deteriorate through some debilitating influence or lack of use: *he allowed his talent to rust over the years.* [OE *rūst*] — **'rustless** *adj.*

rustic ('rʌstɪk) *adj.* **1.** of, characteristic of, or living in the country; rural. **2.** having qualities ascribed to country life or people; simple; unsophisticated: *rustic pleasures.* **3.** crude, awkward, or uncouth. **4.** made of untrimmed branches: *a rustic seat.* **5.** (of masonry, etc.) having a rusticated finish. ~*n.* **6.** a person who comes from or

lives in the country. **7.** an unsophisticated, simple, or clownish person from the country. **8.** Also called: **rusticwork.** brick or stone having a rough finish. [C16: from OF *rustique*, from L *rūsticus*, from *rūs* the country] — **'rustically** *adv.* — **rusticity** (rʌ'stɪsɪtɪ) *n.*

rusticate ('rʌstɪˌkeɪt) *vb.* **1.** to banish or retire to the country. **2.** to make or become rustic in style, etc. **3.** (*tr.*) *Architect.* to finish (an exterior wall) with large blocks of masonry separated by deep joints. **4.** (*tr.*) *Brit.* to send down from university for a specified time as a punishment. [C17: from L *rūsticārī*, from *rūs* the country] — **,rusti'cation** *n.* — **'rusti,cator** *n.*

rusticated ('rʌstɪˌkeɪtɪd) *or* **rusticating** ('rʌstɪˌkeɪtɪŋ) *n.* (in New Zealand) a wide type of weatherboarding used in older houses.

rustle[1] ('rʌs³l) *vb.* **1.** to make or cause to make a low crisp whispering or rubbing sound, as of dry leaves or paper. **2.** to move with such a sound. ~*n.* **3.** such a sound or sounds. [OE *hrūxlian*]

rustle[2] ('rʌs³l) *vb.* **1.** *Chiefly U.S. & Canad.* to steal (cattle, horses, etc.). **2.** *Inf., U.S. & Canad.* to move swiftly and energetically. [C19: prob. special use of RUSTLE[1](in the sense: to move with a quiet sound)] — **'rustler** *n.*

rustle up *vb.* (*tr., adv.*) *Inf.* **1.** to prepare (a meal, etc.) rapidly, esp. at short notice. **2.** to forage for and obtain.

rustproof ('rʌst,pruːf) *adj.* treated against rusting.

rusty ('rʌstɪ) *adj.* **rustier, rustiest. 1.** covered with, affected by, or consisting of rust: *a rusty machine.* **2.** of the colour rust. **3.** discoloured by age: *a rusty coat.* **4.** (of the voice) tending to croak. **5.** old-fashioned in appearance: *a rusty old gentleman.* **6.** impaired in skill or knowledge by inaction or neglect. **7.** (of plants) affected by the rust fungus. — **'rustily** *adv.* — **'rustiness** *n.*

rut[1] (rʌt) *n.* **1.** a groove or furrow in a soft road, caused by wheels. **2.** a narrow or predictable way of life; dreary or undeviating routine (esp. in **in a rut**). ~*vb.* **rutting, rutted. 3.** (*tr.*) to make a rut in. [C16: prob. from F *route* road]

rut[2] (rʌt) *n.* **1.** a recurrent period of sexual excitement and reproductive activity in certain male ruminants. ~*vb.* **rutting, rutted. 2.** (*intr.*) (of male ruminants) to be in a period of sexual excitement and activity. [C15: from OF *rut* noise, roar, from L *rugītus*, from *rugīre* to roar]

rutabaga (,ruːtə'beɪgə) *n.* the U.S. and Canad. name for **swede.** [C18: from Swedish dialect *rotabagge*, lit.: root bag]

rutaceous (ruː'teɪʃəs) *adj.* of, relating to, or belonging to a family of tropical and temperate flowering plants many of which have aromatic leaves. The family includes rue, citrus trees, and dittany. [C19: from NL *Rutaceae*, from L *rūta* RUE[2]]

ruth (ruːθ) *n.* *Arch.* **1.** pity; compassion. **2.** repentance; remorse. [C12: from *rewen* to RUE[1]]

Ruth (ruːθ) *n.* **1.** *Old Testament.* **a.** a Moabite woman, who left her own people to remain with her mother-in-law Naomi, and became the wife of Boaz; an ancestress of David. **b.** the book in which these events are recounted. **2. George Herman.** nicknamed *Babe.* 1895–1948, U.S. professional baseball player from 1914 to 1935.

Ruthenia (ruː'θiːnɪə) *n.* a region of E Europe on the south side of the Carpathian Mountains: belonged to Hungary from the 14th century, to Czechoslovakia from 1918 to 1939, and was ceded to the Soviet Union in 1945; now forms the Transcarpathian Region of the Ukrainian SSR. Also called: **Carpatho-Ukraine.** — **Ru'thenian** *adj., n.*

ruthenium (ruː'θiːnɪəm) *n.* a hard brittle white element of the platinum metal group. It is used to harden platinum and palladium. Symbol: Ru; atomic no.: 44; atomic wt.: 101.07. [C19: from Med. L *Ruthenia* Russia, where it was discovered]

rutherford ('rʌðəfəd) *n.* a unit of activity equal to the quantity of a radioactive nuclide required to produce one million disintegrations per second. Abbrev.: **rd.** [C20: after Ernest RUTHERFORD]

Rutherford ('rʌðəfəd) *n.* **Ernest,** 1st Baron Rutherford. 1871–1937, British physicist, born in New Zealand, who discovered the atomic nucleus (1909). Nobel prize for chemistry 1908.

rutherfordium (,rʌðə'fɔːdɪəm) *n.* the U.S. name for the element with the atomic no. 104, known in the USSR as kurchatovium. Symbol: Rf [C20: after E. RUTHERFORD]

ruthful ('ruːθfʊl) *adj.* *Arch.* full of or causing sorrow or pity. — **'ruthfully** *adv.* — **'ruthfulness** *n.*

ruthless ('ruːθlɪs) *adj.* feeling or showing no mercy; hardhearted. —'**ruthlessly** *adv.* —'**ruthlessness** *n.*

rutile ('ruːtaɪl) *n.* a mineral consisting of titanium(IV) oxide (TiO$_2$) in tetragonal crystalline form. It is an important source of titanium. [C19: via F from G *Rutil*, from L *rutilus* red, glowing]

Rutland ('rʌtlənd) *n.* a former inland county of central England: the smallest English county. It became part of Leicestershire in 1974.

ruttish ('rʌtɪʃ) *adj.* **1.** (of an animal) in a condition of rut. **2.** lascivious or salacious. —'**ruttishly** *adv.* —'**ruttishness** *n.*

rutty ('rʌtɪ) *adj.* **-tier, -tiest.** full of ruts or holes: *a rutty track.* —'**ruttily** *adv.* —'**ruttiness** *n.*

Ruwenzori (ˌruːwɛnˈzɔːrɪ) *n.* a mountain range in central Africa, on the Ugandan-Zaïrese border between Lakes Edward and Albert: generally thought to be Ptolemy's "Mountains of the Moon". Highest peak: Mount Stanley, 5109 m (16 763 ft.).

Ruysdael ('riːzdɑːl, -deɪl, 'raɪz-; *Dutch* 'rœizdaːl) *n.* a variant spelling of **Ruisdael.**

Ruyter ('raɪtə; *Dutch* 'rœitər) *n.* **Michiel Adriaanszoon de** (miːˈxiːl ˌaːdriˈaːnsun də). 1607–76, Dutch admiral, noted for actions in the Anglo-Dutch wars in 1652–53, 1665–67, 1672, and 1673, when he prevented an Anglo-French invasion.

RV *abbrev. for* Revised Version (of the Bible).

Rwanda (rʊˈændə) *n.* a republic in central Africa: part of German East Africa from 1899 until 1917, when Belgium took over the administration; became a republic in 1961 after the successful Hutu revolt against the Tutsi (1959). Official languages: Rwanda and French. Currency: Rwanda franc. Capital: Kigali. Pop.: 6 324 000 (1986 est.). Area: 26 338 sq. km (10 169 sq. miles). Former name (until 1962): **Ruanda.**

-ry *suffix forming nouns.* a variant of **-ery:** *dentistry.*

Ryazan (*Russian* rɪˈzanj) *n.* a city in the W central Soviet Union: capital of a medieval principality; oil refineries and engineering industries. Pop.: 508 000 (1987).

Rybinsk (*Russian* 'ribinsk) *n.* a former name (1957–84) for **Andropov.**

Rydal ('raɪdəl) *n.* a village in NW England, in Cumbria on **Rydal Water** (a small lake). **Rydal Mount,** home of Wordsworth from 1813 to 1850, is situated here.

rye (raɪ) *n.* **1.** a tall hardy widely cultivated annual grass having bristly flower spikes and light brown grain. **2.** the grain of this grass, used in making flour and whisky, and as a livestock food. **3.** Also called: (esp. U.S.): **rye whiskey.** whisky distilled from rye. **4.** *U.S.* short for **rye bread.** [OE *ryge*]

rye bread *n.* any of various breads made entirely or partly from rye flour, often with caraway seeds.

rye-grass *n.* any of various grasses native to Europe, N Africa, and Asia, and widely cultivated as forage crops. They have flattened flower spikes and hairless leaves.

Ryle (raɪl) *n.* Sir **Martin.** 1918–84, English astronomer, noted for his research on radio astronomy: Astronomer Royal 1972–82; shared the Nobel prize for physics in 1974.

Ryswick ('rɪzwɪk) *n.* the English name for **Rijswijk.**

Ryukyu Islands (rɪˈuːkjuː) *pl. n.* a chain of 55 islands in the W Pacific, extending almost 650 km (400 miles) from S Japan to N Taiwan: an ancient kingdom, under Chinese rule from the late 14th century, Japanese supremacy from 1872 to 1945, and U.S. control from 1945 to 1972; now part of Japan again. They are subject to frequent typhoons. Chief town: Naha City (on Okinawa). Pop.: 1 179 000 (1985). Area: 2196 sq. km (849 sq. miles).

Ryurik ('rʊərɪk) *n.* a variant spelling of **Rurik.**

S

s or **S** (ɛs) *n., pl.* **s's, S's,** or **Ss. 1.** the 19th letter of the English alphabet. **2.** a speech sound represented by this letter, either voiceless, as in *sit,* or voiced, as in *dogs.* **3. a.** something shaped like an S. **b.** (*in combination*): *an S-bend in a road.*

s *symbol for* second (of time).

S *symbol for:* **1.** small. **2.** Society. **3.** South. **4.** *Chem.* sulphur. **5.** *Physics.* **a.** entropy. **b.** siemens. **c.** strangeness. **6.** *Currency.* Schilling.

s. *abbrev. for:* **1.** shilling. **2.** singular. **3.** son. **4.** succeeded.

s. or **S.** *Music. abbrev. for* soprano.

S. *abbrev. for:* **1.** sabbath. **2.** (*pl.* **SS**) Saint. **3.** Saturday. **4.** Saxon. **5.** school. **6.** September. **7.** Signor. **8.** Sunday.

-s[1] or **-es** *suffix.* forming the plural of most nouns: *boys; boxes.* [from OE *-as,* pl. nominative and accusative ending of some masc. nouns]

-s[2] or **-es** *suffix.* forming the third person singular present indicative tense of verbs: *he runs.* [from OE (northern dialect) *-es, -s,* orig. the ending of the second person singular]

-'s *suffix.* **1.** forming the possessive singular of nouns and some pronouns: *man's; one's.* **2.** forming the possessive plural of nouns whose plurals do not end in *-s: children's.* (The possessive plural of nouns ending in *s* and of some singular nouns is formed by the addition of an apostrophe after the final *s: girls'; for goodness' sake.*) **3.** forming the plural of numbers, letters, or symbols: *20's.* **4.** *Inf.* contraction of *is* or *has: it's gone.* **5.** *Inf.* contraction of *us* with *let: let's.* **6.** *Inf.* contraction of *does* in some questions: *what's he do?* [senses 1, 2: assimilated contraction from ME *-es,* from OE, masc. and neuter genitive sing.; sense 3, equivalent to -s[1]]

SA *abbrev. for:* **1.** Salvation Army. **2.** South Africa. **3.** South America. **4.** South Australia. **5.** *Sturmabteilung:* the Nazi terrorist militia.

Saadi (sɑːˈdiː) *n.* a variant spelling of **Sadi.**

Saar (sɑː; *German* zaːr) *n.* **1.** a river in W Europe, rising in the Vosges Mountains and flowing north to the Moselle River in West Germany. Length: 246 km (153 miles). French name: **Sarre. 2. the Saar.** another name for **Saarland.**

Saarbrücken (*German* zaːrˈbrykən) *n.* an industrial city in W West Germany, capital of Saarland state, on the Saar River. Pop.: 185 100 (1986).

Saarinen (ˈsɑːrɪnən) *n.* **Eero** (ˈeɪrəʊ). 1910–61, U.S. architect, born in Finland. His works include the U.S. Embassy, London (1960).

Saarland (*German* ˈzaːrlant) *n.* a state of W West Germany: formed in 1919; under League of Nations administration until 1935; occupied by France (1945–57); contains rich coal deposits and is a major industrial region. Capital: Saarbrücken. Pop.: 1 043 400 (1986). Area: 2567 sq. km (991 sq. miles).

Saba (ˈsɑːbə) *n.* **1.** an island in the NE West Indies, in the Netherlands Antilles. Pop.: 965 (1981). Area: 13 sq. km (5 sq. miles). **2.** another name for **Sheba** (sense 1).

Sabadell (*Spanish* saβaˈðel) *n.* a town in NE Spain, near Barcelona: textile manufacturing. Pop.: 186 123 (1981).

sabadilla (ˌsæbəˈdɪlə) *n.* **1.** a tropical American liliaceous plant. **2.** the bitter brown seeds of this plant, which contain the alkaloid veratrine used in insecticides. [C19: from Sp. *cebadilla,* dim. of *cebada* barley, from L *cibāre* to feed, from *cibus* food]

Sabaean or **Sabean** (səˈbiːən) *n.* **1.** an inhabitant or native of ancient Saba. **2.** the ancient Semitic language of Saba. ~*adj.* **3.** of or relating to ancient Saba, its inhabitants, or their language. [C16: from L *Sabaeus,* from Gk *Sabaios* belonging to Saba (Sheba)]

Sabah (ˈsɑːbɑː) *n.* a state of Malaysia, occupying N Borneo and offshore islands in the South China and Sulu Seas: became a British protectorate in 1888; gained independence and joined Malaysia in 1963. Capital: Kota Kinabalu. Pop.: 1 222 718 (1985 est.). Area: 76 522 sq. km (29 545 sq. miles). Former name (until 1963): **North Borneo.**

Sabatier (*French* sabatje) *n.* **Paul** (pɔl). 1854–1941, French chemist, who discovered a process for the hydrogenation of organic compounds: shared the Nobel prize for chemistry (1912).

sabbat (ˈsæbæt, -ət) *n.* another word for **Sabbath** (sense 4).

Sabbatarian (ˌsæbəˈtɛərɪən) *n.* **1.** a person advocating the strict religious observance of Sunday. **2.** a person who observes Saturday as the Sabbath. ~*adj.* **3.** of the Sabbath or its observance. [C17: from LL *sabbatārius* a Sabbath-keeper] — ˌSabba'tarianism *n.*

Sabbath (ˈsæbəθ) *n.* **1.** the seventh day of the week, Saturday, devoted to worship and rest from work in Judaism and in certain Christian Churches. **2.** Sunday, observed by Christians as the day of worship and rest. **3.** (*not cap.*) a period of rest. **4.** Also called: **sabbat, witches' Sabbath.** a midnight meeting for practitioners of witchcraft or devil worship. [OE *sabbat,* from L, from Gk *sabbaton,* from Heb. *shabbath* to rest]

sabbatical (səˈbætɪkəl) *adj.* **1.** denoting a period of leave granted to university staff, teachers, etc., esp. originally every seventh year: *a sabbatical year.* ~*n.* **2.** any sabbatical period. [C16: from Gk *sabbatikos;* see SABBATH]

Sabbatical (səˈbætɪkəl) *adj.* of, relating to, or appropriate to the Sabbath as a day of rest and religious observance.

SABC *abbrev. for* South African Broadcasting Corporation.

saber (ˈseɪbə) *n., vb.* the U.S. spelling of **sabre.**

sabin (ˈseɪbɪn, ˈseɪ-) *n. Physics.* a unit of acoustic absorption. [C20: introduced by Wallace C. *Sabine* (1868–1919), U.S. physicist]

Sabin (ˈseɪbɪn) *n.* **Albert Bruce.** born 1906, U.S. microbiologist, born in Poland. He developed the **Sabin vaccine** (1955), taken orally to immunize against poliomyelitis.

Sabine (ˈsæbaɪn) *n.* **1.** a member of an ancient people who lived in central Italy. ~*adj.* **2.** of or relating to this people or their language.

sable (ˈseɪbəl) *n., pl.* **-bles** or **-ble. 1.** a marten of N Asian forests, with dark brown luxuriant fur. **2. a.** the highly valued fur of this animal. **b.** (*as modifier*): *a sable coat.* **3. American sable.** the brown, slightly less valuable fur of the American marten. **4.** a dark brown to yellowish-brown colour. ~*adj.* **5.** of the colour of sable fur. **6.** black; dark. **7.** (*usually postpositive*) *Heraldry.* of the colour black. [C15: from OF, from OHG *zobel,* of Slavic origin]

Sable (ˈseɪbəl) *n.* **Cape. 1.** a cape at the S tip of Florida: the southernmost point of continental U.S. **2.** the southernmost point of Nova Scotia, Canada.

sable antelope *n.* a large black E African antelope with long backward-curving horns.

sabot (ˈsæbəʊ) *n.* **1.** a shoe made from a single block of wood. **2.** a shoe with a wooden sole and a leather or cloth upper. **3.** *Austral.* a small sailing boat with a shortened bow. [C17: from F, prob. from OF *savate* an old shoe, also infl. by *bot* BOOT[1]]

sabotage (ˈsæbəˌtɑːʒ) *n.* **1.** the deliberate destruction, disruption, or damage of equipment, a public service, etc., as by enemy agents, dissatisfied employees, etc. **2.** any similar action. ~*vb.* **3.** (*tr.*) to destroy or disrupt, esp. by secret means. [C20: from F, from *saboter* to spoil through clumsiness (lit.: to clatter in sabots)]

saboteur (ˌsæbəˈtɜː) *n.* a person who commits sabotage. [C20: from F]

sabra (ˈsɑːbrə) *n.* a Jew born in Israel. [from Heb. *Sabēr* prickly pear, common plant in the coastal areas of the country]

sabre or *U.S.* **saber** (ˈseɪbə) *n.* **1.** a stout single-edged cavalry sword, having a curved blade. **2.** a sword used in fencing, having a narrow V-shaped blade. ~*vb.* **3.** (*tr.*) to injure or kill with a sabre. [C17: via F from G (dialect) *Sabel,* from MHG *sebel,* ?from Magyar *szablya*]

sabre-rattling *n., adj. Inf.* seeking to intimidate by an aggressive display of military power.

sabre-toothed tiger *or* **cat** *n.* any of various extinct felines with long curved upper canine teeth.

sac (sæk) *n.* a pouch, bag, or pouchlike part in an animal or plant. [C18: from F, from L *saccus*; see SACK¹] —**saccate** ('sækɪt, -eɪt) *adj.* —'**sac,like** *adj.*

saccharide ('sækə,raɪd) *n.* any sugar or other carbohydrate, esp. a simple sugar.

saccharimeter (,sækə'rɪmɪtə) *n.* any instrument for measuring the strength of sugar solutions. —,**saccha'rimetry** *n.*

saccharin ('sækərɪn) *n.* a very sweet white crystalline slightly soluble powder used as a nonfattening sweetener. [C19: from SACCHARO- + -IN]

saccharine ('sækə,ri:n) *adj.* **1.** excessively sweet; sugary: *a saccharine smile.* **2.** of the nature of or containing sugar or saccharin.

saccharo- *or before a vowel* **sacchar-** *combining form.* sugar. [via L from Gk *sakkharon*, ult. from Sansk. *śarkarā* sugar]

saccharose ('sækə,rəʊz, -,rəʊs) *n.* a technical name for **sugar** (sense 1).

Sacco ('sækəʊ) *n.* **Nicola** (ni'kɔ:la). 1891–1927, U.S. radical agitator, born in Italy. With Bartolomeo Vanzetti, he was executed for murder (1927) despite suspicions that their political opinions influenced the verdict: the case caused international protests.

saccule ('sækju:l) *or* **sacculus** ('sækjʊləs) *n.* **1.** a small sac. **2.** the smaller of the two parts of the membranous labyrinth of the internal ear. Cf. **utricle.** [C19: from L *sacculus* dim. of *saccus* SACK¹]

sacerdotal (,sæsə'dəʊt³l) *adj.* of, relating to, or characteristic of priests. [C14: from L *sacerdōtālis*, from *sacerdōs* priest, from *sacer* sacred] —,**sacer'dota,lism** *n.* —,**sacer'dotally** *adv.*

sachem ('seɪtʃəm) *n.* **1.** *U.S.* a leader of a political party or organization. **2.** another name for **sagamore.** [C17: from Amerind *sáchim* chief]

sachet ('sæʃeɪ) *n.* **1.** a small sealed envelope, usually made of plastic, for containing shampoo, etc. **2. a.** a small soft bag containing perfumed powder, placed in drawers to scent clothing. **b.** the powder contained in such a bag. [C19: from OF: a little bag, from *sac* bag; see SACK¹]

Sachs (*German* zaks) *n.* **Hans** (hans). 1494–1576, German master shoemaker and Meistersinger, portrayed by Wagner in *Die Meistersinger von Nürnberg.*

Sachsen ('zaksən) *n.* the German name for **Saxony.**

sack¹ (sæk) *n.* **1.** a large bag made of coarse cloth, thick paper, etc., used as a container. **2.** Also called: **sackful.** the amount contained in a sack. **3. a.** a woman's loose tube-shaped dress. **b.** Also called: **sacque** (sæk). a woman's full loose hip-length jacket. **4. the sack.** *Inf.* dismissal from employment. **5.** a slang word for **bed. 6. hit the sack.** *Sl.* to go to bed. *~vb.* (*tr.*) **7.** *Inf.* to dismiss from employment. **8.** to put into a sack or sacks. [OE *sacc*, from L *saccus* bag, from Gk *sakkos*] —'**sack,like** *adj.*

sack² (sæk) *n.* **1.** the plundering of a place by an army or mob. *~vb.* **2.** (*tr.*) to plunder and partially destroy (a place). [C16: from F *mettre à sac*, lit.: to put (loot) in a sack, from L *saccus* SACK¹] —'**sacker** *n.*

sack³ (sæk) *n.* *Arch. except in trademarks.* any dry white wine from SW Europe. [C16 *wyne seck*, from F *vin sec* dry wine, from L *siccus* dry]

sackbut ('sæk,bʌt) *n.* a medieval form of trombone. [C16: from F *saqueboute*, from OF *saquer* to pull + *bouter* to push]

sackcloth ('sæk,klɒθ) *n.* **1.** coarse cloth such as sacking. **2.** garments made of such cloth, worn formerly to indicate mourning. **3. sackcloth and ashes.** a public display of extreme grief.

sacking ('sækɪŋ) *n.* coarse cloth used for making sacks, woven from flax, hemp, jute, etc.

sack race *n.* a race in which the competitors' legs and often bodies are enclosed in sacks.

Sackville ('sækvɪl) *n.* **Thomas,** 1st Earl of Dorset. 1536–1608, English poet, dramatist, and statesman. He collaborated with Thomas Norton on the early blank-verse tragedy *Gorboduc* (1561).

sacral¹ ('seɪkrəl) *adj.* of or associated with sacred rites. [C19: from L *sacrum* sacred object]

sacral² ('seɪkrəl) *adj.* of or relating to the sacrum. [C18: from NL *sacrālis* of the SACRUM]

sacrament ('sækrəmənt) *n.* **1.** an outward sign combined with a prescribed form of words and regarded as conferring grace upon those who receive it. The Protestant sacraments are baptism and the Lord's Supper. In the Roman Catholic and Eastern Churches they are baptism, penance, confirmation, the Eucharist, holy orders, matrimony, and the anointing of the sick (formerly extreme unction). **2.** (*often cap.*) the Eucharist. **3.** the consecrated elements of the Eucharist, esp. the bread. **4.** something regarded as possessing a sacred significance. **5.** a pledge. [C12: from Church L *sacrāmentum* vow, from L *sacrāre* to consecrate]

sacramental (,sækrə'mɛnt³l) *adj.* **1.** of or having the nature of a sacrament. *~n.* **2.** *R.C. Church.* a sacrament-like ritual action, such as the sign of the cross or the use of holy water. —,**sacra'menta,lism** *n.* —**sacramentality** (,sækrəmɛn'tælɪtɪ) *n.*

Sacramento (,sækrə'mɛntəʊ) *n.* **1.** an inland port in N central California, capital of the state at the confluence of the American and Sacramento Rivers: became a boom town in the gold rush of the 1850s. Pop.: 323 550 (1986 est.). **2.** a river in N California, flowing generally south to San Francisco Bay. Length: 615 km (382 miles).

sacrarium (sæ'krɛərɪəm) *n.*, *pl.* **-craria** (-'krɛərɪə). **1.** the sanctuary of a church. **2.** *R.C. Church.* a place near the altar of a church where materials used in the sacred rites are deposited or poured away. [C18: from L, from *sacer* sacred]

sacred ('seɪkrɪd) *adj.* **1.** exclusively devoted to a deity or to some religious ceremony or use. **2.** worthy of or regarded with reverence and awe. **3.** connected with or intended for religious use: *sacred music.* **4. sacred to.** dedicated to. [C14: from L *sacrāre* to set apart as holy, from *sacer* holy] —'**sacredly** *adv.* —'**sacredness** *n.*

sacred cow *n.* *Inf.* a person, custom, etc., held to be beyond criticism. [alluding to the Hindu belief that cattle are sacred]

sacred mushroom *n.* **1.** any of various hallucinogenic mushrooms that have been eaten in rituals in various parts of the world. **2.** a mescal button, used in a similar way.

sacrifice ('sækrɪ,faɪs) *n.* **1.** a surrender of something of value as a means of gaining something more desirable or of preventing some evil. **2.** a ritual killing of a person or animal with the intention of propitiating or pleasing a deity. **3.** a symbolic offering of something to a deity. **4.** the person, animal, or object killed or offered. **5.** loss entailed by giving up or selling something at less than its value. **6.** *Chess.* the act or an instance of sacrificing a piece. *~vb.* **7.** to make a sacrifice (of). **8.** *Chess.* to permit or force one's opponent to capture a piece freely, as in playing a gambit: *he sacrificed his queen and checkmated his opponent on the next move.* [C13: via OF from L *sacrificium*, from *sacer* holy + *facere* to make] —'**sacri,ficer** *n.*

sacrifice paddock *n.* *N.Z.* a grassed field which is allowed to be grazed completely, so that it can be cultivated and sown later.

sacrificial (,sækrɪ'fɪʃəl) *adj.* used in or connected with a sacrifice. —,**sacri'ficially** *adv.*

sacrilege ('sækrɪlɪdʒ) *n.* **1.** the misuse or desecration of anything regarded as sacred or as worthy of extreme respect. **2.** the act or an instance of taking anything sacred for secular use. [C13: from OF, from L, from *sacrilegus* temple-robber, from *sacra* sacred things + *legere* to take] —**sacrilegist** (,sækrɪ'li:dʒɪst) *n.*

sacrilegious (,sækrɪ'lɪdʒəs) *adj.* **1.** of, relating to, or involving sacrilege. **2.** guilty of sacrilege. —,**sacri'legiously** *adv.*

sacring bell ('seɪkrɪŋ) *n.* *Chiefly R.C. Church.* a small bell rung at the elevation of the Host and chalice during Mass.

sacristan ('sækrɪstən) *or* **sacrist** ('sækrɪst, 'seɪ-) *n.* **1.** a person who has charge of the contents of a church. **2.** a less common word for **sexton** (sense 1). [C14: from Med. L *sacristānus*, ult. from *sacer* holy]

sacristy ('sækrɪstɪ) *n.*, *pl.* **-ties.** a room attached to a church or chapel where the sacred vessels, vestments, etc., are kept. [C17: from Med. L *sacristia*; see SACRISTAN]

sacroiliac (,seɪkrəʊ'ɪlɪ,æk) *Anat.* *~adj.* **1.** of or relating to the sacrum and ilium or their articulation. *~n.* **2.** the joint where these bones meet.

sacrosanct ('sækrəʊ,sæŋkt) *adj.* very sacred or holy. [C17: from L *sacrōsanctus* made holy by sacred rite, from *sacer* holy + *sanctus*, from *sancīre* to hallow] —,**sacro'sanctity** *n.*

sacrum ('seɪkrəm) *n., pl.* **-cra** (-krə). the large wedge-shaped bone, consisting of five fused vertebrae, in the lower part of the back. [C18: from L *os sacrum* holy bone, because it was used in sacrifices, from *sacer* holy]

sad (sæd) *adj.* **sadder, saddest. 1.** feeling sorrow; unhappy. **2.** causing, suggestive, or expressive of such feelings: *a sad story.* **3.** unfortunate; shabby: *her clothes were in a sad state.* [OE *sæd* weary] —**'sadly** *adv.* —**'sadness** *n.*

SAD *abbrev. for* seasonal affective disorder.

Sadat (sə'dæt) *n.* (**Mohammed**) **Anwar El** ('ænwɑ: ɛl). 1918–81, Egyptian statesman: president of Egypt (1970–81); assassinated.

sadden ('sæd³n) *vb.* to make or become sad.

saddle ('sæd³l) *n.* **1.** a seat for a rider, usually made of leather, placed on a horse's back and secured with a girth under the belly. **2.** a similar seat on a bicycle, tractor, etc. **3.** a back pad forming part of the harness of a packhorse. **4.** anything that resembles a saddle in shape, position, or function. **5.** a cut of meat, esp. mutton, consisting of both loins. **6.** the part of a horse or similar animal on which a saddle is placed. **7.** the part of the back of a domestic chicken that is nearest to the tail. **8.** another word for **col** (sense 1). **9. in the saddle.** in a position of control. ~*vb.* **10.** (sometimes foll. by *up*) to put a saddle on (a horse). **11.** (*intr.*) to mount into the saddle. **12.** (*tr.*) to burden: *I didn't ask to be saddled with this job.* [OE *sadol, sædel*] —**'saddle-,like** *adj.*

saddleback ('sæd³l,bæk) *n.* a marking resembling a saddle on the backs of various animals. —**'saddle-,backed** *adj.*

saddlebag ('sæd³l,bæg) *n.* a pouch or small bag attached to the saddle of a horse, bicycle, etc.

saddlebill ('sæd³l,bɪl) *n.* a large black-and-white stork of tropical Africa, having a heavy red bill with a black band around the middle. Also called: **jabiru.**

saddlebow ('sæd³l,bəʊ) *n.* the pommel of a saddle.

saddlecloth ('sæd³l,klɒθ) *n.* a light cloth put under a horse's saddle, so as to prevent rubbing.

saddle horse *n.* a lightweight horse kept for riding only.

saddler ('sædlə) *n.* a person who makes, deals in, or repairs saddles and other leather equipment for horses.

saddle roof *n.* a roof that has a ridge and two gables.

saddlery ('sædlərɪ) *n., pl.* **-dleries. 1.** saddles, harness, and other leather equipment for horses collectively. **2.** the business, work, or place of work of a saddler.

saddle soap *n.* a soft soap containing neat's-foot oil used to preserve and clean leather.

saddletree ('sæd³l,tri:) *n.* the frame of a saddle.

Sadducee ('sædjʊ,si:) *n. Judaism.* a member of an ancient Jewish sect that was opposed to the Pharisees, denying the resurrection of the dead and the validity of oral tradition. [OE *saddūcēas*, via L & Gk from LHeb. *sāddūqi*, prob. from *Sadoq* Zadok, high priest and supposed founder of the sect] —,**Saddu'cean** *adj.*

Sade (sɑ:d) *n.* Comte **Donatien Alphonse François de** (dɔnasjɛ̃ alfɔ̃s frɑ̃swa də), known as the *Marquis de Sade.* 1740–1814, French soldier and writer, whose exposition of sexual perversion gave rise to the term sadism.

sadhu *or* **saddhu** ('sɑ:du:) *n.* a Hindu wandering holy man. [Sansk., from *sādhu* good]

Sadi *or* **Saadi** (sɑ:'di:) *n.* original name *Sheikh Muslih Addin.* ?1184–1292, Persian poet. His best-known works are *Gulistān* (Flower Garden) and *Būstān* (Tree Garden), long moralistic poems in prose and verse.

sadiron ('sæd,aɪən) *n.* a heavy iron, pointed at both ends for pressing clothes. [C19: from SAD (in the obs. sense: heavy) + IRON]

sadism ('seɪdɪzəm) *n.* the gaining of pleasure or sexual gratification from the infliction of pain and mental suffering on another person. Cf. **masochism.** [C19: from F, after the Marquis de SADE] —**'sadist** *n.* —**sadistic** (sə'dɪstɪk) *adj.* —**sa'distically** *adv.*

Sadler's Wells ('sædləz wɛlz) *n. (functioning as sing.)* a theatre in London. It was renovated in 1931 by Lilian Bayliss and became the home of the Sadler's Wells Opera Company and the Sadler's Wells Ballet (now the Royal Ballet). [named after the medicinal *wells* on the site and

its owner Thomas *Sadler*, who founded the original theatre on the site]

sadomasochism (,seɪdəʊ'mæsə,kɪzəm) *n.* the combination of sadistic and masochistic elements in one person. —,**sadomaso'chistic** *adj.*

Sadowa ('sɑ:dəʊvə) *n.* a village in W Czechoslovakia, in NE Bohemia: scene of the decisive battle of the Austro-Prussian war (1866) in which the Austrians were defeated by the Prussians. Czech name: **Sadová** ('sadɔva:).

s.a.e. *abbrev. for* stamped addressed envelope.

safari (sə'fɑ:rɪ) *n., pl.* **-ris. 1.** an overland journey or hunting expedition, esp. in Africa. **2.** the people, animals, etc., that go on the expedition. [C19: from Swahili: journey, from Ar., from *safara* to travel]

safari park *n.* an enclosed park in which lions and other wild animals are kept uncaged in the open and can be viewed by the public from cars, etc.

safari suit *n.* an outfit made of tough cotton, denim, etc., consisting of a bush jacket with matching trousers, shorts, or skirt.

safe (seɪf) *adj.* **1.** affording security or protection from harm: *a safe place.* **2.** (*postpositive*) free from danger: *you'll be safe here.* **3.** secure from risk: *a safe investment.* **4.** worthy of trust: *a safe companion.* **5.** tending to avoid controversy or risk: *a safe player.* **6.** not dangerous: *water safe to drink.* **7. on the safe side.** as a precaution. ~*adv.* **8.** in a safe condition: *the children are safe in bed now.* **9. play safe.** to act in a way least likely to cause danger, controversy, or defeat. ~*n.* **10.** a strong container, usually of metal and provided with a secure lock, for storing money or valuables. **11.** a small cupboard-like container for storing food. [C13: from OF *salf*, from L *salvus*] —**'safely** *adv.* —**'safeness** *n.*

safe-breaker *n.* a person who breaks open and robs safes. Also called: **safe-cracker.**

safe-conduct *n.* **1.** a document giving official permission to travel through a region, esp. in time of war. **2.** the protection afforded by such a document.

safe-deposit *or* **safety-deposit** *n.* **a.** a place with facilities for the safe storage of money. **b.** (*as modifier*): *a safe-deposit box.*

safeguard ('seɪf,gɑ:d) *n.* **1.** a person or thing that ensures protection against danger, injury, etc. **2.** a safe-conduct. ~*vb.* **3.** (*tr.*) to protect.

safe house *n.* a place used secretly by undercover agents, terrorists, etc., as a refuge.

safekeeping ('seɪf'ki:pɪŋ) *n.* the act of keeping or state of being kept in safety.

safe period *n. Inf.* the period during the menstrual cycle when conception is considered least likely to occur.

safe seat *n.* a Parliamentary seat that at an election is sure to be held by the same party as held it before.

safe sex *n.* sexual intercourse using physical protection, such as a condom, or nonpenetrative methods to prevent the spread of such diseases as AIDS.

safety ('seɪftɪ) *n., pl.* **-ties. 1.** the quality of being safe. **2.** freedom from danger or risk of injury. **3.** a contrivance designed to prevent injury. **4.** *American football.* Also called: **safetyman.** the defensive player furthest back in the field.

safety belt *n.* **1.** another name for **seat belt** (sense 1). **2.** a belt or strap worn by a person working at a great height to prevent him from falling.

safety curtain *n.* a curtain made of fireproof material that can be lowered to separate the auditorium and stage in a theatre to prevent the spread of a fire.

safety factor *n.* the ratio of the breaking stress of a material to the calculated maximum stress in use. Also called: **factor of safety.**

safety glass *n.* glass that if broken will not shatter.

Safety Islands *pl. n.* a group of three small French islands in the Atlantic, off the coast of French Guiana. French name: **Îles du Salut.**

safety lamp *n.* an oil-burning miner's lamp in which the flame is surrounded by a metal gauze to prevent it from igniting combustible gas.

safety match *n.* a match that will light only when struck against a specially prepared surface.

safety net *n.* **1.** a net used in a circus to catch high-wire and trapeze artistes if they fall. **2.** any means of protection from hardship or loss.

safety pin *n.* a spring wire clasp with a covering catch, made so as to shield the point when closed.

safety razor *n.* a razor with a guard over the blade or blades to prevent deep cuts.

safety valve *n.* **1.** a valve in a pressure vessel that allows fluid to escape at excess pressure. **2.** a harmless outlet for emotion, etc.

saffian ('sæfɪən) *n.* leather tanned with sumach and usually dyed a bright colour. [C16: via Russian & Turkish from Persian *sakhtiyān* goatskin, from *sakht* hard]

safflower ('sæflaʊə) *n.* **1.** a thistle-like Eurasian annual plant having large heads of orange-yellow flowers and yielding a dye and an oil used in paints, medicines, etc. **2.** a red dye used for cotton and for colouring foods and cosmetics. [C16: via Du. *saffloer* or G *safflor* from OF *saffleur*]

saffron ('sæfrən) *n.* **1.** an Old World crocus having purple or white flowers with orange stigmas. **2.** the dried stigmas of this plant, used to flavour or colour food. **3. meadow saffron.** another name for **autumn crocus. 4. a.** an orange to orange-yellow colour. **b.** (*as adj*): *a saffron dress* [C13: from OF *safran*, from Med. L *safranum*, from Ar. *za'farān*]

Safi (*French* safi) *n.* a port in W Morocco, 170 km (105 miles) northwest of Marrakech, to which it is the nearest port. Pop.: 197 309 (1982).

Safid Rud (sæ'fiːd 'ruːd) *n.* a river in N Iran, flowing northeast to a delta on the Caspian Sea. Length: about 785 km (490 miles).

S.Afr. *abbrev. for* South Africa(n).

safranine *or* **safranin** ('sæfrənɪn) *n.* any of a class of azine dyes used for textiles. [C19: from F *safran* SAFFRON + -INE²]

sag (sæg) *vb.* **sagging, sagged.** (*mainly intr.*) **1.** (*also tr.*) to sink or cause to sink in parts, as under weight or pressure: *the bed sags in the middle.* **2.** to fall in value: *prices sagged to a new low.* **3.** to hang unevenly. **4.** (of courage, etc.) to weaken. ~*n.* **5.** the act or an instance of sagging: *a sag in profits.* **6.** *Naut.* the extent to which a vessel's keel sags at the centre. [C15: from ON] —**'saggy** *adj.*

saga ('sɑːgə) *n.* **1.** any of several medieval prose narratives written in Iceland and recounting the exploits of a hero or a family. **2.** any similar heroic narrative. **3.** a series of novels about several generations or members of a family. **4.** *Inf.* a series of events or a story stretching over a long period. [C18: from ON: a narrative]

sagacious (sə'geɪʃəs) *adj.* having or showing sagacity; wise. [C17: from L *sagāx*, from *sāgīre* to be astute] —**sa'gaciously** *adv.*

sagacity (sə'gæsɪtɪ) *n.* foresight, discernment, or keen perception; ability to make good judgments.

sagamore ('sægə,mɔː) *n.* (among some North American Indians) a chief or eminent man. [C17: from Amerind *sāgimau*, lit.: he overcomes]

sage¹ (seɪdʒ) *n.* **1.** a man revered for his profound wisdom. ~*adj.* **2.** profoundly wise or prudent. [C13: from OF, from L *sapere* to be sensible] —**'sagely** *adv.* —**'sageness** *n.*

sage² (seɪdʒ) *n.* **1.** a perennial Mediterranean plant having grey-green leaves and purple, blue, or white flowers. **2.** the leaves of this plant, used in cooking for flavouring. **3.** short for **sagebrush.** [C14: from OF *saulge*, from L *salvia*, from *salvus* in good health (from its curative properties)]

sagebrush ('seɪdʒ,brʌʃ) *n.* any of a genus of aromatic plants of W North America, having silver-green leaves and large clusters of small white flowers.

saggar *or* **sagger** ('sægə) *n.* a clay box in which ceramic wares are placed during firing. [C17: ? alteration of SAFE-GUARD]

Saghalien (sə'gɑːljən) *n.* a variant of **Sakhalin.**

sagittal suture ('sædʒɪt³l) *n.* a serrated line on the top of the skull that marks the junction of the two parietal bones.

Sagittarius (,sædʒɪ'tɛərɪəs) *n.*, *Latin genitive* **Sagittarii** (,sædʒɪ'tɛərɪ,aɪ). **1.** *Astron.* a S constellation. **2.** Also called: the **Archer.** *Astrol.* the ninth sign of the zodiac. The sun is in this sign between Nov. 22 and Dec. 21. [C14: from L: an archer, from *sagitta* an arrow] —**Sagittarian** (,sædʒɪ'tɛərɪən) *adj.*

sagittate ('sædʒɪ,teɪt) *adj.* (esp. of leaves) shaped like the head of an arrow. [C18: from NL *sagittātus*, from L *sagitta* arrow]

sago ('seɪgəʊ) *n.* a starchy cereal obtained from the powdered pith of a palm (**sago palm**), used for puddings and as a thickening agent. [C16: from Malay *sāgū*]

saguaro (sə'gwɑːrəʊ) *n.*, *pl.* **-ros.** a giant cactus of desert regions of Arizona, S California, and Mexico. [Mexican Sp., var. of *sahuaro*, an Indian name]

Saguenay (,sægə'neɪ) *n.* a river in SE Canada in S Quebec, rising as the Péribonca River on the central plateau and flowing south, then east to the St. Lawrence. Length: 764 km (475 miles).

Sagunto (*Spanish* sa'ɣunto) *n.* an industrial town in E Spain, near Valencia: allied to Rome and made a heroic resistance to the Carthaginian attack led by Hannibal (219–218 B.C.). Pop.: 54 759 (1981). Ancient name: **Saguntum** (sə'gʊntəm).

Sahara (sə'hɑːrə) *n.* a desert in N Africa, extending from the Atlantic to the Red Sea and from the Mediterranean to central Mali, Niger, Chad, and the Sudan: the largest desert in the world, occupying over a quarter of Africa; rises to over 3300 m (11 000 ft.) in the central mountain system of the Ahaggar and Tibesti massifs; large reserves of iron ore, oil, and natural gas. Area: 9 100 000 sq. km (3 500 000 sq. miles). Average annual rainfall: less than 254 mm (10 in.). Highest recorded temperature: 58°C (136.4°F). —**Sa'haran** *n.*, *adj.*

sahib ('sɑːhɪb) *n.* (in India) a form of address placed after a man's name, used as a mark of respect. [C17: from Urdu, from Ar. *çāhib*, lit.: friend]

said¹ (sɛd) *adj.* **1.** (*prenominal*) (in contracts, etc.) aforesaid. ~*vb.* **2.** the past tense and past participle of **say.**

said² ('sɑːɪd) *n.* a variant of **sayyid.**

Saida ('sɑːɪdə) *n.* a port in SW Lebanon, on the Mediterranean: on the site of ancient Sidon; terminal of the Trans-Arabian pipeline from Saudi Arabia. Pop.: 24 740 (1980 est.).

saiga ('saɪgə) *n.* either of two antelopes of the plains of central Asia, having a slightly elongated nose. [C19: from Russian]

Saigon (saɪ'gɒn) *n.* the former name (until 1976) of **Ho Chi Minh City.**

sail (seɪl) *n.* **1.** an area of fabric, usually Terylene or nylon (formerly canvas), with fittings for holding it in any suitable position to catch the wind, used for propelling certain kinds of vessels, esp. over water. **2.** a voyage on such a vessel: *a sail down the river.* **3.** a vessel with sails or such vessels collectively: *to travel by sail.* **4.** a ship's sails collectively. **5.** something resembling a sail in shape, position, or function, such as the part of a windmill that is turned by the wind. **6. in sail.** having the sail set. **7. make sail. a.** to run up the sail or to run up more sail. **b.** to begin a voyage. **8. set sail. a.** to embark on a voyage by ship. **b.** to hoist sail. **9. under sail. a.** with sail hoisted. **b.** under way. ~*vb.* (*mainly intr.*) **10.** to travel in a boat or ship: *we sailed to Le Havre.* **11.** to begin a voyage: *we sail at 5 o'clock.* **12.** (of a vessel) to move over the water. **13.** (*tr.*) to manoeuvre or navigate a vessel: *he sailed the schooner up the channel.* **14.** (*tr.*) to sail over: *she sailed the Atlantic single-handed.* **15.** (often foll. by *over*, *through*, etc.) to move fast or effortlessly: *we sailed through customs.* **16.** to move along smoothly; glide. **17.** (often foll. by *in* or *into*) *Inf.* **a.** to begin (something) with vigour. **b.** to make an attack (on) violently. [OE *segl*] —**'sailable** *adj.* —**'sailless** *adj.*

sailboard ('seɪl,bɔːd) *n.* the craft used for windsurfing, consisting of a moulded board to which a mast bearing a single sail is attached.

sailcloth ('seɪl,klɒθ) *n.* **1.** any of various fabrics from which sails are made. **2.** a canvas-like cloth used for clothing, etc.

sailer ('seɪlə) *n.* a vessel, with specified sailing characteristics: *a good sailer.*

sailfish ('seɪl,fɪʃ) *n.*, *pl.* **-fish** *or* **-fishes. 1.** any of several large game fishes of warm and tropical seas. They have an elongated upper jaw and a long sail-like dorsal fin. **2.** another name for **basking shark.**

sailing ship *n.* a large sailing vessel.

sailor ('seɪlə) *n.* **1.** any member of a ship's crew, esp. one below the rank of officer. **2.** a person who sails, esp. with reference to the likelihood of his becoming seasick: *a good sailor.*

sailplane ('seɪl,pleɪn) *n.* a high-performance glider.

sainfoin ('sænfɔɪn) *n.* a Eurasian perennial plant, widely grown as a forage crop, having pale pink flowers and curved pods. [C17: from F, from Med. L *sānum faenum* wholesome hay, referring to its former use as a medicine]

saint (seɪnt; *unstressed* sənt) *n.* **1.** a person who after death is formally recognized by a Christian Church as having attained a specially exalted place in heaven and the right to veneration. **2.** a person of exceptional holiness. **3.** (*pl.*) *Bible.* the collective body of those who are righteous in God's sight. ~*vb.* **4.** (*tr.*) to recognize formally as a saint. [C12: from OF, from L *sanctus* holy, from *sancīre* to hallow] —**'sainthood** *n.* —**'saintlike** *adj.*

Saint Agnes' Eve *n.*, *usually abbreviated to* **St Agnes' Eve.** the night of Jan. 20, when according to tradition a woman can discover the identity of her future husband by performing certain rites.

Saint Albans ('ɔːlbənz) *n.*, *usually abbreviated to* **St Albans.** a city in SE England, in W Hertfordshire: founded in 948 A.D. around the Benedictine abbey first built in Saxon times on the site of the martyrdom (about 303 A.D.) of St Alban; present abbey built in 1077; Roman ruins. Pop.: 50 888 (1981). Latin name: **Verulamium.**

Saint Andrews *n.*, *usually abbreviated to* **St Andrews.** a city in E Scotland, in Fife region on the North Sea: the oldest university in Scotland (1411); famous golf links. Pop.: 16 000 (1985 est.).

Saint Andrew's Cross *n.*, *usually abbreviated to* **St Andrew's Cross.** **1.** a diagonal cross with equal arms. **2.** a white diagonal cross on a blue ground.

Saint Anthony's fire *n.*, *usually abbreviated to* **St Anthony's fire.** *Pathol.* another name for **ergotism** or **erysipelas.**

Saint Augustine ('ɔːgəs,tiːn) *n.*, *usually abbreviated to* **St Augustine.** a resort in NE Florida, on the Intracoastal Waterway: the oldest town in North America (1565); the northernmost outpost of the Spanish colonial empire for over 200 years. Pop.: 11 985 (1980).

Saint Austell ('ɔːstəl) *n.*, *usually abbreviated to* **St Austell.** a town in SW England, in S Cornwall on **St Austell Bay** (an inlet of the English Channel): china clay industry; administratively part of St Austell with Fowey since 1968. Pop. (with Fowey): 39 240 (1985 est.).

Saint Bernard *n.*, *usually abbreviated to* **St Bernard.** a large breed of dog with a dense red-and-white coat, formerly used as a rescue dog in mountainous areas.

Saint Bernard Pass *n.*, *usually abbreviated to* **St Bernard Pass.** either of two passes over the Alps: the **Great St Bernard Pass,** 2472 m (8110 ft.) high, east of Mont Blanc between Italy and Switzerland, or the **Little St Bernard Pass,** 2157 m (7077 ft.) high, south of Mont Blanc between Italy and France.

Saint-Brieuc (*French* sēbriø) *n.*, *usually abbreviated to* **St-Brieuc.** a market town in NW France, near the N coast of Brittany. Pop.: 52 243 (1983 est.).

Saint Catharines *n.*, *usually abbreviated to* **St Catharines.** an industrial city in S central Canada, in S Ontario on the Welland Canal. Pop.: 123 455 (1986).

Saint Christopher *n.*, *usually abbreviated to* **St Christopher.** another name for **Saint Kitts.**

Saint Christopher-Nevis *n.*, *usually abbreviated to* **St Christopher-Nevis.** the official name of **Saint Kitts-Nevis.**

Saint Clair (klɛə) *n.*, *usually abbreviated to* **St Clair. Lake.** a lake between SE Michigan and Ontario: linked with Lake Huron by the **St Clair River** and with Lake Erie by the Detroit River. Area: 1191 sq. km (460 sq. miles).

Saint-Cloud (*French* sēklu) *n.*, *usually abbreviated to* **St-Cloud.** a residential suburb of Paris: former royal palace; Sèvres porcelain factory. Pop.: 28 760 (1982).

Saint Croix (krɔɪ) *n.*, *usually abbreviated to* **St Croix.** an island in the West Indies, the largest of the Virgin Islands of the U.S.: purchased by the U.S. in 1917. Chief town: Christiansted. Pop.: 55 300 (1985). Area: 207 sq. km (80 sq. miles). Also called: **Santa Cruz** ('sæntə 'kruːz).

Saint Croix River *n.*, *usually abbreviated to* **St Croix River.** a river on the border between the northeast U.S. and SE Canada, flowing from the Chiputneticook Lakes to Passamaquoddy Bay, forming the border between Maine, U.S., and New Brunswick, Canada. Length: 121 km (75 miles).

Saint David's *n.*, *usually abbreviated to* **St David's.** a town in SW Wales, in Dyfed: its cathedral was a place of pilgrimage in medieval times. Pop.: 1595 (1984).

Saint-Denis (*French* sēdəni) *n.*, *usually abbreviated to* **St-Denis. 1.** a town in N France, on the Seine: 12th-century Gothic abbey church, containing the tombs of many French monarchs; an industrial suburb of Paris. Pop.: 96 000 (1983 est.). **2.** the capital of the French overseas region of Réunion, a port on the N coast. Pop.: 109 072 (1982).

Sainte-Beuve (*French* sētbœv) *n.* **Charles Augustin** (ʃarl ogystɛ̃). 1804–69, French critic, best known for his collections of essays *Port Royal* (1840–59) and *Les Causeries du Lundi* (1851–62).

sainted ('seɪntɪd) *adj.* **1.** canonized. **2.** like a saint in character or nature. **3.** hallowed or holy.

Sainte Foy (seɪnt 'fɔɪ, sənt) *n.*, *usually abbreviated to* **Ste Foy.** a SW suburb of Quebec, on the St Lawrence River. Pop.: 68 883 (1981).

Saint Elias Mountains *pl. n.*, *usually abbreviated to* **St Elias Mountains.** a mountain range between SE Alaska and the SW Yukon, Canada. Highest peak: Mount Logan, 6050 m (19 850 ft.).

Saint Elmo's fire ('ɛlməʊz) *n.*, *usually abbreviated to* **St Elmo's fire.** (not in technical usage) a luminous region that sometimes appears around church spires, the masts of ships, etc.

Saint-Étienne (*French* sētetjɛn) *n.*, *usually abbreviated to* **St-Étienne.** a town in E central France: a major producer of textiles and armaments. Pop.: 219 855 (1983 est.).

Saint-Exupéry (*French* sētɛgzyperi) *n.* **Antoine de** (ãtwan də). 1900–44, French novelist and aviator. His novels of aviation include *Vol de nuit* (1931) and *Terre des hommes* (1939). He also wrote the fairy tale *Le petit prince* (1943).

Saint Gall (*French* sē gal) *n.*, *usually abbreviated to* **St Gall. 1.** a canton of NE Switzerland. Capital: St Gall. Pop.: 403 900 (1986 est.). Area: 2012 sq. km (777 sq. miles). **2.** a town in NE Switzerland, capital of St Gall canton: an important educational centre in the Middle Ages. Pop.: 73 200 (1985). ~German name: **Sankt Gallen** (zaŋkt 'galən).

Saint George's *n.*, *usually abbreviated to* **St George's.** the capital of Grenada, a port in the southwest. Pop.: 4788 (1981).

Saint George's Channel *n.*, *usually abbreviated to* **St George's Channel.** a strait between Wales and Ireland, linking the Irish Sea with the Atlantic. Length: about 160 km (100 miles). Width: up to 145 km (90 miles).

Saint Gotthard ('gotəd) *n.*, *usually abbreviated to* **St Gotthard. 1.** a range of the Lepontine Alps in SE central Switzerland. **2.** a pass over the St Gotthard mountains, in S Switzerland. Height: 2114 m (6935 ft.).

Saint Helena (,sɛntɪ'liːnə) *n.*, *usually abbreviated to* **St Helena.** a volcanic island in the SE Atlantic, forming (with its dependencies Tristan da Cunha and Ascension) a British colony: discovered by the Portuguese in 1502 and annexed by England in 1651; scene of Napoleon's exile and death. Capital: Jamestown. Pop.: 5895 (1985). Area: 122 sq. km (47 sq. miles).

Saint Helens *n.*, *usually abbreviated to* **St Helens. 1.** a town in NW England, in Merseyside: glass industry. Pop.: 98 769 (1981). **2. Mount.** a volcanic peak in S Washington state; it erupted in 1980 after lying dormant from 1857.

Saint Helier ('hɛliə) *n.*, *usually abbreviated to* **St Helier.** a market town and resort in the Channel Islands, on the S coast of Jersey. Pop.: 25 698 (1981).

Saint James's Palace *n.*, *usually abbreviated to* **St James's Palace.** a palace in Pall Mall, London: residence of British monarchs from 1697 to 1837.

Saint John *n.*, *usually abbreviated to* **St John. 1.** a port in E Canada, at the mouth of the St John River: the largest city in New Brunswick. Pop.: 76 381 (1986). **2.** an island in the West Indies, in the Virgin Islands of the U.S. Pop.: 2360 (1980). Area: 49 sq. km (19 sq. miles). **3. Lake.** a lake in Canada, in S Quebec: drained by the Saguenay River. Area: 971 sq. km (375 sq. miles). **4.** a river in E North America, rising in Maine, U.S., and flowing northeast to New Brunswick, Canada, then generally southeast to the Bay of Fundy. Length: 673 km (418 miles).

Saint John's *n.*, *usually abbreviated to* **St John's. 1.** a port in Canada, capital of Newfoundland, on the E coast of the Avalon Peninsula. Pop.: 96 216 (1986). **2.** the capital of Antigua and Barbuda: a port on the NW coast of the island of Antigua. Pop.: 30 000 (1982 est.).

Saint John's wort *n., usually abbreviated to* **St John's wort.** any of a genus of shrubs or herbaceous plants, having yellow flowers.

Saint-Just (*French* sɛ̃ʒyst) *n.* **Louis Antoine Léon de** (lwi ɑ̃twan leɔ̃ də). 1767–94, French Revolutionary leader and orator. A member of the Committee of Public Safety (1793–94), he was guillotined with Robespierre.

Saint Kilda ('kɪldə) *n., usually abbreviated to* **St Kilda.** a small island in the Atlantic, in the Outer Hebrides: uninhabited since 1930; bird sanctuary.

Saint Kitts (kɪts) *n., usually abbreviated to* **St Kitts.** an island in the E Caribbean, in the Leeward Islands: part of the state of St Kitts-Nevis. Capital: Basseterre. Pop.: 33 881 (1983). Area: 168 sq. km (65 sq. miles). Also called: **Saint Christopher.**

Saint Kitts-Nevis *n., usually abbreviated to* **St Kitts-Nevis.** an independent state in the E Caribbean, in the West Indies; comprises the two islands of St Kitts and Nevis: with the island of Anguilla formed a colony (1882–1967) and a British associated state (1967–83); Anguilla formally separated from the group in 1983; gained full independence in 1983.

Saint Laurent (*French* sɛ̃ lɔrɑ̃) *n., usually abbreviated to* **St Laurent.** a W suburb of Montreal. Pop.: 65 900 (1981).

Saint-Laurent (*French* sɛ̃lɔrɑ̃) *n.* **Yves** (iv), full name *Yves-Mathieu.* born 1936, French couturier: popularized trousers for women for all occasions.

Saint Lawrence *n., usually abbreviated to* **St Lawrence.**
1. a river in SE Canada, flowing northeast from Lake Ontario, forming part of the border between Canada and the U.S., to the Gulf of St Lawrence: commercially one of the most important rivers in the world as the easternmost link of the St Lawrence Seaway. Length: 1207 km (750 miles). Width at mouth: 145 km (90 miles). **2. Gulf of.** a deep arm of the Atlantic off the E coast of Canada between Newfoundland and the mainland coasts of Quebec, New Brunswick, and Nova Scotia.

Saint Lawrence Seaway *n., usually abbreviated to* **St Lawrence Seaway.** an inland waterway of North America, passing through the Great Lakes, the St Lawrence River, and connecting canals and locks: one of the most important waterways in the world. Length: 3993 km (2480 miles).

Saint Leger ('lɛdʒə) *n., usually abbreviated to* **St Leger. the.** an annual horse race run at Doncaster, England, since 1776.

Saint Leonard ('lɛnəd) *n., usually abbreviated to* **St Leonard.** a N suburb of Montreal. Pop.: 82 200 (1981).

Saint-Lô (*French* sɛ̃lo) *n., usually abbreviated to* **St-Lô.** a market town in NW France: a Calvinist stronghold in the 16th century. Pop.: 24 792 (1982).

Saint Louis (luɪs) *n., usually abbreviated to* **St Louis.** a port in E Missouri, on the Mississippi River near its confluence with the Missouri: the largest city in the state; university; major industrial centre. Pop.: 429 300 (1986 est.).

Saint-Louis (*French* sɛ̃lwi) *n., usually abbreviated to* **St-Louis.** a port in NW Senegal, on an island at the mouth of the Senegal River: the first French settlement in W Africa (1689); capital of Senegal until 1958. Pop.: 96 594 (1979 est.).

Saint Lucia ('luːʃə) *n., usually abbreviated to* **St Lucia.** an island state in the Caribbean, in the Windward Islands group of the Lesser Antilles: a volcanic island; gained self-government in 1967 as a British Associated State; attained full independence within the British Commonwealth in 1979. Capital: Castries. Pop.: 143 600 (1987). Area: 616 sq. km (238 sq. miles).

saintly ('seɪntlɪ) *adj.* like, relating to, or suitable for a saint. **—'saintlily** *adv.* **—'saintliness** *n.*

Saint Martin *n., usually abbreviated to* **St Martin.** an island in the E West Indies, in the Leeward Islands: administratively divided since 1648, the north belonging to France (as a dependency of Guadeloupe) and the south belonging to the Netherlands (as part of the Netherlands Antilles); salt industry. Pop.: (French) 8072 (1982); (Dutch) 15 926 (1983). Areas: (French) 52 sq. km (20 sq. miles); (Dutch) 33 sq. km (13 sq. miles). Dutch name: **Sint Maarten.**

Saint-Maur-des-Fossés (*French* sɛ̃mɔrdefose) *n., usually abbreviated to* **St-Maur-des-Fossés.** a town in N France, on the River Marne: a residential suburb of SE Paris. Pop.: 80 816 (1983 est.).

Saint Moritz (məˈrɪts) *n., usually abbreviated to* **St Moritz.** a village in E Switzerland, in Graubünden canton in

the Upper Engadine, at an altitude of 1856 m (6089 ft.): sports and tourist centre. Pop.: 5900 (1980).

Saint-Nazaire (*French* sɛ̃nazɛr) *n., usually abbreviated to* **St-Nazaire.** a port in NW France, at the mouth of the River Loire: German submarine base in World War II; shipbuilding. Pop.: 69 176 (1983 est.).

Saint-Ouen (*French* sɛ̃twɛ̃) *n., usually abbreviated to* **St-Ouen.** a town in N France, on the Seine: an industrial suburb of Paris; famous flea market. Pop.: 43 571 (1983 est.).

Saint Paul *n., usually abbreviated to* **St Paul.** a port in SE Minnesota, capital of the state, at the head of navigation of the Mississippi: now contiguous with Minneapolis (the Twin Cities). Pop.: 263 680 (1986 est.).

saintpaulia (sənt'pɔːlɪə) *n.* another name for **African violet.** [C20: NL, after Baron W. von *Saint Paul*, G soldier (died 1910), who discovered it]

Saint Paul's *n., usually abbreviated to* **St Paul's.** a cathedral in central London, built between 1675 and 1710 to replace an earlier cathedral destroyed during the Great Fire (1666): regarded as Wren's masterpiece.

Saint Peter's *n., usually abbreviated to* **St Peter's.** the basilica of the Vatican City, built between 1506 and 1615 to replace an earlier church: the largest church in the world, 188 m (615 ft.) long, and chief pilgrimage centre of Europe; designed by many architects, notably Bramante, Raphael, Sangallo, Michelangelo, and Bernini.

Saint Petersburg ('piːtəzˌbɜːg) *n., usually abbreviated to* **St Petersburg. 1.** the former name (1703–1914) of **Leningrad. 2.** a city and resort in W Florida, on Tampa Bay. Pop.: 243 090 (1986 est.).

Saint Pierre (*French* sɛ̃ pjɛr) *n., usually abbreviated to* **St Pierre.** a former town on the coast of the French island of Martinique, destroyed by the eruption of Mont Pelée in 1902.

Saint-Pierre (*French* sɛ̃pjɛr) *n.* **Jacques Henri Bernardin de** (ʒak ɑ̃ri bɛrnardɛ̃ də). 1737–1814, French author; his work, which was greatly influenced by the writings of Rousseau, includes *Voyage à l'Île de France* (1773), *Études de la nature* (1784, 1788), and *La chaumière indienne* (1791).

Saint Pierre and Miquelon (ˌmɪkə'lɒn; *French* miklɔ̃) *n., usually abbreviated to* **St Pierre and Miquelon.** an archipelago in the Atlantic, just off the S coast of Newfoundland: administratively an overseas department of France and the only remaining French possession in North America; consists of the islands of St Pierre, with most of the population, and Miquelon, about ten times as large; fishing industries. Capital: St Pierre. Pop.: 6300 (1987 est.). Area: 242 sq. km (94 sq. miles).

Saint Pölten ('pɜːltən) *n.* See **Sankt Pölten.**

Saint-Quentin (*French* sɛ̃kɑ̃tɛ̃) *n., usually abbreviated to* **St-Quentin.** a town in N France, on the River Somme: textile industry. Pop.: 67 087 (1983 est.).

Saint-Saëns (*French* sɛ̃sɑ̃s) *n.* (**Charles**) **Camille** (kamij). 1835–1921, French composer, pianist, and organist. His works include the symphonic poem *Danse Macabre* (1874), the opera *Samson and Delilah* (1877), the humorous orchestral suite *Carnival of Animals* (1886), five symphonies, and five piano concertos.

Saintsbury ('seɪntsbərɪ, -brɪ) *n.* **George Edward Bateman.** 1845–1933, English literary critic and historian; author of many works on English and French literature.

saint's day *n. Christianity.* a day in the church calendar commemorating a saint.

Saint-Simon (*French* sɛ̃simɔ̃) *n.* **1. Comte de** (kɔ̃t də), title of *Claude Henri de Rouvroy.* 1760–1825, French social philosopher, generally regarded as the founder of French socialism. He thought society should be reorganized along industrial lines and that scientists should be the new spiritual leaders. His most important work is *Nouveau Christianisme* (1825). **2. Duc de** (dyk də), title of *Louis de Rouvroy.* 1675–1755, French soldier, statesman, and writer: his *Mémoires* are an outstanding account of the period 1694–1723, during the reigns of Louis XIV and Louis XV.

Saint Thomas *n., usually abbreviated to* **St Thomas. 1.** an island in the E West Indies, in the Virgin Islands of the U.S. Capital: Charlotte Amalie. Pop.: 52 660 (1985). Area: 83 sq. km (28 sq. miles). **2.** the former name (1921–37) of **Charlotte Amalie.**

Saint Vincent *n., usually abbreviated to* **St Vincent. 1. Cape.** a headland at the SW extremity of Portugal: scene of several important naval battles, notably in 1797, when the British defeated the French and Spanish. **2. Gulf.** a shallow inlet of SE South Australia, between Yorke Peninsula and the mainland: salt industry.

Saint Vincent and the Grenadines *n., usually abbreviated to* **St Vincent and the Grenadines.** an island state in the Caribbean, in the Windward Islands of the Lesser Antilles: comprises the island of St Vincent and the Northern Grenadines; formerly a British associated state (1969–79); gained full independence in 1979. Language: English. Religion: Christian majority. Currency: East Caribbean dollar. Capital: Kingstown. Pop.: 112 000 (1987). Area: 389 sq. km (150 sq. miles).

Saint Vitus's dance ('vaɪtəsɪz) *n., usually abbreviated to* **St Vitus's dance.** *Pathol.* a nontechnical name for **Sydenham's chorea.**

Saipan (saɪ'pæn) *n.* an island in the W Pacific, in the S central Mariana Islands: administrative centre of the U.S. Trust Territory of the Pacific Islands; captured by the Americans and used as a leading air base until the end of World War II; administered by the U.S. since 1946. Pop.: 16 532 (1983 est.). Area: 180 sq. km (70 sq. miles).

Saïs ('seɪɪs) *n.* (in ancient Egypt) a city in the W Nile delta; the royal capital of the 24th dynasty (about 730–715 B.C.) and the 26th dynasty (about 664–525 B.C.). —**Saïte** ('seɪaɪt) *n.* —**Saïtic** (seɪ'ɪtɪk) *adj.*

saith (sɛθ) *vb.* (used with *he, she,* or *it*) *Arch.* a form of the present tense of **say.**

saithe (seɪθ) *n. Brit.* another name for **coalfish.** [C19: from ON]

Sakai (sɑː'kaɪ) *n.* a port in S Japan, on S Honshu on Osaka Bay: a major port in the 16th century; an industrial satellite of Osaka. Pop.: 818 000 (1985).

sake[1] (seɪk) *n.* **1.** benefit or interest (esp. in **for (someone's** *or* **one's own) sake). 2.** the purpose of obtaining or achieving (esp. in **for the sake of (something)). 3.** used in various exclamations of impatience, urgency, etc.: *for heaven's sake.* [C13 (in the phrase *for the sake of,* prob. from legal usage): from OE *sacu* lawsuit (hence, a cause)]

sake[2], **saké,** *or* **saki** ('sækɪ) *n.* a Japanese alcoholic drink made from fermented rice. [C17: from Japanese]

saker ('seɪkə) *n.* a large falcon of E Europe and Asia. [C14 *sagre,* from OF *sacre,* from Ar. *saqr*]

Sakhalin (*Russian* səxa'lin) *or* **Saghalien** *n.* an island in the Sea of Okhotsk, off the SE coast of the Soviet Union north of Japan: fishing, forestry, and mineral resources (coal and petroleum). Capital: Yuzhno-Sakhalinsk. Pop.: 660 000 (1983 est.). Area: 76 000 sq. km (29 300 sq. miles). Japanese name (1905–24): **Karafuto.**

Sakharov (*Russian* za'xarəf) *n.* **Andrei** (an'drjej). born 1921, Soviet nuclear physicist and human-rights campaigner: Nobel peace prize 1975.

saki ('sɑːkɪ) *n.* **1.** any of several small mostly arboreal New World monkeys having a long bushy tail. **2.** another name for **sake**[2]. [sense 1: C20: F, from Tupi *saqi*]

Saki ('sɑːkɪ) *n.* pen name of (Hector Hugh) **Munro.**

sal (sæl) *n.* a pharmacological term for **salt** (sense 3). [L: salt]

salaam (sə'lɑːm) *n.* **1.** a Muslim salutation consisting of a deep bow with the right palm on the forehead. **2.** a salutation signifying peace. ~*vb.* **3.** to make a salaam (to). [C17: from Ar. *salām* peace, from *assalām 'alaikum* peace be to you]

salable ('seɪləbᵊl) *adj.* the U.S. spelling of **saleable.**

salacious (sə'leɪʃəs) *adj.* **1.** having an excessive interest in sex. **2.** (of books, etc.) erotic, bawdy, or lewd. [C17: from L *salax* fond of leaping, from *salīre* to leap] —**sa'laciously** *adv.* —**sa'laciousness** *or* **salacity** (sə'læsɪtɪ) *n.*

salad ('sæləd) *n.* **1.** a dish of raw vegetables, such as lettuce, tomatoes, etc., served as a separate course with cold meat, eggs, etc., or as part of a main course. **2.** any dish of cold vegetables or fruit served with a dressing: *potato salad.* **3.** any green vegetable or herb used in such a dish. [C15: from OF *salade,* from OProvençal *salada,* from *salar* to season with salt, from L *sal* salt]

salad days *pl. n.* a period of youth and inexperience.

salad dressing *n.* a sauce for salad, such as oil and vinegar or mayonnaise.

salade niçoise (sæ'lɑːd niː'swɑːz) *n.* a cold dish consisting of a variety of ingredients, usually including hardboiled eggs, anchovy fillets, olives, tomatoes, and sometimes tuna fish. [C20: from F, lit.: salad of or from NICE]

Saladin ('sælədɪn) *n.* Arabic name *Salah-ed-Din Yusuf ibn-Ayyub.* ?1137–93, sultan of Egypt and Syria and opponent of the Crusaders. He defeated the Christians near Tiberias (1187) and captured Acre, Jerusalem, and Ashkelon. He fought against Richard I of England and Philip II of France during the Third Crusade (1189–92).

Salado (*Spanish* sa'laðo) *n.* **1.** a river in N Argentina, rising in the Andes as the Juramento and flowing southeast to the Paraná River. Length: 2012 km (1250 miles). **2.** a river in W Argentina, rising near the Chilean border as the Desaguadero and flowing south to the Colorado River. Length: about 1365 km (850 miles).

Salamanca (*Spanish* sala'maŋka) *n.* a city in W Spain: a leading cultural centre of Europe till the end of the 16th century; market town. Pop.: 152 766 (1986 est.).

salamander ('sælə,mændə) *n.* **1.** any of various amphibians of central and S Europe. They have an elongated body, and only return to water to breed. **2.** *Chiefly U.S. & Canad.* any amphibian with a tail, as the newt. **3.** a mythical reptilian creature supposed to live in fire. **4.** an elemental fire-inhabiting being. [C14: from OF *salamandre,* from L *salamandra,* from Gk]

Salambria (sə'læmbrɪə, ˌsɑːlɑːm'brɪə) *n.* a river in N Greece, in Thessaly, rising in the Pindus Mountains and flowing southeast and east to the Gulf of Salonika. Length: about 200 km (125 miles). Ancient name: **Peneus.** Modern Greek name: **Piniós.**

salami (sə'lɑːmɪ) *n.* a highly seasoned type of sausage, usually flavoured with garlic. [C19: from It., pl. of *salame,* from Vulgar L *salāre* (unattested) to salt, from L *sal* salt]

Salamis ('sæləmɪs) *n.* an island in the Saronic Gulf, Greece: scene of the naval battle in 480 B.C., in which the Greeks defeated the Persians. Pop.: 20 000 (1985 est.). Area: 95 sq. km (37 sq. miles).

sal ammoniac *n.* another name for **ammonium chloride.**

salaried ('sælərɪd) *adj.* earning or yielding a salary: *a salaried worker; salaried employment.*

salary ('sælərɪ) *n., pl.* **-ries. 1.** a fixed payment made by an employer, often monthly, for professional or office work. Cf. **wage.** ~*vb.* **-rying, -ried. 2.** (*tr.*) to pay a salary to. [C14: from Anglo-Norman *salarie,* from L *salārium* the sum given to Roman soldiers to buy salt, from *sal* salt]

Salazar (*Portuguese* sələ'zar) *n.* **Antonio de Oliveira** (ən'tɔnju 'dɔː oli'vəɪrə). 1889–1970, Portuguese statesman; dictator (1932–68).

salchow ('sɔːlkaʊ) *n. Figure skating.* a jump from the inner backward edge of one foot with one, two, or three full turns in the air, returning to the outer backward edge of the opposite foot. [C20: after Ulrich *Salchow* (1877–1949), Swedish figure skater, who originated it]

Salduba (sæl'duːbə, 'sældəbə) *n.* the pre-Roman (Celtiberian) name for **Zaragoza.**

sale (seɪl) *n.* **1.** the exchange of goods, property, or services for an agreed sum of money or credit. **2.** the amount sold. **3.** the opportunity to sell: *there was no sale for luxuries.* **4. a.** an event at which goods are sold at reduced prices, usually to clear old stocks. **b.** (*as modifier*): *sale bargains.* **5.** an auction. [OE *sala,* from ON *sala*]

Sale (seɪl) *n.* **1.** a town in NW England, in Greater Manchester: a residential suburb of Manchester. Pop.: 57 824 (1981). **2.** a city in SE Australia, in SE Victoria: centre of an agricultural region. Pop.: 12 968 (1981).

Salé (*French* sale) *n.* a port in NW Morocco, on the Atlantic adjoining Rabat. Pop.: 289 391 (1982).

saleable *or U.S.* **salable** ('seɪləbᵊl) *adj.* fit for selling or capable of being sold. —**salea'bility** *or U.S.* ˌ**sala'bility** *n.*

Salem ('seɪləm) *n.* **1.** a city in S India, in Tamil Nadu: textile industries. Pop.: 361 177 (1981). **2.** a city in NE Massachusetts, on the Atlantic: scene of the execution of 19 witches after the witch hunts of 1692. Pop.: 89 233 (1980). **3.** an Old Testament name for **Jerusalem.** (Genesis 14:18; Psalms 76:2).

sale of work *n.* a sale of articles, often handmade, the proceeds of which benefit a charity or charities.

sale or return *n.* an arrangement by which a retailer pays only for goods sold, returning those that are unsold.

Salerno (*Italian* sa'lɛrno) *n.* a port in SW Italy, in Campania on the **Gulf of Salerno:** first medical school of medieval Europe. Pop.: 154 848 (1986).

saleroom ('seɪlˌruːm, -ˌrʊm) n. Chiefly Brit. a room where objects are displayed for sale, esp. by auction.

salesclerk ('seɪlzˌklɑːk) n. U.S. & Canad. a shop assistant.

salesman ('seɪlzmən) n., pl. **-men**. **1.** Also called: **saleswoman** (fem.), **salesgirl** (fem.), or **salesperson**. a person who sells merchandise or services in a shop. **2.** short for **travelling salesman**.

salesmanship ('seɪlzmənˌʃɪp) n. **1.** the technique of, skill, or ability in selling. **2.** the work of a salesman.

sales resistance n. opposition of potential customers to selling, esp. aggressive selling.

sales talk or **pitch** n. an argument or other persuasion used in selling.

sales tax n. a tax levied on retail sales receipts and added to selling prices by retailers.

sales trader n. Stock Exchange. a person employed by a market maker, or his firm, to find clients.

Salford ('sɔːlfəd, 'sɒl-) n. a city in NW England in Greater Manchester, on the Manchester Ship Canal: a major centre of the cotton industry in the 19th century; extensive docks. Pop.: 98 024 (1981).

Salian ('seɪlɪən) adj. **1.** denoting or relating to a group of Franks (the **Salii**) who settled in the Netherlands in the 4th century A.D. — n. **2.** a member of this group.

salicin ('sælɪsɪn) n. a crystalline water-soluble glucoside obtained from the bark of poplar trees and used as a medical analgesic. [C19: from F, from L salix willow]

Salic law ('sælɪk) n. History. **1.** the code of laws of the Salian Franks and other Germanic tribes. **2.** a law excluding women from succession to the throne in certain countries, such as France.

salicylate (sə'lɪsɪˌleɪt) n. any salt or ester of salicylic acid.

salicylic acid (ˌsælɪ'sɪlɪk) n. a white crystalline substance with a sweet taste and bitter aftertaste, used in the manufacture of aspirin, and as a fungicide.

salient ('seɪlɪənt) adj. **1.** conspicuous or striking: a salient feature. **2.** projecting outwards at an angle of less than 180°. **3.** (esp. of animals) leaping. ~n. **4.** Mil. a projection of the forward line into enemy-held territory. **5.** a salient angle. [C16: from L salīre to leap] —**'salience** or **'saliency** n. —**'saliently** adv.

salientian (ˌseɪlɪ'ɛnʃɪən) n. **1.** any of an order of vertebrates with no tail and long hind legs adapted for hopping, as the frog or the toad. ~adj. **2.** of or belonging to this order. [C19: from NL Salientia, lit.: leapers, from L salīre to leap]

salina (sə'laɪnə) n. a salt marsh or lake. [C17: from Sp., from Med. L: salt pit, from LL salīnus SALINE]

saline ('seɪlaɪn) adj. **1.** of, consisting of, or containing common salt: a saline taste. **2.** Med. of or relating to a saline. **3.** of, consisting of, or containing any chemical salt, esp. sodium chloride. ~n. **4.** Med. a solution of sodium chloride and water. [C15: from LL salīnus, from L sal salt] —**salinity** (sə'lɪnɪtɪ) n.

Salinger ('sælɪndʒə) n. **J(erome) D(avid)**. born 1919, U.S. writer, noted particularly for his novel of adolescence The Catcher in the Rye (1951).

salinometer (ˌsælɪ'nɒmɪtə) n. a hydrometer for determining the amount of salt in a solution. —ˌsali'nometry n.

Salisbury[1] ('sɔːlzbərɪ, -brɪ) n. **1.** the former name (until 1982) of **Harare**. **2.** a city in S Australia: an industrial suburb of N Adelaide. Pop.: 88 230 (1981). **3.** a city in S England, in SE Wiltshire: nearby Old Sarum was the site of an Early Iron Age hill fort; its cathedral (1220–58) has the highest spire in England. Pop.: 35 355 (1981). Ancient name: **Sarum**. Official name: **New Sarum**.

Salisbury[2] ('sɔːlzbərɪ, -brɪ) n. **Robert Gascoyne Cecil** ('gæskɔɪn), 3rd Marquess of Salisbury. 1830–1903, British statesman; Conservative prime minister (1885–86; 1886–92; 1895–1902). His greatest interest was in foreign and imperial affairs.

Salisbury Plain n. an open chalk plateau in S England, in Wiltshire: site of Stonehenge; military training area. Average height: 120 m (400 ft.).

saliva (sə'laɪvə) n. the secretion of salivary glands, consisting of a clear usually slightly acid aqueous fluid of variable composition. [C17: from L, from ?] —**salivary** (sə'laɪvərɪ) adj.

salivary gland n. any of the glands in mammals that secrete saliva.

salivate ('sælɪˌveɪt) vb. **1.** (intr.) to secrete saliva, esp. an excessive amount. **2.** (tr.) to cause (an animal, etc.) to produce saliva, as by the administration of mercury. —ˌsali'vation n.

Salk (sɔːlk) n. **Jonas Edward**. born 1914, U.S. virologist: developed an injected vaccine against poliomyelitis (1954).

sallee ('sælɪ) n. Austral. **1.** a SE Australian eucalyptus tree with pale grey bark. **2.** any of various acacia trees. [prob. from Abor.]

sallow[1] ('sæləʊ) adj. **1.** (esp. of human skin) of an unhealthy pale or yellowish colour. ~vb. **2.** (tr.) to make sallow. [OE salu] —**'sallowish** adj. —**'sallowness** n.

sallow[2] ('sæləʊ) n. **1.** any of several small willow trees, esp. the common sallow, which has large catkins that appear before the leaves. **2.** a twig or the wood of any of these trees. [OE sealh] —**'sallowy** adj.

Sallust ('sæləst) n. full name **Gaius Sallustius Crispus**. 86–?34 B.C., Roman historian and statesman, noted for his histories of the Catiline conspiracy and the Roman war against Jugurtha.

sally ('sælɪ) n., pl. **-lies**. **1.** a sudden sortie, esp. by troops. **2.** a sudden outburst or emergence into action or expression. **3.** an excursion. **4.** a jocular retort. ~vb. **-lying**, **-lied**. (intr.) **5.** to make a sudden violent sortie. **6.** (often foll. by forth) to go out on an expedition, etc. **7.** to come or set out in an energetic manner. **8.** to rush out suddenly. [C16: from OF saillie, from saillir to dash forwards, from L salīre to leap]

Sally Lunn (lʌn) n. a flat round cake made from a sweet yeast dough. [C19: said to be after an 18th-century E baker who invented it]

salmagundi (ˌsælmə'gʌndɪ) n. **1.** a mixed salad dish of cooked meats, eggs, beetroot, etc., popular in 18th-century England. **2.** a miscellany. [C17: from F salmigondis, ?from It. salami conditi pickled salami]

salmon ('sæmən) n., pl. **-ons** or **-on**. **1.** a soft-finned fish of the Atlantic and the Pacific, which is an important food fish. Salmon occur in cold and temperate waters and many species migrate to fresh water to spawn. **2.** Austral. any of several unrelated fish. [C13: from OF saumon, from L salmō] —**'salmo,noid** adj.

salmonella (ˌsælmə'nɛlə) n., pl. **-lae** (-ˌliː). any of a genus of rod-shaped aerobic bacteria including many species which cause food poisoning. [C19: NL, after Daniel E. Salmon (1850–1914), U.S. veterinary surgeon]

salmon ladder n. a series of steps designed to enable salmon to move upstream to their breeding grounds.

Salome (sə'ləʊmɪ) n. New Testament. the daughter of Herodias, at whose instigation she beguiled Herod by her seductive dancing into giving her the head of John the Baptist.

salon ('sælɒn) n. **1.** a room in a large house in which guests are received. **2.** an assembly of guests in a fashionable household, esp. a gathering of major literary, artistic, and political figures. **3.** a commercial establishment in which hairdressers, etc., carry on their businesses. **4. a.** a hall for exhibiting works of art. **b.** such an exhibition, esp. one showing the work of living artists. [C18: from F, from It. salone, augmented form of sala hall, of Gmc origin]

Salonika or **Salonica** (sə'lɒnɪkə) n. the English name for **Thessaloníki**.

saloon (sə'luːn) n. **1.** Also called: **saloon bar**. Brit. another word for **lounge** (sense 5). **2.** a large public room on a passenger ship. **3.** any large public room used for a purpose: a dancing saloon. **4.** Chiefly U.S. & Canad. a place where alcoholic drink is sold and consumed. **5.** a closed two-door or four-door car with four to six seats. U.S., Canad., and N.Z. name: **sedan**. [C18: from F SALON]

Salop ('sæləp) n. a former name (1974–80) of **Shropshire**. — **Salopian** (sə'ləʊpjən) n., adj.

salopettes (ˌsælə'pɛts) pl. n. a garment worn for skiing, consisting of quilted trousers held up by shoulder straps. [C20: from F]

salpiglossis (ˌsælpɪ'glɒsɪs) n. any of a genus of plants, some species of which are cultivated for their bright funnel-shaped flowers. [C19: NL, from Gk salpinx trumpet + glōssa tongue]

salpinx ('sælpɪŋks) n., pl. **salpinges** (sæl'pɪndʒiːz). Anat. another name for **Fallopian tube** or **Eustachian tube**. [C19: from Gk: trumpet] —**salpingectomy** (ˌsælpɪn'dʒɛktəmɪ) n. —**salpingitis** (ˌsælpɪn'dʒaɪtɪs) n.

salsa ('sælsə) n. **1.** a type of Puerto Rican big-band dance music. **2.** a dance performed to this.

salsify ('sælsɪfɪ) n., pl. **-fies. 1.** Also called: **oyster plant, vegetable oyster.** a Mediterranean plant having grasslike leaves, purple flower heads, and a long white edible taproot. **2.** the root of this plant, which tastes of oysters and is eaten as a vegetable. [C17: from F, from It. *sassefrica*, from LL, from L *saxum* rock + *fricāre* to rub]

sal soda n. the crystalline decahydrate of sodium carbonate, $Na_2CO_3.10H_2O$.

salt (sɔːlt) n. **1.** a white powder or colourless crystalline solid, consisting mainly of sodium chloride and used for seasoning and preserving food. **2.** (*modifier*) preserved in, flooded with, containing, or growing in salt or salty water: *salt pork.* **3.** *Chem.* any of a class of crystalline solid compounds that are formed from, or can be regarded as formed from, an acid and a base. **4.** liveliness or pungency: *his wit added salt to the discussion.* **5.** dry or laconic wit. **6.** an experienced sailor. **7.** short for **saltcellar. 8. rub salt into someone's wounds.** to make someone's pain, shame, etc., even worse. **9. salt of the earth.** a person or group of people regarded as the finest of their kind. **10. with a grain** (*or* **pinch**) **of salt.** with reservations. **11. worth one's salt.** worthy of one's pay. ~*vb.* (*tr.*) **12.** to season or preserve with salt. **13.** to scatter salt over (an iced road, etc.) to melt the ice. **14.** to add zest to. **15.** (often foll. by *down* or *away*) to preserve or cure with salt. **16.** *Chem.* to treat with salt. **17.** to give a false appearance of value to, esp. to introduce valuable ore fraudulently into (a mine, sample, etc.). ~*adj.* **18.** not sour, sweet, or bitter; salty. ~See also **salt away, salts.** [OE *sealt*] —**'salt,like** adj. —**'saltness** n.

SALT (sɔːlt) n. acronym for Strategic Arms Limitation Talks *or* Treaty.

Salta (*Spanish* 'salta) n. a city in NW Argentina: thermal springs. Pop.: 260 000 (1980).

saltation (sæl'teɪʃən) n. **1.** *Biol.* an abrupt variation in the appearance of an organism, species, etc. **2.** *Geol.* the leaping movement of sand or soil particles carried in water or by the wind. **3.** a sudden abrupt movement. [C17: from L *saltātiō* a dance, from *saltāre* to leap about] —**saltatorial** (,sæltə'tɔːrɪəl) *or* **'saltatory** adj.

salt away *or* (*less commonly*) **down** vb. (*tr., adv.*) to hoard or save (money, valuables, etc.).

saltbush ('sɔːlt,bʊʃ) n. any of certain shrubs that grow in alkaline desert regions.

salt cake n. an impure form of sodium sulphate used in the manufacture of detergents, glass, and ceramic glazes.

saltcellar ('sɔːlt,selə) n. **1.** a small container for salt used at the table. **2.** *Brit. inf.* either of the two hollows formed above the collarbones. [changed (through infl. of cellar) from C15 *salt saler; saler* from OF *saliere* container for salt, from L *salārius* belonging to salt, from *sal* salt]

salt dome *or* **plug** n. a domelike structure of stratified rocks containing a central core of salt.

salted ('sɔːltɪd) adj. seasoned, preserved, or treated with salt.

salt flat n. a flat expanse of salt left by the total evaporation of a body of water.

saltigrade ('sæltɪ,greɪd) adj. (of animals) adapted for moving in a series of jumps. [C19: from NL *Saltigradae*, name formerly applied to jumping spiders, from L *saltus* a leap + *gradī* to move]

Saltillo (*Spanish* sal'tiʎo) n. a city in N Mexico, capital of Coahuila state: resort and commercial centre of a mining region. Pop.: 321 758 (1980).

saltings ('sɔːltɪŋz) pl. n. meadow land or marsh that is periodically flooded by sea water.

saltire *or* **saltier** ('sɔːl,taɪə) n. *Heraldry.* an ordinary consisting of a diagonal cross on a shield. [C14 *sawturoure*, from OF *sauteour* cross-shaped barricade, from *saulter* to jump, from L *saltāre*]

Salt Lake City n. a city in N central Utah, near the Great Salt Lake at an altitude of 1330 m (4300 ft.): state capital; founded in 1847 by the Mormons as world capital of the Mormon Church; University of Utah (1850). Pop.: 158 440 (1986 est.).

salt lick n. **1.** a place where wild animals go to lick salt deposits. **2.** a block of salt given to domestic animals to lick. **3.** *Austral. & N.Z.* a soluble cake of minerals used to supplement the diet of farm animals.

Salto (*Spanish* 'salto) n. a port in NW Uruguay, on the Uruguay River: Uruguay's second largest city. Pop.: 77 400 (1985).

saltpan ('sɔːlt,pæn) n. a shallow basin, usually in a desert region, containing salt, gypsum, etc., that was deposited from an evaporated salt lake.

saltpetre *or U.S.* **saltpeter** (,sɔːlt'piːtə) n. **1.** another name for **potassium nitrate. 2.** short for **Chile saltpetre.** [C16: from OF *salpetre*, from L *sal petrae* salt of rock]

salt pork n. pork, esp. taken from the back and belly, that has been cured with salt.

salts (sɔːlts) pl. n. **1.** *Med.* any of various mineral salts, such as magnesium sulphate, for use as a cathartic. **2.** short for **smelling salts. 3. like a dose of salts.** *Inf.* very quickly.

saltus ('sæltəs) n., pl. **-tuses.** a break in the continuity of a sequence. [L: a leap]

saltwater ('sɔːlt,wɔːtə) adj. of or inhabiting salt water, esp. the sea: *saltwater fishes.*

saltworks ('sɔːlt,wɜːks) n. (*functioning as sing.*) a building or factory where salt is produced.

saltwort ('sɔːlt,wɜːt) n. any of various plants, of beaches and salt marshes, having prickly leaves, striped stems, and small green flowers. Also called: **glasswort, kali.**

salty ('sɔːltɪ) adj. **saltier, saltiest. 1.** of, tasting of, or containing salt. **2.** (esp. of humour) sharp. **3.** relating to life at sea. —**'saltiness** n.

salubrious (sə'luːbrɪəs) adj. conducive or favourable to health. [C16: from L, from *salūs* health] —**sa'lubriously** adv. —**sa'lubrity** n.

Saluki (sə'luːkɪ) n. a tall breed of hound with a smooth coat and long fringes on the ears and tail. [C19: from Ar. *salūqīy* of Saluq, an ancient Arabian city]

salutary ('sæljutərɪ) adj. **1.** promoting or intended to promote an improvement: *a salutary warning.* **2.** promoting or intended to promote health. [C15: from L *salūtāris* wholesome, from *salūs* safety] —**'salutarily** adv.

salutation (,sæljuː'teɪʃən) n. **1.** an act, phrase, gesture, etc., that serves as a greeting. **2.** a form of words used as an opening to a speech or letter, such as *Dear Sir.* [C14: from L *salūtātiō*, from *salūtāre* to greet; see SALUTE]

salutatory (sə'luːtətərɪ) adj. of, relating to, or resembling a salutation. —**sa'lutatorily** adv.

salute (sə'luːt) vb. **1.** (*tr.*) to address or welcome with friendly words or gestures of respect, such as bowing. **2.** (*tr.*) to acknowledge with praise: *we salute your gallantry.* **3.** *Mil.* to pay formal respect, as by raising the right arm. ~*n.* **4.** the act of saluting. **5.** a formal military gesture of respect. [C14: from L *salūtāre* to greet, from *salūs* wellbeing] —**sa'luter** n.

salvable ('sælvəbəl) adj. capable of or suitable for being saved or salvaged. [C17: from LL *salvāre* to save, from *salvus* safe]

Salvador ('sælvə,dɔː; *Portuguese* salva'dor) n. a port in E Brazil, capital of Bahia state: founded in 1549 as capital of the Portuguese colony, which it remained until 1763; a major centre of the African slave trade in colonial times. Pop.: 1 811 367 (1985). Former name: **Bahia.** Official name: **São Salvador da Bahia de Todos os Santos** (səu salva'dor 'də: ba'ia 'də: 'toːduʃ uʃ 'səntuʃ). —,**Salva'dorian** n., adj.

salvage ('sælvɪdʒ) n. **1.** the act, process, or business of rescuing vessels or their cargoes from loss at sea. **2. a.** the act of saving any goods or property in danger of damage or destruction. **b.** (*as modifier*): *a salvage operation.* **3.** the goods or property so saved. **4.** compensation paid for the salvage of a vessel or its cargo. **5.** the proceeds from the sale of salvaged goods. ~*vb.* (*tr.*) **6.** to save or rescue (goods or property) from fire, shipwreck, etc. **7.** to gain (something beneficial) from a failure. [C17: from OF, from Med. L *salvāgium*, from *salvāre* to SAVE[1]] —**'salvageable** adj. —**'salvager** n.

salvation (sæl'veɪʃən) n. **1.** the act of preserving or the state of being preserved from harm. **2.** a person or thing that is the means of preserving from harm. **3.** *Christianity.* deliverance by redemption from the power of sin. [C13: from OF, from LL *salvātiō*, from L *salvātus* saved, from *salvāre* to SAVE[1]]

Salvation Army n. a Christian body founded in 1865 by William Booth and organized on quasi-military lines for evangelism and social work among the poor.

salvationist (sæl'veɪʃənɪst) n. **1.** a member of an evangelical sect emphasizing the doctrine of salvation. **2.** (*often cap.*) a member of the Salvation Army.

salve (sælv, saːv) *n.* **1.** an ointment for wounds, etc. **2.** anything that heals or soothes. ~*vb.* (*tr.*) **3.** to apply salve to (a wound, etc.). **4.** to soothe, comfort, or appease. [OE *sealf*]

salver ('sælvə) *n.* a tray, esp. one of silver, on which food, letters, visiting cards, etc., are presented. [C17: from F *salve*, from Sp. *salva* tray from which the king's taster sampled food, from L *salvāre* to SAVE[1]]

salvia ('sælvɪə) *n.* any of a genus of herbaceous plants or small shrubs, such as the sage, grown for their medicinal or culinary properties or for ornament. [C19: from L: SAGE[2]]

salvo ('sælvəʊ) *n., pl.* **-vos** *or* **-voes.** **1.** a discharge of fire from weapons in unison, esp. on a ceremonial occasion. **2.** concentrated fire from many weapons, as in a naval battle. **3.** an outburst, as of applause. [C17: from It. *salva*, from OF *salve*, from L *salvē!* greetings!, ult. from *salvus* safe]

Salvo ('sælvəʊ) *n., pl.* **-vos.** *Austral. sl.* a member of the Salvation Army.

sal volatile (vɒ'lætɪlɪ) *n.* a solution of ammonium carbonate in alcohol and aqueous ammonia, used as smelling salts. Also called: **spirits of ammonia.** [C17: from NL: volatile salt]

Salween ('sælwiːn) *n.* a river in SW Asia, rising in the Tibetan Plateau and flowing east and south through SW China and Burma to the Gulf of Martaban. Length: 2400 km (1500 miles).

Salzburg ('sæltsbɜːg; *German* 'zaltsburk) *n.* **1.** a city in W Austria, capital of Salzburg province: 7th-century Benedictine abbey; a centre of music since the Middle Ages and birthplace of Mozart; tourist centre. Pop.: 138 213 (1981). **2.** a province of W Austria. Pop.: 441 842 (1981). Area: 7154 sq. km (2762 sq. miles).

Salzgitter (*German* zalts'gɪtər) *n.* an industrial city in West Germany, in SE Lower Saxony. Pop.: 113 600 (1980 est.).

SAM (sæm) *n. acronym for* surface-to-air missile.

Sam. *Bible. abbrev. for* Samuel.

Samar ('saːmə) *n.* an island in the E central Philippines, separated from S Luzon by the San Bernardino Strait: the third largest island in the republic. Capital: Catbalogan. Pop.: 1 200 592 (1980). Area: 13 080 sq. km (5050 sq. miles).

samara (sə'maːrə) *n.* a dry winged one-seeded fruit: occurs in the ash, maple, etc. Also called: **key fruit.** [C16: from NL, from L: seed of an elm]

Samara (*Russian* sa'marə) *n.* the former name (until 1935) of **Kuibyshev.**

Samarang (sə'maːraːŋ) *n.* a variant spelling of **Semarang.**

Samaria (sə'mɛərɪə) *n.* **1.** the region of ancient Palestine that extended from Judaea to Galilee and from the Mediterranean to the River Jordan; the N kingdom of Israel. **2.** the capital of this kingdom; constructed northwest of Shechem in the 9th century B.C.

Samaritan (sə'mærɪtᵊn) *n.* **1.** a native or inhabitant of Samaria. **2.** short for **Good Samaritan. 3.** a member of a voluntary organization (**the Samaritans**) whose aim is to help people in distress or despair.

samarium (sə'mɛərɪəm) *n.* a silvery metallic element of the lanthanide series used in carbon-arc lighting, as a doping agent in laser crystals, and as a neutron-absorber. Symbol: Sm; atomic no.: 62; atomic wt.: 150.35. [C19: from NL, from mineral, *samarskite*, after Col. von *Samarski*, 19th-century Russian inspector of mines + -IUM]

Samarkand ('sæmə,kænd; *Russian* səmar'kant) *n.* a city in the S central Soviet Union, in the Uzbek SSR: under Tamerlane it became the chief economic and cultural centre of central Asia, on trade routes from China and India (the "silk road"). Pop.: 388 000 (1987). Ancient name: **Maracanda.**

samba ('sæmbə) *n., pl.* **-bas. 1.** a modern ballroom dance from Brazil in bouncy duple time. **2.** a piece of music composed for or in the rhythm of this dance. ~*vb.* **-baing, -baed. 3.** (*intr.*) to perform such a dance. [Port., of African origin]

sambar *or* **sambur** ('sæmbə) *n., pl.* **-bars, -bar** *or* **-burs, -bur.** a S Asian deer with three-tined antlers. [C17: from Hindi, from Sansk. *śambarra*, from ?]

Sambre (*French* sābrə) *n.* a river in W Europe, rising in N France and flowing east into Belgium to join the Meuse at Namur. Length: 190 km (118 miles).

Sam Browne belt (,sæm 'braʊn) *n.* a military officer's wide belt supported by a strap passing from the left side of the belt over the right shoulder. [C20: after Sir *Samuel J. Browne* (1824–1901), British general, who invented it]

same (seɪm) *adj.* (usually preceded by *the*) **1.** being the very one: *she is wearing the same hat.* **2. a.** being the one previously referred to. **b.** (*as n.*): *a note received about same.* **3. a.** identical in kind, quantity, etc.: *two girls of the same age.* **b.** (*as n.*): *we'd like the same.* **4.** unchanged in character or nature: *his attitude is the same as ever.* **5. all the same. a.** Also: **just the same.** nevertheless; yet. **b.** immaterial: *it's all the same to me.* ~*adv.* **6.** in an identical manner. [C12: from ON *samr*] —'**sameness** *n.*

▷ **Usage.** The use of *same* exemplified in *if you send us your order for the materials, we will deliver same tomorrow* is common in business and official English. In general English, however, this use of the word is avoided: *may I borrow your book? I'll return it* (not *same*) *tomorrow.*

samfoo ('sæmfuː) *n.* a style of dress worn by Chinese women, consisting of a waisted blouse and trousers. [from Chinese *sam* dress + *foo* trousers]

Samian ('seɪmɪən) *adj.* **1.** of or relating to Samos, an island in the Aegean, or its inhabitants. ~*n.* **2.** a native or inhabitant of Samos.

Samian ware *n.* a fine earthenware pottery, reddish-brown or black in colour, found in large quantities on Roman sites. [C19: after the island of SAMOS, source of a reddish earth similar to that from which the pottery was made]

samisen ('sæmɪ,sɛn) *n.* a Japanese plucked stringed instrument with a long neck and a rectangular soundbox. [Japanese, from Chinese *san-hsien*, from *san* three + *hsien* string]

samite ('sæmaɪt) *n.* a heavy fabric of silk, often woven with gold or silver threads, used in the Middle Ages. [C13: from OF *samit*, from Med. L *examitum*, from Gk, from *hexamitos* having six threads]

samizdat (*Russian* səmiz'dat) *n.* (in the Soviet Union) **a.** a system of clandestine printing and distribution of banned literature. **b.** (*as modifier*): *a samizdat publication.* [from Russian]

Samnium ('sæmnɪəm) *n.* an ancient country of central Italy inhabited by Oscan-speaking Samnites: corresponds to the present-day region of Abruzzi e Molise and part of Campania.

Samoa (sə'məʊə) *n. or* **Samoa Islands** *pl. n.* a group of islands in the S Pacific, northeast of Fiji: an independent kingdom until the mid 19th century, when it was divided administratively into **American Samoa** (in the east) and **German Samoa** (in the west); the latter was mandated to New Zealand in 1919 and gained full independence in 1962 as **Western Samoa.** Area: 3038 sq. km (1173 sq. miles). —**Sa'moan** *adj., n.*

Samos ('seɪmɒs) *n.* an island in the E Aegean Sea, off the SW coast of Turkey: a leading commercial centre of ancient Greece. Pop.: 40 519 (1981). Area: 492 sq. km (190 sq. miles).

samosa (sə'məʊsə) *n., pl.* **-sas** *or* **-sa.** (in Indian cookery) a small, fried, triangular spiced meat or vegetable pasty. [C20: from Hindi]

Samothrace ('sæmə,θreɪs) *n.* a Greek island in the NE Aegean Sea: mountainous. Pop.: 4000 (1984 est.).

samovar ('sæmə,vaː) *n.* (esp. in Russia) a metal urn for making tea, in which the water is usually heated by an inner container. [C19: from Russian, from *samo-* self + *varit'* to boil]

Samoyed (,sæmə'jɛd) *n.* **1.** (*pl.* **-yed** *or* **-yeds**) a member of a group of peoples who live chiefly in the area of the N Urals: related to the Finns. **2.** the languages of these peoples. **3.** (sə'mɔɪed) a white or cream breed of dog having a dense coat and a tightly curled tail. [C17: from Russian *Samoed*]

samp (sæmp) *n. S. African.* crushed maize used for porridge. [from Amerind *nasaump* corn mush, soup]

sampan ('sæmpæn) *n.* a small skiff, widely used in the Orient, that is propelled by oars. [C17: from Chinese, from *san* three + *pan* board]

samphire ('sæm,faɪə) *n.* **1.** an umbelliferous plant of Eurasian coasts, having fleshy divided leaves and clusters of small white flowers. **2. golden samphire.** a Eurasian coastal plant with fleshy leaves and yellow flower heads. **3. marsh samphire.** another name for **glasswort** (sense

1). **4.** any of several other plants of coastal areas. [C16 *sampiere*, from F *herbe de Saint Pierre* Saint Peter's herb]

sample ('sɑ:mpᵊl) *n.* **1. a.** a small part of anything, intended as representative of the whole. **b.** (*as modifier*): *a sample bottle.* **2.** Also called: **sampling**. *Statistics.* a set of individuals or items selected from a population and analysed to test hypotheses about or yield estimates of the population. ~*vb.* **3.** (*tr.*) to take a sample or samples of. **4.** *Music.* **a.** to take a short extract from (one record) and mix it into a different backing track. **b.** to record (a sound) and feed it into a computerized synthesizer so that it can be reproduced at any pitch. [C13: from OF *essample*, from L *exemplum* EXAMPLE]

sampler ('sɑ:mplə) *n.* **1.** a person who takes samples. **2.** a piece of embroidery done to show the embroiderer's skill in using many different stitches.

sampling ('sɑ:mplɪŋ) *n.* **1.** the process of selecting a random sample. **2.** a variant of **sample** (sense 2).

sampling distribution *n. Statistics.* the distribution of a random, experimentally obtained sample.

Samson ('sæmsən) *n.* **1.** a judge of Israel, who performed herculean feats of strength until he was betrayed by his mistress Delilah (Judges 13–16). **2.** any man of outstanding physical strength.

Samsun (*Turkish* 'samsun) *n.* a port in N Turkey, on the Black Sea. Pop.: 280 068 (1985). Ancient name: **Amisus** (əmi:səs).

Samuel ('sæmjʊəl) *n. Old Testament.* **1.** a Hebrew prophet, seer, and judge, who anointed the first two kings of the Israelites (I Samuel 1–3; 8–15). **2.** either of the two books named after him, **I** and **II Samuel**.

samurai ('sæmʊ,raɪ) *n., pl.* **-rai. 1.** the Japanese warrior caste from the 11th to the 19th centuries. **2.** a member of this aristocratic caste. [C19: from Japanese]

San (sɑ:n) *n.* a river in E central Europe, rising in the W Soviet Union and flowing northwest across SE Poland to the Vistula River. Length: about 450 km (280 miles).

San'a *or* **Sanaa** (sɑ:'nɑ:) *n.* the capital of North Yemen, on the central plateau at an altitude of 2350 m (7700 ft.): became capital of Yemen when Turkish rule ended in 1918. Pop.: 427 185 (1986).

San Antonio (sæn æn'təʊnɪ,əʊ) *n.* a city in S Texas: site of the Alamo; the leading town in Texas until about 1930. Pop.: 914 350 (1986 est.). —**San Antonian** *adj., n.*

sanative ('sænətɪv) *adj., n.* a less common word for **curative**. [C15: from Med. L *sānātīvus*, from L *sānāre* to heal, from *sānus* healthy]

sanatorium (,sænə'tɔ:rɪəm) *or U.S.* **sanitarium** *n., pl.* **-riums** *or* **-ria** (-rɪə). **1.** an institution for the medical care and recuperation of persons who are chronically ill. **2.** *Brit.* a room as in a boarding school where sick pupils may be treated. [C19: from NL, from L *sānāre* to heal]

San Bernardino (sæn ,bɜ:nə'di:nəʊ) *n.* a city in SE California: founded in 1851 by Mormons from Salt Lake City. Pop.: 138 610 (1986 est.).

San Bernardino Pass *n.* a pass over the Lepontine Alps in SE Switzerland. Highest point: 2062 m (6766 ft.).

San Blas ('sɑ:n 'blɑ:s) *n.* **1. Isthmus of.** the narrowest part of the Isthmus of Panama. Width: about 50 km (30 miles). **2. Gulf of.** an inlet of the Caribbean on the N coast of Panama.

San Cristóbal (*Spanish* saŋ kri'stoβal) *n.* **1.** Also called: **Chatham Island.** an island in the Pacific, in the Galápagos Islands. Area: 505 sq. km (195 sq. miles). **2.** a city in SW Venezuela: founded in 1561 by Spanish conquistadores. Pop.: 234 905 (1987 est.).

sanctified ('sæŋktɪ,faɪd) *adj.* **1.** consecrated or made holy. **2.** sanctimonious.

sanctify ('sæŋktɪ,faɪ) *vb.* **-fying, -fied.** (*tr.*) **1.** to make holy. **2.** to free from sin. **3.** to sanction (an action or practice) as religiously binding: *to sanctify a marriage.* **4.** to declare or render (something) productive of or conductive to holiness or grace. [C14: from L *sanctificāre*, from L *sanctus* holy + *facere* to make] —,**sanctifi'cation** *n.* —'**sancti,fier** *n.*

sanctimonious (,sæŋktɪ'məʊnɪəs) *adj.* affecting piety or making a display of holiness. [C17: from L *sanctimonia* sanctity, from *sanctus* holy] —,**sancti'moniously** *adv.* —,**sancti'moniousness** *or* '**sanctimony** *n.*

sanction ('sæŋkʃən) *n.* **1.** authorization. **2.** aid or encouragement. **3.** something, such as an ethical principle,

that imparts binding force to a rule, oath, etc. **4.** the penalty laid down in a law for contravention of its provisions. **5.** (*often pl.*) a coercive measure, esp. one taken by one or more states against another guilty of violating international law. ~*vb.* (*tr.*) **6.** to give authority to. **7.** to confirm. [C16: from L *sanctiō* the establishment of an inviolable decree, from *sancīre* to decree]

sanctitude ('sæŋktɪ,tju:d) *n.* saintliness; holiness.

sanctity ('sæŋktɪtɪ) *n., pl.* **-ties. 1.** the condition of being sanctified; holiness. **2.** anything regarded as sanctified or holy. **3.** the condition of being inviolable: *the sanctity of marriage.* [C14: from OF *saincteté*, from L *sanctitās*, from *sanctus* holy]

sanctuary ('sæŋktjʊərɪ) *n., pl.* **-aries. 1.** a holy place. **2.** a consecrated building or shrine. **3.** *Old Testament.* **a.** the Israelite temple at Jerusalem. **b.** the tabernacle in which the Ark was enshrined. **4.** the chancel, or that part of a sacred building surrounding the main altar. **5. a.** a sacred building where fugitives were formerly entitled to immunity from arrest or execution. **b.** the immunity so afforded. **6.** a place of refuge. **7.** a place, protected by law, where animals can live and breed without interference. [C14: from OF *sainctuarie*, from LL *sanctuārium* repository for holy things, from *sanctus* holy]

sanctuary lamp *n. Christianity.* a lamp, usually red, placed in a prominent position in the sanctuary of a church, which, when lit, indicates the presence of the Blessed Sacrament.

sanctum ('sæŋktəm) *n., pl.* **-tums** *or* **-ta** (-tə). **1.** a sacred or holy place. **2.** a room or place of total privacy. [C16: from L, from *sanctus* holy]

sanctum sanctorum (sæŋk'tɔ:rəm) *n.* **1.** *Bible.* another term for the **holy of holies**. **2.** *Often facetious.* an especially private place. [C14: from L, lit.: holy of holies, rendering Heb. *qōdesh haqqodāshīm*]

Sanctus ('sæŋktəs) *n.* **1.** *Liturgy.* the hymn that occurs immediately after the preface in the celebration of the Eucharist. **2.** a musical setting of this. [C14: from the hymn, *Sanctus sanctus sanctus* Holy, holy, holy, from L *sancīre* to consecrate]

Sanctus bell *n. Chiefly R.C. Church.* a bell rung as the opening words of the Sanctus are pronounced.

sand (sænd) *n.* **1.** loose material consisting of rock or mineral grains, esp. rounded grains of quartz. **2.** (*often pl.*) a sandy area, esp. on the seashore or in a desert. **3. a.** a greyish-yellow colour. **b.** (*as adj.*): *sand upholstery.* **4.** the grains of sandlike material in an hourglass. **5.** *U.S. inf.* courage. **6. the sands are running out.** there is not much time left before the end. ~*vb.* **7.** (*tr.*) to smooth or polish the surface of with sandpaper or sand. **8.** (*tr.*) to sprinkle or cover with or as if with sand. **9.** to fill or cause to fill with sand: *the channel sanded up.* [OE] —'**sand,like** *adj.*

Sand (*French* sɑ̃d) *n.* **George** (ʒɔrʒ), pen name of *Amandine Aurore Lucie Dupin.* 1804–76, French novelist, best known for such pastoral novels as *La Mare au diable* (1846) and *François le Champi* (1847–48) and for her works for women's rights to independence.

Sandakan (sɑ:n'dɑ:kɑ:n) *n.* a port in Malaysia, on the NE coast of Sabah: capital (until 1947) of North Borneo. Pop.: 70 420 (1980).

sandal ('sændᵊl) *n.* **1.** a light shoe consisting of a sole held on the foot by thongs, straps, etc. **2.** a strap passing over the instep or around the ankle to keep a low shoe on the foot. **3.** another name for **sandalwood**. [C14: from L *sandalium*, from Gk, from *sandalon* sandal] —'**sandalled** *adj.*

sandalwood ('sændᵊl,wʊd) *or* **sandal** *n.* **1.** any of a genus of evergreen trees, esp. the **white sandalwood**, of S Asia and Australia, having hard light-coloured heartwood. **2.** the wood of any of these trees, which is used for carving, is burned as incense, and yields an aromatic oil used in perfumery. **3.** any of various similar trees or their wood, esp. a leguminous tree of SE Asia having dark red wood used as a dye. [C14 *sandal*, from Med. L, from LGk *sandanon*, from Sansk. *candana* sandalwood]

Sandalwood Island *n.* the former name for **Sumba**.

sandarac *or* **sandarach** ('sændə,ræk) *n.* **1.** a pinaceous tree of NW Africa, having hard fragrant dark wood. **2.** a brittle pale yellow transparent resin obtained from the bark of this tree and used in making varnish and incense. [C16 *sandaracha*, from L *sandaraca* red pigment, from Gk *sandarakē*]

sandbag ('sænd,bæg) *n.* **1.** a sack filled with sand used for protection against gunfire, floodwater, etc., or as ballast in a balloon, etc. **2.** a bag filled with sand and used as a weapon. ~*vb.* **-bagging, -bagged.** (*tr.*) **3.** to protect or strengthen with sandbags. **4.** to hit with or as if with a sandbag. —**'sand,bagger** *n.*

sandbank ('sænd,bæŋk) *n.* a bank of sand in a sea or river, that may be exposed at low tide.

sand bar *n.* a ridge of sand in a river or sea, built up by the action of tides, currents, etc., and often exposed at low tide.

sandblast ('sænd,blɑːst) *n.* **1.** a jet of sand blown from a nozzle under air or steam pressure. ~*vb.* **2.** (*tr.*) to clean or decorate (a surface) with a sandblast. —**'sand,blaster** *n.*

sand-blind *adj.* not completely blind. Cf. **stone-blind.** [C15: changed (through infl. of SAND) from OE *samblind* (unattested), from *sam-* half, + BLIND] —**'sand-,blindness** *n.*

sandbox ('sænd,bɒks) *n.* **1.** a container on a railway locomotive from which sand is released onto the rails to assist the traction. **2.** a container of sand for small children to play in.

sandboy ('sænd,bɔɪ) *n.* **happy** (*or* **jolly**) **as a sandboy.** very happy; high-spirited.

Sandburg ('sændbɜːg, 'sænbɜːg) *n.* **Carl.** 1878–1967, U.S. writer, noted esp. for his poetry, often written in free verse.

sand castle *n.* a mass of sand moulded into a castle-like shape, esp. by a child on the beach.

sand eel *or* **lance** *n.* a silvery eel-like marine spiny-finned fish found burrowing in sand or shingle. Popular name: **launce.**

sander ('sændə) *n.* **1.** a power-driven tool for smoothing surfaces by rubbing with an abrasive disc. **2.** a person who uses such a device.

sanderling ('sændəlɪŋ) *n.* a small sandpiper that frequents sandy shores. [C17: ?from SAND + OE *erthling, eorthling* inhabitant of earth]

sand flea *n.* another name for the **chigoe** or **sand hopper.**

sandfly ('sænd,flaɪ) *n.*, *pl.* **-flies. 1.** any of various small mothlike dipterous flies: the bloodsucking females transmit diseases including leishmaniasis. **2.** any of various similar flies.

sandgrouse ('sænd,graʊs) *n.* a bird of dry regions of the Old World, having very short feet, a short bill, and long pointed wings and tail.

sand hopper *n.* any of various small hopping crustaceans, common in intertidal regions of seashores. Also called: **beach flea, sand flea.**

Sandhurst ('sænd,hɜːst) *n.* a village in S England, in Berkshire: seat of the Royal Military Academy for the training of officer cadets in the British Army. Pop.: 17 832 (1985 est.).

San Diego (,sæn dɪ'eɪgəʊ) *n.* a port in S California, on the Pacific: naval base; two universities. Pop.: 1 015 190 (1986 est.).

sandman ('sænd,mæn) *n.*, *pl.* **-men.** (in folklore) a magical person supposed to put children to sleep by sprinkling sand in their eyes.

sand martin *n.* a small brown European songbird with white underparts: it nests in tunnels bored in sand, river banks, etc.

sandpaper ('sænd,peɪpə) *n.* **1.** a strong paper coated with sand or other abrasive material for smoothing and polishing. ~*vb.* **2.** (*tr.*) to polish or grind (a surface) with or as if with sandpaper.

sandpiper ('sænd,paɪpə) *n.* **1.** any of numerous N hemisphere shore birds having a long slender bill and legs and cryptic plumage. **2.** any other bird of the family which includes snipes and woodcocks.

sandpit ('sænd,pɪt) *n.* **1.** a shallow pit or container holding sand for children to play in. **2.** a pit from which sand is extracted.

Sandringham ('sændrɪŋəm) *n.* a village in E England, in Norfolk near the E shore of the Wash: site of **Sandringham House,** a residence of the royal family.

Sandrocottus (,sændrəʊ'kɒtəs) *n.* the Greek name of **Chandragupta.**

sandshoes ('sænd,ʃuːz) *pl. n.* light canvas shoes with rubber soles.

sandstone ('sænd,stəʊn) *n.* any of a group of common sedimentary rocks consisting of sand grains consolidated with such materials as quartz, haematite, and clay minerals.

sandstorm ('sænd,stɔːm) *n.* a strong wind that whips up clouds of sand, esp. in a desert.

sand trap *n.* another name (esp. U.S.) for **bunker** (sense 2).

sand viper *n.* a S European viper having a yellowish-brown coloration with a zigzag pattern along the back.

sandwich ('sænwɪdʒ, -wɪtʃ) *n.* **1.** two or more slices of bread, usually buttered, with a filling of meat, cheese, etc. **2.** anything that resembles a sandwich in arrangement. ~*vb.* (*tr.*) **3.** to insert tightly between two other things. **4.** to put into a sandwich. **5.** to place between two dissimilar things. [C18: after 4th Earl of *Sandwich* (1718–92), who ate sandwiches rather than leave the gambling table for meals]

sandwich board *n.* one of two connected boards that are hung over the shoulders in front of and behind a person to display advertisements.

sandwich course *n.* any of several courses consisting of alternate periods of study and industrial work.

Sandwich Islands *pl. n.* the former name of **Hawaii.**

sandwich man *n.* a man who carries sandwich boards.

sandwort ('sænd,wɜːt) *n.* **1.** any of various plants which grow in dense tufts on sandy soil and have white or pink solitary flowers. **2.** any of various related plants.

sandy ('sændɪ) *adj.* **sandier, sandiest. 1.** consisting of, containing, or covered with sand. **2.** (esp. of hair) reddish-yellow. **3.** resembling sand in texture. —**'sandiness** *n.*

sand yacht *n.* a wheeled boat with sails, built to be propelled over sand by the wind.

sandy blight *n. Austral. inf.* any inflammation and irritation of the eye.

sane (seɪn) *adj.* **1.** free from mental disturbance. **2.** having or showing reason or sound sense. [C17: from L *sānus* healthy] —**'sanely** *adv.* —**'saneness** *n.*

San Fernando (*Spanish* san fɛr'nando) *n.* **1.** a port in SW Trinidad, on the Gulf of Paria: the second largest town in the country. Pop.: 32 600 (1986). **2.** an inland port in W Venezuela, on the Apure River. Pop.: 54 000 (1980 est.). Official name: **San Fernando de Apure. 3.** a port in SW Spain, on the Isla de León SE of Cádiz; site of an arsenal (founded 1790) and of the most southerly observatory in Europe. Pop.: 71 846 (1981).

Sanforize *or* **-rise** ('sænfə,raɪz) *vb.* (*tr.*) *Trademark.* to preshrink (a fabric) using a patented process.

San Francisco (,sæn fræn'sɪskəʊ) *n.* a port in W California, situated around the Golden Gate: developed rapidly during the California gold rush; a major commercial centre and one of the world's finest harbours. Pop.: 749 000 (1986 est.). —**San Franciscan** *n.*, *adj.*

San Francisco Bay *n.* an inlet of the Pacific in W California, linked with the open sea by the Golden Gate strait. Length: about 80 km (50 miles). Greatest width: 19 km (12 miles).

sang (sæŋ) *vb.* the past tense of **sing.**
▷ **Usage.** See at **ring**[2].

Sanger ('sæŋə) *n.* **1. Frederick.** born 1918, English biochemist, who determined the molecular structure of insulin: awarded two Nobel prizes for chemistry (1958; 1980). **2. Margaret** (**Higgins**). 1883–1966, U.S. leader of the birth-control movement.

sang-froid (*French* sɑ̃frwa) *n.* composure; self-possession. [C18: from F, lit.: cold blood]

sangoma (sæŋ'gəʊmə) *n.*, *pl.* **-mas.** *S. African.* a witch doctor. [from Bantu]

Sangraal (sæŋ'greɪl), **Sangrail,** *or* **Sangreal** ('sæŋgrɪəl) *n.* another name for the **Holy Grail.**

Sangre de Cristo Mountains ('sæŋgrɪ də 'krɪstəʊ) *pl. n.* a mountain range in S Colorado and N New Mexico: part of the Rocky Mountains. Highest peak: Blanca Peak, 4364 m (14 317 ft.).

sangria (sæŋ'griːə) *n.* a Spanish drink of red wine, sugar, and orange or lemon juice, sometimes laced with brandy. [Sp.: a bleeding]

sanguinary ('sæŋgwɪnərɪ) *adj.* **1.** accompanied by much bloodshed. **2.** bloodthirsty. **3.** consisting of or stained with blood. [C17: from L *sanguinārius*] —**'sanguinarily** *adv.* —**'sanguinariness** *n.*

sanguine ('sæŋgwɪn) *adj.* **1.** cheerful and confident; optimistic. **2.** (esp. of the complexion) ruddy in appearance. **3.** blood-red. ~*n.* **4.** a red pencil containing ferric oxide, used in drawing. [C14: from L *sanguineus* bloody, from *sanguis* blood] —**'sanguinely** *adv.* —**'sanguineness** *n.*

sanguineous (sæŋ'gwɪnɪəs) *adj.* **1.** of, containing, or associated with blood. **2.** a less common word for **sanguine.** —**san'guineousness** *n.*

Sanhedrin ('sænɪdrɪn) *n. Judaism.* the supreme judicial, ecclesiastical, and administrative council of the Jews in New Testament times. [C16: from LHeb., from Gk *sunedrion* council, from *sun*-SYN- + *hedra* seat]

sanies ('seɪnɪˌiːz) *n. Pathol.* a thin greenish foul-smelling discharge from a wound, ulcer, etc., containing pus and blood. [C16: from L, from ?]

San Ildefonso (*Spanish* san ilde'fɔnso) *n.* a town in central Spain, near Segovia: site of the 18th-century summer palace of the kings of Spain. Also called: **La Granja.**

sanitarium (ˌsænɪ'tɛərɪəm) *n., pl.* **-riums** *or* **-ria** (-rɪə). the U.S. word for **sanatorium.** [C19: from L *sānitās* health]

sanitary ('sænɪtərɪ) *adj.* **1.** of or relating to health and measures for the protection of health. **2.** free from dirt, germs, etc.; hygienic. [C19: from F *sanitaire,* from L *sānitās* health] —**sanitarian** (ˌsænɪ'tɛərɪən) *n.* —**'sanitariness** *n.*

sanitary engineering *n.* the branch of civil engineering associated with the supply of water, disposal of sewage, and other public health services. —**sanitary engineer** *n.*

sanitary towel *or esp. U.S.* **napkin** *n.* an absorbent pad worn externally by women during menstruation to absorb the menstrual flow.

sanitation (ˌsænɪ'teɪʃən) *n.* the study and use of practical measures for the preservation of public health.

sanitize *or* **-tise** ('sænɪˌtaɪz) *vb.* (*tr.*) *Chiefly U.S. & Canad.* to make hygienic, as by sterilizing. —ˌsaniti'zation *or* -ti'sation *n.*

sanity ('sænɪtɪ) *n.* **1.** the state of being sane. **2.** good sense or soundness of judgment. [C15: from L *sānitās* health, from *sānus* healthy]

San Jose (ˌsæn həʊ'zeɪ) *n.* a city in W central California: a leading world centre of the fruit drying and canning industry. Pop.: 712 080 (1986 est.).

San José (*Spanish* saŋ xo'se) *n.* the capital of Costa Rica, on the central plateau: a major centre of coffee production in the mid-19th century; University of Costa Rica (1843). Pop.: 241 464 (1984 est.).

San Juan (*Spanish* saŋ 'xwan) *n.* **1.** the capital and chief port of Puerto Rico, on the NE coast; University of Puerto Rico; manufacturing centre. Pop.: 424 600 (1980). **2.** a city in W Argentina: almost completely destroyed by an earthquake in 1944. Pop.: 428 900 (1984 est.).

San Juan Bautista (*Spanish* saŋ 'xwan bau'tista) *n.* the former name of **Villahermosa.**

San Juan Islands (sæn 'wɑːn, 'hwɑːn) *pl. n.* a group of islands between NW Washington, U.S., and SE Vancouver Island, Canada: administratively part of Washington.

San Juan Mountains *pl. n.* a mountain range in SW Colorado and N New Mexico: part of the Rocky Mountains. Highest peak: Uncompahgre Peak, 4363 m (14 314 ft.).

sank (sæŋk) *vb.* the past tense of **sink.**

Sankey ('sæŋkɪ) *n.* **Ira David.** 1840–1908, U.S. evangelist and hymnodist, noted for his revivalist campaigns in Britain and the U.S. with D. L. Moody.

Sankt Pölten (*German* zaŋkt 'pœltən) *n., usually abbreviated to* **St. Pölten.** a city in NE Austria, in Lower Austria province. Pop.: 51 102 (1981).

San Luis Potosí (*Spanish* san 'lwis poto'si) *n.* **1.** a state of central Mexico: mainly high plateau; economy based on mining (esp. silver) and agriculture. Capital: San Luis Potosí. Pop.: 1 670 637 (1980). Area: 62 849 sq. km (24 266 sq. miles). **2.** an industrial city in central Mexico, capital of San Luis Potosí state, at an altitude of 1850 m (6000 ft.). Pop.: 327 333 (1979 est.).

San Marino (ˌsæn məˈriːnəʊ) *n.* a republic in S central Europe in the Apennines, forming an enclave in Italy: the smallest republic in Europe, according to tradition founded by St Marinus in the 4th century. Language: Italian. Religion: Roman Catholic. Currency: lira. Capital: San Marino. Pop.: 22 100 (1987). Area: 62 sq. km (24 sq. miles). —**San Marinese** (ˌsæn ˌmærɪ'niːz) *or* **Sammarinese** (sə,mærɪ'niːz) *adj., n.*

San Martín (*Spanish* san mar'tin) *n.* **José de** (xo'se de). 1778–1850, South American patriot, who played an important part in gaining independence for Argentina, Chile, and Peru. He was protector of Peru (1821–22).

Sanmicheli (*Italian* sanmi'kɛːli) *n.* **Michele** (mi'kɛːle). ?1484–1559, Italian mannerist architect.

San Pedro Sula (*Spanish* san 'peðro 'sula) *n.* a city in NW Honduras: the country's chief industrial centre. Pop.: 372 800 (1985).

San Remo (*Italian* san 'rɛːmo) *n.* a port and resort in NW Italy, in Liguria on the slopes of the Maritime Alps; flower market. Pop.: 62 711 (1981 est.).

sans (sænz) *prep.* an archaic word for **without.** [C13: from OF *sanz,* from L *sine* without, but prob. also infl. by L *absentiā* in the absence of]

Sans. *or* **Sansk.** *abbrev. for* Sanskrit.

San Salvador (sæn 'sælvəˌdɔː; *Spanish* san salβa'ðɔr) *n.* the capital of El Salvador, situated in the SW central part: became capital in 1841; ruined by earthquakes in 1854 and 1873; university (1841). Pop.: 459 902 (1985 est.).

San Salvador Island *n.* an island in the central Bahamas: the first land in the New World seen by Christopher Columbus (1492). Area: 156 sq. km (60 sq. miles). Also called: **Watling Island.**

sans-culotte (ˌsænzkjʊ'lɒt) *n.* **1.** (during the French Revolution) **a.** (originally) a revolutionary of the poorer class. **b.** (later) any revolutionary. **2.** any revolutionary extremist. [C18: from F, lit.: without knee breeches, because the revolutionaries wore pantaloons or trousers rather than knee breeches]

San Sebastián (ˌsæn sə'bæstjən; *Spanish* san seβas'tjan) *n.* a port and resort in N Spain on the Bay of Biscay: former summer residence of the Spanish court. Pop.: 172 303 (1981).

sansevieria (ˌsænsɪ'vɪərɪə) *n.* any of a genus of herbaceous perennial plants of Old World tropical regions: some are cultivated as house plants for their bayonet-like leaves; others yield a useful fibre. [NL, after Raimondo di Sangro (1710–71), It. scholar and prince of *San Seviero*]

Sanskrit ('sænskrɪt) *n.* an ancient language of India. It is the oldest recorded member of the Indic branch of the Indo-European family of languages. Although it is used only for religious purposes, it is one of the official languages of India. [C17: from Sansk. *samskrta* perfected, lit.: put together] —**San'skritic** *adj.*

sans serif *or* **sanserif** (sæn'sɛrɪf) *n.* a style of printer's typeface in which the characters have no serifs.

San Stefano (ˌsæn stɪ'fɑːnəʊ) *n.* a village in NW Turkey, near Istanbul on the Sea of Marmara: scene of the signing (1878) of the treaty ending the Russo-Turkish War. Turkish name: **Yeşilköy.**

Santa Ana *n.* **1.** (*Spanish* 'santa 'ana). a city in NW El Salvador: the second largest city in the country; coffee-processing industry. Pop.: 137 879 (1985 est.). **2.** ('sæntə 'ænə). a city in SW California: commercial and processing centre of a rich agricultural region. Pop.: 203 713 (1980).

Santa Anna *or* **Santa Ana** (*Spanish* 'santa 'ana) *n.* **Antonio López de** (a'tonjo 'lopeθ de). ?1795–1876, Mexican general, revolutionary, and president (1833–36, 1841–?45, 1847–48, 1853–55). In 1836, he captured the Alamo in an attempt to crush the Texan Revolution but was then defeated at San Jacinto.

Santa Catalina ('sæntə ˌkætə'liːnə) *n.* an island in the Pacific, off the coast of SW California: part of Los Angeles county: resort. Area: 181 sq. km (70 sq. miles). Also called: **Catalina Island.**

Santa Catarina (*Portuguese* 'santə kətə'rinə) *n.* a state of S Brazil, on the Atlantic: consists chiefly of the Great Escarpment. Capital: Florianópolis. Pop.: 3 631 368 (1980). Area: 95 985 sq. km (37 060 sq. miles).

Santa Clara (*Spanish* 'santa 'klara) *n.* a city in W central Cuba: sugar and tobacco industries. Pop.: 178 300 (1986 est.).

Santa Claus ('sæntə ˌklɔːz) *n.* the legendary patron saint of children, commonly identified with Saint Nicholas, who brings presents to children on Christmas Eve. Often shortened to **Santa.** Also called: **Father Christmas.**

Santa Cruz ('sæntə 'kruːz; *Spanish* 'santa 'kruθ) *n.* **1.** a province of S Argentina, on the Atlantic: consists of a large part of Patagonia, with the forested foothills of the Andes in the west. Capital: Río Gallegos. Pop.: 114 941 (1980). Area: 243 940 sq. km (94 186 sq. miles). **2.** a city in

E Bolivia: the second largest town in Bolivia. Pop.: 441 717 (1985 est.). **3.** another name for **Saint Croix.**

Santa Cruz de Tenerife ('sæntə 'kruːz də ˌtɛnə'riːf; *Spanish* 'santa 'kruθ de tene'rife) *n.* a port and resort in the W Canary Islands, on NE Tenerife: oil refinery. Pop.: 185 899 (1981).

Santa Fe *n.* **1.** ('sæntə 'feɪ). a city in N central New Mexico, capital of the state: one of the oldest European settlements in North America, founded in 1610 as the capital of the Kingdom of New Mexico; developed trade with the U.S. by the Santa Fe Trail in the early 19th century. Pop.: 55 980 (1986 est.). **2.** (*Spanish* 'santa 'fe). an inland port in E Argentina, on the Salado River: University of the Littoral (1920). Pop.: 287 000 (1980). — **'Santa 'Fean** *adj., n.*

Santa Gertrudis ('sæntə gə'truːdɪs) *n.* one of a breed of red beef cattle developed in Texas.

Santa Isabel (*Spanish* 'santa isa'βɛl) *n.* the former name (until 1973) of **Malabo.**

Santa María *n.* **1.** (*Portuguese* 'səntə ma'ria) a city in S Brazil, in Rio Grande do Sul state. Pop.: 151 202 (1980). **2.** (*Spanish* 'santa ma'ria) an active volcano in SW Guatemala. Height: 3768 m (12 362 ft.).

Santa Marta (*Spanish* 'santa 'marta) *n.* a port in NW Colombia, on the Caribbean: the oldest city in Colombia, founded in 1525; terminus of the Atlantic railway from Bogotá (opened 1961). Pop.: 225 936 (1985).

Santa Maura ('santa 'maura) *n.* the Italian name for **Levkás.**

Santander (*Spanish* santan'dɛr) *n.* a port and resort in N Spain, on an inlet of the Bay of Biscay: noted for its prehistoric collection from nearby caves; shipyards and an oil refinery. Pop.: 179 694 (1981).

Santarém (*Portuguese* sentə'rəj) *n.* a port in N Brazil, in Pará state where the Tapajós River flows into the Amazon. Pop.: 101 534 (1980).

Santa Rosa de Copán (*Spanish* 'santa 'rɔsa de ko'pan) *n.* a village in W Honduras: noted for the ruined Mayan city of Copán, which lies to the west.

Santayana (ˌsæntɪ'ænə) *n.* **George.** 1863–1952, U.S. philosopher, poet, and critic, born in Spain. His works include *The Life of Reason* (1905–06) and *The Realms of Being* (1927–40).

Santee (sæn'tiː) *n.* a river in SE central South Carolina, formed by the union of the Congaree and Wateree Rivers: flows southeast to the Atlantic; part of the **Santee-Wateree-Catawba River System,** an inland waterway 866 km (538 miles) long. Length: 230 km (143 miles).

Santiago (ˌsæntɪ'ɑːgəʊ; *Spanish* san'tjaɣo) *n.* **1.** the capital of Chile, at the foot of the Andes: commercial and industrial centre; two universities. Pop.: 4 318 305 (1985 est.). Official name: **Santiago de Chile** (de 'tʃile). **2.** a city in the N Dominican Republic. Pop.: 285 000 (1983 est.). Official name: **Santiago de los Caballeros** (de los kaβa'ʎeros).

Santiago de Compostela (*Spanish* de kɔmpɔs'tela) *n.* a city in NW Spain: place of pilgrimage since the 9th century and the most visited (after Jerusalem and Rome) in the Middle Ages; cathedral built over the tomb of the apostle St. James. Pop.: 93 695 (1981). Latin name: **Campus Stellae** ('kæmpəs 'steliː).

Santiago de Cuba (*Spanish* de 'kuβa) *n.* a port in SE Cuba, on **Santiago Bay** (a large inlet of the Caribbean): capital of Cuba until 1589; university (1947); industrial centre. Pop.: 358 800 (1986 est.).

Santiago del Estero (*Spanish* del es'tero) *n.* a city in N Argentina: the oldest continuous settlement in Argentina, founded in 1553 by Spaniards from Peru. Pop.: 148 000 (1980).

Santo Domingo ('sæntəʊ də'mɪŋgəʊ; *Spanish* 'santo ðo'mingo) *n.* **1.** the capital and chief port of the Dominican Republic, on the S coast: the oldest continuous European settlement in the Americas, founded in 1496; university (1538). Pop. (capital district): 1 410 000 (1983 est.). Former name (1936–61): **Ciudad Trujillo. 2.** the former name (until 1844) of the **Dominican Republic. 3.** another name (esp. in colonial times) for **Hispaniola.**

santonica (sæn'tɒnɪkə) *n.* **1.** an oriental wormwood plant. **2.** the dried flower heads of this plant, formerly used as a vermifuge. ~Also called: **wormseed.** [C17: NL, from LL *herba santonica* herb of the *Santones* (prob. wormwood), from *Santonī* a people of Aquitania]

santonin ('sæntənɪn) *n.* a white crystalline soluble substance extracted from the dried flower heads of santonica

and used in medicine as an anthelmintic. [C19: from SANTONICA + -IN]

Santos (*Portuguese* 'sɒntuʃ) *n.* a port in S Brazil, in São Paulo state: the world's leading coffee port. Pop.: 461 096 (1985).

Santos-Dumont (*French* sãtodymɔ̃) *n.* **Alberto** (albɛrto). 1873–1932, Brazilian aeronaut, living in France. He constructed dirigibles and aircraft, including a monoplane (1909).

São Francisco (*Portuguese* səu frə'sisku) *n.* a river in E Brazil, rising in SW Minas Gerais state and flowing northeast, then southeast to the Atlantic northeast of Aracajú. Length: 3200 km (1990 miles).

São Luís (*Portuguese* səu 'lwis) or **São Luíz** ('lwiʃ) *n.* a port in NE Brazil, capital of Maranhão state, on the W coast of São Luís Island: founded in 1612 by the French and taken by the Portuguese in 1615. Pop.: 182 466 (1980).

São Miguel (*Portuguese* səu mi'ɣɛl) *n.* an island in the E Azores: the largest of the group. Pop.: 159 000 (1970). Area: 854 sq. km (333 sq. miles).

Saône (*French* son) *n.* a river in E France, rising in Lorraine and flowing generally south to join the Rhône at Lyon, as its chief tributary: canalized for 375 km (233 miles) above Lyon; linked by canals with the Rhine, Marne, Seine, and Loire Rivers. Length: 480 km (298 miles).

Saône-et-Loire (*French* sonelwar) *n.* a department of central France, in Burgundy region. Capital: Mâcon. Pop.: 571 852 (1982). Area: 8627 sq. km (3365 sq. miles).

São Paulo (*Portuguese* səum 'paulu) *n.* **1.** a state of SE Brazil: consists chiefly of tableland draining west into the Paraná River. Capital: São Paulo. Pop.: 25 036 171 (1980). Area: 247 239 sq. km (95 459 sq. miles). **2.** a city in S Brazil, capital of São Paulo state: the largest city and industrial centre in Brazil, with one of the busiest airports in the world; three universities; rapidly expanding population. Pop.: 25 000 (1874); 2 017 025 (1950); 10 099 086 (1985).

Saorstat Eireann ('sɛəstɑːt 'ɛərən) *n.* the Gaelic name for the **Irish Free State.**

São Salvador (*Portuguese* səu salva'dor) *n.* short for **São Salvador da Bahia de Todos os Santos,** the official name for **Salvador.**

São Tomé e Principe (*Portuguese* səun tu'mɛ 'ɛ: 'prĩsipə) *n.* a republic in the Gulf of Guinea, off the W coast of Africa, on the Equator: consists of the islands of Principe and São Tomé; colonized by the Portuguese in the late 15th century; became independent in 1975. Capital: São Tomé. Pop.: 113 000 (1987 UN est.). Area: 964 sq. km (372 sq. miles).

sap[1] (sæp) *n.* **1.** a solution of mineral salts, sugars, etc., that circulates in a plant. **2.** any vital body fluid. **3.** energy; vigour. **4.** *Sl.* a gullible person. **5.** another name for **sapwood.** ~*vb.* **sapping, sapped.** (*tr.*) **6.** to drain of sap. [OE *sæp*]

sap[2] (sæp) *n.* **1.** a deep and narrow trench used to approach or undermine an enemy position. ~*vb.* **sapping, sapped. 2.** to undermine (a fortification, etc.) by digging saps. **3.** (*tr.*) to weaken. [C16 *zappe*, from It. *zappa* spade, from ?]

sapele (sə'piːlɪ) *n.* **1.** any of various W African trees yielding a hard timber resembling mahogany. **2.** the timber of such a tree, used to make furniture. [C20: West African name]

sapid ('sæpɪd) *adj.* **1.** having a pleasant taste. **2.** agreeable or engaging. [C17: from L *sapidus*, from *sapere* to taste] —**sapidity** (sə'pɪdɪtɪ) *n.*

sapient ('seɪpɪənt) *adj. Often used ironically.* wise or sagacious. [C15: from L *sapere* to taste] —**'sapience** *n.* —**'sapiently** *adv.*

sapiential (ˌseɪpɪ'ɛnʃəl) *adj.* showing, having, or providing wisdom.

Sapir (sə'pɪə, 'seɪˌpɪə) *n.* **Edward.** 1884–1939, U.S. anthropologist and linguist, noted for his study of the ethnology and languages of North American Indians.

sapling ('sæplɪŋ) *n.* **1.** a young tree. **2.** *Literary.* a youth.

sapodilla (ˌsæpə'dɪlə) *n.* **1.** a large tropical American evergreen tree, the latex of which yields chicle. **2.** Also called: **sapodilla plum.** the edible brown rough-skinned fruit of this tree. [C17: from Sp. *zapotillo*, dim. of *zapote* sapodilla fruit, from Nahuatl *tsapotl*]

saponaceous (ˌsæpəʊˈneɪʃəs) *adj.* resembling soap. [C18: from NL, from L *sāpō* soap]

saponify (səˈpɒnɪˌfaɪ) *vb.* **-fying, -fied.** *Chem.* **1.** to undergo or cause to undergo a process in which a fat is converted into a soap by treatment with alkali. **2.** to undergo or cause to undergo a reaction in which an ester is hydrolysed to an acid and an alcohol as a result of treatment with an alkali. [C19: from F *saponifier*, from L *sāpō* soap] —**sa,ponifiˈcation** *n.*

saponin (ˈsæpənɪn) *n.* any of a group of plant glycosides with a steroid structure that foam when shaken and are used in detergents. [C19: from F *saponine*, from L *sāpō* soap]

sappanwood *or* **sapanwood** (ˈsæpənˌwʊd) *n.* **1.** a small tree of S Asia producing wood that yields a red dye. **2.** the wood of this tree. [C16: *sapan*, via Du. from Malay *sapang*]

sapper (ˈsæpə) *n.* **1.** a soldier who digs trenches, etc. **2.** (in the British Army) a private of the Royal Engineers.

Sapphic (ˈsæfɪk) *adj.* **1.** *Prosody.* denoting a metre associated with Sappho. **2.** of or relating to Sappho or her poetry. **3.** lesbian. ~*n.* **4.** *Prosody.* a verse, line, or stanza written in the Sapphic form of classical lyric poetry.

Sapphira (sæˈfaɪrə) *n. New Testament.* the wife of Ananias, who together with her husband was struck dead for fraudulently concealing their wealth from the Church (Acts 5).

sapphire (ˈsæfaɪə) *n.* **1. a.** any precious corundum gemstone that is not red, esp. the highly valued transparent blue variety. **b.** (*as modifier*): *a sapphire ring.* **2. a.** the blue colour of sapphire. **b.** (*as adj.*): *sapphire eyes.* **3.** (*modifier*) denoting a forty-fifth anniversary: *our sapphire wedding.* [C13 *safir*, from OF, from L *sapphirus*, from Gk *sappheiros*, ?from Sansk. *śanipriya*, lit.: beloved of the planet Saturn]

Sappho (ˈsæfəʊ) *n.* 6th century B.C., Greek lyric poetess of Lesbos.

Sapporo (ˈsɑːpəʊˌrəʊ) *n.* a city in N Japan, on W Hokkaido: commercial centre; university (1918). Pop.: 1 543 000 (1985).

sappy (ˈsæpɪ) *adj.* **-pier, -piest. 1.** (of plants) full of sap. **2.** full of energy or vitality.

sapro- *or before a vowel* **sapr-** *combining form.* indicating dead or decaying matter: *saprogenic.* [from Gk *sapros* rotten]

saprogenic (ˌsæprəʊˈdʒɛnɪk) *or* **saprogenous** (sæˈprɒdʒɪnəs) *adj.* **1.** producing or resulting from decay. **2.** growing on decaying matter.

saprophyte (ˈsæprəʊˌfaɪt) *n.* any plant, esp. a fungus, that lives and feeds on dead organic matter. —**saprophytic** (ˌsæprəʊˈfɪtɪk) *adj.*

saprozoic (ˌsæprəʊˈzəʊɪk) *adj.* (of animals or plants) feeding on dead organic matter.

sapsucker (ˈsæpˌsʌkə) *n.* either of two North American woodpeckers that have white wing patches and feed on the sap from trees.

sapwood (ˈsæpˌwʊd) *n.* the soft wood, just beneath the bark in tree trunks, that consists of living tissue.

saraband *or* **sarabande** (ˈsærəˌbænd) *n.* **1.** a decorous 17th-century courtly dance. **2.** a piece of music composed for or in the rhythm of this dance, in slow triple time. [C17: from F *sarabande*, from Sp. *zarabanda*, from ?]

Saracen (ˈsærəsᵊn) *n.* **1.** *History.* a member of one of the nomadic Arabic tribes, esp. of the Syrian desert. **2. a.** a Muslim, esp. one who opposed the crusades. **b.** (in later use) any Arab. ~*adj.* **3.** of or relating to Arabs of either of these periods, regions, or types. [C13: from OF *Sarrazin*, from LL *Saracēnus*, from LGk *Sarakēnos*, ?from Ar. *sharq* sunrise] —**Saracenic** (ˌsærəˈsɛnɪk) *adj.*

Saragossa (ˌsærəˈgɒsə) *n.* the English name for **Zaragoza.**

Sarah (ˈsɛərə) *n. Old Testament.* the wife of Abraham and mother of Isaac (Genesis 17:15–22).

Sarajevo (*Serbo-Croatian* ˈsarajɛvɔ) *or* **Serajevo** *n.* a city in central Yugoslavia, capital of Bosnia and Herzegovina: developed as a Turkish town in the 15th century; capital of the Turkish and Austro-Hungarian administrations in 1850 and 1878 respectively; scene of the assassination of Archduke Francis Ferdinand in 1914, precipitating World War I. Pop.: 448 500 (1982).

Saransk (*Russian* saˈransk) *n.* a city in the W central Soviet Union, capital of the Mordovian ASSR: university (1957). Pop.: 323 000 (1987).

Saratov (*Russian* saˈratəf) *n.* an industrial city in the W Soviet Union, on the River Volga: university (1919). Pop.: 918 000 (1987).

Sarawak (səˈrɑːwək) *n.* a state of Malaysia, on the NW coast of Borneo on the South China Sea: granted to Sir James Brooke by the Sultan of Brunei in 1841 as a reward for helping quell a revolt; mainly agricultural. Capital: Kuching. Pop.: 1 477 428 (1985 est.). Area: about 121 400 sq. km (48 250 sq. miles).

sarcasm (ˈsɑːkæzəm) *n.* **1.** mocking or ironic language intended to convey scorn or insult. **2.** the use or tone of such language. [C16: from LL *sarcasmus*, from Gk, from *sarkazein* to rend the flesh, from *sarx* flesh]

sarcastic (sɑːˈkæstɪk) *adj.* **1.** characterized by sarcasm. **2.** given to the use of sarcasm. —**sarˈcastically** *adv.*

sarcenet *or* **sarsenet** (ˈsɑːsnɪt) *n.* a fine soft silk fabric used for clothing, ribbons, etc. [C15: from OF *sarzinet*, from *Sarrazin* SARACEN]

sarco- *or before a vowel* **sarc-** *combining form.* indicating flesh: *sarcoma.* [from Gk *sark-, sarx* flesh]

sarcocarp (ˈsɑːkəʊˌkɑːp) *n. Bot.* the fleshy mesocarp of such fruits as the peach or plum.

sarcoma (sɑːˈkəʊmə) *n., pl.* **-mata** (-mətə) *or* **-mas.** *Pathol.* a usually malignant tumour arising from connective tissue. [C17: via NL from Gk *sarkōma* fleshy growth] —**sarˈcomatous** *adj.*

sarcomatosis (sɑːˌkəʊməˈtəʊsɪs) *n. Pathol.* a condition characterized by the development of several sarcomas at various bodily sites. [C19: see SARCOMA, -OSIS]

sarcophagus (sɑːˈkɒfəgəs) *n., pl.* **-gi** (-ˌgaɪ) *or* **-guses.** a stone or marble coffin or tomb, esp. one bearing sculpture or inscriptions. [C17: via L from Gk *sarkophagos* flesh-devouring; from the type of stone used, which was believed to destroy the flesh of corpses]

sarcous (ˈsɑːkəs) *adj.* (of tissue) muscular or fleshy. [C19: from Gk *sarx* flesh]

sard (sɑːd) *or* **sardius** (ˈsɑːdɪəs) *n.* a red or brown variety of chalcedony. [C14: from L *sarda*, from Gk *sardios* stone from Sardis]

Sardanapalus (ˌsɑːdəˈnæpələs) *n.* the Greek name for **Ashurbanipal.**

sardar *or* **sirdar** (səˈdɑː) *n.* (in India) **1.** a title used before the name of Sikh men. **2.** a leader. [Hindi, from Persian]

Sardegna (sarˈdeɲɲa) *n.* the Italian name for **Sardinia.**

sardine[1] (sɑːˈdiːn) *n., pl.* **-dine** *or* **-dines. 1.** any of various small food fishes of the herring family, esp. a young pilchard. **2. like sardines.** very closely crowded together. [C15: via OF from L *sardina*, dim. of *sarda* a fish suitable for pickling]

sardine[2] (ˈsɑːdiːn) *n.* another name for **sard.** [C14: from LL *sardinus*, from Gk *sardinos lithos* Sardian stone, from *Sardeis* Sardis]

Sardinia (sɑːˈdɪnɪə) *n.* the second largest island in the Mediterranean: forms, with offshore islands, an administrative region of Italy; ceded to Savoy by Austria in 1720 in exchange for Sicily and formed the Kingdom of Sardinia with Piedmont; became part of Italy in 1861. Capital: Cagliari. Pop.: 1 643 789 (1985 est.). Area: 24 089 sq. km (9301 sq. miles). Italian name: **Sardegna.**

Sardinian (sɑːˈdɪnɪən) *adj.* **1.** of or relating to Sardinia, its inhabitants, or their language. ~*n.* **2.** a native or inhabitant of Sardinia. **3.** the spoken language of Sardinia, sometimes regarded as a dialect of Italian but containing many loan words from Spanish.

Sardis (ˈsɑːdɪs) *or* **Sardes** (ˈsɑːdiːz) *n.* an ancient city of W Asia Minor: capital of Lydia.

sardonic (sɑːˈdɒnɪk) *adj.* characterized by irony, mockery, or derision. [C17: from F, from L, from Gk *sardonios* derisive, lit.: of Sardinia, alteration of Homeric *sardanios* scornful (laughter or smile)] —**sarˈdonically** *adv.*

sardonyx (ˈsɑːdənɪks) *n.* a variety of chalcedony with alternating reddish-brown and white parallel bands. [C14: via L from Gk *sardonux*, ?from *sardion* SARD + *onux* nail]

Sardou (*French* sardu) *n.* **Victorien** (viktɔrjɛ̃). 1831–1908, French dramatist. His plays include *Fédora* (1882) and *La Tosca* (1887), the source of Puccini's opera.

Sargasso Sea *n.* a calm area of the N Atlantic, between the West Indies and the Azores, where there is an abundance of floating seaweed of the genus *Sargassum.*

sargassum (sɑːˈɡæsəm) *n.* a floating brown seaweed having ribbon-like fronds containing air sacs, esp. abundant in the Sargasso Sea. [C16: from Port. *sargaço* from ?]

sarge (sɑːdʒ) *n. Inf.* sergeant.

Sargent (ˈsɑːdʒənt) *n.* **1.** Sir (**Harold**) **Malcolm** (**Watts**). 1895–1967, English conductor. **2. John Singer.** 1856–1925, U.S. painter, esp. of society portraits; in London from 1885.

Sargeson (ˈsɑːdʒəsən) *n.* **Frank.** 1903–82, New Zealand short-story writer and novelist. His work includes the short-story collection *That Summer and Other Stories* (1946) and the novel *I Saw in my Dream* (1949).

Sargodha (sɑːˈɡəʊdə) *n.* a city in NE Pakistan: grain market. Pop.: 294 000 (1981 est.).

Sargon II (ˈsɑːɡɒn) *n.* died 705 B.C., king of Assyria (722–705). He developed a policy of transporting conquered peoples to distant parts of his empire.

sari *or* **saree** (ˈsɑːrɪ) *n., pl.* **-ris** *or* **-rees.** the traditional dress of women of India, Pakistan, etc., consisting of a very long piece of cloth swathed around the body. [C18: from Hindi *sārī,* from Sansk. *śātī*]

Sark (sɑːk) *n.* an island in the English Channel in the Channel Islands, consisting of **Great Sark** and **Little Sark,** connected by an isthmus: ruled by a hereditary seigneur or dame. Pop.: 560 (1981). Area: 5 sq. km (2 sq. miles). French name: **Sercq.**

Sarka (ˈzɑːkə) *n.* a variant spelling of **Zarga.**

sarking (ˈsɑːkɪŋ) *n. Scot., northern English, & N.Z.* flat planking supporting the roof cladding of a building. [C15 in England: from Scot. *sark* shirt]

sarky (ˈsɑːkɪ) *adj.* **-kier, -kiest.** *Brit. inf.* sarcastic.

Sarmatia (sɑːˈmeɪʃɪə) *n.* the ancient name of a region of present-day Poland and the SW Soviet Union, between the Volga and Vistula Rivers. —**Sarˈmatian** *n., adj.* —**Sarmatic** (sɑːˈmætɪk) *adj.*

sarmentose (sɑːˈmɛntəʊs) *or* **sarmentous** (sɑːˈmɛntəs) *adj.* (of plants such as the strawberry) having stems in the form of runners. [C18: from L *sarmentōsus* full of twigs, from *sarmentum* brushwood, from *sarpere* to prune]

Sarnen (*German* ˈzarnən) *n.* a town in central Switzerland, capital of Obwalden demicanton: resort. Pop.: 7200 (1980).

Sarnia (ˈsɑːnɪə) *n.* an inland port in S central Canada, in SW Ontario at the S end of Lake Huron: oil refineries. Pop.: 50 892 (1981).

sarnie (ˈsɑːnɪ) *n. Brit. inf.* a sandwich. [C20: prob. from N or dialect pronunciation of first syllable of *sandwich*]

sarod (sæˈrəʊd) *n.* an Indian stringed musical instrument that may be played with a bow or plucked. [C19: from Hindi]

sarong (səˈrɒŋ) *n.* a skirtlike garment worn by men and women in the Malay Archipelago, Sri Lanka, etc. [C19: from Malay, lit.: sheath]

Saronic Gulf (səˈrɒnɪk) *n.* an inlet of the Aegean on the SE coast of Greece. Length: about 80 km (50 miles). Width: about 48 km (30 miles). Also called: (**Gulf of**) **Aegina.**

saros (ˈseɪrɒs) *n.* a cycle of about 18 years 11 days (6585.32 days) in which eclipses of the sun and moon occur in the same sequence. [C19: from Gk, from Babylonian *šāru* 3600 (years); modern use apparently based on mistaken interpretation of *šāru* as a period of 18½ years]

Saros (ˈsɑːrɒs) *n.* **Gulf of.** an inlet of the Aegean in NW Turkey, north of the Gallipoli Peninsula. Length: 59 km (37 miles). Width: 35 km (22 miles).

Sarpedon (sɑːˈpiːdɒn) *n. Greek myth.* a son of Zeus and Laodameia, or perhaps Europa, and king of Lycia. He was slain by Patroclus while fighting on behalf of the Trojans.

Sarraute (*French* sarot) *n.* **Nathalie** (natali). born 1902, French novelist, noted as an exponent of the anti-novel. Her novels include *Portrait of a Man Unknown* (1947) and *Martereau* (1954).

Sarre (sar) *n.* the French name for the **Saar.**

sarrusophone (səˈruːzəˌfəʊn) *n.* a wind instrument resembling the oboe but made of brass. [C19: after *Sarrus,* F bandmaster, who invented it (1856)]

sarsaparilla (ˌsɑːsəpəˈrɪlə) *n.* **1.** any of a genus of tropical American prickly climbing plants having large aromatic roots and heart-shaped leaves. **2.** the dried roots of any of these plants, formerly used in medicine to treat

psoriasis, etc. **3.** a nonalcoholic drink prepared from these roots. [C16: from Sp. *sarzaparrilla,* from *zarza* a bramble + *-parrilla,* from *parra* a climbing plant]

sarsen (ˈsɑːsᵊn) *n.* **1.** *Geol.* a boulder of silicified sandstone, probably of Tertiary age. **2.** such a stone used in a megalithic monument. [C17: prob. a var. of SARACEN]

sarsenet (ˈsɑːsnɪt) *n.* a variant spelling of **sarcenet.**

Sarthe (*French* sart) *n.* a department of NW France, in Pays de la Loire region. Capital: Le Mans. Pop.: 504 768 (1982). Area: 6245 sq. km (2436 sq. miles).

Sarto (*Italian* ˈsarto) *n.* **Andrea del** (anˈdrɛːa del). 1486–1531, Florentine painter. His works include *The Nativity of the Virgin* (1514) in the church of Sant' Annunziata, Florence.

sartorial (sɑːˈtɔːrɪəl) *adj.* **1.** of or relating to a tailor or to tailoring. **2.** *Anat.* of the sartorius. [C19: from LL *sartōrius* from L *sartor* a patcher, from *sarcīre* to patch] —**sarˈtorially** *adv.*

sartorius (sɑːˈtɔːrɪəs) *n., pl.* **-torii** (-ˈtɔːrɪˌaɪ). *Anat.* a long ribbon-shaped muscle that aids in flexing the knee. [C18: NL, from *sartorius musculus,* lit.: tailor's muscle, because it is used when one sits in the cross-legged position in which tailors traditionally sat while sewing]

Sartre (*French* sartrə) *n.* **Jean-Paul** (ʒɑ̃pɔl). 1905–80, French philosopher, novelist, and dramatist; chief French exponent of atheistic existentialism. His works include the philosophical essay *Being and Nothingness* (1943), the novels *Nausea* (1938) and *Les Chemins de la liberté* (1945–49), a trilogy, and the plays *Les Mouches* (1943), *Huis clos* (1944), and *Les Mains sales* (1948).

Sarum (ˈsɛərəm) *n.* the ancient name of **Salisbury**¹(sense 3).

Sarum use *n.* the distinctive local rite or system of rites used at Salisbury cathedral in late medieval times.

SAS *abbrev. for* Special Air Service.

Sasebo (ˈsɑːsəˌbəʊ) *n.* a port in SW Japan, on NW Kyushu on Omura Bay: naval base. Pop.: 251 000 (1985).

sash¹ (sæʃ) *n.* a long piece of ribbon, etc., worn around the waist or over one shoulder, as a symbol of rank. [C16: from Ar. *shāsh* muslin]

sash² (sæʃ) *n.* **1.** a frame that contains the panes of a window or door. **2.** a complete frame together with panes of glass. ~*vb.* **3.** (*tr.*) to furnish with a sash, sashes, or sash windows. [C17: orig. pl. *sashes,* var. of *shashes,* from CHASSIS]

sashay (sæˈʃeɪ) *vb.* (*intr.*) *Inf., chiefly U.S. & Canad.* **1.** to move, walk, or glide along casually. **2.** to move or walk in a showy way; parade. [C19: from an alteration of *chassé,* a gliding dance step]

sash cord *n.* a strong cord connecting a sash weight to a sliding sash.

sashimi (ˈsæʃɪmɪ) *n.* a Japanese dish of thin fillets of raw fish. [C19: from Japanese *sashi* pierce + *mi* flesh]

sash weight *n.* a weight used to counterbalance the weight of a sliding sash in a sash window and thus hold it in position at any height.

sash window *n.* a window consisting of two sashes placed one above the other so that they can be slid past each other.

Saskatchewan (sæsˈkætʃɪwən) *n.* **1.** a province of W Canada: consists of Canadian Shield in the north and open prairie in the south; economy based chiefly on agriculture and mineral resources. Capital: Regina. Pop.: 1 009 613 (1986). Area: 651 900 sq. km (251 700 sq. miles). Abbrevs.: **Sask., SK. 2.** a river in W Canada, formed by the confluence of the North and South Saskatchewan Rivers: flows east to Lake Winnipeg. Length: 596 km (370 miles). —**Saskatchewanian** (sæsˌkætʃəˈwɒnɪən) *n., adj.*

Saskatoon (ˌsæskəˈtuːn) *n.* a city in W Canada, in S Saskatchewan on the South Saskatchewan River: oil refining; university (1907). Pop.: 177 641 (1986).

sasquatch (ˈsæsˌkwætʃ) *n.* (in Canadian folklore) in British Columbia, a hairy beast or manlike monster said to leave huge footprints. [from Amerind]

sass (sæs) *U.S. & Canad. inf.* ~*n.* **1.** impudent talk or behaviour. ~*vb.* (*intr.*) **2.** to talk or answer back in such a way. [C20: back formation from SASSY]

sassaby (ˈsæsəbɪ) *n., pl.* **-bies.** an African antelope of grasslands and semideserts, having angular curved horns. [C19: from Bantu *tshêsêbê*]

sassafras (ˈsæsəˌfræs) *n.* **1.** an aromatic deciduous tree of North America, having three-lobed leaves and dark blue fruits. **2.** the aromatic dried root bark of this tree, used as a flavouring, and yielding **sassafras oil**. **3.** *Austral.* any of several unrelated trees having a similar fragrant bark. [C16: from Sp. *sasafras*, from ?]

Sassari (*Italian* 'sassari) *n.* a city in NW Sardinia, Italy: the second largest city on the island; university (1565). Pop.: 120 152 (1986).

Sassenach ('sæsə,næx) *n. Scot. & occasionally Irish.* an English person or Lowland Scot. [C18: from Gaelic *Sassunach*, from LL *saxonēs* Saxons]

Sassoon (sæ'su:n) *n.* **Siegfried (Lorraine)**. 1886–1967, English poet and novelist, best known for his poems of the horrors of war collected in *Counterattack* (1918) and *Satirical Poems* (1926). He also wrote a semi-fictitious autobiographical trilogy *The Memoirs of George Sherston* (1928–36).

sassy ('sæsɪ) *adj.* **-sier, -siest.** *U.S. & Canad. inf.* insolent; impertinent. [C19: var. of SAUCY] —'**sassily** *adv.* —'**sassiness** *n.*

sat (sæt) *vb.* the past tense and past participle of **sit**.

Sat. *abbrev. for:* **1.** Saturday. **2.** Saturn.

Satan ('seɪt³n) *n.* the devil, adversary of God, and tempter of mankind: sometimes identified with Lucifer (Luke 4:5–8). [C16: from LL, from Gk, from Heb.: plotter, from *sātan* to plot against]

satanic (sə'tænɪk) *adj.* **1.** of or relating to Satan. **2.** supremely evil or wicked. —**sa'tanically** *adv.*

Satanism ('seɪt³,nɪzəm) *n.* **1.** the worship of Satan. **2.** a form of such worship which includes blasphemous parodies of Christian prayers, etc. **3.** a satanic disposition. —'**Satanist** *n., adj.*

SATB *abbrev. for* soprano, alto, tenor, bass: a combination of voices in choral music.

satchel ('sætʃəl) *n.* a rectangular bag, usually made of leather or cloth and provided with a shoulder strap, used for carrying school books. [C14: from OF *sachel*, from LL *saccellus*, from L *saccus* SACK¹] —'**satchelled** *adj.*

sate¹ (seɪt) *vb.* (*tr.*) **1.** to satisfy (a desire or appetite) fully. **2.** to supply beyond capacity or desire. [OE *sadian*]

sate² (sæt, seɪt) *vb. Arch.* a past tense and past participle of **sit**.

sateen (sæ'ti:n) *n.* a glossy linen or cotton fabric that resembles satin. [C19: changed from SATIN, on the model of VELVETEEN]

satellite ('sæt³,laɪt) *n.* **1.** a celestial body orbiting around a planet or star: *the earth is a satellite of the sun.* **2.** a man-made device orbiting around the earth, moon, or another planet transmitting to earth scientific information or used for communication. **3.** a country or political unit under the domination of a foreign power. **4.** a subordinate area that is dependent upon a larger adjacent town. **5.** (*modifier*) dependent upon another: *a satellite nation.* **6.** (*modifier*) of, used in, or relating to the transmission of television signals from a satellite to the house: *a satellite dish aerial.* [C16: from L *satelles* an attendant, prob. of Etruscan origin]

satiable ('seɪʃɪəb³l) *adj.* capable of being satiated. —**satia'bility** *n.* —'**satiably** *adv.*

satiate ('seɪʃɪ,eɪt) *vb.* (*tr.*) **1.** to fill or supply beyond capacity or desire. **2.** to supply to capacity. [C16: from L *satiāre* to satisfy, from *satis* enough] —**,sati'ation** *n.*

Satie (*French* sati) *n.* **Erik (Alfred Leslie)** (erik). 1866–1925, French composer, noted for his eccentricity, experimentalism, and his direct and economical style. His music, including numerous piano pieces and several ballets, exercised a profound influence upon other composers, such as Debussy and Ravel.

satiety (sə'taɪɪtɪ) *n.* the state of being satiated. [C16: from L *satietās*, from *satis* enough]

satin ('sætɪn) *n.* **1.** a fabric of silk, rayon, etc., closely woven to show much of the warp, giving a smooth glossy appearance. **2.** (*modifier*) like satin in texture: *a satin finish.* [C14: via OF from Ar. *zaitūnī*, Ar. rendering of Chinese *Tseutung* (now *Tsinkiang*), port from which the cloth was prob. first exported] —'**satiny** *adj.*

satinet *or* **satinette** (,sætɪ'nɛt) *n.* a thin satin or satin-like fabric. [C18: from F: small satin]

satinflower ('sætɪn,flaʊə) *n.* another name for **greater stitchwort** (see **stitchwort**).

satinwood ('sætɪn,wʊd) *n.* **1.** a tree that occurs in the East Indies and has hard wood with a satiny texture. **2.** the wood of this tree, used in veneering, marquetry, etc.

satire ('sætaɪə) *n.* **1.** a novel, play, etc., in which topical issues, folly, or evil are held up to scorn by means of ridicule. **2.** the genre constituted by such works. **3.** the use of ridicule, irony, etc., to create such an effect. [C16: from L *satira* a mixture, from *satur* sated, from *satis* enough]

satirical (sə'tɪrɪk³l) *or* **satiric** *adj.* **1.** of, relating to, or containing satire. **2.** given to the use of satire. —**sa'tirically** *adv.*

satirist ('sætərɪst) *n.* **1.** a person who writes satire. **2.** a person given to the use of satire.

satirize *or* **-rise** ('sætə,raɪz) *vb.* to deride (a person or thing) by means of satire. —,**satiri'zation** *or* **-ri'sation** *n.*

satisfaction (,sætɪs'fækʃən) *n.* **1.** the act of satisfying or state of being satisfied. **2.** the fulfilment of a desire. **3.** the pleasure obtained from such fulfilment. **4.** a source of fulfilment. **5.** compensation for a wrong done or received. **6.** *R.C. Church, Church of England.* the performance of a penance. **7.** *Christianity.* the atonement for sin by the death of Christ.

satisfactory (,sætɪs'fæktərɪ) *adj.* **1.** adequate or suitable; acceptable. **2.** giving satisfaction. **3.** constituting or involving atonement or expiation for sin. —,**satis'factorily** *adv.*

satisfy ('sætɪs,faɪ) *vb.* **-fying, -fied.** (*mainly tr.*) **1.** (*also intr.*) to fulfil the desires or needs of (a person). **2.** to provide amply for (a need or desire). **3.** to convince. **4.** to dispel (a doubt). **5.** to make reparation to or for. **6.** to discharge or pay off (a debt) to (a creditor). **7.** to fulfil the requirements of; comply with: *you must satisfy the terms of your lease.* **8.** *Maths, logic.* to fulfil the conditions of (a theorem, assumption, etc.); to yield a truth by substitution of the given value. [C15: from OF *satisfier*, from L *satisfacere*, from *satis* enough + *facere* to make] —'**satis,fiable** *adj.* —'**satis,fying** *adj.* —'**satis,fyingly** *adv.*

satori (sə'tɔːrɪ) *n. Zen Buddhism.* a state of sudden intuitive enlightenment. [from Japanese]

satrap ('sætrəp) *n.* **1.** (in ancient Persia) a provincial governor. **2.** a subordinate ruler. [C14: from L *satrapa*, from Gk *satrapēs*, from OPersian *khshathrapāvan*, lit.: protector of the land]

satrapy ('sætrəpɪ) *n., pl.* **-trapies.** the province, office, or period of rule of a satrap.

satsuma (sæt'su:mə) *n.* **1.** a small citrus tree cultivated, esp. in Japan, for its edible fruit. **2.** the fruit of this tree, which has easily separable segments. [from SATSUMA]

Satsuma ('sætsʊ,ma:) *n.* a former province of SW Japan, on S Kyushu: famous for its porcelain.

saturable ('sætʃərəb³l) *adj. Chem.* capable of being saturated. —,**satura'bility** *n.*

saturate *vb.* ('sætʃə,reɪt). **1.** to fill, soak, or imbue totally. **2.** to make (a chemical compound, solution, etc.) saturated or (of a compound, etc.) to become saturated. **3.** (*tr.*) *Mil.* to bomb or shell heavily. ~*adj.* ('sætʃərɪt, -,reɪt). **4.** saturated. [C16: from L *saturāre*, from *satur* sated, from *satis* enough]

saturated ('sætʃə,reɪtɪd) *adj.* **1.** (of a solution or solvent) containing the maximum amount of solute that can normally be dissolved at a given temperature and pressure. **2.** (of a chemical compound) containing no multiple bonds: *a saturated hydrocarbon.* **3.** (of a fat) containing a high proportion of fatty acids having single bonds. **4.** (of a vapour) containing the maximum amount of gaseous material at a given temperature and pressure.

saturation (,sætʃə'reɪʃən) *n.* **1.** the act of saturating or the state of being saturated. **2.** *Chem.* the state of a chemical compound, solution, or vapour when it is saturated. **3.** *Meteorol.* the state of the atmosphere when it can hold no more water vapour at its particular temperature and pressure. **4.** the attribute of a colour that enables an observer to judge its proportion of pure chromatic colour. **5.** the level beyond which demand for a product or service is not expected to rise. ~*modifier.* **6.** denoting the maximum possible intensity of coverage of an area: *saturation bombing.*

saturation point *n.* the point at which no more can be absorbed, accommodated, used, etc.

Saturday ('sætədɪ) *n.* the seventh and last day of the week: the Jewish Sabbath. [OE *sæternes dæg*, translation of L *Saturnī diēs* day of Saturn]

Saturn¹ ('sætɜːn) *n.* the Roman god of agriculture and vegetation.

Saturn[2] ('sætɜːn) *n.* **1.** the sixth planet from the sun, around which revolve planar concentric rings (**Saturn's rings**) consisting of small frozen particles. **2.** the alchemical name for lead[2]. —**Saturnian** (sæ'tɜːnɪən) *adj.*

Saturnalia (ˌsætə'neɪlɪə) *n., pl.* **-lia** *or* **-lias. 1.** an ancient Roman festival celebrated in December: renowned for its general merrymaking. **2.** (*sometimes not cap.*) a period or occasion of wild revelry. [C16: from L *Sāturnālis* relating to SATURN[1]] —ˌSatur'nalian *adj.*

saturnine ('sætəˌnaɪn) *adj.* **1.** having a gloomy temperament. **2.** *Arch.* **a.** of or relating to lead. **b.** having lead poisoning. [C15: from F *saturnin*, from Med. L *sāturnīnus* (unattested), from L *Sāturnus* Saturn, from the gloomy influence attributed to the planet Saturn] —ˈsaturˌninely *adv.*

satyagraha ('sʌtjɑːˌgrɑːhɑː) *n.* the policy of nonviolent resistance adopted by Mahatma Gandhi to oppose British rule in India. [via Hindi from Sansk., lit.: insistence on truth, from *satya* truth + *agraha* fervour]

satyr ('sætə) *n.* **1.** *Greek myth.* one of a class of sylvan deities, represented as goatlike men who drank and danced in the train of Dionysus and chased the nymphs. **2.** a man who has strong sexual desires. **3.** any of various butterflies, having dark wings often marked with eyespots. [C14: from L *satyrus*, from Gk *saturos*] —**satyric** (sə'tɪrɪk) *adj.*

satyriasis (ˌsætɪ'raɪəsɪs) *n.* a neurotic compulsion in men to have sexual intercourse with many women without being able to have lasting relationships with them. [C17: via NL from Gk *saturiasis*]

sauce (sɔːs) *n.* **1.** any liquid or semiliquid preparation eaten with food to enhance its flavour. **2.** anything that adds piquancy. **3.** *U.S. & Canad.* stewed fruit. **4.** *Inf.* impudent language or behaviour. ~*vb.* (*tr.*) **5.** to prepare (food) with sauce. **6.** to add zest to. **7.** *Inf.* to be saucy to. [C14: via OF from L *salsus* salted, from *sal* salt]

saucepan ('sɔːspən) *n.* a metal or enamel pan with a long handle and often a lid, used for cooking food.

saucer ('sɔːsə) *n.* **1.** a small round dish on which a cup is set. **2.** any similar dish. [C14: from OF *saussier* container for SAUCE] —ˈsaucerful *n.*

saucy ('sɔːsɪ) *adj.* **saucier, sauciest. 1.** impertinent. **2.** pert; jaunty: *a saucy hat.* —ˈsaucily *adv.* —ˈsauciness *n.*

Saud (saʊd) *n.* full name **Saud ibn Abdul-Aziz.** 1902–69, king of Saudi Arabia (1953–64); son of Ibn Saud. He was deposed by his brother Faisal.

Saudi Arabia ('sɔːdɪ, 'saʊ-) *n.* a kingdom in SW Asia, occupying most of the Arabian peninsula between the Persian Gulf and the Red Sea: founded in 1932 by Ibn Saud, who united Hejaz and Nejd; consists mostly of desert plateau; large reserves of petroleum and natural gas. Language: Arabic. Religion: Sunni Muslim. Currency: riyal. Capital: Riyadh (royal), Jidda (administrative). Pop.: 12 483 000 (1987). Area: 2 260 353 sq. km (872 722 sq. miles). —**Saudi** *or* **Saudi Arabian** *adj., n.*

sauerkraut ('saʊəˌkraʊt) *n.* finely shredded cabbage which has been fermented in brine. [G, from *sauer* sour + *Kraut* cabbage]

sauger ('sɔːgə) *n.* a small North American pikeperch with a spotted dorsal fin: valued as a food and game fish. [C19: from ?]

Saul (sɔːl) *n.* **1.** *Old Testament.* the first king of Israel (?1020–1000 B.C.). He led Israel successfully against the Philistines, but was in continual conflict with the high priest Samuel. He became afflicted with madness and died by his own hand; succeeded by David. **2.** *New Testament.* the name borne by Paul prior to his conversion (Acts 9: 1–30).

sault (suː) *n. Canad.* a waterfall or rapids. [C17: from Canad. F, from F *saut* a leap]

Sault Sainte Marie ('suː seɪnt mə'riː) *n., usually abbreviated to* **Sault Ste Marie. 1.** an inland port in central Canada, in Ontario on the St. Mary's River, which links Lake Superior and Lake Huron, opposite Sault Ste Marie, Michigan: canal by-passing the rapids completed in 1895. Pop.: 82 697 (1981). **2.** an inland port in NE Michigan, opposite Sault Ste. Marie, Ontario: canal around the rapids completed in 1855, enlarged and divided in 1896 and 1919 (popularly called **Soo Canals**). Pop.: 14 448 (1980).

sauna ('sɔːnə) *n.* **1.** an invigorating bath originating in Finland in which the bather is subjected to hot steam, usually followed by a cold plunge. **2.** the place in which such a bath is taken. [C20: from Finnish]

Saunders ('sɔːndəz) *n.* Dame **Cicely.** born 1918, British philanthropist: founded St Christopher's Hospice in 1967 for the care of the terminally ill, upon which the modern hospice movement is modelled. Her books include *Living with Dying* (1983).

saunter ('sɔːntə) *vb.* **1.** (*intr.*) to walk in a casual manner; stroll. ~*n.* **2.** a leisurely pace or stroll. [C17 (meaning: to wander aimlessly), C15 (to muse): from ?] —ˈsaunterer *n.*

-saur *or* **-saurus** *n. combining form.* lizard: dinosaur. [from NL *saurus*]

saurian ('sɔːrɪən) *adj.* **1.** of or resembling a lizard. ~*n.* **2.** a former name for **lizard.** [C15: from NL *Sauria*, from Gk *sauros*]

saury ('sɔːrɪ) *n., pl.* **-ries.** a fish of tropical and temperate seas, having an elongated body and long toothed jaws. Also called: **skipper.** [C18: ?from LL *saurus*, from ?]

sausage ('sɒsɪdʒ) *n.* **1.** finely minced meat, esp. pork or beef, mixed with fat, cereal, and seasonings (**sausage meat**), and packed into a tube-shaped edible casing. **2.** *Scot.* sausage meat. **3.** an object shaped like a sausage. **4. not a sausage.** nothing at all. [C15: from OF *saussiche*, from LL *salsicia*, from L *salsus* salted; see SAUCE]

sausage dog *n.* an informal name for **dachshund.**

sausage roll *n. Brit.* a roll of sausage meat in pastry.

Saussure (French sosyr) *n.* **Ferdinand de** (fɛrdinɑ̃ də). 1857–1913, Swiss linguist. He pioneered structuralism in linguistics and the separation of scientific language description from historical philological studies. —**Saus'surean** *adj., n.*

sauté ('səʊteɪ) *vb.* **-téing** *or* **téeing, -téed. 1.** to fry (food) quickly in a little fat. ~*n.* **2.** a dish of sautéed food, esp. meat that is browned and then cooked in a sauce. ~*adj.* **3.** sautéed until lightly brown: *sauté potatoes.* [C19: from F: tossed, from *sauter* to jump, from L, from *salire* to spring]

Sava ('sɑːvə) *or* **Save** (sɑːv) *n.* a river in N Yugoslavia, flowing east to the Danube at Belgrade: the longest river wholly in Yugoslavia. Length: 940 km (584 miles).

savage ('sævɪdʒ) *adj.* **1.** wild; untamed: *savage beasts.* **2.** ferocious in temper: *a savage dog.* **3.** uncivilized; crude: *savage behaviour.* **4.** (of peoples) nonliterate or primitive: *a savage tribe.* **5.** (of terrain) rugged and uncultivated. ~*n.* **6.** a member of a nonliterate society, esp. one regarded as primitive. **7.** a fierce or vicious person or animal. ~*vb.* (*tr.*) **8.** to criticize violently. **9.** to attack ferociously and wound. [C13: from OF *sauvage*, from L *silvāticus* belonging to a wood, from *silva* a wood] —ˈsavagely *adv.* —ˈsavageness *n.*

Savage ('sævɪdʒ) *n.* **Michael Joseph.** 1872-1940, New Zealand statesman; prime minister of New Zealand (1935-40).

Savage Island *n.* another name for **Niue.**

savagery ('sævɪdʒrɪ) *n., pl.* **-ries. 1.** an uncivilized condition. **2.** a savage act or nature. **3.** savages collectively.

Savaii (sɑː'vaɪɪ) *n.* the largest island in Western Samoa: mountainous and volcanic. Pop.: 42 218 (1981). Area: 1174 sq. km (662 sq. miles).

savanna *or* **savannah** (sə'vænə) *n.* open grasslands, usually with scattered bushes or trees, characteristic of much of tropical Africa. [C16: from Sp. *zavana*, from Amerind *zabana*]

Savannah (sə'vænə) *n.* **1.** a port in E Georgia, near the mouth of the Savannah River: port of departure of the *Savannah* for Liverpool (1819), the first steamship to cross the Atlantic. Pop.: 146 800 (1986 est.). **2.** a river in the southeastern U.S., formed by the confluence of the Tugaloo and Seneca Rivers in NW South Carolina: flows southeast to the Atlantic. Length: 505 km (314 miles).

savant ('sævənt) *n.* a man of great learning; sage. [C18: from F, from *savoir* to know, from L *sapere* to be wise] —ˈsavante *fem. n.*

savate (sə'væt) *n.* a form of boxing in which blows may be delivered with the feet as well as the hands. [C19: from F, lit.: old worn-out shoe]

save[1] (seɪv) *vb.* **1.** (*tr.*) to rescue, preserve, or guard (a person or thing) from danger or harm. **2.** to avoid the spending, waste, or loss of (money, possessions, etc.). **3.** (*tr.*) to deliver from sin; redeem. **4.** (often foll. by *up*) to set aside or reserve (money, goods, etc.) for future use. **5.** (*tr.*) to treat with care so as to avoid or lessen wear or degeneration. **6.** (*tr.*) to prevent the necessity for; obviate the trouble of. **7.** (*tr.*) *Soccer, hockey, etc.* to prevent (a goal) by stopping (a struck ball or puck). ~*n.* **8.** *Soccer, hockey, etc.* the act of saving a goal. **9.** *Computers.* an instruction to write information from the memory onto a tape or disk. [C13: from OF *salver*, via LL from L *salvus* safe] —'**savable** *or* '**saveable** *adj.* —'**saver** *n.*

save[2] (seɪv) *Arch.* ~*prep.* **1.** (often foll. by *for*) Also: **saving.** with the exception of. ~*conj.* **2.** but. [C13 *sauf*, from OF, from L *salvō*, from *salvus* safe]

save as you earn *n.* (in Britain) a savings scheme operated by the government, in which monthly contributions earn tax-free interest. Abbrev.: **SAYE.**

saveloy ('sævɪˌlɔɪ) *n.* a smoked sausage made from salted pork, coloured red with saltpetre. [C19: prob. via F from It. *cervellato*, from *cervello* brain, from L, from *cerebrum* brain]

savin *or* **savine** ('sævɪn) *n.* **1.** a small spreading juniper bush of Europe, N Asia, and North America. **2.** the oil derived from the shoots and leaves of this plant, formerly used in medicine to treat rheumatism, etc. [C14: from OF *savine*, from L *herba Sabīna* the Sabine plant]

saving ('seɪvɪŋ) *adj.* **1.** tending to save or preserve. **2.** redeeming or compensating (esp. in **saving grace**). **3.** thrifty or economical. **4.** *Law.* denoting or relating to an exception or reservation: *a saving clause in an agreement.* ~*n.* **5.** preservation or redemption. **6.** economy or avoidance of waste. **7.** reduction in cost or expenditure. **8.** anything saved. **9.** (*pl.*) money saved for future use. ~*prep.* **10.** with the exception of. ~*conj.* **11.** except. —'**savingly** *adv.*

savings bank *n.* a bank that accepts the savings of depositors and pays interest on them.

saviour *or U.S.* **savior** ('seɪvjə) *n.* a person who rescues another person or a thing from danger or harm. [C13 *saveour*, from OF, from Church L *Salvātor* the Saviour]

Saviour *or U.S.* **Savior** ('seɪvjə) *n. Christianity.* Jesus Christ regarded as the saviour of men from sin.

Savoie (*French* savwa) *n.* **1.** a department of E France, in Rhône-Alpes region. Capital: Chambéry. Pop.: 323 675 (1982). Area: 6188 sq. km (2413 sq. miles). **2.** the French name for **Savoy**[1].

savoir-faire ('sævwɑː'fɛə) *n.* the ability to do the right thing in any situation. [F, lit.: a knowing how to do]

Savona (*Italian* sa'voːna) *n.* a port in NW Italy, in Liguria on the Mediterranean: an important centre of the Italian iron and steel industry. Pop.: 75 353 (1981).

Savonarola (*Italian* savona'rɔːla) *n.* **Girolamo** (dʒiˈrɔːlamo). 1452–98, Italian religious and political reformer. As a Dominican prior in Florence he preached against contemporary sinfulness and moral corruption. When the Medici were expelled from the city (1494) he instituted a severely puritanical republic but lost the citizens' support after being excommunicated (1497). He was hanged and burned as a heretic.

savory ('seɪvərɪ) *n., pl.* -**vories. 1.** any of numerous aromatic plants, including the **winter savory** and **summer savory,** of the Mediterranean region, having narrow leaves and white, pink, or purple flowers. **2.** the leaves of any of these plants, used as a potherb. [C14: prob. from OE *sætherie*, from L *saturēia*, from ?]

savour *or U.S.* **savor** ('seɪvə) *n.* **1.** the quality in a substance that is perceived by the sense of taste or smell. **2.** a specific taste or smell: *the savour of lime.* **3.** a slight but distinctive quality or trace. **4.** the power to excite interest: *the savour of wit has been lost.* ~*vb.* **5.** (*intr.*; often foll. by *of*) to possess the taste or smell (of). **6.** (*intr.*; often foll. by *of*) to have a suggestion (of). **7.** (*tr.*) to season. **8.** (*tr.*) to taste or smell, esp. appreciatively. **9.** (*tr.*) to relish or enjoy. [C13: from OF *savour*, from L *sapor* taste, from *sapere* to taste] —'**savourless** *or U.S.* '**savorless** *adj.*

savoury *or U.S.* **savory** ('seɪvərɪ) *adj.* **1.** attractive to the sense of taste or smell. **2.** salty or spicy: *a savoury dish.* **3.** pleasant. **4.** respectable. ~*n., pl.* -**vouries. 5.** *Chiefly Brit.* a savoury dish served as an hors d'oeuvre or dessert. [C13 *savure*, from OF, from *savourer* to SAVOUR] —'**savouriness** *or U.S.* '**savoriness** *n.*

savoy (sə'vɔɪ) *n.* a cultivated variety of cabbage having a compact head and wrinkled leaves. [C16: after the SAVOY region]

Savoy[1] (sə'vɔɪ) *n.* an area of SE France, bordering on Italy, mainly in the Savoy Alps: a duchy in the late Middle Ages and part of the Kingdom of Sardinia from 1720 to

1860, when it became part of France. French name: **Savoie.**

Savoy[2] (sə'vɔɪ) *n.* a noble family of Italy that ruled over the duchy of Savoy and became the royal house of Italy (1861–1946): the oldest reigning dynasty in Europe before the dissolution of the Italian monarchy.

Savoy Alps *pl. n.* a range of the Alps in SE France. Highest peak: Mont Blanc, 4807 m (15 772 ft.).

Savoyard (sə'vɔɪɑːd; *French* savwajar) *n.* **1.** a native of Savoy. **2.** the dialect of French spoken in Savoy. ~*adj.* **3.** of or relating to Savoy, its inhabitants, or their dialect.

savvy ('sævɪ) *Sl.* ~*vb.* -**vying,** -**vied. 1.** to understand or get the sense of (an idea, etc.). ~*n.* **2.** comprehension. ~*adj.* -**vier,** -**viest. 3.** *Chiefly U.S.* shrewd. [C18: corruption of Sp. *sabe* (*usted*) (you) know, from *saber* to know, from L *sapere* to be wise]

saw[1] (sɔː) *n.* **1.** any of various hand tools for cutting wood, metal, etc., having a blade with teeth along one edge. **2.** any of various machines or devices for cutting by use of a toothed blade, such as a power-driven toothed band of metal. ~*vb.* **sawing, sawed; sawed** *or* **sawn. 3.** to cut with a saw. **4.** to form by sawing. **5.** to cut as if wielding a saw: *to saw the air.* **6.** to move (an object) from side to side as if moving a saw. [OE *sagu*: rel. to L *secare* to cut] —'**sawer** *n.* —'**saw,like** *adj.*

saw[2] (sɔː) *vb.* the past tense of **see**[1].

saw[3] (sɔː) *n.* a wise saying, maxim, or proverb. [OE *sagu* a saying]

sawbones ('sɔːˌbəʊnz) *n., pl.* -**bones** *or* -**boneses.** *Sl.* a surgeon or doctor.

sawdust ('sɔːˌdʌst) *n.* particles of wood formed by sawing.

sawfish ('sɔːˌfɪʃ) *n., pl.* -**fish** *or* -**fishes.** a sharklike ray of subtropical coastal waters, having a serrated bladelike mouth.

sawfly ('sɔːˌflaɪ) *n., pl.* -**flies.** any of various hymenopterous insects, the females of which have a sawlike ovipositor.

sawhorse ('sɔːˌhɔːs) *n.* a stand for timber during sawing.

sawmill ('sɔːˌmɪl) *n.* an industrial establishment where timber is sawn into planks, etc.

sawn (sɔːn) *vb.* a past participle of **saw**[1].

sawn-off *or esp. U.S.* **sawed-off** *adj.* (*prenominal*) (of a shotgun) having the barrel cut short, mainly to facilitate concealment of the weapon.

saw set *n.* a tool used for setting the teeth of a saw, consisting of a clamp used to bend each tooth at a slight angle to the plane of the saw, alternate teeth being bent in the same direction.

sawyer ('sɔːjə) *n.* a person who saws timber for a living. [C14 *sawier*, from SAW[1] + -*ier*, from OF -ER[1]]

sax (sæks) *n. Inf.* short for **saxophone.**

Saxe[1] (saks) *n.* the French name for **Saxony.**

Saxe[2] (*French* saks) *n.* **Hermann Maurice** (ɛrman mɔris) comte de Saxe. 1696–1750, French marshal born in Saxony: he distinguished himself in the War of the Austrian Succession (1740–48).

saxe blue (sæks) *n.* **a.** a light greyish-blue colour. **b.** (*as adj.*): *a saxe-blue dress.* [C19: from F *Saxe* Saxony, source of a dye of this colour]

Saxe-Coburg-Gotha (sæks'kəʊbɜːg'gəʊθə) *n.* the ruling house of the former German duchy of Saxe-Coburg-Gotha (until 1918) and the name of the British royal family (1901–17) through Prince Albert.

saxhorn ('sæksˌhɔːn) *n.* a valved brass instrument used chiefly in brass and military bands, having a tube of conical bore. It resembles the tuba. [C19: after Adolphe Sax (see SAXOPHONE), who invented it (1845)]

saxicolous (sæk'sɪkələs) *adj.* living on or among rocks: *saxicolous plants.* Also: **saxatile** ('sæksəˌtaɪl). [C19: from NL *saxicolus*, from L *saxum* rock + *colere* to dwell]

saxifrage ('sæksɪˌfreɪdʒ) *n.* a plant having small white, yellow, purple, or pink flowers. [C15: from LL *saxifraga*, lit.: rock-breaker, from L *saxum* rock + *frangere* to break]

Saxo Grammaticus ('sæksəʊ grə'mætɪkəs) *n.* ?1150–?1220, Danish chronicler, noted for his *Gesta Danorum,* a history of Denmark down to 1185, written in Latin, which is partly historical and partly mythological, and contains the Hamlet (Amleth) legend.

Saxon ('sæksən) *n.* **1.** a member of a West Germanic people who raided and settled parts of S Britain in the fifth and sixth centuries A.D. **2.** a native or inhabitant of

Saxony. **3. a.** the Low German dialect of Saxony. **b.** any of the West Germanic dialects spoken by the ancient Saxons. ~*adj.* **4.** of or characteristic of the ancient Saxons, the Anglo-Saxons, or their descendants. **5.** of or characteristic of Saxony, its inhabitants, or their Low German dialect. [C13 (replacing OE *Seaxe*): via OF from LL *Saxon-, Saxo*, from Gk; of Gmc origin]

Saxony ('sæksənɪ) *n.* a region in S East Germany around the upper Elbe River: referred at various times to those places inhabited by Saxons or ruled by Saxon princes. German name: **Sachsen.** French name: **Saxe.**

saxophone ('sæksə,fəun) *n.* a keyed single-reed wind instrument of mellow tone colour, used mainly in jazz and dance music. Often shortened to **sax.** [C19: after Adolphe *Sax* (1814–94), Belgian musical-instrument maker, who invented it (1846)] —**saxophonic** (,sæksə'fɒnɪk) *adj.* —**saxophonist** (sæk'sɒfənɪst) *n.*

say (seɪ) *vb.* **saying, said.** (*mainly tr.*) **1.** to speak, pronounce, or utter. **2.** (*also intr.*) to express (an idea, etc.) in words; tell. **3.** (*also intr.; may take a clause as object*) to state (an opinion, fact, etc.) positively. **4.** to recite: *to say grace.* **5.** (*may take a clause as object*) to report or allege: *they say we shall have rain today.* **6.** (*may take a clause as object*) to suppose: *let us say that he is lying.* **7.** (*may take a clause as object*) to convey by means of artistic expression. **8.** to make a case for: *there is much to be said for it.* **9. go without saying.** to be so obvious as to need no explanation. **10. I say!** *Inf., chiefly Brit.* an exclamation of surprise. **11. not to say.** even. **12. that is to say.** in other words. **13. to say the least.** at the very least. ~*adv.* **14.** approximately: *there were, say, 20 people present.* **15.** for example: *choose a number, say, four.* ~*n.* **16.** the right or chance to speak: *let him have his say.* **17.** authority, esp. to influence a decision: *he has a lot of say.* **18.** a statement of opinion: *you've had your say.* ~*interj.* **19.** *U.S. & Canad. inf.* an exclamation to attract attention or express surprise. [OE *secgan*] —**'sayer** *n.*

Sayan Mountains (sɑː'jæn) *pl. n.* a mountain range in the SE Soviet Union, in S Siberia. Highest peak: Munku-Sardyk, 3437 m (11 457 ft.).

SAYE (in Britain) *abbrev. for* save as you earn.

Sayers ('seɪəz) *n.* **Dorothy L(eigh).** 1893–1957, English detective-story writer.

saying ('seɪɪŋ) *n.* a maxim, adage, or proverb.

say-so *n. Inf.* **1.** an arbitrary assertion. **2.** an authoritative decision. **3.** the authority to make a final decision.

sayyid ('saɪɪd) *or* **said** *n.* **1.** a Muslim claiming descent from Mohammed's grandson Husain. **2.** a Muslim honorary title. [C17: from Ar.: lord]

Sb *the chemical symbol for* antimony. [from NL *stibium*]

sc *Printing. abbrev. for* small capitals.

Sc *the chemical symbol for* scandium.

SC *abbrev. for:* **1.** *Austral. & N.Z.* School Certificate. **2.** Signal Corps. **3.** *Canad.* Social Credit.

sc. *abbrev. for:* **1.** scale. **2.** scene. **3.** science. **4.** scilicet. **5.** screw. **6.** scruple (unit of weight).

scab (skæb) *n.* **1.** the dried crusty surface of a healing skin wound or sore. **2.** a contagious disease of sheep resembling mange, caused by a mite. **3.** a fungal disease of plants characterized by crusty spots on the fruits, leaves, etc. **4.** *Derog.* **a.** Also called: **blackleg.** a person who refuses to support a trade union's actions, esp. strikes. **b.** (*as modifier*): *scab labour.* **c.** a despicable person. ~*vb.* **scabbing, scabbed.** (*intr.*) **5.** to become covered with a scab. **7.** to replace a striking worker. [OE *sceabb*]

scabbard ('skæbəd) *n.* a holder for a bladed weapon such as a sword or bayonet. [C13 *scauberc*, from Norman F *escaubers*, (pl.) of Gmc origin]

scabby ('skæbɪ) *adj.* **-bier, -biest. 1.** *Pathol.* having an area of the skin covered with scabs. **2.** *Pathol.* having scabies. **3.** *Inf.* despicable. —**'scabbily** *adv.* —**'scabbiness** *n.*

scabies ('skeɪbiːz) *n.* a contagious skin infection caused by a mite, characterized by intense itching and inflammation. [C15: from L: scurf, from *scabere* to scratch]

scabious [1] ('skeɪbɪəs) *adj.* **1.** having or covered with scabs. **2.** of, relating to, or resembling scabies. [C17: from L *scabiōsus*, from SCABIES]

scabious [2] ('skeɪbɪəs) *n.* any of a genus of plants of the Mediterranean region, having blue, red, or whitish dome-shaped flower heads. [C14: from Med. L *scabiōsa herba* the scabies plant, referring to its use in treating scabies]

scabrous ('skeɪbrəs) *adj.* **1.** roughened because of small projections. **2.** indecent or salacious: *scabrous humour.* **3.** difficult to deal with. [C17: from L *scaber* rough] —**'scabrously** *adv.*

scad (skæd) *n., pl.* **scad** *or* **scads.** any of various marine fishes having a deeply forked tail, such as the large mackerel. [C17: from ?]

scads (skædz) *pl. n. Inf.* a large amount or number. [C19: from ?]

Scafell Pike (skɔː'fɛl) *n.* a mountain in NW England, in Cumbria in the Lake District: the highest peak in England. Height: 978 m (3209 ft.).

scaffold ('skæfəld) *n.* **1.** a temporary framework that is used to support workmen and materials during the erection, repair, etc., of a building. **2.** a raised wooden platform on which plays are performed, tobacco, etc., is dried, or (esp. formerly) criminals are executed. ~*vb.* (*tr.*) **3.** to provide with a scaffold. **4.** to support by means of a scaffold. [C14: from OF *eschaffaut*, from Vulgar L *catafalicum* (unattested)] —**'scaffolder** *n.*

scaffolding ('skæfəldɪŋ) *n.* **1.** a scaffold or system of scaffolds. **2.** the building materials used to make scaffolds.

Scala ('skɑːla) *n. La.* See **La Scala.**

scalable ('skeɪləbəl) *adj.* capable of being climbed. —**'scalableness** *n.* —**'scalably** *adv.*

scalar ('skeɪlə) *n.* **1.** a quantity, such as time or temperature, that has magnitude but not direction. ~*adj.* **2.** having magnitude but not direction. [C17 (meaning: resembling a ladder): from L *scālāris*, from *scāla* ladder]

scalar product *n.* the product of two vectors to form a scalar, whose value is the product of the magnitudes of the vectors and the cosine of the angle between them. Also called: **dot product.**

scalawag ('skælə,wæg) *n.* a variant of **scallywag.**

scald [1] (skɔːld) *vb.* **1.** to burn or be burnt with or as if with hot liquid or steam. **2.** (*tr.*) to subject to the action of boiling water, esp. so as to sterilize. **3.** (*tr.*) to heat (a liquid) almost to boiling point. **4.** to plunge (tomatoes, etc.) into boiling water in order to skin them more easily. ~*n.* **5.** the act or result of scalding. **6.** an abnormal condition in plants, caused by exposure to excessive sunlight, gases, etc. [C13: via OF from LL *excaldāre* to wash in warm water, from *calida (aqua)* warm (water), from *calēre* to be warm] —**'scalder** *n.*

scald [2] (skɔːld) *n.* a variant spelling of **skald.**

scaldfish ('skɔːld,fɪʃ, 'skɑːld-) *n., pl.* **-fish** *or* **-fishes.** a small European flatfish, covered with large fragile scales.

scale [1] (skeɪl) *n.* **1.** any of the numerous plates, made of various substances, covering the bodies of fishes. **2. a.** any of the horny or chitinous plates covering a part or the entire body of certain reptiles and mammals. **b.** any of the numerous minute structures covering the wings of lepidoptera. **3.** a thin flat piece or flake. **4.** a thin flake of dead epidermis shed from the skin. **5.** a specialized leaf or bract, esp. the protective covering of a bud or the dry membranous bract of a catkin. **6.** See **scale insect. 7.** any oxide formed on a metal when heated. **8.** tartar formed on the teeth. ~*vb.* **9.** (*tr.*) to remove the scales or coating from. **10.** to peel off or cause to peel off in flakes or scales. **11.** (*intr.*) to shed scales. **12.** to cover or become covered with scales, incrustation, etc. [C14: from OF *escale*, of Gmc origin]

scale [2] (skeɪl) *n.* **1.** (*often pl.*) a machine or device for weighing. **2.** one of the pans of a balance. **3. tip the scales. a.** to exercise a decisive influence. **b.** (foll. by *at*) to amount in weight (to). ~*vb.* (*tr.*) **4.** to weigh with or as if with scales. [C13: from ON *skāl* bowl]

scale [3] (skeɪl) *n.* **1.** a sequence of marks either at regular intervals, or representing equal steps, used as a reference in making measurements. **2.** a measuring instrument having such a scale. **3. a.** the ratio between the size of something real and that of a representation of it. **b.** (*as modifier*): *a scale model.* **4.** a line, numerical ratio, etc., for showing this ratio. **5.** a progressive or graduated table of things, wages, etc.: *a wage scale for carpenters.* **6.** an established standard. **7.** a relative degree or extent: *he entertained on a grand scale.* **8.** *Music.* a group of notes taken in ascending or descending order, esp. within the compass of one octave. **9.** *Maths.* the notation of a given number system: *the decimal scale.* ~*vb.* **10.** to climb to the top of (a height) by or as if by a ladder. **11.** (*tr.*) to make or draw (a model, etc.) according to a particular ratio of proportionate reduction. **12.** (*tr.*; usually foll. by *up* or *down*) to increase or reduce proportionately in size, etc. **13.** (*intr.*) *Austral. inf.* to ride on public transport without paying a fare. [C15: via It. from L *scāla* ladder]

scaleboard ('skeɪl,bɔːd) *n.* a very thin piece of board, used for backing a picture, etc.

scale insect *n.* a small insect which typically lives and feeds on plants and secretes a protective scale around itself. Many species are pests.

scalene ('skeɪliːn) *adj.* **1.** *Maths.* (of a triangle) having all sides of unequal length. **2.** *Anat.* of or relating to any of the scalenus muscles. [C17: from LL *scalēnus* with unequal sides, from Gk *skalēnos*]

scalenus (skə'liːnəs) *n., pl.* **-ni** (-naɪ). *Anat.* any one of the three muscles situated on each side of the neck extending from the cervical vertebrae to the first or second pair of ribs. [C18: from NL; see SCALENE]

Scaliger ('skælɪdʒə) *n.* **1. Joseph Justus** ('dʒʌstəs). 1540–1609, French scholar, who revolutionized the study of ancient chronology by his work *De Emendatione temporum* (1583). **2.** his father, **Julius Caesar.** 1484–1558, Italian classical scholar, and writer on biology and medicine.

scaling ladder *n.* a ladder used to climb high walls, esp. one used formerly to enter a besieged town, fortress, etc.

scallion ('skæljən) *n.* any of various onions, such as the spring onion, that have a small bulb and long leaves and are eaten in salads. [C14: from Anglo-F *scalun*, from L *Ascalōnia* (*caepa*) Ascalonian (onion), from *Ascalo* Ascalon, a Palestinian port]

scallop ('skɒləp, 'skæl-) *n.* **1.** any of various marine bivalves having a fluted fan-shaped shell. **2.** the edible adductor muscle of certain of these molluscs. **3.** either of the shell valves of any of these molluscs. **4.** a scallop shell in which fish, esp. shellfish, is cooked and served. **5.** one of a series of curves along an edge. **6.** the shape of a scallop shell used as the badge of a pilgrim, esp. in the Middle Ages. **7.** *Chiefly Austral.* a potato cake fried in batter. ~*vb.* **8.** (*tr.*) to decorate (an edge) with scallops. **9.** to bake (food) in a scallop shell or similar dish. [C14: from OF *escalope* shell, of Gmc origin] —'**scalloper** *n.* —'**scalloping** *n.*

scallywag ('skælɪ,wæg) *n. Inf.* a scamp; rascal. ~Also: **scalawag, scallawag.** [C19: (orig. undersized animal): from ?]

scalp (skælp) *n.* **1.** *Anat.* the skin and subcutaneous tissue covering the top of the head. **2.** (among North American Indians) a part of this removed as a trophy from a slain enemy. **3.** a trophy or token signifying conquest. **4.** *Scot. dialect.* a projection of bare rock from vegetation. ~*vb.* (*tr.*) **5.** to cut the scalp from. **6.** *Inf., chiefly U.S.* to purchase and resell (securities) quickly so as to make several small profits. **7.** *Inf.* to buy (tickets) cheaply and resell at an inflated price. [C13: prob. from ON] —'**scalper** *n.*

scalpel ('skælpəl) *n.* a surgical knife with a short thin blade. [C18: from L *scalpellum*, from *scalper* a knife, from *scalpere* to scrape]

scaly ('skeɪlɪ) *adj.* **scalier, scaliest. 1.** resembling or covered in scales. **2.** peeling off in scales. —'**scaliness** *n.*

scaly anteater *n.* another name for **pangolin.**

Scamander (skə'mændə) *n.* the ancient name for the **Menderes** (sense 2).

scamp[1] (skæmp) *n.* **1.** an idle mischievous person. **2.** a mischievous child. [C18: from *scamp* (vb.) to be a highway robber, prob. from MDu. *schampen* to decamp, from OF *escamper*, from L *campus* field] —'**scampish** *adj.*

scamp[2] (skæmp) *vb.* a less common word for **skimp.** —'**scamper** *n.*

scamper ('skæmpə) *vb.* **1.** (*intr.*) to run about playfully. **2.** (often foll. by *through*) to hurry through (a place, task, etc.) ~*n.* **3.** the act of scampering. [C17: prob. from *scamp* (vb.); see SCAMP[1]]

scampi ('skæmpɪ) *n.* (*usually functioning as sing.*) large prawns, usually eaten fried in breadcrumbs. [It.: pl. of *scampo* shrimp, from ?]

scan (skæn) *vb.* **scanning, scanned. 1.** (*tr.*) to scrutinize minutely. **2.** (*tr.*) to glance at quickly. **3.** (*tr.*) *Prosody.* to read or analyse (verse) according to the rules of metre and versification. **4.** (*intr.*) *Prosody.* to conform to the rules of metre and versification. **5.** (*tr.*) *Electronics.* to

move a beam of light, electrons, etc., in a predetermined pattern over (a surface or region) to obtain information, esp. to reproduce a television image. **6.** (*tr.*) to examine data stored on (magnetic tape, etc.), usually in order to retrieve information. **7.** to examine or search (a prescribed region) by systematically varying the direction of a radar or sonar beam. **8.** *Med.* to obtain an image of (a part of the body) by means of ultrasound or a scanner. ~*n.* **9.** the act or an instance of scanning. [C14: from LL *scandere* to scan (verse), from L: to climb] —'**scannable** *adj.*

Scand. *or* **Scan.** *abbrev. for* Scandinavia(n).

scandal ('skændəl) *n.* **1.** a disgraceful action or event: *his negligence was a scandal.* **2.** censure or outrage arising from an action or event. **3.** a person whose conduct causes reproach or disgrace. **4.** malicious talk, esp. gossip. **5.** *Law.* a libellous action or statement. [C16: from LL *scandalum* stumbling block, from Gk *skandalon* a trap] —'**scandalous** *adj.* —'**scandalously** *adv.*

scandalize *or* **-ise** ('skændə,laɪz) *vb.* (*tr.*) to shock, as by improper behaviour. —,**scandali'zation** *or* **-i'sation** *n.*

scandalmonger ('skændəl,mʌŋgə) *n.* a person who spreads or enjoys scandal, gossip, etc.

Scanderbeg ('skændə,bɛg) *n.* original name *George Castriota;* Turkish name *Iskender Bey.* ?1403–68, Albanian patriot. He was an army commander for the sultan of Turkey until 1443, when he changed sides and drove the Turks from Albania.

Scandinavia (,skændɪ'neɪvɪə) *n.* **1.** Also called: **the Scandinavian Peninsula.** the peninsula of N Europe occupied by Norway and Sweden. **2.** the countries of N Europe, esp. considered as a cultural unit and including Norway, Sweden, Denmark, and often Finland, Iceland, and the Faeroe Islands. —,**Scandi'navian** *adj., n.*

scandium ('skændɪəm) *n.* a rare silvery-white metallic element occurring in minute quantities in numerous minerals. Symbol: Sc; atomic no.: 21; atomic wt.: 44.96. [C19: from NL, from L *Scandia* Scandinavia, where discovered]

scanner ('skænə) *n.* **1.** a person or thing that scans. **2.** a device, usually electronic, used to measure or sample the distribution of some quantity or condition in a particular system, region, or area. **3.** an aerial or similar device designed to transmit or receive signals, esp. radar signals, inside a given solid angle of space. **4.** any device used in medical diagnosis to obtain an image of an internal organ or part.

scanning electron microscope *n.* a type of electron microscope that produces a three-dimensional image.

scansion ('skænʃən) *n.* the analysis of the metrical structure of verse. [C17: from L: climbing up, from *scandere* to climb]

scant (skænt) *adj.* **1.** scarcely sufficient: *he paid her scant attention.* **2.** (*prenominal*) bare: *a scant ten inches.* **3.** (*postpositive;* foll. by *of*) having a short supply (of). ~*vb.* (*tr.*) **4.** to limit in size or quantity. **5.** to provide with a limited supply of. **6.** to treat in an inadequate manner. ~*adv.* **7.** scarcely; barely. [C14: from ON *skamt,* from *skammr* short] —'**scantly** *adv.*

scantling ('skæntlɪŋ) *n.* **1.** a piece of sawn timber, such as a rafter, that has a small cross section. **2.** the dimensions of a piece of building material or the structural parts of a ship or aircraft. **3.** a building stone. **4.** a small quantity or amount. [C16: changed (through infl. of SCANT & -LING[1]) from earlier *scantillon* a carpenter's gauge, from OF *escantillon,* ult. from L *scandere* to climb]

scanty ('skæntɪ) *adj.* **scantier, scantiest. 1.** limited; barely enough. **2.** inadequate. **3.** lacking fullness. —'**scantily** *adv.* —'**scantiness** *n.*

Scapa Flow ('skæpə) *n.* an extensive landlocked anchorage off the N coast of Scotland, in the Orkney Islands: major British naval base in both World Wars. Length: about 24 km (15 miles). Width: 13 km (8 miles).

scape *or* '**scape** (skeɪp) *vb., n.* an archaic word for **escape.**

-scape *suffix forming nouns.* indicating a scene or view of something: *seascape.* [from LANDSCAPE]

scapegoat ('skeɪp,gəʊt) *n.* **1.** a person made to bear the blame for others. **2.** *Bible.* a goat symbolically laden with the sins of the Israelites and sent into the wilderness. [C16: from ESCAPE + GOAT, coined by William Tyndale to translate Biblical Heb. *azāzēl* (prob.) goat for Azazel, mistakenly thought to mean "goat that escapes"]

scapegrace ('skeɪp,greɪs) *n.* a mischievous person. [C19: from SCAPE + GRACE, alluding to a person who lacks God's grace]

scaphoid ('skæfɔɪd) *adj. Anat.* an obsolete word for **navicular**. [C18: via NL from Gk *skaphoeidēs*, from *skaphē* boat]

scapula ('skæpjʊlə) *n., pl.* **-lae** (-liː) *or* **-las.** either of two large flat triangular bones, one on each side of the back part of the shoulder in man. Nontechnical name: **shoulder blade.** [C16: from LL: shoulder]

scapular ('skæpjʊlə) *adj.* **1.** *Anat.* of or relating to the scapula. ~*n.* **2.** part of the monastic habit worn by members of many Christian religious orders, consisting of a piece of woollen cloth worn over the shoulders, and hanging down to the ankles. **3.** two small rectangular pieces of cloth joined by tapes passing over the shoulders and worn in token of affiliation to a religious order. **4.** any of the small feathers of a bird that lie along the shoulder. ~Also called (for senses 2 and 3): **scapulary.**

scar[1] (skɑː) *n.* **1.** any mark left on the skin or other tissue following the healing of a wound, etc. **2.** a permanent change in a person's character resulting from emotional distress. **3.** the mark on a plant indicating the former point of attachment of a part. **4.** a mark of damage. ~*vb.* **scarring, scarred.** **5.** to mark or become marked with a scar. **6.** (*intr.*) to heal leaving a scar. [C14: via LL from Gk *eskhara* scab]

scar[2] (skɑː) *n.* a bare craggy rock formation. [C14: from ON *sker* low reef]

scarab ('skærəb) *n.* **1.** any scarabaeid beetle, esp. the **sacred scarab**, regarded by the ancient Egyptians as divine. **2.** the scarab as represented on amulets, etc. [C16: from L *scarabaeus*]

scarabaeid (,skærə'biːɪd) *n.* **1.** any of a family of beetles including the sacred scarab and other dung beetles, the chafers, and rhinoceros beetles. ~*adj.* **2.** of or belonging to this family. [C19: from NL]

Scaramouch ('skærə,maʊtʃ) *n.* a stock character who appears as a boastful coward in commedia dell'arte. [C17: via F from It. *Scaramuccia*, from *scaramuccia* a SKIRMISH]

Scarborough ('skɑːbrə) *n.* a fishing port and resort in NE England, in North Yorkshire on the North Sea: developed as a spa after 1660; ruined 12th-century castle. Pop.: 43 103 (1981).

scarce (skɛəs) *adj.* **1.** rarely encountered. **2.** insufficient to meet the demand. **3. make oneself scarce.** *Inf.* to go away. ~*adv.* **4.** *Arch. or literary.* scarcely. [C13: from OF *scars*, from Vulgar L *excarpsus* (unattested) plucked out, from L *excerpere* to select] —'**scarceness** *n.*

scarcely ('skɛəslɪ) *adv.* **1.** hardly at all. **2.** *Often used ironically.* probably or definitely not: *that is scarcely justification for your actions.*
▷ **Usage.** See at **hardly.**

scarcity ('skɛəsɪtɪ) *n., pl.* **-ties.** **1.** inadequate supply. **2.** rarity or infrequent occurrence.

scare (skɛə) *vb.* **1.** to fill or be filled with fear or alarm. **2.** (*tr.*; often foll. by *away* or *off*) to drive (away) by frightening. ~*n.* **3.** a sudden attack of fear or alarm. **4.** a period of general fear or alarm. ~*adj.* **5.** causing (needless) fear or alarm: *a scare story.* [C12: from ON *skirra*] —'**scarer** *n.*

scarecrow ('skɛə,krəʊ) *n.* **1.** an object, usually in the shape of a man, made out of sticks and old clothes to scare birds away from crops. **2.** a person or thing that appears frightening. **3.** an untidy-looking person.

scaremonger ('skɛə,mʌŋgə) *n.* a person who delights in spreading rumours of disaster. —'**scare,mongering** *n.*

scarf[1] (skɑːf) *n., pl.* **scarfs** *or* **scarves.** a rectangular, triangular, or long narrow piece of cloth worn around the head, neck, or shoulders for warmth or decoration. [C16: from ?]

scarf[2] (skɑːf) *n., pl.* **scarfs.** **1.** Also called: **scarf joint, scarfed joint.** a lapped joint between two pieces of timber made by notching the ends and strapping or gluing the two pieces together. **2.** the end of a piece of timber shaped to form such a joint. **3.** *Whaling.* an incision made along a whale before stripping off the blubber. ~*vb.* (*tr.*) **4.** to join (two pieces of timber) by means of a scarf. **5.** to make a scarf on (a piece of timber). **6.** to cut a scarf in (a whale). [C14: prob. from ON]

scarfskin ('skɑːf,skɪn) *n.* the outermost layer of the skin; epidermis or cuticle. [C17: from SCARF[1] (in the sense: an outer covering)]

scarify ('skɛərɪ,faɪ, 'skærɪ-) *vb.* **-fying, -fied.** (*tr.*) **1.** *Surgery.* to make tiny punctures or superficial incisions in (the skin or other tissue), as for inoculating. **2.** *Agriculture.* to break up and loosen (soil) to a shallow depth. **3.** to wound with harsh criticism. [C15: via OF from L *scarifāre* to scratch open, from Gk *skariphasthai* to draw, from *skariphos* a pencil] —,**scarifi'cation** *n.* —'**scari,fier** *n.*

scarlatina (,skɑːlə'tiːnə) *n.* the technical name for **scarlet fever.** [C19: from NL, from It. *scarlattina*, dim. of *scarlatto* scarlet]

Scarlatti (skɑː'lætɪ) *n.* **1. Alessandro** (ales'sandro). ?1659–1725, Italian composer; regarded as the founder of modern opera. **2.** his son, (**Giuseppe**) **Domenico** (do'me:niko). 1685–1757, Italian composer and harpsichordist, in Portugal and Spain from 1720. He wrote over 550 single-movement sonatas for harpsichord, many of them exercises in virtuoso technique.

scarlet ('skɑːlɪt) *n.* **1.** a vivid orange-red colour. **2.** cloth or clothing of this colour. ~*adj.* **3.** of the colour scarlet. **4.** sinful or immoral. [C13: from OF *escarlate* fine cloth, from ?]

scarlet fever *n.* an acute communicable disease characterized by fever, strawberry-coloured tongue, and a rash starting on the neck and chest and spreading to the abdomen and limbs. Technical name: **scarlatina.**

scarlet letter *n.* (esp. among U.S. Puritans) a scarlet letter *A* formerly worn by a person convicted of adultery.

scarlet pimpernel *n.* a plant, related to the primrose, having small red, purple, or white star-shaped flowers that close in bad weather. Also called: **shepherd's** (or **poor man's) weatherglass.**

scarlet runner *n.* a climbing perennial bean plant of tropical America, having scarlet flowers: widely cultivated for its long green edible pods containing edible seeds. Also: **runner bean.**

scarlet woman *n.* **1.** a sinful woman described in the Bible (Rev. 17), interpreted as a symbol of pagan Rome or of the Roman Catholic Church. **2.** any sexually promiscuous woman.

scarp (skɑːp) *n.* **1.** a steep slope, esp. one formed by erosion or faulting. **2.** *Fortifications.* the side of a ditch cut nearest to a rampart. ~*vb.* **3.** (*tr.; often passive*) to wear or cut so as to form a steep slope. [C16: from It. *scarpa*]

scarper ('skɑːpə) *Brit. sl.* ~*vb.* **1.** (*intr.*) to depart in haste. ~*n.* **2.** a hasty departure. [from ?]

Scarron (*French* skɑrɔ̃) *n.* **Paul** (pɔl). 1610–60, French comic dramatist and novelist, noted particularly for his picaresque novel *Le Roman comique* (1651–57).

scarves (skɑːvz) *n.* a plural of **scarf**[1].

scary ('skɛərɪ) *adj.* **scarier, scariest.** *Inf.* **1.** causing fear or alarm. **2.** timid.

scat[1] (skæt) *vb.* **scatting, scatted.** (*intr.; usually imperative*) *Inf.* to go away in haste. [C19: ?from a hiss + *cat*, used to frighten away cats]

scat[2] (skæt) *n.* **1.** a type of jazz singing characterized by improvised vocal sounds instead of words. ~*vb.* **scatting, scatted.** **2.** (*intr.*) to sing jazz in this way. [C20: ? imit.]

scathe (skeɪð) *vb.* (*tr.*) **1.** *Rare.* to attack with severe criticism. **2.** *Arch. or dialect.* to injure. ~*n.* **3.** *Arch. or dialect.* harm. [OE *sceatha*]

scathing ('skeɪðɪŋ) *adj.* **1.** harshly critical; scornful. **2.** damaging. —'**scathingly** *adv.*

scatology (skæ'tɒlədʒɪ) *n.* **1.** the scientific study of excrement, esp. in medicine and in palaeontology. **2.** obscenity or preoccupation with obscenity, esp. in the form of references to excrement. [C19: from Gk *skat-* excrement + -LOGY] —**scatological** (,skætə'lɒdʒɪkəl) *adj.*

scatter ('skætə) *vb.* **1.** (*tr.*) to throw about in various directions. **2.** to separate and move or cause to separate and move in various directions. **3.** to deviate or cause to deviate in many directions, as in the refraction of light. ~*n.* **4.** the act of scattering. **5.** a substance or a number of objects scattered about. [C13: prob. a var. of SHATTER] —'**scatterer** *n.*

scatterbrain ('skætə,breɪn) *n.* a person who is incapable of serious thought or concentration. —'**scatter,brained** *adj.*

scatter diagram *n. Statistics.* a representation by a Cartesian graph of the correlation between two quantities, such as height and weight.

scattering ('skætərɪŋ) *n.* **1.** a small amount. **2.** *Physics.* the process in which particles, atoms, etc., are deflected as a result of collision.

scatty ('skætɪ) *adj.* **-tier, -tiest.** *Brit. inf.* **1.** emptyheaded or thoughtless. **2.** (distracted (esp. in **drive someone scatty**). [C20: from SCATTERBRAINED] —'**scattily** *adv.* —'**scattiness** *n.*

scaup *or* **scaup duck** (skɔːp) *n.* either of two diving ducks, the **greater scaup** or the **lesser scaup**, of Europe and America, having a black-and-white plumage in the male. [C16: Scot. var. of SCALP]

scavenge ('skævɪndʒ) *vb.* **1.** to search for (anything usable) among discarded material. **2.** *(tr.)* to purify (a molten metal) by bubbling a suitable gas through it. **3.** to clean up filth from (streets, etc.).

scavenger ('skævɪndʒə) *n.* **1.** a person who collects things discarded by others. **2.** any animal that feeds on decaying organic matter. **3.** a person employed to clean the streets. [C16: from Anglo-Norman *scawager*, from OF *escauwage* examination, from *escauwer* to scrutinize, of Gmc origin] —'**scavengery** *n.*

ScD *abbrev. for* Doctor of Science.

SCE (in Scotland) *abbrev. for* Scottish Certificate of Education: either of two public examinations in specific subjects taken as school-leaving qualifications or as qualifying examinations for entry into a university, college, etc.

scena ('ʃeɪnə) *n., pl.* **-ne** (-,neɪ) a solo vocal piece of dramatic style and large scope, esp. in opera. [C19: It., from L *scēna* scene]

scenario (sɪ'nɑːrɪ,əʊ) *n., pl.* **-narios. 1.** a summary of the plot of a play, etc., including information about its characters, scenes, etc. **2.** a predicted sequence of events. [C19: via It. from L *scēnārium*, from *scēna;* see SCENE]

scene (siːn) *n.* **1.** the place where an action or event, real or imaginary, occurs. **2.** the setting for the action of a play, novel, etc. **3.** an incident or situation, real or imaginary, esp. as described or represented. **4. a.** a subdivision of an act of a play, in which the setting is fixed. **b.** a single event, esp. a significant one, in a play. **5.** *Films.* a shot or series of shots that constitutes a unit of the action. **6.** the backcloths, etc., for a play or film set. **7.** the prospect of a place, landscape, etc. **8.** a display of emotion. **9.** *Inf.* the environment for a specific activity: *the fashion scene.* **10.** *Inf.* interest or chosen occupation: *classical music is not my scene.* **11.** *Rare.* the stage. **12. behind the scenes.** out of public view. [C16: from L *scēna* theatrical stage, from Gk *skēnē* tent, stage]

scene dock *or* **bay** *n.* a place in a theatre where scenery is stored, usually near the stage.

scenery ('siːnərɪ) *n., pl.* **-eries. 1.** the natural features of a landscape. **2.** *Theatre.* the painted backcloths, etc., used to represent a location in a theatre or studio. [C18: from It. SCENARIO]

scenic ('siːnɪk) *adj.* **1.** of or relating to natural scenery. **2.** having beautiful natural scenery: *a scenic drive.* **3.** of or relating to the stage or stage scenery. **4.** (in painting, etc.) representing a scene. —'**scenically** *adv.*

scenic railway *n.* a miniature railway used for amusement in a park, zoo, etc.

scenic reserve *n. N.Z.* an area of natural beauty, set aside for public recreation.

scent (sɛnt) *n.* **1.** a distinctive smell, esp. a pleasant one. **2.** a smell left in passing, by which a person or animal may be traced. **3.** a trail, clue, or guide. **4.** an instinctive ability for detecting. **5.** another word (esp. Brit.) for **perfume.** ~*vb.* **6.** *(tr.)* to recognize by or as if by the smell. **7.** *(tr.)* to have a suspicion of: *I scent foul play.* **8.** *(tr.)* to fill with odour or fragrance. **9.** *(intr.)* (of hounds, etc.) to hunt by the sense of smell. **10.** to smell (at): *the dog scented the air.* [C14: from OF *sentir* to sense, from L *sentīre* to feel] —'**scented** *adj.*

sceptic *or arch. & U.S.* **skeptic** ('skɛptɪk) *n.* **1.** a person who habitually doubts the authenticity of accepted beliefs. **2.** a person who mistrusts people, ideas, etc., in general. **3.** a person who doubts the truth of religion. [C16: from L *scepticus*, from Gk *skeptikos* one who reflects upon, from *skeptesthai* to consider] —'**sceptical** *or arch. & U.S.* '**skeptical** *adj.* —'**sceptically** *or arch. & U.S.*

'**skeptically** *adv.* —'**scepticism** *or arch. & U.S.* '**skepticism** *n.*

Sceptic *or arch. & U.S.* **Skeptic** ('skɛptɪk) *n.* **1.** a member of one of the ancient Greek schools of philosophy, esp. that of Pyrrho, who believed that real knowledge of things is impossible. ~*adj.* **2.** of or relating to the Sceptics. —'**Scepticism** *or arch. & U.S.* '**Skepticism** *n.*

sceptre *or U.S.* **scepter** ('sɛptə) *n.* **1.** a ceremonial staff held by a monarch as the symbol of authority. **2.** imperial authority; sovereignty. [C13: from OF *sceptre*, from L, from Gk *skeptron* staff] —'**sceptred** *or U.S.* '**sceptered** *adj.*

Schaerbeek (*Flemish* 'sxaːrbeːk) *n.* a city in central Belgium, in Brabant province: an industrial suburb of Brussels. Pop.: 105 905 (1982).

Schaffhausen (*German* ʃaf'hauzən) *n.* **1.** a small canton of N Switzerland. Pop.: 69 413 (1980). Area: 298 sq. km (115 sq. miles). **2.** a town in N Switzerland, capital of Schaffhausen canton, on the Rhine. Pop.: 34 396 (1983 est.). French name: **Schaffhouse.**

Schaumburg-Lippe (*German* 'ʃaumburk'lɪpə) *n.* a former state of NW Germany, between Westphalia and Hanover: part of Lower Saxony since 1946.

schedule ('ʃɛdjuːl; *also, esp. U.S.* 'skɛdʒuəl) *n.* **1.** a plan of procedure for a project. **2.** a list of items: *a schedule of fixed prices.* **3.** a list of times; timetable. **4.** a list of tasks to be performed, esp. within a set period. **5.** *Law.* a list or inventory. ~*vb.* *(tr.)* **6.** to make a schedule of or place in a schedule. **7.** to plan to occur at a certain time. [C14: earlier *cedule, sedule* via OF from LL *schedula* small piece of paper, from L *scheda* sheet of paper]

scheduled castes *pl. n.* certain classes in Indian society officially granted special concessions. See **Harijan.**

scheduled territories *pl. n.* **the.** another name for **sterling area.**

Scheel (*German* ʃeːl) *n.* **Walter** ('valtər). born 1919, West German statesman; president of West Germany (1974–79).

Scheele (*Swedish* 'ʃeːlə) *n.* **Karl Wilhelm** (kɑːrl 'vɪlhɛlm). 1742–86, Swedish chemist. He discovered oxygen, independently of Priestley, and many other substances.

scheelite ('ʃiːlaɪt) *n.* a white, brownish, or greenish mineral, usually fluorescent, consisting of calcium tungstate with some tungsten often replaced by molybdenum. It is an important source of tungsten. [C19: from G *Scheelit*, after K. W. SCHEELE]

Scheldt (ʃɛlt, skɛlt) *n.* a river in W Europe, rising in NE France and flowing north and northeast through W Belgium to Antwerp, then northwest to the North Sea in the SW Netherlands. Length: 435 km (270 miles). Flemish and Dutch name: **Schelde** ('sxɛldə). French name: **Escaut.**

Schelling (*German* 'ʃɛlɪŋ) *n.* **Friedrich Wilhelm Joseph von** ('friːdrɪç 'vɪlhɛlm 'joːzɛf fɔn). 1775–1854, German philosopher. He expanded Fichte's idea that there is one reality, the infinite and absolute Ego, by regarding nature as an absolute being working towards self-consciousness. His works include *Ideas towards a Philosophy of Nature* (1797) and *System of Transcendental Idealism* (1800). —**Schellingian** (ʃɛ'lɪŋɪən) *adj.*

schema ('skiːmə) *n., pl.* **-mata** (-mətə). **1.** a plan, diagram, or scheme. **2.** (in the philosophy of Kant) a rule or principle that enables the understanding to unify experience. **3.** *Logic.* **a.** a syllogistic figure. **b.** a representation of the form of an inference. [C19: from Gk: form]

schematic (skɪ'mætɪk) *adj.* **1.** of or relating to the nature of a diagram, plan, or schema. ~*n.* **2.** a schematic diagram, esp. of an electrical circuit, etc. —**sche'matically** *adv.*

schematize *or* **-ise** ('skiːmə,taɪz) *vb.* *(tr.)* to form into or arrange in a scheme. —'**schema,tism** *n.* —,**schemati'zation** *or* **-i'sation** *n.*

scheme (skiːm) *n.* **1.** a systematic plan for a course of action. **2.** a systematic arrangement of parts. **3.** a secret plot. **4.** a chart, diagram, or outline. **5.** an astrological diagram giving the aspects of celestial bodies. **6.** *Chiefly Brit.* a plan formally adopted by a commercial enterprise or governmental body, as for pensions, etc. **7.** Short for **housing scheme.** ~*vb.* **8.** *(tr.)* to devise a system for. **9.** to form intrigues (for) in an underhand manner. [C16: from L *schema*, from Gk *skhēma* form] —'**schemer** *n.*

scheming ('ski:mɪŋ) *adj.* **1.** given to making plots; cunning. ~*n.* **2.** intrigues.

scherzando (skɛə'tsændəʊ) *Music.* ~*adj.*, *adv.* **1.** to be performed in a light-hearted manner. ~*n.*, *pl.* **-di** (-di:) *or* **-dos. 2.** a movement, passage, etc., directed to be performed in this way. [It., lit.: joking; see SCHERZO]

scherzo ('skɛətsəʊ) *n.*, *pl.* **-zos** *or* **-zi** (-tsi:). a brisk lively movement, developed from the minuet, with a contrastive middle section (a trio). [It.: joke, of Gmc origin]

Schiaparelli (*Italian* skjapa'rɛlli) *n.* **1. Elsa** ('ɛlsa). 1896–1973, Italian couturière, noted esp. for the dramatic colours of her designs. **2. Giovanni Virginio** (dʒo'vanni vir'dʒiːnjo). 1835–1910, Italian astronomer, who discovered the asteroid Hesperia (1861) and the so-called canals of Mars (1877).

Schick test (ʃɪk) *n. Med.* a skin test to determine immunity to diphtheria. [C20: after Bela *Schick* (1877–1967), U.S. paediatrician]

Schiedam (*Dutch* sxi:'dɑm) *n.* a port in the SW Netherlands, in South Holland province west of Rotterdam: gin distilleries. Pop.: 69 349 (1987).

Schiele (*German* 'ʃiːlə) *n.* **Egon** ('eːgɔn). 1890–1918, Austrian painter and draughtsman: a leading exponent of Austrian expressionism.

Schiller (*German* 'ʃɪlər) *n.* **Johann Christoph Friedrich von** (jo'han 'krɪstɔf 'friːdrɪç fɔn). 1759–1805, German poet, dramatist, historian, and critic. His concern with the ideal freedom of the human spirit to rise above the constraints placed upon it is reflected in his great trilogy *Wallenstein* (1800) and in *Maria Stuart* (1800).

schilling ('ʃɪlɪŋ) *n.* the standard monetary unit of Austria. [C18: from G: SHILLING]

schism ('sɪzəm, 'skɪz-) *n.* **1.** the division of a group into opposing factions. **2.** the factions so formed. **3.** division within or separation from an established Church, not necessarily involving differences in doctrine. [C14: from Church L *schisma*, from Gk *skhisma* a cleft, from *skhizein* to split]

schismatic (sɪz'mætɪk, skɪz-) *or* **schismatical** *adj.* **1.** of or promoting schism. ~*n.* **2.** a person who causes schism or belongs to a schismatic faction. —**schis'matically** *adv.*

schist (ʃɪst) *n.* any metamorphic rock that can be split into thin layers. [C18: from F *schiste*, from L *lapis schistos* stone that may be split, from Gk *skhizein* to split] —'**schistose** *adj.*

schistosome ('ʃɪstə,səʊm) *n.* any of a genus of blood flukes which cause disease in man and domestic animals. Also called: **bilharzia.** [C19: from NL *Schistosoma*; see SCHIST, -SOME³]

schistosomiasis (,ʃɪstəsəʊ'maɪəsɪs) *n.* a disease caused by infestation of the body with schistosomes. Also called: **bilharziasis.**

schizanthus (skɪz'ænθəs) *n.* a flowering annual plant, native to Chile, that has finely divided leaves. [C19: NL from Gk *skhizein* to cut + *anthos* flower]

schizo ('skɪtsəʊ) *Inf.* ~*adj.* **1.** schizophrenic. ~*n.*, *pl.* **-os. 2.** a schizophrenic person.

schizo- *or before a vowel* **schiz-** *combining form.* indicating a cleavage, split, or division: *schizophrenia*. [from Gk *skhizein* to split]

schizocarp ('skɪzə,kɑːp) *n. Bot.* a dry fruit that splits into two or more one-seeded portions at maturity. —,**schizo'carpous** *adj.*

schizoid ('skɪtsɔɪd) *adj.* **1.** *Psychol.* denoting a personality disorder characterized by extreme shyness and over-sensitivity. **2.** *Inf.* characterized by conflicting or contradictory ideas, attitudes, etc. ~*n.* **3.** a person who has a schizoid personality.

schizomycete (,skɪtsəʊmaɪ'siːt) *n.* any microscopic organism of the class *Schizomycetes*, which includes the bacteria.

schizophrenia (,skɪtsəʊ'friːnɪə) *n.* **1.** any of a group of psychotic disorders characterized by progressive deterioration of the personality, withdrawal from reality, hallucinations, emotional instability, etc. **2.** *Inf.* behaviour that seems to be motivated by contradictory or conflicting principles. [C20: from SCHIZO- + Gk *phrēn* mind] —,**schiz-o'phrenic** *adj.*, *n.*

schizothymia (,skɪtsəʊ'θaɪmɪə) *n. Psychiatry.* the condition of being schizoid or introverted. It encompasses elements of schizophrenia. [C20: NL, from SCHIZO- + -*thymia*, from Gk *thumos* spirit] —,**schizo'thymic** *adj.*

Schlegel (*German* 'ʃleːgəl) *n.* **1. August Wilhelm von** ('august 'vɪlhɛlm fɔn). 1767–1845, German romantic critic and scholar, noted particularly for his translations of Shakespeare. **2.** his brother, **Friedrich von** ('friːdrɪç fɔn). 1772–1829, German philosopher and critic; a founder of the romantic movement in Germany.

Schleiermacher (*German* 'ʃlaiər,maxər) *n.* **Friedrich Ernst Daniel** ('friːdrɪç ɛrnst 'daːnjeːl). 1768–1834, German Protestant theologian and philosopher. His works include *The Christian Faith* (1821–22).

Schlesien ('ʃleːziən) *n.* the German name for **Silesia.**

Schleswig (*German* 'ʃleːsvɪç) *n.* **1.** a fishing port in N West Germany, in Schleswig-Holstein state: on an inlet of the Baltic. Pop.: 30 000 (1985 est.). **2.** a former duchy, in the S Jutland Peninsula: annexed by Prussia in 1864; N part returned to Denmark after a plebiscite in 1920; S part forms part of the West German state of Schleswig-Holstein. Danish name: **Slesvig.**

Schleswig-Holstein (*German* 'ʃleːsvɪç'hɔlʃtain) *n.* a state of N West Germany: drained chiefly by the River Elbe; mainly agricultural. Capital: Kiel. Pop.: 2 612 700 (1986). Area: 15 658 sq. km (6045 sq. miles).

Schlieffen (*German* 'ʃliːfən) *n.* **Alfred** ('alfreːt), Count von Schlieffen. 1833–1913, German field marshal, who devised the **Schlieffen Plan** (1905): it was intended to ensure German victory over a Franco-Russian alliance by holding off Russia with minimal strength and swiftly defeating France by a massive flanking movement through the Low Countries. In a modified form, it was unsuccessfully employed in World War I (1914).

Schliemann (*German* 'ʃliːman) *n.* **Heinrich** ('hainrɪç). 1822–90, German archaeologist, who discovered nine superimposed city sites of Troy (1871–90). He also excavated the site of Mycenae (1876).

schlieren ('ʃliːrən) *n.* **1.** *Physics.* visible streaks produced in a transparent fluid as a result of variations in the fluid's density. **2.** streaks or platelike masses of mineral in a rock mass. [G, pl. of *Schliere* streak]

schmaltz *or* **schmalz** (ʃmælts, ʃmɔːlts) *n.* excessive sentimentality, esp. in music. [C20: from G (*Schmalz*) & Yiddish: melted fat, from OHG *smalz*] —'**schmaltzy** *or* '**schmalzy** *adj.*

Schmidt (ʃmɪt) *n.* **Helmut (Heinrich Waldemar)** ('hɛlmuːt). born 1918, West German statesman; chancellor of West Germany (1974–82).

Schmidt telescope *or* **camera** (ʃmɪt) *n.* a type of reflecting telescope incorporating a camera. Wide areas of the sky can be photographed in one exposure. [C20: after B. *Schmidt* (1879–1935), Swedish-born G inventor]

Schnabel ('ʃnɑːbəl) *n.* **Artur** ('artʊr). 1882–1951, U.S. pianist and composer, born in Austria.

schnapper ('ʃnæpə) *n.* a variant spelling of **snapper** (senses 1, 2).

schnapps *or* **schnaps** (ʃnæps) *n.* **1.** a Dutch spirit distilled from potatoes. **2.** (in Germany) any strong spirit. [C19: from G *Schnaps*, from *schnappen* to SNAP]

schnauzer ('ʃnautsə) *n.* a wire-haired breed of dog of the terrier type, originally from Germany, with a greyish coat. [C19: from G *Schnauze* snout]

schnitzel ('ʃnɪtsəl) *n.* a thin slice of meat, esp. veal. [G: cutlet, from *schnitzen* to carve, *schnitzeln* to whittle]

Schnitzler (*German* 'ʃnɪtslər) *n.* **Arthur** ('artʊr). 1862–1931, Austrian dramatist and novelist. His best-known work is *Anatol* (1893), a series of one-act plays that reveal his psychological insight and preoccupation with sexuality.

schnorkle ('ʃnɔːkəl) *n.*, *vb.* a less common variant of **snorkel.**

schnozzle ('ʃnɒzəl) *n. Chiefly U.S.* a slang word for **nose.** [alteration of Yiddish *shnoitsl*, from G *Schnauze* snout]

Schoenberg *or* **Schönberg** ('ʃɜːnbɜːg; *German* 'ʃøːnbɛrk) *n.* **Arnold** ('arnɔlt). 1874–1951, Austrian composer and musical theorist, in the U.S. after 1933. The harmonic idiom of such early works as the string sextet *Verklärte Nacht* (1899) gave way to his development of atonality, as in the song cycle *Pierrot Lunaire* (1912), and later of the twelve-tone technique. He wrote many choral, orchestral, and chamber works and the unfinished opera *Moses and Aaron.*

scholar ('skɒlə) *n.* **1.** a learned person, esp. in the humanities. **2.** a person, esp. a child, who studies; pupil. **3.** a student receiving a scholarship. [C14: from OF *escoler*, via LL from L *schola* SCHOOL[1]] —'**scholarly** *adj.* —'**scholariness** *n.*

scholarship ('skɒləʃɪp) *n.* **1.** academic achievement; learning. **2. a.** financial aid provided for a scholar because of academic merit. **b.** the position of a student who gains this financial aid. **c.** (*as modifier*): *a scholarship student*. **3.** the qualities of a scholar.

scholastic (skə'læstɪk) *adj.* **1.** of or befitting schools, scholars, or education. **2.** pedantic or precise. **3.** (*often cap.*) characteristic of or relating to the medieval Schoolmen. ~*n.* **4.** a student or pupil. **5.** a person who is given to logical subtleties. **6.** (*often cap.*) a disciple or adherent of scholasticism; Schoolman. **7.** a Jesuit student who is undergoing a period of probation prior to commencing his theological studies. [C16: via L from Gk *skholastikos* devoted to learning, ult. from *skholē* SCHOOL[1]] —**scho'lastically** *adv.*

scholasticism (skə'læstɪ,sɪzəm) *n.* (*sometimes cap.*) the system of philosophy, theology, and teaching that dominated medieval western Europe and was based on the writings of the Church Fathers and Aristotle.

scholiast ('skəʊlɪ,æst) *n.* a medieval annotator, esp. of classical texts. [C16: from LGk, ult. from Gk *skholē* school] —,**scholi'astic** *adj.*

Schönberg ('ʃɜːnbɜːg; *German* 'ʃøːnbɛrk) *n.* See Schoenberg.

Schongauer (*German* 'ʃoːngauər) *n.* **Martin** ('martiːn). ?1445–91, German painter and engraver.

school[1] (skuːl) *n.* **1. a.** an institution or building at which children and young people receive education. **b.** (*as modifier*): *school day.* **c.** (*in combination*): *schoolwork.* **2.** any educational institution or building. **3.** a faculty or department specializing in a particular subject: *a law school.* **4.** the staff and pupils of a school. **5.** the period of instruction in a school or one session of this: *he stayed after school to do extra work.* **6.** a place or sphere of activity that instructs: *the school of hard knocks.* **7.** a body of people or pupils adhering to a certain set of principles, doctrines, or methods. **8.** a group of artists, writers, etc., linked by the same style, teachers, or aims. **9.** a style of life: *a gentleman of the old school.* **10.** *Inf.* a group assembled for a common purpose, esp. gambling or drinking. ~*vb.* (*tr.*) **11.** to train or educate in or as in a school. **12.** to discipline or control. [OE *scōl*, from L *schola* school, from Gk *skholē* leisure spent in the pursuit of knowledge]

school[2] (skuːl) *n.* **1.** a group of fish or other aquatic animals that swim together. ~*vb.* **2.** (*intr.*) to form such a group. [OE *scolu* SHOAL[2]]

school board *n.* **1.** *English History.* an elected board of ratepayers who provided elementary schools (**board schools**). **2.** (in the U.S. and Canada) a local board of education.

schoolboy ('skuːl,bɔɪ) *or* (*fem.*) **schoolgirl** *n.* a child attending school.

schoolhouse ('skuːl,haʊs) *n.* **1.** a building used as a school. **2.** a house attached to a school.

schoolie ('skuːlɪ) *n. Austral. sl.* a schoolteacher.

schooling ('skuːlɪŋ) *n.* **1.** education, esp. when received at school. **2.** the process of teaching or being taught in a school. **3.** the training of an animal, esp. of a horse for dressage.

schoolman ('skuːlmən) *n., pl.* **-men.** (*sometimes cap.*) a scholar versed in the learning of the **Schoolmen**, the masters in the universities of the Middle Ages who were versed in scholasticism.

schoolmarm ('skuːl,mɑːm) *n. Inf.* **1.** a woman schoolteacher. **2.** any woman considered to be prim or old-fashioned. —'**school,marmish** *adj.*

schoolmaster ('skuːl,mɑːstə) *or* (*fem.*) **schoolmistress** *n.* **1.** a person who teaches in or runs a school. **2.** a person or thing that acts as an instructor.

schoolmate ('skuːl,meɪt) *or* **schoolfellow** *n.* a companion at school; fellow pupil.

school of arts *n. Austral.* a public building in a small town: orig. one used for adult education.

Schools (skuːlz) *pl. n.* **1. the Schools.** the medieval Schoolmen collectively. **2.** (at Oxford University) **a.** the University building in which examinations are held. **b.** *Inf.* the Second Public Examination for the degree of Bachelor of Arts.

schoolteacher ('skuːl,tiːtʃə) *n.* a person who teaches in a school. —'**school,teaching** *n.*

school year *n.* **1.** a twelve-month period, usually of three terms, during which pupils remain in the same class. **2.** the time during this period when the school is open.

schooner ('skuːnə) *n.* **1.** a sailing vessel with at least two masts, with lower sails rigged fore-and-aft. **2.** *Brit.* a large glass for sherry. **3.** *U.S., Canad., Austral., & N.Z.* a large glass for beer. [C18: from ?]

Schopenhauer (*German* 'ʃoːpənhauər) *n.* **Arthur** ('artur). 1788–1860, German pessimist philosopher. In his chief work, *The World as Will and Idea* (1819), he expounded the view that will is the creative primary factor and idea the secondary receptive factor. —**Schopenhauerian** (,ʃəʊpən'hauərɪən) *adj.* —'**Schopen,hauer,ism** *n.*

schottische (ʃɒ'tiːʃ) *n.* **1.** a 19th-century German dance resembling a slow polka. **2.** a piece of music composed for or in the manner of this dance. [C19: from G *der schottische Tanz* the Scottish dance]

Schouten Islands (*German* 'ʃaʊtᵊn) *pl. n.* a group of islands in the Pacific, off the N coast of Irian Jaya. Pop.: 25 487 (1966). Area: 3185 sq. km (1230 sq. miles).

Schrödinger (*German* 'ʃrøːdɪŋər) *n.* **Erwin** ('ɛrviːn). 1887–1961, Austrian physicist, who discovered the wave equation: shared the Nobel prize for physics 1933.

Schrödinger equation *n.* an equation used in wave mechanics to describe a physical system.

Schubert ('ʃuːbət) *n.* **Franz** (**Peter**) (frants). 1797–1828, Austrian composer; the originator and supreme exponent of the modern German lied. His many songs include the cycles *Die Schöne Müllerin* (1823) and *Die Winterreise* (1827). His other works include symphonies and much piano and chamber music including string quartets and the *Trout* piano quintet (1819).

Schumacher (*German* 'ʃuːmaxər) *n.* **Ernst Friedrich** (ɛrnst 'friːdrɪç). 1911–77, British economist, born in Germany. He is best known for his book *Small is Beautiful* (1973).

Schuman *n.* **1.** (*French* ʃumɑ̃). **Robert** (rɔbɛr). 1886–1963, French statesman; prime minister (1947–48). He proposed (1950) pooling the coal and steel resources of W Europe. **2.** ('ʃuːmən). **William** (**Howard**). born 1910, U.S. composer.

Schumann ('ʃuːmən) *n.* **1. Elisabeth** (e'liːzabɛt). 1885–1952, German soprano, noted esp. for her interpretations of lieder. **2. Robert Alexander** ('roːbɛrt alɛ'ksandər). 1810–56, German romantic composer, noted esp. for his piano music, such as *Carneval* (1835) and *Kreisleriana* (1838), his songs, and four symphonies.

schuss (ʃʊs) *Skiing.* ~*n.* **1.** a straight high-speed downhill run. ~*vb.* **2.** (*intr.*) to perform a schuss. [G: SHOT[1]]

Schütz (*German* ʃyts) *n.* **Heinrich** ('hainrɪç). 1585–1672, German composer, esp. of church music and madrigals.

schwa *or* **shwa** (ʃwɑː) *n.* **1.** a central vowel represented in the International Phonetic Alphabet by (ə). The sound occurs in unstressed syllables in English, as in *around* and *sofa*. **2.** the symbol (ə) used to represent this sound. [C19: via G from Heb. *shewā*, a diacritic indicating lack of a vowel sound]

Schwaben ('ʃvaːbən) *n.* the German name for **Swabia**.

Schwann (*German* ʃvan) *n.* **Theodor** ('teːodoːr). 1810–82, German physiologist, who founded the theory that all animals consist of cells or cell products.

Schwarzkopf (*German* 'ʃvartskɔpf) *n.* **Elisabeth** (e'liːzabɛt). born 1915, German operatic soprano.

Schwarzwald ('ʃvartsvalt) *n.* the German name for the **Black Forest**.

Schweinfurt (*German* 'ʃvainfurt) *n.* a city in central West Germany, in N Bavaria on the River Main. Pop.: 51 500 (1984 est.).

Schweitzer ('ʃwaɪtsə, 'ʃvaɪt-) *n.* **Albert**. 1875–1965, Franco-German medical missionary, philosopher, theologian, and organist, born in Alsace. He took up medicine in 1905 and devoted most of his life after 1913 to a medical mission at Lambaréné, Gabon: Nobel peace prize 1952.

Schweiz (ʃvaits) *n.* the German name for **Switzerland**.

Schwerin (*German* ʃve'riːn) *n.* a city in N East Germany, on **Lake Schwerin**: capital of the former state of Mecklenburg. Pop.: 127 823 (1986).

Schwitters (*German* 'ʃvɪtərs) *n.* **Kurt** (kurt). 1887–1948, German dadaist painter and poet, noted for his collages composed of discarded materials.

Schwyz (*German* ʃviːts) *n.* **1.** a canton of central Switzerland: played an important part in the formation of the Swiss confederation, to which it gave its name. Capital:

Schwyz. Pop.: 97 354 (1980). Area: 908 sq. km (351 sq. miles). **2.** a town in E central Switzerland, capital of Schwyz canton: tourism. Pop.: 12 336 (1983 est.).

sci. *abbrev. for:* **1.** science. **2.** scientific.

sciatic (saɪˈætɪk) *adj.* **1.** *Anat.* of or relating to the hip or the hipbone. **2.** of or afflicted with sciatica. [C16: from F, from LL, from L *ischiadicus* relating to pain in the hip, from Gk, from *iskhia* hip-joint]

sciatica (saɪˈætɪkə) *n.* a form of neuralgia characterized by intense pain along the body's longest nerve (**sciatic nerve**), extending from the back of the thigh down to the calf of the leg. [C15: from LL *sciatica*; see SCIATIC]

science (ˈsaɪəns) *n.* **1.** the systematic study of the nature and behaviour of the material and physical universe, based on observation, experiment, and measurement. **2.** the knowledge so obtained or the practice of obtaining it. **3.** any particular branch of this knowledge: *the applied sciences.* **4.** any body of knowledge organized in a systematic manner. **5.** skill or technique. **6.** *Arch.* knowledge. [C14: via OF from L *scientia* knowledge, from *scīre* to know]

science fiction *n.* **a.** a literary genre that makes imaginative use of scientific knowledge. **b.** (*as modifier*): *a science-fiction writer.*

science park *n.* an area where scientific research and commercial development are carried on in cooperation.

scienter (saɪˈɛntə) *adv. Law.* knowingly; wilfully. [from L]

sciential (saɪˈɛnʃəl) *adj.* **1.** of or relating to science. **2.** skilful or knowledgeable.

scientific (ˌsaɪənˈtɪfɪk) *adj.* **1.** (*prenominal*) of, derived from, or used in science: *scientific equipment.* **2.** (*prenominal*) occupied in science: *scientific manpower.* **3.** conforming with the methods used in science. — **scien'tifically** *adv.*

scientism (ˈsaɪənˌtɪzəm) *n.* **1.** the application of the scientific method. **2.** the uncritical application of scientific methods to inappropriate fields of study. — **scien'tistic** *adj.*

scientist (ˈsaɪəntɪst) *n.* a person who studies or practises any of the sciences or who uses scientific methods.

Scientology (ˌsaɪənˈtɒlədʒɪ) *n. Trademark.* a cult, founded in the early 1950s, based on the belief that self-awareness is paramount. [C20: from L *scient(ia)* SCIENCE + -LOGY] — **Scien'tologist** *n.*

sci-fi (ˈsaɪˈfaɪ) *n.* short for **science fiction.**

scilicet (ˈsɪlɪˌsɛt) *adv.* namely: used esp. in explaining an obscure text or supplying a missing word. [L: from *scīre licet* it is permitted to know]

scilla (ˈsɪlə) *n.* any of a genus of liliaceous plants having small bell-shaped flowers. See also **squill** (sense 3). [C19: via L from Gk *skilla*]

Scilly Isles, Scilly Islands (ˈsɪlɪ), *or* **Scillies** (ˈsɪlɪz) *pl. n.* a group of about 140 small islands (only five inhabited) off the extreme SW coast of England: administratively part of the county of Cornwall; tourist centre. Capital: Hugh Town. Pop.: 2628 (1981). Area: 16 sq. km (6 sq. miles). — **Scillonian** (sɪˈləʊnɪən) *adj., n.*

scimitar (ˈsɪmɪtə) *n.* an oriental sword with a curved blade broadening towards the point. [C16: from OIt., prob. from Persian *shimshīr*, from ?]

scintigraphy (ˌsɪnˈtɪgrəfɪ) *n. Med.* a diagnostic technique using a radioactive tracer and scintillation counter for producing pictures (**scintigrams**) of internal parts of the body. [C20: from SCINTI(LLATION) + -GRAPHY]

scintilla (sɪnˈtɪlə) *n.* a minute amount; hint, trace, or particle. [C17: from L: a spark]

scintillate (ˈsɪntɪˌleɪt) *vb.* (*mainly intr.*) **1.** (*also tr.*) to give off (sparks); sparkle. **2.** to be animated or brilliant. **3.** *Physics.* to give off flashes of light as a result of the impact of photons. [C17: from L *scintillāre*, from *scintilla* a spark] — **'scintillant** *adj.* — **'scintilˌlating** *adj.*

scintillation (ˌsɪntɪˈleɪʃən) *n.* **1.** the act of scintillating. **2.** a spark or flash. **3.** the twinkling of stars. **4.** *Physics.* a flash of light produced when a material scintillates.

scintillation counter *n.* an instrument for detecting and measuring the intensity of high-energy radiation. It consists of a phosphor with which particles collide producing flashes of light that are converted into pulses of electric current that are counted by electronic equipment.

sciolism (ˈsaɪəˌlɪzəm) *n. Rare.* the practice of opinionating on subjects of which one has only superficial knowledge. [C19: from LL *sciolus* someone with a smattering of

knowledge, from L *scīre* to know] — **'sciolist** *n.* — **ˌsci-o'listic** *adj.*

scion (ˈsaɪən) *n.* **1.** a descendant or young member of a family. **2.** a shoot of a plant used to form a graft. [C14: from OF *cion*, of Gmc origin]

Scipio (ˈskɪpɪˌəʊ, ˈsɪpɪˌəʊ) *n.* **1.** full name *Publius Cornelius Scipio Africanus Major.* 237–183 B.C., Roman general. He commanded the Roman invasion of Carthage in the Second Punic War, defeating Hannibal at Zama (202). **2.** full name *Publius Cornelius Scipio Aemilianus Africanus Minor.* ?185–129 B.C., Roman statesman and general; the grandson by adoption of Scipio Africanus Major. He commanded an army against Carthage in the last Punic War and razed the city to the ground (146). He became the leader (132) of the opposition in Rome to popular reforms.

scirrhus (ˈsɪrəs) *n., pl.* **-rhi** (-raɪ) *or* **-rhuses.** *Pathol.* a firm cancerous growth composed of fibrous tissues. [C17: from NL, from L *scirros*, from Gk, from *skiros* hard] — **scirrhoid** (ˈsɪrɔɪd) *adj.*

scission (ˈsɪʃən) *n.* the act or an instance of cutting, splitting, or dividing. [C15: from LL *scissiō*, from *scindere* to split]

scissor (ˈsɪzə) *vb.* to cut (an object) with scissors.

scissors (ˈsɪzəz) *pl. n.* **1.** Also called: **pair of scissors.** a cutting instrument used for cloth, hair, etc., having two crossed pivoted blades that cut by a shearing action. **2.** a wrestling hold in which a wrestler wraps his legs round his opponent's body or head and squeezes. **3.** any gymnastic feat in which the legs cross and uncross in a scissor-like movement. [C14 *sisoures*, from OF *cisoires*, from Vulgar L *cīsōria* (unattested), ult. from L *caedere* to cut]

scissors kick *n.* a type of swimming kick in which one leg is moved forward and the other bent back and they are then brought together again in a scissor-like action.

sciurine (ˈsaɪjʊrɪn, -ˌraɪn) *adj.* of or belonging to a family of rodents inhabiting most parts of the world except Australia and southern South America: includes squirrels, marmots, and chipmunks. [C19: from L *sciūrus*, from Gk *skiouros* squirrel, from *skia* a shadow + *oura* a tail]

sclera (ˈsklɪərə) *n.* the firm white fibrous membrane that forms the outer covering of the eyeball. Also called: **sclerotic.** [C19: from NL, from Gk *sklēros* hard] — **scle'ritis** *n.*

sclerenchyma (sklɪəˈrɛŋkɪmə) *n.* a supporting tissue in plants consisting of dead cells with very thick lignified walls. [C19: from SCLERO- + PARENCHYMA]

sclero- *or before a vowel* **scler-** *combining form.* **1.** indicating hardness: *sclerosis.* **2.** of the sclera: *sclerotomy.* [from Gk *sklēros* hard]

scleroderma (ˌsklɪərəʊˈdɜːmə) *or* **sclerodermia** (ˌsklɪərəʊˈdɜːmɪə) *n.* a chronic disease common among women, characterized by thickening and hardening of the skin.

scleroma (sklɪəˈrəʊmə) *n., pl.* **-mata** (-mətə). *Pathol.* any small area of abnormally hard tissue, esp. in a mucous membrane. [C17: from NL, from Gk *sklēroun* to harden, from *sklēros* hard]

scleroprotein (ˌsklɪərəʊˈprəʊtiːn) *n.* any of a group of insoluble stable proteins such as keratin that occur in skeletal and connective tissues.

sclerosis (sklɪəˈrəʊsɪs) *n., pl.* **-ses** (-siːz). **1.** *Pathol.* a hardening or thickening of organs, tissues, or vessels from inflammation, degeneration, or (esp. on the inner walls of arteries) deposition of fatty plaques. **2.** the hardening of a plant cell wall or tissue. [C14: via Med. L from Gk *sklērōsis* a hardening]

sclerotic (sklɪəˈrɒtɪk) *adj.* **1.** of or relating to the sclera. **2.** of, relating to, or having sclerosis. ~*n.* **3.** another name for **sclera.** [C16: from Med. L *sclērōticus*, from Gk; see SCLEROMA]

sclerous (ˈsklɪərəs) *adj. Anat., pathol.* hard; bony; indurated. [C19: from Gk *sklēros* hard]

SCM (in Britain) *abbrev. for:* **1.** State Certified Midwife. **2.** Student Christian Movement.

scoff[1] (skɒf) *vb.* **1.** (*intr.; often foll. by at*) to speak contemptuously (about); mock. **2.** (*tr.*) *Obs.* to regard with derision. ~*n.* **3.** an expression of derision. **4.** an object of derision. [C14: prob. from ON] — **'scoffer** *n.* — **'scoffing** *adj., n.*

scoff[2] (skɒf) *Inf., chiefly Brit.* ~*vb.* **1.** to eat (food) fast and greedily. ~*n.* **2.** food or rations. [C19: var of *scaff* food]

Scofield ('skəufiːld) n. (**David**) **Paul.** born 1922, English stage and film actor.

scold (skəuld) vb. **1.** to find fault with or reprimand (a person) harshly. **2.** (intr.) to use harsh or abusive language. ~n. **3.** a person, esp. a woman, who constantly finds fault. [C13: from ON SKALD] —'**scolder** n. —'**scolding** n.

scoliosis (ˌskɒlɪ'əusɪs) n. Pathol. an abnormal lateral curvature of the spine. [C18: from NL, from Gk: a curving, from skolios bent] —**scoliotic** (ˌskɒlɪ'ɒtɪk) adj.

scollop ('skɒləp) n., vb. a variant spelling of **scallop**.

scombroid ('skɒmbrɔɪd) adj. **1.** of, relating to, or belonging to the Scombroidea, a suborder of marine spiny-finned fishes having a forked powerful tail: includes the mackerels, tunnies, and sailfish. ~n. **2.** any fish belonging to the suborder Scombroidea. [C19: from Gk skombros a mackerel; see -OID]

sconce[1] (skɒns) n. **1.** a bracket fixed to a wall for holding candles or lights. **2.** a flat candlestick with a handle. [C14: from OF esconse hiding place, lantern, or from LL sconsa, from absconsa dark lantern]

sconce[2] (skɒns) n. a small protective fortification, such as an earthwork. [C16: from Du. schans, from MHG schanze bundle of brushwood]

scone (skəun, skɒn) n. a light plain doughy cake made from flour with very little fat, cooked in an oven or (esp. originally) on a griddle. [C16: Scot., ?from MDu. schoonbrot fine bread]

Scone (skuːn) n. a parish in E Scotland near Perth, consisting of the two villages of New Scone and Old Scone, which was the Pictish capital: original site of the stone upon which medieval Scottish kings were crowned. The stone was removed to Westminster Abbey by Edward I in 1296.

scoop (skuːp) n. **1.** a utensil used as a shovel or ladle, esp. a small shovel with deep sides and a short handle, used for taking up flour, etc. **2.** a utensil with a long handle and round bowl used for dispensing liquids, etc. **3.** anything that resembles a scoop in action, such as the bucket on a dredge. **4.** a utensil used for serving mashed potatoes, ice cream, etc. **5.** a spoonlike surgical instrument for extracting foreign matter, etc., from the body. **6.** the quantity taken up by a scoop. **7.** the act of scooping, dredging, etc. **8.** a hollow cavity. **9.** Sl. a large quick gain, as of money. **10.** a news story reported in one newspaper before all the others. ~vb. (mainly tr.) **11.** (often foll. by up) to take up and remove (an object or substance) with or as if with a scoop. **12.** (often foll. by out) to hollow out with or as if with a scoop. **13.** to make (a large sudden profit). **14.** to beat (rival newspapers) in uncovering a news item. [C14: via MDu. schôpe from Gmc] —'**scooper** n. —'**scoop,ful** n.

scoot (skuːt) vb. **1.** to go or cause to go quickly or hastily; dart or cause to dart off or away. ~n. **2.** the act of scooting. [C19 (U.S.): from ?]

scooter ('skuːtə) n. **1.** a child's vehicle consisting of a low footboard mounted between two small wheels with a handlebar. **2.** See **motor scooter**.

Scopas ('skəupəs) n. 4th century B.C., Greek sculptor and architect.

scope (skəup) n. **1.** opportunity for exercising the faculties or abilities. **2.** range of view or grasp. **3.** the area covered by an activity, topic, etc.: the scope of his thesis was vast. **4.** Naut. slack left in an anchor cable. **5.** Logic. the part of a formula that follows a quantifier or an operator. **6.** Inf. short for **telescope, microscope, oscilloscope**, etc. **7.** Arch. purpose. [C16: from It. scopo goal, from L scopus, from Gk skopos target]

-scope n. combining form. indicating an instrument for observing or detecting: microscope. [from NL -scopium, from Gk -skopion, from skopein to look at] —**scopic** adj. combining form.

scopolamine (skə'pɒlə,miːn) n. a colourless viscous liquid alkaloid extracted from certain plants, such as henbane: used in preventing travel sickness and as a sedative and truth serum. Also called: **hyoscine**. [C20: scopol- from NL scopolia Japonica Japanese belladonna (from which the alkaloid is extracted), after G. A. Scopoli (1723–88), It. naturalist, + AMINE]

Scopus ('skəupəs) n. **Mount.** a mountain in central Israel, east of Jerusalem: a N extension of the Mount of Olives; site of the Hebrew University (1925). Height: 834 m (2736 ft.).

-scopy n. combining form. indicating a viewing or observation: microscopy. [from Gk -skopia, from skopein to look at]

scorbutic (skɔː'bjuːtɪk) adj. of or having scurvy. [C17: from NL scorbūticus, from Med. L scorbūtus, prob. of Gmc origin] —**scor'butically** adv.

scorch (skɔːtʃ) vb. **1.** to burn or become burnt, esp. so as to affect the colour, taste, etc. **2.** to wither or parch or cause to wither from exposure to heat. **3.** (intr.) Inf. to be very hot: it is scorching outside. **4.** (tr.) Inf. to criticize harshly. ~n. **5.** a slight burn. **6.** a mark caused by the application of too great heat. **7.** Horticulture. a mark on fruit, etc., caused by pests or insecticides. [C15: prob. from ON skorpna to shrivel up] —'**scorching** adj.

scorched earth policy n. the policy in warfare of removing or destroying everything that might be useful to an invading enemy.

scorcher ('skɔːtʃə) n. **1.** a person or thing that scorches. **2.** something caustic. **3.** Inf. a very hot day. **4.** Brit. inf. something remarkable.

score (skɔː) n. **1.** a numerical record of a competitive game or match. **2.** the total number of points made by a side or individual in a game. **3.** the act of scoring, esp. a point or points. **4. the score.** Inf. the actual situation. **5.** a group or set of twenty: three score years and ten. **6.** (usually pl.; foll. by of) lots: I have scores of things to do. **7.** Music. **a.** the printed form of a composition in which the instrumental or vocal parts appear on separate staves vertically arranged on large pages (**full score**) or in a condensed version, usually for piano (**short score**) or voices and piano (**vocal score**). **b.** the incidental music for a film or play. **c.** the songs, music, etc., for a stage or film musical. **8.** a mark or notch, esp. one made in keeping a tally. **9.** an account of amounts due. **10.** an amount recorded as due. **11.** a reason: the book was rejected on the score of length. **12.** a grievance. **13. a.** a line marking a division or boundary. **b.** (as modifier): score line. **14. over the score.** Inf. excessive; unfair. **15. settle** or **pay off a score. a.** to avenge a wrong. **b.** to repay a debt. ~vb. **16.** to gain (a point or points) in a game or contest. **17.** (tr.) to make a total score of. **18.** to keep a record of the score (of). **19.** (tr.) to be worth (a certain amount) in a game. **20.** (tr.) to record by making notches in. **21.** to make (cuts, lines, etc.) in or on. **22.** (intr.) Sl. to obtain something desired, esp. to purchase an illegal drug. **23.** (intr.) Sl. (of men) to be successful in seducing a person. **24.** (tr.) **a.** to arrange (a piece of music) for specific instruments or voices. **b.** to write the music for (a film, play, etc.). **25.** to achieve (success or an advantage): your idea scored with the boss. [OE scora] —'**scorer** n.

scoreboard ('skɔː,bɔːd) n. Sport, etc. a board for displaying the score of a game or match.

scorecard ('skɔː,kɑːd) n. **1.** a card on which scores are recorded, as in golf. **2.** a card identifying the players in a sports match, esp. cricket.

score off vb. (intr., prep.) to gain an advantage at someone else's expense.

scoria ('skɔːrɪə) n., pl. **-riae** (-rɪ,iː). **1.** a mass of solidified lava containing many cavities. **2.** refuse obtained from smelted ore. [C17: from L: dross, from Gk skōria, from skōr excrement]

scorify ('skɔːrɪ,faɪ) vb. **-fying, -fied.** to remove (impurities) from metals by forming scoria. —,**scorifi'cation** n. —'**scori,fier** n.

scoring ('skɔːrɪŋ) n. another name for **orchestration** (see **orchestrate**).

scorn (skɔːn) n. **1.** open contempt for a person or thing. **2.** an object of contempt or derision. ~vb. **3.** to treat with contempt or derision. **4.** (tr.) to reject with contempt. [C12 schornen, from OF escharnir, of Gmc origin] —'**scorner** n. —'**scornful** adj. —'**scornfully** adv.

Scorpio ('skɔː,pɪˌəu) n. **1.** Also called: **Scorpius**. Astron. a large S constellation. **2.** Also called: **the Scorpion**. Astrol. the eighth sign of the zodiac. The sun is in this sign between about Oct. 23 and Nov. 21. [L: SCORPION]

scorpion ('skɔː,pɪən) n. **1.** an arachnid of warm dry regions, having a segmented body with a long tail terminating in a venomous sting. **2. false scorpion**. a small nonvenomous arachnid that superficially resembles the scorpion but lacks the long tail. **3.** Bible. a barbed scourge (I Kings 12:11). [C13: via OF from L scorpiō, from Gk skorpios, from ?]

Scorpion ('skɔːpɪən) *n.* **the.** the constellation Scorpio, the eighth sign of the zodiac.

scorpion fish *n.* any of a genus of fish of temperate and tropical seas, having venomous spines on the dorsal and anal fins.

Scot (skɒt) *n.* **1.** a native or inhabitant of Scotland. **2.** a member of a tribe of Celtic raiders from northern Ireland who eventually settled in N Britain during the 5th and 6th centuries.

Scot. *abbrev. for:* **1.** Scotch (whisky). **2.** Scotland. **3.** Scottish.

scot and lot *n. Brit. history.* a municipal tax paid by burgesses that came to be regarded as a qualification for the borough franchise in parliamentary elections. [C13 *scot* tax, from Gmc]

scotch[1] (skɒtʃ) *vb.* (*tr.*) **1.** to put an end to; crush: *bad weather scotched our plans.* **2.** *Obs.* to cut or score. ~*n.* **3.** *Arch.* a gash. **4.** a line marked down, as for hopscotch. [C15: from ?]

scotch[2] (skɒtʃ) *vb.* **1.** (*tr.*) to block, prop, or prevent from moving with or as if with a wedge. ~*n.* **2.** a block or wedge to prevent motion. [C17: from ?]

Scotch[1] (skɒtʃ) *adj.* **1.** another word for **Scottish.** ~*n.* **2.** the Scots or their language.

▷ **Usage.** In the north of England and in Scotland, *Scotch* is not used outside fixed expressions such as *Scotch whisky.* The use of *Scotch* for *Scots* or *Scottish* is otherwise felt to be incorrect, esp. when applied to persons.

Scotch[2] (skɒtʃ) *n.* whisky distilled from fermented malted barley and made in Scotland. Also called: **Scotch whisky.**

Scotch broth *n. Brit.* a thick soup made from mutton or beef stock, vegetables, and pearl barley.

Scotch egg *n. Brit.* a hard-boiled egg enclosed in a layer of sausage meat, covered in egg and crumbs, and fried.

Scotchman ('skɒtʃmən) *or* (*fem.*) **Scotchwoman** *n., pl.* **-men** *or* **-women.** (*regarded as bad usage by the Scots*) another word for **Scotsman** or **Scotswoman.**

Scotch mist *n.* **1.** a heavy wet mist. **2.** drizzle.

Scotch snap *n. Music.* a rhythmical pattern consisting of a short note followed by a long one. Also called: **Scotch catch.**

Scotch terrier *n.* another name for **Scottish terrier.**

scoter ('skəʊtə) *n., pl.* **-ters** *or* **-ter.** a sea duck of northern regions. The male plumage is black with white patches around the head and eyes. [C17: from ?]

scot-free *adv., adj.* (*predicative*) without harm, loss, or penalty. [C16: see SCOT AND LOT]

Scotland ('skɒtlənd) *n.* a country that is part of the United Kingdom, occupying the north of Great Britain: the English and Scottish thrones were united under one monarch in 1603 and the parliaments in 1707. It consists of the Highlands in the north, the central Lowlands, and hilly uplands in the south; has a deeply indented coastline, about 800 offshore islands (mostly in the west), and many lochs. Capital: Edinburgh. Pop.: 5 121 000 (1986 est.). Area: 78 768 sq. km (30 412 sq. miles).

Scotland Yard *n.* the headquarters of the police force of metropolitan London. Official name: **New Scotland Yard.**

scotoma (skɒ'təʊmə) *n., pl.* **-mas** *or* **-mata** (-mətə). **1.** *Pathol.* a blind spot. **2.** *Psychol.* a mental blind spot. [C16: via Med. L from Gk *skotōma* giddiness, from *skotoun* to make dark, from *skotos* darkness]

Scots (skɒts) *adj.* **1.** of or characteristic of Scotland, its people, their English dialects, or their Gaelic language. ~*n.* **2.** any of the English dialects spoken or written in Scotland.

Scotsman ('skɒtsmən) *or* (*fem.*) **Scotswoman** *n., pl.* **-men** *or* **-women.** a native or inhabitant of Scotland.

Scots pine *or* **Scotch pine** *n.* **1.** a coniferous tree of Europe and W and N Asia, having blue-green needle-like leaves and brown cones with a small prickle on each scale. **2.** the wood of this tree.

Scott (skɒt) *n.* **1.** Sir **George Gilbert.** 1811–78, English architect, prominent in the Gothic revival. He restored many churches and cathedrals and designed the Albert Memorial (1863) and St Pancras Station (1865). **2.** **Paul** (**Mark**). 1920–78, English novelist, who is best known for the series of novels known as the "Raj Quartet": *The Jewel in the Crown* (1966), *The Day of the Scorpion* (1968), *The Towers of Silence* (1972), *A Division of the Spoils* (1975), and *Staying On* (1977) which won the Booker Prize. **3.**

Robert Falcon. 1868–1912, English naval officer and explorer of the Antarctic. He commanded two Antarctic expeditions (1901–04; 1910–12) and reached the South Pole on Jan. 18, 1912, shortly after Amundsen; he and the rest of his party died on the return journey. **4.** Sir **Walter.** 1771–1832, Scottish romantic novelist and poet. He is remembered chiefly for his tales inspired by Scottish history and folklore, esp. the "Waverley" novels, including *Waverley* (1814), *Rob Roy* (1817), *The Heart of Midlothian* (1818), *Ivanhoe* (1819), *Kenilworth* (1821), *Quentin Durward* (1823), and *Redgauntlet* (1824). His narrative poems include *The Lay of the Last Minstrel* (1805), *Marmion* (1808), and *The Lady of the Lake* (1810).

Scotticism ('skɒtɪˌsɪzəm) *n.* a Scottish idiom, word, etc.

Scottie *or* **Scotty** ('skɒtɪ) *n., pl.* **-ties.** **1.** See **Scottish terrier.** **2.** *Inf.* a Scotsman.

Scottish ('skɒtɪʃ) *adj.* of, relating to, or characteristic of Scotland, its people, their Gaelic language, or their English dialects.

Scottish Certificate of Education *n.* See **SCE.**

Scottish Gaelic *n.* the Goidelic language of the Celts of Scotland, used esp. in the Highlands and Western Isles.

Scottish National Party *n.* a political party advocating the independence of Scotland. Abbrev.: **SNP.**

Scottish terrier *n.* a small but sturdy long-haired breed of terrier, usually with a black coat.

Scotus ('skəʊtəs) *n.* See **Duns Scotus.**

scoundrel ('skaʊndrəl) *n.* a worthless or villainous person. [C16: from ?]

scour[1] ('skaʊə) *vb.* **1.** to clean or polish (a surface) by washing and rubbing. **2.** to remove dirt from or have the dirt removed from. **3.** (*tr.*) to clear (a channel) by the force of water. **4.** (*tr.*) to remove by or as if by rubbing. **5.** (*tr.*) to cause (livestock) to purge their bowels. ~*n.* **6.** the act of scouring. **7.** the place scoured, esp. by running water. **8.** something that scours, such as a cleansing agent. **9.** (*often pl.*) prolonged diarrhoea in livestock, esp. cattle. [C13: via MLow G *schüren,* from OF *escurer,* from LL *excūrāre* to cleanse, from *cūrāre;* see CURE] —'**scourer** *n.*

scour[2] ('skaʊə) *vb.* **1.** to range over (territory), as in making a search. **2.** to move swiftly or energetically over (territory). [C14: from ON *skūr*]

scourge (skɜːdʒ) *n.* **1.** a person who harasses or causes destruction. **2.** a means of inflicting punishment or suffering. **3.** a whip used for inflicting punishment or torture. ~*vb.* (*tr.*) **4.** to whip. **5.** to punish severely. [C13: from Anglo-F, from OF *escorgier* (unattested) to lash, from *es-* EX-[1] + L *corrigia* whip] —'**scourger** *n.*

scourings ('skaʊərɪŋz) *pl. n.* **1.** the residue left after cleaning grain. **2.** residue that remains after scouring.

scouse (skaʊs) *n. Liverpool dialect.* a stew made from left-over meat. [C19: shortened from LOBSCOUSE]

Scouse (skaʊs) *Brit. inf.* ~*n.* **1.** a person who comes from Liverpool. **2.** the dialect spoken by such a person. ~*adj.* **3.** of or from Liverpool. [C20: from SCOUSE]

scout[1] (skaʊt) *n.* **1.** a person, ship, or aircraft sent out to gain information. **2.** *Mil.* a person or unit despatched to reconnoitre the position of the enemy, etc. **3.** the act or an instance of scouting. **4.** (esp. at Oxford University) a college servant. **5.** *Inf.* a fellow. ~*vb.* **6.** to examine or observe (anything) in order to obtain information. **7.** (*tr.;* sometimes foll. by *out* or *up*) to seek. **8.** (*intr.;* foll. by *about* or *around*) to go in search (for). [C14: from OF *ascouter* to listen to, from L *auscultāre* to AUSCULTATE] —'**scouter** *n.*

scout[2] (skaʊt) *vb.* to reject (a person, etc.) with contempt. [C17: from ON *skūta* derision]

Scout (skaʊt) *n.* (*sometimes not cap.*) a boy or (in the U.S.) a girl who is a member of a worldwide movement (the **Scout Association**) founded as the Boy Scouts in England in 1908 by Lord Baden-Powell. British female counterpart: **Guide.** — '**Scouting** *n.*

Scouter ('skaʊtə) *n.* the leader of a troop of Scouts. Also called (esp. formerly): **Scoutmaster.**

scow (skaʊ) *n.* an unpowered barge used for freight, etc.; lighter. [C18: via Du. *schouw* from Low G *schalde*]

scowl (skaʊl) *vb.* **1.** (*intr.*) to contract the brows in a threatening or angry manner. ~*n.* **2.** a gloomy or threatening expression. [C14: prob. from ON] — '**scowler** *n.*

SCPS (in Britain) *abbrev. for* Society of Civil and Public Servants.

scrabble ('skræbᵊl) vb. **1.** (intr.; often foll. by about or at) to scrape (at) or grope (for), as with hands or claws. **2.** to struggle (with). **3.** (intr.; often foll. by for) to struggle to gain possession. **4.** to scribble. ~n. **5.** the act or an instance of scrabbling. **6.** a scribble. **7.** a disorderly struggle. [C16: from MDu. shrabbelen, frequentative of shrabben to scrape] —'**scrabbler** n.

Scrabble ('skræbᵊl) n. Trademark. a game in which words are formed by placing lettered tiles in a pattern similar to a crossword puzzle.

scrag (skræg) n. **1.** a thin or scrawny person or animal. **2.** the lean end of a neck of veal or mutton. **3.** Inf. the neck of a human being. ~vb. **scragging, scragged. 4.** (tr.) Inf. to wring the neck of. [C16: ? var. of CRAG]

scraggly ('skræglı) adj. **-glier, -gliest.** Chiefly U.S. untidy or irregular.

scraggy ('skrægı) adj. **-gier, -giest. 1.** lean or scrawny. **2.** rough; unkempt. — '**scraggily** adv. — '**scragginess** n.

scram¹ (skræm) vb. **scramming, scrammed.** (intr.; often imperative) Inf. to go away hastily. [C20: from SCRAMBLE]

scram² (skræm) n. **1.** an emergency shutdown of a nuclear reactor. ~vb. **2.** (of a nuclear reactor) to shut down or be shut down in an emergency. [C20: ?from SCRAM¹]

scramble ('skræmbᵊl) vb. **1.** (intr.) to climb or crawl, esp. by using the hands to aid movement. **2.** to proceed hurriedly or in a disorderly fashion. **3.** (intr.; often foll. by for) to compete with others, esp. in a disordered manner. **4.** (intr.; foll. by through) to deal with hurriedly. **5.** (tr.) to throw together in a haphazard manner. **6.** (tr.) to collect in a hurried or disorganized manner. **7.** (tr.) to cook (eggs that have been whisked up with milk) in a pan containing a little melted butter. **8.** Mil. to order (a crew or aircraft) to take off immediately or (of a crew or aircraft) to take off immediately. **9.** (tr.) to render (speech) unintelligible during transmission by means of an electronic scrambler. ~n. **10.** the act of scrambling. **11.** a climb or trek over difficult ground. **12.** a disorderly struggle, esp. to gain possession. **13.** Mil. an immediate preparation for action, as of crew, aircraft, etc. **14.** Brit. a motorcycle rally in which competitors race across rough open ground. [C16: blend of SCRABBLE & RAMP]

scrambler ('skræmblə) n. an electronic device that renders speech unintelligible during transmission, by altering frequencies.

Scranton ('skræntən) n. an industrial city in NE Pennsylvania: university (1888). Pop.: 88 117 (1980).

scrap¹ (skræp) n. **1.** a small piece of something larger; fragment. **2.** an extract from something written. **3. a.** waste material or used articles, esp. metal, often collected and reprocessed. **b.** (as modifier): scrap iron. **4.** (pl.) pieces of discarded food. ~vb. **scrapping, scrapped.** (tr.) **5.** to discard as useless. [C14: from ON skrap]

scrap² (skræp) Inf. ~n. **1.** a fight or argument. ~vb. **scrapping, scrapped. 2.** (intr.) to quarrel or fight. [C17: ?from SCRAPE]

scrapbook ('skræp,bʊk) n. a book or album of blank pages in which to mount newspaper cuttings, pictures, etc.

scrape (skreɪp) vb. **1.** to move (a rough or sharp object) across (a surface), esp. to smooth or clean. **2.** (tr.; often foll. by away or off) to remove (a layer) by rubbing. **3.** to produce a harsh or grating sound by rubbing against (a surface, etc.). **4.** (tr.) to injure or damage by rough contact: to scrape one's knee. **5.** (intr.) to be very economical (esp. in **scrimp and scrape**). **6.** (intr.) to draw the foot backwards in making a bow. **7. scrape acquaintance with.** to contrive an acquaintance with. ~n. **8.** the act of scraping. **9.** a scraped place. **10.** a harsh or grating sound. **11.** Inf. an awkward or embarrassing predicament. **12.** Inf. a conflict or struggle. [OE scrapian] — '**scraper** n.

scraperboard ('skreɪpə,bɔːd) n. thin card covered with a layer of china clay and a top layer of Indian ink, which can be scraped away with a special tool to leave a white line.

scrape through vb. (adv.) **1.** (intr.) to manage or survive with difficulty. **2.** to succeed in with difficulty or by a narrow margin.

scrape together or **up** vb. (tr., adv.) to collect with difficulty: to scrape together money for a new car.

scrapheap ('skræp,hiːp) n. **1.** a pile of discarded material. **2. on the scrapheap.** (of people or things) having outlived their usefulness.

scrappy ('skræpɪ) adj. **-pier, -piest.** fragmentary; disjointed. — '**scrappily** adv.

scratch (skrætʃ) vb. **1.** to mark or cut (the surface of something) with a rough or sharp instrument. **2.** (often foll. by at, out, off, etc.) to scrape (the surface of something), as with claws, nails, etc. **3.** to scrape (the surface of the skin) with the nails, as to relieve itching. **4.** to chafe or irritate (a surface, esp. the skin). **5.** to make or cause to make a grating sound. **6.** (tr.; sometimes foll. by out) to erase by or as if by scraping. **7.** (tr.) to write or draw awkwardly. **8.** (intr.; sometimes foll. by along) to earn a living, manage, etc., with difficulty. **9.** to withdraw (an entry) from a race, (U.S.) election, etc. ~n. **10.** the act of scratching. **11.** a slight injury. **12.** a mark made by scratching. **13.** a slight grating sound. **14.** (in a handicap sport) a competitor or the status of a competitor who has no allowance. **15. a.** the line from which competitors start in a race. **b.** (formerly) a line drawn on the floor of a prize ring at which the contestants stood to begin fighting. **16.** Billiards, etc. a lucky shot. **17. from scratch.** Inf. from the very beginning. **18. up to scratch.** (usually used with a negative) Inf. up to standard. ~adj. **19.** Sport. (of a team) assembled hastily. **20.** (in a handicap sport) with no allowance or penalty. **21.** Inf. rough or haphazard. [C15: via OF escrater from Gmc] — '**scratcher** n. — '**scratchy** adj.

scratching ('skrætʃɪŋ) n. a percussive effect obtained by rotating a gramophone record manually: a disc-jockey and dub technique.

scratch pad n. Chiefly U.S. a notebook, esp. one with detachable leaves.

scratch video n. the recycling of images from films or television to make collages.

scrawl (skrɔːl) vb. **1.** to write or draw (words, etc.) carelessly or hastily. ~n. **2.** careless or scribbled writing or drawing. [C17: ? a blend of SPRAWL & CRAWL¹] — '**scrawly** adj.

scrawny ('skrɔːnɪ) adj. **scrawnier, scrawniest. 1.** very thin and bony. **2.** meagre or stunted. [C19: var. of dialect scranny] — '**scrawnily** adv. — '**scrawniness** n.

scream (skriːm) vb. **1.** to utter or emit (a sharp piercing cry or similar sound), esp. as of fear, pain, etc. **2.** (intr.) to laugh wildly. **3.** (intr.) to speak, shout, or behave in a wild manner. **4.** (tr.) to bring (oneself) into a specified state by screaming: she screamed herself hoarse. **5.** (intr.) to be extremely conspicuous: these orange curtains scream; you need something more restful. ~n. **6.** a sharp piercing cry or sound, esp. one denoting fear or pain. **7.** Inf. a person or thing that causes great amusement. [C13: from Gmc]

screamer ('skriːmə) n. **1.** a person or thing that screams. **2.** a goose-like aquatic bird, such as the **crested screamer** of tropical and subtropical South America. **3.** Inf. (in printing) an exclamation mark. **4.** someone or something that raises screams of laughter or astonishment. **5.** U.S. & Canad. sl. a sensational headline. **6.** Austral. sl. a person or thing that is excellent of its kind.

scree (skriː) n. an accumulation of rock fragments at the foot of a cliff or hillside, often forming a sloping heap. [OE scríthan to slip; rel. to ON skrítha to slide]

screech¹ (skriːtʃ) n. **1.** a shrill or high-pitched sound or cry. ~vb. **2.** to utter with or produce a screech. [C16: var. of earlier scritch, imit.] — '**screecher** n. — '**screechy** adj.

screech² (skriːtʃ) n. Canad. sl. **1.** a dark rum. **2.** any strong cheap drink. [?from SCREECH¹]

screech owl n. **1.** Brit. another name for **barn owl. 2.** a small North American owl having a reddish-brown or grey plumage.

screed (skriːd) n. **1.** a long or prolonged speech or piece of writing. **2.** a strip of wood, plaster, or metal placed on a surface to act as a guide to the thickness of the cement or plaster coat to be applied. **3.** a mixture of cement, sand, and water applied to a concrete slab, etc., to give a smooth surface finish. [C14: prob. var. of OE scréade shred]

screen (skriːn) n. **1.** a light movable frame, panel, or partition serving to shelter, divide, hide, etc. **2.** anything that serves to shelter, protect, or conceal. **3.** a frame containing a mesh that is placed over a window to keep out insects. **4.** a decorated partition, esp. in a church around the choir. **5.** a sieve. **6.** the wide end of a cathode-ray tube, esp. in a television set, on which a visible image is formed. **7.** a white or silvered surface, placed in front of a projector to receive the enlarged image of a film or of slides. **8. the screen.** the film industry or films collectively. **9.** *Photog.* a plate of ground glass in some types of camera on which the image of a subject is focused. **10.** men or ships deployed around and ahead of a larger military formation to warn of attack. **11.** *Electronics.* See **screen grid.** ~*vb.* (*tr.*) **12.** (sometimes foll. by *off*) to shelter, protect, or conceal. **13.** to sieve or sort. **14.** to test or check (an individual or group) so as to determine suitability for a task, etc. **15.** to examine for the presence of a disease, weapons, etc. **16.** to provide with a screen or screens. **17.** to project (a film) onto a screen, esp. for public viewing. [C15: from OF *escren* (F *écran*)] —'**screenable** *adj.* —'**screener** *n.*

screen grid *n.* *Electronics.* an electrode placed between the control grid and anode of a valve which acts as an electrostatic shield, thus increasing the stability of the device. Sometimes shortened to **screen.**

screenings ('skriːnɪŋz) *pl. n.* refuse separated by sifting.

screening test *n.* a simple test performed on a large number of people to identify those who have or are likely to develop a specified disease.

screenplay ('skriːn,pleɪ) *n.* the script for a film, including instructions for sets and camera work.

screen process *n.* a method of printing using a fine mesh of silk, nylon, etc., treated with an impermeable coating except in the areas through which ink is subsequently forced onto the paper behind. Also called: **silk-screen printing.**

screenwriter ('skriːn,raɪtə) *n.* a person who writes screenplays.

screw (skruː) *n.* **1.** a device used for fastening materials together, consisting of a threaded shank that has a slotted head by which it may be rotated so as to cut its own thread. **2.** Also called: **screw-bolt.** a threaded cylindrical rod that engages with a similarly threaded cylindrical hole. **3.** a thread in a cylindrical hole corresponding with that on the screw with which it is designed to engage. **4.** anything resembling a screw in shape or spiral form. **5.** a twisting movement of or resembling that of a screw. **6.** Also called: **screw-back.** *Billiards, etc.* a stroke in which the cue ball moves backward after striking the object ball. **7.** another name for **propeller** (sense 1). **8.** *Sl.* a prison guard. **9.** *Brit. sl.* salary, wages, or earnings. **10.** *Brit.* a small amount of salt, tobacco, etc., in a twist of paper. **11.** *Sl.* a person who is mean with money. **12.** *Sl.* an old or worthless horse. **13.** (*often pl.*) *Sl.* force or compulsion (esp. in **put the screws on**). **14.** *Taboo sl.* sexual intercourse. **15. have a screw loose.** *Inf.* to be insane. ~*vb.* **16.** (*tr.*) to rotate (a screw or bolt) so as to drive it into or draw it out of a material. **17.** (*tr.*) to cut a screw thread in (a rod or hole) with a tap or die or on a lathe. **18.** to turn or cause to turn in the manner of a screw. **19.** (*tr.*) to attach or fasten with a screw or screws. **20.** (*tr.*) *Inf.* to take advantage of; cheat. **21.** (*tr.; often foll. by *up*) *Inf.* to distort or contort: *he screwed his face into a scowl.* **22.** (*tr.; often foll. by *from* or *out of*) *Inf.* to coerce or force out; extort. **23.** *Taboo sl.* to have sexual intercourse (with). **24.** (*tr.*) *Sl.* to burgle. **25. have one's head screwed on the right way.** *Inf.* to be sensible. ~See also **screw up.** [C15: from F *escroe*, from Med. L *scrōfa* screw, from L: sow, presumably because the thread of the screw is like the spiral of the sow's tail] —'**screwer** *n.*

screwball ('skruː,bɔːl) *Sl., chiefly U.S. & Canad.* ~*n.* **1.** an odd or eccentric person. ~*adj.* **2.** odd; eccentric.

screwdriver ('skruː,draɪvə) *n.* **1.** a tool used for turning screws, usually having a steel shank with a flattened square-cut tip that fits into a slot in the head of the screw. **2.** an alcoholic beverage consisting of orange juice and vodka.

screwed (skruːd) *adj.* **1.** fastened by a screw or screws. **2.** having spiral grooves like a screw. **3.** twisted or distorted. **4.** *Brit. sl.* drunk.

screw eye *n.* a wood screw with its shank bent into a ring.

screw pine *n.* any of various tropical Old World plants having a spiral mass of pineapple-like leaves and conelike fruits.

screw propeller *n.* an early form of ship's propeller in which an Archimedes' screw is used to produce thrust by accelerating a flow of water.

screw top *n.* **1.** a bottle top that screws onto the bottle, allowing the bottle to be resealed after use. **2.** a bottle with such a top. —'**screw-,top** *adj.*

screw up *vb.* (*tr., adv.*) **1.** to twist out of shape or distort. **2.** to summon up: *to screw up one's courage.* **3.** *Inf.* to mishandle or bungle.

screwy ('skruːɪ) *adj.* **screwier, screwiest.** *Inf.* odd, crazy, or eccentric.

Scriabin ('skrɪəbɪn; *Russian* 'skrjabin) *n.* **Aleksandr Nikolayevich** (alɪk'sandr nika'lajɪvɪtʃ). 1872–1915, Russian composer, whose works came increasingly to express his theosophic beliefs. He wrote many piano works; his orchestral compositions include *Prometheus* (1911).

scribble ('skrɪbᵊl) *vb.* **1.** to write or draw in a hasty or illegible manner. **2.** to make meaningless or illegible marks (on). **3.** *Derog. or facetious.* to write poetry, novels, etc. ~*n.* **4.** hasty careless writing or drawing. **5.** meaningless or illegible marks. [C15: from Med. L *scribillāre* to write hastily, from L *scrībere* to write] —'**scribbler** *n.* —'**scribbly** *adj.*

scribbly gum *n.* *Austral.* a eucalypt with smooth white bark, marked with random patterns made by wood-boring insects.

scribe (skraɪb) *n.* **1.** a person who, copies documents, esp. a person who made handwritten copies before the invention of printing. **2.** a clerk or public copyist. **3.** *Bible.* a recognized scholar and teacher of the Jewish Law. ~*vb.* **4.** to score a line on (a surface) with a pointed instrument, as in metalworking. [(in the senses: writer, etc.) C14: from L *scrība* clerk, from *scrībere* to write; C17 (vb.): ?from INSCRIBE] —'**scribal** *adj.*

Scribe (*French* skrib) *n.* **Augustin Eugène** (ogystɛ̃ ɵ̃ʒɛn). 1791–1861, French author or coauthor of over 350 vaudevilles, comedies, and libretti for light opera.

scriber ('skraɪbə) *n.* a pointed steel tool used to score materials as a guide to cutting, etc. Also called: **scribe.**

scrim (skrɪm) *n.* a fine open-weave fabric, used in upholstery, lining, building, and in the theatre to create the illusion of a solid wall. [C18: from ?]

scrimmage ('skrɪmɪdʒ) *n.* **1.** a rough or disorderly struggle. **2.** *American football.* the period of a game from the time the ball goes into play to the time it is declared dead. ~*vb.* **3.** (*intr.*) to engage in a scrimmage. **4.** (*tr.*) to put (the ball) into a scrimmage. [C15: from earlier *scrimish,* var. of SKIRMISH] —'**scrimmager** *n.*

scrimp (skrɪmp) *vb.* **1.** (when *intr.*, sometimes foll. by *on*) to be very sparing in the use (of) (esp. in **scrimp and scrape**). **2.** (*tr.*) to treat meanly: *he is scrimping his children.* [C18: Scot., from ?] —'**scrimpy** *adj.* —'**scrimpiness** *n.*

scrimshank ('skrɪm,ʃæŋk) *vb.* (*intr.*) *Brit. mil. sl.* to shirk work. [C19: from ?]

scrimshaw ('skrɪm,ʃɔː) *n.* **1.** the art of decorating or carving shells, bone, ivory, etc., done by sailors as a leisure activity. **2.** an article or articles made in this manner. [C19: from ?]

scrip (skrɪp) *n.* **1.** a written certificate, list, etc. **2.** a small scrap, esp. of paper with writing on it. **3.** *Finance.* **a.** a certificate representing a claim to part of a share of stock. **b.** the shares issued by a company (**scrip** or **bonus issue**) without charge and distributed among existing shareholders. [C18: in some senses, prob. from SCRIPT; otherwise, short for *subscription receipt*]

script (skrɪpt) *n.* **1.** handwriting as distinguished from print. **2.** the letters, characters, or figures used in writing by hand. **3.** any system or style of writing. **4.** written copy for the use of performers in films and plays. **5.** *Law.* an original or principal document. **6.** an answer paper in an examination. ~*vb.* **7.** (*tr.*) to write a script for. [C14: from L *scriptum* something written, from *scrībere* to write]

Script. *abbrev. for* Scripture(s).

scriptorium (skrɪp'tɔːrɪəm) *n., pl.* **-riums** *or* **-ria** (-rɪə) a room, esp. in a monastery, set apart for the copying of manuscripts. [from Med. L]

scripture ('skrɪptʃə) *n.* a sacred, solemn, or authoritative book or piece of writing. [C13: from L *scriptūra* written material, from *scrībere* to write] —'**scriptural** *adj.*

Scripture ('skrɪptʃə) *n.* **1.** Also called: **Holy Scripture, Holy Writ, the Scriptures.** *Christianity.* the Old and New Testaments. **2.** any book or body of writings, esp. when regarded as sacred by a particular religious group.

scriptwriter ('skrɪpt,raɪtə) *n.* a person who prepares scripts, esp. for a film. —'**script,writing** *n.*

scrivener ('skrɪvɪnə) *n. Arch.* **1.** a person who writes out deeds, etc. **2.** a notary. [C14: from *scrivein* clerk, from OF *escrivain*, ult. from L *scrība* SCRIBE]

scrod (skrɒd) *n. U.S.* a young cod or haddock. [C19: ? from obs. Du. *schrood*, from MDu. *schrode* SHRED (n.); the name perhaps refers to the method of preparing the fish for cooking]

scrofula ('skrɒfjʊlə) *n. Pathol.* (*no longer in technical use*) tuberculosis of the lymphatic glands. Also called (formerly): (the) **king's evil.** [C14: from Med. L, from LL *scrófulae* swollen glands in the neck, lit.: little sows (sows were thought to be particularly prone to the disease), from L *scrófa* sow] —'**scrofulous** *adj.*

scroll (skrəʊl) *n.* **1.** a roll of parchment, etc., usually inscribed with writing. **2.** an ancient book in the form of a roll of parchment, papyrus, etc. **3.** a decorative carving or moulding resembling a scroll. ~*vb.* **4.** (*tr.*) to saw into scrolls. **5.** to roll up like a scroll. **6.** *Computers.* to move (text) on a screen in order to view a section that cannot be fitted into a single display. [C15 *scrowle*, from *scrowe*, from OF *escroe* scrap of parchment, but also infl. by ROLL]

scroll saw *n.* a saw with a narrow blade for cutting intricate ornamental curves in wood.

scrollwork ('skrəʊl,wɜːk) *n.* ornamental work in scroll-like patterns.

Scrooge (skruːdʒ) *n.* a mean or miserly person. [C19: after a character in Dickens' story *A Christmas Carol* (1843)]

scrophulariaceous (,skrɒfjʊ,lɛərɪ'eɪʃəs) *adj.* of or belonging to the *Scrophulariaceae*, a family of plants including figwort, snapdragon, foxglove, and mullein. [C19: from NL (*herba*) *scrophularia* scrofula (plant), from the use of such plants in treating scrofula]

scrotum ('skrəʊtəm) *n., pl.* -**ta** (-tə) *or* -**tums.** the pouch of skin containing the testes in most mammals. [C16: from L] —'**scrotal** *adj.*

scrounge (skraʊndʒ) *vb. Inf.* **1.** (when *intr.*, sometimes foll. by *around*) to search in order to acquire (something) without cost. **2.** to obtain or seek to obtain (something) by begging. [C20: var. of dialect *scrunge* to steal, from ?] —'**scrounger** *n.*

scrub[1] (skrʌb) *vb.* **scrubbing, scrubbed. 1.** to rub (a surface, etc.) hard, with or as if with a brush, soap, and water, in order to clean it. **2.** to remove (dirt) by rubbing, esp. with a brush and water. **3.** (*intr.*; foll. by *up*) (of a surgeon) to wash the hands and arms thoroughly before operating. **4.** (*tr.*) to purify (a gas) by removing impurities. **5.** (*tr.*) *Inf.* to delete or cancel. ~*n.* **6.** the act of or an instance of scrubbing. [C14: from MLow G *schrubben*, or MDu. *schrobben*]

scrub[2] (skrʌb) *n.* **1. a.** vegetation consisting of stunted trees, bushes, and other plants growing in an arid area. **b.** (*as modifier*): *scrub vegetation.* **2.** an area of arid land covered with such vegetation. **3. a.** an animal of inferior breeding or condition. **b.** (*as modifier*): *a scrub bull.* **4.** a small person. **5.** anything stunted or inferior. **6.** *Sport, U.S.* **a.** a player not in the first team. **b.** a team composed of such players. **7. the scrub.** *Austral. inf.* a remote or uncivilized place. ~*adj.* (*prenominal*) **8.** small or inferior. **9.** *Sport, U.S.* **a.** (of a player) not in the first team. **b.** (of a team) composed of such players. [C16: var. of SHRUB[1]]

scrubber ('skrʌbə) *n.* **1.** a person or thing that scrubs. **2.** an apparatus for purifying a gas. **3.** *Derog. sl.* a promiscuous girl.

scrubby ('skrʌbɪ) *adj.* -**bier, -biest. 1.** covered with or consisting of scrub. **2.** (of trees, etc.) stunted in growth. **3.** *Brit. inf.* messy.

scrubland ('skrʌb,lænd) *n.* an area of scrub vegetation.

scrub turkey *n.* another term for **megapode.**

scrub typhus *n.* a disease characterized by severe headache, skin rash, chills, and swelling of the lymph nodes, caused by the bite of mites infected with a microorganism: occurs mainly in Asia and Australia.

scruff[1] (skrʌf) *n.* the nape of the neck (esp. in **by the scruff of the neck**). [C18: var. of *scuft*, ?from ON *skoft* hair]

scruff[2] (skrʌf) *n. Inf.* **1.** an untidy scruffy person. **2.** a disreputable person; ruffian.

scruffy ('skrʌfɪ) *adj.* **scruffier, scruffiest.** unkempt or shabby.

scrum (skrʌm) *n.* **1.** *Rugby.* the act or method of restarting play when the two opposing packs of forwards group together with heads down and arms interlocked and push to gain ground while the scrum half throws the ball in and the hookers attempt to scoop it out to their own team. **2.** *Inf.* a disorderly struggle. ~*vb.* **scrumming, scrummed. 3.** (*intr.*; usually foll. by *down*) *Rugby.* to form a scrum. [C19: from SCRUMMAGE]

scrum half *n. Rugby.* **1.** a player who puts in the ball at scrums and tries to get it away to his three-quarter backs. **2.** this position in a team.

scrummage ('skrʌmɪdʒ) *n., vb.* **1.** *Rugby.* another word for **scrum. 2.** a variant of **scrimmage.** [C19: var. of SCRIMMAGE]

scrump (skrʌmp) *vb. Dialect.* to steal (apples) from an orchard or garden. [var. of PREENP]

scrumptious ('skrʌmpʃəs) *adj. Inf.* very pleasing; delicious. [C19: prob. changed from SUMPTUOUS] —'**scrumptiously** *adv.*

scrumpy ('skrʌmpɪ) *n.* a rough dry cider, brewed esp. in the West Country of England. [from *scrump*, var. of SCRIMP (in obs. sense: withered), referring to the apples used]

scrunch (skrʌntʃ) *vb.* **1.** to crumple or crunch or to be crumpled or crunched. ~*n.* **2.** the act or sound of scrunching. [C19: var. of CRUNCH]

scruple ('skruːpəl) *n.* **1.** (*often pl.*) a doubt or hesitation as to what is morally right in a certain situation. **2.** *Arch.* a very small amount. **3.** a unit of weight equal to 20 grains (1.296 grams). ~*vb.* **4.** (*obs. when tr.*) to have doubts (about), esp. from a moral compunction. [C16: from L *scrúpulus* a small weight, from *scrúpus* rough stone]

scrupulous ('skruːpjʊləs) *adj.* **1.** characterized by careful observation of what is morally right. **2.** very careful or precise. [C15: from L *scrúpulōsus* punctilious] —'**scrupulously** *adv.* —'**scrupulousness** *n.*

scrutineer (,skruːtɪ'nɪə) *n.* a person who examines, esp. one who scrutinizes the conduct of an election poll.

scrutinize *or* -**nise** ('skruːtɪ,naɪz) *vb.* (*tr.*) to examine carefully or in minute detail. —'**scruti,nizer** *or* -,**niser** *n.*

scrutiny ('skruːtɪnɪ) *n., pl.* -**nies. 1.** close or minute examination. **2.** a searching look. **3.** (in the early Christian Church) a formal testing that catechumens had to undergo before being baptized. [C15: from LL *scrútinium* an investigation, from *scrútāri* to search (orig. referring to rag-and-bone men), from *scrúta* rubbish]

scry (skraɪ) *vb.* **scrying, scried.** (*intr.*) to divine, esp. by crystal gazing. [C16: from DESCRY]

scuba ('skjuːbə) *n.* an apparatus used in skin diving, consisting of a cylinder or cylinders containing compressed air attached to a breathing apparatus. [C20: from the initials of *self-contained underwater breathing apparatus*]

scud (skʌd) *vb.* **scudding, scudded.** (*intr.*) **1.** (esp. of clouds) to move along swiftly and smoothly. **2.** *Naut.* to run before a gale. ~*n.* **3.** the act of scudding. **4. a.** a formation of low ragged clouds driven by a strong wind beneath rain-bearing clouds. **b.** a sudden shower or gust of wind. [C16: prob. of Scand. origin]

Scudamore ('skuːdəmɔː) *n.* **Peter.** born 1958, British champion jockey.

scuff (skʌf) *vb.* **1.** to drag (the feet) while walking. **2.** to scratch (a surface) or (of a surface) to become scratched. **3.** (*tr.*) *U.S.* to poke at (something) with the foot. ~*n.* **4.** the act or sound of scuffing. **5.** a rubbed place caused by scuffing. **6.** a backless slipper. [C19: prob. imit.]

scuffle ('skʌfəl) *vb.* (*intr.*) **1.** to fight in a disorderly manner. **2.** to move by shuffling. ~*n.* **3.** a disorderly struggle. **4.** the sound made by scuffling. [C16: of Scand. origin; cf. Swedish *skuff, skuffa* to push]

scull (skʌl) *n.* **1.** a single oar moved from side to side over the stern of a boat to propel it. **2.** one of a pair of short-handled oars, both of which are pulled by one oarsman. **3.** a racing shell propelled by a single oarsman pulling two oars. **4.** an act, instance, period, or distance of sculling. ~*vb.* **5.** to propel (a boat) with a scull. [C14: from ?] —'**sculler** *n.*

scullery ('skʌlərɪ) *n., pl.* -**leries.** *Chiefly Brit.* a small room or part of a kitchen where washing-up, vegetable preparation, etc., is done. [C15: from Anglo-Norman *squillerie*, from OF, from *escuele* a bowl, from L *scutella*, from *scutra* a flat tray]

Scullin ('skʌlɪn) *n.* **James Henry.** 1876–1953, Australian statesman; prime minister of Australia (1929–31).

scullion ('skʌljən) n. 1. a mean or despicable person. 2. Arch. a servant employed to work in a kitchen. [C15: from OF escouillon cleaning cloth, from escouve a broom, from L scōpa a broom, twig]

sculpt (skʌlpt) vb. 1. a variant of **sculpture**. 2. (intr.) to practise sculpture. ~Also: **sculp**. [C19: from F sculpter, from L sculpere to carve]

sculptor ('skʌlptə) or (fem.) **sculptress** n. a person who practises sculpture.

sculpture ('skʌlptʃə) n. 1. the art of making figures or designs in relief or the round by carving wood, moulding plaster, etc., or casting metals, etc. 2. works or a work made in this way. 3. ridges or indentations as on a shell, formed by natural processes. ~vb. (mainly tr.) 4. (also intr.) to carve, cast, or fashion (stone, bronze, etc.) three-dimensionally. 5. to portray (a person, etc.) by means of sculpture. 6. to form in the manner of sculpture. 7. to decorate with sculpture. [C14: from L sculptūra a carving] — '**sculptural** adj.

sculpturesque (ˌskʌlptʃə'rɛsk) adj. resembling sculpture. — ˌ**sculptur'esquely** adv.

scum (skʌm) n. 1. a layer of impure matter that forms on the surface of a liquid, often as the result of boiling or fermentation. 2. the greenish film of algae and similar vegetation surface of a stagnant pond. 3. the skin of oxides or impurities on the surface of a molten metal. 4. waste matter. 5. a worthless person or group of people. ~vb. **scumming**, **scummed**. 6. (tr.) to remove scum from. 7. (intr.) Rare. to form a layer of or become covered with scum. [C13: of Gmc origin] — '**scummy** adj.

scumbag ('skʌm,bæg) n. Sl an offensive or despicable person. [C20: ?from earlier U.S. sense: condom, from U.S. slang scum semen + bag]

scumble ('skʌmbəl) vb. 1. (in painting and drawing) to soften or blend (an outline or colour) with an upper coat of opaque colour, applied very thinly. 2. to produce an effect of broken colour on doors, panelling, etc., by exposing coats of paint below the top coat. ~n. 3. the upper layer of colour applied in this way. [C18: prob. from SCUM]

scuncheon ('skʌntʃən) n. the inner part of a door jamb or window frame. [C15: from OF escoinson, from coin angle]

scungy ('skʌndʒɪ) adj. **scungier**, **scungiest**. Austral. & N.Z. sl. miserable; sordid. [C20: from ?]

scunner ('skʌnə) vb. Dialect, chiefly Scot. 1. (intr.) to feel aversion. 2. (tr.) to produce a feeling of aversion in. ~n. 3. a strong aversion (often in **take a scunner**). 4. an object of dislike; nuisance. [C14: from Scot. skunner, from ?]

Scunthorpe ('skʌn,θɔːp) n. a town in E England, in Humberside: developed rapidly after the discovery of local iron ore (1871); iron and steel centre. Pop.: 66 353 (1981).

scup (skʌp) n. a common fish of American coastal regions of the Atlantic. [C19: from Amerind mishcup, from mishe big + kuppe close together; from the form of the scales]

scupper[1] ('skʌpə) n. Naut. a drain or spout allowing water on the deck of a vessel to flow overboard. [C15 skopper, from ?]

scupper[2] ('skʌpə) vb. (tr.) Brit. sl. 1. to overwhelm, ruin, or disable. 2. to sink (one's ship) deliberately. [C19: from ?]

scurf (skɜːf) n. 1. another name for **dandruff**. 2. flaky or scaly matter adhering to or peeling off a surface. [OE scurf] — '**scurfy** adj.

scurrilous ('skʌrɪləs) adj. 1. grossly or obscenely abusive or defamatory. 2. characterized by gross or obscene humour. [C16: from L scurrīlis derisive, from scurra buffoon] — **scurrility** (skə'rɪlɪtɪ) n. — '**scurrilously** adv.

scurry ('skʌrɪ) vb. **-rying**, **-ried**. 1. to move about hurriedly. 2. (intr.) to whirl about. ~n., pl. **-ries**. 3. the act or sound of scurrying. 4. a brisk light whirling movement, as of snow. [C19: prob. from hurry-scurry, from HURRY]

scurvy ('skɜːvɪ) n. 1. a disease caused by a lack of vitamin C, characterized by anaemia, spongy gums, and bleeding beneath the skin. ~adj. **-vier**, **-viest**. 2. mean or despicable. [C16: see SCURF] — '**scurvily** adv. — '**scurviness** n.

scurvy grass n. any of various plants of Europe and North America, formerly used to treat scurvy.

scut (skʌt) n. the short tail of animals such as the deer and rabbit. [C15: prob. from ON]

scutage ('skjuːtɪdʒ) n. (in feudal society) a payment sometimes exacted by a lord from his vassal in lieu of military service. [C15: from Med. L scūtāgium, lit.: shield dues, from L scūtum a shield]

Scutari n. 1. ('skuːtərɪ, skuː'tɑːrɪ). the former name of **Üskÿdar**. 2. (skuˈtari). the Italian name for **Shkodër**.

scutate ('skjuːteɪt) adj. 1. (of animals) covered with large bony or horny plates. 2. Bot. shaped like a round shield. [C19: from L scūtātus armed with a shield, from scūtum a shield]

scutcheon ('skʌtʃən) n. 1. a variant of **escutcheon**. 2. any rounded or shield-shaped structure.

scutch grass (skʌtʃ) n. another name for **couch grass**. [var. of COUCH GRASS]

scute (skjuːt) n. Zool. a horny plate that makes up part of the exoskeleton in armadillos, turtles, etc. [C14 (the name of a F coin; C19 in zoological sense): from L scūtum shield]

scutellum (skjuːˈtɛləm) n., pl. **-la** (-lə). Biol. 1. the last of three plates into which an insect's thorax is divided. 2. one of the scales on the tarsus of a bird's leg. 3. the cotyledon of a developing grass seed. [C18: from NL: a little shield, from L scūtum a shield] — **scutellate** ('skjuːtɪˌleɪt, -lɪt) adj.

scutter ('skʌtə) vb., n. Brit. inf. scurry. [C18: prob. from SCUTTLE[2], with -ER[1] as in SCATTER]

scuttle[1] ('skʌtəl) n. 1. See **coal scuttle**. 2. Dialect, chiefly Brit. a shallow basket, esp. for carrying vegetables. 3. the part of a motorcar body lying immediately behind the bonnet. [OE scutel trencher, from L scutella bowl, dim. of scutra platter]

scuttle[2] ('skʌtəl) vb. 1. (intr.) to run or move about with short hasty steps. ~n. 2. a hurried pace or run. [C15: ?from SCUD, infl. by SHUTTLE]

scuttle[3] ('skʌtəl) vb. (tr.) 1. Naut. to cause (a vessel) to sink by opening the seacocks or making holes in the bottom. 2. to give up (hopes, plans, etc.). ~n. 3. Naut. a small hatch or its cover. [C15 (n.): via OF from Sp. escotilla a small opening, from escote opening in a piece of cloth, from escotar to cut out]

scuttlebutt ('skʌtəl,bʌt) n. Naut. 1. a drinking fountain. 2. (formerly) a cask of drinking water aboard a ship. 3. Chiefly U.S. sl. gossip.

scutum ('skjuːtəm) n., pl. **-ta** (-tə). 1. the middle of three plates into which an insect's thorax is divided. 2. another word for **scute**. [L: shield]

scuzzy ('skʌzɪ) adj. **-zier**, **-ziest**. Sl., chiefly U.S. unkempt, dirty, or squalid. [C20: ?from disgusting or ?from blend of scum & fuzz]

Scylla ('sɪlə) n. 1. Greek myth. a sea nymph transformed into a sea monster believed to drown sailors navigating the Straits of Messina. Cf. **Charybdis**. 2. **between Scylla and Charybdis**. in a predicament in which avoidance of either of two dangers means exposure to the other.

Scyros ('skɪrɔs) n. a variant spelling of **Skyros**.

scythe (saɪð) n. 1. a long-handled implement for cutting grass, etc., having a curved sharpened blade that moves in a plane parallel to the ground. ~vb. 2. (tr.) to cut (grass, etc.) with a scythe. [OE sigthe]

Scythia ('sɪðɪə) n. an ancient region of SE Europe and Asia, north of the Black Sea: now part of the Soviet Union. — '**Scythian** adj., n.

SDI abbrev. for Strategic Defense Initiative. See **Star Wars**.

SDLP abbrev. for Social and Democratic Labour Party (of Ulster).

SDP abbrev. for Social Democratic Party.

SDRs Finance. abbrev. for special drawing rights.

Se the chemical symbol for selenium.

SE symbol for southeast(ern).

sea (siː) n. 1. a. (usually preceded by the) the mass of salt water on the earth's surface as differentiated from the land. Related adjs.: **marine**, **maritime**. b. (as modifier): sea air. 2. (cap. when part of place name) a. one of the smaller areas of ocean: the Irish Sea. b. a large inland area of water: the Caspian Sea. 3. turbulence or swell: heavy seas. 4. (cap. when part of a name) Astron. any of many huge dry plains on the surface of the moon: Sea of Serenity. See also **mare**[2]. 5. anything resembling the sea in size or apparent limitlessness. 6. **at sea. a.** on the ocean. **b.** in a state of confusion. **7. go to sea.** to become a sailor. **8. put (out) to sea.** to embark on a sea voyage. [OE *sæ*]

sea anchor *n. Naut.* any device, such as a bucket, dragged in the water to keep a vessel heading into the wind or reduce drifting.

sea anemone *n.* any of various coelenterates having a polypoid body with oral rings of tentacles.

sea bag *n.* a canvas bag used by a seaman for his belongings.

sea bass (bæs) *n.* any of various American coastal fishes having an elongated body with a long spiny dorsal fin almost divided into two.

sea bird *n.* a bird such as a gull, that lives on the sea.

seaboard ('si:,bɔːd) *n.* land bordering on the sea.

Seaborg ('si:bɔːg) *n.* **Glenn Theodore.** born 1912, U.S. chemist and nuclear physicist. With E. M. McMillan, he discovered several transuranic elements, including plutonium (1940), curium, and americium (1944), and shared a Nobel prize for chemistry 1951.

seaborne ('si:,bɔːn) *adj.* **1.** carried on or by the sea. **2.** transported by ship.

sea bream *n.* a fish of European seas, valued as a food fish.

sea breeze *n.* a wind blowing from the sea to the land, esp. during the day when the land surface is warmer.

sea change *n.* a seemingly magical change. [from Ariel's song "Full Fathom Five" in *The Tempest*]

seacoast ('si:,kəust) *n.* land bordering on the sea; a coast.

seacock ('si:,kɒk) *n. Naut.* a valve in the hull of a vessel below the water line for admitting sea water or for pumping out bilge water.

sea cow *n.* **1.** a dugong or manatee. **2.** an archaic name for the **walrus.**

sea cucumber *n.* an echinoderm having an elongated body covered with a leathery skin and a cluster of tentacles at the oral end.

sea dog *n.* an experienced or old sailor.

sea eagle *n.* any of various fish-eating eagles of coastal areas, esp. the **European sea eagle,** having a brown plumage and white tail.

seafarer ('si:,fɛərə) *n.* **1.** a traveller who goes by sea. **2.** a sailor.

seafaring ('si:,fɛərɪŋ) *adj.* (*prenominal*) **1.** travelling by sea. **2.** working as a sailor. ~*n.* **3.** the act of travelling by sea. **4.** the work of a sailor.

seafood ('si:,fu:d) *n.* edible saltwater fish or shellfish.

seafront ('si:,frʌnt) *n.* a built-up area facing the sea.

sea-girt *adj. Literary.* surrounded by the sea.

seagoing ('si:,gəuɪŋ) *adj.* intended for or used at sea.

sea green *n.* **a.** a moderate green colour, sometimes with a bluish or yellowish tinge. **b.** (*as adj.*): *a sea-green carpet.*

sea gull *n.* **1.** a popular name for the **gull** (the bird). **2.** *Austral. & N.Z. inf.* a casual dock worker.

sea holly *n.* a European plant of sandy shores, having bluish-green stems and blue flowers.

sea horse *n.* **1.** a marine teleost fish of temperate and tropical waters, having a bony-plated body, a prehensile tail, and a horselike head and swimming in an upright position. **2.** an archaic name for the **walrus. 3.** a fabled sea creature with the tail of a fish and the front parts of a horse.

sea-island cotton *n.* **1.** a cotton plant of the Sea Islands, off the Florida coast, widely cultivated for its fine long fibres. **2.** the fibre of this plant or the material woven from it.

Sea Islands *pl. n.* a chain of islands in the Atlantic off the coasts of South Carolina, Georgia, and Florida.

sea kale *n.* a European coastal plant with broad fleshy leaves and white flowers: cultivated for its edible asparagus-like shoots. Cf. **kale.**

seal[1] (si:l) *n.* **1.** a device impressed on a piece of wax, etc., fixed to a letter, etc., as a mark of authentication. **2.** a stamp, ring, etc., engraved with a device to form such an impression. **3.** a substance, esp. wax, so placed over an envelope, etc., that it must be broken before the object can be opened or used. **4.** any substance or device used to close or fasten tightly. **5.** a small amount of water contained in the trap of a drain to prevent the passage of foul smells. **6.** anything that gives a pledge or confirmation. **7.** a token; sign: *seal of death.* **8.** a decorative stamp sold in aid of charity. **9.** *R.C. Church.* Also called: **seal of**

confession. the obligation never to reveal anything said in confession. **10. set one's seal on** (*or* **to**). **a.** to mark with one's sign or seal. **b.** to endorse. ~*vb.* (*tr.*) **11.** to affix a seal to, as proof of authenticity, etc. **12.** to stamp with or as if with a seal. **13.** to approve or authorize. **14.** (sometimes foll. by *up*) to close or secure with or as if with a seal: *to seal one's lips.* **15.** (foll. by *off*) to enclose (a place) with a fence, etc. **16.** to decide irrevocably. **17.** to close tightly so as to render airtight or watertight. **18.** to subject (the outside of meat, etc.) to fierce heat so as to retain the juices during cooking. **19.** to paint (a porous material) with a nonporous coating. **20.** *Austral.* to cover (a road) with bitumen, asphalt, tarmac, etc. [C13 *seel*, from OF, from L *sigillum* little figure, from *signum* a sign] —'**sealable** *adj.*

seal[2] (si:l) *n.* **1.** a fish-eating mammal with four flippers which is aquatic but comes on shore to breed. **2.** sealskin. ~*vb.* **3.** (*intr.*) to hunt for seals. [OE *seolh*] —'**sealer** *n.* —'**seal-,like** *adj.*

sea lane *n.* an established route for ships.

sealant ('si:lənt) *n.* **1.** any substance, such as wax, used for sealing documents, bottles, etc. **2.** any of a number of substances used for stopping leaks, waterproofing wood, etc.

sea lavender *n.* any of various plants found on temperate salt marshes, having spikes of white, pink, or mauve flowers.

sealed-beam *adj.* (esp. of a car headlight) having a lens and prefocused reflector sealed in the lamp vacuum.

sealed road *n. Austral. & N.Z.* a road surfaced with bitumen or some other hard material.

sea legs *pl. n. Inf.* **1.** the ability to maintain one's balance on board ship. **2.** the ability to resist seasickness.

sea level *n.* the level of the surface of the sea with respect to the land, taken to be the mean level between high and low tide.

sea lily *n.* any of various echinoderms in which the body consists of a long stalk bearing a central disc with delicate radiating arms.

sealing wax *n.* a hard material made of shellac, turpentine, and pigment that softens when heated.

sea lion *n.* any of various large eared seals, such as the **Californian sea lion,** of the N Pacific, often used as a performing animal.

Sea Lord *n.* (in Britain) either of the two serving naval officers (**First** and **Second Sea Lords**) who sit on the admiralty board of the Ministry of Defence.

seal ring *n.* another term for **signet ring.**

sealskin ('si:l,skɪn) *n.* **a.** the skin or pelt of a fur seal, esp. when dressed with the outer hair removed and the under-fur dyed dark brown. **b.** (*as modifier*): *a sealskin coat.*

Sealyham terrier ('si:lɪəm) *n.* a short-legged wire-haired breed of terrier with a medium-length white coat. [C19: after *Sealyham*, village in S Wales]

seam (si:m) *n.* **1.** the line along which pieces of fabric, etc., are joined, esp. by stitching. **2.** a ridge or line made by joining two edges. **3.** a stratum of coal, ore, etc. **4.** a linear indentation, such as a wrinkle or scar. **5.** (*modifier*) *Cricket.* of or relating to a style of bowling in which the bowler utilizes the stitched seam round the ball in order to make it swing in flight and after touching the ground: *a seam bowler.* **6. bursting at the seams.** full to overflowing. ~*vb.* **7.** (*tr.*) to join or sew together by or as if by a seam. **8.** to mark or become marked with or as if with a seam or wrinkle. [OE] —'**seamer** *n.* —'**seamless** *adj.*

seaman ('si:mən) *n., pl.* **-men. 1.** a naval rating trained in seamanship. **2.** a man who serves as a sailor. **3.** a person skilled in seamanship. —'**seamanly** *adj., adv.* —'**seaman-,like** *adj.*

seamanship ('si:mənʃɪp) *n.* skill in and knowledge of the work of navigating, maintaining, and operating a vessel.

Seami (si:'ɑːmɪ) *n.* a variant spelling of **Zeami.**

sea mile *n.* an Imperial unit of length, formerly used in navigation, equal to 6000 feet or 1000 fathoms. It is equivalent to 1828.8 metres.

sea mouse *n.* any of various large worms having a broad flattened body covered dorsally with a dense mat of iridescent hairlike setae.

seamstress ('sɛmstrɪs) *or* (*rarely*) **sempstress** ('sɛmpstrɪs) *n.* a woman who sews and makes clothes, esp. professionally.

seamy ('si:mɪ) *adj.* **seamier, seamiest.** showing the least pleasant aspect; sordid. —**'seaminess** *n.*

Seanad Éireann ('ʃænəð 'e:rən) *n.* (in the Republic of Ireland) the upper chamber of parliament. [from Irish, lit.: senate of Ireland]

seance *or* **séance** ('seɪɑ̃s) *n.* a meeting at which spiritualists attempt to receive messages from the spirits of the dead. [C19: from F, lit.: a sitting, from OF *seoir* to sit, from L *sedēre*]

sea otter *n.* a large marine otter of N Pacific coasts, formerly hunted for its thick brown fur.

sea pink *n.* another name for **thrift** (the plant).

seaplane ('si:,pleɪn) *n.* any aircraft that lands on and takes off from water.

seaport ('si:,pɔ:t) *n.* **1.** a port or harbour accessible to seagoing vessels. **2.** a town or city located at such a place.

SEAQ ('si:,æk) *n. acronym for* Stock Exchange Automated Quotations: an electronic system that collects and displays information needed to trade in equities.

sear (sɪə) *vb.* (*tr.*) **1.** to scorch or burn the surface of. **2.** to brand with a hot iron. **3.** to cause to wither. **4.** *Rare.* to make unfeeling. ~*adj.* **5.** *Poetic.* dried up. [OE *sēarian* to become withered, from *sēar* withered]

search (sɜːtʃ) *vb.* **1.** to look through (a place, etc.) thoroughly in order to find someone or something. **2.** (*tr.*) to examine (a person) for concealed objects. **3.** to look at or examine (something) closely: *to search one's conscience.* **4.** (*tr.*; foll. by *out*) to discover by investigation. **5.** *Surgery.* to probe (a wound, etc.). **6.** *Computers.* to review (a file) to locate specific information. **7.** *Arch.* to penetrate. **8. search me.** *Inf.* I don't know. ~*n.* **9.** the act or an instance of searching. **10.** the examination of a vessel by the right of search. **11. right of search.** *International law.* the right possessed by the warships of a belligerent state to search merchant vessels to ascertain whether ship or cargo is liable to seizure. [C14: from OF *cerchier*, from LL *circāre* to go around, from L *circus* circle] —**'searchable** *adj.* —**'searcher** *n.*

searching ('sɜːtʃɪŋ) *adj.* keenly penetrating: *a searching look.* —**'searchingly** *adv.*

searchlight ('sɜːtʃ,laɪt) *n.* **1.** a device that projects a powerful beam of light in a particular direction. **2.** the beam of light produced by such a device.

search party *n.* a group of people taking part in an organized search, as for a lost, missing, or wanted person.

search warrant *n.* a written order issued by a justice of the peace authorizing a constable to enter and search premises for stolen goods, etc.

seascape ('si:,skeɪp) *n.* a sketch, etc., of the sea.

sea scorpion *n.* any of various northern marine fishes having a tapering body and a large head covered with bony plates and spines.

Sea Scout *n.* a Scout belonging to any of a number of Scout troops whose main activities are canoeing, sailing, etc.

sea serpent *n.* a huge legendary creature of the sea resembling a snake or dragon.

seashell ('si:,ʃɛl) *n.* the empty shell of a marine mollusc.

seashore ('si:,ʃɔː) *n.* **1.** land bordering on the sea. **2.** *Law.* the land between the marks of high and low water.

seasick ('si:,sɪk) *adj.* suffering from nausea and dizziness caused by the motion of a ship at sea. —**'sea,sickness** *n.*

seaside ('si:,saɪd) *n.* **a.** any area bordering on the sea, esp. one regarded as a resort. **b.** (*as modifier*): *a seaside hotel.*

sea snail *n.* a small spiny-finned fish of cold seas, having a soft scaleless tadpole-shaped body with the pelvic fins fused into a sucker.

sea snake *n.* a venomous snake of tropical seas that swims by means of a laterally compressed oarlike tail.

season ('si:z°n) *n.* **1.** one of the four equal periods into which the year is divided by the equinoxes and solstices. These periods (spring, summer, autumn, and winter) have characteristic weather conditions, and occur at opposite times of the year in the N and S hemispheres. **2.** a period of the year characterized by particular conditions or activities: *the rainy season.* **3.** the period during which any particular species of animal, bird, or fish is legally permitted to be caught or killed: *open season on red deer.* **4.** a period during which a particular entertainment, sport, etc., takes place: *the football season.* **5.** any definite or indefinite period. **6.** any of the major periods into which

the ecclesiastical calendar is divided, such as Lent or Easter. **7.** fitting or proper time. **8. in good season.** early enough. **9. in season. a.** (of game) permitted to be killed. **b.** (of fresh food) readily available. **c.** Also: **in** *or* **on heat.** (of some female mammals) sexually receptive. **d.** appropriate. ~*vb.* **10.** (*tr.*) to add herbs, salt, pepper, or spice to (food). **11.** (*tr.*) to add zest to. **12.** (in the preparation of timber) to undergo or cause to undergo drying. **13.** (*tr.*; *usually passive*) to make or become experienced: *seasoned troops.* **14.** (*tr.*) to mitigate or temper. [C13: from OF *seson*, from L *satiō* a sowing, from *serere* to sow] —**'seasoned** *adj.* —**'seasoner** *n.*

seasonable ('si:zənəb°l) *adj.* **1.** suitable for the season: *a seasonable Christmas snow scene.* **2.** taking place at the appropriate time. —**'seasonableness** *n.* —**'seasonably** *adv.*

seasonal ('si:zən°l) *adj.* of, relating to, or occurring at a certain season or certain seasons of the year: *seasonal labour.* —**'seasonally** *adv.*

seasonal affective disorder *n.* a state of depression sometimes experienced by people in winter, thought to be related to lack of sunlight. Abbrev.: **SAD.**

seasoning ('si:zənɪŋ) *n.* **1.** something that enhances the flavour of food, such as salt or herbs. **2.** another term (not now in technical usage) for **drying.**

season ticket *n.* a ticket for a series of events, number of journeys, etc., within a limited time, usually obtained at a reduced rate.

sea squirt *n.* a minute primitive marine animal, most of which are sedentary, having a saclike body with openings through which water enters and leaves.

sea swallow *n.* a popular name for **tern.**

seat (si:t) *n.* **1.** a piece of furniture designed for sitting on, such as a chair or sofa. **2.** the part of a chair, bench, etc., on which one sits. **3.** a place to sit, esp. one that requires a ticket: *I have two seats for the film tonight.* **4.** the buttocks. **5.** the part of a garment covering the buttocks. **6.** the part or area serving as the base of an object. **7.** the part or surface on which the base of an object rests. **8.** the place or centre in which something is located: *a seat of government.* **9.** a place of abode, esp. a country mansion. **10.** a membership or the right to membership in a legislative or similar body. **11.** *Chiefly Brit.* a parliamentary constituency. **12.** the manner in which a rider sits on a horse. ~*vb.* **13.** (*tr.*) to bring to or place on a seat. **14.** (*tr.*) to provide with seats. **15.** (*tr.*; *often passive*) to place or centre: *the ministry is seated in the capital.* **16.** (*tr.*) to set firmly in place. **17.** (*tr.*) to fix or install in a position of power. **18.** (*intr.*) (of garments) to sag in the area covering the buttocks: *your skirt has seated badly.* [OE *gesete*]

seat belt *n.* **1.** Also called: **safety belt.** a belt or strap worn in a car to restrain forward motion in the event of a collision. **2.** a similar belt or strap worn in an aircraft at takeoff and landing.

seating ('si:tɪŋ) *n.* **1.** the act of providing with a seat or seats. **2. a.** the provision of seats, as in a theatre, etc. **b.** (*as modifier*): *seating arrangements.* **3.** material used for covering seats. **4.** a surface on which a part, such as a valve, is supported.

SEATO ('si:təʊ) *n. acronym for* South East Asia Treaty Organization; a former anti-Communist defence association for the Far East and the W Pacific (1954–77).

Seaton Valley ('si:t°n) *n.* a region in NE England, in SE Northumberland: consists of a group of coal-mining villages. Pop.: 46 141 (1981).

sea trout *n.* a silvery marine variety of the brown trout that migrates to fresh water to spawn.

Seattle (sɪ'æt°l) *n.* a port in W Washington, on the isthmus between Lake Washington and Puget Sound: the largest city in the state and chief commercial centre of the Northwest; two universities. Pop.: 486 200 (1986 est.).

sea urchin *n.* any echinoderm such as the **edible sea urchin,** having a globular body enclosed in a rigid spiny test and occurring in shallow marine waters.

sea wall *n.* a wall or embankment built to prevent encroachment or erosion by the sea.

seaward ('si:wəd) *adv.* **1.** Also called: **seawards.** towards the sea. ~*adj.* **2.** directed or moving towards the sea. **3.** (esp. of a wind) coming from the sea.

seaway ('si:,weɪ) *n.* **1.** a waterway giving access to an inland port. **2.** a vessel's progress. **3.** a route across the sea.

seaweed ('si:,wi:d) *n.* any of numerous multicellular marine algae that grow on the seashore, in salt marshes, in brackish water, or submerged in the ocean.

seaworthy ('si:,wɜ:ðɪ) *adj.* in a fit condition or ready for a sea voyage. —'**sea,worthiness** *n.*

sebaceous (sɪ'beɪʃəs) *adj.* **1.** of or resembling sebum, fat, or tallow. **2.** secreting fat. [C18: from LL *sēbāceus*, from SEBUM]

sebaceous glands *pl. n.* the small glands in the skin that secrete sebum onto hair follicles and onto most of the body surface except the soles of the feet and the palms of the hands.

Sebastian (sɪ'bæstjən) *n.* **Saint.** died ?288 A.D., Christian martyr. According to tradition, he was first shot with arrows and then beaten to death. Feast day: Jan. 20.

Sebastopol (sɪ'bæstəpəl) *n.* the English name for **Sevastopol.**

seborrhoea *or esp. U.S.* **seborrhea** (,sɛbə'rɪə) *n.* a disease of the sebaceous glands characterized by excessive secretion of sebum.

sebum ('si:bəm) *n.* the oily secretion of the sebaceous glands that acts as a lubricant for the hair and skin and provides some protection against bacteria. [C19: from NL, from L: tallow]

sec[1] (sɛk) *adj.* **1.** (of wines) dry. **2.** (of champagne) of medium sweetness. [C19: from F, from L *siccus*]

sec[2] (sɛk) *n. Inf.* short for **second**[2]: *wait a sec.*

sec[3] (sɛk) *adv.* abbrev. for secant.

sec. *abbrev. for:* **1.** second (of time). **2.** secondary. **3.** secretary. **4.** section. **5.** sector.

secant ('si:kənt) *n.* **1.** (of an angle) a trigonometric function that in a right-angled triangle is the ratio of the length of the hypotenuse to that of the adjacent side; the reciprocal of cosine. Abbrev.: **sec.** **2.** a line that intersects a curve. [C16: from L *secāre* to cut]

secateurs ('sɛkətəz) *pl. n. Chiefly Brit.* a small pair of shears for pruning, having a pair of pivoted handles and usually a single cutting blade that closes against a flat surface. [C19: pl. of F *sécateur*, from L *secāre* to cut]

secede (sɪ'si:d) *vb.* (*intr.*; often foll. by *from*) (of a person, section, etc.) to make a formal withdrawal of membership, as from a political alliance, etc. [C18: from L *sēcēdere* to withdraw, from *sē-* apart + *cēdere* to go] —se'ceder *n.*

secession (sɪ'sɛʃən) *n.* **1.** the act of seceding. **2.** (*often cap.*) *Chiefly U.S.* the withdrawal in 1860–61 of 11 Southern states from the Union to form the Confederacy, precipitating the American Civil War. [C17: from L *sēcessiō* a withdrawing, from *sēcēdere* to SECEDE] —se'cession,ism *n.* —se'cessionist *n., adj.*

sech (ʃɛk, sɛtʃ, 'sɛk'eɪtʃ) *n.* hyperbolic secant.

seclude (sɪ'klu:d) *vb.* (*tr.*) **1.** to remove from contact with others. **2.** to shut off or screen from view. [C15: from L *sēclūdere* to shut off, from *sē-* + *claudere* to imprison]

secluded (sɪ'klu:dɪd) *adj.* **1.** kept apart from the company of others: *a secluded life.* **2.** private. —se'cludedly *adv.* —se'cludedness *n.*

seclusion (sɪ'klu:ʒən) *n.* **1.** the act of secluding or the state of being secluded. **2.** a secluded place. [C17: from Med. L *sēclūsiō;* see SECLUDE]

second[1] ('sɛkənd) *adj.* (*usually prenominal*) **1. a.** coming directly after the first in numbering or counting order, position, time, etc.; being the ordinal number of *two*: often written 2nd. **b.** (*as n.*): *the second in line.* **2.** graded or ranked between the first and third levels. **3.** alternate: *every second Thursday.* **4.** extra: *a second opportunity.* **5.** resembling a person or event from an earlier period of history: *a second Wagner.* **6.** of lower quality; inferior. **7.** denoting the lowest but one forward ratio of a gearbox in a motor vehicle. **8.** *Music.* denoting a musical part, voice, or instrument subordinate to or lower in pitch than another (the first): *the second tenors.* **9. at second hand.** by hearsay. ~*n.* **10.** *Brit. education.* an honours degree of the second class, usually further divided into an upper and lower designation. Full term: **second-class honours degree.** **11.** the lowest but one forward ratio of a gearbox in a motor vehicle. **12.** (in boxing, duelling, etc.) an attendant who looks after a competitor. **13.** a speech seconding a motion or the person making it. **14.** *Music.* the interval between one note and another lying next above or below it in the diatonic scale. **15.** (*pl.*) goods of inferior quality. **16.** (*pl.*) *Inf.* a second helping of food.

17. (*pl.*) the second course of a meal. ~*vb.* (*tr.*) **18.** to give aid or backing to. **19.** (in boxing, etc.) to act as second to (a competitor). **20.** to express formal support for (a motion already proposed). ~*adv.* **21.** Also: **secondly.** in the second place. ~*sentence connector.* **22.** Also: **secondly.** as the second point. [C13: via OF from L *secundus* coming next in order, from *sequī* to follow] —'seconder *n.*

▷ **Usage.** See at **important.**

second[2] ('sɛkənd) *n.* **1. a.** 1/60 of a minute of time. **b.** the basic SI unit of time: the duration of 9 192 631 770 periods of radiation corresponding to the transition between two hyperfine levels of the ground state of caesium-133. Symbol: s **2.** 1/60 of a minute of angle. Symbol: ″ **3.** a very short period of time. [C14: from OF, from Med. L *pars minūta secunda* the second small part (a minute being the first small part of an hour); see SECOND[1]]

second[3] (sɪ'kɒnd) *vb.* (*tr.*) *Brit.* **1.** to transfer (an employee) temporarily to another branch, etc. **2.** *Mil.* to transfer (an officer) to another post. [C19: from F *en second* in second rank (or position)] —se'condment *n.*

secondary ('sɛkəndərɪ) *adj.* **1.** one grade or step after the first. **2.** derived from or depending on what is primary or first: *a secondary source.* **3.** below the first in rank, importance, etc. **4.** (*prenominal*) of or relating to the education of young people between the ages of 11 and 18: *secondary education.* **5.** (of the flight feathers of a bird's wing) growing from the ulna. **6. a.** being the part of an electric circuit, such as a transformer or induction coil, in which a current is induced by a changing current in a neighbouring coil: *a secondary coil.* **b.** (of a current) flowing in such a circuit. **7.** *Chem.* **a.** (of an amine) containing the group NH. **b.** (of a salt) derived from a tribasic acid by replacement of two acidic hydrogen atoms with metal atoms. ~*n., pl.* **-aries.** **8.** a person or thing that is secondary. **9.** a subordinate, deputy, or inferior. **10.** a secondary coil, winding, inductance, or current in an electric circuit. **11.** *Ornithol.* any of the flight feathers that grow from the ulna of a bird's wing. **12.** *Astron.* a celestial body that orbits around a specified primary body: *the moon is the secondary of the earth.* **13.** short for **secondary colour.** —'secondarily *adv.* —'secondariness *n.*

secondary cell *n.* an electric cell that can be recharged and can therefore be used to store electrical energy in the form of chemical energy.

secondary colour *n.* a colour formed by mixing two primary colours.

secondary emission *n. Physics.* the emission of electrons (**secondary electrons**) from a solid as a result of bombardment with a beam of electrons, ions, or metastable atoms.

secondary picketing *n.* the picketing by striking workers of a factory, distribution outlet, etc., that supplies goods to or distributes goods from their employer.

secondary sexual characteristic *n.* any of various features distinguishing individuals of different sex but not directly concerned in reproduction. Examples are the antlers of a stag and the beard of a man.

second ballot *n.* an electoral procedure in which, after a first ballot, candidates at the bottom of the poll are eliminated and another ballot is held among the remaining candidates.

second-best *adj.* **1.** next to the best. **2. come off second best.** *Inf.* to be worsted by someone. ~*n.* **3. second best.** an inferior alternative.

second chamber *n.* the upper house of a bicameral legislative assembly.

second childhood *n.* dotage; senility (esp. in **in his, her,** etc., **second childhood**).

second class *n.* **1.** the class or grade next in value, quality, etc., to the first. ~*adj.* (**second-class** *when prenominal*). **2.** of the class or grade next to the best in quality, etc. **3.** shoddy or inferior. **4.** of or denoting the class of accommodation in a hotel or on a train, etc., lower in quality and price than first class. **5.** (in Britain) of letters that are handled more slowly than first-class letters. **6.** *Education.* See **second**[1](sense 10). ~*adv.* **7.** by second-class mail, transport, etc.

second-class citizen *n.* a person whose rights and opportunities are treated as less important than those of other people in the same society.

Second Coming *n.* the prophesied return of Christ to earth at the Last Judgment.

second cousin *n.* the child of a first cousin of either of one's parents.

second-degree burn *n. Pathol.* a burn in which blisters appear on the skin.

seconde (sɪˈkɒnd) *n.* the second of eight positions from which a parry or attack can be made in fencing. [C18: from F *seconde parade* the second parry]

Second Empire *n.* the style of furniture and decoration of the Second Empire in France (1852–70), reviving the Empire style, but with fussier ornamentation.

second fiddle *n. Inf.* **1. a.** the second violin in a string quartet or an orchestra. **b.** the musical part assigned to such an instrument. **2.** a person who has a secondary status.

second floor *n. Brit.* the storey of a building immediately above the first and two floors up from the ground. U.S. and Canad. term: **third floor.**

second generation *n.* **1.** offspring of parents born in a given country. **2.** (*modifier*) of a refined stage of development in manufacture: *a second-generation robot.*

second growth *n.* natural regrowth of a forest after fire, cutting, etc.

second hand *n.* a pointer on the face of a timepiece that indicates the seconds.

second-hand *adj.* **1.** previously owned or used. **2.** not from an original source or experience. **3.** dealing in or selling goods that are not new: *a second-hand car dealer.* ~*adv.* **4.** from a source of previously owned or used goods: *he prefers to buy second-hand.* **5.** not directly: *he got the news second-hand.*

Second International *n.* an international association of socialist parties and trade unions that began in Paris in 1889 and collapsed during World War I.

second language *n.* **1.** a language other than the mother tongue used for business transactions, teaching, debate, etc. **2.** a language that is officially recognized in a country, other than the main national language.

second lieutenant *n.* an officer holding the lowest commissioned rank in the armed forces of certain nations.

secondly (ˈsɛkəndlɪ) *adv.* another word for **second**[1], usually used to precede the second item in a list of topics.

second nature *n.* a habit, characteristic, etc., long practised or acquired so as to seem innate.

second person *n.* a grammatical category of pronouns and verbs used when referring to or describing the individual or individuals being addressed.

second-rate *adj.* **1.** not of the highest quality; mediocre. **2.** second in importance, etc.

second reading *n.* the second presentation of a bill in a legislative assembly, as to approve its general principles (in Britain), or to discuss a committee's report on it (in the U.S.).

second sight *n.* the alleged ability to foresee the future, see actions taking place elsewhere, etc. —ˈ**second-ˈsighted** *adj.*

second string *n.* **1.** *Chiefly Brit.* an alternative course of action, etc., intended to come into use should the first fail (esp. in **a second string to one's bow**). **2.** *Chiefly U.S. & Canad.* a substitute or reserve player or team.

second thought *n.* (*usually pl.*) a revised opinion or idea on a matter already considered.

second wind (wɪnd) *n.* **1.** the return of the ability to breathe at a normal rate, esp. following a period of exertion. **2.** renewed ability to continue in an effort.

secrecy (ˈsiːkrɪsɪ) *n., pl.* **-cies.** **1.** the state or quality of being secret. **2.** the state of keeping something secret. **3.** the ability or tendency to keep things secret.

secret (ˈsiːkrɪt) *adj.* **1.** kept hidden or separate from the knowledge of others. Related adj.: **cryptic.** **2.** known only to initiates: *a secret password.* **3.** hidden from general view or use: *a secret garden.* **4.** able or tending to keep things private or to oneself. **5.** operating without the knowledge of outsiders: *a secret society.* ~*n.* **6.** something kept or to be kept hidden. **7.** something unrevealed; a mystery. **8.** an underlying explanation, reason, etc.: *the secret of success.* **9.** a method, plan, etc., known only to initiates. **10.** *Liturgy.* a prayer said by the celebrant of the Mass after the offertory and before the preface. [C14: via OF from L *sēcrētus* concealed, from *sēcernere* to sift] —ˈ**secretly** *adv.*

secret agent *n.* a person employed in espionage.

secretaire (ˌsɛkrɪˈtɛə) *n.* an enclosed writing desk, usually having an upper cabinet section. [C19: from F; see SECRETARY]

secretariat (ˌsɛkrɪˈtɛərɪət) *n.* **1. a.** an office responsible for the secretarial, clerical, and administrative affairs of a legislative body or international organization. **b.** the staff of such an office. **2.** a body of secretaries. **3.** a secretary's place of work; office. **4.** the position of a secretary. [C19: via F from Med. L *sēcrētāriātus,* from *sēcrētārius* SECRETARY]

secretary (ˈsɛkrətrɪ) *n., pl.* **-taries.** **1.** a person who handles correspondence, keeps records, and does general clerical work for an individual, organization, etc. **2.** the official manager of the day-to-day business of a society or board. **3.** (in Britain) a senior civil servant who assists a government minister. **4.** (in the U.S.) the head of a government administrative department. **5.** (in Britain) See **secretary of state.** **6.** Another name for **secretaire.** [C14: from Med. L *sēcrētārius,* from L *sēcrētum* something hidden; see SECRET] —**secretarial** (ˌsɛkrɪˈtɛərɪəl) *adj.* —ˈ**secretaryship** *n.*

secretary bird *n.* a large African long-legged bird of prey having a crest and tail of long feathers and feeding chiefly on snakes.

secretary-general *n., pl.* **secretaries-general.** a chief administrative official, as of the United Nations.

secretary of state *n.* **1.** (in Britain) the head of any of several government departments. **2.** (in the U.S.) the head of the government department in charge of foreign affairs (**State Department**).

secrete[1] (sɪˈkriːt) *vb.* (of a cell, organ, etc.) to synthesize and release (a secretion). [C18: back formation from SECRETION] —**seˈcretor** *n.* —**seˈcretory** *adj.*

secrete[2] (sɪˈkriːt) *vb.* (*tr.*) to put in a hiding place. [C18: var. of obs. *secret* to hide away]

secretion (sɪˈkriːʃən) *n.* **1.** a substance that is released from a cell, esp. a glandular cell. **2.** the process involved in producing and releasing such a substance from the cell. [C17: from Med. L *sēcrētiō,* from L: a separation]

secretive (ˈsiːkrɪtɪv) *adj.* inclined to secrecy. —ˈ**secretively** *adv.* —ˈ**secretiveness** *n.*

secretory (sɪˈkriːtərɪ) *adj.* of, relating to, or producing a secretion: *secretory function.*

secret police *n.* a police force that operates relatively secretly to check subversion or political dissent.

secret service *n.* a government agency or department that conducts intelligence or counterintelligence operations.

sect (sɛkt) *n.* **1.** a subdivision of a larger religious group (esp. the Christian Church as a whole) the members of which have to some extent diverged from the rest by developing deviating beliefs, practices, etc. **2.** *Often disparaging.* **a.** a schismatic religious body. **b.** a religious group regarded as extreme or heretical. **3.** a group of people with a common interest, doctrine, etc. [C14: from L *secta* faction, from *sequī* to follow]

-sect *vb. combining form.* to cut or divide, esp. into a specified number of parts: *trisect.* [from L *sectus* cut, from *secāre* to cut]

sectarian (sɛkˈtɛərɪən) *adj.* **1.** of, relating to, or characteristic of sects or sectaries. **2.** adhering to a particular sect, faction, or doctrine. **3.** narrow-minded, esp. as a result of adherence to a particular sect. ~*n.* **4.** a member of a sect or faction, esp. one who is intolerant towards other sects, etc. —**secˈtarianˌism** *n.*

sectary (ˈsɛktərɪ) *n., pl.* **-taries.** **1.** a member of a sect, esp. a religous sect. **2.** a member of a Nonconformist denomination, esp. one that is small. [C16: from Med. L *sectārius,* from L *secta* SECT]

section (ˈsɛkʃən) *n.* **1.** a part cut off or separated from the main body of something. **2.** a part or subdivision of a piece of writing, book, etc.: *the sports section of the newspaper.* **3.** one of several component parts. **4.** a distinct part of a country, community, etc. **5.** *U.S. & Canad.* an area one mile square. **6.** *N.Z.* a plot of land for building, esp. in a suburban area. **7.** the section of a railway track that is controlled by a particular signal box. **8.** the act or process of cutting or separating by cutting. **9.** a representation of an object cut by an imaginary vertical plane so as to show its construction and interior. **10.** *Geom.* a plane surface formed by cutting through a solid. **11.** a thin slice of biological tissue, etc., prepared for examination by microscope. **12.** a segment of an orange or other citrus fruit. **13.** a small military formation. **14.** *Austral. & N.Z.* a fare stage on a bus, tram, etc. **15.** *Music.* **a.** an extended division of a composition or movement: *the development section.* **b.** a division in an orchestra, band, etc., containing instruments belonging to the same class: *the brass section.* **16.** Also called: **signature, gathering.** a folded printing sheet or sheets ready for gathering and binding. ~*vb.* (*tr.*) **17.** to cut or divide into sections. **18.** to cut through so as to reveal a section. **19.** (in drawing, esp. mechanical drawing) to shade so as to indicate sections. [C16: from L *sectiō*, from *secāre* to cut]

sectional ('sɛkʃənᵊl) *adj.* **1.** composed of several sections. **2.** of or relating to a section. —'**sectiona,lize** *or* **-ise** *vb.* (*tr.*) —'**sectionally** *adv.*

sectionalism ('sɛkʃənə,lɪzəm) *n.* excessive or narrow-minded concern for local or regional interests. —'**sectionalist** *n.*, *adj.*

sector ('sɛktə) *n.* **1.** a part or subdivision, esp. of a society or an economy: *the private sector.* **2.** *Geom.* either portion of a circle included between two radii and an arc. **3.** a measuring instrument consisting of two graduated arms hinged at one end. **4.** a part or subdivision of an area of military operations. [C16: from LL: sector, from L: a cutter, from *secāre* to cut] —'**sectoral** *adj.*

sectorial (sɛk'tɔːrɪəl) *adj.* **1.** of or relating to a sector. **2.** *Zool.* adapted for cutting: *the sectorial teeth of carnivores.*

secular ('sɛkjʊlə) *adj.* **1.** of or relating to worldly as opposed to sacred things. **2.** not concerned with or related to religion. **3.** not within the control of the Church. **4.** (of an education, etc.) having no particular religious affinities. **5.** (of clerics) not bound by religious vows to a monastic or other order. **6.** occurring or appearing once in an age or century. **7.** lasting for a long time. **8.** *Astron.* occurring slowly over a long period of time. ~*n.* **9.** a member of the secular clergy. [C13: from OF *seculer*, from LL *saeculāris* temporal, from L: concerning an age, from *saeculum* an age] —**secularity** (,sɛkjʊ'lærɪtɪ) *n.* —'**secularly** *adv.*

secularism ('sɛkjʊlə,rɪzəm) *n.* **1.** *Philosophy.* a doctrine that rejects religion, esp. in ethics. **2.** the attitude that religion should have no place in civil affairs. —'**secularist** *n.*, *adj.*

secularize *or* **-rise** ('sɛkjʊlə,raɪz) *vb.* (*tr.*) **1.** to change from religious or sacred to secular functions, etc. **2.** to dispense from allegiance to a religious order. **3.** *Law.* to transfer (property) from ecclesiastical to civil possession or use. —,**seculari'zation** *or* **-ri'sation** *n.*

secund (sɪ'kʌnd) *adj. Bot.* having parts arranged on or turned to one side of the axis. [C18: from L *secundus* following, from *sequī* to follow]

Secunderabad (sə'kʌndərə,bæd, -,bɑːd) *n.* a former town in S central India, in N Andra Pradesh: one of the largest British military stations in India: now part of Hyderabad city.

secure (sɪ'kjʊə) *adj.* **1.** free from danger, damage, etc. **2.** free from fear, care, etc. **3.** in safe custody. **4.** not likely to fail, become loose, etc. **5.** able to be relied on: *a secure investment.* **6.** *Arch.* overconfident. ~*vb.* **7.** (*tr.*) to obtain: *I will secure some good seats.* **8.** (when *intr.*, often foll. by *against*) to make or become free from danger, fear, etc. **9.** (*tr.*) to make fast or firm. **10.** (when *intr.*, often foll. by *against*) to make or become certain: *this plan will secure your happiness.* **11.** (*tr.*) to assure (a creditor) of payment, as by giving security. **12.** (*tr.*) to make (a military position) safe from attack. **13.** *Naut.* to make (a vessel or its contents) safe or ready by battening down hatches, etc. [C16: from L *secūrus* free from care] —se'**curable** *adj.* —se'**curely** *adv.* —se'**curement** *n.* —se'**curer** *n.*

securitization *or* **-tisation** (sɪ,kjʊərɪtaɪ'zeɪʃən) *n. Stock Exchange.* the packaging of a number of instruments (stocks, bonds, debts, etc.) into one instrument that can be treated as a single security or bond.

security (sɪ'kjʊərɪtɪ) *n.*, *pl.* **-ties. 1.** the state of being secure. **2.** assured freedom from poverty or want: *he needs the security of a permanent job.* **3.** a person or thing that secures, guarantees, etc. **4.** precautions taken to ensure against theft, espionage, etc. **5.** (*often pl.*) **a.** a certificate of creditorship or property carrying the right to receive interest or dividend, such as shares or bonds. **b.** the financial asset represented by such a certificate. **6.**

the specific asset that a creditor can claim in the event of default on an obligation. **7.** something given or pledged to secure the fulfilment of a promise or obligation. **8.** the protection of data to ensure that only authorised personnel have access to computer files.

security blanket *n.* **1.** a policy of temporary secrecy by police or those in charge of security, in order to protect a person, place, etc., threatened with danger, from further risk. **2.** a baby's blanket, soft toy, etc., to which a baby or young child becomes very attached, using it as a comforter. **3.** *Inf.* anything used or thought of as providing reassurance.

Security Council *n.* an organ of the United Nations established to maintain world peace.

security guard *n.* someone employed to protect buildings, people, etc., and to collect and deliver large sums of money.

security risk *n.* a person deemed to be a threat to state security in that he could be open to pressure, have subversive political beliefs, etc.

secy. *or* **sec'y.** *abbrev. for* secretary.

sedan (sɪ'dæn) *n.* **1.** *U.S., Canad., & N.Z.* a saloon car. **2.** short for **sedan chair.** [C17: from ?]

Sedan (*French* sədɑ̃; *English* sɪ'dæn) *n.* a town in NE France, on the River Meuse: passed to France in 1642; a Protestant stronghold (16th–17th centuries); scene of a French defeat (1870) during the Franco-Prussian War and of a battle (1940) in World War II, which began the German invasion of France. Pop.: 23 357 (1982).

sedan chair *n.* a closed chair for one passenger, carried on poles by two bearers, commonly used in the 17th and 18th centuries.

sedate[1] (sɪ'deɪt) *adj.* **1.** habitually calm and composed in manner. **2.** sober or decorous. [C17: from L *sēdāre* to soothe] —se'**dately** *adv.* —se'**dateness** *n.*

sedate[2] (sɪ'deɪt) *vb.* (*tr.*) to administer a sedative to. [C20: back formation from SEDATIVE]

sedation (sɪ'deɪʃən) *n.* **1.** a state of calm or reduced nervous activity. **2.** the administration of a sedative.

sedative ('sɛdətɪv) *adj.* **1.** having a soothing or calming effect. ~*n.* **2.** of or relating to sedation. ~*n.* **3.** *Med.* a sedative drug or agent. [C15: from Med. L *sēdātīvus*, from L *sēdātus* assuaged; see SEDATE[1]]

Seddon ('sɛdⁿn) *n.* **Richard John,** known as *King Dick.* 1845–1906, New Zealand statesman, born in England; prime minister of New Zealand (1893–1906).

sedentary ('sɛdⁿntərɪ) *adj.* **1.** characterized by or requiring a sitting position: *sedentary work.* **2.** tending to sit about without taking much exercise. **3.** (of animals) moving about very little. **4.** (of birds) not migratory. [C16: from L *sedentārius*, from *sedēre* to sit] —'**sedentarily** *adv.* —'**sedentariness** *n.*

Seder ('seɪdə) *n. Judaism.* a ceremonial meal on the first night or first two nights of Passover. [from Heb. *sēdher* order]

sedge (sɛdʒ) *n.* a grasslike plant growing on wet ground and having rhizomes, triangular stems, and minute flowers in spikelets. [OE *secg*] —'**sedgy** *adj.*

sedge warbler *n.* a European songbird of reed beds and swampy areas, having a streaked brownish plumage with white eye stripes.

Sedgwick ('sɛdʒwɪk) *n.* **Adam.** 1785–1873, English geologist; played a major role in establishing parts of the geological time scale, esp. the Cambrian and Devonian periods.

sedilia (sɛ'daɪlɪə) *n.* (*functioning as sing.*) the group of three seats, each called a **sedile** (sɛ'daɪlɪ) on the south side of a sanctuary where the celebrant and ministers sit during High Mass. [C18: from L, from *sedīle* a chair, from *sedēre* to sit]

sediment ('sɛdɪmənt) *n.* **1.** matter that settles to the bottom of a liquid. **2.** material that has been deposited from water, ice, or wind. [C16: from L *sedimentum* a settling, from *sedēre* to sit] —,**sedimen'tation** *n.*

sedimentary (,sɛdɪ'mɛntərɪ) *adj.* **1.** characteristic of, resembling, or containing sediment. **2.** (of rocks) formed by the accumulation of mineral and organic fragments that have been deposited by water, ice, or wind. —,**sedi'mentarily** *adv.*

sedition (sɪ'dɪʃən) *n.* **1.** speech or behaviour directed against the peace of a state. **2.** an offence that tends to undermine the authority of a state. **3.** an incitement to public disorder. [C14: from L *sēditiō* discord, from *sēd-*

apart + *itiō* a going, from *īre* to go] —**se'ditionary** *n.*, *adj.*

seditious (sɪ'dɪʃəs) *adj.* **1.** of, like, or causing sedition. **2.** inclined to or taking part in sedition.

seduce (sɪ'djuːs) *vb.* (*tr.*) **1.** to persuade to engage in sexual intercourse. **2.** to lead astray, as from the right action. **3.** to win over, attract, or lure. [C15: from L *sēdūcere* to lead apart] —**se'ducible** *adj.*

seducer (sɪ'djuːsə) *or* (*fem.*) **seductress** (sɪ'dʌktrɪs) *n.* a person who entices, allures, or seduces, esp. one who entices another to engage in sexual intercourse.

seduction (sɪ'dʌkʃən) *n.* **1.** the act of seducing or the state of being seduced. **2.** a means of seduction.

seductive (sɪ'dʌktɪv) *adj.* tending to seduce or capable of seducing; enticing; alluring. —**se'ductively** *adv.* —**se'ductiveness** *n.*

sedulous ('sɛdjʊləs) *adj.* assiduous; diligent. [C16: from L *sēdulus*, from ?] —**sedulity** (sɪ'djuːlɪtɪ) *or* **'sedulousness** *n.* —**'sedulously** *adv.*

sedum ('siːdəm) *n.* a rock plant having thick fleshy leaves and clusters of white, yellow, or pink flowers. [C15: from L: houseleek]

see[1] (siː) *vb.* **seeing, saw, seen. 1.** to perceive with the eyes. **2.** (when *tr.*, *may take a clause as object*) to understand: *I explained the problem but he could not see it.* **3.** (*tr.*) to perceive with any or all of the senses: *I hate to see you so unhappy.* **4.** (*tr.*; *may take a clause as object*) to foresee: *I can see what will happen if you don't help.* **5.** (when *tr.*, *may take a clause as object*) to ascertain or find out (a fact): *see who is at the door.* **6.** (when *tr.*, takes a clause as object; when *intr.*, foll. by *to*) to make sure (of something) or take care (of something): *see that he gets to bed early.* **7.** (when *tr.*, *may take a clause as object*) to consider, deliberate, or decide: *see if you can come next week.* **8.** (*tr.*) to have experience of: *he had seen much unhappiness in his life.* **9.** (*tr.*) to allow to be in a specified condition: *I cannot stand by and see a child in pain.* **10.** (*tr.*) to be characterized by: *this period of history has seen much unrest.* **11.** (*tr.*) to meet or pay a visit to: *to see one's solicitor.* **12.** (*tr.*) to receive: *the Prime Minister will see the deputation now.* **13.** (*tr.*) to frequent the company of: *she is seeing a married man.* **14.** (*tr.*) to accompany: *I saw her to the door.* **15.** (*tr.*) to refer to or look up: *for further information see the appendix.* **16.** (in gambling, esp. in poker) to match (another player's bet) or match the bet of (another player) by staking an equal sum. **17. as far as I can see.** to the best of my judgment. **18. see fit.** (*takes an infinitive*) to consider proper, etc.: *I don't see fit to allow her to come here.* **19. see (someone) hanged** *or* **damned first.** *Inf.* to refuse absolutely to do what one has been asked. **20. see you, see you later,** *or* **be seeing you.** an expression of farewell. ~See also **see about, see into,** etc. [OE *sēon*]

see[2] (siː) *n.* the diocese of a bishop, or the place within it where his cathedral is situated. [C13: from OF *sed*, from L *sēdēs* a seat]

see about *vb.* (*intr.*, *prep.*) **1.** to take care of: *he couldn't see about the matter because he was ill.* **2.** to investigate: *to see about a new car.*

Seebeck effect ('siːbɛk) *n.* the phenomenon in which a current is produced in a circuit containing two or more different metals when the junctions between the metals are maintained at different temperatures. Also called: **thermoelectric effect.** [C19: after Thomas *Seebeck* (1770–1831), G physicist]

seed (siːd) *n.* **1.** *Bot.* a mature fertilized plant ovule, consisting of an embryo and its food store surrounded by a protective seed coat (testa). Related adj.: **seminal. 2.** the small hard seedlike fruit of plants such as wheat. **3.** any propagative part of a plant, such as a tuber, spore, or bulb. **4.** the source, beginning, or germ of anything: *the seeds of revolt.* **5.** *Chiefly Bible.* descendants: *the seed of Abraham.* **6.** an archaic term for **sperm** or **semen. 7.** *Sport.* a seeded player. **8.** *Chem.* a small crystal added to a supersaturated solution to induce crystallization. **9. go** *or* **run to seed. a.** (of plants) to produce and shed seeds. **b.** to lose vigour, usefulness, etc. ~*vb.* **10.** to plant (seeds, grain, etc.) in (soil): *we seeded this field with oats.* **11.** (*intr.*) (of plants) to form or shed seeds. **12.** (*tr.*) to remove the seeds from (fruit, etc.). **13.** (*tr.*) *Chem.* to add a small crystal to (a supersaturated solution) in order to cause crystallization. **14.** (*tr.*) to scatter certain substances, such as silver iodide, in (clouds) in order to cause

rain. **15.** (*tr.*) to arrange (the draw of a tournament) so that outstanding teams or players will not meet in the early rounds. [OE *sǣd*] —**'seeder** *n.* —**'seedless** *adj.*

seedbed ('siːd,bɛd) *n.* **1.** a plot of land in which seedlings are grown before being transplanted. **2.** the place where something develops.

seedcake ('siːd,keɪk) *n.* a sweet cake flavoured with caraway seeds and lemon rind or essence.

seed coral *n.* small pieces of coral used in jewellery, etc.

seed corn *n.* **1.** the good quality ears or kernels of corn that are used as seed. **2.** assets that are expected to provide future benefits.

seed leaf *n.* the nontechnical name for **cotyledon.**

seedling ('siːdlɪŋ) *n.* a plant produced from a seed, esp. a very young plant.

seed money *n.* money used for the establishment of an enterprise.

seed oyster *n.* a young oyster, esp. a cultivated oyster, ready for transplantation.

seed pearl *n.* a tiny pearl weighing less than a quarter of a grain.

seed pod *n.* a carpel or pistil enclosing the seeds of a plant, esp. a flowering plant.

seed potato *n.* a potato tuber used for planting.

seed vessel *n.* *Bot.* a dry fruit, such as a capsule.

seedy ('siːdɪ) *adj.* **seedier, seediest. 1.** shabby in appearance: *seedy clothes.* **2.** (of a plant) at the stage of producing seeds. **3.** *Inf.* not physically fit. —**'seedily** *adv.* —**'seediness** *n.*

Seeger ('siːgə) *n.* **Pete.** born 1919. U.S. folk singer and songwriter, noted for his protest songs, which include "We shall Overcome" (1960), "Where have all the Flowers gone?" (1961), "If I had a Hammer" (1962), and "Little Boxes" (1962).

seeing ('siːɪŋ) *n.* **1.** the sense or faculty of sight. **2.** *Astron.* the condition of the atmosphere with respect to observation of stars, planets, etc. ~*conj.* **3.** (*subordinating*; often foll. by *that*) in light of the fact (that).

see into *vb.* (*intr.*, *prep.*) to discover the true nature of: *I can't see into your thoughts.*

seek (siːk) *vb.* **seeking, sought. 1.** (when *intr.*, often foll. by *for* or *after*) to try to find by searching: *to seek a solution.* **2.** (*also intr.*) to try to obtain or acquire: *to seek happiness.* **3.** to attempt (to do something): *I'm only seeking to help.* **4.** (*also intr.*) to inquire about or request (something). **5.** to resort to: *to seek the garden for peace.* [OE *sēcan*] —**'seeker** *n.*

seek out *vb.* (*tr.*, *adv.*) to search hard for and find a specific person or thing: *she sought out her friend from amongst the crowd.*

Seeland ('zeːlant) *n.* the German name for **Sjælland.**

seem (siːm) *vb.* (*may take an infinitive*) **1.** (*copula*) to appear to the mind or eye; look: *the car seems to be running well.* **2.** to appear to be: *there seems no need for all this nonsense.* **3.** used to diminish the force of a following infinitive to be polite, more noncommittal, etc.: *I can't seem to get through to you.* [C12: ?from ON *soma* to beseem, from *sœmr* befitting]

seeming ('siːmɪŋ) *adj.* **1.** (*prenominal*) apparent but not actual or genuine. ~*n.* **2.** outward or false appearance. —**'seemingly** *adv.*

seemly ('siːmlɪ) *adj.* **-lier, -liest. 1.** proper or fitting. **2.** *Obs.* pleasing in appearance. ~*adv.* **3.** *Arch.* decorously. [C13: from ON *sœmiligr*, from *sœmr* befitting]

seen (siːn) *vb.* the past participle of **see**[1].

see off *vb.* (*tr.*, *adv.*) **1.** to be present at the departure of (a person making a journey). **2.** *Inf.* to cause to leave or depart, esp. by force.

seep (siːp) *vb.* **1.** (*intr.*) to pass gradually or leak as if through small openings. ~*n.* **2.** a small spring or place where water, oil, etc., has oozed through the ground. [OE *sipian*] —**'seepage** *n.*

seer[1] (sɪə) *n.* **1.** a person who can supposedly see into the future. **2.** a person who professes supernatural powers. **3.** a person who sees.

seer[2] (sɪə) *n.* a varying unit of weight used in India, usually about two pounds or one kilogram. [from Hindi]

seersucker ('sɪə,sʌkə) *n.* a light cotton, linen, or other fabric with a crinkled surface and often striped. [C18: from Hindi *sīrsakar*, from Persian *shīr o shakkar*, lit.: milk and sugar]

seesaw ('siː,sɔː) *n.* **1.** a plank balanced in the middle so that two people seated on the ends can ride up and down by pushing on the ground with their feet. **2.** the pastime of riding up and down on a seesaw. **3.** an up-and-down or back-and-forth movement. ~*vb.* **4.** (*intr.*) to move up and down or back and forth in such a manner. [C17: reduplication of SAW[1], alluding to the movement from side to side, as in sawing]

seethe (siːð) *vb.* **1.** (*intr.*) to boil or to foam as if boiling. **2.** (*intr.*) to be in a state of extreme agitation, esp. through anger. **3.** (*tr.*) to soak in liquid. **4.** (*tr.*) *Arch.* to cook by boiling. [OE *sēothan*] —'**seething** *adj.* —'**seethingly** *adv.*

see through *vb.* **1.** (*tr.*) to help out in time of need or trouble. **2.** (*tr., adv.*) to remain with until the end or completion: *let's see the job through.* **3.** (*intr., prep.*) to perceive the true nature of: *I can see through your evasion.* ~*adj.* **see–through**. **4.** partly or wholly transparent or translucent, esp. (of clothes) in a titillating way.

Seferis (sə'fɛərɪs) *n.* **George.** pen name of *Georgios Seferiades.* 1900–71, Greek poet and diplomat: Nobel prize for literature 1963.

segment *n.* ('sɛgmənt). **1.** *Maths.* **a.** a part of a line or curve between two points. **b.** a part of a plane or solid figure cut off by an intersecting line, plane, or planes. **2.** one of several parts or sections into which an object is divided. **3.** *Zool.* any of the parts into which the body or appendages of an annelid or arthropod are divided. **4.** *Linguistics.* a speech sound considered in isolation. ~*vb.* (sɛg'mɛnt). **5.** to cut or divide (a whole object) into segments. [C16: from L *segmentum*, from *secāre* to cut] —**seg'mental** *adj.* —**segmentary** ('sɛgməntərɪ) *adj.*

segmentation (,sɛgmɛn'teɪʃən) *n.* **1.** the act or an instance of dividing into segments. **2.** *Embryol.* another name for **cleavage** (sense 4).

Segovia[1] (sɪ'gəʊvɪə; *Spanish* se'ɣoβja) *n.* a town in central Spain: site of a Roman aqueduct, still in use, and the fortified palace of the kings of Castile (the Alcázar). Pop.: 54 568 (1982 est.).

Segovia[2] (sɪ'gəʊvɪə; *Spanish* se'ɣoβja) *n.* **Andrés** (an'dres), Marquis of Salobreña. 1893–1987, Spanish classical guitarist.

segregate ('sɛgrɪ,geɪt) *vb.* **1.** to set or be set apart from others or from the main group. **2.** (*tr.*) to impose segregation on (a racial or minority group). **3.** *Genetics.* to undergo or cause to undergo segregation. [C16: from L *sēgregāre*, from *sē-* apart + *grex* a flock] —'**segre,gative** *adj.* —'**segre,gator** *n.*

segregation (,sɛgrɪ'geɪʃən) *n.* **1.** the act of segregating or state of being segregated. **2.** *Sociol.* the practice or policy of creating separate facilities within the same society for the use of a particular group. **3.** *Genetics.* the separation at meiosis of the two members of any pair of alleles into separate gametes. —,**segre'gational** *adj.* —,**segre'gationist** *n.*

segue ('seɪgwɪ) *vb.* (*intr.*) **segueing, segued. 1.** (often foll. by *into*) to proceed from one piece of music to another without a break. ~*n.* **2.** the practice or an instance of segueing. [from It: follows, from *seguire* to follow, from L *sequī*]

seguidilla (,sɛgɪ'diːljə) *n.* **1.** a Spanish dance in a fast triple rhythm. **2.** a piece of music composed for or in the rhythm of this dance. [Sp.: a little dance, from *seguida* a dance, from *seguir* to follow, from L *sequī*]

seiche (seɪʃ) *n.* a tide-like movement of a body of water caused by barometric pressure, earth tremors, etc. [C19: from Swiss F, from ?]

Seidlitz powder *or* **powders** ('sɛdlɪts) *n.* a laxative consisting of two powders, tartaric acid and a mixture of sodium bicarbonate and Rochelle salt. [C19: after *Seidlitz*, a village in Bohemia with mineral springs having similar laxative effects]

seif dune (seɪf) *n.* (in deserts, esp. the Sahara) a long ridge of blown sand, often several miles long. [*seif*, from Ar.: sword, from the shape of the dune]

seigneur (sɛ'njɜː; *French* sɛɲœr) *n.* a feudal lord, esp. in France. [C16: from OF, from Vulgar L *senior*, from L: an elderly man; see SENIOR] —**sei'gneurial** *adj.*

seigneury ('seɪnjərɪ) *n., pl.* **-gneuries.** the estate of a seigneur.

seignior ('seɪnjə) *n.* **1.** a less common name for a **seigneur. 2.** (in England) the lord of a seigniory. [C14: from Anglo-F *segnour*] —**seigniorial** (seɪ'njɔːrɪəl) *adj.*

seigniory ('seɪnjərɪ) *or* **signory** ('siːnjərɪ) *n., pl.* **-gniories** *or* **-gnories. 1.** less common names for a **seigneury. 2.** (in England) the fee or manor of a seignior; a feudal domain. **3.** the authority of a seignior.

seine (seɪn) *n.* **1.** a large fishing net that hangs vertically in the water by means of floats at the top and weights at the bottom. ~*vb.* **2.** to catch (fish) using this net. [OF *segne*, from L *sagēna*, from Gk *sagēnē*]

Seine (seɪn; *French* sɛn) *n.* a river in N France, rising on the Plateau de Langres and flowing northwest through Paris to the English Channel: the second longest river in France, linked by canal with the Rivers Somme, Scheldt, Meuse, Rhine, Saône, and Loire. Length: 776 km (482 miles).

Seine-et-Marne (*French* sɛnemarn) *n.* a department of N central France, in Île-de-France region. Capital: Melun. Pop.: 887 112 (1982). Area: 5931 sq. km (2313 sq. miles).

Seine-Maritime (*French* sɛnmaritim) *n.* a department of N France, in Haute-Normandie region. Capital: Rouen. Pop.: 1 193 039 (1982). Area: 6342 sq. km (2473 sq. miles).

Seine-Saint-Denis (*French* sɛnsɛdni) *n.* a department of N central France, in Île-de-France region. Capital: Bobigny. Pop.: 1 324 301 (1982). Area: 236 sq. km (92 sq. miles).

seise *or U.S.* **seize** (siːz) *vb.* to put into legal possession of (property, etc.). —**seiser** *n.*

seisin *or U.S.* **seizin** ('siːzɪn) *n. Property law.* feudal possession of an estate in land. [C13: from OF *seisine*, from *seisir* to SEIZE]

seismic ('saɪzmɪk) *adj.* relating to or caused by earthquakes or artificially produced earth tremors.

seismo- *or before a vowel* **seism-** *combining form.* earthquake: *seismology.* [from Gk *seismos*]

seismograph ('saɪzmə,grɑːf) *n.* an instrument that registers and records earthquakes. A **seismogram** is the record from such an instrument. —**seismographic** (,saɪzmə'græfɪk) *adj.* —**seismographer** (saɪz'mɒgrəfə) *n.* —**seis'mography** *n.*

seismology (saɪz'mɒlədʒɪ) *n.* the branch of geology concerned with the study of earthquakes. —**seismologic** (,saɪzmə'lɒdʒɪk) *or* ,**seismo'logical** *adj.* —,**seismo'logically** *adv.* —**seis'mologist** *n.*

seize[1] (siːz) *vb.* (*mainly tr.*) **1.** (also *intr.*, foll. by *on*) to take hold of quickly; grab. **2.** (sometimes foll. by *on* or *upon*) to grasp mentally, esp. rapidly: *she immediately seized his idea.* **3.** to take mental possession of: *alarm seized the crowd.* **4.** to take possession of rapidly and forcibly: *the thief seized the woman's purse.* **5.** to take legal possession of. **6.** to take by force or capture: *the army seized the undefended town.* **7.** to take immediate advantage of: *to seize an opportunity.* **8.** *Naut.* to bind (two ropes together). **9.** (*intr.;* often foll. by *up*) (of mechanical parts) to become jammed, esp. because of excessive heat. [C13 *saisen*, from OF *saisir*, from Med. L *sacīre* to position, of Gmc origin] —'**seizable** *adj.*

seize[2] (siːz) *vb.* the U.S. spelling of **seise.**

seizure ('siːʒə) *n.* **1.** the act or an instance of seizing or the state of being seized. **2.** *Pathol.* a sudden manifestation or recurrence of a disease, such as an epileptic convulsion.

Sekondi (,sɛkɒn'diː) *n.* a port in SW Ghana, 8 km (5 miles) northeast of Takoradi: linked administratively with Takoradi in 1946. Pop. (with Takoradi): 93 900 (1984).

selachian (sɪ'leɪkɪən) *adj.* of or belonging to a large subclass of cartilaginous fishes including the sharks, rays, dogfish, and skates. [C19: from NL *Selachii*, from Gk *selakhē* a shark]

Selangor (sə'læŋə) *n.* a state of Peninsular Malaysia, on the Strait of Malacca: established as a British protectorate in 1874; tin producer. Capital: Shah Alam. Pop.: 1 731 090 (1985 est.). Area: 8203 sq. km (3167 sq. miles).

Selden ('sɛldən) *n.* **John.** 1584–1654, English antiquary and politician. As a member of Parliament, he was twice imprisoned for opposing the king.

seldom ('sɛldəm) *adv.* rarely. [OE *seldon*]

select (sɪ'lɛkt) *vb.* **1.** to choose (someone or something) in preference to another or others. ~*adj.* also **selected. 2.** chosen in preference to others. **3.** of particular quality. **4.** limited as to membership or entry: *a select gathering.* ~*n. Austral. history.* **5.** a piece of land acquired by a free-selector. **6.** the process of free-selection. [C16: from L *sēligere* to sort, from *sē-* apart + *legere* to choose] —**se'lectness** *n.* —**se'lector** *n.*

select committee *n.* (in Britain) a small committee of members of parliament, set up to investigate and report on a specified matter.

selection (sɪ'lɛkʃən) *n.* **1.** the act or an instance of selecting or the state of being selected. **2.** a thing or number of things that have been selected. **3.** a range from which something may be selected: *a good selection of clothes.* **4.** *Biol.* the process by which certain organisms or characters are reproduced and perpetuated in the species in preference to others.

selective (sɪ'lɛktɪv) *adj.* **1.** of or characterized by selection. **2.** tending to choose carefully or characterized by careful choice. **3.** *Electronics.* occurring at or operating at a particular frequency or band of frequencies. —**se'lectively** *adv.*

selectivity (sɪ,lɛk'tɪvɪtɪ) *n.* **1.** the state or quality of being selective. **2.** the degree to which a radio receiver, etc., can respond to the frequency of a desired signal.

Selene (sɪ'liːnɪ) *n.* the Greek goddess of the moon. Roman counterpart: **Luna.**

selenite ('sɛlɪ,naɪt) *n.* a colourless glassy variety of gypsum.

selenium (sɪ'liːnɪəm) *n.* a nonmetallic element that exists in several allotropic forms. The common form is a grey crystalline solid that is photoconductive, photovoltaic, and semiconducting: used in photocells, solar cells, and in xerography. Symbol: Se; atomic no.: 34; atomic wt.: 78.96. [C19: from NL, from Gk *selēnē* moon; by analogy to TELLURIUM (from L *tellus* earth)]

seleno- *or before a vowel* **selen-** *combining form.* denoting the moon: *selenography.* [from Gk *selēnē* moon]

selenography (,siːlɪ'nɒgrəfɪ) *n.* the branch of astronomy concerned with the description and mapping of the surface features of the moon. —,**sele'nographer** *n.* —**selenographic** (sɪ,liːnəʊ'græfɪk) *adj.*

Seleucia (sɪ'luːʃɪə) *n.* **1.** an ancient city in Mesopotamia, on the River Tigris: founded by Seleucus Nicator in 312 B.C.; became the chief city of the Seleucid empire; sacked by the Romans around 162 A.D. **2.** an ancient city in SE Asia Minor, on the River Calycadnus (modern Goksu Nehri): captured by the Turks in the 13th century; site of present-day Silifke (Turkey). Official name: **Seleucia Tracheotis** (,trækɪ'əʊtɪs) or **Trachea** (trə'kɪə). **3.** an ancient port in Syria, on the River Orontes: the port of Antioch, of military importance during the wars between the Ptolemies and Seleucids; largely destroyed by earthquake in 526; site of present-day Samandağ (Turkey). Official name: **Seleucia Pieria** (paɪ'iːrɪə).

Seleucus I (sɪ'luːkəs) *n.* surname *Nicator.* ?358–280 B.C., Macedonian general under Alexander the Great, who founded the Seleucid kingdom. 1635.

self (sɛlf) *n., pl.* **selves. 1.** the distinct individuality or identity of a person or thing. **2.** a person's typical bodily make-up or personal characteristics: *she's looking her old self again.* **3.** one's own welfare or interests: *he only thinks of self.* **4.** an individual's consciousness of his own identity or being. **5.** a bird, animal, etc., that is a single colour throughout. ~*pron.* **6.** *Not standard.* myself, yourself, etc.: *seats for self and wife.* ~*adj.* **7.** of the same colour or material. **8.** *Obs.* the same. [OE *seolf*]

self- *combining form.* **1.** of oneself or itself: *self-defence.* **2.** by, to, in, due to, for, or from the self: *self-employed; self-respect.* **3.** automatic or automatically: *self-propelled.*

self-abnegation *n.* the denial of one's own interests in favour of the interests of others.

self-absorption *n.* **1.** preoccupation with oneself to the exclusion of others. **2.** *Physics.* the process in which some of the radiation emitted by a material is absorbed by the material itself.

self-abuse *n.* **1.** disparagement or misuse of one's own abilities, etc. **2.** a censorious term for **masturbation.**

self-acting *adj.* not requiring an external influence or control to function; automatic.

self-addressed *adj.* **1.** addressed for return to the sender. **2.** directed to oneself: *a self-addressed remark.*

self-aggrandizement *n.* the act of increasing one's own power, importance, etc. —,**self-ag'gran,dizing** *adj.*

self-appointed *adj.* having assumed authority without the agreement of others: *a self-appointed critic.*

self-assertion *n.* the act or an instance of putting forward one's own opinions, etc., esp. in an aggressive or conceited manner. —,**self-as'serting** *adj.* —,**self-as'sertive** *adj.*

self-assurance *n.* confidence in the validity, value, etc., of one's own ideas, opinions, etc. —,**self-as'sured** *adj.* —,**self-as'suredly** *adv.*

self-centred *adj.* totally preoccupied with one's own concerns. —,**self-'centredness** *n.*

self-certification *n.* (in Britain) a formal assertion by a worker to his employer that absence from work for up to seven days was due to sickness.

self-coloured *adj.* **1.** having only a single and uniform colour: *a self-coloured dress.* **2.** (of cloth, etc.) having its natural or original colour.

self-command *n.* another term for **self-control.**

self-confessed *adj.* according to one's own testimony or admission: *a self-confessed liar.*

self-confidence *n.* confidence in one's own powers, judgment, etc. —,**self-'confident** *adj.* —,**self-'confidently** *adv.*

self-conscious *adj.* **1.** unduly aware of oneself as the object of the attention of others. **2.** conscious of one's existence. —,**self-'consciously** *adv.* —,**self-'consciousness** *n.*

self-contained *adj.* **1.** containing within itself all parts necessary for completeness. **2.** (of a flat) having its own kitchen, bathroom, and lavatory not shared by others. **3.** able or tending to keep one's feelings, thoughts, etc., to oneself. —,**self-con'tainedness** *n.*

self-contradictory *adj.* *Logic.* (of a proposition) both asserting and denying a given proposition.

self-control *n.* the ability to exercise restraint or control over one's feelings, emotions, reactions, etc. —,**self-con'trolled** *adj.*

self-deception *or* **self-deceit** *n.* the act or an instance of deceiving oneself. —,**self-de'ceptive** *adj.*

self-defence *n.* **1.** the act of defending oneself, one's actions, ideas, etc. **2.** boxing as a means of defending the person (esp. in **noble art of self-defence**). **3.** *Law.* the right to defend one's person, family, or property against attack or threat of attack. —,**self-de'fensive** *adj.*

self-denial *n.* the denial or sacrifice of one's own desires. —,**self-de'nying** *adj.*

self-determination *n.* **1.** the ability to make a decision for oneself without influence from outside. **2.** the right of a nation or people to determine its own form of government. —,**self-de'termined** *adj.* —,**self-de'termining** *adj.*

self-discipline *n.* the act of disciplining or power to discipline one's own feelings, desires, etc. —,**self-'disciplined** *adj.*

self-drive *adj.* denoting or relating to a hired car that is driven by the hirer.

self-educated *adj.* **1.** educated through one's own efforts without formal instruction. **2.** educated at one's own expense.

self-effacement *n.* the act of making oneself, one's actions, etc., inconspicuous, esp. because of timidity. —,**self-ef'facing** *adj.*

self-employed *adj.* earning one's living in one's own business or through freelance work, rather than as the employee of another. —,**self-em'ployment** *n.*

self-esteem *n.* **1.** respect for or a favourable opinion of oneself. **2.** an unduly high opinion of oneself.

self-evident *adj.* containing its own evidence or proof without need of further demonstration. —,**self-'evidence** *n.* —,**self-'evidently** *adv.*

self-existent *adj.* *Philosophy.* existing independently of any other being or cause.

self-explanatory *adj.* understandable without explanation; self-evident.

,**self-a'basement** *n.*	,**self-a'ware** *adj.*	,**self-condem'nation** *n.*	,**self-degra'dation** *n.*
,**self-ab'horrence** *n.*	,**self-'catering** *adj.*	,**self-con,gratu'lation** *n.*	,**self-de'lusion** *n.*
,**self-ab'sorbed** *adj.*	,**self-'censorship** *n.*	,**self-con'sistency** *n.*	,**self-de'struct** *vb.*
,**self-ad'hesive** *adj.*	,**self-'cleaning** *adj.*	,**self-con'sistent** *adj.*	,**self-'doubt** *n.*
,**self-ad'vancement** *n.*	,**self-'closing** *adj.*	,**self-de'feating** *adj.*	,**self-ex,ami'nation** *n.*
,**self-a'nalysis** *n.*	,**self-con'ceit** *n.*		

self-expression n. the expression of one's own personality, feelings, etc., as in painting or poetry. —,self-ex'pressive adj.

self-government n. **1.** the government of a country, nation, etc., by its own people. **2.** the state of being self-controlled. —,self-'governed adj. —,self-'governing adj.

selfheal ('sɛlf,hiːl) n. **1.** a low-growing European herbaceous plant with tightly clustered violet-blue flowers and reputedly having healing powers. **2.** any of several other plants thought to have healing powers.

self-help n. the act or state of providing the means to help oneself without relying on the assistance of others.

self-image n. one's own idea of oneself or sense of one's worth.

self-important adj. having or showing an unduly high opinion of one's own abilities, importance, etc. —,self-im'portantly adv. —,self-im'portance n.

self-improvement n. the improvement of one's status, position, education, etc., by one's own efforts.

self-induced adj. **1.** induced or brought on by oneself or itself. **2.** Electronics. produced by self-induction.

self-induction n. the production of an electromotive force in a circuit when the magnetic flux linked with the circuit changes as a result of a change in current in the same circuit.

self-indulgent adj. tending to indulge one's own desires, etc. —,self-in'dulgence n.

self-interest n. **1.** one's personal interest or advantage. **2.** the act or an instance of pursuing one's own interest. —,self-'interested adj.

selfish ('sɛlfɪʃ) adj. **1.** chiefly concerned with one's own interest, advantage, etc., esp. to the exclusion of the interests of others. **2.** relating to or characterized by self-interest. —'selfishly adv. —'selfishness n.

self-justification n. the act or an instance of justifying or providing excuses for one's own behaviour, etc.

selfless ('sɛlflɪs) adj. having little concern for one's own interests. —'selflessly adv. —'selflessness n.

self-loading adj. (of a firearm) utilizing some of the force of the explosion to eject the empty shell and replace it with a new one. —,self-'loader n.

self-love n. the instinct to seek one's own well-being or to further one's own interest.

self-made adj. **1.** having achieved wealth, status, etc., by one's own efforts. **2.** made by oneself.

self-opinionated adj. **1.** having an unduly high regard for oneself or one's own opinions. **2.** clinging stubbornly to one's own opinions.

self-pity n. the act or state of pitying oneself, esp. in an exaggerated or self-indulgent manner. —,self-'pitying adj. —,self-'pityingly adv.

self-pollination n. the transfer of pollen from the anthers to the stigma of the same flower. —,self-'polli,nated adj.

self-possessed adj. having control of one's emotions, etc. —,self-pos'session n.

self-preservation n. the preservation of oneself from danger or injury.

self-pronouncing adj. (in a phonetic transcription) of or denoting a word that, except for marks of stress, keeps the letters of its ordinary orthography to represent its pronunciation.

self-propelled adj. (of a vehicle) provided with its own source of tractive power rather than requiring an external means of propulsion. —,self-pro'pelling adj.

self-raising adj. (of flour) having a raising agent, such as baking powder, already added.

self-realization n. the realization or fulfilment of one's own potential or abilities.

self-regard n. **1.** concern for one's own interest. **2.** proper esteem for oneself.

self-reliance n. reliance on one's own abilities, decisions, etc. —,self-re'liant adj.

self-reproach n. the act of finding fault with or blaming oneself. —,self-re'proachful adj.

self-respect n. a proper sense of one's own dignity and integrity. —,self-re'specting adj.

self-restraint n. restraint imposed by oneself on one's own feelings, desires, etc.

self-righteous adj. having an exaggerated awareness of one's own virtuousness. —,self-'righteously adv. —,self-'righteousness n.

self-rule n. another term for **self-government** (sense 1).

self-sacrifice n. the sacrifice of one's own desires, etc., for the sake of duty or for the well-being of others. —,self-'sacri,ficing adj.

selfsame ('sɛlf,seɪm) adj. (prenominal) the very same.

self-satisfied adj. having or showing a complacent satisfaction with oneself, one's own actions, behaviour, etc. —,self-,satis'faction n.

self-sealing adj. (esp. of an envelope) designed to become sealed with the application of pressure only.

self-seeking n. **1.** the act or an instance of seeking one's own profit or interest. ~adj. **2.** having or showing an exclusive preoccupation with one's own profit or interest: a self-seeking attitude. —,self-'seeker n.

self-service adj. **1.** of or denoting a shop, restaurant, etc., where the customer serves himself. ~n. **2.** the practice of serving oneself, as in a shop, etc.

self-serving adj. habitually seeking one's own advantage, esp. at the expense of others.

self-sown adj. (of plants) growing from seed dispersed by any means other than by the agency of man or animals. Also: **self-seeded**.

self-starter n. **1.** an electric motor used to start an internal-combustion engine. **2.** the switch that operates this motor. **3.** a person who is strongly motivated and shows initiative, esp. at work.

self-styled adj. (prenominal) claiming to be of a specified nature, quality, profession, etc.: a self-styled expert.

self-sufficient or **self-sufficing** adj. **1.** able to provide for or support oneself without the help of others. **2.** Rare. having undue confidence in oneself. —,self-suf'ficiency n. —,self-suf'ficiently adv.

self-supporting adj. **1.** able to support or maintain oneself without the help of others. **2.** able to stand up or hold firm without support, props, attachments, etc.

self-will n. stubborn adherence to one's own will, desires, etc., esp. at the expense of others. —,self-'willed adj.

self-winding adj. (of a wrist watch) having a mechanism in which a rotating or oscillating weight rewinds the mainspring.

Seljuk (sɛl'dʒuːk) n. **1.** a member of any of the pre-Ottoman Turkish dynasties ruling over large parts of Asia in the 11th, 12th, and 13th centuries A.D. ~adj. **2.** of or relating to these dynasties. [C19: from Turkish]

Selkirk ('sɛl,kɜːk) n. **Alexander**. original name Alexander Selcraig. 1676–1721, Scottish sailor, who was marooned on one of the islets of Juan Fernández and is regarded as the prototype of Defoe's Robinson Crusoe.

Selkirk Mountains pl. n. a mountain range in SW Canada, in SE British Columbia. Highest peak: Mount Sir Sandford, 3533 m (11 590 ft.).

Selkirkshire ('sɛlkɜːk,ʃɪə, -ʃə) n. (until 1975) a county of SE Scotland, now part of Borders region.

sell (sɛl) vb. **selling, sold. 1.** to dispose of or transfer or be disposed of or transferred to a purchaser in exchange for money or other consideration. **2.** to deal in (objects, property, etc.): he sells used cars. **3.** (tr.) to give up or surrender for a price or reward: to sell one's honour. **4.** to promote or facilitate the sale of (objects, property, etc.): publicity sells many products. **5.** to gain acceptance of: to sell an idea. **6.** (intr.) to be in demand on the market: these dresses sell well. **7.** (tr.) Inf. to deceive. **8.** sell down the river. Inf. to betray. **9.** sell oneself. **a.** to convince someone else of one's potential or worth. **b.** to give up one's moral standards, etc. **10.** sell short. **a.** Inf. to belittle. **b.** Finance. to sell securities or goods without owning them in anticipation of buying them before delivery at a lower price. ~n. **11.** the act or an instance of selling: *a soft sell.* **12.** *Inf.* a hoax or deception. ~See also **sell off, sell out,** etc. [OE *sellan* to lend, deliver] — '**sellable** *adj.* — '**seller** *n.*

Sellafield ('sɛlə,fiːld) *n.* the site of an atomic power station in NW England, in W Cumbria. Former name: **Windscale.**

Sellers ('sɛləz) *n.* **Peter.** 1925–80, English radio, stage, and film actor and comedian: noted for his gift of precise vocal mimicry, esp. in *The Goon Show* (with Spike Milligan and Harry Secombe; BBC Radio, 1952–60). His films include *The Lady Killers* (1955), *I'm All Right, Jack* (1959), *The Millionairess* (1961), *Only Two Can Play* (1962), *The Pink Panther* (1963), *Dr Strangelove* (1964), and *Being There* (1979).

selling race or **plate** *n.* a horse race in which the winner must be offered for sale at auction.

sell off *vb.* (*tr., adv.*) to sell (remaining or unprofitable items), esp. at low prices.

Sellotape ('sɛlə,teɪp) *n.* **1.** *Trademark.* a type of transparent adhesive tape. ~*vb.* (*tr.*) **2.** to seal or stick using adhesive tape.

sell out *vb.* (*adv.*) **1.** Also (*chiefly Brit.*): **sell up.** to dispose of (something) completely by selling. **2.** (*tr.*) *Inf.* to betray. ~*n.* **sellout.** **3.** *Inf.* a performance for which all tickets are sold. **4.** a commercial success. **5.** *Inf.* a betrayal.

sell up *vb.* (*adv.*) *Chiefly Brit.* **1.** (*tr.*) to sell all (the possessions) of (a bankrupt debtor) in order to discharge his debts. **2.** (*intr.*) to sell a business.

selsyn ('sɛlsɪn) *n.* another name for **synchro.** [from SEL(F-) + SYN(CHRONOUS)]

Seltzer ('sɛltsə) *n.* **1.** a natural effervescent water with a high content of minerals. **2.** a similar synthetic water, used as a beverage. [C18: changed from G *Selterser Wasser* water from (*Nieder*) *Selters,* district where mineral springs are located, near Wiesbaden, Germany]

selva ('sɛlvə) *n.* **1.** dense equatorial forest, esp. in the Amazon basin, characterized by tall broad-leaved evergreen trees. **2.** a tract of such forest. [C19: from Sp. & Port., from L *silva* forest]

selvage or **selvedge** ('sɛlvɪdʒ) *n.* **1.** the finished non-fraying edge of a length of woven fabric. **2.** a similar strip of material allowed in fabricating a metal or plastic article. [C15: from SELF + EDGE] — '**selvaged** *adj.*

selves (sɛlvz) *n.* **a.** the plural of **self.** **b.** (*in combination*): *ourselves, yourselves, themselves.*

Sem. *abbrev. for:* **1.** Seminary. **2.** Semitic.

semantic (sɪ'mæntɪk) *adj.* **1.** of or relating to the meanings of different words or symbols. **2.** of or relating to semantics. [C19: from Gk *sēmantikos* having significance, from *sēmainein* to signify, from *sēma* a sign] — **se'mantically** *adv.*

semantics (sɪ'mæntɪks) *n.* (*functioning as sing.*) **1.** the branch of linguistics that deals with the study of meaning. **2.** the study of the relationships between signs and symbols and what they represent. **3.** *Logic.* the principles that determine the truth-values of the formulas in a logical system. — **se'manticist** *n.*

semaphore ('sɛmə,fɔː) *n.* **1.** an apparatus for conveying information by means of visual signals, as with flags, etc. **2.** a system of signalling by holding a flag in each hand and moving the arms to designated positions for each letter of the alphabet. ~*vb.* **3.** to signal (information) by means of semaphore. [C19: via F, from Gk *sēma* a signal + -PHORE] — **semaphoric** (,sɛmə'fɒrɪk) *adj.*

Semarang or **Samarang** (sə'mɑːraːŋ) *n.* a port in S Indonesia, in N Java on the Java Sea. Pop.: 1 077 000 (1984).

semasiology (sɪ,meɪsɪ'ɒlədʒɪ) *n.* another name for **semantics.** [C19: from Gk *sēmasia* meaning, from *sēmainein* to signify + -LOGY]

sematic (sɪ'mætɪk) *adj.* (of the conspicuous coloration of certain animals) acting as a warning. [C19: from Gk *sēma* a sign]

semblance ('sɛmbləns) *n.* **1.** outward appearance, esp. without any inner substance. **2.** a resemblance. [C13: from OF, from *sembler* to seem, from L *simulāre* to imitate, from *similis* like]

Semele ('sɛmɪlɪ) *n. Greek myth.* mother of Dionysus by Zeus.

sememe ('siːmiːm) *n. Linguistics.* the meaning of a morpheme. [C20 (coined in 1933 by L. Bloomfield, U.S. linguist): from Gk *sēma* a sign + -EME]

semen ('siːmɛn) *n.* **1.** the thick whitish fluid containing spermatozoa that is ejaculated from the male genital tract. **2.** another name for **sperm**[1]. [C14: from L: seed]

Semeru or **Semeroe** (sə'mɛruː) *n.* a volcano in Indonesia: the highest peak in Java. Height: 3676 m (12 060 ft.).

semester (sɪ'mɛstə) *n.* **1.** *Chiefly U.S. & Canad.* either of two divisions of the academic year. **2.** (in German universities) a session of six months. [C19: via G from L *sēmestris* half-yearly, from *sex* six + *mensis* a month]

semi ('sɛmɪ) *n., pl.* **semis.** *Inf.* **1.** *Brit.* short for **semidetached (house).** **2.** short for **semifinal.**

semi- *prefix.* **1.** half: *semicircle.* **2.** partially, partly, or almost: *semiprofessional.* **3.** occurring twice in a specified period of time: *semiweekly.* [from L]

▷ **Usage.** See at **bi-.**

semiannual (,sɛmɪ'ænjʊəl) *adj.* **1.** occurring every half-year. **2.** lasting for half a year. — **,semi'annually** *adv.*

semiarid (,sɛmɪ'ærɪd) *adj.* characterized by scanty rainfall and scrubby vegetation, often occurring in continental interiors.

semiautomatic (,sɛmɪ,ɔːtə'mætɪk) *adj.* **1.** partly automatic. **2.** (of a firearm) self-loading but firing only one shot at each pull of the trigger. ~*n.* **3.** a semiautomatic firearm. — **,semi,auto'matically** *adv.*

semibreve ('sɛmɪ,briːv) *n. Music.* a note, now the longest in common use, having a time value that may be divided by any power of 2 to give all other notes. Usual U.S. and Canad. name: **whole note.**

semicircle ('sɛmɪ,sɜːk³l) *n.* **1. a.** one half of a circle. **b.** half the circumference of a circle. **2.** anything having the shape or form of half a circle. — **semicircular** (,sɛmɪ'sɜːkjʊlə) *adj.*

semicircular canal *n. Anat.* any of the three looped fluid-filled membranous tubes, at right angles to one another, that comprise the labyrinth of the ear.

semicolon (,sɛmɪ'kəʊlən) *n.* the punctuation mark (;) used to indicate a pause intermediate in value or length between that of a comma and that of a full stop.

semiconductor (,sɛmɪkən'dʌktə) *n.* **1.** a substance, such as germanium or silicon, that has an electrical conductivity that increases with temperature. **2. a.** a device, such as a transistor or integrated circuit, that depends on the properties of such a substance. **b.** (*as modifier*): *a semiconductor diode.*

semiconscious (,sɛmɪ'kɒnʃəs) *adj.* not fully conscious. — **,semi'consciously** *adv.* — **,semi'consciousness** *n.*

semidetached (,sɛmɪdɪ'tætʃt) *adj.* **a.** (of a building) joined to another building on one side by a common wall. **b.** (*as n.*): *they live in a semidetached.*

semifinal (,sɛmɪ'faɪn³l) *n.* **a.** the round before the final in a competition. **b.** (*as modifier*): *the semifinal draw.* — **,semi'finalist** *n.*

semifluid (,sɛmɪ'fluːɪd) *adj.* **1.** having properties between those of a liquid and those of a solid. ~*n.* **2.** a substance that has such properties because of high viscosity: *tar is a semifluid.* ~Also: **semiliquid.**

semiliterate (,sɛmɪ'lɪtərɪt) *adj.* **1.** hardly able to read or write. **2.** able to read but not to write.

semilunar (,sɛmɪ'luːnə) *adj.* shaped like a crescent or half-moon.

semilunar valve *n. Anat.* either of two crescent-shaped valves, one in the aorta and one in the pulmonary artery, that prevent regurgitation of blood into the heart.

seminal ('sɛmɪnəl) *adj.* **1.** potentially capable of development. **2.** highly original and important. **3.** rudimentary or unformed. **4.** of or relating to semen: *seminal fluid.* **5.** *Biol.* of or relating to seed. [C14: from LL

,semi,agri'cultural *adj.*	,semi'darkness *n.*	'semi,dome *n.*	,semi-in'dustrial *adj.*
,semia'quatic *adj.*	,semidi'rect *adj.*	,semi'dry *adj.*	,semi-'invalid *n.*
,semi,autobio'graphical *adj.*	,semidi'vine *adj.*	,semiel'liptical *adj.*	,semi'legendary *adj.*
,semiau'tonomous *adj.*	,semi,docu'mentary *n., adj.*	,semi'hard *adj.*	,semima'ture *adj.*
,semi'classical *adj.*		,semi-,inde'pendent *adj.*	

...ging to seed, from L *sēmen* seed] —'**sem**-

...**nɪ**,**nɑː**) *n.* **1.** a small group of students meet-
...y under the guidance of a tutor, professor, etc.
...**h meeting or the place in which it is held. **3.** a
hu...ourse for postgraduates. **4.** any group or meeting
for h...ding discussions or exchanging information. [C19:
via G from L *sēminārium* SEMINARY]
seminary ('sɛmɪnərɪ) *n.*, *pl.* **-naries. 1.** an academy for
the training of priests, etc. **2.** *Arch.* a private secondary
school, esp. for girls. [C15: from L *sēminārium* a nursery
garden, from *sēmen* seed] —,**semi**'**narial** *adj.* —**semi**-
narian (,sɛmɪ'nɛərɪən) *n.*
seminiferous (,sɛmɪ'nɪfərəs) *adj.* **1.** containing, conveying, or producing semen. **2.** (of plants) bearing or producing seeds.
semiotics (,sɛmɪ'ɒtɪks) *n.* (*functioning as sing.*) **1.** the
study of signs and symbols, esp. the relations between
written or spoken signs and their referents in the physical
world or the world of ideas. **2.** the scientific study of the
symptoms of disease. ~Also called: **semiology**. [from Gk
sēmeiōtikos, from *sēmeion* a sign] —,**semi**'**otic** *adj.*
Semipalatinsk (*Russian* sɪmipa'latinsk) *n.* a city in the S
Soviet Union, in the NE Kazakh SSR on the Irtysh River.
Pop.: 330 000 (1987).
semipermeable (,sɛmɪ'pɜːmɪəb³l) *adj.* (esp. of a cell
membrane) selectively permeable. —,**semi**,**permea**-
'**bility** *n.*
semiprecious (,sɛmɪ'prɛʃəs) *adj.* (of certain stones) having less value than a precious stone.
semiprofessional (,sɛmɪprə'fɛʃən³l) *adj.* **1.** (of a person) engaged in an activity or sport part-time but for pay.
2. (of an activity or sport) engaged in by semiprofessional
people. **3.** of or relating to a person whose activities are
professional in some respects. ~*n.* **4.** a semiprofessional
person. —,**semipro**'**fessionally** *adv.*
semiquaver ('sɛmɪ,kweɪvə) *n.* *Music.* a note having the
time value of one-sixteenth of a semibreve. Usual U.S. and
Canad. name: **sixteenth note.**
Semiramis (sɛ'mɪrəmɪs) *n.* the legendary founder of Babylon and wife of Ninus, king of Assyria, which she ruled
with great skill after his death.
semirigid (,sɛmɪ'rɪdʒɪd) *adj.* **1.** partly but not wholly
rigid. **2.** (of an airship) maintaining shape by means of a
main supporting keel and internal gas pressure.
semiskilled (,sɛmɪ'skɪld) *adj.* partly skilled or trained but
not sufficiently so to perform specialized work.
semisolid (,sɛmɪ'sɒlɪd) *adj.* having a viscosity and rigidity intermediate between that of a solid and a liquid.
Semite ('siːmaɪt) *n.* a member of the group of peoples
who speak a Semitic language, including the Jews and
Arabs as well as the ancient Babylonians, Assyrians, and
Phoenicians. [C19: from NL *sēmita* descendant of Shem,
via Gk *Sēm*, from Heb. SHEM]
Semitic (sɪ'mɪtɪk) *n.* **1.** a branch or subfamily of the Afro-
Asiatic family of languages that includes Arabic, Hebrew,
Aramaic, and such ancient languages as Phoenician.
~*adj.* **2.** denoting or belonging to this group of languages. **3.** denoting or characteristic of any of the peoples speaking a Semitic language, esp. the Jews or the
Arabs. **4.** another word for **Jewish.**
semitone ('sɛmɪ,təʊn) *n.* an interval denoting the pitch
difference between certain adjacent degrees of the diatonic scale (**diatonic semitone**) or between one note and
its sharpened or flattened equivalent (**chromatic semitone**); minor second. Also called (U.S. and Canad.): **half
step.** Cf. **whole tone.** — **semitonic** (,sɛmɪ'tɒnɪk) *adj.*
semitrailer (,sɛmɪ'treɪlə) *n.* a type of trailer or articulated
lorry that has wheels only at the rear, the front end being
supported by the towing vehicle.
semitropical (,sɛmɪ'trɒpɪk³l) *adj.* partly tropical.
— ,**semi**'**tropics** *pl. n.*
semivowel ('sɛmɪ,vaʊəl) *n.* *Phonetics.* a vowel-like sound
that acts like a consonant. In English and many other languages the chief semivowels are (w) in *well* and (j), represented as *y*, in *yell.* Also called: **glide.**

semiyearly (,sɛmɪ'jɪəlɪ) *adj.* another word for **semiannual.**
semolina (,sɛmə'liːnə) *n.* the large hard grains of wheat
left after flour has been bolted, used for puddings, soups,
etc. [C18: from It. *semolino*, dim. of *semola* bran, from L
simila very fine wheat flour]
Sempach (*German* 'zɛmpax) *n.* a village in central Switzerland, in Lucerne canton on **Lake Sempach:** scene of
the victory (1386) of the Swiss over the Hapsburgs.
sempervivum (,sɛmpə'vaɪvəm) *n.* any of a genus of
hardy perennials including the houseleek. [C16 (used of
the houseleek, adopted C18 by Linnaeus (1707-78), Swedish botanist, for the genus): L, from *sempervivus* everliv-
ing]
sempiternal (,sɛmpɪ'tɜːn³l) *adj.* *Literary.* everlasting;
eternal. [C15: from OF, from LL *sempiternālis*, from L,
from *semper* always + *aeternus* ETERNAL] —,**sempi**'**ternally** *adv.*
semplice ('sɛmplɪtʃɪ) *adj.*, *adv.* *Music.* to be performed
in a simple manner. [It.: simple, from L *simplex*]
sempre ('sɛmprɪ) *adv.* *Music.* (preceding a tempo or dynamic marking) always; consistently. It is used to indicate
that a specified volume, tempo, etc., is to be sustained
throughout a piece or passage. [It.: always, from L
semper]
sempstress ('sɛmpstrɪs) *n.* a rare word for **seamstress.**
SEN (in Britain) *abbrev. for* State Enrolled Nurse.
Sen. *or* **sen.** *abbrev. for:* **1.** senate. **2.** senator. **3.** senior.
senate ('sɛnɪt) *n.* **1.** any legislative body considered to
resemble a Senate. **2.** the main governing body at some
universities. [C13: from L *senātus* council of the elders,
from *senex* an old man]
Senate ('sɛnɪt) *n.* (*sometimes not cap.*) **1.** the upper
chamber of the legislatures of the U.S., Canada, Australia,
and many other countries. **2.** the legislative council of
ancient Rome.
senator ('sɛnətə) *n.* **1.** (*often cap.*) a member of a Senate
or senate. **2.** any legislator. —**senatorial** (,sɛnə'tɔːrɪəl)
adj.
send (sɛnd) *vb.* **sending, sent. 1.** (*tr.*) to cause or order
(a person or thing) to be taken, directed, or transmitted to
another place: *to send a letter.* **2.** (when *intr.*, foll. by *for;*
when *tr.*, *takes an infinitive*) to dispatch a request or
command (for something or to do something): *he sent for
a bottle of wine.* **3.** (*tr.*) to direct or cause to go to a place
or point: *his blow sent the champion to the floor.* **4.** (*tr.*)
to bring to a state or condition: *this noise will send me
mad.* **5.** (*tr.*; often foll. by *forth, out,* etc.) to cause to
issue: *his cooking sent forth a lovely smell.* **6.** (*tr.*) to
cause to happen or come: *misery sent by fate.* **7.** to
transmit (a message) by radio. **8.** (*tr.*) *Sl.* to move to excitement or rapture: *this music really sends me.* ~*n.* **9.**
another word for **swash** (sense 4). [OE *sendan*] —'**send-
able** *adj.* —'**sender** *n.*
Sendai (sɛn'daɪ) *n.* a city in central Japan, on NE Honshu:
university (1907). Pop.: 700 000 (1985).
send down *vb.* (*tr.*, *adv.*) **1.** *Brit.* to expel from a university. **2.** *Inf.* to send to prison.
sendoff ('sɛnd,ɒf) *n.* *Inf.* **1.** a demonstration of good
wishes to a person about to set off on a journey, etc. ~*vb.*
send off. (*tr.*, *adv.*) **2.** to cause to depart. **3.** *Soccer,
rugby, etc.* (of the referee) to dismiss (a player) from the
field of play for some offence. **4.** *Inf.* to give a sendoff to.
send up *vb.* (*tr.*, *adv.*) **1.** *Sl.* to send to prison. **2.** *Brit.
inf.* to make fun of, esp. by doing an imitation or parody
of. ~*n.* **send-up. 3.** *Brit. inf.* a parody or imitation.
Seneca ('sɛnɪkə) *n.* **1. Lucius Annaeus** (ə'niːəs), called
the Younger. ?4 B.C.–65 A.D., Roman philosopher, statesman, and dramatist; tutor and adviser to Nero. He was implicated in a plot to murder Nero and committed suicide.
His works include Stoical essays on ethical subjects and
tragedies that had a considerable influence on Elizabethan drama. **2.** his father, **Marcus** ('mɑːkəs) *or* **Lucius
Annaeus**, called *the Elder* or *the Rhetorician.* ?55 B.C.–
?39 A.D., Roman writer on oratory and history.
Senegal (,sɛnɪ'gɔːl) *n.* a republic in West Africa, on the
Atlantic: made part of French West Africa in 1895; became

,**semi**'**nude** *adj.*	,**semipo**'**litical** *adj.*	,**semi**'**rural** *adj.*	,**semitrans**'**lucent** *adj.*
,**semiof**'**ficial** *adj.*	,**semi**'**porous** *adj.*	,**semi**'**serious** *adj.*	,**semitrans**'**parent** *adj.*
,**semi**,**para**'**sitic** *adj.*	,**semi**'**private** *adj.*	,**semi**'**sweet** *adj.*	,**semi**'**truthful** *adj.*
,**semi**'**permanent** *adj.*	,**semi**'**public** *adj.*	,**semi**'**trained** *adj.*	,**semi**'**urban** *adj.*
,**semi**'**plastic** *adj.*	,**semire**'**tired** *adj.*		

fully independent in 1960; mostly low-lying, with semidesert in the north and tropical forest in the southwest. Official language: French. Religion: Muslim majority. Currency: franc. Capital: Dakar. Pop.: 6 793 000 (1987). Area: 197 160 sq. km (76 124 sq. miles). —**Senegalese** (ˌsɛnɪɡəˈliːz) *adj., n.*

Senegambia (ˌsɛnəˈɡæmbɪə) *n.* a region of W Africa, between the Senegal and Gambia Rivers: now mostly in Senegal.

senescent (sɪˈnɛsənt) *adj.* **1.** growing old. **2.** characteristic of old age. [C17: from L *senēscere* to grow old, from *senex* old] —**seˈnescence** *n.*

seneschal (ˈsɛnɪʃəl) *n.* **1.** a steward of the household of a medieval prince or nobleman. **2.** *Brit.* a cathedral official. [C14: from OF, from Med. L *siniscalcus*, of Gmc origin]

Senghor (*French* sāɡɔr) *n.* **Léopold Sédar** (leɔpɔl sedar). born 1906, Senegalese statesman and writer; president of Senegal (1960–80).

senile (ˈsiːnaɪl) *adj.* **1.** of or characteristic of old age. **2.** mentally or physically weak or infirm on account of old age. [C17: from L *senīlis*, from *senex* an old man] —**senility** (sɪˈnɪlɪtɪ) *n.*

senior (ˈsiːnjə) *adj.* **1.** higher in rank or length of service. **2.** older in years: *senior citizens.* **3.** of or relating to maturity or old age: *senior privileges.* **4.** *Education.* **a.** of or designating more advanced or older pupils. **b.** of or relating to a secondary school. **c.** *U.S.* denoting a student in the last year of school or university. ~*n.* **5.** a senior person. **6.** a senior pupil, student, etc. [C14: from L: older, from *senex* old]

Senior (ˈsiːnjə) *adj. Chiefly U.S.* being the older: used to distinguish the father from the son: *Charles Parker, Senior.* Abbrevs.: **Sr., Sen.**

senior aircraftman *n.* a rank in the Royal Air Force comparable to that of a private in the army, though not the lowest rank in the Royal Air Force.

senior citizen *n. Euphemistic.* an old age pensioner.

senior common room *n.* (in British universities, colleges, etc.) a common room for the use of academic staff.

seniority (ˌsiːnɪˈɒrɪtɪ) *n., pl.* -**ties. 1.** the state of being senior. **2.** precedence in rank, etc., due to senior status.

senior service *n. Brit.* the Royal Navy.

senna (ˈsɛnə) *n.* **1.** any of a genus of tropical plants having typically yellow flowers and long pods. **2. senna leaf.** the dried leaflets of any of these plants, used as a cathartic and laxative. **3. senna pods.** the dried fruits of any of these plants, used as a cathartic and laxative. [C16: via NL from Ar. *sanā*]

Sennacherib (sɛˈnækərɪb) *n.* died 681 B.C., king of Assyria (705–681); son of Sargon II. He invaded Judah twice, defeated Babylon, and rebuilt Nineveh.

Sennar (sɛnɑː, sɛˈnɑː) *n.* **1.** a region of the E Sudan, between the White Nile and the Blue Nile: a kingdom from the 16th to 19th centuries. **2.** a town in this region, on the Blue Nile: the nearby **Sennar Dam** (1925) supplies irrigation water to Gezira. Pop.: 8000 (1984 est.).

sennight *or* **se'nnight** (ˈsɛnaɪt) *n.* an archaic word for **week.** [OE *seofan nihte;* see SEVEN, NIGHT]

señor (sɛˈnjɔː; *Spanish* seˈɲor) *n., pl.* -**ñors** *or* -**ñores** (*Spanish* -ˈɲores). a Spaniard: a title of address equivalent to *Mr* when placed before a name or *sir* when used alone. [Sp., from L *senior* an older man, SENIOR]

señora (sɛˈnjɔːrə; *Spanish* seˈɲora) *n., pl.* -**ras** (-rəz; *Spanish* -ras). a married Spanish woman: a title of address equivalent to *Mrs* when placed before a name or *madam* when used alone.

señorita (ˌsɛnjɔːˈriːtə; *Spanish* ˌseɲoˈrita) *n., pl.* -**tas** (-təz; *Spanish* -tas). an unmarried Spanish woman: title of address equivalent to *Miss* when placed before a name or *madam* or *miss* when used alone.

sensation (sɛnˈseɪʃən) *n.* **1.** the power of perceiving through the senses. **2.** a physical experience resulting from the stimulation of one of the sense organs. **3.** a general feeling or awareness: *a sensation of fear.* **4.** a state of widespread public excitement: *his announcement caused a sensation.* **5.** anything that causes such a state: *your speech was a sensation.* [C17: from Med. L, from LL *sensātus* endowed with SENSE]

sensational (sɛnˈseɪʃənəl) *adj.* **1.** causing or intended to cause intense feelings, esp. of curiosity, horror, etc.: *sensational disclosures in the press.* **2.** *Inf.* extremely good:

a sensational skater. **3.** of or relating to the faculty of sensation. —**senˈsationally** *adv.*

sensationalism (sɛnˈseɪʃənəˌlɪzəm) *n.* **1.** the use of sensational language, etc., to arouse an intense emotional response. **2.** such sensational matter itself. **3.** *Philosophy.* the doctrine that knowledge cannot go beyond the analysis of experience. —**senˈsationalist** *n.* —**senˌsationalˈistic** *adj.*

sense (sɛns) *n.* **1.** any of the faculties by which the mind receives information about the external world or the state of the body. The five traditional senses are sight, hearing, touch, taste, and smell. **2.** the ability to perceive. **3.** a feeling perceived through one of the senses: *a sense of warmth.* **4.** a mental perception or awareness: *a sense of happiness.* **5.** moral discernment: *a sense of right and wrong.* **6.** (*sometimes pl.*) sound practical judgment or intelligence. **7.** reason or purpose: *what is the sense of going out?* **8.** meaning: *what is the sense of this proverb?* **9.** specific meaning; definition: *in what sense are you using the word?* **10.** an opinion or consensus. **11.** *Maths.* one of two opposite directions in which a vector can operate. **12. make sense.** to be understandable. **13. take leave of one's senses.** *Inf.* to go mad. ~*vb.* (*tr.*) **14.** to perceive through one or more of the senses. **15.** to apprehend or detect without or in advance of the evidence of the senses. **16.** to understand. **17.** *Computers.* **a.** to test or locate the position of (a part of computer hardware). **b.** to read (data). [C14: from L *sēnsus*, from *sentīre* to feel]

sense datum *n.* a unit of sensation, such as a sharp pain, detached both from any information it may convey and from its putative source in the external world.

senseless (ˈsɛnslɪs) *adj.* **1.** foolish: *a senseless plan.* **2.** lacking in feeling; unconscious. **3.** lacking in perception. —**ˈsenselessly** *adv.* —**ˈsenselessness** *n.*

sense organ *n.* a structure in animals that is specialized for receiving external or internal stimuli and transmitting them in the form of nervous impulses to the brain.

sensibility (ˌsɛnsɪˈbɪlɪtɪ) *n., pl.* -**ties. 1.** the ability to perceive or feel. **2.** (*often pl.*) the capacity for responding to emotion, etc. **3.** (*often pl.*) the capacity for responding to aesthetic stimuli. **4.** discernment; awareness. **5.** (*usually pl.*) emotional or moral feelings: *cruelty offends most people's sensibilities.*

sensible (ˈsɛnsɪbəl) *adj.* **1.** having or showing good sense or judgment. **2.** (of clothing) serviceable; practical. **3.** having the capacity for sensation; sensitive. **4.** capable of being apprehended by the senses. **5.** perceptible to the mind. **6.** (sometimes foll. by *of*) having perception; aware: *sensible of your kindness.* **7.** readily perceived: *a sensible difference.* [C14: from OF, from LL *sēnsibilis*, from L *sentīre* to sense] —**ˈsensibleness** *n.* —**ˈsensibly** *adv.*

sensitive (ˈsɛnsɪtɪv) *adj.* **1.** having the power of sensation. **2.** easily irritated; delicate. **3.** affected by external conditions or stimuli. **4.** easily offended. **5.** of or relating to the senses or the power of sensation. **6.** capable of registering small differences or changes in amounts, etc.: *a sensitive instrument.* **7.** *Photog.* responding readily to light: *a sensitive emulsion.* **8.** *Chiefly U.S.* connected with matters affecting national security. **9.** (of a stock market or prices) quickly responsive to external influences. [C14: from Med. L *sēnsitīvus*, from L *sentīre* to feel] —**ˈsensitively** *adv.* —**ˌsensiˈtivity** *n.*

sensitive plant *n.* a tropical American mimosa plant, the leaflets and stems of which fold if touched.

sensitize *or* -**tise** (ˈsɛnsɪˌtaɪz) *vb.* **1.** to make or become sensitive. **2.** (*tr.*) to render (an individual) sensitive to a drug, etc. **3.** (*tr.*) *Photog.* to make (a material) sensitive to light by coating it with a photographic emulsion often containing special chemicals, such as dyes. —ˌsensitiˈzation *or* -tiˈsation *n.* —ˈsensiˌtizer *or* -ˌtiser *n.*

sensitometer (ˌsɛnsɪˈtɒmɪtə) *n.* an instrument for measuring the sensitivity to light of a photographic material over a range of exposures.

sensor (ˈsɛnsə) *n.* anything, such as a photoelectric cell, that receives a signal or stimulus and responds to it. [C19: from L *sēnsus* perceived, from *sentīre* to observe]

sensorimotor (ˌsɛnsərɪˈməʊtə) *or* **sensomotor** (ˌsɛnsəˈməʊtə) *adj.* of or relating to both the sensory and motor functions of an organism or to the nerves controlling them.

sensorium (sɛn'sɔːrɪəm) n., pl. **-riums** or **-ria** (-rɪə). **1.** the area of the brain considered responsible for receiving and integrating sensations from the outside world. **2.** Physiol. the entire sensory and intellectual apparatus of the body. [C17: from LL, from L sēnsus felt, from sentīre to perceive]

sensory ('sɛnsərɪ) adj. of or relating to the senses or the power of sensation. [C18: from L sensōrius, from sentīre to feel]

sensual ('sɛnsjʊəl) adj. **1.** of or relating to any of the senses or sense organs; bodily. **2.** strongly or unduly inclined to gratification of the senses. **3.** tending to arouse the bodily appetites, esp. the sexual appetite. [C15: from LL sensuālis, from L sēnsus SENSE] —'**sensually** adv.

sensualism ('sɛnsjʊə,lɪzəm) n. **1.** the quality or state of being sensual. **2.** the doctrine that the ability to gratify the senses is the only criterion of goodness.

sensuality (,sɛnsjʊ'ælɪtɪ) n., pl. **-ties. 1.** the quality or state of being sensual. **2.** excessive indulgence in sensual pleasures. —**sensualist** ('sɛnsjʊəlɪst) n.

sensuous ('sɛnsjʊəs) adj. **1.** aesthetically pleasing to the senses. **2.** appreciative of qualities perceived by the senses. **3.** of or derived from the senses. [C17, but not common until C19: apparently coined by Milton to avoid the sexual overtones of SENSUAL] —'**sensuously** adv. —'**sensuousness** n.

sent (sɛnt) vb. the past tense and past participle of **send**.

sentence ('sɛntəns) n. **1.** a sequence of words capable of standing alone to make an assertion, ask a question, or give a command, usually consisting of a subject and a predicate. **2.** the judgment formally pronounced upon a person convicted in criminal proceedings, esp. the decision as to what punishment is to be imposed. **3.** Music. a passage or division of a piece of music, usually consisting of two or more contrasting musical phrases and ending in a cadence. **4.** Arch. a proverb, maxim, or aphorism. ~vb. **5.** (tr.) to pronounce sentence on (a convicted person) in a court of law. [C13: via OF from L sententia a way of thinking, from sentīre to feel] —**sentential** (sɛn'tɛnʃəl) adj.

sentence connector n. a word or phrase that introduces a clause or sentence and serves as a transition between it and a previous clause or sentence, as for example also in I'm buying eggs and also I'm looking for a dessert for tonight.

sentence substitute n. a word or phrase, esp. one traditionally classified as an adverb, that is used in place of a finite sentence, such as yes, no, certainly, and never.

sententious (sɛn'tɛnʃəs) adj. **1.** characterized by or full of aphorisms or axioms. **2.** constantly using aphorisms, etc. **3.** tending to indulge in pompous moralizing. [C15: from L sententiōsus full of meaning, from sententia; see SENTENCE] —**sen'tentiously** adv. —**sen'tentiousness** n.

sentient ('sɛntɪənt) adj. **1.** having the power of sense perception or sensation; conscious. ~n. **2.** Rare. a sentient person or thing. [C17: from L sentiēns feeling, from sentīre to perceive] —**sentience** ('sɛnʃəns) n.

sentiment ('sɛntɪmənt) n. **1.** susceptibility to tender or romantic emotion: she has too much sentiment to be successful. **2.** (often pl.) a thought, opinion, or attitude. **3.** exaggerated or mawkish feeling or emotion. **4.** an expression of response to deep feeling, esp. in art. **5.** a feeling or awareness: a sentiment of pity. **6.** a mental attitude determined by feeling: there is a strong revolutionary sentiment in his country. **7.** a feeling conveyed, or intended to be conveyed, in words. [C17: from Med. L sentimentum, from L sentīre to feel]

sentimental (,sɛntɪ'mɛntəl) adj. **1.** tending to indulge the emotions excessively. **2.** making a direct appeal to the emotions, esp. to romantic feelings. **3.** relating to or characterized by sentiment. —,**senti'menta,lism** n. —,**senti'mentalist** n. —,**senti'mentally** adv.

sentimentality (,sɛntɪmɛn'tælɪtɪ) n., pl. **-ties. 1.** the state, quality, or an instance of being sentimental. **2.** an act, statement, etc., that is sentimental.

sentimentalize or **-lise** (,sɛntɪ'mɛntə,laɪz) vb. to make sentimental or behave sentimentally. —,**senti,mentali'zation** or **-li'sation** n.

sentimental value n. the value of an article in terms of its sentimental associations for a particular person.

sentinel ('sɛntɪnəl) n. **1.** a person, such as a sentry, assigned to keep guard. ~vb. **-nelling, -nelled.** (tr.) **2.** to guard as a sentinel. **3.** to post as a sentinel. [C16: from OF sentinelle, from OIt., from sentina watchfulness, from sentire to notice, from L]

sentry ('sɛntrɪ) n., pl. **-tries.** a soldier who guards or prevents unauthorized access to a place, etc. [C17: ? shortened from obs. centrinel, C16 var. of SENTINEL]

sentry box n. a small shelter with an open front in which a sentry may stand to be sheltered from the weather.

senza ('sɛntsɑː) prep. Music. omitting. [It.]

Seoul (səʊl) n. the capital of South Korea, in the west on the Han River: capital of Korea from 1392 to 1910, then seat of the Japanese administration until 1945; became capital of South Korea in 1948; cultural centre, with four universities. Pop.: 9 465 824 (1985). Also called: **Kyongsong.** Japanese name: **Keijo.**

Sep. abbrev. for: **1.** September. **2.** Septuagint.

sepal ('sɛpəl) n. any of the separate parts of the calyx of a flower. [C19: from NL sepalum: sep- from Gk skepē a covering + -alum, from NL petalum PETAL]

-sepalous adj. combining form. having sepals of a specified type or number: polysepalous. —**-sepaly** n. combining form.

separable ('sɛpərəbəl) adj. able to be separated, divided, or parted. —,**separa'bility** or '**separableness** n. —'**separably** adv.

separate vb. ('sɛpə,reɪt). **1.** (tr.) to act as a barrier between: a range of mountains separates the two countries. **2.** to part or be parted from a mass or group. **3.** (tr.) to discriminate between: to separate the men and the boys. **4.** to divide or be divided into component parts. **5.** to sever or be severed. **6.** (intr.) (of a married couple) to cease living together. ~adj. ('sɛprɪt, 'sɛpərɪt). **7.** existing or considered independently: a separate problem. **8.** disunited or apart. **9.** set apart from the main body or mass. **10.** distinct, individual, or particular. **11.** solitary or withdrawn. [C15: from L sēparāre, from sē- apart + parāre to obtain] —'**separately** adv. —'**separateness** n. —'**separative** adj. —'**sepa,rator** n.

separates ('sɛprɪts, 'sɛpərɪts) pl. n. women's outer garments that only cover part of the body; skirts, blouses, jackets, trousers, etc.

separate school n. **1.** (in certain Canadian provinces) a school for a large religious minority financed by provincial grants in addition to the education tax. **2.** a Roman Catholic school.

separation (,sɛpə'reɪʃən) n. **1.** the act of separating or state of being separated. **2.** the place or line where a separation is made. **3.** a gap that separates. **4.** Family law. the cessation of cohabitation between a man and wife, either by mutual agreement or under a decree of a court.

separatist ('sɛpərətɪst) n. **a.** a person who advocates secession from an organization, federation, union, etc. **b.** (as modifier): a separatist movement. —'**separa,tism** n.

Sephardi (sɪ'fɑːdiː) n., pl. **-dim** (-dɪm). Judaism. **1.** a Jew of Spanish, Portuguese, or North African descent. **2.** the pronunciation of Hebrew used by these Jews, and of Modern Hebrew as spoken in Israel. ~Cf. **Ashkenazi.** [C19: from LHeb., from Heb. sepharad a region mentioned in Obadiah 20, thought to have been Spain] —**Se'phardic** adj.

sepia ('siːpɪə) n. **1.** a dark reddish-brown pigment obtained from the inky secretion of the cuttlefish. **2.** a brownish tone imparted to a photograph, esp. an early one. **3.** a brownish-grey to dark yellowish-brown colour. **4.** a drawing or photograph in sepia. ~adj. **5.** of the colour sepia or done in sepia: a sepia print. [C16: from L: a cuttlefish, from Gk]

sepoy ('siːpɔɪ) n. (formerly) an Indian soldier in the service of the British. [C18: from Port. sipaio, from Urdu sipāhī, from Persian: horseman, from sipāh army]

seppuku (sɛ'puːkuː) n. another word for **hara-kiri.** [from Japanese, from Chinese ch'ieh to cut + fu bowels]

sepsis ('sɛpsɪs) n. the presence of pus-forming bacteria in the body. [C19: via NL from Gk sēpsis a rotting]

sept (sɛpt) n. **1.** Anthropol. a clan that believes itself to be descended from a common ancestor. **2.** a branch of a tribe, esp. in Ireland or Scotland. [C16: ? a var. of SECT]

Sept. abbrev. for: **1.** September. **2.** Septuagint.

septa ('sɛptə) n. the plural of **septum.**

septal ('sɛptəl) adj. of or relating to a septum.

September (sɛp'tɛmbə) n. the ninth month of the year, consisting of 30 days. [OE, from L: the seventh (month) according to the calendar of ancient Rome, from *septem* seven]

septenary ('sɛptɪnərɪ) *adj.* **1.** of or relating to the number seven. **2.** forming a group of seven. ~*n., pl.* **-naries. 3.** the number seven. **4.** a group of seven things. **5.** a period of seven years. [C16: from L *septēnārius*, from *septēnī* seven each, from *septem* seven]

septennial (sɛp'tɛnɪəl) *adj.* **1.** occurring every seven years. **2.** relating to or lasting seven years. [C17: from L, from *septem* seven + *annus* a year]

septet (sɛp'tɛt) *n.* **1.** *Music.* a group of seven singers or instrumentalists or a piece of music composed for such a group. **2.** a group of seven people or things. [C19: from G, from L *septem* seven]

septic ('sɛptɪk) *adj.* **1.** of or caused by sepsis. **2.** of or caused by putrefaction. ~*n.* **3.** *Austral. & N.Z. inf.* short for **septic tank.** [C17: from L *sēpticus*, from Gk, from *sēptos* decayed, from *sēpein* to make rotten] —'**septically** *adv.* —**septicity** (sɛp'tɪsɪtɪ) *n.*

septicaemia *or* **septicemia** (,sɛptɪ'siːmɪə) *n.* any of various diseases caused by microorganisms in the blood. Nontechnical name: **blood poisoning.** [C19: from NL, from Gk *sēptik(os)* SEPTIC + -AEMIA] —,**septi'caemic** *or* ,**septi'cemic** *adj.*

septic tank *n.* a tank, usually below ground, for containing sewage to be decomposed by anaerobic bacteria. Also called (Austral.): **septic system.**

septillion (sɛp'tɪljən) *n., pl.* **-lions** *or* **-lion. 1.** (in Britain, France, and Germany) the number represented as one followed by 42 zeros (10^{42}). **2.** (in the U.S. and Canada) the number represented as one followed by 24 zeros (10^{24}). Brit. word: **quadrillion.** [C17: from F, from *sept* seven + *-illion*, on the model of *million*] —**sep'tillionth** *adj., n.*

septime ('sɛptiːm) *n.* the seventh of eight basic positions from which a parry or attack can be made in fencing. [C19: from L *septimus* seventh, from *septem* seven]

septuagenarian (,sɛptjuədʒɪ'nɛərɪən) *n.* **1.** a person who is from 70 to 79 years old. ~*adj.* **2.** being between 70 and 79 years old. **3.** of or relating to a septuagenarian. [C18: from L, from *septuāgintā* seventy]

Septuagesima (,sɛptjuə'dʒɛsɪmə) *n.* the third Sunday before Lent. [C14: from Church L *septuāgēsima (diēs)* the seventieth (day)]

Septuagint ('sɛptjuə,dʒɪnt) *n.* the principal Greek version of the Old Testament, including the Apocrypha, believed to have been translated by 70 or 72 scholars. [C16: from L *septuāgintā* seventy]

septum ('sɛptəm) *n., pl.* **-ta.** *Biol., anat.* a dividing partition between two tissues or cavities. [C18: from L *saeptum* wall, from *saepīre* to enclose]

septuple ('sɛptjupəl) *adj.* **1.** seven times as much or as many. **2.** consisting of seven parts or members. ~*vb.* **3.** (*tr.*) to multiply by seven. [C17: from L *septuplus*, from *septem* seven] —**septuplicate** (sɛp'tjuːplɪkət) *n., adj.*

sepulchral (sɪ'pʌlkrəl) *adj.* **1.** suggestive of a tomb; gloomy. **2.** of or relating to a sepulchre. —**se'pulchrally** *adv.*

sepulchre *or U.S.* **sepulcher** ('sɛpəlkə) *n.* **1.** a burial vault, tomb, or grave. **2.** Also called: **Easter sepulchre.** an alcove in some churches in which the Eucharistic elements were kept from Good Friday until Easter. ~*vb.* **3.** (*tr.*) to bury in a sepulchre. [C12: from OF *sépulcre*, from L *sepulcrum*, from *sepelīre* to bury]

sepulture ('sɛpəltʃə) *n.* the act of placing in a sepulchre. [C13: via OF from L *sepultūra*, from *sepultus* buried, from *sepelīre* to bury]

seq. *abbrev. for:* **1.** sequel. **2.** sequens. [L: the following (one)]

sequel ('siːkwəl) *n.* **1.** anything that follows from something else. **2.** a consequence. **3.** a novel, play, etc., that continues a previously related story. [C15: from LL *sequēla*, from L *sequī* to follow]

sequela (sɪ'kwiːlə) *n., pl.* **-lae** (-liː). (*often pl.*) *Med.* **1.** any abnormal bodily condition or disease arising from a pre-existing disease. **2.** any complication of a disease. [C18: from L: SEQUEL]

sequence ('siːkwəns) *n.* **1.** an arrangement of two or more things in a successive order. **2.** the successive order of two or more things: *chronological sequence.* **3.** an action or event that follows another or others. **4. a.** *Cards.* a set of three or more consecutive cards, usually of the same suit. **b.** *Bridge.* a set of two or more consecutive cards. **5.** *Music.* an arrangement of notes or chords repeated several times at different pitches. **6.** *Maths.* an ordered set of numbers or other mathematical entities in one-to-one correspondence with the integers 1 to *n.* **7.** a section of a film constituting a single continuous uninterrupted episode. **8.** *Biochem.* the unique order of amino acids in a protein or of nucleotides in DNA or RNA. [C14: from Med. L *sequentia* that which follows, from L *sequī* to follow]

sequence of tenses *n. Grammar.* the sequence according to which the tense of a subordinate verb in a sentence is determined by the tense of the principal verb, as in *I believe he is lying, I believed he was lying,* etc.

sequent ('siːkwənt) *adj.* **1.** following in order or succession. **2.** following as a result. ~*n.* **3.** something that follows. [C16: from L *sequēns*, from *sequī* to follow] —'**sequently** *adv.*

sequential (sɪ'kwɛnʃəl) *adj.* **1.** characterized by or having a regular sequence. **2.** another word for **sequent.** —**sequentiality** (sɪ,kwɛnʃɪ'ælɪtɪ) *n.* —**se'quentially** *adv.*

sequential access *n.* a method of reading data from a computer file by reading through the file from the beginning.

sequester (sɪ'kwɛstə) *vb.* (*tr.*) **1.** to remove or separate. **2.** (*usually passive*) to retire into seclusion. **3.** *Law.* to take (property) temporarily out of the possession of its owner, esp. until creditors are satisfied or a court order is complied with. **4.** *International law.* to appropriate (enemy property). [C14: from LL *sequestrāre* to surrender for safekeeping, from L *sequester* a trustee]

sequestrate (sɪ'kwɛstreɪt) *vb.* (*tr.*) *Law.* a variant of **sequester** (sense 3). [C16: from LL *sequestrāre* to SEQUESTER] —**sequestrator** ('siːkwɛs,treɪtə) *n.*

sequestration (,siːkwɛ'streɪʃən) *n.* **1.** the act of sequestering or state of being sequestered. **2.** *Law.* the sequestering of property. **3.** *Chem.* the effective removal of ions from a solution by coordination with another type of ion or molecule to form complexes.

sequestrum (sɪ'kwɛstrəm) *n., pl.* **-tra** (-trə). *Pathol.* a detached piece of dead bone that often migrates to a wound, etc. [C19: from NL, from L: something deposited] —**se'questral** *adj.*

sequin ('siːkwɪn) *n.* **1.** a small piece of shiny often coloured metal foil, usually round, used to decorate garments, etc. **2.** a gold coin formerly minted in Italy. [C17: via F from It. *zecchino*, from *zecca* mint, from Ar. *sikkah* die for striking coins] —'**sequined** *adj.*

sequoia (sɪ'kwɔɪə) *n.* either of two giant Californian coniferous trees, the **redwood,** or the **big tree** or **giant sequoia.** [C19: NL, after *Sequoya,* known also as George Guess, (?1770–1843), American Indian scholar and leader]

sérac ('sɛræk) *n.* a pinnacle of ice among crevasses on a glacier, usually on a steep slope. [C19: from Swiss F: a variety of white cheese (hence the ice that resembles it), from Med. L *serācium*, from L *serum* whey]

seraglio (sɛ'rɑːlɪ,əʊ) *or* **serail** (sə'raɪ) *n., pl.* **-raglios** *or* **-rails. 1.** the harem of a Muslim house or palace. **2.** a sultan's palace, esp. in the former Turkish empire. [C16: from It. *serraglio* animal cage, from Med. L *serrāculum* bolt, from L *sera* a door bar; associated also with Turkish *seray* palace]

Serajevo (*Serbo-Croatian* 'sɛrajɛvɔ) *n.* a variant of **Sarajevo.**

Seram *or* **Ceram** (sɪ'ræm) *n.* an island in Indonesia, in the Moluccas, separated from New Guinea by the **Ceram Sea:** mountainous and densely forested. Area: 17 150 sq. km (6622 sq. miles). Also called: **Serang** (sə'ræŋ).

seraph ('sɛrəf) *n., pl.* **-aphs** *or* **-aphim** (-əfɪm). *Theol.* a member of the highest order of angels in the celestial hierarchies, often depicted as the winged head of a child. [C17: back formation from pl. *seraphim,* via LL from Heb.] —**seraphic** (sɪ'ræfɪk) *adj.*

Serapis ('sɛrəpɪs) *n.* a Graeco-Egyptian god combining attributes of Apis and Osiris.

Serb (sɜːb) *n., adj.* another word for **Serbian.** [C19: from Serbian *Srb*]

Serbia ('sɜːbɪə) *n.* a constituent republic of SE Yugoslavia: includes the autonomous regions of Vojvodina and Kosovo-Metohija; declared a kingdom in 1882; precipitated World War I by the conflict with Austria; became part of the Kingdom of the Serbs, Croats, and Slovenes (later called Yugoslavia) in 1918. Capital: Belgrade. Pop.:

9 313 677 (1981). Area: 88 361 sq. km (34 109 sq. miles). Former name: **Servia**. Serbian name: **Srbija**.

Serbian ('sɜːbɪən) *adj.* **1.** of, relating to, or characteristic of Serbia, its people, or their dialect of Serbo-Croatian. ~*n.* **2.** the dialect of Serbo-Croatian spoken in Serbia. **3.** a native or inhabitant of Serbia.

Serbo-Croatian *or* **Serbo-Croat** *n.* **1.** the chief official language of Yugoslavia. The Serbian dialect is usually written in the Cyrillic alphabet, the Croatian in Roman. ~*adj.* **2.** of or relating to this language.

SERC (in Britain) *abbrev. for* Science and Engineering Research Council.

Sercq (sɛrk) *n.* the French name for **Sark**.

sere[1] (sɪə) *adj.* **1.** *Arch.* dried up. ~*vb.*, *n.* **2.** a rare spelling of **sear**. [OE *sēar*]

sere[2] (sɪə) *n.* the series of changes occurring in the ecological succession of a particular community. [C20: from SERIES]

Seremban (sə'rɛmbən) *n.* a town in Peninsular Malaysia, capital of Negri Sembilan state. Pop.: 136 252 (1980).

serenade (ˌsɛrɪ'neɪd) *n.* **1.** a piece of music characteristically played outside the house of a woman. **2.** a piece of music suggestive of this. **3.** an extended composition in several movements similar to the modern suite. ~*vb.* **4.** (*tr.*) to play a serenade for (someone). **5.** (*intr.*) to play a serenade. [C17: from F *sérénade*, from It. *serenata*, from *sereno* peaceful, from L *serēnus;* also infl. in meaning by It. *sera* evening, from L *sērus* late] —**sere'nader** *n.*

serendipity (ˌsɛrən'dɪpɪtɪ) *n.* the faculty of making fortunate discoveries by accident. [C18: coined by Horace Walpole, from the Persian fairytale *The Three Princes of Serendip*, in which the heroes possess this gift] —**seren'dipitous** *adj.*

serene (sɪ'riːn) *adj.* **1.** peaceful or tranquil; calm. **2.** clear or bright: *a serene sky.* **3.** (*often cap.*) honoured: *His Serene Highness.* [C16: from L *serēnus*] —**se'renely** *adv.* —**serenity** (sɪ'rɛnɪtɪ) *n.*

serf (sɜːf) *n.* (esp. in medieval Europe) an unfree person, esp. one bound to the land. [C15: from OF, from L *servus* a slave] —**serfdom** *or* **serfhood** *n.*

serge (sɜːdʒ) *n.* **1.** a twill-weave woollen or worsted fabric used for clothing. **2.** a similar twilled cotton, silk, or rayon fabric. [C14: from OF *sarge*, from Vulgar L *sārica* (unattested), from L *sēricum*, from Gk *sērikon* silk, ult. from *sēr* silkworm]

sergeant ('sɑːdʒənt) *n.* **1.** a noncommissioned officer in certain armies, air forces, and marine corps, usually ranking immediately above a corporal. **2. a.** (in Britain) a police officer ranking between constable and inspector. **b.** (in the U.S.) a police officer ranking below a captain. **3.** a court or municipal officer who has ceremonial duties. ~*Also:* **serjeant**. [C12: from OF *sergent*, from L *serviēns*, lit.: serving, from *servīre* to SERVE]

sergeant at arms *n.* an officer of a legislative or fraternal body responsible for maintaining internal order. Also: **sergeant, serjeant at arms.**

Sergeant Baker ('beɪkə) *n.* a large brightly coloured Australian sea fish.

sergeant major *n.* the chief administrative noncommissioned officer of a military headquarters. See also **warrant officer.**

Sergipe (*Portuguese* ser'ʒipi) *n.* a state of NE Brazil; the smallest Brazilian state; a centre of resistance to Dutch conquest (17th century). Capital: Aracajú. Pop.: 1 313 000 (1986 est.). Area: 13 672 sq. km (8492 sq. miles).

Sergt *abbrev. for* Sergeant.

serial ('sɪərɪəl) *n.* **1.** a novel, film, etc., presented in instalments at regular intervals. **2.** a publication, regularly issued and consecutively numbered. ~*adj.* **3.** of or resembling a series. **4.** published or presented as a serial. **5.** of or relating to such publication or presentation. **6.** *Computers.* of or operating on items of information, etc., in the order in which they occur. **7.** of or using the techniques of serialism. [C19: from NL *seriālis*, from L *seriēs* SERIES] —**serially** *adv.*

serialism ('sɪərɪəˌlɪzəm) *n.* (in 20th-century music) the use of a sequence of notes in a definite order as a thematic basis for a composition. See also **twelve-tone.**

serialize *or* **-lise** ('sɪərɪəˌlaɪz) *vb.* (*tr.*) to publish or present in the form of a serial. —**ˌseriali'zation** *or* **-li'sation** *n.*

serial number *n.* any of the consecutive numbers assigned to machines, tools, books, etc.

seriate ('sɪərɪɪt) *adj.* forming a series.

seriatim (ˌsɪərɪ'ætɪm) *adv.* one after another in order. [C17: from Med. L, from L *seriēs* SERIES]

sericeous (sɪ'rɪʃəs) *adj. Bot.* **1.** covered with a layer of small silky hairs: *a sericeous leaf.* **2.** silky. [C18: from LL *sēriceus* silken, from L *sēricus;* see SERGE]

sericulture ('sɛrɪˌkʌltʃə) *n.* the rearing of silkworms for the production of raw silk. [C19: via F; *seri-* from L *sēricum* silk, ult. from Gk *sēr* a silkworm] —**ˌseri'cultural** *adj.* —**ˌseri'culturist** *n.*

series ('sɪəriːz) *n., pl.* **-ries.** **1.** a group or succession of related things, usually arranged in order. **2.** a set of radio or television programmes having the same characters but different stories. **3.** a set of books having the same format, related content, etc., published by one firm. **4.** a set of stamps, coins, etc., issued at a particular time. **5.** *Maths.* the sum of a finite or infinite sequence of numbers or quantities. **6.** *Electronics.* a configuration of two or more components connected in a circuit so that the same current flows in turn through each of them (esp. in **in series**). Cf. **parallel** (sense 10). **7.** *Geol.* a stratigraphical unit that represents the rocks formed during an epoch. [C17: from L: a row, from *serere* to link]

series-wound ('sɪəriːzˌwaʊnd) *adj.* (of a motor or generator) having the field and armature circuits connected in series.

serif ('sɛrɪf) *n. Printing.* a small line at the extremities of a main stroke in a type character. [C19: ?from Du. *schreef* dash, prob. of Gmc origin]

serigraph ('sɛrɪˌɡrɑːf) *n.* a colour print made by an adaptation of the silk-screen process. [C19: from *seri-*, from L *sēricum* silk + -GRAPH] —**serigraphy** (sə'rɪɡrəfɪ) *n.*

serin ('sɛrɪn) *n.* any of various small yellow-and-brown finches of parts of Europe. [C16: from F, ?from OProvençal *sirena* a bee-eater, from L *sīrēn*, a kind of bird, from SIREN]

seringa (sə'rɪŋɡə) *n.* **1.** any of a Brazilian genus of trees that yield rubber. **2.** a deciduous tree of southern Africa with a graceful shape. [C18: from Port., var. of SYRINGA]

Seringapatam (sə,rɪŋɡəpə'tæm) *n.* a small town in S India, in Karnataka on **Seringapatam Island** in the Cauvery River: capital of Mysore from 1610 to 1799, when it was besieged and captured by the British. Pop.: 18 137 (1981).

seriocomic (ˌsɪərɪəʊ'kɒmɪk) *adj.* mixing serious and comic elements. —**ˌserio'comically** *adv.*

serious ('sɪərɪəs) *adj.* **1.** grave in nature or disposition: *a serious person.* **2.** marked by deep feeling; sincere: *is he serious or joking?* **3.** concerned with important matters: *a serious conversation.* **4.** requiring effort or concentration: *a serious book.* **5.** giving rise to fear or anxiety: *a serious illness.* [C15: from LL *sēriōsus*, from L *sērius*] —**seriously** *adv.* —**seriousness** *n.*

serjeant ('sɑːdʒənt) *n.* a variant spelling of **sergeant.**

serjeant at law *n.* (formerly, in England) a barrister of a special rank. Also: **serjeant, sergeant at law, sergeant.**

sermon ('sɜːmən) *n.* **1. a.** an address of religious instruction or exhortation, often based on a passage from the Bible, esp. one delivered during a church service. **b.** a written version of such an address. **2.** a serious speech, esp. one administering reproof. [C12: via OF from L *sermō* discourse, prob. from *serere* to join together]

sermonize *or* **-ise** ('sɜːməˌnaɪz) *vb.* to address (a person or audience) as if delivering a sermon. —**'sermonˌizer** *or* **-ˌiser** *n.*

Sermon on the Mount *n. Bible.* the first major discourse delivered by Christ (Matthew 5–7).

sero- *combining form.* indicating a serum: *serology.*

serology (sɪ'rɒlədʒɪ) *n.* the branch of science concerned with serums. —**serologic** (ˌsɪərə'lɒdʒɪk) *or* **ˌsero'logical** *adj.*

seropositive (ˌsɪərəʊ'pɒzɪtɪv) *adj.* (of a person whose blood has been tested for a specific disease, such as AIDS) showing a serological reaction indicating the presence of the disease.

serotine ('sɛrəˌtaɪn) *adj.* **1.** *Biol.* produced, flowering, or developing late in the season. ~*n.* **2.** a reddish-coloured European insectivorous bat. [C16: from L *sērōtinus* late, from *sērus* late; applied to the bat because it flies late in the evening]

serotonin (ˌsɛrə'təʊnɪn) *n.* a compound that occurs in the brain, intestines, and blood platelets and induces vasoconstriction.

serous ('sɪərəs) *adj.* of, producing, or containing serum. [C16: from L *serōsus*] —**serosity** (sɪ'rɒsɪtɪ) *n.*

serous fluid *n.* a thin watery fluid found in many body cavities.

serous membrane *n.* any of the smooth moist delicate membranes, such as the pleura, that line the closed cavities of the body.

serow ('sɛrəʊ) *n.* either of two antelopes of mountainous regions of S and SE Asia, having a dark coat and conical backward-pointing horns. [C19: from native name *sá-ro* Tibetan goat]

serpent ('sɜːpənt) *n.* **1.** a literary word for **snake.** **2.** *Bible.* a manifestation of Satan as a guileful tempter (Genesis 3:1–5). **3.** a sly or unscrupulous person. **4.** an obsolete wind instrument resembling a snake in shape. [C14: via OF from L *serpēns* a creeping thing, from *serpere* to creep]

serpentine[1] ('sɜːpən,taɪn) *adj.* **1.** of, relating to, or resembling a serpent. **2.** twisting; winding. [C14: from LL *serpentīmus*, from *serpēns* SERPENT]

serpentine[2] ('sɜːpən,taɪn) *n.* any of several secondary minerals, consisting of hydrated magnesium silicate, that are green to brown in colour and greasy to the touch. [C15 *serpentyn*, from Med. L *serpentīnum* SERPENTINE[1]; referring to the snakelike patterns of these minerals]

serpigo (sɜː'paɪgəʊ) *n. Pathol.* any progressive skin eruption, such as ringworm or herpes. [C14: from Med. '., from L *serpere* to creep]

SERPS *or* **Serps** (sɜːps) *n.* (in Britain) *acronym for* state earnings-related pension scheme.

serrate *adj.* ('sɛrɪt, -eɪt). **1.** (of leaves) having a margin of forward pointing teeth. **2.** having a notched or sawlike edge. ~*vb.* (sɛ'reɪt). **3.** (*tr.*) to make serrate. [C17: from L *serrātus* saw-shaped, from *serra* a saw] —**ser'rated** *adj.*

serration (sɛ'reɪʃən) *n.* **1.** the state or condition of being serrated. **2.** a row of toothlike projections on an edge. **3.** a single notch.

serried ('sɛrɪd) *adj.* in close or compact formation: *serried ranks of troops.* [C17: from OF *serré* close-packed, from *serrer* to shut up]

serriform ('sɛrɪ,fɔːm) *adj. Biol.* resembling a notched or sawlike edge. [*serri-*, from L *serra* saw]

serrulate ('sɛru,leɪt, -lɪt) *adj.* (esp. of leaves) minutely serrate. [C18: from NL *serrulātus*, from *serrula* dim. of *serra* a saw] —**,serru'lation** *n.*

Sertorius (sɜː'tɔːrɪəs) *n.* **Quintus** ('kwɪntəs). ?123–72 B.C., Roman soldier who fought with Marius in Gaul (102) and led an insurrection in Spain against Sulla until he was assassinated.

serum ('sɪərəm) *n.*, *pl.* -**rums** *or* -**ra** (-rə). **1.** Also called: **blood serum.** blood plasma from which the clotting factors have been removed. **2.** antitoxin obtained from the blood serum of immunized animals. **3.** *Physiol.*, *zool.* clear watery fluid, esp. that exuded by serous membranes. **4.** a less common word for **whey.** [C17: from L: whey]

serum albumin *n.* the principal protein of the blood. See also **albumin.**

serum hepatitis *n.* an acute infectious viral disease characterized by inflammation of the liver, fever, and jaundice: transmitted by means of injection with a contaminated needle or transfusion of contaminated blood.

serum sickness *n.* an allergic reaction, such as vomiting, skin rash, etc., that sometimes follows injection of a foreign serum.

serval ('sɜːv³l) *n.*, *pl.* -**vals** *or* -**val.** a slender feline mammal of the African bush, having an orange-brown coat with black spots. [C18: via F from LL *cervālis* staglike, from L *cervus* a stag]

servant ('sɜːv³nt) *n.* **1.** a person employed to work for another, esp. one who performs household duties. **2.** See **public servant.** [C13: via OF from *servant* serving, from *servir* to SERVE]

serve (sɜːv) *vb.* **1.** to be in the service of (a person). **2.** to render or be of service to (a person, cause, etc.); help. **3.** to attend to (customers) in a shop, etc. **4.** (*tr.*) to provide (guests, etc.) with food, drink, etc.: *she served her guests with cocktails.* **5.** to distribute or provide (food, etc.) for guests, etc.: *do you serve coffee?* **6.** (*tr.*; sometimes foll. by *up*) to present (food, etc.) in a specified manner: *duck served with orange sauce.* **7.** (*tr.*) to provide with a regular supply of. **8.** (*tr.*) to work actively for: *to serve the government.* **9.** (*tr.*) to pay homage to: *to serve God.* **10.** to suit: *this will serve my purpose.* **11.** (*intr.*; *may take*

an infinitive) to function: *this wood will serve to build a fire.* **12.** to go through (a period of service, enlistment, etc.). **13.** (*intr.*) (of weather, conditions, etc.) to be suitable. **14.** (*tr.*) Also: **service.** (of a male animal) to copulate with (a female animal). **15.** *Tennis, squash, etc.* to put (the ball) into play. **16.** (*tr.*) to deliver (a legal document) to (a person). **17.** (*tr.*) *Naut.* to bind (a rope, etc.) with fine cord to protect it from chafing, etc. **18.** **serve (a person) right.** *Inf.* to pay (a person) back, esp. for wrongful or foolish treatment or behaviour. ~*n.* **19.** *Tennis, squash, etc.* short for **service. 20.** *Austral. inf.* hostile or critical remarks. [C13: from OF *servir*, from L *servīre*, from *servus* a slave] —'**servable** *or* '**serveable** *adj.*

server ('sɜːvə) *n.* **1.** a person who serves. **2.** *R.C. Church.* a person who assists the priest at Mass. **3.** something that is used in serving food and drink. **4.** the player who serves in racket games.

Servetus (sɜː'viːtəs) *n.* **Michael,** Spanish name *Miguel Serveto.* 1511–53, Spanish theologian and physician. He was burnt at the stake by order of Calvin for denying the doctrine of the Trinity and the divinity of Christ.

Servia ('sɜːvɪə) *n.* the former name of **Serbia.** —'**Servian** *adj.*, *n.*

service ('sɜːvɪs) *n.* **1.** an act of help or assistance. **2.** an organized system of labour and material aids used to supply the needs of the public: *telephone service.* **3.** the supply, installation, or maintenance of goods carried out by a dealer. **4.** the state of availability for use by the public (esp. in **into** *or* **out of service**). **5.** a periodic overhaul made on a car, etc. **6.** the act or manner of serving guests, customers, etc., in a shop, hotel, etc. **7.** a department of public employment and its employees: *civil service.* **8.** employment in or performance of work for another: *in the service of his firm.* **9. a.** one of the branches of the armed forces. **b.** (*as modifier*): *service life.* **10.** the state or duties of a domestic servant (esp. in **in service**). **11.** the act or manner of serving food. **12.** a set of dishes, cups, etc., for use at table. **13.** public worship carried out according to certain prescribed forms: *divine service.* **14.** the prescribed form according to which a specific kind of religious ceremony is to be carried out: *the burial service.* **15.** *Tennis, squash, etc.* **a.** the act, manner, or right of serving a ball. **b.** the game in which a particular player serves: *he has lost his service.* **16.** the serving of a writ, summons, etc., upon a person. **17.** (of male animals) the act of mating. **18.** (*modifier*) of or for the use of servants or employees. **19.** (*modifier*) serving the public rather than producing goods: *service industry.* ~*vb.* (*tr.*) **20.** to provide service or services to. **21.** to make fit for use. **22.** to supply with assistance. **23.** to overhaul (a car, machine, etc.). **24.** (of a male animal) to mate with (a female). **25.** *Brit.* to meet interest on (debt). ~See also **services.** [C12 *servise*, from OF, from L *servitium* condition of a slave, from *servus* a slave]

serviceable ('sɜːvɪsəb³l) *adj.* **1.** capable of or ready for service. **2.** capable of giving good service. —**,service-a'bility** *n.* —'**serviceably** *adv.*

service area *n.* a place on a motorway providing garage services, restaurants, toilet facilities, etc.

service car *n. N.Z.* a bus operating on a long-distance route.

service charge *n.* a percentage of a bill, as at a hotel, added to the total to pay for service.

serviceman ('sɜːvɪsmən) *n.*, *pl.* -**men. 1.** a person who serves in the armed services of a country. **2.** a man employed to service and maintain equipment. —'**service,woman** *fem. n.*

service road *n. Brit.* a narrow road running parallel to a main road and providing access to houses, shops, etc., situated along its length.

services ('sɜːvɪsɪz) *pl. n.* **1.** work performed for remuneration. **2.** (usually preceded by *the*) the armed forces. **3.** (*sometimes sing.*) *Econ.* commodities, such as banking, that are mainly intangible and usually consumed concurrently with their production. **4.** a system of providing the public with gas, water, etc.

service station *n.* a place that supplies fuel, oil, etc., for motor vehicles and often carries out repairs, servicing, etc.

service tree *n.* **1.** Also called: **sorb.** a Eurasian rosaceous tree, cultivated for its white flowers and brown edible apple-like fruits. **2. wild service tree.** a similar and related Eurasian tree. [*service* from OE *syrfe*, from Vulgar L *sorbea* (unattested), from L *sorbus* sorb]

serviette (ˌsɜːvɪˈɛt) *n. Chiefly Brit.* a small square of cloth or paper used while eating to protect the clothes, etc. [C15: from OF, from *servir* to SERVE; on the model of OUBLIETTE]

servile ('sɜːvaɪl) *adj.* **1.** obsequious or fawning in attitude or behaviour. **2.** of or suitable for a slave. **3.** existing in or relating to a state of slavery. **4.** (when *postpositive*, foll. by *to*) submitting or obedient. [C14: from L *servīlis*, from *servus* slave] —**servility** (sɜːˈvɪlɪtɪ) *n.*

serving ('sɜːvɪŋ) *n.* a portion or helping of food or drink.

servitor ('sɜːvɪtə) *n. Arch.* a person who serves another. [C14: from OF, from LL, from L *servīre* to SERVE]

servitude ('sɜːvɪˌtjuːd) *n.* **1.** the state or condition of a slave. **2.** the state or condition of being subjected to or dominated by a person or thing. **3.** *Law.* a burden attaching to an estate for the benefit of an adjoining estate or of some definite person. See also **easement.** [C15: via OF from L *servitūdō*, from *servus* a slave]

servo ('sɜːvəʊ) *adj.* **1.** (*prenominal*) of or activated by a servomechanism: *servo brakes.* ~*n.*, *pl.* **-vos.** **2.** *Inf.* short for **servomechanism.** [from *servomotor* from F, from L *servus* slave + F *moteur* motor]

servomechanism ('sɜːvəʊˌmɛkəˌnɪzəm) *n.* a mechanical or electromechanical system for control of the position or speed of an output transducer.

servomotor ('sɜːvəʊˌməʊtə) *n.* any motor that supplies power to a servomechanism.

sesame ('sɛsəmɪ) *n.* **1.** a tropical herbaceous plant of the East Indies, cultivated, esp. in India, for its small oval seeds. **2.** the seeds of this plant, used in flavouring bread and yielding an edible oil (**benne oil** or **gingili**). [C15: from L *sēsamum*, from Gk *sēsamon*, *sēsamē*, of Semitic origin]

sesamoid ('sɛsəˌmɔɪd) *adj. Anat.* **1.** of or relating to various small bones formed in tendons, such as the patella. **2.** of or relating to any of various small cartilages, esp. those of the nose. [C17: from L *sēsamoīdes* like sesame (seed), from Gk]

sesqui- *prefix.* **1.** indicating one and a half: *sesquicentennial.* **2.** (in a chemical compound) indicating a ratio of two to three. [from L, contraction of SEMI- + as AS² + *-que* and]

sesquicentennial (ˌsɛskwɪsɛnˈtɛnɪəl) *adj.* **1.** of a period of 150 years. ~*n.* **2.** a period of 150 years. **3.** a 150th anniversary or its celebration. —**ˌsesquicenˈtennially** *adv.*

sessile ('sɛsaɪl) *adj.* **1.** (of flowers or leaves) having no stalk. **2.** (of animals such as the barnacle) permanently attached. [C18: from L *sessilis* concerning sitting, from *sedēre* to sit] —**sessility** (sɛˈsɪlɪtɪ) *n.*

sessile oak *n.* another name for the **durmast.**

session ('sɛʃən) *n.* **1.** the meeting of a court, legislature, judicial body, etc., for the execution of its function or the transaction of business. **2.** a single continuous meeting of such a body. **3.** a series or period of such meetings. **4.** *Education.* **a.** the time during which classes are held. **b.** a school or university year. **5.** *Presbyterian Church.* the body presiding over a local congregation and consisting of the minister and elders. **6.** any period devoted to an activity. [C14: from L *sessiō* a sitting, from *sedēre* to sit] —**'sessional** *adj.*

Sessions ('sɛʃənz) *n.* **Roger** (**Huntington**). 1896–1985, U.S. composer.

sesterce ('sɛstəs) *or* **sestertius** (sɛˈstɜːtɪəs) *n.* a silver or, later, bronze coin of ancient Rome worth a quarter of a denarius. [C16: from L *sēstertius* a coin worth two and a half asses, from *sēmis* half + *tertius* a third]

sestet (sɛˈstɛt) *n.* **1.** *Prosody.* the last six lines of a sonnet. **2.** another word for **sextet** (sense 1). [C19: from It., from *sesto* sixth, from L, from *sex* six]

sestina (sɛˈstiːnə) *n.* an elaborate verse form of Italian origin in which the six final words of the lines in the first stanza are repeated in a different order in each of the remaining five stanzas. [C19: from It., from *sesto* sixth, from L *sextus*]

Sestos ('sɛstɒs) *n.* a ruined town in NW Turkey, at the narrowest point of the Dardanelles: N terminus of the bridge of boats built by Xerxes in 481 B.C. for the crossing of his armies of invasion.

set[1] (sɛt) *vb.* **setting, set.** (*mainly tr.*) **1.** to put or place in position or into a specified state or condition: *to set someone free.* **2.** (*also intr.; foll. by* to *or* on) to put or be put (to); apply or be applied: *he set fire to the house.* **3.** to put into order or readiness for use: *to set the table for dinner.* **4.** (*also intr.*) to put, form, or be formed into a jelled, firm, or rigid state: *the jelly set in three hours.* **5.** (*also intr.*) to put or be put into a position that will restore a normal state: *to set a broken bone.* **6.** to adjust (a clock or other instrument) to a position. **7.** to establish: *we have set the date for our wedding.* **8.** to prescribe (an undertaking, course of study, etc.): *the examiners have set "Paradise Lost".* **9.** to arrange in a particular fashion, esp. an attractive one: *she set her hair.* **10.** Also: **set to music.** to provide music for (a poem or other text to be sung). **11.** Also: **set up.** *Printing.* to arrange or produce (type, film, etc.) from (text or copy). **12.** to arrange (a stage, television studio, etc.) with scenery and props. **13.** to describe (a scene or the background to a literary work, etc.) in words: *his novel is set in Russia.* **14.** to present as a model of good or bad behaviour (esp. in **set an example**). **15.** (foll. by *on* or *by*) to value (something) at a specified price or estimation of worth: *he set a high price on his services.* **16.** (*also intr.*) to give or be given a particular direction: *his course was set to the East.* **17.** (*also intr.*) to rig (a sail) or (of a sail) to be rigged so as to catch the wind. **18.** (*intr.*) (of the sun, moon, etc.) to disappear beneath the horizon. **19.** to leave (dough, etc.) in one place so that it may prove. **20.** to sink (the head of a nail) below the surface surrounding it by using a nail set. **21.** *Computers.* to give (a binary circuit) the value 1. **22.** (of plants) to produce (fruits, seeds, etc.) after pollination or (of fruits or seeds) to develop after pollination. **23.** to plant (seeds, seedlings, etc.). **24.** to place (a hen) on (eggs) for the purpose of incubation. **25.** (*intr.*) (of a gun dog) to turn in the direction of game. **26.** *Bridge.* to defeat (one's opponents) in their attempt to make a contract. **27.** a dialect word for **sit.** ~*n.* **28.** the act of setting or the state of being set. **29.** a condition of firmness or hardness. **30.** bearing, carriage, or posture: *the set of a gun dog when pointing.* **31.** the scenery and other props used in a dramatic production, film, etc. **32.** Also called: **set width.** *Printing.* **a.** the width of the body of a piece of type. **b.** the width of the lines of type in a page or column. **33.** *Psychol.* a temporary bias disposing an organism to react to a stimulus in one way rather than in others. **34.** a seedling, cutting, or similar part that is ready for planting: *onion sets.* **35.** a variant spelling of **sett.** ~*adj.* **36.** fixed or established by authority or agreement: *set hours of work.* **37.** (*usually postpositive*) rigid or inflexible: *she is set in her ways.* **38.** unmoving; fixed: *a set expression on his face.* **39.** conventional, artificial, or stereotyped: *she made her apology in set phrases.* **40.** (*postpositive*; foll. by *on* or *upon*) resolute in intention: *he is set upon marrying.* **41.** (of a book, etc.) prescribed for students' preparation for an examination. ~*See also* **set about, set against,** etc. [OE *settan*, causative of *sittan* to SIT]

set[2] (sɛt) *n.* **1.** a number of objects or people grouped or belonging together, often having certain features or characteristics in common: *a set of coins.* **2.** a group of people who associate together, etc.: *he's part of the jet set.* **3.** *Maths.* a collection of numbers, objects, etc., that are treated as an entity: {3, the moon} is the set the two members of which are the number 3 and the moon. **4.** any apparatus that receives or transmits television or radio signals. **5.** *Tennis, squash, etc.* one of the units of a match, in tennis, one in which one player or pair of players must win at least six games. **6. a.** the number of couples required for a formation dance. **b.** a series of figures that make up a formation dance. **7. a.** a band's or performer's concert repertoire on a given occasion: *the set included no new songs.* **b.** a continuous performance: *the Who played two sets.* **8. make a dead set at. a.** to attack by arguing or ridiculing. **b.** (of a woman) to try to gain the affections of (a man). ~*vb.* **setting, set.** **9.** (*intr.*) (in square and country dancing) to perform a sequence of steps while facing towards another dancer. **10.** (*usually tr.*) to divide into sets: *in this school we set our older pupils for English.* [C14 (in the obs. sense: a religious sect): from OF *sette*, from L *secta* SECT; later sense infl. by the verb SET[1]]

seta ('si:tə) *n.*, *pl.* **-tae** (-ti:). (in invertebrates and plants) any bristle or bristle-like appendage. [C18: from L] —**setaceous** (sɪ'teɪʃəs) *adj.*

set about *vb.* (*intr.*, *prep.*) **1.** to start or begin. **2.** to attack physically or verbally.

set against *vb.* (*tr.*, *prep.*) **1.** to balance or compare. **2.** to cause to be unfriendly to.

set aside *vb.* (*tr.*, *adv.*) **1.** to reserve for a special purpose. **2.** to discard or quash.

set back *vb.* (*tr.*, *adv.*) **1.** to hinder; impede. **2.** *Inf.* to cost (a person) a specified amount. ~*n.* **setback. 3.** anything that serves to hinder or impede. **4.** a recession in the upper part of a high building. **5.** a steplike shelf where a wall is reduced in thickness.

set down *vb.* (*tr.*, *adv.*) **1.** to record. **2.** to judge or regard: *he set him down as an idiot.* **3.** (foll. by *to*) to attribute: *his attitude was set down to his illness.* **4.** to rebuke. **5.** to snub. **6.** *Brit.* to allow (passengers) to alight from a bus, etc.

set forth *vb.* (*adv.*) *Formal or arch.* **1.** (*tr.*) to state, express, or utter. **2.** (*intr.*) to start out on a journey.

Seth (sɛθ) *n. Old Testament.* Adam's third son, given by God in place of the murdered Abel (Genesis 4:25).

setiferous (sɪ'tɪfərəs) *or* **setigerous** (sɪ'tɪdʒərəs) *adj. Biol.* bearing bristles. [C19: see SETA, -FEROUS, -GEROUS]

set in *vb.* (*intr.*, *adv.*) **1.** to become established: *the winter has set in.* **2.** (of wind) to blow or (of current) to move towards shore. ~*adj.* **set-in. 3.** (of a part) made separately and then added to a larger whole: *a set-in sleeve.*

setline ('sɛt,laɪn) *n.* any of various types of fishing line that consist of a long suspended line having shorter hooked and baited lines attached.

set off *vb.* (*adv.*) **1.** (*intr.*) to embark on a journey. **2.** (*tr.*) to cause (a person) to act or do something, such as laugh. **3.** (*tr.*) to cause to explode. **4.** (*tr.*) to act as a foil or contrast to: *that brooch sets your dress off well.* **5.** (*tr.*) *Accounting.* to cancel a credit on (one account) against a debit on another. ~*n.* **setoff. 6.** anything that serves as a counterbalance. **7.** anything that serves to contrast with or enhance something else; foil. **8.** a cross claim brought by a debtor that partly offsets the creditor's claim.

set-off *n. Printing.* a fault in which ink is transferred from a heavily inked or undried printed sheet to the sheet next to it in a pile.

set on *vb.* **1.** (*prep.*) Also: **set upon.** to attack or cause to attack: *they set the dogs on him.* **2.** (*tr.*, *adv.*) to instigate or incite; urge.

Seton ('si:t³n) *n.* **Ernest Thompson.** 1860–1946, U.S. author and illustrator of animal books, born in England.

Seto Naikai ('sɛtəʊ 'naɪkaɪ) *n.* transliteration of the Japanese name for the **Inland Sea.**

setose ('si:təʊs) *adj. Biol.* covered with setae; bristly. [C17: from L *saetōsus*, from *saeta* a bristle]

set out *vb.* (*adv.*, *mainly tr.*) **1.** to present, arrange, or display. **2.** to give a full account of: *he set out the matter in full.* **3.** to plan or lay out (a garden, etc.). **4.** (*intr.*) to begin or embark on an undertaking, esp. a journey.

set piece *n.* **1.** a work of literature, music, etc., often having a conventional or prescribed theme, intended to create an impressive effect. **2.** a display of fireworks. **3.** *Sport.* a rehearsed team manoeuvre usually attempted at a restart of play.

setscrew ('sɛt,skru:) *n.* a screw that fits into the boss or hub of a wheel, coupling, cam, etc., and prevents motion of the part relative to the shaft on which it is mounted.

set square *n.* a thin flat piece of plastic, metal, etc., in the shape of a right-angled triangle, used in technical drawing.

sett *or* **set** (sɛt) *n.* **1.** a small rectangular paving block made of stone. **2.** the burrow of a badger. **3. a.** a square in a pattern of tartan. **b.** the pattern itself. [C19: var. of SET¹ (*n.*)]

settee (sɛ'ti:) *n.* a seat, for two or more people, with a back and usually with arms. [C18: changed from SETTLE²]

setter ('sɛtə) *n.* any of various breeds of large long-haired gun dog trained to point out game by standing rigid.

set theory *n. Maths.* the branch of mathematics concerned with the properties and interrelationships of sets.

setting ('sɛtɪŋ) *n.* **1.** the surroundings in which something is set. **2.** the scenery, properties, or background used to create the location for a stage play, film, etc. **3.**

Music. a composition consisting of a certain text and music arranged for it. **4.** the metal mounting and surround of a gem. **5.** the tableware, cutlery, etc., for a single place at table. **6.** any of a set of points on a scale or dial that can be selected to control the speed, temperature, etc., at which a machine operates.

settle¹ ('sɛt³l) *vb.* **1.** (*tr.*) to put in order: *he settled his affairs before he died.* **2.** to arrange or be arranged in a fixed or comfortable position: *he settled himself by the fire.* **3.** (*intr.*) to come to rest or a halt: *a bird settled on the hedge.* **4.** to take up or cause to take up residence: *the family settled in the country.* **5.** to establish or become established in a way of life, job, etc. **6.** (*tr.*) to migrate to and form a community; colonize. **7.** to make or become quiet, calm, or stable. **8.** to cause (sediment) to sink to the bottom, as in a liquid, or (of sediment) to sink thus. **9.** to subside or cause to subside: *the dust settled.* **10.** (sometimes foll. by *up*) to pay off or account for (a bill, debt, etc.). **11.** (*tr.*) to decide or dispose of: *to settle an argument.* **12.** (*intr.*; often foll. by *on* or *upon*) to agree or fix: *to settle upon a plan.* **13.** (*tr.*; usually foll. by *on* or *upon*) to secure (title, property, etc.) to a person: *he settled his property on his wife.* **14.** to determine (a legal dispute, etc.) by agreement of the parties without resort to court action (esp. in **settle out of court**). [OE *setlan*] —**'settleable** *adj.*

settle² ('sɛt³l) *n.* a seat, for two or more people, usually made of wood with a high back and arms, and sometimes having a storage space in the boxlike seat. [OE *setl*]

settle down *vb.* (*adv.*, *mainly intr.*) **1.** (*also tr.*) to make or become quiet and orderly. **2.** (often foll. by *to*) to apply oneself diligently: *please settle down to work.* **3.** to adopt an orderly and routine way of life, esp. after marriage.

settle for *vb.* (*intr.*, *prep.*) to accept or agree to in spite of dispute or dissatisfaction.

settlement ('sɛt³lmənt) *n.* **1.** the act or state of settling or being settled. **2.** the establishment of a new region; colonization. **3.** a place newly settled; colony. **4.** a community formed by members of a group, esp. of a religious sect. **5.** a public building used to provide educational and general welfare facilities for persons living in deprived areas. **6.** a subsidence of all or part of a structure. **7.** an agreement reached in matters of finance, business, etc. **8.** *Law.* **a.** a conveyance, usually to trustees, of property to be enjoyed by several persons in succession. **b.** the deed conveying such property.

settler ('sɛtlə) *n.* a person who settles in a new country or a colony.

settlings ('sɛtlɪŋz) *pl. n.* any matter that has settled at the bottom of a liquid.

set to *vb.* (*intr.*, *adv.*) **1.** to begin working. **2.** to start fighting. ~*n.* **set-to. 3.** *Inf.* a brief disagreement or fight.

Setúbal (*Portuguese* sə'tuβal) *n.* a port in SW Portugal, on **Setúbal Bay** south of Lisbon: an earthquake in 1755 destroyed most of the old town. Pop.: 77 885 (1984).

set up *vb.* (*adv.*, *mainly tr.*) **1.** (*also intr.*) to put into a position of power, etc. **2.** (*also intr.*) to begin or enable (someone) to begin a (new venture), as by acquiring or providing means, etc. **3.** to build or construct: *to set up a shed.* **4.** to raise or produce: *to set up a wail.* **5.** to advance or propose: *to set up a theory.* **6.** to restore the health of: *the sea air will set you up again.* **7.** to establish (a record). **8.** *Inf.* to cause (a person) to be blamed, accused, etc. ~*n.* **setup. 9.** *Inf.* the way in which anything is organized or arranged. **10.** *Sl.*, *chiefly U.S. & Canad.* an event the result of which is prearranged: *it's a setup.* **11.** a prepared arrangement of materials, machines, etc., for a job or undertaking. ~*adj.* **set-up. 12.** physically well-built.

Seurat (*French* sœra) *n.* **Georges** (ʒɔrʒ). 1859–91, French neoimpressionist painter. He developed the pointillist technique of painting, characterized by brilliant luminosity, as in *Dimanche à la Grande-Jatte* (1886).

Sevan (sɛ'vɑːn) *n.* **Lake.** a lake in the SW Soviet Union, in the N Armenian SSR at an altitude of 1914 m (6279 ft.). Area: 1417 sq. km (547 sq. miles).

Sevastopol (*Russian* sıvas'təpəlj) *n.* a port and resort in the SW Soviet Union, in the S Ukrainian SSR on the Black Sea: captured and destroyed by British, French, and Turkish forces after a siege of 11 months (1854–55) during the Crimean War; taken by the Germans after a siege of 8 months (1942) during World War II. Pop.: 350 000 (1987). English name: **Sebastopol.**

seven ('sɛvᵊn) n. **1.** the cardinal number that is the sum of six and one and is a prime number. **2.** a numeral, 7, VII, etc., representing this number. **3.** the amount or quantity that is one greater than six. **4.** anything representing, represented by, or consisting of seven units, such as a playing card with seven symbols on it. **5.** Also called: **seven o'clock.** seven hours after noon or midnight. ~*determiner.* **6. a.** amounting to seven: *seven swans a-swimming.* **b.** (*as pron.*): *you've eaten seven already.* ~See also **sevens.** [OE *seofon*]

Seven against Thebes *pl. n. Greek myth.* the seven members of an expedition undertaken to regain for Polynices, a son of Oedipus, his share in the throne of Thebes from his usurping brother Eteocles. The seven are usually listed as Polynices, Adrastus, Amphiaraus, Capaneus, Hippomedon, Tydeus, and Parthenopaeus. The campaign failed and the warring brothers killed each other in single combat before the Theban walls. See also **Adrastus.**

seven deadly sins *pl. n.* a fuller name for the **deadly sins.**

sevenfold ('sɛvᵊn,fəʊld) *adj.* **1.** equal to or having seven times as many or as much. **2.** composed of seven parts. ~*adv.* **3.** by or up to seven times as many or as much.

Seven Hills of Rome *pl. n.* the hills on which the ancient city of Rome was built: the Palatine, Capitoline, Quirinal, Caelian, Aventine, Esquiline, and Viminal.

sevens ('sɛvᵊnz) n. (*functioning as sing.*) a rugby union match or competition played with seven players on each side.

seven seas *pl. n.* the oceans of the world considered as the N and S Pacific, the N and S Atlantic, and the Arctic, Antarctic, and Indian Oceans.

Seven Sleepers *pl. n.* seven Christian youths from Ephesus who were walled up in a cave by the Emperor Decius in 250 A.D. and, according to legend, slept for 187 years.

seventeen ('sɛvᵊn'tiːn) n. **1.** the cardinal number that is the sum of ten and seven and is a prime number. **2.** a numeral, 17, XVII, etc., representing this number. **3.** the amount or quantity that is seven more than ten. **4.** something represented by, representing, or consisting of 17 units. ~*determiner.* **5. a.** amounting to seventeen: *seventeen attempts.* **b.** (*as pron.*): *seventeen were sold.* [OE *seofontiene*] —'seven'teenth *adj., n.*

seventh ('sɛvᵊnθ) *adj.* **1.** (*usually prenominal*) **a.** coming after the sixth and before the eighth in numbering, position, etc.; being the ordinal number of *seven:* often written 7th. **b.** (*as n.*): *she left on the seventh.* ~*n.* **2. a.** one of seven equal parts of an object, quantity, measurement, etc. **b.** (*as modifier*): *a seventh part.* **3.** the fraction equal to one divided by seven (1/7). **4.** *Music.* **a.** the interval between one note and another seven notes away from it in a diatonic scale. **b.** one of two notes constituting such an interval in relation to the other. ~*adv.* **5.** Also: **seventhly.** after the sixth person, event, etc.

Seventh-Day Adventist *n.* a member of that branch of the Adventists which constituted itself as a separate body after the expected Second Coming of Christ failed to be realized in 1844. They believe that Christ's coming is imminent and observe Saturday instead of Sunday as their Sabbath.

seventh heaven *n.* **1.** the final state of eternal bliss. **2.** a state of supreme happiness.

seventy ('sɛvᵊntɪ) n., pl. **-ties. 1.** the cardinal number that is the product of ten and seven. **2.** a numeral, 70, LXX, etc., representing this number. **3.** (*pl.*) the numbers 70–79, esp. the 70th to the 79th year of a person's life or of a particular century. **4.** the amount or quantity that is seven times as big as ten. **5.** something represented by, representing, or consisting of 70 units. ~*determiner.* **6. a.** amounting to seventy: *the seventy varieties of fabric.* **b.** (*as pron.*): *to invite seventy to the wedding.* —'seventieth *adj., n.*

Seven Wonders of the World *pl. n.* the seven structures considered by ancient and medieval scholars to be the most wondrous of the ancient world. The list varies, but generally consists of the Pyramids of Egypt, the Hanging Gardens of Babylon, Phidias's statue of Zeus at Olympia, the temple of Artemis at Ephesus, the mausoleum of Halicarnassus, the Colossus of Rhodes, and the Pharos (or lighthouse) of Alexandria.

sever ('sɛvə) vb. **1.** to put or be put apart. **2.** to divide or be divided into parts. **3.** (*tr.*) to break off or dissolve (a tie, relationship, etc.). [C14 *severen*, from OF, from L *sēparāre* to SEPARATE] —'severable *adj.*

several ('sɛvrəl) *determiner.* **1. a.** more than a few: *several people objected.* **b.** (*as pronoun; functioning as pl.*): *several of them know.* ~*adj.* **2.** (*prenominal*) various; separate: *the members with their several occupations.* **3.** (*prenominal*) distinct; different: *three several times.* **4.** *Law.* capable of being dealt with separately. [C15: via Anglo-F from Med. L *sēparālis*, from L *sēpar*, from *sēparāre* to SEPARATE]

severally ('sɛvrəlɪ) *adv. Arch. or literary.* **1.** separately or distinctly. **2.** each in turn.

severalty ('sɛvrəltɪ) n., pl. **-ties. 1.** the state of being several or separate. **2.** (*usually preceded by in*) *Property law.* the tenure of property, esp. land, in a person's own right.

severance ('sɛvərəns) n. **1.** the act of severing or state of being severed. **2.** a separation. **3.** *Law.* the division into separate parts of a joint estate, contract, etc.

severance pay *n.* compensation paid by a firm to employees for loss of employment.

severe (sɪ'vɪə) *adj.* **1.** rigorous or harsh in the treatment of others: *a severe parent.* **2.** serious in appearance or manner. **3.** critical or dangerous: *a severe illness.* **4.** causing discomfort by its harshness: *severe weather.* **5.** strictly restrained in appearance: *a severe way of dressing.* **6.** hard to perform or accomplish: *a severe test.* [C16: from L *sevērus*] —se'verely *adv.* —severity (sɪ'vɛrɪtɪ) n.

Severn ('sɛvᵊn) n. **1.** a river in E Wales and W England, rising in Powys and flowing northeast and east into England, then south to the Bristol Channel. Length: about 290 km (180 miles). **2.** a river in SE central Canada, in Ontario, flowing northeast to Hudson Bay. Length: about 676 km (420 miles).

Severnaya Zemlya (*Russian* 'sjevɪrnəjə zɪm'lja) n. an archipelago in the Arctic Ocean off the coast of the N central Soviet Union.

Severus (sɪ'vɪərəs) n. **Lucius Septimius** (sɛp'tɪmɪəs). 146–211 A.D., Roman soldier and emperor (193–211). He waged war successfully against the Parthians (197–202) and spent his last years in Britain (208–11).

Sévigné (*French* sevɪɲe) n. **Marquise de,** title of *Marie de Rabutin-Chantal.* 1626–96, French letter writer. Her correspondence with her daughter and others provides a vivid account of society during the reign of Louis XIV.

Seville (sə'vɪl) n. a port in SW Spain, on the Guadalquivir River: chief town of S Spain under the Vandals and Visigoths (5th–8th centuries); centre of Spanish colonial trade (16th–17th centuries); tourist centre. Pop.: 651 299 (1986 est.). Ancient name: **Hispalis.** Spanish name: **Sevilla** (se'βiʎa).

Seville orange *n.* **1.** an orange tree of tropical and semitropical regions: grown for its bitter fruit, which is used to make marmalade. **2.** the fruit of this tree.

Sèvres (*French* sɛvrə) n. porcelain ware manufactured at Sèvres, near Paris, from 1756, characterized by the use of clear colours and elaborate decorative detail.

sew (səʊ) vb. **sewing, sewed; sewn** *or* **sewed. 1.** to join or decorate (pieces of fabric, etc.) by means of a thread repeatedly passed through with a needle. **2.** (*tr.; often foll. by on or up*) to attach, fasten, or close by sewing. **3.** (*tr.*) to make (a garment, etc.) by sewing. ~See also **sew up.** [OE *sēowan*]

sewage ('suːɪdʒ) n. waste matter from domestic or industrial establishments that is carried away in sewers or drains. [C19: back formation from SEWER[1]]

sewage farm *n.* a place where sewage is treated, esp. for use as manure.

Seward ('sjuːəd) n. **William Henry.** 1801–72, U.S. statesman; secretary of state (1861–69). He was a leading opponent of slavery and was responsible for the purchase of Alaska (1867).

Seward Peninsula *n.* a peninsula of W Alaska, on the Bering Strait. Length: about 290 km (180 miles).

Sewell ('suːəl) n. **Henry.** 1807–79, New Zealand statesman, born in England: first prime minister of New Zealand (1856).

sewer[1] (suə) n. **1.** a drain or pipe, esp. one that is underground, used to carry away surface water or sewage. ~*vb.* **2.** (*tr.*) to provide with sewers. [C15: from OF, from *essever* to drain, from Vulgar L *exaquāre* (unattested), from L EX-[1] + *aqua* water]

sewer² ('səʊə) *n.* a person or thing that sews.

sewerage ('sʊərɪdʒ) *n.* **1.** an arrangement of sewers. **2.** the removal of surface water or sewage by means of sewers. **3.** another word for **sewage.**

sewing ('səʊɪŋ) *n.* **a.** a piece of cloth, etc., that is sewn or to be sewn. **b.** (*as modifier*): *sewing basket.*

sewing machine *n.* any machine designed to sew material. It is now usually driven by electric motor but is sometimes operated by a foot treadle or by hand.

sewn (səʊn) *vb.* a past participle of **sew.**

sew up *vb.* (*tr., adv.*) **1.** to fasten or mend completely by sewing. **2.** *U.S.* to acquire sole use or control of. **3.** *Inf.* to complete or negotiate successfully: *to sew up a deal.*

sex (sɛks) *n.* **1.** the sum of the characteristics that distinguish organisms on the basis of their reproductive function. **2.** either of the two categories, male or female, into which organisms are placed on this basis. **3.** short for **sexual intercourse. 4.** feelings or behaviour resulting from the urge to gratify the sexual instinct. **5.** sexual matters in general. ~*modifier.* **6.** of or concerning sexual matters: *sex education.* **7.** based on or arising from the difference between the sexes: *sex discrimination.* ~*vb.* **8.** (*tr.*) to ascertain the sex of. [C14: from L *sexus*]

sex- *combining form.* six: *sexcentenary.* [from L]

sexagenarian (ˌsɛksədʒɪ'nɛərɪən) *n.* **1.** a person from 60 to 69 years old. ~*adj.* **2.** being from 60 to 69 years old. **3.** of or relating to a sexagenarian. [C18: from L, from *sexāgēnī* sixty each, from *sexāgintā* sixty]

Sexagesima (ˌsɛksə'dʒɛsɪmə) *n.* the second Sunday before Lent. [C16: from L: sixtieth, from *sexāgintā* sixty]

sexagesimal (ˌsɛksə'dʒɛsɪməl) *adj.* **1.** relating to or based on the number 60: *sexagesimal measurement of angles.* ~*n.* **2.** a fraction in which the denominator is some power of 60.

sex appeal *n.* the quality or power of attracting the opposite sex.

sexcentenary (ˌsɛksɛn'tiːnərɪ) *adj.* **1.** of or relating to 600 or a period of 600 years. **2.** of or celebrating a 600th anniversary. ~*n., pl.* **-naries. 3.** a 600th anniversary or its celebration. [C18: from L *sexcentēnī* six hundred each]

sex chromosome *n.* either of the chromosomes determining the sex of animals.

sexed (sɛkst) *adj.* **1.** (*in combination*) having a specified degree of sexuality: *undersexed.* **2.** of, relating to, or having sexual differentiation.

sex hormone *n.* an animal hormone affecting development and growth of reproductive organs and related parts.

sexism ('sɛksɪzəm) *n.* discrimination on the basis of sex, esp. the oppression of women by men. —'**sexist** *n., adj.*

sexless ('sɛkslɪs) *adj.* **1.** having or showing no sexual differentiation. **2.** having no sexual desires. **3.** sexually unattractive.

sex linkage *n. Genetics.* the condition in which a gene is located on a sex chromosome so that the character controlled by the gene is associated with either of the sexes. —'**sex,linked** *adj.*

sex object *n.* someone, esp. a woman, regarded only from the point of view of someone else's sexual desires.

sexology (sɛk'splədʒɪ) *n.* the study of sexual behaviour in human beings. —**sex'ologist** *n.* —**sexological** (ˌsɛksə'lɒdʒɪkʰl) *adj.*

sexpartite (sɛks'pɑːtaɪt) *adj.* **1.** (esp. of vaults, arches, etc.) divided into or composed of six parts. **2.** involving six participants.

sex shop *n.* a shop selling aids to sexual activity, pornographic material, etc.

sext (sɛkst) *n. Chiefly R.C. Church.* the fourth of the seven canonical hours of the divine office or the prayers prescribed for it. [C15: from Church L *sexta hōra* the sixth hour]

sextan ('sɛkstən) *adj.* (of a fever) marked by paroxysms that recur every fifth day. [C17: from Med. L *sextana* (*febris*) (fever) of the sixth (day)]

sextant ('sɛkstənt) *n.* **1.** an instrument used in navigation and consisting of a telescope through which a sighting of a heavenly body is taken, with protractors for determining its angular distance above the horizon. **2.** a sixth part of a circle. [C17: from L *sextāns* one sixth of a unit]

sextet *or* **sextette** (sɛks'tɛt) *n.* **1.** *Music.* a group of six singers or instrumentalists or a piece of music composed for such a group. **2.** a group of six people or things. [C19: var. of SESTET]

sextillion (sɛks'tɪljən) *n., pl.* **-lions** *or* **-lion. 1.** (in Britain, France, and Germany) the number represented as one followed by 36 zeros (10^{36}). **2.** (in the U.S. and Canada) the number represented as one followed by 21 zeros (10^{21}). [C17: from F, from SEX- + *-illion*, on the model of SEPTILLION]

sexton ('sɛkstən) *n.* **1.** a man employed to act as caretaker of a church and often also as a bell-ringer, gravedigger, etc. **2.** another name for the **burying beetle.** [C14: from OF, from Med. L *sacristānus* SACRISTAN]

sextuple ('sɛkstjʊpˤl) *n.* **1.** a quantity or number six times as great as another. ~*adj.* **2.** six times as much or as many. **3.** consisting of six parts or members. [C17: L *sextus* sixth + *-uple*, as in QUADRUPLE]

sextuplet ('sɛkstjʊplɪt) *n.* **1.** one of six offspring at one birth. **2.** a group of six. **3.** *Music.* a group of six notes played in a time value of four.

sexual ('sɛksjʊəl) *adj.* **1.** of or characterized by sex. **2.** (of reproduction) characterized by the union of male and female gametes. Cf. **asexual** (sense 2). [C17: from LL *sexuālis*] —**sexuality** (ˌsɛksjʊ'ælɪtɪ) *n.* —'**sexually** *adv.*

sexual harassment *n.* the persistent unwelcome directing of sexual remarks, looks, etc., at a woman, esp. in the workplace.

sexual intercourse *n.* the sexual act in which the male's erect penis is inserted into the female's vagina; copulation; coitus.

sexually transmitted disease *n.* any of various diseases, such as syphilis or gonorrhoea, transmitted by sexual intercourse. Also called: **venereal disease.**

sexual selection *n.* an evolutionary process in animals, in which selection by females of males with certain characters results in the preservation of these characters in the species.

sexy ('sɛksɪ) *adj.* **sexier, sexiest.** *Inf.* **1.** provoking or intended to provoke sexual interest: *a sexy dress.* **2.** feeling sexual interest; aroused. **3.** interesting, exciting, or trendy: *a sexy project; a sexy new car.* —'**sexily** *adv.* —'**sexiness** *n.*

Seychelles (seɪ'ʃɛl, -'ʃɛlz) *pl. n.* a group of volcanic islands in the W Indian Ocean: taken by the British from the French in 1744: became an independent republic within the Commonwealth in 1976, incorporating the British Indian Ocean Territory islands of Aldabra, Farquhar and Desroches. Official languages: English and French. Currency: rupee. Capital: Victoria. Pop.: 67 000 (1987 est.). Area: 375 sq. km (145 sq. miles).

Seyhan (seɪ'hɑːn) *n.* another name for **Adana.**

Seymour ('siːmɔː) *n.* **Jane.** ?1509–37, third wife of Henry VIII of England; mother of Edward VI.

sf *or* **sfz** *Music. abbrev. for* sforzando.

SF *or* **sf** *abbrev. for* science fiction.

SFA *abbrev. for:* **1.** Scottish Football Association. **2.** sweet Fanny Adams. See **fanny adams.**

Sfax (sfæks) *n.* a port in E Tunisia, on the Gulf of Gabès: the second largest town in Tunisia; commercial centre of a phosphate region. Pop.: 231 911 (1984).

Sforza (*Italian* 'sfɔrtsa) *n.* **1.** Count **Carlo** ('karlo). 1873–1952, Italian statesman; leader of the anti-Fascist opposition. **2. Francesco** (fran'tʃesko). 1401–66, duke of Milan (1450–66). **3.** his father **Giacomuzzo** (dʒako'muttso) *or* **Muzio** ('muttsjo), original name *Attendolo.* 1369–1424, Italian condottiere and founder of the dynasty that ruled Milan (1450–1535). **4. Lodovico** (lodo'viːko), called *the Moor.* 1451–1508, duke of Milan (1494–1500), but effective ruler from 1480; patron of Leonardo da Vinci.

sforzando (sfɔː'tsaːndəʊ) *or* **sforzato** (sfɔː'tsaːtəʊ) *Music.* ~*adj., adv.* **1.** to be played with strong initial attack. Abbrevs.: **sf, sfz.** ~*n.* **2.** a symbol, mark, etc., indicating this. [C19: from It., from *sforzare* to force, from Vulgar L *fortiāre* (unattested) to FORCE]

SG *abbrev. for* solicitor general.

sgd *abbrev. for* signed.

S. Glam *abbrev. for* South Glamorgan.

sgraffito (sgræ'fiːtəʊ) *n., pl.* **-ti** (-tɪ). **1.** a technique in mural or ceramic decoration in which the top layer of glaze, plaster, etc., is incised with a design to reveal parts of the ground. **2.** such a decoration. [C18: from It., from *sgraffire* to scratch]

's Gravenhage (sxraːvən'haːxə) *n.* the Dutch name for (The) **Hague.**

Sgt *abbrev. for* Sergeant.

sh (*spelling pron.* ʃʃʃ) *interj.* an exclamation to request silence or quiet.

sh. *abbrev. for:* **1.** *Stock Exchange.* share. **2.** sheep. **3.** *Bookbinding.* sheet.

Shaanxi (ˈʃænˈʃiː) *or* **Shensi** *n.* a province of NW China: one of the earliest centres of Chinese civilization; largely mountainous. Capital: Xi An. Pop.: 26 000 000 (1985). Area: 195 800 sq. km (75 598 sq. miles).

Shaba (ˈʃɑːbə) *n.* a province of SE Zaïre: important for hydroelectric power and rich mineral resources (copper and tin ore). Capital: Lubumbashi. Pop.: 3 874 019 (1984). Area: 496 964 sq. km (191 878 sq. miles). Former name (until 1972): **Katanga.**

shabby (ˈʃæbɪ) *adj.* **-bier, -biest. 1.** threadbare or dilapidated in appearance. **2.** wearing worn and dirty clothes. **3.** mean or unworthy: *shabby treatment.* **4.** dirty or squalid. [C17: from OE *sceabb* scab] —ˈ**shabbily** *adv.* —ˈ**shabbiness** *n.*

Shache (ˈʃæˈtʃeɪ), Soche, *or* **So-ch'e** *n.* a town in W China, in the W Xinjiang Uygur AR: a centre of the caravan trade between China, India, and Transcaspian Soviet areas. Also called: **Yarkand.**

shack (ʃæk) *n.* **1.** a roughly built hut. ~*vb.* **2.** See **shack up.** [C19: ?from dialect *shackly* ramshackle, from dialect *shack* to shake]

shackle (ˈʃækəl) *n.* **1.** (*often pl.*) a metal ring or fastening, usually part of a pair used to secure a person's wrists or ankles. **2.** (*often pl.*) anything that confines or restricts freedom. **3.** a U-shaped bracket, the open end of which is closed by a bolt (**shackle pin**), used for securing ropes, chains, etc. ~*vb.* (*tr.*) **4.** to confine with or as if with shackles. **5.** to fasten or connect with a shackle. [OE *sceacel*] —ˈ**shackler** *n.*

Shackleton (ˈʃækəltən) *n.* Sir **Ernest Henry.** 1874–1922, British explorer. He commanded three expeditions to the Antarctic (1907–09; 1914–17; 1921–22), during which the south magnetic pole was located (1909).

shack up *vb.* (*intr., adv.;* usually foll. by *with*) *Sl.* to live, esp. with a lover.

shad (ʃæd) *n., pl.* **shad** *or* **shads.** any of various herring-like food fishes that migrate from the sea to fresh water to spawn. [OE *sceadd*]

Shadbolt (ˈʃæd͵bəʊlt) *n.* **Maurice.** born 1932, New Zealand novelist.

shaddock (ˈʃædək) *n.* another name for **pomelo** (sense 1). [C17: after Captain *Shaddock*, who brought its seed from the East Indies to Jamaica in 1696]

shade (ʃeɪd) *n.* **1.** relative darkness produced by the blocking out of light. **2.** a place made relatively darker or cooler than other areas by the blocking of light, esp. sunlight. **3.** a position of relative obscurity. **4.** something used to provide a shield or protection from a direct source of light, such as a lampshade. **5.** a darker area indicated in a painting, drawing, etc., by shading. **6.** a colour that varies slightly from a standard colour: *a darker shade of green.* **7.** a slight amount: *a shade of difference.* **8.** *Literary.* a ghost. ~*vb.* (*mainly tr.*) **9.** to screen or protect from heat, light, view, etc. **10.** to make darker or dimmer. **11.** to represent (a darker area) in (a painting, etc.), by means of hatching, etc. **12.** (*also intr.*) to change or cause to change slightly. **13.** to lower (a price) slightly. [OE *sceadu*] —ˈ**shadeless** *adj.*

shades (ʃeɪdz) *pl. n.* **1.** gathering darkness at nightfall. **2.** *Sl.* sunglasses. **3.** (*often cap.;* preceded by *the*) a literary term for **Hades. 4.** (foll. by *of*) undertones: *shades of my father!*

shading (ˈʃeɪdɪŋ) *n.* the graded areas of tone, lines, dots, etc., indicating light and dark in a painting or drawing.

shadoof (ʃəˈduːf) *n.* a mechanism for raising water, consisting of a pivoted pole with a bucket at one end and a counterweight at the other, esp. as used in Egypt. [C19: from Egyptian Ar.]

shadow (ˈʃædəʊ) *n.* **1.** a dark image or shape cast on a surface by the interception of light rays by an opaque body. **2.** an area of relative darkness. **3.** the dark portions of a picture. **4.** a hint or faint semblance: *beyond a shadow of a doubt.* **5.** a remnant or vestige: *a shadow of one's past self.* **6.** a reflection. **7.** a threatening influence: *a shadow over one's happiness.* **8.** a spectre. **9.** an inseparable companion. **10.** a person who trails another in secret, such as a detective. **11.** *Med.* a dark area on an x-ray film representing an opaque structure or part. **12.**

Arch. shelter. **13.** (*modifier*) *Brit.* designating a member or members of the main opposition party in Parliament who would hold ministerial office if their party were in power: *shadow cabinet.* ~*vb.* (*tr.*) **14.** to cast a shadow over. **15.** to make dark or gloomy. **16.** to shade from light. **17.** to follow or trail secretly. **18.** (often foll. by *forth*) to represent vaguely. [OE *sceadwe*, oblique case of *sceadu* shade] —ˈ**shadower** *n.*

shadow-box *vb.* (*intr.*) *Boxing.* to practise blows and footwork against an imaginary opponent. —ˈ**shadow͵boxing** *n.*

shadowgraph (ˈʃædəʊ͵grɑːf) *n.* **1.** a silhouette made by casting a shadow on a lighted surface. **2.** another name for **radiograph.**

shadow play *n.* a theatrical entertainment using shadows thrown by puppets or actors onto a lighted screen.

shadowy (ˈʃædəʊɪ) *adj.* **1.** dark; shady. **2.** resembling a shadow in faintness. **3.** illusory or imaginary. —ˈ**shadowiness** *n.*

Shadrach (ˈʃædræk, ˈʃeɪ-) *n. Old Testament.* one of Daniel's three companions, who, together with Meshach and Abednego, was miraculously saved from destruction in Nebuchadnezzar's fiery furnace (Daniel 3:12–30).

Shadwell (ˈʃædwəl) *n.* **Thomas.** ?1642–92, English dramatist; poet laureate (1688–92). He was satirized by Dryden.

shady (ˈʃeɪdɪ) *adj.* **shadier, shadiest. 1.** shaded. **2.** affording or casting a shade. **3.** quiet or concealed. **4.** *Inf.* questionable as to honesty or legality. —ˈ**shadily** *adv.* —ˈ**shadiness** *n.*

SHAEF (ʃeɪf) *n.* acronym for Supreme Headquarters Allied Expeditionary Forces.

Shaffer (ˈʃæfə) *n.* **Peter.** born 1926, British dramatist. His plays include *The Royal Hunt of the Sun* (1964), *Equus* (1973), and *Amadeus* (1979).

shaft (ʃɑːft) *n.* **1.** the long narrow pole that forms the body of a spear, arrow, etc. **2.** something directed at a person in the manner of a missile. **3.** a ray or streak, esp. of light. **4.** a rod or pole forming the handle of a hammer, golf club, etc. **5.** a revolving rod that transmits motion or power. **6.** one of the two wooden poles by which an animal is harnessed to a vehicle. **7.** *Anat.* the middle part of a long bone. **8.** the middle part of a column or pier, between the base and the capital. **9.** *Archit.* a column that supports a vaulting rib, sometimes one of a set. **10.** a vertical passageway through a building, as for a lift. **11.** a vertical passageway into a mine. **12.** *Ornithol.* the central rib of a feather. **13.** an archaic or literary word for **arrow.** ~*vb.* **14.** *U.S. & Canad. sl.* to trick or cheat. [OE *sceaft*]

Shaftesbury (ˈʃɑːftsbərɪ, -brɪ) *n.* **1. 1st Earl of,** title of *Anthony Ashley Cooper.* 1621–83, English statesman; a major figure in the Whig opposition to Charles II. **2. 7th Earl of,** title of *Anthony Ashley Cooper.* 1801–85, English evangelical churchman and social reformer. He promoted measures to improve conditions in mines (1842), factories (1833; 1847; 1850), and schools.

shag[1] (ʃæg) *n.* **1.** a matted tangle, esp. of hair, etc. **2.** a napped fabric, usually a rough wool. **3.** shredded coarse tobacco. [OE *sceacga*]

shag[2] (ʃæg) *n.* another name for **cormorant,** esp. (in Britain) the **green cormorant.** [C16: special use of SHAG[1], with reference to its crest]

shag[3] (ʃæg) *Brit. sl.* ~*vb.* **shagging, shagged. 1.** *Taboo.* to have sexual intercourse with (a person). **2.** (*tr.;* often foll. by *out; usually passive*) to exhaust. ~*n.* **3.** *Taboo.* an act of sexual intercourse. [C20: from ?]

shaggy (ˈʃægɪ) *adj.* **-gier, -giest. 1.** having or covered with rough unkempt fur, hair, wool, etc.: *a shaggy dog.* **2.** rough or unkempt. —ˈ**shaggily** *adv.* —ˈ**shagginess** *n.*

shaggy dog story *n. Inf.* a long rambling joke ending in a deliberate anticlimax, such as a pointless punch line.

shagreen (ʃæˈgriːn) *n.* **1.** the rough skin of certain sharks and rays, used as an abrasive. **2.** a rough grainy leather made from certain animal hides. [C17: from F *chagrin,* from Turkish *çagri* rump]

shah (ʃɑː) *n.* a ruler of certain Middle Eastern countries, esp. (formerly) Iran. [C16: from Persian: king] —ˈ**shahdom** *n.*

Shah Jahan (dʒɑˈhɑːn) *n.* 1592–1666, Mogul emperor (1628–58). During his reign the finest monuments of Mogul architecture in India were built, including the Taj Mahal and the Pearl Mosque at Agra.

Shahjahanpur (ˌʃɑːdʒəˌhɑːnˈpʊə) *n.* a city in N India, in central Uttar Pradesh: founded in 1647 in the reign of Shah Jahan. Pop.: 187 934 (1981).

Shaka *or* **Chaka** (ˈʃaka) *n.* died 1828, Zulu military leader, who founded the Zulu Empire in southern Africa.

shake (ʃeɪk) *vb.* **shaking, shook, shaken. 1.** to move or cause to move up and down or back and forth with short quick movements. **2.** to sway or totter or cause to sway or totter. **3.** to clasp or grasp (the hand) of (a person) in greeting, agreement, etc.: *he shook John's hand.* **4. shake hands.** to clasp hands in greeting, agreement, etc. **5. shake on it.** *Inf.* to shake hands in agreement, reconciliation, etc. **6.** to bring or come to a specified condition by or as if by shaking: *he shook free and ran.* **7.** (*tr.*) to wave or brandish: *he shook his sword.* **8.** (*tr.*; often foll. by *up*) to rouse or agitate. **9.** (*tr.*) to shock, disturb, or upset: *he was shaken by the news.* **10.** (*tr.*) to undermine or weaken: *the crisis shook his faith.* **11.** to mix (dice) by rattling in a cup or the hand before throwing. **12.** *Austral. sl.* to steal. **13.** (*tr.*) *U.S. & Canad. inf.* to get rid of. **14.** *Music.* to perform a trill on (a note). **15. shake in one's shoes.** to tremble with fear or apprehension. **16. shake one's head.** to indicate disagreement or disapproval by moving the head from side to side. ~*n.* **17.** the act or an instance of shaking. **18.** a tremor or vibration. **19. the shakes.** a state of uncontrollable trembling or a condition that causes it, such as a fever. **20.** *Inf.* a very short period of time: *in half a shake.* **21.** a fissure or crack in timber or rock. **22.** an instance of shaking dice before casting. **23.** *Music.* another word for **trill¹** (sense 1). **24.** an informal name for **earthquake. 25.** short for **milk shake. 26. no great shakes.** *Inf.* of no great merit or value. ~See also **shake down, shake off, shake up.** [OE *sceacan*] —ˈshakable *or* ˈshakeable *adj.*

shake down *vb.* (*adv.*) **1.** to fall or settle or cause to fall or settle by shaking. **2.** (*tr.*) *U.S. sl.* to extort money from, esp. by blackmail. **3.** (*tr.*) *Inf.*, *chiefly U.S.* to submit (a vessel, etc.) to a shakedown test. **4.** (*intr.*) to go to bed, esp. to a makeshift bed. ~*n.* **shakedown. 5.** *U.S. sl.* a swindle or act of extortion. **6.** a makeshift bed, esp. of straw, blankets, etc. **7.** *Inf.*, *chiefly U.S.* **a.** a voyage to test the performance of a ship or aircraft or to familiarize the crew with their duties. **b.** (*as modifier*): *a shakedown run.*

shake off *vb.* (*adv.*) **1.** to remove or be removed with or as if with a quick movement: *she shook off her depression.* **2.** (*tr.*) to escape from; elude: *they shook off the police.*

shaker (ˈʃeɪkə) *n.* **1.** a person or thing that shakes. **2.** a container from which a condiment is shaken. **3.** a container in which the ingredients of alcoholic drinks are shaken together.

Shakers (ˈʃeɪkəz) *pl. n.* **the.** an American millenarian sect, founded in 1747 as an offshoot of the Quakers, given to ecstatic shaking and practising common ownership of property.

Shakespeare (ˈʃeɪkspɪə) *n.* **William.** 1564–1616, English dramatist and poet. He was born and died at Stratford-upon-Avon but spent most of his life as an actor and playwright in London. His plays with approximate dates of composition are: *Henry VI, Parts I–III* (1590); *Richard III* (1592); *The Comedy of Errors* (1592); *Titus Andronicus* (1593); *The Taming of the Shrew* (1593); *The Two Gentlemen of Verona* (1594); *Love's Labour's Lost* (1594); *Romeo and Juliet* (1594); *Richard II* (1595); *A Midsummer Night's Dream* (1595); *King John* (1595); *The Merchant of Venice* (1596); *Henry IV, Parts I–II* (1597); *Much Ado about Nothing* (1598); *Henry V* (1598); *Julius Caesar* (1599); *As You Like It* (1599); *Twelfth Night* (1599); *Hamlet* (1600); *The Merry Wives of Windsor* (1600); *Troilus and Cressida* (1601); *All's Well that ends Well* (1602); *Measure for Measure* (1604); *Othello* (1604); *King Lear* (1605); *Macbeth* (1605); *Antony and Cleopatra* (1606); *Coriolanus* (1607); *Timon of Athens* (1607); *Pericles* (1608); *Cymbeline* (1609); *The Winter's Tale* (1610); *The Tempest* (1611); and, possibly in collaboration with John Fletcher, *Two Noble Kinsmen* (1612) and *Henry VIII* (1612). His *Sonnets*, variously addressed to a fair young man and a dark lady, were published in 1609.

Shakespearean *or* **Shakespearian** (ʃeɪkˈspɪərɪən) *adj.* **1.** of, relating to, or characteristic of Shakespeare or his works. ~*n.* **2.** a student of or specialist in Shakespeare's works.

Shakespearean sonnet *n.* a sonnet form developed in 16th-century England and employed by Shakespeare, having the rhyme scheme a b a b c d c d e f e f g g.

shake up *vb.* (*tr.*, *adv.*) **1.** to shake in order to mix. **2.** to reorganize drastically. **3.** to stir. **4.** to restore the shape of (a pillow, etc.). **5.** *Inf.* to shock mentally or physically. ~*n.* **shake-up. 6.** *Inf.* a radical reorganization.

Shakhty (*Russian* ˈʃaxtɪ) *n.* an industrial city in the SW Soviet Union, in Rostov Region: the chief town of the E Donets Basin. Pop.: 225 000 (1987).

shako (ˈʃækəʊ) *n.*, *pl.* **shakos** *or* **shakoes.** a tall usually cylindrical military headdress, having a plume and often a peak. [C19: via F from Hungarian *csákó*, from MHG *zacke* a sharp point]

shaky (ˈʃeɪkɪ) *adj.* **shakier, shakiest. 1.** tending to shake or tremble. **2.** liable to prove defective. **3.** uncertain or questionable: *your arguments are very shaky.* —ˈshakily *adv.* —ˈshakiness *n.*

shale (ʃeɪl) *n.* a dark fine-grained sedimentary rock formed by compression of successive layers of clay. [OE *scealu* shell] —ˈshaly *adj.*

shale oil *n.* an oil distilled from shales and used as fuel.

shall (ʃæl; *unstressed* ʃəl) *vb. past* **should.** (takes an infinitive without *to* or an implied infinitive) used as an auxiliary: **1.** (esp. with *I* or *we* as subject) to make the future tense: *we shall see you tomorrow.* Cf. **will¹** (sense 1). **2.** (with *you, he, she, it, they,* or a noun as subject) **a.** to indicate determination on the part of the speaker, as in issuing a threat: *you shall pay for this!* **b.** to indicate compulsion, now esp. in official documents. **c.** to indicate certainty or inevitability: *our day shall come.* **3.** (*with any noun or pronoun as subject, esp. in conditional clauses or clauses expressing doubt*) to indicate nonspecific futurity: *I don't think I shall ever see her again.* [OE *sceal*]

▷ **Usage.** The usual rule given for the use of *shall* and *will* is that where the meaning is one of simple futurity, *shall* is used for the first person of the verb and *will* for the second and third: *I shall go tomorrow; they will be there now.* Where the meaning involves command, obligation, or determination, the positions are reversed: *it shall be done; I will definitely go.* However, *shall* has come to be largely neglected in favour of *will.*

shallop (ˈʃæləp) *n.* a light boat used for rowing in shallow water. [C16: from F *chaloupe*, from Du. *sloep* sloop]

shallot (ʃəˈlɒt) *n.* **1.** an alliaceous plant cultivated for its edible bulb. **2.** the bulb of this plant, which divides into small sections and is used in cooking for flavouring. [C17: from OF, from *eschaloigne*, from L *Ascalōnia caepa* Ascalonian onion, from *Ascalon*, a Palestinian town]

shallow (ˈʃæləʊ) *adj.* **1.** having little depth. **2.** lacking intellectual or mental depth or subtlety. ~*n.* **3.** (*often pl.*) a shallow place in a body of water. ~*vb.* **4.** to make or become shallow. [C15: rel. to OE *sceald* shallow] —ˈshallowly *adv.* —ˈshallowness *n.*

shalom aleichem *Hebrew.* (ʃaˈlɔm aˈlexɛm) *sentence substitute.* peace be to you: used by Jews as a greeting or farewell. Often shortened to **shalom.**

shalt (ʃælt) *vb. Arch. or dialect.* (used with the pronoun *thou*) a singular form of the present tense (indicative mood) of **shall.**

sham (ʃæm) *n.* **1.** anything that is not what it appears to be. **2.** something false or fictitious that purports to be genuine. **3.** a person who pretends to be something other than he is. ~*adj.* **4.** counterfeit or false. ~*vb.* **shamming, shammed. 5.** to assume the appearance of (something); counterfeit: *to sham illness.* [C17: ? a N English dialect var. of SHAME]

shaman (ˈʃæmən) *n.* **1.** a priest of shamanism. **2.** a medicine man of a similar religion, esp. among certain tribes of North American Indians. [C17: from Russian *shaman*, ult. from Sansk. *śrama* religious exercise]

shamanism (ˈʃæməˌnɪzəm) *n.* **1.** the religion of certain peoples of northern Asia, based on the belief that the world is pervaded by good and evil spirits who can be influenced or controlled only by the shamans. **2.** any similar religion involving forms of spiritualism. —ˈshamanist *n., adj.*

Shamash (ˈʃɑːmæʃ) *n.* the sun god of Assyria ˙and Babylonia. [from Akkadian: sun]

shamateur (ˈʃæmətə) *n.* a sportsperson who is officially an amateur but accepts payment. [C20: from *sham* + *amateur*]

shamble ('ʃæmbəl) *vb.* **1.** (*intr.*) to walk or move along in an awkward or unsteady way. ~*n.* **2.** an awkward or unsteady walk. [C17: from *shamble* (adj.) ungainly, ?from *shamble legs* legs resembling those of a meat vendor's table; see SHAMBLES] —'**shambling** *adj.*, *n.*

shambles ('ʃæmbəlz) *n.* (*functioning as sing. or pl.*) **1.** a place of great disorder: *the room was a shambles after the party.* **2.** a place where animals are brought to be slaughtered. **3.** any place of slaughter or execution. [C14 *shamble* table used by meat vendors, from OE *sceamel* stool, from LL *scamellum* a small bench, from L *scamnum* stool]

shambolic (ʃæm'bɒlɪk) *adj. Inf.* completely disorganized; chaotic. [C20: from SHAMBLES]

shame (ʃeɪm) *n.* **1.** a painful emotion resulting from an awareness of having done something dishonourable, unworthy, etc. **2.** capacity to feel such an emotion. **3.** ignominy or disgrace. **4.** a person or thing that causes this. **5.** an occasion for regret, disappointment, etc.: *it's a shame you can't come with us.* **6. put to shame. a.** to disgrace. **b.** to surpass totally. ~*vb.* (*tr.*) **7.** to cause to feel shame. **8.** to bring shame on. **9.** (often foll. by *into*) to compel through a sense of shame. ~*interj.* **10.** *S. African sl.* a general exclamation of delight, sympathy, etc. [OE *scamu*] —'**shamable** *or* '**shameable** *adj.*

shamefaced ('ʃeɪm,feɪst) *adj.* **1.** bashful or modest. **2.** showing a sense of shame. [C16: alteration of earlier *shamefast*, from OE *sceamfaest*] —**shamefacedly** (ʃeɪm'feɪsɪdlɪ) *adv.*

shameful ('ʃeɪmfʊl) *adj.* causing or deserving shame. —'**shamefully** *adv.* —'**shamefulness** *n.*

shameless ('ʃeɪmlɪs) *adj.* **1.** having no sense of shame. **2.** without decency or modesty. —'**shamelessly** *adv.* —'**shamelessness** *n.*

Shamir (ʃæ'mɪə) *n.* **Yitzhak** ('jɪtʒæk). born 1915, Israeli statesman, born in Poland: prime minister (1983–84) and from 1986.

shammy ('ʃæmɪ) *n.*, *pl.* -**mies.** *Inf.* another word for **chamois** (sense 3). Also called: **shammy leather.** [C18: variant of CHAMOIS]

Shamo (ʃɑ:'məʊ) *n.* transliteration of the Chinese name for the **Gobi.**

shampoo (ʃæm'pu:) *n.* **1.** a preparation of soap or detergent to wash the hair. **2.** a similar preparation for washing carpets, etc. **3.** the process of shampooing. ~*vb.* -**pooing, -pooed.** (*tr.*) **4.** to wash (the hair, etc.) with such a preparation. [C18: from Hindi, from *chāmpnā* to knead]

shamrock ('ʃæm,rɒk) *n.* a plant having leaves divided into three leaflets: the national emblem of Ireland. [C16: from Irish Gaelic *seamróg*, dim. of *seamar* clover]

shamus ('ʃɑ:məs, 'ʃeɪ-) *n.*, *pl.* -**muses.** *U.S. sl.* a police or private detective. [prob. from *shammes* caretaker of a synagogue, infl. by Irish *Séamas* James]

Shandong ('ʃæn'dʌŋ) *or* **Shantung** *n.* a province of NE China, on the Yellow Sea and the Gulf of Chihli: part of the earliest organized state of China (1520–1030 B.C.); consists chiefly of the fertile plain of the lower Yellow River, with mountains over 1500 m (5000 ft.) high in the centre. Capital: Jinan. Pop.: 76 370 000 (1982). Area: 153 300 sq. km (59 189 sq. miles).

shandy ('ʃændɪ) *n.*, *pl.* -**dies.** an alcoholic drink made of beer and ginger beer or lemonade. [C19: from ?]

Shang (ʃæŋ) *n.* **1.** the dynasty ruling in China from about the 18th to the 12th centuries B.C. ~*adj.* **2.** of or relating to the pottery produced during the Shang dynasty.

shanghai ('ʃænhaɪ, ʃæŋ'haɪ) *Sl.* ~*vb.* -**haiing, -haied.** (*tr.*) **1.** to kidnap (a man or seaman) for enforced service at sea. **2.** to force or trick (someone) into doing something, etc. **3.** *Austral. & N.Z.* to shoot with a catapult. ~*n.* **4.** *Austral. & N.Z.* a catapult. [C19: from the city of SHANGHAI; from the forceful methods formerly used to collect crews for voyages to the Orient]

Shanghai ('ʃæŋ'haɪ) *n.* a port in E China, in SE Jiangsu near the estuary of the Yangtze: the largest city in China and one of the largest ports in the world; a major cultural and industrial centre, with two universities. Pop.: 6 980 000 (1986).

Shangri-la (,ʃæŋgrɪ'lɑ:) *n.* a remote or imaginary utopia. [C20: from the name of an imaginary valley in the Himalayas, from *Lost Horizon* (1933), a novel by James Hilton]

shank (ʃæŋk) *n.* **1.** *Anat.* the shin. **2.** the corresponding part of the leg in vertebrates other than man. **3.** a cut of meat from the top part of an animal's shank. **4.** the main part of a tool, between the working part and the handle. **5.** the part of a bolt between the thread and the head. **6.** the ring or stem on the back of some buttons. **7.** the stem or long narrow part of a key, hook, spoon handle, nail, etc. **8.** the band of a ring as distinguished from the setting. **9.** the part of a shoe connecting the wide part of the sole with the heel. **10.** *Printing.* the body of a piece of type. ~*vb.* **11.** (*intr.*) (of fruits, roots, etc.) to show disease symptoms, esp. discoloration. **12.** (*tr.*) *Golf.* to mishit (the ball) with the foot of the shaft. [OE *scanca*]

Shankar ('ʃænkɑ:) *n.* **Ravi** ('rɑ:vi:). born 1920, Indian sitarist.

Shankaracharya (,ʃʌnkərɑ:'tʃɑ:rjə) *or* **Shankara** ('ʃʌnkərə) *n.* 9th century A.D., Hindu philosopher and teacher; chief exponent of Vedanta philosophy.

shanks's pony *or U.S.* **shanks's mare** ('ʃæŋksɪz) *n. Inf.* one's own legs as a means of transportation.

Shannon[1] ('ʃænən) *n.* a river in the Republic of Ireland, rising in NW Co. Cavan and flowing south to the Atlantic by an estuary 113 km (70 miles) long: the longest river in the Republic of Ireland. Length: 260 km (161 miles).

Shannon[2] ('ʃænən) *n.* **Claude (Elwood).** born 1916, U.S. mathematician, who was responsible for the development of information theory.

shanny ('ʃænɪ) *n.*, *pl.* -**nies.** a European blenny of rocky coastal waters. [C19: from ?]

Shansi ('ʃæn'si:) *n.* a variant transliteration of the Chinese name for **Shanxi.**

Shan State (ʃɑ:n, ʃæn) *n.* an administrative division of E Burma: formed in 1947 from the joining of the Federation of Shan States with the Wa States; consists of the **Shan plateau,** crossed by forested mountain ranges reaching over 2100 m (7000 ft.). Pop.: 3 718 706 (1983). Area: 149 743 sq. km (57 816 sq. miles).

shan't (ʃɑ:nt) *contraction of* shall not.

Shantou *or* **Shantow** ('ʃæn'taʊ) *n.* a port in SE China, in E Guangdong near the mouth of the Han River: became a treaty port in 1869. Pop.: 476 600 (1985 est.). Also called: **Swatow.**

shantung (,ʃæn'tʌŋ) *n.* **1.** a heavy silk fabric with a knobbly surface. **2.** a cotton or rayon imitation of this. [C19: after SHANTUNG]

Shantung ('ʃæn'tʌŋ) *n.* a variant transliteration of the Chinese name for **Shandong.**

shanty[1] ('ʃæntɪ) *n.*, *pl.* -**ties.** **1.** a ramshackle hut; crude dwelling. **2.** *Austral. & N.Z.* a public house, esp. an unlicensed one. [C19: from Canad. F *chantier* cabin built in a lumber camp, from OF *gantier* GANTRY]

shanty[2] ('ʃæntɪ) *or* **chanty** *n.*, *pl.* -**ties.** a song originally sung by sailors, esp. a rhythmical one forming an accompaniment to work. [C19: from F *chanter* to sing; see CHANT]

shantytown ('ʃæntɪ,taʊn) *n.* a town or section of a town or city inhabited by very poor people living in shanties.

Shanxi *or* **Shansi** ('ʃæn'ʃi:) *n.* a province of N China: China's richest coal reserves and much heavy industry. Capital: Taiyuan. Pop.: 25 291 389 (1982). Area: 157 099 sq. km (60 656 sq. miles).

shape (ʃeɪp) *n.* **1.** the outward form of an object defined by outline. **2.** the figure or outline of the body of a person. **3.** a phantom. **4.** organized or definite form: *my plans are taking shape.* **5.** the form that anything assumes. **6.** pattern; mould. **7.** condition or state of efficiency: *to be in good shape.* **8. out of shape. a.** in bad physical condition. **b.** bent, twisted, or deformed. **9. take shape.** to assume a definite form. ~*vb.* **10.** (when *intr.,* often foll. by *into* or *up*) to receive or cause to receive shape or form. **11.** (*tr.*) to mould into a particular pattern or form. **12.** (*tr.*) to plan, devise, or prepare: *to shape a plan of action.* ~See also **shape up.** [OE *gesceap,* lit.: that which is created, from *scieppan* to create] —'**shapable** *or* '**shapeable** *adj.* —'**shaper** *n.*

SHAPE (ʃeɪp) *n. acronym for* Supreme Headquarters Allied Powers Europe.

-**shaped** (ʃeɪpt) *adj. combining form.* having the shape of: *an L-shaped room;* or *pear-shaped figure.*

shapeless ('ʃeɪplɪs) *adj.* **1.** having no definite shape or form: *a shapeless mass.* **2.** lacking a symmetrical or aesthetically pleasing shape: *a shapeless figure.* —'**shapelessness** *n.*

shapely ('ʃeɪplɪ) *adj.* **-lier, -liest.** (esp. of a woman's body or legs) pleasing or attractive in shape. —'**shapeliness** *n.*

shape up *vb.* (*intr., adv.*) *Inf.* **1.** to proceed or develop satisfactorily. **2.** to develop a definite or proper form.

shard (ʃɑːd) *or* **sherd** *n.* **1.** a broken piece or fragment of a brittle substance, esp. of pottery. **2.** *Zool.* a tough sheath, scale, or shell, esp. the elytra of a beetle. [OE *sceard*]

share[1] (ʃɛə) *n.* **1.** a part or portion of something owned or contributed by a person or group. **2.** (*often pl.*) any of the equal parts, usually of low par value, into which the capital stock of a company is divided. **3. go shares.** *Inf.* to share (something) with another or others. ~*vb.* **4.** (*tr.; often foll. by out*) to divide or apportion, esp. equally. **5.** (when *intr.,* often foll. by *in*) to receive or contribute a portion of: *we can share the cost of the petrol.* **6.** to join with another or others in the use of (something): *can I share your umbrella?* [OE *scearu*] —'**sharable** *or* '**shareable** *adj.* —'**sharer** *n.*

share[2] (ʃɛə) *n.* short for **ploughshare.** [OE *scear*]

sharecrop ('ʃɛə,krɒp) *vb.* **-cropping, -cropped.** *Chiefly U.S.* to cultivate (farmland) as a sharecropper.

sharecropper ('ʃɛə,krɒpə) *n. Chiefly U.S.* a farmer, esp. a tenant farmer, who pays over a proportion of a crop or crops as rent.

shared ownership *n.* (in Britain) a form of house purchase whereby the purchaser buys a proportion of the dwelling, usually from a local authority or housing association, and rents the rest.

share-farmer *n. Chiefly Austral.* a farmer who pays a fee to another in return for use of land to raise crops, etc.

shareholder ('ʃɛə,həʊldə) *n.* the owner of one or more shares in a company.

share-milker *n.* (in New Zealand) a person who lives on a dairy farm and milks the farmer's herd in return for an agreed share of the profits.

share option *n.* a scheme whereby employees may take out an option to buy, at a favourable price, shares in the company they work for.

share premium *n. Brit.* the excess of the amount actually subscribed for an issue of corporate capital over its par value.

share shop *n.* a high-street shop or a department within a store that is run by a stockbroking firm, where the public can buy and sell shares quickly, with little formality and no investment advice.

Shari ('ʃɑːrɪ) *n.* a variant spelling of **Chari** (the river).

sharia *or* **sheria** (ʃə'riːə) *n.* the body of doctrines that regulate the lives of those who profess Islam. [Ar.]

shark[1] (ʃɑːk) *n.* any of various usually ferocious fishes, with a long body, two dorsal fins, and rows of sharp teeth. [C16: from ?] —'**shark,like** *adj.*

shark[2] (ʃɑːk) *n.* a person who preys on or victimizes others, esp. by swindling or extortion. [C18: prob. from G *Schurke* rogue]

sharkskin ('ʃɑːk,skɪn) *n.* a smooth glossy fabric of acetate rayon, used for sportswear, etc.

Sharon ('ʃærən) *n.* **Plain of.** a plain in W Israel, between the Mediterranean and the hills of Samaria, extending from Haifa to Tel Aviv.

sharp (ʃɑːp) *adj.* **1.** having a keen edge suitable for cutting. **2.** having an edge or point. **3.** involving a sudden change, esp. in direction: *a sharp bend.* **4.** moving, acting, or reacting quickly, etc.: *sharp reflexes.* **5.** clearly defined. **6.** mentally acute; keen-witted; attentive. **7.** sly or artful: *sharp practice.* **8.** bitter or harsh: *sharp words.* **9.** shrill or penetrating: *a sharp cry.* **10.** having an acrid taste. **11.** keen; biting: *a sharp wind.* **12.** *Music.* **a.** (*immediately postpositive*) denoting a note that has been raised in pitch by one chromatic semitone: *B sharp.* **b.** (of an instrument, voice, etc.) out of tune by being too high in pitch. Cf. **flat**[1] (sense 19). **13.** *Inf.* **a.** stylish. **b.** too smart. **14. at the sharp end.** involved in the most competitive or difficult aspect of any activity. ~*adv.* **15.** in a sharp manner. **16.** exactly: *six o'clock sharp.* **17.** *Music.* **a.** higher than a standard pitch. **b.** out of tune by being too high in pitch: *she sings sharp.* Cf. **flat**[1] (sense 24). ~*n.* **18.** *Music.* **a.** an accidental that raises the pitch of a note by one chromatic semitone. Usual symbol: ♯ **b.** a note affected by this accidental. Cf. **flat**[1] (sense 30). **19.** a thin needle with a sharp point. **20.** *Inf.* a sharper. ~*vb.*

21. (*tr.*) *Music.* the usual U.S. and Canad. word for **sharpen.** [OE *scearp*] —'**sharply** *adv.* —'**sharpness** *n.*

sharpen ('ʃɑːpən) *vb.* **1.** to make or become sharp or sharper. **2.** *Music.* to raise the pitch of (a note), esp. by one semitone. —'**sharpener** *n.*

sharper ('ʃɑːpə) *n.* a person who cheats or swindles; fraud.

sharpish ('ʃɑːpɪʃ) *adj.* **1.** rather sharp. ~*adv.* **2.** *Inf.* quickly; fairly sharply: *quick sharpish.*

sharp-set *adj.* **1.** set to give an acute cutting angle. **2.** keenly hungry. **3.** keen or eager.

sharpshooter ('ʃɑːp,ʃuːtə) *n.* an expert marksman. —'**sharp,shooting** *n.*

sharp-tongued *adj.* bitter or critical in speech; sarcastic.

sharp-witted *adj.* having or showing a keen intelligence; perceptive. —,**sharp-'wittedly** *adv.* —,**sharp-'wittedness** *n.*

Shasta daisy ('ʃæstə) *n.* a plant widely cultivated for its large white daisy-like flowers.

shastra ('ʃɑːstrə), **shaster** ('ʃɑːstə), *or* **sastra** ('ʃɑːstrə) *n.* any of the sacred writings of Hinduism. [C17: from Sansk. *śāstra,* from *śās* to teach]

Shatt-al-Arab ('ʃætæl'ærəb) *n.* a river in SE Iraq, formed by the confluence of the Tigris and Euphrates Rivers; flows southeast as part of the border between Iraq and Iran to the Persian Gulf. Length: 193 km (120 miles).

shatter ('ʃætə) *vb.* **1.** to break or be broken into many small pieces. **2.** (*tr.*) to impair or destroy: *his nerves were shattered by the torture.* **3.** (*tr.*) to dumbfound or thoroughly upset: *she was shattered by the news.* **4.** (*tr.*) *Inf.* to cause to be tired out or exhausted. [C12: ? obscurely rel. to SCATTER] —'**shattered** *adj.* —'**shattering** *adj.* —'**shatteringly** *adv.*

shatterproof ('ʃætə,pruːf) *adj.* designed to resist shattering.

shave (ʃeɪv) *vb.* **shaving, shaved; shaved** *or* **shaven.** (*mainly tr.*) **1.** (*also intr.*) to remove (the beard, hair, etc.) from (the face, head, or body) by scraping the skin with a razor. **2.** to cut or trim very closely. **3.** to reduce to shavings. **4.** to remove thin slices from (wood, etc.) with a sharp cutting tool. **5.** to touch or graze in passing. **6.** *Inf.* to reduce (a price) by a slight amount. ~*n.* **7.** the act or an instance of shaving. **8.** any tool for scraping. **9.** a thin slice or shaving. [OE *sceafan*] —'**shavable** *or* '**shaveable** *adj.*

shaveling ('ʃeɪvlɪŋ) *n. Arch.* **1.** *Derog.* a priest or clergyman with a shaven head. **2.** a young fellow; youth.

shaven ('ʃeɪvən) *adj.* **a.** closely shaved or tonsured. **b.** (*in combination*): *clean-shaven.*

shaver ('ʃeɪvə) *n.* **1.** a person or thing that shaves. **2.** Also called: **electric razor, electric shaver.** an electrically powered implement for shaving, having rotating blades behind a fine metal comb. **3.** *Inf.* a youngster, esp. a young boy.

Shavian ('ʃeɪvɪən) *adj.* **1.** of or like George Bernard Shaw (1856–1950), Irish dramatist, his works, ideas, etc. ~*n.* **2.** an admirer of Shaw or his works.

shaving ('ʃeɪvɪŋ) *n.* **1.** a thin paring or slice, esp. of wood, that has been shaved from something. ~*modifier.* **2.** used when shaving the face, etc.: *shaving cream.*

Shaw (ʃɔː) *n.* **1. George Bernard,** often known as *GBS.* 1856–1950, Irish dramatist and critic, in England from 1876. He was an active socialist and became a member of the Fabian Society but his major works are effective as satiric attacks rather than political tracts. These include *Arms and the Man* (1894), *Candida* (1894), *Man and Superman* (1903), *Major Barbara* (1905), *Pygmalion* (1913), *Back to Methuselah* (1921), and *St. Joan* (1923): Nobel prize for literature 1925. **2. Richard Norman.** 1831–1912, English architect. **3. Thomas Edward.** the name assumed by (T. E.) **Lawrence** after 1927.

shawl (ʃɔːl) *n.* a piece of fabric or knitted or crocheted material worn around the shoulders by women or wrapped around a baby. [C17: from Persian *shāl*]

shawm (ʃɔːm) *n. Music.* a medieval form of the oboe with a conical bore and flaring bell. [C14 *shalmye,* from OF *chalemie,* ult. from L *calamus* a reed, from Gk *kalamos*]

shay (ʃeɪ) *n.* a dialect word for **chaise.** [C18: back formation from CHAISE, mistaken for pl.]

Shays (ʃeɪz) *n.* **Daniel.** ?1747–1825, American soldier and revolutionary leader of a rebellion of Massachusetts farmers against the U.S. government (1786–87).

Shcheglovsk (*Russian* ʃtʃɪg'lɔfsk) *n.* the former name (until 1932) of **Kemerovo**.

Shcherbakov (*Russian* ʃtʃɪrba'kɔf) *n.* the former name (from the Revolution until 1957) of **Andropov**.

she (ʃiː) *pron.* (*subjective*) **1.** refers to a female person or animal: *she is an actress.* **2.** refers to things personified as feminine, such as cars, ships, and nations. **3.** *Austral. & N.Z.* a pronoun often used instead of *it*, as in **she'll be right** (it will be all right). ~*n.* **4. a.** a female person or animal. **b.** (*in combination*): *she-cat.* [OE *sīe*, accusative of *sēo*, fem. demonstrative pron.]

shea (ʃɪə) *n.* **1.** a tropical African tree with oily seeds. **2. shea butter.** the white butter-like fat obtained from the seeds of this plant and used as food, etc. [C18: from W African *si*]

sheading ('ʃiːdɪŋ) *n.* any of the six subdivisions of the Isle of Man. [var. of *shedding*]

sheaf (ʃiːf) *n.*, *pl.* **sheaves. 1.** a bundle of reaped but unthreshed corn tied with one or two bonds. **2.** a bundle of objects tied together. **3.** the arrows contained in a quiver. ~*vb.* **4.** (*tr.*) to bind or tie into a sheaf. [OE *scēaf*]

shear (ʃɪə) *vb.* **shearing, sheared** *or arch., Austral., & N.Z. sometimes* **shore; sheared** *or* **shorn. 1.** (*tr.*) to remove (the fleece or hair) of (sheep, etc.) by cutting or clipping. **2.** to cut or cut through (something) with shears or a sharp instrument. **3.** *Engineering.* to cause (a part, member, etc.) to deform or fracture or (of a part, etc.) to deform or fracture as a result of excess torsion. **4.** (*tr.*, often foll. by *of*) to strip or divest: *to shear someone of his power.* **5.** (when *intr.*, foll. by *through*) to move through (something) by or as if by cutting. ~*n.* **6.** the act, process, or an instance of shearing. **7.** a shearing of a sheep or flock of sheep: *a sheep of two shears.* **8.** a form of deformation or fracture in which parallel planes in a body slide over one another. **9.** *Physics.* the deformation of a body, part, etc., expressed as the lateral displacement between two points in parallel planes divided by the distance between the planes. **10.** either one of the blades of a pair of shears, scissors, etc. ~See also **shears.** [OE *sceran*] — **'shearer** *n.*

shearling ('ʃɪəlɪŋ) *n.* **1.** a young sheep after its first shearing. **2.** the skin of such an animal.

shear pin *n.* an easily replaceable pin in a machine designed to break and stop the machine if the stress becomes too great.

shears (ʃɪəz) *pl. n.* **1. a.** large scissors, as for cutting cloth, jointing poultry, etc. **b.** a large scissor-like and usually hand-held cutting tool with flat blades, as for cutting hedges. **2.** any of various analogous cutting implements.

shearwater ('ʃɪə,wɔːtə) *n.* any of several oceanic birds specialized for an aerial or aquatic existence.

sheatfish ('ʃiːt,fɪʃ) *n.*, *pl.* **-fish** *or* **-fishes.** another name for **European catfish** (see **silurid** (sense 1)). [C16: var. of *sheathfish;* ? infl. by G *Schaid* sheatfish]

sheath (ʃiːθ) *n.*, *pl.* **sheaths** (ʃiːðz). **1.** a case or covering for the blade of a knife, sword, etc. **2.** any similar close-fitting case. **3.** *Biol.* an enclosing or protective structure. **4.** the protective covering on an electric cable. **5.** a figure-hugging dress with a narrow tapering skirt. **6.** another name for **condom**. [OE *scēath*]

sheathe (ʃiːð) *vb.* (*tr.*) **1.** to insert (a knife, sword, etc.) into a sheath. **2.** (esp. of cats) to retract (the claws). **3.** to surface with or encase in a sheath or sheathing.

sheathing ('ʃiːðɪŋ) *n.* **1.** any material used as an outer layer, as on a ship's hull. **2.** boarding, etc., used to cover a timber frame.

sheath knife *n.* a knife carried in or protected by a sheath.

sheave¹ (ʃiːv) *vb.* (*tr.*) to gather or bind into sheaves.

sheave² (ʃiːv) *n.* a wheel with a grooved rim, esp. one used as a pulley. [C14: of Gmc origin]

sheaves (ʃiːvz) *n.* the plural of **sheaf.**

Sheba¹ ('ʃiːbə) *n.* **1.** Also called: **Saba.** the ancient kingdom of the Sabeans: a rich trading nation dealing in gold, spices, and precious stones (I Kings 10). **2.** the region inhabited by this nation, located in the SW corner of the Arabian peninsula: modern Yemen.

Sheba² ('ʃiːbə) *n.* **Queen of.** *Old Testament.* a queen of the Sabeans, who visited Solomon (I Kings 10:1–13).

shebang (ʃɪ'bæŋ) *n. Sl., chiefly U.S. & Canad.* a situation or affair (esp. in **the whole shebang**). [C19: from ?]

shebeen *or* **shebean** (ʃə'biːn) *n.* **1.** *Irish, Scot., & S. African.* a place where alcoholic drink is sold illegally. **2.**

(in Ireland) alcohol, esp. home-distilled whiskey, sold without a licence. **3.** (in South Africa) a place where Black African men engage in social drinking. [C18: from Irish Gaelic *sibín* beer of poor quality]

shebeen king *or* (*fem.*) **shebeen queen** *n.* (in South Africa) the proprietor of a shebeen.

Shechem ('ʃɛkəm, -ɛm) *n.* the ancient name of **Nablus**.

shed¹ (ʃɛd) *n.* **1.** a small building or lean-to of light construction, used for storage, shelter, etc. **2.** a large roofed structure, esp. one with open sides, used for storage, repairing locomotives, etc. **3.** *Austral. & N.Z.* the building in which sheep are shorn. [OE *sced;* prob. var. of *scead* shelter]

shed² (ʃɛd) *vb.* **shedding, shed.** (*mainly tr.*) **1.** to pour forth or cause to pour forth: *to shed tears.* **2. shed light on** *or* **upon.** to clarify (a problem, etc.). **3.** to cast off or lose: *the snake shed its skin.* **4.** to repel: *this coat sheds water.* **5.** *N.Z.* to separate or divide a group of sheep: *a good dog can shed his sheep in minutes.* **6.** *Dialect.* to make a parting in (the hair). ~*n.* **7.** short for **watershed. 8.** *N.Z.* the action of separating or dividing a group of sheep: *the old dog was better at the shed than the young one.* [OE *sceadan*] — **'shedable** *or* **'sheddable** *adj.*

she'd (ʃiːd) *contraction of* she had *or* she would.

shedder¹ ('ʃɛdə) *n.* **1.** a person or thing that sheds. **2.** an animal, such as a llama, snake, or lobster, that moults.

shedder² ('ʃɛdə) *n. N.Z.* a person who milks cows in a cow shed.

shed hand *n. Chiefly Austral.* an unskilled worker in a sheepshearing shed.

shed out *vb.* (*tr.*, *adv.*) *N.Z.* to separate off (sheep that have lambed) and move them to better pasture.

sheen (ʃiːn) *n.* **1.** a gleaming or glistening brightness; lustre. **2.** *Poetic.* splendid clothing. ~*adj.* **3.** *Rare.* beautiful. [OE *sciene*] — **'sheeny** *adj.*

Sheene (ʃiːn) *n.* **Barry,** real name *Stephen Frank Sheene*. born 1950, English racing motorcyclist: 500 cc. world champion (1976, 1977).

sheep (ʃiːp) *n.*, *pl.* **sheep. 1.** any of a genus of ruminant mammals having transversely ribbed horns and a narrow face. **2. Barbary sheep.** another name for **aoudad. 3.** a meek or timid person. **4. separate the sheep from the goats.** to pick out the members of a group who are superior in some respects. [OE *scēap*] — **'sheep,like** *adj.*

sheepcote ('ʃiːp,kəʊt) *n. Chiefly Brit.* another word for **sheepfold.**

sheep-dip *n.* **1.** any of several liquid disinfectants and insecticides in which sheep are immersed. **2.** a deep trough containing such a liquid.

sheepdog ('ʃiːp,dɒg) *n.* **1.** a dog used for herding sheep. **2.** any of various breeds of dog reared originally for herding sheep. See **Old English sheepdog, Shetland sheepdog.**

sheepdog trial *n.* (*often pl.*) a competition in which sheepdogs are tested in their tasks.

sheepfold ('ʃiːp,fəʊld) *n.* a pen or enclosure for sheep.

sheepish ('ʃiːpɪʃ) *adj.* **1.** abashed or embarrassed, esp. through looking foolish. **2.** resembling a sheep in timidity. — **'sheepishly** *adv.* — **'sheepishness** *n.*

sheepo ('ʃiːpəʊ) *n.*, *pl.* **sheepos.** *N.Z.* a person employed to bring sheep to the catching pen in a shearing shed.

sheep's eyes *pl. n. Old-fashioned.* amorous or inviting glances.

sheepshank ('ʃiːp,ʃæŋk) *n.* a knot made in a rope to shorten it temporarily.

sheepskin ('ʃiːp,skɪn) *n.* **a.** the skin of a sheep, esp. when used for clothing, etc. **b.** (*as modifier*): *a sheepskin coat.*

sheepwalk ('ʃiːp,wɔːk) *n. Chiefly Brit.* a tract of land for grazing sheep.

sheer¹ (ʃɪə) *adj.* **1.** perpendicular; very steep: *a sheer cliff.* **2.** (of textiles) so fine as to be transparent. **3.** (*prenominal*) absolute: *sheer folly.* **4.** *Obs.* bright. ~*adv.* **5.** steeply. **6.** completely or absolutely. [OE *scīr*] — **'sheerly** *adv.* — **'sheerness** *n.*

sheer² (ʃɪə) *vb.* (foll. by *off* or *away* (*from*)). **1.** to deviate or cause to deviate from a course. **2.** (*intr.*) to avoid an unpleasant person, thing, topic, etc. ~*n.* **3.** *Naut.* the position of a vessel relative to its mooring. [C17: ? var. of SHEAR]

sheerlegs *or* **shearlegs** ('ʃɪə,lɛgz) *n.* (*functioning as sing.*) a device for lifting weights consisting of two spars lashed together at the upper ends from which a lifting tackle is suspended. Also called: **shears**. [C19: var. of *shear legs*]

Sheerness (ˌʃɪəˈnɛs) *n.* a port and resort in SE England, in N Kent at the junction of the Medway estuary and the Thames: administratively part of Queenborough in Sheppey since 1968.

sheet[1] (ʃiːt) *n.* **1.** a large rectangular piece of cloth, generally one of a pair used as inner bedclothes. **2. a.** a thin piece of a substance such as paper or glass, usually rectangular in form. **b.** (*as modifier*): *sheet iron*. **3.** a broad continuous surface: *a sheet of water*. **4.** a newspaper, esp. a tabloid. **5.** a piece of printed paper to be folded into a section for a book. ~*vb.* **6.** (*tr.*) to provide with, cover, or wrap in a sheet. [OE *sciete*]

sheet[2] (ʃiːt) *n. Naut.* a line or rope for controlling the position of a sail relative to the wind. [OE *scēata* corner of a sail]

sheet anchor *n.* **1.** *Naut.* a large strong anchor for use in emergency. **2.** a person or thing to be relied on in an emergency. [C17: from earlier *shute anker*, from *shoot* (obs.) the sheet of a sail]

sheet bend *n.* a knot used esp. for joining ropes of different sizes.

sheeting (ˈʃiːtɪŋ) *n.* fabric from which sheets are made.

sheet lightning *n.* lightning that appears as a broad sheet, caused by the reflection of more distant lightning.

sheet metal *n.* metal in the form of a sheet, the thickness being intermediate between that of plate and that of foil.

sheet music *n.* **1.** the printed or written copy of a short composition or piece. **2.** music in its written or printed form.

Sheffield (ˈʃɛfiːld) *n.* a city in N England, in South Yorkshire on the River Don: important centre of steel manufacture and of the cutlery industry; university (1905). Pop.: 538 700 (1986).

sheik *or* **sheikh** (ʃeɪk) *n.* (in Muslim countries) **a.** the head of an Arab tribe, village, etc. **b.** a religious leader. [C16: from Ar. *shaykh* old man] — **ˈsheikdom** *or* **ˈsheikhdom** *n.*

sheila (ˈʃiːlə) *n. Austral. & N.Z.* an informal word for **girl** or **woman**. [C19: from the girl's name *Sheila*]

shekel (ˈʃɛkᵊl) *n.* **1.** any of several former coins and units of weight of the Near East. **2.** (*often pl.*) *Inf.* any coin or money. [C16: from Heb. *sheqel*]

shelduck (ˈʃɛlˌdʌk) *or* (*masc.*) **sheldrake** (ˈʃɛlˌdreɪk) *n.*, *pl.* **-ducks, -duck** *or* **-drakes, -drake.** any of various large usually brightly coloured gooselike ducks of the Old World. [C14: *shel*, prob. from dialect *sheld* pied]

shelf (ʃɛlf) *n., pl.* **shelves. 1.** a thin flat plank of wood, metal, etc., fixed horizontally against a wall, etc., for the purpose of supporting objects. **2.** something resembling this in shape or function. **3.** the objects placed on a shelf: *a shelf of books.* **4.** a projecting layer of ice, rock, etc., on land or in the sea. **5. off the shelf.** readily available from existing stock. **6. on the shelf.** put aside or abandoned; used esp. of unmarried women considered to be past the age of marriage. [OE *scylfe* ship's deck] — **ˈshelfˌlike** *adj.*

shelf life *n.* the length of time a packaged food, etc., will last without deteriorating.

shell (ʃɛl) *n.* **1.** the protective outer layer of an egg, esp. a bird's egg. **2.** the hard outer covering of many molluscs. **3.** any other hard outer layer, such as the exoskeleton of many arthropods. **4.** the hard outer layer of some fruits, esp. of nuts. **5.** any hard outer case. **6.** a hollow artillery projectile filled with explosive primed to explode either during flight or on impact. **7.** a small-arms cartridge. **8.** a pyrotechnic cartridge designed to explode in the air. **9.** *Rowing.* a very light narrow racing boat. **10.** the external structure of a building, esp. one that is unfinished. **11.** *Physics.* a class of electron orbits in an atom in which the electrons have the same principal quantum number and little difference in their energy levels. **12. come** (*or* **bring**) **out of one's shell.** to become (or help to become) less shy and reserved. ~*vb.* **13.** to divest or be divested of a shell, husk, etc. **14.** to separate or be separated from an ear, husk, etc. **15.** (*tr.*) to bombard with artillery shells. ~See also **shell out.** [OE *sciell*] — **ˈshell-less** *adj.* — **ˈshellˌlike** *adj.* — **ˈshelly** *adj.*

she'll (ʃiːl; *unstressed* ʃɪl) *contraction of* she will *or* she shall.

shellac (ʃəˈlæk, ˈʃɛlæk) *n.* **1.** a yellowish resin secreted by the lac insect, from esp. a commercial preparation of this used in varnishes, polishes, etc. **2.** Also called: **shellac**

varnish. a varnish made by dissolving shellac in ethanol or a similar solvent. ~*vb.* **-lacking, -lacked.** (*tr.*) **3.** to coat (an article) with a shellac varnish. [C18: SHELL + LAC[1], translation of F *laque en écailles*, lit.: lac in scales, that is, in thin plates]

shellback (ˈʃɛlˌbæk) *n.* an experienced or old sailor.

Shelley (ˈʃɛlɪ) *n.* **1. Mary Wollstonecraft (Godwin)** (ˈwʊlstən,krɑːft). 1797–1851, English writer; author of *Frankenstein* (1818); eloped with Percy Bysshe Shelley. **2. Percy Bysshe** (bɪʃ). 1792–1822, English Romantic poet. His major works include *Queen Mab* (1813), *The Revolt of Islam* (1817), and the verse drama *Prometheus Unbound* (1820). He wrote an elegy on the death of Keats, *Adonais* (1821), and shorter lyrics, including the odes *To the West Wind* and *To a Skylark* (both 1820). He was drowned in the Ligurian Sea while sailing from Leghorn to La Spezia.

shellfire (ˈʃɛl,faɪə) *n.* the firing of artillery shells.

shellfish (ˈʃɛl,fɪʃ) *n., pl.* **-fish** *or* **-fishes.** any aquatic invertebrate having a shell or shell-like carapace, esp. such an animal used as human food. Examples are crustaceans such as crabs and lobsters and molluscs such as oysters.

shell out *vb.* (*adv.*) *Inf.* to pay out or hand over (money).

shell program *n. Computers.* a basic low-cost computer program that provides a framework within which the user can develop the program to suit his personal requirements.

shellproof (ˈʃɛl,pruːf) *adj.* designed, intended, or able to resist shellfire.

shell shock *n.* loss of sight, etc., resulting from psychological strain during prolonged engagement in warfare. — **ˈshell-ˌshocked** *adj.*

Shelta (ˈʃɛltə) *n.* a secret language used by some itinerant tinkers in Ireland and parts of Britain, based on Gaelic. [C19: from earlier *sheldrū*, ? an arbitrary alteration of OIrish *bēlre* speech]

shelter (ˈʃɛltə) *n.* **1.** something that provides cover or protection, as from weather or danger. **2.** the protection afforded by such a cover. **3.** the state of being sheltered. ~*vb.* **4.** (*tr.*) to provide with or protect by a shelter. **5.** (*intr.*) to take cover, as from rain. **6.** (*tr.*) to act as a shelter for. [C16: from ?] — **ˈshelterer** *n.*

sheltered (ˈʃɛltəd) *adj.* **1.** protected from wind or weather. **2.** protected from outside influences: *a sheltered upbringing.* **3.** specially designed to provide a safe environment for the elderly, handicapped, or disabled: *sheltered housing.*

sheltie *or* **shelty** (ˈʃɛltɪ) *n., pl.* **-ties.** another name for **Shetland pony** *or* **Shetland sheepdog.** [C17: prob. from Orkney dialect *sjalti*, from ON *Hjalti* Shetlander, from *Hjaltland* Shetland]

shelve[1] (ʃɛlv) *vb.* (*tr.*) **1.** to place on a shelf. **2.** to provide with shelves. **3.** to put aside or postpone from consideration. **4.** to dismiss or cause to retire. — **ˈshelver** *n.*

shelve[2] (ʃɛlv) *vb.* (*intr.*) to slope away gradually.

shelves (ʃɛlvz) *n.* the plural of **shelf.**

shelving (ˈʃɛlvɪŋ) *n.* **1.** material for making shelves. **2.** a set of shelves; shelves collectively.

Shem (ʃɛm) *n. Old Testament.* the eldest of Noah's three sons (Genesis 10:21). Douay spelling: **Sem** (sɛm).

shemozzle (ʃɪˈmɒzᵊl) *n. Inf.* a noisy confusion or dispute; uproar. [C19: ?from Yiddish *shlimazl* misfortune]

shenanigan (ʃɪˈnænɪgən) *n. Inf.* **1.** (*usually pl.*) roguishness; mischief. **2.** an act of treachery; deception. [C19: from ?]

Shensi (ˈʃɛnˈsiː) *n.* a variant transliteration of the Chinese name for **Shaanxi.**

Shenyang (ˈʃɛnˈjæŋ) *n.* a walled city in NE China in S Manchuria, capital of Liaoning province: capital of the Manchu dynasty from 1644–1912; seized by the Japanese in 1931. Pop.: 4 200 000 (1986). Former name: **Mukden.**

she-oak *n.* any of various Australian trees of the genus *Casuarina*. See **casuarina.** [C18: *she* (in the sense: inferior) + OAK]

Sheol (ˈʃiːəʊl, -ɒl) *n. Bible.* **1.** the abode of the dead. **2.** (*often not cap.*) hell. [C16: from Heb. *shĕ'ōl*]

Shepard (ˈʃɛpəd) *n.* **Alan Bartlett, Jr.** born 1923, U.S. naval officer; first U.S. astronaut in space (1961).

shepherd (ˈʃɛpəd) *n.* **1.** a person employed to tend sheep. Fem. equivalent: **shepherdess. 2.** a person, such as a clergyman, who watches over a group of people. ~*vb.* (*tr.*) **3.** to guide or watch over in the manner of a shepherd. **4.** *Australian Rules football, rugby, etc.* to prevent opponents from tackling (a member of one's own team) by blocking their path: illegal in rugby.

shepherd dog *n.* another term for **sheepdog** (sense 1).

shepherd's pie *n. Chiefly Brit.* a baked dish of minced meat covered with mashed potato.

shepherd's-purse *n.* a plant having small white flowers and flattened triangular seed pods.

shepherd's weatherglass *n. Brit.* another name for the **scarlet pimpernel.**

Sheppey ('ʃɛpɪ) *n.* **Isle of.** an island in SE England, off the N coast of Kent in the Thames estuary: separated from the mainland by **The Swale,** a narrow channel. Chief towns: Sheerness, Minister. Pop.: 31 854 (1971). Area: 80 sq. km (30 sq. miles).

Sheraton[1] ('ʃɛrətən) *n.* **Thomas.** 1751–1806, English furniture maker, author of the influential *Cabinet-Maker and Upholsterer's Drawing Book* (1791).

Sheraton[2] ('ʃɛrətən) *adj.* denoting furniture made by or in the style of Thomas Sheraton, characterized by lightness, elegance, and the extensive use of inlay.

sherbet ('ʃɜːbət) *n.* **1.** a fruit-flavoured slightly effervescent powder, eaten as a sweet or used to make a drink. **2.** another word (esp. U.S. and Canad.) for **sorbet** (sense 1). [C17: from Turkish, from Persian, from Ar. *sharbah* drink, from *shariba* to drink]

Sherbrooke ('ʃɜː,brʊk) *n.* a city in E Canada, in S Quebec: industrial and commercial centre. Pop.: 74 438 (1986).

sherd (ʃɜːd) *n.* another word for **shard.**

Sheridan ('ʃɛrɪdən) *n.* **1. Philip Henry.** 1831–88, American Union cavalry commander in the Civil War. He forced Lee's surrender to Grant (1865). **2. Richard Brinsley** ('brɪnzlɪ). 1751–1816, Irish dramatist, politician, and orator, noted for his comedies of manners *The Rivals* (1775), *School for Scandal* (1777), and *The Critic* (1779).

sherif *or* **shereef** (ʃɛ'riːf) *n. Islam.* **1.** a descendant of Mohammed through his daughter Fatima. **2.** an honorific title accorded to any Muslim ruler. [C16: from Ar. *sharīf* noble]

sheriff ('ʃɛrɪf) *n.* **1.** (in the U.S.) the chief elected law-enforcement officer in a county. **2.** (in Canada) a municipal official who enforces court orders, escorts convicted criminals to prison, etc. **3.** (in England and Wales) the chief executive officer of the Crown in a county, having chiefly ceremonial duties. **4.** (in Scotland) a judge in any of the sheriff courts. [OE *scīrgerēfa,* from *scīr* SHIRE + *gerēfa* REEVE[1]] —'**sheriffdom** *n.*

sheriff court *n.* (in Scotland) a court having jurisdiction to try all but the most serious crimes and to deal with most civil actions.

Sherman ('ʃɜːmən) *n.* **William Tecumseh** (tɪ'kʌmsə). 1820–91, American Union commander during the Civil War. He led the victorious march through Georgia (1864), becoming commander of the army in 1869.

Sherpa ('ʃɜːpə) *n., pl.* **-pas** *or* **-pa.** a member of a people of Mongolian origin living on the southern slopes of the Himalayas in Nepal, noted as mountaineers.

Sherrington ('ʃɛrɪŋtən) *n.* **Sir Charles Scott.** 1857–1952, English physiologist, noted for his work on reflex action, published in *The Integrative Action of the Nervous System* (1906): shared the Nobel prize for physiology or medicine with Adrian (1932).

sherry ('ʃɛrɪ) *n., pl.* **-ries.** a fortified wine, originally only from the Jerez region of southern Spain. [C16: from earlier *sherris* (assumed to be pl.), from Sp. *Xeres,* now *Jerez*]

sherwani (ʃɛə'wɑːnɪ) *n.* a long coat closed up to the neck, worn by men in India. [Hindi]

Sherwood ('ʃɜː,wʊd) *n.* **Robert Emmet.** 1896–1955, U.S. dramatist. His plays include *The Petrified Forest* (1935), *Idiot's Delight* (1936), and *There shall be no Night* (1940).

Sherwood Forest *n.* an ancient forest in central England, in Nottinghamshire: formerly a royal hunting ground and much more extensive; famous as the home of Robin Hood.

she's (ʃiːz) *contraction of* she is *or* she has.

Shetland *or* **Shetland Islands** ('ʃɛtlənd) *pl. n.* a group of about 100 islands (fewer than 20 inhabited), off the N coast of Scotland, which constitute an island authority of Scotland: a Norse dependency from the 8th century until 1472; noted for the breeding of Shetland ponies, knitwear manufacturing, and fishing; oil-based industries. Administrative centre: Lerwick. Pop.: 23 580 (1986 est.). Area: 1426 sq. km (550 sq. miles). Official name (until 1974): **Zetland.**

Shetland pony *n.* a very small sturdy breed of pony with a long shaggy mane and tail.

Shetland sheepdog *n.* a small dog similar in appearance to a collie.

shew (ʃəʊ) *vb.* **shewing, shewed; shewn** *or* **shewed.** an archaic spelling of **show.**

shewbread *or* **showbread** ('ʃəʊ,brɛd) *n. Bible.* the loaves of bread placed every Sabbath on the table beside the altar of incense in the tabernacle or temple of ancient Israel.

SHF *or* **shf** *Radio. abbrev. for* superhigh frequency.

Shiah *or* **Shia** ('ʃiːə) *n.* **1.** one of the two main branches of Islam, now mainly in Iran, which regards Mohammed's cousin Ali and his successors as the true imams. ~*adj.* **2.** designating or characteristic of this sect or its beliefs and practices. [C17: from Ar. *shī'ah* sect, from *shā'a* to follow]

shibboleth ('ʃɪbə,lɛθ) *n.* **1.** a slogan or catch phrase, usually considered outworn, characteristic of a particular party or sect. **2.** a custom, phrase, or use of language that acts as a test of belonging to, or as a stumbling block to joining a particular social class, profession, etc. [C14: from Heb., lit.: ear of grain; the word is used in the Old Testament by the Gileadites as a test word for the Ephraimites, who could not pronounce the sound *sh*]

shickered ('ʃɪkəd) *adj. Austral. & N.Z. sl.* drunk; intoxicated. [via Yiddish from Heb.]

shied (ʃaɪd) *vb.* the past tense and past participle of **shy**[1] and **shy**[2].

shield (ʃiːld) *n.* **1.** any protection used to intercept blows, missiles, etc., such as a tough piece of armour carried on the arm. **2.** any similar protective device. **3.** *Heraldry.* a pointed stylized shield used for displaying armorial bearings. **4.** anything that resembles a shield in shape, such as a prize in a sports competition. **5.** *Physics.* a structure of concrete, lead, etc., placed around a nuclear reactor. **6.** a broad stable plateau of ancient Precambrian rocks forming the rigid nucleus of a particular continent. **7. the shield.** *N.Z.* the Bledisloe Shield, a trophy competed for by provincial rugby teams. ~*vb.* (*tr.*) **8.** to protect, hide, or conceal (something) from danger or harm. [OE *scield*] —'**shield,like** *adj.*

Shield (ʃiːld) *n.* **the.** *Canad.* another term for the **Canadian Shield.**

Shield cricket *n.* **1.** *Austral.* the interstate cricket competition held for the Sheffield Shield. **2.** *N.Z.* the cricket competition held between provinces for the Ranfurly Shield.

shieling ('ʃiːlɪŋ) *or* **shiel** (ʃiːl) *n. Chiefly Scot.* **1.** a temporary shelter used by people tending cattle on high or remote ground. **2.** pasture land for the grazing of cattle in summer. [C16: from earlier *shiel,* from ME *shale* hut, from ?]

shier ('ʃaɪə) *adj.* a comparative of **shy**[1].

shiest ('ʃaɪɪst) *adj.* a superlative of **shy**[1].

shift (ʃɪft) *vb.* **1.** to move or cause to move from one place or position to another. **2.** (*tr.*) to change for another or others. **3.** to change (gear) in a motor vehicle. **4.** (*intr.*) (of a sound or set of sounds) to alter in a systematic way. **5.** (*intr.*) to provide for one's needs (esp. in **shift for oneself**). **6.** to remove or be removed, esp. with difficulty: *no detergent can shift these stains.* **7.** (*intr.*) *Sl.* to move quickly. ~*n.* **8.** the act or an instance of shifting. **9.** a group of workers who work for a specific period. **10.** the period of time worked by such a group. **11.** an expedient, contrivance, or artifice. **12.** an underskirt or dress with little shaping. [OE *sciftan*] —'**shifter** *n.*

shiftless ('ʃɪftlɪs) *adj.* lacking in ambition or initiative. —'**shiftlessness** *n.*

shifty ('ʃɪftɪ) *adj.* **shiftier, shiftiest.** **1.** given to evasions. **2.** furtive in character or appearance. —'**shiftily** *adv.* —'**shiftiness** *n.*

shigella (ʃɪ'gɛlə) *n.* any of a genus of rod-shaped bacteria, some species of which cause dysentery. [C20: after K. *Shiga* (1870–1957), Japanese bacteriologist, who discovered them]

Shiite ('ʃiːaɪt) *or* **Shiah** *Islam.* ~*n.* **1.** an adherent of Shiah. ~*adj.* **2.** of or relating to Shiah. —**Shiism** ('ʃiːɪzəm) *n.* —**Shiitic** (ʃi:'ɪtɪk) *adj.*

Shijiazhuang ('ʃiːdʒɑː'dʒwæŋ), **Shihchiachuang,** *or* **Shihkiachwang** (,ʃiːtʃjɑː'tʃwæŋ) *n.* a city in NE China, capital of Hebei province: textile manufacturing. Pop.: 1 160 000 (1986).

Shikoku ('ʃiːkəʊˌkuː) *n.* the smallest of the four main islands of Japan, separated from Honshu by the Inland Sea: mostly forested and mountainous. Pop.: 4 227 400 (1985). Area: 17 759 sq. km (6857 sq. miles).

shillelagh *or* **shillala** (ʃəˈleɪlə, -lɪ) *n.* (in Ireland) a stout club or cudgel. [C18: from Irish Gaelic *sail* cudgel + *éille* leash, thong]

shilling ('ʃɪlɪŋ) *n.* **1.** a British silver or (later) cupronickel coin worth one twentieth of a pound, replaced by the 5p piece in 1970. Abbrev.: **s., sh. 2.** the standard monetary unit of Kenya, Uganda, the Somali Republic, and Tanzania. [OE *scilling*]

Shillong (ʃɪˈlɒŋ) *n.* a city in NE India, capital of Meghalaya: situated on the **Shillong Plateau** at an altitude of 1520 m (4987 ft.); destroyed by earthquake in 1897 and rebuilt. Pop.: 109 244 (1981).

shillyshally ('ʃɪlɪˌʃælɪ) *Inf.* ~*vb.* -lying, -lied. **1.** (*intr.*) to be indecisive, esp. over unimportant matters. ~*adv.* **2.** in an indecisive manner. ~*adj.* **3.** indecisive or hesitant. ~*n., pl.* -lies. **4.** vacillation. [C18: from *shill I shall I*, by reduplication of *shall I*] —'shilly,shallier *n.*

Shiloh ('ʃaɪləʊ) *n.* a town in central ancient Palestine, in Canaan on the E slope of Mount Ephraim: keeping place of the tabernacle and the ark; destroyed by the Philistines.

shily ('ʃaɪlɪ) *adv.* a less common spelling of shyly. See shy¹.

shim (ʃɪm) *n.* **1.** a thin washer or strip often used with a number of similar washers or strips to adjust a clearance for gears, etc. ~*vb.* **shimming, shimmed. 2.** (*tr.*) to modify clearance on (a gear, etc.) by use of shims. [C18: from ?]

shimmer ('ʃɪmə) *vb.* **1.** (*intr.*) to shine with a glistening or tremulous light. ~*n.* **2.** a faint, glistening, or tremulous light. [OE *scimerian*] —'shimmering *or* 'shimmery *adj.*

shimmy ('ʃɪmɪ) *n., pl.* -mies. **1.** an American ragtime dance with much shaking of the hips and shoulders. **2.** abnormal wobbling motion in a motor vehicle, esp. in the front wheels or steering. ~*vb.* -mying, -mied. (*intr.*) **3.** to dance the shimmy. **4.** to vibrate or wobble. [C19: changed from CHEMISE, mistaken for pl.]

Shimonoseki (ˌʃɪmənəʊˈsɛkɪ) *n.* a port in SW Japan, on SW Honshu: scene of the peace treaty (1895) ending the Sino-Japanese War; a heavy industrial centre. Pop.: 269 000 (1985).

shin (ʃɪn) *n.* **1.** the front part of the lower leg. **2.** the front edge of the tibia. **3.** *Chiefly Brit.* a cut of beef, the lower foreleg. ~*vb.* **shinning, shinned. 4.** (when *intr.*, often foll. by *up*) to climb (a pole, tree, etc.) by gripping with the hands or arms and the legs and hauling oneself up. **5.** (*tr.*) to kick (a person) in the shins. [OE *scinu*]

Shinar ('ʃaɪnə) *n. Old Testament.* the southern part of the valley of the Tigris and Euphrates, often identified with Sumer; Babylonia.

shinbone ('ʃɪnˌbəʊn) *n.* the nontechnical name for tibia (sense 1).

shindig ('ʃɪnˌdɪg) *or* **shindy** ('ʃɪndɪ) *n., pl.* -digs *or* -dies. *Sl.* **1.** a noisy party, dance, etc. **2.** a quarrel or commotion. [C19: var. of SHINTY]

shine (ʃaɪn) *vb.* **shining, shone. 1.** (*intr.*) to emit light. **2.** (*intr.*) to glow or be bright with reflected light. **3.** (*tr.*) to direct the light of (a lamp, etc.): *he shone the torch in my eyes.* **4.** (*tr.; p.t. & p.p.* **shined**) to cause to gleam by polishing: *to shine shoes.* **5.** (*intr.*) to excel: *she shines at tennis.* **6.** (*intr.*) to appear clearly. ~*n.* **7.** the state or quality of shining; sheen; lustre. **8.** *Inf.* a liking or fancy (esp. in take a shine to). [OE *scīnan*]

shiner ('ʃaɪnə) *n.* **1.** something that shines, such as a polishing device. **2.** any of numerous small North American freshwater cyprinid fishes. **3.** *Inf.* a black eye. **4.** *N.Z. old-fashioned inf.* a tramp.

shingle¹ ('ʃɪŋgᵊl) *n.* **1.** a thin rectangular tile, esp. one made of wood, that is laid with others in overlapping rows to cover a roof or a wall. **2.** a woman's short-cropped hairstyle. **3.** *U.S. & Canad.* a small signboard fixed outside the office of a doctor, lawyer, etc. ~*vb.* (*tr.*) **4.** to cover (a roof or a wall) with shingles. **5.** to cut (the hair) in a short-cropped style. [C12 *scingle*, from LL *scindula*, split piece of wood, from L *scindere* to split] —'shingler *n.*

shingle² ('ʃɪŋgᵊl) *n.* **1.** coarse gravel, esp. the pebbles found on beaches. **2.** a place or area strewn with shingle. [C16: of Scand. origin] —'shingly *adj.*

shingles ('ʃɪŋgᵊlz) *n.* (*functioning as sing.*) an acute viral disease characterized by inflammation, pain, and skin eruptions along the course of affected nerves. Technical names: **herpes zoster, zoster.** [C14: from Med. L *cingulum* girdle, rendering Gk *zōnē* zone]

Shinto ('ʃɪntəʊ) *n.* the indigenous religion of Japan, incorporating the worship of a number of ethnic divinities. [C18: from Japanese: the way of the gods, from Chinese *shén* gods + *tao* way] —'Shintoism *n.* —'Shintoist *n., adj.*

shinty ('ʃɪntɪ) *n.* **1.** a game resembling hockey played with a ball and sticks curved at the lower end. **2.** (*pl.* -ties) the stick used in this game. [C17: prob. from the cry *shin ye* in the game]

shiny ('ʃaɪnɪ) *adj.* **shinier, shiniest. 1.** glossy or polished; bright. **2.** (of clothes or material) worn to a smooth and glossy state, as by continual rubbing. —'shininess *n.*

ship (ʃɪp) *n.* **1.** a vessel propelled by engines or sails for navigating on the water, esp. a large vessel. **2.** *Naut.* a large sailing vessel with three or more square-rigged masts. **3.** the crew of a ship. **4.** short for **airship** or **spaceship. 5.** when one's ship comes in (*or* home). when one has become successful. ~*vb.* **shipping, shipped. 6.** to place, transport, or travel on any conveyance, esp. aboard a ship. **7.** (*tr.*) *Naut.* to take (water) over the side. **8.** to bring or go aboard a vessel: *to ship oars.* **9.** (*tr.; often foll. by off*) *Inf.* to send away: *they shipped the children off to boarding school.* **10.** (*intr.*) to engage to serve aboard a ship: *I shipped aboard a Liverpool liner.* [OE *scip*] —'shippable *adj.*

-ship *suffix forming nouns.* **1.** indicating state or condition: *fellowship.* **2.** indicating rank, office, or position: *lordship.* **3.** indicating craft or skill: *scholarship.* [OE *-scipe*]

shipboard ('ʃɪpˌbɔːd) *n.* (*modifier*) taking place, used, or intended for use aboard a ship: *a shipboard encounter.*

shipbuilder ('ʃɪpˌbɪldə) *n.* a person or business engaged in building ships. —'ship,building *n.*

ship chandler *n.* a person or business dealing in supplies for ships. —**ship chandlery** *n.*

Shipka Pass ('ʃɪpkə) *n.* a pass over the Balkan Mountains in central Bulgaria: scene of a bloody Turkish defeat in the Russo-Turkish War (1877–78). Height: 1334 m (4376 ft.).

shipload ('ʃɪpˌləʊd) *n.* the quantity carried by a ship.

shipmaster ('ʃɪpˌmɑːstə) *n.* the master or captain of a ship.

shipmate ('ʃɪpˌmeɪt) *n.* a sailor who serves on the same ship as another.

shipment ('ʃɪpmənt) *n.* **1. a.** goods shipped together as part of the same lot: *a shipment of grain.* **b.** (*as modifier*): *a shipment schedule.* **2.** the act of shipping cargo.

ship money *n. English history.* a tax levied to finance the fitting out of warships: abolished 1640.

ship of the line *n. Naut.* (formerly) a warship large enough to fight in the first line of battle.

shipowner ('ʃɪpˌəʊnə) *n.* a person who owns or has shares in a ship or ships.

shipper ('ʃɪpə) *n.* a person or company in the business of shipping freight.

shipping ('ʃɪpɪŋ) *n.* **1. a.** the business of transporting freight, esp. by ship. **b.** (*as modifier*): *a shipping magnate.* **2.** ships collectively: *there is a lot of shipping in the Channel.*

ship's biscuit *n.* another name for **hardtack.**

shipshape ('ʃɪpˌʃeɪp) *adj.* **1.** neat; orderly. ~*adv.* **2.** in a neat and orderly manner.

shipworm ('ʃɪpˌwɜːm) *n.* any of a genus of wormlike marine bivalve molluscs that bore into wooden piers, ships, etc., by means of drill-like shell valves.

shipwreck ('ʃɪpˌrɛk) *n.* **1.** the partial or total destruction of a ship at sea. **2.** a wrecked ship or part of such a ship. **3.** ruin or destruction: *the shipwreck of all my hopes.* ~*vb.* (*tr.*) **4.** to wreck or destroy (a ship). **5.** to bring to ruin or destruction. [OE *scipwræc*, from SHIP + *wræc* something driven by the sea]

shipwright ('ʃɪpˌraɪt) *n.* an artisan skilled in one or more of the tasks required to build vessels.

shipyard ('ʃɪpˌjɑːd) *n.* a place or facility for the building, maintenance, and repair of ships.

shiralee (ˌʃɪrəˈliː) *n. Austral. sl.* a swagman's bundle. [from ?]

Shiraz (ʃɪəˈrɑːz) n. a city in SW Iran, at an altitude of 1585 m (5200 ft.): an important Muslim cultural centre in the 14th century; university (1948); noted for fine carpets. Pop.: 848 011 (1986).

shire (ˈʃaɪə) n. **1. a.** one of the British counties. **b.** (in combination): Yorkshire. **2.** (in Australia) a rural district having its own local council. **3.** See **shire horse**. **4. the Shires**. the Midland counties of England, famous for hunting, etc. [OE scīr office]

Shiré (ˈʃɪəreɪ) n. a river in E central Africa, flowing from Lake Malawi through Malawi and Mozambique to the Zambezi. Length: 402 km (370 miles).

Shiré Highlands pl. n. an upland area of S Malawi. Average height: 900 m (3000 ft.).

shire horse n. a large heavy breed of carthorse with long hair on the fetlocks.

shirk (ʃɜːk) vb. **1.** to avoid discharging (work, a duty, etc.); evade. ~n. also **shirker**. **2.** a person who shirks. [C17: prob. from G Schurke rogue]

shirr (ʃɜː) vb. **1.** to gather (fabric) into two or more parallel rows to decorate a dress, blouse, etc., often using elastic thread. **2.** (tr.) to bake (eggs) out of their shells. ~n. also **shirring**. **3.** a series of gathered rows decorating a dress, blouse, etc. [C19: from ?]

shirt (ʃɜːt) n. **1.** a garment worn on the upper part of the body, esp. by men, usually having a collar and sleeves and buttoning up the front. **2.** short for **nightshirt**. **3. keep your shirt on**. Inf. refrain from losing your temper. **4. put** or **lose one's shirt on**. Inf. to bet or lose all one has on (a horse, etc.). [OE scyrte]

shirting (ˈʃɜːtɪŋ) n. fabric used in making men's shirts.

shirtsleeve (ˈʃɜːtˌsliːv) n. **1.** the sleeve of a shirt. **2. in one's shirtsleeves**. not wearing a jacket.

shirt-tail n. the part of a shirt that extends below the waist.

shirtwaister (ˈʃɜːtˌweɪstə) or U.S. **shirtwaist** n. a woman's dress with a tailored bodice resembling a shirt.

shirty (ˈʃɜːtɪ) adj. **shirtier, shirtiest**. Sl., chiefly Brit. bad-tempered or annoyed. [C19: ? based on such phrases as to get someone's shirt out to annoy someone] —**ˈshirtily** adv.

shish kebab (ˈʃiːʃ kəˈbæb) n. the full term for **kebab**. [from Turkish şiş kebab, from şiş skewer; see KEBAB]

shit (ʃɪt) Taboo. ~vb. **shitting; shitted** or **shit**. **1.** to defecate. ~n. **2.** faeces; excrement. **3.** Sl. rubbish; nonsense. **4.** Sl. an obnoxious or worthless person. ~interj. **5.** Sl. an exclamation expressing anger, disgust, etc. [OE scite (unattested) dung, scītan to defecate, of Gmc origin] —**ˈshitty** adj.

Shittim (ˈʃɪtɪm) n. Old Testament. the site to the east of the Jordan and northeast of the Dead Sea where the Israelites encamped before crossing the Jordan (Numbers 25:1–9).

shiv (ʃɪv) n. a variant of **chiv**.

Shiva (ˈʃiːvə, ˈʃɪvə) n. a variant spelling of **Siva**.

shivaree (ˌʃɪvəˈriː) n. a variant spelling (esp. U.S. and Canad.) of **charivari**.

shiver [1] (ˈʃɪvə) vb. (intr.) **1.** to shake or tremble, as from cold or fear. ~n. **2.** the act of shivering; a tremulous motion. **3. the shivers**. an attack of shivering, esp. through fear or illness. [C13 chiveren, ? var. of chevelen to shiver (used of teeth), from OE ceafl jowl] —**ˈshiverer** n. —**ˈshivering** n., adj. —**ˈshivery** adj.

shiver [2] (ˈʃɪvə) vb. **1.** to break or cause to break into fragments. ~n. **2.** a splintered piece. [C13: of Gmc origin]

shivoo (ʃɪˈvuː) n., pl. **shivoos**. Austral. sl. a party or celebration. [C19: from E dialect]

Shizuoka (ˌʃiːzuːˈəʊkə) n. a city in central Japan, on S Honshu: a centre for green tea; university (1949). Pop.: 468 000 (1985).

Shkodër (Albanian ˈʃkodər) n. a market town in NW Albania, on **Lake Shkodër**: an Illyrian capital in the first millennium B.C. Pop.: 71 000 (1983). Italian name: **Scutari**.

Shoa (ˈʃəʊə) n. a province of central Ethiopia: high plateau country, with the Great Rift Valley in the east and southeast. Capital: Addis Ababa. Pop.: 6 362 200 (1980 est.). Area: 65 483 sq. km (25 283 sq. miles).

shoal [1] (ʃəʊl) n. **1.** a stretch of shallow water. **2.** a sandbank or rocky area, esp. one that is visible at low water. ~vb. **3.** to make or become shallow. **4.** (intr.) Naut. to sail into shallower water. ~adj. also **shoaly**. **5.** a less common word for **shallow**. [OE sceald shallow]

shoal [2] (ʃəʊl) n. **1.** a large group of fish. **2.** a large group of people or things. ~vb. **3.** (intr.) to collect together in such a group. [OE scolu]

shock [1] (ʃɒk) vb. **1.** to experience or cause to experience extreme horror, disgust, surprise, etc.: the atrocities shocked us. **2.** to cause a state of shock in (a person). **3.** to come or cause to come into violent contact. ~n. **4.** a sudden and violent jarring blow or impact. **5.** something that causes a sudden and violent disturbance in the emotions. **6.** Pathol. a state of bodily collapse, as from severe bleeding, burns, fright, etc. [C16: from OF choc, from choquier to make violent contact with, of Gmc origin] —**ˈshockable** adj. —ˌshockaˈbility n.

shock [2] (ʃɒk) n. **1.** a number of sheaves set on end in a field to dry. **2.** a pile or stack of unthreshed corn. ~vb. **3.** (tr.) to set up (sheaves) in shocks. [C14: prob. of Gmc origin]

shock [3] (ʃɒk) n. a thick bushy mass, esp. of hair. [C19: ?from SHOCK [2]]

shock absorber n. any device designed to absorb mechanical shock, esp. one fitted to a motor vehicle to damp the recoil of the road springs.

shocker (ˈʃɒkə) n. Inf. **1.** a person or thing that shocks. **2.** a sensational novel, film, or play.

shockheaded (ˈʃɒkˌhɛdɪd) adj. having a head of bushy or tousled hair.

shocking (ˈʃɒkɪŋ) adj. **1.** causing shock, horror, or disgust. **2. shocking pink. a.** of a garish shade of pink. **b.** (as n.): dressed in shocking pink. **3.** Inf. very bad or terrible: shocking weather. —**ˈshockingly** adv.

shockproof (ˈʃɒkˌpruːf) adj. capable of absorbing shock without damage.

shock therapy or **treatment** n. the treatment of certain psychotic conditions by injecting drugs or by passing an electric current through the brain (**electroconvulsive therapy**) to produce convulsions or coma.

shock troops pl. n. soldiers specially trained and equipped to carry out an assault.

shock wave n. a region across which there is a rapid pressure, temperature, and density rise caused by a body moving supersonically in a gas or by a detonation. See also **sonic boom**.

shod (ʃɒd) vb. the past participle of **shoe**.

shoddy (ˈʃɒdɪ) adj. **-dier, -diest**. **1.** imitating something of better quality. **2.** of poor quality. ~n., pl. **-dies**. **3.** a yarn or fabric made from wool waste or clippings. **4.** anything of inferior quality that is designed to simulate superior quality. [C19: from ?] —**ˈshoddily** adv. —**ˈshoddiness** n.

shoe (ʃuː) n. **1. a.** one of a matching pair of coverings shaped to fit the foot, esp. one ending below the ankle, having an upper of leather, plastic, etc., on a sole and heel of heavier material. **b.** (as modifier): shoe cleaner. **2.** anything resembling a shoe in shape, function, position, etc., such as a horseshoe. **3.** a band of metal or wood on the bottom of the runner of a sledge. **4.** Engineering. a lining to protect from wear: see **brake shoe**. **5. be in (a person's) shoes**. Inf. to be in (another person's) situation. ~vb. **shoeing, shod**. (tr.) **6.** to furnish with shoes. **7.** to fit (a horse) with horseshoes. **8.** to furnish with a hard cover, such as a metal plate, for protection against friction or bruising. [OE scōh]

shoeblack (ˈʃuːˌblæk) n. (esp. formerly) a person who shines boots and shoes.

shoehorn (ˈʃuːˌhɔːn) n. **1.** a smooth curved implement of horn, metal, plastic, etc., inserted at the heel of a shoe to ease the foot into it. ~vb. (tr.) **2.** to cram (people or things) into a small space.

shoelace (ˈʃuːˌleɪs) n. a cord or lace for fastening shoes.

shoe leather n. **1.** leather used to make shoes. **2. save shoe leather**. to avoid wearing out shoes, as by taking a bus rather than walking.

shoemaker (ˈʃuːˌmeɪkə) n. a person who makes or repairs shoes or boots. —**ˈshoeˌmaking** n.

shoer (ˈʃuːə) n. Rare. a person who shoes horses.

shoeshine (ˈʃuːˌʃaɪn) n. the act or an instance of polishing a pair of shoes.

shoestring (ˈʃuːˌstrɪŋ) n. **1.** another word for **shoelace**. **2.** Inf. a very small or petty amount of money (esp. in **on a shoestring**).

shoetree (ˈʃuːˌtriː) n. a wooden or metal form inserted into a shoe or boot to stretch it or preserve its shape.

shofar *or* **shophar** (*Hebrew* ʃɔ'faːr) *n., pl.* **-fars, -phars** *or* **-froth, -phroth** (*Hebrew* -'frɔt). *Judaism.* a ram's horn sounded on certain religious occasions. [from Heb. *shōphār* ram's horn]

shogun ('ʃəʊˌguːn) *n. Japanese history.* (from about 1192 to 1867) any of a line of hereditary military dictators who relegated the emperors to a position of purely theoretical supremacy. [C17: from Japanese, from Chinese *chiang chün* general, from *chiang* to lead + *chün* army] — **'shogunate** *n.*

Sholapur ('ʃəʊləˌpʊə) *n.* a city in SW India, in S Maharashtra: major textile centre. Pop.: 510 707 (1981).

Sholokhov (*Russian* 'ʃɔləxəf) *n.* **Mikhail Aleksandrovich** (mixa'il alık'sandrəvitʃ). 1905–84, Soviet author, noted particularly for *And Quiet flows the Don* (1934) and *The Don flows Home to the Sea* (1940), describing the effect of the Revolution and civil war on the life of the Cossacks: Nobel prize for literature 1965.

shone (ʃɒn; *U.S.* ʃəʊn) *vb.* a past tense and past participle of **shine**.

shoo (ʃuː) *sentence substitute.* **1.** go away!: used to drive away unwanted or annoying people, animals, etc. ~*vb.* **shooing, shooed. 2.** (*tr.*) to drive away by or as if by crying "shoo". **3.** (*intr.*) to cry "shoo". [C15: imit.]

shoo-in *n. U.S. & Canad.* a person or thing that is certain to win or succeed.

shook[1] (ʃʊk) *n.* **1.** a set of parts ready for assembly, esp. of a barrel. **2.** a group of sheaves piled together on end; shock. [C18: from ?]

shook[2] (ʃʊk) *vb.* the past tense of **shake**.

shoon (ʃuːn) *n. Dialect, chiefly Scot.* a plural of **shoe**.

shoot (ʃuːt) *vb.* **shooting, shot. 1.** (*tr.*) to hit, wound, damage, or kill with a missile discharged from a weapon. **2.** to discharge (a missile or missiles) from a weapon. **3.** to fire (a weapon) or (of a weapon) to be fired. **4.** to send out or be sent out as if from a weapon: *he shot questions at her.* **5.** (*intr.*) to move very rapidly. **6.** (*tr.*) to slide or push into or out of a fastening: *to shoot a bolt.* **7.** to emit (a ray of light) or (of a ray of light) to be emitted. **8.** (*tr.*) to go or pass quickly over or through: *to shoot rapids.* **9.** (*intr.*) to hunt game with a gun for sport. **10.** (*tr.*) to pass over (an area) in hunting game. **11.** (*intr.*) (of a plant) to produce (buds, branches, etc.). **12.** to photograph or record (a sequence, etc.). **13.** (*tr.; usually passive*) to variegate or streak, as with colour. **14.** *Soccer, hockey, etc.* to hit or propel (the ball, etc.) towards the goal. **15.** (*tr.*) *Sport, chiefly U.S. & Canad.* to score (strokes, etc.): *he shot 72 on the first round.* **16.** (*tr.*) to measure the altitude of (a celestial body). **17.** (*often foll. by up*) *Sl.* to inject (someone, esp. oneself) with (a drug, esp. heroin). **18. shoot a line.** *Sl.* **a.** to boast. **b.** to tell a lie. **19. shoot oneself in the foot.** *Inf.* to damage one's own cause inadvertently. ~*n.* **20.** the act of shooting. **21.** the action or motion of something that is shot. **22.** the first aerial part of a plant to develop from a germinating seed. **23.** any new growth of a plant, such as a bud, etc. **24.** *Chiefly Brit.* a meeting or party organized for hunting game with guns. **25.** an area where game can be hunted with guns. **26.** a steep descent in a stream; rapid. **27. the whole shoot.** *Sl.* everything. ~*interj.* **28.** *U.S. & Canad.* an exclamation expressing disbelief, scepticism, etc. ~See also **shoot down, shoot through.** [OE *scēotan*] — **'shooter** *n.*

shoot down *vb.* (*tr., adv.*) **1.** to shoot callously. **2.** to defeat or disprove: *he shot down her argument.*

shooting box *n.* a small country house providing accommodation for a shooting party. Also called: **shooting lodge.**

shooting brake *n. Brit.* another name for **estate car.**

shooting star *n. Inf.* a meteor.

shooting stick *n.* a device that resembles a walking stick, having a spike at one end and a folding seat at the other.

shoot through *vb.* (*intr., adv.*) *Austral. inf.* to leave; go away.

shop (ʃɒp) *n.* **1.** a place, esp. a small building, for the retail sale of goods and services. **2.** an act or instance of shopping. **3.** a place for the performance of a specified type of work; workshop. **4. all over the shop.** *Inf.* **a.** in disarray: *his papers were all over the shop.* **b.** in every direction: *I've searched for it all over the shop.* **5. shut up shop.** to close business at the end of the day or permanently. **6. talk shop.** *Inf.* to discuss one's business, profession, etc., esp. on a social occasion. ~*vb.* **shopping, shopped. 7.** (*intr.; often foll. by for*) to visit a shop or shops in search of (goods) with the intention of buying them. **8.** (*tr.*) *Sl., chiefly Brit.* to inform on (someone), esp. to the police. [OE *sceoppa* stall] — **'shopping** *n.*

shop around *vb.* (*intr., adv.*) *Inf.* **1.** to visit a number of shops or stores to compare goods and prices. **2.** to consider a number of possibilities before making a choice.

shop assistant *n.* a person who serves in a shop.

shop floor *n.* **1.** the part of a factory housing the machines and men directly involved in production. **2.** workers, esp. factory workers organized in a union.

shopkeeper ('ʃɒpˌkiːpə) *n.* a person who owns or manages a shop or small store. — **'shop,keeping** *n.*

shoplifter ('ʃɒpˌlɪftə) *n.* a customer who steals goods from a shop. — **'shop,lifting** *n.*

shopper ('ʃɒpə) *n.* **1.** a person who buys goods in a shop. **2.** a bag for shopping.

shopping centre *n.* **1.** the area of a town where most of the shops are situated. **2.** a complex of stores, restaurants, etc., with an adjoining car park.

shopping mall *n. U.S., Canad., & Austral.* a large enclosed shopping centre, often with central heating and air conditioning.

shopping plaza *n. Chiefly U.S. & Canad.* a shopping centre, esp. a small group of stores built as a strip.

shopsoiled ('ʃɒpˌsɔild) *adj.* worn, faded, etc., from being displayed in a shop or store.

shop steward *n.* an elected representative of the union workers in a shop, factory, etc.

shoptalk ('ʃɒpˌtɔːk) *n.* conversation concerning one's work, esp. when carried on outside business hours.

shopwalker ('ʃɒpˌwɔːkə) *n. Brit.* a person employed by a departmental store to supervise sales personnel, assist customers, etc.

shoran ('ʃɔːræn) *n.* a short-range radar system by which an aircraft, ship, etc., can accurately determine its position. [C20: *sho(rt-)ra(nge) n(avigation)*]

shore[1] (ʃɔː) *n.* **1.** the land along the edge of a sea, lake, or wide river. Related adj.: **littoral. 2. a.** land, as opposed to water. **b.** (*as modifier*): *shore duty.* **3.** *Law.* the tract of coastland lying between the ordinary marks of high and low water. **4.** (*often pl.*) a country: *his native shores.* [C14: prob. from MLow G, MDu. *schōre*]

shore[2] (ʃɔː) *n.* **1.** a prop or beam used to support a wall, building, etc. ~*vb.* **2.** (*tr.; often foll. by up*) to make safe with or as if with a shore. [C15: from MDu. *schōre*] — **'shoring** *n.*

shore[3] (ʃɔː) *vb. Arch., Austral., & N.Z.* a past tense of **shear.**

shore bird *n.* any of various birds that live close to water, esp. plovers, sandpipers, etc. Also called (Brit.): **wader.**

shore leave *n. Naval.* **1.** permission to go ashore, esp. when granted to an officer. **2.** time spent ashore during leave.

shoreless ('ʃɔːlɪs) *adj.* **1.** without a shore suitable for landing. **2.** *Poetic.* boundless; vast.

shoreline ('ʃɔːˌlaɪn) *n.* the edge of a body of water.

shoreward ('ʃɔːwəd) *adj.* **1.** near or facing the shore. ~*adv. also* **shorewards. 2.** towards the shore.

shorn (ʃɔːn) *vb.* a past participle of **shear.**

short (ʃɔːt) *adj.* **1.** of little length; not long. **2.** of little height; not tall. **3.** of limited duration. **4.** deficient: *the number of places laid at the table was short by four.* **5.** (*postpositive; often foll. by of or on*) lacking (in) or needful (of): *I'm always short of money.* **6.** concise; succinct. **7.** (of drinks) consisting chiefly of a spirit, such as whisky. **8.** *Cricket.* (of a fielding position) near the batsman: *short leg.* **9.** lacking in the power of retentiveness: *a short memory.* **10.** abrupt to the point of rudeness: *the sales-girl was very short with him.* **11.** (of betting odds) almost even. **12.** *Finance.* **a.** not possessing the securities or commodities that have been sold under contract and therefore obliged to make a purchase before the delivery date. **b.** of or relating to such sales, which depend on falling prices for profit. **13.** *Phonetics.* **a.** denoting a vowel of relatively brief temporal duration. **b.** (in popular usage) denoting the qualities of the five English vowels represented orthographically in the words *pat, pet, pit, pot, put,* and *putt.* **14.** *Prosody.* **a.** denoting a vowel that is phonetically short or a syllable containing such a vowel. **b.** (of a vowel or syllable in verse) not carrying emphasis or accent. **15.** (of pastry) crumbly in texture. **16. in short supply.** scarce. **17. short and sweet.** unexpectedly brief. **18. short for.** an abbreviation for. ~*adv.* **19.**

abruptly: *to stop short.* **20.** briefly or concisely. **21.** rudely or curtly. **22.** *Finance.* without possessing the securities or commodities at the time of their contractual sale: *to sell short.* **23. caught** *or* **taken short.** having a sudden need to urinate or defecate. **24. go short.** not to have a sufficient amount, etc. **25. short of.** except: *nothing short of a miracle can save him now.* ~*n.* **26.** anything that is short. **27.** a drink of spirits. **28.** *Phonetics, prosody.* a short vowel or syllable. **29.** *Finance.* **a.** a short contract or sale. **b.** a short seller. **30.** a short film, usually of a factual nature. **31.** See **short circuit. 32. for short.** *Inf.* as an abbreviation: *he is called J.R. for short.* **33. in short. a.** as a summary. **b.** in a few words. ~*vb.* **34.** See **short circuit** (sense 2). ~See also **shorts.** [OE *scort*] —'**shortness** *n.*

shortage ('fɔːtɪdʒ) *n.* a deficiency or lack in the amount needed, expected, or due; deficit.

shortbread ('fɔːt,brɛd) *n.* a rich crumbly biscuit made with a large proportion of butter.

shortcake ('fɔːt,keɪk) *n.* **1.** shortbread. **2.** a dessert made of layers of biscuit or cake filled with fruit and cream.

short-change *vb.* (*tr.*) **1.** to give less than correct change to. **2.** *Sl.* to cheat or swindle.

short circuit *n.* **1.** a faulty or accidental connection between two points of different potential in an electric circuit, establishing a path of low resistance through which an excessive current can flow. ~*vb.* **short-circuit.** **2.** to develop or cause to develop a short circuit. **3.** (*tr.*) to bypass (a procedure, etc.). **4.** (*tr.*) to hinder or frustrate (plans, etc.). ~Sometimes (for senses 1, 2) shortened to **short.**

shortcoming ('fɔːt,kʌmɪŋ) *n.* a failing, defect, or deficiency.

short covering *n.* the purchase of securities or commodities by a short seller to meet delivery requirements.

shortcrust pastry ('fɔːt,krʌst) *n.* a basic type of pastry that has a crisp but crumbly texture. Also: **short pastry.**

short cut *n.* **1.** a route that is shorter than the usual one. **2.** a means of saving time or effort. ~*vb.* **short-cut, -cutting, -cut.** **3.** (*intr.*) to use a short cut.

short-dated *adj.* (of a gilt-edged security) having less than five years to run before redemption. Cf. **medium-dated, long-dated.**

short-day *adj.* (of plants) able to flower only if exposed to short periods of daylight, each followed by a long dark period. Cf. **long-day.**

shorten ('fɔːtⁿn) *vb.* **1.** to make or become short or shorter. **2.** (*tr.*) *Naut.* to reduce the area of (sail). **3.** (*tr.*) to make (pastry, etc.) short, by adding fat. **4.** *Gambling.* to cause (the odds) to lessen or (of odds) to become less.

shortening ('fɔːtⁿnɪŋ) *n.* butter or other fat, used in a dough, etc., to make the mixture short.

Shorter Catechism *n. Chiefly Presbyterian Church.* the more widely used of two catechisms of religious instruction drawn up in 1647.

shortfall ('fɔːt,fɔːl) *n.* **1.** failure to meet a goal or a requirement. **2.** the amount of such a failure.

shorthand ('fɔːt,hænd) *n.* **a.** a system of rapid handwriting employing simple strokes and other symbols to represent words or phrases. **b.** (*as modifier*): *a shorthand typist.*

short-handed *adj.* lacking the usual or necessary number of assistants, workers, etc.

shorthand typist *n. Brit.* a person skilled in the use of shorthand and in typing. U.S. and Canad. name: **stenographer.**

short head *n. Horse racing.* a distance shorter than the length of a horse's head.

shorthorn ('fɔːt,hɔːn) *n.* a short-horned breed of cattle with several regional varieties.

shortie *or* **shorty** ('fɔːtɪ) *n., pl.* **shorties.** *Inf.* **a.** a person or thing that is extremely short. **b.** (*as modifier*): *a shortie nightdress.*

short list *Chiefly Brit.* ~*n.* **1.** Also called (Scot.): **short leet.** a list of suitable applicants for a job, post, etc., from which the successful candidate will be selected. ~*vb.* **short-list.** (*tr.*) **2.** to put (someone) on a short list.

short-lived *adj.* living or lasting only for a short time.

shortly ('fɔːtlɪ) *adv.* **1.** in a short time; soon. **2.** briefly. **3.** in a curt or rude manner.

short-order *adj. Chiefly U.S.* of or connected with food that is easily and quickly prepared.

short-range *adj.* of small or limited extent in time or distance: *a short-range forecast.*

shorts (fɔːts) *pl. n.* **1.** trousers reaching the top of the thigh or partway to the knee, worn by both sexes for sport, etc. **2.** *Chiefly U.S. & Canad.* men's underpants that usually reach mid-thigh. **3.** short-dated gilt-edged securities. **4.** short-term bonds. **5.** a livestock feed containing a large proportion of bran and wheat germ.

short shrift *n.* **1.** brief and unsympathetic treatment. **2.** (formerly) a brief period allowed to a condemned prisoner to make confession. **3. make short shrift of.** to dispose of quickly.

short-sighted *adj.* **1.** relating to or suffering from myopia. **2.** lacking foresight: *a short-sighted plan.* —,short-'sightedly *adv.* —,short-'sightedness *n.*

short-spoken *adj.* tending to be abrupt in speech.

short story *n.* a prose narrative of shorter length than the novel.

short-tempered *adj.* easily moved to anger.

short-term *adj.* **1.** of, for, or extending over a limited period. **2.** *Finance.* extending over or maturing within a short period of time, usually twelve months: *short-term credit.*

short time *n.* the state or condition of working less than the normal working week, esp. because of a business recession.

short ton *n.* the full name for **ton**¹ (sense 2).

short-waisted *adj.* unusually short from the shoulders to the waist.

short wave *n.* **a.** a radio wave with a wavelength in the range 10–100 metres. **b.** (*as modifier*): *a short-wave broadcast.*

short-winded *adj.* **1.** tending to run out of breath, esp. after exertion. **2.** (of speech or writing) terse or abrupt.

Shostakovich (,fɒstə'kəʊvɪtʃ; *Russian* ʃəsta'kɔvitʃ) *n.* **Dmitri Dmitriyevich** ('dmitrij 'dmitrijivitʃ). 1906–75, Soviet composer, noted esp. for his 15 symphonies and his chamber music.

shot¹ (fɒt) *n.* **1.** the act or an instance of discharging a projectile. **2.** (*pl.* **shot**) a solid missile, such as an iron ball or a lead pellet, discharged from a firearm. **3. a.** small round pellets of lead collectively, as used in cartridges. **b.** metal in the form of coarse powder or small pellets. **4.** the distance that a discharged projectile travels or is capable of travelling. **5.** a person who shoots, esp. with regard to his ability: *he is a good shot.* **6.** *Inf.* an attempt. **7.** *Inf.* a guess. **8.** any act of throwing or hitting something, as in certain sports. **9.** the launching of a rocket, etc., esp. to a specified destination: *a moon shot.* **10. a.** a single photograph. **b.** a length of film taken by a single camera without breaks. **11.** *Inf.* an injection, as of a vaccine or narcotic drug. **12.** *Inf.* a glass of alcoholic drink, esp. spirits. **13.** *Sport.* a heavy metal ball used in the shot put. **14. call the shots.** *Sl.* to have control over an organization, etc. **15. have a shot at.** *Inf.* to attempt. **16. like a shot.** very quickly, esp. willingly. **17. shot in the arm.** *Inf.* anything that regenerates, increases confidence or efficiency, etc. **18. shot in the dark.** a wild guess. [OE *scot*]

shot² (fɒt) *vb.* **1.** the past tense and past participle of **shoot.** ~*adj.* **2.** (of textiles) woven to give a changing colour effect. **3.** streaked with colour.

shotgun ('fɒt,gʌn) *n.* **1.** a shoulder firearm with unrifled bore used mainly for hunting small game. ~*adj.* **2.** *Chiefly U.S.* involving coercion or duress: *a shotgun merger.*

shotgun wedding *n. Inf.* a wedding into which one or both partners are coerced, usually because the woman is pregnant.

shot put *n.* an athletic event in which contestants hurl or put a heavy metal ball or shot as far as possible. —'shot,putter *n.*

shotten ('fɒtⁿn) *adj.* **1.** (of fish, esp. herring) having recently spawned. **2.** *Arch.* worthless. [C15: from obs. p.p. of SHOOT]

shot tower *n.* a building formerly used in the production of shot, in which molten lead was graded and dropped into water, thus cooling it and forming the shot.

should (fʊd) *vb.* the past tense of **shall:** used as an auxiliary verb to indicate that an action is considered by the speaker to be obligatory (*you should go*) or to form the subjunctive mood with *I* or *we* (*I should like to see you*). [OE *sceold*]

▷ **Usage.** Should has, as its most common meaning in modern English, the sense *ought to* as in *I should go to the graduation, but I don't see how I can*. However, the older sense of the subjunctive of *shall* is often used with *I* or *we* to indicate a more polite form than *would*: *I should like to go, but I can't*. In much speech and writing, *should* has been replaced by *would* in contexts of this kind, but it remains in conditional subjunctives: *should* (never *would*) *I go, I should* (or *would*) *wear my black dress*.

shoulder ('ʃəʊldə) *n.* **1.** the part of the vertebrate body where the arm or a corresponding forelimb joins the trunk. **2.** the joint at the junction of the forelimb with the pectoral girdle. **3.** a cut of meat including the upper part of the foreleg. **4.** *Printing.* the flat surface of a piece of type from which the face rises. **5.** the part of a garment that covers the shoulder. **6.** anything that resembles a shoulder in shape or position. **7.** the strip of unpaved land that borders a road. **8. a shoulder to cry on.** a person one turns to for sympathy with one's troubles. **9. give (someone) the cold shoulder.** *Inf.* **a.** to treat in a cold manner; snub. **b.** to ignore or shun. **10. put one's shoulder to the wheel.** *Inf.* to work very hard **11. rub shoulders with.** *Inf.* to mix with socially or associate with. **12. shoulder to shoulder. a.** side by side. **b.** in a corporate effort. ~*vb.* **13.** (*tr.*) to bear or carry (a burden, etc.) as if on one's shoulders. **14.** to push (something) with or as if with the shoulder. **15.** (*tr.*) to lift or carry on the shoulders. **16. shoulder arms.** *Mil.* to bring the rifle vertically close to the right side with the muzzle uppermost. [OE *sculdor*]

shoulder blade *n.* the nontechnical name for **scapula.**

shoulder strap *n.* a strap over the shoulders, as to hold up a garment or to support a bag, etc.

shouldn't ('ʃʊd²nt) *contraction of* should not.

shouldst (ʃʊdst) *or* **shouldest** ('ʃʊdɪst) *vb. Arch. or dialect.* (used with the pronoun *thou*) a form of the past tense of **shall.**

shout (ʃaʊt) *n.* **1.** a loud cry, esp. to convey emotion or a command. **2.** *Inf.* **a.** a round, esp. of drinks. **b.** one's turn to buy a round of drinks. ~*vb.* **3.** to utter (something) in a loud cry. **4.** (*intr.*) to make a loud noise. **5.** (*tr.*) *Austral. & N.Z. inf.* to treat (someone) to (something), esp. a round of drinks. [C14: prob. from ON *skúta* taunt] — 'shouter *n.*

shout down *vb.* (*tr., adv.*) to drown, overwhelm, or silence by talking loudly.

shove (ʃʌv) *vb.* **1.** to give a thrust or push to (a person or thing). **2.** (*tr.*) to give a violent push to. **3.** (*intr.*) to push one's way roughly. **4.** (*tr.*) *Inf.* to put (something) somewhere: *shove it in the bin.* ~*n.* **5.** the act or an instance of shoving. ~See also **shove off.** [OE *scúfan*] — 'shover *n.*

shove-halfpenny *n. Brit.* a game in which players try to propel coins, originally old halfpennies, with the hand into lined sections of a wooden board.

shovel ('ʃʌv²l) *n.* **1.** an instrument for lifting or scooping loose material, such as earth, coal, etc., consisting of a curved blade or a scoop attached to a handle. **2.** any machine or part resembling a shovel in action. **3.** Also called: **shovelful.** the amount that can be contained in a shovel. ~*vb.* **-elling, -elled** *or U.S.* **-eling, -eled.** **4.** to lift (earth, etc.) with a shovel. **5.** (*tr.*) to clear or dig (a path) with or as if with a shovel. **6.** (*tr.*) to gather, load, or unload in a hurried or careless way. [OE *scofl*] — 'shoveller *or U.S.* 'shoveler *n.*

shoveler ('ʃʌvələ) *n.* a duck of ponds and marshes, having a spoon-shaped bill, a blue patch on each wing, and in the male a green head, white breast, and reddish-brown body.

shovelhead ('ʃʌv²l,hɛd) *n.* a common shark of the Atlantic and Pacific Oceans, having a shovel-shaped head.

shove off *vb.* (*intr., adv.; often imperative*) **1.** to move from the shore in a boat. **2.** *Inf.* to go away; depart.

show (ʃəʊ) *vb.* **showing, showed; shown** *or* **showed. 1.** to make, be, or become visible or noticeable: *to show one's dislike.* **2.** (*tr.*) to exhibit: *he showed me a picture.* **3.** (*tr.*) to indicate or explain; prove: *to show that the earth moves round the sun.* **4.** (*tr.*) to present (oneself or itself) in a specific character: *to show oneself to be trustworthy.* **5.** (*tr.*; foll. by *how* and an infinitive) to instruct

by demonstration: *show me how to swim.* **6.** (*tr.*) to indicate: *a barometer shows changes in the weather.* **7.** (*tr.*) to grant or bestow: *to show favour to someone.* **8.** (*intr.*) to appear: *to show to advantage.* **9.** to exhibit, display, or offer (goods, etc.) for sale: *three artists were showing at the gallery.* **10.** (*tr.*) to allege, as in a legal document: *to show cause.* **11.** to present (a film, etc.) or (of a play, etc.) to be presented, as at a theatre or cinema. **12.** (*tr.*) to guide or escort: *please show me to my room.* **13. show in** *or* **out.** to conduct a person into or out of a room or building by opening the door for him. **14.** (*intr.*) *Inf.* to arrive. ~*n.* **15.** a display or exhibition. **16.** a public spectacle. **17.** an ostentatious display. **18.** a theatrical or other entertainment. **19.** a trace or indication. **20.** *Obstetrics.* a discharge of blood at the onset of labour. **21.** *U.S., Austral., & N.Z. inf.* a chance (esp. in **give someone a show**). **22.** *Sl., chiefly Brit.* a thing or affair (esp. in **good show, bad show,** etc.). **23. for show.** in order to attract attention. **24. run the show.** *Inf.* to take charge of or manage an affair, business, etc. **25. steal the show.** *Inf.* to be looked upon as the most interesting, popular, etc., esp. unexpectedly. ~See also **show off, show up.** [OE *scēawian*]

showboat ('ʃəʊ,bəʊt) *n.* a paddle-wheel river steamer with a theatre and a repertory company.

showbread ('ʃəʊ,brɛd) *n.* a variant spelling of **shewbread.**

show business *n.* the entertainment industry, including theatre, films, television, and radio. Informal term: **show biz.**

show card *n. Commerce.* a card containing a tradesman's advertisement; poster.

showcase ('ʃəʊ,keɪs) *n.* **1.** a glass case used to display objects in a museum or shop. **2.** a setting in which anything may be displayed to best advantage. ~*vb.* **3.** (*tr.*) to display or exhibit.

showdown ('ʃəʊ,daʊn) *n.* **1.** *Inf.* an action that brings matters to a head or acts as a conclusion. **2.** *Poker.* the exposing of the cards in the players' hands at the end of the game.

shower[1] ('ʃaʊə) *n.* **1.** a brief period of rain, hail, sleet, or snow. **2.** a sudden abundant fall or downpour, as of tears, sparks, or light. **3.** a rush: *a shower of praise.* **4. a.** a kind of bath in which a person stands upright and is sprayed with water from a nozzle. **b.** the room, booth, etc., containing such a bath. Full name: **shower bath. 5.** *Brit. sl.* a derogatory term applied to a person or group. **6.** *U.S., Canad., Austral., & N.Z.* a party held to honour and present gifts to a person, as to a prospective bride. **7.** a large number of particles formed by the collision of a cosmic-ray particle with a particle in the atmosphere. **8.** *N.Z.* a light fabric put over a tea table to protect the food from flies, etc. ~*vb.* **9.** (*tr.*) to sprinkle or spray with or as if with a shower. **10.** (often with *it* as subject) to fall or cause to fall in the form of a shower. **11.** (*tr.*) to give (gifts, etc.) in abundance or present (a person) with (gifts, etc.): *they showered gifts on him.* **12.** (*intr.*) to take a shower. [OE *scúr*] — 'showery *adj.*

shower[2] ('ʃəʊə) *n.* a person or thing that shows.

showgirl ('ʃəʊ,gɜːl) *n.* a girl who appears in variety shows, nightclub acts, etc.

show house *n.* a house on a newly built estate that is decorated and furnished for prospective buyers to view.

showing ('ʃəʊɪŋ) *n.* **1.** a presentation, exhibition, or display. **2.** manner of presentation.

showjumping ('ʃəʊ,dʒʌmpɪŋ) *n.* the riding of horses in competitions to demonstrate skill in jumping over or between various obstacles. — 'show-,jumper *n.*

showman ('ʃəʊmən) *n., pl.* **-men. 1.** a person who presents or produces a theatrical show, etc. **2.** a person skilled at presenting anything in an effective manner. — 'showmanship *n.*

shown (ʃəʊn) *vb.* a past participle of **show.**

show off *vb.* (*adv.*) **1.** (*tr.*) to exhibit or display so as to invite admiration. **2.** (*intr.*) *Inf.* to behave in such a manner as to make an impression. ~*n.* **show-off. 3.** *Inf.* a person who makes a vain display of himself.

showpiece ('ʃəʊ,piːs) *n.* **1.** anything displayed or exhibited. **2.** anything prized as a very fine example of its type.

showplace ('ʃəʊ,pleɪs) *n.* a place exhibited or visited for its beauty, historic interest, etc.

showroom ('ʃəʊ,ruːm, -,rʊm) *n.* a room in which goods for sale, such as cars, are on display.

show up vb. (adv.) **1.** to reveal or be revealed clearly. **2.** (tr.) to expose or reveal the faults or defects of by comparison. **3.** (tr.) Inf. to put to shame; embarrass. **4.** (intr.) Inf. to appear or arrive.

showy ('ʃəʊɪ) adj. **showier, showiest. 1.** gaudy or ostentatious. **2.** making an imposing display. —'**showily** adv. —'**showiness** n.

shrank (ʃræŋk) vb. a past tense of **shrink.**

shrapnel ('ʃræpnªl) n. **1.** a projectile containing a number of small pellets or bullets exploded before impact. **2.** fragments from this type of shell. [C19: after H. *Shrapnel* (1761–1842), E army officer, who invented it]

shred (ʃrɛd) n. **1.** a long narrow strip or fragment torn or cut off. **2.** a very small piece or amount. ~vb. **shredding, shredded** or **shred. 3.** (tr.) to tear or cut into shreds. [OE *scread*] —'**shredder** n.

Shreveport ('ʃriːvˌpɔːt) n. a city in NW Louisiana, on the Red River: centre of an oil and natural-gas region. Pop.: 220 380 (1986 est.).

shrew (ʃruː) n. **1.** Also called: **shrewmouse.** a small mouselike long-snouted insectivorous mammal. **2.** a bad-tempered or mean-spirited woman. [OE *scrēawa*]

shrewd (ʃruːd) adj. **1.** astute and penetrating, often with regard to business. **2.** artful: *a shrewd politician.* **3.** Obs. piercing: *a shrewd wind.* [C14: from *shrew* (obs. vb.) to curse, from SHREW] —'**shrewdly** adv. —'**shrewdness** n.

shrewish ('ʃruːɪʃ) adj. (esp. of a woman) bad-tempered and nagging.

Shrewsbury ('ʃrəʊzbərɪ, -brɪ, 'ʃruːz-) n. a city in W central England, administrative centre of Shropshire, on the River Severn: strategically situated near the Welsh border; market town. Pop.: 87 300 (1985).

shriek (ʃriːk) n. **1.** a shrill and piercing cry. ~vb. **2.** to produce or utter (words, sounds, etc.) in a shrill piercing tone. [C16: prob. from ON *skrǣkja* to screech] —'**shrieker** n.

shrieval ('ʃriːvªl) adj. of or relating to a sheriff.

shrievalty ('ʃriːvəltɪ) n., pl. **-ties. 1.** the office or term of office of a sheriff. **2.** the jurisdiction of a sheriff. [C16: from arch. *shrieve* sheriff, on the model of *mayoralty*]

shrift (ʃrɪft) n. Arch. the act or an instance of shriving or being shriven. See also **short shrift.** [OE *scrift*, from L *scriptum* SCRIPT]

shrike (ʃraɪk) n. an Old World songbird having a heavy hooked bill and feeding on smaller animals which it sometimes impales on thorns, etc. Also called: **butcherbird.** [OE *scríc* thrush]

shrill (ʃrɪl) adj. **1.** sharp and high-pitched in quality. **2.** emitting a sharp high-pitched sound. ~vb. **3.** to utter (words, sounds, etc.) in a shrill tone. [C14: prob. from OE *scralletan*] —'**shrillness** n. —'**shrilly** adv.

shrimp (ʃrɪmp) n. **1.** any of a genus of chiefly marine decapod crustaceans having a slender flattened body with a long tail and a single pair of pincers. **2.** Inf. a diminutive person, esp. a child. ~vb. **3.** (intr.) to fish for shrimps. [C14: prob. of Gmc origin] —'**shrimper** n.

shrine (ʃraɪn) n. **1.** a place of worship hallowed by association with a sacred person or object. **2.** a container for sacred relics. **3.** the tomb of a saint or other holy person. **4.** a place or site venerated for its association with a famous person or event. **5.** R.C. Church. a building, alcove, or shelf arranged as a setting for a statue, picture, etc., of Christ, the Virgin Mary, or a saint. ~vb. **6.** short for **enshrine.** [OE *scrín*, from L *scrínium* bookcase] —'**shrine,like** adj.

shrink (ʃrɪŋk) vb. **shrinking; shrank** or **shrunk; shrunk** or **shrunken. 1.** to contract or cause to contract as from wetness, heat, cold, etc. **2.** to become or cause to become smaller in size. **3.** (intr.; often foll. by *from*) **a.** to recoil or withdraw: *to shrink from the sight of blood.* **b.** to feel great reluctance (at). ~n. **4.** the act or an instance of shrinking. **5.** a slang word for **psychiatrist.** [OE *scrincan*] —'**shrinkable** adj. —'**shrinker** n. —'**shrinking** adj.

shrinkage ('ʃrɪŋkɪdʒ) n. **1.** the act or fact of shrinking. **2.** the amount by which anything decreases in value, weight, etc.

shrinking violet n. Inf. a shy person.

shrink-wrap vb. **-wrapping, -wrapped.** (tr.) to package a product in a flexible plastic wrapping designed to shrink about its contours to protect and seal it.

shrive (ʃraɪv) vb. **shriving; shrove** or **shrived; shriven** ('ʃrɪvªn) or **shrived.** Chiefly R.C. Church. **1.** to hear the confession of (a penitent). **2.** (tr.) to impose a penance upon (a penitent) and grant him absolution. **3.** (intr.) to confess one's sins to a priest in order to obtain forgiveness. [OE *scrífan*, from L *scríbere* to write] —'**shriver** n.

shrivel ('ʃrɪvªl) vb. **-elling, -elled** or U.S. **-eling, -eled. 1.** to make or become shrunken and withered. **2.** to lose or cause to lose vitality. [C16: prob. of Scand. origin]

Shropshire ('ʃrɒp,ʃɪə, -ʃə) n. a county of W central England: mainly agricultural. Administrative centre: Shrewsbury. Pop.: 392 700 (1986 est.). Area: 3490 sq. km (1347 sq. miles).

shroud (ʃraʊd) n. **1.** a garment or piece of cloth used to wrap a dead body. **2.** anything that envelops like a garment: *a shroud of mist.* **3.** a protective covering for a piece of equipment. **4.** Naut. one of a pattern of ropes or cables used to stay a mast. ~vb. (tr.) **5.** to wrap in a shroud. **6.** to cover, envelop, or hide. [OE *scrúd* garment] —'**shroudless** adj.

shrove (ʃrəʊv) vb. a past tense of **shrive.**

Shrovetide ('ʃrəʊv,taɪd) n. the Sunday, Monday, and Tuesday before Ash Wednesday, formerly a time when confessions were made for Lent.

shrub[1] (ʃrʌb) n. a woody perennial plant, smaller than a tree, with several major branches arising from near the base of the main stem. [OE *scrybb*] —'**shrub,like** adj.

shrub[2] (ʃrʌb) n. a mixed drink of rum, fruit juice, sugar, and spice. [C18: from Ar. *sharāb*, var. of *shurb* drink; see SHERBET]

shrubbery ('ʃrʌbərɪ) n., pl. **-beries. 1.** a place where a number of shrubs are planted. **2.** shrubs collectively.

shrubby ('ʃrʌbɪ) adj. **-bier, -biest. 1.** consisting of, planted with, or abounding in shrubs. **2.** resembling a shrub. —'**shrubbiness** n.

shrug (ʃrʌg) vb. **shrugging, shrugged. 1.** to draw up and drop (the shoulders) abruptly in a gesture expressing indifference, ignorance, etc. ~n. **2.** the gesture so made. [C14: from ?]

shrug off vb. (tr., adv.) **1.** to minimize the importance of; dismiss. **2.** to get rid of.

shrunk (ʃrʌŋk) vb. a past participle and past tense of **shrink.**

shrunken ('ʃrʌŋkªn) vb. **1.** a past participle of **shrink.** ~adj. **2.** (usually prenominal) reduced in size.

shtoom (ʃtʊm) adj. Sl. silent, dumb (esp. in **keep shtoom).** [from Yiddish, from G *stumm* silent]

shuck (ʃʌk) n. **1.** the outer covering of something, such as the husk of a grain of maize, a pea pod, or an oyster shell. ~vb. (tr.) **2.** to remove the shucks from. [C17: U.S. dialect, from ?] —'**shucker** n.

shucks (ʃʌks) interj. U.S. & Canad. inf. an exclamation of disappointment, annoyance, etc.

shudder ('ʃʌdə) vb. **1.** (intr.) to shake or tremble suddenly and violently, as from horror, fear, aversion, etc. ~n. **2.** a convulsive shiver. [C18: from MLow G *schöderen*] —'**shuddering** adj. —'**shudderingly** adv. —'**shuddery** adj.

shuffle ('ʃʌfªl) vb. **1.** to walk or move (the feet) with a slow dragging motion. **2.** to change the position of (something), esp. in order to deceive others. **3.** (tr.) to mix together in a careless manner: *he shuffled the papers nervously.* **4.** to mix up (cards in a pack) to change their order. **5.** (intr.) to behave in an evasive or underhand manner. **6.** (when intr., often foll. by *into* or *out of*) to move or cause to move clumsily: *he shuffled out of the door.* ~n. **7.** the act or an instance of shuffling. **8.** a rearrangement: *a Cabinet shuffle.* **9.** a dance or dance step with short dragging movements of the feet. [C16: prob. from Low G *schüffeln*] —'**shuffler** n.

shuffleboard ('ʃʌfªl,bɔːd) n. a game in which players push wooden or plastic discs with a long cue towards numbered scoring sections marked on a floor, esp. a ship's deck.

shuffle off vb. (tr., adv.) to thrust off or put aside.

shufty or **shufti** ('ʃʊftɪ, 'ʃʌftɪ) n., pl. **-ties.** Brit. sl. a look; peep. [C20: from Ar.]

Shufu or **Sufu** ('ʃuː'fuː) n. transliteration of the Chinese name for Kashi.

shun (ʃʌn) vb. **shunning, shunned.** (tr.) to avoid deliberately. [OE *scunian*, from ?]

shunt (ʃʌnt) vb. **1.** to turn or cause to turn to one side. **2.** Railways. to transfer (rolling stock) from track to track.

3. *Electronics.* to divert or be diverted through a shunt. **4.** (*tr.*) to evade by putting off onto someone else. ~*n.* **5.** the act or an instance of shunting. **6.** a railway point. **7.** *Electronics.* a low-resistance conductor connected in parallel across a part of a circuit to provide an alternative path for a known fraction of the current. **8.** *Med.* a channel that bypasses the normal circulation of the blood. **9.** *Sl.* a car crash. [C13: ?from *shunen* to SHUN]

shunt-wound (ˈʃʌnt‚waʊnd) *adj. Electrical engineering.* (of a motor or generator) having the field and armature circuits connected in parallel.

shush (ʃʊʃ) *interj.* **1.** be quiet! hush! ~*vb.* **2.** to silence or calm (someone) by or as if by saying "shush". [C20: reduplication of SH, infl. by HUSH]

Shushan (ˈʃuːʃæn) *n.* the Biblical name for **Susa.**

shut (ʃʌt) *vb.* **shutting, shut.** **1.** to move (something) so as to cover an aperture: *to shut a door.* **2.** to close (something) by bringing together the parts: *to shut a book.* **3.** (*tr.*; often foll. by *up*) to close or lock the doors of: *to shut up a house.* **4.** (*tr.*; foll. by *in, out*, etc.) to confine, enclose, or exclude. **5.** (*tr.*) to prevent (a business, etc.) from operating. **6. shut the door on. a.** to refuse to think about. **b.** to render impossible. ~*adj.* **7.** closed or fastened. ~*n.* **8.** the act or time of shutting. ~See also **shutdown, shut-off,** etc. [OE *scyttan*]

shutdown (ˈʃʌt‚daʊn) *n.* **1.** the closing of a factory, shop, etc. ~*vb.* **shut down.** (*adv.*) **2.** to cease or cause to cease operation. **3.** (*tr.*) to close by lowering.

Shute (ʃuːt) *n.* Nevil, real name *Nevil Shute Norway.* 1899–1960, English novelist, in Australia after World War II: noted for his novels set in Australia, esp. *A Town like Alice* (1950) and *On the Beach* (1957).

shuteye (ˈʃʌt‚aɪ) *n.* a slang term for **sleep.**

shut-in *n.* **a.** *Chiefly U.S.* a person confined indoors by illness. **b.** (*as modifier*): *a shut-in patient.*

shut-off *n.* **1.** a device that shuts something off, esp. a machine control. **2.** a stoppage or cessation. ~*vb.* **shut off.** (*tr., adv.*) **3.** to stem the flow of. **4.** to block off the passage through. **5.** to isolate or separate.

shutout (ˈʃʌt‚aʊt) *n.* **1.** a less common word for a **lockout. 2.** *Sport.* a match in which the opposition does not score. ~*vb.* **shut out.** (*tr., adv.*) **3.** to keep out or exclude. **4.** to conceal from sight: *we planted trees to shut out the view of the road.*

shutter (ˈʃʌtə) *n.* **1.** a hinged doorlike cover, often louvred and usually one of a pair, for closing off a window. **2. put up the shutters.** to close business at the end of the day or permanently. **3.** *Photog.* an opaque shield in a camera that, when tripped, admits light to expose the film or plate for a predetermined period, usually a fraction of a second. **4.** *Music.* one of the louvred covers over the mouths of organ pipes, operated by the swell pedal. **5.** a person or thing that shuts. ~*vb.* (*tr.*) **6.** to close with a shutter or shutters. **7.** to equip with a shutter or shutters.

shuttering (ˈʃʌtərɪŋ) *n.* another word (esp. Brit.) for **formwork.**

shuttle (ˈʃʌtᵊl) *n.* **1.** a bobbin-like device used in weaving for passing the weft thread between the warp threads. **2.** a small bobbin-like device used to hold the thread in a sewing machine, etc. **3.** a bus, train, aircraft, etc., that plies between two points. **4. a.** the movement between various countries of a diplomat in order to negotiate with rulers who refuse to meet each other. **b.** (*as modifier*): *shuttle diplomacy.* **5.** *Badminton, etc.* short for **shuttlecock.** ~*vb.* **6.** to move or cause to move by or as if by a shuttle. [OE *scytel* bolt]

shuttlecock (ˈʃʌtᵊl‚kɒk) *n.* **1.** a light cone consisting of a cork stub with feathered flights, struck to and fro in badminton and battledore. **2.** anything moved to and fro, as in an argument.

shut up *vb.* (*adv.*) **1.** (*tr.*) to prevent all access to. **2.** (*tr.*) to confine or imprison. **3.** *Inf.* to cease to talk or make a noise or cause to cease to talk or make a noise: often used in commands.

shwa (ʃwɑː) *n.* a variant spelling of **schwa.**

shy¹ (ʃaɪ) *adj.* **shyer, shyest** *or* **shier, shiest. 1.** not at ease in the company of others. **2.** easily frightened; timid. **3.** (often foll. by *of*) watchful or wary. **4.** (foll. by *of*) *Inf., chiefly U.S. & Canad.* short (of). **5.** (*in combination*) showing reluctance or disinclination: *workshy.* ~*vb.* **shying, shied.** (*intr.*) **6.** to move suddenly, as from fear: *the*

horse *shied at the snake in the road.* **7.** (usually foll. by *off* or *away*) to draw back. ~*n.*, *pl.* **shies. 8.** a sudden movement, as from fear. [OE *sceoh*] —ˈshyer *n.* —ˈshyly *adv.* —ˈshyness *n.*

shy² (ʃaɪ) *vb.* **shying, shied. 1.** to throw (something) with a sideways motion. ~*n.*, *pl.* **shies. 2.** a quick throw. **3.** *Inf.* a gibe. **4.** *Inf.* an attempt. [C18: of Gmc origin] —ˈshyer *n.*

Shylock (ˈʃaɪ‚lɒk) *n.* a heartless or demanding creditor. [C19: after *Shylock*, the heartless usurer in Shakespeare's *The Merchant of Venice* (1595)]

shyster (ˈʃaɪstə) *n. Sl., chiefly U.S.* a person, esp. a lawyer or politician, who uses discreditable methods. [C19: prob. based on *Scheuster*, a disreputable 19th-cent. New York lawyer]

si (siː) *n. Music.* a variant of **te.**

Si¹ (ʃiː) *or* **Si Kiang** *n.* a variant transliteration of the Chinese name for the **Xi.**

Si² *the chemical symbol for* silicon.

SI See **SI unit.**

sial (ˈsaɪəl) *n.* the silicon-rich and aluminium-rich rocks of the earth's continental upper crust. [C20: *si(licon)* + *al(uminium)*] —**sialic** (saɪˈælɪk) *adj.*

Sialkot (sɪˈælkɒt) *n.* a city in NE Pakistan: shrine of Guru Nanak. Pop.: 296 000 (1981).

Siam (saɪˈæm, ˈsaɪæm) *n.* **1.** the former name (until 1939 and 1945–49) of **Thailand. 2. Gulf of.** an arm of the South China Sea between the Malay Peninsula and Indochina.

siamang (ˈsaɪə‚mæŋ) *n.* a large black gibbon of Sumatra and the Malay Peninsula, having the second and third toes united. [C19: from Malay]

Siamese (‚saɪəˈmiːz) *n., pl.* **-mese. 1.** See **Siamese cat.** ~*adj.* **2.** characteristic of, relating to, or being a Siamese twin. ~*adj., n., pl.* **-mese. 3.** another word for **Thai.**

Siamese cat *n.* a short-haired breed of cat with a tapering tail, blue eyes, and dark ears, mask, tail, and paws.

Siamese fighting fish *n.* a brightly coloured labyrinth fish of Thailand and Malaysia: the males are very pugnacious.

Siamese twins *pl. n.* twin babies born joined together at some point, such as at the hips.

Sian (ʃjɑːn) *n.* a variant transliteration of the Chinese name for **Xi An.**

Siang (ʃjɑːŋ) *n.* a variant transliteration of the Chinese name for the **Xiang.**

Siangtan (ˈʃjɑːŋˈtɑːn) *n.* a variant transliteration of the Chinese name for **Xiangtan.**

sib (sɪb) *n.* **1.** a blood relative. **2.** kinsmen collectively; kindred. [OE *sibb*]

SIB (in Britain) *abbrev. for* Securities and Investments Board: a body that regulates financial dealings in the City of London.

Sibelius (sɪˈbeɪlɪəs) *n.* Jean (ʒɑ̃). 1865–1957, Finnish composer, noted for the nationalism of his music, as in his symphonies, his symphonic poems, such as *Finlandia* (1900), and his violin concerto (1905).

Siberia (saɪˈbɪərɪə) *n.* a vast region of the Soviet Union: extends from the Ural Mountains to the Pacific and from the Arctic Ocean to the borders with China and the Mongolian People's Republic; colonized rapidly after the building of the Trans-Siberian Railway. Area: 13 807 037 sq. km (5 330 896 sq. miles). —**Si'berian** *n., adj.*

sibilant (ˈsɪbɪlənt) *adj.* **1.** *Phonetics.* relating to or denoting the consonants (s, z, ʃ, ʒ), all pronounced with a characteristic hissing sound. **2.** having a hissing sound. ~*n.* **3.** a sibilant consonant. [C17: from L *sībilāre* to hiss, imit.] —ˈsibilance *or* ˈsibilancy *n.* —ˈsibilantly *adv.*

sibilate (ˈsɪbɪ‚leɪt) *vb.* to pronounce or utter (words or speech) with a hissing sound. —‚sibiˈlation *n.*

Sibiu (*Romanian* siˈbiu) *n.* an industrial town in W central Romania: originally a Roman city, refounded by German colonists in the 12th century. Pop.: 176 928 (1985). German name: **Hermannstadt.** Hungarian name: **Nagyszeben.**

sibling (ˈsɪblɪŋ) *n.* **a.** a person's brother or sister. **b.** (*as modifier*): *sibling rivalry.* [C19: specialized modern use of OE *sibling* relative, from SIB]

sibyl (ˈsɪbɪl) *n.* **1.** (in ancient Greece and Rome) any of a number of women believed to be oracles or prophetesses. **2.** a witch, fortune-teller, or sorceress. [C13: ult. from Gk *Sibulla*, from ?] —**sibylline** (ˈsɪbɪ‚laɪn) *adj.*

sic¹ (sɪk) *adv.* so or thus: inserted in brackets in a text to indicate that an odd or questionable reading is in fact accurate. [L]

sic² (sɪk) *vb.* **sicking, sicked.** (*tr.*) **1.** to attack: used only in commands, as to a dog. **2.** to urge (a dog) to attack. [C19: dialect var. of SEEK]

siccative ('sɪkətɪv) *n.* a substance added to a liquid to promote drying: used in paints and some medicines. [C16: from LL *siccātīvus*, from L *siccāre* to dry up, from *siccus* dry]

Sichuan ('sɪ'tʃwɑːn) *or* **Szechwan** *n.* a province of SW China: the most populous administrative division in the country, esp. in the central Red Basin, where it is crossed by three main tributaries of the Yangtze. Capital: Chengdu. Pop.: 101 120 000 (1985). Area: about 569 800 sq. km (220 000 sq. miles).

Sicilia (si'tʃiːlja) *n.* the Latin and Italian name for **Sicily**.

siciliano (ˌsiːtʃiː'ljɑːnəʊ) *n., pl.* **-lianos. 1.** an old dance in six-beat or twelve-beat time. **2.** a piece of music composed for or in the rhythm of this dance. [It.]

Sicily ('sɪsɪlɪ) *n.* the largest island in the Mediterranean, separated from the tip of SW Italy by the Strait of Messina: administratively an autonomous region of Italy; settled by Phoenicians, Greeks, and Carthaginians before the Roman conquest of 241 B.C.; under Normans (12th–13th centuries); formed the **Kingdom of the Two Sicilies** with Naples in 1815; mountainous and volcanic. Capital: Palermo. Pop.: 5 112 073 (1981). Area: 25 460 sq. km (9830 sq. miles). Latin names: **Sicilia, Trinacria.** Italian name: **Sicilia.** —**Sicilian** (sɪ'sɪljən) *adj., n.*

sick¹ (sɪk) *adj.* **1.** inclined or likely to vomit. **2. a.** suffering from ill health. **b.** (*as collective n.; preceded by the*): *the sick.* **3. a.** of or used by people who are unwell: *sick benefits.* **b.** (*in combination*): *a sickroom.* **4.** deeply affected with a mental or spiritual feeling akin to physical sickness: *sick at heart.* **5.** mentally or spiritually disturbed. **6.** *Inf.* delighting in or catering for the macabre: *sick humour.* **7.** Also: **sick and tired.** (often foll. by *of*) *Inf.* disgusted or weary: *I am sick of his everlasting laughter.* **8.** (often foll. by *for*) weary with longing: *I am sick for my own country.* **9.** pallid or sickly. **10.** not in working order. ~*n., adj.* **11.** an informal word for **vomit.** [OE *sēoc*] —**'sickish** *adj.*

sick² (sɪk) *vb.* a variant spelling of **sic².**

sickbay ('sɪkˌbeɪ) *n.* a room for the treatment of the sick or injured, as on board a ship.

sick building syndrome *n.* a group of symptoms, such as headaches, eye irritation, and lethargy, that may be experienced by workers in offices that are totally air-conditioned.

sicken ('sɪkən) *vb.* **1.** to make or become nauseated or disgusted. **2.** (*intr.; often foll. by for*) to show symptoms (of an illness). —**'sickener** *n.*

sickening ('sɪkənɪŋ) *adj.* **1.** causing sickness or revulsion. **2.** *Inf.* extremely annoying. —**'sickeningly** *adv.*

Sickert ('sɪkət) *n.* **Walter Richard.** 1860–1942, British impressionist painter, esp. of scenes of London music halls.

sick headache *n.* **1.** a headache accompanied by nausea. **2.** a nontechnical name for **migraine.**

sickie ('sɪkɪ) *n. Austral. & N.Z. inf.* a day of sick leave from work. [C20: from SICK¹ + -IE]

sickle ('sɪkˀl) *n.* an implement for cutting grass, corn, etc., having a curved blade and a short handle. [OE *sicol*, from L *sēcula*]

sick leave *n.* leave of absence from work through illness.

sicklebill ('sɪkˀlˌbɪl) *n.* any of various birds having a markedly curved bill, such as certain hummingbirds and birds of paradise.

sickle-cell anaemia *n.* a hereditary form of anaemia occurring mainly in Black populations, in which a large number of red blood cells become sickle-shaped.

sick list *n.* **1.** a list of the sick, esp. in the army or navy. **2. on the sick list.** ill.

sickly ('sɪklɪ) *adj.* **-lier, -liest. 1.** disposed to frequent ailments; not healthy; weak. **2.** of or caused by sickness. **3.** (of a smell, taste, etc.) causing revulsion or nausea. **4.** (of light or colour) faint or feeble. **5.** mawkish; insipid. ~*adv.* **6.** in a sick or sickly manner. —**'sickliness** *n.*

sick-making *adj. Inf.* galling; sickening.

sickness ('sɪknɪs) *n.* **1.** an illness or disease. **2.** nausea or queasiness. **3.** the state or an instance of being sick.

sick pay *n.* wages paid to an employee while he is on sick leave.

sic transit gloria mundi *Latin.* ('sɪk 'trænsɪt 'ɡlɔːrɪˌɑː 'mʊndiː) thus passes the glory of the world.

Sicyon ('sɪsɪˌɒn, 'sɪsɪən) *n.* an ancient city in S Greece, in the NE Peloponnese near Corinth: declined after 146 B.C.

sidalcea (sɪ'dælsɪə) *n.* any of a genus of hardy perennial plants with pink flowers. Also called **Greek mallow.** [from NL]

Siddhartha (sɪ'dɑːtə) *n.* the personal name of the **Buddha.**

Siddons ('sɪdˀnz) *n.* **Sarah.** 1755–1831, English tragedienne.

side (saɪd) *n.* **1.** a line or surface that borders anything. **2.** *Geom.* **a.** any line segment forming part of the perimeter of a plane geometric figure. **b.** another name for **face** (sense 13). **3.** either of two parts into which an object, surface, area, etc., can be divided: *the right side and the left side.* **4.** either of the two surfaces of a flat object: *the right and wrong side of the cloth.* **5.** a surface or part of an object that extends vertically: *the side of a cliff.* **6.** either half of a human or animal body, esp. the area around the waist: *I have a pain in my side.* **7.** the area immediately next to a person or thing: *he stood at her side.* **8.** a district, point, or direction within an area identified by reference to a central point: *the south side of the city.* **9.** the area at the edge of a room, etc. **10.** aspect or part: *look on the bright side.* **11.** one of two or more contesting factions, teams, etc. **12.** a page in an essay, etc. **13.** a position, opinion, etc., held in opposition to another in a dispute. **14.** line of descent: *he gets his brains from his mother's side.* **15.** *Inf.* a television channel. **16.** *Billiards, etc.* spin imparted to a ball by striking it off-centre with the cue. **17.** *Brit. sl.* insolence or pretentiousness: *to put on side.* **18. on one side.** set apart from the rest, as provision for emergencies, etc. **19. on the side. a.** apart from or in addition to the main object. **b.** as a sideline. **c.** *U.S.* as a side dish. **20. take sides.** to support one group, opinion, etc., as against another. ~*adj.* **21.** being on one side; lateral. **22.** from or viewed as if from one side. **23.** directed towards one side. **24.** subordinate or incidental: *side road.* ~*vb.* **25.** (*intr.;* usually foll. by *with*) to support or associate oneself (with a faction, interest, etc.). [OE *sīde*]

side arms *pl. n.* weapons carried on the person, by belt or holster, such as a sword, pistol, etc.

sideband ('saɪdˌbænd) *n.* the frequency band either above (**upper sideband**) or below (**lower sideband**) the carrier frequency, within which fall the components produced by modulation of a carrier wave.

sideboard ('saɪdˌbɔːd) *n.* a piece of furniture intended to stand at the side of a dining room, with drawers, cupboards, and shelves to hold silver, china, linen, etc.

sideboards ('saɪdˌbɔːdz) *pl. n. Brit.* a man's whiskers grown down either side of the face in front of the ears. U.S. and Canad. term: **sideburns.**

sideburns ('saɪdˌbɜːnz) *pl. n.* another term (esp. U.S. and Canad.) for **sideboards.**

sidecar ('saɪdˌkɑː) *n.* a small car attached on one side to a motorcycle, the other side being supported by a single wheel.

side chain *n. Chem.* a group of atoms bound to an atom, usually a carbon atom, that forms part of a larger chain or ring in a molecule.

-sided *adj.* (*in combination*) having a side or sides as specified: *three-sided; many-sided.*

side dish *n.* a portion of food served in addition to the main dish.

side drum *n.* a small double-headed drum carried at the side with snares that produce a rattling effect.

side effect *n.* **1.** any unwanted nontherapeutic effect caused by a drug. **2.** any secondary effect, esp. an undesirable one.

sidekick ('saɪdˌkɪk) *n. Inf.* a close friend or follower who accompanies another on adventures, etc.

sidelight ('saɪdˌlaɪt) *n.* **1.** light coming from the side. **2.** a side window. **3.** either of the two navigational running lights used by vessels at night, a red light on the port and a green on the starboard. **4.** *Brit.* either of two small lights on the front of a motor vehicle. **5.** additional or incidental information.

sideline ('saɪdˌlaɪn) *n.* **1.** *Sport.* a line that marks the side boundary of a playing area. **2.** a subsidiary interest or source of income. **3.** an auxiliary business activity or line of merchandise. ~*vb.* **4.** (*tr.*) *Chiefly U.S. & Canad.* to prevent (a player) from taking part in a game.

sidelines ('saɪd,laɪnz) *pl. n.* **1.** *Sport.* the area immediately outside the playing area, where substitute players sit. **2.** the peripheral areas of any region, organization, etc.

sidelong ('saɪd,lɒŋ) *adj.* (*prenominal*) **1.** directed or inclining to one side. **2.** indirect or oblique. ~*adv.* **3.** from the side; obliquely.

sidereal (saɪ'dɪərɪəl) *adj.* **1.** of or involving the stars. **2.** determined with reference to one or more stars: *the sidereal day.* [C17: from L *sīdereus*, from *sīdus* a star] —**si'dereally** *adv.*

sidereal day *n.* See **day** (sense 5).

sidereal time *n.* time based upon the rotation of the earth with respect to a particular star, the **sidereal day** being the unit of measurement.

sidereal year *n.* See **year** (sense 5).

siderite ('saɪdə,raɪt) *n.* **1.** a pale yellow to brownish-black mineral consisting chiefly of iron(II) carbonate. It occurs mainly in ore veins and sedimentary rocks and is an important source of iron. Formula: $FeCO_3$. **2.** a meteorite consisting principally of metallic iron.

sidero- *or before a vowel* **sider-** *combining form.* indicating iron: *siderolite.* [from Gk *sídēros*]

siderolite ('saɪdərə,laɪt) *n.* a meteorite consisting of a mixture of iron, nickel, and such ferromagnesian minerals as olivine.

siderosis (,saɪdə'rəʊsɪs) *n.* a lung disease caused by breathing in fine particles of iron or other metallic dust.

siderostat ('saɪdərəʊ,stæt) *n.* an astronomical instrument consisting of a plane mirror rotated by a clock mechanism about two axes so that light from a celestial body, esp. the sun, is reflected along a constant direction for a long period of time. [C19: from *sidero-*, from L *sīdus* a star + -STAT]

side-saddle *n.* **1.** a riding saddle originally designed for women riders in skirts who sit with both legs on the near side of the horse. ~*adv.* **2.** on or as if on a side-saddle.

sideshow ('saɪd,ʃəʊ) *n.* **1.** a small show or entertainment offered in conjunction with a larger attraction, as at a circus or fair. **2.** a subordinate event or incident.

sideslip ('saɪd,slɪp) *n.* **1.** a sideways skid, as of a motor vehicle. ~*vb.* **-slipping, -slipped. 2.** another name for **slip**[1] (sense 11).

sidesman ('saɪdzmən) *n., pl.* **-men.** *Church of England.* a man elected to help the parish church-warden.

side-splitting *adj.* **1.** producing great mirth. **2.** (of laughter) uproarious or very hearty.

sidestep ('saɪd,stɛp) *vb.* **-stepping, -stepped. 1.** to step aside from or out of the way of (something). **2.** (*tr.*) to dodge or circumvent. ~*n.* **side step. 3.** a movement to one side, as in dancing, boxing, etc. —**'side,stepper** *n.*

sidestroke ('saɪd,strəʊk) *n.* a type of swimming stroke in which the swimmer lies sideways in the water making a scissors kick with his legs.

sideswipe ('saɪd,swaɪp) *n.* **1.** a glancing blow or hit along or from the side. ~*vb.* **2.** to strike (someone) with such a blow. —**'side,swiper** *n.*

sidetrack ('saɪd,træk) *vb.* **1.** to distract or be distracted from a main subject or topic. ~*n.* **2.** *U.S. & Canad.* a railway siding. **3.** a digression.

side-valve engine *n.* a type of internal-combustion engine in which the inlet and exhaust valves are in the cylinder block at the side of the pistons.

sidewalk ('saɪd,wɔːk) *n.* the U.S. and Canad. word for **pavement.**

sidewall ('saɪd,wɔːl) *n.* either of the sides of a pneumatic tyre between the tread and the rim.

sideward ('saɪdwəd) *adj.* **1.** directed or moving towards one side. ~*adv. also* **sidewards. 1.** towards one side.

sideways ('saɪd,weɪz) *adv.* **1.** moving, facing, or inclining towards one side. **2.** from one side; obliquely. **3.** with one side forward. ~*adj.* (*prenominal*) **4.** moving or directed to or from one side. **5.** towards or from one side.

side whiskers *pl. n.* another name for **sideboards.**

sidewinder ('saɪd,waɪndə) *n.* **1.** a North American rattlesnake that moves forwards by a sideways looping motion. **2.** *Boxing, U.S.* a heavy swinging blow from the side.

Sidi-bel-Abbès (*French* sidibɛlabɛs) *n.* a city in NW Algeria: headquarters of the Foreign Legion until Algerian independence (1962). Pop.: 186 978 (1983).

siding ('saɪdɪŋ) *n.* **1.** a short stretch of railway track connected to a main line, used for storing rolling stock. **2.** a short railway line giving access to the main line for freight from a factory, etc. **3.** *U.S. & Canad.* material attached to the outside of a building to make it weatherproof.

sidle ('saɪd³l) *vb.* (*intr.*) **1.** to move in a furtive or stealthy manner. **2.** to move along sideways. [C17: back formation from obs. *sideling* sideways]

Sidney *or* **Sydney** ('sɪdnɪ) *n.* Sir **Philip.** 1554–86, English poet, courtier, and soldier. His works include the pastoral romance *Arcadia* (1590), the sonnet sequence *Astrophel and Stella* (1591), and *The Defence of Poesie* (1595), one of the earliest works of literary criticism in English.

Sidon ('saɪd³n) *n.* the chief city of ancient Phoenicia: founded in the third millennium B.C.; wealthy through trade and the making of glass and purple dyes; now the Lebanese city of Saïda. —**Sidonian** (saɪ'dəʊnɪən) *adj., n.*

Sidra ('sɪdrə) *n.* **Gulf of.** a wide inlet of the Mediterranean on the N coast of Libya.

SIDS *abbrev. for* sudden infant death syndrome. See **cot death.**

Siegbahn ('siːgbɑːn) *n.* **1. Kai** ('kaɪ). born 1918, Swedish physicist who worked on electron spectroscopy: Nobel prize for physics 1981. **2.** his father, **Karl Manne Georg** (kɑːrl 'manə 'jeːɔrj). 1886–1978, Swedish physicist, who discovered the M series in x-ray spectroscopy: Nobel prize for physics 1924.

siege (siːdʒ) *n.* **1. a.** the offensive operations carried out to capture a fortified place by surrounding it and deploying weapons against it. **b.** (*as modifier*): *siege warfare.* **2.** a persistent attempt to gain something. **3.** *Obs.* a seat or throne. **4. lay siege to. a.** to besiege. **b.** to importune. [C13: from OF *sege* a seat, from Vulgar L *sēdicāre* (unattested) to sit down, from L *sedēre*]

Siegfried ('siːgfriːd; *German* 'ziːkfriːt) *n. German myth.* a German prince, the son of Sigmund and husband of Kriemhild, who, in the *Nibelungenlied*, assumes possession of the treasure of the Nibelungs by slaying the dragon that guards it, wins Brunhild for King Gunther, and is eventually slain by Hagen. Norse equivalent: **Sigurd.**

siemens ('siːmənz) *n., pl.* **siemens.** the derived SI unit of electrical conductance equal to 1 reciprocal ohm. Symbol: S Formerly called: **mho.**

Siemens ('siːmənz) *n.* **1. Ernst Werner von** (ɛrnst 'vɛrnər fɔn). 1816–92, German engineer, inventor, and pioneer in telegraphy. Among his inventions are the self-excited dynamo and an electrolytic refining process. **2.** his brother, Sir **William,** original name *Karl Wilhelm Siemens.* 1823–83, British engineer, born in Germany, who invented the open-hearth process for making steel.

Siena (sɪ'ɛnə; *Italian* 'sjɛːna) *n.* a walled city in central Italy, in Tuscany: founded by the Etruscans; important artistic centre (13th–14th centuries); university (13th century). Pop.: 60 670 (1985 est.).

Sienkiewicz (*Polish* ʃɛŋ'kjɛvitʃ) *n.* **Henryk** ('xɛnrɪk). 1846–1916, Polish novelist. His best-known works are *Quo Vadis* (1896), set in Nero's Rome, and the war trilogy *With Fire and Sword* (1884), *The Deluge* (1886), and *Pan Michael* (1888), set in 17th-century Poland: Nobel prize for literature 1905.

sienna (sɪ'ɛnə) *n.* **1.** a natural earth containing ferric oxide used as a yellowish-brown pigment when untreated (**raw sienna**) or a reddish-brown pigment when roasted (**burnt sienna**). **2.** the colour of this pigment. [C18: from It. *terra di Siena* earth of SIENA]

sierra (sɪ'ɛərə) *n.* a range of mountains with jagged peaks, esp. in Spain or America. [C17: from Sp., lit.: saw, from L *serra*] —**si'erran** *adj.*

Sierra Leone (sɪ'ɛərə lɪ'əʊnɪ, lɪ'əʊn) *n.* a republic in West Africa, on the Atlantic: became a British colony in 1808 and gained independence (within the Commonwealth) in 1961; declared a republic in 1971; consists of coastal swamps rising to a plateau in the east. Official language: English. Religion: animist majority and Muslim. Currency: leone. Capital: Freetown. Pop.: 3 666 000 (1987 est.). Area: 72 326 sq. km (27 925 sq. miles). —**Sierra Leonean** *adj., n.*

Sierra Madre (*Spanish* 'sjɛrra 'maðre) *n.* (*functioning as sing.*) the main mountain system of Mexico, extending for 2500 km (1500 miles) southeast from the N border: consists of the **Sierra Madre Oriental** in the east, the **Sierra Madre Occidental** in the west, and the **Sierra Madre**

del Sur in the south. Highest peak: Citlaltépetl, 5699 m (18 698 ft.).

Sierra Morena (*Spanish* 'sjɛrra mo'rena) n. (*functioning as sing.*) a mountain range in SW Spain, between the Guadiana and Guadalquivir Rivers. Highest peak: Estrella, 1299 m (4262 ft.).

Sierra Nevada n. (*functioning as sing.*) **1.** (sɪ'ɛərənɪ'vɑːdə). a mountain range in E California, parallel to the Coast Ranges. Highest peak: Mount Whitney, 4418 m (14 495 ft.). **2.** (*Spanish* 'sjɛrra ne'βaða). a mountain range in SE Spain, mostly in Granada and Almería provinces. Highest peak: Cerro de Mulhacén, 3478 m (11 411 ft.).

siesta (sɪ'ɛstə) n. a rest or nap, usually taken in the early afternoon, as in hot countries. [C17: from Sp., from L *sexta hōra* the sixth hour, i.e. noon]

sieve (sɪv) n. **1.** a device for separating lumps from powdered material, straining liquids, etc., consisting of a container with a mesh or perforated bottom through which the material is shaken or poured. ~vb. **2.** to pass or cause to pass through a sieve. **3.** (*tr.; often foll. by out*) to separate or remove (lumps, materials, etc.) by use of a sieve. [OE *sife*] — **'sieve,like** adj.

Sieyès (*French* sjejɛs) n. **Emmanuel Joseph** (ɛmanɥɛl ʒɔzɛf), called *Abbé Sieyès*. 1748–1836, French statesman, political theorist, and churchman, who became prominent during the Revolution following the publication of his pamphlet *Qu'est-ce que le tiers état?* (1789). He was instrumental in bringing Napoleon I to power (1799).

sift (sɪft) vb. **1.** (*tr.*) to sieve (sand, flour, etc.) in order to remove the coarser particles. **2.** to scatter (something) over a surface through a sieve. **3.** (*tr.*) to separate with or as if with a sieve. **4.** (*tr.*) to examine minutely: *to sift evidence.* **5.** (*intr.*) to move as if through a sieve. [OE *siftan*] — **'sifter** n.

siftings ('sɪftɪŋz) pl. n. material or particles separated out by or as if by a sieve.

sigh (saɪ) vb. **1.** (*intr.*) to draw in and exhale audibly a deep breath as an expression of weariness, relief, etc. **2.** (*intr.*) to make a sound resembling this. **3.** (*intr.; often foll. by for*) to yearn, long, or pine. **4.** (*tr.*) to utter or express with sighing. ~n. **5.** the act or sound of sighing. [OE *sīcan*, from ?] — **'sigher** n.

sight (saɪt) n. **1.** the power or faculty of seeing; vision. Related adj.: **visual. 2.** the act or an instance of seeing. **3.** the range of vision: *within sight of land.* **4.** point of view; judgment: *in his sight she could do no wrong.* **5.** a glimpse or view (esp. in **catch** or **lose sight of**). **6.** anything that is seen. **7.** (*often pl.*) anything worth seeing: *the sights of London.* **8.** *Inf.* anything unpleasant or undesirable to see: *his room was a sight!* **9.** any of various devices or instruments used to assist the eye in making alignments or directional observations, esp. such a device used in aiming a gun. **10.** an observation or alignment made with such a device. **11. a sight.** *Inf.* a great deal: *she's a sight too good for him.* **12. a sight for sore eyes.** a person or thing that one is pleased or relieved to see. **13. at** or **on sight. a.** as soon as seen. **b.** on presentation: *a bill payable at sight.* **14. know by sight.** to be familiar with the appearance of without having personal acquaintance. **15. not by a long sight.** *Inf.* on no account. **16. set one's sights on.** to have (a specified goal) in mind. **17. sight unseen.** without having seen the object at issue: *to buy a car sight unseen.* ~vb. **18.** (*tr.*) to see, view, or glimpse. **19.** (*tr.*) **a.** to furnish with a sight or sights. **b.** to adjust the sight of. **20.** to aim (a firearm) using the sight. [OE *sihth*] — **'sightable** adj.

sighted ('saɪtɪd) adj. **1.** not blind. **2.** (*in combination*) having sight of a specified kind: *short-sighted.*

sightless ('saɪtlɪs) adj. **1.** blind. **2.** invisible. — **'sightlessly** adv. — **'sightlessness** n.

sightly ('saɪtlɪ) adj. **-lier, -liest.** pleasing or attractive to see. — **'sightliness** n.

sight-read ('saɪt,riːd) vb. **-reading, -read** (-,rɛd). to sing or play (music in a printed or written form) without previous preparation. — **'sight-,reader** n. — **'sight-,reading** n.

sightscreen ('saɪt,skriːn) n. *Cricket.* a large white screen placed near the boundary behind the bowler to help the batsman see the ball.

sightsee ('saɪt,siː) vb. **-seeing, -saw, -seen.** *Inf.* to visit the famous or interesting sights of (a place). — **'sight,seeing** n. — **'sight,seer** n.

Sigismund ('sɪgɪsmənd) n. 1368–1437, king of Hungary (1387–1437) and of Bohemia (1419–37); Holy Roman Emperor (1411–37). He helped to end the Great Schism in the Church; implicated in the death of Huss.

sigla ('sɪglə) n. the list of symbols used in a book, usually collected together as part of the preliminaries. [L: pl. of *siglum*, dim. of *signum* sign]

sigma ('sɪgmə) n. **1.** the 18th letter in the Greek alphabet (Σ, σ, or, when final, ς), a consonant, transliterated as *S.* **2.** *Maths.* the symbol Σ, indicating summation. [C17: from Gk]

sigma notation n. an algebraic notation in which a capital Greek sigma (Σ) is used to indicate that all values of the expression following the sigma are to be added together (usually for values of a variable between specified limits).

sigmoid ('sɪgmɔɪd) adj. *also* **sigmoidal. 1.** shaped like the letter S. **2.** of or relating to the sigmoid flexure of the large intestine. ~n. **3. sigmoid flexure.** the S-shaped bend in the final portion of the large intestine. [C17: from Gk *sigmoeidēs* sigma-shaped]

Sigmund ('sɪgmənd, 'siːgmʊnd; *German* 'ziːkmʊnt) n. **1.** *Norse myth.* the father of the hero Sigurd. **2.** Also called: **Siegmund** (*German* 'ziːkmʊnt). *German myth.* king of the Netherlands, father of Siegfried.

sign (saɪn) n. **1.** something that indicates a fact, condition, etc., that is not immediately or outwardly observable. **2.** an action or gesture intended to convey information, a command, etc. **3. a.** a board, placard, etc., displayed in public and intended to inform, warn, etc. **b.** (*as modifier*): *a sign painter.* **4.** an arbitrary mark or device that stands for a word, phrase, etc. **5.** *Maths, logic.* **a.** any symbol used to indicate an operation: *a plus sign.* **b.** the positivity or negativity of a number, expression, etc. **6.** an indication or vestige: *the house showed no signs of being occupied.* **7.** a portentous or significant event. **8.** the scent or spoor of an animal. **9.** *Med.* any objective evidence of the presence of a disease or disorder. **10.** *Astrol.* See **sign of the zodiac.** ~vb. **11.** to write (one's name) as a signature to (a document, etc.) in attestation, confirmation, etc. **12.** (*intr.; often foll. by to*) to make a sign. **13.** to engage or be engaged by written agreement, as a player for a team, etc. **14.** (*tr.*) to outline in gestures a sign over, esp. the sign of the cross. **15.** (*tr.*) to indicate by or as if by a sign; betoken. ~See also **sign away, sign in**, etc. [C13: from OF, from L *signum* BIGR

Signac (*French* siɲak) n. **Paul** (pɔl). 1863–1935, French neoimpressionist painter, influenced by Seurat.

signal ('sɪgnəl) n. **1.** any sign, gesture, etc., that serves to communicate information. **2.** anything that acts as an incitement to action: *the rise in prices was a signal for rebellion.* **3. a.** a variable parameter, such as a current or electromagnetic wave, by which information is conveyed through an electronic circuit, etc. **b.** the information so conveyed. **c.** (*as modifier*): *a signal generator.* ~adj. **4.** distinguished or conspicuous. **5.** used to give or act as a signal. ~vb. **-nalling, -nalled** or *U.S.* **-naling, -naled. 6.** to communicate (a message, etc.) to (a person). [C16: from OF *seignal*, from Med. L *signāle*, from L *signum* sign] — **'signaller** or *U.S.* **'signaler** n.

signal box n. **1.** a building containing signal levers for all the railway lines in its section. **2.** a control point for a large area of a railway system.

signalize or **-lise** ('sɪgnə,laɪz) vb. (*tr.*) **1.** to make noteworthy. **2.** to point out carefully.

signally ('sɪgnəlɪ) adv. conspicuously or especially.

signalman ('sɪgnəlmən) n., pl. **-men.** a railway employee in charge of the signals and points within a section.

signal-to-noise ratio n. the ratio of one parameter, such as power of a wanted signal, to the same parameter of the noise at a specified point in an electronic circuit, etc.

signatory ('sɪgnətərɪ, -trɪ) n., pl. **-ries. 1.** a person who has signed a document such as a treaty or an organization, state, etc., on whose behalf such a document has been signed. ~adj. **2.** having signed a document, treaty, etc. [C17: from L *signātōrius* concerning sealing, from *signāre* to seal, from *signum* a mark]

signature ('sɪgnɪtʃə) n. **1.** the name of a person or a mark or sign representing his name. **2.** the act of signing one's name. **3.** a distinctive mark, characteristic, etc., that identifies a person or thing. **4.** *Music.* See **key signature, time signature. 5.** *Printing.* **a.** a sheet of paper printed with several pages that upon folding will become a section or sections of a book. **b.** such a sheet so folded. **c.** a mark, esp. a letter, printed on the first page of a signature. [C16: from OF, from Med. L *signātura*, from L *signāre* to sign]

signature tune *n. Brit.* a melody used to introduce or identify a television or radio programme, a dance band, a performer, etc.

sign away *vb.* (*tr., adv.*) to dispose of by or as if by signing a document.

signboard ('saɪn,bɔːd) *n.* a board carrying a sign or notice, esp. one used to advertise a product, event, etc.

signet ('sɪgnɪt) *n.* **1.** a small seal, esp. one as part of a finger ring. **2.** a seal used to stamp or authenticate documents. **3.** the impression made by such a seal. [C14: from Med. L *signētum* a little seal, from L *signum* a sign]

signet ring *n.* a finger ring bearing a signet.

significance (sɪg'nɪfɪkəns) *n.* **1.** consequence or importance. **2.** something expressed or intended. **3.** the state or quality of being significant. **4.** *Statistics.* a measure of the confidence that can be placed in a result as not being merely a matter of chance.

significant (sɪg'nɪfɪkənt) *adj.* **1.** having or expressing a meaning. **2.** having a covert or implied meaning. **3.** important or momentous. **4.** *Statistics.* of or relating to a difference between a result derived from a hypothesis and its observed value that is too large to be attributed to chance. [C16: from L *significāre* to SIGNIFY] —**sig'nificantly** *adv.*

significant figures *pl. n.* **1.** the figures of a number that express a magnitude to a specified degree of accuracy: *3.141 59 to four significant figures is 3.142.* **2.** the number of such figures: *3.142 has four significant figures.*

signification (,sɪgnɪfɪ'keɪʃən) *n.* **1.** meaning or sense. **2.** the act of signifying.

signify ('sɪgnɪ,faɪ) *vb.* **-fying, -fied.** (when *tr., may take a clause as object*) **1.** (*tr.*) to indicate or suggest. **2.** (*tr.*) to imply or portend: *the clouds signified the coming storm.* **3.** (*tr.*) to stand as a symbol, sign, etc. (for). **4.** (*intr.*) to be important. [C13: from OF, from L *significāre*, from *signum* a mark + *facere* to make] —**sig'nificative** *adj.* —**'signi,fier** *n.*

sign in *vb.* (*adv.*) **1.** to sign or cause to sign a register, as at a hotel, club, etc. **2.** to make or become a member, as of a club.

sign language *n.* any system of communication by manual signs or gestures, such as one used by the deaf.

sign off *vb.* (*adv.*) **1.** (*intr.*) to announce the end of a radio or television programme, esp. at the end of a day. **2.** (*tr.*) (of a doctor) to declare unfit for work, because of illness.

sign of the zodiac *n.* any of the 12 equal areas into which the zodiac can be divided, named after the 12 zodiacal constellations. In astrology, it is thought that a person's attitudes to life can be correlated with the sign in which the sun lay at the moment of his birth.

sign on *vb.* (*adv.*) **1.** (*tr.*) to hire or employ. **2.** (*intr.*) to commit oneself to a job, activity, etc. **3.** (*intr.*) *Brit.* to register and report regularly at an unemployment benefit office.

signor or **signior** ('siːnjɔː; *Italian* siɲ'ɲor) *n., pl.* **-gnors** or **-gnori** (*Italian* -'ɲori). an Italian man: usually used before a name as a title equivalent to *Mr.*

signora (siːn'jɔːrə; *Italian* siɲ'ɲora) *n., pl.* **-ras** or **-re** (*Italian* -re). a married Italian woman: a title of address equivalent to *Mrs* when placed before a name or *madam* when used alone. [It., fem. of SIGNORE]

signore (siːn'jɔːreɪ; *Italian* siɲ'ɲore) *n., pl.* **-ri** (-rɪ; *Italian* -ri). an Italian man: a title of respect equivalent to *sir* when used alone. [It., ult. from L *senior* an elder, from *senex* an old man]

Signorelli (*Italian* siɲɲo'rɛlli) *n.* **Luca** ('luːka). ?1441–1523, Italian painter, noted for his frescoes.

signorina (,siːnjɔː'riːnə; *Italian* siɲɲo'rina) *n., pl.* **-nas** or **-ne** (*Italian* -ne). an unmarried Italian woman: a title of address equivalent to *Miss* when placed before a name or *madam* or *miss* when used alone. [It., dim. of SIGNORA]

signory ('siːnjərɪ) *n., pl.* **-gnories.** a variant spelling of **seigniory.**

sign out *vb.* (*adv.*) to sign to sign (one's name) to indicate that one is leaving a place: *he signed out for the evening.*

signpost ('saɪn,pəʊst) *n.* **1.** a post bearing a sign that shows the way, as at a roadside. **2.** something that serves

as a clue or indication. ~*vb.* (*tr.; usually passive*) **3.** to mark with signposts. **4.** to indicate direction towards.

sign up *vb.* (*adv.*) to enlist or cause to enlist, as for military service.

Sigurd ('sɪgʊəd; *German* 'ziːɡʊrt) *n. Norse myth.* a hero who killed the dragon Fafnir to gain the treasure of Andvari, won Brynhild for Gunnar by deception, and then was killed by her when she discovered the fraud. His wife was Gudrun. German counterpart: **Siegfried.**

Sihanouk ('sɪənʊk) *n.* Prince **Norodom** (,nɒrə'dɒm). born 1922, Kampuchean statesman; king of Cambodia (1941–55); prime minister (1955–60), after which he became head of state. He was deposed in 1970 but reinstated (1975–76) following the victory of the Khmer Rouge in the civil war. Head of state in exile of the Government of Democratic Kampuchea from (1982–87).

sika ('siːkə) *n.* a Japanese forest-dwelling deer, now introduced into Britain, having a brown coat and a large white patch on the rump. [from Japanese *shika*]

Sikang ('ʃiː'kæŋ) *n.* a former province of W China: established in 1928 from part of W Sichuan and E Tibet; dissolved in 1955.

Sikh (siːk) *n.* **1.** a member of an Indian religion that separated from Hinduism and was founded in the 16th century, that teaches monotheism and rejects the authority of the Vedas. ~*adj.* **2.** of or relating to the Sikhs or their religious beliefs. [C18: from Hindi, lit.: disciple, from Sansk. *śiksati* he studies] —**'Sikh,ism** *n.*

Si Kiang ('ʃiː 'kjæŋ, kaɪ'æŋ) *n.* See **Xi.**

Siking ('siː'kɪŋ) *n.* a former name for **Xi An.**

Sikkim ('sɪkɪm) *n.* a state of NE India: under British control (1861–1947); became an Indian protectorate in 1950 and an Indian state in 1975; lies in the Himalayas, rising to 8600 m (28 216 ft.) at Kanchenjunga in the north. Capital: Gangtok. Pop.: 315 682 (1981). Area: 7325 sq. km (2828 sq. miles). —,**Sikki'mese** *adj., n.*

Sikorsky (sɪ'kɔːskɪ) *n.* **Igor.** 1889–1972, U.S. aeronautical engineer, born in Russia. He designed and flew the first four-engined aircraft (1913) and designed the first successful helicopter (1939).

silage ('saɪlɪdʒ) *n.* any crop harvested while green for fodder and kept succulent by partial fermentation in a silo. Also called: **ensilage.** [C19: alteration (infl. by SILO) of EN-SILAGE]

sild (sɪld) *n.* any of various small young herrings, esp. when prepared and canned in Norway. [Norwegian]

silence ('saɪləns) *n.* **1.** the state or quality of being silent. **2.** the absence of sound or noise. **3.** refusal or failure to speak, etc., when expected: *his silence on their promotion was alarming.* **4.** a period of time without noise. **5.** oblivion or obscurity. ~*vb.* (*tr.*) **6.** to bring to silence. **7.** to put a stop to: *to silence all complaint.*

silencer ('saɪlənsə) *n.* **1.** any device designed to reduce noise, esp. the device in the exhaust system of a motor vehicle. U.S. and Canad. name: **muffler.** **2.** a device fitted to the muzzle of a firearm to deaden the report. **3.** a person or thing that silences.

silene (saɪ'liːnɪ) *n.* any of a genus of plants with pink or white flowers and slender leaves. [C18: NL, from L]

silent ('saɪlənt) *adj.* **1.** characterized by an absence or near absence of noise or sound: *a silent house.* **2.** tending to speak very little or not at all. **3.** unable to speak. **4.** failing to speak, communicate, etc., when expected: *the witness chose to remain silent.* **5.** not spoken or expressed. **6.** (of a letter) used in the orthography of a word but no longer pronounced in that word: *the "k" in "know" is silent.* **7.** denoting a film that has no accompanying soundtrack. [C16: from L *silēns*, from *silēre* to be quiet] —**'silently** *adv.* —**'silentness** *n.*

silent cop *n. Austral. sl.* a small raised hemispherical marker in the middle of a crossroads.

silent majority *n.* a presumed moderate majority of the citizens who are too passive to make their views known.

Silenus (saɪ'liːnəs) *n. Greek myth.* **1.** chief of the satyrs and foster father to Dionysus. **2.** (*often not cap.*) one of a class of woodland deities, closely similar to the satyrs.

Silesia (saɪ'liːʃɪə) *n.* a region of central Europe around the upper and middle Oder valley: mostly annexed by Prussia in 1742 but became almost wholly Polish in 1945; rich coal and iron-ore deposits. Polish name: **Śląsk.** Czech name: **Slezsko.** German name: **Schlesien.** —**Si'lesian** *adj., n.*

silex ('sailɛks) n. a type of heat-resistant glass made from fused quartz. [C16: from L: hard stone]

silhouette (ˌsɪluː'ɛt) n. 1. the outline of a solid figure as cast by its shadow. 2. an outline drawing filled in with black, often a profile portrait cut out of black paper and mounted on a light ground. ~vb. 3. (tr.) to cause to appear in silhouette. [C18: after Étienne de *Silhouette* (1709–67), F politician]

silica ('sɪlɪkə) n. the dioxide of silicon (SiO₂), occurring naturally as quartz. It is a refractory insoluble material used in the manufacture of glass, ceramics, and abrasives. [C19: NL, from L *silex* hard stone]

silica gel n. an amorphous form of silica capable of absorbing large quantities of water: used esp. in drying gases and oils.

silicate ('sɪlɪkɪt, -ˌkeɪt) n. a salt or ester that can be regarded as derived from silicic acid. Silicates constitute a large proportion of the earth's minerals and are present in cement and glass.

siliceous or **silicious** (sɪ'lɪʃəs) adj. 1. of, relating to, or containing silica: *a siliceous clay.* 2. (of plants) growing in soil rich in silica.

silicic (sɪ'lɪsɪk) adj. of or containing silicon or an acid obtained from silicon.

silicic acid n. a white gelatinous substance obtained by adding an acid to a solution of sodium silicate. It is best regarded as hydrated silica.

silicify (sɪ'lɪsɪˌfaɪ) vb. -**fying**, -**fied**. to convert or be converted into silica: *silicified wood.* —**si,licifi'cation** n.

silicon ('sɪlɪkən) n. **a.** a brittle metalloid element that exists in two allotropic forms; occurs principally in sand, quartz, granite, feldspar, and clay. It is usually a grey crystalline solid but is also found as a brown amorphous powder. It is used in transistors, solar cells, and alloys. Its compounds are widely used in glass manufacture and the building industry. Symbol: Si; atomic no.: 14; atomic wt.: 28.09. **b.** (*modifier; sometimes cap.*) denoting an area of a country that contains much high-technology industry. [C19: from SILICA, on the model of *boron, carbon*]

silicon carbide n. an extremely hard bluish-black insoluble crystalline substance produced by heating carbon with sand at a high temperature and used as an abrasive and refractory material. Very pure crystals are used as semiconductors. Formula: SiC.

silicon chip n. another term for **chip** (sense 7).

silicon controlled rectifier n. a semiconductor rectifier whose forward current between two electrodes, the anode and cathode, is initiated by means of a signal applied to a third electrode, the gate. The current subsequently becomes independent of the signal. Also called: **thyristor**.

silicone ('sɪlɪˌkəʊn) n. *Chem.* **a.** any of a large class of polymeric synthetic materials that usually have resistance to temperature, water, and chemicals, and good insulating and lubricating properties, making them suitable for wide use as oils, water repellents, resins, etc. **b.** (*as modifier*): *silicone rubber.*

Silicon Valley n. any area in which industries associated with information technology are concentrated.

silicosis (ˌsɪlɪ'kəʊsɪs) n. *Pathol.* a form of pneumoconiosis caused by breathing in tiny particles of silica, quartz, or slate, and characterized by shortness of breath.

siliqua (sɪ'liːkwə, 'sɪlɪkwə) or **silique** (sɪ'liːk, 'sɪlɪk) n., pl. -**liquae** (-'liːkwiː), -**liquas**, or -**liques**. the long dry dehiscent fruit of cruciferous plants, such as the wallflower. [C18: via F from L *siliqua* a pod] —**siliquose** ('sɪlɪˌkwəʊs) or **siliquous** ('sɪlɪkwəs) adj.

silk (sɪlk) n. 1. the very fine soft lustrous fibre produced by a silkworm to make its cocoon. 2. **a.** thread or fabric made from this fibre. **b.** (*as modifier*): *a silk dress.* 3. **a.** garment made of this. 4. a very fine fibre produced by a spider to build its web, nest, or cocoon. 5. the tuft of long fine styles on an ear of maize. 6. *Brit.* **a.** the gown worn by a Queen's (or King's) Counsel. **b.** *Inf.* a Queen's (or King's) Counsel. **c. take silk.** to become a Queen's (or King's) Counsel. [OE *sioluc*; ult. from Chinese *ssŭ* silk] —**'silk,like** adj.

silk cotton n. another name for **kapok**.

silk-cotton tree n. any of a genus of tropical trees having seeds covered with silky hairs from which kapok is obtained. Also called: **kapok tree**.

silken ('sɪlkən) adj. 1. made of silk. 2. resembling silk in smoothness or gloss. 3. dressed in silk. 4. soft and delicate.

silk hat n. a man's top hat covered with silk.

silkworm ('sɪlk,wɜːm) n. 1. the larva of the Chinese moth that feeds on the leaves of the mulberry tree: widely cultivated as a source of silk. 2. any of various similar or related larvae.

silky ('sɪlkɪ) adj. **silkier**, **silkiest**. 1. resembling silk in texture; glossy. 2. made of silk. 3. (of a voice, manner, etc.) suave; smooth. 4. *Bot.* covered with long fine soft hairs: *silky leaves.* —**'silkily** adv. —**'silkiness** n.

silky oak n. any of an Australian genus of trees having divided leaves and showy clusters of orange, red, or white flowers: cultivated in the tropics as shade trees.

sill (sɪl) n. 1. a shelf at the bottom of a window inside a room. 2. a horizontal piece along the outside lower member of a window, that throws water clear of the wall below. 3. the lower horizontal member of a window or door frame. 4. a horizontal member placed on top of a foundation wall in order to carry a timber framework. 5. a mass of igneous rock, situated between two layers of older sedimentary rock. [OE *syll*]

sillabub ('sɪlə,bʌb) n. a variant spelling of **syllabub**.

Sillanpää (*Finnish* 'sɪlɑmpæː) n. **Frans Eemil** (frans 'eːmil). 1888–1964, Finnish writer, noted for his novels *Meek Heritage* (1919) and *The Maid Silja* (1931): Nobel prize for literature 1939.

Sillitoe ('sɪlɪtəʊ) n. **Alan.** born 1928, British novelist. His best-known works include *Saturday Night and Sunday Morning* (1958) and *The Loneliness of the Long Distance Runner* (1959).

silly ('sɪlɪ) adj. -**lier**, -**liest**. 1. lacking in good sense; absurd. 2. frivolous, trivial, or superficial. 3. feebleminded. 4. dazed, as from a blow. ~n. 5. (*modifier*) *Cricket.* (of a fielding position) near the batsman's wicket: *silly mid-on.* 6. (*pl.* -**lies**) Also called: **silly-billy**. *Inf.* a foolish person. [C15 (in the sense: pitiable, hence the later senses: foolish): from OE *sǣlig* (unattested) happy, from *sǣl* happiness] —**'silliness** n.

silly season n. *Brit.* a period, usually during the summer months, when journalists fill space reporting on frivolous events and activities.

silo ('saɪləʊ) n., pl. -**los**. 1. a pit, trench, or tower, often cylindrical in shape, in which silage is made and stored. 2. an underground position in which missile systems are sited for protection. [C19: from Sp., ? of Celtic origin]

Siloam (saɪ'ləʊəm, sɪ-) n. *Bible.* a pool in Jerusalem where Jesus cured a man of his blindness (John 9).

Silone (*Italian* si'loːne) n. **Ignazio** (iɲ'ɲattsjo). 1900–78, Italian writer, noted for his humanitarian socialistic novels, *Fontamara* (1933) and *Bread and Wine* (1937).

silt (sɪlt) n. 1. a fine deposit of mud, clay, etc., esp. one in a river or lake. ~vb. 2. (usually foll. by *up*) to fill or become filled with silt; choke. [C15: from ON] —**sil'tation** n. —**'silty** adj.

Silurian (saɪ'lʊərɪən) adj. 1. of or formed in the third period of the Palaeozoic era, during which fishes first appeared. ~n. 2. **the.** the Silurian period or rock system. [C19: from *Silures* a Welsh tribe who opposed the Romans]

silurid (saɪ'lʊərɪd) n. 1. any freshwater teleost fish of the family Siluridae, such as the European catfish, which has an elongated body, naked skin, and a long anal fin. ~adj. 2. of, relating to, or belonging to the family Siluridae. [C19: from L *silūrus*, from Gk *silouros* a river fish]

silva ('sɪlvə) n. a variant spelling of **sylva**.

silvan ('sɪlvən) adj. a variant spelling of **sylvan**.

Silvanus or **Sylvanus** (sɪl'veɪnəs) n. *Roman myth.* the Roman god of woodlands, fields, and flocks. Greek counterpart: **Pan**. [L: from *silva* woodland]

silver ('sɪlvə) n. 1. **a.** a ductile malleable brilliant greyish-white element having the highest electrical and thermal conductivity of any metal. It occurs free and in argentite and other ores: used in jewellery, tableware, coinage, electrical contacts, and electroplating. Symbol: Ag; atomic no.: 47; atomic wt.: 107.870. **b.** (*as modifier*): *a silver coin.* Related adj.: **argent.** 2. coin made of this metal. 3. cutlery, whether made of silver or not. 4. any household articles made of silver. 5. short for **silver medal.** 6. **a.** a brilliant or light greyish-white colour. **b.** (*as adj.*): *silver hair.* ~adj. 7. well-articulated: *silver speech.* 8. (*prenominal*) denoting the 25th in a series: *a silver wedding* *anniversary.* ~*vb.* **9.** (*tr.*) to coat with silver or a silvery substance: *to silver a spoon.* **10.** to become or cause to become silvery in colour. [OE *siolfor*] —'**silvering** *n.*

silver age *n.* **1.** (in Greek and Roman mythology) the second of the world's major epochs, inferior to the preceding golden age. **2.** the postclassical period of Latin literature, occupying the early part of the Roman imperial era.

silver beet *n.* an Australian and New Zealand variety of beet, cultivated for its edible spinach-like leaves with white stems.

silver bell *n.* any of various deciduous trees of North America and China, having white bell-shaped flowers. Also called: **snowdrop tree.**

silver birch *n.* a tree of N temperate regions of the Old World, having silvery-white peeling bark.

silver bromide *n.* a yellowish powder that darkens when exposed to light: used in making photographic emulsions. Formula: AgBr.

silver chloride *n.* a white powder that darkens on exposure to light: used in making photographic emulsions and papers. Formula: AgCl.

silver-eye *n. Austral. & N.Z.* another name for **waxeye** or **white-eye.**

silver fern *n. N.Z.* **1.** another name for **ponga.** **2.** a formalized spray of fern leaf, silver on a black background: the symbol of New Zealand sporting teams.

silver fir *n.* any of various fir trees the leaves of which have a silvery undersurface.

silverfish ('sɪlvə,fɪʃ) *n., pl.* **-fish** or **-fishes.** **1.** a silver variety of the goldfish. **2.** any of various other silvery fishes, such as the moonfish. **3.** any of various small primitive wingless insects that have long antennae and tail appendages and occur in buildings, feeding on food scraps, book-bindings, etc.

silver fox *n.* **1.** an American red fox in a colour phase in which the fur is black with long silver-tipped hairs. **2.** the valuable fur or pelt of this animal.

silver-gilt *n.* silver covered with a thin film of gold.

silver iodide *n.* a yellow powder that darkens on exposure to light: used in photography and artificial rainmaking. Formula: AgI.

silver lining *n.* a hopeful aspect of an otherwise desperate or unhappy situation.

silver medal *n.* a medal of silver awarded to a competitor who comes second in a contest or race.

silver nitrate *n.* a white crystalline soluble poisonous substance used in making photographic emulsions and as a medical antiseptic and astringent. Formula: $AgNO_3$.

silver plate *n.* **1.** a thin layer of silver deposited on a base metal. **2.** articles, esp. tableware, made of silver plate. ~*vb.* **silver-plate.** **3.** (*tr.*) to coat (a metal, object, etc.) with silver, as by electroplating.

silver screen *n.* **the.** *Inf.* **1.** films collectively or the film industry. **2.** the screen onto which films are projected.

silver service *n.* (in restaurants) a style of serving food using a spoon and fork in one hand like a pair of tongs.

silverside ('sɪlvə,saɪd) *n.* **1.** *Brit. & N.Z.* a cut of beef below the aitchbone and above the leg. **2.** a small marine or freshwater teleost fish related to the grey mullets.

silversmith ('sɪlvə,smɪθ) *n.* a craftsman who makes or repairs articles of silver. —'**silver,smithing** *n.*

silverware ('sɪlvə,wɛə) *n.* articles, esp. tableware, made of or plated with silver.

silverweed ('sɪlvə,wiːd) *n.* **1.** a rosaceous perennial creeping plant with silvery pinnate leaves and yellow flowers. **2.** any of various twining shrubs of SE Asia and Australia, having silvery leaves and showy purple flowers.

silvery ('sɪlvərɪ) *adj.* **1.** of or having the appearance of silver: *the silvery moon.* **2.** containing or covered with silver. **3.** having a clear ringing sound. —'**silveriness** *n.*

silviculture ('sɪlvɪ,kʌltʃə) *n.* the branch of forestry that is concerned with the cultivation of trees. [C20: *silvi-*, from L *silva* woodland + CULTURE] —,**silvi'cultural** *adj.* —,**silvi'culturist** *n.*

sima ('saɪmə) *n.* **1.** the silicon-rich and magnesium-rich rocks of the earth's oceanic crust. **2.** the earth's continental lower crust. [C20: from SI(LICA) + MA(GNESIA)]

Simbirsk (*Russian* sim'birsk) *n.* the former name (until 1924) of **Ulyanovsk.**

Simenon ('sɪmənɒn; *French* simnɔ̃) *n.* **Georges** (ʒɔrʒ). born 1903, Belgian novelist. He wrote over two hundred novels, including the detective series featuring Maigret.

Simeon ('sɪmɪən) *n.* **1. a.** *Old Testament.* the second son of Jacob and Leah. **b.** the tribe descended from him. **c.** the territory once occupied by this tribe in the extreme south of the land of Canaan. **2.** *New Testament.* a devout Jew, who recognized the infant Jesus as the Messiah and uttered the canticle *Nunc Dimittis* over him in the Temple (Luke 2:25–35).

Simeon Stylites (staɪ'laɪtiːz) *n.* **Saint.** ?390–459 A.D., Syrian monk, first of the ascetics who lived on pillars. Feast day: Jan. 5.

Simferopol (*Russian* simfɪ'rɔpəlj) *n.* a city in the SW Soviet Union, in the S Ukrainian SSR on the S Crimean Peninsula: a Scythian town in the 1st century B.C.; seized by the Russians in 1736. Pop.: 338 000 (1987).

simian ('sɪmɪən) *adj.* **1.** of or resembling a monkey or ape. ~*n.* **2.** a monkey or ape. [C17: from L *sīmia* an ape, prob. from Gk *sīmos* flat-nosed]

similar ('sɪmɪlə) *adj.* **1.** showing resemblance in qualities, characteristics, or appearance. **2.** *Geom.* (of two or more figures) having corresponding angles equal and all corresponding sides in the same ratio. [C17: from OF, from L *similis*] —**similarity** (,sɪmɪ'lærɪtɪ) *n.* —'**similarly** *adv.*

▷ *Usage.* Careful writers prefer not to use *similarly* where *correspondingly* would be appropriate: *if our competitors raise their prices, we must correspondingly* (not *similarly*) *make increases in ours.*

simile ('sɪmɪlɪ) *n.* a figure of speech that expresses the resemblance of one thing to another of a different category, usually introduced by *as* or *like.* Cf. **metaphor.** [C14: from L *simile* something similar, from *similis* like]

similitude (sɪ'mɪlɪ,tjuːd) *n.* **1.** likeness. **2.** a thing or sometimes a person that is like or the counterpart of another. **3.** *Arch.* a simile or parable. [C14: from L *similitūdō*, from *similis* like]

Simla ('sɪmlə) *n.* a city in N India, capital of Himachal Pradesh state: summer capital of India (1865–1939); hill resort and health centre. Pop.: 70 604 (1981).

simmer ('sɪmə) *vb.* **1.** to cook (food) gently at or just below the boiling point. **2.** (*intr.*) to be about to break out in rage or excitement. ~*n.* **3.** the act, sound, or state of simmering. [C17: ? imit.]

simmer down *vb.* (*adv.*) **1.** (*intr.*) *Inf.* to grow calmer, as after intense rage. **2.** (*tr.*) to reduce the volume of (a liquid) by boiling slowly.

simnel cake ('sɪmnəl) *n. Brit.* a fruit cake covered with a layer of marzipan, traditionally eaten during Lent or at Easter. [C13 *simenel*, from OF, from L *simila* fine flour, prob. of Semitic origin]

Simon ('saɪmən) *n.* **1.** the original name of (Saint) **Peter.** **2.** *New Testament.* **a.** See **Simon Zelotes.** **b.** a relative of Jesus, who may have been identical with Simon Zelotes (Matthew 13:55). **c.** Also called: **Simon the Tanner.** a Christian of Joppa with whom Peter stayed (Acts of the Apostles 9:43). **3.** **John** (**Allsebrook**), 1st Viscount Simon. 1873–1954, British statesman and lawyer. He was Liberal home secretary (1915–16) and, as a leader of the National Liberals, foreign secretary (1931–35), home secretary (1935–37), Chancellor of the Exchequer (1937–40), Lord Chancellor (1940–45). **4. Paul.** born 1942, U.S. pop singer and songwriter. His recordings include: with Art Garfunkel (born 1941), "The Sounds of Silence" (1965), "Mrs Robinson" (1968), and *Bridge over Troubled Water* (1970); and, solo, "50 Ways to Leave your Lover" (1975), and *Hearts and Bones* (1983).

Simonides (saɪ'mɒnɪ,diːz) *n.* ?556–?468 B.C., Greek lyric poet and epigrammatist, noted for his odes to victory.

Simon Magus *n. New Testament.* a Samaritan sorcerer, probably from Gitta, of the 1st century A.D. After being converted to Christianity, he tried to buy miraculous powers from the apostles (Acts of the Apostles 8:9–24). He is also identified as the founder of a Gnostic sect.

Simon Peter *n. New Testament.* the full name of the apostle Peter, a combination of his original name and the name given him by Christ (Matthew 16:17–18).

simon-pure ('saɪmən-) *adj. Rare.* real; authentic. [C19: from *the real Simon Pure*, a character in the play *A Bold Stroke for a Wife* (1717) by Susannah Centlivre (1669-1723), who is impersonated by another character in some scenes]

simony ('saɪmənɪ) *n. Christianity.* the practice, now usually regarded as a sin, of buying or selling spiritual or Church benefits such as pardons, relics, etc. [C13: from

OF *simonie*, from LL *sīmōnia*, from SIMON MAGUS] —'**simonist** *n.*

Simon Zelotes (zɪ'lɒutiːz) *n.* one of the 12 apostles, who had probably belonged to the Zealot party before becoming a Christian (Luke 6:15). Owing to a misinterpretation of two similar Aramaic words he is also, but mistakenly, called *the Canaanite* (Matthew 10:4).

simoom (sɪ'muːm) *or* **simoon** (sɪ'muːn) *n.* a strong suffocating sand-laden wind of the deserts of Arabia and North Africa. [from Ar. *samūm* poisonous, from Aramaic *sammā* poison]

simpatico (sɪm'pɑːtɪˌkəʊ) *adj. Inf.* 1. pleasant or congenial. 2. of similar mind or temperament. [It.: from *simpatia* SYMPATHY]

simper ('sɪmpə) *vb.* 1. (*intr.*) to smile coyly, affectedly, or in a silly self-conscious way. 2. (*tr.*) to utter (something) in such a manner. ~*n.* 3. a simpering smile; smirk. [C16: prob. from Du. *simper* affected] —'**simpering** *adj.* —'**simperingly** *adv.*

simple ('sɪmpəl) *adj.* 1. easy to understand or do: *a simple problem.* 2. plain; unadorned: *a simple dress.* 3. not combined or complex: *a simple mechanism.* 4. unaffected or unpretentious: *although he became famous, he remained a simple man.* 5. sincere; frank: *her simple explanation was readily accepted.* 6. of humble condition or rank: *the peasant was of simple birth.* 7. feeble-minded. 8. (*prenominal*) without additions or modifications: *the witness told the simple truth.* 9. (*prenominal*) straightforward: *a simple case of mumps.* 10. *Chem.* (of a substance) consisting of only one chemical compound. 11. *Maths.* (of an equation) containing variables to the first power only. 12. *Biol.* **a.** not divided into parts: *a simple leaf.* **b.** formed from only one ovary: *simple fruit.* 13. *Music.* relating to or denoting a time where the number of beats per bar may be two, three, or four. ~*n.* *Arch.* 14. a simpleton. 15. a plant having medicinal properties. [C13: via OF from L *simplex* plain] —**simplicity** (sɪm'plɪsɪtɪ) *n.*

simple fraction *n.* a fraction in which the numerator and denominator are both integers. Also called: **common fraction, vulgar fraction.**

simple fracture *n.* a fracture in which the broken bone does not pierce the skin.

simple harmonic motion *n.* a form of periodic motion of a particle, etc., in which the acceleration is always directed towards some equilibrium point and is proportional to the displacement from this point. Abbrev.: **SHM.**

simple-hearted *adj.* free from deceit; frank.

simple interest *n.* interest paid on the principal alone. Cf. **compound interest.**

simple machine *n.* a simple device for altering the magnitude or direction of a force. The six basic types are the lever, wheel and axle, pulley, screw, wedge, and inclined plane.

simple-minded *adj.* 1. stupid; foolish; feeble-minded. 2. mentally defective. 3. unsophisticated; artless. —**simple-'mindedly** *adv.* —**simple-'mindedness** *n.*

simple sentence *n.* a sentence consisting of a single main clause.

simpleton ('sɪmpəltən) *n.* a foolish or ignorant person.

simplify ('sɪmplɪˌfaɪ) *vb.* **-fying, -fied.** (*tr.*) 1. to make less complicated or easier. 2. *Maths.* to reduce (an equation, fraction, etc.) to its simplest form. [C17: via F from Med. L *simplificāre*, from L *simplus* simple + *facere* to make] —**simplifi'cation** *n.*

simplistic (sɪm'plɪstɪk) *adj.* 1. characterized by extreme simplicity. 2. making unrealistically simple judgments or analyses. —'**simplism** *n.* —**sim'plistically** *adv.*

Simplon Pass ('sɪmplɒn) *n.* a pass over the Lepontine Alps in S Switzerland, between Brig (Switzerland) and Iselle (Italy). Height: 2009 m (6590 ft.).

simply ('sɪmplɪ) *adv.* 1. in a simple manner. 2. merely. 3. absolutely; altogether: *a simply wonderful holiday.* 4. (*sentence modifier*) frankly.

Simpson ('sɪmpsən, 'sɪmsən) *n.* Sir **James Young.** 1811–70, Scottish obstetrician, who pioneered the use of chloroform as an anaesthetic.

Simpson Desert ('sɪmpsən) *n.* an uninhabited arid region in central Australia, mainly in the Northern Territory. Area: about 145 000 sq. km (56 000 sq. miles).

simulacrum (ˌsɪmjʊ'leɪkrəm) *n.*, *pl.* **-cra** (-krə). *Arch.* 1. any image or representation of something. 2. a superficial likeness. [C16: from L: likeness, from *simulāre* to imitate, from *similis* like]

simulate *vb.* ('sɪmjʊˌleɪt). (*tr.*) 1. to make a pretence of: *to simulate anxiety.* 2. to reproduce the conditions of (a situation, etc.), as in carrying out an experiment: *to simulate weightlessness.* 3. to have the appearance of. ~*adj.* ('sɪmjʊlɪt, -ˌleɪt). 4. *Arch.* assumed. [C17: from L *simulāre* to copy, from *similis* like] —ˌsimu'lation *n.* —'**simulative** *adj.*

simulated ('sɪmjʊˌleɪtɪd) *adj.* 1. (of fur, leather, pearls, etc.) being an imitation of the genuine article, usually made from cheaper material. 2. (of actions, emotions, etc.) imitated; feigned.

simulator ('sɪmjʊˌleɪtə) *n.* 1. any device that simulates specific conditions for the purposes of research or operator training: *space simulator.* 2. a person who simulates.

simulcast ('sɪməlˌkɑːst) *vb.* 1. (*tr.*) to broadcast (a programme, etc.) simultaneously on radio and television. ~*n.* 2. a programme, etc., so broadcast. [C20: from SIMUL(TANEOUS) + (BROAD)CAST]

simultaneous (ˌsɪməl'teɪnɪəs) *adj.* occurring, existing, or operating at the same time. [C17: on the model of INSTANTANEOUS from L *simul* at the same time] —ˌsimul'taneously *adv.* —ˌsimul'taneousness *or* simultaneity (ˌsɪməltə'niːɪtɪ) *n.*

▷ *Usage.* See at **unique.**

simultaneous equations *pl. n.* a set of equations that are all satisfied by the same values of the variables, the number of variables being equal to the number of equations.

sin[1] (sɪn) *n.* 1. **a.** transgression of God's known will or any principle or law regarded as embodying this. **b.** the condition of estrangement from God arising from such transgression. 2. any serious offence, as against a religious or moral principle. 3. any offence against a principle or standard. 4. **live in sin.** *Inf.* (of an unmarried couple) to live together. ~*vb.* (*intr.*) **sinning, sinned.** 5. to commit a sin. 6. (usually foll. by *against*) to commit an offence (against a person, etc.). [OE *synn*] —'**sinner** *n.*

sin[2] (saɪn) *Maths. abbrev. for* sine.

SIN (in Canada) *abbrev. for* Social Insurance Number.

Sinai ('saɪnaɪ) *n.* 1. a mountainous peninsula of NE Egypt at the N end of the Red Sea, between the Gulf of Suez and the Gulf of Aqaba: occupied by Israel in 1967; fully restored by 1982. 2. **Mount.** the mountain where Moses received the Law from God (Exodus 19–20): often identified as Jebel Musa, sometimes as Jebel Serbal, both on the S Sinai Peninsula. —**Sinaitic** (ˌsaɪnɪ'ɪtɪk) *or* **Sinaic** (saɪ'neɪɪk) *adj.*

Sinaloa (ˌsiːnɑː'ləʊə, ˌsɪn-; *Spanish* sina'loa) *n.* a state of W Mexico. Capital: Culiacán. Pop.: 1 880 098 (1980). Area: 58 092 sq. km (22 425 sq. miles).

sinanthropus (sɪn'ænθrəpəs) *n.* a primitive apelike man of the genus *Sinanthropus*, now considered a subspecies of *Homo erectus*. [C20: from NL, from LL *Sīnae* the Chinese + *-anthropus*, from Gk *anthrōpos* man]

Sinatra (sɪ'nɑːtrə) *n.* **Francis Albert,** known as *Frank*. born 1915, U.S. popular singer and film actor. His recordings include "One for my Baby (and one More for the Road)" (1955) and "My Way" (1969).

sin bin *n.* 1. *Sl.* (in ice hockey, etc.) an area off the field of play where a player who has committed a foul can be sent to sit for a specified period. 2. *Inf.* a separate unit for disruptive schoolchildren.

since (sɪns) *prep.* 1. during or throughout the period of time after: *since May it has only rained once.* ~*conj.* (*subordinating*) 2. (sometimes preceded by *ever*) continuously from or starting from the time when. 3. seeing that; because. ~*adv.* 4. since that time: *I haven't seen him since.* [OE *siththan*, lit.: after that]

▷ *Usage.* See at **ago.**

sincere (sɪn'sɪə) *adj.* 1. not hypocritical or deceitful; genuine: *sincere regret.* 2. *Arch.* pure; unmixed. [C16: from L *sincērus*] —**sin'cerely** *adv.* —**sincerity** (sɪn'sɛrɪtɪ) *or* **sin'cereness** *n.*

sinciput ('sɪnsɪˌpʌt) *n.*, *pl.* **sinciputs** *or* **sincipita** (sɪn'sɪpɪtə). *Anat.* the forward upper part of the skull. [C16: from L: half a head, from SEMI- + *caput* head] —**sin'cipital** *adj.*

Sinclair (sɪŋ'klɛə, 'sɪŋklɛə) *n.* **Upton** (**Beall**). 1878–1968, U.S. novelist, whose *The Jungle* (1906) exposed the working and sanitary conditions of the Chicago meat-packing industry and prompted the passage of food inspection laws.

Sind (sɪnd) *n.* a province of SE Pakistan, mainly in the lower Indus valley: formerly a province of British India; became a province of Pakistan in 1947; divided in 1955 between Hyderabad and Khairpur; reunited as a province in 1970. Capital: Karachi. Pop.: 21 682 000 (1985 est.). Area: 140 914 sq. km (54 407 sq. miles).

sine[1] (saɪn) *n.* (of an angle) a trigonometric function that in a right-angled triangle is the ratio of the length of the opposite side to that of the hypotenuse. [C16: from L *sinus* a bend; in NL, *sinus* was mistaken as a translation of Ar. *jiba* sine (from Sansk. *jīva*, lit.: bowstring) because of confusion with Ar. *jaib* curve]

sine[2] ('saɪnɪ) *prep.* (esp. in Latin phrases or legal terms) lacking; without.

sinecure ('saɪnɪˌkjʊə) *n.* **1.** a paid office or post involving minimal duties. **2.** a Church benefice to which no spiritual charge is attached. [C17: from Med. L (*beneficium*) *sine cūrā* (benefice) without cure (of souls), from L *sine* without + *cūra* cure] —'**sine,curism** *n.* —'**sine,curist** *n.*

sine curve (saɪn) *n.* a curve of the equation $y = \sin x$. Also called: **sinusoid.**

sine die *Latin.* ('saɪnɪ 'daɪɪ) *adv., adj.* without a day fixed. [lit.: without a day]

sine qua non *Latin.* ('saɪnɪ kweɪ 'nɒn) *n.* an essential requirement. [lit.: without which not]

sinew ('sɪnjuː) *n.* **1.** *Anat.* another name for **tendon. 2.** (*often pl.*) **a.** a source of strength or power. **b.** a literary word for **muscle.** [OE *sionu*] —'**sinewless** *adj.*

sine wave (saɪn) *n.* any oscillation, such as an alternating current, whose waveform is that of a sine curve.

sinewy ('sɪnjʊɪ) *adj.* **1.** consisting of or resembling a tendon or tendons. **2.** muscular. **3.** (esp. of language, style, etc.) forceful. **4.** (of meat, etc.) tough. —'**sinewiness** *n.*

sinfonia (ˌsɪnfə'nɪə) *n., pl.* **-nie** (-'niːeɪ) *or* **-nias. 1.** another word for **symphony** (senses 2, 3). **2.** (*cap. when part of a name*) a symphony orchestra. [It.]

sinfonietta (ˌsɪnfən'jɛtə) *n.* **1.** a short or light symphony. **2.** (*cap. when part of a name*) a small symphony orchestra. [It.: a little symphony]

sinful ('sɪnfʊl) *adj.* **1.** having committed or tending to commit sin: *a sinful person.* **2.** characterized by or being a sin: *a sinful act.* —'**sinfully** *adv.* —'**sinfulness** *n.*

sing (sɪŋ) *vb.* **singing, sang, sung. 1.** to produce or articulate (sounds, words, a song, etc.) with musical intonation. **2.** (when *intr.*, often foll. by *to*) to perform (a song) to the accompaniment (of): *to sing to a guitar.* **3.** (*intr.*; foll. by *of*) to tell a story in song (about): *I sing of a maiden.* **4.** (*intr.*) to perform songs for a living. **5.** (*intr.*) (esp. of certain birds and insects) to utter calls or sounds reminiscent of music. **6.** (when *intr.*, usually foll. by *of*) to tell (something), esp. in verse: *the poet who sings of the Trojan dead.* **7.** (*intr.*) to make a whining, ringing, or whistling sound: *the arrow sang past his ear.* **8.** (*intr.*) (of the ears) to experience a continuous ringing. **9.** (*tr.*) to bring to a given state by singing: *to sing a child to sleep.* **10.** (*intr.*) *Sl.*, chiefly *U.S.* to confess or act as an informer. ~*n.* **11.** *Inf.* an act or performance of singing. ~See also **sing out.** [OE *singan*] —'**singable** *adj.* —'**singer** *n.* —'**singing** *adj., n.*
▷ **Usage.** See at **ring**[2].

sing. *abbrev. for* singular.

Singapore (ˌsɪŋə'pɔː, ˌsɪŋgə-) *n.* **1.** a republic in SE Asia, occupying one main island and about 40 small islands at the S end of the Malay Peninsula: established as a British trading post in 1819 and became part of the Straits Settlements in 1826; occupied by the Japanese (1942–45); a British colony from 1946, becoming self-governing in 1959; part of the Federation of Malaysia from 1963 to 1965, when it became an independent republic (within the Commonwealth). Languages: Malay, English, Chinese, and Tamil. Currency: Singapore dollar. Capital: Singapore. Pop.: 2 616 000 (1987). Area: 580 sq. km (224 sq. miles). **2.** the capital of the republic of Singapore: a major international port. Pop.: 2 413 945 (1980). —ˌ**Singa'porean** *adj., n.*

singe (sɪndʒ) *vb.* **1.** to burn or be burnt superficially; scorch: *to singe one's clothes.* **2.** (*tr.*) to burn the ends of

(hair, etc.). **3.** (*tr.*) to expose (a carcass) to flame to remove bristles or hair. ~*n.* **4.** a superficial burn. [OE *sengan*]

Singer ('sɪŋə) *n.* **1. Isaac Bashevis.** born 1904, U.S. writer of Yiddish novels and short stories; born in Poland. His works include *Satan in Goray* (1935), *The Family Moskrat* (1950), and the autobiographical *In my Father's Court* (1966): Nobel prize for literature 1978. **2. Isaac Merrit.** 1811–75, U.S. inventor, who originated and developed an improved chain-stitch sewing machine (1852).

Singh (sɪŋ) *n.* a title assumed by a Sikh when he becomes a full member of the community. [from Hindi, from Sansk. *sinhā* a lion]

Singhalese (ˌsɪŋə'liːz) *n., pl.* **-leses** *or* **-lese,** *adj.* a variant spelling of **Sinhalese.**

singing telegram *n.* a service by which a person is employed to present greetings or congratulations by singing.

single ('sɪŋg²l) *adj.* (*usually prenominal*) **1.** existing alone; solitary: *upon the hill stood a single tower.* **2.** distinct from other things. **3.** composed of one part. **4.** designed or sufficient for one user: *a single bed.* **5.** (*also postpositive*) unmarried. **6.** connected with the condition of being unmarried: *he led a single life.* **7.** (esp. of combat) involving two individuals. **8.** even one: *there wasn't a single person on the beach.* **9.** (of a flower) having only one set or whorl of petals. **10.** single-minded: *a single devotion to duty.* **11.** *Rare.* honest or sincere. ~*n.* **12.** something forming one individual unit. **13.** (*often pl.*) **a.** an unmarried person. **b.** (*as modifier*): *singles bar.* **14.** a gramophone record with a short recording, usually of pop music, on each side. **15.** *Cricket.* a hit from which one run is scored. **16. a.** *Brit.* a pound note. **b.** *U.S. & Canad.* a dollar note. **17.** See **single ticket.** ~*vb.* **18.** (*tr.*; usually foll. by *out*) to select from a group of people or things: *he singled him out for special mention.* ~See also **singles.** [C14: from OF *sengle*, from L *singulus* individual] —'**singleness** *n.*

single-acting *adj.* (of a reciprocating engine or pump) having a piston or pistons pressurized on one side only.

single-breasted *adj.* (of a garment) having the fronts overlapping only slightly and with one row of fastenings.

single cream *n.* cream having a low fat content that does not thicken with beating.

single-decker *n. Brit. inf.* a bus with only one passenger deck.

single-end *n. Scot.* accommodation consisting of a single room.

single entry *n.* **a.** a book-keeping system in which transactions are entered in one account only. **b.** (*as modifier*): *a single-entry account.*

single file *n.* a line of persons, animals, or things ranged one behind the other.

single-foot *n.* **1.** a rapid showy gait of a horse in which each foot strikes the ground separately. ~*vb.* **2.** to move or cause to move at this gait.

single-handed *adj., adv.* **1.** unaided or working alone: *a single-handed crossing of the Atlantic.* **2.** having or operated by one hand or one person only. —ˌ**single-'handedly** *adv.* —ˌ**single-'handedness** *n.*

single-lens reflex *n.* See **reflex camera.**

single-minded *adj.* having but one aim or purpose; dedicated. —ˌ**single-'mindedly** *adv.* —ˌ**single-'mindedness** *n.*

single-parent family *n.* another term for **one-parent family.**

singles ('sɪŋg²lz) *pl. n. Tennis, etc.* a match played with one person on each side.

singles bar *n.* a bar or club that is a social meeting place for single people.

single-sex *adj.* (of schools, etc.) admitting members of one sex only.

single sideband transmission *n.* a method of transmitting radio waves in which either the upper or the lower sideband is transmitted, the carrier being either wholly or partially suppressed.

singlestick ('sɪŋg²lˌstɪk) *n.* **1.** a wooden stick used instead of a sword for fencing. **2.** fencing with such a stick. **3.** any short heavy stick.

singlet ('sɪŋglɪt) *n. Chiefly Brit.* **1.** a man's sleeveless vest. **2.** a garment worn with shorts by athletes, boxers, etc. [C18: from SINGLE, on the model of *doublet*]

single ticket *n. Brit.* a ticket entitling a passenger to travel only to his destination, without returning.

singleton ('sɪŋɡəltən) n. **1.** Bridge, etc. an original holding of one card only in a suit. **2.** a single object, etc., distinguished from a pair or group. **3.** Maths. a set containing only one member. [C19: from SINGLE, on the model of SIMPLETON]

single-track adj. **1.** (of a railway) having only a single pair of lines, so that trains can travel in only one direction at a time. **2.** (of a road) only wide enough for one vehicle.

singletree ('sɪŋɡəl,triː) n. U.S. & Austral. another word for **swingletree**.

singly ('sɪŋɡlɪ) adv. **1.** one at a time; one by one. **2.** apart from others; separately; alone.

sing out vb. (tr., adv.) to call out in a loud voice; shout.

singsong ('sɪŋ,sɒŋ) n. **1.** an accent or intonation that is characterized by an alternately rising and falling rhythm, such as in a person's voice. **2.** Brit. an informal session of singing, esp. of popular songs. ~adj. **3.** having a monotonous rhythm: a singsong accent.

singular ('sɪŋɡjʊlə) adj. **1.** remarkable; extraordinary: a singular feat. **2.** unusual; odd: a singular character. **3.** unique. **4.** denoting a word or an inflected form of a word indicating that one referent is being referred to or described. **5.** Logic. (of a proposition) referring to a specific thing or person. ~n. **6.** Grammar. **a.** the singular number. **b.** a singular form of a word. [C14: from L singulāris single] —'**singularly** adv.

singularity (,sɪŋɡjʊ'lærɪtɪ) n., pl. -ties. **1.** the state or quality of being singular. **2.** something distinguishing a person or thing from others. **3.** something unusual. **4.** Maths. a point at which a function is not differentiable although it is differentiable in a neighbourhood of that point. **5.** Astron. a hypothetical point in space at which matter is infinitely compressed to infinitesimal volume. Cf. **black hole**.

singularize or **-rise** ('sɪŋɡjʊlə,raɪz) vb. (tr.) **1.** to make (a word, etc.) singular. **2.** to make conspicuous. —,singulari'**zation** or -ri'**sation** n.

singultus (sɪŋ'ɡʌltəs) n. a technical name for **hiccup**. [C18: from L, lit.: a sob]

sinh (ʃaɪn, sɪnʃ) n. hyperbolic sine. [C20: from SIN(E)[1] + H(YPERBOLIC)]

Sinhailien ('ʃɪn'haɪ'ljɛn) n. a variant transliteration of the Chinese name for **Lianyungang**.

Sinhalese (,sɪnhə'liːz) or **Singhalese** n. **1.** (pl. -leses or -lese) a member of a people living chiefly in Sri Lanka, where they constitute the majority of the population. **2.** the language of this people: the official language of Sri Lanka. ~adj. **3.** of or relating to this people or their language.

Sining ('ʃiː'nɪŋ) n. variant transliteration of the Chinese name for **Xining**.

sinister ('sɪnɪstə) adj. **1.** threatening or suggesting evil or harm: a sinister glance. **2.** evil or treacherous. **3.** (usually postpositive) Heraldry. of, on, or starting from the left side from the bearer's point of view. **4.** Arch. located on the left side. [C15: from L sinister on the left-hand side, considered by Roman augurers to be the unlucky one] —'**sinisterly** adv. —'**sinisterness** n.

sinistral ('sɪnɪstrəl) adj. **1.** of or located on the left side, esp. the left side of the body. **2.** a technical term for **left-handed**. **3.** (of the shells of certain molluscs) coiling in a clockwise direction from the apex. —'**sinistrally** adv.

sinistrorse ('sɪnɪ,strɔːs, ,sɪnɪ'strɔːs) adj. (of some climbing plants) growing upwards in a spiral from right to left. [C19: from L sinistrōrsus turned towards the left, from sinister on the left + vertere to turn] —,sinis'**trorsal** adj.

Sinitic (sɪ'nɪtɪk) n. **1.** a branch of the Sino-Tibetan family of languages, consisting of the various dialects of Chinese. ~adj. **2.** belonging to this group of languages.

sink (sɪŋk) vb. **sinking**, **sank** or **sunk**; **sunk** or **sunken**. **1.** to descend or cause to descend, esp. beneath the surface of a liquid. **2.** (intr.) to appear to move down towards or descend below the horizon. **3.** (intr.) to slope downwards. **4.** (intr.; often foll. by in or into) to pass into a specified lower state or condition: to sink into apathy. **5.** to make or become lower in volume, pitch, etc. **6.** to make or become lower in value, price, etc. **7.** (intr.) to become weaker in health, strength, etc. **8.** (intr.) to seep or penetrate. **9.** (tr.) to dig, cut, drill, bore, or excavate (a hole, shaft, etc.). **10.** (tr.) to drive into the ground: to sink a stake. **11.** (tr.; usually foll. by in or into) **a.** to invest (money). **b.** to lose (money) in an unwise investment. **12.** (tr.) to pay (a debt). **13.** (intr.) to become hollow: his cheeks had sunk during his illness. **14.** (tr.) to hit or propel (a ball) into a hole, pocket, etc.: he sank a 15-foot putt. **15.** (tr.) Brit. inf. to drink, esp. quickly: he sank three pints in half an hour. **16. sink or swim.** to take risks where the alternatives are loss or success. ~n. **17.** a fixed basin, esp. in a kitchen, made of stone, metal, etc., used for washing. **18.** a place of vice or corruption. **19.** an area of ground below that of the surrounding land, where water collects. **20.** Physics. a device by which energy is removed from a system: a heat sink. [OE sincan] —'**sinkable** adj.

sinker ('sɪŋkə) n. **1.** a weight attached to a fishing line, net, etc., to cause it to sink in water. **2.** a person who sinks shafts, etc.

sinkhole ('sɪŋk,həʊl) n. **1.** Also called (esp. in Britain): **swallow hole**. a depression in the ground surface, esp. in limestone, where a surface stream disappears underground. **2.** a place into which foul matter runs.

Sinkiang-Uighur Autonomous Region ('sɪn'kjæŋ 'wiːɡʊə) n. a variant transliteration of the Chinese name for the **Xinjiang Uygur Autonomous Region**.

sink in vb. (intr., adv.) to enter or penetrate the mind: eventually the news sank in.

sinking ('sɪŋkɪŋ) n. **a.** a feeling in the stomach caused by hunger or uneasiness. **b.** (as modifier): a sinking feeling.

sinking fund n. a fund accumulated out of a business enterprise's earnings or a government's revenue and invested to repay a long-term debt.

sinless ('sɪnlɪs) adj. free from sin or guilt; pure. —'**sinlessly** adv. —'**sinlessness** n.

Sinn Féin ('ʃɪn 'feːn) n. an Irish republican political movement founded about 1905 and linked to the revolutionary Irish Republican Army. [C20: from Irish Gaelic: we ourselves] —**Sinn 'Feiner** n. —**Sinn 'Feinism** n.

Sino- combining form. Chinese: Sino-Tibetan; Sinology. [from F, from LL Sīnae the Chinese, from LGk, from Ar. Sīn China, prob. from Chinese Ch'in]

Sinology (saɪ'nɒlədʒɪ) n. the study of Chinese history, language, culture, etc. —**Sinological** (,saɪnə'lɒdʒɪk³l) adj. —**Si'nologist** n. —**Sinologue** ('saɪnə,lɒɡ) n.

Sino-Tibetan ('saɪnəʊ-) n. **1.** a family of languages that includes most of the languages of China, as well as Tibetan, Burmese, and possibly Thai. ~adj. **2.** belonging or relating to this family of languages.

sinsemilla (,sɪnsə'mɪːljə) n. **1.** a type of marijuana with a very high narcotic content. **2.** the plant from which it is obtained, a strain of Cannabis sativa. [C20: from American Sp., lit.: without seed]

sinter ('sɪntə) n. **1.** a whitish porous incrustation, usually consisting of silica, that is deposited from hot springs. **2.** the product of a sintering process. ~vb. **3.** (tr.) to form large particles, lumps, or masses from (metal powders) by heating or pressure or both. [C18: from G Sinter CINDER]

Sint Maarten (sɪnt 'maːrtə) n. the Dutch name for **Saint Martin**.

sinuate ('sɪnjʊɪt, -,eɪt) adj. **1.** Also: **sinuous**. (of leaves) having a strongly waved margin. **2.** another word for **sinuous**. [C17: from L sinuātus curved] —'**sinuately** adv.

Sinŭiju (sɪ,nuːɪ'dʒuː) n. a port in North Korea, on the Yalu River opposite Andong, China: developed by the Japanese during their occupation (1910–45); industrial centre. Pop.: 305 000 (1981).

sinuous ('sɪnjʊəs) adj. **1.** full of turns or curves. **2.** devious; not straightforward. **3.** supple. [C16: from L sinuōsus winding, from sinus a curve] —'**sinuously** adv. —**sinuosity** (,sɪnjʊ'ɒsɪtɪ) n.

sinus ('saɪnəs) n., pl. -nuses. **1.** Anat. **a.** any bodily cavity or hollow space. **b.** a large channel for venous blood, esp. between the brain and the skull. **c.** any of the air cavities in the cranial bones. **2.** Pathol. a passage leading to a cavity containing pus. [C16: from L: a curve]

sinusitis (,saɪnə'saɪtɪs) n. inflammation of the membrane lining a sinus, esp. a nasal sinus.

sinusoid ('saɪnə,sɔɪd) n. another name for **sine curve**. —,sinu'**soidal** adj.

sinusoidal projection n. an equal-area map projection on which all parallels are straight lines and all except the prime meridian are sine curves, often used to show tropical latitudes.

Sion *n.* **1.** (*French* sjɔ̃). a town in SW Switzerland, capital of Valais canton, on the River Rhône. Pop.: 22 877 (1980). Latin name: **Sedunum**. **2.** ('saɪən). a variant of **Zion**.

Siouan ('suːən) *n.* a family of North American Indian languages, including Sioux.

Sioux (suː) *n.* **1.** (*pl.* **Sioux** (suː, suːz)) a member of a group of North American Indian peoples. **2.** any of the languages of the Sioux. [from F, shortened from *Nadowessioux*]

sip (sɪp) *vb.* **sipping, sipped**. **1.** to drink (a liquid) by taking small mouthfuls. ~*n.* **2.** a small quantity of a liquid taken into the mouth and swallowed. **3.** an act of sipping. [C14: prob. from Low G *sippen*] —'**sipper** *n.*

siphon *or* **syphon** ('saɪfˀn) *n.* **1.** a tube placed with one end at a certain level in a vessel of liquid and the other end outside the vessel below this level, so that atmospheric pressure forces the liquid through the tube and out of the vessel. **2.** See **soda siphon**. **3.** *Zool.* any of various tubular organs in different aquatic animals, such as molluscs, through which water passes. ~*vb.* **4.** (often foll. by *off*) to draw off through or as if through a siphon. [C17: from L *siphō*, from Gk *siphōn*] —'**siphonal** *or* **siphonic** (saɪ'fɒnɪk) *adj.*

siphon bottle *n.* another name (esp. U.S.) for **soda siphon**.

siphonophore ('saɪfənəˌfɔː) *n.* any of an order of marine colonial hydrozoans, including the Portuguese man-of-war. [C19: from NL, from Gk *siphōnophoros* tube-bearing]

Siple ('saɪpˀl) *n.* **Mount**. a mountain in Antarctica, on the coast of Byrd Land. Height: 3100 m (10 171 ft.).

sippet ('sɪpɪt) *n.* a small piece of something, esp. a piece of toast or fried bread eaten with soup or gravy. [C16: used as dim. of SOP]

Siqueiros (*Spanish* si'kɛjrɒs) *n.* **David Alfaro** (da'βið al'faro). 1896–1974, Mexican painter, noted for his murals expressing a revolutionary message.

sir (sɜː) *n.* **1.** a polite term of address for a man. **2.** *Arch.* a gentleman of high social status. [C13: var. of SIRE]

Sir (sɜː) *n.* **1.** a title of honour placed before the name of a knight or baronet: *Sir Walter Raleigh.* **2.** *Arch.* a title placed before the name of a figure from ancient history.

Siracusa (sira'kuːza) *n.* the Italian name for **Syracuse**.

Siraj-ud-daula (sɪˈrɑːdʒʊdˈdaʊlə) *n.* ?1728–57, Indian leader who became the Great Mogul's deputy in Bengal (1756); opponent of English colonization. He captured Calcutta (1756) from the English and many of his prisoners suffocated in a crowded room that became known as the Black Hole of Calcutta. He was defeated (1757) by a group of Indian nobles in alliance with Robert Clive.

sirdar ('sɜːdɑː) *n.* **1.** a general or military leader in Pakistan and India. **2.** (formerly) the title of the British commander in chief of the Egyptian Army. **3.** a variant of **sardar**. [from Hindi *sardār*, from Persian, from *sar* head + *dār* possession]

sire ('saɪə) *n.* **1.** a male parent, esp. of a horse or other domestic animal. **2.** a respectful term of address, now used only in addressing a male monarch. ~*vb.* **3.** (*tr.*) (esp. of a domestic animal) to father. [C13: from OF, from L *senior* an elder, from *senex* an old man]

siren ('saɪərən) *n.* **1.** a device for emitting a loud wailing sound, esp. as a warning or signal, consisting of a rotating perforated metal drum through which air or steam is passed under pressure. **2.** (*sometimes cap.*) *Greek myth.* one of several sea nymphs whose singing was believed to lure sailors to destruction on the rocks the nymphs inhabited. **3.** a woman considered to be dangerously alluring or seductive. **4.** an aquatic eel-like salamander of North America, having external gills, no hind limbs, and reduced forelimbs. [C14: from OF *sereine*, from L *sīren*, from Gk *seirēn*]

sirenian (saɪˈriːnɪən) *adj.* **1.** of or belonging to the Sirenia, an order of aquatic herbivorous placental mammals having forelimbs modified as paddles and a horizontally flattened tail: contains only the dugong and manatees. ~*n.* **2.** an animal belonging to this order; sea cow.

Siret (sɪˈrɛt) *n.* a river in SE Europe, rising in the Ukrainian SSR of the Soviet Union and flowing southeast through E Romania to the Danube. Length: about 450 km (280 miles).

Sirius ('sɪrɪəs) *n.* the brightest star in the sky, lying in the constellation Canis Major. Also called: the **Dog Star**. [C14: via L from Gk *Seirios*, from ?]

sirloin ('sɜːˌlɔɪn) *n.* a prime cut of beef from the loin, esp. the upper part. [C16 *surloyn*, from OF *surlonge*, from *sur* above + *longe*, from *loigne* LOIN]

sirocco (sɪˈrɒkəʊ) *n., pl.* **-cos**. a hot oppressive and often dusty wind usually occurring in spring, beginning in N Africa and reaching S Europe. [C17: from It., from Ar. *sharq* east wind]

sironize *or* **-ise** ('saɪrəˌnaɪz) *vb.* (*tr.*) *Austral.* to treat (a woollen fabric) chemically to prevent it wrinkling after being washed. [C20: from (C)SIRO + *-n-* + *-IZE*]

siroset ('saɪrəˌsɛt) *adj. Austral.* of or relating to the chemical treatment of woollen fabrics to give a permanent-press effect, or a garment so treated.

sirrah ('sɪrə) *n. Arch.* a contemptuous term used in addressing a man or boy. [C16: prob. var. of SIRE]

sirree (sə'riː) *interj.* (*sometimes cap.*) *U.S. inf.* an exclamation used with *yes* or *no*.

sirup ('sɪrəp) *n. U.S.* a less common spelling of **syrup**.

sis (sɪs) *n. Inf.* short for **sister**.

sisal ('saɪsˀl) *n.* **1.** a Mexican agave plant cultivated for its large fleshy leaves, which yield a stiff fibre used for making rope. **2.** the fibre of this plant. ~Also called: **sisal hemp**. [C19: from Mexican Sp., after *Sisal*, a port in Yucatán, Mexico]

Sisera ('sɪsərə) *n.* a defeated leader of the Canaanites, who was assassinated by Jael (Judges 5:26).

siskin ('sɪskɪn) *n.* **1.** a yellow-and-black Eurasian finch. **2. pine siskin.** a North American finch, having a streaked yellowish-brown plumage. [C16: from MDu. *siseken*, from MLow G *sisek*]

Sisley ('sɪslɪ; *French* sislɛ) *n.* **Alfred** (alfrɛd). 1839–99, French painter, esp. of landscapes; one of the originators of impressionism.

Sismondi (sɪs'mɒndɪ; *French* sismɔ̃di) *n.* **Jean Charles Léonard Simonde de** (ʒɑ̃ ʃarl leɔnar simɔ̃d də). 1773–1842, Swiss historian and economist. His *Histoire des républiques italiennes du moyen âge* (1807–18) contributed to the movement for Italian unification.

sissy *or* **cissy** ('sɪsɪ) *n., pl.* **-sies**. **1.** an effeminate, weak, or cowardly boy or man. ~*adj.* **2.** effeminate, weak, or cowardly.

sister ('sɪstə) *n.* **1.** a female person having the same parents as another person. **2.** a female person who belongs to the same group, trade union, etc., as another or others. **3.** a senior nurse. **4.** *Chiefly R.C. Church.* a nun or a title given to a nun. **5.** a woman fellow member of a religious body. **6.** (*modifier*) belonging to the same class, fleet, etc., as another or others: *a sister ship.* [OE *sweostor*]

sisterhood ('sɪstəˌhʊd) *n.* **1.** the state of being related as a sister or sisters. **2.** a religious body or society of sisters.

sister-in-law *n., pl.* **sisters-in-law**. **1.** the sister of one's husband or wife. **2.** the wife of one's brother. **3.** the wife of the brother of one's husband or wife.

sisterly ('sɪstəlɪ) *adj.* of or suitable to a sister, esp. in showing kindness. —'**sisterliness** *n.*

Sistine Chapel ('sɪstaɪn, -tiːn) *n.* the chapel of the pope in the Vatican at Rome, built for Sixtus IV and decorated with frescoes by Michelangelo and others. [Sistine, from It. *Sistino* relating to *Sisto* Sixtus (Pope Sixtus IV)]

sistrum ('sɪstrəm) *n., pl.* **-tra** (-trə). a musical instrument of ancient Egypt consisting of a metal rattle. [C14: via L from Gk *seistron*, from *seiein* to shake]

Sisyphean (ˌsɪsɪ'fiːən) *adj.* **1.** relating to Sisyphus. **2.** actually or seemingly endless and futile.

Sisyphus ('sɪsɪfəs) *n. Greek myth.* a king of Corinth, punished in Hades for his misdeeds by eternally having to roll a heavy stone up a hill: every time he approached the top, the stone escaped his grasp and rolled to the bottom.

sit (sɪt) *vb.* **sitting, sat**. (*mainly intr.*) **1.** (*also tr.*; when *intr.*, often foll. by *down*, *in*, or *on*) to adopt a posture in which the body is supported on the buttocks and the torso is more or less upright: *to sit on a chair.* **2.** (*tr.*) to cause to adopt such a posture. **3.** (of an animal) to adopt or rest in a posture with the hindquarters lowered to the ground. **4.** (of a bird) to perch or roost. **5.** (of a hen or other bird) to cover eggs to hatch them. **6.** to be situated or located. **7.** (of the wind) to blow from the direction specified. **8.** to adopt and maintain a posture for one's portrait to be painted, etc. **9.** to occupy or be entitled to a seat in some official capacity, as a judge, etc. **10.** (of a deliberative body) to be in session. **11.** to remain inactive or unused: *his car sat in the garage.* **12.** (of a garment) to fit or hang as specified: *that dress sits well on you.* **13.**

to weigh, rest, or lie as specified: *greatness sits easily on him.* **14.** (*tr.*) *Chiefly Brit.* to take (an examination): *he's sitting his bar finals.* **15.** (usually foll. by *for*) *Chiefly Brit.* to be a candidate (for a qualification): *he's sitting for a BA.* **16.** to keep watch over an invalid, a baby, etc. **17.** (*tr.*) to have seating capacity for. **18. sit tight.** *Inf.* **a.** to wait patiently. **b.** to maintain one's stand, opinion, etc., firmly. ~See also **sit back, sit down,** etc. [OE *sittan*]

sitar (sɪ'tɑː) *n.* a stringed musical instrument, esp. of India, having a long neck, a rounded body, and movable frets. [from Hindi *sitār*, lit.: three-stringed] —**si'tarist** *n.*

sit back *vb.* (*intr., adv.*) to relax, as when action should be taken: *many people just sit back and ignore the problems of today.*

sitcom ('sɪt,kɒm) *n.* an informal term for **situation comedy.**

sit down *vb.* (*adv.*) **1.** to adopt or cause (oneself or another) to adopt a sitting posture. **2.** (*intr.; foll. by under*) to suffer (insults, etc.) without protests or resistance. ~*n.* **sit-down. 3.** a form of civil disobedience in which demonstrators sit down in a public place. **4.** See **sit-down strike.** ~*adj.* **sit-down. 5.** (of a meal, etc.) eaten while sitting down at a table.

sit-down strike *n.* a strike in which workers refuse to leave their place of employment until a settlement is reached.

site (saɪt) *n.* **1. a.** the piece of land where something was, is, or is intended to be located: *a building site.* **b.** (*as modifier*): *site office.* ~*vb.* **2.** (*tr.*) to locate or install (something) in a specific place. [C14: from L, from *sinere* to be placed]

sith (sɪθ) *adv., conj., prep.* an archaic word for **since.** [OE *siththa*]

sit-in *n.* **1.** a form of civil disobedience in which demonstrators occupy seats in a public place and refuse to move. **2.** another term for **sit-down strike.** ~*vb.* **sit in.** (*intr., adv.*) **3.** (often foll. by *for*) to deputize (for). **4.** (foll. by *on*) to take part (in) as a visitor or guest. **5.** to organize or take part in a sit-in.

Sitka ('sɪtkə) *n.* a town in SE Alaska, in the Alexander Archipelago on W Baranof Island: capital of Russian America (1804–67) and of Alaska (1867–1906). Pop.: 8350 (1984).

sitkamer ('sɪt,kɑːmə) *n. S. African.* a sitting room. [from Afrik.]

sitka spruce ('sɪtkə) *n.* a tall North American spruce tree having yellowish-green needle-like leaves. [from SITKA]

sit on *vb.* (*intr., prep.*) **1.** to be a member of (a committee, etc.). **2.** *Inf.* to suppress. **3.** *Inf.* to check or rebuke.

sit out *vb.* (*tr., adv.*) **1.** to endure to the end: *I sat out the play although it was terrible.* **2.** to remain seated throughout (a dance, etc.).

Sitsang (si:'tsæŋ) *n.* a Chinese name for **Tibet.**

sitter ('sɪtə) *n.* **1.** a person or animal that sits. **2.** a person who is posing for his or her portrait to be painted, etc. **3.** a broody hen that is sitting on its eggs to hatch them. **4.** See **baby-sitter. 5.** anything that is extremely easy, such as an easy catch in cricket.

Sitter ('sɪtə) *n.* **Willem de** ('wɪləm də). 1872–1934, Dutch astronomer, who calculated the size of the universe and conceived of it as expanding.

sitting ('sɪtɪŋ) *n.* **1.** a continuous period of being seated: *I read his novel at one sitting.* **2.** such a period in a restaurant, canteen, etc.: *dinner will be served in two sittings.* **3.** the act or period of posing for one's portrait to be painted, etc. **4.** a meeting, esp. of an official body, to conduct business. **5.** the incubation period of a bird's eggs during which the mother sits on them. ~*adj.* **6.** in office: *a sitting councillor.* **7.** seated: *in a sitting position.*

Sitting Bull *n.* ?1831–90, American Indian chief of the Teton Dakota Sioux. Resisting white encroachment on his people's hunting grounds, he led the Sioux tribes against the U.S. Army in the Sioux War (1876–77) in which Custer was killed. The hunger of the Sioux, whose food came from the diminishing buffalo, forced his surrender (1881). He was killed during renewed strife.

sitting duck *n. Inf.* a person or thing in a defenceless or vulnerable position. Also called: **sitting target.**

sitting room *n.* a room in a private house or flat used for relaxation and entertainment of guests.

sitting tenant *n.* a tenant occupying a house, flat, etc.

situate ('sɪtjʊ,eɪt) *vb.* **1.** (*tr.; often passive*) to place. ~*adj.* **2.** (now used esp. in legal contexts) situated. [C16: from LL *situāre* to position, from L *situs* a SITE]

situation (,sɪtjʊ'eɪʃən) *n.* **1.** physical placement, esp. with regard to the surroundings. **2. a.** state of affairs. **b.** a complex or critical state of affairs in a novel, play, etc. **3.** social or financial status, position, or circumstances. **4.** a position of employment. —,situ'ational *adj.*

situation comedy *n.* (on television or radio) a comedy series involving the same characters in various day-to-day situations which are developed as separate stories for each episode. Also called: **sitcom.**

sit up *vb.* (*adv.*) **1.** to raise (oneself or another) from a recumbent to an upright posture. **2.** (*intr.*) to remain out of bed and awake, esp. until a late hour. **3.** (*intr.*) *Inf.* to become suddenly interested: *devaluation of the dollar made the money market sit up.* ~*n.* **sit-up. 4.** *Gymnastics.* another name for **trunk curl.**

Sitwell ('sɪtwəl) *n.* **1.** Dame **Edith.** 1887–1964, English poet and critic, noted esp. for her collection *Façade* (1922). **2.** her brother, Sir **Osbert.** 1892–1969, English writer, best known for his five autobiographical books (1944–50). **3.** his brother, Sir **Sacheverell** (sə'ʃevərəl). born 1897, English poet and writer of books on art, architecture, music, and travel.

sitz bath (sɪts, zɪts) *n.* a bath in which the buttocks and hips are immersed in hot water. [half translation of G *Sitzbad*, from *Sitz* seat + *Bad* bath]

SI unit *n.* any of the units adopted for international use under the Système International d'Unités, now employed for all scientific and most technical purposes. There are seven fundamental units: the metre, kilogram, second, ampere, kelvin, candela, and mole; and two supplementary units: the radian and the steradian. All other units are derived by multiplication or division of these units.

Siva ('si:və) *n. Hinduism.* the destroyer, one of the three chief divinities of the later Hindu pantheon. [from Sansk. *Siva,* lit.: the auspicious (one)] —'Siva,ism *n.*

Sivas (*Turkish* 'sivas) *n.* a city in central Turkey, at an altitude of 1347 m (4420 ft.): one of the chief cities in Asia Minor in ancient times; scene of the national congress (1919) leading to the revolution that established modern Turkey. Pop.: 197 266 (1985).

six (sɪks) *n.* **1.** the cardinal number that is the sum of five and one. **2.** a numeral, 6, VI, etc., representing this number. **3.** something representing, represented by, or consisting of six units, such as a playing card with six symbols on it. **4.** Also: **six o'clock.** six hours after noon or midnight. **5.** *Cricket.* **a.** a stroke from which the ball crosses the boundary without bouncing. **b.** the six runs scored for such a shot. **6.** a division of a Brownie Guide or Cub Scout pack. **7. at sixes and sevens. a.** in disagreement. **b.** in a state of confusion. **8. knock (someone) for six.** *Inf.* to upset or overwhelm (someone) completely. **9. six of one and half a dozen of the other.** a situation in which the alternatives are considered equivalent. ~*determiner.* **10. a.** amounting to six: *six nations.* **b.** (*as pron.*): *set the table for six.* [OE *siex*]

Six (*French* sis) *n.* **Les** (le). a group of six young composers in France, who from about 1916 formed a temporary association as a result of interest in neoclassicism and in the music of Satie and the poetry of Cocteau. Its members were Darius Milhaud, Arthur Honegger, Francis Poulenc, Georges Auric, Louis Durey, and Germaine Tailleferre.

Six Counties *pl. n.* the former counties of Northern Ireland.

sixer ('sɪksə) *n.* the leader of a group of six Cub Scouts or Brownie Guides.

sixfold ('sɪks,fəʊld) *adj.* **1.** equal to or having six times as many or as much. **2.** composed of six parts. ~*adv.* **3.** by or up to six times as many or as much.

sixmo ('sɪksməʊ) *n., pl.* **-mos.** a book size resulting from folding a sheet of paper into six leaves or twelve pages, each one sixth the size of the sheet. Often written: **6mo,** **6°.** Also called: **sexto.**

Six Nations *pl. n.* (in North America) the Indian confederacy of the Cayugas, Mohawks, Oneidas, Onondagas, Senecas, and Tuscaroras. Also called: **Iroquois.** See also **Five Nations.**

sixpence ('sɪkspəns) *n.* (formerly) a small British cupronickel coin with a face value of six old pennies, worth 2½ pence.

six-shooter *n. U.S. inf.* a revolver with six chambers. Also called: **six-gun.**

sixte (sɪkst) *n.* the sixth of eight basic positions from which a parry or attack can be made in fencing. [from F: (the) sixth (parrying position), from L *sextus* sixth]

sixteen (ˈsɪksˈtiːn) *n.* 1. the cardinal number that is the sum of ten and six. 2. a numeral, 16, XVI, etc., representing this number. 3. something represented by, representing, or consisting of 16 units. ~*determiner.* 4. a. amounting to sixteen: *sixteen tons.* b. (*as pron.*): *sixteen are known to the police.* —ˈsix'teenth *adj., n.*

sixteenmo (ˈsɪksˈtiːnməʊ) *n., pl.* -**mos.** a book size resulting from folding a sheet of paper into 16 leaves or 32 pages. Often written: **16mo, 16°.** Also called: **sextodecimo.**

sixteenth note *n.* the usual U.S. and Canad. name for **semiquaver.**

sixth (sɪksθ) *adj.* 1. (*usually prenominal*) a. coming after the fifth and before the seventh in numbering, position, time, etc.; being the ordinal number of *six*: often written 6th. b. (*as n.*): *the sixth to go.* ~*n.* 2. a. one of six parts of an object, quantity, measurement, etc. b. (*as modifier*): *a sixth part.* 3. the fraction equal to one divided by six (1/6). 4. *Music.* a. the interval between one note and another six notes away from it in the diatonic scale. b. one of two notes constituting such an interval in relation to the other. ~*adv.* 5. Also: **sixthly.** after the fifth person, position, etc. ~*sentence connector.* 6. Also: **sixthly.** as the sixth point.

sixth form *n.* a. (in England and Wales) the most senior level in a secondary school to which pupils, usually above the legal leaving age, may proceed to take A levels, retake O levels, etc. b. (*as modifier*): *a sixth-form college.* —ˈsixth-,former *n.*

sixth sense *n.* any supposed means of perception, such as intuition, other than the five senses of sight, hearing, touch, taste, and smell.

Sixtus V (ˈsɪkstəs) *n.* original name *Felice Peretti.* 1520–90, Italian ecclesiastic; pope (1585–90). He is noted for vigorous administrative reforms that contributed to the Counter-Reformation.

sixty (ˈsɪkstɪ) *n., pl.* -**ties.** 1. the cardinal number that is the product of ten and six. 2. a numeral, 60, LX, etc., representing sixty. 3. something represented by, representing, or consisting of 60 units. ~*determiner.* 4. a. amounting to sixty: *sixty soldiers.* b. (*as pron.*): *sixty are dead.* [OE *sixtig*] —ˈsixtieth *adj., n.*

sixty-fourmo (ˌsɪkstɪˈfɔːməʊ) *n., pl.* -**mos.** a book size resulting from folding a sheet of paper into 64 leaves or 128 pages, each one sixty-fourth the size of the sheet. Often written **64mo, 64°.**

sixty-fourth note *n.* the usual U.S. and Canad. name for **hemidemisemiquaver.**

sixty-nine *n.* another term for **soixante-neuf.**

sizable *or* **sizeable** (ˈsaɪzəbªl) *adj.* quite large. —ˈsizably *or* ˈsizeably *adv.*

size¹ (saɪz) *n.* 1. the dimensions, amount, or extent of something. 2. large dimensions, etc. 3. one of a series of graduated measurements, as of clothing: *she takes size 4 shoes.* 4. *Inf.* state of affairs as summarized: *he's bankrupt, that's the size of it.* ~*vb.* 5. to sort according to size. 6. (*tr.*) to cut to a particular size or sizes. [C13: from OF *sise*, shortened from *assise* ASSIZE] —ˈsizer *n.*

size² (saɪz) *n.* 1. Also called: **sizing.** a thin gelatinous mixture, made from glue, clay, or wax, that is used as a sealer on paper or plaster surfaces. ~*vb.* 2. (*tr.*) to treat or coat (a surface) with size. [C15: ?from OF *sise*; see SIZE¹]

sized (saɪzd) *adj.* of a specified size: *medium-sized.*

size up *vb.* (*adv.*) 1. (*tr.*) *Inf.* to make an assessment of (a person, problem, etc.). 2. to conform to or make so as to conform to certain specifications of dimension.

sizzle (ˈsɪzªl) *vb.* (*intr.*) 1. to make the hissing sound characteristic of frying fat. 2. *Inf.* to be very hot. 3. *Inf.* to be very angry. ~*n.* 4. a hissing sound. [C17: imit.] —ˈsizzler *n.* —ˈsizzling *adj.*

SJ *abbrev. for* Society of Jesus.

SJA *abbrev. for* Saint John's Ambulance (Brigade *or* Association).

Sjælland (*Danish* ˈsjɛlan) *n.* the largest island of Denmark, separated from the island of Fyn by the Great Belt and from S Sweden by the Sound. Chief town: Copenhagen. Pop.: 1 987 549 (1976 est.). Area: 7016 sq. km (2709 sq. miles). English name: **Zealand.** German name: **Seeland.**

sjambok (ˈʃæmbʌk) *n.* (in South Africa) a heavy whip of rhinoceros or hippopotamus hide. [C19: from Afrik., ult. from Urdu *chābuk* horsewhip]

ska (skɑː) *n.* a type of West Indian pop music: a precursor of reggae. [C20: from ?]

skaapsteker (ˈskɑːpˌstɪəkə) *n.* any of several back-fanged venomous South African snakes. [from Afrik. *skaap* sheep + *steek* to pierce]

Skagen (ˈskɑːgən) *n.* **Cape.** another name for the **Skaw.**

Skagerrak (ˈskægəˌræk) *n.* an arm of the North Sea between Denmark and Norway, merging with the Kattegat in the southeast.

skald *or* **scald** (skɔːld) *n.* (in ancient Scandinavia) a bard or minstrel. [from ON, from ?] —ˈskaldic *or* ˈscaldic *adj.*

Skara Brae (ˈskærə) *n.* a neolithic village in NE Scotland, in the Orkney Islands: one of Europe's most perfectly preserved Stone Age villages, buried by a sand dune until uncovered by a storm in 1850.

skat (skæt) *n.* a three-handed card game using 32 cards, popular in German-speaking communities. [C19: from G, from It. *scarto* played cards, from *scartare* to discard, from L *charta* CARD¹]

skate¹ (skeɪt) *n.* 1. See **roller skate, ice skate.** 2. the steel blade or runner of an ice skate. 3. such a blade fitted with straps for fastening to a shoe. 4. **get one's skates on.** to hurry. ~*vb.* (*intr.*) 5. to glide swiftly on skates. 6. to slide smoothly over a surface. 7. **skate on thin ice.** to place oneself in a dangerous situation. [C17: via Du. from OF *éschasse* stilt, prob. of Gmc origin] —ˈskater *n.*

skate² (skeɪt) *n., pl.* **skate** *or* **skates.** any of a family of large rays of temperate and tropical seas, having two dorsal fins, a short spineless tail, and a long snout. [C14: from ON *skata*]

skateboard (ˈskeɪtˌbɔːd) *n.* 1. a plank mounted on roller-skate wheels, usually ridden while standing up. ~*vb.* 2. (*intr.*) to ride on a skateboard. —ˈskate,boarder *n.* —ˈskate,boarding *n.*

skate over *vb.* (*intr., prep.*) 1. to cross on or as if on skates. 2. to avoid dealing with (a matter) fully.

Skaw (skɔː) *n.* **the.** a cape at the N tip of Denmark. Also called: (Cape) **Skagen.**

skean-dhu (ˌskiːənˈduː) *n.* a dirk worn in the stocking as part of Highland dress. [C19: from Gaelic *sgian dubh* black knife]

skedaddle (skɪˈdædªl) *Inf.* ~*vb.* 1. (*intr.*) to run off hastily. ~*n.* 2. a hasty retreat. [C19: from ?]

skeet (skiːt) *n.* a form of clay-pigeon shooting in which targets are hurled from two traps at varying speeds and angles. [C20: changed from ON *skeyti* a thrown object, from *skjóta* to shoot]

skein (skeɪn) *n.* 1. a length of yarn, etc., wound in a long coil. 2. something resembling this, such as a lock of hair. 3. a flock of geese flying. [C15: from OF *escaigne*, from ?]

skeleton (ˈskɛlɪtən) *n.* 1. a hard framework consisting of inorganic material that supports and protects the soft parts of an animal's body: may be internal, as in vertebrates, or external, as in arthropods. 2. *Inf.* a very thin emaciated person or animal. 3. the essential framework of any structure, such as a building or leaf. 4. an outline consisting of bare essentials: *the skeleton of a novel.* 5. (*modifier*) reduced to a minimum: *a skeleton staff.* 6. **skeleton in the cupboard** *or U.S. & Canad.* **closet.** a scandalous fact or event in the past that is kept secret. [C16: via NL from Gk: something desiccated, from *skellein* to dry up] —ˈskeletal *or* ˈskeleton-,like *adj.*

skeletonize *or* **-nise** (ˈskɛlɪtəˌnaɪz) *vb.* (*tr.*) 1. to reduce to a minimum framework or outline. 2. to create the essential framework of.

skeleton key *n.* a key with the serrated edge filed down so that it can open numerous locks. Also called: **passkey.**

Skelmersdale (ˈskɛlməzˌdeɪl) *n.* a town in NW England, in Lancashire: designated a new town in 1962. Pop.: 41 800 (1985).

Skelton (ˈskɛltən) *n.* **John.** ?1460–1529, English poet celebrated for his short rhyming lines using the rhythms of colloquial speech.

skep (skɛp) *n.* 1. a beehive, esp. one constructed of straw. 2. *Now chiefly dialect.* a large basket of wickerwork or straw. [OE *sceppe*]

skeptic ('skɛptɪk) *n., adj.* an archaic and the usual U.S. spelling of **sceptic**.

skerrick ('skɛrɪk) *n. U.S., Austral., & N.Z. inf.* a small fragment or amount (esp. in **not a skerrick**). [C20: N English dialect, prob. of Scand. origin]

skerry ('skɛrɪ) *n., pl.* **-ries.** *Chiefly Scot.* **1.** a small rocky island. **2.** a reef. [C17: Orkney dialect, from ON *sker* scar (rock formation)]

sketch (skɛtʃ) *n.* **1.** a rapid drawing or painting. **2.** a brief usually descriptive essay or other literary composition. **3.** a short play, often comic, forming part of a revue. **4.** a short evocative piece of instrumental music. **5.** any brief outline. ~*vb.* **6.** to make a rough drawing (of). **7.** (*tr.; often foll. by out*) to make a brief description of. [C17: from Du. *schets*, via It. from L *schedius* hastily made, from Gk *skhedios* unprepared] — **'sketcher** *n.*

sketchbook ('skɛtʃˌbʊk) *n.* **1.** a book of plain paper containing sketches or for making sketches in. **2.** a book of literary sketches.

sketchy ('skɛtʃɪ) *adj.* **sketchier, sketchiest.** **1.** existing only in outline. **2.** superficial or slight. — **'sketchily** *adv.* — **'sketchiness** *n.*

skew (skjuː) *adj.* **1.** placed in or turning into an oblique position or course. **2.** *Machinery.* having a component that is at an angle to the main axis of an assembly: *a skew bevel gear.* **3.** *Maths.* composed of or being elements that are neither parallel nor intersecting. **4.** (of a statistical distribution) not having equal probabilities above and below the mean. **5.** distorted or biased. ~*n.* **6.** an oblique, slanting, or indirect course or position. ~*vb.* **7.** to take or cause to take an oblique course or direction. **8.** (*intr.*) to look sideways. **9.** (*tr.*) to distort. [C14: from OF *escuer* to shun, of Gmc origin] — **'skewness** *n.*

skewback ('skjuːˌbæk) *n. Archit.* the sloping surface on both sides of a segmental arch that takes the thrust.

skewbald ('skjuːˌbɔːld) *adj.* **1.** marked or spotted in white and any colour except black. ~*n.* **2.** a horse with this marking. [C17: see SKEW, PIEBALD]

skewer (skjuə) *n.* **1.** a long pin for holding meat in position while being cooked, etc. **2.** a similar pin having some other function. ~*vb.* **3.** (*tr.*) to drive a skewer through or fasten with a skewer. [C17: prob. from dialect *skiver*]

skewwhiff ('skjuːˈwɪf) *adj.* (*postpositive*) *Brit. inf.* not straight. [C20: prob. infl. by ASKEW]

ski (skiː) *n., pl.* **skis** *or* **ski.** **1. a.** one of a pair of wood, metal, or plastic runners that are used for gliding over snow. **b.** (*as modifier): a ski boot.* **2.** a water-ski. ~*vb.* **skiing; skied** *or* **ski'd.** **3.** (*intr.*) to travel on skis. [C19: from Norwegian, from ON *skith* snowshoes] — **'skier** *n.* — **'skiing** *n.*

skibob ('skiːˌbɒb) *n.* a vehicle made of two short skis, the forward one having a steering handle and the rear one supporting a low seat, for gliding down snow slopes. — **'skibobber** *n.*

skid (skɪd) *vb.* **skidding, skidded.** **1.** to cause (a vehicle) to slide sideways or (of a vehicle) to slide sideways while in motion, esp. out of control. **2.** (*intr.*) to slide without revolving, as the wheel of a moving vehicle after sudden braking. ~*n.* **3.** an instance of sliding, esp. sideways. **4.** a support on which heavy objects may be stored and moved short distances by sliding. **5.** a shoe or drag used to apply pressure to the metal rim of a wheel to act as a brake. [C17: ? of Scand. origin]

skidoo ('skɪduː) *Canad.* ~*n., pl.* **-doos.** **1.** a snowmobile. ~*vb.* (*intr.*) **2.** to travel using a snowmobile. [C20: from *Ski-Doo*, orig. a trademark]

skid row (rəʊ) *or* **skid road** *n. Sl., chiefly U.S. & Canad.* a dilapidated section of a city inhabited by vagrants, etc.

skied[1] (skaɪd) *vb.* the past tense and past participle of **sky**.

skied[2] (skiːd) *vb.* a past tense and past participle of **ski**.

Skien (Norwegian 'ʃeːən) *n.* a port in S Norway, on the **Skien River**: one of the oldest towns in Norway; lumber industry. Pop.: 47 318 (1980).

skiff (skɪf) *n.* any of various small boats propelled by oars, sail, or motor. [C18: from F *esquif*, from OIt. *schifo* a boat, of Gmc origin]

skiffle ('skɪfəl) *n.* a style of popular music of the 1950s, played chiefly on guitars and improvised percussion instruments. [C20: from ?]

skijoring (skiː'dʒɔːrɪŋ, -'jɔːrɪŋ) *n.* a sport in which a skier is pulled over snow or ice, usually by a horse. [Norwegian *skikjöring*, lit.: ski-driving] — **ski'jorer** *n.*

ski jump *n.* **1.** a high ramp overhanging a slope from which skiers compete to make the longest jump. ~*vb.* **ski-jump. 2.** (*intr.*) to perform a ski jump. — **ski jumper** *n.*

Skikda ('skɪkdɑː) *n.* a port in NE Algeria, on an inlet of the Mediterranean: founded by the French in 1838 on the site of a Roman city. Pop.: 141 159 (1983). Former name: **Philippeville.**

skilful *or U.S.* **skillful** ('skɪlfʊl) *adj.* **1.** possessing or displaying accomplishment or skill. **2.** involving or requiring accomplishment or skill. — **'skilfully** *or U.S.* **'skillfully** *adv.*

ski lift *n.* any device for carrying skiers up a slope, such as a chair lift.

skill (skɪl) *n.* **1.** special ability in a sport, etc., esp. ability acquired by training. **2.** something, esp. a trade or technique, requiring special training or manual proficiency. [C12: from ON *skil* distinction] — **'skill-less** *or* **'skilless** *adj.*

skilled (skɪld) *adj.* **1.** demonstrating accomplishment or special training. **2.** (*prenominal*) involving skill or special training: *a skilled job.*

skillet ('skɪlɪt) *n.* **1.** a small frying pan. **2.** *Chiefly Brit.* a saucepan. [C15: prob. from *skele* bucket, from ON]

skilly ('skɪlɪ) *n. Chiefly Brit.* a thin soup or gruel. [C19: from *skilligallee*, from ?]

skim (skɪm) *vb.* **skimming, skimmed. 1.** (*tr.*) to remove floating material from the surface of (a liquid), as with a spoon: *to skim milk.* **2.** to glide smoothly or lightly over (a surface). **3.** (*tr.*) to throw (something) in a path over a surface, so as to bounce or ricochet: *to skim stones over water.* **4.** (when *intr.*, usually foll. by *through*) to read (a book) in a superficial manner. ~*n.* **5.** the act or process of skimming. **6.** material skimmed off a liquid, esp. off milk. **7.** any thin layer covering a surface. [C15 *skimmen*, prob. from *scumen* to skim]

skimmer ('skɪmə) *n.* **1.** a person or thing that skims. **2.** any of several mainly tropical coastal aquatic birds having a bill with an elongated lower mandible for skimming food from the surface of the water. **3.** a flat perforated spoon used for skimming fat from liquids.

skimmia ('skɪmɪə) *n.* any of a genus of rutaceous shrubs grown for their ornamental red berries and evergreen foliage. [C18: NL from Japanese (*mijama-*) *shikimi*, a native name of the plant]

skim milk *n.* milk from which the cream has been removed. Also called: **skimmed milk.**

skimp (skɪmp) *vb.* **1.** to be extremely sparing or supply (someone) sparingly. **2.** to perform (work, etc.) carelessly or with inadequate materials. [C17: ? a combination of SCANT & SCRIMP]

skimpy ('skɪmpɪ) *adj.* **skimpier, skimpiest. 1.** made of too little material. **2.** excessively thrifty; mean. — **'skimpily** *adv.* — **'skimpiness** *n.*

skin (skɪn) *n.* **1.** the tissue forming the outer covering of the vertebrate body: it consists of two layers, the outermost of which may be covered with hair, scales, feathers, etc. **2.** a person's complexion: *a fair skin.* **3.** any similar covering in a plant or lower animal. **4.** any coating or film, such as one that forms on the surface of a liquid. **5.** the outer covering of a fur-bearing animal, dressed and finished with the hair on. **6.** a container made from animal skin. **7.** the outer covering surface of a vessel, rocket, etc. **8.** a person's skin regarded as his life: *to save one's skin.* **9.** (*often pl.*) *Inf.* (in jazz or pop use) a drum. **10.** *Inf.* short for **skinhead. 11. by the skin of one's teeth.** only just. **12. get under one's skin.** *Inf.* to irritate. **13. no skin off one's nose.** *Inf.* not a matter that affects one adversely. **14. skin and bone.** extremely thin. **15. thick (*or* thin) skin.** an insensitive (*or* sensitive) nature. ~*vb.* **skinning, skinned. 16.** (*tr.*) to remove the outer covering from (fruit, etc.). **17.** (*tr.*) to scrape a small piece of skin from (a part of oneself) in falling, etc.: *he skinned his knee.* **18.** (often foll. by *over*) to cover (something) with skin or a skinlike substance or (of something) to become covered in this way. **19.** (*tr.*) *Sl.* to swindle. ~*adj.* **20.** of or for the skin: *skin cream.* [OE *scinn*] — **'skinless** *adj.* — **'skin,like** *adj.*

skin-deep *adj.* **1.** superficial; shallow. ~*adv.* **2.** superficially.

skin diving *n.* the sport or activity of underwater swimming using breathing apparatus. — **'skin-,diver** *n.*

skin flick *n. Sl.* a film containing much nudity and explicit sex for sensational purposes.

skinflint ('skɪn,flɪnt) *n.* an ungenerous or niggardly person. [C18: referring to a person so avaricious that he would skin (swindle) a flint]

skinful ('skɪn,fʊl) *n., pl.* **-fuls.** *Sl.* sufficient alcoholic drink to make one drunk.

skin graft *n.* a piece of skin removed from one part of the body and surgically grafted at the site of a severe burn or similar injury.

skinhead ('skɪn,hɛd) *n. Brit.* one of a gang of White boys characterized by closely cropped hair, heavy boots, and braces.

skink (skɪŋk) *n.* any of a family of lizards commonest in tropical Africa and Asia, having an elongated body covered with smooth scales. [C16: from L *scincus* a lizard, from Gk *skinkos*]

skinned (skɪnd) *adj.* **1.** stripped of the skin. **2. a.** having a skin as specified. **b.** (*in combination*): *thick-skinned.*

Skinner ('skɪnə) *n.* **B**(**urrhus**) **F**(**rederic**). born 1904. U.S. behavioural psychologist. His "laws of learning", derived from experiments with animals, have been widely applied to education and behaviour therapy.

skinny ('skɪnɪ) *adj.* **-nier, -niest.** **1.** lacking in flesh; thin. **2.** consisting of or resembling skin.

skint (skɪnt) *adj.* (*usually postpositive*) *Brit. sl.* without money. [var. of *skinned*, p.p. of SKIN]

skin test *n. Med.* any test to determine immunity to a disease or hypersensitivity by introducing a small amount of the test substance beneath the skin.

skintight ('skɪn'taɪt) *adj.* (of garments) fitting tightly over the body; clinging.

skip[1] (skɪp) *vb.* **skipping, skipped.** **1.** (when *intr.*, often foll. by *over, into*, etc.) to spring or move lightly, esp. to move by hopping from one foot to the other. **2.** (*intr.*) to jump over a skipping-rope. **3.** to cause (a stone, etc.) to skim over a surface or (of a stone) to move in this way. **4.** to omit (intervening matter): *he skipped a chapter of the book.* **5.** (*intr.*; foll. by *through*) *Inf.* to read or deal with quickly or superficially. **6. skip it!** *Inf.* it doesn't matter! **7.** (*tr.*) *Inf.* to miss deliberately: *to skip school.* **8.** (*tr.*) *Inf., chiefly U.S. & Canad.* to leave (a place) in haste: *to skip town.* ~*n.* **9.** a skipping movement or gait. **10.** the act of passing over or omitting. [C13: prob. from ON]

skip[2] (skɪp) *n., vb.* **skipping, skipped.** *Inf.* short for **skipper**[1].

skip[3] (skɪp) *n.* **1.** a large open container for transporting building materials, etc. **2.** a cage used as a lift in mines, etc. [C19: var. of SKEP]

ski pants *pl. n.* stretch trousers, worn for skiing or as a fashion garment, kept taut by a strap under the foot.

skip distance *n.* the shortest distance between a transmitter and a receiver that will permit reception of radio waves of a specified frequency by one reflection from the ionosphere.

skipjack ('skɪp,dʒæk) *n., pl.* **-jack** or **-jacks.** **1.** Also called: **skipjack tuna.** an important food fish that has a striped abdomen and occurs in all tropical seas. **2. black skipjack.** a small spotted tuna of Indo-Pacific seas.

skiplane ('skiː,pleɪn) *n.* an aircraft fitted with skis to enable it to land on and take off from snow.

skipper[1] ('skɪpə) *n.* **1.** the captain of any vessel. **2.** the captain of an aircraft. **3.** a leader, as of a sporting team. ~*vb.* **4.** to act as skipper (of). [C14: from MLow G, MDu. *schipper* shipper]

skipper[2] ('skɪpə) *n.* **1.** a person or thing that skips. **2.** a small butterfly having a hairy mothlike body and erratic darting flight.

skipping ('skɪpɪŋ) *n.* the act of jumping over a rope that is held either by the person jumping or by two other people, as a game or for exercise.

skipping-rope *n. Brit.* a cord, usually having handles at each end, that is held in the hands and swung round and down so that the holder or others can jump over it.

Skipton ('skɪptən) *n.* a market town in N England, in North Yorkshire: 11th-century castle. Pop.: 13 246 (1981).

skip zone *n.* a region surrounding a broadcasting station that cannot receive transmissions either directly or by reflection off the ionosphere.

skirl (skɜːl) *Scot. & N English dialect.* ~*vb.* **1.** (*intr.*) (esp. of bagpipes) to emit a shrill sound. ~*n.* **2.** the sound of bagpipes. [C14: prob. from ON]

skirmish ('skɜːmɪʃ) *n.* **1.** a minor short-lived military engagement. **2.** any brisk clash or encounter. ~*vb.* **3.** (*intr.*; often foll. by *with*) to engage in a skirmish. [C14: from OF *eskirmir*, of Gmc origin] —**'skirmisher** *n.*

Skíros ('skɪrɔs) *n.* transliteration of the Modern Greek name for **Skyros.**

skirt (skɜːt) *n.* **1.** a garment hanging from the waist, worn chiefly by women and girls. **2.** the part of a dress below the waist. **3.** Also called: **apron.** a circular flap, as round the base of a hovercraft. **4.** the flaps on a saddle. **5.** *Brit.* a cut of beef from the flank. **6.** (*often pl.*) an outlying area. **7. bit of skirt.** *Sl.* a girl or woman. ~*vb.* **8.** (*tr.*) to form the edge of. **9.** (*tr.*) to provide with a border. **10.** (when *intr.*, foll. by *around, along*, etc.) to pass (by) or be situated (near) the outer edge of (an area, etc.). **11.** (*tr.*) to avoid (a difficulty, etc.): *he skirted the issue.* **12.** *Chiefly Austral. & N.Z.* to trim the ragged edges from (a fleece). [C13: from ON *skyrta* shirt] —**'skirted** *adj.*

skirting ('skɜːtɪŋ) *n.* **1.** a border, esp. of wood or tiles, fixed round the base of an interior wall to protect it. **2.** material used for skirts.

skirting board *n.* a skirting made of wood.

skirtings ('skɜːtɪŋz) *pl. n. Austral. & N.Z.* ragged edges trimmed from the fleece of a sheep.

ski stick or **pole** *n.* a stick, usually with a metal point, used by skiers to gain momentum and maintain balance.

skit (skɪt) *n.* **1.** a brief satirical theatrical sketch. **2.** a short satirical piece of writing. [C18: rel. to earlier verb *skit* to move rapidly, hence to score a satirical hit, prob. of Scand. origin]

skite[1] (skaɪt) *Scot. dialect.* ~*vb.* **1.** (*intr.*) to slide or slip, as on ice. **2.** (*tr.*) to strike with a sharp blow. ~*n.* **3.** an instance of slipping or sliding. **4.** a sharp blow. [C18: from ?]

skite[2] (skaɪt) *Austral. & N.Z. inf.* ~*vb.* (*intr.*) **1.** to boast. ~*n.* **2.** boastful talk. **3.** a person who boasts. [C19: from Scot. & N English dialect]

ski tow *n.* a device for pulling skiers uphill, usually a motor-driven rope grasped by the skier while riding on his skis.

skitter ('skɪtə) *vb.* **1.** (*intr.*; often foll. by *off*) to move or run rapidly or lightly. **2.** to skim or cause to skim lightly and rapidly. **3.** (*intr.*) *Angling.* to draw a bait lightly over the surface of water. [C19: prob. from dialect *skite* to dash about]

skittish ('skɪtɪʃ) *adj.* **1.** playful, lively, or frivolous. **2.** difficult to handle or predict. [C15: prob. from ON] —**'skittishly** *adv.* —**'skittishness** *n.*

skittle ('skɪt²l) *n.* **1.** a wooden or plastic pin, typically widest just above the base. **2.** (*pl.; functioning as sing.*) Also called (esp. U.S.): **ninepins.** a bowling game in which players knock over as many skittles as possible by rolling a wooden ball at them. [C17: from ?]

skive[1] (skaɪv) *vb.* (*tr.*) to shave or remove the surface of (leather). [C19: of Scand. origin, from *skifa*] —**'skiver** *n.*

skive[2] (skaɪv) *vb.* (when *intr.*, often foll. by *off*) *Brit. inf.* to evade (work or responsibility). [C20: from ?] —**'skiver** *n.*

skivvy[1] ('skɪvɪ) *n., pl.* **-vies.** **1.** *Chiefly Brit., often contemptuous.* a servant, esp. a female; drudge. ~*vb.* **-vying, -vied.** **2.** (*intr.*) *Brit.* to work as a skivvy. [C20: from ?]

skivvy[2] ('skɪvɪ) *n., pl.* **-vies.** *Austral. & N.Z.* a lightweight sweater-like garment with long sleeves and a polo neck. [from ?]

skol (skɒl) or **skoal** (skɔʊl) *sentence substitute* good health! (a drinking toast). [C16: from Danish *skaal* bowl, of Scand. origin, from *skal*]

skookum ('skuːkəm) *adj. W Canad.* large or big. [from Chinook Jargon]

Skopje ('skɔːpjɛ) *n.* a city in S Yugoslavia, capital of Macedonia on the Vardar River: became capital of Serbia in 1346 and of Macedonia in 1945; suffered a severe earthquake in 1963. Pop.: 503 449 (1981). Serbo-Croatian name: **Skoplje** ('skɔplje). Turkish name (1392–1913): **Üsküb.**

Skt, Skt., Skr, or **Skr.** *abbrev. for* Sanskrit.

skua ('skjuːə) *n.* any of various predatory aquatic gull-like birds having a dark plumage and long tail. [C17: from NL, from Faeroese *skúgvur*, of Scand. origin, from *skúfr*]

skulduggery or *U.S.* **skullduggery** (skʌl'dʌgərɪ) *n. Inf.* underhand dealing; trickery. [C18: from earlier Scot. *skulduddery*, from ?]

skulk (skʌlk) *vb.* (*intr.*) **1.** to move stealthily so as to avoid notice. **2.** to lie in hiding; lurk. **3.** to shirk duty or evade responsibilities. ~n. **4.** a person who skulks. **5.** *Obs.* a pack of foxes. [C13: from ON] —'**skulker** n.

skull (skʌl) n. **1.** the bony skeleton of the head of vertebrates. **2.** *Often derog.* the head regarded as the mind or intelligence: *to have a dense skull.* **3.** a picture of a skull used to represent death or danger. [C13: from ON]

skull and crossbones n. a picture of the human skull above two crossed thighbones, formerly on the pirate flag, now used as a warning of danger or death.

skullcap ('skʌl,kæp) n. **1.** a rounded brimless hat fitting the crown of the head. **2.** the top part of the skull. **3.** any of a genus of perennial plants, that have helmet-shaped flowers.

skunk (skʌŋk) n., pl. **skunk** or **skunks**. **1.** any of various American mammals having a black-and-white coat and bushy tail: they eject an unpleasant-smelling fluid from the anal gland when attacked. **2.** *Inf.* a despicable person. [C17: of Amerind origin]

skunk cabbage n. a low-growing fetid aroid swamp plant of E North America, having broad leaves and minute flowers enclosed in a greenish spathe.

sky (skaɪ) n., pl. **skies**. **1.** (*sometimes pl.*) the apparently dome-shaped expanse extending upwards from the horizon that is blue or grey during the day and black at night. **2.** outer space, as seen from the earth. **3.** (*often pl.*) weather, as described by the appearance of the upper air: *sunny skies.* **4.** heaven. **5.** *Inf.* the highest level of attainment: *the sky's the limit.* **6. to the skies.** extravagantly. ~vb. **skying, skied. 7.** *Rowing.* to lift (the blade of an oar) too high before a stroke. **8.** (*tr.*) *Inf.* to hit (a ball) high in the air. [C13: from ON *ský*]

sky blue n., adj. (of) a light or pale blue colour.

skydiving ('skaɪ,daɪvɪŋ) n. the sport of parachute jumping, in which participants perform manoeuvres before opening the parachute. —'**sky,dive** vb. (*intr.*) —'**sky,diver** n.

Skye (skaɪ) n. a mountainous island off the NW coast of Scotland, the largest island of the Inner Hebrides: tourist centre. Chief town: Portree. Pop.: 7500 (1985 est.). Area: 1735 sq. km (670 sq. miles).

Skye terrier n. a short-legged long-bodied breed of terrier with long wiry hair and erect ears.

sky-high adj., adv. **1.** at or to an unprecedented level: *prices rocketed sky-high.* ~adv. **2.** high into the air. **3. blow sky-high.** to destroy.

skyjack ('skaɪ,dʒæk) vb. (*tr.*) to hijack (an aircraft). [C20: from SKY + HIJACK]

skylark ('skaɪ,lɑ:k) n. **1.** an Old World lark, noted for singing while hovering at a great height. ~vb. **2.** (*intr.*) *Inf.* to romp or play jokes.

skylight ('skaɪ,laɪt) n. a window placed in a roof or ceiling to admit daylight. Also called: **fanlight.**

skyline ('skaɪ,laɪn) n. **1.** the line at which the earth and sky appear to meet. **2.** the outline of buildings, trees, etc., seen against the sky.

sky pilot n. *Sl.* a clergyman, esp. a chaplain.

skyrocket ('skaɪ,rɒkɪt) n. **1.** another word for **rocket** (sense 1). ~vb. **2.** (*intr.*) *Inf.* to rise rapidly, as in price.

Skyros or **Scyros** ('skɪːrɒs) n. a Greek island in the Aegean, the largest island in the N Sporades. Pop.: 2757 (1981). Area: 199 sq. km (77 sq. miles). Modern Greek name: **Skíros.**

skysail ('skaɪ,seɪl) n. *Naut.* a square sail set above the royal on a square-rigger.

skyscraper ('skaɪ,skreɪpə) n. a very tall multistorey building.

skyward ('skaɪwəd) adj. **1.** directed or moving towards the sky. ~adv. **2.** Also: **skywards.** towards the sky.

skywriting ('skaɪ,raɪtɪŋ) n. **1.** the forming of words in the sky by the release of smoke or vapour from an aircraft. **2.** the words so formed. —'**sky,writer** n.

slab (slæb) n. **1.** a broad flat thick piece of wood, stone, or other material. **2.** a thick slice of cake, etc. **3.** any of the outside parts of a log that are sawn off while the log is being made into planks. **4.** *Austral. & N.Z.* **a.** a roughhewn wooden plank. **b.** (*as modifier*): *a slab hut.* **5.** *Inf., chiefly Brit.* an operating or mortuary table. ~vb. **slabbing, slabbed.** (*tr.*) **6.** to cut or make into a slab or slabs. **7.** to saw slabs from (a log). [C13: from ?]

slack[1] (slæk) adj. **1.** not tight, tense, or taut. **2.** negligent or careless. **3.** (esp. of water, etc.) moving slowly. **4.** (of trade, etc.) not busy. **5.** *Phonetics.* another term for **lax** (sense 4). ~adv. **6.** in a slack manner. ~n. **7.** a part of a rope, etc., that is slack: *take in the slack.* **8.** a period of decreased activity. ~vb. **9.** to neglect (one's duty, etc.). **10.** (often foll. by *off*) to loosen. ~See also **slacks.** [OE *slæc, sleac*] —'**slackly** adv. —'**slackness** n.

slack[2] (slæk) n. small pieces of coal with a high ash content. [C15: prob. from MLow G *slecke*]

slacken ('slækən) vb. (often foll. by *off*) **1.** to make or become looser. **2.** to make or become slower, less intense, etc.

slacker ('slækə) n. a person who evades work or duty; shirker.

slacks (slæks) pl. n. informal trousers worn by both sexes.

slack water n. the period of still water around the turn of the tide, esp. at low tide.

slag (slæg) n. **1.** Also called: **cinder.** the fused material formed during the smelting or refining of metals. It usually consists of a mixture of silicates with calcium, phosphorus, sulphur, etc. **2.** the mass of rough fragments of rock derived from volcanic lava. **3.** a mixture of shale, clay, coal dust, etc., produced during coal mining. ~vb. **slagging, slagged. 4.** to convert into or become slag. **5.** (*tr.*; sometimes foll. by *off*) *Sl.* to make disparaging comments about; slander. [C16: from MLow G *slagge*, ?from *slagen* to slay] —'**slagging** n. —'**slaggy** adj.

slag heap n. a hillock of waste matter from coal mining, etc.

slain (sleɪn) vb. the past participle of **slay.**

slake (sleɪk) vb. **1.** (*tr.*) *Literary.* to satisfy (thirst, desire, etc.). **2.** (*tr.*) *Poetic.* to cool or refresh. **3.** to undergo or cause to undergo the process in which lime reacts with water to produce calcium hydroxide. [OE *slacian*, from *slæc* SLACK[1]] —'**slakable** or '**slakeable** adj.

slaked lime n. another name for **calcium hydroxide.**

slalom ('slɑːləm) n. *Skiing, canoeing, etc.* a race over a winding course marked by artificial obstacles. [Norwegian, from *slad* sloping + *lom* path]

slam[1] (slæm) vb. **slamming, slammed. 1.** to cause (a door or window) to close noisily or (of a door, etc.) to close in this way. **2.** (*tr.*) to throw (something) down violently. **3.** (*tr.*) *Sl.* to criticize harshly. **4.** (*intr.*; usually foll. by *into* or *out of*) *Inf.* to go (into or out of a room, etc.) in violent haste or anger. **5.** (*tr.*) to strike with violent force. **6.** (*tr.*) *Inf.* to defeat easily. ~n. **7.** the act or noise of slamming. [C17: of Scand. origin]

slam[2] (slæm) n. **a.** the winning of all (**grand slam**) or all but one (**little** or **small slam**) of the 13 tricks at bridge or whist. **b.** the bid to do so in bridge. [C17: from ?]

slammer ('slæmə) n. **the.** *Sl.* prison.

slander ('slɑːndə) n. **1.** *Law.* **a.** defamation in some transient form, as by spoken words, gestures, etc. **b.** a slanderous statement, etc. **2.** any defamatory words spoken about a person. ~vb. **3.** (*tr.*) to utter or circulate slander (about). [C13: via Anglo-F from OF *escandle*, from LL *scandalum* a cause of offence; see SCANDAL] —'**slanderer** n. —'**slanderous** adj.

slang (slæŋ) n. **1. a.** vocabulary, idiom, etc., that is not appropriate to the standard form of a language or to formal contexts and may be restricted as to social status or distribution. **b.** (*as modifier*): *a slang word.* ~vb. **2.** to abuse (someone) with vituperative language. [C18: from ?] —'**slangy** adj. —'**slangily** adv. —'**slanginess** n.

slant (slɑːnt) vb. **1.** to incline or be inclined at an oblique or sloping angle. **2.** (*tr.*) to write or present (news, etc.) with a bias. **3.** (*intr.*; foll. by *towards*) (of a person's opinions) to be biased. ~n. **4.** an inclined or oblique line or direction. **5.** a way of looking at something. **6.** a bias or opinion, as in an article. **7. on a** (or **the**) **slant.** sloping. ~adj. **8.** oblique; sloping. [C17: short for ASLANT, prob. of Scand. origin] —'**slanting** adj.

slantwise ('slɑːnt,waɪz) or **slantways** adv., adj. (*prenominal*) in a slanting or oblique direction.

slap (slæp) n. **1.** a sharp blow or smack, as with the open hand, something flat, etc. **2.** the sound made by or as if by such a blow. **3.** (**a bit of**) **slap and tickle.** *Brit. inf.* sexual play. **4. a slap in the face.** an insult or rebuff. **5. a slap on the back.** congratulation. ~vb. **slapping, slapped. 6.** (*tr.*) to strike (a person or thing) sharply, as with the open hand or something flat. **7.** (*tr.*) to bring down (the hand, etc.) sharply. **8.** (when *intr.*, usually foll. by *against*) to strike (something) with or as if with a slap. **9.** (*tr.*) *Inf., chiefly Brit.* to apply in large quantities, haphazardly, etc.: *she slapped butter on the bread.* **10. slap on**

the back. to congratulate. ~*adv. Inf.* **11.** exactly: *slap on time.* **12.** forcibly or abruptly: *to fall slap on the floor.* [C17: from Low G *slapp*, G *Schlappe*, imit.]

slapdash ('slæp,dæʃ) *adv.* **1.** in a careless, hasty, or haphazard manner. ~*adj.* **2.** careless, hasty, or haphazard. ~*n.* **3.** slapdash activity or work.

slaphappy ('slæp,hæpɪ) *adj.* **-pier, -piest.** *Inf.* **1.** cheerfully irresponsible or careless. **2.** dazed or giddy from or as if from repeated blows.

slapstick ('slæp,stɪk) *n.* **1. a.** comedy characterized by horseplay and physical action. **b.** (*as modifier*): *slapstick humour.* **2.** a pair of paddles formerly used in pantomime to strike a blow with a loud sound but without injury.

slap-up *adj.* (*prenominal*) *Brit. inf.* (esp. of meals) lavish; excellent; first-class.

slash (slæʃ) *vb.* (*tr.*) **1.** to cut or lay about (a person or thing) with sharp sweeping strokes, as with a sword, etc. **2.** to lash with a whip. **3.** to make large gashes in: *to slash tyres.* **4.** to reduce (prices, etc.) drastically. **5.** to criticize harshly. **6.** to slit (the outer fabric of a garment) so that the lining material is revealed. ~*n.* **7.** a sharp sweeping stroke, as with a sword or whip. **8.** a cut or rent made by such a stroke. **9.** a decorative slit in a garment revealing the lining material. **10.** *North American.* littered wood chips that remain after trees have been cut down. **11.** another name for **solidus. 12.** *Brit. sl.* the act of urinating. [C14 *slaschen*, ?from OF *esclachier* to break]

slasher ('slæʃə) *n.* **1.** a person or thing that slashes. **2.** *N.Z.* a tool used for cutting scrub or undergrowth in the bush.

slashing ('slæʃɪŋ) *adj.* aggressively or harshly critical (esp. in **slashing attack**).

Śląsk (ʃlõsk) *n.* the Polish name for **Silesia.**

slat (slæt) *n.* **1.** a narrow thin strip of wood or metal, as used in a Venetian blind, etc. **2.** a movable or fixed aerofoil attached to the leading edge of an aircraft wing to increase lift. [C14: from OF *esclat* splinter, from *esclater* to shatter]

slate[1] (sleɪt) *n.* **1. a.** a compact fine-grained metamorphic rock that can be split into thin layers and is used as a roofing and paving material. **b.** (*as modifier*): *a slate tile.* **2.** a roofing tile of slate. **3.** (formerly) a writing tablet of slate. **4.** a dark grey colour. **5.** *Chiefly U.S. & Canad.* a list of candidates in an election. **6. clean slate.** a record without dishonour. **7. on the slate.** *Brit. inf.* on credit. ~*vb.* (*tr.*) **8.** to cover (a roof) with slates. **9.** *Chiefly U.S.* to enter (a person's name) on a list, esp. on a political slate. ~*adj.* **10.** of the colour slate. [C14: from OF *esclate*, from *esclat* a fragment] —'**slaty** *adj.*

slate[2] (sleɪt) *vb.* (*tr.*) *Inf., chiefly Brit.* to criticize harshly. [C19: prob. from SLATE[1]] —'**slating** *n.*

slater ('sleɪtə) *n.* **1.** a person trained in laying roof slates. **2.** another name for **woodlouse.**

slather ('slɑːðə) *n.* **1.** (*usually pl.*) *Inf., chiefly U.S. & Canad.* a large quantity. **2. open slather.** *Austral. & N.Z. sl.* a free-for-all. [C19: from ?]

slattern ('slætən) *n.* a slovenly woman or girl. [C17: prob. from *slattering*, from dialect *slatter* to slop] —'**slatternly** *adj.* —'**slatternliness** *n.*

slaughter ('slɔːtə) *n.* **1.** the killing of animals, esp. for food. **2.** the savage killing of a person. **3.** the indiscriminate or brutal killing of large numbers of people, as in war. ~*vb.* (*tr.*) **4.** to kill (animals), esp. for food. **5.** to kill in a brutal manner. **6.** to kill indiscriminately or in large numbers. [OE *sleaht*] —'**slaughterer** *n.* —'**slaughterous** *adj.*

slaughterhouse ('slɔːtə,haʊs) *n.* a place where animals are butchered for food; abattoir.

Slav (slɑːv) *n.* a member of any of the peoples of E Europe or Soviet Asia who speak a Slavonic language. [C14: from Med. L *Sclāvus* a captive Slav; see SLAVE]

slave (sleɪv) *n.* **1.** a person legally owned by another and having no freedom of action or right to property. **2.** a person who is forced to work for another against his will. **3.** a person under the domination of another person or some habit or influence. **4.** a drudge. **5.** a device that is controlled by or that duplicates the action of another similar device. ~*vb.* **6.** (*intr.*; often foll. by *away*) to work like a slave. [C13: via OF from Med. L *Sclāvus* a Slav, one held in bondage, from the Slavonic races were frequently conquered in the Middle Ages, from LGk *Sklabos* a Slav]

Slave Coast *n.* the coast of W Africa between the Volta River and Mount Cameroon, chiefly along the Bight of Benin: the main source of African slaves (16th–19th centuries).

slave cylinder *n.* a small cylinder containing a piston that operates the brake shoes or pads in hydraulic brakes or the working part in any other hydraulically operated system.

slave-driver *n.* **1.** (esp. formerly) a person forcing slaves to work. **2.** an employer who demands excessively hard work from his employees.

slaveholder ('sleɪv,həʊldə) *n.* a person who owns slaves. —'**slave,holding** *n.*

slaver[1] ('sleɪvə) *n.* **1.** an owner of or dealer in slaves. **2.** another name for **slave ship.**

slaver[2] ('slævə) *vb.* (*intr.*) **1.** to dribble saliva. **2.** (often foll. by *over*) **a.** to fawn or drool (over someone). **b.** to show great desire (for). ~*n.* **3.** saliva dribbling from the mouth. **4.** *Inf.* drivel. [C14: prob. from Low Du.] —'**slaverer** *n.*

Slave River *n.* a river in W Canada, in the Northwest Territories and NE Alberta, flowing from Lake Athabaska northwest to Great Slave Lake. Length: about 420 km (260 miles). Also called: **Great Slave River.**

slavery ('sleɪvərɪ) *n.* **1.** the state or condition of being a slave. **2.** the subjection of a person to another person, esp. in being forced into work. **3.** the condition of being subject to some influence or habit. **4.** work done in harsh conditions for low pay.

slave ship *n.* a ship used to transport slaves, esp. formerly from Africa to the New World.

Slave State *n.* *U.S. history.* any of the 15 Southern states in which slavery was legal until the Civil War.

slave trade *n.* the business of trading in slaves, esp. the transportation of Black Africans to America from the 16th to 19th centuries. —'**slave-,trader** *n.* —'**slave-,trading** *n.*

slavey ('sleɪvɪ) *n. Brit. inf.* a female general servant.

Slavic ('slɑːvɪk) *n., adj.* another word (esp. U.S.) another word (esp. U.S.) for **Slavonic.**

slavish ('sleɪvɪʃ) *adj.* **1.** of or befitting a slave. **2.** being or resembling a slave. **3.** unoriginal; imitative. —'**slavishly** *adv.*

Slavkov ('slafkɔf) *n.* the Czech name for **Austerlitz.**

Slavonia (slə'vəʊnɪə) *n.* a region of N Yugoslavia, in Croatia, mainly between the Drava and Sava Rivers. —**Sla'vonian** *adj., n.*

Slavonic (slə'vɒnɪk) *or esp. U.S.* **Slavic** *n.* **1.** a branch of the Indo-European family of languages, usually divided into three subbranches: **South Slavonic** (including Bulgarian), **East Slavonic** (including Russian), and **West Slavonic** (including Polish and Czech). ~*adj.* **2.** of or relating to this group of languages. **3.** of or relating to the people who speak these languages.

slaw (slɔː) *n. Chiefly U.S. & Canad.* short for **coleslaw.** [C19: from Danish *sla*, short for *salade* SALAD]

slay (sleɪ) *vb.* **slaying, slew, slain.** (*tr.*) **1.** *Arch. or literary.* to kill, esp. violently. **2.** *Sl.* to impress (someone of the opposite sex). [OE *slēan*] —'**slayer** *n.*

SLD *abbrev. for* Social and Liberal Democratic Party.

sleaze (sliːz) *n. Inf.* sleaziness.

sleazy ('sliːzɪ) *adj.* **-zier, -ziest. 1.** disreputable: *a sleazy nightclub.* **2.** flimsy, as cloth. [C17: from ?] —'**sleazily** *adv.* —'**sleaziness** *n.*

sledge[1] (slɛdʒ) *or esp. U.S. & Canad.* **sled** (slɛd) *n.* **1. a.** a vehicle mounted on runners, drawn by horses or dogs, for transporting people or goods, esp. over snow. **2.** a light wooden frame used, esp. by children, for sliding over snow. ~*vb.* **3.** to convey, travel, or go by sledge. [C17: from MDu. *sleedse*; C14 *sled*, from MLow G, from ON *slethi*] —'**sledger** *n.*

sledge[2] (slɛdʒ) *n.* short for **sledgehammer.**

sledge[3] (slɛdʒ) *vb.* (*tr.*) *Austral.* to bait (an opponent, esp. a batsman in cricket) in order to upset his concentration. [from ?]

sledgehammer ('slɛdʒ,hæmə) *n.* **1.** a large heavy hammer with a long handle used with both hands for heavy work such as breaking rocks, etc. **2.** (*modifier*) resembling the action of a sledgehammer in power, etc.: *a sledgehammer blow.* [C15: *sledge*, from OE *slecg* a large hammer]

sleek (sliːk) *adj.* **1.** smooth and shiny. **2.** polished in speech or behaviour. **3.** (of an animal or bird) having a shiny healthy coat or feathers. **4.** (of a person) having a prosperous appearance. ~*vb.* (*tr.*) **5.** to make smooth and glossy, as by grooming, etc. **6.** (usually foll. by *over*) to gloss (over). [C16: var. of SLICK] —'**sleekness** *n.* —'**sleeky** *adj.*

sleep (sli:p) *n.* **1.** a periodic state of physiological rest during which consciousness is suspended. **2.** *Bot.* the nontechnical name for **nyctitropism**. **3.** a period spent sleeping. **4.** a state of quiescence or dormancy. **5.** a poetic word for **death**. ~*vb.* **sleeping, slept**. **6.** (*intr.*) to be in or as in the state of sleep. **7.** (*intr.*) (of plants) to show nyctitropism. **8.** (*intr.*) to be inactive or quiescent. **9.** (*tr.*) to have sleeping accommodation for (a certain number): *the boat could sleep six.* **10.** (*tr.*; foll. by *away*) to pass (time) sleeping. **11.** (*intr.*) *Poetic.* to be dead. **12. sleep on it.** to give (something) extended consideration, esp. overnight. ~See also **sleep around, sleep in,** etc. [OE *slǣpan*]

sleep around *vb.* (*intr., adv.*) *Inf.* to be sexually promiscuous.

sleeper ('sli:pə) *n.* **1.** a person, animal, or thing that sleeps. **2.** a railway sleeping car or compartment. **3.** *Brit.* one of the blocks supporting the rails on a railway track. **4.** a heavy timber beam, esp. one that is laid horizontally on the ground. **5.** *Chiefly Brit.* a small plain gold circle worn in a pierced ear lobe to prevent the hole from closing up. **6.** *Inf., chiefly U.S. & Canad.* a person or thing that achieves unexpected success. **7.** a spy planted in advance for future use.

sleep in *vb.* (*intr., adv.*) **1.** *Brit.* to sleep longer than usual. **2.** to sleep at the place of one's employment.

sleeping bag *n.* a large well-padded bag designed for sleeping in, esp. outdoors.

sleeping car *n.* a railway carriage fitted with compartments containing bunks for people to sleep in.

sleeping partner *n.* a partner in a business who does not play an active role. Also called: **silent partner**.

sleeping pill *n.* a pill or tablet containing a sedative drug, such as a barbiturate, used to induce sleep.

sleeping policeman *n.* a bump built across a road to deter motorists from speeding. Official name: **road hump**.

sleeping sickness *n.* **1.** Also called: **African sleeping sickness.** an African disease transmitted by the bite of tsetse fly, characterized by fever and sluggishness. **2.** Also called: **sleepy sickness.** an epidemic viral form of encephalitis characterized by extreme drowsiness. Technical name: **encephalitis lethargica**.

sleepless ('sli:plɪs) *adj.* **1.** without sleep or rest: *a sleepless journey.* **2.** unable to sleep. **3.** always alert. **4.** *Chiefly poetic.* always active or moving. —'**sleeplessly** *adv.* —'**sleeplessness** *n.*

sleep off *vb.* (*tr., adv.*) *Inf.* to lose by sleeping: *to sleep off a hangover.*

sleep out *vb.* (*intr., adv.*) **1.** (esp. of a tramp) to sleep in the open air. **2.** to sleep away from the place of one's employment. ~*n.* **sleep-out**. **3.** *Austral. & N.Z.* an area of a veranda partitioned off so that it may be used as a bedroom.

sleepwalk ('sli:p,wɔ:k) *vb.* (*intr.*) to walk while asleep. —'**sleep,walker** *n.* —'**sleep,walking** *n., adj.*

sleep with *vb.* (*intr., prep.*) to have sexual intercourse and (usually) spend the night with. Also: **sleep together**.

sleepy ('sli:pɪ) *adj.* **sleepier, sleepiest**. **1.** inclined to or needing sleep. **2.** characterized by or exhibiting drowsiness, etc. **3.** conducive to sleep. **4.** without activity or bustle: *a sleepy town.* —'**sleepily** *adv.* —'**sleepiness** *n.*

sleet (sli:t) *n.* **1.** partly melted falling snow or hail or (esp. U.S.) partly frozen rain. **2.** *Chiefly U.S.* the thin coat of ice that forms when sleet or rain freezes on cold surfaces. ~*vb.* **3.** (*intr.*) to fall as sleet. [C13: of Gmc origin] —'**sleety** *adj.*

sleeve (sli:v) *n.* **1.** the part of a garment covering the arm. **2.** a tubular piece that is shrunk into a cylindrical bore to reduce its bore or to line it with a different material. **3.** a tube fitted externally over two cylindrical parts in order to join them. **4.** a flat cardboard container to protect a gramophone record. U.S. name: **jacket**. **5. (have a few tricks) up one's sleeve.** (to have options, etc.) secretly ready. **6. roll up one's sleeves.** to prepare oneself for work, a fight, etc. ~*vb.* **7.** (*tr.*) to provide with a sleeve or sleeves. [OE *slīf, slēf*] —'**sleeveless** *adj.* —'**sleeve,like** *adj.*

sleeve board *n.* a small ironing board for pressing sleeves, fitted onto an ironing board or table.

sleeving ('sli:vɪŋ) *n. Electronics, chiefly Brit.* tubular flexible insulation into which bare wire can be inserted.

sleigh (sleɪ) *n.* **1.** another name for **sledge**[1](sense 1). ~*vb.* **2.** (*intr.*) to travel by sleigh. [C18: from Du. *slee*, var. of *slede* SLEDGE[1]]

sleight (slaɪt) *n. Arch.* **1.** skill; dexterity. **2.** a trick or stratagem. **3.** cunning. [C14: from ON *slǣgth*, from *slǣgr* SLY]

sleight of hand *n.* **1.** manual dexterity used in performing conjuring tricks. **2.** the performance of such tricks.

slender ('slɛndə) *adj.* **1.** of small width relative to length or height. **2.** (esp. of a person's figure) slim and well-formed. **3.** small or inadequate in amount, size, etc.: *slender resources.* **4.** (of hopes, etc.) feeble. **5.** very small: *a slender margin.* [C14 *slendre*, from ?] —'**slenderly** *adv.* —'**slenderness** *n.*

slenderize *or* -**rise** ('slɛndə,raɪz) *vb. Chiefly U.S. & Canad.* to make or become slender.

slept (slɛpt) *vb.* the past tense and past participle of **sleep**.

Slesvig ('slesvi) *n.* the Danish name for **Schleswig**.

sleuth (slu:θ) *n.* **1.** an informal word for **detective**. **2.** short for **sleuthhound** (sense 1). ~*vb.* **3.** (*tr.*) to follow. [C19: short for *sleuthhound*, from C12 *sleuth* trail, from ON *sloth*]

sleuthhound ('slu:θ,haʊnd) *n.* **1.** a dog trained to track people, esp. a bloodhound. **2.** an informal word for **detective**.

S level *n. Brit.* the Special level of a subject taken for the General Certificate of Education: usually taken at the same time as A levels as an additional qualification.

slew[1] (slu:) *vb.* the past tense of **slay**.

slew[2] *or esp. U.S.* **slue** (slu:) *vb.* **1.** to twist or be twisted sideways, esp. awkwardly. **2.** *Naut.* to cause (a mast) to rotate in its step or (of a mast) to rotate in its step. ~*n.* **3.** the act of slewing. [C18: from ?]

slew[3] (slu:) *n.* a variant spelling (esp. U.S.) of **slough**[1] (sense 2).

slew[4] *or* **slue** (slu:) *n. U.S. & Canad. inf.* a great number. [C20: from Irish Gaelic *sluagh*]

Slezsko ('slɛskɔ) *n.* the Czech name for **Silesia**.

slice (slaɪs) *n.* **1.** a thin flat piece cut from something having bulk: *a slice of pork.* **2.** a share or portion: *a slice of the company's revenue.* **3.** any of various utensils having a broad flat blade and resembling a spatula. **4.** (in golf, tennis, etc.) **a.** the flight of a ball that travels obliquely. **b.** the action of hitting such a shot. **c.** the shot so hit. ~*vb.* **5.** to divide or cut (something) into parts or slices. **6.** (when *intr.*, usually foll. by *through*) to cut in a clean and effortless manner. **7.** (when *intr.*, foll. by *into* or *through*) to move or go (through something) like a knife. **8.** (usually foll. by *off, from, away*, etc.) to cut or be cut (from) a larger piece. **9.** (*tr.*) to remove by use of a slicing implement. **10.** to hit (a ball) with a slice. [C14: from OF *esclice* a piece split off, from *esclicier* to splinter] —'**sliceable** *adj.* —'**slicer** *n.*

slick (slɪk) *adj.* **1.** flattering and glib: *a slick salesman.* **2.** adroitly devised or executed: *a slick show.* **3.** *Inf., chiefly U.S. & Canad.* shrewd; sly. **4.** *Inf.* superficially attractive: *a slick publication.* **5.** *Chiefly U.S. & Canad.* slippery. ~*n.* **6.** a slippery area, esp. a patch of oil floating on water. ~*vb.* (*tr.*) **7.** *Chiefly U.S. & Canad.* to make smooth or sleek. [C14: prob. from ON] —'**slickly** *adv.* —'**slickness** *n.*

slicker ('slɪkə) *n.* **1.** *Inf.* a sly or untrustworthy person (esp. in **city slicker**). **2.** *U.S. & Canad.* a shiny raincoat, esp. an oilskin.

slide (slaɪd) *vb.* **sliding, slid** (slɪd); **slid** *or* **slidden** ('slɪd'n). **1.** to move or cause to move smoothly along a surface in continual contact with it: *doors that slide open.* **2.** (*intr.*) to lose grip or balance: *he slid on his back.* **3.** (*intr.*; usually foll. by *into, out of, away from*, etc.) to pass or move unobtrusively: *she slid into the room.* **4.** (*intr.*; usually foll. by *into*) to go (into a specified condition) by degrees, etc.: *he slid into loose living.* **5.** (foll. by *in, into*, etc.) to move (an object) unobtrusively or (of an object) to move in this way: *he slid the gun into his pocket.* **6. let slide.** to allow to deteriorate: *to let things slide.* ~*n.* **7.** the act or an instance of sliding. **8.** a smooth surface, as of ice or mud, for sliding on. **9.** a construction incorporating an inclined smooth slope for sliding down in playgrounds, etc. **10.** a small glass plate on which specimens are mounted for microscopic study. **11.** Also called: **transparency.** a positive photograph on a transparent base, mounted in a frame, that can be viewed by means of a slide projector. **12.** Also called: **hair slide.** *Chiefly Brit.* an ornamental clip to hold hair in place. **13.** *Machinery.* a sliding part or member. **14.** *Music.* a portamento. **15.** *Music.* the sliding curved tube of a trombone that is moved in or out. **16.** *Music* **a.** a tube placed over a finger held against the frets of a guitar to produce a portamento. **b.** the style of guitar playing using a slide. **17.** *Geol.* **a.** the downward movement of a large mass of earth, rocks, etc. **b.** the mass of material involved in this descent. See also **landslide.** [OE *slīdan*] —'**slidable** *adj.* —'**slider** *n.*

slide over *vb.* (*intr., prep.*) **1.** to cross as if by sliding. **2.** to avoid dealing with (a matter) fully.

slide rule *n.* a mechanical calculating device consisting of two strips, one sliding along a central groove in the other, each graduated in two or more logarithmic scales of numbers, trigonometric functions, etc.

sliding scale *n.* a variable scale according to which specified wages, prices, etc., fluctuate in response to changes in some other factor.

slier ('slaɪə) *adj.* a comparative of **sly.**

sliest ('slaɪɪst) *adj.* a superlative of **sly.**

slight (slaɪt) *adj.* **1.** small in quantity or extent. **2.** of small importance. **3.** slim and delicate. **4.** lacking in strength or substance. ~*vb.* (*tr.*) **5.** to show disregard for (someone); snub. **6.** to treat as unimportant or trifling. **7.** *U.S.* to devote inadequate attention to (work, duties, etc.). ~*n.* **8.** an act or omission indicating supercilious neglect. [C13: from OE *slĕttr* smooth] —'**slightingly** *adv.* —'**slightly** *adv.* —'**slightness** *n.*

Sligo ('slaɪgəʊ) *n.* **1.** a county of NW Ireland, on the Atlantic: has a deeply indented low-lying coast; livestock and dairy farming. County town: Sligo. Pop.: 55 979 (1986). Area: 1795 sq. km (693 sq. miles). **2.** a port in NW Ireland, county town of Co. Sligo on **Sligo Bay.** Pop.: 17 232 (1981).

slily ('slaɪlɪ) *adv.* a variant spelling of **slyly.**

slim (slɪm) *adj.* **slimmer, slimmest. 1.** small in width relative to height or length. **2.** poor; meagre: *slim chances of success.* ~*vb.* **3.** to make or become slim, esp. by diets and exercise. **4.** (*tr.*) to reduce in size: *the workforce was slimmed.* [C17: from Du.: crafty, from MDu. *slimp* slanting] —'**slimmer** *n.* —'**slimming** *n.* —'**slimness** *n.*

Slim (slɪm) *n.* the E African name for **AIDS.** [from its wasting effects]

Slim (slɪm) *n.* **William Joseph,** 1st Viscount. 1891–1970, British field marshal, who commanded (1943–45) the 14th Army in the reconquest of Burma from the Japanese; governor general of Australia (1953–60).

slime (slaɪm) *n.* **1.** soft thin runny mud or filth. **2.** any moist viscous fluid, esp. when noxious or unpleasant. **3.** a mucous substance produced by various organisms, such as fish, slugs, and fungi. ~*vb.* (*tr.*) **4.** to cover with slime. [OE *slīm*]

slimline ('slɪm,laɪn) *adj.* slim or conducive to slimness.

slimy ('slaɪmɪ) *adj.* **slimier, slimiest. 1.** characterized by, covered with, secreting, or resembling slime. **2.** offensive or repulsive. **3.** *Chiefly Brit.* characterized by servility.

sling[1] (slɪŋ) *n.* **1.** a simple weapon consisting of a loop of leather, etc., in which a stone is whirled and then let fly. **2.** a rope or strap by which something may be secured or lifted. **3.** *Med.* a wide piece of cloth suspended from the neck for supporting an injured hand or arm. **4.** a loop or band attached to an object for carrying. **5.** the act of slinging. ~*vb.* **slinging, slung. 6.** (*tr.*) to hurl with or as if with a sling. **7.** to attach a sling or slings to (a load, etc.). **8.** (*tr.*) to carry or hang loosely from or as if from a sling: *to sling washing from the line.* **9.** (*tr.*) *Inf.* to throw. [C13: ?from ON] —'**slinger** *n.*

sling[2] (slɪŋ) *n.* a mixed drink with a spirit base, usually sweetened. [C19: from ?]

slingback ('slɪŋ,bæk) *n.* a shoe with a strap instead of a full covering for the heel.

sling off *vb.* (*intr., adv.; often foll. by at*) *Austral. & N.Z. inf.* to mock; deride; jeer (at).

slingshot ('slɪŋ,ʃɒt) *n.* **1.** the U.S. and Canad. name for **catapult** (sense 1). **2.** another name for **sling**[1](sense 1).

slink (slɪŋk) *vb.* **slinking, slunk. 1.** (*intr.*) to move or act in a furtive manner from or as if from fear, guilt, etc. **2.** (*intr.*) to move in a sinuous alluring manner. **3.** (*tr.*) of animals, esp. cows) to give birth to prematurely. ~*n.* **4.** an animal, esp. a calf, born prematurely. [OE *slincan*]

slinky ('slɪŋkɪ) *adj.* **slinkier, slinkiest.** *Inf.* **1.** moving in a sinuously graceful or provocative way. **2.** (of clothes) figure-hugging. —'**slinkily** *adv.* —'**slinkiness** *n.*

slip[1] (slɪp) *vb.* **slipping, slipped. 1.** to move or cause to move smoothly and easily. **2.** (*tr.*) to place, insert, or convey quickly or stealthily. **3.** (*tr.*) to put on or take off easily or quickly: *to slip on a sweater.* **4.** (*intr.*) to lose balance and slide unexpectedly: *he slipped on the ice.* **5.** to let loose or be let loose. **6.** to be released from (something). **7.** (*tr.*) to let go (mooring or anchor lines) over the side. **8.** (when *intr.*, often foll. by *from* or *out of*) to pass out of (the mind or memory). **9.** (*intr.*) to move or pass swiftly or unperceived: *to slip quietly out of the room.* **10.** (*intr.*; sometimes foll. by *up*) to make a mistake. **11.** Also: **sideslip.** to cause (an aircraft) to slide sideways or (of an aircraft) to slide sideways. **12.** (*intr.*) to decline in health, mental ability, etc. **13.** (*intr.*) (of an intervertebral disc) to become displaced from the normal position. **14.** (*tr.*) to dislocate (a bone). **15.** (of animals) to give birth to (offspring) prematurely. **16.** (*tr.*) to pass (a stitch) from one needle to another without knitting it. **17. a.** (*tr.*) to operate (the clutch of a motor vehicle) so that it partially disengages. **b.** (*intr.*) (of the clutch of a motor vehicle) to fail to engage, esp. as a result of wear. **18. let slip. a.** to allow to escape. **b.** to say unintentionally. ~*n.* **19.** the act or an instance of slipping. **20.** a mistake or oversight: *a slip of the pen.* **21.** a moral lapse or failing. **22.** a woman's sleeveless undergarment, worn as a lining for a dress. **23.** a pillowcase. **24.** See **slipway. 25.** *Cricket.* **a.** the position of the fielder who stands a little way behind and to the offside of the wicketkeeper. **b.** the fielder himself. **26.** the relative movement of rocks along a fault plane. **27.** *Metallurgy, crystallog.* the deformation of a metallic crystal caused when one part glides over another part along a plane. **28.** a landslide. **29.** the deviation of a propeller from its helical path through a fluid. **30.** another name for **sideslip** (sense 1). **31. give someone the slip.** to elude or escape from someone. ~See also **slip up.** [C13: from MLow G or Du. *slippen*] —'**slipless** *adj.*

slip[2] (slɪp) *n.* **1.** a narrow piece; strip. **2.** a small piece of paper: *a receipt slip.* **3.** a part of a plant that, when detached from the parent, will grow into a new plant; cutting. **4.** a young slender person: *a slip of a child.* **5.** *Printing.* **a.** a long galley. **b.** a galley proof. ~*vb.* **slipping, slipped. 6.** (*tr.*) to detach (portions of stem, etc.) from (a plant) for propagation. [C15: prob. from MLow G, MDu. *slippe* to cut, strip]

slip[3] (slɪp) *n.* clay mixed with water to a creamy consistency, used for decorating or patching a ceramic piece. [OE *slyppe* slime]

slipcase ('slɪp,keɪs) *n.* a protective case for a book or set of books that is open at one end so that only the spines of the books are visible.

slipcover ('slɪp,kʌvə) *n. U.S. & Canad.* **1.** a loose cover. **2.** a book jacket; dust cover.

slipe (slaɪp) *n. N.Z.* **a.** wool removed from the pelt of a slaughtered sheep by immersion in a chemical bath. **b.** (*as modifier*): *slipe wool.* [C14 in England: from *slype* to strip, skin]

slipknot ('slɪp,nɒt) *n.* **1.** Also called: **running knot.** a nooselike knot tied so that it will slip along the rope round which it is made. **2.** a knot that can be easily untied by pulling one free end.

slip-on *adj.* **1.** (of a garment or shoe) made so as to be easily and quickly put on or taken off. ~*n.* **2.** a slip-on garment or shoe.

slipover ('slɪp,əʊvə) *adj.* **1.** of or denoting a garment that can be put on easily over the head. ~*n.* **2.** such a garment, esp. a sleeveless pullover.

slippage ('slɪpɪdʒ) *n.* **1.** the act or an instance of slipping. **2.** the amount of slipping or the extent to which slipping occurs. **3. a.** an instance of not reaching a target, etc. **b.** the extent of this.

slipped disc n. Pathol. a herniated intervertebral disc, often resulting in pain because of pressure on the spinal nerves.

slipper ('slɪpə) n. **1.** a light shoe of some soft material, for wearing around the house. **2.** a woman's evening shoe. ~vb. **3.** (tr.) Inf. to hit or beat with a slipper. —'**slippered** adj.

slipper bath n. a bath in the shape of a slipper, with a covered end.

slipperwort ('slɪpə,wɜːt) n. another name for **calceolaria**.

slippery ('slɪpərɪ, -prɪ) adj. **1.** causing or tending to cause objects to slip: a slippery road. **2.** liable to slip from the grasp, etc. **3.** not to be relied upon: a slippery character. **4.** (esp. of a situation) unstable. [C16: prob. coined by Coverdale to translate G schlipfferig in Luther's Bible (Psalm 35:6)] —'**slipperiness** n.

slippery elm n. **1.** a North American tree, having notched winged fruits and a mucilaginous inner bark. **2.** the bark of this tree, used medicinally as a demulcent. ~Also called: **red elm**.

slippy ('slɪpɪ) adj. -**pier**, -**piest**. **1.** Inf. or dialect. another word for **slippery** (senses 1, 2). **2.** Brit. inf. alert; quick. —'**slippiness** n.

slip rail n. Austral. & N.Z. a rail in a fence that can be slipped out of place to make an opening.

slip road n. Brit. a short road connecting a motorway to another road.

slipshod ('slɪp,ʃɒd) adj. **1.** (of an action) negligent; careless. **2.** (of a person's appearance) slovenly; down-at-heel. [C16: from SLIP[1] + SHOD]

slip-slop n. S. African. the usual name for **flip-flop** (sense 5).

slipstream ('slɪp,striːm) n. Also called: **airstream. a.** the stream of air forced backwards by an aircraft propeller. **b.** a stream of air behind any moving object.

slip up Inf. ~vb. (intr., adv.) **1.** to make a blunder or mistake. ~n. **slip-up. 2.** a mistake or mishap.

slipware ('slɪp,wɛə) n. pottery that has been decorated with slip and glazed.

slipway ('slɪp,weɪ) n. **1.** the sloping area in a shipyard, containing the ways. **2.** the ways on which a vessel is launched.

slit (slɪt) vb. **slitting, slit**. (tr.) **1.** to make a straight long incision in. **2.** to cut into strips lengthwise. ~n. **3.** a long narrow cut. **4.** a long narrow opening. [OE slītan to slice] —'**slitter** n.

slither ('slɪðə) vb. **1.** to move or slide or cause to move or slide unsteadily, as on a slippery surface. **2.** (intr.) to travel with a sliding motion. ~n. **3.** a slithering motion. [OE slidrian, from slidan to slide] —'**slithery** adj.

slit trench n. Mil. a narrow trench dug for the protection of a small number of people.

sliver ('slɪvə) n. **1.** a thin piece that is cut or broken off lengthwise. **2.** a loose fibre obtained by carding. ~vb. **3.** to divide or be divided into splinters. **4.** (tr.) to form (wool, etc.) into slivers. [C14: from sliven to split]

Sloan (sləʊn) n. **John**. 1871–1951, U.S. painter and etcher, a leading member of the group of realistic painters known as the Ash Can School. His pictures of city scenes include McSorley's Bar (1912) and Backyards, Greenwich Village (1914).

Sloane Ranger (sləʊn) n. (in Britain) Inf. a young upper-class person having a home in London and in the country, characterized as wearing expensive informal clothes. Also called: **Sloane**. [C20: pun on Sloane Square, London, and Lone Ranger, cowboy cartoon character]

slob (slɒb) n. **1.** Inf. a stupid or coarse person. **2.** Irish. mire. [C19: from Irish Gaelic slab mud]

slobber ('slɒbə) or **slabber** vb. **1.** to dribble (saliva, food, etc.) from the mouth. **2.** (intr.) to speak or write mawkishly. **3.** (tr.) to smear with matter dribbling from the mouth. ~n. **4.** liquid or saliva spilt from the mouth. **5.** maudlin language or behaviour. [C15: from MLow G, MDu. slubberen] —'**slobberer** or '**slabberer** n. —'**slobbery** or '**slabbery** adj.

sloe (sləʊ) n. **1.** the small sour blue-black fruit of the blackthorn. **2.** another name for **blackthorn**. [OE slāh]

sloe-eyed adj. having dark slanted or almond-shaped eyes.

sloe gin n. gin flavoured with sloe juice.

slog (slɒg) vb. **slogging, slogged. 1.** to hit with heavy blows, as in boxing. **2.** (intr.) to work hard; toil. **3.**

(intr.; foll. by down, up, along, etc.) to move with difficulty. **4.** Cricket. to take large swipes at the ball. ~n. **5.** a tiring walk. **6.** long exhausting work. **7.** a heavy blow or swipe. [C19: from ?] —'**slogger** n.

slogan ('sləʊgən) n. **1.** a distinctive or topical phrase used in politics, advertising, etc. **2.** Scot. history. a Highland battle cry. [C16: from Gaelic sluagh-ghairm war cry]

sloop (sluːp) n. a single-masted sailing vessel, rigged fore-and-aft. [C17: from Du. sloep]

sloot (sluːt) n. S. African. a ditch for irrigation or drainage. [from Afrik., from Du. sluit, sluis SLUICE]

slop[1] (slɒp) vb. **slopping, slopped. 1.** (when intr., often foll. by about) to cause (liquid) to splash or spill or (of liquid) to splash or spill. **2.** (intr.; foll. by along, through, etc.) to tramp (through) mud or slush. **3.** (tr.) to feed slop or swill to: to slop the pigs. **4.** (tr.) to ladle or serve, esp. clumsily. **5.** (intr.; foll. by over) Inf., chiefly U.S. & Canad. to be unpleasantly effusive. ~n. **6.** a puddle of spilt liquid. **7.** (pl.) wet feed, esp. for pigs, made from kitchen waste, etc. **8.** (pl.) waste food or liquid refuse. **9.** (often pl.) Inf. liquid or semiliquid food of low quality. **10.** soft mud, snow, etc. [C14: prob. from OE -sloppe in cūsloppe COWSLIP]

slop[2] (slɒp) n. **1.** (pl.) sailors' clothing and bedding issued from a ship's stores. **2.** any loose article of clothing, esp. a smock. **3.** (pl.) shoddy manufactured clothing. [OE oferslop surplice]

slop basin n. a bowl or basin into which the dregs from teacups are emptied at the table.

slope (sləʊp) vb. **1.** to lie or cause to lie at a slanting or oblique angle. **2.** (intr.) (esp. of natural features) to follow an inclined course: many paths sloped down the hillside. **3.** (intr.; foll. by off, away, etc.) to go furtively. **4.** (tr.) Mil. (formerly) to hold (a rifle) in the sloping position. ~n. **5.** an inclined portion of ground. **6.** (pl.) hills or foothills. **7.** any inclined surface or line. **8.** the degree or amount of such inclination. **9.** Maths. (of a line) the tangent of the angle between the line and another line parallel to the x-axis. **10.** (formerly) the position adopted for military drill when the rifle is rested on the shoulder. [C15: short for aslope, ?from the p.p. of OE āslūpan to slip away] —'**sloper** n. —'**sloping** adj.

slop out vb. (intr., adv.) (of prisoners) to empty chamber pots and collect water for washing.

sloppy ('slɒpɪ) adj. -**pier**, -**piest**. **1.** (esp. of the ground, etc.) wet; slushy. **2.** Inf. careless; untidy. **3.** Inf. mawkishly sentimental. **4.** (of food or drink) watery and unappetizing. **5.** splashed with slops. **6.** (of clothes) loose; baggy. —'**sloppily** adv. —'**sloppiness** n.

slosh (slɒʃ) n. **1.** watery mud, snow, etc. **2.** Brit. sl. **4.** a heavy blow. **3.** the sound of splashing liquid. ~vb. **4.** (tr.; foll. by around, on, in, etc.) Inf. to throw or pour (liquid). **5.** (when intr., often foll. by about or around) Inf. **a.** to shake or stir (something) in a liquid. **b.** (of a person) to splash (around) in water, etc. **6.** (tr.) Brit. sl. to deal a heavy blow to. **7.** (usually foll. by about or around) Inf. to shake (a container of liquid) or (of liquid within a container) to be shaken. [C19: var. of SLUSH, infl. by SLOP[1]] —'**sloshy** adj.

sloshed (slɒʃt) adj. Chiefly Brit. sl. drunk.

slot[1] (slɒt) n. **1.** an elongated aperture or groove, such as one in a vending machine for inserting a coin. **2.** Inf. a place in a series or scheme. ~vb. **slotting, slotted. 3.** (tr.) to furnish with a slot or slots. **4.** (usually foll. by in or into) to fit or adjust in a slot. **5.** Inf. to situate or be situated in a series. [C13: from OF esclot the depression of the breastbone, from ?] —'**slotter** n.

slot[2] (slɒt) n. the trail of an animal, esp. a deer. [C16: from OF esclot horse's hoofprint, prob. of Scand. origin]

sloth (sləʊθ) n. **1.** any of a family of shaggy-coated arboreal edentate mammals, such as the three-toed sloth or ai or the two-toed sloth or unau, of Central and South America. They are slow-moving, hanging upside down by their long arms and feeding on vegetation. **2.** reluctance to exert oneself. [OE slǣwth, from slǣw, var. of slāw slow]

sloth bear n. a bear of forests of S India and Sri Lanka, having an elongated snout specialized for feeding on termites.

slothful ('sləʊθfʊl) adj. lazy; indolent. —'**slothfully** adv. —'**slothfulness** n.

slot machine n. a machine, esp. one for gambling, activated by placing a coin in a slot.

slouch (slaʊtʃ) vb. **1.** (intr.) to sit or stand with a drooping bearing. **2.** (intr.) to walk or move with an awkward slovenly gait. **3.** (tr.) to cause (the shoulders) to droop. ~n. **4.** a drooping carriage. **5.** (usually used in negative constructions) Inf. an incompetent or slovenly person: he's no slouch at football. [C16: from ?] — **'slouching** adj.

slouch hat n. any soft hat with a brim that can be pulled down over the ears, esp. an Australian army hat with the left side of the brim turned up.

slough[1] (slaʊ) n. **1.** a hollow filled with mud; bog. **2.** (sluː) North American. a large hole where water collects or a marshy inlet. **3.** despair or degradation. [OE slōh] — **'sloughy** adj.

slough[2] (slʌf) n. **1.** any outer covering that is shed, such as the dead outer layer of the skin of a snake, the cellular debris in a wound, etc. ~vb. **2.** (often foll. by off) to shed (a skin, etc.) or (of a skin, etc.) to be shed. [C13: of Gmc origin] — **'sloughy** adj.

Slough (slaʊ) n. an industrial town in SE central England, in NE Berkshire. Pop.: 97 008 (1981).

slough off (slʌf) vb. (tr., adv.) to cast off (cares, etc.).

Slovak ('sləʊvæk) adj. **1.** of or characteristic of Slovakia, its people, or their language. ~n. **2.** one of the two official languages of Czechoslovakia. Czech and Slovak are closely related and mutually intelligible. **3.** a native or inhabitant of Slovakia.

Slovakia (sləʊ'vækɪə) n. a region of E Czechoslovakia: part of Hungary from the 11th century until 1918, when it united with Bohemia and Moravia to form Czechoslovakia. Area: 49 009 sq. km (18 922 sq. miles). — **Slo'vakian** adj., n.

sloven ('slʌv³n) n. a person who is habitually negligent in appearance, hygiene, or work. [C15: prob. rel. to Flemish sloef dirty, Du. slof negligent]

Slovene (sləʊ'viːn) adj. **1.** of or characteristic of Slovenia, its people, or their language. ~n. **2.** the Slavonic language spoken in Slovenia. **3.** a native or inhabitant of Slovenia.

Slovenia (sləʊ'viːnɪə) n. a constituent republic of NW Yugoslavia: settled by the Slovenes in the 6th century; joined Yugoslavia in 1918 and became an autonomous republic in 1946; rises over 2800 m (9000 ft.) in the Julian Alps. Capital: Ljubljana. Pop.: 1 930 000 (1985). Area: 20 251 sq. km (7819 sq. miles). — **Slo'venian** adj., n.

slovenly ('slʌvənlɪ) adj. **1.** frequently or habitually unclean or untidy. **2.** negligent and careless: slovenly manners. ~adv. **3.** in a negligent or slovenly manner. — **'slovenliness** n.

slow (sləʊ) adj. **1.** performed or occurring during a comparatively long interval of time. **2.** lasting a comparatively long time: a slow journey. **3.** characterized by lack of speed: a slow walker. **4.** (prenominal) adapted to or productive of slow movement: the slow lane of a motorway. **5.** (of a clock, etc.) indicating a time earlier than the correct time. **6.** not readily responsive to stimulation: a slow mind. **7.** dull or uninteresting: the play was very slow. **8.** not easily aroused: a slow temperament. **9.** lacking promptness or immediacy: a slow answer. **10.** unwilling to perform an action or enter into a state: slow to anger. **11.** behind the times. **12.** (of trade, etc.) unproductive; slack. **13.** (of a fire) burning weakly. **14.** (of an oven) cool. **15.** Photog. requiring a relatively long time of exposure to produce a given density: a slow lens. **16.** Sport. (of a court, track, etc.) tending to reduce the speed of the ball or the competitors. **17.** Cricket. (of a bowler, etc.) delivering the ball slowly, usually with spin. ~adv. **18.** in a manner characterized by lack of speed; slowly. ~vb. **19.** (often foll. by up, down, etc.) to decrease or cause to decrease in speed, efficiency, etc. [OE slāw sluggish] — **'slowly** adv. — **'slowness** n.

slowcoach ('sləʊ‚kəʊtʃ) n. Brit. inf. a person who moves or works slowly. U.S. and Canad. equivalent: **slowpoke**.

slow handclap n. Brit. slow rhythmic clapping, esp. used by an audience to indicate dissatisfaction or impatience.

slow march n. Mil. a march in **slow time,** usually 65 or 75 paces to the minute.

slow match or **fuse** n. a match or fuse that burns slowly without flame.

slow motion n. **1.** Films, television, etc. action that is made to appear slower than normal by passing the film through the camera at a faster rate or by replaying a video recording more slowly. ~adj. **slow-motion. 2.** of or relating to such action. **3.** moving or functioning at considerably less than usual speed.

slow virus n. a type of virus that is present in the body for a long time before it becomes active or infectious.

slowworm ('sləʊ‚wɜːm) n. a Eurasian legless lizard with a brownish-grey snakelike body. Also called: **blindworm**.

SLR abbrev. for single-lens reflex: see **reflex camera.**

slub (slʌb) n. **1.** a lump in yarn or fabric, often made intentionally to give a knobbly effect. **2.** a loosely twisted roll of fibre prepared for spinning. ~vb. **slubbing, slubbed. 3.** (tr.) to draw out and twist (a sliver of fibre). ~adj. **4.** (of material) having an irregular appearance. [C18: from ?]

sludge (slʌdʒ) n. **1.** soft mud, snow, etc. **2.** any deposit or sediment. **3.** a surface layer of ice that is not frozen solid but has a slushy appearance. **4.** (in sewage disposal) the solid constituents of sewage that are removed for purification. [C17: prob. rel. to SLUSH] — **'sludgy** adj.

slue[1] (sluː) n., vb. a variant spelling (esp. U.S.) of **slew**[2].

slue[2] (sluː) n. a variant spelling of **slough**[1](sense 2).

slug[1] (slʌg) n. **1.** any of various terrestrial gastropod molluscs in which the body is elongated and the shell is absent or very much reduced. **2.** any of various other invertebrates having a soft slimy body, esp. the larvae of certain sawflies. [C15 (in the sense: a slow person or animal): prob. from ON]

slug[2] (slʌg) n. **1.** an fps unit of mass; the mass that will acquire an acceleration of 1 foot per second per second when acted upon by a force of 1 pound. **2.** Metallurgy. a metal blank from which small forgings are worked. **3.** a bullet. **4.** Chiefly U.S. & Canad. a metal token for use in slot machines, etc. **5.** Printing. **a.** a thick strip of type metal that is used for spacing. **b.** a metal strip containing a line of characters as produced by a Linotype machine. **6.** a draught of alcoholic drink, esp. spirits. [C17 (bullet), C19 (printing): ?from SLUG[1], with allusion to the shape of the animal]

slug[3] (slʌg) vb. **slugging, slugged. 1.** Chiefly U.S. & Canad. to hit very hard and solidly. **2.** (tr.) Austral. & N.Z. inf. to charge (someone) an exorbitant price. ~n. **3.** U.S. & Canad. a heavy blow. **4.** Austral. & N.Z. inf. an exorbitant price. [C19: ?from SLUG[2] (bullet)]

sluggard ('slʌgəd) n. **1.** a person who is habitually indolent. ~adj. **2.** lazy. [C14 slogarde] — **'sluggardly** adj.

sluggish ('slʌgɪʃ) adj. **1.** lacking energy; inactive. **2.** functioning at below normal rate or level. **3.** exhibiting poor response to stimulation. — **'sluggishly** adv. — **'sluggishness** n.

sluice (sluːs) n. **1.** Also called: **sluiceway.** a channel that carries a rapid current of water, esp. one that has a sluicegate to control the flow. **2.** the body of water controlled by a sluicegate. **3.** See **sluicegate. 4.** Mining. an inclined trough for washing ore. **5.** an artificial channel through which logs can be floated. ~vb. **6.** (tr.) to draw out or drain (water, etc.) from (a pond, etc.) by means of a sluice. **7.** (tr.) to wash or irrigate with a stream of water. **8.** (tr.) Mining. to wash in a sluice. **9.** (tr.) to send (logs, etc.) down a sluice. **10.** (intr.; often foll. by away or out) (of water, etc.) to run or flow from or as if from a sluice. **11.** (tr.) to provide with a sluice. [C14: from OF escluse, from LL exclūsa aqua water shut out, from L exclūdere to shut out] — **'sluice‚like** adj.

sluicegate ('sluːs‚geɪt) n. a valve or gate fitted to a sluice to control the rate of flow of water. See also **floodgate** (sense 1).

slum (slʌm) n. **1.** a squalid overcrowded house, etc. **2.** (often pl.) a squalid section of a city, characterized by inferior living conditions. **3.** (modifier) of or characteristic of slums: slum conditions. ~vb. **slumming, slummed. (intr.) 4.** to visit slums, esp. for curiosity. **5.** Also: **slum it.** to suffer conditions below those to which one is accustomed. [C19: orig. sl., from ?] — **'slummy** adj.

slumber ('slʌmbə) vb. **1.** (intr.) to sleep, esp. peacefully. **2.** (intr.) to be quiescent or dormant. **3.** (tr.; foll. by away) to spend (time) sleeping. ~n. **4.** (sometimes pl.) sleep. **5.** a dormant or quiescent state. [OE slūma sleep (n.)] — **'slumberer** n. — **'slumbering** adj.

slumberous ('slʌmbərəs) adj. Chiefly poetic. **1.** sleepy; drowsy. **2.** inducing sleep. — **'slumberously** adv. — **'slumberousness** n.

slump (slʌmp) vb. (intr.) **1.** to sink or fall heavily and suddenly. **2.** to relax ungracefully. **3.** (of business activity, etc.) to decline suddenly. **4.** (of health, interest, etc.) to deteriorate or decline suddenly. ~n. **5.** a sudden or marked decline or failure, as in progress or achievement. **6.** a decline in commercial activity, prices, etc.; depression. **7.** the act of slumping. [C17: prob. of Scand. origin]

slung (slʌŋ) vb. the past tense and past participle of **sling**[1].

slunk (slʌŋk) vb. the past tense and past participle of **slink**.

slur (slɜː) vb. **slurring, slurred.** (mainly tr.) **1.** (often foll. by over) to treat superficially, hastily, or without due deliberation. **2.** (also intr.) to pronounce or utter (words, etc.) indistinctly. **3.** to speak disparagingly of. **4.** Music. to execute (a melodic interval of two or more notes) smoothly, as in legato performance. ~n. **5.** an indistinct sound or utterance. **6.** a slighting remark. **7.** a stain or disgrace, as upon one's reputation. **8.** Music. **a.** a performance or execution of a melodic interval of two or more notes in a part. **b.** the curved line (⌢ or ⌣) indicating this. [C15: prob. from MLow G]

slurp (slɜːp) Inf. ~vb. **1.** to eat or drink (something) noisily. ~n. **2.** a sound produced in this way. [C17: from MDu. slorpen to sip]

slurry ('slʌrɪ) n., pl. **-ries.** a suspension of solid particles in a liquid, as in a mixture of cement, manure, or coal dust with water. [C15 slory]

slush (slʌʃ) n. **1.** any watery muddy substance, esp. melting snow. **2.** Inf. sloppily sentimental language. ~vb. **3.** (intr.; often foll. by along) to make one's way through or as if through slush. [C17: rel. to Danish slus sleet, Norwegian slusk slops] — **'slushiness** n. — **'slushy** adj.

slush fund n. a fund for financing political or commercial corruption.

slushy ('slʌʃɪ) adj. **slushier, slushiest.** of, resembling, or consisting of slush.

slut (slʌt) n. **1.** a dirty slatternly woman. **2.** an immoral woman. [C14: from ?] — **'sluttish** adj. — **'sluttishness** n.

sly (slaɪ) adj. **slyer, slyest** or **slier, sliest. 1.** crafty; artful: a sly dodge. **2.** insidious; furtive: a sly manner. **3.** roguish: sly humour. ~n. **4. on the sly.** in a secretive manner. [C12: from ON slœgr clever, lit.: able to strike, from slā to slay] — **'slyly** or **'slily** adv. — **'slyness** n.

slype (slaɪp) n. a covered passage in a church that connects the transept to the chapterhouse. [C19: prob. from MFlemish slijpen to slip]

Sm the chemical symbol for samarium.

SM abbrev. for sergeant major.

smack[1] (smæk) n. **1.** a smell or flavour that is distinctive though faint. **2.** a distinctive trace: the smack of corruption. **3.** a small quantity, esp. a taste. **4.** a slang word for heroin. ~vb. (intr.; foll. by of) **5.** to have the characteristic smell or flavour (of something): to smack of the sea. **6.** to have an element suggestive (of something): his speeches smacked of bigotry. [OE smæc]

smack[2] (smæk) vb. **1.** (tr.) to strike or slap smartly, with or as if with the open hand. **2.** to strike or send forcibly or loudly or to be struck or sent forcibly or loudly. **3.** to open and close (the lips) loudly, esp. to show pleasure. ~n. **4.** a sharp resounding slap or blow with something flat, or the sound of such a blow. **5.** a loud kiss. **6.** a sharp sound made by the lips, as in enjoyment. **7. have a smack at.** Inf., chiefly Brit. to attempt. **8. smack in the eye.** Inf., chiefly Brit. a snub or setback. ~adv. Inf. **9.** directly; squarely. **10.** sharply and unexpectedly. [C16: from MLow G or MDu. smacken, prob. imit.]

smack[3] (smæk) n. a sailing vessel, usually sloop-rigged, used in coasting and fishing along the British coast. [C17: from Low G smack or Du. smak, from ?]

smacker ('smækə) n. Sl. **1.** a loud kiss; smack. **2.** a pound note or dollar bill.

small (smɔːl) adj. **1.** limited in size, number, importance, etc. **2.** of little importance or on a minor scale: a small business. **3.** lacking in moral or mental breadth or depth: a small mind. **4.** modest or humble: small beginnings. **5.** of low or inferior status, esp. socially. **6. feel small.** to be humiliated. **7.** (of a child or animal) young; not mature. **8.** unimportant; trivial: a small matter. **9.** of or designating the ordinary modern minuscule letter used in printing and cursive writing. **10.** lacking great strength or force: a small effort. **11.** in fine particles: small gravel. ~adv. **12.** into small pieces: cut it small. **13.** in a small

or soft manner. ~n. **14.** (often preceded by the) an object, person, or group considered to be small: the small or the large? **15.** a small slender part, esp. of the back. **16.** (pl.) Inf., chiefly Brit. items of personal laundry, such as underwear. [OE smæl] — **'smallish** adj. — **'smallness** n.

small arms pl. n. portable firearms of relatively small calibre.

small beer n. **1.** Inf., chiefly Brit. people or things of no importance. **2.** Now rare. weak beer.

small change n. **1.** coins, esp. those of low value. **2.** a person or thing that is not outstanding or important.

small circle n. a circular section of a sphere that does not contain the centre of the sphere.

small claims court n. Brit. a local court administered by the county court with jurisdiction to try civil actions involving small claims.

small fry pl. n. **1.** people or things regarded as unimportant. **2.** young children. **3.** young or small fishes.

small goods pl. n. Austral. & N.Z. meats bought from a delicatessen, such as sausages.

smallholding ('smɔːl,həʊldɪŋ) n. a holding of agricultural land smaller than a small farm. — **'small,holder** n.

small hours pl. n. **the.** the early hours of the morning, after midnight and before dawn.

small intestine n. the longest part of the alimentary canal, in which digestion is completed. Cf. **large intestine.**

small-minded adj. narrow-minded; intolerant. — **,small-'mindedly** adv. — **,small-'mindedness** n.

smallpox ('smɔːl,pɒks) n. a highly contagious viral disease characterized by high fever and a rash changing to pustules, which dry up and form scabs that are cast off, leaving pitted depressions. Technical name: **variola.**

small print n. matter in a contract, etc., printed in small type, esp. when considered to be a trap for the unwary.

small-scale adj. **1.** of limited size or scope. **2.** (of a map, model, etc.) giving a relatively small representation of something.

small screen n. an informal name for **television.**

small slam n. Bridge. another name for **little slam.**

small talk n. light conversation for social occasions.

small-time adj. Inf. insignificant; minor: a small-time criminal. — **'small-'timer** n.

smalt (smɔːlt) n. **1.** a type of silica glass coloured deep blue with cobalt oxide. **2.** a pigment made by crushing this glass, used in colouring enamels. [C16: via F from It. smalto coloured glass, of Gmc origin]

smarm (smɑːm) vb. Brit. inf. **1.** (tr.; often foll. by down) to flatten (the hair, etc.) with grease. **2.** (when intr., foll. by up to) to ingratiate oneself (with). [C19: from ?]

smarmy ('smɑːmɪ) adj. **smarmier, smarmiest.** Brit. inf. obsequiously flattering or unpleasantly suave. — **'smarmily** adv. — **'smarminess** n.

smart (smɑːt) adj. **1.** astute, as in business. **2.** quick, witty, and often impertinent in speech: a smart talker. **3.** fashionable; chic: a smart hotel. **4.** well-kept; neat. **5.** causing a sharp stinging pain. **6.** vigorous or brisk. **7.** (of systems) operating as if by human intelligence by using automatic computer control. **8.** (of a bomb, etc.) containing a device which enables it to be guided to its target. ~vb. (mainly intr.) **9.** to feel, cause, or be the source of a sharp stinging physical pain or keen mental distress: he smarted under their abuse. **10.** (often foll. by for) to suffer a harsh penalty. ~n. **11.** a stinging pain or feeling. ~adv. **12.** in a smart manner. ~See also **smarts.** [OE smeortan] — **'smartly** adv. — **'smartness** n.

smart aleck ('ælɪk) n. Inf. **a.** an irritatingly oversmart person. **b.** (as modifier): a smart-aleck remark. [C19: from Aleck, Alec, short for Alexander] — **'smart-,alecky** adj.

smart card n. another name for **intelligent card.**

smarten ('smɑːtᵊn) vb. (usually foll. by up) **1.** (intr.) to make oneself neater. **2.** (tr.) to make quicker or livelier.

smart money n. U.S. **1.** money bet or invested by experienced gamblers or investors. **2.** money paid in order to extricate oneself from an unpleasant situation or agreement, esp. from military service. **3.** Law. damages awarded to a plaintiff where the wrong was aggravated by fraud, malice, etc.

smarts (smɑːts) pl. n. Sl., chiefly U.S. know-how, intelligence, or wits: street smarts.

smart set n. (functioning as sing. or pl.) fashionable people considered as a group.

smash (smæʃ) vb. **1.** to break into pieces violently and usually noisily. **2.** (when intr., foll. by against, through, into, etc.) to throw or crash (against) vigorously, causing shattering: he smashed the equipment. **3.** (tr.) to hit forcefully and suddenly. **4.** (tr.) Tennis, etc. to hit (the ball) fast and powerfully, esp. with an overhead stroke. **5.** (tr.) to defeat (persons, theories, etc.). **6.** to make or become bankrupt. **7.** (intr.) to collide violently; crash. ~n. **8.** an act, instance, or sound of smashing or the state of being smashed. **9.** a violent collision, esp. of vehicles. **10.** a total failure or collapse, as of a business. **11.** Tennis, etc. a fast and powerful overhead stroke. **12.** Inf. **a.** something having popular success. **b.** (in combination): smash-hit. ~adv. **13.** with a smash. ~See also **smash-up.** [C18: prob. from SM(ACK² + M)ASH] —'**smashable** adj.

smash-and-grab adj. Inf. of or relating to a robbery in which a shop window is broken and the contents removed.

smashed (smæʃt) adj. Sl. drunk or under the influence of a drug.

smasher ('smæʃə) n. Inf., chiefly Brit. a person or thing that is very attractive or outstanding.

smashing ('smæʃɪŋ) adj. Inf., chiefly Brit. excellent or first-rate: we had a smashing time.

smash-up Inf. ~n. **1.** a bad collision, esp of cars. ~vb. **smash up. 2.** (tr., adv.) to damage to the point of complete destruction: they smashed the place up.

smatter ('smætə) n. **1.** a smattering. ~vb. **2.** (tr.) Arch. to dabble in. [C14 (in the sense: to prattle): from ?] —'**smatterer** n.

smattering ('smætərɪŋ) n. **1.** a slight or superficial knowledge. **2.** a small amount.

smear (smɪə) vb. (mainly tr.) **1.** to bedaub or cover with oil, grease, etc. **2.** to rub over or apply thickly. **3.** to rub so as to produce a smudge. **4.** to slander. **5.** (intr.) to be or become smeared or dirtied. ~n. **6.** a dirty mark or smudge. **7. a.** a slanderous attack. **b.** (as modifier): smear tactics. **8.** a preparation of blood, secretions, etc., smeared onto a glass slide for examination under a microscope. [OE smeoru (n.)] —'**smeary** adj. —'**smearily** adv. —'**smeariness** n.

smear test n. Med. another name for **Pap test.**

smectic ('smɛktɪk) adj. Chem. (of a substance) existing in or having a mesomorphic state in which the molecules are oriented in layers. [C17: via L from Gk smēktikos, from smēkhein to wash; from the soaplike consistency of a smectic substance]

smegma ('smɛgmə) n. Physiol. sebum. [C19: via L from Gk smēgma detergent, from smekhein to wash]

smell (smɛl) vb. **smelling, smelt** or **smelled. 1.** (tr.) to perceive the scent of (a substance) by means of the olfactory nerves. **2.** (copula) to have a specified smell: the curry smells very spicy. **3.** (intr.; foll. by of) to emit an odour (of): the park smells of flowers. **4.** (intr.) to emit an unpleasant odour. **5.** (tr.; often foll. by out) to detect through shrewdness or instinct. **6.** (intr.) to have or use the sense of smell; sniff. **7.** (intr.; foll. by of) to give indications (of): he smells of money. **8.** (intr.; foll. by around, about, etc.) to search, investigate, or pry. **9.** (copula) to be or seem to be untrustworthy. ~n. **10.** that sense (olfaction) by which scents or odours are perceived. Related adj.: **olfactory. 11.** anything detected by the sense of smell. **12.** a trace or indication. **13.** the act or an instance of smelling. [C12: from ?] —'**smeller** n.

▷ Usage. Smell in its neutral sense of emitting an odour is followed by an adjective rather than by an adverb: this flower smells good (rather than well). Smell in the sense of emitting an unpleasant odour is followed by an adverb.

smelling salts pl. n. a pungent preparation containing crystals of ammonium carbonate that has a stimulant action when sniffed in cases of faintness, headache, etc.

smelly ('smɛlɪ) adj. **smellier, smelliest.** having a strong or nasty smell. —'**smelliness** n.

smelt¹ (smɛlt) vb. (tr.) to extract (a metal) from (an ore) by heating. [C15: from MLow G, MDu. smelten]

smelt² (smɛlt) n., pl. **smelt** or **smelts.** a marine or freshwater salmonoid food fish having a long silvery body and occurring in temperate and cold northern waters. [OE smylt]

smelt³ (smɛlt) vb. a past tense and past participle of **smell.**

smelter ('smɛltə) n. **1.** a person engaged in smelting. **2.** Also called: **smeltery.** an industrial plant in which smelting is carried out.

Smetana (Czech 'smɛtana) n. **Bedřich** ('bɛdrʒix). 1824–84, Czech composer, founder of his country's national school of music. His works include My Fatherland (1874–79), a cycle of six symphonic poems, and the opera The Bartered Bride (1866).

smew (smju:) n. a merganser of N Europe and Asia, having a male plumage of white with black markings. [C17: from ?]

smidgen or **smidgin** ('smɪdʒən) n. Inf., chiefly U.S. a very small amount. [C20: from ?]

smilax ('smaɪlæks) n. **1.** any of a genus of climbing shrubs having slightly lobed leaves, small greenish or yellow flowers, and berry-like fruits: includes the sarsaparilla plant and greenbrier. **2.** a fragile, much branched vine of southern Africa: cultivated for its glossy green foliage. [C17: via L from Gk: bindweed]

smile (smaɪl) n. **1.** a facial expression characterized by an upturning of the corners of the mouth, usually showing amusement, friendliness, etc. **2.** favour or blessing: the smile of fortune. ~vb. **3.** (intr.) to wear or assume a smile. **4.** (intr.; foll. by at) **a.** to look (at) with a kindly expression. **b.** to look derisively (at). **c.** to bear (troubles, etc.) patiently. **5.** (intr.; foll. by on or upon) to show approval. **6.** (tr.) to express by means of a smile: she smiled a welcome. **7.** (tr.; often foll. by away) to drive away or change by smiling. **8. come up smiling.** to recover cheerfully from misfortune. [C13: prob. from ON] —'**smiler** n. —'**smiling** adj. —'**smilingly** adv.

Smiles (smaɪlz) n. **Samuel.** 1812–1904, British writer: author of the didactic work Self-Help (1859).

smirch (smɜ:tʃ) vb. (tr.) **1.** to dirty; soil. ~n. **2.** the act of smirching or state of being smirched. **3.** a smear or stain. [C15 smorchen, from ?]

smirk (smɜ:k) n. **1.** a smile expressing scorn, smugness, etc., rather than pleasure. ~vb. **2.** (intr.) to give such a smile. **3.** (tr.) to express with such a smile. [OE smearcian] —'**smirker** n. —'**smirking** adj. —'**smirkingly** adv.

smite (smaɪt) vb. **smiting, smote; smitten** or **smit** (smɪt). (mainly tr.) Now arch. in most senses. **1.** to strike with a heavy blow. **2.** to damage with or as if with blows. **3.** to affect severely: smitten with flu. **4.** to afflict in order to punish. **5.** (intr.; foll. by on) to strike forcibly or abruptly: the sun smote down on him. [OE smitan] —'**smiter** n.

smith (smɪθ) n. **1. a.** a person who works in metal. **b.** (in combination): a silversmith. **2.** See **blacksmith.** [OE]

Smith (smɪθ) n. **1. Adam.** 1723–90, Scottish economist and philosopher, whose influential book The Wealth of Nations (1776) advocated free trade and private enterprise and opposed state interference. **2. Bessie,** known as Empress of the Blues. 1894–1937, U.S. blues singer and songwriter. **3. F. E.** See (1st Earl of) **Birkenhead. 4. Ian (Douglas).** born 1919, Zimbabwean statesman; prime minister of Rhodesia (1964–79). He declared independence from Britain unilaterally (1965). **5. John.** ?1580–1631, English explorer and writer, who helped found the North American colony of Jamestown, Virginia. He was reputedly saved by the Indian chief's daughter Pocahontas from execution by her tribe. Among his works is a Description of New England (1616). **6. Joseph.** 1805–44, U.S. religious leader; founder of the Mormon Church. **7. Maggie.** born 1934, British actress. Her films include The VIPs (1963), The Prime of Miss Jean Brodie (1969), and The Lonely Passion of Judith Hearne (1988). **8. Stevie,** real name Florence Margaret Smith. 1902–71, British poet. Her works include Novel on Yellow Paper (1936), and the poems A Good Time was had by All (1937) and Not Waving but Drowning (1957). **9. Sydney.** 1771–1845, English clergyman and writer, noted for The Letters of Peter Plymley (1807–08), in which he advocated Catholic emancipation. **10. William.** 1769–1839, English geologist, who founded the science of stratigraphy by proving that rock strata could be dated by the fossils they contained.

smithereens (ˌsmɪðə'ri:nz) pl. n. little shattered pieces or fragments. [C19: from Irish Gaelic smidirín, from smiodar]

smithery ('smɪθərɪ) n., pl. **-eries. 1.** the trade or craft of a blacksmith. **2.** a rare word for **smithy.**

Smithson ('smiθsən) *n.* **James.** original name *James Lewes Macie.* 1765–1829, English chemist and mineralogist, who left a bequest to found the Smithsonian Institution.

smithy ('smiði) *n., pl.* **smithies.** a place in which metal, usually iron or steel, is worked by heating and hammering; forge. [OE *smiththe*]

smitten ('smit³n) *vb.* **1.** a past participle of **smite.** ~*adj.* **2.** (*postpositive*) affected by love (for).

smock (smɒk) *n.* **1.** any loose protective garment, worn by artists, laboratory technicians, etc. **2.** a woman's loose blouselike garment, reaching to below the waist, worn over slacks, etc. **3.** Also called: **smock frock.** a loose protective overgarment decorated with smocking, worn formerly esp. by farm workers. **4.** *Arch.* a woman's loose undergarment. ~*vb.* **5.** to ornament (a garment) with smocking. [OE *smocc*] —'**smock,like** *adj.*

smocking ('smɒkɪŋ) *n.* ornamental needlework used to gather and stitch material in a honeycomb pattern so that the part below the gathers hangs in even folds.

smog (smɒg) *n.* a mixture of smoke, fog, and chemical fumes. [C20: from SM(OKE + F)OG¹] —'**smoggy** *adj.*

smoke (smอʊk) *n.* **1.** the product of combustion, consisting of fine particles of carbon carried by hot gases and air. **2.** any cloud of fine particles suspended in a gas. **3. a.** the act of smoking tobacco, esp. as a cigarette. **b.** the duration of smoking such substances. **4.** *Inf.* a cigarette or cigar. **5.** something with no concrete or lasting substance: *everything turned to smoke.* **6.** a thing or condition that obscures. **7. go** *or* **end up in smoke. a.** to come to nothing. **b.** to burn up vigorously. **c.** to flare up in anger. ~*vb.* **8.** (*intr.*) to emit smoke or the like, sometimes excessively or in the wrong place. **9.** to draw in on (a burning cigarette, etc.) and exhale the smoke. **10.** (*tr.*) to bring (oneself) into a specified state by smoking. **11.** (*tr.*) to subject or expose to smoke. **12.** (*tr.*) to cure (meat, fish, etc.) by treating with smoke. **13.** (*tr.*) to fumigate or purify the air of (rooms, etc.). **14.** (*tr.*) to darken (glass, etc.) by exposure to smoke. ~See also **smoke out.** [OE *smoca* (n.)] —'**smokable** *or* '**smokeable** *adj.*

Smoke (smอʊk) *n.* **the.** *Brit. & Austral. sl.* a big city, esp. (in Britain) London. Also called: **the big smoke.**

smoke-dried *adj.* (of fish, etc.) cured in smoke.

smoked rubber *n.* a type of crude natural rubber in the form of brown sheets obtained by coagulating latex with an acid, rolling it into sheets, and drying over open wood fires. It is the main raw material for natural rubber products.

smokeho ('smอʊkอʊ) *n.* a variant spelling of **smoko.**

smokehouse ('smอʊk,haʊs) *n.* a building or special construction for curing meat, fish, etc., by smoking.

smokeless ('smอʊklɪs) *adj.* having or producing little or no smoke: *smokeless fuel.*

smokeless zone *n.* an area where only smokeless fuels are permitted to be used.

smoke out *vb.* (*tr., adv.*) **1.** to subject to smoke in order to drive out of hiding. **2.** to bring into the open: *they smoked out the plot.*

smoker ('smอʊkə) *n.* **1.** a person who habitually smokes tobacco. **2.** Also called: **smoking compartment.** a compartment of a train where smoking is permitted. **3.** an informal social gathering, as at a club.

smoke screen *n.* **1.** *Mil.* a cloud of smoke produced to obscure movements. **2.** something said or done in order to hide the truth.

smokestack ('smอʊk,stæk) *n.* **1.** a tall chimney that conveys smoke into the air. **2.** (*modifier*) relating to heavy industry.

smoking jacket *n.* (formerly) a man's comfortable jacket of velvet, etc., closed by a tie belt or fastenings, worn at home.

smoko *or* **smokeho** ('smอʊkอʊ) *n., pl.* **-kos** *or* **-hos.** *Austral. & N.Z. inf.* **1.** a short break from work for tea, a cigarette, etc. **2.** refreshment taken during this break.

smoky ('smอʊkɪ) *adj.* **smokier, smokiest. 1.** emitting or resembling smoke. **2.** emitting smoke excessively or in the wrong place: *a smoky fireplace.* **3.** having the flavour of having been cured by smoking. **4.** made dirty or hazy by smoke. —'**smokily** *adv.* —'**smokiness** *n.*

Smoky Mountains *pl. n.* See **Great Smoky Mountains.**

smolder ('smอʊldə) *vb., n.* the U.S. spelling of **smoulder.**

Smolensk (*Russian* smɑ'ljɛnsk; *English* 'smɒlɛnsk) *n.* a city in the W Soviet Union, on the Dnieper River: a major commercial centre in medieval times; scene of severe fighting (1941 and 1943) in World War II. Pop.: 338 000 (1987).

Smollett ('smɒlɪt) *n.* **Tobias George.** 1721–71, Scottish novelist, whose picaresque satires include *Roderick Random* (1748), *Peregrine Pickle* (1751), and *Humphry Clinker* (1771).

smolt (smอʊlt) *n.* a young salmon at the stage when it migrates from fresh water to the sea. [C14: Scot., from ?]

smooch (smuːtʃ) *Sl.* ~*vb.* (*intr.*) **1.** Also (*Austral.* and *N.Z.*): **smoodge, smooge.** (of two people) to kiss and cuddle. **2.** *Brit.* to dance very slowly and amorously with one's arms around another person or (of two people) to dance together in such a way. ~*n.* **3.** the act of smooching. [C20: var. of dialect *smouch,* imit.]

smoodge *or* **smooge** (smuːdʒ) *vb.* (*intr.*) *Austral. & N.Z.* **1.** another word for **smooch** (sense 1). **2.** to seek to ingratiate oneself.

smooth (smuːð) *adj.* **1.** without bends or irregularities. **2.** silky to the touch: *smooth velvet.* **3.** lacking roughness of surface; flat. **4.** tranquil or unruffled: *smooth temper.* **5.** lacking obstructions or difficulties. **6. a.** suave or persuasive, esp. as suggestive of insincerity. **b.** (*in combination*): *smooth-tongued.* **7.** (of the skin) free from hair. **8.** of uniform consistency: *smooth batter.* **9.** free from jolts: *smooth driving.* **10.** not harsh or astringent: *a smooth wine.* **11.** having all projections worn away: *smooth tyres.* **12.** *Phonetics.* without preliminary aspiration. **13.** *Physics.* (of a plane, etc.) regarded as being frictionless. ~*adv.* **14.** in a calm or even manner. ~*vb.* (*mainly tr.*) **15.** (*also intr.;* often foll. by *down*) to make or become flattened or without roughness. **16.** (often foll. by *out* or *away*) to take or rub (away) in order to make smooth: *she smoothed out the creases in her dress.* **17.** to make calm; soothe. **18.** to make easier: *smooth his path.* ~*n.* **19.** the smooth part of something. **20.** the act of smoothing. **21.** *Tennis, etc.* the side of a racket on which the binding strings form a continuous line. ~See also **smooth over.** [OE *smôth*] —'**smoother** *n.* —'**smoothly** *adv.* —'**smoothness** *n.*

smoothbore ('smuːð,bɔː) *n.* (*modifier*) (of a firearm) having an unrifled bore: *a smoothbore shotgun.* —'**smooth,bored** *adj.*

smooth breathing *n.* (in Greek) the sign (') placed over an initial vowel, indicating that (in ancient Greek) it was not pronounced with an *h.*

smoothen ('smuːðən) *vb.* to make or become smooth.

smooth hound *n.* any of several small sharks of North Atlantic coastal regions.

smoothie *or* **smoothy** ('smuːðɪ) *n., pl.* **smoothies.** *Sl.,* usually derog. a person, esp. a man, who is suave or slick, esp. in speech, dress, or manner.

smoothing iron *n.* a former name for **iron** (sense 3).

smooth muscle *n.* muscle that is capable of slow rhythmic involuntary contractions: occurs in the walls of the blood vessels, etc.

smooth over *vb.* (*tr.*) to ease or gloss over: *to smooth over a difficulty.*

smooth snake *n.* any of several slender nonvenomous European snakes having very smooth scales and a reddish-brown coloration.

smooth-spoken *adj.* speaking or spoken in a gently persuasive or competent manner.

smooth-tongued *adj.* suave or persuasive in speech.

smorgasbord ('smɔː'gəs,bɔːd) *n.* a variety of cold or hot savoury dishes served in Scandinavia as hors d'oeuvres or as a buffet meal. [Swedish, from *smörgås* sandwich + *bord* table]

smote (smอʊt) *vb.* the past tense of **smite.**

smother ('smʌðə) *vb.* **1.** to suffocate or stifle by cutting off or being cut off from the air. **2.** (*tr.*) to surround (with) or envelop (in): *he smothered her with love.* **3.** (*tr.*) to extinguish (a fire) by covering so as to cut it off from the air. **4.** to be or cause to be suppressed or stifled: *smother a giggle.* **5.** (*tr.*) to cook or serve (food) thickly covered with sauce, etc. ~*n.* **6.** anything, such as a cloud of smoke, that stifles. **7.** a profusion or turmoil. [OE *smorian* to suffocate] —'**smothery** *adj.*

smothered mate *n.* *Chess.* checkmate given by a knight when the king is prevented from moving by surrounding men.

smoulder *or U.S.* **smolder** ('smอʊldə) *vb.* (*intr.*) **1.** to burn slowly without flame, usually emitting smoke. **2.**

(esp. of anger, etc.) to exist in a suppressed state. **3.** to have strong repressed feelings, esp. anger. ~*n.* **4.** a smouldering fire. [C14: from *smolder* (n.), from ?]

smudge (smʌdʒ) *vb.* **1.** to smear or soil or cause to do so. **2.** (*tr.*) *Chiefly U.S. & Canad.* to fill (an area) with smoke in order to drive insects away. ~*n.* **3.** a smear or dirty mark. **4.** a blurred form or area: *that smudge in the distance is a quarry.* **5.** *Chiefly U.S. & Canad.* a smoky fire for driving insects away or protecting plants from frost. [C15: from ?] —'**smudgy** *adj.* —'**smudgily** *adv.* —'**smudginess** *n.*

smug (smʌg) *adj.* **smugger, smuggest.** excessively self-satisfied or complacent. [C16: of Gmc origin] —'**smugly** *adv.* —'**smugness** *n.*

smuggle ('smʌgᵊl) *vb.* **1.** to import or export (prohibited or dutiable goods) secretly. **2.** (*tr.*; often foll. by *into* or *out of*) to bring or take secretly, as against the law or rules. [C17: from Low G *smukkelen* & Du. *smokkelen,* ?from OE *smūgen* to creep] —'**smuggler** *n.* —'**smuggling** *n.*

smut (smʌt) *n.* **1.** a small dark smudge or stain, esp. one caused by soot. **2.** a speck of soot or dirt. **3.** something obscene or indecent. **4. a.** any of various fungal diseases of flowering plants, esp. cereals, in which black sooty masses of spores cover the affected parts. **b.** any parasitic fungus that causes such a disease. ~*vb.* **smutting, smutted. 5.** to mark or become marked or smudged, as with soot. **6.** to affect (grain, etc.) or (of grain) to be affected with smut. [OE *smitte;* associated with SMUDGE, SMUTCH] —'**smutty** *adj.* —'**smuttily** *adv.* —'**smuttiness** *n.*

smutch (smʌtʃ) *vb.* **1.** (*tr.*) to smudge; mark. ~*n.* **2.** a mark; smudge. **3.** soot; dirt. [C16: prob. from MHG *smutzen* to soil] —'**smutchy** *adj.*

Smuts (smʌts) *n.* **Jan Christiaan** (jan 'kristi,an). 1870–1950, South African statesman; prime minister (1919–24; 1939–48). He fought for the Boers during the Boer War, then worked for Anglo-Boer reconciliation and served the Allies during World Wars I and II.

Smyrna ('smɜːnə) *n.* an ancient city on the W coast of Asia Minor: a major trading centre in the ancient world; a centre of early Christianity. Modern name: **Izmir.**

Sn *the chemical symbol for* tin. [from NL *stannum*]

snack (snæk) *n.* **1.** a light quick meal eaten between or in place of main meals. **2.** a sip or bite. ~*vb.* **3.** (*intr.*) to eat a snack. [C15: prob. from MDu. *snacken,* var. of *snappen* to snap]

snack bar *n.* a place where light meals or snacks can be obtained, often with a self-service system.

snaffle ('snæfᵊl) *n.* **1.** Also called: **snaffle bit.** a simple jointed bit for a horse. ~*vb.* (*tr.*) **2.** *Brit. inf.* to steal or take for oneself. **3.** to equip or control with a snaffle. [C16: from ?]

snafu (snæ'fuː) *Sl., chiefly mil.* ~*n.* **1.** confusion or chaos regarded as the normal state. ~*adj.* **2.** (*postpositive*) confused or muddled up, as usual. ~*vb.* **-fuing, -fued. 3.** (*tr.*) *U.S. & Canad.* to throw into chaos. [C20: from *s(ituation) n(ormal): a(ll) f(ucked) u(p)*]

snag[1] (snæg) *n.* **1.** a difficulty or disadvantage: *the snag is that I have nothing suitable to wear.* **2.** a sharp protuberance, such as a tree stump. **3.** a small loop or hole in a fabric caused by a sharp object. **4.** a tree stump in a riverbed that is dangerous to navigation. ~*vb.* **snagging, snagged. 5.** (*tr.*) to hinder or impede. **6.** (*tr.*) to tear or catch (fabric). **7.** (*intr.*) to develop a snag. **8.** (*intr.*) *Chiefly U.S. & Canad.* (of a boat) to strike a snag. **9.** (*tr.*) *Chiefly U.S. & Canad.* to clear (a stretch of water) of snags. **10.** (*tr.*) *U.S.* to seize (an opportunity, etc.). [C16: of Scand. origin] —'**snaggy** *adj.*

snag[2] (snæg) *n.* (*usually pl.*) *Austral. sl.* a sausage. [from ?]

snaggletooth ('snægᵊl,tuːθ) *n., pl.* **-teeth.** a tooth that is broken or projecting.

snail (sneɪl) *n.* **1.** any of numerous terrestrial or freshwater gastropod molluscs with a spirally coiled shell, esp. the **garden snail. 2.** any other gastropod with a spirally coiled shell, such as a whelk. **3.** a slow-moving person or animal. [OE *snægl*] —'**snail-,like** *adj.*

snail's pace *n.* a very slow speed or rate.

snake (sneɪk) *n.* **1.** a reptile having a scaly cylindrical limbless body, fused eyelids, and a jaw modified for swallowing large prey: includes venomous forms such as cobras and rattlesnakes, large nonvenomous constrictors

(boas and pythons), and small harmless types such as the grass snake. **2.** Also: **snake in the grass.** a deceitful or treacherous person. **3.** anything resembling a snake in appearance or action. **4.** a group of currencies, any one of which can only fluctuate within narrow limits, but each can fluctuate more against other currencies. **5.** a tool in the form of a long flexible wire for unblocking drains. ~*vb.* **6.** (*intr.*) to glide or move like a snake. **7.** (*tr.*) to move in or follow (a sinuous course). [OE *snaca*] —'**snake,like** *adj.*

snakebird ('sneɪk,bɜːd) *n.* another name for **darter** (the bird).

snakebite ('sneɪk,baɪt) *n.* **1.** a bite inflicted by a snake, esp. a venomous one. **2.** a drink of cider and lager.

snake charmer *n.* an entertainer, esp. in Asia, who charms or appears to charm snakes by playing music.

Snake River *n.* a river in the northwestern U.S., rising in NW Wyoming and flowing west through Idaho, turning north as part of the border between Idaho and Oregon, and flowing west to the Columbia River near Pasco, Washington. Length: 1670 km (1038 miles).

snakeroot ('sneɪk,ruːt) *n.* **1.** any of various North American plants the roots or rhizomes of which have been used as a remedy for snakebite. **2.** the rhizome or root of any such plant.

snakes and ladders *n.* (*functioning as sing.*) a board game in which players move counters along a series of squares by means of dice. A ladder provides a short cut to a square nearer the finish and a snake obliges a player to return to a square nearer the start.

snake's head *n.* a European fritillary plant of damp meadows, having purple-and-white flowers.

snakeskin ('sneɪk,skɪn) *n.* the skin of a snake, esp. when made into a leather valued for handbags, shoes, etc.

snaky ('sneɪkɪ) *adj.* **snakier, snakiest. 1.** of or like a snake. **2.** treacherous or insidious. **3.** infested with snakes. **4.** *Austral. & N.Z. sl.* angry or bad-tempered. —'**snakily** *adv.* —'**snakiness** *n.*

snap (snæp) *vb.* **snapping, snapped. 1.** to break or cause to break suddenly, esp. with a sharp sound. **2.** to make or cause to make a sudden sharp cracking sound. **3.** (*intr.*) to give way or collapse suddenly, esp. from strain. **4.** to move, close, etc., or cause to move, close, etc., with a sudden sharp sound. **5.** to move or cause to move in a sudden or abrupt way. **6.** (*intr.*; often foll. by *at* or *up*) to seize something suddenly or quickly. **7.** (when *intr.*, often foll. by *at*) to bite at (something) bringing the jaws rapidly together. **8.** to speak (words) sharply or abruptly. **9.** to take a snapshot of (something). **10.** (*tr.*) *American football.* to put (the ball) into play by sending it back from the line of scrimmage. **11. snap one's fingers.** *Inf.* **a.** to dismiss with contempt. **b.** to defy. **12. snap out of it.** *Inf.* to recover quickly, esp. from depression or anger. ~*n.* **13.** the act of breaking suddenly or the sound produced by a sudden breakage. **14.** a sudden sharp sound, esp. of bursting, popping, or cracking. **15.** a catch, clasp, or fastener that operates with a snapping sound. **16.** a sudden grab or bite. **17.** a thin crisp biscuit: *ginger snaps.* **18.** *Inf.* See **snapshot. 19.** *Inf.* vigour, liveliness, or energy. **20.** *Inf.* a task or job that is easy or profitable to do. **21.** a short spell or period, esp. of cold weather. **22.** *Brit.* a card game in which the word *snap* is called when two cards of equal value are turned up on the separate piles dealt by each player. **23.** (*modifier*) done on the spur of the moment: *a snap decision.* **24.** (*modifier*) closed or fastened with a snap. ~*adv.* **25.** with a snap. ~*interj.* **26. a.** *Cards.* the word called while playing snap. **b.** an exclamation used to draw attention to the similarity of two things. ~See also **snap up.** [C15: from MLow G or MDu. *snappen* to seize] —'**snapless** *adj.* —'**snappingly** *adv.*

snapdragon ('snæp,drægən) *n.* any of several plants of the genus *Antirrhinum* having spikes of showy white, yellow, pink, red, or purplish flowers. Also called: **antirrhinum.**

snap fastener *n.* another name for **press stud.**

snapper ('snæpə) *n., pl.* **-per** *or* **-pers. 1.** any large sharp-toothed percoid food fish of warm and tropical coastal regions. See also **red snapper. 2.** a food fish of Australia and New Zealand that has a pinkish body covered with blue spots. **3.** another name for the **snapping turtle. 4.** a person or thing that snaps. ~Also (for sense 1, 2): **schnapper.**

snapping turtle *n.* any large aggressive North American river turtle having powerful hooked jaws and a rough shell. Also called: **snapper.**

snappy ('snæpɪ) *adj.* **-pier, -piest. 1.** Also: **snappish.** apt to speak sharply or irritably. **2.** Also: **snappish.** apt to snap or bite. **3.** crackling in sound: *a snappy fire.* **4.** brisk, sharp, or chilly: *a snappy pace.* **5.** smart and fashionable: *a snappy dresser.* **6. make it snappy.** *Sl.* hurry up! —'**snappily** *adv.* —'**snappiness** *n.*

snap ring *n. Mountaineering.* another name for **karabiner.**

snapshot ('snæp.ʃɒt) *n.* an informal photograph taken with a simple camera. Often shortened to **snap.**

snap up *vb.* (*tr., adv.*) **1.** to avail oneself of eagerly and quickly: *she snapped up the bargains.* **2.** to interrupt abruptly.

snare[1] (snɛə) *n.* **1.** a device for trapping birds or small animals, esp. a flexible loop that is drawn tight around the prey. **2.** a surgical instrument for removing certain tumours, consisting of a wire loop that may be drawn tight around their base to sever them. **3.** anything that traps or entangles someone or something unawares. ~*vb.* (*tr.*) **4.** to catch (birds or small animals) with a snare. **5.** to catch or trap in or as if in a snare. [OE *sneare*] —'**snarer** *n.*

snare[2] (snɛə) *n. Music.* a set of gut strings wound with wire fitted against the lower drumhead of a snare drum. They produce a rattling sound when the drum is beaten. [C17: from MDu. *snaer* or MLow G *snare* string]

snare drum *n. Music.* a cylindrical drum with two drumheads, the upper of which is struck and the lower fitted with a snare. See **snare**[2].

snarl[1] (snɑ:l) *vb.* **1.** (*intr.*) (of an animal) to growl viciously, baring the teeth. **2.** to speak or express (something) viciously. ~*n.* **3.** a vicious growl or facial expression. **4.** the act of snarling. [C16: of Gmc origin] —'**snarler** *n.* —'**snarling** *adj.* —'**snarly** *adj.*

snarl[2] (snɑ:l) *n.* **1.** a tangled mass of thread, hair, etc. **2.** a complicated or confused state or situation. **3.** a knot in wood. ~*vb.* **4.** (often foll. by *up*) to be, become, or make tangled or complicated. **5.** (*tr.;* often foll. by *up*) to confuse mentally. **6.** (*tr.*) to emboss (metal) by hammering on a tool held against the under surface. [C14: from ON] —'**snarler** *n.* —'**snarly** *adj.*

snarl-up *n. Inf., chiefly Brit.* a confusion, obstruction, or tangle, esp. a traffic jam.

snatch (snætʃ) *vb.* **1.** (*tr.*) to seize or grasp (something) suddenly or peremptorily: *he snatched the chocolate.* **2.** (*intr.;* usually foll. by *at*) to seize or attempt to seize suddenly. **3.** (*tr.*) to take hurriedly: *to snatch some sleep.* **4.** (*tr.*) to remove suddenly: *she snatched her hand away.* **5.** (*tr.*) to gain, win, or rescue, esp. narrowly: *they snatched victory in the closing seconds.* ~*n.* **6.** an act of snatching. **7.** a fragment or incomplete part: *snatches of conversation.* **8.** a brief spell: *snatches of time off.* **9.** *Weightlifting.* a lift in which the weight is raised in one quick motion from the floor to an overhead position. **10.** *Sl., chiefly U.S.* an act of kidnapping. **11.** *Brit. sl.* a robbery: *a diamond snatch.* [C13 *snacchen*] —'**snatcher** *n.*

snatchy ('snætʃɪ) *adj.* **snatchier, snatchiest.** disconnected or spasmodic. —'**snatchily** *adv.*

snazzy ('snæzɪ) *adj.* **-zier, -ziest.** *Inf.* (esp. of clothes) stylishly and often flashily attractive. [C20: ?from SN(APPY + J)AZZY] —'**snazzily** *adv.* —'**snazziness** *n.*

sneak (sni:k) *vb.* **1.** (*intr.;* often foll. by *along, off, in,* etc.) to move furtively. **2.** (*intr.*) to behave in a cowardly or underhand manner. **3.** (*tr.*) to bring, take, or put stealthily. **4.** (*intr.*) *Inf., chiefly Brit.* to tell tales (esp. in schools). **5.** (*tr.*) *Inf.* to steal. **6.** (*intr.;* foll. by *off, out, away,* etc.) *Inf.* to leave unobtrusively. ~*n.* **7.** a person who acts in an underhand or cowardly manner, esp. as an informer. **8. a.** a stealthy act. **b.** (*as modifier*): *a sneak attack.* [OE *snican* to creep] —'**sneaky** *adj.* —'**sneakily** *adv.* —'**sneakiness** *n.*

sneakers ('sni:kəz) *pl. n. Chiefly U.S. & Canad.* canvas shoes with rubber soles worn informally.

sneaking ('sni:kɪŋ) *adj.* **1.** acting in a furtive or cowardly way. **2.** secret: *a sneaking desire to marry a millionaire.* **3.** slight but nagging (esp. in **a sneaking suspicion**). —'**sneakingly** *adv.*

sneak thief *n.* a person who steals paltry articles from premises, which he enters through open doors, windows, etc.

sneer (snɪə) *n.* **1.** a facial expression of scorn or contempt, typically with the upper lip curled. **2.** a scornful or contemptuous remark or utterance. ~*vb.* **3.** (*intr.*) to assume a facial expression of scorn or contempt. **4.** to say or utter (something) in a scornful manner. [C16: ?from Low Du.] —'**sneerer** *n.* —'**sneering** *adj., n.*

sneeze (sni:z) *vb.* **1.** (*intr.*) to expel air from the nose involuntarily, esp. as the result of irritation of the nasal mucous membrane. ~*n.* **2.** the act or sound of sneezing. [OE *fnēosan* (unattested)] —'**sneezer** *n.* —'**sneezy** *adj.*

sneeze at *vb.* (*intr., prep.*) usually with a negative) *Inf.* to dismiss lightly: *his offer is not to be sneezed at.*

sneezewood ('sni:z.wʊd) *n.* **1.** a South African tree. **2.** its exceptionally hard wood, used for furniture, gateposts and railway sleepers.

sneezewort ('sni:z.wɜ:t) *n.* a Eurasian plant having daisy-like flowers and long grey-green leaves, which cause sneezing when powdered.

snick (snɪk) *n.* **1.** a small cut; notch. **2.** *Cricket.* **a.** a glancing blow off the edge of the bat. **b.** the ball so hit. ~*vb.* (*tr.*) **3.** to cut a small corner or notch in (material, etc.). **4.** *Cricket.* to hit (the ball) with a snick. [C18: prob. of Scand. origin]

snicker ('snɪkə) *n., vb.* **1.** another word (esp. U.S. and Canad.) for **snigger.** ~*vb.* **2.** (*intr.*) (of a horse) to whinny. [C17: prob. imit.]

snide (snaɪd) *adj.* **1.** (of a remark, etc.) maliciously derogatory. **2.** counterfeit. ~*n.* **3.** *Sl.* sham jewellery. [C19: from ?] —'**snidely** *adv.* —'**snideness** *n.*

sniff (snɪf) *vb.* **1.** to inhale through the nose, usually in short rapid audible inspirations, as for clearing a congested nasal passage or for taking a drug. **2.** (when *intr.*, often foll. by *at*) to perceive or attempt to perceive (a smell) by inhaling through the nose. ~*n.* **3.** the act or sound of sniffing. **4.** a smell perceived by sniffing, esp. a faint scent. [C14: prob. rel. to *snivelen* to snivel] ~See also **sniff at, sniff out.** —'**sniffer** *n.* —'**sniffing** *n., adj.*

sniff at *vb.* (*intr., prep.*) to express contempt or dislike for.

sniffer dog *n.* a police dog trained to detect drugs or explosives by smell.

sniffle ('snɪfʰl) *vb.* **1.** (*intr.*) to breathe audibly through the nose, as when the nasal passages are congested. ~*n.* **2.** the act, sound, or an instance of sniffling. —'**sniffler** *n.* —'**sniffly** *adj.*

sniffles ('snɪfʰlz) or **snuffles** *pl. n. Inf.* **the.** a cold in the head.

sniff out *vb.* (*tr., adv.*) to detect through shrewdness or instinct.

sniffy ('snɪfɪ) *adj.* **-fier, -fiest.** *Inf.* contemptuous or disdainful. —'**sniffily** *adv.* —'**sniffiness** *n.*

snifter ('snɪftə) *n.* **1.** a pear-shaped glass with a bowl that narrows towards the top so that the aroma of brandy or a liqueur is retained. **2.** *Inf.* a small quantity of alcoholic drink. [C19: ?from dialect *snifter* to sniff, ? of Scand. origin]

snig *vb.* **snigging, snigged.** (*tr.*) *N.Z.* to drag (a felled log) by a chain or cable. [from E dialect]

snigger ('snɪgə) *n.* **1.** a sly or disrespectful laugh, esp. one partly stifled. ~*vb.* (*intr.*) **2.** to utter such a laugh. [C18: var. of SNICKER] —'**sniggering** *n., adj.*

snigging chain *Austral. & N.Z.* a chain attached to a log when being hauled out of the bush.

snip (snɪp) *vb.* **snipping, snipped. 1.** to cut or clip with a small quick stroke or a succession of small quick strokes, esp. with scissors or shears. ~*n.* **2.** the act of snipping. **3.** the sound of scissors or shears closing. **4.** Also called: **snipping.** a small piece of anything. **5.** a small cut made by snipping. **6.** *Chiefly Brit.* an informal word for **bargain. 7.** *Inf.* something easily done; cinch. ~See also **snips.** [C16: from Low G, Du. *snippen*]

snipe (snaɪp) *n., pl.* **snipe** or **snipes. 1.** any of a genus of birds, such as the common snipe, of marshes and river banks, having a long straight bill. **2.** a shot, esp. a gunshot, fired from a place of concealment. ~*vb.* **3.** (when *intr.*, often foll. by *at*) to attack (a person or persons) with a rifle from a place of concealment. **4.** (*intr.;* often foll. by *at*) to criticize a person or persons from a position of security. **5.** (*intr.*) to hunt or shoot snipe. [C14: from ON *snipa*] —'**sniper** *n.*

snipefish ('snaɪp.fɪʃ) *n., pl.* **-fish** or **fishes.** a teleost fish of tropical and temperate seas, having a deep body, long snout, and a single long dorsal fin. Also called: **bellows fish.**

snippet ('snɪpɪt) n. a small scrap or fragment of fabric, news, etc. —'**snippetiness** n. —'**snippety** adj.

snips (snɪps) pl. n. a small pair of shears used for cutting sheet metal.

snitch (snɪtʃ) Sl. ~vb. **1.** (tr.) to steal; take, esp. in an underhand way. **2.** (intr.) to act as an informer. ~n. **3.** an informer. **4.** the nose. [C17: from ?]

snitchy ('snɪtʃɪ) adj. **snitchier, snitchiest.** N.Z. inf. bad-tempered or irritable.

snivel ('snɪvəl) vb. **-elling, -elled** or U.S. **-eling, -eled. 1.** (intr.) to sniffle as a sign of distress. **2.** to utter (something) tearfully; whine. **3.** (intr.) to have a runny nose. ~n. **4.** an instance of snivelling. [C14 snivelen] —'**sniveller** n. —'**snivelling** adj., n.

SNO abbrev. for Scottish National Orchestra.

snob (snɒb) n. **1. a.** a person who strives to associate with those of higher social status and who behaves condescendingly to others. **b.** (as modifier): snob appeal. **2.** a person having similar pretensions with regard to his tastes, etc.: an intellectual snob. [C18 (in the sense: shoemaker; hence, C19: a person without those of higher station, etc.): from ?] —'**snobbery** n. —'**snobbish** adj. —'**snobbishly** adv.

SNOBOL ('snəʊbɒl) n. String Oriented Symbolic Language: a computer-programming language for handling strings of symbols.

Sno-Cat ('snəʊˌkæt) n. Trademark. a type of snowmobile.

snoek (snʊk) n. a South African edible marine fish. [from Afrik., from Du. snoek pike]

snog (snɒg) Brit. sl. ~vb. **snogging, snogged. 1.** (intr.) to kiss and cuddle. ~n. **2.** the act of kissing and cuddling. [from ?]

snood (snu:d) n. **1.** a pouchlike hat, often of net, loosely holding a woman's hair at the back. **2.** a headband, esp. one formerly worn by young unmarried women in Scotland. [OE snōd; from ?]

snook[1] (snu:k) n., pl. **snook** or **snooks. 1.** any of a genus of large game fishes of tropical American marine and fresh waters. **2.** Austral. the sea pike. [C17: from Du. snoek pike]

snook[2] (snu:k) n. Brit. a rude gesture, made by putting one thumb to the nose with the fingers of the hand outstretched (esp. in **cock a snook**). [C19: from ?]

snooker ('snu:kə) n. **1.** a game played on a billiard table with 15 red balls, six balls of other colours, and a white cue ball. The object is to pot the balls in a certain order. **2.** a shot in which the cue ball is left in a position such that another ball blocks the target ball. ~vb. (tr.) **3.** to leave (an opponent) in an unfavourable position by playing a snooker. **4.** to place (someone) in a difficult situation. **5.** (often passive) to thwart; defeat. [C19: from ?]

snoop (snu:p) Inf. ~vb. **1.** (intr.; often foll. by about or around) to pry into the private business of others. ~n. **2.** a person who pries into the business of others. **3.** an act or instance of snooping. [C19: from Du. snoepen to eat furtively] —'**snooper** n. —'**snoopy** adj.

snooperscope ('snu:pəˌskəʊp) n. Mil., U.S. an instrument that enables the user to see objects in the dark by illuminating the object with infrared radiation.

snoot (snu:t) n. Sl. the nose. [C20: var. of SNOUT]

snooty ('snu:tɪ) adj. **snootier, snootiest.** Inf. **1.** aloof or supercilious. **2.** snobbish: a snooty restaurant. —'**snootily** adv. —'**snootiness** n.

snooze (snu:z) Inf. ~vb. **1.** (intr.) to take a brief light sleep. ~n. **2.** a nap. [C18: from ?] —'**snoozer** n. —'**snoozy** adj.

snore (snɔ:) vb. **1.** (intr.) to breathe through the mouth and nose while asleep with snorting sounds caused by the soft palate vibrating. ~n. **2.** the act or sound of snoring. [C14: imit.] —'**snorer** n.

snorkel ('snɔ:kəl) n. **1.** a device allowing a swimmer to breathe while face down on the surface of the water, consisting of a bent tube fitting into the mouth and projecting above the surface. **2.** (on a submarine) a retractable vertical device containing air-intake and exhaust pipes for the engines and general ventilation. ~vb. **-kelling, -kelled** or U.S. **-keling, -kelled. 3.** (intr.) to swim with a snorkel. [C20: from G Schnorchel]

Snorri Sturluson ('snɔ:rɪ 'stɜ:ləsən) n. 1179–1241, Icelandic historian and poet; author of Younger or Prose Edda (?1222), containing a collection of Norse myths and a treatise on poetry, and the Heimskringla sagas of the Norwegian kings from their mythological origins to the 12th century.

snort (snɔ:t) vb. **1.** (intr.) to exhale forcibly through the nostrils, making a characteristic noise. **2.** (intr.) (of a person) to express contempt or annoyance by such an exhalation. **3.** (tr.) to utter in a contemptuous or annoyed manner. **4.** Sl. to inhale (a powdered drug) through the nostrils. ~n. **5.** a forcible exhalation of air through the nostrils. **6.** Sl. (of persons) as a noise of contempt. **6.** Sl. an instance of snorting a drug. [C14 snorten] —'**snorting** n., adj. —'**snortingly** adv.

snorter ('snɔ:tə) n. **1.** a person or animal that snorts. **2.** Brit. sl. something outstandingly impressive or difficult.

snot (snɒt) n. (usually considered vulgar) **1.** nasal mucus or discharge. **2.** Sl. a contemptible person. [OE gesnot]

snotty ('snɒtɪ) adj. **-tier, -tiest.** (considered vulgar) **1.** dirty with nasal discharge. **2.** Sl. contemptible; nasty. **3.** snobbish; conceited. —'**snottily** adv. —'**snottiness** n.

snout (snaʊt) n. **1.** the part of the head of a vertebrate, esp. a mammal, consisting of the nose, jaws, and surrounding region. **2.** the corresponding part of the head of such insects as weevils. **3.** anything projecting like a snout, such as a nozzle. **4.** Sl. a person's nose. **5.** Brit. sl. a cigarette or tobacco. **6.** Sl. an informer. [C13: of Gmc origin] —'**snouted** adj. —'**snoutless** adj. —'**snout,like** adj.

snout beetle n. another name for **weevil.**

snow (snəʊ) n. **1.** precipitation from clouds in the form of flakes of ice crystals formed in the upper atmosphere. **2.** a layer of snowflakes on the ground. **3.** a fall of such precipitation. **4.** anything resembling snow in whiteness, softness, etc. **5.** the random pattern of white spots on a television or radar screen, occurring when the signal is weak. **6.** Sl. cocaine. ~vb. **7.** (intr., with it as subject) to be the case that snow is falling. **8.** (tr.; usually passive, foll. by over, under, in, or up) to cover or confine with a heavy fall of snow. **9.** (often with it as subject) to fall or cause to fall as or like snow. **10.** (tr.) U.S. & Canad. sl. to overwhelm with elaborate often insincere talk. **11. be snowed under.** to be overwhelmed, esp. with paperwork. [OE snāw] —'**snowless** adj. —'**snow,like** adj.

Snow (snəʊ) n. C(harles) P(ercy), Baron Snow. 1905–80, English novelist and physicist. His novels include the series Strangers and Brothers (1949–70).

snowball ('snəʊˌbɔ:l) n. **1.** snow pressed into a ball for throwing, as in play. **2.** a drink made of advocaat and lemonade. ~vb. **3.** (intr.) to increase rapidly in size, importance, etc. **4.** (tr.) to throw snowballs at.

snowball tree n. any of several shrubs of the genus Viburnum, with spherical clusters of white or pinkish flowers.

snowberry ('snəʊbərɪ) n., pl. **-ries. 1.** a shrub cultivated for its small pink flowers and white berries. **2.** Also called: **waxberry.** any of the berries of such a plant.

snow-blind adj. having temporarily impaired vision because of the intense reflection of sunlight from snow. —**snow blindness** n.

snowblower ('snəʊˌbləʊə) n. a snow-clearing machine that draws the snow in and blows it away.

snowbound ('snəʊˌbaʊnd) adj. confined to one place by heavy falls or drifts of snow; snowed in.

snow bunting n. a bunting of northern and arctic regions, having a white plumage with dark markings on the wings, back, and tail.

snowcap ('snəʊˌkæp) n. a cap of snow, as on top of a mountain. —'**snow,capped** adj.

Snowdon ('snəʊdən) n. a mountain in NW Wales, in Gwynedd: the highest peak in Wales. Height: 1085 m (3560 ft.).

Snowdonia (snəʊ'dəʊnɪə) n. **1.** a massif in NW Wales, in Gwynedd, the highest peak being Snowdon. **2.** a national park in NW Wales, in Gwynedd and Clwyd: includes the Snowdonia massif in the north. Area: 2189 sq. km (845 sq. miles).

snowdrift ('snəʊˌdrɪft) n. a bank of deep snow driven together by the wind.

snowdrop ('snəʊˌdrɒp) n. a Eurasian plant having drooping white bell-shaped flowers that bloom in early spring.

snowfall ('snəʊˌfɔ:l) n. **1.** a fall of snow. **2.** Meteorol. the amount of snow received in a specified place and time.

snow fence n. a lath-and-wire fence put up in winter beside windy roads to prevent snowdrifts.

snowfield ('snəʊ,fiːld) n. a large area of permanent snow.

snowflake ('snəʊ,fleɪk) n. **1.** one of the mass of small thin delicate arrangements of ice crystals that fall as snow. **2.** any of various European plants that have white nodding bell-shaped flowers.

snow goose n. a North American goose having a white plumage with black wing tips.

snow gum n. any of several eucalypts of mountainous regions of SE Australia.

snow-in-summer n. a plant of SE Europe and Asia having white flowers and downy stems and leaves: cultivated as a rock plant.

snow leopard n. a large feline mammal of mountainous regions of central Asia, closely related to the leopard but having a long pale brown coat marked with black rosettes.

snow lily n. Canad. another name for **dogtooth violet.**

snow line n. the altitudinal or latitudinal limit of permanent snow.

snowman ('snəʊ,mæn) n., pl. **-men.** a figure resembling a man, made of packed snow.

snowmobile ('snəʊmə,biːl) n. a motor vehicle for travelling on snow, esp. one with caterpillar tracks and front skis.

snowplough or esp. U.S. **snowplow** ('snəʊ,plaʊ) n. an implement or vehicle for clearing away snow.

snowshoe ('snəʊ,ʃuː) n. **1.** a device to facilitate walking on snow, esp. a racket-shaped frame with a network of thongs stretched across it. ~vb. **-shoeing, -shoed. 2.** (intr.) to walk or go using snowshoes. — **'snow,shoer** n.

snowstorm ('snəʊ,stɔːm) n. a storm with heavy snow.

snow tyre n. a motor-vehicle tyre with deep treads to give improved grip on snow and ice.

snow-white adj. **1.** white as snow. **2.** pure as white snow.

snowy ('snəʊɪ) adj. **snowier, snowiest. 1.** covered with or abounding in snow: snowy hills. **2.** characterized by snow: snowy weather. **3.** resembling snow in whiteness, purity, etc. — **'snowily** adv. — **'snowiness** n.

Snowy Mountains pl. n. a mountain range in SE Australia, part of the Australian Alps: famous hydroelectric scheme. Also called (Austral. informal): **the Snowy, the Snowies. —Snowy Mountain** adj.

snowy owl n. a large owl of tundra regions, having a white plumage flecked with brown.

Snowy River n. a river in SE Australia, rising in SE New South Wales: waters diverted through a system of dams and tunnels across the watershed into the Murray and Murrumbidgee Rivers for hydroelectric power and to provide water for irrigation. Length: 426 km (265 miles).

SNP abbrev. for Scottish National Party.

Snr or **snr** abbrev. for senior.

snub (snʌb) vb. **snubbing, snubbed.** (tr.) **1.** to insult (someone) deliberately. **2.** to stop or check the motion of (a boat, horse, etc.) by taking turns of a rope around a post. ~n. **3.** a deliberately insulting act or remark. **4.** Naut. an elastic shock absorber attached to a mooring line. ~adj. **5.** short and blunt. See also **snub-nosed.** [C14: from ON snubba to scold] — **'snubber** n. — **'snubby** adj.

snub-nosed adj. **1.** having a short turned-up nose. **2.** (of a pistol) having an extremely short barrel.

snuff¹ (snʌf) vb. **1.** (tr.) to inhale through the nose. **2.** (when intr., often foll. by at) (esp. of an animal) to examine by sniffing. ~n. **3.** an act or the sound of snuffing. [C16: prob. from MDu. snuffen to snuffle, ult. imit.] — **'snuffer** n.

snuff² (snʌf) n. **1.** finely powdered tobacco, esp. for sniffing up the nostrils. **2.** a small amount of this. **3. up to snuff.** Inf. **a.** in good health or in good condition. **b.** Chiefly Brit. not easily deceived. ~vb. **4.** (intr.) to use or inhale snuff. [C17: from Du. snuf, shortened from snuftabake, lit.: tobacco for snuffing]

snuff³ (snʌf) vb. (tr.) **1.** (often foll. by out) to extinguish (a light from a candle). **2.** to cut off the charred part of (the wick of a candle, etc.). **3.** (usually foll. by out) Inf. to put an end to. **4. snuff it.** Brit. inf. to die. ~n. **5.** the burned portion of the wick of a candle. [C14 snoffe, from ?]

snuffbox ('snʌf,bɒks) n. a container, often of elaborate ornamental design, for holding small quantities of snuff.

snuff-dipping n. the practice of absorbing nicotine by holding in one's mouth, between the cheek and the gum, a small amount of tobacco.

snuffer ('snʌfə) n. **1.** a cone-shaped implement for extinguishing candles. **2.** (pl.) an instrument resembling a pair of scissors for trimming the wick or extinguishing the flame of a candle.

snuffle ('snʌfᵊl) vb. **1.** (intr.) to breathe noisily or with difficulty. **2.** to say or speak in a nasal tone. **3.** (intr.) to snivel. ~n. **4.** an act or the sound of snuffling. **5.** a nasal voice. **6. the snuffles.** a condition characterized by snuffling. [C16: from Low G or Du. snuffelen] — **'snuffly** adj.

snuff movie or **film** n. Sl. a pornographic film in which an unsuspecting actress or actor is murdered as the climax of the film.

snuffy ('snʌfɪ) adj. **snuffier, snuffiest. 1.** of or resembling snuff. **2.** covered with or smelling of snuff. **3.** disagreeable. — **'snuffiness** n.

snug (snʌg) adj. **snugger, snuggest. 1.** comfortably warm and well protected; cosy: the children were snug in bed. **2.** small but comfortable: a snug cottage. **3.** well ordered; compact: a snug boat. **4.** sheltered and secure: a snug anchorage. **5.** fitting closely and comfortably. **6.** offering safe concealment. ~n. **7.** (in Britain and Ireland) one of the bars in certain pubs, offering intimate seating for only a few persons. ~vb. **snugging, snugged. 8.** to make or become comfortable and warm. [C16 (in the sense: prepared for storms (used of a ship))] — **'snugly** adv. — **'snugness** n.

snuggery ('snʌgərɪ) n., pl. **-geries. 1.** a cosy and comfortable place or room. **2.** another name for **snug** (sense 7).

snuggle ('snʌgᵊl) vb. **1.** (usually intr.; usually foll. by down, up, or together) to nestle into or draw close to (somebody or something) for warmth or from affection. ~n. **2.** the act of snuggling. [C17: frequentative of SNUG (vb.)]

so¹ (səʊ) adv. **1.** (foll. by an adjective or adverb and a correlative clause often introduced by that) to such an extent: the river is so dirty that it smells. **2.** (used with a negative; it replaces the first as in an equative comparison) to the same extent as: she is not so old as you. **3.** (intensifier): it's so lovely. **4.** in the state or manner expressed or implied: they're happy and will remain so. **5.** (not used with a negative; foll. by an auxiliary verb or do, have, or be used as main verbs) also: I can speak Spanish and so can you. **6.** Dialect. indeed: used to contradict a negative statement: "you didn't phone her." "I did so!" **7.** Arch. provided that. **8. and so on** or **forth.** and continuing similarly. **9. or so.** approximately: fifty or so people came to see me. **10. so be it.** used to express agreement or resignation. **11. so much. a.** a certain degree or amount (of). **b.** a lot (of): it's just so much nonsense. **12. so much for. a.** no more can or need be said about. **b.** used to express contempt for something that has failed. ~conj. (subordinating; often foll. by that) **13.** in order (that): to die so that you might live. **14.** with the consequence (that): she was late home, so that there was trouble. **15. so as.** (takes an infinitive) in order (to): to diet so as to lose weight. ~sentence connector. **16.** in consequence: when that wasn't needed, so she left. **17.** thereupon: and so we ended up in France. **18. so what!** Inf. what importance does that have? ~pron. **19.** used to substitute for a clause or sentence, which may be understood: you'll stop because I said so. ~adj. **20.** (used with is, was, etc.) factual: it can't be so. ~interj. **21.** an exclamation of surprise, etc. [OE swā]
▷ **Usage.** Careful writers of formal English consider it poor style to use so as a conjunction, to indicate either purpose (he did it so he could feel happier) or result (he could not do it so he did not try). In the former case in order to should be used instead and in the latter case and so or and therefore would be more acceptable.

so² (səʊ) n. Music. a variant spelling of **soh.**

So. abbrev. for south(ern).

soak (səʊk) vb. **1.** to make, become, or be thoroughly wet or saturated, esp. by immersion in a liquid. **2.** (when intr., usually foll. by in or into) (of a liquid) to penetrate or permeate. **3.** (tr.; usually foll. by in or up) (of a permeable solid) to take in (a liquid) by absorption: the earth soaks up rainwater. **4.** (tr.; foll. by out or out of) to remove by immersion in a liquid: she soaked the stains out *of the dress.* **5.** *Inf.* to drink excessively or make or become drunk. **6.** (*tr.*) *Sl.* to overcharge. ~*n.* **7.** the act of immersing in a liquid or the period of immersion. **8.** the liquid in which something may be soaked. **9.** *Austral.* a natural depression holding rainwater, esp. just beneath the surface of the ground. **10.** *Sl.* a person who drinks to excess. [OE *sócian* to cook] — 'soaker *n.* — 'soaking *n.*, *adj.* — 'soakingly *adv.*

soakaway ('səʊkə,weɪ) *n.* a pit filled with rubble, etc., into which waste water drains.

so-and-so *n., pl.* **so-and-sos.** *Inf.* **1.** a person whose name is forgotten or ignored. **2.** *Euphemistic.* a person or thing regarded as unpleasant: *which so-and-so broke my razor?*

soap (səʊp) *n.* **1.** a cleaning agent made by reacting animal or vegetable fats or oils with potassium or sodium hydroxide. Soaps act by emulsifying grease and lowering the surface tension of water, so that it more readily penetrates open materials such as textiles. **2.** any metallic salt of a fatty acid, such as palmitic or stearic acid. **3.** *Sl.* flattery or persuasive talk (esp. in **soft soap**). **4.** *Inf.* short for **soap opera**. **5. no soap.** *Sl.* not possible. ~*vb.* (*tr.*) **6.** to apply soap to. **7.** (often foll. by *up*) *Sl.* to flatter. [OE *sápe*] — 'soapless *adj.* — 'soap,like *adj.*

soapberry ('səʊp,bɛrɪ) *n., pl.* **-ries. 1.** any of various chiefly tropical American trees having pulpy fruit containing saponin. **2.** the fruit of any of these trees.

soapbox ('səʊp,bɒks) *n.* **1.** a box or crate for packing soap. **2.** a crate used as a platform for speech-making. **3.** a child's home-made racing cart.

soap opera *n.* a serialized drama, usually dealing with domestic themes, broadcast on radio or television. [C20: so called because manufacturers of soap were typical sponsors]

soapstone ('səʊp,stəʊn) *n.* a massive compact soft variety of talc, used for making table tops, hearths, ornaments, etc. Also called: **steatite.**

soapsuds ('səʊp,sʌdz) *pl. n.* foam or lather made from soap. — 'soap,sudsy *adj.*

soapwort ('səʊp,wɜːt) *n.* a Eurasian plant having rounded clusters of fragrant pink or white flowers and leaves that were formerly used as a soap substitute. Also called: **bouncing Bet.**

soapy ('səʊpɪ) *adj.* **soapier, soapiest. 1.** containing or covered with soap: *soapy water.* **2.** resembling or characteristic of soap. **3.** *Sl.* flattering. — 'soapily *adv.* — 'soapiness *n.*

soar (sɔː) *vb.* (*intr.*) **1.** to rise or fly upwards into the air. **2.** (of a bird, aircraft, etc.) to glide while maintaining altitude by the use of ascending air currents. **3.** to rise or increase in volume, size, etc.: *soaring prices.* [C14: from OF *essorer*, from Vulgar L *exaurāre* (unattested) to expose to the breezes, from L EX-[1] + *aura* breeze] — 'soarer *n.* — 'soaring *n., adj.* — 'soaringly *adv.*

Soares (*Portuguese* 'swarɪʃ) *n.* **Mário** ('mərju). born 1924, Portuguese statesman; prime minister of Portugal (1976–77; 1978–80; 1983–86; president of Portugal from 1986).

sob (sɒb) *vb.* **sobbing, sobbed. 1.** (*intr.*) to weep with convulsive gasps. **2.** (*tr.*) to utter with sobs. **3.** to cause (oneself) to be in a specified state by sobbing: *to sob oneself to sleep.* ~*n.* **4.** a convulsive gasp in weeping. [C12: prob. from Low G] — 'sobbing *adj.*

sober ('səʊbə) *adj.* **1.** not drunk. **2.** not given to excessive indulgence in drink or any other activity. **3.** sedate and rational: *a sober attitude to a problem.* **4.** (of colours) plain and dull or subdued. **5.** free from exaggeration or speculation: *he told us the sober truth.* ~*vb.* **6.** (usually foll. by *up*) to make or become less intoxicated. [C14 *sobre*, from OF, from L *sōbrius*] — 'sobering *n., adj.* — 'soberly *adv.*

Sobers ('səʊbəz) *n.* Sir **Garfield St. Aubrun,** known as *Gary.* born 1936, West Indian cricketer; one of the finest all-rounders of all time.

sobriety (səʊ'braɪətɪ) *n.* **1.** the state or quality of being sober. **2.** the quality of refraining from excess. **3.** the quality of being serious or sedate.

sobriquet or **soubriquet** ('səʊbrɪ,keɪ) *n.* a humorous epithet, assumed name, or nickname. [C17: from F *soubriquet*, from ?]

sob story *n.* a tale of personal distress intended to arouse sympathy.

Soc. or **soc.** *abbrev. for:* **1.** socialist. **2.** society.

soca ('səʊkə) *n.* a mixture of soul and calypso music typical of the E Caribbean. [C20: a blend of *soul* + *calypso*]

socage ('sɒkɪdʒ) *n. English legal history.* the tenure of land by certain services, esp. of an agricultural nature. [C14: from Anglo-F, from *soc* SOKE]

so-called *adj.* **a.** (*prenominal*) designated or styled by the name or word mentioned, esp. (in the speaker's opinion) incorrectly: *a so-called genius.* **b.** (also used parenthetically after a noun): *these experts, so-called, are no help.*

soccer ('sɒkə) *n.* **a.** a game in which two teams of eleven players try to kick or head a ball into their opponents' goal, only the goalkeeper on either side being allowed to touch the ball with his hands and arms, except in the case of throw-ins. **b.** (*as modifier*): *a soccer player.* ~Also called: **Association Football.** [C19: from *Assoc(iation Football)* + -ER[1]]

socceroo (,sɒkə'ruː) *n., pl.* **-ceroos.** *Austral. sl.* a member of the Australian national soccer team. [C20: from SOCCER + (KANGAR)OO]

Soche or **So-ch'e** ('səʊ'tʃe) *n.* a variant transliteration of the Chinese name for **Shache.**

Sochi (*Russian* 'sɔtʃi) *n.* a city and resort in the SW Soviet Union, in the Krasnodar Territory on the Black Sea: hot mineral springs. Pop.: 317 000 (1987).

sociable ('səʊʃəbªl) *adj.* **1.** friendly or companionable. **2.** (of an occasion) providing the opportunity for friendliness and conviviality. ~*n.* **3.** *Chiefly U.S.* a social. **4.** a type of open carriage with two seats facing each other. [C16: via F from L, from *sociāre* to unite, from *socius* an associate] — ,socia'bility *n.* — 'sociably *adv.*

social ('səʊʃəl) *adj.* **1.** living or preferring to live in a community rather than alone. **2.** denoting or relating to human society or any of its subdivisions. **3.** of or characteristic of the behaviour and interaction of persons forming groups. **4.** relating to or having the purpose of promoting companionship, communal activities, etc.: *a social club.* **5.** relating to or engaged in social services: *a social worker.* **6.** relating to or considered appropriate to a certain class of society. **7.** (esp. of certain species of insects) living together in organized colonies: *social bees.* **8.** (of plant species) growing in clumps. ~*n.* **9.** an informal gathering, esp. of an organized group. [C16: from L *sociālis* companionable, from *socius* a comrade] — 'socially *adv.*

Social and Liberal Democratic Party *n.* (in Britain) a centrist political party formed in 1988 by the merging of the Liberal Party and part of the Social Democratic Party.

social anthropology *n.* the branch of anthropology that deals with cultural and social phenomena such as kinship systems or beliefs.

social climber *n.* a person who seeks advancement to a higher social class, esp. by obsequious behaviour. — **social climbing** *n.*

social contract or **compact** *n.* (in the theories of Rousseau and others) an agreement, entered into by individuals, that results in the formation of the state, the prime motive being the desire for protection, which entails the surrender of some personal liberties.

Social Credit *n.* **1.** (esp. in Canada) a right-wing Populist political party, movement, or doctrine. **2. Social Credit League.** (in New Zealand) a middle-of-the-road political party, in favour of free enterprise. **3. Social Credit Rally.** (in Canada) a political party formed in 1963 from a splinter group of the Social Credit Party.

social democrat *n.* **1.** any socialist who believes in the gradual transformation of capitalism into democratic socialism. **2.** (*usually cap.*) a member of a Social Democratic Party. — **social democracy** *n.*

Social Democratic Party *n.* **1.** (in Britain) a centre political party founded in 1981 by ex-members of the Labour Party. It formed an alliance with the Liberal Party and continued in a reduced form after many members left to join the Social and Liberal Democratic Party in 1988. **2.** one of the two major political parties in West Germany, favouring gradual reform. **3.** any of the parties in many other countries similar to that of West Germany.

social fund *n.* (in Britain) a social security fund from which loans or payments may be made to people in cases of extreme need.

social insurance *n.* government insurance providing coverage for the unemployed, the injured, the old, etc.:

usually financed by contributions from employers and employees.

Social Insurance Number *n. Canad.* an identification number issued to individuals by the government in connection with income tax and social insurance.

socialism ('səʊʃə,lɪzəm) *n.* **1.** an economic theory or system in which the means of production, distribution, and exchange are owned by the community collectively, usually through the state. Cf. **capitalism. 2.** any of various social or political theories or movements in which the common welfare is to be achieved through the establishment of a socialist economic system. **3.** (in Marxist theory) a transitional stage in the development of a society from capitalism to communism: characterized by the distribution of income according to work rather than need.

socialist ('səʊʃəlɪst) *n.* **1.** a supporter or advocate of socialism or any party promoting socialism (**socialist party**). ~*adj.* **2.** of, implementing, or relating to socialism. **3.** (*sometimes cap.*) of or relating to socialists or a socialist party. — ,socia'listic *adj.*

Socialist International *n.* an international association of largely anti-Communist Social Democratic Parties founded in Frankfurt in 1951.

socialite ('səʊʃə,laɪt) *n.* a person who is or seeks to be prominent in fashionable society.

sociality (,səʊʃɪ'ælɪtɪ) *n., pl.* **-ties. 1.** the tendency of groups and persons to develop social links and live in communities. **2.** the quality or state of being social.

socialize *or* **-lise** ('səʊʃə,laɪz) *vb.* **1.** (*intr.*) to behave in a friendly or sociable manner. **2.** (*tr.*) to prepare for life in society. **3.** (*tr.*) *Chiefly U.S.* to alter or create so as to be in accordance with socialist principles.

social science *n.* **1.** the study of society and of the relationship of individual members within society, including economics, history, political science, psychology, anthropology, and sociology. **2.** any of these subjects studied individually. — **social scientist** *n.*

social secretary *n.* **1.** a member of an organization who arranges its social events. **2.** a personal secretary who deals with private correspondence, etc.

social security *n.* **1.** public provision for the economic welfare of the aged, unemployed, etc., esp. through pensions and other monetary assistance. **2.** (*often cap.*) a government programme designed to provide such assistance.

social services *pl. n.* welfare activities organized by the state or a local authority and carried out by trained personnel.

social studies *n.* (*functioning as sing.*) the study of how people live and organize themselves in society, embracing geography, history, economics, and other subjects.

social welfare *n.* **1.** social services provided by a state for the benefit of its citizens. **2.** (*caps.*) (in New Zealand) a government department concerned with pensions and benefits for the elderly, the sick, etc.

social work *n.* any of various social services designed to alleviate the conditions of the poor and aged and to increase the welfare of children. — **social worker** *n.*

societal (sə'saɪət³l) *adj.* of or relating to society, esp. human society. — **so'cietally** *adv.*

society (sə'saɪətɪ) *n., pl.* **-ties. 1.** the totality of social relationships among organized groups of human beings or animals. **2.** a system of human organizations generating distinctive cultural patterns and institutions. **3.** such a system with reference to its mode of social and economic organization or its dominant class: *middle-class society.* **4.** those with whom one has companionship. **5.** an organized group of people associated for some specific purpose or on account of some common interest: *a learned society.* **6. a.** the privileged class of people in a community, esp. as considered superior or fashionable. **b.** (*as modifier*): *a society woman.* **7.** the social life and intercourse of such people: *to enter society.* **8.** companionship: *I enjoy her society.* **9.** *Ecology.* a small community of plants within a larger association. [C16: via OF *societé* from L *societās*, from *socius* a comrade]

Society Islands *pl. n.* a group of islands in the S Pacific: administratively part of French Polynesia; consists of the Windward Islands and the Leeward Islands; became a French protectorate in 1843 and a colony in 1880. Pop.: 142 129 (1983). Area: 1595 sq. km (616 sq. miles).

Society of Friends *n.* the official name for the **Quakers.**
Society of Jesus *n.* the religious order of the Jesuits, founded by Ignatius Loyola.

Socinus (səʊ'saɪnəs) *n.* **Faustus** ('fɔːstəs), Italian name *Fausto Sozzini*, 1539–1604, and his uncle, **Laelius** ('liːlɪəs), Italian name *Lelio Sozzini*, 1525–62, Italian Protestant theologians and reformers.

socio- *combining form.* denoting social or society: *socioeconomic; sociopolitical; sociology.*

sociobiology (,səʊsɪəʊbaɪ'ɒlədʒɪ) *n.* the study of social behaviour in animals and humans.

socioeconomic (,səʊsɪəʊ,iːkə'nɒmɪk, ,ɛkə-) *adj.* of, relating to, or involving both economic and social factors. — ,socio,eco'nomically *adv.*

sociolinguistics (,səʊsɪəʊlɪŋ'gwɪstɪks) *n.* (*functioning as sing.*) the study of language in relation to its social context. — ,socio'linguist *n.*

sociology (,səʊsɪ'ɒlədʒɪ) *n.* the study of the development, organization, functioning, and classification of human societies. — **sociological** (,səʊsɪə'lɒdʒɪk³l) *adj.* — ,soci'ologist *n.*

sociometry (,səʊsɪ'ɒmɪtrɪ) *n.* the study of sociological relationships within groups. — **sociometric** (,səʊsɪə'mɛtrɪk) *adj.* — ,soci'ometrist *n.*

sociopath ('səʊsɪə,pæθ) *n. Psychiatry.* another term for **psychopath.** — ,socio'pathic *adj.* — **sociopathy** (,səʊsɪ'ɒpəθɪ) *n.*

sociopolitical (,səʊsɪəʊpə'lɪtɪk³l) *adj.* of or involving both political and social factors.

sock[1] (sɒk) *n.* **1.** a cloth covering for the foot, reaching to between the ankle and knee and worn inside a shoe. **2.** an insole put in a shoe, as to make it fit better. **3.** a light shoe worn by actors in ancient Greek and Roman comedy. **4. pull one's socks up.** *Brit. inf.* to make a determined effort, esp. in order to regain control of a situation. **5. put a sock in it.** *Brit. sl.* be quiet! [OE *socc* a light shoe, from L *soccus*, from Gk *sukkhos*]

sock[2] (sɒk) *Sl.* ~*vb.* **1.** (*usually tr.*) to hit with force. **2. sock it to.** *Sl.* to make a forceful impression on. ~*n.* **3.** a forceful blow. [C17: from ?]

socket ('sɒkɪt) *n.* **1.** a device into which an electric plug can be inserted in order to make a connection in a circuit. **2.** *Chiefly Brit.* such a device mounted on a wall and connected to the electricity supply; power point. **3.** a part with an opening or hollow into which some other part can be fitted. **4.** *Anat.* **a.** a bony hollow into which a part or structure fits: *an eye socket.* **b.** the receptacle of a ball-and-socket joint. ~*vb.* **5.** (*tr.*) to furnish with or place into a socket. [C13: from Anglo-Norman *soket* a little ploughshare, from *soc*, of Celtic origin]

sockeye ('sɒk,aɪ) *n.* a Pacific salmon having red flesh and valued as a food fish. Also called: **red salmon.** [by folk etymology from *sukkegh*, of Amerind origin]

socle ('səʊk³l) *n.* another name for **plinth** (sense 1). [C18: via F from It. *zoccolo*, from L *socculus* a little shoe, from *soccus* a SOCK[1]]

Socotra, Sokotra, *or* **Suqutra** (sə'kəʊtrə) *n.* an island in the Indian Ocean, about 240 km (150 miles) off Cape Guardafui, Somalia: administratively part of South Yemen. Capital: Tamrida. Area: 3100 sq. km (1200 sq. miles).

Socrates ('sɒkrə,tiːz) *n.* ?470–399 B.C., Athenian philosopher, whose beliefs are known only through the writings of his pupils Plato and Xenophon. He taught that virtue was based on knowledge, which was attained by a dialectical process that took into account many aspects of a stated hypothesis. He was indicted for impiety and corruption of youth (399) and was condemned to death. He refused to flee and died by drinking hemlock.

Socratic (sɒ'krætɪk) *adj.* **1.** of or relating to Socrates, his methods, etc. ~*n.* **2.** a person who follows the teachings of Socrates. — **So'cratically** *adv.* — **So'crati,cism** *n.* — **Socratist** ('sɒkrətɪst) *n.*

Socratic irony *n. Philosophy.* a means by which the feigned ignorance of a questioner leads the person answering to expose his own ignorance.

Socratic method *n. Philosophy.* the method of instruction by question and answer used by Socrates in order to elicit from his pupils truths he considered to be implicitly known by all rational beings.

sod[1] (sɒd) *n.* **1.** a piece of grass-covered surface soil held together by the roots of the grass; turf. **2.** *Poetic.* the ground. ~*vb.* **sodding, sodded. 3.** (*tr.*) to cover with sods. [C15: from Low G]

sod[2] (sɒd) *Sl.*, *chiefly Brit.* ~*n.* **1.** a person considered to be obnoxious. **2.** a jocular word for a **person.** **3. sod all.** *Sl.* nothing. ~*interj.* **4.** a strong exclamation of annoyance. [C19: shortened from SODOMITE] —'**sodding** *adj.*

soda ('səʊdə) *n.* **1.** any of a number of simple inorganic compounds of sodium, such as sodium carbonate (**washing soda**), sodium bicarbonate (**baking soda**), and sodium hydroxide (**caustic soda**). **2.** See **soda water.** **3.** *U.S. & Canad.* a fizzy drink. [C16: from Med. L, from *sodanum* barilla, a plant that was burned to obtain a type of sodium carbonate, ?from Ar.]

soda ash *n.* the anhydrous commercial form of sodium carbonate.

soda bread *n.* a type of bread leavened with sodium bicarbonate combined with milk and cream of tartar.

soda fountain *n.* *U.S. & Canad.* **1.** a counter that serves drinks, snacks, etc. **2.** an apparatus dispensing soda water.

sodality (səʊ'dælɪtɪ) *n.*, *pl.* **-ties.** **1.** *R.C. Church.* a religious society. **2.** fellowship. [C16: from L *sodālitās* fellowship, from *sodālis* a comrade]

sodamide ('səʊdə,maɪd) *n.* a white crystalline compound used as a dehydrating agent and in making sodium cyanide. Formula: $NaNH_2$.

soda siphon *n.* a sealed bottle containing and dispensing soda water. The water is forced up a tube reaching to the bottom of the bottle by the pressure of gas above the water.

soda water *n.* an effervescent beverage made by charging water with carbon dioxide under pressure. Sometimes shortened to **soda.**

sodden ('sɒd³n) *adj.* **1.** completely saturated. **2. a.** dulled, esp. by excessive drinking. **b.** (*in combination*): *a drink-sodden mind.* **3.** doughy, as bread is when improperly cooked. ~*vb.* **4.** to make or become sodden. [C13 *soden,* p.p. of SEETHE] —'**soddenness** *n.*

Soddy ('sɒdɪ) *n.* **Frederick.** 1877–1956, English chemist, whose work on radioactive disintegration led to the discovery of isotopes: Nobel prize for chemistry 1921.

sodium ('səʊdɪəm) *n.* **a.** a very reactive soft silvery-white element of the alkali metal group occurring principally in common salt, Chile saltpetre, and cryolite. It is used in the production of chemicals, in metallurgy, and, alloyed with potassium, as a cooling medium in nuclear reactors. Symbol: Na; atomic no.: 11; atomic wt.: 22.99. **b.** (*as modifier*): *sodium light.* [C19: NL, from SODA + -IUM]

sodium amytal *n.* another name for **Amytal.**

sodium benzoate *n.* a white crystalline soluble compound used in preserving food (**E 211**), as an antiseptic, and in making dyes.

sodium bicarbonate *n.* a white crystalline soluble compound used in effervescent drinks, baking powders, fire-extinguishers, and in medicine as an antacid; sodium hydrogen carbonate. Formula: $NaHCO_3$. Systematic name: **sodium hydrogencarbonate.** Also called: **bicarbonate of soda, baking soda.**

sodium carbonate *n.* a colourless or white odourless soluble crystalline compound used in the manufacture of glass, ceramics, soap, and paper, and as a cleansing agent. Formula: Na_2CO_3.

sodium chlorate *n.* a colourless crystalline soluble compound used as a bleaching agent, antiseptic, and weedkiller. Formula: $NaClO_3$.

sodium chloride *n.* common table salt; a soluble colourless crystalline compound widely used as a seasoning and preservative for food and in the manufacture of chemicals, glass, and soap. Formula: NaCl. Also called: **salt.**

sodium cyanide *n.* a white odourless crystalline soluble poisonous compound used for extracting gold and silver from their ores and for case-hardening steel. Formula: NaCN.

sodium glutamate ('glu:tə,meɪt) *n.* another name for **monosodium glutamate.**

sodium hydrogencarbonate *n.* the systematic name for **sodium bicarbonate.**

sodium hydroxide *n.* a white strongly alkaline solid used in the manufacture of rayon, paper, aluminium, soap, and sodium compounds. Formula: NaOH. Also called: **caustic soda.**

sodium hyposulphite *n.* another name (not in technical usage) for **sodium thiosulphate.**

sodium lamp *n.* another name for **sodium-vapour lamp.**

sodium nitrate *n.* a white crystalline soluble solid compound used in matches, explosives, and rocket propellants, as a fertilizer, and as a curing salt for preserving food (**E 251**). Formula: $NaNO_3$.

Sodium Pentothal *n. Trademark.* another name for **thiopentone sodium.**

sodium silicate *n.* **1.** Also called: **soluble glass.** See **water glass.** **2.** any sodium salt of a silicic acid.

sodium sulphate *n.* a solid white substance used in making glass, detergents, and pulp. Formula: Na_2SO_4. See **salt cake** and **Glauber's salt.**

sodium thiosulphate *n.* a white soluble substance used in photography as a fixer to dissolve unchanged silver halides and also to remove excess chlorine from chlorinated water. Formula: $Na_2S_2O_3$. Also called (not in technical usage): **sodium hyposulphite, hypo.**

sodium-vapour lamp *n.* a type of electric lamp consisting of a glass tube containing neon and sodium vapour at low pressure through which an electric current is passed to give an orange light: used in street lighting.

sod off *Brit. taboo sl.* ~*interj.* **1.** a forceful expression of dismissal. ~*vb.* **sodding, sodded. 2.** (*intr., adv.*) to go away.

Sodom ('sɒdəm) *n.* **1.** *Old Testament.* a city destroyed by God for its wickedness that, with Gomorrah, traditionally typifies depravity (Genesis 19:24). **2.** this city as representing homosexuality. **3.** any place notorious for depravity.

sodomite ('sɒdə,maɪt) *n.* a person who practises sodomy.

sodomy ('sɒdəmɪ) *n.* anal intercourse committed by a man with another man or a woman. [C13: via OF *sodomie* from L (Vulgate) *Sodoma* Sodom]

Sod's law (sɒdz) *n. Inf.* a facetious precept stating that if something can go wrong or turn out inconveniently it will.

Soekarno (su:'kɑ:nəʊ) *n.* a variant spelling of (Achmed) **Sukarno.**

Soemba ('su:mbə) *n.* a variant spelling of **Sumba.**

Soembawa (su:m'bɑ:wə) *n.* a variant spelling of **Sumbawa.**

Soenda Islands ('su:ndə) *pl. n.* a variant spelling of **Sunda Islands.**

Soenda Strait *n.* a variant spelling of **Sunda Strait.**

Soerabaja (,suərə'baɪə) *n.* a variant spelling of **Surabaya.**

soever (səʊ'ɛvə) *adv.* in any way at all: used to emphasize or make less precise a word or phrase, usually in combination with *what, where, when, how,* etc., or else separated by intervening words. Cf. **whatsoever.**

sofa ('səʊfə) *n.* an upholstered seat with back and arms for two or more people. [C17 (in the sense: dais upholstered as a seat): from Ar. *suffah*]

soffit ('sɒfɪt) *n.* the underside of a part of a building or a structural component, such as an arch, beam, stair, etc. [C17: via F from It. *soffitto,* from L *suffixus* something fixed underneath, from *suffigere,* from *sub-* under + *figere* to fasten]

Sofia ('səʊfɪə) *n.* the capital of Bulgaria, in the west: colonized by the Romans in 29 A.D.; became capital of Bulgaria in 1879; university (1880). Pop.: 1 114 962 (1985). Ancient name: **Serdica.** Bulgarian name: **Sofiya** ('sɔfɪ,ja).

S. of Sol. *Bible. abbrev. for* Song of Solomon.

soft (sɒft) *adj.* **1.** easy to dent, work, or cut without shattering; malleable. **2.** not hard; giving little or no resistance to pressure or weight. **3.** fine, light, smooth, or fluffy to the touch. **4.** gentle; tranquil. **5.** (of music, sounds, etc.) low and pleasing. **6.** (of light, colour, etc.) not excessively bright or harsh. **7.** (of a breeze, climate, etc.) temperate, mild, or pleasant. **8.** slightly blurred; not sharply outlined: *soft focus.* **9.** (of a diet) consisting of easily digestible foods. **10.** kind or lenient, often excessively so. **11.** easy to influence or impose upon. **12.** prepared to compromise; not doctrinaire: *the soft left.* **13.** *Inf.* feeble or silly; simple (often in **soft in the head**). **14.** unable to endure hardship, esp. through pampering. **15.** physically out of condition; flabby: *soft muscles.* **16.** loving; tender: *soft words.* **17.** *Inf.* requiring little exertion; easy: *a soft job.* **18.** *Chem.* (of water) relatively free of mineral salts and therefore easily able to make soap lather. **19.** (of a drug such as cannabis) nonaddictive. **20.** *Phonetics.* (not in technical usage) denoting the consonants *c* and *g* in English when they are pronounced as palatal or alveolar fricatives or affricates (s, dʒ, ʃ, ð, tʃ) before *e* and *i*, rather than as velar stops (k, g). **21.** *Finance, chiefly U.S.* (of prices, a market, etc.) unstable and tending to decline. **22.** (of currency) relatively unstable in exchange value. **23.** (of radiation, such as x-rays and ultraviolet radiation) having low energy and not capable of deep penetration of materials. **24. soft on** *or* **about. a.** gentle, sympathetic, or lenient towards. **b.** feeling affection or infatuation for. ~*adv.* **25.** in a soft manner: *to speak soft.* ~*n.* **26.** a soft object, part, or piece. **27.** *Inf.* See **softy.** ~*sentence substitute. Arch.* **28.** quiet! **29.** wait! [OE *sōfte*] — **'softly** *adv.* — **'softness** *n.*

softa ('sɒftə) *n.* a Muslim student of divinity and jurisprudence, esp. in Turkey. [C17: from Turkish, from Persian *sōkhtah* aflame (with love of learning)]

softball ('sɒft,bɔːl) *n.* a variation of baseball using a larger softer ball, pitched underhand.

soft ball *n. Cookery.* a term used for sugar syrup boiled to a consistency at which it may be rubbed into balls after dipping in cold water.

soft-boiled *adj.* (of an egg) boiled for a short time so that the yolk is still soft.

soft coal *n.* another name for **bituminous coal.**

soft-core *adj.* (of pornography) suggestive and titillating through not being totally explicit.

soft-cover *adj.* a less common word for **paperback.**

soft drink *n.* a nonalcoholic drink.

soften ('sɒfᵊn) *vb.* **1.** to make or become soft or softer. **2.** to make or become more gentle. — **'softener** *n.*

softening of the brain *n.* an abnormal softening of the tissues of the cerebrum characterized by mental impairment.

soft-focus lens *n. Photog.* a lens designed to produce an image that is slightly out of focus: typically used for portrait work.

soft furnishings *pl. n. Brit.* curtains, hangings, rugs, etc.

soft goods *pl. n.* textile fabrics and related merchandise.

soft-headed *adj.* **1.** *Inf.* feeble-minded; stupid; simple. **2.** (of a stick or hammer for playing a percussion instrument) having a soft head. — **,soft-'headedness** *n.*

softhearted (,sɒft'hɑːtɪd) *adj.* easily moved to pity. — **,soft'heartedly** *adv.* — **,soft'heartedness** *n.*

soft landing *n.* a landing by a spacecraft on the moon or a planet at a sufficiently low velocity for the equipment or occupants to remain unharmed.

soft option *n.* in a number of choices, the one involving the least difficulty or exertion.

soft palate *n.* the posterior fleshy portion of the roof of the mouth.

soft paste *n.* **a.** artificial porcelain made from clay, bone ash, etc. **b.** (*as modifier*): *softpaste porcelain.*

soft-pedal *vb.* **-alling, -alled** *or U.S.* **-aling, -aled.** (*tr.*) **1.** to mute the tone of (a piano) by depressing the soft pedal. **2.** *Inf.* to make (something, esp. something unpleasant) less obvious by deliberately failing to emphasize or allude to it. ~*n.* **soft pedal. 3.** a foot-operated lever on a piano, the left one of two, that either moves the whole action closer to the strings so that the hammers strike with less force or causes fewer of the strings to sound.

soft porn *n. Inf.* soft-core pornography.

soft sell *n.* a method of selling based on indirect suggestion or inducement.

soft shoulder *or* **verge** *n.* a soft edge along the side of a road that is unsuitable for vehicles to drive on.

soft soap *n.* **1.** *Med.* Also called: **green soap.** a soft or liquid alkaline soap used in treating certain skin disorders. **2.** *Inf.* flattering, persuasive, or cajoling talk. ~*vb.* **soft-soap. 3.** *Inf.* to use such talk on (a person).

soft-spoken *adj.* **1.** speaking or said with a soft gentle voice. **2.** able to persuade or impress by glibness of tongue.

soft spot *n.* a sentimental fondness (esp. in **have a soft spot for**).

soft touch *n. Inf.* a person easily persuaded or imposed on, esp. to lend money.

software ('sɒft,wɛə) *n. Computers.* the programs that can be used with a particular computer system. Cf. **hardware** (sense 2).

softwood ('sɒft,wʊd) *n.* **1.** the open-grained wood of any of numerous coniferous trees, such as pine and cedar. **2.** any tree yielding this wood.

softy *or* **softie** ('sɒftɪ) *n., pl.* **softies.** *Inf.* a person who is sentimental, weakly foolish, or lacking in physical endurance.

SOGAT ('səʊgæt) *n.* (in Britain) *acronym for* Society of Graphical and Allied Trades.

Sogdiana (,sɒgdɪ'ɑːnə) *n.* a region of ancient central Asia. Its chief city was Samarkand. — **'Sogdian** *adj., n.*

soggy ('sɒgɪ) *adj.* **-gier, -giest. 1.** soaked with liquid. **2.** (of bread, pastry, etc.) moist and heavy. **3.** *Inf.* lacking in spirit or positiveness. [C18: prob. from dialect *sog* marsh, from ?] — **'soggily** *adv.* — **'sogginess** *n.*

soh *or* **so** (səʊ) *n. Music.* (in tonic sol-fa) the name used for the fifth note or dominant of any scale. [C13: see GAMUT]

Soho ('səʊhəʊ) *n.* a district of central London, in the City of Westminster: a foreign quarter since the late 17th century, now chiefly known for restaurants, nightclubs, striptease clubs, etc.

soi-disant French. (swadizã) *adj.* so-called; self-styled. [lit.: calling oneself]

soigné *or (fem.)* **soignée** ('swɑːnjeɪ) *adj.* well-groomed; elegant. [F, from *soigner* to take good care of, of Gmc origin]

soil[1] (sɔɪl) *n.* **1.** the top layer of the land surface of the earth that is composed of disintegrated rock particles, humus, water, and air. **2.** a type of this material having specific characteristics: *loamy soil.* **3.** land, country, or region: *one's native soil.* **4. the soil.** life and work on a farm; land: *he belonged to the soil.* **5.** any place or thing encouraging growth or development. [C14: from Anglo-Norman, from L *solium* a seat, but confused with L *solum* the ground]

soil[2] (sɔɪl) *vb.* **1.** to make or become dirty or stained. **2.** (*tr.*) to pollute with sin or disgrace; sully; defile. ~*n.* **3.** the state or result of soiling. **4.** refuse, manure, or excrement. [C13: from OF *soillier* to defile, from *soil* pigsty, prob. from L *sūs* a swine]

soil[3] (sɔɪl) *vb.* (*tr.*) to feed (livestock) green fodder to fatten or purge them. [C17: ?from obs. vb. (C16) *soil* to manure, from SOIL[2] (*n.*)]

soil pipe *n.* a pipe that conveys sewage or waste water from a toilet, etc., to a soil drain or sewer.

soiree ('swɑːreɪ) *n.* an evening party or gathering, usually at a private house, esp. where guests listen to, play, or dance to music. [C19: from F, from OF *soir* evening, from L *sērum* a late time, from *sērus* late]

Soissons (*French* swasɔ̃) *n.* a city in N France, on the Aisne River: has Roman remains and an 11th-century abbey. Pop.: 32 236 (1982).

soixante-neuf French. (swasãtnœf) *n.* a sexual activity in which two people simultaneously stimulate each other's genitalia with their mouths. Also called: **sixty-nine.** [lit.: sixty-nine, from the position adopted by the participants]

sojourn ('sɒdʒɜːn, 'sʌdʒ-) *n.* **1.** a temporary stay. ~*vb.* **2.** (*intr.*) to stay or reside temporarily. [C13: from OF *sojorner*, from Vulgar L *subdiurnāre* (unattested) to spend a day, from L *sub-* during + LL *diurnum* day] — **'sojourner** *n.*

soke (səʊk) *n. English legal history.* **1.** the right to hold a local court. **2.** the territory under the jurisdiction of a particular court. [C14: from Med. L *sōca*, from OE *sōcn* a seeking]

Sokoto ('səʊkə,təʊ) *n.* **1.** a state of NW Nigeria: the country's largest state, formed in 1976 from part of North-Western State. Capital: Sokoto. Pop.: 7 608 900 (1984). Area: 149 066 sq. km (57 542 sq. miles). **2.** a town in NW Nigeria, capital of Sokoto state: capital of the Fulah Empire in the 19th century; Muslim place of pilgrimage. Pop.: 148 000 (1983).

Sokotra (sə'kəʊtrə) *n.* a variant spelling of **Socotra.**

sol[1] (sɒl) *n. Music.* another name for **soh.** [C14: see GAMUT]

sol[2] (sɒl) *n.* a colloid that has a continuous liquid phase, esp. one in which a solid is suspended in a liquid. [C20: shortened from SOLUTION]

Sol (sɒl) *n.* **1.** the Roman god personifying the sun. **2.** a poetic word for the **sun.**

sol. *abbrev. for:* **1.** soluble. **2.** solution.

Sol. *Bible abbrev. for* Solomon.

sola Latin. ('səʊlə) *adj.* the feminine form of *solus.*

solace ('sɒlɪs) *n.* **1.** comfort in misery, disappointment, etc. **2.** something that gives comfort or consolation. ~*vb.*

(*tr.*) **3.** to give comfort or cheer to (a person) in time of sorrow, distress, etc. **4.** to alleviate (sorrow, misery, etc.). [C13: from OF *solas*, from L *sōlātium* comfort, from *sōlārī* to console] —**'solacer** *n.*

solan *or* **solan goose** ('səʊlən) *n.* an archaic name for the **gannet.** [C15 *soland*, from ON]

solanaceous (ˌsɒlə'neɪʃəs) *adj.* of or relating to the Solanaceae, a family of plants having typically tubular flowers, protruding anthers, and often poisonous or narcotic properties: includes the potato, tobacco, and several nightshades. [C19: from NL *Solānāceae*, from L *sōlānum* nightshade]

solanum (səʊ'leɪnəm) *n.* any tree, shrub, or herbaceous plant of the mainly tropical solanaceous genus *Solanum*: includes the potato and certain nightshades. [C16: from L: nightshade]

solar ('səʊlə) *adj.* **1.** of or relating to the sun. **2.** operating by or utilizing the energy of the sun: *solar cell.* **3.** *Astron.* determined from the motion of the earth relative to the sun: *solar year.* **4.** *Astrol.* subject to the influence of the sun. [C15: from L *sōlāris*, from *sōl* the sun]

solar cell *n.* a cell that produces electricity from the sun's rays, used esp. in spacecraft.

solar constant *n.* the rate at which the sun's energy is received per unit area on the earth's surface when the sun is at its mean distance from the earth and atmospheric absorption has been corrected for.

solar day *n.* See under **day** (sense 6).

solar flare *n.* a brief powerful eruption of intense high-energy radiation from the sun's surface, associated with sunspots and causing radio and magnetic disturbances on earth.

solarium (səʊ'lɛərɪəm) *n.*, *pl.* **-laria** (-'lɛərɪə) *or* **-lariums.** **1.** a room built largely of glass to afford exposure to the sun. **2.** a bed equipped with ultraviolet lights used for acquiring an artificial suntan. **3.** an establishment offering such facilities. [C19: from L: a terrace, from *sōl* sun]

solar month *n.* See under **month** (sense 4).

solar plexus *n.* **1.** *Anat.* the network of nerves situated behind the stomach that supply the abdominal organs. **2.** (not in technical usage) the part of the stomach beneath the diaphragm; pit of the stomach. [C18: referring to resemblance between the radial network of nerves & ganglia & the rays of the sun]

solar system *n.* the system containing the sun and the bodies held in its gravitational field, including the planets (Mercury, Venus, earth, Mars, Jupiter, Saturn, Uranus, Neptune, Pluto), the asteroids, and comets.

solar wind (wɪnd) *n.* the stream of charged particles, such as protons, emitted by the sun at high velocities, its intensity increasing during periods of solar activity.

solar year *n.* See under **year** (sense 4).

solatium (səʊ'leɪʃɪəm) *n.*, *pl.* **-tia** (-ʃɪə) compensation awarded for injury to the feelings as distinct from physical suffering and pecuniary loss. [C19: from L: see SOLACE]

sold (səʊld) *vb.* **1.** the past tense and past participle of **sell.** ~*adj.* **2. sold on.** *Sl.* uncritically attached to or enthusiastic about.

solder ('sɒldə; *U.S.* 'sɒdər) *n.* **1.** an alloy for joining two metal surfaces by melting the alloy so that it forms a thin layer between the surfaces. **2.** something that joins things together firmly; a bond. ~*vb.* **3.** to join or mend or be joined or mended with or as if with solder. [C14: via OF from L *solidāre* to strengthen, from *solidus* solid] —**'solderable** *adj.* —**'solderer** *n.*

soldering iron *n.* a hand tool consisting of a handle fixed to an iron or copper tip that is heated and used to melt and apply solder.

soldier ('səʊldʒə) *n.* **1. a.** a person who serves or has served in an army. **b.** Also called: **common soldier.** a noncommissioned member of an army as opposed to a commissioned officer. **2.** a person who works diligently for a cause. **3.** *Zool.* an individual in a colony of social insects, esp. ants, that has powerful jaws adapted for defending the colony, crushing food, etc. ~*vb.* **5.** (*intr.*) to serve as a soldier. [C13: from OF *soudier*, from *soude* (army) pay, from LL *solidus* a gold coin, from L: firm] —**'soldierly** *adj.*

soldier of fortune *n.* a man who seeks money or adventure as a soldier; mercenary.

soldier on *vb.* (*intr., adv.*) to persist in one's efforts in spite of difficulties, pressure, etc.

soldiery ('səʊldʒərɪ) *n.*, *pl.* **-dieries. 1.** soldiers collectively. **2.** a group of soldiers. **3.** the profession of being a soldier.

sole[1] (səʊl) *adj.* **1.** (*prenominal*) being the only one; only. **2.** (*prenominal*) of or relating to one individual or group and no other: *sole rights.* **3.** *Law.* having no wife or husband. **4.** an archaic word for **solitary.** [C14: from OF *soule*, from L *sōlus* alone] —**'soleness** *n.*

sole[2] (səʊl) *n.* **1.** the underside of the foot. **2.** the underside of a shoe. **3. a.** the bottom of a furrow. **b.** the bottom of a plough. **4.** the underside of a golf-club head. ~*vb.* (*tr.*) **5.** to provide (a shoe) with a sole. [C14: via OF from L *solea* sandal]

sole[3] (səʊl) *n.*, *pl.* **sole** *or* **soles.** any of various tongue-shaped flatfishes, esp. the **European sole:** most common in warm seas and highly valued as food fishes. [C14: via OF from Vulgar L *sola* (unattested), from L *solea* a sandal (from the fish's shape)]

solecism ('sɒlɪˌsɪzəm) *n.* **1. a.** the nonstandard use of a grammatical construction. **b.** any mistake, incongruity, or absurdity. **2.** a violation of good manners. [C16: from L *soloecismus*, from Gk, from *soloikos* speaking incorrectly, from *Soloi* an Athenian colony of Cilicia where the inhabitants spoke a corrupt form of Greek] —**'solecist** *n.* —ˌsole'cistic *adj.* —ˌsole'cistically *adv.*

solely ('səʊllɪ) *adv.* **1.** only; completely. **2.** without others; singly. **3.** for one thing only.

solemn ('sɒləm) *adj.* **1.** characterized or marked by seriousness or sincerity: *a solemn vow.* **2.** characterized by pomp, ceremony, or formality. **3.** serious, glum, or pompous. **4.** inspiring awe: *a solemn occasion.* **5.** performed with religious ceremony. **6.** gloomy or sombre: *solemn colours.* [C14: from OF *solempne*, from L *sōllemnis* appointed, ?from *sollus* whole] —**'solemnly** *adv.* —**'solemnness** *or* **'solemness** *n.*

solemnify (sə'lɛmnɪˌfaɪ) *vb.* **-fying, -fied.** (*tr.*) to make serious or grave. —**soˌlemnifi'cation** *n.*

solemnity (sə'lɛmnɪtɪ) *n.*, *pl.* **-ties. 1.** the state or quality of being solemn. **2.** (*often pl.*) solemn ceremony, observance, etc. **3.** *Law.* a formality necessary to validate a deed, contract, etc.

solemnize *or* **-ise** ('sɒləmˌnaɪz) *vb.* (*tr.*) **1.** to celebrate or observe with rites or formal ceremonies, as a religious occasion. **2.** to celebrate or perform the ceremony of (marriage). **3.** to make solemn or serious. **4.** to perform or hold (ceremonies, etc.) in due manner. —ˌsolemni'zation *or* **-i'sation** *n.* —**'solemˌnizer** *or* **-iser** *n.*

solenodon (sə'lɛnədən) *n.* either of two rare shrewlike nocturnal mammals of the West Indies having a long hairless tail and an elongated snout. [C19: from NL, from L *sōlēn* sea mussel (from Gk: pipe) + Gk *odōn* tooth]

solenoid ('səʊlɪˌnɔɪd) *n.* **1.** a coil of wire, usually cylindrical, in which a magnetic field is set up by passing a current through it. **2.** a coil of wire, partially surrounding an iron core, that is made to move inside the coil by the magnetic field set up by a current: used to convert electrical to mechanical energy, as in the operation of a switch. [C19: from F *solénoïde*, from Gk *sōlēn* a tube] —ˌsole'noidal *adj.*

Solent ('səʊlənt) *n.* **the.** a strait of the English Channel between the mainland coast of Hampshire, England, and the Isle of Wight. Width: up to 6 km (4 miles).

Soleure (sɒlœr) *n.* the French name for **Solothurn.**

sol-fa ('sɒl'fɑː) *n.* **1.** short for **tonic sol-fa.** ~*vb.* **-faing, -faed. 2.** *U.S.* to use tonic sol-fa syllables in singing (a tune). [C16: see GAMUT]

solfatara (ˌsɒlfə'tɑːrə) *n.* a volcanic vent emitting only sulphurous gases and water vapour or sometimes hot mud. [C18: from It.: a sulphurous volcano near Naples, from *solfo* sulphur]

solfeggio (sɒl'fɛdʒɪəʊ) *or* **solfège** (sɒl'fɛʒ) *n.*, *pl.* **-feggi** (-'fɛdʒiː), **-feggios,** *or* **-fèges.** *Music.* **1.** a voice exercise in which runs, scales, etc., are sung to the same syllable or syllables. **2.** solmization, esp. the French or Italian system, in which the names correspond to the notes of the scale of C major. [C18: from It. *solfeggiare* to use the syllables sol-fa; see GAMUT]

soli ('səʊlɪ) *adj., adv. Music.* (of a piece or passage) (to be performed) by or with soloists.

solicit (sə'lɪsɪt) *vb.* **1.** (when *intr.,* foll. by *for*) to make a request, application, etc., to (a person for business, support, etc.). **2.** to accost (a person) with an offer of sexual relations in return for money. **3.** to provoke or incite (a person) to do something wrong or illegal. [C15: from OF *solliciter* to disturb, from L *sollicitāre* to harass, from *sollus* whole + *ciēre* to excite] —**so,lici'tation** *n.*

solicitor (sə'lɪsɪtə) *n.* **1.** (in Britain) a lawyer who advises clients on matters of law, draws up legal documents, prepares cases for barristers, etc. **2.** (in the U.S.) an officer responsible for the legal affairs of a town, city, etc. **3.** a person who solicits. —**so'licitor,ship** *n.*

Solicitor General *n., pl.* **Solicitors General. 1.** (in Britain) the law officer of the Crown ranking next to the Attorney General (in Scotland to the Lord Advocate) and acting as his assistant. **2.** (in New Zealand) the government's chief lawyer.

solicitous (sə'lɪsɪtəs) *adj.* **1.** showing consideration, concern, attention, etc. **2.** keenly anxious or willing; eager. [C16: from L *sollicitus* anxious; see SOLICIT] —**so'licitousness** *n.*

solicitude (sə'lɪsɪ,tjuːd) *n.* **1.** the state or quality of being solicitous. **2.** (*often pl.*) something that causes anxiety or concern. **3.** anxiety or concern.

solid ('sɒlɪd) *adj.* **1.** of, concerned with, or being a substance in a physical state in which it resists changes in size and shape. **2.** consisting of matter all through. **3.** of the same substance all through: *solid rock.* **4.** sound; proved or provable: *solid facts.* **5.** reliable or sensible; upstanding: *a solid citizen.* **6.** firm, strong, compact, or substantial: *a solid table; solid ground.* **7.** (of a meal or food) substantial. **8.** (*often postpositive*) without interruption or respite: *solid bombardment.* **9.** financially sound or solvent: *a solid institution.* **10.** strongly linked or consolidated: *a solid relationship.* **11. solid for.** unanimously in favour of. **12.** *Geom.* having or relating to three dimensions. **13.** (of a word composed of two or more elements) written or printed as a single word without a hyphen. **14.** *Printing.* with no space or leads between lines of type. **15.** (of a writer, work, etc.) adequate; sensible. **16.** of or having a single uniform colour or tone. **17.** *Austral. & N.Z. inf.* excessively severe or unreasonable. —*n.* **18.** *Geom.* **a.** a closed surface in three-dimensional space. **b.** such a surface together with the volume enclosed by it. **19.** a solid substance, such as wood, iron, or diamond. [C14: from OF *solide*, from L *solidus* firm] —**solidity** (sə'lɪdɪtɪ) *n.* —'**solidly** *adv.* —'**solidness** *n.*

solidago (,sɒlɪ'deɪɡəʊ) *n., pl.* **-gos.** any plant of a chiefly American genus, which includes the goldenrods. [C18: via NL from Med. L *soldago* a plant reputed to have healing properties, from *soldāre* to strengthen, from L *solidāre*, from *solidus* solid]

solid angle *n.* an area subtended in three dimensions by lines intersecting at a point on a sphere whose radius is the distance to the point. See also **steradian.**

solidarity (,sɒlɪ'dærɪtɪ) *n., pl.* **-ties.** unity of interests, sympathies, etc., as among members of the same class.

solid fuel *n.* **1.** a fuel, such as coal or coke, that is a solid rather than an oil or gas. **2.** Also called: **solid propellant.** a rocket fuel that is a solid rather than a liquid or a gas.

solid geometry *n.* the branch of geometry concerned with three-dimensional geometric figures.

solidify (sə'lɪdɪ,faɪ) *vb.* **-fying, -fied. 1.** to make or become solid or hard. **2.** to make or become strong, united, determined, etc. —**so,lidifi'cation** *n.* —**so'lidi,fier** *n.*

solid-state *n.* (*modifier*) **1.** (of an electronic device) activated by a semiconductor component in which current flow is through solid material rather than in a vacuum. **2.** of, concerned with, characteristic of, or consisting of solid matter.

solid-state physics *n.* (*functioning as sing.*) the branch of physics concerned with the properties of solids, such as superconductivity, photoconductivity, and ferromagnetism.

solidus ('sɒlɪdəs) *n., pl.* **-di** (-,daɪ). **1.** Also called: **diagonal, separatrix, shilling mark, slash, stroke, virgule.** a short oblique stroke used in text to separate items of information, such as days, months, and years in dates (*18/7/80*), alternative words (*and/or*), numerator from denominator in fractions (*55/103*), etc. **2.** a gold coin of the Byzantine empire. [C14: from LL *solidus* (*nummus*) a gold coin (from *solidus* solid); in Med. L, *solidus* referred to a shilling and was indicated by a long *s*, which ult. became the virgule]

solifluction *or* **solifluxion** ('sɒlɪ,flʌkʃən, ,səʊlɪ-) *n.* slow downhill movement of soil, saturated with meltwater,

over a permanently frozen subsoil in tundra regions. [C20: from L *solum* soil + *fluctio* act of flowing]

Solihull (,səʊlɪ'hʌl) *n.* a town in central England, in the S West Midlands near Birmingham: mainly residential. Pop.: 111 541 (1981).

soliloquize *or* **-ise** (sə'lɪlə,kwaɪz) *vb.* to utter (something) in soliloquy. —**so'liloquist** *n.* —**so'lilo,quizer** *or* **-iser** *n.*

soliloquy (sə'lɪləkwɪ) *n., pl.* **-quies. 1.** the act of speaking alone or to oneself, esp. as a theatrical device. **2.** a speech in a play that is spoken in soliloquy. [C17: via LL *sōliloquium*, from L *sōlus* sole + *loqui* to speak]

Soliman ('sɒlɪmən) *n.* a variant spelling of **Suleiman I.**

Solimões (suli'mõəʃ) *n.* **the.** the Brazilian name for the Amazon from the Peruvian border to the Rio Negro.

Solingen (*German* 'zoːlɪŋən) *n.* a city in West Germany, in North Rhine-Westphalia: a major European centre of the cutlery industry. Pop.: 158 000 (1986).

solipsism ('sɒlɪp,sɪzəm) *n. Philosophy.* the extreme form of scepticism which denies the possibility of any knowledge other than of one's own existence. [C19: from L *sōlus* alone + *ipse* self] —'**solipsist** *n., adj.* —,**solip'sistic** *adj.*

solitaire ('sɒlɪ,tɛə, ,sɒlɪ'tɛə) *n.* **1.** Also called: **pegboard.** a game played by one person, esp. one involving moving and taking pegs in a pegboard with the object of being left with only one. **2.** the U.S. name for **patience** (the card game). **3.** a gem, esp. a diamond, set alone in a ring. **4.** any of several extinct birds related to the dodo. **5.** any of several dull grey North American songbirds. [C18: from OF: SOLITARY]

solitary ('sɒlɪtərɪ, -trɪ) *adj.* **1.** following or enjoying a life of solitude: *a solitary disposition.* **2.** experienced or performed alone: *a solitary walk.* **3.** (of a place) unfrequented. **4.** (*prenominal*) single; sole: *a solitary cloud.* **5.** having few companions; lonely. **6.** (of animals) not living in organized colonies or large groups: *solitary bees.* **7.** (of flowers) growing singly. ~*n., pl.* **-taries. 8.** a person who lives in seclusion; hermit. **9.** *Inf.* short for **solitary confinement.** [C14: from L *sōlitārius*, from *sōlus* SOLE[1]] —'**solitarily** *adv.* —'**solitariness** *n.*

solitary confinement *n.* isolation imposed on a prisoner, as by confinement in a special cell.

solitude ('sɒlɪ,tjuːd) *n.* **1.** the state of being solitary or secluded. **2.** *Poetic.* a solitary place. [C14: from L *sōlitūdō*, from *sōlus* alone, SOLE[1]] —,**soli'tudinous** *adj.*

solmization *or* **-isation** (,sɒlmɪ'zeɪʃən) *n. Music.* a system of naming the notes of a scale by syllables instead of letters, which assigns the names *ut* (or *do*), *re, mi, fa, sol, la, si* (or *ti*) to the degrees of the major scale of C (**fixed system**) or (excluding the syllables *ut* and *si*) to the major scale in any key (**movable system**). See also **tonic sol-fa.** [C18: from F *solmisation*, from *solmiser* to use the sol-fa syllables, from SOL[1] + MI]

solo ('səʊləʊ) *n., pl.* **-los. 1.** (*pl.* **-los** *or* **-li** (-liː)). a musical composition for one performer with or without accompaniment. **2.** any of various card games in which each person plays on his own, such as solo whist. **3.** a flight in which an aircraft pilot is unaccompanied. **4. a.** any performance carried out by an individual without assistance. **b.** (*as modifier*): *a solo attempt.* ~*adj.* **5.** *Music.* unaccompanied: *a sonata for cello solo.* ~*adv.* **6.** by oneself; alone: *to fly solo.* ~*vb.* **7.** (*intr.*) to operate an aircraft alone. [C17: via It. from L *sōlus* alone] —**soloist** ('səʊləʊɪst) *n.*

Solomon ('sɒləmən) *n.* any person credited with great wisdom. [after 10th-cent. B.C. king of Israel] —**Solomonic** (,sɒlə'mɒnɪk) *adj.*

Solomon Islands *pl. n.* an independent state in the SW Pacific comprising an archipelago extending for almost 1450 km (900 miles) in a northwest–southeast direction: the northernmost islands of the archipelago (Buka and Bougainville) form part of Papua New Guinea; the main islands are Guadalcanal, Malaita, San Cristobal, New Georgia, Santa Isabel, and Choiseul: a member of the Commonwealth. Official language: English. Religion: Christian majority. Currency: Solomon Islands dollar. Capital: Honiara. Pop.: 291 800 (1987). Area: 29 785 sq. km (11 500 sq. miles).

Solomon's seal *n.* **1.** another name for **Star of David. 2.** any of several plants of N temperate regions, having greenish or yellow paired flowers, long narrow waxy leaves, and prominent leaf scars. [C16: translation of Med.

L *sigillum Solomonis*, ?from resemblance of the leaf scars to seals]

Solon ('səʊlən) *n.* ?638–?559 B.C., Athenian statesman, who introduced economic, political, and legal reforms. —**Solonian** (səʊ'ləʊnɪən) *or* **Solonic** (səʊ'lɒnɪk) *adj.*

so long *sentence substitute.* **1.** *Inf.* farewell; goodbye. ~*adv.* **2.** *S. African sl.* for the time being; meanwhile.

Solothurn (*German* 'zo:lotʊrn) *n.* **1.** a canton of NW Switzerland. Capital: Solothurn. Pop.: 218 102 (1980). Area: 793 sq. km (306 sq. miles). **2.** a town in NW Switzerland, capital of Solothurn canton, on the Aare River. Pop.: 15 400 (1984 est.). —French name: **Soleure**.

solo whist *n.* a version of whist for four players acting independently, each of whom may bid to win or lose a fixed number of tricks.

solstice ('sɒlstɪs) *n.* **1.** either the shortest day of the year (**winter solstice**) or the longest day of the year (**summer solstice**). **2.** either of the two points on the ecliptic at which the sun is overhead at the tropic of Cancer or Capricorn at the summer and winter solstices. [C13: via OF from L *sōlstitium*, lit.: the (apparent) standing still of the sun, from *sōl* sun + *sistere* to stand still] —**solstitial** (sɒl'stɪʃəl) *adj.*

Solti ('ʃɒltɪ) *n.* Sir **Georg** ('ge:ɔrk). born 1912, British conductor, born in Hungary.

soluble ('sɒljʊbᵊl) *adj.* **1.** (of a substance) capable of being dissolved, esp. easily dissolved. **2.** capable of being solved or answered. [C14: from LL *solūbilis*, from L *solvere* to dissolve] —,**solu'bility** *n.* —'**solubly** *adv.*

solus *Latin.* ('səʊlʊs) *or* (*fem.*) **sola** *adj.* alone; by oneself (formerly used in stage directions).

solute (sɒ'lju:t) *n.* **1.** the substance in a solution that is dissolved. ~*adj.* **2.** *Bot.* loose or unattached; free. [C16: from L *solūtus* free, from *solvere* to release]

solution (sə'lu:ʃən) *n.* **1.** a homogeneous mixture of two or more substances in which the molecules or atoms of the substances are completely dispersed. **2.** the act or process of forming a solution. **3.** the state of being dissolved (esp. in **in solution**). **4.** a mixture of substances in which one or more components are present as small particles with colloidal dimension: *a colloidal solution.* **5.** a specific answer to or way of answering a problem. **6.** the act or process of solving a problem. **7.** *Maths.* **a.** the unique set of values that yield a true statement when substituted for the variables in an equation. **b.** a member of a set of assignments of values to variables under which a given statement is satisfied; a member of a solution set. [C14: from L *solūtiō* an unloosing, from *solūtus*; see SOLUTE]

solution set *n.* another name for **truth set.**

Solutrean (sə'lu:trɪən) *adj.* of or relating to an Upper Palaeolithic culture of Europe. [C19: after *Solutré*, village in central France where traces of this culture were orig. found]

solvation (sɒl'veɪʃən) *n.* the process in which there is some chemical association between the molecules of a solute and those of the solvent.

Solvay process ('sɒlveɪ) *n.* an industrial process for manufacturing sodium carbonate. Carbon dioxide is passed into a solution of sodium chloride saturated with ammonia. Sodium bicarbonate is precipitated and heated to form the carbonate. [C19: after Ernest *Solvay* (1838–1922), Belgian chemist who invented it]

solve (sɒlv) *vb.* (*tr.*) **1.** to find the explanation for or solution to (a mystery, problem, etc.). **2.** *Maths.* **a.** to work out the answer to (a problem). **b.** to obtain the roots of (an equation). [C15: from L *solvere* to loosen] —'**solvable** *adj.*

solvent ('sɒlvənt) *adj.* **1.** capable of meeting financial obligations. **2.** (of a substance, esp. a liquid) capable of dissolving another substance. ~*n.* **3.** a liquid capable of dissolving another substance. **4.** something that solves. [C17: from L *solvēns* releasing, from *solvere* to free] —'**solvency** *n.*

solvent abuse *n.* the deliberate inhaling of intoxicating fumes given off by certain solvents.

Solway Firth ('sɒlweɪ) *n.* an inlet of the Irish Sea between SW Scotland and NW England. Length: about 56 km (35 miles).

Solyman ('sɒlɪmən) *n.* a variant spelling of **Suleiman I.**

Solzhenitsyn (*Russian* səlʒə'nitsin; ,sɒlʒə'nɪtsɪn) *n.* **Alexander Isayevich** (alɪk'sandr i'sajɪvɪtʃ). born 1918,

exiled Soviet novelist. His books include *One Day in the Life of Ivan Denisovich* (1962), *The First Circle* (1968), *Cancer Ward* (1968), *August 1914* (1971), and *The Gulag Archipelago* (1974). His works are critical of the injustices of the Soviet regime and he was imprisoned (1945–53) and exiled to Siberia (1953–56). He was deported to the West from the Soviet Union in 1974: Nobel prize for literature 1970.

Som. *abbrev. for* Somerset.

soma[1] ('səʊmə) *n.*, *pl.* -**mata** (-mətə) *or* -**mas.** the body of an organism, as distinct from the germ cells. [C19: via NL from Gk *sōma* the body]

soma[2] ('səʊmə) *n.* an intoxicating plant juice drink used in Vedic rituals. [from Sansk.]

Somali (səʊ'mɑ:lɪ) *n.* **1.** (*pl.* -**lis** *or* -**li**) a member of a tall dark-skinned people inhabiting Somalia. **2.** the Cushitic language of this people. ~*adj.* **3.** of, relating to, or characteristic of Somalia, the Somalis, or their language.

Somalia (səʊ'mɑ:lɪə) *n.* a republic in NE Africa, on the Indian Ocean and the Gulf of Aden: the north became a British protectorate in 1884; the east and south were established as an Italian protectorate in 1889; gained independence and united as the Somali Republic in 1960. Languages: Arabic, Italian, English, and Somali. Religion: chiefly Sunni Muslim. Currency: Somali shilling. Capital: Mogadiscio. Pop.: 6 110 000 (1987 est.). Area: 637 541 sq. km (246 154 sq. miles). Official name: **Somali Democratic Republic.** —**So'malian** *adj.*, *n.*

Somaliland (səʊ'mɑ:lɪˌlænd) *n.* a former region of E Africa, between the equator and the Gulf of Aden: includes Somalia, Djibouti, and SE Ethiopia.

somatic (səʊ'mætɪk) *adj.* **1.** of or relating to the soma: *somatic cells.* **2.** of or relating to an animal body or body wall as distinct from the viscera, limbs, and head. **3.** of or relating to the human body as distinct from the mind: *a somatic disease.* [C18: from Gk *sōmatikos* concerning the body, from *sōma* the body] —**so'matically** *adv.*

somato- *or before a vowel* **somat-** *combining form.* body: *somatotype.* [from Gk *sōma, sōmat-* body]

somatotype ('səʊmətəˌtaɪp) *n.* a type or classification of physique or body build. See **endomorph, mesomorph, ectomorph.**

sombre *or U.S.* **somber** ('sɒmbə) *adj.* **1.** dismal; melancholy: *a sombre mood.* **2.** dim, gloomy, or shadowy. **3.** (of colour, clothes, etc.) sober, dull, or dark. [C18: from F, from Vulgar L *subumbrāre* (unattested) to shade, from L *sub* beneath + *umbra* shade] —'**sombrely** *or U.S.* '**somberly** *adv.* —'**sombreness** *or U.S.* '**somberness** *n.* —**sombrous** ('sɒmbrəs) *adj.*

sombrero (sɒm'brɛərəʊ) *n.*, *pl.* -**ros.** a hat with a wide brim, as worn in Mexico. [C16: from Sp., from *sombrero de sol* shade from the sun]

some (sʌm; *unstressed* səm) *determiner.* **1. a.** (a) certain unknown or unspecified: *some people never learn.* **b.** (*as pron.; functioning as sing. or pl.*): *some can teach and others can't.* **2. a.** an unknown or unspecified quantity or amount of: *there's some rice on the table; he owns some horses.* **b.** (*as pron.; functioning as sing. or pl.*): *we'll buy some.* **3. a.** a considerable number or amount of: *he lived some years afterwards.* **b.** a little: *show him some respect.* **4.** (*usually stressed*) *Inf.* an impressive or remarkable: *that was some game!* ~*adv.* **5.** about; approximately: *some thirty pounds.* **6.** a certain amount (more) (in **some more** and (*inf.*) **and then some**). **7.** *U.S.*, *not standard.* to a certain degree or extent: *I like him some.* [OE *sum*]

-some[1] *suffix forming adjectives.* characterized by; tending to: *awesome; tiresome.* [OE -*sum*]

-some[2] *suffix forming nouns.* indicating a group of a specified number of members: *threesome.* [OE *sum*, special use of SOME (determiner)]

-some[3] (-səʊm) *n. combining form.* a body: *chromosome.* [from Gk *sōma* the body]

somebody ('sʌmbədɪ) *pron.* **1.** some person; someone. ~*n.*, *pl.* -**bodies. 2.** a person of great importance: *he is somebody in this town.*
▷ *Usage.* See at **everyone.**

someday ('sʌmˌdeɪ) *adv.* at some unspecified time in the (distant) future.

somehow ('sʌmˌhaʊ) *adv.* **1.** in some unspecified way. **2.** Also: **somehow or other.** by any means that are necessary.

someone ('sʌm,wʌn, -wən) *pron.* some person; somebody.
▷ *Usage.* See at **everyone.**

someplace ('sʌm,pleɪs) *adv. U.S. & Canad inf.* in, at, or to some unspecified place or region.

somersault *or* **summersault** ('sʌmə,sɔːlt) *n.* **1. a.** a forward roll in which the head is placed on the ground and the trunk and legs are turned over it. **b.** a similar roll in a backward direction. **2.** an acrobatic feat in which either of these rolls is performed in midair, as in diving or gymnastics. **3.** a complete reversal of opinion, policy, etc. ~*vb.* **4.** (*intr.*) to perform a somersault. [C16: from OF *soubresault*, prob. from OProvençal *sobresaut*, from *sobre* over (from L *super*) + *saut* a jump, leap (from L *saltus*)]

Somerset ('sʌməsɪt, -,sɛt) *n.* a county of SW England, on the Bristol Channel: the Mendip Hills lie in the north and Exmoor in the west; mainly agricultural (esp. dairying and fruit). Administrative centre: Taunton. Pop.: 448 900 (1986 est.). Area: 3451 sq. km (1332 sq. miles).

something ('sʌmθɪŋ) *pron.* **1.** an unspecified or unknown thing; some thing: *take something warm with you.* **2. something or other.** one unspecified thing or an alternative thing. **3.** an unspecified or unknown amount: *something less than a hundred.* **4.** an impressive or important person, thing, or event: *isn't that something?* ~*adv.* **5.** to some degree; a little; somewhat: *to look something like me.* **6.** (foll. by an *adj.*) *Inf.* (intensifier): *it hurts something awful.* **7. something else.** *Sl.*, *chiefly U.S.* a remarkable person or thing.

sometime ('sʌm,taɪm) *adv.* **1.** at some unspecified point of time. ~*adj.* **2.** (*prenominal*) having been at one time; former: *the sometime President.*

sometimes ('sʌm,taɪmz) *adv.* **1.** now and then; from time to time. **2.** *Obs.* formerly; sometime.

someway ('sʌm,weɪ) *adv.* in some unspecified manner.

somewhat ('sʌm,wɒt) *adv.* (*not used with a negative*) rather; a bit: *she found it somewhat odd.*

somewhere ('sʌm,wɛə) *adv.* **1.** in, to, or at some unknown or unspecified place or point: *somewhere in England; somewhere between 3 and 4 o'clock.* **2. get somewhere.** *Inf.* to make progress.

Somme (*French* sɔm) *n.* **1.** a department of N France, in Picardy region. Capital: Amiens. Pop.: 544 570 (1982). Area: 6277 sq. km (2448 sq. miles). **2.** a river in N France, rising in Aisne department and flowing west to Amiens, then northwest to the English Channel: scene of heavy fighting in World War I. Length: 245 km (152 miles).

sommelier ('sʌməl,jeɪ) *n.* a wine waiter. [F: butler, via OF from OProvençal *saumalier* pack-animal driver, from LL *sagma* a packsaddle, from Gk]

somnambulate (sɒm'næmbjʊ,leɪt) *vb.* (*intr.*) to walk while asleep. [C19: from L *somnus* sleep + *ambulāre* to walk] —**som'nambulance** *n.* —**som'nambulant** *adj., n.* —**som,nambu'lation** *n.* —**som'nambu,lator** *n.*

somnambulism (sɒm'næmbjʊ,lɪzəm) *n.* a condition characterized by walking while asleep or in a hypnotic trance. Also called: **noctambulism.** —**som'nambulist** *n.*

somniferous (sɒm'nɪfərəs) *or* **somnific** *adj. Rare.* tending to induce sleep.

somnolent ('sɒmnələnt) *adj.* **1.** drowsy; sleepy. **2.** causing drowsiness. [C15: from L *somnus* sleep] —**'somnolence** *or* **'somnolency** *n.* —**'somnolently** *adv.*

Somnus ('sɒmnəs) *n.* the Roman god of sleep. Greek counterpart: **Hypnos.**

son (sʌn) *n.* **1.** a male offspring; a boy or man in relation to his parents. **2.** a male descendant. **3.** (*often cap.*) a familiar term of address for a boy or man. **4.** a male from a certain country, environment, etc.: *a son of the circus.* ~Related adj.: **filial.** [OE *sunu*] —**'sonless** *adj.*

Son (sʌn) *n. Christianity.* the second person of the Trinity, Jesus Christ.

sonant ('səʊnənt) *adj.* **1.** *Phonetics.* denoting a voiced sound capable of forming a syllable or syllabic nucleus. **2.** inherently possessing, exhibiting, or producing a sound. **3.** *Rare.* resonant; sounding. ~*n.* **4.** *Phonetics.* a voiced sound belonging to the class of frictionless continuants or nasals (l, r, m, n, ŋ) considered from the point of view of being a vowel and, in this capacity, able to form a syllable or syllabic nucleus. [C19: from L *sonāns* sounding, from *sonāre* to make a noise, resound] —**'sonance** *n.*

sonar ('səʊnɑː) *n.* a communication and position-finding device used in underwater navigation and target detection using echolocation. [C20: from *so(und) na(vigation and) r(anging)*]

sonata (sə'nɑːtə) *n.* **1.** an instrumental composition, usually in three or more movements, for piano alone (**piano sonata**) or for any other instrument with or without piano accompaniment (**violin sonata, cello sonata,** etc.). See also **sonata form.** **2.** a one-movement keyboard composition of the baroque period. [C17: from It., from *sonare* to sound, from L]

sonata form *n.* a musical structure consisting of an expanded ternary form whose three sections (exposition, development, and recapitulation), followed by a coda, are characteristic of the first movement in a sonata, symphony, string quartet, concerto, etc.

sondage (sɒn'dɑːʒ) *n., pl.* **-dages** (-'dɑːʒɪz, -'dɑːʒ). *Archaeol.* a deep trial trench for inspecting stratigraphy. [C20: from F: a sounding, from *sonder* to sound]

sonde (sɒnd) *n.* a rocket, balloon, or probe used for observing in the upper atmosphere. [C20: from F: plummet, plumb line; see SOUND³]

Sondheim ('sɒndhaɪm) *n.* **Stephen (Joshua).** born 1930, U.S. songwriter. He wrote the lyrics for *West Side Story* (1957), the score for *Company* (1971), and both for *A Little Night Music* (1973).

sone (səʊn) *n.* a unit of loudness equal to 40 phons. [C20: from L *sonus* a sound]

son et lumière ('sɒn eɪ 'luːmɪˌɛə) *n.* an entertainment staged at night at a famous building, historical site, etc., whereby the history of the location is presented by means of lighting effects, sound effects, and narration. [F, lit.: sound and light]

song (sɒŋ) *n.* **1. a.** a piece of music, usually employing a verbal text, composed for the voice, esp. one intended for performance by a soloist. **b.** the whole repertory of such pieces. **c.** (*as modifier*): *a song book.* **2.** poetical composition; poetry. **3.** the characteristic tuneful call or sound made by certain birds or insects. **4.** the act or process of singing: *they raised their voices in song.* **5. for a song.** at a bargain price. **6. on song.** *Brit. inf.* performing at peak efficiency or ability. [OE *sang*]

Song (sɒŋ) *n.* the Pinyin transliteration of the Chinese name for **Sung.**

song and dance *n. Inf.* **1.** *Brit.* a fuss, esp. one that is unnecessary. **2.** *U.S. & Canad.* a long or elaborate story or explanation.

songbird ('sɒŋ,bɜːd) *n.* **1.** any of a suborder of passerine birds having highly developed vocal organs and, in most, a musical call. **2.** any bird having a musical call.

song cycle *n.* any of several groups of songs written during and after the Romantic period, each series relating a story or grouped around a central motif.

Songhua ('sʌŋ'wɑː) *n.* a river in NE China, rising in SE Jilin province and flowing north and northeast to the Amur River near Tongjiang: the chief river of Manchuria and largest tributary of the Amur; frozen from November to April. Length: over 1300 km (800 miles). Also called: **Sungari.**

Song Koi *or* **Song Coi** ('sɒŋ 'kɔɪ) *n.* transliteration of the Vietnamese name for the **Red River** (sense 3).

songololo (,sɒŋɡə'lɒlə) *n., pl.* **-los.** *S. African.* a millipede. [from Bantu, from *ukusonga* to roll up]

songster ('sɒŋstə) *n.* **1.** a singer or poet. **2.** a singing bird; songbird. —**'songstress** *fem. n.*

song thrush *n.* a common Old World thrush with a spotted breast, noted for its song.

songwriter ('sɒŋ,raɪtə) *n.* a person who composes songs in a popular idiom.

sonic ('sɒnɪk) *adj.* **1.** of, involving, or producing sound. **2.** having a speed about equal to that of sound in air. [C20: from L *sonus* sound]

sonic barrier *n.* another name for **sound barrier.**

sonic boom *n.* a loud explosive sound caused by the shock wave of an aircraft, etc., travelling at supersonic speed.

sonic depth finder *n.* an instrument for detecting the depth of water or of a submerged object by means of sound waves; Fathometer.

son-in-law *n., pl.* **sons-in-law.** the husband of one's daughter.

sonnet ('sɒnɪt) *Prosody.* ~*n.* **1.** a verse form consisting of 14 lines in iambic pentameter with a fixed rhyme scheme, usually divided into octave and sestet or, in the English form, into three quatrains and a couplet. ~*vb.* **2.**

(*intr.*) to compose sonnets. **3.** (*tr.*) to celebrate in a sonnet. [C16: via It. from OProvençal *sonet* a little poem, from *son* song, from L *sonus* a sound]

sonneteer (ˌsɒnɪˈtɪə) *n.* a writer of sonnets.

sonny (ˈsʌnɪ) *n.*, *pl.* **-nies.** *Often patronizing.* a familiar term of address to a boy or man.

sonobuoy (ˈsəʊnəˌbɔɪ) *n.* a buoy equipped to detect underwater noises and transmit them by radio. [SONIC + BUOY]

Son of Man *n. Bible.* a title of Jesus Christ.

Sonora (*Spanish* soˈnora) *n.* a state of NW Mexico, on the Gulf of California: consists of a narrow coastal plain rising inland to the Sierra Madre Occidental; an important mining area in colonial times. Capital: Hermosillo. Pop.: 1 661 898 (1983 est.). Area: 184 934 sq. km (71 403 sq. miles).

sonorant (ˈsɒnərənt) *n. Phonetics.* **1.** one of the frictionless continuants or nasals (l, r, m, n, ŋ) having consonantal or vocalic functions depending on its situation within the syllable. **2.** either of the two consonants represented in English orthography by *w* or *y* and regarded as either consonantal or vocalic articulations of the vowels (iː) and (uː).

sonorous (səˈnɔːrəs, ˈsɒnərəs) *adj.* **1.** producing or capable of producing sound. **2.** (of language, sound, etc.) deep or resonant. **3.** (esp. of speech) high-flown; grandiloquent. [C17: from L *sonōrus* loud, from *sonor* a noise] —**sonority** (səˈnɒrɪtɪ) *n.* —**soˈnorously** *adv.* —**soˈnorousness** *n.*

sonsy *or* **sonsie** (ˈsɒnsɪ) *adj.* **-sier, -siest.** *Scot., Irish, & English dialect.* **1.** plump; buxom. **2.** cheerful; good-natured. **3.** lucky. [C16: from Gaelic *sonas* good fortune]

Soo Canals (suː) *pl. n.* **the.** the two ship canals linking Lakes Superior and Huron. There is a canal on the Canadian and on the U.S. side of the rapids of the St Mary's River. See also **Sault Sainte Marie.**

Soochow (ˈsuːˈtʃaʊ) *n.* a variant transliteration of the Chinese name for **Suzhou.**

sook (sʊk) *n.* **1.** *SW English dialect.* a baby. **2.** *Derog.* a coward. [?from OE *sūcan* to suck, infl. by Welsh *swci swead* tame]

sool (suːl) *vb.* (*tr.*) *Austral. & N.Z. sl.* **1.** to incite (esp. a dog) to attack. **2.** to attack. —**ˈsooler** *n.*

soon (suːn) *adv.* **1.** in or after a short time; in a little while; before long. **2. as soon as.** at the very moment that: *as soon as she saw him.* **3. as soon ... as.** used to indicate that the second alternative is not preferable to the first: *I'd just as soon go by train as drive.* [OE *sōna*]

sooner (ˈsuːnə) *adv.* **1.** the comparative of **soon:** *he came sooner than I thought.* **2.** rather; in preference: *I'd sooner die than give up.* **3. no sooner ... than.** immediately after or when: *no sooner had he got home than the rain stopped.* **4. sooner or later.** eventually; inevitably.

Soong *or* **Song** (sʊŋ) *n.* an influential Chinese family, notably **Soong Ch'ing-ling** (1890–1981), who married **Sun Yat-sen** and became a vice-chairman of the People's Republic of China (1959); and **Soong Mei-ling** (born 1898), who married **Chiang Kai-shek.**

soot (sʊt) *n.* **1.** finely divided carbon deposited from flames during the incomplete combustion of organic substances such as coal. ~*vb.* **2.** (*tr.*) to cover with soot. [OE *sōt*]

sooth (suːθ) *Arch. or poetic.* ~*n.* **1.** truth or reality (esp. in **in sooth**). **2.** true or real. [OE *sōth*]

soothe (suːð) *vb.* **1.** (*tr.*) to make calm or tranquil. **2.** (*tr.*) to relieve or assuage (pain, longing, etc.). **3.** (*intr.*) to bring tranquillity or relief. [C16 (in the sense: to mollify): from OE *sōthian* to prove] —**ˈsoother** *n.* —**ˈsoothing** *adj.* —**ˈsoothingly** *adv.* —**ˈsoothingness** *n.*

soothsayer (ˈsuːθˌseɪə) *n.* a seer or prophet.

sooty (ˈsʊtɪ) *adj.* **sootier, sootiest.** **1.** covered with soot. **2.** resembling or consisting of soot. —**ˈsootily** *adv.* —**ˈsootiness** *n.*

sop (sɒp) *n.* **1.** (*often pl.*) food soaked in a liquid before being eaten. **2.** a concession, bribe, etc., given to placate or mollify: *a sop to one's feelings.* **3.** *Inf.* a stupid or weak person. ~*vb.* **sopping, sopped.** **4.** (*tr.*) to dip or soak (food) in liquid. **5.** (when *intr.*, often foll. by *in*) to soak or be soaked. **6.** (*tr.*; often foll. by *up*) to mop or absorb (liquid) as with a sponge. [OE *sopp*]

SOP *abbrev. for* standard operating procedure.

sop. *abbrev. for* soprano.

sophism (ˈsɒfɪzəm) *n.* an instance of sophistry. Cf. **paralogism.** [C14: from L *sophisma*, from Gk: ingenious trick, from *sophizesthai* to use clever deceit, from *sophos* wise]

sophist (ˈsɒfɪst) *n.* **1.** a person who uses clever or quibbling but unsound arguments. **2.** one of the pre-Socratic philosophers who were prepared to enter into debate on any subject however specious. [C16: from L *sophista*, from Gk *sophistēs* a wise man, from *sophizesthai* to act craftily]

sophistic (səˈfɪstɪk) *or* **sophistical** *adj.* **1.** of or relating to sophists or sophistry. **2.** consisting of sophisms or sophistry; specious. —**soˈphistically** *adv.*

sophisticate *vb.* (səˈfɪstɪˌkeɪt). **1.** (*tr.*) to make (someone) less natural or innocent, as by education. **2.** to pervert or corrupt (an argument, etc.) by sophistry. **3.** (*tr.*) to make more complex or refined. **4.** *Rare.* to falsify (a text, etc.) by alterations. ~*n.* (səˈfɪstɪˌkeɪt, -kɪt). **5.** a sophisticated person. [C14: from Med. L *sophisticāre*, from L *sophisticus* sophistic] —**soˌphistiˈcation** *n.* —**soˈphistiˌcator** *n.*

sophisticated (səˈfɪstɪˌkeɪtɪd) *adj.* **1.** having refined or cultured tastes and habits. **2.** appealing to sophisticates: *a sophisticated restaurant.* **3.** unduly refined or cultured. **4.** pretentiously or superficially wise. **5.** (of machines, methods, etc.) complex and refined.

sophistry (ˈsɒfɪstrɪ) *n.*, *pl.* **-ries.** **1. a.** a method of argument that is seemingly plausible though actually invalid and misleading. **b.** the art of using such arguments. **2.** subtle but unsound or fallacious reasoning. **3.** an instance of this.

Sophocles (ˈsɒfəˌkliːz) *n.* ?496–406 B.C., Greek dramatist; author of seven extant tragedies–*Ajax, Antigone, Oedipus Rex, Trachiniae, Electra, Philoctetes,* and *Oedipus at Colonus.* —**Sophoclean** (ˌsɒfəˈkliːən) *adj.*

sophomore (ˈsɒfəˌmɔː) *n. Chiefly U.S. & Canad.* a second-year student. [C17: ?from earlier *sophumer*, from *sophum*, var. of SOPHISM, + -ER[1]]

Sophy *or* **Sophi** (ˈsəʊfɪ) *n.*, *pl.* **-phies.** (formerly) a title of the Persian monarchs. [C16: from L *sophī* wise men, from Gk *sophos* wise]

-sophy *n. combining form.* indicating knowledge or an intellectual system: *philosophy.* [from Gk, from *sophia* wisdom, from *sophos* wise] —**-sophic** *or* **-sophical** *adj. combining form.*

soporific (ˌsɒpəˈrɪfɪk) *adj. also* (*arch.*) **soporiferous.** **1.** inducing sleep. **2.** drowsy; sleepy. ~*n.* **3.** a drug or other agent that induces sleep. [C17: from F, from L *sopor* sleep + -FIC]

sopping (ˈsɒpɪŋ) *adj.* completely soaked; wet through. Also: **sopping wet.**

soppy (ˈsɒpɪ) *adj.* **-pier, -piest.** **1.** wet or soggy. **2.** *Brit. inf.* silly or sentimental. **3. soppy on.** *Brit. inf.* foolishly charmed or affected by. —**ˈsoppily** *adv.* —**ˈsoppiness** *n.*

sopranino (ˌsɒprəˈniːnəʊ) *n.*, *pl.* **-nos. a.** the instrument with the highest possible pitch in a family of instruments. **b.** (*as modifier*): *a sopranino recorder.* [It., dim. of SOPRANO]

soprano (səˈprɑːnəʊ) *n.*, *pl.* **-pranos** *or* **-prani** (-ˈprɑːniː). **1.** the highest adult female voice. **2.** the voice of a young boy before puberty. **3.** a singer with such a voice. **4.** the highest part of a piece of harmony. **5. a.** the highest or second highest instrument in a family of instruments. **b.** (*as modifier*): *a soprano saxophone.* ~See also **treble.** [C18: from It., from *sopra* above, from L *suprā*]

soprano clef *n.* the clef that establishes middle C as being on the bottom line of the staff.

Sorata (*Spanish* soˈrata) *n. Mount.* a mountain in W Bolivia, in the Andes: the highest mountain in the Cordillera Real, with two peaks, Ancohuma, 6550 m (21 490 ft.), and Illampu, 6485 m (21 276 ft.).

sorb (sɔːb) *n.* **1.** another name for **service tree.** **2.** any of various related trees, esp. the mountain ash. This is also called: **sorb apple.** the fruit of any of these trees. [C16: from L *sorbus*]

sorbefacient (ˌsɔːbɪˈfeɪʃənt) *adj.* **1.** inducing absorption. ~*n.* **2.** a sorbefacient drug. [C19: from L *sorbē(re)* to absorb + -FACIENT]

sorbet (ˈsɔːbeɪ, -beɪ) *n.* **1.** a water ice made from fruit juice, egg whites, etc. **2.** a U.S. word for **sherbet** (sense 1). [C16: from F, from OIt. *sorbetto*, from Turkish *şerbet*, from Ar. *sharbah* a drink]

sorbic acid ('sɔ:bɪk) *n.* a white crystalline carboxylic acid found in berries of the mountain ash and used to inhibit the growth of moulds and as an additive (**E 200**) for certain synthetic coatings. [C19: from SORB (the tree), from its discovery in berries of the mountain ash]

sorbitol ('sɔ:bɪ,tɒl) *n.* a white crystalline alcohol, found in certain fruits and berries and manufactured by the catalytic hydrogenation of sucrose: used as a sweetener (**E 420**) and in the manufacture of ascorbic acid and synthetic resins. [C19: from SORB + -ITOL]

Sorbonne (*French* sɔrbɔn) *n.* **the.** a part of the University of Paris containing the faculties of science and literature: founded in 1253 by Robert de Sorbon as a theological college; given to the university in 1808.

sorbo rubber ('sɔ:bəʊ) *n. Brit.* a spongy form of rubber. [C20: from ABSORB]

sorcerer ('sɔ:sərə) *or* (*fem.*) **sorceress** ('sɔ:sərɪs) *n.* a person who seeks to control and use magic powers; a wizard or magician. [C16: from OF *sorcier*, from Vulgar L *sortiārius* (unattested) caster of lots, from L *sors* lot]

sorcery ('sɔ:sərɪ) *n., pl.* **-ceries.** the art, practices, or spells of magic, esp. black magic. [C13: from OF *sorcerie*, from *sorcier* SORCERER]

Sordello (*Italian* sor'dɛllo) *n.* born ?1200, Italian troubadour.

sordid ('sɔ:dɪd) *adj.* **1.** dirty, foul, or squalid. **2.** degraded; vile; base. **3.** selfish and grasping: *sordid avarice.* [C16: from L *sordidus*, from *sordēre* to be dirty] — 'sordidly *adv.* —'sordidness *n.*

sordino (sɔ:'di:nəʊ) *n., pl.* **-ni** (-ni:). **1.** a mute for a stringed or brass musical instrument. **2.** any of the dampers in a piano. **3. con sordino** *or* **sordini.** a musical direction to play with a mute. **4. senza sordino** *or* **sordini.** a musical direction to remove or play without the mute or (on the piano) with the sustaining pedal pressed down. [It.: from *sordo* deaf, from L *surdus*]

sore (sɔ:) *adj.* **1.** (esp. of a wound, injury, etc.) painfully sensitive; tender. **2.** causing annoyance: *a sore point.* **3.** resentful; irked. **4.** urgent; pressing: *in sore need.* **5.** (*postpositive*) grieved; distressed. **6.** causing grief or sorrow. ~*n.* **7.** a painful or sensitive wound, injury, etc. **8.** any cause of distress or vexation. ~*adv.* **9.** *Arch.* direly; sorely (now only in such phrases as **sore afraid**). [OE *sār*] — 'soreness *n.*

sorehead ('sɔ:,hɛd) *n. Inf., chiefly U.S. & Canad.* a peevish or disgruntled person.

sorely ('sɔ:lɪ) *adv.* **1.** painfully or grievously: *sorely wounded.* **2.** pressingly or greatly: *to be sorely taxed.*

sorghum ('sɔ:gəm) *n.* any grass of the Old World genus *Sorghum,* having glossy seeds: cultivated for grain, hay, and as a source of syrup. [C16: from NL, from It. *sorgo,* prob. from Vulgar L *Syricum grānum* (unattested) Syrian grain]

Sorocaba (*Portuguese* soro'kaba) *n.* a city in S Brazil, in São Paulo state: industrial centre. Pop.: 254 718 (1980).

soroptimist (sə'rɒptɪmɪst) *n.* a member of Soroptimist International, an organization of clubs for professional and executive businesswomen.

sorority (sə'rɒrɪtɪ) *n., pl.* **-ties.** *Chiefly U.S.* a social club or society for university women. [C16: from Med. L *sorōritās,* from L *soror* sister]

sorption ('sɔ:pʃən) *n.* the process in which one substance takes up or holds another; adsorption or absorption. [C20: back formation from ABSORPTION, ADSORPTION]

sorrel[1] ('sɒrəl) *n.* **1. a.** a light brown to brownish-orange colour. **b.** (*as adj.*): *a sorrel carpet.* **2.** a horse of this colour. [C15: from OF *sorel,* from *sor* a reddish brown, of Gmc origin]

sorrel[2] ('sɒrəl) *n.* **1.** any of several plants of Eurasia and North America, having acid-tasting leaves used in salads and sauces. **2.** short for **wood sorrel.** [C14: from OF *surele,* from *sur* sour, of Gmc origin]

Sorrento (sə'rɛntəʊ; *Italian* sor'rɛnto) *n.* a port in SW Italy, in Campania on a mountainous peninsula between the Bay of Naples and the Gulf of Salerno: a resort since Roman times. Pop.: 17 301 (1981 est.).

sorrow ('sɒrəʊ) *n.* **1.** the feeling of sadness, grief, or regret associated with loss, bereavement, sympathy for another's suffering, etc. **2.** a particular cause or source of this. **3.** Also called: **sorrowing.** the outward expression of grief or sadness. ~*vb.* **4.** (*intr.*) to mourn or grieve. [OE *sorg*] —'sorrowful *adj.* —'sorrowfully *adv.* —'sorrowfulness *n.*

sorry ('sɒrɪ) *adj.* **-rier, -riest.** **1.** (*usually postpositive; often foll. by for*) feeling or expressing pity, sympathy, grief, or regret: *I feel sorry for him.* **2.** pitiful, wretched, or deplorable: *a sorry sight.* **3.** poor; paltry: *a sorry excuse.* **4.** affected by sorrow; sad. **5.** causing sorrow or sadness. ~*interj.* **6.** an exclamation expressing apology. [OE *sārig*] —'sorrily *adv.* —'sorriness *n.*

sort (sɔ:t) *n.* **1.** a class, group, kind, etc., as distinguished by some common quality or characteristic. **2.** *Inf.* a type of character, nature, etc.: *he's a good sort.* **3.** *Austral. sl.* a person, esp. a girl. **4.** a more or less definable or adequate example: *it's a sort of review.* **5.** (*often pl.*) *Printing.* any of the individual characters making up a fount of type. **6.** *Arch.* manner; way: *in this sort we struggled home.* **7. after a sort.** to some extent. **8. of sorts** *or* **of a sort. a.** of an inferior kind. **b.** of an indefinite kind. **9. out of sorts.** not in normal good health, temper, etc. **10. sort of.** in some way or other; as it were; rather. ~*vb.* **11.** (*tr.*) to arrange according to class, type, etc. **12.** (*tr.*) to put (something) into working order. **13.** to arrange (computer information) by machine in an order convenient to the user. **14.** (*intr.*) *Arch.* to agree; accord. [C14: from OF, from Med. L *sors* kind, from L: fate] —'sortable *adj.* —'sorter *n.*

▷ **Usage.** See at **kind**[2].

sortie ('sɔ:tɪ) *n.* **1. a.** (of troops, etc.) the act of attacking from a contained or besieged position. **b.** the troops doing this. **2.** an operational flight made by one aircraft. ~*vb.* **-tieing, -tied. 3.** (*intr.*) to make a sortie. [C17: from F: a going out, from *sortir* to go out]

sortilege ('sɔ:tɪlɪdʒ) *n.* the act or practice of divination by drawing lots. [C14: via OF from Med. L *sortilegium,* from L *sortilegus* a soothsayer, from *sors* fate + *legere* to select]

sort out *vb.* (*tr., adv.*) **1.** to find a solution to (a problem, etc.), esp. to make clear or tidy: *to sort out the mess.* **2.** to take or separate, as from a larger group: *to sort out the likely ones.* **3.** to organize into an orderly and disciplined group. **4.** *Inf.* to beat or punish.

SOS *n.* **1.** an internationally recognized distress signal in which the letters SOS are repeatedly spelt out, as by radiotelegraphy: used esp. by ships and aircraft. **2.** a message broadcast in an emergency for people otherwise unobtainable. **3.** *Inf.* a call for help.

sosatie (sə'sɑ:tɪ) *n. S. African.* curried meat on skewers. [from Afrik., from Du.]

Sosnowiec (*Polish* sɔs'nɔvjɛts) *n.* an industrial town in S Poland. Pop.: 255 000 (1985).

so-so *Inf.* ~*adj.* **1.** (*postpositive*) neither good nor bad. ~*adv.* **2.** in an average or indifferent manner.

sostenuto (,sɒstə'nu:təʊ) *adj., adv. Music.* to be performed in a smooth sustained manner. [C18: from It., from *sostenere* to sustain, from L *sustinēre*]

sot (sɒt) *n.* **1.** a habitual or chronic drunkard. **2.** a person stupefied by or as if by drink. [OE, from Med. L *sottus*] —'sottish *adj.*

soteriology (sɒ,tɪərɪ'ɒlədʒɪ) *n. Christian theol.* the doctrine of salvation. [C19: from Gk *sōtēria* deliverance (from *sōtēr* a saviour) + -LOGY]

sotto voce ('sɒtəʊ 'vəʊtʃɪ) *adv.* in an undertone. [C18: from It.: under (one's) voice]

sou (su:) *n.* **1.** a former French coin of low denomination. **2.** a very small amount of money: *I haven't a sou.* [C19: from F, from OF *sol,* from L: SOLIDUS]

soubrette (su:'brɛt) *n.* **1.** a minor female role in comedy, often that of a pert lady's maid. **2.** any pert or flirtatious girl. [C18: from F: maidservant, from Provençal, from *soubret* conceited, from *soubra* to exceed, from L *superāre* to surmount]

soubriquet ('su:brɪ,keɪ) *n.* a variant spelling of **sobriquet.**

Soudan (sudã) *n.* the French name for the **Sudan.**

soufflé ('su:fleɪ) *n.* **1.** a light fluffy dish made with beaten egg whites combined with cheese, fish, etc. **2.** a similar sweet or savoury cold dish, set with gelatin. ~*adj. also* **souffléed. 3.** made light and puffy, as by beating and cooking. [C19: from F, from *souffler* to blow, from L *sufflāre*]

Soufrière (*French* sufrjɛr) *n.* **1.** a volcano on N St Vincent: erupted in 1902, killing about 2000 people. Height: 1234 m (4048 ft.). **2.** a volcano in the West Indies, on S Montserrat: the highest point on the island. Height: 915 m

(3002 ft.). **3.** a volcano in the French West Indies, on Guadeloupe. Height: 1484 m (4869 ft.).

sough (sau) *vb.* **1.** (*intr.*) (esp. of the wind) to make a sighing sound. ~*n.* **2.** a soft continuous murmuring sound. [OE *swōgan* to resound]

sought (sɔːt) *vb.* the past tense and past participle of **seek.**

souk (suːk) *n.* an open-air marketplace in Muslim countries, esp. North Africa and the Middle East. [from Ar.]

soul (səʊl) *n.* **1.** the spirit or immaterial part of man, the seat of human personality, intellect, will, and emotions: regarded as an entity that survives the body after death. **2.** *Christianity.* the spiritual part of a person, capable of redemption from sin through divine grace. **3.** the essential part or fundamental nature of anything. **4.** a person's feelings or moral nature. **5. a.** Also called: **soul music.** a type of Black music resulting from the addition of jazz, gospel, and pop elements to the urban blues style. **b.** (*as modifier*): *a soul singer.* **6.** (*modifier*) of or relating to Black Americans and their culture: *soul food.* **7.** nobility of spirit or temperament: *a man of great soul.* **8.** an inspiring or leading figure, as of a movement. **9. the life and soul.** *Inf.* a person regarded as the main source of gaiety, merriment, etc.: *the life and soul of the party.* **10.** a person regarded as typifying some characteristic or quality: *the soul of discretion.* **11.** a person; individual: *an honest soul.* **12. upon my soul!** an exclamation of surprise. [OE *sāwol*]

soul-destroying *adj.* (of an occupation, situation, etc.) unremittingly monotonous.

soul food *n. Inf.* food, such as chitterlings, yams, etc., traditionally eaten by U.S. Blacks.

soulful ('səʊlfʊl) *adj.* expressing profound thoughts or feelings. —'**soulfully** *adv.* —'**soulfulness** *n.*

soulless ('səʊllɪs) *adj.* **1.** lacking humanizing qualities or influences; mechanical: *soulless work.* **2.** (of a person) lacking in sensitivity or nobility. —'**soullessness** *n.*

soul mate *n.* a person for whom one has a deep affinity, esp. a lover, wife, husband, etc.

soul-searching *n.* **1.** deep or critical examination of one's motives, actions, beliefs, etc. ~*adj.* **2.** displaying the characteristics of this.

Soult (*French* sult) *n.* **Nicolas Jean de Dieu** (nikɔla ʒɑ̃ dɔdyø). 1769–1851, French marshal under Napoleon I. Under Louis-Philippe he was minister of war (1830–34; 1840–44).

sound[1] (saʊnd) *n.* **1. a.** a periodic disturbance in the pressure or density of a fluid or in the elastic strain in a solid, produced by a vibrating object. It travels as longitudinal waves. **b.** (*as modifier*): *a sound wave.* **2.** the sensation produced by such a periodic disturbance in the organs of hearing. **3.** anything that can be heard. **4.** (*modifier*) of or relating to radio as distinguished from television: *sound broadcasting.* **5.** a particular instance or type of sound: *the sound of running water.* **6.** volume or quality of sound: *a radio with poor sound.* **7.** the area or distance over which something can be heard: *within the sound of Big Ben.* **8.** impression or implication: *I don't like the sound of that.* **9.** (*often pl.*) *Sl.* music, esp. rock, jazz, or pop. ~*vb.* **10.** to cause (an instrument, etc.) to make a sound or (of an instrument, etc.) to emit a sound. **11.** to announce or be announced by a sound: *to sound the alarm.* **12.** (*intr.*) (of a sound) to be heard. **13.** (*intr.*) to resonate with a certain quality or intensity: *to sound loud.* **14.** (*copula*) to give the impression of being as specified: *to sound reasonable.* **15.** (*tr.*) to pronounce distinctly or audibly: *to sound one's consonants.* [C13: from OF *suner* to make a sound, from L *sonāre*, from *sonus* a sound] —'**soundable** *adj.*

sound[2] (saʊnd) *adj.* **1.** free from damage, injury, decay, etc. **2.** firm; substantial: *a sound basis.* **3.** financially safe or stable: *a sound investment.* **4.** showing good judgment or reasoning; wise: *sound advice.* **5.** valid, logical, or justifiable: *a sound argument.* **6.** holding approved beliefs; ethically correct; honest. **7.** (of sleep) deep; peaceful; unbroken. **8.** thorough: *a sound examination.* ~*adv.* **9.** soundly; deeply: now archaic except when applied to sleep. [OE *sund*] —'**soundly** *adv.* —'**soundness** *n.*

sound[3] (saʊnd) *vb.* **1.** to measure the depth of (a well, the sea, etc.) by plumb line, sonar, etc. **2.** to seek to discover (someone's views, etc.), as by questioning. **3.** (*intr.*) (of a whale, etc.) to dive downwards swiftly and deeply. **4.**

Med. **a.** to probe or explore (a bodily cavity or passage) by means of a sound. **b.** to examine (a patient) by means of percussion and auscultation. ~*n.* **5.** *Med.* an instrument for insertion into a bodily cavity or passage to dilate strictures, dislodge foreign material, etc. ~See also **sound out.** [C14: from OF *sonder*, from *sonde* sounding line, prob. of Gmc origin] —'**sounder** *n.*

sound[4] (saʊnd) *n.* **1.** a relatively narrow channel between two larger areas of sea or between an island and the mainland. **2.** an inlet or deep bay of the sea. **3.** the air bladder of a fish. [OE *sund* swimming, narrow sea]

Sound (saʊnd) *n.* **the.** a strait between SW Sweden and Sjælland (Denmark), linking the Kattegat with the Baltic: busy shipping lane. Length: 113 km (70 miles). Narrowest point: 5 km (3 miles). Swedish and Danish name: **Øresund.**

sound barrier *n.* (not in technical usage) a hypothetical barrier to flight at or above the speed of sound, when a sudden large increase in drag occurs. Also called: **sonic barrier.**

soundbox ('saʊnd,bɒks) *n.* the resonating chamber of the hollow body of a violin, guitar, etc.

sound effect *n.* any sound artificially produced, reproduced from a recording, etc., to create a theatrical effect, as in plays, films, etc.

sounding[1] ('saʊndɪŋ) *adj.* **1.** resounding; resonant. **2.** having an imposing sound and little content; pompous: *sounding phrases.*

sounding[2] ('saʊndɪŋ) *n.* **1.** (*sometimes pl.*) the act or process of measuring depth of water or examining the bottom of a river, lake, etc., as with a sounding line. **2.** an observation or measurement of atmospheric conditions, as made using a sonde. **3.** (*often pl.*) measurements taken by sounding. **4.** (*pl.*) a place where a sounding line will reach the bottom, esp. less than 100 fathoms in depth.

sounding board *n.* **1.** Also called: **soundboard.** a thin wooden board in a violin, piano, etc., serving to amplify the vibrations produced by the strings passing across it. **2.** Also called: **soundboard.** a thin screen suspended over a pulpit, stage, etc., to reflect sound towards an audience. **3.** a person, group, experiment, etc., used to test a new idea, policy, etc.

sounding line *n.* a line marked off to indicate its length and having a **sounding lead** at one end. It is dropped over the side of a vessel to determine the depth of the water.

soundless ('saʊndlɪs) *adj.* extremely still or silent. —'**soundlessness** *n.*

sound out *vb.* (*tr., adv.*) to question (someone) in order to discover (opinions, facts, etc.).

soundpost ('saʊnd,pəʊst) *n. Music.* a small wooden post in guitars, violins, etc., that joins the front to the back and helps support the bridge.

soundproof ('saʊnd,pruːf) *adj.* **1.** not penetrable by sound. ~*vb.* **2.** (*tr.*) to render soundproof.

sound spectrograph *n.* an electronic instrument that produces a record (**sound spectrogram**) of the frequencies and intensities of the components of a sound.

sound system *n.* **1.** any system of sounds, as in the speech of a language. **2.** integrated equipment for producing amplified sound, as in a hi-fi or mobile disco, or a public-address system on stage.

soundtrack ('saʊnd,træk) *n.* **1.** the recorded sound accompaniment to a film. **2.** a narrow strip along the side of a spool of film, which carries the sound accompaniment.

sound wave *n.* a wave that propagates sound.

soup (suːp) *n.* **1.** a liquid food made by boiling or simmering meat, fish, vegetables, etc. **2.** *Inf.* a photographic developer. **3.** *Inf.* anything resembling soup, esp. thick fog. **4.** a slang name for **nitroglycerin. 5. in the soup.** *Sl.* in trouble or difficulties. [C17: from OF *soupe*, from LL *suppa*, of Gmc origin] —'**soupy** *adj.*

soupçon *French* (supsɔ̃) *n.* a slight amount; dash. [C18: from F, ult. from L *suspicio* SUSPICION]

Souphanouvong (,suːfænuːˈvɒŋ) *n.* **Prince.** born 1902, Laotian statesman; president of Laos from 1975.

soup kitchen *n.* **1.** a place or mobile stall where food and drink, esp. soup, is served to destitute people. **2.** *Mil.* a mobile kitchen.

soup plate *n.* a deep plate with a wide rim, used esp. for drinking soup.

soup up *vb.* (*tr., adv.*) *Sl.* to modify (a car or motorcycle engine) in order to increase its power. Also: **hot up,** (esp. U.S. and Canad.) **hop up.**

sour ('sauə) *adj.* **1.** having or denoting a sharp biting taste like that of lemon juice or vinegar. **2.** made acid or bad, as in the case of milk, by the action of microorganisms. **3.** having a rancid or unwholesome smell. **4.** (of a person's temperament) sullen, morose, or disagreeable. **5.** (esp. of the weather) harsh and unpleasant. **6.** disagreeable; distasteful: *a sour experience.* **7.** (of land, etc.) lacking in fertility, esp. due to excessive acidity. **8.** (of petrol, gas, etc.) containing a relatively large amount of sulphur compounds. **9. go** *or* **turn sour.** to become unfavourable or inharmonious: *his marriage went sour.* ~*n.* **10.** something sour. **11.** *Chiefly U.S.* an iced drink usually made with spirits, lemon juice, and ice: *a whiskey sour.* **12.** an acid used in bleaching clothes or in curing skins. ~*vb.* **13.** to make or become sour. [OE *sūr*] —'**sourish** *adj.* —'**sourly** *adv.* —'**sourness** *n.*

Sour (suə) *n.* a variant spelling of **Sur.**

source (sɔ:s) *n.* **1.** the point or place from which something originates. **2. a.** a spring that forms the starting point of a stream. **b.** the area where the headwaters of a river rise. **3.** a person, group, etc., that creates, issues, or originates something: *the source of a complaint.* **4. a.** any person, book, organization, etc., from which information, evidence, etc., is obtained. **b.** (*as modifier*): *source material.* **5.** anything, such as a story or work of art, that provides a model or inspiration for a later work. **6. at source.** at the point of origin. ~*vb.* **7.** (*tr.*) to establish an originator or source of (a product, etc.). [C14: from OF *sors*, from *sourdre* to spring forth, from L *surgere* to rise]

source program *n.* an original computer program written by a programmer that is converted into the equivalent object program, written in machine language.

sour cherry *n.* **1.** a Eurasian tree with white flowers: cultivated for its tart red fruits. **2.** the fruit.

sour cream *n.* cream soured by lactic acid bacteria, used in making salads, dips, etc.

sourdough ('sauə,dəʊ) *Dialect.* ~*adj.* **1.** (of bread) made with fermented dough used as leaven. ~*n.* **2.** (in the Western U.S., Canada, and Alaska) an old-time prospector or pioneer.

sour gourd *n.* **1.** a large tree of N Australia, having gourdlike fruit. **2.** the acid-tasting fruit. **3.** the fruit of the baobab tree.

sour grapes *n.* (*functioning as sing.*) the attitude of affecting to despise something because one cannot have it oneself.

sourpuss ('sauə,pus) *n. Inf.* a person who is habitually gloomy or sullen.

sourveld ('sauə,felt) *n.* (in South Africa) a type of grazing characterized by long coarse grass. [from Afrik. *suur* sour + *veld* grassland]

Sousa ('su:zə) *n.* **John Philip.** 1854–1932, U.S. bandmaster and composer of military marches, such as *The Stars and Stripes Forever* (1897) and *The Liberty Bell* (1893).

sousaphone ('su:zə,fəʊn) *n.* a large tuba that encircles the player's body and has a bell facing forwards. [C20: after J. P. SOUSA] —'**sousa,phonist** *n.*

souse (saus) *vb.* **1.** to plunge (something) into water or other liquid. **2.** to drench or be drenched. **3.** (*tr.*) to pour or dash (liquid) over (a person or thing). **4.** to steep or cook (food) in a marinade. **5.** (*tr.*) *Sl.* to make drunk. ~*n.* **6.** the liquid used in pickling. **7.** the act or process of sousing. **8.** *Sl.* a drunkard. [C14: from OF *sous*, of Gmc origin]

Sousse (su:s), **Susa,** *or* **Susah** *n.* a port in E Tunisia, on the Mediterranean: founded by the Phoenicians in the 9th century B.C. Pop.: 322 491 (1984). Ancient name: **Hadrumetum** (,hædrə'mi:təm).

soutane (su:'tæn) *n. R.C. Church.* a priest's cassock. [C19: from F, from OIt. *sottana*, from Med. L *subtanus* (adj.) (worn) beneath, from L *subtus* below]

souterrain ('su:tə,rein) *n. Archaeol.* an underground chamber or passage. [C18: from F]

south (sauθ) *n.* **1.** one of the four cardinal points of the compass, at 180° from north and 90° clockwise from east and anticlockwise from west. **2.** the direction along a meridian towards the South Pole. **3. the south.** (*often cap.*) any area lying in or towards the south. **4.** (*usually cap.*) *Cards.* the player or position corresponding to south on the compass. ~*adj.* **5.** in, towards, or facing the south. **6.** (esp. of the wind) from the south. ~*adv.* **7.** in, to, or towards the south. [OE *sūth*]

South (sauθ) *n.* **the. 1.** the southern part of England, generally regarded as lying to the south of an imaginary line between the Wash and the Severn. **2.** (in the U.S.) **a.** the states south of the Mason-Dixon Line that formed the Confederacy during the Civil War. **b.** the Confederacy itself. **3.** the countries of the world that are not economically and technically advanced. ~*adj.* **4.** of or denoting the southern part of a specified country, area, etc.

South Africa *n.* **Republic of.** a republic occupying the southernmost part of the African continent: the Dutch Cape Colony (1652) was acquired by Britain in 1806 and British victory in the Boer War resulted in the formation of the Union of South Africa in 1910, which left the Commonwealth and became a republic in 1961; implementation of the apartheid system began in 1948; mainly plateau with mountains in the south and east. Mineral production includes gold, diamonds, coal, and copper. Official languages: Afrikaans and English. Religion: chiefly Christian. Currency: rand. Capitals: Cape Town (legislative) and Pretoria (administrative). Pop.: 28 881 000 (1987). Area: 1 221 044 sq. km (471 445 sq. miles). Former name (1910–61): **Union of South Africa.** —**South African** *adj., n.*

South America *n.* the fourth largest of the continents, bordering on the Caribbean in the north, the Pacific in the west, and the Atlantic in the east and joined to Central America by the Isthmus of Panama. It is dominated by the Andes Mountains, which extend over 7250 km (4500 miles) and include many volcanoes; ranges from dense tropical jungle, desert, and temperate plains to the cold wet windswept region of Tierra del Fuego. It comprises chiefly developing countries undergoing great changes. Pop.: 263 300 000 (1985). Area: 17 816 600 sq. km (6 879 000 sq. miles). —**South American** *adj., n.*

Southampton (sauθ'æmptən, -'hæmp-) *n.* a port in S England, in Hampshire on **Southampton Water** (an inlet of the English Channel): chief English passenger port; university (1952); shipyards and oil refinery. Pop.: 204 406 (1981).

Southampton Island *n.* an island in N Canada, in the Northwest Territories at the entrance to Hudson Bay: inhabited chiefly by Inuit. Area: 49 470 sq. km (19 100 sq. miles).

South Arabia *n.* **Federation of.** the former name (1959–67) of **South Yemen.** —**South Arabian** *adj., n.*

South Australia *n.* a state of S central Australia, on the Great Australian Bight: generally arid, with the Great Victoria Desert in the west central part, the Lake Eyre basin in the northeast, and the Flinders Ranges, Murray River basin, and salt lakes in the southeast. Capital: Adelaide. Pop.: 1 345 945 (1986). Area: 984 395 sq. km (380 070 sq. miles). —**South Australian** *adj., n.*

South Bend *n.* a city in N Indiana: university (1842). Pop.: 109 727 (1980).

southbound ('sauθ,baund) *adj.* going or leading towards the south.

south by east *n.* **1.** one point on the compass east of south. ~*adj., adv.* **2.** in, from, or towards this direction.

south by west *n.* **1.** one point on the compass west of south. ~*adj., adv.* **2.** in, from, or towards this direction.

South Carolina *n.* a state of the southeastern U.S., on the Atlantic: the first state to secede from the Union in 1860; consists largely of low-lying coastal plains, rising in the northwest to the Blue Ridge Mountains; the largest U.S. textile producer. Capital: Columbia. Pop.: 3 376 000 (1986 est.). Area: 78 282 sq. km (30 225 sq. miles). Abbrev.: **SC** —**South Carolinian** *adj., n.*

South China Sea *n.* part of the Pacific surrounded by SE China, Vietnam, the Malay Peninsula, Borneo, and the Philippines.

South Dakota *n.* a state of the western U.S.: lies mostly in the Great Plains; the chief U.S. producer of gold and beryl. Capital: Pierre. Pop.: 708 000 (1986 est.). Area: 196 723 sq. km (75 955 sq. miles). Abbrevs.: **S. Dak.** or (with zip code) **SD** —**South Dakotan** *adj., n.*

Southdown ('sauθ,daun) *n.* an English breed of sheep with short wool and a greyish-brown face and legs. [C18: so called because it was originally bred on the SOUTH DOWNS]

South Downs *pl. n.* a range of low hills in S England, extending from W Dorset to East Sussex.

southeast (,sauθ'i:st; *Naut.* ,sau'i:st) *n.* **1.** the point of the compass or the direction midway between south and east. ~*adj.* also ,**south'eastern. 2.** (*sometimes cap.*) of or denoting the southeastern part of a specified country, area, etc. **3.** in, towards, or facing the southeast. **4.** (esp. of the wind) from the southeast. ~*adv.* **5.** in, to, or towards the southeast. —**south'easternmost** *adj.*

Southeast (ˌsaʊθ'iːst) *n.* (usually preceded by *the*) the southeastern part of Britain, esp. the London area.

Southeast Asia *n.* a region including Brunei, Burma, Indonesia, Kampuchea, Laos, Malaysia, the Philippines, Thailand, and Vietnam. —**Southeast Asian** *adj., n.*

southeast by east *n.* **1.** one point on the compass north of southeast. ~*adj., adv.* **2.** in, from, or towards this direction.

southeast by south *n.* **1.** one point on the compass south of southeast. ~*adj., adv.* **2.** in, from, or towards this direction.

southeaster (ˌsaʊθ'iːstə; *Naut.* ˌsaʊ'iːstə) *n.* a strong wind or storm from the southeast.

southeasterly (ˌsaʊθ'iːstəlɪ; *Naut.* ˌsaʊ'iːstəlɪ) *adj., adv.* **1.** in, towards, or (esp. of the wind) from the southeast. ~*n., pl.* **-lies. 2.** a strong wind or storm from the southeast.

southeastward (ˌsaʊθ'iːstwəd; *Naut.* ˌsaʊ'iːstwəd) *adj.* **1.** towards or (esp. of a wind) from the southeast. ~*n.* **2.** a direction towards or area in the southeast. ~*adv.* **3.** Also: **southeastwards.** towards the southeast.

Southend-on-Sea (ˌsaʊθ'end-) *n.* a town in SE England, in SE Essex on the Thames estuary: one of England's largest resorts, extending for about 11 km (7 miles) along the coast. Pop.: 156 683 (1981).

souther ('saʊðə) *n.* a strong wind or storm from the south.

southerly ('sʌðəlɪ) *adj.* **1.** of or situated in the south. ~*adv., adj.* **2.** towards the south. **3.** from the south. ~*n., pl.* **-lies. 4.** a wind from the south. —**'southerliness** *n.*

southern ('sʌðən) *adj.* **1.** in or towards the south. **2.** (of a wind, etc.) coming from the south. **3.** native to or inhabiting the south. —**'southern,most** *adj.*

Southern ('sʌðən) *adj.* of, relating to, or characteristic of the south of a particular region or country.

Southern Alps *pl. n.* a mountain range in New Zealand, on South Island: the highest range in Australasia. Highest peak: Mount Cook, 3764 m (12 349 ft.).

Southern Cross *n.* a small constellation in the S hemisphere whose four brightest stars form a cross. It is represented on the national flags of Australia and New Zealand.

Southerner ('sʌðənə) *n.* (*sometimes not cap.*) a native or inhabitant of the south of any specified region, esp. the South of England or the Southern states of the U.S.

southern hemisphere *n.* (*often caps.*) that half of the earth lying south of the equator.

Southern Ireland *n.* See **Ireland**[1] (sense 2).

southern lights *pl. n.* another name for **aurora australis.**

Southern Rhodesia *n.* the former name (until 1964) of **Zimbabwe.** —**Southern Rhodesian** *adj., n.*

Southern Uplands *pl. n.* a hilly region extending across S Scotland: includes the Lowther, Moorfoot, and Lammermuir hills.

Southey ('saʊðɪ, 'sʌðɪ) *n.* **Robert.** 1774–1843, English poet, a friend of Wordsworth and Coleridge, attacked by Byron; poet laureate (1813–43).

South Georgia *n.* an island in the S Atlantic, about 1300 km (800 miles) southeast of the Falkland Islands, of which it is a dependency. Area: 3755 sq. km (1450 sq. miles). —**South Georgian** *adj.*

South Glamorgan *n.* a county of S Wales, formed in 1974 from part of Glamorgan, two parishes from Monmouthshire, and the county borough of Cardiff. Administrative centre: Cardiff. Pop.: 395 700 (1986 est.). Area: 416 sq. km (161 sq. miles).

South Holland *n.* a province of the SW Netherlands, on the North Sea: lying mostly below sea level, it has a coastal strip of dunes and is drained chiefly by distributaries of the Rhine, with large areas of reclaimed land; the most densely populated province in the country, intensively cultivated and industrialized. Capital: The Hague. Pop.: 3 186 249 (1987). Area: 3196 sq. km (1234 sq. miles). Dutch name: **Zuidholland.**

southing ('saʊðɪŋ) *n.* **1.** *Navigation.* movement, deviation, or distance covered in a southerly direction. **2.** *Astron.* a south or negative declination.

South Island *n.* (usually preceded by *the*) the largest island of New Zealand, separated from North Island by Cook Strait. Pop.: 850 500 (1983). Area: 153 947 sq. km (59 439 sq. miles).

South Korea *n.* a republic in NE Asia: established as a republic in 1948; invaded by North Korea and Chinese Communists in 1950 but division remained unchanged at the end of the war (1953); includes over 3000 islands; rapid industrialization. Language: Korean. Religions: Buddhist, Confucianist, Shamanist, and Chondokyo. Currency: won. Capital: Seoul. Pop.: 41 826 706 (1987 est.). Area: 98 477 sq. km (38 022 sq. miles). Korean name: **Hanguk.** —**South Korean** *adj., n.*

South Orkney Islands *pl. n.* a group of islands in the S Atlantic, southeast of Cape Horn: formerly a dependency of the Falkland Islands; part of British Antarctic Territory since 1962. Area: 621 sq. km (240 sq. miles).

South Ossetian Autonomous Region (ə'siːʃən) *n.* an administrative division of the S Soviet Union, in the Georgian SSR on the S slopes of the Caucasus Mountains. Capital: Tskhinvali. Pop.: 99 000 (1986). Area: 3900 sq. km (1500 sq. miles).

southpaw ('saʊθ,pɔː) *Inf.* ~*n.* **1.** a left-handed boxer. **2.** any left-handed person. ~*adj.* **3.** of or relating to a southpaw.

South Pole *n.* **1.** the southernmost point on the earth's axis, at the latitude of 90°S. **2.** *Astron.* the point of intersection of the earth's extended axis and the southern half of the celestial sphere. **3.** (*usually not caps.*) the south-seeking pole of a freely suspended magnet.

Southport ('saʊθ,pɔːt) *n.* a town and resort in NW England, in Merseyside on the Irish Sea. Pop.: 89 745 (1981).

South Saskatchewan *n.* a river in S central Canada, rising in S Alberta and flowing east and northeast to join the North Saskatchewan River, forming the Saskatchewan River. Length: 1392 km (865 miles).

South Sea Bubble *n. Brit. history.* the financial crash that occurred in 1720 after the **South Sea Company** had taken over the national debt in return for a monopoly of trade with the South Seas, causing feverish speculation in their stocks.

South Sea Islands *pl. n.* the islands in the S Pacific.

South Seas *pl. n.* the seas south of the equator.

South Shetland Islands *pl. n.* a group of islands in the S Atlantic, north of the Antarctic Peninsula: formerly a dependency of the Falkland Islands; part of British Antarctic Territory since 1962. Area: 4662 sq. km (1800 sq. miles).

South Shields *n.* a port in NE England, in Tyne and Wear on the Tyne estuary opposite North Shields: shipbuilding and marine engineering industries. Pop.: 87 203 (1981).

south-southeast *n.* **1.** the point on the compass or the direction midway between southeast and south. ~*adj., adv.* **2.** in, from, or towards this direction.

south-southwest *n.* **1.** the point on the compass or the direction midway between south and southwest. ~*adj., adv.* **2.** in, from, or towards this direction.

South Tyrol *or* **Tirol** *n.* a former part of the Austrian state of Tyrol: ceded to Italy in 1919, becoming the Bolzano and Trento provinces of the Trentino-Alto Adige Autonomous Region. Area: 14 037 sq. km (5420 sq. miles).

South Vietnam *n.* a region of S Vietnam, on the South China Sea and the Gulf of Siam: an independent republic (1955–76). —**South Vietnamese** *n.*

southward ('saʊθwəd; *Naut.* 'sʌðəd) *adj.* **1.** situated, directed, or moving towards the south. ~*n.* **2.** the southward part, direction, etc. ~*adv.* **3.** Also: **southwards.** towards the south.

Southwark ('sʌðək) *n.* a borough of S central Greater London, on the River Thames: site of the Globe Theatre; docks and warehouses. Pop.: 216 000 (1986 est.).

southwest (ˌsaʊθ'west; *Naut.* ˌsaʊ'west) *n.* **1.** the point of the compass or the direction midway between west and south. ~*adj. also* ˌsouth'western. **2.** (*sometimes cap.*) of or denoting the southwestern part of a specified country, area, etc.: *southwest Italy.* **3.** in or towards the southwest. **4.** (esp. of the wind) from the southwest. ~*adv.* **5.** in, to, or towards the southwest. —ˌsouth'westernmost *adj.*

Southwest (ˌsaʊθ'west) *n.* (usually preceded by *the*) the southwestern part of Britain, esp. Cornwall, Devon, and Somerset.

South West Africa *n.* another name for **Namibia**.

southwest by south *n.* **1.** one point on the compass south of southwest. ~*adj., adv.* **2.** in, from, or towards this direction.

southwest by west *n.* **1.** one point on the compass north of southwest. ~*adj., adv.* **2.** in, from, or towards this direction.

southwester (ˌsaʊθ'wɛstə; *Naut.* ˌsaʊ'wɛstə) *n.* a strong wind or storm from the southwest.

southwesterly (ˌsaʊθ'wɛstəlɪ; *Naut.* ˌsaʊ'wɛstəlɪ) *adj., adv.* **1.** in, towards, or (esp. of a wind) from the southwest. ~*n., pl.* **-lies. 2.** a wind or storm from the southwest.

southwestward (ˌsaʊθ'wɛstwəd; *Naut.* ˌsaʊ'wɛstwəd) *adj.* **1.** from or towards the southwest. ~*adv.* **2.** Also: **southwestwards.** towards the southwest. ~*n.* **3.** a direction towards or area in the southwest.

South Yemen *n.* a republic in SW Asia, on the Gulf of Aden: separated from Turkish-occupied Yemen in 1914; became a republic in 1967. Official language: Arabic. Religion: mostly Sunni Moslem. Currency: dinar. Capital: Madinat ash Sha'b (administrative) and Aden (national). Pop.: 2 278 000 (1987 est.). Area: about 240 275 sq. km (112 075 sq. miles). Former name (1959–67): (Federation of) **South Arabia.** Official name: **People's Democratic Republic of Yemen.** —**South 'Yemen,ite** *or* '**Yemeni** *adj., n.*

South Yorkshire *n.* (1974–86) a metropolitan county of N England, comprising the districts of Barnsley, Doncaster, Sheffield, and Rotherham. Administrative centre: Barnsley. Pop.: 1 301 813 (1981). Area: 1560 sq. km (602 sq. miles).

Soutine (*French* sutin) *n.* **Chaim** ('xaɪɪm). 1893–1943, French expressionist painter, born in Russia; noted for his portraits and still lifes, esp. of animal carcasses.

souvenir (ˌsuːvə'nɪə, 'suːvəˌnɪə) *n.* **1.** an object that recalls a certain place, occasion, or person; memento. **2.** *Rare.* a thing recalled. ~*vb.* **3.** (*tr.*) *Austral. & N.Z., sl.* to steal or keep for one's own use; purloin. [C18: from F, from (*se*) *souvenir* to remember, from L *subvenīre* to come to mind]

sou'wester (saʊ'wɛstə) *n.* a waterproof hat having a very broad rim behind, worn esp. by seamen. [C19: a contraction of SOUTHWESTER]

sovereign ('sɒvrɪn) *n.* **1.** a person exercising supreme authority, esp. a monarch. **2.** a former British gold coin worth one pound sterling. ~*adj.* **3.** supreme in rank or authority: *a sovereign lord.* **4.** excellent or outstanding: *a sovereign remedy.* **5.** of or relating to a sovereign. **6.** independent of outside authority: *a sovereign state.* [C13: from OF *soverain*, from Vulgar L *superānus* (unattested), from L *super* above; also infl. by REIGN] —'**sovereignly** *adv.*

sovereignty ('sɒvrəntɪ) *n., pl.* **-ties. 1.** supreme and unrestricted power, as of a state. **2.** the position, dominion, or authority of a sovereign. **3.** an independent state.

Sovetsk (*Russian* sa'vjɛtsk) *n.* a town in the W Soviet Union, in the Kaliningrad Region on the Neman River: scene of the signing of the treaty (1807) between Napoleon I and Tsar Alexander I; passed from East Prussia to the Soviet Union in 1945. Former name (until 1945): **Tilsit.**

soviet ('səʊvɪət, 'sɒv-) *n.* **1.** (in the Soviet Union) an elected government council at the local, regional, and national levels, culminating in the Supreme Soviet. ~*adj.* **2.** of or relating to a soviet. [C20: from Russian *sovyet* council, from ORussian *sŭvětŭ*] —'**sovie,tism** *n.*

Soviet ('səʊvɪət, 'sɒv-) *adj.* of or relating to the Soviet Union, its people, or its government.

Soviet Central Asia *n.* the region of the Soviet Union occupied by the Kazakh, Kirghiz, Tadzhik, Turkmen, and Uzbek SSRs. Also called: **Russian Turkestan, West Turkestan.**

sovietize *or* **-ise** ('səʊvɪɪˌtaɪz, 'sɒv-) *vb.* (*tr.*) (*often cap.*) **1.** to bring (a country, person, etc.) under Soviet control or influence. **2.** to cause (a country) to conform to the Soviet model in its social, political, and economic structure. — ,sovieti'zation *or* -i'sation *n.*

Soviet Russia *n.* another name for the **Russian Soviet Federated Socialist Republic** or the **Soviet Union.**

Soviets ('səʊvɪəts, 'sɒv-) *pl. n.* the people or government of the Soviet Union.

Soviet Union *n.* a federal republic in E Europe and central and N Asia: the revolution of 1917 achieved the overthrow of the monarchy and the USSR was established in 1922. It is the largest country in the world, occupying a seventh of the total land surface, and consists chiefly of plains, crossed by the Ural Mountains, with the Caucasus to the south and mountains rising over 7350 m (24 500 ft.) in the extreme southwest. Languages: Russian and many national minority languages. Currency: rouble. Capital: Moscow. Pop.: 284 500 000 (1988). Area: 22 402 202 sq. km (8 649 489 sq. miles). Official name: **Union of Soviet Socialist Republics.** Also called: **Russia, Soviet Russia.** Abbrev.: **USSR.**

Soviet Zone *n.* that part of Germany occupied by the Soviet forces from 1945: transformed into the German Democratic Republic in 1949–50. Also called: **Russian Zone.**

sow[1] (səʊ) *vb.* **sowing, sowed; sown** *or* **sowed. 1.** to scatter or place (seed, a crop, etc.) in or on (a piece of ground, field, etc.) so that it may grow: *to sow wheat; to sow a strip of land.* **2.** (*tr.*) to implant or introduce: *to sow a doubt in someone's mind.* [OE *sāwan*] —'**sower** *n.*

sow[2] (saʊ) *n.* **1.** a female adult pig. **2.** the female of certain other animals, such as the mink. **3.** *Metallurgy.* **a.** the channels for leading molten metal to the moulds in casting pig iron. **b.** iron that has solidified in these channels. [OE *sugu*; rel. to ON *sỹr*, OHG *sū*, L *sūs*, Norwegian *sugga*, Du. *zeug*: see SWINE]

Soweto (sə'wɛtəʊ, -'weɪtəʊ) *n.* a contiguous group of Black African townships southwest of Johannesburg, South Africa: the largest purely Black African urban settlement in southern Africa: scene of riots (1976) following protests against the use of Afrikaans in schools for Black African children. Area: 62 sq. km (24 sq. miles). Pop.: 915 872 (1983). [C20: from *so(uth) we(st) to(wnship)*]

sown (səʊn) *vb.* a past participle of **sow**[1].

sow thistle (saʊ) *n.* any of various plants of an Old World genus, having milky juice, prickly leaves, and heads of yellow flowers.

soya bean ('sɔɪə) *or U.S. & Canad.* **soybean** ('sɔɪˌbiːn) *n.* **1.** an Asian bean plant cultivated for its nutritious seeds, for forage, and to improve the soil. **2.** the seed, used as food, forage, and as the source of an oil. [C17 *soya*, via Du. from Japanese *shōyu*, from Chinese *chiang yu*, from *chiang* paste + *yu* sauce]

Soyinka (sɔ'jɪŋkə) *n.* **Wole** ('wɔːle). born 1934, Nigerian dramatist, novelist, and literary critic. His works include the plays *The Strong Breed* (1963), *The Road* (1965), and *Kongi's Harvest* (1966), and the novels *The Interpreters* (1965) and *Aké* (1982). Nobel prize for literature 1986.

soy sauce (sɔɪ) *n.* a salty dark brown sauce made from fermented soya beans, used esp. in Chinese cookery. Also called: **soya sauce.**

sozzled ('sɒzəld) *adj.* an informal word for **drunk.** [C19: ?from obs. *sozzle* stupor]

SP *abbrev. for* starting price.

sp. *abbrev. for:* **1.** special. **2.** (*pl.* **spp.**) species. **3.** specific. **4.** specimen. **5.** spelling.

Sp. *abbrev. for:* **1.** Spain. **2.** Spaniard. **3.** Spanish.

spa (spɑː) *n.* a mineral spring or a place or resort where such a spring is found. [C17: after SPA]

Spa (spɑː) *n.* a town in E Belgium, in Liège province: a resort with medicinal mineral springs (discovered in the 14th century). Pop.: 9636 (1982).

Spaak (spɑːk) *n.* **Paul Henri** (pɔl ɑ̃ri). 1899–1972, Belgian statesman, first socialist premier of Belgium (1937–38); a leading advocate of European unity, he was president of the consultative assembly of the Council of Europe (1949–51) and secretary-general of NATO (1957–61).

space (speɪs) *n.* **1.** the unlimited three-dimensional expanse in which all material objects are located. Related adj.: **spatial. 2.** an interval of distance or time between two points, objects, or events. **3.** a blank portion or area. **4. a.** an unoccupied area or room: *there is no space for a table.* **b.** (*in combination*): *space-saving.* Related adj.: **spacious. 5. a.** the region beyond the earth's atmosphere containing other planets, stars, galaxies, etc.; universe. **b.** (*as modifier*): *a space probe.* **6.** a seat or place, as on a train, aircraft, etc. **7.** *Printing.* a piece of metal, less than type-high, used to separate letters or words. **8.** *Music.* any of the gaps between the lines that make up the staff. **9.** Also called: **spacing.** *Telegraphy.* the period of time that separates characters in Morse code. ~*vb.* (*tr.*)

10. to place or arrange at intervals or with spaces between. **11.** to divide into or by spaces: *to space one's time evenly.* **12.** *Printing.* to separate (letters, words, or lines) by the insertion of spaces. [C13: from OF *espace*, from L *spatium*] —'**spacer** *n.*

space age *n.* **1.** the period in which the exploration of space has become possible. ~*adj.* **space-age. 2.** (*usually prenominal*) futuristic or ultramodern.

space-bar *n.* a horizontal bar on a typewriter that is depressed in order to leave a space between words, letters, etc.

space capsule *n.* a vehicle, sometimes carrying men or animals, designed to obtain scientific information from space, planets, etc., and be recovered on returning to earth.

spacecraft ('speɪsˌkrɑːft) *n.* a manned or unmanned vehicle designed to orbit the earth or travel to celestial objects.

spaced out *adj. Sl.* intoxicated through taking a drug. Often shortened to **spaced.**

Space Invaders *n. Trademark.* a video game, the object of which is to obliterate a series of symbols moving down a television screen by operating levers or buttons.

spaceman ('speɪsˌmæn) *or* (*fem.*) **spacewoman** *n., pl.* **-men** *or* (*fem.*) **-women.** a person who travels in outer space.

space platform *n.* another name for **space station.**

spaceport ('speɪsˌpɔːt) *n.* a base equipped to launch, maintain, and test spacecraft.

space probe *n.* a vehicle, such as a satellite, equipped to obtain scientific information, normally transmitted back to earth by radio, about a planet, conditions in space, etc.

spaceship ('speɪsˌʃɪp) *n.* a manned spacecraft.

space shuttle *n.* a manned reusable spacecraft designed for making regular orbital flights.

space station *n.* any large manned artificial satellite designed to orbit the earth during a long period of time thus providing a base for scientific research in space and a construction site, launching pad, and docking arrangements for spacecraft.

spacesuit ('speɪsˌsuːt, -ˌsjuːt) *n.* a sealed and pressurized suit worn by astronauts providing an artificial atmosphere, acceptable temperature, radiocommunication link, and protection from radiation.

space-time *or* **space-time continuum** *n. Physics.* the four-dimensional continuum having three spatial coordinates and one time coordinate that together completely specify the location of a particle or an event.

spacewalk ('speɪsˌwɔːk) *n.* **1.** the act or an instance of floating and manoeuvring in space, outside but attached by a lifeline to a spacecraft. Technical name: **extravehicular activity.** ~*vb.* **2.** (*intr.*) to engage in this activity.

spacial ('speɪʃəl) *adj.* a variant spelling of **spatial.**

spacing ('speɪsɪŋ) *n.* **1.** the arrangement of letters, words, spaces, etc., on a page. **2.** the arrangement of objects in a space.

spacious ('speɪʃəs) *adj.* having a large capacity or area. —'**spaciously** *adv.* —'**spaciousness** *n.*

spade[1] (speɪd) *n.* **1.** a tool for digging, typically consisting of a flat rectangular steel blade attached to a long wooden handle. **2.** something resembling a spade. **3.** a cutting tool for stripping the blubber from a whale or skin from a carcass. **4. call a spade a spade.** to speak plainly and frankly. ~*vb.* **5.** (*tr.*) to use a spade on. [OE *spadu*] —'**spader** *n.*

spade[2] (speɪd) *n.* **1. a.** the black symbol on a playing card resembling a heart-shaped leaf with a stem. **b.** a card with one or more of these symbols or (*when pl.*) the suit of cards so marked, usually the highest ranking of the four. **2.** a derogatory word for a **Negro. 3. in spades.** *Inf.* in an extreme or emphatic way. [C16: from It. *spada* sword, used as an emblem on playing cards, from L *spatha*, from Gk *spathē* blade]

spadework ('speɪdˌwɜːk) *n.* dull or routine preparatory work.

spadix ('speɪdɪks) *n., pl.* **spadices** (speɪ'daɪsiːz). a spike of small flowers on a fleshy stem, the whole being enclosed in a spathe. [C18: from L: pulled-off branch of a palm, with its fruit, from Gk: torn-off frond]

spaghetti (spə'gɛtɪ) *n.* pasta in the form of long strings. [C19: from It.: little cords, from *spago* a cord]

spaghetti junction *n.* a junction, usually between motorways, in which there are a large number of intersecting roads used by a large volume of high-speed traffic. [C20: from the nickname given to the Gravelly Hill Interchange, Birmingham, where the M6, A38M, A38, and A5127 intersect]

spaghetti western *n.* a cowboy film made in Europe, esp. by an Italian director.

spahi *or* **spahee** ('spɑːhiː, 'spɑːiː) *n., pl.* **-his** *or* **-hees. 1.** (formerly) an irregular cavalryman in the Turkish army. **2.** (formerly) a member of a body of native Algerian cavalry in the French army. [C16: from OF, from Turkish *sipahi*, from Persian *sipāhī* soldier]

Spain (speɪn) *n.* a kingdom of SW Europe, occupying the Iberian peninsula between the Mediterranean and the Atlantic: a leading European power in the 16th century, with many overseas possessions, esp. in the New World; became a republic in 1931; under the fascist dictatorship of Franco following the Civil War (1936–39) until his death in 1975. It consists chiefly of a central plateau (the Meseta), with the Pyrenees and the Cantabrian Mountains in the north and the Sierra Nevada in the south. Language: Spanish, with Catalan, Galician, and Basque regional minority languages. Religion: Roman Catholic. Currency: peseta. Capital: Madrid. Pop.: 38 832 000 (1987). Area: 504 748 sq. km (194 883 sq. miles). Spanish name: **España.**

spake (speɪk) *vb. Arch.* a past tense of **speak.**

Spalato ('spɑːlato) *n.* the Italian name for **Split.**

Spam (spæm) *n. Trademark.* a kind of tinned luncheon meat, made largely from pork.

span[1] (spæn) *n.* **1.** the interval, space, or distance between two points, such as the ends of a bridge or arch. **2.** the complete duration or extent: *the span of his life.* **3.** *Psychol.* the amount of material that can be processed in a single mental act: *span of attention.* **4.** short for **wingspan. 5.** a unit of length based on the width of an expanded hand, usually taken as nine inches. ~*vb.* **spanning, spanned.** (*tr.*) **6.** to stretch or extend across, over, or around. **7.** to provide with something that spans: *to span a river with a bridge.* **8.** to measure or cover, esp. with the extended hand. [OE *spann*]

span[2] (spæn) *n.* a team of horses or oxen, esp. two matched animals. [C16 (in the sense: yoke): from MDu.: something stretched, from *spannen* to stretch]

span[3] (spæn) *vb. Arch. or dialect.* a past tense of **spin.**

Span. *abbrev. for* Spanish.

spandrel *or* **spandril** ('spændrəl) *n. Archit.* **1.** an approximately triangular surface bounded by the outer curve of an arch and the adjacent wall. **2.** the surface area between two adjacent arches and the horizontal cornice above them. [C15 *spaundrell*, from Anglo-F *spaundre*, from OF *spandre* to spread]

spangle ('spæŋgəl) *n.* **1.** a small thin piece of metal or other shiny material used as a decoration, esp. on clothes; sequin. **2.** any glittering or shiny spot or object. ~*vb.* **3.** (*intr.*) to glitter or shine with or like spangles. **4.** (*tr.*) to cover with spangles. [C15: dim. of *spange*, ?from MDu.: clasp] —'**spangly** *adj.*

Spaniard ('spænjəd) *n.* a native or inhabitant of Spain.

spaniel ('spænjəl) *n.* **1.** any of several breeds of gundog with long drooping ears and a silky coat. **2.** an obsequiously devoted person. [C14: from OF *espaigneul* Spanish (dog), from OProvençal *espanhol*, ult. from L *Hispāniolus* Spanish]

Spanish ('spænɪʃ) *n.* **1.** the official language of Spain, Mexico, and most countries of South and Central America except Brazil. Spanish is an Indo-European language belonging to the Romance group. **2. the Spanish.** (*functioning as pl.*) the natives, citizens, or inhabitants of Spain. ~*adj.* **3.** of or relating to the Spanish language or its speakers. **4.** of or relating to Spain or Spaniards.

Spanish America *n.* the parts of America colonized by Spaniards and now chiefly Spanish-speaking: includes most of South and Central America, Mexico, and much of the West Indies.

Spanish-American *adj.* **1.** of or relating to any of the Spanish-speaking countries or peoples of the Americas. ~*n.* **2.** a native or inhabitant of Spanish America. **3.** a Spanish-speaking person in the U.S.

Spanish fly *n.* **1.** a European blister beetle, the dried body of which yields cantharides. **2.** another name for **cantharides.**

Spanish Guinea *n.* the former name (until 1964) of **Equatorial Guinea.**

Spanish guitar *n.* the classic form of the guitar; a six-stringed instrument with a waisted body and a central sound hole.

Spanish Main *n.* **1.** the mainland of Spanish America, esp. the N coast of South America. **2.** the Caribbean Sea, the S part of which in colonial times was the haunt of pirates.

Spanish Morocco *n.* a former Spanish colony on the N coast of Morocco: part of the kingdom of Morocco since 1956. —**Spanish Moroccan** *adj., n.*

Spanish moss *n.* **1.** an epiphytic plant growing in tropical and subtropical regions as long bluish-grey strands suspended from the branches of trees. **2.** a tropical lichen growing as long trailing green threads from the branches of trees.

Spanish omelette *n.* an omelette containing green peppers, onions, tomato, etc.

Spanish rice *n.* rice cooked with tomatoes, onions, green peppers, etc.

Spanish Sahara *n.* the former name (until 1975) of **Western Sahara.**

Spanish West Africa *n.* a former overseas territory of Spain in NW Africa: divided in 1958 into the overseas provinces of Ifni and Spanish Sahara. —**Spanish West African** *adj., n.*

spank[1] (spæŋk) *vb.* **1.** (*tr.*) to slap with the open hand, esp. on the buttocks. ~*n.* **2.** one or a series of these slaps. [C18: prob. imit.]

spank[2] (spæŋk) *vb.* (*intr.*) to go at a quick and lively pace. [C19: back formation from SPANKING[2]]

spanker ('spæŋkə) *n.* **1.** a person or thing that spanks. **2.** *Naut.* a fore-and-aft sail or a mast that is aftermost in a sailing vessel. **3.** *Inf.* something outstandingly fine or large.

spanking[1] ('spæŋkɪŋ) *n.* a series of spanks, usually as a punishment for children.

spanking[2] ('spæŋkɪŋ) *adj.* (*prenominal*) **1.** *Inf.* outstandingly fine, smart, large, etc. **2.** quick and energetic. **3.** (esp. of a breeze) fresh and brisk.

spanner ('spænə) *n.* **1.** a steel hand tool with jaws or a hole, designed to grip a nut or bolt head. **2. spanner in the works.** *Brit. inf.* an impediment or annoyance. [C17: from G, from *spannen* to stretch]

span roof *n.* a roof consisting of two equal sloping sides.

spanspek ('spæn,spɛk) *n. S. African.* the sweet melon. [from Afrik., from early Du.]

spar[1] (spɑ:) *n.* **1.** any piece of nautical gear resembling a pole and used as a mast, boom, gaff, etc. **2.** a principal supporting structural member of an aerofoil that runs from tip to tip or root to tip. [C13: from ON *sperra* beam]

spar[2] (spɑ:) *vb.* **sparring, sparred.** (*intr.*) **1.** *Boxing.* to box using light blows, as in training. **2.** to dispute or argue. **3.** (of gamecocks, etc.) to fight with the feet or spurs. ~*n.* **4.** an unaggressive fight. **5.** an argument or wrangle. [OE, ? from SPUR]

spar[3] (spɑ:) *n.* any of various minerals, such as feldspar, that are light-coloured, crystalline, and easily cleavable. [C16: from MLow G *spar*]

sparaxis (spər'æksɪs) *n.* a South African plant of the iris family, having lacerated spathes and showy flowers. [C19: NL, from Gk, from *sparassō* to tear]

spare (spɛə) *vb.* **1.** (*tr.*) to refrain from killing, punishing, or injuring. **2.** (*tr.*) to release or relieve, as from pain, suffering, etc. **3.** (*tr.*) to refrain from using: *spare the rod, spoil the child.* **4.** (*tr.*) to be able to afford or give: *I can't spare the time.* **5.** (*usually passive*) (esp. of Providence) to allow to survive: *I'll see you next year if we are spared.* **6.** (*intr.*) *Now rare.* to act or live frugally. **7. not spare oneself.** to exert oneself to the full. **8. to spare.** more than is required: *two minutes to spare.* ~*adj.* **9.** (*often immediately postpositive*) in excess of what is needed; additional. **10.** able to be used when needed: *a spare part.* **11.** (of a person) thin and lean. **12.** scanty or meagre. **13.** (*postpositive*) *Brit. sl.* upset, angry, or distracted (esp. in **go spare**). ~*n.* **14.** a duplicate kept as a replacement in case of damage or loss. **15.** a spare tyre. **16.** *Tenpin bowling.* **a.** the act of knocking down all the pins with the two bowls of a single frame. **b.** the score thus made. [OE *sparian* to refrain from injuring] —**'sparely** *adv.* —**'spareness** *n.* —**'sparer** *n.*

spare-part surgery *n.* surgical replacement of defective or damaged organs by transplant or insertion of artficial devices.

sparerib (,spɛə'rɪb) *n.* a cut of pork ribs with most of the meat trimmed off.

spare tyre *n.* **1.** an additional tyre carried by a motor vehicle in case of puncture. **2.** *Brit. sl.* a deposit of fat just above the waist.

sparing ('spɛərɪŋ) *adj.* **1.** (sometimes foll. by *of*) economical or frugal (with). **2.** scanty; meagre. **3.** merciful or lenient. —**'sparingly** *adv.* —**'sparingness** *n.*

spark[1] (spɑ:k) *n.* **1.** a fiery particle thrown out or left by burning material or caused by the friction of two hard surfaces. **2. a.** a momentary flash of light accompanied by a sharp crackling noise, produced by a sudden electrical discharge through the air or some other insulating medium between two points. **b.** the electrical discharge itself. **c.** (*as modifier*): *a spark gap.* **3.** anything that serves to animate or kindle. **4.** a trace or hint: *a spark of interest.* **5.** vivacity, enthusiasm, or humour. **6.** a small piece of diamond, as used in cutting glass. ~*vb.* **7.** (*intr.*) to give off sparks. **8.** (*intr.*) (of the sparking plug or ignition system of an internal-combustion engine) to produce a spark. **9.** (*tr.*; often foll. by *off*) to kindle or animate. ~See also **sparks.** [OE *spearca*]

spark[2] (spɑ:k) *n.* **1.** *Rare.* a fashionable or gallant young man. **2. bright spark.** *Brit., usually ironic.* a person who appears clever or witty. [C16 (in the sense: beautiful or witty woman): ? of Scand. origin] —**'sparkish** *adj.*

Spark (spɑ:k) *n.* **Muriel.** born 1918, Scottish novelist; her works include *Memento Mori* (1959), *The Prime of Miss Jean Brodie* (1961), *The Takeover* (1976), and *The Only Problem* (1984).

spark gap *n.* the space between two electrodes across which a spark can jump.

sparking plug *n.* a device screwed into the cylinder head of an internal-combustion engine to ignite the explosive mixture by means of an electric spark. Also called: **spark plug.**

sparkle ('spɑ:k³l) *vb.* **1.** to issue or reflect or cause to issue or reflect bright points of light. **2.** (*intr.*) (of wine, mineral water, etc.) to effervesce. **3.** (*intr.*) to be vivacious or witty. ~*n.* **4.** a point of light, spark, or gleam. **5.** vivacity or wit. [C12 *sparklen*, frequentative of *sparken* to SPARK[1]]

sparkler ('spɑ:klə) *n.* **1.** a type of firework that throws out sparks. **2.** *Inf.* a sparkling gem.

sparkling wine *n.* a wine made effervescent by carbon dioxide gas added artificially or produced naturally by secondary fermentation.

spark plug *n.* another name for **sparking plug.**

sparks (spɑ:ks) *n.* (*functioning as sing.*) *Inf.* **1.** an electrician. **2.** a radio officer, esp. on a ship.

sparky ('spɑ:kɪ) *adj.* **sparkier, sparkiest.** lively, vivacious, spirited.

sparring partner ('spɑ:rɪŋ) *n.* **1.** a person who practises with a boxer during training. **2.** a person with whom one has friendly arguments.

sparrow ('spærəʊ) *n.* **1.** any of various weaverbirds, esp. the house sparrow, having a brown or grey plumage and feeding on seeds or insects. **2.** *U.S. & Canad.* any of various North American finches, such as the chipping sparrow, that have a dullish streaked plumage. ~See also **hedge sparrow, tree sparrow.** [OE *spearwa*]

sparrowgrass ('spærəʊ,grɑ:s) *n.* a dialect or popular name for **asparagus.**

sparrowhawk ('spærəʊ,hɔ:k) *n.* any of several small hawks of Eurasia and N Africa that prey on smaller birds.

sparrow hawk *n.* a very small North American falcon, closely related to the kestrels.

sparse (spɑ:s) *adj.* scattered or scanty; not dense. [C18: from L *sparsus*, from *spargere* to scatter] —**'sparsely** *adv.* —**'sparseness** *or* **'sparsity** *n.*

Sparta ('spɑ:tə) *n.* an ancient Greek city in the S Peloponnese, famous for the discipline and military prowess of its citizens and for their austere way of life.

Spartacus ('spɑ:təkəs) *n.* died 71 B.C., Thracian slave, who led an ultimately unsuccessful revolt of gladiators against Rome (73–71 B.C.).

Spartan ('spɑ:t³n) *adj.* **1.** of or relating to Sparta or its citizens. **2.** (*sometimes not cap.*) very strict or austere: *a Spartan upbringing.* **3.** (*sometimes not cap.*) possessing courage and resolve. ~*n.* **4.** a citizen of Sparta. **5.** (*sometimes not cap.*) a disciplined or brave person.

spasm ('spæzəm) *n.* **1.** an involuntary muscular contraction, esp. one resulting in cramp or convulsion. **2.** a sudden burst of activity, emotion, etc. [C14: from L *spasmus*, from Gk *spasmos* a cramp, from *span* to tear]

spasmodic (spæz'mɒdɪk) *or* (*rarely*) **spasmodical** *adj.* **1.** taking place in sudden brief spells. **2.** of or characterized by spasms. [C17: NL, from Gk *spasmos* SPASM] —**spas'modically** *adv.*

Spassky ('spæskɪ; *Russian* 'spaskij) *n.* **Boris** (ba'ris). born 1937, Soviet chess player; world champion (1969–72).

spastic ('spæstɪk) *n.* **1.** a person who has cerebral palsy. **2.** *Derog. sl.* a clumsy, incapable, or incompetent person. ~*adj.* **3.** affected by or resembling spasms. **4.** *Derog. sl.* clumsy, incapable, or incompetent. [C18: from L *spasticus*, from Gk, from *spasmos* SPASM] —'**spastically** *adv.*

spat[1] (spæt) *n.* **1.** *Now rare.* a slap or smack. **2.** a slight quarrel. ~*vb.* **spatting, spatted.** **3.** *Rare.* to slap (someone). **4.** (*intr.*) *U.S., Canad., & N.Z.* to have a slight quarrel. [C19: prob. imit.]

spat[2] (spæt) *vb.* a past tense and past participle of **spit**[1].

spat[3] (spæt) *n.* another name for **gaiter** (sense 2). [C19: short for SPATTERDASH]

spat[4] (spæt) *n.* **1.** a larval oyster or similar bivalve mollusc. **2.** such oysters or other molluscs collectively. [C17: from Anglo-Norman *spat*]

spatchcock ('spætʃ,kɒk) *n.* **1.** a chicken or game bird split down the back and grilled. ~*vb.* (*tr.*) **2.** to interpolate (words, a story, etc.) into a sentence, narrative, etc., esp. inappropriately. [C18: ? var. of *spitchcock* eel when prepared & cooked]

spate (speɪt) *n.* **1.** a fast flow, rush, or outpouring: *a spate of words.* **2.** *Chiefly Brit.* a sudden flood: *the rivers were in spate.* **3.** *Chiefly Brit.* a sudden heavy downpour. [C15 (Scot. & N English): from ?]

spathe (speɪð) *n.* a large bract that encloses the inflorescence of several members of the lily family. [C18: from L *spatha*, from Gk *spathē* a blade] —**spathaceous** (spə'θeɪʃəs) *adj.*

spathic ('spæθɪk) *or* **spathose** ('spæθəʊs) *adj.* (of minerals) resembling spar, esp. in having good cleavage. [C18: from G *Spat* SPAR[3]]

spatial *or* **spacial** ('speɪʃəl) *adj.* **1.** of or relating to space. **2.** existing or happening in space. —**spatiality** (,speɪʃɪ'ælɪtɪ) *n.* —'**spatially** *adv.*

spatiotemporal (,speɪʃɪəʊ'tɛmpərəl) *adj.* **1.** of or existing in both space and time. **2.** of or concerned with space-time. —**spatio'temporally** *adv.*

spatter ('spætə) *vb.* **1.** to scatter or splash (a substance, esp. a liquid) or (of a substance) to splash (something) in scattered drops: *to spatter mud on the car; mud spattered in her face.* **2.** (*tr.*) to sprinkle, cover, or spot (with a liquid). **3.** (*tr.*) to slander or defame. **4.** (*intr.*) to shower or rain down: *bullets spattered around them.* ~*n.* **5.** the sound of spattering. **6.** something spattered, such as a spot or splash. **7.** the act or an instance of spattering. [C16: imit.]

spatterdash ('spætə,dæʃ) *n.* **1.** *U.S.* another name for **roughcast.** **2.** (*pl.*) long leather leggings worn in the 18th century, as to protect from mud when riding. [C17: see SPATTER, DASH[1]]

spatula ('spætjʊlə) *n.* a utensil with a broad flat blade, used for lifting, spreading, or stirring foods, etc. [C16: from L: a broad piece, from *spatha* a flat wooden implement; see SPATHE] —'**spatular** *adj.*

spatulate ('spætjʊlɪt) *adj.* **1.** shaped like a spatula; having thickened rounded ends: *spatulate fingers.* **2.** Also: **spathulate.** *Bot.* having a narrow base and a broad rounded apex.

spavin ('spævɪn) *n.* enlargement of the hock of a horse by a bony growth (**bony spavin**) or distension of the ligament (**bog spavin**), often resulting in lameness. [C15: from OF *espavin*, from ?] —'**spavined** *adj.*

spawn (spɔːn) *n.* **1.** the mass of eggs deposited by fish, amphibians, or molluscs. **2.** *Often derog.* offspring, product, or yield. **3.** *Bot.* the nontechnical name for **mycelium.** ~*vb.* **4.** (of fish, amphibians, etc.) to produce or deposit (eggs). **5.** *Often derog.* (of people) to produce (offspring). **6.** (*tr.*) to produce or engender. [C14: from Anglo-Norman *espaundre*, from OF *spandre* to spread out] —'**spawner** *n.*

spay (speɪ) *vb.* (*tr.*) to remove the ovaries from (a female animal). [C15: from OF *espeer* to cut with the sword, from *espee* sword, from L *spatha*]

SPCK (in Britain) *abbrev. for* Society for Promoting Christian Knowledge.

speak (spiːk) *vb.* **speaking, spoke, spoken.** **1.** to make (verbal utterances); utter (words). **2.** to communicate or express (something) in or as if in words. **3.** (*intr.*) to deliver a speech, discourse, etc. **4.** (*tr.*) to know how to talk in (a language or dialect): *he does not speak German.* **5.** (*intr.*) to make a characteristic sound: *the clock spoke.* **6.** (*intr.*) (of hounds used in hunting) to give tongue; bark. **7.** (*tr.*) *Naut.* to hail and communicate with (another vessel) at sea. **8.** (*intr.*) (of a musical instrument) to produce a sound. **9.** (*intr.; foll. by for*) to be a representative or advocate (of). **10. on speaking terms.** on good terms; friendly. **11. so to speak.** in a manner of speaking; as it were. **12. speak one's mind.** to express one's opinions frankly and plainly. **13. to speak of.** of a significant or worthwhile nature: *no support to speak of.* ~See also **speak for, speak out, speak to.** [OE *specan*] —'**speakable** *adj.*

speakeasy ('spiːk,iːzɪ) *n., pl.* -**easies.** *U.S.* a place where alcoholic drink was sold illicitly during Prohibition.

speaker ('spiːkə) *n.* **1.** a person who speaks, esp. at a formal occasion. **2.** See **loudspeaker.** —'**speakership** *n.*

Speaker ('spiːkə) *n.* the presiding officer in any of numerous legislative bodies.

speak for *vb.* (*intr., prep.*) **1.** to speak as a representative of (other people). **2. speak for itself.** to be so evident that no further comment is necessary. **3. speak for yourself.** *Inf.* (used as an imperative) do not presume that other people agree with you.

speaking ('spiːkɪŋ) *adj.* **1.** (*prenominal*) eloquent, impressive, or striking. **2. a.** able to speak. **b.** (*in combination*) able to speak a particular language: *French-speaking.*

speaking clock *n. Brit.* a telephone service that gives a verbal statement of the time.

speaking in tongues *n.* another term for **gift of tongues.**

speaking tube *n.* a tube for conveying a person's voice from one room or building to another.

speak out *or* **up** *vb.* (*intr., adv.*) **1.** to state one's beliefs, objections, etc., bravely and firmly. **2.** to speak more loudly and clearly.

speak to *vb.* (*intr., prep.*) **1.** to address (a person). **2.** to reprimand. **3.** *Formal.* to give evidence of or comments on (a subject).

spear[1] (spɪə) *n.* **1.** a weapon consisting of a long shaft with a sharp pointed end of metal, stone, or wood that may be thrown or thrust. **2.** a similar implement used to catch fish. **3.** another name for **spearman.** ~*vb.* **4.** to pierce (something) with or as if with a spear. [OE *spere*]

spear[2] (spɪə) *n.* a shoot, stalk, or blade, as of grass. [C16: prob. var. of SPIRE[1], infl. by SPEAR[1]]

spear grass *n.* **1.** Also called: **wild Spaniard.** a New Zealand grass with sharp leaves that grows on mountains. **2.** any of various other grasses with sharp stiff blades or seeds.

spear gun *n.* a device for shooting spears underwater.

spearhead ('spɪə,hɛd) *n.* **1.** the pointed head of a spear. **2.** the leading force in a military attack. **3.** any person or thing that leads or initiates an attack, campaign, etc. ~*vb.* **4.** (*tr.*) to lead or initiate (an attack, campaign, etc.).

spearman ('spɪəmən) *n., pl.* -**men.** a soldier armed with a spear.

spearmint ('spɪəmɪnt) *n.* a purple-flowered mint plant of Europe, having leaves that yield an oil used for flavouring.

spec (spɛk) *n.* **1. on spec.** *Inf.* as a speculation or gamble: *all the tickets were sold so I went to the theatre on spec.* ~*adj.* **2.** (*prenominal*) *Austral. & N.Z. inf.* speculative: *a spec developer.*

spec. *abbrev. for:* **1.** special. **2.** specification. **3.** speculation.

special ('spɛʃəl) *adj.* **1.** distinguished from, set apart from, or excelling others of its kind. **2.** (*prenominal*) designed or reserved for a particular purpose. **3.** not usual or commonplace. **4.** (*prenominal*) particular or primary: *his special interest was music.* **5.** of or relating to the education of handicapped children: *a special school.* ~*n.* **6.** a special person or thing, such as an extra edition of a newspaper or a train reserved for a particular purpose. **7.** a dish or meal given prominence, esp. at a low price, in a café, etc. **8.** short for **special constable. 9.** *U.S.*, *Canad.*, *Austral.*, *& N.Z. inf.* an item in a store advertised at a reduce price. ~*vb.* **-cialling, -cialled.** (*tr.*) **10.** (of a nurse) to give (a gravely ill patient) constant individual care. **11.** *N.Z. inf.* to advertise and sell (an item) at a reduced price. [C13: from OF *especial*, from L *specialis* individual, special, from *species* appearance] —'**specially** *adv.* —'**specialness** *n.*

▷ **Usage.** See at **especial.**

Special Branch *n.* (in Britain) the department of the police force that is concerned with political security.

special constable *n.* a person recruited for temporary or occasional police duties, esp. in time of emergency.

special delivery *n.* the delivery of a piece of mail outside the time of a scheduled delivery.

special drawing rights *pl. n.* (*sometimes caps.*) the reserve assets of the International Monetary Fund on which member nations may draw.

specialist ('spɛʃəlɪst) *n.* a person who specializes in a particular activity, field of research, etc. —'**special,ism** *n.* —,**special'istic** *adj.*

speciality (,spɛʃɪ'ælɪtɪ) *or esp. U.S. & Canad.* **specialty** *n., pl.* **-ties. 1.** a special interest or skill. **2. a.** a service or product specialized in, as at a restaurant. **b.** (*as modifier*): *a speciality dish.* **3.** a special feature or characteristic.

specialize *or* **-ise** ('spɛʃə,laɪz) *vb.* **1.** (*intr.*) to train in or devote oneself to a particular area of study, occupation, or activity. **2.** (*usually passive*) to cause (organisms or parts) to develop in a way most suited to a particular environment or way of life or (of organisms, etc.) to develop in this way. **3.** (*tr.*) to modify for a special use or purpose. —,**speciali'zation** *or* **-i'sation** *n.*

special licence *n. Brit.* a licence permitting a marriage to take place by dispensing with the usual legal conditions.

special pleading *n. Law.* **1.** a pleading that alleges new facts that offset those put forward by the other side rather than directly admitting or denying those facts. **2.** a pleading that emphasizes the favourable aspects of a case while omitting the unfavourable.

special school *n. Brit.* a school for children who are unable to benefit from ordinary schooling because they are educationally subnormal, handicapped, etc.

specialty ('spɛʃəltɪ) *n., pl.* **-ties. 1.** *Law.* a formal contract or obligation expressed in a deed. **2.** a variant (esp. U.S. and Canad.) of **speciality.**

speciation (,spiːʃɪ'eɪʃən) *n.* the evolutionary development of a biological species.

specie ('spiːʃiː) *n.* **1.** coin money, as distinguished from bullion or paper money. **2. in specie. a.** (of money) in coin. **b.** in kind. [C16: from L *in specie* in kind]

species ('spiːʃiːz; *Latin* 'spiːʃɪ,iːz) *n., pl.* **-cies. 1.** *Biol.* **a.** any of the taxonomic groups into which a genus is divided, the members of which are capable of interbreeding. **b.** the animals of such a group. **c.** any group of related animals or plants not necessarily of this taxonomic rank. **2.** (*modifier*) denoting a plant that is a natural member of a species rather than a hybrid or cultivar: *a species clematis.* **3.** *Logic.* a group of objects or individuals, all sharing common attributes, that forms a subdivision of a genus. **4.** a kind, sort, or variety: *a species of treachery.* **5.** *Chiefly R.C. Church.* the outward form of the bread and wine in the Eucharist. **6.** *Obs.* an outward appearance or form. [C16: from L: appearance, from *specere* to look]

specif. *abbrev. for* **specifically.**

specific (spɪ'sɪfɪk) *adj.* **1.** explicit, particular, or definite. **2.** relating to a specified or particular thing: *a specific treatment for arthritis.* **3.** of or relating to a biological species. **4.** (of a disease) caused by a particular pathogenic agent. **5.** *Physics.* **a.** characteristic of a property of a substance, esp. in relation to the same property of a standard reference substance: *specific gravity.* **b.** characteristic of a property of a substance per unit mass, length, area, etc.: *specific heat.* **c.** (of an extensive physical quantity) divided by mass: *specific volume.* **6.** denoting a tariff levied at a fixed sum per unit of weight, quantity, volume, etc., irrespective of value. ~*n.* **7.** (*sometimes pl.*) a designated quality, thing, etc. **8.** *Med.* any drug used to treat a particular disease. [C17: from

Med. L *specificus*, from L SPECIES] —spe'**cifically** *adv.* —**specificity** (,spɛsɪ'fɪsɪtɪ) *n.*

specification (,spɛsɪfɪ'keɪʃən) *n.* **1.** the act or an instance of specifying. **2.** (in patent law) a written statement accompanying an application for a patent that describes the nature of an invention. **3.** a detailed description of the criteria for the constituents, construction, appearance, performance, etc., of a material, apparatus, etc., or of the standard of workmanship required in its manufacture. **4.** an item, detail, etc., specified.

specific gravity *n.* the ratio of the density of a substance to that of water.

specific heat capacity *n.* the heat required to raise unit mass of a substance by unit temperature interval under specified conditions, such as constant pressure. Also called: **specific heat.**

specific volume *n. Physics.* the volume of matter per unit mass.

specify ('spɛsɪ,faɪ) *vb.* **-fying, -fied.** (*tr.; may take a clause as object*) **1.** to refer to or state specifically. **2.** to state as a condition. **3.** to state or include in the specification of. [C13: from Med. L *specificāre* to describe] —'**speci,fiable** *adj.* —**specificative** ('spɛsɪfɪ,keɪtɪv) *adj.*

specimen ('spɛsɪmɪn) *n.* **1. a.** an individual, object, or part regarded as typical of its group or class. **b.** (*as modifier*): *a specimen page.* **2.** *Med.* a sample of tissue, blood, urine, etc., taken for diagnostic examination or evaluation. **3.** the whole or a part of an organism, plant, rock, etc., collected and preserved as an example of its class, species, etc. **4.** *Inf., often derog.* a person. [C17: from L: mark, proof, from *specere* to look at]

specious ('spiːʃəs) *adj.* **1.** apparently correct or true, but actually wrong or false. **2.** deceptively attractive in appearance. [C14 (orig.: fair): from L *speciōsus* plausible, from *speciēs* outward appearance, from *specere* to look at] —'**speciously** *adv.* —,**speci'osity** (,spiːʃɪ'ɒsɪtɪ) *or* '**speciousness** *n.*

speck (spɛk) *n.* **1.** a very small mark or spot. **2.** a small or tiny piece of something. ~*vb.* **3.** (*tr.*) to mark with specks or spots. [OE *specca*]

speckle ('spɛk³l) *n.* **1.** a small mark usually of a contrasting colour, as on the skin, eggs, etc. ~*vb.* **2.** (*tr.*) to mark with or as if with speckles. [C15: from MDu. *spekkel*] —'**speckled** *adj.*

specs (spɛks) *pl. n. Inf.* **1.** short for **spectacles. 2.** short for **specifications.**

spectacle ('spɛktək³l) *n.* **1.** a public display or performance, esp. a showy or ceremonial one. **2.** a thing or person seen, esp. an unusual or ridiculous one: *he makes a spectacle of himself.* **3.** a strange or interesting object or phenomenon. [C14: via OF from L *spectaculum* a show, from *spectāre* to watch, from *specere* to look at]

spectacles ('spɛktək³lz) *pl. n.* a pair of glasses for correcting defective vision. Often (informal) shortened to **specs.** —'**spectacled** *adj.*

spectacular (spɛk'tækjʊlə) *adj.* **1.** of or resembling a spectacle; impressive, grand, or dramatic. **2.** unusually marked or great: *a spectacular increase.* ~*n.* **3.** a lavishly produced performance. —**spec'tacularly** *adv.*

spectate (spɛk'teɪt) *vb.* (*intr.*) to be a spectator; watch. [C20: back formation from SPECTATOR]

spectator (spɛk'teɪtə) *n.* a person viewing anything; onlooker; observer. [C16: from L, from *spectāre* to watch; see SPECTACLE]

spectator sport *n.* a sport that attracts people as spectators rather than as participants.

Spector ('spɛktə) *n. Phil.* born 1940, U.S. record producer and songwriter, noted for the densely orchestrated "Wall of Sound" in his work with groups such as the Ronettes and the Crystals.

spectra ('spɛktrə) *n.* the plural of **spectrum.**

spectral ('spɛktrəl) *adj.* **1.** of or like a spectre. **2.** of or relating to a spectrum. —**spectrality** (spɛk'trælɪtɪ) *n.* —'**spectrally** *adv.*

spectral type *or* **class** *n.* any of various groups into which stars are classified according to characteristic spectral lines and bands.

spectre *or U.S.* **specter** ('spɛktə) *n.* **1.** a ghost; phantom; apparition. **2.** an unpleasant or menacing mental image: *the spectre of redundancy.* [C17: from L *spectrum*, from *specere* to look at]

spectro- *combining form.* indicating a spectrum: *spectrogram.*

spectrograph ('spɛktrəʊˌgrɑːf) *n.* a spectroscope or spectrometer that produces a photographic record (**spectrogram**) of a spectrum. See also **sound spectrograph.** —ˌspectro'graphic *adj.* —ˌspectro'graphically *adv.* —**spectrography** (spɛk'trɒgrəfɪ) *n.*

spectroheliograph (ˌspɛktrəʊ'hiːlɪəˌgrɑːf) *n.* an instrument used to take a photograph (**spectroheliogram**) of the sun in light of a particular wavelength, usually that of calcium or hydrogen, to show the distribution of the element over the surface and in the atmosphere. —ˌspectroˌhelio'graphic *adj.*

spectrometer (spɛk'trɒmɪtə) *n.* any instrument for producing a spectrum, esp. one in which wavelength, energy, intensity, etc., can be measured. See also **mass spectrometer.** —**spectrometric** (ˌspɛktrəʊ'mɛtrɪk) *adj.* —spec'trometry *n.*

spectrophotometer (ˌspɛktrəʊfəʊ'tɒmɪtə) *n.* an instrument for producing or recording a spectrum and measuring the photometric intensity of each wavelength present. —**spectrophotometric** (ˌspɛktrəʊˌfəʊtə'mɛtrɪk) *adj.* —ˌspectropho'tometry *n.*

spectroscope ('spɛktrəˌskəʊp) *n.* any of a number of instruments for dispersing electromagnetic radiation and thus forming or recording a spectrum. —**spectroscopic** (ˌspɛktrə'skɒpɪk) *or* ˌspectro'scopical *adj.*

spectroscopy (spɛk'trɒskəpɪ) *n.* the science and practice of using spectrometers and spectroscopes and of analysing spectra. —spec'troscopist *n.*

spectrum ('spɛktrəm) *n., pl* **-tra.** **1.** the distribution of colours produced when white light is dispersed by a prism or diffraction grating. There is a continuous change in wavelength from red, the longest wavelength, to violet, the shortest. Seven colours are usually distinguished: violet, indigo, blue, green, yellow, orange, and red. **2.** the whole range of electromagnetic radiation with respect to its wavelength or frequency. **3.** any particular distribution of electromagnetic radiation often showing lines or bands characteristic of the substance emitting the radiation or absorbing it. **4.** any similar distribution or record of the energies, velocities, masses, etc., of atoms, ions, electrons, etc.: *a mass spectrum.* **5.** any range or scale, as of capabilities, emotions, or moods. **6.** another name for an **afterimage.** [C17: from L: image, from *spectāre* to observe, from *specere* to look at]

spectrum analysis *n.* the analysis of a spectrum to determine the properties of its source.

specular ('spɛkjʊlə) *adj.* **1.** of, relating to, or having the properties of a mirror. **2.** of or relating to a speculum. [C16: from L *speculāris,* from *speculum* a mirror, from *specere* to look at]

speculate ('spɛkjʊˌleɪt) *vb.* **1.** (when *tr.,* takes a clause *as object*) to conjecture without knowing the complete facts. **2.** (*intr.*) to buy or sell securities, property, etc., in the hope of deriving capital gains. **3.** (*intr.*) to risk loss for the possibility of considerable gain. **4.** (*intr.*) *N.Z.* in rugby football, to make an emergency undirected forward kick at the ball. [C16: from L *speculārī* to spy out, from *specula* a watchtower, from *specere* to look at]

speculation (ˌspɛkjʊ'leɪʃən) *n.* **1.** the act or an instance of speculating. **2.** a supposition, theory, or opinion arrived at through speculating. **3.** investment involving high risk but also possible high profits. —'speculative *adj.*

speculator ('spɛkjʊˌleɪtə) *n.* **1.** a person who speculates. **2.** *N.Z. rugby.* an undirected kick of the ball.

speculum ('spɛkjʊləm) *n., pl* **-la** (-lə) *or* **-lums.** **1.** a mirror, esp. one made of polished metal for use in a telescope, etc. **2.** *Med.* an instrument for dilating a bodily cavity or passage to permit examination of its interior. **3.** a patch of distinctive colour on the wing of a bird. [C16: from L: mirror, from *specere* to look at]

sped (spɛd) *vb.* a past tense and past participle of **speed.**

speech (spiːtʃ) *n.* **1. a.** the act or faculty of speaking. **b.** (*as modifier*): *speech therapy.* **2.** that which is spoken; utterance. **3.** a talk or address delivered to an audience. **4.** a person's characteristic manner of speaking. **5.** a national or regional language or dialect. **6.** *Linguistics.* another word for **parole.** [OE *spēc*]

speech day *n. Brit.* (in schools) an annual day on which prizes are presented, speeches are made by guest speakers, etc.

speechify ('spiːtʃɪˌfaɪ) *vb.* **-fying, -fied.** (*intr.*) **1.** to make a speech or speeches. **2.** to talk pompously and boringly. —'speechiˌfier *n.*

speechless ('spiːtʃlɪs) *adj.* **1.** not able to speak. **2.** temporarily deprived of speech. **3.** not expressed or able to be expressed in words: *speechless fear.* —'speechlessly *adv.* —'speechlessness *n.*

speed (spiːd) *n.* **1.** the act or quality of acting or moving fast; rapidity. **2.** the rate at which something moves, is done, or acts. **3.** *Physics.* **a.** a scalar measure of the rate of movement of a body expressed either as the distance travelled divided by the time taken (**average speed**) or the rate of change of position with respect to time at a particular point (**instantaneous speed**). **b.** another word for **velocity** (sense 2). **4.** a rate of rotation, usually expressed in revolutions per unit time. **5. a.** a gear ratio in a motor vehicle, bicycle, etc. **b.** (*in combination*): *a three-speed gear.* **6.** *Photog.* a numerical expression of the sensitivity to light of a particular type of film, paper, or plate. **7.** *Photog.* a measure of the ability of a lens to pass light from an object to the image position. **8.** a slang word for **amphetamine.** **9.** *Arch.* prosperity or success. **10. at speed.** quickly. ~*vb.* **speeding; sped** *or* **speeded.** **11.** to move or go or cause to move or go quickly. **12.** (*intr.*) to drive (a motor vehicle) at a high speed, esp. above legal limits. **13.** (*tr.*) to help further the success or completion of. **14.** (*intr.*) *Sl.* to take or be under the influence of amphetamines. **15.** (*intr.*) to operate or run at a high speed. **16.** *Arch.* **a.** (*intr.*) to prosper or succeed. **b.** (*tr.*) to wish success to. ~See also **speed up.** [OE *spēd* (orig. in the sense: success)] —'speeder *n.*

speedball ('spiːdˌbɔːl) *n. Sl.* a mixture of heroin with amphetamine or cocaine.

speedboat ('spiːdˌbəʊt) *n.* a high-speed motorboat.

speed chess *n.* a form of chess in which each player's game is limited to a total stipulated time, usually half an hour; the first player to exceed the time limit loses.

speed limit *n.* the maximum permitted speed at which a vehicle may travel on certain roads.

speedo ('spiːdəʊ) *n., pl* **speedos.** an informal name for **speedometer.**

speedometer (spɪ'dɒmɪtə) *n.* a device fitted to a vehicle to measure and display the speed of travel. See also **mileometer.**

speed up *vb.* (*adv.*) **1.** to increase or cause to increase in speed or rate; accelerate. ~*n.* **speed-up. 2.** an instance of this; acceleration.

speedway ('spiːdˌweɪ) *n.* **1.** the sport of racing on light powerful motorcycles round cinder tracks. **2.** the track or stadium where such races are held. **3.** *U.S. & Canad.* **a.** a racetrack for cars. **b.** a road on which fast driving is allowed.

speedwell ('spiːdˌwɛl) *n.* any of various temperate plants, such as the **common speedwell** and the **germander speedwell,** having small blue or pinkish-white flowers.

speedy ('spiːdɪ) *adj.* **speedier, speediest. 1.** characterized by speed. **2.** done or decided without delay. —'speedily *adv.* —'speediness *n.*

spek (spɛk) *n. S. African.* bacon. [from Afrik., from Du.]

speleology *or* **spelaeology** (ˌspiːlɪ'ɒlədʒɪ) *n.* **1.** the scientific study of caves. **2.** the sport or pastime of exploring caves. [C19: from L *spēlaeum* cave] —**speleological** *or* **spelaeological** (ˌspiːlɪə'lɒdʒɪkəl) *adj.* —ˌspele'ologist *or* ˌspelae'ologist *n.*

spell[1] (spɛl) *vb.* **spelling; spelt** *or* **spelled. 1.** to write or name in correct order the letters that comprise the conventionally accepted form of (a word). **2.** (*tr.*) (of letters) to go to make up the conventionally established form of (a word) when arranged correctly: *d-o-g spells dog.* **3.** (*tr.*) to indicate or signify: *such actions spell disaster.* ~See also **spell out.** [C13: from OF *espeller,* of Gmc origin] —'spellable *adj.*

spell[2] (spɛl) *n.* **1.** a verbal formula considered as having magical force. **2.** any influence that can control the mind or character; fascination. **3.** a state induced as by the pronouncing of a spell; trance: *to break the spell.* **4. under a spell.** held in or as if in a spell. [OE *spell* speech]

spell[3] (spɛl) *n.* **1.** an indeterminate, usually short, period of time: *a spell of cold weather.* **2.** a period or tour of duty after which one person or group relieves another. **3.** *Scot., Austral., & N.Z.* a period or interval of rest. ~*vb.* **4.** (*tr.*) to take over from (a person) for an interval of time;

relieve temporarily. [OE *spelian* to take the place of, from ?]

spellbind ('spɛl,baɪnd) *vb.* **-binding, -bound.** (*tr.*) to cause to be spellbound; entrance or enthral. —'**spell,binder** *n.*

spellbound ('spɛl,baʊnd) *adj.* having one's attention held as though one is bound by a spell.

speller ('spɛlə) *n.* **1.** a person who spells words in the manner specified: *a bad speller.* **2.** a book designed to teach or improve spelling.

spelling ('spɛlɪŋ) *n.* **1.** the act or process of writing words by using the letters conventionally accepted for their formation; orthography. **2.** the art or study of orthography. **3.** the way in which a word is spelt. **4.** the ability of a person to spell.

spelling bee *n.* a contest in which players are required to spell words.

spell out *vb.* (*tr., adv.*) **1.** to make clear, distinct, or explicit; clarify in detail: *let me spell out the implications.* **2.** to read laboriously or with difficulty, working out each word letter by letter. **3.** to discern by study; puzzle out.

spelt[1] (spɛlt) *vb.* a past tense and past participle of **spell**[1].

spelt[2] (spɛlt) *n.* a species of wheat that was formerly much cultivated and was used to develop present-day cultivated wheats. [OE]

spelter ('spɛltə) *n.* impure zinc. [C17: prob. from MDu. *speauter*, from ?]

spelunker (spɪ'lʌŋkə) *n.* a person whose hobby is the exploration of caves. [C20: from L *spēlunca*, from Gk *spēlunx* a cave] —**spe'lunking** *n.*

Spence (spɛns) *n.* Sir **Basil** (**Unwin**). 1907–76, Scottish architect, born in India; designed Coventry Cathedral (1951).

spencer[1] ('spɛnsə) *n.* **1.** a short fitted coat or jacket. **2.** a woman's knitted vest. [C18: after Earl *Spencer* (1758–1834)]

spencer[2] ('spɛnsə) *n. Naut.* a large loose-footed gaffsail on a square-rigger or barque. [C19: ?from a proper name]

Spencer ('spɛnsə) *n.* **1. Herbert.** 1820–1903, English philosopher, who applied evolutionary theory to the study of society, favouring laissez-faire doctrines. **2.** Sir **Stanley.** 1891–1959, English painter, noted esp. for his paintings of Christ in a contemporary English setting.

Spencer Gulf *n.* an inlet of the Indian Ocean in S Australia, between the Eyre and Yorke Peninsulas. Length: about 320 km (200 miles). Greatest width: about 145 km (90 miles).

spend (spɛnd) *vb.* **spending, spent. 1.** to pay out (money, wealth, etc.). **2.** (*tr.*) to concentrate (time, effort, etc.) upon an object, activity, etc. **3.** (*tr.*) to pass (time) in a specific way, place, etc. **4.** (*tr.*) to use up completely: *the hurricane spent its force.* **5.** (*tr.*) to give up (one's blood, life, etc.) in a cause. [OE *spendan*, from L *expendere;* infl. also by OF *despendre* to spend; see EXPEND, DISPENSE] —'**spendable** *adj.* —'**spender** *n.*

Spender ('spɛndə) *n.* Sir **Stephen.** born 1909, English poet and critic, who played an important part in the left-wing literary movement of the 1930s: coeditor of *Horizon* (1939–41) and of *Encounter* (1953–67). His works include *Journals 1939–83* (1985), *Collected Poems* (1985), and the novel *The Temple* (1988).

spendthrift ('spɛnd,θrɪft) *n.* **1.** a person who spends money in an extravagant manner. ~*adj.* **2.** (*usually prenominal*) of or like a spendthrift.

Spengler ('spɛŋlə; German 'ʃpɛŋlər) *n.* **Oswald** ('ɔsvalt). 1880–1936, German philosopher of history, noted for *The Decline of the West* (1918–22), which argues that civilizations go through natural cycles of growth and decay.

Spenser ('spɛnsə) *n.* **Edmund.** ?1552–99, English poet celebrated for *The Faerie Queene* (1590; 1596), an allegorical romance. His other verse includes the collection of eclogues *The Shepherd's Calendar* (1579) and the marriage poem *Epithalamion* (1594).

Spenserian (spɛn'sɪərɪən) *adj.* **1.** relating to or characteristic of Edmund Spenser or his poetry. ~*n.* **2.** a student or imitator of Edmund Spenser.

Spenserian stanza *n. Prosody.* the stanza form used by the poet Spenser in his poem *The Faerie Queene*, consisting of eight lines in iambic pentameter and a concluding Alexandrine, rhyming a b a b b c b c c.

spent (spɛnt) *vb.* **1.** the past tense and past participle of **spend.** ~*adj.* **2.** used up or exhausted; consumed. **3.** (of a fish) exhausted by spawning.

sperm[1] (spɜːm) *n.* **1.** another name for **semen. 2.** a male reproductive cell; male gamete. [C14: from LL *sperma*, from Gk]

sperm[2] (spɜːm) *n.* short for **sperm whale, spermaceti,** or **sperm oil.**

-sperm *n. combining form.* (in botany) a seed: *gymnosperm.* —**-spermous** or **-spermal** *adj. combining form.*

spermaceti (,spɜːmə'sɛtɪ, -'siːtɪ) *n.* a white waxy substance obtained from oil from the head of the sperm whale. [C15: from Med. L *sperma cētī* whale's sperm, from *sperma* SPERM + L *cētus* whale, from Gk *kētos*]

spermatic (spɜː'mætɪk), **spermic** ('spɜːmɪk), or **spermous** ('spɜːməs) *adj.* **1.** of or relating to spermatozoa: *spermatic fluid.* **2.** of or relating to the testis: *the spermatic artery.* [C16: from LL *spermaticus*, from Gk *spermatikos* concerning seed, from *sperma* seed] —**sper'matically** *adv.*

spermatid ('spɜːmətɪd) *n. Zool.* any of four immature male gametes that are formed from a spermatocyte, each of which develops into a spermatozoon.

spermato-, spermo- *or before a vowel* **spermat-, sperm-** *combining form.* **1.** indicating sperm: *spermatozoon.* **2.** indicating seed: *spermatophyte.* [from Gk *sperma, spermat-* seed]

spermatocyte ('spɜːmətəʊ,saɪt) *n.* an immature male germ cell.

spermatogenesis (,spɜːmətəʊ'dʒɛnɪsɪs) *n.* the formation and maturation of spermatozoa in the testis. —**spermatogenetic** (,spɜːmətəʊdʒɪ'nɛtɪk) *adj.*

spermatogonium (,spɜːmətə'gəʊnɪəm) *n., pl.* **-nia** (-nɪə). *Zool.* an immature male germ cell that divides to form many spermatocytes.

spermatophyte ('spɜːmətəʊ,faɪt) *or* **spermophyte** *n.* any seed-bearing plant. Former name: **phanerogam.** —**spermatophytic** (,spɜːmətəʊ'fɪtɪk) *adj.*

spermatozoon (,spɜːmətəʊ'zəʊɒn) *n., pl.* **-zoa** (-zəʊə). any of the male reproductive cells released in the semen during ejaculation. Also called: **sperm, zoosperm.** —,**spermato'zoal,** ,**spermato'zoan,** *or* ,**spermato'zoic** *adj.*

spermicide ('spɜːmɪ,saɪd) *n.* any agent that kills spermatozoa. —,**spermi'cidal** *adj.*

sperm oil *n.* an oil obtained from the head of the sperm whale, used as a lubricant.

spermous ('spɜːməs) *adj.* **1.** of or relating to the sperm whale or its products. **2.** another word for **spermatic.**

sperm whale *n.* a large toothed whale, having a square-shaped head and hunted for sperm oil, spermaceti, and ambergris. Also called: **cachalot.** [C19: short for SPERMACETI *whale*]

spew (spjuː) *vb.* **1.** to eject (the contents of the stomach) involuntarily through the mouth; vomit. **2.** to spit (spittle, phlegm, etc.) out of the mouth. **3.** (usually foll. by *out*) to send or be sent out in a stream: *flames spewed out.* ~*n.* **4.** something ejected from the mouth. ~Also (archaic): **spue.** [OE *spīwan*] —'**spewer** *n.*

Spey (speɪ) *n.* a river in E Scotland, flowing generally northeast through the Grampian Mountains to the Moray Firth: salmon fishing. Length: 172 km (107 miles).

Speyer (German 'ʃpaɪər) *n.* a port in SW West Germany, in Rhineland-Palatinate on the Rhine: the scene of 50 imperial diets. Pop.: 43 800 (1984 est.). English name: **Spires.**

sp. gr. *abbrev. for* specific gravity.

sphagnum ('sfægnəm) *n.* any moss of the genus *Sphagnum*, of temperate bogs: layers of these mosses decay to form peat. Also called: **peat moss, bog moss.** [C18: from NL, from Gk *sphagnos* a variety of moss] —'**sphagnous** *adj.*

sphairee (sfaɪˈriː) *n. Austral.* a game resembling tennis played with wooden bats and a perforated plastic ball. [from Gk *sphaira* a ball]

sphalerite ('sfælə,raɪt, 'sfeɪlə-) *n.* a yellow to brownish-black mineral consisting mainly of zinc sulphide in cubic crystalline form: the chief source of zinc. Formula: ZnS. Also called: **zinc blende.** [C19: from Gk *sphaleros* deceitful, from *sphallein* to cause to stumble]

sphene (sfiːn) *n.* a brown, yellow, green, or grey lustrous mineral consisting of calcium titanium silicate in monoclinic crystalline form. Also called: **titanite.** [C19: from F *sphène*, from Gk *sphēn* a wedge, alluding to its crystals]

sphenoid ('sfiːnɔɪd) *adj.* *also* **sphenoidal.** **1.** wedge-shaped. **2.** of or relating to the sphenoid bone. ~*n.* **3.** See **sphenoid bone.**
sphenoid bone *n.* the large butterfly-shaped compound bone at the base of the skull.
sphere (sfɪə) *n.* **1.** *Maths.* **a.** a three-dimensional closed surface such that every point on the surface is equidistant from a given point, the centre. **b.** the solid figure bounded by this surface or the space enclosed by it. **2.** any object having approximately this shape; a globe. **3.** the night sky considered as a vaulted roof; firmament. **4.** any heavenly object such as a planet, natural satellite, or star. **5.** (in the Ptolemaic or Copernican systems of astronomy) one of a series of revolving hollow globes, arranged concentrically, on whose transparent surfaces the sun, the moon, the planets, and fixed stars were thought to be set. **6.** a particular field of activity; environment. **7.** a social class or stratum of society. ~*vb.* (*tr.*) *Chiefly poetic.* **8.** to surround or encircle. **9.** to place aloft or in the heavens. [C14: from LL *sphēra*, from L *sphaera* globe, from Gk *sphaira*] —**'spheral** *adj.*
-sphere *n. combining form.* **1.** having the shape or form of a sphere: *bathysphere.* **2.** indicating a spherelike enveloping mass: *atmosphere.* —**-spheric** *adj. combining form.*
spherical ('sfɛrɪkᵊl) *or* **spheric** *adj.* **1.** shaped like a sphere. **2.** of or relating to a sphere: *spherical geometry.* **3.** *Geom.* formed on the surface of or inside a sphere: *a spherical triangle.* **4. a.** of or relating to heavenly bodies. **b.** of or relating to the spheres of the Ptolemaic or the Copernican system. —**'spherically** *adv.* —**'sphericalness** *n.*
spherical aberration *n. Physics.* a defect of optical systems that arises when light striking a mirror or lens near its edge is focused at different points on the axis to the light striking near the centre. The effect occurs when the mirror or lens has spherical surfaces.
spherical angle *n.* an angle formed at the intersection of two great circles of a sphere.
spherical coordinates *pl. n.* three coordinates that define the location of a point in space in terms of its radius vector, r, the angle, θ, which this vector makes with one axis, and the angle, ϕ, which the plane of this vector makes with a mutually perpendicular axis.
spherical trigonometry *n.* the branch of trigonometry concerned with the measurement of the angles and sides of spherical triangles.
spheroid ('sfɪərɔɪd) *n.* **1.** another name for **ellipsoid of revolution.** ~*adj.* **2.** shaped like but not exactly a sphere. —**spher'oidal** *adj.* —**ˌspheroid'icity** *n.*
spherometer (sfɪə'rɒmɪtə) *n.* an instrument for measuring the curvature of a surface.
spherule ('sfɛruːl) *n.* a very small sphere. [C17: from LL *sphaerula*] —**'spherular** *adj.*
spherulite ('sfɛrʊˌlaɪt) *n.* any of several spherical masses of radiating needle-like crystals of one or more minerals occurring in rocks such as obsidian. —**spherulitic** (ˌsfɛrʊ'lɪtɪk) *adj.*
sphincter ('sfɪŋktə) *n. Anat.* a ring of muscle surrounding the opening of a hollow organ or body and contracting to close it. [C16: from LL, from Gk *sphinktēr*, from *sphingein* to grip tightly] —**'sphincteral** *adj.*
sphinx (sfɪŋks) *n.*, *pl.* **sphinxes** *or* **sphinges** ('sfɪndʒiːz). **1.** any of a number of huge stone statues built by the ancient Egyptians, having the body of a lion and the head of a man. **2.** an inscrutable person.
Sphinx (sfɪŋks) *n.* **the. 1.** *Greek myth.* a monster with a woman's head and a lion's body. She lay outside Thebes, asking travellers a riddle and killing them when they failed to answer it. Oedipus answered the riddle and the Sphinx then killed herself. **2.** the huge statue of a sphinx near the pyramids at El Gîza in Egypt. [C16: via L from Gk, apparently from *sphingein* to hold fast]
sphragistics (sfrə'dʒɪstɪks) *n.* (*functioning as sing.*) the study of seals and signet rings. [C19: from Gk *sphragistikos*, from *sphragizein* to seal, from *sphragis* a seal] —**sphra'gistic** *adj.*
sphygmo- *or before a vowel* **sphygm-** *combining form.* indicating the pulse: *sphygmograph.* [from Gk *sphugmos* pulsation, from *sphuzein* to throb]
sphygmograph ('sfɪgməʊˌgrɑːf) *n. Med.* an instrument for making a recording (**sphygmogram**) of variations in blood pressure and pulse. —**sphygmographic** (ˌsfɪgməʊ'græfɪk) *adj.* —**sphygmography** (sfɪg'mɒgrəfɪ) *n.*
sphygmomanometer (ˌsfɪgməʊmə'nɒmɪtə) *n. Med.* an instrument for measuring arterial blood pressure.
spicate ('spaɪkeɪt) *adj. Bot.* having, arranged in, or relating to spikes: *a spicate inflorescence.* [C17: from L *spīcātus* having spikes, from *spīca* a point]
spiccato (spɪ'kɑːtəʊ) *Music.* ~*n.* **1.** a style of playing a bowed stringed instrument in which the bow bounces lightly off the strings. ~*adj.*, *adv.* **2.** (to be played) in this manner. [It.: detached]
spice (spaɪs) *n.* **1. a.** any of a variety of aromatic vegetable substances, such as ginger, cinnamon, or nutmeg, used as flavourings. **b.** these substances collectively. **2.** something that represents or introduces zest, charm, or gusto. **3.** *Rare.* a small amount. ~*vb.* (*tr.*) **4.** to prepare or flavour (food) with spices. **5.** to introduce charm or zest into. [C13: from OF *espice*, from LL *speciēs* (pl.) spices, from L *speciēs* (sing.) kind; also associated with LL *spīcea* (unattested) fragrant herb, from L *spīceus* having spikes of foliage]
spicebush ('spaɪsˌbʊʃ) *n.* a North American shrub having aromatic leaves and bark.
Spice Islands *pl. n.* the former name of the **Moluccas.**
spick-and-span *or* **spic-and-span** ('spɪkən'spæn) *adj.* **1.** extremely neat and clean. **2.** new and fresh. [C17: shortened from *spick-and-span-new*, from obs. *spick* spike + *span-new*, from ON *spānnȳr* absolutely new]
spicule ('spɪkjuːl) *n.* **1.** Also called: **spiculum.** a small slender pointed structure or crystal, esp. any of the calcareous or siliceous elements of the skeleton of sponges, corals, etc. **2.** *Astron.* a spiked ejection of hot gas above the sun's surface. [C18: from L *spiculum* small, sharp point] —**spiculate** ('spɪkjʊˌleɪt, -lɪt) *adj.*
spicy ('spaɪsɪ) *adj.* **spicier, spiciest. 1.** seasoned with or containing spice. **2.** highly flavoured; pungent. **3.** *Inf.* suggestive of scandal or sensation. —**'spicily** *adv.* —**'spiciness** *n.*
spider ('spaɪdə) *n.* **1.** any of various predatory silk-producing arachnids, having four pairs of legs and a rounded unsegmented body. **2.** any of various similar or related arachnids. **3.** any implement or tool having the shape of a spider. **4.** any part of a machine having a number of radiating spokes, tines, or arms. **5.** Also called: **octopus.** *Brit.* a cluster of elastic straps fastened at a central point and used to hold a load on a car rack, motorcycle, etc. **6.** *Snooker, etc.* a rest having long legs, used to raise the cue above the level of the height of the ball. [OE *spīthra*] —**'spidery** *adj.*
spider crab *n.* any of various crabs having a small triangular body and very long legs.
spiderman ('spaɪdəˌmæn) *n.*, *pl.* **-men.** *Inf.*, *chiefly Brit.* a person who erects the steel structure of a building.
spider mite *n.* any of various plant-feeding mites, esp. the **red spider mite,** which is a serious orchard pest.
spider monkey *n.* **1.** any of several arboreal New World monkeys of Central and South America, having very long legs, a long prehensile tail, and a small head. **2. woolly spider monkey.** a rare related monkey of SE Brazil.
spider plant *n.* a house plant having long narrow leaves with a light central stripe.
spiderwort ('spaɪdəˌwɜːt) *n.* **1.** any of various American plants having blue, purplish, or pink flowers and widely grown as house plants. See also **tradescantia. 2.** any of various similar or related plants.
spiel (ʃpiːl) *n.* **1.** glib plausible talk, associated esp. with salesmen. ~*vb.* **2.** (*intr.*) to deliver a prepared spiel. **3.** (*tr.;* usually foll. by *off*) to recite (a prepared oration). [C19: from G *Spiel* play] —**'spieler** *n.*
spier ('spaɪə) *n. Arch.* a person who spies or scouts.
spiffing ('spɪfɪŋ) *adj. Brit. sl.*, *old-fashioned.* excellent; splendid. [C19: prob. from dialect *spiff* spruce, smart]
spiffy ('spɪfɪ) *adj.* **-fier, -fiest.** *U.S. & Canad. sl.* smart; stylish. [C19: from dialect *spiff* smartly dressed] —**'spiffily** *adv.*
spigot ('spɪgət) *n.* **1.** a stopper for the vent hole of a cask. **2.** a tap, usually of wood, fitted to a cask. **3.** a U.S. name for **tap**² (sense 1). **4.** a short projection on one component designed to fit into a hole on another, esp. the male part of a joint between two pipes. [C14: prob. from OProvençal *espiga* a head of grain, from L *spīca* a point]
spike¹ (spaɪk) *n.* **1.** a sharp point. **2.** any sharp-pointed object, esp. one made of metal. **3.** a long metal nail. **4.**

(*pl.*) shoes with metal projections on the sole and heel for greater traction, as used by athletes. **5.** *Brit. sl.* another word for **dosshouse.** ~*vb.* (*tr.*) **6.** to secure or supply with or as with spikes. **7.** to render ineffective or block the intentions of; thwart. **8.** to impale on a spike. **9.** to add alcohol to (a drink). **10.** *Volleyball.* to hit (a ball) sharply downwards with an overarm motion from the front of one's own court into the opposing court. **11.** (formerly) to render (a cannon) ineffective by blocking its vent with a spike. **12. spike (someone's) guns.** to thwart (someone's) purpose. [C13 *spyk*] —'**spiky** *adj.*

spike² (spaık) *n. Bot.* **1.** an inflorescence consisting of a raceme of sessile flowers. **2.** an ear of wheat, etc. [C14: from L *spica* ear of corn]

spikelet ('spaıklıt) *n. Bot.* a small spike, esp. the inflorescence of most grasses and sedges.

spikenard ('spaıknɑːd, 'spaıkə,nɑːd) *n.* **1.** an aromatic Indian plant, having rose-purple flowers. **2.** an aromatic ointment obtained from this plant. **3.** any of various similar or related plants. **4.** a North American plant having small green flowers and an aromatic root. ~Also called (for senses 1, 2): **nard.** [C14: from Med. L *spica nardi;* see SPIKE², NARD]

spile (spaıl) *n.* **1.** a heavy timber stake or pile. **2.** *U.S.* a spout for tapping sap from the sugar maple tree. **3.** a plug or spigot. ~*vb.* (*tr.*) **4.** to provide or support with a spile. **5.** *U.S.* to tap (a tree) with a spile. [C16: prob. from MDu. *spile* peg]

spill¹ (spıl) *vb.* **spilling; spilt** *or* **spilled.** (*mainly tr.*) **1.** (when *intr.,* usually foll. by *from, out of,* etc.) to fall or cause to fall from or as from a container, esp. unintentionally. **2.** to disgorge (contents, occupants, etc.) or (of contents, occupants, etc.) to be disgorged. **3.** to shed (blood). **4.** Also: **spill the beans.** *Inf.* to divulge something confidential. **5.** *Naut.* to let (wind) escape from a sail or (of the wind) to escape from a sail. ~*n.* **6.** *Inf.* a fall or tumble. **7.** short for **spillway. 8.** a spilling of liquid, etc., or the amount spilt. **9.** *Austral.* the declaring of several political jobs vacant when one higher up becomes so. [OE *spillan* to destroy] —'**spillage** *n.* —'**spiller** *n.*

spill² (spıl) *n.* a splinter of wood or strip of twisted paper with which pipes, fires, etc., are lit. [C13: of Gmc origin]

spillikin, spilikin ('spılıkın), *or* **spellican** ('spɛlıkən) *n.* a thin strip of wood, cardboard, or plastic, esp. one used in spillikins.

spillikins ('spılıkınz) *n.* (*functioning as sing.*) *Brit.* a game in which players try to pick each spillikin from a heap without moving any of the others. Also called: **jack-straws.**

spill over *vb.* **1.** (*intr., adv.*) to overflow or be forced out of an area, container, etc. ~*n.* **spillover.** *Chiefly U.S. & Canad.* **2.** the act of spilling over. **3.** the excess part of something.

spillway ('spıl,weı) *n.* a channel that carries away surplus water, as from a dam.

spilt (spılt) *vb.* a past tense and past participle of **spill¹.**

spin (spın) *vb.* **spinning, spun. 1.** to rotate or cause to rotate rapidly, as on an axis. **2. a.** to draw out and twist (natural fibres, as of silk or cotton) into a long continuous thread. **b.** to make such a thread or filament from (synthetic resins, etc.), usually by forcing through a nozzle. **3.** (of spiders, silkworms, etc.) to form (webs, cocoons, etc.) from a silky fibre exuded from the body. **4.** (*tr.*) to shape (metal) into a rounded form on a lathe. **5.** (*tr.*) *Inf.* to tell (a tale, story, etc.) by drawing it out at great length (esp. in **spin a yarn**). **6.** to bowl, pitch, hit, or kick (a ball) so that it rotates in the air and changes direction or speed on bouncing, or (of a ball) to be projected in this way. **7.** (*intr.*) (of wheels) to revolve rapidly without causing propulsion. **8.** to cause (an aircraft) to dive in a spiral descent or (of an aircraft) to dive in a spiral descent. **9.** (*intr.;* foll. by *along*) to drive or travel swiftly. **10.** (*tr.*) Also: **spin-dry.** to rotate (clothes) in a washing machine in order to extract surplus water. **11.** (*intr.*) to reel or grow dizzy, as from turning around: *my head is spinning.* **12.** (*intr.*) to fish by drawing a revolving lure through the water. ~*n.* **13.** a swift rotating motion; instance of spinning. **14.** *Physics.* **a.** the intrinsic angular momentum of an elementary particle or atomic nucleus. **b.** a quantum number determining values of this angular momentum. **15.** a condition of loss of control of an aircraft or an intentional flight manoeuvre in which the aircraft performs a

continuous spiral descent. **16.** a spinning motion imparted to a ball, etc. **17.** *Inf.* a short or fast drive, ride, etc., esp. in a car, for pleasure. **18. flat spin.** *Inf., chiefly Brit.* a state of agitation or confusion. **19.** *Austral. & N.Z. inf.* a period of a specified kind of fortune: *a bad spin.* ~See also **spin out.** [OE *spinnan*]

spina bifida ('spaınə 'bıfıdə) *n.* a congenital condition in which the meninges of the spinal cord protrude through a gap in the backbone, sometimes causing enlargement of the skull and paralysis. [NL; see SPINE, BIFID]

spinach ('spınıdʒ, -ıtʃ) *n.* **1.** an annual plant cultivated for its dark green edible leaves. **2.** the leaves, eaten as a vegetable. [C16: from OF *espinache,* from OSp., from Ar. *isfānākh,* from Persian]

spinal ('spaın³l) *adj.* **1.** of or relating to the spine or the spinal cord. ~*n.* **2.** short for **spinal anaesthesia.** —'**spinally** *adv.*

spinal anaesthesia *n.* **1.** anaesthesia of the lower half of the body produced by injecting an anaesthetic beneath the arachnoid membrane. **2.** loss of sensation in part of the body as the result of injury of the spinal cord.

spinal canal *n.* the passage through the spinal column that contains the spinal cord.

spinal column *n.* a series of contiguous or interconnecting bony or cartilaginous segments that surround and protect the spinal cord. Also called: **spine, vertebral column.** Nontechnical name: **backbone.**

spinal cord *n.* the thick cord of nerve tissue within the spinal canal, which together with the brain forms the central nervous system.

spin bowler *n.* another name for **spinner** (sense 2).

spindle ('spınd³l) *n.* **1.** a rod or stick that has a notch in the top, used to draw out natural fibres for spinning into thread, and a long narrow body around which the thread is wound when spun. **2.** one of the thin rods or pins bearing bobbins upon which spun thread is wound in a spinning machine. **3.** any of various parts in the form of a rod, esp. a rotating rod that acts as an axle, etc. **4.** a piece of wood that has been turned, such as a table leg. **5.** a small square metal shaft that passes through the lock of a door and to which the door knobs or handles are fixed. **6.** *Biol.* a spindle-shaped structure formed in a cell during mitosis or meiosis which draws the duplicated chromosomes apart during cell division. **7.** a device consisting of a sharp upright spike on a pedestal on which bills, order forms, etc., are impaled. ~*vb.* **8.** (*tr.*) to form into a spindle or equip with spindles. **9.** (*intr.*) *Rare.* (of a plant, stem, shoot, etc.) to grow rapidly and become elongated and thin. [OE *spinel*]

spindlelegs ('spınd³l,lɛgz) *or* **spindleshanks** *n.* **1.** (*functioning as pl.*) long thin legs. **2.** (*functioning as sing.*) a person who has such legs.

spindle tree *n.* any of various shrubs or trees of Europe and W Asia, typically having red fruits and yielding a hard wood formerly used in making spindles.

spindly ('spındlı) *adj.* **-dlier, -dliest.** tall, slender, and frail; attenuated.

spindrift ('spın,drıft) *n.* spray blown up from the sea. Also: **spoondrift.** [C16: Scot. var. of *spoondrift,* from *spoon* to scud + DRIFT]

spin-dry *vb.* **-drying, -dried.** (*tr.*) to dry (clothes, etc.) in a spin-dryer.

spin-dryer *n.* a device that extracts water from clothes, etc., by spinning them in a perforated drum.

spine (spaın) *n.* **1.** the spinal column. **2.** the sharply pointed tip or outgrowth of a leaf, stem, etc. **3.** *Zool.* a hard pointed process or structure, such as the quill of a porcupine. **4.** the back of a book, record sleeve, etc. **5.** a ridge, esp. of a hill. **6.** strength of endurance, will, etc. **7.** anything resembling the spinal column in function or importance; main support or feature. [C14: from OF *espine* spine, from L *spina* thorn, backbone] —**spined** *adj.*

spine-chiller *n.* a book, film, etc., that arouses terror. —'**spine-,chilling** *adj.*

spinel (spı'nɛl) *n.* any of a group of hard glassy minerals of variable colour consisting of oxides of aluminium, magnesium, iron, zinc, or manganese: used as gemstones. [C16: from F *spinelle,* from It. *spinella,* dim. of *spina* a thorn, from L; so called from the shape of the crystals]

spineless ('spaınlıs) *adj.* **1.** lacking a backbone. **2.** having no spiny processes: *spineless stems.* **3.** lacking character, resolution, or courage. —'**spinelessly** *adv.* —'**spinelessness** *n.*

spinet (spɪ'nɛt, 'spɪnɪt) *n.* a small type of harpsichord having one manual. [C17: from It. *spinetta*, ? from Giovanni *Spinetti*, 16th-cent. It. maker of musical instruments & its supposed inventor]

spinifex ('spɪnɪˌfɛks) *n.* **1.** any of various Australian grasses having pointed leaves and spiny seed heads. **2.** Also called: **porcupine grass.** *Austral.* any of various coarse spiny-leaved inland grasses. [C19: from NL, from L *spīna* a thorn + *-fex* maker, from *facere* to make]

spinnaker ('spɪnəkə; *Naut.* 'spæŋkə) *n.* a large light triangular racing sail set from the foremast of a yacht. [C19: prob. from SPIN + (MO)NIKER, but traditionally from *Sphinx*, the yacht that first adopted this type of sail]

spinner ('spɪnə) *n.* **1.** a person or thing that spins. **2.** *Cricket.* **a.** a ball that is bowled with a spinning motion. **b.** a bowler who specializes in bowling such balls. **3.** a streamlined fairing that fits over the hub of an aircraft propeller. **4.** a fishing lure with a fin or wing that revolves.

spinneret ('spɪnəˌrɛt) *n.* **1.** any of several organs in spiders and certain insects through which silk threads are exuded. **2.** a finely perforated dispenser through which a liquid is extruded in the production of synthetic fibres.

spinney ('spɪnɪ) *n. Chiefly Brit.* a small wood or copse. [C16: from OF *espinei*, from *espine* thorn, from L *spīna*]

spinning ('spɪnɪŋ) *n.* **1.** the act or process of spinning. **2.** the act or technique of casting and drawing a revolving lure through the water so as to imitate a live fish, etc.

spinning jenny *n.* an early type of spinning frame with several spindles, invented in 1764.

spinning wheel *n.* a wheel-like machine for spinning at home, having one hand- or foot-operated spindle.

spin-off *n.* any product or development derived incidentally from the application of existing knowledge or enterprise.

spinose ('spaɪnəʊs, spaɪ'nəʊs) *adj.* (esp. of plants) bearing many spines. [C17: from L *spīnōsus* prickly, from *spīna* a thorn]

spin out *vb.* (*tr., adv.*) **1.** to extend or protract (a story, etc.) by including superfluous detail. **2.** to spend or pass (time). **3.** to contrive to cause (money, etc.) to last as long as possible.

Spinoza (spɪ'nəʊzə) *n.* **Baruch** (bə'ruːk). 1632–77, Dutch philosopher who constructed a holistic metaphysical system derived from a series of hypotheses that he judged self-evident. His chief work is *Ethics* (1677).

spinster ('spɪnstə) *n.* **1.** an unmarried woman. **2.** a woman regarded as being beyond the age of marriage. **3.** (formerly) a woman who spins thread for her living. [C14 (in the sense: a person, esp. a woman, whose occupation is spinning; C17: a woman still unmarried): from SPIN + -STER] —'spinster,hood *n.* —'spinsterish *adj.*

spiny ('spaɪnɪ) *adj.* **spinier, spiniest. 1.** (of animals) having or covered with quills or spines. **2.** (of plants) covered with spines; thorny. **3.** troublesome; puzzling. —'spininess *n.*

spiny anteater *n.* another name for **echidna.**

spiny-finned *adj.* (of certain fishes) having fins that are supported by stiff bony spines.

spiny lobster *n.* any of various large edible marine decapod crustaceans having a very tough spiny carapace. Also called: **rock lobster, crawfish, langouste.**

spiracle ('spaɪərək²l, 'spaɪrə-) *n.* **1.** any of several paired apertures in the cuticle of an insect, by which air enters and leaves the trachea. **2.** a small paired rudimentary gill slit in skates, rays, and related fishes. **3.** any similar respiratory aperture, such as the blowhole in whales. [C14 (orig.: breath): from L *spīrāculum* vent, from *spīrāre* to breathe] —**spiracular** (spɪ'rækjʊlə) *adj.* —**spi'raculate** *adj.*

spiraea *or esp. U.S.* **spirea** (spaɪ'rɪə) *n.* any of various rosaceous plants having sprays of small white or pink flowers. See also **meadowsweet** (sense 2). [C17: via L from Gk *speiraia*, from *speira* SPIRE²]

spiral ('spaɪərəl) *n.* **1.** *Geom.* one of several plane curves formed by a point winding about a fixed point at an ever-increasing distance from it. **2.** a curve that lies on a cylinder or cone, at a constant angle to the line segments making up the surface; helix. **3.** something that pursues a winding, usually upward, course or that displays a twisting form or shape. **4.** a flight manoeuvre in which an aircraft descends describing a helix of comparatively large

radius with the angle of attack within the normal flight range. **5.** *Econ.* a continuous upward or downward movement in economic activity or prices, caused by interaction between prices, wages, demand, and production. ~*adj.* **6.** having the shape of a spiral. ~*vb.* **-ralling, -ralled** *or U.S.* **-raling, -raled. 7.** to assume or cause to assume a spiral course or shape. **8.** (*intr.*) to increase or decrease with steady acceleration: *prices continue to spiral.* [C16: via F from Med. L *spīrālis*, from L *spīra* a coil; see SPIRE²] —'spirally *adv.*

spiral galaxy *n.* a galaxy consisting of an ellipsoidal nucleus of old stars from opposite sides of which arms, containing younger stars, spiral outwards around the nucleus.

spirant ('spaɪrənt) *adj.* **1.** *Phonetics.* another word for **fricative.** ~*n.* **2.** a fricative consonant. [C19: from L *spīrāns* breathing, from *spīrāre* to breathe]

spire¹ ('spaɪə) *n.* **1.** Also called: **steeple.** a tall structure that tapers upwards to a point, esp. one on a tower or roof or one that forms the upper part of a steeple. **2.** a slender tapering shoot or stem, such as a blade of grass. **3.** the apical part of any tapering formation; summit. ~*vb.* **4.** (*intr.*) to assume the shape of a spire; point up. **5.** (*tr.*) to furnish with a spire or spires. [OE *spīr* blade] —'spiry *adj.*

spire² ('spaɪə) *n.* **1.** any of the coils or turns in a spiral structure. **2.** the apical part of a spiral shell. [C16: from L *spīra* a coil, from Gk *speira*]

Spires (spaɪəz) *n.* the English name for **Speyer.**

spirillum (spaɪ'rɪləm) *n., pl.* **-la** (-lə). **1.** any bacterium having a curved or spirally twisted rodlike body. **2.** any bacterium of the genus *Spirillum*, such as *S. minus*, which causes ratbite fever. [C19: from NL, lit.: a little coil, from *spīra* a coil]

spirit¹ ('spɪrɪt) *n.* **1.** the force or principle of life that animates the body of living things. **2.** temperament or disposition: *truculent in spirit.* **3.** liveliness; mettle: *they set to it with spirit.* **4.** the fundamental, emotional, and activating principle of a person; will: *the experience broke his spirit.* **5.** a sense of loyalty or dedication: *team spirit.* **6.** the prevailing element; feeling: *a spirit of joy pervaded the atmosphere.* **7.** state of mind or mood; attitude: *he did it in the wrong spirit.* **8.** (*pl.*) an emotional state, esp. with regard to exaltation or dejection: *in high spirits.* **9.** a person characterized by some activity, quality, or disposition: *a leading spirit of the movement.* **10.** the deeper more significant meaning as opposed to a pedantic interpretation: *the spirit of the law.* **11.** a person's intangible being as contrasted with his physical presence: *I shall be with you in spirit.* **12. a.** an incorporeal being, esp. the soul of a dead person. **b.** (*as modifier*): *spirit world.* ~*vb.* (*tr.*) **13.** (usually foll. by *away* or *off*) to carry off mysteriously or secretly. **14.** (often foll. by *up*) to impart animation or courage to. [C13: from OF *esperit*, from L *spīritus* breath, spirit] —'spiritless *adj.*

spirit² ('spɪrɪt) *n.* **1.** (*often pl.*) any distilled alcoholic liquor, such as whisky or gin. **2.** *Chem.* **a.** an aqueous solution of ethanol, esp. one obtained by distillation. **b.** the active principle or essence of a substance, extracted as a liquid, esp. by distillation. **3.** *Pharmacol.* a solution of a volatile substance, esp. a volatile oil, in alcohol. **4.** *Alchemy.* any of the four substances sulphur, mercury, sal ammoniac, or arsenic. [C14: special use of SPIRIT¹, name applied to alchemical substances (as in sense 4), hence extended to distilled liquids]

Spirit ('spɪrɪt) *n.* **the.** **a.** another name for the **Holy Spirit.** **b.** God, esp. when regarded as transcending material limitations.

spirited ('spɪrɪtɪd) *adj.* **1.** displaying animation, vigour, or liveliness. **2.** (*in combination*) characterized by mood, temper, or disposition as specified: *high-spirited; public-spirited.* —'spiritedly *adv.* —'spiritedness *n.*

spirit gum *n.* a glue made from gum dissolved in ether used to affix a false beard, etc.

spiritism ('spɪrɪˌtɪzəm) *n.* a less common word for **spiritualism.** —'spiritist *n.* —,spirit'istic *adj.*

spirit lamp *n.* a lamp that burns methylated or other spirits instead of oil.

spirit level *n.* a device for setting horizontal surfaces, consisting of a block of material in which a sealed tube partially filled with liquid is set so that the air bubble rests between two marks on the tube when the block is horizontal.

spiritous ('spirɪtəs) *adj.* a variant spelling of **spirituous**.

spirits of ammonia *n.* (*functioning as sing. or pl.*) another name for **sal volatile**.

spirits of hartshorn *n.* (*functioning as sing. or pl.*) a solution of ammonia gas in water. See **ammonium hydroxide**. Also called: **aqueous ammonia**.

spirits of salt *n.* (*functioning as sing. or pl.*) a solution of hydrochloric acid in water.

spiritual ('spirɪtjʊəl) *adj.* **1.** relating to the spirit or soul and not to physical nature or matter; intangible. **2.** of or relating to sacred things, the Church, religion, etc. **3.** standing in a relationship based on communication between souls or minds: *a spiritual father*. **4.** having a mind or emotions of a high and delicately refined quality. ~*n.* **5.** Also called: **Negro spiritual**. a type of religious song originating among Black slaves in the American South. **6.** (*often pl.*) the sphere of religious, spiritual, or ecclesiastical matters, or such matters in themselves. — ˌspiritu'ality *n.* — 'spiritually *adv.*

spiritualism ('spirɪtjʊəˌlɪzəm) *n.* **1.** the belief that the disembodied spirits of the dead, surviving in another world, can communicate with the living in this world, esp. through mediums. **2.** the doctrines and practices associated with this belief. **3.** *Philosophy.* the belief that because reality is to some extent immaterial it is therefore spiritual. **4.** any doctrine that prefers the spiritual to the material. — 'spiritualist *n.*

spiritualize *or* **-ise** ('spirɪtjʊəˌlaɪz) *vb.* (*tr.*) to make spiritual or infuse with spiritual content. — ˌspirituali'zation *or* **-i'sation** *n.* — 'spiritualˌizer *or* **-iser** *n.*

spirituel (ˌspirɪtjʊ'el) *adj.* having a refined and lively mind or wit. Also (*fem.*): **spirituelle**. [C17: from F]

spirituous ('spirɪtjʊəs) *adj.* **1.** characterized by or containing alcohol. **2.** (of a drink) being a spirit. — **spirituosity** (ˌspirɪtjʊ'ɒsɪtɪ) *or* **'spirituousness** *n.*

spirochaete *or U.S.* **spirochete** ('spaɪrəʊˌkiːt) *n.* any of a group of spirally coiled rodlike bacteria that includes the causative agent of syphilis. [C19: from NL, from *spiro-*, from L *spira*, from Gk *speira* a coil + *chaeta*, from Gk *khaitē* long hair]

spirograph ('spaɪrəˌgrɑːf) *n. Med.* an instrument for recording the movements of breathing. [C20: NL, from *spiro-*, from L *spirāre* to breathe + -GRAPH] — ˌspiro'graphic *adj.*

spirogyra (ˌspaɪrəʊ'dʒaɪrə) *n.* any of various green freshwater multicellular algae containing spirally coiled chloroplasts. [C20: from NL, from *spiro-*, from L *spira*, from Gk *speira* a coil + Gk *guros* a circle]

spirt (spɜːt) *n.* a variant spelling of **spurt**.

spiry ('spaɪərɪ) *adj. Poetic.* of spiral form; helical.

spit[1] (spit) *vb.* **spitting, spat** *or* **spit. 1.** (*intr.*) to expel saliva from the mouth; expectorate. **2.** (*intr.*) *Inf.* to show disdain or hatred by spitting. **3.** (of a fire, hot fat, etc.) to eject (sparks, etc.) violently and with an explosive sound. **4.** (*intr.*) to rain very lightly. **5.** (*tr.;* often foll. by *out*) to eject or discharge (something) from the mouth: *he spat the food out*. **6.** (*tr.;* often foll. by *out*) to utter (short sharp words or syllables), esp. in a violent manner. **7. spit it out!** *Brit. inf.* a command given to someone that he should speak forthwith. ~*n.* **8.** another name for **spittle**. **9.** a light or brief fall of rain, snow, etc. **10.** the act or an instance of spitting. **11.** *Inf.*, chiefly *Brit.* another word for **spitting image**. [OE *spittan*] — 'spitter *n.*

spit[2] (spit) *n.* **1.** a pointed rod on which meat is skewered and roasted before or over an open fire. **2.** Also called: **rotisserie, rotating spit.** a similar device fitted onto a cooker. **3.** an elongated often hooked strip of sand or shingle projecting from a shore. ~*vb.* **spitting, spitted. 4.** (*tr.*) to impale on or transfix with or as if with a spit. [OE *spitu*]

spit and polish *n. Inf.* punctilious attention to neatness, discipline, etc., esp. in the armed forces.

spite (spaɪt) *n.* **1.** maliciousness; venomous ill will. **2.** an instance of such malice; grudge. **3. in spite of.** (*prep.*) in defiance of; regardless of; notwithstanding. ~*vb.* (*tr.*) **4.** to annoy in order to vent spite. [C13: var. of DESPITE] — 'spiteful *adj.*

spitfire ('spit,faɪə) *n.* a person given to outbursts of spiteful temper, esp. a woman or girl.

Spithead (ˌspit'hɛd) *n.* an extensive anchorage between the mainland of England and the Isle of Wight, off Portsmouth.

Spitsbergen ('spits,bɜːgən) *n.* another name for **Svalbard**.

spitting image *n. Inf.* a person who bears a strong physical resemblance to another. Also called: **spit, spit and image**. [C19: modification of *spit and image*, from SPIT[1] (as in *the very spit of* the exact likeness of)]

spitting snake *n.* another name for the **ringhals**.

spittle ('spit²l) *n.* **1.** the fluid secreted in the mouth; saliva. **2.** Also called: **cuckoo spit, frog spit.** the frothy substance secreted on plants by the larvae of certain froghoppers. [OE *spǣtl* saliva]

spittoon (spi'tuːn) *n.* a receptacle for spittle, usually in a public place.

spitz (spits) *n.* any of various breeds of dog characterized by a stocky build, a pointed muzzle, erect ears, and a tightly-curled tail. [C19: from G *Spitz*, from *spitz* pointed]

Spitz (spits) *n.* **Mark.** born 1950, U.S. swimmer, who won seven gold medals at the 1972 Olympic Games.

spiv (spiv) *n. Brit. sl.* a person who makes a living by underhand dealings or swindling; black marketeer. [C20: back formation from dialect *spiving* small] — 'spivvy *adj.*

splake (spleɪk) *n.* a type of hybrid trout bred by Canadian zoologists. [from *sp(eckled)* + *lake (trout)*]

splanchnic ('splæŋknɪk) *adj.* of or relating to the viscera: *a splanchnic nerve.* [C17: from NL *splanchnicus*, from Gk, from *splankhna* the entrails]

splash (splæʃ) *vb.* **1.** to scatter (liquid) about in blobs; spatter. **2.** to descend or cause to descend upon in scattered blobs: *he splashed his jacket; rain splashed against the window.* **3.** to make (one's way) by or as if by splashing: *he splashed through the puddle.* **4.** (*tr.*) to print (a story or photograph) prominently in a newspaper. ~*n.* **5.** an instance or sound of splashing. **6.** an amount splashed. **7.** a mark or patch created by or as if by splashing. **8.** *Inf.* an extravagant display, usually for effect (esp. in **make a splash**). **9.** a small amount of soda water, etc., added to an alcoholic drink. [C18: alteration of PLASH] — 'splashy *adj.*

splashdown ('splæʃ,daʊn) *n.* **1.** the controlled landing of a spacecraft on water at the end of a space flight. **2.** the time scheduled for this event. ~*vb.* **splash down. 3.** (*intr., adv.*) (of a spacecraft) to make a splashdown.

splat[1] (splæt) *n.* a wet slapping sound. [C19: imit.]

splat[2] (splæt) *n.* a wide flat piece of wood, esp. one that is the upright central part of a chair back. [C19: ? rel. to OE *splātan* to split]

splatter ('splætə) *vb.* **1.** to splash with small blobs. ~*n.* **2.** a splash of liquid, mud, etc.

splay (spleɪ) *adj.* **1.** spread out; broad and flat. **2.** turned outwards in an awkward manner. ~*vb.* **3.** to spread out; turn out or expand. ~*n.* **4.** a surface of a wall that forms an oblique angle to the main flat surfaces, esp. at a doorway or window opening. [C14: short for DISPLAY]

splayfoot ('spleɪ,fʊt) *n., pl.* **-feet.** *Pathol.* another word for **flatfoot**. — 'splay,footed *adj.*

spleen (spliːn) *n.* **1.** a spongy highly vascular organ situated near the stomach in man. It forms lymphocytes, produces antibodies, and filters bacteria and foreign particles from the blood. **2.** the corresponding organ in other animals. **3.** spitefulness or ill humour: *to vent one's spleen.* **4.** *Arch.* the organ in the human body considered to be the seat of the emotions. **5.** *Arch.* another word for **melancholy**. [C13: from OF *esplen*, from L *splēn*, from Gk] — 'spleenish *or* 'spleeny *adj.*

spleenwort ('spliːn,wɜːt) *n.* any of various ferns that often grow on walls.

splendent ('splɛndənt) *adj. Arch.* **1.** shining brightly; lustrous: *a splendent sun.* **2.** famous; illustrious. [C15: from L *splendēns* brilliant, from *splendēre* to shine]

splendid ('splɛndɪd) *adj.* **1.** brilliant or fine, esp. in appearance. **2.** characterized by magnificence. **3.** glorious or illustrious: *a splendid reputation.* **4.** brightly gleaming; radiant: *splendid colours.* **5.** very good or satisfactory: *a splendid time.* [C17: from L *splendidus*, from *splendēre* to shine] — 'splendidly *adv.* — 'splendidness *n.*

splendiferous (splɛn'dɪfərəs) *adj. Facetious.* grand; splendid: *a really splendiferous meal.* [C15: from Med. L *splendiferus*, from L *splendor* radiance + *ferre* to bring]

splendour or U.S. **splendor** ('splɛndə) n. 1. the state or quality of being splendid. 2. **sun in splendour.** Heraldry. a representation of the sun with rays and a human face.

splenetic (splɪ'nɛtɪk) adj. 1. of or relating to the spleen. 2. spiteful or irritable; peevish. ~n. 3. a spiteful or irritable person. —**sple'netically** adv.

splenic ('splɛnɪk, 'spliː-) adj. 1. of, relating to, or in the spleen. 2. having a disease or disorder of the spleen.

splenius ('spliːnɪəs) n., pl. -**nii** (-nɪˌaɪ). either of two muscles at the back of the neck that rotate, flex, and extend the head and neck. [C18: via NL from Gk splénion a plaster] —**splenial** adj.

splenomegaly (ˌspliːnəʊ'mɛgəlɪ) n. abnormal enlargement of the spleen. [C20: NL, from Gk splḗn spleen + megal-, stem of megas big]

splice (splaɪs) vb. (tr.) 1. to join (two ropes) by intertwining the strands. 2. to join up the trimmed ends of (two pieces of wire, film, etc.) with solder or an adhesive material. 3. to join (timbers) by overlapping and binding or bolting the ends together. 4. (passive) Inf. to enter into marriage: the couple got spliced. 5. **splice the mainbrace.** Naut. to issue and partake of an extra allocation of alcoholic spirits. ~n. 6. a join made by splicing. 7. the place where such a join occurs. 8. the wedge-shaped end of a cricket-bat handle that fits into the blade. [C16: prob. from MDu. splissen] —**splicer** n.

spline (splaɪn) n. 1. any one of a series of narrow keys formed longitudinally around a shaft that fit into corresponding grooves in a mating part: used to prevent movement between two parts, esp. in transmitting torque. 2. a long narrow strip of wood, metal, etc.; slat. 3. a thin narrow strip made of wood, metal, or plastic fitted into a groove in the edge of a board, tile, etc., to connect it to another. ~vb. 4. (tr.) to provide (a shaft, part, etc.) with splines. [C18: East Anglian dialect; ? rel. to OE splin spindle]

splint (splɪnt) n. 1. a rigid support for restricting movement of an injured part, esp. a broken bone. 2. a thin sliver of wood, esp. one used to light cigars, a fire, etc. 3. a thin strip of wood woven with others to form a chair seat, basket, etc. 4. Vet. science. a bony enlargement of the cannon bone of a horse. ~vb. 5. to apply a splint to (a broken arm, etc.). [C13: from MLow G splinte]

splinter ('splɪntə) n. 1. a small thin sharp piece of wood, glass, etc., broken off from a whole. 2. a metal fragment from a shell, bomb, etc., thrown out during an explosion. ~vb. 3. to reduce or be reduced to sharp fragments. 4. to break or be broken off in small sharp fragments. [C14: from MDu. splinter; see SPLINT] —**splintery** adj.

splinter group n. a number of members of an organization, political party, etc., who split from the main body and form an independent association of their own.

split (splɪt) vb. **splitting, split.** 1. to break or cause to break, esp. forcibly, by cleaving into separate pieces, often into two roughly equal pieces. 2. to separate or be separated from a whole: he split a piece of wood from the block. 3. to separate or be separated into factions, usually through discord. 4. (often foll. by up) to separate or cause to separate through a disagreement. 5. (when tr., often foll. by up) to divide or be divided among two or more persons: split up the pie among us. 6. Sl. to depart; leave: let's split. 7. (tr.) to separate (something) into its components by interposing something else: to split a word with hyphens. 8. (intr.; usually foll. by on) Sl. to betray; inform: he split on me to the cops. 9. (tr.) U.S. politics. to mark (a ballot, etc.) so as to vote for the candidates of more than one party: he split the ticket. 10. **split one's sides.** to laugh very heartily. ~n. 11. the act or process of splitting. 12. a gap or rift caused or a piece removed by the process of splitting. 13. a breach or schism in a group or the faction resulting from such a breach. 14. a dessert of sliced fruit and ice cream, covered with whipped cream, nuts, etc.: banana split. 15. See **Devonshire split.** 16. Tenpin bowling. a formation of the pins after the first bowl in which there is a large gap between two pins or groups of pins. 17. Inf. an arrangement or process of dividing up loot or money. ~adj. 18. having been split; divided: split logs. 19. having a split or splits: hair with split ends. ~See also **splits, split up.** [C16: from MDu. splitten to cleave] —**splitter** n.

Split (Serbo-Croatian split) n. a port and resort in W Yugoslavia, in Croatia on the Adriatic: became part of Yugoslavia in 1918 after Austrian rule since 1797: remains of the palace of Diocletian (295–305). Pop.: 235 922 (1981). Italian name: **Spalato.**

split infinitive n. (in English grammar) an infinitive used with another word between to and the verb itself, as in to really finish it.
▷**Usage.** The traditional rule against placing an adverb between to and its verb is gradually disappearing. Although it is true that a split infinitive may result in a clumsy sentence, this is not enough to justify the absolute condemnation that this practice has attracted. Indeed, very often the most natural position of the adverb is between to and the verb (he decided to really try) and to change it would result in an artificial and awkward construction (he really decided to try). The current view is therefore that the split infinitive is not a grammatical error. Nevertheless, many writers prefer to avoid splitting infinitives in formal English, since readers with a more traditional point of view are likely to interpret this as incorrect.

split-level adj. (of a house, room, etc.) having the floor level of one part about half a storey above the floor level of an adjoining part.

split pea n. a pea dried and split and used in soups, pease pudding, or as a vegetable.

split personality n. 1. the tendency to change rapidly in mood or temperament. 2. a nontechnical term for **multiple personality.**

splits (splɪts) n. (functioning as sing.) (in gymnastics, etc.) the act of sinking to the floor to achieve a sitting position in which both legs are straight, pointing in opposite directions, and at right angles to the body.

split-screen technique n. a cinematic device by which two or more complete images are projected simultaneously onto separate parts of the screen. Also called: **split screen.**

split second n. 1. an infinitely small period of time; instant. ~adj. **split-second.** (prenominal) 2. made or arrived at in an infinitely short time: a split-second decision. 3. depending upon minute precision: split-second timing.

split shift n. a work period divided into two parts that are separated by an interval longer than a normal rest period.

splitting ('splɪtɪŋ) adj. 1. (of a headache) intolerably painful; acute. 2. (of the head) assailed by an overpowering unbearable pain.

split up vb. (adv.) 1. (tr.) to separate out into parts; divide. 2. (intr.) to become parted through disagreement: they split up after years of marriage. 3. to break down or be capable of being broken down into constituent parts. ~n. **split-up.** 4. the act or an instance of separating.

splodge (splɒdʒ) n. 1. a large irregular spot or blot. ~vb. 2. (tr.) to mark (something) with such a blot or blots. [C19: alteration of earlier SPLOTCH] —**splodgy** adj.

splotch (splɒtʃ) n., vb. the usual U.S. word for **splodge.** [C17: ? a blend of SPOT + BLOTCH] —**splotchy** adj.

splurge (splɜːdʒ) n. 1. an ostentatious display, esp. of wealth. 2. a bout of unrestrained extravagance. ~vb. 3. (often foll. by on) to spend (money) extravagantly. [C19: from ?]

splutter ('splʌtə) vb. 1. to spit out (saliva, food particles, etc.) from the mouth in an explosive manner, as through choking or laughing. 2. to utter (words) with spitting sounds, as through rage or choking. 3. to eject or be ejected in an explosive manner: sparks spluttered from the fire. 4. (tr.) to bespatter (a person) with tiny particles explosively ejected. ~n. 5. the process or noise of spluttering. 6. spluttering incoherent speech. 7. anything ejected through spluttering. [C17: var. of SPUTTER, infl. by SPLASH] —**splutterer** n.

Spock (spɒk) n. **Benjamin,** known as Dr Spock. born 1903, U.S. paediatrician, whose The Common Sense Book of Baby and Child Care (1946) has influenced the upbringing of children throughout the world.

spode (spəʊd) n. (sometimes cap.) china or porcelain manufactured by Josiah Spode (1754–1827), English potter, or his company.

spoil (spɔɪl) vb. **spoiling, spoilt** or **spoiled.** 1. (tr.) to cause damage to (something), in regard to its value, beauty, usefulness, etc. 2. (tr.) to weaken the character of (a child) by complying unrestrainedly with its desires.

3. (*intr.*) (of perishable substances) to become unfit for consumption or use. **4.** (*intr.*) *Sport.* to disrupt the play or style of an opponent, as to prevent him from settling into a rhythm. **5.** *Arch.* to strip (a person or place) of (property) by force. **6. be spoiling for.** to have an aggressive desire for (a fight, etc.). ~*n.* **7.** waste material thrown up by an excavation. **8.** any treasure accumulated by a person. **9.** *Obs.* the act of plundering. ~See **spoils.** [C13: from OF *espoillier*, from L *spoliāre* to strip, from *spolium* booty]

spoilage ('spɔɪlɪdʒ) *n.* **1.** the act or an instance of spoiling or the state or condition of being spoilt. **2.** an amount of material that has been wasted by being spoilt: *considerable spoilage.*

spoiler ('spɔɪlə) *n.* **1.** a plunderer or robber. **2.** a person or thing that causes spoilage or corruption. **3.** a device fitted to an aircraft wing to increase drag and reduce lift. **4.** a similar device fitted to a car. **5.** *Sport.* a competitor who adopts spoiling tactics.

spoils (spɔɪlz) *pl. n.* **1.** (*sometimes sing.*) valuables seized by violence, esp. in war. **2.** *Chiefly U.S.* the rewards and benefits of public office regarded as plunder for the winning party or candidate. See also **spoils system.**

spoilsport ('spɔɪl‚spɔːt) *n. Inf.* a person who spoils the pleasure of other people.

spoils system *n. Chiefly U.S.* the practice of filling appointive public offices with friends and supporters of the ruling political party.

spoilt (spɔɪlt) *vb.* a past tense and past participle of **spoil.**

Spokane (spəʊ'kæn) *n.* a city in E Washington: commercial centre of an agricultural region. Pop.: 172 890 (1986 est.).

spoke[1] (spəʊk) *vb.* **1.** the past tense of **speak.** **2.** *Arch. or dialect.* a past participle of **speak.**

spoke[2] (spəʊk) *n.* **1.** a radial member of a wheel, joining the hub to the rim. **2.** a radial projection from the rim of a wheel, as in a ship's wheel. **3.** a rung of a ladder. **4. put a spoke in someone's wheel.** *Brit.* to thwart someone's plans. ~*vb.* **5.** (*tr.*) to equip with or as if with spokes. [OE *spaca*]

spoken ('spəʊkən) *vb.* **1.** the past participle of **speak.** ~*adj.* **2.** uttered in speech. **3.** (*in combination*) having speech as specified: *soft-spoken.* **4. spoken for.** engaged or reserved.

spokeshave ('spəʊk‚ʃeɪv) *n.* a small plane with two handles, one on each side of its blade, used for shaping or smoothing cylindrical wooden surfaces, such as spokes.

spokesman ('spəʊksmən), **spokesperson** ('spəʊks‚pɜːsn), *or* **spokeswoman** ('spəʊks‚wʊmən) *n., pl.* **-men, -persons** *or* **-people,** *or* **-women.** a person authorized to speak on behalf of another person or group.

spoliation (‚spəʊlɪ'eɪʃən) *n.* **1.** the act or an instance of despoiling or plundering. **2.** the authorized plundering of neutral vessels on the seas by a belligerent state in time of war. **3.** *Law.* the material alteration of a document so as to render it invalid. **4.** *English ecclesiastical law.* the taking of the fruits of a benefice by a person not entitled to them. [C14: from L *spoliātiō*, from *spoliāre* to SPOIL] —**spoliatory** ('spəʊlɪətərɪ, -trɪ) *adj.*

spondee ('spɒndiː) *n. Prosody.* a metrical foot consisting of two long syllables (‾ ‾). [C14: from OF *spondee*, from L *spondēus*, from Gk, from *spondē* ritual libation; from use of spondee in the music for such ceremonies] —**spondaic** (spɒn'deɪɪk) *adj.*

spondylitis (‚spɒndɪ'laɪtɪs) *n.* inflammation of the vertebrae. [C19: from NL, from Gk *spondulos* vertebra; see -ITIS]

sponge (spʌndʒ) *n.* **1.** any of various multicellular typically marine animals, usually occurring in complex sessile colonies, in which the porous body is supported by a fibrous, calcareous, or siliceous skeletal framework. **2.** a piece of the light porous highly absorbent elastic skeleton of certain sponges, used in bathing, cleaning, etc. **3.** any of a number of materials resembling a sponge. **4.** another word for **sponger** (sense 1). **5.** *Inf.* a person who indulges in heavy drinking. **6.** leavened dough, esp. before kneading. **7.** See **sponge cake. 8.** Also called: **sponge pudding.** *Brit.* a light steamed or baked spongy pudding. **9.** porous metal capable of absorbing large quantities of gas: *platinum sponge.* **10.** a rub with a sponge. **11. throw in** (*or* **up**) **the sponge** (*or* **towel**). See **throw in** (sense 3). ~*vb.* **12.** (*tr.*; often foll. by *off* or *down*) to

clean (something) by wiping or rubbing with a damp or wet sponge. **13.** (*tr.*; usually foll. by *off, away, out,* etc.) to remove (marks, etc.) by rubbing with a damp or wet sponge or cloth. **14.** (when *tr.*, often foll. by *up*) to absorb (liquids, esp. when spilt) in the manner of a sponge. **15.** (*intr.*) to go collecting sponges. **16.** (foll. by *off*) to get something from (someone) by presuming on his generosity: *to sponge a meal off someone.* **17.** (foll. by *off* or *on*) to obtain one's subsistence, etc., unjustifiably (from): *he sponges off his friends.* [OE, from L *spongia,* from Gk] —'**spongy** *adj.*

sponge bag *n.* a small waterproof bag made of plastic, etc., that holds toilet articles, used esp. when travelling.

sponge bath *n.* a washing of the body with a wet sponge or cloth, without immersion in water.

sponge cake *n.* a light porous cake, made of eggs, sugar, flour, and flavourings, without any fat.

sponger ('spʌndʒə) *n.* **1.** *Inf.* a person who lives off other people by continually taking advantage of their generosity; parasite or scrounger. **2.** a person or ship employed in collecting sponges.

sponsion ('spɒnʃən) *n.* **1.** the act or process of becoming surety; sponsorship. **2.** (*often pl.*) *International law.* an unauthorized agreement made by a public officer, requiring ratification by his government. **3.** any act or promise, esp. one made on behalf of someone else. [C17: from L *sponsiō,* from *spondēre* to pledge]

sponson ('spɒnsən) *n.* **1.** *Naval.* an outboard support for a gun, etc. **2.** a structural projection from the side of a paddle steamer for supporting a paddle wheel. **3.** a structural unit attached to a helicopter fuselage by struts, housing the landing gear and flotation bags. [C19: ?from EXPANSION]

sponsor ('spɒnsə) *n.* **1.** a person or group that promotes either another person or group in an activity or the activity itself, either for profit or charity. **2.** *Chiefly U.S. & Canad.* a person or business firm that pays the costs of a radio or television programme in return for advertising time. **3.** a legislator who presents and supports a bill, motion, etc. **4.** Also called: **godparent. a.** an authorized witness who makes the required promises on behalf of a person to be baptized and thereafter assumes responsibility for his Christian upbringing. **b.** a person who presents a candidate for confirmation. ~*vb.* **5.** (*tr.*) to act as a sponsor for. [C17: from L, from *spondēre* to promise solemnly] —**sponsorial** (spɒn'sɔːrɪəl) *adj.* —'**spon sor‚ship** *n.*

sponsored ('spɒnsəd) *adj.* denoting an activity organized to raise money for a charity in which sponsors agree to donate money on completion of the activity by participants.

spontaneity (‚spɒntə'niːɪtɪ, -'neɪ-) *n., pl.* **-ties. 1.** the state or quality of being spontaneous. **2.** (*often pl.*) the exhibiting of spontaneous actions, impulses, or behaviour.

spontaneous (spɒn'teɪnɪəs) *adj.* **1.** occurring, produced, or performed through natural processes without external influence. **2.** arising from an unforced personal impulse; voluntary; unpremeditated. **3.** (of plants) growing naturally; indigenous. [C17: from LL *spontaneus,* from L *sponte* voluntarily] —**spon'taneously** *adv.* —**spon'taneousness** *n.*

spontaneous combustion *n.* the ignition of a substance or body as a result of internal oxidation processes, without the application of an external source of heat.

spontaneous generation *n.* another name for **abiogenesis.**

spoof (spuːf) *Inf.* ~*n.* **1.** a mildly satirical mockery or parody; lampoon. **2.** a good-humoured deception or trick. ~*vb.* **3.** to indulge in a spoof of (a person or thing). [C19: coined by A. Roberts (1852–1933), E comedian] —'**spoofer** *n.*

spook (spuːk) *Inf.* ~*n.* **1.** a ghost or a person suggestive of this. **2.** *U.S. & Canad.* a spy. ~*vb.* (*tr.*) *U.S. & Canad.* **3.** to frighten: *to spook horses; to spook a person.* **4.** (of a ghost) to haunt. [C19: Du. *spook,* from MLow G *spōk* ghost] —'**spooky** *adj.*

spool (spuːl) *n.* **1.** a device around which magnetic tape, film, cotton, etc., can be wound, with plates at top and bottom to prevent it from slipping off. **2.** anything round which other materials, esp. thread, are wound. ~*vb.* **3.** (sometimes foll. by *up*) to wind or be wound onto a spool. [C14: of Gmc origin]

spoon (spu:n) *n.* **1.** a utensil having a shallow concave part, usually elliptical in shape, attached to a handle, used in eating or serving food, stirring, etc. **2.** Also called: **spoonbait.** an angling lure consisting of a bright piece of metal which swivels on a trace to which are attached a hook or hooks. **3.** a golf club with a shorter shaft and shallower face than a brassie. **4. be born with a silver spoon in one's mouth.** to inherit wealth or social standing. **5.** *Rowing.* a type of oar blade that is curved at the edges and tip. ~*vb.* **6.** (*tr.*) to scoop up or transfer (food, liquid, etc.) from one container to another with or as if with a spoon. **7.** (*intr.*) *Old-fashioned sl.* to kiss and cuddle. **8.** *Sport.* to hit (a ball) with a weak lifting motion, as in golf, cricket, etc. [OE *spōn* splinter]

spoonbill ('spu:n,bɪl) *n.* any of several wading birds of warm regions, having a long horizontally flattened bill.

spoondrift ('spu:n,drɪft) *n.* a less common spelling of **spindrift.**

spoonerism ('spu:nə,rɪzəm) *n.* the transposition of the initial consonants or consonant clusters of a pair of words, often resulting in an amusing ambiguity, such as *hush my brat* for *brush my hat.* [C20: after W. A. *Spooner* (1844–1930), E clergyman renowned for this]

spoon-feed *vb.* **-feeding, -fed.** (*tr.*) **1.** to feed with a spoon. **2.** to overindulge or spoil. **3.** to provide (a person) with ready-made opinions, judgments, etc.

spoonful ('spu:n,ful) *n., pl.* **-fuls. 1.** the amount that a spoon is able to hold. **2.** a small quantity.

spoony *or* **spooney** ('spu:nɪ) *Sl., rare old-fashioned.* ~*adj.* **spoonier, spooniest. 1.** foolishly or stupidly amorous. ~*n., pl.* **spoonies. 2.** a fool or silly person, esp. one in love.

spoor (spuə, spɔ:) *n.* **1.** the trail of an animal or person, esp. as discernible to the eye. ~*vb.* **2.** to track (an animal) by following its trail. [C19: from Afrik., from MDu. *spor*; rel. to OE *spor* track]

Sporades ('spɒrə,di:z) *pl. n.* two groups of Greek islands in the Aegean: the **Northern Sporades,** lying northeast of Euboea, and the **Southern Sporades,** which include the Dodecanese and lie off the SW coast of Turkey.

sporadic (spə'rædɪk) *adj.* **1.** occurring at irregular points in time; intermittent: *sporadic firing.* **2.** scattered; isolated: *a sporadic disease.* [C17: from Med. L *sporadicus,* from Gk, from *sporas* scattered] —**spo'radically** *adv.*

sporangium (spə'rændʒɪəm) *n., pl.* **-gia** (-dʒɪə). any organ, esp. in fungi, in which asexual spores are produced. [C19: from NL, from SPORO- + Gk *angeion* receptacle] —**spo'rangial** *adj.*

spore (spɔ:) *n.* **1.** a reproductive body, produced by some protozoans and many plants, that develops into a new individual. A **sexual spore** is formed after the fusion of gametes and an **asexual spore** is the result of asexual reproduction. **2.** a germ cell, seed, dormant bacterium, or similar body. ~*vb.* **3.** (*intr.*) to produce, carry, or release spores. [C19: from NL *spora,* from Gk: a sowing; rel. to Gk *speirein* to sow]

spore case *n.* the nontechnical name for **sporangium.**

sporo- *or before a vowel* **spor-** *combining form.* spore: *sporophyte.* [from NL *spora*]

sporogenesis (,spɔ:rəʊ'dʒɛnɪsɪs, ,spɒ-) *n.* the process of spore formation in plants and animals. —**sporogenous** (spɔ:'rɒdʒɪnəs, spɒ-) *adj.*

sporogonium (,spɔ:rəʊ'gəʊnɪəm, ,spɒ-) *n., pl.* **-nia** (-nɪə). a structure in mosses and liverworts consisting of a spore-bearing capsule on a short stalk that arises from the parent plant.

sporophyll *or* **sporophyl** ('spɔ:rəʊfɪl, 'spɒ-) *n.* a leaf in mosses, ferns, and related plants that bears the sporangia.

sporophyte ('spɔ:rəʊ,faɪt, 'spɒ-) *n.* the diploid form of plants that have alternation of generations. It produces asexual spores. —**sporophytic** (,spɔ:rə'fɪtɪk, ,spɒ-) *adj.*

-sporous *adj. combining form.* (in botany) having a specified type or number of spores.

sporozoan (,spɔ:rə'zəʊən, ,spɒ-) *n.* **1.** any parasitic protozoan of a class that includes the malaria parasite. ~*adj.* **2.** of or relating to the sporozoans.

sporran ('spɒrən) *n.* a large pouch, usually of fur, worn hanging from a belt in front of the kilt in Scottish Highland dress. [C19: from Scot. Gaelic *sporan* purse]

sport (spɔ:t) *n.* **1.** an individual or group activity pursued for exercise or pleasure, often taking a competitive form. **2.** such activities considered collectively. **3.** any pastime

indulged in for pleasure. **4.** the pleasure derived from a pastime, esp. hunting, shooting, or fishing. **5.** playful or good-humoured joking: *to say a thing in sport.* **6.** derisive mockery or the object of such mockery: *to make sport of someone.* **7.** someone or something that is controlled by external influences: *the sport of fate.* **8.** *Inf.* (sometimes qualified by *good, bad,* etc.) a person who reacts cheerfully in the face of adversity, esp. a good loser. **9.** *Inf.* a person noted for being scrupulously fair and abiding by the rules of a game. **10.** *Inf.* a person who leads a merry existence, esp. a gambler: *he's a bit of a sport.* **11.** *Austral. & N.Z. inf.* a form of address used esp. between males. **12.** *Biol.* **a.** an animal or plant that differs conspicuously from other organisms of the same species, usually because of a mutation. **b.** an anomalous characteristic of such an organism. ~*vb.* **13.** (*tr.*) *Inf.* to wear or display in an ostentatious or proud manner: *she was sporting a new hat.* **14.** (*intr.*) to skip about or frolic happily. **15.** to amuse (oneself), esp. in outdoor physical recreation. **16.** (*intr.;* often foll. by *with*) *Arch.* to make fun (of). **17.** (*intr.*) *Biol.* to produce or undergo a mutation. ~See also **sports.** [C15 *sporten,* var. of *disporten* to DISPORT] —**'sporter** *n.* —**'sportful** *adj.* —**'sportfully** *adv.* —**'sportfulness** *n.*

sporting ('spɔ:tɪŋ) *adj.* **1.** (*prenominal*) of, relating to, or used or engaged in a sport or sports. **2.** characteristic of or conforming to sportsmanship; fair. **3.** of or relating to gambling. **4.** willing to take a risk. —**'sportingly** *adv.*

sportive ('spɔ:tɪv) *adj.* **1.** playful or joyous. **2.** done in jest rather than seriously. —**'sportively** *adv.* —**'sportiveness** *n.*

sports (spɔ:ts) *n.* **1.** (*modifier*) relating to, concerned with, or used in sports: *sports equipment.* **2.** Also called: **sports day.** *Brit.* a meeting held at a school or college for competitions in various athletic events.

sports car *n.* a production car designed for speed and manoeuvrability, having a low body and usually seating only two persons.

sportscast ('spɔ:ts,kɑ:st) *n. U.S.* a broadcast consisting of sports news. —**'sports,caster** *n.*

sports jacket *n.* a man's informal jacket, made esp. of tweed. Also called (U.S., Austral. & N.Z.): **sports coat.**

sportsman ('spɔ:tsmən) *n., pl.* **-men. 1.** a man who takes part in sports, esp. of the outdoor type. **2.** a person who exhibits fairness, generosity, observance of the rules, and good humour when losing. —**'sportsman-,like** *or* **'sportsmanly** *adj.* —**'sportsman,ship** *n.*

sports medicine *n.* the branch of medicine concerned with injuries sustained through sport.

sportswear ('spɔ:ts,wɛə) *n.* clothes worn for sport or outdoor leisure wear.

sportswoman ('spɔ:ts,wʊmən) *n., pl.* **-women.** a woman who takes part in sports, esp. of the outdoor type.

sporty ('spɔ:tɪ) *adj.* **sportier, sportiest. 1.** vulgarly ostentatious; stylish, loud, or gay. **2.** relating to or appropriate to a sportsman or sportswoman. **3.** (of women) amorous or wanton; lusty. —**'sportily** *adv.* —**'sportiness** *n.*

sporule ('spɒru:l) *n.* a very small spore. [C19: from NL *sporula*]

spot (spɒt) *n.* **1.** a small mark on a surface, such as a circular patch or stain, differing in colour or texture from its surroundings. **2.** a location: *this is the exact spot.* **3.** a blemish of the skin, esp. a pimple or one occurring through some disease. **4.** a blemish on the character of a person; moral flaw. **5.** *Inf.* a place of entertainment: *a night spot.* **6.** *Inf., chiefly Brit.* a small quantity or amount: *a spot of lunch.* **7.** *Inf.* an awkward situation: *that puts me in a spot.* **8.** a short period between regular television or radio programmes that is used for advertising. **9.** a position or length of time in a show assigned to a specific performer. **10.** short for **spotlight. 11.** (in billiards) **a.** Also called: **spot ball.** the white ball that is distinguished from the plain by a mark or spot. **b.** the player using this ball. **12.** *Billiards, snooker, etc.* one of the marked places where the ball is placed. **13.** (*modifier*) **a.** to be paid or delivered immediately: *spot cash.* **b.** involving immediate cash payment: *spot sales.* **14. change one's spots.** (*used mainly in negative constructions*) to reform one's character. **15. high spot.** an outstanding event: *the high spot of the holiday.* **16. knock spots off.** to outstrip or outdo with ease. **17. on the spot. a.** immediately. **b.** at the place in question. **c.** in the best position to deal with a situation. **d.** in an awkward predicament. **e.** (*as modifier*): *our on-the-spot reporter.* **18. soft spot.** a special sympathetic affection or weakness for a person or thing. **19. tight spot.** a serious, difficult, or dangerous situation. **20. weak spot. a.** some aspect of a character or situation that is susceptible to criticism. **b.** a flaw in a person's knowledge. ~*vb.* **spotting, spotted.** **21.** (*tr.*) to observe or perceive suddenly; discern. **22.** to put stains or spots upon (something). **23.** (*intr.*) (of some fabrics) to be susceptible to spotting by or as if by water: *silk spots easily.* **24.** *Billiards.* to place (a ball) on one of the spots. **25.** to look out for and note (trains, talent, etc.). **26.** (*intr.*) to rain slightly; spit. [C12 (in the sense: moral blemish): from G] —**'spotless** *adj.* —**'spotlessly** *adv.* —**'spotlessness** *n.*

spot check *n.* **1.** a quick random examination. **2.** a check made without prior warning. ~*vb.* **spot-check.** **3.** (*tr.*) to perform a spot check on.

spot height *n.* a mark on a map indicating the height of a hill, mountain, etc.

spotlight ('spɒt,laɪt) *n.* **1.** a powerful light focused so as to illuminate a small area. **2. the.** the focus of attention. ~*vb.* **-lighting, -lit** *or* **-lighted.** (*tr.*) **3.** to direct a spotlight on. **4.** to focus attention on.

spot-on *adj. Brit. inf.* absolutely correct; very accurate.

spotted ('spɒtɪd) *adj.* **1.** characterized by spots or marks, esp. in having a pattern of spots. **2.** stained or blemished; soiled or bespattered.

spotted dick *or* **dog** *n. Brit.* a steamed or boiled suet pudding containing dried fruit and shaped into a roll.

spotted fever *n.* any of various severe febrile diseases characterized by small irregular spots on the skin.

spotter ('spɒtə) *n.* **1. a.** a person or thing that watches or observes. **b.** (*as modifier*): *a spotter plane.* **2.** a person who makes a hobby of watching for and noting numbers or types of trains, buses, etc.: *a train spotter.* **3.** *Mil.* a person who advises adjustment of fire on a target by observations. **4.** a person, esp. one engaged in civil defence, who watches for enemy aircraft.

spottie ('spɒtɪ) *n. N.Z.* a young deer of up to three months of age.

spotty ('spɒtɪ) *adj.* **-tier, -tiest.** **1.** abounding in or characterized by spots or marks, esp. on the skin. **2.** not consistent or uniform; irregular or uneven. —**'spottily** *adv.* —**'spottiness** *n.*

spot-weld *vb.* **1.** (*tr.*) to join (two pieces of metal) by small circular welds by means of heat, usually electrically generated, and pressure. ~*n.* **2.** a weld so formed. —**'spot-welder** *n.*

spousal ('spaʊzªl) *n.* **1.** (*often pl.*) **a.** the marriage ceremony. **b.** a wedding. ~*adj.* **2.** of or relating to marriage. —**'spousally** *adv.*

spouse *n.* (spaʊs, spaʊz). **1.** a person's partner in marriage. Related adj.: **spousal.** ~*vb.* (spaʊz, spaʊs). **2.** (*tr.*) *Obs.* to marry. [C12: from OF *spus* (masc.), *spuse* (fem.), from L *sponsus, sponsa* betrothed man or woman, from *spondēre* to promise solemnly]

spout (spaʊt) *vb.* **1.** to discharge (a liquid) in a continuous jet or in spurts, esp. through a narrow gap or under pressure, or (of a liquid) to gush thus. **2.** (of a whale, etc.) to discharge air through the blowhole in a spray at the surface of the water. **3.** *Inf.* to utter (a stream of words) on a subject. ~*n.* **4.** a tube, pipe, chute, etc., allowing the passage or pouring of liquids, grain, etc. **5.** a continuous stream or jet of liquid. **6.** short for **waterspout.** **7. up the spout.** *Sl.* **a.** ruined or lost: *any hope of rescue is right up the spout.* **b.** pregnant. [C14: ?from MDu. *spouten*, from ON *spyta* to spit] —**'spouter** *n.*

spouting ('spaʊtɪŋ) *n. N.Z.* **a.** a rainwater downpipe on the exterior of a building. **b.** such pipes collectively.

SPQR *abbrev. for* Senatus Populusque Romanus. [L: the Senate and People of Rome]

sprag (spræg) *n.* **1.** a chock or steel bar used to prevent a vehicle from running backwards on an incline. **2.** a support or post used in mining. [C19: from ?]

sprain (spreɪn) *vb.* **1.** (*tr.*) to injure (a joint) by a sudden twisting or wrenching of its ligaments. ~*n.* **2.** the injury, characterized by swelling and temporary disability. [C17: from ?]

sprang (spræŋ) *vb.* a past tense of **spring.**

sprat (spræt) *n.* **1.** Also called: **brisling.** a small marine food fish of the herring family. **2.** any of various small or young herrings. [C16: var. of OE *sprott*]

sprawl (sprɔːl) *vb.* **1.** (*intr.*) to sit or lie in an ungainly manner with one's limbs spread out. **2.** to fall down or knock down with the limbs spread out in an ungainly way. **3.** to spread out or cause to spread out in a straggling fashion: *his handwriting sprawled all over the paper.* ~*n.* **4.** the act or an instance of sprawling. **5.** a sprawling posture or arrangement of items. [OE *spreawlian*] —**'sprawling** *or* **'sprawly** *adj.*

spray[1] (spreɪ) *n.* **1.** fine particles of a liquid. **2. a.** a liquid, such as perfume, paint, etc., designed to be discharged from an aerosol or atomizer: *hair spray.* **b.** the aerosol or atomizer itself. **3.** a quantity of small objects flying through the air: *a spray of bullets.* ~*vb.* **4.** to scatter (liquid) in the form of fine particles. **5.** to discharge (a liquid) from an aerosol or atomizer. **6.** (*tr.*) to treat or bombard with a spray: *to spray the lawn.* [C17: from MDu. *spräien*] —**'sprayer** *n.*

spray[2] (spreɪ) *n.* **1.** a single slender shoot, twig, or branch that bears buds, leaves, flowers, or berries. **2.** an ornament or floral design like this. [C13: of Gmc origin]

spray gun *n.* a device that sprays a fluid in a finely divided form by atomizing it in an air jet.

spread (sprɛd) *vb.* **spreading, spread.** **1.** to extend or unfold or be extended or unfolded to the fullest width: *she spread the map.* **2.** to extend or cause to extend over a larger expanse: *the milk spread all over the floor; the political unrest spread over several years.* **3.** to apply or be applied in a coating: *butter does not spread very well when cold.* **4.** to distribute or be distributed over an area or region. **5.** to display or be displayed in its fullest extent: *the landscape spread before us.* **6.** (*tr.*) to prepare (a table) for a meal. **7.** (*tr.*) to lay out (a meal) on a table. **8.** to send or be sent out in all directions; disseminate or be disseminated: *someone was spreading rumours; the disease spread quickly.* **9.** (of rails, wires, etc.) to force or be forced apart. **10.** to increase the breadth of (a part), esp. to flatten the head of a rivet by pressing, hammering, or forging. **11.** (*tr.*) *Agriculture.* **a.** to lay out (hay) in a relatively thin layer to dry. **b.** to scatter (seed, manure, etc.) over an area. **12.** (*tr.; often foll. by around*) *Inf.* to make (oneself) agreeable to a large number of people. ~*n.* **13.** the act or process of spreading; diffusion, dispersion, expansion, etc. **14.** *Inf.* the wingspan of an aircraft. **15.** an extent of space or time; stretch: *a spread of 50 years.* **16.** *Inf., chiefly U.S. & Canad.* a ranch or large tract of land. **17.** the limit of something fully extended: *the spread of a bird's wings.* **18.** a covering for a table or bed. **19.** *Inf.* a large meal or feast, esp. when it is laid out on a table. **20.** a food which can be spread on bread, etc.: *salmon spread.* **21.** two facing pages in a book or other publication. **22.** a widening of the hips and waist: *middle-age spread.* ~*adj.* **23.** extended or stretched out, esp. to the fullest extent. [OE *sprædan*] —**'spreadable** *adj.* —**'spreader** *n.*

spread eagle *n.* **1.** the representation of an eagle with outstretched wings, used as an emblem of the U.S. **2.** an acrobatic skating figure.

spread-eagle *adj. also* **spread-eagled.** **1.** lying or standing with arms and legs outstretched. ~*vb.* **2.** to assume or cause to assume the shape of a spread eagle. **3.** (*intr.*) *Skating.* to execute a spread eagle.

spreadsheet ('sprɛd,ʃiːt) *n.* a computer program that allows easy entry and manipulation of text: used esp. for financial planning.

sprechgesang (*German* 'ʃprɛçgəzaŋ) *n. Music.* a type of vocalization between singing and recitation. [C20: from G *Sprechgesang*, lit.: speaking-song]

spree (spriː) *n.* **1.** a session of considerable overindulgence, esp. in drinking, squandering money, etc. **2.** a romp. [C19: ? changed from Scot. *spreath* plundered cattle, ult. from L *praeda* booty]

sprig (sprɪg) *n.* **1.** a shoot, twig, or sprout of a tree, shrub, etc.; spray. **2.** an ornamental device resembling a spray of leaves or flowers. **3.** Also called: **dowel pin.** a small wire nail without a head. **4.** *Inf., rare.* a youth. **5.** *Inf., rare.* a person considered as the descendant of an established family, social class, etc. **6.** *N.Z.* another word for **stud**[1] (sense 5). ~*vb.* **sprigging, sprigged.** (*tr.*) **7.** to fasten or secure with sprigs. **8.** to ornament (fabric, etc.) with a design of sprigs. [C15: prob. of Gmc origin] —**'sprigger** *n.* —**'spriggy** *adj.*

sprightly ('spraɪtlɪ) *adj.* **-lier, -liest.** **1.** full of vitality; lively and gay. ~*adv.* **2.** *Obs.* in a gay or lively manner.

[C16: from *spright*, var. of SPRITE + -LY[1]] —'**sprightliness** *n.*

spring (sprɪŋ) *vb.* **springing, sprang** *or* **sprung; sprung**. **1.** to move or cause to move suddenly upwards or forwards in a single motion. **2.** to release or be released from a forced position by elastic force: *the bolt sprang back.* **3.** (*tr.*) to leap or jump over. **4.** (*intr.*) to come or arise suddenly. **5.** (*intr.*) (of a part of a mechanism, etc.) to jump out of place. **6.** to make (wood, etc.) warped or split or (of wood, etc.) to become warped or split. **7.** to happen or cause to happen unexpectedly: *to spring a surprise.* **8.** (*intr.*; usually foll. by *from*) to originate; be descended: *the idea sprang from a chance meeting; he sprang from peasant stock.* **9.** (*intr.*; often foll. by *up*) to come into being or appear suddenly: *factories springing up.* **10.** (*tr.*) (of a gundog) to rouse (game) from cover. **11.** (*intr.*) (of game or quarry) to start or rise suddenly from cover. **12.** to explode (a mine) or (of a mine) to explode. **13.** (*tr.*) to provide with a spring or springs. **14.** (*tr.*) *Inf.* to arrange the escape of (someone) from prison. **15.** (*intr.*) *Arch. or poetic.* (of daylight or dawn) to begin to appear. ~*n.* **16.** the act or an instance of springing. **17.** a leap, jump, or bound. **18. a.** the quality of resilience; elasticity. **b.** (*as modifier*): *spring steel.* **19.** the act or an instance of moving rapidly back from a position of tension. **20. a.** a natural outflow of ground water, as forming the source of a stream. **b.** (*as modifier*): *spring water.* **21. a.** a device, such as a coil or strip of steel, that stores potential energy when it is compressed, stretched, or bent and releases it when the restraining force is removed. **b.** (*as modifier*): *a spring mattress.* **22.** a structural defect such as a warp or bend. **23. a.** (*sometimes cap.*) the season of the year between winter and summer, astronomically from the March equinox to the June solstice in the N hemisphere and from the September equinox to the December solstice in the S hemisphere. **b.** (*as modifier*): *spring showers.* Related adj.: **vernal. 24.** the earliest or freshest time of something. **25.** a source or origin. **26.** Also called: **spring line.** *Naut.* a mooring line, usually one of a pair that cross amidships. [OE *springan*] —'**springless** *adj.* —'**spring- like** *adj.*

spring balance *or esp. U.S.* **spring scale** *n.* a device in which an object to be weighed is attached to the end of a helical spring, the extension of which indicates the weight of the object on a calibrated scale.

springboard ('sprɪŋ,bɔːd) *n.* **1.** a flexible board, usually projecting low over the water, used for diving. **2.** a similar board used for gaining height or momentum in gymnastics. **3.** *Austral. & N.Z.* a board inserted into the trunk of a tree at some height above the ground on which a lumberjack stands to chop down the tree. **4.** anything that serves as a point of departure or initiation.

springbok ('sprɪŋ,bʌk) *n.*, *pl.* **-bok** *or* **-boks**. an antelope of semidesert regions of southern Africa, which moves in leaps. [C18: from Afrik., from Du. *springen* to spring + *bok* goat]

Springbok ('sprɪŋ,bʌk, -,bɒk) *n.* an amateur athlete who has represented South Africa in international competitions.

spring chicken *n.* **1.** *Chiefly U.S.* a young chicken, tender for cooking, esp. one from two to ten months old. **2.** *Inf.* a young, inexperienced, or unsophisticated person (esp. in **no spring chicken**).

spring-clean *vb.* **1.** to clean (a house) thoroughly: traditionally at the end of winter. ~*n.* **2.** an instance of this. —,**spring-'cleaning** *n.*

springe (sprɪndʒ) *n.* **1.** a snare set to catch small wild animals or birds and consisting of a loop attached to a bent twig or branch under tension. ~*vb.* **2.** (*tr.*) to catch (animals or birds) with this. [C13: rel. to OE *springan* to spring]

springer ('sprɪŋə) *n.* **1.** a person or thing that springs. **2.** short for **springer spaniel. 3.** *Archit.* **a.** the first and lowest stone of an arch. **b.** the impost of an arch.

springer spaniel *n.* either of two breeds of spaniel with a slightly domed head and ears of medium length.

Springfield ('sprɪŋ,fiːld) *n.* **1.** a city in S Massachusetts, on the Connecticut River: the site of the U.S. arsenal and armoury (1794–1968), which developed the Springfield and Garand rifles. Pop.: 149 410 (1986 est.). **2.** a city in SW Missouri. Pop.: 139 360 (1986 est.). **3.** a city in central

Illinois, capital of the state: the home and burial place of Abraham Lincoln. Pop.: 100 290 (1986 est.).

springhaas ('sprɪŋ,hɑːs) *n.*, *pl.* **-haas** *or* **-hase** (-,hɑːzə). a small S and E African nocturnal kangaroo-like rodent. [from Afrik.: spring hare]

springing ('sprɪŋɪŋ) *n. Archit.* the level where an arch or vault rises from a support.

spring lock *n.* a type of lock having a spring-loaded bolt, a key being required only to unlock it.

spring onion *n.* an immature form of the onion, widely cultivated for its tiny bulb and long green leaves which are eaten in salads, etc. Also called: **scallion.**

spring roll *n.* a Chinese dish consisting of a savoury mixture rolled up in a thin pancake and fried.

Springs (sprɪŋz) *n.* a city in E South Africa, in the Transvaal: developed around a coal mine established in 1885 and later became a major world gold-mining centre, now with uranium extraction. Pop.: 153 974 (1980).

Springsteen ('sprɪŋ,stiːn) *n.* **Bruce.** born 1949, U.S. rock singer, songwriter, and guitarist. His albums with the E Street Band include *Born to Run* (1975), *Darkness on the Edge of Town* (1978), and *Born in the U.S.A.* (1984).

springtail ('sprɪŋ,teɪl) *n.* any of various primitive wingless insects having a forked springing organ.

spring tide *n.* **1.** either of the two tides that occur at or just after new moon and full moon: the greatest rise and fall in tidal level. Cf. **neap tide. 2.** any great rush or flood.

springtime ('sprɪŋ,taɪm) *n.* **1.** Also called: **springtide.** the season of spring. **2.** the earliest, usually the most attractive, period of the existence of something.

springy ('sprɪŋɪ) *adj.* **springier, springiest. 1.** possessing or characterized by resilience or bounce. **2.** (of a place) having many springs of water. —'**springily** *adv.* —'**springiness** *n.*

sprinkle ('sprɪŋkᵊl) *vb.* **1.** to scatter (liquid, powder, etc.) in tiny particles or droplets over (something). **2.** (*tr.*) to distribute over (something): *the field was sprinkled with flowers.* **3.** (*intr.*) to drizzle slightly. ~*n.* **4.** the act or an instance of sprinkling or a quantity that is sprinkled. **5.** a slight drizzle. [C14: prob. from MDu. *sprenkelen*] —'**sprinkler** *n.*

sprinkler system *n.* a fire-extinguishing system that releases water from overhead nozzles opened automatically by a temperature rise.

sprinkling ('sprɪŋklɪŋ) *n.* a small quantity or amount: *a sprinkling of common sense.*

sprint (sprɪnt) *n.* **1.** *Athletics.* a short race run at top speed. **2.** a fast finishing speed at the end of a longer race, as in running or cycling, etc. **3.** any quick run. ~*vb.* **4.** (*intr.*) to go at top speed, as in running, cycling, etc. [C16: of Scand. origin] —'**sprinter** *n.*

sprit (sprɪt) *n. Naut.* a light spar pivoted at the mast and crossing a fore-and-aft quadrilateral sail diagonally to the peak. [OE *spreot*]

sprite (spraɪt) *n.* **1.** (in folklore) a nimble elflike creature, esp. one associated with water. **2.** a small dainty person. [C13: from OF *esprit*, from L *spiritus* SPIRIT[1]]

spritsail ('sprɪt,seɪl; *Naut.* 'sprɪtsəl) *n. Naut.* a sail mounted on a sprit or bowsprit.

spritzer ('sprɪtsə) *n.* a drink, usually white wine, with soda water added. [from G *spritzen* to splash]

sprocket ('sprɒkɪt) *n.* **1.** Also called: **sprocket wheel.** a relatively thin wheel having teeth projecting radially from the rim, esp. one that drives or is driven by a chain. **2.** an individual tooth on such a wheel. **3.** a cylindrical wheel with teeth on one or both rims for pulling film through a camera or projector. [C16: from ?]

sprout (spraʊt) *vb.* **1.** (of a plant, seed, etc.) to produce (new leaves, shoots, etc.). **2.** (*intr.*; often foll. by *up*) to begin to grow or develop. ~*n.* **3.** a new shoot or bud. **4.** something that grows like a sprout. **5.** See **Brussels sprout.** [OE *sprūtan*]

spruce[1] (spruːs) *n.* **1.** any coniferous tree of a N temperate genus, cultivated for timber and for ornament. They grow in a pyramidal shape and have needle-like leaves and light-coloured wood. See also **Norway spruce. 2.** the wood of any of these trees. [C17: short for *Spruce fir*, from C14 *Spruce* Prussia, changed from *Pruce*, via OF from L *Prussia*]

spruce[2] (spruːs) *adj.* neat, smart, and trim. [C16: ?from *Spruce leather*, a fashionable leather imported from Prussia; see SPRUCE[1]] —'**sprucely** *adv.* —'**spruceness** *n.*

spruce beer *n.* an alcoholic drink made of fermented molasses flavoured with spruce twigs and cones.

spruce up *vb.* (*adv.*) to make (oneself, a person, or thing) smart and neat.

sprue[1] (spru:) *n.* **1.** a vertical channel in a mould through which plastic or molten metal is introduced or out of which it flows when the mould is filled. **2.** plastic or metal that solidifies in a sprue. [C19: from ?]

sprue[2] (spru:) *n.* a chronic disease, esp. of tropical climates, characterized by diarrhoea and emaciation. [C19: from Du. *spruw*]

spruik ('spru:ik) *vb.* (*intr.*) *Austral. sl.* to describe or hold forth like a salesman; spiel or advertise loudly. [C20: from ?] —**'spruiker** *n.*

spruit (spreit) *n. S. African.* a small tributary stream or watercourse. [Afrik.]

sprung (sprʌŋ) *vb.* a past tense and past participle of **spring.**

sprung rhythm *n. Prosody.* a type of poetic rhythm characterized by metrical feet of irregular composition, each having one strongly stressed syllable, often the first, and an indefinite number of unstressed syllables.

spry (sprai) *adj.* **spryer, spryest** *or* **sprier, spriest.** active and brisk; nimble. [C18: ? of Scand. origin] —**'spryly** *adv.* —**'spryness** *n.*

spud (spʌd) *n.* **1.** an informal word for **potato. 2.** a narrow-bladed spade for cutting roots, digging up weeds, etc. ~*vb.* **spudding, spudded. 3.** (*tr.*) to eradicate (weeds) with a spud. **4.** (*intr.*) to drill the first foot of an oil well. [C15 *spudde* short knife, from ?; applied later to a digging tool, & hence to a potato]

Spud Island *n.* a slang name for **Prince Edward Island.**

spue (spju:) *vb.* **spuing, spued.** an archaic spelling of **spew.** —**'spuer** *n.*

spume (spju:m) *n.* **1.** foam or surf, esp. on the sea; froth. ~*vb.* **2.** (*intr.*) to foam or froth. [C14: from OF *espume*, from L *spūma*] —**'spumous** *or* **'spumy** *adj.*

spun (spʌn) *vb.* the past tense and past participle of **spin.** ~*adj.* **1.** formed or manufactured by spinning: *spun gold; spun glass.*

spunk (spʌŋk) *n.* **1.** *Inf.* courage or spirit. **2.** *Brit. taboo sl.* semen. **3.** touchwood or tinder. [C16 (in the sense: a spark): from Scot. Gaelic *spong* tinder, sponge, from L *spongia* sponge] —**'spunky** *adj.* —**'spunkily** *adv.*

spun silk *n.* shiny yarn or fabric made from silk waste.

spur (sp3:) *n.* **1.** a pointed device or sharp spiked wheel fixed to the heel of a rider's boot to enable him to urge his horse on. **2.** anything serving to urge or encourage. **3.** a sharp horny projection from the leg in male birds, such as the domestic cock. **4.** a pointed process in any of various animals. **5.** a tubular extension at the base of the corolla in flowers such as larkspur. **6.** a short or stunted branch of a tree. **7.** a ridge projecting laterally from a mountain or mountain range. **8.** another name for **groyne. 9.** Also called: **spur track.** a railway branch line or siding. **10.** a short side road leading off a main road. **11.** a sharp cutting instrument attached to the leg of a gamecock. **12. on the spur of the moment.** on impulse. **13. win one's spurs. a.** to prove one's ability; gain distinction. **b.** *History.* to earn knighthood. ~*vb.* **spurring, spurred. 14.** (*tr.*) to goad or urge with or as if with spurs. **15.** (*intr.*) to go or ride quickly; press on. **16.** (*tr.*) to provide with a spur or spurs. [OE *spura*]

spurge (sp3:dʒ) *n.* any of various plants that have milky sap and small flowers typically surrounded by conspicuous bracts. [C14: from OF *espurge*, from *espurgier* to purge, from L *expurgāre* to cleanse]

spur gear *or* **wheel** *n.* a gear having involuted teeth either straight or helically cut on a cylindrical surface.

spurious ('spjʊəriəs) *adj.* **1.** not genuine or real. **2.** (of a plant part or organ) resembling another part in appearance only; false: *a spurious fruit.* **3.** *Rare.* illegitimate. [C17: from L *spurius* of illegitimate birth] —**'spuriously** *adv.* —**'spuriousness** *n.*

spurn (sp3:n) *vb.* **1.** to reject (a person or thing) with contempt. **2.** (when *intr.*, often foll. by *against*) *Arch.* to kick (at). ~*n.* **3.** an instance of spurning. **4.** *Arch.* a kick or thrust. [OE *spurnan*] —**'spurner** *n.*

spurt *or* **spirt** (sp3:t) *vb.* **1.** to gush or cause to gush forth in a sudden stream or jet. **2.** (*intr.*) to make a sudden effort. ~*n.* **3.** a sudden stream or jet. **4.** a short burst of activity, speed, or energy. [C16: ? rel. to MHG *sprützen* to squirt]

sputnik ('spʊtnɪk, 'spʌt-) *n.* any of a series of Soviet artificial satellites, **Sputnik 1** (launched in 1957) being the first man-made satellite to orbit the earth. [C20: from Russian, lit.: fellow traveller, from *s-* with + *put* path + *-nik,* suffix indicating agent]

sputter ('spʌtə) *vb.* **1.** another word for **splutter** (senses 1-3). **2.** *Physics.* **a.** to undergo or cause to undergo a process in which atoms of a solid are removed from its surface by the impact of high-energy ions. **b.** to coat (a metal) onto (a solid surface) by this process. ~*n.* **3.** the process or noise of sputtering. **4.** incoherent stammering speech. **5.** something ejected while sputtering. [C16: from Du. *sputteren,* imit.] —**'sputterer** *n.*

sputum ('spju:təm) *n., pl.* **-ta** (-tə). saliva ejected from the mouth, esp. mixed with mucus. [C17: from L: spittle, from *spuere* to spit out]

spy (spai) *n., pl.* **spies. 1.** a person employed by a state or institution to obtain secret information from rival countries, organizations, companies, etc. **2.** a person who keeps secret watch on others. **3.** *Obs.* a close view. ~*vb.* **spying, spied. 4.** (*intr.*; usually foll. by *on*) to keep a secret or furtive watch (on). **5.** (*intr.*) to engage in espionage. **6.** (*tr.*) to catch sight of; descry. [C13 *spien,* from OF *espier,* of Gmc origin]

spyglass ('spai,glɑ:s) *n.* a small telescope.

spy out *vb.* (*tr., adv.*) **1.** to discover by careful observation. **2.** to make a close scrutiny of.

sq. *abbrev. for:* **1.** sequence. **2.** square. **3.** (*pl.* **sqq.**) the following one. [from L *sequens*]

Sq. *abbrev. for:* **1.** Squadron. **2.** Square.

squab (skwɒb) *n., pl.* **squabs** *or* **squab. 1.** a young unfledged bird, esp. a pigeon. **2.** a short fat person. **3. a.** a well-stuffed bolster or cushion. **b.** a sofa. ~*adj.* **4.** (of birds) unfledged. **5.** short and fat. [C17: prob. of Gmc origin] —**'squabby** *adj.*

squabble ('skwɒbᵊl) *vb.* **1.** (*intr.*) to quarrel over a small matter. ~*n.* **2.** a petty quarrel. [C17: prob. of Scand. origin] —**'squabbler** *n.*

squad (skwɒd) *n.* **1.** the smallest military formation, typically a dozen soldiers, esp. a drill formation. **2.** any small group of people engaged in a common pursuit. **3.** *Sport.* a number of players from which a team is to be selected. [C17: from OF *esquade,* from OSp. *escuadra,* from *escuadrar* to SQUARE, from the square formations used]

squaddie *or* **squaddy** ('skwɒdɪ) *n., pl.* **-dies.** *Brit. sl.* a private soldier. [C20: from SQUAD]

squadron ('skwɒdrən) *n.* **1.** a subdivision of a naval fleet detached for a particular task. **2.** a cavalry unit comprising two or more troops. **3.** the basic tactical and administrative air force unit comprising two or more flights. [C16: from It. *squadrone* soldiers drawn up in square formation, from *squadro* square]

squadron leader *n.* an officer holding commissioned rank, between flight lieutenant and wing commander in the air forces of Britain and certain other countries.

squalene ('skwei,li:n) *n. Biochemistry.* a terpene first found in the liver of sharks but also present in the livers of most higher animals. [C20: from NL *squalus,* genus name of the shark]

squalid ('skwɒlɪd) *adj.* **1.** dirty and repulsive, esp. as a result of neglect or poverty. **2.** sordid. [C16: from L *squālidus,* from *squālēre* to be stiff with dirt] —**squa'lidity** *or* **'squalidness** *n.* —**'squalidly** *adv.*

squall[1] (skwɔ:l) *n.* **1.** a sudden strong wind or brief turbulent storm. **2.** any sudden commotion. ~*vb.* **3.** (*intr.*) to blow in a squall. [C18: ? a special use of SQUALL[2]] —**'squally** *adj.*

squall[2] (skwɔ:l) *vb.* **1.** (*intr.*) to cry noisily; yell. ~*n.* **2.** a shrill or noisy yell or howl. [C17: prob. of Scand. origin] —**'squaller** *n.*

squalor ('skwɒlə) *n.* the condition or quality of being squalid; disgusting filth. [C17: from L]

squama ('skweimə) *n., pl.* **-mae** (-mi:). *Biol.* a scale or scalelike structure. [C18: from L] —**squamate** ('skweimeit) *adj.* —**squa'mation** *n.* —**'squamose** *or* **'squamous** *adj.*

squander ('skwɒndə) *vb.* (*tr.*) to spend wastefully or extravagantly; dissipate. [C16: from ?] —**'squanderer** *n.*

square (skwɛə) *n.* **1.** a plane geometric figure having four equal sides and four right angles. **2.** any object, part, or arrangement having this or a similar shape. **3.** an open area in a town, sometimes including the surrounding buildings, which may form a square. **4.** *Maths.* the product of two equal factors; the second power: *9 is the square of 3, written 3*². **5.** an instrument having two strips of wood, metal, etc., set in the shape of a T or L, used for constructing or testing right angles. **6.** *Inf.* a person who is old-fashioned in views, customs, appearance, etc. **7.** *Obs.* a standard, pattern, or rule. **8. back to square one.** indicating a return to the starting point because of failure, lack of progress, etc. **9. on the square. a.** at right angles. **b.** *Inf.* honestly and openly. **10. out of square. a.** not at right angles or not having a right angle. **b.** not in order or agreement. ~*adj.* **11.** being a square in shape or section. **12.** having or forming one or more right angles or being at right angles to something. **13. a.** (*prenominal*) denoting a measure of area of any shape: *a circle of four square feet.* **b.** (*immediately postpositive*) denoting a square having a specified length on each side: *a board four feet square.* **14.** fair and honest (esp. in a **square deal**). **15.** straight, even, or level: *a square surface.* **16.** *Cricket.* at right angles to the wicket: *square leg.* **17.** *Soccer, hockey, etc.* in a straight line across the pitch: *a square pass.* **18.** *Naut.* (of the sails of a square-rigged ship) set at right angles to the keel. **19.** *Inf.* old-fashioned. **20.** stocky or sturdy: *square shoulders.* **21.** (*postpositive*) having no remaining debts or accounts to be settled. **22.** (*prenominal*) unequivocal or straightforward: *a square contradiction.* **23.** (*postpositive*) neat and tidy. **24.** *Maths.* (of a matrix) having the same number of rows and columns. **25. all square.** on equal terms; even in score. **26. square peg (in a round hole).** *Inf.* a person or thing that is a misfit. ~*vb.* (*mainly tr.*) **27.** to make into a square or similar shape. **28.** *Maths.* to raise (a number or quantity) to the second power. **29.** to test or adjust for deviation with respect to a right angle, plane surface, etc. **30.** (sometimes foll. by *off*) to divide into squares. **31.** to position so as to be rectangular, straight, or level: *to square the shoulders.* **32.** (sometimes foll. by *up*) to settle (debts, accounts, etc.). **33.** to level (the score) in a game, etc. **34.** (*also intr.*; often foll. by *with*) to agree or cause to agree: *your ideas don't square with mine.* **35.** to arrange (something) or come to an arrangement with (someone) as by bribery. **36. square the circle.** to attempt the impossible (in reference to the insoluble problem of constructing a square having exactly the same area as a given circle). ~*adv.* **37.** in order to be square. **38.** at right angles. **39.** *Soccer, hockey, etc.* in a straight line across the pitch: *to pass the ball square.* **40.** *Inf.* squarely. ~*See also* **square away, square off, square up.** [C13: from OF *esquare*, from Vulgar L *exquadra* (unattested), from L *quadrāre* to make square] —**'squareness** *n.* —**'squarer** *n.*

square away *vb.* (*adv.*) **1.** to set the sails of (a square-rigged ship) at right angles to the keel. **2.** (*tr.*) *U.S. & Canad.* to make neat and tidy.

square-bashing *n.* *Brit. mil. sl.* drill on a barracks square.

square bracket *n.* **1.** either of a pair of characters [ ], used to enclose a section of writing or printing to separate it from the main text. **2.** Also called: **bracket.** either of these characters used as a sign of aggregation in mathematical or logical expressions.

square dance *n.* **1.** any of various formation dances in which the couples form squares. ~*vb.* **square-dance. 2.** (*intr.*) to perform such a dance. —**'square-,dancer** *n.*

square knot *n.* another name for **reef knot.**

square leg *n.* *Cricket.* **1.** a fielding position on the on side approximately at right angles to the batsman. **2.** a person who fields in this position.

squarely ('skwɛəlɪ) *adv.* **1.** in a direct way; straight: *he hit me squarely on the nose.* **2.** in an honest, frank, and just manner. **3.** at right angles.

square meal *n.* a substantial meal consisting of enough to satisfy.

square measure *n.* a unit or system of units for measuring areas.

square number *n.* an integer, such as 1, 4, 9, or 16, that is the square of an integer.

square off *vb.* (*intr., adv.*) to assume a posture of offence or defence, as in boxing.

square of opposition *n.* *Logic.* the diagrammatic representation of the relationships between the four types of proposition found in the syllogism.

square-rigged *adj.* *Naut.* rigged with square sails. See **square sail.**

square root *n.* a number or quantity that when multiplied by itself gives a given number or quantity: *the square roots of 4 are 2 and −2.*

square sail *n.* *Naut.* a rectangular or square sail set on a horizontal yard rigged more or less at right angles to the keel.

square shooter *n.* *Inf., chiefly U.S.* an honest or frank person. —**square shooting** *adj.*

square up *vb.* (*adv.*) **1.** to pay or settle (bills, debts, etc.). **2.** *Inf.* to arrange or be arranged satisfactorily. **3.** (*intr.*; foll. by *to*) to prepare to be confronted (with), esp. courageously. **4.** (*tr.*; foll. by *to*) to adopt a position of readiness to fight (an opponent). **5.** *Scot.* to tidy up.

squarrose ('skwærəʊz, 'skwɒ-) *adj.* **1.** *Biol.* having a rough surface, caused by projecting hairs, scales, etc. **2.** *Bot.* having or relating to overlapping parts that are pointed or recurved. [C18: from L *squarrōsus* scabby]

squash¹ (skwɒʃ) *vb.* **1.** to press or squeeze or be pressed or squeezed in or down so as to crush, distort, or pulp. **2.** (*tr.*) to suppress or overcome. **3.** (*tr.*) to humiliate or crush (a person), esp. with a disconcerting retort. **4.** (*intr.*) to make a sucking, splashing, or squelching sound. **5.** (often foll. by *in* or *into*) to enter or insert in a confined space. ~*n.* **6.** *Brit.* a still drink made from fruit juice or fruit syrup diluted with water. **7.** a crush, esp. of people in a confined space. **8.** something squashed. **9.** the act or sound of squashing or the state of being squashed. **10.** Also called: **squash rackets.** a game for two or four players played in an enclosed court with a small rubber ball and light long-handled rackets. **11.** Also called: **squash tennis.** a similar game played with larger rackets and a larger pneumatic ball. [C16: from OF *esquasser*, from Vulgar L *exquassāre* (unattested), from L EX-¹ + *quassāre* to shatter] —**'squasher** *n.*

squash² (skwɒʃ) *n., pl.* **squashes** *or* **squash.** *U.S. & Canad.* **1.** any of various marrow-like plants, the fruits of which have a hard rind surrounding edible flesh. **2.** the fruit, eaten as a vegetable. [C17: of Amerind origin, from *askutasquash*, lit.: green vegetable eaten green]

squashy ('skwɒʃɪ) *adj.* **squashier, squashiest. 1.** easily squashed; pulpy: *a squashy peach.* **2.** soft and wet; marshy: *squashy ground.* —**'squashily** *adv.* —**'squashiness** *n.*

squat (skwɒt) *vb.* **squatting, squatted.** (*intr.*) **1.** to rest in a crouching position with the knees bent and the weight on the feet. **2.** to crouch down, esp. in order to hide. **3.** *Law.* to occupy land or property to which the occupant has no legal title. ~*adj.* **4.** Also: **squatty.** short and broad. ~*n.* **5.** a squatting position. **6.** a house occupied by squatters. [C13: from OF *esquater*, from *es-* EX-¹ + *catir* to press together, from Vulgar L *coactīre* (unattested), from L *cōgere* to compress] —**'squatly** *adv.* —**'squatness** *n.*

squatter ('skwɒtə) *n.* **1.** (in Britain) a person who occupies land or property wrongfully. **2.** (in Australia) **a.** a grazier with extensive holdings. **b.** *History.* a person occupying land as tenant of the Crown. **3.** (in New Zealand) a 19th-century settler who took up large acreage on a crown lease.

squattocracy (skwɒ'tɒkrəsɪ) *n. Austral.* squatters collectively, regarded as rich and influential. See **squatter** (sense 2a). [C19: from SQUATTER + -CRACY]

squaw (skwɔ:) *n.* **1.** *Offens.* a North American Indian woman. **2.** *Sl., usually facetious.* a woman or wife. [C17: of Amerind origin]

squawk (skwɔ:k) *n.* **1.** a loud raucous cry; screech. **2.** *Inf.* a loud complaint. ~*vb.* **3.** to utter (with) a squawk. **4.** (*intr.*) *Inf.* to complain loudly. [C19: imit.] —**'squawker** *n.*

squaw man *n. Derog.* a White man married to a North American Indian woman.

squeak (skwi:k) *n.* **1.** a short shrill cry or high-pitched sound. **2.** *Inf.* an escape (esp. in **narrow squeak, near squeak**). **3.** *Inf.* (*usually used with a negative*) a word; a slight sound. ~*vb.* **4.** to make or cause to make a squeak. **5.** (*intr.*; usually foll. by *through* or *by*) to pass with only a narrow margin: *to squeak through an examination.* **6.** (*intr.*) *Inf.* to confess information about oneself or another. **7.** (*tr.*) to utter with a squeak. [C17: prob. of Scand. origin] —**'squeaky** *adj.* —**'squeakily** *adv.* —**'squeakiness** *n.*

squeaky-clean adj. **1.** (of hair) washed so clean that wet strands squeak when rubbed. **2.** completely clean. **3.** above reproach: his squeaky-clean image.

squeal (skwi:l) n. **1.** a high shrill yelp, as of pain. **2.** a screaming sound. ~vb. **3.** to utter (with) a squeal. **4.** (intr.) Sl. to confess information about another. **5.** (intr.) Inf., chiefly Brit. to complain loudly. [C13 squelen, imit.] —'**squealer** n.

squeamish ('skwi:mɪʃ) adj. **1.** easily sickened or nauseated. **2.** easily shocked; prudish. **3.** easily frightened: squeamish about spiders. [C15: from Anglo-F escoymous, from ?] —'**squeamishly** adv. —'**squeamishness** n.

squeegee ('skwi:dʒi:) n. **1.** an implement with a rubber blade used for wiping away surplus water from a surface, such as a windowpane. **2.** any of various similar devices used in photography for pressing water out of wet prints or negatives or for squeezing prints onto a glazing surface. ~vb. **-geeing, -geed. 3.** to remove (liquid) from (something) by use of a squeegee. [C19: prob. imit., infl. by SQUEEZE]

squeeze (skwi:z) vb. (mainly tr.) **1.** to grip or press firmly, esp. so as to crush or distort. **2.** to crush or press (something) so as to extract (a liquid): to squeeze juice from an orange; to squeeze an orange. **3.** to apply gentle pressure to, as in affection or reassurance: he squeezed her hand. **4.** to push or force in a confined space: to squeeze six lettuces into one box; to squeeze through a crowd. **5.** to hug closely. **6.** to oppress with exacting demands, such as excessive taxes. **7.** to exert pressure on (someone) in order to extort (something): to squeeze money out of a victim by blackmail. **8.** Bridge, whist. to lead a card that forces (opponents) to discard potentially winning cards. ~n. **9.** the act or an instance of squeezing or of being squeezed. **10.** a hug or handclasp. **11.** a crush of people in a confined space. **12.** Chiefly Brit. a condition of restricted credit imposed by a government to counteract price inflation. **13.** an amount extracted by squeezing: a squeeze of lemon juice. **14.** Inf. pressure brought to bear in order to extort something (esp. in **put the squeeze on**). **15.** Also called: **squeeze play**. Bridge, whist. a manoeuvre that forces opponents to discard potentially winning cards. [C16: from ME queysen to press, from OE cwȳsan] —'**squeezable** adj. —'**squeezer** n.

squelch (skwɛltʃ) vb. **1.** (intr.) to walk laboriously through soft wet material or with wet shoes, making a sucking noise. **2.** (intr.) to make such a noise. **3.** (tr.) to crush completely; squash. **4.** (tr.) Inf. to silence, as by a crushing retort. ~n. **5.** a squelching sound. **6.** something that has been squelched. **7.** Inf. a crushing remark. [C17: imit.] —'**squelcher** n. —'**squelchy** adj.

squib (skwɪb) n. **1.** a firework that burns with a hissing noise and culminates in a small explosion. **2.** a short witty attack; lampoon. **3. damp squib**. something intended but failing to impress. ~vb. **squibbing, squibbed. 4.** (intr.) to sound, move, or explode like a squib. **5.** (intr.) to let off or shoot a squib. **6.** to write a squib against (someone). [C16: prob. imit. of a light explosion]

squid (skwɪd) n., pl. **squid** or **squids**. any of various ten-limbed pelagic cephalopod molluscs of most seas, having a torpedo-shaped body ranging from about 10 centimetres to 16.5 metres long. See also **cuttlefish**. [C17: from ?]

squiffy ('skwɪfɪ) adj. **-fier, -fiest**. Brit. inf. slightly drunk. [C19: from ?]

squiggle ('skwɪgᵊl) n. **1.** a mark or movement in the form of a wavy line; curlicue. **2.** an illegible scrawl. ~vb. **3.** (intr.) to wriggle. **4.** (intr.) to·form or draw squiggles. **5.** (tr.) to make into squiggles. [C19: ? a blend of SQUIRM + WIGGLE] —'**squiggler** n. —'**squiggly** adj.

squilgee ('skwɪldʒi:) n. a variant spelling of **squeegee**. [C19: ?from SQUEEGEE, infl. by SQUELCH]

squill (skwɪl) n. **1.** Also called: **sea squill**. a Mediterranean plant of the lily family. **2.** any of various related Old World plants. **3.** the bulb of the sea squill, which is sliced, dried, and used medicinally, as an expectorant. [C14: from L squilla sea onion, from Gk skilla, from ?]

squinch (skwɪntʃ) n. a small arch, corbelling, etc., across an internal corner of a tower, used to support a spire, etc. Also called: **squinch arch**. [C15: from obs. scunch, from ME sconcheon, from OF escoinson, from es- EX-¹ + coin corner]

squint (skwɪnt) vb. **1.** (usually intr.) to cross or partly close (the eyes). **2.** (intr.) to have a squint. **3.** (intr.) to

look or glance sideways or askance. ~n. **4.** the nontechnical name for **strabismus. 5.** the act or an instance of squinting; glimpse. **6.** a narrow oblique opening in a wall or pillar of a church to permit a view of the main altar from a side aisle or transept. **7.** Inf. a quick look; glance. ~adj. **8.** having a squint. **9.** Inf. askew; crooked. [C14: short for ASQUINT] —'**squinter** n. —'**squinty** adj.

squire ('skwaɪə) n. **1.** a country gentleman in England, esp. the main landowner in a rural community. **2.** Feudal history. a young man of noble birth, who attended upon a knight. **3.** Rare. a man who courts or escorts a woman. **4.** Inf., chiefly Brit. a term of address used by one man to another. ~vb. **5.** (tr.) (of a man) to escort a woman. [C13: from OF esquier; see ESQUIRE]

squirearchy or **squirarchy** ('skwaɪə‚rɑ:kɪ) n., pl. **-chies. 1.** government by squires. **2.** squires collectively, esp. as a political or social force. —**squire'archal**, **squir'archal** or **squire'archical, squir'archical** adj.

squireen (skwaɪ'ri:n) or **squireling** ('skwaɪəlɪŋ) n. Rare. a petty squire. [C19: from SQUIRE + -een, Anglo-Irish dim. suffix]

squirm (skw3:m) vb. (intr.) **1.** to move with a wriggling motion; writhe. **2.** to feel deep mental discomfort, guilt, embarrassment, etc. ~n. **3.** a squirming movement. [C17: imit. (? infl. by WORM)] —'**squirmer** n. —'**squirmy** adj.

squirrel ('skwɪrəl) n., pl. **-rels** or **-rel. 1.** any of various arboreal rodents having a bushy tail and feeding on nuts, seeds, etc. **2.** any of various related rodents, such as a ground squirrel or a marmot. **3.** the fur of such an animal. **4.** Inf. a person who hoards things. ~vb. **-relling, -relled** or (esp. U.S.) **-reling, -reled. 5.** (tr ; usually foll. by away) Inf. to store for future use; hoard. [C14: from OF esquireul, from LL sciūrus, from Gk skiouros, from skia shadow + oura tail]

squirrel cage n. **1.** a cage consisting of a cylindrical framework that is made to rotate by a small animal running inside the framework. **2.** a repetitive purposeless task, way of life, etc. **3.** Also called: **squirrel-cage motor**. Electrical engineering. the rotor of an induction motor with a cylindrical winding having copper bars around the periphery parallel to the axis.

squirt (skw3:t) vb. **1.** to force (a liquid) or (of a liquid) to be forced out of a narrow opening. **2.** (tr.) to cover or spatter with liquid so ejected. ~n. **3.** a jet or amount of liquid so ejected. **4.** the act or an instance of squirting. **5.** an instrument used for squirting. **6.** Inf. **a.** a person regarded as insignificant or contemptible. **b.** a short person. [C15: imit.] —'**squirter** n.

squirting cucumber n. a hairy plant of the Mediterranean region, having a fruit that discharges seeds explosively when ripe.

squish (skwɪʃ) vb. **1.** (tr.) to crush, esp. so as to make a soft splashing noise. **2.** (intr.) (of mud, etc.) to make a splashing noise. ~n. **3.** a soft squashing sound. [C17: imit.] —'**squishy** adj.

squit (skwɪt) n. Brit. sl. **1.** an insignificant person. **2.** nonsense. [C19: var. of SQUIRT]

squiz (skwɪz) n., pl. **squizzes**. Austral. & N.Z. sl. a look or glance, esp. an inquisitive one. [C20: ? blend of SQUINT + QUIZ]

sr Maths. abbrev. for steradian.

Sr abbrev. for: **1.** (after a name) senior. **2.** Señor. **3.** Sir. **4.** Sister (religious). **5.** the chemical symbol for strontium.

Sra abbrev. for Señora.

Srbija ('sᵊrbija) n. the Serbian name for **Serbia**.

SRC (in Britain) abbrev. for Science Research Council.

Sri Lanka (‚sri: 'læŋkə) n. a republic in S Asia, occupying the island of Ceylon: settled by the Sinhalese from S India in about 550 B.C.; became a British colony 1802; gained independence in 1948, becoming a republic within the Commonwealth in 1972. Exports include tea, cocoa, cinnamon, and copra. Languages: Sinhalese, Tamil, and English. Religion: Hinayana Buddhist majority. Currency: Sri Lanka rupee. Capital: Colombo. Pop.: 16 353 000 (1987). Area: 65 610 sq. km (25 332 sq. miles). Official name (since 1978): **Democratic Socialist Republic of Sri Lanka**. Former name (until 1972): **Ceylon**.

Srinagar (sri:'nʌgə) n. a city in N India, the summer capital of the state of Jammu and Kashmir, at an altitude of 1600 m (5250 ft.) on the Jhelum River: seat of the University of Jammu and Kashmir (1948). Pop.: 520 000 (1981 est.).

SRN (in Britain) *abbrev. for* State Registered Nurse.
SRO *abbrev. for:* **1.** standing room only. **2.** (in Britain) Statutory Rules and Orders.
Srta *abbrev. for* Señorita.
SS *abbrev. for:* **1.** Saints. **2.** a paramilitary organization within the Nazi party that provided Hitler's bodyguard, security forces, concentration-camp guards, etc. [G *Schutzstaffel* protection squad] **3.** steamship.
SSE *symbol for* south-southeast.
SSR *abbrev. for* Soviet Socialist Republic.
SSRC (in Britain, formerly) *abbrev. for* Social Science Research Council.
SST *abbrev. for* supersonic transport.
SSW *symbol for* south-southwest.
St *abbrev. for:* **1.** Saint (all entries that are usually preceded by *St* are in this dictionary listed alphabetically under **Saint**). **2.** statute. **3.** Strait. **4.** Street.
-st *suffix.* a variant of **-est**[2].
st. *abbrev. for:* **1.** stanza. **2.** statute. **3.** stone. **4.** *Cricket.* stumped by.
s.t. *abbrev. for* short ton.
stab (stæb) *vb.* **stabbing, stabbed. 1.** (*tr.*) to pierce or injure with a sharp pointed instrument. **2.** (*tr.*) (of a sharp pointed instrument) to pierce or wound. **3.** (when *intr.*, often foll. by *at*) to make a thrust (at); jab. **4.** (*tr.*) to inflict with a sharp pain. **5. stab in the back. a.** (*vb.*) to damage the reputation of (a person, esp. a friend) in a surreptitious way. **b.** (*n.*) a treacherous action or remark that causes the downfall of or injury to a person. ~*n.* **6.** the act or an instance of stabbing. **7.** an injury or rift made by stabbing. **8.** a sudden sensation, esp. an unpleasant one: *a stab of pity.* **9.** *Inf.* an attempt (esp. in **make a stab at**). [C14: from *stabbe* stab wound] —'**stabber** *n.*
Stabat Mater ('stɑːbæt 'mɑːtə) *n.* **1.** *R.C. Church.* a Latin hymn commemorating the sorrows of the Virgin Mary at the crucifixion. **2.** a musical setting of this hymn. [from opening words, lit.: the mother was standing]
stabile ('steɪbaɪl) *n.* **1.** *Arts.* a stationary abstract construction, usually of wire, metal, wood, etc. ~*adj.* **2.** fixed; stable. **3.** resistant to chemical change. [C18: from L *stabilis*]
stability (stə'bɪlɪtɪ) *n., pl.* **-ties. 1.** the quality of being stable. **2.** the ability of an aircraft to resume its original flight path after inadvertent displacement.
stabilize *or* **-ise** ('steɪbɪˌlaɪz) *vb.* **1.** to make or become stable or more stable. **2.** to keep or be kept stable. **3.** (*tr.*) to put or keep (an aircraft, vessel, etc.) in equilibrium by one or more special devices or (of an aircraft, etc.) to become stable. — ˌstabili'zation *or* -i'sation *n.*
stabilizer *or* **-iser** ('steɪbɪˌlaɪzə) *n.* **1.** any device for stabilizing an aircraft. **2.** a substance added to something to maintain it in a stable or unchanging state, such as an additive that preserves the texture of food. **3.** *Naut.* **a.** a system of pairs of fins projecting from the hull of a ship and controllable to counteract roll. **b.** See **gyrostabilizer. 4.** a person or thing that stabilizes. **5.** either of a pair of small wheels fitted to the back wheel of a bicycle to help a beginner to maintain balance.
stable[1] ('steɪbᵊl) *n.* **1.** a building, usually consisting of stalls, for the lodging of horses or other livestock. **2.** the animals lodged in such a building, collectively. **3. a.** the racehorses belonging to a particular establishment or owner. **b.** the establishment itself. **c.** (*as modifier*): *stable companion.* **4.** *Inf.* a source of training, such as a school, theatre, etc.: *the two athletes were out of the same stable.* **5.** a number of people considered as a source of a particular talent: *a stable of writers.* **6.** (*modifier*) of, relating to, or suitable for a stable: *stable door.* ~*vb.* **7.** to put, keep, or be kept in a stable. [C13: from OF *estable* cowshed, from L *stabulum* shed, from *stāre* to stand]
stable[2] ('steɪbᵊl) *adj.* **1.** steady in position or balance; firm. **2.** lasting: *a stable relationship.* **3.** steadfast or firm of purpose. **4.** (of an elementary particle, etc.) not undergoing decay; not radioactive. **5.** (of a chemical compound) not readily partaking in a chemical change. [C13: from OF *estable*, from L *stabilis* steady, from *stāre* to stand] —'**stableness** *n.* —'**stably** *adv.*
stableboy ('steɪbᵊlˌbɔɪ), **stablegirl** ('steɪbᵊlˌgɜl), *or* **stableman** ('steɪbᵊlˌmæn, -mən) *n., pl.* **-boys, -girls,** *or* **-men.** a boy, girl, or man who works in a stable.
stable door *n.* a door with an upper and lower leaf that may be opened separately. U.S. and Canad. equivalent: **Dutch door.**

stable lad *n.* a person who looks after the horses in a racing stable.
stabling ('steɪblɪŋ) *n.* stable buildings or accommodation.
stablish ('stæblɪʃ) *vb.* an archaic variant of **establish.**
Stabroek (*Dutch* 'staːbruːk) *n.* the former name (until 1812) of **Georgetown** (sense 1).
staccato (stə'kɑːtəʊ) *adj.* **1.** *Music.* (of notes) short, clipped, and separate. **2.** characterized by short abrupt sounds, as in speech: *a staccato command.* ~*adv.* **3.** (esp. used as a musical direction) in a staccato manner. [C18: from It., from *staccare* to detach, shortened from *distaccare*]
stachys ('steɪkɪs) *n.* any plant of the herbaceous genus *Stachys.* See also **woundwort.** [C16: from L, from Gk: ear of corn]
stack (stæk) *n.* **1.** an ordered pile or heap. **2.** a large orderly pile of hay, straw, etc., for storage in the open air. **3.** (*often pl.*) compactly spaced bookshelves, used to house collections of books in an area usually prohibited to library users. **4.** a number of aircraft circling an airport at different altitudes, awaiting their signal to land. **5.** a large amount. **6.** *Mil.* a pile of rifles or muskets in the shape of a cone. **7.** *Brit.* a measure of coal or wood equal to 108 cubic feet. **8.** See **chimney stack, smokestack. 9.** a vertical pipe, such as the funnel of a ship or the soil pipe attached to the side of a building. **10.** a high column of rock, esp. one isolated from the mainland by the erosive action of the sea. **11.** an area in a computer memory for temporary storage. ~*vb.* (*tr.*) **12.** to place in a stack; pile. **13.** to load or fill up with piles of something: *to stack a lorry with bricks.* **14.** to control a number of aircraft waiting to land at an airport so that each flies at a different altitude. **15. stack the cards.** to prearrange the order of a pack of cards secretly so as to cheat. [C13: from ON *stakkr* haystack, of Gmc origin] —'**stacker** *n.*
stacked (stækt) *adj. Sl.* a variant of **well-stacked.**
stadholder *or* **stadtholder** ('stæd,həʊldə) *n.* **1.** the chief magistrate of the former Dutch republic or any of its provinces (from about 1580 to 1802). **2.** a viceroy or governor of a province. [C16: from Du. *stad houder*, from *stad* city + *houder* holder]
stadia[1] ('steɪdɪə) *n.* **1.** measurement of distance using a telescopic surveying instrument and a graduated staff calibrated to correspond with the distance from the observer. **2.** the two parallel cross hairs or **stadia hairs** in the eyepiece of the instrument used. **3.** the staff used. [C19: prob. from STADIA[2]]
stadia[2] ('steɪdɪə) *n.* a plural of **stadium.**
stadium ('steɪdɪəm) *n., pl.* **-diums** *or* **-dia. 1.** a sports arena with tiered seats for spectators. **2.** (in ancient Greece) a course for races, usually located between two hills providing slopes for tiers of seats. **3.** an ancient Greek measure of length equivalent to about 607 feet or 184 metres. [C16: via L from Gk *stadion*, changed from *spadion* racecourse, from *spān* to pull; infl. by Gk *stadios* steady]
Staël (*French* stal) *n.* **Madame de.** full name *Baronne Anne Louise Germaine (née Necker) de Staël-Holstein.* 1766–1817, French writer, whose works, esp. *De l'Allemagne* (1810), anticipated French romanticism.
staff[1] (stɑːf) *n., pl.* **staffs** *for senses 1–4;* **staffs** *or* **staves** *for senses 5–9.* **1.** a group of people employed by a company, individual, etc., for executive, clerical, sales work, etc. **2.** (*modifier*) attached to or provided for the staff of an establishment: *a staff doctor.* **3.** the body of teachers or lecturers at an educational institution. **4.** *Mil.* the officers appointed to assist a commander, service, or central headquarters organization. **5.** a stick with some special use, such as a walking stick or an emblem of authority. **6.** something that sustains or supports: *bread is the staff of life.* **7.** a pole on which a flag is hung. **8.** *Chiefly Brit.* a graduated rod used in surveying, esp. for sighting to with a levelling instrument. **9.** Also called: **stave.** *Music.* **a.** the system of horizontal lines grouped into sets of five (four in plainsong) upon which music is written. The spaces between them are employed in conjunction with a clef in order to give a graphic indication of pitch. **b.** any set of five lines in this system together with its clef: *the treble staff.* ~*vb.* **10.** (*tr.*) to provide with a staff. [OE *stæf*]
staff[2] (stɑːf) *n. U.S.* a mixture of plaster and hair used to cover the external surface of temporary structures and for decoration. [C19: from ?]

Staffa ('stæfə) *n.* an island in W Scotland, in the Inner Hebrides west of Mull: site of Fingal's Cave.

staff corporal *n.* a noncommissioned rank in the British Army above that of staff sergeant and below that of warrant officer.

staff nurse *n.* a qualified nurse ranking immediately below a sister.

staff officer *n.* a commissioned officer serving on the staff of a commander, service, or central headquarters.

Stafford[1] ('stæfəd) *n.* a market town in central England, administrative centre of Staffordshire. Pop.: 62 978 (1984 est.).

Stafford[2] ('stæfəd) *n.* Sir **Edward William.** 1819–1901, New Zealand statesman, born in Scotland: prime minister of New Zealand (1856–61; 1865–69; 1872).

Staffordshire ('stæfəd,ʃɪə, -ʃə) *n.* a county of central England: coalfields lie in the east and south and the Pennine uplands in the north; important in the history of industry, coal and iron having been worked at least since the 13th century. Administrative centre: Stafford. Pop.: 1 021 000 (1986 est.). Area: 2716 sq. km (1048 sq. miles).

Staffordshire bull terrier *n.* a breed of smooth-coated terrier with a stocky frame and generally a pied or brindled coat.

Staffs. (stæfs) *abbrev. for* Staffordshire.

staff sergeant *n. Mil.* **1.** *Brit.* a noncommissioned officer holding a rank between sergeant and warrant officer and employed on administrative duties. **2.** *U.S.* a noncommissioned officer who ranks: **a.** (in the Army) above sergeant and below sergeant first class. **b.** (in the Air Force) above airman first class and below technical sergeant. **c.** (in the Marine Corps) above sergeant and below gunnery sergeant.

stag (stæg) *n.* **1.** the adult male of a deer. **2.** a man unaccompanied by a woman at a social gathering. **3.** *Stock Exchange, Brit.* a speculator who buys heavily on a new share issue in anticipation of a rise in its price and thus a quick profit on its resale. **4.** *(modifier)* (of a social gathering) attended by men only. ~*adv.* **5.** without a female escort. [OE *stagga* (unattested); rel. to ON *steggr* male bird]

stag beetle *n.* any of various beetles, the males of which have large branched mandibles.

stage (steɪdʒ) *n.* **1.** a distinct step or period of development, growth, or progress. **2.** a raised area or platform. **3.** the platform in a theatre where actors perform. **4. the.** the theatre as a profession. **5.** any scene regarded as a setting for an event or action. **6.** a portion of a journey or a stopping place after such a portion. **7.** short for **stagecoach. 8.** *Brit.* a division of a bus route for which there is a fixed fare. **9.** one of the separate propulsion units of a rocket that can be jettisoned when it has burnt out. **10.** a small stratigraphical unit; a subdivision of a rock series or system. **11.** the platform on a microscope on which the specimen is mounted for examination. **12.** *Electronics.* a part of a complex circuit, esp. a transistor with the associated elements required to amplify a signal in an amplifier. **13. by** *or* **in easy stages.** not hurriedly: *he learnt French by easy stages.* ~*vb.* (*tr.*) **14.** to perform (a play), esp. on a stage: *to stage "Hamlet".* **15.** to set the action of (a play) in a particular time or place. **16.** to plan, organize, and carry out (an event). [C13: from OF *estage* position, from Vulgar L *staticum* (unattested), from L *stāre* to stand]

stagecoach ('steɪdʒ,kəʊtʃ) *n.* a large four-wheeled horse-drawn vehicle formerly used to carry passengers, mail, etc., on a regular route.

stagecraft ('steɪdʒ,krɑːft) *n.* skill in or the art of writing or staging plays.

stage direction *n.* an instruction to an actor or director, written into the script of a play.

stage door *n.* a door at a theatre leading backstage.

stage fright *n.* nervousness or panic that may beset a person about to appear in front of an audience.

stagehand ('steɪdʒ,hænd) *n.* a person who sets the stage, moves props, etc., in a theatrical production.

stage left *n.* the part of the stage to the left of a performer facing the audience.

stage-manage *vb.* **1.** to work as stage manager (for a play, etc.). **2.** (*tr.*) to arrange, present, or supervise from behind the scenes.

stage manager *n.* a person who supervises the stage arrangements of a theatrical production.

stager ('steɪdʒə) *n.* **1.** a person of experience; veteran (esp. in **old stager**). **2.** an archaic word for **actor.**

stage right *n.* the part of the stage to the right of a performer facing the audience.

stage-struck *adj.* infatuated with the glamour of theatrical life, esp. with the desire to act.

stage whisper *n.* **1.** a loud whisper from one actor to another onstage intended to be heard by the audience. **2.** any loud whisper that is intended to be overheard.

stagflation (stæg'fleɪʃən) *n.* a situation in which inflation is combined with stagnant or falling output and employment. [C20: blend of *stagnation* + *inflation*]

stagger ('stægə) *vb.* **1.** (*usually intr.*) to walk or cause to walk unsteadily as if about to fall. **2.** (*tr.*) to astound or overwhelm, as with shock: *I am staggered by his ruthlessness.* **3.** (*tr.*) to place or arrange in alternating or overlapping positions or time periods to prevent confusion or congestion: *a staggered junction; to stagger holidays.* **4.** (*intr.*) to falter or hesitate: *his courage staggered in the face of the battle.* ~*n.* **5.** the act or an instance of staggering. [C13: from dialect *stacker*, from ON *staka* to push] —**'staggerer** *n.* —**'staggering** *adj.* —**'staggeringly** *adv.*

staggers ('stægəz) *n.* (*functioning as sing. or pl.*) **1.** a form of vertigo associated with decompression sickness. **2.** Also called: **blind staggers.** a disease of horses and some other domestic animals characterized by a swaying unsteady gait, caused by infection or lesions of the central nervous system.

staging ('steɪdʒɪŋ) *n.* any temporary structure used in the process of building, esp. the horizontal platforms supported by scaffolding.

staging area *n.* a checkpoint or regrouping area for military formations in transit.

staging post *n.* a place where a journey is usually broken, esp. a stopover on a flight.

Stagira (stə'dʒaɪrə) *n.* an ancient city on the coast of Chalcidice in Macedonia: the birthplace of Aristotle.

stagnant ('stægnənt) *adj.* **1.** (of water, etc.) standing still; without flow or current. **2.** brackish and foul from standing still. **3.** stale, sluggish, or dull from inaction. **4.** not growing or developing; static. [C17: from L *stagnāns*, from *stagnāre* to be stagnant, from *stagnum* a pool] —**'stagnancy** *n.*

stagnate (stæg'neɪt) *vb.* (*intr.*) to be or become stagnant. —**stag'nation** *n.*

stag party *n.* a party for men only, esp. one held for a man just before he is married.

stagy *or U.S.* **stagey** ('steɪdʒɪ) *adj.* **stagier, stagiest.** excessively theatrical or dramatic. —**'stagily** *adv.* —**'staginess** *n.*

staid (steɪd) *adj.* of a settled, sedate, and steady character. [C16: obs. p.p. of STAY[1]] —**'staidly** *adv.* —**'staidness** *n.*

stain (steɪn) *vb.* (*mainly tr.*) **1.** to mark or discolour with patches of something that dirties. **2.** to dye with a penetrating dyestuff or pigment. **3.** to bring disgrace or shame on: *to stain one's honour.* **4.** to colour (specimens) for microscopic study by treatment with a dye or similar reagent. **5.** (*intr.*) to produce indelible marks or discoloration: *does ink stain?* ~*n.* **6.** a spot, mark, or discoloration. **7.** a moral taint; blemish or slur. **8.** a dye or similar reagent, used to colour specimens for microscopic study. **9.** a solution or liquid used to penetrate the surface of a material, esp. wood, and impart a rich colour without covering up the surface or grain. **10.** any dye used to colour textiles and hides. [C14 *steynen* (vb.), shortened from *disteynen* to remove colour from, from OF *desteindre* to discolour, ult. from L *tingere* to tinge] —**'stainable** *adj.* —**,staina'bility** *n.* —**'stainer** *n.*

stained glass *n.* **a.** glass that has been coloured, as by fusing with a film of metallic oxide or burning pigment into the surface. **b.** (*as modifier*): *a stained-glass window.*

Staines (steɪnz) *n.* a town in SE England, in N Surrey on the River Thames. Pop.: 53 823 (1981).

stainless ('steɪnlɪs) *adj.* **1.** resistant to discoloration, esp. that resulting from corrosion; rust-resistant: *stainless steel.* **2.** having no blemish: *stainless reputation.* —**'stainlessly** *adv.*

stainless steel *n.* **a.** a type of steel resistant to corrosion as a result of the presence of large amounts of chromium. **b.** (*as modifier*): *stainless-steel cutlery.*

stair (stɛə) *n.* **1.** one of a flight of stairs. **2.** a series of steps: *a narrow stair.* ~See also **stairs.** [OE *stæger*]

staircase ('stɛə,keɪs) *n.* a flight of stairs, its supporting framework, and, usually, a handrail or banisters.

stairs (stɛəz) *pl. n.* **1.** a flight of steps leading from one storey or level to another, esp. indoors. **2. below stairs.** *Brit.* in the servants' quarters.

stairway ('stɛə,weɪ) *n.* a means of access consisting of stairs; staircase or flight of steps.

stairwell ('stɛə,wɛl) *n.* a vertical shaft or opening that contains a staircase.

stake[1] (steɪk) *n.* **1.** a stick or metal bar driven into the ground as a marker, part of a fence, support for a plant, etc. **2.** one of a number of vertical posts that fit into sockets around a flat truck or railway wagon to hold the load in place. **3.** a method or the practice of executing a person by binding him to a stake in the centre of a pile of wood that is then set on fire. **4. pull up stakes.** to leave one's home or resting place and move on. ~*vb.* (*tr.*) **5.** to tie, fasten, or tether with or to a stake. **6.** (often foll. by *out* or *off*) to fence or surround with stakes. **7.** (often foll. by *out*) to lay (a claim) to land, rights, etc. **8.** to support with a stake. [OE *staca* pin]

stake[2] (steɪk) *n.* **1.** the money or valuables that a player must hazard in order to buy into a gambling game or make a bet. **2.** an interest, often financial, held in something: *a stake in the company's future.* **3.** (*often pl.*) the money that a player has available for gambling. **4.** (*often pl.*) a prize in a race, etc., esp. one made up of contributions from contestants or owners. **5.** (*pl.*) a horse race in which all owners of competing horses contribute to the prize. **6.** *U.S. & Canad. inf.* short for **grubstake.** **7. at stake.** at risk: *lives are at stake.* ~*vb.* (*tr.*) **8.** to hazard (money, etc.) on a result. **9.** to invest in or support with money, etc.: *to stake a business.* [C16: from ?]

Staked Plain *n.* another name for the **Llano Estacado.**

stakeout ('steɪkaʊt) *Chiefly U.S. & Canad. sl.* ~*n.* **1.** a police surveillance. **2.** an area or house kept under such surveillance. ~*vb.* **stake out. 3.** (*tr., adv.*) to keep under surveillance.

Stakhanovism (stæ'kænə,vɪzəm) *n.* (in the Soviet Union) a system designed to raise production by offering incentives to efficient workers. [C20: after A. G. *Stakhanov* (1906–77), Soviet miner, the worker first rewarded under the system in 1935] —**Sta'khanov,ite** *n., adj.*

stalactite ('stælək,taɪt) *n.* a cylindrical mass of calcium carbonate hanging from the roof of a limestone cave: formed by precipitation from continually dripping water. Cf. **stalagmite.** [C17: from NL *stalactites,* from Gk *stalaktos* dripping, from *stalassein* to drip] —**stalacti-form** (stə'læktɪ,fɔːm) *adj.* —**stalactitic** (,stælək'tɪtɪk) *or* ,**stalac'titical** *adj.*

stalag ('stælæg) *n.* a German prisoner-of-war camp in World War II, esp. for men from the ranks. [short for *Stammlager* base camp]

stalagmite ('stæləg,maɪt) *n.* a cylindrical mass of calcium carbonate projecting upwards from the floor of a limestone cave: formed by precipitation from continually dripping water. Cf. **stalactite.** [C17: from NL *stalagmites,* from Gk *stalagmos* dripping; rel. to Gk *stalassein* to drip] —**stalagmitic** (,stæləg'mɪtɪk) *or* ,**stalag'mitical** *adj.*

stale[1] (steɪl) *adj.* **1.** (esp. of food) hard, musty, or dry from being kept too long. **2.** (of beer, etc.) flat and tasteless from being kept open too long. **3.** (of air) stagnant; foul. **4.** uninteresting from overuse: *stale clichés.* **5.** no longer new: *stale news.* **6.** lacking in energy or ideas through overwork or lack of variety. **7.** *Law.* (of a claim, etc.) having lost its effectiveness or force, as by failure to act or by the lapse of time. ~*vb.* **8.** to make or become stale. [C13 (orig. applied to liquor in the sense: well matured): prob. from OF *estale* (unattested) motionless, of Frankish origin] —**'staleness** *n.*

stale[2] (steɪl) *vb.* **1.** (*intr.*) (of livestock) to urinate. ~*n.* **2.** the urine of horses or cattle. [C15: ?from OF *estaler* to stand in one position]

stalemate ('steɪl,meɪt) *n.* **1.** a chess position in which any of a player's possible moves would place his king in check: in this position the game ends in a draw. **2.** a situation in which two opposing forces find that further action is impossible or futile; deadlock. ~*vb.* **3.** (*tr.*) to subject to a stalemate. [C18: from obs. *stale,* from OF *estal* STALL[1] + (CHECK)MATE]

Stalin[1] ('staːlɪn) *n.* **1.** Also called: **Stalino.** a former name (from after the Revolution until 1961) of **Donetsk.** **2.** the former name (1950–61) of **Braşov.** **3.** the former name (1949–56) of **Varna.**

Stalin[2] ('staːlɪn) *n.* **Joseph.** original name *Iosif Vissarionovich Dzhugashvili.* 1879–1953, Soviet leader; general secretary of the Communist Party of the Soviet Union (1922–53). He succeeded Lenin as head of the party and created a totalitarian state, crushing all opposition, esp. in the great purges of 1934–37. He instigated rapid industrialization and the collectivization of agriculture and established the Soviet Union as a world power.

Stalinabad (*Russian* stəlina'bat) *n.* the former name (1929–61) of **Dushanbe.**

Stalingrad ('staːlɪn,græd; *Russian* stəlin'grat) *n.* the former name (1925–61) of **Volgograd.**

Stalinism ('staːlɪ,nɪzəm) *n.* the theory and form of government associated with Joseph Stalin: a variant of Marxism-Leninism characterized by totalitarianism, rigid bureaucracy, and loyalty to the Soviet state. —**'Stalinist** *n., adj.*

Stalinogrod (*Polish* stali'nɔgrɔt) *n.* the former name (1953–56) for **Katowice.**

Stalin Peak *n.* a former name for **Kommunizma Peak.**

Stalinsk (*Russian* 'stalinsk) *n.* the former name (1932–61) of **Novokuznetsk.**

stalk[1] (stɔːk) *n.* **1.** the main stem of a herbaceous plant. **2.** any of various subsidiary plant stems, such as a leaf-stalk or flower stalk. **3.** a slender supporting structure in animals such as crinoids and barnacles. **4.** any long slender supporting shaft or column. [C14: prob. dim. from OE *stalu* upright piece of wood] —**stalked** *adj.* —**'stalk-,like** *adj.*

stalk[2] (stɔːk) *vb.* **1.** to follow or approach (game, prey, etc.) stealthily and quietly. **2.** to spread over (a place) in a menacing or grim manner: *fever stalked the camp.* **3.** (*intr.*) to walk in a haughty, stiff, or threatening way. **4.** to search (a piece of land) for prey. ~*n.* **5.** the act of stalking. **6.** a stiff or threatening stride. [OE *bestealcian* to walk stealthily] —**'stalker** *n.*

stalking-horse *n.* **1.** a horse or an imitation one used by a hunter to hide behind while stalking. **2.** something serving as a means of concealing plans; pretext. **3.** *Chiefly U.S.* a candidate put forward to divide the opposition or mask the candidacy of another person for whom the stalking-horse would then withdraw.

stalky ('stɔːkɪ) *adj.* **stalkier, stalkiest. 1.** like a stalk; slender and tall. **2.** having or abounding in stalks. —**'stalkily** *adv.* —**'stalkiness** *n.*

stall[1] (stɔːl) *n.* **1. a.** a compartment in a stable or shed for a single animal. **b.** another name for **stable**[1]. **2.** a small often temporary stand or booth for the sale of goods. **3.** (in a church) **a.** one of a row of seats usually divided by armrests or a small screen, for the choir or clergy. **b.** a pen. **4.** an instance of an engine stalling. **5.** a condition of an aircraft in flight in which a reduction in speed or an increase in the aircraft's angle of attack causes a sudden loss of lift resulting in a downward plunge. **6.** any small room or compartment. **7.** *Brit.* **a.** a seat in a theatre or cinema, usually fixed to the floor. **b.** (*pl.*) the area of seats on the ground floor of a theatre or cinema nearest to the stage or screen. **8.** a tubelike covering for a finger. **9.** (*pl.*) short for **starting stalls.** ~*vb.* **10.** to cause (a motor vehicle or its engine) to stop, usually by incorrect use of the clutch or incorrect adjustment of the fuel mixture, or (of an engine or motor vehicle) to stop, usually for these reasons. **11.** to cause (an aircraft) to go into a stall or (of an aircraft) to go into a stall. **12.** to stick or cause to stick fast, as in mud or snow. **13.** (*tr.*) to confine (an animal) in a stall. [OE *steall* a place for standing]

stall[2] (stɔːl) *vb.* **1.** to employ delaying tactics towards (someone); to be evasive. ~*n.* **2.** an evasive move; pretext. [C16: from Anglo-F *estale* bird used as a decoy, infl. by STALL[1]]

stall-feed *vb.* **-feeding, -fed.** (*tr.*) to keep and feed (an animal) in a stall, esp. as an intensive method of fattening it for slaughter.

stallion ('stæljən) *n.* an uncastrated male horse, esp. one used for breeding. [C14 *staloun,* from OF *estalon,* of Gmc origin]

stalwart ('stɔːlwət) *adj.* **1.** strong and sturdy; robust. **2.** solid, dependable, and courageous. **3.** resolute and firm. ~*n.* **4.** a stalwart person, esp. a supporter. [OE *stælwirthe* serviceable, from *stæl*, from *stathol* support + *wierthe* worth] —'**stalwartly** *adv.* —'**stalwartness** *n.*

Stambul *or* **Stamboul** (stæm'bu:l) *n.* the old part of Istanbul, Turkey, south of the Golden Horn: the site of ancient Byzantium; sometimes used as a name for the whole city.

stamen ('steimɛn) *n., pl.* **stamens** *or* **stamina.** the male reproductive organ of a flower, consisting of a stalk (filament) bearing an anther in which pollen is produced. [C17: from L: the warp in an upright loom, from *stāre* to stand] —**staminiferous** (,stæmi'nifərəs) *adj.*

Stamford ('stæmfəd) *n.* a city in SW Connecticut, on Long Island Sound: major chemical research laboratories. Pop.: 102 453 (1980).

stamina[1] ('stæminə) *n.* enduring energy, strength, and resilience. [C19: identical with STAMINA[2], from L *stāmen* thread, hence the threads of life spun out by the Fates, hence energy, etc.]

stamina[2] ('stæminə) *n.* a plural of **stamen.**

staminate ('stæminit, -,neit) *adj.* (of plants) having stamens, esp. having stamens but no carpels; male.

stammer ('stæmə) *vb.* **1.** to speak or say (something) in a hesitant way, esp. as a result of a speech disorder or through fear, stress, etc. ~*n.* **2.** a speech disorder characterized by involuntary repetitions and hesitations. [OE *stamerian*] —'**stammerer** *n.* —'**stammering** *n., adj.*

stamp (stæmp) *vb.* **1.** (when *intr.*, often foll. by *on*) to bring (the foot) down heavily (on the ground, etc.). **2.** (*intr.*) to walk with heavy or noisy footsteps. **3.** (*intr.*; foll. by *on*) to repress or extinguish: *he stamped on criticism.* **4.** (*tr.*) to impress or mark (a device or sign) on (something). **5.** to mark (something) with an official seal or device: *to stamp a passport.* **6.** (*tr.*) to fix or impress permanently: *the date was stamped on her memory.* **7.** (*tr.*) to affix a postage stamp to. **8.** (*tr.*) to distinguish or reveal: *that behaviour stamps him as a cheat.* **9.** to pound or crush (ores, etc.). ~*n.* **10.** the act or an instance of stamping. **11. a.** See **postage stamp. b.** a mark applied to postage stamps for cancellation. **12.** a similar piece of gummed paper used for commercial or trading purposes. **13.** a block, die, etc., used for imprinting a design or device. **14.** a design, device, or mark that has been stamped. **15.** a characteristic feature or trait; hallmark: *the stamp of authenticity.* **16.** a piece of gummed paper or other mark applied to official documents to indicate payment, validity, ownership, etc. **17.** *Brit. inf.* a national insurance contribution, formerly recorded by means of a stamp on an official card. **18.** type or class: *men of his stamp.* **19.** an instrument or machine for crushing or pounding ores, etc., or the pestle in such a device. ~See also **stamp out.** [OE *stampe*] —'**stamper** *n.*

stamp duty *or* **tax** *n.* a tax on legal documents, publications, etc., the payment of which is certified by the attaching or impressing of official stamps.

stampede (stæm'pi:d) *n.* **1.** an impulsive headlong rush of startled cattle or horses. **2.** headlong rush of a crowd. **3.** any sudden large-scale action, such as a rush of people to support a candidate. **4.** *Canad.* a rodeo. ~*vb.* **5.** to run away or cause to run away in a stampede. [C19: from American Sp. *estampida*, from Sp.: a din, from *estampar* to stamp, of Gmc origin] —**stam'peder** *n.*

stamping ground *n.* a habitual or favourite meeting or gathering place.

stamp mill *n.* a machine for crushing ore.

stamp out *vb.* (*tr., adv.*) **1.** to put out or extinguish by stamping: *to stamp out a fire.* **2.** to suppress by force: *to stamp out a rebellion.*

stance (stæns, stɑ:ns) *n.* **1.** the manner and position in which a person or animal stands. **2.** *Sport.* the posture assumed when about to play the ball, as in golf, cricket, etc. **3.** emotional or intellectual attitude: *a leftist stance.* **4.** *Chiefly Scot.* a place where a vehicle waits: *taxi stance.* [C16: via F from It. *stanza* place for standing, from L *stāns*, from *stāre* to stand]

stanch (stɑ:ntʃ) *or* **staunch** (stɔ:ntʃ) *vb.* **1.** to stem the flow of (a liquid, esp. blood) or (of a liquid) to stop flowing. **2.** to prevent the flow of (a liquid, esp. blood, from (a hole, wound, etc.). [C14: from OF *estanchier*, from Vulgar L *stanticāre* (unattested) to cause to stand, from L *stāre* to halt] —'**stanchable** *or* '**staunchable** *adj.* —'**stancher** *or* '**stauncher** *n.*

stanchion ('stɑ:nʃən) *n.* **1.** any vertical pole, beam, rod, etc., used as a support. ~*vb.* **2.** (*tr.*) to provide or support with a stanchion or stanchions. [C15: from OF *estanchon*, from *estance*, from Vulgar L *stantia* (unattested) a standing, from L *stāre* to stand]

stand (stænd) *vb.* **standing, stood.** (*mainly intr.*) **1.** (*also tr.*) to be or cause to be in an erect or upright position. **2.** to rise to, assume, or maintain an upright position. **3.** (*copula*) to have a specified height when standing: *to stand six feet tall.* **4.** to be situated or located: *the house stands in the square.* **5.** to be in a specified state or condition: *to stand in awe of someone.* **6.** to adopt or remain in a resolute position or attitude. **7.** (*may take an infinitive*) to be in a specified position: *I stand to lose money in this venture.* **8.** to remain in force or continue in effect: *my orders stand.* **9.** to come to a stop or halt, esp. temporarily. **10.** (of water, etc.) to collect and remain without flowing. **11.** (often foll. by *at*) (of a score, account, etc.) to indicate the specified position: *the score stands at 20 to 1.* **12.** (*also tr.*; when *intr.*, foll. by *for*) to tolerate or bear: *I won't stand for your nonsense; I can't stand spiders.* **13.** (*tr.*) to resist; survive: *to stand the test of time.* **14.** (*tr.*) to submit to: *to stand trial.* **15.** (often foll. by *for*) *Chiefly Brit.* to be or become a candidate: *stand for Parliament.* **16.** to navigate in a specified direction: *we were standing for Madeira.* **17.** (of a gun dog) to point at game. **18.** to halt, esp. to give action, repel attack, or disrupt an enemy advance when retreating. **19.** (*tr.*) *Inf.* to bear the cost of; pay for: *to stand someone a drink.* **20. stand a chance.** to have a hope or likelihood of winning, succeeding, etc. **21. stand fast.** to maintain one's position firmly. **22. stand one's ground.** to maintain a stance or position in the face of opposition. **23. stand still. a.** to remain motionless. **b.** (foll. by *for*) *U.S.* to tolerate: *I won't stand still for your threats.* ~*n.* **24.** the act or an instance of standing. **25.** an opinion, esp. a resolutely held one: *he took a stand on capital punishment.* **26.** a halt or standstill. **27.** a place where a person or thing stands. **28.** *Austral. & N.Z.* **a.** a position on the floor of a shearing shed allocated to one shearer. **b.** the shearer's equipment. **29.** a structure on which people can sit or stand. **30.** a frame or rack on which such articles as coats and hats may be hung. **31.** a small table or piece of furniture where articles may be placed or stored: *a music stand.* **32.** a supporting framework, esp. for a tool or instrument. **33.** a stall, booth, or counter from which goods may be sold. **34.** a halt to give action, etc., esp. during a retreat and having some duration or success. **35.** *Cricket.* an extended period at the wicket by two batsmen. **36.** a growth of plants in a particular area, esp. trees in a forest or a crop in a field. **37.** a stop made by a touring theatrical company, pop group, etc., to give a performance (esp. in **one-night stand**). **38.** (of a gun dog) the act of pointing at game. ~See also **stand by, stand down,** etc. [OE *standan*] —'**stander** *n.*

standard ('stændəd) *n.* **1.** an accepted or approved example of something against which others are judged or measured. **2.** (*often pl.*) a principle of propriety, honesty, and integrity. **3.** a level of excellence or quality. **4.** any distinctive flag or device, etc., as of a nation, sovereign, or special cause, etc., or the colours of a cavalry regiment. **5.** a flag or emblem formerly used to show the central or rallying point of an army in battle. **6.** the commodity or commodities in which is stated the value of a basic monetary unit: *the gold standard; the silver standard.* **7.** an authorized model of a unit of measure or weight. **8.** a unit of board measure equal to 1980 board feet. **9.** (in coinage) the prescribed proportion by weight of precious metal and base metal that each coin must contain. **10.** an upright pole or beam, esp. one used as a support. **11. a.** a piece of furniture consisting of an upright pole or beam on a base or support. **b.** (*as modifier*): *a standard lamp.* **12. a.** a plant, esp. a fruit tree, that is trained so that it has an upright stem free of branches. **b.** (*as modifier*): *a standard cherry.* **13.** a song or piece of music that has remained popular for many years. **14.** a form or grade in an elementary school. ~*adj.* **15.** of the usual, regularized, medium, or accepted kind: *a standard size.* **16.** of recognized authority, competence, or excellence: *the standard work on Greece.* **17.** denoting or characterized by idiom, vocabulary, etc., that is regarded as correct and acceptable by educated native speakers. **18.** *Brit.* (formerly) (of eggs) of a size that is smaller than *large* and larger than *medium.* [C12: from OF *estandart* gathering place, flag to mark such a place, prob. of Gmc origin]

standard-bearer *n.* **1.** a man who carries a standard. **2.** a leader of a cause or party.

standard cell *n.* a voltaic cell producing a constant and accurately known electromotive force that can be used to calibrate voltage-measuring instruments.

standard cost *n.* the predetermined budgeted cost of a manufacturing process against which actual costs are compared.

standard deviation *n. Statistics.* a measure of dispersion obtained by extracting the square root of the mean of the squared deviations of the observed values from their mean in a frequency distribution.

standard error of the mean *n. Statistics.* the standard deviation of the distribution of means of samples chosen from a larger population; equal to the standard deviation of the whole population divided by the square root of the sample size.

standard gauge *n.* **1.** a railway track with a distance of 4 ft. 8½ in. (1.435 m) between the lines; used on most railways. ~*adj.* **standard-gauge** *or* **standard-gauged.** **2.** of, relating to, or denoting a railway with a standard gauge.

Standard Grade *n.* (in Scotland) a new type of examination designed to test skills and the application of knowledge, which will gradually replace O grade.

standardize *or* **-ise** ('stændə,daɪz) *vb.* **1.** to make or become standard. **2.** (*tr.*) to test by or compare with a standard. — ,standardi'zation *or* -i'sation *n.* — 'standard,izer *or* -,iser *n.*

standard of living *n.* a level of subsistence or material welfare of a community, class, or person.

standard time *n.* the official local time of a region or country determined by the distance from Greenwich of a line of longitude passing through the area.

stand by *vb.* (*intr.*) **1.** (*adv.*) to be available and ready to act if needed. **2.** (*adv.*) to be present as an onlooker or without taking any action: *he stood by at the accident.* **3.** (*prep.*) to be faithful to: *to stand by one's principles.* ~*n.* **stand-by.** **4. a.** a person or thing that is ready for use or can be relied on in an emergency. **b.** (*as modifier*): *stand-by provisions.* **5. on stand-by.** in a state of readiness for action or use. ~*adj.* **stand-by.** **6.** not booked in advance but awaiting or subject to availability: *a stand-by ticket.*

stand down *vb.* (*adv.*) **1.** (*intr.*) to resign or withdraw, esp. in favour of another. **2.** (*intr.*) to leave the witness box in a court of law after giving evidence. **3.** *Chiefly Brit.* to go or be taken off duty.

stand for *vb.* (*intr., prep.*) **1.** to represent or mean. **2.** *Chiefly Brit.* to be or become a candidate for. **3.** to support or recommend. **4.** *Inf.* to tolerate or bear: *he won't stand for it.*

stand in *vb.* **1.** (*intr., adv.; usually foll. by for*) to act as a substitute. **2. stand (someone) in good stead.** to be of benefit or advantage to (someone). ~*n.* **stand-in. 3. a.** a person or thing that serves as a substitute. **b.** (*as modifier*): *a stand-in teacher.* **4.** a person who substitutes for an actor during intervals of waiting or in dangerous stunts.

standing ('stændɪŋ) *n.* **1.** social or financial position, status, or reputation: *a man of some standing.* **2.** length of existence, experience, etc. **3.** (*modifier*) used to stand in or on: *standing room.* ~*adj.* **4.** *Athletics.* **a.** (of the start of a race) begun from a standing position. **b.** (of a jump, leap, etc.) performed from a stationary position without a run-up. **5.** (*prenominal*) permanent, fixed, or lasting. **6.** (*prenominal*) still or stagnant: *a standing pond.* **7.** *Printing.* (of type) set and stored for future use.

standing army *n.* a permanent army of paid soldiers maintained by a nation.

standing order *n.* **1.** Also called: **banker's order.** an instruction to a bank by a depositor to pay a stated sum at regular intervals. **2.** a rule or order governing the procedure, conduct, etc., of an organization. **3.** *Mil.* one of a number of orders which have long-term validity.

standing rigging *n.* the stays, shrouds, and other more or less fixed, though adjustable, ropes that support the masts of a sailing vessel.

standing wave *n. Physics.* a wave that has unchanging amplitude at each point along its axis. Also called: **stationary wave.**

Standish ('stændɪʃ) *n.* **Myles** (or **Miles**). ?1584–1656, English military leader of the Pilgrim Fathers at Plymouth, New England.

standoff ('stænd,ɒf) *n.* **1.** *U.S. & Canad.* the act or an instance of standing off or apart. **2.** a deadlock or stalemate. **3.** *Rugby.* short for **stand-off half.** ~*vb.* **stand off.** (*adv.*). **4.** (*intr.*) to navigate a vessel so as to avoid the shore, an obstruction, etc. **5.** (*tr.*) to keep or cause to keep at a distance. **6.** (*intr.*) to reach a deadlock or stalemate. **7.** (*tr.*) to dismiss (workers), esp. temporarily.

stand-off half *n. Rugby.* **1.** a player who acts as a link between his scrum half and three-quarter backs and who marks the opposing scrum half. **2.** this position. ~Also called: **fly half.**

standoffish (,stænd'ɒfɪʃ) *adj.* reserved, haughty, or aloof. — ,stand'offishness *n.*

stand on *vb.* (*intr.*) **1.** (*adv.*) to continue to navigate a vessel on the same heading. **2.** (*prep.*) to insist on: *to stand on ceremony.*

stand out *vb.* (*intr., adv.*) **1.** to be distinctive or conspicuous. **2.** to refuse to agree or comply: *they stood out for a better price.* **3.** to protrude or project. **4.** to navigate a vessel away from a port, harbour, etc. ~*n.* **standout. 5.** *U.S. & Canad. inf.* a person or thing that is distinctive or outstanding.

stand over *vb.* (*tr. prep.*) **1.** to supervise closely. **2.** *Austral. & N.Z. inf.* to threaten or intimidate.

standpipe ('stænd,paɪp) *n.* **1.** a vertical pipe, open at the upper end, attached to a pipeline or tank serving to limit the pressure head to that of the height of the pipe. **2.** a temporary freshwater outlet installed in a street when household water supplies are cut off.

standpoint ('stænd,pɔɪnt) *n.* a physical or mental position from which things are viewed.

standstill ('stænd,stɪl) *n.* a complete cessation of movement; halt: *come to a standstill.*

stand to *vb.* **1.** (*adv.*) *Mil.* to assume positions or cause to assume positions to resist a possible attack. **2. stand to reason.** to conform with the dictates of reason: *it stands to reason.*

stand up *vb.* (*adv.*) **1.** (*intr.*) to rise to the feet. **2.** (*intr.*) to resist or withstand wear, criticism, etc. **3.** (*tr.*) *Inf.* to fail to keep an appointment with, esp. intentionally. **4. stand up for.** to support, side with, or defend. **5. stand up to. a.** to confront or resist courageously. **b.** to withstand or endure (wear, criticism, etc.). ~*adj.* **stand-up.** (*prenominal*) **6.** having or being in an erect position: *a stand-up collar.* **7.** done, taken, etc., while standing: *a stand-up meal.* **8.** (of a comedian) telling jokes, stories, etc., directly to the audience.

Stanford-Binet test ('stænfədbɪ'neɪ) *n. Psychol.* a revision, esp. for U.S. use, of the Binet-Simon scale designed to measure mental ability by comparing the performance of an individual with the average performance for his age group. See also **Binet-Simon scale, intelligence test.** [C20: after *Stanford University,* California, & Alfred *Binet* (1857–1911), F psychologist]

stanhope ('stænəp) *n.* a light one-seater carriage with two or four wheels. [C18: after Fitzroy *Stanhope* (1787–1864), E clergyman for whom it was first built]

Stanislavsky *or* **Stanislavski** (,stænɪ'slævskɪ; *Russian* stəni'slafskij) *n.* **Konstantin** (kənstan'tin). 1863–1938, Russian actor and director, cofounder of the Moscow Art Theatre (1897). He is famous for his theory of acting, known as the Method, which directs the actor to find the truth within himself about the role he is playing.

stank (stæŋk) *vb.* a past tense of **stink.**

Stanley[1] ('stænlɪ) *n.* **1.** a town in NE England, in N Durham. Pop.: 41 210 (1981). **2. Mount.** a mountain in central Africa, between Uganda and Zaïre: the highest peak of the Ruwenzori range. Height: 5109 m (16 763 ft.). Zaïrese name: **Ngaliema Mountain.**

Stanley[2] ('stænlɪ) *n.* **Sir Henry Morton.** 1841–1904, British explorer and journalist, who led an expedition to Africa in search of Livingstone, whom he found on Nov. 10, 1871. He led three further expeditions in Africa (1874–77; 1879–84; 1887–89) and was instrumental in securing Belgian sovereignty over the Congo Free State.

Stanley Falls *pl. n.* the former name of **Boyoma Falls.**

Stanley Pool *n.* a lake between Zaïre and the Congo, formed by a widening of the River Congo. Area: 829 sq. km (320 sq. miles). Zaïrese name: **Pool Malebo.**

Stanleyville ('stænlɪ,vɪl) *n.* the former name (until 1966) of **Kisangani.**

stann- *combining form.* denoting tin: *stannite.* [from LL *stannum* tin]

Stannaries ('stænərɪz) *n.* (*sometimes functioning as sing.*) **the.** a tin-mining district of Devon and Cornwall, under the jurisdiction of special courts.

stannary ('stænərɪ) *n., pl.* **-ries.** a place or region where tin is mined or worked. [C15: from Med. L *stannāria*, from LL *stannum* tin]

stannic ('stænɪk) *adj.* of or containing tin, esp. in the tetravalent state; designating a tin(IV) compound. [C18: from LL *stannum* tin]

stannite ('stænaɪt) *n.* a grey metallic mineral that consists of a sulphide of tin, copper, and iron and is a source of tin. Formula: Cu_2FeSnS_4. [C19: from LL *stannum* tin + -ITE[1]]

stannous ('stænəs) *adj.* of or containing tin, esp. in the divalent state; designating a tin(II) compound.

Stanovoi Range *or* **Stanovoy Range** (*Russian* stəna'vɔj) *n.* a mountain range in the SE Soviet Union: forms part of the watershed between rivers flowing to the Arctic and the Pacific. Highest peak: Mount Skalisty, 2482 m (8143 ft.).

Stans (*German* ʃtans) *n.* a town in central Switzerland, capital of Nidwalden demicanton, 11 km (7 miles) southeast of Lucerne: tourist centre. Pop.: 5700 (1980).

stanza ('stænzə) *n.* **1.** *Prosody.* a fixed number of verse lines arranged in a definite metrical pattern, forming a unit of a poem. **2.** *U.S. & Austral.* a half or a quarter in a football match. [C16: from It.: halting place, from Vulgar L *stantia* (unattested) station, from L *stāre* to stand] — **'stanzaed** *adj.* — **stanzaic** (stæn'zeɪɪk) *adj.*

stapelia (stə'piːlɪə) *n.* any of various fleshy cactus-like leafless African plants having large fetid flowers. [C18: from NL, after J. B. van *Stapel* (died 1636), Du. botanist]

stapes ('steɪpiːz) *n., pl.* **stapes** *or* **stapedes** (stæ'piːdiːz). the stirrup-shaped bone that is the innermost of three small bones in the middle ear of mammals. Nontechnical name: **stirrup bone.** Cf. **incus, malleus.** [C17: via NL from Med. L, ? var. of *stapeda* stirrup, infl. by L *stāre* to stand + *pes* a foot]

staphylo- *combining form.* **1.** uvula: *staphyloplasty.* **2.** resembling a bunch of grapes: *staphylococcus.* [from Gk *staphulē* bunch of grapes, uvula]

staphylococcus (,stæfɪləʊ'kɒkəs) *n., pl.* **-cocci** (-'kɒksaɪ). any spherical Gram-positive bacterium of the genus *Staphylococcus*, typically occurring in clusters and causing boils, infection in wounds, and septicaemia. Often shortened to **staph.** — ,staphylo'coccal *adj.*

staphyloplasty ('stæfɪləʊ,plæstɪ) *n.* plastic surgery or surgical repair involving the soft palate or the uvula. — ,staphylo'plastic *adj.*

staple[1] ('steɪpᵊl) *n.* **1.** a short length of thin wire bent into a square U-shape, used to fasten papers, cloth, etc. **2.** a short length of stiff wire formed into a U-shape with pointed ends, used for holding a hasp to a post, securing electric cables, etc. ~*vb.* **3.** (*tr.*) to secure (papers, wire, etc.) with staples. [OE *stapol* prop, of Gmc origin] — **'stapler** *n.*

staple[2] ('steɪpᵊl) *adj.* **1.** of prime importance; principal: *staple foods.* **2.** (of a commodity) forming a predominant element in the product, consumption, or trade of a nation, region, etc. ~*n.* **3.** a staple commodity. **4.** a main constituent; integral part. **5.** *Chiefly U.S. & Canad.* a principal raw material produced or grown in a region. **6.** the fibre of wool, cotton, etc., graded as to length and degree of fineness. ~*vb.* **7.** (*tr.*) to arrange or sort (wool, cotton, etc.) according to length and fineness. [C15: from MDu. *stapel* warehouse]

staple gun *n.* a mechanism that fixes staples to a surface.

star (stɑː) *n.* **1.** any of a vast number of celestial objects visible in the clear night sky as points of light. **2. a.** a hot gaseous mass, such as the sun, that radiates energy, esp. as heat and light, and in some cases as radio waves and x-rays. **b.** (*as modifier*): *a star catalogue.* Related adjs.: **astral, sidereal, stellar. 3.** *Astrol.* a celestial body, esp. a planet, supposed to influence events, personalities, etc. **b.** (*pl.*) another name for **horoscope** (sense 1). **4.** an emblem shaped like a conventionalized star, often used as a symbol of rank, an award, etc. **5.** a small white blaze on the forehead of an animal, esp. a horse. **6. a.** a distinguished or glamorous celebrity, often from the entertainment world. **b.** (*as modifier*): *star quality.* **7.** another

word for **asterisk. 8. see stars.** to see or seem to see bright moving pinpoints of light, as from a blow on the head, increased blood pressure, etc. ~*vb.* **starring, starred. 9.** (*tr.*) to mark or decorate with a star or stars. **10.** to feature or be featured as a star: *"Greed" starred Erich von Stroheim; Olivier starred in "Hamlet".* [OE *steorra*] — **'starless** *adj.* — **star,like** *adj.*

Stara Zagora (*Bulgarian* 'stara za'gɔra) *n.* a city in central Bulgaria: ceded to Bulgaria by Turkey in 1877. Pop.: 150 906 (1985).

starboard ('stɑːbəd, -,bɔːd) *n.* **1.** the right side of an aeroplane or vessel when facing the nose or bow. Cf. **port**[2]. ~*adj.* **2.** relating to or on the starboard. ~*vb.* **3.** to turn or be turned towards the starboard. [OE *stēorbord*, lit.: steering side, from *stēor* steering paddle + *bord* side; from the fact that boats were formerly steered by a paddle held over the right-hand side]

starch (stɑːtʃ) *n.* **1.** a polysaccharide composed of glucose units that occurs widely in plant tissues in the form of storage granules. **2.** a starch obtained from potatoes and some grain: it is fine white powder that, in solution with water, is used to stiffen fabric. **3.** any food containing a large amount of starch, such as rice and potatoes. **4.** stiff or pompous formality. ~*vb.* **5.** (*tr.*) to stiffen with or soak in starch. [OE *stercan* (unattested except by the p.p. *sterced*) to stiffen] — **'starcher** *n.*

Star Chamber *n.* **1.** *English history.* the Privy Council sitting as a court of equity; abolished 1641. **2.** (*sometimes not caps.*) any arbitrary tribunal dispensing summary justice. **3.** (*sometimes not caps.*) (in Britain, in a Conservative government) a group of senior ministers who make the final decision on the public spending of each government department.

starch-reduced *adj.* (of food, esp. bread) having the starch content reduced, as in proprietary slimming products.

starchy ('stɑːtʃɪ) *adj.* **starchier, starchiest. 1.** of or containing starch. **2.** extremely formal, stiff, or conventional: *a starchy manner.* **3.** stiffened with starch. — **'starchily** *adv.* — **'starchiness** *n.*

star connection *n.* a connection used in a polyphase electrical device or system of devices in which the windings each have one end connected to a common junction, the **star point,** and the other end to a separate terminal.

star-crossed *adj.* dogged by ill luck; destined to misfortune.

stardom ('stɑːdəm) *n.* **1.** the fame and prestige of being a star in films, sport, etc. **2.** the world of celebrities.

stardust ('stɑː,dʌst) *n.* **1.** a large number of distant stars appearing to the observer as a cloud of dust. **2.** a dreamy romantic or sentimental quality or feeling.

stare (stɛə) *vb.* **1.** (*intr.*) (often foll. by *at*) to look or gaze fixedly, often with hostility or rudeness. **2.** (*intr.*) to stand out as obvious; glare. **3. stare one in the face.** to be glaringly obvious or imminent. ~*n.* **4.** the act or an instance of staring. [OE *starian*] — **'starer** *n.*

starfish ('stɑː,fɪʃ) *n., pl.* **-fish** *or* **-fishes.** any of various echinoderms, typically having a flattened body covered with a flexible test and five arms radiating from a central disc.

star fruit *n.* another name for **carambola.**

stargaze ('stɑː,geɪz) *vb.* (*intr.*) **1.** to observe the stars. **2.** to daydream. — **'star,gazer** *n.* — **'star,gazing** *n., adj.*

stark (stɑːk) *adj.* **1.** (*usually prenominal*) devoid of any elaboration; blunt: *the stark facts.* **2.** grim; desolate: *a stark landscape.* **3.** (*usually prenominal*) utter; absolute: *stark folly.* **4.** *Arch.* severe; violent. **5.** *Arch. or poetic.* rigid, as in death (esp. in **stiff and stark, stark dead). 6.** short for **stark-naked.** ~*adv.* **7.** completely: *stark mad.* **8.** *Rare.* starkly. [OE *stearc* stiff] — **'starkly** *adv.* — **'starkness** *n.*

Stark (stɑːk; *German* ʃtark) *n.* **Johannes** (joˈhanəs). 1874–1957, German physicist, who discovered the splitting of the lines of a spectrum when the source of light is subjected to a strong electrostatic field (**Stark effect,** 1913): Nobel prize for physics 1919.

stark-naked *adj.* completely naked. Informal word (*postpositive*): **starkers.** [C13 *stert naket*, lit.: tail naked; *stert*, from OE *steort* tail]

starlet ('stɑːlɪt) *n.* **1.** a young actress who is projected as a potential star. **2.** a small star.

starlight ('stɑː,laɪt) n. **1.** the light emanating from the stars. ~adj. also **starlighted. 2.** of or like starlight. **3.** Also: **starlit** ('stɑː,lɪt). illuminated by starlight.

starling ('stɑːlɪŋ) n. any gregarious passerine songbird of an Old World family, esp. the **common starling**, which has a blackish iridescent plumage and a short tail. [OE *stærlinc*, from *stær* starling + *-line* -LING¹]

star-of-Bethlehem n. **1.** Also: **starflower.** a Eurasian liliaceous plant having narrow leaves and starlike white flowers. **2.** any of several similar and related plants.

Star of David n. an emblem symbolizing Judaism and consisting of a six-pointed star formed by superimposing one inverted equilateral triangle upon another of equal size.

starry ('stɑːrɪ) adj. **-rier, -riest. 1.** filled, covered with, or illuminated by stars. **2.** of, like, or relating to a star or stars. —'**starriness** n.

starry-eyed adj. given to naive wishes, judgments, etc.; full of unsophisticated optimism.

Stars and Stripes n. (*functioning as sing.*) **the.** the national flag of the United States of America, consisting of 50 white stars representing the present states on a blue field and seven red and six white horizontal stripes representing the original states. Also called: the **Star-Spangled Banner.**

star sapphire n. a sapphire showing a starlike figure in reflected light because of its crystalline structure.

Star-Spangled Banner n. **the. 1.** the national anthem of the United States of America. **2.** another term for the **Stars and Stripes.**

star stream n. one of two main streams of stars that, because of the rotation of the Milky Way, appear to move in opposite directions.

star-studded adj. featuring a large proportion of well-known performers: *a star-studded cast.*

start (stɑːt) vb. **1.** to begin or cause to begin (something or to do something); come or cause to come into being, operation, etc.: *he started a quarrel; they started to work.* **2.** (when *intr.*, sometimes foll. by *on*) to make or cause to make a beginning (of a process, series of actions, etc.): *they started on the project.* **3.** (sometimes foll. by *up*) to set or be set in motion: *he started up the machine.* **4.** (*intr.*) to make a sudden involuntary movement, as from fright; jump. **5.** (*intr.*; sometimes foll. by *up, away,* etc.) to spring or jump suddenly from a position or place. **6.** to establish or be established; set up: *to start a business.* **7.** (*tr.*) to support (someone) in the first part of a venture, career, etc. **8.** to work or cause to work loose. **9.** to enter or be entered in a race. **10.** (*intr.*) to flow violently from a source: *wine started from a hole in the cask.* **11.** (*tr.*) to rouse (game) from a hiding place, lair, etc. **12.** (*intr.*) (esp. of eyes) to bulge; pop. **13.** (*intr.*) Brit. inf. to commence quarrelling or causing a disturbance. **14. to start with.** in the first place. ~n. **15.** the first or first part of a series of actions, a journey, etc. **16.** the place or time of starting, as of a race or performance. **17.** a signal to proceed, as in a race. **18.** a lead or advantage, either in time or distance, in a competitive activity: *he had an hour's start on me.* **19.** a slight involuntary movement, as through fright, surprise, etc.: *she gave a start as I entered.* **20.** an opportunity to enter a career, undertake a project, etc. **21.** Inf. a surprising incident. **22. for a start.** in the first place. ~See also **start in, start off,** etc. [OE *styrtan*]

starter ('stɑːtə) n. **1.** Also called: **self-starter.** a device for starting an internal-combustion engine, usually consisting of a powerful electric motor that engages with the flywheel. **2.** a person who supervises and signals the start of a race. **3.** a competitor who starts in a race or contest. **4.** Austral. inf. an acceptable or practicable proposition, plan, idea, etc. **5.** Chiefly Brit. the first course of a meal. **6. for starters.** Sl. in the first place. **7. under starter's orders. a.** (of horses in a race) awaiting the start signal. **b.** (of a person) eager or ready to begin.

start in vb. (adv.) to undertake (something or doing something); commence or begin.

starting block n. one of a pair of adjustable devices with pads or blocks against which a sprinter braces his feet in crouch starts.

starting gate n. **1.** a movable barrier so placed on the starting line of a racecourse that the raising of it releases all the contestants simultaneously. **2.** the U.S. name for **starting stalls.**

starting grid n. Motor racing. a marked section of the track at the start where the cars line up according to their times in practice, the fastest occupying the front position.

starting price n. (esp. in horse racing) the latest odds offered by bookmakers at the start of a race.

starting stalls pl. n. Brit. a line of stalls in which horses are enclosed at the start of a race and from which they are released by the simultaneous springing open of retaining barriers at the front of each stall.

startle ('stɑːt³l) vb. to be or cause to be surprised or frightened, esp. so as to start involuntarily. [OE *steartlian* to stumble] —'**startler** n. —'**startling** adj.

start off vb. (adv.) **1.** (*intr.*) to set out on a journey. **2.** to be or make the first step in (an activity); initiate: *he started the show off with a lively song.* **3.** (*tr.*) to cause (a person) to act or do something, such as to laugh, to tell stories, etc.

start on vb. (*intr., prep.*) Brit. inf. to pick a quarrel with; upbraid.

start out vb. (*intr., adv.*) **1.** to set out on a journey. **2.** to take the first steps, as in life, one's career, etc.: *he started out as a salesman.* **3.** to take the first actions in an activity in a particular way or with a specified aim: *they started out wanting a house, but eventually bought a flat.*

start up vb. (adv.) **1.** to come or cause to come into being for the first time; originate. **2.** (*intr.*) to spring or jump suddenly. **3.** to set in or go into motion, activity, etc.: *he started up the engine.* ~n. **start-up. 4.** the setting up of a new business.

starve (stɑːv) vb. **1.** to die or cause to die from lack of food. **2.** to deprive (a person or animal) or (of a person, etc.) to be deprived of food. **3.** (*intr.*) Inf. to be very hungry. **4.** (foll. by *of* or *for*) to deprive or be deprived (of something), esp. so as to cause suffering or malfunctioning: *the engine was starved of fuel.* **5.** (*tr.*; foll. by *into*) to bring (to) a specified condition by starving: *to starve someone into submission.* **6.** Arch. or dialect. to be or cause to be extremely cold. [OE *steorfan* to die] —**star'vation** n.

starveling ('stɑːvlɪŋ) Arch. ~n. **1. a.** a starving or poorly fed person, animal, etc. **b.** (*as modifier*): *a starveling child.* ~adj. **2.** insufficient; meagre; scant.

Star Wars n. (*functioning as sing.*) (in the U.S.) a proposed system of artificial satellites armed with lasers to destroy enemy missiles in space. [C20: popularly named after the science-fiction film *Star Wars* (1977)]

starwort ('stɑː,wɜːt) n. **1.** any of several plants with star-shaped flowers, esp. the stitchwort. **2.** any of several aquatic plants having a star-shaped rosette of floating leaves.

stash (stæʃ) vb. **1.** (*tr.*; often foll. by *away*) Inf. to put or store (money, valuables, etc.) in a secret place, as for safekeeping. ~n. **2.** Inf., chiefly U.S. & Canad. a secret store or the place where this is hidden. **3.** Sl. drugs kept for personal consumption. [C20: from ?]

stasis ('steɪsɪs) n. **1.** Pathol. a stagnation in the normal flow of bodily fluids, such as the blood or urine. **2.** a state or condition in which there is no action or progress. [C18: via NL from Gk: a standing, from *histanai* to cause to stand]

-stat n. combining form. indicating a device that causes something to remain stationary or constant: *thermostat.* [from Gk *-statēs*, from *histanai* to cause to stand]

state (steɪt) n. **1.** the condition of a person, thing, etc., with regard to main attributes. **2.** the structure or form of something: *a solid state.* **3.** any mode of existence. **4.** position in life or society; estate. **5.** ceremonious style, as befitting wealth and dignity: *to live in state.* **6.** a sovereign political power or community. **7.** the territory occupied by such a community. **8.** the sphere of power in such a community: *affairs of state.* **9.** (*often cap.*) one of a number of areas or communities having their own governments and forming a federation under a sovereign government, as in the U.S. **10.** (*often cap.*) the body politic of a particular sovereign power, esp. as contrasted with a rival authority such as the Church. **11.** Obs. a class or order; estate. **12.** Inf. a nervous, upset, or excited condition (esp. in **in a state**). **13. lie in state.** (of a body) to be placed on public view before burial. **14. state of affairs.** a situation; circumstances or condition. ~modifier. **15.** controlled or financed by a state: *state university.* **16.** of, relating to, or concerning the State: *State trial.* **17.** involving ceremony or concerned with a ceremonious occasion: *state visit.* *~vb.* (*tr.; may take a clause as object*) **18.** to articulate in words; utter. **19.** to declare formally or publicly. [C13: from OF *estat*, from L *status* a standing, from *stāre* to stand] —'**statable** *or* 'stateable *adj.* —'statehood *n.*

state bank *n.* (in the U.S.) a commercial bank incorporated under a State charter and not required to be a member of the Federal Reserve System.

statecraft ('steɪt,krɑːft) *n.* the art of conducting public affairs; statesmanship.

State Enrolled Nurse *n.* a nurse who has trained and is qualified to perform many nursing services.

state house *n. N.Z.* a house built by the government and rented to a **state tenant.** Brit. equivalent: **council house.**

Statehouse ('steɪt,haʊs) *n.* (in the U.S.) the building which houses a state legislature.

stateless ('steɪtlɪs) *adj.* **1.** without nationality: *stateless persons.* **2.** without a state or states. —'**statelessness** *n.*

stately ('steɪtlɪ) *adj.* **-lier, -liest. 1.** characterized by a graceful, dignified, and imposing appearance or manner. *~adv.* **2.** in a stately manner. —'**stateliness** *n.*

stately home *n. Brit.* a large mansion, esp. one open to the public.

statement ('steɪtmənt) *n.* **1.** the act of stating. **2.** something that is stated, esp. a formal prepared announcement or reply. **3.** *Law.* a declaration of matters of fact. **4.** an account containing a summary of bills or invoices and displaying the total amount due. **5.** an account prepared by a bank for a client, usually at regular intervals, to show all credits and debits and the balance at the end of the period. **6.** a computer instruction written in a source language, such as FORTRAN, which is converted into one or more machine-code instructions by a compiler. **7.** *Logic.* the content of a sentence that affirms or denies something and may be true or false.

statement of claim *n. Law.* (in England) the first pleading made by the plaintiff in a High Court action.

Staten Island ('stæt²n) *n.* an island in SE New York State, in New York Harbor: forms the Richmond borough of New York city; heavy industry. Pop.: 352 121 (1980). Area: 155 sq. km (60 sq. miles).

state of the art *n.* **1.** the level of knowledge and development achieved in a technique, science, etc., esp. at present. *~adj.* **state-of-the-art.** (*prenominal*) **2.** the most recent and therefore considered the best; up-to-the-minute: *a state-of-the-art amplifier.*

State Registered Nurse *n.* a nurse who has had extensive training and is qualified to perform all nursing services.

stateroom ('steɪt,ruːm, -,rʊm) *n.* **1.** a private cabin or room on a ship, train, etc. **2.** *Chiefly Brit.* a large room in a palace or other building for use on state occasions.

States (steɪts) *n.* (*functioning as sing. or pl.*) **the.** an informal name for the **United States of America.**

state school *n.* any school maintained by the state, in which education is free.

stateside ('steɪt,saɪd) *adj., adv. U.S.* of, in, to, or towards the U.S.

statesman ('steɪtsmən) *n., pl.* **-men. 1.** a political leader whose wisdom, integrity, etc., win great respect. **2.** a person active and influential in the formulation of high government policy. —'**statesman-,like** *or* 'statesmanly *adj.* —'statesmanship *n.* —'states,woman *fem. n.*

state socialism *n.* a variant of socialism in which the power of the state is employed for the purpose of creating an egalitarian society by means of public control of major industries, banks, etc. —**state socialist** *n.*

state trooper *n. U.S.* a state policeman.

static ('stætɪk) *adj. also* **statical. 1.** not active or moving; stationary. **2.** (of a weight, force, or pressure) acting but causing no movement. **3.** of or concerned with forces that do not produce movement. **4.** relating to or causing stationary electric charges; electrostatic. **5.** of or relating to interference in the reception of radio or television transmissions. **6.** of or concerned with statics. **7.** *Computers.* (of a memory) not needing its contents refreshed periodically. *~n.* **8.** random hissing or crackling or a speckled picture caused by interference in the reception of radio or television transmissions. **9.** electric sparks or crackling produced by friction. [C16: from NL *staticus,*

from Gk *statikos* causing to stand, from *histanai* to stand] —'statically *adv.*

statice ('stætɪsɪ) *n.* another name for **sea lavender.**

static electricity *n.* electricity that is not dynamic or flowing as a current.

statics ('stætɪks) *n.* (*functioning as sing.*) the branch of mechanics concerned with the forces that produce a state of equilibrium in a system.

station ('steɪʃən) *n.* **1.** the place or position at which a thing or person stands. **2. a.** a place along a route or line at which a bus, train, etc., stops for fuel or to pick up or let off passengers or goods, esp. one with ancillary buildings and services. **b.** (*as modifier*): *a station buffet.* **3. a.** the headquarters or local offices of an organization such as the police or fire services. **b.** (*as modifier*): *a station sergeant.* See **police station, fire station. 4.** a building, depot, etc., with special equipment for some particular purpose: *power station; petrol station.* **5.** *Mil.* a place of duty: *an action station.* **6.** *Navy.* **a.** a location to which a ship or fleet is assigned for duty. **b.** an assigned location for a member of a ship's crew. **7.** a television or radio channel. **8.** a position or standing, as in a particular society or organization. **9.** the type of one's occupation; calling. **10.** (in British India) a place where the British district officials or garrison officers resided. **11.** *Biol.* the habitat occupied by a particular animal or plant. **12.** *Austral. & N.Z.* a large sheep or cattle farm. **13.** (*sometimes cap.*) *R.C. Church.* **a.** one of the stations of the Cross. **b.** any of the churches (**station churches**) in Rome used as points of assembly for religious processions and ceremonies on particular days (**station days**). *~vb.* **14.** (*tr.*) to place in or assign to a station. [C14: via OF from L *statiō* a standing still, from *stāre* to stand]

stationary ('steɪʃənərɪ) *adj.* **1.** not moving; standing still. **2.** not able to be moved. **3.** showing no change: *the doctors said his condition was stationary.* **4.** tending to remain in one place. [C15: from L *statiōnārius*, from *statiō* STATION]

stationary orbit *n. Astronautics.* a synchronous orbit lying in or approximately in the plane of the equator.

stationary wave *n.* another name for **standing wave.**

stationer ('steɪʃənə) *n.* a person who sells stationery or a shop where stationery is sold. [C14: from Med. L *stationarius* a person having a regular station, hence a shopkeeper (esp. a bookseller) as distinguished from an itinerant tradesman; see STATION]

stationery ('steɪʃənərɪ) *n.* any writing materials, such as paper, envelopes, pens, ink, rulers, etc.

station house *n. Chiefly U.S.* a house that is situated by or serves as a station, esp. as a police or fire station.

stationmaster ('steɪʃən,mɑːstə) *n.* the senior official in charge of a railway station.

stations of the Cross *pl. n. R.C. Church.* **1.** a series of 14 crosses, often accompanied by 14 pictures or carvings, arranged around the walls of a church, to commemorate 14 stages in Christ's journey to Calvary. **2.** a devotion of 14 prayers relating to each of these stages.

station wagon *n.* another name (less common in Britain) for **estate car.**

statism ('steɪtɪzəm) *n.* the theory or practice of concentrating economic and political power in the state. —'statist *n.*

statistic (stə'tɪstɪk) *n.* a datum capable of exact numerical representation, such as the correlation coefficient of two series or the standard deviation of a sample. —sta'tistical *adj.* —sta'tistically *adv.* —statistician (,stætɪ'stɪʃən) *n.*

statistical mechanics *n.* (*functioning as sing.*) the study of the properties of physical systems as predicted by the statistical behaviour of their constituent particles.

statistics (stə'tɪstɪks) *n.* **1.** (*functioning as sing.*) a science concerned with the collection, classification, and interpretation of quantitative data and with the application of probability theory to the analysis and estimation of population parameters. **2.** the quantitative data themselves. [C18 (orig. "science dealing with facts of a state"): via G *Statistik*, from NL *statisticus* concerning state affairs, from L *status* STATE]

Statius ('steɪʃɪəs) *n.* **Publius Papinius** ('pʌblɪəs pə'pɪnɪəs). ?45—96 A.D., Roman poet; author of the collection *Silvae* and of two epics, *Thebais* and the unfinished *Achilleis.*

stator ('steɪtə) *n.* the stationary part of a rotary machine or device, esp. of a motor or generator. [C20: from L: one who stands (by), from *stāre* to stand]

statoscope ('stætə,skəʊp) *n.* a very sensitive form of aneroid barometer used to detect and measure small variations in atmospheric pressure, such as one used in an aircraft to indicate small changes in altitude.

statuary ('stætjʊərɪ) *n.* **1.** statues collectively. **2.** the art of making statues. ~*adj.* **3.** of or for statues. [C16: from L *statuārius*]

statue ('stætjuː) *n.* a wooden, stone, metal, plaster, or other sculpture of a human or animal figure, usually lifesize or larger. [C14: via OF from L *statua*, from *statuere* to set up; cf. STATUTE]

statuesque (,stætjʊ'ɛsk) *adj.* like a statue, esp. in possessing great formal beauty or dignity. —,**statu'esquely** *adv.* —,**statu'esqueness** *n.*

statuette (,stætjʊ'ɛt) *n.* a small statue.

stature ('stætʃə) *n.* **1.** height, esp. of a person or animal when standing. **2.** the degree of development of a person: *the stature of a champion.* **3.** intellectual or moral greatness: *a man of stature.* [C13: via OF from L *statūra*, from *stāre* to stand]

status ('steɪtəs) *n., pl.* -**tuses.** **1.** a social or professional position, condition, or standing. **2.** the relative position or standing of a person or thing. **3.** a high position or standing: *he has acquired a new status in that job.* **4.** the legal standing or condition of a person. **5.** a state of affairs. [C17: from L: *posture*, from *stāre* to stand]

status quo (kwəʊ) *n.* (usually preceded by *the*) the existing state of affairs. [lit.: the state in which]

status symbol *n.* a possession which is regarded as proof of the owner's social position, wealth, prestige, etc.

statute ('stætjuːt) *n.* **1. a.** an enactment of a legislative body expressed in a formal document. **b.** this document. **2.** a permanent rule made by a body or institution. [C13: from OF *estatut*, from LL *statūtum*, from L *statuere* to set up, decree, ult. from *stāre* to stand]

statute book *n. Chiefly Brit.* a register of enactments passed by the legislative body of a state: *not on the statute book.*

statute law *n.* **1.** a law enacted by a legislative body. **2.** a particular example of this. ~Cf. **common law, equity.**

statute mile *n.* a legal or formal name for **mile** (sense 1).

statute of limitations *n.* a legislative enactment prescribing the period of time within which proceedings must be instituted to enforce a right or bring an action at law.

statutory ('stætjʊtərɪ, -trɪ) *adj.* **1.** of, relating to, or having the nature of a statute. **2.** prescribed or authorized by statute. **3.** (of an offence) **a.** recognized by statute. **b.** subject to a punishment or penalty prescribed by statute. —'**statutorily** *adv.*

staunch[1] (stɔːntʃ) *adj.* **1.** loyal, firm, and dependable: *a staunch supporter.* **2.** solid or substantial in construction. **3.** *Rare.* (of a ship, etc.) watertight; seaworthy. [C15 (orig.: watertight): from OF *estanche*, from *estanchier* to STANCH] —'**staunchly** *adv.* —'**staunchness** *n.*

staunch[2] (stɔːntʃ) *vb., n.* a variant spelling of **stanch.**

Stavanger (*Norwegian* sta'vaŋər) *n.* a port in SW Norway: canning and shipbuilding industries. Pop.: 95 437 (1987).

stave (steɪv) *n.* **1.** any one of a number of long strips of wood joined together to form a barrel, bucket, boat hull, etc. **2.** any of various bars, slats, or rods, usually of wood, such as a rung of a ladder. **3.** any stick, staff, etc. **4.** a stanza or verse of a poem. **5.** *Music.* **a.** *Brit.* an individual group of five lines and four spaces used in staff notation. **b.** another word for **staff**[1] (sense 9). ~*vb.* **staving, staved** *or* **stove.** **6.** (often foll. by *in*) to break or crush (the staves of a boat, barrel, etc.) *or* (of the staves of a boat) to be broken or crushed. **7.** (*tr.;* usually foll. by *in*) to burst or force (a hole in something). **8.** (*tr.*) to provide (a ladder, chair, etc.) with staves. [C14: back formation from *staves,* pl. of STAFF[1]]

stave off *vb.* (*tr., adv.*) to avert or hold off, esp. temporarily: *to stave off hunger.*

staves (steɪvz) *n.* a plural of **staff**[1] *or* **stave.**

stavesacre ('steɪvz,eɪkə) *n.* **1.** a Eurasian ranunculaceous plant having poisonous seeds. **2.** the seeds, which have strong emetic and cathartic properties. [C14 *staphisagre,* from L *staphis agria,* from Gk, from *staphis* raisin + *agria* wild]

Stavropol (*Russian* 'stavrəpəlj) *n.* **1.** a city in the SW Soviet Union: founded as a fortress in 1777. Pop.: 271 000 (1981 est.). Former name (1940–44): **Voroshilovsk. 2.** the former name (until 1964) of **Togliatti.**

stay[1] (steɪ) *vb.* **1.** (*intr.*) to continue or remain in a certain place, position, etc.: *to stay outside.* **2.** (*copula*) to continue to be; remain: *to stay awake.* **3.** (*intr.;* often foll. by *at*) to reside temporarily: *to stay at a hotel.* **4.** (*tr.*) to remain for a specified period: *to stay the weekend.* **5.** (*intr.*) *Scot. & S. African.* to reside permanently or habitually; live. **6.** *Arch.* to stop or cause to stop. **7.** (*intr.*) to wait, pause, or tarry. **8.** (*tr.*) to delay or hinder. **9.** (*tr.*) **a.** to discontinue or suspend (a judicial proceeding). **b.** to hold in abeyance or restrain from enforcing (an order, decree, etc.). **10.** to endure (something testing or difficult, such as a race): *stay the course.* **11.** (*tr.*) to hold back or restrain: *to stay one's anger.* **12.** (*tr.*) to satisfy or appease (an appetite, etc.) temporarily. ~*n.* **13.** the act of staying or sojourning in a place or the period during which one stays. **14.** the act of stopping or restraining or state of being stopped, etc. **15.** the suspension of a judicial proceeding, etc.: *stay of execution.* [C15 *staien,* from Anglo-F *estaier* to stay, from OF *ester* to stay, from L *stāre* to stand] —'**stayer** *n.*

stay[2] (steɪ) *n.* **1.** anything that supports or steadies, such as a prop or buttress. **2.** a thin strip of metal, plastic, bone, etc., used to stiffen corsets, etc. See also **stays** (sense 1). ~*vb.* (*tr.*) *Arch.* **3.** (often foll. by *up*) to prop or hold. **4.** (often foll. by *up*) to comfort or sustain. **5.** (foll. by *on* or *upon*) to cause to rely or depend. [C16: from OF *estaye,* of Gmc origin]

stay[3] (steɪ) *n.* a rope, cable, or chain, usually one of a set, used for bracing uprights, such as masts, funnels, flagpoles, chimneys, etc.; guy. ~See also **stays** (senses 2, 3). [OE *stæg*]

stay-at-home *adj.* **1.** (of a person) enjoying a quiet, settled, and unadventurous use of leisure. ~*n.* **2.** a stay-at-home person.

staying power *n.* endurance; stamina.

stays (steɪz) *pl. n.* **1.** old-fashioned corsets with bones in them. **2.** a position of a sailing vessel relative to the wind so that the sails are luffing or aback. **3. miss** *or* **refuse stays.** (of a sailing vessel) to fail to come about.

staysail ('steɪ,seɪl; *Naut.* 'steɪs'l) *n.* an auxiliary sail, often triangular, set on a stay.

STD *abbrev. for:* **1.** Doctor of Sacred Theology. **2.** sexually transmitted disease. **3.** subscriber trunk dialling.

STD code *n. Brit.* a code of two or more digits, other than those comprising a subscriber's local telephone number, that determines the routing of a call. [C20: s(*ubscriber*) *t*(*runk*) *d*(*ialling*)]

Ste *abbrev. for* Saint (female). [F *Sainte*]

stead (stɛd) *n.* **1.** (preceded by *in*) *Rare.* the place, function, or position that should be taken by another: *to come in someone's stead.* **2. stand** (**someone**) **in good stead.** to be useful or of good service to (someone). ~*vb.* **3.** (*tr.*) *Arch.* to help or benefit. [OE *stede*]

Stead (stɛd) *n.* **Christina** (**Ellen**). 1902–83, Australian novelist. Her works include *Seven Poor Men of Sydney* (1934), *The Man who Loved Children* (1940), and *Cotters' England* (1966).

steadfast *or* **stedfast** ('stɛdfəst, -,fɑːst) *adj.* **1.** (esp. of a person's gaze) fixed in intensity or direction; steady. **2.** unwavering or determined in purpose, loyalty, etc.: *steadfast resolve.* —'**steadfastly** *or* '**stedfastly** *adv.* —'**steadfastness** *or* '**stedfastness** *n.*

steading ('stɛdɪŋ) *n.* another name for **farmstead.**

steady ('stɛdɪ) *adj.* **steadier, steadiest. 1.** not able to be moved or disturbed easily; stable. **2.** free from fluctuation. **3.** not easily excited; imperturbable. **4.** staid; sober. **5.** regular; habitual: *a steady drinker.* **6.** continuous: *a steady flow.* **7.** *Naut.* (of a vessel) keeping upright, as in heavy seas. ~*vb.* **steadying, steadied. 8.** to make or become steady. ~*adv.* **9.** in a steady manner. **10. go steady.** *Inf.* to date one person regularly. ~*n., pl.* **steadies. 11.** *Inf.* one's regular boyfriend or girlfriend. ~*interj.* **12.** *Naut.* an order to the helmsman to stay on a steady course. **13.** a warning to keep calm, be careful, etc. **14.** *Brit.* a command to get set to start, as in a race: *ready, steady, go!* [C16: from STEAD + -Y[1]] —'**steadily** *adv.* —'**steadiness** *n.* —'**steadying** *adj.*

steady state *n. Physics.* the condition of a system when some or all of the quantities describing it are independent of time but not necessarily in thermodynamic or chemical equilibrium.

steady-state theory *n.* a theory postulating that the universe exists throughout time in a steady state such that the average density of matter does not vary with distance or time. Matter is continuously created in the space left by the receding stars and galaxies of the expanding universe. Cf. **big-bang theory.**

steak (steɪk) *n.* **1.** See **beefsteak. 2.** any of various cuts of beef, for braising, stewing, etc. **3.** a thick slice of pork, veal, cod, salmon, etc. **4.** minced meat prepared in the same way as steak: *hamburger steak.* [C15: from ON *steik* roast]

steakhouse ('steɪk,haʊs) *n.* a restaurant that has steaks as its speciality.

steak tartare (tɑː'tɑː) *or* **tartar** *n.* raw minced steak, mixed with onion, seasonings, and raw egg. Also called: **tartare steak, tartar steak.**

steal (stiːl) *vb.* **stealing, stole, stolen. 1.** to take (something) from someone, etc. without permission or unlawfully, esp. in a secret manner. **2.** (*tr.*) to obtain surreptitiously. **3.** (*tr.*) to appropriate (ideas, etc.) without acknowledgment, as in plagiarism. **4.** to move or convey stealthily: *they stole along the corridor.* **5.** (*intr.*) to pass unnoticed: *the hours stole by.* **6.** (*tr.*) to win or gain by strategy or luck, as in various sports: *to steal a few yards.* ~*n. Inf.* **7.** the act of stealing. **8.** *U.S. & Canad.* something stolen or acquired easily or at little cost. [OE *stelan*] —'**stealer** *n.*

stealth (stelθ) *n.* **1.** the act or characteristic of moving with extreme care and quietness, esp. so as to avoid detection. **2.** cunning or underhand procedure or dealing. [C13 *stelthe;* see STEAL, -TH[1]] —'**stealthy** *adj.*

steam (stiːm) *n.* **1.** the gas or vapour into which water is changed when boiled. **2.** the mist formed when such gas or vapour condenses in the atmosphere. **3.** any vaporous exhalation. **4.** *Inf.* power, energy, or speed. **5. get up steam. a.** (of a ship, etc.) to work up a sufficient head of steam in a boiler to drive an engine. **b.** *Inf.* to go quickly. **6. let off steam.** *Inf.* to release pent-up energy, feelings, etc. **7. under one's own steam.** without the assistance of others. **8.** (*modifier*) driven, operated, heated, powered, etc., by steam: *a steam radiator.* **9.** (*modifier*) treated by steam: *steam-ironed.* **10.** (*modifier*) *Humorous.* old-fashioned; outmoded: *steam radio.* ~*vb.* **11.** to emit or be emitted as steam. **12.** (*intr.*) to generate steam, as a boiler, etc. **13.** (*intr.*) to move or travel by steam power, as a ship, etc. **14.** (*intr.*) *Inf.* to proceed quickly and sometimes forcefully. **15.** to cook or be cooked in steam. **16.** (*tr.*) to treat with steam or apply steam to, as in cleaning, pressing clothes, etc. ~See also **steam up.** [OE]

steam bath *n.* **1.** a room or enclosure that can be filled with steam in which people bathe to induce sweating and refresh or cleanse themselves. **2.** an act of taking such a bath.

steamboat ('stiːm,bəʊt) *n.* a boat powered by a steam engine.

steam boiler *n.* a vessel in which water is boiled to generate steam.

steam engine *n.* an engine that uses steam to produce mechanical work, esp. one in which steam from a boiler is expanded in a cylinder to drive a reciprocating piston.

steamer ('stiːmə) *n.* **1.** a boat or ship driven by steam engines. **2.** a vessel used to cook food by steam. **3.** *Austral. sl.* a rough clash between sports teams.

steam iron *n.* an electric iron that emits steam from channels in the iron face to facilitate pressing and ironing, the steam being produced from water contained within the iron.

steam jacket *n. Engineering.* a jacket containing steam that surrounds and heats a cylinder.

steam organ *n.* a type of organ powered by steam, once common at fairgrounds, played either by a keyboard or by a moving punched card. U.S. name: **calliope.**

steam point *n.* the temperature at which the maximum vapour pressure of water is equal to one atmosphere $(1.01325 \times 10^5 \text{ N/m}^2)$. It has the value of 100° on the Celsius scale.

steamroller ('stiːm,rəʊlə) *n.* **1. a.** a steam-powered vehicle with heavy rollers used for compressing road surfaces during road-making. **b.** another word for **roadroller. 2.**

a. an overpowering force or person that overcomes all opposition. **b.** (*as modifier*): *steamroller tactics.* ~*vb.* **3.** (*tr.*) to crush (opposition, etc.) by overpowering force.

steamship ('stiːm,ʃɪp) *n.* a ship powered by one or more steam engines.

steam shovel *n.* a steam-driven mechanical excavator.

steam turbine *n.* a turbine driven by steam.

steam up *vb.* (*adv.*) **1.** to cover (windows, etc.) or (of windows, etc.) to become covered with a film of condensed steam. **2.** (*tr.; usually passive*) *Sl.* to excite or make angry: *he's all steamed up about the delay.*

steamy ('stiːmɪ) *adj.* **steamier, steamiest. 1.** of, resembling, full of, or covered with steam. **2.** *Inf.* lustful or erotic: *steamy nightlife.* —'**steaminess** *n.*

steapsin (stɪ'æpsɪn) *n. Biochem.* a pancreatic lipase. [C19: from Gk *stear* fat + PEPSIN]

stearic (stɪ'ærɪk) *adj.* **1.** of or relating to suet or fat. **2.** of, consisting of, containing, or derived from stearic acid.

stearic acid *n.* a colourless odourless insoluble waxy carboxylic acid used for making candles and suppositories. Formula: $CH_3(CH_2)_{16}COOH$. Systematic name: **octadecanoic acid.**

stearin *or* **stearine** ('stɪərɪn) *n.* **1.** Also called: **tristearin.** a colourless crystalline ester of glycerol and stearic acid, present in fats and used in soap and candles. **2.** another name for **stearic acid. 3.** fat in its solid form. [C19: from F *stéarine,* from Gk *stear* fat + -IN]

steatite ('stɪə,taɪt) *n.* another name for **soapstone.** [C18: from L *steatitēs,* from Gk *stear* fat + -ITE[1]] —**steatitic** (,stɪə'tɪtɪk) *adj.*

steato- *combining form.* denoting fat. [from Gk *stear, steat-*fat, tallow]

steatolysis (,stɪə'tɒlɪsɪs) *n. Physiol.* **1.** the digestive process whereby fats are emulsified and then hydrolysed to fatty acids and glycerin. **2.** the breaking down of fat.

steatopygia (,stɪətəʊ'pɪdʒɪə, -'paɪ-) *or* **steatopyga** (,stɪətəʊ'paɪɡə) *n.* excessive fatness of the buttocks. [C19: from NL, from STEATO- + Gk *pugē* the buttocks] —**steato'pygic** *or* **steatopygous** (,stɪə'tɒpɪɡəs) *adj.*

Stębark ('stɛmbark) *n.* the Polish name for **Tannenberg.**

stedfast ('stɛdfəst, -,fɑːst) *adj.* a less common spelling of **steadfast.**

steed (stiːd) *n. Arch. or literary.* a horse, esp. one that is spirited or swift. [OE *stēda* stallion]

steel (stiːl) *n.* **1. a.** any of various alloys based on iron containing carbon and often small quantities of other elements such as sulphur, manganese, chromium, and nickel. Steels exhibit a variety of properties, such as strength, malleability, etc., depending on their composition and the way they have been treated. See also **stainless steel. b.** (*as modifier*): *steel girders.* See also **stainless steel. 2.** something that is made of steel. **3.** a steel stiffener in a corset, etc. **4.** a ridged steel rod used for sharpening knives. **5.** the quality of hardness, esp. with regard to a person's character or attitudes. **6.** *Canad.* a railway track or line. **7. cold steel.** bladed weapons. ~*vb.* (*tr.*) **8.** to fit, plate, edge, or point with steel. **9.** to make hard and unfeeling: *he steeled his heart against her sorrow; he steeled himself for the blow.* [OE *stēli*] —'**steely** *adj.* —'**steeliness** *n.*

Steel (stiːl) *n.* **David (Martin Scott).** born 1938, British politician; leader of the Liberal Party (1976–88).

steel band *n. Music.* a type of band, popular in the Caribbean Islands, consisting mainly of percussion instruments made from oil drums, hammered or embossed to obtain different notes.

steel blue *n.* **a.** a dark bluish-grey colour. **b.** (*as adj.*): *steel-blue eyes.*

Steele (stiːl) *n.* **Sir Richard.** 1672–1729, British essayist and dramatist, born in Ireland; with Joseph Addison he was the chief contributor to the periodicals *The Tatler* (1709–11) and *The Spectator* (1711–12).

steel engraving *n.* **a.** a method or art of engraving (letters, etc.) on a steel plate. **b.** a print made from such a plate.

steel grey *n.* **a.** a dark grey colour, usually slightly purple. **b.** (*as adj.*): *a steel-grey suit.*

steelhead ('stiːl,hɛd) *n., pl.* **-heads** *or* **-head.** a silvery North Pacific variety of the rainbow trout.

steel wool *n.* a tangled or woven mass of fine steel fibres, used for cleaning or polishing.

steelworks ('stiːl,wɜːks) *n.* (*functioning as sing. or pl.*) a plant in which steel is made from iron ore and rolled or forged into bars, sheets, etc. —'**steel,worker** *n.*

steelyard ('sti:l,jɑ:d) *n.* a portable balance consisting of a pivoted bar with two unequal arms. The load is suspended from the shorter one and the bar is returned to the horizontal by sliding a weight along the longer, graduated arm.

Steen (stein) *n.* **Jan** (jɑn). 1626–79, Dutch genre painter.

steenbok ('sti:n,bɒk) *n.*, *pl.* **-boks** *or* **-bok.** a small antelope of central and southern Africa, having a reddish-brown coat and straight horns. [C18: from Afrik., from Du. *steen* stone + *bok* BUCK[1]]

steep[1] (sti:p) *adj.* **1. a.** having or being a slope or gradient approaching the perpendicular. **b.** (*as n.*): *the steep.* **2.** *Inf.* (of a fee, price, demand, etc.) unduly high; unreasonable (esp. in **that's a bit steep**). **3.** *Inf.* excessively demanding or ambitious: *a steep task.* **4.** *Brit. inf.* (of a statement) extreme or far-fetched. [OE *steap*] —'**steeply** *adv.* —'**steepness** *n.*

steep[2] (sti:p) *vb.* **1.** to soak or be soaked in a liquid in order to soften, cleanse, extract an element, etc. **2.** (*tr.; usually passive*) to saturate; imbue: *steeped in ideology.* ~*n.* **3.** an instance or the process of steeping or the condition of being steeped. **4.** a liquid or solution used for the purpose of steeping something. [OE *stēpan*] —'**steeper** *n.*

steepen ('sti:pᵊn) *vb.* to become or cause to become steep or steeper.

steeple ('sti:pᵊl) *n.* **1.** a tall ornamental tower that forms the superstructure of a church, temple, etc. **2.** such a tower with the spire above it. **3.** any spire or pointed structure. [OE *stēpel*] —'**steepled** *adj.*

steeplechase ('sti:pᵊl,tʃeɪs) *n.* **1.** a horse race over a course equipped with obstacles to be jumped. **2.** a track race in which the runners have to leap hurdles, a water jump, etc. **3.** *Arch.* **a.** a horse race across a stretch of open countryside including obstacles to be jumped. **b.** a rare word for **point-to-point.** ~*vb.* **4.** (*intr.*) to take part in a steeplechase. —'**steeple,chaser** *n.* — '**steeple,chasing** *n.*

steeplejack ('sti:pᵊl,dʒæk) *n.* a person trained and skilled in the construction and repair of steeples, chimneys, etc.

steer[1] (stɪə) *vb.* **1.** to direct the course of (a vehicle or vessel) with a steering wheel, rudder, etc. **2.** (*tr.*) to guide with tuition: *his teachers steered him through his exams.* **3.** (*tr.*) to direct the movements or course of (a person, conversation, etc.). **4.** to pursue (a specified course). **5.** (*intr.*) (of a vessel, vehicle, etc.) to admit of being guided in a specified fashion: *this boat does not steer properly.* **6. steer clear of.** to keep away from; shun. ~*n.* **7.** *Chiefly U.S.* guidance; information (esp. in **a bum steer**). [OE *stieran*] —'**steerable** *adj.* —'**steerer** *n.*

steer[2] (stɪə) *n.* a castrated male ox or bull; bullock. [OE *stēor*]

steerage ('stɪərɪdʒ) *n.* **1.** the cheapest accommodation on a passenger ship, originally the compartments containing steering apparatus. **2.** an instance or the practice of steering and its effect on a vessel or vehicle.

steerageway ('stɪərɪdʒ,weɪ) *n.* *Naut.* enough forward movement to allow a vessel to be steered.

steering committee *n.* a committee set up to prepare and arrange topics to be discussed, the order of business, etc., for a legislative assembly or other body.

steering wheel *n.* a wheel turned by the driver of a motor vehicle, ship, etc., when he wishes to change direction.

steersman ('stɪəzmən) *n.*, *pl.* **-men.** the helmsman of a vessel.

Stefansson ('stɛfənsən) *n.* **Vilhjalmur** ('vɪl,hjaʊmɛr) 1879–1962, Canadian explorer, noted for his books on the Inuit.

Steffens ('stɛfənz) *n.* (**Joseph**) **Lincoln.** 1866–1936, U.S. political analyst, known for his exposure of political corruption.

stegosaur ('stɛgə,sɔ:) *or* **stegosaurus** (,stɛgə'sɔ:rəs) *n.* any of various quadrupedal herbivorous dinosaurs of Jurassic and early Cretaceous times, having an armour of bony plates. [C19: from Gk *stegos* roof + -SAUR]

Steier (*German* 'ʃtaɪər) *n.* a variant spelling of **Steyr.**

Steiermark ('ʃtaɪər,mark) *n.* the German name for **Styria.**

stein (staɪn) *n.* an earthenware beer mug, esp. of a German design. [from G *Stein*, lit.: stone]

Stein *n.* **1.** (staɪn). **Gertrude.** 1874–1946, U.S. writer, resident in Paris (1903–1946). Her works include *Three Lives* (1908) and *The Autobiography of Alice B. Toklas* (1933). **2.** (*German* ʃtaɪn). **Heinrich Friedrich Carl** ('haɪnrɪç 'fri:drɪç karl), Baron Stein. 1757–1831, Prussian statesman, who contributed greatly to the modernization of Prussia and played a major role in the European coalition against Napoleon (1813–15).

Steinbeck ('staɪnbɛk) *n.* **John** (**Ernst**). 1902–68, U.S. writer, noted for his novels about agricultural workers, esp. *The Grapes of Wrath* (1939): Nobel prize for literature 1962.

steinbok ('staɪn,bɒk) *n.*, *pl.* **-boks** *or* **-bok.** a variant of **steenbok.**

Steiner ('staɪnə; *German* 'ʃtaɪnər) *n.* **Rudolf** ('ru:dɔlf). 1861–1925, Austrian philosopher, founder of anthroposophy. He was particularly influential in education. See also **anthroposophy.**

Steinitz ('staɪnɪts; *German* 'ʃtaɪnɪts) *n.* **Wilhelm** ('vɪlhɛlm). 1836–1900, U.S. chess player, born in Prague; world champion (1866–94).

stele ('sti:lɪ, sti:l) *n.*, *pl.* **stelae** ('sti:li:) *or* **steles. 1.** an upright stone slab or column decorated with figures or inscriptions, common in prehistoric times. **2.** a prepared vertical surface that has a commemorative inscription or design, esp. one on the face of a building. **3.** the conducting tissue of the stems and roots of plants, which is in the form of a cylinder. ~Also called (for senses 1, 2): **stela.** [C19: from Gk *stēlē*] —'**stelar** *adj.*

stellar ('stɛlə) *adj.* **1.** of, relating to, or resembling a star or stars. **2.** of or relating to star entertainers. [C17: from LL *stellāris*, from L *stella* star]

stellate ('stɛlɪt, -eɪt) *or* **stellated** *adj.* resembling a star in shape; radiating from the centre: *a stellate arrangement of petals.* [C16: from L *stellātus* starry, from *stellāre* to stud with stars, from *stella* a star] —'**stellately** *adv.*

stellular ('stɛljʊlə) *adj.* **1.** displaying or abounding in small stars: *a stellular pattern.* **2.** resembling a little star or little stars. [C18: from LL *stellula*, dim. of L *stella* star] —'**stellularly** *adv.*

stem[1] (stɛm) *n.* **1.** the main axis of a plant, which bears the leaves, axillary buds, and flowers and contains a hollow cylinder of vascular tissue. **2.** any similar subsidiary structure in such plants that bears a flower, fruit, or leaf. **3.** a corresponding structure in algae and fungi. **4.** any long slender part, such as the hollow part of a tobacco pipe between the bit and the bowl. **5.** the main line of descent or branch of a family. **6.** any shank or cylindrical pin or rod, such as the pin that carries the winding knob on a watch. **7.** *Linguistics.* the form of a word that remains after removal of all inflectional affixes. **8.** the main, usually vertical, stroke of a letter or of a musical note such as a minim. **9. a.** the main upright timber or structure at the bow of a vessel. **b.** the very forward end of a vessel (esp. in **from stem to stern**). ~*vb.* **stemming, stemmed. 10.** (*intr.; usually foll. by from*) to be derived; originate. **11.** (*tr.*) to make headway against (a tide, wind, etc.). **12.** (*tr.*) to remove or disengage the stem or stems from. [OE *stemn*] —'**stem,like** *adj.*

stem[2] (stɛm) *vb.* **stemming, stemmed. 1.** (*tr.*) to restrain or stop (the flow of something) by or as if by damming up. **2.** (*tr.*) to pack tightly or stop up. **3.** *Skiing.* to manoeuvre (a ski or skis), as in performing a stem. ~*n.* **4.** *Skiing.* a technique in which the heel of one ski or both skis is forced outwards from the direction of movement in order to slow down or turn. [C15 *stemmen*, from ON *stemma*]

stem cell *n.* *Histology.* an undifferentiated cell that gives rise to specialized cells, such as blood cells.

stem ginger *n.* choice pieces of the underground stem of the ginger plant which are crystallized or preserved in syrup and eaten as a sweetmeat.

stemma ('stɛmə) *n.* a family tree; pedigree. [C19: via L from Gk *stema* garland, wreath, from *stephein* to crown, wreathe]

stemmed (stɛmd) *adj.* **1. a.** having a stem. **b.** (*in combination*): *a long-stemmed glass.* **2.** having had the stem or stems removed.

stem turn *n.* *Skiing.* a turn in which the heel of one ski is stemmed and the other ski is brought parallel. Also called: **stem.**

stench (stɛntʃ) *n.* a strong and extremely offensive odour; stink. [OE *stenc*]

stencil ('stɛnsᵊl) *n.* **1.** a device for applying a design, characters, etc., to a surface, consisting of a thin sheet of plastic, metal, etc., in which the design or characters have been cut so that ink or paint can be applied through the incisions onto the surface. **2.** a design or characters produced in this way. ~*vb.* **-cilling, -cilled** *or U.S.* **-ciling, -ciled.** (*tr.*) **3.** to mark (a surface) with a stencil. **4.** to produce (characters or a design) with a stencil. [C14 *stanselen* to decorate with bright colours, from OF *estenceler*, from *estencele* a spark, from L *scintilla*]

Stendhal (*French* stε̃dal) *n.* original name *Marie Henri Beyle.* 1783–1842, French writer, who anticipated later novelists in his psychological analysis of character. His two chief novels are *Le Rouge et le noir* (1830) and *La Chartreuse de Parme* (1839).

Sten gun (stεn) *n.* a light 9mm sub-machine-gun formerly used in the British Army. [C20: from *S* & *T* (initials of Shepherd & Turpin, the inventors) + *-en,* as in BREN GUN]

steno- *or before a vowel* **sten-** *combining form.* indicating narrowness or contraction: *stenography; stenosis.* [from Gk *stenos* narrow]

stenograph ('stεnə,grɑːf) *n.* **1.** any of various keyboard machines for writing in shorthand. **2.** any character used in shorthand. ~*vb.* **3.** (*tr.*) to record (minutes, letters, etc.) in shorthand.

stenographer (stə'nɒgrəfə) *n.* the U.S. & Canad. name for **shorthand typist.**

stenography (stə'nɒgrəfı) *n.* **1.** the act or process of writing in shorthand by hand or machine. **2.** matter written in shorthand. —**stenographic** (,stεnə'græfık) *adj.*

stenosis (stı'nəusıs) *n., pl.* **-ses** (-siːz). *Pathol.* an abnormal narrowing of a bodily canal or passage. [C19: via NL from Gk *stenōsis,* ult. from *stenos* narrow] —**stenotic** (stı'nɒtık) *adj.*

Stenotype ('stεnə,taıp) *n.* **1.** *Trademark.* a machine with a keyboard for recording speeches, etc., in a phonetic shorthand. **2.** any machine resembling this. **3.** the phonetic symbol typed in one stroke of such a machine.

stenotypy ('stεnə,taıpı) *n.* a form of shorthand in which alphabetic combinations are used to represent groups of sounds or short common words. —'**steno,typist** *n.*

Stentor ('stεntɔː) *n.* **1.** *Greek myth.* a Greek herald with a powerful voice who died after he lost a shouting contest with Hermes, herald of the gods. **2.** (*not cap.*) any person with an unusually loud voice.

stentorian (stεn'tɔːrıən) *adj.* (of the voice, etc.) uncommonly loud: *stentorian tones.* [C17: after STENTOR]

step (stεp) *n.* **1.** the act of raising the foot and setting it down again in coordination with the transference of the weight of the body. **2.** the distance or space covered by such a motion. **3.** the sound made by such a movement. **4.** the impression made by such movement of the foot; footprint. **5.** the manner of walking or moving the feet; gait: *a proud step.* **6.** a sequence of foot movements that make up a particular dance or part of a dance: *the steps of the waltz.* **7.** any of several paces or rhythmic movements in marching, dancing, etc.: *the goose step.* **8.** (*pl.*) a course followed by a person in walking or as walking: *they followed in their leader's steps.* **9.** one of a sequence of separate consecutive stages in the progression towards some goal. **10.** a rank or grade in a series or scale. **11.** an object or device that offers support for the foot when ascending or descending. **12.** (*pl.*) a flight of stairs, esp. out of doors. **13.** (*pl.*) another name for **stepladder. 14.** a very short easily walked distance: *it is only a step.* **15.** *Music.* a melodic interval of a second. **16.** an offset or change in the level of a surface similar to the step of a stair. **17.** a strong block or frame bolted onto the keel of a vessel and fitted to receive the base of a mast. **18.** a ledge cut in mining or quarrying excavations. **19. break step.** to cease to march in step. **20. in step. a.** marching, dancing, etc., in conformity with a specified pace or moving in unison with others. **b.** *Inf.* in agreement or harmony. **21. keep step.** to remain walking, marching, dancing, etc., in unison or in a specified rhythm. **22. out of step. a.** not moving in conformity with a specified pace or in accordance with others. **b.** *Inf.* not in agreement; out of harmony. **23. step by step.** with care and deliberation; gradually. **24. take steps.** to undertake measures (to do something). **25. watch one's step. a.** *Inf.* to conduct oneself with caution and good behaviour. **b.** to walk or move carefully. ~*vb.* **stepping, stepped. 26.** (*intr.*) to move by raising the foot and then setting it down in a different position, transferring the weight of the body to this foot and repeating the process with the other foot. **27.** (*intr.;* often foll. by *in, out,* etc.) to move or go on foot, esp. for a short distance: *step this way.* **28.** (*intr.*)

Inf., chiefly U.S. to move, often in an attractive graceful manner, as in dancing: *he can really step around.* **29.** (*intr.;* usually foll. by *on* or *upon*) to place or press the foot; tread: *to step on the accelerator.* **30.** (*intr.;* usually foll. by *into*) to enter (into a situation) apparently with ease: *she stepped into a life of luxury.* **31.** (*tr.*) to walk or take (a number of paces, etc.): *to step ten paces.* **32.** (*tr.*) to perform the steps of: *they step the tango well.* **33.** (*tr.*) to set or place (the foot). **34.** (*tr.;* usually foll. by *off* or *out*) to measure (some distance of ground) by stepping. **35.** (*tr.*) to arrange in or supply with a series of steps so as to avoid coincidence or symmetry. **36.** (*tr.*) to raise (a mast) and fit it into its step. ~See also **step down, step in,** etc. [OE *stepe, stæpe*] —'**step,like** *adj.*

step- *combining form.* indicating relationship through the previous marriage of a spouse or parent: *stepson; stepfather.* [OE *stēop-*]

stepbrother ('stεp,brʌðə) *n.* a son of one's stepmother or stepfather by a union with someone other than one's father or mother.

stepchild ('stεp,tʃaıld) *n., pl.* **-children.** a stepson or stepdaughter.

stepdaughter ('stεp,dɔːtə) *n.* a daughter of one's husband or wife by a former union.

step down *vb.* (*adv.*) **1.** (*tr.*) to reduce gradually. **2.** (*intr.*) *Inf.* to resign or abdicate (from a position). **3.** (*intr.*) *Inf.* to assume an inferior or less senior position. ~*adj.* **step-down.** (*prenominal*) **4.** (of a transformer) reducing a high voltage to a lower voltage. Cf. **step-up** (sense 3). ~*n.* **step-down. 5.** *Inf.* a decrease in quantity or size.

stepfather ('stεp,fɑːðə) *n.* a man who has married one's mother after the death or divorce of one's father.

stephanotis (,stεfə'nəutıs) *n.* any of various climbing shrubs of Madagascar and Malaya, cultivated for their fragrant white waxy flowers. [C19: via NL from Gk: fit for a crown, from *stephanos* a crown]

Stephen ('stiːvən) *n.* **1.** ?1097–1154, king of England (1135–54); grandson of William the Conqueror. He seized the throne on the death of Henry I, causing civil war with Henry's daughter Matilda. He eventually recognized her son (later Henry II) as his successor. **2. Saint.** died ?35 A.D., the first Christian martyr. Feast day: Dec. 26. **3. Saint,** Hungarian name *Istvân.* ?975–1038 A.D., first king of Hungary as Stephen I (997–1038). Feast day: Aug. 16. **4.** called *Saint Stephen I.* died 257 A.D.; pope (254–57). Feast day: Aug. 2. **5.** Sir **Leslie.** 1832–1904, English biographer, critic, and first editor of the *Dictionary of National Biography;* father of the novelist Virginia Woolf.

Stephenson ('stiːvənsən) *n.* **1. George.** 1781–1848, English inventor of the first successful steam locomotive (1814); constructed the first railway line to carry passengers, the Stockton and Darlington Railway (opened 1825). **2.** his son, **Robert.** 1803–59, English engineer, noted for his construction of railway bridges and viaducts, esp. the tubular bridge over the Menai Straits.

step in *vb.* **1.** (*intr., adv.*) *Inf.* to intervene or involve oneself. ~*adj.* **step-in. 2.** (*prenominal*) (of garments, etc.) put on by being stepped into; without fastenings. **3.** (of a ski binding) engaging automatically when the boot is positioned on the ski. ~*n.* **step-in. 4.** (*often pl.*) a step-in garment, esp. underwear.

stepladder ('stεp,lædə) *n.* a folding portable ladder that is made of broad flat steps fixed to a supporting frame hinged at the top to another supporting frame.

stepmother ('stεp,mʌðə) *n.* a woman who has married one's father after the death or divorce of one's mother.

step on *vb.* (*intr., prep.*) **1.** to place or press the foot on. **2.** *Inf.* to behave harshly or contemptuously towards. **3. step on it.** *Inf.* to go more quickly; hurry up.

step out *vb.* (*intr., adv.*) **1.** to go outside or leave a room, etc., esp. briefly. **2.** to begin to walk more quickly and take longer strides. **3.** *U.S. & Canad. inf.* to withdraw from involvement.

step-parent ('stεp,pεərənt) *n.* a stepfather or stepmother. —'**step-,parenting** *n.*

steppe (stεp) *n.* (*often pl.*) an extensive grassy plain usually without trees. [C17: from ORussian *step* lowland]

stepper ('stεpə) *n.* a person who or animal that steps, esp. a horse or a dancer.

Steppes (stεps) *pl. n.* **the. 1.** the huge grasslands of Eurasia, chiefly in the Soviet Union. **2.** another name for **Kirghiz Steppe.**

stepping stone n. **1.** one of a series of stones acting as footrests for crossing streams, marshes, etc. **2.** a circumstance that assists progress towards some goal.

stepsister ('stɛp,sɪstə) n. a daughter of one's stepmother or stepfather by a union with someone other than one's father or mother.

stepson ('stɛp,sʌn) n. a son of one's husband or wife by a former union.

step up vb. (adv.) Inf. **1.** (tr.) to increase or raise by stages; accelerate. **2.** (intr.) to make progress or effect an advancement; be promoted. ~adj. **step-up.** (prenominal) **3.** (of a transformer) increasing a low voltage to a higher voltage. Cf. **step-down** (sense 4). ~n. **step-up. 4.** Inf. an increment in quantity, size, etc.

-ster suffix forming nouns. **1.** indicating a person who is engaged in a certain activity: prankster; songster. **2.** indicating a person associated with or being something specified: mobster; youngster. [OE -estre]

steradian (stə'reɪdɪən) n. an SI unit of solid angle; the angle that, having its vertex in the centre of a sphere, cuts off an area of the surface of the sphere equal to the square of the length of the radius. Symbol: sr [C19: from STEREO- + RADIAN]

stercoraceous (,stɜːkə'reɪʃəs) adj. of, relating to, or consisting of dung or excrement. [C18: from L stercus dung + -ACEOUS]

stere (stɪə) n. a unit used to measure volumes of stacked timber equal to one cubic metre (35.315 cubic feet). [C18: from F stère, from Gk stereos solid]

stereo ('stɛrɪəʊ, 'stɪər-) adj. **1.** short for **stereophonic** or **stereoscopic.** ~n., pl. **stereos. 2.** stereophonic sound: to broadcast in stereo. **3.** a stereophonic record player, tape recorder, etc. **4.** Photog. **a.** stereoscopic photography. **b.** a stereoscopic photograph. **5.** Printing. short for **stereotype.** [C20: shortened form]

stereo- or sometimes before a vowel **stere-** combining form. indicating three-dimensional quality or solidity: stereoscope. [from Gk stereos solid]

stereochemistry (,stɛrɪəʊ'kɛmɪstrɪ, ,stɪər-) n. the study of the spatial arrangement of atoms in molecules and its effect on chemical properties.

stereograph ('stɛrɪə,grɑːf, 'stɪər-) n. two almost identical pictures, or one special picture, that when viewed through special glasses or a stereoscope form a single three-dimensional image. Also called: **stereogram.**

stereoisomer (,stɛrɪəʊ'aɪsəmə, ,stɪər-) n. Chem. an isomer that exhibits stereoisomerism.

stereoisomerism (,stɛrɪəʊaɪ'somə,rɪzəm, ,stɪər-) n. Chem. isomerism caused by differences in the spatial arrangement of atoms in molecules.

stereophonic (,stɛrɪə'fɒnɪk, ,stɪər-) adj. (of a system for recording, reproducing, or broadcasting sound) using two or more separate microphones to feed two or more loudspeakers through separate channels in order to give a spatial effect to the sound. Often shortened to **stereo.** —,stereo'phonically adv. —**stereophony** (,stɛrɪ'ɒfənɪ, ,stɪər-) n.

stereoscope ('stɛrɪə,skəʊp, 'stɪər-) n. an optical instrument for viewing two-dimensional pictures, giving an illusion of depth and relief. It has a binocular eyepiece through which two slightly different pictures of an object are viewed, one with each eye. —**stereoscopic** (,stɛrɪə'skɒpɪk, ,stɪər-) adj.

stereoscopy (,stɛrɪ'ɒskəpɪ, ,stɪər-) n. **1.** the viewing or appearance of objects in or as if in three dimensions. **2.** the study and use of the stereoscope. —,stereo'scopic adj.

stereospecific (,stɛrɪəʊspɪ'sɪfɪk, ,stɪər-) adj. Chem. relating to or having fixed position in space, as in the spatial arrangements of atoms in certain polymers.

stereotype ('stɛrɪə,taɪp, 'stɪər-) n. **1. a.** a method of producing cast-metal printing plates from a mould made from a forme of type. **b.** the plate so made. **2.** another word for **stereotypy. 3.** an idea, convention, etc., that has grown stale through fixed usage. **4.** a standardized image or conception of a type of person, etc. ~vb. (tr.) **5. a.** to make a stereotype of. **b.** to print from a stereotype. **6.** to impart a fixed usage or convention to. —'stereo,typer or 'stereo,typist n.

stereotyped ('stɛrɪə,taɪpt, 'stɪər-) adj. **1.** lacking originality or individuality; conventional; trite. **2.** reproduced from or on a stereotype printing plate.

stereotypy ('stɛrɪə,taɪpɪ, 'stɪər-) n. **1.** the act or process of making stereotype printing plates. **2.** a tendency to think or act in rigid, repetitive, and often meaningless patterns.

stereovision ('stɛrɪəʊ,vɪʒən, 'stɪər-) n. the perception or exhibition of three-dimensional objects in three dimensions.

steric ('stɛrɪk, 'stɪər-) or **sterical** adj. Chem. of or caused by the spatial arrangement of atoms in a molecule. [C19: from STEREO- + -IC]

sterile ('stɛraɪl) adj. **1.** unable to produce offspring; permanently infertile. **2.** free from living, esp. pathogenic, microorganisms. **3.** (of plants or their parts) not producing or bearing seeds, fruit, spores, stamens, or pistils. **4.** lacking inspiration or vitality; fruitless. [C16: from L sterilis] —'sterilely adv. —**sterility** (stɛ'rɪlɪtɪ) n.

sterilize or **-ise** ('stɛrɪ,laɪz) vb. (tr.) to render sterile; make infertile or barren. —,sterili'zation or **-i'sation** n. —'steri,lizer or **-iser** n.

sterling ('stɜːlɪŋ) n. **1. a.** British money: pound sterling. **b.** (as modifier): sterling reserves. **2.** the official standard of purity of British coins. **3. a.** short for **sterling silver. b.** (as modifier): a sterling bracelet. **4.** an article or articles manufactured from sterling silver. ~adj. **5.** (prenominal) genuine and reliable: first-class: sterling quality. [C13: prob. from OE steorra star + -LING[1]; referring to a small star on early Norman pennies]

sterling area n. a group of countries that use sterling as a medium of international payments. Also called: **scheduled territories.**

sterling silver n. **1.** an alloy containing not less than 92.5 per cent of silver. **2.** sterling-silver articles collectively.

Sterlitamak (Russian stjerlitə'mak) n. an industrial city in the W central Soviet Union, in the Bashkir ASSR. Pop.: 228 000 (1981 est.).

stern[1] (stɜːn) adj. **1.** showing uncompromising or inflexible resolve; firm or authoritarian. **2.** lacking leniency or clemency. **3.** relentless; unyielding: the stern demands of parenthood. **4.** having an austere or forbidding appearance or nature. [OE styrne] —'sternly adv. —'sternness n.

stern[2] (stɜːn) n. **1.** the rear or after part of a vessel, opposite the bow or stem. **2.** the rear part of any object. ~adj. **3.** relating to or located at the stern. [C13: from ON stjörn steering]

Stern (stɜːn) n. **Isaac.** born 1920, U.S. concert violinist, born in Russia.

Sternberg ('stɜːn,bɜːg, 'ʃtɜːn-) n. See (Joseph) **von Sternberg.**

Sterne (stɜːn) n. **Laurence.** 1713–68, English novelist, born in Ireland, author of The Life and Opinions of Tristram Shandy, Gentleman (1759–67) and A Sentimental Journey through France and Italy (1768).

sternforemost ('stɜːn'fɔːməʊst) adv. Naut. backwards.

sternmost ('stɜːn,məʊst) adj. Naut. **1.** farthest to the stern; aftmost. **2.** nearest the stern.

sternpost ('stɜːn,pəʊst) n. Naut. the main upright timber or structure at the stern of a vessel.

stern sheets pl. n. Naut. the part of an open boat near the stern.

sternum ('stɜːnəm) n., pl. **-na** (-nə) or **-nums. 1.** (in man) a long flat vertical bone in front of the thorax, to which are attached the collarbone and the first seven pairs of ribs. Nontechnical name: **breastbone. 2.** the corresponding part in many other vertebrates. [C17: via NL from Gk sternon breastbone] —'sternal adj.

sternutation (,stɜːnjʊ'teɪʃən) n. a sneeze or the act of sneezing. [C16: from LL sternūtāre to sneeze, from sternuere to sputter (of a light)]

sternutator ('stɜːnjʊ,teɪtə) n. a substance that causes sneezing, coughing, and tears; used in chemical warfare. —sternutatory (stɜː'njuːtətərɪ, -trɪ) adj., n.

sternwards ('stɜːnwədz) or **sternward** adv. Naut. towards the stern; astern.

sternway ('stɜːn,weɪ) n. Naut. movement of a vessel sternforemost.

stern-wheeler n. a vessel, esp. a river boat, propelled by a large paddle wheel at the stern.

steroid ('stɪərɔɪd) n. Biochem. any of a large group of organic compounds containing a characteristic chemical ring system, including sterols, bile acids, many hormones, and the D vitamins. [C20: from STEROL + -OID] —ste'roidal adj.

sterol ('stɛrɒl) *n. Biochem.* any of a group of natural steroid alcohols, such as cholesterol and ergosterol, that are waxy insoluble substances. [C20: shortened from CHOLESTEROL, ERGOSTEROL, etc.]

stertorous ('stɜːtərəs) *adj.* **1.** marked by heavy snoring. **2.** breathing in this way. [C19: from L *stertere* to snore] —'**stertorously** *adv.* —'**stertorousness** *n.*

stet (stɛt) *n.* **1.** a word or mark indicating that certain deleted typeset or written matter is to be retained. ~*vb.* **stetting, stetted. 2.** (*tr.*) to mark (matter) thus. [L, lit.: let it stand]

stethoscope ('stɛθə,skəʊp) *n. Med.* an instrument for listening to the sounds made within the body, typically consisting of a hollow disc that transmits the sound through hollow tubes to earpieces. [C19: from F, from Gk *stēthos* breast + -SCOPE] —**stethoscopic** (,stɛθə'skɒpɪk) *adj.* —**stethoscopy** (stɛ'θɒskəpɪ) *n.*

stetson ('stɛtsªn) *n.* a man's felt slouch hat with a broad brim and high crown. [C20: after John *Stetson* (1830–1906), American hat-maker]

Stettin (ʃtɛ'tiːn) *n.* the German name for **Szczecin.**

stevedore ('stiːvɪ,dɔː) *n.* **1.** a person employed to load or unload ships. ~*vb.* **2.** to load or unload (a ship, ship's cargo, etc.). [C18: from Sp. *estibador* a packer, from *estibar* to load (a ship), from L *stipāre* to pack full]

Stevenage ('stiːvənɪdʒ) *n.* a town in SE England, in N Hertfordshire on the Great North Road: developed chiefly as the first of the new towns (1946). Pop.: 74 381 (1981).

Stevens ('stiːvªnz) *n.* **1. Thaddeus** ('θædɪəs). 1792–1868, U.S. Radical Republican politician. An opponent of slavery, he supported Reconstruction and entered the resolution calling for the impeachment of President Andrew Johnson. **2. Wallace.** 1879–1955, U.S. poet, whose books include the collections *Harmonium* (1923), *The Man with the Blue Guitar* (1937), and *Transport to Summer* (1947).

Stevenson ('stiːvªnsən) *n.* **1. Adlai Ewing** ('ædleɪ 'juːɪŋ). 1900–68, U.S. statesman: twice defeated as Democratic presidential candidate (1952; 1956); U.S. delegate at the United Nations (1961–65). **2. Robert Louis (Balfour).** 1850–94, Scottish writer: his novels include *Treasure Island* (1883), *Kidnapped* (1886), and *The Master of Ballantrae* (1889).

stew¹ (stjuː) *n.* **1. a.** a dish of meat, fish, or other food, cooked by stewing. **b.** (*as modifier*): *stew pot.* **2.** *Inf.* a difficult or worrying situation or a troubled state (esp. in **in a stew**). **3.** a heterogeneous mixture: *a stew of people of every race.* **4.** (*usually pl.*) *Arch.* a brothel. ~*vb.* **5.** to cook or cause to cook by long slow simmering. **6.** (*intr.*) *Inf.* to be troubled or agitated. **7.** (*intr.*) *Inf.* to be oppressed with heat or crowding. **8.** to cause (tea) to become bitter or (of tea) to become bitter through infusing for too long. **9. stew in one's own juice.** to suffer unaided the consequences of one's actions. [C14 *stuen* to take a very hot bath, from OF *estuver*, from Vulgar L *extūfāre* (unattested), from EX-¹ + (unattested) *tūfus* vapour, from Gk *tuphos*]

stew² (stjuː) *n. Brit.* **1.** a fishpond or fishtank. **2.** an artificial oyster bed. [C14: from OF *estui*, from *estoier* to confine, ult. from L *studium* STUDY]

steward ('stjʊəd) *n.* **1.** a person who administers the property, house, finances, etc., of another. **2.** a person who manages the eating arrangements, staff, or service at a club, hotel, etc. **3.** a waiter on a ship or aircraft. **4.** a mess attendant in a naval mess. **5.** a person who helps to supervise some event or proceedings in an official capacity. **6.** short for **shop steward. 7.** to act or serve as a steward (of something). [OE *stigweard*, from *stig* hall + *weard* WARD] —'**stewardship** *n.*

stewardess ('stjʊədɪs, ,stjʊə'dɛs) *n.* a woman steward on an aircraft or ship.

Stewart ('stjʊət) *n.* **1.** the usual spelling for the royal house of **Stuart** before the reign of Mary Queen of Scots (Mary Stuart). **2. Jackie,** full name *John Young Stewart.* born 1939, Scottish motor-racing driver: world champion 1969, 1971, and 1973. **3. Rod.** born 1945, English rock singer: vocalist with the Faces (1969–75). His albums include *Gasoline Alley* (1970), *Every Picture Tells a Story* (1971), and *Atlantic Crossing* (1975).

Stewart Island *n.* the third largest island of New Zealand, in the SW Pacific off the S tip of South Island. Pop.: 600 (1981). Area: 1735 sq. km (670 sq. miles).

stewed (stjuːd) *adj.* **1.** (of meat, fish, etc.) cooked by stewing. **2.** *Brit.* (of tea) bitter through having been left to infuse for too long. **3.** a slang word for **drunk** (sense 1).

Steyr *or* **Steier** (*German* 'ʃtaɪər) *n.* an industrial city in N central Austria, in Upper Austria. Pop.: 38 967 (1981).

stg *abbrev. for* sterling.

sthenic ('sθɛnɪk) *adj.* abounding in energy or bodily strength; active or strong. [C18: from NL *sthenicus*, from Gk *sthenos* force, on the model of *asthenic*]

Stheno ('sθiːnəʊ, 'sθɛnəʊ) *n. Greek myth.* one of the three Gorgons.

stibine ('stɪbaɪn) *n.* **1.** a colourless poisonous gas with an offensive odour: made by the action of hydrochloric acid on an alloy of antimony and zinc. **2.** any one of a class of stibine derivatives in which one or more hydrogen atoms have been replaced by organic groups. [C19: from L *stibium* antimony + -INE²]

stibnite ('stɪbnaɪt) *n.* a soft greyish mineral consisting of antimony sulphide in crystalline form: the chief ore of antimony. [C19: from obs. *stibine* stibnite + -ITE¹]

-stichous *adj. combining form.* having a certain number of rows. [from LL *-stichus*, from Gk *-stikhos*, from *stikhos* row]

stick¹ (stɪk) *n.* **1.** a small thin branch of a tree. **2. a.** any long thin piece of wood. **b.** such a piece of wood having a characteristic shape for a special purpose: *a walking stick; a hockey stick.* **c.** a baton, wand, staff, or rod. **3.** an object or piece shaped like a stick: *a stick of celery.* **4.** In full: **control stick.** the lever by which a pilot controls the movements of an aircraft. **5.** *Inf.* the lever used to change gear in a motor vehicle. **6.** *Naut.* a mast or yard. **7. a.** a group of bombs arranged to fall at intervals across a target. **b.** a number of paratroops jumping in sequence. **8.** *Sl.* **a.** verbal abuse, criticism: *I got some stick for that blunder.* **b.** physical power, force (esp. in **give it some stick**). **9.** (*usually pl.*) a piece of furniture: *these few sticks are all I have.* **10.** (*pl.*) *Inf.* a rural area considered remote or backward (esp. in **in the sticks**). **11.** (*pl.*) *Hockey.* a declaration made by the umpire if a player's stick is above the shoulders. **12.** (*pl.*) *Austral.* goal posts. **13.** *Inf.* a dull boring person. **14.** (usually preceded by *old*) *Inf.* a familiar name for a person: *not a bad old stick.* **15.** punishment; beating. **16. in a cleft stick.** in a difficult position. **17. wrong end of the stick.** a complete misunderstanding of a situation, explanation, etc. ~*vb.* **sticking, sticked. 18.** to support (a plant) with sticks; stake. [OE *sticca*]

stick² (stɪk) *vb.* **sticking, stuck. 1.** (*tr.*) to pierce or stab with or as if with something pointed. **2.** to thrust or push (a sharp or pointed object) or (of a sharp or pointed object) to be pushed into or through another object. **3.** (*tr.*) to fasten in position by pushing or forcing a point into something: *to stick a peg in a hole.* **4.** (*tr.*) to fasten in position by or as if by pins, nails, etc.: *to stick a picture on the wall.* **5.** (*tr.*) to transfix or impale on a pointed object. **6.** (*tr.*) to cover with objects piercing or set in the surface. **7.** (when *intr.*, foll. by *out, up, through*, etc.) to put forward or be put forward; protrude or cause to protrude: *to stick one's head out.* **8.** (*tr.*) to place or put in a specified position: *stick your coat on this chair.* **9.** to fasten or be fastened by or as if by an adhesive substance: *stick the pages together; they won't stick.* **10.** (*tr.*) *Inf.* to cause to become sticky. **11.** (when *tr.*, usually passive) to come or cause to come to a standstill: *stuck in a traffic jam; the wheels stuck.* **12.** (*intr.*) to remain for a long time: *the memory sticks in my mind.* **13.** (*tr.*) *Sl.*, chiefly *Brit.* to tolerate; abide: *I can't stick that man.* **14.** (*intr.*) to be reluctant. **15.** (*tr.*; usually passive) *Inf.* to cause to be at a loss; baffle or puzzle: *I was totally stuck for an answer.* **16.** (*tr.*) *Sl.* to force or impose something unpleasant on: *they stuck me with the bill.* **17.** (*tr.*) to kill by piercing or stabbing. **18. stick to the ribs.** *Inf.* (of food) to be hearty and satisfying. ~*n.* **19.** the state or condition of adhering. **20.** *Inf.* a substance causing adhesion. **21.** *Obs.* something that causes delay or stoppage. ~See also **stick around, stick by**, etc. [OE *stician*]

stick around *or* **about** *vb.* (*intr.*, *adv.*) *Inf.* to remain in a place, esp. awaiting something.

stick by *vb.* (*intr.*, *prep.*) to remain faithful to; adhere to.

sticker ('stɪkə) *n.* **1.** an adhesive label, poster, or paper. **2.** a person or thing that sticks. **3.** a persevering or industrious person. **4.** something prickly, such as a thorn, that

clings to one's clothing, etc. **5.** *Inf.* something that perplexes. **6.** *Inf.* a knife used for stabbing or piercing.
sticking plaster *n.* a thin cloth with an adhesive substance on one side, used for covering slight or superficial wounds.
stick insect *n.* any of various mostly tropical insects that have an elongated cylindrical body and long legs and resemble twigs.
stick-in-the-mud *n. Inf.* a conservative person who lacks initiative or imagination.
stickle ('stɪkªl) *vb. (intr.)* **1.** to dispute stubbornly, esp. about minor points. **2.** to refuse to agree or concur, esp. by making petty stipulations. [C16 *stightle* (in the sense: to arbitrate): frequentative of OE *stihtan* to arrange]
stickleback ('stɪkªl,bæk) *n.* any of various small fishes that have a series of spines along the back and occur in cold and temperate northern regions. [C15: from OE *stickel* prick, sting + BACK[1]]
stickler ('stɪklə) *n.* **1.** (usually foll. by *for*) a person who makes insistent demands: *a stickler for accuracy.* **2.** a problem or puzzle.
stick out *vb. (adv.)* **1.** to project or cause to project. **2.** *(tr.) Inf.* to endure (something disagreeable) (esp. in **stick it out**). **3. stick out a mile** *or* **like a sore thumb.** *Inf.* to be extremely obvious. **4. stick out for.** to insist on (a demand), refusing to yield until it is met.
stick to *vb. (prep., mainly intr.)* **1.** *(also tr.)* to adhere or cause to adhere to. **2.** to continue constantly at. **3.** to remain faithful to. **4.** not to move or digress from: *the speaker stuck closely to his subject.* **5. stick to someone's fingers.** *Inf.* to be stolen by someone.
stick-up *n.* **1.** *Sl., chiefly U.S.* a robbery at gunpoint; hold-up. *~vb.* **stick up.** *(adv.)* **2.** *(tr.) Sl., chiefly U.S.* to rob, esp. at gunpoint. **3.** *(intr.;* foll. by *for) Inf.* to support or defend: *stick up for oneself.*
sticky ('stɪkɪ) *adj.* **stickier, stickiest.** **1.** covered or daubed with an adhesive or viscous substance: *sticky fingers.* **2.** having the property of sticking to a surface. **3.** (of weather or atmosphere) warm and humid; muggy. **4.** *Inf.* difficult, awkward, or painful: *a sticky business. ~vb.* **stickying, stickied.** **5.** *(tr.) Inf.* to make sticky. —'**stickily** *adv.* —'**stickiness** *n.*
stickybeak ('stɪkɪ,biːk) *Austral. & N.Z. inf. ~n.* **1.** an inquisitive person. *~vb.* **2.** *(intr.)* to pry.
sticky end *n. Inf.* an unpleasant finish or death (esp. in **come to** *or* **meet a sticky end**).
sticky wicket *n.* **1.** a cricket pitch that is rapidly being dried by the sun after rain and is particularly conducive to spin. **2.** *Inf.* a difficult or awkward situation.
stiff (stɪf) *adj.* **1.** not easily bent; rigid; inflexible. **2.** not working or moving easily or smoothly: *a stiff handle.* **3.** difficult to accept in its severity or harshness: *a stiff punishment.* **4.** moving with pain or difficulty; not supple: *a stiff neck.* **5.** difficult; arduous: *a stiff climb.* **6.** unrelaxed or awkward; formal. **7.** firmer than liquid in consistency; thick or viscous. **8.** powerful; strong: *a stiff breeze; a stiff drink.* **9.** excessively high: *a stiff price.* **10.** lacking grace or attractiveness. **11.** stubborn or stubbornly maintained: *a stiff fight.* **12.** *Obs.* tightly stretched; taut. **13.** *Sl.* intoxicated. **14. stiff with.** *Inf.* amply provided with. *~n.* **15.** *Sl.* a corpse. *~adv.* **16.** completely or utterly: *bored stiff; frozen stiff.* [OE *stif*] —'**stiffish** *adj.* —'**stiffly** *adv.* —'**stiffness** *n.*
stiffen ('stɪfªn) *vb.* **1.** to make or become stiff or stiffer. **2.** *(intr.)* to become suddenly tense or unyielding. —'**stiffener** *n.*
stiff-necked *adj.* haughtily stubborn or obstinate.
stifle ('staɪfªl) *vb.* **1.** *(tr.)* to smother or suppress: *stifle a cough.* **2.** to feel or cause to feel discomfort and difficulty in breathing. **3.** to prevent or be prevented from breathing so as to cause death. **4.** *(tr.)* to crush or stamp out. [C14: var. of *stuflen,* prob. from OF *estouffer* to smother]
stigma ('stɪgmə) *n., pl.* **stigmas** *or* **stigmata** ('stɪgmətə, stɪg'mɑːtə). **1.** a distinguishing mark of social disgrace: *the stigma of having been in prison.* **2.** a small scar or mark such as a birthmark. **3.** *Pathol.* any mark on the skin, such as one characteristic of a specific disease. **4.** *Bot.* the terminal part of the ovary, at the end of the style, where deposited pollen enters the gynoecium. **5.** *Zool.* **a.** a pigmented eyespot in some invertebrates. **b.** the spiracle of an insect. **6.** *Arch.* a mark branded on the skin. **7.** *(pl.) Christianity.* marks resembling the wounds of the

crucified Christ, believed to appear on the bodies of certain individuals. [C16: via L from Gk: brand, from *stizein* to tattoo]
stigmatic (stɪg'mætɪk) *adj.* **1.** relating to or having a stigma or stigmata. **2.** another word for **anastigmatic.** *~n. also* **stigmatist** ('stɪgmətɪst). **3.** *Chiefly R.C. Church.* a person marked with the stigmata.
stigmatism ('stɪgmə,tɪzəm) *n.* **1.** *Physics.* the state or condition of being anastigmatic. **2.** *Pathol.* the condition resulting from or characterized by stigmata.
stigmatize *or* **-ise** ('stɪgmə,taɪz) *vb. (tr.)* **1.** to mark out or describe (as something bad). **2.** to mark with a stigma or stigmata. —,**stigmati'zation** *or* **-i'sation** *n.* —'**stigma,tizer** *or* **-iser** *n.*
stilbene ('stɪlbiːn) *n.* a colourless or slightly yellow crystalline unsaturated hydrocarbon used in the manufacture of dyes. [C19: from Gk *stilbos* glittering + -ENE]
stilboestrol *or U.S.* **stilbestrol** (stɪl'biːstrɒl) *n.* a synthetic hormone having derivatives with oestrogenic properties. Also called: **diethylstilboestrol.** [C20: from STILBENE + OESTRUS + -OL[1]]
stile[1] (staɪl) *n.* **1.** a set of steps or rungs in a wall or fence to allow people, but not animals, to pass over. **2.** short for **turnstile.** [OE *stigel*]
stile[2] (staɪl) *n.* a vertical framing member in a door, window frame, etc. [C17: prob. from Du. *stijl* pillar, ult. from L *stilus* writing instrument]
stiletto (stɪ'lɛtəʊ) *n., pl.* **-tos.** **1.** a small dagger with a slender tapered blade. **2.** a sharply pointed tool used to make holes in leather, cloth, etc. **3.** Also called: **spike heel, stiletto heel.** a very high heel on a woman's shoe, tapering to a very narrow tip. *~vb.* **-toeing, -toed.** **4.** *(tr.)* to stab with a stiletto. [C17: from It., from *stilo* a dagger, from L *stilus* a stake, pen]
Stilicho ('stɪlɪkəʊ) *n.* **Flavius** ('fleɪvɪəs). ?365–408 A.D., Roman general and statesman, born a Vandal. As the guardian of Emperor Theodosius' son Honorius, he was effective ruler of the Western Roman Empire (395–408), which he defended against the Visigoths.
still[1] (stɪl) *adj.* **1.** *(usually predicative)* motionless; stationary. **2.** undisturbed or tranquil; silent and calm. **3.** not sparkling or effervescent. **4.** gentle or quiet; subdued. **5.** *Obs.* (of a child) dead at birth. *~adv.* **6.** continuing now or in the future as in the past: *do you still love me?* **7.** up to this or that time; yet: *I still don't know your name.* **8.** (often used with a comparative) even or yet: *still more insults.* **9.** quiet or without movement: *sit still.* **10.** *Poetic & dialect.* always. *~n.* **11.** *Poetic.* silence or tranquillity: *the still of the night.* **12. a.** a still photograph, esp. of a scene from a film. **b.** *(as modifier):* a *still camera. ~vb.* **13.** to make or become still, quiet, or calm. **14.** *(tr.)* to allay or relieve: *her fears were stilled. ~sentence connector.* **15.** even then; nevertheless: *the child has some new toys and still cries.* [OE *stille*] —'**stillness** *n.*
still[2] (stɪl) *n.* an apparatus for carrying out distillation, used esp. in the manufacture of spirits. [C16: from OF *stiller* to drip, from L *stillāre,* from *stilla* a drip]
stillborn ('stɪl,bɔːn) *adj.* **1.** (of a fetus) dead at birth. **2.** (of an idea, plan, etc.) fruitless; abortive; unsuccessful. —'**still,birth** *n.*
still life *n., pl.* **still lifes.** **1. a.** a painting or drawing of inanimate objects, such as fruit, flowers, etc. **b.** *(as modifier):* a *still-life painting.* **2.** the genre of such paintings.
still room *n. Brit.* **1.** a room in which distilling is carried out. **2.** a pantry or storeroom, as in a large house.
Stillson wrench ('stɪlsªn) *n. Trademark.* a large wrench having jaws that tighten as the pressure on the handle is increased.
stilly *adv.* ('stɪlɪ). **1.** *Arch. or literary.* quietly or calmly. *~adj.* ('stɪlɪ). **2.** *Poetic.* still, quiet, or calm.
stilt (stɪlt) *n.* **1.** either of a pair of two long poles with footrests on which a person stands and walks, as used by circus clowns. **2.** a long post or column that is used with others to support a building above ground level. **3.** any of several shore birds similar to the avocets but having a straight bill. *~vb.* **4.** *(tr.)* to raise or place on or as if on stilts. [C14 (in the sense: crutch, handle of a plough): rel. to Low G *stilte* pole]
stilted ('stɪltɪd) *adj.* **1.** (of speech, writing, etc.) formal, pompous, or bombastic. **2.** not flowing continuously or naturally: *stilted conversation.* **3.** *Archit.* (of an arch)

having vertical piers between the impost and the springing. —'**stiltedly** *adv.* —'**stiltedness** *n.*

Stilton ('stɪltən) *n. Trademark.* either of two rich cheeses, blue-veined (**blue Stilton**) or white (**white Stilton**), both very strong in flavour. [C18: named after *Stilton*, Cambridgeshire, where it was orig. sold]

stimulant ('stɪmjʊlənt) *n.* **1.** a drug or similar substance that increases physiological activity, esp. of a particular organ. **2.** any stimulating agent or thing. ~*adj.* **3.** stimulating. [C18: from L *stimulāns* goading, from *stimulāre* to urge on]

stimulate ('stɪmjʊ,leɪt) *vb.* **1.** (*tr.*) to arouse or quicken the activity or senses of. **2.** (*tr.*) *Physiol.* to excite (a nerve, organ, etc.) with a stimulus. **3.** (*intr.*) to act as a stimulant or stimulus. [C16: from L *stimulāre*] —'**stimu,lating** *adj.* —,**stimu'lation** *n.* —'**stimulative** *adj., n.* —'**stimu,lator** *n.*

stimulus ('stɪmjʊləs) *n., pl.* -**li** (-,laɪ, -,liː). **1.** something that stimulates or acts as an incentive. **2.** any drug, agent, electrical impulse, or other factor able to cause a response in an organism. [C17: from L: a cattle goad]

sting (stɪŋ) *vb.* **stinging, stung.** **1.** (of certain animals and plants) to inflict a wound on (an organism) by the injection of poison. **2.** to feel or cause to feel a sharp mental or physical pain. **3.** (*tr.*) to goad or incite (esp. in **sting into action**). **4.** (*tr.*) *Inf.* to cheat, esp. by overcharging. ~*n.* **5.** a skin wound caused by the poison injected by certain insects or plants. **6.** pain caused by or as if by the sting of a plant or animal. **7.** a mental pain or pang: *a sting of conscience.* **8.** a sharp pointed organ, such as the ovipositor of a wasp, by which poison can be injected. **9.** the ability to sting: *a sharp sting in his criticism.* **10.** something as painful or swift of action as a sting: *the sting of death.* **11.** a sharp stimulus or incitement. **12.** *Sl.* a deceptive ruse. [OE *stingan*] —'**stinger** *n.* —'**stinging** *adj.*

stinging nettle *n.* See **nettle** (sense 1).

stingray ('stɪŋ,reɪ) *n.* any of various rays having a whiplike tail bearing a serrated venomous spine capable of inflicting painful weals.

stingy[1] ('stɪndʒɪ) *adj.* -**gier, -giest.** **1.** unwilling to spend or give. **2.** insufficient or scanty. [C17 (? in the sense: ill-tempered): ?from *stinge*, dialect var. of STING] —'**stingily** *adv.* —'**stinginess** *n.*

stingy[2] ('stɪŋɪ) *adj.* **stingier, stingiest.** *Inf.* stinging or capable of stinging.

stink (stɪŋk) *n.* **1.** a strong foul smell; stench. **2.** *Sl.* a great deal of trouble (esp. in **make** *or* **raise a stink**). **3.** **like stink.** intensely; furiously. ~*vb.* **stinking, stank** *or* **stunk; stunk.** (*mainly intr.*) **4.** to emit a foul smell. **5.** *Sl.* to be thoroughly bad or abhorrent: *this town stinks.* **6.** *Inf.* to have a very bad reputation: *his name stinks.* **7.** to be of poor quality. **8.** (foll. by *of* or *with*) *Sl.* to have or appear to have an excessive amount (of money). **9.** (*tr.; usually foll. by up*) *Inf.* to cause to stink. ~See also **stink out.** [OE *stincan*]

stink bomb *n.* a small glass globe used by practical jokers: it releases a liquid with an offensive smell when broken.

stinker ('stɪŋkə) *n.* **1.** a person or thing that stinks. **2.** *Sl.* a difficult or very unpleasant person or thing. **3.** *Sl.* something of very poor quality. **4.** *Inf.* any of several fulmars or related birds that feed on carrion.

stinkhorn ('stɪŋk,hɔːn) *n.* any of various fungi having an offensive odour.

stinking ('stɪŋkɪŋ) *adj.* **1.** having a foul smell. **2.** *Inf.* unpleasant or disgusting. **3.** (*postpositive*) *Sl.* very drunk. **4. cry stinking fish.** to decry something, esp. one's own products. ~*adv.* **5.** *Inf.* (intensifier, expressing contempt): *stinking rich.* —'**stinkingly** *adv.* —'**stinkingness** *n.*

stinko ('stɪŋkəʊ) *adj.* (*postpositive*) *Sl.* drunk.

stink out *vb.* (*tr., adv.*) **1.** to drive out or away by a foul smell. **2.** *Brit.* to cause to stink: *the smell of orange peel stinks out the room.*

stinkweed ('stɪŋk,wiːd) *n.* **1.** Also called: **wall mustard.** a cruciferous plant, naturalized in Britain and S and central Europe, having pale yellow flowers and a disagreeable smell when bruised. **2.** any of various other ill-smelling plants.

stinkwood ('stɪŋk,wʊd) *n.* **1.** any of various trees having offensive-smelling wood, esp. a southern African lauraceous tree yielding a hard wood used for furniture. **2.** the heavy durable wood of any of these trees.

stint[1] (stɪnt) *vb.* **1.** to be frugal or miserly towards (someone) with (something). **2.** *Arch.* to stop or check (something). ~*n.* **3.** an allotted or fixed amount of work. **4.** a limitation or check. [OE *styntan* to blunt] —'**stinter** *n.*

stint[2] (stɪnt) *n.* any of various small sandpipers of a chiefly northern genus. [OE]

stipe (staɪp) *n.* **1.** a stalk in plants that bears reproductive structures, esp. the stalk bearing the cap of a mushroom. **2.** the stalk that bears the leaflets of a fern or the thallus of a seaweed. **3.** *Zool.* any stalklike part; stipes. [C18: via F from L *stīpes* tree trunk]

stipel ('staɪpəl) *n.* a small paired leaflike structure at the base of certain leaflets; secondary stipule. [C19: via NL from L *stipula*, dim. of *stīpes* a log] —**stipellate** (staɪ'pɛlɪt, -eɪt) *adj.*

stipend ('staɪpɛnd) *n.* a fixed or regular amount of money paid as a salary or allowance, as to a clergyman. [C15: from OF *stipende*, from L *stīpendium* tax, from *stips* a contribution + *pendere* to pay out]

stipendiary (staɪ'pɛndɪərɪ) *adj.* **1.** receiving or working for regular pay: *a stipendiary magistrate.* **2.** paid for by a stipend. ~*n., pl.* -**aries.** **3.** a person who receives regular payment. [C16: from L *stīpendiārius* concerning tribute, from *stīpendium* STIPEND]

stipes ('staɪpiːz) *n., pl.* **stipites** ('stɪpɪ,tiːz). *Zool.* **1.** the second maxillary segment in insects and crustaceans. **2.** the eyestalk of a crab or similar crustacean. **3.** any similar stemlike structure. [C18: from L; see STIPE] —**stipiform** ('staɪpɪ,fɔːm) *or* **stipitiform** ('stɪpɪtɪ,fɔːm) *adj.*

stipple ('stɪpəl) *vb.* (*tr.*) **1.** to draw, engrave, or paint using dots or flecks. **2.** to apply paint, powder, etc., to (something) with many light dabs. ~*n. also* **stippling.** **3.** the technique of stippling or a picture produced by or using stippling. [C18: from Du. *stippelen*, from *stippen* to prick, from *stip* point] —'**stippler** *n.*

stipulate ('stɪpjʊ,leɪt) *vb.* **1.** (*tr.; may take a clause as object*) to specify, often as a condition of an agreement. **2.** (*intr.; foll. by for*) to insist (on) as a term of an agreement. **3.** (*tr.; may take a clause as object*) to guarantee or promise. [C17: from L *stipulārī*, prob. from OL *stipulus* firm] —,**stipu'lation** *n.* —'**stipu,lator** *n.*

stipule ('stɪpjuːl) *n.* a small paired usually leaflike outgrowth occurring at the base of a leaf or its stalk. [C18: from L STIPE] —**stipular** ('stɪpjʊlə) *adj.*

stir[1] (stɜː) *vb.* **stirring, stirred.** **1.** to move an implement such as a spoon around in (a liquid) so as to mix up the constituents. **2.** to change or cause to change position; disturb or be disturbed. **3.** (*intr.; often foll. by from*) to venture or depart (from one's usual or preferred place). **4.** (*intr.*) to be active after a rest; be up and about. **5.** (*tr.*) to excite or stimulate, esp. emotionally. **6.** to move (oneself) briskly or vigorously; exert (oneself). **7.** (*tr.*) to rouse or awaken: *to stir someone from sleep; to stir memories.* **8.** (when *tr.*, foll. by *up*) to cause or incite others to cause (trouble, arguments, etc.). **9. stir one's stumps.** to move or become active. ~*n.* **10.** the act or an instance of stirring or the state of being stirred. **11.** a strong reaction, esp. of excitement: *his publication caused a stir.* **12.** a slight movement. **13.** *N.Z. inf.* a noisy party. ~See also **stir up.** [OE *styrian*]

stir[2] (stɜː) *n.* **1.** a slang word for **prison:** *in stir.* **2. stir-crazy.** *Sl., chiefly U.S. & Canad.* mentally disturbed as a result of being in prison. [C19: from ?]

stir-fry ('stɜː'fraɪ) *vb.* -**frying, -fried.** **1.** to cook (chopped meat, vegetables, etc.) rapidly by stirring them in a wok or frying pan over a high heat. ~*n., pl.* -**fries.** **2.** a dish cooked in this way.

stirk (stɜːk) *n.* **1.** a heifer of 6 to 12 months old. **2.** a yearling heifer or bullock. [OE *stierc*]

Stirling ('stɜːlɪŋ) *n.* a town in central Scotland, administrative centre of the Central region, on the River Forth: its castle was a regular residence of many Scottish monarchs between the 12th century and 1603. Pop.: 29 238 (1985 est.).

Stirlingshire ('stɜːlɪŋ,ʃɪə, -ʃə) *n.* (until 1975) a county of central Scotland, now part of Central and Strathclyde regions.

stirps (stɜːps) *n., pl.* **stirpes** ('stɜːpiːz). **1.** *Genealogy.* a line of descendants from an ancestor. **2.** *Bot.* a race or variety. [C17: from L: root, family origin]

stirrer ('stɜːrə) *n.* **1.** a person or thing that stirs. **2.** *Inf.* a person who deliberately causes trouble. **3.** *Austral. & N.Z. inf.* a political activist or agitator.

stirring ('stɜːrɪŋ) *adj.* **1.** exciting the emotions; stimulating. **2.** active, lively, or busy. —'**stirringly** *adv.*

stirrup ('stɪrəp) *n.* **1.** Also called: **stirrup iron.** either of two metal loops on a riding saddle, with a flat footpiece through which a rider puts his foot for support. They are attached to the saddle by **stirrup leathers. 2.** a U-shaped support or clamp. **3.** *Naut.* one of a set of ropes fastened to a yard at one end and having a thimble at the other through which a footrope is reeved for support. [OE *stigráp*, from *stíg* step + *ráp* rope]

stirrup cup *n.* a cup containing an alcoholic drink offered to a horseman ready to ride away.

stirrup pump *n.* a hand-operated pump, the base of the cylinder of which is placed in a bucket of water: used in fighting fires.

stir up *vb.* (*tr., adv.*) to set in motion; instigate or be instigated: *he stirred up trouble.*

stitch (stɪtʃ) *n.* **1.** a link made by drawing a thread through material by means of a needle. **2.** a loop of yarn formed around an implement used in knitting, crocheting, etc. **3.** a particular method of stitching or shape of stitch. **4.** a sharp spasmodic pain in the side resulting from running or exercising. **5.** (*usually used with a negative*) *Inf.* the least fragment of clothing: *he wasn't wearing a stitch.* **6.** *Agriculture.* the ridge between two furrows. **7. drop a stitch.** to allow a loop of wool to fall off a knitting needle accidentally while knitting. **8. in stitches.** *Inf.* laughing uncontrollably. ~*vb.* **9.** (*tr.*) to sew, fasten, etc., with stitches. **10.** (*intr.*) to be engaged in sewing. **11.** (*tr.*) to bind together (the leaves of a book, pamphlet, etc.) with wire staples or thread. ~*n., vb.* **12.** an informal word for **suture** (senses 1b, 5). [OE *stice* sting] —'**stitcher** *n.*

stitchwort ('stɪtʃˌwɜːt) *n.* any of several low-growing N temperate herbaceous plants having small white star-shaped flowers.

stiver ('staɪvə) *n.* **1.** a former Dutch coin worth one twentieth of a guilder. **2.** a small amount, esp. of money. [C16: from Du. *stuiver*]

St John ('sɪndʒən) *n.* **Henry.** See (1st Viscount) **Bolingbroke.**

stoa ('stəʊə) *n., pl.* **stoae** ('stəʊiː) *or* **stoas.** a covered walk that has a colonnade on one or both sides, esp. as in ancient Greece. [C17: from Gk]

stoat (stəʊt) *n.* a small Eurasian mammal, closely related to the weasels, having a brown coat and a black-tipped tail: in the northern parts of its range it has a white winter coat and is then known as an ermine. [C15: from ?]

stochastic (stɒ'kæstɪk) *adj.* **1.** *Statistics.* **a.** (of a random variable) having a probability distribution, usually with finite variance. **b.** (of a process) involving a random variable the successive values of which are not independent. **c.** (of a matrix) square with non-negative elements that add to unity in each row. **2.** *Rare.* involving conjecture. [C17: from Gk *stokhastikos* capable of guessing, from *stokhazesthai* to aim at, conjecture, from *stokhos* a target]

stock (stɒk) *n.* **1. a.** (*sometimes pl.*) the total goods or raw material kept on the premises of a shop or business. **b.** (*as modifier*): *a stock book.* **2.** a supply of something stored for future use. **3.** *Finance.* **a.** the capital raised by a company through the issue and subscription of shares entitling their holders to dividends, partial ownership, and usually voting rights. **b.** the proportion of such capital held by an individual shareholder. **c.** the shares of a specified company or industry. **4.** standing or status. **5. a.** farm animals, such as cattle and sheep, bred and kept for their meat, skins, etc. **b.** (*as modifier*): *stock farming.* **6.** the trunk or main stem of a tree or other plant. **7.** *Horticulture.* **a.** a rooted plant into which a scion is inserted during grafting. **b.** a plant or stem from which cuttings are taken. **8.** the original type from which a particular race, family, group, etc., is derived. **9.** a race, breed, or variety of animals or plants. **10.** (*often pl.*) a small pen in which a single animal can be confined. **11.** a line of descent. **12.** any of the major subdivisions of the human species; race or ethnic group. **13.** the part of a rifle, etc., into which the barrel is set: held by the firer against the

shoulder. **14.** the handle of something, such as a whip or fishing rod. **15.** the main body of a tool, such as the block of a plane. **16.** short for **diestock, gunstock,** or **rolling stock. 17.** (formerly) the part of a plough to which the irons and handles were attached. **18.** the main upright part of a supporting structure. **19.** a liquid or broth in which meat, fish, bones, or vegetables have been simmered for a long time. **20.** film material before exposure and processing. **21.** Also called: **gillyflower.** any of several cruciferous plants such as **evening** or **night-scented stock,** of the Mediterranean region: cultivated for their brightly coloured flowers. **22. Virginian stock.** a similar and related North American plant. **23.** a long usually white neckcloth wrapped around the neck, worn in the 18th century and as part of modern riding dress. **24. a.** the repertoire of plays available to a repertory company. **b.** (*as modifier*): *a stock play.* **25.** a log or block of wood. **26.** See **laughing stock. 27. in stock. a.** stored on the premises or available for sale or use. **b.** supplied with goods of a specified kind. **28. out of stock. a.** not immediately available for sale or use. **b.** not having goods of a specified kind immediately available. **29. take stock. a.** to make an inventory. **b.** to make a general appraisal, esp. of prospects, resources, etc. **30. take stock in.** to attach importance to. ~*adj.* **31.** staple; standard: *stock sizes in clothes.* **32.** (*prenominal*) being a cliché; hackneyed: *a stock phrase.* ~*vb.* **33.** (*tr.*) to keep (goods) for sale. **34.** (*intr.*; usually foll. by *up* or *up on*) to obtain a store of (something) for future use or sale: *to stock up on beer.* **35.** (*tr.*) to supply with live animals, fish, etc.: *to stock a farm.* **36.** (*intr.*) (of a plant) to put forth new shoots. **37.** (*tr.*) *Obs.* to punish by putting in the stocks. ~See also **stocks.** [OE *stocc* trunk (of a tree), stem, stick (the various senses developed from these meanings, as trunk of a tree, hence line of descent; structures made of timber; a store of timber or other goods for future use, hence an aggregate of goods, animals, etc.)] —'**stocker** *n.*

stockade (stɒ'keɪd) *n.* **1.** an enclosure or barrier of stakes and timbers. ~*vb.* **2.** (*tr.*) to surround with a stockade. [C17: from Sp. *estacada,* from *estaca* a stake, of Gmc origin]

stockbreeder ('stɒkˌbriːdə) *n.* a person who breeds or rears livestock as an occupation. —'**stock,breeding** *n.*

stockbroker ('stɒkˌbrəʊkə) *n.* a person who buys and sells securities on a commission basis for customers. —'**stock,brokerage** *or* '**stock,broking** *n.*

stockbroker belt *n. Brit. inf.* the area outside a city, esp. London, in which rich commuters live.

stock car *n.* **1.** a car, usually a production saloon, strengthened and modified for a form of racing in which the cars often collide. **2.** *U.S. & Canad.* a railway wagon for carrying livestock.

stock dove *n.* a European dove, smaller than the wood pigeon and having a grey plumage.

stock exchange *n.* **1.** Also called: **stock market. a.** a highly organized market facilitating the purchase and sale of securities and operated by professional stockbrokers and stockjobbers according to fixed rules. **b.** a place where securities are regularly traded. **c.** (*as modifier*): *a stock-exchange operator; stock-exchange prices.* **2.** the prices or trading activity of a stock exchange: *the stock exchange fell heavily today.*

stockfish ('stɒkˌfɪʃ) *n., pl.* **-fish** *or* **-fishes.** fish cured by splitting and drying in the air.

Stockhausen (*German* 'ʃtɒkhaʊzən) *n.* **Karlheinz** (karl-'haints). born 1928, German composer, whose avant-garde music exploits advanced serialization, electronic sounds, group improvization, and vocal and instrumental timbres and techniques. Works include *Gruppen* (1959) for three orchestras, *Stimmung* (1968) for six vocalists, and *Ylem* (1972) for instrumental ensemble and tape.

stockholder ('stɒkˌhəʊldə) *n.* **1.** an owner of corporate capital stock. **2.** *Austral.* a person who keeps livestock. —'**stock,holding** *n.*

Stockholm ('stɒkhəʊm; *Swedish* 'stɔkhɔlm) *n.* the capital of Sweden, a port in the E central part at the outflow of Lake Mälar into the Baltic: situated partly on the mainland and partly on islands; traditionally founded about 1250; university (1877). Pop.: 663 217 (1986).

stockhorse ('stɒkˌhɔːs) *n. Austral.* a stockman's horse.

stockinet (ˌstɒkɪ'nɛt) *n.* a machine-knitted elastic fabric used, esp. formerly, for stockings, underwear, etc. [C19: ?from earlier *stocking-net*]

stocking ('stɒkɪŋ) *n.* **1.** one of a pair of close-fitting garments made of knitted yarn to cover the foot and part or all of the leg. **2.** something resembling this in position, function, etc. **3. in (one's) stocking** *or* **stockinged feet.** wearing stockings or socks but no shoes. [C16: from dialect *stock* stocking + -ING[1]] —'**stockinged** *adj.*

stocking cap *n.* a conical knitted cap, often with a tassel.

stocking filler *n. Brit.* a present of a size suitable for inclusion in a Christmas stocking.

stock in trade *n.* **1.** goods in stock necessary for carrying on a business. **2.** anything constantly used by someone as a part of his profession, occupation, or trade: *friendliness is the salesman's stock in trade.*

stockist ('stɒkɪst) *n. Commerce, Brit.* a dealer who undertakes to maintain stocks of a specified product at or above a certain minimum in return for favourable buying terms granted by the manufacturer of the product.

stockjobber ('stɒk,dʒɒbə) *n.* **1.** *Brit.* before Big Bang, a wholesale dealer on a stock exchange who operates as an intermediary between brokers without transacting directly with the public and derives his income from the spread between the bid and offered prices. See **market maker.** **2.** *U.S., disparaging.* a stockbroker, esp. one dealing in worthless securities. —'**stock jobbery** *or* '**stock jobbing** *n.*

stockman ('stɒkmən, -,mæn) *n., pl.* **-men.** **1. a.** a man engaged in the rearing or care of farm livestock, esp. cattle. **b.** an owner of cattle or other livestock. **2.** *U.S. & Canad.* a man employed in a warehouse or stockroom.

stock market *n.* another name for **stock exchange.**

stockpile ('stɒk,paɪl) *vb.* **1.** to acquire and store a large quantity of (something). ~*n.* **2.** a large store or supply accumulated for future use. — '**stock,piler** *n.*

Stockport ('stɒk,pɔːt) *n.* a town in NW England, in Greater Manchester: an early textile centre and scene of several labour disturbances in the early 19th century. Pop.: 136 496 (1981).

stockpot ('stɒk,pɒt) *n. Chiefly Brit.* a pot in which stock for soup, etc., is made or kept.

stockroom ('stɒk,ruːm, -,rʊm) *n.* a room in which a stock of goods is kept, as in a shop or factory.

stock route *n. Austral. & N.Z.* a route designated for droving stock, avoiding traffic.

stocks (stɒks) *pl. n.* **1.** *History.* an instrument of punishment consisting of a heavy wooden frame with holes in which the feet, hands, or head of an offender were locked. **2.** a frame used to support a boat while under construction. **3.** *Naut.* a vertical post or shaft at the forward edge of a rudder, extended upwards for attachment to the steering controls. **4. on the stocks.** in preparation or under construction.

stock-still *adv.* absolutely still; motionless.

stocktaking ('stɒk,teɪkɪŋ) *n.* **1.** the examination, counting, and valuing of goods on hand in a shop or business. **2.** a reassessment of one's current situation, progress, prospects, etc.

Stockton ('stɒktən) *n.* an inland port in central California, on the San Joaquin River: seat of the University of the Pacific (1851). Pop.: 183 430 (1986 est.).

Stockton-on-Tees *n.* a port in NE England, in Cleveland on the River Tees: industrial centre, famous for the **Stockton-Darlington Railway** (1825), the first passenger-carrying railway in the world. Pop.: 154 585 (1981).

stock whip *n.* a whip with a long lash and a short handle, used to herd cattle, etc.

Stockwood ('stɒkwʊd) *n.* (**Arthur**) **Mervyn.** born 1913, English Anglican prelate; bishop of Southwark (1959–80).

stocky ('stɒkɪ) *adj.* **stockier, stockiest.** (usually of a person) thickset; sturdy. — '**stockily** *adv.* — '**stockiness** *n.*

stockyard ('stɒk,jɑːd) *n.* a large yard with pens or covered buildings where farm animals are assembled, sold, etc.

stodge (stɒdʒ) *Inf.* ~*n.* **1.** heavy filling starchy food. **2.** a dull person or subject. ~*vb.* **3.** to stuff (oneself or another) with food. [C17: ? blend of STUFF + *podge*, from *podgy* fat]

stodgy ('stɒdʒɪ) *adj.* **stodgier, stodgiest.** **1.** (of food) heavy or uninteresting. **2.** excessively formal and conventional. [C19: from STODGE] — '**stodgily** *adv.* — '**stodginess** *n.*

stoep (stuːp) *n.* (in South Africa) a veranda. [from Afrik., from Du.]

stoic ('stəʊɪk) *n.* **1.** a person who maintains stoical qualities. ~*adj.* **2.** a variant of **stoical.**

Stoic ('stəʊɪk) *n.* **1.** a member of the ancient Greek school of philosophy founded by Zeno, holding that virtue and happiness can be attained only by submission to destiny and the natural law. ~*adj.* **2.** of or relating to the doctrines of the Stoics. [C16: via L from Gk *stōikos*, from *stoa*, the porch in Athens where Zeno taught]

stoical ('stəʊɪkᵊl) *adj.* characterized by impassivity or resignation. — '**stoically** *adv.*

stoichiometry *or* **stoicheiometry** (,stɔɪkɪ'ɒmɪtrɪ) *n.* the branch of chemistry concerned with the proportions in which elements are combined in compounds and the quantitative relationships between reactants and products in chemical reactions. [C19: from Gk *stoikheion* element + -METRY] — ,**stoichio'metric** *or* ,**stoicheio'metric** *adj.*

stoicism ('stəʊɪ,sɪzəm) *n.* **1.** indifference to pleasure and pain. **2.** (*cap.*) the philosophy of the Stoics.

stoke (stəʊk) *vb.* **1.** to feed, stir, and tend (a fire, furnace, etc.). **2.** (*tr.*) to tend the furnace of; act as a stoker for. [C17: back formation from STOKER]

stokehold ('stəʊk,həʊld) *n. Naut.* **1.** a coal bunker for a ship's furnace. **2.** the hold for a ship's boilers; fire room.

stokehole ('stəʊk,həʊl) *n.* **1.** another word for **stokehold.** **2.** a hole in a furnace through which it is stoked.

Stoke-on-Trent *n.* a city in central England, in N Staffordshire on the River Trent: a major centre of the pottery industry. Pop.: 252 351 (1981).

stoker ('stəʊkə) *n.* a person employed to tend a furnace, as on a steamship. [C17: from Du., from *stoken* to stoke]

stoke up *vb.* (*adv.*) **1.** to feed and tend (a fire, etc.) with fuel. **2.** (*intr.*) to fill oneself with food.

Stokowski (stə'kɒfskɪ) *n.* **Leopold.** 1887–1977, U.S. conductor, born in Britain. He did much to popularize classical music with orchestral transcriptions and film appearances, esp. in *Fantasia* (1940).

STOL (stɒl) *n.* **1.** a system in which an aircraft can take off and land in a short distance. **2.** an aircraft using this system. Cf. **VTOL.** [C20: *s(hort)* *t(ake)o(ff and)* *l(anding)*]

stole[1] (stəʊl) *vb.* the past tense of **steal.**

stole[2] (stəʊl) *n.* **1.** a long scarf or shawl, worn by women. **2.** a long narrow scarf worn by various officiating clergymen. [OE *stole*, from L *stola*, from Gk *stolē* clothing]

stolen ('stəʊlən) *vb.* the past participle of **steal.**

stolid ('stɒlɪd) *adj.* showing little or no emotion or interest. [C17: from L *stolidus* dull] —**stolidity** (stɒ'lɪdɪtɪ) *or* '**stolidness** *n.* — '**stolidly** *adv.*

stolon ('stəʊlən) *n.* **1.** another name for **runner** (sense 9). **2.** a branching structure in lower animals, esp. the anchoring rootlike part of colonial organisms. [C17: from L *stolō* shoot] —**stoloniferous** (,stəʊlə'nɪfərəs) *adj.*

stoma ('stəʊmə) *n., pl.* **stomata.** **1.** *Bot.* an epidermal pore in plant leaves, that controls the passage of gases into and out of a plant. **2.** *Zool., anat.* a mouth or mouthlike part. [C17: via NL from Gk: mouth]

stomach ('stʌmək) *n.* **1.** (in vertebrates) the enlarged muscular saclike part of the alimentary canal in which food is stored until it has been partially digested. Related adj.: **gastric.** **2.** the corresponding organ in invertebrates. **3.** the abdominal region. **4.** desire, appetite, or inclination: *I have no stomach for arguments.* ~*vb.* (*tr.; used mainly in negative constructions*) **5.** to tolerate; bear: *I can't stomach his bragging.* **6.** to eat or digest: *he cannot stomach oysters.* [C14: from OF *stomaque*, from L *stomachus*, from Gk *stomakhos*, from *stoma* mouth]

stomachache ('stʌmək,eɪk) *n.* pain in the stomach, as from acute indigestion. Also called: **stomach upset, upset stomach.**

stomacher ('stʌmək ə) *n.* a decorative V-shaped panel of stiff material worn over the chest and stomach by men and women in the 16th century, later only by women.

stomachic (stə'mækɪk) *adj. also* **stomachical.** **1.** stimulating gastric activity. **2.** of or relating to the stomach. ~*n.* **3.** a stomachic medicine.

stomach pump *n. Med.* a suction device for removing stomach contents via an orally inserted tube.

stomata ('stəʊmətə, 'stɒm-, stəʊ'mɑːtə) *n.* the plural of **stoma.**

stomatitis (,stəʊmə'taɪtɪs, ,stɒm-) *n.* inflammation of the mouth. —**stomatitic** (,stəʊmə'tɪtɪk, ,stɒm-) *adj.*

stomato- *or before a vowel* **stomat-** *combining form.* indicating the mouth or a mouthlike part: *stomatology.* [from Gk *stoma, stomat-*]

stomatology (ˌstəʊməˈtɒlədʒɪ) *n.* the branch of medicine concerned with the mouth. **—stomatological** (ˌstəʊmətəˈlɒdʒɪkᵊl) *adj.*

-stome *n. combining form.* indicating a mouth or opening resembling a mouth: *peristome.* [from Gk *stoma* mouth, & *stomion* little mouth]

-stomous *adj. combining form.* having a specified type of mouth.

stomp (stɒmp) *vb.* **1.** (*intr.*) to tread or stamp heavily. ~*n.* **2.** a rhythmical stamping jazz dance. [var. of STAMP] **—'stomper** *n.*

-stomy *n. combining form.* indicating a surgical operation performed to make an artificial opening into or for a specified part: *cytostomy.* [from Gk *-stomia,* from *stoma* mouth]

stone (stəʊn) *n.* **1.** the hard compact nonmetallic material of which rocks are made. **2.** a small lump of rock; pebble. **3.** short for **gemstone. 4. a.** a piece of rock designed or shaped for some particular purpose. **b.** (*in combination*): *gravestone; millstone.* **5. a.** something that resembles a stone. **b.** (*in combination*): *hailstone.* **6.** the woody central part of such fruits as the peach and plum, that contains the seed; endocarp. **7.** any similar hard part of a fruit, such as the stony seed of a date. **8.** (*pl.* **stone**) *Brit.* a unit of weight, used esp. to express human body weight, equal to 14 pounds or 6.350 kilograms. **9.** Also called: **granite.** the rounded heavy mass of granite or iron used in the game of curling. **10.** *Pathol.* a nontechnical name for **calculus. 11.** *Printing.* a table with a very flat iron or stone surface upon which pages are composed. **12.** (*modifier*) relating to or made of stone: *a stone house.* **13.** (*modifier*) made of stoneware: *a stone jar.* **14. cast a stone** (**at**). cast aspersions (upon). **15. heart of stone.** an obdurate or unemotional nature. **16. leave no stone unturned.** to do everything possible to achieve an end. ~*vb.* (*tr.*) **17.** to throw stones at, esp. to kill. **18.** to remove the stones from. **19.** to furnish or provide with stones. [OE *stān*] **—'stoner** *n.*

stone- *prefix.* very, completely: *stone-blind, stone-cold.* [from STONE in sense of "like a stone"]

Stone Age *n.* **1.** a period in human culture identified by the use of stone implements. ~*modifier.* **Stone-Age. 2.** (*sometimes not caps.*) of or relating to this period.

stone-blind *adj.* completely blind. Cf. **sand-blind.**

stonechat ('stəʊnˌtʃæt) *n.* an Old World songbird having a black plumage with a reddish-brown breast. [C18: from its cry, which sounds like clattering pebbles]

stone-cold *adj.* **1.** completely cold. **2. stone-cold sober.** completely sober.

stonecrop ('stəʊnˌkrɒp) *n.* any of various N temperate plants having fleshy leaves and typically red, yellow, or white flowers.

stone curlew *n.* any of several brownish shore birds having a large head and eyes. Also called: **thick-knee.**

stonecutter ('stəʊnˌkʌtə) *n.* **1.** a person who is skilled in cutting and carving stone. **2.** a machine used to dress stone. **—'stoneˌcutting** *n.*

stoned (stəʊnd) *adj. Sl.* under the influence of drugs or alcohol.

stone-deaf *adj.* completely deaf.

stonefish ('stəʊnˌfɪʃ) *n., pl.* **-fish** *or* **-fishes.** a venomous tropical marine fish that resembles a piece of rock on the seabed.

stonefly ('stəʊnˌflaɪ) *n., pl.* **-flies.** any of various insects, in which the larvae are aquatic, living beneath stones.

stone fruit *n.* the nontechnical name for **drupe.**

Stonehenge (ˌstəʊnˈhɛndʒ) *n.* a prehistoric ruin in S England, in Wiltshire on Salisbury Plain: constructed over the period of roughly 2500–1500 B.C.; one of the most important megalithic monuments in Europe; believed to have had religious and astronomical purposes.

stonemason ('stəʊnˌmeɪsᵊn) *n.* a person who is skilled in preparing stone for building. **—'stoneˌmasonry** *n.*

stone pine *n.* a pine tree with a short bole and radiating branches forming an umbrella shape.

Stones (stəʊnz) *pl. n.* **the.** See **Rolling Stones.**

stone's throw *n.* a short distance.

stonewall (ˌstəʊnˈwɔːl) *vb.* **1.** (*intr.*) *Cricket.* (of a batsman) to play defensively. **2.** to obstruct or hinder (parliamentary business). **—ˌstoneˈwaller** *n.*

stoneware ('stəʊnˌwɛə) *n.* **1.** a hard opaque pottery, fired at a very high temperature. ~*adj.* **2.** made of stoneware.

stonewashed ('stəʊnˌwɒʃt) *adj.* (of clothes or fabric) given a worn faded look by being subjected to the abrasive action of many small pieces of pumice.

stonework ('stəʊnˌwɜːk) *n.* **1.** any structure or part of a building made of stone. **2.** the process of dressing or setting stones. **—'stoneˌworker** *n.*

stonkered ('stɒŋkəd) *adj. Sl.* completely exhausted or beaten. [C20: from *stonker* to beat, from ?]

stony *or* **stoney** ('stəʊnɪ) *adj.* **stonier, stoniest. 1.** of or resembling stone. **2.** abounding in stone or stones. **3.** unfeeling or obdurate. **4.** short for **stony-broke.** **—'stonily** *adv.* **—'stoniness** *n.*

stony-broke *adj. Brit. sl.* completely without money; penniless.

stony-hearted *adj.* unfeeling; hardhearted. **—ˌstony-'heartedness** *n.*

stood (stʊd) *vb.* the past tense and past participle of **stand.**

stooge (stuːdʒ) *n.* **1.** an actor who feeds lines to a comedian or acts as his butt. **2.** *Sl.* someone who is taken advantage of by another. ~*vb.* **3.** (*intr.*) *Sl.* to act as a stooge. [C20: from ?]

stook (stuːk) *n.* **1.** a number of sheaves set upright in a field to dry with their heads together. ~*vb.* **2.** (*tr.*) to set up (sheaves) in stooks. [C15: var. of *stouk,* of Gmc origin] **—'stooker** *n.*

stool (stuːl) *n.* **1.** a simple seat or footrest consisting of a small flat piece of wood, etc., resting on three or four legs, a pedestal, etc. **2.** a rootstock or base of a plant from which shoots, etc., are produced. **3.** a cluster of shoots growing from such a base. **4.** *Chiefly U.S.* a decoy used in hunting. **5.** waste matter evacuated from the bowels. **6.** a lavatory seat. **7.** (in W Africa, esp. Ghana) a chief's throne. **8. fall between two stools.** to fail through vacillation between two alternatives. ~*vb.* (*intr.*) **9.** (of a plant) to send up shoots from the base of the stem, rootstock, etc. **10.** to lure wildfowl with a decoy. [OE *stōl*]

stool ball *n.* a game resembling cricket, still played by girls and women in Sussex, England.

stool pigeon *n.* **1.** an informer for the police. **2.** *U.S. sl.* a person acting as a decoy. [C19: from use of pigeon fixed to a stool as a decoy]

stoop¹ (stuːp) *vb.* (*mainly intr.*) **1.** (*also tr.*) to bend (the body) forward and downward. **2.** to carry oneself with head and shoulders habitually bent forward. **3.** (often foll. by *to*) to abase or degrade oneself. **4.** (often foll. by *to*) to condescend; deign. **5.** (of a bird of prey) to swoop down. ~*n.* **6.** the act, position, or characteristic of stooping. **7.** a lowering from a position of dignity or superiority. **8.** a downward swoop, esp. of a bird of prey. [OE *stūpan*] **—'stooping** *adj.*

stoop² (stuːp) *n. U.S.* an open porch or small platform with steps leading up to it at the entrance to a building. [C18: from Du. *stoep,* of Gmc origin]

stop (stɒp) *vb.* **stopping, stopped. 1.** to cease from doing or being (something); discontinue. **2.** to cause (something moving) to halt or (of something moving) to come to a halt. **3.** (*tr.*) to prevent the continuance or completion of. **4.** (*tr.*; often foll. by *from*) to prevent or restrain: *to stop George from fighting.* **5.** (*tr.*) to keep back: *to stop supplies.* **6.** (*tr.*) to intercept or hinder in transit: *to stop a letter.* **7.** (*tr.*; often foll. by *up*) to block or plug, esp. so as to close: *to stop up a pipe.* **8.** (*tr.*; often foll. by *up*) to fill a hole or opening in: *to stop up a wall.* **9.** (*tr.*) to staunch or stem: *to stop a wound.* **10.** (*tr.*) to instruct a bank not to honour (a cheque). **11.** (*tr.*) to deduct (money) from pay. **12.** (*tr.*) *Brit.* to provide with punctuation. **13.** (*tr.*) *Boxing.* to beat (an opponent) by a knockout. **14.** (*tr.*) *Inf.* to receive (a blow, hit, etc.). **15.** (*intr.*) to stay or rest: *we stopped at the Robinsons'.* **16.** (*tr.*) *Rare.* to defeat, beat, or kill. **17.** (*tr.*) *Music.* **a.** to alter the vibrating length of (a string on a violin, guitar, etc.) by pressing down on it at some point with the finger. **b.** to alter the vibrating length of an air column in a wind instrument by closing (a finger hole, etc.). **c.** to produce (a note) in this manner. **18.** *Bridge.* to have a protecting card or winner in (a suit in which one's opponents are strong). **19. stop at nothing.** to be prepared to do anything; be unscrupulous or ruthless. ~*n.* **20.** an arrest of movement or progress. **21.** the act of stopping or the state of being stopped. **22.** a place where something halts or pauses: *a bus stop.* **23.** a stay in or as if in the course of a journey. **24.** the act or an instance of blocking or obstructing. **25.** a plug or stopper. **26.** a block, screw, etc., that prevents, limits, or terminates the motion of a mechanism or moving part. **27.** *Brit.* a punctuation mark, esp. a full stop. **28.** *Music.* **a.** the act of stopping the string, finger hole, etc., of an instrument. **b.** a set of organ pipes or harpsichord strings that may be allowed to sound as a group by muffling or silencing all other such sets. **c.** a knob, lever, or handle on an organ, etc., that is operated to allow sets of pipes to sound. **d.** an analogous device on a harpsichord or other instrument with variable registers, such as an electronic instrument. **29. pull out all the stops. a.** to play at full volume. **b.** to spare no effort. **30.** Also called: **stop consonant.** *Phonetics.* any of a class of consonants articulated by first making a complete closure at some point of the vocal tract and then releasing it abruptly with audible plosion. **31.** Also called: **f-stop.** *Photog.* **a.** a setting of the aperture of a camera lens, calibrated to the corresponding f-number. **b.** another name for **diaphragm** (sense 4). **32.** Also called: **stopper.** *Bridge.* a protecting card or winner in a suit in which one's opponents are strong. ~See also **stop off, stop out, stopover.** [C14: from OE *stoppian* (unattested), as in *forstoppian* to plug the ear, ult. from LL *stuppāre* to stop with tow, from L *stuppa* tow, from Gk *stuppē*] —'**stoppable** *adj.*

stopbank ('stɒpbæŋk) *n. N.Z.* an embankment to prevent flooding.

stop bath *n.* a weakly acidic solution used to stop the action of a developer on a film, plate, or paper before the material is immersed in fixer.

stopcock ('stɒp,kɒk) *n.* a valve used to control or stop the flow of a fluid in a pipe.

stope (stəʊp) *n.* **1.** a steplike excavation made in a mine to extract ore. ~*vb.* **2.** to mine (ore, etc.) in stopes. [C18: prob. from Low G *stope*]

Stopes (stəʊps) *n.* **Marie Carmichael.** 1880–1958, English pioneer of birth control, who established the first birth-control clinic in Britain (1921).

stopgap ('stɒp,gæp) *n.* **a.** a temporary substitute. **b.** (*as modifier*): *a stopgap programme.*

stop-go *adj. Brit.* (of economic policy) characterized by deliberate alternate expansion and contraction of aggregate demand in an effort to curb inflation and eliminate balance-of-payments deficits, and yet maintain full employment.

stoplight ('stɒp,laɪt) *n.* **1.** a red light on a traffic signal indicating that vehicles or pedestrians coming towards it should stop. **2.** another word for **brake light.**

stop off *vb. also* **stop in,** (esp. U.S.) **stop by. 1.** (*intr., adv.;* often foll. by *at*) to halt and call somewhere, as on a visit or errand, esp. en route to another place. ~*n.* **stop-off. 2. a.** a break in a journey. **b.** (*as modifier*): *stopoff point.*

stop out *vb.* (*adv.*) **1.** (*tr.*) to cover (part of the area) of a piece of cloth, printing plate, etc., to prevent it from being dyed, etched, etc. **2.** (*intr.*) to remain out of a house, esp. overnight.

stopover ('stɒp,əʊvə) *n.* **1.** a stopping place on a journey. ~*vb.* **stop over. 2.** (*intr., adv.*) to make a stopover.

stoppage ('stɒpɪdʒ) *n.* **1.** the act of stopping or the state of being stopped. **2.** something that stops or blocks. **3.** a deduction of money, as from pay. **4.** an organized cessation of work, as during a strike.

Stoppard ('stɒpɑːd) *n.* **Tom.** born 1937, British playwright, born in Czechoslovakia: his works include *Rosencrantz and Guildenstern are Dead* (1967), *Jumpers* (1972), *Travesties* (1974), *Night and Day* (1978), and *Hapgood* (1988).

stopped (stɒpt) *adj.* (of a pipe, esp. an organ pipe) closed at one end and thus sounding an octave lower than an open pipe of the same length.

stopper ('stɒpə) *n.* **1.** Also called: **stopple.** a plug or bung for closing a bottle, pipe, duct, etc. **2.** a person or thing that stops or puts an end to something. **3.** *Bridge.* another name for **stop** (sense 32). ~*vb.* **4.** (*tr.*) Also: **stopple.** to close or fit with a stopper.

stopping ('stɒpɪŋ) *n.* **1.** *Brit. inf.* a dental filling. ~*adj.* **2.** *Chiefly Brit.* making many stops in a journey: *a stopping train.*

stop press *n. Brit.* **1.** news items inserted into a newspaper after the printing has been started. **2.** the space regularly left blank for this.

stopwatch ('stɒp,wɒtʃ) *n.* a type of watch used for timing sporting events, etc., accurately, having a device for stopping the hands instantly.

storage ('stɔːrɪdʒ) *n.* **1.** the act of storing or the state of being stored. **2.** space or an area reserved for storing. **3.** a charge made for storing. **4.** *Computers.* **a.** the act or process of storing information in a computer memory or on a disk, etc. **b.** (*as modifier*): *storage capacity.*

storage battery *n.* another name (esp. U.S.) for **accumulator** (sense 1).

storage capacity *n.* the maximum number of bits, bytes, words, etc., that can be held in a memory system such as that of a computer or of the brain.

storage device *n.* a piece of computer equipment, such as a magnetic tape, disk, drum, etc., in or on which information can be stored.

storage heater *n.* an electric device capable of accumulating and radiating heat generated by off-peak electricity.

storax ('stɔːræks) *n.* **1.** any of numerous trees or shrubs of tropical and subtropical regions, having drooping showy white flowers. **2.** a vanilla-scented solid resin obtained from one of these trees, formerly used as incense and in perfumery and medicine. **3.** a liquid aromatic balsam obtained from liquidambar trees and used in perfumery and medicine. [C14: via LL from Gk *sturax*]

store (stɔː) *vb.* **1.** (*tr.*) to keep, set aside, or accumulate for future use. **2.** (*tr.*) to place in a warehouse, depository, etc., for safekeeping. **3.** (*tr.*) to supply, provide, or stock. **4.** (*intr.*) to be put into storage. **5.** *Computers.* to enter or retain (information) in a storage device. ~*n.* **6. a.** an establishment for the retail sale of goods and services. **b.** (*in combination*): *storefront.* **7.** a large supply or stock kept for future use. **8.** short for **department store. 9. a.** a storage place such as a warehouse or depository. **b.** (*in combination*): *storeman.* **10.** the state of being stored (esp. **in in store**). **11.** a large amount or quantity. **12.** *Computers, chiefly Brit.* another name for **memory** (sense 7). **13. in store.** forthcoming or imminent. **14. lay, put,** *or* **set store by.** to value or reckon as important. ~*adj.* **15.** (of cattle, sheep, etc.) bought lean to be fattened up for market. ~See also **stores.** [C13: from OF *estor*, from *estorer* to restore, from L *instaurāre* to refresh] —'**storable** *adj.*

Store Bælt ('sdoːrə 'bɛld) *n.* the Danish name for the **Great Belt.**

storehouse ('stɔː,haʊs) *n.* a place where things are stored.

storekeeper ('stɔː,kiːpə) *n.* a manager, owner, or keeper of a store. —'**store,keeping** *n.*

storeroom ('stɔː,ruːm, -,rʊm) *n.* **1.** a room in which things are stored. **2.** room for storing.

stores (stɔːz) *pl. n.* supply or stock of something, esp. essentials, for a specific purpose.

storey *or U.S.* **story** ('stɔːrɪ) *n., pl.* **-reys** *or* **-ries. 1.** a floor or level of a building. **2.** a set of rooms on one level. [C14: from Anglo-L *historia*, picture, from L: narrative, prob. from the pictures on medieval windows]

Storey ('stɔːrɪ) *n.* **David.** born 1933, British novelist and dramatist. His best-known works include the novel *This Sporting Life* (1960), and the plays *In Celebration* (1969) and *Home* (1970).

storeyed *or U.S.* **storied** ('stɔːrɪd) *adj.* **a.** having a storey or storeys. **b.** (*in combination*): *a two-storeyed house.*

storied ('stɔːrɪd) *adj.* **1.** recorded in history or in a story. **2.** decorated with narrative scenes.

stork (stɔːk) *n.* any of a family of large wading birds, chiefly of warm regions of the Old World, having very long legs and a long stout pointed bill, and typically having a white-and-black plumage. [OE *storc*]

storksbill ('stɔːks,bɪl) *n.* a plant related to the geranium, having pink or reddish-purple flowers and fruits with a beaklike process.

storm (stɔːm) *n.* **1. a.** a violent weather condition of strong winds, rain, hail, thunder, lightning, blowing sand, snow, etc. **b.** (*as modifier*): *storm cloud.* **c.** (*in combination*): *stormproof.* **2.** *Meteorol.* a wind of force 10 on the Beaufort scale, reaching speeds of 55 to 63 mph. **3.** a violent disturbance or quarrel. **4.** a direct assault on a stronghold. **5.** a heavy discharge or rain, as of bullets or missiles. **6.** short for **storm window. 7. storm in a tea-cup.** *Brit.* a violent fuss or disturbance over a trivial matter. **8. take by storm. a.** to capture or overrun by a violent assault. **b.** to overwhelm and enthral. ~*vb.* **9.** to attack or capture (something) suddenly and violently. **10.** (*intr.*) to be vociferously angry. **11.** (*intr.*) to move or rush violently or angrily. **12.** (*intr.; with it as subject*) to rain, hail, or snow hard and be very windy, often with thunder and lightning. [OE]

stormbound ('stɔːm‚baʊnd) *adj.* detained or harassed by storms.

storm centre *n.* **1.** the centre of a cyclonic storm, etc., where pressure is lowest. **2.** the centre of any disturbance or trouble.

storm cloud *n.* **1.** a heavy dark cloud presaging rain or a storm. **2.** a herald of disturbance, anger, etc.: *the storm clouds of war.*

storm-cock *n.* another name for **mistle thrush.**

storm cone *n. Brit.* a canvas cone hoisted as a warning of high winds.

storm door *n.* an additional door outside an ordinary door, providing extra insulation against wind, cold, rain, etc.

storm lantern *n.* another name for **hurricane lamp.**

storm trooper *n.* **1.** a member of the Nazi SA. **2.** a member of a force of shock troops.

storm window *n.* **1.** an additional window fitted outside an ordinary window to provide insulation against wind, cold, rain, etc. **2.** a type of dormer window.

stormy ('stɔːmɪ) *adj.* **stormier, stormiest. 1.** characterized by storms. **2.** involving or characterized by violent disturbance or emotional outburst. —'**stormily** *adv.* —'**storminess** *n.*

stormy petrel *n.* **1.** Also called: **storm petrel.** any of various small petrels typically having dark plumage and paler underparts. **2.** a person who brings or portends trouble.

Stornoway ('stɔːnə‚weɪ) *n.* a port in NW Scotland, on the E coast of Lewis in the Outer Hebrides, administrative centre of the Western Isles. Pop.: 8660 (1981).

Storting *or* **Storthing** ('stɔːtɪŋ) *n.* the parliament of Norway. [C19: Norwegian, from *stor* great + *thing* assembly]

story[1] ('stɔːrɪ) *n., pl.* **-ries. 1.** a narration of a chain of events told or written in prose or verse. **2.** Also called: **short story.** a piece of fiction, briefer and usually less detailed than a novel. **3.** Also called: **story line.** the plot of a book, film, etc. **4.** an event that could be the subject of a narrative. **5.** a report or statement on a matter or event. **6.** the event or material for such a report. **7.** *Inf.* a lie, fib, or untruth. **8. cut** (*or* **make**) **a long story short.** to leave out details in a narration. **9. the same old story.** *Inf.* the familiar or regular course of events. **10. the story goes.** it is commonly said or believed. ~*vb.* **-rying, -ried.** (*tr.*) **11.** to decorate (a pot, wall, etc.) with scenes from history or legends. [C13: from Anglo-F *estorie,* from L *historia;* see HISTORY]

story[2] ('stɔːrɪ) *n., pl.* **-ries.** another spelling (esp. U.S.) of **storey.**

storyboard ('stɔːrɪ‚bɔːd) *n.* (in films, television, etc.) a series of sketches or photographs showing the sequence of shots or images planned for a film.

storybook ('stɔːrɪ‚bʊk) *n.* **1.** a book containing stories, esp. for children. ~*adj.* **2.** unreal or fantastic: *a story-book world.*

storyteller ('stɔːrɪ‚tɛlə) *n.* **1.** a person who tells stories. **2.** *Inf.* a liar. —'**story‚telling** *n.*

stoup *or* **stoop** (stuːp) *n.* **1.** a small basin for holy water. **2.** *Dialect.* a bucket or cup. [C14 (in the sense: bucket): from ON]

Stourbridge ('staʊə‚brɪdʒ) *n.* an industrial town in W central England, in the West Midlands. Pop.: 54 661 (1981).

stoush (staʊʃ) *Austral. & N.Z. sl.* ~*vb.* **1.** (*tr.*) to hit or punch. ~*n.* **2.** fighting, violence, or a fight. [C19: from ?]

stout (staʊt) *adj.* **1.** solidly built or corpulent. **2.** (*prenominal*) resolute or valiant: *stout fellow.* **3.** strong, substantial, and robust. **4. a stout heart.** courage; resolution. ~*n.* **5.** strong porter highly flavoured with malt. [C14: from OF *estout* bold, of Gmc origin] —'**stoutly** *adv.* —'**stoutness** *n.*

Stout (staʊt) *n.* Sir **Robert.** 1844–1930, New Zealand statesman, born in Scotland: prime minister of New Zealand (1884–87).

stouthearted (‚staʊt'hɑːtɪd) *adj.* valiant; brave. —‚stout'**heartedly** *adv.* —‚stout'**heartedness** *n.*

stove[1] (stəʊv) *n.* **1.** another word for **cooker** (sense 1). **2.** any heating apparatus, such as a kiln. [OE *stofa* bathroom]

stove[2] (stəʊv) *vb.* a past tense and past participle of **stave.**

stove enamel *n.* a type of enamel made heatproof by treatment in a stove.

stovepipe ('stəʊv‚paɪp) *n.* **1.** a pipe that serves as a flue to a stove. **2.** Also called: **stovepipe hat.** a man's tall silk hat.

stow (stəʊ) *vb.* (*tr.*) **1.** (often foll. by *away*) to pack or store. **2.** to fill by packing. **3.** *Naut.* to pack or put away (cargo, sails, etc.). **4.** to have enough room for. **5.** (*usually imperative*) *Brit. sl.* to cease from: *stow your noise!* [OE *stōwian* to keep, from *stōw* a place]

Stow (stəʊ) *n.* **John.** 1525–1605, English antiquary, noted for his *Survey of London and Westminster* (1598; 1603).

stowage ('stəʊɪdʒ) *n.* **1.** space, room, or a charge for stowing goods. **2.** the act or an instance of stowing or the state of being stowed. **3.** something that is stowed.

stowaway ('stəʊə‚weɪ) *n.* **1.** a person who hides aboard a vehicle, ship, or aircraft in order to gain free passage. ~*vb.* **stow away. 2.** (*intr., adv.*) to travel in such a way.

Stowe (stəʊ) *n.* **Harriet Elizabeth Beecher.** 1811–96, U.S. writer, whose best-selling novel *Uncle Tom's Cabin* (1852) contributed to the antislavery cause.

STP *abbrev. for:* **1.** Professor of Sacred Theology. [from L: *Sanctae Theologiae Professor*] **2.** *Trademark.* scientifically treated petroleum: an oil substitute promising renewed power for an internal-combustion engine. **3.** standard temperature and pressure. ~*n.* **4.** a synthetic hallucinogenic drug related to mescaline. [from humorous reference to the extra power resulting from scientifically treated petroleum]

strabismus (strə'bɪzməs) *n.* abnormal alignment of one or both eyes, characterized by a turning inwards or outwards from the nose: caused by paralysis of an eye muscle, etc. Also called: **squint.** [C17: via NL from Gk *strabismos,* from *strabizein* to squint, from *strabos* cross-eyed] —**stra'bismal, stra'bismic,** *or* **stra'bismical** *adj.*

Strabo ('streɪbəʊ) *n.* ?63 B.C.–?23 A.D., Greek geographer and historian, noted for his *Geographica.*

Strachey ('streɪtʃɪ) *n.* **(Giles) Lytton.** 1880–1932, English biographer and critic, best known for *Eminent Victorians* (1918) and *Queen Victoria* (1921).

straddle ('strædᵊl) *vb.* **1.** (*tr.*) to have one leg, part, or support on each side of. **2.** (*tr.*) *U.S. & Canad. inf.* to be in favour of both sides of (something). **3.** (*intr.*) to stand, walk, or sit with the legs apart. **4.** (*tr.*) to spread (the legs) apart. **5.** *Gunnery.* to fire a number of shots slightly beyond and slightly short of (a target) to determine the correct range. **6.** (*intr.*) (in poker, of the second player after the dealer) to double the ante before looking at one's cards. ~*n.* **7.** the act or position of straddling. **8.** a noncommittal attitude or stand. **9.** *Stock Exchange.* a contract or option permitting its purchaser either to sell securities to or buy securities from the maker of the contract within a specified period of time. **10.** *Athletics.* a high-jumping technique in which the body is parallel with the bar and the legs straddle it at the highest point of the jump. **11.** (in poker) the stake put up after the ante in poker by the second player after the dealer. [C16: from obs. *strad-* (OE *strode*), past stem of STRIDE] —'**straddler** *n.*

Stradivari (‚strædɪ'vɑːrɪ) *n.* **Antonio** (an'tɔːnjo). ?1644–1737, Italian violin, viola, and cello maker.

Stradivarius (‚strædɪ'vɛərɪəs) *n.* any of a number of violins manufactured by Antonio Stradivari or his family. Often shortened to (informal) **Strad.**

strafe (streɪf, strɑːf) *vb.* (*tr.*) **1.** to machine-gun (troops, etc.) from the air. **2.** *Sl.* to punish harshly. ~*n.* **3.** an act or instance of strafing. [C20: from G *strafen* to punish] —'**strafer** *n.*

Strafford ('stræfəd) *n.* **Thomas Wentworth,** Earl of. 1593–1641, English statesman. As lord deputy of Ireland (1632–39) and a chief adviser to Charles I, he was a leading proponent of the king's absolutist rule. He was impeached by Parliament and executed.

straggle ('strægᵊl) *vb.* (*intr.*) **1.** to go, come, or spread in a rambling or irregular way. **2.** to linger behind or wander from a main line or part. [C14: from ?] —**'strag- gler** n. —**'straggly** adj.

straight (streɪt) adj. **1.** not curved or crooked; continuing in the same direction without deviating. **2.** straightforward, outright, or candid: *a straight rejection.* **3.** even, level, or upright. **4.** in keeping with the facts; accurate. **5.** honest, respectable, or reliable. **6.** accurate or logical: *straight reasoning.* **7.** continuous; uninterrupted. **8.** (esp. of an alcoholic drink) undiluted; neat. **9.** not crisp, kinked, or curly: *straight hair.* **10.** correctly arranged; orderly. **11.** (of a play, acting style, etc.) straightforward or serious. **12.** *Boxing.* (of a blow) delivered with an unbent arm: *a straight left.* **13.** (of the cylinders of an internal-combustion engine) in line, rather than in a V-formation or in some other arrangement: *a straight eight.* **14.** a slang word for **heterosexual. 15.** *Inf.* no longer owing or being owed something: *if you buy the next round we'll be straight.* **16.** *Sl.* conventional in views, customs, appearance, etc. **17.** *Sl.* not using narcotics. ~*adv.* **18.** in a straight line or direct course. **19.** immediately; at once: *he came straight back.* **20.** in an even, level, or upright position. **21.** without cheating, lying, or unreliability: *tell it to me straight.* **22.** continuously; uninterruptedly. **23.** (often foll. by *out*) frankly; candidly: *he told me straight out.* **24. go straight.** *Inf.* to reform after having been dishonest or a criminal. ~n. **25.** the state of being straight. **26.** a straight line, form, part, or position. **27.** *Brit.* a straight part of a racetrack. **28.** *Poker.* **a.** five cards that are in sequence irrespective of suit. **b.** a hand containing such a sequence. **c.** (*as modifier*): *a straight flush.* **29.** *Sl.* a conventional person. **30.** a slang word for a **heterosexual. 31.** *Sl.* a cigarette containing only tobacco, without marijuana, etc. [C14: from p.p. of OE *streccan* to stretch] —**'straightly** adv. —**'straightness** n.

straight and narrow n. *Inf.* the proper, honest, and moral path of behaviour.

straight angle n. an angle of 180°.

straightaway adv. (ˌstreɪtəˈweɪ). also **straight away. 1.** at once. ~n. (ˈstreɪtəˌweɪ). **2.** the U.S. word for **straight** (sense 27).

straight chair n. a straight-backed side chair.

straightedge (ˈstreɪtˌɛdʒ) n. a stiff strip of wood or metal with one edge straight, used for ruling and testing straight lines.

straighten (ˈstreɪtᵊn) vb. (sometimes foll. by *up* or *out*) **1.** to make or become straight. **2.** (tr.) to make neat or tidy. —**'straightener** n.

straighten out vb. (adv.) **1.** to make or become less complicated or confused. **2.** *U.S. & Canad.* to reform or become reformed.

straight face n. a serious facial expression, esp. one that conceals the impulse to laugh. —**'straight-'faced** adj.

straight fight n. a contest between two candidates only.

straight flush n. (in poker) five consecutive cards of the same suit.

straightforward (ˌstreɪtˈfɔːwəd) adj. **1.** (of a person) honest, frank, or simple. **2.** *Chiefly Brit.* (of a task, etc.) simple; easy. ~adv., adj. **3.** in a straight course. —ˌstraight'forwardly adv. —ˌstraight'forwardness n.

straightjacket (ˈstreɪtˌdʒækɪt) n. a less common spelling of **straitjacket.**

straight-laced adj. a variant spelling of **strait-laced.**

straight man n. a subsidiary actor who acts as stooge to a comedian.

straight-out adj. *U.S. inf.* **1.** complete; thoroughgoing. **2.** frank or honest.

straight razor n. another name for **cutthroat** (sense 2).

straightway (ˈstreɪtˌweɪ) adv. *Arch.* at once.

strain[1] (streɪn) vb. **1.** to draw or be drawn taut; stretch tight. **2.** to exert, tax, or use (resources) to the utmost extent. **3.** to injure or damage or be injured or damaged by overexertion: *he strained himself.* **4.** to deform or be deformed as a result of a stress. **5.** (intr.) to make intense or violent efforts; strive. **6.** to subject or be subjected to mental tension or stress. **7.** to pour or pass (a substance) or (of a substance) to be poured or passed through a sieve, filter, or strainer. **8.** (tr.) to draw off or remove (one part of a substance or mixture from another) by or as if by filtering. **9.** (tr.) to clasp tightly; hug. **10.** (intr.; foll. by *at*) to push, pull, or work with violent exertion (upon). ~n. **11.** the act or an instance of straining. **12.** the damage resulting from excessive exertion. **13.** an intense physical or mental effort. **14.** (often pl.) *Music.* a

theme, melody, or tune. **15.** a great demand on the emotions, resources, etc. **16.** a way of speaking; tone of voice: *don't go on in that strain.* **17.** tension or tiredness resulting from overwork, worry, etc.; stress. **18.** *Physics.* the change in dimension of a body under load expressed as the ratio of the total deflection or change in dimension to the original unloaded dimension. [C13: from OF *estreindre* to press together, from L *stringere* to bind tightly]

strain[2] (streɪn) n. **1.** the main body of descendants from one ancestor. **2.** a group of organisms within a species or variety, distinguished by one or more minor characteristics. **3.** a variety of bacterium or fungus, esp. one used for a culture. **4.** a streak; trace. **5.** *Arch.* a kind, type, or sort. [OE *strēon*]

strained (streɪnd) adj. **1.** (of an action, expression, etc.) not natural or spontaneous. **2.** (of an atmosphere, relationship, etc.) not relaxed; tense.

strainer (ˈstreɪnə) n. **1.** a sieve used for straining sauces, vegetables, tea, etc. **2.** a gauze or simple filter used to strain liquids.

strait (streɪt) n. **1.** (often pl.) a narrow channel of the sea linking two larger areas of sea. **2.** (often pl.) a position of acute difficulty (often in **in dire** or **desperate straits**). **3.** *Arch.* a narrow place or passage. ~adj. **4.** *Arch.* (of spaces, etc.) affording little room. [C13: from OF *estreit* narrow, from L *strictus* constricted, from *stringere* to bind tightly] —**'straitly** adv. —**'straitness** n.

straiten (ˈstreɪtᵊn) vb. **1.** (tr.; usually passive) to embarrass or distress, esp. financially. **2.** (tr.) to limit, confine, or restrict. **3.** *Arch.* to make or become narrow.

straitjacket (ˈstreɪtˌdʒækɪt) n. **1.** Also: **straightjacket.** a jacket made of strong canvas material with long sleeves for binding the arms of violent prisoners or mental patients. **2.** a restriction or limitation. ~vb. **3.** (tr.) to confine in or as if in a straitjacket.

strait-laced or **straight-laced** adj. prudish or puritanical.

Straits Settlements (streɪts) n. (formerly) a British crown colony of SE Asia that included Singapore, Penang, Malacca, Labuan, and some smaller islands.

strake (streɪk) n. **1. a.** a curved metal plate forming part of the metal rim on a wooden wheel. **b.** any metal plate let into a rubber tyre. **2.** Also called: **streak.** *Naut.* one of a continuous range of planks or plates forming the side of a vessel. [C14: rel. to OE *streccan* to stretch]

Stralsund (German ˈʃtraːlzʊnt) n. a port in N East Germany, on a strait of the Baltic: one of the leading towns of the Hanseatic League. Pop.: 75 070 (1981 est.).

stramonium (strəˈməʊnɪəm) n. **1.** a preparation of the dried leaves and flowers of the thorn apple, containing hyoscyamine and used as a drug to treat nervous disorders. **2.** another name for **thorn apple** (sense 1). [C17: from NL, from ?]

strand[1] (strænd) vb. **1.** to leave or drive (ships, fish, etc.) aground or ashore or (of ships, etc.) to be left or driven ashore. **2.** (tr.; usually passive) to leave helpless, as without transport, money, etc. ~n. **3.** *Chiefly poetic.* a shore or beach. [OE]

strand[2] (strænd) n. **1.** a set of or one of the individual fibres or threads of string, wire, etc., that form a rope, cable, etc. **2.** a single length of string, hair, wool, wire, etc. **3.** a string of pearls or beads. **4.** a constituent element of something. ~vb. **5.** (tr.) to form (a rope, cable, etc.) by winding strands together. [C15: from ?]

Strand (strænd) n. **the.** a street in W central London, parallel to the Thames: famous for its hotels and theatres.

strange (streɪndʒ) adj. **1.** odd, unusual, and extraordinary; peculiar. **2.** not known, seen, or experienced before; unfamiliar. **3.** not easily explained. **4.** (usually foll. by *to*) inexperienced (in) or unaccustomed (to): *strange to a task.* **5.** not of one's own kind, locality, etc.; alien; foreign. **6.** shy; distant; reserved. **7. strange to say.** it is unusual or surprising (that). ~adv. **8.** *Not standard.* in a strange manner. [C13: from OF *estrange*, from L *extrāneus* foreign; see EXTRANEOUS] —**'strangely** adv.

strangeness (ˈstreɪndʒnɪs) n. **1.** the state or quality of being strange. **2.** *Physics.* a property of certain elementary particles characterized by a quantum number (**strangeness number**) conserved in strong but not in weak interactions.

strange particle n. *Physics.* an elementary particle having a nonzero strangeness number.

stranger ('streɪndʒə) n. **1.** any person whom one does not know. **2.** a person who is new to a particular locality, from another region, town, etc. **3.** a guest or visitor. **4.** (foll. by *to*) a person who is unfamiliar (with) or new (to) something: *he is no stranger to computers.*

strangle ('stræŋgᵊl) vb. (tr.) **1.** to kill by compressing the windpipe; throttle. **2.** to prevent or inhibit the growth or development of: *to strangle originality.* **3.** to suppress (an utterance) by or as if by swallowing suddenly: *to strangle a cry.* ~See also **strangles.** [C13: via OF, ult. from Gk *strangalē* a halter] —'**strangler** n.

stranglehold ('stræŋgᵊl,həʊld) n. **1.** a wrestling hold in which a wrestler's arms are pressed against his opponent's windpipe. **2.** complete power or control over a person or situation.

strangles ('stræŋgᵊlz) n. (functioning as sing.) an acute infectious bacterial disease of horses, characterized by inflammation of the respiratory tract. Also called: **equine distemper.**

strangulate ('stræŋgjʊ,leɪt) vb. (tr.) **1.** to constrict (a hollow organ, vessel, etc.) so as to stop the flow of air, blood, etc., through it. **2.** another word for **strangle.** —,**strangu'lation** n.

strangury ('stræŋgjʊrɪ) n. Pathol. painful excretion of urine, drop by drop. [C14: from L *stranguria*, from Gk, from *stranx* a drop squeezed out + *ouron* urine]

Stranraer (stræn'rɑː) n. a market town in SW Scotland, in W Dumfries and Galloway region: fishing port with a steamer service to Northern Ireland. Pop.: 10 170 (1984 est.).

strap (stræp) n. **1.** a long strip of leather or similar material, for binding trunks, baggage, etc. **2.** a strip of leather or similar material used for carrying, lifting, or holding. **3.** a loop of leather, rubber, etc., suspended from the roof in a bus or train for standing passengers to hold on to. **4.** a razor strop. **5.** short for **shoulder strap. 6. the strap.** a beating with a strap as a punishment. ~vb. **strapping, strapped.** (tr.) **7.** to tie or bind with a strap. **8.** to beat with a strap. **9.** to sharpen with a strap or strop. [C16: var. of STROP]

straphanger ('stræp,hæŋə) n. Inf. a passenger in a bus, train, etc., who has to travel standing, esp. holding on to a strap. —'**strap,hanging** n.

strapping ('stræpɪŋ) adj. (prenominal) tall and sturdy. [C17: from STRAP (in the arch. sense: to work vigorously)]

strap work n. Archit. decorative work resembling interlacing straps.

Strasbourg (French strasbur; English 'stræzbɜːg) n. a city in NE France, on the Rhine: the chief French inland port; under German rule (1870–1918); university (1567); seat of the Council of Europe and of the European Parliament. Pop.: 252 300 (1983 est.). German name: **Strassburg** ('ʃtraːsburk).

strata ('strɑːtə) n. a plural of **stratum.**

▷ **Usage.** In careful usage, *strata* is the standard plural of *stratum* and is not treated as singular.

stratagem ('strætɪdʒəm) n. a plan or trick, esp. to deceive an enemy. [C15: ult. from Gk *stratēgos* a general, from *stratos* an army + *agein* to lead]

strategic (strə'tiːdʒɪk) or **strategical** adj. **1.** of or characteristic of strategy. **2.** important to strategy. **3.** (of weapons, esp. missiles) directed against an enemy's homeland rather than used on a battlefield. Cf. **tactical.** —**stra'tegically** adv.

strategics (strə'tiːdʒɪks) n. (functioning as sing.) strategy, esp. in a military sense.

strategist ('strætɪdʒɪst) n. a specialist or expert in strategy.

strategy ('strætɪdʒɪ) n., pl. **-gies. 1.** the art or science of the planning and conduct of a war. **2.** a particular longterm plan for success, esp. in politics, business, etc. **3.** a plan or stratagem. [C17: from F *stratégie*, from Gk *stratēgia* function of a general; see STRATAGEM]

Stratford-on-Avon or **Stratford-upon-Avon** ('strætfəd) n. a market town in central England, in SW Warwickshire on the River Avon: the birthplace and burial place of William Shakespeare and home of the Royal Shakespeare Company; tourist centre. Pop.: 20 858 (1981).

strath (stræθ) n. Scot. a flat river valley. [C16: from Scot. & Irish Gaelic *srath*]

Strathclyde (,stræθ'klaɪd) n. a local government region in W Scotland, formed in 1975 from Glasgow, Renfrewshire, Lanarkshire, Buteshire, Dunbartonshire, and parts

of Argyllshire, Ayrshire, and Stirlingshire. Administrative centre: Glasgow. Pop.: 2 344 585 (1986 est.). Area: 13 727 sq. km (5300 sq. miles).

strathspey (,stræθ'speɪ) n. **1.** a Scottish dance with gliding steps, slower than a reel. **2.** a piece of music composed for or in the rhythm of this dance. [after *Strathspey*, valley of the river Spey]

strati- combining form. indicating stratum or strata: *stratigraphy.*

straticulate (strə'tɪkjʊlɪt, -,leɪt) adj. (of a rock formation) composed of very thin even strata. [C19: from NL *strāticulum* (unattested), dim. of L *strātum* something strewn; see STRATUS] —**stra,ticu'lation** n.

stratify ('strætɪ,faɪ) vb. **-fying, -fied. 1.** to form or be formed in layers or strata. **2.** Sociol. to divide (a society) into status groups or (of a society) to develop such groups. [C17: from F *stratifier*, from NL *stratificāre*, from L STRATUM] —,**stratifi'cation** n. —'**strati,fied** adj.

stratigraphy (strə'tɪgrəfɪ) n. **1.** the study of the composition, relative positions, etc., of rock strata in order to determine their geological history. **2.** Archaeol. a vertical section through the earth showing the relative positions of the human artefacts and therefore the chronology of successive levels of occupation. —**stratigraphic** (,strætɪ'græfɪk) or ,**strati'graphical** adj.

stratocumulus (,strætəʊ'kjuːmjʊləs) n., pl. **-li** (-,laɪ). Meteorol. a uniform stretch of cloud containing dark grey globular masses.

stratopause ('strætə,pɔːz) n. Meteorol. the transitional zone of maximum temperature between the stratosphere and the mesosphere.

stratosphere ('strætə,sfɪə) n. the atmospheric layer lying between the troposphere and the mesosphere, in which temperature generally increases with height. —**stratospheric** (,strætə'sfɛrɪk) or ,**strato'spherical** adj.

stratum ('strɑːtəm) n., pl. **-ta** or **-tums. 1.** (usually pl.) any of the distinct layers into which sedimentary rocks are divided. **2.** Biol. a single layer of tissue or cells. **3.** a layer of any material, esp. one of several parallel layers. **4.** a layer of ocean or atmosphere either naturally or arbitrarily demarcated. **5.** a level of a social hierarchy. [C16: via NL from L: something strewn, from *sternere* to scatter] —'**stratal** adj.

stratus ('streɪtəs) n., pl. **-ti** (-taɪ). a grey layer cloud. [C19: via NL from L: strewn, from *sternere* to extend]

Straus (straus) n. Oscar ('ɔskar). 1870–1954, French composer, born in Austria, noted for such operettas as *Waltz Dream* (1907) and *The Chocolate Soldier* (1908).

Strauss (straus; German ʃtraus) n. **1. David Friedrich** ('daːfɪt 'friːdrɪç). 1808–74, German Protestant theologian: in his *Life of Jesus* (1835–36) he treated the supernatural elements of the story as myth. **2. Johann** (joʊ'han). 1804–49, Austrian composer, noted for his waltzes. **3.** his son, **Johann,** called the *Waltz King*. 1825–99, Austrian composer, whose works include *The Blue Danube Waltz* (1867) and the operetta *Die Fledermaus* (1874). **4. Richard** ('rɪçart). 1864–1949, German composer, noted esp. for his symphonic poems, including *Don Juan* (1889) and *Till Eulenspiegel* (1895), his operas, such as *Elektra* (1909) and *Der Rosenkavalier* (1911), and his *Four Last Songs* (1948).

Stravinsky (Russian stra'vinskij) n. **Igor Fyodorovich** ('iːgɔr 'fjɔːdərəvɪtʃ). 1882–1971, U.S. composer, born in Russia. He created ballet scores, such as *The Firebird* (1910), *Petrushka* (1911), and *The Rite of Spring* (1913), for Diaghilev. These were followed by neoclassical works, including *Oedipus Rex* (1927) and the *Symphony of Psalms* (1930). The 1950s saw him reconciled to serial techniques, which he employed in such works as the *Canticum Sacrum* (1955), the ballet *Agon* (1957), and *Requiem Canticles* (1966).

straw (strɔː) n. **1. a.** stalks of threshed grain, esp. of wheat, rye, oats, or barley, used in plaiting hats, baskets, etc., or as fodder. **b.** (as modifier): *a straw hat.* **2.** a single dry or ripened stalk, esp. of a grass. **3.** a long thin hollow paper or plastic tube, used for sucking up liquids into the mouth. **4.** (usually used with a negative) anything of little value or importance: *I wouldn't give a straw for our chances.* **5.** a measure or remedy that one turns to in desperation (esp. in **clutch** or **grasp at a straw** or **straws**). **6. a.** a pale yellow colour. **b.** (as adj.): *straw hair.* **7. draw the short straw.** to be the person to whom an unpleasant task falls. **8. straw in the wind.** a hint or indication. **9. the last straw.** a small incident, setback, etc., that coming after others proves insufferable. [OE *streaw*] —'**strawy** *adj.*

strawberry ('strɔ:bəri, -bri) *n., pl.* **-ries. 1.** any of various low-growing rosaceous plants which have red edible fruits and spread by runners. **2. a.** the fruit of any of these plants, consisting of a sweet fleshy receptacle bearing small seedlike parts (the true fruits). **b.** (*as modifier*): *strawberry ice cream.* **3. a.** a purplish-red colour. **b.** (*as adj.*): *strawberry shoes.* [OE *strawberige;* ?from the strawlike appearance of the runners]

strawberry blonde *adj.* **1.** (of hair) reddish blonde. ~*n.* **2.** a woman with such hair.

strawberry mark *n.* a soft vascular red birthmark. Also called: **strawberry.**

strawberry tomato *n.* **1.** a tropical annual plant having bell-shaped whitish-yellow flowers and small edible round yellow berries. **2.** the fruit of this plant, eaten fresh or made into preserves or pickles. ~Also called: **Cape gooseberry.**

strawberry tree *n.* a S European evergreen tree having white or pink flowers and red strawberry-like berries. See also **arbutus.**

strawboard ('strɔ:,bɔ:d) *n.* a board made of compressed straw and adhesive.

strawflower ('strɔ:,flaʊə) *n.* an Australian plant in which the coloured bracts retain their colour when the plant is dried. See also **immortelle.**

straw man *n. Chiefly U.S.* **1.** a figure of a man made from straw. **2.** a person of little substance. **3.** a person used as a cover for some dubious plan or enterprise.

straw poll *or esp. U.S., Canad., & N.Z.* **vote** *n.* an unofficial poll or vote taken to determine the opinion of a group or the public on some issue.

stray (streɪ) *vb.* (*intr.*) **1.** to wander away, as from the correct path or from a given area. **2.** to wander haphazardly. **3.** to digress from the point, lose concentration, etc. **4.** to deviate from certain moral standards. ~*n.* **5. a.** a domestic animal, fowl, etc., that has wandered away from its place of keeping and is lost. **b.** (*as modifier*): *stray dogs.* **6.** a lost or homeless person, esp. a child: *waifs and strays.* **7.** an occurrence, specimen, etc., that is out of place or outside the usual pattern. ~*adj.* **8.** scattered, random, or haphazard. [C14: from OF *estraier*, from Vulgar L *estragāre* (unattested), from L *extrā-* outside + *vagāri* to roam] —'**strayer** *n.*

strays (streɪz) *pl. n.* **1.** Also called: **stray capacitance.** *Electronics.* undesired capacitance in equipment. **2.** another word for **static** (sense 8).

streak (stri:k) *n.* **1.** a long thin mark, stripe, or trace of some contrasting colour. **2.** (of lightning) a sudden flash. **3.** an element or trace, as of some quality or characteristic. **4.** a strip, vein, or layer. **5.** a short stretch or run, esp. of good or bad luck. **6.** *Inf.* an act or the practice of running naked through a public place. ~*vb.* **7.** (*tr.*) to mark or daub with a streak or streaks. **8.** (*intr.*) to form streaks or become streaked. **9.** (*intr.*) to move rapidly in a straight line. **10.** (*intr.*) *Inf.* to run naked through a public place in order to shock or amuse. [OE *strica*] —**streaked** *adj.* —'**streaker** *n.* —'**streak,like** *adj.*

streaky ('stri:kɪ) *adj.* **streakier, streakiest. 1.** marked with streaks. **2.** occurring in streaks. **3.** (of bacon) having alternate layers of meat and fat. **4.** of varying or uneven quality. —'**streakiness** *n.*

stream (stri:m) *n.* **1.** a small river; brook. **2.** any steady flow of water or other fluid. **3.** something that resembles a stream in moving continuously in a line or particular direction. **4.** a rapid or unbroken flow of speech, etc.: *a stream of abuse.* **5.** *Brit.* any of several parallel classes of schoolchildren, or divisions of children within a class, grouped together because of similar ability. **6. go** (*or* **drift**) **with the stream.** to conform to the accepted standards. **7. on** (*or* **off**) **stream.** (of an industrial plant, manufacturing process, etc.) in (*or* not in) operation or production. ~*vb.* **8.** to emit or be emitted in a continuous flow: *his nose streamed blood.* **9.** (*intr.*) to move in unbroken succession, as a crowd of people, vehicles, etc. **10.** (*intr.*) to float freely or with a waving motion: *bunting streamed in the wind.* **11.** (*tr.*) to unfurl (a flag, etc.). **12.** *Brit. education.* to group or divide (children) in streams. [OE] —'**streamlet** *n.*

streamer ('stri:mə) *n.* **1.** a long narrow flag or part of a flag. **2.** a long narrow coiled ribbon of coloured paper

that becomes unrolled when tossed. **3.** a stream of light, esp. one appearing in some forms of the aurora. **4.** *Journalism.* a large heavy headline printed across the width of a page. **5.** *Computers.* an electromechanical device that enables a hard disk to copy data byte by byte onto magnetic tape for security or storage.

streamline ('stri:m,laɪn) *n.* **1.** a contour on a body that offers the minimum resistance to a gas or liquid flowing around it. ~*vb.* **2.** (*tr.*) to make streamlined.

streamlined ('stri:m,laɪnd) *adj.* **1.** offering or designed to offer the minimum resistance to the flow of a gas or liquid. **2.** made more efficient, esp. by simplifying.

stream of consciousness *n.* **1.** *Psychol.* the continuous flow of ideas, thoughts, and feelings forming the content of an individual's consciousness. **2.** a literary technique that reveals the flow of thoughts and feelings of characters through long passages of soliloquy.

streamy ('stri:mɪ) *adj.* **streamier, streamiest.** *Chiefly poetic.* **1.** (of an area, land, etc.) having many streams. **2.** flowing or streaming.

street (stri:t) *n.* **1. a.** a public road that is usually lined with buildings, esp. in a town: *Oxford Street.* **b.** (*as modifier*): *a street directory.* **2.** the buildings lining a street. **3.** the part of the road between the pavements, used by vehicles. **4.** the people living, working, etc., in a particular street. **5.** (*modifier*) of or relating to the urban counterculture. **6. man in the street.** an ordinary or average citizen. **7. on the streets. a.** earning a living as a prostitute. **b.** homeless. **8. (right) up one's street.** *Inf.* (just) what one knows or likes best. **9. streets ahead of.** *Inf.* superior to, more advanced than, etc. **10. streets apart.** *Inf.* markedly different. [OE *strǣt*, from L *via strāta* paved way (*strāta*, from *strātus*, p.p. of *sternere* to stretch out)]

street Arab *n.* a homeless child, esp. one who survives by begging and stealing; urchin.

streetcar ('stri:t,kɑː) *n.* the usual U.S. and Canad. name for **tram** (sense 1).

street credibility *n.* a command of the style, knowledge, etc., associated with urban counter-culture. Sometimes shortened to **street cred.** —,**street-'credible** *adj.*

street cry *n.* (*often pl.*) the cry of a street hawker.

street value *n.* the monetary worth of a commodity, usually an illicit one, considered as the price it would fetch when sold to the ultimate user.

streetwalker ('stri:t,wɔ:kə) *n.* a prostitute who solicits on the streets. —'**street,walking** *n., adj.*

streetwise ('stri:t,waɪz) *adj.* adept at surviving in an urban, poor, and often criminal environment.

Streisand ('straɪsænd) *n.* **Barbra.** born 1942, U.S. singer and film actress: her films include *Funny Girl* (1968), *A Star is born* (1976), and *Yentl* (1983).

strelitzia (strɛ'lɪtsɪə) *n.* any of various southern African perennial herbaceous plants, cultivated for their showy flowers: includes the bird-of-paradise flower. [C18: after Charlotte of Mecklenburg-*Strelitz* (1744–1818), queen of Great Britain & Ireland]

strength (strɛŋθ) *n.* **1.** the state or quality of being physically or mentally strong. **2.** the ability to withstand or exert great force, stress, or pressure. **3.** something regarded as beneficial or a source of power: *their chief strength is technology.* **4.** potency, as of a drink, drug, etc. **5.** power to convince; cogency: *the strength of an argument.* **6.** degree of intensity or concentration of colour, light, sound, flavour, etc. **7.** the full or part of the full complement as specified: *at full strength; below strength.* **8. from strength to strength.** with ever-increasing success. **9. in strength.** in large numbers. **10. on the strength of.** on the basis of or relying upon. **11. the strength of.** *Austral. & N.Z. inf.* the essential facts about. [OE *strengthu*]

strengthen ('strɛŋθən) *vb.* to make or become stronger. —'**strengthener** *n.*

strenuous ('strɛnjʊəs) *adj.* **1.** requiring or involving the use of great energy or effort. **2.** characterized by great activity, effort, or endeavour. [C16: from L *strēnuus* brisk] —'**strenuously** *adv.* —'**strenuousness** *n.*

strep (strɛp) *n. Inf.* short for **streptococcus.**

streptoso (,strɛpɪ'taʊsəʊ) *adv. Music.* boisterously. [It.]

strepto- *combining form.* **1.** indicating a shape resembling a twisted chain: *streptococcus.* **2.** indicating streptococcus. [from Gk *streptos* twisted, from *strephein* to twist]

streptocarpus (ˌstrɛptəʊˈkɑːpəs) n. any of various mostly African plants having spirally-twisted capsules. [C19: from NL, from Gk *streptos* twisted + *karpos* fruit]

streptococcus (ˌstrɛptəʊˈkɒkəs) n., pl. **-cocci** (-ˈkɒkaɪ). any spherical bacterium of the genus *Streptococcus*, typically occurring in chains and including many pathogenic species. Often shortened to **strep.** —**streptococcal** (ˌstrɛptəʊˈkɒkᵊl) or **streptococcic** (ˌstrɛptəʊˈkɒksɪk) adj.

streptomycin (ˌstrɛptəʊˈmaɪsɪn) n. an antibiotic obtained from the bacterium *Streptomyces griseus*: used in the treatment of tuberculosis and other bacterial infections.

streptothricin (ˌstrɛptəʊˈθraɪsɪn) n. an antibiotic produced by the bacterium *Streptomyces lavendulae*.

stress (strɛs) n. **1.** special emphasis or significance. **2.** mental, emotional, or physical strain or tension. **3.** emphasis placed upon a syllable by pronouncing it more loudly than those that surround it. **4.** such emphasis as part of a rhythm in music or poetry. **5.** a syllable so emphasized. **6.** *Physics.* **a.** force or a system of forces producing deformation or strain. **b.** the force acting per unit area. ~vb. (tr.) **7.** to give emphasis or prominence to. **8.** to pronounce (a word or syllable) more loudly than those that surround it. **9.** to subject to stress. [C14 *stresse*, shortened from DISTRESS] —**ˈstressful** adj.

-stress suffix forming nouns. indicating a woman who performs or is engaged in a certain activity: *songstress; seamstress.* [from -ST(E)R + -ESS]

stretch (strɛtʃ) vb. **1.** to draw out or extend or be drawn out or extended in length, area, etc. **2.** to extend or be extended to an undue degree, esp. so as to distort or lengthen permanently. **3.** to extend (the limbs, body, etc.). **4.** (tr.) to reach or suspend (a rope, etc.) from one place to another. **5.** (tr.) to draw tight; tighten. **6.** (often foll. by *out, forward,* etc.) to reach or hold (out); extend. **7.** (intr.; usually foll. by *over*) to extend in time: *the course stretched over three months.* **8.** (intr.; foll. by *for, over,* etc.) (of a region, etc.) to extend in length or area. **9.** (intr.) (esp. of a garment) to be capable of expanding, as to a larger size: *socks that will stretch.* **10.** (tr.) to put a great strain upon or extend to the limit. **11.** to injure (a muscle, tendon, etc.) by means of a strain or sprain. **12.** (tr.; often foll. by *out*) to make do with (limited resources): *to stretch one's budget.* **13.** (tr.) Inf. to expand or elaborate (a story, etc.) beyond what is credible or acceptable. **14.** (tr.; often passive) to extend, as to the limit of one's abilities or talents. **15.** Arch. or sl. to hang or be hanged by the neck. **16. stretch a point. a.** to make a concession or exception not usually made. **b.** to exaggerate. ~n. **17.** the act of stretching or state of being stretched. **18.** a large or continuous expanse or distance: *a stretch of water.* **19.** extent in time, length, area, etc. **20. a.** capacity for being stretched, as in some garments. **b.** (as modifier): *stretch pants.* **21.** the section or sections of a racecourse that are straight, esp. the final section leading to the finishing line. **22.** Sl. a term of imprisonment. **23. at a stretch.** Chiefly Brit. **a.** with some difficulty; by making a special effort. **b.** if really necessary or in extreme circumstances. **c.** at one time: *he sometimes read for hours at a stretch.* [OE *streccan*] —**ˈstretchable** adj. —**ˌstretchaˈbility** n.

stretcher (ˈstrɛtʃə) n. **1.** a device for transporting the ill, wounded, or dead, consisting of a frame covered by canvas or other material. **2.** a strengthening often decorative member joining the legs of a chair, table, etc. **3.** the wooden frame on which canvas is stretched and fixed for oil painting. **4.** a tie beam or brace used in a structural framework. **5.** a brick or stone laid horizontally with its length parallel to the length of a wall. **6.** Rowing. a fixed board across a boat on which an oarsman braces his feet. **7.** Austral. & N.Z. a camp bed. ~vb. (tr.) **8.** to transport (a sick or injured person) on a stretcher.

stretcher-bearer n. a person who helps to carry a stretcher, esp. in wartime.

stretchmarks (ˈstrɛtʃˌmɑːks) pl. n. marks that remain visible on the abdomen after its distension in pregnancy.

stretchy (ˈstrɛtʃɪ) adj. **stretchier, stretchiest.** characterized by elasticity. —**ˈstretchiness** n.

Stretford (ˈstrɛtfəd) n. an industrial town in NW England, in Greater Manchester. Pop.: 47 600 (1981).

stretto (ˈstrɛtəʊ) n., pl. **-tos** or **-ti** (-tiː). **1.** (in a fugue) the close overlapping of two parts or voices, the second one

entering before the first has completed its statement. **2.** Also called: **stretta.** a concluding passage, played at a faster speed than earlier material. [C17: from It., from L *strictus* tightly bound; see STRICT]

strew (struː) vb. **strewing, strewed, strewn** or **strewed.** to spread or scatter or be spread or scattered, as over a surface or area. [OE *streowian*] —**ˈstrewer** n.

strewth (struːθ) interj. an expression of surprise or dismay. [C19: alteration of *God's truth*]

stria (ˈstraɪə) n., pl. **striae** (ˈstraɪiː). (often pl.) **1.** Also called: **striation.** Geol. any of the parallel scratches or grooves on the surface of a rock over which a glacier has flowed or on the surface of a crystal. **2.** Biol., anat. a narrow band of colour or a ridge, groove, or similar linear mark. **3.** Archit. a narrow channel, such as a flute on the shaft of a column. [C16: from L: a groove]

striate adj. (ˈstraɪɪt), also **striated.** **1.** marked with striae; striped. ~vb. (ˈstraɪeɪt). **2.** (tr.) to mark with striae. [C17: from L *striāre* to make grooves]

striation (straɪˈeɪʃən) n. **1.** an arrangement or pattern of striae. **2.** the condition of being striate. **3.** another word for **stria** (sense 1).

stricken (ˈstrɪkən) adj. **1.** laid low, as by disease or sickness. **2.** deeply affected, as by grief, love, etc. **3.** Arch. wounded or injured. **4. stricken in years.** made feeble by age. [C14: p.p. of STRIKE] —**ˈstrickenly** adv.

strict (strɪkt) adj. **1.** adhering closely to specified rules, ordinances, etc. **2.** complied with or enforced stringently; rigorous: *a strict code of conduct.* **3.** severely correct in attention to conduct or morality: *a strict teacher.* **4.** (of a punishment, etc.) harsh; severe. **5.** (prenominal) complete; absolute: *strict secrecy.* [C16: from L *strictus*, from *stringere* to draw tight] —**ˈstrictly** adv. —**ˈstrictness** n.

strict implication n. Logic. a form of implication in which the proposition "if A then B" is true only when B is deducible from A.

stricture (ˈstrɪktʃə) n. **1.** a severe criticism; censure. **2.** Pathol. an abnormal constriction of a tubular organ or part. [C14: from L *strictūra* contraction; see STRICT] —**ˈstrictured** adj.

stride (straɪd) n. **1.** a long step or pace. **2.** the space measured by such a step. **3.** a striding gait. **4.** an act of forward movement by an animal. **5.** progress or development (esp. in **make rapid strides**). **6.** a regular pace or rate of progress: *to get into one's stride; to be put off one's stride.* **7.** Also: **stride piano.** Jazz. a piano style characterized by single bass notes on the first and third beats and chords on the second and fourth. **8.** (pl.) Inf., chiefly Austral. men's trousers. **9. take (something) in one's stride.** to do (something) without difficulty or effort. ~vb. **striding, strode, stridden. 10.** (intr.) to walk with long regular or measured paces, as in haste, etc. **11.** (tr.) to cover or traverse by striding: *he strode thirty miles.* **12.** (often foll. by *over, across,* etc.) to cross (over a space, obstacle, etc.) with a stride. **13.** Arch. or poetic. to straddle or bestride. [OE *strīdan*] —**ˈstrider** n.

strident (ˈstraɪdᵊnt) adj. **1.** (of a shout, voice, etc.) loud or harsh. **2.** urgent, clamorous, or vociferous: *strident demands.* [C17: from L *strīdēns*, from *strīdēre* to make a grating sound] —**ˈstridence** or **ˈstridency** n. —**ˈstridently** adv.

stridor (ˈstraɪdɔː) n. **1.** Pathol. a high-pitched whistling sound made during respiration, caused by obstruction of the air passages. **2.** Chiefly literary. a harsh or shrill sound. [C17: from L; see STRIDENT]

stridulate (ˈstrɪdjʊˌleɪt) vb. (intr.) (of insects such as the cricket) to produce sounds by rubbing one part of the body against another. [C19: back formation from *stridulation*, from L *strīdulus* creaking, from *strīdēre* to make a harsh noise] —**ˌstriduˈlation** n. —**ˈstriduˌlator** n.

stridulous (ˈstrɪdjʊləs) or **stridulant** adj. **1.** making a harsh, shrill, or grating noise. **2.** Pathol. of, relating to, or characterized by stridor. —**ˈstridulousness** or **ˈstridulance** n.

strife (straɪf) n. **1.** angry or violent struggle; conflict. **2.** rivalry or contention, esp. of a bitter kind. **3.** Austral. & N.Z. inf. trouble or discord of any kind. **4.** Arch. striving. [C13: from OF *estrif*, prob. from *estriver* to STRIVE]

strigil (ˈstrɪdʒɪl) n. a curved blade used by the ancient Romans and Greeks to scrape the body after bathing. [C16: from L *strigilis*, from *stringere* to graze]

strigose (ˈstraɪɡəʊs) adj. **1.** Bot. bearing stiff hairs or bristles. **2.** Zool. marked with fine closely set grooves or ridges. [C18: via NL *strigōsus*, from *striga* a bristle, from L: grain cut down]

strike (straɪk) *vb.* **striking, struck. 1.** to deliver (a blow or stroke) to (a person). **2.** to come or cause to come into sudden or violent contact (with). **3.** (*tr.*) to make an attack on. **4.** to produce (fire, sparks, etc.) or (of fire, sparks, etc.) to be produced by ignition. **5.** to cause (a match) to light by friction or (of a match) to be lighted. **6.** to press (the key of a piano, organ, etc.) or to sound (a specific note) in this or a similar way. **7.** to indicate (a specific time) by the sound of a hammer striking a bell or by any other percussive sound. **8.** (of a venomous snake) to cause injury by biting. **9.** (*tr.*) to affect or cause to affect deeply, suddenly, or radically: *her appearance struck him as strange.* **10.** (*past participle* **struck** *or* **stricken**) (*tr.; passive;* usually foll. by *with*) to render incapable or nearly so: *stricken with grief.* **11.** (*tr.*) to enter the mind of: *it struck me that he had become very quiet.* **12.** (*past participle* **struck** *or* **stricken**) to render: *struck dumb.* **13.** (*tr.*) to be perceived by; catch: *the glint of metal struck his eye.* **14.** to arrive at or come upon (something), esp. suddenly or unexpectedly: *to strike the path for home; to strike upon a solution.* **15.** (*intr.*; sometimes foll. by *out*) to set (out) or proceed, esp. upon a new course: *to strike out for the coast.* **16.** (*tr.; usually passive*) to afflict with a disease, esp. unexpectedly: *he was struck with polio.* **17.** (*tr.*) to discover or come upon a source of (ore, petroleum, etc.). **18.** (*tr.*) (of a plant) to produce or send down (a root or roots). **19.** (*tr.*) to take apart or pack up; break (esp. in **strike camp**). **20.** (*tr.*) to take down or dismantle (a stage set, etc.). **21.** (*tr.*) *Naut.* **a.** to lower or remove (a specified piece of gear). **b.** to haul down or dip (a flag, sail, etc.) in salute or in surrender. **22.** to attack (an objective). **23.** to impale the hook in the mouth of (a fish) by suddenly tightening or jerking the line after the bait has been taken. **24.** (*tr.*) to form or impress (a coin, metal, etc.) by or as if by stamping. **25.** to level (a surface) by use of a flat board. **26.** (*tr.*) to assume or take up (an attitude, posture, etc.). **27.** (*intr.*) (of workers in a factory, etc.) to cease work collectively as a protest against working conditions, low pay, etc. **28.** (*tr.*) to reach by agreement: *to strike a bargain.* **29.** (*tr.*) to form (a jury, esp. a special jury) by cancelling certain names among those nominated for jury service until only the requisite number remains. **30. strike home. a.** to deliver an effective blow. **b.** to achieve the intended effect. **31. strike it rich.** *Inf.* **a.** to discover an extensive deposit of a mineral, petroleum, etc. **b.** to have an unexpected financial success. ~*n.* **32.** an act or instance of striking. **33.** a cessation of work, as a protest against working conditions or low pay: *on strike.* **34.** a military attack, esp. an air attack on a surface target: *air strike.* **35.** *Baseball.* a pitched ball judged good but missed or not swung at, three of which cause a batter to be out. **36.** Also called: **ten-strike.** *Tenpin bowling.* **a.** the act or an instance of knocking down all the pins with the first bowl of a single frame. **b.** the score thus made. **37.** a sound made by striking. **38.** the mechanism that makes a clock strike. **39.** the discovery of a source of ore, petroleum, etc. **40.** the horizontal direction of a fault, rock stratum, etc. **41.** *Angling.* the act or an instance of striking. **42.** *Inf.* an unexpected or complete success, esp. one that brings financial gain. **43. take strike.** *Cricket.* (of a batsman) to prepare to play a ball delivered by the bowler. ~See also **strike down, strike off,** etc. [OE *strīcan*]

strikebound ('straɪk,baʊnd) *adj.* (of a factory, etc.) closed or made inoperative by a strike.

strikebreaker ('straɪk,breɪkə) *n.* a person who tries to make a strike ineffectual by working or by taking the place of those on strike. —'**strike,breaking** *n., adj.*

strike down *vb.* (*tr., adv.*) to cause to die, esp. suddenly: *he was struck down in his prime.*

strike off *vb.* (*tr.*) **1.** to remove or erase from (a list, record, etc.) by or as if by a stroke of the pen. **2.** (*adv.*) to cut off or separate by or as if by a blow: *she was struck off from the inheritance.*

strike out *vb.* (*adv.*) **1.** (*tr.*) to remove or erase. **2.** (*intr.*) to start out or begin: *to strike out on one's own.* **3.** *Baseball.* to put out or be put out on strikes. **4.** (*intr.*) *U.S. inf.* to fail utterly.

strike pay *n.* money paid to strikers from the funds of a trade union.

striker ('straɪkə) *n.* **1.** a person who is on strike. **2.** the hammer in a timepiece that rings a bell or alarm. **3.** any part in a mechanical device that strikes something, such as the firing pin of a gun. **4.** *Soccer, inf.* an attacking player, esp. one who generally positions himself near his opponent's goal in the hope of scoring. **5.** *Cricket.* the batsman who is about to play a ball.

strike up *vb.* (*adv.*) **1.** (of a band, orchestra, etc.) to begin to play or sing. **2.** (*tr.*) to bring about; cause to begin: *to strike up a friendship.*

striking ('straɪkɪŋ) *adj.* **1.** attracting attention; fine; impressive: *a striking beauty.* **2.** conspicuous; noticeable: *a striking difference.* —'**strikingly** *adv.* —'**strikingness** *n.*

striking circle *n. Hockey.* the semicircular area in front of each goal, which an attacking player must have entered before scoring a goal.

Strimon ('strimɔn) *n.* a transliteration of the Greek name for the **Struma.**

Strindberg ('strɪndbɜ:g; *Swedish* 'strɪndbærj) *n.* **August** ('august). 1849–1912, Swedish dramatist and novelist, whose plays include *The Father* (1887), *Miss Julie* (1888), and *The Ghost Sonata* (1907).

Strine (straɪn) *n.* a humorous transliteration of Australian pronunciation, as in *Gloria Soame* for *glorious home.* [C20: a jocular rendering of the Australian pronunciation of *Australian*]

string (strɪŋ) *n.* **1.** a thin length of cord, twine, fibre, or similar material used for tying, hanging, binding, etc. **2.** a group of objects threaded on a single strand: *a string of beads.* **3.** a series or succession of things, events, etc.: *a string of oaths.* **4.** a number, chain, or group of similar things, animals, etc., owned by or associated with one person or body: *a string of girlfriends.* **5.** a tough fibre or cord in a plant. **6.** *Music.* a tightly stretched wire, cord, etc., found on stringed instruments, such as the violin, guitar, and piano. **7.** short for **bowstring. 8.** *Archit.* short for **string-course** or **stringer** (sense 1). **9.** (*pl.;* usually preceded by *the*) **a.** violins, violas, cellos, and double basses collectively. **b.** the section of a symphony orchestra constituted by such instruments. **10.** a group of characters that can be treated as a unit by a computer program. **11.** (*pl.*) complications or conditions (esp. in **no strings attached**). **12.** (*modifier*) composed of string-like strands woven in a large mesh: *a string bag; a string vest.* **13. first (second,** *etc.***) string.** a person or thing regarded as a primary (secondary, etc.) source of strength. **14. keep on a string.** to have control or a hold over (a person), esp. emotionally. **15. pull strings.** *Inf.* to exert power or influence, esp. secretly or unofficially. **16. pull the strings.** to have real or ultimate control of something. ~*vb.* **stringing, strung. 17.** (*tr.*) to provide with a string or strings. **18.** (*tr.*) to suspend or stretch from one point to another. **19.** (*tr.*) to thread on a string. **20.** (*tr.*) to form or extend in a line or series. **21.** (foll. by *out*) to space or spread out at intervals. **22.** (*tr.; usually* foll. by *up*) *Inf.* to kill (a person) by hanging. **23.** (*tr.*) to remove the stringy parts from (vegetables, esp. beans). **24.** (*intr.*) (esp. of viscous liquids) to become stringy or ropy. **25.** (often foll. by *up*) to cause to be tense or nervous. [OE *streng*] —'**string,like** *adj.*

string along *vb.* (*adv.*) *Inf.* **1.** (*intr.*; often foll. by *with*) to agree or appear to be in agreement (with). **2.** (*intr.*; often foll. by *with*) to accompany. **3.** to deceive or hoax, esp. in order to gain time.

stringboard ('strɪŋ,bɔ:d) *n.* a skirting that covers the ends of the steps in a staircase. Also called: **stringer.**

string course *n. Archit.* an ornamental projecting band or continuous moulding along a wall. Also called: **cordon.**

stringed (strɪŋd) *adj.* (of musical instruments) having or provided with strings.

stringendo (strɪn'dʒɛndəʊ) *adj., adv. Music.* to be performed with increasing speed. [It., from *stringere* to compress, from L: to draw tight]

stringent ('strɪndʒənt) *adj.* **1.** requiring strict attention to rules, procedure, detail, etc. **2.** *Finance.* characterized by or causing a shortage of credit, loan capital, etc. [C17: from L *stringere* to bind] —'**stringency** *n.* —'**stringently** *adv.*

stringer ('strɪŋə) *n.* **1.** *Archit.* **a.** a long horizontal timber beam that is used for structural purposes. **b.** another name for **stringboard. 2.** *Naut.* a longitudinal structural brace for strengthening the hull of a vessel. **3.** a journalist retained by a newspaper or news service on a part-time basis to cover a particular town or area.

stringhalt ('strɪŋ,hɔːlt) *n. Vet. science.* a sudden spasmodic lifting of the hind leg of a horse. Also called: **springhalt.** [C16: prob. STRING + HALT²]

stringpiece ('strɪŋ,piːs) *n.* a long horizontal timber beam used to strengthen or support a framework.

string quartet *n. Music.* **1.** an instrumental ensemble consisting of two violins, one viola, and one cello. **2.** a piece of music for such a group.

string tie *n.* a very narrow tie.

stringy ('strɪŋɪ) *adj.* **stringier, stringiest. 1.** made of strings or resembling strings. **2.** (of meat, etc.) fibrous. **3.** (of a person's build) wiry; sinewy. **4.** (of liquids) forming in strings. —**'stringily** *adv.* —**'stringiness** *n.*

stringy-bark *n. Austral.* any of several eucalyptus trees having fibrous bark.

strip¹ (strɪp) *vb.* **stripping, stripped. 1.** to take or pull (the covering, clothes, etc.) off (oneself, another person, or thing). **2.** (*intr.*) **a.** to remove all one's clothes. **b.** to perform a striptease. **3.** (*tr.*) to denude or empty completely. **4.** (*tr.*) to deprive: *he was stripped of his pride.* **5.** (*tr.*) to rob or plunder. **6.** (*tr.*) to remove (paint, etc.) from (a surface, furniture, etc.): *stripped pine.* **7.** (*tr.*) to pull out the old coat of hair from (dogs of certain long- and wire-haired breeds). **8. a.** to remove the leaves from the stalks of (tobacco, etc.). **b.** to separate the leaves from the stems of (tobacco, etc.). **9.** (*tr.*) *Agriculture.* to draw the last milk from (a cow). **10.** to dismantle (an engine, mechanism, etc.). **11.** to tear off or break (the thread) from (a screw, bolt, etc.) or (the teeth) from (a gear). **12.** (often foll. by *down*) to remove the accessories from (a motor vehicle): *his car was stripped down.* ~*n.* **13.** the act or an instance of undressing or of performing a striptease. [OE *bestrīepan* to plunder]

strip² (strɪp) *n.* **1.** a relatively long, flat, narrow piece of something. **2.** short for **airstrip. 3.** the clothes worn by the members of a team, esp. a football team. **4. tear (someone) off a strip.** *Inf.* to rebuke (someone) angrily. ~*vb.* **stripping, stripped. 5.** to cut or divide into strips. [C15: from MDu. *stripe* STRIPE¹]

strip cartoon *n.* a sequence of drawings in a newspaper, magazine, etc., relating a humorous story or an adventure. Also called: **comic strip.**

strip club *n.* a small club in which striptease performances take place.

stripe¹ ('straɪp) *n.* **1.** a relatively long band of colour or texture that differs from the surrounding material or background. **2.** a fabric having such bands. **3.** a strip, band, or chevron worn on a uniform, etc., esp. to indicate rank. **4.** *Chiefly U.S. & Canad.* kind; type: *a man of a certain stripe.* ~*vb.* **5.** (*tr.*) to mark with stripes. [C17: prob. from MDu. *stripe*] —**striped** *adj.*

stripe² ('straɪp) *n.* a stroke from a whip, rod, cane, etc. [C15: ?from MLow G *strippe*]

striped muscle *n.* a type of contractile tissue that is marked by transverse striations. Also called: **striated muscle.**

strip lighting *n.* electric lighting by means of long glass tubes that are fluorescent lamps or that contain long filaments.

stripling ('strɪplɪŋ) *n.* a lad. [C13: from STRIP² + -LING¹]

strip mining *n.* another term (esp. U.S.) for **opencast mining.**

stripper ('strɪpə) *n.* **1.** a striptease artiste. **2.** a person or thing that strips. **3.** a device or substance for removing paint, varnish, etc.

strip-searching *n.* the practice by police or customs officials of stripping a prisoner or suspect naked and searching him or her for contraband, narcotics, etc. —**'strip-,search** *n., vb.*

striptease ('strɪp,tiːz) *n.* **a.** a form of erotic entertainment in which a person gradually undresses to music. **b.** (*as modifier*): *a striptease club.* —**'strip,teaser** *n.*

stripy ('straɪpɪ) *adj.* **stripier, stripiest.** marked by or with stripes; striped.

strive (straɪv) *vb.* **striving, strove, striven. 1.** (*may take a clause as object or an infinitive*) to make a great and tenacious effort. **2.** (*intr.*) to fight; contend. [C13: from OF *estriver*, of Gmc origin] —**'striver** *n.*

strobe (strəub) *n.* short for **strobe lighting** or **stroboscope.**

strobe lighting *n.* **1.** a high-intensity flashing beam of light produced by rapid electrical discharges in a tube or by a perforated disc rotating in front of an intense light source. **2.** the use of or the apparatus for producing such light. Sometimes shortened to **strobe.**

strobilus ('strəʊbɪləs) *or* **strobile** ('strəʊbaɪl) *n., pl.* **-bi-luses, -bili** (-bɪlaɪ), *or* **-biles.** *Bot.* the technical name for **cone** (sense 3). [C18: via LL from Gk *strobilos* a fir cone]

stroboscope ('strəʊbə,skəʊp) *n.* **1.** an instrument producing an intense flashing light, the frequency of which can be synchronized with some multiple of the frequency of rotation, vibration, or operation of an object, etc., making it appear stationary. Sometimes shortened to **strobe. 2.** a similar device synchronized with the shutter of a camera so that a series of still photographs can be taken of a moving object. [C19: from *strobo-*, from Gk *strobos* a whirling + -SCOPE] —**stroboscopic** (,strəʊbə'skɒpɪk) *or* **,strobo'scopical** *adj.*, **,strobo'scopically** *adv.*

strode (strəʊd) *vb.* the past tense of **stride.**

stroganoff ('strɒgə,nɒf) *n.* a dish of sliced beef cooked with onions and mushrooms, served in a sour-cream sauce. Also called: **beef stroganoff.** [C19: after Count *Stroganoff*, 19th-century Russian diplomat]

Stroheim ('strəʊ,haɪm, 'ʃtrəʊ-) *n.* See (Erich) **von Stroheim.**

stroke (strəʊk) *n.* **1.** the act or an instance of striking; a blow, knock, or hit. **2.** a sudden action, movement, or occurrence: *a stroke of luck.* **3.** a brilliant or inspired act or feat: *a stroke of genius.* **4.** *Pathol.* apoplexy; rupture of a blood vessel in the brain resulting in loss of consciousness, often followed by paralysis, or embolism or thrombosis affecting a cerebral vessel. **5. a.** the striking of a clock. **b.** the hour registered by this: *on the stroke of three.* **6.** a mark made by a writing implement. **7.** another name for **solidus** (sense 1), used esp. when dictating or reading aloud. **8.** a light touch or caress, as with the fingers. **9.** a pulsation, esp. of the heart. **10.** a single complete movement or one of a series of complete movements. **11.** *Sport.* the act or manner of striking the ball with a club, bat, etc. **12.** any one of the repeated movements used by a swimmer. **13.** a manner of swimming, esp. one of several named styles such as the crawl. **14. a.** any one of a series of linear movements of a reciprocating part, such as a piston. **b.** the distance travelled by such a part from one end of its movement to the other. **15.** a single pull on an oar or oars in rowing. **16.** manner or style of rowing. **17.** the oarsman who sits nearest the stern of a shell, facing the cox, and sets the rate of rowing. **18. a stroke (of work).** (*usually used with a negative*) a small amount of work. **19. at a stroke.** with one action. **20. off one's stroke.** performing or working less well than usual. **21. on the stroke.** punctually. ~*vb.* **22.** (*tr.*) to touch, brush, etc. lightly or gently. **23.** (*tr.*) to mark a line or a stroke on or through. **24.** to act as the stroke of (a racing shell). **25.** (*tr.*) *Sport.* to strike (a ball) with a smooth swinging blow. [OE *strācian*]

stroke play *n. Golf.* **a.** scoring by counting the strokes taken. **b.** (*as modifier*): *a strokeplay tournament.* ~Also called: **medal play.** Cf. **match play.**

stroll (strəʊl) *vb.* **1.** to walk about in a leisurely manner. **2.** (*intr.*) to wander about. ~*n.* **3.** a leisurely walk. [C17: prob. from dialect G *strollen*, from ?]

stroller ('strəʊlə) *n.* the usual U.S., Canad., and Austral. word for **pushchair.**

stroma ('strəʊmə) *n., pl.* **-mata** (-mətə). *Biol.* **1.** the dense colourless framework of a chloroplast and certain cells. **2.** the fibrous connective tissue forming the matrix of the mammalian ovary and testis. **3.** a dense mass of hyphae that is produced by certain fungi and gives rise to spore-producing bodies. [C19: via NL from LL: a mattress, from Gk] —**stromatic** (strəʊ'mætɪk) *or* **'stromatous** *adj.*

Stromboli ('strɒmbəlɪ) *n.* an island in the Tyrrhenian Sea, in the Lipari Islands off the N coast of Sicily: famous for its active volcano, 927 m (3040 ft.) high.

strong (strɒŋ) *adj.* **stronger** ('strɒŋgə), **strongest** ('strɒŋgɪst). **1.** involving or possessing strength. **2.** solid or robust; not easily broken or injured. **3.** resolute or morally firm. **4.** intense in quality; not faint or feeble: *a strong voice; a strong smell.* **5.** easily defensible; incontestable or formidable. **6.** concentrated; not weak or diluted. **7. a.** (*postpositive*) containing or having a specified number: *a navy 40 000 strong.* **b.** (*in combination*): *a 40 000-strong navy.* **8.** having an unpleasantly powerful taste or smell. **9.** having an extreme or drastic effect: *strong discipline.* **10.** emphatic or immoderate: *strong language.* **11.** convincing, effective, or cogent. **12.** (of a colour) having a high degree of saturation or purity; produced by a concentrated quantity of colouring agent. **13.** *Grammar.* **a.** of or denoting a class of verbs, in certain languages including the Germanic languages, whose conjugation shows vowel gradation, as *sing, sang, sung.* **b.** belonging to any part-of-speech class, in various languages, whose inflections follow the less regular of two possible patterns. Cf. **weak** (sense 10). **14.** (of a wind, current, etc.) moving fast. **15.** (of a syllable) accented or stressed. **16.** (of an industry, etc.) firm in price or characterized by firm or increasing prices. **17.** (of certain acids and bases) producing high concentrations of hydrogen or hydroxide ions in aqueous solution. **18. have a strong stomach.** not to be prone to nausea. ~*adv.* **19.** *Inf.* in a strong way; effectively: *going strong.* **20. come on strong.** to make a forceful or exaggerated impression. [OE *strang*] —'**strongly** *adv.* —'**strongness** *n.*

strong-arm *Inf.* ~*n.* **1.** (*modifier*) of or involving physical force or violence: *strong-arm tactics.* ~*vb.* **2.** (*tr.*) to show violence towards.

strongbox ('strɒŋ,bɒks) *n.* a box or safe in which valuables are locked for safety.

strong breeze *n. Meteorol.* a wind of force 6 on the Beaufort scale, reaching speeds of 25 to 31 mph.

strong drink *n.* alcoholic drink.

strong-eye dog *n. N.Z.* See **eye dog.**

strong gale *n. Meteorol.* a wind of force 9 on the Beaufort scale, reaching speeds of 47 to 54 mph.

stronghold ('strɒŋ,həuld) *n.* **1.** a defensible place; fortress. **2.** a major centre or area of predominance.

strong interaction *n. Physics.* an interaction between elementary particles responsible for the forces between nucleons in the nucleus. Cf. **weak interaction.**

strong-minded *adj.* having strength of mind; firm, resolute, and determined. —,**strong-'mindedly** *adv.* —,**strong-'mindedness** *n.*

strong point *n.* something at which one excels; forte.

strongroom ('strɒŋ,ru:m, -,rum) *n.* a specially designed room in which valuables are locked for safety.

strong-willed *adj.* having strength of will.

strontium ('strɒntɪəm) *n.* a soft silvery-white element of the alkaline earth group of metals. The radioisotope **strontium-90,** with a half-life of 28.1 years, is used in nuclear power sources and is a hazardous nuclear fallout product. Symbol: Sr; atomic no.: 38; atomic wt.: 87.62. [C19: from NL, after *Strontian,* in the Highlands of Scotland where discovered]

strontium unit *n.* a unit expressing the concentration of strontium-90 in an organic medium, such as soil, bone, etc., relative to the concentration of calcium in the medium.

strop (strɒp) *n.* **1.** a leather strap or an abrasive strip for sharpening razors. **2.** a rope or metal band around a block or deadeye for support. ~*vb.* **stropping, stropped.** **3.** (*tr.*) to sharpen (a razor, etc.) on a strop. [C14 (in nautical use: a strip of rope): via MLow G or MDu. *strop,* ult. from L *stroppus,* from Gk *strophos* cord]

strophanthin (strəʊ'fænθɪn) *n.* a toxic glycoside or mixture of glycosides obtained from the ripe seeds of certain species of strophanthus. [C19: NL, from STROPHANTH(US) + -IN]

strophanthus (strəʊ'fænθəs) *n.* **1.** any of various small trees or shrubs of tropical Africa and Asia, having strap-shaped twisted petals. **2.** the seeds of any of these plants. [C19: NL, from Gk *strophos* twisted cord + *anthos* flower]

strophe ('strəʊfɪ) *n. Prosody.* (in ancient Greek drama) **a.** the first of two movements made by a chorus during the performance of a choral ode. **b.** the first part of a choral ode sung during this movement. ~See **antistrophe, epode.** [C17: from Gk: a verse, lit.: a turning, from *strephein* to twist] —'**strophic** ('strɒfɪk, 'strəʊ-) *adj.*

stroppy ('strɒpɪ) *adj.* **-pier, -piest.** *Brit. inf.* angry or awkward. [C20: changed & shortened from OBSTREPEROUS] —'**stroppily** *adv.* —'**stroppiness** *n.*

strove (strəʊv) *vb.* the past tense of **strive.**

strow (strəʊ) *vb.* **strowing, strowed; strown** *or* **strowed.** an archaic variant of **strew.**

struck (strʌk) *vb.* **1.** the past tense and past participle of **strike.** ~*adj.* **2.** *Chiefly U.S. & Canad.* (of an industry, factory, etc.) shut down or otherwise affected by a labour strike.

structural ('strʌktʃərəl) *adj.* **1.** of, relating to, or having structure or a structure. **2.** of, relating to, or forming part of the structure of a building. **3.** of or relating to the structure of the earth's crust. **4.** of or relating to the structure of organisms. **5.** *Chem.* of or involving the arrangement of atoms in molecules. —'**structurally** *adv.*

structural formula *n.* a chemical formula showing the composition and structure of a molecule.

structuralism ('strʌktʃərə,lɪzəm) *n.* **1.** an approach to social sciences and to literature in terms of oppositions, contrasts, and hierarchical structures, esp. as they might reflect universal mental characteristics or organizing principles. **2.** an approach to linguistics that analyses and describes the structure of language, as distinguished from its comparative and historical aspects. —'**structuralist** *n., adj.*

structural linguistics *n.* (*functioning as sing.*) a descriptive approach to an analysis of language on the basis of its structure as reflected by irreducible units of phonological, morphological, and semantic features.

structure ('strʌktʃə) *n.* **1.** a complex construction or entity. **2.** the arrangement and interrelationship of parts in a construction. **3.** the manner of construction or organization. **4.** *Chem.* the arrangement of atoms in a molecule of a chemical compound. **5.** *Geol.* the way in which a mineral, rock, etc., is made up of its component parts. ~*vb.* (*tr.*) **6.** to impart a structure to. [C15: from L *structūra,* from *struere* to build]

strudel ('stru:dəl) *n.* a thin sheet of filled dough rolled up and baked: *apple strudel.* [G, from MHG *strodel* whirlpool, from the way the pastry is rolled]

struggle ('strʌgᵊl) *vb.* **1.** (*intr.;* usually foll. by *for* or *against; may take an infinitive*) to exert strength, energy, and force; work or strive. **2.** (*intr.*) to move about strenuously so as to escape from something confining. **3.** (*intr.*) to contend, battle, or fight. **4.** (*intr.*) to go or progress with difficulty. ~*n.* **5.** a laboured or strenuous exertion or effort. **6.** a fight or battle. **7.** the act of struggling. [C14: from ?] —'**struggling** *adj.*

strum (strʌm) *vb.* **strumming, strummed.** **1.** to sound (the strings of a guitar, etc.) with a downward or upward sweep of the thumb or of a plectrum. **2.** to play (chords, a tune, etc.) in this way. [C18: prob. imit.] —'**strummer** *n.*

struma ('stru:mə) *n., pl.* **-mae** (-mi:). **1.** an abnormal enlargement of the thyroid gland; goitre. **2.** *Bot.* a swelling, esp. at the base of a moss capsule. **3.** another word for **scrofula.** [C16: from L: scrofulous tumour, from *struere* to heap up] —**strumous** ('stru:məs) *or* **strumose** ('stru:məʊs) *adj.*

Struma ('stru:mə) *n.* a river in S Europe, rising in SW Bulgaria near Sofia and flowing generally southeast through Greece to the Aegean. Length: 362 km (225 miles). Greek names: **Strimon, Strymon.**

strumpet ('strʌmpɪt) *n. Arch.* a prostitute or promiscuous woman. [C14: from ?]

strung (strʌŋ) *vb.* **1.** a past tense and past participle of **string.** ~*adj.* **2. a.** (of a piano, etc.) provided with strings. **b.** (*in combination*): *gut-strung.* **3. highly strung.** very nervous or volatile in character.

strung up *adj.* (*postpositive*) *Inf.* tense or nervous.

strut (strʌt) *vb.* **strutting, strutted.** **1.** (*intr.*) to walk in a pompous manner; swagger. **2.** (*tr.*) to support or provide with struts. ~*n.* **3.** a structural member, esp. as part of a framework. **4.** an affected, proud, or stiff walk. [C14 *strouten* (in the sense: swell, stand out; C16: to walk stiffly), from OE *strūtian* to stand stiffly] —'**strutter** *n.* —'**strutting** *adj.* —'**struttingly** *adv.*

struthious ('stru:θɪəs) *adj.* **1.** (of birds) related to or resembling the ostrich. **2.** of, relating to, or designating all flightless birds. [C18: from LL *strūthiō,* from Gk *strouthiōn,* from *strouthos* ostrich]

strychnine ('strɪkni:n) *n.* a white crystalline very poisonous alkaloid, obtained from the plant nux vomica: used in small quantities as a stimulant. [C19: via F from NL *Strychnos,* from Gk *strukhnos* nightshade]

Strymon ('straɪmən) *n.* transliteration of the Greek name for the **Struma.**

Stuart ('stjʊət) *n.* **1.** the royal house that ruled in Scotland from 1371 to 1714 and in England from 1603 to 1714.

See also **Stewart** (sense 1). **2. Charles Edward,** called *the Young Pretender* or *Bonnie Prince Charlie.* 1720–88, pretender to the British throne. He led the Jacobite Rebellion (1745–46) in an attempt to re-establish the Stuart succession. **3.** his father, **James Francis Edward,** called *the Old Pretender.* 1688–1766, pretender to the British throne; son of James II (James VII of Scotland) and his second wife, Mary of Modena. He made two unsuccessful attempts to realize his claim to the throne (1708; 1715). **4. Mary.** See **Mary Queen of Scots.**

stub (stʌb) *n.* **1.** a short piece remaining after something has been cut, removed, etc.: *a cigar stub.* **2.** the residual piece or section of a receipt, ticket, cheque, etc. **3.** the usual U.S. and Canad. word for **counterfoil.** **4.** any short projection or blunted end. **5.** the stump of a tree or plant. ~*vb.* **stubbing, stubbed.** (*tr.*) **6.** to strike (one's toe, foot, etc.) painfully against a hard surface. **7.** (usually foll. by *out*) to put (out a cigarette or cigar) by pressing the end against a surface. **8.** to clear (land) of stubs. **9.** to dig up (the roots) of (a tree or bush). [OE *stubb*]

stub axle *n.* a short axle that carries one of the front steered wheels of a motor vehicle.

stubble ('stʌbᵊl) *n.* **1. a.** the stubs of stalks left in a field where a crop has been harvested. **b.** (*as modifier*): *a stubble field.* **2.** any bristly growth. [C13: from OF *estuble*, from L *stupula,* var. of *stipula* stalk] —'**stubbled** *or* '**stubbly** *adj.*

stubble-jumper *n. Canad. sl.* a prairie grain farmer.

stubborn ('stʌbᵊn) *adj.* **1.** refusing to comply, agree, or give in. **2.** difficult to handle, treat, or overcome. **3.** persistent and dogged. [C14 *stoborne,* from ?] —'**stubbornly** *adv.* —'**stubbornness** *n.*

Stubbs (stʌbz) *n.* **George.** 1724–1806, English painter, noted esp. for his pictures of horses.

stubby ('stʌbɪ) *adj.* **-bier, -biest.** **1.** short and broad; stumpy or thickset. **2.** bristling and stiff. ~*n.* **3.** *Austral. sl.* a small bottle of beer. —'**stubbily** *adv.* —'**stubbiness** *n.*

stucco ('stʌkəʊ) *n., pl.* **-coes** *or* **-cos.** **1.** a weather-resistant mixture of dehydrated lime, powdered marble, and glue, used in decorative mouldings on buildings. **2.** any of various types of cement or plaster used for coating outside walls. **3.** Also called: **stuccowork.** decorative work moulded in stucco. ~*vb.* **-coing, -coed.** **4.** (*tr.*) to apply stucco to. [C16: from It., of Gmc origin]

stuck (stʌk) *vb.* **1.** the past tense and past participle of **stick²**. ~*adj.* **2.** *Inf.* baffled or nonplussed. **3.** (foll. by *on*) *Sl.* keen (on) or infatuated (with). **4. get stuck in** *or* **into.** *Inf.* **a.** to perform (a task) with determination. **b.** to attack (a person).

stuck-up *adj. Inf.* conceited, arrogant, or snobbish. —'**stuck-'upness** *n.*

stud¹ (stʌd) *n.* **1.** a large-headed nail or other projection protruding from a surface, usually as decoration. **2.** a type of fastener consisting of two discs at either end of a short shank, used to fasten shirtfronts, collars, etc. **3.** a vertical member used with others to construct the framework of a wall. **4.** the crossbar in the centre of a link of a heavy chain. **5.** one of a number of rounded projections on the sole of a boot or shoe to give better grip, as on a football boot. ~*vb.* **studding, studded.** (*tr.*) **6.** to provide, ornament, or make with studs. **7.** to dot or cover with: *the park was studded with daisies.* **8.** to provide or support (a wall, partition, etc.) with studs. [OE *studu*]

stud² (stʌd) *n.* **1.** a group of pedigree animals, esp. horses, kept for breeding purposes. **2.** any male animal kept principally for breeding purposes, esp. a stallion. **3.** a farm or stable where a stud is kept. **4.** the state or condition of being kept for breeding purposes: *at stud; put to stud.* **5.** (*modifier*) of or relating to such animals or the place where they are kept: *a stud farm; a stud horse.* **6.** *Sl.* a virile or sexually active man. **7.** short for **stud poker.** [OE *stōd*]

studbook ('stʌd,bʊk) *n.* a written record of the pedigree of a purebred stock, esp. of racehorses.

studding ('stʌdɪŋ) *n.* **1.** studs collectively, esp. as used to form a wall or partition. **2.** material used to form or serve as studs.

studdingsail ('stʌdɪŋ,seɪl; *Naut.* 'stʌnsᵊl) *n. Naut.* a light auxiliary sail set outboard on spars on either side of a square sail. Also called: **stunsail, stuns'l.** [C16: *studding,* ?from MLow G, MDu. *stōtinge,* from *stōten* to thrust]

student ('stjuːd⁰nt) *n.* **1. a.** a person following a course of study, as in a school, college, university, etc. **b.** (*as modifier*): *student teacher.* **2.** a person who makes a thorough study of a subject. [C15: from L *studēns* diligent, from *studēre* to be zealous]

Student's t *n.* a statistic often used to test the hypothesis that a random sample of normally distributed observations has a given mean. [after *Student,* pen name of W. S. Gosset (1876–1937), E mathematician]

studhorse ('stʌd,hɔːs) *n.* another word for **stallion.**

studied ('stʌdɪd) *adj.* carefully practised, designed, or premeditated: *a studied reply.* —'**studiedly** *adv.* —'**studiedness** *n.*

studio ('stjuːdɪəʊ) *n., pl.* **-dios.** **1.** a room in which an artist, photographer, or musician works. **2.** a room used to record television or radio programmes, make films, etc. **3.** (*pl.*) the premises of a radio, television, or film company. [C19: from It., lit.: study, from L *studium* diligence]

studio couch *n.* an upholstered couch, usually backless, convertible into a double bed.

studio flat *n.* a flat with one main room.

studious ('stjuːdɪəs) *adj.* **1.** given to study. **2.** of a serious, thoughtful, and hard-working character. **3.** showing deliberation, care, or precision. [C14: from L *studiōsus* devoted to, from *studium* assiduity] —'**studiously** *adv.* —'**studiousness** *n.*

stud poker *n.* a variety of poker in which the first card is dealt face down before each player and the next four are dealt face up (**five-card stud**) or in which the first two cards and the last card are dealt face down and the intervening four cards are dealt face up (**seven-card stud**).

study ('stʌdɪ) *vb.* **studying, studied.** **1.** to apply the mind to the learning or understanding of (a subject), esp. by reading. **2.** (*tr.*) to investigate or examine, as by observation, research, etc. **3.** (*tr.*) to look at minutely; scrutinize. **4.** (*tr.*) to give much careful or critical thought to. **5.** to take a course in (a subject), as at a college. **6.** (*tr.*) to try to memorize: *to study a part for a play.* **7.** (*intr.*) to meditate or contemplate; reflect. ~*n., pl.* **studies.** **8. a.** the act or process of studying. **b.** (*as modifier*): *study group.* **9.** a room used for studying, reading, writing, etc. **10.** (*often pl.*) work relating to a particular discipline: *environmental studies.* **11.** an investigation and analysis of a subject, institution, etc. **12.** a product of studying, such as a written paper or book. **13.** a drawing, sculpture, etc., executed for practice or in preparation for another work. **14.** a musical composition intended to develop one aspect of performing technique. **15. in a brown study.** in a reverie or daydream. [C13: from OF *estudie,* from L *studium* zeal, from *studēre* to be diligent]

stuff (stʌf) *vb.* (*mainly tr.*) **1.** to pack or fill completely; cram. **2.** (*intr.*) to eat large quantities. **3.** to force, shove, or squeeze: *to stuff money into a pocket.* **4.** to fill (food such as poultry or tomatoes) with a stuffing. **5.** to fill (an animal's skin) with material so as to restore the shape of the live animal. **6.** *Taboo sl.* to have sexual intercourse with (a woman). **7.** *U.S. & Canad.* to fill (a ballot box) with fraudulent votes. ~*n.* **8.** the raw material or fabric of something. **9.** woollen cloth or fabric. **10.** any general or unspecified substance or accumulation of objects. **11.** stupid or worthless actions, speech, etc. **12.** subject matter, skill, etc.: *he knows his stuff.* **13.** a slang word for **money.** **14.** *Sl.* a drug, esp. cannabis. **15.** *Inf.* **do one's stuff.** to do what is expected of one. **16. that's the stuff.** that is what is needed. **17.** *Brit. sl.* a girl or woman considered sexually (esp. in **bit of stuff**). [C14: from OF *estoffe,* from *estoffer* to furnish, of Gmc origin] —'**stuffer** *n.*

stuffed (stʌft) *adj.* **1.** filled with something, esp. (of poultry and other food) filled with stuffing. **2.** (foll. by *up*) (of the nasal passages) blocked with mucus. **3. get stuffed!** *Brit. taboo sl.* an exclamation of contemptuous anger or annoyance against another person.

stuffed shirt *n. Inf.* a pompous person.

stuff gown *n. Brit.* a woollen gown worn by a barrister who has not taken silk.

stuffing ('stʌfɪŋ) *n.* **1.** the material with which something is stuffed. **2.** a mixture of ingredients with which poultry, meat, etc., is stuffed before cooking. **3. knock the stuffing out of** (**someone**). to defeat (someone) utterly.

stuffing box *n.* a small chamber in which packing is compressed around a reciprocating or rotating rod or shaft to form a seal.

stuffy ('stʌfɪ) *adj.* **-ier, -iest. 1.** lacking fresh air. **2.** excessively dull, staid, or conventional. **3.** (of the nasal passages) blocked with mucus. —'**stuffily** *adv.* —'**stuffiness** *n.*

stultify ('stʌltɪˌfaɪ) *vb.* **-fying, -fied.** (*tr.*) **1.** to make useless, futile, or ineffectual, esp. by routine. **2.** to cause to appear absurd or inconsistent. [C18: from L *stultus* stupid + *facere* to make] —ˌ**stultifi'cation** *n.* —'**stulti,fier** *n.*

stum (stʌm) (in wine-making) ~*n.* **1.** a less common word for **must**². **2.** partly fermented wine added to fermented wine as a preservative. ~*vb.* **stumming, stummed. 3.** to preserve (wine) by adding stum. [C17: from Du. *stom* dumb]

stumble ('stʌmbʰl) *vb.* (*intr.*) **1.** to trip or fall while walking or running. **2.** to walk in an awkward, unsteady, or unsure way. **3.** to make mistakes or hesitate in speech or actions. **4.** (foll. by *across* or *upon*) to come (across) by accident. ~*n.* **5.** a false step, trip, or blunder. **6.** the act of stumbling. [C14: rel. to Norwegian *stumla*, Danish dialect *stumle*] —'**stumbler** *n.* —'**stumbling** *adj.* —'**stumblingly** *adv.*

stumbling block *n.* any impediment or obstacle.

stumer ('stjuːmə) *n.* **1.** *Sl.* a forgery or cheat. **2.** *Irish dialect.* a poor bargain. **3.** *Scot.* a stupid person. **4. come a stumer.** *Austral. sl.* to crash financially. [from ?]

stump (stʌmp) *n.* **1.** the base of a tree trunk left standing after the tree has been felled or has fallen. **2.** the part of something, such as a tooth, limb, or blade, that remains after a larger part has been removed. **3.** (*often pl.*) *Inf., facetious.* a leg (esp. in **stir one's stumps**). **4.** *Cricket.* any of three upright wooden sticks that, with two bails laid across them, form a wicket (the **stumps**). **5.** Also called: **tortillon.** a short sharply-pointed stick of cork or rolled paper or leather, used in drawing and shading. **6.** a heavy tread or the sound of heavy footsteps. **7.** a platform used by an orator when addressing a meeting. ~*vb.* **8.** (*tr.*) to stop, confuse, or puzzle. **9.** (*intr.*) to plod or trudge heavily. **10.** (*tr.*) *Cricket.* to dismiss (a batsman) by breaking his wicket with the ball or with the ball in the hand while he is out of his crease. **11.** *Chiefly U.S. & Canad.* to campaign or canvass (an area), esp. by political speech-making. [C14: from MLow G *stump*] —'**stumper** *n.*

stump up *vb.* (*adv.*) *Brit. inf.* to give (the money required).

stumpy ('stʌmpɪ) *adj.* **stumpier, stumpiest. 1.** short and thickset like a stump; stubby. **2.** full of stumps. —'**stumpiness** *n.*

stun (stʌn) *vb.* **stunning, stunned.** (*tr.*) **1.** to render unconscious, as by a heavy blow or fall. **2.** to shock or overwhelm. **3.** to surprise or astound. ~*n.* **4.** the state or effect of being stunned. [C13 *stunen*, from OF *estoner* to daze, ult. from L EX-¹ + *tonāre* to thunder]

stung (stʌŋ) *vb.* the past tense and past participle of **sting.**

stunk (stʌŋk) *vb.* a past tense and past participle of **stink.**

stunner ('stʌnə) *n. Inf.* a person or thing of great beauty, quality, size, etc.

stunning ('stʌnɪŋ) *adj. Inf.* very attractive, impressive, astonishing, etc. —'**stunningly** *adv.*

stunsail *or* **stuns'l** ('stʌnsʰl) *n.* another word for **studdingsail.**

stunt¹ (stʌnt) *vb.* **1.** (*tr.*) to prevent or impede (the growth or development) of (a plant, animal, etc.). ~*n.* **2.** the act or an instance of stunting. **3.** a person, animal, or plant that has been stunted. [C17 (as vb.: to check the growth of): ?from C15 *stont* of short duration, from OE *stunt* foolish; sense prob. infl. by ON *stuttr* dwarfed] —'**stunted** *adj.* —'**stuntedness** *n.*

stunt² (stʌnt) *n.* **1.** a feat of daring or skill. **2. a.** an acrobatic or dangerous piece of action in a film, etc. **b.** (*as modifier*): *a stunt man.* **3.** anything spectacular or unusual done for attention. ~*vb.* **4.** (*intr.*) to perform a stunt or stunts. [C19: U.S. student slang, from ?]

stupa ('stuːpə) *n.* a domed edifice housing Buddhist or Jain relics. [C19: from Sansk.: dome]

stupe (stjuːp) *n. Med.* a hot damp cloth, usually sprinkled with an irritant, applied to the body to relieve pain by counterirritation. [C14: from L *stuppa* flax, from Gk *stuppē*]

stupefacient (ˌstjuːpɪ'feɪʃɪənt) *n.* **1.** a drug that causes stupor. ~*adj.* **2.** of, relating to, or designating this type of drug. [C17: from L *stupefaciēns*, from *stupēre* to be stunned + *facere* to make]

stupefaction (ˌstjuːpɪ'fækʃən) *n.* **1.** astonishment. **2.** the act of stupefying or the state of being stupefied.

stupefy ('stjuːpɪˌfaɪ) *vb.* **-fying, -fied.** (*tr.*) **1.** to render insensitive or lethargic. **2.** to confuse or astound. [C16: from OF *stupefier*, from L *stupefacere*; see STUPEFACIENT] —'**stupe,fying** *adj.*

stupendous (stjuː'pɛndəs) *adj.* astounding, wonderful, huge, etc. [C17: from L *stupēre* to be amazed] —**stu'pendously** *adv.* —**stu'pendousness** *n.*

stupid ('stjuːpɪd) *adj.* **1.** lacking in common sense, perception, or intelligence. **2.** (*usually postpositive*) dazed or stupefied: *stupid from lack of sleep.* **3.** slow-witted. **4.** trivial, silly, or frivolous. ~*n.* **5.** *Inf.* a stupid person. [C16: from F *stupide*, from L *stupidus* silly, from *stupēre* to be amazed] —**stu'pidity** *or* '**stupidness** *n.*

stupor ('stjuːpə) *n.* **1.** a state of unconsciousness. **2.** mental dullness; torpor. [C17: from L, from *stupēre* to be aghast] —'**stuporous** *adj.*

sturdy ('stɜːdɪ) *adj.* **-dier, -diest. 1.** healthy, strong, and vigorous. **2.** strongly built; stalwart. [C13 (in the sense: rash, harsh): from OF *estordi* dazed, from *estordir* to stun] —'**sturdily** *adv.* —'**sturdiness** *n.*

sturgeon ('stɜːdʒən) *n.* any of various primitive bony fishes of temperate waters of the N hemisphere, having an elongated snout and rows of spines along the body. [C13: from OF *estourgeon*, of Gmc origin]

Sturt (stɜːt) *n.* **Charles.** 1795–1869, English explorer, who led three expeditions (1828–29; 1829; 1844–45) into the Australian interior, discovering the Darling River (1828).

Sturt's desert pea (stɜːts) *n.* another name for **desert pea.**

stutter ('stʌtə) *vb.* **1.** to speak (a word, phrase, etc.) with recurring repetition of consonants, esp. initial ones. **2.** to make (an abrupt sound) repeatedly: *the gun stuttered.* ~*n.* **3.** the act or habit of stuttering. **4.** a stuttering sound. [C16] —'**stutterer** *n.* —'**stuttering** *n., adj.* —'**stutteringly** *adv.*

Stuttgart (*German*: 'ʃtʊtgart) *n.* an industrial city in W West Germany, capital of Baden-Württemberg state, on the River Neckar: developed around a stud farm (*Stuotgarten*) of the Counts of Württemberg. Pop.: 564 500 (1986).

Stuyvesant ('staɪvɪsʰnt) *n.* **Peter.** ?1610–72, Dutch colonial administrator of New Netherland (later New York) (1646–64).

sty¹ (staɪ) *n., pl.* **sties. 1.** a pen in which pigs are housed. **2.** any filthy or corrupt place. ~*vb.* **stying, stied. 3.** to enclose or be enclosed in a sty. [OE *stig*]

sty² *or* **stye** (staɪ) *n., pl.* **sties** *or* **styes.** inflammation of a sebaceous gland of the eyelid. [C15 *styanye* (mistaken as *sty on eye*), from OE *stīgend* rising, hence swelling, + *ye* eye]

Stygian ('stɪdʒɪən) *adj.* **1.** of or relating to the Styx. **2.** *Chiefly literary.* dark, gloomy, or hellish. [C16: from L *Stygius*, from Gk *Stugios*, from *Stux* STYX]

style (staɪl) *n.* **1.** a form of appearance, design, or production; type or make. **2.** the way in which something is done: *good style.* **3.** the manner in which something is expressed or performed, considered as separate from its intrinsic content, meaning, etc. **4.** a distinctive, formal, or characteristic manner of expression in words, music, painting, etc. **5.** elegance or refinement of manners, dress, etc. **6.** prevailing fashion in dress, looks, etc. **7.** a fashionable or ostentatious mode of existence: *to live in style.* **8.** the particular mode of orthography, punctuation, design, etc., followed in a book, journal, etc., or in a printing or publishing house. **9.** *Chiefly Brit.* the distinguishing title or form of address of a person or firm. **10.** *Bot.* the long slender extension of the ovary, bearing the stigma. **11.** a method of expressing or calculating dates. See Old Style, New Style. **12.** another word for **stylus** (sense 1). **13.** the arm of a sundial. ~*vb.* (*mainly tr.*) **14.** to design, shape, or tailor: *to style hair.* **15.** to adapt or make suitable for. **16.** to make consistent or correct according to a printing or publishing style. **17.** to name or call; designate: *to style a man a fool.* [C13: from L *stylus, stilus* writing implement, hence characteristics of the writing, style] —'**stylar** *adj.* —'**styler** *n.*

stylebook ('staɪl,bʊk) n. a book containing rules and examples of punctuation, typography, etc., for the use of writers, editors, and printers.

stylet ('staɪlɪt) n. Surgery. 1. a wire for insertion into a catheter, etc., to maintain its rigidity during passage. 2. a slender probe. [C17: from F stilet, from OIt. STILETTO; infl. by L stylus style]

styling mousse n. a light foamy substance applied to the hair before styling in order to retain the style.

stylish ('staɪlɪʃ) adj. having style; smart; fashionable. —'**stylishly** adv. —'**stylishness** n.

stylist ('staɪlɪst) n. 1. a person who performs, writes, or acts with attention to style. 2. a designer of clothes, décor, etc. 3. a hairdresser who styles hair.

stylistic (staɪ'lɪstɪk) adj. of or relating to style, esp. artistic or literary style. —**sty'listically** adv.

stylite ('staɪlaɪt) n. Christianity. one of a class of recluses who in ancient times lived on the top of high pillars. [C17: from LGk stulitēs, from Gk stulos a pillar] —**stylitic** (staɪ'lɪtɪk) adj.

stylize or **-ise** ('staɪlaɪz) vb. (tr.) to give a conventional or established stylistic form to. —**styli'zation** or **-i'sation** n.

stylo- or before a vowel **styl-** combining form. 1. (in biology) a style. 2. indicating a column or point: stylobate; stylograph. [from Gk stulos column]

stylobate ('staɪlə,beɪt) n. a continuous horizontal course of masonry that supports a colonnade. [C17: from L stylobatēs, from Gk stulos pillar + -batēs, from bainein to walk]

stylograph ('staɪlə,grɑːf) n. a fountain pen having a fine hollow tube as the writing point instead of a nib. [C19: from STYL(US) + -GRAPH]

styloid ('staɪlɔɪd) adj. 1. resembling a stylus. 2. Anat. of or relating to a projecting process of the temporal bone. [C18: from NL styloides, from Gk stuloeidēs like a stylus; infl. by Gk stulos pillar]

stylops ('staɪlɒps) n., pl. **-lopes** (-lə,piːz). any of various insects living as a parasite in other insects, esp. bees and wasps. [C19: NL, from Gk, from stulos a pillar + ōps an eye, from the fact that the male has stalked eyes]

stylus ('staɪləs) n., pl. **-li** (-laɪ) or **-luses**. 1. Also called: **style**. a pointed instrument for engraving, drawing, or writing. 2. a tool used in ancient times for writing on wax tablets, which was pointed at one end and blunt at the other for erasing. 3. a device attached to the cartridge in the pick-up arm of a record player that rests in the groove in the record, transmitting the vibrations to the sensing device in the cartridge. [C18: from L, var. of stilus writing implement]

stymie or **stymy** ('staɪmɪ) vb. **-mieing, -mied** or **-mying, -mied.** (tr.; often passive) 1. to hinder or thwart. 2. Golf. to impede with a stymie. ~n., pl. **-mies.** 3. Golf. (formerly) a situation in which an opponent's ball is blocking the line between the hole and the ball about to be played. 4. a situation of obstruction. [C19: from ?]

styptic ('stɪptɪk) adj. 1. contracting the blood vessels or tissues. ~n. 2. a styptic drug. [C14: via LL, from Gk stuptikos capable of contracting, from stuphein to contract]

styrene ('staɪriːn) n. a colourless oily volatile flammable liquid made from ethylene and benzene. It readily polymerizes and is used in making synthetic plastics and rubbers. Formula: $C_6H_5CH:CH_2$. Systematic name: **phenylethene.** [C20: from Gk sturax tree of the genus Styrax + -ENE]

Styria ('stɪrɪə) n. a mountainous province of SE Austria: rich mineral resources. Capital: Graz. Pop.: 1 182 599 (1986). Area: 16 384 sq. km (6326 sq. miles). German name: **Steiermark.**

Styx (stɪks) n. Greek myth. a river in Hades across which Charon ferried the souls of the dead. [from Gk Stux; related to stugein to hate]

suable ('sjuːəb⁾l) adj. liable to be sued in a court. —**su-a'bility** n.

Suakin ('suːɑːkɪn) n. a port in the NE Sudan, on the Red Sea: formerly the chief port of the African Red Sea; now obstructed by a coral reef. Pop.: 5511 (1973).

Suárez (Spanish 'swarεθ) n. **Adolfo** (a'ðɔlfɔ). born 1932, Spanish statesman; prime minister (1976–78).

suasion ('sweɪʒən) n. a rare word for **persuasion.** [C14: from L suāsiō, from suādēre to PERSUADE] —'**suasive** adj.

suave (swɑːv) adj. (esp. of a man) displaying smoothness and sophistication in manner; urbane. [C16: from L suāvis sweet] —'**suavely** adv. —**suavity** ('swɑːvɪtɪ) or '**suaveness** n.

sub (sʌb) n. 1. short for several words beginning with sub-, such as **subeditor, submarine, subordinate, subscription,** and **substitute.** 2. Brit. inf. an advance payment of wages or salary. Formal term: **subsistence allowance.** ~vb. **subbing, subbed.** 3. (intr.) to serve or act as a substitute. 4. Brit. inf. to grant or receive (an advance payment of wages or salary). 5. (tr.) Inf. short for **subedit.**

sub. abbrev. for: 1. subeditor. 2. Music. subito. 3. subscription. 4. substitute.

sub- prefix. 1. situated under or beneath: subterranean. 2. secondary in rank; subordinate: subeditor. 3. falling short of; less than or imperfectly: subarctic; subhuman. 4. forming a subdivision or subordinate part: subcommittee. 5. (in chemistry) **a.** indicating that a compound contains a relatively small proportion of a specified element: suboxide. **b.** indicating that a salt is basic salt: subacetate. [from L sub]

subacid (sʌb'æsɪd) adj. (esp. of some fruits) moderately acid or sour. —**subacidity** (,sʌbə'sɪdɪtɪ) or **sub'acidness** n.

subadar or **subahdar** ('suːbə,dɑː) n. (formerly) the chief native officer of a company of Indian soldiers in the British service. [C17: via Urdu from Persian, from sūba province + -dār holding]

subalpine (sʌb'ælpaɪn) adj. 1. situated in or relating to the regions at the foot of mountains. 2. (of plants) growing below the tree line in mountainous regions.

subaltern ('sʌb⁾ltən) n. 1. a commissioned officer below the rank of captain in certain armies, esp. the British. ~adj. 2. of inferior position or rank. 3. Logic. (of a proposition) particular, esp. in relation to a universal of the same quality. [C16: from LL subalternus, from L SUB- + alternus alternate, from alter the other]

subalternation (,sʌbɔːltə'neɪʃən) n. Logic. the relation between a universal and a particular proposition of the same quality where the universal proposition implies the particular proposition.

subantarctic (,sʌbænt'ɑːktɪk) adj. of or relating to latitudes immediately north of the Antarctic Circle.

subaqua (,sʌb'ækwə) adj. of or relating to underwater sport: subaqua swimming.

subaqueous (sʌb'eɪkwɪəs, -'ækwɪ-) adj. occurring, formed, or used under water.

subarctic (sʌb'ɑːktɪk) adj. of or relating to latitudes immediately south of the Arctic Circle.

subatomic (,sʌbə'tɒmɪk) adj. 1. of, relating to, or being a particle making up an atom or a process occurring within atoms. 2. having dimensions smaller than atomic dimensions.

subbasement ('sʌb,beɪsmənt) n. a storey of a building beneath the main basement.

subclass ('sʌb,klɑːs) n. 1. a principal subdivision of a class. 2. Biol. a taxonomic group that is a subdivision of a class. 3. Maths. another name for **subset.**

subclavian (sʌb'kleɪvɪən) adj. Anat. (of an artery, vein, etc.) below the clavicle. [C17: from NL subclāvius, from L SUB- + clavis key]

subclinical (sʌb'klɪnɪk⁾l) adj. Med. of or relating to the stage in the course of a disease before the symptoms are first noted. —**sub'clinically** adv.

subconscious (sʌb'kɒnʃəs) adj. 1. acting or existing without one's awareness. ~n. 2. Psychol. that part of the mind on the fringe of consciousness which contains material it is possible to become aware of by redirecting attention. —**sub'consciously** adv. —**sub'consciousness** n.

ˌsubab'dominal adj.	'sub,average adj.	'sub,clause n.
ˌsuba'cute adj.	ˌsubax'illary adj.	'sub,chapter n.	'subcom,mission n.
sub'agent n.	'sub,branch n.	'sub,chief n.	ˌsubcom'missioner n.
ˌsuba'quatic adj.	sub'category n.	ˌsubclassifi'cation n.	'subcom,mittee n.
'sub,article n.	'sub,cell n.	sub'classiˌfy vb.	

subcontinent (sʌbˈkɒntɪnənt) *n.* a large land mass that is a distinct part of a continent, such as India is of Asia. —**subcontinental** (ˌsʌbkɒntɪˈnɛntəl) *adj.*

subcontract *n.* (sʌbˈkɒntrækt). **1.** a subordinate contract under which the supply of materials, labour, etc. is let out to someone other than a party to the main contract. ~*vb.* (ˌsʌbkənˈtrækt). **2.** (*intr.; often foll. by for*) to enter into or make a subcontract. **3.** (*tr.*) to let out (work) on a subcontract. —**subcon'tractor** *n.*

subcontrary (sʌbˈkɒntrərɪ) *Logic.* ~*adj.* **1.** (of a pair of propositions) related such that they cannot both be false at once, although they may be true together. ~*n., pl.* **-ries. 2.** a statement which cannot be false when a given statement is false.

subcritical (sʌbˈkrɪtɪkəl) *adj. Physics.* (of a nuclear reaction, power station, etc.) having or involving a chain reaction that is not self-sustaining; not yet critical.

subculture (ˈsʌbˌkʌltʃə) *n.* a subdivision of a national culture or an enclave within it with a distinct integrated network of behaviour, beliefs, and attitudes. —**sub'cultural** *adj.*

subcutaneous (ˌsʌbkjuːˈteɪnɪəs) *adj. Med.* situated, used, or introduced beneath the skin. —**subcu'taneously** *adv.*

subdeacon (sʌbˈdiːkən) *n. Chiefly R.C. Church.* **1.** a cleric who assists at High Mass. **2.** (formerly) a person ordained to the lowest of the major orders. —**subdeaconate** (sʌbˈdiːkənɪt) *n.*

subdivide (ˌsʌbdɪˈvaɪd, ˈsʌbdɪˌvaɪd) *vb.* to divide (something) resulting from an earlier division. —**'subdiˌvision** *n.*

subdominant (sʌbˈdɒmɪnənt) *Music.* ~*n.* **1.** the fourth degree of a major or minor scale. **2.** a key or chord based on this. ~*adj.* **3.** of or relating to the subdominant.

subdue (səbˈdjuː) *vb.* **-duing, -dued.** (*tr.*) **1.** to establish ascendancy over by force. **2.** to overcome and bring under control, as by intimidation or persuasion. **3.** to hold in check or repress (feelings, etc.). **4.** to render less intense or less conspicuous. [C14 *sobdue,* from OF *soduire* to mislead, from L *subdūcere* to remove; infl. by L *subdere* to subject] —**sub'duable** *adj.* —**sub'dual** *n.*

subdued (səbˈdjuːd) *adj.* **1.** cowed, passive, or shy. **2.** gentle or quiet: *a subdued whisper.* **3.** (of colours, lighting, etc.) not harsh or bright.

subedit (sʌbˈɛdɪt) *vb.* to edit and correct (written or printed material).

subeditor (sʌbˈɛdɪtə) *n.* a person who checks and edits copy, esp. on a newspaper.

subequatorial (sʌbˌɛkwəˈtɔːrɪəl) *adj.* in or characteristic of regions immediately north or south of equatorial regions.

suberose (ˈsjuːbəˌrəʊs), **subereous** (sjuːˈbɛrɪəs), *or* **suberic** (sjuːˈbɛrɪk) *adj. Bot.* relating to, resembling, or consisting of cork; corky. [C19: from L *sūber* cork + -OSE[1]]

subfamily (ˈsʌbˌfæmɪlɪ) *n., pl.* **-lies. 1.** *Biol.* a taxonomic group that is a subdivision of a family. **2.** a subdivision of a family of languages.

subfusc (ˈsʌbfʌsk) *adj.* **1.** devoid of brightness or appeal; drab, dull, or dark. ~*n.* **2.** (at Oxford University) formal academic dress. [C18: from L *subfuscus* dusky, from *fuscus* dark]

subgenus (ˈsʌbˌdʒiːnəs, -ˌdʒɛn-) *n., pl.* **-genera** (-ˈdʒɛnərə) *or* **-genuses.** *Biol.* a subdivision of a genus that is of higher rank than a species. —**subgeneric** (ˌsʌbdʒəˈnɛrɪk) *adj.*

subheading (ˈsʌbˌhɛdɪŋ) *or* **subhead** *n.* **1.** the heading or title of a subdivision or subsection of a printed work. **2.** a division subordinate to a main heading or title.

subhuman (sʌbˈhjuːmən) *adj.* **1.** of or designating animals below man (*Homo sapiens*) in evolutionary development. **2.** less than human.

subindex (sʌbˈɪndɛks) *n., pl.* **-dices** (-dɪˌsiːz) *or* **-dexes.** another word for **subscript** (sense 2).

subito (ˈsuːbɪˌtəʊ) *adv. Music.* suddenly; immediately. [C18: via It. from L: suddenly, from *subitus* sudden, from *subīre* to approach]

subj. *abbrev. for:* **1.** subject. **2.** subjective(ly). **3.** subjunctive.

subjacent (sʌbˈdʒeɪsənt) *adj.* **1.** forming a foundation; underlying. **2.** lower than. [C16: from L *subjacēre* to lie close, be under] —**sub'jacency** *n.* —**sub'jacently** *adv.*

subject *n.* (ˈsʌbdʒɪkt). **1.** the predominant theme or topic, as of a book, discussion, etc. **2.** any branch of learning considered as a course of study. **3.** *Grammar, logic.* a word, phrase, etc., about which something is predicated or stated in a sentence; for example, *the cat* in the sentence *The cat catches mice.* **4.** a person or thing that undergoes experiment, treatment, etc. **5.** a person under the rule of a monarch, government, etc. **6.** an object, figure, scene, etc., as portrayed by an artist or photographer. **7.** *Philosophy.* **a.** that which thinks or feels as opposed to the object of thinking and feeling; the self or the mind. **b.** a substance as opposed to its attributes. **8.** Also called: **theme.** *Music.* the principal motif of a fugue, the basis from which the musical material is derived in a sonata-form movement, or the recurrent figure in a rondo. **9.** *Logic.* the term of a proposition about which something is asserted. **10.** an originating motive. **11. change the subject.** to select a new topic of conversation. ~*adj.* (ˈsʌbdʒɪkt). (*usually postpositive; foll. by to*) **12.** being under the power or sovereignty of a ruler, government, etc.: *subject peoples.* **13.** showing a tendency (towards): *a child subject to indiscipline.* **14.** exposed or vulnerable: *subject to ribaldry.* **15.** conditional upon: *the results are subject to correction.* ~*adv.* (ˈsʌbdʒɪkt). **16. subject to.** (*prep.*) under the condition that: *we accept, subject to her agreement.* ~*vb.* (səbˈdʒɛkt). (*tr.*) **17.** (foll. by *to*) to cause to undergo: *they subjected him to torture.* **18.** (*often passive; foll. by to*) to expose or render vulnerable or liable (to some experience): *he was subjected to great danger.* **19.** (foll. by *to*) to bring under the control or authority (of): *to subject a soldier to discipline.* **20.** *Rare.* to present for consideration; submit. [C14: from L *subjectus* brought under, from *subicere* to place under, from SUB- + *jacere* to throw] —**sub'jectable** *adj.* —**sub'jection** *n.*

subjective (səbˈdʒɛktɪv) *adj.* **1.** of, proceeding from, or relating to the mind of the thinking subject and not the nature of the object being considered. **2.** of, relating to, or emanating from a person's emotions, prejudices, etc. **3.** relating to the inherent nature of a person or thing; essential. **4.** existing only as perceived and not as a thing in itself. **5.** *Med.* (of a symptom, condition, etc.) experienced only by the patient and incapable of being recognized or studied by anyone else. **6.** *Grammar.* denoting a case of nouns and pronouns, esp. in languages having only two cases, that identifies the subject of a finite verb and (in formal use in English) is selected for predicate complements, as in *It is I.* ~*n.* **7.** *Grammar.* **a.** the subjective case. **b.** a subjective word or speech element. Cf. **objective.** —**sub'jectively** *adv.* —**ˌsubjec'tivity** *or* **sub'jectiveness** *n.*

subjectivism (səbˈdʒɛktɪˌvɪzəm) *n. Philosophy.* the doctrine that there are no absolute moral values but that these are variable in the same way that taste is. —**sub'jectivist** *n.*

subjoin (sʌbˈdʒɔɪn) *vb.* (*tr.*) to add or attach at the end of something spoken, written, etc. [C16: from F *subjoindre,* from L *subjungere* to add to, from *sub-* in addition + *jungere* to join] —**sub'joinder** *n.*

sub judice (ˈdʒuːdɪsɪ) *adj.* (*usually postpositive*) before a court of law or a judge; under judicial consideration. [L]

subjugate (ˈsʌbdʒʊˌgeɪt) *vb.* (*tr.*) **1.** to bring into subjection. **2.** to make subservient or submissive. [C15: from LL *subjugāre* to subdue, from L SUB- + *jugum* yoke] —**subjugable** (ˈsʌbdʒəgəbəl) *adj.* —**ˌsubju'gation** *n.* —**'subju,gator** *n.*

subjunctive (səbˈdʒʌŋktɪv) *Grammar.* ~*adj.* **1.** denoting a mood of verbs used when the content of the clause is being doubted, supposed, feared true, etc., rather than being asserted. In the following sentence, *were* is in the subjunctive: *I'd think seriously about it if I were you.* Cf. **indicative.** ~*n.* **2. a.** the subjunctive mood. **b.** a verb in this mood. [C16: via LL *subjunctīvus,* from L *subjungere* to SUBJOIN] —**sub'junctively** *adv.*

sublease *n.* (ˈsʌbˌliːs). **1.** a lease of property made by a lessee or tenant of that property. ~*vb.* (sʌbˈliːs). **2.** to

---

sub'cranial *adj.*	**'sub,file** *n.*
'sub,depot *n.*	**'sub,floor** *n.*
sub'entry *n.*	

sub'foreman *n.*	**'sub,function** *n.*
sub'freezing *adj.*	**'sub,group** *n.*

grant a sublease of (property); sublet. **3.** (*tr.*) to obtain or hold by sublease. —**sublessee** (ˌsʌbləˈsiː) *n.* —**sublessor** (ˌsʌblɛˈsɔː) *n.*

sublet (sʌbˈlɛt) *vb.* **-letting, -let. 1.** to grant a sublease of (property). **2.** to let out (work, etc.) under a subcontract.

sublieutenant (ˌsʌbləˈtɛnənt) *n.* the most junior commissioned officer in the Royal Navy and certain other navies. —ˌsubˈlieuˈtenancy *n.*

sublimate (ˈsʌblɪˌmeɪt) *vb.* **1.** *Psychol.* to direct the energy of (a primitive impulse) into activities that are socially more acceptable. **2.** (*tr.*) to make purer; refine. ~*n.* **3.** *Chem.* the material obtained when a substance is sublimed. [C16: from L *sublīmāre* to elevate, from *sublīmis* lofty; see SUBLIME] —ˌsubliˈmation *n.*

sublime (səˈblaɪm) *adj.* **1.** of high moral, intellectual, or spiritual value; noble; exalted. **2.** inspiring deep veneration or awe. **3.** unparalleled; supreme. **4.** *Poetic.* of proud bearing or aspect. **5.** *Arch.* raised up. ~*n.* **the sublime. 6.** something that is sublime. **7.** the ultimate degree or perfect example: *the sublime of folly.* ~*vb.* **8.** (*tr.*) to make higher or purer. **9.** to change or cause to change directly from a solid to a vapour or gas without first melting. **10.** to undergo or cause to undergo this process followed by a reverse change directly from a vapour to a solid: *to sublime iodine onto glass.* [C14: from L *sublīmis* lofty, ?from *sub-* up to + *līmen* lintel] —subˈlimely *adv.* —sublimity (səˈblɪmɪtɪ) *n.*

subliminal (sʌbˈlɪmɪnəl) *adj.* **1.** resulting from processes of which the individual is not aware. **2.** (of stimuli) less than the minimum intensity or duration required to elicit a response. [C19: from L *sub-* below + *līmen* threshold] —subˈliminally *adv.*

subliminal advertising *n.* advertising on film or television that employs subliminal images to influence the viewer unconsciously.

sublingual (sʌbˈlɪŋɡwəl) *adj. Anat.* situated beneath the tongue.

sublunary (sʌbˈluːnərɪ) *adj.* **1.** between the moon and the earth. **2.** of or relating to the earth. [C16: via LL, from L SUB- + *lūna* moon]

sub-machine-gun *n.* a portable automatic or semiautomatic light gun with a short barrel, designed to be fired from the hip or shoulder.

submarginal (sʌbˈmɑːdʒɪnəl) *adj.* **1.** below the minimum requirements. **2.** (of land) infertile and unprofitable. —subˈmarginally *adv.*

submarine (ˈsʌbməˌriːn, ˌsʌbməˈriːn) *n.* **1.** a vessel, esp. a warship, capable of operating below the surface of the sea. **2.** (*modifier*) **a.** of or relating to a submarine: *a submarine captain.* **b.** below the surface of the sea: *a submarine cable.* —**submariner** (sʌbˈmærɪnə) *n.*

submaxillary gland (ˌsʌbmækˈsɪlərɪ) *n.* (in mammals) either of a pair of salivary glands situated on each side behind the lower jaw.

submediant (sʌbˈmiːdɪənt) *Music.* ~*n.* **1.** the sixth degree of a major or minor scale. **2.** a key or chord based on this. ~*adj.* **3.** of or relating to the submediant.

submerge (səbˈmɜːdʒ) *or* **submerse** (səbˈmɜːs) *vb.* **1.** to plunge, sink, or dive or cause to plunge, sink, or dive below the surface of water, etc. **2.** (*tr.*) to cover with water or other liquid. **3.** (*tr.*) to hide; suppress. **4.** (*tr.*) to overwhelm, as with work, etc. [C17: from L *submergere*] —subˈmergence *or* subˈmersion *n.*

submersible (səbˈmɜːsɪbəl) *or* **submergible** (səbˈmɜːdʒɪbəl) *adj.* **1.** able to be submerged. **2.** capable of operating under water, etc. ~*n.* **3.** a vessel designed to operate under water for short periods. **4.** a submarine designed and equipped to carry out work below the level that divers can work. —subˌmersiˈbility *or* subˌmergiˈbility *n.*

subminiature (sʌbˈmɪnɪətʃə) *adj.* smaller than miniature.

subminiature camera *n.* a pocket-sized camera, usually using 16 millimetre film.

submission (səbˈmɪʃən) *n.* **1.** an act or instance of submitting. **2.** something submitted; a proposal, etc. **3.** the quality or condition of being submissive. **4.** the act of referring a document, etc., for the consideration of someone else.

submissive (səbˈmɪsɪv) *adj.* of, tending towards, or indicating submission, humility, or servility. —subˈmissively *adv.* —subˈmissiveness *n.*

submit (səbˈmɪt) *vb.* **-mitting, -mitted. 1.** (often foll. by *to*) to yield (oneself), as to the will of another person, a superior force, etc. **2.** (foll. by *to*) to subject or be voluntarily subjected (to analysis, treatment, etc.). **3.** (*tr.*; often foll. by *to*) to refer (something to someone) for judgment or consideration. **4.** (*tr.*; *may take a clause as object*) to state, contend, or propose deferentially. **5.** (*intr.*; often foll. by *to*) to defer or accede (to the decision, etc., of another). [C14: from L *submittere* to place under] —subˈmittable *or* subˈmissible *adj.* —subˈmittal *n.* —subˈmitter *n.*

submultiple (sʌbˈmʌltɪpəl) *n.* **1.** a number that can be divided into another number an integral number of times without a remainder: *three is a submultiple of nine.* ~*adj.* **2.** being a submultiple of a quantity or number.

subnormal (sʌbˈnɔːməl) *adj.* **1.** less than the normal. **2.** having a low intelligence. ~*n.* **3.** a subnormal person. —**subnormality** (ˌsʌbnɔːˈmælɪtɪ) *n.*

subnuclear (sʌbˈnjuːklɪə) *adj.* in or smaller than the nucleus of an atom.

suborbital (sʌbˈɔːbɪtəl) *adj.* **1.** (of a rocket, missile, etc.) having a flight path that is less than an orbit of the earth or other celestial body. **2.** *Anat.* situated beneath the orbit of the eye.

suborder (ˈsʌbˌɔːdə) *n. Biol.* a subdivision of an order. —subˈordinal *adj.*

subordinate *adj.* (səˈbɔːdɪnɪt). **1.** of lesser order or importance. **2.** under the authority or control of another: *a subordinate functionary.* ~*n.* (səˈbɔːdɪnɪt). **3.** a person or thing that is subordinate. ~*vb.* (səˈbɔːdɪˌneɪt). (*tr.*) usually foll. by *to*) **4.** to put in a lower rank or position (than). **5.** to make subservient: *to subordinate mind to heart.* [C15: from Med. L *subordināre*, from L SUB- + *ordō* rank] —subˈordinately *adv.* —subˌordiˈnation *n.* —subˈordinative *adj.*

subordinate clause *n. Grammar.* a clause with an adjectival, adverbial, or nominal function, rather than one that functions as a separate sentence in its own right.

subordinating conjunction *n.* a conjunction that introduces subordinate clauses, such as *if, because, although,* and *until.*

suborn (səˈbɔːn) *vb.* (*tr.*) **1.** to bribe, incite, or instigate (a person) to commit a wrongful act. **2.** *Law.* to induce (a witness) to commit perjury. [C16: from L *subornāre*, from *sub-* secretly + *ornāre* to furnish] —**subornation** (ˌsʌbɔːˈneɪʃən) *n.* —**subornative** (sʌˈbɔːnətɪv) *adj.* —subˈorner *n.*

Subotica (*Serbo-Croatian* ˈsubɔtitsa) *n.* a town in NE Yugoslavia, in Serbia near the border with Hungary: agricultural and industrial centre. Pop.: 154 611 (1981 est.). Hungarian name: **Szabadka.**

suboxide (sʌbˈɒksaɪd) *n.* an oxide of an element containing less oxygen than the common oxide formed by the element: *carbon suboxide,* C_2O_3.

subplot (ˈsʌbˌplɒt) *n.* a subordinate or auxiliary plot in a novel, play, film, etc.

subpoena (səbˈpiːnə) *n.* **1.** a writ issued by a court of justice requiring a person to appear before the court at a specified time. ~*vb.* **-naing, -naed. 2.** (*tr.*) to serve with a subpoena. [C15: from L: under penalty]

subrogate (ˈsʌbrəˌɡeɪt) *vb.* (*tr.*) *Law.* to put (one person or thing) in the place of another in respect of a right or claim. [C16: from L *subrogāre*, from *sub-* in place of + *rogāre* to ask] —ˌsubroˈgation *n.*

sub rosa (ˈrəʊzə) *adv.* in secret. [L, lit.: under the rose; from use of the rose in ancient times as a token of secrecy]

subroutine (ˈsʌbruːˌtiːn) *n.* a section of a computer program that is stored only once but can be used at several different points in the program. Also called: **procedure.**

subscribe (səbˈskraɪb) *vb.* **1.** (usually foll. by *to*) to pay or promise to pay (money) as a contribution (to a fund, for a magazine, etc.), esp. at regular intervals. **2.** to sign (one's name, etc.) at the end of a document. **3.** (*intr.*; foll. by *to*) to give support or approval: *to subscribe to the theory of reincarnation.* [C15: from L *subscribere* to write underneath] —subˈscriber *n.*

ˌsubmicroˈscopic *adj.*   subˈparaˌgraph *n.*   subˈregion *n.*   subˈscapular *adj., n.*
ˌsubmoˈlecular *adj.*   subˈphylum *n.*   ˌsubsatuˈration *n.*

subscriber trunk dialling *n. Brit.* a service by which telephone subscribers can obtain trunk calls by dialling direct without the aid of an operator. Abbrev.: **STD**.

subscript ('sʌbskrɪpt) *adj.* **1.** *Printing.* (of a character) written or printed below the base line. Cf. **superscript**. ~*n.* **2.** Also called: **subindex**. a subscript character.

subscription (səb'skrɪpʃən) *n.* **1.** a payment or promise of payment for consecutive issues of a magazine, newspaper, book, etc., over a specified period of time. **2. a.** the advance purchase of tickets for a series of concerts, etc. **b.** (*as modifier*): *a subscription concert.* **3.** money paid or promised, as to a charity, or the fund raised in this way. **4.** an offer to buy shares or bonds issued by a company. **5.** the act of signing one's name to a document, etc. **6.** a signature or other appendage attached to the bottom of a document, etc. **7.** agreement or acceptance expressed by or as if by signing one's name. **8.** a signed document, statement, etc. **9.** *Chiefly Brit.* the membership dues or fees paid to a society or club. **10.** an advance order for a new product. **11. a.** the sale of books, etc., prior to publishing. **b.** (*as modifier*): *a subscription edition.* —**sub'scriptive** *adj.* —**sub'scriptively** *adv.*

subsequence ('sʌbsɪkwəns) *n.* **1.** the fact or state of being subsequent. **2.** a subsequent incident or occurrence.

subsequent ('sʌbsɪkwənt) *adj.* occurring after; succeeding. [C15: from L *subsequēns* following on, from *subsequi*, from *sub-* near + *sequi* to follow] —**'subsequently** *adv.* —**'subsequentness** *n.*

subserve (səb'sɜːv) *vb.* (*tr.*) to be helpful or useful to. [C17: from L *subservīre* to be subject to, from SUB- + *servīre* to serve]

subservient (səb'sɜːvɪənt) *adj.* **1.** obsequious. **2.** serving as a means to an end. **3.** a less common word for **subordinate** (sense 2). [C17: from L *subserviēns* complying with, from *subservīre* to SUBSERVE] —**sub'serviently** *adv.* —**sub'servience** or **sub'serviency** *n.*

subset ('sʌb,sɛt) *n.* a mathematical set contained within a larger set.

subshrub ('sʌb,ʃrʌb) *n.* a small bushy plant that is woody except for the tips of the branches.

subside (səb'saɪd) *vb.* (*intr.*) **1.** to become less loud, excited, violent, etc.; abate. **2.** to sink or fall to a lower level. **3.** (of the surface of the earth, etc.) to cave in; collapse. **4.** (of sediment, etc.) to sink or descend to the bottom; settle. [C17: from L *subsīdere* to settle down] —**sub'sider** *n.*

subsidence (səb'saɪdⁿns, 'sʌbsɪdⁿns) *n.* **1.** the act or process of subsiding or the condition of having subsided. **2.** *Geol.* the gradual sinking of landforms to a lower level.

subsidiary (səb'sɪdɪərɪ) *adj.* **1.** serving to aid or supplement; auxiliary. **2.** of lesser importance; subordinate. ~*n., pl.* -**aries**. **3.** a subsidiary person or thing. **4.** Also called: **subsidiary company**. a company with at least half of its capital stock owned by another company. [C16: from L *subsidiārius* supporting, from *subsidium* SUBSIDY] —**sub'sidiarily** *adv.* —**sub'sidiariness** *n.*

subsidize or **-ise** ('sʌbsɪ,daɪz) *vb.* (*tr.*) **1.** to aid or support with a subsidy. **2.** to obtain the aid of by means of a subsidy. —**,subsidi'zation** or **-i'sation** *n.* —**'subsi,dizer** or **iser** *n.*

subsidy ('sʌbsɪdɪ) *n., pl.* -**dies**. **1.** a financial aid supplied by a government, as to industry, for public welfare, the balance of payments, etc. **2.** *English history.* a financial grant made originally for special purposes by Parliament to the Crown. **3.** any monetary aid, grant, or contribution. [C14: from Anglo-Norman *subsidie*, from L *subsidium* assistance, from *subsidēre* to remain, from *sub-* down + *sedēre* to sit]

subsist (səb'sɪst) *vb.* (*mainly intr.*) **1.** (often foll. by *on*) to be sustained; manage to live: *to subsist on milk.* **2.** to continue in existence. **3.** (foll. by *in*) to lie or reside by virtue (of); consist. **4.** (*tr.*) *Obs.* to provide with support. [C16: from L *subsistere* to stand firm] —**sub'sistent** *adj.*

subsistence (səb'sɪstəns) *n.* **1.** the means by which one maintains life. **2.** the act or condition of subsisting.

subsistence farming *n.* a type of farming in which most of the produce is consumed by the farmer and his family.

subsistence level *n.* a standard of living barely adequate to support life.

subsoil ('sʌb,sɔɪl) *n.* **1.** Also called: **undersoil**. the layer of soil beneath the surface soil and overlying the bedrock.

~*vb.* **2.** (*tr.*) to plough (land) to a depth so as to break up the subsoil.

subsonic (sʌb'sɒnɪk) *adj.* being, having, or travelling at a velocity below that of sound.

subspecies ('sʌb,spiːʃiːz) *n., pl.* -**cies**. *Biol.* a subdivision of a species: usually occurs because of isolation within a species.

substance ('sʌbstəns) *n.* **1.** the tangible basic matter of which a thing consists. **2.** a specific type of matter, esp. a homogeneous material with definite or fairly definite chemical composition. **3.** the essence, meaning, etc., of a discourse, thought, or written article. **4.** solid or meaningful quality: *an education of substance.* **5.** material density or body: *free space has no substance.* **6.** material possessions or wealth: *a man of substance.* **7.** *Philosophy.* the supposed immaterial substratum of anything that can receive modifications and in which attributes and accidents inhere. **8. in substance.** with regard to the salient points. [C13: via OF from L *substantia*, from *substāre*, from SUB- + *stāre* to stand]

substandard (sʌb'stændəd) *adj.* **1.** below an established or required standard. **2.** another word for **nonstandard**.

substantial (səb'stænʃəl) *adj.* **1.** of a considerable size or value: *substantial funds.* **2.** worthwhile; important; telling: *a substantial reform.* **3.** having wealth or importance: *a substantial member of the community.* **4.** (of food or a meal) sufficient and nourishing. **5.** solid or strong: *a substantial door.* **6.** real; actual; true: *substantial evidence.* **7.** of or relating to the basic or fundamental substance or aspects of a thing. ~*n.* **8.** (*often pl.*) *Rare.* an essential or important element. —**substantiality** (səb,stænʃɪ'ælɪtɪ) or **sub'stantialness** *n.* —**sub'stantially** *adv.*

substantialism (səb'stænʃə,lɪzəm) *n. Philosophy.* the doctrine that a substantial reality underlies phenomena. —**sub'stantialist** *n.*

substantiate (səb'stænʃɪ,eɪt) *vb.* (*tr.*) **1.** to establish as valid or genuine. **2.** to give form or real existence to. [C17: from NL *substantiāre*, from L *substantia* SUBSTANCE] —**sub,stanti'ation** *n.*

substantive ('sʌbstəntɪv) *n.* **1.** *Grammar.* a noun or pronoun used in place of a noun. ~*adj.* **2.** of, relating to, containing, or being the essential element of a thing. **3.** having independent function, resources, or existence. **4.** of substantial quantity. **5.** solid in foundation or basis. **6.** *Grammar.* denoting, relating to, or standing in place of a noun. **7.** (səb'stæntɪv). (of a dye or colour) staining the material directly without use of a mordant. [C15: from LL *substantīvus*, from L *substāre* to stand beneath] —**substantival** (,sʌbstən'taɪvᵊl) *adj.* —**,substan'tivally** *adv.* —**'substantively** *adv.*

substantive rank *n.* a permanent rank in the armed services.

substation ('sʌb,steɪʃən) *n.* **1.** a subsidiary station. **2.** an installation at which electrical energy is received from one or more power stations for conversion from alternating to direct current, stepping down the voltage, or switching before distribution by a low-tension network.

substituent (sʌb'stɪtjʊənt) *n.* **1.** *Chem.* an atom or group that replaces another atom or group in a molecule or can be regarded as replacing an atom in a parent compound. ~*adj.* **2.** substituted or substitutable. [C19: from L *substituere* to SUBSTITUTE]

substitute ('sʌbstɪ,tjuːt) *vb.* **1.** (often foll. by *for*) to serve or cause to serve in place of another person or thing. **2.** *Chem.* to replace (an atom or group in a molecule) with (another atom or group). ~*n.* **3. a.** a person or thing that serves in place of another, such as a player in a game who takes the place of an injured colleague. **b.** (*as modifier*): *a substitute goalkeeper.* [C16: from L *substituere*, from *sub-* in place of + *statuere* to set up] —,**sub'stitutable** *adj.* —**'substi,tutive** *adj.*

substitution (,sʌbstɪ'tjuːʃən) *n.* **1.** the act of substituting or state of being substituted. **2.** something or someone substituted.

substrate ('sʌbstreɪt) *n.* **1.** *Biochem.* the substance upon which an enzyme acts. **2.** another word for **substratum**.

substratum (sʌb'strɑːtəm, -'streɪ-) *n., pl.* -**strata** (-'strɑːtə, -'streɪtə). **1.** any layer or stratum lying underneath another. **2.** a basis or foundation; groundwork.

---

sub'section *n.*   **sub'series** *n.*

[C17: from NL, from L *substrātus* strewn beneath, from *substernere* to spread under] —**sub'strative** *or* **sub'stratal** *adj.*

substructure ('sʌb,strʌktʃə) *n.* **1.** a structure, pattern, etc., that forms the basis of anything. **2.** a structure forming a foundation or framework for a building or other construction. —**sub'structural** *adj.*

subsume (səb'sjuːm) *vb.* (*tr.*) **1.** to incorporate (an idea, case, etc.) under a comprehensive or inclusive classification. **2.** to consider (an instance of something) as part of a general rule. [C16: from NL *subsumere*, from L SUB- + *sumere* to take] —**sub'sumable** *adj.* —**subsumption** (səb'sʌmpʃən) *n.*

subtemperate (sʌb'tɛmpərɪt) *adj.* of or relating to the colder temperate regions.

subtenant (sʌb'tɛnənt) *n.* a person who rents or leases property from a tenant. —**sub'tenancy** *n.*

subtend (səb'tɛnd) *vb.* (*tr.*) **1.** *Geom.* to be opposite to and delimit (an angle or side). **2.** (of a bract, stem, etc.) to have (a bud or similar part) growing in its axil. [C16: from L *subtendere* to extend beneath]

subterfuge ('sʌbtə,fjuːdʒ) *n.* a stratagem employed to conceal something, evade an argument, etc. [C16: from LL *subterfugium*, from L *subterfugere* to escape by stealth, from *subter* secretly + *fugere* to flee]

subterminal (sʌb'tɜːmɪnᵊl) *adj.* almost at an end.

subterranean (,sʌbtə'reɪnɪən) *adj.* **1.** Also: **subterraneous, subterrestrial.** situated, living, or operating below the surface of the earth. **2.** existing or operating in concealment. [C17: from L *subterrāneus*, from SUB- + *terra* earth] —**,subter'raneanly** *or* **,subter'raneously** *adv.*

subtile ('sʌtᵊl) *adj.* a rare spelling of **subtle.** —'**subtilely** *adv.* —**subtility** (sʌb'tɪlɪtɪ) *or* '**subtileness** *n.* —'**subtilty** *n.*

subtilize *or* **-ise** ('sʌtɪ,laɪz) *vb.* **1.** (*tr.*) to bring to a purer state; refine. **2.** to debate subtly. **3.** (*tr.*) to make (the mind, etc.) keener. —**,subtili'zation** *or* **-i'sation** *n.*

subtitle ('sʌb,taɪtᵊl) *n.* **1.** an additional subordinate title given to a literary or other work. **2.** (*often pl.*) Also called: **caption.** *Films.* **a.** a written translation superimposed on a film that has foreign dialogue. **b.** explanatory text on a silent film. ~*vb.* **3.** (*tr.; usually passive*) to provide a subtitle for.

subtle ('sʌtᵊl) *adj.* **1.** not immediately obvious or comprehensible. **2.** difficult to detect or analyse, often through being delicate or highly refined: *a subtle scent.* **3.** showing or making or capable of showing or making fine distinctions of meaning. **4.** marked by or requiring mental acuteness or ingenuity; discriminating. **5.** delicate or faint: *a subtle shade.* **6.** cunning or wily: *a subtle rogue.* **7.** operating or executed in secret: *a subtle intrigue.* [C14: from OF *soutil*, from L *subtīlis* finely woven] —'**subtleness** *n.* —'**subtly** *adv.*

subtlety ('sʌtᵊltɪ) *n., pl.* **-ties. 1.** the state or quality of being subtle; delicacy. **2.** a fine distinction. **3.** something subtle.

subtonic (sʌb'tɒnɪk) *n. Music.* the seventh degree of a major or minor scale.

subtotal (sʌb'təʊtᵊl, 'sʌb,təʊtᵊl) *n.* **1.** the total made up by a column of figures, etc., forming part of the total made up by a larger column. ~*vb.* **-talling, -talled** *or U.S.* **-taling, -taled. 2.** to work out a subtotal for (a column, etc.).

subtract (səb'trækt) *vb.* **1.** to calculate the difference between (two numbers or quantities) by subtraction. **2.** to remove (a part of a thing, quantity, etc.) from the whole. [C16: from L *subtractus* withdrawn, from *subtrahere* to draw away from beneath] —**sub'tracter** *n.* —**sub'tractive** *adj.*

subtraction (səb'trækʃən) *n.* **1.** the act or process of subtracting. **2.** a mathematical operation in which the difference between two numbers or quantities is calculated.

subtrahend ('sʌbtrə,hɛnd) *n.* the number to be subtracted from another number (the **minuend**). [C17: from L *subtrahendus*, from *subtrahere* to SUBTRACT]

subtropics (sʌb'trɒpɪks) *pl. n.* the region lying between the tropics and temperate lands. —**sub'tropical** *adj.*

subulate ('suːbjʊlɪt, -,leɪt) *adj.* (esp. of plant parts) tapering to a point; awl-shaped. [C18: from NL *subulatus* like an awl, from L *sūbula* awl]

suburb ('sʌbɜːb) *n.* a residential district situated on the outskirts of a city or town. [C14: from L *suburbium*, from *sub-* close to + *urbs* a city]

suburban (sə'bɜːbᵊn) *adj.* **1.** of, in, or inhabiting a suburb or the suburbs. **2.** characteristic of a suburb or the suburbs. **3.** *Mildly derog.* narrow or unadventurous in outlook. ~*n.* **4.** Also called: **suburbanite.** a person who lives in a suburb. —**su'burba,nize** *or* **-ise** *vb.(tr.)*

suburbia (sə'bɜːbɪə) *n.* **1.** suburbs or the people living in them considered as an identifiable community or class in society. **2.** the life, customs, etc., of suburbanites.

subvention (səb'vɛnʃən) *n.* a grant, aid, or subsidy, as from a government. [C15: from LL *subventiō* assistance, from L *subvenīre*, from *sub-* under + *venīre* to come]

subversion (səb'vɜːʃən) *n.* **1.** the act or an instance of subverting a legally constituted government, institution, etc. **2.** the state of being subverted; destruction or ruin. [C14: from LL *subversiō* destruction, from L *subvertere* to overturn]

subversive (səb'vɜːsɪv) *adj.* **1.** liable to subvert or overthrow a government, legally constituted institution, etc. ~*n.* **2.** a person engaged in subversive activities, etc. —**sub'versively** *adv.* —**sub'versiveness** *n.*

subvert (səb'vɜːt) *vb.* (*tr.*) **1.** to bring about the complete downfall or ruin of (something existing by a system of law, etc.). **2.** to undermine the moral principles of (a person, etc.). [C14: from L *subvertere* to overturn] —**sub'verter** *n.*

subway ('sʌb,weɪ) *n.* **1.** *Brit.* an underground tunnel enabling pedestrians to cross a road, railway, etc. **2.** an underground tunnel for traffic, power supplies, etc. **3.** an underground railway.

succedaneum (,sʌksɪ'deɪnɪəm) *n., pl.* **-nea** (-nɪə). something that is used as a substitute, esp. any medical drug or agent that may be taken or prescribed in place of another. [C17: from L *succēdāneus* following after; see SUCCEED] —**,succe'daneous** *adj.*

succeed (sək'siːd) *vb.* **1.** (*intr.*) to accomplish an aim, esp. in the manner desired. **2.** (*intr.*) to happen in the manner desired: *the plan succeeded.* **3.** (*intr.*) to acquit oneself satisfactorily or do well, as in a specified field. **4.** (when *intr.*, often foll. by *to*) to come next in order (after someone or something). **5.** (when *intr.*, often foll. by *to*) to take over an office, post, etc. (from a person). **6.** (*intr.;* usually foll. by *to*) to come into possession (of property, etc.); inherit. **7.** (*intr.*) to have a result according to a specified manner: *the plan succeeded badly.* [C15: from L *succēdere* to follow after] —**suc'ceeder** *n.* —**suc'ceedingly** *adv.*

success (sək'sɛs) *n.* **1.** the favourable outcome of something attempted. **2.** the attainment of wealth, fame, etc. **3.** an action, performance, etc., that is characterized by success. **4.** a person or thing that is successful. [C16: from L *successus* an outcome; see SUCCEED]

successful (sək'sɛsfʊl) *adj.* **1.** having succeeded in one's endeavours. **2.** marked by a favourable outcome. **3.** having obtained fame, wealth, etc. —**suc'cessfully** *adv.* —**suc'cessfulness** *n.*

succession (sək'sɛʃən) *n.* **1.** the act or an instance of one person or thing following another. **2.** a number of people or things following one another in order. **3.** the act, process, or right by which one person succeeds to the office, etc., of another. **4.** the order that determines how one person or thing follows another. **5.** a line of descent to a title, etc. **6. in succession.** in a manner such that one thing is followed uninterruptedly by another. [C14: from L *successio;* see SUCCEED] —**suc'cessional** *adj.*

successive (sək'sɛsɪv) *adj.* **1.** following another without interruption. **2.** of or involving succession: *a successive process.* —**suc'cessively** *adv.* —**suc'cessiveness** *n.*

successor (sək'sɛsə) *n.* a person or thing that follows, esp. a person who succeeds another.

succinct (sək'sɪŋkt) *adj.* marked by brevity and clarity; concise. [C15: from L *succinctus* girt about, from *succingere* to gird from below] —**suc'cinctly** *adv.* —**suc'cinctness** *n.*

succinic acid (sʌk'sɪnɪk) *n.* a colourless odourless water-soluble acid found in plant and animal tissues, deriving from amber. Formula: $HOOC(CH_2)_2COOH$. Systematic name: **butanedioic acid.** [C19: from L *succinum* amber]

---

sub'surface *adj.*   '**sub,system** *n.*   **sub'zero** *adj.*

succotash ('sʌkə,tæʃ) n. U.S. & Canad. a mixture of cooked sweet corn kernels and lima beans, served as a vegetable. [C18: of Amerind origin, from *msiquatash*, lit.: broken pieces]

succour or U.S. **succor** ('sʌkə) n. **1.** help or assistance, esp. in time of difficulty. **2.** a person or thing that provides help. ~vb. **3.** (tr.) to give aid to. [C13: from OF *sucurir*, from L *succurrere* to hurry to help]

succubus ('sʌkjʊbəs) n., pl. **-bi** (-,baɪ). **1.** Also called: **succuba.** a female demon fabled to have sexual intercourse with sleeping men. Cf. **incubus. 2.** any evil demon. [C16: from Med. L, from LL *succuba* harlot, from L *succubāre* to lie beneath]

succulent ('sʌkjʊlənt) adj. **1.** juicy. **2.** (of plants) having thick fleshy leaves or stems. ~n. **3.** a plant that can exist in arid conditions by using water stored in its fleshy tissues. [C17: from L *succulentus*, from *sūcus* juice] —'**succulence** or '**succulency** n. —'**succulently** adv.

succumb (sə'kʌm) vb. (intr.; often foll. by to) **1.** to give way to the force (of) or desire (for). **2.** to be fatally overwhelmed (by disease, etc.). (the (of). [C15: from L *succumbere* to be overcome, from SUB- + -*cumbere*, from *cubāre* to lie down]

succursal (sʌ'kɜːsᵊl) adj. **1.** (esp. of a religious establishment) subsidiary. ~n. **2.** a subsidiary establishment. [C19: from F, from Med. L *succursus*, from L *succurrere* to SUCCOUR]

such (sʌtʃ) (often foll. by a corresponding subordinate clause introduced by *that* or *as*) ~determiner. **1. a.** of the sort specified or understood: *such books.* **b.** (as pronoun): *such is life; robbers, rapists, and such.* **2.** so great; so much: *such a help.* **3. a. as such.** in the capacity previously specified or understood: *a judge as such hasn't so much power.* **b.** in itself or themselves: *intelligence as such can't guarantee success.* **4. such and such.** specific, but not known or named: *at such and such a time.* **5. such as. a.** for example: *animals, such as tigers.* **b.** of a similar kind as; like: *people such as your friend.* **c.** of the (usually small) amount, etc.: *the food, such as there was, was excellent.* **6. such that.** so that: used to express purpose or result: *power such that it was effortless.* ~adv. **7.** (intensifier): *such a nice person.* [OE *swilc*]

suchlike ('sʌtʃ,laɪk) adj. **1.** (prenominal) of such a kind; similar: *John, Ken, and other suchlike idiots.* ~n. **2.** such or similar persons or things: *hyenas, jackals, and suchlike.*

Su-chou ('suː'tʃaʊ) n. a variant transliteration of the Chinese name for **Suzhou.**

Süchow ('ʃuː'tʃaʊ) n. a variant transliteration of the Chinese name for **Xuzhou.**

suck (sʌk) vb. **1.** to draw (a liquid or other substance) into the mouth by creating a partial vacuum in the mouth. **2.** to draw in (fluid, etc.) by or as if by a similar action: *plants suck moisture from the soil.* **3.** to drink milk from (a mother's breast); suckle. **4.** (tr.) to extract fluid content from (a solid food): *to suck a lemon.* **5.** (tr.) to take into the mouth and moisten, dissolve, or roll around with the tongue: *to suck one's thumb.* **6.** (tr.; often foll. by *down, in,* etc.) to draw by using irresistible force. **7.** (intr.) (of a pump) to draw in air because of a low supply level or leaking valves, etc. **8.** (tr.) to assimilate or acquire (knowledge, comfort, etc.). ~n. **9.** the act or an instance of sucking. **10.** something that is sucked, esp. milk from the mother's breast. **11. give suck to.** to give (a baby or young animal) milk from the breast or udder. **12.** an attracting or sucking force. **13.** a sound caused by sucking. ~See also **suck in, sucks, suck up to.** [OE *sūcan*]

sucker ('sʌkə) n. **1.** a person or thing that sucks. **2.** Sl. a person who is easily deceived or swindled. **3.** Sl. a person who cannot resist the attractions of a particular type of person or thing: *he's a sucker for blondes.* **4.** a young animal that is not yet weaned. **5.** Zool. an organ specialized for sucking or adhering. **6.** a cup-shaped device, generally made of rubber, that may be attached to articles allowing them to adhere to a surface by suction. **7.** Bot. **a.** a strong shoot that arises in a mature plant from a root, rhizome, or the base of the main stem. **b.** a short branch of a parasitic plant that absorbs nutrients from the host. **8.** a pipe or tube through which a fluid is drawn by suction. **9.** any of various small mainly North American cyprinoid fishes having a large sucking mouth. **10.** any of

certain fishes that have sucking discs, esp. the sea snail. **11.** a piston in a suction pump or the valve in such a piston. ~vb. **12.** (tr.) to strip the suckers from (a plant). **13.** (intr.) (of a plant) to produce suckers.

suck in vb. (adv.) **1.** (tr.) to attract by using an inexorable force, inducement, etc. **2.** to draw in (one's breath) sharply.

suckle ('sʌkᵊl) vb. **1.** to give (a baby or young animal) milk from the breast or (of a baby, etc.) to suck milk from the breast. **2.** (tr.) to bring up; nurture. [C15: prob. back formation from SUCKLING] —'**suckler** n.

suckling ('sʌklɪŋ) n. **1.** an infant or young animal that is still taking milk from the mother. **2.** a very young child. [C15: see SUCK, -LING¹]

Suckling ('sʌklɪŋ) n. Sir **John.** 1609–42, English Cavalier poet and dramatist.

sucks (sʌks) interj. Sl. **1.** an expression of disappointment. **2.** an exclamation of defiance or derision (esp. in **yah boo sucks to you**).

suck up to vb. (intr., adv. + prep.) Inf. to flatter for one's own profit; toady.

sucrase ('sjuːkreɪz) n. another name for **invertase.** [C19: from F *sucre* sugar + -ASE]

sucre (Spanish 'sukre) n. the standard monetary unit of Ecuador. [C19: after Antonio José de SUCRE]

Sucre¹ (Spanish 'sukre) n. the legal capital of Bolivia, in the south central part of the country in the E Andes: university (1624). Pop.: 86 609 (1985 est.). Former name (until 1839): **Chuquisaca.**

Sucre² (Spanish 'sukre) n. **Antonio José de** (an'tonjo xo'se de). 1795–1830, South American liberator, born in Venezuela, who assisted Bolivar in the colonial revolt against Spain; first president of Bolivia (1826–28).

sucrose ('sjuːkrəʊz, -krəʊs) n. the technical name for **sugar** (sense 1). [C19: F *sucre* sugar + -OSE²]

suction ('sʌkʃən) n. **1.** the act or process of sucking. **2.** the force produced by a pressure difference, as the force holding a suction cap onto a surface. **3.** the act or process of producing such a force. [C17: from LL *suctiō* a sucking, from L *sūgere* to suck] —'**suctional** adj.

suction pump n. a pump for raising water or a similar fluid by suction. It usually consists of a cylinder containing a piston fitted with a flap valve.

suctorial (sʌk'tɔːrɪəl) adj. **1.** specialized for sucking or adhering. **2.** relating to or possessing suckers or suction. [C19: from NL *suctōrius*, from L *sūgere* to suck]

Sudan (suː'dɑːn, -'dæn) n. **the. 1.** a republic in NE Africa, on the Red Sea: the largest country in Africa; conquered by Mehemet Ali of Egypt (1820–22) and made an Anglo-Egyptian condominium in 1899 after joint forces defeated the Mahdist revolt; became a republic in 1956. It consists mainly of a plateau, with the Nubian Desert in the north. Official language: Arabic. Religion: Muslim majority. Currency: Sudanese pound. Capital: Khartoum. Pop.: 25 550 000 (1987 est.). Area: 2 505 805 sq. km (967 491 sq. miles). Former name (1899–1956): **Anglo-Egyptian Sudan.** French name: **Soudan. 2.** a region stretching across Africa south of the Sahara and north of the tropical zone: inhabited chiefly by Negro tribes rather than Arabs. —**Sudanese** (,suːdᵊ'niːz) adj., n.

sudarium (sjʊ'dɛərɪəm) n., pl. **-daria** (-'dɛərɪə). another word for **sudatorium.** [C17: from L, from *sūdāre* to sweat]

sudatorium (,sjuːdə'tɔːrɪəm) or **sudatory** n., pl. **-toria** (-'tɔːrɪə) or **-tories.** a room, esp. in a Roman bathhouse, where sweating is induced by heat. [C18: from L, from *sūdāre* to sweat]

sudatory ('sjuːdətərɪ, -trɪ) adj. **1.** relating to or producing sweating. ~n., pl. **-ries. 2.** a sudatory agent. **3.** another word for **sudatorium.**

Sudbury ('sʌdbərɪ, -brɪ) n. a city in central Canada, in Ontario: a major nickel-mining centre. Pop.: 88 717 (1986).

sudd (sʌd) n. floating masses of reeds and weeds that occur on the White Nile and obstruct navigation. [C19: from Ar., lit.: obstruction]

sudden ('sʌdᵊn) adj. **1.** occurring or performed quickly and without warning. **2.** marked by haste; abrupt. **3.** Rare. rash; precipitate. ~n. **4.** Arch. an abrupt occurrence (in **on a sudden**). **5. all of a sudden.** without warning; unexpectedly. [C13: via F from LL *subitāneus*, from L *subitus* unexpected, from *subīre* to happen unexpectedly, from *sub-* secretly + *īre* to go] —'**suddenly** adv. —'**suddenness** n.

sudden death n. **1.** (in sports, etc.) an extra game or contest to decide the winner of a tied competition. **2.** an unexpected or quick death.

sudden infant death syndrome n. a technical name for **cot death.**

Sudetenland (suː'deɪtᵊn,lænd) n. a mountainous region of N and NW Czechoslovakia: annexed by Germany in 1938; returned to Czechoslovakia in 1945. Also called: **the Sudeten.**

Sudetes (suː'diːtiːz) or **Sudeten Mountains** pl. n. a mountain range in E central Europe, along the N border of Czechoslovakia, extending into East Germany and Poland: rich in minerals, esp. coal. Highest peak: Schneekoppe, 1603 m (5259 ft.).

sudor ('sjuːdɔː) n. a technical name for **sweat.** [L] —**sudoral** ('sjuːdərəl) adj.

sudoriferous (,sjuːdə'rɪfərəs) adj. producing or conveying sweat. [C16: via NL from SUDOR + L ferre to bear] —,**sudor'iferousness** n.

sudorific (,sjuːdə'rɪfɪk) adj. **1.** producing or causing sweating. ~n. **2.** a sudorific agent. [C17: from NL sūdōrificus, from SUDOR + L facere to make]

suds (sʌdz) pl. n. **1.** the bubbles on the surface of water in which soap, detergents, etc., have been dissolved; lather. **2.** soapy water. [C16: prob. from MDu. sudse marsh] —'**sudsy** adj.

sue (sjuː, suː) vb. **suing, sued. 1.** to institute legal proceedings (against). **2.** to make suppliant requests of (someone for something). [C13: from OF sivre, from L sequī to follow] —'**suer** n.

Sue (French sy) n. **Eugène** (øʒɛn). original name Marie-Joseph Sue. 1804–57, French novelist, whose works, notably Les mystères de Paris (1842–43) and Le juif errant (1844–45), were among the first to reflect the impact of the industrial revolution on France.

suede (sweɪd) n. **a.** a leather with a fine velvet-like nap on the flesh side, produced by abrasive action. **b.** (as modifier): a suede coat. [C19: from F gants de Suède, lit.: gloves from Sweden]

suet ('suːɪt, 'sjuːɪt) n. a hard waxy fat around the kidneys and loins in sheep, cattle, etc., used in cooking and making tallow. [C14: from OF seu, from L sēbum] —'**suety** adj.

Suetonius (swiː'təʊnɪəs) n. full name Gaius Suetonius Tranquillus. 75–150 A.D., Roman biographer and historian, whose chief works were Concerning Illustrious Men and The Lives of the Caesars (from Julius Caesar to Domitian).

suet pudding n. Brit. any of a variety of puddings made with suet and steamed or boiled.

Suez ('suːɪz) n. **1.** a port in NE Egypt, at the head of the Gulf of Suez at the S end of the Suez Canal: an ancient trading site and a major naval station under the Ottoman Empire; port of departure for pilgrims to Mecca; oil-refining centre. It suffered severely in the Arab–Israeli conflicts of 1967 and 1973. Pop.: 254 000 (1985). **2. Isthmus of.** a strip of land in NE Egypt, between the Mediterranean and the Red Sea: links Africa and Asia and is crossed by the Suez Canal. **3. Gulf of.** the NW arm of the Red Sea: linked with the Mediterranean by the Suez Canal.

Suez Canal n. a sea-level canal in NE Egypt, crossing the Isthmus of Suez and linking the Mediterranean with the Red Sea: built (1854–69) by de Lesseps with French and Egyptian capital; nationalized in 1956 by the Egyptians. Length: 163 km (101 miles).

suffer ('sʌfə) vb. **1.** to undergo or be subjected to (pain, punishment, etc.). **2.** (tr.) to undergo or experience (anything): to suffer a change of management. **3.** (intr.) to be set at a disadvantage: this author suffers in translation. **4.** (tr.) Arch. to tolerate; permit (someone to do something): suffer the little children to come unto me. **5. suffer from. a.** to be ill with, esp. recurrently. **b.** to be given to: he suffers from a tendency to exaggerate. [C13: from OF soffrir, from L sufferre, from SUB- + ferre to bear] —'**sufferer** n. —'**suffering** n.

sufferable ('sʌfərəbᵊl, 'sʌfrə-) adj. able to be tolerated or suffered; endurable.

sufferance ('sʌfərəns, 'sʌfrəns) n. **1.** tolerance arising from failure to prohibit; tacit permission. **2.** capacity to endure pain, injury, etc. **3.** the state or condition of suffering. **4. on sufferance.** tolerated with reluctance. [C13: via OF from LL sufferentia endurance, from L sufferre to SUFFER]

suffice (sə'faɪs) vb. **1.** to be adequate or satisfactory for (something). **2. suffice it to say that.** (takes a clause as object) let us say no more than that; I shall just say that. [C14: from OF suffire, from L sufficere from sub- below + facere to make]

sufficiency (sə'fɪʃənsɪ) n., pl. -cies. **1.** the quality or condition of being sufficient. **2.** an adequate amount. **3.** Arch. efficiency.

sufficient (sə'fɪʃənt) adj. **1.** enough to meet a need or purpose; adequate. **2.** Logic. (of a condition) assuring the truth of a statement; requiring but not necessarily caused by some other state of affairs. Cf. **necessary** (sense 3b). **3.** Arch. competent; capable. ~n. **4.** a sufficient quantity. [C14: from L sufficiens supplying the needs of, from sufficere to SUFFICE] —**suf'ficiently** adv.

suffix n. ('sʌfɪks). **1.** Grammar. an affix that follows the stem to which it is attached, as for example -s and -ness in dogs and softness. Cf. **prefix** (sense 1). **2.** anything added at the end of something else. ~vb. ('sʌfɪks, sə'fɪks). **3.** (tr.) Grammar. to add (a morpheme) as a suffix to a word. [C18: from NL suffixum, from L suffixus fastened below, from suffigere to fasten below]

suffocate ('sʌfə,keɪt) vb. **1.** to kill or be killed by the deprivation of oxygen, as by obstruction of the air passage. **2.** to block the air passages or have the air passages blocked. **3.** to feel or cause to feel discomfort from heat and lack of air. [C16: from L suffōcāre, from SUB- + faucēs throat] —'**suffo,cating** adj. —,**suffo'cation** n.

Suffolk ('sʌfək) n. a county of SE England, on the North Sea: its coast is flat and marshy, indented by broad tidal estuaries. Administrative centre: Ipswich. Pop.: 628 600 (1986 est.). Area: 3800 sq. km (1467 sq. miles).

Suffolk punch n. a breed of draught horse with a chestnut coat and short legs.

suffragan ('sʌfrəgən) adj. **1. a.** (of any bishop of a diocese) subordinate to and assisting his superior archbishop or metropolitan. **b.** (of any assistant bishop) assisting the bishop of his diocese but having no ordinary jurisdiction in that diocese. ~n. **2.** a suffragan bishop. [C14: from Med. L suffragāneus, from suffrāgium assistance, from L: suffrage] —'**suffraganship** n.

suffrage ('sʌfrɪdʒ) n. **1.** the right to vote, esp. in public elections; franchise. **2.** the exercise of such a right; casting a vote. **3.** a short intercessory prayer. [C14: from L suffrāgium]

suffragette (,sʌfrə'dʒɛt) n. a female advocate of the extension of the franchise to women, esp. a militant one, as in Britain at the beginning of the 20th century. [C20: from SUFFRAG(E) + -ETTE]

suffragist ('sʌfrədʒɪst) n. an advocate of the extension of the franchise, esp. to women. —'**suffragism** n.

suffruticose (sə'fruːtɪ,kəʊz) adj. (of a plant) having a permanent woody base and herbaceous branches. [C18: from NL suffruticōsus, from L SUB- + frutex shrub]

suffuse (sə'fjuːz) vb. (tr.; usually passive) to spread or flood through or over (something). [C16: from L suffūsus overspread with, from suffundere, from SUB- + fundere to pour] —**suffusion** (sə'fjuːʒən) n. —**suf'fusive** adj.

Sufu ('ʃuː'fuː) n. a variant spelling of **Shufu.**

sug (sʌg) vb. **sugging, sugged.** (intr.) to use the pretence of conducting a survey in order to try to sell something to a person. [C20: from selling under the guise (of market research)] —'**sugging** n.

sugar ('ʃʊgə) n. **1.** Also called: **sucrose, saccharose.** a white crystalline sweet carbohydrate, a disaccharide, found in many plants: used esp. as a sweetening agent in food and drinks. Related adj.: **saccharine. 2.** any of a class of simple water-soluble carbohydrates, such as sucrose, lactose, and fructose. **3.** Inf., chiefly U.S. & Canad. a term of affection, esp. for one's sweetheart. ~vb. **4.** (tr.) to add sugar to; make sweet. **5.** (tr.) to cover or sprinkle with sugar. **6.** (intr.) to produce sugar. **7. sugar the pill** or **medicine.** to make something unpleasant more agreeable by adding something pleasant. [C13 suker, from OF çucre, from Med. L zuccārum, ult. from Sansk. śarkarā] —'**sugared** adj.

sugar beet n. a variety of beet cultivated for its white roots from which sugar is obtained.

sugar candy n. **1.** Also called: **rock candy.** large crystals of sugar formed by suspending strings in a strong sugar solution that hardens on the strings, used chiefly for sweetening coffee. **2.** Chiefly U.S. confectionery; sweets.

sugar cane *n.* a coarse perennial grass of Old World tropical regions, having tall stout canes that yield sugar: cultivated chiefly in the West Indies and the southern U.S.

sugar-coat *vb.* (*tr.*) **1.** to coat or cover with sugar. **2.** to cause to appear more attractive.

sugar diabetes *n.* an informal name for **diabetes mellitus** (see **diabetes**).

sugar glider *n.* a common Australian possum that glides from tree to tree feeding on insects and nectar.

sugaring off *n. Canad.* the boiling down of maple sap to produce sugar, traditionally a social event in early spring.

sugar loaf *n.* **1.** a large conical mass of hard refined sugar. **2.** something resembling this.

Sugar Loaf Mountain *n.* a mountain in SE Brazil, in Rio de Janeiro on Guanabara Bay. Height: 390 m (1280 ft.). Portuguese name: **Pão de Açúcar**.

sugar maple *n.* a North American maple tree, grown as a source of sugar, which is extracted from the sap, and for its hard wood.

sugar of lead (lɛd) *n.* another name for **lead acetate**.

sugarplum ('ʃʊgə,plʌm) *n.* a crystallized plum.

sugary ('ʃʊgərɪ) *adj.* **1.** of, like, or containing sugar. **2.** excessively sweet. **3.** deceptively pleasant; insincere. —'**sugariness** *n.*

suggest (sə'dʒɛst) *vb.* (*tr.; may take a clause as object*) **1.** to put forward (a plan, idea, etc.) for consideration: *I suggest Smith for the post; a plan suggested itself.* **2.** to evoke (a person, thing, etc.) in the mind by the association of ideas: *that painting suggests home to me.* **3.** to give an indirect or vague hint of: *his face always suggests his peace of mind.* [C16: from L *suggerere* to bring up] —**sug'gester** *n.*

suggestible (sə'dʒɛstɪbəl) *adj.* **1.** easily influenced by ideas provided by other persons. **2.** characteristic of something that can be suggested. —**sug,gesti'bility** *n.*

suggestion (sə'dʒɛstʃən) *n.* **1.** something that is suggested. **2.** a hint or indication: *a suggestion of the odour of violets.* **3.** *Psychol.* the process whereby the mere presentation of an idea to a receptive individual leads to the acceptance of that idea. See also **autosuggestion**.

suggestive (sə'dʒɛstɪv) *adj.* **1.** (*postpositive; foll. by of*) conveying a hint (of something). **2.** tending to suggest something improper or indecent. —**sug'gestively** *adv.* —**sug'gestiveness** *n.*

Suharto (sʊ'hɑːtəʊ) *n.* **T. N. J.** born 1921, Indonesian general and statesman; president from 1968.

suicidal (,suːɪ'saɪdəl, ,sjuː-) *adj.* **1.** involving, indicating, or tending towards suicide. **2.** liable to result in suicide: *a suicidal attempt.* **3.** liable to destroy one's own interests or prospects; dangerously rash. —,**sui'cidally** *adv.*

suicide ('suːɪ,saɪd, 'sjuː-) *n.* **1.** the act or an instance of killing oneself intentionally. **2.** the self-inflicted ruin of one's own prospects or interests: *a merger would be financial suicide.* **3.** a person who kills himself intentionally. **4.** (*modifier*) reckless; extremely dangerous: *a suicide mission.* **5.** (*modifier*) (of an action) undertaken or (of a person) undertaking an action in the knowledge that it will result in the death of the person performing it in order that maximum damage may be inflicted: *suicide bomber.* [C17: from NL *suīcīdium*, from L *suī* of oneself + -*cīdium*, from *caedere* to kill]

sui generis (,suːaɪ 'dʒɛnərɪs) *adj.* unique. [L, lit.: of its own kind]

suint ('suːɪnt, swɪnt) *n.* a water-soluble substance found in the fleece of sheep, formed from dried perspiration. [C18: from F *suer* to sweat, from L *sūdāre*]

Suisse (syis) *n.* the French name for **Switzerland**.

suit (suːt, sjuːt) *n.* **1.** any set of clothes of the same or similar material designed to be worn together, now usually (for men) a jacket with matching trousers or (for women) a jacket with matching or contrasting skirt or trousers. **2.** (*in combination*) any outfit worn for a specific purpose: *a spacesuit.* **3.** any set of items, such as parts of personal armour. **4.** any of the four sets of 13 cards in a pack of playing cards, being spades, hearts, diamonds, and clubs. **5.** a civil proceeding; lawsuit. **6.** the act or process of suing in a court of law. **7.** a petition or appeal made to a person of superior rank or status or the act of making such a petition. **8.** a man's courting of a woman. **9. follow suit. a.** to play a card of the same suit as the card played immediately before it. **b.** to act in the same way as someone else. **10. strong** *or* **strongest suit.** something that one excels in. ~*vb.* **11.** to make or

be fit or appropriate for: *that dress suits your figure.* **12.** to meet the requirements or standards (of). **13.** to be agreeable or acceptable to (someone). **14. suit oneself.** to pursue one's own intentions without reference to others. [C13: from OF *sieute* set of things, from *sivre* to follow]

suitable ('suːtəbəl, 'sjuːt-) *adj.* appropriate; proper; fit. —,**suita'bility** *or* '**suitableness** *n.* —'**suitably** *adv.*

suitcase ('suːt,keɪs, 'sjuːt-) *n.* a portable rectangular travelling case for clothing, etc.

suite (swiːt) *n.* **1.** a series of items intended to be used together; set. **2.** a set of connected rooms in a hotel. **3.** a matching set of furniture, esp. of two armchairs and a settee. **4.** a number of attendants or followers. **5.** *Music.* **a.** an instrumental composition consisting of several movements in the same key based on or derived from dance rhythms, esp. in the baroque period. **b.** an instrumental composition in several movements less closely connected than a sonata. [C17: from F, from OF *sieute*; see SUIT]

suiting ('suːtɪŋ, 'sjuːt-) *n.* a fabric used for suits.

suitor ('suːtə, 'sjuːt-) *n.* **1.** a man who courts a woman; wooer. **2.** *Law.* a person who brings a suit in a court of law; plaintiff. [C13: from Anglo-Norman *suter*, from L *secūtor* follower, from *sequī* to follow]

Suiyüan ('swiːr'yɑːn) *n.* a former province in N China: now part of the Inner Mongolian Autonomous Region.

Sukarnapura (sʊ,kɑːnə'pʊərə) *n.* a former name of **Jayapura**.

Sukarno *or* **Soekarno** (suː'kɑːnəʊ) *n.* **Achmed** ('ɑːkmɛd). 1901–70, Indonesian statesman; first president of the Republic of Indonesia (1945–67).

Sukarno Peak *n.* a former name of (Mount) **Jaya**.

Sukhumi (*Russian* su'xumi) *n.* a port and resort in the SW Soviet Union, in the Georgian SSR on the Black Sea: site of an ancient Greek colony. Pop.: 122 000 (1987).

sukiyaki (,suːkɪ'jɑːkɪ) *n.* a Japanese dish consisting of very thinly sliced beef or other meat, vegetables, and seasonings cooked together quickly, usually at the table. [from Japanese]

Sulawesi (,suːlɔ'weɪsɪ) *n.* an island in E Indonesia: mountainous and forested, with volcanoes and hot springs. Pop.: 11 803 100 (1986 est.). Area (including adjacent islands): 229 108 sq. km (88 440 sq. miles). Also called: **Celebes**.

sulcate ('sʌlkeɪt) *adj. Biol.* marked with longitudinal parallel grooves. [C18: via L *sulcātus* from *sulcāre* to plough, from *sulcus* a furrow]

sulcus ('sʌlkəs) *n., pl.* -**ci** (-saɪ). **1.** a linear groove, furrow, or slight depression. **2.** any of the narrow grooves on the surface of the brain that mark the cerebral convolutions. [C17: from L]

Suleiman I (,suːlɪ'mɑːn, -leɪ-), **Soliman,** *or* **Solyman** *n.* called the *Magnificent*. ?1495–1566, sultan of the Ottoman Empire (1520–66), whose reign was noted for its military power and cultural achievements.

sulf- *combining form.* a U.S. variant of **sulph-**.

sulfur ('sʌlfə) *n.* the U.S. spelling of **sulphur**.

sulk (sʌlk) *vb.* **1.** (*intr.*) to be silent and resentful because of a wrong done to one; brood sullenly: *the child sulked after being slapped.* ~*n.* **2.** (*often pl.*) a state or mood of feeling resentful or sullen: *he's in a sulk; he's got the sulks.* **3.** Also: **sulker.** a person who sulks. [C18: back formation from SULKY[1]]

sulky[1] ('sʌlkɪ) *adj.* **sulkier, sulkiest. 1.** sullen, withdrawn, or moody through or as if through resentment. **2.** dull or dismal: *sulky weather.* [C18: ?from obs. *sulke* sluggish] —'**sulkily** *adv.* —'**sulkiness** *n.*

sulky[2] ('sʌlkɪ) *n., pl.* **sulkies.** a light two-wheeled vehicle for one person, usually drawn by one horse. [C18: from SULKY[1]]

Sulla ('sʌlə) *n.* full name *Lucius Cornelius Sulla Felix.* 138–78 B.C., Roman general and dictator (82–79). He introduced reforms to strengthen the power of the Senate.

sullage ('sʌlɪdʒ) *n.* **1.** filth or waste, esp. sewage. **2.** sediment deposited by running water. [C16: ?from F *souiller* to sully]

sullen ('sʌlən) *adj.* **1.** unwilling to talk or be sociable; sulky; morose. **2.** sombre; gloomy: *a sullen day.* ~*n.* **3.** (*pl.*) *Arch.* a sullen mood. [C16: ?from Anglo-F *solain* (unattested), ult. rel. to L *sōlus* alone] —'**sullenly** *adv.* —'**sullenness** *n.*

Sullivan ('sʌlɪvən) *n.* **1.** Sir **Arthur** (**Seymour**). 1842–1900, English composer who wrote operettas, such as

H.M.S. Pinafore (1878) and *The Mikado* (1885), with W. S. Gilbert as librettist. **2. Louis (Henri).** 1856–1924, U.S. pioneer of modern architecture: he coined the slogan "form follows function".

Sullom Voe ('sʌləm vəʊ) *n.* a deep coastal inlet in the Shetland Islands, on the N coast of Mainland. It is used for the storage and transshipment of oil.

sully ('sʌlɪ) *vb.* **-lying, -lied.** (*tr.*) to stain or tarnish (a reputation, etc.) or (of a reputation) to become stained or tarnished. [C16: prob. from F *souiller* to soil]

Sully ('sʌlɪ; *French* sylli) *n.* **Maximilien de Béthune** (maksimiljɛ̃ də betyn), Duc de Sully. 1559–1641, French statesman; minister of Henry IV. He helped restore the finances of France after the Wars of Religion.

Sully-Prudhomme (*French* sylli prydɔm) *n.* **René François Armand** (rənə frɑ̃swa armɑ̃). 1839–1907, French poet: Nobel prize for literature 1901.

sulph- *or U.S.* **sulf-** *combining form.* containing sulphur: *sulphate.*

sulpha *or U.S.* **sulfa drug** ('sʌlfə) *n.* any of a group of sulphonamides that inhibit the activity of bacteria and are used to treat bacterial infections.

sulphadiazine *or U.S.* **sulfadiazine** (ˌsʌlfə'daɪəˌziːn) *n.* an important sulpha drug used chiefly in combination with an antibiotic. [from SULPH- + DIAZ(O) + -INE[2]]

sulphanilamide *or U.S.* **sulfanilamide** (ˌsʌlfə-'nɪləˌmaɪd) *n.* a white crystalline compound formerly used in the treatment of bacterial infections. [from SULPH- + ANIL(INE) + AMIDE]

sulphate *or U.S.* **sulfate** ('sʌlfeɪt) *n.* **1.** any salt or ester of sulphuric acid. ~*vb.* **2.** (*tr.*) to treat with a sulphate or convert into a sulphate. **3.** to undergo or cause to undergo the formation of a layer of lead sulphate on the plates of an accumulator. [C18: from NL *sulfātum*] —**sul'phation** *or U.S.* **sul'fation** *n.*

sulphide *or U.S.* **sulfide** ('sʌlfaɪd) *n.* a compound of sulphur with a more electropositive element.

sulphite *or U.S.* **sulfite** ('sʌlfaɪt) *n.* any salt or ester of sulphurous acid. —**sulphitic** *or U.S.* **sulfitic** (sʌl'fɪtɪk) *adj.*

sulphonamide *or U.S.* **sulfonamide** (sʌl'fɒnəˌmaɪd) *n.* any of a class of organic compounds that are amides of sulphonic acids containing the group -SO₂NH₂ or a group derived from this. An important class of sulphonamides are the sulpha drugs.

sulphone *or U.S.* **sulfone** ('sʌlfəʊn) *n.* any of a class of organic compounds containing the divalent group SO₂ linked to two other organic groups.

sulphonic *or U.S.* **sulfonic acid** (sʌl'fɒnɪk) *n.* any of a large group of strong organic acids that contain the group -SO₂OH and are used in the manufacture of dyes and drugs.

sulphonmethane *or U.S.* **sulfonmethane** (ˌsʌlfɒn-'miːθeɪn) *n.* a colourless crystalline compound used medicinally as a hypnotic. Formula: $C_7H_{16}O_4S_2$.

sulphur *or U.S.* **sulfur** ('sʌlfə) *n.* **a.** an allotropic nonmetallic element, occurring free in volcanic regions and in combined state in gypsum, pyrite, and galena. It is used in the production of sulphuric acid, in the vulcanization of rubber, and in fungicides. Symbol: S; atomic no.: 16; atomic wt.: 32.064. **b.** (*as modifier*): *sulphur springs.* [C14 *soufre,* from OF, from L *sulfur*] —**sulphuric** *or U.S.* **sulfuric** (sʌl'fjʊərɪk) *adj.*

sulphurate *or U.S.* **sulfurate** ('sʌlfjʊˌreɪt) *vb.* (*tr.*) to combine or treat with sulphur or a sulphur compound. —ˌsulphu'ration *or U.S.* ˌsulfu'ration *n.*

sulphur-bottom *n.* another name for **blue whale.**

sulphur dioxide *n.* a colourless soluble pungent gas. It is both an oxidizing and a reducing agent and is used in the manufacture of sulphuric acid, the preservation of foodstuffs (**E 220**), bleaching, and disinfecting. Formula: SO_2. Systematic name: **sulphur(IV) oxide.**

sulphureous *or U.S.* **sulfureous** (sʌl'fjʊərɪəs) *adj.* **1.** another word for **sulphurous** (sense 1). **2.** of the yellow colour of sulphur.

sulphuretted *or U.S.* **sulfureted hydrogen** ('sʌlfjʊ-ˌrɛtɪd) *n.* another name for **hydrogen sulphide.**

sulphuric acid *n.* a colourless dense oily corrosive liquid used in accumulators and in the manufacture of fertilizers, dyes, and explosives. Formula: H_2SO_4. Systematic name: **tetraoxosulphuric(VI) acid.**

sulphurize, -ise, *or U.S.* **sulfurize** ('sʌlfjʊˌraɪz) *vb.* (*tr.*) to combine or treat with sulphur or a sulphur compound. —ˌsulphuri'zation, -i'sation, *or U.S.* ˌsulfuri'zation *n.*

sulphurous *or U.S.* **sulfurous** ('sʌlfərəs) *adj.* **1.** Also: **sulphureous.** of, relating to, or resembling sulphur: *a sulphurous colour.* **2.** of or containing sulphur in the divalent state: *sulphurous acid.* **3.** of or relating to hellfire. **4.** hot-tempered. —'sulphurously *or U.S.* 'sulfurously *adv.* —'sulphurousness *or U.S.* 'sulfurousness *n.*

sulphurous acid *n.* an unstable acid produced when sulphur dioxide dissolves in water: used as a preservative for food and a bleaching agent. Formula: H_2SO_3. Systematic name: **sulphuric(IV) acid.**

sulphur trioxide *n.* a colourless reactive fuming solid that forms sulphuric acid with water. Formula: SO_3. Systematic name: **sulphur(VI) oxide.**

sultan ('sʌltən) *n.* **1.** the sovereign of a Muslim country, esp. of the former Ottoman Empire. **2.** a small domestic fowl with a white crest and heavily feathered legs and feet: originated in Turkey. [C16: from Med. L *sultānus,* from Ar. *sultān* rule, from Aramaic *salita* to rule]

sultana (sʌl'tɑːnə) *n.* **1. a.** the dried fruit of a small white seedless grape, originally produced in SW Asia; seedless raisin. **b.** the grape itself. **2.** Also called: **sultaness.** a wife, concubine, or female relative of a sultan. **3.** a mistress; concubine. [C16: from It., fem. of *sultano* SULTAN]

sultanate ('sʌltəˌneɪt) *n.* **1.** the territory or a country ruled by a sultan. **2.** the office, rank, or jurisdiction of a sultan.

sultry ('sʌltrɪ) *adj.* **-trier, -triest. 1.** (of weather or climate) oppressively hot and humid. **2.** characterized by or emitting oppressive heat. **3.** displaying or suggesting passion; sensual: *sultry eyes.* [C16: from obs. *sulter* to swelter + -Y[1]] —'sultrily *adv.* —'sultriness *n.*

Sulu Archipelago ('suːluː) *n.* a chain of over 500 islands in the SW Philippines, separating the Sulu Sea from the Celebes Sea: formerly a sultanate, ceded to the Philippines in 1940. Capital: Jolo. Pop.: 555 239 (1980). Area: 2686 sq. km (1037 sq. miles).

Sulu Sea *n.* part of the W Pacific between Borneo and the central Philippines.

sum (sʌm) *n.* **1.** the result of the addition of numbers, quantities, objects, etc. **2.** one or more columns or rows of numbers to be added, subtracted, multiplied, or divided. **3.** *Maths.* the limit of the first *n* terms of a converging infinite series as *n* tends to infinity. **4.** a quantity, esp. of money: *he borrows enormous sums.* **5.** the essence or gist of a matter (esp. in **in sum, in sum and substance**). **6.** a less common word for **summary. 7.** (*modifier*) complete or final (esp. in **sum total**). ~*vb.* **summing, summed. 8.** (often foll. by *up*) to add or form a total of (something). **9.** (*tr.*) to calculate the sum of (the terms in a sequence). ~See also **sum up.** [C13 *summe,* from OF, from L *summa* the top, sum, from *summus* highest, from *super* above]

sumach *or U.S.* **sumac** ('suːmæk, 'ʃuː-) *n.* **1.** any of various temperate or subtropical shrubs or small trees, having compound leaves and red hairy fruits. See also **poison sumach. 2.** a preparation of powdered leaves of certain species of sumach, used in dyeing and tanning. **3.** the wood of any of these plants. [C14: via OF from Ar. *summāq*]

Sumatra (sʊ'mɑːtrə) *n.* a mountainous island in W Indonesia, in the Greater Sunda Islands, separated from the Malay Peninsula by the Strait of Malacca: Dutch control began in the 16th century; joined Indonesia in 1945. Pop.: 19 105 900 (1986 est.). Area: 473 606 sq. km (182 821 sq. miles). —**Su'matran** *adj., n.*

Sumba *or* **Soemba** ('suːmbə) *n.* an island in Indonesia, in the Lesser Sunda Islands, separated from Flores by the **Sumba Strait:** formerly important for sandalwood exports. Pop.: 355 073 (1980). Area: 11 153 sq. km (4306 sq. miles). Former name: **Sandalwood Island.**

Sumbawa *or* **Soembawa** (suːm'bɑːwə) *n.* a mountainous island in Indonesia, in the Lesser Sunda Islands, between Lombok and Flores Islands. Pop.: 320 000 (1980). Area: 14 750 sq. km (5695 sq. miles).

Sumer ('suːmə) *n.* the S region of Babylonia; seat of a civilization of city-states that reached its height in the 3rd millennium B.C.

Sumerian (suː'mɪərɪən, -'mɛər-) *n.* **1.** a member of a people who established a civilization in Sumer during the 4th millennium B.C. **2.** the extinct language of this people.

~*adj.* **3.** of or relating to ancient Sumer, its inhabitants, or their language or civilization.

summa cum laude ('sʊmɑː kʊm 'laʊdeɪ) *adv., adj. Chiefly U.S.* with the utmost praise: the highest designation for achievement in examinations. In Britain it is sometimes used to designate a first-class honours degree. [from L]

summarize *or* **-ise** ('sʌməˌraɪz) *vb.* (*tr.*) to make or be a summary of; express concisely. —ˌsummari'zation *or* -i'sation *n.* —'summaˌrizer, -iser, *or* 'summarist *n.*

summary ('sʌmərɪ) *n., pl.* **-maries. 1.** a brief account giving the main points of something. ~*adj.* (*usually prenominal*). **2.** performed arbitrarily and quickly, without formality: *a summary execution.* **3.** (of legal proceedings) short and free from the complexities and delays of a full trial. **4. summary jurisdiction.** the right a court has to adjudicate immediately upon some matter. **5.** giving the gist or essence. [C15: from L *summārium*, from *summa* SUM] —'summarily *adv.* —'summariness *n.*

summary offence *n.* an offence that is triable in a magistrates' court.

summation (sʌ'meɪʃən) *n.* **1.** the act or process of determining a sum; addition. **2.** the result of such an act or process. **3.** a summary. **4.** *U.S. law.* the concluding statements made by opposing counsel in a case before a court. [C18: from Med. L *summātiō*, from *summāre* to total, from L *summa* SUM] —sum'mational *adj.*

summer ('sʌmə) *n.* **1.** (*sometimes cap.*) **a.** the warmest season of the year, between spring and autumn, astronomically from the June solstice to the September equinox in the N hemisphere and at the opposite time of year in the S hemisphere. **b.** (*as modifier*): *summer flowers.* Related adj.: **aestival. 2.** the period of hot weather associated with the summer. **3.** a time of blossoming, greatest happiness, etc. **4.** *Chiefly poetic.* a year represented by this season: *a child of nine summers.* ~*vb.* **5.** (*intr.*) to spend the summer (at a place). **6.** (*tr.*) to keep or feed (farm animals) during the summer: *they summered their cattle on the mountain slopes.* [OE *sumor*] —'summerly *adj.* —'summery *adj.*

summerhouse ('sʌməˌhaʊs) *n.* a small building in a garden or park, used for shade or recreation in the summer.

summer pudding *n. Brit.* a pudding made by filling a bread-lined basin with a purée of fruit.

summersault ('sʌməˌsɔːlt) *n., vb.* a variant spelling of **somersault.**

summer school *n.* a school, academic course, etc., held during the summer.

summer solstice *n.* **1.** the time at which the sun is at its northernmost point in the sky (southernmost point in the S hemisphere). It occurs about June 21 (December 22 in the S hemisphere). **2.** *Astron.* the point on the celestial sphere, opposite the **winter solstice,** at which the ecliptic is furthest north from the celestial equator.

summertime ('sʌməˌtaɪm) *n.* the period or season of summer.

summer time *n. Brit.* any daylight-saving time, esp. British Summer Time.

summerweight ('sʌməˌweɪt) *adj.* (of clothes) suitable in weight for wear in the summer.

summing-up *n.* **1.** a review or summary of the main points of an argument, speech, etc. **2.** concluding statements made by a judge to the jury before they retire to consider their verdict.

summit ('sʌmɪt) *n.* **1.** the highest point or part, esp. of a mountain; top. **2.** the highest possible degree or state; peak or climax: *the summit of ambition.* **3.** the highest level, importance, or rank: *a meeting at the summit.* **4. a.** a meeting of chiefs of governments or other high officials. **b.** (*as modifier*): *a summit conference.* [C15: from OF *somet*, dim. of *som,* from L *summum;* see SUM]

summon ('sʌmən) *vb.* (*tr.*) **1.** to order to come; send for, esp. to attend court, by issuing a summons. **2.** to order or instruct (to do something) or call (to something): *the bell summoned them to their work.* **3.** to call upon to meet or convene. **4.** (often foll. by *up*) to muster or gather (one's strength, courage, etc.). **5.** *Arch.* to call upon to surrender. [C13: from L *summonēre* to give a discreet reminder, from *monēre* to advise]

summons ('sʌmənz) *n., pl.* **-monses. 1.** a call, signal, or order to do something, esp. to attend at a specified place or time. **2. a.** an official order requiring a person to attend court, either to answer a charge or to give evidence.

b. the writ making such an order. **3.** a call or command given to the members of an assembly to convene a meeting. ~*vb.* **4.** to take out a summons against (a person). [C13: from OF *somonse,* from *somondre* to SUMMON]

summum bonum *Latin.* ('sʊmʊm 'bɒnʊm) *n.* the principle of goodness in which all moral values are included or from which they are derived; highest or supreme good.

sumo ('suːməʊ) *n.* the national style of wrestling of Japan, the object of which is to force one's opponent to touch the ground with any part of his body except the soles of his feet or to step out of the ring. [from Japanese *sumō*]

sump (sʌmp) *n.* **1.** a receptacle, as in the crankcase of an internal-combustion engine, into which liquids, esp. lubricants, can drain to form a reservoir. **2.** another name for **cesspool** (sense 1). **3.** *Mining.* a depression at the bottom of a shaft where water collects. [C17: from MDu. *somp* marsh]

sumpter ('sʌmptə) *n. Arch.* a packhorse, mule, or other beast of burden. [C14: from OF *sometier* driver of a baggage horse, from Vulgar L *sagmatārius* (unattested), from LL *sagma* packsaddle]

sumptuary ('sʌmptjʊərɪ) *adj.* relating to or controlling expenditure or extravagance. [C17: from L *sumptuārius* concerning expense, from *sumptus* expense, from *sūmere* to spend]

sumptuous ('sʌmptjʊəs) *adj.* **1.** expensive or extravagant: *sumptuous costumes.* **2.** magnificent; splendid: *a sumptuous scene.* [C16: from OF *somptueux,* from L *sumptuōsus* costly, from *sumptus;* see SUMPTUARY] —'sumptuously *adv.* —'sumptuousness *n.*

sum up *vb.* (*adv.*) **1.** to summarize (the main points of an argument, etc.). **2.** (*tr.*) to form a quick opinion of: *I summed him up in five minutes.*

Sumy (*Russian* 'sumi) *n.* a city in the SW Soviet Union, in the NE Ukrainian SSR: site of early Slav settlements. Pop.: 240 000 (1981 est.).

sun (sʌn) *n.* **1.** the star that is the source of heat and light for the planets in the solar system. Related adj.: **solar. 2.** any star around which a planetary system revolves. **3.** the sun as it appears at a particular time or place: *the winter sun.* **4.** the radiant energy, esp. heat and light, received from the sun; sunshine. **5.** a person or thing considered as a source of radiant warmth, glory, etc. **6.** a pictorial representation of the sun, often depicted with a human face. **7.** *Poetic.* a year or a day. **8.** *Poetic.* a climate. **9.** *Arch.* sunrise or sunset (esp. in **from sun to sun**). **10. catch the sun.** to become slightly sunburnt. **11. place in the sun.** a prominent or favourable position. **12. take** *or* **shoot the sun.** *Naut.* to measure the altitude of the sun in order to determine latitude. **13. touch of the sun.** slight sunstroke. **14. under** *or* **beneath the sun.** on earth; at all: *nobody under the sun eats more than you.* ~*vb.* **sunning, sunned. 15.** to expose (oneself) to the sunshine. **16.** (*tr.*) to expose to the sunshine in order to warm, etc. [OE *sunne*]

Sun. *abbrev. for* Sunday.

sunbaked ('sʌnˌbeɪkt) *adj.* **1.** (esp. of roads, etc.) dried or cracked by the sun's heat. **2.** baked hard by the heat of the sun: *sunbaked bricks.*

sun bath *n.* the exposure of the body to the rays of the sun or a sun lamp, esp. in order to get a suntan.

sunbathe ('sʌnˌbeɪð) *vb.* (*intr.*) to bask in the sunshine, esp. in order to get a suntan. —'sunˌbather *n.*

sunbeam ('sʌnˌbiːm) *n.* a beam, ray, or stream of sunlight.

Sunbelt ('sʌnˌbelt) *n.* the southern states of the U.S.A.

sunbird ('sʌnˌbɜːd) *n.* any of various small songbirds of tropical regions of the Old World, esp. Africa, having a long slender curved bill and a bright plumage in the males.

sunbonnet ('sʌnˌbɒnɪt) *n.* a hat that shades the face and neck from the sun, esp. one of cotton with a projecting brim, now worn esp. by babies.

sunburn ('sʌnˌbɜːn) *n.* **1.** inflammation of the skin caused by overexposure to the sun. **2.** another word for **suntan.** —'sunˌburnt *or* 'sunˌburned *adj.*

sunburst ('sʌnˌbɜːst) *n.* **1.** a burst of sunshine, as through a break in the clouds. **2.** a pattern or design resembling that of the sun. **3.** a jewelled brooch with this pattern.

Sunbury-on-Thames ('sʌnbərɪ, -brɪ) *n.* a town in SE England, in N Surrey. Pop.: 39 075 (1981).

sun-cured *adj.* cured or preserved by exposure to the sun.

sundae ('sʌndɪ, -deɪ) n. ice cream topped with a sweet sauce, nuts, whipped cream, etc. [C20: from ?]

Sunda Islands ('sʌndə) or **Soenda Islands** pl. n. a chain of islands in the Malay Archipelago, consisting of the **Greater Sunda Islands** (chiefly Sumatra, Java, Borneo, and Sulawesi) and **Nusa Tenggara** (formerly the Lesser Sunda Islands).

Sunda Strait or **Soenda Strait** n. a strait between Sumatra and Java, linking the Java Sea with the Indian Ocean. Narrowest point: about 26 km (16 miles).

Sunday ('sʌndɪ) n. the first day of the week and the Christian day of worship. [OE sunnandæg, translation of L diēs sōlis day of the sun, translation of Gk hēmera hēliou]

Sunday best n. one's best clothes, esp. regarded as those most suitable for churchgoing.

Sunday school n. **1. a.** a school for the religious instruction of children on Sundays, usually held in a church. **b.** (as modifier): a Sunday-school outing. **2.** the members of such a school.

sunder ('sʌndə) Arch. or literary. ~vb. **1.** to break or cause to break apart or in pieces. ~n. **2. in sunder.** into pieces; apart. [OE sundrian]

Sunderland ('sʌndələnd) n. a port in NE England, in Tyne and Wear at the mouth of the River Wear: shipbuilding and marine engineering. Pop.: 196 152 (1981).

sundew ('sʌn,dju:) n. any of several bog plants having leaves covered with sticky hairs that trap and digest insects. [C16: translation of L ros solis]

sundial ('sʌn,daɪəl) n. a device indicating the time during the hours of sunlight by means of a stationary arm (the **gnomon**) that casts a shadow onto a plate or surface marked in hours.

sun disc n. a disc symbolizing the sun, esp. one flanked by two serpents and the extended wings of a vulture: a religious figure in ancient Egypt.

sundog ('sʌn,dɒg) n. another word for **parhelion**.

sundown ('sʌn,daʊn) n. another name for **sunset**.

sundowner ('sʌn,daʊnə) n. **1.** Austral. sl. a tramp, esp. one who seeks food and lodging at sundown when it is too late to work. **2.** Inf., chiefly Brit. an alcoholic drink taken at sunset.

sundress ('sʌn,drɛs) n. a dress for hot weather that exposes the shoulders, arms, and back.

sun-dried adj. dried or preserved by exposure to the sun.

sundry ('sʌndrɪ) determiner. **1.** several or various; miscellaneous. ~pron. **2. all and sundry.** everybody, individually and collectively. ~n., pl. **-dries. 3.** (pl.) miscellaneous unspecified items. **4.** the Austral. term for **extra** (sense 6). [OE syndrig separate]

Sundsvall (Swedish 'sundsval) n. a port in E Sweden, on the Gulf of Bothnia: icebound in winter; cellulose industries. Pop.: 92 795 (1986).

sunfast ('sʌn,fɑːst) adj. Chiefly U.S. & Canad. not fading in sunlight.

sunfish ('sʌn,fɪʃ) n., pl. **-fish** or **-fishes. 1.** any of various large fishes of temperate and tropical seas, esp. one which has a large rounded compressed body, long pointed dorsal and anal fins, and a fringelike tail fin. **2.** any of various small predatory North American freshwater percoid fishes, typically having a compressed brightly coloured body.

sunflower ('sʌn,flaʊə) n. **1.** any of several American plants having very tall thick stems, large flower heads with yellow rays, and seeds used as food, esp. for poultry. See also **Jerusalem artichoke. 2. sunflower seed oil.** the oil extracted from sunflower seeds, used as a salad oil, in margarine, etc.

sung (sʌŋ) vb. **1.** the past participle of **sing**. ~adj. **2.** produced by singing: a sung syllable.

▷ **Usage.** See at **ring²**.

Sung or **Song** (sʊŋ) n. an imperial dynasty of China (960–1279 A.D.), notable for its art, literature, and philosophy.

Sungari ('sʊŋgərɪ) n. another name for the **Songhua**.

Sungkiang ('sʊŋ'kjæŋ, -kaɪ'æŋ) n. a former province of NE China: now part of the Inner Mongolian AR.

sunglass ('sʌn,glɑːs) n. another name for **burning glass**.

sunglasses ('sʌn,glɑːsɪz) pl. n. glasses with darkened or polarizing lenses that protect the eyes from the sun's glare.

sun-god n. **1.** the sun considered as a personal deity. **2.** a deity associated with the sun or controlling its movements.

sunk (sʌŋk) vb. **1.** a past tense and past participle of **sink**. ~adj. **2.** Inf. with all hopes dashed; ruined.

sunken ('sʌŋkən) vb. **1.** a past participle of **sink**. ~adj. **2.** unhealthily hollow: sunken cheeks. **3.** situated at a lower level than the surrounding or usual one: a sunken bath. **4.** situated under water; submerged. **5.** depressed; low: sunken spirits.

sunk fence n. a ditch, one side of which is made into a retaining wall so as to enclose an area of land while remaining hidden in the total landscape. Also called: **ha-ha.**

Sun King n. **the.** an epithet of **Louis XIV.**

sun lamp n. **1.** a lamp that generates ultraviolet rays, used for obtaining an artificial suntan, for muscular therapy, etc. **2.** a lamp used in film studios, etc., to give an intense beam of light by means of parabolic mirrors.

sunless ('sʌnlɪs) adj. **1.** without sun or sunshine. **2.** gloomy; depressing. —'**sunlessly** adv.

sunlight ('sʌnlaɪt) n. **1.** the light emanating from the sun. **2.** an area or the time characterized by sunshine. —'**sunlit** adj.

sun lounge or U.S. **sun parlor** n. a room with large windows positioned to receive as much sunlight as possible.

Sunna ('sʊnə) n. the body of traditional Islamic law accepted by most orthodox Muslims as based on the words and acts of Mohammed. [C18: from Ar. sunnah rule]

Sunni ('sʊnɪ) n. **1.** one of the two main branches of orthodox Islam (the other being the Shiah), consisting of those who acknowledge the authority of the Sunna. **2.** (pl. **-ni**) a less common word for **Sunnite**.

Sunnite ('sʌnaɪt) n. an adherent of the Sunni.

sunny ('sʌnɪ) adj. **-nier, -niest. 1.** full of or exposed to sunlight. **2.** radiating good humour. **3.** of or resembling the sun. —'**sunnily** adv. —'**sunniness** n.

sunrise ('sʌn,raɪz) n. **1.** the daily appearance of the sun above the horizon. **2.** the atmospheric phenomena accompanying this appearance. **3.** Also called (esp. U.S.): **sunup.** the time at which the sun rises at a particular locality.

sunrise industry n. any of the high-technology industries, such as electronics, that hold promise of future development.

sunset ('sʌn,sɛt) n. **1.** the daily disappearance of the sun below the horizon. **2.** the atmospheric phenomena accompanying this disappearance. **3.** Also called: **sundown.** the time at which the sun sets at a particular locality. **4.** the final stage or closing period, as of a person's life.

sunshade ('sʌn,ʃeɪd) n. a device, esp. a parasol or awning, serving to shade from the sun.

sunshine ('sʌn,ʃaɪn) n. **1.** the light received directly from the sun. **2.** the warmth from the sun. **3.** a sunny area. **4.** a light-hearted or ironic term of address. —'**sun,shiny** adj.

sunshine roof or **sunroof** ('sʌn,ru:f) n. a panel in the roof of a car that may be opened by sliding it back.

sunspot ('sʌn,spɒt) n. **1.** any of the dark cool patches that appear on the surface of the sun and last about a week. **2.** Inf. a sunny holiday resort. **3.** Austral. a small cancerous spot produced by overexposure to the sun.

sunstroke ('sʌn,strəʊk) n. heatstroke caused by prolonged exposure to intensely hot sunlight.

sunsuit ('sʌn,su:t, -,sju:t) n. a child's outfit consisting of a brief top and shorts or skirt.

suntan ('sʌn,tæn) n. **a.** a brownish colouring of the skin caused by the formation of the pigment melanin within the skin on exposure to the ultraviolet rays of the sun or a sunlamp. Often shortened to **tan. b.** (as modifier): suntan oil. —'sun,tanned adj.

suntrap ('sʌn,træp) n. a very sunny sheltered place.

sunward ('sʌnwəd) adj. **1.** directed or moving towards the sun. ~adv. **2.** Also: **sunwards.** towards the sun.

Sun Yat-sen ('sʊn 'jɑːt'sɛn) n. 1866–1925, Chinese statesman, who was instrumental in the overthrow of the Manchu dynasty and was the first president of the Republic of China (1911). He reorganized the Kuomintang.

Suomi ('suomi) n. the Finnish name for **Finland**.

sup¹ (sʌp) vb. **supping, supped.** (intr.) Arch. to have supper. [C13: from OF soper]

sup² (sʌp) vb. **supping, supped. 1.** to partake of (liquid) by swallowing a little at a time. **2.** Scot. & N English dialect. to drink. ~n. **3.** a sip. [OE sūpan]

sup. *abbrev. for:* **1.** above. [from L *supra*] **2.** superior. **3.** *Grammar.* superlative. **4.** supplement. **5.** supplementary. **6.** supply.

super (su:pə) *adj.* **1.** *Inf.* outstanding; exceptional. ~*n.* **2.** petrol with a high octane rating. **3.** *Inf.* a supervisor. **4.** *Austral. & N.Z. inf.* superannuation benefits. **5.** *Austral & N.Z. inf.* superphosphate. ~*interj.* **6.** *Brit. inf.* an enthusiastic expression of approval. [from L: above]

super. *abbrev. for:* **1.** superfine. **2.** superior.

super- *prefix.* **1.** placed above or over: *superscript.* **2.** surpassing others; outstanding: *superstar.* **3.** of greater size, extent, quality, etc.: *supermarket.* **4.** beyond a standard or norm: *supersonic.* **5.** indicating that a chemical compound contains a specified element in a higher proportion than usual: *superphosphate.* [from L *super* above]

superable ('su:pərəb³l) *adj.* able to be surmounted or overcome. [C17: from L *superābilis*, from *superāre* to overcome] —,**supera'bility** *or* '**superableness** *n.* —'**superably** *adv.*

superannuate (,su:pər'ænju,eɪt) *vb.* (*tr.*) **1.** to pension off. **2.** to discard as obsolete or old-fashioned.

superannuated (,su:pər'ænju,eɪtɪd) *adj.* **1.** discharged, esp. with a pension, owing to age or illness. **2.** too old to serve usefully. **3.** obsolete. [C17: from Med. L *superannātus* aged more than one year, from L SUPER- + *annus* a year]

superannuation (,su:pər,ænju'eɪʃən) *n.* **1. a.** the amount deducted regularly from employees' incomes in a contributory pension scheme. **b.** the pension finally paid. **2.** the act or process of superannuating or the condition of being superannuated.

superb (sʊ'pɜ:b, sjʊ-) *adj.* **1.** surpassingly good; excellent. **2.** majestic or imposing. **3.** magnificently rich; luxurious. [C16: from OF *superbe*, from L *superbus* distinguished, from *super* above] —su'**perbly** *adv.* —su'**perbness** *n.*

Super Bowl *n. American football.* the championship game held annually between the best team of the American Football Conference and that of the National Football Conference.

supercalender (,su:pə'kæləndə) *n.* **1.** a calender that gives a high gloss to paper. ~*vb.* **2.** (*tr.*) to finish (paper) in this way. —,**super'calendered** *adj.*

supercargo (,su:pə'ka:gəʊ) *n., pl.* -**goes.** an officer on a merchant ship who supervises commercial matters and is in charge of the cargo. [C17: changed from Sp. *sobrecargo*, from *sobre* over + *cargo* CARGO]

supercharge ('su:pə,tʃɑ:dʒ) *vb.* (*tr.*) **1.** to increase the intake pressure of (an internal-combustion engine) with a supercharger; boost. **2.** to charge (the atmosphere, a remark, etc.) with an excess amount of (tension, emotion, etc.). **3.** to apply pressure to (a fluid); pressurize.

supercharger ('su:pə,tʃɑ:dʒə) *n.* a device that increases the mass of air drawn into an internal-combustion engine by raising the intake pressure. Also called: **blower, booster.**

superciliary (,su:pə'sɪlɪərɪ) *adj.* over the eyebrow or a corresponding region in lower animals. [C18: from NL *superciliaris*, from L, from SUPER- + *cilium* eyelid]

supercilious (,su:pə'sɪlɪəs) *adj.* displaying arrogant pride, scorn, or indifference. [C16: from L, from *supercilium* eyebrow] —,**super'ciliously** *adv.* —,**super'ciliousness** *n.*

superclass ('su:pə,klɑ:s) *n.* a taxonomic group that is a subdivision of a subphylum.

supercolumnar (,su:pəkə'lʌmnə) *adj. Archit.* **1.** having one colonnade above another. **2.** placed above a colonnade or a column. —,**supercol,umni'ation** *n.*

superconductivity (,su:pə,kɒndʌk'tɪvɪtɪ) *n. Physics.* the property of certain substances that have almost no electrical resistance at very low temperatures. —**superconduction** (,su:pəkən'dʌkʃən) *n.* —,**supercon'ductive** *or* ,**supercon'ducting** *adj.* —,**supercon'ductor** *n.*

supercool (,su:pə'ku:l) *vb. Chem.* to cool or be cooled without freezing or crystallization to a temperature below that at which freezing or crystallization should occur.

superdense theory (,su:pə'dɛns) *n. Astron.* another name for the **big-bang theory.**

super-duper ('su:pə'du:pə) *adj. Inf.* extremely pleasing, impressive, etc.: often used as an exclamation.

superego (,su:pər'i:gəʊ, -'ɛgəʊ) *n., pl.* -**gos.** *Psychoanal.* that part of the unconscious mind that acts as a conscience for the ego.

superelevation (,su:pər,ɛlɪ'veɪʃən) *n.* **1.** another name for **bank²** (sense 8). **2.** the difference between the heights of the sides of a road or railway track on a bend.

supereminent (,su:pər'ɛmɪnənt) *adj.* of distinction, dignity, or rank superior to that of others; pre-eminent. —,**super'eminence** *n.* —,**super'eminently** *adv.*

supererogation (,su:pər,ɛrə'geɪʃən) *n.* **1.** the performance of work in excess of that required or expected. **2.** *R.C. Church.* supererogatory prayers, devotions, etc.

supererogatory (,su:pərɛ'rɒgətərɪ, -trɪ) *adj.* **1.** performed to an extent exceeding that required or expected. **2.** exceeding what is needed; superfluous. **3.** *R.C. Church.* of or relating to prayers, good works, etc., performed over and above those prescribed as obligatory. [C16: from Med. L *superērogātōrius*, from L *superērogāre* to spend over and above]

superfamily ('su:pə,fæmɪlɪ) *n., pl.* -**lies. 1.** *Biol.* a subdivision of a suborder. **2.** any analogous group, such as a group of related languages.

superfecundation (,su:pə,fi:kən'deɪʃən) *n. Physiol.* the fertilization of two or more ova, produced during the same menstrual cycle, by sperm ejaculated during two or more acts of sexual intercourse.

superfetation (,su:pəfi:'teɪʃən) *n. Physiol.* the presence in the uterus of two fetuses developing from ova fertilized at different times. [C17 *superfetate*, from L *superfētāre* to fertilize when already pregnant, from *fētus* offspring]

superficial (,su:pə'fɪʃəl) *adj.* **1.** of, near, or forming the surface: *superficial bruising.* **2.** displaying a lack of thoroughness or care: *a superficial inspection.* **3.** only outwardly apparent rather than genuine or actual: *the similarity was merely superficial.* **4.** of little substance or significance: *superficial differences.* **5.** lacking profundity: *the film's plot was quite superficial.* **6.** (of measurements) involving only the surface area. [C14: from LL *superficiālis* of the surface, from L SUPERFICIES] —**superficiality** (,su:pə,fɪʃɪ'ælɪtɪ) *n.* —,**super'ficially** *adv.*

superficies (,su:pə'fɪʃi:z) *n., pl.* -**cies. 1.** a surface or outer face. **2.** the outward form of a thing. [C16: from L: upper side]

superfine (,su:pə'faɪn) *adj.* **1.** of exceptional fineness or quality. **2.** excessively refined. —,**super'fineness** *n.*

superfix ('su:pə,fɪks) *n. Linguistics.* a type of feature distinguishing the meaning or grammatical function of one word or phrase from that of another, as stress does for example between the noun *conduct* and the verb *conduct.*

superfluid (,su:pə'flu:ɪd) *n.* **1.** *Physics.* a fluid in a state characterized by a very low viscosity, high thermal conductivity, high capillarity, etc. The only known example is that of liquid helium at temperatures close to absolute zero. ~*adj.* **2.** being or relating to a superfluid. —,**super'fluidity** *n.*

superfluity (,su:pə'flu:ɪtɪ) *n.* **1.** the condition of being superfluous. **2.** a quantity or thing that is in excess of what is needed. **3.** a thing that is not needed. [C14: from OF *superfluité*, via LL from L *superfluus* SUPERFLUOUS]

superfluous (su:'pɜ:fluəs) *adj.* **1.** exceeding what is sufficient or required. **2.** not necessary or relevant; uncalled for. [C15: from L *superfluus* overflowing, from *fluere* to flow] —su'**perfluously** *adv.* —su'**perfluousness** *n.*

supergiant ('su:pə,dʒaɪənt) *n.* any of a class of extremely bright stars which have expanded to a diameter hundreds or thousands of times greater than that of the sun and have an extremely low mean density.

superglue ('su:pə,glu:) *n.* any of various adhesives that quickly make an exceptionally strong bond.

supergrass ('su:pə,grɑ:s) *n.* an informer whose information implicates a large number of people.

superheat (,su:pə'hi:t) *vb.* (*tr.*) **1.** to heat (a vapour, esp. steam) to a temperature above its saturation point for a given pressure. **2.** to heat (a liquid) to a temperature above its boiling point without boiling occurring. **3.** to heat excessively; overheat. —,**super'heater** *n.*

superheterodyne receiver (,su:pə'hɛtərə,daɪn) *n.* a radio receiver that combines two radio-frequency signals by heterodyne action, to produce a signal above the audible

---

,**supera'bound** *vb.*
,**supera'bundant** *adj.*

,**superce'lestial** *adj.*
,**super'confident** *adj.*

,**super'critical** *adj.*
,**super'dose** *n.*

,**superef'ficient** *adj.*
,**super'fatted** *adj.*

frequency limit. Sometimes shortened to **superhet.** [C20: from SUPER(SONIC) + HETERODYNE]

superhigh frequency (ˌsuːpəˌhaɪ) *n.* a radio-frequency band or radio frequency lying between 30 000 and 3000 megahertz.

superhuman (ˌsuːpəˈhjuːmən) *adj.* **1.** having powers above and beyond those of mankind. **2.** exceeding normal human ability or experience. — **ˌsuper'humanly** *adv.*

superimpose (ˌsuːpərɪmˈpəʊz) *vb.* (*tr.*) **1.** to set or place on or over something else. **2.** (usually foll. by *on* or *upon*) to add (to). — **ˌsuper,impo'sition** *n.*

superinduce (ˌsuːpərɪnˈdjuːs) *vb.* (*tr.*) to introduce as an additional feature, factor, etc. — **superinduction** (ˌsuːpərɪnˈdʌkʃən) *n.*

superintend (ˌsuːpərɪnˈtɛnd) *vb.* to undertake the direction or supervision (of); manage. [C17: from Church L *superintendere*, from L SUPER- + *intendere* to give attention to] — **ˌsuperin'tendence** *n.*

superintendent (ˌsuːpərɪnˈtɛndənt) *n.* **1.** a person who directs and manages an organization, office, etc. **2.** (in Britain) a senior police officer higher in rank than an inspector but lower than a chief superintendent. **3.** (in the U.S.) the head of a police department. **4.** *Chiefly U.S. & Canad.* a caretaker, esp. of a block of apartments. ~*adj.* **5.** of or relating to supervision; superintending. [C16: from Church L *superintendens* overseeing] — **ˌsuperin'tendency** *n.*

superior (suːˈpɪərɪə) *adj.* **1.** greater in quality, quantity, etc. **2.** of high or extraordinary worth, merit, etc. **3.** higher in rank or status. **4.** displaying a conscious sense of being above or better than others; supercilious. **5.** (*often postpositive*; foll. by *to*) not susceptible (to) or influenced (by). **6.** placed higher up; further from the base. **7.** *Astron.* (of a planet) having an orbit further from the sun than the orbit of the earth. **8.** (of a plant ovary) situated above the calyx and other floral parts. **9.** *Printing.* (of a character) written or printed above the line; superscript. ~*n.* **10.** a person or thing of greater rank or quality. **11.** *Printing.* a character set in a superior position. **12.** (*often cap.*) the head of a community in a religious order. [C14: from L, from *superus* placed above, from *super* above] — **su'perioress** *fem. n.* — **superiority** (suːˌpɪərɪˈɒrɪtɪ) *n.*

Superior (suːˈpɪərɪə, sjuː-) *n.* **Lake.** a lake in the N central U.S. and S Canada: one of the largest freshwater lakes in the world and westernmost of the Great Lakes. Area: 82 362 sq. km (31 800 sq. miles).

superior court *n.* **1.** (in England) a higher court not subject to control by any other court except by way of appeal. See also **Supreme Court of Judicature. 2.** (in several states of the U.S.) a court of general jurisdiction ranking above the inferior courts and below courts of last resort.

superiority complex *n. Inf.* an inflated estimate of one's own merit, usually manifested in arrogance.

superior planet *n.* any of the six planets (Mars, Jupiter, Saturn, Uranus, Neptune, and Pluto) whose orbit lies outside that of the earth.

superl. *abbrev. for* superlative.

superlative (suːˈpɜːlətɪv) *adj.* **1.** of outstanding quality, degree, etc.; supreme. **2.** *Grammar.* denoting the form of an adjective or adverb that expresses the highest or a very high degree of quality. In English this is usually marked by the suffix *-est* or the word *most*, as in *loudest* or *most loudly.* **3.** (of language or style) excessive; exaggerated. ~*n.* **4.** a thing that excels all others or is of the highest quality. **5.** *Grammar.* the superlative form of an adjective. **6.** the highest degree; peak. [C14: from OF *superlatif*, via LL from L *superlātus* extravagant, from *superferre* to carry beyond] — **su'perlatively** *adv.* — **su'perlativeness** *n.*

superlunar (ˌsuːpəˈluːnə) *adj.* beyond the moon; celestial. — **ˌsuper'lunary** *adj.*

superman (ˈsuːpəˌmæn) *n., pl.* **-men. 1.** (in the philosophy of Nietzsche) an ideal man who would rise above good and evil and who represents the goal of human evolution. **2.** any man of apparently superhuman powers.

supermarket (ˈsuːpəˌmɑːkɪt) *n.* a large self-service store selling food and household supplies.

supermundane (ˌsuːpəˈmʌndeɪn) *adj.* elevated above earthly things.

supernal (suːˈpɜːnᵊl, sjuː-) *adj. Literary.* **1.** divine; celestial. **2.** of, from above, or from the sky. [C15: from Med. L *supernālis*, from L *supernus* that is on high, from *super* above] — **su'pernally** *adv.*

supernatant (ˌsuːpəˈneɪtᵊnt) *adj.* **1.** floating on the surface or over something. **2.** *Chem.* (of a liquid) lying above a sediment or settled precipitate. [C17: from L *supernatāre* to float, from SUPER- + *natāre* to swim] — **ˌsuperna'tation** *n.*

supernatural (ˌsuːpəˈnætʃərəl) *adj.* **1.** of or relating to things that cannot be explained according to natural laws. **2.** of or caused as if by a god; miraculous. **3.** of or involving occult beings. **4.** exceeding the ordinary; abnormal. ~*n.* **5. the supernatural.** supernatural forces, occurrences, and beings collectively. — **ˌsuper'naturally** *adv.* — **ˌsuper'naturalness** *n.*

supernaturalism (ˌsuːpəˈnætʃərəlɪzəm) *n.* **1.** the quality or condition of being supernatural. **2.** belief in supernatural forces or agencies as producing effects in this world. — **ˌsuper'naturalist** *n., adj.* — **ˌsuper,natural'istic** *adj.*

supernormal (ˌsuːpəˈnɔːməl) *adj.* greatly exceeding the normal. — **supernormality** (ˌsuːpənɔːˈmælɪtɪ) *n.* — **su'per'normally** *adv.*

supernova (ˌsuːpəˈnəʊvə) *n., pl.* **-vae** (-viː) *or* **-vas.** a star that explodes owing to instabilities following the exhaustion of its nuclear fuel, becoming for a few days up to one hundred million times brighter than the sun. Cf. **nova.**

supernumerary (ˌsuːpəˈnjuːmərərɪ) *adj.* **1.** exceeding a regular or proper number; extra. **2.** functioning as a substitute or assistant with regard to a regular body or staff. ~*n., pl.* **-aries. 3.** a person or thing that exceeds the required or regular number. **4.** a substitute or assistant. **5.** an actor who has no lines, esp. a nonprofessional one. [C17: from LL *supernumerārius*, from L SUPER- + *numerus* number]

superorder (ˈsuːpərˌɔːdə) *n. Biol.* a subdivision of a subclass.

superordinate *adj.* (ˌsuːpərˈɔːdᵊnɪt). **1.** of higher status or condition. ~*n.* (ˌsuːpərˈɔːdɪnɪt) **2.** a person or thing that is superordinate. **3.** a word the meaning of which includes the meaning of another word or words: *"red" is the superordinate of "scarlet" and "crimson".*

superphosphate (ˌsuːpəˈfɒsfeɪt) *n.* **1.** a mixture of the diacid calcium salt of orthophosphoric acid with calcium sulphate and small quantities of other phosphates: used as a fertilizer. **2.** a salt of phosphoric acid formed by incompletely replacing its acidic hydrogen atoms.

superpose (ˌsuːpəˈpəʊz) *vb.* (*tr.*) *Geom.* to transpose (the coordinates of one geometric figure) to coincide with those of another. [C19: from F *superposer*, from L *superpōnere*, from *pōnere* to place]

superposition (ˌsuːpəpəˈzɪʃən) *n.* **1.** the act of superposing or state of being superposed. **2.** *Geol.* the principle that in any sequence of sedimentary rocks that has not been disturbed the lowest strata are the oldest.

superpower (ˈsuːpəˌpaʊə) *n.* **1.** an extremely powerful state, such as the U.S. **2.** extremely high power, esp. electrical or mechanical. — **'super,powered** *adj.*

supersaturated (ˌsuːpəˈsætʃəˌreɪtɪd) *adj.* **1.** (of a solution) containing more solute than a saturated solution. **2.** (of a vapour) containing more material than a saturated vapour. — **ˌsuper,satu'ration** *n.*

superscribe (ˌsuːpəˈskraɪb) *vb.* (*tr.*) to write (an inscription, name, etc.) above, on top of, or outside. [C16: from L *superscrībere*, from *scrībere* to write] — **superscription** (ˌsuːpəˈskrɪpʃən) *n.*

superscript (ˈsuːpəˌskrɪpt) *adj.* **1.** *Printing.* (of a character) written or printed above the line; superior. Cf. **subscript.** ~*n.* **2.** a superscript or superior character. [C16: from L *superscrīptus*]

supersede (ˌsuːpəˈsiːd) *vb.* (*tr.*) **1.** to take the place of (something old-fashioned or less appropriate); supplant. **2.** to replace in function, office, etc.; succeed. **3.** to discard or set aside or cause to be set aside as obsolete or inferior. [C15: via OF from L *supersedēre* to sit above] — **ˌsuper'sedence**, **supersedure** (ˌsuːpəˈsiːdʒə) *n.* — **supersession** (ˌsuːpəˈsɛʃən) *n.*

supersex (ˈsuːpəˌsɛks) *n. Genetics.* a sterile organism in which the ratio between the sex chromosomes is disturbed.

ˌsuperin'telligent *adj.*   **ˌsuper'pure** *adj.*   **ˌsuper'rich** *adj.*   **ˌsuper'sensitive** *adj.*
ˌsuper'polymer *n.*   **ˌsuperre'fine** *vb.*

supersonic (ˌsuːpəˈsɒnɪk) *adj.* being, having, or capable of a velocity in excess of the velocity of sound. —ˌsuperˈsonically *adv.*

supersonics (ˌsuːpəˈsɒnɪks) *n.* (*functioning as sing.*) **1.** the study of supersonic motion. **2.** a less common name for **ultrasonics.**

superstar ('suːpəˌstɑː) *n.* an extremely popular film star, pop star, etc.

superstition (ˌsuːpəˈstɪʃən) *n.* **1.** irrational belief usually founded on ignorance or fear and characterized by obsessive reverence for omens, charms, etc. **2.** a notion, act, or ritual that derives from such belief. **3.** any irrational belief, esp. with regard to the unknown. [C15: from L *superstitiō*, from *superstāre* to stand still by something (as in amazement)]

superstitious (ˌsuːpəˈstɪʃəs) *adj.* **1.** disposed to believe in superstition. **2.** of or relating to superstition. —ˌsuperˈstitiously *adv.* —ˌsuperˈstitiousness *n.*

superstore ('suːpəˌstɔː) *n.* a large supermarket.

superstratum (ˌsuːpəˈstrɑːtəm, -ˈstreɪ-) *n., pl.* **-ta** (-tə) *or* **-tums.** *Geol.* a layer or stratum overlying another layer or similar structure.

superstructure ('suːpəˌstrʌktʃə) *n.* **1.** the part of a building above its foundation. **2.** any structure or concept erected on something else. **3.** *Naut.* any structure above the main deck of a ship with sides flush with the sides of the hull. **4.** the part of a bridge supported by the piers and abutments. —ˌsuperˈstructural *adj.*

supertanker ('suːpəˌtæŋkə) *n.* a large fast tanker of more than 275 000 tons capacity.

supertax ('suːpəˌtæks) *n.* a tax levied in addition to the basic or normal tax, esp. a surtax on incomes above a certain level.

supertonic (ˌsuːpəˈtɒnɪk) *n.* *Music.* **1.** the second degree of a major or minor scale. **2.** a key or chord based on this.

supervene (ˌsuːpəˈviːn) *vb.* (*intr.*) **1.** to follow closely; ensue. **2.** to occur as an unexpected or extraneous development. [C17: from L *supervenīre* to come upon] —ˌsuperˈvenience *or* **supervention** (ˌsuːpəˈvɛnʃən) *n.* —ˌsuperˈvenient *adj.*

supervise ('suːpəˌvaɪz) *vb.* (*tr.*) **1.** to direct or oversee the performance or operation of. **2.** to watch over so as to maintain order, etc. [C16: from Med. L *supervidēre*, from L SUPER- + *vidēre* to see] —**supervision** (ˌsuːpəˈvɪʒən) *n.*

supervisor ('suːpəˌvaɪzə) *n.* **1.** a person who manages or supervises. **2.** a foreman or forewoman. **3.** (in some British universities) a tutor supervising the work, esp. research work, of a student. **4.** (in some U.S. schools) an administrator running a department of teachers. —ˌsuperˌvisorship *n.* —ˌsuperˈvisory *adj.*

supinate ('suːpɪˌneɪt, 'sjuː-) *vb.* to turn (the hand and forearm) so that the palm faces up or forwards. [C19: from L *supīnāre* to lay on the back, from *supīnus* supine] —ˌsupiˈnation *n.*

supine *adj.* (suːˈpaɪn, sjuː-; 'suːpaɪn, 'sjuː-). **1.** lying or resting on the back with the face, palm, etc., upwards. **2.** displaying no interest or animation; lethargic. ~*n.* ('suːpaɪn, 'sjuː-). **3.** *Grammar.* a noun form derived from a verb in Latin, often used to express purpose with verbs of motion. [C15: from L *supīnus* rel. to *sub* under, up; (in grammatical sense) from L *verbum supīnum* supine word (from ?)] —**suˈpinely** *adv.* —**suˈpineness** *n.*

supp. *or* **suppl.** *abbrev. for* supplement(ary).

supper ('sʌpə) *n.* **1.** an evening meal, esp. a light one. **2.** an evening social event featuring a supper. **3. sing for one's supper.** to obtain something by performing a service. [C13: from OF *soper*] —**'supperless** *adj.*

supplant (səˈplɑːnt) *vb.* (*tr.*) to take the place of, often by trickery or force. [C13: via OF from L *supplantāre* to trip up, from *sub-* from below + *planta* sole of the foot] —**supˈplanter** *n.*

supple ('sʌp²l) *adj.* **1.** bending easily without damage. **2.** capable of or showing easy or graceful movement; lithe. **3.** mentally flexible; responding readily. **4.** disposed to agree, sometimes to the point of servility. ~*vb.* **5.** *Rare.* to make or become supple. [C13: from OF *souple*, from L *supplex* bowed] —**'suppleness** *n.*

supplejack ('sʌp²lˌdʒæk) *n.* **1.** a North American twining woody vine that has greenish-white flowers and purple fruits. **2.** a bush plant of New Zealand having tough climbing vines. **3.** a tropical American woody vine having strong supple wood. **4.** any of various other vines with strong supple stems. **5.** *U.S.* a walking stick made from the wood of the tropical supplejack.

supplement *n.* ('sʌplɪmənt). **1.** an addition designed to complete, make up for a deficiency, etc. **2.** a section appended to a publication to supply further information, correct errors, etc. **3.** a magazine or section inserted into a newspaper or periodical, such as one issued every week. **4.** *Geom.* **a.** either of a pair of angles whose sum is 180°. **b.** an arc of a circle that when added to another arc forms a semicircle. ~*vb.* ('sʌplɪˌmɛnt). **5.** (*tr.*) to provide a supplement to, esp. in order to remedy a deficiency. [C14: from L *supplēmentum*, from *supplēre* to SUPPLY] —**supplemenˈtation** *n.*

supplementary (ˌsʌplɪˈmɛntərɪ) *adj.* **1.** Also (*less commonly*): **supplemental** (ˌsʌpləˈmɛntl). forming or acting as a supplement. ~*n., pl.* **-ries.** **2.** a person or thing that is a supplement. —ˌsuppleˈmentarily *or* (*less commonly*) ˌsuppleˈmentally *adv.*

supplementary angle *n.* either of two angles whose sum is 180°.

supplementary benefit *n.* (in Britain) a weekly allowance paid to various groups of people by the state to bring their incomes up to minimum levels established by law.

suppliant ('sʌplɪənt) *adj.* **1.** expressing entreaty or supplication. ~*n., adj.* **2.** another word for **supplicant.** [C15: from F *supplier* to beseech, from L *supplicāre* to kneel in entreaty] —**'suppliantly** *adv.*

supplicant ('sʌplɪkənt) *or* **suppliant** *n.* **1.** a person who supplicates. ~*adj.* **2.** entreating humbly; supplicating. [C16: from L *supplicāns* beseeching]

supplicate ('sʌplɪˌkeɪt) *vb.* **1.** to make a humble request to (someone); plead. **2.** (*tr.*) to ask for or seek humbly. [C15: from L *supplicāre* to beg on one's knees] —ˌsuppliˈcation *n.* —'suppliˌcatory *adj.*

supply[1] (səˈplaɪ) *vb.* **-plying, -plied. 1.** (*tr.; often foll. by with*) to furnish with something required. **2.** (*tr.; often foll. by to or for*) to make available or provide (something desired or lacking): *to supply books to the library.* **3.** (*tr.*) to provide for adequately; satisfy: *who will supply their needs?* **4.** to serve as a substitute, usually temporary, in (another's position, etc.): *there are no clergymen to supply the pulpit.* **5.** (*tr.*) *Brit.* to fill (a vacancy, position, etc.). ~*n., pl.* **-plies. 6. a.** the act of providing or something provided. **b.** (*as modifier*): *a supply dump.* **7.** (*often pl.*) an amount available for use; stock. **8.** (*pl.*) food, equipment, etc., needed for a campaign or trip. **9.** *Econ.* **a.** willingness and ability to offer goods and services for sale. **b.** the amount of a commodity that producers are willing and able to offer for sale at a specified price. Cf. **demand** (sense 9). **10.** *Mil.* **a.** the management and disposal of food and equipment. **b.** (*as modifier*): *supply routes.* **11.** (*often pl.*) a grant of money voted by a legislature for government expenses. **12.** (in Parliament and similar legislatures) the money voted annually for the expenses of the civil service and armed forces. **13. a.** a person who acts as a temporary substitute, esp. a clergyman. **b.** (*as modifier*): *a supply teacher.* **14.** a source of electricity, gas, etc. [C14: from OF *souppleier*, from L *supplēre* to complete, from *sub-* up + *plēre* to fill] —**supˈpliable** *adj.* —**supˈplier** *n.*

supply[2] ('sʌplɪ) *or* **supplely** ('sʌp²lɪ) *adv.* in a supple manner.

supply-side economics *n.* (*functioning as sing.*) the theory that reductions in taxation lead to greater investment in industry, which is seen as the driving force of the economy, rather than to demand for consumer goods and services.

support (səˈpɔːt) *vb.* (*tr.*) **1.** to carry the weight of. **2.** to bear (pressure, weight, etc.). **3.** to provide the necessities of life for (a family, person, etc.). **4.** to tend to establish (a theory, statement, etc.) by providing new facts. **5.** to speak in favour of (a motion). **6.** to give aid or courage to. **7.** to give approval to (a cause, principle, etc.); subscribe to. **8.** to endure with forbearance: *I will no longer support bad behaviour.* **9.** to give strength to; maintain: *to support a business.* **10.** (*tr.*) (in a concert) to perform earlier than (the main attraction). **11.** *Films, theatre.* **a.** to play a subordinate role to. **b.** to accompany (the feature) in a film programme. **12.** to act or perform (a role or character). ~n. **13.** the act of supporting or the condition of being supported. **14.** a thing that bears the weight or part of the weight of a construction. **15.** a person who or thing that furnishes aid. **16.** the means of maintenance of a family, person, etc. **17.** a band or entertainer not topping the bill. **18.** (often preceded by *the*) an actor or group of actors playing subordinate roles. **19.** *Med.* an appliance worn to ease the strain on an injured bodily structure or part. **20.** Also: **athletic support.** a more formal term for **jockstrap**. [C14: from OF *supporter*, from L *supportāre* to bring, from *sub-* up + *portāre* to carry] —**sup'portable** *adj.* —**sup'portive** *adj.*

supporter (sə'pɔːtə) *n.* **1.** a person or thing that acts as a support. **2.** a person who backs a sports team, politician, etc. **3.** a garment or device worn to ease the strain on or restrict the movement of a bodily structure or part. **4.** *Heraldry.* a figure or beast in a coat of arms depicted as holding up the shield.

supporting (sə'pɔːtɪŋ) *adj.* **1.** (of a role) being a fairly important but not leading part. **2.** (of an actor or actress) playing a supporting role.

suppose (sə'pəʊz) *vb.* (*tr.; may take a clause as object*) **1.** to presume (something) to be true without certain knowledge: *I suppose he meant to kill her.* **2.** to consider as a possible suggestion for the sake of discussion, etc.: *suppose that he wins.* **3.** (of theories, etc.) to imply the inference or assumption (of): *your policy supposes full employment.* [C14: from OF *supposer*, from Med. L *suppōnere*, from L: to substitute, from SUB- + *pōnere* to put] —**sup'posable** *adj.* —**sup'poser** *n.*

supposed (sə'pəʊzd, -'pəʊzɪd) *adj.* **1.** (*prenominal*) presumed to be true without certain knowledge. **2.** (*prenominal*) believed to be true on slight grounds; highly doubtful. **3.** (sə'pəʊzd). (*postpositive*; foll. by *to*) expected or obliged (to): *I'm supposed to be there.* **4.** (*postpositive*; used in negative; foll. by *to*) expected or obliged not (to): *you're not supposed to walk on the grass.* —**supposedly** (sə'pəʊzɪdlɪ) *adv.*

supposition (,sʌpə'zɪʃən) *n.* **1.** the act of supposing. **2.** a fact, theory, etc., that is supposed. —**,suppo'sitional** *adj.* —**,suppo'sitionally** *adv.*

suppositious (,sʌpə'zɪʃəs) *or* **supposititious** (sə,pɒzɪ'tɪʃəs) *adj.* **1.** deduced from supposition; hypothetical. **2.** substituted with intent to mislead or deceive. —**,suppo'sitiously** *or* **sup,posi'titiously** *adv.* —**,suppo'sitiousness** *or* **sup,posi'titiousness** *n.*

suppositive (sə'pɒzɪtɪv) *adj.* **1.** of, involving, or arising out of supposition. **2.** *Grammar.* denoting a conjunction introducing a clause expressing a supposition, as for example *if, supposing,* or *provided that.* ~*n.* **3.** *Grammar.* a suppositive conjunction. —**sup'positively** *adv.*

suppository (sə'pɒzɪtərɪ, -trɪ) *n., pl.* -**ries.** *Med.* a solid medication for insertion into the vagina, rectum, or urethra, where it melts and releases the active substance. [C14: from Med. L *suppositōrium*, from L *suppositus* placed beneath]

suppress (sə'prɛs) *vb.* (*tr.*) **1.** to put an end to; prohibit. **2.** to hold in check; restrain: *I was obliged to suppress a smile.* **3.** to withhold from circulation or publication: *to suppress seditious pamphlets.* **4.** to stop the activities of; crush: *to suppress a rebellion.* **5.** *Electronics.* **a.** to reduce or eliminate (unwanted oscillations) in a circuit. **b.** to eliminate (a particular frequency or frequencies) in a signal. **6.** *Psychiatry.* to resist consciously (an idea or a desire entering one's mind). [C14: from L *suppressus* held down, from *supprimere* to restrain, from *sub-* down + *premere* to press] —**sup'pressible** *adj.* —**sup'pressive** *adj.* —**sup'pressor** *or* **sup'presser** *n.*

suppression (sə'prɛʃən) *n.* **1.** the act or process of suppressing or the condition of being suppressed. **2.** *Psychiatry.* the conscious avoidance of unpleasant thoughts.

suppurate ('sʌpjʊ,reɪt) *vb.* (*intr.*) *Pathol.* (of a wound, sore, etc.) to discharge pus; fester. [C16: from L *suppūrāre*, from SUB- + *pūs* pus] —**,suppu'ration** *n.* —**'suppurative** *adj.*

supra- *prefix.* over, above, beyond, or greater than: *supranational.* [from L *suprā* above]

supraliminal (,suːprə'lɪmɪnəl, ,sjuː-) *adj.* of or relating to any stimulus that is above the threshold of sensory awareness. —**,supra'liminally** *adv.*

supramolecular (,suːprəmə'lɛkjʊlə, ,sjuː-) *adj.* **1.** more complex than a molecule. **2.** consisting of more than one molecule.

supranational (,suːprə'næʃnəl, ,sjuː-) *adj.* involving or relating to more than one nation. —**,supra'nationalism** *n.*

supraorbital (,suːprə'ɔːbɪtəl, ,sjuː-) *adj.* *Anat.* situated above the orbit.

suprarenal (,suːprə'riːnəl, ,sjuː-) *adj.* *Anat.* situated above a kidney.

suprarenal gland *n.* another name for **adrenal gland.**

supremacist (sʊ'prɛməsɪst, sjʊ-) *n.* **1.** a person who promotes or advocates the supremacy of any particular group. ~*adj.* **2.** characterized by belief in the supremacy of any particular group. —**su'prematism** *n.*

supremacy (sʊ'prɛməsɪ, sjʊ-) *n.* **1.** supreme power; authority. **2.** the quality or condition of being supreme.

supreme (sʊ'priːm, sjʊ-) *adj.* **1.** of highest status or power. **2.** (*usually prenominal*) of highest quality, importance, etc. **3.** greatest in degree; extreme: *supreme folly.* **4.** (*prenominal*) final or last; ultimate: *the supreme judgment.* [C16: from L *suprēmus* highest, from *superus* that is above, from *super* above] —**su'premely** *adv.*

Supreme Being *n.* God.

Supreme Court *n.* (in the U.S.) **1.** the highest Federal court. **2.** (in many states) the highest state court.

Supreme Court of Judicature *n.* (in England) a court formed in 1873 by the amalgamation of several superior courts into two divisions, the High Court of Justice and the Court of Appeal.

supreme sacrifice *n.* **the.** the sacrifice of one's life.

Supreme Soviet *n.* (in the Soviet Union) **1.** the bicameral legislature, comprising the **Soviet of the Union** and the **Soviet of the Nationalities.** **2.** a similar legislature in each republic.

supremo (sʊ'priːməʊ, sjʊ-) *n., pl.* -**mos.** *Brit. inf.* a person in overall authority. [C20: from SUPREME]

Supt *or* **supt** *abbrev. for* superintendent.

Suqutra (sə'kəʊtrə) *n.* a variant spelling of **Socotra.**

Sur *or* **Sour** (sʊə) *n.* transliteration of the Arabic name for **Tyre.**

sur-[1] *prefix.* over; above; beyond: *surcharge; surrealism.* Cf. **super-.** [from OF, from L SUPER-]

sur-[2] *prefix.* a variant of **sub-** before *r: surrogate.*

sura ('sʊərə) *n.* any of the 114 chapters of the Koran. [C17: from Ar. *sūrah* section]

Surabaya, Surabaja, *or* **Soerabaja** (,sʊərə'baɪə) *n.* a port in Indonesia, on E Java on the **Surabaya Strait:** the country's second port and chief naval base; university (1954); fishing and ship-building industries; oil refinery. Pop.: 2 345 000 (1985).

surah ('sʊərə) *n.* a twill-weave fabric of silk or rayon. [C19: from F pronunciation of *Surat*, a port in W India where orig. made]

Surakarta (,sʊərə'kɑːtə) *n.* a town in Indonesia, on central Java: textile manufacturing. Pop.: 469 888 (1980).

sural ('sjʊərəl) *adj.* *Anat.* of or relating to the calf of the leg. [C17: via NL from L *sūra* calf]

Surat (sʊ'ræt, 'sʊərət) *n.* a port in W India, in W Gujarat: a major port in the 17th century; textile manufacturing. Pop.: 775 711 (1981).

surbase ('sɜː,beɪs) *n.* the uppermost part, such as a moulding, of a pedestal, base, or skirting.

surcease (sɜː'siːs) *Arch.* ~*n.* **1.** cessation or intermission. ~*vb.* **2.** to desist from (some action). **3.** to cease or cause to cease. [C16: from earlier *sursesen*, from OF *surseoir*, from L *supersedēre* to sit above]

surcharge *n.* ('sɜː,tʃɑːdʒ). **1.** a charge in addition to the usual payment, tax, etc. **2.** an excessive sum charged, esp. when unlawful. **3.** an extra and usually excessive burden or supply. **4.** an overprint that alters the face value of a postage stamp. ~*vb.* (sɜː'tʃɑːdʒ, 'sɜː,tʃɑːdʒ). (*tr.*) **5.** to charge an additional sum, tax, etc. **6.** to overcharge (a person) for something. **7.** to put an extra physical burden upon; overload. **8.** to fill to excess; overwhelm. **9.** *Law.* to insert credits that have been omitted in (an account). **10.** to overprint a surcharge on (a stamp).

surcingle ('sɜː,sɪŋɡəl) *n.* a girth for a horse which goes around the body, used esp. with a racing saddle. [C14: from OF *surcengle*, from *sur-* over + *cengle* a belt, from L *cingulum*]

surcoat ('sɜː,kəʊt) *n.* **1.** a tunic, often embroidered with heraldic arms, worn by a knight over his armour during the Middle Ages. **2.** (formerly) an outer coat or other garment.

surculose ('sɜːkjʊ,ləʊs) adj. (of a plant) bearing suckers. [C19: from L surculōsus woody, from surculus twig, from sūrus a branch]

surd (sɜːd) n. **1.** Maths. a number containing an irrational root, such as 2√3; irrational number. **2.** Phonetics. a voiceless consonant, such as (t). ~adj. **3.** of or relating to a surd. [C16: from L surdus muffled]

sure (ʃʊə, ʃɔː) adj. **1.** (sometimes foll. by of) free from hesitancy or uncertainty (with regard to a belief, conviction, etc.): we are sure of the accuracy of the data; I am sure that he is lying. **2.** (foll. by of) having no doubt, as of the occurrence of a future state or event: sure of success. **3.** always effective; unfailing: a sure remedy. **4.** reliable in indication or accuracy: a sure criterion. **5.** (of persons) worthy of trust or confidence: a sure friend. **6.** not open to doubt: sure proof. **7.** admitting of no vacillation or doubt: he is sure in his beliefs. **8.** bound to be or occur; inevitable: victory is sure. **9.** (postpositive) bound inevitably (to be or do something); certain: she is sure to be there. **10.** physically secure or dependable: a sure footing. **11. be sure.** (usually imperative or dependent imperative; takes a clause as object or an infinitive, sometimes with to replaced by and) to be careful or certain: be sure and shut the door; be sure to shut the door. **12. for sure.** without a doubt; surely. **13. make sure. a.** (takes a clause as object) to make certain; ensure. **b.** (foll. by of) to establish or confirm power or possession (over). **14. sure enough.** Inf. as might have been confidently expected; definitely: often used as a sentence substitute. **15. to be sure. a.** without doubt; certainly. **b.** it has to be acknowledged; admittedly. ~adv. **16.** (sentence modifier) U.S. & Canad. inf. without question; certainly. **17.** (sentence substitute) U.S. & Canad. inf. willingly; yes. [C14: from OF seur, from L sēcūrus SECURE] —'**sureness** n.

sure-fire adj. (usually prenominal) Inf. certain to succeed or meet expectations; assured.

sure-footed adj. **1.** unlikely to fall, slip, or stumble. **2.** not likely to err or fall. —,sure-'footedly adv. —,sure-'footedness n.

surely ('ʃʊəlɪ, 'ʃɔː-) adv. **1.** without doubt; assuredly. **2.** without fail; inexorably (esp. in **slowly but surely**). **3.** (sentence modifier) am I not right in thinking that?; I am sure that: surely you don't mean it? **4.** Rare. in a sure manner. **5.** Arch. safely; securely. **6.** (sentence substitute) Chiefly U.S. & Canad. willingly; yes.

sure thing Inf. **1.** (sentence substitute) Chiefly U.S. used to express enthusiastic assent. ~n. **2.** something guaranteed to be successful.

surety ('ʃʊətɪ, 'ʃʊərɪtɪ) n., pl. -ties. **1.** a person who assumes legal responsibility for the fulfilment of another's debt or obligation and himself becomes liable if the other defaults. **2.** security given against loss or damage or as a guarantee that an obligation will be met. **3.** Obs. the quality or condition of being sure. **4. stand surety.** to act as a surety. [C14: from OF seurte, from L sēcūritās security] —'**suretyship** n.

surf (sɜːf) n. **1.** waves breaking on the shore or on a reef. **2.** foam caused by the breaking of waves. ~vb. **3.** (intr.) to take part in surfing. [C17: prob. var. of SOUGH] —'**surfy** adj.

surface ('sɜːfɪs) n. **1. a.** the exterior face of an object or one such face. **b.** (as modifier): surface gloss. **2.** the area or size of such a face. **3.** material resembling such a face, with length and width but without depth. **4. a.** the superficial appearance as opposed to the real nature. **b.** (as modifier): a surface resemblance. **5.** Geom. **a.** the complete boundary of a solid figure. **b.** a continuous two-dimensional configuration. **6. a.** the uppermost level of the land or sea. **b.** (as modifier): surface transportation. **7. come to the surface.** to emerge; become apparent. **8. on the surface.** to all appearances. ~vb. **9.** to rise or cause to rise to or as if to the surface (of water, etc.). **10.** (tr.) to treat the surface of, as by polishing, smoothing, etc. **11.** (tr.) to furnish with a surface. **12.** (intr.) to become apparent; emerge. **13.** (intr.) Inf. **a.** to wake up. **b.** to get up. [C17: from F, from sur on + face FACE] —'**surfacer** n.

surface-active adj. (of a substance, esp. a detergent) capable of lowering the surface tension of a liquid. See also **surfactant.**

surface mail n. mail transported by land or sea. Cf. **air mail.**

surface structure n. Generative grammar. a representation of a string of words or morphemes as they occur in a sentence, together with labels and brackets that represent syntactic structure. Cf. **deep structure.**

surface tension n. **1.** a property of liquids caused by intermolecular forces near the surface leading to the apparent presence of a surface film and to capillarity, etc. **2.** a measure of this.

surface-to-air adj. of or relating to a missile launched from the surface of the earth against airborne targets.

surfactant (sɜː'fæktənt) n. a substance, such as a detergent, that can reduce the surface tension of a liquid and thus allow it to foam or penetrate solids; a wetting agent. Also called: **surface-active agent.** [C20: surf(ace)-act(ive) a(ge)nt]

surfboard ('sɜːf,bɔːd) n. a long narrow board used in surfing.

surfboat ('sɜːf,bəʊt) n. a boat with a high bow and stern and flotation chambers, equipped for use in rough surf.

surfcasting ('sɜːf,kɑːstɪŋ) n. fishing from the shore by casting into the surf. —'**surf,caster** n.

surfeit ('sɜːfɪt) n. **1.** (usually foll. by of) an excessive amount. **2.** overindulgence, esp. in eating or drinking. **3.** disgust, nausea, etc., caused by such overindulgence. ~vb. **4.** (tr.) to supply or feed excessively; satiate. **5.** Arch. to eat, drink, or be supplied to excess. [C13: from F sourfait, from sourfaire to overdo, from SUR-1 + faire, from L facere to do]

surfie ('sɜːfɪ) n. Austral. & N.Z. sl. a young person whose main interest in life is surfing.

surfing ('sɜːfɪŋ) n. the sport of riding towards shore on the crest of a wave by standing or lying on a surfboard. —'**surfer** or '**surf,rider** n.

surg. abbrev. for: **1.** surgeon. **2.** surgery. **3.** surgical.

surge (sɜːdʒ) n. **1.** a strong rush or sweep; sudden increase: a surge of anger. **2.** the rolling swell of the sea. **3.** a heavy rolling motion or sound: the surge of the trumpets. **4.** an undulating rolling surface, as of hills. **5.** a billowing cloud or volume. **6.** Naut. a temporary release or slackening of a rope or cable. **7.** a large momentary increase in the voltage or current in an electric circuit. **8.** an instability or unevenness in the power output of an engine. ~vb. **9.** (intr.) (of waves, the sea, etc.) to rise or roll with a heavy swelling motion. **10.** (intr.) to move like a heavy sea. **11.** Naut. to slacken or temporarily release (a rope or cable) from a capstan or (of a rope, etc.) to be slackened or released and slip back. **12.** (intr.) (of an electric current or voltage) to undergo a large momentary increase. **13.** (tr.) Rare. to cause to move in or as if in a wave or waves. [C15: from L surgere to rise, from sub- up + regere to lead] —'**surger** n.

surgeon ('sɜːdʒən) n. **1.** a medical practitioner who specializes in surgery. **2.** a medical officer in the Royal Navy. [C14: from Anglo-Norman surgien, from OF cirurgien; see SURGERY]

surgeonfish ('sɜːdʒən,fɪʃ) n., pl. -**fish** or -**fishes.** any of various tropical marine spiny-finned fishes, having a compressed brightly coloured body with knifelike spines at the base of the tail.

surgeon general n., pl. **surgeons general. 1.** (esp. in the British and U.S. armies and navies) the senior officer of the medical service. **2.** the head of the U.S. public health service.

surgery ('sɜːdʒərɪ) n., pl. -**geries. 1.** the branch of medicine concerned with manual or operative procedures, esp. incision into the body. **2.** the performance of such procedures by a surgeon. **3.** Brit. a place where, or time when, a doctor, dentist, etc., can be consulted. **4.** Brit. an occasion when an MP, lawyer, etc., is available for consultation. **5.** U.S. & Canad. an operating theatre. [C14: via OF from L chirurgia, from Gk kheirurgia, from kheir hand + ergon work]

surgical ('sɜːdʒɪkᵊl) adj. of, relating to, involving, or used in surgery. —'**surgically** adv.

surgical boot n. a specially designed boot or shoe that compensates for deformities of the foot or leg.

surgical spirit n. methylated spirit used medically for sterilizing.

Suribachi (,sʊərɪ'bɑːtʃɪ) n. **Mount.** a volcanic hill in the Volcano Islands, on Iwo Jima: site of a U.S. victory (1945) over the Japanese in World War II.

suricate ('sjuəri,keit) *n.* another name for **slender-tailed meerkat** (see **meerkat**). [C18: from F *surikate*, prob. from a native South African word]

Surinam (,suəri'næm) *n.* a republic in NE South America, on the Atlantic: became a self-governing part of the Netherlands in 1954 and fully independent in 1975; a leading exporter of bauxite. Languages: Dutch and English. Currency: guilder. Capital: Paramaribo. Pop.: 415 000 (1987). Area: 163 820 sq. km (63 251 sq. miles). Former names: **Dutch Guiana, Netherlands Guiana.**

surly ('sɜːli) *adj.* **-lier, -liest.** **1.** sullenly ill-tempered or rude. **2.** (of an animal) ill-tempered or refractory. [C16: from obs. *sirly* haughty] —**'surlily** *adv.* —**'surliness** *n.*

surmise *vb.* (sɜː'maiz). **1.** (when *tr.*, *may take a clause as object*) to infer (something) from incomplete or uncertain evidence. ~*n.* (sɜː'maiz, 'sɜːmaiz). **2.** an idea inferred from inconclusive evidence. [C15: from OF, from *surmettre* to accuse, from L *supermittere* to throw over] —**surmisedly** (sɜː'maizidli) *adv.*

surmount (sɜː'maunt) *vb.* (*tr.*) **1.** to prevail over; overcome. **2.** to ascend and cross to the opposite side of. **3.** to lie on top of or rise above. **4.** to put something on top of or above. [C14: from OF *surmonter*, from SUR-[1] + *monter* to mount] —**sur'mountable** *adj.*

surname ('sɜː,neim) *n.* **1.** Also called: **last name, second name.** a family name as opposed to a Christian name. **2.** (formerly) a descriptive epithet attached to a person's name to denote a personal characteristic, profession, etc.; nickname. ~*vb.* **3.** (*tr.*) to furnish with or call by a surname. —**'sur,namer** *n.*

surpass (sɜː'pɑːs) *vb.* (*tr.*) **1.** to be greater than in degree, extent, etc. **2.** to be superior to in achievement or excellence. **3.** to overstep the limit or range of: *the theory surpasses my comprehension.* [C16: from F *surpasser*, from SUR-[1] + *passer* to PASS] —**sur'passable** *adj.*

surpassing (sɜː'pɑːsiŋ) *adj.* **1.** exceptional; extraordinary. ~*adv.* **2.** *Obs. or poetic.* (intensifier): *surpassing fair.* —**sur'passingly** *adv.*

surplice ('sɜːplis) *n.* a loose wide-sleeved liturgical vestment of linen, reaching to the knees, worn over the cassock by clergymen, choristers, and acolytes. [C13: from OF *sourpelis*, from Med. L *superpellicium*, from SUPER- + *pellicium* coat made of skins, from L *pellis* a skin]

surplus ('sɜːpləs) *n.*, *pl.* **-pluses.** **1.** a quantity or amount in excess of what is required. **2.** *Accounting.* **a.** an excess of total assets over total liabilities. **b.** an excess of actual net assets over the nominal value of capital stock. **c.** an excess of revenues over expenditures. **3.** *Econ.* **a.** an excess of government revenues over expenditures. **b.** an excess of receipts over payments on the balance of payments. ~*adj.* **4.** being in excess; extra. [C14: from OF, from Med. L *superplūs*, from L SUPER- + *plūs* more]

surprise (sə'praiz) *vb.* (*tr.*) **1.** to cause to feel amazement or wonder. **2.** to encounter or discover unexpectedly or suddenly. **3.** to capture or assault suddenly and without warning. **4.** to present with something unexpected, such as a gift. **5.** (foll. by *into*) to provoke (someone) to unintended action by a trick, etc. **6.** (often foll. by *from*) to elicit by unexpected behaviour or by a trick: *to surprise information from a prisoner.* ~*n.* **7.** the act or an instance of surprising; the act of taking unawares. **8.** a sudden or unexpected event, gift, etc. **9.** the feeling or condition of being surprised; astonishment. **10.** (*modifier*) causing, characterized by, or relying upon surprise: *a surprise move.* **11. take by surprise. a.** to come upon suddenly and without warning. **b.** to capture unexpectedly or catch unprepared. **c.** to astonish; amaze. [C15: from OF, from *surprendre* to overtake, from SUR-[1] + L *prehendere* to grasp] —**sur'prisal** *n.* —**sur'prised** *adj.* —**surprisedly** (sə'praizidli) *adv.*

surprising (sə'praiziŋ) *adj.* causing surprise; unexpected or amazing. —**sur'prisingly** *adv.*

surra ('suərə) *n.* a tropical febrile disease of cattle, horses, camels, and dogs. [from Marathi, a language of India]

surrealism (sə'riə,lizəm) *n.* (*sometimes cap.*) a movement in art and literature in the 1920s, which developed esp. from Dada, characterized by the evocative juxtaposition of incongruous images in order to include unconscious and dream elements. [C20: from F *surréalisme*, from SUR-[1] + *réalisme* realism] —**sur'real** *adj.* —**sur'realist** *n.*, *adj.* —**sur,real'istic** *adj.*

surrebutter (,sɜːri'bʌtə) *n.* *Law.* (in pleading) the plaintiff's reply to the defendant's rebutter. —**,surre'buttal** *n.*

surrejoinder (,sɜːri'dʒɔində) *n.* *Law.* (in pleading) the plaintiff's reply to the defendant's rejoinder.

surrender (sə'rɛndə) *vb.* **1.** (*tr.*) to relinquish to another under duress or on demand: *to surrender a city.* **2.** (*tr.*) to relinquish or forego (an office, position, etc.), esp. as a voluntary concession to another: *he surrendered his place to a lady.* **3.** to give (oneself) up physically, as to an enemy. **4.** to allow (oneself) to yield, as to a temptation, influence, etc. **5.** (*tr.*) to give up (hope, etc.) **6.** (*tr.*) *Law.* to give up or restore (an estate), esp. to give up a lease before expiration of the term. **7. surrender to bail.** to present oneself at court at the appointed time after having been on bail. ~*n.* **8.** the act or instance of surrendering. **9.** *Insurance.* the voluntary discontinuation of a life policy by its holder in return for a consideration (the **surrender value**). **10.** *Law.* **a.** the yielding up or restoring of an estate, esp. the giving up of a lease before its term has expired. **b.** the giving up to the appropriate authority of a fugitive from justice. **c.** the act of surrendering or being surrendered to bail. **d.** the deed by which a legal surrender is effected. [C15: from OF *surrendre* to yield]

surreptitious (,sʌrəp'tiʃəs) *adj.* **1.** done, acquired, etc., in secret or by improper means. **2.** operating by stealth. [C15: from L *surreptīcius* furtive, from *surripere* to steal, from *sub-* secretly + *rapere* to snatch] —**,surrep'titiously** *adv.* —**,surrep'titiousness** *n.*

surrey ('sʌri) *n.* a light four-wheeled horse-drawn carriage having two or four seats. [C19: from *Surrey cart*, after SURREY[1] where orig. made]

Surrey[1] ('sʌri) *n.* a county of SE England, on the River Thames: urban in the northeast; crossed from east to west by the North Downs and drained by tributaries of the Thames. Administrative centre: Kingston upon Thames. Pop.: 1 011 400 (1986 est.). Area: 1679 sq. km (648 sq. miles).

Surrey[2] ('sʌri) *n.* **Earl of,** title of *Henry Howard.* ?1517–47, English courtier and poet; one of the first in England to write sonnets. He was beheaded for high treason.

surrogate *n.* ('sʌrəgit). **1.** a person or thing acting as a substitute. **2.** *Chiefly Brit.* a deputy, such as a clergyman appointed to deputize for a bishop in granting marriage licences. **3.** (in some U.S. states) a judge with jurisdiction over the probate of wills, etc. **4.** (*modifier*) of, relating to, or acting as a surrogate: *a surrogate pleasure.* ~*vb.* ('sʌrə,geit). (*tr.*) **5.** to put in another's position as a deputy, substitute, etc. [C17: from L *surrogāre* to substitute] —**'surrogateship** *n.* —**,surro'gation** *n.*

surrogate motherhood *or* **surrogacy** ('sʌrəgəsi) *n.* the role of a woman who bears a child on behalf of a childless couple, either by artificial insemination or implantation of an embryo. —**surrogate mother** *n.*

surround (sə'raund) *vb.* (*tr.*) **1.** to encircle or enclose or cause to be encircled or enclosed. **2.** to deploy forces on all sides of (a place or military formation), so preventing access or retreat. **3.** to exist around: *the people who surround her.* ~*n.* **4.** *Chiefly Brit.* a border, esp. the area of uncovered floor between the walls of a room and the carpet or around an opening or panel. **5.** *Chiefly U.S.* **a.** a method of capturing wild beasts by encircling the area in which they are believed to be. **b.** the area so encircled. [C15 *surrounden* to overflow, from OF *suronder*, from LL, from L SUPER- + *undāre* to abound, from *unda* a wave] —**sur'rounding** *adj.*

surroundings (sə'raundiŋz) *pl. n.* the conditions, scenery, etc., around a person, place, or thing; environment.

sursum corda ('sɜːsəm 'kɔːdə) *n.* **1.** *R.C. Church.* a Latin versicle meaning *Lift up your hearts,* said by the priest at Mass. **2.** a cry of exhortation, hope, etc.

surtax ('sɜː,tæks) *n.* **1.** a tax, usually highly progressive, levied on the amount by which a person's income exceeds a specific level. **2.** an additional tax on something that has already been taxed. ~*vb.* **3.** (*tr.*) to assess for liability to surtax; charge with an extra tax.

surtitles ('sɜː,taitəlz) *pl. n.* brief translations of the text of an opera that is being sung in a foreign language, projected above the stage.

surtout ('sɜː'tuː) *n.* a man's overcoat resembling a frock coat, popular in the late 19th century. [C17: from F, from *sur* over + *tout* all]

surveillance (sɜː'veiləns) *n.* close observation or supervision over a person, group, etc., esp. one in custody or under suspicion. [C19: from F, from *surveiller* to watch over, from SUR-[1] + *veiller* to keep watch (from L *vigilāre;* see VIGIL)] —**sur'veillant** *adj., n.*

survey *vb.* (sɜː'veɪ, 'sɜːveɪ). **1.** (*tr.*) to view or consider in a comprehensive or general way. **2.** (*tr.*) to examine carefully, as or as if to appraise value. **3.** to plot a detailed map of (an area of land) by measuring or calculating distances and height. **4.** *Brit.* to inspect a building to determine its condition and value. **5.** to examine a vessel thoroughly in order to determine its seaworthiness. **6.** (*tr.*) to run a statistical survey on (incomes, opinions, etc.). ~*n.* ('sɜːveɪ). **7.** a comprehensive or general view. **8.** a critical, detailed, and formal inspection. **9.** *Brit.* an inspection of a building to determine its condition and value. **10.** a report incorporating the results of such an inspection. **11. a.** a body of surveyors. **b.** an area surveyed. [C15: from F *surveoir*, from SUR-[1] + *veoir* to see, from L *vidēre*]

surveying (sɜː'veɪɪŋ) *n.* **1.** the study or practice of making surveys of land. **2.** the setting out on the ground of the positions of proposed construction or engineering works.

surveyor (sɜː'veɪə) *n.* **1.** a person whose occupation is to survey land or buildings. See also **quantity surveyor. 2.** *Chiefly Brit.* a person concerned with the official inspection of something for purposes of measurement and valuation. **3.** a person who carries out surveys, esp. of ships (**marine surveyor**) to determine seaworthiness, etc. **4.** a customs official. **5.** *Arch.* a supervisor. —**sur'veyorship** *n.*

surveyor's measure *n.* the system of measurement based on the **surveyor's chain** (66 feet) as a unit.

survival (sə'vaɪvəl) *n.* **1.** a person or thing that survives, such as a custom. **2. a.** the act or fact of surviving or condition of having survived. **b.** (*as modifier*): *survival kit.*

survival bag *n.* a large plastic bag carried by climbers for use in an emergency as protection against exposure.

survival of the fittest *n.* a popular term for **natural selection.**

survive (sə'vaɪv) *vb.* **1.** (*tr.*) to live after the death of (another). **2.** to continue in existence or use after (a passage of time, adversity, etc.). **3.** *Inf.* to endure (something): *I don't know how I survive such an awful job.* [C15: from OF *sourvivre*, from L *supervīvere*, from SUPER- + *vīvere* to live] —**sur'vivor** *n.*

sus (sʌs) *Brit. sl.* ~*n.* **1.** short for **suspicion,** with reference to former police powers (**sus laws**) of detaining for questioning, searching, etc. any person suspected of criminal intent: *he was picked up on sus.* ~*vb.* **2.** a variant spelling of **suss.**

Susa ('suːsə) *n.* an ancient city north of the Persian Gulf: capital of Elam and of the Persian Empire; flourished as a Greek polis under the Seleucids and Parthians. Biblical name: **Shushan.**

Susah *or* **Susa** ('suːzə) *n.* other names for **Sousse.**

Susanna (suː'zænə) *n. Apocrypha.* **1.** the wife of Joachim, who was condemned to death for adultery because of a false accusation, but saved by Daniel's sagacity. **2.** the book of the Apocrypha containing this story.

susceptance (sə'sɛptəns) *n. Physics.* the imaginary component of the admittance. [C19: from *suscept*(*ibility*) + -ANCE]

susceptibility (sə,sɛptə'bɪlɪtɪ) *n., pl.* **-ties. 1.** the quality or condition of being susceptible. **2.** the ability or tendency to be impressed by emotional feelings. **3.** (*pl.*) emotional sensibilities; feelings. **4.** *Physics.* **a.** Also called: **electric susceptibility.** (of a dielectric) the amount by which the relative permittivity differs from unity. **b.** Also called: **magnetic susceptibility.** (of a magnetic medium) the amount by which the relative permeability differs from unity.

susceptible (sə'sɛptəb[ə]l) *adj.* **1.** (*postpositive;* foll. by *of* or *to*) yielding readily (to); capable (of): *hypotheses susceptible of refutation; susceptible to control.* **2.** (*postpositive;* foll. by *to*) liable to be afflicted (by): *susceptible to colds.* **3.** easily impressed emotionally. [C17: from LL *susceptibilis*, from L *suscipere* to take up] —**sus'ceptibly** *adv.*

sushi ('suːʃɪ) *n.* a Japanese dish consisting of small cakes of cold rice with a topping, esp. of raw fish. [Japanese]

suslik ('sʌslɪk) *or* **souslik** *n.* a central Eurasian ground squirrel having large eyes and small ears. [from Russian]

suspect *vb.* (sə'spɛkt). **1.** (*tr.*) to believe guilty of a specified offence without proof. **2.** (*tr.*) to think false, questionable, etc.: *she suspected his sincerity.* **3.** (*tr.; may take a clause as object*) to surmise to be the case; think probable: *to suspect fraud.* **4.** (*intr.*) to have suspicion. ~*n.* ('sʌspɛkt). **5.** a person under suspicion. ~*adj.* ('sʌspɛkt). **6.** causing or open to suspicion. [C14: from L *suspicere* to mistrust, from SUB- + *specere* to look]

suspend (sə'spɛnd) *vb.* **1.** (*tr.*) to hang from above. **2.** (*tr.; passive*) to cause to remain floating or hanging: *a cloud of smoke was suspended over the town.* **3.** (*tr.*) to render inoperative or cause to cease, esp. temporarily. **4.** (*tr.*) to hold in abeyance; postpone action on. **5.** (*tr.*) to debar temporarily from privilege, office, etc., as a punishment. **6.** (*tr.*) *Chem.* to cause (particles) to be held in suspension in a fluid. **7.** (*tr.*) *Music.* to continue (a note) until the next chord is sounded, with which it usually forms a dissonance. See **suspension** (sense 11). **8.** (*intr.*) to cease payment, as from incapacity to meet financial obligations. [C13: from L *suspendere* from SUB- + *pendere* to hang] —**sus'pendible** *or* **sus'pensible** *adj.* —**sus,pendi'bility** *n.*

suspended animation *n.* a temporary cessation of the vital functions, as by freezing an organism.

suspended sentence *n.* a sentence of imprisonment that is not served by an offender unless he commits a further offence during its currency.

suspender (sə'spɛndə) *n.* **1.** (*often pl.*) *Brit.* **a.** an elastic strap attached to a belt or corset having a fastener at the end, for holding up women's stockings. **b.** a similar fastener attached to a garter worn by men in order to support socks. **2.** (*pl.*) the U.S. and Canad. name for **braces. 3.** a person or thing that suspends, such as one of the vertical cables in a suspension bridge.

suspender belt *n.* a belt with suspenders hanging from it to hold up women's stockings.

suspense (sə'spɛns) *n.* **1.** the condition of being insecure or uncertain. **2.** mental uncertainty; anxiety: *their father's illness kept them in a state of suspense.* **3.** excitement felt at the approach of the climax: *a play of terrifying suspense.* **4.** the condition of being suspended. [C15: from Med. L *suspensum* delay, from L *suspendere* to hang up] —**sus'penseful** *adj.*

suspense account *n.* an account in which entries are made until determination of their proper disposition.

suspension (sə'spɛnʃən) *n.* **1.** an interruption or temporary revocation: *the suspension of a law.* **2.** a temporary debarment, as from position, privilege, etc. **3.** a deferment, esp. of a decision, judgment, etc. **4.** *Law.* a postponement of execution of a sentence or the deferring of a judgment, etc. **5.** cessation of payment of business debts, esp. as a result of insolvency. **6.** the act of suspending or the state of being suspended. **7.** a system of springs, shock absorbers, etc., that supports the body of a wheeled or tracked vehicle and insulates it from shocks transmitted by the wheels. **8.** a device or structure, usually a wire or spring, that serves to suspend or support something, such as the pendulum of a clock. **9.** *Chem.* a dispersion of fine solid or liquid particles in a fluid, the particles being supported by buoyancy. See also **colloid. 10.** the process by which eroded particles of rock are transported in a river. **11.** *Music.* one or more notes of a chord that are prolonged until a subsequent chord is sounded, usually to form a dissonance.

suspension bridge *n.* a bridge suspended from cables or chains that hang between two towers and are anchored at both ends.

suspensive (sə'spɛnsɪv) *adj.* **1.** having the power of deferment; effecting suspension. **2.** causing, characterized by, or relating to suspense. —**sus'pensively** *adv.* —**sus'pensiveness** *n.*

suspensory (sə'spɛnsərɪ) *n., pl.* **-ries. 1.** Also called: **suspensor.** *Anat.* a ligament or muscle that holds a structure or part in position. **2.** *Med.* a bandage, sling, etc., for supporting a dependent part. ~*adj.* **3.** suspending or supporting. **4.** *Anat.* (of a ligament or muscle) supporting or holding a structure or part in position.

suspicion (sə'spɪʃən) *n.* **1.** the act or an instance of suspecting; belief without sure proof, esp. that something is wrong. **2.** the feeling of mistrust of a person who suspects. **3.** the state of being suspected: *to be shielded from suspicion.* **4.** a slight trace. **5. above suspicion.** in such a position that no guilt may be thought or implied, esp.

through having an unblemished reputation. **6. on suspicion.** as a suspect. **7. under suspicion.** regarded with distrust. [C14: from OF *sospeçon*, from L *suspīciō* distrust, from *suspicere;* see SUSPECT] —**sus'picional** *adj.*

suspicious (sə'spɪʃəs) *adj.* **1.** exciting or liable to excite suspicion; questionable. **2.** disposed to suspect something wrong. **3.** indicative or expressive of suspicion. —**sus'piciously** *adv.* —**sus'piciousness** *n.*

Susquehanna (ˌsʌskwɪ'hænə) *n.* a river in the eastern U.S., rising in Otsego Lake and flowing generally south to Chesapeake Bay at Havre de Grace: the longest river in the eastern U.S. Length: 714 km (444 miles).

suss (sʌs) *vb.* (*tr.*) *Brit. & N.Z. sl.* **1.** (often foll. by *out*) to attempt to work out (a situation, person's character, etc.), esp. using one's intuition. **2.** Also: **sus.** to become aware of; suspect (esp. in **suss it**). [C20: shortened from SUSPECT]

Sussex ('sʌsɪks) *n.* **1.** (until 1974) a county of SE England, now divided into the separate counties of East Sussex and West Sussex. **2.** (in Anglo-Saxon England) the kingdom of the South Saxons, which became a shire of the kingdom of Wessex in the early 9th century A.D. **3.** a breed of red beef cattle originally from Sussex. **4.** a heavy and long-established breed of domestic fowl used principally as a table bird.

sustain (sə'steɪn) *vb.* (*tr.*) **1.** to hold up under; withstand: *to sustain great provocation.* **2.** to undergo (an injury, loss, etc.); suffer: *to sustain a broken arm.* **3.** to maintain or prolong: *to sustain a discussion.* **4.** to support physically from below. **5.** to provide for or give support to, esp. by supplying necessities: *to sustain one's family.* **6.** to keep up the vitality or courage of. **7.** to uphold or affirm the justice or validity of: *to sustain a decision.* **8.** to establish the truth of; confirm. —*n.* **9.** *Music.* the prolongation of a note, by playing technique or electronics. [C13: via OF from L *sustinēre* to hold up] —**sus'tainable** *adj.* —**sus'tained** *adj.* —**sustainedly** (sə'steɪnɪdlɪ) *adv.* —**sus'tainer** *n.* —**sus'taining** *adj.* —**sus'tainment** *n.*

sustaining pedal *n. Music.* a foot-operated lever on a piano that keeps the dampers raised from the strings when keys are released, allowing them to continue to vibrate.

sustenance ('sʌstənəns) *n.* **1.** means of sustaining health or life; nourishment. **2.** means of maintenance; livelihood. **3.** Also: **sustention** (sə'stɛnʃən). the act or process of sustaining or the quality of being sustained. [C13: from OF *sostenance*, from *sustenir* to SUSTAIN]

sustentation (ˌsʌstɛn'teɪʃən) *n.* a less common word for **sustenance.** [C14: from L *sustentātiō*, from *sustentāre*, frequentative of *sustinēre* to SUSTAIN]

susurrate ('sjuːsəˌreɪt) *vb.* (*intr.*) *Literary.* to make a soft rustling sound; whisper; murmur. [C17: from L *susurrāre* to whisper] —ˌsusur'ration *or* 'susurrus *n.*

Sutcliffe ('sʌtˌklɪf) *n.* Herbert. 1894–1978, English cricketer, who played for Yorkshire; scorer of 149 centuries and 1000 runs in a season 24 times.

Sutherland[1] ('sʌðələnd) *n.* (until 1975) a county of N Scotland, now part of the Highland region.

Sutherland[2] ('sʌðələnd) *n.* **1. Graham.** 1903–80, English artist, noted for his work as an official war artist (1941–44) and for his tapestry *Christ in Majesty* (1962) in Coventry Cathedral. **2. Dame Joan,** known as *La Stupenda.* born 1926, Australian operatic soprano.

Sutherland Falls *n.* a waterfall in New Zealand, on SW South Island. Height: 580 m (1904 ft.).

Sutlej ('sʌtlɪdʒ) *n.* a river in S Asia, rising in SW Tibet and flowing west through the Himalayas: crosses Himachal Pradesh and the Punjab (India), enters Pakistan, and joins the Chenab west of Bahawalpur: the longest of the five rivers of the Punjab. Length: 1368 km (850 miles).

sutler ('sʌtlə) *n.* (formerly) a merchant who accompanied an army in order to sell provisions to the soldiers. [C16: from obs. Du. *soeteler*, ult. from MHG *sudelen* to do dirty work]

sutra ('suːtrə) *n.* **1.** *Hinduism.* Sanskrit sayings or collections of sayings on Vedic doctrine dating from about 200 A.D. onwards. **2.** (*modifier*) *Hinduism.* **a.** of or relating to the last of the Vedic literary periods, from about 500 to 100 B.C.: *the sutra period.* **b.** of or relating to the sutras or compilations of sutras of about 200 A.D. onwards. **3.** *Buddhism.* collections of dialogues and discourses of classic Mahayana Buddhism dating from the 2nd to the 6th century A.D. [C19: from Sansk.: list of rules]

suttee (sʌ'tiː, 'sʌti:) *n.* **1.** the former Hindu custom whereby a widow burnt herself to death on her husband's funeral pyre. **2.** a widow performing this. [C18: from Sansk. *sati* virtuous woman, from *sat* good] —**sut'tee-ism** *n.*

Sutton ('sʌtᵊn) *n.* a borough of S Greater London. Pop.: 168 700 (1986 est.).

Sutton Coldfield (-'kəʊld,fiːld) *n.* a town in central England, in the N West Midlands. Pop.: 86 494 (1981).

Sutton-in-Ashfield (-'æʃˌfiːld) *n.* a market town in N central England, in W Nottinghamshire. Pop.: 40 420 (1985 est.).

suture ('suːtʃə) *n.* **1.** *Surgery.* **a.** catgut, silk thread, or wire used to stitch together two bodily surfaces. **b.** the surgical seam formed after stitching. **2.** *Anat.* a type of immovable joint, esp. between the bones of the skull (**cranial suture**). **3.** a seam or joining, as in sewing. **4.** *Zool.* a line of junction in a molluscan shell. ~*vb.* **5.** (*tr.*) *Surgery.* to join (the edges of a wound, etc.) by means of sutures. [C16: from L *sūtūra*, from *suere* to sew] —'**sutural** *adj.*

Suva ('suːvə) *n.* the capital and chief port of Fiji, on the SE coast of Viti Levu. Pop.: 69 481 (1986).

Suvorov (*Russian* su'vɔrəf) *n.* **Aleksandr Vasilyevich** (alık'sandr va'siljvɪtʃ). 1729–1800, Russian field marshal, who fought successfully against the Turks (1787–91), the Poles (1794), and the French in Italy (1798–99).

Suwannee (su'wɒnɪ) *or* **Swanee** *n.* a river in the southeastern U.S., rising in SE Georgia and flowing across Florida to the Gulf of Mexico at **Suwannee Sound.** Length: about 400 km (250 miles).

suzerain ('suːzəˌreɪn) *n.* **1. a.** a state or sovereign exercising some degree of dominion over a dependent state, usually controlling its foreign affairs. **b.** (*as modifier*): *a suzerain power.* **2. a.** a feudal overlord. **b.** (*as modifier*): *suzerain lord.* [C19: from F, from *sus* above (from L *sursum* turned upwards) + *-erain*, as in *souverain* sovereign]

suzerainty ('suːzərəntɪ) *n., pl.* **-ties. 1.** the position, power, or dignity of a suzerain. **2.** the relationship between suzerain and subject.

Suzhou ('suː'dʒəʊ), **Su-chou,** *or* **Soochow** *n.* a city in E China, in S Jiangsu on the Grand Canal: noted for its gardens; produces chiefly silk. Pop.: 611 500 (1985 est.). Also called: **Wuhsien.**

sv *abbrev. for:* **1.** sailing vessel. **2.** side valve. **3.** sub verbo *or* voce. [L: under the word]

Svalbard (*Norwegian* 'sva:lbar) *n.* a Norwegian archipelago in the Arctic Ocean, about 650 km (400 miles) north of Norway: consists of the main group (Spitsbergen, North East Land, Edge Island, Barents Island, and Prince Charles Foreland) and a number of outlying islands; sovereignty long disputed but granted to Norway in 1920; coal mining. Administrative centre: Longyearbyen. Area: 62 050 sq. km (23 958 sq. miles). Also called: **Spitsbergen.**

svelte (svɛlt, sfɛlt) *adj.* attractively or gracefully slim; slender. [C19: from F, from It. *svelto*, from *svellere* to pull out, from L *ēvellere*]

Sverdlovsk (*Russian* svɪr'dlɔfsk) *n.* a city in the W central Soviet Union, in the Ural Mountains: scene of the execution (1918) of Nicholas II and his family; university (1920); one of the largest centres of heavy engineering in the Soviet Union. Pop.: 1 331 000 (1987). Former name (until 1924): **Yekaterinburg.**

Sverige (*sværjə*) *n.* the Swedish name for **Sweden.**

Svizzera ('zvittsera) *n.* the Italian name for **Switzerland.**

SW 1. *symbol for* southwest(ern). **2.** *abbrev. for* short wave.

Sw. *abbrev. for:* **1.** Sweden. **2.** Swedish.

swab (swɒb) *n.* **1.** *Med.* **a.** a small piece of cotton, gauze, etc., for use in applying medication, cleansing a wound, or obtaining a specimen of a secretion, etc. **b.** the specimen so obtained. **2.** a mop for cleaning floors, decks, etc. **3.** a brush used to clean a firearm's bore. **4.** *Sl.* an uncouth or worthless fellow. ~*vb.* **swabbing, swabbed. 5.** (*tr.*) to clean or medicate with or as if with a swab. **6.** (*tr.*; foll. by *up*) to take up with a swab. [C16: prob. from MDu. *swabbe* mop] —'**swabber** *n.*

Swabia ('sweɪbɪə) *n.* a region and former duchy (from the 10th century to 1313) of SW West Germany: now part of Baden-Württemberg and Bavaria. German name: **Schwaben** ('ʃva:bᵊn).—'**Swabian** *adj., n.*

swaddle ('swɒdᵊl) *vb.* (*tr.*) **1.** to wind a bandage round. **2.** to wrap (a baby) in swaddling clothes. **3.** to restrain as if by wrapping with bandages; smother. ~*n.* **4.** *Chiefly U.S.* swaddling clothes. [C15: from OE *swæthel* swaddling clothes]

swaddling clothes *pl. n.* **1.** long strips of linen or other cloth formerly wrapped round a newly born baby. **2.** restrictions or supervision imposed on the immature.

swaddy *or* **swaddie** ('swɒdɪ) *n. Brit. sl., old-fashioned.* a soldier. [C19: from E dialect *swad* country bumpkin, soldier]

swag (swæg) *n.* **1.** *Sl.* property obtained by theft or other illicit means. **2.** *Sl.* goods; valuables. **3.** an ornamental festoon of fruit, flowers, or drapery or a representation of this. **4.** a swaying movement; lurch. **5.** *Austral. & N.Z. inf.* a swagman's pack containing personal belongings, etc. **6. swags of.** *Austral. & N.Z. inf.* lots of. ~*vb.* **swagging, swagged. 7.** *Chiefly Brit.* to lurch or sag or cause to lurch or sag. **8.** (*tr.*) to adorn or arrange with swags. [C17: ? of Scand. origin]

swage (sweɪdʒ) *n.* **1.** a shaped tool or die used in forming cold metal by hammering, pressing, etc. ~*vb.* **2.** (*tr.*) to form (metal) with a swage. [C19: from F *souage*, from ?] —'**swager** *n.*

swage block *n.* an iron block with holes, grooves, etc., to assist in the cold-working of metal.

swagger ('swægə) *vb.* **1.** (*intr.*) to walk or behave in an arrogant manner. **2.** (*intr.;* often foll. by *about*) to brag loudly. ~*n.* **3.** an arrogant gait or manner. ~*adj.* **4.** *Brit. inf., rare.* elegantly fashionable. [C16: prob. from SWAG] —'**swaggerer** *n.* —'**swaggering** *adj.* —'**swaggeringly** *adv.*

swagger stick *or esp. Brit.* **swagger cane** *n.* a short cane or stick carried on occasion mainly by army officers.

swaggie ('swægɪ) *n. Austral. sl.* short for **swagman.**

swagman ('swæg,mæn, -mən) *n., pl.* **-men.** *Austral. & N.Z. inf.* a tramp or vagrant worker who carries his possessions on his back. Also called: **swaggie.**

Swahili (swɑːˈhiːlɪ) *n.* **1.** a language of E Africa that is an official language of Kenya and Tanzania and is widely used as a lingua franca throughout E and central Africa. **2.** (*pl.* **-lis** *or* **-li**) a member of a people speaking this language, living chiefly in Zanzibar. ~*adj.* **3.** of or relating to the Swahilis or their language. [C19: from Ar. *sawāhil* coasts] —**Swa'hilian** *adj.*

swain (sweɪn) *n. Arch. or poetic.* **1.** a male lover or admirer. **2.** a country youth. [OE *swān* swineherd]

swallow[1] ('swɒləʊ) *vb.* (*mainly tr.*) **1.** to pass (food, drink, etc.) through the mouth to the stomach by means of the muscular action of the oesophagus. **2.** (often foll. by *up*) to engulf or destroy as if by ingestion. **3.** *Inf.* to believe gullibly: *he will never swallow such an excuse.* **4.** to refrain from uttering or manifesting: *to swallow one's disappointment.* **5.** to endure without retaliation. **6.** to enunciate (words, etc.) indistinctly; mutter. **7.** (often foll. by *down*) to eat or drink reluctantly. **8.** (*intr.*) to perform or simulate the act of swallowing, as in gulping. ~*n.* **9.** the act of swallowing. **10.** the amount swallowed at any single time; mouthful. **11.** *Rare.* another word for **throat** or **gullet.** [OE *swelgan*] —'**swallowable** *adj.* —'**swallower** *n.*

swallow[2] ('swɒləʊ) *n.* any of various passerine songbirds having long pointed wings, a forked tail, short legs, and a rapid flight. [OE *swealwe*]

swallow dive *n.* a type of dive in which the diver arches back while in the air, keeping his legs straight and together and his arms outstretched, finally entering the water headfirst. U.S. and Canad. equivalent: **swan dive.**

swallow hole *n. Chiefly Brit.* another word for **sinkhole** (sense 1).

swallowtail ('swɒləʊ,teɪl) *n.* **1.** any of various butterflies of Europe, having a tail-like extension of each hind wing. **2.** the forked tail of a swallow or similar bird. **3.** short for **swallow-tailed coat.** —'**swallow-,tailed** *adj.*

swallow-tailed coat *n.* another name for **tail coat.**

swam (swæm) *vb.* the past tense of **swim.**

swami ('swɑːmɪ) *n., pl.* **-mies** *or* **-mis.** (in India) a title of respect for a Hindu saint or religious teacher. [C18: from Hindi *svāmī*, from Sansk. *svāmin* master, from *sva* one's own]

swamp (swɒmp) *n.* **1.** permanently waterlogged ground that is usually overgrown and sometimes partly forested. Cf. **marsh.** ~*vb.* **2.** to drench or submerge or be drenched or submerged. **3.** *Naut.* to cause (a boat) to sink or fill with water or (of a boat) to sink or fill with

water. **4.** to overburden or overwhelm or be overburdened or overwhelmed, as by excess work or great numbers. **5.** (*tr.*) to render helpless. [C17: prob. from MDu. *somp*] —'**swampy** *adj.*

swamp boat *n.* a shallow-draught boat powered by an aeroplane engine mounted on a raised structure for use in swamps. Also called: **airboat.**

swamp cypress *n.* a North American deciduous coniferous tree that grows in swamps. Also called: **bald cypress.**

swamp fever *n.* **1.** Also called: **equine infectious anaemia.** a viral disease of horses. **2.** *U.S.* another name for **malaria.**

swampland ('swɒmp,lænd) *n.* a permanently waterlogged area; marshland.

swan (swɒn) *n.* **1.** any of various large aquatic birds having a long neck and usually a white plumage. **2.** *Rare, literary.* **a.** a poet. **b.** (*cap. when part of a title or epithet*): *the Swan of Avon* (Shakespeare). ~*vb.* **swanning, swanned. 3.** (*intr.;* usually foll. by *around* or *about*) *Inf.* to wander idly. [OE] —'**swan,like** *adj.*

Swan[1] (swɒn) *n.* a river in SW Western Australia, rising as the Avon northeast of Narrogin and flowing northwest and west to the Indian Ocean below Perth. Length: about 240 km (150 miles).

Swan[2] (swɒn) *n.* Sir **Joseph Wilson.** 1828–1914, English physicist and chemist, who developed the incandescent electric light (1880) independently of Edison.

swan dive *n.* the U.S. and Canad. name for **swallow dive.**

Swanee ('swɒnɪ) *n.* a variant spelling of **Suwannee.**

swank (swæŋk) *Inf.* ~*vb.* **1.** (*intr.*) to show off or swagger. ~*n.* **2.** Also called: **swankpot.** *Brit.* a swaggering or conceited person. **3.** *Chiefly U.S.* showy elegance or style. **4.** swagger; ostentation. ~*adj.* **5.** another word (esp. U.S.) for **swanky.** [C19: ?from MHG *swanken* to sway]

swanky ('swæŋkɪ) *adj.* **swankier, swankiest.** *Inf.* **1.** expensive and showy; stylish: *a swanky hotel.* **2.** boastful or conceited. —'**swankily** *adv.* —'**swankiness** *n.*

swan neck *n.* a tube, rail, etc., curved like a swan's neck.

swannery ('swɒnərɪ) *n., pl.* **-neries.** a place where swans are kept and bred.

swan's-down *n.* **1.** the fine soft down feathers of a swan, used to trim powder puffs, clothes, etc. **2.** a thick soft fabric of wool with silk, cotton, or rayon, used for infants' clothing, etc. **3.** a cotton fabric with a heavy nap.

Swansea ('swɒnzɪ) *n.* a port in S Wales, in West Glamorgan on an inlet of the Bristol Channel (**Swansea Bay**); a metallurgical and oil-refining centre; university (1920). Pop.: 167 796 (1981).

swan song *n.* **1.** the last act, publication, etc., of a person before retirement or death. **2.** the song that a dying swan is said to sing.

swan-upping *n. Brit.* **1.** the practice or action of marking nicks in swans' beaks as a sign of ownership. **2.** the annual swan-upping of royal cygnets on the River Thames.

swap *or* **swop** (swɒp) ~*vb.* **swapping, swapped** *or* **swopping, swopped. 1.** to trade or exchange (something or someone) for another. ~*n.* **2.** an exchange. **3.** something that is exchanged. [C14 (in the sense: to shake hands on a bargain, strike): prob. imit.] —'**swapper** *or* '**swopper** *n.*

SWAPO *or* **Swapo** ('swɑːpəʊ) *n. acronym for* South-West Africa People's Organization.

swaraj (swəˈrɑːdʒ) *n.* (in British India) self-government; independence. [C20: from Sansk. *svarāj*, from *sva* self + *rājya* rule] —**swa'rajism** *n.* —**swa'rajist** *n., adj.*

sward (swɔːd) *n.* **1.** turf or grass or a stretch of turf or grass. ~*vb.* **2.** to cover or become covered with grass. [OE *sweard* skin]

swarf (swɔːf, swɑːf) *n.* material removed by cutting or grinding in the machining of metals, stone, etc. [C16: of Scand. origin]

swarm[1] (swɔːm) *n.* **1.** a group of bees, led by a queen, that has left the parent hive to start a new colony. **2.** a large mass of small animals, esp. insects. **3.** a throng or mass, esp. when moving or in turmoil. ~*vb.* **4.** (*intr.*) (of small animals, esp. bees) to move in or form a swarm. **5.** (*intr.*) to congregate, move about or proceed in large numbers. **6.** (when *intr.*, often foll. by *with*) to overrun or be overrun (with): *swarming with rats.* **7.** (*tr.*) to cause to swarm. [OE *swearm*]

swarm[2] (swɔːm) *vb.* (when *intr.*, usually foll. by *up*) to climb (a ladder, etc.) by gripping with the hands and feet: *the boys swarmed up the rigging.* [C16: from ?]

swart (swɔːt) *or* **swarth** (swɔːθ) *adj. Arch. or dialect.* swarthy. [OE *sweart*]

swarthy ('swɔːðɪ) *adj.* **swarthier, swarthiest.** dark-hued or dark-complexioned. [C16: from obs. *swarty*] —'**swarthily** *adv.* —'**swarthiness** *n.*

swash (swɒʃ) *vb.* **1.** (*intr.*) (esp. of water or things in water) to wash or move with noisy splashing. **2.** (*tr.*) to dash (a liquid, esp. water) against or upon. **3.** (*intr.*) *Arch.* to swagger. ~*n.* **4.** Also called: **send.** the dashing movement or sound of water, as of waves on a beach. **5.** Also called: **swash channel.** a channel of moving water cutting through or running behind a sandbank. **6.** *Arch.* swagger or bluster. [C16: prob. imit.]

swashbuckler ('swɒʃˌbʌklə) *n.* a swaggering or dare-devil adventurer or bully. [C16: from SWASH (in archaic sense: to make the noise of a sword striking a shield) + BUCKLER]

swashbuckling ('swɒʃˌbʌklɪŋ) *adj.* (*usually prenominal*) **1.** of or characteristic of a swashbuckler. **2.** (esp. of films in period costume) full of adventure and excitement.

swash letter *n. Printing.* a decorative letter, esp. an ornamental italic capital. [C17: from *aswash* aslant]

swastika ('swɒstɪkə) *n.* **1.** a primitive religious symbol or ornament in the shape of a Greek cross, usually having the ends of the arms bent at right angles. **2.** this symbol with clockwise arms, the emblem of Nazi Germany. [C19: from Sansk. *svastika*, from *svasti* prosperity; from belief that it brings good luck]

swat (swɒt) *vb.* **swatting, swatted.** (*tr.*) **1.** to strike or hit sharply: *to swat a fly.* ~*n.* **2.** a sharp or violent blow. ~Also: **swot.** [C17: N English dialect & U.S. var. of SQUAT] —'**swatter** *n.*

Swat (swɒt) *n.* **1.** a former princely state of NW India: passed to Pakistan in 1947. **2.** a river in Pakistan, rising in the north and flowing south to the Kabul River north of Peshawar. Length: about 640 km (400 miles).

swatch (swɒtʃ) *n.* **1.** a sample of cloth or other material. **2.** a number of such samples, usually fastened together in book form. [C16: Scot. & N English, from ?]

swath (swɔːθ) *or* **swathe** (sweɪð) *n., pl.* **swaths** (swɔːðz) *or* **swathes.** **1.** the width of one sweep of a scythe or of the blade of a mowing machine. **2.** the strip cut by these in one course. **3.** the quantity of cut grass, hay, etc., left in one such course. **4.** a long narrow strip or belt. [OE *swæth*]

swathe (sweɪð) *vb.* (*tr.*) **1.** to bandage (a wound, limb, etc.), esp. completely. **2.** to wrap a band, garment, etc., around, esp. so as to cover completely; swaddle. **3.** to envelop. ~*n.* **4.** a bandage or wrapping. **5.** a variant spelling of **swath.** [OE *swathian*]

Swatow ('swɒ'taʊ) *n.* a variant transliteration of the Chinese name for **Shantou.**

sway (sweɪ) *vb.* **1.** (*usually intr.*) to swing or cause to swing to and fro: *the door swayed in the wind.* **2.** (*usually intr.*) to lean or incline or cause to lean or incline to one side or in different directions in turn. **3.** (*usually intr.*) to vacillate or cause to vacillate between two or more opinions. **4.** to be influenced or swerve or influence or cause to swerve to or from a purpose or opinion. **5.** *Arch. or poetic.* to rule or wield power (over). ~*n.* **6.** control; power. **7.** a swinging or leaning movement. **8.** *Arch.* dominion; governing authority. **9. hold sway.** to be master; reign. [C16: prob. from ON *sveigja* to bend]

sway-back *n.* an abnormal sagging or concavity of the spine in horses. —'**sway-,backed** *adj.*

Swaziland ('swɑːzɪˌlænd) *n.* a kingdom in southern Africa: made a protectorate of the Transvaal by Britain in 1894; gained independence in 1968; a member of the Commonwealth. Official languages: English and Swazi. Currency: rand. Capital: Mbabane. Pop.: 716 000 (1987). Area: 17 363 sq. km (6704 sq. miles).

Swazi Territory *n.* the former name of **KaNgwane.**

swear (swɛə) *vb.* **swearing, swore, sworn. 1.** to declare or affirm (a statement) as true, esp. by invoking a deity, etc., as witness. **2.** (foll. by *by*) **a.** to invoke (a deity), esp. by name as a witness or guarantee to an oath. **b.** to trust implicitly; have complete confidence (in). **3.** (*intr.*; often foll. by *at*) to curse, blaspheme, or use swearwords. **4.** (when *tr.*, *may take a clause as object or an infinitive*) to

promise solemnly on oath; vow. **5.** (*tr.*) to assert or affirm with great emphasis or earnestness. **6.** (*intr.*) to give evidence or make any statement or solemn declaration on oath. **7.** to take an oath in order to add force or solemnity to (a statement or declaration). ~*n.* **8.** a period of swearing. [OE *swerian*] —'**swearer** *n.*

swear in *vb.* (*tr., adv.*) to administer an oath to (a person) on his assuming office, entering the witness box to give evidence, etc.

swear off *vb.* (*intr., prep.*) to promise to abstain from something: *to swear off drink.*

swearword ('swɛəˌwɜːd) *n.* a socially taboo word of a profane, obscene, or insulting character.

sweat (swɛt) *n.* **1.** the secretion from the sweat glands, esp. when profuse and visible, as during strenuous activity, from excessive heat, etc.; perspiration. **2.** the act or process of secreting this fluid. **3.** the act of inducing the exudation of moisture. **4.** drops of moisture given forth or gathered on the surface of something. **5.** *Inf.* a state or condition of worry or eagerness (esp. in **in a sweat**). **6.** *Sl.* drudgery or hard labour: *mowing lawns is a real sweat!* **7.** *Sl., chiefly Brit.* a soldier, esp. one who is old and experienced. **8. no sweat!** *Sl.* an expression conveying consent or assurance. ~*vb.* **sweating; sweat** *or* **sweated. 9.** to secrete (sweat) through the pores of the skin, esp. profusely; perspire. **10.** (*tr.*) to make wet or stain with perspiration. **11.** to give forth or cause to give forth (moisture) in droplets: *the maple sweats sap.* **12.** (*intr.*) to collect and condense moisture on an outer surface: *a glass of beer sweating.* **13.** (*intr.*) (of a liquid) to pass through a porous surface in droplets. **14.** (of tobacco leaves, hay, etc.) to exude moisture and, sometimes, begin to ferment or to cause (tobacco leaves, etc.) to exude moisture. **15.** (*tr.*) to heat (food, esp. vegetables) slowly in butter in a tightly closed saucepan. **16.** (*tr.*) to join (pieces of metal) by pressing together and heating. **17.** (*tr.*) to heat (solder) until it melts. **18.** (*tr.*) to heat (partially fused metal) to extract an easily fusible constituent. **19.** *Inf.* to suffer anxiety, impatience, or distress. **20.** *Inf.* to overwork or be overworked. **21.** (*tr.*) *Inf.* to employ at very low wages and under bad conditions. **22.** (*tr.*) *Inf.* to extort, esp. by torture: *to sweat information out of a captive.* **23.** (*intr.*) *Inf.* to suffer punishment: *you'll sweat for this!* **24. sweat blood.** *Inf.* **a.** to work very hard. **b.** to be filled with anxiety or impatience. ~See also **sweat off, sweat out, sweats.** [OE *swǣtan* to sweat, from *swāt* sweat]

sweatband ('swɛtˌbænd) *n.* **1.** a band of material set in a hat or cap to protect it from sweat. **2.** a piece of cloth tied around the forehead to keep sweat out of the eyes or around the wrist to keep the hands dry, as in sports.

sweated ('swɛtɪd) *adj.* **1.** made by exploited labour: *sweated goods.* **2.** (of workers, etc.) forced to work in poor conditions for low pay.

sweater ('swɛtə) *n.* **1.** a garment made of knitted or crocheted material covering the upper part of the body, esp. a heavy one worn for warmth. **2.** a person or thing that sweats. **3.** an employer who overworks and underpays his employees.

sweat gland *n.* any of the coiled tubular subcutaneous glands that secrete sweat.

sweating sickness *n.* an acute infectious febrile disease that was widespread in Europe during the late 15th century, characterized by profuse sweating.

sweat off *or* **away** *vb.* (*tr., adv.*) *Inf.* to get rid of (weight) by strenuous exercise or sweating.

sweat out *vb.* (*tr., adv.*) **1.** to cure or lessen the effects of (a cold, respiratory infection, etc.) by sweating. **2.** *Inf.* to endure (hardships) for a time (often in **sweat it out**). **3. sweat one's guts out.** *Inf.* to work extremely hard.

sweats (swɛts) *pl. n.* sweat shirts and sweat-suit trousers: *jeans and sweats.*

sweat shirt *n.* a long-sleeved knitted cotton sweater worn by athletes, etc.

sweatshop ('swɛtˌʃɒp) *n.* a workshop where employees work long hours under bad conditions for low wages.

sweat suit *n.* a suit worn by athletes for training comprising knitted cotton trousers and a light cotton sweater.

sweaty ('swɛtɪ) *adj.* **sweatier, sweatiest. 1.** covered with perspiration; sweating. **2.** smelling of or like sweat. **3.** causing sweat. —'**sweatily** *adv.* —'**sweatiness** *n.*

swede (swiːd) *n.* **1.** a Eurasian plant cultivated for its bulbous edible root, which is used as a vegetable and as cattle fodder. **2.** the root of this plant. ~Also called: **Swedish turnip.** [C19: so called after being introduced into Scotland from Sweden in the 18th century]

Swede ('swiːd) n. a native, citizen, or inhabitant of Sweden.

Sweden ('swiːdᵊn) n. a kingdom in NW Europe, occupying the E part of the Scandinavian Peninsula, on the Gulf of Bothnia and the Baltic: first united during the Viking period (8th–11th centuries). About 50 per cent of the total area is forest and 9 per cent lakes. Exports include timber, pulp, paper, iron ore, and steel. Language: Swedish. Religion: mostly Lutheran. Currency: krona. Capital: Stockholm. Pop.: 8 387 000 (1987). Area: 449 793 sq. km (173 665 sq. miles). Swedish name: **Sverige.**

Swedenborg ('swiːdᵊnˌbɔːg; Swedish 'sveːdɘnbɔrj) n. **Emanuel** (e'manuel). original surname *Svedberg.* 1688–1772, Swedish scientist and theologian, whose mystical ideas became the basis of a religious movement.

Swedish ('swiːdɪʃ) adj. **1.** of, relating to, or characteristic of Sweden, its people, or their language. ~n. **2.** the official language of Sweden.

Sweelinck (Dutch 'sweːlɪŋk) n. **Jan Pieterszoon** (jɑn 'piːtərˌzoːn). 1562–1621, Dutch composer and organist, whose organ works are important for being the first to incorporate independent parts for the pedals.

sweep (swiːp) vb. **sweeping, swept.** **1.** to clean or clear (a space, chimney, etc.) with a brush, broom, etc. **2.** (often foll. by *up*) to remove or collect (dirt, rubbish, etc.) with a brush, broom, etc. **3.** to move in a smooth or continuous manner, esp. quickly or forcibly: *cars swept along the road.* **4.** to move in a proud or dignified fashion: *she swept past.* **5.** to spread or pass rapidly across, through, or along (a region, area, etc.): *the news swept through the town.* **6.** (tr.) to direct (the gaze, line of fire, etc.) over; survey. **7.** (tr.; foll. by *away* or *off*) to overwhelm emotionally: *she was swept away by his charm.* **8.** (tr.) to brush or lightly touch (a surface, etc.): *the dress swept along the ground.* **9.** (tr.; often foll. by *away*) to convey, clear, or abolish, esp. with strong or continuous movements: *the sea swept the sandcastle away; secondary modern schools were swept away.* **10.** (intr.) to extend gracefully or majestically, esp. in a wide circle: *the plains sweep down to the sea.* **11.** to search (a body of water) for mines, etc., by dragging. **12.** (tr.) to win overwhelmingly, esp. in an election: *Labour swept the country.* **13.** (tr.) to propel (a boat) with sweeps. **14. sweep the board. a.** (in gambling) to win all the cards or money. **b.** to win every event or prize in a contest. **15. sweep (something) under the carpet.** to conceal (something, esp. a problem) in the hope that it will be overlooked by others. ~n. **16.** the act or an instance of sweeping; removal by or as if by a brush or broom. **17.** a swift or steady movement, esp. in an arc. **18.** the distance, arc, etc., through which something, such as a pendulum, moves. **19.** a wide expanse or scope: *the sweep of the plains.* **20.** any curving line or contour. **21.** short for **sweepstake.** **22. a.** a long oar used on an open boat. **b.** *Austral.* a person steering a surf boat with such an oar at the stern. **23.** any of the sails of a windmill. **24.** *Electronics.* a steady horizontal or circular movement of an electron beam across or around the fluorescent screen of a cathode-ray tube. **25.** a curving driveway. **26.** *Chiefly Brit.* See **chimney sweep.** **27.** another name for **swipe** (sense 4). **28. clean sweep. a.** an overwhelming victory or success. **b.** a complete change; purge: *to make a clean sweep.* [C13 *swepen*] —'**sweepy** adj.

sweeper ('swiːpə) n. **1.** a person employed to sweep, such as a roadsweeper. **2.** any device for sweeping: *a carpet sweeper.* **3.** *Inf., soccer.* a player who supports the main defenders, as by intercepting loose balls, etc.

sweep hand n. *Horology.* a long hand that registers seconds or fractions of seconds on the perimeter of the dial.

sweeping ('swiːpɪŋ) adj. **1.** comprehensive and wide-ranging: *sweeping reforms.* **2.** indiscriminate or without reservations: *sweeping statements.* **3.** decisive or overwhelming: *a sweeping victory.* **4.** taking in a wide area: *a sweeping glance.* **5.** driving steadily onwards, esp. over a large area: *a sweeping attack.* —'**sweepingly** adv. —'**sweepingness** n.

sweepstake ('swiːpˌsteɪk) or esp. U.S. **sweepstakes** n. **1. a.** a lottery in which the stakes of the participants constitute the prize. **b.** the prize itself. **2.** any event involving such a lottery, esp. a horse race. ~Often shortened to **sweep.** [C15: orig. referring to someone who *sweeps* or takes all the stakes in a game]

sweet (swiːt) adj. **1.** having or denoting a pleasant taste like that of sugar. **2.** agreeable to the senses or the mind: *sweet music.* **3.** having pleasant manners; gentle: *a sweet child.* **4.** (of wine, etc.) having a relatively high sugar content; not dry. **5.** (of foods) not decaying or rancid: *sweet milk.* **6.** not salty: *sweet water.* **7.** free from unpleasant odours: *sweet air.* **8.** containing no corrosive substances: *sweet soil.* **9.** (of petrol) containing no sulphur compounds. **10.** sentimental or unrealistic. **11.** *Jazz.* performed with a regular beat, with the emphasis on clearly outlined melody and little improvisation. **12.** *Arch.* respected; dear (used in polite forms of address): *sweet sir.* **13.** smooth and precise; perfectly executed: *a sweet shot.* **14. at one's own sweet will.** as it suits oneself alone. **15. keep (someone) sweet.** to ingratiate oneself in order to ensure cooperation. **16. sweet on.** fond of or infatuated with. ~adv. **17.** *Inf.* in a sweet manner. ~n. **18.** a sweet taste or smell; sweetness in general. **19.** (often pl.) *Brit.* any of numerous kinds of confectionery consisting wholly or partly of sugar, esp. of sugar boiled and crystallized (**boiled sweets**). **20.** *Brit.* any sweet dish served as a dessert. **21.** dear; sweetheart (used as a form of address). **22.** anything that is sweet. **23.** (often pl.) a pleasurable experience, state, etc.: *the sweets of success.* [OE *swēte*] —'**sweetish** adj. —'**sweetly** adv. —'**sweetness** n.

Sweet n. **Henry.** 1845–1912, English philologist; a pioneer of modern phonetics. His books include *A History of English Sounds* (1874).

sweet alyssum n. a Mediterranean plant having clusters of small fragrant white or violet flowers. See also **alyssum.**

sweet-and-sour adj. (of food) cooked in a sauce made from sugar and vinegar and other ingredients.

sweet bay n. **1.** a small tree of SE North America, belonging to the magnolia family and having large fragrant white flowers. **2.** another name for **bay⁴** (sense 1).

sweetbread ('swiːtˌbrɛd) n. the pancreas or the thymus gland of an animal, used for food. [C16: SWEET + BREAD, ? from OE *brǣd* meat]

sweetbrier ('swiːtˌbraɪə) n. a Eurasian rose having a tall bristly stem, fragrant leaves, and single pink flowers. Also called: **eglantine.**

sweet cherry n. either of two types of cherry tree that are cultivated for their edible sweet fruit.

sweet chestnut n. See **chestnut** (sense 1).

sweet cicely n. **1.** Also called: **myrrh.** an aromatic European plant, having compound leaves and clusters of small white flowers. **2.** the leaves, formerly used in cookery for their flavour of aniseed. **3.** any of various related plants of Asia and America, having aromatic roots.

sweet corn n. **1.** a variety of maize whose kernels are rich in sugar and eaten as a vegetable when young. **2.** the unripe ears of maize, esp. the sweet kernels removed from the cob, cooked as a vegetable.

sweeten ('swiːtᵊn) vb. (mainly tr.) **1.** (also intr.) to make or become sweet or sweeter. **2.** to mollify or soften (a person). **3.** to make more agreeable. **4.** (also intr.) *Chem.* to free or be freed from unpleasant odours, acidic or corrosive substances, or the like.

sweetener ('swiːtᵊnə) n. **1.** a sweetening agent, esp. one that does not contain sugar. **2.** a slang word for **bribe.**

sweetening ('swiːtᵊnɪŋ) n. something that sweetens.

sweet flag n. an aroid marsh plant, having swordlike leaves, small greenish flowers, and aromatic roots. Also called: **calamus.**

sweet gale n. a shrub of northern swamp regions, having yellow catkin-like flowers and aromatic leaves. Also called: **bog myrtle.** Often shortened to **gale.**

sweet gum n. **1.** a North American liquidambar tree, having prickly spherical fruit clusters and fragrant sap: the wood is used to make furniture. **2.** the wood or sap of this tree.

sweetheart ('swiːtˌhɑːt) n. **1.** a person loved by another. **2.** *Inf.* a lovable, generous, or obliging person. **3.** a term of endearment.

sweetheart agreement *n. Austral. inf.* an industrial agreement on pay and conditions concluded without resort to arbitration.

sweetie ('swiːtɪ) *n. Inf.* **1.** sweetheart; darling: used as a term of endearment. **2.** *Brit.* another word for **sweet** (sense 19). **3.** *Chiefly Brit.* an endearing person.

sweeting ('swiːtɪŋ) *n.* **1.** a variety of sweet apple. **2.** an archaic word for **sweetheart.**

sweet marjoram *n.* another name for **marjoram** (sense 1).

sweetmeat ('swiːt,miːt) *n.* a sweetened delicacy, such as a preserve, sweet, or, formerly, a cake or pastry.

sweet pea *n.* a climbing plant of S Europe, widely cultivated for its butterfly-shaped fragrant flowers of delicate pastel colours.

sweet pepper *n.* **1.** a pepper plant with large bell-shaped fruits that are eaten unripe (**green pepper**) or ripe (**red pepper**). **2.** the fruit of this plant.

sweet potato *n.* **1.** a twining plant of tropical America, cultivated in the tropics for its edible fleshy yellow root. **2.** the root of this plant.

sweet shop *n. Chiefly Brit.* a shop solely or largely selling sweets, esp. boiled sweets.

sweetsop ('swiːt,sɒp) *n.* **1.** a small West Indian tree, having yellowish-green fruit. **2.** the fruit, which has a sweet edible pulp. ~Also called: **custard apple.**

sweet-talk *Inf.* ~*vb.* **1.** to coax, flatter, or cajole (someone). ~*n.* **sweet talk. 2.** cajolery; coaxing.

sweet tooth *n.* a strong liking for sweet foods.

sweetveld ('swiːt,fɛlt) *n.* (in South Africa) a type of grazing characterized by high-quality grass. [pron. from Afrik. *soetveld*]

sweet william *n.* a widely cultivated Eurasian plant with flat clusters of white, pink, red, or purple flowers.

swell (swɛl) *vb.* **swelling, swelled; swollen** *or* **swelled. 1.** to grow or cause to grow in size, esp. as a result of internal pressure. **2.** to expand or cause to expand at a particular point or above the surrounding level; protrude. **3.** to grow or cause to grow in size, amount, intensity, or degree: *the party is swelling with new recruits.* **4.** to puff or be puffed up with pride or another emotion. **5.** (*intr.*) (of seas or lakes) to rise in waves. **6.** (*intr.*) to well up or overflow. **7.** (*tr.*) to make (a musical phrase) increase gradually in volume and then diminish. ~*n.* **8. a.** the undulating movement of the surface of the open sea. **b.** a succession of waves or a single large wave. **9.** a swelling or being swollen; expansion. **10.** an increase in quantity or degree; inflation. **11.** a bulge; protuberance. **12.** a gentle hill. **13.** *Inf.* a person very fashionably dressed. **14.** *Inf.* a man of high social or political standing. **15.** *Music.* a crescendo followed by an immediate diminuendo. **16.** Also called: **swell organ.** *Music.* **a.** a set of pipes on an organ housed in a box (**swell box**) fitted with a shutter operated by a pedal, which can be opened or closed to control the volume. **b.** the manual on an organ controlling this. ~*adj.* **17.** *Inf.* stylish or grand. **18.** *Sl.* excellent; first-class. [OE *swellan*]

swelled head *or* **swollen head** *Inf. n.* **1.** an inflated view of one's own worth, often caused by sudden success. ~*adj.* **swelled-headed, swell-headed,** *or* **swollenheaded. 2.** conceited.

swelling ('swɛlɪŋ) *n.* **1.** the act of expansion or inflation. **2.** the state of being or becoming swollen. **3.** a swollen or inflated part or area. **4.** an abnormal enlargement of a bodily structure or part, esp. as the result of injury. ~ Related adj.: **tumescent.**

swelter ('swɛltə) *vb.* **1.** (*intr.*) to suffer under oppressive heat, esp. to perspire and feel faint. **2.** (*tr.*) *Rare.* to cause to suffer under oppressive heat. ~*n.* **3.** a sweltering condition (esp. in **in a swelter**). **4.** oppressive humid heat. [C15 *swelten*, from OE *sweltan* to die]

sweltering ('swɛltərɪŋ) *adj.* oppressively hot and humid: *a sweltering day.* —'**swelteringly** *adv.*

swept (swɛpt) *vb.* the past tense of **sweep.**

sweptback ('swɛpt,bæk) *adj.* (of an aircraft wing) inclined backwards towards the rear of the fuselage.

sweptwing ('swɛpt,wɪŋ) *adj.* (of an aircraft, etc.) having wings swept (usually) backwards.

swerve (swɜːv) *vb.* **1.** to turn or cause to turn aside, usually sharply or suddenly, from a course. ~*n.* **2.** the act, instance, or degree of swerving. [OE *sweorfan* to scour] —'**swervable** *adj.* —'**swerver** *n.* —'**swerving** *adj.*

Sweyn (sweɪn) *n.* known as *Sweyn Forkbeard.* died 1014, king of Denmark (?986–1014). He conquered England, forcing Ethelred II to flee (1013); father of Canute.

SWG *abbrev. for* Standard Wire Gauge; a notation for the diameters of metal rods or thickness of metal sheet ranging from 16 mm to 0.02 mm or from 0.5 inch to 0.001 inch.

swift (swɪft) *adj.* **1.** moving or able to move quickly; fast. **2.** occurring or performed quickly or suddenly; instant. **3.** (*postpositive;* foll. by *to*) prompt to act or respond: *swift to take revenge.* ~*adv.* **4. a.** swiftly or quickly. **b.** (*in combination*): *swift-moving.* ~*n.* **5.** any of various insectivorous birds of the Old World. They have long narrow wings and spend most of the time on the wing. **6.** any of certain North American lizards of the iguana family that can run very rapidly. **7.** the main cylinder in a carding machine. **8.** an expanding circular frame used to hold skeins of silk, wool, etc. [OE, from *swīfan* to turn] —'**swiftly** *adv.* —'**swiftness** *n.*

Swift (swɪft) *n.* **Jonathan.** 1667–1745, Anglo-Irish satirist and churchman, who became dean of St. Patrick's, Dublin, in 1713. His works include *A Tale of a Tub* (1704) and *Gulliver's Travels* (1726).

swiftlet ('swɪftlɪt) *n.* any of various small swifts of an Asian genus that often live in caves and use echolocation.

swig (swɪg) *Inf.* ~*n.* **1.** a large swallow or deep drink, esp. from a bottle. ~*vb.* **swigging, swigged. 2.** to drink (some liquid) deeply, esp. from a bottle. [C16: from ?] —'**swigger** *n.*

swill (swɪl) *vb.* **1.** to drink large quantities of (liquid, esp. alcoholic drink); guzzle. **2.** (*tr.;* often foll. by *out*) *Chiefly Brit.* to drench or rinse in large amounts of water. **3.** (*tr.*) to feed swill to (pigs, etc.). ~*n.* **4.** wet feed, esp. for pigs, consisting of kitchen waste, skim milk, etc. **5.** refuse, esp. from a kitchen. **6.** a deep drink, esp. beer. **7.** any liquid mess. **8.** the act of swilling. [OE *swilian* to wash out] —'**swiller** *n.*

swim (swɪm) *vb.* **swimming, swam, swum. 1.** (*intr.*) to move along in water, etc., by means of movements of the body, esp. the arms and legs, or (in the case of fish) tail and fins. **2.** (*tr.*) to cover (a distance or stretch of water) in this way. **3.** (*tr.*) to compete in (a race) in this way. **4.** (*intr.*) to be supported by and on a liquid; float. **5.** (*tr.*) to use (a particular stroke) in swimming. **6.** (*intr.*) to move smoothly, usually through air or over a surface. **7.** (*intr.*) to reel or seem to reel: *my head swam; the room swam around me.* **8.** (*intr.;* often foll. by *in* or *with*) to be covered or flooded with water or other liquid. **9.** (*intr.;* often foll. by *in*) to be liberally supplied (with): *he's swimming in money.* **10.** (*tr.*) to cause to float or swim. **11. swim with** (*or* **against**) **the stream** *or* **tide.** to conform to (or resist) prevailing opinion. ~*n.* **12.** the act, an instance, or period of swimming. **13.** any graceful gliding motion. **14.** a condition of dizziness; swoon. **15.** a pool in a river good for fishing. **16. in the swim.** *Inf.* fashionable or active in social or political activities. [OE *swimman*] —'**swimmable** *adj.* —'**swimmer** *n.* —'**swimming** *n., adj.*

swim bladder *n. Ichthyol.* another name for **air bladder** (sense 1).

swimmeret ('swɪmə,rɛt) *n.* any of the small paired appendages on the abdomen of crustaceans, used chiefly in locomotion.

swimming bath *n.* (*often pl.*) an indoor swimming pool.

swimming costume *or* **bathing costume** *n. Chiefly Brit.* any garment worn for swimming or sunbathing, such as a woman's one-piece garment covering most of the torso but not the limbs.

swimmingly ('swɪmɪŋlɪ) *adv.* successfully, effortlessly, or well (esp. in **go swimmingly**).

swimming pool *n.* an artificial pool for swimming.

swimsuit ('swɪm,suːt, -,sjuːt) *n.* a woman's one-piece swimming garment that leaves the arms and legs bare.

Swinburne ('swɪn,bɜːn) *n.* **Algernon Charles.** 1837–1909, English lyric poet and critic.

swindle ('swɪndəl) *vb.* **1.** to cheat (someone) of money, etc.; defraud. **2.** (*tr.*) to obtain (money, etc.) by fraud. ~*n.* **3.** a fraudulent scheme or transaction. [C18: back formation from G *Schwindler*, from *schwindeln*, from OHG *swintilōn*, from *swintan* to disappear] —'**swindler** *n.*

swindle sheet *n.* a slang term for **expense account.**

Swindon ('swɪndən) *n.* a town in S England, in NE Wiltshire: railway workshops. Pop.: 129 300 (1985 est.).

swine (swaɪn) *n., pl.* **swine**. **1.** a coarse or contemptible person. **2.** another name for a **pig**. [OE *swīn*] —'**swinish** *adj.* —'**swinishly** *adv.* —'**swinishness** *n.*

swine fever *n.* an infectious viral disease of pigs, characterized by fever and diarrhoea.

swineherd ('swaɪn,hɜːd) *n.* a person who looks after pigs.

swing (swɪŋ) *vb.* **swinging, swung**. **1.** to move or cause to move rhythmically to and fro, as a free-hanging object; sway. **2.** (*intr.*) to move, walk, etc., with a relaxed and swaying motion. **3.** to pivot or cause to pivot, as on a hinge. **4.** to move or cause to move in a curve: *the car swung around the bend.* **5.** to move or cause to move by suspending or being suspended. **6.** to hang or be hung so as to be able to turn freely. **7.** (*intr.*) *Sl.* to be hanged: *he'll swing for it.* **8.** to alter or cause to alter habits, a course, etc. **9.** (*tr.*) *Inf.* to influence or manipulate successfully: *I hope he can swing the deal.* **10.** (*tr.*; foll. by *up*) to raise or hoist, esp. in a sweeping motion. **11.** (*intr.*; often foll. by *at*) to hit out or strike (at), esp. with a sweeping motion. **12.** (*tr.*) to wave (a weapon, etc.) in a sweeping motion; flourish. **13.** to arrange or play (music) with the rhythmically flexible and compulsive quality associated with jazz. **14.** (*intr.*) (of popular music, esp. jazz, or of the musicians who play it) to have this quality. **15.** *Sl.* to be lively and modern. **16.** (*intr.*) *Cricket.* to bowl (a ball) with swing or (of a ball) to move with a swing. **17. swing the lead**. *Inf.* to malinger or make up excuses. ~*n.* **18.** the act or manner of swinging or the distance covered while swinging: *a wide swing.* **19.** a sweeping stroke or blow. **20.** *Boxing.* a wide punch from the side similar to but longer than a hook. **21.** *Cricket.* the lateral movement of a bowled ball through the air. **22.** any free swaying motion. **23.** any curving movement; sweep. **24.** something that swings or is swung, esp. a suspended seat on which a person may swing back and forth. **25.** a kind of popular dance music influenced by jazz, usually played by big bands and originating in the 1930s. **26.** *Prosody.* a steady distinct rhythm or cadence in prose or verse. **27.** *Inf.* the normal round or pace: *the swing of things.* **28.** a fluctuation, as in some business activity, voting pattern, etc. **29.** *Canad.* (in the North) a train of freight sleighs or canoes. **30.** *Chiefly U.S.* a circular tour. **31. go with a swing**. to go well; be successful. **32. in full swing**. at the height of activity. [OE *swingan*]

swingboat ('swɪŋ,bəʊt) *n.* a piece of fairground equipment consisting of a boat-shaped carriage for swinging in.

swing bridge *n.* a low bridge that can be rotated about a vertical axis to permit the passage of ships, etc.

swinge (swɪndʒ) *vb.* **swingeing** *or* **swingeing, swinged**. (*tr.*) *Arch.* to beat, flog, or punish. [OE *swengan*]

swingeing ('swɪndʒɪŋ) *adj. Chiefly Brit.* punishing; severe.

swinger ('swɪŋə) *n. Sl.* a person regarded as being modern and lively. —'**swinging** *adj.* —'**swingingly** *adv.*

swingle ('swɪŋgəl) *n.* **1.** a flat-bladed wooden instrument used for beating and scraping flax or hemp to remove coarse matter from it. ~*vb.* **2.** to use a swingle on. [OE *swingel* stroke]

swingletree ('swɪŋgəl,triː) *n.* a crossbar in a horse's harness to which the ends of the traces are attached. Also called: **whippletree**.

swing shift *n. U.S. & Canad. inf.* the evening work shift, usually from mid-afternoon until midnight. —**swing shifter** *n.*

swing-wing *adj.* **1.** of or relating to an aircraft equipped with wings that are automatically swept back close to the fuselage when flying at high speed and are brought forward for landing and takeoff. ~*n.* **2. a.** an aircraft fitted with such wings. **b.** either of the two wings of such an aircraft.

swingy ('swɪŋɪ) *adj.* **swingier, swingiest.** (of a garment, esp. a skirt) styled so that it swings as the wearer moves.

swipe (swaɪp) *vb.* **1.** (when *intr.*, usually foll. by *at*) *Inf.* to hit hard with a sweeping blow. **2.** (*tr.*) *Sl.* to steal. ~*n.* **3.** *Inf.* a hard blow. **4.** Also called: **sweep**. a type of lever for raising and lowering a weight, such as a bucket in a well. [C19: ? rel. to SWEEP]

swirl (swɜːl) *vb.* **1.** to turn or cause to turn in a twisting spinning fashion. **2.** (*intr.*) to be dizzy; swim: *my head was swirling.* ~*n.* **3.** a whirling or spinning motion, esp. in water. **4.** a whorl; curl. **5.** the act of swirling or stirring. **6.** dizzy confusion or disorder. [C15: prob. from Du. *zwirrelen*] —'**swirling** *adj.* —'**swirly** *adj.*

swish (swɪʃ) *vb.* **1.** to move with or make or cause to move with or make a whistling or hissing sound. **2.** (*intr.*) (esp. of fabrics) to rustle. **3.** (*tr.*) *Sl., now rare.* to whip; flog. **4.** (*tr.*; foll. by *off*) to cut with a swishing blow. ~*n.* **5.** a hissing or rustling sound or movement. **6.** a rod for flogging or a blow from this. ~*adj.* **7.** *Inf., chiefly Brit.* fashionable; smart. [C18: imit.] —'**swishy** *adj.*

Swiss (swɪs) *adj.* **1.** of, relating to, or characteristic of Switzerland, its inhabitants, or their dialects of German, French, and Italian. ~*n.* **2.** a native, inhabitant, or citizen of Switzerland.

Swiss chard *n.* another name for **chard**.

Swiss cheese plant *n.* See **monstera**.

swiss roll *n.* a sponge cake spread with jam, cream, or some other filling, and rolled up.

switch (swɪtʃ) *n.* **1.** a mechanical, electrical, or electronic device for opening or closing a circuit or for diverting a current from one part of a circuit to another. **2.** a swift and usually sudden shift or change. **3.** an exchange or swap. **4.** a flexible rod or twig, used esp. for punishment. **5.** the sharp movement or blow of such an instrument. **6.** a tress of false hair used to give added length or bulk to a woman's own hair-style. **7.** the tassel-like tip of the tail of cattle and certain other animals. **8.** any of various card games in which the suit is changed during play. **9.** *U.S. & Canad.* a railway siding. **10.** *U.S. & Canad.* a railway point. **11.** *Austral. inf.* short for **switchboard** (sense 1). ~*vb.* **12.** to shift, change, turn aside, or change the direction of (something). **13.** to exchange (places); replace (something by something else). **14.** *Chiefly U.S. & Canad.* to transfer (rolling stock) from one railway track to another. **15.** (*tr.*) to cause (an electric current) to start or stop flowing or to change its path by operating a switch. **16.** (*tr.*) to lash or whip with or as if with a switch. ~See also **switch off, switch on**. [C16: ?from MDu. *swijch* twig] —'**switcher** *n.*

switchback ('swɪtʃ,bæk) *n.* **1.** a steep mountain road, railway, or track with hairpin bends or a hairpin bend on such a road, etc. **2.** another word (esp. Brit.) for **big dipper**.

switchblade *or* **switchblade knife** ('swɪtʃ,bleɪd) *n.* another name (esp. U.S. and Canad.) for **flick knife**.

switchboard ('swɪtʃ,bɔːd) *n.* **1.** an installation in a telephone exchange, office, etc., at which the interconnection of telephone lines is manually controlled. **2.** a similar installation by which certain electrical equipment is operated.

switchman ('swɪtʃmən) *n., pl.* **-men**. the U.S. and Canad. name for **pointsman**.

switch off *vb.* (*adv.*) **1.** to cause (a device) to stop operating as by moving a switch, knob, or lever. **2.** *Inf.* to cease to interest or be interested; make or become bored, alienated, etc.

switch on *vb.* (*adv.*) **1.** to cause (a device) to operate as by moving a switch, knob, or lever. **2.** (*tr.*) *Inf.* to produce (charm, tears, etc.) suddenly or automatically. **3.** (*tr.*) *Inf.* (now dated) to make up-to-date, esp. in outlook, dress, etc.

swither ('swɪðə) *Scot.* ~*vb.* (*intr.*) **1.** to hesitate; vacillate; be perplexed. ~*n.* **2.** hesitation; perplexity; agitation. [C16: from ?]

Swithin *or* **Swithun** ('swɪðɪn, 'swɪθ-) *n.* **Saint.** died 862 A.D., English ecclesiastic: bishop of Winchester (?852–862). Feast day: July 15.

Switzer ('switsə) *n.* a less common word for **Swiss**. [C16: from MHG, from *Swiz* Switzerland]

Switzerland ('switsələnd) *n.* a federal republic in W central Europe: the cantons of Schwyz, Uri, and Unterwalden formed a defensive league against the Hapsburgs in 1291, later joined by other cantons; gained independence in 1499; adopted a policy of permanent neutrality from 1516; a leading centre of the Reformation in the 16th century. It lies in the Jura Mountains and the Alps, with a plateau between the two ranges. Languages: German, French, Italian, and Romansch. Religion: mostly Protestant and Roman Catholic. Currency: Swiss franc. Capital: Bern. Pop.: 6 586 000 (1987). Area: 41 288 sq. km (15 941 sq. miles). German name: **Schweiz**. French name: **Suisse**. Italian name: **Svizzera**.

swivel ('swɪvəl) *n.* **1.** a coupling device which allows an attached object to turn freely. **2.** such a device made of two parts which turn independently, such as a compound link of a chain. **3. a.** a pivot on which is mounted a gun that may be swung horizontally from side to side. **b.** Also called: **swivel gun.** the gun itself. ~*vb.* **-elling, -elled** *or* U.S. **-eling, -eled.** **4.** to turn or swing on or as if on a pivot. **5.** (*tr.*) to provide with, secure by, or support with a swivel. [C14: from OE *swifan* to turn]

swivel chair *n.* a chair, the seat of which is joined to the legs by a swivel and which thus may be spun round.

swivel pin *n.* another name for **kingpin** (sense 2).

swizzle ('swɪz²l) *n.* **1.** an alcoholic drink containing gin or rum. **2.** Also called: **swizz.** *Brit. inf.* a swindle or disappointment. ~*vb.* **3.** (*tr.*) to stir a swizzle stick in (a drink). **4.** *Brit. inf.* to swindle; cheat. [C19: from ?]

swizzle stick *n.* a small rod used to agitate an effervescent drink to facilitate the escape of carbon dioxide.

swob (swɒb) *n., vb.,* **swobbing, swobbed.** a less common word for **swab.**

swollen ('swəʊlən) *vb.* **1.** a past participle of **swell.** ~*adj.* **2.** tumid or enlarged as by swelling. **3.** turgid or bombastic. —'**swollenness** *n.*

swoon (swuːn) *vb.* (*intr.*) **1.** a literary word for **faint.** **2.** to become ecstatic. ~*n.* **3.** an instance of fainting. ~Also (archaic or dialect): **swound** (swaʊnd). [OE *geswōgen* insensible, p.p. of *swōgan* (unattested except in compounds) suffocate] —'**swooning** *adj.*

swoop (swuːp) *vb.* **1.** (*intr.*; usually foll. by *down, on,* or *upon*) to sweep or pounce suddenly. **2.** (*tr.*; often foll. by *up, away,* or *off*) to seize or scoop suddenly. ~*n.* **3.** the act of swooping. **4.** a swift descent. [OE *swāpan* to sweep]

swoosh (swuːʃ) *vb.* **1.** to make or cause to make a rustling or swirling sound, esp. when moving or pouring out. ~*n.* **2.** a swirling or rustling sound or movement. [C20: imit.]

swop (swɒp) *n., vb.,* **swopping, swopped.** a variant spelling of **swap.**

sword (sɔːd) *n.* **1.** a thrusting, striking, or cutting weapon with a long blade having one or two cutting edges, a hilt, and usually a crosspiece or guard. **2.** such a weapon worn on ceremonial occasions as a symbol of authority. **3.** something resembling a sword, such as the snout of a swordfish. **4. the sword. a.** violence or power, esp. military power. **b.** death; destruction: *to put to the sword.* [OE *sweord*]

swordbearer ('sɔːd,bɛərə) *n.* an official who carries a ceremonial sword.

sword dance *n.* a dance in which the performers dance nimbly over swords on the ground or brandish them in the air. —**sword dancer** *n.* —**sword dancing** *n.*

swordfish ('sɔːd,fɪʃ) *n., pl.* **-fish** *or* **-fishes.** a large fish with a very long upper jaw: valued as a food and game fish.

sword grass *n.* any of various grasses and other plants having sword-shaped sharp leaves.

sword knot *n.* a loop on the hilt of a sword by which it was attached to the wrist, now purely decorative.

sword lily *n.* another name for **gladiolus.**

Sword of Damocles *n.* a closely impending disaster. [see DAMOCLES]

swordplay ('sɔːd,pleɪ) *n.* **1.** the action or art of fighting with a sword. **2.** verbal sparring.

swordsman ('sɔːdzmən) *n., pl.* **-men.** one who uses or is skilled in the use of a sword. —'**swordsmanship** *n.*

swordstick ('sɔːd,stɪk) *n.* a hollow walking stick containing a short sword or dagger.

swordtail ('sɔːd,teɪl) *n.* any of several small freshwater fishes of Central America having a long swordlike tail.

swore (swɔː) *vb.* the past tense of **swear.**

sworn (swɔːn) *vb.* **1.** the past participle of **swear.** ~*adj.* **2.** bound, pledged, or made inveterate, by or as if by an oath: *a sworn statement; he was sworn to God.*

swot[1] (swɒt) *Brit. inf.* ~*vb.* **swotting, swotted.** **1.** (often foll. by *up*) to study (a subject) intensively, as for an examination; cram. ~*n.* **2.** Also called: **swotter.** a person who works or studies hard. **3.** hard work or grind. ~Also: **swat.** [C19: var. of SWEAT (n.)]

swot[2] (swɒt) *vb.* **swotting, swotted,** *n.* a variant of **swat.**

swounds *or* '**swounds** (zwaʊndz, zaʊndz) *interj. Arch.* less common spellings of **zounds.**

swum (swʌm) *vb.* the past participle of **swim.**

swung (swʌŋ) *vb.* the past tense and past participle of **swing.**

swy (swaɪ) *n. Austral.* another name for **two-up.** [C20: from G *zwei* two]

Sybaris ('sɪbərɪs) *n.* a Greek colony in S Italy, on the Gulf of Taranto: notorious for its luxurious living, founded about 720 B.C. and sacked in 510. —'**Sybarite** *n.* —**Sybaritic** (,sɪbə'rɪtɪk) *adj.*

sybarite ('sɪbə,raɪt) *n.* **1.** (*sometimes cap.*) a devotee of luxury and the sensual vices. ~*adj.* **2.** luxurious; sensuous. [C16: from L *Sybarīta,* from Gk *Subarītēs* inhabitant of SYBARIS] —**sybaritic** (,sɪbə'rɪtɪk) *adj.* —,**syba'ritically** *adv.* —'**sybaritism** *n.*

sycamore ('sɪkə,mɔː) *n.* **1.** a Eurasian maple tree, naturalized in Britain and North America, having five-lobed leaves and two-winged fruits. **2.** *U.S. & Canad.* an American plane tree. See **plane tree.** **3.** a tree of N Africa and W Asia, having an edible figlike fruit. [C14: from OF *sicamor,* from L *sȳcomorus,* from Gk, from *sukon* fig + *moron* mulberry]

syconium (saɪ'kəʊnɪəm) *n., pl.* **-nia** (-nɪə). *Bot.* the fleshy fruit of the fig, consisting of an enlarged receptacle. [C19: from NL, from Gk *sukon* fig]

sycophant ('sɪkəfənt) *n.* a person who uses flattery to win favour from individuals wielding influence; toady. [C16: from L *sȳcophanta,* from Gk *sukophantēs,* lit.: person showing a fig, apparently referring to the fig sign used in accusation, from *sukon* fig + *phainein* to show; sense prob. developed from "accuser" to "informer, flatterer"] —'**sycophancy** *n.* —**sycophantic** (,sɪkə'fæntɪk) *adj.* —,**syco'phantically** *adv.*

sycosis (saɪ'kəʊsɪs) *n.* chronic inflammation of the hair follicles, esp. those of the beard. [C16: via NL from Gk *sukōsis,* from *sukon* fig]

Sydenham's chorea ('sɪdənəmz) *n.* a form of chorea affecting children, often associated with rheumatic fever. Nontechnical name: **Saint Vitus's dance.** [after T. Sydenham (1624–89), E physician]

Sydney[1] ('sɪdnɪ) *n.* **1.** a port in SE Australia, capital of New South Wales, on an inlet of the S Pacific: the largest city in Australia and the first British settlement, established as a penal colony in 1788; developed rapidly after 1820 with the discovery of gold in its hinterland; large wool market; three universities. Pop.: 3 430 600 (1986 est.). **2.** a port in SE Canada, in Nova Scotia on NE Cape Breton Island: capital of Cape Breton Island until 1820, when the island united administratively with Nova Scotia. Pop.: 27 754 (1986).

Sydney[2] ('sɪdnɪ) *n.* a variant spelling of (Sir Philip) **Sidney.**

Syene (saɪ'iːnɪ) *n.* transliteration of the Ancient Greek name for **Aswan.**

syenite ('saɪə,naɪt) *n.* a light-coloured coarse-grained igneous rock consisting of feldspars with hornblende. [C18: from F, from L *syēnītēs lapis* stone from *Syene* (Aswan), where orig. quarried] —**syenitic** (,saɪə'nɪtɪk) *adj.*

Syktyvkar (*Russian* siktif'kar) *n.* a city in the NW Soviet Union, capital of the Komi ASSR: timber industry. Pop.: 224 000 (1987).

syllabary ('sɪləbərɪ) *n., pl.* **-baries.** **1.** a table or list of syllables. **2.** a set of symbols used in certain writing systems, such as one used for Japanese, in which each symbol represents a spoken syllable. [C16: from NL *syllabārium,* from L *syllaba* SYLLABLE]

syllabi ('sɪlə,baɪ) *n.* a plural of **syllabus.**

syllabic (sɪ'læbɪk) *adj.* **1.** of or relating to syllables or the division of a word into syllables. **2.** denoting a kind of verse line based on a specific number of syllables rather than being regulated by stresses or quantities. **3.** (of a consonant) constituting a syllable. ~*n.* **4.** a syllabic consonant. —**syl'labically** *adv.*

syllabify (sɪ'læbɪ,faɪ) *or* **syllabicate** *vb.* **-fying, -fied** *or* **-cating, -cated.** (*tr.*) to divide (a word) into its constituent syllables. —**syl,labifi'cation** *or* **syl,labi'cation** *n.*

syllable ('sɪləb²l) *n.* **1.** a combination or set of one or more units of sound in a language that must consist of a sonorous element (a sonant or vowel) and may or may not contain less sonorous elements (consonants or semivowels) flanking it: for example "paper" has two syllables. **2.** (in the writing systems of certain languages, esp. ancient ones) a symbol or set of symbols standing for a syllable. **3.** the least mention: *don't breathe a syllable of it.* **4. in words of one syllable.** simply; bluntly. ~*vb.* **5.** to pronounce syllables of (a text); articulate. **6.** (*tr.*) to write down in syllables. [C14: via OF from L *syllaba,* from Gk *sullabē,* from *sullambanein* to collect together]

syllabub *or* **sillabub** ('sɪlə,bʌb) *n.* **1.** a spiced drink made of milk with rum, port, brandy, or wine, often hot. **2.** *Brit.* a cold dessert made from milk or cream beaten with sugar, wine, and lemon juice. [C16: from ?]

syllabus ('sɪləbəs) *n., pl.* **-buses** *or* **-bi** (-,baɪ). **1.** an outline of a course of studies, text, etc. **2.** *Brit.* **a.** the subjects studied for a particular course. **b.** a list of these subjects. [C17: from LL, erroneously from L *sittybus* parchment strip giving title and author, from Gk *sittuba*]

syllepsis (sɪ'lɛpsɪs) *n., pl.* **-ses** (-siːz). **1.** (in grammar or rhetoric) the use of a single sentence construction in which a verb, adjective, etc., is made to cover two syntactical functions, as *have* in *she and they have promised to come.* **2.** another word for **zeugma.** [C16: from LL, from Gk *sullēpsis*, from *sul- lēpsis*, from *lambanein* to take] —**syl'leptic** *adj.* —**syl'leptically** *adv.*

syllogism ('sɪlə,dʒɪzəm) *n.* **1.** a deductive inference consisting of two premises and a conclusion, all of which are categorical propositions. The subject of the conclusion is the **minor term** and its predicate the **major term;** the **middle term** occurs in both premises but not the conclusion. There are 256 such arguments but only 24 are valid. *Some men are mortal; some men are angelic; so some mortals are angelic* is invalid, while *some temples are in ruins; all ruins are fascinating; so some temples are fascinating* is valid. Here *fascinating, in ruins,* and *temples* are respectively major, middle, and minor terms. **2.** a piece of deductive reasoning from the general to the particular. [C14: via L from Gk *sullogismos*, from *sullogizesthai* to reckon together, from *logos* a discourse] —**syllo'gistic** *adj.* —**syllo,gize** *or* **-ise** *vb.*

sylph (sɪlf) *n.* **1.** a slender graceful girl or young woman. **2.** any of a class of imaginary beings assumed to inhabit the air. [C17: from NL *sylphus*, prob. coined from L *silva* wood + Gk *numphē* nymph] —**'sylph,like** *adj.*

sylva *or* **silva** ('sɪlvə) *n., pl.* **-vas** *or* **-vae** (-viː). the trees growing in a particular region. [C17: from L *silva* a wood]

sylvan *or* **silvan** ('sɪlvən) *Chiefly poetic.* ~*adj.* **1.** of or consisting of woods or forests. **2.** in woods or forests. **3.** idyllically rural or rustic. ~*n.* **4.** an inhabitant of the woods, esp. a spirit. [C16: from L *silvānus*, from *silva* forest]

sylvanite ('sɪlvə,naɪt) *n.* a silver-white mineral consisting of a compound of tellurium with gold and silver in the form of elongated crystals. [C18: from (TRAN)SYLVAN(IA) + -ITE[1], with reference to the region where first found]

Sylvanus (sɪl'veɪnəs) *n.* a variant spelling of **Silvanus.**

sylviculture ('sɪlvɪ,kʌltʃə) *n.* a variant spelling of **silviculture.**

sym- *prefix.* a variant of **syn-** before *b, p,* and *m.*

symbiont ('sɪmbɪ,ɒnt) *n.* an organism living in a state of symbiosis. [C19: from Gk *sumbioun* to live together, from *bioun* to live] —**,symbi'ontic** *adj.* —**,symbi'ontically** *adv.*

symbiosis (,sɪmbɪ'əusɪs) *n.* **1.** a close association of two interdependent animal or plant species. **2.** a similar relationship between persons or groups. [C19: via NL from Gk: a living together] —**,symbi'otic** *adj.*

symbol ('sɪmbˀl) *n.* **1.** something that represents or stands for something else, usually by convention or association, esp. a material object used to represent something abstract. **2.** an object, person, etc., used in a literary work, film, etc., to stand for or suggest something else with which it is associated. **3.** a letter, figure, or sign used in mathematics, music, etc., to represent a quantity, phenomenon, operation, function, etc. ~*vb.* **-bolling, -bolled** *or U.S.* **-boling, -boled.** **4.** (*tr.*) another word for **symbolize.** [C15: from Church L *symbolum*, from Gk *sumbolon* sign, from *sumballein* to throw together, from SYN- + *ballein* to throw]

symbolic (sɪm'bɒlɪk) *or* **symbolical** *adj.* **1.** of or relating to a symbol or symbols. **2.** serving as a symbol. **3.** characterized by the use of symbols or symbolism. —**sym'bolically** *adv.*

symbolic logic *n.* another name for **formal logic.**

symbolism ('sɪmbə,lɪzəm) *n.* **1.** the representation of something in symbolic form or the attribution of symbolic character to something. **2.** a system of symbols or symbolic representation. **3.** a symbolic significance or quality. **4.** (*often cap.*) a late 19th-century movement in art that sought to express mystical or abstract ideas through the symbolic use of images.

symbolist ('sɪmbəlɪst) *n.* **1.** a person who uses or can interpret symbols, esp. as a means to revealing aspects of truth and reality. **2.** an artist or writer who practises symbolism in his work. **3.** (*usually cap.*) a writer associated with the symbolist movement. **4.** (*often cap.*) an artist associated with the symbolism movement. ~*adj.* **5.** of, relating to, or characterizing symbolism or symbolists. —**,symbol'istic** *adj.* —**,symbol'istically** *adv.*

symbolist movement *n.* (*usually cap.*) a movement beginning in French and Belgian poetry towards the end of the 19th century with Mallarmé, Valéry, Verlaine, Rimbaud, and others, and seeking to express states of mind rather than objective reality by the power of words and images to suggest as well as denote.

symbolize *or* **-ise** ('sɪmbə,laɪz) *vb.* **1.** (*tr.*) to serve as or be a symbol of. **2.** (*tr.;* usually foll. by *by*) to represent by a symbol or symbols. **3.** (*intr.*) to use symbols. **4.** (*tr.*) to treat or regard as symbolic. —**,symboli'zation** *or* **-i'sation** *n.*

symmetrical (sɪ'mɛtrɪkˀl) *adj.* possessing or displaying symmetry.

symmetry ('sɪmɪtrɪ) *n., pl.* **-tries.** **1.** similarity, correspondence, or balance among systems or parts of a system. **2.** *Maths.* an exact correspondence in position or form about a given point, line, or plane. **3.** beauty or harmony of form based on a proportionate arrangement of parts. [C16: from L *symmetria*, from Gk *summetria* proportion, from SYN- + *metron* measure]

Symonds ('sɪməndz) *n.* **John Addington** ('ædɪŋtən). 1840–93, English writer, noted for his *Renaissance in Italy* (1875–86) and for studies of homosexuality.

Symons ('saɪmənz) *n.* **Arthur.** 1865–1945, English poet and critic, who helped to introduce the French symbolists to England.

sympathectomy (,sɪmpə'θɛktəmɪ) *n., pl.* **-mies.** the surgical excision or chemical destruction (**chemical sympathectomy**) of one or more parts of the sympathetic nervous system. [C20: from SYMPATHETIC + -ECTOMY]

sympathetic (,sɪmpə'θɛtɪk) *adj.* **1.** characterized by, feeling, or showing sympathy; understanding. **2.** in accord with the subject's personality or mood; congenial: *a sympathetic atmosphere.* **3.** (when *postpositive,* often foll. by *to* or *towards*) showing agreement (with) or favour (towards). **4.** *Anat., physiol.* of or relating to the division of the autonomic nervous system that acts in opposition to the parasympathetic system accelerating the heartbeat, dilating the bronchi, inhibiting the smooth muscles of the digestive tract, etc. Cf. **parasympathetic.** **5.** relating to vibrations occurring as a result of similar vibrations in a neighbouring body: *sympathetic strings on a sitar.* —**,sympa'thetically** *adv.*

sympathetic magic *n.* a type of magic in which it is sought to produce a large-scale effect, often at a distance, by performing some small-scale ceremony resembling it, such as the pouring of water on an altar to induce rainfall.

sympathize *or* **-ise** ('sɪmpə,θaɪz) *vb.* (*intr.;* often foll. by *with*) **1.** to feel or express compassion or sympathy (for); commiserate: *he sympathized with my troubles.* **2.** to share or understand the sentiments or ideas (of); be in sympathy (with). —**'sympa,thizer** *or* **-iser** *n.*

sympatholytic (,sɪmpəθəʊ'lɪtɪk) *Med.* ~*adj.* **1. a.** inhibiting or antagonistic to nerve impulses of the sympathetic nervous system. **b.** of or relating to such inhibition. ~*n.* **2.** a sympatholytic drug. Cf. **sympathomimetic.** [C20: from SYMPATH(ETIC) + -LYTIC]

sympathomimetic (,sɪmpəθəʊmɪ'mɛtɪk) *Med.* ~*adj.* **1.** causing a physiological effect similar to that produced by stimulation of the sympathetic nervous system. ~*n.* **2.** a sympathomimetic drug. Cf. **sympatholytic.** [C20: from SYMPATH(ETIC) + MIMETIC]

sympathy ('sɪmpəθɪ) *n., pl.* **-thies.** **1.** the sharing of another's emotions, esp. of sorrow or anguish; compassion. **2.** affinity or harmony, usually of feelings or interests, between persons or things: *to be in sympathy with someone.* **3.** mutual affection or understanding arising from such a relationship. **4.** the condition of a physical system or body when its behaviour is similar or corresponds to that of a different system that influences it, such as the vibration of sympathetic strings. **5.** (*sometimes pl.*) a feeling of loyalty, support, or accord, as for an idea, cause, etc. **6.** *Physiol.* the relationship between two organs or parts whereby a change in one affects the other.

[C16: from L *sympathia*, from Gk, from *sumpathēs*, from SYN- + *pathos* suffering]

sympathy strike *n.* a strike organized in support of another strike or cause. Also called: **sympathetic strike.**

symphonic poem *n. Music.* an extended orchestral composition, originated by Liszt, based on nonmusical material, such as a work of literature or folk tale. Also called: **tone poem.**

symphony ('sɪmfənɪ) *n., pl.* **-nies. 1.** an extended large-scale orchestral composition, usually with several movements, at least one of which is in sonata form. **2.** a piece of instrumental music in up to three very short movements, used as an overture to or interlude in a baroque opera. **3.** any purely orchestral movement in a vocal work, such as a cantata or oratorio. **4.** short for **symphony orchestra. 5.** anything distinguished by a harmonious composition: *the picture was a symphony of green.* **6.** *Arch.* harmony in general; concord. [C13: from OF *symphonie*, from L *symphōnia* concord, from Gk, from SYN- + *phōnē* sound] —**symphonic** (sɪm'fɒnɪk) *adj.* —**sym'phonically** *adv.*

symphony orchestra *n. Music.* an orchestra capable of performing symphonies, esp. a large orchestra comprising strings, brass, woodwind, harp and percussion.

symphysis ('sɪmfɪsɪs) *n., pl.* **-ses** (-ˌsiːz). **1.** *Anat., bot.* a growing together of parts or structures, such as two bony surfaces joined by an intermediate layer of fibrous cartilage. **2.** a line marking this growing together. **3.** *Pathol.* an abnormal adhesion of two or more parts or structures. [C16: via NL from Gk *sumphusis*, from *sumphuein*, from SYN- + *phuein* to grow] —**symphysial** or **symphyseal** (sɪm'fɪzɪəl) *adj.*

sympodium (sɪm'pəʊdɪəm) *n., pl.* **-dia** (-dɪə). the main axis of growth in the grapevine and similar plants: a number of lateral branches that arise from just behind the apex of the main stem, which ceases to grow. [C19: from NL, from SYN- + Gk *podion* a little foot] —**sym'podial** *adj.* —**sym'podially** *adv.*

symposium (sɪm'pəʊzɪəm) *n., pl.* **-siums** or **-sia** (-zɪə). **1.** a conference or meeting for the discussion of some subject, esp. an academic topic or social problem. **2.** a collection of scholarly contributions on a given subject. **3.** (in classical Greece) a drinking party with intellectual conversation, music, etc. [C16: via L from Gk *sumposion*, from *sumpinein* to drink together]

symptom ('sɪmptəm) *n.* **1.** *Med.* any sensation or change in bodily function experienced by a patient that is associated with a particular disease. **2.** any phenomenon or circumstance accompanying something and regarded as evidence of its existence; indication. [C16: from LL *symptōma*, from Gk *sumptōma* chance, from *sumpiptein* to occur, from SYN- + *piptein* to fall]

symptomatic (ˌsɪmptə'mætɪk) *adj.* **1.** (often foll. by *of*) being a symptom; indicative: *symptomatic of insanity.* **2.** of, relating to, or according to symptoms: *a symptomatic analysis.* —**ˌsympto'matically** *adv.*

symptomatology (ˌsɪmptəmə'tɒlədʒɪ) *n.* the branch of medicine concerned with the study and classification of the symptoms of disease.

syn. *abbrev. for* synonym(ous).

syn- *prefix.* **1.** with or together: *synecology.* **2.** fusion: *syngamy.* [from Gk *sun* together]

synaeresis (sɪ'nɪərɪsɪs) *n.* a variant spelling of **syneresis.**

synaesthesia or *U.S.* **synesthesia** (ˌsɪniːs'θiːzɪə) *n.* **1.** *Physiol.* a sensation experienced in a part of the body other than that stimulated. **2.** *Psychol.* the subjective sensation of a sense other than the one being stimulated. [C19: from NL, from SYN- + *-esthesia*, from Gk *aisthēsis* sensation] —**synaesthetic** or *U.S.* **synesthetic** (ˌsɪniːs'θɛtɪk) *adj.*

synagogue ('sɪnəˌgɒg) *n.* **1. a.** a building for Jewish religious services and religious instruction. **b.** (*as modifier*): *synagogue services.* **2.** a congregation of Jews who assemble for worship or religious study. **3.** the religion of Judaism as organized in such congregations. [C12: from OF, from LL *synagōga*, from Gk *sunagōgē* a gathering, from *sunagein* to bring together] —**synagogical** (ˌsɪnə'gɒdʒɪkəl) or **synagogal** ('sɪnəˌgɒgəl) *adj.*

synapse ('saɪnæps) *n.* the point at which a nerve impulse is relayed from the terminal portion of an axon to the dendrites of an adjacent neuron.

synapsis (sɪ'næpsɪs) *n., pl.* **-ses** (-siːz). **1.** *Cytology.* the association in pairs of homologous chromosomes at the start of meiosis. **2.** another word for **synapse.** [C19: from NL, from Gk *sunapsis* junction, from *sunaptein* to join together] —**synaptic** (sɪ'næptɪk) *adj.* —**syn'aptically** *adv.*

synarthrosis (ˌsɪnɑː'θrəʊsɪs) *n., pl.* **-ses** (-siːz). *Anat.* any of various joints which lack a synovial cavity and are virtually immovable; a fixed joint. [C16: via NL from Gk *sunarthrōsis*, from *sunarthrousthai* to be connected by joints, from *sun-*SYN- + *arthron* a joint] —**ˌsynar'thro-dial** *adj.*

sync or **synch** (sɪŋk) *Films, television, computers.* ~*vb.* **1.** an informal word for **synchronize.** ~*n.* **2.** an informal word for **synchronization** (esp. in **in** or **out of sync**).

syncarp ('sɪnkɑːp) *n. Bot.* a fleshy multiple fruit, formed from two or more carpels of one flower or the aggregated fruits of several flowers. [C19: from NL *syncarpium*, from SYN- + Gk *karpos* fruit]

syncarpous (sɪn'kɑːpəs) *adj.* **1.** (of the ovaries of certain flowering plants) consisting of united carpels. **2.** of or relating to a syncarp.

synchro ('sɪŋkrəʊ) *n., pl.* **-chros.** any of a number of electrical devices in which the angular position of a rotating part is transformed into a voltage, or vice versa. Also called: **selsyn.**

synchro- *combining form.* indicating synchronization: *synchromesh.*

synchrocyclotron (ˌsɪŋkrəʊ'saɪkləˌtrɒn) *n.* a cyclotron in which the frequency of the electric field is modulated to allow for relativistic effects at high velocities and thus produce higher energies.

synchromesh (ˈsɪŋkrəʊˌmɛʃ) *adj.* **1.** (of a gearbox, etc.) having a system of clutches that synchronizes the speeds of the driving and driven members before engagement to avoid shock in gear changing and to reduce noise and wear. ~*n.* **2.** a gear system having these features. [C20: shortened from *synchronized mesh*]

synchronic (sɪn'krɒnɪk) *adj.* **1.** concerned with the events or phenomena at a particular period without considering historical antecedents: *synchronic linguistics.* Cf. **diachronic. 2.** synchronous. —**syn'chronically** *adv.* —**synchronicity** (ˌsɪnkrə'nɪsɪtɪ) *n.*

synchronism ('sɪŋkrəˌnɪzəm) *n.* **1.** the quality or condition of being synchronous. **2.** a chronological list of historical persons and events, arranged to show parallel or synchronous occurrence. **3.** the representation in a work of art of one or more incidents that occurred at separate times. [C16: from Gk *sunkhronismos*] —**ˌsynchro'nistic** or **ˌsynchro'nistical** *adj.* —**ˌsynchro'nistically** *adv.*

synchronize or **-ise** ('sɪŋkrəˌnaɪz) *vb.* **1.** (when *intr.*, usually foll. by *with*) to occur or recur or cause to occur or recur at the same time or in unison. **2.** to indicate or cause to indicate the same time: *synchronize your watches.* **3.** (*tr.*) *Films.* to establish (the picture and soundtrack records) in their correct relative position. **4.** (*tr.*) to designate (events) as simultaneous. —**ˌsynchroni'zation** or **-i'sation** *n.* —**'synchro,nizer** or **-iser** *n.*

synchronized swimming *n.* a sport in which swimmers move in patterns in time to music.

synchronous ('sɪŋkrənəs) *adj.* **1.** occurring at the same time. **2.** *Physics.* (of periodic phenomena, such as voltages) having the same frequency and phase. **3.** occurring or recurring exactly together and at the same rate. [C17: from LL *synchronus*, from Gk *sunkhronos*, from SYN- + *khronos* time] —**'synchronously** *adv.* —**'synchronous-ness** *n.* —**'synchrony** *n.*

synchronous machine *n.* an electrical machine whose rotating speed is proportional to the frequency of the alternating-current supply and independent of the load.

synchronous motor *n.* an alternating-current motor that runs at a speed that is equal to or is a multiple of the frequency of the supply.

synchrotron ('sɪŋkrəˌtrɒn) *n.* a particle accelerator having an electric field of fixed frequency and a changing magnetic field. [C20: from SYNCHRO- + (ELEC)TRON]

syncline ('sɪŋklaɪn) *n.* a downward fold of stratified rock in which the strata slope towards a vertical axis. [C19: from SYN- + Gk *klīnein* to lean] —**syn'clinal** *adj.*

Syncom ('sɪn,kɒm) *n.* a communications satellite in stationary orbit. [C20: from *syn*(*chronous*) *com*(*munication*)]

syncopate ('sıŋkə,peıt) vb. (tr.) **1.** Music. to modify or treat (a beat, rhythm, note, etc.) by syncopation. **2.** to shorten (a word) by omitting sounds or letters from the middle. [C17: from Med. L syncopāre to omit a letter or syllable, from LL syncopa SYNCOPE] —'**synco,pator** n.

syncopation (,sıŋkə'peıʃən) n. **1.** Music. **a.** the displacement of the usual rhythmical accent away from a strong beat onto a weak beat. **b.** a note, beat, rhythm, etc., produced by syncopation. **2.** another word for **syncope** (sense 2).

syncope ('sıŋkəpı) n. **1.** a technical word for a **faint**. **2.** the omission of sounds or letters from the middle of a word. [C16: from LL syncopa, from Gk sunkopē a cutting off, from SYN- + koptein to cut] —**syncopic** (sıŋ'kɒpık) or '**syncopal** adj.

syncretism ('sıŋkrı,tızəm) n. **1.** the tendency to syncretize. **2.** the historical tendency of languages to reduce their use of inflection, as in the development of Old English into Modern English. [C17: from NL syncrētismus, from Gk sunkrētismos alliance of Cretans, from sunkrētizein to join forces (in the manner of the Cretan towns), from SYN- + Krēs a Cretan] —**syncretic** (sıŋ'krɛtık) or ,**syncre'tistic** adj. —'**syncretist** n.

syncretize or **-ise** ('sıŋkrı,taız) vb. to attempt to combine the characteristic teachings, beliefs, or practices of (differing systems of religion or philosophy). —,**syncreti'zation** or **-i'sation** n.

syndactyl (sın'dæktıl) adj. **1.** (of certain animals) having two or more digits growing fused together. ~n. **2.** an animal with this arrangement of digits. —**syn'dactylism** n.

syndesmosis (,sındɛs'məʊsıs) n., pl. **-ses** (-siːz). Anat. a type of joint in which the articulating bones are held together by a ligament of connective tissue. [C18: NL, from Gk sundein to bind together] —**syndesmotic** (,sındɛs'mɒtık) adj.

syndetic (sın'dɛtık) adj. denoting a grammatical construction in which two clauses are connected by a conjunction. [C17: from Gk sundetikos, from sundetos bound together] —**syndesis** (sın'diːsıs) n. —**syn'detically** adv.

syndic ('sındık) n. **1.** Brit. a business agent of some universities or other bodies. **2.** (in several countries) a government administrator or magistrate with varying powers. [C17: via OF from LL syndicus, from Gk sundikos defendant's advocate, from SYN- + dikē justice] —'**syndical** adj.

syndicalism ('sındıkə,lızəm) n. **1.** a revolutionary movement and theory advocating seizure of the means of production and distribution by syndicates of workers, esp. by a general strike. **2.** an economic system resulting from such action. —'**syndical** adj. —'**syndicalist** adj., n. —,**syndical'istic** adj.

syndicate n. ('sındıkıt). **1.** an association of business enterprises or individuals organized to undertake a joint project. **2.** a news agency that sells articles, photographs, etc., to a number of newspapers for simultaneous publication. **3.** any association formed to carry out an enterprise of common interest to its members. **4.** a board of syndics or the office of syndic. ~vb. ('sındı,keıt). **5.** (tr.) to sell (articles, photographs, etc.) to several newspapers for simultaneous publication. **6.** (tr.) U.S. to sell (a programme or programmes) to several local commercial stations. **7.** to form a syndicate of (people). [C17: from OF syndicat office of a SYNDIC] —,**syndi'cation** n.

syndrome ('sındrəʊm) n. **1.** Med. any combination of signs and symptoms that are indicative of a particular disease or disorder. **2.** a symptom, characteristic, or set of symptoms or characteristics indicating the existence of a condition, problem, etc. [C16: via NL from Gk sundromē, lit.: a running together, from SYN- + dramein to run] —**syndromic** (sın'drɒmık) adj.

syne or **syn** (saın) adv., prep., conj. a Scottish word for **since**. [C14: prob. rel. to OE sīth since]

synecdoche (sın'ɛkdəkı) n. a figure of speech in which a part is substituted for a whole or a whole for a part, as in 50 head of cattle for 50 cows, or the army for a soldier. [C14: via L from Gk sunekdokhē, from SYN- + ekdokhē interpretation, from dekhesthai to accept] —**synecdochic** (,sınɛk'dɒkık) or ,**synec'dochical** adj.

synecious (sı'niːʃəs) adj. a variant spelling of **synoecious**.

synecology (,sını'kɒlədʒı) n. the ecological study of communities of plants and animals. —**synecologic**

(sın,ɛkə'lɒdʒık) or **syn,eco'logical** adj. —**syn,eco'logically** adv.

syneresis or **synaeresis** (sı'nıərısıs) n. **1.** Chem. the process in which a gel contracts on standing and exudes liquid, as in the separation of whey in cheese-making. **2.** the contraction of two vowels into a diphthong. [C16: via LL from Gk sunairesis a shortening, from sunairein to draw together, from SYN- + hairein to take]

synergism ('sınə,dʒızəm, sı'nɜː-) n. the working together of two or more drugs, muscles, etc., to produce an effect greater than the sum of their individual effects. Also called: **synergy**. [C18: from NL synergismus, from Gk sunergos, from SYN- + ergon work] —,**syner'getic** adj. —**syn'ergic** adj. —**synergist** ('sınədʒıst, sı'nɜː-) n., adj.

synesis ('sınısıs) n. a grammatical construction in which the inflection or form of a word is conditioned by the meaning rather than the syntax, as for example the plural form have with the singular noun group in the sentence the group have already assembled. [via NL from Gk sunesis union, from sunienai to bring together, from SYN- + hienai to send]

synesthesia (,sınıs'θiːzıə) n. the usual U.S. spelling of **synaesthesia**.

syngamy ('sıŋgəmı) or **syngenesis** (sın'dʒɛnısıs) n. reproduction involving the fusion of a male and female haploid gamete. Also called: **sexual reproduction**. —**syngamic** (sıŋ'gæmık) or **syngamous** ('sıŋgəməs) adj.

Synge (sıŋ) n. **John Millington.** 1871–1909, Irish playwright. His plays, marked by vivid colloquial Irish speech, include Riders to the Sea (1904) and The Playboy of the Western World, produced amidst uproar at the Abbey Theatre, Dublin, in 1907.

synod ('sınəd, 'sınɒd) n. **1.** a local or special ecclesiastical council, esp. of a diocese, formally convened to discuss ecclesiastical affairs. **2.** Rare. any council, esp. for discussion. [C14: from LL synodus, from Gk sunodos, from SYN- + hodos a way] —'**synodal** adj.

synodic (sı'nɒdık) adj. relating to or involving a conjunction or two successive conjunctions of the same star, planet, or satellite: the synodic month.

synoecious or **synecious** (sı'niːʃəs) adj. (of plants) having male and female organs on the same flower or structure. [C19: SYN- + -oecious, from Gk oikion dim. of oikos house]

synonym ('sınənım) n. **1.** a word that means the same or nearly the same as another word, such as bucket and pail. **2.** a word or phrase used as another name for something, such as Hellene for a Greek. —,**syno'nymic** or ,**syno'nymical** adj. —,**syno'nymity** n.

synonymous (sı'nɒnıməs) adj. **1.** (often foll. by with) being a synonym (of). **2.** (postpositive; foll. by with) closely associated (with) or suggestive (of): his name was synonymous with greed. —**syn'onymously** adv. —**syn'onymousness** n.

synonymy (sı'nɒnımı) n., pl. **-mies. 1.** the study of synonyms. **2.** the character of being synonymous; equivalence. **3.** a list or collection of synonyms, esp. one in which their meanings are discriminated.

synopsis (sı'nɒpsıs) n., pl. **-ses** (-siːz). a brief review of a subject; summary. [C17: via LL from Gk sunopsis, from SYN- + opsis view]

synopsize or **-ise** (sı'nɒpsaız) vb. (tr.) **1.** U.S. variants of **epitomize**. **2.** U.S. & Canad. to make a synopsis of.

synoptic (sı'nɒptık) adj. **1.** of or relating to a synopsis. **2.** (often cap.) Bible. **a.** (of the Gospels of Matthew, Mark, and Luke) presenting the narrative of Christ's life, ministry, etc., from a point of view held in common by all three, and with close similarities in content, order, etc. **b.** of or relating to these three Gospels. **3.** Meteorol. concerned with the distribution of meteorological conditions over a wide area at a given time: a synoptic chart. ~n. **4.** (often cap.) Bible. **a.** any of the three synoptic Gospels. **b.** any of the authors of these. [C18: from Gk sunoptikos] —**syn'optically** adv. —**syn'optist** n.

synovia (saı'nəʊvıə, sı-) n. a transparent viscid lubricating fluid, secreted by the membrane lining joints, tendon sheaths, etc. [C17: from NL, prob. from SYN- + L ōvum egg] —**syn'ovial** adj.

synovitis (,saınəʊ'vaıtıs, ,sın-) n. inflammation of the membrane surrounding a joint. —**synovitic** (,saınəʊ'vıtık, ,sın-) adj.

synroc ('sɪn,rɒk) n. a titanium-ceramic substance that can incorporate nuclear waste in its crystals. [from *syn(thetic)* + *roc(k)*]

syntactics (sɪn'tæktɪks) n. (*functioning as sing.*) the branch of semiotics that deals with the formal properties of symbol systems; proof theory.

syntagma (sɪn'tægmə) or **syntagm** ('sɪn,tæm) n., pl. **-tagmata** (-'tægmətə) or **-tagms**. 1. a word or phrase forming a syntactic unit. 2. a systematic collection of statements or propositions. [C17: from LL, from Gk, from *suntassein* to put in order; see SYNTAX] —**syntag'matic** *adj.*

syntax ('sɪntæks) n. 1. the branch of linguistics that deals with the grammatical arrangement of words and morphemes in sentences. 2. the totality of facts about the grammatical arrangement of words in a language. 3. a systematic statement of the rules governing the grammatical arrangement of words and morphemes in a language. 4. a systematic statement of the rules governing the properly formed formulas of a logical system. [C17: from LL *syntaxis*, from Gk *suntaxis*, from *suntassein* to put in order, from SYN- + *tassein* to arrange] —**syn'tactic** or **syn'tactical** *adj.* —**syn'tactically** *adv.*

synth (sɪnθ) n. short for **synthesizer**.

synthesis ('sɪnθɪsɪs) n., pl. **-ses** (-,siːz). 1. the process of combining objects or ideas into a complex whole. 2. the combination or whole produced by such a process. 3. the process of producing a compound by a chemical reaction or series of reactions, usually from simpler starting materials. 4. *Linguistics.* the use of inflections rather than word order and function words to express the syntactic relations in a language. [C17: via L from Gk *sunthesis*, from *suntithenai* to put together, from SYN- + *tithenai* to place] —**'synthesist** n.

synthesize ('sɪnθɪ,saɪz), **synthetize** or **-sise, -tise** vb. 1. to combine or cause to combine into a whole. 2. (*tr.*) to produce by synthesis. —**synthesi'zation, syntheti'zation** or **-si'sation, -ti'sation** n.

synthesizer ('sɪnθɪ,saɪzə) n. 1. an electronic musical instrument, usually operated by means of a keyboard, in which sounds are produced by oscillators, filters, and amplifiers. 2. a person or thing that synthesizes.

synthetic (sɪn'θɛtɪk) *adj.* also **synthetical**. 1. (of a substance or material) made artificially by chemical reaction. 2. not genuine; insincere: *synthetic compassion.* 3. denoting languages, such as Latin, whose morphology is characterized by synthesis. 4. *Philosophy.* **a.** (of a proposition) having a truth-value that is not determined solely by virtue of the meanings of the words, as in *all men are arrogant.* **b.** contingent. ~n. 5. a synthetic substance or material. [C17: from NL *syntheticus*, from Gk *sunthetikos* expert in putting together, from *suntithenai* to put together; see SYNTHESIS] —**syn'thetically** *adv.*

syphilis ('sɪfɪlɪs) n. a venereal disease caused by infection with the microorganism *Treponema pallidum:* characterized by an ulcerating chancre, usually on the genitals and progressing through the lymphatic system to nearly all tissues of the body, producing serious clinical manifestations. [C18: from NL *Syphilis (sive Morbus Gallicus)* "Syphilis (or the French disease)", title of a poem (1530) by G. Fracastoro, It. physician and poet, in which a shepherd *Syphilus* is portrayed as the first victim of the disease] —**syphilitic** (,sɪfɪ'lɪtɪk) *adj.* —**'syphi,loid** *adj.*

syphon ('saɪfən) n. a variant spelling of **siphon**.

Syracuse n. 1. ('saɪrə,kjuːz) a port in SW Italy, in SE Sicily on the Ionian Sea: founded in 734 B.C. by Greeks from Corinth and taken by the Romans in 212 B.C., after a siege of three years. Pop.: 122 857 (1986). Italian name: **Siracusa**. 2. ('sɪrə,kjuːs) a city in central New York State, on Lake Onondaga: site of the capital of the Iroquois Indian federation. Pop.: 160 750 (1986 est.).

Syr Darya (*Russian* si darj'ja) n. a river in the S central Soviet Union, formed from two headstreams rising in the Tian Shan: flows generally west to the Aral Sea: the longest river in central Asia. Length: (from the source of the Naryn) 2900 km (1800 miles). Ancient name: **Jaxartes**.

Syria ('sɪrɪə) n. 1. a republic in W Asia, on the Mediterranean: ruled by the Ottoman Turks (1516–1918); made a French mandate in 1920; became independent in 1944; joined Egypt in the United Arab Republic (1958–61). Language: Arabic. Religion: Muslim majority. Currency: Syrian pound. Capital: Damascus. Pop.: 10 969 000 (1987). Area: 185 180 sq. km (71 498 sq. miles). 2. (formerly) the region between the Mediterranean, the Euphrates, the Taurus, and the Arabian Desert.

Syriac ('sɪrɪ,æk) n. a dialect of Aramaic spoken in Syria until about the 13th century A.D.

Syrian ('sɪrɪən) *adj.* 1. of or relating to Syria, its people, or their dialect of Arabic. ~n. 2. a native or inhabitant of Syria.

syringa (sɪ'rɪŋgə) n. another name for **mock orange** (sense 1) or **lilac** (sense 1). [C17: from NL, from Gk *surinx* tube, from use of its hollow stems for pipes]

syringe ('sɪrɪndʒ, sɪ'rɪndʒ) n. 1. *Med.* a hypodermic syringe or a rubber ball with a slender nozzle, for use in withdrawing or injecting fluids, cleaning wounds, etc. 2. any similar device for injecting, spraying, or extracting liquids by means of pressure or suction. ~vb. 3. (*tr.*) to cleanse, inject, or spray with a syringe. [C15: from LL, from L: SYRINX]

syringomyelia (sə,rɪŋgəʊmaɪ'iːlɪə) n. a chronic progressive disease of the spinal cord in which cavities form in the grey matter: characterized by loss of the sense of pain and temperature. [C19: *syringo-*, from Gk: SYRINX + *-myelia* from Gk *muelos* marrow] —**syringomyelic** (sə,rɪŋgəʊmaɪ'ɛlɪk) *adj.*

syrinx ('sɪrɪŋks) n., pl. **syringes** (sɪ'rɪndʒiːz) or **syrinxes**. 1. the vocal organ of a bird, situated in the lower part of the trachea. 2. (in classical Greek music) a panpipe or set of panpipes. [C17: via L from Gk *surinx* pipe] —**syringeal** (sɪ'rɪndʒɪəl) *adj.*

Syrinx ('sɪrɪŋks) n. *Greek myth.* a nymph who was changed into a reed to save her from the amorous pursuit of Pan. From this reed Pan then fashioned his musical pipes.

syrup ('sɪrəp) n. 1. a solution of sugar dissolved in water and often flavoured with fruit juice: used for sweetening fruit, etc. 2. any of various thick sweet liquids prepared for cooking or table use from molasses, sugars, etc. 3. *Inf.* cloying sentimentality. 4. a liquid medicine containing a sugar solution for flavouring or preservation. ~Also: **sirup**. [C15: from Med. L *syrupus*, from Ar. *sharāb* a drink, from *shariba* to drink] —**'syrupy** *adj.*

syssarcosis (,sɪsɑː'kəʊsɪs) n., pl. **-ses** (-siːz). *Anat.* the union or articulation of bones by muscle. [C17: from NL, from Gk *sussarkōsis*, from *sus-* SYN- + *sarkoun* to become fleshy, from *sarx* flesh] —**syssarcotic** (,sɪsɑː'kɒtɪk) *adj.*

systaltic (sɪ'stæltɪk) *adj.* (esp. of the action of the heart) of, relating to, or characterized by alternate contractions and dilations; pulsating. [C17: from LL *systalticus*, from Gk, from *sustellein* to contract, from SYN- + *stellein* to place]

system ('sɪstəm) n. 1. a group or combination of interrelated, interdependent, or interacting elements forming a collective entity; a methodical or coordinated assemblage of parts, facts, etc. 2. any scheme of classification or arrangement. 3. a network of communications, transportation, or distribution. 4. a method or complex of methods: *he has a perfect system at roulette.* 5. orderliness; an ordered manner. 6. **the system.** (*often cap.*) society seen as an environment exploiting, restricting, and repressing individuals. 7. an organism considered as a functioning entity. 8. any of various bodily parts or structures that are anatomically or physiologically related: *the digestive system.* 9. one's physiological or psychological constitution: *get it out of your system.* 10. any assembly of electronic, mechanical, etc., components with interdependent functions, usually forming a self-contained unit: *a brake system.* 11. a group of celestial bodies that are associated as a result of natural laws, esp. gravitational attraction: *the solar system.* 12. a point of view or doctrine used to interpret a branch of knowledge. 13. *Mineralogy.* one of a group of divisions into which crystals may be placed on the basis of the lengths and inclinations of their axes. 14. *Geol.* a stratigraphical unit for the rock strata formed during a period of geological time. [C17: from F, from LL *systēma*, from Gk *sustēma*, from SYN- + *histanai* to cause to stand]

systematic (,sɪstɪ'mætɪk) *adj.* 1. characterized by the use of order and planning; methodical: *a systematic administrator.* 2. comprising or resembling a system: *systematic theology.* 3. Also: **systematical**. *Biol.* of or relating to taxonomic classification. —**,system'atically** *adv.* —**'systema,tism** n. —**'systematist** n.

systematics (ˌsɪstɪˈmætɪks) *n.* (*functioning as sing.*) the study of systems and the principles of classification and nomenclature.

systematize (ˈsɪstɪməˌtaɪz), **systemize** *or* **-tise, -mise** *vb.* (*tr.*) to arrange in a system. —ˌsystematiˈzation, **-iˈsation** *or* ˌsystemiˈzation, **-iˈsation** *n.* —ˈsystemaˌtizer, **-iser** *or* ˈsystemˌizer, **-ˌiser** *n.*

Système International d'Unités (*French* sistɛm ɛtɛrnasjɔnal dynite) *n.* the International System of units. See **SI unit.**

systemic (sɪˈstɛmɪk, -ˈstiː-) *adj.* **1.** another word for **systematic** (senses 1, 2). **2.** *Physiol.* (of a poison, disease, etc.) affecting the entire body. **3.** (of an insecticide, fungicide, etc.) designed to be absorbed by a plant into its tissues. ~*n.* **4.** a systemic insecticide, fungicide, etc. —sysˈtemically *adv.*

systems analysis *n.* the analysis of the requirements of a task and the expression of these in a form that permits the assembly of computer hardware and software to perform the task. —**systems analyst** *n.*

systems engineering *n.* the branch of engineering, based on systems analysis and information theory, concerned with the design of integrated systems.

systole (ˈsɪstəlɪ) *n.* contraction of the heart, during which blood is pumped into the aorta and the arteries. Cf. **diastole.** [C16: via LL from Gk *sustolē*, from *sustellein* to contract; see SYSTALTIC] —**systolic** (sɪˈstɒlɪk) *adj.*

Syzran (*Russian* ˈsizrənj) *n.* a port in the W central Soviet Union, in Kuibyshev Region on the Volga River: oil refining. Pop.: 169 000 (1981 est.).

syzygy (ˈsɪzɪdʒɪ) *n., pl.* **-gies. 1.** either of the two positions (conjunction or opposition) of a celestial body when sun, earth, and the body lie in a straight line: *the moon is at syzygy when full.* **2.** *Rare.* any pair, usually of opposites. [C17: from LL, from Gk *suzugia*, from *suzugos* yoked together, from SYN- + *zugon* a yoke] —**syzygial** (sɪˈzɪdʒɪəl), **syzygetic** (ˌsɪzɪˈdʒɛtɪk), *or* **syzygal** (ˈsɪzɪgªl) *adj.* —ˌsyzyˈgetically *adv.*

Szabadka (ˈsɔbɔtkɔ) *n.* the Hungarian name for **Subotica.**

Szczecin (*Polish* ˈʃtʃɛtʃin) *n.* a port in NW Poland, on the River Oder: the busiest Polish port and leading coal exporter; shipbuilding. Pop.: 387 659 (1980 est.). German name: **Stettin.**

Szechwan (ˈseɪˈtʃwɑːn) *n.* a variant transliteration of the Chinese name for **Sichuan.**

Szeged (*Hungarian* ˈsɛgɛd) *n.* an industrial city in S Hungary, on the Tisza River. Pop.: 186 000 (1986 est.).

Szell (sɛl) *n.* **George.** 1897–1970, U.S. conductor, born in Hungary.

Szombathely (*Hungarian* ˈsombɔthɛj) *n.* a city in W Hungary: site of the Roman capital of Pannonia. Pop.: 85 251 (1982 est.).

Szymanowski (*Polish* ʃimaˈnɔfski) *n.* **Karol** (ˈkarɔl). 1882–1937, Polish composer, whose works include the opera *King Roger* (1926), two violin concertos, symphonies, piano music, and songs.

T

t *or* **T** (tiː) *n., pl.* **t's, T's,** *or* **Ts.** **1.** the 20th letter of the English alphabet. **2.** a speech sound represented by this letter. **3.** something shaped like a T. **4. to a T.** in every detail; perfectly.

t *symbol for:* **1.** *Statistics.* distribution. **2.** tonne(s). **3.** troy (weight).

T *symbol for:* **1.** absolute temperature. **2.** surface tension. **3.** tera-. **4.** tesla. **5.** *Chem.* tritium.

t. *abbrev. for:* **1.** *Commerce.* tare. **2.** teaspoon(ful). **3.** temperature. **4.** *Music.* tempo. **5.** *Music.* Also: **T.** tenor. **6.** *Grammar.* tense. **7.** ton(s). **8.** transitive.

't *contraction of* it.

ta (taː) *interj. Brit. inf.* thank you. [C18: imit. of baby talk]

Ta the chemical symbol *for* tantalum.

TA (in Britain) *abbrev. for* Territorial Army (now superseded by **TAVR**).

TAA *abbrev. for* Trans-Australia Airlines.

Taal[1] (taːl) *n.* **the.** another name for **Afrikaans.** [Du.: speech]

Taal[2] (taːˈaːl) *n.* an active volcano in the Philippines, on S Luzon on an island in the centre of **Lake Taal.** Height: 300 m (984 ft.). Area of lake: 243 sq. km (94 sq. miles).

tab[1] (tæb) *n.* **1.** a small flap of material, esp. one on a garment for decoration or for fastening to a button. **2.** any similar flap, such as a piece of paper attached to a file for identification. **3.** *Brit. mil.* the insignia on the collar of a staff officer. **4.** *Chiefly U.S. & Canad.* a bill, esp. for a meal or drinks. **5. keep tabs on.** *Inf.* to keep a watchful eye on. ~*vb.* **tabbing, tabbed.** **6.** (*tr.*) to supply with a tab or tabs. [C17: from ?]

tab[2] (tæb) *n.* short for **tabulator** or **tablet.**

TAB *abbrev. for:* **1.** *Austral. & N.Z.* Totalizator Agency Board. **2.** typhoid-paratyphoid A and B (vaccine).

tabard (ˈtæbəd) *n.* a sleeveless or short-sleeved jacket, esp. one worn by a herald, bearing a coat of arms, or by a knight over his armour. [C13: from OF *tabart*, from ?]

tabaret (ˈtæbərɪt) *n.* a hard-wearing fabric of silk or similar cloth with stripes of satin or moire, used esp. for upholstery. [C19: ?from TABBY]

Tabasco[1] (təˈbæskəʊ) *n. Trademark.* a very hot red sauce made from matured capsicums.

Tabasco[2] (*Spanish* taˈβasko) *n.* a state in SE Mexico, on the Gulf of Campeche: mostly flat and marshy with extensive jungles; hot and humid climate. Capital: Villahermosa. Pop.: 1 149 756 (1980). Area: 24 661 sq. km (9520 sq. miles).

tabby (ˈtæbɪ) *adj.* **1.** (esp. of cats) brindled with dark stripes or wavy markings on a lighter background. **2.** having a wavy or striped pattern, particularly in colours of grey and brown. ~*n., pl.* **-bies.** **3.** a tabby cat. **4.** any female domestic cat. **5.** a fabric with a watered pattern, esp. silk or taffeta. [C17: from OF *tabis* silk cloth, from Ar. *al-'attabiya*, lit.: the quarter of (Prince) 'Attab, the part of Baghdad where the fabric was first made]

tabernacle (ˈtæbəˌnækəl) *n.* **1.** (*often cap.*) *Old Testament.* **a.** the portable sanctuary in which the ancient Israelites carried the Ark of the Covenant. **b.** the Jewish Temple. **2.** any place of worship that is not called a church. **3.** *R.C. Church.* a receptacle in which the Blessed Sacrament is kept. **4.** *Chiefly R.C. Church.* a canopied niche. **5.** *Naut.* a strong framework for holding the foot of a mast, allowing it to be swung down to pass under low bridges, etc. [C13: from L *tabernāculum* a tent, from *taberna* a hut] —**taberˈnacular** *adj.*

tabes (ˈteɪbiːz) *n., pl.* **tabes.** **1.** a wasting of a bodily organ or part. **2.** short for **tabes dorsalis.** [C17: from L: a wasting away] —**tabetic** (təˈbɛtɪk) *adj.*

tabescent (təˈbɛsənt) *adj.* **1.** progressively emaciating; wasting away. **2.** of, relating to, or having tabes. [C19: from L *tābēscere*, from TABES] —**taˈbescence** *n.*

tabes dorsalis (dɔːˈsaːlɪs) *n.* a former type of late syphilis that attacks the spinal cord causing degeneration of the nerve fibres, paralysis of the leg muscles, acute abdominal pain, etc. [NL, lit.: tabes of the back]

tabla (ˈtʌblə, ˈtɑːbluː) *n.* a musical instrument of India

consisting of a pair of drums whose pitches can be varied. [Hindu, from Ar. *tabla* drum]

tablature (ˈtæblətʃə) *n. Music.* any of a number of forms of musical notation, esp. for playing the lute, consisting of letters and signs indicating rhythm and fingering. [C16: from F, ult. from L *tabulātum* wooden floor, from *tabula* a plank]

table (ˈteɪbəl) *n.* **1.** a flat horizontal slab or board supported by one or more legs. **2. a.** such a slab or board on which food is served. **b.** (*as modifier*): *table linen.* **3.** food as served in a particular household, etc.: *a good table.* **4.** such a piece of furniture specially designed for any of various purposes: *a bird table.* **5. a.** a company of persons assembled for a meal, game, etc. **b.** (*as modifier*): *table talk.* **6.** any flat or level area, such as a plateau. **7.** a rectangular panel set below or above the face of a wall. **8.** *Archit.* another name for **string course. 9.** any of various flat surfaces, as an upper horizontal facet of a cut gem. **10.** *Music.* the sounding board of a violin, guitar, etc. **11. a.** an arrangement of words, numbers, or signs, usually in parallel columns. **b.** See **multiplication table. 12.** a tablet on which laws were inscribed by the ancient Romans, the Hebrews, etc. **13. turn the tables.** to cause a complete reversal of circumstances. **14. under the table. a.** (**under-the-table** *when prenominal*) done illicitly and secretly. **b.** *Sl.* drunk. ~*vb.* (*tr.*) **15.** to place on a table. **16.** *Brit.* to submit (a bill, etc.) for consideration by a legislative body. **17.** *U.S.* to suspend discussion of (a bill, etc.) indefinitely. **18.** to enter in or form into a list. [C12: via OF from L *tabula* a writing tablet]

tableau (ˈtæbləʊ) *n., pl.* **-leaux** (-ləʊ, -ləʊz) *or* **-leaus. 1.** See **tableau vivant. 2.** a pause on stage when all the performers briefly freeze in position. **3.** any dramatic group or scene. [C17: from F, from OF *tablel* a picture, dim. of TABLE]

tableau vivant *French.* (tablo ˌvivɑ̃) *n., pl.* **tableaux vivants** (tablo vivɑ̃). a representation of a scene by a person or group posed silent and motionless. [C19, lit.: living picture]

Table Bay *n.* the large bay on which Cape Town is situated, on the SW coast of South Africa.

tablecloth (ˈteɪbəlˌklɒθ) *n.* a cloth for covering the top of a table, esp. during meals.

table d'hôte (ˈtɑːbəl ˈdəʊt) *adj.* **1.** (of a meal) consisting of a set number of courses with limited choice of dishes offered at a fixed price. Cf. **à la carte.** ~*n., pl.* **tables d'hôte** (ˈtɑːbəlz ˈdəʊt). **2.** a table d'hôte meal or menu. [C17: from F, lit.: the host's table]

tableland (ˈteɪbəlˌlænd) *n.* flat elevated land.

table licence *n.* a licence authorizing the sale of alcoholic drinks with meals only.

Table Mountain *n.* a mountain in SW South Africa, in Cape Province overlooking Cape Town and Table Bay: flat-topped and steep-sided. Height: 1087 m (3567 ft.).

tablespoon (ˈteɪbəlˌspuːn) *n.* **1.** a spoon, larger than a dessertspoon, used for serving food, etc. **2.** Also called: **tablespoonful.** the amount contained in such a spoon. **3.** a unit of capacity used in cooking, etc., equal to half a fluid ounce.

tablet (ˈtæblɪt) *n.* **1.** a pill made of a compressed medicinal substance. **2.** a flattish cake of some substance, such as soap. **3.** a slab of stone, wood, etc., esp. one used for inscriptions. **4. a.** a rigid sheet, as of bark, etc., used for similar purposes. **b.** (*often pl.*) a set of these fastened together. **5.** a pad of writing paper. **6.** *Scot.* a sweet made from butter, sugar, and condensed milk, usually shaped into flat oblong cakes. [C14: from OF *tablete* a little table, from L *tabula* a board]

table tennis *n.* a miniature form of tennis played on a table with bats and a hollow ball.

table-turning *n.* the movement of a table attributed by spiritualists to the power of spirits.

tableware (ˈteɪbəlˌwɛə) *n.* articles such as dishes, plates, knives, forks, etc., used at meals.

tabloid ('tæblɔɪd) *n.* **1.** a newspaper with pages about 30 cm (12 inches) by 40 cm (16 inches), usually with many photographs and a concise and often sensational style. **2.** something in a condensed or summarized form. [C20: from earlier *Tabloid*, a trademark for a medicine in tablet form]

taboo *or* **tabu** (tə'buː) *adj.* **1.** forbidden or disapproved of: *taboo words.* **2.** (in Polynesia) marked off as sacred and forbidden. ~*n.*, *pl.* **-boos** *or* **-bus.** **3.** any prohibition resulting from social or other conventions. **4.** ritual restriction or prohibition, esp. of something that is considered holy or unclean. ~*vb.* **5.** (*tr.*) to place under a taboo. [C18: from Tongan *tabu*]

tabor *or* **tabour** ('teɪbə) *n.* a small drum used esp. in the Middle Ages, struck with one hand while the other held a pipe. [C13: from OF *tabour*, ?from Persian *tabîr*]

Tabor ('teɪbə) *n.* **Mount.** a mountain in N Israel, near Nazareth: traditionally regarded as the mountain where the Transfiguration took place. Height: 588 m (1929 ft.).

taboret *or* **tabouret** ('tæbərɪt) *n.* **1.** a low stool. **2.** a frame for stretching out cloth while it is being embroidered. **3.** a small tabor. [C17: from F *tabouret*, dim. of TABOR]

Tabriz (tæ'briːz) *n.* a city in NW Iran: an ancient city, situated in a volcanic region of hot springs; university (1947); carpet manufacturing. Pop.: 994 377 (1986). Ancient name: **Tauris** ('tɔːrɪs).

tabular ('tæbjʊlə) *adj.* **1.** arranged in systematic or table form. **2.** calculated from or by means of a table. **3.** like a table in form; flat. [C17: from L *tabulāris* concerning boards, from *tabula* a board] —'**tabularly** *adv.*

tabula rasa ('tæbjʊlə 'rɑːsə) *n.*, *pl.* **tabulae rasae** ('tæbjuːliː 'rɑːsiː). **1.** the mind in its uninformed original state. **2.** an opportunity for a fresh start; clean slate. [L: a scraped tablet]

tabulate *vb.* ('tæbjʊˌleɪt). (*tr.*) **1.** to set out, arrange, or write in tabular form. **2.** to form or cut with a flat surface. ~*adj.* ('tæbjʊlɪt, -ˌleɪt). **3.** having a flat surface. [C18: from L *tabula* a board] —'**tabulable** *adj.* —ˌtabu'lation *n.*

tabulator ('tæbjʊˌleɪtə) *n.* **1.** a device for setting the stops that locate the column margins on a typewriter. **2.** *Computers.* a machine that reads data from one medium, such as punched cards, producing lists, tabulations, or totals.

tacamahac ('tækəməˌhæk) *or* **tacmahack** *n.* **1.** any of several strong-smelling resinous gums used in ointments, incense, etc. **2.** any tree yielding this resin. [C16: from Sp. *tacamahaca*, from Nahuatl *tecomahca* aromatic resin]

tacet ('teɪsɛt, 'tæs-) *vb.* (*intr.*) (on a musical score) a direction indicating that a particular instrument or singer does not take part. [C18: from L: it is silent, from *tacēre* to be quiet]

tacheometer (ˌtækɪ'ɒmɪtə) *or* **tachymeter** *n.* *Surveying.* a type of theodolite designed for the rapid measurement of distances, elevations, and directions. —ˌtache'ometry *n.*

tachisme ('tɑːʃɪzəm) *n.* a type of action painting in which haphazard dabs and blots of colour are treated as a means of unconscious expression. [C20: F, from *tache* stain]

tachistoscope (tə'kɪstəˌskəʊp) *n.* an instrument for displaying visual images for very brief intervals, usually a fraction of a second. [C20: from Gk *takhistos* swiftest + -SCOPE] —**tachistoscopic** (tæˌkɪstə'skɒpɪk) *adj.*

tacho- *combining form.* speed: *tachograph; tachometer.* [from Gk *takhos*]

tachograph ('tækəˌgrɑːf) *n.* a tachometer that produces a record (**tachogram**) of its readings, esp. a device for recording the speed of and distance covered by a vehicle.

tachometer (tæ'kɒmɪtə) *n.* any device for measuring speed, esp. the rate of revolution of a shaft. Tachometers are often fitted to cars to indicate the number of revolutions per minute of the engine. —ta'chometry *n.*

tachy- *or* **tacheo-** *combining form.* swift or accelerated: *tachyon.* [from Gk *takhus* swift]

tachycardia (ˌtækɪ'kɑːdɪə) *n.* abnormally rapid beating of the heart.

tachygraphy (tæ'kɪgrəfɪ) *n.* shorthand, esp. as used in ancient Rome or Greece.

tachymeter (tæ'kɪmɪtə) *n.* another name for **tacheometer.**

tachyon ('tækɪˌɒn) *n.* *Physics.* a hypothetical elementary particle capable of travelling faster than the velocity of light. [C20: from TACHY- + -ON]

tachyphylaxis (ˌtækɪfɪ'læksɪs) *n.* very rapid development of tolerance or immunity to the effects of a drug. [NL, from TACHY- + *phylaxis* on the model of *prophylaxis*; see PROPHYLACTIC]

tacit ('tæsɪt) *adj.* implied or inferred without direct expression; understood: *a tacit agreement.* [C17: from L *tacitus*, p.p. of *tacēre* to be silent] —'**tacitly** *adv.*

taciturn ('tæsɪˌtɜːn) *adj.* habitually silent, reserved, or uncommunicative. [C18: from L *taciturnus*, from *tacēre* to be silent] —ˌtaci'turnity *n.* —'**taci**ˌ**turnly** *adv.*

Tacitus ('tæsɪtəs) *n.* **Publius Cornelius** ('pʌblɪəs kɔː'niːljəs). ?55–?120 A.D., Roman historian and orator, famous as a prose stylist. His works include the *Histories*, dealing with the period 68–96, and the *Annals*, dealing with the period 14–68.

tack[1] (tæk) *n.* **1.** a short sharp-pointed nail, with a large flat head. **2.** *Brit.* a long loose temporary stitch used in dressmaking, etc. **3.** See **tailor's-tack.** **4.** a temporary fastening. **5.** stickiness. **6.** *Naut.* the heading of a vessel sailing to windward, stated in terms of the side of the sail against which the wind is pressing. **7.** *Naut.* **a.** a course sailed with the wind blowing from forward of the beam. **b.** one such course or a zigzag pattern of such courses. **8.** *Naut.* **a.** a sheet for controlling the weather clew of a course. **b.** the weather clew itself. **9.** *Naut.* the forward lower clew of a fore-and-aft sail. **10.** a course of action or policy. **11. on the wrong tack.** under a false impression. ~*vb.* **12.** (*tr.*) to secure by a tack or tacks. **13.** *Brit.* to sew (something) with long loose temporary stitches. **14.** (*tr.*) to attach or append. **15.** *Naut.* to change the heading of (a sailing vessel) to the opposite tack. **16.** *Naut.* to steer (a sailing vessel) on alternate tacks. **17.** (*intr.*) *Naut.* (of a sailing vessel) to proceed on a different tack or to alternate tacks. **18.** (*intr.*) to follow a zigzag route; keep changing one's course of action. [C14 *tak* fastening, nail] —'**tacker** *n.*

tack[2] (tæk) *n.* riding harness for horses, such as saddles, bridles, etc. [C20: shortened from TACKLE]

tack hammer *n.* a light hammer for driving tacks.

tackies ('tækɪz) *pl. n.*, *sing.* **tacky.** *S. African inf.* tennis shoes or plimsolls. [C20: prob. from TACKY[1], from their nonslip rubber soles]

tackle ('tækəl) *n.* **1.** an arrangement of ropes and pulleys designed to lift heavy weights. **2.** the equipment required for a particular occupation, etc. **3.** *Naut.* the halyards and other running rigging aboard a vessel. **4.** *Sport.* a physical challenge to an opponent, as to prevent his progress with the ball. ~*vb.* **5.** (*tr.*) to undertake (a task, etc.). **6.** (*tr.*) to confront (esp. an opponent) with a difficult proposition. **7.** *Sport.* to challenge (an opponent) with a tackle. [C13: rel. to MLow G *takel* ship's rigging] —'**tackler** *n.*

tacky[1] ('tækɪ) *adj.* **tackier, tackiest.** slightly sticky or adhesive. [C18: from TACK[1] (in the sense: stickiness)] —'**tackily** *adv.* —'**tackiness** *n.*

tacky[2] ('tækɪ) *adj.* **tackier, tackiest.** *Inf.* **1.** shabby or shoddy. **2.** ostentatious and vulgar. **3.** *U.S.* (of a person) dowdy; seedy. [C19: from dialect *tacky* an inferior horse, from ?] —'**tackiness** *n.*

Tacna-Arica (*Spanish* 'taknaa'rika) *n.* a coastal desert region of W South America, long disputed by Chile and Peru: divided in 1929 into the Peruvian department of Tacna and the Chilean department of Arica.

tacnode ('tækˌnəʊd) *n.* another name for **osculation** (sense 1). [C19: from L *tactus* touch (from *tangere* to touch) + NODE]

Tacoma (tə'kəʊmə) *n.* a port in W Washington, on Puget Sound: industrial centre. Pop.: 158 950 (1986 est.).

tact (tækt) *n.* **1.** a sense of what is fitting and considerate in dealing with others, so as to avoid giving offence. **2.** skill in handling difficult situations; diplomacy. [C17: from L *tactus* a touching, from *tangere* to touch] —'**tactful** *adj.* —'**tactfulness** *n.* —'**tactless** *adj.* —'**tactlessness** *n.*

tactic ('tæktɪk) *n.* a piece of tactics; tactical move. See also **tactics.**

-tactic *adj. combining form.* having a specified kind of pattern or arrangement or having an orientation determined by a specified force: *syndiotactic; phototactic.* [from Gk *taktikos* relating to order; see TACTICS]

tactical ('tæktɪkᵊl) *adj.* **1.** of, relating to, or employing tactics: *a tactical error.* **2.** (of missiles, bombing, etc.) for use in or supporting limited military operations; short-range. **3.** skilful, adroit, or diplomatic. — '**tactically** *adv.*
tactical voting *n.* (in an election) the practice of casting one's vote not for the party of one's choice but for the second strongest contender in a constituency in order to defeat the likeliest winner.
tactics ('tæktɪks) *pl. n.* **1.** (*functioning as sing.*) *Mil.* the art and science of the detailed direction and control of movement of forces in battle to achieve an aim or task. **2.** the manoeuvres used to achieve an aim or task. **3.** plans followed to achieve a particular short-term aim. [C17: from NL *tactica*, from Gk, from *taktikos* concerning arrangement, from *taktos* arranged (for battle), from *tassein* to arrange] — **tac'tician** *n.*
tactile ('tæktaɪl) *adj.* **1.** of, relating to, affecting, or having a sense of touch. **2.** *Now rare.* capable of being touched; tangible. [C17: from L *tactilis*, from *tangere* to touch] — **tactility** (tæk'tɪlɪtɪ) *n.*
Tadmor ('tædmɔː) *n.* the biblical name for **Palmyra.**
tadpole ('tæd,pəʊl) *n.* the aquatic larva of frogs, toads, etc., which develops from a limbless tailed form with external gills into a form with internal gills, limbs, and a reduced tail. [C15 *taddepol*, from *tadde* toad + *pol* head]
Tadzhik Soviet Socialist Republic *n.* an administrative division of the S central Soviet Union: mountainous. Capital: Dushanbe. Pop.: 4 807 000 (1987). Area: 143 100 sq. km (55 240 sq. miles). Also called: **Tadzhikistan** (taː,dʒɪkɪ'staːn).
taedium vitae ('tiːdɪəm 'viːtaɪ, 'vaɪtɪ:) *n.* the feeling that life is boring and dull. [L, lit.: weariness of life]
Taegu (tɛ'guː) *n.* a city in SE South Korea: textile and agricultural trading centre. Pop.: 2 030 649 (1985).
Taejon (tɛ'dʒɒn) *n.* a city in W South Korea: market centre of an agricultural region. Pop.: 866 303 (1985).
tael (teɪl) *n.* **1.** a unit of weight, used in the Far East. **2.** (formerly) a Chinese monetary unit. [C16: from Port., from Malay *tahil* weight, ?from Sansk.]
ta'en (teɪn) *vb.* a Scot. or poetic contraction of **taken.**
taenia *or U.S.* **tenia** ('tiːnɪə) *n., pl.* **-niae** (-nɪ,iː). **1.** (in ancient Greece) a headband. **2.** *Archit.* the fillet between the architrave and frieze of a Doric entablature. **3.** *Anat.* any bandlike structure or part. **4.** any of a genus of tapeworms. [C16: via L from Gk *tainia* narrow strip]
taeniasis *or U.S.* **teniasis** (tiː'naɪəsɪs) *n. Pathol.* infestation with tapeworms of the genus *Taenia.*
taffeta ('tæfɪtə) *n.* a thin crisp lustrous plain-weave fabric of silk, rayon, etc., used esp. for women's clothes. [C14: from Med. L *taffata*, from Persian *tāftah* spun, from *tāftan* to spin]
taffrail ('tæf,reɪl) *n. Naut.* a rail at the stern of a vessel. [C19: changed from earlier *tafferel*, from Du. *taffereel* panel (hence applied to the part of a vessel decorated with carved panels), from *tafel* table]
Taffy ('tæfɪ) *n., pl.* **-fies.** a slang word or nickname for a **Welshman.** [C17: from the supposed Welsh pronunciation of *Davy* (from *David*, Welsh *Dafydd*), a common Welsh Christian name]
tafia *or* **taffia** ('tæfɪə) *n.* a type of rum, esp. from Guyana or the West Indies. [C18: from F, from West Indian Creole, prob. from RATAFIA]
Tafilelt (tæ'fiːlɛlt) *or* **Tafilalet** (,tæfɪ'laːlɛt) *n.* an oasis in SE Morocco, the largest in the Sahara. Area: about 1300 sq. km (500 sq. miles).
Taft (tæft) *n.* **William Howard.** 1857–1930, U.S. statesman; 27th president of the U.S. (1909–13).
tag¹ (tæg) *n.* **1.** a piece of paper, leather, etc., for attaching to something as a mark or label: *a price tag.* **2.** a small piece of material hanging from a part or piece. **3.** a point of metal, etc., at the end of a cord or lace. **4.** an epithet or verbal appendage, the refrain of a song, the moral of a fable, etc. **5.** a brief quotation. **6.** an ornamental flourish. **7.** the tip of an animal's tail. **8.** a matted lock of wool or hair. ~*vb.* **tagging, tagged.** (*mainly tr.*) **9.** to mark with a tag. **10.** to add or append as a tag. **11.** to supply (prose or blank verse) with rhymes. **12.** (*intr.*; usually foll. by *on* or *along*) to trail (behind). **13.** to name or call (someone something). **14.** to cut the tags of wool or hair from (an animal). [C15: from ?]
tag² (tæg) *n.* **1.** Also called: **tig.** a children's game in which one player chases the others in an attempt to catch one of them who will then become the chaser. **2.** the act

of tagging one's partner in tag wrestling. **3.** (*modifier*) denoting a wrestling contest between two teams of two wrestlers, in which only one from each team may be in the ring at one time. The contestant outside the ring may change places with his team-mate inside the ring after touching his hand. ~*vb.* **tagging, tagged.** (*tr.*) **4.** to catch (another child) in the game of tag. **5.** (in tag wrestling) to touch the hand of (one's partner). [C18: ?from TAG¹]
Tagalog (tə'gɑːlɒg) *n.* **1.** (*pl.* **-logs** *or* **-log**). a member of a people of the Philippines. **2.** the language of this people. ~*adj.* **3.** of or relating to this people or their language.
Taganrog (*Russian* təgan'rɔk) *n.* a port in the S Soviet Union, on the **Gulf of Taganrog** (an inlet of the Sea of Azov): founded in 1698 as a naval base and fortress by Peter the Great: industrial centre. Pop.: 295 000 (1987).
tag end *n.* **1.** *Chiefly U.S. & Canad.* the last part of something. **2.** a loose end of cloth, thread, etc.
tagetes (tæ'dʒiːtiːz) *n., pl.* **-tes.** any of a genus of plants with yellow or orange flowers, including the French and African marigolds. [from NL, from *Tages*, an Etruscan god]
tagliatelle (,tæljə'tɛlɪ) *n.* a form of pasta made in narrow strips. [It., from *tagliare* to cut]
Tagore (tə'gɔː) *n.* **Rabindranath** (rə'biːndrə,naːt). 1861–1941, Indian poet and philosopher. His verse collections, written in Bengali and English, include *Gitanjali* (1910; 1912): Nobel prize for literature 1913.
Tagus ('teɪgəs) *n.* a river in SW Europe, rising in E central Spain and flowing west to the border with Portugal, then southwest to the Atlantic at Lisbon: the longest river of the Iberian Peninsula. Length: 1007 km (626 miles). Portuguese name: **Tejo.** Spanish name: **Tajo.**
Tahiti (tə'hiːtɪ) *n.* an island in the S Pacific, in the Windward group of the Society Islands: the largest and most important island in French Polynesia; became a French protectorate in 1842 and a colony in 1880. Capital: Papeete. Pop.: 116 000 (1983 est.). Area: 1005 sq. km (388 sq. miles). — **Tahitian** (tə'hiːtɪən, tə'hiːʃɪən) *adj., n.*
Tahoe (tə'həʊ, 'teɪ-) *n.* **Lake.** a lake between E California and W Nevada, in the Sierra Nevada Mountains at an altitude of 1899 m (6229 ft.). Area: about 520 sq. km (200 sq. miles).
tahr *or* **thar** (taː) *n.* any of several goatlike mammals of S and SW Asia, having a shaggy coat and curved horns. [from Nepali *thār*]
tahsil (tə'siːl) *n.* an administrative division in certain states in India. [Urdu, from Ar.: collection]
Tai (taɪ) *adj., n.* a variant spelling of **Thai.**
taiaha ('taɪə,haː) *n. N.Z.* a carved weapon in the form of a staff, now used in Maori ceremonial oratory. [from Maori]
t'ai chi ch'uan ('taɪ dʒiː 'tʃwaːn) *n.* a Chinese system of callisthenics characterized by coordinated and rhythmic movements. Often shortened to **t'ai chi** ('taɪ 'dʒiː). [Chinese, lit.: great art of boxing]
Taichung *or* **T'ai-chung** ('taɪ'tʃʊŋ) *n.* a city in the W Republic of China (Taiwan): commercial centre of an agricultural region. Pop.: 607 738 (1981 est.).
taiga ('taɪgɑː) *n.* the coniferous forests extending across much of subarctic North America and Eurasia. [from Russian, of Turkic origin]
taihoa ('taɪhəʊə) *sentence substitute. N.Z.* hold on! no hurry!
tail¹ (teɪl) *n.* **1.** the rear part of the vertebrate body that contains an elongation of the vertebral column, esp. forming a flexible appendage. **2.** anything resembling such an appendage; the bottom, lowest, or rear part. **3.** the last part or parts: *the tail of the storm.* **4.** the rear part of an aircraft including the fin, tailplane, and control surfaces. **5.** *Astron.* the luminous stream of gas and dust particles driven from the head of a comet when close to the sun. **6.** the rear portion of a bomb, rocket, missile, etc., usually fitted with guiding or stabilizing vanes. **7.** a line of people or things. **8.** a long braid or tress of hair: *a pigtail.* **9.** a final short line in a stanza. **10.** *Inf.* a person employed to follow and spy upon another. **11.** an informal word for **buttocks.** **12.** *Taboo sl.* **a.** the female genitals. **b.** a woman considered sexually (esp. in **piece of tail, bit of tail**). **13.** the foot of a page. **14.** the lower end of a pool or part of a stream. **15.** *Inf.* the course or track of a fleeing person or animal. **16.** (*modifier*) coming from or situated in the rear: *a tail wind.* **17. turn tail.** to run away;

escape. **18. with one's tail between one's legs.** in a state of utter defeat or confusion. ~*vb.* **19.** to form or cause to form the tail. **20.** to remove the tail of (an animal). **21.** (*tr.*) to remove the stalk of. **22.** (*tr.*) to connect (objects, ideas, etc.) together by or as if by the tail. **23.** (*tr.*) *Inf.* to follow stealthily. **24.** (*intr.*) (of a vessel) to assume a specified position, as when at a mooring. **25.** to build the end of (a brick, joist, etc.) into a wall or (of a brick, etc.) to have one end built into a wall. ~See also **tail off, tail out, tails.** [OE *tægel*] —'**tailless** *adj.*

tail[2] (teɪl) *Law.* ~*n.* **1.** the limitation of an estate or interest to a person and the heirs of his body. ~*adj.* **2.** (*immediately postpositive*) limited in this way. [C15: from OF *taille* a division; see TAILOR] —'**tailless** *adj.*

tailback ('teɪl,bæk) *n.* a queue of traffic stretching back from an obstruction.

tailboard ('teɪl,bɔːd) *n.* a board at the rear of a lorry, etc., that can be removed or let down.

tail coat *n.* **1.** a man's black coat having a horizontal cut over the hips and a tapering tail with a vertical slit up to the waist. **2.** a cutaway frock coat, part of morning dress.

tail covert *n.* any of the covert feathers of a bird covering the bases of the tail feathers.

tail end *n.* the last, endmost, or final part.

tailgate ('teɪl,geɪt) *n.* **1.** another name for **tailboard.** ~*vb.* **2.** to drive very close behind (a vehicle).

tail gate *n.* a gate that is used to control the flow of water at the lower end of a lock.

tailing ('teɪlɪŋ) *n.* the part of a beam, rafter, projecting brick, etc., embedded in a wall.

tailings ('teɪlɪŋz) *pl. n.* waste left over after certain processes, such as from an ore-crushing plant or in milling grain.

taillight ('teɪl,laɪt) *or* **taillamp** *n.* the U.S. and Canad. names for **rear light.**

tail off *or* **away** *vb.* (*adv.; usually intr.*) to decrease or cause to decrease in quantity, degree, etc., esp. gradually.

tailor ('teɪlə) *n.* **1.** a person who makes, repairs, or alters outer garments, esp. menswear. Related adj.: **sartorial.** **2.** a voracious and active marine food fish of Australia. ~*vb.* **3.** to cut or style (material, etc.) to satisfy certain requirements. **4.** (*tr.*) to adapt so as to make suitable. **5.** (*intr.*) to work as a tailor. [C13: from Anglo-Norman *taillour*, from OF *taillier* to cut, from L *tālea* a cutting] —'**tailored** *adj.*

tailorbird ('teɪlə,bɜːd) *n.* any of several tropical Asian warblers that build nests by sewing together large leaves using plant fibres.

tailor-made *adj.* **1.** made by a tailor to fit exactly. **2.** perfectly meeting a particular purpose. ~*n.* **3.** a tailor-made garment. **4.** *Inf.* a factory-made cigarette.

tailor's chalk *n.* pipeclay used by tailors and dressmakers to mark seams, darts, etc., on material.

tailor's-tack *n.* one of a series of loose looped stitches used to transfer markings for seams, darts, etc., from a paper pattern to material.

tail out *vb.* (*tr., adv.*) *N.Z.* to guide (timber) as it emerges from a circular saw.

tailpiece ('teɪl,piːs) *n.* **1.** an extension or appendage that lengthens or completes something. **2.** a decorative design at the foot of a page or end of a chapter. **3.** *Music.* a piece of wood to which the strings of a violin, etc., are attached at their lower end. **4.** a short beam or rafter that has one end embedded in a wall.

tailpipe ('teɪl,paɪp) *n.* a pipe from which exhaust gases are discharged, esp. the terminal pipe of the exhaust system of a motor vehicle.

tailplane ('teɪl,pleɪn) *n.* a small horizontal wing at the tail of an aircraft to provide longitudinal stability. Also called (esp. U.S.): **horizontal stabilizer.**

tailrace ('teɪl,reɪs) *n.* a channel that carries water away from a water wheel, turbine, etc.

tail rotor *n.* a small propeller fitted to the rear of a helicopter to counteract the torque reaction of the main rotor and thus prevent the body of the helicopter from rotating in an opposite direction.

tails (teɪlz) *pl. n.* **1.** an informal name for **tail coat.** ~*interj., adv.* **2.** with the reverse side of a coin uppermost.

tailskid ('teɪl,skɪd) *n.* **1.** a runner under the tail of an aircraft. **2.** a rear-wheel skid of a motor vehicle.

tailspin ('teɪl,spɪn) *n.* **1.** *Aeronautics.* another name for **spin** (sense 15). **2.** *Inf.* a state of confusion or panic.

tailstock ('teɪl,stɒk) *n.* a casting that slides on the bed of a lathe and is locked in position to support the free end of a workpiece.

tailwind ('teɪl,wɪnd) *n.* a wind blowing in the same direction as the course of an aircraft or ship.

Taimyr Peninsula (*Russian* taj'mir) *n.* a large peninsula of the N central Soviet Union, between the Kara Sea and the Laptev Sea. Also called: **Taymyr Peninsula.**

Tainan *or* **T'ai-nan** ('taɪ'næn) *n.* a city in the SW Republic of China (Taiwan): an early centre of Chinese emigration from the mainland; largest city and capital of the island (1638–1885); Chengkung University. Pop.: 633 607 (1985).

Tainaron ('tɛnarɒn) *n.* transliteration of the Modern Greek name for (Cape) **Matapan.**

Taine (*French* tɛn) *n.* **Hippolyte Adolphe** (ipɔlit a'dɔlf). 1828–93, French literary critic and historian. He applied determinist criteria to the study of literature, art, history, and psychology, regarding them as products of environment and race. His works include *Histoire de la littérature anglaise* (1863–64) and *Les Origines de la France contemporaine* (1875–93).

Taino ('taɪnəʊ) *n.* **1.** (*pl.* **-nos** *or* **-no**) a member of an extinct American Indian people of the West Indies. **2.** the language of this people.

taint (teɪnt) *vb.* **1.** to affect or be affected by pollution or contamination. **2.** to tarnish (someone's reputation, etc.) ~*n.* **3.** a defect or flaw. **4.** a trace of contamination or infection. [C14: (infl. by *attaint* infected, from ATTAIN) from OF *teindre* to dye, from L *tingere*] —'**taintless** *adj.*

taipan ('taɪ,pæn) *n.* a large highly venomous Australian snake. [C20: from Abor.]

Taipei *or* **T'ai-pei** ('taɪ'peɪ) *n.* the capital of the Republic of China (Taiwan), at the N tip of the island: became capital in 1885; industrial centre; two universities. Pop.: 2 500 000 (1985 est.).

Taisho (taɪ'ʃəʊ) *n.* **1.** the period of Japanese history and artistic style associated with the reign of Emperor Yoshihito (1912–26). **2.** the throne name of Yoshihito (1879–1926), emperor of Japan (1912–26).

Taiwan ('taɪ'wɑːn) *n.* an island in SE Asia between the East China Sea and the South China Sea, off the SE coast of the People's Republic of China: the principal territory of the Republic of China. Pop.: 19 630 000 (1987). Former name: **Formosa.** —,**Taiwan'ese** *adj., n.*

Taiwan Strait *n.* another name for **Formosa Strait.**

Taiyuan *or* **T'ai-yüan** ('taɪjuː'ɑːn) *n.* a city in N China, capital of Shanxi: founded before 450 A.D.; an industrial centre, surrounded by China's largest reserves of high-grade bituminous coal. Pop.: 1 880 000 (1986).

Ta'izz (tæ'ɪz, teɪ'iːz) *n.* a town in SW North Yemen: agricultural trading centre. Pop.: 119 572 (1980).

taj (tɑːdʒ) *n.* a tall conical cap worn as a mark of distinction by Muslims. [via Ar. from Persian: crown]

Taj Mahal ('tɑːdʒ məˈhɑːl) *n.* a white marble mausoleum in central India, in Agra on the Jumna River: built (1632–43) by the emperor Shah Jahan in memory of his beloved wife, Mumtaz Mahal; regarded as the finest example of Mogul architecture. [Urdu, lit.: crown of buildings]

Tajo ('taxo) *n.* the Spanish name for the **Tagus.**

takahe ('tɑːkə,hiː) *n.* a rare flightless New Zealand rail. Also called: **notornis.** [from Maori]

Takamatsu (,tækə'mætsuː) *n.* a port in SW Japan, on NE Shikoku on the Inland Sea. Pop.: 316 662 (1985).

Takao (tæ'kaʊ) *n.* the Japanese name for **Kaohsiung.**

take (teɪk) *vb.* **taking, took, taken.** (*mainly tr.*) **1.** (*also intr.*) to gain possession of (something) by force or effort. **2.** to appropriate or steal. **3.** to receive or accept into a relationship with oneself: *to take a wife.* **4.** to pay for or buy. **5.** to rent or lease. **6.** to obtain by regular payment. **7.** to win. **8.** to obtain or derive from a source. **9.** to assume the obligations of: *to take office.* **10.** to endure, esp. with fortitude: *to take punishment.* **11.** to adopt as a symbol of duty, etc.: *to take the veil.* **12.** to receive in a specified way: *she took the news very well.* **13.** to adopt as one's own: *to take someone's part in a quarrel.* **14.** to receive and make use of: *to take advice.* **15.** to receive into the body, as by eating, inhaling, etc. **16.** to eat, drink, etc., esp. habitually. **17.** to have or be engaged in for one's benefit or use: *to take a rest.* **18.** to work at or study: *to take economics at college.* **19.** to make, do, or perform (an action). **20.** to make use of: *to take an opportunity.* **21.** to put into effect: *to take measures.* **22.** (*also intr.*) to make a photograph of or admit of being photographed. **23.** to act or perform. **24.** to write down or copy: *to take notes.* **25.** to experience or feel: *to take offence.* **26.** to consider or regard: *I take him to be honest.* **27.** to accept as valid: *I take your point.* **28.** to hold or maintain in the mind: *his father took a dim view of his career.* **29.** to deal or contend with. **30.** to use as a particular case: *take hotels for example.* **31.** (*intr.;* often foll. by *from*) to diminish or detract: *the actor's bad performance took from the effect of the play.* **32.** to confront successfully: *the horse took the jump at the third attempt.* **33.** (*intr.*) to have or produce the intended effect: *her vaccination took.* **34.** (*intr.*) (of plants, etc.) to start growing successfully. **35.** to aim or direct: *he took a swipe at his opponent.* **36.** to deal a blow to in a specified place. **37.** *Arch.* to have sexual intercourse with (a woman). **38.** to remove from a place. **39.** to carry along or have in one's possession. **40.** to convey or transport. **41.** to use as a means of transport: *I shall take the bus.* **42.** to conduct or lead. **43.** to escort or accompany. **44.** to bring or deliver to a state, position, etc.: *his ability took him to the forefront.* **45.** to seek: *to take cover.* **46.** to ascertain by measuring, etc.: *to take a pulse.* **47.** (*intr.*) (of a mechanism) to catch or engage (a part). **48.** to put an end to: *she took her own life.* **49.** to come upon unexpectedly. **50.** to contract: *he took a chill.* **51.** to affect or attack: *the fever took him one night.* **52.** (*copula*) to become suddenly or be rendered (ill): *he was taken sick.* **53.** (*also intr.*) to absorb or become absorbed by something: *to take a polish.* **54.** (*usually passive*) to charm: *she was very taken with the puppy.* **55.** (*intr.*) to be or become popular; win favour. **56.** to require: *that task will take all your time.* **57.** to subtract or deduct. **58.** to hold: *the suitcase won't take all your clothes.* **59.** to quote or copy. **60.** to proceed to occupy: *to take a seat.* **61.** (often foll. by *to*) to use or employ: *to take steps to ascertain the answer.* **62.** to win or capture (a trick, piece, etc.). **63.** *Sl.* to cheat, deceive, or victimize. **64. take five** (or **ten**). *Inf., chiefly U.S. & Canad.* to take a break of five (or ten) minutes. **65. take it. a.** to assume; believe. **b.** *Inf.* to stand up to or endure criticism, harsh treatment, etc. **66. take one's time.** to use as much time as is needed. **67. take** (**someone's**) **name in vain. a.** to use a name, esp. of God, disrespectfully or irreverently. **b.** *Jocular.* to say (someone's) name. **68. take upon oneself.** to assume the right to do or responsibility for something. ~*n.* **69.** the act of taking. **70.** the number of quarry killed or captured. **71.** *Inf., chiefly U.S.* the amount of anything taken, esp. money. **72.** *Films, music.* **a.** one of a series of recordings from which the best will be selected. **b.** the process of taking one such recording. **c.** a scene photographed without interruption. ~See also **take after, take apart,** etc. [OE *tacan*] —'**takable** *or* '**takeable** *adj.* —'**taker** *n.*

take after *vb.* (*intr., prep.*) to resemble in appearance, character, behaviour, etc.

take apart *vb.* (*tr., adv.*) **1.** to separate (something) into component parts. **2.** to criticize severely.

take away *vb.* (*tr., adv.*) **1.** to subtract: *take away four from nine to leave five.* ~*prep.* **2.** minus: *nine take away four is five.* ~*adj.* **takeaway.** *Brit., Austral., & N.Z.* **3.** sold for consumption away from the premises: *a takeaway meal.* **4.** selling food for consumption away from the premises: *a takeaway Indian restaurant.* ~*n.* **takeaway.** *Brit., Austral., & N.Z.* **5.** a shop or restaurant that sells such food. **6.** a meal bought at such a shop or restaurant: *we'll have a Chinese takeaway tonight.* ~Scot. word (for senses 3–6): **carry out.** U.S. and Canad. word (for senses 3–6): **takeout.**

take back *vb.* (*adv., mainly tr.*) **1.** to retract or withdraw (something said, promised, etc.). **2.** to regain possession of. **3.** to return for exchange. **4.** to accept (someone) back (into one's home, affections, etc.). **5.** to remind one of the past: *that tune really takes me back.* **6.** (*also intr.*) *Printing.* to move (copy) to the previous line.

take down *vb.* (*tr., adv.*) **1.** to record in writing. **2.** to dismantle or tear down. **3.** to lower or reduce in power, arrogance, etc. (esp. in **take down a peg**). ~*adj.* **takedown. 4.** made or intended to be disassembled.

take for *vb.* (*tr., prep.*) **1.** *Inf.* to consider or suppose to be, esp. mistakenly: *the fake coins were taken for genuine; who do you take me for?* **2. take for granted. a.** to accept or assume without question. **b.** to fail to appreciate the value, merit, etc., of.

take-home pay *n.* the remainder of one's pay after all income tax and other compulsory deductions have been made.

take in *vb.* (*tr., adv.*) **1.** to understand. **2.** to include. **3.** to receive into one's house in exchange for payment: *to take in lodgers.* **4.** to make (clothing, etc.) smaller by altering seams. **5.** *Inf.* to cheat or deceive. **6.** *U.S.* to go to: *let's take in a movie tonight.*

taken ('teɪkən) *vb.* **1.** the past participle of **take.** ~*adj.* **2.** (*postpositive;* foll. by *with*) enthusiastically impressed (by); infatuated (with).

take off *vb.* (*adv.*) **1.** (*tr.*) to remove (a garment). **2.** (*intr.*) (of an aircraft) to become airborne. **3.** *Inf.* to set out or cause to set out on a journey: *they took off for Spain.* **4.** (*tr.*) (of a disease) to kill. **5.** (*tr.*) *Inf.* to mimic. **6.** (*intr.*) *Inf.* to become successful or popular. ~*n.* **take-off. 7.** the act or process of making an aircraft airborne. **8.** the stage of a country's economic development when rapid and sustained economic growth is first achieved. **9.** *Inf.* an act of mimicry.

take on *vb.* (*adv., mainly tr.*) **1.** to employ or hire. **2.** to assume or acquire: *his voice took on a plaintive note.* **3.** to agree to do; undertake. **4.** to compete against; fight. **5.** (*intr.*) *Inf.* to exhibit great emotion, esp. grief.

take out *vb.* (*tr., adv.*) **1.** to extract or remove. **2.** to obtain or secure (a licence, patent, etc.). **3.** to go out with; escort. **4.** *Bridge.* to bid a different suit from (one's partner) in order to rescue him from a difficult contract. **5.** *Sl.* to kill or destroy. **6.** *Austral. inf.* to win, esp. in sport. **7. take it** *or* **a lot out of.** *Inf.* to sap the energy or vitality of. **8. take out on.** *Inf.* to vent (anger, etc.) on. **9. take someone out of himself.** *Inf.* to make someone forget his anxieties, problems, etc. ~*adj.* **takeout. 10.** *Bridge.* of or designating a conventional informatory bid, asking one's partner to bid another suit. ~*adj., n.* **11.** the U.S. and Canad. word for **takeaway** (senses 3–6).

take over *vb.* (*adv.*) **1.** to assume the control or management of. **2.** *Printing.* to move (copy) to the next line. ~*n.* **takeover. 3.** the act of seizing or assuming power, control, etc.

take to *vb.* (*intr., prep.*) **1.** to make for; flee to: *to take to the hills.* **2.** to form a liking for. **3.** to have recourse to: *to take to the bottle.*

take up *vb.* (*adv., mainly tr.*) **1.** to adopt the study, practice, or activity of: *to take up gardening.* **2.** to shorten (a garment). **3.** to pay off (a note, mortgage, etc.). **4.** to agree to or accept (an invitation, etc.). **5.** to pursue further or resume (something): *he took up French where he left off.* **6.** to absorb (a liquid). **7.** to act as a patron to. **8.** to occupy or fill (space or time). **9.** to interrupt, esp. in order to contradict or criticize. **10.** *Austral. & N.Z.* to occupy and break in (uncultivated land): *he took up some hundreds of acres in the back country.* **11. take up on. a.** to argue with (someone): *can I take you up on two points in your talk?* **b.** to accept what is offered by (someone): *let me take you up on your invitation.* **12. take up with. a.** to discuss with (someone); refer to. **b.** (*intr.*) to begin to keep company or associate with. ~*n.* **take-up. 13. a.** the claiming of something, esp. a state benefit. **b.** (*as modifier*): *take-up rate.*

takin ('tɑːkiːn) *n.* a massive bovid mammal of S Asia, having a shaggy coat, short legs, and horns. [C19: from Tibetan native name]

taking ('teɪkɪŋ) *adj.* **1.** charming, fascinating, or intriguing. **2.** *Inf.* infectious; catching. ~*n.* **3.** something taken. **4.** (*pl.*) receipts; earnings. —'**takingly** *adv.* —'**takingness** *n.*

Takoradi (ˌtɑːkəˈrɑːdɪ) *n.* the chief port of Ghana, in the southwest on the Gulf of Guinea: modern harbour opened in 1928. Pop. (with Sekondi): 123 637 (1982 est.).

talapoin ('tæləˌpɔɪn) *n.* **1.** a small W African monkey. **2.** (in Burma and Thailand) a Buddhist monk. [C16: from F, lit.: Buddhist monk, from Port. *talapão;* orig. jocular, from the appearance of the monkey]

talaria (təˈlɛərɪə) *pl. n. Greek myth.* winged sandals. [C16: from L, from *tālāris* belonging to the ankle, from *tālus* ankle]

Talavera de la Reina (*Spanish* talaˈβera ðe la ˈrɛina) *n.* a walled town in central Spain, on the Tagus River: scene of the defeat of the French by British and Spanish forces (1809) during the Peninsular War; agricultural processing centre. Pop.: 64 136 (1981).

talc (tælk) *n. also* **talcum**. **1.** See **talcum powder**. **2.** a soft mineral, consisting of magnesium silicate, used in the manufacture of ceramics and paints and as a filler in talcum powder, etc. ~*vb*. **talcking, talcked** *or* **talcing, talced**. **3.** (*tr*.) to apply talc to. [C16: from Med. L *talcum*, from Ar. *talq* mica, from Persian *talk*] —**'talcose** *or* **'talcous** *adj*.

Talca (*Spanish* 'talka) *n*. a city in central Chile: scene of the declaration of Chilean independence (1818). Pop.: 144 656 (1985 est.).

Talcahuano (*Spanish* talka'wano) *n*. a port in S central Chile, near Concepción on an inlet of the Pacific: oil refinery. Pop.: 220 910 (1985 est.).

talcum powder ('tælkəm) *n*. a powder made of purified talc, usually scented, used for perfuming the body and for absorbing excess moisture. Often shortened to **talcum** or **talc**.

tale (teɪl) *n*. **1.** a report, narrative, or story. **2.** one of a group of short stories. **3. a.** a malicious or meddlesome rumour or piece of gossip. **b.** (*in combination*): *talebearer; taleteller*. **4.** a fictitious or false statement. **5. tell tales. a.** to tell fanciful lies. **b.** to report malicious stories, trivial complaints, etc., esp. to someone in authority. **6. tell a tale.** to reveal something important. **7. tell its own tale.** to be self-evident. **8.** *Arch*. a number; amount. [OE *talu* list]

talent ('tælənt) *n*. **1.** innate ability, aptitude, or faculty; above average ability: *a talent for cooking; a child with talent*. **2.** a person or persons possessing such ability. **3.** any of various ancient units of weight and money. **4.** *Inf.* members of the opposite sex collectively: *the local talent*. [OE *talente*, from L *talenta*, pl. of *talentum* sum of money, from Gk *talanton* unit of money; in Med. L the sense was extended to ability through the infl. of the parable of the talents (Matthew 25:14–30)] —**'talented** *adj*.

talent scout *n*. a person whose occupation is the search for talented sportsmen, performers, etc., for engagements as professionals.

tales ('teɪliːz) *n. Law*. **1.** (*functioning as pl.*) a group of persons summoned to fill vacancies on a jury panel. **2.** (*functioning as sing.*) the writ summoning such jurors. [C15: from Med. L *tālēs dē circumstantibus* such men from among the bystanders, from L *tālis* such] —**'talesman** *n*.

Taliesin (ˌtælɪ'ɛsɪn) *n*. 6th century A.D., Welsh bard; supposed author of 12 heroic poems in the *Book of Taliesin*.

taligrade ('tælɪˌgreɪd) *adj*. (of mammals) walking on the outer side of the foot. [C20: from NL, from L *tālus* ankle, heel + -GRADE]

talion ('tælɪən) *n*. the system or legal principle of making the punishment correspond to the crime; retaliation. [C15: via OF from L *tāliō*, from *tālis* such]

talipes ('tælɪˌpiːz) *n*. **1.** a congenital deformity of the foot by which it is twisted in any of various positions. **2.** a technical name for **club foot**. [C19: NL, from L *tālus* ankle + *pēs* foot]

talipot *or* **talipot palm** ('tælɪˌpɒt) *n*. a palm tree of the East Indies, having large leaves that are used for fans, thatching houses, etc. [C17: from Bengali: palm leaf, from Sansk. *tālī* fan palm + *pattra* leaf]

talisman ('tælɪzmən) *n., pl.* **-mans**. **1.** a stone or other small object, usually inscribed or carved, believed to protect the wearer from evil influences. **2.** anything thought to have magical or protective powers. [C17: via F or Sp. from Ar. *tilsam*, from Med. Gk *telesma* ritual, from Gk: consecration, from *telein* to perform a rite, complete] —**talismanic** (ˌtælɪz'mænɪk) *adj*.

talk (tɔːk) *vb*. **1.** (*intr.;* often foll. by *to* or *with*) to express one's thoughts, feelings, or desires by means of words (to). **2.** (*intr.*) to communicate by other means: *lovers talk with their eyes*. **3.** (*intr.;* usually foll. by *about*) to exchange ideas or opinions (about). **4.** (*intr.*) to articulate words. **5.** (*tr.*) to give voice to; utter: *to talk rubbish*. **6.** (*tr.*) to discuss: *to talk business*. **7.** (*intr.*) to reveal information. **8.** (*tr.*) to know how to communicate in (a language or idiom): *he talks English*. **9.** (*intr.*) to spread rumours or gossip. **10.** (*intr.*) to make sounds suggestive of talking. **11.** (*intr.*) to be effective or persuasive: *money talks*. **12. now you're talking.** *Inf.* at last you're saying something agreeable. **13. talk big.** to boast. **14. you can talk.** *Inf.* **a.** you don't have to worry about doing a particular thing yourself. **b.** Also: **you can't talk.** you yourself are guilty of offending in the very matter you are upholding or decrying. ~*n*. **15.** a speech or lecture. **16.** an exchange of ideas or thoughts. **17.** idle chatter, gossip, or rumour. **18.** a subject of conversation; theme. **19.** (*often pl.*) a conference, discussion, or negotiation. **20.** a specific manner of speaking: *children's talk*. ~See also **talk about, talk back**, etc. [C13 *talkien*] —**'talker** *n*.

talk about *vb*. (*intr., prep.*) **1.** to discuss. **2.** used informally and often ironically to add emphasis to a statement: *all his plays have such ridiculous plots—talk about good drama!*

talkative ('tɔːkətɪv) *adj*. given to talking a great deal. —**'talkatively** *adv*. —**'talkativeness** *n*.

talk back *vb*. (*intr., adv.*) **1.** to answer boldly or impudently. **2.** *N.Z.* to conduct a telephone dialogue for immediate transmission over the air. ~*n*. **talkback**. **3.** *Television, radio*. a system of telephone links enabling spoken directions to be given during the production of a programme. **4.** *N.Z.* a broadcast telephone dialogue.

talk down *vb*. (*adv.*) **1.** (*intr.;* often foll. by *to*) to behave (towards) in a superior manner. **2.** (*tr.*) to override (a person) by continuous or loud talking. **3.** (*tr.*) to give instructions to (an aircraft) by radio to enable it to land.

talkie ('tɔːkɪ) *n. Inf.* an early film with a soundtrack. Full name: **talking picture**.

talking book *n*. a recording of a book, designed to be used by the blind.

talking head *n*. (on television) a person, shown only from the shoulders up, who speaks without illustrative material.

talking-to *n. Inf.* a session of criticism, as of a subordinate by a person in authority.

talk into *vb*. (*tr., prep.*) to persuade to by talking: *I talked him into buying the house*.

talk out *vb*. (*tr., adv.*) **1.** to resolve or eliminate by talking. **2.** *Brit.* to block (a bill, etc.) in a legislative body by lengthy discussion. **3. talk out of.** to dissuade from by talking.

talk round *vb*. **1.** (*tr., adv.*) Also: **talk over.** to persuade to one's opinion. **2.** (*intr., prep.*) to discuss (a subject), esp. without coming to a conclusion.

talk shop *vb*. to talk about one's profession, esp. at a social occasion.

talk show *n*. another name for **chat show**.

tall (tɔːl) *adj*. **1.** of more than average height. **2.** (*postpositive*) having a specified height: *five feet tall*. [C14 (in the sense: big, comely, valiant)] —**'tallness** *n*.

tallage ('tælɪdʒ) *n. English history*. **a.** a tax levied by kings on Crown lands and royal towns. **b.** a toll levied by a lord upon his tenants or by a feudal lord upon his vassals. [C13: from OF *taillage*, from *taillier* to cut; see TAILOR]

Tallahassee (ˌtælə'hæsɪ) *n*. a city in N Florida, capital of the state: two universities. Pop.: 120 023 (1986 est.).

tallboy ('tɔːlˌbɔɪ) *n*. a high chest of drawers made in two sections placed one on top of the other.

Talleyrand-Périgord ('tælɪˌrænd'perɪɡɔː; *French* talɛrɑ̃periɡɔr) *n*. **Charles Maurice** (ʃarl mɔris). 1754–1838, French statesman; foreign minister (1797–1807; 1814–15). He secretly negotiated with the Allies against Napoleon I from 1808 and was France's representative at the Congress of Vienna (1815).

Tallinn *or* **Tallin** ('tælɪn) *n*. a port in the NW Soviet Union, capital of the Estonian SSR, on the Gulf of Finland: founded by the Danes in 1219; naval base. Pop.: 478 000 (1987). German name: **Reval**.

Tallis ('tælɪs) *n*. **Thomas**. ?1505–85, English composer and organist; noted for his arrangements of the liturgical music of the Church of England.

tallith ('tælɪθ) *n*. a shawl with fringed corners worn by Jewish males, esp. during religious services. [C17: from Heb. *tallīt*]

tall order *n. Inf.* a difficult or unreasonable request.

tallow ('tæləʊ) *n*. **1.** a fatty substance extracted chiefly from the suet of sheep and cattle: used for making soap, candles, food, etc. ~*vb*. **2.** (*tr.*) to cover or smear with tallow. [OE *tælg*, a dye] —**'tallowy** *adj*.

tallowwood ('tæləʊˌwʊd) *n. Austral.* a tall eucalyptus tree having soft fibrous bark and a greasy timber.

tall poppy *n. Austral. inf.* a prominent or highly paid person.

tall ship n. any square-rigged sailing ship.

tall story n. Inf. an exaggerated or incredible account.

tally ('tælɪ) vb. **-lying, -lied. 1.** (intr.) to correspond one with the other: *the two stories don't tally.* **2.** (tr.) to supply with an identifying tag. **3.** (intr.) to keep score. **4.** (tr.) Obs. to record or mark. ~n., pl. **-lies. 5.** any record of debit, credit, the score in a game, etc. **6.** Austral. & N.Z. the number of sheep shorn in a specified period. **7.** an identifying label or mark. **8.** a counterpart or duplicate of something. **9.** a stick used (esp. formerly) as a record of the amount of a debt according to the notches cut in it. **10.** a notch or mark made on such a stick. **11.** a mark used to represent a certain number in counting. [C15: from Med. L *tālea*, from L: cutting]

tally clerk n. Austral. & N.Z. a person, esp. on a wharf, who checks the count of goods being loaded or unloaded.

tally-ho (ˌtælɪˈhəʊ) interj. **1.** the cry of a participant at a hunt when the quarry is sighted. ~n., pl. **-hos. 2.** an instance of crying tally-ho. **3.** another name for a **four-in-hand** (sense 1). ~vb. **-hoing, -hoed** or **-ho'd. 4.** (intr.) to make the cry of tally-ho. [C18: ?from F *taïaut* cry used in hunting]

tallyman ('tælɪmən) n., pl. **-men. 1.** a scorekeeper or recorder. **2.** Dialect. a travelling salesman for a firm specializing in hire-purchase. — **'tally,woman** fem. n.

Talmud ('tælmʊd) n. Judaism. the primary source of Jewish religious law, consisting of the Mishnah and the Gemara. [C16: from Heb. *talmūdh*, lit.: instruction, from *lāmadh* to learn] — **Tal'mudic** or **Tal'mudical** adj. — **'Talmudism** n. — **'Talmudist** n.

talon ('tælən) n. **1.** a sharply hooked claw, esp. of a bird of prey. **2.** anything resembling this. **3.** the part of a lock that the key presses on when it is turned. **4.** Piquet, etc. the pile of cards left after the deal. **5.** Archit. another name for **ogee**. [C14: from OF: heel, from L *tālus*] — **'taloned** adj.

Talos ('teɪlɒs) n. Greek myth. the nephew and apprentice of Daedalus, who surpassed his uncle as an inventor and was killed by him out of jealousy.

talus[1] ('teɪləs) n., pl. **-li** (-laɪ). the bone of the ankle that articulates with the leg bones to form the ankle joint; anklebone. [C18: from L: ankle]

talus[2] ('teɪləs) n., pl. **-luses. 1.** Geol. another name for **scree. 2.** Fortifications. the sloping side of a wall. [C17: from F, from L *talūtium* slope, ? of Iberian origin]

tam (tæm) n. short for **tam-o'-shanter.**

tamale (təˈmɑːlɪ) n. a Mexican dish made of minced meat mixed with crushed maize and seasonings, wrapped in maize husks and steamed. [C19: erroneously for *tamal*, from Mexican Sp., from Nahuatl *tamalli*]

tamandua (ˌtæmənˈduə) n. a small arboreal mammal of Central and South America, having a tubular mouth specialized for feeding on termites. Also called: **lesser anteater.** [C17: via Port. from Tupi: ant trapper, from *taixi* ant + *mondé* to catch]

tamarack ('tæməˌræk) n. **1.** any of several North American larches. **2.** the wood of any of these trees. [C19: of Amerind origin]

tamarillo (ˌtæməˈrɪləʊ) n., pl. **-los.** N.Z. another name for **tree tomato.**

tamarin ('tæmərɪn) n. any of numerous small monkeys of South and Central American forests; similar to the marmosets. [C18: via F, of Amerind origin]

tamarind ('tæmərɪnd) n. **1.** a tropical evergreen tree having yellow flowers and brown pods. **2.** the fruit of this tree, used as a food and to make beverages and medicines. **3.** the wood of this tree. [C16: from Med. L *tamarindus*, ult. from Ar. *tamr hindī* Indian date]

tamarisk ('tæmərɪsk) n. any of a genus of trees and shrubs of the Mediterranean region and S and SE Asia, having scalelike leaves, slender branches, and feathery flower clusters. [C15: from LL *tamariscus*, from L *tamarix*]

Tamatave (French tamatav) n. the former name (until 1979) of **Toamasina.**

Tamaulipas (Spanish tamauˈlipas) n. a state of NE Mexico, on the Gulf of Mexico. Capital: Ciudad Victoria. Pop.: 1 924 934 (1980). Area: 79 829 sq. km (30 822 sq. miles).

Tambora ('tæmbəˌrɑː) n. a volcano in Indonesia, on N Sumbawa: violent eruption of 1815 reduced its height from about 4000 m (13 000 ft.) to 2850 m (9400 ft.).

tambour ('tæmbʊə) n. **1.** Real Tennis. the sloping buttress on one side of the receiver's end of the court. **2.** a small embroidery frame, consisting of two hoops over which the fabric is stretched while being worked. **3.** embroidered work done on such a frame. **4.** a sliding door on desks, cabinets, etc., made of thin strips of wood glued onto a canvas backing. **5.** Archit. a wall that is circular in plan, esp. one that supports a dome or one that is surrounded by a colonnade. **6.** a drum. ~vb. **7.** to embroider on a tambour. [C15: from F, from *tabour* TABOR]

tamboura (tæmˈbʊərə) n. a stringed instrument with a long neck used in Indian music to provide a drone. [from Persian *tanbūr*, from Ar. *tunbūr*]

tambourin ('tæmbʊrɪn) n. **1.** an 18th-century Provençal folk dance. **2.** a piece of music composed for or in the rhythm of this dance. **3.** a small drum. [C18: from F: a little drum]

tambourine (ˌtæmbəˈriːn) n. Music. a percussion instrument consisting of a single drumhead of skin stretched over a circular wooden frame hung with pairs of metal discs that jingle when it is struck or shaken. [C16: from MFlemish *tamborijn* a little drum, from OF: TAMBOURIN] — ˌtambou'rinist n.

Tambov (Russian tamˈbɔf) n. an industrial city in the W central Soviet Union: founded in 1636 as a Muscovite fort. Pop.: 305 000 (1987).

Tamburlaine (ˈtæmbəˌleɪn) n. a variant of **Tamerlane.**

tame (teɪm) adj. **1.** changed by man from a wild state into a domesticated or cultivated condition. **2.** (of animals) not fearful of human contact. **3.** meek or submissive. **4.** flat, insipid, or uninspiring. ~vb. (tr.) **5.** to make tame; domesticate. **6.** to break the spirit of, subdue, or curb. **7.** to tone down, soften, or mitigate. [OE *tam*] — **'tamable** or **'tameable** adj. — **'tamely** adv. — **'tameness** n. — **'tamer** n.

Tamerlane ('tæməˌleɪn) or **Tamburlaine** n. Turkic name *Timur* (tiːˈmʊə). ?1336–1405, Mongol conqueror of the area from Mongolia to the Mediterranean; ruler of Samarkand (1369–1405). He defeated the Turks at Angora (1402) and died while invading China.

Tamil ('tæmɪl) n. **1.** (pl. **-ils** or **-il**) a member of a mixed Dravidian and Caucasoid people of S India and Sri Lanka. **2.** the language of this people. ~adj. **3.** of or relating to this people or their language.

Tamil Nadu ('tæmɪl nɑːˈduː) n. a state of SE India, on the Coromandel Coast: reorganized in 1956 and 1960 and made smaller; consists of a coastal plain backed by hills, including the Nilgiri Hills in the west. Capital: Madras. Pop.: 48 297 456 (1981). Area: 130 357 sq. km (50 839 sq. miles). Former name (until 1968): **Madras.**

Tammerfors (tamərˈfɔrs) n. the Swedish name for **Tampere.**

tammy[1] ('tæmɪ) n., pl. **-mies.** another word for **tam-o'-shanter.**

tammy[2] ('tæmɪ) n., pl. **-mies.** (esp. formerly) a woollen cloth used for straining sauces, soups, etc. [C18: changed from F *tamis*, ? of Celtic origin]

tam-o'-shanter (ˌtæmə'ʃæntə) n. a Scottish brimless wool or cloth cap with a bobble in the centre. [C19: after the hero of Burns's poem *Tam o' Shanter* (1790)]

tamp (tæmp) vb. (tr.) **1.** to force or pack down firmly by repeated blows. **2.** to pack sand, earth, etc., into (a drill hole) over an explosive. [C17: prob. back formation from *tampin* (obs. var. of TAMPION), taken as a present participle *tamping*]

Tampa ('tæmpə) n. a port and resort in W Florida, on **Tampa Bay** (an arm of the Gulf of Mexico): two universities. Pop.: 278 755 (1986 est.).

tamper[1] ('tæmpə) vb. (intr.) **1.** (usually foll. by with) to interfere or meddle. **2.** to use bribery or blackmail. **3.** (usually foll. by with) to attempt to influence, esp. by bribery. [C16: alteration of TEMPER (vb.)] — **'tamperer** n.

tamper[2] ('tæmpə) n. **1.** a person or thing that tamps, esp. an instrument for packing down tobacco in a pipe. **2.** a casing around the core of a nuclear weapon to increase its efficiency by reflecting neutrons and delaying the expansion.

Tampere (Finnish 'tampɛrɛ) n. a city in SW Finland: the second largest town in Finland; textile manufacturing. Pop.: 169 994 (1986). Swedish name: **Tammerfors.**

Tampico (Spanish tamˈpiko) n. a port and resort in E Mexico, in Tamaulipas on the Pánuco River: oil refining. Pop.: 267 957 (1980).

tampion ('tæmpɪən) *or* **tompion** *n.* a plug placed in a gun's muzzle when the gun is not in use. [C15: from F: TAMPON]

tampon ('tæmpɒn) *n.* **1.** a plug of lint, cotton wool, etc., inserted into a wound or body cavity to stop the flow of blood, absorb secretions, etc. ~*vb.* **2.** (*tr.*) to plug (a wound, etc.) with a tampon. [C19: via F from OF *tapon* a little plug, of Gmc origin] — **tamponage** ('tæmpənɪdʒ) *n.*

tam-tam *n.* another name for **gong** (sense 1). [from Hindi; see TOM-TOM]

Tamworth ('tæmwəθ) *n.* **1.** a market town in W central England, in SE Staffordshire. Pop.: 64 315 (1981). **2.** a city in SE Australia, in E central New South Wales: industrial centre of an agricultural region. Pop.: 33 900 (1985 est.).

tan[1] (tæn) *n.* **1.** the brown colour produced by the skin after exposure to ultraviolet rays, esp. those of the sun. **2.** a yellowish-brown colour. **3.** short for **tanbark**. ~*vb.* **tanning, tanned. 4.** to go brown or cause to go brown after exposure to ultraviolet rays. **5.** to convert (a skin or hide) into leather by treating it with a tanning agent. **6.** (*tr.*) *Sl.* to beat or flog. ~*adj.* **tanner, tannest. 7.** of the colour tan. [OE *tannian* (unattested as infinitive, attested as *getanned*, p.p.), from Med. L *tannāre*, from *tannum* tanbark, ? of Celtic origin] — **'tannable** *adj.* — **'tannish** *adj.*

tan[2] (tæn) *abbrev. for* tangent (sense 2).

Tana ('tɑːnə) *n.* **1. Lake.** Also called: (Lake) **Tsana.** a lake in NW Ethiopia, on a plateau 1800 m (6000 ft.) high: the largest lake of Ethiopia; source of the Blue Nile. Area: 3673 sq. km (1418 sq. miles). **2.** a river in E Kenya, rising in the Aberdare Range and flowing in a wide curve east to the Indian Ocean: the longest river in Kenya. Length: 708 km (440 miles). **3.** a river in NE Norway, flowing generally northeast as part of the border between Norway and Finland to the Arctic Ocean by Tana Fjord. Length: about 320 km (200 miles). Finnish name: **Teno.**

tanager ('tænədʒə) *n.* any of a family of American songbirds having a short thick bill and, in the male, a brilliantly coloured plumage. [C19: from NL *tanagra*, based on Amerind *tangara*]

Tanagra ('tænəgrə) *n.* a town in ancient Boeotia, famous for terracotta figurines of the same name, first discovered in its necropolis.

Tanana ('tænənɑ) *n.* a river in central Alaska, rising in the Wrangell Mountains and flowing northwest to the Yukon River. Length: about 765 km (475 miles).

Tananarive (*French* tananariv) *n.* the former name of **Antananarivo.**

tanbark ('tæn,bɑːk) *n.* the bark of certain trees, esp. the oak, used as a source of tannin.

Tancred ('tæŋkrɪd) *n.* died 1112, Norman hero of the First Crusade, who played a prominent part in the capture of Jerusalem (1099).

T & E *abbrev. for* tired and emotional.

tandem ('tændəm) *n.* **1.** a bicycle with two sets of pedals and two saddles, arranged one behind the other for two riders. **2.** a two-wheeled carriage drawn by two horses harnessed one behind the other. **3.** a team of two horses so harnessed. **4.** any arrangement of two things in which one is placed behind the other. ~*adj.* **5.** *Brit.* used as, used in, or routed through an intermediate automatic telephone exchange. ~*adv.* **6.** one behind the other. [C18: whimsical use of L *tandem* at length, to indicate a long vehicle]

Tandjungpriok *or* **Tanjungpriok** (,tændʒʊŋ'priːɒk) *n.* a port in Indonesia, on the NW coast of Java adjoining the capital, Jakarta: a major shipping and distributing centre for the whole archipelago.

tandoori (tæn'dʊərɪ) *n.* an Indian method of cooking meat or vegetables on a spit in a clay oven. [from Urdu, from *tandoor* an oven]

tang (tæŋ) *n.* **1.** a strong taste or flavour. **2.** a pungent or characteristic smell. **3.** a trace, touch, or hint of something. **4.** the pointed end of a tool, such as a chisel, file, knife, etc., which is fitted into a handle, shaft, or stock. [C14: from ON *tangi* point]

Tang (tæŋ) *n.* the imperial dynasty of China from 618–907 A.D.

Tanga ('tæŋgə) *n.* a port in N Tanzania, on the Indian Ocean: Tanzania's second port. Pop.: 103 409 (1978).

Tanganyika (,tæŋgə'njiːkə) *n.* **1.** a former state in E Africa: became part of German East Africa in 1884; ceded to Britain as a League of Nations mandate in 1919 and as a

UN trust territory in 1946; gained independence in 1961 and united with Zanzibar in 1964 as the United Republic of Tanzania. **2. Lake.** a lake in central Africa between Tanzania and Zaïre, bordering also on Burundi and Zambia, in the Great Rift Valley: the longest freshwater lake in the world. Area: 32 893 sq. km (12 700 sq. miles). Length: 676 km (420 miles). — **,Tangan'yikan** *adj., n.*

Tange ('tæŋgə) *n.* **Kenzo.** born 1913, Japanese architect. His buildings include the Kurashiki city hall (1960) and St Mary's Cathedral in Tokyo (1962–64).

tangent ('tændʒənt) *n.* **1.** a geometric line, curve, plane, or curved surface that touches another curve or surface at one point but does not intersect it. **2.** (of an angle) a trigonometric function that in a right-angled triangle is the ratio of the length of the opposite side to that of the adjacent side; the ratio of sine to cosine. Abbrev.: **tan. 3.** *Music.* a small piece of metal that strikes the string of a clavichord. **4. on** *or* **at a tangent.** on a completely different or divergent course, esp. of thought. ~*adj.* **5. a.** of or involving a tangent. **b.** touching at a single point. **6.** touching. [C16: from L *linea tangēns* the touching line, from *tangere* to touch] — **'tangency** *n.*

tangent galvanometer *n.* a galvanometer having a vertical coil of wire with a horizontal magnetic needle at its centre. The current to be measured is passed through the coil and produces a proportional magnetic field which deflects the needle.

tangential (tæn'dʒɛnʃəl) *adj.* **1.** of, being, or in the direction of a tangent. **2.** *Astron.* (of velocity) in a direction perpendicular to the line of sight of a celestial object. **3.** of superficial relevance only; digressive. — **tan,genti'ality** *n.* — **tan'gentially** *adv.*

tangerine (,tændʒə'riːn) *n.* **1.** an Asian citrus tree cultivated for its small orange-like fruits. **2.** the fruit of this tree, having sweet spicy flesh. **3. a.** a reddish-orange colour. **b.** (*as adj.*): *a tangerine door.* [C19: from TANGIER]

tangi ('tæŋiː) *n.* *N.Z.* **1.** a Maori funeral ceremony. **2.** *Inf.* a lamentation.

tangible ('tændʒɪbªl) *adj.* **1.** capable of being touched or felt. **2.** capable of being clearly grasped by the mind. **3.** having a physical existence: *tangible property.* [C16: from LL *tangibilis*, from L *tangere* to touch] — **,tangi'bility** *or* **'tangibleness** *n.* — **'tangibly** *adv.*

Tangier (tæn'dʒɪə) *n.* a port in N Morocco, on the Strait of Gibraltar: a Phoenician trading post in the 15th century B.C.; a neutral international zone (1923–56); made the summer capital of Morocco and a free port in 1962; commercial and financial centre. Pop.: 266 346 (1982). — **,Tange'rine** *n., adj.*

tangle ('tæŋgªl) *n.* **1.** a confused or complicated mass of hairs, lines, fibres, etc., knotted or coiled together. **2.** a complicated problem, condition, or situation. ~*vb.* **3.** to become or cause to become twisted together in a confused mass. **4.** (*intr.*; often foll. by *with*) to come into conflict; contend. **5.** (*tr.*) to involve in matters which hinder or confuse. **6.** (*tr.*) to ensnare or trap, as in a net. [C14 *tangilen*, var. of *tagilen*, prob. from ON] — **'tangled** *or* **'tangly** *adj.*

tango ('tæŋgəʊ) *n., pl.* **-gos. 1.** a Latin-American dance characterized by long gliding steps and sudden pauses. **2.** a piece of music composed for or in the rhythm of this dance. ~*vb.* **-going, -goed. 3.** (*intr.*) to perform this dance. [C20: from American Sp., prob. of Niger-Congo origin]

tangram ('tæŋgræm) *n.* a Chinese puzzle in which a square, cut into a parallelogram, a square, and five triangles, is formed into figures. [C19: ?from Chinese *t'ang* Chinese + -GRAM]

Tangshan ('tæŋ'ʃæn) *n.* an industrial city in NE China, in Hebei province. Pop.: 1 390 000 (1986).

Tanguy (*French* tɑ̃gi) *n.* **Yves** (iv). 1900–55, U.S. surrealist painter, born in France.

tangy ('tæŋɪ) *adj.* **tangier, tangiest.** having a pungent, fresh, or briny flavour or aroma.

tanh (θæn, tænʃ) *n.* hyperbolic tangent; a hyperbolic function that is the ratio of sinh to cosh. [C20: from TAN(GENT) + H(YPERBOLIC)]

Tanis ('teɪnɪs) *n.* an ancient city located in the E part of the Nile delta: abandoned after the 6th century B.C.; at one time the capital of Egypt. Biblical name: **Zoan.**

Tanjore (tæn'dʒɔː) *n.* the former name of **Thanjavur.**

Tanjungpriok (,tændʒʊŋ'priːɒk) *n.* a variant spelling of **Tandjungpriok.**

tank (tæŋk) *n.* **1.** a large container or reservoir for liquids or gases. **2.** an armoured combat vehicle moving on tracks and armed with guns, etc. **3.** *Brit. or U.S. dialect.* a reservoir, lake, or pond. **4.** *Sl., chiefly U.S.* a jail. **5.** Also called: **tankful.** the quantity contained in a tank. **6.** *Austral.* a reservoir formed by excavation and damming. ~*vb.* **7.** (*tr.*) to put or keep in a tank. **8.** *Sl.* to defeat heavily. ~See also **tank up.** [C17: from Gujarati (a language of W India) *tānkh* artificial lake, but infl. also by Port. *tanque*, from *estanque* pond, ult. from Vulgar L *stanticāre* (unattested) to block]

tanka ('tɑːŋkə) *n., pl.* **-kas** *or* **-ka.** a Japanese verse form consisting of five lines, the first and third having five syllables, the others seven. [C19: from Japanese, from *tan* short + *ka* verse]

tankage ('tæŋkɪdʒ) *n.* **1.** the capacity or contents of a tank or tanks. **2.** the act of storing in a tank or tanks, or a fee charged for this. **3.** *Agriculture.* **a.** fertilizer consisting of the dried and ground residues of animal carcasses. **b.** a protein supplement feed for livestock.

tankard ('tæŋkəd) *n.* a large one-handled drinking vessel sometimes fitted with a hinged lid. [C14]

tank engine *or* **locomotive** *n.* a steam locomotive that carries its water supply in tanks mounted around its boiler.

tanker ('tæŋkə) *n.* a ship, lorry, or aeroplane designed to carry liquid in bulk, such as oil.

tank farming *n.* another name for **hydroponics.** — **tank farmer** *n.*

tank top *n.* a sleeveless upper garment with wide shoulder straps and a low neck. [C20: after *tank suits,* one-piece bathing costumes of the 1920s worn in tanks or swimming pools]

tank up *vb.* (*adv.*) *Chiefly Brit.* **1.** to fill the tank of (a vehicle) with petrol. **2.** *Sl.* to imbibe or cause to imbibe a large quantity of alcoholic drink.

tank wagon *or esp. U.S. & Canad.* **tank car** *n.* a form of railway wagon carrying a tank for the transport of liquids.

tanner[1] ('tænə) *n.* a person who tans skins and hides.

tanner[2] ('tænə) *n. Brit.* an informal word for **sixpence.** [C19: from ?]

tannery ('tænərɪ) *n., pl.* **-neries.** a place or building where skins and hides are tanned.

Tannhäuser ('tæn,hɔɪzə) *n.* 13th-century German minnesinger, commonly identified with a legendary knight who sought papal absolution after years spent in revelry with Venus. The legend forms the basis of an opera by Wagner.

tannic ('tænɪk) *adj.* of, relating to, containing, or produced from tan, tannin, or tannic acid.

tannin ('tænɪn) *n.* any of a class of yellowish compounds found in many plants and used as tanning agents, mordants, medical astringents, etc. Also called: **tannic acid.** [C19: from F *tanin,* from TAN[1]]

Tannoy ('tænɔɪ) *n. Trademark.* a type of public-address system.

tansy ('tænzɪ) *n., pl.* **-sies.** any of numerous plants having yellow flowers in flat-topped clusters and formerly used in medicine and for seasoning. [C15: from OF *tanesie,* from Med. L *athanasia* (from its alleged power to prolong life) from Gk: immortality]

Tanta ('tæntə) *n.* a city in N Egypt, on the Nile delta: noted for its Muslim festivals. Pop.: 364 700 (1985).

tantalite ('tæntə,laɪt) *n.* a heavy brownish mineral: it occurs in coarse granite and is an ore of tantalum. [C19: from TANTALUM + -ITE[1]]

tantalize *or* **-ise** ('tæntə,laɪz) *vb.* (*tr.*) to tease or make frustrated, as by tormenting with the sight of something desired but inaccessible. [C16: from TANTALUS] — **,tantali'zation** *or* **-i'sation** *n.* — **'tanta,lizing** *or* **-ising** *adj.* — **'tanta,lizingly** *or* **-isingly** *adv.*

tantalum ('tæntələm) *n.* a hard greyish-white metallic element: used in electrolytic rectifiers and in alloys to increase hardness and chemical resistance, esp. in surgical instruments. Symbol: Ta; atomic no.: 73; atomic wt.: 180.95. [C19: after TANTALUS, from the metal's incapacity to absorb acids]

tantalus ('tæntələs) *n. Brit.* a case in which bottles may be locked with their contents tantalizingly visible.

Tantalus ('tæntələs) *n. Greek myth.* a king, the father of Pelops, punished in Hades for his misdeeds by having to stand in water that recedes when he tries to drink it and under fruit that moves away as he reaches for it.

tantamount ('tæntə,maʊnt) *adj.* (*postpositive; foll. by to*) as good (as); equivalent in effect (to). [C17: from Anglo-F *tant amunter* to amount to as much]

tantara ('tæntərə, tæn'tɑːrə) *n.* a fanfare or blast, as on a trumpet or horn. [C16: from L *taratantara,* imit. of the sound of the tuba]

tantivy (tæn'tɪvɪ) *adv.* **1.** at full speed; rapidly. ~*n., pl.* **-tivies,** *sentence substitute.* **2.** a hunting cry, esp. at full gallop. [C17: ? imit. of galloping hooves]

tant mieux *French.* (tɑ̃ mjø) so much the better.

tanto ('tæntəʊ) *adv. Music.* too much; excessively. [It.]

tant pis *French.* (tɑ̃ pi) so much the worse.

Tantrism ('tæntrɪzəm) *n.* **1.** a movement within Hinduism combining magical and mystical elements and with sacred writings of its own (**the Tantra**). **2.** a similar movement within Buddhism. [C18: from Sansk. *tantra,* lit.: warp, hence doctrine] — **'Tantric** *adj.* — **'Tantrist** *n.*

tantrum ('tæntrəm) *n.* (*often pl.*) a childish fit of rage; outburst of bad temper. [C18: from ?]

Tanzania (,tænzə'nɪə) *n.* a republic in E Africa, on the Indian Ocean: formed by the union of the independent states of Tanganyika and Zanzibar in 1964; a member of the Commonwealth. Exports include coffee, tea, sisal, and cotton. Official languages: English and Swahili. Religions: Christian, Muslim, and animist. Currency: Tanzanian shilling. Capital: Dodoma. Pop.: 23 200 000 (1987 est.). Area: 945 203 sq. km (364 943 sq. miles). — **,Tanza'nian** *adj., n.*

Tao (taʊ) *n.* (in the philosophy of Taoism) **1.** that in virtue of which all things happen or exist. **2.** the rational basis of human conduct. **3.** the course of life and its relation to eternal truth. [Chinese, lit.: path, way]

Taoiseach ('tiːʃæx) *n.* the prime mininster of the Irish Republic. [from Irish, lit.: leader]

Taoism ('taʊɪzəm) *n.* a system of religion and philosophy based on the teachings of Lao Zi and advocating a simple honest life and noninterference with the course of natural events. — **'Taoist** *n., adj.* — **,Tao'istic** *adj.*

tap[1] (tæp) *vb.* **tapping, tapped. 1.** to strike (something) lightly and usually repeatedly. **2.** (*tr.*) to produce by striking in this way: *to tap a rhythm.* **3.** (*tr.*) to strike lightly with (something): *to tap one's finger on the desk.* **4.** (*intr.*) to walk with a tapping sound. **5.** (*tr.*) to attach reinforcing pieces to (the toe or heel of a shoe). ~*n.* **6.** a light blow or knock, or the sound made by it. **7.** the metal piece attached to the toe or heel of a shoe used for tap-dancing. **8.** short for **tap-dancing.** ~See also **taps.** [C13 *tappen,* prob. from OF *taper,* of Gmc origin]

tap[2] (tæp) *n.* **1.** a valve by which a fluid flow from a pipe can be controlled. U.S. names: **faucet, spigot. 2.** a stopper to plug a cask or barrel. **3.** a particular quality of alcoholic drink, esp. when contained in casks: *an excellent tap.* **4.** *Brit.* short for **taproom. 5.** the withdrawal of fluid from a bodily cavity. **6.** a tool for cutting female screw threads. **7.** *Electronics, chiefly U.S. & Canad.* a connection made at some point between the end terminals of an inductor, resistor, etc. Usual Brit. name: **tapping. 8.** a concealed listening or recording device connected to a telephone or telegraph wire. **9. on tap. a.** *Inf.* ready for use. **b.** (of drinks) on draught. ~*vb.* **tapping, tapped.** (*tr.*) **10.** to furnish with a tap. **11.** to draw off with or as if with a tap. **12.** to cut into (a tree) and draw off sap from it. **13.** *Brit. inf.* **a.** to ask (someone) for money: *he tapped me for a fiver.* **b.** to obtain (money) from someone. **14.** to connect a tap to (a telephone or telegraph wire). **15.** to make a connection to (a pipe, drain, etc.). **16.** to cut a female screw thread in (an object or material) by use of a tap. [OE *tæppa*] — **'tapper** *n.*

tapa ('tɑːpə) *n.* **1.** the inner bark of the paper mulberry. **2.** a cloth made from this in the Pacific islands. [C19: from native Polynesian name]

Tapajós (*Portuguese* tapa'ʒɒs) *n.* a river in N Brazil, rising in N central Mato Grosso and flowing northeast to the Amazon. Length: about 800 km (500 miles).

tap dance *n.* **1.** a step dance in which the performer wears shoes equipped with taps that make a rhythmic sound on the stage as he dances. ~*vb.* **tap-dance.** (*intr.*) **2.** to perform a tap dance. — **'tap-,dancer** *n.* — **'tap,dancing** *n.*

tape (teɪp) *n.* **1.** a long thin strip of cotton, linen, etc., used for binding, fastening, etc. **2.** a long narrow strip of paper, metal, etc. **3.** a string stretched across the track at the end of a race course. **4.** See **magnetic tape, ticker tape, paper tape, tape recording.** ~*vb.* (*mainly tr.*) **5.**

to furnish with tapes. **6.** to bind, measure, secure, or wrap with tape. **7.** (*usually passive*) *Brit. inf.* to take stock of (a person or situation). **8.** (*also intr.*) Also: **tape-record.** to record (speech, music, etc.). [OE *tæppe*] —'**tape,like** *adj.* —'**taper** *n.*

tape deck *n.* the platform supporting the spools, cassettes, or cartridges of a tape recorder, incorporating the motor and the playback, recording, and erasing heads.

tape machine *n.* a telegraphic device that records current stock quotations electronically or on ticker tape. U.S. equivalent: **ticker.**

tape measure *n.* a tape or length of metal marked off in inches, centimetres, etc., used for measuring. Also called (esp. U.S.): **tapeline.**

taper ('teɪpə) *vb.* **1.** to become or cause to become narrower towards one end. **2.** (often foll. by *off*) to become or cause to become smaller or less significant. ~*n.* **3.** a thin candle. **4.** a thin wooden or waxed strip for transferring a flame; spill. **5.** a narrowing. **6.** any feeble light. [OE *tapor*, prob. from L *papȳrus* papyrus (from its use as a wick)] —'**taperer** *n.* —'**tapering** *adj.*

tape recorder *n.* an electrical device used for recording sounds on magnetic tape and usually also for reproducing them.

tape recording *n.* **1.** the act of recording on magnetic tape. **2.** the magnetized tape used for this. **3.** the speech, music, etc., so recorded.

tapestry ('tæpɪstrɪ) *n., pl.* **-tries. 1.** a heavy woven fabric, often in the form of a picture, used for wall hangings, furnishings, etc. **2.** another word for **needlepoint** (sense 1). [C15: from OF *tapisserie* carpeting, from OF *tapiz*; see TAPIS] —'**tapestried** *adj.*

tapeworm ('teɪp,wɜːm) *n.* any of a class of parasitic ribbon-like flatworms. The adults inhabit the intestines of vertebrates.

taphole ('tæp,həʊl) *n.* a hole in a furnace for running off molten metal or slag.

taphouse ('tæp,haʊs) *n. Now rare.* an inn.

tapioca (,tæpɪ'əʊkə) *n.* a beadlike starch obtained from cassava root, used in cooking as a thickening agent, esp. in puddings. [C18: via Port. from Tupi *tipioca* pressed-out juice, from *tipi* residue + *ok* to squeeze out]

tapir ('teɪpə) *n., pl.* **-pirs** *or* **-pir.** any of various mammals of South and Central America and SE Asia, having an elongated snout, three-toed hind legs, and four-toed forelegs. [C18: from Tupi *tapiira*]

tapis ('tæpiː) *n., pl.* **tapis. 1.** tapestry or carpeting, esp. as formerly used to cover a table. **2. on the tapis.** currently under consideration. [C17: from F, from OF *tapiz*, from Gk *tapētion* rug, from *tapēs* carpet]

tappet ('tæpɪt) *n.* a mechanical part that reciprocates to receive or transmit intermittent motion. [C18: from TAP[1] + -ET]

taproom ('tæp,ruːm, -,rʊm) *n.* a bar, as in a hotel or pub.

taproot ('tæp,ruːt) *n.* the main root of plants such as the dandelion, which grows vertically downwards and bears smaller lateral roots.

taps (tæps) *n.* (*functioning as sing.*) **1.** *Chiefly U.S.* **a.** (in army camps, etc.) a signal given on a bugle, drum, etc., indicating that lights are to be put out. **b.** any similar signal, as at a military funeral. **2.** (in the Guide movement) a closing song sung at an evening camp fire or at the end of a meeting.

tapster ('tæpstə) *n.* **1.** *Rare.* a barman. **2.** (in W Africa) a man who taps palm trees. [OE *tæppestre*, fem. of *tæppere*, from *tappian* to TAP[2]]

tap water *n.* water drawn off through taps from pipes in a house, as distinguished from distilled water, mineral water, etc.

tar[1] (tɑː) *n.* **1.** any of various dark viscid substances obtained by the destructive distillation of organic matter such as coal, wood, or peat. **2.** another name for **coal tar.** ~*vb.* **tarring, tarred.** (*tr.*) **3.** to coat with tar. **4. tar and feather.** to punish by smearing tar and feathers over (someone). **5. tarred with the same brush.** having the same faults. [OE *teoru*] —'**tarry** *adj.* —'**tarriness** *n.*

tar[2] (tɑː) *n.* an informal word for **seaman.** [C17: short for TARPAULIN]

Tara ('tærə, 'tɑːrə) *n.* a village in Co. Meath near Dublin, by the **Hill of Tara,** the historic seat of the ancient Irish kings.

Tarabulus el Gharb (tə'rɑːbələs ɛl 'gɑːb) *n.* transliteration of the Arabic name for **Tripoli** (Libya).

Tarabulus esh Sham (tə'rɑːbələs ɛʃ 'ʃæm) *n.* transliteration of the Arabic name for **Tripoli** (Lebanon).

taradiddle ('tærə,dɪd°l) *n.* a variant spelling of **tarradiddle.**

tarakihi *or* **terakihi** ('tærə,kiːhiː) *n., pl.* **-kihis.** a common edible sea fish of New Zealand waters. [from Maori]

taramasalata (,tærəməsə'lɑːtə) *n.* a creamy pale pink paté, made from the roe of grey mullet or smoked cod and served as an hors d'oeuvre. [C20: from Mod. Gk, from *tarama* cod's roe]

tarantass (,tærən'tæs) *n.* a four-wheeled Russian carriage without springs. [C19: from Russian *tarantas*]

tarantella (,tærən'tɛlə) *n.* **1.** a peasant dance from S Italy. **2.** a piece of music composed for or in the rhythm of this dance. [C18: from It., from TARANTO]

tarantism ('tærən,tɪzəm) *n.* a nervous disorder marked by uncontrollable bodily movement, widespread in S Italy during the 15th to 17th centuries: popularly thought to be caused by the bite of a tarantula. [C17: from NL *tarantismus*, from TARANTO]

Taranto (tə'ræntəʊ; *Italian* 'tɑːranto) *n.* a port in SE Italy, in Apulia on the **Gulf of Taranto** (an inlet of the Ionian Sea): the chief city of Magna Graecia; taken by the Romans in 272 B.C. Pop.: 244 997 (1986). Latin name: **Tarentum.**

tarantula (tə'ræntjʊlə) *n., pl.* **-las** *or* **-lae** (-,liː). **1.** any of various large hairy spiders of tropical America. **2.** a large hairy spider of S Europe. [C16: from Med. L, from OIt. *tarantola*, from TARANTO]

Tarawa (tə'rɑːwə) *n.* the capital of Kiribati, occupying a chain of islets surrounding a lagoon in the W central Pacific. Pop.: 25 100 (1983 est.).

taraxacum (tə'ræksəkəm) *n.* **1.** any of a genus of perennial plants of the composite family, such as the dandelion. **2.** the dried root of the dandelion, used as a laxative, diuretic, and tonic. [C18: from Med. L, from Ar. *tarakhshaqūn* wild chicory, ? of Persian origin]

Tarbes (*French* tarb) *n.* a town in SW France: noted for the breeding of Anglo-Arab horses. Pop.: 54 850 (1983).

tarboosh (tɑː'buːʃ) *n.* a felt or cloth brimless cap, usually red and often with a silk tassel, worn by Muslim men. [C18: from Ar. *tarbūsh*]

tarboy ('tɑː,bɔɪ) *n. Austral. & N.Z. inf.* a boy who applies tar to the skin of sheep cut during shearing.

Tardenoisian (,tɑːdə'nɔɪzɪən) *adj.* of or referring to a Mesolithic culture characterized by small flint instruments. [C20: after *Tardenois*, France, where implements were found]

tardigrade ('tɑːdɪ,greɪd) *n.* any of various minute aquatic segmented eight-legged invertebrates occurring in soil, ditches, etc. Popular name: **water bear.** [C17: via L *tardigradus*, from *tardus* sluggish + *gradi* to walk]

tardy ('tɑːdɪ) *adj.* **-dier, -diest. 1.** occurring later than expected. **2.** slow in progress, growth, etc. [C15: from OF *tardif*, from L *tardus* slow] —'**tardily** *adv.* —'**tardiness** *n.*

tare[1] (tɛə) *n.* **1.** any of various vetch plants of Eurasia and N Africa. **2.** the seed of any of these plants. **3.** *Bible.* a weed, thought to be the darnel. [C14: from ?]

tare[2] (tɛə) *n.* **1.** the weight of the wrapping or container in which goods are packed. **2.** a deduction from gross weight to compensate for this. **3.** the weight of an unladen vehicle. ~*vb.* **4.** (*tr.*) to weigh (a package, etc.) in order to calculate the amount of tare. [C15: from OF: waste, from Med. L *tara*, from Ar. *tarhah* something discarded, from *taraha* to reject]

Tarentum (tə'rentəm) *n.* the Latin name of **Taranto.**

targe (tɑːdʒ) *n.* an archaic word for **shield.** [C13: from OF, of Gmc origin]

target ('tɑːgɪt) *n.* **1. a.** an object or area at which an archer or marksman aims, usually a round flat surface marked with concentric rings. **b.** (*as modifier*): *target practice.* **2. a.** any point or area aimed at. **b.** (*as modifier*): *target area.* **3.** a fixed goal or objective. **4.** a person or thing at which an action or remark is directed or the object of a person's feelings. **5.** a joint of lamb consisting of the breast and neck. **6.** (formerly) a small round shield. **7.** *Physics, electronics.* **a.** a substance subjected to bombardment by electrons or other particles, or to irradiation. **b.** an electrode in a television camera tube whose surface is scanned by the electron beam. **8.** *Electronics.* an object detected by the reflection of a radar or sonar signal, etc. ~*vb.* (*tr.*) **9.** to make a target of. **10.** to

direct or aim: *to target benefits at those most in need.*
[C14: from OF *targette* a little shield, from OF TARGE]

tariff ('tærɪf) *n.* **1. a.** a tax levied by a government on imports or occasionally exports. **b.** a system or list of such taxes. **2.** any schedule of prices, fees, fares, etc. **3.** *Chiefly Brit.* **a.** a method of charging for the supply of services such as gas and electricity. **b.** a schedule of such charges. **4.** *Chiefly Brit.* a bill of fare with prices listed; menu. ~*vb.* (*tr.*) **5.** to set a tariff on. **6.** to price according to a schedule of tariffs. [C16: from It. *tariffa*, from Ar. *ta'rīfa* to inform]

Tarim ('tɑː'riːm) *n.* a river in NW China, in Xinjiang Uygur AR: flows east along the N edge of the Taklimakan Shama desert, dividing repeatedly and forming lakes among the dunes, finally disappearing in the Lop Nor depression; the chief river of Xinjiang Uygur AR; drains the great **Tarim Basin** between the Tian Shan and Kunlun mountain systems of central Asia, an area of about 906 500 sq. km (350 000 sq. miles). Length: 2190 km (1360 miles).

Tarkington ('tɑːkɪŋtən) *n.* (**Newton**) **Booth.** 1869–1946, U.S. novelist. His works include the historical romance *Monsieur Beaucaire* (1900), tales of the Middle West, such as *The Magnificent Ambersons* (1918) and *Alice Adams* (1921), and the series featuring the character Penrod.

tarlatan ('tɑːlətən) *n.* an open-weave cotton fabric, used for stiffening garments. [C18: from F *tarlatane*, var. of *tarnatane* type of muslin, ? of Indian origin]

Tarmac ('tɑːmæk) *n.* **1.** *Trademark.* (*often not cap.*) a paving material that consists of crushed stone rolled and bound with a mixture of tar and bitumen, esp. as used for a road, airport runway, etc. Full name: **Tarmacadam** (ˌtɑːməˈkædəm). See also **macadam.** ~*vb.* **-macking, -macked.** (*tr.*) **2.** (*usually not cap.*) to apply tarmac to.

tarn (tɑːn) *n.* a small mountain lake or pool. [C14: from ON]

Tarn (*French* tarn) *n.* **1.** a department of S France, in Midi-Pyrénées region. Capital: Albi. Pop.: 339 345 (1982). Area: 5780 sq. km (2254 sq. miles). **2.** a river in SW France, rising in the Massif Central and flowing generally west to the Garonne River. Length: 375 km (233 miles).

tarnation (tɑːˈneɪʃən) *n.* a euphemism for **damnation.**

Tarn-et-Garonne (*French* tarnegarɔn) *n.* a department of SW France, in Midi-Pyrénées region. Capital: Montauban. Pop.: 190 485 (1982). Area: 3731 sq. km (1455 sq. miles).

tarnish ('tɑːnɪʃ) *vb.* **1.** to lose or cause to lose the shine, esp. by exposure to air or moisture resulting in surface oxidation; discolour. **2.** to stain or become stained; taint. ~*n.* **3.** a tarnished condition, surface, or film. [C16: from OF *ternir* to make dull, from *terne* lustreless of Gmc origin] —**'tarnishable** *adj.*

Tarnopol (tar'nɔpɔl) *n.* the Polish name for **Ternopol.**

Tarnów (*Polish* 'tarnuf) *n.* an industrial city in SE Poland. Pop.: 103 673 (1980 est.).

taro ('tɑːrəʊ) *n.*, *pl.* **-ros. 1.** an Asian plant, cultivated in the tropics for its large edible rootstock. **2.** the rootstock of this plant. [C18: from Tahitian & Maori]

tarot ('tærəʊ) *n.* **1.** one of a special pack of cards, now used mainly for fortune-telling. **2.** a card in a tarot pack with distinctive symbolic design. ~*adj.* **3.** relating to tarot cards. [C16: from F, from OIt. *tarocco*, from ?]

tarpan ('tɑːpæn) *n.* a European wild horse, now extinct. [from Tatar]

tarpaulin (tɑːˈpɔːlɪn) *n.* **1.** a heavy waterproof fabric made of canvas or similar material coated with tar, wax, or paint. **2.** a sheet of this fabric. **3.** a hat made of or covered with this fabric, esp. a sailor's hat. **4.** a rare word for **seaman.** [C17: prob. from TAR¹ + PALL¹ + -ING¹]

Tarpeia (tɑːˈpiːə) *n.* (in Roman legend) a vestal virgin, who betrayed Rome to the Sabines and was killed by them when she requested a reward.

Tarpeian Rock (tɑːˈpiːən) *n.* (in ancient Rome) a cliff on the Capitoline hill from which traitors were hurled.

tarpon ('tɑːpən) *n.*, *pl.* **-pons** *or* **-pon.** a large silvery game fish of warm oceans. [C17: ?from Du. *tarpoen*, from ?]

Tarquin ('tɑːkwɪn) *n.* **1.** Latin name *Lucius Tarquinius Priscus.* fifth legendary king of Rome (616–578 B.C.). **2.** Latin name *Lucius Tarquinius Superbus.* seventh and last legendary king of Rome (534–510 B.C.).

tarradiddle ('tærəˌdɪdªl) *n.* **1.** a trifling lie. **2.** nonsense; twaddle. [C18: from ?]

tarragon ('tærəgən) *n.* **1.** an aromatic plant of the Old World, having leaves which are used as seasoning. **2.** the

leaves of this plant. [C16: from OF *targon*, from Med. L *tarcon*, ? ult. from Gk *drakontion* adderwort]

Tarragona (*Spanish* tarraˈɣona) *n.* a port in NE Spain, on the Mediterranean: one of the richest seaports of the Roman Empire; destroyed by the Moors (714). Pop.: 106 631 (1986 est.). Latin name: **Tarraco** (təˈrɑːkəʊ).

Tarrasa (*Spanish* ta'rrasa) *n.* a city in NE Spain: textile centre. Pop.: 155 360 (1981).

tarry ('tærɪ) *vb.* **-rying, -ried. 1.** (*intr.*) to delay; linger. **2.** (*intr.*) to remain temporarily or briefly. **3.** (*intr.*) to wait or stay. **4.** (*tr.*) *Arch. or poetic.* to await. [C14 *tarien*, from ?] —**'tarrier** *n.*

tarsal ('tɑːsªl) *adj.* **1.** of the tarsus or tarsi. ~*n.* **2.** a tarsal bone.

tarseal ('tɑːˌsiːl) *n.* *N.Z.* **1.** the bitumen surface of a road. **2.** the **tarseal.** the main highway.

Tarshish ('tɑːʃɪʃ) *n.* *Old Testament.* an ancient port, mentioned in I Kings 10:22, situated in Spain or in one of the Phoenician colonies in Sardinia.

tarsia ('tɑːsɪə) *n.* another term for **intarsia.** [C17: from It., from Ar. *tarsi*']

tarsier ('tɑːsɪə) *n.* any of several nocturnal arboreal primates of Indonesia and the Philippines, having huge eyes and long hind legs. [C18: from F, from *tarse* the flat of the foot; see TARSUS]

tarsus ('tɑːsəs) *n.*, *pl.* **-si** (-saɪ). **1.** the bones of the ankle and heel, collectively. **2.** the corresponding part in other mammals and in amphibians and reptiles. **3.** the connective tissue supporting the free edge of each eyelid. **4.** the part of an insect's leg that lies distal to the tibia. [C17: from NL, from Gk *tarsos* flat surface, instep]

Tarsus ('tɑːsəs) *n.* **1.** a city in SE Turkey, on the Tarsus River: site of ruins of ancient Tarsus, capital of Cilicia, and birthplace of St. Paul. Pop.: 121 074 (1980). **2.** a river in SE Turkey, in Cilicia, rising in the Taurus Mountains and flowing south past Tarsus to the Mediterranean. Ancient name: **Cydnus.** Length: 153 km (95 miles).

tart¹ (tɑːt) *n.* **1.** *Chiefly Brit.* a pastry case often having no top crust, with a filling of fruit, jam, custard, etc. **2.** *Chiefly U.S.* a small open pie with a fruit filling. [C14: from OF *tarte*, from ?]

tart² (tɑːt) *adj.* **1.** (of a flavour, etc.) sour; acid. **2.** cutting; sharp: *a tart remark.* [OE *teart* rough] —**'tartly** *adv.* —**'tartness** *n.*

tart³ (tɑːt) *n.* *Inf.* a promiscuous woman, esp. a prostitute. See also **tart up.** [C19: shortened from SWEETHEART] —**'tarty** *adj.*

tartan ('tɑːtªn) *n.* **1. a.** a design of straight lines, crossing at right angles to give a chequered appearance, esp. the distinctive design or designs associated with each Scottish clan. **b.** (*as modifier*): *a tartan kilt.* **2.** a fabric or garment with this design. [C16: ?from OF *tertaine* linsey-woolsey, from OSp. *tiritaña* a fine silk fabric, from *tiritar* to rustle] —**'tartaned** *adj.*

tartar¹ ('tɑːtə) *n.* **1.** a hard deposit on the teeth, consisting of food, cellular debris, and mineral salts. **2.** a brownish-red substance consisting mainly of potassium hydrogen tartrate, deposited during the fermentation of wine. [C14: from Med. L *tartarum*, from Med. Gk *tartaron*]

tartar² ('tɑːtə) *n.* (*sometimes cap.*) a fearsome or formidable person. [C16: special use of TARTAR]

Tartar ('tɑːtə) *n.*, *adj.* a variant spelling of **Tatar.**

Tartarean (tɑːˈtɛərɪən) *adj.* *Literary.* of or relating to Tartarus; infernal.

tartar emetic *n.* antimony potassium tartrate, a poisonous, crystalline salt used as a mordant and in medicine.

tartaric (tɑːˈtærɪk) *adj.* of, containing, or derived from tartar or tartaric acid.

tartaric acid *n.* a colourless crystalline acid which is found in many fruits: used as a food additive (**E 334**) in soft drinks, confectionery, and baking powders, and in tanning and photography. Formula: $(CHOH)_2(COOH)_2$. Systematic name: **2,3-dihydroxybutanedioic acid.**

tartar sauce *n.* a mayonnaise sauce mixed with hard-boiled egg yolks, chopped herbs, capers, etc. [from F *sauce tartare*, from TARTAR]

Tartarus ('tɑːtərəs) *n.* *Greek myth.* **1.** an abyss under Hades where the Titans were imprisoned. **2.** a part of Hades reserved for evildoers. **3.** the underworld; Hades. **4.** a primordial god who became the father of the monster Typhon. [C16: from L, from Gk *Tartaros*, of obscure origin]

Tartary ('tɑːtərɪ) n. a variant spelling of **Tatary**.

tartlet ('tɑːtlɪt) n. Brit. an individual pastry case with a sweet or savoury filling.

tartrate ('tɑːtreɪt) n. any salt or ester of tartaric acid.

tartrated ('tɑːtreɪtɪd) adj. being in the form of a tartrate.

tartrazine ('tɑːtrə,ziːn, -zɪn) n. an azo dye that produces a yellow colour: used as a food additive (**E102**), in drugs, and to dye textiles.

Tartu (Russian 'tartu) n. a city in the W Soviet Union, in the SE Estonian SSR: became Russian in 1704 after successive Russian, Polish, and Swedish rule; university (1632). Pop.: 111 000 (1986 est.). Former name (11th century until 1918): **Yurev**. German name: **Dorpat**.

tart up vb. (tr.; adv.) Brit. inf. **1.** to dress and make (oneself) up in a provocative or promiscuous way. **2.** to reissue or decorate in a cheap and flashy way: to tart up a bar.

tarwhine ('tɑː,waɪn) n. any of various Australian marine food fishes, esp. the sea bream. [?from Abor.]

Tarzan ('tɑːzən) n. (sometimes not cap.) Inf., often ironical. a man with great physical strength, agility, and virility. [C20: after the hero of a series of stories by E. R. BURROUGHS]

Tas. abbrev. for Tasmania.

Tashkent (Russian taʃ'kjent) n. a city in the S central Soviet Union, capital of the Uzbek SSR: one of the oldest and largest cities in central Asia; taken by the Russians in 1865; cotton textile manufacturing. Pop.: 2 124 000 (1987).

tasimeter (tə'sɪmɪtə) n. a device for measuring small temperature changes. It depends on the changes of pressure resulting from expanding or contracting solids. [C19 tasi-, from Gk tasis tension + -METER] —**tasimetric** (,tæsɪ'mɛtrɪk) adj. —**ta'simetry** n.

task (tɑːsk) n. **1.** a specific piece of work required to be done. **2.** an unpleasant or difficult job or duty. **3.** any piece of work. **4.** **take to task.** to criticize or reprove. ~vb. (tr.) **5.** to assign a task to. **6.** to subject to severe strain; tax. [C13: from OF tasche, from Med. L tasca, from taxa tax, from L taxāre to TAX]

task force n. **1.** a temporary grouping of military units formed to undertake a specific mission. **2.** any organization set up to carry out a continuing task.

taskmaster ('tɑːsk,mɑːstə) n. a person, discipline, etc., that enforces work, esp. hard or continuous work. —**'task,mistress** fem. n.

taskwork ('tɑːsk,wɜːk) n. **1.** hard or unpleasant work. **2.** a rare word for **piecework**.

Tasman ('tæzmən) n. **Abel Janszoon** ('ɑbəl 'jansuːn). 1603–59, Dutch navigator, who discovered Tasmania, New Zealand, and the Tonga and Fiji Islands (1642–43).

Tasmania (tæz'meɪnɪə) n. an island in the S Pacific, south of mainland Australia: forms, with offshore islands, the smallest state of Australia; discovered by the Dutch explorer Tasman in 1642; used as a penal colony by the British (1803–53); mostly forested and mountainous. Capital: Hobart. Pop.: 442 111 (1985). Area: 68 332 sq. km (26 383 sq. miles). Former name (1642–1855): **Van Diemen's Land**. —**Tas'manian** adj., n.

Tasmanian devil n. a small ferocious carnivorous marsupial of Tasmania.

Tasmanian wolf or **tiger** n. other names for **thylacine**.

Tasman Sea n. the part of the Pacific between SE Australia and NW New Zealand.

tass (tæs) or **tassie** ('tæsɪ) n. Scot. & N English dialect. **1.** a cup or glass. **2.** its contents. [C15: from OF tasse cup, from Ar. tassah basin, from Persian tast]

Tass (tæs) n. the principal news agency of the Soviet Union. [T(elegrafnoye) a(gentstvo) S(ovetskogo) S(oyuza) Telegraphic Agency of the Soviet Union]

TASS (tæs) n. (in Britain) acronym for Technical, Administrative, and Supervisory Section (of the AEU).

tassel ('tæsəl) n. **1.** a tuft of loose threads secured by a knot or knob, used to decorate soft furnishings, clothes, etc. **2.** anything resembling this, esp. the tuft of stamens at the tip of a maize inflorescence. ~vb. **-selling, -selled** or U.S. **-seling, -seled.** **3.** (tr.) to adorn with tassels. **4.** (intr.) (of maize) to produce stamens in a tuft. [C13: from OF, from Vulgar L tassellus (unattested), changed from L taxillus a small die]

Tasso (Italian 'tasso) n. **Torquato** (tor'kwaːto). 1544–95, Italian poet, noted for his pastoral idyll Aminta (1573) and for Jerusalem Delivered (1581), dealing with the First Crusade.

taste (teɪst) n. **1.** the sense by which the qualities and flavour of a substance are distinguished by the taste buds. **2.** the sensation experienced by means of the taste buds. **3.** the act of tasting. **4.** a small amount eaten, drunk, or tried on the tongue. **5.** a brief experience of something: a taste of the whip. **6.** a preference or liking for something. **7.** the ability to make discerning judgments about aesthetic, artistic, and intellectual matters. **8.** judgment of aesthetic or social matters according to a generally accepted standard: bad taste. **9.** discretion; delicacy: that remark lacks taste. ~vb. **10.** to distinguish the taste of (a substance) by means of the taste buds. **11.** (usually tr.) to take a small amount of (a food, liquid, etc.) into the mouth, esp. in order to test the quality. **12.** (often foll. by of) to have a specific flavour or taste. **13.** (when intr., usually foll. by of) to have an experience of (something): to taste success. **14.** (tr.) an archaic word for **enjoy**. [C13: from OF taster, ult. from L taxāre to appraise] —**'tastable** adj.

taste bud n. any of the elevated sensory organs on the surface of the tongue, by means of which the sensation of taste is experienced.

tasteful ('teɪstfʊl) adj. indicating good taste: a tasteful design. —**'tastefully** adv. —**'tastefulness** n.

tasteless ('teɪstlɪs) adj. **1.** lacking in flavour; insipid. **2.** lacking social or aesthetic taste. —**'tastelessly** adv. —**'tastelessness** n.

taster ('teɪstə) n. **1.** a person who samples food or drink for quality. **2.** any device used in tasting or sampling. **3.** a person employed, esp. formerly, to taste food and drink prepared for a king, etc., to test for poison.

tasty ('teɪstɪ) adj. **tastier, tastiest.** having a pleasant flavour. —**'tastily** adv. —**'tastiness** n.

tat¹ (tæt) vb. **tatting, tatted.** to make (something) by tatting. [C19: from ?]

tat² (tæt) n. **1.** tatty articles or a tatty condition. **2.** tasteless articles. **3.** a tangled mass. [C20: back formation from TATTY]

tat³ (tæt) n. See **tit for tat**.

ta-ta (tæ'tɑː) sentence substitute. Brit. inf. goodbye; farewell. [C19: from ?]

Tatar or **Tartar** ('tɑːtə) n. **1. a.** a member of a Mongoloid people who established a powerful state in central Asia in the 13th century. **b.** a descendant of this people, now scattered throughout the Soviet Union. **2.** any of the Turkic languages spoken by the present-day Tatars. ~adj. **3.** of or relating to the Tatars. [C14: from OF Tartare, from Med. L Tartarus (associated with L Tartarus the underworld), from Persian Tātār] —**Tatarian** (tɑː'tɛərɪən), **Tar'tarian** or **Tataric** (tɑː'tærɪk), **Tar'taric** adj.

Tatar Autonomous Soviet Socialist Republic n. an administrative division of the W central Soviet Union, in the RSFSR around the confluence of the Volga and Kama Rivers. Capital: Kazan. Pop.: 3 537 000 (1986) Area: 68 000 sq. km (26 250 sq. miles).

Tatar Strait n. an arm of the Pacific between the mainland of the SE Soviet Union and Sakhalin Island, linking the Sea of Japan with the Sea of Okhotsk. Length: about 560 km (350 miles). Also called: **Gulf of Tatary**.

Tatary or **Tartary** ('tɑːtərɪ) n. **1.** a historical region (with indefinite boundaries) in E Europe and Asia, inhabited by Bulgars until overrun by the Tatars in the mid-13th century: extended as far east as the Pacific under Genghis Khan. **2. Gulf of.** another name for the **Tatar Strait**.

Tate (teɪt) n. **1. Sir Henry.** 1819–99, English sugar refiner and philanthropist; founder of the Tate Gallery. **2.** (**John Orley**) **Allen.** 1899–1979, U.S. poet and critic.

Tate Gallery n. an art gallery in London, built in 1897.

tater ('teɪtə) n. a dialect word for **potato**.

Tati (French tati) n. **Jacques** (ʒak), real name Jacques Tatischeff. 1908–82, French film director, pantomimist, and comic actor, creator of the character Monsieur Hulot.

tatouay ('tætʊ,eɪ) n. a large armadillo of South America. [C16: from Sp. tatuay, from Guarani, from tatu armadillo + ai worthless (because inedible)]

Tatra Mountains ('tɑːtrə, 'tæt-) pl. n. a mountain range along the border between Czechoslovakia and Poland, extending for about 64 km (40 miles): the highest range of the central Carpathians. Highest peak: Gerlachovka, 2663 m (8737 ft.). Also called: **High Tatra**.

tatter ('tætə) vb. **1.** to make or become ragged or worn to shreds. ~n. **2.** a torn or ragged piece, esp. of material. [C14: from ON]

tatterdemalion (ˌtætədɪˈmeɪljən) *n. Rare.* a person dressed in ragged clothes. [C17: from TATTER + -*demalion*, from ?]

tattersall (ˈtætəˌsɔːl) *n.* a fabric having stripes or bars in a checked or squared pattern. [C19: after *Tattersall's*, a horse market in London founded by Richard *Tattersall* (died 1795), E horseman; the horse blankets at the market orig. had this pattern]

Tattersall's (ˈtætəˌsɔːlz) *n. Austral.* **1.** Also called (*inf.*): **Tatt's.** a lottery now based in Melbourne. **2.** a name used for sportsmen's clubs. [from Richard *Tattersall;* see TATTERSALL]

tatting (ˈtætɪŋ) *n.* **1.** an intricate type of lace made by looping a thread of cotton or linen by means of a hand shuttle. **2.** the act or work of producing this. [C19: from ?]

tattle (ˈtætˀl) *vb.* **1.** (*intr.*) to gossip about another's personal matters. **2.** (*tr.*) to reveal by gossiping. **3.** (*intr.*) to talk idly; chat. ~*n.* **4.** the act or an instance of tattling. **5.** a scandalmonger; gossip. [C15 (in the sense: to stammer, hesitate): from MDu. *tatelen* to prate, imit.] — ˈ**tattler** *n.*

tattletale (ˈtætˀlˌteɪl) *Chiefly U.S. & Canad.* ~*n.* **1.** a scandalmonger or gossip. ~*adj.* telltale.

tattoo[1] (tæˈtuː) *n., pl.* **-toos. 1.** (formerly) a signal by drum or bugle ordering the military to return to their quarters. **2.** a military display or pageant. **3.** any similar beating on a drum, etc. [C17: from Du. *taptoe*, from *tap toe!* turn off the taps! from *tap* tap of a barrel + *toe* to shut]

tattoo[2] (tæˈtuː) *vb.* **-tooing, -tooed. 1.** to make (pictures or designs) on (the skin) by pricking and staining with indelible colours. ~*n., pl.* **-toos. 2.** a design made by this process. **3.** the practice of tattooing. [C18: from Tahitian *tatau*] —ˈ**tattooer** or **tat**ˈ**tooist** *n.*

tatty (ˈtætɪ) *adj.* **-tier, -tiest.** *Chiefly Brit.* worn out, shabby, or unkempt. [C16: of Scot. origin] — ˈ**tattily** *adv.* —ˈ**tattiness** *n.*

Tatum (ˈteɪtəm) *n. Art,* full name *Arthur Tatum.* 1910–56, U.S. jazz pianist.

tau (tɔː, tau) *n.* the 19th letter in the Greek alphabet (T or τ). [C13: from Gk]

tau cross *n.* a cross shaped like the Greek letter tau. Also called: **Saint Anthony's cross.**

taught (tɔːt) *vb.* the past tense and past participle of **teach.**

taunt (tɔːnt) *vb.* (*tr.*) **1.** to provoke or deride with mockery, contempt, or criticism. **2.** to tease; tantalize. ~*n.* **3.** a jeering remark. [C16: from F *tant pour tant* like for like] —ˈ**taunting** *adj.*

Taunton (ˈtɔːntən) *n.* a market town in SW England, in Somerset: scene of Judge Jeffreys' "Bloody Assize" (1685) after the Battle of Sedgemoor. Pop.: 55 600 (1985).

taupe (təup) *n.* **a.** a brownish-grey colour. **b.** (*as adj.*): *a taupe coat.* [C20: from F, lit.: mole, from L *talpa*]

Taupo (ˈtaupəu) *n. Lake.* a lake in New Zealand, on central North Island: the largest lake of New Zealand. Area: 616 sq. km (238 sq. miles).

Tauranga (tauˈræŋə) *n.* a port in New Zealand, on NE North Island on the Bay of Plenty: exports dairy produce, meat, and timber. Pop.: 60 500 (1987).

taurine (ˈtɔːraɪn) *adj.* of or resembling a bull. [C17: from L *taurīnus*, from *taurus* a bull]

tauromachy (tɔːˈrɒməkɪ) *n.* the art or act of bullfighting. [C19: Gk *tauromakhia*, from *tauros* bull + *makhē* fight]

Taurus (ˈtɔːrəs) *n.* **1.** *Astron.* a constellation in the N hemisphere. **2.** *Astrol.* Also called: the **Bull.** the second sign of the zodiac. The sun is in this sign between about April 20 and May 20. [C14: from L: bull]

Taurus Mountains *pl. n.* a mountain range in S Turkey, parallel to the Mediterranean coast: crossed by the Cilician Gates; continued in the northeast by the Anti-Taurus range. Highest peak: Kaldi Daǧ, 3734 m (12 251 ft.).

taut (tɔːt) *adj.* **1.** tightly stretched; tense. **2.** showing nervous strain; stressed. **3.** *Chiefly naut.* in good order; neat. [C14 *tought*] —ˈ**tautly** *adv.* —ˈ**tautness** *n.*

tauten (ˈtɔːtˀn) *vb.* to make or become taut.

tauto- or before a vowel **taut-** *combining form.* identical or same: *tautology.* [from Gk *tauto*, from *to auto*]

tautog (tɔːˈtɒg) *n.* a large dark-coloured food fish of the North American coast of the Atlantic Ocean. [C17: from Narraganset *tautauog*, pl. of *tautau* sheepshead]

tautology (tɔːˈtɒlədʒɪ) *n., pl.* **-gies. 1.** the use of words that merely repeat elements of the meaning already conveyed, as in *Will these supplies be adequate enough?* in

place of *Will these supplies be adequate?* **2.** *Logic.* a statement that is always true, as in *either the sun is out or the sun is not out.* [C16: from LL *tautologia*, from Gk, from *tautologos*] —**tautological** (ˌtɔːtˀˈlɒdʒɪkˀl) or **tau**ˈ**tologous** *adj.*

tautomerism (tɔːˈtɒməˌrɪzəm) *n.* the ability of certain chemical compounds to exist as a mixture of two interconvertible isomers in equilibrium. [C19: from TAUTO- + ISOMERISM] —**tautomer** (ˈtɔːtəmə) *n.* —**tautomeric** (ˌtɔːtəˈmɛrɪk) *adj.*

tautonym (ˈtɔːtənɪm) *n. Biol.* a taxonomic name in which the generic and specific components are the same, as in *Rattus rattus* (black rat). —ˌ**tauto**ˈ**nymic** or **tautonymous** (tɔːˈtɒnəməs) *adj.* —**tau**ˈ**tonymy** *n.*

tavern (ˈtævən) *n.* **1.** a less common word for **pub. 2.** *U.S., Canad., & N.Z.* a place licensed for the sale and consumption of alcoholic drink. [C13: from OF *taverne*, from L *taberna* hut]

taverna (təˈvɜːnə) *n.* **1.** (in Greece) a guesthouse that has its own bar. **2.** a Greek restaurant. [C20: Mod. Gk, from L *taberna*]

Taverner (ˈtævənə) *n.* **John.** ?1495–1545, English composer, esp. of church music.

TAVR *abbrev. for* Territorial and Army Volunteer Reserve.

taw[1] (tɔː) *n.* **1.** a large marble used for shooting. **2.** a game of marbles. **3.** the line from which the players shoot at marbles. **4. back to taws.** *Austral. inf.* back to the beginning. [C18: from ?]

taw[2] (tɔː) *vb.* (*tr.*) to convert (skins) into leather by treatment with alum and salt rather than by normal tanning processes. [OE *tawian*] —ˈ**tawer** *n.*

tawa (ˈtɑːwə) *n.* a New Zealand timber tree with edible berries. [from Maori]

tawdry (ˈtɔːdrɪ) *adj.* **-drier, -driest.** cheap, showy, and of poor quality: *tawdry jewellery.* [C16 *tawdry lace,* shortened & altered from *Seynt Audries lace,* finery sold at the fair of St *Audrey* (Etheldrida), 7th-century queen of Northumbria] —ˈ**tawdrily** *adv.* —ˈ**tawdriness** *n.*

Tawney (ˈtɔːnɪ) *n.* **R**(*ichard*) **H**(*enry*). 1880–1962, English economic historian, born in India. His chief works are *The Acquisitive Society* (1920), *Religion and the Rise of Capitalism* (1926), and *Equality* (1931).

tawny (ˈtɔːnɪ) *n.* **a.** a light brown to brownish-orange colour. **b.** (*as adj.*): *tawny port.* [C14: from OF *tané*, from *taner* to tan] —ˈ**tawniness** *n.*

tawny owl *n.* a European owl having a reddish-brown plumage and a round head.

tawse or **taws** (tɔːz) *n. Chiefly Scot.* a leather strap having one end cut into thongs, formerly used as an instrument of punishment by a schoolteacher. [C16: prob. pl. of obs. *taw* strip of leather; see TAW[2]]

tax (tæks) *n.* **1.** a compulsory financial contribution imposed by a government to raise revenue, levied on income or property, on the prices of goods and services, etc. **2.** a heavy demand on something; strain. ~*vb.* (*tr.*) **3.** to levy a tax on (persons, companies, etc.). **4.** to make heavy demands on; strain. **5.** to accuse or blame. **6.** *Law.* to determine (the amount legally chargeable or allowable to a party to a legal action): *to tax costs.* [C13: from OF *taxer,* from L *taxāre* to appraise, from *tangere* to touch] —ˈ**taxable** *adj.* —ˈ**taxer** *n.*

taxation (tækˈseɪʃən) *n.* **1.** the act or principle of levying taxes or the condition of being taxed. **2. a.** an amount assessed as tax. **b.** a tax rate. **3.** revenue from taxes. —**tax**ˈ**ational** *adj.*

tax avoidance *n.* reduction or minimization of tax liability by lawful methods.

tax-deductible *adj.* legally deductible from income or wealth before tax assessment.

tax disc *n.* a paper disc displayed on the windscreen of a motor vehicle showing that the tax due on it has been paid.

taxeme (ˈtæksiːm) *n. Linguistics.* any element of speech that may differentiate one utterance from another with a different meaning, such as the occurrence of a particular phoneme, the presence of a certain intonation, or a distinctive word order. [C20: from Gk *taxis* order, arrangement + -EME] —**tax**ˈ**emic** *adj.*

tax evasion *n.* reduction or minimization of tax liability by illegal methods.

tax exile *n.* a person having a high income who chooses to live abroad so as to avoid paying high taxes.

tax haven *n.* a country or state having a lower rate of taxation than elsewhere.

taxi ('tæksɪ) *n.*, *pl.* **taxis** *or* **taxies**. **1.** Also called: **cab**, **taxicab**. a car, usually fitted with a taximeter, that may be hired to carry passengers to any specified destination. ~*vb.* **taxiing** *or* **taxying, taxied**. **2.** to cause (an aircraft) to move along the ground, esp. before takeoff and after landing, or (of an aircraft) to move along the ground in this way. **3.** (*intr.*) to travel in a taxi. [C20: shortened from *taximeter cab*]

taxidermy ('tæksɪ,dɜːmɪ) *n.* the art or process of preparing, stuffing, and mounting animal skins so that they have a lifelike appearance. [C19: from Gk *taxis* arrangement + *-dermy*, from Gk *derma* skin] —,**taxi'dermal** *or* ,**taxi'dermic** *adj.* —'**taxi,dermist** *n.*

taximeter ('tæksɪ,miːtə) *n.* a meter fitted to a taxi to register the fare, based on the length of the journey. [C19: from F *taximètre;* see TAX, -METER]

taxing ('tæksɪŋ) *adj.* demanding, onerous, and wearing. —'**taxingly** *adv.*

taxi rank *n.* a place where taxis wait to be hired.

taxis ('tæksɪs) *n.* **1.** the movement of an organism in response to an external stimulus. **2.** *Surgery.* the repositioning of a displaced part by manual manipulation only. [C18: via NL from Gk: arrangement, from *tassein* to place in order]

-taxis *or* **-taxy** *n. combining form.* **1.** indicating movement towards or away from a specified stimulus: *thermotaxis*. **2.** order or arrangement: *phyllotaxis*. [from NL, from Gk *taxis* order] —**-tactic** *or* **-taxic** *adj. combining form.*

taxiway ('tæksɪ,weɪ) *n.* a marked path along which aircraft taxi to or from a runway, parking area, etc.

taxon ('tæksɒn) *n.*, *pl.* **taxa** ('tæksə). *Biol.* any taxonomic group or rank. [C20: back formation from TAXONOMY]

taxonomy (tæk'sɒnəmɪ) *n.* **1.** the branch of biology concerned with the classification of organisms into groups based on similarities of structure, origin, etc. **2.** the science or practice of classification. [C19: from F *taxonomie*, from Gk *taxis* order + -NOMY] —**taxonomic** (,tæksə'nɒmɪk) *or* ,**taxo'nomical** *adj.* —,**taxo'nomically** *adv.* —**tax'onomist** *n.*

taxpayer ('tæks,peɪə) *n.* a person or organization that pays taxes.

tax return *n.* a declaration of personal income used as a basis for assessing an individual's liability for taxation.

tax shelter *n.* a form into which business activities may be organized to minimize taxation.

-taxy *n. combining form.* a variant of **-taxis**.

Tay (teɪ) *n.* **1.** Firth of. the estuary of the River Tay on the North Sea coast of Scotland. Length: 40 km (25 miles). **2.** a river in central Scotland, flowing northeast through Loch Tay, then southeast to the Firth of Tay: the longest river in Scotland; noted for salmon fishing. Length: 193 km (120 miles). **3.** Loch. a lake in central Scotland, in Tayside region. Length: 23 km (14 miles).

Taylor ('teɪlə) *n.* **1. A(lan) J(ohn) P(ercivale)**. born 1906, British historian whose many works include *The Origins of the Second World War* (1961). **2. Brook.** 1685–1731, English mathematician, who laid the foundations of differential calculus. **3. Dennis.** born 1949, Irish snooker player: world champion 1985. **4. Elizabeth.** born 1932, U.S. film actress, born in England: films include *National Velvet* (1944), *Cat on a Hot Tin Roof* (1958), *Suddenly Last Summer* (1959), and *Butterfield 8* (1960) and *Who's Afraid of Virginia Woolf?* (1966), for both of which she won Oscars. **5. Jeremy.** 1613–67, English cleric, best known for his devotional manuals *Holy Living* (1650) and *Holy Dying* (1651). **6. Zachary.** 1784–1850, 12th president of the U.S. (1849–50); hero of the Mexican War.

Taymyr Peninsula (taɪ'mɪə) *n.* a variant spelling of **Taimyr Peninsula**.

Tayside Region ('teɪ,saɪd) *n.* a local government region in E Scotland: formed in 1975 from Angus, Kinross-shire, and most of Perthshire. Administrative centre: Dundee. Pop.: 392 346 (1986 est.). Area: 7511 sq. km (2900 sq. miles).

tazza ('tætsə) *n.* a wine cup with a shallow bowl and a circular foot. [C19: from It., prob. from Ar. *tassah* bowl]

Tb *the chemical symbol for* terbium.

TB *abbrev. for:* **1.** torpedo boat. **2.** Also: **tb.** tuberculosis.

T-bar *n.* **1.** a T-shaped wrench for use with a socket. **2.** a T-shaped bar on a ski tow which skiers hold on to while being pulled up slopes.

Tbilisi (dbɪ'liːsɪ) *n.* a city in the SW Soviet Union, capital of the Georgian SSR, on the Kura River: founded in 458 as capital of Georgia; taken by the Russians in 1801; university (1918). Pop.: 1 194 000 (1987). Russian name: **Tiflis**.

T-bone steak *n.* a large choice steak cut from the sirloin of beef, containing a T-shaped bone.

tbs. *or* **tbsp.** *abbrev. for* tablespoon(ful).

TBT *abbrev. for* tri-*n*-butyl tin: a biocide used in marine paints to prevent fouling.

Tc *the chemical symbol for* technetium.

T-cell *n.* a type of lymphocyte that matures in the thymus gland and is responsible for killing cells infected by a virus. Also called: **T-lymphocyte**.

Tchad (tʃad) *n.* the French name for **Chad**.

Tchaikovsky (tʃaɪ'kɒfskɪ; *Russian* tʃɪj'kɔfskij) *n.* **Pyotr Ilyich** (pjɔtr ilj'jitʃ). 1840–93, Russian composer. His works, which are noted for their expressive melodies, include the *Sixth Symphony* (the *Pathétique;* 1893), ballets, esp. *Swan Lake* (1876) and *The Sleeping Beauty* (1889), and operas, including *Eugene Onegin* (1879) and *The Queen of Spades* (1890), both based on works by Pushkin.

t distribution *n.* See **Student's t**.

te *or* **ti** (tiː) *n. Music.* (in tonic sol-fa) the syllable used for the seventh note or subtonic of any scale. [see GAMUT]

Te *the chemical symbol for* tellurium.

tea (tiː) *n.* **1.** an evergreen shrub of tropical and subtropical Asia, having white fragrant flowers: family *Theaceae*. **2. a.** the dried leaves of this shrub, used to make a beverage by infusion in boiling water. **b.** such a beverage, served hot or iced. **3. a.** any of various similar plants or any plants that are used to make a tealike beverage. **b.** any such beverage. **4.** Also called: **afternoon tea**. *Chiefly Brit.* a light meal eaten in midafternoon, usually consisting of tea and cakes, etc. **5.** Also called (Brit.): **high tea**. *Brit., Austral., & N.Z.* the main evening meal. **6.** *U.S. & Canad. dated sl.* marijuana. [C17: from Chinese (Amoy) *t'e*, from Ancient Chinese *d'a*]

tea bag *n.* a small bag containing tea leaves, infused in boiling water to make tea.

tea ball *n. Chiefly U.S.* a perforated metal ball filled with tea leaves and used to make tea.

teacake ('tiː,keɪk) *n. Brit.* a flat bun, usually eaten toasted and buttered.

teach (tiːtʃ) *vb.* **teaching, taught**. **1.** (*tr.; may take a clause as object or an infinitive;* often foll. by *how*) to help to learn; tell or show (how). **2.** to give instruction or lessons in (a subject) to (a person or animal). **3.** (*tr.; may take a clause as object or an infinitive*) to cause to learn or understand: *experience taught him that he could not be a journalist*. [OE *tǣcan*] —'**teachable** *adj.*

Teach (tiːtʃ) *n.* **Edward**, known as *Blackbeard*. died 1718, English pirate, active in the West Indies and on the Atlantic coast of North America.

teacher ('tiːtʃə) *n.* a person whose occupation is teaching others, esp. children.

teach-in *n.* an informal conference, esp. on a topical subject, usually held at a university or college and involving a panel of visiting speakers, lecturers, students, etc.

teaching ('tiːtʃɪŋ) *n.* **1.** the art or profession of a teacher. **2.** (*sometimes pl.*) something taught; precept. **3.** (*modifier*) denoting a person or institution that teaches: *a teaching hospital*. **4.** (*modifier*) used in teaching: *teaching aids*.

teaching machine *n.* a machine that presents information and questions to the user, registers the answers, and indicates whether these are correct or acceptable.

tea cloth *n.* another name for **tea towel**.

tea cosy *n.* a covering for a teapot to keep the contents hot.

teacup ('tiː,kʌp) *n.* **1.** a cup out of which tea may be drunk. **2.** Also called: **teacupful**. the amount a teacup will hold, about four fluid ounces.

teahouse ('tiː,haʊs) *n.* a restaurant, esp. in Japan or China, where tea and light refreshments are served.

teak (tiːk) *n.* **1.** a large tree of the East Indies. **2.** the hard resinous yellowish-brown wood of this tree, used for furniture making, etc. [C17: from Port. *teca*, from Malayalam *tēkka*]

teakettle ('tiː,kɛtᵊl) *n.* a kettle for boiling water to make tea.

teal (tiːl) *n., pl.* **teals** *or* **teal.** **1.** any of various small freshwater ducks that are related to the mallard. **2.** a greenish-blue colour. [C14]

tea leaf *n.* **1.** the dried leaf of the tea shrub, used to make tea. **2.** (*usually pl.*) shredded parts of these leaves, esp. after infusion.

team (tiːm) *n.* (*sometimes functioning as pl.*) **1.** a group of people organized to work together. **2.** a group of players forming one of the sides in a sporting contest. **3.** two or more animals working together, as to pull a vehicle. **4.** such animals and the vehicle. ~*vb.* **5.** (when *intr.*, often foll. by *up*) to make or cause to make a team. **6.** (*tr.*) *U.S. & Canad.* to drag or transport in or by a team. **7.** (*intr.*) *U.S. & Canad.* to drive a team. [OE *team* offspring]

tea-maker *n.* a spoon with a perforated cover used to infuse tea in a cup of boiling water.

team-mate *n.* a fellow member of a team.

team spirit *n.* willingness to cooperate as part of a team.

teamster ('tiːmstə) *n.* **1.** a driver of a team of horses. **2.** *U.S. & Canad.* the driver of a lorry.

team teaching *n.* a system whereby two or more teachers pool their skills, knowledge, etc., to teach combined classes.

teamwork ('tiːm,wɜːk) *n.* **1.** the cooperative work done by a team. **2.** the ability to work efficiently as a team.

teapot ('tiː,pɒt) *n.* a container with a lid, spout, and handle, in which tea is made and from which it is served.

teapoy ('tiːpɔɪ) *n.* a small table with a tripod base. [C19: from Hindi *tipāī*, from Sansk. *tri* three + *pāda* foot]

tear[1] (tɪə) *n.* **1.** a drop of the secretion of the lacrimal glands. See **tears. 2.** something shaped like a falling drop: *a tear of amber.* ~Also called: **teardrop.** [OE *tēar*] —**'tearless** *adj.*

tear[2] (tɛə) *vb.* **tearing, tore, torn. 1.** to cause to come apart or to come apart; rip. **2.** (*tr.*) to make (a hole or split) in (something). **3.** (*intr.*; often foll. by *along*) to hurry or rush. **4.** (*tr.*; usually foll. by *away* or *from*) to remove or take by force. **5.** (when *intr.*, often foll. by *at*) to cause pain, distress, or anguish (to). **6. tear one's hair.** *Inf.* to be angry, frustrated, very worried, etc. ~*n.* **7.** a hole, cut, or split. **8.** the act of tearing. ~See also **tear away, tear down,** etc. [OE *teran*] —**'tearable** *adj.* —**'tearer** *n.*

tear away (tɛə) *vb.* **1.** (*tr., adv.*) to persuade (oneself or someone else) to leave. ~*n.* **tearaway. 2.** *Brit.* a reckless impetuous unruly person.

tear down (tɛə) *vb.* (*tr., adv.*) to destroy or demolish: *to tear down an argument.*

tear duct (tɪə) *n.* a short tube in the inner corner of the eyelid through which tears drain into the nose. Technical name: **lacrimal duct.**

tearful ('tɪəful) *adj.* **1.** crying or about to cry. **2.** tending to produce tears; sad. —**'tearfully** *adv.* —**'tearfulness** *n.*

tear gas (tɪə) *n.* a gas that makes the eyes smart and water, causing temporary blindness; used in warfare and to control riots.

tearing ('tɛərɪŋ) *adj.* violent or furious (esp. in **tearing hurry** *or* **rush**).

tear into (tɛə) *vb.* (*intr., prep.*) *Inf.* to attack vigorously and damagingly.

tear-jerker ('tɪə,dʒɜːkə) *n. Inf.* an excessively sentimental film, play, book, etc.

tearoom ('tiː,ruːm, -,rʊm) *n. Brit.* a restaurant where tea and light refreshments are served. Also called: **teashop.**

tea rose *n.* any of several varieties of hybrid rose that have pink or yellow flowers with a scent resembling that of tea.

tears (tɪəz) *pl. n.* **1.** the clear salty solution secreted by the lacrimal glands that lubricates and cleanses the surface of the eyeball. **2.** a state of intense frustration (esp. in **bored to tears**). **3. in tears.** weeping.

tear sheet (tɛə) *n.* a page in a newspaper or periodical that is cut or perforated so that it can be easily torn out.

tease (tiːz) *vb.* **1.** to annoy (someone) by deliberately offering something with the intention of delaying or withdrawing the offer. **2.** to vex (someone) maliciously or playfully. **3.** (*tr.*) to separate the fibres of; comb; card. **4.** (*tr.*) to raise the nap of (a fabric) with a teasel. **5.** another word (esp. U.S. and Canad.) for **backcomb. 6.** (*tr.*) to

loosen or pull apart (biological tissues, etc.). ~*n.* **7.** a person or thing that teases. **8.** the act of teasing. [OE *tǣsan*] —**'teaser** *n.* —**'teasing** *adj.* —**'teasingly** *adv.*

teasel, teazel, *or* **teazle** ('tiːzəl) *n.* **1.** any of various plants (esp. the **fuller's teasel**) of Eurasia and N Africa, having prickly leaves and prickly heads of yellow or purple flowers. **2. a.** the dried flower head of the fuller's teasel, used for teasing. **b.** any implement used for the same purpose. ~*vb.* **-selling, -selled** *or U.S.* **-seling, -seled. 3.** (*tr.*) to tease (a fabric). [OE *tǣsel*] —**'teaseller** *n.*

tea service *or* **set** *n.* the china or pottery articles used in serving tea, including a teapot, cups, saucers, etc.

teashop ('tiː,ʃɒp) *n. Brit.* another name for **tearoom.**

teaspoon ('tiː,spuːn) *n.* **1.** a small spoon used for stirring tea, etc. **2.** Also called: **teaspoonful** the amount contained in such a spoon. **3.** a unit of capacity used in cooking, medicine, etc., equal to about one fluid dram.

teat (tiːt) *n.* **1. a.** the nipple of a mammary gland. **b.** (in cows, etc.) any of the projections from the udder. **2.** something resembling a teat such as the rubber mouthpiece of a feeding bottle. [C13: from OF *tete*, of Gmc origin]

tea towel *or* **cloth** *n.* a towel for drying dishes, etc. U.S. name: **dishtowel.**

tea tree *n.* any of various trees of Australia and New Zealand, the leaves of which were formerly used to make tea.

tea trolley *n. Brit.* a trolley from which tea is served.

tech (tɛk) *n. Inf.* a technical college.

tech. *abbrev. for:* **1.** technical. **2.** technology.

technetium (tɛk'niːʃɪəm) *n.* a silvery-grey metallic element, artificially produced by bombardment of molybdenum by deuterons. The radioisotope **technetium-99m** is used in radiotherapy. Symbol: Tc; atomic no.: 43; half-life of most stable isotope, ^{97}Tc: 2.6×10^6 years. [C20: NL, from Gk *tekhnētos* manmade, from *tekhnasthai* to devise artificially, from *tekhnē* skill]

technic *n.* **1.** (tɛk'niːk). another word for **technique. 2.** ('tɛknɪk). another word for **technics.** [C17: from L *technicus*, from Gk *tekhnikos*, from *tekhnē* skill]

technical ('tɛknɪkᵊl) *adj.* **1.** of or specializing in industrial, practical, or mechanical arts and applied sciences: *a technical institute.* **2.** skilled in practical arts rather than abstract thinking. **3.** relating to a particular field of activity: *the technical jargon of linguistics.* **4.** existing by virtue of a strict application of the rules or a strict interpretation of the wording: *a technical loophole in the law.* **5.** of or showing technique: *technical brilliance.* —**'technically** *adv.* —**'technicalness** *n.*

technical college *n. Brit.* an institution for further education that provides courses in technology, art, secretarial skills, agriculture, etc.

technical drawing *n.* the study and practice of the basic techniques of draughtsmanship, as employed in mechanical drawing, architecture, etc.

technicality (,tɛknɪ'kælɪtɪ) *n., pl.* **-ties. 1.** a petty formal point arising from a strict interpretation of rules, etc. **2.** the state or quality of being technical. **3.** technical methods and vocabulary.

technical knockout *n. Boxing.* a judgment of a knockout given when a boxer is in the referee's opinion too badly beaten to continue without risk of serious injury.

technician (tɛk'nɪʃən) *n.* **1.** a person skilled in mechanical or industrial techniques or in a particular technical field. **2.** a person employed in a laboratory, etc., to do mechanical and practical work. **3.** a person having specific artistic or mechanical skill, esp. if lacking flair.

Technicolor ('tɛknɪ,kʌlə) *n. Trademark.* the process of producing colour film by means of superimposing synchronized films of the same scene, each of which has a different colour filter.

technics ('tɛknɪks) *n.* (*functioning as sing.*) the study or theory of industry and industrial arts; technology.

technique (tɛk'niːk) *n.* **1.** a practical method, skill, or art applied to a particular task. **2.** proficiency in a practical or mechanical skill. **3.** special facility; knack. [C19: from F, from *technique* (adj.): see TECHNIC]

techno- *combining form.* **1.** craft or art: *technology; technography.* **2.** technological or technical: *technocracy.* [from Gk *tekhnē* skill]

technocracy (tɛk'nɒkrəsɪ) *n., pl.* **-cies.** government by scientists, engineers, and other such experts. —**technocrat** ('tɛknə,kræt) *n.* —**,techno'cratic** *adj.*

technology (tɛk'nɒlədʒɪ) n., pl. **-gies. 1.** the application of practical or mechanical sciences to industry or commerce. **2.** the methods, theory, and practices governing such application. **3.** the total knowledge and skills available to any human society. [C17: from Gk *tekhnologia* systematic treatment, from *tekhnē* skill] —**technological** (ˌtɛknə'lɒdʒɪkªl) adj. —**tech'nologist** n.

techy ('tɛtʃɪ) adj. **techier, techiest.** a variant spelling of **tetchy.** — 'techily adv. — 'techiness n.

tectonic (tɛk'tɒnɪk) adj. **1.** denoting or relating to building. **2.** Geol. **a.** (of landforms, etc.) resulting from distortion of the earth's crust due to forces within it. **b.** (of processes, movements, etc.) occurring within the earth's crust and causing structural deformation. [C17: from LL *tectonicus*, from Gk *tektonikos* belonging to carpentry, from *tektōn* a builder]

tectonics (tɛk'tɒnɪks) n. (functioning as sing.) **1.** the art and science of construction or building. **2.** the study of the processes by which the earth's surface has attained its present structure.

tectrix ('tɛktrɪks) n., pl. **tectrices** ('tɛktrɪˌsiːz). (usually pl.) Ornithol. another name for **covert** (sense 5). [C19: NL, from L *tector* plasterer, from *tegere* to cover] —**tectricial** (tɛk'trɪʃəl) adj.

Tecumseh (tɪ'kʌmsə) n. ?1768–1813, American Indian chief of the Shawnee tribe. He attempted to unite western Indian tribes against the Whites, but was defeated at Tippecanoe (1811). He was killed while fighting for the British in the War of 1812.

ted¹ (tɛd) vb. **tedding, tedded.** to shake out (hay), so as to dry it. [C15: from ON *tethja*]

ted² (tɛd) n. Inf. short for **teddy boy.**

tedder ('tɛdə) n. **1.** a machine equipped with a series of small rotating forks for tedding hay. **2.** a person who teds.

Tedder ('tɛdə) n. **Arthur William,** 1st Baron Tedder of Glenguin. 1890–1967, British marshal of the Royal Air Force; deputy commander under Eisenhower of the Allied Expeditionary Force (1944–45).

teddy ('tɛdɪ) n., pl. **-dies.** a woman's one-piece undergarment, incorporating a chemise top and panties.

teddy bear n. a stuffed toy bear. Often shortened to **teddy.** [C20: from *Teddy*, from *Theodore*, after Theodore ROOSEVELT, well known as a hunter of bears]

teddy boy n. **1.** (in Britain, esp. in the mid-1950s) one of a cult of youths who wore mock Edwardian fashions. **2.** any tough or delinquent youth. [C20: from *Teddy*, from *Edward*, referring to the Edwardian dress]

Te Deum (ˌtiː 'diːəm) n. **1.** an ancient Latin hymn in rhythmic prose. **2.** a musical setting of this hymn. **3.** a service of thanksgiving in which the recital of this hymn forms a central part. [from the L canticle beginning *Tē Deum laudāmus*, lit.: Thee, God, we praise]

tedious ('tiːdɪəs) adj. causing fatigue or tedium; monotonous. —'**tediousness** n.

tedium ('tiːdɪəm) n. the state of being bored or the quality of being boring; monotony. [C17: from L *taedium*, from *taedēre* to weary]

tee¹ (tiː) n. **1.** a pipe fitting in the form of a letter *T*, used to join three pipes. **2.** a metal section with a cross section in the form of a letter *T*.

tee² (tiː) Golf. ~n. **1.** an area from which the first stroke of a hole is made. **2.** a support for a golf ball, usually a small wooden or plastic peg, used when teeing off or in long grass, etc. ~vb. **teeing, teed. 3.** (when intr., often foll. by *up*) to position (the ball) ready for striking, on or as if on a tee. ~See also **tee off.** [C17 *teaz*, from ?]

tee³ (tiː) n. a mark used as a target in certain games such as curling and quoits. [C18: ?from T-shaped marks, which may have orig. been used in curling]

tee-hee or **te-hee** ('tiː'hiː) interj. **1.** an exclamation of laughter, esp. when mocking. ~n. **2.** a chuckle. ~vb. **-heeing, -heed. 3.** (intr.) to snigger or laugh, esp. derisively. [C14: imit.]

teem¹ (tiːm) vb. (intr.; usually foll. by *with*) to be prolific or abundant (in). [OE *tēman* to produce offspring; rel. to West Saxon *tīeman*; see TEAM]

teem² (tiːm) vb. **1.** (intr.; often foll. by *down* or *with rain*) to pour in torrents. **2.** (tr.) to pour or empty out. [C15 *temen* to empty, from ON *tœma*]

teen (tiːn) adj. Inf. another word for **teenage.**

teenage ('tiːnˌeɪdʒ) adj. also **teenaged.** (prenominal) of or relating to the time in a person's life between the ages of 13 and 19.

teenager ('tiːnˌeɪdʒə) n. a person between the ages of 13 and 19 inclusive.

teens (tiːnz) pl. n. **1.** the years of a person's life between the ages of 13 and 19 inclusive. **2.** all the numbers that end in -*teen.*

teeny ('tiːnɪ) adj. **-nier, -niest.** extremely small; tiny. Also: **teeny-weeny** ('tiːnɪ'wiːnɪ) or **teensy-weensy** ('tiːnzɪ'wiːnzɪ). [C19: var. of TINY]

teenybopper ('tiːnɪˌbɒpə) n. Sl. a young teenager, usually a girl, who avidly follows fashions in clothes and pop music. [C20: *teeny*, from *teenage* + -*bopper*; see BOP]

tee off vb. (adv.) **1.** Golf. to strike (the ball) from a tee. **2.** Inf. to begin; start.

teepee ('tiːpiː) n. a variant spelling of **tepee.**

Tees (tiːz) n. a river in N England, rising in the N Pennines and flowing southeast and east to the North Sea at Middlesbrough. Length: 113 km (70 miles).

tee shirt n. a variant of **T-shirt.**

Teesside ('tiːzˌsaɪd) n. the industrial region around the lower Tees valley and estuary: a county borough, containing Middlesbrough, from 1968 to 1974.

teeter ('tiːtə) vb. **1.** to move or cause to move unsteadily; wobble. ~n., vb. **2.** another word for **seesaw.** [C19: from ME *titeren*]

teeth (tiːθ) n. **1.** the plural of **tooth. 2.** the most violent part: *the teeth of the gale.* **3.** the power to produce a desired effect: *that law has no teeth.* **4. get one's teeth into.** to become engrossed in. **5. in the teeth of.** in direct opposition to; against. **6. to the teeth.** to the greatest possible degree: *armed to the teeth.* **7. show one's teeth.** to threaten.

teethe (tiːð) vb. (intr.) to cut one's baby (deciduous) teeth.

teething ring n. a hard ring on which babies may bite while teething.

teething troubles pl. n. the problems that arise during the initial stages of a project, etc.

teetotal (tiː'təʊtªl) adj. **1.** of or practising abstinence from alcoholic drink. **2.** Dialect. complete. [C19: allegedly coined in 1833 by Richard Turner, E advocate of total abstinence from alcohol; prob. from TOTAL, with emphatic reduplication] —**tee'totaller** n. —**tee'totalism** n.

teetotum (tiː'təʊtəm) n. Arch. a spinning top bearing letters of the alphabet on its four sides. [C18: from *T totum*, from *T* initial on one of the faces + *totum* the name of the toy, from L *tōtum* the whole]

teff (tɛf) n. an annual grass of NE Africa, grown for its grain. [C18: from Amharic *tēf*]

TEFL abbrev. for Teaching (of) English as a Foreign Language.

Teflon ('tɛflɒn) n. a trademark for **polytetrafluoroethylene.**

teg (tɛg) n. **1.** a two-year-old sheep. **2.** the fleece of a two-year-old sheep. [C16: from ?]

tegmen ('tɛgmən) n., pl. **-mina** (-mɪnə). **1.** either of the leathery forewings of the cockroach and related insects. **2.** the delicate inner covering of a seed. **3.** any similar covering or layer. [C19: from L: a cover, from *tegere* to cover] —'**tegminal** adj.

Tegucigalpa (Spanish teɣuθi'ɣalpa) n. the capital of Honduras, in the south on the Choluteca River: founded about 1579; university (1847). Pop.: 571 400 (1985).

tegument ('tɛgjʊmənt) n. a less common word for **integument.** [C15: from L *tegumentum* a covering, from *tegere* to cover]

te-hee (tiː'hiː) interj., n., vb. a variant of **tee-hee.**

Tehran or **Teheran** (tɛə'rɑːn, -'ræn) n. the capital of Iran, at the foot of the Elburz Mountains: built on the site of the ancient capital Ray, destroyed by Mongols in 1220; became capital in the 1790s; three universities. Pop.: 6 022 078 (1986).

Tehuantepec (tə'wɑːntəˌpɛk) n. **Isthmus of.** the narrowest part of S Mexico, with the Bay of Campeche on the north coast and the **Gulf of Tehuantepec** (an inlet of the Pacific) on the south coast.

Teide or **Teyde** (Spanish 'tɛɪðe) n. **Pico de** ('piko de). a volcanic mountain in the Canary Islands, on Tenerife. Height: 3718 m (12 198 ft.).

te igitur *Latin.* (teɪ 'ɪɡɪ,tuə; *English* teɪ 'ɪdʒɪtuə) *n. R.C. Church.* the first prayer of the canon of the Mass, which begins *Te igitur clementissime Pater* (Thee, therefore, most merciful Father).

Teilhard de Chardin (*French* tɛjar də ʃardɛ̃) *n.* **Pierre** (pjɛr). 1881–1955, French Jesuit priest, palaeontologist, and philosopher. In *The Phenomenon of Man* (1938–40), he explored the mystery of man's evolution and cites his scientific findings as proof of the existence of God.

Tejo ('təʒu) *n.* the Portuguese name for the **Tagus**.

Te Kanawa (teɪ 'kɑːnəwə) *n.* Dame **Kiri** ('kɪrɪ). born 1944, New Zealand operatic soprano.

tektite ('tɛktaɪt) *n.* a small dark glassy object found in several areas around the world, thought to be a product of meteorite impact. [C20: from Gk *tēktos* molten]

tel. *abbrev. for:* **1.** telegram. **2.** telegraph(ic). **3.** telephone.

tel- *combining form.* a variant of **tele-** and **telo-**before a vowel.

telaesthesia *or U.S.* **telesthesia** (,tɛlɪs'θiːzɪə) *n.* the alleged perception of events that are beyond the normal range of perceptual processes. —**telaesthetic** *or U.S.* **telesthetic** (,tɛlɪs'θɛtɪk) *adj.*

telamon ('tɛləmən) *n., pl.* **-mones** (-'məʊniːz) *or* **-mons.** a column in the form of a male figure, used to support an entablature. [C18: via L from Gk, from *tlēnai* to bear]

Telamon ('tɛləmən, -,mɒn) *n. Greek myth.* a king of Salamis; brother of Peleus and father of Teucer and Ajax.

Telanaipura (,tɛlənaɪ'pʊərə) *n.* another name for **Jambi.**

telangiectasis (tɪ,lændʒɪ'ɛktəsɪs) *or* **telangiectasia** (tɪ,lændʒɪɛk'teɪzɪə) *n., pl.* **-ses** (-,siːz). *Pathol.* an abnormal dilation of the capillaries or terminal arteries producing blotched red spots, esp. on the face or thighs. [C19: NL, from Gk *telos* end + *angeion* vessel + *ektasis* dilation] —**telangiectatic** (tɪ,lændʒɪɛk'tætɪk) *adj.*

Tel Aviv ('tɛl ə'viːv) *n.* a city in W Israel, on the Mediterranean: the largest city and chief financial centre in Israel; incorporated the city of Jaffa in 1950; university (1953). Pop.: 320 300 (1986). Official name: **Tel Aviv-Jaffa** ('tɛl ə'viːv'dʒæfə).

tele- *combining form.* **1.** at or over a distance; distant: *telescope; telekinesis.* **2.** television: *telecast.* **3.** by means of or via telephone or television: *teleshopping.* [from Gk *tele* far]

telecast ('tɛlə,kɑːst) *vb.* **-casting, -cast** *or* **-casted.** **1.** to broadcast by television. ~*n.* **2.** a television broadcast. —**'tele,caster** *n.*

telecom ('tɛlɪ,kɒm) *or* **telecoms** ('tɛlɪ,kɒmz) *n.* (*functioning as sing.*) short for **telecommunications.**

telecommunications (,tɛlɪkə,mjuːnɪ'keɪʃənz) *n.* (*functioning as sing.*) the science and technology of communications by telephony, radio, television, etc.

teledu ('tɛlɪ,duː) *n.* a badger of SE Asia and Indonesia, having dark brown hair with a white stripe along the back and producing a fetid secretion when attacked. [C19: from Malay]

telegenic (,tɛlɪ'dʒɛnɪk) *adj.* having or showing a pleasant television image. [C20: from TELE(VISION) + (PHOTO)GENIC] —**,tele'genically** *adv.*

telegnosis (,tɛlə'nəʊsɪs, ,tɛlɒɡ-) *n.* knowledge about distant events alleged to have been obtained without the use of any normal sensory mechanism. [C20: from TELE- + -*gnosis*, from Gk *gnōsis* knowledge]

Telegonus (tɪ'lɛɡənəs) *n. Greek myth.* a son of Odysseus and Circe, who sought his father and mistakenly killed him, later marrying Odysseus' widow Penelope.

telegony (tɪ'lɛɡənɪ) *n. Genetics.* the supposed influence of a previous sire on offspring borne by a female to other sires. —**telegonic** (,tɛlɪ'ɡɒnɪk) *or* **te'legonous** *adj.*

telegram ('tɛlɪ,ɡræm) *n.* a communication transmitted by telegraph.

telegraph ('tɛlɪ,ɡrɑːf) *n.* **1. a.** a device, system, or process by which information can be transmitted over a distance, esp. using radio signals or coded electrical signals sent along a transmission line. **b.** (*as modifier*): *telegraph pole.* ~*vb.* **2.** to send a telegram to (a person or place); wire. **3.** (*tr.*) to transmit or send by telegraph. **4.** (*tr.*) to give advance notice of (anything), esp. unintentionally. **5.** (*tr.*) *Canad. inf.* to cast (votes) illegally by impersonating registered voters. —**telegrapher** (tɪ'lɛɡrəfə) *or* **te'legraphist** *n.* —**,tele'graphic** *adj.*

telegraph plant *n.* a small tropical Asian shrub having small leaflets that turn in various directions during the day and droop at night.

telegraphy (tɪ'lɛɡrəfɪ) *n.* **1.** a system of telecommunications involving any process providing reproduction at a distance of written, printed, or pictorial matter. **2.** the skill or process of operating a telegraph.

Telegu ('tɛlə,ɡuː) *n., adj.* a variant spelling of **Telugu.**

telekinesis (,tɛlɪkaɪ'niːsɪs) *n.* **1.** the movement of a body caused by thought or willpower without the application of a physical force. **2.** the ability to cause such movement. —**telekinetic** (,tɛlɪkɪ'nɛtɪk) *adj.*

Telemachus (tɪ'lɛməkəs) *n. Greek myth.* the son of Odysseus and Penelope, who helped his father slay his mother's suitors.

Telemann (*German* 'teːləman) *n.* **Georg Philipp** ('geːɔrk 'fiːlɪp). 1681–1767, German composer, noted for his prolific output.

telemark ('tɛlɪ,mɑːk) *n. Skiing.* a turn in which one ski is placed far forward of the other and turned gradually inwards. [C20: after *Telemark,* county in Norway]

Telemessage ('tɛlɪ,mɛsɪdʒ) *n. Trademark.* a message sent by telephone or telex and delivered in printed form.

telemeter (tɪ'lɛmɪtə) *n.* **1.** any device for recording or measuring a distant event and transmitting the data to a receiver. **2.** any device used to measure a distance without directly comparing it with a measuring rod, etc. ~*vb.* **3.** (*tr.*) to obtain and transmit (data) from a distant source. —**telemetric** (,tɛlɪ'mɛtrɪk) *adj.*

telemetry (tɪ'lɛmɪtrɪ) *n.* **1.** the use of radio waves, telephone lines, etc., to transmit the readings of measuring instruments to a device on which the readings can be indicated or recorded. **2.** the measurement of linear distance using a tellurometer.

telencephalon (,tɛlɛn'sɛfə,lɒn) *n.* the cerebrum together with related parts of the hypothalamus and the third ventricle. —**telencephalic** ('tɛlɛnsɪ'fælɪk) *adj.*

teleology (,tɛlɪ'ɒlədʒɪ, ,tiːlɪ-) *n.* **1.** *Philosophy.* **a.** the doctrine that there is evidence of purpose or design in the universe, and esp. that this provides proof of the existence of a Designer. **b.** the belief that certain phenomena are best explained in terms of purpose rather than cause. **2.** *Biol.* the belief that natural phenomena have a predetermined purpose and are not determined by mechanical laws. [C18: from NL *teleologia,* from Gk *telos* end + -LOGY] —**teleological** (,tɛlɪə'lɒdʒɪkəl, ,tiːlɪ-) *adj.* —**,tele'ologist** *n.*

teleost ('tɛlɪ,ɒst, 'tiːlɪ-) *n.* any of a subclass of bony fishes having rayed fins and a swim bladder, as herrings, carps, eels, cod, perches, etc. [C19: from NL *teleosteī* (pl.) creatures having complete skeletons, from Gk *teleos* complete + *osteon* bone]

telepathy (tɪ'lɛpəθɪ) *n.* the communication between people of thoughts, feelings, etc., involving mechanisms that cannot be understood in terms of known scientific laws. —**telepathic** (,tɛlɪ'pæθɪk) *adj.* —**te'lepathist** *n.* —**te'lepa,thize** *or* **-ise** *vb.* (*intr.*).

telephone ('tɛlɪ,fəʊn) *n.* **1.** an electrical device for transmitting speech, consisting of a microphone and receiver mounted on a handset. **2. a.** a worldwide system of communications using telephones. The microphone in one telephone converts sound waves into electrical oscillations that are transmitted along a telephone wire or by radio to one or more distant ones. **b.** (*as modifier*): *a telephone exchange.* ~*vb.* **3.** to call or talk to (a person) by telephone. **4.** to transmit (a message, etc.) by telephone. —**'tele,phoner** *n.* —**telephonic** (,tɛlɪ'fɒnɪk) *adj.*

telephone box *n.* a soundproof enclosure from which a paid telephone call can be made. Also called: **telephone kiosk, telephone booth.**

telephone directory *n.* a book listing the names, addresses, and telephone numbers of subscribers in a particular area.

telephone number *n.* a set of figures identifying the telephone of a particular subscriber, and used in making connections to that telephone.

telephonist (tɪ'lɛfənɪst) *n. Brit.* a person who operates a telephone switchboard. Also called (esp. U.S.): **telephone operator.**

telephony (tɪ'lɛfənɪ) *n.* a system of telecommunications for the transmission of speech or other sounds.

telephotography (ˌtɛlɪfəˈtɒɡrəfɪ) n. the process or technique of photographing distant objects using a telephoto lens.

telephoto lens (ˈtɛlɪˌfəʊtəʊ) n. a compound camera lens in which the focal length is greater than that of a simple lens and thus produces a magnified image of a distant object.

teleprinter (ˈtɛlɪˌprɪntə) n. 1. a telegraph apparatus consisting of a keyboard transmitter, which converts a typed message into coded pulses for transmission along a wire or cable, and a printing receiver, which converts incoming signals and prints out the message. U.S. name: **teletypewriter**. 2. a network of such devices. 3. a similar device used for direct input/output of data into a computer at a distant location.

Teleprompter (ˈtɛlɪˌprɒmptə) n. *Trademark.* a device for displaying a television script so that the speaker can read it while appearing to look at the camera.

Teleran (ˈtɛləˌræn) n. *Trademark.* an electronic navigational aid in which the image of a ground-based radar system is televised to aircraft. [C20: from *Tele(vision) R(adar) A(ir) N(avigation)*]

telesales (ˈtɛlɪˌseɪlz) pl. n. the selling of a commodity or service by a salesperson who makes an initial approach by telephone.

telescope (ˈtɛlɪˌskəʊp) n. 1. an optical instrument for making distant objects appear closer by use of a combination of lenses (**refracting telescope**) or lenses and curved mirrors (**reflecting telescope**). 2. any instrument, such as a **radio telescope**, for collecting, focusing, and detecting electromagnetic radiation from space. ~vb. 3. to crush together or be crushed together, as in a collision. 4. to fit together like a set of cylinders that slide into one another, thus allowing extension and shortening. 5. to make or become smaller or shorter. [C17: from It. *telescopio* or NL *telescopium*, lit.: far-seeing instrument]

telescopic (ˌtɛlɪˈskɒpɪk) adj. 1. of or relating to a telescope. 2. seen through or obtained by means of a telescope. 3. visible only with a telescope. 4. able to see far. 5. having parts that telescope. —ˌtele'scopically adv.

telescopic sight n. a telescope mounted on a rifle, etc., used for sighting.

telescopy (tɪˈlɛskəpɪ) n. the branch of astronomy concerned with the use and design of telescopes.

telespectroscope (ˌtɛlɪˈspɛktrəˌskəʊp) n. a combination of a telescope and a spectroscope, used for spectroscopic analysis of radiation from stars and other celestial bodies.

telestereoscope (ˌtɛlɪˈstɪərɪəˌskəʊp, -ˈstɛrɪə-) n. an optical instrument for obtaining stereoscopic images of distant objects.

telestich (tɪˈlɛstɪk, ˈtɛlɪˌstɪk) n. a short poem in which the last letters of each successive line form a word. [C17: from Gk *telos* end + *stikhos* row]

teletext (ˈtɛlɪˌtɛkst) n. a videotext service in which the consumer is not able to interact with the computer. Cf. **viewdata**.

telethon (ˈtɛləˌθɒn) n. *U.S.* a lengthy television programme to raise charity funds, etc. [C20: from TELE- + MARATHON]

Teletype (ˈtɛlɪˌtaɪp) n. 1. *Trademark.* a type of teleprinter. 2. (*sometimes not cap.*) a network of such devices. ~vb. 3. (*sometimes not cap.*) to transmit (a message) by Teletype.

teletypewriter (ˌtɛlɪˈtaɪpˌraɪtə, ˈtɛlɪˌtaɪp-) n. a U.S. name for **teleprinter**.

televangelist (ˌtɛlɪˈvændʒəlɪst) n. *U.S.* an evangelical preacher who appears regularly on television, preaching the gospel and appealing for donations from viewers. [C20: from TELE(VISION + E)VANGELIST)]

televise (ˈtɛlɪˌvaɪz) vb. 1. to put on television. 2. (*tr.*) to transmit by television.

television (ˈtɛlɪˌvɪʒən) n. 1. the system or process of producing on a distant screen a series of transient visible images, usually with an accompanying sound signal. Electrical signals, converted from optical images by a camera tube, are transmitted by radio waves or by cable and reconverted into optical images by means of a television tube inside a television set. 2. Also called: **television set**. a device designed to receive and convert incoming electrical signals into a series of visible images on a screen together with accompanying sound. 3. the content, etc., of television programmes. 4. the occupation or

profession concerned with any aspect of the broadcasting of television programmes. 5. (*modifier*) of, relating to, or used in the transmission or reception of video and audio UHF or VHF radio signals: *a television transmitter*. ~Abbrev.: **TV**.

television tube n. a cathode-ray tube designed for the reproduction of television pictures. Sometimes shortened to **tube**.

televisual (ˌtɛlɪˈvɪʒʊəl, -zjʊ-) adj. relating to or suitable for production on television.

telex (ˈtɛlɛks) n. 1. an international telegraph service in which teleprinters are rented out to subscribers. 2. a teleprinter used in such a service. 3. a message transmitted or received by telex. ~vb. 4. to transmit (a message) to (a person, etc.) by telex. [C20: from *tel(eprinter) ex(change)*]

Telford[1] (ˈtɛlfəd) n. a town in W central England, in Shropshire: designated a new town in 1963. Pop.: 103 786 (1981).

Telford[2] (ˈtɛlfəd) n. **Thomas.** 1757–1834, Scottish civil engineer, known esp. for his roads and such bridges as the Menai suspension bridge (1825).

Telidon (ˈtɛlɪˌdɒn) n. *Trademark.* a Canadian interactive viewdata service.

tell[1] (tɛl) vb. **telling, told.** 1. (when *tr., may take a clause as object*) to let know or notify. 2. (*tr.*) to order or instruct. 3. (when *intr.*, usually foll. by *of*) to give an account or narration (of). 4. (*tr.*) to communicate by words; utter: *to tell the truth.* 5. (*tr.*) to make known: *to tell fortunes.* 6. (*intr.*; often foll. by *of*) to serve as an indication: *her blush told of her embarrassment.* 7. (*tr.*; used with *can*, etc.; *may take a clause as object*) to discover or discern: *I can tell what is wrong.* 8. (*tr.*; used with *can*, etc.) to distinguish or discriminate: *he couldn't tell chalk from cheese.* 9. (*intr.*) to have or produce an impact, effect, or strain: *every step told on his bruised feet.* 10. (*intr.*; sometimes foll. by *on*) *Inf.* to reveal secrets or gossip (about). 11. (*tr.*) to assure: *I tell you, I've had enough!* 12. (*tr.*) to count (votes). 13. **tell the time**, to read the time from a clock. 14. **you're telling me.** *Sl.* I know that very well. ~See also **tell apart, tell off.** [OE *tellan*] —**'tellable** adj.

tell[2] (tɛl) n. a large mound resulting from the accumulation of rubbish on a long-settled site, esp. in the Middle East. [C19: from Ar. *tall*]

Tell (tɛl) n. **William,** German name *Wilhelm Tell.* a legendary Swiss patriot, who, traditionally, lived in the early 14th century and was compelled by an Austrian governor to shoot an apple from his son's head with one shot of his crossbow. He did so without mishap.

tell apart vb. (*tr., adv.*) to distinguish between.

Tell el Amarna (ˈtɛl ɛl əˈmɑːnə) n. a group of ruins and rock tombs in Upper Egypt, on the Nile below Asyut: site of the capital of Amenhotep IV, built about 1375 B.C.; excavated from 1891 onwards.

teller (ˈtɛlə) n. 1. a bank cashier. 2. a person appointed to count votes. 3. a person who tells; narrator.

Teller (ˈtɛlə) n. **Edward.** born 1908, U.S. nuclear physicist, born in Hungary: a major contributor to the development of the hydrogen bomb (1952).

telling (ˈtɛlɪŋ) adj. 1. having a marked effect or impact. 2. revealing. —**'tellingly** adv.

tell off vb. (*tr., adv.*) 1. *Inf.* to reprimand; scold. 2. to count and appoint for duty.

telltale (ˈtɛlˌteɪl) n. 1. a person who tells tales about others. 2. a. an outward indication of something concealed. b. (*as modifier*): *a telltale paw mark.* 3. a device used to monitor a process, machine, etc.

tellurian (tɛˈlʊərɪən) adj. 1. of the earth. ~n. 2. (esp. in science fiction) an inhabitant of the earth. [C19: from L *tellūs* the earth]

telluric[1] (tɛˈlʊərɪk) adj. of or originating on or in the earth or soil; terrestrial. [C19: from L *tellūs* the earth]

telluric[2] (tɛˈlʊərɪk) adj. of or containing tellurium, esp. in a high valence state. [C20: from TELLUR(IUM) + -IC]

tellurion *or* **tellurian** (tɛˈlʊərɪən) n. an instrument that shows how day and night and the seasons result from the earth's rotation on its axis, etc. [C19: from L *tellūs* the earth]

tellurium (tɛˈlʊərɪəm) n. a brittle silvery-white nonmetallic element. Symbol: Te; atomic no.: 52; atomic wt.: 127.60. [C19: NL, from L *tellūs* the earth, by analogy with URANIUM]

tellurometer (ˌtɛljʊˈrɒmɪtə) *n. Surveying.* an electronic instrument for measuring distances by the transmission of radio waves. [C20: from L *tellūs* the earth + -METER]

Tellus ('tɛləs) *n.* the Roman goddess of the earth; protectress of marriage, fertility, and the dead.

telly ('tɛlɪ) *n., pl.* **-lies.** *Inf., chiefly Brit.* short for **television.**

telo- *or before a vowel* **tel-** *combining form.* **1.** complete; final; perfect. **2.** end; at the end. [from Gk *telos* end]

telpherage ('tɛlfərɪdʒ) *n.* an overhead transport system in which an electrically driven truck runs along a rail or cable, the load being suspended in a car beneath. Also called: **telpher.** [C19: changed from *telephore*, from TELE- + -PHORE + -AGE]

telson ('tɛlsən) *n.* the last segment or an appendage on the last segment of the body of crustaceans and arachnids. [C19: from Gk: a boundary]

Telugu *or* **Telegu** ('tɛləˌguː) *n.* **1.** a language of SE India, belonging to the Dravidian family of languages. **2.** (*pl.* **-gus** *or* **-gu**) a member of the people who speak this language. ~*adj.* **3.** of or relating to this people or their language.

Telukbetung *or* **Teloekbetoeng** (təˌlʊkbəˈtʊŋ) *n.* a port in Indonesia, in S Sumatra on the Sunda Strait. Pop.: 284 275 (1980).

Tema ('tiːmə) *n.* a port in SE Ghana on the Atlantic: new harbour opened in 1962; oil-refining. Pop.: 99 608 (1984).

Témbi ('tɛmbiː) *n.* transliteration of the Modern Greek name for **Tempe.**

temerity (tɪˈmɛrɪtɪ) *n.* rashness or boldness. [C15: from L *temeritās* accident, from *temere* at random] —**temerarious** (ˌtɛməˈrɛərɪəs) *adj.*

Temesvár ('tɛmɛʃvaːr) *n.* the Hungarian name for **Timişoara.**

temp (tɛmp) *Inf.* ~*n.* **1.** a person, esp. a typist or other office worker, employed on a temporary basis. ~*vb.* (*intr.*) **2.** to work as a temp.

temp. *abbrev. for:* **1.** temperature. **2.** temporary. **3.** tempore. [L: in the time of]

Tempe ('tɛmpɪ) *n.* **Vale of.** a wooded valley in E Greece, in Thessaly between the mountains Olympus and Ossa. Modern Greek name: **Témbi.**

temper ('tɛmpə) *n.* **1.** a frame of mind; mood or humour. **2.** a sudden outburst of anger. **3.** a tendency to exhibit anger; irritability. **4.** a mental condition of moderation and calm (esp. in **keep one's temper** *or* **lose one's temper**). **5.** the degree of hardness, elasticity, etc., of a metal. ~*vb.* (*tr.*) **6.** to make more acceptable or suitable by adding something else; moderate: *he tempered his criticism with sympathy.* **7.** to strengthen or toughen (a metal), as by heating and quenching. **8.** *Music.* **a.** to adjust the frequency differences between the notes of a scale on (a keyboard instrument). **b.** to make such an adjustment to the pitches of notes in (a scale). [OE *temprian* to mingle, from L *temperāre* to mix, prob. from *tempus* time] —**'temperable** *adj.* —**'temperer** *n.*

tempera ('tɛmpərə) *n.* **1.** a painting medium for powdered pigments, consisting usually of egg yolk and water. **2. a.** any emulsion used as a painting medium, with casein, glue, wax, etc., as a base. **b.** the paint made from this. **3.** the technique of painting with tempera. [C19: from It. *pingere a tempera* painting in tempera, from *temperare* to mingle; see TEMPER]

temperament ('tɛmpərəmənt) *n.* **1.** a person's character, disposition, and tendencies. **2.** excitability, moodiness, or anger. **3.** the characteristic way an individual behaves, esp. towards other people. **4. a.** an adjustment made to the frequency differences between notes on a keyboard instrument to allow modulation to other keys. **b.** any of several systems of such adjustment, esp. **equal temperament,** a system giving a scale based on an octave divided into twelve exactly equal semitones. **5.** *Obs.* the characteristic way an individual behaves, viewed as the result of the influence of the four humours. [C15: from L *temperāmentum* a mixing in proportion, from *temperāre* to TEMPER]

temperamental (ˌtɛmpərəˈmɛntəl) *adj.* **1.** easily upset or irritated; excitable. **2.** of or caused by temperament. **3.** *Inf.* working erratically and inconsistently; unreliable. —ˌtempera'mentally *adv.*

temperance ('tɛmpərəns) *n.* **1.** restraint or moderation, esp. in yielding to one's appetites or desires. **2.** abstinence from alcoholic drink. [C14: from L *temperantia*, from *temperāre* to regulate]

temperate ('tɛmpərɪt) *adj.* **1.** having a climate intermediate between tropical and polar; moderate or mild in temperature. **2.** mild in quality or character; exhibiting temperance. [C14: from L *temperātus*] —'temperately *adv.* —'temperateness *n.*

Temperate Zone *n.* those parts of the earth's surface lying between the Arctic Circle and the tropic of Cancer and between the Antarctic Circle and the tropic of Capricorn.

temperature ('tɛmprɪtʃə) *n.* **1.** the degree of hotness of a body, substance, or medium, esp. as measured on a scale that has one or more fixed reference points. **2.** *Inf.* body temperature in excess of the normal. [C16 (orig.: a mingling): from L *temperātūra* proportion, from *temperāre* to TEMPER]

temperature gradient *n.* the rate of change in temperature in a given direction.

temperature-humidity index *n.* an index of the effect on human comfort of temperature and humidity levels, 65 being the highest comfortable level.

tempered ('tɛmpəd) *adj.* **1.** *Music.* adjusted in accordance with a system of temperament. **2.** (*in combination*) having a temper or temperament as specified: *ill-tempered.*

tempest ('tɛmpɪst) *n.* **1.** *Chiefly literary.* a violent wind or storm. **2.** a violent commotion, uproar, or disturbance. [C13: from OF *tempeste*, from L *tempestās* storm, from *tempus* time]

tempestuous (tɛmˈpɛstjʊəs) *adj.* **1.** of or relating to a tempest. **2.** violent or stormy. —**tem'pestuously** *adv.* —**tem'pestuousness** *n.*

tempi ('tɛmpiː) *n.* (in musical senses) the plural of **tempo.**

Templar ('tɛmplə) *n.* **1.** a member of a military religious order (**Knights of the Temple of Solomon**) founded by Crusaders in Jerusalem around 1118; suppressed in 1312. **2.** (*sometimes not cap.*) *Brit.* a lawyer who has chambers in the Temple in London. [C13: from Med. L *templārius* of the temple, from L *templum* temple; first applied to the knightly order because their house was near the site of the Temple of Solomon]

template *or* **templet** ('tɛmplɪt) *n.* **1.** a gauge or pattern, cut out in wood or metal, used in woodwork, etc., to help shape something accurately. **2.** a pattern cut out in card or plastic, used to reproduce shapes. **3.** a short beam that is used to spread a load, as over a doorway. **4.** *Biochem.* the molecular structure of a compound that serves as a pattern for the production of another compound. [C17 *templet* (later spelling infl. by PLATE), prob. from F, dim. of TEMPLE³]

temple¹ ('tɛmpəl) *n.* **1.** a building or place dedicated to the worship of a deity or deities. **2.** a Mormon church. **3.** *U.S.* another name for a **synagogue. 4.** a Christian church. **5.** any place or object regarded as a shrine where God makes himself present. **6.** a building regarded as the focus of an activity, interest, or practice: *a temple of the arts.* [OE *tempel*, from L *templum*]

temple² ('tɛmpəl) *n.* the region on each side of the head in front of the ear and above the cheek bone. [C14: from OF *temple*, from L *tempora* the temples, from *tempus* temple of the head]

temple³ ('tɛmpəl) *n.* the part of a loom that keeps the cloth being woven stretched to the correct width. [C15: from F, from L *templum* a small timber]

Temple¹ ('tɛmpəl) *n.* **1.** a building in London that belonged to the Templars: it now houses two law societies. **2.** any of three buildings erected by the Jews in ancient Jerusalem for the worship of Jehovah.

Temple² ('tɛmpəl) *n.* **1. Shirley,** married name *Shirley Temple Black.* born 1928, U.S. film actress and politician. Her films as a child star include *Little Miss Marker* (1934), *Wee Willie Winkie* (1937), and *Heidi* (1937). She was appointed U.S. ambassador to Ghana in 1974. **2.** Sir **William.** 1628–99, English diplomat and essayist. He negotiated the Triple Alliance (1668) and the marriage of William of Orange to Mary II. **3. William.** 1881–1944, English prelate and advocate of social reform; archbishop of Canterbury (1942–44).

Temple of Artemis *n.* the large temple at Ephesus, on the W coast of Asia Minor: one of the Seven Wonders of the World.

tempo ('tɛmpəʊ) *n., pl.* **-pos** *or* **-pi** (-piː). **1.** the speed at which a piece of music is meant to be played. **2.** rate or pace. [C18: from It., from L *tempus* time]

temporal[1] ('tɛmpərəl) *adj.* **1.** of or relating to time. **2.** of secular as opposed to spiritual or religious affairs. **3.** lasting for a relatively short time. **4.** *Grammar.* of or relating to tense or the linguistic expression of time. [C14: from L *temporālis*, from *tempus* time] —**'temporally** *adv.*

temporal[2] ('tɛmpərəl) *adj. Anat.* of or near the temple or temples. [C16: from LL *temporālis* belonging to the temples; see TEMPLE[2]]

temporal bone *n.* either of two compound bones forming the sides of the skull.

temporality (ˌtɛmpəˈrælɪtɪ) *n., pl.* **-ties. 1.** the state or quality of being temporal. **2.** something temporal. **3.** (*often pl.*) a secular possession or revenue belonging to a Church.

temporal lobe *n.* the laterally protruding portion of each cerebral hemisphere, situated below the parietal lobe and associated with sound perception and interpretation.

temporary ('tɛmpərərɪ) *adj.* **1.** not permanent; provisional. **2.** lasting only a short time. ~*n., pl.* **-raries. 3.** a person employed on a temporary basis. [C16: from L *temporārius*, from *tempus* time] —**'temporarily** *adv.* —**'temporariness** *n.*

temporize *or* **-ise** ('tɛmpəˌraɪz) *vb.* (*intr.*) **1.** to delay, act evasively, or protract a negotiation, etc., esp. in order to gain time or effect a compromise. **2.** to adapt oneself to the circumstances, as by temporary or apparent agreement. [C16: from F *temporiser*, from Med. L *temporizāre*, from L *tempus* time] —,**tempori'zation** *or* **-i'sation** *n.* —**'tempo,rizer** *or* **-iser** *n.*

tempt (tɛmpt) *vb.* (*tr.*) **1.** to entice to do something, esp. something morally wrong or unwise. **2.** to allure or attract. **3.** to give rise to a desire in (someone) to do something; dispose. **4.** to risk provoking (esp. in **tempt fate**). [C13: from OF *tempter*, from L *temptāre* to test] —**'temptable** *adj.* —**'tempter** *n.* —**'temptress** *fem. n.*

temptation (tɛmp'teɪʃən) *n.* **1.** the act of tempting or the state of being tempted. **2.** a person or thing that tempts.

tempting ('tɛmptɪŋ) *adj.* attractive or inviting: *a tempting meal.* —**'temptingly** *adv.*

tempus fugit *Latin.* ('tɛmpəs 'fjuːdʒɪt) time flies.

Temuco (*Spanish* teˈmuko) *n.* a city in S Chile: agricultural trading centre. Pop.: 171 831 (1985 est.).

ten (tɛn) *n.* **1.** the cardinal number that is the sum of nine and one. It is the base of the decimal number system and the base of the common logarithm. **2.** a numeral, 10, X, etc., representing this number. **3.** something representing or consisting of ten units. **4.** Also called: **ten o'clock.** ten hours after noon or midnight. ~*determiner.* **5.** amounting to ten. ~Related adj.: **decimal.** [OE *tēn*]

ten. *Music. abbrev. for:* **1.** tenor. **2.** tenuto.

tenable ('tɛnəbᵊl) *adj.* able to be upheld, believed, maintained, or defended. [C16: from OF, from *tenir* to hold, from L *tenēre*] —,**tena'bility** *or* **'tenableness** *n.* —**'tenably** *adv.*

tenace ('tɛneɪs) *n. Bridge, whist.* a holding of two nonconsecutive high cards of a suit, such as the ace and queen. [C17: from F, from Sp. *tenaza* forceps, ult. from L *tenāx* holding fast, from *tenēre* to hold]

tenacious (tɪˈneɪʃəs) *adj.* **1.** holding firmly: *a tenacious grip.* **2.** retentive: *a tenacious memory.* **3.** stubborn or persistent. **4.** holding together firmly; cohesive. **5.** tending to stick or adhere. [C16: from L *tenāx*, from *tenēre* to hold] —**te'naciously** *adv.* —**te'naciousness** *or* **tenacity** (tɪˈnæsɪtɪ) *n.*

tenaculum (tɪˈnækjʊləm) *n., pl.* **-la** (-lə). a hooked surgical instrument for grasping and holding parts. [C17: from LL, from L *tenēre* to hold]

tenancy ('tɛnənsɪ) *n., pl.* **-cies. 1.** the temporary possession or holding by a tenant of lands or property owned by another. **2.** the period of holding or occupying such property. **3.** the period of holding office, a position, etc.

tenant ('tɛnənt) *n.* **1.** a person who holds, occupies, or possesses land or property, esp. from a landlord. **2.** a person who has the use of a house, etc., subject to the payment of rent. **3.** any holder or occupant. ~*vb.* **4.** (*tr.*) to hold as a tenant. [C14: from OF, lit.: (one who is) holding, from *tenir* to hold, from L *tenēre*] —**'tenantable** *adj.* —**'tenantless** *adj.*

tenant farmer *n.* a person who farms land rented from another, the rent usually taking the form of crops or livestock.

tenantry ('tɛnəntrɪ) *n.* **1.** tenants collectively. **2.** the status or condition of being a tenant.

tench (tɛntʃ) *n.* a European freshwater game fish of the carp family. [C14: from OF *tenche*, from LL *tinca*]

Ten Commandments *pl. n.* **the.** *Old Testament.* the commandments summarizing the basic obligations of man towards God and his fellow men, delivered to Moses on Mount Sinai engraved on two tables of stone (Exodus 20:1–17).

tend[1] (tɛnd) *vb.* (when *intr.*, usually foll. by *to* or *towards*) **1.** (when *tr.*, *takes an infinitive*) to have a general disposition (to do something); be inclined: *children tend to prefer sweets to meat.* **2.** (*intr.*) to have or be an influence (towards a specific result). **3.** (*intr.*) to go or move (in a particular direction): *to tend to the south.* [C14: from OF *tendre*, from L *tendere* to stretch]

tend[2] (tɛnd) *vb.* **1.** (*tr.*) to care for. **2.** (when *intr.*, often foll. by *on* or *to*) to attend (to). **3.** (*tr.*) to handle or control. **4.** (*intr.*; often foll. by *to*) *Inf., chiefly U.S. & Canad.* to pay attention. [C14: var. of ATTEND]

tendency ('tɛndənsɪ) *n., pl.* **-cies. 1.** (often foll. by *to*) an inclination, predisposition, propensity, or leaning. **2.** the general course, purport, or drift of something, esp. a written work. [C17: from Med. L *tendentia*, from L *tendere* to TEND[1]]

tendentious *or* **tendencious** (tɛnˈdɛnʃəs) *adj.* having or showing an intentional tendency or bias, esp. a controversial one. [C20: from TENDENCY] —**ten'dentiously** *or* **ten'denciously** *adv.* —**ten'dentiousness** *or* **ten'denciousness** *n.*

tender[1] ('tɛndə) *adj.* **1.** easily broken, cut, or crushed; soft. **2.** easily damaged; vulnerable or sensitive: *at a tender age.* **3.** having or expressing warm feelings. **4.** kind or sympathetic: *a tender heart.* **5.** arousing warm feelings; touching. **6.** gentle and delicate: *a tender breeze.* **7.** requiring care in handling: *a tender question.* **8.** painful or sore. **9.** sensitive to moral or spiritual feelings. **10.** (*postpositive*; foll. by *of*) protective: *tender of one's emotions.* [C13: from OF *tendre*, from L *tener* delicate] —**'tenderly** *adv.* —**'tenderness** *n.*

tender[2] ('tɛndə) *vb.* **1.** (*tr.*) to give, present, or offer: *to tender a bid.* **2.** (*intr.*; foll. by *for*) to make a formal offer or estimate (for a job or contract). **3.** (*tr.*) *Law.* to offer (money or goods) in settlement of a debt or claim. ~*n.* **4.** the act or an instance of tendering; offer. **5.** a formal offer to supply specified goods or services at a stated cost or rate. **6.** something, esp. money, used as an official medium of payment: *legal tender.* [C16: from Anglo-F *tendre*, from L *tendere* to extend] —**'tenderer** *n.*

tender[3] ('tɛndə) *n.* **1.** a small boat towed or carried by a ship. **2.** a vehicle drawn behind a steam locomotive to carry the fuel and water. **3.** a person who tends. [C15: var. of *attender*]

tenderfoot ('tɛndəˌfʊt) *n., pl.* **-foots** *or* **-feet. 1.** a newcomer, esp. to the mines or ranches of the southwestern U.S. **2.** (formerly) a beginner in the Scouts or Guides.

tenderhearted (ˌtɛndəˈhɑːtɪd) *adj.* having a compassionate, kindly, or sensitive disposition.

tenderize *or* **-ise** ('tɛndəˌraɪz) *vb.* (*tr.*) to make (meat) tender, as by pounding it or adding a substance to break down the fibres. —,**tenderi'zation** *or* **-i'sation** *n.* —**'tender,izer** *or* **-,iser** *n.*

tenderloin ('tɛndəˌlɔɪn) *n.* a tender cut of pork or other meat from between the sirloin and ribs.

tendon ('tɛndən) *n.* a cord or band of tough tissue that attaches a muscle to a bone or some other part; sinew. [C16: from Med. L *tendō*, from L *tendere* to stretch]

tendril ('tɛndrɪl) *n.* a threadlike leaf or stem that attaches climbing plants to a support by twining or adhering. [C16: ?from OF *tendron* tendril (confused with OF *tendron* bud), from Med. L *tendō* TENDON]

tenebrism ('tɛnəˌbrɪzəm) *n.* (*sometimes cap.*) a school, style, or method of painting, adopted chiefly by 17th-century Spanish and Neapolitan painters, characterized by large areas of dark colours, usually relieved with a shaft of light. —**'tenebrist** *n., adj.*

tenebrous ('tɛnəbrəs) *or* **tenebrious** (təˈnɛbrɪəs) *adj.* gloomy, shadowy, or dark. [C15: from L *tenebrōsus* from *tenebrae* darkness]

Tenedos ('tɛnɪˌdɒs) *n.* an island in the NE Aegean, near the entrance to the Dardanelles: in Greek legend the base of the Greek fleet during the siege of Troy. Modern Turkish name: **Bozcaada.**

tenement ('tɛnəmənt) *n.* **1.** Also called: **tenement building.** a large building divided into rooms or flats. **2.** a dwelling place or residence. **3.** *Chiefly Brit.* a room or flat for rent. **4.** *Property law.* any form of permanent property, such as land, dwellings, offices, etc. [C14: from Med. L *tenementum*, from L *tenēre* to hold] —**tenemental** (ˌtɛnə'mɛntᵊl) *adj.*

Tenerife (ˌtɛnə'riːf; *Spanish* tene'rife) *n.* a Spanish island in the Atlantic, off the NW coast of Africa: the largest of the Canary Islands; volcanic and mountainous; tourism and agriculture. Capital: Santa Cruz. Pop.: 557 191 (1981). Area: 2058 sq. km (795 sq. miles).

tenesmus (tɪ'nɛzməs) *n.* an ineffective painful straining to empty the bowels or bladder. [C16: from Med. L, from L *tēnesmos*, from Gk, from *teinein* to strain] —**te'nesmic** *adj.*

tenet ('tɛnɪt, 'tiːnɪt) *n.* a belief, opinion, or dogma. [C17: from L, lit.: he (it) holds, from *tenēre* to hold]

tenfold ('tɛnˌfəʊld) *adj.* **1.** equal to or having 10 times as many or as much. **2.** composed of 10 parts. ~*adv.* **3.** by or up to 10 times as many or as much.

ten-gallon hat *n.* (in the U.S.) a cowboy's broad-brimmed felt hat with a very high crown.

Teng Hsiao-ping ('tɛŋ sjaʊ 'pɪŋ) *n.* a variant transliteration of the Chinese name for **Deng Xiaoping.**

Tengri Khan ('tɛŋgrɪ 'kɑːn) *n.* a mountain in central Asia, on the border between the Kirghiz SSR of the Soviet Union and the Xinjiang Uygur AR of W China. Height: 6995 m (22 951 ft.).

Tengri Nor ('tɛŋgrɪ 'nɔː) *n.* another name for **Nam Co.**

Teniers ('tɛnɪəz) *n.* **David** ('daːvɪt), called *the Elder,* 1582–1649, and his son **David,** called *the Younger,* 1610–90, Flemish painters.

tenner ('tɛnə) *n. Inf.* **1.** *Brit.* **a.** a ten-pound note. **b.** the sum of ten pounds. **2.** *U.S.* a ten-dollar bill.

Tennessee (ˌtɛnɪ'siː) *n.* **1.** a state of the E central U.S.: consists of a plain in the west, rising to the Appalachians and the Cumberland Plateau in the east. Capital: Nashville. Pop.: 4 803 000 (1986 est.). Area: 109 412 sq. km (42 244 sq. miles). Abbrevs.: **Tenn.** or (with zip code) **TN 2.** a river in the E central U.S., flowing southwest from E Tennessee into N Alabama, then west and north to the Ohio River at Paducah: the longest tributary of the Ohio; includes a series of dams and reservoirs under the Tennessee Valley Authority. Length: 1049 km (652 miles). —ˌTennes'sean *adj., n.*

Tenniel ('tɛnjəl) *n.* Sir **John.** 1820–1914, English caricaturist, noted for his illustrations to Lewis Carroll's *Alice* books and for his political cartoons in *Punch* (1851–1901).

tennis ('tɛnɪs) *n.* **a.** a racket game played between two players or pairs of players who hit a ball to and fro over a net on a rectangular court of grass, asphalt, clay, etc. See also **lawn tennis, real tennis, table tennis. b.** (*as modifier*): *tennis court; tennis racket.* [C14: prob. from Anglo-F *tenetz* hold (imperative), from OF *tenir* to hold, from L *tenēre*]

tennis elbow *n.* inflammation of the elbow caused by exertion in playing tennis, etc.

tennis shoe *n.* a rubber-soled canvas shoe tied with laces.

Tennyson ('tɛnɪsᵊn) *n.* **Alfred,** Lord Tennyson. 1809–92, English poet; poet laureate (1850–92). His poems include *The Lady of Shalott* (1832), *Morte d'Arthur* (1842), the collection *In Memoriam* (1850), *Maud* (1855), and *Idylls of the King* (1859). —**Tennysonian** (ˌtɛnɪ'səʊnɪən) *adj., n.*

Teno ('tɛnɔ) *n.* the Finnish name for **Tana** (sense 3).

teno- *or before a vowel* **ten-** *combining form.* tendon: *tenosynovitis.* [from Gk *tenōn*]

Tenochtitlán (tɛˌnɔːtʃtiː'tlɑːn) *n.* an ancient city and capital of the Aztec empire on the present site of Mexico City; razed by Cortés in 1521.

tenon ('tɛnən) *n.* **1.** the projecting end of a piece of wood formed to fit into a corresponding mortise in another piece. ~*vb.* **2.** to form a tenon on (a piece of wood). **3.** to join with a tenon and mortise. [C15: from OF, from *tenir* to hold, from L *tenēre*] —'**tenoner** *n.*

tenon saw *n.* a small fine-toothed saw with a strong back, used esp. for cutting tenons.

tenor ('tɛnə) *n.* **1.** *Music.* **a.** the male voice intermediate between alto and baritone. **b.** a singer with such a voice. **c.** a saxophone, horn, etc., intermediate between the alto and baritone or bass. **2.** general drift of thought; purpose. **3.** a settled course of progress. **4.** *Arch.* general tendency. **5.** *Law.* **a.** the exact words of a deed, etc. **b.** an exact copy. [C13 (orig.: general sense): from OF *tenour,* from L *tenor* a holding to a course, from *tenēre* to hold; musical sense via It. *tenore,* referring to the voice part that was continuous, that is, to which the melody was assigned]

tenor clef *n.* the clef that establishes middle C as being on the fourth line of the staff.

tenorrhaphy (tɪ'nɒrəfɪ) *n., pl.* -**phies.** *Surgery.* the union of torn or divided tendons by means of sutures. [C19: from TENO- + Gk *raphē* a sewing]

tenosynovitis ('tɛnəʊˌsaɪnəʊ'vaɪtɪs) *n.* painful swelling and inflammation of tendons, usually of the wrist, often the result of repetitive movements such as typing.

tenotomy (tə'nɒtəmɪ) *n., pl.* -**mies.** surgical incision into a tendon. —**te'notomist** *n.*

tenpin bowling ('tɛnˌpɪn) *n.* a bowling game in which bowls are rolled down a lane to knock over the ten target pins. Also called (esp. U.S. and Canad.): **tenpins.**

tenrec ('tɛnrɛk) *n.* any of a family of small mammals of Madagascar resembling hedgehogs or shrews. [C18: via F from Malagasy *tràndraka*]

tense¹ (tɛns) *adj.* **1.** stretched or stressed tightly; taut or rigid. **2.** under mental or emotional strain. **3.** producing mental or emotional strain: *a tense day.* **4.** *Phonetics.* pronounced with considerable muscular effort, as the vowel (iː) *in "beam".* ~*vb.* (often foll. by *up*) **5.** to make or become tense. [C17: from L *tensus* taut, from *tendere* to stretch] —**'tensely** *adv.* —**'tenseness** *n.*

tense² (tɛns) *n. Grammar.* a category of the verb or verbal inflections, such as present, past, and future, that expresses the temporal relations between what is reported in a sentence and the time of its utterance. [C14: from OF *tens* time, from L *tempus*] —**'tenseless** *adj.*

tense logic *n. Logic.* the study of temporal relations between propositions, usually pursued by considering the logical properties of symbols representing the tenses of natural languages.

tensile ('tɛnsaɪl) *adj.* **1.** of or relating to tension. **2.** sufficiently ductile to be stretched or drawn out. [C17: from NL *tensilis,* from L *tendere* to stretch] —**tensility** (tɛn'sɪlɪtɪ) *or* '**tensileness** *n.*

tensile strength *n.* a measure of the ability of a material to withstand a longitudinal stress, expressed as the greatest stress that the material can stand without breaking.

tensimeter (tɛn'sɪmɪtə) *n.* a device that measures differences in vapour pressures. [C20: from TENSI(ON) + -METER]

tensiometer (ˌtɛnsɪ'ɒmɪtə) *n.* **1.** an instrument for measuring the tensile strength of a wire, beam, etc. **2.** an instrument used to compare the vapour pressures of two liquids. **3.** an instrument for measuring the surface tension of a liquid. **4.** an instrument for measuring the moisture content of soil.

tension ('tɛnʃən) *n.* **1.** the act of stretching or the state or degree of being stretched. **2.** mental or emotional strain; stress. **3.** a situation or condition of hostility, suspense, or uneasiness. **4.** *Physics.* a force that tends to produce an elongation of a body or structure. **5.** *Physics.* voltage, electromotive force, or potential difference. **6.** a device for regulating the tension in a part, string, thread, etc., as in a sewing machine. **7.** the degree of tightness or looseness with which a person knits. [C16: from L *tensiō,* from *tendere* to strain] —'**tensional** *adj.* —'**tensionless** *adj.*

tensor ('tɛnsə, -sɔː) *n.* **1.** *Anat.* any muscle that can cause a part to become firm or tense. **2.** *Maths.* a set of components, functions of the coordinates of any point in space, that transform linearly between coordinate systems. [C18: from NL, lit.: a stretcher] —**tensorial** (tɛn'sɔːrɪəl) *adj.*

tent (tɛnt) *n.* **1.** a portable shelter of canvas, plastic, etc., supported on poles and fastened to the ground by pegs and ropes. **2.** something resembling this in function or shape. ~*vb.* **3.** (*intr.*) to camp in a tent. **4.** (*tr.*) to cover with or as if with a tent or tents. **5.** (*tr.*) to provide with a tent as shelter. [C13: from OF *tente,* from L *tentōrium* something stretched out, from *tendere* to stretch] —'**tentage** *n.* —'**tented** *adj.*

tentacle ('tɛntək³l) *n.* **1.** any of various elongated flexible organs that occur near the mouth in many invertebrates and are used for feeding, grasping, etc. **2.** any of the hairs on the leaf of an insectivorous plant that are used to capture prey. [C18: from NL *tentāculum*, from L *tentāre*, vars. of *temptāre* to feel] —'**tentacled** *adj.* —**tentacular** (tɛn'tækjʊlə) *adj.*

tentation (tɛn'teɪʃən) *n.* a method of achieving the correct adjustment of a mechanical device by a series of trials. [C14: from L *tentātiō*, variant of *temptātiō* TEMPTATION]

tentative ('tɛntətɪv) *adj.* **1.** provisional or experimental. **2.** hesitant, uncertain, or cautious. [C16: from Med. L *tentātivus*, from L *tentāre* to test] —'**tentatively** *adv.* —'**tentativeness** *n.*

tenter ('tɛntə) *n.* **1.** a frame on which cloth is stretched in order that it may retain its shape while drying. **2.** a person who stretches cloth on a tenter. ~*vb.* **3.** (*tr.*) to stretch (cloth) on a tenter. [C14: from Med. L *tentōrium*, from L *tentus* stretched, from *tendere* to stretch]

tenterhook ('tɛntə,hʊk) *n.* **1.** one of a series of hooks used to hold cloth on a tenter. **2. on tenterhooks.** in a state of tension or suspense.

tenth (tɛnθ) *adj.* **1.** (*usually prenominal*) **a.** coming after the ninth in numbering, position, etc.; being the ordinal number of *ten*: often written 10th. **b.** (*as n.*): *see you on the tenth.* ~*n.* **2.** one of 10 equal parts of something. **b.** (*as modifier*): *a tenth part.* **3.** the fraction equal to one divided by ten (1/10). ~*adv.* **4.** Also: **tenthly.** after the tenth person, position, event, etc. [C12 *tenthe*, from OE *tēotha*]

tent stitch *n.* another term for **petit point.** [C17: from ?]

tenuis ('tɛnjʊɪs) *n.*, *pl.* **tenues** ('tɛnjʊ,iːz). (in classical Greek) a voiceless stop (k, p, t). [C17: from L: thin]

tenuous ('tɛnjʊəs) *adj.* **1.** insignificant or flimsy: *a tenuous argument.* **2.** slim, fine, or delicate: *a tenuous thread.* **3.** diluted or rarefied in consistency or density: *a tenuous fluid.* [C16: from L *tenuis*] —**tenuity** (tɛ'njuːɪtɪ) *or* '**tenuousness** *n.* —'**tenuously** *adv.*

tenure ('tɛnjʊə, 'tɛnjə) *n.* **1.** the possession or holding of an office or position. **2.** the length of time an office, position, etc., lasts. **3.** *U.S. & Canad.* the improved security status of a person after having been in the employ of the same company or institution for a specified period. **4. a.** the holding of property, esp. realty, in return for services rendered, etc. **b.** the duration of such holding. [C15: from OF, from Med. L *tenitūra*, ult. from L *tenēre* to hold] —**ten'urial** *adj.*

tenuto (tɪ'njuːtəʊ) *adj., adv. Music.* (of a note) to be held for or beyond its full time value. [from It., lit.: held, from *tenere* to hold, from L *tenēre*]

Tenzing Norgay ('tɛnsɪŋ 'nɔːgeɪ) *n.* 1914–86, Nepalese mountaineer. With Sir Edmund Hillary, he was the first to reach the summit of Mount Everest (1953).

teocalli (,tiːəʊ'kælɪ) *n.*, *pl.* **-lis.** any of various truncated pyramids built by the Aztecs as bases for their temples. [C17: from Nahuatl, from *teotl* god + *calli* house]

tepee *or* **teepee** ('tiːpiː) *n.* a cone-shaped tent of animal skins used by certain American Indians. [C19: from Siouan *tīpī*, from *ti* to dwell + *pi* used for]

tephra ('tɛfrə) *n. Chiefly U.S.* solid matter ejected during a volcanic eruption. [C20: Gk, lit.: ashes]

Tepic (*Spanish* te'pik) *n.* a city in W central Mexico, capital of Nayarit state: agricultural, trading and processing centre. Pop.: 117 007 (1980).

tepid ('tɛpɪd) *adj.* **1.** slightly warm; lukewarm. **2.** relatively unenthusiastic or apathetic. [C14: from L *tepidus*, from *tepēre* to be lukewarm] —**tepidity** (tɛ'pɪdɪtɪ) *or* '**tepidness** *n.* —'**tepidly** *adv.*

tequila (tɪ'kiːlə) *n.* **1.** a spirit that is distilled in Mexico from an agave plant and forms the basis of many mixed drinks. **2.** the plant from which this drink is made. [C19: from Mexican Sp., from *Tequila*, district in Mexico]

ter. *abbrev. for:* **1.** terrace. **2.** territory.

ter- *combining form.* three, third, or three times. [from L *ter* thrice]

tera- *prefix.* denoting 10^{12}: *terameter.* Symbol: T [from Gk *teras* monster]

Terai (tə'raɪ) *n.* **1.** (in India) a belt of marshy land at the foot of mountains, esp. at the foot of the Himalayas in Uttar Pradesh. **2.** a felt hat with a wide brim worn in subtropical regions.

terat- *or* **terato-** *combining form.* indicating a monster or something abnormal: *teratism.* [from Gk *terat-*, *teras* monster, prodigy]

teratism ('tɛrə,tɪzəm) *n.* a malformed animal or human, esp. in the fetal stage; monster.

teratogenic (,tɛrətəʊ'dʒɛnɪk) *adj.* producing malformation in a fetus.

teratoid ('tɛrə,tɔɪd) *adj. Biol.* resembling a monster.

teratology (,tɛrə'tɒlədʒɪ) *n.* **1.** the branch of biology concerned with the structure, development, etc., of monsters. **2.** a collection of tales about mythical or fantastic creatures, monsters, etc. —,**tera'tologist** *n.*

teratoma (,tɛrə'təʊmə) *n.*, *pl.* **-mata** (-mətə) *or* **-mas.** a tumour composed of tissue foreign to the site of growth.

terbium ('tɜːbɪəm) *n.* a soft malleable silvery-grey element of the lanthanide series of metals. Symbol: Tb; atomic no.: 65; atomic wt.: 158.925. [C19: from NL, after *Ytterby*, Sweden, village where discovered] —'**terbic** *adj.*

terbium metal *n. Chem.* any of a group of related lanthanides, including terbium, europium, and gadolinium.

Ter Borch *or* **Terborch** (*Dutch* tɛr 'bɔrx) *n.* **Gerard** ('xeːrɑrt). 1617–81, Dutch genre and portrait painter.

terce (tɜːs) *or* **tierce** *n. Chiefly R.C. Church.* the third of the seven canonical hours, originally fixed at the third hour of the day, about 9 a.m. [C14: var. of TIERCE]

Terceira (*Portuguese* tər'səirə) *n.* an island in the N Atlantic, in the Azores: NATO military air base. Pop.: 59 204 (1981). Area: 397 sq. km (153 sq. miles).

tercel ('tɜːsəl) *or* **tiercel** *n.* a male falcon or hawk, esp. as used in falconry. [C14: from OF, from Vulgar L *tertiolus* (unattested), from L *tertius* third, from the tradition that only one egg in three hatched a male chick]

tercentenary (,tɜːsɛn'tiːnərɪ) *or* **tercentennial** *adj.* **1.** of a period of 300 years. **2.** of a 300th anniversary. ~*n.*, *pl.* **-tenaries** *or* **-tennials.** **3.** an anniversary of 300 years.

tercet ('tɜːsɪt, tɜː'sɛt) *n.* a group of three lines of verse that rhyme together or are connected by rhyme with adjacent groups of three lines. [C16: from F, from It. *terzetto*, dim. of *terzo* third, from L *tertius*]

terebene ('tɛrə,biːn) *n.* a mixture of hydrocarbons prepared from oil of turpentine and sulphuric acid, used to make paints and varnishes and medicinally as an expectorant and antiseptic. [C19: from TEREB(INTH) + -ENE]

terebinth ('tɛrɪbɪnθ) *n.* a small Mediterranean tree that yields a turpentine. [C14: from L *terebinthus*, from Gk *terebinthos* turpentine tree]

terebinthine (,tɛrɪ'bɪnθaɪn) *adj.* **1.** of or relating to terebinth or related plants. **2.** of, consisting of, or resembling turpentine.

teredo (tɛ'riːdəʊ) *n.*, *pl.* **-dos** *or* **-dines** (-dɪ,niːz). any of a genus of marine bivalve molluscs. See **shipworm.** [C17: via L from Gk *terēdōn* wood-boring worm]

Terence ('tɛrəns) *n.* Latin name *Publius Terentius Afer.* ?190–159 B.C., Roman comic dramatist. His six comedies, *Andria, Hecyra, Heauton Timoroumenos, Eunuchus, Phormio,* and *Adelphoe,* are based on Greek originals by Menander.

Teresa *or* **Theresa** (tə'riːzə; *Spanish* te'resa) *n.* **1. Saint,** known as *Teresa of Avila.* 1515–82, Spanish nun and mystic. She reformed the Carmelite order and founded 17 convents. Her writings include a spiritual autobiography and *The Way to Perfection.* Feast day: Oct. 15. **2. Mother,** original name *Agnes Gonxha Bojaxhiu.* born 1910, Indian Roman Catholic missionary, born in Yugoslavia of Albanian parents: noted for her work among the starving in Calcutta; Nobel peace prize 1979. ~See also **Thérèse de Lisieux.**

Tereshkova (*Russian* tɪrɪʃ'kɔvə) *n.* **Valentina Vladimirovna** (vəlɪn'tinə vla'dimirəvnə). born 1937, Soviet cosmonaut; first woman in space (1963).

Teresina (*Portuguese* tere'zina) *n.* an inland port in NE Brazil, capital of Piauí state, on the Parnaíba River: chief commercial centre of the Parnaíba valley. Pop.: 339 264 (1980). Former name: **Therezina.**

terete ('tɛriːt) *adj.* (esp. of plant parts) cylindrical and tapering. [C17: from L *teres* smooth, from *terere* to rub]

Tereus ('tɪərɪəs) *n. Greek myth.* a prince of Thrace, who raped Philomela, sister of his wife Procne, and was punished by being turned into a hoopoe.

tergiversate ('tɜːdʒɪvəˌseɪt) *vb.* (*intr.*) **1.** to change sides or loyalties. **2.** to be evasive or ambiguous. [C17: from L *tergiversārī* to turn one's back, from *tergum* back + *vertere* to turn] —ˌtergiverˈsation *n.* —ˈtergiverˌsator *n.*

tergum ('tɜːgəm) *n., pl.* -ga (-gə). a cuticular plate covering the dorsal surface of a body segment of an arthropod. [C19: from L: the back] —ˈtergal *adj.*

term (tɜːm) *n.* **1.** a name, expression, or word used for some particular thing, esp. in a specialized field of knowledge: *a medical term.* **2.** any word or expression. **3.** a limited period of time: *a prison term.* **4.** any of the divisions of the academic year during which a school, college, etc., is in session. **5.** a point in time determined for an event or for the end of a period. **6.** the period at which childbirth is imminent. **7.** *Law.* **a.** an estate or interest in land limited to run for a specified period. **b.** the duration of an estate, etc. **c.** a period of time during which sessions of courts of law are held. **d.** time allowed to a debtor to settle. **8.** *Maths.* any distinct quantity making up a fraction or proportion, or contained in a polynominal, sequence, series, etc. **9.** *Logic.* **a.** the word or phrase that forms either the subject or predicate of a proposition. **b.** a name or variable, as opposed to a predicate. **c.** any of the three subjects or predicates occurring in a syllogism. **10.** *Archit.* a sculptured post, esp. one in the form of an armless bust or an animal on the top of a square pillar. ~*vb.* **11.** (*tr.*) to designate; call: *he was termed a thief.* ~See also **terms.** [C13: from OF *terme*, from L *terminus* end] —ˈtermly *adj., adv.*

termagant ('tɜːməgənt) *n. Rare.* a shrewish woman; scold. [C13: from earlier *Tervagaunt*, from OF *Tervagan*, from It. *Trivigante*; after an arrogant character in medieval mystery plays who was supposed to be a Muslim deity]

-termer *n.* (*in combination*) a person serving a specified length of time in prison: *a short-termer.*

terminable ('tɜːmɪnəbəl) *adj.* **1.** able to be terminated. **2.** terminating after a specific period or event. —ˌterminaˈbility *or* ˈterminableness *n.* —ˈterminably *adv.*

terminal ('tɜːmɪnəl) *adj.* **1.** of, being, or situated at an end, terminus, or boundary. **2.** of or occurring after or in a term: *terminal examinations.* **3.** (of a disease) terminating in death. **4.** *Inf.* extreme: *terminal boredom.* **5.** of or relating to the storage or delivery of freight at a warehouse. ~*n.* **6.** a terminating point, part, or place. **7. a.** a point at which current enters or leaves an electrical device, such as a battery or a circuit. **b.** a conductor by which current enters or leaves at such a point. **8.** *Computers.* a device having input/output links with a computer. **9.** *Archit.* **a.** an ornamental carving at the end of a structure. **b.** another name for **term** (sense 10). **10. a.** a point or station at the end of the line of a railway or at an airport, serving as an important access point for passengers or freight. **b.** a less common name for **terminus** (sense 2). **11.** a reception and departure building at the terminus of a bus, sea, or air transport route. **11.** a site where raw material is unloaded and processed, esp. an onshore installation designed to receive offshore oil or gas. [C15: from L *terminālis*, from *terminus* end] —ˈterminally *adv.*

terminal velocity *n.* **1.** the constant maximum velocity reached by a body falling under gravity through a fluid, esp. the atmosphere. **2.** the velocity of a missile or projectile when it reaches its target. **3.** the maximum velocity attained by a rocket, missile, or shell flying in a parabolic flight path. **4.** the maximum velocity that an aircraft can attain.

terminate ('tɜːmɪˌneɪt) *vb.* (when *intr.*, often foll. by *in* or *with*) to form, be, or put an end (to); conclude. [C16: from L *terminātus* limited, from *termināre* to set boundaries, from *terminus* end] —ˈterminative *adj.* —ˈtermiˌnator *n.*

termination (ˌtɜːmɪˈneɪʃən) *n.* **1.** the act of terminating or the state of being terminated. **2.** something that terminates. **3.** a final result.

terminology (ˌtɜːmɪˈnɒlədʒɪ) *n., pl.* -gies. **1.** the body of specialized words relating to a particular subject. **2.** the

study of terms. [C19: from Med. L *terminus* term from L: end] —**terminological** (ˌtɜːmɪnəˈlɒdʒɪkəl) *adj.* —ˌtermiˈnologist *n.*

term insurance *n.* life assurance, usually low in cost and offering no cash value, that provides for the payment of a specified sum of money only if the insured dies within a stipulated time.

terminus ('tɜːmɪnəs) *n., pl.* -ni (-naɪ) *or* -nuses. **1.** the last or final part or point. **2.** either end of a railway, bus route, etc., or a station or town at such a point. **3.** a goal aimed for. **4.** a boundary or boundary marker. **5.** *Archit.* another name for **term** (sense 10). [C16: from L: end]

Terminus ('tɜːmɪnəs) *n.* the Roman god of boundaries.

terminus ad quem *Latin.* ('tɜːmɪˌnʊs æd 'kwɛm) *n.* the aim or terminal point. [lit.: the end to which]

terminus a quo *Latin.* ('tɜːmɪˌnʊs ɑː 'kwəʊ) *n.* the starting point; beginning. [lit.: the end from which]

termitarium (ˌtɜːmɪˈtɛərɪəm) *n., pl.* -ia (-ɪə). the nest of a termite colony. [C20: from TERMITE + -ARIUM]

termite ('tɜːmaɪt) *n.* any of an order of whitish antlike social insects of warm and tropical regions. Some species feed on wood, causing damage to buildings, trees, etc. [C18: from NL *termitēs* white ants, pl. of *termes*, from L: a woodworm] —**termitic** (tɜːˈmɪtɪk) *adj.*

termless ('tɜːmlɪs) *adj.* **1.** without limit or boundary. **2.** unconditional. **3.** an archaic word for **indescribable.**

termor *or* **termer** ('tɜːmə) *n. Property law.* a person who holds an estate for a term of years or until he dies.

terms (tɜːmz) *pl. n.* **1.** (usually specified prenominally) the actual language or mode of presentation used: *he described the project in loose terms.* **2.** conditions of an agreement. **3.** a sum of money paid for a service. **4.** (usually preceded by *on*) mutual relationship or standing: *they were on affectionate terms.* **5. bring to terms.** to cause to agree or submit. **6. come to terms.** to reach acceptance or agreement. **7. in terms of.** as expressed by; regarding: *in terms of money he was no better off.*

terms of trade *pl. n. Economics, Brit.* the ratio of export prices to import prices.

tern (tɜːn) *n.* any of several aquatic birds related to the gulls, having a forked tail, long narrow wings, and a typically black-and-white plumage. [C18: from ON *therna*]

ternary ('tɜːnərɪ) *adj.* **1.** consisting of three or groups of three. **2.** *Maths.* (of a number system) to the base three. [C14: from L *ternārius*, from *ternī* three each]

ternary form *n.* a musical structure consisting of two contrasting sections followed by a repetition of the first; the form *aba.*

ternate ('tɜːnɪt, -neɪt) *adj.* **1.** (esp. of a leaf) consisting of three leaflets or other parts. **2.** (esp. of plants) having groups of three members. [C18: from NL *ternātus*, from Med. L *ternāre* to increase threefold] —**ternately** *adv.*

terne (tɜːn) *n.* **1.** an alloy of lead containing tin and antimony. **2.** Also called: **terne plate.** steel plate coated with this alloy. [C16: ?from F *terne* dull, from OF *ternir* to TARNISH]

Terni (*Italian* 'tɛrni) *n.* an industrial city in central Italy, in Umbria: site of waterfalls created in Roman times. Pop.: 111 157 (1987).

Ternopol (*Russian* tɪrˈnɔpəlj) *n.* a town in the SW Soviet Union, in the W Ukrainian SSR: formerly under Polish rule. Pop.: 156 000 (1981 est.). Polish name: **Tarnopol.**

terotechnology (ˌtɪərəʊtɛkˈnɒlədʒɪ, tɛr-) *n.* a branch of technology that utilizes management, financial, and engineering expertise in the installation, efficient operation, and maintenance of equipment and machinery. [C20: from Gk *tērein* to care for + TECHNOLOGY]

terpene ('tɜːpiːn) *n.* any one of a class of unsaturated hydrocarbons, such as pinene and the carotenes, that are found in the essential oils of many plants, esp. conifers. [C19: *terp*-from obs. *terpentine* turpentine + -ENE]

terpineol (tɜːˈpɪnɪˌɒl) *n.* a terpene alcohol with an odour of lilac, existing in three isomeric forms that occur in several essential oils. [C20: from TERPENE + -INE² + -OL¹]

Terpsichore (tɜːpˈsɪkərɪ) *n.* the Muse of the dance and of choral song. [C18: via L from Gk, from *terpsikhoros* delighting in the dance, from *terpein* to delight + *khoros* dance]

Terpsichorean (ˌtɜːpsɪkəˈrɪən, -ˈkɔːrɪən) *Often used facetiously.* ~*adj. also* **Terpsichoreal.** **1.** of or relating to dancing. ~*n.* **2.** a dancer.

terra ('tɛrə) n. (in legal contexts) earth or land. [from L]

terra alba ('ælbə) n. **1.** a white finely powdered form of gypsum, used to make paints, paper, etc. **2.** any of various other white earthy substances, such as kaolin, pipeclay, and magnesia. [from L, lit.: white earth]

terrace ('tɛrəs) n. **1.** a horizontal flat area of ground, often one of a series in a slope. **2. a.** a row of houses, usually identical and having common dividing walls, or the street onto which they face. **b.** (cap. when part of a street name): Grosvenor Terrace. **3.** a paved area alongside a building, serving partly as a garden. **4.** a balcony or patio. **5.** the flat roof of a house built in a Spanish or Oriental style. **6.** a flat area bounded by a short steep slope formed by the down-cutting of a river or by erosion. **7.** (usually pl.) unroofed tiers around a football pitch on which the spectators stand. ~vb. (tr.) **8.** to make into or provide with a terrace or terraces. [C16: from OF terrasse, from OProvençal terrassa pile of earth, from terra earth, from L]

terraced house n. Brit. a house that is part of a terrace. U.S. and Canad. name: **row house.**

terra cotta ('kɒtə) n. **1.** a hard unglazed brownish-red earthenware, or the clay from which it is made. **2.** something made of terra cotta, such as a sculpture. **3.** a strong reddish-brown to brownish-orange colour. [C18: from It., lit.: baked earth] —**terra-'cotta** adj.

terra firma ('fɜːmə) n. the solid earth; firm ground. [C17: from L]

terrain (tə'reɪn) n. a piece of ground, esp. with reference to its physical character or military potential: a rocky terrain. [C18: from F, ult. from L terrēnum ground, from terra earth]

terra incognita Latin. ('tɛrə ɪn'kɒgnɪtə) n. an unexplored or unknown land, region, or area.

Terramycin (ˌtɛrə'maɪsɪn) n. Trademark. a broad-spectrum antibiotic used in treating various infections.

terrapin ('tɛrəpɪn) n. any of various web-footed reptiles that live on land and in fresh water and feed on small aquatic animals. Also called: **water tortoise.** [C17: of Amerind origin]

terrarium (tɛ'rɛərɪəm) n., pl. **-rariums** or **-raria** (-'rɛərɪə). **1.** an enclosure for small land animals. **2.** a glass container, often a globe, in which plants are grown. [C19: NL, from L terra earth]

terra sigillata (ˌsɪdʒɪ'lɑːtə) n. **1.** a reddish-brown clayey earth found on the Aegean island of Lemnos: formerly used as an astringent and in the making of earthenware pottery. **2.** earthenware pottery made from this or a similar earth, esp. Samian ware. [from L: sealed earth]

terrazzo (tɛ'rætsəʊ) n., pl. **-zos.** a floor made by setting marble chips into a layer of mortar and polishing the surface. [C20: from It.: TERRACE]

Terre Adélie (French tɛr adeli) n. the French name for **Adélie Land.**

terrene (tɛ'riːn) adj. **1.** of the earth; worldly; mundane. **2.** Rare. of earth; earthy. ~n. **3.** a land. **4.** a rare word for **earth.** [C14: from Anglo-Norman, from L terrēnus, from terra earth]

terreplein ('tɛrəˌpleɪn) n. the top of a rampart where guns are placed behind the parapet. [C16: from F, from Med. L terrā plēnus filled with earth]

terrestrial (tə'rɛstrɪəl) adj. **1.** of the earth. **2.** of the land as opposed to the sea or air. **3.** (of animals and plants) living or growing on the land. **4.** earthly, worldly, or mundane. **5.** Television. denoting or using signals sent over the earth's surface from a transmitter on land, rather than by satellite. ~n. **6.** an inhabitant of the earth. [C15: from L terrestris, from terra earth] —**ter'restrially** adv.

terrestrial telescope n. a telescope for use on earth rather than for making astronomical observations. Such telescopes contain an additional lens or prism system to produce an erect image.

terret ('tɛrɪt) n. **1.** either of the two rings on a harness through which the reins are passed. **2.** the ring on a dog's collar for attaching the lead. [C15: var. of toret, from OF, dim. of tor loop]

terre-verte ('tɛəˌvɜːt) n. **1.** a greyish-green pigment used in paints. It is made from a mineral found in greensand and similar rocks. ~adj. **2.** of a greyish-green colour. [C17: from F, lit.: green earth]

terrible ('tɛrəbᵊl) adj. **1.** very serious or extreme. **2.** Inf. of poor quality; unpleasant or bad. **3.** causing terror. **4.** causing awe. [C15: from L terribilis, from terrēre to terrify] —**'terribleness** n. —**'terribly** adv.

terricolous (tɛ'rɪkələs) adj. living on or in the soil. [C19: from L terricola, from terra earth + colere to inhabit]

terrier¹ ('tɛrɪə) n. any of several usually small, active, and short-bodied breeds of dog, originally trained to hunt animals living underground. [C15: from OF chien terrier earth dog, from Med. L terrārius belonging to the earth, from L terra earth]

terrier² ('tɛrɪə) n. English legal history. a register or survey of land. [C15: from OF, from Med. L terrārius of the land, from L terra land]

terrific (tə'rɪfɪk) adj. **1.** very great or intense. **2.** Inf. very good; excellent. **3.** very frightening. [C17: from L terrificus, from terrēre to frighten] —**ter'rifically** adv.

terrify ('tɛrɪˌfaɪ) vb. **-fying, -fied.** (tr.) to inspire fear or dread in; frighten greatly. [C16: from L terrificāre, from terrēre to alarm + facere to cause] —**'terri,fying** adj. —**'terri,fyingly** adv.

terrigenous (tɛ'rɪdʒɪnəs) adj. **1.** of or produced by the earth. **2.** (of geological deposits) formed in the sea from material derived from the land by erosion. [C17: from L terrigenus, from terra earth + gignere to beget]

terrine (tɛ'riːn) n. **1.** an oval earthenware cooking dish with a tightly fitting lid used for pâtés, etc. **2.** the food cooked or served in such a dish, esp. pâté. [C18: earlier form of TUREEN]

territorial (ˌtɛrɪ'tɔːrɪəl) adj. **1.** of or relating to a territory or territories. **2.** restricted to or owned by a particular territory. **3.** local or regional. **4.** Zool. establishing and defending a territory. **5.** pertaining to a territorial army, providing a reserve of trained men for use in emergency. —ˌterri,tori'ality n. —ˌterri'torially adv.

Territorial (ˌtɛrɪ'tɔːrɪəl) n. a member of a Territorial Army.

Territorial Army n. (in Britain) a standing reserve army originally organized between 1907 and 1908. Full name: **Territorial and Volunteer Reserve.**

Territorial Council n. (in Canada) an elected body responsible for local government in the Northwest Territories or the Yukon.

territorial waters pl. n. the waters over which a nation exercises jurisdiction and control.

territory ('tɛrɪtəri) n., pl. **-ries. 1.** any tract of land; district. **2.** the geographical domain under the jurisdiction of a political unit, esp. of a sovereign state. **3.** the district for which an agent, etc., is responsible. **4.** an area inhabited and defended by an animal or a pair of animals. **5.** an area of knowledge. **6.** (in football, hockey, etc.) the area defended by a team. **7.** (often cap.) a region of a country, esp. of a federal state, that enjoys less autonomy and a lower status than most constituent parts of the state. **8.** (often cap.) a protectorate or other dependency of a country. [C15: from L territōrium land surrounding a town, from terra land]

Territory ('tɛrɪtəri, -trɪ) n. **the.** Austral. See **Northern Territory.**

terror ('tɛrə) n. **1.** great fear, panic, or dread. **2.** a person or thing that inspires great dread. **3.** Inf. a troublesome person or thing, esp. a child. **4.** terrorism. [C14: from OF terreur, from L terror, from terrēre to frighten] —**'terrorful** adj. —**'terrorless** adj.

terrorism ('tɛrəˌrɪzəm) n. **1.** the systematic use of violence and intimidation to achieve some goal. **2.** the act of terrorizing. **3.** the state of being terrorized. —**'terrorist** n., adj.

terrorize or **-ise** ('tɛrəˌraɪz) vb. (tr.) **1.** to coerce or control by violence, fear, threats, etc. **2.** to inspire with dread; terrify. —ˌterrori'zation or -i'sation n. —**'terror,izer** or **,iser** n.

terror-stricken or **terror-struck** adj. in a state of terror.

terry ('tɛrɪ) n., pl. **-ries. 1.** an uncut loop in the pile of towelling or a similar fabric. **2.** a fabric with such a pile. [C18: ? var. of TERRET]

Terry ('tɛrɪ) n. Dame Ellen. 1847–1928, English actress, noted for her Shakespearean roles opposite Sir Henry Irving and for her correspondence with George Bernard Shaw.

terse (tɜːs) adj. **1.** neatly brief and concise. **2.** curt; abrupt. [C17: from L tersus precise, from tergēre to polish] —**'tersely** adv. —**'terseness** n.

tertial ('tɜ:ʃəl) *adj., n.* another word for **tertiary** (senses 5, 6). [C19: from L *tertius* third, from *ter* thrice, from *trēs* three]

tertian ('tɜ:ʃən) *adj.* 1. (of a fever) occurring every other day. ~*n.* 2. a tertian fever. [C14: from L *febris tertiāna* fever occurring every third day, from *tertius* third]

tertiary ('tɜ:ʃərɪ) *adj.* 1. third in degree, order, etc. 2. (of an industry) involving services as opposed to extraction or manufacture, such as transport, finance, etc. 3. *R.C. Church.* of or relating to a Third Order. 4. *Chem.* **a.** (of an organic compound) having a functional group attached to a carbon atom that is attached to three other groups. **b.** (of an amine) having three organic groups attached to a nitrogen atom. **c.** (of a salt) derived from a tribasic acid by replacement of all its acidic hydrogen atoms with metal atoms or electropositive groups. 5. *Ornithol., rare.* of or designating any of the small flight feathers attached to the part of the humerus nearest to the body. ~*n., pl.* **-tiaries.** 6. *Ornithol., rare.* any of the tertiary feathers. 7. *R.C. Church.* a member of a Third Order. [C16: from L *tertiārius* containing one third, from *tertius* third]

Tertiary ('tɜ:ʃərɪ) *adj.* 1. of, denoting, or formed in the first period of the Cenozoic era. ~*n.* 2. **the.** the Tertiary period or rock system.

tertiary college *n. Brit.* a college system incorporating the secondary school sixth form and vocational courses.

tertium quid ('tɜ:tɪəm) *n.* an unknown or indefinite thing related in some way to two known or definite things, but distinct from both. [C18: from LL, rendering Gk *triton ti* some third thing]

Tertullian (tɜ:'tʌlɪən) *n.* Latin name *Quintus Septimius Florens Tertullianus.* ?160–?220 A.D., Carthaginian Christian theologian, who wrote in Latin rather than Greek and originated much of Christian terminology.

Teruel (*Spanish* te'rwɛl) *n.* a city in E central Spain: 15th-century cathedral; scene of fierce fighting during the Spanish Civil War. Pop.: 25 935 (1981).

tervalent (tɜ:'veɪlənt) *adj. Chem.* another word for **trivalent. —ter'valency** *n.*

Terylene ('tɛrɪ,li:n) *n. Trademark.* a synthetic polyester fibre or fabric. U.S. name (trademark): **Dacron.**

terza rima ('tɛətsə 'ri:mə) *n., pl.* **terze rime** ('tɛətseɪ 'ri:meɪ). a verse form consisting of a series of tercets in which the middle line of one tercet rhymes with the first and third lines of the next. [C19: from It., lit.: third rhyme]

TESL *abbrev. for* Teaching (of) English as a Second Language.

tesla ('tɛslə) *n.* the derived SI unit of magnetic flux density equal to a flux of 1 weber in an area of 1 square metre. Symbol: T [C20: after Nikola TESLA]

Tesla ('tɛslə) *n.* **Nikola** ('nɪkələ). 1857–1943, U.S. electrical engineer and inventor, born in Yugoslavia. His inventions include a transformer, generators, and dynamos.

tesla coil *n.* a step-up transformer with an air core, used for producing high voltages at high frequencies.

tessellate ('tɛsɪ,leɪt) *vb.* 1. (*tr.*) to construct, pave, or inlay with a mosaic of small tiles. 2. (*intr.*) (of identical shapes) to fit together exactly. [C18: from L *tessellātus* checked, from *tessella* small stone cube, from TESSERA]

tessera ('tɛsərə) *n., pl.* **-serae** (-sə,ri:). 1. a small square tile of stone, glass, etc., used in mosaics. 2. a die, tally, etc., used in classical times, made of bone or wood. [C17: from L, from Ionic Gk *tesseres* four] **—'tesseral** *adj.*

Tessin (tɛ'si:n) *n.* the German name for **Ticino.**

tessitura (,tɛsɪ'tʊərə) *n. Music.* the general pitch level of a piece of vocal music. [It.: texture, from L *textura;* see TEXTURE]

test[1] (tɛst) *vb.* 1. to ascertain (the worth, capability, or endurance) of (a person or thing) by subjection to certain examinations, etc.; try. 2. (often foll. by *for*) to carry out an examination on (a substance, material, or system) to indicate the presence of a substance or the possession of a property: *to test food for arsenic.* ~*n.* 3. a method, practice, or examination designed to test a person or thing. 4. a series of questions or problems designed to test a specific skill or knowledge. 5. a standard of judgment; criterion. 6. **a.** a chemical reaction or physical procedure for testing a substance, material, etc. **b.** a chemical reagent used in such a procedure. **c.** the result of the procedure or the evidence gained from it. 7. *Sport.* See **test match.** 8. *Arch.* a declaration of truth, loyalty, etc. 9. (*modifier*) performed as a test: *test drive.* [C14 (in

the sense: vessel used in treating metals): from L *testum* earthen vessel] **—'testable** *adj.* **—'testing** *adj.*

test[2] (tɛst) *n.* the hard outer covering of certain invertebrates and tunicates. [C19: from L *testa* shell]

testa ('tɛstə) *n., pl.* **-tae** (-ti:). the hard outer layer of a seed. [C18: from L: shell]

testaceous (tɛ'steɪʃəs) *adj. Biol.* 1. of or possessing a test or testa. 2. of the reddish-brown colour of terra cotta. [C17: from L *testāceus,* from TESTA]

testament ('tɛstəmənt) *n.* 1. *Law.* a will (esp. in **last will and testament**). 2. a proof, attestation, or tribute. 3. **a.** a covenant instituted between God and man. **b.** a copy of either the Old or the New Testament, or of the complete Bible. [C14: from L: a will, from *testārī* to bear witness, from *testis* a witness] **—,testa'mental** *adj.* **—,testa'mentary** *adj.*

Testament ('tɛstəmənt) *n.* 1. either of the two main parts of the Bible; the Old Testament or the New Testament. 2. the New Testament as distinct from the Old.

testate ('tɛsteɪt, 'tɛstɪt) *adj.* 1. having left a legally valid will at death. ~*n.* 2. a person who dies testate. [C15: from L *testārī* to make a will; see TESTAMENT] **—testacy** ('tɛstəsɪ) *n.*

testator (tɛ'steɪtə) *or* (*fem.*) **testatrix** (tɛ'steɪtrɪks) *n.* a person who makes a will, esp. one who dies testate. [C15: from Anglo-F *testatour,* from LL *testātor,* from L *testārī* to make a will]

test ban *n.* an agreement among nations to forgo tests of nuclear weapons.

test-bed *n. Engineering.* an area used for testing machinery, etc., under working conditions.

test case *n.* a legal action that serves as a precedent in deciding similar succeeding cases.

test-drive *vb.* (*tr.*) **-driving, -drove, -driven.** to drive (a car or other motor vehicle) for a limited period in order to assess it.

tester[1] ('tɛstə) *n.* a person or thing that tests.

tester[2] ('tɛstə) *n.* a canopy over a bed. [C14: from Med. L *testerium,* from LL *testa* a skull, from L: shell]

testes ('tɛsti:z) *n.* the plural of **testis.**

testicle ('tɛstɪk³l) *n.* either of the two male reproductive glands, in most mammals enclosed within the scrotum, that produce spermatozoa. [C15: from L *testiculus,* dim. of *testis*] **—testicular** (tɛ'stɪkjʊlə) *adj.*

testiculate (tɛ'stɪkjʊlɪt) *adj. Bot.* having an oval shape: *the testiculate tubers of certain orchids.* [C18: from LL *testiculātus;* see TESTICLE]

testify ('tɛstɪ,faɪ) *vb.* **-fying, -fied.** 1. (when *tr., may take a clause as object*) to state (something) formally as a declaration of fact. 2. *Law.* to declare or give (evidence) under oath, esp. in court. 3. (when *intr.,* often foll. by *to*) to be evidence (of); serve as witness (to). 4. (*tr.*) to declare or acknowledge openly. [C14: from L *testificārī,* from *testis* witness] **—,testifi'cation** *n.* **—'testi,fier** *n.*

testimonial (,tɛstɪ'məʊnɪəl) *n.* 1. a recommendation of the character, ability, etc., of a person or of the quality of a product or service. 2. a formal statement of truth or fact. 3. a tribute given for services or achievements. ~*adj.* 4. of or relating to a testimony or testimonial.

testimony ('tɛstɪmənɪ) *n., pl.* **-nies.** 1. a declaration of truth or fact. 2. *Law.* evidence given by a witness, esp. in court under oath. 3. evidence testifying to something: *her success was a testimony to her good luck.* 4. *Old Testament.* the Ten Commandments. [C15: from L *testimōnium,* from *testis* witness]

testis ('tɛstɪs) *n., pl.* **-tes.** another word for **testicle.** [C17: from L, lit.: witness (to masculinity)]

test match *n.* (in various sports, esp. cricket) any of a series of international matches.

testosterone (tɛ'stɒstə,rəʊn) *n.* a potent steroid hormone secreted mainly by the testes. [C20: from TESTIS + STEROL + -ONE]

test paper *n.* 1. *Chem.* paper impregnated with an indicator for use on chemical tests. 2. **a.** the question sheet of a test. **b.** the paper completed by a test candidate.

test pilot *n.* a pilot who flies aircraft of new design to test their performance in the air.

test tube *n.* 1. a cylindrical round-bottomed glass tube open at one end: used in scientific experiments. 2. (*modifier*) made synthetically in, or as if in, a test tube: *a test-tube product.*

test-tube baby *n.* **1.** a fetus that has developed from an ovum fertilized in an artificial womb. **2.** a baby conceived by artificial insemination.

testudinal (tɛ'stjuːdɪnəl) *adj.* of or resembling a tortoise. [C19: from L TESTUDO]

testudo (tɛ'stjuːdəʊ) *n., pl.* **-dines** (-dɪˌniːz). a form of shelter used by the ancient Roman Army as protection against attack from above, consisting of a mobile arched structure or of overlapping shields held by the soldiers over their heads. [C17: from L: a tortoise, from *testa* a shell]

testy ('tɛstɪ) *adj.* **-tier, -tiest.** irritable or touchy. [C14: from Anglo-Norman *testif* headstrong, from OF *teste* head, from LL *testa* skull, from L: shell] —'**testily** *adv.* —'**testiness** *n.*

tetanus ('tɛtənəs) *n.* **1.** Also called: **lockjaw.** an acute infectious disease in which sustained muscular spasm, contraction, and convulsion are caused by the release of toxins from a bacterium. **2.** *Physiol.* any tense contraction of a muscle. [C16: via L from Gk *tetanos,* ult. from *teinein* to stretch] —'**tetanal** *adj.* —'**teta,noid** *adj.*

tetany ('tɛtənɪ) *n.* an abnormal increase in the excitability of nerves and muscles caused by a deficiency of parathyroid secretion. [C19: from F; see TETANUS]

tetchy ('tɛtʃɪ) *adj.* **tetchier, tetchiest.** being or inclined to be cross, irritable, or touchy. [C16: prob. from obs. *tetch* defect, from OF *tache* spot, of Gmc origin] —'**tetchily** *adv.* —'**tetchiness** *n.*

tête-à-tête (ˌteɪtɑːˈteɪt) *n., pl.* **-têtes** *or* **-tête.** **1. a.** a private conversation between two people. **b.** (*as modifier*): *a tête-à-tête conversation.* **2.** a small sofa for two people, esp. one that is S-shaped in plan so that the sitters are almost face to face. ~*adv.* **3.** intimately; in private. [C17: from F, lit.: head to head]

tête-bêche (tɛtˈbɛʃ) *adj. Philately.* (of an unseparated pair of stamps) printed so that one is inverted in relation to the other. [C19: from F, from *tête* head + *bêche,* from obs. *béchevet* double-headed (orig. of a bed)]

tether ('tɛðə) *n.* **1.** a rope, chain, etc., by which an animal is tied to a particular spot. **2.** the range of one's endurance, etc. **3. at the end of one's tether.** distressed or exasperated to the limit of one's endurance. ~*vb.* **4.** (*tr.*) to tie with or as if with a tether. [C14: from ON *tjothr*]

Tethys[1] ('tiːθɪs, 'tɛθ-) *n. Greek myth.* a Titaness and sea goddess, wife of Oceanus.

Tethys[2] ('tiːθɪs, 'tɛθ-) *n.* the sea that lay between the two ancient supercontinents, Laurasia and Gondwanaland, and which can be regarded as the predecessor of today's smaller Mediterranean.

Teton Range ('tiːtᵊn) *n.* a mountain range in the N central U.S., mainly in NW Wyoming. Highest peak: Grand Teton, 4196 m (13 766 ft.).

tetra- *or before a vowel* **tetr-** *combining form.* four: *tetrameter.* [from Gk]

tetrabasic (ˌtɛtrəˈbeɪsɪk) *adj.* (of an acid) containing four replaceable hydrogen atoms. —**tetrabasicity** (ˌtɛtrəbeɪˈsɪsɪtɪ) *n.*

tetrachloromethane ('tɛtrəklɔːrəʊˌmiːˈθeɪn) *n.* the systematic name for **carbon tetrachloride.**

tetrachord ('tɛtrəˌkɔːd) *n. Music.* any of several groups of four notes in descending order, in which the first and last notes form a perfect fourth. [C17: from Gk *tetrakhordos* four-stringed] —'**tetra,chordal** *adj.*

tetracyclic (ˌtɛtrəˈsaɪklɪk) *adj. Chem.* containing four rings in its molecular structure.

tetracycline (ˌtɛtrəˈsaɪklaɪn, -klɪn) *n.* an antibiotic synthesized from chlortetracycline or derived from a bacterium. [C20: from TETRA- + CYCL(IC) + -INE[2]]

tetrad ('tɛtræd) *n.* a group or series of four. [C17: from Gk *tetras,* from *tettares* four]

tetraethyl lead (ˌtɛtrəˈiːθaɪl lɛd) *n.* a colourless oily insoluble liquid used in petrol to prevent knocking. Systematic name: **lead tetraethyl.**

tetrafluoroethylene ('tɛtrəˌflʊərəʊˈɛθɪˌliːn) *n. Chem.* a dense colourless gas that is polymerized to make plastics. [C20: from TETRA- + FLUORO- + ETHYLENE]

tetragon ('tɛtrəˌgɒn) *n.* a less common name for **quadrilateral** (sense 2). [C17: from Gk *tetragōnon*]

tetragonal (tɛ'trægᵊnᵊl) *adj.* **1.** *Crystallog.* relating or belonging to the crystal system characterized by three mutually perpendicular axes of which only two are equal. **2.** of or shaped like a quadrilateral. —**te'tragonally** *adv.*

Tetragrammaton (ˌtɛtrəˈgræmətᵊn) *n. Bible.* the Hebrew name for God consisting of the four consonants Y H V H (or Y H W H). It is usually transliterated as *Jehovah* or *Yahweh.* Sometimes shortened to **Tetragram.** [C14: from Gk, from *tetragrammatos* having four letters]

tetrahedron (ˌtɛtrəˈhiːdrən) *n., pl.* **-drons** *or* **-dra** (-drə). a solid figure having four plane faces. A **regular tetrahedron** has faces that are equilateral triangles. [C16: from NL, from LGk *tetraedron*] —ˌ**tetra'hedral** *adj.*

tetralogy (tɛ'trælədʒɪ) *n., pl.* **-gies.** a series of four related works, as in drama or opera. [C17: from Gk *tetralogia*]

tetramerous (tɛ'træmərəs) *adj. Biol.* having or consisting of four parts. [C19: from NL *tetramerus,* from Gk *tetramerēs*]

tetrameter (tɛ'træmɪtə) *n. Prosody.* **1.** a line of verse consisting of four metrical feet. **2.** a verse composed of such lines.

tetraplegia (ˌtɛtrəˈpliːdʒɪə) *n.* another name for **quadriplegia.** —ˌ**tetra'plegic** *adj.*

tetraploid ('tɛtrəˌplɔɪd) *Genetics.* ~*adj.* **1.** having four times the haploid number of chromosomes in the nucleus. ~*n.* **2.** a tetraploid organism, nucleus, or cell.

tetrapod ('tɛtrəˌpɒd) *n.* **1.** any vertebrate that has four limbs. **2.** a device consisting of four arms radiating from a central point: three arms form a supporting tripod and the fourth is vertical.

tetrapterous (tɛ'træptərəs) *adj.* having four wings. [C19: from NL *tetrapterus,* from Gk *tetrapteros,* from TETRA- + *pteron* wing]

tetrarch ('tɛtrɑːk) *n.* **1.** the ruler of one fourth of a country. **2.** a subordinate ruler. **3.** any of four joint rulers. [C14: from Gk *tetrarkhēs;* see TETRA-, -ARCH] —**tetrarchate** (tɛ'trɑːˌkeɪt, -kɪt) *n.* —**te'trarchic** *adj.* —'**tetrarchy** *n.*

tetrastich ('tɛtrəˌstɪk) *n.* a poem, stanza, or strophe that consists of four lines. [C16: via L from Gk *tetrastikhon,* from TETRA- + *stikhos* row] —**tetrastichic** (ˌtɛtrəˈstɪkɪk) *or* **tetrastichal** (tɛ'træstɪkᵊl) *adj.*

tetravalent (ˌtɛtrəˈveɪlənt) *adj. Chem.* **1.** having a valency of four. **2.** Also: **quadrivalent.** having four valencies. —ˌ**tetra'valency** *n.*

Tetrazzini (*Italian* tetrat'tsiːni) *n.* **Luisa** (lu'iːza). 1871–1940, Italian coloratura soprano.

tetrode ('tɛtrəʊd) *n.* an electronic valve having four electrodes.

tetroxide (tɛ'trɒksaɪd) *n.* any oxide that contains four oxygen atoms per molecule.

tetryl ('tɛtrɪl) *n.* a yellow crystalline explosive solid, trinitrophenylmethylnitramine used in detonators.

Tetuán (tɛ'twɑːn) *n.* a city in N Morocco: capital of Spanish Morocco (1912–56). Pop.: 199 615 (1982).

Tetzel *or* **Tezel** ('tɛtsᵊl) *n.* **Johann** (jo'han). ?1465–1519, German Dominican monk. His preaching on papal indulgences provoked Luther's 95 theses at Wittenberg (1517).

Teucer ('tjuːsə) *n. Greek myth.* **1.** a Cretan leader, who founded Troy. **2.** a son of Telamon and Hesione, who distinguished himself by his archery on the side of the Greeks in the Trojan War.

Teucrian ('tjuːkrɪən) *n., adj.* another word for **Trojan.**

Teut. *abbrev. for* Teuton(ic).

Teutoburger Wald (*German* 'tɔytobʊrgər valt) *n.* a low wooded mountain range in N West Germany: possible site of the annihilation of three Roman legions by Germans under Arminius in 9 A.D.

Teuton ('tjuːtən) *n.* **1.** a member of an ancient Germanic people from Jutland who migrated to S Gaul in the 2nd century B.C. **2.** a member of any people speaking a Germanic language, esp. a German. ~*adj.* **3.** Teutonic. [C18: from L *Teutoni* the Teutons, of Gmc origin]

Teutonic (tjuː'tɒnɪk) *adj.* **1.** characteristic of or relating to the German people. **2.** of the ancient Teutons. **3.** (not used in linguistics) of or relating to the Germanic languages.

Tevere ('teːvere) *n.* the Italian name for the **Tiber.**

Tewkesbury ('tjuːksbərɪ, -brɪ) *n.* a town in W England, in N Gloucestershire at the confluence of the Rivers Severn and Avon: scene of a decisive battle (1471) of the Wars of the Roses in which the Yorkists defeated the Lancastrians; 12th-century abbey. Pop.: 9554 (1981).

Texas ('tɛksəs) *n.* a state of the southwestern U.S., on the Gulf of Mexico: the second largest state; part of Mexico from 1821 to 1836, when it was declared an independent republic; joined the U.S. in 1845; consists chiefly of a plain, with a wide flat coastal belt rising up to the semi-arid Sacramento and Davis Mountains of the southwest; a major producer of cotton, rice, and livestock; the chief U.S. producer of oil and gas; a leading world supplier of sulphur. Capital: Austin. Pop.: 16 370 000 (1985 est.). Area: 678 927 sq. km (262 134 sq. miles). Abbrevs.: **Tex.** or (with zip code) **TX** —'**Texan** *n.*, *adj.*

Tex-Mex ('tɛks,mɛks) *adj.* of, relating to, or denoting the Texan version of something Mexican, such as music, food, or language.

text (tɛkst) *n.* **1.** the main body of a printed or written work as distinct from commentary, notes, illustrations, etc. **2.** the words of something printed, written, or displayed on a visual display unit. **3.** the original exact wording of a work as distinct from a revision or translation. **4.** a short passage of the Bible used as a starting point for a sermon. **5.** the topic or subject of a discussion or work. **6.** short for **textbook. 7.** any novel, play, etc., prescribed as part of a course of study. [C14: from Med. L *textus* version, from L *textus* texture, from *texere* to compose]

textbook ('tɛkst,bʊk) *n.* a book used as a standard source of information on a particular subject. —'**text,bookish** *adj.*

textile ('tɛkstaɪl) *n.* **1.** any fabric or cloth, esp. woven. **2.** raw material suitable to be made into cloth. ~*adj.* **3.** of or relating to fabrics. [C17: from L *textilis* woven, from *texere* to weave]

textual ('tɛkstjʊəl) *adj.* **1.** of or relating to a text or texts. **2.** based on a text. —'**textually** *adv.*

textual criticism *n.* **1.** the scholarly study of manuscripts, esp. of the Bible, in an effort to establish the original text. **2.** literary criticism emphasizing a close analysis of the text.

textualism ('tɛkstjʊə,lɪzəm) *n.* **1.** doctrinaire adherence to a text, esp. of the Bible. **2.** textual criticism, esp. of the Bible. —'**textualist** *n.*, *adj.*

texture ('tɛkstʃə) *n.* **1.** the surface of a material, esp. as perceived by the sense of touch. **2.** the structure, appearance, and feel of a woven fabric. **3.** the general structure and disposition of the constituent parts of something: *the texture of a cake.* **4.** the distinctive character or quality of something: *the texture of life in America.* ~*vb.* **5.** (*tr.*) to give a distinctive texture to. [C15: from L *textūra* web, from *texere* to weave] —'**textural** *adj.* —'**texturally** *adv.*

Teyde (*Spanish* 'teiðe) *n.* a variant spelling of **Teide.**

Tezel ('tɛtsᵊl) *n.* a variant spelling of (Johann) **Tetzel.**

TGWU (in Britain) *abbrev. for* Transport and General Workers' Union.

Th *the chemical symbol for* thorium.

Th. *abbrev. for* Thursday.

-th¹ *suffix forming nouns.* **1.** (*from verbs*) indicating an action or its consequence: *growth.* **2.** (*from adjectives*) indicating a quality: *width.* [from OE *-thu*, *-tho*]

-th² *or* **-eth** *suffix.* forming ordinal numbers: *fourth; thousandth.* [from OE *-(o)tha*, *-(o)the*]

Thabana-Ntlenyana (tɑː'bɑːnᵊn'tleɪnjənə) *n.* a mountain in Lesotho: the highest peak of the Drakensberg Mountains. Height: 3482 m (11 425 ft.). Also called: **Thadentsonyane, Thabantshonyana.**

Thackeray ('θækərɪ) *n.* **William Makepeace.** 1811–63, English novelist, born in India. His novels, originally serialized, include *Vanity Fair* (1848), *Pendennis* (1850), *Henry Esmond* (1852), and *The Newcomes* (1855).

Thaddeus *or* **Thadeus** ('θædɪəs) *n. New Testament.* one of the 12 apostles (Matthew 10:3; Mark 3:18), traditionally identified with Jude.

Thadentsonyane (,tɑːdən'tsɒnjənə) *n.* another name for **Thabana-Ntlenyana.**

Thai (taɪ) *adj.* **1.** of Thailand, its people, or their language. ~*n.* **2.** (*pl.* **Thais** *or* **Thai**) a native or inhabitant of Thailand. **3.** the language of Thailand, sometimes classified as belonging to the Sino-Tibetan family.

Thailand ('taɪ,lænd) *n.* a kingdom in SE Asia: on the Andaman Sea and the Gulf of Siam: united as a kingdom in 1350 and became a major SE Asian power; consists chiefly of a central plain around the Chao Phraya river system, mountains rising over 2400 m (8000 ft.) in the northwest, and rainforest the length of the S peninsula. Official language: Thai. Religion: mostly Hinayana Buddhist. Currency: baht. Capital: Bangkok. Pop.: 53 722 000

(1987). Area: 513 998 sq. km (198 455 sq. miles). Former name (until 1939 and 1945–49): **Siam.**

Thaïs ('θeɪɪs) *n.* 4th-century B.C. Athenian courtesan; mistress of Alexander the Great.

thalamus ('θæləməs) *n., pl.* **-mi** (-,maɪ). **1.** either of the two contiguous egg-shaped masses of grey matter at the base of the brain. **2.** both of these masses considered as a functional unit. **3.** the receptacle or torus of a flower. [C18: from L, from Gk *thalamos* inner room] —**thalamic** (θə'læmɪk) *adj.*

thalassaemia *or U.S.* **thalassemia** (,θælə'siːmɪə) *n.* a hereditary disease resulting from defects in the synthesis of the red blood pigment haemoglobin. [NL, from Gk *thalassa* sea + -AEMIA, it being esp. prevalent round the eastern Mediterranean]

thalassic (θə'læsɪk) *adj.* of or relating to the sea, esp. to small or inland seas. [C19: from F *thalassique*, from Gk *thalassa* sea]

thaler ('tɑːlə) *n., pl.* **-ler** *or* **-lers.** a former German, Austrian, or Swiss silver coin. [from G; see DOLLAR]

Thales ('θeɪliːz) *n.* ?624–?546 B.C., Greek philosopher, mathematician, and astronomer, born in Miletus. He held that water was the origin of all things and he predicted the solar eclipse of May 28, 585 B.C.

Thalia (θə'laɪə) *n. Greek myth.* **1.** the Muse of comedy and pastoral poetry. **2.** one of the three Graces. [C17: via L from Gk, from *thaleia* blooming]

thalidomide (θə'lɪdə,maɪd) *n.* **a.** a drug formerly used as a sedative and hypnotic but withdrawn from use when found to cause abnormalities in developing fetuses. **b.** (*as modifier*): *a thalidomide baby.* [C20: from *thali(mi)do(glutari)mide*]

thallium ('θælɪəm) *n.* a soft malleable highly toxic white metallic element. Symbol: Tl; atomic no.: 81; atomic wt.: 204.37. [C19: from NL, from Gk *thallos* a green shoot; from the green line in its spectrum]

thallophyte ('θælə,faɪt) *n.* any of a group of plants lacking true stems, leaves, and roots: includes the algae, fungi, lichens, and bacteria. [C19: from NL *thallophyta*, from Gk *thallos* a young shoot + *phuton* a plant] —**thallophytic** (,θælə'fɪtɪk) *adj.*

thallus ('θæləs) *n., pl.* **thalli** ('θælaɪ) *or* **thalluses.** the undifferentiated plant body of algae, fungi, and lichens. [C19: from L, from Gk *thallos* green shoot, from *thallein* to bloom] —'**thalloid** *adj.*

thalweg *or* **talweg** ('tɑːlvɛg) *n. Geog., rare.* **1.** the longitudinal outline of a riverbed from source to mouth. **2.** the line of steepest descent from any point on the land surface. [C19: from G *Thal* or *Tal* valley + *Weg* way]

Thames *n.* **1.** (tɛmz). a river in S England, rising in the Cotswold Hills in several headstreams and flowing generally east through London to the North Sea by a large estuary. Length: 338 km (210 miles). Ancient name: **Tamesis** ('tæməsɪs). **2.** (teɪmz, θeɪmz). a river in SE Canada, in Ontario, flowing south to London, then southwest to Lake St Clair. Length: 217 km (135 miles).

than (ðæn; *unstressed* ðən) *conj.* (*coordinating*), *prep.* **1.** used to introduce the second element of a comparison, the first element of which expresses difference: *shorter than you.* **2.** used after adverbs such as *rather* or *sooner* to introduce a rejected alternative in an expression of preference: *rather than be imprisoned, I shall die.* [OE *thanne*]

▷**Usage.** In sentences such as *he does it far better than I,* *than* is usually regarded in careful usage as a conjunction governing an unexpressed verb: *he does it far better than I* (*do it*). The case of any pronoun therefore depends on whether it is the subject or the object of that unexpressed verb: *she likes him more than I* (*like him*); *she likes him more than* (*she likes*) *me.* However, in informal usage *than* is often treated as a preposition and any pronoun is therefore used in its objective form, so that *she likes him more than me* is ambiguous.

thanatology (,θænə'tɒlədʒɪ) *n.* the scientific study of death and its related phenomena. [C19: from Gk *thanatos* death + -LOGY]

thanatopsis (,θænə'tɒpsɪs) *n.* a meditation on death, as in a poem. [C19: from Gk *thanatos* death + *opsis* a view]

Thanatos ('θænə,tɒs) *n.* the Greek personification of death: son of Nyx, goddess of night. Roman counterpart: **Mors.** Thanatos was the name chosen by Freud to represent a universal death instinct. Compare **Eros.** —**Thanatotic** (,θænə'tɒtɪk) *adj.*

thane or (less commonly) **thegn** (θeɪn) n. **1.** (in Anglo-Saxon England) a member of an aristocratic class who held land from the king or from another nobleman in return for certain services. **2.** (in medieval Scotland) a person of rank holding land from the king. [OE thegn] —**thanage** ('θeɪnɪdʒ) n.

Thanet ('θænɪt) n. **Isle of.** an island in SE England, in NE Kent, separated from the mainland by two branches of the River Stour: scene of many Norse invasions. Area: 109 sq. km (42 sq. miles).

Thanjavur (ˌtʌndʒəˈvʊə) n. a city in SE India, in E Tamil Nadu: headquarters of the earliest Protestant missions in India. Pop.: 184 015 (1981). Former name: **Tanjore.**

thank (θæŋk) vb. (tr.) **1.** to convey feelings of gratitude to. **2.** to hold responsible: he has his creditors to thank for his bankruptcy. [OE thancian]

thankful ('θæŋkfʊl) adj. grateful and appreciative. —'**thankfully** adv. —'**thankfulness** n.

thankless ('θæŋklɪs) adj. **1.** receiving no thanks or appreciation. **2.** ungrateful. —'**thanklessly** adv. —'**thank-lessness** n.

thanks (θæŋks) pl. n. **1.** an expression of appreciation or gratitude. **2. thanks to.** because of: thanks to him we lost the match. ~interj. **3.** Inf. an exclamation expressing gratitude.

thanksgiving ('θæŋks,gɪvɪŋ; U.S. θæŋks'gɪv-) n. **1.** the act of giving thanks. **2.** a formal public expression of thanks to God.

Thanksgiving Day n. an annual day of holiday celebrated in thanksgiving to God on the fourth Thursday of November in the United States, and on the second Monday of October in Canada. Often shortened to **Thanksgiving.**

Thant (θænt) n. **U** (uː). 1909–74, Burmese diplomat; secretary-general of the United Nations (1962–71).

thar (tɑː) n. a variant spelling of **tahr.**

Thar Desert (tɑː) n. a desert in NW India, mainly in NW Rajasthan state and extending into Pakistan. Area: over 260 000 sq. km (100 000 sq. miles). Also called: **Indian Desert, Great Indian Desert.**

Thásos ('θɑːsɒs) n. a Greek island in N Aegean: colonized by Greeks from Paros in the 7th century B.C. as a gold-mining centre; under Turkish rule (1455–1912). Pop.: 13 110 (1981). Area: 379 sq. km (146 sq. miles).

that (ðæt; unstressed ðət) determiner. (used before a sing. n.) **1. a.** used preceding a noun that has been mentioned or is understood: that idea of yours. **b.** (as pronoun): don't eat that. **2. a.** used preceding a noun that denotes something more remote or removed: that building over there is for sale. **b.** (as pronoun): that is John and this is his wife. **3.** used to refer to something that is familiar: that old chap from across the street. **4. and (all) that.** Inf. everything connected with the subject mentioned: he knows a lot about building and that. **5. at that.** (completive-intensive) additionally, all things considered, or nevertheless: I might decide to go at that. **6. like that. a.** effortlessly: he gave me the answer just like that. **b.** of such a nature, character, etc.: he paid for all our tickets—he's like that. **7. that is. a.** to be precise. **b.** in other words. **c.** for example. **8. that's that.** there is no more to be done, discussed, etc. ~conj. (subordinating) **9.** used to introduce a noun clause: I believe that you'll come. **10.** used to introduce: **a.** a clause of purpose: they fought that others might have peace. **b.** a clause of result: he laughed so hard that he cried. **c.** a clause after an understood sentence expressing desire, indignation, or amazement: oh, that I had never lived! ~adv. **11.** used to reinforce the specification of a precise degree already mentioned: go just that fast and you should be safe. **12.** Also: **all that.** (usually used with a negative) Inf. (intensifier): he wasn't that upset at the news. **13.** Dialect. (intensifier): the cat was that weak after the fight. ~pron. **14.** used to introduce a restrictive relative clause: the book that we want. **15.** used to introduce a clause with the verb to be to emphasize the extent to which the preceding noun is applicable: genius that she is, she outwitted the computer. [OE thæt]

▷ **Usage.** Precise stylists maintain a distinction between that and which: that is used as a relative pronoun in restrictive clauses and which in nonrestrictive clauses. In the book that is on the table is mine, the clause that is on the table is used to distinguish one particular book (the one on the table) from another or others (which may be anywhere, but not on the table). In the book, which is on the table, is mine, the which clause is merely descriptive or incidental. The more formal the level of language, the more important it is to preserve the distinction between the two relative pronouns; but in informal or colloquial usage, the words are often used interchangeably.

thatch (θætʃ) n. **1. a.** Also called: **thatching.** a roofing material that consists of straw, reed, etc. **b.** a roof made of such a material. **2.** anything resembling this, such as the hair of the head. **3.** Also called: **thatch palm.** any of various palms with leaves suitable for thatching. ~vb. **4.** to cover with thatch. [OE theccan to cover] —'**thatcher** n.

Thatcher ('θætʃə) n. **Margaret (Hilda)** (née Roberts). born 1925, British stateswoman; leader of the Conservative Party from 1975; prime minister from 1979.

Thatcherism ('θætʃər,ɪzəm) n. the policies of monetarism, privatization, and self-help promoted by Margaret Thatcher. —**Thatcherite** ('θætʃəraɪt) n., adj.

thaumatology (ˌθɔːməˈtɒlədʒɪ) n. the study of or a treatise on miracles. [C19: from Gk thaumato- combining form of thauma a wonder, marvel + -LOGY]

thaumatrope ('θɔːmə,trəʊp) n. a toy in which partial pictures on the two sides of a card appear to merge when the card is twirled rapidly. [C19: from Gk thaumato- (see THAUMATOLOGY) + -TROPE] —**thaumatropical** (ˌθɔːməˈtrɒpɪkəl) adj.

thaumaturge ('θɔːmə,tɜːdʒ) n. Rare. a performer of miracles; magician. [C18: from Med. L thaumaturgus, from Gk thaumatourgos miracle-working] —,**thauma'turgic** adj. —'**thauma,turgy** n.

thaw (θɔː) vb. **1.** to melt or cause to melt: the snow thawed. **2.** to become or cause to become unfrozen; defrost. **3.** (intr.) to be the case that the ice or snow is melting: it's thawing fast. **4.** (intr.) to become more relaxed or friendly. ~n. **5.** the act or process of thawing. **6.** a spell of relatively warm weather, causing snow or ice to melt. **7.** an increase in relaxation or friendliness. [OE thawian]

ThD abbrev. for Doctor of Theology.

the[1] (stressed or emphatic ðiː; unstressed before a consonant ðə; unstressed before a vowel ðɪ) determiner. (article) **1.** used preceding a noun that has been previously specified: the pain should disappear soon. Cf. **a**[1]. **2.** used to indicate a particular person, object, etc.: ask the man standing outside. Cf. **a**[1]. **3.** used preceding certain nouns associated with one's culture, society, or community: to go to the doctor; to listen to the news. **4.** used preceding present participles and adjectives when they function as nouns: the singing is awful. **5.** used preceding titles and certain uniquely specific or proper nouns: the United States; the Chairman. **6.** used preceding a qualifying adjective or noun in certain names or titles: Edward the First. **7.** used preceding a noun to make it refer to its class generically: the white seal is hunted for its fur. **8.** used instead of my, your, her, etc., with parts of the body: take me by the hand. **9.** (usually stressed) the best, only, or most remarkable: Harry's is the club in this town. **10.** used with proper nouns when qualified: written by the young Hardy. **11.** another word for **per:** fifty pence the pound. **12.** Often facetious or derog. my; our: the wife goes out on Thursdays. **13.** used preceding a unit of time in phrases or titles indicating an outstanding person, event, etc.: housewife of the year. [ME, from OE thē, a demonstrative adjective that later superseded sē (masculine singular) and sēo, sio (feminine singular)]

the[2] (ðə, ðɪ) adv. **1.** (often foll. by for) used before comparative adjectives or adverbs for emphasis: she looks happier for her trip. **2.** used correlatively before each of two comparative adjectives or adverbs to indicate equality: the sooner you come, the better; the more I see you, the more I love you. [OE thī, thȳ]

theanthropism (θiːˈænθrə,pɪzəm) n. **1.** the ascription of human traits or characteristics to a god or gods. **2.** Christian theol. the doctrine of the union of the divine and human natures in the single person of Christ. [C19: from Ecclesiastical Gk theanthrōpos (from theos god + anthrōpos man) + -ISM] —**theanthropic** (ˌθiːænˈθrɒpɪk) adj.

thearchy ('θiːɑːkɪ) n., pl. **-chies.** rule or government by God or gods; theocracy. [C17: from Church Gk thearkhia; see THEO-, -ARCHY]

theatre or U.S. **theater** ('θɪətə) n. **1.** a building designed for the performance of plays, operas, etc. **2.** a large room or hall, usually with a raised platform and tiered seats for an audience. **3.** a room in a hospital equipped for surgical operations. **4.** plays regarded collectively as a form of art. **5. the theatre.** the world of actors, theatrical companies, etc. **6.** a setting for dramatic or important events. **7.** writing that is suitable for dramatic presentation: a good piece of theatre. **8.** U.S., Austral., & N.Z. the usual word for **cinema** (sense 1). **9.** a major area of military activity. **10.** a circular or semicircular open-air building with tiers of seats. [C14: from L theātrum, from Gk theatron place for viewing, from theasthai to look at]

theatre-in-the-round n., pl. **theatres-in-the-round.** a theatre with seats arranged around a central acting area.

theatre of cruelty n. a type of theatre that seeks to communicate a sense of pain, suffering, and evil, using gesture, movement, sound, and symbolism rather than language.

theatre of the absurd n. drama in which normal conventions and dramatic structure are modified in order to present life as irrational.

theatrical (θɪ'ætrɪk³l) adj. **1.** of or relating to the theatre or dramatic performances. **2.** exaggerated and affected in manner or behaviour; histrionic. **— the,atri'cality** or **the'atricalness** n. **— the'atrically** adv.

theatricals (θɪ'ætrɪk³lz) pl. n. dramatic performances, esp. as given by amateurs.

theatrics (θɪ'ætrɪks) n. (functioning as sing.) **1.** the art of staging plays. **2.** exaggerated mannerisms or displays of emotions.

Thebaid ('θiːbeɪɪd, -bɪ-) n. the territory around ancient Thebes in Egypt, or sometimes around Thebes in Greece.

thebaine ('θiːbəˌiːn) n. a poisonous white crystalline alkaloid, extracted from opium. [C19: from NL thebaia opium of Thebes (with reference to Egypt as a chief source of opium) + -INE²]

Thebes (θiːbz) n. **1.** (in ancient Greece) the chief city of Boeotia, destroyed by Alexander the Great (336 B.C.). **2.** (in ancient Egypt) a city on the Nile: at various times capital of Upper Egypt or of the entire country. **— Thebaic** (θɪ'beɪɪk) adj. **— 'Theban** adj., n.

theca ('θiːkə) n., pl. **-cae** (-siː). **1.** Bot. an enclosing organ, cell, or spore case. **2.** Zool. a hard outer covering, such as the container of a coral polyp. [C17: from L thēca, from Gk thēkē case] **— 'thecate** adj.

thecodont ('θiːkəˌdɒnt) adj. **1.** (of mammals and certain reptiles) having teeth that grow in sockets. **2.** of or relating to teeth of this type. ~n. **3.** any of various extinct reptiles of Triassic times, having teeth set in sockets: they gave rise to the dinosaurs, crocodiles, pterodactyls, and birds. [C20: NL Thecodontia, from Gk thēkē case + -ODONT]

thé dansant French. (te dɑ̃sɑ̃) n., pl. **thés dansant** (te dɑ̃sɑ̃). a dance held while afternoon tea is served, popular in the 1920s and 1930s. [lit.: dancing tea]

thee (ðiː) pron. **1.** the objective form of thou¹. **2.** (subjective) Rare. refers to the person addressed: used mainly by members of the Society of Friends. [OE thē]

theft (θɛft) n. **1.** the dishonest taking of property belonging to another person with the intention of depriving the owner permanently of its possession. **2.** Rare. something stolen. [OE thēofth]

thegn (θeɪn) n. a less common variant of **thane.**

theine ('θiːiːn, -ɪn) n. caffeine, esp. when present in tea. [C19: from NL thea tea + -INE²]

their (ðɛə) determiner. **1.** of or associated in some way with them: their own clothes; she tried to combat their mocking her. **2.** belonging to or associated with people in general: in many countries they wash their clothes in the river. **3.** belonging to or associated with an indefinite antecedent such as one, whoever, or anybody: everyone should bring their own lunch. [C12: from ON theira]

▷ **Usage.** The use of their and similar plural forms as in sense 3 is sometimes regarded as unacceptable in formal contexts, though it has existed in the language for at least five centuries and is common in informal contexts.

theirs (ðɛəz) pron. **1.** something or someone belonging to or associated with them: theirs is difficult. **2.** something or someone belonging to or associated with an indefinite antecedent such as one, whoever, or anybody:

everyone thinks theirs is best. **3. of theirs.** belonging to or associated with them.

▷ **Usage.** See at **their.**

theism ('θiːɪzəm) n. **1.** the belief in one God as the creator and ruler of the universe. **2.** the belief in the existence of a God or gods. **— 'theist** n., adj. **— the'istic** or **the'istical** adj.

them (ðɛm; unstressed ðəm) pron. **1.** (objective) refers to things or people other than the speaker or people addressed: I'll kill them; what happened to them? ~determiner. **2.** a nonstandard word for **those:** three of them oranges. [OE thǣm, infl. by ON theim]

▷ **Usage.** See at **me.**

theme (θiːm) n. **1.** an idea or topic expanded in a discourse, discussion, etc. **2.** (in literature, music, art, etc.) a unifying idea, image, or motif, repeated or developed throughout a work. **3.** Music. a group of notes forming a recognizable melodic unit, often used as the basis of the musical material in a composition. **4.** a short essay, esp. one set as an exercise for a student. **5.** Grammar. another word for **root¹** or **stem¹** (sense 7). **6.** (modifier) planned or designed round one unifying subject, image, etc.: a theme holiday. ~vb. (tr.) **7.** to design, decorate, etc., in accordance with a theme. [C13: from L thema, from Gk: deposit, from tithenai to lay down] **— thematic** (θɪ'mætɪk) adj.

theme park n. an area planned as a leisure attraction, in which all the displays, buildings, activities, etc., are based on one subject.

theme song n. **1.** a melody used, esp. in a film score, to set a mood, introduce a character, etc. **2.** another term for **signature tune.**

Themis ('θiːmɪs) n. Greek myth. the goddess personifying justice.

Themistocles (θə'mɪstəˌkliːz) n. ?527–?460 B.C., Athenian statesman, who was responsible for the Athenian victory against the Persians at Salamis (480). He was ostracized in 470.

themselves (ðəm'sɛlvz) pron. **1. a.** the reflexive form of they or them. **b.** (intensifier): the team themselves voted on it. **2.** (preceded by a copula) their normal or usual selves: they don't seem themselves any more. **3.** Also: **themself.** Not standard. a reflexive form of an indefinite antecedent such as one, whoever, or anybody: everyone has to look after themselves.

▷ **Usage.** See at **myself.**

then (ðɛn) adv. **1.** at that time; over that period of time. **2.** (sentence modifier) in that case; that being so: then why don't you ask her? go on then, take it. ~sentence connector. **3.** after that; with that: then John left the room. ~n. **4.** that time: from then on. ~adj. **5.** (prenominal) existing, functioning, etc., at that time: the then prime minister. [OE thenne]

thenar ('θiːnɑː) n. **1.** the palm of the hand. **2.** the fleshy area of the palm at the base of the thumb. [C17: via NL from Gk]

thence (ðɛns) adv. **1.** from that place. **2.** Also: **thenceforth** ('ðɛns'fɔːθ). from that time or event; thereafter. **3.** therefore. [C13 thannes, from thanne, from OE thanon]

thenceforward ('ðɛns'fɔːwəd) or **thenceforwards** adv. from that time or place on.

theo- or before a vowel **the-** combining form. indicating God or gods: theology. [from Gk theos god]

theobromine (ˌθiːəʊ'brəʊmiːn, -mɪn) n. a white crystalline alkaloid that occurs in tea and cacao: used to treat coronary heart disease and headaches. [C18: from NL theobroma genus of trees, lit.: food of the gods]

theocentric (ˌθiːə'sɛntrɪk) adj. Theol. having God as the focal point of attention.

theocracy (θɪ'ɒkrəsɪ) n., pl. **-cies. 1.** government by a deity or by a priesthood. **2.** a community under such government. **— 'theo,crat** n. **— ,theo'cratic** adj.

theocrasy (θɪ'ɒkrəsɪ) n. **1.** a mingling into one of deities or divine attributes previously regarded as distinct. **2.** the union of the soul with God in mysticism. [C19: from Gk theokrasia, from THEO- + -krasia from krasis a blending]

Theocritus (θɪ'ɒkrɪtəs) n. ?310–?250 B.C., Greek poet, born in Syracuse. He wrote the first pastoral poems in Greek literature and was closely imitated by Virgil. **— The'ocritan** or **Theo'critean** (θɪˌɒkrɪ'tiːən) adj., n.

theodicy (θɪ'ɒdɪsɪ) n., pl. **-cies.** the branch of theology concerned with defending the attributes of God against objections resulting from the existence of physical and

moral evil. [C18: coined by Leibnitz in F as *théodicée*, from THEO- + Gk *dikē* justice] —**the‚odi'cean** *adj.*

theodolite (θɪ'ɒdə‚laɪt) *n.* a surveying instrument for measuring horizontal and vertical angles, consisting of a small tripod-mounted telescope. Also called (in the U.S. and Canada): **transit.** [C16: from NL *theodolitus*, from ?] —**theodolitic** (θɪ‚ɒdə'lɪtɪk) *adj.*

Theodora (‚θɪə'dɔːrə) *n.* ?500–548 A.D., Byzantine empress; wife and counsellor of Justinian I.

Theodorakis (*Greek* θεɔðɔ'rakis) *n.* **Mikis** ('mikis). born 1925, Greek composer: wrote the music for the film *Zorba the Greek* (1965).

Theodoric *or* **Theoderic** (θɪ'ɒdərɪk) *n.* called *the Great.* ?454–526 A.D., king of the Ostrogoths and founder of the Ostrogothic kingdom in Italy after his murder of Odoacer (493).

Theodosius I (‚θɪə'dəʊsɪəs) *n.* called *the Great.* ?346–395 A.D., Roman emperor of the Eastern Roman Empire (379–95) and of the Western Roman Empire (392–95).

theogony (θɪ'ɒgənɪ) *n., pl.* **-nies.** 1. the origin and descent of the gods. 2. an account of this. [C17: from Gk *theogonia*] —**theogonic** (‚θɪə'gɒnɪk) *adj.* —**the'ogonist** *n.*

theol. *abbrev. for:* 1. theologian. 2. theological. 3. theology.

theologian (‚θɪə'ləʊdʒɪən) *n.* a person versed in or engaged in the study of theology.

theological (‚θɪə'lɒdʒɪkəl) *adj.* of, relating to, or based on theology. —‚**theo'logically** *adv.*

theological virtues *pl. n.* those virtues that are infused into man by a special grace of God, specifically faith, hope, and charity.

theologize *or* **-ise** (θɪ'ɒlə‚dʒaɪz) *vb.* 1. (*intr.*) to speculate upon theological subjects or engage in theological study or discussion. 2. (*tr.*) to render theological or treat from a theological point of view. —**the‚ologi'zation** *or* **-i'sation** *n.* —**the'olo‚gizer** *or* **-iser** *n.*

theology (θɪ'ɒlədʒɪ) *n., pl.* **-gies.** 1. the systematic study of the existence and nature of the divine and its relationship to other beings. 2. the systematic study of Christian revelation concerning God's nature and purpose. 3. a specific system, form, or branch of this study. [C14: from LL *theologia*, from L] —**the'ologist** *n.*

theomachy (θɪ'ɒməkɪ) *n., pl.* **-chies.** a battle among the gods or against them. [C16: from Gk *theomakhia*, from THEO- + *makhē* battle]

theomancy ('θiːəʊmænsɪ) *n.* divination or prophecy by an oracle or by people directly inspired by a god.

theomania (‚θɪə'meɪnɪə) *n.* religious madness, esp. when it takes the form of believing oneself to be a god. —‚**the·o'mani‚ac** *n.*

theophany (θɪ'ɒfənɪ) *n., pl.* **-nies.** a visible manifestation of a deity to man. [C17: from LL *theophania*, from LGk, from THEO- + *phainein* to show] —**theophanic** (‚θɪə'fænɪk) *adj.*

Theophrastus (‚θɪə'fræstəs) *n.* ?372–?287 B.C., Greek Peripatetic philosopher, noted esp. for his *Characters*, a collection of sketches of moral types.

theophylline (‚θɪə'fɪliːn, -ɪn) *n.* a white crystalline alkaloid that is an isomer of theobromine: it occurs in plants such as tea. [C19: from THEO(BROMINE) + PHYLLO- + -INE[2]]

theorem ('θɪərəm) *n.* a statement or formula that can be deduced from the axioms of a formal system by means of its rules of inference. [C16: from LL *theōrēma*, from Gk: something to be viewed, from *theōrein* to view] —**theorematic** (‚θɪərə'mætɪk) *or* **theoremic** (‚θɪə'remɪk) *adj.*

theoretical (‚θɪə'rɛtɪkəl) *or* **theoretic** *adj.* 1. of or based on theory. 2. lacking practical application or actual existence; hypothetical. 3. using or dealing in theory; impractical. —‚**theo'retically** *adv.*

theoretician (‚θɪərɪ'tɪʃən) *n.* a student or user of the theory rather than the practical aspects of a subject.

theoretics (‚θɪə'rɛtɪks) *n.* (*functioning as sing. or pl.*) the theory of a particular subject.

theorize *or* **-ise** ('θɪə‚raɪz) *vb.* (*intr.*) to produce or use theories; speculate. —'**theorist** *n.* —‚**theori'zation** *or* **-i'sation** *n.* —'**theo‚rizer** *or* **-iser** *n.*

theory ('θɪərɪ) *n., pl.* **-ries.** 1. a system of rules, procedures, and assumptions used to produce a result. 2. abstract knowledge or reasoning. 3. a conjectural view or idea: *I have a theory about that.* 4. an ideal or hypothetical situation (esp. in **in theory**). 5. a set of hypotheses related by logical or mathematical arguments to explain a

wide variety of connected phenomena in general terms: *the theory of relativity.* 6. a nontechnical name for **hypothesis.** [C16: from LL *theōria*, from Gk: a sight, from *theōrein* to gaze upon]

theory of games *n.* a mathematical theory concerned with the optimum choice of strategy in situations involving a conflict of interest. Also called: **game theory.**

theosophy (θɪ'ɒsəfɪ) *n.* 1. any of various religious or philosophical systems claiming to be based on or to express an intuitive insight into the divine nature. 2. the system of beliefs of the Theosophical Society founded in 1875, claiming to be derived from the sacred writings of Brahmanism and Buddhism. [C17: from Medieval L *theosophia*, from LGk; see THEO-, -SOPHY] —**theosophical** (‚θɪə'sɒfɪkəl) *or* ‚**theo'sophic** *adj.* —**the'osophist** *n.*

therapeutic (‚θɛrə'pjuːtɪk) *adj.* 1. of or relating to the treatment of disease; curative. 2. serving or performed to maintain health: *therapeutic abortion.* [C17: from NL *therapeuticus*, from Gk, from *therapeuein* to minister to, from *theraps* an attendant] —‚**thera'peutically** *adv.*

therapeutics (‚θɛrə'pjuːtɪks) *n.* (*functioning as sing.*) the branch of medicine concerned with the treatment of disease.

therapy ('θɛrəpɪ) *n., pl.* **-pies. a.** the treatment of physical, mental, or social disorders or disease. **b.** (*in combination*): *physiotherapy.* [C19: from NL *therapia*, from Gk *therapeia* attendance; see THERAPEUTIC] —'**therapist** *n.*

Theravada (‚θɛrə'vɑːdə) *n.* the southern school of Buddhism, the name preferred by Hinayana Buddhists for their doctrines. [from Pali: doctrine of the elders]

there (ðɛə) *adv.* 1. in, at, or to that place, point, case, or respect: *we never go there; I agree with you there.* ~*pron.* 2. used as a grammatical subject with some verbs, esp. *be*, when the true subject follows the verb: *there is a girl in that office.* ~*adj.* 3. (*postpositive*) who or which is in that place or position: *that boy there did it.* 4. **all there.** (*predicative*) of normal intelligence. 5. **so there.** an exclamation that usually follows a declaration of refusal or defiance. 6. **there you are. a.** an expression used when handing a person something requested or desired. **b.** an exclamation of triumph. ~*n.* 7. that place: *near there.* ~*interj.* 8. an expression of sympathy, as in consoling a child: *there, there, dear.* [OE *thǣr*]

▷ **Usage.** Careful writers and speakers ensure that the verb agrees with the number of the subject in such constructions as *there is a man waiting* and *there are several people waiting.* However, where the subject is compound even careful speakers frequently use the singular as in *there is a pen and a book on the table.*

thereabouts ('ðɛərə‚baʊts) *or U.S.* **thereabout** *adv.* near that place, time, amount, etc.

thereafter (‚ðɛər'ɑːftə) *adv.* from that time on or after that time.

thereat (‚ðɛər'æt) *adv. Rare.* 1. at that point or time. 2. for that reason.

thereby (‚ðɛə'baɪ, 'ðɛə‚baɪ) *adv.* 1. by that means; because of that. 2. *Arch.* thereabouts.

therefor (‚ðɛə'fɔː) *adv. Arch.* for this, that, or it.

therefore ('ðɛə‚fɔː) *sentence connector.* 1. thus; hence: *those people have their umbrellas up; therefore, it must be raining.* 2. consequently; as a result.

therefrom (‚ðɛə'frɒm) *adv. Arch.* from that or there: *the roads that lead therefrom.*

therein (‚ðɛər'ɪn) *adv. Formal or law.* in or into that place, thing, etc.

thereinto (‚ðɛər'ɪntuː) *adv. Formal or law.* into that place, circumstance, etc.

thereof (‚ðɛər'ɒv) *adv. Formal or law.* 1. of or concerning that or it. 2. from or because of that.

thereon (‚ðɛər'ɒn) *adv. Arch.* thereupon.

Theresa (tə'riːzə; *Spanish* te'resa) *n.* See (Saint) **Teresa.**

Thérèse de Lisieux (*French* terɛz də lizjø) *n.* **Saint,** known as *the Little Flower of Jesus.* 1873–97, French Carmelite nun, noted for her autobiography, *The Story of a Soul* (1897). Feast day: Oct. 3.

thereto (‚ðɛə'tuː) *adv.* 1. *Formal or law.* to that or it. 2. *Obs.* in addition to that.

theretofore (‚ðɛətʊ'fɔː) *adv. Formal or law.* before that time; previous to that.

thereunder (‚ðɛər'ʌndə) *adv. Formal or law.* 1. (in documents, etc.) below that or it; subsequently in that; thereafter. 2. under the terms or authority of that.

thereupon (ˌðɛərə'pɒn) adv. **1.** immediately after that; at that point. **2.** Formal or law. upon that thing, point, subject, etc.

therewith (ˌðɛə'wɪθ, -'wɪð) or **therewithal** adv. **1.** Formal or law. with or in addition to that. **2.** a less common word for **thereupon** (sense 1). **3.** Arch. by means of or on account of that.

Therezina (Portuguese tere'zina) n. the former name of **Teresina**.

therianthropic (ˌθɪərɪən'θrɒpɪk) adj. **1.** (of certain mythical creatures or deities) having a partly animal, partly human form. **2.** of or relating to such creatures or deities. [C19: from Gk thērion wild animal + anthrōpos man] **— therianthropism** (ˌθɪərɪ'ænθrəˌpɪzəm) n.

theriomorphic (ˌθɪərɪəʊ'mɔːfɪk) adj. (esp. of a deity) possessing or depicted in the form of a beast. [C19: from Gk thēriomorphos, from thērion wild animal + morphē shape]

therm (θɜːm) n. Brit. a unit of heat equal to 1 0 British thermal units. One therm is equal to $1.055\,056 \times 10^8$ joules. [C19: from Gk thermē heat]

thermae ('θɜːmiː) pl. n. public baths or hot springs, esp. in ancient Greece or Rome. [C17: from L, from Gk thermai, pl. of thermē heat]

thermal ('θɜːməl) adj. **1.** Also: **thermic**. of, caused by, or generating heat. **2.** hot or warm: thermal baths. **3.** (of garments) specially made so as to have exceptional heat-retaining qualities: thermal underwear. ~n. **4.** a column of rising air caused by local unequal heating of the land surface, and used by gliders and birds to gain height. **5.** (pl.) thermal garments, esp. underclothes. — '**thermally** adv.

thermal barrier n. an obstacle to flight at very high speeds as a result of the heating effect of air friction. Also called: **heat barrier**.

thermal conductivity n. a measure of the ability of a substance to conduct heat.

thermal efficiency n. the ratio of the work done by a heat engine to the energy supplied to it.

thermal equator n. an imaginary line round the earth running through the point on each meridian with the highest average temperature.

thermalize or **-ise** ('θɜːməˌlaɪz) vb. Physics. to undergo or cause to undergo a process in which neutrons lose energy in a moderator and become thermal neutrons. — ˌthermali'zation or -i'sation n.

thermal neutrons pl. n. slow neutrons that are approximately in thermal equilibrium with a moderator.

thermal reactor n. a nuclear reactor in which most of the fission is caused by thermal neutrons.

thermal shock n. a fluctuation in temperature causing stress in a material. It often results in fracture, esp. in brittle materials such as ceramics.

thermion ('θɜːmɪən) n. Physics. an electron or ion emitted by a body at high temperature.

thermionic (ˌθɜːmɪ'ɒnɪk) adj. of, relating to, or operated by electrons emitted from materials at high temperatures: a thermionic valve.

thermionic current n. an electric current produced between two electrodes as a result of electrons emitted by thermionic emission.

thermionic emission n. the emission of electrons from very hot solids or liquids.

thermionics (ˌθɜːmɪ'ɒnɪks) n. (functioning as sing.) the branch of electronics concerned with the emission of electrons by hot bodies and with devices based on this effect.

thermionic valve or esp. U.S. & Canad. **tube** n. an electronic valve in which electrons are emitted from a heated rather than a cold cathode.

thermistor (θɜː'mɪstə) n. a semiconductor device having a resistance that decreases rapidly with an increase in temperature. It is used for temperature measurement and control. [C20: from THERMO- + (RES)ISTOR]

Thermit ('θɜːmɪt) or **Thermite** ('θɜːmaɪt) n. Trademark. a mixture of aluminium powder and a metal oxide, which when ignited produces great heat: used for welding and in incendiary bombs.

thermo- or before a vowel **therm-** combining form. related to, caused by, or measuring heat: thermodynamics; thermophile. [from Gk thermos hot, thermē heat]

thermobarograph (ˌθɜːməʊ'bærəˌɡrɑːf) n. a device that simultaneously records the temperature and pressure of the atmosphere.

thermobarometer (ˌθɜːməʊbə'rɒmɪtə) n. an apparatus that provides an accurate measurement of pressure by observation of the change in the boiling point of a fluid.

thermochemistry (ˌθɜːməʊ'kɛmɪstrɪ) n. the branch of chemistry concerned with the study and measurement of the heat evolved or absorbed during chemical reactions. — ˌthermo'chemical adj. — ˌthermo'chemist n.

thermocline ('θɜːməʊˌklaɪn) n. a temperature gradient in a thermally stratified body of water, such as a lake.

thermocouple ('θɜːməʊˌkʌpəl) n. **1.** a device for measuring temperature consisting of a pair of wires of different metals or semiconductors joined at both ends. One junction is at the temperature to be measured, the second at a fixed temperature. The electromotive force generated depends upon the temperature difference. **2.** a similar device with only one junction between two dissimilar metals or semiconductors.

thermodynamic (ˌθɜːməʊdaɪ'næmɪk) or **thermodynamical** adj. **1.** of or concerned with thermodynamics. **2.** determined by or obeying the laws of thermodynamics.

thermodynamic equilibrium n. the condition of a system in which the quantities that specify its properties, such as pressure, temperature, etc., all remain unchanged.

thermodynamics (ˌθɜːməʊdaɪ'næmɪks) n. (functioning as sing.) the branch of physical science concerned with the interrelationship and interconversion of different forms of energy.

thermodynamic temperature n. temperature defined in terms of the laws of thermodynamics and not in terms of the properties of any real material: usually expressed in the Kelvin scale.

thermoelectric (ˌθɜːməʊɪ'lɛktrɪk) or **thermoelectrical** adj. **1.** of, relating to, used in, or operated by the conversion of heat energy to electrical energy. **2.** of, relating to, used in, or operated by the conversion of electrical energy.

thermoelectric effect n. another name for the **Seebeck effect**.

thermoelectricity (ˌθɜːməʊɪlɛk'trɪsɪtɪ) n. **1.** electricity generated by a thermocouple. **2.** the study of the relationship between heat and electrical energy.

thermoelectron (ˌθɜːməʊɪ'lɛktrɒn) n. an electron emitted at high temperature, such as one produced in a thermionic valve.

thermogenesis (ˌθɜːməʊ'dʒɛnɪsɪs) n. the production of heat by metabolic processes.

thermograph ('θɜːməʊˌɡrɑːf) n. a type of thermometer that produces a continuous record (**thermogram**) of a fluctuating temperature.

thermojunction (ˌθɜːməʊ'dʒʌŋkʃən) n. a point of electrical contact between two dissimilar metals across which a voltage appears, the magnitude of which depends on the temperature of the contact and the nature of the metals.

thermolabile (ˌθɜːməʊ'leɪbɪl) adj. easily decomposed or subject to a loss of characteristic properties by the action of heat.

thermoluminescence (ˌθɜːməʊˌluːmɪ'nɛsəns) n. phosphorescence of certain materials or objects as a result of heating.

thermolysis (θɜː'mɒlɪsɪs) n. **1.** Physiol. loss of heat from the body. **2.** the dissociation of a substance as a result of heating. — **thermolytic** (ˌθɜːməʊ'lɪtɪk) adj.

thermomagnetic (ˌθɜːməʊmæg'nɛtɪk) adj. of or concerned with the relationship between heat and magnetism, esp. the change in temperature of a body when it is magnetized or demagnetized.

thermometer (θə'mɒmɪtə) n. an instrument used to measure temperature, esp. one in which a thin column of liquid, such as mercury, expands and contracts within a graduated sealed tube. — **ther'mometry** n.

thermonuclear (ˌθɜːməʊ'njuːklɪə) adj. **1.** involving nuclear fusion. **2.** involving thermonuclear weapons.

thermonuclear reaction n. a nuclear fusion reaction occurring at a very high temperature: responsible for the energy produced in the sun, nuclear weapons, and fusion reactors.

thermophile ('θɜːməʊˌfaɪl) or **thermophil** ('θɜːməʊˌfɪl) n. **1.** an organism, esp. a bacterium or plant, that thrives under warm conditions. ~adj. **2.** thriving under warm conditions. — ˌthermo'philic adj.

thermopile ('θɜːməʊˌpaɪl) n. an instrument for detecting and measuring heat radiation or for generating a thermo-electric current. It consists of a number of thermocouple junctions.

thermoplastic (ˌθɜːməʊˈplæstɪk) adj. 1. (of a material, esp. a synthetic plastic) becoming soft when heated and rehardening on cooling without appreciable change of properties. ~n. 2. a synthetic plastic or resin, such as polystyrene, with these properties.

Thermos or **Thermos flask** ('θɜːməs) n. Trademark. a type of stoppered vacuum flask used to preserve the temperature of its contents.

thermosetting (ˌθɜːməʊˈsɛtɪŋ) adj. (of a material, esp. a synthetic plastic) hardening permanently after one application of heat and pressure.

thermosiphon (ˌθɜːməʊˈsaɪfən) n. a system in which a coolant is circulated by convection caused by a difference in density between the hot and cold portions of the liquid.

thermosphere ('θɜːməˌsfɪə) n. an atmospheric layer lying between the mesosphere and the exosphere.

thermostable (ˌθɜːməʊˈsteɪbəl) adj. capable of withstanding moderate heat without loss of characteristic properties.

thermostat ('θɜːməˌstæt) n. 1. a device that maintains a system at a constant temperature. 2. a device that sets off a sprinkler, etc., at a certain temperature. —ˌthermoˈstatic adj. —ˌthermoˈstatically adv.

thermostatics (ˌθɜːməˈstætɪks) n. (functioning as sing.) the branch of science concerned with thermal equilibrium.

thermotaxis (ˌθɜːməʊˈtæksɪs) n. the directional movement of an organism in response to the stimulus of heat. —ˌthermoˈtaxic adj.

thermotropism (ˌθɜːməʊˈtrəʊpɪzəm) n. the directional growth of a plant in response to the stimulus of heat. —ˌthermoˈtropic adj.

-thermy n. combining form. indicating heat: diathermy. [from NL -thermia, from Gk thermē] —-thermic or -thermal adj. combining form.

theroid ('θɪərɔɪd) adj. of, relating to, or resembling a beast. [C19: from Gk thēroeidēs, from thēr wild animal; see -OID]

Thersites (θɜːˈsaɪtiːz) n. the ugliest and most evil-tongued fighter on the Greek side in the Trojan War, killed by Achilles when he mocked him.

thesaurus (θɪˈsɔːrəs) n., pl. **-ri** (-raɪ) or **-ruses**. 1. a book containing systematized lists of synonyms and related words. 2. a dictionary of selected words or topics. 3. Rare. a treasury. [C18: from L, Gk: TREASURE]

these (ðiːz) determiner. **a.** the form of **this** used before a plural noun: these men. **b.** (as pronoun): I don't much care for these.

Theseus ('θiːsɪəs) n. Greek myth. a hero of Attica, noted for his many great deeds, among them the slaying of the Minotaur, the conquest of the Amazons, whose queen he married, participation in the Calydonian hunt, and the search for the Golden Fleece. —**Thesean** (θɪˈsiːən) adj.

thesis ('θiːsɪs) n., pl. **-ses** (-siːz). 1. a dissertation resulting from original research, esp. when submitted for a degree or diploma. 2. a doctrine maintained in argument. 3. a subject for a discussion or essay. 4. an unproved statement put forward as a premise in an argument. [C16: via LL from Gk: a placing, from tithenai to place]

Thespian ('θɛspɪən) adj. 1. of or relating to Thespis. 2. of or relating to drama and the theatre; dramatic. ~n. 3. Often facetious. an actor or actress.

Thespis ('θɛspɪs) n. 6th century B.C., Greek poet, regarded as the founder of tragic drama.

Thess. Bible. abbrev. for Thessalonians.

Thessaloníki (Greek θɛsaˈlɒniki) n. a port in NE Greece, in central Macedonia at the head of the **Gulf of Salonika** (an inlet of the Aegean): capital of the Roman province of Macedonia; university (1926). Pop.: 402 443 (1981). Latin name: **Thessalonica** (ˌθɛsəˈlɒnɪkə). English name: **Salonika** or **Salonica**.

Thessaly ('θɛsəlɪ) n. a region of E Central Greece, on the Aegean: an extensive fertile plain, edged with mountains. Pop.: 695 654 (1981). Area: 13 973 sq. km (5395 sq. miles). Modern Greek name: **Thessalía** (ˌθɛsaˈljia). —**Thessalian** (θɛˈseɪlɪən) adj., n.

theta ('θiːtə) n. the eighth letter of the Greek alphabet (Θ, θ). [C17: from Gk]

Thetford Mines ('θɛtfəd) n. a city in SE Canada, in S Quebec: asbestos industry. Pop.: 19 965 (1981).

Thetis ('θiːtɪs) n. one of the Nereids and mother of Achilles by Peleus.

theurgy ('θiːˌɜːdʒɪ) n., pl. **-gies**. 1. the intervention of a divine or supernatural agency in the affairs of man. 2. beneficent magic as taught by Egyptian Neoplatonists. [C16: from LL theūrgia, from LGk theourgia the practice of magic, from theo- THEO- + -urgia, from ergon work] —**theˈurgic** or **theˈurgical** adj. —**ˈtheurgist** n.

thew (θjuː) n. 1. muscle, esp. if strong or well-developed. 2. (pl.) muscular strength. [OE thēaw] —**ˈthewless** adj. —**ˈthewy** adj.

they (ðeɪ) pron. (subjective) 1. refers to people or things other than the speaker or people addressed: they fight among themselves. 2. refers to people in general: in Australia they have Christmas in the summer. 3. refers to an indefinite antecedent such as one, whoever, or anybody: if anyone objects, they can go. [C12 thei from ON their, masc. nominative pl., equivalent to OE thā]

▷ **Usage.** See at **their.**

they'd (ðeɪd) contraction of they would or they had.

they'll (ðeɪl) contraction of they will or they shall.

they're (ðɛə, 'ðeɪə) contraction of they are.

they've (ðeɪv) contraction of they have.

thi- combining form. a variant of **thio-**.

thiamine ('θaɪəˌmiːn, -mɪn) or **thiamin** ('θaɪəmɪn) n. a white crystalline vitamin that occurs in the outer coat of rice and other grains. It forms part of the vitamin B complex: deficiency leads to nervous disorders and to the disease beriberi. Also called: **vitamin B₁, aneurin**. [C20: THIO- + (VIT)AMIN]

thiazine ('θaɪəˌziːn, -ˌzaɪn) n. any of a group of organic compounds containing a ring system composed of four carbon atoms, a sulphur atom, and a nitrogen atom.

thiazole ('θaɪəˌzəʊl) n. 1. a colourless liquid that contains a ring system composed of three carbon atoms, a sulphur atom, and a nitrogen atom. 2. any of a group of compounds derived from this substance that are used in dyes.

thick (θɪk) adj. 1. of relatively great extent from one surface to the other: a thick slice of bread. 2. **a.** (postpositive) of specific fatness: ten centimetres thick. **b.** (in combination): a six-inch-thick wall. 3. having a dense consistency: thick soup. 4. abundantly covered or filled: a piano thick with dust. 5. impenetrable; dense: a thick fog. 6. stupid, slow, or insensitive. 7. throaty or badly articulated: a voice thick with emotion. 8. (of accents, etc.) pronounced. 9. Inf. very friendly (esp. in **thick as thieves**). 10. a bit thick. Brit. unfair or excessive. ~adv. 11. in order to produce something thick: to slice bread thick. 12. profusely; in quick succession (esp. in **thick and fast**). 13. lay it on thick. Inf. **a.** to exaggerate a story, etc. **b.** to flatter excessively. ~n. 14. a thick piece or part. 15. the thick. the most intense or active part. 16. through thick and thin. in good times and bad. [OE thicce] —**ˈthickish** adj. —**ˈthickly** adv.

thicken ('θɪkən) vb. 1. to make or become thick or thicker. 2. (intr.) to become more involved: the plot thickened. —**ˈthickener** n.

thickening ('θɪkənɪŋ) n. 1. something added to a liquid to thicken it. 2. a thickened part or piece.

thicket ('θɪkɪt) n. a dense growth of small trees, shrubs, and similar plants. [OE thiccet]

thickhead ('θɪkˌhɛd) n. 1. a stupid or ignorant person; fool. 2. any of a family of Australian and SE Asian songbirds. —**ˌthickˈheaded** adj.

thickie or **thicky** ('θɪkɪ) n., pl. **-ies**. Brit. sl. a slow-witted unintelligent person.

thick-knee n. another name for **stone curlew**.

thickness ('θɪknɪs) n. 1. the state or quality of being thick. 2. the dimension through an object, as opposed to length or width. 3. a layer.

thickset (ˌθɪkˈsɛt) adj. 1. stocky in build; sturdy. 2. densely planted or placed. ~n. 3. a rare word for **thicket**.

thick-skinned adj. insensitive to criticism or hints; not easily upset or affected.

thick-witted or **thick-skulled** adj. stupid, dull, or slow to learn. —**ˌthick-ˈwittedly** adv. —**ˌthick-ˈwittedness** n.

thief (θiːf) n., pl. **thieves** (θiːvz). a person who steals something from another. [OE thēof] —**ˈthievish** adj.

Thiers (*French* tjɛr) *n.* **Louis Adolphe** (lwi adɔlf). 1797–1877, French statesman and historian. After the Franco-Prussian war, he suppressed the Paris Commune and became first president of the Third Republic (1871–73). His policies made possible the paying off of the war indemnity exacted by Germany.

thieve (θiːv) *vb.* to steal (someone's possessions). [OE *thēofian*, from *thēof* thief] — '**thievery** *n.* — '**thieving** *adj.*

thigh (θaɪ) *n.* **1.** the part of the leg between the hip and the knee in man. **2.** the corresponding part in other vertebrates and insects. ~Related adj.: **femoral.** [OE *thēh*]

thighbone ('θaɪ,bəʊn) *n.* a nontechnical name for the **femur.**

thimble ('θɪmbəl) *n.* **1.** a cap of metal, plastic, etc., used to protect the end of the finger when sewing. **2.** any small metal cap resembling this. **3.** *Naut.* a loop of metal having a groove at its outer edge for a rope or cable. [OE *thŷmel* thumbstall, from *thūma* thumb]

thimbleful ('θɪmbəl,fʊl) *n.* a very small amount, esp. of a liquid.

thimblerig ('θɪmbəl,rɪg) *n.* a game in which the operator rapidly moves about three inverted thimbles, often with sleight of hand, one of which conceals a token, the other player betting on which thimble the token is under. [C19: from THIMBLE + RIG (in obs. sense meaning a trick, scheme)] — '**thimble,rigger** *n.*

Thimbu ('θɪmbuː) *or* **Thimphu** ('θɪmfuː) *n.* the capital of Bhutan, in the west in the foothills of the E Himalayas: became the official capital in 1962. Pop.: 15 000 (1987).

thin (θɪn) *adj.* **thinner, thinnest. 1.** of relatively small extent from one side or surface to the other. **2.** slim or lean. **3.** sparsely placed; meagre: *thin hair.* **4.** of low density: *a thin liquid.* **5.** weak; poor: *a thin disguise.* **6. thin on the ground.** few in number; scarce. ~*adv.* **7.** in order to produce something thin: *to cut bread thin.* ~*vb.* **thinning, thinned. 8.** to make or become thin or sparse. [OE *thynne*] — '**thinly** *adv.* — '**thinness** *n.*

thine (ðaɪn) *determiner. Arch.* **a.** (*preceding a vowel*) of or associated with you (thou): *thine eyes.* **b.** (*as pronoun*): *thine is the greatest burden.* [OE *thīn*]

thin-film *adj.* (of an electronic component, etc.) composed of one or more extremely thin layers of metal, semiconductor, etc.

thing (θɪŋ) *n.* **1.** an object, fact, affair, circumstance, or concept considered as being a separate entity. **2.** any inanimate object. **3.** an object or entity that cannot or need not be precisely named. **4.** *Inf.* a person or animal: *you poor thing.* **5.** an event or act. **6.** a thought or statement. **7.** *Law.* property. **8.** a device, means, or instrument. **9.** (*often pl.*) a possession, article of clothing, etc. **10.** *Inf.* a preoccupation or obsession (esp. in **have a thing about**). **11.** an activity or mode of behaviour satisfying to one's personality (esp. in **do one's (own) thing**). **12. make a thing of.** exaggerate the importance of. **13. the thing.** the latest fashion. [OE *thing* assembly]

thing-in-itself *n.* (in the philosophy of Immanuel Kant) reality regarded apart from human knowledge and perception.

thingumabob *or* **thingamabob** ('θɪŋəmə,bɒb) *n. Inf.* a person or thing the name of which is unknown, temporarily forgotten, or deliberately overlooked. Also: **thingumajig, thingamajig,** *or* **thingummy.** [C18: from THING, with humorous suffix]

think (θɪŋk) *vb.* **thinking, thought. 1.** (*tr.; may take a clause as object*) to consider, judge, or believe: *he thinks my ideas impractical.* **2.** (*intr.; often foll. by about*) to exercise the mind as in order to make a decision; ponder. **3.** (*intr.*) to be capable of conscious thought: *man is the only animal that thinks.* **4.** to remember; recollect. **5.** (*intr.;* foll. by *of*) to make the mental choice (of): *think of a number.* **6.** (*may take a clause as object or an infinitive*) **a.** to expect; suppose. **b.** to be considerate enough (to do something): *he did not think to thank them.* **7.** (*intr.*) to focus the attention on being: *think big.* **8. think twice.** to consider carefully before deciding. ~*n.* **9.** *Inf.* a careful, open-minded assessment. **10.** (*modifier*) *Inf.* characterized by or involving thinkers, thinking, or thought. ~See also **think over, think up.** [OE *thencan*] — '**thinkable** *adj.* — '**thinker** *n.*

thinking ('θɪŋkɪŋ) *n.* **1.** opinion or judgment. **2.** the process of thought. ~*adj.* **3.** (*prenominal*) using or capable

of using intelligent thought: *thinking people.* **4. put on one's thinking cap.** to ponder a matter or problem.

think over *vb.* (*tr., adv.*) to ponder or consider.

think-tank *n. Inf.* a group of specialists commissioned to undertake intensive study and research into specified problems.

think up *vb.* (*tr., adv.*) to invent or devise.

thinner ('θɪnə) *n.* (*often pl., functioning as sing.*) a solvent, such as turpentine, added to paint or varnish to dilute it, reduce its opacity or viscosity, or increase its penetration.

thin-skinned *adj.* sensitive to criticism or hints; easily upset or affected.

thio- *or before a vowel* **thi-** *combining form.* sulphur, esp. denoting the replacement of an oxygen atom with a sulphur atom: *thiol; thiosulphate.* [from Gk *theion* sulphur]

thiol ('θaɪɒl) *n.* any of a class of sulphur-containing organic compounds with the formula RSH, where R is an organic group.

thionine ('θaɪəʊ,niːn, -,naɪn) *or* **thionin** ('θaɪənɪn) *n.* **1.** a crystalline derivative of thiazine used as a violet dye to stain microscope specimens. **2.** any of a class of related dyes. [C19: by shortening, from *ergothioneine*]

thiopentone sodium (,θaɪəʊ'pɛntəʊn) *or* **thiopental sodium** (,θaɪəʊ'pɛntæl) *n.* a barbiturate drug used as an intravenous general anaesthetic. Also called: **Sodium Pentothal.**

thiophen ('θaɪəʊ,fɛn) *or* **thiophene** ('θaɪəʊ,fiːn) *n.* a colourless liquid heterocyclic compound found in the benzene fraction of coal tar and manufactured from butane and sulphur.

thiosulphate (,θaɪəʊ'sʌlfeɪt) *n.* any salt of thiosulphuric acid.

thiosulphuric acid (,θaɪəʊsʌl'fjʊərɪk) *n.* an unstable acid known only in solutions and in the form of its salts. Formula: $H_2S_2O_3$.

thiouracil (,θaɪəʊ'jʊərəsɪl) *n.* a white crystalline water-insoluble substance with an intensely bitter taste, used in medicine to treat hyperthyroidism. [from THIO- + *uracil* (URO- + AC(ETIC) + -IL(E))]

thiourea (,θaɪəʊ'jʊərɪə) *n.* a white crystalline substance used in photographic fixing, rubber vulcanization, and the manufacture of synthetic resins.

third (θɜːd) *adj.* (*usually prenominal*) **1. a.** coming after the second in numbering, position, etc.; being the ordinal number of *three*: often written 3rd. **b.** (*as n.*): *the third got a ring.* **2.** rated, graded, or ranked below the second level. **3.** denoting the third from lowest forward ratio of a gearbox in a motor vehicle. ~*n.* **4. a.** one of three equal parts of an object, quantity, etc. **b.** (*as modifier*): *a third part.* **5.** the fraction equal to one divided by three (1/3). **6.** the forward ratio above second of a gearbox in a motor vehicle. **7. a.** the interval between one note and another three notes away from it counting inclusively along the diatonic scale. **b.** one of two notes constituting such an interval in relation to the other. **8.** *Brit.* an honours degree of the third and usually the lowest class. Full term: **third class honours degree.** ~*adv.* **9.** Also: **thirdly.** in the third place. [OE *thirda,* var. of *thridda;* rel. to OFrisian *thredda,* OSaxon *thriddio*] — '**thirdly** *adv.*

Third Age *n.* **the.** old age, esp. when viewed as a period of opportunity for learning something new or for other new developments.

third class *n.* **1.** the class or grade next in value, quality, etc., to the second. ~*adj.* (**third-class** *when prenominal*). **2.** of the class or grade next in value, quality, etc., to the second. ~*adv.* **3.** by third-class transport, etc.

third degree *n. Inf.* torture or bullying, esp. used to extort confessions or information.

third-degree burn *n. Pathol.* the most severe type of burn, involving the destruction of both epidermis and dermis.

third dimension *n.* the dimension of depth by which a solid object may be distinguished from a two-dimensional drawing or picture of it.

third eyelid *n.* another name for **nictitating membrane.**

Third International *n.* another name for **Comintern.**

third man *n. Cricket.* a fielding position on the off side near the boundary behind the batsman's wicket.

Third Market *n. Stock Exchange.* a new small market designed to meet the needs of young growing British companies for raising capital.

third party n. **1.** a person who is involved by chance or only incidentally in a legal proceeding, agreement, or other transaction. ~*adj.* **2.** *Insurance.* providing protection against liability caused by accidental injury or death of other persons.

third person n. a grammatical category of pronouns and verbs used when referring to objects or individuals other than the speaker or his addressee or addressees.

third-rate *adj.* mediocre or inferior.

third reading n. (in a legislative assembly) **1.** *Brit.* the process of discussing the committee's report on a bill. **2.** *U.S.* the final consideration of a bill.

Third World n. the countries of Africa, Asia, and Latin America collectively, esp. when viewed as underdeveloped.

Thirlmere ('θɜːlmɪə) n. a lake in NW England, in Cumbria in the Lake District: provides part of Manchester's water supply. Length: 6 km (4 miles).

thirst (θɜːst) n. **1.** a craving to drink, accompanied by a feeling of dryness in the mouth and throat. **2.** an eager longing, craving, or yearning. ~*vb.* (*intr.*) **3.** to feel a thirst. [OE *thyrstan*, from *thurst*]

thirsty ('θɜːstɪ) *adj.* **thirstier, thirstiest. 1.** feeling a desire to drink. **2.** dry; arid. **3.** (foll. by *for*) feeling an eager desire. **4.** causing thirst. — '**thirstily** *adv.* — '**thirstiness** n.

thirteen (ˌθɜːˈtiːn) n. **1.** the cardinal number that is the sum of ten and three and is a prime number. **2.** a numeral, 13, XIII, etc., representing this number. **3.** something representing or consisting of 13 units. ~*determiner.* **4. a.** amounting to thirteen. **b.** (*as pronoun*): *thirteen of them fell.* [OE *threotēne*] — '**thir'teenth** *adj., n.*

thirteenth chord n. a chord much used in jazz and pop, consisting of a major or minor triad upon which are superimposed the seventh, ninth, eleventh, and thirteenth above the root. Often shortened to **thirteenth.**

thirty ('θɜːtɪ) n., pl. **-ties. 1.** the cardinal number that is the product of ten and three. **2.** a numeral, 30, XXX, etc., representing this number. **3.** (*pl.*) the numbers 30-39, esp. the 30th to the 39th year of a person's life or of a century. **4.** the amount or quantity that is three times as big as ten. **5.** something representing or consisting of 30 units. ~*determiner.* **6. a.** amounting to thirty. **b.** (*as pronoun*): *thirty are broken.* [OE *thritig*] — '**thirtieth** *adj., n.*

Thirty-nine Articles *pl.* n. a set of formulas defining the doctrinal position of the Church of England, drawn up in the 16th century.

thirty-second note n. the usual U.S. and Canad. name for **demisemiquaver.**

thirty-twomo (ˌθɜːtɪˈtuːməʊ) n., pl. **-mos.** a book size resulting from folding a sheet of paper into 32 leaves or 64 pages.

this (ðɪs) *determiner.* (*used before a sing.* n.) **1. a.** used preceding a noun referring to something or someone that is closer: *look at this picture.* **b.** (*as pronoun*): *take this.* **2. a.** used preceding a noun that has just been mentioned or is understood: *this plan of yours won't work.* **b.** (*as pronoun*): *I first saw this on Sunday.* **3. a.** used to refer to something about to be said, read, etc.: *consider this argument.* **b.** (*as pronoun*): *listen to this.* **4. a.** the present or immediate: *this time you'll know better.* **b.** (*as pronoun*): *before this, I was mistaken.* **5.** *Inf.* an emphatic form of **a** or **the**[1]: *I saw this big brown bear.* **6. this and that.** various unspecified and trivial actions, matters, objects, etc. **7. with** (*or* **at**) **this.** after this. ~*adv.* **8.** used with adjectives and adverbs to specify a precise degree that is about to be mentioned: *go just this fast and you'll be safe.* [OE *thēs, thēos, this* (masc., fem., neuter sing.)]

Thisbe ('θɪzbɪ) n. See **Pyramus and Thisbe.**

thistle ('θɪsᵊl) n. **1.** any of a genus of plants of the composite family, having prickly-edged leaves, dense flower heads, and feathery hairs on the seeds: the national emblem of Scotland. **2.** any of various similar or related plants. [OE *thistel*] — '**thistly** *adj.*

thistledown ('θɪsᵊlˌdaʊn) n. the mass of feathery plumed seeds produced by a thistle.

thither ('ðɪðə) *or* **thitherward** *adv. Obs. or formal.* to or towards that place; in that direction. [OE *thider*, var. of *thæder*, infl. by *hider* hither]

thitherto (ˌðɪðəˈtuː; ˈðɪðə,tuː) *adv. Obs. or formal.* until that time.

thixotropic (ˌθɪksəˈtrɒpɪk) *adj.* (of fluids and gels) having a reduced viscosity when stress is applied, as when

stirred: *thixotropic paints.* [from Gk *thixis* the act of touching + -TROPIC] —**thixotropy** (θɪkˈsɒtrəpɪ) n.

tho *or* **tho'** (ðəʊ) *conj., adv. U.S. or poetic.* a variant spelling of **though.**

thole[1] (θəʊl) *or* **tholepin** ('θəʊl,pɪn) n. a wooden pin or one of a pair, set upright in the gunwales of a rowing boat to serve as a fulcrum in rowing. [OE *tholl*]

thole[2] (θəʊl) *vb.* **1.** (*tr.*) *Scot. & N English dialect.* to put up with; bear. **2.** an archaic word for **suffer.** [OE *tholian*]

tholos ('θəʊlɒs) n., pl. **-loi** (-lɔɪ). a dry-stone beehive-shaped tomb associated with the Mycenaean culture of Greece from the 16th to the 12th centuries B.C. [C17: from Gk]

Thomas ('tɒməs) n. **1.** Also called: **doubting Thomas.** one of the twelve apostles, who refused to believe in Christ's resurrection until he had seen his wounds (John 20:24-29). **2.** (*French* tɔma). **Ambroise** (ābrwaz). 1811-96, French composer of light operas, including *Mignon* (1866). **3. Dylan** (**Marlais**) ('dɪlən). 1914-53, Welsh poet and essayist. His works include the prose *Portrait of the Artist as a Young Dog* (1940), the verse collection *Deaths and Entrances* (1946), and his play for voices *Under Milk Wood* (1954). **4.** (**Philip**) **Edward,** pen name *Edward Eastaway.* 1878-1917, English nature poet and critic.

Thomas à Kempis n. See (Thomas à) **Kempis.**

Thomas Becket n. **Saint.** See (Saint Thomas) **Becket.**

Thomas of Erceldoune ('ɜːsᵊl,duːn) n. called *Thomas the Rhymer.* ?1220-?97, Scottish seer and poet; reputed author of a poem on the Tristan legend.

Thomas of Woodstock n. 1355-97, youngest son of Edward III, who led opposition to his nephew Richard II (1386-89); arrested in 1397, he died in prison.

Thomism ('təʊmɪzəm) n. the system of philosophy and theology developed by Saint Thomas Aquinas in the 13th century.

Thompson ('tɒmpsən, 'tɒmsən) n. **1. Benjamin,** Count Rumford. 1753-1814, Anglo-American physicist, noted for his work on the nature of heat. **2. Daley.** born 1958, English athlete: Olympic decathlon champion (1980, 1984). **3. Francis.** 1859-1907, English poet, best known for the mystical poem *The Hound of Heaven* (1893).

Thompson sub-machine-gun n. *Trademark.* a .45 calibre sub-machine-gun. [C20: after John T. *Thompson* (1860-1940), U.S. Army officer, its co-inventor]

Thomson ('tɒmsən) n. **1. Sir George Paget,** son of Joseph John Thomson. 1892-1975, English physicist, who discovered (1927) the diffraction of electrons by crystals: shared the Nobel prize for physics (1937). **2. James.** 1700-48, Scottish poet. He anticipated the romantics' feeling for nature in *The Seasons* (1726-30). **3. James,** pen name *B.V.* 1834-82, British poet, born in Scotland, noted esp. for *The City of Dreadful Night* (1874), reflecting man's isolation and despair. **4. Sir Joseph John.** 1856-1940, English physicist. He discovered the electron (1897) and his work on the nature of positive rays led to the discovery of isotopes: Nobel prize for physics 1906. **5. Roy,** 1st Baron Thomson of Fleet. 1894-1976, British newspaper proprietor, born in Canada. **6. Sir William.** See (1st Baron) **Kelvin.**

-thon *suffix forming nouns.* indicating a large-scale event or operation of a specified kind: *telethon.* [C20: on the pattern of MARATHON]

Thonburi (ˌtɒnbuˈriː) n. a city in central Thailand, part of Bankok Metropolis on the Chao Phraya River; the national capital (1767-82).

thong (θɒŋ) n. **1.** a thin strip of leather or other material. **2.** a whip or whiplash, esp. one made of leather. **3.** *U.S., Canad., Austral., & N.Z.* the usual name for **flip-flop** (sense 5). [OE *thwang*]

Thor (θɔː) n. *Norse myth.* the god of thunder, depicted as wielding a hammer, emblematic of the thunderbolt. [OE *Thōr,* from ON *thōrr* THUNDER]

thoracic (θɔːˈræsɪk) *adj.* of, near, or relating to the thorax.

thoracic duct n. the major duct of the lymphatic system, beginning below the diaphragm and ascending in front of the spinal column to the base of the neck.

thoraco- *or before a vowel* **thorac-** *combining form.* thorax: *thoracotomy.*

thoracoplasty ('θɔːrəkəʊˌplæstɪ) n., pl. **-ties. 1.** plastic surgery of the thorax. **2.** surgical removal of several ribs or a part of them to permit the collapse of a diseased lung.

thorax ('θɔ:ræks) n., pl. **thoraxes** or **thoraces** ('θɔ:rə,si:z, θɔ:'reɪsi:z). **1.** the part of the human body enclosed by the ribs. **2.** the corresponding part in other vertebrates. **3.** the part of an insect's body between the head and abdomen. [C16: via L from Gk *thōrax* breastplate, chest]

Thorburn ('θɔ:bɜ:n) n. **Cliff.** born 1948, Canadian snooker player.

Thoreau ('θɔ:rəʊ, θɔ:'rəʊ) n. **Henry David.** 1817–62, U.S. writer, noted esp. for *Walden, or Life in the Woods* (1854), an account of his experiment in living in solitude. A powerful social critic, his essay *Civil Disobedience* (1849) influenced such dissenters as Gandhi.

thorium ('θɔ:rɪəm) n. a silvery-white radioactive metallic element. It is used in electronic equipment and as a nuclear power source. Symbol: Th; atomic no.: 90; atomic wt.: 232.04. [C19: NL, THOR + -IUM] —'**thoric** adj.

thorium dioxide n. a white powder used in incandescent mantles. Also called: **thoria.**

thorium series n. a radioactive series that starts with thorium–232 and ends with lead–208.

thorn (θɔ:n) n. **1.** a sharp pointed woody extension of a stem or leaf. Cf. **prickle** (sense 1). **2.** any of various trees or shrubs having thorns, esp. the hawthorn. **3.** a Germanic character of runic origin (þ) used in Icelandic to represent the sound of *th*, as in *thin, bath*. **4.** this same character as used in Old and Middle English to represent this sound. **5.** a source of irritation (esp. in **a thorn in one's side** or **flesh**). [OE] —'**thornless** adj.

Thorn[1] (tɔːrn) n. the German name for **Toruń.**

Thorn[2] (θɔ:n) n. **Willie.** born 1954, British snooker player.

thorn apple n. **1.** a poisonous plant of the N hemisphere, having white funnel-shaped flowers and spiny fruits. U.S. name: **jimson weed. 2.** the fruit of certain types of hawthorn.

thornbill ('θɔ:n,bɪl) n. **1.** any of various South American hummingbirds having a thornlike bill. **2.** Also called: **thornbill warbler.** any of various Australasian wrens. **3.** any of various other birds with thornlike bills.

Thorndike ('θɔ:n,daɪk) n. **1. Edward Lee.** 1874–1949, U.S. psychologist, who worked on animals and proposed that all learnt behaviour is regulated by rewards and punishments. **2. Dame Sybil.** 1882–1976, English actress.

thorny ('θɔ:nɪ) adj. **thornier, thorniest. 1.** bearing or covered with thorns. **2.** difficult or unpleasant. **3.** sharp. —'**thornily** adv. —'**thorniness** n.

thoron ('θɔ:rɒn) n. a radioisotope of radon that is a decay product of thorium. Symbol: Tn or [220]Rn; atomic no.: 86; half-life: 54.5s. [C20: from THORIUM + -ON]

thorough ('θʌrə) adj. **1.** carried out completely and carefully. **2.** (*prenominal*) utter: *a thorough bore.* **3.** painstakingly careful. [OE *thurh*] —'**thoroughly** adv. —'**thoroughness** n.

thorough bass (beɪs) n. a bass part underlying a piece of concerted music. Also called: **basso continuo, continuo.** See also **figured bass.**

thoroughbred ('θʌrə,brɛd) adj. **1.** purebred. ~n. **2.** a pedigree animal; purebred. **3.** a person regarded as being of good breeding.

Thoroughbred ('θʌrə,brɛd) n. a British breed of horse the ancestry of which can be traced to English mares and Arab sires.

thoroughfare ('θʌrə,fɛə) n. **1.** a road from one place to another, esp. a main road. **2.** way through, access, or passage: *no thoroughfare.*

thoroughgoing ('θʌrə,gəʊɪŋ) adj. **1.** extremely thorough. **2.** (*usually prenominal*) absolute; complete: *thoroughgoing incompetence.*

thoroughpaced ('θʌrə,peɪst) adj. **1.** (of a horse) showing performing ability in all paces. **2.** thoroughgoing.

thorp or **thorpe** (θɔ:p) n. *Obs. except in place names.* a small village. [OE]

Thorpe (θɔ:p) n. **Jeremy.** born 1929, British politician; leader of the Liberal party (1967–76).

Thorshavn (*Danish* 'tɔːrshaun) n. the capital of the Faeroe Islands, a port on the northernmost island. Pop.: 13 757 (1980).

Thorvaldsen or **Thorwaldsen** (*Danish* 'tɔrvalsən) n. **Bertel** ('bɛrtəl). 1770–1884, Danish neoclassical sculptor.

those (ðəʊz) *determiner.* the form of **that** used before a plural noun. [OE *thās,* pl. of THIS]

Thoth (θəʊθ, təʊt) n. (in Egyptian mythology) a moon deity, scribe of the gods and protector of learning and the arts.

thou[1] (ðaʊ) *pron.* (*subjective*) **1.** *Arch.* or *dialect.* refers to the person addressed: used mainly in familiar address. **2.** (*usually cap.*) refers to God when addressed in prayer, etc. [OE *thū*]

▷ **Usage.** Although *thou* has now disappeared from general use in English and is restricted to certain dialects, it was part of standard English until the 18th century. *Thou* was a form of address reserved for God, friends, family, and those inferior in age and status and was therefore similar in meaning and use to the modern French *tu. You* was the more formal mode of address until the disappearance of *thou.*

thou[2] (ðaʊ) n., pl. **thous** or **thou. 1.** one thousandth of an inch. **2.** *Inf.* short for **thousand.**

though (ðəʊ) *conj.* (*subordinating*) **1.** (sometimes preceded by *even*) despite the fact that: *though he tries hard, he always fails.* ~adv. **2.** nevertheless; however: *he can't dance; he sings well, though.* [OE *theah*]

thought (θɔ:t) vb. **1.** the past tense and past participle of **think.** ~n. **2.** the act or process of thinking. **3.** a concept, opinion, or idea. **4.** ideas typical of a particular time or place: *German thought in the 19th century.* **5.** application of mental attention; consideration. **6.** purpose or intention: *I have no thought of giving up.* **7.** expectation: *no thought of reward.* **8.** a small amount; trifle: *you could be a thought more enthusiastic.* **9.** kindness or regard. [OE *thōht*]

thoughtful ('θɔ:tful) adj. **1.** considerate in the treatment of other people. **2.** showing careful thought. **3.** pensive; reflective. —'**thoughtfully** adv. —'**thoughtfulness** n.

thoughtless ('θɔ:tlɪs) adj. **1.** inconsiderate. **2.** having or showing lack of thought. —'**thoughtlessly** adv. —'**thoughtlessness** n.

thought-out adj. conceived and developed by careful thought: *a well thought-out scheme.*

thought transference n. *Psychol.* another name for **telepathy.**

thousand ('θaʊzənd) n. **1.** the cardinal number that is the product of 10 and 100. **2.** a numeral, 1000, 10^3, M, etc., representing this number. **3.** (*often pl.*) a very large but unspecified number, amount, or quantity. **4.** something representing or consisting of 1000 units. ~determiner. **5. a.** amounting to a thousand. **b.** (*as pronoun*): *a thousand is hardly enough.* ~Related adj.: **millenary.** [OE *thūsend*] —'**thousandth** adj., n

Thousand Guineas n. (*functioning as sing.*), usually written **1,000 Guineas.** an annual horse race, restricted to fillies, run at Newmarket in England since 1814.

Thousand Island dressing n. a salad dressing made from mayonnaise with ketchup, chopped gherkins, etc.

Thousand Islands pl. n. a group of about 1500 islands on the border between the U.S. and Canada, in the upper St Lawrence River: administratively divided between the U.S. and Canada. —**Thousand Island** adj.

Thrace (θreɪs) n. **1.** an ancient country in the E Balkan Peninsula: successively under the Persians, Macedonians, and Romans. **2.** a region of SE Europe, corresponding to the S part of the ancient country: divided by the Maritsa River into **Western Thrace** (Greece) and **Eastern Thrace** (Turkey).

Thracian ('θreɪʃɪən) n. **1.** a member of an ancient Indo-European people who lived in Thrace. **2.** the ancient language spoken by this people. ~adj. **3.** of or relating to Thrace, its inhabitants, or the extinct Thracian language.

Thrale (θreɪl) n. **Hester Lynch,** known as **Mrs Thrale** or (later) *Mrs Piozzi* (née *Salusbury*). 1741–1821, English writer of memoirs, noted for her friendship with Dr Johnson. Her works include *Anecdotes of the late Samuel Johnson* (1786) and *Letters to and from the late Samuel Johnson* (1788).

thrall (θrɔ:l) n. **1.** Also: **thraldom** or *U.S.* **thralldom** ('θrɔ:ldəm). the state or condition of being in the power of another person. **2.** a person who is in such a state. **3.** a person totally subject to some need, desire, appetite, etc. ~vb. **4.** (*tr.*) to enslave or dominate. [OE *thrǣl* slave]

thrash (θræʃ) vb. **1.** (*tr.*) to beat soundly, as with a whip or stick. **2.** (*tr.*) to defeat totally; overwhelm. **3.** (*intr.*) to beat or plunge about in a wild manner. **4.** to sail (a boat) against the wind or tide or (of a boat) to sail in this way. **5.** another word for **thresh.** ~n. **6.** the act of thrashing; beating. **7.** *Inf.* a party. ~See also **thrash out.** [OE *threscan*]

thrasher[1] ('θræʃə) *n.* another name for **thresher** (the shark).

thrasher[2] ('θræʃə) *n.* any of various brown thrushlike American songbirds.

thrashing ('θræʃɪŋ) *n.* a physical assault; flogging.

thrash out *vb.* (*tr., adv.*) to discuss fully or vehemently, esp. in order to come to an agreement.

thrasonical (θrə'sɒnɪkəl) *adj. Rare.* bragging; boastful. [C16: from L *Thrasō* name of boastful soldier in *Eunuchus*, a play by Terence, from Gk *Thrasōn*, from *thrasus* forceful] —**thra'sonically** *adv.*

thrawn (θrɔːn) *adj. Scot. & N English dialect.* **1.** crooked or twisted. **2.** stubborn; perverse. [N English dialect, var. of *thrown*, from OE *thrāwan* to twist about, throw]

thread (θrɛd) *n.* **1.** a fine strand, filament, or fibre of some material. **2.** a fine cord of twisted filaments, esp. of cotton, used in sewing, etc. **3.** any of the filaments of which a spider's web is made. **4.** any fine line, stream, mark, or piece. **5.** the helical ridge on a screw, bolt, nut, etc. **6.** a very thin seam of coal or vein of ore. **7.** something acting as the continuous link or theme of a whole: *the thread of the story.* **8.** the course of an individual's life believed in Greek mythology to be spun, measured, and cut by the Fates. ~*vb.* **9.** (*tr.*) to pass (thread, film, tape, etc.) through (something). **10.** (*tr.*) to string on a thread: *she threaded the beads.* **11.** to make (one's way) through or over (something). **12.** (*tr.*) to produce a screw thread. **13.** (*tr.*) to pervade: *hysteria threaded his account.* **14.** (*intr.*) (of boiling syrup) to form a fine thread when poured from a spoon. [OE *thrǣd*] —'**threader** *n.* —'**thread,like** *adj.*

threadbare ('θrɛd,bɛə) *adj.* **1.** (of cloth, clothing, etc.) having the nap worn off so that the threads are exposed; worn out. **2.** meagre or poor. **3.** hackneyed: *a threadbare argument.* **4.** wearing threadbare clothes; shabby.

thread mark *n.* a mark put into paper money to prevent counterfeiting, consisting of a pattern of silk fibres.

threadworm ('θrɛd,wɜːm) *n.* any of various nematodes, esp. the pinworm.

thready ('θrɛdɪ) *adj.* **threadier, threadiest. 1.** of or resembling a thread. **2.** (of the pulse) barely perceptible; weak. **3.** sounding thin, weak, or reedy. —'**threadiness** *n.*

threat (θrɛt) *n.* **1.** a declaration of the intention to inflict harm, pain, or misery. **2.** an indication of imminent harm, danger, or pain. **3.** a person or thing that is regarded as dangerous or likely to inflict pain or misery. [OE]

threaten ('θrɛtᵊn) *vb.* **1.** (*tr.*) to be a threat to. **2.** to be a menacing indication of (something); portend. **3.** (when *tr., may take a clause as object*) to express a threat to (a person or people). —'**threatening** *adj.* —'**threateningly** *adv.*

three (θriː) *n.* **1.** the cardinal number that is the sum of two and one and is a prime number. **2.** a numeral, 3, III, (iii), representing this number. **3.** something representing or consisting of three units. **4.** Also called: **three o'clock.** three hours after noon or midnight. ~*determiner.* **5. a.** amounting to three. **b.** (*as pronoun*): *three were killed.* ~Related adjs.: **ternary, tertiary, treble, triple.** [OE *thrēo*]

three-card trick *n.* a game in which players bet on which of three playing cards is the queen.

three-colour *adj.* of or comprising a colour print or a photomechanical process in which a picture is reproduced by superimposing three prints from half-tone plates in inks corresponding to the three primary colours.

three-D *or* **3-D** *n.* a three-dimensional effect.

three-decker *n.* **1. a.** anything having three levels or layers. **b.** (*as modifier*): *a three-decker sandwich.* **2.** a warship with guns on three decks.

three-dimensional *adj.* **1.** of, having, or relating to three dimensions. **2.** simulating the effect of depth. **3.** having volume. **4.** lifelike.

threefold ('θriː,fəʊld) *adj.* **1.** equal to or having three times as many or as much; triple. **2.** composed of three parts. ~*adv.* **3.** by or up to three times as many or as much.

three-legged race *n.* a race in which pairs of competitors run with their adjacent legs tied together.

threepenny bit *or* **thrupenny bit** ('θrʌpnɪ, -ənɪ, 'θrɛp-) *n.* a twelve-sided British coin valued at three old pence, obsolete since 1971.

three-phase *adj.* (of an electrical circuit, etc.) having or using three alternating voltages of the same frequency, displaced in phase by 120°.

three-ply *adj.* **1.** having three layers or thicknesses. **2.** (of wool, etc.) three-stranded.

three-point landing *n.* an aircraft landing in which the main wheels and the nose or tail wheel touch the ground simultaneously.

three-point turn *n.* a complete turn of a motor vehicle using forward and reverse gears alternately, and completed after only three movements.

three-quarter *adj.* **1.** being three quarters of something. **2.** being of three quarters the normal length. ~*n.* **3.** *Rugby.* any of the players between the fullback and the forwards.

three-ring circus *n. U.S.* **1.** a circus with three rings for simultaneous performances. **2.** a situation of confusion, characterized by a bewildering variety of events or activities.

Three Rivers *n.* the English name for **Trois Rivières.**

three Rs *pl. n.* **the. the** three skills regarded as the fundamentals of education; reading, writing, and arithmetic. [from the humorous spelling *reading, 'riting,* and *'rithmetic*]

threescore ('θriː'skɔː) *determiner.* an archaic word for **sixty.**

threesome ('θriːsəm) *n.* **1.** a group of three. **2.** *Golf.* a match in which a single player playing his own ball competes against two others playing on the same ball. **3.** any game, etc., for three people. **4.** (*modifier*) performed by three.

thremmatology (,θrɛmə'tɒlədʒɪ) *n.* the science of breeding domesticated animals and plants. [C19: from Gk *thremma* nursling + -LOGY]

threnody ('θrɛnədɪ, 'θriː-) *or* **threnode** ('θriːnəʊd, 'θrɛn-) *n., pl.* **threnodies** *or* **threnodes.** an ode, song, or speech of lamentation, esp. for the dead. [C17: from Gk *thrēnōidia*, from *thrēnos* dirge + *ōidē* song] —**threnodic** (θrɪ'nɒdɪk) *adj.* —**threnodist** ('θrɛnədɪst, 'θriː-) *n.*

thresh (θrɛʃ) *vb.* **1.** to beat stalks of ripe corn, etc., either with a hand implement or a machine to separate the grain from the husks and straw. **2.** (*tr.*) to beat or strike. **3.** (*intr.;* often foll. by *about*) to toss and turn; thrash. [OE *threscan*]

thresher ('θrɛʃə) *n.* **1.** a person who threshes. **2.** short for **threshing machine. 3.** any of a genus of large sharks occurring in tropical and temperate seas. They have a very long whiplike tail.

threshing machine *n.* a machine for threshing crops.

threshold ('θrɛʃəʊld, 'θrɛʃ,həʊld) *n.* **1.** a sill, esp. one made of stone or hardwood, placed at a doorway. **2.** any doorway or entrance. **3.** the starting point of an experience, event, or venture. **4.** *Psychol.* the strength at which a stimulus is just perceived: *the threshold of consciousness.* **5.** a point at which something would stop, take effect, etc. **6.** the minimum intensity or value of a signal, etc., that will produce a response or specified effect. **7.** (*modifier*) of a pay agreement, clause, etc., that raises wages to compensate for increases in the cost of living. ~Related adj.: **liminal.** [OE *therscold*]

threw (θruː) *vb.* the past tense of **throw.**

thrice (θraɪs) *adv.* **1.** three times. **2.** threefold. **3.** *Arch.* greatly. [OE *thrīwa, thrīga*]

thrift (θrɪft) *n.* **1.** wisdom and caution in the management of money. **2.** Also called: **sea pink.** any of a genus of perennial low-growing plants of Europe, W Asia, and North America, having narrow leaves and round heads of pink or white flowers. [C13: from ON: success; see THRIVE] —'**thriftless** *adj.* —'**thriftlessly** *adv.*

thrifty ('θrɪftɪ) *adj.* **thriftier, thriftiest. 1.** showing thrift; economical or frugal. **2.** *Rare.* thriving or prospering. —'**thriftily** *adv.* —'**thriftiness** *n.*

thrill (θrɪl) *n.* **1.** a sudden sensation of excitement and pleasure. **2.** a situation producing such a sensation. **3.** a trembling sensation caused by fear or emotional shock. **4.** *Pathol.* an abnormal slight tremor. ~*vb.* **5.** to feel or cause to feel a thrill. **6.** to tremble or cause to tremble; vibrate or quiver. [OE *thȳrlian* to pierce, from *thyrel* hole] —'**thrilling** *adj.*

thriller ('θrɪlə) n. a book, film, play, etc., depicting crime, mystery, or espionage in an atmosphere of excitement and suspense.

thrips (θrɪps) n., pl. **thrips**. any of various small slender-bodied insects typically having piercing mouthparts and feeding on plant sap. [C18: via NL from Gk: woodworm]

thrive (θraɪv) vb. **thriving; thrived** or **throve; thrived** or **thriven** ('θrɪvᵊn). (intr.) **1.** to grow strongly and vigorously. **2.** to do well; prosper. [C13: from ON thrífask to grasp for oneself, from ?]

thro' or **thro** (θruː) prep., adv. Inf. or poetic. variant spellings of **through**.

throat (θrəʊt) n. **1. a.** that part of the alimentary and respiratory tracts extending from the back of the mouth to just below the larynx. **b.** the front part of the neck. **2.** something resembling a throat, esp. in shape or function: the throat of a chimney. **3. cut one's (own) throat.** to bring about one's own ruin. **4. ram** or **force (something) down someone's throat.** to insist that someone listen to or accept (something). ~Related adjs.: **guttural, laryngeal.** [OE throtu]

throaty ('θrəʊtɪ) adj. **throatier, throatiest. 1.** indicating a sore throat; hoarse: a throaty cough. **2.** of or produced in the throat. **3.** deep, husky, or guttural. —'**throatily** adv.

throb (θrɒb) vb. **throbbing, throbbed.** (intr.) **1.** to pulsate or beat repeatedly, esp. with increased force. **2.** (of engines, drums, etc.) to have a strong rhythmic vibration or beat. ~n. **3.** a throbbing, esp. a rapid pulsation as of the heart: a throb of pleasure. [C14: ? imit.]

throes (θrəʊz) pl. n. **1.** a condition of violent pangs, pain, or convulsions: death throes. **2. in the throes of.** struggling with great effort with. [OE thráwu threat]

thrombin ('θrɒmbɪn) n. Biochem. an enzyme that acts on fibrinogen in blood causing it to clot. [C19: from THROMB(US) + -IN]

thrombocyte ('θrɒmbə,saɪt) n. another name for **platelet.** —**thrombocytic** (,θrɒmbə'sɪtɪk) adj.

thromboembolism (,θrɒmbəʊ'ɛmbə,lɪzəm) n. the obstruction of a blood vessel by a thrombus that has become detached from its original site.

thrombose ('θrɒmbəʊz) vb. to become or affect with a thrombus. [C19: back formation from THROMBOSIS]

thrombosis (θrɒm'bəʊsɪs) n., pl. **-ses** (-siːz). **1.** the formation or presence of a thrombus. **2.** Inf. short for **coronary thrombosis.** [C18: from NL, from Gk: curdling, from thrombousthai to clot, from thrombos THROMBUS] —**thrombotic** (θrɒm'bɒtɪk) adj.

thrombus ('θrɒmbəs) n., pl. **-bi** (-baɪ). a clot of coagulated blood that forms within a blood vessel or inside the heart, often impeding the flow of blood. [C17: from NL, from Gk thrombos lump, from ?]

throne (θrəʊn) n. **1.** the ceremonial seat occupied by a monarch, bishop, etc., on occasions of state. **2.** the power or rank ascribed to a royal person. **3.** a person holding royal rank. **4.** (pl.; often cap.) the third of the nine orders into which the angels are divided in medieval angelology. ~vb. **5.** to place or be placed on a throne. [C13: from OF trone, from L thronus, from Gk thronos]

throng (θrɒŋ) n. **1.** a great number of people or things crowded together. ~vb. **2.** to gather in or fill (a place) in large numbers; crowd. **3.** (tr.) to hem in (a person); jostle. [OE gethrang]

throstle ('θrɒsᵊl) n. **1.** a poetic name for the **song thrush. 2.** a spinning machine for wool or cotton in which the fibres are twisted and wound continuously. [OE]

throttle ('θrɒtᵊl) n. **1.** Also called: **throttle valve.** any device that controls the quantity of fuel or fuel and air mixture entering an engine. **2.** an informal or dialect word for **throat.** ~vb. (tr.) **3.** to kill or injure by squeezing the throat. **4.** to suppress. **5.** to control or restrict (a flow of fluid) by means of a throttle valve. [C14: throtelen, from throte THROAT] —'**throttler** n.

through (θruː) prep. **1.** going in at one side and coming out at the other side of: a path through the wood. **2.** occupying or visiting several points scattered around in (an area). **3.** as a result of; by means of. **4.** Chiefly U.S. up to and including: Monday through Friday. **5.** during: through the night. **6.** at the end of; having completed. **7. through with.** having finished with (esp. when dissatisfied with). ~adj. **8.** (postpositive) having successfully completed some specified activity. **9.** (on a telephone line) connected. **10.** (postpositive) no longer able to function successfully in some specified capacity: as a journalist, you're through. **11.** (prenominal) (of a route, journey, etc.) continuous or unbroken: a through train. ~adv. **12.** through some specified thing, place, or period of time. **13. through and through.** thoroughly; completely. [OE thurh]

throughout (θruː'aʊt) prep. **1.** right through; through the whole of (a place or a period of time): throughout the day. ~adv. **2.** throughout some specified period or area.

throughput ('θruː,pʊt) n. the quantity of raw material processed in a given period, esp. by a computer.

throughway ('θruː,weɪ) n. U.S. a thoroughfare, esp. a motorway.

throve (θrəʊv) vb. a past tense of **thrive.**

throw (θrəʊ) vb. **throwing, threw, thrown.** (mainly tr.) **1.** (also intr.) to project (something) through the air, esp. with a rapid motion of the arm. **2.** (foll. by in, on, onto, etc.) to put or move suddenly, carelessly, or violently. **3.** to bring to or cause to be in a specified state or condition, esp. suddenly: the news threw them into a panic. **4.** to direct or cast (a shadow, light, etc.). **5.** to project (the voice) so as to make it appear to come from other than its source. **6.** to give or hold (a party). **7.** to cause to fall or be upset: the horse threw his rider. **8. a.** to tip (dice) out onto a flat surface. **b.** to obtain (a specified number) in this way. **9.** to shape on a potter's wheel. **10.** to move (a switch or lever) to engage or disengage a mechanism. **11.** to be subjected to (a fit). **12.** to turn (wood, etc.) on a lathe. **13.** Inf. to baffle or astonish; confuse: the question threw me. **14.** Boxing. to deliver (a punch). **15.** Wrestling. to hurl (an opponent) to the ground. **16.** Inf. to lose (a contest, etc.) deliberately. **17. a.** to play (a card). **b.** to discard (a card). **18.** (of an animal) to give birth to (young). **19.** to twist or spin (filaments) into thread. **20.** Austral. inf. (often foll. by at) to mock or poke fun. **21. throw oneself at.** to strive actively to attract the attention or affection of. **22. throw oneself into.** to involve oneself enthusiastically in. **23. throw oneself on.** to rely entirely upon. ~n. **24.** the act or an instance of throwing. **25.** the distance over which anything may be thrown: a stone's throw. **26.** Inf. a chance or try. **27.** an act or result of throwing dice. **28. a.** the eccentricity of a cam. **b.** the radial distance between the central axis of a crankshaft and the axis of a crankpin forming part of the shaft. **29.** Chiefly U.S. & Canad. a decorative blanket or cover. **30.** Geol. the vertical displacement of rock strata at a fault. **31.** Physics. the deflection of a measuring instrument as a result of a fluctuation. ~See also **throwaway, throwback, throw in,** etc. [OE thráwan to turn, torment] —'**thrower** n.

throwaway ('θrəʊə,weɪ) adj. **1.** (prenominal) Chiefly Brit. said or done incidentally, esp. for rhetorical effect; casual: a throwaway remark. **2.** designed to be discarded after use rather than reused, refilled, etc.: a throwaway carton. ~n. **3.** Chiefly U.S. & Canad. a handbill. ~vb. **throw away.** (tr., adv.) **4.** to get rid of; discard. **5.** to fail to make good use of; waste.

throwback ('θrəʊ,bæk) n. **1. a.** a person, animal, or plant that has the characteristics of an earlier or more primitive type. **b.** a reversion to such an organism. ~vb. **throw back.** (adv.) **2.** (intr.) to revert to an earlier or more primitive type. **3.** (tr.; foll. by on) to force to depend (on): the crisis threw her back on her faith in God.

throw in vb. (tr., adv.) **1.** to add at no additional cost. **2.** to contribute or interpose (a remark, argument, etc.). **3. throw in the towel** (or sponge). to give in; accept defeat. ~n. **throw-in. 4.** Soccer. the method of putting the ball into play after it has gone into touch by throwing it to a team-mate.

thrown (θrəʊn) vb. the past participle of **throw.**

throw off vb. (adv., mainly tr.) **1.** to free oneself of; discard. **2.** to produce or utter in a casual manner. **3.** to escape from or elude. **4.** to confuse or disconcert. **5.** (intr.; often foll. by at) Austral. & N.Z. inf. to deride or ridicule.

throw out vb. (tr., adv.) **1.** to discard or reject. **2.** to expel or dismiss, esp. forcibly. **3.** to construct (something projecting or prominent). **4.** to put forward or offer. **5.** to utter in a casual or indirect manner. **6.** to confuse or disconcert. **7.** to give off or emit. **8.** Cricket. (of a fielder) to put (the batsman) out by throwing the ball to hit the wicket. **9.** *Baseball.* to make a throw to a teammate who in turn puts out (a base runner).

throw over *vb.* (*tr., adv.*) to forsake or abandon; jilt.

throw together *vb.* (*tr., adv.*) **1.** to assemble hurriedly. **2.** to cause to become casually acquainted.

throw up *vb.* (*adv., mainly tr.*) **1.** to give up; abandon. **2.** to construct hastily. **3.** to reveal; produce. **4.** (*also intr.*) *Inf.* to vomit.

thru (θruː) *prep., adv., adj. Chiefly U.S.* a variant spelling of **through.**

thrum[1] (θrʌm) *vb.* **thrumming, thrummed. 1.** to strum rhythmically but without expression on (a musical instrument). **2.** (*intr.*) to drum incessantly: *rain thrummed on the roof.* ~*n.* **3.** a repetitive strumming. [C16: imit.]

thrum[2] (θrʌm) *n.* **1. a.** any of the unwoven ends of warp thread remaining on the loom when the web has been removed. **b.** such ends of thread collectively. **2.** a fringe or tassel of short unwoven threads. ~*vb.* **thrumming, thrummed. 3.** (*tr.*) to trim with thrums. [C14: from OE]

thrush[1] (θrʌʃ) *n.* any of a subfamily of songbirds, esp. those having a brown plumage with a spotted breast, such as the mistle thrush and song thrush. [OE *thrȳsce*]

thrush[2] (θrʌʃ) *n.* **1.** a fungal disease, esp. of infants, characterized by the formation of whitish spots. **2.** a vaginal infection caused by the same fungus. **3.** a softening of the frog of a horse's hoof characterized by inflammation and a thick foul discharge. [C17: from ?]

thrust (θrʌst) *vb.* **1.** (*tr.*) to push (someone or something) with force. **2.** (*tr.*) to force upon (someone) or into (some condition or situation): *they thrust responsibilities upon her.* **3.** (*tr.;* foll. by *through*) to pierce; stab. **4.** (*intr.;* usually foll. by *through* or *into*) to force a passage. **5.** to make a stab or lunge at. ~*n.* **6.** a forceful drive, push, stab, or lunge. **7.** a force, esp. one that produces motion. **8. a.** a propulsive force produced by the fluid pressure or the change of momentum of the fluid in a jet engine, rocket engine, etc. **b.** a similar force produced by a propeller. **9.** a continuous pressure exerted by one part of an object, structure, etc., against another. **10.** force, impetus, or drive. **11.** the essential or most forceful part: *the thrust of the argument.* [C12: from ON *thrysta*]

thruster ('θrʌstə) *n.* **1.** a person or thing that thrusts. **2.** a small rocket engine, esp. one used to correct the altitude or course of a spacecraft.

thrust fault *n.* a fault in which the rocks on the lower side of an inclined fault plane have been displaced downwards; a reverse fault.

Thucydides (θuːˈsɪdɪˌdiːz) *n.* ?460–?395 B.C., Greek historian and politician, distinguished for his *History of the Peloponnesian War.* —**Thu,cydi'dean** *adj.*

thud (θʌd) *n.* **1.** a dull heavy sound. **2.** a blow or fall that causes such a sound. ~*vb.* **thudding, thudded. 3.** to make or cause to make such a sound. [OE *thyddan* to strike]

thug (θʌg) *n.* **1.** a tough and violent man, esp. a criminal. **2.** (*sometimes cap.*) (formerly) a member of an organization of robbers and assassins in India. [C19: from Hindi *thag* thief, from Sansk. *sthaga* scoundrel, from *sthagati* to conceal] —'**thuggery** *n.* —'**thuggish** *adj.*

thuja *or* **thuya** ('θuːjə) *n.* any of a genus of coniferous trees of North America and East Asia, having scalelike leaves, small cones, and an aromatic wood. [C18: from NL, from Med. L *thuia,* ult. from Gk *thua* an African tree]

Thule ('θjuːlɪ) *n.* **1.** Also called: **ultima Thule.** a region believed by ancient geographers to be the northernmost land in the inhabited world: sometimes thought to have been Iceland, Norway, or one of the Shetland Islands. **2.** an Eskimo settlement in NW Greenland: a Danish trading post, founded in 1910, and U.S. air force base.

thulium ('θjuːlɪəm) *n.* a malleable ductile silvery-grey element. The radioisotope **thulium-170** is used as an electron source in portable x-ray units. Symbol: Tm; atomic no.: 69; atomic wt.: 168.93. [C19: NL, from THULE + -IUM]

thumb (θʌm) *n.* **1.** the first and usually shortest and thickest of the digits of the hand. **2.** the corresponding digit in other vertebrates. **3.** the part of a glove shaped to fit the thumb. **4. all thumbs.** clumsy. **5. thumbs down.** an indication of refusal or disapproval. **6. thumbs up.** an indication of encouragement or approval. **7. under someone's thumb.** at someone's mercy or command. ~*vb.* **8.** (*tr.*) to touch, mark, or move with the thumb. **9.** to attempt to obtain (a lift or ride) by signalling with the thumb. **10.** (when *intr.,* often foll. by *through*) to flip the pages of (a book, etc.) in order to glance at the contents. **11. thumb one's nose at.** to deride or mock, esp. by placing the thumb on the nose with fingers extended. [OE *thūma*]

thumb index *n.* **1.** a series of indentations cut into the fore-edge of a book to facilitate quick reference. ~*vb.* **thumb-index. 2.** (*tr.*) to furnish with a thumb index.

thumbnail ('θʌm,neɪl) *n.* **1.** the nail of the thumb. **2.** (*modifier*) concise and brief: *a thumbnail sketch.*

thumbnut ('θʌm,nʌt) *n.* a wing nut.

thumbscrew ('θʌm,skruː) *n.* **1.** an instrument of torture that pinches or crushes the thumbs. **2.** a screw with projections on its head enabling it to be turned by the thumb and forefinger.

thumbtack ('θʌm,tæk) *n.* the U.S. and Canad. name for **drawing pin.**

thump (θʌmp) *n.* **1.** the sound of a heavy solid body hitting a comparatively soft surface. **2.** a heavy blow with the hand. ~*vb.* **3.** (*tr.*) to strike or beat heavily; pound. **4.** (*intr.*) to throb, beat, or pound violently. [C16] —'**thumper** *n.*

thumping ('θʌmpɪŋ) *adj.* (*prenominal*) *Sl.* huge or excessive: *a thumping loss.*

Thun (German tuːn) *n.* **1.** a town in central Switzerland, in Bern canton on Lake Thun. Pop.: 36 496 (1983 est.). **2. Lake.** a lake in central Switzerland, formed by a widening of the Aar River. Length: about 17 km (11 miles). Width: 3 km (2 miles). German name: **Thuner See.**

thunbergia (θʌnˈbɜːdʒɪə) *n.* any of various climbing or dwarf plants of tropical and subtropical Africa and Asia. [C19: after K. P. *Thunberg* (1743–1822), Swedish botanist]

thunder ('θʌndə) *n.* **1.** a loud cracking or deep rumbling noise caused by the rapid expansion of atmospheric gases which are suddenly heated by lightning. **2.** any loud booming sound. **3.** *Rare.* a violent threat or denunciation. **4. steal someone's thunder.** to lessen the effect of someone's idea or action by anticipating it. ~*vb.* **5.** to make (a loud sound) or utter (words) in a manner suggesting thunder. **6.** (*intr.;* with *it* as subject) to be the case that thunder is being heard. **7.** (*intr.*) to move fast and heavily: *the bus thundered downhill.* **8.** (*intr.*) to utter vehement threats or denunciation; rail. [OE *thunor*] —'**thundery** *adj.* —'**thunderer** *n.*

Thunder Bay *n.* a port in central Canada, in Ontario on Lake Superior: formed in 1970 by the amalgamation of Fort William and Port Arthur; the head of the St Lawrence Seaway for Canada. Pop.: 122 217 (1986).

thunderbolt ('θʌndə,bəʊlt) *n.* **1.** a flash of lightning accompanying thunder. **2.** the imagined agency of destruction produced by a flash of lightning. **3.** (in mythology) the destructive weapon wielded by several gods, esp. the Greek god Zeus. **4.** something very startling.

thunderclap ('θʌndə,klæp) *n.* **1.** a loud outburst of thunder. **2.** something as violent or unexpected as a clap of thunder.

thundercloud ('θʌndə,klaʊd) *n.* a towering electrically charged cumulonimbus cloud associated with thunderstorms.

thunderhead ('θʌndə,hɛd) *n. Chiefly U.S.* the anvil-shaped top of a cumulonimbus cloud.

thundering ('θʌndərɪŋ) *adj.* (*prenominal*) *Sl.* very great or excessive: *a thundering idiot.*

thunderous ('θʌndərəs) *adj.* **1.** threatening; angry. **2.** resembling thunder, esp. in loudness.

thunderstorm ('θʌndə,stɔːm) *n.* a storm with thunder and lightning and usually heavy rain or hail.

thunderstruck ('θʌndə,strʌk) *or* **thunderstricken** ('θʌndə,strɪkən) *adj.* **1.** completely taken aback; amazed or shocked. **2.** *Rare.* struck by lightning.

Thurber ('θɜːbə) *n.* **James (Grover).** 1894–1961, U.S. humorist and illustrator. He contributed drawings and stories to the *New Yorker* and his books include *Is Sex Necessary?* (1929), written with E. B. White.

Thurgau (German 'tuːrgaʊ) *n.* a canton of NE Switzerland, on Lake Constance: annexed by the confederated Swiss states in 1460. Capital: Frauenfeld. Pop.: 183 795 (1980). Area: 1007 sq. km (389 sq. miles). French name: **Thurgovie** (tyrgɔvi).

thurible ('θjʊərɪb³l) *n.* another word for **censer.** [C15: from L *tūribulum* censer, from *tūs* incense]

Thuringia (θjʊˈrɪndʒɪə) *n.* a region of SW East Germany: a former state of central Germany (1920–45). German name: **Thüringen** ('tyːrɪŋən). —**Thu'ringian** *adj., n.*

Thuringian Forest *n.* a forested mountainous region in central East Germany, rising over 900 m (3000 ft.). German name: **Thüringer Wald** ('ty:rɪŋər 'valt).

Thurs. *abbrev. for* Thursday.

Thursday ('θɜ:zdɪ) *n.* the fifth day of the week; fourth day of the working week. [OE *Thursdæg*, lit.: Thor's day]

Thursday Island *n.* an island in Torres Strait, between NE Australia and New Guinea: administratively part of Queensland, Australia. Area: 4 sq. km (1.5 sq. miles).

thus (ðʌs) *adv.* **1.** in this manner: *do it thus.* **2.** to such a degree: *thus far and no further.* *~sentence connector.* **3.** therefore: *We have failed. Thus we have to take the consequences.* [OE]

thuya ('θu:jə) *n.* a variant spelling of **thuja.**

thwack (θwæk) *vb.* **1.** to beat, esp. with something flat. *~n.* **2. a.** a blow with something flat. **b.** the sound made by it. [C16: imit.]

thwart (θwɔ:t) *vb.* **1.** to oppose successfully or prevent; frustrate. **2.** *Obs.* to be or move across. *~n.* **3.** an oarsman's seat lying across a boat. *~adj.* **4.** passing or being situated across. *~prep., adv.* **5.** *Obs.* across. [C13: from ON *thvert*, from *thverr* transverse]

thy (ðaɪ) *determiner.* (*usually preceding a consonant*) *Arch. or Brit. dialect.* belonging to or associated in some way with you (thou): *thy goodness and mercy.* [C12: var. of THINE]

Thyestes (θaɪ'ɛsti:z) *n. Greek myth.* son of Pelops and brother of Atreus, with whose wife he committed adultery. In revenge, Atreus killed Thyestes' sons and served them to their father at a banquet. —**Thyestean** *or* **Thyestian** (θaɪ'ɛstɪən, θaɪ'sti:ən) *adj.*

thylacine ('θaɪlə,saɪn) *n.* an extinct or very rare doglike carnivorous marsupial of Tasmania. Also called: **Tasmanian wolf.** [C19: from NL *thylacīnus*, from Gk *thulakos* pouch]

thyme (taɪm) *n.* any of various small shrubs having a strong odour, small leaves, and white, pink, or red flowers. [C14: from OF *thym*, from L *thymum*, from Gk, from *thuein* to make a burnt offering] —**'thymy** *adj.*

-thymia *n. combining form.* indicating a certain emotional condition, mood, or state of mind: *cyclothymia.* [NL, from Gk *thumos* temper]

thymine ('θaɪmi:n) *n.* a white crystalline base found in DNA. [C19: from THYMIC + -INE²]

thymol ('θaɪmɒl) *n.* a white crystalline substance obtained from thyme and used as a fungicide, antiseptic, etc. [C19: from THYME + -OL²]

thymus ('θaɪməs) *n., pl.* **-muses** *or* **-mi** (-maɪ). a glandular organ of vertebrates, consisting in man of two lobes situated below the thyroid. It atrophies with age and is almost nonexistent in the adult. [C17: from NL, from Gk *thumos* sweetbread]

thyratron ('θaɪrə,trɒn) *n.* an electronic relay consisting of a gas-filled tube, usually a triode, in which a signal applied to the control grid initiates a transient anode current but subsequently loses control over it. [C20: orig. a trademark, from Gk *thura* door, valve + -TRON]

thyristor (θaɪ'rɪstə) *n.* another name for **silicon controlled rectifier.** [C20: from THYR(ATRON) + (TRANS)ISTOR]

thyroid ('θaɪrɔɪd) *adj.* **1.** of or relating to the thyroid gland. **2.** of or relating to the largest cartilage of the larynx. *~n.* **3.** See **thyroid gland.** **4.** a preparation of the thyroid gland of certain animals, used to treat hypothyroidism. [C18: from NL *thyroīdes*, from Gk *thureoeidēs*, from *thureos* oblong (lit.: door-shaped), from *thura* door]

thyroid gland *n.* an endocrine gland of vertebrates, consisting in man of two lobes near the base of the neck. It secretes hormones that control metabolism and body growth.

thyrotropin (,θaɪrəʊ'trəʊpɪn) *or* **thyrotrophin** *n.* a hormone secreted by the pituitary gland: it stimulates the activity of the thyroid gland. [C20: from *thyro*- thyroid + -TROPE + -IN]

thyroxine (θaɪ'rɒksi:n, -sɪn) *or* **thyroxin** (θaɪ'rɒksɪn) *n.* the principal hormone produced by the thyroid gland. [C19: from *thyro*- thyroid + OXY-² + -INE²]

thyrse (θɜ:s) *or* **thyrsus** ('θɜ:səs) *n., pl.* **thyrses** *or* **thyrsi** ('θɜ:saɪ). *Bot.* a type of inflorescence, occurring in the lilac and grape, in which the main branch is racemose and the lateral branches cymose. [C17: from F: THYRSUS]

thyrsus ('θɜ:səs) *n., pl.* **-si** (-saɪ). **1.** *Greek myth.* a staff, usually one tipped with a pine cone, borne by Dionysus

(Bacchus) and his followers. **2.** a variant spelling of **thyrse.** [C18: from L, from Gk *thursos* stalk]

thyself (ðaɪ'sɛlf) *pron. Arch.* **a.** the reflexive form of *thou* or *thee.* **b.** (intensifier): *thou, thyself, wouldst know.*

ti (ti:) *n. Music.* a variant spelling of **te.**

Ti the chemical symbol for titanium.

Tia Juana ('tɪə 'wɑ:nə; *Spanish* 'tia 'xwana) *n.* a variant spelling of **Tijuana.**

Tianjin ('tjɛn'dʒɪn), **Tientsin,** *or* **T'ien-ching** *n.* an industrial city in NE China, in Hebei province, on the Grand Canal, 51 km (32 miles) from the Yellow Sea: the third largest city in China; seat of Nankai University (1919). Pop.: 5 380 000 (1986).

Tian Shan *or* **Tien Shan** ('tjɛn'ʃɑ:n) *n.* a great mountain system of central Asia, in the Kirghiz SSR of the Soviet Union and the Xinjiang Uygur AR of W China, extending for about 2500 km (1500 miles). Highest peak: Pobeda Peak, 7439 m (24 406 ft.). Russian name: **Tyan-Shan.**

tiara (tɪ'ɑ:rə) *n.* **1.** a woman's semicircular jewelled headdress for formal occasions. **2.** a high headdress worn by Persian kings in ancient times. **3.** a headdress worn by the pope, consisting of a beehive-shaped diadem surrounded by three coronets. [C16: via L from Gk, of Oriental origin] —**ti'araed** *adj.*

Tiber ('taɪbə) *n.* a river in central Italy, rising in the Tuscan Apennines and flowing south through Rome to the Tyrrhenian Sea. Length: 405 km (252 miles). Ancient name: **Tiberis** ('ti:bərɪs). Italian name: **Tevere.**

Tiberias (taɪ'bɪərɪ,æs) *n.* **Lake.** another name for the (Sea of) **Galilee.**

Tiberius (taɪ'bɪərɪəs) *n.* full name *Tiberius Claudius Nero Caesar Augustus.* 42 B.C.–37 A.D., Roman emperor (14–37 A.D.). He succeeded his father-in-law Augustus after a brilliant military career. He became increasingly tyrannical.

Tibesti *or* **Tibesti Massif** (tɪ'bɛstɪ) *pl. n.* a mountain range of volcanic origin in NW Chad, in the central Sahara: extending for about 480 km (300 miles). Highest peak: Emi Koussi, 3415 m (11 204 ft.).

Tibet (tɪ'bɛt) *n.* an autonomous region of SW China: Europeans strictly excluded in the 19th century; invaded by China in 1950; rebellion (1959) against Chinese rule suppressed and the Dalai Lama fled to India; consists largely of a vast high plateau between the Himalayas and Kunlun Mountains; formerly a theocracy and the centre of Lamaism. Capital: Lhasa. Pop.: 1 970 000 (1985). Area: 1 221 601 sq. km (471 660 sq. miles). Chinese names: **Xizang Autonomous Region, Sitsang.**

Tibetan (tɪ'bɛtᵊn) *adj.* **1.** of or characteristic of Tibet, its people, or their language. *~n.* **2.** a native or inhabitant of Tibet. **3.** the language of Tibet.

tibia ('tɪbɪə) *n., pl.* **tibiae** ('tɪbɪ,i:) *or* **tibias.** **1.** the inner and thicker of the two bones of the human leg below the knee; shinbone. **2.** the corresponding bone in other vertebrates. **3.** the fourth segment of an insect's leg. [C16: from L: leg, pipe] —**'tibial** *adj.*

Tibullus (tɪ'bʌləs) *n.* **Albius** ('ælbɪəs). ?54–?19 B.C., Roman elegiac poet.

Tibur ('taɪbə) *n.* the ancient name for **Tivoli.**

tic (tɪk) *n.* spasmodic twitching of a particular group of muscles. [C19: from F, from ?]

tic douloureux ('tɪk ,du:lə'ru:) *n.* a condition of momentary stabbing pain along the trigeminal nerve. [C19: from F, lit.: painful tic]

Ticino (*Italian* ti'tʃi:no) *n.* **1.** a canton in S Switzerland: predominantly Italian-speaking and Roman Catholic; mountainous. Capital: Bellinzona. Pop.: 265 899 (1980). Area: 2810 sq. km (1085 sq. miles). German name: **Tessin. 2.** a river in S central Europe, rising in S central Switzerland and flowing southeast and west to Lake Maggiore, then southeast to the River Po. Length: 248 km (154 miles).

tick¹ (tɪk) *n.* **1.** a recurrent metallic tapping or clicking sound, such as that made by a clock. **2.** *Brit. inf.* a moment or instant. **3.** a mark (✓) used to check off or indicate the correctness of something. *~vb.* **4.** to produce a recurrent tapping sound or indicate by such a sound: *the clock ticked the minutes away.* **5.** (when *tr.*, often foll. by *off*) to mark or check with a tick. **6. what makes someone tick.** *Inf.* the basic drive or motivation of a person. *~See also* **tick off, tick over.** [C13: from Low G *tikk* touch]

tick[2] (tɪk) *n.* any of a large group of small parasitic arachnids typically living on the skin of warm-blooded animals and feeding on the blood and tissues of their hosts. [OE *ticca*]

tick[3] (tɪk) *n.* **1.** the strong covering of a pillow, mattress, etc. **2.** *Inf.* short for **ticking**. [C15: prob. from MDu. *tīke*]

tick[4] (tɪk) *n. Brit. inf.* account or credit (esp. in **on tick**). [C17: shortened from TICKET]

tick bird *n.* another name for **oxpecker**.

ticker ('tɪkə) *n.* **1.** *Sl.* **a.** the heart. **b.** a watch. **2.** a person or thing that ticks. **3.** the U.S. word for **tape machine**.

ticker tape *n.* a continuous paper ribbon on which a tape machine prints current stock quotations.

ticket ('tɪkɪt) *n.* **1. a.** a piece of paper, cardboard, etc., showing that the holder is entitled to certain rights, such as travel on a train or bus, entry to a place of public entertainment, etc. **b.** (*modifier*) concerned with the issue, sale, or checking of tickets: *a ticket collector*. **2.** a piece of card, cloth, etc., attached to an article showing information such as its price, size, etc. **3.** a summons served for a parking or traffic offence. **4.** *Inf.* the certificate of competence issued to a ship's captain or an aircraft pilot. **5.** *U.S. & N.Z.* the group of candidates nominated by one party in an election; slate. **6.** *Chiefly U.S.* the declared policy of a political party at an election. **7.** *Brit. inf.* a certificate of discharge from the armed forces. **8.** *Inf.* the right or appropriate thing: *that's the ticket*. **9. have** (**got**) **tickets on oneself.** *Austral. inf.* to be conceited. ~*vb.* (*tr.*) **10.** to issue or attach a ticket or tickets to. [C17: from OF *etiquet*, from *estiquier* to stick on, from MDu. *steken* to stick]

ticket day *n. Stock Exchange.* the day before settling day, when the stockbrokers are given the names of the purchasers.

ticket of leave *n.* (formerly, in Britain) a permit allowing a convict (**ticket-of-leave man**) to leave prison, after serving only part of his sentence, with certain restrictions placed on him.

tick fever *n.* any acute infectious febrile disease caused by the bite of an infected tick.

ticking ('tɪkɪŋ) *n.* a strong cotton fabric, often striped, used esp. for mattress and pillow covers. [C17: from TICK[3]]

tickle ('tɪk³l) *vb.* **1.** to touch or stroke, so as to produce pleasure, laughter, or a twitching sensation. **2.** (*tr.*) to excite pleasurably; gratify. **3.** (*tr.*) to delight or entertain (often in **tickle one's fancy**). **4.** (*intr.*) to itch or tingle. **5.** (*tr.*) to catch (a fish, esp. a trout) with the hands. **6. tickle pink** *or* **to death.** *Inf.* to please greatly. ~*n.* **7.** a sensation of light stroking or itching. **8.** the act of tickling. **9.** *Canad.* (in the Atlantic Provinces) a narrow strait. [C14]

tickler ('tɪklə) *n.* **1.** *Inf., chiefly Brit.* a difficult problem. **2.** Also called: **tickler file.** *U.S.* a memorandum book. **3.** a person or thing that tickles.

ticklish ('tɪklɪʃ) *adj.* **1.** sensitive to being tickled. **2.** delicate or difficult. **3.** easily upset or offended. —**ticklishly** *adv.* —**ticklishness** *n.*

tick off *vb.* (*tr., adv.*) **1.** to mark with a tick. **2.** *Inf., chiefly Brit.* to scold; reprimand.

tick over *vb.* (*intr., adv.*) **1.** Also: **idle.** *Brit.* (of an engine) to run at low speed with the throttle control closed and the transmission disengaged. **2.** to run smoothly without any major changes.

ticktack ('tɪk,tæk) *n.* **1.** *Brit.* a system of sign language, mainly using the hands, by which bookmakers transmit their odds to each other at race courses. **2.** *U.S.* a ticking sound. [from TICK[1]]

ticktock ('tɪk,tɒk) *n.* **1.** a ticking sound as made by a clock. ~*vb.* **2.** (*intr.*) to make a ticking sound.

tidal ('taɪd³l) *adj.* **1.** relating to, characterized by, or affected by tides. **2.** dependent on the tide: *a tidal ferry.* —**tidally** *adv.*

tidal wave *n.* **1.** a name (not in technical usage) for **tsunami**. **2.** an unusually large incoming wave, often caused by high winds and spring tides. **3.** a forceful and widespread movement in public opinion, action, etc.

tidbit ('tɪd,bɪt) *n.* the usual U.S. spelling of **titbit**.

tiddler ('tɪdlə) *n. Brit. inf.* **1.** a very small fish, esp. a stickleback. **2.** a small child. [C19: from *tittlebat*, childish var. of STICKLEBACK, infl. by TIDDLY[1]]

tiddly[1] ('tɪdlɪ) *adj.* **-dlier, -dliest.** *Brit.* small; tiny. [C19: childish var. of LITTLE]

tiddly[2] ('tɪdlɪ) *adj. Sl., chiefly Brit.* slightly drunk. [C19 (meaning: a drink): from ?]

tiddlywinks ('tɪdlɪ,wɪŋks) *n.* (*functioning as sing.*) a game in which players try to flick discs of plastic into a cup by pressing them with other larger discs. [C19: prob. from TIDDLY[1] + dialect *wink*, var. of WINCH[1]]

tide (taɪd) *n.* **1.** the cyclic rise and fall of sea level caused by the gravitational pull of the sun and moon. There are usually two high tides and two low tides in each lunar day. **2.** the current, ebb, or flow of water at a specified place resulting from these changes in level. **3.** See **ebb** (sense 3) and **flood** (sense 3). **4.** a widespread tendency or movement. **5.** a critical point in time; turning point. **6.** *Arch. except in combination.* a season or time: *Christmastide.* **7.** *Arch.* a favourable opportunity. **8. the tide is in** (*or* **out**). the sea has reached its highest (*or* lowest) level. ~*vb.* **9.** to carry or be carried with or as if with the tide. **10.** (*intr.*) to ebb and flow like the tide. [OE *tīd* time] —**tideless** *adj.*

tideland ('taɪd,lænd) *n. U.S.* land between high-water and low-water marks.

tidemark ('taɪd,mɑːk) *n.* **1.** a mark left by the highest or lowest point of a tide. **2.** *Chiefly Brit.* a mark showing a level reached by a liquid: *a tidemark on the bath.* **3.** *Inf., chiefly Brit.* a dirty mark on the skin, indicating the extent to which someone has washed.

tide over *vb.* (*tr., adv.*) to help to get through (a period of) difficulty, distress, etc.).

tide-rip *n.* another word for **riptide** (sense 1).

tidewaiter ('taɪd,weɪtə) *n.* (formerly) a customs officer who boarded and inspected incoming ships.

tidewater ('taɪd,wɔːtə) *n.* **1.** water that advances and recedes with the tide. **2.** *U.S.* coastal land drained by tidal streams.

tideway ('taɪd,weɪ) *n.* a strong tidal current or its channel, esp. the tidal part of a river.

tidings ('taɪdɪŋz) *pl. n.* information or news. [OE *tīdung*]

tidy ('taɪdɪ) *adj.* **-dier, -diest.** **1.** characterized by or indicating neatness and order. **2.** *Inf.* considerable: *a tidy sum of money.* ~*vb.* **-dying, -died.** **3.** (when *intr.*, usually foll. by *up*) to put (things) in order; neaten. ~*n., pl.* **-dies.** **4. a.** a small container for odds and ends. **b. sink tidy.** a container to retain rubbish that might clog the plughole. **5.** *Chiefly U.S. & Canad.* an ornamental protective covering for the back or arms of a chair. [C13 (in the sense: timely, excellent): from TIDE + -Y[1]] —**tidily** *adv.* —**tidiness** *n.*

tie (taɪ) *vb.* **tying, tied.** **1.** (when *tr.*, often foll. by *up*) to fasten or be fastened with string, thread, etc. **2.** to make (a knot or bow) in (something). **3.** (*tr.*) to restrict or secure. **4.** to equal (the score) of a competitor, etc. **5.** (*tr.*) *Inf.* to unite in marriage. **6.** *Music.* **a.** to execute (two successive notes) as though they formed one note. **b.** to connect (two printed notes) with a tie. ~*n.* **7.** a bond, link, or fastening. **8.** a restriction or restraint. **9.** a string, wire, etc., with which something is tied. **10.** a long narrow piece of material worn, esp. by men, under the collar of a shirt, tied in a knot close to the throat with the ends hanging down the front. U.S. name: **necktie.** **11. a.** an equality in score, attainment, etc., in a contest. **b.** the match or competition in which such a result is attained. **12.** a structural member such as a tie beam or tie rod. **13.** *Sport, Brit.* a match or game in an eliminating competition: *a cup tie.* **14.** (*usually pl.*) a shoe fastened by means of laces. **15.** the U.S. and Canad. name for **sleeper** (on a railway track). **16.** *Music.* a slur connecting two notes of the same pitch indicating that the sound is to be prolonged for their joint time value. ~See also **tie in, tie up.** [OE *tīgan* to tie]

tie beam *n.* a horizontal beam that serves to prevent two other structural members from separating, esp. one that connects two corresponding rafters in a roof or roof truss.

tiebreaker ('taɪ,breɪkə) *n.* any method of deciding quickly the result of a drawn contest, esp. an extra game, question, etc.

Tieck (*German* tiːk) *n.* **Ludwig** ('luːtvɪç). 1773–1853, German romantic writer, noted esp. for his fairy tales.

tie clasp *n.* a clip which holds a tie in place against a shirt. Also called: **tie clip.**

tied (taɪd) *adj. Brit.* **1.** (of a public house) obliged to sell only the beer of a particular brewery. **2.** (of a house) rented out to the tenant for as long as he is employed by the owner.

tie-dyeing, tie-dye or **tie and dye** n. a method of dyeing textiles to produce patterns by tying sections of the cloth together so that they will not absorb the dye. — **'tie-,dyed** adj.

tie in vb. (adv.) **1.** to come or bring into a certain relationship; coordinate. ~n. **tie-in. 2.** a link, relationship, or co-ordination. **3.** publicity material, a book, etc., linked to a film, etc. **4.** U.S. **a.** a sale or advertisement offering products of which a purchaser must buy one or more in addition to his purchase. **b.** an item sold or advertised in this way. **c.** (as modifier): a tie-in sale.

tie line n. a telephone line between two private branch exchanges or private exchanges that may or may not pass through a main exchange.

Tien Shan ('tjɛn'ʃɑːn) n. a variant transliteration of the Chinese name for the **Tian Shan**.

Tientsin ('tjɛn'tsɪn) n. a variant transliteration of the Chinese name for **Tianjin**.

tiepin ('taɪ,pɪn) n. an ornamental pin of various shapes used to pin the two ends of a tie to a shirt.

Tiepolo (Italian 'tjɛ:polo; English ti:'ɛpə,ləʊ) n. **Giovanni Battista** (dʒo'vanni bat'tista). 1696–1770, Italian rococo painter, esp. of frescoes as in Residenz at Würzburg.

tier[1] (tɪə) n. **1.** one of a set of rows placed one above and behind the other, such as theatre seats. **2. a.** a layer or level. **b.** (in combination): a three-tier cake. ~vb. **3.** to be or arrange in tiers. [C16: from OF tire rank, of Gmc origin]

tier[2] ('taɪə) n. a person or thing that ties.

tierce (tɪəs) n. **1.** a variant of **terce. 2.** the third of eight positions from which a parry or attack can be made in fencing. **3.** (tɜːs). a sequence of three cards. **4.** an obsolete measure of capacity equal to 42 wine gallons. [C15: from OF, fem. of tiers third, from L tertius]

tiercel ('tɪəs²l) n. a variant of **tercel**.

Tierra del Fuego (Spanish 'tjɛrra ðɛl 'fweɣo) n. an archipelago at the S extremity of South America, separated from the mainland by the Strait of Magellan: the west and south belong to Chile, the east to Argentina, and several islands are disputed. Area: 73 643 sq. km (28 434 sq. miles).

tie up vb. (adv.) **1.** (tr.) to bind securely with or as if with string, rope, etc. **2.** to moor (a vessel). **3.** (tr.; often passive) to engage the attentions of. **4.** (tr.; often passive) to conclude (the organization of something). **5.** to come or bring to a complete standstill. **6.** (tr.) to commit (funds, etc.) and so make unavailable for other uses. **7.** (tr.) to subject (property) to conditions that prevent sale, alienation, etc. ~n. **tie-up. 8.** a link or connection. **9.** Chiefly U.S. & Canad. a standstill. **10.** Chiefly U.S. & Canad. an informal term for **traffic jam**.

tiff (tɪf) n. **1.** a petty quarrel. **2.** a fit of ill humour. ~vb. **3.** (intr.) to have or be in a tiff. [C18: from ?]

tiffany ('tɪfənɪ) n., pl. **-nies.** a sheer fine gauzy fabric. [C17 (in the sense: a fine dress worn on Twelfth Night): from OF tifanie, from ecclesiastical L theophania Epiphany]

tiffin ('tɪfɪn) n. (in India) a light meal, esp. at midday. [C18: prob. from obs. tiffing, from tiff to sip]

Tiflis (tɪf'liːs) n. transliteration of the Russian name for **Tbilisi**.

tig (tɪg) n., vb. **tigging, tigged.** another word for **tag**[2](senses 1, 4).

tiger ('taɪgə) n. **1.** a large feline mammal of forests in most of Asia, having a tawny yellow coat with black stripes. **2.** a dynamic, forceful, or cruel person. [C13: from OF tigre, from L tigris, from Gk, of Iranian origin] — **'tigerish** or **'tigrish** adj.

tiger beetle n. any of a family of active predatory beetles, chiefly of warm dry regions, having powerful mandibles and long legs.

tiger cat n. a medium-sized feline mammal of Central and South America, having a dark-striped coat.

tiger lily n. a lily plant of China and Japan cultivated for its flowers, which have black-spotted orange petals.

tiger moth n. any of various moths having wings that are conspicuously marked with stripes and spots.

tiger's-eye or **tigereye** ('taɪgər,aɪ) n. a semiprecious golden-brown stone.

tiger shark n. a voracious omnivorous requiem shark of tropical waters, having a striped or spotted body.

tiger snake n. a highly venomous and aggressive Australian snake, usually with dark bands on the back.

tight (taɪt) adj. **1.** stretched or drawn so as not to be loose; taut. **2.** fitting in a close manner. **3.** held, made, fixed, or closed firmly and securely: a tight knot. **4. a.** of close and compact construction or organization, esp. so as to be impervious to water, air, etc. **b.** (in combination): airtight. **5.** unyielding or stringent. **6.** cramped or constricted: a tight fit. **7.** mean or miserly. **8.** difficult and problematic: a tight situation. **9.** hardly profitable: a tight bargain. **10.** Econ. **a.** (of a commodity) difficult to obtain. **b.** (of funds, money, etc.) difficult and expensive to borrow. **c.** (of markets) characterized by excess demand or scarcity. **11.** (of a match or game) very close or even. **12.** (of a team or group, esp. of a pop group) playing well together, in a disciplined coordinated way. **13.** Inf. drunk. **14.** Inf. (of a person) showing tension. ~adv. **15.** in a close, firm, or secure way. [C14: prob. var. of thight, from ON théttr close] — **'tightly** adv. — **'tightness** n.

tighten ('taɪt²n) vb. to make or become tight or tighter.

tightfisted (,taɪt'fɪstɪd) adj. mean; miserly.

tightknit (,taɪt'nɪt) adj. **1.** closely integrated: a tightknit community. **2.** organized carefully.

tight-lipped adj. **1.** secretive or taciturn. **2.** with the lips pressed tightly together, as through anger.

tightrope ('taɪt,rəʊp) n. a rope stretched taut on which acrobats walk or perform balancing feats. — **tightrope walker** n.

tights (taɪts) pl. n. **1.** Also called: (U.S.) **panty hose,** (Canad. and N.Z.) **pantyhose,** (Austral. and N.Z.) **pantihose.** a one-piece clinging garment covering the body from the waist to the feet, worn by women and also by acrobats, dancers, etc. **2.** a similar garment formerly worn by men, as in the 16th century with a doublet.

Tiglath-pileser I ('tɪglæθpɪ'liːzə, -paɪ-) n. king of Assyria (?1116–?1093 B.C.), who extended his kingdom to the upper Euphrates and defeated the king of Babylonia.

Tiglath-pileser III n. known as Pulu. died ?727 B.C., king of Assyria (745–727), who greatly extended his empire, subjugating Syria and Palestine.

tiglic acid ('tɪglɪk) n. a syrupy liquid or crystalline unsaturated carboxylic acid, found in croton oil and used in perfumery. [C19 tiglic, from NL Croton tiglium (the croton plant), from ?]

tigon ('taɪgən) or **tiglon** ('tɪglɒn) n. the hybrid offspring of a male tiger and a female lion.

Tigré ('tiːgreɪ) n. a province of N Ethiopia, bordering on Eritrea: formerly a separate kingdom. Capital: Mekele. Pop.: 2 044 400 (1981 est.). Area: 65 900 sq. km (25 444 sq. miles).

tigress ('taɪgrɪs) n. **1.** a female tiger. **2.** a fierce, cruel, or wildly passionate woman.

tigridia (taɪ'grɪdɪə) n. any of various bulbous plants of Mexico, Central America, and tropical S America. [C19: from Mod. L, from Gk tigris tiger (alluding to the spotted flowers of these plants)]

Tigris ('taɪgrɪs) n. a river in SW Asia, rising in E Turkey and flowing southeast through Baghdad to the Euphrates in SE Iraq, forming the delta of the Shatt-al-Arab, which flows into the Persian Gulf: part of a canal and irrigation system as early as 2400 B.C., with many ancient cities (including Nineveh) on its banks. Length: 1900 km (1180 miles).

Tihwa or **Tihua** ('tiː'hwɑː) n. a former name for **Urumqi**.

Tijuana (tiː'wɑːnə; Spanish ti'xwana) or **Tia Juana** n. a city and resort in NW Mexico, in Baja California. Pop.: 461 257 (1980).

tike (taɪk) n. a variant spelling of **tyke**.

tiki ('tiːkiː) n. a Maori greenstone neck ornament in the form of a fetus. Also called: **heitiki.** [from Maori heitiki figure worn round neck]

Tilburg ('tɪlbɜːg; Dutch 'tɪlbyrx) n. a city in the S Netherlands, in North Brabant: textile industries. Pop.: 153 675 (1987).

tilbury ('tɪlbərɪ, -brɪ) n., pl. **-buries.** a light two-wheeled horse-drawn open carriage, seating two people. [C19: prob. after the inventor]

Tilbury ('tɪlbərɪ, -brɪ) n. an area in Essex, on the River Thames: extensive docks; principal container port of the Port of London.

tilde ('tɪldə) n. the diacritical mark (˜) placed over a letter to indicate a nasal sound, as in Spanish señor. [C19: from Sp., from L titulus title]

Tilden ('tıldᵊn) n. **Bill**, full name *William Tatem Tilden*, known as *Big Bill*. 1893–1953, U.S. tennis player: won the U.S. singles championship (1920–25, 1929) and the British singles championship (1920–21, 1930).

tile (taıl) n. **1.** a flat thin slab of fired clay, rubber, linoleum, etc., used with others to cover a roof, floor, wall, etc. **2.** a short pipe made of earthenware, plastic, etc., used with others to form a drain. **3.** tiles collectively. **4.** a rectangular block used as a playing piece in mahjong and other games. **5. on the tiles.** *Inf.* on a spree, esp. of drinking or debauchery. ~vb. **6.** (tr.) to cover with tiles. [OE *tigele*, from L *tēgula*] — '**tiler** n.

tiling ('taılıŋ) n. **1.** tiles collectively. **2.** something made of or surfaced with tiles.

till[1] (tıl) conj., prep. short for **until**. Also (not standard): '**til**. [OE *til*]

▷ *Usage. Till* is a variant of *until* that is acceptable at all levels of language. *Until* is, however, often preferred at the beginning of a sentence in formal writing.

till[2] (tıl) vb. (tr.) **1.** to cultivate and work (land) for the raising of crops. **2.** to plough. [OE *tilian* to try, obtain] — '**tillable** adj. — '**tiller** n.

till[3] (tıl) n. a box, case, or drawer into which money taken from customers is put, now usually part of a cash register. [C15 *tylle*, from ?]

till[4] (tıl) n. a glacial deposit consisting of rock fragments of various sizes. The most common is boulder clay. [C17: from ?]

tillage ('tılıdʒ) n. **1.** the act, process, or art of tilling. **2.** tilled land.

tiller[1] ('tılə) n. *Naut.* a handle fixed to the top of a rudderpost to serve as a lever in steering it. [C14: from Anglo-F *teiler* beam of a loom, from Med. L *tēlārium*, from L *tēla* web] — '**tillerless** adj.

tiller[2] ('tılə) n. **1.** a shoot that arises from the base of the stem in grasses. **2.** a less common name for **sapling**. ~vb. **3.** (intr.) (of a plant) to produce tillers. [OE *telgor* twig]

Tillich ('tılık) n. **Paul Johannes.** 1886–1965, U.S. Protestant theologian and philosopher, born in Germany. His works include *The Courage to Be* (1952) and *Systematic Theology* (1951–63).

Tilly ('tılı) n. Count **Johan Tserclaes von** (jo'hɑn tsɛr'klɑs fɔn). 1559–1632, Flemish soldier, who commanded the army of The Catholic League (1618–32) and the imperial forces (1630–32) in the Thirty Years' War.

Tilsit ('tılzıt) n. the former name (until 1945) of **Sovetsk**.

tilt (tılt) vb. **1.** to incline or cause to incline at an angle. **2.** (usually intr.) to attack or overthrow (a person) in a tilt or joust. **3.** (when intr., often foll. by *at*) to aim or thrust: *to tilt a lance.* **4.** (tr.) to forge with a tilt hammer. ~n. **5.** a slope or angle: *at a tilt.* **6.** the act of tilting. **7.** (esp. in medieval Europe) **a.** a jousting contest. **b.** a thrust with a lance or pole delivered during a tournament. **8.** any dispute or contest. **9.** See **tilt hammer**. **10.** (**at**) **full tilt.** at full speed or force. [OE *tealtian*] — '**tilter** n.

tilth (tılθ) n. **1.** the act or process of tilling land. **2.** the condition of soil or land that has been tilled. [OE *tilthe*]

tilt hammer n. a drop hammer with a heavy head; used in forging.

tiltyard ('tılt,jɑːd) n. (formerly) an enclosed area for tilting.

Tim. *Bible.* abbrev. for Timothy.

Timaru ('tımə,ruː) n. a port and resort in S New Zealand, on E South Island. Pop.: 28 500 (1987).

timbal or **tymbal** ('tımbᵊl) n. *Music.* a type of kettledrum. [C17: from F *timbale*, from OF *tamballe*, (associated also with *cymbale* cymbal), from OSp. *atabal*, from Ar. *at-tabl* the drum]

timbale (tæm'bɑːl) n. **1.** a mixture of meat, fish, etc., cooked in a mould lined with potato or pastry. **2.** a straight-sided mould in which such a dish is prepared. [C19: from F: kettledrum]

timber ('tımbə) n. **1. a.** wood, esp. when regarded as a construction material. **b.** (as modifier): *a timber cottage.* Usual U.S. and Canad. word: **lumber**. **2. a.** trees collectively. **b.** *Chiefly U.S.* woodland. **3.** a piece of wood used in a structure. **4.** *Naut.* a frame in a wooden vessel. ~vb. **5.** (tr.) to provide with timbers. ~sentence substitute. **6.** a lumberjack's shouted warning when a tree is about to fall. [OE] — '**timbered** adj. — '**timbering** n.

timber hitch n. a knot used for tying a rope round a spar, log, etc., for haulage.

timber limit n. *Canad.* **1.** the area to which rights of cutting timber, granted by a government licence, are limited. **2.** another term for **timber line**.

timber line n. the altitudinal or latitudinal limit of tree growth. Also called: **tree line**.

timber wolf n. a wolf with a grey brindled coat found in forested northern regions, esp. of North America.

timberyard ('tımbə,jɑːd) n. *Brit.* an establishment where timber, etc., is stored or sold. U.S. and Canad. word: **lumberyard**.

timbre ('tımbə, 'tæmbə) n. **1.** *Phonetics.* the distinctive tone quality differentiating one vowel or sonant from another. **2.** *Music.* tone colour or quality of sound. [C19: from F: note of a bell, from OF: drum, from Med. Gk *timbanon*, from Gk *tumpanon*]

timbrel ('tımbrəl) n. *Chiefly biblical.* a tambourine. [C16: from OF; see TIMBRE]

Timbuktu (,tımbʌk'tuː) n. **1.** a town in central Mali, on the River Niger: terminus of a trans-Saharan caravan route; a great Muslim centre (14th–16th centuries). Pop.: 19 165 (1976). French name: **Tombouctou**. **2.** any distant or outlandish place: *from here to Timbuktu.*

time (taım) n. **1.** the continuous passage of existence in which events pass from a state of potentiality in the future, through the present, to a state of finality in the past. Related adj.: **temporal**. **2.** *Physics.* a quantity measuring duration, usually with reference to a periodic process such as the rotation of the earth or the vibration of electromagnetic radiation emitted from certain atoms. Time is considered as a fourth coordinate required to specify an event. See **space-time continuum**. **3.** a specific point on this continuum expressed in hours and minutes: *the time is four o'clock.* **4.** a system of reckoning for expressing time: *Greenwich Mean Time.* **5. a.** a definite and measurable portion of this continuum. **b.** (as modifier): *time limit.* **6. a.** an accepted period such as a day, season, etc. **b.** (in combination): *springtime.* **7.** an unspecified interval; a while. **8.** (often pl.) a period or point marked by specific attributes or events: *the Victorian times.* **9.** a sufficient interval or period: *have you got time to help me?* **10.** an instance or occasion: *I called you three times.* **11.** an occasion or period of specified quality: *have a good time.* **12.** the duration of human existence. **13.** the heyday of human life: *in her time she was a great star.* **14.** a suitable moment: *it's time I told you.* **15.** the expected interval in which something is done. **16.** a particularly important moment, esp. childbirth or death: *her time had come.* **17.** (pl.) indicating a degree or amount calculated by multiplication with the number specified: *ten times three is thirty.* **18.** (often pl.) the fashions, thought, etc., of the present age (esp. in **ahead of one's time, behind the times**). **19.** *Brit.* Also: **closing time**. the time at which bars, pubs, etc., are legally obliged to stop selling alcoholic drinks. **20.** *Inf.* a term in jail (esp. in **do time**). **21. a.** a customary or full period of work. **b.** the rate of pay for this period. **22.** Also: (esp. U.S.): **metre. a.** the system of combining beats or pulses in music into successive groupings by which the rhythm of the music is established. **b.** a specific system having a specific number of beats in each grouping or bar: *duple time.* **23.** *Music.* short for **time value**. **24. against time.** in an effort to complete something in a limited period. **25. ahead of time.** before the deadline. **26. at one time. a.** once; formerly. **b.** simultaneously. **27. at the same time. a.** simultaneously. **b.** nevertheless; however. **28. at times.** sometimes. **29. beat time.** to indicate the tempo of a piece of music by waving a baton, hand, etc. **30. for the time being.** for the moment; temporarily. **31. from time to time.** at intervals; occasionally. **32. have no time for.** to have no patience with; not tolerate. **33. in good time. a.** early. **b.** quickly. **34. in no time.** very quickly. **35. in one's own time. a.** outside paid working hours. **b.** at one's own rate. **36. in time. a.** early or at the appointed time. **b.** eventually. **c.** *Music.* at a correct metrical or rhythmical pulse. **37. keep time.** to observe correctly the accent or rhythmical pulse of a piece of music in relation to tempo. **38. make time. a.** to find an opportunity. **b.** (often foll. by *with*) *U.S. inf.* to succeed in seducing. **39. on time. a.** at the expected or scheduled time. **b.** *U.S.* payable in instalments. **40. pass the time of day.** to exchange casual greetings (with an acquaintance). **41. time and again.** frequently. **42. time off.** a period when one is absent from work for a holiday, through sickness, etc. **43. time of one's life.** a memorably enjoyable time. **44. time out of mind.** from time immemorial. **45.** (*modifier*) operating automatically at or for a set time: *time lock; time switch.* ~*vb.* (*tr.*) **46.** to ascertain the duration or speed of. **47.** to set a time for. **48.** to adjust to keep accurate time. **49.** to pick a suitable time for. **50.** *Sport.* to control the execution or speed of (an action). ~*sentence substitute.* **51.** the word called out by a publican signalling that it is closing time. [OE *tīma*]

time and a half *n.* the rate of pay equalling one and a half times the normal rate, often offered for overtime work.

time and motion study *n.* the analysis of industrial or work procedures to determine the most efficient methods of operation. Also: **time and motion, time study, motion study.**

time bomb *n.* a bomb containing a timing mechanism that determines the time at which it will detonate.

time capsule *n.* a container holding articles, documents, etc., representative of the current age, buried for discovery in the future.

time clock *n.* a clock which records, by punching or stamping **timecards** inserted into it, the time of arrival or departure of people, such as employees in a factory.

time-consuming *adj.* taking up or involving a great deal of time.

time exposure *n.* **1.** an exposure of a photographic film for a relatively long period, usually a few seconds. **2.** a photograph produced by such an exposure.

time-honoured *adj.* having been observed for a long time and sanctioned by custom.

time immemorial *n.* the distant past beyond memory or record.

timekeeper ('taɪmˌkiːpə) *n.* **1.** a person or thing that keeps or records time. **2.** an employee who maintains a record of the hours worked by the other employees. **3.** an employee whose record of punctuality is of a specified nature: *a bad timekeeper.* —'time,keeping *n.*

time-lag *n.* an interval between two connected events.

time-lapse photography *n.* the technique of recording a very slow process on film by exposing single frames at regular intervals. The film is then projected at normal speed.

timeless ('taɪmlɪs) *adj.* **1.** unaffected or unchanged by time; ageless. **2.** eternal. —'timelessly *adv.* —'timelessness *n.*

timely ('taɪmlɪ) *adj.* **-lier, -liest,** *adv.* at the right or an opportune or appropriate time.

time machine *n.* (in science fiction) a machine in which people or objects can be transported into the past or the future.

time-out *n. Chiefly U.S. & Canad.* **1.** *Sport.* an interruption in play during which players rest, discuss tactics, etc. **2.** a period of rest; break.

timepiece ('taɪmˌpiːs) *n.* any of various devices, such as a clock, watch, or chronometer, which measure and indicate time.

timer ('taɪmə) *n.* **1.** a device for measuring, recording, or indicating time. **2.** a switch or regulator that causes a mechanism to operate at a specific time. **3.** a person or thing that times.

timesaving ('taɪmˌseɪvɪŋ) *adj.* shortening the length of time required for an operation, activity, etc. —'time,saver *n.*

timescale ('taɪmˌskeɪl) *n.* the span of time within which certain events occur or are scheduled in relation to any broader period of time.

time-served *adj.* (of a craftsman or tradesman) having completed an apprenticeship; fully trained and competent.

timeserver ('taɪmˌsɜːvə) *n.* a person who compromises and changes his opinions, way of life, etc., to suit the current fashions.

time sharing *n.* **1.** a system of part ownership of a property for use as a holiday home whereby each participant owns the property for a particular period every year. **2.** a system by which users at different terminals of a computer can, because of its high speed, apparently communicate with it at the same time.

time signal *n.* an announcement of the correct time, esp. on radio or television.

time signature *n. Music.* a sign usually consisting of two figures, one above the other, the upper figure representing

the number of beats per bar and the lower one the time value of each beat: it is placed after the key signature.

timetable ('taɪmˌteɪbᵊl) *n.* **1.** a list or table of events arranged according to the time when they take place; schedule. ~*vb.* (*tr.*) **2.** to include in or arrange according to a timetable.

time value *n. Music.* the duration of a note relative to other notes in a composition and considered in relation to the basic tempo.

time warp *n.* an imagined distortion of the progress of time so that, for instance, events from the past may appear to be happening in the present.

timeworn ('taɪmˌwɔːn) *adj.* **1.** showing the adverse effects of overlong use or of old age. **2.** hackneyed; trite.

time zone *n.* a region throughout which the same standard time is used. There are 24 time zones in the world, demarcated approximately by meridians at 15° intervals, an hour apart.

timid ('tɪmɪd) *adj.* **1.** easily frightened or upset, esp. by human contact; shy. **2.** indicating shyness or fear. [C16: from L *timidus,* from *timēre* to fear] —ti'midity *or* 'timidness *n.* —'timidly *adv.*

timing ('taɪmɪŋ) *n.* the regulation of actions or remarks in relation to others to produce the best effect, as in music, the theatre, etc.

Timişoara (*Romanian* timiˈʃwara) *n.* a city in W Romania: under Turkish and later Hapsburg rule, being allotted to Romania in 1920. Pop.: 318 955 (1985). Hungarian name: **Temesvár.**

timocracy (taɪˈmɒkrəsɪ) *n., pl.* **-cies.** **1.** a political system in which possession of property is a requirement for participation in government. **2.** a political system in which love of honour is deemed the guiding principle of government. [C16: from OF *tymocracie,* ult. from Gk *timokratia,* from *timē* worth, honour, + -CRACY]

Timor ('tiːmɔː, 'taɪ-) *n.* an island in Indonesia in the Malay Archipelago, the largest and easternmost of the Lesser Sunda Islands: the east, together with an enclave on the NW coast, formed the Portuguese overseas province of Portuguese Timor until civil war in 1975 led to its annexation by Indonesia; made an Indonesian province of East Timor in 1976. Area: 30 775 sq. km (11 883 sq. miles).

timorous ('tɪmərəs) *adj.* **1.** fearful or timid. **2.** indicating fear or timidity. [C15: from OF *temoros,* from Med. L, from L *timor* fear, from *timēre* to be afraid] —'timorously *adv.* —'timorousness *n.*

Timor Sea *n.* an arm of the Indian Ocean between Australia and Timor. Width: about 480 km (300 miles).

Timoshenko (ˌtɪməˈʃɛŋkəʊ; *Russian* tima'ʃɛnkə) *n.* **Semyon Konstantinovich** (sɪ'mjɒn kənstan'tinavitʃ). 1895–1970, Soviet general in World War II.

Timothy ('tɪməθɪ) *n. New Testament.* **1.** a disciple of Paul, who became leader of the Christian community at Ephesus. **2.** either of the two books addressed to him (in full **The First and Second Epistles of Paul the Apostle to Timothy**), containing advice on pastoral matters.

timothy grass *or* **timothy** *n.* a perennial grass of temperate regions having erect stiff stems: grown for hay and pasture. [C18: apparently after a *Timothy Hanson,* who brought it to colonial Carolina]

timpani *or* **tympani** ('tɪmpənɪ) *pl. n.* (*sometimes functioning as sing.*) a set of kettledrums. [from It., pl. of *timpano* kettledrum, from L: TYMPANUM] —'timpanist *or* 'tympanist *n.*

Timur *or* **Timour** (tiː'mʊə) *n.* See **Tamerlane.**

tin (tɪn) *n.* **1.** a malleable silvery-white metallic element. It is used extensively in alloys, esp. bronze and pewter, and as a noncorroding coating for steel. Symbol: Sn; atomic no.: 50; atomic wt.: 118.69. **2.** Also called (esp. U.S. and Canad.): **can.** an airtight sealed container of thin sheet metal coated with tin, used for preserving and storing food or drink. **3.** any container made of metallic tin. **4.** Also called: **tinful.** the contents of a tin. **5.** *Brit., Austral., & N.Z.* galvanized iron: *a tin roof.* **6.** any metal regarded as cheap or flimsy. **7.** *Brit.* a loaf of bread with a rectangular shape. **8.** *N.Z.* a receptacle for home-baked biscuits, etc. (esp. in **to fill her tins** to bake a supply of biscuits, etc.). ~*vb.* **tinning, tinned.** (*tr.*) **9.** to put (food, etc.) into a tin or tins; preserve in a tin. **10.** to plate or coat with tin. **11.** to prepare (a metal) for soldering or brazing by applying a thin layer of solder to the surface. ~**Related adjs.: stannic, stannous.** [OE]

tinamou ('tɪnə,muː) *n.* any of various birds of Central and South America, having small wings and a heavy body. [C18: via F from Carib *tinamu*]

Tinbergen ('tɪn,bɜːgən) *n.* **Nikolaas** ('nɪkələs). born 1907, British zoologist, born in the Netherlands; studied animal behaviour, esp. instincts, and was one of the founders of ethology; Nobel prize for medicine, 1973.

tin can *n.* a metal food container, esp. when empty.

tinctorial (tɪŋk'tɔːrɪəl) *adj.* of or relating to colouring, staining, or dyeing. [C17: from L *tinctōrius*, from *tingere* to tinge]

tincture ('tɪŋktʃə) *n.* **1.** a medicinal extract in a solution of alcohol. **2.** a tint, colour, or tinge. **3.** a slight flavour, aroma, or trace. **4.** a colour or metal used on heraldic arms. **5.** *Obs.* a dye. ~*vb.* **6.** (*tr.*) to give a tint or colour to. [C14: from L *tinctūra* a dyeing, from *tingere* to dye]

Tindal *or* **Tindale** ('tɪndəl) *n.* variant spellings of (William) **Tyndale.**

tinder ('tɪndə) *n.* **1.** dry wood or other easily combustible material used for lighting a fire. **2.** anything inflammatory or dangerous. [OE *tynder*] —'**tindery** *adj.*

tinderbox ('tɪndə,bɒks) *n.* **1.** a box used formerly for holding tinder, esp. one fitted with a flint and steel. **2.** a person or thing that is particularly touchy or explosive.

tine (taɪn) *n.* **1.** a slender prong, esp. of a fork. **2.** any of the sharp terminal branches of a deer's antler. [OE *tind*] —**tined** *adj.*

tinea ('tɪnɪə) *n.* any fungal skin disease, esp. ringworm. [C17: from L: worm] —'**tineal** *adj.*

tinfoil ('tɪn,fɔɪl) *n.* **1.** thin foil made of tin or an alloy of tin and lead. **2.** thin foil made of aluminium; used for wrapping foodstuffs.

ting (tɪŋ) *n.* **1.** a high metallic sound such as that made by a small bell. ~*vb.* **2.** to make or cause to make such a sound. [C15: imit.]

ting-a-ling ('tɪŋə'lɪŋ) *n.* the sound of a small bell.

tinge (tɪndʒ) *n.* **1.** a slight tint or colouring. **2.** any slight addition. ~*vb.* **tingeing** *or* **tinging, tinged.** (*tr.*) **3.** to colour or tint faintly. **4.** to impart a slight trace to: *her thoughts were tinged with nostalgia.* [C15: from L *tingere* to colour]

tingle ('tɪŋgəl) *vb.* **1.** (*usually intr.*) to feel or cause to feel a prickling, itching, or stinging sensation of the flesh, as from a cold plunge. ~*n.* **2.** a sensation of tingling. [C14: ? a var. of TINKLE] —'**tingler** *n.* —'**tingling** *adj.* —'**tingly** *adj.*

tin god *n.* **1.** a self-important person. **2.** a person erroneously regarded as holy or venerable.

tin hat *n.* *Inf.* a steel helmet worn by military personnel.

tinker ('tɪŋkə) *n.* **1.** (esp. formerly) a travelling mender of pots and pans. **2.** a clumsy worker. **3.** the act of tinkering. **4.** *Scot. & Irish.* a Gypsy. ~*vb.* **5.** (*intr.; foll. by with*) to play, fiddle, or meddle (with machinery, etc.), esp. while undertaking repairs. **6.** to mend (pots and pans) as a tinker. [C13 *tinkere*, ?from *tink* tinkle, imit.] —'**tinkerer** *n.*

tinker's damn *or* **cuss** *n.* *Sl.* the slightest heed (esp. in **not give a tinker's damn** *or* **cuss**).

tinkle ('tɪŋkəl) *vb.* **1.** to ring with a high tinny sound like a small bell. **2.** (*tr.*) to announce or summon by such a ringing. **3.** (*intr.*) *Brit. inf.* to urinate. ~*n.* **4.** a high clear ringing sound. **5.** the act of tinkling. **6.** *Brit. inf.* a telephone call. [C14: imit.] —'**tinkly** *adj.*

tin lizzie ('lɪzɪ) *n.* *Inf.* an old or decrepit car.

tinned (tɪnd) *adj.* **1.** plated, coated, or treated with tin. **2.** *Chiefly Brit.* preserved or stored in airtight tins. **3.** coated with a layer of solder.

tinned dog *n.* *Sl., chiefly Austral.* tinned meat.

tinnitus (tɪ'naɪtəs) *n.* *Pathol.* a ringing, hissing, or booming sensation in one or both ears, caused by infection of the ear, a side effect of certain drugs, etc. [C19: from L, from *tinnīre* to ring]

tinny ('tɪnɪ) *adj.* -**nier, -niest. 1.** of or resembling tin. **2.** cheap or shoddy. **3.** (of a sound) high, thin, and metallic. **4.** (of food or drink) flavoured with metal, as from a container. **5.** *Austral. inf.* lucky. ~*n., pl.* -**nies. 6.** *Austral. sl.* a can of beer. —'**tinnily** *adv.* —'**tinniness** *n.*

tin-opener *n.* a small tool for opening tins.

Tin Pan Alley *n.* **1.** originally, a district in New York concerned with the production of popular music. **2.** the commercial side of show business and pop music.

tin plate *n.* **1.** thin steel sheet coated with a layer of tin that protects the steel from corrosion. ~*vb.* **tin-plate. 2.** (*tr.*) to coat with a layer of tin.

tinpot ('tɪn,pɒt) *adj.* (*prenominal*) *Brit. inf.* **1.** inferior, cheap, or worthless. **2.** petty; unimportant.

tinsel ('tɪnsəl) *n.* **1.** a decoration consisting of a piece of string with thin strips of metal foil attached along its length. **2.** a yarn or fabric interwoven with strands of glittering thread. **3.** anything cheap, showy, and gaudy. ~*vb.* -**selling, -selled** *or U.S.* -**seling, -seled.** (*tr.*) **4.** to decorate with or as if with tinsel: *snow tinsels the trees.* **5.** to give a gaudy appearance to. ~*adj.* **6.** made of or decorated with tinsel. **7.** showily but cheaply attractive; gaudy. [C16: from OF *estincele* a spark, from L *scintilla*] —'**tinselly** *adj.*

Tinseltown ('tɪnsəl,taʊn) *n.* an informal name for **Hollywood,** esp. as the home of the film industry. [C20: from the insubstantial glitter of the film world]

tinsmith ('tɪn,smɪθ) *n.* a person who works with tin or tin plate.

tin soldier *n.* a miniature toy soldier, usually made of lead.

tinstone ('tɪn,stəʊn) *n.* another name for **cassiterite.**

tint (tɪnt) *n.* **1.** a shade of a colour, esp. a pale one. **2.** a colour that is softened by the addition of white. **3.** a tinge. **4.** a dye for the hair. **5.** a trace or hint. **6.** *Engraving.* uniform shading, produced esp. by hatching. ~*vb.* **7.** (*tr.*) to colour or tinge. **8.** (*intr.*) to acquire a tint. [C18: from earlier *tinct*, from L *tingere* to colour] —'**tinter** *n.*

Tintagel Head (tɪn'tædʒəl) *n.* a promontory in SW England, on the W coast of Cornwall: ruins of **Tintagel Castle,** legendary birthplace of King Arthur.

tintinnabulation (,tɪntɪ,næbjʊ'leɪʃən) *n.* the act or an instance of the ringing or pealing of bells. [from L, from *tintinnāre* to tinkle, from *tinnīre* to ring]

Tintoretto (,tɪntə'rɛtəʊ; *Italian* tinto'retto) *n.* **Il** (il). original name *Jacopo Robusti.* 1518–94, Italian painter of the Venetian school. His works include *Susanna bathing* (?1550) and the fresco cycle in the Scuola di San Rocco, Venice (from 1564).

tinware ('tɪn,wɛə) *n.* objects made of tin plate.

tin whistle *n.* another name for **penny whistle.**

tinworks ('tɪn,wɜːks) *n.* (*functioning as sing. or pl.*) a place where tin is mined, smelted, or rolled.

tiny ('taɪnɪ) *adj.* **tinier, tiniest.** very small. [C16 *tine*, from ?] —'**tinily** *adv.* —'**tininess** *n.*

-tion *suffix forming nouns.* indicating state, condition, action, process, or result: *election; prohibition.* [from OF, from L -*tiō*, -*tiōn*-]

tip¹ (tɪp) *n.* **1.** a narrow or pointed end of something. **2.** the top or summit. **3.** a small piece forming an end: *a metal tip on a cane.* ~*vb.* **tipping, tipped.** (*tr.*) **4.** to adorn or mark the tip of. **5.** to cause to form a tip. [C15: from ON *typpa*] —'**tipless** *adj.*

tip² (tɪp) *vb.* **tipping, tipped. 1.** to tilt or cause to tilt. **2.** (usually foll. by *over* or *up*) to tilt or cause to tilt, so as to overturn or fall. **3.** *Brit.* to dump (rubbish, etc.). **4. tip one's hat.** to raise one's hat in salutation. ~*n.* **5.** a tipping or being tipped. **6.** *Brit.* a dump for refuse, etc. [C14: from ?] —'**tipper** *n.*

tip³ (tɪp) *n.* **1.** a payment given for services in excess of the standard charge; gratuity. **2.** a helpful hint or warning. **3.** a piece of inside information, esp. in betting or investing. ~*vb.* **tipping, tipped. 4.** to give a tip to. [C18: ?from TIP⁴] —'**tipper** *n.*

tip⁴ (tɪp) *vb.* **tipping, tipped.** (*tr.*) **1.** to hit or strike lightly. ~*n.* **2.** a light blow. [C13: ?from Low G *tippen*]

tip-off *n.* **1.** a warning or hint, esp. given confidentially and based on inside information. **2.** *Basketball.* the act or an instance of putting the ball in play by the referee throwing it high between two opposing players. ~*vb.* **tip off. 3.** (*tr., adv.*) to give a hint or warning to.

Tipperary (,tɪpə'rɛərɪ) *n.* a county of S Ireland, in Munster province: mountainous. County town: Clonmel. Pop.: 136 504 (1986). Area: 4255 sq. km (1643 sq. miles).

tipper truck *or* **lorry** *n.* a truck or lorry the rear platform of which can be raised at the front end to enable the load to be discharged.

tippet ('tɪpɪt) *n.* **1.** a woman's fur cape for the shoulders. **2.** the long stole of Anglican clergy worn during a service. **3.** a long streamer-like part to a sleeve, hood, etc., esp. in the 16th century. [C14: ?from TIP¹]

Tippett ('tɪpɪt) *n.* Sir **Michael.** born 1905, English composer, whose works include the oratorio *A Child of Our Time* (1941) and the operas *The Midsummer Marriage* (1952), *King Priam* (1961), *The Knot Garden* (1970), and *The Ice Break* (1976).

tipple ('tɪpəl) *vb.* **1.** to make a habit of taking (alcoholic drink), esp. in small quantities. ~*n.* **2.** alcoholic drink. [C15: back formation from obs. *tippler* tapster, from ?] —'**tippler** *n.*

tipstaff ('tɪp,stɑːf) *n.* **1.** a court official. **2.** a metal-tipped staff formerly used as a symbol of office. [C16 *tipped staff*]

tipster ('tɪpstə) *n.* a person who sells tips on horse racing, the stock market, etc.

tipsy ('tɪpsɪ) *adj.* **-sier, -siest. 1.** slightly drunk. **2.** slightly tilted or tipped; askew. [C16: from TIP²] —'**tipsily** *adv.* —'**tipsiness** *n.*

tipsy cake *n. Brit.* a kind of trifle made from a sponge cake soaked with wine or sherry and decorated with almonds and crystallized fruit.

tiptoe ('tɪp,təʊ) *vb.* **-toeing, -toed.** (*intr.*) **1.** to walk with the heels off the ground. **2.** to walk silently or stealthily. ~*n.* **3. on tiptoe. a.** on the tips of the toes or on the ball of the foot and the toes. **b.** eagerly anticipating something. **c.** stealthily or silently. ~*adv.* **4.** on tiptoe. ~*adj.* **5.** walking or standing on tiptoe.

tiptop (,tɪp'tɒp) *adj., adv.* **1.** at the highest point of health, excellence, etc. **2.** at the topmost point. ~*n.* **3.** the best in quality: **4.** the topmost point.

tip-up *adj.* (*prenominal*) able to be turned upwards around a hinge or pivot: *a tip-up seat.*

Tipu Sahib *or* **Tippoo Sahib** ('tɪpuː 'sɑːɪb) *n.* ?1750–99, sultan of Mysore (1782–99): killed fighting the British.

TIR *abbrev. for* Transports Internationaux Routiers. [F: International Road Transport]

tirade (taɪ'reɪd) *n.* a long angry speech or denunciation. [C19: from F, lit.: a pulling, from It. *tirata*, from *tirare* to pull, from ?]

Tiran (tɪ'rɑːn) *n.* **Strait of.** a strait between the Gulf of Aqaba and the Red Sea. Length: 16 km (10 miles). Width: 8 km (5 miles).

Tirana (tɪ'rɑːnə) *or* **Tiranë** (*Albanian* tɪ'ranə) *n.* the capital of Albania, in the central part 32 km (20 miles) from the Adriatic: founded in the early 17th century by Turks; became capital in 1920; the country's largest city and industrial centre. Pop.: 206 000 (1983).

tire¹ ('taɪə) *vb.* **1.** (*tr.*) to reduce the energy of, esp. by exertion; weary. **2.** (*tr.; often passive*) to reduce the tolerance of; bore or irritate: *I'm tired of the children's chatter.* **3.** (*intr.*) to become wearied or bored; flag. [OE *tēorian*, from ?] —'**tiring** *adj.*

tire² ('taɪə) *n., vb.* the U.S. spelling of **tyre.**

tired ('taɪəd) *adj.* **1.** weary; fatigued. **2.** no longer fresh; hackneyed. **3. tired and emotional.** *Euphemistic.* drunk.

Tiree (taɪ'riː) *n.* an island off the W coast of Scotland, in the Inner Hebrides. Pop.: 1054 (1971). Area: 78 sq. km (30 sq. miles).

tireless ('taɪəlɪs) *adj.* unable to be tired. —'**tirelessly** *adv.* —'**tirelessness** *n.*

Tiresias (taɪ'riːsɪˌæs) *n.* a blind soothsayer of Thebes, who revealed to Oedipus that the latter had murdered his father and married his mother.

tiresome ('taɪəsəm) *adj.* boring and irritating. —'**tiresomely** *adv.* —'**tiresomeness** *n.*

tirewoman ('taɪə,wʊmən) *n., pl.* **-women.** an obsolete term for a lady's maid. [C17: from *tire* (obs.) to ATTIRE]

Tîrgu Mureş (*Romanian* 'tirgu 'mureʃ) *n.* a city in central Romania: manufacturing and cultural centre. Pop.: 136 679 (1978 est.).

Tirich Mir ('tɪərɪtʃ 'mɪə) *n.* a mountain in N Pakistan: highest peak of the Hindu Kush. Height: 7690 m (25 230 ft.).

tiring room *n. Arch.* a dressing room.

tiro ('taɪrəʊ) *n., pl.* **-ros.** a variant spelling of **tyro.**

Tirol (tɪ'rəʊl, 'tɪrəʊl; *German* ti'roːl) *n.* a variant spelling of **Tyrol.** —**Tirolese** (,tɪrə'liːz) *or* ,**Tiro'lean** *adj., n.*

Tirpitz (*German* 'tɪrpɪts) *n.* **Alfred von** ('alfreːt fɔn). 1849–1930, German admiral: as secretary of state for the Imperial Navy (1897–1916), he created the modern German navy, which challenged British supremacy at sea.

Tirso de Molina (*Spanish* 'tirso ðe mo'lina) *n.* pen name of *Gabriel Téllez.* ?1571–1648, Spanish dramatist; author

of the first dramatic treatment of the Don Juan legend *El Burlador de Sevilla* (1630).

Tiruchirapalli (,tɪrətʃɪrə'pʌlɪ, tɪ,ruːtʃɪ'rɑːpəlɪ) *or* **Trichinopoly** *n.* an industrial city in S India, in central Tamil Nadu on the Cauvery River: dominated by a rock fortress 83 m (273 ft.). high. Pop.: 360 919 (1981).

Tirunelveli (,tɪruː'nelvɛlɪ) *n.* a city in S India, in Tamil Nadu: site of St Francis Xavier's first preaching in India; textile manufacturing. Pop.: 608 000 (1981).

'tis (tɪz) *Poetic or dialect. contraction of* it is.

Tisa ('tisa) *n.* the Slavonic and Romanian name for the **Tisza.**

tisane (tɪ'zæn) *n.* an infusion of leaves or flowers. [C19: from F, from L *ptisana* barley water]

Tishri *Hebrew.* (tɪʃ'riː) *n.* (in the Jewish calendar) the seventh month of the year according to biblical reckoning and the first month of the civil year, falling in September and October. [C19: from Heb.]

Tisiphone (tɪ'sɪfənɪ) *n. Greek myth.* one of the three Furies; the others are Alecto and Megaera.

tissue ('tɪsjuː, 'tɪʃuː) *n.* **1.** a part of an organism consisting of a large number of cells having a similar structure and function: nerve tissue. **2.** a thin piece of soft absorbent paper used as a disposable handkerchief, towel, etc. **3.** See **tissue paper. 4.** an interwoven series: *a tissue of lies.* **5.** a woven cloth, esp. of a light gauzy nature. ~*vb.* (*tr.*) **6.** to decorate or clothe with tissue or tissue paper. [C14: from OF *tissu* woven cloth, from *tistre* to weave, from L *texere*]

tissue culture *n.* **1.** the growth of small pieces of animal or plant tissue in a sterile controlled medium. **2.** the tissue produced.

tissue paper *n.* very thin soft delicate paper used to wrap breakable goods, as decoration, etc.

Tisza (*Hungarian* 'tisɔ) *n.* a river in S central Europe, rising in the W Ukrainian SSR of the Soviet Union and flowing west, forming part of the border between the Soviet Union and Romania, then southwest across Hungary into Yugoslavia to the Danube north of Belgrade. Slavonic and Romanian name: **Tisa.**

tit¹ (tɪt) *n.* any of numerous small active Old World songbirds, esp. the bluetit, great tit, etc. They have a short bill and feed on insects and seeds. [C16: ? imit., applied to small animate or inanimate objects]

tit² (tɪt) *n.* **1.** *Sl.* a female breast. **2.** a teat or nipple. **3.** *Derog.* a young woman. **4.** *Taboo sl.* a despicable or unpleasant person. [OE *titt*]

Tit. *Bible. abbrev. for* Titus.

titan ('taɪt²n) *n.* a person of great strength or size. [after TITAN]

Titan ('taɪt²n) *or* (*fem.*) **Titaness** *n. Greek myth.* **1.** any of a family of primordial gods, the sons and daughters of Uranus (sky) and Gaea (earth). **2.** any of the offspring of the children of Uranus and Gaea. —**Titanesque** (,taɪtə'nɛsk) *adj.*

Titania (tɪ'tɑːnɪə) *n.* **1.** (in medieval folklore) the queen of the fairies and wife of Oberon. **2.** (in classical antiquity) a poetic epithet used variously to characterize Circe, Diana, Latona, or Pyrrha.

titanic (taɪ'tænɪk) *adj.* possessing or requiring colossal strength: *a titanic battle.*

titanium (taɪ'teɪnɪəm) *n.* a strong malleable white metallic element, which is very corrosion-resistant. It is used in the manufacture of strong lightweight alloys, esp. aircraft parts. Symbol: Ti; atomic no.: 22; atomic wt.: 47.90. [C18: NL; see TITAN, -IUM]

titanium dioxide *n.* a white powder used chiefly as a pigment. Formula: TiO_2. Also called: **titanium oxide, titanic oxide, titania.**

titbit ('tɪt,bɪt) *or esp. U.S.* **tidbit** *n.* **1.** a tasty small piece of food; dainty. **2.** a pleasing scrap of anything, such as scandal. [C17: ?from dialect *tid* tender, from ?]

titchy *or* **tichy** ('tɪtʃɪ) *adj.* **-chier, -chiest.** *Brit. sl.* very small; tiny. [C20: from *tich* or *titch* a small person, from *Little Tich,* stage name of Harry Relph (1867–1928), E actor noted for his small stature]

titfer ('tɪtfə) *n. Brit. sl.* a hat. [from rhyming slang *tit for tat*]

tit for tat *n.* an equivalent given in return or retaliation; blow for blow. [C16: from earlier *tip for tap*]

tithe (taɪð) *n.* **1.** (*often pl.*) a tenth part of produce, income, or profits, contributed for the support of the church or clergy. **2.** any levy, esp. of one tenth. **3.** a tenth or very small part of anything. ~*vb.* **4.** (*tr.*) **a.** to exact or demand a tithe from. **b.** to levy a tithe upon. **5.** (*intr.*) to pay a tithe or tithes. [OE *teogoth*] —'**tithable** *adj.*

tithe barn *n.* a large barn where, formerly, the agricultural tithe of a parish was stored.

Tithonus (tɪ'θəʊnəs) *n. Greek myth.* the son of Laomedon of Troy who was loved by the goddess Eos. She asked that he be made immortal but forgot to ask that he be made eternally young. When he aged she turned him into a grasshopper.

titi ('tiːtiː) *n.*, *pl.* **-tis.** any of a genus of small New World monkeys of South America, having beautifully coloured fur and a long tail. [via Sp. from Aymara, lit.: little cat]

Titian ('tɪʃən) *n.* original name *Tiziano Vecellio.* ?1490–1576, Italian painter of the Venetian school, noted for his religious and mythological works, such as *Bacchus and Ariadne* (1523), and his portraits. —,**Titian'esque** *adj.*

Titian red *n.* a reddish-yellow colour, as in the hair colour in many of the works of Titian.

Titicaca (*Spanish* titi'kaka) *n.* **Lake.** a lake between S Peru and W Bolivia, in the Andes: the highest large lake in the world; drained by the Desaguadero River flowing into Lake Poopó. Area: 8135 sq. km (3141 sq. miles). Altitude: 3809 m (12 497 ft.). Depth: 370 m (1214 ft.).

titillate ('tɪtɪˌleɪt) *vb.* (*tr.*) **1.** to arouse or excite pleasurably. **2.** to cause a tickling or tingling sensation in, esp. by touching. [C17: from L *titillāre*] —'**titil,lating** *adj.* —,**titil'lation** *n.*

titivate *or* **tittivate** ('tɪtɪˌveɪt) *vb.* to smarten up; spruce up. [C19: earlier *tidivate*, ? based on TIDY & CULTIVATE] —,**titi'vation** *or* ,**titti'vation** *n.*

titlark ('tɪtˌlɑːk) *n.* another name for **pipit**, esp. the meadow pipit. [C17: from TIT¹ + LARK¹]

title ('taɪt³l) *n.* **1.** the distinctive name of a work of art, musical or literary composition, etc. **2.** a descriptive name or heading of a section of a book, speech, etc. **3.** See **title page.** **4.** a name or epithet signifying rank, office, or function. **5.** a formal designation, such as *Mr.* **6.** an appellation designating nobility. **7.** *Films.* **a.** short for **subtitle.** **b.** written material giving credits in a film or television programme. **8.** *Sport.* a championship. **9.** *Law.* **a.** the legal right to possession of property, esp. real property. **b.** the basis of such right. **c.** the documentary evidence of such right: *title deeds.* **10. a.** any customary or established right. **b.** a claim based on such a right. **11.** a definite spiritual charge or office in the church as a prerequisite for ordination. **12.** *R.C. Church.* a titular church. ~*vb.* **13.** (*tr.*) to give a title to. [C13: from OF, from L *titulus*]

title deed *n.* a document evidencing a person's legal right or title to property, esp. real property.

titleholder ('taɪt³l,həʊldə) *n.* a person who holds a title, esp. a sporting championship.

title page *n.* the page in a book that gives the title, author, publisher, etc.

title role *n.* the role of the character after whom a play, etc., is named.

titmouse ('tɪt,maʊs) *n.*, *pl.* **-mice.** another name for **tit¹**. [C14 *titemous*, from *tite* (see TIT¹) + MOUSE]

Tito ('tiːtəʊ) *n.* Marshal. original name *Josip Broz.* 1892–1980, Yugoslav statesman, who led the communist guerrilla resistance to German occupation during World War II; prime minister of Yugoslavia (1945–53) and president (1953–80).

Titograd (*Serbo-Croatian* 'titɔgraːd) *n.* a city in S Yugoslavia, capital of Montenegro: under Turkish rule (1474–1878). Pop.: 132 290 (1981). Former name (until 1946): **Podgorica.**

titrate ('taɪtreɪt) *vb.* (*tr.*) to measure the volume or concentration of (a solution) by titration. [C19: from F *titrer*; see TITRE] —**ti'tratable** *adj.*

titration (taɪ'treɪʃən) *n.* an operation in which a measured amount of one solution is added to a known quantity of another solution until the reaction between the two is complete. If the concentration of one solution is known, that of the other can be calculated.

titre *or U.S.* **titer** ('taɪtə) *n.* the concentration of a solution as determined by titration. [C19: from F *titre* proportion of gold or silver in an alloy, from OF *title* TITLE]

titter ('tɪtə) *vb.* (*intr.*) **1.** to snigger, esp. derisively or in a suppressed way. ~*n.* **2.** a suppressed laugh, chuckle, or snigger. [C17: imit.] —'**titterer** *n.* —'**tittering** *adj.*

tittle ('tɪt³l) *n.* **1.** a small mark in printing or writing, esp. a diacritic. **2.** a jot; particle. [C14: from Med. L *titulus* label, from L: title]

tittle-tattle *n.* **1.** idle chat or gossip. ~*vb.* **2.** (*intr.*) to chatter or gossip. —'**tittle-,tattler** *n.*

tittup ('tɪtəp) *vb.* **-tupping, -tupped** *or U.S.* **-tuping, -tuped.** **1.** (*intr.*) to prance or frolic. ~*n.* **2.** a caper. [C18 (in the sense: a horse's gallop): prob. imit.]

titubation (,tɪtjʊ'beɪʃən) *n. Pathol.* a disordered gait characterized by stumbling or staggering, often caused by a lesion of the cerebellum. [C17: from L *titubātiō*, from *titubāre* to reel]

titular ('tɪtjʊlə) *adj.* **1.** of, relating to, or of the nature of a title. **2.** in name only. **3.** bearing a title. **4.** *R.C. Church.* designating any of certain churches in Rome to whom cardinals or bishops are attached as their nominal incumbents. ~*n.* **5.** the bearer of a title. **6.** the bearer of a nominal office. [C18: from F *titulaire*, from L *titulus* title]

Titus ('taɪtəs) *n.* **1.** *New Testament.* **a.** a Greek disciple and helper of Saint Paul. **b.** the book written to him (in full **The Epistle of Paul the Apostle to Titus**), containing advice on pastoral matters. **2.** full name *Titus Flavius Sabinus Vespasianus.* ?40–81 A.D., Roman emperor (78–81 A.D.).

Tiu ('tiːuː) *n.* (in Anglo-Saxon mythology) the god of war and the sky. Norse counterpart: **Tyr.**

Tivoli ('tɪvəlɪ; *Italian* 'tiːvoli) *n.* a town in central Italy, east of Rome: a summer resort in Roman times; contains the Renaissance Villa d'Este and the remains of Hadrian's Villa. Pop.: 51 528 (1981 est.). Ancient name: **Tibur.**

tizzy ('tɪzɪ) *n.*, *pl.* **-zies.** *Inf.* a state of confusion or excitement. Also called: **tizz, tiz-woz.** [C19: from ?]

Tjirebon *or* **Cheribon** ('tʃɪərə,bɒn) *n.* a port in S central Indonesia, on N Java on the Java Sea: scene of the signing of the **Tjirebon Agreement** of Indonesian independence (1946) by the Netherlands. Pop.: 223 776 (1980).

T-junction *n.* a road junction in which one road joins another at right angles but does not cross it.

TKO *Boxing. abbrev. for* technical knockout.

Tl *the chemical symbol for* thallium.

Tlaxcala (*Spanish* tlas'kala) *n.* **1.** a state of S central Mexico: the smallest Mexican state; formerly an Indian principality, the chief Indian ally of Cortés in the conquest of Mexico. Capital: Tlaxcala. Pop.: 547 261 (1980). Area: 3914 sq. km (1511 sq. miles). **2.** a city in E central Mexico, capital of Tlaxcala state: the church of San Francisco (founded 1521 by Cortés) is the oldest in the Americas. Pop.: 13 000 (1980). Official name: **Tlaxcala de Xicohténcatl.**

Tlemcen (*French* tlɛm'sɛn) *n.* a city in NW Algeria: capital of an Arab kingdom from the 12th to the late 14th century. Pop.: 146 089 (1983).

Tm *the chemical symbol for* thulium.

TM *abbrev. for* transcendental meditation.

tmesis (tə'miːsɪs) *n.* interpolation of a word or words between the parts of a compound word, as in *every-bloom-ing-where.* [C16: via L from Gk, lit.: a cutting, from *temnein* to cut]

TNT *n.* 2,4,6-trinitrotoluene; a yellow solid: used chiefly as a high explosive.

T-number *or* **T number** *n. Photog.* a function of the f-number of a lens that takes into account the light transmitted by the lens. [from T(*otal Light Transmission*) *Number*]

to (tuː; *unstressed* tʊ, tə) *prep.* **1.** used to indicate the destination of the subject or object of an action: *he climbed to the top.* **2.** used to mark the indirect object of a verb: *telling stories to children.* **3.** used to mark the infinitive of a verb: *he wanted to go.* **4.** as far as; until: *working from Monday to Friday.* **5.** used to indicate equality: *16 ounces to the pound.* **6.** against; upon; onto: *put your ear to the wall.* **7.** before the hour of: *five to four.* **8.** accompanied by: *dancing to loud music.* **9.** as compared with, as against: *the score was eight to three.* **10.** used to indicate a resulting condition: *they starved to death.* ~*adv.* **11.** towards a fixed position, esp. (of a door) closed. [OE *tō*]

▷ **Usage.** In formal usage, *to* is always used with an infinitive and never omitted as in *come see the show.* The use of *and* instead of *to* (*try and come*) is very common in informal speech but is avoided by careful writers.

toad (təud) n. **1.** any of a group of amphibians similar to frogs but more terrestrial, having a drier warty skin. **2.** a loathsome person. [OE *tādige*, from ?] —'**toadish** adj.

toadfish ('təud,fɪʃ) n., pl. **-fish** or **-fishes.** any of various spiny-finned marine fishes of tropical and temperate seas.

toadflax ('təud,flæks) n. a perennial plant having narrow leaves and spurred two-lipped yellow-orange flowers. Also called: **butter-and-eggs.**

toad-in-the-hole n. Brit. a dish made of sausages baked in a batter.

toadstone ('təud,stəun) n. an intrusive volcanic rock occurring in limestone. [C18: ?from a supposed resemblance to a toad's spotted skin]

toadstool ('təud,stu:l) n. (not in technical use) any basidiomycetous fungus with a capped spore-producing body that is poisonous. Cf. **mushroom.**

toady ('təudɪ) n., pl. **toadies. 1.** Also: **toadeater.** a person who flatters and ingratiates himself in a servile way; sycophant. ~vb. **toadying, toadied. 2.** to fawn on and flatter (someone). [C19: shortened from *toadeater*, orig. a quack's assistant who pretended to eat toads, hence a flatterer] —'**toadyish** adj. —'**toadyism** n.

Toamasina (Portuguese təuma'sinə) n. a port in E Madagascar, on the Indian Ocean: the country's chief commercial centre. Pop.: 82 907 (1982 est.). Former name (until 1979): **Tamatave.**

to and fro adj., **to-and-fro** adv. **1.** back and forth. **2.** here and there. —'**toing and 'froing** n.

toast[1] (təust) n. **1. a.** sliced bread browned by exposure to heat. **b.** (as modifier): a toast rack. ~vb. **2.** (tr.) to brown under a grill or over a fire: to toast cheese. **3.** to warm or be warmed: to toast one's hands by the fire. [C14: from OF *toster*, from L *tōstus* parched, from *torrēre* to dry with heat]

toast[2] (təust) n. **1.** a tribute or proposal of health, success, etc., given to a person or thing and marked by people raising glasses and drinking together. **2.** a person or thing honoured by such a tribute or proposal. **3.** (esp. formerly) an attractive woman to whom such tributes are frequently made. ~vb. **4.** to propose or drink a toast to (a person or thing). **5.** (intr.) to add vocal effects to a prerecorded track: a disc-jockey technique. [C17 (in the sense: a lady to whom the company is asked to drink): from TOAST[1], from the idea that the name of the lady would flavour the drink like a piece of spiced toast] —'**toaster** n.

toaster ('təustə) n. a device, esp. an electrical device, for toasting bread.

toastmaster ('təust,mɑːstə) n. a person who introduces speakers, proposes toasts, etc., at public dinners. —'**toast,mistress** fem. n.

toasty or **toastie** ('təustɪ) n., pl. **toasties.** a toasted sandwich.

Tob. abbrev. for Tobit.

tobacco (tə'bækəu) n., pl. **-cos** or **-coes. 1.** any of a genus of plants having mildly narcotic properties, one species of which is cultivated as the chief source of commercial tobacco. **2.** the leaves of certain of these plants dried and prepared for snuff, chewing, or smoking. [C16: from Sp. *tabaco*, ?from Taino: leaves rolled for smoking, assumed by the Spaniards to be the name of the plant]

tobacco mosaic virus n. the virus that causes mosaic disease in tobacco and related plants: its discovery provided the first evidence of the existence of viruses. Abbrev.: **TMV.**

tobacconist (tə'bækənɪst) n. Chiefly Brit. a person or shop that sells tobacco, cigarettes, pipes, etc.

Tobago (tə'beɪgəu) n. an island in the SE West Indies, northeast of Trinidad: ceded to Britain in 1814; joined with Trinidad in 1888 as a British colony; part of the independent republic of Trinidad and Tobago. Pop.: 40 700 (1980). —**Tobagonian** (,təubə'gəunɪən) adj., n.

-to-be adj. (in combination) about to be; future: a mother-to-be; the bride-to-be.

Tobey ('təubɪ) n. **Mark.** 1890–1976, U.S. painter. Influenced by Chinese calligraphy, he devised a style of improvisatory abstract painting called "white writing".

Tobit ('təubɪt) n. Old Testament. **1.** a pious Jew who was released from blindness through the help of the archangel Raphael. **2.** a book of the Apocrypha relating this story.

toboggan (tə'bɒgən) n. **1.** a light wooden frame on runners used for sliding over snow and ice. **2.** a long narrow sledge made of a thin board curved upwards at the front.

~vb. (intr.) **3.** to ride on a toboggan. [C19: from Canad. F, of Amerind origin] —**to'bogganer** or **to'bogganist** n.

Tobol (Russian ta'bɔl) n. a river in the central Soviet Union, rising in the N Kazakh SSR and flowing northeast to the Irtysh River. Length: about 1300 km (800 miles).

Tobolsk (Russian ta'bɔljsk) n. a town in the central Soviet Union, at the confluence of the Irtysh and Tobol Rivers: the chief centre for the early Russian colonization of Siberia. Pop.: 69 000 (1983 est.).

Tobruk (tə'bruk, təu-) n. a small port in NE Libya, in E Cyrenaica on the Mediterranean coast road: scene of severe fighting in World War II: taken from the Italians by the British in January 1941, from the British by the Germans in June 1942, and finally taken by the British in November 1942.

toby ('təubɪ) n., pl. **-bies.** N.Z. a water stopcock at the boundary of a street and house section.

toby jug n. a beer mug or jug in the form of a stout seated man wearing a three-cornered hat and smoking a pipe. Also called: **toby.** [C19: from the familiar form of the name *Tobias*]

Tocantins (Portuguese tokã'tĩs) n. a river in E Brazil, rising in S central Goiás state and flowing generally north to the Pará River. Length: about 2700 km (1700 miles).

toccata (tə'kɑːtə) n. a rapid keyboard composition for organ, harpsichord, etc., usually in a rhythmically free style. [C18: from It., lit.: touched, from *toccare* to play (an instrument)]

Toc H ('tɒk 'eɪtʃ) n. a society formed after World War I to encourage Christian comradeship. [C20: from the obs. telegraphic code for *T.H.*, initials of Talbot House, Poperinge, Belgium, the original headquarters of the society]

Tocharian or **Tokharian** (tɒ'kɑːrɪən) n. **1.** a member of an Asian people who lived in the Tarim Basin until around 800 A.D. **2.** the language of this people, known from records in a N Indian script of the 7th and 8th centuries A.D. [C20: ult. from Gk *Tokharoi*, from ?]

tocopherol (tɒ'kɒfə,rɒl) n. any of a group of fat-soluble alcohols that occur in wheat-germ oil, lettuce, egg yolk, etc. Also called: **vitamin E.** [C20: from *toco-*, from Gk *tokos* offspring + *-pher-*, from *pherein* to bear + -OL[1]]

Tocqueville ('təukvɪl, 'tɒk-; French tɔkvil) n. **Alexis Charles Henri Maurice Clérel de** (alɛksi ʃarl ɑːri mɔris klerɛl də). 1805–59, French politician and political writer. His chief works are De la Démocratie en Amérique (1835–40) and L'Ancien régime et la révolution (1856).

tocsin ('tɒksɪn) n. **1.** an alarm or warning signal, esp. one sounded on a bell. **2.** an alarm bell. [C16: from F, from OF *toquassen*, from OProvençal, from *tocar* to touch + *senh* bell, from L *signum*]

tod (tɒd) n. **on one's tod.** Brit. sl. on one's own. [C19: rhyming sl. Tod Sloan/alone, after Tod Sloan, a jockey]

today (tə'deɪ) n. **1.** this day, as distinct from yesterday or tomorrow. **2.** the present age. ~adv. **3.** during or on this day. **4.** nowadays. [OE *tō dæge*, lit.: on this day]

Todd (tɒd) n. Baron **Alexander Robertus.** born 1907, Scottish chemist, noted for his research into the structure of nucleic acids: Nobel prize for chemistry 1957.

toddle ('tɒdᵊl) vb. (intr.) **1.** to walk with short unsteady steps, as a child. **2.** (foll. by off) Jocular. to depart. **3.** (foll. by round, over, etc.) Jocular. to stroll. ~n. **4.** the act or an instance of toddling. [C16 (Scot. & N English): from ?]

toddler ('tɒdlə) n. a young child, usually between the ages of one and two and a half.

toddy ('tɒdɪ) n., pl. **-dies. 1.** a drink made from spirits, esp. whisky, hot water, sugar, and usually lemon juice. **2.** the sap of various palm trees used as a beverage. [C17: from Hindi *tārī* juice of the palmyra palm, from *tār* palmyra palm, from Sansk. *tāra*]

to-do (tə'duː) n., pl. **-dos.** a commotion, fuss, or quarrel.

toe (təu) n. **1.** any one of the digits of the foot. **2.** the corresponding part in other vertebrates. **3.** the part of a shoe, etc., covering the toes. **4.** anything resembling a toe in shape or position. **5. on one's toes.** alert. **6. tread on someone's toes.** to offend a person, esp. by trespassing on his field of responsibility. ~vb. **toeing, toed. 7.** (tr.) to touch, kick, or mark with the toe. **8.** (tr.) to drive (a nail, etc.) obliquely. **9.** (intr.) to walk with the toes pointing in a specified direction: to toe inwards. **10. toe the line** or **mark.** to conform to expected attitudes, standards, etc. [OE *tā*]

toe and heel *n.* a technique used by racing drivers on sharp bends, in which the brake and accelerator are operated simultaneously by the toe and heel of the right foot.

toecap ('təʊ,kæp) *n.* a reinforced covering for the toe of a boot or shoe.

toed (təʊd) *adj.* **1.** having a part resembling a toe. **2.** fixed by nails driven in at the foot. **3.** (*in combination*) having a toe or toes as specified: *five-toed; thick-toed.*

toehold ('təʊ,həʊld) *n.* **1.** a small foothold to facilitate climbing. **2.** any means of gaining access, support, etc. **3.** a wrestling hold in which the opponent's toe is held and his leg twisted.

toe-in *n.* a slight forward convergence given to the wheels of motor vehicles to improve steering.

toenail ('təʊ,neɪl) *n.* **1.** a thin horny translucent plate covering part of the surface of the end joint of each toe. **2.** *Carpentry.* a nail driven obliquely. ~*vb.* **3.** (*tr.*) *Carpentry.* to join (beams) by driving nails obliquely.

toerag ('təʊ,ræg) *n. Brit. sl.* a contemptible or despicable person. [C20: orig., a beggar, tramp: from the rags wrapped round their feet]

toey ('təʊɪ) *adj. Austral. sl.* nervous and restless; anxious.

toff (tɒf) *n. Brit. sl.* a well-dressed or upper-class person, esp. a man. [C19: ? var. of TUFT, nickname for a commoner at Oxford University]

toffee *or* **toffy** ('tɒfɪ) *n.*, *pl.* **-fees** *or* **-fies**. **1.** a sweet made from sugar or treacle boiled with butter, nuts, etc. **2. for toffee.** (preceded by *can't*) *Inf.* to be incompetent at: *he can't sing for toffee.* [C19: var. of earlier *taffy*]

toffee-apple *n.* an apple fixed on a stick and coated with a thin layer of toffee.

toffee-nosed *adj. Sl., chiefly Brit.* pretentious or supercilious; used esp. of snobbish people.

toft (tɒft) *n. British history.* **1.** a homestead. **2.** a homestead and its arable land. [OE]

tofu ('təʊ,fuː) *n.* unfermented soya-bean curd, a food with a soft cheeselike consistency. [from Japanese]

tog[1] (tɒg) *Inf.* ~*vb.* **togging, togged. 1.** (often foll. by *up* or *out*) to dress oneself, esp. in smart clothes. ~*n.* **2.** See **togs.** [C18: ?from obs. cant *togemans* coat, from L *toga* TOGA + *-mans*, from ?]

tog[2] (tɒg) *n.* a unit of thermal resistance used to measure the power of insulation of a fabric, garment, quilt, etc. **b.** (*as modifier*): *tog-rating.* [C20: arbitrary coinage from TOG[1] (n.)]

toga ('təʊgə) *n.* **1.** a garment worn by citizens of ancient Rome, consisting of a piece of cloth draped around the body. **2.** a robe of office. [C16: from L] —**togaed** ('təʊgəd) *adj.*

together (tə'gɛðə) *adv.* **1.** with cooperation and interchange between constituent elements, members, etc.: *we worked together.* **2.** in or into contact with each other: *to stick papers together.* **3.** in or into one place; with each other: *the people are gathered together.* **4.** at the same time. **5.** considered collectively: *all our wages put together couldn't buy that car.* **6.** continuously: *working for eight hours together.* **7.** closely or compactly united or held: *water will hold the dough together.* **8.** mutually or reciprocally: *to multiply seven and eight together.* **9.** *Inf.* organized: *to get things together.* ~*adj.* **10.** *Sl.* self-possessed, competent, and well-organized. **11. together with.** in addition to. [OE *tōgædre*]
▷ **Usage.** See at **plus.**

togetherness (tə'gɛðənɪs) *n.* a feeling of closeness or affection from being united with other people.

toggery ('tɒgərɪ) *n. Inf.* clothes; togs.

toggle ('tɒg°l) *n.* **1.** a peg or rod at the end of a rope, chain, or cable, for fastening by insertion through an eye in another rope, chain, etc. **2.** a bar-shaped button inserted through a loop for fastening. **3.** a toggle joint or a device having such a joint. ~*vb.* **4.** (*tr.*) to supply or fasten with a toggle. [C18: from ?]

toggle joint *n.* a device consisting of two arms pivoted at a common joint and at their outer ends and used to apply pressure by straightening the angle between the two arms.

toggle switch *n.* **1.** an electric switch having a projecting lever that is manipulated in a particular way to open or close a circuit. **2.** a computer device used to turn a feature on or off.

Togliatti (,tɒlɪ'ætɪ) *n.* a city in the W central Soviet Union, on the Volga River: automobile industry: renamed in honour of Palmiro Togliatti, an Italian communist. Pop.: 627 000 (1987). Former name (until 1964): **Stavropol.** Russian name: **Tol'yatti.**

Togo[1] ('təʊgəʊ) *n.* a republic in West Africa, on the Gulf of Guinea: became French Togoland (a League of Nations mandate) after the division of German Togoland in 1922; independent since 1960. Official language: French. Religion: animist majority. Currency: franc. Capital: Lomé. Pop.: 3 158 000 (1987 est.). Area: 56 700 sq. km (20 900 sq. miles). —**Togolese** (,təʊgə'liːz) *adj.*, *n.*

Togo[2] ('təʊgəʊ) *n.* Marquis **Heihachiro** (,heɪhɑː'tʃiːrəʊ) 1847–1934, Japanese admiral, who commanded the Japanese fleet in the war with Russia (1904–05).

Togoland ('təʊgəʊ,lænd) *n.* a former German protectorate in West Africa on the Gulf of Guinea: divided in 1922 into the League of Nations mandates of British Togoland (west) and French Togoland (east); the former joined Ghana in 1957; the latter became independent as Togo in 1960. —**'Togo,lander** *n.*

togs (tɒgz) *pl. n. Inf.* **1.** clothes. **2.** *Austral. & N.Z.* a swimming costume. [from TOG[1]]

toheroa (,təʊə'rəʊə) *n.* a large edible bivalve mollusc of New Zealand with a distinctive flavour. [from Maori]

tohunga ('tɒhʊŋə) *n. N.Z.* a Maori priest, the repository of traditional lore.

toil[1] (tɔɪl) *n.* **1.** hard or exhausting work. ~*vb.* (*intr.*) **2.** to labour. **3.** to progress with slow painful movements. [C13: from Anglo-F *toiler* to struggle, from OF *toeillier* to confuse, from L *tudiculāre* to stir, ult. from *tundere* to beat] —**'toiler** *n.*

toil[2] (tɔɪl) *n.* **1.** (*often pl.*) a net or snare. **2.** *Arch.* a trap for wild beasts. [C16: from OF *toile*, from L *tēla* loom]

toile (twɑːl) *n.* **1.** a transparent linen or cotton fabric. **2.** a garment of exclusive design made up in cheap cloth so that alterations can be made. [C19: from F, from L *tēla* loom]

toilet ('tɔɪlɪt) *n.* **1.** another word for **lavatory. 2.** the act of dressing and preparing oneself. **3.** a dressing table. **4.** *Rare.* costume. **5.** the cleansing of a wound, etc., after an operation or childbirth. [C16: from F *toilette* dress, from TOILE]

toilet paper *or* **tissue** *n.* thin absorbent paper, often wound in a roll round a cardboard cylinder (**toilet roll**), used for cleaning oneself after defecation or urination.

toiletry ('tɔɪlɪtrɪ) *n.*, *pl.* **-ries.** an object or cosmetic used in making up, dressing, etc.

toilet set *n.* a matching set consisting of a hairbrush, comb, mirror, and clothes brush.

toilette (twɑː'lɛt) *n.* another word for **toilet** (sense 2). [C16: from F; see TOILET]

toilet water *n.* a form of liquid perfume lighter than cologne.

toilsome ('tɔɪlsəm) *or* **toilful** *adj.* laborious. —**'toil-somely** *adv.* —**'toilsomeness** *n.*

toitoi ('tɔɪtɔɪ) *n.* a tall New Zealand grass with feathery seed-heads. [from Maori]

Tojo ('təʊdʒəʊ) *n.* **Hideki** ('hiːdɛ,kiː). 1885–1948, Japanese soldier and statesman; minister of war (1940–41) and premier (1941–44); hanged as a war criminal.

tokamak ('təʊkə,mæk) *n. Physics.* a toroidal-shaped thermonuclear reactor designed for nuclear fusion in which strong magnetic fields keep the plasma from contacting the container walls. [C20: from Russian acronym, from *toroidalnaya kamera s magnitnym polem*, toroidal chamber with magnetic field]

Tokay (təʊ'keɪ) *n.* **1.** a sweet wine made near Tokaj, Hungary. **2.** a variety of grape used to make this. **3.** a similar wine made elsewhere.

Tokelau Islands ('təʊkə,laʊ) *pl. n.* an island group in the South Pacific composed of three atolls, Nukunono, Atafu, and Fakaofo, which in 1948 was included within the territorial boundaries of New Zealand. Area: about 11 sq. km (4 sq. miles).

token ('təʊkən) *n.* **1.** an indication, warning, or sign of something. **2.** a symbol or visible representation of something. **3.** something that indicates authority, proof, etc. **4.** a metal or plastic disc, such as a substitute for currency for use in slot machines. **5.** a memento. **6.** a gift voucher that can be used as payment for goods of a specified value. **7.** (*modifier*) as a matter of form only; nominal: *a token increase in salary.* ~*vb.* **8.** (*tr.*) to act or serve as a warning or symbol of; betoken. [OE *tācen*]

tokenism ('təυkə,nɪzəm) n. the practice of making only a token effort or doing no more than the minimum, esp. in order to comply with a law. —'**toke,nist** adj.

token money n. coins having greater face value than the value of their metal content.

token strike n. a brief strike intended to convey strength of feeling on a disputed issue.

token vote n. a Parliamentary vote of money in which the amount quoted is not binding.

tokoloshe (,tɒkɒ'lɒʃ, -'lɒʃɪ) n. (in Bantu folklore) a malevolent mythical manlike animal. Also called: **tikoloshe**. [from Xhosa uthikoloshe]

toktokkie ('tɒk,tɒkɪ) n. a large S. African beetle. [from Afrik., from Du. tokken to tap]

Tokugawa Ieyasu (,təυkuː'gɑːwə ,iːjeɪ'jɑːsuː) n. See (Tokugawa) **Ieyasu**.

Tokyo ('təυkjəυ, -kɪ,əυ) n. the capital of Japan, a port on SE Honshu on **Tokyo Bay** (an inlet of the Pacific): the largest city in the world since the 18th century, with a conurbation of over 25 million people; major industrial centre and the chief cultural centre of Japan. Pop.: 8 379 385 (1986 est.).

tolbooth ('təυl,buːθ, -,buːð, 'tɒl-) n. **1.** Chiefly Scot. a town hall. **2.** a variant spelling of **tollbooth**.

tolbutamide (tɒl'bjuːtə,maɪd) n. a synthetic crystalline compound used in the treatment of diabetes to lower blood glucose levels. [C20: from TOL(UENE) + BUT(YRIC ACID) + AMIDE]

told (təυld) vb. **1.** the past tense and past participle of **tell**[1]. ~adj. **2.** See **all told**.

tole (təυl) n. enamelled or lacquered metal ware, popular in the 18th century. [from F tôle sheet metal, from F (dialect): table, from L tabula table]

Toledo n. **1.** (tɒ'leɪdəυ; Spanish to'leðo). a city in central Spain, on the River Tagus: capital of Visigothic Spain, and of Castile from 1087 to 1560; famous for steel and swords since the first century. Pop.: 61 813 (1982 est.). Ancient name: **Toletum** (tə'liːtəm). **2.** (tə'liːdəυ). an inland port in NW Ohio, on Lake Erie: one of the largest coal-shipping ports in the world; transportation and industrial centre; university (1872). Pop.: 340 680 (1986 est.). **3.** a fine-tapered sword or sword blade.

tolerable ('tɒlərəb³l) adj. **1.** able to be tolerated; endurable. **2.** permissible. **3.** Inf. fairly good. —,**tolera'bility** n. —'**tolerably** adv.

tolerance ('tɒlərəns) n. **1.** the state or quality of being tolerant. **2.** capacity to endure something, esp. pain or hardship. **3.** the permitted variation in some characteristic of an object or workpiece. **4.** the capacity to endure the effects of a poison or other substance, esp. after it has been taken over a prolonged period.

tolerant ('tɒlərənt) adj. **1.** able to tolerate the beliefs, actions, etc., of others. **2.** permissive. **3.** able to withstand extremes. **4.** exhibiting tolerance to a drug. —'**tolerantly** adv.

tolerate ('tɒlə,reɪt) vb. (tr.) **1.** to treat with indulgence or forbearance. **2.** to permit. **3.** to be able to bear; put up with. **4.** to have tolerance for (a drug, etc.). [C16: from L tolerāre to sustain]

toleration (,tɒlə'reɪʃən) n. **1.** the act or practice of tolerating. **2.** freedom to hold religious opinions that differ from the established religion of a country. —,**toler'a-tionist** n.

Tolima (Spanish to'lima) n. a volcano in W Colombia, in the Andes. Height: 5215 m (17 110 ft.).

Tolkien ('tɒlkiːn) n. **J(ohn) R(onald) R(euel)**. 1892–1973, British philologist and writer, born in South Africa. He is best known for The Hobbit (1937), the trilogy The Lord of the Rings (1954–55), and the posthumously published Silmarillion (1977).

toll[1] (təυl) vb. **1.** to ring slowly and recurrently. **2.** (tr.) to summon or announce by tolling. **3.** U.S. & Canad. to decoy (game, esp. ducks). ~n. **4.** the act or sound of tolling. [C15: ? rel. to OE -tyllan, as in fortyllan to attract]

toll[2] (təυl, tɒl) n. **1. a.** an amount of money levied, esp. for the use of certain roads, bridges, etc. **b.** (as modifier): toll road; toll bridge. **2.** loss or damage incurred through a disaster, etc.: the war took its toll of the inhabitants. **3.** (formerly) the right to levy a toll. [OE toln]

tollbooth or **tolbooth** ('təυl,buːθ, -,buːð, 'tɒl-) n. a booth or kiosk at which a toll is collected.

Toller (German 'tɒlər) n. **Ernst** (ɛrnst). 1893–1939, German dramatist and revolutionary, noted particularly for his expressionist plays, esp. Masse Mensch (1921).

tollgate ('təυl,geɪt, 'tɒl-) n. a gate across a toll road or bridge at which travellers must pay.

tollhouse ('təυl,haυs, 'tɒl-) n. a small house at a tollgate occupied by a toll collector.

tollie ('tɒlɪ) n., pl. **-lies**. S. African. a castrated calf. [C19: from Xhosa ithole calf on which the horns have begun to appear]

Tolstoy ('tɒlstɔɪ; Russian tal'stɔj) n. **Leo**, Russian name Count Lev Nikolayevich Tolstoy. 1828–1910, Russian novelist, short-story writer, and philosopher; author of the two monumental novels War and Peace (1865–69) and Anna Karenina (1875–77). Following a spiritual crisis in 1879, he adopted a form of Christianity based on a doctrine of nonresistance to evil.

Toltec ('tɒltɛk) n., pl. **-tecs** or **-tec**. **1.** a member of a Central American Indian people who dominated the valley of Mexico until they were overrun by the Aztecs. ~adj. also **Toltecan**. **2.** of or relating to this people.

tolu (tɒ'luː) n. an aromatic balsam obtained from a South American tree. [C17: after Santiago de Tolu, Colombia, from which it was exported]

Toluca (Spanish to'luka) n. **1.** a city in S central Mexico, capital of Mexico state, at an altitude of 2640 m (8660 ft.). Pop.: 234 000 (1980). Official name: **Toluca de Lerdo** ('lɛrdo). **2. Nevado de** (ne'βaðo de). a volcano in central Mexico, in Mexico state near Toluca: crater partly filled by a lake. Height: 4577 m (15 017 ft.).

toluene ('tɒljυ,iːn) n. a colourless volatile flammable liquid obtained from petroleum and coal tar and used as a solvent and in the manufacture of many organic chemicals. [C19: from TOLU + -ENE, since it was previously obtained from tolu]

toluic acid (tɒ'luːɪk) n. a white crystalline derivative of toluene used in synthetic resins and as an insect repellent. [C19: from TOLU(ENE) + -IC]

toluidine (tɒ'ljuː,diːn) n. an amine derived from toluene, used in making dyes. [C19: from TOLU(ENE) + -IDE + -INE[2]]

tom (tɒm) n. **a.** the male of various animals, esp. the cat. **b.** (as modifier): a tom turkey. **c.** (in combination): a tomcat. [C16: special use of the short form of Thomas, applied to any male, often implying a common or ordinary type of person, etc.]

Tom, Dick, and (or) Harry n. an ordinary, undistinguished, or common person (esp. in **every Tom, Dick, and Harry; any Tom, Dick, or Harry**).

tomahawk ('tɒmə,hɔːk) n. a fighting axe with a stone or iron head, used by the North American Indians. [C17: from Algonquian tamahaac]

tomato (tə'mɑːtəυ) n., pl. **-toes**. **1.** a South American plant widely cultivated for its red fleshy many-seeded fruits. **2.** the fruit of this plant, eaten in salads, as a vegetable, etc. [C17 tomate, from Sp., from Nahuatl tomatl]

tomb (tuːm) n. **1.** a place, esp. a vault beneath the ground, for the burial of a corpse. **2.** a monument to the dead. **3. the tomb**. a poetic term for death. [C13: from OF tombe, from LL tumba burial mound, from Gk tumbos]

tombac ('tɒmbæk) n. any of various alloys containing copper and zinc: used for making cheap jewellery, etc. [C17: from F, from Du. tombak, from Malay tambāga copper, apparently from Sansk. tāmraka, from tāmra dark coppery red]

tombola (tɒm'bəυlə) n. Brit. a type of lottery, esp. at a fête, in which tickets are drawn from a revolving drum. [C19: from It., from tombolare to somersault]

Tombouctou (tɔbuktu) n. the French name for **Timbuktu**.

tomboy ('tɒm,bɔɪ) n. a girl who acts or dresses in a boyish way, liking rough outdoor activities. —'**tom,boyish** adj. —'**tom,boyishly** adv.

tombstone ('tuːm,stəυn) n. another word for **gravestone**.

Tom Collins n. a long drink consisting of gin, lime or lemon juice, sugar, and soda water.

tome (təυm) n. **1.** a large weighty book. **2.** one of the several volumes of a work. [C16: from F, from L tomus section of larger work, from Gk tomos a slice, from temnein to cut]

-tome *n. combining form.* indicating an instrument for cutting: *osteotome.* [from Gk *tomē* a cutting, *tomos* a slice, from *temnein* to cut]

tomentum (tə'mɛntəm) *n., pl.* **-ta** (-tə). **1.** a covering of downy hairs on leaves and other plant parts. **2.** a network of minute blood vessels occurring in the human brain. [C17: NL, from L: stuffing for cushions] —**to'mentose** *adj.*

tomfool (,tom'fuːl) *n.* **a.** a fool. **b.** (*as modifier*): *tomfool ideas.* —,**tom'foolishness** *n.*

tomfoolery (,tom'fuːlərɪ) *n., pl.* **-eries.** **1.** foolish behaviour. **2.** utter nonsense; rubbish.

tommy ('tomɪ) *n., pl.* **-mies.** (*often cap.*) *Brit. inf.* a private in the British Army. [C19: orig. *Thomas Atkins,* name representing typical private in specimen forms]

Tommy gun *n.* an informal name for **Thompson sub-machine-gun.**

tommyrot ('tomɪ,rot) *n.* utter nonsense.

tomography (tə'mogrəfɪ) *n.* a technique used to obtain an x-ray photograph of a plane section of the human body or some other object. [C20: from Gk *tomē* a cutting + -GRAPHY]

tomorrow (tə'morəʊ) *n.* **1.** the day after today. **2.** the future. ~*adv.* **3.** on the day after today. **4.** at some time in the future. [OE *tō morgenne,* from *to* on + *morgenne,* dative of *morgen* morning]

Tomsk (*Russian* tomsk) *n.* a city in the central Soviet Union: formerly an important gold-mining town and administrative centre for a large area of Siberia; university (1888); engineering industries. Pop.: 489 000 (1987).

Tom Thumb *n.* **1. General,** stage name of *Charles Stratton.* 1838–83, U.S. midget, exhibited in P. T. Barnum's circus. **2.** a dwarf; midget. [after *Tom Thumb,* the tiny hero of several English folk tales]

tomtit ('tom,tɪt) *n. Brit.* any of various tits, esp. the bluetit.

tom-tom *n.* a drum usually beaten with the hands as a signalling instrument. [C17: from Hindi *tamtam,* imit.]

-tomy *n. combining form.* indicating a surgical cutting of a specified part or tissue: *lobotomy.* [from Gk *-tomia*]

ton[1] (tʌn) *n.* **1.** Also called: **long ton.** *Brit.* a unit of weight equal to 2240 pounds or 1016.046 909 kilograms. **2.** Also called: **short ton, net ton.** *U.S. & Canad.* a unit of weight equal to 2000 pounds or 907.184 kilograms. **3.** See **metric ton, tonne.** a unit of weight equal to 1000 kilograms. **4.** Also called: **freight ton, measurement ton.** a unit of volume or weight used for charging or measuring freight in shipping. It is usually equal to 40 cubic feet, 1 cubic metre, or 1000 kilograms. **5.** Also called: **displacement ton.** a unit used for measuring the displacement of a ship, equal to 35 cubic feet of sea water or 2240 pounds. **6.** Also called: **register ton.** a unit of internal capacity of ships equal to 100 cubic feet. ~*adv.* **7. tons.** (*intensifier*): *the new flat is tons better than the old one.* [C14: var. of TUN]

ton[2] (tʌn) *n. Sl., chiefly Brit.* a score or achievement of a hundred, esp. a hundred miles per hour, as on a motorcycle. [C20: special use of TON[1] applied to quantities of one hundred]

tonal ('təʊnəl) *adj.* **1.** of or relating to tone. **2.** of or utilizing the diatonic system; having an established key. **3.** (of an answer in a fugue) not having the same melodic intervals as the subject, so as to remain in the original key. —'**tonally** *adv.*

tonality (təʊ'nælɪtɪ) *n., pl.* **-ties.** **1.** *Music.* **a.** the presence of a musical key in a composition. **b.** the system of major and minor keys prevalent in Western music. **2.** the overall scheme of colours and tones in a painting.

Tonbridge ('tʌn,brɪdʒ) *n.* a market town in SE England, in SW Kent on the River Medway. Pop.: 30 375 (1981).

tondo ('tondəʊ) *n., pl.* **-di** (-diː). a circular easel painting or relief carving. [C19: from It.: a circle, shortened from *rotondo* round]

tone (təʊn) *n.* **1.** sound with reference to quality, pitch, or volume. **2.** short for **tone colour. 3.** *U.S. & Canad.* another word for **note** (sense 10). **4.** an interval of a major second; whole tone. **5.** Also called: **Gregorian tone.** any of several plainsong melodies or other chants used in the singing of psalms. **6.** *Linguistics.* any of the pitch levels or pitch contours at which a syllable may be pronounced, such as high tone, falling tone, etc. **7.** the quality or character of a sound: *a nervous tone of voice.* **8.** general aspect, quality, or style. **9.** high quality or style: *to lower the*

tone of a place. **10.** the quality of a given colour, as modified by mixture with white or black; shade; tint. **11.** *Physiol.* **a.** the normal tension of a muscle at rest. **b.** the natural firmness of the tissues and normal functioning of bodily organs in health. **12.** the overall effect of the colour values and gradations of light and dark in a picture. **13.** *Photog.* a colour of a particular area on a negative or positive that can be distinguished from surrounding areas. ~*vb.* **14.** (*intr.; often foll. by with*) to be of a matching or similar tone (to). **15.** (*tr.*) to give a tone to or correct the tone of. **16.** (*tr.*) *Photog.* to soften or change the colour of the tones of (a photographic image). ~See also **tone down, tone up.** [C14: from L *tonus,* from Gk *tonos* tension, tone, from *teinein* to stretch] —'**toneless** *adj.* —'**tonelessly** *adv.*

tone arm *n.* another name for **pick-up.**

tone colour *n.* the quality of a musical sound that is conditioned or distinguished by the upper partials or overtones present in it.

tone-deaf *adj.* unable to distinguish subtle differences in musical pitch. —**tone deafness** *n.*

tone down *vb.* (*adv.*) to moderate or become moderated in tone: *to tone down an argument.*

tone language *n.* a language, such as Chinese, in which differences in tone may make differences in meaning.

toneme ('təʊniːm) *n. Linguistics.* a phoneme that is distinguished from another phoneme only by its tone. [C20] —**to'nemic** *adj.*

tone poem *n.* another term for **symphonic poem.**

toner ('təʊnə) *n.* **1.** a person or thing that tones. **2.** a cosmetic preparation that is applied to produce a desired effect, such as to reduce the oiliness of the skin. **3.** *Photog.* a chemical solution that softens or alters the tones of a photographic image.

tone row *or* **series** *n. Music.* a group of notes having a characteristic pattern that forms the basis of the musical material in a serial composition, esp. one consisting of the twelve notes of the chromatic scale.

tone up *vb.* (*adv.*) to make or become more vigorous, healthy, etc.

tong (toŋ) *n.* (formerly) a secret society of Chinese Americans. [C20: from Chinese (Cantonese) *t'ong* meeting place]

tonga ('toŋgə) *n.* a light two-wheeled vehicle used in rural areas of India. [C19: from Hindi *tāngā*]

Tonga ('toŋə, 'toŋgə) *n.* a kingdom occupying an archipelago of more than 150 volcanic and coral islands in the SW Pacific, east of Fiji: inhabited by Polynesians; became a British protectorate in 1900 and gained independence in 1970; a member of the Commonwealth. Languages: Tongan and English. Religion: Christian. Currency: pa'anga. Capital: Nuku'alofa. Pop.: 94 800 (1987). Area: 675 sq. km (261 sq. miles). Also called: **Friendly Islands.** —'**Tongan** *adj., n.*

tongs (toŋz) *pl. n.* a tool for grasping or lifting, consisting of a hinged, sprung, or pivoted pair of arms or levers, joined at one end. Also called: **pair of tongs.** [pl. of OE *tange*]

tongue (tʌŋ) *n.* **1.** a movable mass of muscular tissue attached to the floor of the mouth in most vertebrates. It is used in tasting, eating, and (in man) speaking. Related adj.: **lingual. 2.** an analogous organ in invertebrates. **3.** the tongue of certain animals used as food. **4.** a language, dialect, or idiom: *the English tongue.* **5.** the ability to speak: *to lose one's tongue.* **6.** a manner of speaking: *a glib tongue.* **7.** utterance or voice (esp. in **give tongue**). **8.** anything which resembles a tongue in shape or function. **9.** a promontory or spit of land. **10.** a flap of leather on a shoe. **11.** *Music.* the reed of an oboe or similar instrument. **12.** the clapper of a bell. **13.** the harnessing pole of a horse-drawn vehicle. **14.** a projection on a machine part that serves as a guide for assembly, etc. **15.** a projecting strip along an edge of a board that is made to fit a groove in another board. **16. hold one's tongue.** to keep quiet. **17. on the tip of one's tongue.** about to come to mind. **18. with (one's) tongue in (one's) cheek.** Also: **tongue in cheek.** with insincere or ironical intent. ~*vb.* **19.** to articulate (notes on a wind instrument) by tonguing. **20.** (*tr.*) to lick, feel, or touch with the tongue. **21.** (*tr.*) to provide (a board) with a tongue. **22.** (*intr.*) (of a piece of land) to project into a body of water. [OE *tunge*] —'**tongueless** *adj.* —'**tongue,like** *adj.*

tongue-and-groove joint *n.* a joint made between two boards by means of a tongue along the edge of one board that fits into a groove along the edge of the other board.

tongued (tʌŋd) *adj.* **1.** having a tongue or tongues. **2.** (*in combination*) having a manner of speech as specified: *sharp-tongued.*

tongue-lash *vb.* (*tr.*) to reprimand severely; scold. —'**tongue-,lashing** *n., adj.*

tongue-tie *n.* a congenital condition in which the tongue has restricted mobility as the result of an abnormally short fraenum.

tongue-tied *adj.* **1.** speechless, esp. with embarrassment or shyness. **2.** having a condition of tongue-tie.

tongue twister *n.* a sentence or phrase that is difficult to articulate clearly and quickly, such as *Peter Piper picked a peck of pickled pepper.*

tonguing ('tʌŋɪŋ) *n.* a technique of playing (any nonlegato passage) on a wind instrument by obstructing and uncovering the air passage through the lips with the tongue.

tonic ('tɒnɪk) *n.* **1.** a medicinal preparation that improves the functioning of the body or increases the feeling of wellbeing. **2.** anything that enlivens or strengthens. **3.** Also called: **tonic water.** a mineral water, usually carbonated and containing quinine and often mixed with gin or other alcoholic drinks. **4.** *Music.* **a.** the first degree of a major or minor scale and the tonal centre of a piece composed in a particular key. **b.** a key or chord based on this. ~*adj.* **5.** serving to enliven and invigorate: *a tonic wine.* **6.** of or relating to a tone or tones. **7.** *Music.* of the first degree of a major or minor scale. **8.** of or denoting the general effect of colour and light and shade in a picture. **9.** *Physiol.* of or affecting normal muscular or bodily tone: *a tonic spasm.* [C17: from NL *tonicus*, from Gk *tonikos* concerning tone, from *tonos* TONE] —'**tonically** *adv.*

tonic accent *n.* **1.** emphasis imparted to a note by virtue of its having a higher pitch. **2.** (in some languages) an accent in which emphatic syllables are pronounced on a higher musical pitch.

tonicity (təʊ'nɪsɪtɪ) *n.* **1.** the condition or quality of being tonic. **2.** another name for **tonus.**

tonic sol-fa *n.* a method of teaching music, by which syllables are used as names for the notes of the major scale in any key.

tonight (tə'naɪt) *n.* **1.** the night or evening of this present day. ~*adv.* **2.** in or during the night or evening of this day. **3.** *Obs.* last night. [OE *tōniht*]

tonka bean ('tɒŋkə) *n.* **1.** a tall tree of tropical America. **2.** the seeds of this tree, used in the manufacture of perfumes, snuff, etc. [C18: prob. from Tupi *tonka*]

Tonkin ('tɒn'kɪn) *or* **Tongking** ('tɒŋ'kɪŋ) *n.* **1.** a former state of N French Indochina (1883–1946), on the Gulf of Tonkin: forms the largest part of N Vietnam. **2. Gulf of.** an arm of the South China Sea, bordered by N Vietnam, the Leizhou Peninsula of SW China, and Hainan Island. Length: about 500 km (300 miles).

Tonle Sap ('tɒnlɪ 'sæp) *n.* a lake in W central Kampuchea, linked to the Mekong River by the **Tonle Sap River.** Area: (dry season) about 2600 sq. km (1000 sq. miles); (rainy season) up to 24 600 sq. km (9500 sq. miles).

tonnage *or* **tunnage** ('tʌnɪdʒ) *n.* **1.** the capacity of a merchant ship expressed in tons. **2.** the weight of the cargo of a merchant ship. **3.** the total amount of shipping of a port or nation. **4.** a duty on ships based either on their capacity or their register tonnage. [C15: from OF, from *tonne* barrel]

tonne (tʌn) *n.* a unit of mass equal to 1000 kg or 2204.6 pounds. Also called (not in technical use): **metric ton.** [from F]

tonneau ('tɒnəʊ) *n., pl.* **-neaus** *or* **-neaux** (-nəʊ, -nəʊz). **1.** a detachable cover to protect empty passenger seats in an open vehicle. **2.** *Rare.* the part of an open car in which the rear passengers sit. [C20: from F: special type of vehicle body, from OF *tonnel* cask, from *tonne* tun]

tonometer (təʊ'nɒmɪtə) *n.* **1.** an instrument for measuring the pitch of a sound, esp. one consisting of a set of tuning forks. **2.** any of various types of instrument for measuring pressure or tension, such as the blood pressure, vapour pressure, etc. [C18: from Gk *tonos* TONE + -METER] —**tonometric** (,tɒnə'mɛtrɪk, ,təʊ-) *adj.*

tonsil ('tɒnsəl) *n.* either of two small masses of lymphatic tissue situated one on each side of the back of the mouth.

[C17: from L *tōnsillae* (pl.) tonsils, from ?] —'**tonsillar** *adj.*

tonsillectomy (,tɒnsɪ'lɛktəmɪ) *n., pl.* **-mies.** surgical removal of the tonsils.

tonsillitis (,tɒnsɪ'laɪtɪs) *n.* inflammation of the tonsils. —**tonsillitic** (,tɒnsɪ'lɪtɪk) *adj.*

tonsorial (tɒn'sɔːrɪəl) *adj. Often facetious.* of barbering or hairdressing. [C19: from L *tōnsōrius* concerning shaving, from *tondēre* to shave]

tonsure ('tɒnʃə) *n.* **1.** (in certain religions and monastic orders) **a.** the shaving of the head or the crown of the head only. **b.** the part of the head left bare by shaving. ~*vb.* **2.** (*tr.*) to shave the head of. [C14: from L *tōnsūra* a clipping, from *tondēre* to shave] —'**tonsured** *adj.*

tontine ('tɒnti:n, tɒn'ti:n) *n.* an annuity scheme by which several subscribers accumulate and invest a common fund out of which they receive an annuity that increases as subscribers die until the last survivor takes the whole. [C18: from F, after Lorenzo *Tonti,* Neapolitan banker who devised the scheme]

ton-up *Brit. inf.* ~*adj.* (*prenominal*) **1.** (esp. of a motorcycle) capable of speeds of a hundred miles per hour or more. **2.** liking to travel at such speeds: *a ton-up boy.* ~*n.* **3.** a person who habitually rides at such speeds.

tonus ('təʊnəs) *n.* the normal tension of a muscle at rest; tone. [C19: from L, from Gk *tonos* TONE]

too (tu:) *adv.* **1.** as well; in addition; also: *can I come too?* **2.** in or to an excessive degree: *I have too many things to do.* **3.** extremely: *you're too kind.* **4.** *U.S. & Canad. inf.* indeed: used to reinforce a command: *you will too do it!* [OE *tō*]

▷ **Usage.** See at **very.**

took (tʊk) *vb.* the past tense of **take.**

tool (tu:l) *n.* **1. a.** an implement, such as a hammer, saw, or spade, that is used by hand. **b.** a power-driven instrument; machine tool. **c.** (*in combination*): *a toolkit.* **2.** the cutting part of such an instrument. **3.** any of the instruments used by a bookbinder to impress a design on a book cover. **4.** anything used as a means of achieving an end. **5.** a person used to perform dishonourable or unpleasant tasks for another. **6.** a necessary medium for or adjunct to one's profession: *numbers are the tools of the mathematician's trade.* ~*vb.* **7.** to work, cut, or form (something) with a tool. **8.** (*tr.*) to decorate (a book cover) with a bookbinder's tool. **9.** (*tr.*; often foll. by *up*) to furnish with tools. [OE *tōl*] —'**tooler** *n.*

tooling ('tu:lɪŋ) *n.* **1.** any decorative work done with a tool, esp. a design stamped onto a book cover, etc. **2.** the selection, provision, and setting up of tools for a machining operation.

tool-maker *n.* a person who specializes in the production or reconditioning of precision tools, cutters, etc. —'**tool,making** *n.*

toolroom ('tu:lru:m, -rʊm) *n.* a room, such as in a machine shop, where tools are made, stored, etc.

toot (tu:t) *vb.* **1.** to give or cause to give (a short blast, hoot, or whistle). ~*n.* **2.** the sound made by or as if by a horn, whistle, etc. **3.** *Sl.* any drug for snorting, esp. cocaine. **4.** *U.S. & Canad. sl.* a drinking spree. **5.** *Austral. sl.* a lavatory. [C16: from MLow G *tuten,* imit.] —'**tooter** *n.*

tooth (tu:θ) *n., pl.* **teeth** (ti:θ). **1.** any of various bonelike structures set in the jaws of most vertebrates and used for biting, tearing, or chewing. Related adj.: **dental. 2.** any of various similar structures in invertebrates. **3.** anything resembling a tooth in shape, prominence, or function: *the tooth of a comb.* **4.** any of the indentations on the margin of a leaf, petal, etc. **5.** any of the projections on a gear, sprocket, rack, etc. **6.** taste or appetite (esp. in **sweet tooth**). **7. long in the tooth.** old or ageing. **8. tooth and nail.** with ferocity and force. ~*vb.* (tu:ð, tu:θ). **9.** (*tr.*) to provide with a tooth or teeth. **10.** (*intr.*) (of two gearwheels) to engage. [OE *tōth*] —'**toothless** *adj.* —'**tooth,like** *adj.*

toothache ('tu:θ,eɪk) *n.* a pain in or about a tooth. Technical name: **odontalgia.**

toothbrush ('tu:θ,brʌʃ) *n.* a small brush, usually with a long handle, for cleaning the teeth.

toothed (tu:θt) *adj.* **a.** having a tooth or teeth. **b.** (*in combination*): *sabre-toothed; six-toothed.*

toothed whale *n.* any of a suborder of whales having simple teeth and feeding on fish, smaller mammals, etc.: includes dolphins and porpoises.

toothpaste ('tu:θ,peɪst) *n.* a paste used for cleaning the teeth, applied with a toothbrush.

toothpick ('tu:θ,pɪk) *n.* a small sharp sliver of wood, plastic, etc., used for extracting pieces of food from between the teeth.

tooth powder *n.* a powder used for cleaning the teeth, applied with a toothbrush.

tooth shell *n.* another name for the **tusk shell.**

toothsome ('tu:θsəm) *adj.* of delicious or appetizing appearance, flavour, or smell.

toothwort ('tu:θ,wɜ:t) *n.* **1.** a European plant having scaly stems and pinkish flowers and a rhizome covered with toothlike scales. **2.** any of a genus of North American or Eurasian plants having rhizomes covered with toothlike projections.

toothy ('tu:θɪ) *adj.* **toothier, toothiest.** having or showing numerous, large, or projecting teeth: *a toothy grin.* — 'toothily *adv.* — 'toothiness *n.*

tootle ('tu:t⁰l) *vb.* **1.** to toot or hoot softly or repeatedly. ~*n.* **2.** a soft hoot or series of hoots. [C19: from TOOT] — 'tootler *n.*

Toowoomba (tə'wʊmbə) *n.* a city in E Australia, in SE Queensland: agricultural and industrial centre. Pop.: 75 060 (1986 est.).

top[1] (tɒp) *n.* **1.** the highest or uppermost part of anything: *the top of a hill.* **2.** the most important or successful position: *the top of the class.* **3.** the part of a plant that is above ground: *carrot tops.* **4.** a thing that forms or covers the uppermost part of anything, esp. a lid or cap. **5.** the highest degree or point: *at the top of his career.* **6.** the most important person. **7.** the best part of anything. **8.** the loudest or highest pitch (esp. in **top of one's voice**). **9.** another name for **top gear** (sense 1). **10.** *Cards.* the highest card of a suit in a player's hand. **11.** *Sport.* **a.** a stroke that hits the ball above its centre. **b.** short for **topspin. 12.** a platform around the head of a lower mast of a sailing vessel. **13.** a garment, esp. for a woman, that extends from the shoulders to the waist or hips. **14. off the top of one's head.** with no previous preparation; extempore. **15. on top of. a.** in addition to. **b.** *Inf.* in complete control of (a difficult situation, etc.). **16. over the top. a.** over the parapet or leading edge of a trench. **b.** over the limit; lacking restraint or a sense of proportion. **17. the top of the morning.** a morning greeting regarded as characteristic of Irishmen. ~*adj.* **18.** of, relating to, serving as, or situated on the top. ~*vb.* **topping, topped.** (*mainly tr.*) **19.** to form a top on (something): *to top a cake with cream.* **20.** to remove the top of or from. **21.** to reach or pass the top of. **22.** to be at the top of: *he tops the team.* **23.** to exceed or surpass. **24.** *Sl.* to kill, esp. by hanging. **25.** (*also intr.*) *Sport.* **a.** to hit (a ball) above the centre. **b.** to make (a stroke) by hitting the ball in this way. ~See also **top off, top out, tops, top up.** [OE *topp*]

top[2] (tɒp) *n.* **1.** a toy that is spun on its pointed base. **2. sleep like a top.** to sleep very soundly. [OE, from ?]

topaz ('təʊpæz) *n.* **1.** a hard glassy mineral consisting of a silicate of aluminium and fluorine in crystalline form. It is yellow, pink, or colourless, and is a valuable gemstone. **2. oriental topaz.** a yellowish-brown variety of sapphire. **3. false topaz.** another name for **citrine. 4.** either of two South American hummingbirds. [C13: from OF *topaze*, from L *topazus*, from Gk *topazos*]

top boot *n.* a high boot, often with a decorative or contrasting upper section.

top brass *n.* (*functioning as pl.*) *Inf.* the most important or high-ranking officials or leaders.

topcoat ('tɒp,kəʊt) *n.* an outdoor coat worn over a suit, etc.

top dog *n.* *Inf.* the leader or chief of a group.

top drawer *n.* people of the highest standing, esp. socially (esp. in **out of the top drawer**).

top dressing *n.* a surface application of some material, such as fertilizer. — 'top-,dress *vb.* (*tr.*)

tope[1] (təʊp) *vb.* to consume (alcoholic drink) as a regular habit, usually in large quantities. [C17: from F *toper* to keep an agreement, from Sp. *topar* to take a bet; prob. because a wager was generally followed by a drink] — 'toper *n.*

tope[2] (təʊp) *n.* a small grey shark of European coastal waters. [C17: from ?]

topee *or* **topi** ('təʊpi:, -pɪ) *n., pl.* **-pees** *or* **-pis.** another name for **pith helmet.** [C19: from Hindi *topi* hat]

Topeka (tə'pi:kə) *n.* a city in E central Kansas, capital of the state, on the Kansas River: university (1865). Pop.: 118 580 (1986 est.).

Top End *n.* **the.** *Austral.* the northern part of the Northern Territory.

top-flight *adj.* of superior or excellent quality.

topgallant (,tɒp'gælənt; *Naut.* tə'gælənt) *n.* **1.** a mast on a square-rigger above a topmast or an extension of a topmast. **2.** a sail set on a yard of a topgallant mast. **3.** (*modifier*) of or relating to a topgallant.

top gear *n.* **1.** Also called: **top.** the highest forward ratio of a gearbox in a motor vehicle. **2.** the highest speed, greatest energy, etc.

top hat *n.* a man's hat with a tall cylindrical crown and narrow brim, often made of silk, now worn for some formal occasions.

top-heavy *adj.* **1.** unstable through being overloaded at the top. **2.** *Finance.* characterized by too much debt capital in relation to revenue or profit; overcapitalized.

Tophet *or* **Topheth** ('təʊfɛt) *n. Old Testament.* a place in the valley immediately to the southwest of Jerusalem; the Shrine of Moloch, where human sacrifices were offered. [from Heb. *Tōpheth*]

top-hole *interj., adj. Brit. old-fashioned inf.* excellent; splendid.

tophus ('təʊfəs) *n., pl.* **-phi** (-faɪ). a deposit of sodium urate in the ear or surrounding a joint: a diagnostic of gout. [C16: from L, var. of *tōfus* TUFA, TUFF]

topi *n., pl.* **-pis. 1.** ('təʊpɪ). an African antelope. **2.** ('təʊpi:, -pɪ). another name for **pith helmet.** [C19: from Hindi: hat]

topiary ('təʊpɪərɪ) *adj.* **1.** of, relating to, or characterized by the trimming or training of trees or bushes into artificial decorative shapes. **2.** (*pl.* **-aries**) **a.** topiary work. **b.** a topiary garden. **3.** the art of topiary. [C16: from F *topiaire*, from L *topia* decorative garden work, from Gk *topion* little place, from *topos* place] — 'topiarist *n.*

topic ('tɒpɪk) *n.* **1.** a subject or theme of a speech, book, etc. **2.** a subject of conversation. [C16: from L *topica* translating Gk *ta topika*, lit.: matters relating to commonplaces, title of a treatise by Aristotle, from *topoi*, pl. of *topos* place]

topical ('tɒpɪk⁰l) *adj.* **1.** of, relating to, or constituting current affairs. **2.** relating to a particular place; local. **3.** of or relating to a topic or topics. **4.** (of a drug, ointment, etc.) for application to the body surface; local. — **topicality** (,tɒpɪ'kælɪtɪ) *n.* — 'topically *adv.*

topknot ('tɒp,nɒt) *n.* **1.** a crest, tuft, decorative bow, chignon, etc., on the top of the head. **2.** any of several European flatfishes.

topless ('tɒplɪs) *adj.* **1.** having no top. **2. a.** denoting a costume which has no covering for the breasts. **b.** wearing such a costume.

top-level *n.* (*modifier*) of, involving, or by those on the highest level of influence or authority: *top-level talks.*

toplofty ('tɒp,lɒftɪ) *adj. Inf.* haughty or pretentious. — 'top,loftiness *n.*

topmast ('tɒp,mɑːst; *Naut.* 'tɒpməst) *n.* the mast next above a lower mast on a sailing vessel.

topmost ('tɒp,məʊst) *adj.* at or nearest the top.

topnotch ('tɒp'nɒtʃ) *adj. Inf.* excellent; superb. — 'top'notcher *n.*

topo- *or before a vowel* **top-** *combining form.* indicating place or region: *topography; topology.* [from Gk *topos* a place]

top off *vb.* (*tr., adv.*) to finish or complete, esp. with some decisive action.

topography (tə'pɒɡrəfɪ) *n., pl.* **-phies. 1.** the study or detailed description of the surface features of a region. **2.** the detailed mapping of the configuration of a region. **3.** the land forms or surface configuration of a region. **4.** the surveying of a region's surface features. **5.** the study or description of the configuration of any object. — **to'pographer** *n.* — **topographic** (,tɒpə'ɡræfɪk) *or* ,topo'graph-ical *adj.*

topological group *n. Maths.* a group, such as the set of all real numbers, that constitutes a topological space and in which multiplication and inversion are continuous.

topological space *n. Maths.* a set *S* with an associated family of subsets τ that is closed under set union and finite intersection.

topology (tə'pɒlədʒɪ) n. 1. the branch of mathematics concerned with generalization of the concepts of continuity, limit, etc. 2. a branch of geometry describing the properties of a figure that are unaffected by continuous distortion. 3. *Maths.* a family of subsets of a given set *S*, such that *S* is a topological space. 4. the study of the topography of a given place. 5. the anatomy of any specific bodily area, structure, or part. —**topologic** (,tɒpə'lɒdʒɪk) or ,**topo'logical** *adj.* —,**topo'logically** *adv.* —**to'pologist** n.

top out vb. (adv.) to place the highest part of a building in position.

topper ('tɒpə) n. 1. an informal name for **top hat**. 2. a person or thing that tops or excels.

topping ('tɒpɪŋ) n. 1. something that tops something else, esp. a sauce or garnish for food. ~adj. 2. high or superior in rank, degree, etc. 3. *Brit. sl.* excellent; splendid.

topple ('tɒpᵊl) vb. 1. to tip over or cause to tip over, esp. from a height. 2. (intr.) to lean precariously or totter. [C16: frequentative of TOP¹ (vb.)]

tops (tɒps) *Sl.* ~n. 1. **the tops.** a person or thing of top quality. ~adj. 2. (*postpositive*) excellent.

topsail ('tɒp,seɪl; *Naut.* 'tɒpsᵊl) n. a square sail carried on a yard set on a topmast.

top-secret *adj.* classified as needing the highest level of secrecy and security.

topside ('tɒp,saɪd) n. 1. the uppermost side of anything. 2. *Brit. & N.Z.* a lean cut of beef from the thigh containing no bone. 3. (*often pl.*) **a.** the part of a ship's sides above the water line. **b.** the parts of a ship above decks.

topsoil ('tɒp,sɔɪl) n. the surface layer of soil.

topspin ('tɒp,spɪn) n. *Tennis, etc.* a spin imparted to make a ball bounce or travel exceptionally far, high, or quickly.

topsy-turvy ('tɒpsɪ'tɜːvɪ) *adj.* 1. upside down. 2. in a state of confusion. ~adv. 3. in a topsy-turvy manner. ~n. 4. a topsy-turvy state. [C16: prob. from *tops*, pl. of TOP¹ + obs. *tervy* to turn upside down]

top up vb. (tr., adv.) *Brit.* to raise the level of (a liquid, powder, etc.) in (a container), usually bringing it to the brim of the container.

toque (təʊk) n. 1. a woman's small round brimless hat. 2. a chef's tall white hat. 3. *Canad.* a knitted cap with a round tassel on top. 4. a small plumed hat popular in the 16th century. [C16: from F, from OSp. *toca* headdress, prob. from Basque *tauka* hat]

tor (tɔː) n. a high hill, esp. a bare rocky one. [OE *torr*]

Torah ('təʊrə) n. 1. **a.** the Pentateuch. **b.** the scroll on which this is written. 2. the whole body of traditional Jewish teaching, including the Oral Law. [C16: from Heb.: precept, from *yārāh* to instruct]

Torbay (,tɔː'beɪ) n. 1. a resort and former county borough in SW England, in Devon, formed in 1968 by the amalgamation of Torquay with two neighbouring coastal towns. Pop.: 117 300 (1986 est.). 2. **Tor Bay.** an inlet of the English Channel on the coast of SW England, near Torquay.

torc (tɔːk) n. a variant of **torque** (sense 1).

torch (tɔːtʃ) n. 1. a small portable electric lamp powered by batteries. U.S. and Canad. word: **flashlight.** 2. a wooden or tow shaft dipped in wax or tallow and set alight. 3. anything regarded as a source of enlightenment, guidance, etc. 4. any apparatus with a hot flame for welding, brazing, etc. 5. **carry a torch for.** to be in love with, esp. unrequitedly. [C13: from OF *torche* handful of twisted straw, from Vulgar L *torca* (unattested), from L *torquēre* to twist]

torchbearer ('tɔːtʃ,bɛərə) n. 1. a person or thing that carries a torch. 2. a person who leads or inspires.

torchère (tɔː'ʃɛə) n. a tall stand for holding a candelabrum. [C20: from F, from *torche* TORCH]

torchier or **torchiere** ('tɔːtʃɪə) n. a standing lamp with a bowl for casting light upwards. [C20: from TORCHÈRE]

torch song n. a sentimental song, usually sung by a woman. [C20: from *to carry a torch for* (*someone*)] —**torch singer** n.

tore (tɔː) vb. the past tense of **tear².**

toreador ('tɒrɪə,dɔː) n. a bullfighter. [C17: from Sp., from *torear* to take part in bullfighting, from *toro* a bull, from L *taurus*]

torero (tɒ'rɛərəʊ) n., pl. **-ros.** a bullfighter, esp. one who fights on foot. [C18: from Sp., from LL *taurārius*, from L *taurus* a bull]

toric lens ('tɒrɪk) n. a lens used to correct astigmatism, having one of its surfaces shaped like part of a torus so that its focal lengths are different in different meridians.

torii ('tɔːrɪ,iː) n., pl. **-rii.** a gateway at the entrance to a Shinto temple. [C19: from Japanese, lit.: a perch for birds]

Torino (tɔ'riːno) n. the Italian name for **Turin.**

torment vb. (tɔː'mɛnt). (tr.) 1. to afflict with great pain, suffering, or anguish; torture. 2. to tease or pester in an annoying way. ~n. ('tɔːmɛnt). 3. physical or mental pain. 4. a source of pain, worry, annoyance, etc. [C13: from OF, from L *tormentum*, from *torquēre*] —**tor'mented** *adj.* —**tor'menting** *adj., n.* —**tor'mentor** n.

tormentil ('tɔːməntɪl) n. a perennial plant of Europe and W Asia, having yellow flowers, and an astringent root used in medicine, tanning, and dyeing. [C15: from OF *tormentille*, from Med. L *tormentilla*, from L *tormentum* agony; from its use in relieving pain]

torn (tɔːn) vb. 1. the past participle of **tear².** 2. **that's torn it.** *Brit. sl.* an unexpected event or circumstance has upset one's plans. ~adj. 3. split or cut. 4. divided or undecided, as in preference: *torn between staying and leaving.*

tornado (tɔː'neɪdəʊ) n., pl. **-does** or **-dos.** 1. a violent storm with winds whirling around a small area of extremely low pressure, usually characterized by a dark funnel-shaped cloud causing damage along its path. 2. a small but violent squall or whirlwind. 3. any violently active or destructive person or thing. [C16: prob. alteration of Sp. *tronada* thunderstorm (from *tronar* to thunder, from L *tonāre*) through infl. of *tornar* to turn, from L *tornāre* to turn in a lathe] —**tornadic** (tɔː'nædɪk) *adj.*

toroid ('tɔːrɔɪd) n. 1. *Geom.* a surface generated by rotating a closed plane curve about a coplanar line that does not intersect the curve. 2. the solid enclosed by such a surface. See also **torus.** —**to'roidal** *adj.*

Toronto (tə'rɒntəʊ) n. a city in S central Canada, capital of Ontario, on Lake Ontario: the second largest city and the major industrial centre of Canada; two universities. Pop.: 599 217 (1981), with a conurbation of 3 427 168 (1986). —**Toron'tonian** *adj., n.*

torpedo (tɔː'piːdəʊ) n., pl. **-does.** 1. a cylindrical self-propelled weapon carrying explosives that is launched from aircraft, ships, or submarines and follows an underwater path to hit its target. 2. *Obs.* a submarine mine. 3. *U.S. & Canad.* a firework with a percussion cap. 4. an electric ray. ~vb. **-doing, -doed.** (tr.) 5. to attack or hit (a ship, etc.) with one or a number of torpedoes. 6. to destroy or wreck: *to torpedo the administration's plan.* [C16: from L: crampfish (whose electric discharges can cause numbness), from *torpēre* to be inactive] —**tor'pedo-,like** *adj.*

torpedo boat n. (formerly) a small high-speed warship designed to carry out torpedo attacks.

torpedo tube n. the tube from which a torpedo is discharged from submarines or ships.

torpid ('tɔːpɪd) *adj.* 1. apathetic; sluggish. 2. (of a hibernating animal) dormant. 3. unable to move or feel. [C17: from L *torpidus*, from *torpēre* to be numb] —**tor'pidity** n. —**'torpidly** *adv.*

torpor ('tɔːpə) n. a state of torpidity. [C17: from L: inactivity, from *torpēre* to be motionless]

Torquay (,tɔː'kiː) n. a town and resort in SW England, in S Devon: administratively part of Torbay since 1968.

torque (tɔːk) n. 1. a necklace or armband made of twisted metal. 2. any force that causes rotation. [C19: from L *torquēs* necklace & *torquēre* to twist]

torque converter n. a device for the transmission of power in which an engine-driven impeller transmits its momentum to a fluid held in a sealed container, which in turn drives a rotor.

Torquemada (*Spanish* tɔrke'maða) n. **Tomás de** (to'mas de). 1420–98, Spanish Dominican monk. As first Inquisitor-General of Spain (1483–98), he was responsible for the burning of some 2000 heretics.

torques ('tɔːkwiːz) n. a distinctive band of hair, feathers, skin, or colour around the neck of an animal; a collar. [C17: from L: necklace, from *torquēre* to twist] —**torquate** ('tɔːkwɪt, -kweɪt) *adj.*

torque wrench n. a type of wrench with a gauge attached to indicate the torque applied.

torr (tɔː) *n., pl.* **torr.** a unit of pressure equal to one millimetre of mercury (133.322 newtons per square metre). [C20: after E. TORRICELLI]

Torrance ('tɒrəns) *n.* a city in SW California, southwest of Los Angeles: developed rapidly with the discovery of oil. Pop.: 129 881 (1980).

Torre del Greco (*Italian* 'torre del 'grɛːko) *n.* a city in SW Italy, in Campania near Vesuvius on the Bay of Naples: damaged several times by eruptions. Pop.: 102 621 (1980 est.).

torrefy ('tɒrɪ,faɪ) *vb.* **-fying, -fied.** (*tr.*) to dry (drugs, ores, etc.) by heat. [C17: from F *torréfier,* from L *torrefacere,* from *torrēre* to parch + *facere* to make] —**torrefaction** (,tɒrɪ'fækʃən) *n.*

Torrens ('tɒrənz) *n.* **Lake.** a shallow salt lake in E central South Australia, about 8 m (25 ft.) below sea level. Area: 5776 sq. km (2230 sq. miles).

Torrens title *n. Austral.* legal title to land based on record of registration rather than on title deeds. [from Sir Robert Richard *Torrens* (1814–84), who introduced the system as premier of South Australia in 1857]

torrent ('tɒrənt) *n.* **1.** a fast or violent stream, esp. of water. **2.** an overwhelming flow of thoughts, words, sound, etc. [C17: from F, from L *torrēns* (n.), from *torrēns* (adj.) burning, from *torrēre* to burn] —**torrential** (tɒ'rɛnʃəl) *adj.*

Torreón (*Spanish* tɔrre'ɔn) *n.* an industrial city in N Mexico, in Coahuila state. Pop.: 363 886 (1980).

Torres Strait ('tɒrɪz, 'tɒr-) *n.* a strait between NE Australia and S New Guinea, linking the Arafura Sea with the Coral Sea. Width: about 145 km (90 miles).

Torricelli (,tɒrɪ'tʃɛlɪ) *n.* **Evangelista** (evandʒe'lista). 1608–47, Italian physicist and mathematician, who discovered the principle of the barometer.

Torricellian tube (,tɒrɪ'sɛlɪən) *n.* a vertical glass tube partly evacuated and partly filled with mercury, used to measure atmospheric pressure. [C17: after E. TORRICELLI]

torrid ('tɒrɪd) *adj.* **1.** so hot and dry as to parch or scorch. **2.** arid or parched. **3.** highly charged emotionally: *a torrid love scene.* [C16: from L *torridus,* from *torrēre* to scorch] —**tor'ridity** *or* '**torridness** *n.* —**'torridly** *adv.*

Torrid Zone *n. Rare.* that part of the earth's surface lying between the tropics of Cancer and Capricorn.

torsion ('tɔːʃən) *n.* **1. a.** the twisting of a part by application of equal and opposite torques. **b.** the condition of twist and shear stress produced by a torque on a part or component. **2.** a twisting or being twisted. [C15: from OF, from Medical L *torsió* griping pains, from L *torquēre* to twist, torture] —**'torsional** *adj.* —**'torsionally** *adv.*

torsion balance *n.* an instrument used to measure small forces, esp. electric or magnetic forces, by the torsion they produce in a thin wire.

torsion bar *n.* a metal bar acting as a torsional spring.

torsk (tɔːsk) *n., pl.* **torsks** *or* **torsk.** a food fish of northern coastal waters. Usual U.S. name: **cusk.** [C17: of Scand. origin]

torso ('tɔːsəʊ) *n., pl.* **-sos** *or* **-si** (-sɪ). **1.** the trunk of the human body. **2.** a statue of a nude human trunk, esp. without the head or limbs. [C18: from It.: stalk, stump, from L: THYRSUS]

tort (tɔːt) *n. Law.* a civil wrong or injury arising out of an act or failure to act, independently of any contract, for which an action for damages may be brought. [C14: from OF, from Med. L *tortum,* lit.: something twisted, from L *torquēre* to twist]

torte (tɔːt) *n.* a rich cake usually decorated or filled with cream, fruit, etc. [C16: ult. ?from LL *tõrta* a round loaf, from ?]

Tortelier (*French* tɔrtəlje) *n.* **Paul** (pɔl). born 1914, French cellist and composer.

torticollis (,tɔːtɪ'kɒlɪs) *n. Pathol.* an abnormal position of the head, usually with the neck bent to one side. [C19: NL, from L *tortus* twisted (from *torquēre* to twist) + *collum* neck]

tortilla (tɔː'tiːə) *n. Mexican cookery.* a kind of thin pancake made from corn meal. [C17: from Sp.: a little cake, from *torta* a round cake, from LL]

tortoise ('tɔːtəs) *n.* **1.** any of a family of herbivorous reptiles having a heavy dome-shaped shell and clawed limbs. **2.** a slow-moving person. **3.** another word for **testudo.** [C15: prob. from OF *tortue* (infl. by L *tortus* twisted), from Med. L *tortūca,* from LL *tartarūcha* coming from Tartarus

(in the underworld), from Gk *tartaroukhos;* from belief that the tortoise originated in the underworld]

tortoiseshell ('tɔːtəs,ʃɛl) *n.* **1.** the horny yellow-and-brown mottled shell of the hawksbill turtle: used for making ornaments, jewellery, etc. **2.** a similar synthetic substance. **3.** a breed of domestic cat having black, cream, and brownish markings. **4.** any of several butterflies having orange-brown wings with black markings. **5. a.** a yellowish-brown mottled colour. **b.** (*as adj.*): *a tortoiseshell décor.* **6.** (*modifier*) made of tortoiseshell.

Tortola (tɔː'təʊlə) *n.* an island in the NE West Indies, in the Leeward Islands group: chief island of the British Virgin Islands. Pop.: 9322 (1980). Area: 62 sq. km (24 sq. miles).

tortricid ('tɔːtrɪsɪd) *n.* any of a family of moths, the larvae of which live in leaves, which they roll or tie together. [C19: from NL *Tortricidae,* from *tortrix,* fem. of *tortor,* lit.: twister, from the leaf-rolling of the larvae, from *torquēre* to twist]

Tortuga (tɔː'tuːgə) *n.* an island in the West Indies, off the NW coast of Haiti: haunt of pirates in the 17th century. Area: 180 sq. km (70 sq. miles). French name: **La Tortue** (la tɔrty).

tortuous ('tɔːtjʊəs) *adj.* **1.** twisted or winding. **2.** devious or cunning. **3.** intricate. —**tortuosity** (,tɔːtjʊ'ɒsɪtɪ) *n.* —**'tortuously** *adv.* —**'tortuousness** *n.*

torture ('tɔːtʃə) *vb.* (*tr.*) **1.** to cause extreme physical pain to, esp. to extract information, etc.: *to torture prisoners.* **2.** to give mental anguish to. **3.** to twist into a grotesque form. ~*n.* **4.** physical or mental anguish. **5.** the practice of torturing a person. **6.** a cause of mental agony. [C16: from LL *tortūra* a twisting, from *torquēre* to twist] —**'torturer** *n.* —**'torturous** *adj.* —**'torturously** *adv.*

Toruń (*Polish* 'tɔrunj) *n.* an industrial city in N Poland, on the River Vistula: developed around a castle that was founded by the Teutonic Knights in 1230; under Prussian rule (1793–1919). Pop.: 186 000 (1985). German name: **Thorn.**

torus ('tɔːrəs) *n., pl.* **-ri** (-raɪ). **1.** a large convex moulding semicircular in cross section, esp. one used on the base of a column. **2.** *Geom.* a ring-shaped surface generated by rotating a circle about a coplanar line that does not intersect the circle. **3.** *Bot.* another name for **receptacle** (sense 2). [C16: from L: a swelling, from ?] —**toric** ('tɒrɪk) *adj.*

Torvill and Dean ('tɔːvɪl) *n.* two British ice dancers, **Jayne Torvill,** born 1957, and **Christopher Dean,** born 1958. They won the world championships in 1981–83, the European Championships in 1981–82 and 1984, and the gold medal in the 1984 Olympic Games.

Tory ('tɔːrɪ) *n., pl.* **-ries. 1.** a member of the Conservative Party in Great Britain or Canada. **2.** a member of the English political party that opposed the exclusion of James, Duke of York from the royal succession (1679–80). Tory remained the label for conservative interests until they gave birth to the Conservative Party in the 1830s. **3.** an American supporter of the British cause; loyalist. Cf. **Whig. 4.** (*sometimes not cap.*) an ultraconservative or reactionary. ~*adj.* **5.** of, characteristic of, or relating to Tories. **6.** (*sometimes not cap.*) ultraconservative or reactionary. [C17: from Irish *tóraidhe* outlaw, from MIrish *tóir* pursuit] —**'Toryish** *adj.* —**'Toryism** *n.*

Toscana (tos'kaːna) *n.* the Italian name for **Tuscany.**

Toscanini (,tɔskə'niːnɪ) *n.* **Arturo** (ar'tuːro). 1867–1957, Italian conductor.

tosh (tɒʃ) *n. Sl., chiefly Brit.* nonsense; rubbish. [C19: from ?]

toss (tɒs) *vb.* **1.** (*tr.*) to throw lightly, esp. with the palm of the hand upwards. **2.** to fling or be flung about, esp. in an agitated or violent way: *a ship tosses in a storm.* **3.** to discuss or put forward for discussion in an informal way. **4.** (*tr.*) (of a horse, etc.) to throw (its rider). **5.** (*tr.*) (of an animal) to butt with the head or the horns and throw into the air. **6.** (*tr.*) to shake or disturb. **7.** to toss up a coin with (someone) in order to decide something. **8.** (*intr.*) to move away angrily or impatiently. ~*n.* **9.** an abrupt movement. **10.** a rolling or pitching motion. **11.** the act or an instance of tossing. **12.** the act of tossing up a coin. See **toss up. 13.** a fall from a horse. [C16: of Scand. origin] —**'tosser** *n.*

toss off *vb.* (*adv.*) **1.** (*tr.*) to perform, write, etc., quickly and easily. **2.** (*tr.*) to drink at one draught. **3.** (*intr.*) *Brit.* taboo. to masturbate.

toss up *vb.* (*adv.*) **1.** to spin (a coin) in the air in order to decide between alternatives by guessing which side will fall uppermost. ~*n.* **toss-up. 2.** an instance of tossing up a coin. **3.** *Inf.* an even chance or risk.

tot[1] (tɒt) *n.* **1.** a young child; toddler. **2.** *Chiefly Brit.* a small amount of anything. **3.** a small measure of spirits. [C18: ? short for *totter*; see TOTTER]

tot[2] (tɒt) *vb.* **totting, totted.** (usually foll. by *up*) *Chiefly Brit.* to total; add. [C17: shortened from TOTAL or from L *totum* all]

total ('təʊt²l) *n.* **1.** the whole, esp. regarded as the complete sum of a number of parts. ~*adj.* **2.** complete; absolute. **3.** (*prenominal*) being or related to a total. ~*vb.* **-talling, -talled** or *U.S.* **-taling, -taled. 4.** (when *intr.*, sometimes foll. by *to*) to amount: *to total six pounds.* **5.** (*tr.*) to add up. **6.** (*tr.*) *Sl.* to kill or destroy. [C14: from OF, from Med. L *totālis*, from L *totus* all] — 'totally *adv.*

total internal reflection *n. Physics.* the complete reflection of a light ray at the boundary of two media, when the ray is in the medium with greater refractive index.

totalitarian (təʊ,tælɪ'tɛərɪən) *adj.* of, denoting, relating to, or characteristic of a dictatorial one-party state that regulates every realm of life. — **to,tali'tarianism** *n.*

totality (təʊ'tælɪtɪ) *n., pl.* **-ties. 1.** the whole amount. **2.** the state of being total.

totalizator ('təʊt²laɪ,zeɪtə), **totalizer** or **totalisator, totaliser** *n.* **1.** a system of betting on horse races in which the aggregate stake, less tax, etc., is paid out to winners in proportion to their stake. **2.** the machine that records bets in this system and works out odds, pays out winnings, etc. ~U.S. and Canad. term: **pari-mutuel.**

totaquine ('təʊtə,kwiːn, -kwɪn) *n.* a mixture of quinine and other alkaloids derived from cinchona bark, used as a substitute for quinine in treating malaria. [C20: from NL *totaquina*, from TOTA(L) + Sp. *quina* cinchona bark; see QUININE]

totara ('təʊtərə) *n.* a tall coniferous forest tree of New Zealand with durable wood.

tote[1] (təʊt) *Inf.* ~*vb.* **1.** (*tr.*) to carry, convey, or drag. ~*n.* **2.** the act of or an instance of toting. **3.** something toted. [C17: from ?] — 'toter *n.*

tote[2] (təʊt) *n.* (usually preceded by *the*) *Inf.* short for **totalizator.**

tote bag *n.* a large handbag or shopping bag.

totem ('təʊtəm) *n.* **1.** (in some societies, esp. among North American Indians) an object, animal, plant, etc., symbolizing a clan, family, etc., often having ritual associations. **2.** a representation of such an object. [C18: from Ojibwa *nintotem* mark of my family] — **totemic** (təʊ'tɛmɪk) *adj.* — 'totem,ism *n.*

totem pole *n.* a pole carved or painted with totemic figures set up by certain North American Indians as a tribal symbol, etc.

tother or **t'other** ('tʌðə) *adj., n. Arch. or dialect.* the other. [C13 *the tother*, by mistaken division from *thet other* (*thet*, from OE *thæt*, neuter of THE[1])]

totipalmate (,təʊtɪ'pælmɪt, -,meɪt) *adj.* (of certain birds) having all four toes webbed. [C19: from L *totus* entire + *palmate*, from *palmātus* shaped like a hand, from *palma* PALM[1]]

totter ('tɒtə) *vb.* (*intr.*) **1.** to move in an unsteady manner. **2.** to sway or shake as if about to fall. **3.** to be failing, unstable, or precarious. ~*n.* **4.** the act or an instance of tottering. [C12: ?from OE *tealtrian* to waver, & MDu. *touteren* to stagger] — 'totterer *n.* — 'tottery *adj.*

totting ('tɒtɪŋ) *n. Brit.* the practice of searching through rubbish for usable or saleable items. [C19: from ?]

toucan ('tuːkən) *n.* any of a family of tropical American fruit-eating birds having a large brightly coloured bill and a bright plumage. [C16: from F, from Port. *tucano*, from Tupi *tucana*, prob. imit. of its cry]

touch (tʌtʃ) *n.* **1.** the sense by which the texture and other qualities of objects can be experienced when they come in contact with a part of the body surface, esp. the tips of the fingers. Related adj.: **tactile. 2.** the quality of an object as perceived by this sense; feel; feeling. **3.** the act or an instance of something coming into contact with the body. **4.** a gentle push, tap, or caress. **5.** a small amount; hint: *a touch of sarcasm.* **6.** a noticeable effect; influence: *the house needed a woman's touch.* **7.** any

slight stroke or mark. **8.** characteristic manner or style. **9.** a detail of some work: *she added a few finishing touches to the book.* **10.** a slight attack, as of a disease. **11.** a specific ability or facility. **12.** the state of being aware of a situation or in contact with someone. **13.** the state of being in physical contact. **14.** a trial or test (esp. in **put to the touch**). **15.** *Rugby, soccer, etc.* the area outside the touchlines, beyond which the ball is out of play (esp. in **in touch**). **16.** a scoring hit in fencing. **17.** an estimate of the amount of gold in an alloy as obtained by use of a touchstone. **18.** the technique of fingering a keyboard instrument. **19.** the quality of the action of a keyboard instrument with regard to the ease with which the keys may be depressed. **20.** *Sl.* **a.** the act of asking for money, often by devious means. **b.** the money received. **c.** a person asked for money in this way. ~*vb.* **21.** (*tr.*) to cause or permit a part of the body to come into contact with. **22.** (*tr.*) to tap, feel, or strike. **23.** to come or cause to come into contact with. **24.** (*intr.*) to be in contact. **25.** (*tr.; usually used with a negative*) to take hold of (a person or thing), esp. in violence. **26.** to be adjacent to (each other). **27.** (*tr.*) to move or disturb by handling. **28.** (*tr.*) to have an effect on. **29.** (*tr.*) to produce an emotional response in. **30.** (*tr.*) to affect; concern. **31.** (*tr.; usually used with a negative*) to partake of, eat, or drink. **32.** (*tr.; usually used with a negative*) to handle or deal with: *I wouldn't touch that business.* **33.** (when *intr.*, often foll. by *on*) to allude (to) briefly or in passing. **34.** (*tr.*) to tinge or tint slightly: *brown hair touched with gold.* **35.** (*tr.*) to spoil slightly: *blackfly touched the flowers.* **36.** (*tr.*) to ma:k, as with a brush or pen. **37.** (*tr.*) to compare to in quality or attainment. **38.** (*tr.*) to reach or attain: *he touched the high point in his career.* **39.** (*intr.*) to dock or stop briefly: *the ship touches at Tenerife.* **40.** (*tr.*) *Sl.* to ask for a loan or gift of money from. ~See also **touchdown, touch off, touch up.** [C13: from OF *tochier*, from Vulgar L *toccāre* (unattested) to strike, prob. imit. of a tapping sound] — 'touchable *adj.* — 'toucher *n.*

touch and go *adj.* (**touch-and-go** *when prenominal*) risky or critical.

touchdown ('tʌtʃ,daʊn) *n.* **1.** the moment at which a landing aircraft or spacecraft comes into contact with the landing surface. **2.** *Rugby.* the act of placing or touching the ball on the ground behind the goal line, as in scoring a try. **3.** *American football.* a scoring play for six points achieved by being in possession of the ball in the opponents' end zone. Abbrev.: **TD.** ~*vb.* **touch down.** (*intr., adv.*) **4.** (of an aircraft, etc.) to land. **5.** *Rugby.* to place the ball behind the goal line, as when scoring a try.

touché (tuː'ʃeɪ) *interj.* **1.** an acknowledgment of a scoring hit in fencing. **2.** an acknowledgment of the striking home of a remark, witty reply, etc. [from F, lit.: touched]

touched (tʌtʃt) *adj.* (*postpositive*) **1.** moved to sympathy or emotion. **2.** showing slight insanity.

touchhole ('tʌtʃ,həʊl) *n.* a hole in the breech of early cannon and firearms through which the charge was ignited.

touching ('tʌtʃɪŋ) *adj.* **1.** evoking or eliciting tender feelings. ~*prep.* **2.** on the subject of; relating to. — 'touchingly *adv.*

touch judge *n.* one of the two linesmen in rugby.

touchline ('tʌtʃ,laɪn) *n.* either of the lines marking the side of the playing area in certain games, such as rugby.

touchmark ('tʌtʃ,mɑːk) *n.* a maker's mark stamped on pewter objects.

touch-me-not *n.* an impatiens with yellow spurred flowers and seed pods that burst open at a touch when ripe. Also called: **noli-me-tangere.**

touch off *vb.* (*tr., adv.*) **1.** to cause to explode, as by touching with a match. **2.** to cause (a disturbance, violence, etc.) to begin.

touchpaper ('tʌtʃ,peɪpə) *n.* paper soaked in saltpetre for firing gunpowder.

touchstone ('tʌtʃ,stəʊn) *n.* **1.** a criterion or standard. **2.** a hard dark stone that is used to test gold and silver from the streak they produce on it.

touch-type *vb.* (*intr.*) to type without looking at the keyboard. — 'touch-,typist *n.*

touch up *vb.* (*tr., adv.*) **1.** to put extra or finishing touches to. **2.** to enhance, renovate, or falsify by putting extra touches to. **3.** *Brit. sl.* to touch or caress (someone).

touchwood ('tʌtʃ,wʊd) *n.* something, esp. dry wood or fungus material, used as tinder. [C16: TOUCH (in the sense: to kindle) + WOOD]

touchy ('tʌtʃɪ) *adj.* **touchier, touchiest.** **1.** easily upset or irritated. **2.** extremely risky. **3.** easily ignited. —'**touchily** *adv.* —'**touchiness** *n.*

tough (tʌf) *adj.* **1.** strong or resilient; durable. **2.** not tender. **3.** hardy and fit. **4.** rough or pugnacious. **5.** resolute or intractable. **6.** difficult or troublesome to do or deal with: *a tough problem.* **7.** *Inf.* unfortunate or unlucky: *it's tough on him.* ~*n.* **8.** a rough, vicious, or pugnacious person. ~*adv.* **9.** *Inf.* violently, aggressively, or intractably: *to treat someone tough.* ~*vb.* (*tr.*) **10.** *Sl.* to stand firm, hold out against (a difficulty or difficult situation) (esp. in **tough it out**). [OE *tōh*] —'**toughly** *adv.* —'**toughness** *n.*

toughen ('tʌfən) *vb.* to make or become tough or tougher. —'**toughener** *n.*

tough-minded *adj.* practical, unsentimental, or intractable. —,**tough-'mindedness** *n.*

Toul (tuːl) *n.* a town in NE France: a leading episcopal see in the Middle Ages. Pop.: 16 832 (1975).

Toulon (*French* tulɔ̃) *n.* a fortified port and naval base in SE France, on the Mediterranean: naval arsenal developed by Henry IV and Richelieu, later fortified by Vauban. Pop.: 190 000 (1983).

Toulouse (tuː'luːz) *n.* a city in S France, on the Garonne River: scene of severe religious strife in the early 13th and mid-16th centuries; university (1229). Pop.: 372 159 (1983 est.). Ancient name: **Tolosa** (tə'ləʊsə).

Toulouse-Lautrec (*French* tuluzlotrɛk) *n.* **Henri (Marie Raymond) de** (ɑ̃ri də). 1864–1901, French painter and lithographer, noted for his paintings and posters of the life of Montmartre, Paris.

toupee ('tuːpeɪ) *n.* a hairpiece worn by men to cover a bald place. [C18: apparently from F *toupet* forelock, from OF *toup* top, of Gmc origin]

tour (tʊə) *n.* **1.** an extended journey visiting places of interest along the route. **2.** *Mil.* a period of service, esp. in one place. **3.** a short trip, as for inspection. **4.** a trip made by a theatre company, orchestra, etc., to perform in several places. **5.** an overseas trip made by a cricket or rugby team, etc., to play in several places. ~*vb.* **6.** to make a tour of (a place). [C14: from OF: a turn, from L *tornus* a lathe, from Gk *tornos*]

touraco *or* **turaco** ('tʊərə,kəʊ) *n., pl.* **-cos.** any of a family of brightly coloured crested African birds. [C18: of West African origin]

Touraine (*French* turɛn) *n.* a former province of NW central France: at its height in the 16th century as an area of royal residences, esp. along the Loire. Chief town: Tours.

Tourane (tuː'rɑːn) *n.* the former name of **Da Nang.**

Tourcoing (*French* turkwɛ̃) *n.* a town in NE France: textile manufacturing. Pop.: 102 121 (1983).

tour de force *French.* (tur də fɔrs) *n., pl.* **tours de force** (tur). a masterly or brilliant stroke, creation, effect, or accomplishment. [lit.: feat of skill or strength]

Touré ('tʊəreɪ) *n.* **(Ahmed) Sékou** ('seɪkuː). 1922–84, president of the Republic of Guinea (1958–84).

tourer ('tʊərə) *n.* a large open car with a folding top, usually seating a driver and four passengers. Also called (esp. U.S.): **touring car.**

tourism ('tʊərɪzəm) *n.* tourist travel, esp. when regarded as an industry.

tourist ('tʊərɪst) *n.* **1. a.** a person who travels for pleasure, usually sightseeing and staying in hotels. **b.** (*as modifier*): *tourist attractions.* **2.** a person on an excursion or sightseeing tour. **3.** a member of a touring team. **4.** Also called: **tourist class.** the lowest class of accommodation on a passenger ship. ~*adj.* **5.** of or relating to tourist accommodation. —**tour'istic** *adj.*

touristy ('tʊərɪstɪ) *adj. Inf., often derog.* abounding in or designed for tourists.

tourmaline ('tʊəmə,liːn) *n.* any of a group of hard glassy minerals of variable colour consisting of a complex silicate of boron and aluminium in crystalline form: used in jewellery and optical and electrical equipment. [C18: from G *Turmalin,* from Sinhalese *toramalli* carnelian]

Tournai (*French* turnɛ) *n.* a city in W Belgium, in Hainaut province on the River Scheldt: under several different European rulers until 1814. Pop.: 66 998 (1987 est.). Flemish name: **Doornik.**

tournament ('tʊənəmənt) *n.* **1.** a sporting competition in which contestants play a series of games to determine an overall winner. **2.** a meeting for athletic or other sporting contestants: *an archery tournament.* **3.** *Medieval history.* a martial sport or contest in which mounted combatants fought for a prize. [C13: from OF *torneiement,* from *torneier* to fight on horseback, lit.: to turn, from the constant wheeling round of the combatants; see TOURNEY]

tournedos ('tʊənə,dəʊ) *n., pl.* **-dos** (-,dəʊz). a thick round steak of beef. [from F, from *tourner* to TURN + *dos* back]

Tourneur ('tɜːnə) *n.* **Cyril.** ?1575–1626, English dramatist; author of *The Atheist's Tragedy* (1611) and, reputedly, of *The Revenger's Tragedy* (1607).

tourney ('tʊənɪ, 'tɔː-) *Medieval history.* ~*n.* **1.** a knightly tournament. ~*vb.* **2.** (*intr.*) to engage in a tourney. [C13: from OF *torneier,* from Vulgar L *tornidiāre* (unattested) to turn constantly, from L *tornāre* to TURN (in a lathe); see TOURNAMENT]

tourniquet ('tʊənɪ,keɪ) *n. Med.* any device for constricting an artery of the arm or leg to control bleeding. [C17: from F: device that operates by turning, from *tourner* to TURN]

tour operator *n.* a person or company that specializes in providing package holidays.

Tours (*French* tur) *n.* a town in W central France, on the River Loire: scene of the defeat of the Arabs in 732, ending the advance of Islam in W Europe. Pop.: 139 789 (1983 est.).

tousle ('taʊzʲl) *vb.* (*tr.*) **1.** to tangle, ruffle, or disarrange. **2.** to treat roughly. ~*n.* **3.** a disorderly, tangled, or rumpled state. **4.** a dishevelled or disordered mass, esp. of hair. [C15: from Low G *tūsen* to shake]

Toussaint L'Ouverture (*French* tusɛ̃ luvɛrtyr) *n.* **Pierre Dominique** (pjɛr dɔminik). ?1743–1803, Haitian revolutionary leader. He was made governor of the island by the French Revolutionary government (1794) and expelled the Spanish and British but when Napoleon I proclaimed the re-establishment of slavery he was arrested. He died in prison in France.

tout (taʊt) *vb.* **1.** to solicit (business, customers, etc.) or hawk (merchandise), esp. in a brazen way. **2.** (*intr.*) **a.** to spy on racehorses being trained in order to obtain information for betting purposes. **b.** to sell such information or to take bets, esp. in public places. ~*n.* **3.** a person who touts. **4.** Also: **ticket tout.** a person who sells tickets for a heavily booked event at inflated prices. [C14 (in the sense: to peer, look out): rel. to OE *tȳtan* to peep out] —'**touter** *n.*

tout à fait *French.* (tut a fɛ) *adv.* completely.

tout de suite *French.* (tud sɥit) *adv.* at once.

tout le monde *French.* (tu lə mɔ̃d) *n.* all the world; everyone.

tovarisch, tovarich, *or* **tovarish** (tə'vɑːrɪʃ) *n.* comrade: a term of address. [from Russian]

tow[1] (təʊ) *vb.* **1.** (*tr.*) to pull or drag (a vehicle, boat, etc.), esp. by means of a rope or cable. ~*n.* **2.** the act or an instance of towing. **3.** the state of being towed (esp. in **in tow, on tow**). **4.** something towed. **5.** something used for towing. **6. in tow.** in one's charge or under one's influence. **7.** short for **ski tow.** [OE *togian*] —'**towable** *adj.* —'**towage** *n.*

tow[2] (təʊ) *n.* the coarse and broken fibres of hemp, flax, jute, etc., preparatory to spinning. [OE *tōw*] —'**towy** *adj.*

toward *adj.* ('təʊəd). **1.** *Now rare.* in progress; afoot. **2.** *Obs.* about to happen; imminent. **3.** *Obs.* promising or favourable. ~*prep.* (tə'wɔːd, tɔːd). **4.** a variant of **towards.** [OE *tōweard*]

towards (tə'wɔːdz, tɔːdz) *prep.* **1.** in the direction or vicinity of: *towards London.* **2.** with regard to: *her feelings towards me.* **3.** as a contribution or help to: *money towards a new car.* **4.** just before: *towards noon.* ~Also: **toward.**

towbar ('təʊ,bɑː) *n.* a rigid metal bar or frame used for towing vehicles.

towboat ('təʊ,bəʊt) *n.* another word for **tug** (sense 4).

tow-coloured *adj.* pale yellow; flaxen.

towel ('taʊəl) *n.* **1.** a piece of absorbent cloth or paper used for drying things. **2. throw in the towel.** See **throw in** (sense 3). ~*vb.* **-elling, -elled** *or U.S.* **-eling, -eled.** **3.** (*tr.*) to dry or wipe with a towel. **4.** (*tr.;* often foll. by *up*) *Austral. sl.* to assault or beat (a person). [C13: from OF *toaille,* of Gmc origin]

towelling ('taʊəlɪŋ) n. an absorbent fabric used for making towels, bathrobes, etc.

tower ('taʊə) n. 1. a tall, usually square or circular structure, sometimes part of a larger building and usually built for a specific purpose. 2. a place of defence or retreat. 3. **tower of strength.** a person who gives support, comfort, etc. ~vb. 4. (intr.) to be or rise like a tower; loom. [C12: from OF tur, from L turris, from Gk]

Tower Hamlets n. a borough of Greater London, on the River Thames: contains the main part of the East End. Pop.: 152 800 (1986 est.).

towering ('taʊərɪŋ) adj. 1. very tall; lofty. 2. outstanding, as in importance or stature. 3. (prenominal) very intense: a towering rage.

Tower of London n. a fortress in the City of London, on the River Thames: begun 1078; later extended and used as a palace, the main state prison, and now as a museum containing the crown jewels.

towhead ('taʊ,hɛd) n. 1. a person with blond or yellowish hair. 2. a head of such hair. [from TOW² (flax)] —,tow'headed adj.

towhee ('taʊ,hiː, 'taʊ-) n. any of various North American brownish-coloured sparrows. [C18: imit.]

towline ('taʊ,laɪn) n. another name for **towrope.**

town (taʊn) n. 1. a densely populated urban area, typically smaller than a city and larger than a village. 2. a city, borough, or other urban area. 3. (in the U.S.) a territorial unit of local government that is smaller than a county; township. 4. the nearest town or commercial district. 5. London or the chief city of an area. 6. the inhabitants of a town. 7. **go to town. a.** to make a supreme or unrestricted effort. **b.** Austral. & N.Z. inf. to lose one's temper. 8. **on the town.** seeking out entertainments and amusements. [OE tūn village] —'townish adj.

town clerk n. 1. (in Britain until 1974) the secretary and chief administrative officer of a town or city. 2. (in the U.S.) the official who keeps the records of a town.

town crier n. (formerly) a person employed to make public announcements in the streets.

townee (taʊ'niː) or U.S. **townie** or **towny** ('taʊnɪ) n. Inf., often disparaging. a permanent resident in a town, esp. as distinct from country dwellers or students.

Townes (taʊnz) n. **Charles Hard.** born 1915, U.S. physicist, noted for his research in quantum electronics leading to the invention of the maser and the laser; shared the Nobel prize for physics in 1964.

town gas n. coal gas manufactured for domestic and industrial use.

town hall n. the chief building in which municipal business is transacted, often with a hall for public meetings.

town house n. 1. a terraced house in an urban area, esp. a fashionable one. 2. a person's town residence as distinct from his country residence.

town planning n. the comprehensive planning of the physical and social development of a town. U.S. term: **city planning.**

townscape ('taʊnskeɪp) n. 1. a view of an urban scene. 2. an extensive area of urban development.

Townshend ('taʊnzend) n. 1. **Charles,** 2nd Viscount, nicknamed Turnip Townshend. 1674–1738, English politician and agriculturist. 2. **Pete.** born 1945, English rock guitarist, singer, and songwriter: member of the Who (1964–83) and composer of much of their material.

township ('taʊnʃɪp) n. 1. a small town. 2. (in the Scottish Highlands) a small crofting community. 3. (in the U.S. and Canada) a territorial area, esp. a subdivision of a county: often organized as a unit of local government. 4. (in Canada) a land-survey area, usually 36 square miles (93 square kilometres). 5. (in South Africa) a planned urban settlement of Black Africans or Coloureds. 6. English history. **a.** any of the local districts of a large parish. **b.** the parish itself.

townsman ('taʊnzmən) n., pl. **-men.** 1. an inhabitant of a town. 2. a person from the same town as oneself. —'towns,woman fem. n.

townspeople ('taʊnz,piːpəl) or **townsfolk** ('taʊnz,fəʊk) pl. n. the inhabitants of a town; citizens.

Townsville ('taʊnzvɪl) n. a port in E Australia, in NE Queensland on the Coral Sea: centre of a vast agricultural and mining hinterland. Pop.: 103 660 (1986 est.).

towpath ('taʊ,pɑːθ) n. a path beside a canal or river, used by people or animals towing boats. Also called: **towing path.**

towrope ('taʊ,rəʊp) n. a rope or cable used for towing a vehicle or vessel. Also called: **towline.**

tox-, toxic- or before a consonant **toxo-, toxico-** combining form. indicating poison: toxaemia. [from L toxicum]

toxaemia or U.S. **toxemia** (tɒk'siːmɪə) n. 1. a condition characterized by the presence of bacterial toxins in the blood. 2. the condition in pregnancy of pre-eclampsia or eclampsia. —**tox'aemic** or U.S. **tox'emic** adj.

toxic ('tɒksɪk) adj. 1. of or caused by a toxin or poison. 2. harmful or deadly. [C17: from Medical L toxicus, from L toxicum poison, from Gk toxikon (pharmakon) (poison) used on arrows, from toxon arrow] —'**toxically** adv. —**toxicity** (tɒk'sɪsɪtɪ) n.

toxicant ('tɒksɪkənt) n. 1. a toxic substance; poison. ~adj. 2. poisonous; toxic. [C19: from Med. L toxicāre to poison]

toxicology (,tɒksɪ'kɒlədʒɪ) n. the branch of science concerned with poisons, their effects, antidotes, etc. —**toxicological** (,tɒksɪkə'lɒdʒɪkəl) or ,**toxico'logic** adj. —,**toxi'cologist** n.

toxin ('tɒksɪn) n. 1. any of various poisonous substances produced by microorganisms that stimulate the production of neutralizing substances (antitoxins) in the body. 2. any other poisonous substance of plant or animal origin.

toxin-antitoxin n. a mixture of a toxin and antitoxin. The diphtheria toxin-antitoxin was formerly used for immunization.

toxocariasis (,tɒksəkə'raɪəsɪs) n. the infection of humans with the larvae of a genus of roundworms, Toxocara, of dogs and cats.

toxoid ('tɒksɔɪd) n. a toxin that has been treated to reduce its toxicity and is used in immunization to stimulate production of antitoxins.

toxophilite (tɒk'sɒfɪ,laɪt) Formal. ~n. 1. an archer. ~adj. 2. of archery. [C18: from Toxophilus, the title of a book (1545) by Ascham, designed to mean: a lover of the bow, from Gk toxon bow + philos loving] —**tox'ophily** n.

toxoplasmosis (,tɒksəʊplæz'məʊsɪs) n. a protozoal disease characterized by jaundice and convulsions. —,**toxo'plasmic** adj.

toy (tɔɪ) n. 1. an object designed to be played with. 2. **a.** something that is a nonfunctioning replica of something else, esp. a miniature one. **b.** (as modifier): a toy guitar. 3. any small thing of little value; trifle. 4. **a.** something small or miniature, esp. a miniature variety of a breed of dog. **b.** (as modifier): a toy poodle. ~vb. 5. (intr.; usually foll. by with) to play, fiddle, or flirt. [C16 (in the sense: amorous dalliance): from ?]

Toyama ('tɔʊjɑː,mɑː) n. a city in central Japan, on W Honshu on **Toyama Bay** (an inlet of the Sea of Japan): chemical and textile centre. Pop.: 314 000 (1985).

toy boy n. the much younger male lover of an older woman.

Toynbee ('tɔɪnbɪ) n. 1. **Arnold.** 1852–83, English economist and social reformer. 2. his nephew, **Arnold Joseph.** 1889–1975, English historian. In his chief work, A Study of History (1934–61), he attempted to analyse the principles determining the rise and fall of civilizations.

tr abbrev. for treasurer.

tr. abbrev. for: 1. transitive. 2. translated. 3. translator. 4. Music. trill. 5. trustee.

trabeated ('treɪbɪ,eɪtɪd) or **trabeate** ('treɪbɪɪt, -,eɪt) adj. Archit. constructed with horizontal beams as opposed to arches. [C19: back formation from trabeation, from L trabs a beam]

trabecula (trə'bɛkjʊlə) n., pl. **-lae** (-,liː). Anat., bot. any of various rod-shaped structures that support other organs. [C19: via NL from L: a little beam, from trabs a beam] —**tra'becular** or **tra'beculate** adj.

Trabzon ('trɑːbzɔːn) or **Trebizond** n. a port in NE Turkey, on the Black Sea: founded as a Greek colony in the 8th century B.C. at the terminus of an important trade route from central Europe to Asia. Pop.: 155 960 (1985).

trace¹ (treɪs) n. 1. a mark or other sign that something has been in a place. 2. a scarcely detectable amount or characteristic. 3. a footprint or other indication of the passage of an animal or person. 4. any line drawn by a recording instrument or a record consisting of a number of such lines. 5. something drawn, such as a tracing. 6.

Chiefly U.S. a beaten track or path. ~*vb.* **7.** (*tr.*) to follow, discover, or ascertain the course or development of (something). **8.** (*tr.*) to track down and find, as by following a trail. **9.** to copy (a design, map, etc.) by drawing over the lines visible through a superimposed sheet of transparent paper. **10.** (*tr.; often foll. by out*) **a.** to draw or delineate a plan or diagram of. **b.** to outline or sketch (an idea, etc.). **11.** (*tr.*) to decorate with tracery. **12.** (usually foll. by *back*) to follow or be followed to source; date back: *his ancestors trace back to the 16th century.* [C13: from F *tracier*, from Vulgar L *tractiāre* (unattested) to drag, from L *tractus*, from *trahere*] — **'traceable** *adj.* — **,tracea'bility** *or* **'traceableness** *n.* — **'traceably** *adv.*

trace² (treɪs) *n.* **1.** either of the two side straps that connect a horse's harness to the swingletree. **2.** *Angling.* a length of nylon or, formerly, gut attaching a hook or fly to a line. **3. kick over the traces.** to escape or defy control. [C14 *trais*, from OF *trait*, ult. from L *trahere* to drag]

trace element *n.* any of various chemical elements that occur in very small amounts in organisms and are essential for many physiological and biochemical processes.

tracer ('treɪsə) *n.* **1.** a person or thing that traces. **2.** a projectile that can be observed when in flight by the burning of chemical substances in its base. **3.** *Med.* any radioactive isotope introduced into the body to study metabolic processes, etc., by following its progress with a Geiger counter or other detector. **4.** an investigation to trace missing cargo, mail, etc.

tracer bullet *n.* a round of small arms ammunition containing a tracer.

tracery ('treɪsərɪ) *n., pl.* **-eries. 1.** a pattern of interlacing ribs, esp. as used in the upper part of a Gothic window, etc. **2.** any fine pattern resembling this. — **'traceried** *adj.*

trachea (trə'ki:ə) *n., pl.* **-cheae** (-'ki:i:). **1.** *Anat., zool.* the tube that conveys inhaled air from the larynx to the bronchi. **2.** any of the tubes in insects and related animals that convey air from the spiracles to the tissues. [C16: from Med. L, from Gk *trakheia*, shortened from (*artēria*) *trakheia* rough (artery), from *trakhus* rough] — **tra'cheal** *or* **tra'cheate** *adj.*

tracheitis (,treɪkɪ'aɪtɪs) *n.* inflammation of the trachea.

tracheo- *or before a vowel* **trache-** *combining form.* denoting the trachea.

tracheotomy (,trækɪ'ɒtəmɪ) *n., pl.* **-mies.** surgical incision into the trachea, as performed when the air passage has been blocked.

trachoma (trə'kəʊmə) *n.* a chronic contagious disease of the eye caused by a virus-like organism characterized by inflammation of the conjunctiva and cornea and the formation of scar tissue. [C17: from NL, from Gk *trakhōma* roughness, from *trakhus* rough] — **trachomatous** (trə'kɒmətəs) *adj.*

trachyte ('treɪkaɪt, 'træ-) *n.* a light-coloured fine-grained volcanic rock. [C19: from F, from Gk *trakhutēs*, from *trakhus* rough]

tracing ('treɪsɪŋ) *n.* **1.** a copy made by tracing. **2.** the act of making a trace. **3.** a record made by an instrument.

track (træk) *n.* **1.** the mark or trail left by something that has passed by. **2.** any road or path, esp. a rough one. **3.** a rail or pair of parallel rails on which a vehicle, such as a locomotive, runs. **4.** a course of action, thought, etc.: *don't start on that track again!* **5.** a line of motion or travel, such as flight. **6.** an endless band on the wheels of a tank, tractor, etc., to enable it to move across rough ground. **7. a.** a course for running or racing. **b.** (*as modifier*): *track events.* **8.** *U.S. & Canad.* **a.** sports performed on a track. **b.** track and field events as a whole. **9.** a path on a magnetic recording medium, esp. magnetic tape, on which music or speech is recorded. **10.** Also called: **band.** any of a number of separate sections in the recording on either side of a gramophone record. **11.** the distance between the points of contact with the ground of a pair of wheels, as of a motor vehicle. **12. keep** (*or* **lose**) **track of.** to follow (or fail to follow) the passage, course, or progress of. **13. off the track.** away from what is correct or true. **14. on the track of.** on the scent or trail of; pursuing. ~*vb.* **15.** to follow the trail of (a person, animal, etc.). **16.** to follow the flight path of (a satellite, etc.) by picking up signals transmitted or reflected by it. **17.** *U.S. railways.* **a.** to provide with a track. **b.** to run on a track of (a certain width). **18.** (of a camera or camera-operator) to follow (a moving object) while operating.

19. to follow a track through (a place): *to track the jungles.* **20.** (*intr.*) (of the pick-up, stylus, etc., of a record player) to follow the groove of a record. ~*See also* **tracks.** [C15: from OF *trac*, prob. of Gmc origin] — **'tracker** *n.*

track down *vb.* (*tr., adv.*) to find by tracking or pursuing.

tracker dog *n.* a dog specially trained to search for missing people.

track event *n.* a competition in athletics, such as relay running or sprinting, that takes place on a running track.

tracking station *n.* a station that can use a radio or radar beam to follow the path of an object in space or in the atmosphere.

tracklaying ('træk,leɪɪŋ) *adj. also* **tracked.** (of a vehicle) having an endless jointed metal band around the wheels.

track record *n. Inf.* the past record of the accomplishments and failures of a person, business, etc.

track rod *n.* the rod connecting the two front wheels of a motor vehicle.

tracks (træks) *pl. n.* **1.** (*sometimes sing.*) marks, such as footprints, etc., left by someone or something that has passed. **2. in one's tracks.** on the very spot where one is standing. **3. make tracks.** to leave or depart. **4. make tracks for.** to go or head towards.

track shoe *n.* either of a pair of light running shoes fitted with steel spikes for better grip.

tracksuit ('træk,su:t) *n.* a warm suit worn by athletes, etc., esp. during training.

tract¹ (trækt) *n.* **1.** an extended area, as of land. **2.** *Anat.* a system of organs, glands, etc., that has a particular function: *the digestive tract.* **3.** *Arch.* an extended period of time. [C15: from L *tractus* a stretching out, from *trahere* to drag]

tract² (trækt) *n.* a treatise or pamphlet, esp. a religious or moralistic one. [C15: from L *tractātus* TRACTATE]

tractable ('træktəb²l) *adj.* **1.** easily controlled or persuaded. **2.** readily worked; malleable. [C16: from L *tractābilis*, from *tractāre* to manage, from *trahere* to draw] — **,tracta'bility** *or* **'tractableness** *n.* — **'tractably** *adv.*

Tractarianism (træk'tɛərɪə,nɪzəm) *n.* another name for the **Oxford Movement.** [after the series of tracts, *Tracts for the Times* published between 1833 and 1841, in which the principles of the movement were presented] — **Trac'tarian** *n., adj.*

tractate ('trækteɪt) *n.* a treatise. [C15: from L *tractātus*, from *tractāre* to handle; see TRACTABLE]

traction ('trækʃən) *n.* **1.** the act of drawing or pulling, esp. by motive power. **2.** the state of being drawn or pulled. **3.** *Med.* the application of a steady pull on a limb, etc., using a system of weights and pulleys or splints. **4.** adhesive friction, as between a wheel of a motor vehicle and the road. [C17: from Med. L *tractiō*, from L *tractus* dragged, from *trahere* to drag] — **'tractional** *adj.* — **tractive** ('træktɪv) *adj.*

traction engine *n.* a steam-powered locomotive used, esp. formerly, for drawing heavy loads along roads or over rough ground.

tractor ('træktə) *n.* **1.** a motor vehicle with large rear wheels or endless belt treads, used to pull heavy loads, esp. farm machinery. **2.** a short vehicle with a driver's cab, used to pull a trailer, as in an articulated lorry. [C18: from LL: one who pulls, from *trahere* to drag]

Tracy ('treɪsɪ) *n.* **Spencer.** 1900–67, U.S. film actor. His films include *The Power and the Glory* (1933), *Captains Courageous* (1937) and *Boys' Town* (1938), for both of which he won Oscars, *Adam's Rib* (1949), and *Bad Day at Black Rock* (1955).

trad (træd) *n.* **1.** *Chiefly Brit.* traditional jazz. ~*adj.* **2.** short for **traditional.**

trade (treɪd) *n.* **1.** the act or an instance of buying and selling goods and services. **2.** a personal occupation, esp. a craft requiring skill. **3.** the people and practices of an industry, craft, or business. **4.** exchange of one thing for something else. **5.** the regular clientele of a firm or industry. **6.** amount of custom or commercial dealings; business. **7.** a specified market or business: *the tailoring trade.* **8.** an occupation in commerce, as opposed to a profession. ~*vb.* **9.** (*tr.*) to buy and sell (merchandise). **10.** to exchange (one thing) for another. **11.** (*intr.*) to engage in trade. **12.** (*intr.*) to deal or do business (with). ~*See also* **trade-in, trade on.** [C14 (in the sense: track, hence, a regular business)] —'**tradable** *or* '**tradeable** *adj.*

trade cycle *n.* the recurrent fluctuation between boom and depression in the economic activity of a capitalist country.

trade discount *n.* a sum or percentage deducted from the list price of a commodity allowed to a retailer or by one enterprise to another in the same trade.

trade gap *n.* the amount by which the value of a country's visible imports exceeds that of visible exports; an unfavourable balance of trade.

trade-in *n.* **1. a.** a used article given in part payment for the purchase of a new article. **b.** a transaction involving such part payment. **c.** the valuation put on the article traded in. ~*vb.* **trade in.** **2.** (*tr., adv.*) to give (a used article) as part payment for a new article.

trademark ('treɪd,mɑːk) *n.* **1. a.** the name or other symbol used by a manufacturer or dealer to distinguish his products from those of competitors. **b. Registered Trademark.** one that is officially registered and legally protected. **2.** any distinctive sign or mark of the presence of a person or animal. ~*vb.* (*tr.*) **3.** to label with a trademark. **4.** to register as a trademark.

trade name *n.* **1.** the name used by a trade to refer to a commodity, service, etc. **2.** the name under which a commercial enterprise operates in business.

trade-off *n.* an exchange, esp. as a compromise.

trade on *vb.* (*intr., prep.*) to exploit or take advantage of: *he traded on her endless patience.*

trade plate *n.* a numberplate attached temporarily to a vehicle by a dealer, etc., before the vehicle has been registered.

trader ('treɪdə) *n.* **1.** a person who engages in trade. **2.** a vessel regularly employed in trade. **3.** *Stock Exchange, U.S.* a member who operates mainly on his own account.

tradescantia (,trædɛs'kænʃɪə) *n.* any of a genus of plants widely cultivated for their striped variegated leaves. [C18: NL, after John *Tradescant* (1608–62), E botanist]

trade secret *n.* a secret formula, technique, process, etc., known and used to advantage by only one manufacturer.

tradesman ('treɪdzmən) *n., pl.* **-men. 1.** a man engaged in trade, esp. a retail dealer. **2.** a skilled worker. —'**trades,woman** *fem. n.*

tradespeople ('treɪdz,piːpˀl) *or* **tradesfolk** ('treɪdz- ,fəʊk) *pl. n. Chiefly Brit.* people engaged in trade, esp. shopkeepers.

Trades Union Congress *n.* the major association of British trade unions, which includes all the larger unions. Abbrev.: **TUC**

trade union *or* **trades union** *n.* an association of employees formed to improve their incomes and working conditions by collective bargaining. — **trade unionism** *or* **trades unionism** *n.* — **trade unionist** *or* **trades union- ist** *n.*

trade wind (wɪnd) *n.* a wind blowing obliquely towards the equator either from the northeast in the N hemisphere or the southeast in the S hemisphere, between latitudes 30° N and S. [C17: from *to blow trade* to blow steadily in one direction, from *trade* in the obs. sense: a track]

trading estate *n. Chiefly Brit.* a large area in which a number of commercial or industrial firms are situated.

trading post *n.* a general store in an unsettled or thinly populated region.

tradition (trə'dɪʃən) *n.* **1.** the handing down from generation to generation of customs, beliefs, etc. **2.** the body of customs, thought, etc., belonging to a particular country, people, family, or institution over a long period. **3.** a specific custom or practice of long standing. **4.** *Christianity.* a doctrine regarded as having been established by Christ or the apostles though not contained in Scripture. **5.** (*often cap.*) *Judaism.* a body of laws regarded as having been handed down from Moses orally. **6.** the beliefs and customs of Islam supplementing the Koran. **7.** *Law, chiefly Roman & Scots.* the act of formally transferring ownership of movable property. [C14: from L *trāditiō* a handing down, surrender, from *trādere* to give up, transmit, from TRANS-+ *dāre* to give] —**tra'ditionless** *adj.*

traditional (trə'dɪʃənˀl) *adj.* **1.** of, relating to, or being a tradition. **2.** of the style of jazz originating in New Orleans, characterized by collective improvisation by a front line of trumpet, trombone, and clarinet. — **tra'ditionally** *adv.*

traditionalism (trə'dɪʃənˀ,lɪzəm) *n.* **1.** the doctrine that all knowledge originates in divine revelation and is perpetuated by tradition. **2.** adherence to tradition, esp. in religion. —**tra'ditionalist** *n., adj.* —**tra,ditional'istic** *adj.*

traditional logic *n.* the logic of the late Middle Ages, derived from Aristotelian logic, and concerned esp. with the study of the syllogism.

traduce (trə'djuːs) *vb.* (*tr.*) to speak badly or maliciously of. [C16: from L *trādūcere* to lead over, disgrace] —**tra'ducement** *n.* —**tra'ducer** *n.*

traffic ('træfɪk) *n.* **1. a.** the vehicles coming and going in a street, town, etc. **b.** (*as modifier*): *traffic lights.* **2.** the movement of vehicles, people, etc., in a particular place or for a particular purpose: *sea traffic.* **3.** (usually foll. by *with*) dealings or business. **4.** trade, esp. of an illicit kind: *drug traffic.* **5.** the aggregate volume of messages transmitted through a communications system in a given period. **6.** *Chiefly U.S.* the number of customers patronizing a commercial establishment in a given time period. ~*vb.* **-ficking, -ficked.** (*intr.*) **7.** (often foll. by *in*) to carry on trade or business, esp. of an illicit kind. **8.** (usually foll. by *with*) to have dealings. [C16: from OF *trafique*, from OIt. *traffico*, from *trafficare* to engage in trade] —'**trafficker** *n.*

trafficator ('træfɪ,keɪtə) *n.* (formerly) an illuminated arm on a motor vehicle that was raised to indicate a left or right turn.

traffic island *n.* a raised area in the middle of a road designed as a guide for traffic flow and to provide a stopping place for pedestrians crossing.

traffic light *or* **signal** *n.* one of a set of coloured lights placed at crossroads, junctions, etc., to control the flow of traffic.

traffic pattern *n.* a pattern of permitted lanes in the air around an airport to which an aircraft is restricted.

traffic warden *n. Brit.* a person who is appointed to supervise road traffic and report traffic offences.

tragacanth ('trægə,kænθ) *n.* **1.** any of various spiny plants that yield a substance that is made into a gum. **2.** the gum obtained from these plants, used in the manufacture of pills and lozenges and in calico printing. [C16: from F *tragacante*, from L *tragacantha* goat's thorn, from Gk, from *tragos* goat + *akantha* thorn]

tragedian (trə'dʒiːdɪən) *or* (*fem.*) **tragedienne** (trə,dʒiːdɪ'ɛn) *n.* **1.** an actor who specializes in tragic roles. **2.** a writer of tragedy.

tragedy ('trædʒɪdɪ) *n., pl.* **-dies. 1.** a play in which the protagonist falls to disaster through the combination of a personal failing and circumstances with which he cannot deal. **2.** any dramatic or literary composition dealing with serious or sombre themes and ending with disaster. **3.** the branch of drama dealing with such themes. **4.** the unfortunate aspect of something. **5.** a shocking or sad event; disaster. [C14: from OF *tragédie*, from L *tragoedia*, from Gk, from *tragos* goat + *ōidē* song; ?from the goatsatyrs of Peloponnesian plays]

tragic ('trædʒɪk) *or* (*less commonly*) **tragical** *adj.* **1.** of, relating to, or characteristic of tragedy. **2.** mournful or pitiable. —'**tragically** *adv.*

tragic flaw *n.* the failing of character in a tragic hero.

tragic irony *n.* the use of dramatic irony in a tragedy so that the audience is aware that a character's words or actions will bring about a tragic or fatal result, while the character himself is not.

tragicomedy (,trædʒɪ'kɒmɪdɪ) *n., pl.* **-dies. 1.** a drama in which aspects of both tragedy and comedy are found. **2.** an event or incident having both comic and tragic aspects. [C16: from F, ult. from LL *tragicōmoedia*] —,**trag-i'comic** *or* ,**tragi'comical** *adj.*

tragopan ('trægə,pæn) *n.* any of a genus of pheasants of S and SE Asia, having brightly coloured fleshy processes on the head. [C19: via L from Gk, from *tragos* goat + PAN]

tragus ('treɪgəs) *n., pl.* **-gi** (-dʒaɪ). the fleshy projection that partially covers the entrance to the external ear. [C17: from LL, from Gk *tragos* hairy projection of the ear, lit.: goat]

Traherne (trə'hɜːn) *n.* **Thomas.** 1637–74, English mystical prose writer and poet. His prose works include *Centuries of Meditations*, which was discovered in manuscript in 1896 and published in 1908.

trail (treɪl) *vb.* **1.** to drag, stream, or permit to drag or stream along a surface, esp. the ground. **2.** to make (a track) through (a place). **3.** to follow or hunt (an animal or person) by following marks or tracks. **4.** (when *intr.*, often foll. by *behind*) to lag or linger behind (a person or thing). **5.** (*intr.*) (esp. of plants) to extend or droop over or along a surface. **6.** (*intr.*) to be falling behind in a race: *the favourite is trailing at the last fence.* **7.** (*tr.*) to tow (a caravan, etc.) behind a motor vehicle. **8.** (*tr.*) to carry (a rifle) at the full length of the right arm in a horizontal position, with the muzzle to the fore. **9.** (*intr.*) to move wearily or slowly. **10.** (*tr.*) (on television or radio) to advertise (a future programme) with short extracts. ~*n.* **11.** a print, mark, or scent made by a person, animal, or object. **12.** the act or an instance of trailing. **13.** a path, track, or road, esp. one roughly blazed. **14.** something that trails behind or trails in loops or strands. **15.** the part of a towed gun carriage and limber that connects the two when in movement and rests on the ground as a partial support when unlimbered. [C14: from OF *trailler* to tow, from Vulgar L *tragulāre* (unattested), from L *trāgula* dragnet, from *trahere* to drag]

trail away *or* **off** *vb.* (*intr.*, *adv.*) to make or become fainter, quieter, or weaker.

trailblazer ('treɪl,bleɪzə) *n.* **1.** a leader or pioneer in a particular field. **2.** a person who blazes a trail. —'**trail,blazing** *adj.*, *n.*

trailer ('treɪlə) *n.* **1.** a road vehicle, usually two-wheeled, towed by a motor vehicle: used for transporting boats, etc. **2.** the rear section of an articulated lorry. **3.** a series of short extracts from a film, used to advertise it in a cinema or on television. **4.** a person or thing that trails. **5.** the U.S. and Canad. name for **caravan** (sense 1).

trailing edge *n.* the rear edge of a propeller blade or aerofoil. Cf. **leading edge.**

trail mix *n.* a mixture of nuts, dried fruits, and seeds, eaten as a snack, esp. originally by hikers.

train (treɪn) *vb.* **1.** (*tr.*) to guide or teach (to do something), as by subjecting to various exercises or experiences. **2.** (*tr.*) to control or guide towards a specific goal: *to train a plant up a wall.* **3.** (*intr.*) to do exercises and prepare for a specific purpose. **4.** (*tr.*) to improve or curb by subjecting to discipline: *to train the mind.* **5.** (*tr.*) to focus or bring to bear (on something): *to train a telescope on the moon.* ~*n.* **6.** a line of coaches or wagons coupled together and drawn by a railway locomotive. **7.** a sequence or series: *a train of disasters.* **8.** a procession of people, vehicles, etc., travelling together, such as one carrying equipment in support of a military operation. **9.** a series of interacting parts through which motion is transmitted: *a train of gears.* **10.** a fuse or line of gunpowder to an explosive charge, etc. **11.** something drawn along, such as the long back section of a dress that trails along the floor. **12.** a retinue or suite. [C14: from OF *trahiner*, from Vulgar L *tragināre* (unattested) to draw] —'**trainable** *adj.*

trainband ('treɪn,bænd) *n.* a company of English militia from the 16th to the 18th century. [C17: altered from *trained band*]

trainbearer ('treɪn,bɛərə) *n.* an attendant who holds up the train of a dignitary's robe or bride's gown.

trainee (treɪ'niː) *n.* **a.** a person undergoing training. **b.** (*as modifier*): *a trainee journalist.*

trainer ('treɪnə) *n.* **1.** a person who trains athletes. **2.** a piece of equipment employed in training, such as a simulated aircraft cockpit. **3.** a person who schools racehorses. **4.** (*pl.*) **a.** running shoes for sports training. **b.** casual shoes like these.

training ('treɪnɪŋ) *n.* **1. a.** the process of bringing a person, etc., to an agreed standard of proficiency, etc., by practice and instruction. **b.** (*as modifier*): *training college.* **2. in training. a.** undergoing physical training. **b.** physically fit. **3. out of training.** physically unfit.

train oil *n.* whale oil obtained from blubber. [C16: from earlier *train* or *trane*, from MLow G *trān*, or MDu. *traen* tear, drop]

train spotter *n.* a person who collects the numbers of railway locomotives.

traipse *or* **trapes** (treɪps) *Inf.* ~*vb.* **1.** (*intr.*) to walk heavily or tiredly. ~*n.* **2.** a long or tiring walk; trudge. [C16: from ?]

trait (treɪt, treɪ) *n.* **1.** a characteristic feature or quality distinguishing a particular person or thing. **2.** *Rare.* a touch or stroke. [C16: from F, from OF: a pulling, from L *tractus*, from *trahere* to drag]

traitor ('treɪtə) *n.* a person who is guilty of treason or treachery, in betraying friends, country, a cause, etc. [C13: from OF *traitour*, from L *trāditor*, from *trādere* to hand over] —'**traitorous** *adj.* —'**traitress** *fem. n.*

Trajan ('treɪdʒən) *n.* Latin name *Marcus Ulpius Traianus.* ?53–117 A.D., Roman emperor (98–117). He extended the empire to the east and built many roads, bridges, canals, and towns.

trajectory (trə'dʒɛktərɪ) *n.*, *pl.* **-ries. 1.** the path described by an object moving in air or space, esp. the curved path of a projectile. **2.** *Geom.* a curve that cuts a family of curves or surfaces at a constant angle. [C17: from L *trājectus* cast over, from *trāicere* to throw across]

Tralee (trə'liː) *n.* a market town in SW Ireland, county town of Kerry, near **Tralee Bay** (an inlet of the Atlantic). Pop.: 16 495 (1981).

tram (træm) *n.* **1.** Also called: **tramcar.** an electrically driven public transport vehicle that runs on rails let into the surface of the road. U.S. and Canad. names: **streetcar, trolley car. 2.** a small vehicle on rails for carrying loads in a mine; tub. [C16 (in the sense: shaft of a cart): prob. from Low G *traam* beam] —'**tramless** *adj.*

tramline ('træm,laɪn) *n.* **1.** (*often pl.*) Also called: **tramway.** the tracks on which a tram runs. **2.** the route taken by a tram. **3.** (*often pl.*) the outer markings along the sides of a tennis or badminton court.

trammel ('træməl) *n.* **1.** (*often pl.*) a hindrance to free action or movement. **2.** Also called: **trammel net.** a fishing net in three sections, the two outer nets having a large mesh and the middle one a fine mesh. **3.** *Rare.* a fowling net. **4.** *U.S.* a shackle for a horse. **5.** a device for drawing ellipses consisting of a flat sheet having a cruciform slot in which run two pegs attached to a beam. **6.** (*sometimes pl.*) a beam compass. **7.** a device set in a fireplace to support cooking pots. ~*vb.* **-elling, -elled** *or U.S.* **-eling, -eled.** (*tr.*) **8.** to hinder or restrain. **9.** to catch or ensnare. [C14: from OF *tramail* three-mesh net, from LL *trēmaculum*, from L *trēs* three + *macula* mesh in a net]

tramontane (trə'mɒnteɪn) *adj.* **1.** being or coming from the far side of the mountains, esp. from the other side of the Alps as seen from Italy. ~*n.* **2.** an inhabitant of a tramontane country. **3.** Also called: **tramontana.** a cold dry wind blowing south or southwest from the mountains in Italy and the W Mediterranean. [C16: from It. *tramontano*, from L *trānsmontānus*, from TRANS- + *montānus*, from *mōns* mountain]

tramp (træmp) *vb.* **1.** (*intr.*) to walk long and far; hike. **2.** to walk heavily or firmly across or through (a place). **3.** (*intr.*) to wander about as a vagabond or tramp. **4.** (*tr.*) to traverse on foot, esp. laboriously or wearily. **5.** (*intr.*) to tread or trample. ~*n.* **6.** a person who travels about on foot, living by begging or doing casual work. **7.** a long hard walk; hike. **8.** a heavy or rhythmic tread. **9.** the sound of heavy treading. **10.** a merchant ship that does not run on a regular schedule but carries cargo wherever the shippers desire. **11.** *Sl., chiefly U.S. & Canad.* a prostitute or promiscuous girl or woman. [C14: prob. from MLow G *trampen*] —'**trampish** *adj.*

tramper ('træmpə) *n. N.Z.* a person who tramps, or walks long distances, in the bush.

tramping ('træmpɪŋ) *n. N.Z.* **1.** the leisure activity of walking in the bush. **2.** (*as modifier*): *tramping boots.*

trample ('træmp³l) *vb.* (when *intr.*, usually foll. by *on*, *upon*, or *over*) **1.** to stamp or walk roughly (on). **2.** to encroach (upon) so as to violate or hurt. ~*n.* **3.** the action or sound of trampling. [C14: frequentative of TRAMP] —'**trampler** *n.*

trampoline ('træmpəlɪn, -,liːn) *n.* **1.** a tough canvas sheet suspended by springs or cords from a frame, used by acrobats, gymnasts, etc. ~*vb.* **2.** (*intr.*) to exercise on a trampoline. [C18: via Sp. from It. *trampolino*, from *trampoli* stilts, of Gmc origin] —'**trampoliner** *or* '**trampolinist** *n.*

trance (trɑːns) *n.* **1.** a hypnotic state resembling sleep. **2.** any mental state in which a person is unaware of the environment, characterized by loss of voluntary movement, rigidity, and lack of sensitivity to external stimuli. **3.** a dazed or stunned state. **4.** a state of ecstasy or mystic absorption so intense as to cause a temporary loss of consciousness at the earthly level. **5.** *Spiritualism.* a state in which a medium can supposedly be controlled by an intelligence from without as a means of communication with the dead. ~*vb.* **6.** (*tr.*) to put into or as into a trance.

[C14: from OF *transe*, from *transir* to faint, from L *trānsīre* to go over] —'**trance,like** *adj.*

tranche ('trɑːnʃ) *n.* an instalment or portion of a large sum of money, such as a loan to a government or an issue of shares. [F, lit.: slice]

trannie *or* **tranny** ('trænɪ) *n., pl.* **-nies.** *Inf., chiefly Brit.* a transistor radio.

tranquil ('træŋkwɪl) *adj.* calm, peaceful, or quiet. [C17: from L *tranquillus*] —'**tranquilly** *adv.*

tranquillity *or U.S.* (*sometimes*) **tranquility** (træŋ-'kwɪlɪtɪ) *n.* a state of calm or quietude.

tranquillize, -ise, *or U.S.* **tranquilize** ('træŋkwɪ,laɪz) *vb.* to make or become calm or calmer. —,**tranquilli'zation, -i'sation,** *or U.S.* ,**tranquili'zation** *n.*

tranquillizer, -iser *or U.S.* **tranquilizer** ('træŋkwɪ,laɪzə) *n.* 1. a drug that calms a person. 2. anything that tranquillizes.

tranquillo (,træŋ'kwiːləʊ) *adj. Music.* calm; tranquil. [It.]

trans. *abbrev. for:* 1. transaction. 2. transferred. 3. transitive. 4. translated. 5. translator. 6. transport(ation). 7. transverse.

trans- *prefix.* 1. across, beyond, crossing, on the other side: *transatlantic.* 2. changing thoroughly: *transliterate.* 3. transcending: *transubstantiation.* 4. transversely: *transect.* 5. (*often in italics*) indicating that a chemical compound has a molecular structure in which two identical groups or atoms are on opposite sides of a double bond: *trans*-butadiene. [from L *trāns* across, through, beyond]

transact (træn'zækt) *vb.* to do, conduct, or negotiate (business, a deal, etc.). [C16: from L *trānsactus*, from *trānsigere*, lit.: to drive through] —**trans'actor** *n.*

transactinide (træns'æktɪ,naɪd) *n.* any artificially produced element with an atomic number greater than 103. [C20]

transaction (træn'zækʃən) *n.* 1. something that is transacted, esp. a business deal. 2. a transacting or being transacted. 3. (*pl.*) the records of the proceedings of a society, etc. —**trans'actional** *adj.*

transalpine (trænz'ælpaɪn) *adj.* (*prenominal*) 1. situated in or relating to places beyond the Alps, esp. from Italy. 2. passing over the Alps.

Transalpine Gaul *n.* (in the ancient world) that part of Gaul northwest of the Alps.

transatlantic (,trænzət'læntɪk) *adj.* 1. on or from the other side of the Atlantic. 2. crossing the Atlantic.

Transcaucasia (,trænskɔː'keɪzjə) *n.* a region of the SW Soviet Union, south of the Caucasus Mountains between the Black and Caspian Seas: formerly a constituent republic of the Soviet Union, divided in 1936 into the Georgian, Azerbaijan, and Armenian SSRs. —,**Transcau'casian** *adj., n.*

transceiver (træn'siːvə) *n.* a combined radio transmitter and receiver. [C20: from TRANS(MITTER) + (RE)CEIVER]

transcend (træn'send) *vb.* 1. to go above or beyond (a limit, expectation, etc.), as in degree or excellence. 2. (*tr.*) to be superior to. [C14: from L *trānscendere* to climb over]

transcendent (træn'sendənt) *adj.* 1. exceeding or surpassing in degree or excellence. 2. (in the philosophy of Kant) beyond or before experience. 3. *Theol.* (of God) having existence outside the created world. 4. free from the limitations inherent in matter. —*n.* 5. *Philosophy.* a transcendent thing. —**tran'scendence** *or* **tran'scendency** *n.* —**tran'scendently** *adv.*

transcendental (,trænsen'dentəl) *adj.* 1. transcendent, superior, or surpassing. 2. (in the philosophy of Kant) **a.** (of a judgment or logical deduction) being both synthetic and a priori. **b.** of or relating to knowledge of the presuppositions of thought. 3. *Philosophy.* beyond our experience of phenomena, although not beyond potential knowledge. 4. *Theol.* supernatural or mystical. 5. *Maths.* **a.** (of a number or quantity) not being a root of any polynomial with rational coefficients. **b.** (of a function) not capable of expression in terms of a finite number of arithmetical operations. —,**transcen'dentally** *adv.*

transcendentalism (,trænsen'dentə,lɪzəm) *n.* 1. **a.** any system of philosophy, esp. that of Kant, holding that the key to knowledge of the nature of reality lies in the critical examination of the processes of reason on which depends the nature of experience. **b.** any system of philosophy, esp. that of Emerson, that emphasizes intuition as a means to knowledge or the importance of the

search for the divine. 2. vague philosophical speculation. 3. the state of being transcendental. 4. something, such as thought or language, that is transcendental. —,**tran-scen'dentalist** *n., adj.*

transcendental meditation *n.* a technique, based on Hindu traditions, for relaxing and refreshing the mind and body through the silent repetition of a mantra.

transcontinental (,trænzkɒntɪ'nentəl) *adj.* 1. crossing a continent. 2. on or from the far side of a continent. —,**transconti'nentally** *adv.*

transcribe (træn'skraɪb) *vb.* (*tr.*) 1. to write, type, or print out fully from speech, notes, etc. 2. to transliterate or translate. 3. to make an electrical recording of (a programme or speech) for a later broadcast. 4. *Music.* to rewrite (a piece of music) for an instrument or medium other than that originally intended; arrange. 5. *Computers.* **a.** to transfer (information) from one storage device to another. **b.** to transfer (information) from a computer to an external storage device. [C16: from L *trānscrībere*] —**tran'scribable** *adj.* —**tran'scriber** *n.*

transcript ('trænskrɪpt) *n.* 1. a written, typed, or printed copy or manuscript made by transcribing. 2. *Chiefly U.S. & Canad.* an official record of a student's school progress. 3. any reproduction or copy. [C13: from L *trānscrīptum*, from *trānscrībere* to transcribe]

transcription (træn'skrɪpʃən) *n.* 1. the act or an instance of transcribing or the state of being transcribed. 2. something transcribed. 3. a representation in writing of the actual pronunciation of a speech sound, word, etc., using phonetic symbols. —**tran'scriptional** *or* **tran's-criptive** *adj.*

transducer (trænz'djuːsə) *n.* any device, such as a microphone or electric motor, that converts one form of energy into another. [C20: from L *trānsdūcere* to lead across]

transect *vb.* (træn'sɛkt). (*tr.*) 1. to cut or divide crossways. ~*n.* ('trænsɛkt). 2. a sample strip of land used to monitor plant distribution, animal populations, or some other feature, within a given area. [C17: from L TRANS- + *secāre* to cut] —**tran'section** *n.*

transept ('trænsept) *n.* either of the two wings of a cruciform church at right angles to the nave. [C16: from Anglo-L *trānseptum*, from L TRANS- + *saeptum* enclosure] —**tran'septal** *adj.*

transfer *vb.* (træns'fɜː), **-ferring, -ferred.** 1. to change or go or cause to change or go from one thing, person, or point to another. 2. to change (buses, trains, etc.). 3. *Law.* to make over (property, etc.) to another; convey. 4. to displace (a drawing, design, etc.) from one surface to another. 5. (of a football player) to change clubs or (of a club, manager, etc.) to sell or release (a player) to another club. 6. to leave one school, college, etc., and enrol at another. 7. to change (the meaning of a word, etc.), esp. by metaphorical extension. ~*n.* ('trænsfɜː). 8. the act, process, or system of transferring, or the state of being transferred. 9. a person or thing that transfers or is transferred. 10. a design or drawing that is transferred from one surface to another. 11. *Law.* the passing of title to property or other right from one person to another; conveyance. 12. any document or form effecting or regulating a transfer. 13. *Chiefly U.S. & Canad.* a ticket that allows a passenger to change routes. [C14: from L *trānsferre*, from TRANS-+ *ferre* to carry] —**trans'ferable** *or* **trans'ferrable** *adj.* —**transference** ('trænsfərəns) *n.*

transferable vote *n.* a vote that is transferred to a second candidate indicated by the voter if the first is eliminated from the ballot.

transferee (,trænsfə'riː) *n.* 1. *Property law.* a person to whom property is transferred. 2. a person who is transferred.

transfer fee *n.* a sum of money paid by one football club to another for a transferred player.

transferrin (træns'fɜːrɪn) *n. Biochem.* any of a group of blood proteins that transport iron. [C20: from TRANS- + FERRO- + -IN]

transfer RNA *n. Biochem.* any of several soluble forms of RNA of low molecular weight, each of which transports a specific amino acid to a ribosome during protein synthesis.

transfiguration (,trænsfɪgjʊ'reɪʃən) *n.* a transfiguring or being transfigured.

Transfiguration (,trænsfɪgjʊ'reɪʃən) *n.* 1. *New Testament.* the change in the appearance of Christ that took place before three disciples (Matthew 17:1–9). **2.** the Church festival held in commemoration of this on Aug. 6.

transfigure (træns'fɪgə) *vb. (usually tr.)* **1.** to change or cause to change in appearance. **2.** to become or cause to become more exalted. [C13: from L *trānsfigūrāre*, from TRANS- + *figūra* appearance] —**trans'figurement** *n.*

transfinite number (træns'faɪnaɪt) *n.* a cardinal or ordinal number used in the comparison of infinite sets for which several types of infinity can be classified.

transfix (træns'fɪks) *vb.* **-fixing, -fixed** *or* **-fixt.** (*tr.*) **1.** to render motionless, esp. with horror or shock. **2.** to impale or fix with a sharp weapon or other device. [C16: from L *trānsfīgere* to pierce through] —**transfixion** (træns'fɪkʃən) *n.*

transform *vb.* (træns'fɔːm). **1.** to alter or be altered in form, function, etc. **2.** (*tr.*) to convert (one form of energy) to another form. **3.** (*tr.*) *Maths.* to change the form of (an equation, etc.) by a mathematical transformation. **4.** (*tr.*) to change (an alternating current or voltage) using a transformer. ~*n.* ('træns,fɔːm). **5.** *Maths.* the result of a mathematical transformation. [C14: from L *trānsformāre*] —**trans'formable** *adj.* —**trans'formative** *adj.*

transformation (,trænsfə'meɪʃən) *n.* **1.** a change or alteration, esp. a radical one. **2.** a transforming or being transformed. **3.** *Maths.* **a.** a change in position or direction of the reference axes in a coordinate system without an alteration in their relative angle. **b.** an equivalent change in an expression or equation resulting from the substitution of one set of variables by another. **4.** *Physics.* a change in an atomic nucleus to a different nuclide as the result of the emission of either an alpha-particle or a beta-particle. **5.** *Linguistics.* another word for **transformational rule. 6.** an apparently miraculous change in the appearance of a stage set. —**,transfor'mational** *adj.*

transformational grammar *n.* a grammatical description of a language making essential use of transformational rules.

transformational rule *n. Generative grammar.* a rule that converts one phrase marker into another. Taken together, these rules convert the deep structures of sentences into their surface structures.

transformer (træns'fɔːmə) *n.* **1.** a device that transfers an alternating current from one circuit to one or more other circuits, usually with a change of voltage. **2.** a person or thing that transforms.

transfuse (træns'fjuːz) *vb.* (*tr.*) **1.** to permeate or infuse. **2. a.** to inject (blood, etc.) into a blood vessel. **b.** to give a transfusion to (a patient). [C15: from L *trānsfundere* to pour out] —**trans'fuser** *n.* —**trans'fusible** *or* **trans'fusable** *adj.* —**trans'fusive** *adj.*

transfusion (træns'fjuːʒən) *n.* **1.** a transfusing. **2.** the injection of blood, blood plasma, etc., into the blood vessels of a patient.

transgress (trænz'grɛs) *vb.* **1.** to break (a law, etc.). **2.** to go beyond or overstep (a limit). [C16: from L *trānsgredī*, from TRANS- + *gradī* to step] —**trans'gressive** *adj.* —**trans'gressor** *n.*

transgression (trænz'grɛʃən) *n.* **1.** a breach of a law, etc.; sin or crime. **2.** a transgressing.

tranship (træn'ʃɪp) *vb.* **-shipping, -shipped.** a variant spelling of **transship.**

transhumance (træns'hjuːməns) *n.* the seasonal migration of livestock to suitable grazing grounds. [C20: from F, from *transhumer* to change one's pastures, from Sp. *trashumar*, from L TRANS- + *humus* ground] —**trans'humant** *adj.*

transient ('trænzɪənt) *adj.* **1.** for a short time only; temporary or transitory. ~*n.* **2.** a transient person or thing. [C17: from L *trānsiēns* going over, from *trānsīre* to pass over] —'**transiently** *adv.* —'**transience** *or* '**transiency** *n.*

transistor (træn'zɪstə) *n.* **1.** a semiconductor device, having three or more terminals attached to electrode regions, in which current flowing between two electrodes is controlled by a voltage or current applied to one or more specified electrodes. The device has replaced the valve in most circuits since it is much smaller and works at a much lower voltage. **2.** *Inf.* a transistor radio. [C20: orig. a trademark, from TRANSFER + RESISTOR, from the transfer of electric signals across a resistor]

transistorize *or* **-ise** (træn'zɪstə,raɪz) *vb.* **1.** to convert to the use or manufacture of transistors and other solid-state components. **2.** (*tr.*) to equip with transistors and other solid-state components.

transit ('trænsɪt, 'trænz-) *n.* **1. a.** the passage or conveyance of goods or people. **b.** (*as modifier*): *a transit visa.* **2.** a change or transition. **3.** a route. **4.** *Astron.* **a.** the passage of a celestial body or satellite across the face of a larger body as seen from the earth. **b.** the apparent passage of a celestial body across the meridian. **5. in transit.** while being conveyed; during passage. ~*vb.* **6.** to make a transit through or over (something). [C15: from L *trānsitus* a going over, from *trānsīre* to pass over]

transit camp *n.* a camp in which refugees, soldiers, etc., live temporarily.

transit instrument *n.* an astronomical instrument used to time the transit of a star, etc., across the meridian.

transition (træn'zɪʃən) *n.* **1.** change or passage from one state or stage to another. **2.** the period of time during which something changes. **3.** *Music.* **a.** a movement from one key to another; modulation. **b.** a linking passage between two divisions in a composition; bridge. **4.** a style of architecture in the late 11th and early 12th centuries, characterized by late Romanesque forms combined with early Gothic details. **5.** *Physics.* a change in the configuration of an atomic nucleus, involving either a change in energy level or a transformation to another element or isotope. **6.** a sentence, passage, etc., that links sections of a written work. [C16: from L *transitio*; see TRANSIENT] —**tran'sitional** *adj.* —**tran'sitionally** *adv.*

transition element *n. Chem.* any element belonging to one of three series of elements with atomic numbers between 21 and 30, 39 and 48, and 57 and 80. They have an incomplete penultimate electron shell and tend to form complexes.

transition temperature *n.* the temperature at which a sudden change of physical properties occurs.

transitive ('trænsɪtɪv) *adj.* **1.** *Grammar.* **a.** denoting an occurrence of a verb when it requires a direct object or denoting a verb that customarily requires a direct object. **b.** (*as n.*): *these verbs are transitives.* **2.** *Logic, maths.* having the property that if one object bears a relationship to a second object that also bears the same relationship to a third object, then the first object bears this relationship to the third object: *if x = y and y = z then x = z.* ~Cf. **intransitive.** [C16: from LL *trānsitīvus*, from L *trānsitus* a going over; see TRANSIENT] —'**transitively** *adv.* —,**transi'tivity** *or* '**transitiveness** *n.*

transitory ('trænsɪtərɪ, -trɪ) *adj.* of short duration; transient or ephemeral. [C14: from Church L *trānsitōrius* passing, from L *trānsitus* a crossing over] —'**transitoriness** *n.*

transit theodolite *n.* a theodolite the telescope of which can be rotated completely about its horizontal axis.

Trans-Jordan *n.* the former name (1922–49) of **Jordan.** —,**Trans-Jor'danian** *adj., n.*

Transkei (træn'skaɪ) *n.* a Bantu homeland in South Africa, in E Cape Province: the largest of South Africa's Bantu homelands and the first Bantu self-governing territory (1963); became an independent state in 1976 but this status is not recognized outside South Africa. Capital: Umtata. Pop.: 3 000 000 (1985 est.). Area: 41 002 sq. km (15 831 sq. miles). —**Trans'keian** *adj., n.*

transl. *abbrev. for:* **1.** translated. **2.** translator.

translate (træns'leɪt, trænz-) *vb.* **1.** to express or be capable of being expressed in another language. **2.** (*intr.*) to act as translator. **3.** (*tr.*) to express or explain in simple or less technical language. **4.** (*tr.*) to interpret or infer the significance of (gestures, symbols, etc.). **5.** (*tr.*) to transform or convert: *to translate hope into reality.* **6.** to transfer from one place or position to another. **7.** (*tr.*) *Theol.* to transfer (a person) from one place or plane of existence to another, as from earth to heaven. **8.** (*tr.*) *Maths, physics.* to move (a figure or body) laterally, without rotation, dilation, or angular displacement. [C13: from L *trānslātus* carried over, from *trānsferre* to TRANSFER] —**trans'latable** *adj.* —**trans'lator** *n.*

translation (træns'leɪʃən, trænz-) *n.* **1.** something that is or has been translated. **2.** a translating or being translated. **3.** *Maths.* a transformation in which the origin of a coordinate system is moved to another position so that each axis retains the same direction. —**trans'lational** *adj.*

transliterate (trænz'lɪtəˌreɪt) vb. (tr.) to transcribe (a word, etc.) into corresponding letters of another alphabet. [C19: TRANS- + -literate, from L littera letter] —**translit-er'ation** n. —**trans'literˌator** n.

translocation (ˌtrænzləʊ'keɪʃən) n. 1. Genetics. the transfer of one part of a chromosome to another part of the same or a different chromosome. 2. Bot. the transport of minerals, sugars, etc., in solution within a plant. 3. a movement from one position or place to another.

translucent (trænz'luːs³nt) adj. allowing light to pass through partially or diffusely; semitransparent. [C16: from L trānslūcēre to shine through] —**trans'lucence** or **trans'lucency** n. —**trans'lucently** adv.

translunar (trænz'luːnə) or **translunary** (trænz'luːnərɪ) adj. 1. lying beyond the moon. 2. unworldly or ethereal.

transmigrate (ˌtrænzmaɪ'greɪt) vb. (intr.) 1. to move from one place, state, or stage to another. 2. (of souls) to pass from one body into another at death. —**trans-mi'gration** n. —**trans'migratory** adj.

transmission (trænz'mɪʃən) n. 1. the act or process of transmitting. 2. something that is transmitted. 3. the extent to which a body or medium transmits light, sound, etc. 4. the transference of motive force or power. 5. a system of shafts, gears, etc., that transmits power, esp. the arrangement of such parts that transmits the power of the engine to the driving wheels of a motor vehicle. 6. the act or process of sending a message, picture, or other information by means of radio waves, electrical signals, light signals, etc. 7. a radio or television broadcast. [C17: from L trānsmissiō a sending across] —**trans'missible** adj. —**trans'missive** adj.

transmission density n. Physics. a measure of the extent to which a substance transmits light or other electromagnetic radiation.

transmission line n. a coaxial cable, waveguide, etc., that transfers electrical signals from one location to another.

transmissivity (ˌtrænzmɪ'sɪvɪtɪ) n. Physics. a measure of the ability of a material to transmit radiation.

transmit (trænz'mɪt) vb. -mitting, -mitted. 1. (tr.) to pass or cause to go from one place or person to another; transfer. 2. (tr.) to pass on or impart (a disease, etc.). 3. (tr.) to hand down to posterity. 4. (tr.; usually passive) to pass (an inheritable characteristic) from parent to offspring. 5. to allow the passage of (particles, energy, etc.): radio waves are transmitted through the atmosphere. 6. a. to send out (signals) by means of radio waves or along a transmission line. b. to broadcast (a radio or television programme). 7. (tr.) to transfer (a force, motion, etc.) from one part of a mechanical system to another. [C14: from L trānsmittere to send across] —**trans'mittable** adj. —**trans'mittal** n.

transmittance (trænz'mɪt³ns) n. 1. the act of transmitting. 2. Also called: **transmission factor**. Physics. a measure of the ability of anything to transmit radiation, equal to the ratio of the transmitted flux to the incident flux.

transmitter (trænz'mɪtə) n. 1. a person or thing that transmits. 2. the equipment used for generating and amplifying a radio-frequency carrier, modulating the carrier with information, and feeding it to an aerial for transmission. 3. the microphone in a telephone that converts sound waves into audio-frequency electrical signals. 4. a device that converts mechanical movements into coded electrical signals transmitted along a telegraph circuit. 5. a substance released by nerve endings that transmits impulses across synapses.

transmogrify (trænz'mɒgrɪˌfaɪ) vb. -fying, -fied. (tr.) Jocular. to change or transform into a different shape, esp. a grotesque or bizarre one. [C17: from ?] —**trans,mogrifi'cation** n.

transmontane (ˌtrænzmɒn'teɪn) adj., n. another word for **tramontane**.

transmutation (ˌtrænzmjuː'teɪʃən) n. 1. the act or an instance of transmuting. 2. the change of one chemical element into another by a nuclear reaction. 3. the attempted conversion, by alchemists, of base metals into gold or silver. —,**transmu'tational** or **trans'mutative** adj.

transmute (trænz'mjuːt) vb. (tr.) 1. to change the form, character, or substance of. 2. to alter (an element, metal, etc.) by alchemy. [C15: via OF from L trānsmūtāre to shift, from TRANS- + mūtāre to change] —**trans,mut-a'bility** n. —**trans'mutable** adj.

transnational (trænz'næʃənəl) adj. extending beyond the boundaries, etc., of a single nation.

transoceanic (ˌtrænzˌəʊʃɪ'ænɪk) adj. 1. on or from the other side of an ocean. 2. crossing an ocean.

transom ('trænsəm) n. 1. a horizontal member across a window. 2. a horizontal member that separates a door from a window over it. 3. the usual U.S. name for **fanlight**. 4. Naut. a. a surface forming the stern of a vessel. b. any of several transverse beams used for strengthening the stern of a vessel. [C14: earlier traversayn, from OF traversin, from TRAVERSE] —'**transomed** adj.

transonic (træn'sɒnɪk) adj. of or relating to conditions when travelling at or near the speed of sound.

transparency (træns'pærənsɪ) n., pl. -cies. 1. Also called: **transparence**. the state of being transparent. 2. Also called: **slide**. a positive photograph on a transparent base, usually mounted in a frame or between glass plates. It can be viewed by means of a slide projector.

transparent (træns'pærənt) adj. 1. permitting the uninterrupted passage of light; clear. 2. easy to see through, understand, or recognize; obvious. 3. permitting the free passage of electromagnetic radiation. 4. candid, open, or frank. [C15: from Med. L trānspārēre to show through, from L TRANS- + pārēre to appear] —**trans'parently** adv. —**trans'parentness** n.

transpire (træn'spaɪə) vb. 1. (intr.) to come to light; be known. 2. (intr.) Inf. to happen or occur. 3. Physiol. to give off or exhale (water or vapour) through the skin, a mucous membrane, etc. 4. (of plants) to lose (water), esp. through the stomata of the leaves. [C16: from Med. L trānspīrāre, from L TRANS- + spīrāre to breathe] —**tran-spiration** (ˌtrænspə'reɪʃən) n. —**tran'spiratory** adj.
▷ Usage. It is often maintained that transpire should not be used to mean happen or occur, as in the event transpired late in the evening, and that the word is properly used to mean become known, as in it transpired later that the thief had been caught. The word is, however, widely used in the former sense, esp. in spoken English.

transplant vb. (træns'plɑːnt). 1. (tr.) to remove or transfer (esp. a plant) from one place to another. 2. (intr.) to be capable of being transplanted. 3. Surgery. to transfer (an organ or tissue) from one part of the body or from one person to another. ~n. ('trænsˌplɑːnt). 4. Surgery. a. the procedure involved in such a transfer. b. the organ or tissue transplanted. —**trans'plantable** adj. —,**trans-plan'tation** n.

transponder (træn'spɒndə) n. 1. a type of radio or radar transmitter-receiver that transmits signals automatically when it receives predetermined signals. 2. the receiver and transmitter in a communications satellite, relaying signals back to earth. [C20: from TRANSMITTER + RESPONDER]

transport vb. (træns'pɔːt). (tr.) 1. to carry or cause to go from one place to another, esp. over some distance. 2. to deport or exile to a penal colony. 3. (usually passive) to have a strong emotional effect on. ~n. ('trænsˌpɔːt). 4. a. the business or system of transporting goods or people. b. (as modifier): a modernized transport system. 5. Brit. freight vehicles generally. 6. a. a vehicle used to transport goods or people, esp. troops. b. (as modifier): a transport plane. 7. a transporting or being transported. 8. ecstasy, rapture, or any powerful emotion. 9. a convict sentenced to be transported. [C14: from L trānsportāre, from TRANS- + portāre to carry] —**trans'portable** adj. —**trans'porter** n.

transportation (ˌtrænspɔː'teɪʃən) n. 1. a means or system of transporting. 2. the act of transporting or the state of being transported. 3. (esp. formerly) deportation to a penal colony.

transport café ('trænsˌpɔːt) n. Brit. an inexpensive eating place on a main route, used mainly by long-distance lorry drivers.

transpose (træns'pəʊz) vb. 1. (tr.) to alter the positions of; interchange, as words in a sentence. 2. Music. to play (notes, music, etc.) in a different key from that originally intended. 3. (tr.) Maths. to move (a term) from one side of an equation to the other with a corresponding reversal in sign. [C14: from OF transposer, from L trānspōnere to remove] —**trans'posable** adj. —**trans'posal** n. —**trans'poser** n. —**transposition** (ˌtrænspə'zɪʃən) n.

transposing instrument n. a musical instrument, esp. a horn or clarinet, pitched in a key other than C major, but whose music is written down as if its basic scale were C major.

transputer (trænz'pju:tə) n. Computers. a type of fast powerful microchip that is the equivalent of a 32-bit microprocessor with its own RAM facility. [C20: from TRANS- + (COM)PUTER]

transsexual (trænz'sɛksjʊəl) n. **1.** a person who is completely identified with the opposite sex. **2.** a person who has undergone medical procedures to alter sexual characteristics to those of the opposite sex.

transship (træns'ʃɪp) or **tranship** vb. **-shipping, -shipped.** to transfer or be transferred from one vessel or vehicle to another. —**trans'shipment** or **tran'shipment** n.

transubstantiation (,trænsəb,stænʃɪ'eɪʃən) n. **1.** (esp. in Roman Catholic theology) **a.** the doctrine that the whole substance of the bread and wine changes into the substance of the body and blood of Christ when consecrated in the Eucharist. **b.** the mystical process by which this is believed to take place during consecration. Cf. **consubstantiation. 2.** a substantial change; transmutation. —,**transub,stanti'ationalist** n.

transude (træn'sju:d) vb. (of a fluid) to ooze or pass through interstices, pores, or small holes. [C17: from NL trānsūdāre, from L TRANS- + sūdāre to sweat] —**transudation** (,trænsju'deɪʃən) n.

transuranic (,trænzju'rænɪk), **transuranian** (,trænzjʊ'reɪnɪən), or **transuranium** adj. **1.** (of an element) having an atomic number greater than that of uranium. **2.** of or having the behaviour of transuranic elements. [C20]

Transvaal ('trænzvɑːl) n. a province of NE South Africa: colonized by the Boers after the Great Trek (1836); became a British colony in 1902; joined South Africa in 1910; consists mostly of a plateau sloping down from the Drakensberg in the southeast to the Limpopo River in the north; the world's chief gold producer. Capital: Pretoria. Pop.: 7 532 179 (1985). Area: 283 919 sq. km (109 621 sq. miles). —**'Trans,vaaler** n. —**Trans'vaalian** adj.

transversal (trænz'vɜːsəl) n. **1.** Geom. a line intersecting two or more other lines. ~adj. **2.** a less common word for **transverse.** —**trans'versally** adv.

transverse (trænz'vɜːs) adj. **1.** crossing from side to side; athwart; crossways. ~n. **2.** a transverse piece or object. [C16: from L trānsversus, from trānsvertere to turn across] —**trans'versely** adv.

transverse colon n. Anat. the part of the large intestine passing transversely in front of the liver and stomach.

transverse wave n. a wave, such as an electromagnetic wave, that is propagated in a direction perpendicular to the direction of displacement of the transmitting field or medium.

transvestite (trænz'vɛstaɪt) n. a person who seeks sexual pleasure from wearing clothes of the opposite sex. [C19: from G Transvestit, from TRANS- + L vestitus clothed, from vestīre to clothe] —**trans'vestism** or **trans'vestism** n.

Transylvania (,trænsɪl'veɪnɪə) n. a region of central and NW Romania: belonged to Hungary from the 11th century until 1918; restored finally to Romania in 1947.

Transylvanian Alps (,trænsɪl'veɪnɪən) pl. n. a mountain range in S Romania; a SW extension of the Carpathian Mountains. Highest peak: Mount Negoiu, 2548 m (8360 ft.).

trap[1] (træp) n. **1.** a mechanical device or enclosed place or pit in which something, esp. an animal, is caught or penned. **2.** any device or plan for tricking a person or thing into being caught unawares. **3.** anything resembling a trap or prison. **4.** a fitting for a pipe in the form of a U-shaped or S-shaped bend that contains standing water to prevent the passage of gases. **5.** any similar device. **6.** a device that hurls clay pigeons into the air to be fired at by trapshooters. **7.** Greyhound racing. any one of a line of boxlike stalls in which greyhounds are enclosed before the start of a race. **8.** See **trap door. 9.** a light two-wheeled carriage. **10.** a slang word for **mouth. 11.** Golf. an obstacle or hazard, esp. a bunker. **12.** (pl.) Jazz sl. percussion instruments. **13.** (usually pl.) Austral. sl. a policeman. ~vb. **trapping, trapped. 14.** to catch, take, or pen in a trap. **15.** (tr.) to ensnare by trickery; trick. **16.** (tr.) to provide (a pipe) with a trap. **17.** to set traps in (a place), esp. for animals. [OE træppe] —**'trap,like** adj.

trap[2] (træp) vb. **trapping, trapped.** (tr.; often foll. by out) to dress or adorn. ~See also **traps.** [C11: prob. from OF drap cloth]

trap[3] (træp) or **traprock** ('træp,rɒk) n. **1.** any fine-grained often columnar dark igneous rock, esp. basalt. **2.** any rock in which oil or gas has accumulated. [C18: from Swedish trappa stair (from its steplike formation)]

Trapani (Italian 'traːpani) n. a port in S Italy, in NW Sicily: Carthaginian naval base, ceded to the Romans after the First Punic War. Pop.: 71 759 (1983 est.).

trap door n. a door or flap flush with and covering an opening, esp. in a ceiling.

trap-door spider n. any of various spiders that construct a silk-lined hole in the ground closed by a hinged door of earth and silk.

trapes (treɪps) vb., n. a less common spelling of **traipse.**

trapeze (trə'piːz) n. a free-swinging bar attached to two ropes, used by circus acrobats, etc. [C19: from F trapèze, from NL; see TRAPEZIUM]

trapezium (trə'piːzɪəm) n., pl. **-ziums** or **-zia** (-zɪə). **1.** Chiefly Brit. a quadrilateral having two parallel sides of unequal length. Usual U.S. and Canad. name: **trapezoid. 2.** Chiefly U.S. & Canad. a quadrilateral having neither pair of sides parallel. [C16: via LL from Gk trapezion, from trapeza table] —**tra'pezial** adj.

trapezius (trə'piːzɪəs) n., pl. **-uses.** either of two flat triangular muscles that rotate the shoulder blades. [C18: from NL trapezius (musculus) trapezium-shaped (muscle)]

trapezoid ('træpɪ,zɔɪd) n. **1.** a quadrilateral having neither pair of sides parallel. **2.** the usual U.S. and Canad. name for **trapezium.** [C18: from NL trapezoidēs, from LGk trapezoeidēs trapezium-shaped, from trapeza table]

trapper ('træpə) n. a person who traps animals, esp. for their furs or skins.

trappings ('træpɪŋz) pl. n. **1.** the accessories and adornments that symbolize a condition, office, etc.: the trappings of success. **2.** ceremonial harness for a horse or other animal. [C16: from TRAP[2]]

Trappist ('træpɪst) n. **a.** a member of a branch of the Cistercian order of Christian monks, which originated at La Trappe in France in 1664. They are noted for their rule of silence. **b.** (as modifier): a Trappist monk.

traps (træps) pl. n. belongings; luggage. [C19: prob. shortened from TRAPPINGS]

trapshooting ('træp,ʃuːtɪŋ) n. the sport of shooting at clay pigeons thrown up by a trap. —**'trap,shooter** n.

trash (træʃ) n. **1.** foolish ideas or talk; nonsense. **2.** Chiefly U.S. & Canad. useless or unwanted matter or objects; rubbish. **3.** a literary or artistic production of poor quality. **4.** Chiefly U.S. & Canad. a poor or worthless person or a group of such people. **5.** bits that are broken or lopped off, esp. the trimmings from trees or plants. **6.** the dry remains of sugar cane after the juice has been extracted. ~vb. **7.** to remove the outer leaves and branches from (growing plants, esp. sugar cane). **8.** Sl. to attack or destroy (someone or something) wilfully or maliciously. [C16: from ?]

trashy ('træʃɪ) adj. **trashier, trashiest.** cheap, worthless, or badly made. —**'trashily** adv. —**'trashiness** n.

Trasimene ('træzɪ,miːn) n. **Lake.** a lake in central Italy, in Umbria: the largest lake in central Italy; scene of Hannibal's victory over the Romans in 217 B.C. Area: 128 sq. km (49 sq. miles). Italian name: **Trasimeno.** Also called: (Lake) **Perugia.**

trass (træs) n. a volcanic rock used to make a hydraulic cement. [C18: from Du. tras, tarasse, from It. terrazza worthless earth; see TERRACE]

trattoria (,trætə'rɪə) n. an Italian restaurant. [C19: from It., from trattore innkeeper, from F traiteur, from OF tretier to TREAT]

trauma ('trɔːmə) n., pl. **-mata** (-mətə) or **-mas. 1.** Psychol. a powerful shock that may have long-lasting effects. **2.** Pathol. any bodily injury or wound. [C18: from Gk: a wound] —**traumatic** (trɔː'mætɪk) adj. —**trau'matically** adv.

traumatize or **-ise** ('trɔːmə,taɪz) vb. **1.** (tr.) to wound or injure (the body). **2.** to subject or be subjected to mental trauma. —,**traumati'zation** or **-i'sation** n.

travail ('træveɪl) Literary. ~n. **1.** painful or excessive labour or exertion. **2.** the pangs of childbirth; labour. ~vb. **3.** (intr.) to suffer or labour painfully, esp. in childbirth. [C13: from OF travaillier, from Vulgar L tripaliāre (unattested) to torture, from LL trepālium instrument of torture, from L tripālis having three stakes]

Travancore (ˌtrævənˈkɔː) n. a former princely state of S India which joined with Cochin in 1949 to form **Travancore-Cochin:** part of Kerala state since 1956.

travel (ˈtrævəl) vb. **-elling, -elled** or U.S. **-eling, -eled.** (mainly intr.) **1.** to go, move, or journey from one place to another. **2.** (tr.) to go, move, or journey through or across (an area, region, etc.). **3.** to go, move, or cover a distance. **4.** to go from place to place as a salesman. **5.** (esp. of perishable goods) to withstand a journey. **6.** (of light, sound, etc.) to be transmitted or move. **7.** to progress or advance. **8.** Basketball. to take an excessive number of steps while holding the ball. **9.** (of part of a mechanism) to move in a fixed path. **10.** Inf. to move rapidly. ~n. **11. a.** the act of travelling. **b.** (as modifier): a travel brochure. Related adj.: **itinerant.** **12.** (usually pl.) a tour or journey. **13.** the distance moved by a mechanical part, such as the stroke of a piston. **14.** movement or passage. [C14 travaillen to make a journey, from OF travaillier to TRAVAIL]

travel agency or **bureau** n. an agency that arranges and negotiates flights, holidays, etc., for travellers. —**travel agent** n.

travelled or U.S. **traveled** (ˈtrævəld) adj. having experienced or undergone much travelling.

traveller (ˈtrævlə) n. **1.** a person who travels, esp. habitually. **2.** See **travelling salesman.** **3.** a part of a mechanism that moves in a fixed course. **4.** Austral. a swagman.

traveller's cheque n. a cheque sold by a bank, etc., to the bearer, who signs it on purchase and can cash it abroad by signing it again.

traveller's joy n. a ranunculaceous Old World climbing plant having white flowers and heads of feathery plumed fruits; wild clematis.

travelling people or **folk** pl. n. (sometimes caps.) Brit. Gypsies or other itinerant people: a term used esp. by such people of themselves.

travelling salesman n. a salesman who travels within an assigned territory in order to sell merchandise or to solicit orders for the commercial enterprise he represents by direct personal contact with customers.

travelling wave n. **a.** a wave carrying energy away from its source. **b.** (as modifier): a travelling-wave aerial.

travelogue or U.S. (sometimes) **travelog** (ˈtrævəlɒg) n. a film, lecture, or brochure on travels and travelling.

traverse (ˈtrævɜːs, trəˈvɜːs) vb. **1.** to pass or go over or back and forth over (something); cross. **2.** (tr.) to go against; oppose. **3.** to move sideways or crosswise. **4.** (tr.) to extend or reach across. **5.** to turn (an artillery gun) laterally or (of an artillery gun) to turn laterally. **6.** (tr.) to examine carefully. **7.** (tr.) Law. to deny (an allegation). **8.** Mountaineering. to move across (a face) horizontally. ~n. **9.** something being or lying across, such as a transom. **10.** a gallery or loft inside a building that crosses it. **11.** an obstruction. **12.** a protective bank or other barrier across a trench or rampart. **13.** a railing, screen, or curtain. **14.** the act or an instance of traversing or crossing. **15.** Mountaineering. the act or an instance of moving horizontally across a face. **16.** a path or road across. **17.** Naut. the zigzag course of a vessel tacking frequently. **18.** Law. the formal denial of a fact alleged in the opposite party's pleading. **19.** Surveying. a survey consisting of a series of straight lines, the length of each and the angle between them being measured. ~adj. **20.** being or lying across; transverse. [C14 from OF traverser, from LL trānsversāre, from L trānsversus TRANSVERSE] —**traˈversal** n. —**ˈtraverser** n.

travertine (ˈtrævətɪn) n. a porous rock consisting of calcium carbonate, used for building. [C18: from It. travertino (infl. by tra- TRANS-), from L lapis Tīburtīnus Tiburtine stone, from Tīburs the district around Tibur (now Tivoli)]

travesty (ˈtrævɪstɪ) n., pl. **-ties. 1.** a farcical or grotesque imitation; mockery. ~vb. **-tying, -tied.** (tr.) **2.** to make or be a travesty of. [C17: from F travesti disguised, from travestir to disguise, from It. travestire, from tra-TRANS- + vestire to clothe]

travois (trəˈvɔɪ) n., pl. **-vois** (-ˈvɔɪz). **1.** History. a sled formerly used by the Plains Indians of North America, consisting of two poles joined by a frame and pulled by an animal. **2.** Canad. a similar sled used for dragging logs. [from Canad. F, from F travail beam, from L trabs]

trawl (trɔːl) n. **1.** Also called: **trawl net.** a large net, usually in the shape of a sock or bag, drawn at deep levels behind special boats (trawlers). **2.** Also called: **trawl line.** a long line to which numerous shorter hooked lines are attached, suspended between buoys. **3.** the act of trawling. ~vb. **4.** to catch (fish) with a trawl net or trawl line. **5.** (intr.; foll. by for) to seek or gather (information, etc.) from a wide variety of sources. [C17: from MDu. traghelen to drag, from L trāgula dragnet; see TRAIL]

trawler (ˈtrɔːlə) n. **1.** a vessel used for trawling. **2.** a person who trawls.

tray (treɪ) n. **1.** a thin flat board or plate of metal, plastic, etc., usually with a raised edge, on which things can be carried. **2.** a shallow receptacle for papers, etc., sometimes forming a drawer in a cabinet or box. [OE trieg]

treacherous (ˈtrɛtʃərəs) adj. **1.** betraying or likely to betray faith or confidence. **2.** unstable, unreliable, or dangerous. —**ˈtreacherously** adv. —**ˈtreacherousness** n.

treachery (ˈtrɛtʃərɪ) n., pl. **-eries. 1.** the act or an instance of wilful betrayal. **2.** the disposition to betray. [C13: from OF trecherie, from trechier to cheat]

treacle (ˈtriːkəl) n. **1.** Also called: **black treacle.** Brit. a dark viscous syrup obtained during the refining of sugar. **2.** Brit. another name for **golden syrup. 3.** anything sweet and cloying. [C14: from OF triacle, from L thēriaca antidote to poison] —**ˈtreacly** adj.

tread (trɛd) vb. **treading, trod, trodden** or **trod. 1.** to walk or trample in, on, over, or across (something). **2.** (when intr., foll. by on) to crush or squash by or as if by treading. **3.** (intr.; sometimes foll. by on) to subdue or repress. **4.** (tr.) to do by walking or dancing: to tread a measure. **5.** (tr.) (of a male bird) to copulate with (a female bird). **6. tread lightly.** to proceed with delicacy or tact. **7. tread water.** to stay afloat in an upright position by moving the legs in a walking motion. ~n. **8.** a manner or style of walking, dancing, etc.: a light tread. **9.** the act of treading. **10.** the top surface of a step in a staircase. **11.** the outer part of a tyre or wheel that makes contact with the road, esp. the grooved surface of a pneumatic tyre. **12.** the part of a rail that wheels touch. **13.** the part of a shoe that is generally in contact with the ground. [OE tredan] —**ˈtreader** n.

treadle (ˈtrɛdəl) n. **1.** a lever operated by the foot to drive a machine. ~vb. **2.** to work (a machine) with a treadle. [OE tredel, from trǣde something firm, from tredan to tread]

treadmill (ˈtrɛdˌmɪl) n. **1.** Also called: **treadwheel.** (formerly) an apparatus turned by the weight of men or animals climbing steps on the periphery of a cylinder or wheel. **2.** a dreary round or routine. **3.** an exercise machine that consists of a continuous moving belt on which to walk or jog.

treas. abbrev. for: **1.** treasurer. **2.** treasury.

treason (ˈtriːzən) n. **1.** betrayal of one's sovereign or country, esp. by attempting to overthrow the government. **2.** any treachery or betrayal. [C13: from OF traison, from L trāditiō a handing over; see TRADITION] —**ˈtreasonable** or **ˈtreasonous** adj. —**ˈtreasonably** adv.

treasure (ˈtrɛʒə) n. **1.** wealth and riches, usually hoarded, esp. in the form of money, precious metals, or gems. **2.** a thing or person that is highly prized or valued. ~vb. (tr.) **3.** to prize highly as valuable, rare, or costly. **4.** to store up and save; hoard. [C12: from OF tresor, from L thēsaurus anything hoarded, from Gk thēsauros]

treasure hunt n. a game in which players act upon successive clues to find a hidden prize.

treasurer (ˈtrɛʒərə) n. a person appointed to look after the funds of a society, company, city, or other governing body. —**ˈtreasurership** n.

Treasurer (ˈtrɛʒərə) n. (in Australia) the minister of finance.

treasure-trove n. **1.** Law. any articles, such as coins, etc., found hidden and of unknown ownership. **2.** any valuable discovery. [C16: from Anglo-F tresor trové treasure found, from OF tresor TREASURE + trover to find]

treasury (ˈtrɛʒərɪ) n., pl. **-uries. 1.** a storage place for treasure. **2.** the revenues or funds of a government, private organization, or individual. **3.** a place where funds are kept and disbursed. **4.** a person or thing regarded as a valuable source of information. **5.** a collection of highly valued poems, etc.; anthology. **6.** Also: **treasure house.** a source of valuable items: a treasury of information. [C13: from OF tresorie, from tresor TREASURE]

Treasury ('trɛʒərɪ) n. (in various countries) the government department in charge of finance.

Treasury Bench n. (in Britain) the front bench to the right of the Speaker in the House of Commons, traditionally reserved for members of the Government.

treasury note n. a note issued by a government treasury and generally receivable as legal tender for any debt.

treat (triːt) n. 1. a celebration, entertainment, gift, or feast given for or to someone and paid for by another. 2. any delightful surprise or specially pleasant occasion. 3. the act of treating. ~vb. 4. (tr.) to deal with or regard in a certain manner: *she treats school as a joke.* 5. (tr.) to apply treatment to. 6. (tr.) to subject to a process or to the application of a substance. 7. (often foll. by *to*) to provide (someone) (with) as a treat. 8. (intr.; usually foll. by *of*) to deal (with), as in writing or speaking. 9. (intr.) to discuss settlement; negotiate. [C13: from OF *tretier*, from L *tractāre* to manage, from *trahere* to drag] —'**treatable** adj. —'**treater** n.

treatise ('triːtɪz) n. a formal work on a subject, esp. one that deals systematically with its principles and conclusions. [C14: from Anglo-F *tretiz*, from OF *tretier* to TREAT]

treatment ('triːtmənt) n. 1. the application of medicines, surgery, etc., to a patient. 2. the manner of handling a person or thing, as in a literary or artistic work. 3. the act, practice, or manner of treating. 4. **the treatment.** *Sl.* the usual manner of dealing with a particular type of person (esp. in **give someone the (full) treatment**).

treaty ('triːtɪ) n., pl. **-ties.** 1. a. a formal agreement between two or more states, such as an alliance or trade arrangement. b. the document in which such a contract is written. 2. any pact or agreement. 3. an agreement between two parties concerning the purchase of property at a price privately agreed between them. [C14: from OF *traité*, from Med. L *tractātus*, from L: discussion, from *tractāre* to manage; see TREAT]

treaty port n. *History.* (in China, Japan, and Korea) a city, esp. a port, in which foreigners, esp. Westerners, were allowed by treaty to conduct trade.

Trebizond ('trɛbɪ,zɒnd) n. a variant of **Trabzon.**

treble ('trɛbªl) adj. 1. threefold; triple. 2. of or denoting a soprano voice or part or a high-pitched instrument. ~n. 3. treble the amount, size, etc. 4. a soprano voice or part or a high-pitched instrument. 5. the highest register of a musical instrument. 6. the high-frequency response of an audio amplifier, esp. in a record player or tape recorder. 7. a. the narrow inner ring on a dartboard. b. a hit on this ring. ~vb. 8. to make or become three times as much. [C14: from OF, from L *triplus* threefold] —'**trebly** adv., adj.

treble chance n. a method of betting in football pools in which the chances of winning are related to the number of draws and the number of home and away wins forecast by the competitor.

treble clef n. *Music.* the clef that establishes G a fifth above middle C as being on the second line of the staff. Symbol: 𝄞

trebuchet ('trɛbjʊ,ʃɛt) or **trebucket** ('triː,bʌkɪt) n. a large medieval siege engine consisting of a sling on a pivoted wooden arm set in motion by the fall of a weight. [C13: from OF, from *trebuchier* to stumble, from *tre-* TRANS- + -*buchier* from *buc* trunk of the body, of Gmc origin]

trecento (treɪ'tʃɛntəʊ) n. the 14th century, esp. with reference to Italian art and literature. [C19: shortened from It. *mille trecento* one thousand three hundred] —**tre'centist** n.

tree (triː) n. 1. any large woody perennial plant with a distinct trunk giving rise to branches. Related adj.: **arboreal.** 2. any plant that resembles this. 3. a wooden post, bar, etc. 4. See **family tree, shoetree, saddletree.** 5. *Chem.* a treelike crystal growth. 6. a branching diagrammatic representation of something. 7. **at the top of the tree.** in the highest position of a profession, etc. 8. **up a tree.** *U.S. & Canad. inf.* in a difficult situation; trapped or stumped. ~vb. **treeing, treed.** (tr.) 9. to drive or force up a tree. 10. *U.S. & Canad. inf.* to force into a difficult situation. 11. to stretch on a shoetree. [OE *treo*] —'**treeless** adj. —'**treelessness** n. —'**tree,like** adj.

Tree (triː) n. Sir **Herbert Beerbohm.** 1853–1917, English actor and theatre manager; half-brother of Sir Max Beerbohm. He was noted for his lavish productions of Shakespeare.

tree creeper n. any of a family of small songbirds of the N hemisphere, having a slender downward-curving bill. They creep up trees to feed on insects.

tree diagram n. a diagram in which relationships are represented by lines and nodes having other lines branching off from them.

tree fern n. any of numerous large tropical ferns having a trunklike stem.

tree frog n. any of various arboreal frogs of SE Asia, Australia, and America.

treehopper ('triː,hɒpə) n. any of a family of insects which live among trees and have a large hoodlike thoracic process curving backwards over the body.

tree kangaroo n. any of several arboreal kangaroos of New Guinea and N Australia, having hind legs and forelegs of a similar length.

tree line n. another name for **timber line.**

treen ('triːən) adj. 1. made of wood; wooden. ~n. 2. dishes and other utensils made of wood. [OE *trēowen*, from *trēow* tree] —'**treen,ware** n.

treenail or **trenail** ('triːneɪl, 'trɛnªl) n. a dowel used for pinning planks or timbers together.

tree of heaven n. another name for **ailanthus.**

tree shrew n. any of a family of small arboreal primates of SE Asia having large eyes and resembling squirrels.

tree sparrow n. 1. a small European weaverbird similar to the house sparrow but having a brown head. 2. a small North American finch.

tree surgery n. the treatment of damaged trees by filling cavities, applying braces, etc. —**tree surgeon** n.

tree toad n. a less common name for **tree frog.**

tree tomato n. 1. an arborescent shrub of South America widely cultivated in New Zealand, bearing red egg-shaped edible fruit. 2. the fruit of this plant. ~Also called: **tamarillo.**

tref (treɪf) adj. *Judaism.* ritually unfit to be eaten. [Yiddish, from Heb. *terēphāh*, lit.: torn (i.e., animal meat torn by beasts), from *tāraf* to tear]

trefoil ('trɛfɔɪl) n. 1. any of a genus of leguminous plants having leaves divided into three leaflets. 2. any of various related plants having similar leaves. 3. a flower or leaf having three lobes. 4. *Archit.* an ornament in the form of three arcs arranged in a circle. [C14: from Anglo-F *trifoil*, from L *trifolium* three-leaved herb] —'**trefoiled** adj.

Treitschke (German 'traɪtʃkə) n. **Heinrich von** ('haɪnrɪç fɒn). 1834–96, German historian, noted for his highly nationalistic views.

trek (trɛk) n. 1. a long and often difficult journey. 2. *S. African.* a journey or stage of a journey, esp. a migration by ox wagon. ~vb. **trekking, trekked.** 3. (intr.) to make a trek. [C19: from Afrik., from MDu. *trekken* to travel]

trellis ('trɛlɪs) n. 1. a structure of latticework, esp. one used to support climbing plants. ~vb. (tr.) 2. to interweave (strips of wood, etc.) to make a trellis. 3. to provide or support with a trellis. [C14: from OF *treliz* fabric of open texture, from LL *trilīcius* woven with three threads, from L TRI- + *līcium* thread] —'**trellis,work** n.

trematode ('trɛmə,təʊd, 'triː-) n. any of a class of parasitic flatworms, which includes the flukes. [C19: from NL *Trematoda*, from Gk *trēmatōdēs* full of holes, from *trēma* hole]

tremble ('trɛmbªl) vb. (intr.) 1. to vibrate with short slight movements; quiver. 2. to shake involuntarily, as with cold or fear; shiver. 3. to experience fear or anxiety. ~n. 4. the act or an instance of trembling. [C14: from OF *trembler*, from Med. L *tremulāre*, from L *tremulus* quivering, from *tremere* to quake] —'**trembling** adj. —'**trembly** adj.

trembler ('trɛmblə) n. a device that vibrates to make or break an electrical circuit.

trembles ('trɛmbªlz) n. (functioning as sing.) a disease of cattle and sheep characterized by trembling.

trembling poplar n. another name for **aspen.**

tremendous (trɪ'mɛndəs) adj. 1. vast; huge. 2. *Inf.* very exciting or unusual. 3. *Inf.* (intensifier): *a tremendous help.* 4. *Arch.* terrible or dreadful. [C17: from L *tremendus* terrible, lit.: that is to be trembled at, from *tremere* to quake] —**tre'mendously** *adv.* —**tre-'mendousness** *n.*

tremolo ('trɛmə,ləʊ) *n., pl.* **-los.** *Music.* 1. (in playing the violin, cello, etc.) the rapid reiteration of a note or notes to produce a trembling effect. 2. (in singing) a fluctuation in pitch. 3. a device, as on an organ, that produces a tremolo effect. [C19: from It.: quavering, from Med. L *tremulāre* to TREMBLE]

tremor ('trɛmə) *n.* 1. an involuntary shudder or vibration. 2. any trembling movement. 3. a vibrating or trembling effect, as of sound or light. 4. a minor earthquake. ~*vb.* 5. (*intr.*) to tremble. [C14: from L: a shaking, from *tremere* to tremble] —**'tremorous** *adj.*

tremulous ('trɛmjʊləs) *adj.* 1. vibrating slightly; quavering; trembling. 2. showing or characterized by fear, anxiety, excitement, etc. [C17: from L *tremulus*, from *tremere* to shake] —**'tremulously** *adv.* —**'tremulousness** *n.*

trenail ('triːneɪl, 'trɛnªl) *n.* a variant spelling of **treenail.**

trench (trɛntʃ) *n.* 1. a deep ditch. 2. a ditch dug as a fortification, having a parapet of earth. ~*vb.* 3. to make a trench in (a place). 4. (*tr.*) to fortify with a trench. 5. to slash or be slashed. 6. (*intr.;* foll. by *on* or *upon*) to encroach or verge. [C14: from OF *trenche* something cut, from *trenchier* to cut, from L *truncāre* to cut off]

trenchant ('trɛntʃənt) *adj.* 1. keen or incisive: *trenchant criticism.* 2. vigorous and effective: *a trenchant foreign policy.* 3. distinctly defined. 4. *Arch. or poetic.* sharp. [C14: from OF *trenchant* cutting, from *trenchier* to cut; see TRENCH] —**'trenchancy** *n.* —**'trenchantly** *adv.*

trench coat *n.* a belted waterproof coat resembling a military officer's coat.

trencher ('trɛntʃə) *n.* 1. (esp. formerly) a wooden board on which food was served or cut. 2. Also called: **trencher cap.** a mortarboard. [C14 *trenchour* knife, plate for carving on, from OF *trencheoir*, from *trenchier* to cut; see TRENCH]

trencherman ('trɛntʃəmən) *n., pl.* **-men.** a person who enjoys food; hearty eater.

trench fever *n.* an acute infectious disease characterized by fever and muscular aches and pains and transmitted by lice.

trench foot *n.* a form of frostbite affecting persons standing for long periods in cold water.

trench mortar *or* **gun** *n.* a portable mortar used in trench warfare to shoot projectiles at a high trajectory over a short range.

trench warfare *n.* a type of warfare in which opposing armies face each other in entrenched positions.

trend (trɛnd) *n.* 1. general tendency or direction. 2. fashion; mode. ~*vb.* 3. (*intr.*) to take a certain trend. [OE *trendan* to turn]

trendsetter ('trɛnd,sɛtə) *n.* a person or thing that creates, or may create, a new fashion. —**'trend,setting** *adj.*

trendy ('trɛndɪ) *Brit. inf.* ~*adj.* **trendier, trendiest.** 1. consciously fashionable. ~*n., pl.* **trendies.** 2. a trendy person. —**'trendily** *adv.* —**'trendiness** *n.*

Trengganu (trɛŋ'gɑːnuː) *n.* a state of E Peninsular Malaysia, on the South China Sea: under Thai suzerainty until becoming a British protectorate in 1909; joined the Federation of Malaya in 1948; an isolated forested region; mainly agricultural. Capital: Kuala Trengganu. Pop.: 638 830 (1985 est.). Area: 13 020 sq. km (5027 sq. miles).

Trent (trɛnt) *n.* 1. a river in central England, rising in Staffordshire and flowing generally northeast into the Humber: the chief river of the Midlands. Length: 270 km (170 miles). 2. Also: **Trient.** the German name for **Trento.**

trente et quarante (*French* trɑ̃t e karɑ̃t) *n. Cards.* another name for **rouge et noir.** [C17: F, lit.: thirty and forty; from the rule that forty is the maximum number that may be dealt and the winning colour is the one closest to thirty-one]

Trentino-Alto Adige (trɛn'tiːnəʊ'ɑːltəʊ 'ɑːdɪ,dʒeɪ) *n.* a region of N Italy: consists of the part of the Tyrol south of the Brenner Pass, ceded by Austria after World War I. Pop.: 880 237 (1985 est.). Area: 13 613 sq. km (5256 sq. miles). Former name (until 1947): **Venezia Tridentina.**

Trento (*Italian* 'trɛnto) *n.* a city in N Italy, in Trentino-Alto Adige region on the Adige River: Roman military base; seat of the Council of Trent. Pop.: 100 202 (1987). Latin name: **Tridentum.** German name: **Trent.**

Trenton ('trɛntən) *n.* a city in W New Jersey, capital of the state, on the Delaware River: settled by English Quakers

in 1679; scene of the defeat of the British by Washington (1776) during the War of American Independence. Pop.: 92 124 (1980).

trepan (trɪ'pæn) *n.* 1. *Surgery.* an instrument resembling a carpenter's brace and bit formerly used to remove circular sections of bone from the skull. 2. a tool for cutting out circular blanks or for making grooves around a fixed centre. ~*vb.* **-panning, -panned.** (*tr.*) 3. to cut (a hole or groove) with a trepan. 4. *Surgery.* another word for **trephine.** [C14: from Med. L *trepanum* rotary saw, from Gk *trupanon* auger, from *trupan* to bore, from *trupa* a hole] —**trepanation** (,trɛpə'neɪʃən) *n.*

trepang (trɪ'pæŋ) *n.* any of various large sea cucumbers of tropical Oriental seas, the dried body walls of which are used as food by the Chinese. [C18: from Malay *tĕripang*]

trephine (trɪ'fiːn) *n.* 1. a surgical sawlike instrument for removing circular sections of bone esp. from the skull. ~*vb.* 2. (*tr.*) to remove a circular section of bone from (esp. the skull). [C17: from F *tréphine*, from obs. E *trefine* TREPAN, allegedly from L *trēs fīnēs*, lit.: three ends] —**trephination** (,trɛfɪ'neɪʃən) *n.*

trepidation (,trɛpɪ'deɪʃən) *n.* 1. a state of fear or anxiety. 2. a condition of quaking or palpitation, esp. one caused by anxiety. [C17: from L *trepidātiō*, from *trepidāre* to be in a state of alarm]

trespass ('trɛspəs) *vb.* (*intr.*) 1. (often foll. by *on* or *upon*) to go or intrude (on the property, privacy, or preserves of another) with no right or permission. 2. *Law.* to commit trespass. 3. *Arch.* (often foll. by *against*) to sin or transgress. ~*n.* 4. *Law.* **a.** any unlawful act committed with force, which causes injury to another person, his property or his rights. **b.** a wrongful entry upon another's land. 5. an intrusion on another's privacy or preserves. 6. a sin or offence. [C13: from OF *trespas* a passage, from *trespasser* to pass through, ult. from L *passus* a PACE[1]] —**'trespasser** *n.*

tress (trɛs) *n.* 1. (*often pl.*) a lock of hair, esp. a long lock of woman's hair. 2. a plait or braid of hair. ~*vb.* (*tr.*) 3. to arrange in tresses. [C13: from OF *trece;* from ?] —**'tressy** *adj.*

trestle ('trɛsªl) *n.* 1. a framework in the form of a horizontal member supported at each end by a pair of splayed legs, used to carry scaffold boards, a table top, etc. 2. **a.** a framework of timber, metal, or reinforced concrete that is used to support a bridge or ropeway. **b.** a bridge constructed of such frameworks. [C14: from OF *trestel*, ult. from L *trānstrum* transom]

trestlework ('trɛsªl,wɜːk) *n.* an arrangement of trestles, esp. one that supports a bridge.

trevally (trɪ'vælɪ) *n., pl.* **-lies.** *Austral. & N.Z.* any of various food and game fishes of the genus *Caranx.* [C19: prob. alteration of *cavally*, from *cavalla* species of tropical fish, from Sp. *caballa* horse]

Trevelyan (trɪ'vɛljən, -'vɪl-) *n.* 1. **George Macaulay.** 1876–1962, English historian, noted for his *English Social History* (1944). 2. his father, Sir **George Otto.** 1838–1928, English historian and biographer. His works include a biography of his uncle Lord Macaulay (1876).

Trèves (trɛv) *n.* the French name for **Trier.**

Trevino (trə'viːnəʊ) *n.* **Lee.** born 1939, U.S. professional golfer: winner of the U.S. Open Championship (1968; 1971) and the British Open Championship (1971; 1972).

Treviso (*Italian* tre'viːzo) *n.* a city in N Italy, in Veneto region: agricultural market centre. Pop.: 87 696 (1981).

trews (truːz) *pl. n. Chiefly Brit.* close-fitting trousers of tartan cloth. [C16: from Scot. Gaelic *triubhas*, from OF *trebus*]

trey (treɪ) *n.* any card or dice throw with three spots. [C14: from OF *treis* three, from L *trēs*]

tri- *prefix.* 1. three or thrice: *triaxial; trigon; trisect.* 2. occurring every three: *trimonthly.* [from L *trēs*, Gk *treis*]

triable ('traɪəbªl) *adj.* 1. subject to trial in a court of law. 2. *Rare.* able to be tested.

triacid (traɪ'æsɪd) *adj.* capable of reacting with three molecules of a monobasic acid.

triad ('traɪæd) *n.* 1. a group of three; trio. 2. *Chem.* an atom, element, group, or ion that has a valency of three. 3. *Music.* a three-note chord consisting of a note and the third and fifth above it. 4. an aphoristic literary form used in medieval Welsh and Irish literature. [C16: from LL *trias*, from Gk] —**tri'adic** *adj.* —**'triadism** *n.*

Triad ('traɪæd) n. any of several Chinese secret societies, esp. one involved in criminal activities, such as drug trafficking.

triage ('triːɑːdʒ) n. **1.** the action of sorting casualties, etc. according to priority. **2.** the allocating of limited resources on a basis of expediency rather than moral principles. [C18: from F; see TRY, -AGE]

trial ('traɪəl, traɪl) n. **1. a.** the act or an instance of trying or proving; test or experiment. **b.** (as modifier): a trial run. **2.** Law. **a.** the judicial examination and determination of the issues in a civil or criminal cause by a competent tribunal. **b.** the determination of an accused person's guilt or innocence after hearing evidence and the judicial examination of the issues involved. **c.** (as modifier): trial proceedings. **3.** an effort or attempt to do something. **4.** trouble or grief. **5.** an annoying or frustrating person or thing. **6.** (often pl.) a competition for individuals: sheepdog trials. **7. on trial. a.** undergoing trial, esp. before a court of law. **b.** being tested, as before a commitment to purchase. [C16: from Anglo-F, from trier to TRY]

trial and error n. a method of discovery, solving problems, etc., based on practical experiment and experience rather than on theory: he learnt to cook by trial and error.

trial balance n. Book-keeping. a statement of all the debit and credit balances in the ledger of a double-entry system, drawn up to test their equality.

triangle ('traɪ,æŋɡəl) n. **1.** Geom. a three-sided polygon that can be classified by angle, as in an acute triangle, or by side, as in an equilateral triangle. **2.** any object shaped like a triangle. **3.** any situation involving three parties or points of view. **4.** Music. a percussion instrument consisting of a sonorous metal bar bent into a triangular shape, beaten with a metal stick. **5.** a group of three. [C14: from L triangulum (n.), from triangulus (adj.), from TRI- + angulus corner] —**triangular** (traɪ'æŋɡjʊlə) adj.

triangle of forces n. Physics. a triangle whose sides represent the magnitudes and directions of three forces in equilibrium.

triangulate vb. (traɪ'æŋɡjʊ,leɪt). (tr.) **1. a.** to survey by the method of triangulation. **b.** to calculate trigonometrically. **2.** to divide into triangles. **3.** to make triangular. ~adj. (traɪ'æŋɡjʊlɪt, -,leɪt). **4.** marked with or composed of triangles. —**tri'angulately** adv.

triangulation (traɪ,æŋɡjʊ'leɪʃən) n. a method of surveying in which an area is divided into triangles, one side (the base line) and all angles of which are measured and the lengths of the other lines calculated trigonometrically.

triangulation station n. a point on a hilltop, etc., used for triangulation by a surveyor.

Triassic (traɪ'æsɪk) adj. **1.** of or formed in the first period of the Mesozoic era. ~n. **2. the.** Also called: **Trias.** the Triassic period or rock system. [C19: from L trias triad, from the three subdivisions]

triathlon (traɪ'æθlɒn) n. an athletic contest in which each athlete competes in three different events, swimming, cycling, and horse riding. [C20: from TRI- + Gk athlon contest]

triatomic (,traɪə'tɒmɪk) adj. Chem. having three atoms in the molecule.

tribade ('trɪbɑːd) n. a lesbian who practises tribadism. [C17: from L tribas, from Gk tribein to rub]

tribadism ('trɪbədɪzəm) n. a lesbian practice in which one partner lies on top of the other and simulates the male role in heterosexual intercourse.

tribalism ('traɪbə,lɪzəm) n. **1.** the state of existing as a tribe. **2.** the customs and beliefs of a tribal society. **3.** loyalty to a tribe. —**'tribalist** n., adj. —,**tribal'istic** adj.

tribasic (traɪ'beɪsɪk) adj. **1.** (of an acid) containing three replaceable hydrogen atoms in the molecule. **2.** (of a molecule) containing three monovalent basic atoms or groups.

tribe (traɪb) n. **1.** a social division of a people, esp. of a preliterate people, defined in terms of common descent, territory, culture, etc. **2.** an ethnic or racial division of ancient cultures, esp.: **a.** one of the political divisions of ancient Rome people. **b.** any of the 12 divisions of ancient Israel, each of which was believed to be descended from one of the 12 patriarchs. **3.** Inf. **a.** a large number of persons, animals, etc. **b.** a specific class or group of persons. **c.** a family, esp. a large one. **4.** Biol. a taxonomic group

that is a subdivision of a subfamily. [C13: from L tribus] —'**tribal** adj.

tribesman ('traɪbzmən) n., pl. -**men.** a member of a tribe.

tribo- combining form. indicating friction: triboelectricity. [from Gk tribein to rub]

triboelectricity (,traɪbəʊɪlɛk'trɪsɪtɪ, -,iːlɛk-) n. electricity generated by friction.

tribology (traɪ'bɒlədʒɪ) n. the study of friction, lubrication, and wear between moving surfaces.

triboluminescence (,traɪbəʊ,luːmɪ'nɛsəns) n. luminescence produced by friction, such as the emission of light when certain crystals are crushed. —,**tribo,lumi'nescent** adj.

tribrach ('traɪbræk, 'trɪb-) n. a metrical foot of three short syllables. [C16: from L tribrachys, from Gk, from TRI- + brakhus short]

tribromoethanol (traɪ,brəʊməʊ'εθə,nɒl) n. a soluble white crystalline compound with a slight aromatic odour, used as a general anaesthetic.

tribulation (,trɪbjʊ'leɪʃən) n. **1.** a cause of distress. **2.** a state of suffering or distress. [C13: from OF, from Church L tribulātiō, from L tribulāre to afflict, from tribulum a threshing board, from terere to rub]

tribunal (traɪ'bjuːnəl, trɪ-) n. **1.** a court of justice. **2.** (in England) a special court, convened by the government to inquire into a specific matter. **3.** a raised platform containing the seat of a judge. [C16: from L tribūnus TRIBUNE[1]]

tribune[1] ('trɪbjuːn) n. **1.** (in ancient Rome) **a.** an officer elected by the plebs to protect their interests. **b.** a senior military officer. **2.** a person who upholds public rights. [C14: from L tribunus, prob. from tribus tribe] —**tribunate** ('trɪbjʊnɪt) or **'tribuneship** n.

tribune[2] ('trɪbjuːn) n. **1. a.** the apse of a Christian basilica that contains the bishop's throne. **b.** the throne itself. **2.** a gallery or raised area in a church. **3.** Rare. a raised platform; dais. [C17: via F from It. tribuna, from Med. L tribūna, var. of L tribūnal TRIBUNAL]

tributary ('trɪbjʊtərɪ) n., pl. -**taries. 1.** a stream, river, or glacier that feeds another larger one. **2.** a person, nation, or people that pays tribute. ~adj. **3.** (of a stream, etc.) feeding a larger stream. **4.** given or owed as a tribute. **5.** paying tribute. —'**tributarily** adv.

tribute ('trɪbjuːt) n. **1.** a gift or statement made in acknowledgment, gratitude, or admiration. **2.** a payment by one ruler or state to another, usually as an acknowledgment of submission. **3.** the obligation to pay tribute. [C14: from L tribūtum, from tribuere to grant (orig.: to distribute among the tribes), from tribus tribe]

trice (traɪs) n. a moment; instant (esp. in **in a trice**). [C15 (in at or in a trice, in the sense: at one tug): apparent substantive use of trice to haul up, from MDu. trīse pulley]

tricentenary (,traɪsɛn'tiːnərɪ) or **tricentennial** (,traɪsɛn'tɛnɪəl) adj. **1.** of a period of 300 years. **2.** of a 300th anniversary. ~n., pl. -**naries. 3.** an anniversary of 300 years.

triceps ('traɪsɛps) n., pl. -**cepses** (-sɛpsɪz) or -**ceps.** any muscle having three heads, esp. the one that extends the forearm. [C16: from L, from TRI- + caput head]

trichiasis (trɪ'kaɪəsɪs) n. Pathol. an abnormal position of the eyelashes that causes irritation when they rub against the eyeball. [C17: via LL from Gk trikhiasis, from thrix a hair]

trichina (trɪ'kaɪnə) n., pl. -**nae** (-niː). a parasitic nematode worm occurring in the intestines of pigs, rats, and man and producing larvae that form cysts in skeletal muscle. [C19: from NL, from Gk trikhinos relating to hair, from thrix a hair] —**trichinous** ('trɪkɪnəs) adj.

Trichinopoly (,trɪkɪ'nɒpəlɪ) n. another name for **Tiruchirapalli.**

trichinosis (,trɪkɪ'nəʊsɪs) n. a disease characterized by nausea, fever, diarrhoea, and swelling of the muscles, caused by ingestion of pork infected with trichina larvae. [C19: from NL TRICHINA]

trichloride (traɪ'klɔːraɪd) n. any compound that contains three chlorine atoms per molecule.

tricho- or before a vowel **trich-** combining form. indicating hair or a part resembling hair: trichocyst. [from Gk thrix (genitive trikhos) hair]

trichology (trɪ'kɒlədʒɪ) n. the branch of medicine concerned with the hair and its diseases. —**tri'chologist** n.

trichomoniasis (ˌtrɪkəʊmə'naɪəsɪs) *n.* inflammation of the vagina caused by infection with parasitic protozoa. [C19: NL]

trichopteran (traɪ'kɒptərən) *n.* **1.** any insect of the order *Trichoptera*, which comprises the caddis flies. ~*adj.* **2.** Also: **trichopterous** (trɪ'kɒptərəs). of or belonging to the order *Trichoptera*. [C19: from NL *Trichoptera*, lit.: having hairy wings, from Gk *thrix* a hair + *pteron* wing]

trichosis (trɪ'kəʊsɪs) *n.* any abnormal condition or disease of the hair. [C19: via NL from Gk *trikhōsis* growth of hair]

trichotomy (traɪ'kɒtəmɪ) *n.*, *pl.* **-mies. 1.** division into three categories. **2.** *Theol.* the division of man into body, spirit, and soul. [C17: prob. from NL *trichotomia*, from Gk *trikhotomein* to divide into three] —**trichotomic** (ˌtrɪkə'tɒmɪk) *or* **tri'chotomous** *adj.*

trichroism ('traɪkrəʊˌɪzəm) *n.* a property of biaxial crystals as a result of which they show a difference in colour when viewed along three different axes. [C19: from Gk *trikhroos* three-coloured, from TRI- + *khrōma* colour]

trichromatic (ˌtraɪkrəʊ'mætɪk) *or* **trichromic** (traɪ-'krəʊmɪk) *adj.* **1.** involving the combination of three primary colours. **2.** of or having normal colour vision. **3.** having or involving three colours. —**tri'chroma,tism** *n.*

trick (trɪk) *n.* **1.** a deceitful or cunning action or plan. **2. a.** a mischievous, malicious, or humorous action or plan; joke. **b.** (*as modifier*): *a trick spider*. **3.** an illusory or magical feat. **4.** a simple feat learned by an animal or person. **5.** an adroit or ingenious device; knack: *a trick of the trade*. **6.** a habit or mannerism. **7.** a turn of duty. **8.** *Cards.* a batch of cards containing one from each player, usually played in turn and won by the player or side that plays the card with the highest value. **9. do the trick.** *Inf.* to produce the desired result. **10. how's tricks?** *Sl.* how are you? ~*vb.* **11.** (*tr.*) to defraud, deceive, or cheat (someone). ~See also **trick out.** [C15: from OF *trique*, from *trikier* to deceive, ult. from L *tricārī* to play tricks]

trick cyclist *n.* **1.** a cyclist who performs tricks, such as in a circus. **2.** a slang term for **psychiatrist.**

trickery ('trɪkərɪ) *n.*, *pl.* **-eries.** the practice or an instance of using tricks.

trickle ('trɪkəl) *vb.* **1.** to run or cause to run in thin or slow streams. **2.** (*intr.*) to move gradually: *the crowd trickled away.* ~*n.* **3.** a thin, irregular, or slow flow of something. **4.** the act of trickling. [C14: ? imit.] —**'trickling** *adj.*

trickle charger *n.* a small mains-operated battery charger, esp. one used by car owners.

trick or treat *n. Chiefly U.S. & Canad.* a customary cry used at Hallowe'en by children dressed in disguises calling at houses, by which they imply that they want a present of sweets, apples, or money and, if refused, will play a trick on the householder.

trick out *or* **up** *vb.* (*tr.*, *adv.*) to dress up; deck out: *tricked out in frilly dresses.*

trickster ('trɪkstə) *n.* a person who deceives or plays tricks.

tricksy ('trɪksɪ) *adj.* **-sier, -siest. 1.** playing tricks habitually; mischievous. **2.** crafty or difficult to deal with. —**'tricksiness** *n.*

tricky ('trɪkɪ) *adj.* **trickier, trickiest. 1.** involving snags or difficulties. **2.** needing careful handling. **3.** sly; wily: *a tricky dealer.* —**'trickily** *adv.* —**'trickiness** *n.*

triclinic (traɪ'klɪnɪk) *adj.* of the crystal system characterized by three unequal axes, no pair of which are perpendicular.

triclinium (traɪ'klɪnɪəm) *n.*, *pl.* **-ia** (-ɪə). (in ancient Rome) **1.** an arrangement of three couches around a table for reclining upon while dining. **2.** a dining room. [C17: from L, from Gk *triklinion*, from TRI- + *klinē* a couch]

tricolour *or U.S.* **tricolor** ('trɪkələ, 'traɪˌkʌlə) *adj. also* **tricoloured** *or U.S.* **tricolored** ('traɪ,kʌləd). **1.** having or involving three colours. ~*n.* **2.** (*often cap.*) the French flag, having three stripes in blue, white, and red. **3.** any flag, badge, etc., with three colours.

tricorn ('traɪ,kɔːn) *n. also* **tricorne. 1.** a cocked hat with opposing brims turned back and caught in three places. ~*adj. also* **tricornered. 2.** having three horns or corners. [C18: from L *tricornis*, from TRI- + *cornu* horn]

tricot ('trɪkəʊ, 'triː-) *n.* **1.** a thin rayon or nylon fabric knitted or resembling knitting, used for dresses, etc. **2.** a type of ribbed dress fabric. [C19: from F, from *tricoter* to knit, from ?]

tricuspid (traɪ'kʌspɪd) *Anat.* ~*adj. also* **tricuspidal. 1.** having three points, cusps, or segments: *a tricuspid tooth; a tricuspid valve.* ~*n.* **2.** a tooth having three cusps.

tricycle ('traɪsɪkəl) *n.* a three-wheeled cycle, esp. one driven by pedals. —**'tricyclist** *n.*

trident ('traɪdənt) *n.* a three-pronged spear. [C16: from L *tridēns* three-pronged, from TRI- + *dēns* tooth]

Trident ('traɪdənt) *n.* a type of U.S. submarine-launched ballistic missile with independently targetable warheads.

tridentate (traɪ'dɛnteɪt) *or* **tridental** *adj.* having three prongs, teeth, or points.

Tridentine (traɪ'dɛntaɪn) *adj.* **1. a.** *History.* of the Council of Trent in the 16th century. **b.** in accord with Tridentine doctrine: *Tridentine mass.* ~*n.* **2.** an orthodox Roman Catholic. [C16: from Med. L *Tridentīnus*, from *Tridentum* TRENT]

Tridentum (traɪ'dɛntəm) *n.* the Latin name for **Trento.**

tried (traɪd) *vb.* the past tense and past participle of **try.**

triella (traɪ'ɛlə) *n.* a cumulative bet on horses in three specified races.

triennial (traɪ'ɛnɪəl) *adj.* **1.** relating to, lasting for, or occurring every three years. ~*n.* **2.** a third anniversary. **3.** a triennial period, thing, or occurrence. [C17: from L TRI-ENNIUM] —**tri'ennially** *adv.*

triennium (traɪ'ɛnɪəm) *n.*, *pl.* **-niums** *or* **-nia** (-nɪə). a period or cycle of three years. [C19: from L, from TRI- + *annus* a year]

Trient (triː'ɛnt) *n.* the German name for **Trento.** Also: **Trent.**

trier ('traɪə) *n.* a person or thing that tries.

Trier (*German* triːr) *n.* a city in W West Germany, in the Rhineland-Palatinate on the Moselle River: one of the oldest towns of central Europe, ancient capital of a Celto-Germanic tribe (the **Treveri**); an early centre of Christianity, ruled by powerful archbishops until the 18th century; wine trade; important Roman remains. Pop.: 94 600 (1984). Latin name: **Augusta Treverorum** (aʊ'guːstə,trɛvə'rɔʊrəm). French name: **Trèves.**

Trieste (triː'ɛst; *Italian* tri'ɛste) *n.* **1.** a port in NE Italy, capital of Friuli-Venezia Giulia region, on the **Gulf of Trieste** at the head of the Adriatic Sea: under Austrian rule (1382–1918); capital of the Free Territory of Trieste (1947–54); important transit port for central Europe. Pop.: 239 031 (1986). Slovene and Serbo-Croatian name: **Trst. 2. Free Territory of.** a former territory on the N Adriatic: established by the UN in 1947; most of the N part passed to Italy and the remainder to Yugoslavia in 1954.

trifacial (traɪ'feɪʃəl) *adj.* another word for **trigeminal.**

trifecta (traɪ'fɛktə) *n. Austral.* a form of betting in which punters select first-, second-, and third-place winners in the correct order.

trifid ('traɪfɪd) *adj.* divided or split into three parts or lobes. [C18: from L *trifidus*, from TRI- + *findere* to split]

trifle ('traɪfəl) *n.* **1.** a thing of little or no value or significance. **2.** a small amount; bit: *a trifle more enthusiasm.* **3.** *Brit.* a cold dessert made with sponge cake spread with jam or fruit, soaked in sherry, covered with custard and cream. ~*vb.* **4.** (*intr.*; usually foll. by *with*) to deal (with) as if worthless; dally: *to trifle with a person's affections.* **5.** to waste (time) frivolously. [C13: from OF *trufle* mockery, from *trufler* to cheat] —**'trifler** *n.*

trifling ('traɪflɪŋ) *adj.* **1.** insignificant or petty. **2.** frivolous or idle. —**'triflingly** *adv.*

trifocal *adj.* (traɪ'fəʊkəl). **1.** having three focuses. **2.** having three focal lengths. ~*n.* (traɪ'fəʊkəl, 'traɪ,fəʊkəl). **3.** (*pl.*) glasses that have trifocal lenses.

triforium (traɪ'fɔːrɪəm) *n.*, *pl.* **-ria** (-rɪə). an arcade above the arches of the nave, choir, or transept of a church. [C18: from Anglo-L, apparently from L TRI- + *foris* a doorway; from the fact that each bay had three openings]

trifurcate ('traɪfɜːkɪt, -ˌkeɪt) *or* **trifurcated** *adj.* having three branches or forks. [C19: from L *trifurcus*, from TRI- + *furca* a fork]

trig (trɪg) *Arch. or dialect.* ~*adj.* **1.** neat or spruce. ~*vb.* **trigging, trigged. 2.** to make or become trim or spruce. [C12: (orig.: trusty): from ON] —**'trigly** *adv.* —**'trigness** *n.*

trig. *abbrev. for:* **1.** trigonometrical. **2.** trigonometry.

trigeminal (traɪ'dʒɛmɪnəl) *adj. Anat.* of or relating to the trigeminal nerve. [C19: from L *trigeminus* triplet, from TRI- + *geminus* twin]

trigeminal nerve *n.* either one of the fifth pair of cranial nerves, which supply the muscles of the mandible and maxilla. Their ophthalmic branches supply the area around the orbit of the eye, the nasal cavity, and the forehead.

trigeminal neuralgia *n. Pathol.* another name for **tic douloureux**.

trigger ('trɪgə) *n.* **1.** a small lever that activates the firing mechanism of a firearm. **2.** a device that releases a spring-loaded mechanism. **3.** any event that sets a course of action in motion. ~*vb.* (*tr.*) **4.** (usually foll. by *off*) to give rise (to); set off. **5.** to fire or set in motion by or as by pulling a trigger. [C17 *tricker*, from Du. *trekker*, from *trekken* to pull]

triggerfish ('trɪgə,fɪʃ) *n.*, *pl.* **-fish** or **-fishes.** any of a family of fishes of tropical and temperate seas. They have erectile spines in the first dorsal fin.

trigger-happy *adj. Inf.* **1.** tending to resort to the use of firearms or violence irresponsibly. **2.** tending to act rashly.

triglyceride (traɪ'glɪsə,raɪd) *n.* any ester of glycerol and one or more carboxylic acids, in which each glycerol molecule has combined with three carboxylic acid molecules.

triglyph ('traɪ,glɪf) *n. Archit.* a stone block in a Doric frieze, having three vertical channels. [C16: via L from Gk *trigluphos*, from TRI- + *gluphē* carving]

trigonal ('trɪgən²l) *adj.* **1.** triangular. **2.** of the crystal system characterized by three equal axes that are equally inclined and not perpendicular to each other. [C16: via L from Gk *trigōnon* triangle]

trigonometric function *n.* any of a group of functions of an angle expressed as a ratio of two of the sides of a right-angled triangle containing the angle. The group includes sine, cosine, tangent, etc.

trigonometry (,trɪgə'nɒmɪtrɪ) *n.* the branch of mathematics concerned with the properties of trigonometric functions and their application to the determination of the angles and sides of triangles: used in surveying, navigation, etc. [C17: from NL *trigōnometria*, from Gk *trigōnon* triangle] —**trigonometric** (,trɪgənə'mɛtrɪk) or ,**trigono'metrical** *adj.*

trig point *n.* an informal name for **triangulation station**. [from *trigonometric*]

trigraph ('traɪ,grɑːf) *n.* a combination of three letters used to represent a single speech sound or phoneme, such as *eau* in French *beau*.

trihedral (traɪ'hiːdrəl) *adj.* **1.** having three plane faces. ~*n.* **2.** a figure formed by the intersection of three lines in different planes.

trihedron (traɪ'hiːdrən) *n.*, *pl.* **-drons** or **-dra** (-drə). a figure determined by the intersection of three planes.

trike (traɪk) *n.* short for **tricycle**.

trilateral (traɪ'lætərəl) *adj.* having three sides.

trilby ('trɪlbɪ) *n.*, *pl.* **-bies.** a man's soft felt hat with an indented crown. [C19: after *Trilby*, the heroine of a dramatized novel (1893) of that title by George Du Maurier]

trilingual (traɪ'lɪŋgwəl) *adj.* **1.** able to speak three languages fluently. **2.** expressed or written in three languages. —**tri'lingualism** *n.*

trilithon (traɪ'lɪθɒn) or **trilith** ('traɪlɪθ) *n.* a structure consisting of two upright stones with a third placed across the top, as at Stonehenge. [C18: from Gk] —**trilithic** (traɪ'lɪθɪk) *adj.*

trill (trɪl) *n.* **1.** *Music.* a rapid alternation between a principal note and the note above it. **2.** a shrill warbling sound, esp. as made by some birds. **3.** the articulation of an (r) sound produced by the rapid vibration of the tongue or the uvula. ~*vb.* **4.** to sound, sing, or play (a trill or with a trill). **5.** (*tr.*) to pronounce (an (r) sound) by the production of a trill. [C17: from It. *trillo*, from *trillare*, apparently from MDu. *trillen* to vibrate]

trillion ('trɪljən) *n.* **1.** (in Britain, France, and Germany) the number represented as one followed by eighteen zeros (10^{18}); a million million million. U.S. and Canad. word: **quintillion. 2.** (in the U.S. and Canada) the number represented as one followed by twelve zeros (10^{12}); a million million. Brit. word: **billion.** ~*determiner.* **3.** (preceded by *a* or a numeral) amounting to a trillion. [C17: from F, on the model of *million*] —**'trillionth** *n.*, *adj.*

trillium ('trɪljəm) *n.* any of a genus of herbaceous plants of Asia and North America, having a whorl of three leaves at the top of the stem with a single white, pink, or purple three-petalled flower. [C18: from NL, modification by Linnaeus of Swedish *trilling* triplet]

trilobate (traɪ'ləʊbeɪt, 'traɪlə,beɪt) *adj.* (esp. of a leaf) consisting of or having three lobes or parts.

trilobite ('traɪlə,baɪt) *n.* any of various extinct marine arthropods abundant in Palaeozoic times, having a segmented exoskeleton divided into three parts. [C19: from NL *Trilobītēs*, from Gk *trilobos* having three lobes] —**trilobitic** (,traɪlə'bɪtɪk) *adj.*

trilogy ('trɪlədʒɪ) *n.*, *pl.* **-gies. 1.** a series of three related works, esp. in literature, etc. **2.** (in ancient Greece) a series of three tragedies performed together. [C19: from Gk *trilogia*]

trim (trɪm) *adj.* **trimmer, trimmest. 1.** neat and spruce in appearance. **2.** slim; slender. **3.** in good condition. ~*vb.* **trimming, trimmed. 1.** to put in good order, esp. by cutting or pruning. **5.** to shape and finish (timber). **6.** to adorn or decorate. **7.** (sometimes foll. by *off* or *away*) to cut so as to remove: *to trim off a branch.* **8.** to cut down to the desired size or shape. **9.** *Naut.* **a.** (*also intr.*) to adjust the balance of (a vessel) or (of a vessel) to maintain an even balance, by distribution of ballast, cargo, etc. **b.** (*also intr.*) to adjust (a vessel's sails) to take advantage of the wind. **10.** to balance (an aircraft) before flight by adjusting the position of the load or in flight by the use of trim tabs, fuel transfer, etc. **11.** (*also intr.*) to modify (one's opinions, etc.) for expediency. **12.** *Inf.* to thrash or beat. **13.** *Inf.* to rebuke. ~*n.* **14.** a decoration or adornment. **15.** the upholstery and decorative facings of a car's interior. **16.** proper order or fitness; good shape. **17.** a haircut that neatens but does not alter the existing hairstyle. **18.** *Naut.* **a.** the general set and appearance of a vessel. **b.** the difference between the draught of a vessel at the bow and at the stern. **c.** the fitness of a vessel. **d.** the position of a vessel's sails relative to the wind. **19.** dress or equipment. **20.** *U.S.* window-dressing. **21.** the attitude of an aircraft in flight when the pilot allows the main control surfaces to take up their own positions. **22.** material that is trimmed off. **23.** decorative mouldings, such as architraves, picture rails, etc. [OE *trymman* to strengthen] —**'trimly** *adv.* —**'trimness** *n.*

trimaran ('traɪmə,ræn) *n.* a vessel, usually of shallow draught, with two hulls flanking the main hull. [C20: from TRI- + (CATA)MARAN]

trimer ('traɪmə) *n.* a polymer or a molecule of a polymer consisting of three identical monomers.

trimerous ('trɪmərəs) *adj.* **1.** having parts in groups of three. **2.** having three parts.

trimester (traɪ'mɛstə) *n.* **1.** a period of three months. **2.** (in some U.S. and Canad. universities or schools) any of the three academic sessions. [C19: from F *trimestre*, from L *trimēstris* of three months] —**tri'mestral** or **tri'mestrial** *adj.*

trimeter ('trɪmɪtə) *Prosody.* ~*n.* **1.** a verse line consisting of three metrical feet. ~*adj.* **2.** designating such a line.

trimethadione (,traɪmɛθə'daɪəʊn) *n.* a crystalline compound with a camphor-like odour, used in the treatment of epilepsy.

trimetric projection (traɪ'mɛtrɪk) *n.* a geometric projection, used in mechanical drawing, in which the three axes are at arbitrary angles, often using different linear scales.

trimmer ('trɪmə) *n.* **1.** a beam attached to truncated joists in order to leave an opening for a staircase, chimney, etc. **2.** a machine for trimming timber. **3.** a variable capacitor of small capacitance used for making fine adjustments, etc. **4.** a person who alters his opinions on the grounds of expediency. **5.** a person who fits out motor vehicles.

trimming ('trɪmɪŋ) *n.* **1.** an extra piece used to decorate or complete. **2.** (*pl.*) usual or traditional accompaniments: *roast turkey with all the trimmings.* **3.** (*pl.*) parts that are cut off.

trimolecular (,traɪmə'lɛkjʊlə) *adj. Chem.* of, formed from, or involving three molecules.

trimonthly (traɪ'mʌnθlɪ) *adj.*, *adv.* every three months.

trimorphism (traɪ'mɔːfɪzəm) *n.* **1.** *Biol.* the property exhibited by certain species of having or occurring in three different forms. **2.** the property of certain minerals of existing in three crystalline forms.

Trinacria (trɪ'neɪkrɪə, traɪ-) *n.* the Latin name for **Sicily**. —**Tri'nacrian** *adj.*

trinary ('traɪnərɪ) *adj.* **1.** made up of three parts; ternary. **2.** going in threes. [C15: from LL *trinārius* of three sorts, from L *trinī* three each, from *trēs* three]

Trincomalee (ˌtrɪŋkəʊmə'liː) n. a port in NE Sri Lanka, on the **Bay of Trincomalee** (an inlet of the Bay of Bengal); British naval base until 1957. Pop.: 44 913 (1981).

trine (traɪn) n. 1. *Astrol.* an aspect of 120° between two planets. 2. anything comprising three parts. ~*adj.* 3. of or relating to a trine. 4. threefold; triple. [C14: from OF *trin*, from L *trīnus* triple, from *trēs* three] — **'trinal** *adj.*

Trinidad ('trɪnɪˌdæd) n. an island in the West Indies, off the NE coast of Venezuela: colonized by the Spanish in the 17th century and ceded to Britain in 1802; joined with Tobago in 1888 as a British colony; now part of the independent republic of Trinidad and Tobago. Pop.: 1 039 100 (1980). — ˌTrini'dadian *adj.*, n.

Trinidad and Tobago n. an independent republic in the West Indies, occupying the two southernmost islands of the Lesser Antilles: became a British colony in 1888 and gained independence in 1962; became a republic in 1976; a member of the Commonwealth. Official language: English. Religion: Christian majority, with a large Hindu minority. Currency: Trinidad and Tobago dollar. Capital: Port-of-Spain. Combined pop.: 1 220 000 (1987 est.). Area: 5128 sq. km (1980 sq. miles).

Trinitarian (ˌtrɪnɪ'tɛərɪən) n. 1. a person who believes in the doctrine of the Trinity. ~*adj.* 2. of or relating to the doctrine of the Trinity or those who uphold it. — ˌTrini'tarianˌism n.

trinitroglycerin (traɪˌnaɪtrəʊ'glɪsərɪn) n. the full name for **nitroglycerin.**

trinitrotoluene (traɪˌnaɪtrəʊ'tɒljuˌiːn) *or* **trinitrotoluol** (traɪˌnaɪtrəʊ'tɒljʊˌɒl) n. the full name for **TNT.**

trinity ('trɪnɪtɪ) n., pl. **-ties.** 1. a group of three. 2. the state of being threefold. [C13: from OF *trinite*, from LL *trīnitās*, from L *trīnus* triple]

Trinity ('trɪnɪtɪ) n. *Christian theol.* the union of three persons, the Father, Son, and Holy Spirit, in one Godhead.

Trinity Brethren pl. n. the members of Trinity House.

Trinity House n. an association that provides lighthouses, buoys, etc., around the British coast.

Trinity Sunday n. the Sunday after Whit Sunday.

Trinity term n. the summer term at certain universities.

trinket ('trɪŋkɪt) n. 1. a small or worthless ornament or piece of jewellery. 2. a trivial object; trifle. [C16: ? from earlier *trenket* little knife, via OF, from L *truncāre* to lop]

trinomial (traɪ'nəʊmɪəl) *adj.* 1. consisting of three terms. ~*n.* 2. *Maths.* a polynomial consisting of three terms, such as $ax^2 + bx + c$. 3. *Biol.* the three-part name of an organism that incorporates its genus, species, and subspecies. [C18: TRI- + *-nomial* on the model of *binomial*]

trio ('triːəʊ) n., pl. **trios.** 1. a group of three. 2. *Music.* a. a group of three singers or instrumentalists or a piece of music composed for such a group. b. a subordinate section in a scherzo, minuet, etc. [C18: from It., ult. from L *trēs* three]

triode ('traɪəʊd) n. 1. an electronic valve having three electrodes, a cathode, an anode, and a grid. 2. any electronic device having three electrodes. [C20: TRI- + ELECTRODE]

trioecious *or* **triecious** (traɪ'iːʃəs) *adj.* (of a plant species) having male, female, and hermaphrodite flowers in three different plants. [C18: from NL *trioecia*, from Gk TRI- + *oikos* house]

triolein (traɪ'əʊlɪɪn) n. a naturally occurring glyceride of oleic acid, found in fats and oils.

triolet ('triːəʊˌlɛt) n. a verse form of eight lines, having the first line repeated as the fourth and seventh and the second line as the eighth, rhyming a b a a a b a b. [C17: from F: a little TRIO]

trioxide (traɪ'ɒksaɪd) n. any oxide that contains three oxygen atoms per molecule.

trip (trɪp) n. 1. an outward and return journey, often for a specific purpose. 2. any journey. 3. a false step; stumble. 4. any slip or blunder. 5. a light step or tread. 6. a manoeuvre or device to cause someone to trip. 7. Also called: **tripper.** any catch on a mechanism that acts as a switch. 8. *Inf.* a hallucinogenic drug experience. 9. *Inf.* any stimulating, profound, etc., experience. ~*vb.* **tripping, tripped.** 10. (often foll. by *up*, or when *intr.*, by *on* or *over*) to stumble or cause to stumble. 11. to make or cause to make a mistake. 12. (*tr.*; often foll. by *up*) to trap or catch in a mistake. 13. (*intr.*) to go on a short journey. 14. (*intr.*) to move or tread lightly. 15. (*intr.*) *Inf.* to experience the effects of a hallucinogenic drug.

16. (*tr.*) to activate a mechanical trip. [C14: from OF *triper* to tread, of Gmc origin]

tripartite (traɪ'pɑːtaɪt) *adj.* 1. divided into or composed of three parts. 2. involving three participants. 3. (esp. of leaves) consisting of three parts formed by divisions extending almost to the base. — **tri'partitely** *adv.*

tripe (traɪp) n. 1. the stomach lining of an ox, cow, etc., prepared for cooking. 2. *Inf.* something silly; rubbish. [C13: from OF, from ?]

triphammer ('trɪpˌhæmə) n. a power hammer that is raised or tilted by a cam and allowed to fall under gravity.

triphibious (traɪ'fɪbɪəs) *adj.* (esp. of military operations) occurring on land, at sea, and in the air. [C20: from TRI- + (AM)PHIBIOUS]

triphthong ('trɪfθɒŋ, 'trɪp-) n. 1. a composite vowel sound during the articulation of which the vocal organs move from one position through a second, ending in a third. 2. a trigraph representing such a composite vowel sound. [C16: via NL from Med. Gk *triphthongos*, from TRI- + *phthongos* sound] — **triph'thongal** *adj.*

tripinnate (traɪ'pɪnɪt, -eɪt) *adj.* (of a leaf) having pinnate leaflets that are bipinnately arranged.

triplane ('traɪˌpleɪn) n. an aeroplane having three wings arranged one above the other.

triple ('trɪpᵊl) *adj.* 1. consisting of three parts; threefold. 2. (of musical time or rhythm) having three beats in each bar. 3. three times as great or as much. ~*n.* 4. a threefold amount. 5. a group of three. ~*vb.* 6. to increase threefold; treble. [C16: from L *triplus*] — **'triply** *adv.*

triple jump n. an athletic event in which the competitor has to perform successively a hop, a step, and a jump in continuous movement.

triple point n. *Chem.* the temperature and pressure at which the three phases of a substance are in equilibrium.

triplet ('trɪplɪt) n. 1. a group or set of three similar things. 2. one of three offspring born at one birth. 3. *Music.* a group of three notes played in a time value of two, four, etc. [C17: from TRIPLE, on the model of *doublet*]

Triplex ('trɪplɛks) n. *Brit. trademark.* a laminated safety glass, as used in car windows.

triplicate *adj.* ('trɪplɪkɪt). 1. triple. ~*vb.* ('trɪplɪˌkeɪt). 2. to multiply or be multiplied by three. ~*n.* ('trɪplɪkɪt). 3. a. a group of three things. b. one of such a group. 4. in triplicate. written out three times. [C15: from L *triplicāre* to triple] — ˌtripli'cation n.

triploid ('trɪplɔɪd) *adj.* 1. having or relating to three times the haploid number of chromosomes: *a triploid organism.* ~*n.* 2. a triploid organism. [C19: from Gk *tripl(oos)* triple + (HAPL)OID]

tripod ('traɪpɒd) n. 1. a three-legged stand to which a camera, etc., can be attached to hold it steady. 2. a stand or table having three legs. — **tripodal** ('trɪpədᵊl) *adj.*

tripoli ('trɪpəlɪ) n. a lightweight porous siliceous rock used in a powdered form as a polish. [C17: after TRIPOLI, in Libya or in Lebanon]

Tripoli ('trɪpəlɪ) n. 1. the capital and chief port of Libya, in the northwest on the Mediterranean: founded by Phoenicians in about the 7th century B.C.; the only city that has survived of the three (Oea, Leptis Magna, and Sabratha) that formed the African Tripolis ("three cities"); fishing and manufacturing centre. Pop.: 980 000 (1982). Ancient name: **Oea** ('iːə). Arabic name: **Tarabulus el Gharb.** 2. a port in N Lebanon, on the Mediterranean: the second largest town in Lebanon; taken by the Crusaders in 1109 after a siege of five years; oil-refining and manufacturing centre. Pop.: 500 000 (1985 est.). Ancient name: **Tripolis.** Arabic name: **Tarabulus esh Sham.**

Tripolitania (ˌtrɪpəlɪ'teɪnɪə) n. the NW part of Libya: established as a Phoenician colony in the 7th century B.C.; taken by the Turks in 1551 and became one of the Barbary states; under Italian rule from 1912 until World War II. — ˌTripoli'tanian *adj.*, n.

tripos ('traɪpɒs) n. *Brit.* the final honours degree examinations at Cambridge University. [C16: from L *tripūs*, infl. by Gk noun ending *-os*]

tripper ('trɪpə) n. 1. *Chiefly Brit.* a tourist. 2. another word for **trip** (sense 7). 3. any device that causes a trip to operate.

triptane ('trɪpteɪn) n. a liquid hydrocarbon used in aviation fuel. [C20: shortened & altered from *trimethylbutane*]

Triptolemus (trɪp'tɒlɪməs) n. *Greek myth.* a favourite of Demeter, sent by her to teach men agriculture.

triptych ('trɪptɪk) n. 1. a set of three pictures or panels, usually hinged so that the two wing panels fold over the larger central one: often used as an altarpiece. 2. a set of three hinged writing tablets. [C18: from Gk *triptukhos*, from TRI- + *ptux* plate]

triptyque (trɪp'tiːk) n. a customs permit for the temporary importation of a motor vehicle. [C20: from F: TRIPTYCH (from its three sections)]

Tripura ('trɪpʊrə) n. a state of NE India: formerly a princely state, ruled by the Maharajahs for over 1300 years; became a union territory in 1956 and a state in 1972; extensive jungles. Capital: Agartala. Pop.: 2 047 351 (1981). Area: 10 453 sq. km (4036 sq. miles).

tripwire ('trɪp,waɪə) n. a wire that activates a trap, mine, etc., when tripped over.

trireme ('traɪriːm) n. an ancient Greek galley with three banks of oars on each side. [C17: from L *triêmis*, from TRI- + *rêmus* oar]

trisect (traɪ'sɛkt) vb. (tr.) to divide into three parts, esp. three equal parts. [C17: TRI- + -sect from L *secâre* to cut] —**trisection** (traɪ'sɛkʃən) n.

trishaw ('traɪ,ʃɔː) n. another name for **rickshaw** (sense 2). [C20: from TRI- + RICKSHAW]

triskelion (trɪ'skɛlɪ,ɒn) n., pl. **triskelia** (trɪ'skɛlɪə). a symbol consisting of three bent limbs or lines radiating from a centre. [C19: from Gk *triskelês* three-legged]

Trismegistus (,trɪsmɪ'dʒɪstəs) n. See **Hermes Trismegistus**.

trismus ('trɪzməs) n. *Pathol.* the state of being unable to open the mouth because of sustained contractions of the jaw muscles, caused by tetanus. Nontechnical name: **lockjaw**. [C17: from NL, from Gk *trismos* a grinding]

Tristan ('trɪstən) or **Tristram** ('trɪstrəm) n. (in medieval romance) the nephew of King Mark of Cornwall who fell in love with his uncle's bride, Iseult, after they mistakenly drank a love potion.

Tristan da Cunha ('trɪstən də 'kuːnjə) n. a group of four small volcanic islands in the S Atlantic, about halfway between South Africa and South America: comprises the main island of Tristan and the uninhabited islands of Gough, Inaccessible, and Nightingale; discovered in 1506 by the Portuguese admiral Tristão da Cunha; annexed to Britain in 1816; whole population of Tristan evacuated for two years after the volcanic eruption of 1961. Pop.: 325 (1982). Area: about 100 sq. km (40 sq. miles).

triste (triːst) adj. an archaic word for **sad**. [from F]

trisyllable (traɪ'sɪləbᵊl) n. a word of three syllables. —**trisyllabic** (,traɪsɪ'læbɪk) adj.

trite (traɪt) adj. hackneyed; dull: *a trite comment*. [C16: from L *tritus* worn down, from *terere* to rub] —**tritely** adv. —**triteness** n.

tritheism ('traɪθɪ,ɪzəm) n. *Theol.* belief in three gods, esp. in the Trinity as consisting of three distinct gods. —**tritheist** n., adj.

triticum ('trɪtɪkəm) n. any of a genus of cereal grasses which includes the wheats. [C19: L, lit.: wheat, prob. from *tritum*, supine of *terere* to grind]

tritium ('trɪtɪəm) n. a radioactive isotope of hydrogen. Symbol: T or ³H; half-life: 12.5 years. [C20: NL, from Gk *tritos* third]

triton[1] ('traɪtᵊn) n. any of various chiefly tropical marine gastropod molluscs having large spiral shells. [C16: via L from Gk *tritôn*]

triton[2] ('traɪtən) n. *Physics.* a nucleus of an atom of tritium, containing two neutrons and one proton. [C20: from TRIT(IUM) + -ON]

Triton ('traɪtᵊn) n. *Greek myth.* a sea god depicted as having the upper parts of a man with a fish's tail.

tritone ('traɪ,təʊn) n. a musical interval consisting of three whole tones.

triturate ('trɪtjʊ,reɪt) vb. 1. (tr.) to grind or rub into a fine powder or pulp. ~n. 2. the powder or pulp resulting from this. [C17: from LL *tritûrâre* to thresh, from L *tritûra* a threshing, from *terere* to grind] —**tritu'ration** n.

triumph ('traɪəmf) n. 1. the feeling of exultation and happiness derived from a victory or major achievement. 2. the act or condition of being victorious; victory. 3. (in ancient Rome) a procession held in honour of a victorious general. ~vb. (intr.) 4. (often foll. by over) to win a victory or control: *to triumph over one's weaknesses*. 5. to rejoice over a victory. 6. to celebrate a Roman triumph.

[C14: from OF *triumphe*, from L *triumphus*, from OL *triumpus*] —**triumphal** (traɪ'ʌmfəl) adj.

triumphant (traɪ'ʌmfənt) adj. 1. experiencing or displaying triumph. 2. exultant through triumph. —**tri'umphantly** adv.

triumvir (traɪ'ʌmvə) n., pl. **-virs** or **-viri** (-vɪ,riː). (esp. in ancient Rome) a member of a triumvirate. [C16: from L: one of three administrators, from *trium virôrum* of three men, from *três* three + *vir* man] —**tri'umviral** adj.

triumvirate (traɪ'ʌmvɪrɪt) n. 1. (in ancient Rome) a board of three officials jointly responsible for some task. 2. joint rule by three men. 3. any group of three men associated in some way. 4. the office of a triumvir.

triune ('traɪjuːn) adj. constituting three in one, esp. the three persons in one God of the Trinity. [C17: TRI- + -une, from L *ûnus* one] —**tri'unity** n.

trivalent (traɪ'veɪlənt, 'trɪvələnt) adj. *Chem.* 1. having a valency of three. 2. having three valencies. ~Also: **tervalent**. —**tri'valency** n.

Trivandrum (trɪ'vændrəm) n. a city in S India, capital of Kerala, on the Malabar Coast: made capital of the kingdom of Travancore in 1745; University of Kerala (1937). Pop.: 482 722 (1981).

trivet ('trɪvɪt) n. 1. a stand, usually three-legged and metal, on which cooking vessels are placed over a fire. 2. a short metal stand on which hot dishes are placed on a table. 3. **as right as a trivet.** in perfect health. [OE *trefet* (infl. by OE *thrîfête* having three feet), from L *tripês* having three feet]

trivia ('trɪvɪə) n. (functioning as sing. or pl.) petty details or considerations; trifles; trivialities. [from NL, pl. of L *trivium* junction of three roads]

trivial ('trɪvɪəl) adj. 1. of little importance; petty or frivolous: *trivial complaints*. 2. ordinary or commonplace; trite: *trivial conversation*. 3. *Biol., chem.* denoting the common name of an organism or substance. 4. *Biol.* denoting the specific name of an organism in binomial nomenclature. [C15: from L *triviâlis* belonging to the public streets, common, from *trivium* junction of three roads] —'**trivially** adv. —'**trivialness** n.

triviality (,trɪvɪ'ælɪtɪ) n., pl. **-ties.** 1. the state or quality of being trivial. 2. something, such as a remark, that is trivial.

trivialize or **-ise** ('trɪvɪə,laɪz) vb. (tr.) to cause to seem trivial or more trivial; minimize. —,**triviali'zation** or **-i'sation** n.

trivium ('trɪvɪəm) n., pl. **-ia** (-ɪə). (in medieval learning) the arts of grammar, rhetoric, and logic. Cf. **quadrivium**. [C19: from Med. L, from L: crossroads]

-trix suffix forming nouns. indicating a feminine agent, corresponding to nouns ending in -tor: *executrix*. [from L]

t-RNA abbrev. for transfer RNA.

Troas ('trəʊæs) n. the region of NW Asia Minor surrounding the ancient city of Troy. Also called: **the Troad** ('trəʊæd).

Trobriand Islands ('trəʊbrɪ,ænd) pl. n. a group of coral islands in the Solomon Sea, north of the E part of New Guinea: part of Papua New Guinea. Area: about 440 sq. km (170 sq. miles). —**Trobriand Islander** n.

trocar ('trəʊkɑː) n. a surgical instrument for removing fluid from bodily cavities. [C18: from F *trocart*, lit.: with three sides, from *trois* three + *carre* side]

trochal ('trəʊkᵊl) adj. *Zool.* shaped like a wheel. [C19: from Gk *trokhos* wheel]

trochanter (trəʊ'kæntə) n. 1. any of several processes on the upper part of the vertebrate femur, to which muscles are attached. 2. the third segment of an insect's leg. [C17: via F from Gk *trokhantêr*, from *trekhein* to run]

troche (trəʊʃ) n. *Med.* another name for **lozenge** (sense 1). [C16: from F *trochisque*, from LL *trochiscus*, from Gk *trokhiskos* little wheel, from *trokhos* wheel]

trochee ('trəʊkiː) n. a metrical foot of two syllables, the first long and the second short. [C16: via L from Gk *trokhaios pous*, lit.: a running foot, from *trekhein* to run] —**trochaic** (trəʊ'keɪɪk) adj.

trochlea ('trɒklɪə) n., pl. **-leae** (-lɪ,iː). any bony or cartilaginous part with a grooved surface over which a bone, etc., may slide or articulate. [C17: from L, from Gk *trokhileia* a sheaf of pulleys]

trochlear nerve ('trɒklɪə) n. either one of the fourth pair of cranial nerves, which supply the superior oblique muscle of the eye.

trochoid ('trəʊkɔɪd) *n.* **1.** the curve described by a fixed point on the radius of a circle as the circle rolls along a straight line. *~adj. also* **trochoidal.** **2.** rotating about a central axis. **3.** *Anat.* (of a structure or part) resembling or functioning as a pivot or pulley. [C18: from Gk *trokhoeidēs* circular, from *trokhos* wheel]

trod (trɒd) *vb.* the past tense and a past participle of **tread.**

trodden ('trɒdⁿ) *vb.* a past participle of **tread.**

trode (trəʊd) *vb. Arch.* a past tense of **tread.**

troglodyte ('trɒglə,daɪt) *n.* **1.** a cave dweller, esp. of prehistoric times. **2.** *Inf.* a person who lives alone and appears eccentric. [C16: via L from Gk *trōglodutēs* one who enters caves, from *trōglē* hole + *duein* to enter] —**troglodytic** (,trɒglə'dɪtɪk) *adj.*

trogon ('trəʊgon) *n.* any of an order of birds of tropical regions of America, Africa, and Asia, having a brilliant plumage and long tail. See also **quetzal** (sense 1). [C18: from NL, from Gk *trōgōn*, from *trōgein* to gnaw]

troika ('trɔɪkə) *n.* **1.** a Russian vehicle drawn by three horses abreast. **2.** three horses harnessed abreast. **3.** a triumvirate. [C19: from Russian, from *troe* three]

Troilus ('trɔɪləs, 'trɔɪlʊs) *n. Greek myth.* the youngest son of King Priam and Queen Hecuba, slain at Troy. In medieval romance he is portrayed as the lover of Cressida.

Trois Rivières (*French* trwɑ rivjɛr) *n.* a port in central Canada, in Quebec on the St Lawrence River: one of the world's largest centres of newsprint production. Pop.: 128 888 (1986). English name: **Three Rivers.**

Trojan ('trəʊdʒən) *n.* **1.** a native or inhabitant of ancient Troy. **2.** a person who is hard-working and determined. *~adj.* **3.** of or relating to ancient Troy or its inhabitants.

Trojan Horse *n.* **1.** *Greek myth.* the huge wooden hollow figure of a horse left outside Troy by the Greeks and dragged inside by the Trojans. The men concealed inside it opened the city to the final Greek assault. **2.** a trap intended to undermine an enemy.

troll¹ (trəʊl) *vb.* **1.** *Angling.* **a.** to draw (a baited line, etc.) through the water. **b.** to fish (a stretch of water) by trolling. **c.** to fish (for) by trolling. **2.** to roll or cause to roll. **3.** *Arch.* to sing (a refrain, chorus, etc.) in a loud hearty voice. **4.** (*intr.*) *Brit. inf.* to walk or stroll. *~n.* **5.** a trolling. **6.** *Angling.* a bait or lure used in trolling. [C14: from OF *troller* to run about] —**'troller** *n.*

troll² (trəʊl) *n.* (in Scandinavian folklore) one of a class of supernatural creatures that dwell in caves or mountains and are depicted either as dwarfs or as giants. [C19: from ON: demon]

trolley ('trɒlɪ) *n.* **1.** *Brit.* a small table on casters used for conveying food, etc. **2.** *Brit.* a wheeled cart or stand used for moving heavy items, such as shopping in a supermarket or luggage at a railway station. **3.** *Brit.* (in a hospital) a bed mounted on casters and used for moving patients who are unconscious, etc. **4.** *Brit.* See **trolley bus.** **5.** *U.S. & Canad.* See **trolley car.** **6.** a device that collects the current from an overhead wire, third rail, etc., to drive the motor of an electric vehicle. **7.** a pulley or truck that travels along an overhead wire in order to support a suspended load. **8.** *Chiefly Brit.* a low truck running on rails, used in factories, mines, etc. **9.** a truck, cage, or basket suspended from an overhead track or cable for carrying loads in a mine, etc. [C19: prob. from TROLL¹]

trolley bus *n.* an electrically driven public-transport vehicle that does not run on rails but takes its power from an overhead wire.

trolley car *n.* a U.S. and Canad. name for **tram**¹ (sense 1).

trollius ('trəʊlɪəs) *n.* another name for **globeflower.** [from G *Trollblume* globeflower]

trollop ('trɒləp) *n.* **1.** a promiscuous woman, esp. a prostitute. **2.** an untidy woman; slattern. [C17: ?from G dialect *Trolle* prostitute] —**'trollopy** *adj.*

Trollope ('trɒləp) *n.* **Anthony.** 1815–82, English novelist. His most successful novels, such as *The Warden* (1855), *Barchester Towers* (1857), and *Dr Thorne* (1858), are those in the Barsetshire series of studies of English provincial life. The Palliser series of political novels includes *Phineas Redux* (1874) and *The Prime Minister* (1876).

trombone (trɒm'bəʊn) *n.* a brass instrument, a low-pitched counterpart of the trumpet, consisting of a tube the effective length of which is varied by means of a U-shaped slide. [C18: from It., from *tromba* a trumpet, from OHG *trumba*] —**trom'bonist** *n.*

trommel ('trɒməl) *n.* a revolving sieve used to screen crushed ore. [C19: from G: a drum]

trompe (trɒmp) *n.* an apparatus for supplying the blast of air in a forge, consisting of a thin column down which water falls, drawing in air through side openings. [C19: from F, lit.: trumpet]

trompe l'oeil (*French* trɔp lœj) *n., pl.* **trompe l'oeils** (trɔp lœj). **1.** a painting, etc., giving a convincing illusion of reality. **2.** an effect of this kind. [from F, lit.: deception of the eye]

Tromsø ('trɒmsəʊ; *Norwegian* 'trumsø) *n.* a port in N Norway, on a small island between Kvaløy and the mainland: fishing and sealing centre. Pop.: 48 829 (1987).

-tron *suffix forming nouns.* **1.** indicating a vacuum tube. **2.** indicating an instrument for accelerating atomic particles. [from Gk, suffix indicating instrument]

Trondheim ('trɒnd,haɪm; *Norwegian* 'trɔnhɛim) *n.* a port in central Norway, on **Trondheim Fjord** (an inlet of the Norwegian Sea): national capital until 1380; seat of the Technical University of Norway. Pop.: 134 496 (1987). Former name (until the 16th century and from 1930 to 1931): **Nidaros.**

tronk (trɒŋk) *n. S. African sl.* a prison. [from Afrik., prob. from Malay *trungku* to imprison]

troop (tru:p) *n.* **1.** a large group or assembly. **2.** a subdivision of a cavalry squadron or artillery battery of about platoon size. **3.** (*pl.*) armed forces; soldiers. **4.** a large group of Scouts comprising several patrols. *~vb.* **5.** (*intr.*) to gather, move, or march in or as if in a crowd. **6.** (*tr.*) *Mil., chiefly Brit.* to parade (the colour or flag) ceremonially. [C16: from F *troupe*, from *troupeau* flock, of Gmc origin]

trooper ('tru:pə) *n.* **1.** a soldier in a cavalry regiment. **2.** *U.S. & Austral.* a mounted policeman. **3.** *U.S.* a state policeman. **4.** a cavalry horse. **5.** *Inf., chiefly Brit.* a troopship.

troopship ('tru:p,ʃɪp) *n.* a ship used to transport military personnel.

tropaeolum (trəʊ'pi:ələm) *n., pl.* **-lums** *or* **-la** (-lə). any of a genus of garden plants, esp. the nasturtium. [C18: from NL, from L *tropaeum* TROPHY; from the shield-shaped leaves and helmet-shaped flowers]

trope (trəʊp) *n.* a word or expression used in a figurative sense. [C16: from L *tropus* figurative use of a word, from Gk *tropos* style, turn]

-trope *n. combining form.* indicating a turning towards, development in the direction of, or affinity to: *heliotrope.* [from Gk *tropos* a turn]

trophic ('trɒfɪk) *adj.* of nutrition. [C19: from Gk *trophikos*, from *trophē* food, from *trephein* to feed]

tropho- *or before a vowel* **troph-** *combining form.* indicating nourishment or nutrition: *trophozoite.* [from Gk *trophē* food, from *trephein* to feed]

trophoblast ('trɒfə,blæst) *n.* a membrane that encloses the embryo of mammals and absorbs nourishment from the uterine fluids.

trophozoite (,trɒfə'zəʊaɪt) *n.* the form of a protozoan, esp. of certain parasites, in the feeding stage.

trophy ('trəʊfɪ) *n., pl.* **-phies.** **1.** an object such as a silver cup that is symbolic of victory in a contest, esp. a sporting contest; prize. **2.** a memento of success, esp. one taken in war or hunting. **3.** (in ancient Greece and Rome) a memorial to a victory, usually consisting of captured arms raised on the battlefield or in a public place. **4.** an ornamental carving that represents a group of weapons, etc. [C16: from F *trophée*, from L *tropaeum*, from Gk *tropaion*, from *tropē* a turning, defeat of the enemy]

-trophy *n. combining form.* indicating a certain type of nourishment or growth: *dystrophy.* [from Gk *-trophia*, from *trophē* nourishment] —**-trophic** *adj. combining form.*

tropic ('trɒpɪk) *n.* **1.** (*sometimes cap.*) either of the parallel lines of latitude at about 23½°N (**tropic of Cancer**) and 23½°S (**tropic of Capricorn**) of the equator. **2. the tropics.** (*often cap.*) that part of the earth's surface between the tropics of Cancer and Capricorn. **3.** *Astron.* either of the two parallel circles on the celestial sphere having the same latitudes and names as the lines on the earth. *~adj.* **4.** tropical. [C14: from LL *tropicus* belonging to a turn, from Gk *tropikos*, from *tropos* a turn; from the belief that the sun turned back at the solstices]

-tropic adj. combining form. turning or developing in response to a certain stimulus: heliotropic. [from Gk tropos a turn]

tropical ('trɒpɪkəl) adj. **1.** situated in, used in, characteristic of, or relating to the tropics. **2.** (of weather) very hot, esp. when humid. **3.** of a trope. —,tropi'cality n. —'tropically adv.

tropicbird ('trɒpɪk,bɜːd) n. any of various tropical aquatic birds having long tail feathers and a white plumage with black markings.

tropism ('trəʊpɪzəm) n. the response of an organism, esp. a plant, to an external stimulus by growth in a direction determined by the stimulus. [from Gk tropos a turn] —,tropis'matic adj.

-tropism or **-tropy** n. combining form. indicating a tendency to turn or develop in response to a stimulus: phototropism. [from Gk tropos a turn]

tropo- combining form. indicating change or a turning: tropophyte. [from Gk tropos a turn]

tropopause ('trɒpə,pɔːz) n. Meteorol. the plane of discontinuity between the troposphere and the stratosphere, characterized by a sharp change in the lapse rate.

troposphere ('trɒpə,sfɪə) n. the lowest atmospheric layer, about 18 kilometres (11 miles) thick at the equator to about 6 km (4 miles) at the Poles, in which air temperature decreases normally with height at about 6.5°C per km.

-tropous adj. combining form. indicating a turning away: anatropous. [from Gk -tropos concerning a turn]

troppo[1] ('trɒpəʊ) adv. Music. too much; excessively. See **non troppo**. [It.]

troppo[2] ('trɒpəʊ) adj. Austral. sl. mentally affected by a tropical climate.

Trossachs ('trɒsəks) n. (functioning as pl. or sing.) **the**. **1.** a narrow wooded valley in central Scotland, between Loch Achray and Loch Katrine: made famous by Sir Walter Scott's descriptions. **2.** (popularly) the area extending northwards from Loch Ard and Aberfoyle to Lochs Katrine, Achray, and Venachar.

trot (trɒt) vb. **trotting, trotted. 1.** to move or cause to move at a trot. ~n. **2.** a gait of a horse in which diagonally opposite legs come down together. **3.** a steady brisk pace. **4.** (in harness racing) a race for horses that have been trained to trot fast. **5.** Chiefly Brit. a small child. **6.** U.S. sl. a student's crib. **7. on the trot**. Inf. **a.** one after the other: to read two books on the trot. **b.** busy, esp. on one's feet. **8. the trots**. Inf. **a.** diarrhoea. **b.** N.Z. trotting races. ~See also **trot out**. [C13: from OF trot, from troter to trot, of Gmc origin]

Trot (trɒt) n. Inf. a follower of Trotsky; Trotskyite.

troth (trəʊθ) n. Arch. **1.** a pledge of fidelity, esp. a betrothal. **2.** truth (esp. in **in troth**). **3.** loyalty; fidelity. [OE tréowth]

trotline ('trɒt,laɪn) n. Angling. a long line suspended across a stream, river, etc., to which shorter hooked and baited lines are attached.

trot out vb. (tr., adv.) Inf. to bring forward, as for approbation or admiration, esp. repeatedly.

Trotsky or **Trotski** ('trɒtskɪ) n. **Leon**, original name Lev Davidovich Bronstein. 1879–1940, Russian revolutionary and Communist theorist. He was a leader of the November Revolution (1917) and, as commissar of foreign affairs and war (1917–24), largely created the Red Army. He was ousted by Stalin after Lenin's death and deported from Russia (1929); assassinated by a Stalinist agent.

Trotskyism ('trɒtskɪ,ɪzəm) n. Trotsky's theory of communism, in which he called for immediate worldwide revolution by the proletariat. —'Trotskyite or 'Trotskyist n., adj.

trotter ('trɒtə) n. **1.** a horse that is specially trained to trot fast. **2.** (usually pl.) the foot of certain animals, esp. of pigs.

troubadour ('truːbə,dʊə) n. any of a class of lyric poets who flourished principally in Provence and N Italy from the 11th to the 13th century, writing chiefly on courtly love. [C18: from F, from OProvençal trobador, from trobar to write verses, ? ult. from L tropus TROPE]

trouble ('trʌbəl) n. **1.** a state of mental distress or anxiety. **2.** a state of disorder or unrest: industrial trouble. **3.** a condition of disease, pain, or malfunctioning: liver trouble. **4.** a cause of distress, disturbance, or pain. **5.** effort or exertion taken to do something. **6.** liability to suffer punishment or misfortune (esp. in **be in trouble**):

he's in trouble with the police. **7.** a personal weakness or cause of annoyance: his trouble is he's too soft. **8.** political unrest. **9.** the condition of an unmarried girl who becomes pregnant (esp. in **in trouble**). ~vb. **10.** (tr.) to cause trouble to. **11.** (intr.; usually with a negative and foll. by about) to put oneself to inconvenience; be concerned: don't trouble about me. **12.** (intr.; usually with a negative) to take pains; exert oneself. **13.** (tr.) to cause inconvenience or discomfort to. **14.** (tr.; usually passive) to agitate or make rough: the seas were troubled. **15.** (tr.) Caribbean. to interfere with. [C13: from OF troubler, from Vulgar L turbulāre (unattested), from LL turbidāre, ult. from turba commotion] —'troubler n.

troublemaker ('trʌbəl,meɪkə) n. a person who makes trouble, esp. between people. —'trouble,making adj., n.

troubleshooter ('trʌbəl,ʃuːtə) n. a person who locates the cause of trouble and removes or treats it. —'trouble,shooting n., adj.

troublesome ('trʌbəlsəm) adj. **1.** causing trouble. **2.** characterized by violence; turbulent. —'troublesomeness n.

troublous ('trʌbləs) adj. Arch. or literary. unsettled; agitated. —'troublously adv.

trough (trɒf) n. **1.** a narrow open container, esp. one in which food or water for animals is put. **2.** a narrow channel, gutter, or gulley. **3.** a narrow depression, as between two waves. **4.** Meteorol. an elongated area of low pressure. **5.** a single or temporary low point; depression. **6.** Physics. the portion of a wave in which the amplitude lies below its average value. **7.** Econ. the lowest point of the trade cycle. [OE trōh]

trounce (traʊns) vb. (tr.) to beat or defeat utterly; thrash. [C16: from ?]

troupe (truːp) n. **1.** a company of actors or other performers, esp. one that travels. ~vb. **2.** (intr.) (esp. of actors) to move or travel in a group. [C19: from F; see TROOP]

trouper ('truːpə) n. **1.** a member of a troupe. **2.** a dependable worker or associate.

trouser ('traʊzə) n. (modifier) of or relating to trousers: trouser buttons.

trousers ('traʊzəz) pl. n. a garment shaped to cover the body from the waist to the ankles or knees with separate tube-shaped sections for both legs. [C17: from earlier trouse, var. of TREWS, infl. by DRAWERS]

trousseau ('truːsəʊ) n., pl. **-seaux** or **-seaus** (-səʊz). the clothes, linen, etc., collected by a bride for her marriage. [C19: from OF, lit.: a little bundle; see TRUSS]

trout (traʊt) n., pl. **trout** or **trouts**. any of various game fishes, mostly of fresh water in northern regions. They are related to the salmon but are smaller and spotted. [OE trüht, from LL tructa, from Gk troktēs sharp-toothed fish]

trouvère (truːˈvɛə) n. any of a group of poets of N France during the 12th and 13th centuries who composed chiefly narrative works. [C19: from F, from OF troveor, from trover to compose]

trove (trəʊv) n. See **treasure-trove**.

trow (trəʊ) vb. Arch. to think, believe, or trust. [OE treow]

Trowbridge ('trəʊ,brɪdʒ) n. a market town in SW England, administrative centre of Wiltshire: woollen manufacturing. Pop.: 22 984 (1981).

trowel ('traʊəl) n. **1.** any of various small hand tools having a flat metal blade attached to a handle, used for scooping or spreading plaster or similar materials. **2.** a similar tool with a curved blade used by gardeners for lifting plants, etc. ~vb. **-elling, -elled** or U.S. **-eling, -eled. 3.** (tr.) to use a trowel on. [C14: from OF truele, from L trulla a scoop, from trua a stirring spoon]

Troy (trɔɪ) n. any of nine ancient cities in NW Asia Minor, each of which was built on the ruins of its predecessor. The seventh was the site of the Trojan War (mid-13th century B.C.). Greek name: Ilion. Latin name: Ilium.

Troyes (French trwa) n. an industrial city in NE France: became prosperous through its great fairs in the early Middle Ages. Pop.: 72 000 (1983 est.).

troy weight or **troy** n. a system of weights used for precious metals and gemstones, based on the grain. 24 grains = 1 pennyweight; 20 pennyweights = 1 (troy) ounce; 12 ounces = 1 (troy) pound. [C14: after TROYES, where first used]

Trst (trst) n. the Slovene and Serbo-Croatian name for **Trieste**.

truant ('tru:ənt) n. 1. a person who is absent without leave, esp. from school. ~adj. 2. being or relating to a truant. ~vb. 3. (intr.) to play truant. [C13: from OF: vagabond, prob. of Celtic origin] —'truancy n.

truce (tru:s) n. 1. an agreement to stop fighting, esp. temporarily. 2. temporary cessation of something unpleasant. [C13: from pl. of OE treow trow]

Trucial States ('tru:ʃəl) pl. n. a former name (until 1971) of the United Arab Emirates. Also called: **Trucial Sheikdoms, Trucial Oman, Trucial Coast.**

truck[1] (trʌk) n. 1. Brit. a vehicle for carrying freight on a railway; wagon. 2. another name (esp. U.S. and Canad.) for **lorry.** 3. Also called: **truckload.** the amount carried by a truck. 4. a frame carrying two or more pairs of wheels attached under an end of a railway coach, etc. 5. Naut. a disc-shaped block fixed to the head of a mast having holes for receiving halyards. 6. any wheeled vehicle used to move goods. ~vb. 7. to convey (goods) in a truck. 8. (intr.) Chiefly U.S. & Canad. to drive a truck. [C17: ? shortened from truckle a small wheel]

truck[2] (trʌk) n. 1. commercial goods. 2. dealings (esp. in **have no truck with**). 3. commercial exchange. 4. payment of wages in kind. 5. miscellaneous articles. 6. Inf. rubbish. 7. U.S. & Canad vegetables grown for market. ~vb. 8. to exchange (goods); barter. 9. (intr.) to traffic or negotiate. [C13: from OF troquer (unattested) to barter, equivalent to Med. L trocare, from ?]

trucker ('trʌkə) n. Chiefly U.S. & Canad. 1. a lorry driver. 2. a person who arranges for the transport of goods by lorry.

truck farm n. U.S. & Canad. a market garden. —**truck farmer** n. —**truck farming** n.

truckie ('trʌkɪ) n. Austral. inf. a truck driver.

trucking ('trʌkɪŋ) n. Chiefly U.S. & Canad. the transportation of goods by lorry.

truckle ('trʌkəl) vb. (intr.; usually foll. by to) to yield weakly; give in. [C17: from obs. truckle to sleep in a truckle bed] —'truckler n.

truckle bed n. a low bed on wheels, stored under a larger bed. [C17: from truckle small wheel, ult. from L trochlea sheaf of a pulley]

truck system n. a system during the early years of the Industrial Revolution of forcing workers to accept payment of wages in kind.

truculent ('trʌkjʊlənt) adj. 1. defiantly aggressive, sullen, or obstreperous. 2. Arch. savage, fierce, or harsh. [C16: from L truculentus, from trux fierce] —'truculence or 'truculency n. —'truculently adv.

Trudeau (tru:'dəʊ) n. Pierre Elliott. born 1919, Canadian statesman; Liberal prime minister (1968–79; 1980–84).

trudge (trʌdʒ) vb. 1. (intr.) to walk or plod heavily or wearily. 2. (tr.) to pass through or over by trudging. ~n. 3. a long tiring walk. [C16: from ?] —'trudger n.

trudgen ('trʌdʒən) n. a type of swimming stroke that uses overarm action, as in the crawl, and a scissors kick. [C19: after John Trudgen, E swimmer, who introduced it]

true (tru:) adj. **truer, truest.** 1. not false, fictional, or illusory; factual; conforming with reality. 2. (prenominal) real; not synthetic. 3. faithful and loyal. 4. conforming to a required standard, law, or pattern: a true aim. 5. exactly in tune. 6. (of a compass bearing) according to the earth's geographical rather than magnetic poles: true north. 7. Biol. conforming to the typical structure of a designated type. 8. Physics. not apparent or relative. ~n. 9. correct alignment (esp. in **in true, out of true**). ~adv. 10. truthfully; rightly. 11. precisely or unswervingly. ~vb. **truing, trued.** 12. (tr.) to adjust so as to make true. [OE triewe] —'trueness n.

true bill n. (formerly in Britain; now U.S.) the endorsement made on a bill of indictment by a grand jury certifying it to be supported by sufficient evidence to warrant a trial.

true-blue adj. 1. unwaveringly or staunchly loyal. ~n. **true blue.** 2. Chiefly Brit. a staunch royalist or Conservative.

true-life adj. directly comparable to reality: a true-life story.

truelove ('tru:,lʌv) n. 1. someone truly loved; sweetheart. 2. another name for **herb Paris.**

truelove knot or **true-lovers' knot** n. a complicated bowknot that is hard to untie, symbolizing ties of love.

true north n. the direction from any point along a meridian towards the North Pole. Also called: **geographic north.** Cf. **magnetic north.**

true rib n. any of the upper seven pairs of ribs in man.

true time n. the time shown by a sundial.

Truffaut (French tryfo) n. **François** (frɑ̃swa). 1932–84, French film director of the New Wave. His films include Les Quatre cents coups (1959), Jules et Jim (1961), Baisers volés (1968), and Le Dernier Métro (1980).

truffle ('trʌfəl) n. 1. any of various edible subterranean European fungi. They have a tuberous appearance and are regarded as a delicacy. 2. Also called: **rum truffle.** Chiefly Brit. a sweet resembling this fungus in shape, flavoured with chocolate or rum. [C16: from F truffe, from OProvençal trufa, ult. from L tüber]

trug (trʌg) n. a long shallow basket for carrying flowers, fruit, etc. [C16: ? var. of TROUGH]

trugo ('tru:gəʊ) n. Austral. a game similar to croquet, originally improvised in Victoria from the rubber discs used as buffers on railway carriages. [from true go, when the wheel is hit between the goal posts]

truism ('tru:ɪzəm) n. an obvious truth; platitude. —**tru'istic** adj.

Trujillo (Spanish tru'xijo) n. a city in NW Peru; founded 1535; university (1824); centre of a district producing rice and sugar cane. Pop.: 476 000 (1987).

Truk Islands (trʌk) pl. n. a group of islands in the W Pacific, in the E Caroline Islands: administratively part of the U.S. Trust Territory of the Pacific Islands from 1947; became self-governing in 1979 as part of the Federated States of Micronesia; consists of 11 chief islands; a major Japanese naval base during World War II. Pop.: 37 742 (1980). Area: 130 sq. km (50 sq. miles).

trull (trʌl) n. Arch. a prostitute; harlot. [C16: from G Trulle]

truly ('tru:lɪ) adv. 1. in a true, just, or faithful manner. 2. (intensifier): a truly great man. 3. indeed; really.

Truman ('tru:mən) n. **Harry S.** 1884–1972, U.S. Democratic statesman; 33rd president of the U.S. (1945–52). He approved the dropping of the two atom bombs on Japan (1945), advocated the postwar loan to Britain, and involved the U.S. in the Korean War.

trumeau (tru'məʊ) n., pl. **-meaux** (-məʊz). Archit. a section of a wall or pillar between two openings. [from F]

trump[1] (trʌmp) n. 1. Also called: **trump card. a.** any card from the suit chosen as trumps. **b.** this suit itself; trumps. 2. a decisive or advantageous move, resource, action, etc. 3. Inf. a fine or reliable person. ~vb. 4. to play a trump card on a suit or a particular card of a suit that is not trumps. 5. (tr.) to outdo or surpass. ~See also **trumps, trump up.** [C16: var. of TRIUMPH]

trump[2] (trʌmp) n. Arch. or literary. 1. a trumpet or the sound produced by one. 2. **the last trump.** the final trumpet call on the Day of Judgment. [C13: from OF trompe, from OHG trumpa trumpet]

trumpery ('trʌmpərɪ) n., pl. **-eries.** 1. foolish talk or actions. 2. a useless or worthless article; trinket. ~adj. 3. useless or worthless. [C15: from OF tromperie deceit, from tromper to cheat]

trumpet ('trʌmpɪt) n. 1. a valved brass instrument of brilliant tone consisting of a narrow tube ending in a flared bell. 2. any similar instrument, esp. a straight instrument used for fanfares, signals, etc. 3. a loud sound such as that of a trumpet, esp. when made by an animal. 4. an eight-foot reed stop on an organ. 5. something resembling a trumpet in shape. 6. short for **ear trumpet.** 7. **blow one's own trumpet.** to boast about one's own skills or good qualities. ~vb. 8. to proclaim or sound loudly. [C13: from OF trompette a little TRUMP[2]]

trumpeter ('trʌmpɪtə) n. 1. a person who plays the trumpet, esp. one whose duty it is to play fanfares, signals, etc. 2. any of three birds of South America, having a rounded body, long legs, and a glossy blackish plumage. 3. (sometimes cap.) a breed of domestic fancy pigeon with a long ruff. 4. a large silvery-grey Australian marine food and game fish that grunts when taken from the water.

trumpeter swan n. a large swan of W North America, having a white plumage and black bill.

trumps (trʌmps) pl. n. 1. (sometimes sing.) Cards. any one of the four suits that outranks all the other suits for the duration of a deal or game. 2. **turn up trumps.** (of a person) to bring about a happy or successful conclusion, esp. unexpectedly.

trump up vb. (tr., adv.) to invent (a charge, accusation, etc.) so as to deceive.

truncate vb. (trʌŋ'keɪt, 'trʌŋkeɪt). **1.** (tr.) to shorten by cutting. ~adj. ('trʌŋkeɪt). **2.** cut short; truncated. **3.** Biol. having a blunt end. [C15: from L truncāre to lop] —**trun'cation** n.

truncated (trʌŋ'keɪtɪd) adj. **1.** (of a cone, prism, etc.) having an apex or end removed by a plane intersection. **2.** shortened by or as if by cutting off; truncate.

truncheon ('trʌntʃən) n. **1.** Chiefly Brit. a short thick club or cudgel carried by a policeman. **2.** a baton of office. [C16: from OF tronchon stump, from L truncus trunk; see TRUNCATE]

trundle ('trʌndᵊl) vb. **1.** to move heavily on or as if on wheels: the bus trundled by. ~n. **2.** a trundling. **3.** a small wheel or roller. [OE tryndel]

trundle bed n. a less common word for **truckle bed.**

trundler ('trʌndlə) n. N.Z. **1.** a trolley for shopping or one for golf clubs. **2.** a child's pushchair.

trunk (trʌŋk) n. **1.** the main stem of a tree. **2.** a large strong case or box used to contain clothes, etc., when travelling and for storage. **3.** the body excluding the head, neck, and limbs; torso. **4.** the elongated nasal part of an elephant. **5.** the U.S. name for **boot¹** (sense 2). **6.** the main stem of a nerve, blood vessel, etc. **7.** Naut. a watertight boxlike cover within a vessel, such as one used to enclose a centreboard. **8.** an enclosed duct or passageway for ventilation, etc. **9.** (modifier) of a main road, railway, etc., in a network: a trunk line. ~See also **trunks.** [C15: from OF tronc, from L truncus, from truncus (adj.) lopped]

trunk call n. Chiefly Brit. a long-distance telephone call.

trunk curl n. a physical exercise in which the body is brought into a sitting position from one of lying on the back. Also called: **sit-up.**

trunkfish ('trʌŋk,fɪʃ) n., pl. **-fish** or **-fishes.** any of a family of fishes having the body encased in bony plates.

trunk hose n. a man's puffed-out breeches reaching to the thighs and worn with tights in the 16th century.

trunk line n. **1.** a direct link between two telephone exchanges or switchboards that are a considerable distance apart. **2.** the main route or routes on a railway.

trunk road n. Brit. a main road, esp. one that is suitable for heavy vehicles.

trunks (trʌŋks) pl. n. **1.** a man's garment used for swimming, extending from the waist to the thigh. **2.** shorts worn for some sports. **3.** Chiefly Brit. men's underpants with legs that reach midthigh.

trunnion ('trʌnjən) n. one of a pair of coaxial projections attached to opposite sides of a container, cannon, etc., to provide a support about which it can turn. [C17: from OF trognon trunk]

Truro ('truərəu) n. a market town in SW England, administrative centre of Cornwall. Pop.: 16 040 (1982).

truss (trʌs) vb. (tr.) **1.** (sometimes foll. by up) to tie, bind, or bundle. **2.** to bind the wings and legs of (a fowl) before cooking. **3.** to support or stiffen (a roof, bridge, etc.) with structural members. **4.** Med. to supply or support with a truss. ~n. **5.** a structural framework of wood or metal used to support a roof, bridge, etc. **6.** Med. a device for holding a hernia in place, typically consisting of a pad held in position by a belt. **7.** a cluster of flowers or fruit growing at the end of a single stalk. **8.** Naut. a metal fitting fixed to a yard at its centre for holding it to a mast. **9.** another name for **corbel.** **10.** a bundle or pack. **11.** Chiefly Brit. a bundle of hay or straw, esp. one having a fixed weight of 36, 56, or 60 pounds. [C13: from OF trousse, from trousser, apparently from Vulgar L torciāre (unattested), from torca (unattested) a bundle]

trust (trʌst) n. **1.** reliance on and confidence in the truth, worth, reliability, etc., of a person or thing; faith. Related adj.: **fiducial.** **2.** a group of commercial enterprises combined to control the market for any commodity. **3.** the obligation of someone in a responsible position. **4.** custody, charge, or care. **5.** a person or thing in which confidence or faith is placed. **6.** commercial credit. **7. a.** an arrangement whereby a person to whom the legal title to property is conveyed (the trustee) holds such property for the benefit of those entitled to the beneficial interest. **b.** property that is the subject of such an arrangement. Related adj.: **fiduciary.** **8.** (modifier) of or relating to a trust or trusts. ~vb. **9.** (tr.; may take a clause as object) to expect, hope, or suppose. **10.** (when tr., may take an infinitive; when intr., often foll. by in or to) to place confidence in (someone to do something); rely (upon). **11.** (tr.) to consign for care. **12.** (tr.) to allow (someone to do something) with confidence in his or her good sense or honesty. **13.** (tr.) to extend business credit to. [C13: from ON traust] —**'trustable** adj. —**'truster** n.

trust account n. **1.** Also called: **trustee account.** a savings account deposited in the name of a trustee who controls it during his lifetime, after which the balance is payable to a prenominated beneficiary. **2.** property under the control of a trustee or trustees.

trustee (trʌ'stiː) n. **1.** a person to whom the legal title to property is entrusted. **2.** a member of a board that manages the affairs of an institution or organization.

trusteeship (trʌ'stiːʃɪp) n. **1.** the office or function of a trustee. **2. a.** the administration or government of a territory by a foreign country under the supervision of the **Trusteeship Council** of the United Nations. **b.** (often cap.) any such dependent territory; trust territory.

trustful ('trʌstfʊl) or **trusting** adj. characterized by a tendency or readiness to trust others. —**'trustfully** or **'trustingly** adv.

trust fund n. money, securities, etc., held in trust.

trust territory n. (sometimes cap.) another name for a **trusteeship** (sense 2).

trustworthy ('trʌst,wɜːðɪ) adj. worthy of being trusted; honest, reliable, or dependable. —**'trust,worthily** adv. —**'trust,worthiness** n.

trusty ('trʌstɪ) adj. **trustier, trustiest. 1.** faithful or reliable. ~n., pl. **trusties. 2.** a trustworthy convict to whom special privileges are granted. —**'trustily** adv. —**'trustiness** n.

truth (truːθ) n. **1.** the quality of being true, genuine, actual, or factual. **2.** something that is true as opposed to false. **3.** a proven or verified fact, principle, etc.: the truths of astronomy. **4.** (usually pl.) a system of concepts purporting to represent some aspect of the world: the truths of ancient religions. **5.** fidelity to a standard or law. **6.** faithful reproduction or portrayal. **7.** honesty. **8.** accuracy, as in the setting of a mechanical instrument. **9.** loyalty. ~Related adjs.: **veritable, veracious.** [OE triewth] —**'truthless** adj.

truth drug or **serum** n. Inf. any of various drugs supposed to have the property of making people tell the truth, as by relaxing them.

truthful ('truːθfʊl) adj. **1.** telling the truth; honest. **2.** realistic: a truthful portrayal of the king. —**'truthfully** adv. —**'truthfulness** n.

truth-function n. Logic. a function that determines the truth-value of a complex sentence solely in terms of the truth-values of the component sentences without reference to their meaning.

truth set n. Logic, maths. the set of values that satisfy an open sentence, equation, inequality, etc., having no unique solution. Also called: **solution set.**

truth table n. **1.** a table, used in logic, indicating the truth-value of a compound statement for every truth-value of its component propositions. **2.** a similar table, used in transistor technology, to indicate the value of the output signal of a logic circuit for every value of input signal.

truth-value n. Logic. either of the values, true or false, that may be taken by a statement.

try (traɪ) vb. **trying, tried. 1.** (when tr., may take an infinitive, sometimes with to replaced by and) to make an effort or attempt. **2.** (tr.; often foll. by out) to sample, test, or give experimental use to (something). **3.** (tr.) to put strain or stress on: he tries my patience. **4.** (tr.; often passive) to give pain, affliction, or vexation to. **5. a.** to examine and determine the issues involved in (a cause) in a court of law. **b.** to hear evidence in order to determine the guilt or innocence of (an accused). **6.** (tr.) to melt (fat, lard, etc.) in order to separate out impurities. ~n., pl. **tries. 7.** an experiment or trial. **8.** an attempt or effort. **9.** Rugby. the act of an attacking player touching the ball down behind the opposing team's goal line. **10.** American football. an attempt made after a touchdown to score an extra point, as by kicking a goal. ~See also **try on, try out.** [C13: from OF trier to sort, from ?]

trying ('traɪɪŋ) adj. upsetting, difficult, or annoying. —**'tryingly** adv.

trying plane n. a plane with a long body for planing the edges of long boards. Also called: **try plane.**

try on vb. (tr., adv.) **1.** to put on (a garment) to find out whether it fits, etc. **2. try it on.** Inf. to attempt to deceive or fool someone. ~n. **try-on. 3.** Brit. inf. something done to test out a person's tolerance, etc.

try out vb. (adv.) **1.** (tr.) to test or put to experimental use. **2.** (when intr., usually foll. by for) U.S. & Canad. (of an athlete, actor, etc.) to undergo a test or to submit (an athlete, actor, etc.) to a test to determine suitability for a place in a team, an acting role, etc. ~n. **tryout. 3.** Chiefly U.S. & Canad. a trial or test, as of an athlete or actor.

trypanosome ('trɪpənəˌsəʊm) n. any of a genus of parasitic protozoa which live in the blood of vertebrates and cause sleeping sickness and certain other diseases. [C19: from NL Trypanosoma, from Gk trupanon borer + sōma body]

trypanosomiasis (ˌtrɪpənəsə'maɪəsɪs) n. any infection of an animal or human with a trypanosome.

trypsin ('trɪpsɪn) n. a digestive enzyme in the pancreatic juice: it catalyses the hydrolysis of proteins to peptides. [C19 tryp-, from Gk tripsis a rubbing, from tribein to rub + -IN; from the fact that it was orig. produced by rubbing the pancreas with glycerin] —**tryptic** ('trɪptɪk) adj.

tryptophan ('trɪptəˌfæn) n. an essential amino acid; a component of proteins necessary for growth. [C20: from trypt(ic), from TRYPSIN + -O- + -phan, var. of -PHANE]

trysail ('traɪˌseɪl; Naut. 'traɪsəl) n. a small fore-and-aft sail set on a sailing vessel in foul weather to help keep her head to the wind.

try square n. a device for testing or laying out right angles, consisting of a grooved metal ruler along which a frame runs, one edge of the frame always being perpendicular to the ruler.

tryst (trɪst, traɪst) n. Arch. or literary. **1.** an appointment to meet, esp. secretly. **2.** the place of such a meeting or the meeting itself. [C14: from OF triste lookout post, apparently from ON]

Tsana ('tsɑːnə) n. Lake. another name for (Lake) **Tana.**

tsar or **czar** (zɑː) n. **1.** (until 1917) the emperor of Russia. **2.** a tyrant; autocrat. **3.** Inf. a person in authority. [C17: from Russian tsar, via Gothic kaisar from L: CAESAR] —'**tsardom** or '**czardom** n.

tsarevitch or **czarevitch** ('zɑːrəvɪtʃ) n. a son of a Russian tsar, esp. the eldest son. [from Russian tsarevich, from TSAR + -evich, masc. patronymic suffix]

tsarevna or **czarevna** (zɑː'rɛvnə) n. **1.** a daughter of a Russian tsar. **2.** the wife of a Russian tsarevitch. [from Russian, from TSAR + -evna, fem. patronymic suffix]

tsarina, czarina (zɑː'riːnə) or **tsaritsa, czaritza** (zɑː'rɪtsə) n. the wife of a Russian tsar; Russian empress. [from Russian, from TSAR + -ina, fem. suffix]

tsarism or **czarism** ('zɑːrɪzəm) n. a system of government by a tsar. —'**tsarist** or '**czarist** n., adj.

Tsaritsyn (Russian tsa'ritsin) n. a former name (until 1925) of **Volgograd.**

TSE (in Canada) abbrev. for Toronto Stock Exchange.

Tselinograd (Russian tsəlɪna'grat) n. a city in the central Soviet Union, in the W Kazakh SSR. Pop.: 276 000 (1987). Former name (until 1961): **Akmolinsk.**

tsetse fly or **tzetze fly** ('tsɛtsɪ) n. any of various bloodsucking African dipterous flies which transmit various diseases, esp. sleeping sickness. [C19: via Afrik. from Tswana]

T-shirt or **tee-shirt** n. a lightweight simple garment for the upper body, usually short-sleeved. [from T-shape formed when laid out flat]

Tshombe ('tʃɒmbɪ) n. Moise (məʊ'iːz). 1919–69, Congolese statesman. He led the secession of Katanga (1960) from the newly independent Congo; forced into exile (1963) but returned (1964–65) as premier of the Congo; died in exile.

Tsinan ('tsiː'næn) n. a variant transliteration of the Chinese name for **Jinan.**

Tsinghai ('tsɪŋ'haɪ) n. **1.** a variant transliteration of the Chinese name for **Qinghai. 2.** a variant transliteration of the Chinese name for **Koko Nor.**

Tsingtao ('tsɪŋ'taʊ) n. a variant transliteration of the Chinese name for **Qingdao.**

Tsingyuan ('tsɪŋ'jwɑːn) or **Ch'ing-yüan** n. the former name of **Baoding.**

tsotsi ('tsɒtsɪ) n., pl. -tsis. S. African inf. a violent usually young criminal who operates mainly in Black African townships and lives by his wits. [C20: from ?]

tsp. abbrev. for teaspoon.

T-square n. a T-shaped ruler used for drawing horizontal lines and to support set squares when drawing vertical and inclined lines.

T-stop n. a setting of the lens aperture on a camera calibrated photometrically and assigned a T-number.

Tsugaru Strait ('tsugaˌru) n. a channel between N Honshu and S Hokkaido islands, Japan. Width: about 30 km (20 miles).

tsunami (tsʊ'nɑːmɪ) n., pl. -mis or -mi. a large, often destructive sea wave produced by a submarine, earthquake, subsidence, or volcanic eruption. [from Japanese, from tsu port + nami wave]

Tsushima ('tsuːˌʃiːˌmɑː) n. a group of five rocky islands between Japan and South Korea, in the Korean Strait: administratively part of Japan; scene of a naval defeat for the Russians (1905) during the Russo-Japanese war. Pop.: 50 810 (1980). Area: 698 sq. km (269 sq. miles).

tsutsugamushi disease (ˌtsʊtsʊgə'muʃɪ) n. one of the five major groups of acute infectious rickettsial diseases affecting man, common in Asia. It is transmitted by the bite of mites. [from Japanese, from tsutsuga disease + mushi insect]

Tswana ('tswɑːnə) n. **1.** (pl. -na or -nas) a member of a mixed Negroid and Bushman people of southern Africa, living chiefly in Botswana. **2.** the language of this people.

TT abbrev. for: **1.** teetotal. **2.** teetotaller. **3.** Tourist Trophy (annual motorcycle races held in the Isle of Man). **4.** tuberculin-tested.

TTL abbrev. for: **1.** transistor transistor logic: a method of constructing electronic logic circuits. **2.** through-the-lens: denoting a system of light metering in cameras.

TU abbrev. for trade union.

Tu. abbrev. for Tuesday.

Tuamotu Archipelago (ˌtuːə'məʊtuː) n. a group of about 80 coral islands in the S Pacific, in French Polynesia. Pop.: 11 793 (1983). Area: 860 sq. km (332 sq. miles). Also called: **Low Archipelago, Paumotu Archipelago.**

tuatara (ˌtuːə'tɑːrə) n. a lizard-like reptile occurring on certain islands near New Zealand. [C19: from Maori, from tua back + tara spine]

tub (tʌb) n. **1.** a low wide open container, typically round: used in a variety of domestic and industrial situations. **2.** a small plastic or cardboard container of similar shape for ice cream, margarine, etc. **3.** another word (esp. U.S.) for **bath**[1](sense 1). **4.** Also called: **tubful.** the amount a tub will hold. **5.** a clumsy slow boat or ship. **6. a.** a small vehicle on rails for carrying loads in a mine. **b.** a container for lifting coal or ore up a mine shaft. ~vb. **tubbing, tubbed. 7.** Brit. inf. to wash (oneself) in a tub. **8.** (tr.) to keep or put in a tub. [C14: from MDu. tubbe] —'**tubbable** adj. —'**tubber** n.

tuba ('tjuːbə) n., pl. -bas or -bae (-biː). **1.** a valved brass instrument of bass pitch, in which the bell points upwards and the mouthpiece projects at right angles. **2.** a powerful reed stop on an organ. [L]

tubal ('tjuːbəl) adj. **1.** of or relating to a tube. **2.** of, relating to, or developing in a Fallopian tube.

Tubal-cain ('tjuːbəlˌkeɪn) n. Old Testament. a son of Lamech, said in Genesis 4:22 to be the first artificer of metals.

tubby ('tʌbɪ) adj. -bier, -biest. **1.** plump. **2.** shaped like a tub. —'**tubbiness** n.

tube (tjuːb) n. **1.** a long hollow cylindrical object, used for the passage of fluids or as a container. **2.** a collapsible cylindrical container of soft metal or plastic closed with a cap, used to hold viscous liquids or pastes. **3.** Anat. short for **Eustachian tube** or **Fallopian tube. 4.** any hollow structure. **5.** (sometimes cap.) Brit. **a. the tube.** an underground railway system, esp. that in London. U.S. and Canad. equivalent: **subway. b.** the tunnels through which the railway runs. **6.** Electronics. **a.** another name for **valve** (sense 3). **b.** See **electron tube, cathode-ray tube, television tube. 7.** Sl., chiefly U.S. a television set. **8.** Austral. sl. a bottle or can of beer. ~vb. (tr.) **9.** to supply with a tube. **10.** to convey in a tube. **11.** to shape like a tube. [C17: from L tubus] —'**tubeless** adj.

tube foot n. any of numerous tubular outgrowths of most echinoderms that are used for locomotion, to aid ingestion of food, etc.

tubeless tyre n. a pneumatic tyre in which the outer casing makes an airtight seal with the rim of the wheel so that an inner tube is unnecessary.

tuber ('tju:bə) n. **1.** a fleshy underground stem or root. **2.** *Anat.* a raised area; swelling. [C17: from L *tūber* hump]

tubercle ('tju:bɜk²l) n. **1.** any small rounded nodule or elevation, esp. on the skin, on a bone, or on a plant. **2.** any small rounded pathological lesion, esp. one characteristic of tuberculosis. [C16: from L *tūberculum* a little swelling]

tubercle bacillus n. a rodlike bacterium that causes tuberculosis.

tubercular (tjʊ'bɜ:kjʊlə) adj. *also* **tuberculous. 1.** of or symptomatic of tuberculosis. **2.** of or relating to a tubercle. **3.** characterized by the presence of tubercles. ~n. **4.** a person with tuberculosis.

tuberculate (tjʊ'bɜ:kjʊlɪt) adj. covered with tubercles. —**tu,bercu'lation** n.

tuberculin (tjʊ'bɜ:kjʊlɪn) n. a sterile liquid prepared from cultures of attenuated tubercle bacillus and used in the diagnosis of tuberculosis.

tuberculin-tested adj. (of milk) produced by cows that have been certified as free of tuberculosis.

tuberculosis (tjʊ,bɜ:kjʊ'ləʊsɪs) n. a communicable disease caused by infection with the tubercle bacillus, most frequently affecting the lungs. [C19: from NL]

tuberose ('tju:bə,rəʊz) n. a perennial Mexican agave plant having a tuberous root and fragrant white flowers. [C17: from L *tūberōsus* full of lumps; from its root]

tuberous ('tju:bərəs) *or* **tuberose** ('tju:bə,rəʊs) adj. **1.** (of plants) forming, bearing, or resembling a tuber or tubers. **2.** *Anat.* of or having warty protuberances or tubers. [C17: from L *tūberōsus* full of knobs]

tube worm n. any of various worms that construct and live in a tube of sand, lime, etc.

tubifex ('tju:bɪ,fɛks) n., pl. **-fex** *or* **-fexes.** any of a genus of small reddish freshwater worms. [C19: from NL, from L *tubus* tube + *facere* to make]

tubing ('tju:bɪŋ) n. **1.** tubes collectively. **2.** a length of tube. **3.** a system of tubes. **4.** fabric in the form of a tube.

Tubman ('tʌbmən) n. **William Vacanarat Shadrach** (və'kænə,ræt 'ʃædræk). 1895–1971, Liberian statesman; president of Liberia (1944–71).

tub-thumper n. a noisy, violent, or ranting public speaker. —**'tub-,thumping** adj., n.

Tubuai Islands (,tu:bu:'aɪ) pl. n. a chain of small islands extending about 1400 km (850 miles) in the S Pacific, in French Polynesia; discovered by Captain Cook in 1777; annexed by France in 1880. Pop.: 6283 (1983). Area: 173 sq. km (67 sq. miles). Also called: **Austral Islands.**

tubular ('tju:bjʊlə) adj. **1.** Also: **tubiform** ('tju:bɪ,fɔ:m). having the form of a tube or tubes. **2.** of or relating to a tube or tubing.

tubular bells pl. n. a set of long tubes of brass tuned for use in an orchestra and struck with a mallet to simulate the sound of bells.

tubule ('tju:bju:l) n. any small tubular structure. [C17: from L *tubulus* a little TUBE]

TUC (in Britain) abbrev. for Trades Union Congress.

tuck (tʌk) n. **1.** (tr.) to push or fold into a small confined space or concealed place or between two surfaces. **2.** (tr.) to thrust the loose ends or sides of (something) into a confining space, so as to make neat and secure. **3.** to make a tuck or tucks in (a garment). **4.** (usually tr.) to draw together, contract, or pucker. ~n. **5.** a tucked object or part. **6.** a pleat or fold in a part of a garment, usually stitched down. **7.** the part of a vessel where the planks meet at the sternpost. **8.** *Brit. inf.* **a.** food, esp. cakes and sweets. **b.** (as modifier): *a tuck box.* **9.** a position of the body, as in certain dives, in which the legs are bent with the knees drawn up against the chest and tightly clasped. ~See also **tuck away, tuck in.** [C14: from OE *tūcian* to torment]

Tuck (tʌk) n. **Friar.** See **Friar Tuck.**

tuck away vb. (tr., adv.) *Inf.* **1.** to eat (a large amount of food). **2.** to store, esp. in a place difficult to find.

tucker[1] ('tʌkə) n. **1.** a person or thing that tucks. **2.** a detachable yoke of lace, linen, etc., often white, worn over the breast, as of a low-cut dress. **3.** *Austral. & N.Z.* an informal word for **food.**

tucker[2] ('tʌkə) vb. (tr.; often passive; usually foll. by out) *Inf., chiefly U.S. & Canad.* to weary or tire.

tucker-bag *or* **tuckerbox** ('tʌkə,bɒks) n. *Austral. sl.* a bag in which food is carried or stored.

tucket ('tʌkɪt) n. *Arch.* a flourish on a trumpet. [C16: from OF *toquer* to sound (on a drum)]

tuck in vb. (adv.) **1.** (tr.) Also: **tuck into.** to put to bed and make snug. **2.** (tr.) to thrust the loose ends or sides of (something) into a confining space: *tuck the blankets in.* **3.** (intr.) Also: **tuck into.** *Inf.* to eat, esp. heartily. ~n. **tuck-in. 4.** *Brit. inf.* a meal, esp. a large one.

tuck shop n. *Chiefly Brit.* a shop, esp. one near a school, where cakes and sweets are sold.

Tucson ('tu:sɒn) n. a city in SE Arizona, at an altitude of 700m (2400 ft.): resort and seat of the University of Arizona (1891). Pop.: 384 385 (1986 est.).

Tucumán (Spanish tuku'man) n. a city in NW Argentina: scene of the declaration (1816) of Argentinian independence from Spain; university (1914). Pop.: 392 888 (1980).

-tude suffix forming nouns. indicating state or condition: *plenitude.* [from L -*tūdō*]

Tudor ('tju:də) n. **1.** an English royal house descended from a Welsh squire, **Owen Tudor** (died 1461), and ruling from 1485 to 1603. Monarchs of the Tudor line were Henry VII, Henry VIII, Edward VI, Mary I, and Elizabeth I. ~adj. **2.** denoting a style of architecture of the late perpendicular period and characterized by half-timbered houses.

Tues. abbrev. for Tuesday.

Tuesday ('tju:zdɪ) n. the third day of the week; second day of the working week. [OE *tīwesdæg*]

tufa ('tju:fə) n. a porous rock formed of calcium carbonate deposited from springs. [C18: from It. *tufo*, from LL *tōfus*] —**tufaceous** (tju:'feɪʃəs) adj.

tuff (tʌf) n. a hard volcanic rock consisting of consolidated fragments of lava. [C16: from OF *tuf*, from It. *tufo*; see TUFA] —**tuffaceous** (tʌ'feɪʃəs) adj.

tuffet ('tʌfɪt) n. a small mound or low seat. [C16: alteration of TUFT]

tuft (tʌft) n. **1.** a bunch of feathers, grass, hair, etc., held together at the base. **2.** a cluster of threads drawn tightly through upholstery, a quilt, etc., to secure the padding. **3.** a small clump of trees or bushes. **4.** (formerly) a gold tassel on the cap worn by titled undergraduates at English universities. ~vb. **5.** (tr.) to provide or decorate with a tuft or tufts. **6.** to form or be formed into tufts. **7.** to secure with tufts. [C14: ?from OF *tufe*, of Gmc origin] —**'tufted** adj. —**'tufty** adj.

tug (tʌg) vb. **tugging, tugged. 1.** (when intr., sometimes foll. by at) to pull or drag with sharp or powerful movements. **2.** (tr.) to tow (a vessel) by means of a tug. ~n. **3.** a strong pull or jerk. **4.** Also called: **tugboat.** a boat with a powerful engine, used for towing barges, ships, etc. **5.** a hard struggle or fight. [C13: rel. to OE *tēon* to TOW[1]] —**'tugger** n.

Tugela (tu:'geɪlə) n. a river in E South Africa, rising in the Drakensberg where it forms the **Tugela Falls,** 856 m (2810 ft.) high, before flowing east to the Indian Ocean: scene of battles during the Zulu War (1879) and the Boer War (1899–1902). Length: about 500 km (312 miles).

tug of love n. a conflict over custody of a child between divorced parents or between natural parents and foster or adoptive parents.

tug of war n. **1.** a contest in which two people or teams pull opposite ends of a rope in an attempt to drag the opposition over a central line. **2.** any hard struggle between two factions.

tui ('tu:i) n., pl. **tuis.** a New Zealand songbird with white feathers at the throat. Also called: **parson bird.** [from Maori]

tuition (tju:'ɪʃən) n. **1.** instruction, esp. that received individually or in a small group. **2.** the payment for instruction, esp. in colleges or universities. [C15: from OF *tuicion*, from L *tuitiō* a guarding, from *tuērī* to watch over] —**tu'itional** adj.

Tula (Russian 'tulə) n. an industrial city in the W central Soviet Union. Pop.: 538 000 (1987).

tularaemia *or* U.S. **tularemia** (,tu:lə'ri:mɪə) n. an infectious disease of rodents, transmitted to man by infected ticks or flies or by handling contaminated flesh. [C19/20: from NL, from *Tulare*, county in California where first observed] —**,tula'raemic** *or* U.S. **,tula'remic** adj.

tulip ('tju:lɪp) n. **1.** any of various spring-blooming bulb plants having long broad pointed leaves and single showy bell-shaped flowers. **2.** the flower or bulb. [C17: from NL *tulipa*, from Turkish *tülbend* turban, which the opened bloom was thought to resemble]

tulip tree n. **1.** Also called: **tulip poplar.** a North American tree having tulip-shaped greenish-yellow flowers and long conelike fruits. **2.** any of various other trees with tulip-shaped flowers, such as the magnolia.

tulipwood ('tjuːlɪpˌwʊd) *n.* **1.** the light soft wood of the tulip tree, used in making furniture and veneer. **2.** any of several woods having streaks of colour.

Tull (tʌl) *n.* **Jethro** ('dʒɛθrəʊ). 1674–1741, English agriculturalist, who invented the seed drill.

tulle (tjuːl) *n.* a fine net fabric of silk, rayon, etc. [C19: from F, from *Tulle*, city in S central France, where first manufactured]

Tully ('tʌlɪ) *n.* the former English name for (Marcus Tullius) **Cicero**.

Tulsa ('tʌlsə) *n.* a city in NE Oklahoma, on the Arkansas River: a major oil centre; two universities. Pop.: 373 000 (1986 est.).

tumble ('tʌmbəl) *vb.* **1.** to fall or cause to fall, esp. awkwardly, precipitately, or violently. **2.** (*intr.; usually foll. by about*) to roll or twist, esp. in playing. **3.** (*intr.*) to perform leaps, somersaults, etc. **4.** to move in a heedless or hasty way. **5.** (*tr.*) to polish (gemstones) in a tumbler. **6.** (*tr.*) to disturb, rumple, or toss around. ~*n.* **7.** a tumbling. **8.** a fall or toss. **9.** an acrobatic feat, esp. a somersault. **10.** a state of confusion. **11.** a confused heap or pile. ~See also **tumble to**. [OE *tumbian*]

tumbledown ('tʌmbəlˌdaʊn) *adj.* falling to pieces; dilapidated; crumbling.

tumble dryer *n.* a machine that dries wet laundry by rotating it in warmed air inside a metal drum. Also called: **tumbler dryer, tumbler**.

tumbler ('tʌmblə) *n.* **1. a.** a flat-bottomed drinking glass with no handle or stem. **b.** Also called: **tumblerful**. its contents. **2.** a person who performs somersaults and other acrobatic feats. **3.** another name for **tumble dryer**. **4.** a box or drum rotated so that the contents (usually gemstones) become smooth and polished. **5.** the part of a lock that retains or releases the bolt and is moved by the action of a key. **6.** a lever in a gunlock that receives the action of the mainspring when the trigger is pressed and thus forces the hammer forwards. **7.** a part that moves a gear in a train of gears into and out of engagement.

tumbler switch *n.* a small electrical switch incorporating a spring, widely used in lighting.

tumble to *vb.* (*intr., prep.*) *Inf.* to understand; become aware of: *she tumbled to his plan quickly.*

tumbleweed ('tʌmbəlˌwiːd) *n.* any of various densely branched American and Australian plants that break off near the ground on withering and are rolled about by the wind.

tumbrel *or* **tumbril** ('tʌmbrəl) *n.* **1.** a farm cart, esp. one that tilts backwards to deposit its load. A cart of this type was used to take condemned prisoners to the guillotine during the French Revolution. **2.** (formerly) a covered cart used to carry ammunition, tools, etc. [C14 *tumberell* ducking stool, from Med. L *tumbrellum*, from OF *tumberel* dump cart, ult. of Gmc origin]

tumefacient (ˌtjuːmɪˈfeɪʃɪənt) *adj.* producing or capable of producing swelling: *a tumefacient drug.* [C16: from L *tumefacere* to cause to swell]

tumefy ('tjuːmɪˌfaɪ) *vb.* **-fying, -fied.** to make or become tumid; swell or puff up. [C16: from F *tuméfier*, from L *tumefacere*] —ˌtume'faction *n.*

tumescent (tjuːˈmɛsənt) *adj.* swollen or becoming swollen. [C19: from L *tumescere* to begin to swell, from *tumēre*] —tu'mescence *n.*

tumid ('tjuːmɪd) *adj.* **1.** enlarged or swollen. **2.** bulging. **3.** pompous or fulsome in style. [C16: from L *tumidus*, from *tumēre* to swell] —tu'midity *or* 'tumidness *n.* —'tumidly *adv.*

tummy ('tʌmɪ) *n., pl.* **-mies.** an informal or childish word for **stomach**. Also called: **tum.**

tumour *or U.S.* **tumor** ('tjuːmə) *n. Pathol.* **a.** any abnormal swelling. **b.** a mass of tissue formed by a new growth of cells. [C16: from L, from *tumēre* to swell] —'tumorous *adj.*

tumult ('tjuːmʌlt) *n.* **1.** a loud confused noise, as of a crowd; commotion. **2.** violent agitation or disturbance. **3.** great emotional agitation. [C15: from L *tumultus*, from *tumēre* to swell up]

tumultuous (tjuːˈmʌltjʊəs) *adj.* **1.** uproarious, riotous, or turbulent. **2.** greatly agitated, confused, or disturbed. **3.** making a loud or unruly disturbance. —tu'multuously *adv.* —tu'multuousness *n.*

tumulus ('tjuːmjʊləs) *n., pl.* **-li** (-liː). *Archaeol.* (*no longer in technical usage*) another word for **barrow**[2]. [C17: from L: a hillock, from *tumēre* to swell up]

tun (tʌn) *n.* **1.** a large beer cask. **2.** a measure of capacity, usually equal to 252 wine gallons. ~*vb.* **tunning, tunned. 3.** (*tr.*) to put into or keep in tuns. [OE *tunne*]

tuna[1] ('tjuːnə) *n., pl.* **-na** *or* **-nas.** another name for **tunny** (sense 1). [C20: from American Sp., from Sp. *atún*, from Ar. *tūn*, from L *thunnus* tunny, from Gk]

tuna[2] ('tjuːnə) *n.* any of various tropical American prickly pear cacti. [C16: via Sp. from Taino]

tunable *or* **tuneable** ('tjuːnəbəl) *adj.* able to be tuned.

Tunbridge Wells ('tʌnˌbrɪdʒ) *n.* a town and resort in SE England, in SW Kent: chalybeate spring discovered in 1606; an important social centre in the 17th and 18th centuries. Pop.: 44 821 (1981). Official name: **Royal Tunbridge Wells.**

tundra ('tʌndrə) *n.* a vast treeless zone lying between the ice cap and the timber line of North America and Eurasia and having a permanently frozen subsoil. [C19: from Russian, from Lapp *tundar* hill]

tune (tjuːn) *n.* **1.** a melody, esp. one for which harmony is not essential. **2.** the condition of producing accurately pitched notes, intervals, etc. (esp. in **in tune, out of tune**). **3.** accurate correspondence of pitch and intonation between instruments (esp. in **in tune, out of tune**). **4.** the correct adjustment of a radio, television, etc., with respect to the required frequency. **5.** a frame of mind; mood. **6. call the tune.** to be in control of the proceedings. **7. change one's tune.** to alter one's attitude or tone of speech. **8. to the tune of.** *Inf.* to the amount or extent of. ~*vb.* **9.** to adjust (a musical instrument) to a certain pitch. **10.** to adjust (a note, etc.) so as to bring it into harmony or concord. **11.** (*tr.*) to adapt or adjust (oneself); attune. **12.** (*tr.; often foll. by up*) to make fine adjustments to (an engine, machine, etc.) to obtain optimum performance. **13.** *Electronics.* to adjust (one or more circuits) for resonance at a desired frequency. ~See also **tune in, tune up.** [C14: var. of TONE] —'tuner *n.*

tuneful ('tjuːnfʊl) *adj.* **1.** having a pleasant tune; melodious. **2.** producing a melody or music. —'tunefully *adv.* —'tunefulness *n.*

tune in *vb.* (*adv.; often foll. by to*) **1.** to adjust (a radio or television) to receive (a station or programme). **2.** *Sl.* to make or become more aware, knowledgeable, etc. (about).

tuneless ('tjuːnlɪs) *adj.* having no melody or tune. —'tunelessly *adv.* —'tunelessness *n.*

tune up *vb.* (*adv.*) **1.** to adjust (a musical instrument) to a particular pitch. **2.** to tune (instruments) to a common pitch. **3.** (*tr.*) to adjust (an engine, etc.) to improve performance. ~*n.* **tune-up. 4.** adjustments made to an engine to improve its performance.

tung oil (tʌŋ) *n.* a fast-drying oil obtained from the seeds of an Asian tree, used in paints, varnishes, etc. [partial translation of Chinese *yu t'ung* tung tree oil, from *yu* oil + *t'ung* tung tree]

tungsten ('tʌŋstən) *n.* a hard malleable ductile greyish-white element. It is used in lamp filaments, electrical contact points, x-ray targets, and, alloyed with steel, in high-speed cutting tools. Symbol: W; atomic no.: 74; atomic wt.: 183.85. [C18: from Swedish *tung* heavy + *sten* stone]

tungsten lamp *n.* a lamp in which light is produced by a tungsten filament heated to incandescence by an electric current.

tungsten steel *n.* any of various hard steels containing tungsten and traces of carbon.

Tungting *or* **Tung-t'ing** (ˌtʊŋˈtɪŋ) *n.* a variant transliteration of the Chinese name for the **Dongting**.

Tungusic (tʊŋˈɡʊsɪk) *n.* a branch or subfamily of the Altaic family of languages, some of which are spoken in NE Asia.

Tunguska (*Russian* tunˈɡuskə) *n.* any of three rivers in the Soviet Union, in central Siberia, all tributaries of the Yenisei: the **Lower** (Nizhnyaya) **Tunguska,** 2690 km (1670 miles) long; the **Stony** (Podkamennaya) **Tunguska,** 1550 km (960 miles) long; the **Upper** (Verkhnyaya) **Tunguska,** which is the lower course of the Angara.

tunic ('tjuːnɪk) *n.* **1.** any of various hip-length or knee-length garments, such as the loose sleeveless garb worn in ancient Greece or Rome, the jacket of some soldiers, or a woman's hip-length garment, worn with a skirt or trousers. **2.** a covering, lining, or enveloping membrane of an organ or part. **3.** Also called: **tunicle**. a short vestment worn by a bishop or subdeacon. [OE *tunice* (unattested except in the accusative case), from L *tunica*]

tunicate ('tju:nɪkɪt, -,keɪt) *n.* **1.** any of various minute primitive marine animals having a saclike unsegmented body enclosed in a cellulose-like outer covering. ~*adj.* also **tunicated.** **2.** (esp. of a bulb) having concentric layers of tissue. [C18: from L *tunicātus* clad in a TUNIC]

tuning ('tju:nɪŋ) *n. Music.* **1.** a set of pitches to which the open strings of a guitar, violin, etc., are tuned. **2.** the accurate pitching of notes and intervals by a choir, orchestra, etc.; intonation.

tuning fork *n.* a two-pronged metal fork that when struck produces a pure note of constant specified pitch. It is used to tune musical instruments and in acoustics.

Tunis ('tju:nɪs) *n.* the capital and chief port of Tunisia, in the northeast on the **Gulf of Tunis** (an inlet of the Mediterranean): dates from Carthaginian times, the ruins of ancient Carthage lying to the northeast; university (1960). Pop.: 556 654 (1984).

Tunisia (tju:'nɪzɪə, -'nɪsɪə) *n.* a republic in N Africa, on the Mediterranean: settled by the Phoenicians in the 12th century B.C.; made a French protectorate in 1881 and gained independence in 1955. It consists chiefly of the Sahara in the south, a central plateau, and the Atlas Mountains in the north. Exports include petroleum, phosphates, and iron ore. Languages: Arabic and French. Religion: mostly Islam. Currency: dinar. Capital: Tunis. Pop.: 7 636 000 (1987). Area: 164 150 sq. km (63 380 sq. miles). —**Tu'nisian** *adj., n.*

tunnage ('tʌnɪdʒ) *n.* a variant spelling of **tonnage.**

tunnel ('tʌnᵊl) *n.* **1.** an underground passageway, esp. one for trains or cars. **2.** any passage or channel through or under something. ~*vb.* **-nelling, -nelled** *or U.S.* **-neling, -neled.** **3.** (*tr.*) to make or force (a way) through or under (something). **4.** (*intr.*; foll. by *through, under,* etc.) to make or force a way (through or under something). [C15: from OF *tonel* cask, from *tonne* tun, from Med. L *tonna* barrel, of Celtic origin] — '**tunneller** *or U.S.* '**tunneler** *n.*

tunnel diode *n.* an extremely stable semiconductor diode, having a very narrow highly doped p-n junction, in which electrons travel across the junction by means of the tunnel effect. Also called: **Esaki diode.**

tunnel effect *n. Physics.* the phenomenon in which an object, usually an elementary particle, tunnels through a potential barrier even though it does not have sufficient energy to surmount it.

tunnel vision *n.* **1.** a condition in which peripheral vision is greatly restricted. **2.** narrowness of viewpoint resulting from concentration on a single idea, opinion, etc.

tunny ('tʌnɪ) *n., pl.* **-nies** *or* **-ny.** Also called: **tuna.** any of a genus of large marine spiny-finned fishes, chiefly of warm waters. They are important food fishes. **2.** any of various similar and related fishes. [C16: from OF *thon,* from OProvençal *ton,* from L *thunnus,* from Gk]

tup (tʌp) *n.* **1.** *Chiefly Brit.* a male sheep; ram. **2.** the head of a pile-driver or steam hammer. ~*vb.* **tupping, tupped.** **3.** (*tr.*) (of a ram) to mate with (a ewe). [C14: from ?]

Tupamaro (,tu:pə'mɑːrəʊ) *n., pl.* **-ros.** any of a group of Marxist urban guerrillas in Uruguay. [C20: after *Tupac Amaru,* 18th-century Peruvian Indian who led a rebellion against the Spaniards]

tupelo ('tju:pɪ,ləʊ) *n., pl.* **-los.** **1.** any of several gum trees of the southern U.S. **2.** the light strong wood of any of these trees. [C18: from Creek *ito opilwa,* from *ito* tree + *opilwa* swamp]

Tupi (tu:'pi:) *n.* **1.** (*pl.* **-pis** *or* **-pi**) a member of a South American Indian people of Brazil and Paraguay. **2.** their language. —**Tu'pian** *adj.*

tupik ('tu:pək) *n. Canad.* a tent of seal or caribou skin used for shelter by the Inuit in summer. [from Eskimo]

tuppence ('tʌpəns) *n. Brit.* a variant spelling of **twopence.** —'**tuppenny** *adj.*

Tupungato (*Spanish* tupuŋ'gato) *n.* a mountain on the border between Argentina and Chile, in the Andes. Height: 6550 m (21 484 ft.).

tuque (tu:k) *n.* (in Canada) a knitted cap with a long tapering end. [from Canad. F, from F: TOQUE]

turaco ('tʊərə,kəʊ) *n., pl.* **-cos.** a variant spelling of **touraco.**

Turanian (tjʊ'reɪnɪən) *n., adj.* another name for **Ural-Altaic.**

turban ('tɜ:bᵊn) *n.* **1.** a man's headdress, worn esp. by Muslims, Hindus, and Sikhs, made by swathing a length of linen, silk, etc., around the head or around a caplike base. **2.** a woman's brimless hat resembling this. **3.** any headdress resembling this. [C16: from Turkish *tülbend,* from Persian *dulband*] —'**turbaned** *adj.*

turbary ('tɜ:bərɪ) *n., pl.* **-ries.** **1.** land where peat or turf is cut. **2.** the legal right to cut peat for fuel on a common. [C14: from OF *turbarie,* from Med. L *turbāria,* from *turba* peat]

turbellarian (,tɜ:bɪ'lɛərɪən) *n.* **1.** any of a class of flatworms having a ciliated epidermis and a simple life cycle. ~*adj.* **2.** of or belonging to this class of flatworms. [C19: from NL *Turbellāria,* from L *turbellae* (pl.) bustle, from *turba* brawl, referring to the swirling motion created in the water]

turbid ('tɜ:bɪd) *adj.* **1.** muddy or opaque, as a liquid clouded with a suspension of particles. **2.** dense, thick, or cloudy: *turbid fog.* **3.** in turmoil or confusion. [C17: from L *turbidus,* from *turbāre* to agitate, from *turba* crowd] —**tur'bidity** *or* '**turbidness** *n.* —'**turbidly** *adv.*

turbinate ('tɜ:bɪnɪt, -,neɪt) *or* **turbinal** ('tɜ:bɪnᵊl) *adj.* also **turbinated.** **1.** *Anat.* of any of the scroll-shaped bones on the walls of the nasal passages. **2.** shaped like a spiral or scroll. **3.** shaped like an inverted cone. ~*n.* **4.** a turbinate bone. **5.** a turbinate shell. [C17: from L *turbō* spinning top] —,**turbi'nation** *n.*

turbine ('tɜ:bɪn, -baɪn) *n.* any of various types of machine in which the kinetic energy of a moving fluid, as water, steam, air, etc., is converted into mechanical energy by causing a bladed rotor to rotate. [C19: from F, from L *turbō* whirlwind, from *turbāre* to throw into confusion]

turbit ('tɜ:bɪt) *n.* a crested breed of domestic pigeon. [C17: from L *turbō* top, from the bird's shape]

turbo- *combining form.* of, relating to, or combining by a turbine: *turbofan.*

turbofan (,tɜ:bəʊ'fæn) *n.* **1.** a type of bypass engine in which a large fan driven by a turbine forces air rearwards around the exhaust gases in order to increase the propulsive thrust. **2.** an aircraft driven by turbofans. **3.** the fan in such an engine.

turbogenerator (,tɜ:bəʊ'dʒɛnə,reɪtə) *n.* an electrical generator driven by a steam turbine.

turbojet (,tɜ:bəʊ'dʒɛt) *n.* **1.** a turbojet engine. **2.** an aircraft powered by turbojet engines.

turbojet engine *n.* a gas turbine in which the exhaust gases provide the propulsive thrust to drive an aircraft.

turboprop (,tɜ:bəʊ'prɒp) *n.* **1.** a gas turbine for driving an aircraft propeller. **2.** an aircraft powered by turboprops.

turbosupercharger (,tɜ:bəʊ'su:pə,tʃɑ:dʒə) *n.* a supercharging device for an internal-combustion engine, consisting of a turbine driven by the exhaust gases.

turbot ('tɜ:bət) *n., pl.* **-bot** *or* **-bots.** **1.** a European flatfish having a speckled scaleless body covered with tubercles. It is highly valued as a food fish. **2.** any of various similar or related fishes. [C13: from OF *tourbot,* from Med. L *turbō,* from L: top, from a fancied similarity in shape]

turbulence ('tɜ:bjʊləns) *n* **1.** a state or condition of confusion, movement, or agitation. **2.** *Meteorol.* instability in the atmosphere causing gusty air currents and cumulonimbus clouds.

turbulent ('tɜ:bjʊlənt) *adj.* **1.** being in a state of turbulence. **2.** wild or insubordinate; unruly. [C16: from L *turbulentus,* from *turba* confusion] —'**turbulently** *adv.*

turd (tɜ:d) *n. Taboo.* **1.** a piece of excrement. **2.** *Sl.* a contemptible person or thing. [OE *tord*]

tureen (tə'ri:n) *n.* a large deep usually rounded dish with a cover, used for serving soups, stews, etc. [C18: from F *terrine* earthenware vessel, from *terrin* made of earthenware, from Vulgar L *terrīnus* (unattested), from L *terra* earth]

Turenne (*French* tyrɛn) *n. Vicomte de,* title of *Henri de la Tour d'Auvergne.* 1611–75, French marshal. He commanded armies during the Thirty Years' War and the wars of the Fronde.

turf (tɜ:f) *n., pl.* **turfs** *or* **turves.** **1.** the surface layer of fields and pastures, consisting of earth containing a dense growth of grasses with their roots; sod. **2.** a piece cut from this layer. **3. the turf. a.** a track where horse races are run. **b.** horse racing as a sport or industry. **4.** another word for **peat.** ~*vb.* **5.** (*tr.*) to cover with pieces of turf. ~See also **turf out.** [OE]

turf accountant *n. Brit.* a formal name for a **bookmaker.**

turfman ('tɜːfmən) *n., pl.* **-men.** *Chiefly U.S.* a person devoted to horse racing.

turf out *vb.* (*tr., adv.*) *Brit. inf.* to throw out or dismiss; eject.

Turgenev (*Russian* tur'gjenɪf) *n.* **Ivan Sergeyevich** (i'van sɪr'gjejɪvitʃ). 1818–83, Russian novelist and dramatist. In *A Sportsman's Sketches* (1852) he pleaded for the abolition of serfdom. His novels, such as *Rudin* (1856) and *Fathers and Sons* (1862), are noted for their portrayal of country life and of the Russian intelligentsia. His plays include *A Month in the Country* (1890).

turgescent (tɜː'dʒɛsᵊnt) *adj.* becoming or being swollen; inflated; tumid. **—tur'gescence** *n.*

turgid ('tɜːdʒɪd) *adj.* **1.** swollen and distended. **2.** (of language) pompous; bombastic. [C17: from L *turgidus,* from *turgēre* to swell] **—tur'gidity** *or* **'turgidness** *n.* **—'turgidly** *adv.*

turgor ('tɜːgə) *n.* the normal rigid state of a cell, caused by pressure of the cell contents against the cell wall or membrane. [C19: from LL: a swelling, from L *turgēre* to swell]

Turgot (*French* tyrgo) *n.* **Anne Robert Jacques** (ɑn rɔbɛr ʒak). 1727–81, French economist and statesman. As controller general of finances (1774–76), he attempted to abolish feudal privileges, incurring the hostility of the aristocracy and his final dismissal.

Turin (tjʊə'rɪn) *n.* a city in NW Italy, capital of Piedmont region, on the River Po: became capital of the Kingdom of Sardinia in 1720; first capital (1861–65) of united Italy; university (1405); a major industrial centre, producing most of Italy's cars. Pop.: 1 035 565 (1987). Italian name: **Torino.**

Turing ('tjʊərɪŋ) *n.* **Alan Mathison.** 1912–54, English mathematician, who was responsible for formal description of abstract automata, and speculation on computer imitation of humans.

Turing machine *n.* a hypothetical universal computing machine able to modify its original instructions by reading, erasing, or writing a new symbol on a moving tape that acts as its program. [C20: after A. M. TURING]

turion ('tʊərɪən) *n.* a scaly shoot produced by many aquatic plants: it detaches from the parent plant and remains dormant until the following spring. [C17: from F *turion,* from L *turio*]

Turishcheva (*Russian* tu'riʃtʃəvə) *n.* **Ludmilla** (lʊd'mɪlə). born 1952, Soviet gymnast: world champion 1970, 1972 (at the Olympic Games), and 1974.

Turk (tɜːk) *n.* **1.** a native, inhabitant, or citizen of Turkey. **2.** a native speaker of any Turkic language. **3.** a brutal or domineering person.

Turk. *abbrev. for:* **1.** Turkey. **2.** Turkish.

Turkana (tɜː'kɑːnə) *n.* **Lake.** a long narrow lake in E Africa, in the Great Rift Valley. Area: 7104 sq. km (2743 sq. miles). Former name: (Lake) **Rudolf.**

Turkestan *or* **Turkistan** (ˌtɜːkɪ'stɑːn) *n.* an extensive region of central Asia between Siberia in the north and Tibet, India, Afghanistan, and Iran in the south: divided into **West** (**Russian**) **Turkestan** (also called Soviet Central Asia), which includes the Turkmen, Uzbek, Tadzhik, and Kirghiz SSRs and the S part of the Kazakh SSR, and **East** (**Chinese**) **Turkestan,** consisting of the Xinjiang Uygur AR. **—,Turke'stani** *adj., n.*

turkey ('tɜːkɪ) *n., pl.* **-keys** *or* **-key.** **1.** a large bird of North America, having a bare wattled head and neck and a brownish plumage. The male has a fan-shaped tail. A domesticated variety is bred for its flesh. **2.** *U.S. & Canad. inf.* something, esp. a theatrical production, that fails. **3.** See **cold turkey. 4. talk turkey.** *Inf., chiefly U.S. and Canad.* to discuss frankly and practically. [C16: shortened from *Turkey cock* (hen), used at first to designate the African guinea fowl (apparently because the bird was brought through Turkish territory), later applied by mistake to the American bird]

Turkey ('tɜːkɪ) *n.* a republic in W Asia and SE Europe, between the Black Sea, the Mediterranean, and the Aegean: one of the oldest inhabited regions of the world; the centre of the Ottoman Empire; became a republic in 1923. The major Asian part, consisting mainly of an arid plateau, is separated from European Turkey by the Bosporus, Sea of Marmara, and Dardanelles. Languages: chiefly Turkish, with Kurdish and Arabic minority languages. Religion: mostly Muslim. Currency: lira. Capital: Ankara. Pop.: 52 845 000 (1987). Area: 780 576 sq. km (301 380 sq. miles).

turkey buzzard *or* **vulture** *n.* a New World vulture having a naked red head.

turkey cock *n.* **1.** a male turkey. **2.** an arrogant person.

Turkey red *n.* **1. a.** a moderate or bright red colour. **b.** (*as adj.*): *a Turkey-red fabric.* **2.** a cotton fabric of a bright red colour.

Turki ('tɜːkɪ) *adj.* **1.** of or relating to the Turkic languages. **2.** of or relating to speakers of these languages. ~*n.* **3.** these languages collectively.

Turkic ('tɜːkɪk) *n.* a branch of the Altaic family of languages, including Turkish, Tatar, etc., members of which are found from Turkey to NE China, esp. in Soviet central Asia.

Turkish ('tɜːkɪʃ) *adj.* **1.** of Turkey, its people, or their language. ~*n.* **2.** the official language of Turkey, belonging to the Turkic branch of the Altaic family.

Turkish bath *n.* **1.** a type of bath in which the bather sweats freely in a steam room, is then washed, often massaged, and has a cold plunge or shower. **2.** (*sometimes pl.*) an establishment where such a bath is obtainable.

Turkish coffee *n.* very strong black coffee.

Turkish delight *n.* a jelly-like sweet flavoured with flower essences, usually cut into cubes and covered in icing sugar.

Turkish towel *n.* a rough loose-piled towel.

Turkmen Soviet Socialist Republic *n.* an administrative division of the S Soviet Union, on the Caspian Sea. Capital: Ashkhabad. Pop.: 3 270 000 (1986). Area: 488 100 sq. km (186 400 sq. miles). Also called: **Turkmenistan** (ˌtɜːkmɛnɪ'stɑːn).

Turks and Caicos Islands *pl. n.* a British colony in the West Indies, southeast of the Bahamas: consists of the eight **Turks Islands,** separated by the **Turks Island Passage** from the Caicos group, which has six main islands. Capital: Grand Turk. Pop.: 7436 (1980). Area: 430 sq. km (166 sq. miles).

Turk's-cap lily *n.* any of several cultivated lilies that have brightly coloured flowers with reflexed petals.

Turk's-head *n.* an ornamental turban-like knot.

Turku (*Finnish* 'turku) *n.* a city and port in SW Finland, on the Gulf of Bothnia: capital of Finland until 1812. Pop.: 161 188 (1986). Swedish name: **Åbo.**

turmeric ('tɜːmərɪk) *n.* **1.** a tropical Asian plant, *Curcuma longa,* having yellow flowers and an aromatic underground stem. **2.** the powdered stem of this plant, used as a condiment and as a yellow dye. [C16: from OF *terre merite,* from Med. L *terra merita,* lit.: meritorious earth, name applied for obscure reasons to curcuma]

turmeric paper *n. Chem.* paper impregnated with turmeric used as a test for alkalis and for boric acid.

turmoil ('tɜːmɔɪl) *n.* violent or confused movement; agitation; tumult. [C16: ?from TURN + MOIL]

turn (tɜːn) *vb.* **1.** to move around an axis: *to turn a knob.* **2.** (sometimes foll. by *round*) to change or cause to change positions by moving through an arc of a circle: *he turned the chair to face the light.* **3.** to change or cause to change in course, direction, etc. **4.** to go or pass to the other side of (a corner, etc.). **5.** to assume or cause to assume a rounded, curved, or folded form: *the road turns here.* **6.** to reverse or cause to reverse position. **7.** (*tr.*) to perform or do by a rotating movement: *to turn a somersault.* **8.** (*tr.*) to shape or cut a thread in (a workpiece) by rotating it on a lathe against a cutting tool. **9.** (when *intr.,* foll. by *into* or *to*) to change or convert or be changed or converted. **10.** (foll. by *into*) to change or cause to change in nature, character, etc.: *the frog turned into a prince.* **11.** (*copula*) to change so as to become: *he turned nasty.* **12.** to cause (foliage, etc.) to change colour or (of foliage, etc.) to change colour. **13.** to cause (milk, etc.) to become rancid or sour or (of milk, etc.) to become rancid or sour. **14.** to change or cause to change in subject, trend, etc.: *the conversation turned to fishing.* **15.** to direct or apply or be directed or applied: *he turned his attention to the problem.* **16.** (*intr.;* usually foll. by *to*) to appeal or apply (to) for help, advice, etc. **17.** to reach, pass, or progress beyond in age, time, etc.: *she has just turned twenty.* **18.** (*tr.*) to cause or allow to go: *to turn an animal loose.* **19.** to affect or be affected with nausea. **20.** to affect or be affected with giddiness: *my* *head is turning.* **21.** (*tr.*) to affect the mental or emotional stability of (esp. in **turn (someone's) head**). **22.** (*tr.*) to release from a container. **23.** (*tr.*) to render into another language. **24.** (usually foll. by *against* or *from*) to transfer or reverse (one's loyalties, affections, etc.). **25.** (*tr.*) to cause (an enemy agent) to become a double agent working for one's own side. **26.** (*tr.*) to bring (soil) from lower layers to the surface. **27.** to blunt (an edge) or (of an edge) to become blunted. **28.** (*tr.*) to give a graceful form to: *to turn a compliment.* **29.** (*tr.*) to reverse (a cuff, collar, etc.). **30.** (*intr.*) *U.S.* to be merchandised as specified: *shirts are turning well this week.* **31.** *Cricket.* to spin (the ball) or (of the ball) to spin. **32. turn a trick.** *Sl.* (of a prostitute) to gain a customer. **33. turn one's hand to.** to undertake (something practical). ~*n.* **34.** a turning or being turned. **35.** a movement of complete or partial rotation. **36.** a change of direction or position. **37.** direction or drift: *his thoughts took a new turn.* **38.** a deviation from a course or tendency. **39.** the place, point, or time at which a deviation or change occurs. **40.** another word for **turning** (sense 1). **41.** the right or opportunity to do something in an agreed order or succession: *now it's George's turn.* **42.** a change in nature, condition, etc.: *his illness took a turn for the worse.* **43.** a period of action, work, etc. **44.** a short walk, ride, or excursion. **45.** natural inclination: *a speculative turn of mind.* **46.** distinctive form or style: *a neat turn of phrase.* **47.** requirement, need, or advantage: *to serve someone's turn.* **48.** a deed that helps or hinders someone. **49.** a twist, bend, or distortion in shape. **50.** *Music.* a melodic ornament that makes a turn around a note, beginning with the note above, in a variety of sequences. **51.** a short theatrical act. **52.** *Stock Exchange, Brit.* the difference between a market maker's bid and offer prices, representing the market maker's income. **53.** *Inf.* a shock or surprise. **54. by turns.** one after another; alternately. **55. turn and turn about.** one after another; alternately. **56. to a turn.** to the proper amount; perfectly. ~See also **turn down, turn in,** etc. [OE *tyrnian,* from OF *torner,* from L *tornāre* to turn in a lathe, from *tornus* lathe, from Gk *tornos* dividers] —'**turner** *n.*

turnabout ('tɜːnə,baʊt) *n.* **1.** the act of turning so as to face a different direction. **2.** a change or reversal of opinion, attitude, etc.

turnaround ('tɜːnə,raʊnd) *n.* another word (esp. U.S. and Canad.) for **turnround.**

turnbuckle ('tɜːn,bʌk³l) *n.* an open mechanical sleeve usually having a swivel at one end and a thread at the other to enable a threaded wire or rope to be tightened.

turncoat ('tɜːn,kəʊt) *n.* a person who deserts one cause or party for the opposite faction.

turncock ('tɜːn,kɒk) *n.* an official employed to turn on the water for the mains supply.

turn down *vb.* (*tr., adv.*) **1.** to reduce (the volume or brightness) of (something). **2.** to reject or refuse. **3.** to fold down (a collar, sheets, etc.). ~*adj.* **turndown.** **4.** (*prenominal*) designed to be folded down.

Turner ('tɜːnə) *n.* **Joseph Mallord William.** 1775–1851, English landscape painter; a master of water colours. He sought to convey atmosphere by means of an innovative use of colour and gradations of light.

turn in *vb.* (*adv.*) *Inf.* **1.** (*intr.*) to go to bed for the night. **2.** (*tr.*) to hand in; deliver. **3.** to give up or conclude (something). **4.** (*tr.*) to record (a score, etc.). **5. turn in on oneself.** to become preoccupied with one's own problems.

turning ('tɜːnɪŋ) *n.* **1.** a road, river, or path that turns off the main way. **2.** the point where such a way turns off. **3.** a bend in a straight course. **4.** an object made on a lathe. **5.** the process or skill of turning objects on a lathe. **6.** (*pl.*) the waste produced in turning on a lathe.

turning circle *n.* the smallest circle in which a vehicle can turn.

turning point *n.* **1.** a moment when the course of events is changed. **2.** a point at which there is a change in direction or motion.

turnip ('tɜːnɪp) *n.* **1.** a widely cultivated plant of the cabbage family with a large yellow or white edible root. **2.** the root of this plant, which is eaten as a vegetable. [C16: from earlier *turnepe,* ?from turn (indicating its rounded shape) + *nepe,* from L *nāpus* turnip]

turnkey ('tɜːn,kiː) *n.* **1.** *Arch.* a keeper of the keys, esp. in a prison; warder or jailer. ~*adj.* **2.** denoting a project, as

in civil engineering, in which a single contractor has responsibility for the complete job from the start to the time of installation or occupancy.

turn off *vb.* **1.** (*intr.*) to leave (a road, etc.). **2.** (*intr.*) (of a road, etc.) to deviate from (another road, etc.). **3.** (*tr., adv.*) to cause (something) to cease operating by turning a knob, pushing a button, etc. **4.** (*tr.*) *Inf.* to cause (a person, etc.) to feel dislike or distaste for (something): *this music turns me off.* **5.** (*tr., adv.*) *Brit. inf.* to dismiss from employment. ~*n.* **turn-off. 6.** a road or other way branching off from the main thoroughfare. **7.** *Inf.* a person or thing that elicits dislike or distaste.

turn on *vb.* **1.** (*tr., adv.*) to cause (something) to operate by turning a knob, etc. **2.** (*intr., prep.*) to depend or hinge on: *the success of the party turns on you.* **3.** (*prep.*) to become hostile to or retaliate: *the dog turned on the children.* **4.** (*tr., adv.*) *Inf.* to produce (charm, tears, etc.) suddenly or automatically. **5.** (*tr., adv.*) *Sl.* to arouse emotionally or sexually. **6.** (*intr., adv.*) *Sl.* to take or become intoxicated by drugs. **7.** (*tr., adv.*) *Sl.* to introduce (someone) to drugs. ~*n.* **turn-on. 8.** *Sl.* a person or thing that causes emotional or sexual arousal.

turn out *vb.* (*adv.*) **1.** (*tr.*) to cause (something, esp. a light) to cease operating by or as if by turning a knob, etc. **2.** (*tr.*) to produce by an effort or process. **3.** (*tr.*) to dismiss, discharge, or expel. **4.** (*tr.*) to empty the contents of, esp. in order to clean, tidy, or rearrange. **5.** (*copula*) to prove to be as specified. **6.** to end up; result: *it all turned out well.* **7.** (*tr.*) to fit as with clothes: *that woman turns her children out well.* **8.** (*intr.*) to assemble or gather. **9.** (of a soldier) to parade or to call (a soldier) to parade. **10.** (*intr.*) *Inf.* to get out of bed. ~*n.* **turnout. 11.** the body of people appearing together at a gathering. **12.** the quantity or amount produced. **13.** an array of clothing or equipment.

turn over *vb.* (*adv.*) **1.** to change or cause to change position, esp. so as to reverse top and bottom. **2.** to start (an engine), esp. with a starting handle, or (of an engine) to start or function correctly. **3.** to shift or cause to shift position, as by rolling from side to side. **4.** (*tr.*) to deliver; transfer. **5.** (*tr.*) to consider carefully. **6.** (*tr.*) **a.** to sell and replenish (stock in trade). **b.** to transact business and so generate gross revenue of (a specified sum). **7.** (*tr.*) to invest and recover (capital). **8.** (*tr.*) *Sl.* to rob. ~*n.* **turnover. 9. a.** the amount of business transacted during a specified period. **b.** the rate at which stock in trade is sold and replenished. **10.** a change or reversal of position. **11.** a small pastry case filled with fruit, jam, etc. **12. a.** the number of workers employed by a firm in a given period to replace those who have left. **b.** the ratio between this number and the average number of employees during the same period. **13.** *Banking.* the amount of capital funds loaned on call during a specified period. ~*adj.* **turnover. 14.** (*prenominal*) designed to be turned over.

turnpike ('tɜːn,paɪk) *n.* **1.** *History.* **a.** a barrier set across a road to prevent passage until a toll had been paid. **b.** a road on which a turnpike was operated. **2.** an obsolete word for **turnstile. 3.** *U.S.* a motorway for use of which a toll is charged. [C15: from TURN + PIKE²]

turnround ('tɜːn,raʊnd) *n.* **1. a.** the act or process in which a ship, aircraft, etc., unloads at the end of a trip and reloads for the next trip. **b.** the time taken for this. **2.** the total time taken by a vehicle in a round trip. **3.** a complete reversal of a situation.

turnspit ('tɜːn,spɪt) *n.* **1.** (formerly) a servant or small dog whose job was to turn a spit. **2.** a spit that can be so turned.

turnstile ('tɜːn,staɪl) *n.* a mechanical barrier with metal arms that are turned to admit one person at a time.

turnstone ('tɜːn,stəʊn) *n.* a shore bird, related to the plovers and sandpipers, that lifts up stones in search of food.

turntable ('tɜːn,teɪb³l) *n.* **1.** the circular platform that rotates a gramophone record while it is being played. **2.** a circular platform used for turning locomotives and cars. **3.** the revolvable platform on a microscope on which specimens are examined.

turntable ladder *n. Brit.* a power-operated extending ladder mounted on a fire engine. U.S. and Canad. name: **aerial ladder.**

turn to vb. (intr., adv.) to set about a task.

turn up vb. (adv.) **1.** (intr.) to arrive or appear. **2.** to find or be found, esp. by accident. **3.** (tr.) to increase the flow, volume, etc., of. ~n. **turn-up. 4.** (often pl.) Brit. the turned-up fold at the bottom of some trouser legs. U.S. and Canad. name: **cuff. 5.** Inf. an unexpected or chance occurrence.

turpentine ('tɜːpˌ°n,taɪn) n. **1.** Also called: **gum turpentine.** any of various oleoresins obtained from various coniferous trees and used as the main source of commercial turpentine. **2.** a sticky oleoresin that exudes from the terebinth tree. **3.** Also called: **oil of turpentine, spirits of turpentine.** a colourless volatile oil distilled from turpentine oleoresin. It is used as a solvent for paints and in medicine. **4.** Also called: **turpentine substitute, white spirit.** (not in technical usage) any one of a number of thinners for paints and varnishes, consisting of fractions of petroleum. Related adj.: **terebinthine.** ~vb. (tr.) **5.** to treat or saturate with turpentine. [C14 terebentyne, from Med. L, from L terebinthīna turpentine, from terebinthus the turpentine tree]

turpentine tree n. **1.** a tropical African tree yielding a hard dark wood and a useful resin. **2.** either of two Australian evergreen trees that yield resin.

turpeth ('tɜːpɪθ) n. **1.** an East Indian plant having roots with purgative properties. **2.** the root of this plant or the drug obtained from it. [C14: from Med. L turbithum, ult. from Ar. turbid]

Turpin ('tɜːpɪn) n. Dick. 1706–39, English highwayman.

turpitude ('tɜːpɪˌtjuːd) n. base character or action; depravity. [C15: from L turpitūdō ugliness, from turpis base]

turps (tɜːps) n. (functioning as sing.) Brit. short for **turpentine** (sense 3).

turquoise ('tɜːkwɔɪz, -kwɑːz) n. **1.** a greenish-blue fine-grained mineral consisting of hydrated copper aluminium phosphate. It is used as a gemstone. **2. a.** the colour of turquoise. **b.** (as adj.): a turquoise dress. [C14: from OF turqueise Turkish (stone)]

turret ('tʌrɪt) n. **1.** a small tower that projects from the wall of a building, esp. a castle. **2. a.** a self-contained structure, capable of rotation, in which weapons are mounted, esp. in tanks and warships. **b.** a similar structure on an aircraft. **3.** (on a machine tool) a turret-like steel structure with tools projecting radially that can be indexed round to bring each tool to bear on the work. [C14: from OF torete, from tor tower, from L turris] —**'turreted** adj.

turret lathe n. another name for **capstan lathe.**

turtle[1] ('tɜːt°l) n. **1.** any of various aquatic reptiles, esp. those having a flattened shell enclosing the body and flipper-like limbs adapted for swimming. **2. turn turtle.** to capsize. [C17: from F tortue TORTOISE (infl. by TURTLE[2])]

turtle[2] ('tɜːt°l) n. an archaic name for **turtledove.** [OE turtla, from L turtur, imit.]

turtleback ('tɜːt°l,bæk) n. an arched projection over the upper deck of a ship for protection in heavy seas.

turtledove ('tɜːt°l,dʌv) n. **1.** any of several Old World doves having a brown plumage with speckled wings and a long dark tail. **2.** a gentle or loving person. [see TURTLE[2]]

turtleneck ('tɜːt°l,nɛk) n. a round high close-fitting neck on a sweater or the sweater itself.

turves (tɜːvz) n. a plural of **turf.**

Tuscan ('tʌskən) adj. **1.** of or relating to Tuscany, its inhabitants, or their dialect of Italian. **2.** of or denoting one of the five classical orders of architecture: characterized by a column with an unfluted shaft and a capital and base with mouldings but no decoration. ~n. **3.** a native or inhabitant of Tuscany. **4.** any of the dialects of Italian spoken in Tuscany.

Tuscany ('tʌskənɪ) n. a region of central Italy, on the Ligurian and Tyrrhenian Seas: corresponds roughly to ancient Etruria; a region of numerous small states in medieval times; united in the 15th and 16th centuries under Florence; united with the rest of Italy in 1861. Capital: Florence. Pop.: 3 571 538 (1985 est.). Area: 22 990 sq. km (8876 sq. miles). Italian name: **Toscana.**

tusche (tʊʃ) n. a substance used in lithography for drawing the design and as a resist in silk-screen printing and lithography. [from G, from tuschen to touch up with colour, from F toucher to touch]

Tusculum ('tʌskjʊləm) n. an ancient city in Latium near Rome. —**'Tusculan** adj.

tush (tʌʃ) interj. Arch. an exclamation of disapproval or contempt. [C15: imit.]

tusk (tʌsk) n. **1.** a pointed elongated usually paired tooth in the elephant, walrus, and certain other mammals. **2.** a tusklike tooth or part. **3.** a sharp pointed projection. ~vb. **4.** to stab, tear, or gore with the tusks. [OE tūsc] —**tusked** adj.

tusker ('tʌskə) n. any animal with long tusks.

tusk shell n. any of various burrowing seashore molluscs that have a long narrow tubular shell open at both ends.

Tussaud (French tyso) n. **Marie** (mari). 1760–1850, Swiss modeller in wax, who founded a permanent exhibition in London of historical and contemporary figures.

tussis ('tʌsɪs) n. the technical name for a **cough.** See **pertussis.** [L: cough] —**'tussive** adj.

tussle ('tʌs°l) vb. **1.** (intr.) to fight or wrestle in a vigorous way. ~n. **2.** a vigorous fight; scuffle; struggle. [C15]

tussock ('tʌsək) n. **1.** a dense tuft of vegetation, esp. of grass. **2.** Austral. & N.Z. **a.** short for **tussock grass** (sense 1). **b. the.** country where tussock grass grows. [C16: from ?] —**'tussocky** adj.

tussock grass n. Austral. & N.Z. **1.** any of several pasture grasses. **2.** a tough grass that is unpalatable to stock.

tussore (tʊˈsɔː, 'tʌsə), **tusser** ('tʌsə), or (Chiefly U.S.) **tussah** ('tʌsə) n. **1.** Also called: **wild silk.** a coarse silk obtained from an oriental silkworm. **2.** the silkworm producing this. [C17: from Hindi tasar shuttle, from Sansk. tasara a wild silkworm]

tut (tʌt) interj., n., vb. **tutting, tutted.** short for **tut-tut.**

Tutankhamen (,tuːtən'kɑːmɛn, -mən) or **Tutankhamun** (,tuːtənkɑː'muːn) n. king (1361–1352 B.C.) of the 18th dynasty of Egypt. His tomb near Luxor, discovered in 1922, contained a wealth of material objects.

tutelage ('tjuːtɪlɪdʒ) n. **1.** the act or office of a guardian or tutor. **2.** instruction or guidance, esp. by a tutor. **3.** the condition of being under the supervision of a guardian or tutor. [C17: from L tūtēla a caring for, from tuērī to watch over]

tutelary ('tjuːtɪlərɪ) or **tutelar** ('tjuːtɪlə) adj. **1.** invested with the role of guardian or protector. **2.** of or relating to a guardian. ~n., pl. **-laries** or **-lars. 3.** a tutelary person, deity, etc.

tutor ('tjuːtə) n. **1.** a teacher, usually instructing individual pupils. **2.** (at universities, colleges, etc.) a member of staff responsible for the teaching and supervision of a certain number of students. ~vb. **3.** to act as a tutor to (someone). **4.** (tr.) to act as guardian to. [C14: from L: a watcher, from tuērī to watch over] —**'tutorage** or **'tutorship** n.

tutorial (tjuːˈtɔːrɪəl) n. **1.** a period of intensive tuition given by a tutor to an individual student or to a small group of students. ~adj. **2.** of or relating to a tutor.

tutsan ('tʌtsən) n. a woodland shrub of Europe and W Asia, having yellow flowers and reddish-purple fruits. [C15: from OF toute-saine (unattested), lit.: all healthy]

tutti ('tʊtɪ) adj., adv. Music. to be performed by the whole orchestra, choir, etc. [C18: from It., pl. of tutto all, from L tōtus]

tutti-frutti ('tuːtɪ'fruːtɪ) n. **1.** (pl. **-fruttis**) an ice cream or a confection containing small pieces of candied or fresh fruits. **2.** a preserve of chopped mixed fruits. **3.** a flavour like that of many fruits combined. [from It., lit.: all the fruits]

tut-tut ('tʌt'tʌt) interj. **1.** an exclamation of mild reprimand, disapproval, or surprise. ~vb. **-tutting, -tutted. 2.** (intr.) to express disapproval by the exclamation of "tut-tut". ~n. **3.** the act of tut-tutting.

tutty ('tʌtɪ) n. impure zinc oxide used as a polishing powder. [C14: from OF tutie, from Ar. tūtiyā, prob. from Persian, from Sansk. tuttha]

tutu ('tuːtuː) n. a very short skirt worn by ballerinas, made of projecting layers of stiffened material. [from F, changed from the nursery word cucu backside, from L cūlus the buttocks]

Tutu ('tuːtuː) n. **Desmond.** born 1931, South African clergyman, noted for his opposition to apartheid. He became Anglican Bishop of Johannesburg in 1984 and Archbishop of Cape Town in 1986; Nobel peace prize 1984.

Tutuila (,tuːtuː'iːlə) n. the largest island of American Samoa, in the SW Pacific. Chief town and port: Pago Pago. Pop.: 30 226 (1980). Area: 135 sq. km (52 sq. miles).

Tuva Autonomous Soviet Socialist Republic ('tuːvə) *n.* an administrative division of the S Soviet Union: mountainous. Capital: Kizyl. Pop.: 284 000 (1986). Area: 170 500 sq. km (65 800 sq. miles). Also called: **Tuvinian ASSR.**

Tuvalu (ˌtuːvəˈluː) *n.* a country in the SW Pacific, comprising a group of nine coral islands: established as a British protectorate in 1892. From 1915 until 1975 the islands formed part of the British colony of the Gilbert and Ellice Islands; achieved full independence in 1978. Official languages: English and Tuvaluan. Religion: mostly Christian. Currency: Australian dollar. Capital: Funafuti. Pop.: 8200 (1987). Area: 26 sq. km (10 sq. miles). Former names: **Lagoon Islands, Ellice Islands.** — ˌTuvaˈluan *adj., n.*

tu-whit tu-whoo (təˈwɪt təˈwuː) *interj.* an imitation of the sound made by an owl.

tuxedo (tʌkˈsiːdəʊ) *n., pl.* **-dos.** the usual U.S. and Canad. name for **dinner jacket.** [C19: after a country club in *Tuxedo Park*, New York]

Tuxtla Gutiérrez (*Spanish* 'tustla guˈtjɛrːeθ) *n.* a city in SE Mexico, capital of Chiapas state: agricultural trading centre. Pop.: 166 476 (1980).

tuyère ('twiːɛə, 'twaɪə) *or* **twyer** ('twaɪə) *n.* a water-cooled nozzle through which air is blown into a cupola, blast furnace, or forge. [C18: from F, from *tuyau* pipe, from OF *tuel*, prob. of Gmc origin]

TV *abbrev. for* television.

TVEI (in Britain) *abbrev. for* technical and vocational educational initiative: a national educational scheme in which pupils gain practical experience in technology and industry often through work placement.

Tver (*Russian* tvjɛr) *n.* the former name (until 1932) of **Kalinin.**

TVP *abbrev. for* textured vegetable protein: protein from soya beans or other vegetables spun into fibres and flavoured: used esp. as a substitute for meat.

twaddle ('twɒdəl) *n.* **1.** silly, trivial, or pretentious talk or writing. ~*vb.* **2.** (*intr.*) to talk or write in a silly or pretentious way. [C16 *twattle*, var. of *twittle* or *tittle*] — **'twaddler** *n.*

twain (tweɪn) *determiner, n.* an archaic word for **two.** [OE *twēgen*]

Twain (tweɪn) *n.* **Mark,** pen name of *Samuel Langhorne Clemens.* 1835–1910, U.S. novelist and humorist, famous for his classics *The Adventures of Tom Sawyer* (1876) and *The Adventures of Huckleberry Finn* (1885).

twang (twæŋ) *n.* **1.** a sharp ringing sound produced by or as if by the plucking of a taut string. **2.** the act of plucking a string to produce such a sound. **3.** a strongly nasal quality in a person's speech. ~*vb.* **4.** to make or cause to make a twang. **5.** to strum (music, a tune, etc.). **6.** to speak with a nasal voice. **7.** (*intr.*) to be released or move with a twang: *the arrow twanged away.* [C16: imit.] — **'twangy** *adj.*

'twas (twɒz; *unstressed* twəz) *Poetic or dialect. contraction of* it was.

twat (twæt, twɒt) *n. Taboo sl.* **1.** the female genitals. **2.** a foolish person. [from ?]

twayblade ('tweɪˌbleɪd) *n.* any of various orchids having a basal pair of unstalked leaves arranged opposite each other. [C16: translation of Med. L *bifolium* having two leaves, from obs. *tway* two + BLADE]

tweak (twiːk) *vb.* **1.** (*tr.*) to twist or pinch with a sharp or sudden movement. ~*n.* **2.** a tweaking. [OE *twiccian*]

twee (twiː) *adj. Brit. inf.* excessively sentimental, sweet, or pretty. [C19: from *tweet*, mincing or affected pronunciation of *sweet*]

tweed (twiːd) *n.* **1.** a thick woollen cloth produced originally in Scotland. **2.** (*pl.*) clothes made of this. [C19: prob. from *tweel*, Scot. var. of TWILL, infl. by TWEED]

Tweed (twiːd) *n.* a river in SE Scotland and NE England, flowing east and forming part of the border between Scotland and England, then crossing into England to enter the North Sea at Berwick. Length: 156 km (97 miles).

Tweeddale ('twiːdˌdeɪl) *n.* another name for **Peeblesshire.**

Tweedledum and Tweedledee (ˌtwiːdəlˈdʌm; ˌtwiːdəlˈdiː) *n.* any two persons or things that differ only slightly from each other; two of a kind. [C19: from the proverbial names of HANDEL and the rival musician Buononcini. The names were popularized by Lewis Carroll's use of them in *Through the Looking Glass* (1872)]

Tweedsmuir ('twiːdzmjʊə) *n.* **Baron.** title of (John) **Buchan.**

tweedy ('twiːdɪ) *adj.* **tweedier, tweediest.** **1.** of, made of, or resembling tweed. **2.** showing a fondness for a hearty outdoor life, usually associated with wearers of tweeds.

'tween (twiːn) *Poetic or dialect. contraction of* between.

'tween deck *or* **decks** *n. Naut.* a space between two continuous decks of a vessel.

tweet (twiːt) *interj.* **1.** an imitation of the thin chirping sound made by small birds. ~*vb.* **2.** (*intr.*) to make this sound. [C19: imit.]

tweeter ('twiːtə) *n.* a loudspeaker used in high-fidelity systems for the reproduction of high audio frequencies. It is usually employed in conjunction with a woofer. [C20: from TWEET]

tweezers ('twiːzəz) *pl. n.* a small pincer-like instrument for handling small objects, plucking out hairs, etc. Also called: **pair of tweezers, tweezer** (esp. U.S.). [C17: pl. of *tweezer* (on the model of *scissors*, etc.), from *tweeze* case of instruments, from F *étuis*, from OF *estuier* to preserve, ult. from L *studēre* to care about]

Twelfth Day *n.* Jan. 6, the twelfth day after Christmas and the feast of the Epiphany.

twelfth man *n.* a reserve player in a cricket team.

Twelfth Night *n.* **a.** the evening of Jan. 5, the eve of Twelfth Day. **b.** the evening of Twelfth Day itself.

twelve (twɛlv) *n.* **1.** the cardinal number that is the sum of ten and two. **2.** a numeral, 12, XII, etc., representing this number. **3.** something representing or consisting of 12 units. **4.** Also called: **twelve o'clock.** noon or midnight. ~*determiner.* **5. a.** amounting to twelve. **b.** (*as pronoun*): *twelve have arrived.* ~Related adj.: **duodecimal.** [OE *twelf*] — **twelfth** *adj., n.*

twelvemo ('twɛlvməʊ) *n., pl.* **-mos.** *Bookbinding.* another word for **duodecimo.**

twelvemonth ('twɛlvˌmʌnθ) *n. Chiefly Brit.* an archaic or dialect word for a **year.**

twelve-tone *adj.* of or denoting the type of serial music which uses as musical material a tone row formed by the 12 semitones of the chromatic scale. See **serialism.**

twenty ('twɛntɪ) *n., pl.* **-ties. 1.** the cardinal number that is the product of ten and two. **2.** a numeral, 20, XX, etc., representing this number. **3.** something representing or consisting of 20 units. ~*determiner.* **4. a.** amounting to twenty: *twenty questions.* **b.** (*as pronoun*): *to order twenty.* — **'twentieth** *adj., n.* [OE *twēntig*]

twenty-twenty *adj. Med.* (of vision) being of normal acuity: usually written 20/20.

'twere (twɜː; *unstressed* twə) *Poetic or dialect. contraction of* it were.

twerp *or* **twirp** (twɜːp) *n. Inf.* a silly, weak-minded, or contemptible person. [C20: from ?]

twibill *or* **twibil** ('twaɪˌbɪl) *n.* **1.** a mattock with a blade shaped like an adze at one end and like an axe at the other. **2.** *Arch.* a double-bladed battle-axe. [OE, from *twi-* double + *bill* sword]

twice (twaɪs) *adv.* **1.** two times; on two occasions or in two cases. **2.** double in degree or quantity: *twice as long.* [OE *twiwa*]

Twickenham ('twɪkənəm) *n.* a former town in SE England, on the River Thames: part of the Greater London borough of Richmond-upon-Thames since 1965; contains the English Rugby Football Union ground.

twiddle ('twɪdəl) *vb.* **1.** (when *intr.*, often foll. by *with*) to twirl or fiddle (with), often in an idle way. **2. twiddle one's thumbs.** to do nothing; be unoccupied. **3.** (*intr.*) to turn, twirl, or rotate. **4.** (*intr.*) *Rare.* to be occupied with trifles. ~*n.* **5.** an act or instance of twiddling. [C16: prob. a blend of TWIRL + FIDDLE] — **'twiddler** *n.*

twig¹ (twɪg) *n.* **1.** any small branch or shoot of a tree. **2.** something resembling this, esp. a minute branch of a blood vessel. [OE *twigge*] — **'twiggy** *adj.*

twig² (twɪg) *vb.* **twigging, twigged.** **1.** to understand (something). **2.** to find out or suddenly comprehend (something): *he hasn't twigged yet.* [C18: ?from Scot. Gaelic *tuig* I understand]

twilight ('twaɪˌlaɪt) *n.* **1.** the soft diffused light occurring when the sun is just below the horizon, esp. following sunset. **2.** the period in which this light occurs. **3.** any faint light. **4.** a period in which strength, importance, etc., are waning. **5.** (*modifier*) of or relating to twilight; dim. [C15: lit.: half light (between day and night), from OE *twi-* half + LIGHT¹] — **twilit** ('twaɪˌlɪt) *adj.*

Twilight of the Gods *n.* another term for **Götterdämmerung.**

twilight sleep *n. Med.* a state of partial anaesthesia in which the patient retains a slight degree of consciousness.

twilight zone *n.* **1.** an inner-city area where houses have become dilapidated. **2.** any indefinite or transitional condition or area.

twill (twɪl) *adj.* **1.** (in textiles) of a weave in which the yarns are worked to produce an effect of parallel diagonal lines or ribs. ~*n.* **2.** any fabric so woven. ~*vb.* **3.** (*tr.*) to weave in this fashion. [OE *twilic* having a double thread]

'twill (twɪl) *Poetic or dialect. contraction of* it will.

twin (twɪn) *n.* **1. a.** either of two persons or animals conceived at the same time. **b.** (*as modifier*): *a twin brother.* See also **identical** (sense 3), **fraternal** (sense 3). **2. a.** either of two persons or things that are identical or very similar. **b.** (*as modifier*): *twin carburettors.* **3.** Also called: **macle.** a crystal consisting of two parts each of which has a definite orientation to the other. ~*vb.* **twinning, twinned. 4.** to pair or be paired together; couple. **5.** (*intr.*) to bear twins. **6.** (*intr.*) (of a crystal) to form into a twin. **7. a.** (*tr.*) to create a reciprocal relation between (two towns in different countries); pair (a town) with another in a different country. **b.** (*intr.*) (of a town) to be paired in a town in a different country. [OE *twinn*] — **'twinning** *n.*

twin bed *n.* one of a pair of matching single beds.

twine (twaɪn) *n.* **1.** string made by twisting together fibres of hemp, cotton, etc. **2.** a twining. **3.** something produced or characterized by twining. **4.** a twist, coil, or convolution. **5.** a knot or tangle. ~*vb.* **6.** (*tr.*) to twist together; interweave. **7.** (*tr.*) to form by or as if by twining. **8.** (when *intr.*, often foll. by *around*) to wind or cause to wind, esp. in spirals. [OE *twin*] — **'twiner** *n.*

twin-engined *adj.* (of an aeroplane) having two engines.

twinge (twɪndʒ) *n.* **1.** a sudden brief darting or stabbing pain. **2.** a sharp emotional pang. ~*vb.* **3.** to have or cause to have a twinge. [OE *twengan* to pinch]

twinkle ('twɪŋkᵊl) *vb.* (*mainly intr.*) **1.** to emit or reflect light in a flickering manner; shine brightly and intermittently; sparkle. **2.** (of the eyes) to sparkle, esp. with amusement or delight. **3.** *Rare.* to move about quickly. ~*n.* **4.** a flickering brightness; sparkle. **5.** an instant. [OE *twinclian*] — **'twinkler** *n.*

twinkling ('twɪŋklɪŋ) *or* **twink** (twɪŋk) *n.* a very short time; instant; moment. Also called: **twinkling of an eye.**

Twins (twɪnz) *pl. n.* **the.** the constellation Gemini, the third sign of the zodiac.

twin-screw *adj.* (of a vessel) having two propellers.

twinset ('twɪn,sɛt) *n. Brit.* a matching jumper and cardigan.

twin town *n. Brit.* a town that has civic associations, such as reciprocal visits and cultural exchanges, with a foreign town.

twin-tub *n.* a type of washing machine that has two revolving drums, one for washing and the other for spin-drying.

twirl (twɜːl) *vb.* **1.** to move around rapidly and repeatedly in a circle. **2.** (*tr.*) to twist, wind, or twiddle, often idly: *she twirled her hair around her finger.* **3.** (*intr.*) often foll. by *around* or *about*) to turn suddenly to face another way. ~*n.* **4.** a rotating or being rotated; whirl or twist. **5.** something wound around or twirled; coil. **6.** a written flourish. [C16: ? a blend of TWIST + WHIRL] — **'twirler** *n.*

twirp (twɜːp) *n.* a variant spelling of **twerp.**

twist (twɪst) *vb.* **1.** to cause (one end or part) to turn or (of one end or part) to turn in the opposite direction from another; coil or spin. **2.** to distort or be distorted. **3.** to wind or twine. **4.** to force or be forced out of the natural form or position. **5.** to change for the worse in character, meaning, etc.; pervert: *she twisted the statement.* **6.** to revolve; rotate. **7.** (*tr.*) to wrench with a turning action. **8.** (*intr.*) to follow a winding course. **9.** (*intr.*) to squirm, as with pain. **10.** (*intr.*) to dance the twist. **11.** (*tr.*) *Brit. inf.* to cheat; swindle. **12. twist someone's arm.** to persuade or coerce someone. ~*n.* **13.** a twisting. **14.** something formed by or as if by twisting. **15.** a decisive change of direction, aim, meaning, or character. **16.** (in a novel, play, etc.) an unexpected event, revelation, etc. **17.** a bend: *a twist in the road.* **18.** a distortion of the original shape or form. **19.** a jerky pull, wrench, or turn. **20.** a strange personal characteristic, esp. a bad one. **21.** a confused tangle made by twisting. **22.** a twisted thread used in sewing where extra strength is needed. **23. the twist.** a dance popular in the 1960s, in which dancers vigorously twist the hips. **24.** a loaf or roll made of pieces of twisted dough. **25.** a thin sliver of peel from a lemon, lime, etc., twisted and added to a drink. **26. a.** a cigar made by twisting three cigars around one another. **b.** chewing tobacco made in the form of a roll by twisting the leaves together. **27.** *Physics.* torsional deformation or shear stress or strain. **28.** *Sport, chiefly U.S. & Canad.* spin given to a ball in various games. **29. round the twist.** *Brit. sl.* mad; eccentric. [OE]

twist drill *n.* a drill bit having two helical grooves running from the point along the shank to clear swarf and cuttings.

twister ('twɪstə) *n.* **1.** *Brit.* a swindling or dishonest person. **2.** a person or thing that twists. **3.** *U.S. & Canad.* an informal name for **tornado.** **4.** a ball moving with a twisting motion.

twist grip *n.* a handlebar control in the form of a ratchet-controlled rotating grip.

twit¹ (twɪt) *vb.* **twitting, twitted. 1.** (*tr.*) to tease, taunt, or reproach, often in jest. ~*n.* **2.** *U.S. & Canad. inf.* a nervous or excitable state. **3.** *Rare.* a reproach; taunt. [OE *ætwītan*, from *æt* against + *witan* to accuse]

twit² (twɪt) *n. Inf., chiefly Brit.* a foolish or stupid person; idiot. [C19: from TWIT¹ (orig. in the sense: a person given to twitting)]

twitch (twɪtʃ) *vb.* **1.** to move in a jerky spasmodic way. **2.** (*tr.*) to pull (something) with a quick jerky movement. **3.** (*intr.*) to hurt with a sharp spasmodic pain. ~*n.* **4.** a sharp jerking movement. **5.** a mental or physical twinge. **6.** a sudden muscular spasm, esp. one caused by a nervous condition. **7.** a loop of cord used to control a horse by drawing it tight about its upper lip. [OE *twiccian* to pluck]

twitcher ('twɪtʃə) *n.* **1.** a person or thing that twitches. **2.** *Inf.* a bird-watcher who tries to spot as many rare varieties as possible.

twitch grass *n.* another name for **couch grass.** Sometimes shortened to **twitch.** [C16: var. of QUITCH GRASS]

twite (twaɪt) *n.* a N European finch with a brown streaked plumage. [C16: imit. of its cry]

twitter ('twɪtə) *vb.* **1.** (*intr.*) (esp. of a bird) to utter a succession of chirping sounds. **2.** (*intr.*) to talk or move rapidly and tremulously. **3.** (*intr.*) to giggle. **4.** (*tr.*) to utter in a chirping way. ~*n.* **5.** a twittering sound. **6.** the act of twittering. **7.** a state of nervous excitement (esp. in **in a twitter**). [C14: imit.] — **'twitterer** *n.* — **'twittery** *adj.*

'twixt *or* **twixt** (twɪkst) *Poetic or dialect. contraction of* betwixt.

two (tuː) *n.* **1.** the cardinal number that is the sum of one and one. **2.** a numeral, 2, II, (ii), etc., representing this number. **3.** something representing or consisting of two units. **4.** Also called: **two o'clock.** two hours after noon or midnight. **5. in two.** in or into two parts. **6. put two and two together.** to make an inference from available evidence, esp. an obvious inference. **7. that makes two of us.** the same applies to me. ~*determiner.* **8. a.** amounting to two: *two nails.* **b.** (*as pronoun*): *he bought two.* ~Related adjs.: **binary, double, dual.** [OE *twā* (fem.)]

two-by-four *n.* **1.** a length of untrimmed timber with a cross section that measures 2 inches by 4 inches. **2.** a trimmed timber joist with a cross section that measures 1½ inches by 3½ inches.

two-dimensional *adj.* **1.** of or having two dimensions. **2.** having an area but not enclosing any volume. **3.** lacking in depth.

two-edged *adj.* **1.** having two cutting edges. **2.** (esp. of a remark) having two interpretations, such as *she looks nice when she smiles.*

two-faced *adj.* deceitful; hypocritical.

twofold ('tuː,fəʊld) *adj.* **1.** equal to twice as many or twice as much. **2.** composed of two parts. ~*adv.* **3.** doubly.

two-handed *adj.* **1.** requiring the use of both hands. **2.** ambidextrous. **3.** requiring the participation or cooperation of two people.

twopence *or* **tuppence** ('tʌpəns) *n. Brit.* **1.** the sum of two pennies. **2.** (*used with a negative*) something of little value (in **not care** *or* **give twopence**). **3.** a former British silver coin.

twopenny or **tuppenny** ('tʌpənɪ) adj. Chiefly Brit. **1.** Also: **twopenny-halfpenny.** cheap or tawdry. **2.** (intensifier): a twopenny damn. **3.** worth two pence.

two-phase adj. (of an electrical circuit, device, etc.) generating or using two alternating voltages of the same frequency, displaced in phase by 90°.

two-piece adj. **1.** consisting of two separate parts, usually matching, as of a garment. ~n. **2.** such an outfit.

two-ply adj. **1.** made of two thicknesses, layers, or strands. ~n., pl. **-plies. 2.** a two-ply wood, knitting yarn, etc.

Two Sicilies pl. n. **the.** a former kingdom of S Italy, consisting of the kingdoms of Sicily and Naples (1061–1860).

two-sided adj. **1.** having two sides or aspects. **2.** controversial; debatable.

twosome ('tuːsəm) n. **1.** two together, esp. two people. **2.** a match between two people.

two-step n. **1.** an old-time dance in duple time. **2.** a piece of music composed for or in the rhythm of this dance.

two-stroke adj. of an internal-combustion engine whose piston makes two strokes for every explosion. U.S. and Canad. word: **two-cycle.**

Two Thousand Guineas n., (functioning as sing.), usually written **2000 Guineas. the.** an annual horse race run at Newmarket since 1809.

two-time vb. Inf. to deceive (someone, esp. a lover) by carrying on a relationship with another. —**,two-'timer** n.

two-tone adj. **1.** of two colours or two shades of the same colour. **2.** (esp. of sirens, car horns, etc.) producing or consisting of two notes.

'twould (twʊd) Poetic or dialect. contraction of it would.

two-up n. Chiefly Austral. a illegal gambling game in which two coins are tossed or spun.

two-way adj. **1.** moving, permitting movement, or operating in either of two opposite directions. **2.** involving two participants. **3.** involving reciprocal obligation or mutual action. **4.** (of a radio, telephone, etc.) allowing communications in two directions using both transmitting and receiving equipment.

two-way mirror n. a half-silvered sheet of glass that functions as a mirror when viewed from one side but is translucent from the other.

-ty[1] suffix of numerals. denoting a multiple of ten: sixty; seventy. [from OE -tig]

-ty[2] suffix forming nouns. indicating state, condition, or quality: cruelty. [from OF -te, -tet, from L -tās, -tāt-]

Tyan-Shan ('tjan'ʃan) n. transliteration of the Russian name for the **Tian Shan.**

Tyburn ('taɪbɜːn) n. (formerly) a place of execution in London, on the River Tyburn.

Tyche ('taɪkɪ) n. Greek myth. the goddess of fortune. Roman counterpart: **Fortuna.**

tychism ('taɪkɪzəm) n. Philosophy. the theory that chance is an objective reality at work in the universe. [from Gk tukhē chance]

tycoon (taɪ'kuːn) n. **1.** a businessman of great wealth and power. **2.** an archaic name for a **shogun.** [C19: from Japanese taikun, from Chinese ta great + chün ruler]

tyke or **tike** (taɪk) n. **1.** a dog, esp. a mongrel. **2.** Inf. a small or cheeky child. **3.** Brit. dialect. a rough ill-mannered person. **4.** Brit. sl. often offens. a person from Yorkshire. **5.** Austral. sl., offens. a Roman Catholic. [C14: from ON tík bitch]

Tyler ('taɪlə) n. **1. John.** 1790–1862, U.S. statesman; tenth president of the U.S. (1841–45). **2. Wat** (wɒt). died 1381, English leader of the Peasants' Revolt (1381).

tylopod ('taɪləʊˌpɒd) n. a mammal having padded, rather than hoofed, digits, such as camels and llamas. [C19: from NL, from Gk tulos knob or tulē cushion + -POD]

tympan ('tɪmpən) n. **1.** a membrane stretched over a frame or cylinder. **2.** Printing. packing interposed between the platen and the paper to be printed in order to provide an even impression. **3.** Archit. another name for **tympanum.** [OE timpana, from L; see TYMPANUM]

tympani ('tɪmpənɪ) pl. n. a variant spelling of **timpani.**

tympanic bone (tɪm'pænɪk) n. the part of the temporal bone that surrounds the auditory canal.

tympanic membrane n. the thin membrane separating the external ear from the middle ear. It transmits vibrations, produced by sound waves, to the cochlea. Nontechnical name: **eardrum.**

tympanites (ˌtɪmpə'naɪtiːz) n. distension of the abdomen caused by an accumulation of gas in the intestinal or peritoneal cavity. [C14: from LL, from Gk tumpanitēs concerning a drum, from tumpanon drum] —**tympanitic** (ˌtɪmpə'nɪtɪk) adj.

tympanitis (ˌtɪmpə'naɪtɪs) n. inflammation of the eardrum.

tympanum ('tɪmpənəm) n., pl. **-nums** or **-na** (-nə). **1. a.** the cavity of the middle ear. **b.** another name for **tympanic membrane. 2.** any diaphragm resembling that in the middle ear in function. **3.** Archit. **a.** the recessed space bounded by the cornices of a pediment, esp. one that is triangular in shape. **b.** the recessed space bounded by an arch and the lintel of a doorway or window below it. **4.** Music. a tympan or drum. **5.** a scoop wheel for raising water. [C17: from L, from Gk tumpanon drum] —**tympanic** (tɪm'pænɪk) adj.

Tyndale, Tindal, or **Tindale** ('tɪndəl) n. **William.** ?1492–1536, English Protestant and humanist, who translated the New Testament (1525), the Pentateuch (1530), and the Book of Jonah (1531) into English. He was burnt at the stake as a heretic.

Tyndall ('tɪndəl) n. **John.** 1820–93, Irish physicist, noted for his work on the radiation of heat by gases, the transmission of sound through the atmosphere, and the scattering of light.

Tyndall effect n. the phenomenon in which light is scattered by particles of matter in its path. [C19: after John TYNDALL]

Tyndareus (tɪn'dærɪəs) n. Greek myth. a Spartan king; the husband of Leda.

Tyne (taɪn) n. a river in N England, flowing east to the North Sea. Length: 48 km (30 miles).

Tyne and Wear n. (1974–86) a metropolitan county of NE England, comprising the districts of Newcastle-upon-Tyne, North Tyneside, Gateshead, South Tyneside, and Sunderland. Administrative centre: Newcastle-upon-Tyne. Pop.: 1 135 500 (1986 est.).

Tynemouth ('taɪnˌmaʊθ) n. a port in NE England, in Tyne and Wear at the mouth of the River Tyne: includes the port and industrial centre of North Shields; fishing, shiprepairing, and marine engineering. Pop.: 60 022 (1981).

Tyneside ('taɪnˌsaɪd) n. the conurbation on the banks of the Tyne from Newcastle to the coast.

Tynwald ('tɪnwəld, 'taɪn-) n. **the.** the Parliament of the Isle of Man. [C15: from ON thingvollr, from thing assembly + vollr field]

typ., typo., or **typog.** abbrev. for: **1.** typographer. **2.** typographic(al). **3.** typography.

typal ('taɪpəl) adj. a rare word for **typical.**

type (taɪp) n. **1.** a kind, class, or category, the constituents of which share similar characteristics. **2.** a subdivision of a particular class; sort: what type of shampoo do you use? **3.** the general form, plan, or design distinguishing a particular group. **4.** Inf. a person who typifies a particular quality: he's the administrative type. **5.** Inf. a person, esp. of a specified kind: he's a strange type. **6. a.** a small block of metal or more rarely wood bearing a letter or character in relief for use in printing. **b.** such pieces collectively. **7.** characters printed from type; print. **8.** Biol. **a.** the taxonomic group the characteristics of which are used for defining the next highest group. **b.** (as modifier): a type genus. **9.** See type specimen. **10.** the characteristic device on a coin. **11.** Chiefly Christian theol. a figure, episode, or symbolic factor resembling some future reality in such a way as to foreshadow or prefigure it. ~vb. **12.** to write (copy) on a typewriter. **13.** (tr.) to be a symbol of; typify. **14.** (tr.) to decide the type of. **15.** (tr.) Med. to determine the blood group of (a blood sample). **16.** (tr.) Chiefly Christian theol. to foreshadow or serve as a symbol of (some future reality). [C15: from L typus figure, from Gk tupos image, from tuptein to strike]

-type n. combining form. **1.** type or form: archetype. **2.** printing type or photographic process: collotype. [from L -typus, from Gk -typos, from tupos TYPE]

typecast ('taɪpˌkɑːst) vb. **-casting, -cast.** (tr.) to cast (an actor) in the same kind of role continually, esp. because of his physical appearance or previous success in such roles.

typeface ('taɪpˌfeɪs) n. another name for **face** (sense 14).

type founder n. a person who casts metallic printer's type. —**type foundry** n.

type metal n. Printing. an alloy of tin, lead, and antimony, from which type is cast.

typescript ('taɪp,skrɪpt) n. **1.** a typed copy of a document, etc. **2.** any typewritten material.

typeset ('taɪp,sɛt) vb. **-setting, -set.** (tr.) Printing. to set (textual matter) in type.

typesetter ('taɪp,sɛtə) n. **1.** a person who sets type; compositor. **2.** a typesetting machine.

type specimen n. Biol. the original specimen from which a description of a new species is made.

typewrite ('taɪp,raɪt) vb. **-writing, -wrote, -written.** to write by means of a typewriter; type. —'**type,writing** n.

typewriter ('taɪp,raɪtə) n. a keyboard machine for writing mechanically in characters resembling print.

typhlitis (tɪf'laɪtɪs) n. inflammation of the caecum. [C19: from NL, from Gk tuphlon the caecum, from tuphlos blind] —**typhlitic** (tɪf'lɪtɪk) adj.

Typhoeus (taɪ'fiːəs) n. Greek myth. the son of Gaea and Tartarus who had a hundred dragon heads, which spurted fire, and a bellowing many-tongued voice. He created the whirlwinds and fought with Zeus before the god hurled him beneath Mount Etna. —**Ty'phoean** adj.

typhoid ('taɪfɔɪd) Pathol. ~adj. also **typhoidal. 1.** resembling typhus. ~n. **2.** short for **typhoid fever.** [C19: from TYPHUS + -OID]

typhoid fever n. an acute infectious disease characterized by high fever, spots, abdominal pain, etc. It is caused by a bacillus ingested with food or water.

Typhon ('taɪfɒn) n. Greek myth. a monster and one of the whirlwinds: later confused with his father Typhoeus.

typhoon (taɪ'fuːn) n. a violent tropical storm or cyclone, esp. in the China Seas and W Pacific. [C16: from Chinese tai fung great wind; infl. by Gk tuphōn whirlwind] —**typhonic** (taɪ'fɒnɪk) adj.

typhus ('taɪfəs) n. any one of a group of acute infectious rickettsial diseases characterized by high fever, skin rash, and severe headache. Also called: **typhus fever.** [C18: from NL typhus, from Gk tuphos fever] —'**typhous** adj.

typical ('tɪpɪkəl) adj. **1.** being or serving as a representative example of a particular type; characteristic. **2.** considered to be an example of some undesirable trait: that is typical of you! **3.** of or relating to a representative specimen or type. **4.** conforming to a type. **5.** Biol. having most of the characteristics of a particular taxonomic group. [C17: from Med. L typicālis, from LL typicus figurative, from Gk tupikos, from tupos TYPE] —'**typically** adv. —'**typicalness** or ,typi'cality n.

typify ('tɪpɪ,faɪ) vb. **-fying, -fied.** (tr.) **1.** to be typical of; characterize. **2.** to symbolize or represent completely, by or as if by a type. [C17; from L typus TYPE] —,typifi'cation n.

typist ('taɪpɪst) n. a person who types, esp. for a living.

typo ('taɪpəʊ) n., pl. **-pos.** Inf. a typographical error. Also called (Brit.): **literal.**

typographer (taɪ'pɒɡrəfə) n. **1.** a person skilled in typography. **2.** a compositor.

typography (taɪ'pɒɡrəfɪ) n. **1.** the art, craft, or process of composing type and printing from it. **2.** the planning, selection, and setting of type for a printed work. —**typographical** (,taɪpə'ɡræfɪkəl) or ,typo'graphic adj. —,typo'graphically adv.

typology (taɪ'pɒlədʒɪ) n. **1.** the study of types in archaeology, biology, etc. **2.** Christian theol. the doctrine that symbols for events, figures, etc., in the New Testament can be found in the Old Testament. —**typological** (,taɪpə'lɒdʒɪkəl) adj. —**ty'pologist** n.

Tyr or **Tyrr** (tjʊə, tɪə) n. Norse myth. the god of war, son of Odin. Anglo-Saxon counterpart: **Tiu.**

tyrannical (tɪ'rænɪkəl) or **tyrannic** adj. characteristic of or relating to a tyrant or to tyranny; oppressive. —**ty'rannically** adv.

tyrannicide (tɪ'rænɪ,saɪd) n. **1.** the killing of a tyrant. **2.** a person who kills a tyrant.

tyrannize or **-ise** ('tɪrə,naɪz) vb. (when intr., often foll. by

over) to rule or exercise power (over) in a cruel or oppressive manner. —'**tyran,nizer** or **-iser** n.

tyrannosaur (tɪ'rænə,sɔː) or **tyrannosaurus** (tɪ,rænə'sɔːrəs) n. any of various large carnivorous two-footed dinosaurs common in North America in Upper Jurassic and Cretaceous times. [C19: from NL Tyrannosaurus, from Gk turannos tyrant + -SAUR]

tyranny ('tɪrənɪ) n., pl. **-nies. 1. a.** government by a tyrant; despotism. **b.** oppressive and unjust government by more than one person. **2.** arbitrary, unreasonable, or despotic behaviour or use of authority. **3.** a tyrannical act. [C14: from OF tyrannie, from Med. L tyrannia, from L tyrannus TYRANT] —'**tyrannous** adj.

tyrant ('taɪrənt) n. **1.** a person who governs oppressively, unjustly, and arbitrarily; despot. **2.** any person who exercises authority in a tyrannical manner. [C13: from OF tyrant, from L tyrannus, from Gk turannos]

tyre or U.S. **tire** ('taɪə) n. **1.** a rubber ring placed over the rim of a wheel of a road vehicle to provide traction and reduce road shocks, esp. a hollow inflated ring (**pneumatic tyre**) consisting of a reinforced outer casing enclosing an inner tube. **2.** a metal band or hoop attached to the rim of a wooden cartwheel. [C18: var. of C15 tire, prob. from archaic var. of ATTIRE]

Tyre or **Tyr** (taɪə) n. a port in S Lebanon, on the Mediterranean: founded about the 15th century B.C.; for centuries a major Phoenician seaport, famous for silks and its Tyrian-purple dye; now a small market town. Pop.: 14 000 (1980 est.). Arabic name: **Sur.** —**Tyrian** ('tɪrɪən) adj., n.

Tyrian purple n. **1.** a deep purple dye obtained from certain molluscs and highly prized in antiquity. **2. a.** a vivid purplish-red colour. **b.** (as adj.): a Tyrian-purple robe.

tyro or **tiro** ('taɪrəʊ) n., pl. **-ros.** a novice or beginner. [C17: from L tiro recruit]

Tyrol or **Tirol** (tɪ'rəʊl, 'tɪrəʊl; German ti'roːl) n. a mountainous province of W Austria: passed to the Hapsburgs in 1363; S part transferred to Italy in 1919. Capital: Innsbruck. Pop.: 605 774 (1986). Area: 12 648 sq. km (4883 sq. miles). —**Tyrolese** (,tɪrə'liːz) or ,Tyro'lean adj., n.

Tyrone (tɪ'rəʊn) n. a former county of W Northern Ireland, occupying almost a quarter of the total area of Northern Ireland.

tyrosinase (,taɪrəʊsɪ'neɪz) n. an enzyme that is a catalyst in the conversion of tyrosine to the pigment melanin.

tyrosine ('taɪrə,siːn, -sɪn, 'tɪrə-) n. an amino acid that is a precursor of the hormones adrenaline and thyroxine and of the pigment melanin. [C19: from Gk turos cheese + -INE²]

tyrothricin (,taɪrəʊ'θraɪsɪn) n. an antibiotic, obtained from a soil bacterium: applied locally for the treatment of ulcers and abscesses. [C20: from NL Tyrothrix (genus name), from Gk turos cheese + thrix hair]

Tyrr (tjʊə, tɪə) n. a variant spelling of **Tyr.**

Tyrrhenian Sea (tɪ'riːnɪən) n. an arm of the Mediterranean between Italy and the islands of Corsica, Sardinia, and Sicily.

Tyson ('taɪsən) n. **Mike.** born 1966, U.S. boxer. World heavyweight champion from 1986.

Tyumen (Russian tju'mjenj) n. a port in the central Soviet Union, on the Tura River: one of the oldest Russian towns in Siberia; industrial centre with nearby oil and natural gas reserves. Pop.: 456 000 (1987).

tzar (zɑː) n. a less common spelling of **tsar.**

tzatziki (tsæt'sɪkɪ) n. a Greek dip made from yoghurt, chopped cucumber, and mint. [C20: from Mod. Gk]

Tzekung ('tsɛ'kʊŋ) or **Tzu-kung** ('tsuː'kʊŋ) n. a variant transliteration of the Chinese name for **Zigong.**

tzetze fly ('tsɛtsɪ) n. a variant spelling of **tsetse fly.**

Tzigane (tsɪ'ɡɑːn, sɪ-) n. **a.** a Gypsy, esp. a Hungarian one. **b.** (as modifier): Tzigane music. [C19: via F from Hungarian czigány Gypsy, from ?]

Tzu-po ('tsuː'pəʊ) or **Tzepo** ('tsɛ'pəʊ) n. a variant transliteration of the Chinese name for **Zibo.**

U

u *or* **U** (juː) *n., pl.* **u's, U's,** *or* **Us.** **1.** the 21st letter and fifth vowel of the English alphabet. **2.** any of several speech sounds represented by this letter, as in *mute, cut,* or *minus.* **3. a.** something shaped like a U. **b.** (*in combination*): *a U-bolt.*

U *symbol for:* **1.** united. **2.** unionist. **3.** university. **4.** (in Britain) **a.** universal (used to describe a category of film certified as suitable for viewing by anyone). **b.** (*as modifier*): *a U certificate film.* **5.** *Chem.* uranium. *~adj.* **6.** *Brit. inf.* (esp. of language habits) characteristic of or appropriate to the upper class.

U. *abbrev. for:* **1.** *Maths.* union. **2.** unit. **3.** united. **4.** university. **5.** upper.

UAE *abbrev. for* United Arab Emirates.

UB40 *n.* (in Britain) **1.** a registration card issued by the Department of Employment to a person registering as unemployed **2.** *Inf.* a person registered as unemployed.

Ubangi (juːˈbæŋgɪ) *n.* a river in central Africa, flowing west and south, forming the border between Zaïre and the Central African Republic and the Republic of the Congo, into the River Congo. Length: (with the Uele) 2250 km (1400 miles). French name: **Oubangui.**

Ubangi-Shari *n.* a former name (until 1958) of the **Central African Republic.**

U-bend *n.* a U-shaped bend in a pipe that traps water in the lower part of the U and prevents the escape of noxious fumes; trap.

ubiety (juːˈbaɪɪtɪ) *n.* the condition of being in a particular place. [C17: from L *ubī* where + *-ety*, on the model of *society*]

ubiquitarian (juːˌbɪkwɪˈtɛərɪən) *n.* **1.** a member of the Lutheran church who holds that Christ is no more present in the elements of the Eucharist than elsewhere, as he is present in all places at all times. *~adj.* **2.** denoting or holding this belief. [C17: from L *ubīque* everywhere] —**u,biqui'tarian,ism** *n.*

ubiquitous (juːˈbɪkwɪtəs) *adj.* having or seeming to have the ability to be everywhere at once. [C14: from L *ubīque* everywhere, from *ubī* where] —**u'biquitously** *adv.* —**u'biquity** *n.*

U-boat *n.* a German submarine, esp. in World Wars I and II. [from G *U-Boot*, short for *Unterseeboot*, lit.: undersea boat]

u.c. *Printing. abbrev. for* upper case.

UCATT (in Britain) *abbrev. for* Union of Construction, Allied Trades and Technicians.

Ucayali (*Spanish* ukaˈjali) *n.* a river in E Peru, flowing north into the Marañón above Iquitos. Length: 1600 km (1000 miles).

UCCA (ˈʌkə) *n.* (in Britain) *acronym for* Universities Central Council on Admissions.

Uccello (*Italian* utˈtʃɛllo) *n.* **Paolo** (ˈpaːolo). 1397–1475, Florentine painter noted esp. for three paintings of *The Battle of San Romano, 1432* (1456–60).

UCW (in Britain) *abbrev. for* Union of Communication Workers.

UDA *abbrev. for* Ulster Defence Association.

Udaipur (uːˈdaɪpʊə, ˈuːdaɪˌpʊə) *n.* **1.** Also called: **Mewar.** a former state of NW India: became part of Rajasthan in 1947. **2.** a city in NW India, in S Rajasthan. Pop.: 232 588 (1981).

udal (ˈjuːdᵊl) *n. Law.* a form of freehold possession of land existing in northern Europe before the introduction of the feudal system and still used in Orkney and Shetland. [C16: Orkney & Shetland dialect, from ON *othal*]

Udall (ˈjuːdᵊl) *or* **Uvedale** (ˈjuːdᵊl, ˈjuːvˌdeɪl) *n.* **Nicholas.** ?1505–56, English dramatist, whose comedy *Ralph Roister Doister* (?1553), modelled on Terence and Plautus, is the earliest known English comedy.

UDC (in Britain) *abbrev. for* Urban District Council.

udder (ˈʌdə) *n.* the large baglike mammary gland of cows, sheep, etc., having two or more teats. [OE *ūder*]

UDF *abbrev. for* United Democratic Front: a federation of South African anti-apartheid groups.

UDI *abbrev. for* Unilateral Declaration of Independence.

Udine (*Italian* ˈuːdine) *n.* a city in NE Italy, in Friuli-Venezia Giulia region: partially damaged in an earthquake in 1976. Pop.: 101 000 (1984).

UDM (in Britain) *abbrev. for* Union of Democratic Mineworkers.

Udmurt Autonomous Soviet Socialist Republic (ˈʊdmʊət) *n.* an administrative division of the W central Soviet Union, in the basin of the middle Kama. Capital: Izhevsk. Pop.: 1 571 000 (1986). Area: 42 100 sq. km (16 250 sq. miles).

udometer (juːˈdɒmɪtə) *n.* another term for **rain gauge.** [C19: from F, from L *ūdus* damp]

UDR *abbrev. for* Ulster Defence Regiment.

UEFA (juːˈeɪfə, ˈjuːfə) *n. acronym for* Union of European Football Associations.

Uele (ˈweɪlə) *n.* a river in central Africa, rising near the border between Zaïre and Uganda and flowing west to join the Bomu River and form the Ubangi River. Length: about 1100 km (700 miles).

uey (ˈjuːɪ) *n., pl.* **ueys.** *Austral. sl.* a U-turn.

Ufa (*Russian* uˈfa) *n.* a city in the W central Soviet Union, capital of the Bashkir ASSR: university (1957). Pop.: 1 092 000 (1987).

Uffizi (juːˈfɪtsɪ) *n.* an art gallery in Florence; built by Giorgio Vasari in the 16th century and opened as a museum in 1765: contains chiefly Italian Renaissance paintings.

UFO (*sometimes* ˈjuːfəʊ) *abbrev. for* unidentified flying object.

ufology (ˌjuːˈfɒlədʒɪ) *n.* the study of UFOs. —**u'fologist** *n.*

Uganda (juːˈgændə) *n.* a republic in East Africa: British protectorate established in 1894–96; gained independence in 1962 and became a republic in 1967; a member of the Commonwealth. It consists mostly of a savanna plateau with part of Lake Victoria in the southeast and mountains in the southwest, reaching 5109 m (16 763 ft.) in the Ruwenzori Range. Official language: English; Swahili, Luganda, and Luo are also widely spoken. Religion: chiefly Christian. Currency: Ugandan shilling. Capital: Kampala. Pop.: 16 789 000 (1987 est.). Area: 235 886 sq. km (91 076 sq. miles). —**U'gandan** *adj., n.*

Ugaritic (ˌuːgəˈrɪtɪk) *n.* **1.** an extinct Semitic language of N Syria. *~adj.* **2.** of or relating to this language. [C19: after *Ugarit* (modern name: Ras Shamra), an ancient Syrian city-state]

UGC (in Britain) *abbrev. for* University Grants Committee.

ugh (ʊx, ʊh, ʌx) *interj.* an exclamation of disgust, annoyance, or dislike.

ugli (ˈʌglɪ) *n., pl.* **-lis** *or* **-lies.** a large juicy yellow-skinned citrus fruit of the West Indies: a cross between a tangerine, grapefruit, and orange. Also called: **ugli fruit.** [C20: prob. an alteration of UGLY, from its wrinkled skin]

uglify (ˈʌglɪˌfaɪ) *vb.* **-fying, -fied.** to make or become ugly or more ugly. —**uglifi'cation** *n.*

ugly (ˈʌglɪ) *adj.* **uglier, ugliest.** **1.** of unpleasant or unsightly appearance. **2.** repulsive or displeasing in any way: *war is ugly.* **3.** ominous or menacing: *an ugly situation.* **4.** bad-tempered or sullen: *an ugly mood.* [C13: from ON *uggligr* dreadful, from *ugga* fear] —**'uglily** *adv.* —**'ugliness** *n.*

ugly duckling *n.* a person or thing, initially ugly or unpromising, that changes into something beautiful or admirable. [from *The Ugly Duckling* by Hans Christian Andersen]

Ugrian (ˈuːgrɪən, ˈjuː-) *adj.* **1.** of or relating to a subdivision of the Turanian people, who include the Samoyeds and Magyars. *~n.* **2.** a member of this group of peoples. **3.** another word for **Ugric.** [C19: from ORussian *Ugre* Hungarians]

Ugric (ˈuːgrɪk, ˈjuː-) *n.* **1.** one of the two branches of the Finno-Ugric family of languages, including Hungarian and some languages of NW Siberia. *~adj.* **2.** of or relating to this group of languages or their speakers.

UHF *Radio. abbrev. for* ultrahigh frequency.

uh-huh *sentence substitute. Inf.* a less emphatic variant of **yes**.

uhlan ('u:lɑ:n) *n. History.* a member of a body of lancers first employed in the Polish army and later in W European armies. [C18: via G from Polish *ulan*, from Turkish *ōlan* young man]

Uhland (*German* 'u:lant) *n.* **Johann Ludwig** (jo'han 'lu:tvɪç). 1787–1862, German romantic poet, esp. of lyrics and ballads.

UHT *abbrev. for* ultra-heat-treated (milk or cream).

uhuru (u:'hu:ru:) *n.* (esp. in E Africa) **1.** national independence. **2.** freedom. [C20: from Swahili]

uillean pipes ('u:lɪən) *pl. n.* bagpipes developed in Ireland and operated by squeezing bellows under the arm. Also called: **Irish pipes, union pipes.** [C19: Irish *píob uilleann*, from *píob* pipe + *uilleann* genetive sing. of *uille* elbow]

Uinta Mountains (ju'ɪntə) *pl. n.* a mountain range in NE Utah: part of the Rocky Mountains. Highest peak: Kings Peak, 4123 m (13 528 ft.).

uitlander ('eɪt,landə, -,læn-) *n.* (*sometimes cap.*) *S. African.* a foreigner. [C19: Afrik.: outlander]

Ujiji (u:'dʒi:dʒi:) *n.* a town in W Tanzania, on Lake Tanganyika: a former slave and ivory centre; the place where Stanley found Livingstone in 1871. Pop.: 21 369 (1967).

Ujjain (u:'dʒeɪn) *n.* a city in W central India, in Madhya Pradesh: one of the seven sacred cities of the Hindus; a major agricultural trade centre. Pop.: 282 000 (1981).

Ujung Pandang ('u:dʒʊŋ pæn'dæŋ) *n.* a port in central Indonesia, on SW Sulawesi: an important native port before Portuguese (16th century) and Dutch (17th century) control; capital of Dutch East Indonesia (1946–49); a major Indonesian distribution and transshipment port. Pop.: 709 000 (1980). Also called: **Makasar, Makassar, Macassar.**

UK *abbrev. for* United Kingdom.

ukase (ju:'keɪz) *n.* **1.** (in imperial Russia) an edict of the tsar. **2.** a rare word for **edict.** [C18: from Russian *ukaz*, from *ukazat* to command]

Ukrainian (ju:'kreɪnɪən) *adj.* **1.** of or relating to the Ukraine, its people, or their language. ~*n.* **2.** the official language of the Ukrainian SSR: an East Slavonic language closely related to Russian. **3.** a native or inhabitant of the Ukraine.

Ukrainian Soviet Socialist Republic *n.* an administrative division of the SE Soviet Union, on the Black Sea and the Sea of Azov: the third largest constituent republic of the Soviet Union and one of the four original republics that formed the USSR in 1922; consists chiefly of lowlands; economy based on rich agriculture and mineral resources (chief Soviet producer of coal) and on the major heavy industries of the Donets Basin. Capital: Kiev. Pop.: 51 201 000 (1987). Area: 603 700 sq. km (231 990 sq. miles). Also called: **the Ukraine.**

ukulele *or* **ukelele** (ˌju:kə'leɪlɪ) *n.* a small four-stringed guitar, esp. of Hawaii. [C19: from Hawaiian, lit.: jumping flea]

Ulan Bator (ʊ'lɑ:n 'bɑ:tɔ:) *n.* the capital of the Mongolian People's Republic, in the N central part: developed in the mid-17th century around the Da Khure monastery, residence until 1924 of successive "living Buddhas" (third in rank of Buddhist-Lamaist leaders), and main junction of caravan routes across Mongolia; university (1942); industrial and commercial centre. Pop.: 479 500 (1984). Former name (until 1924): **Urga.** Chinese name: **Kulun.**

Ulan-Ude (ʊ'lɑ:nʊ'dɛ) *n.* an industrial city in the SE Soviet Union, capital of the Buryat ASSR: an important rail junction. Pop.: 351 000 (1987). Former name (until 1934): **Verkhne-Udinsk.**

Ulbricht (*German* 'ʊlbrɪçt) *n.* **Walter** ('valtər). 1893–1973, East German statesman; largely responsible for the establishment and development of East German communism.

ulcer ('ʌlsə) *n.* **1.** a disintegration of the surface of the skin or a mucous membrane resulting in an open sore that heals very slowly. **2.** a source or element of corruption or evil. [C14: from L *ulcus*]

ulcerate ('ʌlsə,reɪt) *vb.* to make or become ulcerous. —ˌulce'ration *n.* —'ulcerative *adj.*

ulcerous ('ʌlsərəs) *adj.* **1.** relating to or characterized by ulcers. **2.** being or having a corrupting influence. —'ulcerously *adv.*

-ule *suffix forming nouns.* indicating smallness: *globule.* [from L *-ulus*, dim. suffix]

Uleåborg ('u:lɪo,bɔrjə) *n.* the Swedish name for **Oulu.**

ulema ('u:lɪmə) *n.* **1.** a body of Muslim scholars or religious leaders. **2.** a member of this body. [C17: from Ar. *ulamā* scholars, from *alama* to know]

-ulent *suffix forming adjectives.* abundant or full of: *fraudulent.* [from L *-ulentus*]

Ulfilas ('ʊlfɪ,læs), **Ulfila** ('ʊlfɪlə), *or* **Wulfila** *n.* ?311–?382 A.D., Christian bishop of the Goths who translated the Bible from Greek into Gothic.

ullage ('ʌlɪdʒ) *n.* **1.** the volume by which a liquid container falls short of being full. **2. a.** the quantity of liquid lost from a container due to leakage or evaporation. **b.** (in customs terminology) the amount of liquid remaining in a container after such loss. [C15: from OF *ouillage* filling of a cask, from *ouil* eye, from L *oculus* eye]

Ullswater ('ʌlz,wɔ:tə) *n.* a lake in NW England, in Cumbria in the Lake District. Length: 12 km (7.5 miles).

Ulm (*German* ʊlm) *n.* an industrial city in S West Germany, in Baden-Württemberg on the Danube: a free imperial city (1155–1802). Pop.: 100 400 (1986).

ulna ('ʌlnə) *n., pl.* **-nae** (-ni:) *or* **-nas. 1.** the inner and longer of the two bones of the human forearm. **2.** the corresponding bone in other vertebrates. [C16: from L: elbow] —'ulnar *adj.*

ulnar nerve *n.* a nerve situated along the inner side of the arm and passing close to the surface of the skin near the elbow.

ulotrichous (ju:'lɒtrɪkəs) *adj.* having woolly or curly hair. [C19: from NL *Ulotrichī* (classification applied to humans having this type of hair), from Gk *oulothrix*, from *oulos* curly + *thrix* hair]

Ulpian ('ʌlpɪən) *n.* Latin name *Domitius Ulpianus.* died ?228 A.D., Roman jurist, born in Phoenicia.

ulster ('ʌlstə) *n.* a man's heavy double-breasted overcoat with a belt or half-belt. [C19: from ULSTER]

Ulster ('ʌlstə) *n.* **1.** a former kingdom and province of North Ireland: passed to the English Crown in 1461; confiscated land given to English and Scottish Protestant settlers in the 17th century, giving rise to serious long-term conflict; partitioned in 1921 to form the six counties of Northern Ireland and the Ulster province of the Republic of Ireland. **2.** the northernmost province of Ireland, consisting of three counties: Cavan, Monaghan, and Donegal. Pop.: 230 159 (1981). Area: 8013 sq. km (3094 sq. miles). **3.** an informal name for **Northern Ireland.**

Ulster Defence Association *n.* (in Northern Ireland) a Loyalist paramilitary organization. Abbrev.: **UDA.**

Ulsterman ('ʌlstəmən) *n., pl.* **-men.** a native or inhabitant of Ulster. —'Ulster,woman *fem. n.*

ult. *abbrev. for:* **1.** ultimate(ly). **2.** ultimo.

ulterior (ʌl'tɪərɪə) *adj.* **1.** lying beneath or beyond what is revealed or supposed: *ulterior motives.* **2.** succeeding, subsequent, or later. **3.** lying beyond a certain line or point. [C17: from L: further, from *ulter* beyond] —ul'teriorly *adv.*

ultima ('ʌltɪmə) *n.* the final syllable of a word. [from L: the last]

ultimate ('ʌltɪmɪt) *adj.* **1.** conclusive in a series or process; final: *an ultimate question.* **2.** the highest or most significant: *the ultimate goal.* **3.** elemental, fundamental, or essential. ~*n.* **4.** the most significant, highest, or greatest thing. [C17: from LL *ultimāre* to come to an end, from L *ultimus* last, from *ulter* distant] —'ultimately *adv.* —'ultimateness *n.*

ultima Thule ('θju:lɪ) *n.* **1.** a region believed by ancient geographers to be the northernmost land. **2.** any distant or unknown region. **3.** a remote goal or aim. [L: the most distant Thule]

ultimatum (ˌʌltɪ'meɪtəm) *n., pl.* **-tums** *or* **-ta** (-tə). **1.** a final communication by a party setting forth conditions on which it insists, as during negotiations on some topic. **2.** any final or peremptory demand or proposal. [C18: from NL, neuter of *ultimatus* ULTIMATE]

ultimo ('ʌltɪ,məʊ) *adv. Now rare except when abbreviated in formal correspondence.* in or during the previous month: *a letter of the 7th ultimo.* Abbrev.: **ult.** [C16: from L *ultimō* on the last]

ultimogeniture (ˌʌltɪməʊ'dʒɛnɪtʃə) *n. Law.* a principle of inheritance whereby the youngest son succeeds to the estate of his ancestor. [C19: *ultimo-* from L *ultimus* last + LL *genitūra* a birth]

ultra ('ʌltrə) *adj.* **1.** extreme or immoderate, esp. in beliefs or opinions. ~*n.* **2.** an extremist. [C19: from L: beyond, from *ulter* distant]

ultra- *prefix.* **1.** beyond or surpassing a specified extent, range, or limit: *ultramicroscopic.* **2.** extreme or extremely: *ultramodern.* [from L *ultrā* beyond]

ultracentrifuge (ˌʌltrə'sɛntrɪˌfjuːdʒ) *n. Chem.* a high-speed centrifuge used to separate colloidal solutions.

ultraconservative (ˌʌltrəkən'sɜːvətɪv) *adj.* **1.** highly reactionary. ~*n.* **2.** a reactionary person.

ultrafiche ('ʌltrəˌfiːʃ) *n.* a sheet of film, usually the size of a filing card, that is similar to a microfiche but has a much larger number of microcopies. [C20: from ULTRA- + F *fiche* small card]

ultrahigh frequency ('ʌltrəˌhaɪ) *n.* a radio-frequency band or radio frequency lying between 3000 and 300 megahertz. Abbrev.: **UHF.**

ultraism ('ʌltrəˌɪzəm) *n.* extreme philosophy, belief, or action. —'**ultraist** *n., adj.*

ultramarine (ˌʌltrəmə'riːn) *n.* **1.** a blue pigment obtained by powdering natural lapis lazuli or made synthetically: used in paints, printing ink, plastics, etc. **2.** a vivid blue colour. ~*adj.* **3.** of the colour ultramarine. **4.** from across the seas. [C17: from Med. L *ultramarinus,* from *ultrā* beyond + *mare* sea; so called because the lapis lazuli from which the pigment was made was imported from Asia]

ultramicroscope (ˌʌltrə'maɪkrəˌskəʊp) *n.* a microscope used for studying colloids, in which the sample is illuminated from the side and colloidal particles are seen as bright points on a dark background.

ultramicroscopic (ˌʌltrəˌmaɪkrə'skɒpɪk) *adj.* **1.** too small to be seen with an optical microscope. **2.** of or relating to an ultramicroscope.

ultramodern (ˌʌltrə'mɒdən) *adj.* extremely modern. —ˌultra'**modernism** *n.* —ˌultra'**modernist** *n.* —ˌultra,**modern'istic** *adj.*

ultramontane (ˌʌltrəmɒn'teɪn) *adj.* **1.** on the other side of the mountains, esp. the Alps, from the speaker or writer. **2.** of or relating to a movement in the Roman Catholic Church which favours the centralized authority and influence of the pope as opposed to local independence. ~*n.* **3.** a person from beyond the mountains, esp. the Alps. **4.** a member of the ultramontane party of the Roman Catholic Church.

ultramundane (ˌʌltrə'mʌndeɪn) *adj.* extending beyond the world, this life, or the universe.

ultranationalism (ˌʌltrə'næʃnəˌlɪzəm) *n.* extreme devotion to one's own nation. —ˌultra'**national** *adj.* —ˌultra'**nationalist** *adj., n.*

ultrashort (ˌʌltrə'ʃɔːt) *adj.* (of a radio wave) having a wavelength shorter than 10 metres.

ultrasonic (ˌʌltrə'sɒnɪk) *adj.* of, concerned with, or producing waves with the same nature as sound waves but frequencies above audio frequencies. —ˌultra'**sonically** *adv.*

ultrasonics (ˌʌltrə'sɒnɪks) *n. (functioning as sing.)* the branch of physics concerned with ultrasonic waves. Also called: **supersonics.**

ultrasound (ˌʌltrə'saʊnd) *n.* ultrasonic waves at frequencies above the audible range (above about 20 kHz), used in cleaning metallic parts, echo sounding, medical diagnosis and therapy, etc.

ultrasound scan *n.* an examination of an internal bodily structure by the use of ultrasonic waves, esp. for the diagnosis of abnormality in a fetus.

ultrastructure ('ʌltrəˌstrʌktʃə) *n.* the minute structure of an organ, tissue, or cell, as revealed by microscopy.

ultraviolet (ˌʌltrə'vaɪəlɪt) *n.* **1.** the part of the electromagnetic spectrum with wavelengths shorter than light but longer than x-rays; in the range 0.4×10^{-6} and 1×10^{-8} metres. ~*adj.* **2.** of, relating to, or consisting of radiation lying in the ultraviolet: *ultraviolet radiation.*

ultra vires ('vaɪriːz) *adv., adj. (predicative) Law.* beyond the legal power of a person, corporation, agent, etc. [L, lit.: beyond strength]

ultravirus (ˌʌltrə'vaɪrəs) *n.* a virus small enough to pass through the panes of the finest filter.

ululate ('juːljʊˌleɪt) *vb. (intr.)* to howl or wail, as with grief. [C17: from L *ululāre* to howl, from *ulula* screech owl] —'**ululant** *adj.* —ˌulu'**lation** *n.*

Ulyanovsk *(Russian* ulʲɪ'janəfsk) *n.* a city in the W central Soviet Union, on the River Volga: birthplace of Lenin (V. I.

Ulyanov). Pop.: 589 000 (1987). Former name (until 1924): **Simbirsk.**

Ulysses ('juːlɪˌsiːz, juː'lɪsiːz) *n.* the Latin name of **Odysseus.**

Umayyad (uː'maɪjæd) *n.* a variant spelling of **Omayyad.**

umbel ('ʌmbəl) *n.* a racemose inflorescence, characteristic of umbelliferous plants, in which the flowers arise from the same point in the main stem and have stalks of the same length, to give a cluster with the youngest flowers at the centre. [C16: from L *umbella* a sunshade, from *umbra* shade] —**umbellate** ('ʌmbɪlɪt, -ˌleɪt) *or* **umbellar** (ʌm'bɛlə) *adj.* —**umbellule** (ʌm'bɛljuːl) *n.*

umbelliferous (ˌʌmbɪ'lɪfərəs) *adj.* of or belonging to a family of herbaceous plants and shrubs, typically having hollow stems, divided or compound leaves, and flowers in umbels: includes fennel, parsley, carrot, and parsnip. [C17: from NL, from L *umbella* sunshade + *ferre* to bear] —**um'belliferer** *n.*

umber ('ʌmbə) *n.* **1.** any of various natural brown earths containing ferric oxide together with lime and oxides of aluminium, manganese, and silicon. **2.** any of the dark brown to greenish-brown colours produced by this pigment. **3.** *Obs.* shade. ~*adj.* **4.** of, relating to, or stained with umber. [C16: from F *(terre d')ombre* or It. *(terra di) ombra* shadow (earth), from L *umbra* shade]

Umberto I *(Italian* um'bɛrto) *n.* 1844–1900, king of Italy (1878–1900); son of Victor Emmanuel II: assassinated at Monza.

umbilical (ʌm'bɪlɪkəl, ˌʌmbɪ'laɪkəl) *adj.* **1.** of, relating to, or resembling the umbilicus or the umbilical cord. **2.** in the region of the umbilicus: *an umbilical hernia.*

umbilical cord *n.* **1.** the long flexible tubelike structure connecting a fetus with the placenta. **2.** any flexible cord, tube, or cable, as between an astronaut walking in space and his spacecraft.

umbilicate (ʌm'bɪlɪkɪt, -ˌkeɪt) *adj.* **1.** having an umbilicus. **2.** having a central depression: *an umbilicate leaf.* **3.** shaped like a navel, as some bacterial colonies. —um,bili'**cation** *n.*

umbilicus (ʌm'bɪlɪkəs, ˌʌmbɪ'laɪkəs) *n., pl.* **-bilici** (-'bɪlɪˌsaɪ, -bɪ'laɪsaɪ). **1.** *Biol.* a hollow or navel-like structure, such as the cavity at the base of a gastropod shell. **2.** *Anat.* a technical name for the **navel.** [C18: from L: navel, centre]

umble pie ('ʌmbəl) *n.* See **humble pie** (sense 1).

umbles ('ʌmbəlz) *pl. n.* See **numbles.**

umbo ('ʌmbəʊ) *n., pl.* **umbones** (ʌm'bəʊniːz) *or* **umbos.** **1.** *Bot., anat.* a small hump, prominence, or convex area, as in certain mushrooms, bivalve molluscs, and the outer surface of the eardrum. **2.** a large projecting central boss on a shield, esp. on a Saxon shield. [C18: from L: projecting piece] —**umbonate** ('ʌmbənɪt, -ˌneɪt), *or* **umbonal** ('ʌmbənəl), *or* **umbonic** (ʌm'bɒnɪk) *adj.*

umbra ('ʌmbrə) *n., pl.* **-brae** (-briː) *or* **-bras. 1.** a region of complete shadow resulting from the obstruction of light by an opaque object, esp. the shadow cast by the moon onto the earth during a solar eclipse. **2.** the darker inner region of a sunspot. [C16: from L: shade] —'**umbral** *adj.*

umbrage ('ʌmbrɪdʒ) *n.* **1.** displeasure or resentment; offence (in **give** *or* **take umbrage). 2.** the foliage of trees, considered as providing shade. **3.** *Rare.* shadow or shade. [C15: from OF, from L *umbrāticus* relating to shade, from *umbra* shade]

umbrageous (ʌm'breɪdʒəs) *adj.* **1.** shady or shading. **2.** *Rare.* easily offended.

umbrella (ʌm'brɛlə) *n.* **1.** a portable device used for protection against rain, snow, etc., and consisting of a light canopy supported on a collapsible metal frame mounted on a central rod. **2.** the flattened cone-shaped body of a jellyfish. **3.** a protective shield or screen, esp. of aircraft or gunfire. **4.** anything that has the effect of a protective screen, general cover, or organizing agency. [C17: from It. *ombrella,* dim. of *ombra* shade; see UMBRA] —um'**brella-like** *adj.*

umbrella pine *n.* another name for **stone pine.**

umbrella stand *n.* an upright rack or stand for umbrellas.

umbrella tree *n.* **1.** a North American magnolia having long leaves clustered into an umbrella formation at the ends of the branches and having unpleasant-smelling white flowers. **2.** Also called: **umbrella bush.** any of various trees or shrubs having umbrella-shaped leaves or growing in an umbrella-like cluster.

Umbria ('ʌmbrɪə; *Italian* 'umbrja) *n.* a mountainous region of central Italy, in the valley of the Tiber. Pop.: 817 852 (1985 est.). Area: 8456 sq. km (3265 sq. miles).

Umbrian ('ʌmbrɪən) *adj.* **1.** of or relating to Umbria, its inhabitants, or the ancient language once spoken there. **2.** of or relating to a Renaissance school of painting that included Raphael. ~*n.* **3.** a native or inhabitant of Umbria. **4.** an extinct language of ancient S Italy.

umfazi (,um'fɑːʒɪ) *n. S. African.* a Black married woman. [from Bantu]

umiak *or* **oomiak** ('uːmɪ,æk) *n.* a large open boat made of stretched skins, used by Eskimos. [C18: from Eskimo: boat for the use of women]

umlaut ('umlaut) *n.* **1.** the mark (¨) placed over a vowel in some languages, such as German, indicating modification in the quality of the vowel. **2.** (esp. in Germanic languages) the change of a vowel within a word brought about by the assimilating influence of a vowel or semivowel in a preceding or following syllable. [C19: G, from *um* around (in the sense of changing places) + *Laut* sound]

umlungu (,um'luŋgu) *n. S. African.* a White man: used esp. as a term of address. [from Bantu]

umpire ('ʌmpaɪə) *n.* **1.** an official who rules on the playing of a game, as in cricket. **2.** a person who rules on or judges disputes between contesting parties. ~*vb.* **3.** to act as umpire in (a game, dispute, or controversy). [C15: by mistaken division from *a noumpere*, from OF *nomper* not one of a pair, from *nom-, non-* not + *per* equal]

umpteen (,ʌmp'tiːn) *determiner. Inf.* **a.** very many: *umpteen things to do.* **b.** (*as pronoun*): *umpteen of them came.* [C20: from *umpty* a great deal (?from *-enty* as in *twenty*) + *-teen* ten] —**ump'teenth** *n., adj.*

Umtali (um'tɑːlɪ) *n.* the former name (until 1982) of **Mutare.**

UN *abbrev. for* United Nations.

un-1 *prefix. (freely used with adjectives, participles, and their derivative adverbs and nouns: less frequently used with certain other nouns)* not; contrary to; opposite of: *uncertain; untidiness; unbelief; untruth.* [from OE *on-, un-*]

un-2 *prefix forming verbs.* **1.** denoting reversal of an action or state: *uncover; untangle.* **2.** denoting removal from, release, or deprivation: *unharness; unthrone.* **3.** (intensifier): *unloose.* [from OE *un-, on-*]

'un *or* **un** (ən) *pron.* a spelling of **one** intended to reflect a dialectal or informal pronunciation: *that's a big 'un.*

unable (ʌn'eɪbəl) *adj. (postpositive;* foll. by *to)* lacking the necessary power, ability, or authority (to do something); not able.

unaccountable (,ʌnə'kauntəbəl) *adj.* **1.** allowing of no explanation; inexplicable. **2.** extraordinary: *an unaccountable fear of heights.* **3.** not accountable or answerable to. —**unac,counta'bility** *n.* —**unac'countably** *adv.*

unaccustomed (,ʌnə'kʌstəmd) *adj.* **1.** (foll. by *to*) not used (to): *unaccustomed to pain.* **2.** not familiar. —**unac'customedness** *n.*

una corda ('uːnə 'kɔːdə) *adj., adv. Music.* (of the piano) to be played with the soft pedal depressed. [It., lit.: one string; the pedal moves the mechanism so that only one string of the three tuned to each note is struck by the hammer]

unadopted (,ʌnə'dɒptɪd) *adj.* **1.** (of a child) not adopted. **2.** *Brit.* (of a road, etc.) not maintained by a local authority.

unadvised (,ʌnəd'vaɪzd) *adj.* **1.** rash or unwise. **2.** not having received advice. —**unadvisedly** (,ʌnəd'vaɪzɪdlɪ) *adv.* —**unad'visedness** *n.*

unaffected1 (,ʌnə'fɛktɪd) *adj.* unpretentious, natural, or sincere. —**unaf'fectedly** *adv.* —**,unaf'fectedness** *n.*

unaffected2 (,ʌnə'fɛktɪd) *adj.* not affected.

Unalaska Island (,ʌnə'læskə) *n.* a large volcanic island in SW Alaska, in the Aleutian Islands. Length: 120 km (75 miles). Greatest width: about 40 km (25 miles).

unalienable (ʌn'eɪljənəbəl) *adj. Law.* a variant of **inalienable.**

un-American *adj.* **1.** not in accordance with the aims, ideals, customs, etc., of the U.S. **2.** against the interests of the U.S. —**un-A'mericanism** *n.*

Unamuno (*Spanish* una'muno) *n.* **Miguel de** (mi'γɛl de). 1864–1936, Spanish philosopher and writer.

unanimous (juː'nænɪməs) *adj.* **1.** in complete agreement. **2.** characterized by complete agreement: *a unanimous decision.* [C17: from L, from *ūnus* one + *animus* mind] —**u'nanimously** *adv.* —**unanimity** (,juːnə'nɪmɪtɪ) *n.*

unapproachable (,ʌnə'prəutʃəbəl) *adj.* **1.** discouraging intimacy, friendliness, etc.; aloof. **2.** inaccessible. **3.** not to be rivalled. —**,unap'proachableness** *n.* —**,unap'proachably** *adv.*

unappropriated (,ʌnə'prəupri,eɪtɪd) *adj.* **1.** not set aside for specific use. **2.** *Accounting.* designating that portion of the profits of a business enterprise that is retained in the business and not withdrawn by the proprietor. **3.** (of property) not having been taken into any person's possession or control.

unapt (ʌn'æpt) *adj.* **1.** (*usually postpositive;* often foll. by *for*) not suitable or qualified; unfitted. **2.** mentally slow. **3.** (*postpositive; may take an infinitive*) not disposed or likely (to). —**un'aptly** *adv.* —**un'aptness** *n.*

unarm (ʌn'ɑːm) *vb.* a less common word for **disarm.**

unarmed (ʌn'ɑːmd) *adj.* **1.** without weapons. **2.** (of animals and plants) having no claws, prickles, spines, thorns, or similar structures.

unassailable (,ʌnə'seɪləbəl) *adj.* **1.** not able to be attacked. **2.** undeniable or irrefutable. —**,unas'sailableness** *n.* —**,unas'sailably** *adv.*

unassuming (,ʌnə'sjuːmɪŋ) *adj.* modest or unpretentious. —**,unas'sumingly** *adv.* —**,unas'sumingness** *n.*

unattached (,ʌnə'tætʃt) *adj.* **1.** not connected with any specific thing, body, group, etc. **2.** not engaged or married. **3.** (of property) not seized or held as security.

unavailing (,ʌnə'veɪlɪŋ) *adj.* useless or futile. —**,una'vailingly** *adv.*

unavoidable (,ʌnə'vɔɪdəbəl) *adj.* **1.** unable to be avoided. **2.** *Law.* not capable of being declared null and void. —**,una,voida'bility** *or* ,una'voidableness *n.* —**,una'voidably** *adv.*

unaware (,ʌnə'wɛə) *adj.* **1.** (*postpositive*) not aware or conscious (of): *unaware of the danger he ran across the road.* ~*adv.* **2.** a variant of **unawares.** —**,una'wareness** *n.*

▷**Usage.** Careful users of English distinguish between the adjective *unaware* (to be ignorant of) and the adverb *unawares* (by surprise): *they were unaware of the danger; the danger caught them unawares.*

,una'bashed *adj.*	,una'dorned *adj.*	un'ampli,fied *adj.*	,una'shamed *adj.*
,una'bated *adj.*	,una'dulter,ated *adj.*	,una'mused *adj.*	un'asked *adj.*
,unab'brevi,ated *adj.*	,unad'venturous *adj.*	,unan'nounced *adj.*	,una'spi,rated *adj.*
,una'bridged *adj.*	un'adver,tised *adj.*	un'answerable *adj.*	,unas'piring *adj.*
,unac'cented *adj.*	,unad'visable *adj.*	un'answered *adj.*	,unas'sertive *adj.*
,unac'ceptable *adj.*	,unaf'fili,ated *adj.*	,unap'parent *adj.*	,unas'sisted *adj.*
,unac'commo,dating *adj.*	,una'fraid *adj.*	,unap'pealable *adj.*	,unas'sorted *adj.*
,unac'companied *adj.*	un'aided *adj.*	,unap'pealing *adj.*	,unas'sumed *adj.*
,unac'complished *adj.*	,una'ligned *adj.*	un'appe,tizing *or* -,tising	,una'toned *adj.*
,unac'counted *adj.*	,unal'layed *adj.*	*adj.*	,unat'tainable *adj.*
,unac'counted-for *adj.*	,unal'levi,ated *adj.*	,unap'plied *adj.*	,unat'tended *adj.*
,unac'knowledged *adj.*	,unal'lied *adj.*	,unap'preci,ated *adj.*	,unat'tractive *adj.*
,una'quainted *adj.*	,unal'lowable *adj.*	,unap'proved *adj.*	,unaus'picious *adj.*
un'acted *adj.*	,unal'loyed *adj.*	un'arguable *adj.*	,unau'thentic *adj.*
un'actionable *adj.*	un'alterable *adj.*	un'arguably *adv.*	un'author,ized *or* -,ised
,una'daptable *adj.*	,unam'biguous *adj.*	,unar'ticu,lated *adj.*	*adj.*
,una'dapted *adj.*	un'amiable *adj.*	,unar'tistic *adj.*	,una'vailable *adj.*
,unad'dressed *adj.*			

unawares (ˌʌnəˈwɛəz) *adv.* **1.** without prior warning or plan: *she caught him unawares.* **2.** without knowing: *he lost it unawares.*
▷ *Usage.* See at **unaware.**

unbacked (ʌnˈbækt) *adj.* **1.** (of a book, chair, etc.) not having a back. **2.** bereft of support, esp. on a financial basis. **3.** not supported by bets.

unbalance (ʌnˈbæləns) *vb.* (*tr.*) **1.** to upset the equilibrium or balance of. **2.** to disturb the mental stability of (a person or his mind). ~*n.* **3.** imbalance or instability.

unbalanced (ʌnˈbælənst) *adj.* **1.** lacking balance. **2.** irrational or unsound; erratic. **3.** mentally disordered or deranged. **4.** biased; one-sided: *unbalanced reporting.* **5.** (in double-entry book-keeping) not having total debit balances equal to total credit balances.

unbar (ʌnˈbɑː) *vb.* **-barring, -barred.** (*tr.*) **1.** to take away a bar or bars from. **2.** to unfasten bars, locks, etc., from (a door); open.

unbearable (ʌnˈbɛərəbəl) *adj.* not able to be borne or endured. —**un'bearably** *adv.*

unbeatable (ʌnˈbiːtəbəl) *adj.* unable to be defeated or outclassed; surpassingly excellent.

unbeaten (ʌnˈbiːtən) *adj.* **1.** having suffered no defeat. **2.** not worn down; untrodden. **3.** not mixed or stirred by beating: *unbeaten eggs.*

unbecoming (ˌʌnbɪˈkʌmɪŋ) *adj.* **1.** unsuitable or inappropriate, esp. through being unattractive: *an unbecoming hat.* **2.** (when *postpositive,* usually foll. by *of* or an object) not proper or seemly (for): *manners unbecoming a lady.* —, **unbe'comingly** *adv.* —, **unbe'comingness** *n.*

unbeknown (ˌʌnbɪˈnəʊn) *adv.* (*sentence modifier;* foll. by *to*) without the knowledge of (a person): *unbeknown to him she had left the country.* Also (esp. Brit.): **unbeknownst.** [C17: from arch. *beknown* known]

unbelief (ˌʌnbɪˈliːf) *n.* disbelief or rejection of belief.

unbelievable (ˌʌnbɪˈliːvəbəl) *adj.* unable to be believed; incredible. —, **unbe,lieva'bility** *n.* —, **unbe'lievably** *adv.*

unbeliever (ˌʌnbɪˈliːvə) *n.* a person who does not believe, esp. in religious matters.

unbelieving (ˌʌnbɪˈliːvɪŋ) *adj.* **1.** not believing; sceptical. **2.** proceeding from or characterized by scepticism. —, **unbe'lievingly** *adv.*

unbend (ʌnˈbend) *vb.* **-bending, -bent. 1.** to release or be released from the restraints of formality and ceremony. **2.** *Inf.* to relax (the mind) or (of the mind) to become relaxed. **3.** to straighten out from an originally bent shape. **4.** (*tr.*) *Naut.* **a.** to remove (a sail) from a stay, mast, etc. **b.** to untie (a rope, etc.) or cast (a cable) loose.

unbending (ʌnˈbendɪŋ) *adj.* **1.** rigid or inflexible. **2.** characterized by sternness or severity: *an unbending rule.* —**un'bendingly** *adv.* —**un'bendingness** *n.*

unbent (ʌnˈbent) *vb.* **1.** the past tense and past participle of **unbend.** ~*adj.* **2.** not bent or bowed. **3.** not compelled to give way by force.

unbidden (ʌnˈbɪdən) *adj.* **1.** not ordered or commanded; voluntary or spontaneous. **2.** not invited or asked.

unbind (ʌnˈbaɪnd) *vb.* **-binding, -bound.** (*tr.*) **1.** to set free from restraining bonds or chains. **2.** to unfasten or make loose (a bond, etc.).

unblessed (ʌnˈblest) *adj.* **1.** deprived of blessing. **2.** cursed or evil. **3.** unhappy or wretched. —**unblessedness** (ʌnˈblesɪdnɪs) *n.*

unblushing (ʌnˈblʌʃɪŋ) *adj.* immodest or shameless. —**un'blushingly** *adv.*

unbolt (ʌnˈbəʊlt) *vb.* (*tr.*) **1.** to unfasten a bolt of (a door). **2.** to undo (the nut) on a bolt.

unbolted (ʌnˈbəʊltɪd) *adj.* (of grain, meal, or flour) not sifted.

unborn (ʌnˈbɔːn) *adj.* **1.** not yet born or brought to birth. **2.** still to come in the future: *the unborn world.*

unbosom (ʌnˈbʊzəm) *vb.* (*tr.*) to relieve (oneself) of (secrets, etc.) by telling someone. [C16: from UN-[2] + BOSOM (in the sense: seat of the emotions)]

unbounded (ʌnˈbaʊndɪd) *adj.* having no boundaries or limits. —**un'boundedly** *adv.* —**un'boundedness** *n.*

unbowed (ʌnˈbaʊd) *adj.* **1.** not bowed or bent. **2.** free or unconquered.

unbridled (ʌnˈbraɪdəld) *adj.* **1.** with all restraints removed. **2.** (of a horse) wearing no bridle. —**un'bridledly** *adv.* —**un'bridledness** *n.*

unbroken (ʌnˈbrəʊkən) *adj.* **1.** complete or whole. **2.** continuous or incessant. **3.** undaunted in spirit. **4.** (of animals, esp. horses) not tamed; wild. **5.** not disturbed or upset: *the unbroken quiet of the afternoon.* **6.** (of a record, esp. at sport) not improved upon. —**un'brokenly** *adv.* —**un'brokenness** *n.*

unburden (ʌnˈbɜːdən) *vb.* (*tr.*) **1.** to remove a load or burden from. **2.** to relieve or make free (one's mind, oneself, etc.) of a worry, trouble, etc., by revelation or confession.

unbutton (ʌnˈbʌtən) *vb.* to undo by unfastening (the buttons) of (a garment).

unbuttoned (ʌnˈbʌtənd) *adj.* **1.** with buttons not fastened. **2.** *Inf.* uninhibited; unrestrained: *hours of unbuttoned self-revelation.*

uncalled-for (ˌʌnˈkɔːldfɔː) *adj.* unnecessary or unwarranted.

uncanny (ʌnˈkænɪ) *adj.* **1.** characterized by apparently supernatural wonder, horror, etc. **2.** beyond what is normal: *uncanny accuracy.* —**un'cannily** *adv.* —**un'canniness** *n.*

uncap (ʌnˈkæp) *vb.* **-capping, -capped. 1.** (*tr.*) to remove a cap or top from (a container): *to uncap a bottle.* **2.** to remove a cap from (the head).

uncared-for (ʌnˈkɛədfɔː) *adj.* not cared for; neglected.

unceremonious (ˌʌnserɪˈməʊnɪəs) *adj.* without ceremony; informal, abrupt, rude, or undignified. —**uncere'moniously** *adv.* —**uncere'moniousness** *n.*

uncertain (ʌnˈsɜːtən) *adj.* **1.** not able to be accurately known or predicted: *the issue is uncertain.* **2.** (when *postpositive,* often foll. by *of*) not sure or confident (about): *he was uncertain of the date.* **3.** not precisely determined or decided: *uncertain plans.* **4.** not to be depended upon: *an uncertain vote.* **5.** liable to variation; changeable: *the weather is uncertain.* **6. in no uncertain terms. a.** unambiguously. **b.** forcefully. —**un'certainly** *adv.*

uncertainty (ʌnˈsɜːtəntɪ) *n., pl.* **-ties. 1.** Also: **uncertainness.** the state or condition of being uncertain. **2.** an uncertain matter, contingency, etc.

uncertainty principle *n.* **the.** the principle that energy and time or position and momentum, cannot both be accurately measured simultaneously. Also called: **Heisenberg uncertainty principle, indeterminacy principle.**

uncharted (ʌnˈtʃɑːtɪd) *adj.* (of a physical or nonphysical region or area) not yet mapped, surveyed, or investigated: *uncharted waters; the uncharted depths of the mind.*

unchristian (ʌnˈkrɪstʃən) *adj.* **1.** not in accordance with the principles or ethics of Christianity. **2.** non-Christian or pagan. —**un'christianly** *adv.*

unchurch (ʌnˈtʃɜːtʃ) *vb.* (*tr.*) **1.** to excommunicate. **2.** to remove church status from (a building).

uncial (ˈʌnsɪəl) *adj.* **1.** of, relating to, or written in majuscule letters, as used in Greek and Latin manuscripts of the third to ninth centuries, that resemble modern capitals, but are characterized by much greater curvature. ~*n.* **2.** an uncial letter or manuscript. [C17: from LL *unciālēs litterae* letters an inch long, from L *unciālis,* from *uncia* one twelfth, inch] —**'uncially** *adv.*

uncinate (ˈʌnsɪnɪt, -ˌneɪt) *adj. Biol.* shaped like a hook: *the uncinate process of the ribs of certain vertebrates.*

,unbe'fitting *adj.*	un'bound *adj.*	un'caring *adj.*	un'changing *adj.*
,unbe'gotten *adj.*	un'brace *vb.*	un'cashed *adj.*	un'chaper,oned *adj.*
,unbe'holden *adj.*	un'breakable *adj.*	un'caught *adj.*	,uncharacter'istic *adj.*
un'belt *vb.*	un'bridle *vb.*	un'ceasing *adj.*	un'charged *adj.*
un'biased *adj.*	un'bruised *adj.*	un'censored *adj.*	un'charitable *adj.*
un'biblical *adj.*	un'buckle *vb.*	un'censured *adj.*	un'chartered *adj.*
un'bleached *adj.*	un'built *adj.*	un'chain *vb.*	un'chaste *adj.*
un'blemished *adj.*	un'buried *adj.*	un'challenged *adj.*	un'checked *adj.*
un'blinking *adj.*	un'caged *adj.*	un'changed *adj.*	un'chosen *adj.*
un'block *vb.*			

[C18: from L *uncīnātus*, from *uncinus* a hook, from *uncus*]

uncircumcised (ʌnˈsɜːkəmˌsaɪzd) *adj.* **1.** not circumcised. **2.** not Jewish; gentile. **3.** spiritually unpurified. —ˌuncircumˈcision *n.*

uncivil (ʌnˈsɪvəl) *adj.* **1.** lacking civility or good manners. **2.** an obsolete word for **uncivilized.** —**uncivility** (ˌʌnsɪˈvɪlɪtɪ) *n.* —**unˈcivilly** *adv.*

uncivilized *or* **-ised** (ʌnˈsɪvɪˌlaɪzd) *adj.* **1.** (of a tribe or people) not yet civilized, esp. not having developed a written language. **2.** lacking culture or sophistication. —**unˈciviˌlizedness** *or* **-isedness** *n.*

unclad (ʌnˈklæd) *adj.* having no clothes on; naked.

unclasp (ʌnˈklɑːsp) *vb.* **1.** (*tr.*) to unfasten the clasp of (something). **2.** to release one's grip (upon an object).

uncle (ˈʌŋkəl) *n.* **1.** a brother of one's father or mother. **2.** the husband of one's aunt. **3.** a term of address sometimes used by children for a male friend of their parents. **4.** *Sl.* a pawnbroker. ~**Related** *adj.:* **avuncular.** [C13: from OF *oncle*, from L *avunculus*]

unclean (ʌnˈkliːn) *adj.* lacking moral, spiritual, or physical cleanliness. —**unˈcleanness** *n.*

uncleanly[1] (ʌnˈkliːnlɪ) *adv.* in an unclean manner.

uncleanly[2] (ʌnˈklɛnlɪ) *adj.* characterized by an absence of cleanliness. —**unˈcleanliness** *n.*

Uncle Sam (sæm) *n.* a personification of the government of the United States. [C19: apparently a humorous interpretation of the letters stamped on army supply boxes during the War of 1812: *U.S.*]

Uncle Tom (tɒm) *n. Inf., derog.* a Black person whose behaviour towards White people is regarded as servile. [C20: after the main character of H. B. Stowe's novel *Uncle Tom's Cabin* (1852)] —'**Uncle 'Tom,ism** *n.*

unclose (ʌnˈkləʊz) *vb.* **1.** to open or cause to open. **2.** to come or bring to light.

unclothe (ʌnˈkləʊð) *vb.* **-clothing, -clothed** *or* **-clad.** (*tr.*) **1.** to take off garments from; strip. **2.** to uncover or lay bare.

uncoil (ʌnˈkɔɪl) *vb.* to unwind or become unwound; untwist.

uncomfortable (ʌnˈkʌmftəbəl) *adj.* **1.** not comfortable. **2.** feeling or causing discomfort or unease; disquieting. —**unˈcomfortableness** *n.* —**unˈcomfortably** *adv.*

uncommitted (ˌʌnkəˈmɪtɪd) *adj.* not bound or pledged to a specific opinion, course of action, or cause.

uncommon (ʌnˈkɒmən) *adj.* **1.** outside or beyond normal experience, etc. **2.** in excess of what is normal: *an uncommon liking for honey.* ~*adv.* **3.** an archaic word for **uncommonly** (sense 2). —**unˈcommonness** *n.*

uncommonly (ʌnˈkɒmənlɪ) *adv.* **1.** in an uncommon or unusual manner or degree; rarely. **2.** (intensifier): *you're uncommonly friendly.*

uncommunicative (ˌʌnkəˈmjuːnɪkətɪv) *adj.* disinclined to talk or give information or opinions. —ˌ**uncomˈmunicatively** *adv.* —ˌ**uncomˈmunicativeness** *n.*

uncompromising (ʌnˈkɒmprəˌmaɪzɪŋ) *adj.* not prepared to give ground or to compromise. —**unˈcompro,misingly** *adv.*

unconcern (ˌʌnkənˈsɜːn) *n.* apathy or indifference.

unconcerned (ˌʌnkənˈsɜːnd) *adj.* **1.** lacking in concern or involvement. **2.** untroubled. —**unconcernedly** (ˌʌnkənˈsɜːnɪdlɪ) *adv.*

unconditional (ˌʌnkənˈdɪʃənəl) *adj.* without conditions or limitations; total: *unconditional surrender.* —ˌ**unconˈditionally** *adv.*

unconditioned (ˌʌnkənˈdɪʃənd) *adj.* **1.** *Psychol.* characterizing an innate reflex and the stimulus and response

that form parts of it. **2.** *Metaphysics.* unrestricted by conditions; absolute. **3.** without limitations. —ˌ**unconˈditionedness** *n.*

unconformable (ˌʌnkənˈfɔːməbəl) *adj.* **1.** not conformable or conforming. **2.** (of rock strata) consisting of a series of recent strata resting on different, much older rocks. —ˌ**unconˌformaˈbility** *or* ˌ**unconˈformableness** *n.* —ˌ**unconˈformably** *adv.* —ˌ**unconˈformity** *n.*

unconscionable (ʌnˈkɒnʃənəbəl) *adj.* **1.** unscrupulous or unprincipled: *an unconscionable liar.* **2.** immoderate or excessive: *unconscionable demands.* —**unˈconscionably** *adv.*

unconscious (ʌnˈkɒnʃəs) *adj.* **1.** lacking normal sensory awareness of the environment; insensible. **2.** not aware of one's actions, behaviour, etc.: *unconscious of his bad manners.* **3.** characterized by lack of awareness or intention: *an unconscious blunder.* **4.** coming from or produced by the unconscious: *unconscious resentment.* ~*n.* **5.** *Psychoanal.* the part of the mind containing instincts, impulses, images, and ideas that are not available for direct examination. —**unˈconsciously** *adv.* —**unˈconsciousness** *n.*

unconstitutional (ˌʌnkɒnstɪˈtjuːʃənəl) *adj.* at variance with or not permitted by a constitution. —ˌ**unconstiˌtuˈtionality** *n.*

unconventional (ˌʌnkənˈvɛnʃənəl) *adj.* not conforming to accepted rules or standards. —ˌ**unconˌvenˈtionality** *n.* —ˌ**unconˈventionally** *adv.*

uncool (ʌnˈkuːl) *adj. Sl.* **1.** unsophisticated; unfashionable. **2.** excitable; tense; not cool.

uncork (ʌnˈkɔːk) *vb.* (*tr.*) **1.** to draw the cork from (a bottle, etc.). **2.** to release or unleash (emotions, etc.).

uncountable (ʌnˈkaʊntəbəl) *adj.* **1.** too many to be counted; innumerable. **2.** *Linguistics.* denoting a noun that does not refer to an isolable object. See **mass noun.**

uncounted (ʌnˈkaʊntɪd) *adj.* **1.** unable to be counted; innumerable. **2.** not counted.

uncouple (ʌnˈkʌpəl) *vb.* **1.** to disconnect or unfasten or become disconnected or unfastened. **2.** (*tr.*) to set loose; release.

uncouth (ʌnˈkuːθ) *adj.* lacking in good manners, refinement, or grace. [OE *uncūth*, from UN-[1] + *cūth* familiar] —**unˈcouthly** *adv.* —**unˈcouthness** *n.*

uncover (ʌnˈkʌvə) *vb.* **1.** (*tr.*) to remove the cover, cap, top, etc., from. **2.** (*tr.*) to reveal or disclose: *to uncover a plot.* **3.** to take off (one's head covering), esp. as a mark of respect.

uncovered (ʌnˈkʌvəd) *adj.* **1.** not covered; revealed or bare. **2.** not protected by insurance, security, etc. **3.** with hat off, as a mark of respect.

UNCTAD *abbrev. for* United Nations Conference on Trade and Development.

unction (ˈʌŋkʃən) *n.* **1.** *Chiefly R.C. & Eastern Churches.* the act of anointing with oil in sacramental ceremonies, in the conferring of holy orders. **2.** excessive suavity or affected charm. **3.** an ointment or unguent. **4.** anything soothing. [C14: from L *unctiō* an anointing, from *ungere* to anoint] —**unctionless** *adj.*

unctuous (ˈʌŋktjʊəs) *adj.* **1.** slippery or greasy. **2.** affecting an oily charm. [C14: from Med. L *unctuōsus*, from L *unctum* ointment, from *ungere* to anoint] —**unctuosity** (ˌʌŋktjʊˈɒsɪtɪ) *or* **ˈunctuousness** *n.* —**ˈunctuously** *adv.*

uncut (ʌnˈkʌt) *adj.* **1.** (of a book) not having the edges of its pages trimmed or slit. **2.** (of a gemstone) not cut and faceted. **3.** not abridged.

undamped (ʌnˈdæmpt) *adj.* **1.** (of an oscillating system) having unrestricted motion; not damped. **2.** not repressed, discouraged, or subdued.

un'clad *adj.*	,uncom'pleted *adj.*	,uncon'senting *adj.*	,uncor'robo,rated *adj.*
un'claimed *adj.*	un'compli,cated *adj.*	,uncon'sidered *adj.*	un'covenanted *adj.*
un'classi,fied *adj.*	,uncompli'mentary *adj.*	,uncon'stricted *adj.*	,uncre'ative *adj.*
un'clear *adj.*	,uncom'pounded *adj.*	un'consum,mated *adj.*	un'critical *adj.*
un'clog *vb.*	,uncompre'hending *adj.*	,uncon'tami,nated *adj.*	un'crowned *adj.*
un'clouded *adj.*	,uncon'cealed *adj.*	,uncon'tested *adj.*	un'culti,vated *adj.*
un'cluttered *adj.*	,uncon'cluded *adj.*	,uncon'trollable *adj.*	un'cultured *adj.*
un'coloured *adj.*	,uncon'demned *adj.*	,uncon'trolled *adj.*	un'curbed *adj.*
un'combed *adj.*	,uncon'fined *adj.*	,uncontro'versial *adj.*	un'cured *adj.*
,uncom'mercial *adj.*	,uncon'firmed *adj.*	,uncon'verted *adj.*	un'curl *vb.*
un'compen,sated *adj.*	,uncon'nected *adj.*	,uncon'vincing *adj.*	un'damaged *adj.*
,uncom'petitive *adj.*	un'conquered *adj.*	,unco'operative *adj.*	un'dated *adj.*
,uncom'plaining *adj.*	un'conse,crated *adj.*	,unco'ordi,nated *adj.*	

undaunted (ʌn'dɔːntɪd) *adj.* not put off, discouraged, or beaten. —**un'dauntedly** *adv.* —**un'dauntedness** *n.*

undecagon (ʌn'dɛkə,gɒn) *n.* a polygon having eleven sides. [C18: from L *undecim* eleven + -GON]

undeceive (,ʌndɪ'siːv) *vb.* (*tr.*) to reveal the truth to (someone previously misled or deceived). —,**unde'ceivable** *adj.* —**unde'ceiver** *n.*

undecidability (,ʌndɪ,saɪdə'bɪlɪtɪ) *n., pl.* -**ties.** *Maths, logic.* the condition of not being open to formal proof or disproof by logical deduction from the axioms of a system.

undecided (,ʌndɪ'saɪdɪd) *adj.* **1.** not having made up one's mind. **2.** (of an issue, problem, etc.) not agreed or decided upon. —,**unde'cidedly** *adv.* —,**unde'cidedness** *n.*

undeniable (,ʌndɪ'naɪəb³l) *adj.* **1.** unquestionably or obviously true. **2.** of unquestionable excellence: *a man of undeniable character.* **3.** unable to be resisted or denied. —,**unde'niableness** *n.* —,**unde'niably** *adv.*

under ('ʌndə) *prep.* **1.** directly below; on, to, or beneath the underside or base of: *under one's feet.* **2.** less than: *under forty years.* **3.** lower in rank than: *under a corporal.* **4.** subject to the supervision, jurisdiction, control, or influence of. **5.** subject to (conditions); in (certain circumstances). **6.** within a classification of: *a book under theology.* **7.** known by: *under an assumed name.* **8.** planted with: *a field under corn.* **9.** powered by: *under sail.* **10.** *Astrol.* during the period that the sun is in (a sign of the zodiac): *born under Aries.* ~*adv.* **11.** below; to a position underneath something. [OE]

under- *prefix.* **1.** below or beneath: *underarm; underground.* **2.** of lesser importance or lower rank: *undersecretary.* **3.** insufficient or insufficiently: *underemployed.* **4.** indicating secrecy or deception: *underhand.*

underachieve (,ʌndərə'tʃiːv) *vb.* (*intr.*) to fail to achieve a performance appropriate to one's age or talents. —,**undera'chievement** *n.* —,**undera'chiever** *n.*

underact (,ʌndər'ækt) *vb. Theatre.* to play (a role) without adequate emphasis.

underage (,ʌndər'eɪdʒ) *adj.* below the required or standard age, esp. below the legal age for voting or drinking.

underarm ('ʌndər,ɑːm) *adj.* **1.** (of a measurement) extending along the arm from wrist to armpit. **2.** *Cricket, tennis, etc.* denoting a style of throwing, bowling, or serving in which the hand is swung below shoulder level. **3.** below the arm. ~*adv.* **4.** in an underarm style.

underbelly ('ʌndə,bɛlɪ) *n., pl.* -**lies. 1.** the part of an animal's belly nearest to the ground. **2.** a vulnerable or unprotected part, aspect, or region.

underbid (,ʌndə'bɪd) *vb.* -**bidding,** -**bid. 1.** (*tr.*) to submit a bid lower than that of (others): *Irena underbid the other dealers.* **2.** (*tr.*) to submit an excessively low bid for. **3.** *Bridge.* to bid (one's hand) at a lower level than the strength of the hand warrants: *he underbid his hand.* —'**under,bidder** *n.*

underbody ('ʌndə,bɒdɪ) *n., pl.* -**bodies.** the underpart of a body, as of an animal or motor vehicle.

underbred (,ʌndə'brɛd) *adj.* of impure stock; not thoroughbred. —,**under'breeding** *n.*

underbuy (,ʌndə'baɪ) *vb.* -**buying,** -**bought. 1.** to buy (stock in trade) in amounts lower than required. **2.** (*tr.*) to buy at a price below that paid by (others). **3.** (*tr.*) to pay a price less than the true value for.

undercapitalize *or* -**ise** (,ʌndə'kæpɪtə,laɪz) *vb.* to provide or issue capital for (a commercial enterprise) in an amount insufficient for efficient operation.

undercarriage ('ʌndə,kærɪdʒ) *n.* **1.** Also called: **landing gear.** the assembly of wheels, shock absorbers, struts, etc., that supports an aircraft on the ground and enables it to take off and land. **2.** the framework that supports the body of a vehicle, carriage, etc.

undercharge (,ʌndə'tʃɑːdʒ) *vb.* **1.** to charge too little for something. **2.** (*tr.*) to load (a gun, cannon, etc.) with an inadequate charge.

underclass ('ʌndə,klɑːs) *n.* a class beneath the usual social scale consisting of the most disadvantaged people, such as the long-term unemployed.

underclothes ('ʌndə,kləʊðz) *pl. n.* a variant of **underwear.** Also called: **underclothing.**

undercoat ('ʌndə,kəʊt) *n.* **1.** a coat of paint or other substance applied before the top coat. **2.** a coat worn under an overcoat. **3.** *Zool.* another name for **underfur.** ~*vb.* **4.** (*tr.*) to apply an undercoat to (a surface).

undercover (,ʌndə'kʌvə) *adj.* done or acting in secret: *undercover operations.*

undercroft ('ʌndə,krɒft) *n.* an underground chamber, such as a church crypt, often with a vaulted ceiling. [C14: from *croft* a vault, cavern, ult. from L *crypta* CRYPT]

undercurrent ('ʌndə,kʌrənt) *n.* **1.** a current that is not apparent at the surface or lies beneath another current. **2.** an opinion, emotion, etc., lying beneath apparent feeling or meaning. ~Also called: **underflow.**

undercut *vb.* (,ʌndə'kʌt), -**cutting,** -**cut. 1.** to charge less than (a competitor) in order to obtain trade. **2.** to cut away the under part of (something). **3.** *Golf, tennis, etc.* to hit (a ball) in such a way as to impart backspin. ~*n.* ('ʌndə,kʌt). **4.** the act of cutting underneath. **5.** a part that is cut away underneath. **6.** a tenderloin of beef. **7.** *Forestry, chiefly U.S. & Canad.* a notch cut in a tree trunk, to ensure a clean break in felling. **8.** *Tennis, golf, etc.* a stroke that imparts backspin to the ball.

underdevelop (,ʌndədɪ'vɛləp) *vb.* (*tr.*) *Photog.* to process (a film, plate, or paper) in developer for less than the required time, or at too low a temperature, or in an exhausted solution.

underdeveloped (,ʌndədɪ'vɛləpt) *adj.* **1.** immature or undersized. **2.** relating to societies in which both the surplus capital and the social organization necessary to advance are lacking. **3.** *Photog.* (of a film, etc.) processed in developer for less than the required time.

underdog ('ʌndə,dɒg) *n.* **1.** the losing competitor in a fight or contest. **2.** a person in adversity or a position of inferiority.

underdone (,ʌndə'dʌn) *adj.* insufficiently or lightly cooked.

underdressed (,ʌndə'drɛst) *adj.* wearing clothes that are not elaborate or formal enough for a particular occasion.

underemployed (,ʌndərɪm'plɔɪd) *adj.* not fully or adequately employed.

underestimate *vb.* (,ʌndər'ɛstɪ,meɪt). (*tr.*) **1.** to make too low an estimate of: *he underestimated the cost.* **2.** to think insufficiently highly of: *to underestimate a person.* ~*n.* (,ʌndər'ɛstɪmɪt). **3.** too low an estimate. —,**under,esti'mation** *n.*

underexpose (,ʌndərɪk'spəʊz) *vb.* (*tr.*) **1.** *Photog.* to expose (a film, plate, or paper) for too short a period or with insufficient light so as not to produce the required effect. **2.** (*often passive*) to fail to subject to appropriate or expected publicity. —,**underex'posure** *n.*

underfeed (,ʌndə'fiːd) *vb.* -**feeding,** -**fed.** (*tr.*) **1.** to give too little food to. **2.** to supply (a furnace, engine, etc.) with fuel from beneath.

underfelt ('ʌndə,fɛlt) *n.* thick felt laid between floorboards and carpet to increase insulation.

underfloor ('ʌndə,flɔː) *adj.* situated beneath the floor: *underfloor heating.*

underfoot (,ʌndə'fʊt) *adv.* **1.** underneath the feet; on the ground. **2.** in a position of subjugation. **3.** in the way.

underfur ('ʌndə,fɜː) *n.* the layer of dense soft fur occurring beneath the outer coarser fur in certain mammals, such as the otter and seal. Also called: **undercoat.**

undergarment ('ʌndə,gɑːmənt) *n.* any garment worn under the visible outer clothes, usually next to the skin.

undergird (,ʌndə'gɜːd) *vb.* -**girding,** -**girded** *or* -**girt.** (*tr.*) to strengthen or reinforce by passing a rope, cable, or chain around the underside of (an object, load, etc.). [C16: from UNDER- + GIRD¹]

underglaze ('ʌndə,gleɪz) *adj.* **1.** *Ceramics.* applied to pottery or porcelain before the application of glaze. ~*n.* **2.** a pigment, etc., applied in this way.

,**unde'clared** *adj.*
un'deco,rated *adj.*
,**unde'featted** *adj.*
,**unde'fended** *adj.*
,**unde'filed** *adj.*
,**unde'finable** *adj.*

,**unde'manding** *adj.*
,**undemo'cratic** *adj.*
,**unde'monstrative** *adj.*
,**unde'nied** *adj.*
,**unde'pendable** *adj.*

,**under'active** *adj.*
,**under'clad** *adj.*
,**under'clothed** *adj.*
,**under'cook** *vb.*
,**under'do** *vb.*

,**under'eat** *vb.*
,**under'edu,cated** *adj.*
,**under'empha,size** *or* -**ise** *vb.*
,**under'exer,cise** *vb.*

undergo (ˌʌndə'gəʊ) vb. **-going, -went, -gone.** (tr.) to experience, endure, or sustain: *to undergo a change of feelings.* [OE] —'**under,goer** n.

undergraduate (ˌʌndə'grædjʊɪt) n. a person studying in a university for a first degree. Sometimes shortened to **undergrad.**

underground adj. ('ʌndə,graʊnd), adv. (ˌʌndə'graʊnd). 1. occurring, situated, used, or going below ground level: *an underground explosion.* 2. secret; hidden: *underground activities.* ~n. ('ʌndə,graʊnd). 3. a space or region below ground level. 4. a. a movement dedicated to overthrowing a government or occupation forces, as in the European countries occupied by the German army in World War II. b. (as modifier): *an underground group.* 5. (often preceded by the) an electric passenger railway operated in underground tunnels. U.S. and Canad. equivalent: **subway.** 6. (usually preceded by the) a. any avant-garde, experimental, or subversive movement in popular art, films, music, etc. b. (as modifier): *the underground press.*

underground railroad n. (often cap.) (in the pre-Civil War U.S.) the system established by abolitionists to aid escaping slaves.

undergrowth ('ʌndə,grəʊθ) n. small trees, bushes, ferns, etc., growing beneath taller trees in a wood or forest.

underhand ('ʌndə,hænd) adj. also **underhanded.** 1. clandestine, deceptive, or secretive. 2. *Sport.* another word for **underarm.** ~adv. 3. in an underhand manner or style.

underhanded (ˌʌndə'hændɪd) adj. another word for **underhand** or **short-handed.**

underhung (ˌʌndə'hʌŋ) adj. 1. (of the lower jaw) projecting beyond the upper jaw; undershot. 2. (of a sliding door, etc.) supported at its lower edge by a track or rail.

underlay vb. (ˌʌndə'leɪ), **-laying, -laid.** (tr.) 1. to place (something) under or beneath. 2. to support by something laid beneath. 3. to achieve the correct printing pressure all over (a forme block) or to bring (a block) up to type height by adding material, such as paper, beneath it. ~n. ('ʌndə,leɪ). 4. a lining, support, etc., laid underneath something else. 5. *Printing.* material, such as paper, used to underlay a forme or block. 6. felt, rubber, etc., laid beneath a carpet to increase insulation and resilience.

underlie (ˌʌndə'laɪ) vb. **-lying, -lay, -lain.** (tr.) 1. to lie or be placed under or beneath. 2. to be the foundation, cause, or basis of: *careful planning underlies all our decisions.* 3. to be the root or stem from which (a word) is derived: *"happy" underlies "happiest".* —'**under,lier** n.

underline (ˌʌndə'laɪn) vb. (tr.) 1. to put a line under. 2. to state forcibly; emphasize.

underlinen ('ʌndə,lɪnən) n. underclothes, esp. when made of linen.

underling ('ʌndəlɪŋ) n. a subordinate or lackey.

underlying (ˌʌndə'laɪɪŋ) adj. 1. concealed but detectable: *underlying guilt.* 2. fundamental; basic. 3. lying under. 4. *Finance.* (of a claim, liability, etc.) taking precedence; prior.

undermentioned (ˌʌndə'menʃənd) adj. mentioned below or subsequently.

undermine (ˌʌndə'maɪn) vb. (tr.) 1. (of the sea, wind, etc.) to wear away the bottom or base of (land, cliffs, etc.). 2. to weaken gradually or insidiously: *insults undermined her confidence.* 3. to tunnel or dig beneath. —'**under,miner** n.

undermost ('ʌndə,məʊst) adj. 1. being the furthest under; lowest. ~adv. 2. in the lowest place.

underneath (ˌʌndə'ni:θ) prep., adv. 1. under; beneath. ~adj. 2. lower. ~n. 3. a lower part, surface, etc. [OE *underneothan,* from UNDER + *neothan* below]

undernourish (ˌʌndə'nʌrɪʃ) vb. (tr.) to deprive of or fail to provide with nutrients essential for health and growth. —'**under'nourishment** n.

underpants ('ʌndə,pænts) pl. n. a man's undergarment covering the body from the waist or hips to the thighs or ankles. Often shortened to **pants.**

underpass ('ʌndə,pɑːs) n. 1. a section of a road that passes under another road, railway line, etc. 2. another word for **subway** (sense 1).

underpay (ˌʌndə'peɪ) vb. **-paying, -paid.** to pay (someone) insufficiently. —,**under'payment** n.

underpin (ˌʌndə'pɪn) vb. **-pinning, -pinned.** (tr.) 1. to support from beneath, esp. by a prop, while avoiding damaging or weakening the superstructure: *to underpin a wall.* 2. to give corroboration, strength, or support to.

underpinning ('ʌndə,pɪnɪŋ) n. a structure of masonry, concrete, etc., placed beneath a wall to provide support.

underplay (ˌʌndə'pleɪ) vb. 1. to play (a role) with restraint or subtlety. 2. to achieve (an effect) by deliberate lack of emphasis. 3. (intr.) *Cards.* to lead or follow suit with a lower card when holding a higher one.

underprivileged (ˌʌndə'prɪvɪlɪdʒd) adj. lacking the rights and advantages of other members of society; deprived.

underproduction (ˌʌndəprə'dʌkʃən) n. *Commerce.* production below full capacity or below demand.

underproof (ˌʌndə'pru:f) adj. (of a spirit) containing less than 57.1 per cent alcohol by volume.

underquote (ˌʌndə'kwəʊt) vb. 1. to offer for sale (securities, goods, or services) at a price lower than the market price. 2. (tr.) to quote a price lower than that quoted by (another).

underrate (ˌʌndə'reɪt) vb. (tr.) to underestimate.

underscore (ˌʌndə'skɔː) vb. 1. to draw or score a line or mark under. 2. to stress or reinforce.

undersea ('ʌndə,si:) adj., adv. also **underseas** (ˌʌndə'si:z). below the surface of the sea.

underseal ('ʌndə,si:l) *Brit.* ~n. 1. a coating of a tar, etc., applied to the underside of a motor vehicle to retard corrosion. ~vb. 2. (tr.) to apply a coating of underseal to (a vehicle).

undersecretary (ˌʌndə'sekrətrɪ) n., pl. **-taries.** 1. (in Britain) a. any of various senior civil servants in certain government departments. b. short for **undersecretary of state:** any of various high officials subordinate only to the minister in charge of a department. 2. (in the U.S.) a high government official subordinate only to the secretary in charge of a department.

undersell (ˌʌndə'sel) vb. **-selling, -sold.** 1. to sell for less than the usual price. 2. (tr.) to sell at a price lower than that of (another seller). 3. (tr.) to advertise (merchandise) with moderation or restraint. —,**under'seller** n.

undersexed (ˌʌndə'sekst) adj. having weaker sex urges or responses than is considered normal.

undershirt ('ʌndə,ʃɜːt) n. the U.S. and Canad. name for **vest** (sense 1).

undershoot (ˌʌndə'ʃu:t) vb. **-shooting, -shot.** 1. (of a pilot) to cause (an aircraft) to land short of (a runway) or (of an aircraft) to land in this way. 2. to shoot a projectile so that it falls short of (a target).

undershorts ('ʌndə,ʃɔːts) pl. n. another word for **shorts** (sense 2).

undershot ('ʌndə,ʃɒt) adj. 1. (of the lower jaw) projecting beyond the upper jaw; underhung. 2. (of a water wheel) driven by a flow of water that passes under the wheel rather than over it.

underside ('ʌndə,saɪd) n. the bottom or lower surface.

undersigned ('ʌndə,saɪnd) n. 1. **the.** the person or persons who have signed at the foot of a document, statement, etc. ~adj. 2. having signed one's name at the foot of a document, statement, etc.

undersized (ˌʌndə'saɪzd) adj. of less than usual size.

underskirt ('ʌndə,skɜːt) n. any skirtlike garment worn under a skirt or dress; petticoat.

underslung (ˌʌndə'slʌŋ) adj. suspended below a supporting member, esp. (of a motor vehicle chassis) suspended below the axles.

understand (ˌʌndə'stænd) vb. **-standing, -stood.** 1. (may take a clause as object) to know and comprehend the nature or meaning of: *I understand you.* 2. (may take a clause as object) to realize or grasp (something): *he understands your position.* 3. (tr.; may take a clause as object) to assume, infer, or believe: *I understand you are thinking of marrying.* 4. (tr.) to know how to translate or read: *can you understand Spanish?* 5. (tr.; may take a clause as object; often passive) to accept as a condition or proviso: *it is understood that children must be kept* quiet. **6.** (*tr.*) to be sympathetic to or compatible with: *we understand each other.* [OE *understandan*] —,**under'standable** *adj.* —,**under'standably** *adv.*

understanding (,ʌndə'stændɪŋ) *n.* **1.** the ability to learn, judge, make decisions, etc. **2.** personal opinion or interpretation of a subject: *my understanding of your predicament.* **3.** a mutual agreement or compact, esp. an informal or private one. **4.** *Chiefly Brit.* an unofficial engagement to be married. **5. on the understanding that.** providing. ~*adj.* **6.** sympathetic, tolerant, or wise towards people. **7.** possessing judgment and intelligence. —,**under'standingly** *adv.*

understate (,ʌndə'steɪt) *vb.* **1.** to state (something) in restrained terms, often to obtain an ironic effect. **2.** to state that (something, such as a number) is less than it is. —,**under'statement** *n.*

understood (,ʌndə'stʊd) *vb.* **1.** the past tense and past participle of **understand.** ~*adj.* **2.** implied or inferred. **3.** taken for granted.

understudy (,ʌndə,stʌdɪ) *vb.* **-studying, -studied. 1.** (*tr.*) to study (a role or part) so as to be able to replace the usual actor or actress if necessary. **2.** to act as understudy to (an actor or actress). ~*n., pl.* **-studies. 3.** an actor or actress who studies a part so as to be able to replace the usual actor or actress if necessary. **4.** anyone who is trained to take the place of another in case of need.

undertake (,ʌndə'teɪk) *vb.* **-taking, -took, -taken.** (*tr.*) **1.** to contract to or commit oneself to (something) or (to do something): *to undertake a job.* **2.** to attempt to; agree to start. **3.** to take (someone) in charge. **4.** to promise.

undertaker (,ʌndə,teɪkə) *n.* a person whose profession is the preparation of the dead for burial or cremation and the management of funerals; funeral director.

undertaking (,ʌndə,teɪkɪŋ) *n.* **1.** a task, venture, or enterprise. **2.** an agreement to do something. **3.** the business of an undertaker.

underthings (,ʌndə,θɪŋz) *pl. n.* girls' or women's underwear.

underthrust (,ʌndə,θrʌst) *n. Geol.* a reverse fault in which the rocks on the lower surface of a fault plane have moved under the relatively static rocks on the upper surface.

undertone (,ʌndə,təʊn) *n.* **1.** a quiet or hushed tone of voice. **2.** an underlying suggestion in words or actions: *his offer has undertones of dishonesty.*

undertow (,ʌndə,təʊ) *n.* **1.** the seaward undercurrent following the breaking of a wave on the beach. **2.** any strong undercurrent flowing in a different direction from the surface current.

undertrick (,ʌndə,trɪk) *n. Bridge.* a trick by which a declarer falls short of making his or her contract.

undervalue (,ʌndə'væljuː) *vb.* **-valuing, -valued.** (*tr.*) to value at too low a level or price. —,**under,valu'ation** *n.* —,**under'valuer** *n.*

undervest (,ʌndə,vɛst) *n. Brit.* another name for **vest** (sense 1).

underwater (,ʌndə'wɔːtə) *adj.* **1.** being, occurring, or going under the surface of the water, esp. the sea: *underwater exploration.* **2.** *Naut.* below the water line of a vessel. ~*adv.* **3.** beneath the surface of the water.

under way *adj.* (*postpositive*) **1.** in progress; in operation: *the show was under way.* **2.** *Naut.* in motion in the direction headed.

underwear (,ʌndə,wɛə) *n.* clothing worn under the outer garments, usually next to the skin.

underweight (,ʌndə'weɪt) *adj.* weighing less than is average, expected, or healthy.

underwent (,ʌndə'wɛnt) *vb.* the past tense of **undergo.**

underwhelm (,ʌndə'wɛlm) *vb.* (*tr.*) to make no positive impact on; disappoint. [C20: orig. a humorous coinage based on *overwhelm*] —,**under'whelming** *adj.*

underwing (,ʌndə,wɪŋ) *n.* **1.** the hind wing of an insect. **2.** See **red underwing, yellow underwing.**

underwood (,ʌndə,wʊd) *n.* a less common word for **undergrowth.**

underworld (,ʌndə,wɜːld) *n.* **1. a.** criminals and their associates. **b.** (*as modifier*): *underworld connections.* **2.** *Greek & Roman myth.* the regions below the earth's surface regarded as the abode of the dead. **3.** the antipodes.

underwrite (,ʌndə,raɪt, ,ʌndə'raɪt) *vb.* **-writing, -wrote, -written.** (*tr.*) **1.** *Finance.* to undertake to purchase at an agreed price any unsold portion of (a public issue of shares, etc.). **2.** to accept financial responsibility for (a commercial project or enterprise). **3.** *Insurance.* **a.** to sign and issue (an insurance policy) thus accepting liability. **b.** to insure (a property or risk). **c.** to accept liability up to (a specified amount) in an insurance policy. **4.** to write (words, a signature, etc.) beneath (other written matter). **5.** to support.

underwriter (,ʌndə,raɪtə) *n.* **1.** a person or enterprise that underwrites public issues of shares, bonds, etc. **2. a.** a person or enterprise that underwrites insurance policies. **b.** an employee or agent of an insurance company who determines the premiums payable.

undesirable (,ʌndɪ'zaɪərəb³l) *adj.* **1.** not desirable or pleasant; objectionable. ~*n.* **2.** a person or thing considered undesirable. —,**unde,sira'bility** *or* ,**unde'sirableness** *n.* —,**unde'sirably** *adv.*

undetermined (,ʌndɪ'tɜːmɪnd) *adj.* **1.** not yet resolved; undecided. **2.** not known or discovered.

undies (ʌndɪz) *pl. n. Inf.* women's underwear.

undine (ʌndiːn) *n.* any of various female water spirits. [C17: from NL *undina*, from L *unda* a wave]

undistributed (,ʌndɪ'strɪbjʊtɪd) *adj. Logic.* **1.** (of a term) referring only to some members of the class designated by the term, as *doctors* in *some doctors are overworked.* **2. undistributed middle.** the fallacy arising from the failure of the middle term of a syllogism to apply to all members of a class.

undo (ʌn'duː) *vb.* **-doing, -did, -done.** (*mainly tr.*) **1.** (*also intr.*) to untie, unwrap, or open or become untied, unwrapped, etc. **2.** to reverse the effects of. **3.** to cause the downfall of.

undoing (ʌn'duːɪŋ) *n.* **1.** ruin; downfall. **2.** the cause of downfall: *drink was his undoing.*

undone[1] (ʌn'dʌn) *adj.* not done or completed; unfinished.

undone[2] (ʌn'dʌn) *adj.* **1.** ruined; destroyed. **2.** unfastened; untied.

undoubted (ʌn'daʊtɪd) *adj.* beyond doubt; certain or indisputable. —**un'doubtedly** *adv.*

undreamed (ʌn'driːmd) *or* **undreamt** (ʌn'drɛmt) *adj.* (often foll. by *of*) not thought of, conceived, or imagined.

undress (ʌn'drɛs) *vb.* **1.** to take off clothes from (oneself or another). **2.** (*tr.*) to strip of ornamentation. **3.** (*tr.*) to remove the dressing from (a wound). ~*n.* **4.** partial or complete nakedness. **5.** informal or normal working clothes or uniform.

undressed (ʌn'drɛst) *adj.* **1.** partially or completely naked. **2.** (of an animal hide) not fully processed. **3.** (of food, esp. salad) not prepared with sauce or dressing.

Undset (*Norwegian* 'unsɛt) *n.* **Sigrid** ('sigri). 1882–1949, Norwegian novelist, best known for her trilogy *Kristin Lavransdatter* (1920–22): Nobel prize for literature 1928.

undue (ʌn'djuː) *adj.* **1.** excessive or unwarranted. **2.** unjust, improper, or illegal. **3.** (of a debt, bond, etc.) not yet payable.

undulant ('ʌndjʊlənt) *adj. Rare.* resembling waves; undulating. —'**undulance** *n.*

undulant fever *n.* another name for **brucellosis.** [C19: so called because the fever symptoms are intermittent]

undulate *vb.* ('ʌndjʊ,leɪt). **1.** to move or cause to move in waves or as if in waves. **2.** to have or provide with a wavy form or appearance. ~*adj.* ('ʌndjʊlɪt, -,leɪt). **3.** having a wavy or rippled appearance, margin, or form: *an undulate leaf.* [C17: from L from *unda* a wave] —'**undu,lator** *n.* —'**undulatory** *adj.*

---

undulation (ˌʌndjʊˈleɪʃən) n. **1.** the act or an instance of undulating. **2.** any wave or wavelike form, line, etc.

unduly (ʌnˈdjuːlɪ) adv. excessively.

undying (ʌnˈdaɪɪŋ) adj. unending; eternal. —un'dyingly adv.

unearned (ʌnˈ3ːnd) adj. **1.** not deserved. **2.** not yet earned.

unearned income n. income from property, investment, etc., comprising rent, interest, and dividends.

unearth (ʌnˈ3ːθ) vb. (tr.) **1.** to dig up out of the earth. **2.** to reveal or discover, esp. by exhaustive searching.

unearthly (ʌnˈ3ːθlɪ) adj. **1.** ghostly; eerie: unearthly screams. **2.** heavenly; sublime: unearthly music. **3.** ridiculous or unreasonable (esp. in **unearthly hour**). —un'earthliness n.

uneasy (ʌnˈiːzɪ) adj. **1.** (of a person) anxious; apprehensive. **2.** (of a condition) precarious: an uneasy truce. **3.** (of a thought, etc.) disquieting. —un'ease n. —un'easily adv. —un'easiness n.

uneatable (ʌnˈiːtəbəl) adj. (of food) not fit or suitable for eating, esp. because it is rotten or unattractive.
▷ **Usage.** See at **inedible**.

uneconomic (ˌʌniːkəˈnɒmɪk, ˌʌnɛkə-) adj. not economic; not profitable.

uneconomical (ˌʌniːkəˈnɒmɪkəl, -ɛkə-) adj. not economical; wasteful.

unemployable (ˌʌnɪmˈplɔɪəbəl) adj. unable or unfit to keep a job. —ˌunem,ploya'bility n.

unemployed (ˌʌnɪmˈplɔɪd) adj. **1. a.** without remunerative employment; out of work. **b.** (as collective n.; preceded by the): the unemployed. **2.** not being used; idle.

unemployment (ˌʌnɪmˈplɔɪmənt) n. **1.** the condition of being unemployed. **2.** the number of unemployed workers, often as a percentage of the total labour force.

unemployment benefit n. (in the British National Insurance scheme) a regular payment to a person who is out of work and has usually paid a fixed number of insurance contributions. Informal term: **dole**.

unequal (ʌnˈiːkwəl) adj. **1.** not equal in quantity, size, rank, value, etc. **2.** (foll. by to) inadequate; insufficient. **3.** not evenly balanced. **4.** (of character, quality, etc.) irregular; inconsistent. **5.** (of a contest, etc.) having competitors of different ability.

unequalled or U.S. **unequaled** (ʌnˈiːkwəld) adj. not equalled; unrivalled; supreme.

unequivocal (ˌʌnɪˈkwɪvəkəl) adj. not ambiguous; plain. —ˌune'quivocally adv. —ˌune'quivocalness n.

unerring (ʌnˈ3ːrɪŋ) adj. **1.** not missing the mark or target. **2.** consistently accurate; certain. —un'erringly adv. —un'erringness n.

UNESCO (juːˈnɛskəʊ) n. acronym for United Nations Educational, Scientific, and Cultural Organization.

uneven (ʌnˈiːvən) adj. **1.** (of a surface, etc.) not level or flat. **2.** spasmodic or variable. **3.** not parallel, straight, or horizontal. **4.** not fairly matched: an uneven race. **5.** Arch. not equal. —un'evenly adv. —un'evenness n.

uneventful (ˌʌnɪˈvɛntfʊl) adj. ordinary, routine, or quiet. —ˌune'ventfully adv. —ˌune'ventfulness n.

unexampled (ˌʌnɪgˈzɑːmpəld) adj. without precedent or parallel.

unexceptionable (ˌʌnɪkˈsɛpʃənəbəl) adj. beyond criticism or objection. —ˌunex'ceptionably adv.

unexceptional (ˌʌnɪkˈsɛpʃənəl) adj. **1.** usual, ordinary, or normal. **2.** subject to or allowing no exceptions. —ˌunex'ceptionally adv.

unexpected (ˌʌnɪkˈspɛktɪd) adj. surprising or unforeseen. —ˌunex'pectedly adv. —ˌunex'pectedness n.

unfailing (ʌnˈfeɪlɪŋ) adj. **1.** not failing; unflagging. **2.** continuous. **3.** sure; certain. —un'failingly adv. —un'failingness n.

unfair (ʌnˈfɛə) adj. **1.** characterized by inequality or injustice. **2.** dishonest or unethical. —un'fairly adv. —un'fairness n.

unfaithful (ʌnˈfeɪθfʊl) adj. **1.** not true to a promise, vow, etc. **2.** not true to a wife, husband, lover, etc., esp. in having sexual intercourse with someone else. **3.** inaccurate; untrustworthy: unfaithful copy. **4.** Obs. not having religious faith. —un'faithfully adv. —un'faithfulness n.

unfamiliar (ˌʌnfəˈmɪljə) adj. **1.** not known or experienced; strange. **2.** (postpositive; foll. by with) not familiar. —unfamiliarity (ˌʌnfəˌmɪlɪˈærɪtɪ) n. —ˌunfa'miliarly adv.

unfasten (ʌnˈfɑːsən) vb. to undo, untie, or open or become undone, untied, or opened.

unfathered (ʌnˈfɑːðəd) adj. **1.** having no known father. **2.** of unknown or uncertain origin.

unfathomable (ʌnˈfæðəməbəl) adj. **1.** incapable of being fathomed; immeasurable. **2.** incomprehensible. —un'fathomableness n. —un'fathomably adv.

unfavourable or U.S. **unfavorable** (ʌnˈfeɪvərəbəl) adj. not favourable; adverse or inauspicious. —un'favourably or U.S. un'favorably adv.

Unfederated Malay States (ʌnˈfɛdəˌreɪtɪd) pl. n. a former group of native states in the Malay Peninsula that became British protectorates between 1885 and 1909. All except Brunei joined the Malayan Union (later Federation of Malaya) in 1946. Brunei joined the Federation of Malaysia in 1963.

unfeeling (ʌnˈfiːlɪŋ) adj. **1.** without sympathy; callous. **2.** without physical feeling or sensation. —un'feelingly adv. —un'feelingness n.

unfinished (ʌnˈfɪnɪʃt) adj. **1.** incomplete or imperfect. **2.** (of paint, polish, varnish, etc.) without an applied finish; rough. **3.** (of fabric) unbleached or not processed.

unfit (ʌnˈfɪt) adj. **1.** (postpositive; often foll. by for) unqualified, incapable, or incompetent: unfit for military service. **2.** (postpositive; often foll. by for) unsuitable or inappropriate: the ground was unfit for football. **3.** in poor physical condition. ~vb. **-fitting, -fitted. 4.** (tr.) Rare. to render unfit. —un'fitly adv. —un'fitness n.

unfix (ʌnˈfɪks) vb. (tr.) **1.** to unfasten, detach, or loosen. **2.** to unsettle or disturb.

unflappable (ʌnˈflæpəbəl) adj. Inf. hard to upset; calm; composed. —un,flappa'bility n. —un'flappably adv.

unfledged (ʌnˈflɛdʒd) adj. **1.** (of a young bird) not having developed adult feathers. **2.** immature and undeveloped.

unflinching (ʌnˈflɪntʃɪŋ) adj. not shrinking from danger, difficulty, etc. —un'flinchingly adv.

unfold (ʌnˈfəʊld) vb. **1.** to open or spread out or be opened or spread out from a folded state. **2.** to reveal or be revealed: the truth unfolds. **3.** to develop or expand or be developed or expanded. —un'folder n.

unfortunate (ʌnˈfɔːtʃənɪt) adj. **1.** causing or attended by misfortune. **2.** unlucky or unhappy: an unfortunate character. **3.** regrettable or unsuitable: an unfortunate speech. ~n. **4.** an unlucky person. —un'fortunately adv.

unfounded (ʌnˈfaʊndɪd) adj. **1.** (of ideas, allegations, etc.) baseless; groundless. **2.** not yet founded or established. —un'foundedly adv. —un'foundedness n.

un'dutiful adj.	un'enter,prising adj.	,unex'pressed adj.	un'forceable adj.
un'dyed adj.	,unen,thusi'astic adj.	un'expur,gated adj.	un'forced adj.
un'eaten adj.	un'enviable adj.	un'fading adj.	,unfore'seeable adj.
un'edited adj.	,une'quipped adj.	un'fashionable adj.	,unfore'seen adj.
un'educable adj.	,unes'capable adj.	un'fathomed adj.	,unfore'told adj.
un'edu,cated adj.	,unes'corted adj.	un'favoured adj.	,unfor'gettable adj.
,une'lectable adj.	,unes'sential adj.	un'fed adj.	,unfor'givable adj.
,une'manci,pated adj.	un'ethical adj.	un'feder,ated adj.	,unfor'given adj.
,unem'bellished adj.	,unex'agger,ated adj.	un'feigned adj.	,unfor'giving adj.
,une'motional adj.	,unex'cused adj.	,unfer'mented adj.	,unfor'gotten adj.
,unen'cumbered adj.	,unex'perienced adj.	un'ferti,lized or -,lised adj.	un'formed adj.
un'ending adj.	,unex'pired adj.	un'fetter vb.	,unfor'saken adj.
,unen'dowed adj.	,unex'plainable adj.	un'fettered adj.	,unforth'coming adj.
,unen'durable adj.	,unex'plained adj.	un'fitting adj.	un'forti,fied adj.
,unen'gaged adj.	,unex'ploited adj.	un'flattering adj.	un'found adj.
,unen'lightened adj.	,unex'plored adj.	,unfor'bearing adj.	un'framed adj.

unfreeze (ʌn'friːz) *vb.* **-freezing, -froze, -frozen. 1.** to thaw or cause to thaw. **2.** (*tr.*) to relax governmental restrictions on (wages, prices, credit, etc.) or on the manufacture or sale of (goods, etc.).

unfriended (ʌn'frɛndɪd) *adj. Now rare.* without a friend or friends; friendless.

unfriendly (ʌn'frɛndlɪ) *adj.* **-lier, -liest. 1.** not friendly; hostile. **2.** unfavourable or disagreeable. ~*adv.* **3.** *Rare.* in an unfriendly manner. —**un'friendliness** *n.*

unfrock (ʌn'frɒk) *vb.* (*tr.*) to deprive (a person in holy orders) of ecclesiastical status.

unfunded debt (ʌn'fʌndɪd) *n.* a short-term floating debt not represented by bonds.

unfurl (ʌn'fɜːl) *vb.* to unroll, unfold, or spread out or be unrolled, unfolded, or spread out from a furled state.

ungainly (ʌn'geɪnlɪ) *adj.* **-lier, -liest. 1.** lacking grace when moving. **2.** difficult to move or use; unwieldy. [C17: from UN-[1] + obs. or dialect GAINLY graceful] —**un'gainliness** *n.*

Ungaretti (*Italian* uŋga'retti) *n.* **Giuseppe** (dʒu'zɛppe). 1888–1970, Italian poet, best known for his collection of war poems *Allegria di naufragi* (1919).

Ungava (ʊŋ'geɪvə, -'gɑː-) *n.* a sparsely inhabited region of NE Canada, in N Quebec east of Hudson Bay: part of the Labrador peninsula; rich mineral resources. Area: 911 110 sq. km (351 780 sq. miles).

ungodly (ʌn'gɒdlɪ) *adj.* **-lier, -liest. 1. a.** wicked, sinful. **b.** (*as collective n.; preceded by the*): *the ungodly.* **2.** *Inf.* unseemly; outrageous (esp. in **an ungodly hour**). —**un'godliness** *n.*

ungovernable (ʌn'gʌvənəbəl) *adj.* not able to be disciplined, restrained, etc.: *an ungovernable temper.* —**un'governableness** *n.* —**un'governably** *adv.*

ungual ('ʌŋgwəl) *adj.* **1.** of, relating to, or affecting the fingernails or toenails. **2.** of or relating to an unguis. [C19: from L *unguis* nail]

unguarded (ʌn'gɑːdɪd) *adj.* **1.** unprotected; vulnerable. **2.** open; frank. **3.** incautious. —**un'guardedly** *adv.* —**un'guardedness** *n.*

unguent ('ʌŋgwənt) *n.* a less common name for an **ointment**. [C15: from L *unguere* to anoint]

unguiculate (ʌŋ'gwɪkjʊlɪt, -ˌleɪt) *adj.* **1.** (of mammals) having claws or nails. **2.** (of petals) having a clawlike base. ~*n.* **3.** an unguiculate mammal. [C19: from NL *unguiculātus*, from L *unguiculus*, dim. of *unguis* nail]

unguis ('ʌŋgwɪs) *n., pl.* **-gues** (-gwiːz). **1.** a nail, claw, or hoof, or the part of the digit giving rise to it. **2.** the clawlike base of a petal. [C18: from L]

ungulate ('ʌŋgjʊlɪt, -ˌleɪt) *n.* any of a large group of mammals all of which have hooves: divided into odd-toed ungulates (see **perissodactyl**) and even-toed ungulates (see **artiodactyl**). [C19: from LL *ungulātus* having hooves, from *ungula* hoof]

unhallowed (ʌn'hæləʊd) *adj.* **1.** not consecrated or holy: *unhallowed ground.* **2.** sinful.

unhand (ʌn'hænd) *vb.* (*tr.*) *Arch. or literary.* to release from the grasp.

unhappy (ʌn'hæpɪ) *adj.* **-pier, -piest. 1.** not joyful; sad or depressed. **2.** unfortunate or wretched: *an unhappy fellow.* **3.** tactless or inappropriate: *an unhappy remark.* —**un'happily** *adv.* —**un'happiness** *n.*

unhealthy (ʌn'hɛlθɪ) *adj.* **-healthier, -healthiest. 1.** characterized by ill health; sick. **2.** characteristic of, conducive to, or resulting from ill health: *an unhealthy complexion.* **3.** morbid or unwholesome. **4.** *Inf.* dangerous; risky. —**un'healthily** *adv.* —**un'healthiness** *n.*

unheard (ʌn'hɜːd) *adj.* **1.** not heard; not perceived by the ear. **2.** not listened to: *his warning went unheard.* **3.** *Arch.* unheard-of.

unheard-of *adj.* **1.** previously unknown: *an unheard-of actress.* **2.** without precedent: *an unheard-of treatment.* **3.** highly offensive: *unheard-of behaviour.*

unhinge (ʌn'hɪndʒ) *vb.* (*tr.*) **1.** to remove (a door, etc.) from its hinges. **2.** to derange or unbalance (a person, his mind, etc.). **3.** to disrupt or unsettle (a process or state of affairs).

unholy (ʌn'həʊlɪ) *adj.* **-lier, -liest. 1.** not holy or sacred. **2.** immoral or depraved. **3.** *Inf.* outrageous or unnatural: *an unholy alliance.* —**un'holiness** *n.*

unhook (ʌn'hʊk) *vb.* **1.** (*tr.*) to remove (something) from a hook. **2.** (*tr.*) to unfasten the hook of (a dress, etc.). **3.** (*intr.*) to become unfastened or be capable of unfastening: *the dress wouldn't unhook.*

unhorse (ʌn'hɔːs) *vb.* (*tr.*) **1.** (*usually passive*) to knock or throw from a horse. **2.** to overthrow or dislodge, as from a powerful position.

unhouseled (ʌn'haʊzəld) *adj. Arch.* not having received the Eucharist. [C16: from *un-* + obs. *housel* to administer the sacrament, from OE *hūsl* (n.), *hūslian* (vb.), from ?]

uni ('juːnɪ) *n. Inf.* short for **university**.

uni- *combining form.* consisting of, relating to, or having only one: *unilateral.* [from L *ūnus* one]

Uniat ('juːnɪˌæt) *or* **Uniate** ('juːnɪɪt, -ˌeɪt) *adj.* **1.** designating any of the Eastern Churches that retain their own liturgy but submit to papal authority. ~*n.* **2.** a member of one of these Churches. [C19: from Russian *uniyat*, from Polish *unja* union, from LL *ūniō;* see UNION] —'**Uniˌatism** *n.*

uniaxial (ˌjuːnɪ'æksɪəl) *adj.* **1.** (esp. of plants) having an unbranched main axis. **2.** (of a crystal) having only one direction along which double refraction of light does not occur.

unicameral (ˌjuːnɪ'kæmərəl) *adj.* of or characterized by a single legislative chamber. —ˌ**uni'cameralism** *n.* —ˌ**uni'cameralist** *n.* —ˌ**uni'camerally** *adv.*

UNICEF ('juːnɪˌsɛf) *n. acronym for* United Nations Children's Fund (formerly, United Nations International Children's Emergency Fund).

unicellular (ˌjuːnɪ'sɛljʊlə) *adj.* (of organisms, such as protozoans and certain algae) consisting of a single cell. —ˌ**uniˌcellu'larity** *n.*

unicorn ('juːnɪˌkɔːn) *n.* **1.** an imaginary creature usually depicted as a white horse with one long spiralled horn growing from its forehead. **2.** *Old Testament.* a two-horned animal: mistranslation in the Authorized Version of the original Hebrew. [C13: from OF, from L *ūnicornis* one-horned, from *ūnus* one + *cornu* a horn]

unicycle ('juːnɪˌsaɪkəl) *n.* a one-wheeled vehicle driven by pedals, esp. one used in a circus, etc. Also called: **monocycle**. [from UNI- + CYCLE, on the model of TRICYCLE] —'**uniˌcyclist** *n.*

unidirectional (ˌjuːnɪdɪ'rɛkʃənəl) *adj.* having, moving in, or operating in only one direction.

UNIDO (juːˈniːdəʊ) *n. acronym for* United Nations Industrial Development Organization.

Unification Church *n.* a religious sect founded in 1954 by Sun Myung Moon (born 1920), S Korean industrialist and religious leader.

unified field theory *n.* any theory capable of describing in one set of equations the properties of gravitational fields, electromagnetic fields, and strong and weak nuclear interactions. No satisfactory theory has yet been found.

uniform ('juːnɪˌfɔːm) *n.* **1.** a prescribed identifying set of clothes for the members of an organization, such as soldiers or schoolchildren. **2.** a single set of such clothes. **3.** a characteristic feature of some class or group. ~*adj.* **4.** unchanging in form, quality, etc.: *a uniform surface.* **5.** alike or like: *a line of uniform toys.* ~*vb.* (*tr.*) **6.** to fit out (a body of soldiers, etc.) with uniforms. **7.** to make

ˌunfre'quented *adj.*	un'grateful *adj.*	un'harrowed *adj.*	ˌunhis'toric *adj.*
un'fruitful *adj.*	un'grounded *adj.*	un'hatched *adj.*	un'hitch *vb.*
ˌunful'filled *adj.*	un'grudging *adj.*	un'healed *adj.*	un'hoped-for *adj.*
un'furnished *adj.*	un'guided *adj.*	un'heated *adj.*	un'housed *adj.*
un'generous *adj.*	un'hampered *adj.*	un'heeded *adj.*	un'human *adj.*
un'gentlemanly *adj.*	un'handy *adj.*	un'heeding *adj.*	un'hurried *adj.*
un'gifted *adj.*	un'hardened *adj.*	un'helpful *adj.*	un'hurt *adj.*
un'gird *vb.*	un'harmed *adj.*	un'heralded *adj.*	ˌunhy'gienic *adj.*
un'glazed *adj.*	un'harmful *adj.*	ˌunhe'roic *adj.*	un'hyphenˌated *adj.*
un'gracious *adj.*	ˌunhar'monious *adj.*	un'hesiˌtating *adj.*	ˌuni'dentiˌfiable *adj.*
ˌungram'matical *adj.*	un'harness *vb.*	un'hindered *adj.*	ˌuni'dentiˌfied *adj.*

uniform. [C16: from L *ūniformis*, from *ūnus* one + *forma* shape] —'**uni,formly** *adv.* —'**uni,formness** *n.*

uniformitarianism (ˌjuːnɪˌfɔːmɪˈtɛərɪəˌnɪzəm) *n.* the concept that the earth's surface was shaped in the past by gradual processes, such as erosion, and by small sudden changes, such as earthquakes, rather than by sudden divine acts, such as Noah's flood. —ˌuniˌformiˈtarian *n.*, *adj.*

uniformity (ˌjuːnɪˈfɔːmɪtɪ) *n., pl.* -**ties.** 1. a state or condition in which everything is regular, homogeneous, or unvarying. 2. lack of diversity or variation.

unify (ˈjuːnɪˌfaɪ) *vb.* -**fying,** -**fied.** to make or become one; unite. [C16: from Med. L *ūnificāre*, from L *ūnus* one + *facere* to make] —'**uni,fiable** *adj.* —ˌunifiˈcation *n.* —'**uni,fier** *n.*

unilateral (ˌjuːnɪˈlætərəl) *adj.* 1. of, having, affecting, or occurring on only one side. 2. involving or performed by only one party of several: *unilateral disarmament.* 3. *Law.* (of contracts, obligations, etc.) made by, affecting, or binding one party only. 4. *Bot.* having or designating parts situated or turned to one side of an axis. —ˌuniˈlateralism *n.* —ˌuniˈlaterally *adv.*

Unilateral Declaration of Independence *n.* a declaration of independence made by a dependent state without the assent of the protecting state. Abbrev.: **UDI.**

Unimak Island (ˈjuːnɪˌmæk) *n.* an island in SW Alaska, in the Aleutian Islands. Length: 113 km (70 miles).

unimpeachable (ˌʌnɪmˈpiːtʃəb⁰l) *adj.* unquestionable as to honesty, truth, etc. —ˌunimˈpeachably *adv.*

unimproved (ˌʌnɪmˈpruːvd) *adj.* 1. not improved or made better. 2. (of land) not cleared, drained, cultivated, etc. 3. neglected; unused: *unimproved resources.*

uninterested (ʌnˈɪntrɪstɪd) *adj.* indifferent. —un'**interestedly** *adv.* —un'**interestedness** *n.*

▷ **Usage.** See at **disinterested.**

union (ˈjuːnjən) *n.* 1. the condition of being united, the act of uniting, or a conjunction formed by such an act. 2. an association, alliance, or confederation of individuals or groups for a common purpose, esp. political. 3. agreement or harmony. 4. short for **trade union.** 5. the act or state of marriage or sexual intercourse. 6. a device on a flag representing union, such as another flag depicted in the top left corner. 7. a device for coupling pipes. 8. (*often cap.*) **a.** an association of students at a university or college formed to look after the students' interests. **b.** the building or buildings housing the facilities of such an organization. 9. *Maths.* a set containing all members of two given sets. Symbol: ∪ 10. (in 19th-century England) a number of parishes united for the administration of poor relief. 11. *Textiles.* a piece of cloth or fabric consisting of two different kinds of yarn. 12. (*modifier*) of or related to a union, esp. a trade union. [C15: from Church L *ūniō* oneness, from L *ūnus* one]

Union (ˈjuːnjən) *n.* **the.** 1. *Brit.* **a.** the union of the English and Scottish crowns (1603–1707). **b.** the union of England and Scotland from 1707. **c.** the political union of Great Britain and Ireland (1801–1920). **d.** the union of Great Britain and Northern Ireland from 1920. 2. *U.S.* **a.** the United States of America. **b.** the northern states of the U.S. during the Civil War. **c.** (*as modifier*): *Union supporters.*

union catalogue *n.* a catalogue listing every publication held at cooperating libraries.

unionism (ˈjuːnjəˌnɪzəm) *n.* 1. the principles of trade unions. 2. adherence to the principles of trade unions. 3. the principle or theory of any union. —'**unionist** *n., adj.*

Unionist (ˈjuːnjənɪst) *n.* 1. a member or supporter of the Unionist Party. 2. a supporter of the U.S. federal Union, esp. during the Civil War. 3. (*sometimes not cap.*) **a.** (before 1920) a supporter of the union of all Ireland and Great Britain. **b.** (since 1920) a supporter of union between Britain and Northern Ireland. ~*adj.* 4. of, resembling, or relating to Unionists. —'**Union,ism** *n.*

Unionist Party *n.* (in Northern Ireland) formerly, the major Protestant political party, closely identified with the Union with Britain.

unionize *or* -**nise** (ˈjuːnjəˌnaɪz) *vb.* 1. to organize (workers) into a trade union. 2. to join or cause to join a trade union. 3. (*tr.*) to subject to the rules or codes of a trade union. —ˌunioniˈzation *or* -niˈsation *n.*

Union Jack *n.* the national flag of the United Kingdom, being a composite design composed of Saint George's Cross (England), Saint Andrew's Cross (Scotland), and Saint Patrick's Cross (Ireland). Also called: **Union flag.**

Union of South Africa *n.* the former name (1910–61) of the (Republic of) **South Africa.**

Union of Soviet Socialist Republics *n.* the official name of the **Soviet Union.**

union pipes *pl. n.* another name for **uillean pipes.**

union shop *n.* an establishment whose employment policy is governed by a contract between employer and a trade union permitting the employment of nonunion labour only on the condition that such labour joins the union within a specified time period.

unipolar (ˌjuːnɪˈpəʊlə) *adj.* 1. of, concerned with, or having a single magnetic or electric pole. 2. (of a nerve cell) having a single process. 3. (of a transistor) utilizing charge carriers of one polarity only, as in a field-effect transistor. —**unipolarity** (ˌjuːnɪpəʊˈlærɪtɪ) *n.*

unique (juːˈniːk) *adj.* 1. being the only one of a particular type. 2. without equal or like. 3. *Inf.* very remarkable. 4. *Maths.* **a.** leading to only one result: *the sum of two integers is unique.* **b.** having precisely one value: *the unique positive square root of 4 is 2.* [C17: via F from L *ūnicus* unparalleled, from *ūnus* one] —u'**niquely** *adv.* —u'**niqueness** *n.*

▷ **Usage.** Certain words in English, such as *unique*, *perfect*, and *simultaneous*, describe absolute states, that is to say, states that cannot be qualified; something is either *unique* or it is *not unique*, but it cannot be, for example, *rather unique.* Careful users of English therefore avoid the use of comparatives or intensifiers where absolute states are concerned: *that is very exceptional* (not *very unique*); *this one comes nearer to perfection* (not *is more perfect*).

unisex (ˈjuːnɪˌsɛks) *adj.* of or relating to clothing, a hairstyle, hairdressers, etc., that can be worn or used by either sex. [C20: from UNI- + SEX]

unisexual (ˌjuːnɪˈsɛksjʊəl) *adj.* 1. of one sex only. 2. (of some organisms) having either male or female reproductive organs but not both. —ˌuniˌsexuˈality *n.* —ˌuniˈsexually *adv.*

unison (ˈjuːnɪsⁿn) *n.* 1. *Music.* **a.** the interval between two notes of identical pitch. **b.** (*modifier*) played or sung at the same pitch: *unison singing.* 2. complete agreement (esp. in **in unison**). [C16: from LL *ūnisonus*, from UNI- + *sonus* sound] —u'**nisonous, u'nisonal,** *or* u'**nisonant** *adj.*

unit (ˈjuːnɪt) *n.* 1. a single undivided entity or whole. 2. any group or individual, esp. when regarded as a basic element of a larger whole. 3. a mechanical part or assembly of parts that performs a subsidiary function: *a filter unit.* 4. a complete system or establishment that performs a specific function: *a production unit.* 5. a subdivision of a larger military formation. 6. a standard amount of a physical quantity, such as length, mass, energy, etc., specified multiples of which are used to express magnitudes of that physical quantity: *the second is a unit of time.* 7. the amount of a drug, vaccine, etc., needed to produce a particular effect. 8. the digit or position immediately to the left of the decimal point. 9. (*modifier*) having or relating to a value of one: *a unit vector.* 10. *N.Z.* a self-propelled

ˌunil'lumi,nated *adj.*	ˌunim'posing *adj.*	ˌunin'habited *adj.*	ˌunin'telligible *adj.*
ˌunil'lumi,nating *adj.*	ˌunim'pressed *adj.*	ˌunin'hibited *adj.*	ˌunin'tended *adj.*
un'illus,trated *adj.*	ˌunin'closed *adj.*	ˌunin'iti,ated *adj.*	ˌunin'tentional *adj.*
ˌunim'aginable *adj.*	ˌunin'corpo,rated *adj.*	un'injured *adj.*	un'interesting *adj.*
ˌunim'aginably *adv.*	ˌunin'cumbered *adj.*	ˌunin'spired *adj.*	ˌuninter'rupted *adj.*
ˌunim'aginative *adj.*	ˌunin'fected *adj.*	ˌunin'spiring *adj.*	unin'vested *adj.*
ˌunim'aginatively *adv.*	ˌuninflu'ential *adj.*	ˌunin'structed *adj.*	ˌunin'vited *adj.*
ˌunim'paired *adj.*	ˌunin'formative *adj.*	ˌunin'structive *adj.*	ˌunin'viting *adj.*
ˌunim'peded *adj.*	ˌunin'formed *adj.*	ˌunin'sured *adj.*	ˌunin'voked *adj.*
ˌunim'portant *adj.*	ˌunin'habitable *adj.*	ˌunin'telligent *adj.*	un'ironed *adj.*

railcar. **11.** *Austral. & N.Z.* short for **home unit.** [C16: back formation from UNITY, ? on the model of *digit*]

unitarian (ˌjuːnɪˈtɛərɪən) *n.* **1.** a supporter of unity or centralization in politics. ~*adj.* **2.** of or relating to unity or centralization.

Unitarian (ˌjuːnɪˈtɛərɪən) *n.* **1.** a person who believes that God is one being and rejects the doctrine of the Trinity. **2.** a member of the Church (**Unitarian Church**) that embodies this system of belief. ~*adj.* **3.** of or relating to Unitarians or Unitarianism. —ˌ**Uniˈtariaˌnism** *n.*

unitary (ˈjuːnɪtərɪ, -trɪ) *adj.* **1.** of a unit or units. **2.** based on or characterized by unity. **3.** individual; whole.

unit character *n. Genetics.* a character inherited as a single unit and dependent on a single gene.

unit cost *n.* the actual cost of producing one article.

unite[1] (juːˈnaɪt) *vb.* **1.** to make or become an integrated whole or a unity. **2.** to join, unify or be unified in purpose, action, beliefs, etc. **3.** to enter or cause to enter into an association or alliance. **4.** to adhere or cause to adhere; fuse. **5.** (*tr.*) to possess (qualities) in combination or at the same time: *he united charm with severity.* [C15: from LL *ūnīre*, from *ūnus* one]

unite[2] (ˈjuːnaɪt, juːˈnaɪt) *n.* an English gold coin minted in the Stuart period, originally worth 20 shillings. [C17: from obs. *unite* joined, from the union of England & Scotland (1603)]

united (juːˈnaɪtɪd) *adj.* **1.** produced by two or more persons or things in combination or from their union or amalgamation: *a united effort.* **2.** in agreement. **3.** in association or alliance. —**uˈnitedly** *adv.* —**uˈnitedness** *n.*

United Arab Emirates *pl. n.* a group of seven emirates in SW Asia, on the Persian Gulf: consists of Abu Dhabi, Dubai, Sharjah, Ajman, Umm al Qaiwain, Ras el Khaimah, and Fujairah; a former British protectorate; became fully independent in 1971; consists mostly of flat desert, with mountains in the east; rich petroleum resources. Language: Arabic. Religion: Muslim. Currency: dirham. Capital: Abu Dhabi. Pop.: 1 856 000 (1987). Area: 83 600 sq. km (32 300 sq. miles). Former name (until 1971): **Trucial States.** Abbrev.: **UAE.**

United Arab Republic *n.* the official name (1958–71) of **Egypt.**

United Arab States *pl. n.* a federation (1958–61) between the United Arab Republic and Yemen.

United Empire Loyalist *n. Canad. history.* an American colonist who settled in Canada during or after the War of American Independence because of loyalty to the British Crown.

United Kingdom *n.* a kingdom of NW Europe, consisting chiefly of the island of Great Britain together with Northern Ireland: became the world's leading colonial power in the 18th century: the first country to undergo the Industrial Revolution. It became the **United Kingdom of Great Britain and Northern Ireland** in 1921, after the rest of Ireland became autonomous as the Irish Free State. Primarily it is a trading nation, the chief exports being manufactured goods; joined the Common Market in January 1973. Languages: English, with Gaelic and Welsh minority languages. Religion: Christian. Currency: pound sterling. Capital: London. Pop.: 56 878 000 (1987). Area: 244 014 sq. km (94 214 sq. miles). Abbrev.: **UK.** See also **Great Britain.**

United Nations *n.* (*functioning as sing. or pl.*) an international organization of independent states, with its headquarters in New York City, that was formed in 1945 to promote peace and international cooperation and security. Abbrev.: **UN.**

United Provinces *pl. n.* **1.** a Dutch republic (1581–1795) formed by the union of the seven northern provinces of the Netherlands, which were in revolt against their suzerain, Philip II of Spain. **2.** short for **United Provinces of Agra and Oudh:** the former name of **Uttar Pradesh.**

United States of America (*functioning as sing. or pl.*) *n.* a federal republic mainly in North America consisting of 50 states and the District of Columbia: colonized principally by the English and French in the 17th century, the native Indians being gradually displaced; 13 colonies under British rule made the Declaration of Independence in 1776 and became the United States after the War of American Independence. The northern states defeated the South in the Civil War (1861–65). It consists generally of the Rocky Mountains in the west, the Great Plains in the centre, the Appalachians in the east, deserts in the southwest, and coastal lowlands and swamps in the southeast. Language: predominantly English. Religion: Christian majority. Currency: dollar. Capital: Washington, D.C. Pop.: 243 773 000 (1987). Area: 9 363 405 sq. km (3 615 210 sq. miles). Often shortened to: **United States.** Abbrevs.: **U.S., U.S.A.**

unitive (ˈjuːnɪtɪv) *adj.* **1.** tending to unite or capable of uniting. **2.** characterized by unity.

unit-linked policy *n.* a life-assurance policy the benefits of which are directly in proportion to the number of units held by the policyholder.

unit of account *n.* a standard monetary denomination used for keeping accounts in Britain and to express loans and subsidies in the European Economic Community.

unit price *n.* a price for foodstuffs, etc., stated or shown as the cost per unit, as per pound, per kilogram, per dozen, etc.

unit trust *n. Brit.* an investment trust that issues units for public sale, the holders of which are creditors and not shareholders with their interests represented by a trust company independent of the issuing agency. U.S. and Canad. equivalent: **mutual fund.**

unity (ˈjuːnɪtɪ) *n., pl.* **-ties. 1.** the state or quality of being one; oneness. **2.** the act, state, or quality of forming a whole from separate parts. **3.** something whole or complete that is composed of separate parts. **4.** mutual agreement; harmony or concord: *the participants were no longer in unity.* **5.** uniformity or constancy: *unity of purpose.* **6.** *Maths.* **a.** the number or numeral one. **b.** a quantity assuming the value of one: *the area of the triangle was regarded as unity.* **c.** the element of a set producing no change in a number following multiplication. **7.** any one of the three principles of dramatic structure by which the action of a play should be limited to a single plot (unity of action), a single location (unity of place), and a single day (unity of time). [C13: from OF *unité*, from L *ūnitās*, from *ūnus* one]

Univ. *abbrev. for* University.

univalent (ˌjuːnɪˈveɪlənt, juːˈnɪvələnt) *adj.* **1.** (of a chromosome during meiosis) not paired with its homologue. **2.** *Chem.* another word for **monovalent.** —ˌ**uniˈvalency** *n.*

univalve (ˈjuːnɪˌvælv) *Zool.* ~*adj.* **1.** relating to or possessing a mollusc shell that consists of a single piece (valve). ~*n.* **2.** a gastropod mollusc.

universal (ˌjuːnɪˈvɜːsᵊl) *adj.* **1.** of or typical of the whole of mankind or of nature. **2.** common to or proceeding from all in a particular group. **3.** applicable to or affecting many individuals, conditions, or cases. **4.** existing or prevailing everywhere. **5.** applicable or occurring throughout or relating to the universe: *a universal constant.* **6.** (esp. of a language) capable of being used and understood by all. **7.** embracing or versed in many fields of knowledge, activity, interest, etc. **8.** *Machinery.* designed or adapted for a range of sizes, fittings, or uses. **9.** *Logic.* (of a statement or proposition) affirming or denying something about every member of a class, as in *all men are wicked.* Cf. **particular** (sense 6). **10.** *Arch.* entire; whole. ~*n.* **11.** *Philosophy.* a general term or concept or the type such a term signifies. **12.** *Logic.* a universal proposition, statement, or formula. **13.** a characteristic common to every member of a particular culture or to every human being.

universal class *or* **set** *n.* (in Boolean algebra) the class containing all points and including all other classes.

universal gas constant *n.* another name for **gas constant.**

universalism (ˌjuːnɪˈvɜːsəˌlɪzəm) *n.* **1.** a universal feature or characteristic. **2.** another word for **universality.**

Universalism (ˌjuːnɪˈvɜːsəˌlɪzəm) *n.* a system of religious beliefs maintaining that all men are predestined for salvation. —ˌ**Uniˈversalist** *n., adj.*

universality (ˌjuːnɪvɜːˈsælɪtɪ) *n.* the state or quality of being universal.

universalize *or* **-ise** (ˌjuːnɪˈvɜːsəˌlaɪz) *vb.* (*tr.*) to make universal. —ˌ**uniˌversaliˈzation** *or* **-iˈsation** *n.*

universal joint *or* **coupling** *n.* a form of coupling between two rotating shafts allowing freedom of movement in all directions.

universally (ˌjuːnɪˈvɜːsəlɪ) *adv.* everywhere or in every case: *this principle applies universally.*

universal motor n. an electric motor capable of working on either direct current or single-phase alternating current at approximately the same speed and output.

universal time n. another name for **Greenwich Mean Time.**

universe ('juːnɪˌvɜːs) n. **1.** Astron. the aggregate of all existing matter, energy, and space. **2.** human beings collectively. **3.** a province or sphere of thought or activity. [C16: from F, from L *ūniversum* the whole world, from *ūniversus* all together, from UNI- + *vertere* to turn]

universe of discourse n. Logic. the complete range of objects, relations, ideas, etc., that are expressed or implied in a discussion.

university (ˌjuːnɪˈvɜːsɪtɪ) n., pl. **-ties. 1.** an institution of higher education having authority to award bachelors' and higher degrees, usually having research facilities. **2.** the buildings, members, staff, or campus of a university. [C14: from OF, from Med. L *universitās* group of scholars, from LL: guild, body of men, from L: whole]

unjust (ʌnˈdʒʌst) adj. not in accordance with accepted standards of fairness or justice; unfair. —**un'justly** adv. —**un'justness** n.

unkempt (ʌnˈkɛmpt) adj. **1.** (of the hair) uncombed; dishevelled. **2.** ungroomed; slovenly: *unkempt appearance.* [OE *uncembed*; from UN-[1] + *cembed*, p.p. of *cemban* to comb] —**un'kemptly** adv. —**un'kemptness** n.

unkind (ʌnˈkaɪnd) adj. lacking kindness; unsympathetic or cruel. —**un'kindly** adv. —**un'kindness** n.

unknowing (ʌnˈnəʊɪŋ) adj. **1.** not knowing; ignorant. **2.** (*postpositive*; often foll. by *of*) unaware (of). —**un'knowingly** adv.

unknown (ʌnˈnəʊn) adj. **1.** not known, understood, or recognized. **2.** not established, identified, or discovered: *an unknown island.* **3.** not famous: *some unknown artist.* ~n. **4.** an unknown person, quantity, or thing. **5.** Maths. a variable the value of which is to be discovered by solving an equation; a variable in a conditional equation. —**un'knownness** n.

Unknown Soldier or **Warrior** n. (in various countries) an unidentified soldier who has died in battle and for whom a tomb is established as a memorial to the other unidentified dead of the nation's armed forces.

unlace (ʌnˈleɪs) vb. (tr.) **1.** to loosen or undo the lacing of (shoes, etc.). **2.** to unfasten or remove garments, etc., of (oneself or another) by or as if by undoing lacing.

unlawful assembly (ʌnˈlɔːful) n. Law. a meeting of three or more people with the intent of carrying out any unlawful purpose.

unlay (ʌnˈleɪ) vb. **-laying, -laid.** (tr.) to untwist (a rope or cable) to separate its strands.

unleaded (ʌnˈlɛdɪd) adj. (of petrol) containing a reduced amount of tetraethyl lead, in order to reduce environmental pollution.

unlearn (ʌnˈlɜːn) vb. **-learning, -learnt** or **-learned** (-ˈlɜːnd). to try to forget (something learnt) or to discard (accumulated knowledge).

unlearned (ʌnˈlɜːnɪd) adj. ignorant or untaught. —**un'learnedly** adv.

unlearnt (ʌnˈlɜːnt) or **unlearned** (ʌnˈlɜːnd) adj. **1.** denoting knowledge or skills innately present and therefore not learnt. **2.** not learnt or taken notice of: *unlearnt lessons.*

unleash (ʌnˈliːʃ) vb. (tr.) **1.** to release from or as if from a leash. **2.** to free from restraint.

unleavened (ʌnˈlɛvənd) adj. (of bread, etc.) made from a dough containing no yeast or leavening.

unless (ʌnˈlɛs) conj. (*subordinating*) except under the circumstances that; except on the condition that: *they'll sell it unless he hears otherwise.* [C14 *onlesse*, from *on* ON + *lesse* LESS]

▷ **Usage.** Careful writers of English who wish to keep their style clear and concise avoid the use of the expressions *unless and until* and *unless or until.* The difference in meaning of these two words is, in this context, not sufficient to make mentioning them both worthwhile; either would be adequate alone: *Unless* (or *until*, but not *unless and until*) *a candidate is nominated, the election cannot take place.*

unlettered (ʌnˈlɛtəd) adj. uneducated; illiterate.

unlike (ʌnˈlaɪk) adj. **1.** not alike; dissimilar or unequal; different. ~prep. **2.** not like; not typical of: *unlike his father he lacks intelligence.* —**un'likeness** n.

unlikely (ʌnˈlaɪklɪ) adj. not likely; improbable. —**un'likeliness** or **un'likeli,hood** n.

unlimber (ʌnˈlɪmbə) vb. **1.** (tr.) to disengage (a gun) from its limber. **2.** to prepare (something) for use.

unlimited (ʌnˈlɪmɪtɪd) adj. **1.** without limits or bounds: *unlimited knowledge.* **2.** not restricted, limited, or qualified: *unlimited power.* —**un'limitedly** adv. —**un'limitedness** n.

unlisted (ʌnˈlɪstɪd) adj. **1.** not entered on a list. **2.** the U.S. and Canad. word for **ex-directory.**

Unlisted Securities Market n. a market on the London Stock Exchange for trading in shares of smaller companies, who do not wish to comply with the requirements for a full listing. Abbrev.: **USM.**

unload (ʌnˈləʊd) vb. **1.** to remove a load or cargo from (a ship, lorry, etc.). **2.** to discharge (cargo, freight, etc.). **3.** (tr.) to relieve of a burden or troubles. **4.** (tr.) to give vent to (anxiety, troubles, etc.). **5.** (tr.) to get rid of or dispose of (esp. surplus goods). **6.** (tr.) to remove the charge of ammunition from (a firearm). —**un'loader** n.

unlock (ʌnˈlɒk) vb. **1.** (tr.) to unfasten (a lock, door, etc.). **2.** (tr.) to release or let loose. **3.** (tr.) to provide the key to: *unlock a puzzle.* **4.** (intr.) to become unlocked. —**un'lockable** adj.

unlooked-for (ˌʌnˈlʊktfɔː) adj. unexpected; unforeseen.

unloose (ʌnˈluːs) or **unloosen** vb. (tr.) **1.** to set free; release. **2.** to loosen or relax (a hold, grip, etc.). **3.** to unfasten or untie.

unlovely (ʌnˈlʌvlɪ) adj. unpleasant in appearance or character. —**un'loveliness** n.

unlucky (ʌnˈlʌkɪ) adj. **1.** characterized by misfortune or failure: *an unlucky chance.* **2.** ill-omened; inauspicious: *an unlucky date.* **3.** regrettable; disappointing. —**un'luckily** adv. —**un'luckiness** n.

unmake (ʌnˈmeɪk) vb. **-making, -made.** (tr.) **1.** to undo or destroy. **2.** to depose from office or authority. **3.** to alter the nature of.

unman (ʌnˈmæn) vb. **-manning, -manned.** (tr.) **1.** to cause to lose courage or nerve. **2.** to make effeminate. **3.** to remove the men from.

unmanly (ʌnˈmænlɪ) adj. **1.** not masculine or virile. **2.** ignoble, cowardly, or dishonourable. ~adv. **3.** Arch. in an unmanly manner. —**un'manliness** n.

unmanned (ʌnˈmænd) adj. **1.** lacking personnel or crew: *an unmanned ship.* **2.** (of aircraft, spacecraft, etc.) operated by automatic or remote control. **3.** uninhabited.

unmannered (ʌnˈmænəd) adj. **1.** without good manners; rude. **2.** without mannerisms.

unmannerly (ʌnˈmænəlɪ) adj. **1.** lacking manners; discourteous. ~adv. **2.** Arch. rudely; discourteously. —**un'mannerliness** n.

unmask (ʌnˈmɑːsk) vb. **1.** to remove (the mask or disguise) from (someone or oneself). **2.** to appear or cause to appear in true character. —**un'masker** n.

unmeaning (ʌnˈmiːnɪŋ) adj. **1.** having no meaning. **2.** showing no intelligence; vacant: *an unmeaning face.* —**un'meaningly** adv. —**un'meaningness** n.

unmeet (ʌnˈmiːt) adj. Literary or arch. unsuitable. —**un'meetly** adv. —**un'meetness** n.

---

un'joint vb.
un'justi,fiable adj.
un'justi,fied adj.
un'kept adj.
un'kissed adj.
un'knit vb.
un'knowable adj.
un'labelled adj.
un'lade vb.
un'laden adj.

un'lady,like adj.
un'laid adj.
,unla'mented adj.
un'latch vb.
un'lawful adj.
un'liber,ated adj.
un'licensed adj.
un'lighted adj.
un'likable adj.

un'lined adj.
un'lit adj.
un'locked adj.
un'lovable adj.
un'loved adj.
un'made adj.
un'magni,fied adj.
un'manageable adj.
un'marked adj.

un'marketable adj.
un'married adj.
un'matched adj.
,unma'tured adj.
un'meant adj.
un'measured adj.
,unme'lodious adj.
un'melted adj.
un'memorable adj.

unmentionable (ʌnˈmɛnʃənəbəl) *adj.* **a.** unsuitable or forbidden as a topic of conversation. **b.** (*as n.*): *the un-mentionable.* —**un'mentionableness** *n.* —**un'mention-ably** *adv.*
unmentionables (ʌnˈmɛnʃənəbəlz) *pl. n. Chiefly humorous.* underwear.
unmerciful (ʌnˈmɜːsɪful) *adj.* **1.** showing no mercy; relentless. **2.** extreme or excessive. —**un'mercifully** *adv.* —**un'mercifulness** *n.*
unmindful (ʌnˈmaɪndful) *adj.* (*usually postpositive and foll. by of*) careless or forgetful. —**un'mindfully** *adv.* —**un'mindfulness** *n.*
unmistakable *or* **unmistakeable** (ˌʌnmɪsˈteɪkəbəl) *adj.* not mistakable; clear or unambiguous. —**unmis'takably** *or* **unmis'takeably** *adv.*
unmitigated (ʌnˈmɪtɪˌɡeɪtɪd) *adj.* **1.** not diminished in intensity, severity, etc. **2.** (*prenominal*) (intensifier): *an unmitigated disaster.* —**un'miti,gatedly** *adv.*
unmoral (ʌnˈmɒrəl) *adj.* outside morality; amoral. —**un-morality** (ˌʌnmɒˈrælɪtɪ) *n.* —**un'morally** *adv.*
unmurmuring (ʌnˈmɜːmərɪŋ) *adj.* not complaining.
unmuzzle (ʌnˈmʌzəl) *vb.* (*tr.*) **1.** to take the muzzle off (a dog, etc.). **2.** to free from control or censorship.
unnatural (ʌnˈnætʃərəl) *adj.* **1.** contrary to nature; abnormal. **2.** not in accordance with accepted standards of behaviour or right and wrong: *unnatural love.* **3.** uncanny; supernatural: *unnatural phenomena.* **4.** affected or forced: *an unnatural manner.* **5.** inhuman or monstrous: *an unnatural crime.* —**un'naturally** *adv.* —**un'naturalness** *n.*
unnecessary (ʌnˈnɛsɪsərɪ) *adj.* not necessary. —**un'nec-essarily** *adv.* —**un'necessariness** *n.*
unnerve (ʌnˈnɜːv) *vb.* (*tr.*) to cause to lose courage, strength, confidence, self-control, etc.
unnumbered (ʌnˈnʌmbəd) *adj.* **1.** countless; innumerable. **2.** not counted or assigned a number.
UNO *abbrev. for* United Nations Organization.
unoccupied (ʌnˈɒkjʊˌpaɪd) *adj.* **1.** (of a building) without occupants. **2.** unemployed or idle. **3.** (of an area or country) not overrun by foreign troops.
unofficial (ˌʌnəˈfɪʃəl) *adj.* **1.** not official or formal: *an unofficial engagement.* **2.** not confirmed officially: *an unofficial report.* **3.** (of a strike) not approved by the strikers' trade union. —**unof'ficially** *adv.*
unorganized *or* **-nised** (ʌnˈɔːɡəˌnaɪzd) *adj.* **1.** not arranged into an organized system, structure, or unity. **2.** (of workers) not unionized. **3.** nonliving; inorganic.
unpack (ʌnˈpæk) *vb.* **1.** to remove the packed contents of (a case, trunk, etc.). **2.** (*tr.*) to take (something) out of a packed container. **3.** (*tr.*) to unload: *to unpack a mule.* —**un'packer** *n.*
unpaged (ʌnˈpeɪdʒd) *adj.* (of a book) having no page numbers.
unparalleled (ʌnˈpærəˌlɛld) *adj.* unmatched; unequalled.
unparliamentary (ˌʌnpɑːləˈmɛntərɪ) *adj.* not consistent with parliamentary procedure or practice.

—**,unparlia'mentarily** *adv.* —**,unparlia'mentariness** *n.*
unpeg (ʌnˈpɛɡ) *vb.* **-pegging, -pegged.** (*tr.*) **1.** to remove the peg from, esp. to unfasten. **2.** to allow (prices, etc.) to rise and fall freely.
unpeople (ʌnˈpiːpəl) *vb.* (*tr.*) to empty of people.
unperson (ˈʌnpɜːsən) *n.* a person whose existence is officially denied or ignored.
unpick (ʌnˈpɪk) *vb.* (*tr.*) **1.** to undo (the stitches) of (a piece of sewing). **2.** to unravel or undo (a garment, etc.).
unpin (ʌnˈpɪn) *vb.* **-pinning, -pinned.** (*tr.*) **1.** to remove a pin or pins from. **2.** to unfasten by removing pins.
unpleasant (ʌnˈplɛzənt) *adj.* not pleasant or agreeable. —**un'pleasantly** *adv.* —**un'pleasantness** *n.*
unplumbed (ʌnˈplʌmd) *adj.* **1.** unfathomed; unsounded. **2.** not understood in depth. **3.** (of a building) having no plumbing.
unpolled (ʌnˈpəʊld) *adj.* **1.** not included in an opinion poll. **2.** not having voted. **3.** *Arch.* unshorn.
unpopular (ʌnˈpɒpjʊlə) *adj.* not popular with an individual or group of people. —**unpopularity** (ˌʌnpɒpjʊˈlærɪtɪ) *n.* —**un'popularly** *adv.*
unpractical (ʌnˈpræktɪkəl) *adj.* another word for **imprac-tical.** —**,unpracti'cality** *n.* —**un'practically** *adv.*
unpractised *or U.S.* **unpracticed** (ʌnˈpræktɪst) *adj.* **1.** without skill, training, or experience. **2.** not used or done often or repeatedly. **3.** not yet tested.
unprecedented (ʌnˈprɛsɪˌdɛntɪd) *adj.* having no precedent; unparalleled. —**un'prece,dentedly** *adv.*
unprejudiced (ʌnˈprɛdʒʊdɪst) *adj.* not prejudiced or biased; impartial. —**un'prejudicedly** *adv.*
unprincipled (ʌnˈprɪnsɪpəld) *adj.* lacking moral principles; unscrupulous. —**un'principledness** *n.*
unprintable (ʌnˈprɪntəbəl) *adj.* unsuitable for printing for reasons of obscenity, libel, etc. —**un'printableness** *n.* —**un'printably** *adv.*
unprofessional (ˌʌnprəˈfɛʃənəl) *adj.* **1.** contrary to the accepted code of conduct of a profession. **2.** amateur. **3.** not belonging to or having the required qualifications for a profession. —**,unpro'fessionally** *adv.*
unputdownable (ˌʌnpʊtˈdaʊnəbəl) *adj.* (esp. of a novel) so gripping as to be read at one sitting.
unqualified (ʌnˈkwɒlɪˌfaɪd) *adj.* **1.** lacking the necessary qualifications. **2.** not restricted or modified: *an unquali-fied criticism.* **3.** (*usually prenominal*) (intensifier): *an unqualified success.* —**un'quali,fiable** *adj.*
unquestionable (ʌnˈkwɛstʃənəbəl) *adj.* **1.** indubitable or indisputable. **2.** not admitting of exception: *an un-questionable ruling.* —**un,questiona'bility** *n.* —**un'questionably** *adv.*
unquestioned (ʌnˈkwɛstʃənd) *adj.* **1.** accepted without question. **2.** not admitting of doubt or question: *unques-tioned power.* **3.** not questioned or interrogated.

---

un'mentioned *adj.*	,unob'structed *adj.*	,unper'suaded *adj.*	,unpre'scribed *adj.*
un'merchantable *adj.*	,unob'tainable *adj.*	,unper'turbable *adj.*	,unpre'sentable *adj.*
un'merited *adj.*	,unob'tained *adj.*	,unper'turbed *adj.*	un'pressed *adj.*
un'metrical *adj.*	,unob'trusive *adj.*	,unphilo'sophical *adj.*	,unpre'sumptuous *adj.*
,unmis'taken *adj.*	,unof fended *adj.*	un'pitied *adj.*	,unpre'tending *adj.*
un'mixed *adj.*	,unof fensive *adj.*	un'pitying *adj.*	,unpre'tentious *adj.*
un'modi,fied *adj.*	,unof ficious *adj.*	un'placed *adj.*	un'priced *adj.*
un'moor *vb.*	un'opened *adj.*	un'planned *adj.*	,unpro'claimed *adj.*
un'moti,vated *adj.*	,unop'posed *adj.*	un'playable *adj.*	,unpro'ductive *adj.*
un'mounted *adj.*	,unor'dained *adj.*	un'pleasing *adj.*	,unpro fessed *adj.*
un'mourned *adj.*	uno'riginal *adj.*	un'plug *vb.*	un'profitable *adj.*
un'movable *adj.*	un'ortho,dox *adj.*	un'pointed *adj.*	,unpro'hibited *adj.*
un'moved *adj.*	,unosten'tatious *adj.*	un'polar,ized *or* -,ised *adj.*	un'promising *adj.*
un'musical *adj.*	un'paid *adj.*	un'polished *adj.*	un'prompted *adj.*
un'mysti,fied *adj.*	un'paired *adj.*	un'politic *adj.*	,unpro'nounceable *adj.*
un'namable *adj.*	un'palatable *adj.*	un'pol'luted *adj.*	,unpro'nounced *adj.*
un'named *adj.*	un'pardonable *adj.*	un'popu,lated *adj.*	,unpro'pitious *adj.*
un'navigable *adj.*	un'pasteur,ized *or*	un'posed *adj.*	,unpro'tected *adj.*
un'navi,gated *adj.*	-,ised *adj.*	un'practicable *adj.*	,unpro'testing *adj.*
un'needed *adj.*	un'patented *adj.*	,unpre,dicta'bility *or*	un'proved *adj.*
,unne'gotiable *adj.*	un'patri'otic *adj.*	,unpre'dictableness *n.*	un'proven *adj.*
un'neighbourly *adj.*	,unper'ceived *adj.*	,unpre'dictable *adj.*	,unpro'vided *adj.*
un'noticed *adj.*	,unper'ceptive *adj.*	,unpre'dicted *adj.*	,unpro'voked *adj.*
,unob'jectionable *adj.*	,unper'fected *adj.*	,unpre'medi,tated *adj.*	un'published *adj.*
,uno'bliging *adj.*	,unper'fo,rated *adj.*	,unpre'pared *adj.*	un'punished *adj.*
,unob'served *adj.*	,unper'formed *adj.*	,unprepos'sessing *adj.*	un'questioning *adj.*

unquiet (ʌnˈkwaɪət) *Chiefly literary.* ~*adj.* **1.** characterized by disorder or tumult: *unquiet times.* **2.** anxious; uneasy. ~*n.* **3.** a state of unrest. —**un'quietly** *adv.* —**un'quietness** *n.*

unquote (ʌnˈkwəʊt) *interj.* **1.** an expression used parenthetically to indicate that the preceding quotation is finished. ~*vb.* **2.** to close (a quotation), esp. in printing.

unravel (ʌnˈrævəl) *vb.* **-elling, -elled** *or U.S.* **-eling, -eled. 1.** (*tr.*) to reduce (something knitted or woven) to separate strands. **2.** (*tr.*) to explain or solve: *the mystery was unravelled.* **3.** (*intr.*) to become unravelled.

unread (ʌnˈrɛd) *adj.* **1.** (of a book, etc.) not yet read. **2.** (of a person) having read little.

unreadable (ʌnˈriːdəbəl) *adj.* **1.** illegible; undecipherable. **2.** difficult or tedious to read. —**un,reada'bility** *or* **un'readableness** *n.*

unready (ʌnˈrɛdɪ) *adj.* **1.** not ready or prepared. **2.** slow or hesitant to see or act. —**un'readily** *adv.* —**un'readiness** *n.*

unreal (ʌnˈrɪəl) *adj.* **1.** imaginary or fanciful or seemingly so: *an unreal situation.* **2.** having no actual existence or substance. **3.** insincere or artificial. —**unreality** (ˌʌnrɪˈælɪtɪ) *n.* —**un'really** *adv.*

unreason (ʌnˈriːzən) *n.* **1.** irrationality or madness. **2.** something that lacks or is contrary to reason. **3.** lack of order; chaos.

unreasonable (ʌnˈriːznəbəl) *adj.* **1.** immoderate: *unreasonable demands.* **2.** refusing to listen to reason. **3.** lacking judgment. —**un'reasonableness** *n.* —**un'reasonably** *adv.*

unreasoning (ʌnˈriːzənɪŋ) *adj.* not controlled by reason; irrational. —**un'reasoningly** *adv.*

unregenerate (ˌʌnrɪˈdʒɛnərɪt) *adj. also* **unregenerated. 1.** unrepentant; unreformed. **2.** obstinately adhering to one's own views. ~*n.* **3.** an unregenerate person. —ˌun**re'generacy** *n.* —ˌunre'generately *adv.*

unrelenting (ˌʌnrɪˈlɛntɪŋ) *adj.* **1.** refusing to relent or take pity. **2.** not diminishing in determination, speed, effort, force, etc. —ˌunre'lentingly *adv.* —ˌunre'lentingness *n.*

unreligious (ˌʌnrɪˈlɪdʒəs) *adj.* **1.** another word for **irreligious. 2.** secular. —ˌunre'ligiously *adv.*

unremitting (ˌʌnrɪˈmɪtɪŋ) *adj.* never slackening or stopping; unceasing; constant. —ˌunre'mittingly *adv.* —ˌunre'mittingness *n.*

unreserved (ˌʌnrɪˈzɜːvd) *adj.* **1.** without reserve; having an open manner. **2.** without reservation. **3.** not booked or bookable. —**unreservedly** (ˌʌnrɪˈzɜːvɪdlɪ) *adv.* —ˌunre'servedness *n.*

unrest (ʌnˈrɛst) *n.* **1.** a troubled or rebellious state of discontent. **2.** an uneasy or troubled state.

unriddle (ʌnˈrɪdəl) *vb.* (*tr.*) to solve or puzzle out. [C16: from UN-² + RIDDLE¹] —**un'riddler** *n.*

unrig (ʌnˈrɪɡ) *vb.* **-rigging, -rigged. 1.** (*tr.*) to strip (a vessel) of standing and running rigging. **2.** *Arch. or dialect.* to undress (someone or oneself).

unrighteous (ʌnˈraɪtʃəs) *adj.* **1. a.** sinful; wicked. **b.** (*as collective n.; preceded by the*): *the unrighteous.* **2.** not fair or right; unjust. —**un'righteously** *adv.* —**un'righteousness** *n.*

unrip (ʌnˈrɪp) *vb.* **-ripping, -ripped.** (*tr.*) **1.** to rip open. **2.** *Obs.* to reveal; disclose.

unripe (ʌnˈraɪp) *or* **unripened** *adj.* **1.** not fully matured. **2.** not fully prepared or developed; not ready. —**un'ripeness** *n.*

unrivalled *or U.S.* **unrivaled** (ʌnˈraɪvəld) *adj.* having no equal; matchless.

unroll (ʌnˈrəʊl) *vb.* **1.** to open out or unwind (something rolled, folded, or coiled) or (of something rolled, etc.) to become opened out or unwound. **2.** to make or become visible or apparent, esp. gradually; unfold.

unruffled (ʌnˈrʌfəld) *adj.* **1.** unmoved; calm. **2.** still: *the unruffled seas.* —**un'ruffledness** *n.*

unruly (ʌnˈruːlɪ) *adj.* **-lier, -liest.** disposed to disobedience or indiscipline. —**un'ruliness** *n.*

UNRWA (ˈʌnrə) *n. acronym for* United Nations Relief and Works Agency.

unsaddle (ʌnˈsædəl) *vb.* **1.** to remove the saddle from (a horse, mule, etc.). **2.** (*tr.*) to unhorse.

unsaddling enclosure *n.* the area at a racecourse where horses are unsaddled after a race and often where awards are given to owners, trainers, and jockeys.

unsaid (ʌnˈsɛd) *adj.* not said or expressed; unspoken.

unsaturated (ʌnˈsætʃəˌreɪtɪd) *adj.* **1.** not saturated. **2.** (of a chemical compound, esp. an organic compound) containing one or more double or triple bonds and thus capable of undergoing addition reactions. **3.** (of a fat, esp. a vegetable fat) containing a high proportion of fatty acids having double bonds. —ˌunsatu'ration *n.*

unsavoury *or U.S.* **unsavory** (ʌnˈseɪvərɪ) *adj.* **1.** objectionable or distasteful: *an unsavoury character.* **2.** disagreeable in odour or taste. —**un'savourily** *or U.S.* **un'savorily** *adv.* —**un'savouriness** *or U.S.* **un'savoriness** *n.*

unsay (ʌnˈseɪ) *vb.* **-saying, -said.** (*tr.*) to retract or withdraw (something said or written).

unscathed (ʌnˈskeɪðd) *adj.* not harmed or injured.

unscramble (ʌnˈskræmbəl) *vb.* (*tr.*) **1.** to resolve from confusion or disorderliness. **2.** to restore (a scrambled message) to an intelligible form. —**un'scrambler** *n.*

unscrew (ʌnˈskruː) *vb.* **1.** (*tr.*) to remove a screw from (an object). **2.** (*tr.*) to loosen (a screw, lid, etc.) by rotating, usually in an anticlockwise direction. **3.** (*intr.*) (esp. of an engaged threaded part) to become loosened or separated.

unscripted (ʌnˈskrɪptɪd) *adj.* (of a speech, play, etc.) not using or based on a script.

unscrupulous (ʌnˈskruːpjʊləs) *adj.* without scruples; unprincipled. —**un'scrupulously** *adv.* —**un'scrupulousness** *n.*

unseal (ʌnˈsiːl) *vb.* (*tr.*) **1.** to remove or break the seal of. **2.** to free (something concealed or closed as if sealed): *to unseal one's lips.*

unsealed (ʌnˈsiːld) *adj. Austral. & N.Z.* (of a road) surfaced with road metal not bound by bitumen or other sealant.

unseam (ʌnˈsiːm) *vb.* (*tr.*) to open or undo the seam of.

unseasonable (ʌnˈsiːzənəbəl) *adj.* **1.** (esp. of the weather) inappropriate for the season. **2.** untimely; inopportune. —**un'seasonableness** *n.* —**un'seasonably** *adv.*

unseat (ʌnˈsiːt) *vb.* (*tr.*) **1.** to throw or displace from a seat, saddle, etc. **2.** to depose from office or position.

---

un'quotable *adj.*	ˌunre'freshed *adj.*	ˌunre'quited *adj.*	un'salted *adj.*
ˌunreal'istic *adj.*	un're'registered *adj.*	ˌunre'sisting *adj.*	un'sanctioned *adj.*
un're'al,ized *or* -,ised *adj.*	un'regu,lated *adj.*	ˌunre'solved *adj.*	un'sanitary *adj.*
ˌunre'ceptive *adj.*	ˌunre'hearsed *adj.*	ˌunre'sponsive *adj.*	ˌunsatis'factory *adj.*
un'recog,nizable *or* -,nisable *adj.*	un're'lated *adj.*	un'rested *adj.*	un'satis,fied *adj.*
	un're'liable *adj.*	ˌunre'strained *adj.*	un'satis,fying *adj.*
un'recog,nized *or* -,nised *adj.*	ˌunre'markable *adj.*	ˌunre'stricted *adj.*	un'saved *adj.*
	un're'membered *adj.*	ˌunre'vealed *adj.*	un'sayable *adj.*
ˌunrecom'mended *adj.*	ˌunre'morseful *adj.*	ˌunre'vealing *adj.*	un'scented *adj.*
un'recom,pensed *adj.*	un're'newed *adj.*	ˌunre'vised *adj.*	un'scheduled *adj.*
un'recon,ciled *adj.*	un're'nowned *adj.*	ˌunre'warded *adj.*	un'schooled *adj.*
ˌunrecon'structed *adj.*	un're'pealed *adj.*	ˌunre'warding *adj.*	ˌunscien'tific *adj.*
ˌunre'corded *adj.*	un're'peatable *adj.*	un'ridden *adj.*	un'scratched *adj.*
ˌunre'deemable *adj.*	un're'pentant *adj.*	un'ripened *adj.*	un'screened *adj.*
ˌunre'deemed *adj.*	un're'ported *adj.*	ˌunro'mantic *adj.*	un'seasoned *adj.*
un'reel *vb.*	ˌunrepre'sentative *adj.*	un'rounded *adj.*	un'sea,worthy *adj.*
ˌunre'fined *adj.*	ˌunrepre'sented *adj.*	un'ruled *adj.*	ˌunse'cluded *adj.*
ˌunre'flected *adj.*	ˌunre'proved *adj.*	un'safe *adj.*	ˌunse'cured *adj.*
ˌunre'flecting *adj.*	ˌunre'quested *adj.*	un'salaried *adj.*	

unseeded (ʌn'siːdɪd) *adj.* (of players in various sports) not assigned to a preferential position in the preliminary rounds of a tournament.

unseemly (ʌn'siːmlɪ) *adj.* **1.** not in good style or taste. **2.** *Obs.* unattractive. ~*adv.* **3.** *Rare.* in an unseemly manner. —**un'seemliness** *n.*

unseen (ʌn'siːn) *adj.* **1.** not observed or perceived; invisible. **2.** (of passages of writing) not previously seen or prepared. ~*n.* **3.** *Chiefly Brit.* a passage, not previously seen, that is presented to students for translation.

unselfish (ʌn'sɛlfɪʃ) *adj.* not selfish; generous. —**un'selfishly** *adv.* —**un'selfishness** *n.*

unsettle (ʌn'sɛt*ə*l) *vb.* **1.** (*usually tr.*) to change or become changed from a fixed or settled condition. **2.** (*tr.*) to confuse or agitate (emotions, the mind, etc.). —**un'settlement** *n.*

unsettled (ʌn'sɛt*ə*ld) *adj.* **1.** lacking order or stability: *an unsettled era.* **2.** unpredictable: *an unsettled climate.* **3.** constantly changing or moving from place to place: *an unsettled life.* **4.** (of controversy, etc.) not brought to an agreed conclusion. **5.** (of debts, law cases, etc.) not disposed of. —**un'settledness** *n.*

unsex (ʌn'sɛks) *vb.* (*tr.*) *Chiefly literary.* to deprive (a person) of the attributes of his or her sex, esp. to make a woman more callous.

unshapen (ʌn'ʃeɪp*ə*n) *adj.* **1.** having no definite shape; shapeless. **2.** deformed; misshapen.

unsheathe (ʌn'ʃiːð) *vb.* (*tr.*) to draw or pull out (something, esp. a weapon) from a sheath.

unship (ʌn'ʃɪp) *vb.* **-shipping, -shipped. 1.** to be or cause to be unloaded, discharged, or disembarked from a ship. **2.** (*tr.*) *Naut.* to remove from a regular place: *to unship oars.*

unsighted (ʌn'saɪtɪd) *adj.* **1.** not sighted. **2.** not having a clear view. **3.** (of a gun) not equipped with a sight. —**un'sightedly** *adv.*

unsightly (ʌn'saɪtlɪ) *adj.* unpleasant or unattractive to look at; ugly. —**un'sightliness** *n.*

unskilful *or U.S.* **unskillful** (ʌn'skɪlfʊl) *adj.* lacking dexterity or proficiency. —**un'skilfully** *or U.S.* **un'skillfully** *adv.* —**un'skilfulness** *or U.S.* **un'skillfulness** *n.*

unskilled (ʌn'skɪld) *adj.* **1.** not having or requiring any special skill or training: *an unskilled job.* **2.** having no skill; inexpert.

unsling (ʌn'slɪŋ) *vb.* **-slinging, -slung.** (*tr.*) **1.** to remove or release from a slung position. **2.** to remove slings from.

unsnap (ʌn'snæp) *vb.* **-snapping, -snapped.** (*tr.*) to unfasten (the snap or catch) of (something).

unsnarl (ʌn'snɑːl) *vb.* (*tr.*) to free from a snarl or tangle.

unsociable (ʌn'səʊʃəb*ə*l) *adj.* **1.** (of a person) disinclined to associate or fraternize with others. **2.** unconducive to social intercourse: *an unsociable neighbourhood.* —**un,socia'bility** *or* **un'sociableness** *n.*

unsocial (ʌn'səʊʃ*ə*l) *adj.* **1.** not social; antisocial. **2.** (of the hours of work of certain jobs) falling outside the normal working day.

unsophisticated (ˌʌnsə'fɪstɪˌkeɪtɪd) *adj.* **1.** lacking experience or worldly wisdom. **2.** marked by a lack of refinement or complexity: *an unsophisticated machine.* **3.** unadulterated or genuine. —**ˌunso'phisti,catedly** *adv.* —**ˌunso'phisti,catedness** *or* **ˌunso,phisti'cation** *n.*

unsound (ʌn'saʊnd) *adj.* **1.** diseased or unstable: *of unsound mind.* **2.** unreliable or fallacious: *unsound advice.* **3.** lacking strength or firmness: *unsound foundations.* **4.** of doubtful financial or commercial viability: *an unsound enterprise.* —**un'soundly** *adv.* —**un'soundness** *n.*

unsparing (ʌn'spɛərɪŋ) *adj.* **1.** not sparing or frugal; lavish. **2.** showing harshness or severity. —**un'sparingly** *adv.* —**un'sparingness** *n.*

unspeakable (ʌn'spiːkəb*ə*l) *adj.* **1.** incapable of expression in words: *unspeakable ecstasy.* **2.** indescribably bad or evil. **3.** not to be uttered: *unspeakable thoughts.* —**un'speakableness** *n.* —**un'speakably** *adv.*

unstable (ʌn'steɪb*ə*l) *adj.* **1.** lacking stability, fixity, or firmness. **2.** disposed to temperamental or psychological variability. **3.** (of a chemical compound) readily decomposing. **4.** *Physics.* **a.** (of an elementary particle) having a very short lifetime. **b.** spontaneously decomposing by nuclear decay: *an unstable nuclide.* **5.** *Electronics.* (of an electrical circuit, etc.) having a tendency to self-oscillation. —**un'stableness** *n.* —**un'stably** *adv.*

unsteady (ʌn'stɛdɪ) *adj.* **1.** not securely fixed: *an unsteady foothold.* **2.** (of behaviour, etc.) erratic. **3.** without regularity: *an unsteady rhythm.* **4.** (of a manner of walking, etc.) precarious or staggering, as from intoxication. —**un'steadily** *adv.* —**un'steadiness** *n.*

unstep (ʌn'stɛp) *vb.* **-stepping, -stepped.** (*tr.*) *Naut.* to remove (a mast) from its step.

unstick (ʌn'stɪk) *vb.* **-sticking, -stuck.** (*tr.*) to free or loosen (something stuck).

unstop (ʌn'stɒp) *vb.* **-stopping, -stopped.** (*tr.*) **1.** to remove the stop or stopper from. **2.** to free from any stoppage or obstruction. **3.** to draw out the stops on (an organ). —**un'stoppable** *adj.* —**un'stoppably** *adv.*

unstopped (ʌn'stɒpt) *adj.* **1.** not obstructed or stopped up. **2.** *Phonetics.* denoting a speech sound for whose articulation the closure is not complete. **3.** *Prosody.* (of verse) having the sense of the line carried over into the next. **4.** (of an organ pipe or a string on a musical instrument) not stopped.

unstriated (ʌn'straɪˌeɪtɪd) *adj.* (of muscle) composed of elongated cells that do not have striations; smooth.

unstring (ʌn'strɪŋ) *vb.* **-stringing, -strung.** (*tr.*) **1.** to remove the strings of. **2.** (of beads, etc.) to remove from a string. **3.** to weaken emotionally (a person or his nerves).

unstriped (ʌn'straɪpt) *adj.* (esp. of smooth muscle) not having stripes; unstriated.

unstructured (ʌn'strʌktʃəd) *adj.* **1.** without formal structure or systematic organization. **2.** without a preformed shape; (esp. of clothes) loose; untailored.

unstrung (ʌn'strʌŋ) *adj.* **1.** emotionally distressed; unnerved. **2.** (of a stringed instrument) with the strings detached.

unstuck (ʌn'stʌk) *adj.* **1.** freed from being stuck, glued, fastened, etc. **2. come unstuck.** to suffer failure or disaster.

unstudied (ʌn'stʌdɪd) *adj.* **1.** natural. **2.** (foll. by *in*) without knowledge or training.

unsubstantial (ˌʌnsəb'stænʃ*ə*l) *adj.* **1.** lacking weight or firmness. **2.** (of an argument) of doubtful validity. **3.** of no material existence. —**ˌunsub,stanti'ality** *n.* —**ˌunsub'stantially** *adv.*

unsung (ʌn'sʌŋ) *adj.* **1.** not acclaimed or honoured: *unsung deeds.* **2.** not yet sung.

unsuspected (ˌʌnsə'spɛktɪd) *adj.* **1.** not under suspicion. **2.** not known to exist. —**ˌunsus'pectedly** *adv.* —**ˌunsus'pectedness** *n.*

unswerving (ʌn'swɜːvɪŋ) *adj.* not turning aside; constant.

untangle (ʌn'tæŋg*ə*l) *vb.* (*tr.*) **1.** to free from a tangled condition. **2.** to free from confusion.

untaught (ʌn'tɔːt) *adj.* **1.** without training or education. **2.** attained or achieved without instruction.

un'seeing *adj.*	un'shockable *adj.*	un'spoiled *adj.*	ˌunsup'portable *adj.*
un'segre,gated *adj.*	un'shod *adj.*	un'spoken *adj.*	ˌunsup'ported *adj.*
ˌunse'lected *adj.*	un'shrinkable *adj.*	un'sporting *adj.*	un'sure *adj.*
ˌunse'lective *adj.*	un'signed *adj.*	un'spotted *adj.*	ˌunsur'passable *adj.*
ˌunself'conscious *adj.*	un'sinkable *adj.*	un'statesman,like *adj.*	ˌunsur'passed *adj.*
ˌunsenti'mental *adj.*	un'sized *adj.*	un'stinted *adj.*	ˌunsus'ceptible *adj.*
un'set *adj.*	un'smiling *adj.*	un'strained *adj.*	ˌunsus'pecting *adj.*
un'shackle *vb.*	un'sold *adj.*	un'strap *vb.*	ˌunsus'tained *adj.*
un'shakable *adj.*	ˌunso'licited *adj.*	un'subdued *adj.*	un'sweetened *adj.*
un'shaken *adj.*	un'solved *adj.*	unsub'stanti,ated *adj.*	ˌunsympa'thetic *adj.*
un'shared *adj.*	un'sought *adj.*	ˌunsuc'cessful *adj.*	un'tainted *adj.*
un'shaved *adj.*	un'special,ized *or* -,ised *adj.*	un'suitable *adj.*	un'tamed *adj.*
un'shaven *adj.*		un'suited *adj.*	un'tapped *adj.*
un'shed *adj.*	un'speci,fied *adj.*	un'sullied *adj.*	un'tasted *adj.*
un'shielded *adj.*	ˌunspec'tacular *adj.*	un'super,vised *adj.*	un'taxed *adj.*

untenable (ʌn'tɛnəbəl) *adj.* **1.** (of theories, etc.) incapable of being maintained or vindicated. **2.** unable to be maintained against attack. —**un,tena'bility** *or* **un'tenableness** *n.* —**un'tenably** *adv.*

Unterwalden (*German* 'ʊntər,valdən) *n.* a canton of central Switzerland, on Lake Lucerne: consists of the demicantons of **Nidwalden** (east) and **Obwalden** (west). Capitals: (Nidwalden) Stans; (Obwalden) Sarnen. Pop.: (Nidwalden) 31 000 (1986 est.); (Obwalden) 27 600 (1986 est.). Areas: (Nidwalden) 274 sq. km (107 sq. miles); (Obwalden) 492 sq. km (192 sq. miles).

unthinkable (ʌn'θɪŋkəbəl) *adj.* **1.** not to be contemplated; out of the question. **2.** unimaginable; inconceivable. **3.** unreasonable; improbable. —**un'thinkably** *adv.*

unthinking (ʌn'θɪŋkɪŋ) *adj.* **1.** lacking thoughtfulness; inconsiderate. **2.** heedless; inadvertent. **3.** not thinking or able to think. —**un'thinkingly** *adv.* —**un'thinking-ness** *n.*

unthread (ʌn'θrɛd) *vb.* (*tr.*) **1.** to draw out the thread or threads from (a needle, etc.). **2.** to disentangle.

unthrone (ʌn'θrəʊn) *vb.* (*tr.*) a less common word for **dethrone**.

untidy (ʌn'taɪdɪ) *adj.* **-dier, -diest. 1.** not neat; slovenly. ~*vb.* **-dying, -died. 2.** (*tr.*) to make untidy. —**un'tidily** *adv.* —**un'tidiness** *n.*

untie (ʌn'taɪ) *vb.* **-tying, -tied. 1.** to unfasten or free (a knot or something that is tied) or (of a knot, etc.) to become unfastened. **2.** (*tr.*) to free from constraint or restriction.

until (ʌn'tɪl) *conj.* (*subordinating*) **1.** up to (a time) that: *he laughed until he cried.* **2.** (*used with a negative*) before (a time or event): *until you change, you can't go out.* ~*prep.* **3.** (often preceded by *up*) in or throughout the period before: *he waited until six.* **4.** (*used with a negative*) earlier than; before: *he won't come until tomorrow.* [C13 *untill*; see TILL¹]
▷ **Usage.** See at **till¹**.

untimely (ʌn'taɪmlɪ) *adj.* **1.** occurring before the expected, normal, or proper time: *an untimely death.* **2.** inappropriate to the occasion, time, or season: *his joking at the funeral was most untimely.* ~*adv.* **3.** prematurely or inopportunely. —**un'timeliness** *n.*

unto ('ʌntu:) *prep. Arch.* to. [C13: from ON]

untold (ʌn'təʊld) *adj.* **1.** incapable of description: *untold suffering.* **2.** incalculably great in number or quantity: *untold thousands.* **3.** not told.

untouchable (ʌn'tʌtʃəbəl) *adj.* **1.** lying beyond reach. **2.** above reproach, suspicion, or impeachment. **3.** unable to be touched. ~*n.* **4.** a member of the lowest class in India, whom those of the four main castes were formerly forbidden to touch. —**un,toucha'bility** *n.*

untoward (,ʌntə'wɔːd) *adj.* **1.** characterized by misfortune or annoyance. **2.** not auspicious; unfavourable. **3.** unseemly. **4.** out of the ordinary; out of the way. **5.** *Arch.* perverse. **6.** *Obs.* awkward. —**,unto'wardly** *adv.* —**,unto'wardness** *n.*

untrue (ʌn'truː) *adj.* **1.** incorrect or false. **2.** disloyal. **3.** diverging from a rule, standard, or measure; inaccurate. —**un'truly** *adv.*

untruss (ʌn'trʌs) *vb.* **1.** (*tr.*) to release from or as if from a truss; unfasten. **2.** *Obs.* to undress.

untruth (ʌn'truːθ) *n.* **1.** the state or quality of being untrue. **2.** a statement, etc., that is not true.

untruthful (ʌn'truːθfʊl) *adj.* **1.** (of a person) given to lying. **2.** diverging from the truth. —**un'truthfully** *adv.* —**un'truthfulness** *n.*

untuck (ʌn'tʌk) *vb.* to become or cause to become loose or not tucked in: *to untuck the blankets.*

untutored (ʌn'tjuːtəd) *adj.* **1.** without formal education. **2.** lacking sophistication or refinement.

unused *adj.* **1.** (ʌn'juːzd). not being or never having been made use of. **2.** (ʌn'juːst). (*postpositive;* foll. by *to*) not accustomed or used (to something).

unusual (ʌn'juːʒʊəl) *adj.* uncommon; extraordinary: *an unusual design.* —**un'usually** *adv.*

unutterable (ʌn'ʌtərəbəl) *adj.* incapable of being expressed in words. —**un'utterableness** *n.* —**un'utterably** *adv.*

unvarnished (ʌn'vɑːnɪʃt) *adj.* not elaborated upon or glossed; plain and direct: *the unvarnished truth.*

unveil (ʌn'veɪl) *vb.* **1.** (*tr.*) to remove the cover from, esp. in the ceremonial unveiling of a monument, etc. **2.** to remove the veil from (one's own or another person's face). **3.** (*tr.*) to make (something concealed) known or public.

unveiling (ʌn'veɪlɪŋ) *n.* **1.** a ceremony involving the removal of a veil covering a statue, etc., for the first time. **2.** the presentation of something, esp. for the first time.

unvoice (ʌn'vɔɪs) *vb.* (*tr.*) *Phonetics.* **1.** to pronounce without vibration of the vocal cords. **2.** Also: **devoice.** to make (a voiced speech sound) voiceless.

unvoiced (ʌn'vɔɪst) *adj.* **1.** not expressed or spoken. **2.** articulated without vibration of the vocal cords; voiceless.

unwaged (ʌn'weɪdʒd) *adj.* of or denoting a person who is not receiving any pay because of being unemployed or working in the home.

unwarrantable (ʌn'wɒrəntəbəl) *adj.* incapable of vindication or justification. —**un'warrantableness** *n.* —**un'warrantably** *adv.*

unwarranted (ʌn'wɒrəntɪd) *adj.* **1.** lacking justification or authorization. **2.** another word for **unwarrantable.**

unwary (ʌn'wɛərɪ) *adj.* lacking caution or prudence. —**un'warily** *adv.* —**un'wariness** *n.*

unwearied (ʌn'wɪərɪd) *adj.* **1.** not abating or tiring. **2.** not fatigued; fresh. —**un'weariedly** *adv.* —**un'weariedness** *n.*

unweighed (ʌn'weɪd) *adj.* **1.** (of quantities purchased, etc.) not measured for weight. **2.** (of statements, etc.) not carefully considered.

unwell (ʌn'wɛl) *adj.* (*postpositive*) not well; ill.

unwept (ʌn'wɛpt) *adj.* **1.** not wept for or lamented. **2.** *Rare.* (of tears) not shed.

unwholesome (ʌn'həʊlsəm) *adj.* **1.** detrimental to physical or mental health: *an unwholesome climate.* **2.** morally harmful: *unwholesome practices.* **3.** indicative of illness, esp. in appearance. **4.** (esp. of food) of inferior quality. —**un'wholesomeness** *n.*

unwieldy (ʌn'wiːldɪ) *adj.* **1.** too heavy, large, or awkwardly shaped to be easily handled. **2.** ungainly; clumsy. —**un'wieldily** *adv.* —**un'wieldiness** *n.*

unwilled (ʌn'wɪld) *adj.* not intentional; involuntary.

unwilling (ʌn'wɪlɪŋ) *adj.* **1.** reluctant. **2.** performed or said with reluctance. —**un'willingly** *adv.* —**un'willingness** *n.*

unwind (ʌn'waɪnd) *vb.* **-winding, -wound. 1.** to slacken, undo, or unravel or cause to slacken, undo, or unravel. **2.** (*tr.*) to disentangle. **3.** to make or become relaxed: *he finds it hard to unwind.* —**un'windable** *adj.*

unwise (ʌn'waɪz) *adj.* lacking wisdom or prudence. —**un'wisely** *adv.* —**un'wiseness** *n.*

unwish (ʌn'wɪʃ) *vb.* (*tr.*) **1.** to retract or revoke (a wish). **2.** to desire (something) not to be or take place.

unwitting (ʌn'wɪtɪŋ) *adj.* (*usually prenominal*) **1.** not knowing or conscious. **2.** not intentional; inadvertent. [OE *unwitende*, from UN-¹ + *witting*, present participle of *witan* to know] —**un'wittingly** *adv.* —**un'wittingness** *n.*

un'tended *adj.*	,untrans'ferable *adj.*	un'uttered *adj.*	un'washed *adj.*
un'tested *adj.*	un'travelled *adj.*	un'valued *adj.*	un'watched *adj.*
un'tethered *adj.*	un'treated *adj.*	un'vanquished *adj.*	un'wavering *adj.*
un'thanked *adj.*	un'tried *adj.*	un'varied *adj.*	un'weary *adj.*
un'thankful *adj.*	un'trodden *adj.*	un'varying *adj.*	un'wearying *adj.*
un'thoughtful *adj.*	un'troubled *adj.*	un'veri,fiable *adj.*	un'wedded *or* un'wed *adj.*
un'thought-of *adj.*	un'trust,worthy *adj.*	un'veri,fied *adj.*	un'welcome *adj.*
un'tinged *adj.*	un'tucked *adj.*	un'versed *adj.*	un'winking *adj.*
un'tiring *adj.*	un'twine *vb.*	un'viable *adj.*	un'wished *adj.*
un'titled *adj.*	un'twist *vb.*	un'wanted *adj.*	un'wished-for *adj.*
un'touched *adj.*	un'usable *adj.*	un'warmed *adj.*	un'withered *adj.*
un'trained *adj.*	un'uti,lized *or* -,lised *adj.*	un'warned *adj.*	un'witnessed *adj.*
un'trammelled *adj.*			

unwonted (ʌn'wəʊntɪd) *adj.* **1.** out of the ordinary; unusual. **2.** (usually foll. by *to*) *Arch.* unaccustomed; unused. —**un'wontedly** *adv.*

unworldly (ʌn'wɜːldlɪ) *adj.* **1.** not concerned with material values or pursuits. **2.** lacking sophistication; naive. **3.** not of this earth or world. —**un'worldliness** *n.*

unworthy (ʌn'wɜːðɪ) *adj.* **1.** (often foll. by *of*) not deserving or worthy. **2.** (often foll. by *of*) beneath the level considered befitting (to): *that remark is unworthy of you.* **3.** lacking merit or value. **4.** (of treatment) not warranted. —**un'worthily** *adv.* —**un'worthiness** *n.*

unwound (ʌn'waʊnd) *vb.* the past tense and past participle of **unwind.**

unwrap (ʌn'ræp) *vb.* **-wrapping, -wrapped.** to remove the covering or wrapping from (something) or (of something wrapped) to have the covering come off.

unwritten (ʌn'rɪt³n) *adj.* **1.** not printed or in writing. **2.** effective only through custom.

unwritten law *n.* the law based upon custom, usage, and judicial decisions, as distinguished from the enactments of a legislature, orders or decrees in writing, etc.

unyoke (ʌn'jəʊk) *vb.* **1.** to release (an animal, etc.) from a yoke. **2.** (*tr.*) to set free; liberate. **3.** (*tr.*) to disconnect or separate.

unzip (ʌn'zɪp) *vb.* **-zipping, -zipped.** to unfasten the zip of (a garment, etc.) or (of a zip or garment with a zip) to become unfastened: *her skirt unzipped as she sat down.*

up (ʌp) *prep.* **1.** indicating movement from a lower to a higher position: *climbing up a mountain.* **2.** at a higher or further level or position in or on: *a shop up the road.* ~*adv.* **3.** (*often particle*) to an upward, higher, or erect position, esp. indicating readiness for an activity: *up and doing something.* **4.** (*particle*) indicating intensity or completion of an action: *he tore up the cheque.* **5.** to the place referred to or where the speaker is: *the man came up and asked the way.* **6. a.** to a more important place: *up to London.* **b.** to a more northerly place: *up to Scotland.* **c.** (of a member of some British universities) to or at university. **d.** in a particular part of the country: *up north.* **7.** above the horizon: *the sun is up.* **8.** appearing for trial: *up before the magistrate.* **9.** having gained: *ten pounds up on the deal.* **10.** higher in price: *coffee is up again.* **11.** raised (for discussion, etc.): *the plan was up for consideration.* **12.** taught: *well up in physics.* **13.** (*functioning as imperative*) get, stand, etc., up: *up with you!* **14. all up with.** *Inf.* **a.** over; finished. **b.** doomed to die. **15. up with.** (*functioning as imperative*) wanting the beginning or continuation of: *up with the monarchy!* **16. something's up.** *Inf.* something strange is happening. **17. up against a.** touching. **b.** having to cope with: *look what we're up against now.* **18. up for.** as a candidate or applicant for: *he's up for re-election again.* **19. up to. a.** devising or scheming: *she's up to no good.* **b.** dependent or incumbent upon: *the decision is up to you.* **c.** equal to (a challenge, etc.) or capable of (doing, etc.): *are you up to playing in the final?* **d.** as far as: *up to his waist in mud.* **e.** as many as: *up to two years' waiting time.* **f.** comparable with: *not up to your normal standard.* **20. up top.** *Inf.* in the head or mind. **21. up yours.** *Sl.* a vulgar expression of contempt or refusal. **22. what's up?** *Inf.* **a.** what is the matter? **b.** what is happening? ~*adj.* **23.** (*predicative*) of a high or higher position. **24.** (*predicative*) out of bed: *the children aren't up yet.* **25.** (*prenominal*) of or relating to a train or trains to a more important place or one regarded as higher: *the up platform.* ~*vb.* **upping, upped.** **26.** (*tr.*) to increase or raise. **27.** (*intr.*; foll. by *and* with a verb) *Inf.* to do (something) suddenly, etc.: *she upped and married someone else.* ~*n.* **28.** a high point (esp. in **ups and downs**). **29.** *Sl.* another word (esp. U.S.) for **upper** (sense 8). **30. on the up and up. a.** trustworthy or honest. **b.** *Brit.* on the upward trend or movement: *our firm's on the up and up.* [OE *upp*]

up- *prefix.* up, upper, or upwards: *uproot; upmost; upthrust; upgrade; uplift.*

up-anchor *vb.* (*intr.*) *Naut.* to weigh anchor.

up-and-coming *adj.* promising continued or future success; enterprising.

up-and-down *adj.* **1.** moving or formed alternately upwards and downwards. ~*adv., prep.* **up and down.** **2.** backwards and forwards (along).

up-and-over *adj.* (of a door, etc.) opened by being lifted and moved into a horizontal position.

up-and-under *n. Rugby League.* a high kick forwards followed by a charge to the place where the ball lands.

Upanishad (uː'pʌnɪʃəd) *n. Hinduism.* any of a class of the Sanskrit sacred books probably composed between 400 and 200 B.C. and embodying the mystical and esoteric doctrines of ancient Hindu philosophy. [C19: from Sansk. *upanisad* a sitting down near something]

upas ('juːpəs) *n.* **1.** a large tree of Java having whitish bark and poisonous milky sap. **2.** the sap of this tree, used as an arrow poison. ~Also called: **antiar.** [C19: from Malay: poison]

upbeat ('ʌp,biːt) *n.* **1.** *Music.* **a.** a usually unaccented beat, esp. the last in a bar. **b.** the upward gesture of a conductor's baton indicating this. ~*adj.* **2.** *Inf.* marked by cheerfulness or optimism.

upbraid (ʌp'breɪd) *vb.* (*tr.*) **1.** to reprove or reproach angrily. **2.** to find fault with. [OE *upbregdan*] —**up'braider** *n.* —**up'braiding** *n.*

upbringing ('ʌp,brɪŋɪŋ) *n.* the education of a person during his formative years.

upcast ('ʌp,kɑːst) *n.* **1.** material cast or thrown up. **2.** a ventilation shaft through which air leaves a mine. **3.** *Geol.* (in a fault) the section of strata that has been displaced upwards. ~*adj.* **4.** directed or thrown upwards. ~*vb.* **-casting, -cast.** **5.** (*tr.*) to throw or cast up.

upcountry (ʌp'kʌntrɪ) *adj.* **1.** of or coming from the interior of a country or region. ~*n.* **2.** the interior part of a region or country. ~*adv.* **3.** towards, in, or into the interior part of a country or region.

update *vb.* (ʌp'deɪt). (*tr.*) **1.** to bring up to date. ~*n.* ('ʌp,deɪt). **2.** the act of updating or something that is updated. —**up'dateable** *adj.* —**up'dater** *n.*

Updike ('ʌp,daɪk) *n.* **John (Hoyer).** born 1932, U.S. writer. His novels include *Rabbit, Run* (1960), *Couples* (1968), *The Coup* (1979), and *Rabbit is Rich* (1982), which won a Pulitzer prize.

updraught *or U.S.* **updraft** ('ʌp,drɑːft) *n.* an upward movement of air or other gas.

upend (ʌp'end) *vb.* **1.** to turn or set or become turned or set on end. **2.** (*tr.*) to affect or upset drastically.

upfront ('ʌp'frʌnt) *adj.* **1.** open and frank. ~*adv., adj.* **2.** (of money) paid out at the beginning of a business arrangement.

upgrade *vb.* (ʌp'greɪd). (*tr.*) **1.** to assign or promote (a person or job) to a higher professional rank or position. **2.** to raise in value, importance, esteem, etc. **3.** to improve (a breed of livestock) by crossing with a better strain. ~*n.* ('ʌp,greɪd). **4.** *U.S. & Canad.* an upward slope. **5. on the upgrade.** improving or progressing, as in importance, status, health, etc. —**up'grader** *n.*

upheaval (ʌp'hiːv³l) *n.* **1.** a strong, sudden, or violent disturbance, as in politics. **2.** *Geol.* another word for **uplift** (sense 7).

upheave (ʌp'hiːv) *vb.* **-heaving, -heaved** *or* **-hove.** **1.** to heave or rise upwards. **2.** *Geol.* to thrust (land) upwards or (of land) to be thrust upwards. **3.** (*tr.*) to throw into disorder.

upheld (ʌp'held) *vb.* the past tense and past participle of **uphold.**

uphill ('ʌp'hɪl) *adj.* **1.** inclining, sloping, or leading upwards. **2.** requiring protracted effort: *an uphill task.* ~*adv.* **3.** up an incline or slope. **4.** against difficulties. ~*n.* **5.** a rising incline.

uphold (ʌp'həʊld) *vb.* **-holding, -held.** (*tr.*) **1.** to maintain or defend against opposition. **2.** to give moral support to. **3.** *Rare.* to support physically. **4.** to lift up. —**up'holder** *n.*

upholster (ʌp'həʊlstə) *vb.* (*tr.*) to fit (chairs, sofas, etc.) with padding, springs, webbing, and covering. —**up'holstery** *n.*

upholsterer (ʌp'həʊlstərə) *n.* a person who upholsters furniture as a profession. [C17: from *upholster* small furniture dealer]

---

un'workable *adj.*
un'workman,like *adj.*

un'worn *adj.*
un'worried *adj.*

un'wounded *adj.*

un'yielding *adj.*

upkeep ('ʌp,kiːp) n. **1.** the act or process of keeping something in good repair, esp. over a long period. **2.** the cost of maintenance.

upland ('ʌplənd) n. **1.** an area of high or relatively high ground. ~adj. **2.** relating to or situated in an upland.

uplift vb. (ʌp'lɪft). (tr.) **1.** to raise; lift up. **2.** to raise morally, spiritually, etc. **3.** Scot. & N.Z. to collect; pick up (goods, documents, etc.). ~n. ('ʌp,lɪft). **4.** the act, process, or result of lifting up. **5.** the act or process of bettering moral, social, or cultural conditions, etc. **6.** (modifier) designating a brassiere for lifting and supporting the breasts: an uplift bra. **7.** the process or result of land being raised to a higher level, as during a period of mountain building. —**up'lifter** n. —**up'lifting** adj.

uplighter ('ʌp,laɪtə) n. a lamp or wall light designed or positioned to cast its light upwards.

up-market adj. relating to commercial products, services, etc., that are relatively expensive and of superior quality.

upmost ('ʌp,məʊst) adj. another word for **uppermost**.

Upolu (uː'pəʊluː) n. an island in the SW central Pacific, in Western Samoa. Chief town: Apia. Pop.: 113 000 (1981). Area: 1114 sq. km (430 sq. miles).

upon (ə'pɒn) prep. **1.** another word for **on**. **2.** indicating a position reached by going up: climb upon my knee. **3.** imminent for: the weekend was upon us again. [C13: from UP + ON]

upper ('ʌpə) adj. **1.** higher or highest in relation to physical position, wealth, rank, status, etc. **2.** (cap. when part of a name) lying farther upstream, inland, or farther north: the upper valley of the Loire. **3.** (cap. when part of a name) Geol., archaeol. denoting the late part or division of a period, system, etc.: Upper Palaeolithic. **4.** Maths. (of a limit or bound) greater than or equal to one or more numbers or variables. ~n. **5.** the higher of two objects, people, etc. **6.** the part of a shoe above the sole, covering the upper surface of the foot. **7.** on one's uppers. destitute. **8.** Sl. any of various drugs having a stimulant effect.

upper atmosphere n. Meteorol. that part of the atmosphere above the troposphere, esp. at heights that cannot be reached by balloon.

Upper Austria n. a province of N Austria: first divided from Lower Austria in 1251. Capital: Linz. Pop.: 1 270 426 (1981). Area: 11 978 sq. km (4625 sq. miles). German name: **Oberösterreich.**

Upper Burma n. the inland regions of Burma, in the north of the country.

Upper Canada n. **1.** History. (from 1791–1841) the official name of the region of Canada lying southwest of the Ottawa River and north of the lower Great Lakes. Cf. **Lower Canada. 2.** (esp. in E Canada) another name for **Ontario.**

upper case Printing. ~n. **1.** the top half of a compositor's type case in which capital letters, reference marks, and accents are kept. ~adj. (**upper-case** when prenominal). **2.** of or relating to capital letters kept in this case and used in the setting or production of printed or typed matter.

upper chamber n. another name for an **upper house.**

upper class n. **1.** the class occupying the highest position in the social hierarchy, esp. the aristocracy. ~adj. (**upper-class** when prenominal). **2.** of or relating to the upper class.

upper crust n. Inf. the upper class.

uppercut ('ʌpə,kʌt) n. **1.** a short swinging upward blow with the fist delivered at an opponent's chin. ~vb. **-cutting, -cut. 2.** to hit (an opponent) with an uppercut.

Upper Egypt n. one of the two main administrative districts of Egypt: extends south from Cairo to the Sudan.

upper hand n. the. the position of control (esp. in **have** or **get the upper hand**).

upper house n. (often cap.) one of the two houses of a bicameral legislature.

uppermost ('ʌpə,məʊst) adj. also **upmost. 1.** highest in position, power, importance, etc. ~adv. **2.** in or into the highest position, etc.

Upper Palatinate n. See **Palatinate.**

Upper Peninsula n. a peninsula in the northern U.S. between Lakes Superior and Michigan, constituting the N part of the state of Michigan.

upper regions pl. n. the. Chiefly literary. the sky; heavens.

Upper Silesia n. a region of SW Poland, formerly ruled by Germany: coalmining and other heavy industry.

Upper Tunguska n. See **Tunguska.**

Upper Volta ('vɒltə) n. the former name (until 1984) of **Burkina-Faso.**

upper works pl. n. Naut. the parts of a vessel above the water line when fully laden.

uppish ('ʌpɪʃ) adj. Brit. inf. another word for **uppity** (sense 1). [C18: from UP + -ISH] —**'uppishly** adv. —**'uppishness** n.

uppity ('ʌpɪtɪ) adj. Inf. **1.** snobbish, arrogant, or presumptuous. **2.** offensively self-assertive. [from UP + fanciful ending, ? infl. by -ITY]

Uppsala or **Upsala** ('ʌpsɑːlə) n. a city in E central Sweden: the royal headquarters in the 13th century; Gothic cathedral (the largest in Sweden) and Sweden's oldest university (1477). Pop.: 157 675 (1986).

upraise (ʌp'reɪz) vb. (tr.) Chiefly literary. to lift up; elevate. —**up'raiser** n.

uprear (ʌp'rɪə) vb. (tr.) to lift up; raise.

upright ('ʌp,raɪt) adj. **1.** vertical or erect. **2.** honest or just. ~adv. **3.** vertically. ~n. **4.** a vertical support, such as a stake or post. **5.** short for **upright piano. 6.** the state of being vertical. —**'up,rightly** adv. —**'up,rightness** n.

upright piano n. a piano which has a rectangular vertical case.

uprise vb. (ʌp'raɪz), **-rising, -rose, -risen. 1.** (tr.) to rise up. ~n. ('ʌp,raɪz). **2.** another word for **rise** (senses 23, 24). —**up'riser** n.

uprising ('ʌp,raɪzɪŋ, ʌp'raɪzɪŋ) n. **1.** a revolt or rebellion. **2.** Arch. an ascent.

uproar ('ʌp,rɔː) n. a commotion or disturbance characterized by loud noise and confusion.

uproarious (ʌp'rɔːrɪəs) adj. **1.** causing or characterized by an uproar. **2.** extremely funny. **3.** (of laughter, etc.) loud and boisterous. —**up'roariously** adv. —**up'roariousness** n.

uproot (ʌp'ruːt) vb. (tr.) **1.** to pull up by or as if by the roots. **2.** to displace (a person or persons) from native or habitual surroundings. **3.** to remove or destroy utterly. —**up'rooter** n.

uprush ('ʌp,rʌʃ) n. an upward rush, as of consciousness.

upsadaisy ('ʌpsə'deɪzɪ) interj. a variant spelling of **upsy-daisy.**

Upsala ('ʌpsɑːlə) n. a variant spelling of **Uppsala.**

ups and downs pl. n. alternating periods of good and bad fortune, high and low spirits, etc.

upset vb. (ʌp'sɛt), **-setting, -set.** (mainly tr.) **1.** (also intr.) to tip or be tipped over; overturn or spill. **2.** to disturb the normal state or stability of: to upset the balance of nature. **3.** to disturb mentally or emotionally. **4.** to defeat or overthrow, usually unexpectedly. **5.** to make physically ill: seafood always upsets my stomach. **6.** to thicken or spread (the end of a bar, etc.) by hammering. ~n. ('ʌp,sɛt). **7.** an unexpected defeat or reversal, as in a contest or plans. **8.** a disturbance or disorder of the emotions, body, etc. ~adj. (ʌp'sɛt). **9.** overturned or capsized. **10.** emotionally or physically disturbed or distressed. **11.** disordered; confused. **12.** defeated or overthrown. [C14 (in the sense: to erect; C19 in the sense: to overthrow)] —**up'setter** n. —**up'setting** adj. —**up'settingly** adv.

upset price n. Chiefly Scot., U.S., & Canad. the lowest price acceptable for something that is for sale, esp. a house. Cf. **reserve price.**

upshot ('ʌp,ʃɒt) n. **1.** the final result; conclusion; outcome. **2.** Archery. the final shot in a match. [C16: from UP + SHOT[1]]

upside ('ʌp,saɪd) n. the upper surface or part.

upside down adj. **1.** (usually postpositive; **upside-down** when prenominal) turned over completely; inverted. **2.** (**upside-down** when prenominal) Inf. confused; topsy-turvy: an upside-down world. ~adv. **3.** in an inverted fashion. **4.** in a chaotic manner. [C16: var., of earlier upsodown, of earlier upsodown]

upside-down cake n. a sponge cake baked with fruit at the bottom, and inverted before serving.

upsides ('ʌp'saɪdz) adv. Inf., chiefly Brit. (foll. by with) equal or level (with), as through revenge.

upsilon ('ʌpsɪ,lɒn) n. **1.** the 20th letter in the Greek alphabet (Υ or υ), a vowel transliterated as y or u. **2.** a heavy short-lived subatomic particle produced by bombarding beryllium nuclei with high-energy protons. [C17: from Med. Gk u psilon simple u, name adopted for graphic *u* to avoid confusion with graphic *oi*, since pronunciation was the same for both in LGk]

upstage ('ʌp'steɪdʒ) *adv.* **1.** on, at, or to the rear of the stage. ~*adj.* **2.** of or relating to the back half of the stage. **3.** *Inf.* haughty. ~*vb.* (*tr.*) **4.** to move upstage of (another actor), thus forcing him to turn away from the audience. **5.** *Inf.* to draw attention to oneself from (someone else). **6.** *Inf.* to treat haughtily.

upstairs ('ʌp'stɛəz) *adv.* **1.** up the stairs; to or on an upper floor. **2.** *Inf.* to or into a higher rank or office. ~*n.* (*functioning as sing. or pl.*) **3. a.** an upper floor. **b.** (*as modifier*): *an upstairs room.* **4.** *Brit. inf.* the masters of a household collectively, esp. of a large house.

upstanding (ʌp'stændɪŋ) *adj.* **1.** of good character. **2.** upright and vigorous in build. **3. be upstanding. a.** (in a court of law) a direction to all persons present to rise to their feet before the judge enters or leaves the court. **b.** (at a formal dinner) a direction to all persons present to rise to their feet for a toast.

upstart ('ʌp,stɑːt) *n.* **1. a.** a person, group, etc., that has risen suddenly to a position of power. **b.** (*as modifier*): *an upstart family.* **2. a.** an arrogant person. **b.** (*as modifier*): *his upstart ambition.*

upstate ('ʌp'steɪt) *U.S.* ~*adj., adv.* **1.** towards, in, or relating to the outlying or northern sections of a state. ~*n.* **2.** the outlying, esp. northern, sections of a state. —'up'stater *n.*

upstream ('ʌp'striːm) *adv., adj.* in or towards the higher part of a stream; against the current.

upstretched (ʌp'strɛtʃt) *adj.* (esp. of the arms) stretched or raised up.

upstroke ('ʌp,strəʊk) *n.* **1. a.** an upward stroke or movement, as of a pen or brush. **b.** the mark produced by such a stroke. **2.** the upward movement of a piston in a reciprocating engine.

upsurge *vb.* (ʌp'sɜːdʒ). **1.** (*intr.*) *Chiefly literary.* to surge up. ~*n.* ('ʌp,sɜːdʒ). **2.** a rapid rise or swell.

upsweep *n.* ('ʌp,swiːp). **1.** a curve or sweep upwards. ~*vb.* (ʌp'swiːp), **-sweeping, -swept. 2.** to sweep, curve, or brush or be swept, curved, or brushed upwards.

upswing ('ʌp,swɪŋ) *n.* **1.** *Econ.* a recovery period in the trade cycle. **2.** an upward swing or movement or any increase or improvement.

upsy-daisy ('ʌpsɪ'deɪzɪ) *or* **upsadaisy** *interj.* an expression, usually of reassurance, uttered as when someone, esp. a child, stumbles or is being lifted up. [C18 *up-a-daisy*, irregularly formed from UP (adv.)]

uptake ('ʌp,teɪk) *n.* **1.** a pipe, shaft, etc., that is used to convey smoke or gases, esp. one that connects a furnace to a chimney. **2.** lifting up. **3.** the act of accepting something on offer. **4. quick** (*or* **slow**) **on the uptake.** *Inf.* quick (or slow) to understand or learn.

upthrow ('ʌp,θrəʊ) *n.* *Geol.* the upward movement of rocks on one side of a fault plane relative to rocks on the other side.

upthrust ('ʌp,θrʌst) *n.* **1.** an upward push or thrust. **2.** *Geol.* a violent upheaval of the earth's surface.

uptight (ʌp'taɪt) *adj.* *Inf.* **1.** displaying tense repressed nervousness, irritability, or anger. **2.** unable to give expression to one's feelings.

uptime ('ʌp,taɪm) *n.* *Commerce.* time during which a machine, such as a computer, actually operates.

up-to-date *adj.* **a.** modern or fashionable: *an up-to-date magazine.* **b.** (*predicative*): *the magazine is up to date.* —'up-to-'dateness *n.*

uptown ('ʌp'taʊn) *U.S. & Canad.* ~*adj., adv.* **1.** towards, in, or relating to some part of a town that is away from the centre. ~*n.* **2.** such a part of a town, esp. a residential part. —'up'towner *n.*

upturn *vb.* (ʌp'tɜːn). **1.** to turn or cause to turn over or upside down. **2.** (*tr.*) to create disorder. **3.** (*tr.*) to direct upwards. ~*n.* ('ʌp,tɜːn). **4.** an upward trend or improvement. **5.** an upheaval.

UPU *abbrev. for* Universal Postal Union.

upward ('ʌpwəd) *adj.* **1.** directed or moving towards a higher point or level. ~*adv.* **2.** a variant of **upwards.** —'upwardly *adv.* —'upwardness *n.*

upwardly mobile *adj.* (of a person or social group) moving or aspiring to move to a higher social class or status.

upward mobility *n.* movement from a lower to a higher economic and social status.

upwards ('ʌpwədz) *or* **upward** *adv.* **1.** from a lower to a higher place, level, condition, etc. **2.** towards a higher level, standing, etc.

upwind ('ʌp'wɪnd) *adv.* **1.** into or against the wind. **2.** towards or on the side where the wind is blowing; windward. ~*adj.* **3.** going against the wind: *the upwind leg of the course.* **4.** on the windward side.

Ur (ɜː) *n.* an ancient city of Sumer located on a former channel of the Euphrates.

uracil ('jʊərəsɪl) *n.* *Biochem.* a pyrimidine present in all living cells, usually in a combined form, as in RNA. [C20: from URO- + ACETIC + -ILE]

uraemia *or U.S.* **uremia** (jʊ'riːmɪə) *n.* *Pathol.* the accumulation of waste products, normally excreted in the urine, in the blood. [C19: from NL, from Gk *ouron* urine + *haima* blood] —u'raemic *or U.S.* u'remic *adj.*

uraeus (jʊ'riːəs) *n., pl.* **-uses.** the sacred serpent represented on the headdresses of ancient Egyptian kings and gods. [C19: from NL, from Gk *ouraios*, from Egyptian *uro* asp]

Ural ('jʊərəl; *Russian* u'ral) *n.* a river in the central Soviet Union, rising in the S Ural Mountains and flowing south to the Caspian Sea. Length: 2534 km (1575 miles).

Ural-Altaic *n.* **1.** a postulated group of related languages consisting of the Uralic and Altaic families of languages. ~*adj.* **2.** of or relating to this group of languages, characterized by agglutination and vowel harmony.

Uralic (jʊ'rælɪk) *or* **Uralian** (jʊ'reɪlɪən) *n.* **1.** a superfamily of languages consisting of the Finno-Ugric family together with Samoyed. See also **Ural-Altaic.** ~*adj.* **2.** of or relating to these languages.

Ural Mountains *or* **Urals** *pl. n.* a mountain system of the Soviet Union, extending over 2000 km (1250 miles) from the Arctic Ocean towards the Aral Sea: forms part of the geographical boundary between Europe and Asia; one of the richest mineral areas in the world, with many associated major industrial centres. Highest peak: Mount Narodnaya, 1894 m (6214 ft.).

uranalysis (jʊərə'nælɪsɪs) *n., pl.* **-ses** (-,siːz). *Med.* a variant spelling of **urinalysis.**

Urania (jʊ'reɪnɪə) *n. Greek myth.* **1.** the Muse of astronomy. **2.** another name of **Aphrodite.** [C17: from L, from Gk *Ourania*, from *ouranos* heavenly, from *ouranos* heaven] —U'ranian *adj.*

uranide ('jʊərə,naɪd) *n.* any element having an atomic number greater than that of protactinium.

uranism ('jʊərə,nɪzəm) *n. Rare.* homosexuality (esp. male homosexuality). [C20: from G *Uranismus*, from Gk *ouranios* heavenly, i.e. spiritual]

uranium (jʊ'reɪnɪəm) *n.* a radioactive silvery-white metallic element of the actinide series. It occurs in several minerals including pitchblende and is used chiefly as a source of nuclear energy by fission of the radioisotope **uranium-235.** Symbol: U; atomic no.: 92; atomic wt.: 238.03; half-life of most stable isotope, ^{238}U: 4.51×10^9 years. [C18: from NL, from URANUS[2]; from the fact that the element was discovered soon after the planet]

uranium series *n. Physics.* a radioactive series that starts with uranium-238 and proceeds by radioactive decay to lead-206.

urano- *combining form.* denoting the heavens: *uranography.* [from Gk *ouranos*]

uranography (jʊərə'nɒɡrəfɪ) *n.* the branch of astronomy concerned with the description and mapping of the stars, galaxies, etc. —,ura'nographer *n.* —uranographic (,jʊərənə'ɡræfɪk) *adj.*

Uranus[1] (jʊ'reɪnəs, 'jʊərənəs) *n. Greek myth.* the personification of the sky, who, as a god, ruled the universe and fathered the Titans and Cyclopes; overthrown by his son Cronus.

Uranus[2] (jʊ'reɪnəs, 'jʊərənəs) *n.* the seventh planet from the sun, sometimes visible to the naked eye. [C19: from L *Uranus*, from Gk *Ouranos* heaven]

urate ('jʊəreɪt) *n.* any salt or ester of uric acid. —**uratic** (jʊ'rætɪk) *adj.*

urban ('ɜːbən) *adj.* **1.** of, relating to, or constituting a city or town. **2.** living in a city or town. ~Cf. **rural.** [C17: from L *urbānus*, from *urbs* city]

Urban II ('ɜːbən) *n.* original name **Odo** or **Udo.** ?1042–99, French ecclesiastic; pope (1088–99). He inaugurated the First Crusade at the Council of Clermont (1095).

urban area n. (in population censuses) a city area considered as the inner city plus built-up environs, irrespective of local body administrative boundaries.

urban district n. **1.** (in England and Wales from 1888 to 1974 and Northern Ireland from 1898 to 1973) an urban division of an administrative county with an elected council in charge of housing and environmental services. **2.** (in the Republic of Ireland) any of 49 medium-sized towns with their own elected councils.

urbane (ɜːˈbeɪn) adj. characterized by elegance or sophistication. [C16: from L urbānus of the town; see URBAN] —**urˈbanely** adv. —**urˈbaneness** n.

urban guerrilla n. a guerrilla who operates in a town or city, engaging in terrorism, kidnapping, etc.

urbanism (ˈɜːbəˌnɪzəm) n. Chiefly U.S. **a.** the character of city life. **b.** the study of this.

urbanite (ˈɜːbəˌnaɪt) n. a resident of an urban community; city dweller.

urbanity (ɜːˈbænɪtɪ) n., pl. -ties. **1.** the quality of being urbane. **2.** (usually pl.) civilities or courtesies.

urbanize or **-nise** (ˈɜːbəˌnaɪz) vb. (tr.) (usually passive) **a.** to make (esp. a predominantly rural area or country) more industrialized and urban. **b.** to cause the migration of an increasing proportion of (rural dwellers) into cities. —ˌurbaniˈzation or -niˈsation n.

urban renewal n. the process of redeveloping dilapidated or no longer functional urban areas.

urbi et orbi Latin. (ˈɜːbɪ ɛt ˈɔːbɪ) adv. R.C. Church. to the city and the world: a phrase qualifying the solemn papal blessing.

urceolate (ˈɜːsɪəlɪt, -ˌleɪt) adj. Biol. shaped like an urn or pitcher: an urceolate corolla. [C18: via NL from L urceolus, dim. of urceus a pitcher]

urchin (ˈɜːtʃɪn) n. **1.** a mischievous roguish child, esp. one who is young, small, or raggedly dressed. **2.** See **sea urchin**. **3.** Arch., dialect. a hedgehog. **4.** Obs. an elf or sprite. [C13 urchon, from OF heriçon, from L ēricius hedgehog]

Urdu (ˈʊəduː, ˈɜː-) n. an official language of Pakistan, also spoken in India. The script derives primarily from Persia. It belongs to the Indic branch of the Indo-European family of languages, being closely related to Hindi. [C18: from Hindustani (zabāni) urdū (language of the) camp, from Persian urdū camp, from Turkish ordū]

-ure suffix forming nouns. **1.** indicating act, process, or result: seizure. **2.** indicating function or office: legislature; prefecture. [from F, from L -ūra]

urea (ˈjʊərɪə) n. a white water-soluble crystalline compound, produced by protein metabolism and excreted in urine. A synthetic form is used as a fertilizer and animal feed. Formula: $CO(NH_2)_2$. [C19: from NL, from F urée, from Gk ouron urine] —**uˈreal** or **uˈreic** adj.

urea-formaldehyde resin n. any one of a class of rigid odourless synthetic materials that are made from urea and formaldehyde and are used in electrical fittings, adhesives, laminates, and finishes for textiles.

ureide (ˈjʊərɪˌaɪd) n. Chem. **1.** any of a class of organic compounds derived from urea by replacing one or more of its hydrogen atoms by organic groups. **2.** any of a class of derivatives of urea and carboxylic acids, in which one or more of the hydrogen atoms have been replaced by acid radical groups.

-uret suffix of nouns. formerly used to form the names of binary chemical compounds. [from NL -uretum]

ureter (jʊˈriːtə) n. the tube that conveys urine from the kidney to the urinary bladder or cloaca. [C16: via NL from Gk ourētēr, from ourein to urinate] —**uˈreteral** or **ureteric** (ˌjʊərɪˈtɛrɪk) adj.

urethane (ˈjʊərɪˌθeɪn) or **urethan** (ˈjʊərɪˌθæn) n. short for **polyurethane**. [C19: from URO- + ETHYL + -ANE]

urethra (jʊˈriːθrə) n., pl. -thrae (-θriː) or -thras. the canal that in most mammals conveys urine from the bladder out of the body. In human males it also conveys semen. [C17: via LL from Gk ourēthra, from ourein to urinate] —**uˈrethral** adj.

urethritis (ˌjʊərɪˈθraɪtɪs) n. inflammation of the urethra. [C19: from NL, from LL URETHRA] —**urethritic** (ˌjʊərɪˈθrɪtɪk) adj.

urethroscope (jʊˈriːθrəˌskəʊp) n. a medical instrument for examining the urethra. [C20: see URETHRA, -SCOPE] —**urethroscopic** (jʊˌriːθrəˈskɒpɪk) adj. —**urethroscopy** (ˌjʊərɪˈθrɒskəpɪ) n.

uretic (jʊˈrɛtɪk) adj. of or relating to the urine. [C19: via LL from Gk ourētikos, from ouron urine]

Urey (ˈjʊərɪ) n. **Harold Clayton.** 1893–1981, U.S. chemist, who discovered the heavy isotope of hydrogen, deuterium (1932), and worked on methods of separating uranium isotopes: Nobel prize for chemistry 1934.

Urfa (ˈɜːfə) n. a city in SE Turkey: market centre. Pop.: 160 561 (1980). Ancient name: **Edessa**.

Urga (ˈɜːgə) n. the former name (until 1924) of **Ulan Bator**.

urge (ɜːdʒ) vb. (tr.) **1.** to plead, press, or move (someone to do something): we urged him to surrender. **2.** (may take a clause as object) to advocate or recommend earnestly and persistently: to urge the need for safety. **3.** to impel, drive, or hasten onwards: he urged the horses on. ~n. **4.** a strong impulse, inner drive, or yearning. [C16: from L urgēre]

urgent (ˈɜːdʒənt) adj. **1.** requiring or compelling speedy action or attention: the matter is urgent. **2.** earnest and persistent. [C15: via F from L urgent-, urgens, present participle of urgēre to URGE] —**urgency** (ˈɜːdʒənsɪ) n. —**urgently** adv.

-urgy n. combining form. indicating technology concerned with a specified material: metallurgy. [from Gk -urgia, from ergon work]

Uri (German ˈuːrɪ) n. one of the original three cantons of Switzerland, in the centre of the country: mainly German-speaking and Roman Catholic. Capital: Altdorf. Pop.: 33 500 (1986 est.). Area: 1075 sq. km (415 sq. miles).

-uria n. combining form. indicating a diseased or abnormal condition of the urine: pyuria. [from Gk -ouria, from ouron urine] —**-uric** adj. combining form.

Uriah (jʊˈraɪə) n. Old Testament. a Hittite officer, who was killed in battle on instructions from David so that he could marry Uriah's wife Bathsheba (II Samuel 11).

uric (ˈjʊərɪk) adj. of, concerning, or derived from urine. [C18: from URO- + -IC]

uric acid n. a white odourless tasteless crystalline product of protein metabolism, present in the blood and urine. Formula: $C_5H_4N_4O_3$.

uridine (ˈjʊərɪˌdiːn) n. Biochem. a nucleoside present in all living cells in a combined form, esp. in RNA. [C20: from URO- + -IDE + -INE²]

urinal (jʊˈraɪnᵊl, ˈjʊərɪ-) n. **1.** a sanitary fitting, esp. one fixed to a wall, used by men for urination. **2.** a room containing urinals. **3.** any vessel for holding urine prior to its disposal.

urinalysis (ˌjʊərɪˈnælɪsɪs) n., pl. -ses (-ˌsiːz). Med. chemical analysis of the urine to test for the presence of disease.

urinary (ˈjʊərɪnərɪ) adj. **1.** Anat. of or relating to urine or to the organs and structures that secrete and pass urine. ~n., pl. -naries. **2.** a reservoir for urine.

urinary bladder n. a distensible membranous sac in which the urine excreted from the kidneys is stored.

urinate (ˈjʊərɪˌneɪt) vb. (intr.) to excrete or void urine. —ˌuriˈnation n. —**urinative** adj.

urine (ˈjʊərɪn) n. the pale yellow slightly acid fluid excreted by the kidneys, containing waste products removed from the blood. It is stored in the urinary bladder and discharged through the urethra. [C14: via OF from L ūrīna]

urinogenital (ˌjʊərɪnəʊˈdʒɛnɪtᵊl) adj. another word for **urogenital**.

Urmia (ˈɜːmɪə) n. **Lake.** a shallow lake in NW Iran, at an altitude of 1300 m (4250 ft.): the largest lake in Iran, varying in area from 4000–6000 sq. km (1500–2300 sq. miles) between autumn and spring.

Urmston (ˈɜːmstən) n. a town in NW England, in Greater Manchester. Pop.: 44 009 (1981).

urn (ɜːn) n. **1.** a vaselike receptacle or vessel, esp. a large bulbous one with a foot. **2.** a vase used as a receptacle for the ashes of the dead. **3.** a large vessel, usually of metal, with a tap, used for making and holding tea, coffee, etc. [C14: from L ūrna] —**ˈurnˌlike** adj.

urnfield (ˈɜːnˌfiːld) n. **1.** a cemetery full of individual cremation urns. ~adj. **2.** (of a number of Bronze Age cultures) characterized by cremation in urns, which began in E Europe about the second millennium B.C.

uro- or before a vowel **ur-** combining form. indicating urine or the urinary tract: urogenital; urology. [from Gk ouron urine]

urogenital (ˌjʊərəʊˈdʒɛnɪtʰl) *or* **urinogenital** *adj.* of or relating to the urinary and genital organs and their functions. Also: **genitourinary**.

urogenital system *or* **tract** *n. Anat.* the urinary tract and reproductive organs.

urolith (ˈjʊərəʊlɪθ) *n. Pathol.* a calculus in the urinary tract. —ˌuro'lithic *adj.*

urology (jʊˈrɒlədʒɪ) *n.* the branch of medicine concerned with the study and treatment of diseases of the urogenital tract. —**urologic** (ˌjʊərəˈlɒdʒɪk) *adj.* —**u'rologist** *n.*

uropygial gland (ˌjʊərəˈpɪdʒɪəl) *n.* a gland, situated at the base of the tail in most birds, that secretes oil used in preening.

uropygium (ˌjʊərəˈpɪdʒɪəm) *n.* the hindmost part of a bird's body, from which the tail feathers grow. [C19: via NL from Gk *ouropugion*, from *oura* tail + *pugē* rump] —ˌuro'pygial *adj.*

uroscopy (jʊˈrɒskəpɪ) *n. Med.* examination of the urine. See also **urinalysis**. —**uroscopic** (ˌjʊərəˈskɒpɪk) *adj.* —**u'roscopist** *n.*

Urquhart (ˈɜːkət) *n.* Sir **Thomas**. 1611–60, Scottish author and translator of Rabelais' *Gargantua* and *Pantagruel* (1653; 1693).

Ursa Major (ˈɜːsə ˈmeɪdʒə) *n., Latin genitive* **Ursae Majoris** (ˈɜːsiː məˈdʒɔːrɪs). an extensive conspicuous constellation in the N hemisphere. The seven brightest stars form the **Plough**. Also called: the **Great Bear**, the **Bear**. [L: greater bear]

Ursa Minor (ˈɜːsə ˈmaɪnə) *n., Latin genitive* **Ursae Minoris** (ˈɜːsiː mɪˈnɔːrɪs). a small faint constellation, the brightest star of which is the Pole Star. Also called: the **Little Bear**, the **Bear**. [L: lesser bear]

ursine (ˈɜːsaɪn) *adj.* of, relating to, or resembling a bear or bears. [C16: from L *ursus* a bear]

Ursprache German. (ˈuːrʃpraːxə) *n.* any hypothetical extinct and unrecorded language reconstructed from groups of related recorded languages. For example, Indo-European is an Ursprache reconstructed by comparison of the Germanic group, Latin, Sanskrit, etc. [from *ur-* primeval + *Sprache* language]

Ursula (ˈɜːsjʊlə) *n.* **Saint**. a legendary British princess of the fourth or fifth century A.D., said to have been martyred together with 11 000 virgins by the Huns at Cologne.

Ursuline (ˈɜːsjʊˌlaɪn) *n.* **1.** a member of an order of nuns devoted to teaching in the Roman Catholic Church: founded in 1537 at Brescia. ~*adj.* **2.** of or relating to this order. [C16: after St URSULA, patron saint of St Angela Merici, who founded the order]

Urtext German. (ˈuːrtɛkst) *n.* **1.** the earliest form of a text as established by linguistic scholars as a basis for variants in later texts still in existence. **2.** an edition of a musical score showing the composer's intentions without later editorial interpolation. [from *ur-* original + TEXT]

urticaceous (ˌɜːtɪˈkeɪʃəs) *adj.* of or belonging to a family of plants having small flowers and, in many species, stinging hairs: includes the nettles and pellitory. [C18: via NL from L *urtīca* nettle, from *ūrere* to burn]

urticaria (ˌɜːtɪˈkɛərɪə) *n.* a skin condition characterized by the formation of itchy red or whitish raised patches, usually caused by an allergy. Nontechnical names: **hives**, **nettle rash**. [C18: from NL, from L *urtīca* nettle]

urtication (ˌɜːtɪˈkeɪʃən) *n.* **1.** a burning or itching sensation. **2.** another name for **urticaria**.

Uruapan (*Spanish* uˈrwapan) *n.* a city in SW Mexico, in Michoacán state: agricultural trading centre. Pop.: 146 998 (1980).

Uruguay (ˈjʊərəˌgwaɪ) *n.* a republic in South America, on the Atlantic: Spanish colonization began in 1624, followed by Portuguese settlement in 1680; revolted against Spanish rule in 1820 but was annexed by the Portuguese to Brazil; gained independence in 1825. It consists mainly of rolling grassy plains, low hills, and plateaus. Official language: Spanish. Religion: Roman Catholic. Currency: peso. Capital: Montevideo. Pop.: 3 058 000 (1987). Area: 182 427 sq. km (70 435 sq. miles). —ˌUru'guayan *adj., n.*

Urumchi (uːˈruːmtʃɪ), **Urumqi**, *or* **Wu-lu-mu-ch'i** *n.* a city in NW China, capital of Xinjiang Uygur AR: trading centre on a N route between China and the Soviet Union. Pop.: 1 000 000 (1986). Former name: **Tihwa**.

Urundi (uˈrʊndɪ) *n.* the former name (until 1962) of **Burundi**.

urus (ˈjʊərəs) *n., pl.* **uruses**. another name for the **aurochs**. [C17: from *ūrus*, of Gmc origin]

urushiol (ˈuːrʊʃɪˌɒl, uːˈruː-) *n.* a poisonous pale yellow liquid occurring in poison ivy and the lacquer tree. [from Japanese *urushi* lacquer + -OL²]

us (ʌs) *pron.* (*objective*) **1.** refers to the speaker or writer and another person or other people: *don't hurt us*. **2.** refers to all people or people in general: *this table shows us the tides*. **3.** an informal word for **me**: *give us a kiss!* **4.** a formal word for **me** used by editors, monarchs, etc. [OE *ūs*]

▷Usage. See at **me**.

U.S. *or* **US** *abbrev. for* United States.

USA *abbrev. for* United States Army.

U.S.A. *or* **USA** *abbrev. for* United States of America.

usable *or* **useable** (ˈjuːzəbʰl) *adj.* able to be used. —ˌus-a'bility *or* ˌusea'bility *n.*

USAF *abbrev. for* United States Air Force.

usage (ˈjuːsɪdʒ, -zɪdʒ) *n.* **1.** the act or a manner of using; use; employment. **2.** constant use, custom, or habit. **3.** something permitted or established by custom or practice. **4.** what is actually said in a language, esp. as contrasted with what is prescribed. [C14: via OF from L *ūsus* USE (n.)]

usance (ˈjuːzəns) *n. Commerce.* the period of time permitted by commercial usage for the redemption of foreign bills of exchange. [C14: from OF, from Med. L *ūsantia*, from *ūsāre* to USE]

USDAW (ˈʌsdɔː) *n.* (in Britain) *acronym for* Union of Shop, Distributive, and Allied Workers.

use *vb.* (juːz). (*tr.*) **1.** to put into service or action; employ for a given purpose: *to use a spoon to stir with*. **2.** to make a practice or habit of employing; exercise: *he uses his brain*. **3.** to behave towards in a particular way, esp. for one's own ends: *he uses people*. **4.** to consume, expend, or exhaust: *the engine uses very little oil*. **5.** to partake of (alcoholic drink, drugs, etc.) or smoke (tobacco, marijuana, etc.). ~*n.* (juːs). **6.** the act of using or the state of being used: *the carpet wore out through constant use*. **7.** the ability or permission to use. **8.** the occasion to use: *I have no use for this paper*. **9.** an instance or manner of using. **10.** usefulness; advantage: *it is of no use to complain*. **11.** custom; habit: *long use has inured him to it*. **12.** the purpose for which something is used; end. **13.** *Christianity.* a distinctive form of liturgical or ritual observance, esp. one that is traditional. **14.** the enjoyment of property, land, etc., by occupation or by deriving revenue from it. **15.** *Law.* the beneficial enjoyment of property the legal title to which is held by another person as trustee. **16. have no use for. a.** to have no need of. **b.** to have a contemptuous dislike for. **17. make use of. a.** to employ; use. **b.** to exploit (a person). ~See also **use up.** [C13: from OF *user*, from L *ūsus* having used, from *ūtī* to use]

used (juːzd) *adj.* second-hand: *used cars*.

used to (juːst) *adj.* **1.** accustomed to: *I am used to hitchhiking*. ~*vb.* (*tr.*) **2.** (*takes an infinitive or implied infinitive*) used as an auxiliary to express habitual or accustomed actions, states, etc., taking place in the past but not continuing into the present: *I used to fish here every day*.

useful (ˈjuːsfʊl) *adj.* **1.** able to be used advantageously, beneficially, or for several purposes. **2.** *Inf.* commendable or capable: *a useful term's work*. —ˈusefully *adv.* —ˈusefulness *n.*

useless (ˈjuːslɪs) *adj.* **1.** having no practical use or advantage. **2.** *Inf.* ineffectual, weak, or stupid: *he's useless at history*. —ˈuselessly *adv.* —ˈuselessness *n.*

user (ˈjuːzə) *n.* **1.** *Law.* **a.** the continued exercise, use, or enjoyment of a right, esp. in property. **b.** a prescriptive right based on long-continued use: *right of user*. **2.** (*often in combination*) a person or thing that uses: *a road-user*. **3.** *Inf.* a drug addict.

user-friendly *adj.* (**user friendly** *when postpositive*) easy to familiarize oneself with, understand, or use.

use up *vb.* (*tr., adv.*) **1.** to finish (a supply); consume completely. **2.** to exhaust; wear out.

Ushant (ˈʌʃənt) *n.* an island off the NW coast of France, at the tip of Brittany: scene of naval battles in 1778 and 1794 between France and Britain. Area: about 16 sq. km (6 sq. miles). French name: **Ouessant**.

Ushas (ˈuːʃəs) *n.* the Hindu goddess of the dawn.

usher (ˈʌʃə) *n.* **1.** an official who shows people to their seats, as in a church or theatre. **2.** a person who acts as doorkeeper, esp. in a court of law. **3.** (in England) a minor official charged with maintaining order in a court of law. **4.** an officer responsible for preceding persons of rank in a procession. **5.** *Brit., obs.* a teacher. ~*vb.* (*tr.*) **6.** to conduct or escort, esp. in a courteous or obsequious way. **7.** (usually foll. by *in*) to be a precursor or herald (of). [C14: from OF *huissier* doorkeeper, from Vulgar L *ustiārius* (unattested), from L *ostium* door]

Usher ('ʌʃə) *n.* a variant spelling of (James) **Ussher.**

usherette (ˌʌʃəˈrɛt) *n.* a woman assistant in a cinema, etc., who shows people to their seats.

Usk (ʌsk) *n.* a river in SE Wales, flowing southeast and south to the Bristol Channel. Length: 113 km (70 miles).

Üsküb ('ʊskuːb) *n.* the Turkish name (1392–1913) for **Skopje.**

Üsküdar (ˌuːskuˈdɑː) *n.* a town in NW Turkey, across the Bosporus from Istanbul: formerly a terminus of caravan routes from Syria and Asia; base of the British army in the Crimean War. Pop.: 261 141 (1980). Former name: **Scutari.**

USM *Stock Exchange. abbrev. for* unlisted securities market.

USN *abbrev. for* United States Navy.

Usnach *or* **Usnech** ('ʊʃnəx) *n.* (in Irish legend) the father of Naoise.

Uspallata Pass (ˌuːspəˈlɑːtə; *Spanish* uspaˈʎata) *n.* a pass over the Andes in S South America, between Mendoza (Argentina) and Santiago (Chile). Height: 3840 m (12 600 ft.). Also called: **La Cumbre.**

usquebaugh ('ʌskwɪˌbɔː) *n.* **1.** *Irish.* the former name for whiskey. **2.** *Scot.* the former name for **whisky.** [C16: from Irish Gaelic *uisce beathadh* or Scot. Gaelic *uisge beatha* water of life]

USS *abbrev. for:* **1.** United States Senate. **2.** United States Ship.

Ussher *or* **Usher** ('ʌʃə) *n.* **James.** 1581–1656, Irish prelate and scholar. His system of biblical chronology, which dated the creation at 4004 B.C., was for long accepted.

USSR *abbrev. for* Union of Soviet Socialist Republics.

Ussuri (*Russian* ussu'ri) *n.* a river in the SE Soviet Union, flowing north, forming part of the Chinese border, to the Amur River. Length: about 800 km (500 miles).

Ustí nad Labem (*Czech* 'uːstʃi: nad 'labɛm) *n.* a port in NW Czechoslovakia, on the Elbe River: textile and chemical industries. Pop.: 91 000 (1986).

Ustinov ('juːstɪnɒf) *n.* **Peter** (**Alexander**). born 1921, British stage and film actor, director, dramatist, and raconteur.

Ust-Kamenogorsk (*Russian* ustjkəmɪnaˈgɔrsk) *n.* a city in the S Soviet Union, in the E Kazakh SSR: centre of a zinc-, lead-, and copper-mining area Pop.: 321 000 (1987).

Ustyurt *or* **Ust Urt** (*Russian* us'tjurt) *n.* an arid plateau of the S Soviet Union, between the Caspian and Aral seas in the SW Kazakh SSR and the Kara-Kalpak ASSR. Area: about 238 000 sq. km (92 000 sq. miles).

usual ('juːʒʊəl) *adj.* **1.** of the most normal, frequent, or regular type: *that's the usual sort of application to send.* ~*n.* **2.** ordinary or commonplace events (esp. in **out of the usual**). **3. the usual.** *Inf.* the habitual or usual drink, etc. [C14: from LL *ūsuālis* ordinary, from L *ūsus* USE] —**'usually** *adv.* —**'usualness** *n.*

usufruct ('juːsjʊˌfrʌkt) *n.* the right to use and derive profit from a piece of property belonging to another, provided the property itself remains undiminished and uninjured in any way. [C17: from LL *ūsūfrūctus*, from L *ūsus* use + *frūctus* enjoyment] —ˌusu'fructuary *n., adj.*

Usumbura (ˌuːzəmˈbʊərə) *n.* the former name of **Bujumbura.**

usurer ('juːʒərə) *n.* a person who lends funds at an exorbitant rate of interest.

usurp (juː'zɜːp) *vb.* to seize or appropriate (land, a throne, etc.) without authority. [C14: from OF, from L *ūsūrpāre* to take into use, prob. from *ūsus* use + *rapere* to seize] —ˌusur'pation *n.* —u'surper *n.*

usury ('juːʒərɪ) *n., pl.* **-ries. 1.** the practice of loaning money at an exorbitant rate of interest. **2.** an unlawfully high rate of interest. **3.** *Obs.* moneylending. [C14: from Med. L, from L *ūsūra* usage, from *ūsus* USE] —**usurious** (juː'ʒʊərɪəs) *adj.*

USW *Radio. abbrev. for* ultrashort wave.

ut (ʌt, uːt) *n. Music.* the syllable used in the fixed system of solmization for the note C. [C14: from L *ut;* see GAMUT]

UT *abbrev. for:* **1.** universal time. **2.** Utah.

Utah ('juːtɔː, 'juːtɑː) *n.* a state of the western U.S.: settled by Mormons in 1847; situated in the Great Basin and the Rockies, with the Great Salt Lake in the northwest. Capital: Salt Lake City. Pop.: 1 645 000 (1985 est.). Area: 212 628 sq. km (82 096 sq. miles). —**Utahan** (juː'tɔːən, -'tɑːən) *adj., n.*

Utamaro (ˌuːtəˈmɑːrəʊ) *n.* **Kitagawa** (ˌkiːtəˈgɑːwə). 1753–1806, Japanese master of wood-block prints.

ute (juːt) *n. Austral. & N.Z. inf.* short for **utility truck.**

utensil (juː'tɛnsəl) *n.* an implement, tool, or container for practical use: *writing utensils.* [C14 *utensele,* via OF from L *ūtensilia* necessaries, from *ūtēnsilis* available for use, from *ūtī* to use]

uterine ('juːtəˌraɪn) *adj.* **1.** of, relating to, or affecting the uterus. **2.** (of offspring) born of the same mother but not the same father.

uterus ('juːtərəs) *n., pl.* **uteri** ('juːtəˌraɪ). **1.** *Anat.* a hollow muscular organ lying within the pelvic cavity of female mammals. It houses the developing fetus. Nontechnical name: **womb. 2.** the corresponding organ in other animals. [C17: from L]

Utgard ('ʊtgɑːd, 'uːt-) *n. Norse myth.* one of the divisions of Jotunheim, land of the giants, ruled by Utgard-Loki.

Utgard-Loki *n. Norse myth.* the giant king of Utgard.

Uther ('juːθə) *or* **Uther Pendragon** *n.* (in Arthurian legend) a king of Britain and father of Arthur.

Utica ('juːtɪkə) *n.* an ancient city on the N coast of Africa, northwest of Carthage.

utilidor (juː'tɪlədə; *Canad.* -ˌdɔr) *n. Canad.* above-ground insulated casing for pipes carrying water, etc., in permafrost regions.

utilitarian (juːˌtɪlɪ'tɛərɪən) *adj.* **1.** of or relating to utilitarianism. **2.** designed for use rather than beauty. ~*n.* **3.** a person who believes in utilitarianism.

utilitarianism (juːˌtɪlɪ'tɛərɪəˌnɪzəm) *n. Ethics.* **1.** the doctrine that right action consists in the greatest good for the greatest number, that is, in maximizing the total benefit resulting, without regard to the distribution of benefits and burdens. **2.** the theory that the criterion of virtue is utility.

utility (juː'tɪlɪtɪ) *n., pl.* **-ties. 1. a.** the quality of practical use; usefulness. **b.** (*as modifier*): *a utility fabric.* **2.** something useful. **3. a.** a public service, such as the bus system. **b.** (*as modifier*): *utility vehicle.* **4.** *Econ.* the ability of a commodity to satisfy human wants. **5.** *Austral.* short for **utility truck.** [C14: from OF *utelite,* from L *ūtilitās* usefulness, from *ūtī* to use]

utility room *n.* a room, esp. in a private house, used for storage, laundry, etc.

utility truck *n. Austral. & N.Z.* a small truck with an open body and low sides, often with a removable tarpaulin cover; pick-up truck.

utilize *or* **-lise** ('juːtɪˌlaɪz) *vb.* (*tr.*) to make practical or worthwhile use of. —ˈutiˌlizable *or* -ˌlisable *adj.* —ˌutiliˈzation *or* -liˈsation *n.* —ˈutiˌlizer *or* -ˌliser *n.*

utmost ('ʌtˌməʊst) *or* **uttermost** *adj.* (*prenominal*) **1.** of the greatest possible degree or amount: *the utmost degree.* **2.** at the furthest limit: *the utmost town on the peninsula.* ~*n.* **3.** the greatest possible degree, extent, or amount: *he tried his utmost.* [OE *ūtemest,* from *ūte* out + -*mest* MOST]

utmost good faith *n.* a principle used in insurance contracts, legally obliging all parties to reveal to the others any information that might influence the others' decision to enter into the contract. [from L *uberrima fides*]

Utopia (juː'təʊpɪə) *n.* (*sometimes not cap.*) any real or imaginary society, place, state, etc., considered to be perfect or ideal. [C16: from NL *Utopia* (coined by Sir Thomas More in 1516 as the title of his book that described an imaginary island representing the perfect society), lit.: no place: from Gk *ou* not + *topos* a place]

Utopian (juː'təʊpɪən) (*sometimes not cap.*) ~*adj.* **1.** of or relating to a perfect or ideal existence. ~*n.* **2.** an idealistic social reformer. —**U'topianism** *n.*

Utrecht (*Dutch* 'yːtrɛxt; *English* 'juːtrɛkt) *n.* **1.** a province of the W central Netherlands. Capital: Utrecht. Pop.: 953 957 (1987). Area: 1362 sq. km (526 sq. miles). **2.** a city in the central Netherlands, capital of Utrecht province: scene of the signing (1579) of the **Union of Utrecht** (the foundation of the later kingdom of the Netherlands) and of the **Treaty of Utrecht** (1713), ending the War of the Spanish Succession. Pop.: 229 326 (1987).

utricle ('juːtrɪkəl) n. 1. *Anat.* the larger of the two parts of the membranous labyrinth of the internal ear. Cf. **saccule**. 2. *Bot.* the bladder-like one-seeded indehiscent fruit of certain plants. [C18: from L *ūtriculus*, dim. of *ūter* bag] —**u'tricular** *adj.*

utriculitis (juːˌtrɪkjʊ'laɪtɪs) n. inflammation of the inner ear.

Utrillo (*French* ytrijo) n. **Maurice** (mɔris). 1883–1955, French painter, noted for his Parisian street scenes.

Uttar Pradesh ('utə 'praːdɛʃ) n. a state of N India: the most populous state; originated in 1877 with the merging of Agra and Oudh as the United Provinces; augmented by the states of Rampur, Benares, and Tehri-Garhwal in 1949; lies mostly on the Upper Ganges plain but rises over 7500 m (25 000 ft.) in the Himalayas in the northwest; agricultural. Capital: Lucknow. Pop.: 110 885 874 (1981). Area: 294 364 sq. km (113 654 sq. miles).

utter[1] ('ʌtə) vb. 1. to give audible expression to (something): *to utter a growl*. 2. *Criminal law.* to put into circulation (counterfeit coin, forged banknotes, etc.). 3. (*tr.*) to make publicly known; publish: *to utter slander*. [C14: prob. orig. a commercial term, from MDu. *ūteren* (modern Du. *uiteren*) to make known] —**'utterable** *adj.* —**'utterableness** n. —**'utterer** n.

utter[2] ('ʌtə) adj. (*prenominal*) (intensifier): *an utter fool; the utter limit*. [C15: from OE *utera* outer, comp. of *ūte* out (adv.)] —**'utterly** *adv.*

utterance ('ʌtərəns) n. 1. something uttered, such as a statement. 2. the act or power of uttering or ability to utter.

utter barrister n. *Law.* the full title of a barrister who is not a Queen's Counsel.

uttermost ('ʌtəˌməʊst) *adj., n.* a variant of **utmost**.

U-turn n. 1. a turn made by a vehicle in the shape of a U, resulting in a reversal of direction. 2. a complete change in direction of political policy, etc.

UV *abbrev. for* ultraviolet.

UV-A or **UVA** *abbrev. for* ultraviolet radiation with a range of 320-380 nanometres.

uvarovite (uː'vɑːrəˌvaɪt) n. an emerald-green garnet found in chromium deposits. [C19: from G *Uvarovit*; after Count Sergei *Uvarov* (1785–1855), Russian author & statesman]

UV-B or **UVB** *abbrev. for* ultraviolet radiation with a range of 280-320 nanometres.

uvea ('juːvɪə) n. the part of the eyeball consisting of the iris, ciliary body, and choroid. [C16: from Med. L *ūvea*, from L *ūva* grape] —**'uveal** *adj.*

Uvedale ('juːdəl, 'juːvˌdeɪl) n. a variant of (Nicholas) Udall.

UVF *abbrev. for* Ulster Volunteer Force.

uvula ('juːvjʊlə) n., pl. **-las** or **-lae** (-ˌliː). a small fleshy flap of tissue that hangs in the back of the throat and is an extension of the soft palate. [C14: from Med. L, lit.: a little grape, from L *ūva* a grape]

uvular ('juːvjʊlə) adj. 1. of or relating to the uvula. 2. *Phonetics.* articulated with the uvula and the back of the tongue, such as the (r) sound of Parisian French. ~n. 3. a uvular consonant.

Uxbridge ('ʌksˌbrɪdʒ) n. a town in SE England, part of the Greater London borough of Hillingdon since 1965; chiefly residential.

Uxmal (*Spanish* uz'mal) n. an ancient ruined city in SE Mexico, in Yucatán: capital of the later Maya empire.

uxorial (ʌk'sɔːrɪəl) adj. of or relating to a wife: *uxorial influence*. [C19: from L *uxor* wife] —**ux'orially** *adv.*

uxoricide (ʌk'sɔːrɪˌsaɪd) n. 1. the act of killing one's wife. 2. a man who kills his wife. [C19: from L *uxor* wife + -CIDE] —**ux,ori'cidal** *adj.*

uxorious (ʌk'sɔːrɪəs) adj. excessively attached to or dependent on one's wife. [C16: from L *uxōrius* concerning a wife, from *uxor* wife] —**ux'oriously** *adv.* —**ux'oriousness** n.

Uzbek ('uzbɛk, 'ʌz-) n. 1. (*pl.* **-beks** or **-bek**) a member of a Mongoloid people of Uzbekistan. 2. the language of this people.

Uzbek Soviet Socialist Republic n. an administrative division of the SE central Soviet Union, on the Aral Sea. Capital: Tashkent. Pop.: 18 487 000 (1986). Area: 449 600 sq. km (173 546 sq. miles). Also called: **Uzbekistan** (ˌʌzbɛkɪ'staːn).

V

v or **V** (viː) *n., pl.* **v's, V's,** *or* **Vs. 1.** the 22nd letter of the English alphabet. **2.** a speech sound represented by this letter, usually a voiced fricative, as in *vote.* **3. a.** something shaped like a V. **b.** (*in combination*): *a V neck.*

v *symbol. for:* **1.** *Physics.* velocity. **2.** specific volume (of a gas).

V *symbol.for:* **1.** *Chem.* vanadium. **2.** (in transformational grammar) verb. **3.** volume (capacity). **4.** volt. **5.** victory. ~**6.** *the Roman numeral for* five.

v. *abbrev. for:* **1.** ventral. **2.** verb. **3.** verse. **4.** verso. **5.** (*usually italic*) versus. **6.** very. **7.** vide [L: see]. **8.** volume.

V. *abbrev. for:* **1.** Venerable. **2.** (in titles) Very. **3.** (in titles) Vice. **4.** Viscount.

V-1 *n.* a robot bomb invented by the Germans in World War II: used esp. to bombard London. Also called: **doodlebug, buzz bomb, flying bomb.** [from G *Vergeltungswaffe* revenge weapon]

V-2 *n.* a rocket-powered ballistic missile invented by the Germans in World War II: used esp. to bombard London. [see V-1]

V6 *n.* a car or internal-combustion engine having six cylinders arranged in the form of a V.

V8 *n.* a car or internal-combustion engine having eight cylinders arranged in the form of a V.

VA *abbrev. for:* **1.** Vicar Apostolic. **2.** (Order of) Victoria and Albert.

Vaal (vɑːl) *n.* a river in South Africa, rising in the Drakensberg and flowing west as the border between Transvaal and the Orange Free State, then crossing into Cape Province to join the Orange River. Length: 1160 km (720 miles).

Vaasa (*Finnish* 'vɑːsɑ) *n.* a port in W Finland, on the Gulf of Bothnia: the provisional capital of Finland (1918); textile industries. Pop.: 54 253 (1986). Former name: **Nikolainkaupunki.**

vac (væk) *n. Brit. inf.* short for **vacation.**

vacancy ('veɪkənsɪ) *n., pl.* **-cies. 1.** the state or condition of being vacant or unoccupied; emptiness. **2.** an unoccupied post or office: *we have a vacancy in the accounts department.* **3.** an unoccupied room in a hotel, etc.: *put up the "No Vacancies" sign.* **4.** lack of thought or intelligent awareness. **5.** *Obs.* idleness or a period spent in idleness.

vacant ('veɪkənt) *adj.* **1.** without any contents; empty. **2.** (*postpositive;* foll. by *of*) devoid (of something specified). **3.** having no incumbent: *a vacant post.* **4.** having no tenant or occupant: *a vacant house.* **5.** characterized by or resulting from lack of thought or intelligent awareness. **6.** (of time, etc.) not allocated to any activity: *a vacant hour in one's day.* **7.** spent in idleness or inactivity: *a vacant life.* [C13: from L *vacāre* to be empty] —'vacantly *adv.*

vacant possession *n.* ownership of an unoccupied house or property, any previous owner or tenant having departed.

vacate (və'keɪt) *vb.* (*mainly tr.*) **1.** to cause (something) to be empty, esp. by departing from or abandoning it: *to vacate a room.* **2.** (*also intr.*) to give up the tenure, possession, or occupancy of (a place, post, etc.). **3.** *Law.* **a.** to cancel. **b.** to annul. —va'catable *adj.*

vacation (və'keɪʃən) *n.* **1.** *Chiefly Brit.* a period of the year when the law courts or universities are closed. **2.** another word (esp. U.S. and Canad.) for **holiday** (sense 1). **3.** the act of departing from or abandoning property, etc. ~*vb.* **4.** (*intr.*) *U.S. & Canad.* to take a holiday. [C14: from L *vacātiō* freedom, from *vacāre* to be empty] —va'cationer *or* va'cationist *n.*

vaccinate ('væksɪˌneɪt) *vb.* to inoculate (a person) with vaccine so as to produce immunity against a specific disease. —'vacci,nator *n.*

vaccination (ˌvæksɪ'neɪʃən) *n.* **1.** the act of vaccinating. **2.** the scar left following inoculation with a vaccine.

vaccine ('væksiːn) *n. Med.* **1.** a suspension of dead, attenuated, or otherwise modified microorganisms for inoculation to produce immunity to a disease by stimulating the production of antibodies. **2.** a preparation of the virus of cowpox inoculated in humans to produce immunity to smallpox. **3.** (*modifier*) of or relating to vaccination or vaccinia. [C18: from NL *variolae vaccinae* cowpox, title of medical treatise (1798) by Edward Jenner, from L *vacca* a cow] —'vaccinal *adj.*

vaccinia (væk'sɪnɪə) *n.* a technical name for **cowpox.** [C19: NL, from L *vaccīnus* of cows]

vacherin *French.* (vaʃrɛ̃) *n.* a dessert consisting of a meringue shell filled with whipped cream, ice cream, fruit, etc. [also in France a kind of cheese, from F *vache* cow, from L *vacca*]

vacillate ('væsɪˌleɪt) *vb.* (*intr.*) **1.** to fluctuate in one's opinions. **2.** to sway from side to side physically. [C16: from L *vacillāre* to sway, from ?] —ˌvacil'lation *n.* —'vacil,lator *n.*

vacua ('vækjʊə) *n.* a plural of **vacuum.**

vacuity (væ'kjuːɪtɪ) *n., pl.* **-ties. 1.** the state or quality of being vacuous. **2.** an empty space or void. **3.** a lack or absence of something specified: *a vacuity of wind.* **4.** lack of normal intelligence or awareness. **5.** a statement, saying, etc., that is inane or pointless. [C16: from L *vacuitās* empty space, from *vacuus* empty]

vacuole ('vækjʊˌəʊl) *n. Biol.* a fluid-filled cavity in a cell. [C19: from F, lit.: little vacuum, from L VACUUM] —**vacuolar** (ˌvækjʊ'əʊlə) *adj.*

vacuous ('vækjʊəs) *adj.* **1.** empty. **2.** bereft of ideas or intelligence. **3.** characterized by or resulting from vacancy of mind: *a vacuous gaze.* **4.** indulging in no useful mental or physical activity. [C17: from L *vacuus* empty] —'vacuously *adv.*

vacuum ('vækjʊəm) *n., pl.* **vacuums** *or* **vacua. 1.** a region containing no free matter; in technical contexts now often called: **free space. 2.** a region in which gas is present at a low pressure. **3.** the degree of exhaustion of gas within an enclosed space: *a perfect vacuum.* **4.** a feeling of emptiness: *his death left a vacuum in her life.* **5.** short for **vacuum cleaner. 6.** (*modifier*) of, containing, producing, or operated by a low gas pressure: *a vacuum brake.* ~*vb.* **7.** to clean (something) with a vacuum cleaner. [C16: from L: empty space, from *vacuus* empty]

vacuum cleaner *n.* an electrical household appliance used for cleaning floors, carpets, etc., by suction. —**vacuum cleaning** *n.*

vacuum distillation *n.* distillation in which the liquid distilled is enclosed at a low pressure in order to reduce its boiling point.

vacuum flask *n.* an insulating flask that has double walls, usually of silvered glass, with an evacuated space between them. It is used for maintaining substances at high or low temperatures. Also called: **Thermos.**

vacuum gauge *n.* any of a number of instruments for measuring pressures below atmospheric pressure.

vacuum-packed *adj.* packed in an airtight container or packet under low pressure in order to maintain freshness, prevent corrosion, etc.

vacuum pump *n.* a pump for producing a low gas pressure.

vacuum tube *or* **valve** *n.* the U.S. and Canad. name for **valve** (sense 3).

VAD 1. *abbrev. for* Voluntary Aid Detachment. **2.** a member of this organization.

vade mecum ('vɑːdɪ 'meɪkʊm) *n.* a handbook or other aid carried on the person for immediate use when needed. [C17: from L, lit.: go with me]

Vadodara (wə'dəʊdərə) *n.* a city in W India, in SE Gujarat: textile manufacturing. Pop.: 733 656 (1981). Former name (until 1976): **Baroda.**

vadose ('veɪdəʊs) *adj.* of, designating, or derived from water occurring above the water table: *vadose deposits.* [C19: from L *vadōsus* full of shallows, from *vadum* a ford]

Vaduz (*German* fa'dʊts) *n.* the capital of Liechtenstein, in the Rhine valley: an old market town, dominated by a medieval castle, residence of the prince of Liechtenstein. Pop.: 4920 (1986 est.).

vagabond ('vægə,bɒnd) n. **1.** a person with no fixed home. **2.** an idle wandering beggar or thief. **3.** (*modifier*) of or like a vagabond. [C15: from L *vagābundus* wandering, from *vagāri* to roam, from *vagus* VAGUE] —'**vaga,bondage** n.

vagal ('veɪgəl) adj. Anat. of, relating to, or affecting the vagus nerve: *vagal inhibition.*

vagary ('veɪgəri, və'gɛəri) n., pl. -**garies.** an erratic notion or action. [C16: prob. from L *vagāri* to roam; cf. L *vagus* VAGUE]

vagina (və'dʒaɪnə) n., pl. -**nas** or -**nae** (-niː). **1.** the canal in most female mammals that extends from the cervix of the uterus to an external opening between the labia minora. **2.** Anat., biol. any sheath or sheathlike structure. [C17: from L: sheath] —**vag'inal** adj.

vaginate ('vædʒɪnɪt, -,neɪt) adj. (esp. of plant parts) sheathed: *a vaginate leaf.*

vaginectomy (,vædʒɪ'nɛktəmɪ) n., pl. -**mies. 1.** surgical removal of all or part of the vagina. **2.** surgical removal of part of the serous sheath surrounding the testis and epididymis.

vaginismus (,vædʒɪ'nɪzməs) n. painful spasm of the vagina. [C19: from NL, from VAGINA, + -*ismus*; see -ISM]

vaginitis (,vædʒɪ'naɪtɪs) n. inflammation of the vagina.

vagotomy (væ'gɒtəmɪ) n., pl. -**mies.** surgical division of the vagus nerve, performed to limit gastric secretion in patients with severe peptic ulcers. [C19: from VAG(US) + -TOMY]

vagotonia (,veɪgə'təʊnɪə) n. pathological overactivity of the vagus nerve, affecting various bodily functions controlled by this nerve. [C19: from VAG(US) + -*tonia*, from L *tonus* tension, TONE]

vagrancy ('veɪgrənsɪ) n., pl. -**cies. 1.** the state or condition of being a vagrant. **2.** the conduct or mode of living of a vagrant.

vagrant ('veɪgrənt) n. **1.** a person of no settled abode, income, or job; tramp. ~adj. **2.** wandering about. **3.** of or characteristic of a vagrant or vagabond. **4.** moving in an erratic fashion; wayward. **5.** (of plants) showing straggling growth. [C15: prob. from OF *waucrant* (from *wancrer* to roam, of Gmc origin), but also infl. by OF *vagant* vagabond, from L *vagāri* to wander] —'**vagrantly** adv.

vague (veɪg) adj. **1.** (of statements, meaning, etc.) imprecise: *vague promises.* **2.** not clearly perceptible or discernible: *a vague idea.* **3.** not clearly or definitely established or known: *a vague rumour.* **4.** (of a person or his expression) absent-minded. [C16: via F from L *vagus* wandering, from ?] —'**vaguely** adv. —'**vagueness** n.

vagus or **vagus nerve** ('veɪgəs) n., pl. -**gi** (-dʒaɪ). the tenth cranial nerve, which supplies the heart, lungs, and viscera. [C19: from L *vagus* wandering] —'**vagal** adj.

vail (veɪl) Obs. ~vb. (tr.) **1.** to lower (something, such as a weapon), esp. as a sign of deference. **2.** to remove (the hat, etc.) as a mark of respect. ~n. **3.** a tip. [C14 *valen*, from obs. *avalen*, from OF *avaler* to let fall, from L *ad vallem*, lit.: to the valley, i.e., down]

vain (veɪn) adj. **1.** inordinately proud of one's appearance, possessions, or achievements. **2.** given to ostentatious display. **3.** worthless. **4.** senseless or futile. ~n. **5. in vain.** fruitlessly. [C13: via OF from L *vānus*] —'**vainly** adv. —'**vainness** n.

vainglory (,veɪn'glɔːrɪ) n. **1.** boastfulness or vanity. **2.** ostentation. —,**vain'glorious** adj.

vair (vɛə) n. **1.** a fur, probably Russian squirrel, used to trim robes in the Middle Ages. **2.** a fur used on heraldic shields, conventionally represented by white and blue skins in alternate lines. [C13: from OF: of more than one colour, from L *varius* variegated]

Vaisya ('vaɪsjə, 'vaɪʃjə) n. the third of the four main Hindu castes, the traders. [C18: from Sansk., lit.: settler, from *viś* settlement]

Valais (French valɛ) n. a canton of S Switzerland: includes the entire valley of the upper Rhône and the highest peaks in Switzerland; produces a quarter of Switzerland's hydroelectricity. Capital: Sion. Pop.: 232 600 (1986 est.). Area: 5231 sq. km (2020 sq. miles). German name: **Wallis.**

valance ('væləns) n. a short piece of drapery hung along a shelf or bed to hide structural detail. [C15: ? after VALENCE, noted for its textiles] —'**valanced** adj.

Valdai Hills (vɑːl'daɪ) pl. n. a region of hills and plateaus in the NW Soviet Union, between Moscow and Leningrad. Greatest height: 346 m (1135 ft.).

Valdemar I (Danish 'valdəmar) n. a variant spelling of **Waldemar I.**

Val-de-Marne (French valdəmarn) n. a department of N France, in Île-de-France region. Capital: Créteil. Pop.: 1 193 655 (1982). Area: 244 sq. km (95 sq. miles).

Valdivia[1] (Spanish bal'diβja) n. a port in S Chile, on the **Valdivia River** about 19 km (12 miles) from the Pacific: developed chiefly by German settlers in the 1850s; university (1954). Pop.: 119 977 (1985 est.).

Valdivia[2] (Spanish bal'diβja) n. **Pedro de** ('peðro de). ?1500–54, Spanish soldier; conqueror of Chile.

Val-d'Oise (French valdwaz) n. a department of N France, in Île-de-France region. Capital: Pontoise. Pop.: 920 598 (1982). Area: 1249 sq. km (487 sq. miles).

vale[1] (veɪl) n. a literary word for **valley.** [C13: from OF *val*, from L *vallis* valley]

vale[2] Latin. ('vɑːleɪ) sentence substitute. farewell; goodbye.

valediction (,vælɪ'dɪkʃən) n. **1.** the act or an instance of saying goodbye. **2.** any valedictory statement, speech, etc. [C17: from L *valedīcere*, from *valē* farewell + *dīcere* to say]

valedictory (,vælɪ'dɪktərɪ) adj. **1.** saying goodbye. **2.** of or relating to a farewell or an occasion of farewell. ~n., pl. -**ries. 3.** a farewell address or speech.

valence ('veɪləns) n. Chem. **1.** another name (esp. U.S. and Canad.) for **valency. 2.** the phenomenon of forming chemical bonds.

Valence (French valɑ̃s) n. a town in SE France, on the River Rhône. Pop.: 68 382 (1983 est.).

Valencia (Spanish ba'lenθja) n. **1.** a port in E Spain, capital of Valencia province, on the Mediterranean: the third largest city in Spain; capital of the Moorish kingdom of Valencia (1021–1238); university (1501). Pop.: 744 748 (1981). Latin name: **Valentia** (və'lentɪə). **2.** a region and former kingdom of E Spain, on the Mediterranean. **3.** a city in N Venezuela: one of the two main industrial centres in Venezuela. Pop.: 856 455 (1987).

Valenciennes[1] (,vælənsɪ'ɛn) n. a flat bobbin lace typically having scroll and floral designs and originally made of linen. [after VALENCIENNES[2], where orig. made]

Valenciennes[2] (French valɑ̃sjɛn) n. a town in N France, on the River Escaut: a coal-mining and heavy industrial centre. Pop.: 42 068 (1983 est.).

valency ('veɪlənsɪ) or esp. U.S. & Canad. **valence** n., pl. -**cies** or -**ces.** Chem. a property of atoms or groups equal to the number of atoms of hydrogen that the atom or group could combine with or displace in forming compounds. [C19: from L *valentia* strength, from *valēre* to be strong]

valency electron n. Chem. an electron in the outer shell of an atom, responsible for forming chemical bonds.

Valens ('veɪlɛnz) n. ?328–378 A.D., emperor of the Eastern Roman Empire (364–378); appointed by his elder brother Valentinian I, emperor of the Western Empire.

valentine ('vælən,taɪn) n. **1.** a card or gift expressing love or affection, sent, often anonymously, on Saint Valentine's Day. **2.** a sweetheart selected for such a greeting.

Valentine ('vælən,taɪn) n. **Saint.** 3rd century A.D., Christian martyr, associated by historical accident with the custom of sending valentines; bishop of Terni. Feast day: Feb. 14.

Valentinian I (,vælən'tɪnɪən) or **Valentinianus I** (,vælən,tɪnɪ'eɪnəs) n. 321–375 A.D., emperor of the Western Roman Empire (364–375); appointed his brother Valens to rule the Eastern Empire.

Valentinian II or **Valentinianus II** n. 371–392 A.D., emperor of the Western Roman Empire (375–392), reigning jointly with his half brother Gratian until 383.

Valentinian III or **Valentinianus III** n. ?419–455 A.D., emperor of the Western Roman Empire (425–455). His government lost Africa to the Vandals. With Pope Leo I he issued (444) an edict giving the bishop of Rome supremacy over the provincial churches.

Valentino (,vælən'tiːnəʊ) n. **Rudolph,** original name *Rodolpho Guglielmi di Valentina d'Antonguolla.* 1895–1926, U.S. silent-film actor, born in Italy. He is famous for his romantic roles in such films as *The Sheik* (1921).

Valera (və'lɛərə, -'lɪərə) n. See (Eamon) **de Valera.**

valerian (və'lɛərɪən) n. **1.** Also called: **allheal.** a Eurasian plant having small white or pinkish flowers and a medicinal root. **2.** a sedative drug made from the dried roots of this plant. [C14: via OF from Med. L *valeriana* (*herba*) (herb) of *Valerius*, unexplained L personal name]

Valerian (vəˈlɪərɪən) *n.* Latin name *Publius Licinius Valerianus.* died 260 A.D., Roman emperor (253–260): renewed persecution of the Christians; defeated by the Persians.

valeric (vəˈlɛrɪk, -ˈlɪərɪk) *adj.* of, relating to, or derived from valerian.

valeric acid *n.* another name for **pentanoic acid.**

Valéry (*French* valeri) *n.* **Paul** (pɔl). 1871–1945, French poet and essayist, influenced by the symbolists, esp. Mallarmé. He wrote lyric poetry, rich in imagery, as in *La Jeune Parque* (1917) and *Album de vers anciens 1890–1900* (1920).

valet (ˈvælɪt, ˈvæleɪ) *n.* **1.** a manservant who acts as personal attendant to his employer, looking after his clothing, serving his meals, etc. **2.** a manservant who attends to the requirements of patrons in a hotel, etc.; steward. [C16: from OF *vaslet* page, from Med. L *vassus* servant]

valeta (vəˈliːtə) *n.* a variant spelling of **veleta.**

valet de chambre French. (valɛ də ʃɑ̃brə) *n., pl. valets de chambre* (valɛ də ʃɑ̃brə). the full French term for **valet** (sense 1).

Valetta (vəˈlɛtə) *n.* a variant spelling of **Valletta.**

valetudinarian (ˌvælɪˌtjuːdɪˈnɛərɪən) *or* **valetudinary** (ˌvælɪˈtjuːdɪnərɪ) *n., pl.* **-narians** *or* **-naries. 1.** a person who is chronically sick. **2.** a hypochondriac. **3.** an old person who is in good health. ~*adj.* **4.** relating to or resulting from poor health. **5.** being a valetudinarian. [C18: from L *valetūdō* state of health, from *valēre* to be well] **— ˌvaleˌtudiˈnarianism** *n.*

valgus (ˈvælgəs) *adj. Pathol.* twisted away from the midline of the body. [C19: from L: bow-legged]

Valhalla (vælˈhælə), **Walhalla, Valhall** (vælˈhæl, ˈvælhæl), *or* **Walhall** *n. Norse myth.* the great hall of Odin where warriors who die as heroes in battle dwell eternally. [C18: from ON, from *valr* slain warriors + *höll* HALL]

valiant (ˈvæljənt) *adj.* **1.** courageous or intrepid. **2.** marked by bravery or courage: *a valiant deed.* [C14: from OF, from *valoir* to be of value, from L *valēre* to be strong] **— ˈvaliantly** *adv.*

valid (ˈvælɪd) *adj.* **1.** having some foundation; based on truth. **2.** legally acceptable: *a valid licence.* **3. a.** having legal force. **b.** having legal authority. **4.** having some force or cogency: *a valid point in a debate.* **5.** *Logic.* (of an inference or argument) having premises and a conclusion so related that if the premises are true, the conclusion must be true. [C16: from L *validus* robust, from *valēre* to be strong] **—validity** (vəˈlɪdɪtɪ) *n.* **— ˈvalidly** *adv.*

validate (ˈvælɪˌdeɪt) *vb.* (*tr.*) **1.** to confirm or corroborate. **2.** to give legal force or official confirmation to. **— ˌvaliˈdation** *n.*

valine (ˈveɪliːn) *n.* an essential amino acid: a component of proteins. [C19: from VAL(ERIC ACID) + -INE²]

valise (vəˈliːz) *n.* a small overnight travelling case. [C17: via F from It. *valigia*, from ?]

Valium (ˈvælɪəm) *n. Trademark.* a preparation of the drug diazepam used as a tranquillizer.

Valkyrie, Walkyrie (vælˈkɪərɪ, ˈvælkɪərɪ), *or* **Valkyr** (ˈvælkɪə) *n. Norse myth.* any of the beautiful maidens who serve Odin and ride over battlefields to claim the dead heroes and take them to Valhalla. [C18: from ON *Valkyrja*, from *valr* slain warriors + *köri* to CHOOSE] **— Valˈkyrian** *adj.*

Valladolid (Spanish baʎaðoˈlið) *n.* **1.** a city in NW Spain: residence of the Spanish court in the 16th century; university (1346). Pop.: 358 629 (1982 est.). **2.** the former name (until 1828) of **Morelia.**

vallation (vəˈleɪʃən) *n.* **1.** the act or process of building fortifications. **2.** a wall or rampart. [C17: from LL *vallātiō*, from L *vallum* rampart]

vallecula (vəˈlɛkjʊlə) *n., pl.* **-lae** (-ˌliː). **1.** *Anat.* any of various natural depressions or crevices. **2.** *Bot.* a groove or furrow. [C19: from LL: little valley, from L *vallis* valley]

Valle d'Aosta (Italian ˈvalle daˈɔsta) *n.* an autonomous region of NW Italy: under many different rulers until passing to the house of Savoy in the 11th century; established as an autonomous region in 1944. Capital: Aosta. Pop.: 113 855 (1985 est.). Area: 3263 sq. km (1260 sq. miles).

Valletta *or* **Valetta** (vəˈlɛtə) *n.* the capital of Malta, on the NE coast: founded by the Knights Hospitallers, after their

victory over the Turks in 1565; became a major naval base after Malta's annexation by Britain (1814). Pop.: 9263 (1985).

valley (ˈvælɪ) *n.* **1.** a long depression in the land surface, usually containing a river, formed by erosion or by movements in the earth's crust. **2.** the broad area drained by a single river system: *the Thames valley.* **3.** any elongated depression resembling a valley. [C13: from OF *valee*, from L *vallis*]

Valley Forge *n.* an area in SE Pennsylvania, northwest of Philadelphia: winter camp (1777–78) of Washington and the American Revolutionary Army.

Valley of Ten Thousand Smokes *n.* a volcanic region of SW Alaska, formed by the massive eruption of Mount Katmai in 1912; jets of steam issue from vents up to 45 m (150 ft.) across.

Vallombrosa (Italian vallomˈbroːsa) *n.* a village and resort in central Italy, in Tuscany region: 11th-century Benedictine monastery.

vallum (ˈvæləm) *n. Archaeol.* a Roman rampart or earthwork.

Valois¹ (*French* valwa) *n.* a historic region and former duchy of N France.

Valois² (*French* valwa) *n.* a royal house of France, ruling from 1328 to 1589.

Valois³ (ˈvælwɑː) *n.* Dame **Ninette de** (niːˈnɛt də). original name *Edris Stannus.* born 1898, British ballet dancer and choreographer, born in Ireland: a founder of the Vic-Wells Ballet Company (1931), which under her direction became the Royal Ballet (1956).

Valona (vəˈləʊnə) *n.* another name for **Vlorë.**

valonia (vəˈləʊnɪə) *n.* the acorn cups and unripe acorns of the Eurasian oak, used in tanning, dyeing, and making ink. [C18: from It. *vallonia*, ult. from Gk *balanos* acorn]

valorize *or* **-rise** (ˈvælə.raɪz) *vb.* (*tr.*) to fix an artificial price for (a commodity) by governmental action. [C20: back formation from *valorization;* see VALOUR] **—ˌvalori'zation** *or* **-ri'sation** *n.*

valour *or U.S.* **valor** (ˈvælə) *n.* courage or bravery, esp. in battle. [C15: from LL *valor*, from *valēre* to be strong] **— ˈvalorous** *adj.*

Valparaíso (Spanish balparaˈiso) *n.* a port in central Chile, on a wide bay of the Pacific: the third largest city and chief port of Chile; two universities. Pop.: 267 025 (1985 est.).

valse French. (vals) *n.* the French word for **waltz.**

valuable (ˈvæljʊəbəl) *adj.* **1.** having considerable monetary worth. **2.** of considerable importance or quality: *valuable information.* **3.** able to be valued. ~*n.* **4.** (*usually pl.*) a valuable article of personal property, esp. jewellery. **— ˈvaluably** *adv.*

valuate (ˈvæljʊˌeɪt) *vb. U.S.* another word for **value** (senses 10, 12) or **evaluate. — ˈvaluˌator** *n.*

valuation (ˌvæljʊˈeɪʃən) *n.* **1.** the act of valuing, esp. a formal assessment of the worth of property, jewellery, etc. **2.** the price arrived at by the process of valuing: *I set a high valuation on technical ability.* **— ˌvaluˈational** *adj.*

value (ˈvæljuː) *n.* **1.** the desirability of a thing, often in respect of some property such as usefulness or exchangeability. **2.** an amount, price, a material or monetary one, considered to be a fair exchange in return for a thing: *the value of the picture is £10 000.* **3.** satisfaction: *value for money.* **4.** precise meaning or significance. **5.** (*pl.*) the moral principles or accepted standards of a person or group. **6.** *Maths.* a particular magnitude, number, or amount: *the value of the variable was 7.* **7.** *Music.* short for **time value. 8.** (in painting, drawing, etc.) **a.** a gradation of tone from light to dark. **b.** the relation of one of these elements to another or to the whole picture. **9.** *Phonetics.* the quality of the speech sound associated with a written character representing it: *"g" has the value* (dʒ) *in English "gem".* ~*vb.* **-uing, -ued.** (*tr.*) **10.** to assess or estimate the worth, merit, or desirability of. **11.** to have a high regard for, esp. in respect of worth, usefulness, merit, etc. **12.** (foll. by *at*) to fix the financial or material worth of (a unit of currency, work of art, etc.). [C14: from OF, from *valoir*, from L *valēre* to be worth] **— ˈvalued** *adj.* **— ˈvalueless** *adj.* **— ˈvaluer** *n.*

value added *n.* the difference between the total revenues of a firm, industry, etc., and its total purchases from other firms, industries, etc.

value-added tax n. (in Britain) the full name for **VAT**.

valued policy n. an insurance policy in which the amount payable in the event of a valid claim is agreed upon between the company and the policyholder when the policy is issued and is not related to the actual value of a loss.

value judgment n. a subjective assessment based on one's own values or those of one's class.

Valuer General n. Austral. a state official who values properties for rating purposes.

valuta (vəˈluːtə) n. Rare. the value of one currency in terms of its exchange rate with another. [C20: from It., lit.: VALUE]

valvate (ˈvælveɪt) adj. **1.** furnished with a valve or valves. **2.** Bot. **a.** taking place by means of valves: valvate dehiscence. **b.** (of petals) having the margins touching but not overlapping.

valve (vælv) n. **1.** any device that shuts off, starts, regulates, or controls the flow of a fluid. **2.** Anat. a flaplike structure in a hollow organ, such as the heart, that controls the one-way passage of fluid through that organ. **3.** Also called: **tube.** an evacuated electron tube containing a cathode, anode, and, usually, one or more additional control electrodes. When a positive potential is applied to the anode, it produces a one-way flow of current. **4.** Zool. any of the separable pieces that make up the shell of a mollusc. **5.** Music. a device on some brass instruments by which the effective length of the tube may be varied to enable a chromatic scale to be produced. **6.** Bot. any of the several parts that make up a dry dehiscent fruit, esp. a capsule. [C14: from L valva a folding door] —**'valveless** adj. —**'valve,like** adj.

valve-in-head engine n. the U.S. name for **overhead-valve engine.**

valvular (ˈvælvjʊlə) adj. **1.** of, relating to, operated by, or having a valve or valves. **2.** having the shape or function of a valve.

valvulitis (ˌvælvjʊˈlaɪtɪs) n. inflammation of a bodily valve, esp. a heart valve. [C19: from NL valvula dim. of VALVE + -ITIS]

vamoose (vəˈmuːs) vb. (intr.) Sl., chiefly U.S. to leave a place hurriedly; decamp. [C19: from Sp. vamos let us go, from L vādere to go, walk rapidly]

vamp[1] (væmp) Inf. ~n. **1.** a seductive woman who exploits men by use of her sexual charms. ~vb. **2.** to exploit (a man) in the fashion of a vamp. [C20: short for VAMPIRE]

vamp[2] (væmp) n. **1.** something patched up to make it look new. **2.** the reworking of a story, etc. **3.** an improvised accompaniment. **4.** the front part of the upper of a shoe. ~vb. **5.** (tr.; often foll. by up) to make a renovation of. **6.** to improvise (an accompaniment) to (a tune). [C13: from OF avantpié the front part of a shoe (hence, something patched, from avant- fore- + pié foot, from L pēs]

vampire (ˈvæmpaɪə) n. **1.** (in European folklore) a corpse that rises nightly from its grave to drink the blood of the living. **2.** See **vampire bat. 3.** a person who preys mercilessly upon others. [C18: from F, from G, from Magyar] —**vampiric** (væmˈpɪrɪk) adj. —**'vampirism** n.

vampire bat n. a bat of tropical regions of Central and South America, having sharp incisor and canine teeth and feeding on the blood of birds and mammals.

van[1] (væn) n. **1.** short for **caravan** (sense 1). **2.** a motor vehicle for transporting goods, etc., by road. **3.** Brit. a closed railway wagon in which the guard travels, for transporting goods, etc.

van[2] (væn) n. short for **vanguard.**

van[3] (væn) n. Tennis, chiefly Brit. short for **advantage** (sense 3).

van[4] (væn) n. **1.** any device for winnowing corn. **2.** Arch. a wing. [C17: var. of FAN[1]]

Van (vɑːn) n. **1.** a city in E Turkey, on Lake Van. Pop.: 121 306 (1985). **2. Lake.** a salt lake in E Turkey, at an altitude of 1650 m (5400 ft.): fed by melting snow and glaciers. Area: 3737 sq. km (1433 sq. miles).

vanadium (vəˈneɪdɪəm) n. a toxic silvery-white metallic element used in steel alloys and as a catalyst. Symbol: V; atomic no.: 23; atomic wt.: 50.94. [C19: NL, from ON Vanadis, epithet of the goddess Freya + -IUM]

Van Allen belt (væn ˈælən) n. either of two regions of charged particles above the earth, the inner one extending from 2400 to 5600 kilometres above the earth and the outer one from 13 000 to 19 000 kilometres. [C20: after its discoverer, J. A. Van Allen (born 1914), U.S. physicist]

Vanbrugh (ˈvænbrə) n. Sir **John.** 1664–1726, English dramatist and baroque architect. His best-known plays are the Restoration comedies The Relapse (1697) and The Provok'd Wife (1697). As an architect, he is noted esp. for Blenheim Palace.

Van Buren (væn ˈbjʊərən) n. **Martin.** 1782–1862, U.S. Democratic statesman; 8th president of the U.S. (1837–41).

Vancouver[1] (vænˈkuːvə) n. **1.** an island of SW Canada, off the SW coast of British Columbia: separated from the Canadian mainland by the Strait of Georgia and Queen Charlotte Sound, and from the U.S. mainland by Juan de Fuca Strait; the largest island off the W coast of North America. Chief town: Victoria. Pop.: 461 573 (1981). Area: 32 137 sq. km (12 408 sq. miles). **2.** a port in SW Canada, in SW British Columbia: Canada's chief Pacific port and third largest city: university (1908). Pop.: 431 147 (1986). **3. Mount.** a mountain on the border between Canada and Alaska, in the St Elias Mountains. Height: 4785 m (15 700 ft.).

Vancouver[2] (vænˈkuːvə) n. **George.** 1757–98, English navigator, noted for his exploration of the Pacific coast of North America (1792–94).

V and A (in Britain) abbrev. for Victoria and Albert Museum.

vandal (ˈvænd²l) n. a person who deliberately causes damage to personal or public property. [C17: from VANDAL, from L Vandallus, of Gmc origin]

Vandal (ˈvænd²l) n. a member of a Germanic people that raided Roman provinces in the 3rd and 4th centuries A.D. before devastating Gaul, conquering Spain and N Africa, and sacking Rome. —**Vandalic** (vænˈdælɪk) adj.

vandalism (ˈvændə,lɪzəm) n. the deliberate destruction caused by a vandal or an instance of such destruction. —,vandal'istic adj.

vandalize or **-lise** (ˈvændə,laɪz) vb. (tr.) to destroy or damage (something) by an act of vandalism.

Van de Graaff generator (ˈvæn də ˌɡrɑːf) n. a device for producing high electrostatic potentials, consisting of a hollow metal sphere on which a charge is accumulated from a continuous moving belt of insulating material: used in particle accelerators. [C20: after R. J. Van de Graaff (1901–67), U.S. physicist]

Vanderbilt (ˈvændəbɪlt) n. **Cornelius,** known as Commodore Vanderbilt. 1794–1877, U.S. steamship and railway magnate and philanthropist.

Van der Post (ˈvæn də ˌpəʊst) n. Sir **Laurens.** born 1906, South African novelist. His works include the travel books Venture to the Interior (1952) and The Lost World of the Kalahari (1958), and the novels The Hunter and the Whale (1967) and A Story Like the Wind (1972).

Van der Waals Dutch. (van dər ˈwɑːls) n. **Johannes Diderik** (joːˈhɑnəs ˈdiːˌdərɪk). 1837–1923, Dutch physicist, noted for his research on the equations of state of gases and liquids: Nobel prize for physics in 1910.

Van Diemen Gulf (væn ˈdiːmən) n. an inlet of the Timor Sea in N Australia, in the Northern Territory.

Van Diemen's Land (væn ˈdiːmənz) n. the former name (1642–1855) of **Tasmania.** —,Vande'monian n., adj.

Van Dyck or **Vandyke** (væn ˈdaɪk) n. Sir **Anthony.** 1599–1641, Flemish painter; court painter to Charles I of England (1632–41). He is best known for his portraits of the aristocracy.

Vandyke beard (ˈvændaɪk) n. a short pointed beard. Often shortened to **Vandyke.**

Vandyke collar or **cape** n. a large white collar with several very deep points. Often shortened to **Vandyke.**

vane (veɪn) n. **1.** Also called: **weather vane.** a flat plate or blade of metal mounted on a vertical axis in an exposed position to indicate wind direction. **2.** any one of the flat blades or sails forming part of the wheel of a windmill. **3.** any flat or shaped plate used to direct fluid flow, esp. in a turbine, etc. **4.** a fin or plate fitted to a projectile or missile to provide stabilization or guidance. **5.** Ornithol. the flat part of a feather. **6.** Surveying. **a.** a sight on a quadrant or compass. **b.** the movable marker on a levelling staff. [OE fana] —**vaned** adj.

Vane (veɪn) n. Sir **Henry,** known as Sir Harry Vane. 1613–62, English Puritan statesman and colonial administrator; governor of Massachusetts (1636–37). He was executed for high treason after the Restoration.

Vänern (*Swedish* 'vɛːnərn) *n.* **Lake.** a lake in SW Sweden: the largest lake in Sweden and W Europe; drains into the Kattegat. Area: 5585 sq. km (2156 sq. miles).

Van Gogh (væn 'gɒx; *Dutch* vɑn 'xɔx) *n.* **Vincent** (vɪn'sɛnt). 1853–90, Dutch postimpressionist painter, noted for his landscapes and portraits, in which colour is used essentially for its expressive and emotive value.

vanguard ('væn,gɑːd) *n.* **1.** the leading division or units of a military force. **2.** the leading position in any movement or field, or the people who occupy such a position. [C15: from OF *avant-garde*, from *avant-* fore- + *garde* GUARD]

vanilla (və'nɪlə) *n.* **1.** any of a genus of tropical climbing orchids having spikes of large fragrant flowers and long fleshy pods containing the seeds (beans). **2.** the pod or bean of certain of these plants, used to flavour food, etc. **3.** a flavouring extract prepared from vanilla beans and used in cooking. ~*adj.* **4.** flavoured with or as with vanilla: *vanilla ice cream.* **5.** *Computers sl.* ordinary. [C17: from NL, from Sp. *vainilla* pod, from *vaina*, from L *vāgīna* sheath] —**va'nillic** *adj.*

vanillin ('vænɪlɪn, və'nɪlɪn) *n.* a white crystalline aldehyde found in vanilla and many natural balsams and resins. It is a by-product of paper manufacture and is used as a flavouring and in perfumes.

Vanir ('vɑːnɪə) *n. Norse myth.* a race of ancient gods often locked in struggle with the Aesir. The most notable of them are Njord and his children Frey and Freya. [from ON *Vanr*, a fertility god]

vanish ('vænɪʃ) *vb.* (*intr.*) **1.** to disappear, esp. suddenly or mysteriously. **2.** to cease to exist. **3.** *Maths.* to become zero. [C14 *vanissen*, from OF *esvanir*, from L *ēvānēscere* to evaporate, from *ē-* EX-[1] + *vānēscere*, from *vānus* empty] —'**vanisher** *n.*

vanishing cream *n.* a cosmetic cream that is colourless once applied, used as a foundation for powder or as a cleansing cream.

vanishing point *n.* **1.** the point to which parallel lines appear to converge in the rendering of perspective, usually on the horizon. **2.** a point at which something disappears.

vanity ('vænɪtɪ) *n., pl.* -**ties.** **1.** the state or quality of being vain. **2.** ostentation occasioned by ambition or pride. **3.** an instance of being vain or something about which one is vain. **4.** the state or quality of being valueless or futile. [C13: from OF, from L *vānitās* emptiness, from *vānus* empty]

vanity bag, case, or **box** *n.* a woman's small bag or hand case used to carry cosmetics, etc.

vanity unit *n.* a hand basin built into a wooden Formica-covered or tiled top, usually with a built-in cupboard below it. Also called (trademark): **Vanitory unit.**

vanquish ('væŋkwɪʃ) *vb.* (*tr.*) **1.** to defeat or overcome in a battle, contest, etc. **2.** to defeat in argument or debate. **3.** to conquer (an emotion). [C14 *vanquisshen*, from OF *venquis*, from *veintre* to overcome, from L *vincere*] —'**vanquishable** *adj.* —'**vanquisher** *n.*

Vansittart (væn'sɪtət) *n.* **Robert Gilbert,** 1st Baron Vansittart of Denham. 1881–1957, British diplomat and writer; a fierce opponent of Nazi Germany and of Communism.

vantage ('vɑːntɪdʒ) *n.* **1.** a state, position, or opportunity affording superiority or advantage. **2.** superiority or benefit accruing from such a position, etc. **3.** *Tennis.* short for **advantage** (sense 3). [C13: from OF *avantage* ADVANTAGE]

vantage point *n.* a position or place that allows one an overall view of a scene or situation.

Vanua Levu (vɑː'nuːə 'lɛvuː) *n.* the second largest island of Fiji: mountainous. Area: 5535 sq. km (2137 sq. miles).

Vanuatu ('vænuː,ætuː) *n.* a republic comprising a group of islands in the W Pacific, W of Fiji: a condominium under Anglo-French joint rule from 1906; attained partial autonomy in 1978 and full independence in 1980. Economy based chiefly on copra. Capital: Vila (on Efate). Pop.: 141 400 (1987). Area: about 14 760 sq. km (5700 sq. miles). Official name: **Republic of Vanuatu.** Former name (until 1980): **New Hebrides.**

vanward ('vænwəd) *adj., adv.* in or towards the front.

Vanzetti (væn'zɛtɪ) *n.* **Bartolomeo** (bartolo'mɛːo). 1888–1927, U.S. radical agitator, born in Italy: executed with Sacco in a case that had worldwide political repercussions.

vapid ('væpɪd) *adj.* **1.** bereft of strength, sharpness, flavour, etc. **2.** boring or dull: *vapid talk.* [C17: from L *vapidus*] —**va'pidity** *n.* —'**vapidly** *adv.*

vapor ('veɪpə) *n.* the U.S. spelling of **vapour.**

vaporescence (,veɪpə'rɛsəns) *n.* the production or formation of vapour. —,**vapor'escent** *adj.*

vaporetto (,veɪpə'rɛtəʊ) *n., pl.* -**ti** (-tɪ) *or* -**tos.** a steam-powered passenger boat, as used on the canals in Venice. [It., from *vapore* a steamboat]

vaporific (,veɪpə'rɪfɪk) *adj.* **1.** producing, causing, or tending to produce vapour. **2.** of, concerned with, or having the nature of vapour. **3.** tending to become vapour; volatile. [C18: from NL *vaporificus*, from L *vapor* steam + *facere* to make]

vaporimeter (,veɪpə'rɪmɪtə) *n.* an instrument for measuring vapour pressure, used to determine the volatility of oils.

vaporize or **-rise** ('veɪpə,raɪz) *vb.* **1.** to change or cause to change into vapour or into the gaseous state. **2.** to evaporate or disappear or cause to evaporate or disappear, esp. suddenly. **3.** to destroy or be destroyed by turning into a gas as a result of the extreme heat generated by a nuclear explosion. —,**vapori'zation** or **-ri'sation** *n.*

vaporizer or **-riser** ('veɪpə,raɪzə) *n.* **1.** a substance that vaporizes or a device that causes vaporization. **2.** *Med.* a device that produces steam or atomizes medication for inhalation.

vaporous ('veɪpərəs) *adj.* **1.** resembling or full of vapour. **2.** lacking permanence or substance. **3.** given to foolish imaginings. —**vaporosity** (,veɪpə'rɒsɪtɪ) *n.* —'**vaporously** *adv.*

vapour or U.S. **vapor** ('veɪpə) *n.* **1.** particles of moisture or other substance suspended in air and visible as clouds, smoke, etc. **2.** a gaseous substance at a temperature below its critical temperature. **3.** a substance that is in a gaseous state at a temperature below its boiling point. **4. the vapours.** *Arch.* a depressed mental condition believed originally to be the result of vaporous exhalations from the stomach. ~*vb.* **5.** to evaporate or cause to evaporate. **6.** (*intr.*) to make vain empty boasts. [C14: from L *vapor*] —'**vapourer** or U.S. '**vaporer** *n.* —'**vapourish** or U.S. '**vaporish** *adj.* —'**vapour-,like** or U.S. '**vapor-,like** *adj.* —'**vapoury** or U.S. '**vapory** *adj.*

vapour density *n.* the ratio of the density of a gas or vapour to that of hydrogen at the same temperature and pressure.

vapour lock *n.* a stoppage in a pipe carrying a liquid caused by a bubble of gas, esp. in the pipe feeding the carburettor of an internal-combustion engine.

vapour pressure *n. Physics.* the pressure exerted by a vapour in equilibrium with its solid or liquid phase at a particular temperature.

vapour trail *n.* a visible trail left by an aircraft flying at high altitude or through supercold air caused by the deposition of water vapour in the engine exhaust as minute ice crystals.

Var (*French* var) *n.* **1.** a department of SE France, in Provence–Alpes–Côte d'Azur region. Capital: Toulon. Pop.: 708 331 (1982). Area: 6023 sq. km (2349 sq. miles). **2.** a river in SE France, flowing southeast and south to the Mediterranean near Nice. Length: about 130 km (80 miles).

var. *abbrev. for:* **1.** variable. **2.** variant. **3.** variation. **4.** variety. **5.** various.

varactor ('vɛə,ræktə) *n.* a semiconductor diode that acts as a voltage-dependent capacitor, being operated with a reverse bias. [C20: prob. a blend of *variable reactor*]

Varanasi (və'rɑːnəsɪ) *n.* a city in NE India, in SE Uttar Pradesh on the River Ganges: probably dates from the 13th century B.C.; an early centre of Aryan philosophy and religion; a major place of pilgrimage for Hindus, Jains, Sikhs, and Buddhists, with many ghats along the Ganges; seat of the Banaras Hindu University (1916), India's leading university, and the Sanskrit University (1957). Pop.: 704 772 (1981). Former names: **Benares, Banaras.**

Vardar (*Serbo-Croatian* 'vardar) *n.* a river in S Europe, rising in SW Yugoslavia and flowing northeast, then south past Skopje into Greece, where it enters the Aegean at Thessaloniki. Length: about 320 km (200 miles).

Vardon ('vɑ:dən) n. **Harry.** 1870–1937, British golfer.

varec ('værɛk) n. **1.** another name for **kelp. 2.** the ash obtained from kelp. [C17: from F, from ON *wrek* (unattested); see WRECK]

Varese (*Italian* va'reːse) n. a historic city in N Italy, in Lombardy near Lake Varese: manufacturing centre, esp. for leather goods. Pop.: 90 527 (1981).

Varèse (væ'rɛːz) n. **Edgar(d)** (ɛdgar). 1885–1965, U.S. composer, born in France. His works, which combine extreme dissonance with complex rhythms and the use of electronic techniques, include *Ionisation* (1931) and *Poème électronique* (1958).

Vargas (*Portuguese* 'vargas) n. **Getulio Dornelles** (ʒe'tulju dur'nɛləf). 1883–1954, Brazilian statesman; president (1930–45; 1951–54).

variable ('vɛərɪəb²l) adj. **1.** liable to or capable of change: *variable weather.* **2.** (of behaviour, emotions, etc.) lacking constancy. **3.** *Maths.* having a range of possible values. **4.** (of a species, etc.) liable to deviate from the established type. **5.** (of a wind) varying in direction and intensity. **6.** (of an electrical component or device) designed so that a characteristic property, such as resistance, can be varied. ~n. **7.** something that is subject to variation. **8.** *Maths.* **a.** an expression that can be assigned any of a set of values. **b.** a symbol, esp. *x*, *y*, or *z*, representing an unspecified member of a class of objects, numbers, etc. **9.** *Logic.* a symbol, esp. *x*, *y*, or *z*, representing any member of a class of entities. **10.** *Astron.* See **variable star. 11.** a variable wind. **12.** (*pl.*) a region where variable winds occur. [C14: from L *variābilis* changeable, from *variāre* to diversify] —,varia'bility *or* 'variable-ness n. —'variably adv.

variable cost n. a cost that varies directly with output.

variable star n. any star that varies considerably in brightness, either irregularly or in regular periods. **Intrinsic variables,** in which the variation is a result of internal changes, include novae and pulsating stars.

variance ('vɛərɪəns) n. **1.** the act of varying or the quality, state, or degree of being divergent. **2.** an instance of diverging; dissension. **3. at variance. a.** (often foll. by *with*) (of facts, etc.) not in accord. **b.** (of persons) in a state of dissension. **4.** *Statistics.* a measure of dispersion; the square of the standard deviations. **5.** a difference or discrepancy between two steps in a legal proceeding, esp. between a statement and the evidence given to support it. **6.** *Chem.* the number of degrees of freedom of a system, used in the phase rule.

variant ('vɛərɪənt) adj. **1.** liable to or displaying variation. **2.** differing from a standard or type: *a variant spelling.* ~n. **3.** something that differs from a standard or type. **4.** *Statistics.* another word for **variate.** [C14: via OF from L, from *variāre* to diversify, from *varius* VARIOUS]

variate ('vɛərɪɪt) n. *Statistics.* a random variable or a numerical value taken by it. [C16: from L *variāre* to VARY]

variation (,vɛərɪ'eɪʃən) n. **1.** the act, process, condition, or result of changing or varying. **2.** an instance of varying or the amount, rate, or degree of such change. **3.** something that differs from a standard or convention. **4.** *Music.* a repetition of a musical theme in which the rhythm, harmony, or melody is altered or embellished. **5.** *Biol.* a marked deviation from the typical form or function. **6.** *Astron.* any change in or deviation from the mean motion or orbit of a planet, satellite, etc. **7.** another word for **magnetic declination. 8.** *Ballet.* a solo dance. —,vari'ational adj.

varicella (,værɪ'sɛlə) n. the technical name for **chickenpox.** [C18: NL, irregular dim. of VARIOLA]

varices ('værɪ,siːz) pl. n. the plural of **varix.**

varico- *or before a vowel* **varic-** *combining form.* indicating a varix or varicose veins: *varicotomy.* [from L *varix*, *varic-*distended vein]

varicoloured *or U.S.* **varicolored** ('vɛərɪ,kʌləd) adj. having many colours.

varicose ('værɪ,kəʊs) adj. of or resulting from varicose veins: *a varicose ulcer.* [C18: from L *varicōsus*, from VARIX]

varicose veins pl. n. a condition in which the superficial veins, esp. of the legs, become tortuous, knotted, and swollen.

varicosis (,værɪ'kəʊsɪs) n. *Pathol.* any condition characterized by distension of the veins. [C18: from NL, from L: VARIX]

varicosity (,værɪ'kɒsɪtɪ) n., pl. **-ties.** *Pathol.* **1.** the state, condition, or quality of being varicose. **2.** an abnormally distended vein.

varicotomy (,værɪ'kɒtəmɪ) n., pl. **-mies.** surgical excision of a varicose vein.

varied ('vɛərɪd) adj. **1.** displaying or characterized by variety; diverse. **2.** modified or altered: *the amount may be varied without notice.* **3.** varicoloured; variegated. —'variedly adv.

variegate ('vɛərɪ,geɪt) vb. (*tr.*) to alter the appearance of, esp. by adding different colours. [C17: from LL, from L *varius* diverse, VARIOUS + *agere* to make] —,varie'gation n.

variegated ('vɛərɪ,geɪtɪd) adj. **1.** displaying differently coloured spots., streaks, etc. **2.** (of foliage) having pale patches.

varietal (və'raɪɪt²l) adj. **1.** of, characteristic of, designating, or forming a variety, esp. a biological variety. ~n. **2.** a wine labelled with the name of the grape from which it is pressed. —va'rietally adv.

variety (və'raɪɪtɪ) n., pl. **-ties. 1.** the quality or condition of being diversified or various. **2.** a collection of unlike things, esp. of the same general group. **3.** a different form or kind within a general category: *varieties of behaviour.* **4. a.** *Taxonomy.* a race whose distinct characters do not justify classification as a separate species. **b.** *Horticulture, stockbreeding.* a strain of animal or plant produced by artificial breeding. **5. a.** entertainment consisting of a series of short unrelated acts, such as comedy turns, songs, etc. **b.** (*as modifier*): *a variety show.* [C16: from L *varietās*, from VARIOUS]

variform ('vɛərɪ,fɔːm) adj. varying in form or shape. —'vari,formly adv.

variola (və'raɪələ) n. the technical name for **smallpox.** [C18: from Med. L: disease marked by little spots, from L *varius* spotted] —va'riolar adj.

variole ('vɛərɪ,əʊl) n. any of the rounded masses that make up the rock variolite. [C19: from F, from Med. L; see VARIOLA]

variolite ('vɛərɪə,laɪt) n. any basic igneous rock containing rounded bodies (varioles). [C18: from VARIOLA, referring to the pockmarked appearance of the rock] —variolitic (,vɛərɪə'lɪtɪk) adj.

variometer (,vɛərɪ'ɒmɪtə) n. **1.** an instrument for measuring variations in a magnetic field. **2.** *Electronics.* a variable inductor consisting of a movable coil mounted inside and connected in series with a fixed coil.

variorum (,vɛərɪ'ɔːrəm) adj. **1.** containing notes by various scholars or various versions of the text. ~n. **2.** an edition or text of this kind. [C18: from L *ēditiō cum notīs variōrum* edition with the notes of various commentators]

various ('vɛərɪəs) determiner. **1.** several different: *he is an authority on various subjects.* ~adj. **2.** of different kinds, though often within the same general category: *his disguises are many and various.* **3.** (*prenominal*) relating to a collection of separate persons or things: *the various members of the club.* **4.** displaying variety; many-sided: *his various achievements.* [C16: from L *varius* changing] —'variously adv. —'variousness n.

▷ *Usage. Various of,* as in *he wrote to various of his friends,* is not current in good usage. Careful writers prefer *various* or *several of* to *various of: he wrote to various friends; he wrote to several of his friends.*

varistor (və'rɪstə) n. a two-electrode semiconductor device having a voltage-dependent nonlinear resistance. [C20: a blend of *variable resistor*]

Varityper ('vɛərɪ,taɪpə) n. *Trademark.* a justifying typewriter used to produce copy in various type styles.

varix ('vɛərɪks) n., pl. **varices.** *Pathol.* **a.** a tortuous dilated vein. **b.** a similar condition affecting an artery or lymphatic vessel. [C15: from L]

varlet ('vɑːlɪt) n. *Arch.* **1.** a menial servant. **2.** a knight's page. **3.** a rascal. [C15: from OF, var. of *vallet* VALET] —'varletry n.

varmint ('vɑːmɪnt) n. *Inf.* an irritating or obnoxious person or animal. [C16: dialect var. of *varmin* VERMIN]

varna ('vɑːnə) n. any of the four Hindu castes: Brahman, Kshatriya, Vaisya, or Sudra. [from Sansk.: class]

Varna (*Bulgarian* 'varna) n. a port in NE Bulgaria, on the Black Sea: founded by Greeks in the 6th century B.C.; under the Ottoman Turks (1391–1878). Pop.: 466 000 (1985). Former name (1949–56): **Stalin.**

varnish ('vɑːnɪʃ) n. **1.** a preparation consisting of a solvent, a drying oil, and usually resin, rubber, etc., for application to a surface where it yields a hard glossy, usually transparent, coating. **2.** a similar preparation consisting of a substance, such as shellac, dissolved in a volatile solvent, such as alcohol. It hardens to a film on evaporation of the solvent. **3.** the sap of certain trees used to produce such a coating. **4.** a smooth surface, coated with or as with varnish. **5.** an artificial, superficial, or deceptively pleasing manner, covering, etc. **6.** *Chiefly Brit.* another word for **nail polish.** ~*vb.* (*tr.*) **7.** to cover with varnish. **8.** to give a smooth surface to, as if by painting with varnish. **9.** to impart a more attractive appearance to. [C14: from OF, from Med. L *veronix* sandarac, resin, from Med. Gk *berenikē*, ?from Gk *Berenikē*, city in Cyrenaica, Libya where varnishes were used] —'**varnisher** *n.*

varnish tree *n.* any of various trees, such as the lacquer tree, yielding substances used to make varnish or lacquer.

Varro ('værəʊ) *n.* **Marcus Terentius** ('mɑːkəs tə'rɛntɪəs). 116–27 B.C., Roman scholar and satirist.

varsity ('vɑːsɪtɪ) *n., pl.* -**ties.** *Brit. & N.Z. inf.* short for **university.**

Varuna ('værʊnə, 'vʌ-) *n. Hinduism.* the ancient sky god, later the god of the waters and rain-giver. In earlier traditions he was also the all-seeing divine judge.

varus ('vɛərəs) *adj. Pathol.* turned inwards towards the midline of the body. [C19: from L: crooked, bent]

varve (vɑːv) *n. Geol.* a band of sediment deposited in glacial lakes, consisting of a light layer and a dark layer deposited at different seasons. [C20: from Swedish *varv* layer, from *varva*, from ON *hverfa* to turn]

vary ('vɛərɪ) *vb.* **varying, varied. 1.** to undergo or cause to undergo change or modification in appearance, character, form, etc. **2.** to be different or cause to be different; be subject to change. **3.** (*tr.*) to give variety to. **4.** (*intr.;* foll. by *from*) to differ, as from a convention, standard, etc. **5.** (*intr.*) to change in accordance with another variable: *her mood varies with the weather.* [C14: from L, from *varius* VARIOUS] —'**varying** *adj.*

vas (væs) *n., pl.* **vasa** ('veɪsə). *Anat., zool.* a vessel or tube that carries a fluid. [C17: from L: vessel]

Vasari (və'sɑːrɪ; *Italian* va'zaːri) *n.* **Giorgio** ('dʒɔːrdʒo). 1511–74, Italian architect, painter, and art historian, noted for his *Lives of the Most Excellent Italian Architects, Painters, and Sculptors* (1550; 1568), a principal source for the history of Italian Renaissance art.

Vasco da Gama ('væskəʊ də 'gɑːmə) *n.* See (Vasco da) **Gama.**

vascular ('væskjʊlə) *adj. Biol., anat.* of, relating to, or having vessels which conduct and circulate liquids: *a vascular bundle.* [C17: from NL *vāsculāris*, from L *vāsculum*, dim. of *vās* vessel] —**vascularity** (,væskjʊ'lærɪtɪ) *n.* —'**vascularly** *adv.*

vascular bundle *n.* a longitudinal strand of vascular tissue in the stems and leaves of higher plants.

vascular tissue *n.* tissue of plants occurring as a continuous system throughout the plant: it conducts water, mineral salts, and synthesized food, and provides mechanical support.

vas deferens ('væs 'dɛfə,rɛnz) *n., pl.* **vasa deferentia** ('veɪsə ,dɛfə'rɛnʃɪə). *Anat.* the duct within each testis that conveys spermatozoa to the ejaculatory duct. [C16: from NL, from L *vās* vessel + *deferēns*, present participle of *deferre* to bear away]

vase (vɑːz) *n.* a vessel used as an ornament or for holding cut flowers. [C17: via F from L *vās* vessel]

vasectomy (væ'sɛktəmɪ) *n., pl.* -**mies.** surgical removal of all or part of the vas deferens, esp. as a method of contraception.

Vaseline ('væsɪ,liːn) *n.* a trademark for **petrolatum.**

Vashti ('væʃtaɪ) *n. Old Testament.* the wife of the Persian king Ahasuerus: deposed for refusing to display her beauty before his guests (Esther 1–2). Douay spelling: **Vasthi.**

vaso- or before a vowel **vas-** *combining form.* **1.** indicating a blood vessel: *vasodilator.* **2.** indicating the vas deferens: *vasectomy.* [from L *vās* vessel]

vasoconstrictor (,veɪzəʊkən'strɪktə) *n.* a drug, agent, or nerve that causes narrowing of the walls of blood vessels.

vasodilator (,veɪzəʊdaɪ'leɪtə) *n.* a drug, agent, or nerve that can cause dilation of the walls of blood vessels.

vasoinhibitor (,veɪzəʊɪn'hɪbɪtə) *n.* any of a group of drugs that reduce or inhibit the action of the vasomotor nerves.

vasomotor (,veɪzəʊ'məʊtə) *adj.* (of a drug, agent, nerve, etc.) relating to or affecting the diameter of blood vessels.

vasopressin (,veɪzəʊ'prɛsɪn) *n.* a hormone secreted by the pituitary gland. It increases the reabsorption of water by the kidney tubules and increases blood pressure by constricting the arteries. [from *Vasopressin*, a trademark]

vassal ('væsəl) *n.* **1.** (in feudal society) a man who entered into a relationship with a lord to whom he paid homage and fealty in return for protection and often a fief. **2. a.** a person, nation, etc., in a subordinate or dependent position relative to another. **b.** (*as modifier*): *vassal status.* ~*adj.* **3.** of or relating to a vassal. [C14: via OF from Med. L *vassallus*, from *vassus* servant, of Celtic origin] —'**vassalage** *n.*

vast (vɑːst) *adj.* **1.** unusually large in size, degree, or number. **2.** (*prenominal*) (intensifier): *in vast haste.* ~*n.* **3. the vast.** *Chiefly poetic.* immense or boundless space. [C16: from L *vastus* deserted] —'**vastly** *adv.* —'**vastness** *n.*

Västerås (*Swedish* vɛstər'oːs) *n.* a city in central Sweden, on Lake Mälar: Sweden's largest inland port; site of several national parliaments in the 16th century. Pop.: 117 732 (1986).

vasty ('vɑːstɪ) *adj.* **vastier, vastiest.** an archaic or poetic word for **vast.**

vat (væt) *n.* **1.** a large container for holding or storing liquids. **2.** *Chem.* a preparation of reduced vat dye. ~*vb.* **vatting, vatted. 3.** (*tr.*) to place, store, or treat in a vat. [OE *fæt*]

VAT (*sometimes* væt) (in Britain) *abbrev. for* value-added tax: a tax levied on the difference between the cost of materials and the selling price of a commodity or service.

vat dye *n.* a dye, such as indigo, that is applied by first reducing it to its base, which is soluble in alkali, and then regenerating the insoluble dye by oxidation in the fibres of the material. —'**vat-,dyed** *adj.*

vatic ('vætɪk) *adj. Rare.* of, relating to, or characteristic of a prophet; oracular. [C16: from L *vātēs* prophet]

Vatican ('vætɪkən) *n.* **1. a.** the palace of the popes in Rome, which includes administrative offices and is attached to the basilica of St Peter's. **b.** (*as modifier*): *the Vatican Council.* **2. a.** the authority of the Pope and the papal curia. **b.** (*as modifier*): *a Vatican edict.* [C16: from L *Vāticānus mons* Vatican hill, on the western bank of the Tiber, of Etruscan origin]

Vatican City *n.* an independent state forming an enclave in Rome, with extraterritoriality over 12 churches and palaces in Rome: the only remaining Papal State; independence recognized by the Italian government in 1929; contains St Peter's Basilica and Square and the Vatican; the spiritual and administrative centre of the Roman Catholic Church. Languages: Italian and Latin. Currency: lira. Pop.: 1000 (1985 est.). Area: 44 hectares (109 acres). Italian name: **Città del Vaticano.** Also called: the **Holy See.**

Vättern (*Swedish* 'vɛtərn) *n.* **Lake.** a lake in S central Sweden: the second largest lake in Sweden; linked to Lake Vänern by the Göta Canal; drains into the Baltic. Area: 1912 sq. km (738 sq. miles).

Vauban (*French* vobã) *n.* **Sébastien Le Prestre de** (sebastjɛ̃ lə prɛtrə də). 1633–1707, French military engineer and marshal, who greatly developed the science of fortification and devised novel siege tactics using a series of parallel trenches.

Vaucluse (*French* voklyz) *n.* a department of SE France, in Provence–Alpes–Côte d'Azur region. Capital: Avignon. Pop.: 427 343 (1982). Area: 3578 sq. km (1395 sq. miles).

Vaud (*French* vo) *n.* a canton of SW Switzerland: mountainous in the southeast; chief Swiss producer of wine. Capital: Lausanne. Pop.: 550 300 (1986 est.). Area: 3209 sq. km (1240 sq. miles). German name: **Waadt.**

vaudeville ('vəʊdəvɪl, 'vɔː-) *n.* **1.** *Chiefly U.S. & Canad.* variety entertainment consisting of short acts such as acrobatic turns, song-and-dance routines, etc. **2.** a light or comic theatrical piece interspersed with songs and dances. [C18: from F, from *vaudevire* satirical folk song, shortened from *chanson du vau de Vire* song of the valley of Vire, a district in Normandy] —,**vaude'villian** *n., adj.*

Vaudois ('vəʊdwɑː) *pl. n., sing.* -**dois. 1.** another name for the **Waldenses. 2.** the inhabitants of Vaud.

Vaughan (vɔːn) n. **1. Henry.** 1622–95, Welsh mystic poet, best known for his *Silex Scintillans* (1650; 1655). **2.** Dame **Janet (Maria)**. born 1899, English doctor and university official: helped establish a cure for anaemia in the 1920s: helped set up Britain's first National Blood Transfusion Service (1939): after World War II, became Britain's expert on the effects of radiation on humans. As Principal of Somerville, the women's college in Oxford, she was instrumental in raising the number of women and in achieving equal status with the men's colleges in Oxford.

Vaughan Williams ('wɪljəmz) n. **Ralph**. 1872–1958, English composer, inspired by British folk songs and music of the Tudor period. He wrote operas, symphonies, hymns, and choral music.

vault[1] (vɔːlt) n. **1.** an arched structure that forms a roof or ceiling. **2.** a room, esp. a cellar, having an arched roof down to floor level. **3.** a burial chamber, esp. when underground. **4.** a strongroom for the storage of valuables. **5.** an underground room used for the storage of wine, food, etc. **6.** *Anat.* any arched or domed bodily cavity or space: *the cranial vault*. **7.** something suggestive of an arched structure, as the sky. ~*vb.* **8.** (*tr.*) to furnish with or as if with an arched roof. **9.** (*tr.*) to construct in the shape of a vault. **10.** (*intr.*) to curve in the shape of a vault. [C14 *vaute*, from OF, from Vulgar L *volvita* (unattested) a turn, prob. from L *volvere* to roll]

vault[2] (vɔːlt) vb. **1.** to spring over (an object), esp. with the aid of a long pole or with the hands resting on the object. **2.** (*intr.*) to do, achieve, or attain something as if by a leap: *he vaulted to fame.* ~*n.* **3.** the act of vaulting. [C16: from OF *voulter* to turn from It. *voltare*, from Vulgar L *volvitāre* (unattested) to turn, leap; see VAULT[1]] —'**vaulter** n.

vaulting[1] ('vɔːltɪŋ) n. one or more vaults in a building or such structures considered collectively.

vaulting[2] ('vɔːltɪŋ) adj. (*prenominal*) **1.** excessively confident: *vaulting arrogance.* **2.** used to vault: *a vaulting pole.*

vaunt (vɔːnt) vb. **1.** (*tr.*) to describe, praise, or display (one's success, possessions, etc.) boastfully. **2.** (*intr.*) *Rare or literary.* to brag. ~*n.* **3.** a boast. [C14: from OF, from LL *vānitāre*, from L *vānus* VAIN] —'**vaunter** n.

Vauxhall ('vɒks,hɔːl) n. a district in London, on the south bank of the Thames.

vavasor ('vævə,sɔː) or **vavasour** ('vævə,suə) n. (in feudal society) the noble or knightly vassal of a baron or great lord who also has vassals himself. [C13: from OF *vavasour*, ?from Med. L *vassus vassórum* vassal of vassals]

vb abbrev. for verb.

VC abbrev. for: **1.** Vice-chairman. **2.** Vice Chancellor. **3.** Vice Consul. **4.** Victoria Cross.

VCR abbrev. for video cassette recorder.

VD abbrev. for venereal disease.

V-Day n. a day nominated to celebrate victory, as in V-E Day or V-J Day in World War II.

VDU *Computers.* abbrev. for visual display unit.

've contraction of have: *I've; you've.*

veal (viːl) n. the flesh of the calf used as food. [C14: from OF *veel*, from L *vitellus*, dim. of *vitulus* calf]

vealer ('viːlə) n. U.S., Canad., & Austral. a calf bred for veal.

Veblen ('vɛblən) n. **Thorstein** ('θɔːstɪn). 1857–1929, U.S. economist and social scientist, noted for his analysis of social and economic institutions. His works include *The Theory of the Leisure Class* (1899) and *The Theory of Business Enterprise* (1904).

vector ('vɛktə) n. **1.** *Maths.* a variable quantity, such as force, that has magnitude and direction and can be resolved into components that are odd functions of the coordinates. **2.** Also called: **carrier.** *Pathol.* an organism, esp. an insect, that carries a disease-producing microorganism from one host to another. **3.** the course or compass direction of an aircraft. ~*vb.* (*tr.*) **4.** to direct or guide (a pilot, aircraft, etc.) by directions transmitted by radio. **5.** to alter the direction of (the thrust of a jet engine) as a means of steering an aircraft. [C18: from L: carrier, from *vehere* to convey] —**vectorial** (vɛk'tɔːrɪəl) adj.

vector field n. a region of space under the influence of some vector quantity, such as magnetic field strength, in which each point can be described by a vector.

vector product n. the product of two vectors that is a pseudovector, whose magnitude is the product of the

magnitudes of the given vectors and the sine of the angle between them. Its axis is perpendicular to the plane of the given vectors.

vector sum n. a vector whose length and direction are represented by the diagonal of a parallelogram whose sides represent the given vectors.

Veda ('veɪdə) n. any or all of the most ancient sacred writings of Hinduism, esp. the Rig-Veda, Yajur-Veda, Sama-Veda, and Atharva-Veda. [C18: from Sansk.: knowledge]

vedalia (vɪ'deɪlɪə) n. an Australian ladybird introduced elsewhere to control the scale insect, which is a pest of citrus fruits. [C20: from NL]

Vedanta (vɪ'dɑːntə) n. one of the six main philosophical schools of Hinduism, expounding the monism regarded as implicit in the Veda in accordance with the doctrines of the Upanishads. [C19: from Sansk., from VEDA + *ánta* end] —**Ve'dantic** adj. —**Ve'dantist** n.

V-E Day n. the day marking the Allied victory in Europe in World War II (May 8, 1945).

vedette (vɪ'dɛt) n. **1.** *Naval.* a small patrol vessel. **2.** *Mil.* a mounted sentry posted forward of a formation's position. [C17: from F, from It. *vedetta* (infl. by *vedere* to see), from earlier *veletta*, ?from Sp., from L *vigilāre*]

Vedic ('veɪdɪk) adj. **1.** of or relating to the Vedas or the ancient form of Sanskrit in which they are written. ~*n.* **2.** the classical form of Sanskrit; the language of the Vedas.

veer (vɪə) vb. **1.** to alter direction (of). **2.** (*intr.*) to change from one position, opinion, etc., to another. **3.** (*intr.*) (of the wind) to change direction clockwise in the northern hemisphere and anticlockwise in the southern. ~*n.* **4.** a change of course or direction. [C16: from OF *virer*, prob. of Celtic origin]

veg (vɛdʒ) n. *Inf.* a vegetable or vegetables.

Vega[1] ('viːgə) n. the brightest star in the constellation Lyra and one of the most conspicuous in the N hemisphere. [C17: from Med. L, from Ar. (*al nasr*) *al wāqi*, lit.: the falling (vulture), i.e. the constellation Lyra]

Vega[2] ('veɪgə; *Spanish* 'beɣa) n. See **Lope de Vega.**

vegan ('viːgən) n. a person who uses no animal products.

Vegemite ('vɛdʒɪ,maɪt) n. *Austral. trademark.* a yeast extract used as a spread, flavouring for stews, etc.

vegetable ('vɛdʒtəb³l) n. **1.** any of various herbaceous plants having parts that are used as food, such as peas, potatoes, cauliflower, and onions. **2.** *Inf.* a person who has lost control of his mental faculties, limbs, etc., as from an injury, mental disease, etc. **3.** a dull inactive person. **4.** (*modifier*) consisting of or made from edible vegetables: *a vegetable diet.* **5.** (*modifier*) of, characteristic of, derived from, or consisting of plants or plant material: *the vegetable kingdom.* **6.** *Rare.* any member of the plant kingdom. [C14 (adj.): from LL *vegetābilis*, from *vegetāre* to enliven, from L *vegēre* to excite]

vegetable butter n. any of a group of vegetable fats having the consistency of butter.

vegetable ivory n. the hard whitish material obtained from the endosperm of the ivory nut: used to make buttons, ornaments, etc.

vegetable marrow n. **1.** a plant, probably native to America but widely cultivated for its oblong green striped fruit which is eaten as a vegetable. **2.** the fruit of this plant. Often shortened to **marrow.**

vegetable oil n. any of a group of oils that are obtained from plants.

vegetable oyster n. another name for **salsify** (sense 1).

vegetable silk n. any of various silky fibres obtained from the seed pods of certain plants.

vegetable wax n. any of various waxes that occur on parts of certain plants, esp. the trunks of certain palms, and prevent loss of water.

vegetal ('vɛdʒɪt³l) adj. **1.** of or characteristic of vegetables or plant life. **2.** vegetative. [C15: from LL *vegetāre* to quicken]

vegetarian (,vɛdʒɪ'tɛərɪən) n. **1.** a person who advocates or practises the exclusion of meat and fish, and sometimes eggs, milk, and cheese from the diet. ~*adj.* **2.** *Cookery.* strictly, consisting of vegetables and fruit only, but often including milk, cheese, eggs, etc. —,**vege'tarianism** n.

vegetate ('vɛdʒɪ,teɪt) vb. (*intr.*) **1.** to grow like a plant. **2.** to lead a life characterized by monotony, passivity, or mental inactivity. [C17: from LL *vegetāre* to invigorate]

vegetation (ˌvɛdʒɪˈteɪʃən) n. **1.** plant life as a whole, esp. the plant life of a particular region. **2.** the process of vegetating. —ˌvege'tational adj.

vegetative ('vɛdʒɪtətɪv) adj. **1.** of or concerned with plant life or plant growth. **2.** (of reproduction) characterized by asexual processes. **3.** of or relating to functions such as digestion and circulation rather than sexual reproduction. **4.** (of a style of living, etc.) unthinking or passive. —'vegetatively adv.

veggie ('vɛdʒɪ) n., adj. an informal word for **vegetarian**.

veg out vb. **vegging, vegged.** (intr., adv.) Sl., chiefly U.S. to relax in an inert, passive way; vegetate: vegging out in front of the television set.

vehement ('viːɪmənt) adj. **1.** marked by intensity of feeling or conviction. **2.** (of actions, gestures, etc.) characterized by great energy, vigour, or force. [C15: from L vehemēns ardent] —'vehemence n. —'vehemently adv.

vehicle ('viːɪkəl) n. **1.** any conveyance in or by which people or objects are transported, esp. one fitted with wheels. **2.** a medium for the expression or communication of ideas, power, etc. **3.** Pharmacol. a therapeutically inactive substance mixed with the active ingredient to give bulk to a medicine. **4.** Also called: **base.** a painting medium, such as oil, in which pigments are suspended. **5.** (in the performing arts) a play, etc., that enables a particular performer to display his talents. [C17: from L vehiculum, from vehere to carry] —**vehicular** (vɪˈhɪkjʊlə) adj.

Veii ('viːjaɪ) n. an ancient Etruscan city, northwest of Rome: destroyed by the Romans in 396 B.C.

veil (veɪl) n. **1.** a piece of more or less transparent material, usually attached to a hat or headdress, used to conceal or protect a woman's face and head. **2.** part of a nun's headdress falling round the face onto the shoulders. **3.** something that covers, conceals, or separates: a veil of reticence. **4. the veil.** the life of a nun in a religious order. **5. take the veil.** to become a nun. **6.** Also called: **velum.** Bot. a membranous structure, esp. the thin layer of cells covering a young mushroom. ~vb. **7.** (tr.) to cover, conceal, or separate with or as if with a veil. **8.** (intr.) to wear or put on a veil. [C13: from Norman F veile, from L vēla, pl. of vēlum a covering] —'veiler n. —'veil-,like adj.

veiled (veɪld) adj. **1.** disguised: a veiled insult. **2.** (of sound, tone, the voice, etc.) not distinct. —**veiledly** ('veɪldlɪ) adv.

veiling ('veɪlɪŋ) n. a veil or the fabric used for veils.

vein (veɪn) n. **1.** any of the tubular vessels that convey oxygen-depleted blood to the heart. Cf. **pulmonary vein, artery** (sense 1). **2.** any of the hollow branching tubes that form the supporting framework of an insect's wing. **3.** any of the vascular bundles of a leaf. **4.** a clearly defined mass of ore, mineral, etc. **5.** an irregular streak of colour or alien substance in marble, wood, or other material. **6.** a distinctive trait or quality in speech, writing, character, etc.: a vein of humour. **7.** a temporary attitude or temper: the debate entered a frivolous vein. ~vb. (tr.) **8.** to diffuse over or cause to diffuse over in streaked patterns. **9.** to fill, furnish, or mark with or as if with veins. [C13: from OF, from L vēna] —'veinless adj. —'vein-,like adj. —'veiny adj.

veining ('veɪnɪŋ) n. a pattern or network of veins or streaks.

veinlet ('veɪnlɪt) n. any small vein or venule.

velamen (vəˈleɪmɛn) n., pl. **-lamina** (-ˈlæmɪnə). **1.** the thick layer of dead cells that covers the aerial roots of certain orchids. **2.** Anat. another word for **velum.** [C19: from L: veil, from vēlāre to cover]

velar ('viːlə) adj. **1.** of or attached to a velum: velar tentacles. **2.** Phonetics. articulated with the soft palate and the back of the tongue, as in (k) or (ŋ). [C18: from L, from vēlum VEIL]

Velázquez (Spanish beˈlaθkeθ) or **Velásquez** (Spanish beˈlaskeθ) n. **Diego Rodríguez de Silva y** ('djeɣo rɔˈðriɣeθ de 'silβa i). 1599–1660, Spanish painter, remarkable for the realism of his portraits, esp. those of Philip IV of Spain and the royal household.

Velcro ('vɛlkrəʊ) n. Trademark. a fastening consisting of two strips of nylon fabric, one having tiny hooked threads and the other a coarse surface, that form a strong bond when pressed together.

veld or **veldt** (fɛlt, vɛlt) n. elevated open grassland in Southern Africa. [C19: from Afrik., from earlier Du. veldt FIELD]

veldskoen ('fɛlt,skʊn, 'vɛlt-) n. an ankle-length boot of soft but strong rawhide. [from Afrik., lit.: field shoe]

veleta or **valeta** (vəˈliːtə) n. a ballroom dance in triple time. [from Sp.: weather vane]

veliger ('vɛlɪdʒə) n. the free-swimming larva of many molluscs, having a rudimentary shell and a ciliated velum used for feeding and locomotion. [C19: from NL, from VELUM) + -GER(OUS)]

Vellore (vəˈlɔː) n. a town in SE India, in NE Tamil Nadu: medical centre. Pop.: 174 247 (1981).

vellum ('vɛləm) n. **1.** a fine parchment prepared from the skin of a calf, kid, or lamb. **2.** a work printed or written on vellum. **3.** a creamy coloured heavy paper resembling vellum. ~adj. **4.** made of or resembling vellum. [C15: from OF, from velin of a calf, from veel VEAL]

veloce (vɪˈləʊtʃɪ) adj., adv. Music. to be played rapidly. [from It., from L vēlōx quick]

velocipede (vɪˈlɒsɪˌpiːd) n. an early form of bicycle, esp. one propelled by pushing along the ground with the feet. [C19: from F, from L vēlōx swift + pēs foot] —ve'loci,pedist n.

velocity (vɪˈlɒsɪtɪ) n., pl. **-ties. 1.** speed of motion or operation; swiftness. **2.** Physics. a measure of the rate of motion of a body expressed as the rate of change of its position in a particular direction with time. **3.** Physics. (not in technical usage) another word for **speed** (sense 3). [C16: from L vēlōcitās, from vēlōx swift]

velodrome ('viːlə,drəʊm) n. an arena with a banked track for cycle racing. [C20: from F vélodrome, from vélo- (from L vēlōx swift) + -DROME]

velours or **velour** (vɛˈlʊə) n. any of various fabrics with a velvet-like finish, used for upholstery, clothing, etc. [C18: from OF, from OProvençal velos velvet, from L, from villus shaggy hair]

velouté (vəˈluːteɪ) n. a rich white sauce or soup made from stock, egg yolks, and cream. [from F, lit.: velvety, from OF velous; see VELOURS]

Velsen (Dutch 'vɛlsə) n. a port in the W Netherlands, in North Holland at the mouth of the canal connecting Amsterdam with the North Sea: fishing and heavy industrial centre. Pop.: 59 779 (1982 est.).

velum ('viːləm) n., pl. **-la** (-lə). **1.** Zool. any of various membranous structures. **2.** Anat. any of various veil-like bodily structures, esp. the soft palate. **3.** Bot. another word for **veil** (sense 6). [C18: from L: veil]

velure (vəˈlʊə) n. velvet or a similar fabric. [C16: from OF, from velous; see VELOURS]

velutinous (vəˈluːtɪnəs) adj. covered with short dense soft hairs: velutinous leaves. [C19: from NL velūtinus like velvet]

velvet ('vɛlvɪt) n. **1. a.** a fabric of silk, cotton, nylon, etc., with a thick close soft pile. **b.** (as modifier): velvet curtains. **2.** anything with a smooth soft surface. **3. a.** smoothness. **b.** (as modifier): a velvet night. **4.** the furry covering of the newly formed antlers of a deer. **5.** Sl., chiefly U.S. **a.** gambling winnings. **b.** a gain. **6. on velvet.** Sl. in a condition of ease, advantage, or wealth. **7. velvet glove.** gentleness, often concealing strength or determination (esp. in **an iron hand in a velvet glove**). [C14 veluet, from OF, from velu hairy, from Vulgar L villutus (unattested), from L villus shaggy hair] —'velvet-,like adj. —'velvety adj.

velveteen (ˌvɛlvɪˈtiːn) n. **1.** a cotton fabric resembling velvet with a short thick pile, used for clothing, etc. **2.** (pl.) trousers made of velveteen.

Velvet Underground, the. U.S. avant-garde rock group in New York City (formed in 1965; disintegrated 1969–72). See also (Lou) **Reed.**

Ven. abbrev. for Venerable.

vena ('viːnə) n., pl. **-nae** (-niː). Anat. a technical word for **vein.** [C15: from L vēna VEIN]

vena cava ('keɪvə) n., pl. **venae cavae** ('keɪviː). either one of two large veins that convey oxygen-depleted blood to the heart. [L: hollow vein]

venal ('viːnəl) adj. **1.** easily bribed or corrupted: a venal magistrate. **2.** characterized by corruption or bribery. [C17: from L vēnālis, from vēnum sale] —ve'nality n. —'venally adv.

venation (vɪ:'neɪʃən) n. 1. the arrangement of the veins in a leaf or in the wing of an insect. 2. such veins collectively. —**ve'national** adj.

vend (vɛnd) vb. 1. to sell or be sold. 2. to sell (goods) for a living. [C17: from L vendere, from vēnum dare to offer for sale]

Venda ('vɛndə) n. a Bantustan in South Africa, in N Transvaal near the Zimbabwe border; became the third Bantustan to be granted independence in 1979 but this is not recognized outside South Africa. Capital: Thohoyandou. Pop.: 424 000 (1985 est.). Area: 6500 sq. km (2500 sq. miles).

vendace ('vɛndeɪs) n., pl. -daces or -dace. either of two small whitefish occurring in lakes in Scotland and NW England. [C18: from NL vandēsius, from OF vandoise, prob. of Celtic origin]

vendee (vɛn'di:) n. Chiefly law. a person to whom something, esp. real property, is sold.

Vendée (French vɑ̃de) n. a department of W France, in Pays-de-la-Loire region: scene of the **Wars of the Vendée**, a series of peasant-royalist insurrections (1793–95) against the Revolutionary government. Capital: La Roche-sur-Yon. Pop.: 490 300 (1984 est.). Area: 7016 sq. km (2709 sq. miles).

vendetta (vɛn'dɛtə) n. 1. a private feud, originally between Corsican or Sicilian families, in which the relatives of a murdered person seek vengeance by killing the murderer or some member of his family. 2. any prolonged feud. [C19: from It., from L vindicta, from vindicāre to avenge] —**ven'dettist** n.

vendible ('vɛndəb³l) adj. 1. saleable or marketable. ~n. 2. (usually pl.) Rare. a saleable object. —,vendi'bility n.

vending machine n. a machine that automatically dispenses consumer goods such as cigarettes or food, when money is inserted.

Vendôme (French vɑ̃dom) n. **Louis Joseph de** (lwi ʒozɛf də). 1654–1712, French marshal, noted for his command during the War of the Spanish Succession (1701–14).

vendor ('vɛndɔ:) or **vender** ('vɛndə) n. 1. Chiefly law. a person who sells something, esp. real property. 2. another name for **vending machine**.

veneer (vɪ'nɪə) n. 1. a thin layer of wood, plastic, etc., with a decorative or fine finish that is bonded to the surface of a less expensive material, usually wood. 2. a superficial appearance: a veneer of gentility. 3. any facing material that is applied to a different backing material. ~vb. (tr.) 4. to cover (a surface) with a veneer. 5. to conceal (something) under a superficially pleasant surface. [C17: from G furnieren to veneer, from OF fournir to FURNISH] —**ve'neerer** n.

veneering (vɪ'nɪərɪŋ) n. material used as veneer or a veneered surface.

venepuncture ('vɛnɪ,pʌŋktʃə) n. a variant spelling of **venipuncture**.

venerable ('vɛnərəb³l) adj. 1. (esp. of a person) worthy of reverence on account of great age, religious associations, character, etc. 2. (of inanimate objects) hallowed on account of age or historical or religious association. 3. R.C. Church. a title bestowed on a deceased person when the first stage of his canonization has been accomplished. 4. Church of England. a title given to an archdeacon. [C15: from L venerābilis, from venerāri to venerate] —,venera'bility or 'venerableness n. —'venerably adv.

venerate ('vɛnəreɪt) vb. (tr.) 1. to hold in deep respect. 2. to honour in recognition of qualities of holiness, excellence, etc. [C17: from L venerārī, from venus love] —'vener,ator n.

veneration (,vɛnə'reɪʃən) n. 1. a feeling or expression of awe or reverence. 2. the act of venerating or the state of being venerated.

venereal (vɪ'nɪərɪəl) adj. 1. of or infected with venereal disease. 2. (of a disease) transmitted by sexual intercourse. 3. of or involving the genitals. 4. of or relating to sexual intercourse or erotic desire. [C15: from L venereus, from venus sexual love, from VENUS¹]

venereal disease n. another name for **sexually transmitted disease**. Abbrev.: **VD**.

venereology (vɪ,nɪərɪ'ɒlədʒɪ) n. the branch of medicine concerned with the study and treatment of venereal disease. —ve,nere'ologist n.

venery¹ ('vɛnərɪ, 'vi:-) n. Arch. the pursuit of sexual gratification. [C15: from Med. L veneria, from L venus love, VENUS¹]

venery² ('vɛnərɪ, 'vi:-) n. the art, sport, lore, or practice of hunting, esp. with hounds; the chase. [C14: from OF venerie, from vener to hunt, from L vēnārī]

venesection ('vɛnɪ,sɛkʃən) n. surgical incision into a vein. [C17: from NL vēnae sectiō; see VEIN, SECTION]

Venetia (vɪ'ni:ʃə) n. 1. the area of ancient Italy between the lower Po valley and the Alps: later a Roman province. 2. the territorial possessions of the medieval Venetian republic that were at the head of the Adriatic and correspond to the present-day region of Veneto and a large part of Friuli-Venezia Giulia.

Venetian (vɪ'ni:ʃən) adj. 1. of, relating to, or characteristic of Venice or its inhabitants. ~n. 2. a native or inhabitant of Venice. 3. See **Venetian blind**.

Venetian blind n. a window blind consisting of a number of horizontal slats whose angle may be altered to let in more or less light.

Venetian red n. 1. natural or synthetic ferric oxide used as a red pigment. 2. a. a moderate to strong reddish-brown colour. b. (as adj.): a Venetian-red coat.

Veneto (Italian 'vɛ:neto) n. a region of NE Italy, on the Adriatic: mountainous in the north with a fertile plain in the south, crossed by the Rivers Po, Adige, and Piave. Capital: Venice. Pop.: 4 345 047 (1981). Area: 18 377 sq. km (7095 sq. miles). Also called: **Venezia-Euganea** (ve'nɛtsja eu'ga:nea).

Venezia (ve'nɛttsja) n. the Italian name for **Venice**.

Venezia Giulia (Italian 'dʒu:lja) n. a former region of NE Italy at the N end of the Adriatic: divided between Yugoslavia and Italy since World War II.

Venezia Tridentina (Italian triden'ti:na) n. the former name (until 1947) of **Trentino-Alto Adige**.

Venezuela (,vɛnɪ'zweɪlə) n. 1. a republic in South America, on the Caribbean: colonized by the Spanish in the 16th century; independence from Spain declared in 1811 and won in 1819 after a war led by Simón Bolívar. It contains Lake Maracaibo and the northernmost chains of the Andes in the northwest, the Orinoco basin in the central part, and the Guiana Highlands in the south. Exports petroleum, iron ore, and coffee. Official language: Spanish. Religion: Roman Catholic. Currency: bolívar. Capital: Caracas. Pop.: 17 316 740 (1985 est.). Area: 912 050 sq. km (352 142 sq. miles). 2. **Gulf of**. an inlet of the Caribbean in NW Venezuela: continues south as Lake Maracaibo. —,Vene'zuelan adj., n.

vengeance ('vɛndʒəns) n. 1. the act of or desire for taking revenge. 2. **with a vengeance**. (intensifier): he's a coward with a vengeance. [C13: from OF, from venger to avenge, from L vindicāre to punish]

vengeful ('vɛndʒful) adj. 1. desiring revenge. 2. characterized by or indicating a desire for revenge. 3. inflicting or taking revenge: with vengeful blows. —'vengefully adv.

venial ('vi:nɪəl) adj. easily excused or forgiven: a venial error. [C13: via OF from LL veniālis, from L venia forgiveness] —,veni'ality n. —'venially adv.

venial sin n. Christian theol. a sin regarded as involving only a partial loss of grace.

Venice ('vɛnɪs) n. a port in NE Italy, capital of Veneto region, built on over 100 islands and mud flats in the **Lagoon of Venice** (an inlet of the **Gulf of Venice** at the head of the Adriatic): united under the first doge in 697 A.D.; became an independent republic and a great commercial and maritime power, defeating Genoa, the greatest rival, in 1380; contains the Grand Canal and about 170 smaller canals, providing waterways for city transport. Pop.: 331 454 (1986). Italian name: **Venezia**. Related adj.: **Venetian**.

venin ('vɛnɪn) n. any of the poisonous constituents of animal venoms. [C20: from F ven(in) poison + -IN]

venipuncture or **venepuncture** ('vɛnɪ,pʌŋktʃə) n. Med. the puncturing of a vein, esp. to take a sample of venous blood or inject a drug.

venison ('vɛnɪzⁿn, -sⁿn) n. the flesh of a deer, used as food. [C13: from OF venaison, from L vēnātiō hunting, from vēnārī to hunt]

Venite (vɪ'naɪtɪ) n. 1. the opening word of the 95th psalm, an invitatory prayer at matins. 2. a musical setting of this. [L: come ye]

Venizelos (*Greek* vɛni'zɛlɔs) *n.* **Eleutherios** (ɛ,lɛfθɛ-'riɔs). 1864–1936, Greek statesman, who greatly extended Greek territory: prime minister (1910–15; 1917–20; 1924; 1928–32; 1933).

Venlo *or* **Venloo** (*Dutch* 'vɛnloː) *n.* a city in the SE Netherlands, in Limburg on the Maas River. Pop.: 63 598 (1987).

Venn diagram (vɛn) *n. Maths, logic.* a diagram in which mathematical sets or terms of a categorial statement are represented by overlapping circles within a boundary representing the universal set, so that all possible combinations of the relevant properties are represented by the various distinct areas in the diagram. [C19: after John Venn (1834–1923), E logician]

venom ('vɛnəm) *n.* **1.** a poisonous fluid secreted by such animals as certain snakes and scorpions and usually transmitted by a bite or sting. **2.** malice; spite. [C13: from OF, from L *venēnum* poison, love potion] —'**venomous** *adj.* —'**venomously** *adv.* —'**venomousness** *n.*

venose ('viːnəus) *adj.* **1.** having veins; venous. **2.** (of a plant) covered with veins or similar ridges. [C17: via L *vēnōsus*, from *vēna* a VEIN]

venosity (vɪ'nɒsɪtɪ) *n.* **1.** an excessive quantity of blood in the venous system or in an organ or part. **2.** an unusually large number of blood vessels in an organ or part.

venous ('viːnəs) *adj.* **1.** *Physiol.* of or relating to the blood circulating in the veins. **2.** of or relating to the veins. [C17: see VENOSE]

vent[1] (vɛnt) *n.* **1.** a small opening for the escape of fumes, liquids, etc. **2.** the shaft of a volcano through which lava and gases erupt. **3.** the external opening of the urinary or genital systems of lower vertebrates. **4.** a small aperture at the breech of old guns through which the charge was ignited. **5. give vent to.** to release (an emotion, idea, etc.) in an outburst. ~*vb.* (*mainly tr.*) **6.** to release or give expression or utterance to (an emotion, etc.): *he vents his anger on his wife.* **7.** to provide a vent for or make vents in. **8.** to let out (steam, etc.) through a vent. [C14: from OF *esventer* to blow out, from EX-[1] + *venter*, from Vulgar L *ventāre* (unattested), from L *ventus* wind]

vent[2] (vɛnt) *n.* **1.** a vertical slit at the back or both sides of a jacket. ~*vb.* **2.** (*tr.*) to make a vent or vents in (a jacket). [C15: from OF *fente* slit, from *fendre* to split, from L *findere* to cleave]

venter ('vɛntə) *n.* **1.** *Anat., zool.* **a.** the belly or abdomen of vertebrates. **b.** a protuberant structure or part, such as the belly of a muscle. **2.** *Bot.* the swollen basal region of an archegonium. **3.** *Law.* the womb. [C16: from L]

ventilate ('vɛntɪ,leɪt) *vb.* (*tr.*) **1.** to drive foul air out of (an enclosed area). **2.** to provide with a means of airing. **3.** to expose (a question, grievance, etc.) to public discussion. **4.** *Physiol.* to oxygenate (the blood). [C15: from L *ventilāre* to fan, from *ventulus*, dim. of *ventus* wind] —'**ventilable** *adj.* —,**venti'lation** *n.*

ventilator ('vɛntɪ,leɪtə) *n.* **1.** an opening or device, such as a fan, used to ventilate a room, building, etc. **2.** *Med.* a machine that maintains a flow of air into and out of the lungs of a patient unable to breathe normally.

ventral ('vɛntrəl) *adj.* **1.** relating to the front part of the body. **2.** of or situated on the upper or inner side of a plant organ, esp. a leaf, that is facing the axis. [C18: from L *ventrālis*, from *venter* abdomen] —'**ventrally** *adv.*

ventral fin *n.* **1.** another name for **pelvic fin.** **2.** any unpaired median fin situated on the undersurface of fishes.

ventricle ('vɛntrɪk°l) *n. Anat.* **1.** a chamber of the heart that receives blood from the atrium and pumps it to the arteries. **2.** any one of the four main cavities of the vertebrate brain. **3.** any of various other small cavities in the body. [C14: from L *ventriculus*, dim. of *venter* belly] —**ven'tricular** *adj.*

ventricose ('vɛntrɪ,kəus) *adj.* **1.** *Bot., zool., anat.* having a swelling on one side: *the ventricose corolla of many labiate plants.* **2.** another word for **corpulent.** [C18: from NL, from L *venter* belly]

ventriculus (vɛn'trɪkjuləs) *n., pl.* -**li** (-,laɪ). **1.** *Zool.* **a.** the midgut of an insect, where digestion takes place. **b.** the gizzard of a bird. **2.** another word for **ventricle.** [C18: from L, dim. of *venter* belly]

ventriloquism (vɛn'trɪlə,kwɪzəm) *or* **ventriloquy** *n.* the art of producing vocal sounds that appear to come from another source. [C18: from L *venter* belly + *loqui* to speak] —**ventriloquial** (,vɛntrɪ'ləukwɪəl) *adj.* —,**ventri'loquially** *adv.* —**ven'triloquist** *n.* —**ven'trilo,quize** *or* -,**quise** *vb.*

Ventris ('vɛntrɪs) *n.* **Michael George Francis.** 1922–56, English cryptographer, who deciphered the Linear B script, identifying it as an early form of Mycenaean Greek.

venture ('vɛntʃə) *vb.* **1.** (*tr.*) to expose to danger: *he ventured his life.* **2.** (*tr.*) to brave the dangers of (something): *I'll venture the seas.* **3.** (*tr.*) to dare (to do something): *does he venture to object?* **4.** (*tr.; may take a clause as object*) to express in spite of possible criticism: *I venture that he is not that honest.* **5.** (*intr.; often foll. by out, forth,* etc.) to embark on a possibly hazardous journey, etc.: *to venture forth upon the high seas.* ~*n.* **6.** an undertaking that is risky or of uncertain outcome. **7.** a commercial undertaking characterized by risk of loss as well as opportunity for profit. **8.** something hazarded or risked in an adventure. **9. at a venture.** at random. [C15: var. of *aventure* ADVENTURE] —'**venturer** *n.*

venture capital *n.* another name for **risk capital.**

Venture Scout *or* **Venturer** *n. Brit.* a person aged 16–20 who is a member of the senior branch of the Scouts.

venturesome ('vɛntʃəsəm) *or* **venturous** ('vɛntʃərəs) *adj.* **1.** willing to take risks; daring. **2.** hazardous.

Venturi tube (vɛn'tjuərɪ) *n. Physics.* a device for measuring or controlling fluid flow, consisting of a tube so constricted that the pressure differential produced by fluid flowing through the constriction gives a measure of the rate of flow. [C19: after G. B. *Venturi* (1746–1822), It. physicist]

venue ('vɛnjuː) *n.* **1.** *Law.* **a.** the place in which a cause of action arises. **b.** the place fixed for the trial of a cause. **c.** the locality from which the jurors must be summoned. **2.** a meeting place. **3.** any place where an organized gathering, such as a rock concert, is held. [C14: from OF, from *venir* to come, from L *venīre*]

venule ('vɛnjuːl) *n.* **1.** *Anat.* any of the small branches of a vein that receives oxygen-depleted blood from the capillaries and returns it to the heart via the venous system. **2.** any of the branches of a vein in an insect's wing. [C19: from L *vēnula*, dim. of *vēna* VEIN]

Venus[1] ('viːnəs) *n.* the Roman goddess of love. Greek counterpart: **Aphrodite.**

Venus[2] ('viːnəs) *n.* one of the inferior planets and the second nearest to the sun, visible as a bright morning or evening star. —**Venusian** (vɪ'njuːzɪən) *n., adj.*

Venusberg ('viːnəs,bɔːg; *German* 've:nusbɛrk) *n.* a mountain in SW East Germany: contains caverns that, according to medieval legend, housed the palace of the goddess Venus.

Venus's-flytrap *or* **Venus flytrap** *n.* an insectivorous plant having hinged two-lobed leaves that snap closed when the sensitive hairs on the surface are touched.

Venus's looking glass *n.* a purple-flowered plant of Europe, W Asia, and N Africa.

veracious (vɛ'reɪʃəs) *adj.* **1.** habitually truthful or honest. **2.** accurate. [C17: from L *vērax*, from *vērus* true] —**ve'raciously** *adv.* —**ve'raciousness** *n.*

veracity (vɛ'ræsɪtɪ) *n., pl.* -**ties.** **1.** truthfulness or honesty, esp. when consistent or habitual. **2.** accuracy. **3.** a truth. [C17: from Med. L *vērācitās*, from L *vērax*; see VERACIOUS]

Veracruz (,vɛrə'kruːz; *Spanish* bera'kruθ) *n.* **1.** a state of E Mexico, on the Gulf of Mexico: consists of a hot humid coastal strip with lagoons, rising rapidly inland to the central plateau and Sierra Madre Oriental. Capital: Jalapa. Pop.: 6 001 856 (1983). Area: 72 815 sq. km (28 114 sq. miles). **2.** the chief port of Mexico, in Veracruz state on the Gulf of Mexico. Pop.: 305 456 (1980).

veranda *or* **verandah** (və'rændə) *n.* **1.** a porch or portico, sometimes partly enclosed, along the outside of a building. **2.** *N.Z.* a continuous overhead canopy that gives shelter to pedestrians. [C18: from Port. *varanda* railing]

veratrine ('vɛrə,triːn) *or* **veratrin** ('vɛrətrɪn) *n.* a white poisonous mixture obtained from sabadilla, consisting of various alkaloids: formerly used in medicine as a counter-irritant. [C19: from L *vērātrum* hellebore + -INE[2]]

verb (vɜːb) *n.* **1.** (in traditional grammar) any of a large class of words that serve to indicate the occurrence or performance of an action, the existence of a state, etc. Such words as *run, make, do,* etc., are verbs. **2.** (in modern descriptive linguistic analysis) **a.** a word or group of words that functions as the predicate of a sentence or introduces the predicate. **b.** (*as modifier*): *a verb phrase.* ~Abbrev.: **vb,** **v.** [C14: from L *verbum* word]

verbal ('vɜːbᵊl) *adj.* **1.** of, relating to, or using words: *merely verbal concessions.* **2.** oral rather than written: *a verbal agreement.* **3.** verbatim; literal: *an almost verbal copy.* **4.** *Grammar.* of or relating to verbs or a verb. ~See also **verbals.** — **'verbally** *adv.*

verbalism ('vɜːbə,lɪzəm) *n.* **1.** a verbal expression; phrase or word. **2.** an exaggerated emphasis on the importance of words. **3.** a statement lacking real content.

verbalist ('vɜːbəlɪst) *n.* **1.** a person who deals with words alone, rather than facts, ideas, etc. **2.** a person skilled in the use of words.

verbalize *or* **-lise** ('vɜːbə,laɪz) *vb.* **1.** to express (an idea, etc.) in words. **2.** to change (any word) into a verb or derive a verb from (any word). **3.** (*intr.*) to be verbose. —,**verbali'zation** *or* **-li'sation** *n.*

verbal noun *n.* a noun derived from a verb, such as *smoking* in the sentence *smoking is bad for you.*

verbals ('vɜːbᵊlz) *pl. n. Sl.* a criminal's admission of guilt on arrest.

verbascum (vɜː'bæskəm) *n.* any of a genus of hairy plants, mostly biennial, having spikes of yellow, purple, or red flowers. [L: mullein]

verbatim (vɜː'beɪtɪm) *adv., adj.* using exactly the same words; word for word. [C15: from Med. L: word by word, from L *verbum* word]

verbena (vɜː'biːnə) *n.* **1.** any of a genus of plants of tropical and temperate America, having red, white, or purple fragrant flowers: much cultivated as garden plants. **2.** any of various similar plants, esp. the lemon verbena. [C16: via Med. L, from L: sacred bough used by the priest in religious acts]

verbiage ('vɜːbɪɪdʒ) *n.* the excessive and often meaningless use of words. [C18: from F, from OF *verbier* to chatter, from *verbe* word, from L *verbum*]

verbose (vɜː'bəʊs) *adj.* using or containing an excess of words, so as to be pedantic or boring. [C17: from L, from *verbum* word] — **ver'bosely** *adv.* — **verbosity** (vɜː-'bɒsɪtɪ) *n.*

verboten *German.* (fɛr'boːtən) *adj.* forbidden.

verb phrase *n. Grammar.* a constituent of a sentence that contains the verb and any direct and indirect objects but not the subject.

Vercelli (*Italian* ver'tʃɛlli) *n.* a city in NW Italy, in Piedmont: an ancient Ligurian and later Roman city; has an outstanding library of manuscripts (notably the *Codex Vercellensis,* dating from the 10th century). Pop.: 60 000 (1985 est.).

Vercingetorix (,vɜːsɪn'dʒɛtərɪks) *n.* died ?45 B.C., Gallic chieftain and hero, executed for leading a revolt against the Romans under Julius Caesar (52 B.C.).

verdant ('vɜːdᵊnt) *adj.* **1.** covered with green vegetation. **2.** (of plants, etc.) green in colour. **3.** unsophisticated; green. [C16: from OF, from *verdoyer* to become green, from OF *verd* green, from L *viridis*] — **'verdancy** *n.* — **'verdantly** *adv.*

verd antique (vɜːd) *n.* **1.** a dark green mottled impure variety of serpentine marble. **2.** any of various similar marbles or stones. [C18: from F, from It. *verde antico* ancient green]

Verde (vɜːd) *n.* **Cape.** a cape in Senegal, near Dakar: the westernmost point of Africa.

Verdi ('vɛədɪ; *Italian* 'verdi) *n.* **Giuseppe** (dʒu'zɛppe). 1813–1901, Italian composer of operas, esp. *Rigoletto* (1851), *Il Trovatore* (1853), *La Traviata* (1853), and *Aïda* (1871).

verdict ('vɜːdɪkt) *n.* **1.** the findings of a jury on the issues of fact submitted to it for examination and trial. **2.** any decision or conclusion. [C13: from Med. L *vērdictum,* from L *vērē dictum* truly spoken, from *vērus* true + *dicere* to say]

verdigris ('vɜːdɪgrɪs) *n.* **1.** a green or bluish patina formed on copper, brass, or bronze. **2.** a green or blue crystalline substance obtained by the action of acetic acid on copper and used as a fungicide and pigment. [C14: from OF *vert de Grice* green of Greece]

Verdun (*French* vɛrˈdœ; *English* 'vɛədʌn) *n.* a fortified town in NE France, on the Meuse: scene of the longest and most severe battle (1916) of World War I, in which the French repelled a powerful German offensive. Pop.:

24 120 (1982). Ancient name: **Verodunum** (,vɛrə-'djuːnəm).

verdure ('vɜːdʒə) *n.* **1.** flourishing green vegetation or its colour. **2.** a condition of freshness or healthy growth. [C14: from OF *verd* green, from L *viridis*] — **'verdured** *adj.*

Vereeniging (fə'riːnɪkɪŋ, və-) *n.* a city in E South Africa, in the Transvaal: scene of the signing (1902) of the treaty ending the Boer War. Pop.: 129 560 (1983 est.).

verge¹ (vɜːdʒ) *n.* **1.** an edge or rim; margin. **2.** a limit beyond which something occurs: *on the verge of ecstasy.* **3.** *Brit.* a grass border along a road. **4.** *Archit.* the edge of the roof tiles projecting over a gable. **5.** *English legal history.* **a.** the area encompassing the royal court that is subject to the jurisdiction of the Lord High Steward. **b.** a rod or wand carried as a symbol of office or emblem of authority, as in the Church. ~*vb.* **6.** (*intr.*; foll. by *on*) to be near (to): *to verge on chaos.* **7.** (when *intr.*, sometimes foll. by *on*) to serve as the edge of (something): *this narrow strip verges the road.* [C15: from OF, from L *virga* rod]

verge² (vɜːdʒ) *vb.* (*intr.*; foll. by *to* or *towards*) to move or incline in a certain direction. [C17: from L *vergere*]

verger ('vɜːdʒə) *n. Chiefly Church of England.* **1.** a church official who acts as caretaker and attendant. **2.** an official who carries the verge or rod of office before a bishop or dean in ceremonies and processions. [C15: from OF, from *verge,* from L *virga* rod, twig]

Vergil ('vɜːdʒɪl) *n.* a variant spelling of **Virgil.**

verglas ('vɛəglɑː) *n., pl.* **-glases** (-glɑː, -glɑːz) a thin film of ice on rock. [from OF *verre-glaz,* from *verre* glass + *glaz* ice]

veridical (vɪ'rɪdɪkᵊl) *adj.* **1.** truthful. **2.** *Psychol.* of revelations in dreams, etc., that appear to be confirmed by subsequent events. [C17: from L, from *vērus* true + *dīcere* to say] — **ve,ridi'cality** *n.* — **ve'ridically** *adv.*

veriest ('vɛrɪɪst) *adj. Arch.* (intensifier): *the veriest coward.*

verification (,vɛrɪfɪ'keɪʃən) *n.* **1.** establishment of the correctness of a theory, fact, etc. **2.** evidence that provides proof of an assertion, theory, etc. — **'verifi,catory** *adj.*

verify ('vɛrɪ,faɪ) *vb.* **-fying, -fied.** (*tr.*) **1.** to prove to be true; confirm. **2.** to check or determine the correctness or truth of by investigation, etc. **3.** *Law.* to substantiate or confirm (an oath). [C14: from OF, from Med. L *vērificāre,* from L *vērus* true + *facere* to make] — **'veri,fiable** *adj.* — **'veri,fiably** *adv.* — **'veri,fier** *n.*

verily ('vɛrɪlɪ) *adv.* (sentence modifier) *Arch.* in truth; truly: *verily, thou art a man of God.* [C13: from VERY + -LY²]

verisimilar (,vɛrɪ'sɪmɪlə) *adj.* probable; likely. [C17: from L, from *vērus* true + *similis* like]

verisimilitude (,vɛrɪsɪ'mɪlɪ,tjuːd) *n.* **1.** the appearance or semblance of truth or reality. **2.** something that merely seems to be true or real, such as a doubtful statement. [C17: from L, from *vērus* true + *similitūdō* SIMILITUDE]

verism ('vɪərɪzəm) *n.* extreme naturalism in art or literature. [C19: from It. *verismo,* from *vero* true, from L *vērus*] — **'verist** *n., adj.* — **ve'ristic** *adj.*

verismo (vɛ'rɪzməʊ) *n. Music.* a school of composition that originated in Italian opera towards the end of the 19th century, drawing its themes from real life. [C19: from It.; see VERISM]

veritable ('vɛrɪtəbᵊl) *adj.* (prenominal) (intensifier; usually qualifying a word used metaphorically): *he's a veritable swine!* [C15: from OF, from *vérité* truth; see VERITY] — **'veritableness** *n.* — **'veritably** *adv.*

verity ('vɛrɪtɪ) *n., pl.* **-ties. 1.** the quality or state of being true, real, or correct. **2.** a true statement, idea, etc. [C14: from OF from L *vēritās,* from *vērus* true]

verjuice ('vɜː,dʒuːs) *n.* **1.** the acid juice of unripe grapes, apples, or crab apples, formerly much used in making sauces, etc. **2.** *Rare.* sourness or sharpness of temper, looks, etc. [C14: from OF *vert jus* green (unripe) juice]

Verkhne-Udinsk (*Russian* 'vjɛrxnɪʊ'djinsk) *n.* the former name (until 1934) of **Ulan-Ude.**

verkrampte (fə'kramtə) *n.* (in South Africa) **a.** an Afrikaner Nationalist violently opposed to any liberal trends in government policy, particularly those related to race. **b.** (*as modifier*): *verkrampte politics.* [C20: from Afrik. (adj.), lit.: restricted]

Verlaine (*French* vɛrlɛn) *n.* **Paul** (pɔl). 1844–96, French poet. His verse includes *Poèmes saturniens* (1866), *Fêtes galantes* (1869) and *Romances sans paroles* (1874). He was closely associated with Rimbaud and was a precursor of the symbolists.

verligte (fə'lɔxtə) *n.* (in South Africa) **a.** a follower of any White political party who supports liberal trends in government policy. **b.** (*as modifier*): *verligte politics.* [C20: from Afrik. (adj.), lit.: enlightened]

Vermeer (vɛə'mɪə; *Dutch* vər'meːr) *n.* **Jan** (jɑn). full name *Jan van der Meer van Delft.* 1632–75, Dutch genre painter, noted esp. for his masterly treatment of light.

vermeil ('vɜːmeɪl) *n.* **1.** gilded silver, bronze, or other metal, used esp. in the 19th century. **2. a.** vermilion. **b.** (*as adj.*): *vermeil shoes.* [C15: from OF, from LL *vermiculus* insect (of the genus *Kermes*) or the red dye prepared from it, from L: little worm]

vermi- *combining form.* worm: *vermicide; vermiform; vermifuge.* [from L *vermis* worm]

vermicelli (,vɜːmɪ'sɛlɪ, -'tʃɛlɪ) *n.* **1.** very fine strands of pasta, used in soups. **2.** tiny chocolate strands used to coat cakes, etc. [C17: from It.: little worms, from *verme*, from L *vermis*]

vermicide ('vɜːmɪ,saɪd) *n.* any substance used to kill worms. —,vermi'cidal *adj.*

vermicular (vɜː'mɪkjʊlə) *adj.* **1.** resembling the form, motion, or tracks of worms. **2.** of worms or wormlike animals. [C17: from Med. L, from L *vermiculus*, dim. of *vermis* worm] —ver'miculate *adj.* —ver,micu'lation *n.*

vermiculite (vɜː'mɪkjʊ,laɪt) *n.* any of a group of micaceous minerals consisting mainly of hydrated silicate of magnesium, aluminium, and iron: on heating they expand and in this form are used in heat and sound insulation. [C19: from VERMICUL(AR) + -ITE[1]]

vermiform ('vɜːmɪ,fɔːm) *adj.* resembling a worm.

vermiform appendix *n.* a wormlike pouch extending from the lower end of the caecum in some mammals. Also called: **appendix.**

vermifuge ('vɜːmɪ,fjuːdʒ) *n.* any drug or agent able to destroy or expel intestinal worms. —**vermifugal** (,vɜːmɪ'fjuːgəl) *adj.*

vermilion (və'mɪljən) *n.* **1. a.** a bright red to reddish-orange colour. **b.** (*as adj.*): *a vermilion car.* **2.** mercuric sulphide, esp. when used as a bright red pigment; cinnabar. [C13: from OF *vermeillon*, from *vermeil*, from L *vermiculus*, dim. of *vermis* worm]

vermin ('vɜːmɪn) *n.* **1.** (*functioning as pl.*) small animals collectively, esp. insects and rodents, that are troublesome to man, domestic animals, etc. **2.** (*pl.* -**min**) an unpleasant person. [C13: from OF, from L *vermis* worm] —**verminous** *adj.*

vermis ('vɜːmɪs) *n.*, *pl.* -**mes** (-miːz). *Anat.* the middle lobe connecting the two halves of the cerebellum. [C19: via NL: from L: worm]

Vermont (vɜː'mɒnt) *n.* a state in the northeastern U.S.: crossed from north to south by the Green Mountains; bounded on the east by the Connecticut River and by Lake Champlain in the northwest. Capital: Montpelier. Pop.: 541 000 (1986 est.). Area: 2400 sq. km (9267 sq. miles). Abbrevs.: **Vt.** or (with zip code) **VT** —**Ver'monter** *n.*

vermouth ('vɜːməθ) *n.* any of several wines containing aromatic herbs. [C19: from F, from G *Wermut* WORMWOOD (absinthe)]

vernacular (və'nækjʊlə) *n.* **1. the.** the commonly spoken language or dialect of a particular people or place. **2.** a local style of architecture, in which ordinary houses are built: *a true English vernacular.* ~*adj.* **3.** relating to or in the vernacular. **4.** designating or relating to the common name of an animal or plant. **5.** built in the local style of ordinary houses. [C17: from L *vernāculus* belonging to a household slave, from *verna* household slave] —**ver'nacularly** *adv.*

vernal ('vɜːnəl) *adj.* **1.** of or occurring in spring. **2.** *Poetic.* of or characteristic of youth. [C16: from L, from *vēr* spring] —**'vernally** *adv.*

vernal equinox *n.* See at **equinox.**

vernal grass *n.* any of a genus of Eurasian grasses, such as **sweet vernal grass**, having the fragrant scent of coumarin.

vernalize *or* -**lise** ('vɜːnə,laɪz) *vb.* to shorten the period between sowing and flowering in (plants), esp. by subjection of the seeds to low temperatures before planting. —,vernali'zation *or* -li'sation *n.*

vernation (vɜː'neɪʃən) *n.* the way in which leaves are arranged in the bud. [C18: from NL, from L *vernāre* to be springlike, from *vēr* spring]

Verne (vɜːn; *French* vɛrn) *n.* **Jules** (ʒyl). 1828–1905, French writer, esp. of science fiction, such as *Twenty Thousand Leagues under the Sea* (1870) and *Around the World in Eighty Days* (1873).

vernier ('vɜːnɪə) *n.* **1.** a small movable scale running parallel to the main graduated scale in certain measuring instruments, such as theodolites, used to obtain a fractional reading of one of the divisions on the main scale. **2.** (*modifier*) relating to or fitted with a vernier: *a vernier scale.* [C18: after Paul *Vernier* (1580–1637), F mathematician, who described the scale]

vernissage (,vɜːnɪ'sɑːʒ) *n.* a preview or the opening or first day of an exhibition of paintings. [F, from *vernis* VARNISH]

Vernoleninsk (*Russian* vɪrnəlɪ'njiːnsk) *n.* the former name of **Nikolayev.**

Verny (*Russian* 'vjɛrnɪj) *n.* a former name (until 1927) of **Alma-Ata.**

Verona (və'rəʊnə; *Italian* ve'roːna) *n.* a city in N Italy, in Veneto on the Adige River: strategically situated at the junction of major routes between Italy and N Europe; became a Roman colony (89 B.C.); under Austrian rule (1797–1866); many Roman remains. Pop.: 259 151 (1986). —**Veronese** (,vɛrə'niːz) *adj.*, *n.*

Veronal ('vɛrənəl) *n.* a trademark for **barbitone.**

Veronese (*Italian* vero'neːse) *n.* **Paolo** ('paːolo), original name *Paolo Cagliari* or *Caliari.* 1528–88, Italian painter of the Venetian school. His works include *The Marriage at Cana* (1563) and *The Feast of the Levi* (1573).

veronica[1] (və'rɒnɪkə) *n.* any plant of a genus, including the speedwells, of temperate and cold regions, having small blue, pink, or white flowers and flattened notched fruits. [C16: from Med. L, from *Veronica*]

veronica[2] (və'rɒnɪkə) *n.* *Bullfighting.* a pass in which the matador slowly swings the cape away from the charging bull. [from Sp., from the name *Veronica*]

Verrazano *or* **Verrazzano** (*Italian* verra'tsaːno) *n.* **Giovanni da** (dʒo'vanni da). ?1485–?1528, Florentine navigator; the first European to sight what was to become New York (1524).

Verrocchio (və'rəʊkɪ,əʊ; *Italian* ver'rɔkkjo) *n.* **Andrea del** (an'drɛːa del). 1435–88, Italian sculptor, painter, and goldsmith of the Florentine school: noted esp. for the equestrian statue of Bartolommeo Colleoni in Venice.

verruca (vɛ'ruːkə) *n.*, *pl.* -**cae** (-siː) *or* -**cas.** **1.** *Pathol.* a wart, esp. one growing on the hand or foot. **2.** *Biol.* a wartlike outgrowth. [C16: from L: wart]

verrucose ('vɛrʊ,kəʊs) *or* **verrucous** ('vɛrʊkəs, vɛ'ruːkəs) *adj.* *Bot.* covered with warty processes. [C17: from L *verrūcōsus* full of warts, from *verrūca* a wart] —**verrucosity** (,vɛrʊ'kɒsɪtɪ) *n.*

Versailles (vɛə'saɪ, -'seɪlz; *French* vɛrsɑj) *n.* a city in N central France, near Paris: site of an elaborate royal residence built for Louis XIV; seat of the French kings (1682–1789). Pop.: 93 363 (1983 est.).

versant ('vɜːsənt) *n.* **1.** the side or slope of a mountain or mountain range. **2.** the slope of a region. [C19: from F, from *verser* to turn, from L *versāre*]

versatile ('vɜːsə,taɪl) *adj.* **1.** capable of or adapted for many different uses, skills, etc. **2.** variable. **3.** *Bot.* (of an anther) attached to the filament by a small area so that it moves freely in the wind. **4.** *Zool.* able to turn forwards and backwards. [C17: from L *versātilis* moving around, from *versāre* to turn] —'**versa,tilely** *adv.* —**versatility** (,vɜːsə'tɪlɪtɪ) *n.*

verse (vɜːs) *n.* **1.** (not in technical usage) a stanza of a poem. **2.** poetry as distinct from prose. **3. a.** a series of metrical feet forming a rhythmical unit of one line. **b.** (*as modifier*): *verse line.* **4.** a specified type of metre or metrical structure: *iambic verse.* **5.** one of the series of short subsections into which most of the writings in the Bible are divided. **6.** a poem. ~*vb.* **7.** a rare word for **versify.** [OE *vers*, from L *versus* furrow, lit.: a turning (of the plough), from *vertere* to turn]

versed (vɜːst) *adj.* (*postpositive;* foll. by *in*) thoroughly knowledgeable (about), acquainted (with), or skilled (in).

versed sine n. a trigonometric function equal to one minus the cosine of the specified angle. [C16: from NL, from SINE[1] + versus, from vertere to turn]

versicle ('vɜːsɪkəl) n. 1. a short verse. 2. a short sentence recited or sung by a minister and responded to by his congregation. [C14: from L versiculus a little line, from versus VERSE]

versicolour or U.S. **versicolor** ('vɜːsɪˌkʌlə) adj. of variable or various colours. [C18: from L versicolor, from versāre to turn + color COLOUR]

versification (ˌvɜːsɪfɪ'keɪʃən) n. 1. the technique or art of versifying. 2. the form or metrical composition of a poem. 3. a metrical version of a prose text.

versify ('vɜːsɪˌfaɪ) vb. -fying, -fied. 1. (tr.) to render (something) into verse. 2. (intr.) to write in verse. [C14: from OF, from L, from versus VERSE + facere to make] —'versi,fier n.

version ('vɜːʃən) n. 1. an account of a matter from a certain point of view, as contrasted with others: his version of the accident is different from the policeman's. 2. a translation, esp. of the Bible, from one language into another. 3. a variant form of something. 4. an adaptation, as of a book or play into a film. 5. Med. manual turning of a fetus to correct an irregular position within the uterus. [C16: from Med. L versiō a turning, from L vertere to turn] —'versional adj.

vers libre French. (vɛr librə) n. (in French poetry) another term for **free verse**.

verso ('vɜːsəʊ) n., pl. -sos. 1. a. the back of a sheet of printed paper. b. the left-hand pages of a book, bearing the even numbers. 2. the side of a coin opposite to the obverse. [C19: from NL versō foliō the leaf having been turned, from L vertere to turn + folium leaf]

verst (vɜːst) n. a unit of length, used in Russia, equal to 1.067 kilometres (0.6629 miles). [C16: from F or G, from Russian versta line]

versus ('vɜːsəs) prep. 1. (esp. in a competition or lawsuit) against. Abbrev.: **v.**, (esp. U.S.) **vs.** 2. in contrast with. [C15: from L: turned (in the direction of), opposite, from vertere to turn]

vertebra ('vɜːtɪbrə) n., pl. -brae (-briː) or -bras. one of the bony segments of the spinal column. [C17: from L: joint of the spine, from vertere to turn] —'vertebral adj. —'vertebrally adv.

vertebral column n. another name for **spinal column**.

vertebrate ('vɜːtɪˌbreɪt, -brɪt) n. 1. any animal of a subphylum characterized by a bony skeleton and a well-developed brain: the group contains fishes, amphibians, reptiles, birds, and mammals. ~adj. 2. of or belonging to this subphylum.

vertebration (ˌvɜːtɪ'breɪʃən) n. the formation of vertebrae or segmentation resembling vertebrae.

vertex ('vɜːtɛks) n., pl. -texes or -tices. 1. the highest point. 2. Maths. a. the point opposite the base of a figure. b. the point of intersection of two sides of a plane figure or angle. c. the point of intersection of a pencil of lines or three or more planes of a solid figure. 3. Anat. the crown of the head. [C16: from L: whirlpool, from vertere to turn]

vertical ('vɜːtɪkəl) adj. 1. at right angles to the horizon; upright: a vertical wall. 2. extending in a perpendicular direction. 3. directly overhead. 4. Econ. of or relating to associated or consecutive, though not identical, stages of industrial activity: vertical integration. 5. of or relating to the vertex. 6. Anat. of or situated at the top of the head (vertex). ~n. 7. a vertical plane, position, or line. 8. a vertical post, pillar, etc. [C16: from LL verticālis, from L VERTEX] —ˌverti'cality n. —'vertically adv.

vertical angles pl. n. Geom. the pair of equal angles between a pair of intersecting lines.

vertical mobility n. Sociol. the movement of individuals or groups to positions in society that involve a change in class, status, and power.

vertices ('vɜːtɪˌsiːz) n. a plural of **vertex** (in technical and scientific senses only).

verticil ('vɜːtɪsɪl) n. Biol. a circular arrangement of parts about an axis, esp. leaves around a stem. [C18: from L verticillus whorl (of a spindle), from VERTEX] —ver'ticillate adj.

vertiginous (vɜː'tɪdʒɪnəs) adj. 1. of, relating to, or having vertigo. 2. producing dizziness. 3. whirling. 4. changeable; unstable. [C17: from L vertiginōsus, from VERTIGO] —ver'tiginously adv.

vertigo ('vɜːtɪɡəʊ) n., pl. **vertigoes** or **vertigines** (vɜː'tɪdʒɪˌniːz). Pathol. a sensation of dizziness resulting from a disorder of the sense of balance. [C16: from L: a whirling round, from vertere to turn]

vertu (vɜː'tuː) n. a variant spelling of **virtu**.

Vertumnus (vɜː'tʌmnəs) or **Vortumnus** n. a Roman god of gardens, orchards, and seasonal change. [from L, from vertere to turn, change]

Verulamium (ˌvɛrʊ'leɪmɪəm) n. the Latin name of **Saint Albans**.

vervain ('vɜːveɪn) n. any of several plants of the genus Verbena, having square stems and long slender spikes of purple, blue, or white flowers. [C14: from OF verveine, from L verbēna sacred bough]

verve (vɜːv) n. great vitality and liveliness. [C17: from OF: garrulity, from L verba words, chatter]

vervet ('vɜːvɪt) n. a variety of a South African guenon monkey having dark hair on the hands and feet and a reddish patch beneath the tail. [C19: from F, from vert green]

Verwoerd (fə'vʊət, fɛə'vʊət) n. **Hendrik Frensch** ('hɛndrɪk frɛns). 1901–66, South African statesman, born in the Netherlands: prime minister of South Africa (from 1958 until his assassination).

very ('vɛrɪ) adv. 1. (intensifier) used to add emphasis to adjectives that are able to be graded: very good; very tall. ~adj. (prenominal) 2. (intensifier) used with nouns preceded by a definite article or possessive determiner, in order to give emphasis to the significance or relevance of a noun in a particular context, or to give exaggerated intensity to certain nouns: the very man I want to see; the very back of the room. 3. (intensifier) used in metaphors to emphasize the applicability of the image to the situation described: he was a very lion in the fight. 4. Arch. genuine: the very living God. [C13: from OF verai true, from L vērax, from vērus]

▷ **Usage.** In strict usage adverbs of degree such as very, too, quite, really, and extremely are used only to qualify adjectives: he is very happy; she is too sad. By this rule, these words should not be used to qualify past participles that follow the verb to be, since they would then be technically qualifying verbs. With the exception of certain participles, such as tired or disappointed, that have come to be regarded as adjectives, all other past participles are qualified by adverbs such as much, greatly, seriously, or excessively: he has been much (not very) inconvenienced.

very high frequency n. a radio-frequency band or radio frequency lying between 300 and 30 megahertz. Abbrev.: **VHF**.

Very light ('vɛrɪ) n. a coloured flare fired from a special pistol (**Very pistol**) for signalling at night, esp. at sea. [C19: after Edward W. Very (1852–1910), U.S. naval ordnance officer]

very low frequency n. a radio-frequency band or radio frequency lying between 30 and 3 kilohertz. Abbrev.: **VLF**.

Vesalius (vɪ'seɪlɪəs) n. **Andreas** (an'dreːas). 1514–64, Flemish anatomist, whose De Humani Corporis fabrica (1543) formed the basis of modern anatomical research and medicine.

vesica ('vɛsɪkə) n., pl. -cae (-ˌsiː). Anat. a technical name for **bladder** (sense 1). [C17: from L: bladder, sac, blister] —'vesical adj. —**vesiculate** (vɛ'sɪkjʊˌleɪt, -lɪt) vb., adj.

vesicant ('vɛsɪkənt) or **vesicatory** ('vɛsɪˌkeɪtərɪ) n., pl. -cants or -catories. 1. any substance that causes blisters. ~adj. 2. acting as a vesicant. [C19: see VESICA]

vesicate ('vɛsɪˌkeɪt) vb. to blister. [C17: from NL vēsīcāre to blister; see VESICA] —ˌvesi'cation n.

vesicle ('vɛsɪkəl) n. 1. Pathol. a. any small sac or cavity, esp. one containing serous fluid. b. a blister. 2. Geol. a rounded cavity within a rock. 3. Bot. a small bladder-like cavity occurring in certain seaweeds. 4. any small cavity or cell. [C16: from L vēsīcula, dim. of VESICA] —**vesicular** (vɛ'sɪkjʊlə) adj.

Vespasian (vɛs'peɪʒɪən) n. Latin name Titus Flavius Sabinus Vespasianus. 9–79 A.D., Roman emperor (69–79), who consolidated Roman rule, esp. in Britain and Germany. He began the building of the Colosseum.

vesper ('vɛspə) n. 1. an evening prayer, service, or hymn. 2. Arch. evening. 3. (modifier) of or relating to vespers. ~See also **vespers**. [C14: from L: evening, the evening star]

vespers ('vɛspəz) n. (functioning as sing.) **1.** Chiefly R.C. Church. the sixth of the seven canonical hours of the divine office. **2.** another word for **evensong** (sense 1).

vespertine ('vɛspə,taɪn) adj. **1.** Bot., zool. appearing, opening, or active in the evening: vespertine flowers. **2.** occurring in the evening or (esp. of stars) setting in the evening.

vespiary ('vɛspɪərɪ) n., pl. **-aries.** a nest or colony of social wasps or hornets. [C19: from L vespa a wasp, on the model of apiary]

vespid ('vɛspɪd) n. **1.** any of a family of hymenopterous insects, including the common wasp. ~adj. **2.** of or belonging to this family. [C19: from NL, from L vespa a wasp] —'vespine adj.

Vespucci (vɛ'spu:tʃɪ) n. **Amerigo** (ame'ri:go), Latin name Americus Vespucius. ?1454–1512, Florentine navigator in the New World (1499–1500; 1501–02), after whom the continent of America was named.

vessel ('vɛsəl) n. **1.** any object used as a container, esp. for a liquid. **2.** a passenger or freight-carrying ship, boat, etc. **3.** Anat. a tubular structure that transports such body fluids as blood and lymph. **4.** Bot. a tubular element of xylem tissue transporting water. **5.** Rare. a person regarded as a vehicle for some purpose or quality. [C13: from OF, from LL vascellum urn, from L vās vessel]

vest (vɛst) n. **1.** an undergarment covering the body from the shoulders to the hips, made of cotton, nylon, etc. **2.** U.S., Canad., & Austral. a waistcoat. **3.** Obs. any form of dress. ~vb. **4.** (tr.; foll. by in) to place or settle (power, rights, etc., in): power was vested in the committee. **5.** (tr.; foll. by with) to bestow or confer (on): the company was vested with authority. **6.** (usually foll. by in) to confer (a right, title, etc., upon) or (of a right, title, etc.) to pass (to) or devolve (upon). **7.** (tr.) to clothe. **8.** (intr.) to put on clothes, ecclesiastical vestments, etc. [C15: from OF vestir to clothe, from L vestīre, from vestis clothing]

vesta ('vɛstə) n. a short friction match, usually of wood. [C19: after VESTA]

Vesta ('vɛstə) n. the Roman goddess of the hearth and its fire. In her temple a perpetual flame was tended by the vestal virgins. Greek counterpart: **Hestia.**

vestal ('vɛstəl) adj. **1.** chaste or pure. **2.** of or relating to the Roman goddess Vesta. ~n. **3.** a chaste woman, esp. a nun.

vestal virgin n. (in ancient Rome) one of the virgin priestesses whose lives were dedicated to Vesta and to maintaining the sacred fire in her temple.

vested ('vɛstɪd) adj. Property law. having a present right to the immediate or future possession and enjoyment of property.

vested interest n. **1.** Property law. an existing right to the immediate or future possession and enjoyment of property. **2.** a strong personal concern in a state of affairs, etc. **3.** a person or group that has such an interest.

vestiary ('vɛstɪərɪ) n., pl. **-aries.** Obs. a room for storing clothes or dressing in, such as a vestry. [C17: from LL vestiārius, from vestis clothing]

vestibule ('vɛstɪ,bju:l) n. **1.** a small entrance hall or anteroom. **2.** any small bodily cavity at the entrance to a passage or canal. [C17: from L vestibulum]

vestige ('vɛstɪdʒ) n. **1.** a small trace; hint: a vestige of truth. **2.** Biol. an organ or part of an organism that is a small nonfunctioning remnant of a functional organ in an ancestor. [C17: via F from L vestīgium track] —**ves'tigial** adj.

vestment ('vɛstmənt) n. **1.** a garment or robe, esp. one denoting office, authority, or rank. **2.** any of various ceremonial garments worn by the clergy at religious services, etc. [C13: from OF vestiment, from L vestīmentum, from vestīre to clothe] —**vestmental** (vɛst'mɛntəl) adj.

vest-pocket n. (modifier) Chiefly U.S. small enough to fit into a waistcoat pocket.

vestry ('vɛstrɪ) n., pl. **-tries. 1.** a room in or attached to a church in which vestments, sacred vessels, etc., are kept. **2.** a room in or attached to some churches, used for Sunday school, etc. **3. a.** Church of England. a meeting of all the members of a parish or their representatives, to transact the official and administrative business of the parish. **b.** the parish council. [C14: prob. from OF vestiarie; see VEST] —'vestral adj.

vestryman ('vɛstrɪmən) n., pl. **-men.** a member of a church vestry.

vesture ('vɛstʃə) Arch. ~n. **1.** a garment or something that seems like a garment: a vesture of cloud. ~vb. **2.** (tr.) to clothe. [C14: from OF, from vestir, from L vestīre, from vestis clothing] —'vestural adj.

Vesuvius (vɪ'su:vɪəs) n. a volcano in SW Italy, on the Bay of Naples: first recorded eruption in 79 A.D., which destroyed Pompeii, Herculaneum, and Stabiae; numerous eruptions since then. Average height: 1220 m (4003 ft.). Italian name: **Vesuvio** (ve'zu:vjo).

vet¹ (vɛt) n. **1.** short for **veterinary surgeon.** ~vb. **vetting, vetted. 2.** (tr.) Chiefly Brit. to make a prior examination and critical appraisal of (a person, document, etc.): the candidates were well vetted. **3.** to examine, treat, or cure (an animal).

vet² (vɛt) n. U.S. & Canad. short for **veteran** (senses 2, 3).

vet. abbrev. for: **1.** veteran. **2.** veterinarian. **3.** veterinary. ~Also (for senses 2, 3): **veter.**

vetch (vɛtʃ) n. **1.** any of various climbing plants having pinnate leaves, typically blue or purple flowers, and tendrils on the stems. **2.** any of various similar and related plants, such as the kidney vetch. **3.** the beanlike fruit of any of these plants. [C14 fecche, from OF veche, from L vicia]

vetchling ('vɛtʃlɪŋ) n. any of various tendril-climbing plants, mainly of N temperate regions, having winged or angled stems and showy flowers. See also **sweet pea.**

veteran ('vɛtərən) n. **1. a.** a person or thing that has given long service in some capacity. **b.** (as modifier): veteran firemen. **2.** a soldier who has seen considerable active service. **3.** U.S. & Canad. a person who has served in the military forces. [C16: from L, from vetus old]

veteran car n. Brit. a car constructed before 1919, esp. one constructed before 1905.

veterinary ('vɛtərɪnərɪ) adj. of or relating to veterinary science. [C18: from L veterinārius, from veterīnae draught animals]

veterinary science or **medicine** n. the branch of medicine concerned with the health of animals and the treatment of injuries or diseases that affect them.

veterinary surgeon n. Brit. a person qualified to practise veterinary medicine. U.S. and Canad. term: **veterinarian.**

veto ('vi:təʊ) n., pl. **-toes. 1.** the power to prevent legislation or action proposed by others: the presidential veto. **2.** the exercise of this power. ~vb. **-toing, -toed.** (tr.) **3.** to refuse consent to (a proposal, esp. a government bill). **4.** to prohibit, ban, or forbid: her parents vetoed her trip. [C17: from L: I forbid, from vetāre to forbid] —'vetoer n.

vex (vɛks) vb. (tr.) **1.** to anger or annoy. **2.** to confuse; worry. **3.** Arch. to agitate. [C15: from OF vexer, from L vexāre to jolt (in carrying), from vehere to convey] —'vexer n. —'vexing adj.

vexation (vɛk'seɪʃən) n. **1.** the act of vexing or the state of being vexed. **2.** something that vexes.

vexatious (vɛk'seɪʃəs) adj. **1.** vexing or tending to vex. **2.** vexed. **3.** Law. (of a legal action or proceeding) instituted without sufficient grounds, esp. so as to cause annoyance to the defendant. —**vex'atiously** adv.

vexed (vɛkst) adj. **1.** annoyed, confused, or agitated. **2.** much debated (esp. in **a vexed question**). —**vexedly** ('vɛksɪdlɪ) adv.

vexillology (,vɛksɪ'lɒlədʒɪ) n. the study and collection of information about flags. [C20: from L vexillum flag + -LOGY] —**vexil'lologist** n.

vexillum (vɛk'sɪləm) n., pl. **-la** (-lə). **1.** Ornithol. the vane of a feather. **2.** Also called: **standard.** Bot. the largest petal of a papilionaceous flower. [C18: from L: banner, ?from vēlum sail] —**'vexillate** adj.

VF abbrev. for video frequency.

vg abbrev. for very good.

VG abbrev. for Vicar General.

VHF or **vhf** Radio. abbrev. for very high frequency.

VHS abbrev. for video home system: a video cassette recording system using ½″ magnetic tape.

VI abbrev. for: **1.** Vancouver Island. **2.** Virgin Islands.

v.i. abbrev. for vide infra.

via ('vaɪə) prep. by way of; by means of; through: to London via Paris. [C18: from L viā, from via way]

viable ('vaɪəbəl) adj. **1.** capable of becoming actual, etc.: a viable proposition. **2.** (of seeds, eggs, etc.) capable of normal growth and development. **3.** (of a fetus) having reached a stage of development at which further development can occur independently of the mother. [C19: from F, from *vie* life, from L *vīta*] — **via'bility** *n.*

Via Dolorosa ('vi:ə ,dɒlə'rəusə) *n.* the route followed by Christ from the place of his condemnation to Calvary for his crucifixion. [L, lit.: sorrowful road]

viaduct ('vaɪə,dʌkt) *n.* a bridge, esp. for carrying a road or railway across a valley, etc. [C19: from L *via* way + *dūcere* to bring, on the model of *aqueduct*]

vial ('vaɪəl) *n.* a less common variant of **phial.** [C14 *fiole*, from OF, ult. from Gk *phialē*; see PHIAL]

via media *Latin.* ('vaɪə 'mi:dɪə) *n.* a compromise between two extremes.

viand ('vi:ənd) *n.* **1.** a type of food, esp. a delicacy. **2.** (*pl.*) provisions. [C14: from OF, ult. from L *vivenda* things to be lived on, from *vivere* to live]

Viareggio (*Italian* via'reddʒo) *n.* a town and resort in W Italy, in Tuscany on the Ligurian Sea. Pop.: 60 000 (1985 est.).

viaticum (vaɪ'ætɪkəm) *n., pl.* **-ca** (-kə) *or* **-cums.** **1.** *Christianity.* Holy Communion as administered to a person dying or in danger of death. **2.** *Rare.* provisions or a travel allowance for a journey. [C16: from L, from *viaticus* belonging to a journey, from *via* way]

vibes (vaɪbz) *pl. n.* **1.** *Inf.* short for **vibraphone. 2.** *Sl.* short for **vibrations.**

Viborg 1. ('vi:bɔrj). the Swedish name for **Vyborg. 2.** (*Danish* 'vibɔr). a town in N central Denmark, in Jutland: formerly a royal town and capital of Jutland. Pop.: 28 659 (1982 est.).

vibraculum (vaɪ'brækjʊləm) *n., pl.* **-la** (-lə). *Zool.* any of the specialized bristle-like polyps in certain bryozoans, the actions of which prevent parasites from settling on the colony. [C19: from NL, from L *vibrāre* to brandish]

vibrant ('vaɪbrənt) *adj.* **1.** characterized by or exhibiting vibration. **2.** giving an impression of vigour and activity. **3.** caused by vibration; resonant. [C16: from L *vibrāre* to agitate] — **'vibrancy** *n.* — **'vibrantly** *adv.*

vibraphone ('vaɪbrə,fəʊn) *n.* a percussion instrument consisting of a set of metal bars placed over tubular metal resonators, which are made to vibrate electronically. — **'vibra,phonist** *n.*

vibrate (vaɪ'breɪt) *vb.* **1.** to move or cause to move back and forth rapidly. **2.** (*intr.*) to oscillate. **3.** to resonate or cause to resonate. **4.** (*intr.*) to waver. **5.** *Physics.* to undergo or cause to undergo an oscillatory process, as of an alternating current. **6.** (*intr.*) *Rare.* to respond emotionally; thrill. [C17: from L *vibrāre*] — **vibratile** ('vaɪbrə,taɪl) *adj.* — **vi'brating** *adj.* — **vibratory** ('vaɪbrətərɪ) *adj.*

vibration (vaɪ'breɪʃən) *n.* **1.** the act or an instance of vibrating. **2.** *Physics.* **a.** a periodic motion about an equilibrium position, such as in the propagation of sound. **b.** a single cycle of such a motion. **3.** the process or state of vibrating or being vibrated. — **vi'brational** *adj.*

vibrations (vaɪ'breɪʃənz) *pl. n. Sl.* **1.** instinctive feelings supposedly influencing human communication. **2.** a characteristic atmosphere felt to be emanating from places or objects.

vibrato (vɪ'brɑːtəʊ) *n., pl.* **-tos.** *Music.* **1.** a slight, rapid, and regular fluctuation in the pitch of a note produced on a stringed instrument by a shaking movement of the hand stopping the strings. **2.** an oscillatory effect produced in singing by fluctuation in breath pressure or pitch. [C19: from It., from L *vibrāre* to VIBRATE]

vibrator (vaɪ'breɪtə) *n.* **a.** a device for producing a vibratory motion, such as one used in massage. **b.** such a device with a vibrating part or tip, used as a dildo.

vibrissa (vaɪ'brɪsə) *n., pl.* **-sae** (-siː). (*usually pl.*) **1.** any of the bristle-like sensitive hairs on the face of many mammals; a whisker. **2.** any of the specialized bristle-like feathers around the beak in certain insectivorous birds. [C17: from L, prob. from *vibrāre* to shake] — **vi'brissal** *adj.*

viburnum (vaɪ'bɜːnəm) *n.* **1.** any of various temperate and subtropical shrubs or trees having small white flowers and berry-like red or black fruits. **2.** the dried bark of several species of this tree, sometimes used in medicine. [C18: from L: wayfaring tree]

Vic. *Austral. abbrev. for* Victoria (the state).

vicar ('vɪkə) *n.* **1.** *Church of England.* **a.** (in Britain) a clergyman appointed to act as priest of a parish from which, formerly, he did not receive tithes but a stipend. **b.** a clergyman who acts as assistant to or substitute for

the rector of a parish at Communion. **2.** *R.C. Church.* a bishop or priest representing the pope and exercising a limited jurisdiction. **3.** Also called: **lay vicar, vicar choral.** *Church of England.* a member of a cathedral choir appointed to sing certain parts of the services. [C13: from OF, from L *vicārius* (n.) a deputy, from *vicārius* (adj.) VICARIOUS] — **vicarial** (vɪ'kɛərɪəl) *adj.* — **vi'cariate** *n.* — **'vicarly** *adj.*

vicarage ('vɪkərɪdʒ) *n.* the residence or benefice of a vicar.

vicar apostolic *n. R.C. Church.* a titular bishop having jurisdiction in missionary countries.

vicar general *n., pl.* **vicars general.** an official, usually a layman, appointed to assist the bishop of a diocese in discharging his administrative or judicial duties.

vicarious (vɪ'kɛərɪəs, vaɪ-) *adj.* **1.** undergone at second hand through sympathetic participation in another's experiences. **2.** undergone or done as the substitute for another: *vicarious punishment.* **3.** delegated: *vicarious authority.* **4.** taking the place of another. [C17: from L *vicārius* substituted, from *vicis* interchange] — **vi'cariously** *adv.* — **vi'cariousness** *n.*

Vicar of Bray (breɪ) *n.* a vicar (Simon Aleyn) appointed to the parish of Bray in Berkshire during Henry VIII's reign who changed his faith to Catholic when Mary I was on the throne and back to Protestant when Elizabeth I succeeded and so retained his living.

Vicar of Christ *n. R.C. Church.* the pope when regarded as Christ's earthly representative.

vice[1] (vaɪs) *n.* **1.** an immoral, wicked, or evil habit, action, or trait. **2.** frequent indulgence in immoral or degrading practices. **3.** a specific form of pernicious conduct, esp. prostitution or sexual perversion. **4.** an imperfection in character, conduct, etc.: *smoking is his only vice.* **5.** a bad trick or disposition, as of horses, dogs, etc. [C13: via OF from L *vitium* a defect]

vice[2] *or U.S.* (*often*) **vise** (vaɪs) *n.* **1.** an appliance for holding an object while work is done on it, usually having a pair of jaws. *~vb.* **2.** (*tr.*) to grip (something) with or as if with a vice. [C15: from OF *vis* a screw, from L *vītis* vine, plant with spiralling tendrils (hence the later meaning)]

vice[3] (vaɪs) *adj.* **1. a.** (*prenominal*) serving in the place of. **b.** (*in combination*): *viceroy.* *~n.* **2.** *Inf.* a person who serves as a deputy to another. [C18: from L, from *vicis* interchange]

vice[4] ('vaɪsɪ) *prep.* instead of; as a substitute for. [C16: from L, ablative of *vicis* change]

vice admiral *n.* a commissioned officer of flag rank in certain navies, junior to an admiral and senior to a rear admiral.

vice-chairman *n., pl.* **-men.** a person who deputizes for a chairman and serves in his place during his absence. — **,vice-'chairmanship** *n.*

vice chancellor *n.* **1.** the chief executive or administrator at some British universities. **2.** (in the U.S.) a judge in courts of equity subordinate to the chancellor. **3.** (formerly in England) a senior judge of the court of chancery who acted as assistant to the Lord Chancellor. **4.** a person serving as the deputy of a chancellor. — **,vice-'chancellorship** *n.*

vicegerent (,vaɪs'dʒɛrənt) *n.* **1.** a person appointed to exercise all or some of the authority of another. **2.** *R.C. Church.* the pope or any other representative of God or Christ on earth, such as a bishop. *~adj.* **3.** invested with or characterized by delegated authority. [C16: from NL, from VICE[3] + L *gerere* to manage] — **,vice'gerency** *n.*

vicennial (vɪ'sɛnɪəl) *adj.* **1.** occurring every 20 years. **2.** lasting for a period of 20 years. [C18: from LL *vicennium* period of twenty years, from L *viciēs* twenty times + *-ennium*, from *annus* year]

Vicenza (*Italian* vi'tʃɛntsa) *n.* a city in NE Italy, in Veneto: home of the 16th-century architect Andrea Palladio and site of some of his finest works. Pop.: 110 449 (1986).

vice president *n.* an officer ranking immediately below a president and serving as his deputy. A vice president takes the president's place during his absence or incapacity, after his death, and in certain other circumstances. Abbrev.: **VP.** — **,vice-'presidency** *n.*

viceregal (,vaɪs'riːɡ'l) *adj.* **1.** of or relating to a viceroy. **2.** *Chiefly Austral. & N.Z.* of or relating to a governor or governor general. — **,vice'regally** *adv.*

vicereine (ˌvaɪsˈreɪn) *n.* **1.** the wife of a viceroy. **2.** a female viceroy. [C19: from F, from VICE³ + *reine* queen, from L *rēgīna*]

viceroy ('vaɪsrɔɪ) *n.* a governor of a colony, country, or province who acts for and rules in the name of his sovereign or government. Related adj.: **viceregal.** [C16: from F, from VICE³ + *roy* king, from L *rex*] —**'viceroyship** *or* ˌvice'royalty *n.*

vice squad *n.* a police division to which is assigned the enforcement of gaming and prostitution laws.

vice versa ('vaɪsɪ 'vɜːsə) *adv.* the other way around. [C17: from L: relations being reversed, from *vicis* change + *vertere* to turn]

Vichy (*French* viʃi; *English* 'viːʃi:) *n.* a town and spa in central France, on the River Allier: seat of the collaborationist government under Marshal Pétain (1940–44); mineral waters bottled for export. Pop.: 32 114 (1983 est.). Latin name: **Vicus Calidus** ('viːkəs 'kælɪdəs).

vichyssoise (*French* viʃiswaz) *n.* a thick soup made from leeks, potatoes, chicken stock, and cream, usually served chilled. [F, from (*crème*) *vichyssoise* (*glacée*) (ice-cold cream) from Vichy]

vichy water *n.* **1.** (*sometimes cap.*) a natural mineral water from springs at Vichy in France, reputed to be beneficial to the health. **2.** any sparkling mineral water resembling this.

vicinage ('vɪsɪnɪdʒ) *n. Now rare.* **1.** the residents of a particular neighbourhood. **2.** a less common word for **vicinity.** [C14: from OF *vicenage*, from *vicin* neighbouring, from L *vīcīnus*]

vicinal ('vɪsɪnəl) *adj.* **1.** neighbouring. **2.** (esp. of roads) of or relating to a locality or neighbourhood. [C17: from L *vīcīnālis* nearby, from *vīcīnus*, from *vicus* a neighbourhood]

vicinity (vɪˈsɪnɪti) *n., pl.* **-ties. 1.** a surrounding area; neighbourhood. **2.** the fact or condition of being close in space or relationship. [C16: from L, from *vīcīnus* neighbouring, from *vicus* village]

vicious ('vɪʃəs) *adj.* **1.** wicked or cruel: *a vicious thug.* **2.** characterized by violence or ferocity: *a vicious blow.* **3.** *Inf.* unpleasantly severe; harsh: *a vicious wind.* **4.** characterized by malice: *vicious lies.* **5.** (esp. of dogs, horses, etc.) ferocious or hostile. **6.** characterized by or leading to vice. **7.** invalidated by defects; unsound: *a vicious inference.* [C14: from OF, from L *vitiōsus* full of faults, from *vitium* defect] —**'viciously** *adv.* —**'viciousness** *n.*

vicious circle *n.* **1.** a situation in which an attempt to resolve one problem creates new problems that lead back to the original situation. **2.** *Logic.* **a.** a form of reasoning in which a conclusion is inferred from premises the truth of which cannot be established independently of that conclusion. **b.** an explanation given in terms that cannot be understood independently of that which was to be explained.

vicissitude (vɪˈsɪsɪˌtjuːd) *n.* **1.** variation or mutability in nature or life, esp. successive alternation from one condition or thing to another. **2.** a variation in circumstance, fortune, etc. [C16: from L *vicissitūdō*, from *vicis* change; alternation] —**vi·cissi'tudinous** *adj.*

Vicksburg ('vɪksˌbɜːɡ) *n.* a city in W Mississippi, on the Mississippi River: site of one of the most decisive campaigns (1863) of the American Civil War, in which the Confederates were besieged for nearly seven weeks before capitulating. Pop.: 25 434 (1980).

Vicky ('vɪkɪ) *n.* professional name of *Victor Weisz.* 1913–66, British left-wing political cartoonist, born in Germany.

Vico ('viːkəʊ; *Italian* 'viːko) *n.* **Giovanni Battista** (dʒo-'vanni bat'tista). 1668–1744, Italian philosopher. In *Scienza Nuova* (1721) he postulated that civilizations rise and fall in evolutionary cycles, making use of myths, poetry, and linguistics as historical evidence.

victim ('vɪktɪm) *n.* **1.** a person or thing that suffers harm, death, etc.: *victims of tyranny.* **2.** a person who is tricked or swindled. **3.** a living person or animal sacrificed in a religious rite. [C15: from L *victima*]

victimize *or* **-mise** ('vɪktɪˌmaɪz) *vb.* (*tr.*) **1.** to punish or discriminate against selectively or unfairly. **2.** to make a victim of. —ˌvictimi'zation *or* -mi'sation *n.* —'victim,izer *or* -m,iser *n.*

victor ('vɪktə) *n.* **1. a.** a person, nation, etc., that has defeated an adversary in war, etc. **b.** (*as modifier*): *the*

victor army. **2.** the winner of any contest, conflict, or struggle. [C14: from L, from *vincere* to conquer]

Victor Emmanuel II ('vɪktə) *n.* 1820–78, king of Sardinia-Piedmont (1849–78) and first king of Italy from 1861.

Victor Emmanuel III *n.* 1869–1947, last king of Italy (1900–46): dominated after 1922 by Mussolini, whom he appointed as premier; abdicated.

victoria (vɪkˈtɔːrɪə) *n.* **1.** a light four-wheeled horse-drawn carriage with a folding hood, two passenger seats, and a seat in front for the driver. **2.** Also called: **victoria plum.** *Brit.* a large sweet variety of plum, red and yellow in colour. [C19: both after Queen VICTORIA]

Victoria¹ (vɪkˈtɔːrɪə) *n.* **1.** a state of SE Australia: part of New South Wales colony until 1851; semiarid in the northwest, with the Great Dividing Range in the centre and east and the Murray River along the N border. Capital: Melbourne. Pop.: 4 188 300 (1987 est.). Area: 227 620 sq. km (87 884 sq. miles). **2.** Lake. Also called: **Victoria Nyanza.** a lake in East Africa, in Tanzania, Uganda, and Kenya, at an altitude of 1134 m (3720 ft.): the largest lake in Africa and second largest in the world; drained by the Victoria Nile. Area: 69 485 sq. km (26 828 sq. miles). **3.** a port in SW Canada, capital of British Columbia, on Vancouver Island: founded in 1843 by the Hudson's Bay Company; made capital of British Columbia in 1868; university (1963). Pop.: 66 303 (1986). **4.** the capital of the Seychelles, a port on NE Mahé. Pop.: 23 880 (1980 est.). **5.** the capital of Hong Kong, on N Hong Kong Island: financial centre; university (1911). Pop.: 590 771 (1981). **6.** Mount. a mountain in SE Papua New Guinea: the highest peak of the Owen Stanley Range. Height: 4073 m (13 363 ft.).

Victoria² (vɪkˈtɔːrɪə) *n.* 1819–1901, queen of the United Kingdom (1837–1901) and empress of India (1876–1901). She married Prince Albert of Saxe-Coburg-Gotha (1840). Her sense of vocation did much to restore the prestige of the British monarchy.

Victoria³ (vɪkˈtɔːrɪə) *n.* the Roman goddess of victory. Greek counterpart: **Nike.**

Victoria Cross *n.* the highest decoration for gallantry in the face of the enemy awarded to the British and Commonwealth armed forces: instituted in 1856 by Queen Victoria.

Victoria Day *n.* the Monday preceding May 24: observed in Canada as a national holiday in commemoration of the birthday of Queen Victoria.

Victoria Desert *n.* See **Great Victoria Desert.**

Victoria Falls *pl. n.* a waterfall on the border between Zimbabwe and Zambia, on the Zambezi River. Height: about 108 m (355 ft.). Width: about 1400 m (4500 ft.).

Victoria Island *n.* a large island in the Canadian Arctic: part of the Northwest Territories. Area: about 212 000 sq. km (82 000 sq. miles).

Victoria Land *n.* a section of Antarctica, largely in the Ross Dependency on the Ross Sea.

Victorian (vɪkˈtɔːrɪən) *adj.* **1.** of or characteristic of Queen Victoria or the period of her reign. **2.** exhibiting the characteristics popularly attributed to the Victorians, esp. prudery, bigotry, or hypocrisy. Cf. **Victorian values.** **3.** of or relating to Victoria (the state or any of the cities). ~*n.* **4.** a person who lived during the reign of Queen Victoria. **5.** an inhabitant of Victoria (the state or any of the cities). —**Vic'torian,ism** *n.*

Victoriana (vɪkˌtɔːrɪ'ɑːnə) *n.* objects, ornaments, etc., of the Victorian period.

Victoria Nile *n.* See **Nile.**

Victorian values *pl. n.* the qualities of enterprise and initiative, the importance of the family, and the development of charitable voluntary work that are considered to characterize the Victorian period. Cf. **Victorian** (sense 2).

victorious (vɪkˈtɔːrɪəs) *adj.* **1.** having defeated an adversary: *the victorious nations.* **2.** of, indicative of, or characterized by victory: *a victorious conclusion.* —**vic'toriously** *adv.*

victory ('vɪktərɪ) *n., pl.* **-ries. 1.** final and complete superiority in a war. **2.** a successful military engagement. **3.** a success attained in a contest or struggle or over an opponent, obstacle, or problem. **4.** the act of triumphing or state of having triumphed. [C14: from OF *victorie*, from L *victōria*, from *vincere* to subdue]

Victory ('vɪktərɪ) *n.* another name (in English) for the Roman goddess **Victoria** or the Greek **Nike.**

victory roll *n.* a rolling aircraft manoeuvre made by a pilot to announce or celebrate the shooting down of an enemy plane.

victual ('vɪtᵊl) *vb.* **-ualling, -ualled** *or U.S.* **-ualing, -ualed.** to supply with or obtain victuals.~See also **victuals.** [C14: from OF *vitaille,* from LL *victuālia* provisions, from L, from *victus* sustenance, from *vivere* to live] —'**victual-less** *adj.*

victualler ('vɪtələ) *n.* **1.** a supplier of victuals, as to an army. **2.** *Brit.* a licensed purveyor of spirits. **3.** a supply ship, esp. one carrying foodstuffs.

victuals ('vɪtᵊlz) *pl. n. (sometimes sing.)* food or provisions.

vicuña (vɪ'ku:njə) *or* **vicuna** (vɪ'kju:nə, -'ku:njə) *n.* **1.** a tawny-coloured cud-chewing Andean mammal similar to the llama. **2.** the fine light wool obtained from this animal. [C17: from Sp., from Quechuan *wikuña*]

Vidal (vi:'dæl) *n.* **Gore.** born 1925, U.S. novelist and critic. His novels include *Burr* (1974), *Lincoln* (1984), and *Empire* (1987).

vide ('vaɪdɪ) (used to direct a reader to a specified place in a text, another book, etc.) refer to, see (often in **vide ante** (see before), **vide infra** (see below), **vide supra** (see above), etc.) Abbrev.: **v., vid.** [C16: from L]

videlicet (vɪ'di:lɪ,sɛt) *adv.* namely: used to specify items, etc. Abbrev.: **viz.** [C15: from L]

video ('vɪdɪəʊ) *adj.* **1.** relating to or employed in the transmission or reception of a televised image. **2.** of, concerned with, or operating at video frequencies. ~*n., pl.* **-os. 3.** the visual elements of a television broadcast. **4.** a film recorded on a video cassette. **5.** short for **video cassette, video cassette recorder. 6.** *U.S.* an informal name for **television.** ~*vb.* **videoing, videoed. 7.** to record (a television programme, etc.) on a video cassette recorder. [C20: from L *vidēre* to see, on the model of AUDIO]

video cassette *n.* a cassette containing video tape.

video cassette recorder *n.* a tape recorder for vision and sound signals using magnetic tape in closed plastic cassettes: used for recording and playing back television programmes and films. Often shortened to **video** or **video recorder.**

videodisc ('vɪdɪəʊ,dɪsk) *n.* a transparent plastic disc with a metal coating, carrying recorded video material for display on a television screen.

video frequency *n.* the frequency of a signal conveying the image and synchronizing pulses in a television broadcasting system. It lies in the range from about 50 hertz to 8 megahertz.

video game *n.* any of various games that can be played by using an electronic control to move points of light or graphical symbols on the screen of a visual display unit.

video jockey *n.* a person who introduces and plays videos, esp. of pop songs, on a television programme.

video nasty *n., pl.* **nasties.** a film, usually specially made for video, that is explicitly horrific and pornographic.

videophone ('vɪdɪə,fəʊn) *n.* a telephonic device in which there is both verbal and visual communication between parties.

video recorder *n.* short for **video cassette recorder.**

video tape *n.* **1.** magnetic tape used mainly for recording the video-frequency signals of a television programme or film for subsequent transmission. ~*vb.* **video-tape. 2.** to record (a programme, etc.) on video tape.

video tape recorder *n.* a tape recorder for visual signals and sometimes accompanying sound, using magnetic tape on open spools: used in television broadcasting.

videotex ('vɪdɪəʊ,tɛks) *n.* another name for **viewdata.**

videotext ('vɪdɪəʊ,tɛkst) *n.* a means of providing a written or graphical representation of computerized information on a television screen.

vidicon ('vɪdɪ,kɒn) *n.* a small television camera tube, used in closed-circuit television and outside broadcasts, in which incident light forms an electric charge pattern on a photoconductive surface. [C20: from VID(EO) + ICON(O-SCOPE)]

vie (vaɪ) *vb.* **vying, vied.** (*intr.;* foll. by *with* or *for*) to contend for superiority or victory (with) or strive in competition (for). [C15: prob. from OF *envier* to challenge, from L *invītāre* to INVITE] —'**vier** *n.* —'**vying** *adj., n.*

Vienna (vɪ'ɛnə) *n.* the capital and the smallest province of Austria, in the northeast on the River Danube: seat of the Hapsburgs (1278-1918); residence of the Holy Roman Emperor (1558-1806); withstood sieges by Turks in 1529 and 1683; political and cultural centre in the 18th and 19th centuries, having associations with many composers; university (1365). Pop.: 1 481 399 (1986). Area: 1075 sq. km (415 sq. miles). German name: **Wien.** —**Viennese** (,vɪə'ni:z) *adj., n.*

Vienne (*French* vjɛn) *n.* **1.** a department of W central France, in Poitou-Charentes region. Capital: Poitiers. Pop.: 371 428 (1982). Area: 7044 sq. km (2747 sq. miles). **2.** a town in SE France, on the River Rhône: extensive Roman remains. Ancient name: **Vienna. 3.** a river in SW central France, flowing west and north to the Loire below Chinon. Length: over 350 km (200 miles).

Vientiane (,vjɛntɪ'ɑ:n) *n.* the administrative capital of Laos, in the south near the border with Thailand: capital of the kingdom of Vientiane from 1707 until taken by the Thais in 1827. Pop.: 377 409 (1985).

Vierwaldstättersee (fi:r'valtʃtɛtər,ze:) *n.* the German name for (Lake) **Lucerne.**

vies (fɪs) *adj. S. African sl.* angry. [from Afrik., from Du. *vies* nasty, loathsome]

Vietnam (,vjɛt'næm) *or* **Viet Nam** *n.* a republic in SE Asia: an ancient empire, conquered by France in the 19th century; occupied by Japan (1940–45) when the Communist-led Viet-minh began resistance operations that were continued against restored French rule after 1945. In 1954 the country was divided along the 17th parallel, establishing North Vietnam (under the Viet-minh) and South Vietnam (under French control), the latter becoming the independent **Republic of Vietnam** in 1955. From 1959 the country was dominated by war between the Communist Viet-cong, supported by North Vietnam, and the South Vietnamese government; increasing numbers of U.S. forces were brought to the aid of the South Vietnamese army until a peace agreement (1973) led to the withdrawal of U.S. troops; further fighting led to the eventual defeat of the South Vietnamese government in March 1975 and in 1976 an elected National Assembly proclaimed the reunification of the country. Language: Vietnamese. Currency: dong. Capital: Hanoi. Pop.: 62 468 000 (1987). Area: 337 870 sq. km (130 452 sq. miles). Official name: **Socialist Republic of Vietnam.** —,**Vietna'mese** *adj., n.*

vieux jeu *French.* (vjø ʒø) *adj.* old-fashioned. [lit.: old game]

view (vju:) *n.* **1.** the act of seeing or observing. **2.** vision or sight, esp. range of vision: *the church is out of view.* **3.** a scene, esp. of a fine tract of countryside: *the view from the top was superb.* **4.** a pictorial representation of a scene, such as a photograph. **5.** *(sometimes pl.)* opinion: *my own view on the matter differs from yours.* **6.** (foll. by *to*) a desired end or intention: *he has a view to securing further qualifications.* **7.** a general survey of a topic, subject, etc. **8.** visual aspect or appearance: *they look the same in outward view.* **9.** a sight of a hunted animal before or during the chase. **10. in view of.** taking into consideration. **11. on view.** exhibited to the public gaze. **12. take a dim** *or* **poor view of.** to regard (something) with disfavour. **13. with a view to. a.** with the intention of. **b.** in anticipation or hope of. ~*vb.* **14.** (*tr.*) to look at. **15.** (*tr.*) to consider in a specified manner: *they view the growth of Communism with horror.* **16.** (*tr.*) to examine or inspect carefully: *to view the accounts.* **17.** (*tr.*) to contemplate: *to view the difficulties.* **18.** to watch (television). **19.** (*tr.*) to sight (a hunted animal) before or during the chase. [C15: from OF, from *veoir* to see, from L *vidēre*] —'**viewable** *adj.*

viewdata ('vju:,deɪtə) *n.* an interactive videotext service in which the consumer is linked to a computer by telephone and is thus able to select the information required. Cf. **teletext.**

viewer ('vju:ə) *n.* **1.** a person who views something, esp. television. **2.** any optical device by means of which something is viewed, esp. one used for viewing photographic transparencies.

viewfinder ('vju:,faɪndə) *n.* a device on a camera, consisting of a lens system, enabling the user to see what will be included in his photograph.

view halloo *interj.* a huntsman's cry uttered when the quarry is seen breaking cover or shortly afterwards.

viewing ('vju:ɪŋ) *n.* **1.** the act of watching television. **2.** television programmes collectively: *late-night viewing.*

viewless ('vju:lɪs) *adj.* **1.** (of windows, etc.) not affording a view. **2.** having no opinions. **3.** *Poetic.* invisible.

viewpoint ('vjuː,pɔɪnt) n. **1.** the mental attitude that determines a person's judgments. **2.** a place from which something can be viewed.

vigesimal (vaɪ'dʒɛsɪməl) adj. **1.** relating to or based on the number 20. **2.** taking place or proceeding in intervals of 20. **3.** twentieth. [C17: from L vīgēsimus, var. (infl. by vīgintī twenty) of vīcēsimus twentieth]

vigil ('vɪdʒɪl) n. **1.** a purposeful watch maintained, esp. at night, to guard, observe, pray, etc. **2.** the period of such a watch. **3.** R.C. Church, Church of England. the eve of certain major festivals, formerly observed as a night spent in prayer. [C13: from OF, from Med. L vigilia watch preceding a religious festival, from L, from vigil alert, from vigēre to be lively]

vigilance ('vɪdʒɪləns) n. **1.** the fact, quality, or condition of being vigilant. **2.** the abnormal state or condition of being unable to sleep.

vigilance committee n. (in the U.S.) a self-appointed body of citizens organized to maintain order, etc., where an efficient system of courts does not exist.

vigilant ('vɪdʒɪlənt) adj. keenly alert to or heedful of trouble or danger. [C15: from L vigilāns, from vigilāre to be watchful; see VIGIL] —'**vigilantly** adv.

vigilante (,vɪdʒɪ'læntɪ) n. **1.** a self-appointed protector of public order. **2.** U.S. a member of a vigilance committee. [C19: from Sp., from L vigilāre to keep watch]

vigilantism (,vɪdʒɪ'læntɪzəm) n. U.S. the methods, conduct, attitudes, etc., associated with vigilantes, esp. militancy or bigotry.

vignette (vɪ'njɛt) n. **1.** a small illustration placed at the beginning or end of a book or chapter. **2.** a short graceful literary essay or sketch. **3.** a photograph, drawing, etc., with edges that are shaded off. **4.** any small endearing scene, view, etc. ~vb. (tr.) **5.** to finish (a photograph, etc.) with a fading border in the form of a vignette. **6.** to portray in or as in a vignette. [C18: from F, lit.: little vine; with reference to the vine motif frequently used in embellishments to a text] —**vi'gnettist** n.

Vignola (Italian viɲ'ɲɔːla) n. **Giacomo Barozzi da** ('dʒaːkomo ba'rɔttsi da). 1507–73, Italian architect, whose cruciform design for Il Gesù, Rome, greatly influenced later Church architecture.

Vigny (French viɲi) n. **Alfred Victor de** (alfrɛd viktɔr də). 1797–1863, French romantic poet, novelist, and dramatist, noted for his pessimistic lyric verse Poèmes antiques et modernes (1826) and Les Destinées (1864), the novel Cinq-Mars (1826), and the play Chatterton (1835).

Vigo ('viːgəʊ; Spanish 'biɣo) n. a port in NW Spain, in Galicia on **Vigo Bay** (an inlet of the Atlantic): site of a British and Dutch naval victory (1702) over the French and Spanish. Pop.: 258 724 (1981).

vigoro ('vɪgə,rəʊ) n. Austral. a ball game combining elements of cricket and baseball. [C20: from VIGOUR]

vigorous ('vɪgərəs) adj. **1.** endowed with bodily or mental strength or vitality. **2.** displaying, characterized by, or performed with vigour: vigorous growth. —'**vigorously** adv.

vigour or U.S. **vigor** ('vɪgə) n. **1.** exuberant and resilient strength of body or mind. **2.** substantial effective energy or force: the vigour of the tempest. **3.** forcefulness: I was surprised by the vigour of her complaints. **4.** the capacity for survival or strong healthy growth in a plant or animal. **5.** the most active period or stage of life, manhood, etc. [C14: from OF, from L vigor, from vigēre to be lively]

Viipuri ('viːpuri) n. the Finnish name for **Vyborg.**

Vijayawada (,viːdʒaɪə'wɑːdə) n. a town in SE India, in E central Andra Pradesh on the Krishna River: Hindu pilgrimage centre. Pop.: 453 414 (1981). Former name: **Bezwada.**

Viking ('vaɪkɪŋ) n. (sometimes not cap.) **1.** Also called: **Norseman, Northman.** any of the Danes, Norwegians, and Swedes who raided by sea most of N and W Europe from the 8th to the 11th centuries. **2.** (modifier) of, relating to, or characteristic of a Viking or Vikings: a Viking ship. [C19: from ON vīkingr, prob. from vīk creek, sea inlet + -ingr (see -ING³)]

vile (vaɪl) adj. **1.** abominably wicked; shameful or evil. **2.** morally despicable; ignoble: vile accusations. **3.** disgusting to the senses or emotions; foul: a vile smell. **4.** tending to humiliate or degrade: only slaves would perform such vile tasks. **5.** unpleasant or bad: vile weather. [C13:

from OF vil, from L vīlis cheap] —'**vilely** adv. —'**vileness** n.

vilify ('vɪlɪ,faɪ) vb. **-fying, -fied.** (tr.) to revile with abusive language; malign. [C15: from LL, from L vīlis worthless + facere to make] —**vilification** (,vɪlɪfɪ'keɪʃən) n. —'**vili,fier** n.

vilipend ('vɪlɪ,pɛnd) vb. (tr.) Rare. **1.** to treat or regard with contempt. **2.** to speak slanderously of. [C15: from LL, from L vīlis worthless + pendere to esteem] —'**vili,pender** n.

villa ('vɪlə) n. **1.** (in ancient Rome) a country house, usually consisting of farm buildings and residential quarters around a courtyard. **2.** a large country residence. **3.** Brit. a detached or semidetached suburban house. [C17: via It. from L]

Villa ('viːə; Spanish 'biʎa) n. **Francisco** (fran'sisko), called *Pancho Villa*, original name *Doroteo Arango*. ?1877–1923, Mexican revolutionary leader.

Villach (German 'fɪlax) n. a city in S central Austria, on the Drava River: nearby hot mineral springs. Pop.: 52 744 (1981).

village ('vɪlɪdʒ) n. **1.** a small group of houses in a country area, larger than a hamlet. **2.** the inhabitants of such a community collectively. **3.** an incorporated municipality smaller than a town in various parts of the U.S. and Canada. **4.** (modifier) of or characteristic of a village: a village green. [C15: from OF, from ville farm, from L: VILLA] —'**villager** n.

Villahermosa (Spanish biʎaɛr'mosa) n. a town in E Mexico, capital of Tabasco state: university (1959). Pop.: 250 903 (1980). Former name: **San Juan Bautista.**

villain ('vɪlən) n. **1.** a wicked or malevolent person. **2.** (in a novel, play, etc.) the main evil character and antagonist to the hero. **3.** Often jocular. a rogue. **4.** Obs. an uncouth person; boor. [C14: from OF vilein serf, from LL vīllānus worker on a country estate, from L: VILLA] —'**villainess** fem. n.

villainous ('vɪlənəs) adj. **1.** of, like, or appropriate to a villain. **2.** very bad or disagreeable: a villainous climate. —'**villainously** adv. —'**villainousness** n.

villainy ('vɪlənɪ) n., pl. **-lainies. 1.** vicious behaviour or action. **2.** an evil or criminal act or deed. **3.** the fact or condition of being villainous.

Villa-Lobos ('viːlə'ləʊbɒs, 'vɪlə-; Portuguese 'vila'lobus) n. **Heitor** (ej'tor). 1887–1959, Brazilian composer, much of whose work is based on Brazilian folk tunes.

villanelle (,vɪlə'nɛl) n. a verse form of French origin consisting of 19 lines arranged in five tercets and a quatrain. [C16: from F, from It. villanella, from villano rustic]

Villars (French vilar) n. **Claude Louis Hector de** (klod lwi ɛktɔr də). 1653–1734, French marshal, distinguished for his command in the War of the Spanish Succession (1701–14).

-ville n. and adj. combining form. Sl., chiefly U.S. (denoting) a place, condition, or quality with a character as specified: dragsville; squaresville.

villein ('vɪlən) n. (in medieval Europe) a peasant personally bound to his lord, to whom he paid dues and services in return for his land. [C14: from OF vilein serf; see VILLAIN] —'**villeinage** n.

Villeneuve (French vilnœv) n. **Pierre Charles Jean Baptiste Silvestre de** (pjɛr ʃarl ʒã batist silvɛstrədə). 1763–1806, French admiral, defeated by Nelson at the Battle of Trafalgar (1805).

Villeurbanne (French vijœrban) n. a town in E France: an industrial suburb of E Lyons. Pop.: 116 020 (1983 est.).

Villiers ('vɪləz, 'vɪljəz) n. **George.** See (Dukes of) **Buckingham.**

Villiers de l'Isle Adam (French vilje də lil adã) n. **August, Comte de** (ogyst, kɔ̃t də). 1838–89, French poet and dramatist; pioneer of the symbolist movement. His works include Contes cruels (1883) and the play Axel (1885).

villiform ('vɪlɪ,fɔːm) adj. having the form of a villus or a series of villi. [C19: from NL villiformis, from L villus shaggy hair + -FORM]

Villon (French vijɔ̃) n. **1. François** (frãswa). born 1431, French poet. His poems, such as those in Le Petit testament (?1456) and Le Grand testament (1461), are mostly ballades and rondeaux, verse forms that he revitalized. He was banished in 1463, after which nothing more was heard of him. **2. Jacques** (ʒak), real name Gaston

Duchamp. 1875–1963, French cubist painter and engraver.

villus ('vıləs) *n., pl.* **villi** ('vılaı). (*usually pl.*) **1.** *Zool., anat.* any of the numerous finger-like projections of the mucous membrane lining the small intestine of many vertebrates. **2.** any similar membranous process. **3.** *Bot.* any of various hairlike outgrowths. [C18: from L: shaggy hair] **—villosity** (vı'lɒsıtı) *n.* **—'villous** *adj.*

Vilnius *or* **Vilnyus** ('vılnıʊs) *n.* a city in the W Soviet Union, capital of the Lithuanian SSR: passed to Russia in 1795; under Polish rule (1920–39); university (1578). Pop.: 566 000 (1987). Russian name: **Vilna** ('vılna). Polish name: **Wilno.**

vim (vım) *n. Sl.* exuberant vigour and energy. [C19: from L, from *vis;* rel. to Gk *is* strength]

Viminal ('vımın³l) *n.* one of the seven hills on which ancient Rome was built. [from L *Vīminālis Collis* the Viminal Hill, from *vīminālis* of osiers, from *vīmen* an osier, referring to the willow grove on the hill]

vimineous (vı'mınıəs) *adj. Bot.* having, producing, or resembling long flexible shoots. [C17: from L *vimineus* made of osiers, from *vīmen* flexible shoot]

vina ('viːnə) *n.* a stringed musical instrument, esp. of India, related to the sitar. [C18: from Hindi *bīnā,* from Sansk. *vīnā*]

vinaceous (vaı'neıʃəs) *adj.* **1.** of, relating to, or containing wine. **2.** having a colour suggestive of red wine. [C17: from LL *vināceus,* from L *vīnum* wine]

Viña del Mar (*Spanish* 'bıɲa ðɛl 'mar) *n.* a city and resort in central Chile, just north of Valparaíso on the Pacific: the second largest city of Chile. Pop.: 315 947 (1985).

vinaigrette (,vıneı'grɛt) *n.* **1.** Also called: **vinegarette.** a small decorative bottle or box with a perforated top, used for holding smelling salts, etc. **2.** Also called: **vinaigrette sauce.** a salad dressing made from oil and vinegar with seasonings; French dressing. [C17: from F, from *vinaigre* VINEGAR]

Vincennes (*French* vɛ̃sɛn; *English* vın'sɛnz) *n.* a suburb of E Paris: 14th-century castle. Pop.: 44 256 (1983 est.).

Vincent de Paul ('vınsənt də 'pɔːl; *French* vɛ̃sɑ̃ dəpɔl) *n.* **Saint.** ?1581–1660, French Roman Catholic priest, who founded two charitable orders, the Lazarists (1625) and the Sisters of Charity (1634). Feast day: Sept. 27.

Vincent's angina *or* **disease** *n.* an ulcerative bacterial infection of the mouth, esp. involving the throat and tonsils. [C20: after J. H. *Vincent* (died 1950), F bacteriologist]

Vinci ('vıntʃı) *n.* See **Leonardo da Vinci.**

vincible ('vınsıb³l) *adj. Rare.* capable of being defeated or overcome. [C16: from L *vincibilis,* from *vincere* to conquer] **—,vinci'bility** *n.*

vincristine (vın'krıstiːn) *n.* an alkaloid used to treat leukaemia, derived from the tropical shrub Madagascar periwinkle. [C20: from NL *Vinca* genus name of the plant + L *crista* crest + -INE²]

vinculum ('vıŋkjʊləm) *n., pl.* **-la** (-lə). **1.** a horizontal line drawn above a group of mathematical terms, used as an alternative to parentheses in mathematical expressions, as in $x + \overline{y-z}$ which is equivalent to $x + (y - z)$. **2.** *Anat.* any bandlike structure, esp. one uniting two or more parts. [C17: from L: bond, from *vincīre* to bind]

Vindhya Pradesh ('vındjə) *n.* a former state of central India: merged with the reorganized Madhya Pradesh in 1956.

Vindhya Range *or* **Mountains** *n.* a mountain range in central India: separates the Ganges basin from the Deccan, marking the limits of northern and peninsular India. Greatest height: 1113 m (3651 ft.).

vindicable ('vındıkəb³l) *adj.* capable of being vindicated; justifiable. **—,vindica'bility** *n.*

vindicate ('vındı,keıt) *vb.* (*tr.*) **1.** to clear from guilt, blame, etc., as by evidence or argument. **2.** to provide justification for: *his promotion vindicated his unconventional attitude.* **3.** to uphold or defend (a cause, etc.): *to vindicate a claim.* [C17: from L *vindicāre,* from *vindex* claimant] **—'vindi,cator** *n.* **—'vindi,catory** *adj.*

vindication (,vındı'keıʃən) *n.* **1.** the act of vindicating or the condition of being vindicated. **2.** a fact, evidence, etc., that serves to vindicate a claim.

vindictive (vın'dıktıv) *adj.* **1.** disposed to seek vengeance. **2.** characterized by spite or rancour. **3.** *English law.* (of damages) in excess of the compensation due to the plaintiff and imposed in punishment of the defendant.

[C17: from L *vindicta* revenge, from *vindicāre* to VINDICATE] **—vin'dictively** *adv.* **—vin'dictiveness** *n.*

vin du pays *French.* (vɛ̃ du pei) *n., pl.* **vins du pays.** local wine.

vine (vaın) *n.* **1.** any of various plants, esp. the grapevine, having long flexible stems that creep along the ground or climb by clinging to a support by means of tendrils, leafstalks, etc. **2.** the stem of such a plant. [C13: from OF, from L *vīnea* vineyard, from *vīnum* wine] **—'viny** *adj.*

vinedresser ('vaın,drɛsə) *n.* a person who prunes, tends, or cultivates grapevines.

vinegar ('vınıgə) *n.* **1.** a sour-tasting liquid consisting of impure dilute acetic acid, made by fermentation of beer, wine, or cider. It is used as a condiment or preservative. **2.** sourness or peevishness of temper, speech, etc. [C13: from OF, from L *vīnum* WINE + *aigre* sour, from L *acer*] **—'vinegarish** *adj.* **—'vinegary** *adj.*

Vineland ('vaınlənd) *n.* a variant spelling of **Vinland.**

vinery ('vaınərı) *n., pl.* **-eries. 1.** a hothouse for growing grapes. **2.** another name for a **vineyard. 3.** vines collectively.

vineyard ('vınjəd) *n.* a plantation of grapevines, esp. where wine grapes are produced. [OE *wīngeard;* see VINE, YARD²]

vingt-et-un *French.* (vɛ̃ te œ̃) *n.* another name for **pontoon².** [lit.: twenty-one]

vini- *or before a vowel* **vin-** *combining form.* indicating wine: *viniculture.* [from L *vīnum*]

viniculture ('vını,kʌltʃə) *n.* the process or business of growing grapes and making wine. **—,vini'cultural** *adj.* **—,vini'culturist** *n.*

viniferous (vı'nıfərəs) *adj.* wine-producing.

Vinland ('vınlənd) *or* **Vineland** *n.* the stretch of the E coast of North America visited by Leif Ericson and other Vikings from about 1000.

Vinnitsa (*Russian* 'vinnıtsə) *n.* a city in the SW Soviet Union, in the central Ukrainian SSR: passed from Polish to Russian rule in 1793. Pop.: 383 000 (1987).

vino ('viːnəʊ) *n., pl.* **-nos.** an informal word for **wine.** [jocular use of It. or Sp. *vino*]

vin ordinaire *French.* (vɛ̃ ɔrdinɛr) *n., pl.* **vins ordinaires** (vɛ̃z ɔrdinɛr). cheap table wine, esp. French.

vinosity (vı'nɒsıtı) *n.* the distinctive and essential quality and flavour of wine. [C17: from LL *vīnōsitas,* from L *vīnōsus* VINOUS]

vinous ('vaınəs) *adj.* **1.** of or characteristic of wine. **2.** indulging in or indicative of indulgence in wine. [C17: from L *vīnum* wine]

vintage ('vıntıdʒ) *n.* **1.** the wine obtained from a harvest of grapes, esp. in an outstandingly good year. **2.** the harvest from which such a wine is obtained. **3. a.** the harvesting of wine grapes. **b.** the season of harvesting these grapes or for making wine. **4.** a time of origin: *a car of Edwardian vintage.* **5.** *Inf.* a group of people or objects of the same period: *a fashion of last season's vintage.* *~adj.* **6.** (of wine) of an outstandingly good year. **7.** representative of the best and most typical: *vintage Shakespeare.* **8.** of lasting interest and importance; classic: *vintage films.* **9.** old-fashioned; dated. [C15: from OF *vendage* (infl. by *vintener* VINTNER), from L *vindēmia,* from *vīnum* WINE, grape + *dēmere* to take away]

vintage car *n. Chiefly Brit.* an old car, esp. one constructed between 1919 and 1930.

vintager ('vıntıdʒə) *n.* a grape harvester.

vintner ('vıntnə) *n.* a wine merchant. [C15: from OF *vinetier,* from Med. L, from L *vīnētum* vineyard]

vinyl ('vaınıl) *n.* **1.** (*modifier*) of or containing the monovalent group of atoms $CH_2{:}CH-$: *vinyl chloride.* **2.** (*modifier*) of or made of a vinyl resin: *a vinyl raincoat.* **3.** any vinyl resin or plastic, esp. PVC. **4.** (collectively) conventional records made of vinyl as opposed to compact discs. [C19: from VINI- + -YL]

vinyl acetate *n.* a colourless volatile liquid unsaturated ester that polymerizes readily in light and is used for making polyvinyl acetate.

vinyl chloride *n.* a colourless flammable gaseous unsaturated compound made by the chlorination of ethylene and used as a refrigerant and in the manufacture of PVC.

vinyl resin *or* **polymer** *n.* any one of a class of thermoplastic materials, esp. PVC and polyvinyl acetate, made by polymerizing vinyl compounds.

viol ('vaɪəl) *n.* any of a family of stringed musical instruments that preceded the violin family, consisting of a fretted fingerboard, a body rather like that of a violin but having a flat back and six strings, played with a curved bow. [C15: from OF *viole*, from OProvençal *viola;* see VI-OLA[1]]

viola[1] (vɪ'əʊlə) *n.* **1.** a bowed stringed instrument, the alto of the violin family; held beneath the chin when played. **2.** any of various instruments of the viol family, such as the viola da gamba. [C18: from It., prob. from OProvençal, from ?]

viola[2] ('vaɪələ, vaɪ'əʊ-) *n.* any of various temperate perennial herbaceous plants, the flowers of which have showy irregular petals, white, yellow, blue, or mauve in colour. [C15: from L: violet]

viola clef (vɪ'əʊlə) *n.* another term for **alto clef.**

viola da gamba (vɪ'əʊlə də 'gæmbə) *n.* the second largest and lowest member of the viol family. [C18: from It., lit.: viol for the leg]

viola d'amore (vɪ'əʊlə dæ'mɔːrɪ) *n.* an instrument of the viol family having no frets, seven strings, and a set of sympathetic strings. [C18: from It., lit.: viol of love]

violate ('vaɪə,leɪt) *vb.* (*tr.*) **1.** to break, disregard, or infringe (a law, agreement, etc.). **2.** to rape or otherwise sexually assault. **3.** to disturb rudely or improperly. **4.** to treat irreverently or disrespectfully: *he violated a sanctuary.* [C15: from L *violāre* to do violence to, from *vīs* strength] —'**violable** *adj.* —,**vio'lation** *n.* —'**vio,lator** *or* 'vio,**later** *n.*

violence ('vaɪələns) *n.* **1.** the exercise or an instance of physical force, usually effecting or intended to effect injuries, destruction, etc. **2.** powerful, untamed, or devastating force: *the violence of the sea.* **3.** great strength of feeling, as in language, etc. **4.** an unjust, unwarranted, or unlawful display of force. **5. do violence to. a.** to inflict harm upon: *they did violence to the prisoners.* **b.** to distort the sense or intention of: *the reporters did violence to my speech.* [C13: via OF from L *violentia* impetuosity, from *violentus* VIOLENT]

violent ('vaɪələnt) *adj.* **1.** marked or caused by great physical force or violence: *a violent stab.* **2.** (of a person) tending to the use of violence, esp. in order to injure or intimidate others. **3.** marked by intensity of any kind: *a violent clash of colours.* **4.** characterized by an undue use of force. **5.** caused by or displaying strong or undue mental or emotional force. [C14: from L *violentus*, prob. from *vīs* strength] —'**violently** *adv.*

violent storm *n* a wind of force 11 on the Beaufort scale, reaching speeds of 64 to 72 mph.

violet ('vaɪəlɪt) *n.* **1.** any of various temperate perennial herbaceous plants of the genus *Viola,* such as the **sweet** (or **garden**) **violet,** having mauve or bluish flowers with irregular showy petals. **2.** any other plant of the genus *Viola,* such as the wild pansy. **3.** any of various similar but unrelated plants, such as the African violet. **4. a.** any of a group of colours that have a purplish-blue hue. They lie at one end of the visible spectrum. **b.** (*as adj.*): *a violet dress.* **5.** a dye or pigment of or producing these colours. **6.** violet clothing: *dressed in violet.* [C14: from OF *violete* a little violet, from L *viola* violet]

violin (,vaɪə'lɪn) *n.* a bowed stringed instrument, the highest member of the violin family, consisting of a fingerboard, a hollow wooden body with waisted sides, and a sounding board connected to the back by means of a soundpost that also supports the bridge. It has two f-shaped sound holes cut in the belly. [C16: from It. *violino* a little viola, from VIOLA[1]]

violinist (,vaɪə'lɪnɪst) *n.* a person who plays the violin.

violist ('vaɪəlɪst) *n.* a person who plays the viol.

Viollet-le-Duc (*French* vjɔlɛlədyk) *n.* **Eugène Emmanuel** (œʒɛn ɛmanɥɛl). 1814–79, French architect and leader of the Gothic revival in France, noted for his dictionary of French architecture (1854–68) and for his restoration of medieval buildings.

violoncello (,vaɪələn'tʃɛləʊ) *n., pl.* -**los.** the full name for **cello.** [C18: from It., from *violone* large viol + *-cello,* dim. suffix] —,**violon'cellist** *n.*

VIP *abbrev. for* very important person.

viper ('vaɪpə) *n.* **1.** any of a family of venomous Old World snakes having hollow fangs in the upper jaw that are used to inject venom. **2.** any of various other snakes, such as the horned viper. **3.** a malicious or treacherous person. [C16: from L *vīpera,* ?from *vīvus* living + *parere*

to bear, referring to a tradition that the viper was viviparous]

viperous ('vaɪpərəs) *or* **viperish** *adj.* **1.** Also: **viperine** ('vaɪpə,raɪn). of or resembling a viper. **2.** malicious.

viper's bugloss *n.* a Eurasian weed, having blue flowers and pink buds. Also called: (U.S.) **blueweed,** (Austral.) **Paterson's curse.**

virago (vɪ'rɑːgəʊ) *n., pl.* -**goes** *or* -**gos. 1.** a loud, violent, and ill-tempered woman. **2.** *Arch.* a strong or warlike woman. [OE, from L: a manlike maiden, from *vir* a man] —**vi'rago-,like** *adj.*

viral ('vaɪrəl) *adj.* of or caused by a virus.

Virchow (*German* 'fɪrço) *n.* **Rudolf Ludwig Karl** ('ruːdɔlf 'luːtvɪç karl). 1821–1902, German pathologist, who is considered the founder of modern (cellular) pathology.

virelay ('vɪrɪ,leɪ) *n.* an old French verse form, rarely used in English, having stanzas of short lines with two rhymes throughout and two opening lines recurring at intervals. [C14: from OF *virelai,* prob. from *vireli* (associated with *lai* LAY[4]), word used as a refrain]

Viren ('vɪərən) *n.* **Lasse** ('læsɪ). born 1949, Finnish distance runner: winner of the 5000 metres and the 10 000 metres in the 1972 and 1976 Olympic Games.

vireo ('vɪrɪəʊ) *n., pl.* **vireos.** any of a family of insectivorous American songbirds having an olive-grey back with pale underparts. [C19: from L: a bird, prob. a greenfinch; cf. *virēre* to be green]

vires ('vaɪriːz) *n.* the plural of **vis.**

virescent (vɪ'rɛsᵊnt) *adj.* greenish or becoming green. [C19: from L *virescere,* from *virēre* to be green] —**vi'rescence** *n.*

virgate[1] ('vɜːgɪt, -geɪt) *adj.* long, straight, and thin; rod-shaped: *virgate stems.* [C19: from L *virgātus* made of twigs, from *virga* a rod]

virgate[2] ('vɜːgɪt, -geɪt) *n. Brit.* an obsolete measure of land area, usually taken as equivalent to 30 acres. [C17: from Med. L *virgāta (terrae)* a rod's measurement (of land), from L *virga* rod; translation of OE *gierd landes* a yard of land]

Virgil *or* **Vergil** ('vɜːdʒɪl) *n.* Latin name *Publius Vergilius Maro.* 70–19 B.C., Roman poet, patronized by Maecenas. The *Eclogues* (42–37), ten pastoral poems, and the *Georgics* (37–30), four books on the art of farming, established Virgil as the foremost poet of his age. His masterpiece is the *Aeneid* (30–19). —**Vir'gilian** *or* **Ver'gilian** *adj.*

virgin ('vɜːdʒɪn) *n.* **1.** a person, esp. a woman, who has never had sexual intercourse. **2.** an unmarried woman who has taken a religious vow of chastity. **3.** any female animal that has never mated. **4.** a female insect that produces offspring by parthenogenesis. ~*adj.* (*usually prenominal*) **5.** of, suitable for, or characteristic of a virgin or virgins. **6.** pure and natural, uncorrupted or untouched: *virgin purity.* **7.** not yet cultivated, explored, exploited, etc., by man: *the virgin forests.* **8.** being the first or happening for the first time. **9.** (of a metal) made from an ore rather than from scrap. **10.** occurring naturally in a pure and uncombined form: *virgin silver.* [C13: from OF *virgine,* from L *virgō* virgin]

Virgin[1] ('vɜːdʒɪn) *n.* **1. the.** See **Virgin Mary. 2.** a statue or other artistic representation of the Virgin Mary.

Virgin[2] ('vɜːdʒɪn) *n.* **the.** the constellation Virgo, the sixth sign of the zodiac.

virginal[1] ('vɜːdʒɪnᵊl) *adj.* **1.** of, characterized by, or maintaining a state of virginity; chaste. **2.** extremely pure or fresh. [C15: from L *virginālis* maidenly, from *virgō* virgin] —'**virginally** *adv.*

virginal[2] ('vɜːdʒɪnᵊl) *n.* (*often pl.*) a smaller version of the harpsichord, but oblong in shape, having one manual and no pedals. [C16: prob. from L *virginālis* VIRGINAL[1], ? because it was played largely by young ladies] —'**virginalist** *n.*

Virgin Birth *n.* the doctrine that Jesus Christ was conceived solely by the direct intervention of the Holy Spirit so that Mary remained miraculously a virgin during and after his birth.

Virginia (və'dʒɪnɪə) *n.* a state of the eastern U.S., on the Atlantic: site of the first permanent English settlement in North America; consists of a low-lying deeply indented coast rising inland to the Piedmont plateau and the Blue Ridge Mountains. Capital: Richmond. Pop.: 5 787 000

(1986 est.). Area: 103 030 sq. km (39 780 sq. miles). Abbrevs.: **Va.** or (with zip code) **VA** —**Vir'ginian** *adj.*, *n.*

Virginia Beach *n.* a city and resort in SE Virginia, on the Atlantic. Pop.: 262 199 (1980).

Virginia creeper *n.* a woody vine of North America, having tendrils with adhesive tips, bluish-black berry-like fruits, and compound leaves that turn red in autumn: widely planted for ornament.

Virginia stock *n.* a Mediterranean plant cultivated for its white and pink flowers.

Virgin Islands *pl. n.* a group of about 100 small islands (14 inhabited) in the West Indies, east of Puerto Rico: discovered by Columbus (1493); consists of the British Virgin Islands in the east and the Virgin Islands of the United States in the west and south. Area: 497 sq. km (192 sq. miles).

Virgin Islands of the United States *pl. n.* a territory of the U.S. in the Caribbean, consisting of islands west and south of the British Virgin Islands: purchased from Denmark in 1917 for their strategic importance. Capital: Charlotte Amalie. Pop.: 110 800 (1985). Area: 344 sq. km (133 sq. miles). Former name: **Danish West Indies.**

virginity (vǝ'dʒɪnɪtɪ) *n.* **1.** the condition or fact of being a virgin. **2.** the condition of being untouched, unsullied, etc.

virginium (vǝ'dʒɪnɪǝm) *n. Chem.* a former name for **francium.**

Virgin Mary *n.* Mary, the mother of Christ. Also called: the **Virgin.**

virgin's-bower *n.* any of several American varieties of clematis.

virgin wool *n.* wool that is being processed or woven for the first time.

Virgo ('vɜːgǝʊ) *n.*, *Latin genitive* **Virginis** ('vɜːdʒɪnɪs). **1.** *Astron.* a large constellation on the celestial equator. **2.** *Astrol.* Also called: **the Virgin.** the sixth sign of the zodiac. The sun is in this sign between about Aug. 23 and Sept. 22. [C14: from L]

virgo intacta ('vɜːgǝʊ ɪn'tæktǝ) *n.* a girl or woman whose hymen is unbroken. [L, lit.: untouched virgin]

virgule ('vɜːgjuːl) *n. Printing.* another name for **solidus.** [C19: from F: comma, from L *virgula* dim. of *virga* rod]

viridescent (ˌvɪrɪ'dɛsᵊnt) *adj.* greenish or tending to become green. [C19: from LL *viridescere*, from L *viridis* green] —ˌviri'descence *n.*

viridian (vɪ'rɪdɪǝn) *n.* a green pigment consisting of a hydrated form of chromic oxide. [C19: from L *viridis* green]

viridity (vɪ'rɪdɪtɪ) *n.* **1.** the quality or state of being green. **2.** innocence, youth, or freshness. [C15: from L *viriditās*, from *viridis* green]

virile ('vɪraɪl) *adj.* **1.** of or having the characteristics of an adult male. **2.** (of a male) possessing high sexual drive and capacity for sexual intercourse. **3.** of or capable of copulation or procreation. **4.** strong, forceful, or vigorous. [C15: from L *virilis* manly, from *vir* a man; rel. to OE *wer* man] —**virility** (vɪ'rɪlɪtɪ) *n.*

virilism ('vɪrɪˌlɪzǝm) *n. Med.* the abnormal development in a woman of male secondary sex characteristics.

virology (vaɪ'rɒlǝdʒɪ) *n.* the branch of medicine concerned with the study of viruses. —**virological** (ˌvaɪrǝ'lɒdʒɪkᵊl) *adj.*

virtu *or* **vertu** (vɜː'tuː) *n.* **1.** a taste or love for curios or works of fine art. **2.** such objects collectively. **3.** the quality of being appealing to a connoisseur (esp. in **articles of virtu; objects of virtu**). [C18: from It. *virtù*; see VIRTUE]

virtual ('vɜːtʃʊǝl) *adj.* **1.** having the essence or effect but not the appearance or form of: *a virtual revolution.* **2.** *Physics.* being or involving a virtual image: *a virtual focus.* **3.** *Computers.* of or relating to virtual storage: *virtual memory.* [C14: from Med. L *virtuālis* effective, from L *virtūs* VIRTUE] —ˌvirtu'ality *n.*

virtual image *n.* an optical image formed by the apparent divergence of rays from a point, rather than their actual divergence from a point.

virtually ('vɜːtʃʊǝlɪ) *adv.* in effect though not in fact; practically; nearly.

virtual storage *or* **memory** *n.* a computer system in which the size of the memory is increased by transferring sections of a program from a large capacity backing store, such as a disk, into the smaller core memory as they are required.

virtue ('vɜːtjuː) *n.* **1.** the quality or practice of moral excellence or righteousness. **2.** a particular moral excellence: *the virtue of tolerance.* **3.** any of the cardinal virtues (prudence, justice, fortitude, and temperance) or theological virtues (faith, hope, and charity). **4.** any admirable quality or trait. **5.** chastity, esp. in women. **6.** *Arch.* an effective, active, or inherent power. **7. by** *or* **in virtue of.** by reason of. **8. make a virtue of necessity.** to acquiesce in doing something unpleasant with a show of grace because one must do it in any case. [C13 *vertu*, from OF, from L *virtūs* manliness, courage]

virtuoso (ˌvɜːtjʊ'ǝʊzǝʊ, -sǝʊ) *n.*, *pl.* **-sos** *or* **-si** (-siː). **1.** a consummate master of musical technique and artistry. **2.** a person who has a masterly or dazzling skill or technique in any field of activity. **3.** a connoisseur or collector of art objects. **4.** (*modifier*) showing masterly skill or brilliance: *a virtuoso performance.* [C17: from It.: skilled, from LL *virtuōsus* good, virtuous] —**virtuosic** (ˌvɜːtjʊ'ɒsɪk) *adj.* —ˌvirtu'osity *n.*

virtuous ('vɜːtʃʊǝs) *adj.* **1.** characterized by or possessing virtue or moral excellence. **2.** (of women) chaste or virginal. —'**virtuously** *adv.*

virulent ('vɪrʊlǝnt) *adj.* **1. a.** (of a microorganism) extremely infective. **b.** (of a disease) having a violent effect. **2.** extremely poisonous, injurious, etc. **3.** extremely bitter, hostile, etc. [C14: from L *virulentus* full of poison, from *virus* poison] —'**virulence** *or* '**virulency** *n.* —'**virulently** *adv.*

virus ('vaɪrǝs) *n.*, *pl.* **-ruses. 1.** any of a group of submicroscopic entities consisting of a single nucleic acid surrounded by a protein coat and capable of replication only within the cells of animals and plants. **2.** *Inf.* a disease caused by a virus. **3.** any corrupting or infecting influence. **4.** *Computers.* an unauthorized program that inserts itself into a computer system, and then propagates itself to other computers via networks or disks; when activated it interferes with the operation of the computer. [C16: from L: slime, poisonous liquid]

vis *Latin.* (VIS) *n.*, *pl.* ***vires.*** power, force, or strength.

visa ('viːzǝ) *n.*, *pl.* **-sas. 1.** an endorsement in a passport or similar document, signifying that the document is in order and permitting its bearer to travel into or through the country of the government issuing it. ~*vb.* **-saing, -saed. 2.** (*tr.*) to enter a visa into (a passport). [C19: via F from L: things seen, from *visus*, p.p. of *vidēre* to see]

visage ('vɪzɪdʒ) *n. Chiefly literary.* **1.** face or countenance. **2.** appearance. [C13: from OF: aspect, from *vis* face, from L *visus* appearance]

-visaged *adj.* (*in combination*) having a visage as specified: *flat-visaged.*

Visakhapatnam (vɪˌsɑːkǝ'pʌtnǝm) *n.* a variant spelling of **Vishakhapatnam.**

vis-à-vis (ˌviːzɑː'viː) *prep.* **1.** in relation to. **2.** face to face with. ~*adv.*, *adj.* **3.** face to face; opposite. ~*n.*, *pl.* **vis-à-vis. 4.** a person or thing that is situated opposite to another. **5.** a person who corresponds to another in office, capacity, etc. [C18: F, from *vis* face]

Visayan Islands *pl. n.* a group of seven large and several hundred small islands in the central Philippines. Chief islands: Negros and Panay. Pop.: 11 112 523 (1980). Area: about 61 000 sq. km (23 535 sq. miles). Spanish name: **Bisayas.**

Visby (*Swedish* 'viːsbyː) *n.* a port in SE Sweden, on NW Gotland Island in the Baltic: an early member of the Hanseatic League and major N European commercial centre in the Middle Ages. Pop.: 20 442 (1984).

Visc. *abbrev. for* Viscount *or* Viscountess.

viscacha (vɪs'kætʃǝ) *n.* a gregarious burrowing rodent of southern South America, similar to but larger than the chinchillas. [C17: from Sp., from Quechua *wiskácha*]

viscera ('vɪsǝrǝ) *pl. n.*, *sing.* **viscus. 1.** *Anat.* the large internal organs of the body collectively, esp. those in the abdominal cavity. **2.** (less formally) the intestines; guts. [C17: from L: entrails, pl. of *viscus* internal organ]

visceral ('vɪsǝrǝl) *adj.* **1.** of or affecting the viscera. **2.** characterized by instinct rather than intellect. —'**viscerally** *adv.*

viscid ('vɪsɪd) *adj.* **1.** cohesive and sticky. **2.** (esp. of a leaf) covered with a sticky substance. [C17: from LL *viscidus* sticky, from L *viscum* mistletoe, birdlime] —**vis'cidity** *n.*

Visconti (*Italian* vis'konti) *n.* **1.** the ruling family of Milan from 1277 to 1447. **2. Luchino,** real name *Luchino*

Visconti de Modrone. 1906–76, Italian stage and film director, whose films include *Ossessione* (1942). His other films include *The Leopard* (1963), *Death in Venice* (1970), and *The Innocents* (1976).

viscose ('vɪskəʊs) *n.* **1. a.** a viscous orange-brown solution obtained by dissolving cellulose in sodium hydroxide and carbon disulphide. It can be converted back to cellulose by an acid, as in the manufacture of rayon and cellophane. **b.** (*as modifier*): *viscose rayon.* **2.** rayon made from this material. [C19: from LL *viscōsus* full of birdlime, sticky, from *viscum* birdlime]

viscosity (vɪs'kɒsɪtɪ) *n., pl.* **-ties. 1.** the state or property of being viscous. **2.** *Physics.* **a.** the extent to which a fluid resists a tendency to flow. **b.** Also called: **absolute viscosity.** a measure of this resistance, measured in newton seconds per metre squared. Symbol: η

viscount ('vaɪkaʊnt) *n.* **1.** (in the British Isles) a nobleman ranking below an earl and above a baron. **2.** (in various countries) a son or younger brother of a count. **3.** (in medieval Europe) the deputy of a count. [C14: from OF, from Med. L, from LL *vice-* VICE³ + *comes* COUNT²] —'**viscountcy** *or* '**viscounty** *n.*

viscountess ('vaɪkaʊntɪs) *n.* **1.** the wife or widow of a viscount. **2.** a woman who holds the rank of viscount in her own right.

viscous ('vɪskəs) *adj.* **1.** (of liquids) thick and sticky. **2.** having or involving viscosity. [C14: from LL *viscōsus;* see VISCOSE] —'**viscously** *adv.*

viscus ('vɪskəs) *n.* the singular of **viscera.**

vise (vaɪs) *n., vb. U.S.* a variant spelling of **vice².**

Viseu (*Portuguese* vi'zeu) *n.* a city in N central Portugal: 12th-century cathedral. Pop.: 84 576 (1981).

Vishakhapatnam (vɪˌʃɑːkə'pʌtnəm), **Visakhapatnam,** *or* **Vizagapatam** *n.* a port in E India, in NE Andhra Pradesh on the Bay of Bengal: shipbuilding and oil-refining industries. Pop.: 558 117 (1981).

Vishinsky (*Russian* vi'ʃinskij) *n.* a variant spelling of (Andrei Yanuaryevich) **Vyshinsky.**

Vishnu ('vɪʃnuː) *n. Hinduism.* the Pervader or Sustainer, originally a solar deity occupying a secondary place in the Hindu pantheon, later the saviour appearing in many incarnations. [C17: from Sansk.*Visnu,* lit.: the one who works everywhere] —'**Vishnuism** *n.* —'**Vishnuite** *n., adj.*

visibility (ˌvɪzɪ'bɪlɪtɪ) *n.* **1.** the condition or fact of being visible. **2.** clarity of vision or relative possibility of seeing. **3.** the range of vision: *visibility is 500 yards.*

visible ('vɪzɪbəl) *adj.* **1.** capable of being perceived by the eye. **2.** capable of being perceived by the mind: *no visible dangers.* **3.** available: *the visible resources.* **4.** of or relating to the balance of trade: *visible transactions.* [C14: from L *visibilis,* from *vidēre* to see] —'**visibly** *adv.*

visible balance *n.* another name for **balance of trade.**

visible radiation *n.* electromagnetic radiation that causes the sensation of sight; light.

vision ('vɪʒən) *n.* **1.** the act, faculty, or manner of perceiving with the eye; sight. **2. a.** the image on a television screen. **b.** (*as modifier*): *vision control.* **3.** the ability or an instance of great perception, esp. of future developments: *a man of vision.* **4.** mystical or religious experience of seeing some supernatural event, person, etc.: *the vision of St John of the Cross.* **5.** that which is seen, esp. in such a mystical experience. **6.** (*sometimes pl.*) a vivid mental image produced by the imagination: *he had visions of becoming famous.* **7.** a person or thing of extraordinary beauty. [C13: from L *visiō* sight, from *vidēre* to see]

visionary ('vɪʒənərɪ) *adj.* **1.** marked by vision or foresight: *a visionary leader.* **2.** incapable of being realized or effected. **3.** (of people) characterized by idealistic or radical ideas, esp. impractical ones. **4.** given to having visions. **5.** of, of the nature of, or seen in visions. *~n., pl.* **-aries. 6.** a visionary person.

vision mixer *n. Television.* **1.** the person who selects and manipulates the television signals from cameras, film, etc., to make the composite programme. **2.** the equipment used for vision mixing.

visit ('vɪzɪt) *vb.* **1.** to go or come to see (a person, place, etc.). **2.** to stay with (someone) as a guest. **3.** to go or come to (an institution, place, etc.) for the purpose of inspecting or examining. **4.** (*tr.*) (of a disease, disaster, etc.) to afflict. **5.** (*tr.; foll. by upon or on*) to inflict (punishment, etc.). **6.** (often foll. by *with*) *U.S. & Canad. inf.*

to chat (with someone). *~n.* **7.** the act or an instance of visiting. **8.** a stay as a guest. **9.** a professional or official call. **10.** a formal call for the purpose of inspection or examination. **11.** *International law.* the right of an officer of a belligerent state to stop and search neutral ships in war to verify their nationality and ascertain whether they carry contraband. **12.** *U.S. & Canad. inf.* a chat. [C13: from L *visitāre* to go to see, from *visere* to examine, from *vidēre* to see] —'**visitable** *adj.*

visitant ('vɪzɪtənt) *n.* **1.** a ghost; apparition. **2.** a visitor or guest, usually from far away. **3.** Also called: **visitor.** a migratory bird that is present in a particular region only at certain times: *a summer visitant.* [C16: from L *visitāns,* from *visitāre;* see VISIT]

visitation (ˌvɪzɪ'teɪʃən) *n.* **1.** an official call or visit for the purpose of inspecting or examining an institution. **2.** a visiting of punishment or reward from heaven. **3.** any disaster or catastrophe: *a visitation of the plague.* **4.** an appearance or arrival of a supernatural being. **5.** *Inf.* an unduly prolonged social call.

Visitation (ˌvɪzɪ'teɪʃən) *n.* **1. a.** the visit made by the Virgin Mary to her cousin Elizabeth (Luke 1:39–56). **b.** the Church festival commemorating this, held on July 2. **2.** a religious order of nuns, the **Order of the Visitation,** founded in 1610 and dedicated to contemplation.

visiting card *n. Brit.* a small card bearing the name and usually the address of a person, esp. for giving to business or social acquaintances.

visiting fireman *n. U.S. inf.* a visitor whose presence is noticed because he is an important figure, a lavish spender, etc.

visitor ('vɪzɪtə) *n.* **1.** a person who pays a visit. **2.** another name for **visitant** (sense 3).

visitor centre *n.* another term for **interpretive centre.**

Vislinsky Zaliv (*Russian* vis'linski 'zaːlif) *n.* a transliteration of the Russian name for **Vistula** (sense 2).

visor *or* **vizor** ('vaɪzə) *n.* **1.** a piece of armour fixed or hinged to the helmet to protect the face and furnished with slits for the eyes. **2.** another name for **peak** (on a cap). **3.** a small movable screen used as protection against glare from the sun, esp. one attached above the windscreen of a motor vehicle. **4.** *Arch. or literary.* a mask or any other means of disguise. [C14: from Anglo-F *viser,* from OF *visiere,* from *vis* face; see VISAGE] —'**visored** *or* '**vizored** *adj.*

vista ('vɪstə) *n.* **1.** a view, esp. through a long narrow avenue of trees, buildings, etc., or such a passage or avenue itself. **2.** a comprehensive mental view of a distant time or a lengthy series of events. [C17: from It., from *vedere* to see, from L *vidēre*] —'**vistaed** *adj.*

Vistula ('vɪstjʊlə) *n.* **1.** a river in central and N Poland, rising in the Carpathian Mountains and flowing generally north and northwest past Warsaw and Torun, then northeast to enter the Baltic via an extensive delta region. Length: 1090 km (677 miles). Polish name: **Wisla.** German name: **Weichsel. 2. Lagoon.** a shallow lagoon on the SW coast of the Baltic Sea, between Danzig and Kaliningrad, crossed by the border between Poland and the Soviet Union. German name: **Frisches Haff.** Polish name: **Wislany Zalew.** Russian name: **Vislinsky Zaliv.**

visual ('vɪʒʊəl, -zjʊ-) *adj.* **1.** of, done by, or used in seeing: *visual powers.* **2.** another word for **optical. 3.** capable of being seen; visible. **4.** of, occurring as, or induced by a mental image. *~n.* **5.** a sketch to show the proposed layout of an advertisement, as in a newspaper. **6.** (*often pl.*) a photograph, film, or other display material. [C15: from LL *visuālis,* from L *visus* sight, from *vidēre* to see] —'**visually** *adv.*

visual aids *pl. n.* devices, such as films, slides, models, and blackboards, that display in visual form material to be understood or remembered.

visual display unit *n. Computers.* a device that displays characters or line drawings representing data in a computer memory. It usually has a keyboard for the input of information or inquiries. Abbrev.: **VDU.**

visual field *n.* the whole extent of the image falling on the retina when the eye is fixed on a given point.

visualize *or* **-lise** ('vɪʒʊəˌlaɪz) *vb.* to form a mental image of (something incapable of being viewed or not at that moment visible). —ˌvisuali'zation *or* -li'sation *n.*

visual magnitude *n. Astron.* the magnitude of a star as determined by visual observation.

visual purple *n.* another name for **rhodopsin.**

visual violet *n.* another name for **iodopsin.**

visual yellow *n.* another name for **retinene.**

vital ('vaɪtᵊl) *adj.* **1.** essential to maintain life: *the lungs perform a vital function.* **2.** forceful, energetic, or lively: *a vital person.* **3.** of, having, or displaying life: *a vital organism.* **4.** indispensable or essential: *books vital to this study.* **5.** of great importance: *a vital game.* ~*n.* **6.** (*pl.*) the bodily organs, such as the brain, liver, heart, lungs, etc., that are necessary to maintain life. **7.** (*pl.*) the essential elements of anything. [C14: via OF from L *vītālis,* from *vīta* life] —'**vitally** *adv.*

vital capacity *n. Physiol.* the volume of air that can be exhaled from the lungs after the deepest possible breath has been taken.

vital force *n.* (esp. in early biological theory) a hypothetical force, independent of physical and chemical forces, regarded as being the causative factor of the evolution of living organisms.

vitalism ('vaɪtə,lɪzəm) *n.* the philosophical doctrine that the phenomena of life cannot be explained in purely mechanical terms because there is something immaterial which distinguishes living from inanimate matter. —'**vitalist** *n., adj.* —,**vital'istic** *adj.*

vitality (vaɪ'tælɪtɪ) *n., pl.* **-ties.** **1.** physical or mental vigour, energy, etc. **2.** the power or ability to continue in existence, live, or grow: *the vitality of a movement.*

vitalize *or* **-lise** ('vaɪtə,laɪz) *vb.* (*tr.*) to make vital, living, or alive. —,**vitali'zation** *or* **-li'sation** *n.*

vital staining *n.* the technique of treating living cells and tissues with dyes that do not immediately kill them, facilitating observation under a microscope.

vital statistics *pl. n.* **1.** quantitative data concerning human life or the conditions affecting it, such as the death rate. **2.** *Inf.* the measurements of a woman's bust, waist, and hips.

vitamin ('vɪtəmɪn, 'vaɪ-) *n.* any of a group of substances that are essential, in small quantities, for the normal functioning of metabolism in the body. They cannot usually be synthesized in the body but they occur naturally in certain foods. [C20 *vit-* from L *vīta* life + *-amin* from AMINE; so named by Casimir FUNK, who believed the substances to be amines] —,**vita'minic** *adj.*

vitamin A *n.* **1.** Also called: **vitamin A₁, retinol.** a fat-soluble yellow unsaturated alcohol occurring in green and yellow vegetables, butter, egg yolk, and fish-liver oil. It is essential for the prevention of night blindness and the protection of epithelial tissue. **2.** Also called: **vitamin A₂.** a vitamin that occurs in the tissues of freshwater fish and has a function similar to that of vitamin A₁.

vitamin B *n., pl.* **B vitamins.** any of the vitamins in the vitamin B complex.

vitamin B complex *n.* a large group of water-soluble vitamins occurring esp. in liver and yeast: includes thiamine (**vitamin B₁**), riboflavin (**vitamin B₂**), nicotinic acid, pyridoxine (**vitamin B₆**), pantothenic acid, biotin, choline, folic acid, and cyanocobalamin (**vitamin B₁₂**). Sometimes shortened to **B complex.**

vitamin C *n.* another name for **ascorbic acid.**

vitamin D *n., pl.* **D vitamins.** any of the fat-soluble vitamins, including calciferol (**vitamin D₂**) and cholecalciferol (**vitamin D₃**), occurring in fish-liver oils, milk, butter, and eggs: used in the treatment of rickets.

vitamin D₁ *n.* the first isolated form of vitamin D, consisting of calciferol and its precursor, lumisterol.

vitamin E *n.* another name for **tocopherol.**

vitamin G *n.* another name (esp. U.S. and Canad.) for **riboflavin.**

vitamin H *n.* another name (esp. U.S. and Canad.) for **biotin.**

vitamin K *n., pl.* **K vitamins.** any of the fat-soluble vitamins, including phylloquinone (**vitamin K₁**) and the menaquinones (**vitamin K₂**), which are essential for the normal clotting of blood.

vitamin P *n., pl.* **P vitamins.** any of a group of water-soluble crystalline substances occurring mainly in citrus fruits, blackcurrants, and rose-hips: they regulate the permeability of the blood capillaries. Also called: **citrin, bioflavonoid.**

Vitebsk (*Russian* 'vitipsk) *n.* a city in the W Soviet Union, in the Byelorussian SSR: under Russian rule since 1772. Pop.: 347 000 (1987).

vitellin (vɪ'tɛlɪn) *n. Biochem.* a phosphoprotein that is the major protein in egg yolk. [C19: from VITELLUS + -IN]

vitelline membrane (vɪ'tɛlɪn) *n. Zool.* a membrane that surrounds a fertilized ovum and prevents the entry of other spermatozoa.

vitellus (vɪ'tɛləs) *n., pl.* **-luses** *or* **-li** (-laɪ). *Zool., rare.* the yolk of an egg. [C18: from L, lit.: little calf, later: yolk of an egg, from *vitulus* calf]

vitiate ('vɪʃɪ,eɪt) *vb.* (*tr.*) **1.** to make faulty or imperfect. **2.** to debase or corrupt. **3.** to destroy the force or legal effect of (a deed, etc.). [C16: from L *vitiāre* to injure, from *vitium* a fault] —,**viti'ation** *n.* —'**viti,ator** *n.*

viticulture ('vɪtɪ,kʌltʃə) *n.* **1.** the science, art, or process of cultivating grapevines. **2.** the study of grapes and the growing of grapes. [C19: *viti-,* from L *vītis* vine] —,**viti'culturist** *n.*

Viti Levu ('vi:tɪ 'lɛvu:) *n.* the largest island of Fiji: mountainous. Chief town (and capital of the state): Suva. Pop.: 445 422 (1976). Area: 10 386 sq. km (4010 sq. miles).

Vitoria (*Spanish* bi'torja) *n.* a city in NE Spain: scene of Wellington's decisive victory (1813) over Napoleon's forces in the Peninsular War. Pop.: 189 533 (1981).

Vitória (vɪ'tɔːrɪə; *Portuguese* vi'tɔrja) *n.* a port in E Brazil, capital of Espírito Santo state, on an island in the Bay of Espírito Santo. Pop.: 144 143 (1980).

vitreous ('vɪtrɪəs) *adj.* **1.** of or resembling glass. **2.** made of or containing glass. **3.** of or relating to the vitreous humour or vitreous body. [C17: from L *vitreus* made of glass, from *vitrum* glass] —'**vitreously** *adv.*

vitreous humour *or* **body** *n.* a transparent gelatinous substance that fills the interior of the eyeball between the lens and the retina.

vitrescence (vɪ'trɛsəns) *n.* **1.** the quality or condition of being or becoming vitreous. **2.** the process of producing a glass or turning a crystalline material into glass. —**vi'trescent** *adj.*

vitrify ('vɪtrɪ,faɪ) *vb.* **-fying, -fied.** to convert or be converted into glass or a glassy substance. [C16: from F, from L *vitrum* glass] —'**vitri,fiable** *adj.* —**vitrification** (,vɪtrɪfɪ'keɪʃən) *n.*

vitrine ('vɪtriːn) *n.* a glass display case or cabinet for works of art, curios, etc. [C19: from F, from *vitre* pane of glass, from L *vitrum* glass]

vitriol ('vɪtrɪ,ɒl) *n.* **1.** another name for **sulphuric acid. 2.** any one of a number of sulphate salts, such as ferrous sulphate (iron(II) sulphate; **green vitriol**), copper sulphate (**blue vitriol**), or zinc sulphate (**white vitriol**). **3.** speech, writing, etc., displaying vituperation or bitterness. [C14: from Med. L *vitriolum,* from LL, from L *vitrum* glass, referring to the glossy appearance of the sulphates]

vitriolic (,vɪtrɪ'ɒlɪk) *adj.* **1.** (of a strong acid) highly corrosive. **2.** severely bitter or caustic.

vitriolize *or* **-lise** ('vɪtrɪə,laɪz) *vb.* (*tr.*) **1.** to convert into or treat with vitriol. **2.** to injure with vitriol. —,**vitriol'ization** *or* **-li'sation** *n.*

Vitruvius Pollio (vɪ'truːvɪəs 'pɒlɪ,əʊ) *n.* **Marcus** ('mɑːkəs). 1st century B.C., Roman architect, noted for his treatise *De architectura,* the only surviving Roman work on architectural theory and a major influence on Renaissance architects. —**Vi'truvian** *adj.*

vittle ('vɪtᵊl) *n., vb.* an obsolete or dialect spelling of **victual.**

vituperate (vɪ'tjuːpə,reɪt) *vb.* to berate or rail (against) abusively; revile. [C16: from L *vituperāre* to blame, from *vitium* a defect + *parāre* to make] —**vi,tuper'ation** *n.* —**vi'tuper,ator** *n.*

viva¹ ('viːvə) *interj.* long live; up with (a specified person or thing). [C17: from It., lit.: may (he) live! from *vivere* to live, from L *vivere*]

viva² ('vaɪvə) *Brit.* ~*n.* **1.** an oral examination. ~*vb.* **-vaing, -vaed.** (*tr.*) **2.** to examine orally. [shortened from VIVA VOCE]

vivace (vɪ'vɑːtʃɪ) *adj., adv. Music.* to be performed in a brisk lively manner. [C17: from It., from L *vīvax* vigorous, from *vivere* to live]

vivacious (vɪ'veɪʃəs) *adj.* full of high spirits and animation. [C17: from L *vīvax* lively; see VIVACE] —**vi'vaciously** *adv.* —**vi'vaciousness** *n.*

vivacity (vɪ'væsɪtɪ) *n., pl.* **-ties.** the quality or condition of being vivacious.

Vivaldi (vɪ'vældɪ) n. **Antonio** (an'tɔːnjo). ?1675–1741, Italian composer and violinist, noted esp. for his development of the solo concerto. His best-known work is *The Four Seasons* (1725).

vivarium (vaɪ'vɛərɪəm) n., pl. **-iums** or **-ia** (-ɪə). a place where live animals are kept under natural conditions for study, etc. [C16: from L: enclosure where live fish or game are kept, from *vivus* alive]

viva voce ('vaɪvə 'vəʊtʃɪ) adv., adj. **1.** by word of mouth. ~n., vb. **2.** the full form of **viva**². [C16: from Med. L, lit.: with living voice]

vive (viːv) interj. long live; up with (a specified person or thing). [from F]

Vivian ('vɪvɪən) n. (in Arthurian legend) the mistress of Merlin. Also called: the **Lady of the Lake**.

vivid ('vɪvɪd) adj. **1.** (of a colour) very bright; intense. **2.** brilliantly coloured: *vivid plumage*. **3.** conveying to the mind striking realism, freshness, or trueness to life: *a vivid account*. **4.** (of a memory, etc.) remaining distinct in the mind. **5.** (of the imagination, etc.) prolific in the formation of lifelike images. **6.** uttered, operating, or acting with vigour: *vivid expostulations*. **7.** full of life or vitality: *a vivid personality*. [C17: from L *vividus* animated, from *vivere* to live] —**'vividly** adv. —**'vividness** n.

vivify ('vɪvɪˌfaɪ) vb. **-fying, -fied.** (tr.) **1.** to bring to life; animate. **2.** to make more vivid or striking. [C16: from LL *vivificāre*, from L *vivus* alive + *facere* to make] —ˌvivi'fi'cation n.

viviparous (vɪ'vɪpərəs) adj. **1.** (of most mammals) giving birth to living offspring that develop within the uterus of the mother. **2.** (of seeds) germinating before separating from the parent plant. **3.** (of plants) producing bulbils or young plants instead of flowers. [C17: from L, from *vivus* alive + *parere* to bring forth] —**viviparity** (ˌvɪvɪ'pærɪtɪ) or **vi'viparousness** n. —**vi'viparously** adv.

vivisect ('vɪvɪˌsɛkt, ˌvɪvɪ'sɛkt) vb. to subject (an animal) to vivisection. [C19: back formation from VIVISECTION] —'viviˌsector n.

vivisection (ˌvɪvɪ'sɛkʃən) n. the act or practice of performing experiments on living animals, involving cutting into or dissecting the body. [C18: from *vivi-*, from L *vivus* living + SECTION, as in DISSECTION] —ˌvivi'sectional adj.

vivisectionist (ˌvɪvɪ'sɛkʃənɪst) n. a person who practises or advocates vivisection as being useful to science.

vivo ('viːvəʊ) adj., adv. Music. (in combination) with life and vigour: *allegro vivo*. [It.: lively]

vixen ('vɪksən) n. **1.** a female fox. **2.** a quarrelsome or spiteful woman. [C15 *fixen*; rel. to OE *fyxe*, fem. of FOX] —'vixenish adj. —'vixenly adv., adj.

Viyella (vaɪ'ɛlə) n. Trademark. a soft fabric made of wool and cotton.

viz abbrev. for videlicet.

Vizagapatam (vɪˌzægə'pʌtəm) n. a variant spelling of **Vishakhapatnam**.

vizard ('vɪzəd) n. Arch. or literary. a means of disguise. [C16: var. of VISOR] —'vizarded adj.

vizier (vɪ'zɪə) n. a high official in certain Muslim countries, esp. in the former Ottoman Empire. [C16: from Turkish *vezir*, from Ar. *wazīr* from *wazara* to bear a burden] —**vi'zierate** n. —**vi'zierial** adj. —**vi'ziership** n.

vizor ('vaɪzə) n. a variant spelling of **visor**.

vizsla ('vɪʒlə) n. a breed of Hungarian hunting dog with a smooth rusty-gold coat. [C20: after *Vizsla*, town in Hungary]

VJ abbrev. for video jockey.

V-J Day n. the day marking the Allied victory over Japan in World War II (Aug. 15, 1945).

VL abbrev. for Vulgar Latin.

Vlaardingen (Dutch 'vlaːrdɪŋə) n. a port in the W Netherlands, in South Holland west of Rotterdam: the third largest port in the Netherlands. Pop.: 75 430 (1987).

Vladikavkaz (Russian vlədikaf'kas) n. the former name (until 1944) of **Ordzhonikidze**.

Vladimir¹ (Russian vla'dimir) n. a city in the W central Soviet Union: capital of the principality of Vladimir until the court transferred to Moscow in 1328. Pop.: 343 000 (1987).

Vladimir² ('vlædɪˌmɪə; Russian vla'dimir) n. **Saint,** called *the Great*. ?956–1015, grand prince of Kiev (980–1015); first Christian ruler of Russia. Feast day: July 15.

Vladivostok (ˌvlædɪ'vɒstɒk; Russian vlədivas'tɔk) n. a port in the extreme SE Soviet Union, on the Sea of Japan:

terminus of the Trans-Siberian Railway; the main Russian Pacific naval base since 1872 and chief Soviet port in the Far East; university (1956). Pop.: 615 000 (1987).

Vlaminck (French vlamɛ̃k) n. **Maurice de** (mɔris də). 1876–1958, French painter of the Fauve school.

vlei (fleɪ, vleɪ) n. S. African. an area of low marshy ground, esp. one that feeds a stream. [C19: from Afrik.]

VLF or **vlf** Radio. abbrev. for very low frequency.

Vlissingen ('vlɪsɪŋə) n. the Dutch name for **Flushing**.

Vlorë (Albanian 'vlorə) or **Vlonë** (Albanian 'vlonə) n. a port in SW Albania, on the **Bay of Vlorë**: under Turkish rule from 1462 until Albanian independence was declared here in 1912. Pop.: 61 000 (1983). Ancient name: **Avlona**. Also called: **Valona**.

Vltava (Czech 'vltava) n. a river in Czechoslovakia, rising in the Bohemian Forest and flowing generally southeast and then north to the River Elbe near Melnik. Length: 434 km (270 miles). German name: **Moldau**.

V neck n. **a.** a neck on a garment that comes down to a point, resembling the shape of the letter V. **b.** a sweater with such a neck. —'V-ˌneck or 'V-ˌnecked adj.

voc. or **vocat.** abbrev. for vocative.

vocab ('vəʊkæb) n. short for **vocabulary**.

vocable ('vəʊkəbəl) n. any word, either written or spoken, regarded simply as a sequence of letters or spoken sounds. [C16: from L *vocābulum* a designation, from *vocāre* to call] —'vocably adv.

vocabulary (və'kæbjʊlərɪ) n., pl. **-laries. 1.** a listing, either selective or exhaustive, containing the words and phrases of a language, with meanings or translations into another language. **2.** the aggregate of words in the use or comprehension of a specified person, class, etc. **3.** all the words contained in a language. **4.** a range or system of symbols or techniques constituting a means of communication or expression, as any of the arts or crafts: *a wide vocabulary of textures and colours*. [C16: from Med. L *vocābulārium*, from L *vocābulum* VOCABLE]

vocal ('vəʊkəl) adj. **1.** of or designed for the voice: *vocal music*. **2.** produced or delivered by the voice: *vocal noises*. **3.** connected with the production of the voice: *vocal organs*. **4.** frequently disposed to outspoken speech, criticism, etc.: *a vocal minority*. **5.** full of sound or voices: *a vocal assembly*. **6.** endowed with a voice. **7.** Phonetics. **a.** of or relating to a speech sound. **b.** of or relating to a voiced speech sound, esp. a vowel. ~n. **8.** a piece of jazz or pop music that is sung. **9.** a performance of such a piece of music. [C14: from L *vocālis* possessed of a voice, from *vōx* voice] —**vocality** (vəʊ'kælɪtɪ) n. —'vocally adv.

vocal cords pl. n. either of two pairs of membranous folds in the larynx. The upper pair (**false vocal cords**) are not concerned with vocal production; the lower pair (**true vocal cords**) can be made to vibrate and produce sound when air from the lungs is forced over them.

vocalic (vəʊ'kælɪk) adj. Phonetics. of, relating to, or containing a vowel or vowels.

vocalise (ˌvəʊkə'liːz) n. a musical passage sung upon one vowel usually as an exercise to develop flexibility and control of pitch and tone.

vocalism ('vəʊkəˌlɪzəm) n. **1.** the exercise of the voice, as in singing or speaking. **2.** Phonetics. **a.** a voiced speech sound, esp. a vowel. **b.** a system of vowels as used in a language.

vocalist ('vəʊkəlɪst) n. a singer, esp. one who regularly appears with a jazz band or pop group.

vocalize or **-ise** ('vəʊkəˌlaɪz) vb. **1.** to express with or use the voice. **2.** (tr.) to make vocal or articulate. **3.** (tr.) Phonetics. to articulate (a speech sound) with voice. **4.** another word for **vowelize**. **5.** (intr.) to sing a melody on a vowel, etc. —ˌvocali'zation or -i'sation n. —'vocalˌizer or -ˌiser n.

vocal score n. a musical score that shows voice parts in full and orchestral parts in the form of a piano transcription.

vocation (vəʊ'keɪʃən) n. **1.** a specified profession or trade. **2. a.** a special urge or predisposition to a particular calling or career, esp. a religious one. **b.** such a calling or career. [C15: from L *vocātiō*, from *vocāre* to call]

vocational (vəʊ'keɪʃənəl) adj. **1.** of or relating to a vocation or vocations. **2.** of or relating to applied educational courses concerned with skills needed for an occupation, trade, or profession.

vocational guidance *n.* a guidance service based on psychological tests and interviews to find out what career may best suit a person.

vocative ('vɒkətɪv) *Grammar.* ~*adj.* **1.** denoting a case of nouns, in some inflected languages, used when the referent of the noun is being addressed. ~*n.* **2. a.** the vocative case. **b.** a vocative noun or speech element. [C15: from L *vocātīvus cāsus* the calling case, from *vocāre* to call]

voces ('vəʊsiːz) *n.* the plural of **vox**.

vociferate (vəʊ'sɪfə,reɪt) *vb.* to exclaim or cry out about (something) clamorously or insistently. [C17: from L *vōciferārī*, from *vōx* voice + *ferre* to bear] —**vo,cifer'ation** *n.*

vociferous (vəʊ'sɪfərəs) *adj.* **1.** characterized by vehemence or noisiness: *vociferous protests.* **2.** making an outcry: *a vociferous mob.* —**vo'ciferously** *adv.* —**vo'ciferousness** *n.*

vocoder ('vəʊ,kəʊdə) *n. Music.* a type of synthesizer that uses the human voice as an oscillator.

vodka ('vɒdkə) *n.* an alcoholic drink originating in Russia, made from grain, potatoes, etc., usually consisting only of rectified spirit and water. [C19: from Russian, dim. of *voda* water]

voe (vəʊ) *n.* (in Orkney and Shetland) a small bay or narrow creek. [C17: from ON *vagr*]

voetsek ('fʊtsɛk, 'vʊt-) *sentence substitute. S. African sl.* an expletive used when chasing animals away: offensive when addressed to people. [from Afrik., from *voort se ek* away say I]

voetstoets *or* **voetstoots** ('fʊtstʊts, 'vʊt-) *S. African.* ~*adj.* **1.** denoting a sale in which the vendor is freed from all responsibility for the condition of the goods being sold. ~*adv.* **2.** without responsibility for the condition of the goods sold. [Afrik., from Du.]

Vogel ('vəʊɡ°l) *n.* Sir **Julius.** 1835–99, New Zealand statesman; prime minister of New Zealand (1873–75; 1876).

Vogelweide (*German* 'foːɡəlvaidə) *n.* See **Walther von der Vogelweide.**

vogue (vəʊɡ) *n.* **1.** the popular style at a specified time (esp. in **in vogue**). **2.** a period of general or popular usage or favour: *the vogue for such dances is now over.* ~*adj.* **3.** (*usually prenominal*) fashionable: *a vogue word.* [C16: from F: a rowing, fashion, from OIt., from *vogare* to row, from ?] —**'voguish** *adj.*

voice (vɔɪs) *n.* **1.** the sound made by the vibration of the vocal cords, esp. when modified by the tongue and mouth. **2.** the natural and distinctive tone of the speech sounds characteristic of a particular person. **3.** the condition, quality, or tone of such sounds: *a hysterical voice.* **4.** the musical sound of a singing voice, with respect to its quality or tone: *she has a lovely voice.* **5.** the ability to speak, sing, etc.: *he has lost his voice.* **6.** a sound resembling or suggestive of vocal utterance: *the voice of hard experience.* **7.** written or spoken expression, as of feeling, opinion, etc. (esp. in **give voice to**). **8.** a stated choice, wish, or opinion: *to give someone a voice in a decision.* **9.** an agency through which is communicated another's purpose, etc.: *such groups are the voice of our enemies.* **10.** *Music.* **a.** musical notes produced by vibrations of the vocal chords at various frequencies and in certain registers: *a tenor voice.* **b.** (in harmony) an independent melodic line or part: *a fugue in five voices.* **11.** *Phonetics.* the sound characterizing the articulation of several speech sounds, including all vowels or sonants, that is produced when the vocal cords are set in vibration by the breath. **12.** *Grammar.* a category of the verb that expresses whether the relation between the subject and the verb is that of agent and action, action and recipient, or some other relation. **13. in voice.** in a condition to sing or speak well. **14. with one voice.** unanimously. ~*vb.* (*tr.*) **15.** to give expression to: *to voice a complaint.* **16.** to articulate (a speech sound) with voice. **17.** *Music.* to adjust (a wind instrument or organ pipe) so that it conforms to the correct standards of tone colour, pitch, etc. [C13: from OF *voiz*, from L *vōx*] —**'voicer** *n.*

voice box *n.* **1.** another word for the **larynx.** **2.** Also called: **talkbox.** an electronic guitar attachment with a tube into the player's mouth to modulate the sound vocally.

voiced (vɔɪst) *adj.* **1.** declared or expressed by the voice. **2.** (*in combination*) having a voice as specified: *loud-*

voiced. **3.** *Phonetics.* articulated with accompanying vibration of the vocal cords: *in English* (b) *is a voiced consonant.*

voiceless ('vɔɪslɪs) *adj.* **1.** without a voice. **2.** not articulated: *voiceless misery.* **3.** silent. **4.** *Phonetics.* articulated without accompanying vibration of the vocal cords: *In English* (p) *is a voiceless consonant.* —**'voicelessly** *adv.*

voice-over *n.* the voice of an unseen commentator heard during a film, etc.

voiceprint ('vɔɪs,prɪnt) *n.* a graphic representation of a person's voice recorded electronically, usually having time plotted along the horizontal axis and the frequency of the speech on the vertical axis.

void (vɔɪd) *adj.* **1.** without contents. **2.** not legally binding: *null and void.* **3.** (of an office, house, etc.) unoccupied. **4.** (*postpositive;* foll. by *of*) destitute or devoid: *void of resources.* **5.** useless: *all his efforts were rendered void.* **6.** (of a card suit or player) having no cards in a particular suit: *his spades were void.* ~*n.* **7.** an empty space or area: *the huge desert voids of Asia.* **8.** a feeling or condition of loneliness or deprivation. **9.** a lack of any cards in one suit: *to have a void in spades.* ~*vb.* (*mainly tr.*) **10.** to make ineffective or invalid. **11.** to empty (contents, etc.) or make empty of contents. **12.** (*also intr.*) to discharge the contents of (the bowels or urinary bladder). [C13: from OF, from Vulgar L *vocītus* (unattested), from L *vacuus*, from *vacāre* to be empty] —**'voidable** *adj.* —**'voider** *n.*

voidance ('vɔɪdəns) *n.* **1.** an annulment, as of a contract. **2.** the condition of being vacant, as an office, benefice, etc. **3.** the act of voiding or evacuating. [C14: var. of AVOIDANCE]

voile (vɔɪl) *n.* a light semitransparent fabric of silk, rayon, cotton, etc., used for dresses, scarves, shirts, etc. [C19: from F: VEIL]

Voiotia (*Greek* vjɔ'tiːa) *n.* a department of E central Greece: corresponds to ancient Boeotia and part of ancient Phocis. Pop.: 117 175 (1981). Area: 3173 sq. km (1225 sq. miles). Modern Greek name: **Boeotia.**

Vojvodina *or* **Voivodina** (*Serbo-Croatian* 'vɔjvɒdina) *n.* an autonomous region of NE Yugoslavia, in N Serbia: a major agricultural region. Capital: Novi Sad. Pop.: 2 050 000 (1985). Area: 22 489 sq. km (8683 sq. miles).

vol. *abbrev. for:* **1.** volcano. **2.** volume. **3.** volunteer.

volant ('vəʊlənt) *adj.* **1.** (*usually postpositive*) *Heraldry.* in a flying position. **2.** *Rare.* flying or capable of flight. [C16: from F, from *voler* to fly, from L *volāre*]

volar ('vəʊlə) *adj. Anat.* of or relating to the palm of the hand or the sole of the foot. [C19: from L *vola* hollow of the hand, palm, sole of the foot]

volatile ('vɒlə,taɪl) *adj.* **1.** (of a substance) capable of readily changing from a solid or liquid form to a vapour. **2.** (of persons) disposed to caprice or inconstancy. **3.** (of circumstances) liable to sudden change. **4.** lasting only a short time: *volatile business interests.* **5.** *Computers.* (of a memory) not retaining stored information when the power supply is cut off. ~*n.* **6.** a volatile substance. [C17: from L *volātilis* flying, from *volāre* to fly] —**'volatileness** *or* **volatility** (,vɒlə'tɪlɪtɪ) *n.*

volatilize *or* **-lise** (vɒ'læti,laiz) *vb.* to change or cause to change from a solid or liquid to a vapour. —**vo'lati,lizable** *or* **-,lisable** *adj.* —**vo,latiliz'ation** *or* **-lis'ation** *n.*

vol-au-vent (*French* vɔlovɑ̃) *n.* a very light puff pastry case filled with a savoury mixture in a sauce. [C19: from F, lit.: flight in the wind]

volcanic (vɒl'kænɪk) *adj.* **1.** of, produced by, or characterized by the presence of volcanoes: *a volcanic region.* **2.** suggestive of or resembling an erupting volcano: *a volcanic era.* —**vol'canically** *adv.* —**volcanicity** (,vɒlkə'nɪsɪtɪ) *n.*

volcanic glass *n.* any of several glassy volcanic igneous rocks, such as obsidian.

volcanism ('vɒlkə,nɪzəm) *or* **vulcanism** *n.* those processes collectively that result in the formation of volcanoes and their products.

volcano (vɒl'keɪnəʊ) *n., pl.* **-noes** *or* **-nos. 1.** an opening in the earth's crust from which molten lava, rock fragments, ashes, dust, and gases are ejected from below the earth's surface. **2.** a mountain formed from volcanic material ejected from a vent in a central crater. [C17: from It., from L *Volcānus* Vulcan, Roman god of fire and metal-working, whose forges were believed to be responsible for volcanic rumblings]

Volcano Islands *pl. n.* a group of three volcanic islands in the W Pacific, about 1100 km (700 miles) south of Japan: the largest is Iwo Jima, taken by U.S. forces in 1945 and returned to Japan in 1968. Area: about 28 sq. km (11 sq. miles). Japanese name: **Kazan Retto.**

volcanology (,vɒlkə'nɒlədʒɪ) *or* **vulcanology** *n.* the study of volcanoes and volcanic phenomena. —**volcanological** (,vɒlkənə'lɒdʒɪkᵊl) *or* ,**vulcano'logical** *adj.*

vole (vəʊl) *n.* any of various small rodents, mostly of Eurasia and North America, having a stocky body, short tail, and inconspicuous ears. [C19: short for *volemouse*, from ON *vollr* field + *mus* MOUSE]

Volga ('vɒlgə) *n.* a river in the W Soviet Union, rising in the Valdai Range and flowing through a chain of small lakes to the Rybinsk Reservoir and south to the Caspian Sea through Volgograd: the longest river in Europe. Length: 3690 km (2293 miles).

Volgograd (*Russian* vəlgɑ'grat; *English* 'vɒlgə,græd) *n.* a port in the W central Soviet Union, on the River Volga: scene of a major engagement (1918) during the civil war and again in World War II (1942–43), in which the German forces were defeated; major industrial centre. Pop.: 988 000 (1987). Former names: **Tsaritsyn** (until 1925), **Stalingrad** (1925–61).

volitant ('vɒlɪtənt) *adj.* 1. flying or moving about rapidly. 2. capable of flying. [C19: from L *volitāre* to flit, from *volāre* to fly]

volition (və'lɪʃən) *n.* 1. the act of exercising the will: *of one's own volition.* 2. the faculty of conscious choice, decision, and intention. 3. the resulting choice or resolution. [C17: from Med. L *volitiō*, from L *vol-* as in *volō* I will, present stem of *velle* to wish] —**vo'litional** *adj.*

volitive ('vɒlɪtɪv) *adj.* of, relating to, or emanating from the will.

Volk (folk) *n. S. African.* the Afrikaner people. [from Afrik., from Du.]

Volksraad ('folks,rɑːt) *n.* (in South Africa) the former Legislative Assemblies of the Transvaal and Orange Free State republics. [from Afrik., from Du. *volks* people's + *raad* council]

volley ('vɒlɪ) *n.* 1. the simultaneous discharge of several weapons, esp. firearms. 2. the projectiles or missiles so discharged. 3. a burst of oaths, protests, etc., occurring simultaneously or in rapid succession. 4. *Sport.* a stroke, shot, or kick at a moving ball before it hits the ground. 5. *Cricket.* the flight of such a ball or the ball itself. ~*vb.* 6. to discharge (weapons, etc.) in or as if in a volley or (of weapons, etc.) to be discharged. 7. (*tr.*) to utter vehemently. 8. (*tr.*) *Sport.* to strike or kick (a moving ball) before it hits the ground. [C16: from F *volée* a flight, from *voler* to fly, from L *volāre*] —**'volleyer** *n.*

volleyball ('vɒlɪ,bɔːl) *n.* 1. a game in which two teams hit a large ball back and forth over a high net with their hands. 2. the ball used in this game.

Vologda (*Russian* 'vɔləgdə) *n.* an industrial city in the NW central Soviet Union. Pop.: 247 000 (1981 est.).

Vólos (*Greek* 'vɔlɔs) *n.* a port in E Greece, in Thessaly on the Gulf of Volos (an inlet of the Aegean): the third largest port in Greece. Pop.: 70 967 (1981).

volplane ('vɒl,pleɪn) *vb.* 1. (*intr.*) (of an aircraft) to glide without engine power. ~*n.* 2. a glide by an aircraft. [C20: from F *vol plané* a gliding flight]

vols. *abbrev. for* volumes.

Volsung ('vɒlsʊŋ) *n.* 1. a great hero of Norse and Germanic legend and poetry who gave his name to a race of warriors; father of Sigmund and Signy. 2. any member of his family.

volt[1] (vəʊlt) *n.* the derived SI unit of electric potential; the potential difference between two points on a conductor carrying a current of 1 ampere, when the power dissipated between these points is 1 watt. Symbol: V [C19: after Count Alessandro VOLTA]

volt[2] *or* **volte** (vɒlt) *n.* 1. a small circle executed in dressage. 2. a leap made in fencing to avoid an opponent's thrust. [C17: from F, from It. *volta* turn, ult. from L *volvere* to turn]

volta ('vɒltə; *Italian* 'vɔlta) *n., pl.* -**te** (*Italian* -te). 1. an Italian dance popular during the 16th and 17th centuries. 2. a piece of music for or in the rhythm of this dance. [C17: from It.: turn; see VOLT[2]]

Volta[1] ('vɒltə) *n.* 1. a river in W Africa, formed by the confluence of the **Black Volta** and the **White Volta** in N central Ghana: flows south to the Bight of Benin: the chief river of Ghana. Length: 480 km (300 miles); (including the Black Volta) 1600 km (1000 miles). 2. **Lake.** an artificial lake in Ghana, extending 408 km (250 miles) upstream from the **Volta River Dam** on the Volta River: completed in 1966. Area: 8482 sq. km (3275 sq. miles).

Volta[2] ('vɒltə; *Italian* 'vɔlta) *n.* Count **Alessandro** (ales'sandro). 1745–1827, Italian physicist after whom the volt is named. He made important contributions to the theory of current electricity and invented the voltaic pile (1800), the electrophorus (1775), and an electroscope.

voltage ('vəʊltɪdʒ) *n.* an electromotive force or potential difference expressed in volts.

voltaic (vɒl'teɪɪk) *adj.* another word for **galvanic** (sense 1).

voltaic cell *n.* another name for **primary cell.**

voltaic couple *n. Physics.* a pair of dissimilar metals in an electrolyte with a potential difference between the metals resulting from chemical action.

voltaic pile *n.* an early form of battery consisting of a pile of alternate dissimilar metals, such as zinc and copper, separated by pads moistened with an electrolyte.

Voltaire (vɒl'tɛə, vəʊl-; *French* vɔltɛr) *n.* pseudonym of *François Marie Arouet.* 1694–1778, French writer, whose outspoken belief in religious, political, and social liberty made him the embodiment of the 18th-century Enlightenment. His major works include *Lettres philosophiques* (1734) and the satire *Candide* (1759). He also wrote plays, such as *Zaire* (1732), poems, and scientific studies. He suffered several periods of banishment for his radical views. —**Vol'tairean** *or* **Vol'tairian** *adj., n.*

voltameter (vɒl'tæmɪtə) *n.* a device for measuring electric charge. —**voltametric** (,vɒltə'mɛtrɪk) *adj.*

voltammeter (,vəʊlt'æm,miːtə) *n.* a dual-purpose instrument that can measure both potential difference and electric current, usually in volts and amperes respectively.

volt-ampere ('vəʊlt'æmpɛə) *n.* the product of the potential in volts across an electrical circuit and the resultant current in amperes.

Volta Redonda (*Portuguese* 'vɔltə rə'dõdə) *n.* a city in SE Brazil, in Rio de Janeiro state on the Paraíba River: founded in 1941; site of South America's largest steelworks. Pop.: 178 000 (1984 est.).

volte-face ('vɒlt'fɑːs) *n., pl.* **volte-face.** 1. a reversal, as in opinion. 2. a change of position so as to look, lie, etc., in the opposite direction. [C19: from F, from It., from *volta* turn + *faccia* face]

voltmeter ('vəʊlt,miːtə) *n.* an instrument for measuring potential difference or electromotive force.

Volturno (*Italian* vol'turno) *n.* a river in S central Italy, flowing southeast and southwest to the Tyrrhenian Sea: scene of a battle (1860) during the wars for Italian unity, in which Garibaldi defeated the Neapolitans; German line of defence during World War II. Length: 175 km (109 miles).

voluble ('vɒljʊbᵊl) *adj.* 1. talking easily and at length. 2. *Arch.* easily turning or rotating. 3. *Rare.* (of a plant) twining or twisting. [C16: from L *volūbilis* turning readily, from *volvere* to turn] —,**volu'bility** *or* '**volubleness** *n.* —'**volubly** *adv.*

volume ('vɒljuːm) *n.* 1. the magnitude of the three-dimensional space enclosed within or occupied by an object, geometric solid, etc. 2. a large mass or quantity: *the volume of protest.* 3. an amount or total: *the volume of exports.* 4. fullness of sound. 5. the control on a radio, etc., for adjusting the intensity of sound. 6. a bound collection of printed or written pages; book. 7. any of several books either bound in an identical format or part of a series. 8. the complete set of issues of a periodical over a specified period, esp. one year. 9. *History.* a roll of parchment, etc. 10. **speak volumes.** to convey much significant information. [C14: from OF, from L *volūmen* a roll, from *volvere* to roll up]

volumetric (,vɒljʊ'mɛtrɪk) *adj.* of, concerning, or using measurement by volume: *volumetric analysis.* —,**volu'metrically** *adv.*

volumetric analysis *n. Chem.* quantitative analysis of liquids or solutions by comparing the volumes that react with known volumes of standard reagents, usually by titration.

voluminous (vəˈluːmɪnəs) *adj.* **1.** of great size, quantity, or extent. **2.** (of writing) consisting of or sufficient to fill volumes. [C17: from LL *volūminōsus* full of windings, from *volūmen* VOLUME] —**voluminosity** (vəˌluːmɪˈnɒsɪtɪ) *n.* —**voˈluminously** *adv.*

Völund (ˈvø:lʊnd) *n.* the Scandinavian name of **Wayland.**

voluntarism (ˈvɒləntəˌrɪzəm) *n.* **1.** *Philosophy.* the theory that the will rather than the intellect is the ultimate principle of reality. **2.** a doctrine or system based on voluntary participation in a course of action. **3.** another name for **voluntaryism.** —**ˈvoluntarist** *n.*, *adj.*

voluntary (ˈvɒləntərɪ) *adj.* **1.** performed, undertaken, or brought about by free choice or willingly: *a voluntary donation.* **2.** (of persons) serving or acting in a specified function without compulsion or promise of remuneration: *a voluntary social worker.* **3.** done by, composed of, or functioning with the aid of volunteers: *a voluntary association.* **4.** exercising or having the faculty of willing: *a voluntary agent.* **5.** spontaneous: *voluntary laughter.* **6.** *Law.* **a.** acting or done without legal obligation, compulsion, or persuasion. **b.** made without payment or recompense: *a voluntary conveyance.* **7.** (of the muscles of the limbs, neck, etc.) having their action controlled by the will. **8.** maintained by the voluntary actions or contributions of individuals and not by the state: *voluntary schools.* ~*n.*, *pl.* **-taries. 9.** *Music.* a composition or improvisation, usually for organ, played at the beginning or end of a church service. [C14: from L *voluntārius*, from *voluntās* will, from *velle* to wish] —**ˈvoluntarily** *adv.*

voluntaryism (ˈvɒləntərɪˌɪzəm) *or* **voluntarism** *n.* the principle of supporting churches, schools, and various other institutions by voluntary contributions rather than with state funds. —**ˈvoluntaryist** *or* **ˈvoluntarist** *n.*

volunteer (ˌvɒlənˈtɪə) *n.* **1. a.** a person who performs or offers to perform voluntary service. **b.** (*as modifier*): *a volunteer system.* **2.** a person who freely undertakes military service. **3. a.** a plant that grows from seed that has not been deliberately sown. **b.** (*as modifier*): *a volunteer plant.* ~*vb.* **4.** to offer (oneself or one's services) for an undertaking by choice and without request or obligation. **5.** (*tr.*) to perform, give, or communicate voluntarily: *to volunteer help.* **6.** (*intr.*) to enlist voluntarily for military service. [C17: from F, from L *voluntārius;* see VOLUNTARY]

voluptuary (vəˈlʌptjʊərɪ) *n.*, *pl.* **-aries. 1.** a person devoted to luxury and sensual pleasures. ~*adj.* **2.** of or furthering sensual gratification or luxury. [C17: from LL *voluptuārius* delightful, from L *voluptās* pleasure]

voluptuous (vəˈlʌptjʊəs) *adj.* **1.** relating to, characterized by, or consisting of pleasures of the body or senses. **2.** devoted or addicted to sensual indulgence or luxurious pleasures. **3.** sexually alluring, esp. through shapeliness or fullness: *a voluptuous woman.* [C14: from L *voluptuōsus* full of gratification, from *voluptās* pleasure] —**voˈluptuously** *adv.* —**voˈluptuousness** *n.*

volute (ˈvɒljuːt, vəˈluːt) *n.* **1.** a spiral or twisting turn, form, or object. **2.** Also called: **helix.** a carved ornament, esp. as used on an Ionic capital, that has the form of a spiral scroll. **3.** any of the whorls of the spirally coiled shell of a snail or similar gastropod mollusc. **4.** any of a family of tropical marine gastropod molluscs having a spiral shell with beautiful markings. ~*adj.* *also* **voluted** (vəˈluːtɪd). **5.** having the form of a volute; spiral. [C17: from L *volūta* spiral decoration, from *volūtus*, from *volvere* to roll up] —**voˈlution** *n.*

vomer (ˈvəʊmə) *n.* the thin flat bone forming part of the separation between the nasal passages in mammals. [C18: from L: ploughshare]

vomit (ˈvɒmɪt) *vb.* **1.** to eject (the contents of the stomach) through the mouth as the result of involuntary muscular spasms of the stomach and oesophagus. **2.** to eject or be ejected forcefully. ~*n.* **3.** the matter ejected in vomiting. **4.** the act of vomiting. **5.** an emetic. [C14: from L *vomitāre* to vomit repeatedly, from *vomere* to vomit] —**ˈvomiter** *n.*

vomitory (ˈvɒmɪtərɪ) *adj.* **1.** Also: **vomitive** (ˈvɒmɪtɪv). causing vomiting; emetic. ~*n.*, *pl.* **-ries. 2.** a vomitory agent. **3.** Also called: **vomitorium** (ˌvɒmɪˈtɔːrɪəm). a passageway in an ancient Roman amphitheatre that connects an outside entrance to a tier of seats.

Vonnegut (ˈvɒnɪɡʌt) *n.* **Kurt.** born 1922, U.S. novelist. His works include *Cat's Cradle* (1963), *Slaughterhouse Five* (1969), *Palm Sunday* (1981), and *Galapagos* (1985).

von Stroheim (vɒn ˈstrəʊˌhaɪm, ˈʃtrəʊ-; fɒn) *n.* **Erich** (ˈeːrɪç), real name *Hans Erich Maria Stroheim von Nordenwall.* 1885–1957, U.S. film director and actor, born in Austria, whose films include *Foolish Wives* (1921) and *Greed* (1923).

voodoo (ˈvuːduː) *n.*, *pl.* **-doos. 1.** Also called: **voodooism.** a religious cult involving witchcraft, common among Negroes in Haiti and other Caribbean islands. **2.** a person who practises voodoo. **3.** a charm, spell, or fetish involved in voodoo worship. ~*adj.* **4.** relating to or associated with voodoo. ~*vb.* **-dooing, -dooed. 5.** (*tr.*) to affect by or as if by the power of voodoo. [C19: from Louisiana F *voudou*, ult. of West African origin] —**ˈvoodooist** *n.*

voorkamer (ˈfʊəˌkɑːmə) *n.* *S. African.* the front room of a house. [from Afrik., from Du. *voor* fore + *kamer* chamber]

voorlaaier (ˈfʊəˌlaɪə) *n.* *S. African.* a muzzle-loading gun. [from Afrik. *voor* front + *laai* load]

voorskot (ˈfʊəˌskɒt) *n.* (in South Africa) an advance payment made to a farmers' cooperative for a crop or wool clip. [from Afrik., from Du. *voorschieten* to lend, advance (money)]

Voortrekker (ˈfʊəˌtrɛkə) *n.* (in South Africa) **1.** one of the original Afrikaner settlers of the Transvaal and the Orange Free State who migrated from the Cape Colony in the 1830s. **2.** a member of the Afrikaner youth movement founded in 1931. [C19: from Du., from *voor-* FORE- + *trekken* to TREK]

voracious (vɒˈreɪʃəs) *adj.* **1.** devouring or craving food in great quantities. **2.** very eager or unremitting in some activity: *voracious reading.* [C17: from L *vorāx*, from *vorāre* to devour] —**voracity** (vɒˈræsɪtɪ) *or* **voˈraciousness** *n.*

Vorarlberg (German ˈfoːrarlbɛrk) *n.* a mountainous province of W Austria. Capital: Bregenz. Pop.: 305 615 (1981). Area: 2601 sq. km (1004 sq. miles).

Voronezh (Russian vaˈrɔnɪʃ) *n.* a city in the W central Soviet Union: engineering and chemical industries; university (1918). Pop.: 872 000 (1987).

Voroshilov (Russian vərəˈʃiləf) *n.* **Kliment Yefremovich** (ˈklimɪnt jɪˈfrjɛməvɪtʃ). 1881–1969, Soviet military leader; president of the Soviet Union (1953–60).

Voroshilovgrad (Russian vərəˈʃilawˈɡrat) *n.* an industrial city in the SW Soviet Union, in the E Ukrainian SSR, in the Donbass mining region: established in 1795 as an iron-founding centre. Pop.: 501 000 (1987). Former name (until 1935): **Lugansk.**

Voroshilovsk (Russian vərəˈʃiləfsk) *n.* the former name (1940–44) of **Stavropol.**

-vorous *adj. combining form.* feeding on or devouring: *carnivorous.* [from L *-vorus;* rel. to *vorāre* to swallow up] —**-vore** *n. combining form.*

Vorster (ˈfɔːstə, ˈvɔː-) *n.* **Balthazar Johannes,** known as *John.* 1915–83, South African statesman; Nationalist prime minister (1966–78); president (1978).

vortex (ˈvɔːtɛks) *n.*, *pl.* **-texes** *or* **-tices** (-tɪˌsiːz). **1.** a whirling mass or motion of liquid, gas, flame, etc., such as the spiralling movement of water around a whirlpool. **2.** any activity or way of life regarded as irresistibly engulfing. [C17: from L: a whirlpool] —**vortical** (ˈvɔːtɪkəl) *adj.*

vorticella (ˌvɔːtɪˈsɛlə) *n.*, *pl.* **-lae** (-liː). any of a genus of protozoans consisting of a goblet-shaped ciliated cell attached to the substratum by a long contractile stalk. [C18: from NL, lit.: a little eddy, from VORTEX]

vorticism (ˈvɔːtɪˌsɪzəm) *n.* an art movement in England combining the techniques of cubism with the concern for the problems of the machine age evinced in futurism. [C20: referring to the "vortices" of modern life on which the movement was based] —**ˈvorticist** *n.*

Vortumnus (vɔːˈtʌmnəs) *n.* a variant spelling of **Vertumnus.**

Vosges (French vɔʒ) *n.* **1.** a mountain range in E France, west of the Rhine valley. Highest peak: 1423 m (4672 ft.). **2.** a department of NE France, in Lorraine region. Capital: Épinal. Pop.: 395 769 (1982). Area: 5903 sq. km (2302 sq. miles).

votary (ˈvəʊtərɪ) *n.*, *pl.* **-ries,** *also* **votarist. 1.** *R.C. Church, Eastern Churches.* a person, such as a monk or nun, who has dedicated himself or herself to religion by taking vows. **2.** a devoted adherent of a religion, cause, etc. ~*adj.* **3.** ardently devoted to the services or worship of God or a saint. [C16: from L *vōtum* a vow, from *vovēre* to vow] — '**votaress** *fem. n.*

vote (vəʊt) *n.* **1.** an indication of choice, opinion, or will on a question, such as the choosing of a candidate: *10 votes for Jones.* **2.** the opinion of a group of persons as determined by voting: *it was put to the vote.* **3.** a body of votes or voters collectively: *the Jewish vote.* **4.** the total number of votes cast. **5.** the ticket, ballot, etc., by which a vote is expressed. **6. a.** the right to vote; franchise. **b.** a person regarded as the embodiment of this right. **7.** a means of voting, such as a ballot. **8.** *Chiefly Brit.* a grant or other proposition to be voted upon. ~*vb.* **9.** (when *tr.,* takes a clause as object or an infinitive*) to express or signify (one's preference or will) (for or against some question, etc.): *to vote by ballot.* **10.** (*intr.*) to declare oneself as being (something or in favour of something) by exercising one's vote: *to vote socialist.* **11.** (*tr.*; foll. by *into* or *out of,* etc.) to appoint or elect (a person to or from a particular post): *he was voted out of office.* **12.** (*tr.*) to determine the condition of in a specified way by voting: *the court voted itself out of existence.* **13.** (*tr.*) to authorize or allow by voting: *vote us a rise.* **14.** (*tr.*) *Inf.* to declare by common opinion: *the party was voted a failure.* [C15: from L *vōtum* a solemn promise, from *vovēre* to vow] — '**votable** *or* '**voteable** *adj.*

vote down *vb.* (*tr., adv.*) to decide against or defeat in a vote: *the bill was voted down.*

vote of no confidence *n. Parliament.* a vote on a motion put by the Opposition censuring an aspect of the Government's policy; if the motion is carried the Government is obliged to resign. Also called: **vote of censure.**

voter ('vəʊtə) *n.* a person who can or does vote.

voting machine *n.* (esp. in the U.S.) a machine at a polling station that voters operate to register their votes and that mechanically or electronically counts all votes cast.

votive ('vəʊtɪv) *adj.* **1.** given, undertaken, or dedicated in fulfilment of or in accordance with a vow. **2.** *R.C. Church.* having the nature of a voluntary offering: *a votive Mass.* [C16: from L *vōtīvus* promised by a vow, from *vōtum* a vow]

vouch (vaʊtʃ) *vb.* **1.** (*intr.*; usually foll. by *for*) to give personal assurance: *I'll vouch for his safety.* **2.** (when *tr.,* usually takes a clause as object; when *intr.,* usually foll. by *for*) to furnish supporting evidence (for) or function as proof (of). **3.** (*tr.*) *Arch.* to cite (authors, principles, etc.) in support of something. [C14: from OF *vocher* to summon, ult. from L *vocāre* to call]

voucher ('vaʊtʃə) *n.* **1.** a document serving as evidence for some claimed transaction, as the receipt or expenditure of money. **2.** *Brit.* a ticket or card serving as a substitute for cash: *a gift voucher.* **3.** a person or thing that vouches for the truth of some statement, etc. [C16: from Anglo-F, noun use of OF *voucher* to summon; see VOUCH]

vouchsafe (ˌvaʊtʃ'seɪf) *vb.* (*tr.*) **1.** to give or grant or condescend to give or grant: *she vouchsafed no reply.* **2.** (*may take a clause as object or an infinitive*) to agree, promise, or permit, often graciously or condescendingly: *he vouchsafed to come yesterday.* [C14 *vouchen sauf;* see VOUCH, SAFE]

voussoir (vuː'swɑː) *n.* a wedge-shaped stone or brick that is used with others to construct an arch or vault. [C18: from F, from Vulgar L *volsōrium* (unattested), ult. from L *volvere* to turn, roll]

vow (vaʊ) *n.* **1.** a solemn or earnest pledge or promise binding the person making it to perform a specified act or behave in a certain way. **2.** a solemn promise made to a deity or saint, by which the promiser pledges himself to some future act or way of life. **3. take vows.** to enter a religious order and commit oneself to its rule of life by the vows of poverty, chastity, and obedience. ~*vb.* **4.** (*tr.*; may take a clause as object or an infinitive*) to pledge, promise, or undertake solemnly: *he vowed to return.* **5.** (*tr.*) to dedicate or consecrate to God or a saint. **6.** (*tr.*; usually takes a clause as object*) to assert or swear emphatically. **7.** (*intr.*) *Arch.* to declare seriously. [C13: from OF *vou,* from L *vōtum;* see VOTE] — '**vower** *n.*

vowel ('vaʊəl) *n.* **1.** *Phonetics.* a voiced speech sound whose articulation is characterized by the absence of obstruction in the vocal tract, allowing the breath stream free passage. The timbre of a vowel is chiefly determined by the position of the tongue and the lips. **2.** a letter or

character representing a vowel. [C14: from OF, from L *vocālis littera* vowel, from *vocālis,* from *vox* voice] — '**vowel-**, **like** *adj.*

vowel gradation *n.* another name for **ablaut.** See **gradation** (sense 5).

vowelize *or* **-lise** ('vaʊə,laɪz) *vb.* (*tr.*) to mark the vowel points in (a Hebrew word or text). — ,**voweli'zation** *or* **-li'sation** *n.*

vowel mutation *n.* another name for **umlaut.**

vowel point *n.* any of several marks or points placed above or below consonants, esp. those evolved for Hebrew or Arabic, in order to indicate vowel sounds.

vox (vɒks) *n., pl.* **voces.** a voice or sound. [L: voice]

vox pop *n.* interviews with members of the public on a radio or television programme. [C20: shortened from VOX POPULI]

vox populi ('pɒpjʊ,laɪ) *n.* the voice of the people; popular or public opinion. [L]

voyage ('vɔɪɪdʒ) *n.* **1.** a journey, travel, or passage, esp. one to a distant land or by sea or air. ~*vb.* **2.** to travel over or traverse (something): *we will voyage to Africa.* [C13: from OF *veiage,* from L *viāticum* provision for travelling, from *viāticus,* from *via* way] — '**voyager** *n.*

voyageur (ˌvɔɪə'dʒɜː) *n.* (in Canada) a woodsman, guide, trapper, boatman, or explorer, esp. in the North. [C19: F: traveller, from *voyager* to VOYAGE]

voyeur (vwɑ'ɜː) *n.* a person who obtains sexual pleasure from the observation of people undressing, having intercourse, etc. [C20: F, lit.: one who sees, from *voir* to see, from L *vidēre*] — **vo'yeurism** *n.* — ,**voyeur'istic** *adj.*

VP *abbrev. for:* **1.** verb phrase. **2.** Vice President.

VR *abbrev. for:* **1.** variant reading. **2.** Victoria Regina. [L: Queen Victoria]

V. Rev. *abbrev. for* Very Reverend.

Vries (vriːs) *n.* See (Hugo) **De Vries.**

vrou (frəʊ) *n. S. African.* an Afrikaner woman, esp. a married woman. [from Afrik., from Du.]

vrystater ('freɪ,stɑːtə) *n. S. African.* a native inhabitant of the Free State, esp. one who is White. [from Afrik., from Du. *vrij* free + *staat* state]

vs *abbrev. for* versus.

VS *abbrev. for* Veterinary Surgeon.

v.s. *abbrev. for* vide supra (see **vide**).

V-sign *n.* **1.** (in Britain) an offensive gesture made by sticking up the index and middle fingers with the palm of the hand inwards. **2.** a similar gesture with the palm outwards meaning victory or peace.

VSO *abbrev. for:* **1.** very superior old: used to indicate that a brandy, port, etc., is between 12 and 17 years old. **2.** (in Britain) Voluntary Service Overseas: an organization that sends young volunteers to use and teach their skills in developing countries.

VSOP *abbrev. for* very special (*or* superior) old pale: used to indicate that a brandy, port, etc., is between 20 and 25 years old.

VTOL ('viːtɒl) *n.* vertical takeoff and landing; a system in which an aircraft can take off and land vertically. Cf. STOL.

VTR *abbrev. for* video tape recorder.

V-type engine *n.* a type of internal-combustion engine having two cylinder blocks attached to a single crankcase, the angle between the two blocks forming a V.

Vuelta Abajo (*Spanish* 'bwelta a'βaxo) *n.* a region of W Cuba: famous for its tobacco.

vug (vʌg) *n. Mining.* a small cavity in a rock or vein, usually lined with crystals. [C19: from Cornish *vooga* cave] — '**vuggy** *adj.*

Vuillard (*French* vɥijar) *n.* **Jean Édouard** (ʒɑ̃ edwar). 1868–1940, French painter and lithographer.

Vulcan ('vʌlkən) *n.* the Roman god of fire and metalworking. Greek counterpart: **Hephaestus.** — **Vulcanian** (vʌl'keɪnɪən) *adj.*

vulcanian (vʌl'keɪnɪən) *adj. Geol.* of or relating to a volcanic eruption characterized by the explosive discharge of gases, fine ash, and viscous lava that hardens in the crater. [C17: after VULCAN]

vulcanism ('vʌlkə,nɪzəm) *n.* a variant spelling of **volcanism.**

vulcanite ('vʌlkə,naɪt) *n.* a hard usually black rubber produced by vulcanizing natural rubber with sulphur. It is used for electrical insulators, etc. Also called: **ebonite.**

vulcanize *or* **-nise** ('vʌlkə,naɪz) *vb.* (*tr.*) **1.** to treat (rubber) with sulphur under heat and pressure to improve elasticity and strength or to produce a hard substance such as vulcanite. **2.** to treat (substances other than rubber) by a similar process in order to improve their properties. — ˌvulcaniˈzation *or* -niˈsation *n.*

vulcanology (ˌvʌlkəˈnɒlədʒɪ) *n.* a variant spelling of **volcanology.**

Vulg. *abbrev. for* Vulgate.

vulgar ('vʌlgə) *adj.* **1.** marked by lack of taste, culture, delicacy, manners, etc.: *vulgar language.* **2.** (*often cap.; usually prenominal*) denoting a form of a language, esp. of Latin, current among common people, esp. at a period when the formal language is archaic. **3.** *Arch.* of or current among the great mass of common people. [C14: from L *vulgāris,* from *vulgus* the common people] — **'vulgarly** *adv.*

vulgar fraction *n.* another name for **simple fraction.**

vulgarian (vʌlˈgɛərɪən) *n.* a vulgar person, esp. one who is rich or has pretensions to good taste.

vulgarism ('vʌlgəˌrɪzəm) *n.* **1.** a coarse, crude, or obscene expression. **2.** a word or phrase found only in the vulgar form of a language.

vulgarity (vʌlˈgærɪtɪ) *n., pl.* -ties. **1.** the condition of being vulgar; lack of good manners. **2.** a vulgar action, phrase, etc.

vulgarize *or* -rise ('vʌlgəˌraɪz) *vb.* (*tr.*) **1.** to make commonplace or vulgar. **2.** to make (something little known or difficult to understand) widely known or popular among the public. — ˌvulgariˈzation *or* -riˈsation *n.*

Vulgar Latin *n.* any of the dialects of Latin spoken in the Roman Empire other than classical Latin.

vulgate ('vʌlgeɪt, -gɪt) *n. Rare.* **1.** a commonly recognized text or version. **2.** the vernacular.

Vulgate ('vʌlgeɪt, -gɪt) *n.* **a.** (from the 13th century onwards) the fourth-century Latin version of the Bible produced by Jerome. **b.** (*as modifier*): *the Vulgate version.* [C17: from Med. L, from LL *vulgāta editiō* popular version (of the Bible), from L *vulgāre* to make common]

vulnerable ('vʌlnərəbᵊl) *adj.* **1.** capable of being physically or emotionally wounded or hurt. **2.** open to temptation, censure, etc. **3.** *Mil.* exposed to attack. **4.** *Bridge.*

(of a side who have won one game towards rubber) subject to increased bonuses or penalties. [C17: from LL, from L *vulnerāre* to wound, from *vulnus* a wound] — ˌvulneraˈbility *n.* — 'vulnerably *adv.*

vulnerary ('vʌlnərərɪ) *Med.* ~*adj.* **1.** of or used to heal a wound. ~*n., pl.* -aries. **2.** a vulnerary drug or agent. [C16: from L *vulnerārius* from *vulnus* wound]

vulpine ('vʌlpaɪn) *adj.* **1.** of, relating to, or resembling a fox. **2.** crafty, clever, etc. [C17: from L *vulpīnus* foxlike, from *vulpēs* fox]

vulture ('vʌltʃə) *n.* **1.** any of various very large diurnal birds of prey of Africa, Asia, and warm parts of Europe, typically having broad wings and soaring flight and feeding on carrion. **2.** any similar bird of North, Central, and South America. **3.** a person or thing that preys greedily and ruthlessly on others, esp. the helpless. [C14: from OF *voltour,* from L *vultur*] — **vulturine** ('vʌltʃəˌraɪn) *or* 'vulturous *adj.*

vulva ('vʌlvə) *n., pl.* -vae (-viː) *or* -vas. the external genitals of human females, including the labia, mons pubis, clitoris, and the vaginal orifice. [C16: from L: covering, womb, matrix] — 'vulvar *adj.*

vulvitis (vʌlˈvaɪtɪs) *n.* inflammation of the vulva.

vv *abbrev. for* vice versa.

vv. *abbrev. for:* **1.** versus. **2.** *Music.* volumes.

Vyatka (*Russian* 'vjatkə) *n.* the former name (1780–1934) of **Kirov.**

Vyborg (*Russian* 'vibɔrk) *n.* a port in the NW Soviet Union, at the head of **Vyborg Bay** (an inlet of the Gulf of Finland): belonged to Finland (1918–40). Pop.: 79 000 (1983 est.). Finnish name: **Viipuri.** Swedish name: **Viborg.**

Vyshinsky *or* **Vishinsky** (*Russian* viˈʃinskij) *n.* **Andrei Yanuaryevich** (anˈdrjej jənuˈarjɪvitʃ). 1883–1954, Soviet jurist, statesman, and diplomat; foreign minister (1949–53). He was public prosecutor (1935–38) at the trials held to purge Stalin's rivals and was the Soviet representative at the United Nations (1945–49; 1953–54).

W

w *or* **W** ('dʌbªl,juː) *n.,* *pl.* **w's, W's,** *or* **Ws.** **1.** the 23rd letter of the English alphabet. **2.** a speech sound represented by this letter, usually a bilabial semivowel, as in *web*.

W *symbol for:* **1.** *Chem.* tungsten. [from NL *wolframium*, from G *Wolfram*] **2.** watt. **3.** West. **4.** women's (size). **5.** *Physics.* work.

w. *abbrev. for:* **1.** week. **2.** weight. **3.** *Cricket.* **a.** wide. **b.** wicket. **4.** width. **5.** wife. **6.** with.

W. *abbrev. for:* **1.** Wales. **2.** Welsh.

WA *abbrev. for:* **1.** Washington (state). **2.** Western Australia.

WAAAF *abbrev. for* Women's Auxiliary Australian Air Force.

WAAC (wæk) *n.* **1.** *acronym for* Women's Army Auxiliary Corps. **2.** Also called: **Waac.** a member of this corps.

Waadt (vat) *n.* the German name for **Vaud.**

WAAF (wæf) *n.* **1.** *acronym for* Women's Auxiliary Air Force. **2.** Also called: **Waaf.** a member of this force.

Waal (*Dutch* waːl) *n.* a river in the central Netherlands: the S branch of the Lower Rhine. Length: 84 km (52 miles).

Wabash ('wɔːbæʃ) *n.* a river in the E central U.S., rising in W Ohio and flowing west and southwest to join the Ohio River in Indiana. Length: 764 km (475 miles).

wabble ('wɒbªl) *vb., n.* a variant spelling of **wobble.**

Wace (weɪs) *n.* Robert. born ?1100, Anglo-Norman poet; author of the *Roman de Brut* and *Roman de Rou.*

wacke ('wækə) *n. Obs.* any of various soft earthy rocks derived from basalt. [C18: from G: rock, gravel, basalt]

wacky ('wækɪ) *adj.* **wackier, wackiest.** *Sl.* eccentric or unpredictable. [C19 (in dialect sense: a fool): from WHACK (hence, a *whacky*, a person who behaves as if he had been whacked on the head)] —'**wackily** *adv.* —'**wackiness** *n.*

wad (wɒd) *n.* **1.** a small mass or ball of fibrous or soft material, such as cotton wool, used esp. for packing or stuffing. **2. a.** a plug of paper, cloth, leather, etc., pressed against a charge to hold it in place in a muzzle-loading cannon. **b.** a disc of paper, felt, etc., used to hold in place the powder and shot in a shotgun cartridge. **3.** a roll or bundle of something, esp. of banknotes. ~*vb.* **wadding, wadded.** **4.** to form (something) into a wad. **5.** (*tr.*) to roll into a wad or bundle. **6.** (*tr.*) **a.** to hold (a charge) in place with a wad. **b.** to insert a wad into (a gun). **7.** (*tr.*) to pack or stuff with wadding. [C14: from LL *wadda*]

Wadai (waː'daɪ) *n.* a former independent sultanate of NE central Africa: now the E part of Chad.

Waddenzee (*Dutch* 'wadənzeː) *n.* the part of the North Sea between the Dutch mainland and the West Frisian Islands.

wadding ('wɒdɪŋ) *n.* **1. a.** any fibrous or soft substance used as padding, stuffing, etc. **b.** a piece of this. **2.** material for wads used in cartridges or guns.

waddle ('wɒdªl) *vb.* (*intr.*) **1.** to walk with short steps, rocking slightly from side to side. ~*n.* **2.** a swaying gait or motion. [C16: prob. frequentative of WADE] —'**waddler** *n.* —'**waddling** *adj.*

waddy ('wɒdɪ) *n., pl.* **-dies.** **1.** a heavy wooden club used as a weapon by Australian Aborigines. ~*vb.* **-dying, -died.** **2.** (*tr.*) to hit with a waddy. [C19: from Abor., ? based on E WOOD]

wade (weɪd) *vb.* **1.** to walk with the feet immersed in (water, a stream, etc.). **2.** (*intr.;* often foll. by *through*) to proceed with difficulty: *to wade through a book.* **3.** (*intr.;* foll. by *in* or *into*) to attack energetically. ~*n.* **4.** the act or an instance of wading. [OE *wadan*] —'**wadable** *or* '**wadeable** *adj.*

wader ('weɪdə) *n.* **1.** a person or thing that wades. **2.** Also called: **wading bird.** any of various long-legged birds, esp. herons, storks, etc., that live near water and feed on fish, etc. **3.** a Brit. name for **shore bird.**

waders ('weɪdəz) *pl. n.* long waterproof boots, sometimes extending to the chest like trousers, worn by anglers.

wadi *or* **wady** ('wɒdɪ) *n., pl.* **-dies.** a watercourse in N Africa and Arabia, dry except in the rainy season. [C19: from Ar.]

Wadi Halfa ('wɒdɪ 'hælfə) *n.* a town in the N Sudan that was partly submerged by Lake Nasser: an important archaeological site.

Wad Medani (waːd mɪ'daːniː) *n.* a town in the E Sudan, on the Blue Nile: headquarters of the Gezira irrigation scheme; agricultural research centre. Pop.: 141 065 (1984 est.).

wafer ('weɪfə) *n.* **1.** a thin crisp sweetened biscuit, served with ice cream, etc. **2.** *Christianity.* a thin disc of unleavened bread used in the Eucharist. **3.** *Pharmacol.* an envelope of rice paper enclosing a medicament. **4.** *Electronics.* a small thin slice of semiconductor material, such as silicon, that is separated into numerous individual components or circuits. **5.** a small thin disc of adhesive material used to seal letters, etc. ~*vb.* **6.** (*tr.*) to seal or fasten with a wafer. [C14: from OF *waufre*, from MLow G *wāfel*] —'**wafery** *adj.*

waffle[1] ('wɒfªl) *n. Chiefly U.S. & Canad.* **a.** a crisp golden-brown pancake with deep indentations on both sides. **b.** (*as modifier*): *waffle iron.* [C19: from Du. *wafel* (earlier *wæfel*), of Gmc origin]

waffle[2] ('wɒfªl) *Inf., chiefly Brit.* ~*vb.* **1.** (*intr.;* often foll. by *on*) to speak or write in a vague and wordy manner. ~*n.* **2.** vague and wordy speech or writing. [C19: from ?] —'**waffling** *adj., n.*

waft (waːft, wɒft) *vb.* **1.** to carry or be carried gently on or as if on the air or water. ~*n.* **2.** the act or an instance of wafting. **3.** something, such as a scent, carried on the air. **4.** *Naut.* (formerly) a signal flag hoisted furled to signify various messages depending on where it was flown. [C16 (in obs. sense: to convey by ship): back formation from C15 *wafter* a convoy vessel, from MDu. *wachter* guard]

wag[1] (wæg) *vb.* **wagging, wagged.** **1.** to move or cause to move rapidly and repeatedly from side to side or up and down. **2.** to move (the tongue) or (of the tongue) to be moved rapidly in talking, esp. in gossip. **3.** to move (the finger) or (of the finger) to be moved from side to side, in or as in admonition. **4.** *Sl.* to play truant (esp. in **wag it**). ~*n.* **5.** the act or an instance of wagging. [C13: from OE *wagian* to shake]

wag[2] (wæg) *n.* a humorous or jocular person; wit. [C16: from ?] —'**waggish** *adj.*

wage (weɪdʒ) *n.* **1.** (*often pl.*) payment in return for work or services, esp. that made to workmen on a daily, hourly, weekly, or piecework basis. Cf. **salary.** **2.** (*pl.*) *Econ.* the portion of the national income accruing to labour as earned income, as contrasted with the unearned income accruing to capital in the form of rent, interest, and dividends. **3.** (*often pl.*) recompense, return, or yield. ~*vb.* (*tr.*) **4.** to engage in. [C14: from OF *wagier* to pledge, from *wage*, of Gmc origin] —'**wageless** *adj.*

wage earner *n.* **1.** a person who works for wages. **2.** the person who earns money to support a household by working.

wage freeze *n.* a statutory restriction on wage increases.

wage indexation *n.* a linking of wage rises to increases in the cost of living usually in order to maintain real wages during periods of high inflation.

wager ('weɪdʒə) *n.* **1.** an agreement to pay an amount of money as a result of the outcome of an unsettled matter. **2.** an amount staked on the outcome of such an event. **3. wager of battle.** (in medieval Britain) a pledge to do battle to decide guilt or innocence by single combat. **4. wager of law.** *English legal history.* a form of trial in which the accused offered to make oath of his innocence, supported by the oaths of 11 of his neighbours declaring their belief in his statements. ~*vb.* **5.** (when *tr.,* *may take a clause as object*) to risk or bet (something) on the outcome of an unsettled matter. [C14: from Anglo-F *wageure* a pledge, from OF *wagier* to pledge; see WAGE] —'**wagerer** *n.*

wage slave *n. Ironical.* a person dependent on a wage or salary.

wagga ('wɒgə) *n. Austral.* a blanket or bed covering made out of sacks stitched together. [C19: after WAGGA WAGGA]

Wagga Wagga ('wɒgə 'wɒgə) n. a city in SE Australia, in New South Wales on the Murrumbidgee River: agricultural trading centre. Pop. 50 900 (1985 est.).

waggle ('wæg°l) vb. **1.** to move or cause to move with a rapid shaking or wobbling motion. ~n. **2.** a rapid shaking or wobbling motion. [C16: from WAG¹] —'**waggly** adj.

waggon ('wægən) n. a variant spelling (esp. Brit.) of **wagon.**

wag-n-bietjie ('va:x°n,bɪkɪ) n. S. African. any of various thorn bushes or trees. [from Afrik. wag wait + n a + bietjie bit]

Wagner ('va:gnə) n. **(Wilhelm) Richard** ('rɪçart). 1813–83, German romantic composer noted chiefly for his invention of the music drama. His cycle of four such dramas The Ring of the Nibelung was produced at his own theatre in Bayreuth in 1876. His other operas include Tannhäuser (1845; revised 1861), Tristan and Isolde (1865), and Parsifal (1882).

Wagnerian (va:g'nɪərɪən) adj. **1.** of or suggestive of the dramatic musical compositions of Richard Wagner, their massive scale, dramatic and emotional intensity, etc. ~n. also **Wagnerite** ('va:gnə,raɪt). **2.** a follower or disciple of the music or theories of Richard Wagner.

wagon or **waggon** ('wægən) n. **1.** any of various types of wheeled vehicles, ranging from carts to lorries, esp. a vehicle with four wheels drawn by a horse, tractor, etc., and used for carrying heavy loads. **2.** Brit. a railway freight truck, esp. an open one. **3.** an obsolete word for **chariot. 4. on** (or off) **the wagon.** Inf. abstaining (or no longer abstaining) from alcoholic drinks. [C16: from Du. wagen WAIN] —'**wagonless** or '**waggonless** adj.

wagoner or **waggoner** ('wægənə) n. a person who drives a wagon.

wagonette or **waggonette** (,wægə'nɛt) n. a light four-wheeled horse-drawn vehicle with two lengthwise seats facing each other behind a crosswise driver's seat.

wagon-lit (French vagɔ̃li) n., pl. **wagons-lits** (vagɔ̃li). **1.** a sleeping car on a European railway. **2.** a compartment on such a car. [C19: from F, from wagon railway coach + lit bed]

wagonload or **waggonload** ('wægən,ləud) n. the load that is or can be carried by a wagon.

wagon train n. a supply train of horses and wagons, esp. one going over rough terrain.

wagon vault n. another name for **barrel vault.**

Wagram (German 'va:gram) n. a village in NE Austria: scene of the defeat of the Austrians by Napoleon in 1809.

wagtail ('wæg,teɪl) n. any of various passerine songbirds of Eurasia and Africa, having a very long tail that wags when the bird walks.

Wahhabi or **Wahabi** (wə'ha:bɪ) n., pl. **-bis.** a member of a strictly conservative Muslim sect founded in the 18th century. —**Wah'habism** or **Wa'habism** n.

wahine (wa:'hi:nɪ) n. **1.** N.Z. a Maori woman. **2.** a Polynesian woman. [from Maori & Hawaiian]

wahoo (wa:'hu:, 'wa:hu:) n., pl. **-hoos.** a large fast-moving food and game fish of tropical seas. [from ?]

wah-wah ('wa:,wa:) n. **1.** the sound made by a trumpet, cornet, etc., when the bell is alternately covered and uncovered. **2.** an electronic attachment for an electric guitar, etc., that simulates this effect. [C20: imit.]

waif (weɪf) n. **1.** a person, esp. a child, who is homeless, friendless, or neglected. **2.** anything found and not claimed, the owner being unknown. [C14: from Anglo-Norman, var. of OF gaif, from ON] —'**waif,like** adj.

Waikaremoana (waɪ'kɒrəməu,a:nə) n. **Lake.** a lake in the North Island of New Zealand in a dense bush setting. Area: about 55 sq. km (21 sq. miles).

Waikato ('waɪ,ka:təu) n. the longest river in New Zealand, flowing northwest across North Island to the Tasman Sea. Length: 350 km (220 miles).

Waikiki ('waɪkɪ,ki:, ,waɪkɪ'ki:) n. a resort area in Hawaii, on SE Oahu: a suburb of Honolulu.

wail (weɪl) vb. **1.** (intr.) to utter a prolonged high-pitched cry, as of grief or misery. **2.** (intr.) to make a sound resembling such a cry: the wind wailed in the trees. **3.** (tr.) to lament, esp. with mournful sounds. ~n. **4.** a prolonged high-pitched mournful cry or sound. [C14: from ON] —'**wailer** n.

Wailing Wall n. a wall in Jerusalem, the last extant part of the Temple of Herod, held sacred by Jews as a place of prayer and pilgrimage. Also called (in Judaism): **Western Wall.**

wain (weɪn) n. Chiefly poetic. a farm wagon or cart. [OE wægn]

wainscot ('weɪnskət) n. **1.** Also called: **wainscoting** or **wainscotting.** a lining applied to the walls of a room, esp. one of wood panelling. **2.** the lower part of the walls of a room, esp. when finished in a material different from the upper part. **3.** fine-quality oak used as wainscot. ~vb. **4.** (tr.) to line (a wall of a room) with a wainscot. [C14: from MLow G wagenschot, ?from wagen WAGON + schot planking]

wainwright ('weɪn,raɪt) n. a person who makes wagons.

waist (weɪst) n. **1.** Anat. the constricted part of the trunk between the ribs and hips. **2.** the part of a garment covering the waist. **3.** the middle part of an object that resembles the waist in narrowness or position. **4.** the middle part of a ship. **5.** the middle section of an aircraft fuselage. **6.** the constriction between the thorax and abdomen in wasps and similar insects. [C14: from ?] —'**waistless** adj.

waistband ('weɪst,bænd) n. an encircling band of material to finish and strengthen a skirt or trousers at the waist.

waistcoat ('weɪs,kəut) n. **1.** a man's sleeveless waistlength garment worn under a suit jacket, usually buttoning up the front. **2.** a similar garment worn by women. ~U.S. and Canad. name: **vest.** —'**waist,coated** adj.

waistline ('weɪst,laɪn) n. **1.** a line around the body at the narrowest part of the waist. **2.** the intersection of the bodice and the skirt of a dress, etc., or the level of this.

wait (weɪt) vb. **1.** (when intr., often foll. by for, until, or to) to stay in one place or remain inactive in expectation (of something). **2.** to delay temporarily or be temporarily delayed: that work can wait. **3.** (when intr., usually foll. by for) (of things) to be ready or at hand; be in store (for a person): supper was waiting for them when they got home. **4.** (intr.) to act as a waiter or waitress. ~n. **5.** the act or an instance of waiting. **6.** a period of waiting. **7.** (pl.) Rare. a band of musicians who go around the streets, esp. at Christmas, singing and playing carols. **8. lie in wait.** to prepare an ambush (for someone). ~See also **wait on, wait up.** [C12: from OF waitier]

wait-a-bit n. any of various mainly tropical plants having sharp hooked thorns.

waiter ('weɪtə) n. **1.** a man whose occupation is to serve at table, as in a restaurant. **2.** a person who waits. **3.** a tray or salver.

waiting game n. the postponement of action or decision in order to gain the advantage.

waiting list n. a list of people waiting to obtain some object, treatment, status, etc.

waiting room n. a room in which people may wait, as at a railway station, doctor's or dentist's surgery, etc.

wait on vb. (intr., prep.) **1.** to serve at the table of. **2.** to act as an attendant to. ~sentence substitute. **3.** N.Z. stop! hold on! ~Also (for senses 1, 2): **wait upon.**

waitress ('weɪtrɪs) n. a woman who serves at table, as in a restaurant.

wait up vb. (intr., adv.) to delay going to bed in order to await some event.

waive (weɪv) vb. (tr.) **1.** to set aside or relinquish: to waive one's right to something. **2.** to refrain from enforcing or applying (a law, penalty, etc.). **3.** to defer. [C13: from OF weyver, from waif abandoned; see WAIF]

waiver ('weɪvə) n. **1.** the voluntary relinquishment, expressly or by implication, of some claim or right. **2.** the act or an instance of relinquishing a claim or right. **3.** a formal statement in writing of such relinquishment. [C17: from OF weyver to relinquish]

Wajda (Polish 'vajda) n. **Andrei** or **Andrzej** ('andʒɛj). born 1926, Polish film director. His best-known films include Ashes and Diamonds (1958), The Wedding (1972), Man of Iron (1980), and Danton (1982).

Wakayama (,wækə'ja:mə) n. an industrial city in S Japan, on S Honshu. Pop.: 401 462 (1980).

wake¹ (weɪk) vb. **waking, woke, woken. 1.** (often foll. by up) to rouse or become roused from sleep. **2.** (often foll. by up) to rouse or become roused from inactivity. **3.** (intr.; often foll. by to or up to) to become conscious or aware: at last he woke up to the situation. **4.** (intr.) to be or remain awake. ~n. **5.** a watch or vigil held over the body of a dead person during the night before burial. **6.** (in Ireland) festivities held after a funeral. **7.** the patronal or dedication festival of English parish churches. **8.** a solemn or ceremonial vigil. **9.** (*usually pl.*) an annual holiday in various towns in Northern England, when the local factories close. [OE *wacian*] —'**waker** *n.*

▷ **Usage.** Where there is an object and the sense is the literal one *wake* (*up*) and *waken* are the commonest forms: *I wakened him; I woke him* (*up*). Both verbs are also commonly used without an object: *I woke up. Awake* and *awaken* are preferred to other forms of *wake* where the sense is a figurative one: *he awoke to the danger.*

wake² (weɪk) *n.* **1.** the waves or track left by a vessel or other object moving through water. **2.** the track or path left by anything that has passed: *wrecked houses in the wake of the hurricane.* [C16: of Scand. origin]

Wakefield ('weɪk,fiːld) *n.* a city in N England, administrative centre of West Yorkshire: important since medieval times as an agricultural and textile centre. Pop.: 60 540 (1981).

wakeful ('weɪkfʊl) *adj.* **1.** unable or unwilling to sleep. **2.** sleepless. **3.** alert. —'**wakefully** *adv.* —'**wakefulness** *n.*

Wake Island *n.* an atoll in the N central Pacific: claimed by the U.S. in 1899; developed as a civil and naval air station in the late 1930s. Area: 8 sq. km (3 sq. miles).

wakeless ('weɪklɪs) *adj.* (of sleep) unbroken.

waken ('weɪkən) *vb.* to rouse or be roused from sleep or some other inactive state.

▷ **Usage.** See at **wake¹**.

wake-robin *n.* any of a genus of North American herbaceous plants having a whorl of three leaves and three-petalled solitary flowers.

wake-up *n.* **a wake-up to.** *Austral. sl.* fully alert to (a person, thing, action, etc.).

Waksman ('wæksmən) *n.* **Selman Abraham.** 1888–1973, U.S. microbiologist, born in Russia. He discovered streptomycin: Nobel prize for physiology or medicine 1952.

Walachia *or* **Wallachia** (wɒ'leɪkɪə) *n.* a former principality of SE Europe: a vassal state of the Ottoman Empire from the 15th century until its union with Moldavia in 1859, subsequently forming present-day Romania. —**Wa'lachian** *or* **Wal'lachian** *n., adj.*

Walbrzych (*Polish* 'vaubʒix) *n.* an industrial city in SW Poland. Pop.: 138 700 (1986 est.). German name: **Waldenburg.**

Walcheren (*Dutch* 'vɑlxərə) *n.* an island in the SW Netherlands, in the Scheldt estuary: administratively part of Zeeland province; suffered severely in World War II, when the dykes were breached, and again in the floods of 1953. Area: 212 sq. km (82 sq. miles).

Waldemar I *or* **Valdemar I** ('vældɪ,mɑː) *n.* known as *Waldemar the Great.* 1131–82, king of Denmark (1157–82). He conquered the Wends (1169), increased the territory of Denmark, and established the hereditary rule of his line.

Waldenburg ('valdənbʊrk) *n.* the German name for **Walbrzych.**

Waldenses (wɒl'dɛnsiːz) *pl. n.* the members of a small sect founded as a reform movement within the Roman Catholic Church by Peter Waldo, a merchant of Lyons, in the late 12th century. —**Wal'densian** *n., adj.*

Waldheim (*German* 'valthaɪm) *n.* **Kurt** (kʊrt). born 1918, Austrian diplomat; secretary-general of the United Nations (1972–81); president of Austria from 1986.

Waldo ('wɔːldəʊ) *n., pl.* **-dos, -does.** a gadget for manipulating objects by remote control. [C20: after *Waldo* F. Jones, an inventor, in a science fiction story by Robert Heinlein]

Waldstein (*German* 'valtʃtaɪn) *n.* a variant of (Albrecht Wenzel Eusebius von) **Wallenstein.**

wale (weɪl) *n.* **1.** the raised mark left on the skin after the stroke of a rod or whip. **2.** the weave or texture of a fabric, such as the ribs in corduroy. **3.** *Naut.* a ridge of planking along the rail of a ship. ~*vb.* **4.** (*tr.*) to raise a wale or wales on by striking. **5.** to weave with a wale. [OE *walu* weal]

Wales (weɪlz) *n.* a principality that is part of the United Kingdom, in the west of Great Britain; conquered by the English in 1282; parliamentary union with England took place in 1536. It consists mainly of moorlands and mountains and has an economy that is chiefly agricultural, with an industrial and coal-mining area in the south. Capital: Cardiff. Pop.: 2 821 000 (1986 est.). Area: 20 768 sq. km

(8017 sq. miles). Welsh name: **Cymru.** Medieval Latin name: **Cambria.**

Walesa (væ'wɛnsə) *n.* **Lech** (lɛç). born 1943, Polish trade unionist; leader of the independent trade union Solidarity (1980–81); Nobel peace prize 1983.

Waley ('weɪlɪ) *n.* **Arthur.** real name *Arthur Schloss.* 1889–1966, English orientalist, best known for his translations of Chinese poetry.

Walfish Bay ('wɔːlfɪʃ) *n.* a variant spelling of **Walvis Bay.**

Walhalla (wæl'hælə, væl-) *or* **Walhall** (wæl'hæl, væl-) *n.* variants of **Valhalla.**

walk (wɔːk) *vb.* **1.** (*intr.*) to move along or travel on foot at a moderate rate; advance in such a manner that at least one foot is always on the ground. **2.** (*tr.*) to pass through, on, or over on foot, esp. habitually. **3.** (*tr.*) to cause, assist, or force to move along at a moderate rate: *to walk a dog.* **4.** (*tr.*) to escort or conduct by walking: *to walk someone home.* **5.** (*intr.*) (of ghosts, spirits, etc.) to appear or move about in visible form. **6.** (*intr.*) to follow a certain course or way of life: *to walk in misery.* **7.** (*tr.*) to bring into a certain condition by walking: *I walked my shoes to shreds.* **8.** to disappear or be stolen: *where's my pencil? It seems to have walked.* **9. walk it.** to win easily. **10. walk on air.** to be delighted or exhilarated. **11. walk tall.** *Chiefly U.S. & Canad. inf.* to have self-respect or pride. **12. walk the streets. a.** to be a prostitute. **b.** to wander round a town, esp. when looking for work or when homeless. ~*n.* **13.** the act or an instance of walking. **14.** the distance or extent walked. **15.** a manner of walking; gait. **16.** a place set aside for walking; promenade. **17.** a chosen profession or sphere of activity (esp. in **walk of life**). **18. a.** an arrangement of trees or shrubs in widely separated rows. **b.** the space between such rows. **19.** an enclosed ground for the exercise or feeding of domestic animals, esp. horses. **20.** *Chiefly Brit.* the route covered in the course of work, as by a tradesman or postman. **21.** a procession; march: *Orange walk.* **22.** *Obs.* the section of a forest controlled by a keeper. ~See also **walk away, walk into,** etc. [OE *wealcan*] —'**walkable** *adj.*

walkabout ('wɔːkə,baʊt) *n.* **1.** a periodic nomadic excursion into the Australian bush made by an Aborigine. **2.** an occasion when celebrities, royalty, etc., walk among and meet the public.

walk away *vb.* (*intr., adv.*) **1.** to leave, esp. disregarding someone else's distress. **2. walk away with.** to achieve or win easily.

walker ('wɔːkə) *n.* **1.** a person who walks. **2.** Also called: **baby walker.** a tubular frame on wheels or casters to support a baby learning to walk. **3.** a similar support for walking, often with rubber feet, for use by disabled or infirm people.

Walker ('wɔːkə) *n.* **John.** born 1952, New Zealand middle-distance runner, the first athlete to run one hundred sub-four-minute miles.

walkie-talkie *or* **walky-talky** (,wɔːkɪ'tɔːkɪ) *n., pl.* **-talkies.** a small combined radio transmitter and receiver that can be carried around by one person: widely used by the police, medical services, etc.

walk-in *adj.* **1.** (of a cupboard) large enough to allow a person to enter and move about in. **2.** (of a flat or house) in a suitable condition for immediate occupation.

walking papers *pl. n. Sl., chiefly U.S. & Canad.* notice of dismissal.

walking stick *n.* **1.** a stick or cane carried in the hand to assist walking. **2.** the usual U.S. name for **stick insect.**

walk into *vb.* (*intr., prep.*) to meet with unwittingly: *to walk into a trap.*

Walkman ('wɔːkmən) *n., pl.* **-mans.** *Trademark.* a small portable cassette player with headphones.

walk off *vb.* **1.** (*intr.*) to depart suddenly. **2.** (*tr., adv.*) to get rid of by walking: *to walk off an attack of depression.* **3. walk (a person) off his feet.** to make (a person) walk so fast that he is exhausted. **4. walk off with. a.** to steal. **b.** to win, esp. easily.

walk-on *n.* **a.** a small part in a play or theatrical entertainment, esp. one without any lines. **b.** (*as modifier*): *a walk-on part.*

walk out *vb.* (*intr., adv.*) **1.** to leave without explanation, esp. in anger. **2.** to go on strike. **3. walk out on.** *Inf.* to abandon or desert. **4. walk out with.** *Brit., obs. or dialect.* to court or be courted by. ~*n.* **walkout.** **5.** a strike by workers. **6.** the act of leaving a meeting, conference, etc., as a protest.

walkover ('wɔːk,əʊvə) n. **1.** Inf. an easy or unopposed victory. **2.** Horse racing. **a.** the running or walking over the course by the only contestant entered in a race at the time of starting. **b.** a race won in this way. ~vb. **walk over.** (intr., mainly prep.) **3.** (also adv.) to win a race by a walkover. **4.** Inf. to beat (an opponent) conclusively or easily.

walk socks pl. n. the N.Z. name for **pop socks.**

walk through Theatre. ~vb. **1.** (tr.) to act or recite (a part) in a perfunctory manner, as at a first rehearsal. ~n. **walk-through. 2.** a rehearsal of a part.

walkway ('wɔːk,weɪ) n. **1.** a path designed and sometimes landscaped for pedestrian use. **2.** a passage or path, esp. one for walking over machinery, connecting buildings, etc.

Walkyrie (væl'kɪərɪ, 'vælkɪərɪ) n. a variant spelling of **Valkyrie.**

wall (wɔːl) n. **1. a.** a vertical construction made of stone, brick, wood, etc., with a length and height much greater than its thickness, used to enclose, divide, or support. **b.** (as modifier): wall hangings. Related adj.: **mural. 2.** (often pl.) a structure or rampart built to protect and surround a position or place for defensive purposes. **3.** Anat. any lining, membrane, or investing part that encloses or bounds a bodily cavity or structure: abdominal wall. Technical name: **paries.** Related adj.: **parietal. 4.** anything that suggests a wall in function or effect: a wall of fire. **5. drive** (or **push**) **to the wall.** to force into an awkward situation. **6. go to the wall.** Inf. to be ruined. **7. go** (or **drive**) **up the wall.** Sl. to become (or cause to become) crazy or furious. **8. have one's back to the wall.** to be in a very difficult situation. ~vb. (tr.) **9.** to protect, provide, or confine with or as if with a wall. **10.** (often foll. by up) to block (an opening) with a wall. **11.** (often foll. by in or up) to seal by or within a wall or recess. [OE weall, from L vallum palisade, from vallus stake] **—walled** adj. **—'wall-less** adj.

wallaby ('wɒləbɪ) n., pl. **-bies** or **-by.** any of various herbivorous marsupials of Australia and New Guinea, similar to but smaller than kangaroos. [C19: from Abor. wolabā]

Wallaby ('wɒləbɪ) n., pl. **-bies.** a member of the international rugby union football team of Australia.

Wallace ('wɒlɪs) n. **1. Alfred Russel.** 1823–1913, British naturalist, whose work on the theory of natural selection influenced Charles Darwin. **2. Edgar.** 1875–1932, English crime novelist. **3. Sir Richard.** 1818–90, English art collector and philanthropist. His bequest to the nation forms the Wallace Collection, London. **4. Sir William.** ?1272–1305, Scottish patriot, who defeated the army of Edward I of England at Stirling (1297) but was routed at Falkirk (1298) and later executed.

Wallace's line n. the hypothetical boundary between the Oriental and Australasian zoogeographical regions, which runs through Indonesia and SE of the Philippines. [C20: after A. R. WALLACE]

Wallachia (wɒ'leɪkɪə) n. a variant spelling of **Walachia.**

wallah or **walla** ('wɒlə) n. (usually in combination) Inf. a person involved with or in charge of (a specified thing): the book wallah. [C18: from Hindi -wālā from Sansk. pāla protector]

wallaroo (,wɒlə'ruː) n., pl. **-roos** or **-roo.** a large stocky Australian kangaroo of rocky or mountainous regions. [C19: from Abor. wolarū]

Wallasey ('wɒləsɪ) n. a town in NW England, in Merseyside on the Wirral Peninsula near the mouth of the River Mersey, opposite Liverpool. Pop.: 90 057 (1981).

wall bars pl. n. a series of horizontal bars attached to a wall and used in gymnastics.

wallboard ('wɔːl,bɔːd) n. a thin board made of materials, such as compressed wood fibres or gypsum plaster, between stiff paper, and used to cover walls, partitions, etc.

wall creeper n. a pink-and-grey woodpecker-like songbird of Eurasian mountain regions.

walled plain n. any of the largest of the lunar craters, having diameters between 50 and 300 kilometres.

Wallenstein (German 'valənʃtaɪn) or **Waldstein** n. **Albrecht Wenzel Eusebius von** ('albrɛçt 'vɛntsəl ɔy'zeːbius fɔn), duke of Friedland and Mecklenburg, prince of Sagan. 1583–1634, German general and statesman, born in Bohemia. As leader of the Hapsburg forces

in the Thirty Years' War he won many successes until his defeat at Lützen (1632) by Gustavus Adolphus.

Waller ('wɒlə) n. **1. Edmund.** 1606–87, English poet and politician, famous for his poem Go, Lovely Rose. **2. Fats,** real name Thomas Waller. 1904–43, U.S. jazz pianist and singer.

wallet ('wɒlɪt) n. **1.** a small folding case, usually of leather, for holding paper money, documents, etc. **2.** Arch., chiefly Brit. a rucksack or knapsack. [C14: of Gmc origin]

walleye ('wɔːl,aɪ) n., pl. **-eyes** or **-eye. 1.** a divergent squint. **2.** opacity of the cornea. **3.** an eye having a white or light-coloured iris. **4.** Also called: **walleyed pike.** a North American pikeperch valued as a food and game fish. [back formation from earlier walleyed, from ON vagleygr, from vage ? a film over the eye + -eygr -eyed, from auga eye; infl. by WALL] **—'wall,eyed** adj.

wallflower ('wɔːl,flaʊə) n. **1.** Also called: **gillyflower.** a cruciferous plant of S Europe, grown for its clusters of yellow, orange, brown, red, or purple fragrant flowers and naturalized on old walls, cliffs, etc. **2.** Inf. a person who stays on the fringes of a dance or party on account of lacking a partner or being shy.

Wallis[1] ('valɪs) n. the German name for **Valais.**

Wallis[2] ('wɒlɪs) n. **Sir Barnes** (**Neville**). 1887–1979, English aeronautical engineer. He designed the airship R100, the Wellesley and Wellington bombers, and the bouncing bomb (1943), which was used to destroy the Ruhr dams during World War II.

Wallis and Futuna Islands ('wɒlɪs; fuː'tjuːnə) pl. n. a French overseas territory in the SW Pacific, west of Samoa. Capital: Mata-Utu. Pop.: 14 800 (1987 est.). Area: 367 sq. km (143 sq. miles).

wall of death n. (at a fairground) a giant cylinder round the inside vertical walls of which a motorcyclist rides.

Walloon (wɒ'luːn) n. **1.** a member of a French-speaking people living chiefly in S Belgium and adjacent parts of France. **2.** the French dialect of Belgium. ~adj. **3.** of or characteristic of the Walloons or their dialect. [C16: from OF Wallon, from Med. L: foreigner, of Gmc origin]

wallop ('wɒləp) vb. **1.** (tr.) Inf. to beat soundly; strike hard. **2.** (tr.) Inf. to defeat utterly. **3.** (intr.) (of liquids) to boil violently. ~n. **4.** Inf. a hard blow. **5.** Inf. the ability to hit powerfully, as of a boxer. **6.** Inf. a forceful impression. **7.** Brit. sl. beer. [C14: from OF waloper to gallop, from OF galoper, from ?]

walloper ('wɒləpə) n. **1.** a person or thing that wallops. **2.** Austral. sl. a policeman.

walloping ('wɒləpɪŋ) Inf. ~n. **1.** a thrashing. ~adj. **2.** (intensifier): a walloping drop in sales.

wallow ('wɒləʊ) vb. (intr.) **1.** (esp. of certain animals) to roll about in mud, water, etc., for pleasure. **2.** to move about with difficulty. **3.** to indulge oneself in possessions, emotion, etc.: to wallow in self-pity. ~n. **4.** the act or an instance of wallowing. **5.** a muddy place where animals wallow. [OE wealwian to roll (in mud)] **—'wallower** n.

wallpaper ('wɔːl,peɪpə) n. **1.** paper usually printed or embossed with designs for pasting onto walls and ceilings. ~vb. **2.** to cover (a surface) with wallpaper.

wall pepper n. a small Eurasian plant having yellow flowers and acrid-tasting leaves.

wall plate n. a horizontal timber member placed along the top of a wall to support the ends of joists, rafters, etc., and distribute the load.

wallposter ('wɔːl,pəʊstə) n. (in China) a bulletin or political message painted in large characters on a wall.

wall rocket n. any of several yellow-flowered European cruciferous plants that grow on old walls and in waste places.

wall rue n. a delicate fern that grows in rocky crevices and walls in North America and Eurasia.

Wallsend ('wɔːlz,ɛnd) n. a town in NE England, in Tyne and Wear on the River Tyne: situated at the E end of Hadrian's Wall; shipbuilding. Pop.: 44 699 (1981).

Wall Street n. a street in lower Manhattan, New York, where the Stock Exchange and major banks are situated, regarded as the embodiment of American finance.

wall-to-wall adj. **1.** (esp. of carpeting) completely covering a floor. **2.** Inf. nonstop; widespread: wall-to-wall sales.

wally ('wɒlɪ) n., pl. **-lies.** Sl. a stupid person. [C20: shortened from the name Walter]

walnut ('wɔːl,nʌt) n. **1.** any of a genus of deciduous trees of America, SE Europe, and Asia. They have aromatic leaves and flowers in catkins and are grown for their edible nuts and for their wood. **2.** the nut of any of these trees, having a wrinkled two-lobed seed and a hard wrinkled shell. **3.** the wood of any of these trees, used in making furniture, etc. **4.** a light yellowish-brown colour. ~adj. **5.** made from the wood of a walnut tree: *a walnut table.* **6.** of the colour walnut. [OE *walh-hnutu,* lit.: foreign nut]

Walpole ('wɔːl,pəʊl) n. **1. Horace,** 4th Earl of Orford. 1717–97, English writer, noted for his letters and for his delight in the Gothic, as seen in his house Strawberry Hill and his novel *The Castle of Otranto* (1764). **2.** his father, Sir **Robert,** 1st Earl of Orford. 1676–1745, English Whig statesman. As first lord of the Treasury and Chancellor of the Exchequer (1721–42) he was effectively Britain's first prime minister.

Walpurgis Night (væl'pʊəgɪs) n. the eve of May 1, believed in German folklore to be the night of a witches' sabbath on the Brocken, in the Harz Mountains. [C19: translation of G *Walpurgisnacht,* the eve of the feast day of St Walpurga, 8th-cent. abbess in Germany]

walrus ('wɔːlrəs, 'wɒl-) n., pl. **-ruses** or **-rus.** a mammal of northern seas, having a tough thick skin, upper canine teeth enlarged as tusks, and coarse whiskers, and feeding mainly on shellfish. [C17: prob. from Du., of Scand. origin]

walrus moustache n. a long thick moustache drooping at the ends.

Walsall ('wɔːlsɔːl) n. an industrial town in central England, in the West Midlands. Pop.: 178 909 (1981).

Walsingham ('wɔːlsɪŋəm) n. Sir **Francis.** ?1530–90, English statesman. As secretary of state (1573–90) to Elizabeth I he developed a system of domestic and foreign espionage and uncovered several plots against the Queen.

Walter n. **1.** (*German* 'valtər). **Bruno** ('bruːno), real name *Bruno Walter Schlesinger.* 1876–1962, U.S. conductor, born in Germany: famous for his performances of Haydn, Mozart, and Mahler. **2.** ('wɔːltə). **John.** 1739–1812, English publisher; founded *The Daily Universal Register* (1785), which in 1788 became *The Times.*

Waltham Forest ('wɔːlθəm) n. a borough of NE Greater London. Pop.: 215 800 (1986 est.).

Walther von der Vogelweide (*German* 'valtər fɔn der 'foːgəlvaidə) n. ?1170–?1230, German minnesinger, noted for his lyric verse on political and moral themes.

Walton ('wɔːltᵊn) n. **1. Ernest Thomas Sinton.** born 1903, Irish physicist. He succeeded in producing the first artificial transmutation of an atomic nucleus (1932) with Sir John Cockcroft, with whom he shared the Nobel prize for physics 1951. **2. Izaak** ('aɪzək). 1593–1683, English writer, best known for *The Compleat Angler* (1653; enlarged 1676). **3.** Sir **William (Turner).** 1902–83, English composer. His works include *Façade* (1923), a setting of satirical verses by Edith Sitwell, the *Viola Concerto* (1929), and the oratorio *Belshazzar's Feast* (1931).

waltz (wɔːls) n. **1.** a ballroom dance in triple time in which couples spin around as they progress round the room. **2.** a piece of music composed for or in the rhythm of this dance. ~vb. **3.** to dance or lead (someone) in or as in a waltz. **4.** (*intr.*) to move in a sprightly and self-assured manner. **5.** (*intr.*) *Inf.* to succeed easily. **6. waltz Matilda** *Austral.* See **Matilda.** [C18: from G *Walzer,* from MHG *walzen* to roll]

waltzer ('wɔːlsə) n. **1.** a person who waltzes. **2.** a fairground roundabout on which people are spun round and moved up and down as it revolves.

Walvis Bay ('wɔːlvɪs) or **Walfish Bay** n. a port in Namibia, on the Atlantic: forms an exclave of Cape Province, South Africa, covering an area of 1124 sq. km (434 sq. miles) with its hinterland, but has been administered by Namibia since 1922; chief port of Namibia and rich fishing centre. Pop.: 24 600 (1983 est.).

wampum ('wɒmpəm) n. (formerly) money used by North American Indians, made of cylindrical shells strung or woven together. Also called: **peag, peage.** [C17: of Amerind origin, short for *wampumpeag,* from *wampompeag,* from *wampan* light + *api* string + -*ag* pl. suffix]

wan (wɒn) adj. **wanner, wannest. 1.** unnaturally pale, esp. from sickness, grief, etc. **2.** suggestive of ill health, unhappiness, etc. **3.** (of light, stars, etc.) faint or dim. [OE *wann* dark] —'**wanly** adv. —'**wanness** n.

Wanchüan or **Wan-ch'uan** (,wæntʃʊ'aːn) n. a former name of **Zhangjiakou.**

wand (wɒnd) n. **1.** a slender supple stick or twig. **2.** a thin rod carried as a symbol of authority. **3.** a rod used by a magician, etc. **4.** *Inf.* a conductor's baton. **5.** *Archery.* a marker used to show the distance at which the archer stands for the target. [C12: from ON *vöndr*]

wander ('wɒndə) vb. (*mainly intr.*) **1.** (*also tr.*) to move or travel about, in, or through (a place) without any definite purpose or destination. **2.** to proceed in an irregular course. **3.** to go astray, as from a path or course. **4.** (of thoughts, etc.) to lose concentration. **5.** to think or speak incoherently or illogically. ~n. **6.** the act or an instance of wandering. [OE *wandrian*] —'**wanderer** n. —'**wandering** adj., n.

wandering albatross n. a large albatross having a very wide wingspan and a white plumage with black wings.

wandering Jew n. any of several related creeping or trailing plants of tropical America, such as tradescantia.

Wandering Jew n. (in medieval legend) a character condemned to roam the world eternally because he mocked Christ on the day of the Crucifixion.

wanderlust ('wɒndə,lʌst) n. a great desire to travel and rove about. [from G *Wanderlust,* lit.: wander desire]

wanderoo (,wɒndə'ruː) n., pl. **-deroos.** a macaque monkey of India and Sri Lanka, having black fur with a ruff of long greyish fur on each side of the face. [C17: from Sinhalese *vanduru* monkeys, lit.: forest-dwellers]

wandoo (wɒn'duː) n. a eucalyptus tree of W Australia, having white bark and durable wood. [from Abor.]

Wandsworth ('wɒnzwəθ) n. a borough of S Greater London, on the River Thames. Pop.: 257 100 (1986 est.).

wane (weɪn) vb. (*intr.*) **1.** (of the moon) to show a gradually decreasing portion of illuminated surface, between full moon and new moon. **2.** to decrease gradually in size, strength, power, etc. **3.** to draw to a close. ~n. **4.** a decrease, as in size, strength, power, etc. **5.** the period during which the moon wanes. **6.** a drawing to a close. **7.** a rounded surface or defective edge of a plank, where the bark was. **8. on the wane.** in a state of decline. [OE *wanian* (vb.)] —'**waney** or '**wany** adj.

Wanganui (,wɒŋə'nuːɪ) n. a port in New Zealand, on SW North Island: centre for a dairy-farming and sheep-rearing district. Pop.: 40 900 (1987 est.).

wangle ('wæŋgəl) *Inf.* ~vb. **1.** (*tr.*) to use devious methods to get or achieve (something) for (oneself or another): *he wangled himself a salary increase.* **2.** to manipulate or falsify (a situation, etc.). ~n. **3.** the act or an instance of wangling. [C19: orig. printers' sl., ? a blend of WAGGLE & dialect *wankle* wavering, from OE *wancol*] —'**wangler** n.

Wanhsien or **Wan-Hsien** ('wæn'jɛn) n. a variant transliteration of the Chinese name for **Wanxian.**

wanigan or **wannigan** ('wɒnɪgən) n. *Canad.* **1.** a lumberjack's chest or box. **2.** a cabin, caboose, or houseboat. [C19: from Algonquian]

wank (wæŋk) *Taboo sl.* ~vb. **1.** (*intr.*) to masturbate. ~n. **2.** an instance of wanking. [from ?]

wankel engine ('wæŋkəl) n. a type of rotary internal-combustion engine without reciprocating parts. It consists of a curved triangular-shaped piston rotating in an elliptical combustion chamber. [C20: after Felix *Wankel* (born 1902), G engineer who invented it]

wanker ('wæŋkə) n. *Sl.* **1.** *Taboo.* a person who wanks; masturbator. **2.** *Derog.* a worthless fellow.

Wankie ('wɑːŋkɪ) n. the former name (until 1982) of **Hwange.**

Wanne-Eickel (*German* 'vanə'aikəl) n. an industrial town in W West Germany, in North Rhine-Westphalia on the Rhine-Herne Canal: formed in 1926 by the merging of two townships. Pop.: 98 800 (1970).

want (wɒnt) vb. **1.** (*tr.*) to feel a need or longing for: *I want a new hat.* **2.** (when *tr.,* may take a clause as object or an *infinitive*) to wish, need, or desire (something or to do something): *he wants to go home.* **3.** (*intr.;* usually used with a negative and often foll. by *for*) to be lacking or deficient (in something necessary or desirable): *the child wants for nothing.* **4.** (*tr.*) to feel the absence of: *lying on the ground makes me want my bed.* **5.** (*tr.*) to fall short by (a specified amount). **6.** (*tr.*) *Chiefly Brit.* to have need of or require (doing or being something): *your shoes want cleaning.* **7.** (*intr.*) to be destitute. **8.** (*tr.; often passive*) to seek or request the presence of: *you're wanted upstairs.* **9.** (*tr.; takes an infinitive*) *Inf.* should or ought (to do something): *you don't want to go out so late.* ~*n.* **10.** the act or an instance of wanting. **11.** anything that is needed, desired, or lacked: *to supply someone's wants.* **12.** a lack, shortage, or absence: *for want of common sense.* **13.** the state of being in need: *the state should help those in want.* **14.** a sense of lack; craving. [C12 (vb., in the sense: it is lacking), C13 (n.): from ON *vanta* to be deficient] —'**wanter** *n.*

want ad *n. Inf.* a classified advertisement in a newspaper, magazine, etc., for something wanted, such as property or employment.

wanting ('wɒntɪŋ) *adj.* (*postpositive*) **1.** lacking or absent. **2.** not meeting requirements or expectations: *you have been found wanting.*

wanton ('wɒntən) *adj.* **1.** dissolute, licentious, or immoral. **2.** without motive, provocation, or justification: *wanton destruction.* **3.** maliciously and unnecessarily cruel. **4.** unrestrained: *wanton spending.* **5.** *Arch. or poetic.* playful or capricious. **6.** *Arch.* (of vegetation, etc.) luxuriant. ~*n.* **7.** a licentious person, esp. a woman. ~*vb.* **8.** (*intr.*) to behave in a wanton manner. [C13 *wantowen* (in the obs. sense: unruly): from *wan-* (prefix equivalent to UN-¹) + *-towen*, from OE *togen* brought up, from *tēon* to bring up] —'**wantonly** *adv.* —'**wantonness** *n.*

Wanxian, Wanhsien, or **Wan-Hsien** ('wæn'ʃjɛn) *n.* an inland port in central China, in E Sichuan province, on the Yangtze River.

wapentake ('wɒpən,teɪk, 'wæp-) *n. English legal history.* a subdivision of certain shires or counties, esp. in the Midlands and North of England, corresponding to the hundred in other shires. [OE *wǣpen(ge)tæc*]

wapiti ('wɒpɪtɪ) *n., pl.* **-tis.** a large North American deer with large much-branched antlers, now also found in New Zealand. [C19: of Amerind origin, lit.: white deer, from *wap* (unattested) white; from the animal's white tail and rump]

war (wɔː) *n.* **1.** open armed conflict between two or more parties, nations, or states. Related adj.: **belligerent** (see sense 2). **2.** a particular armed conflict: *the 1973 war in the Middle East.* **3.** the techniques of armed conflict as a study, science, or profession. **4.** any conflict or contest: *the war against crime.* **5.** (*modifier*) of, resulting from, or characteristic of war: *war damage; a war story.* **6. in the wars.** *Inf.* (esp. of a child) hurt or knocked about, esp. as a result of quarrelling and fighting. ~*vb.* **warring, warred. 7.** (*intr.*) to conduct a war. [C12: from ONorthern F *werre* (var. of OF *guerre*), of Gmc origin]

War. *abbrev. for* Warwickshire.

Warangal ('wʌrəŋgəl) *n.* a city in S central India, in N Andhra Pradesh: capital of a 12th-century Hindu kingdom. Pop.: 336 018 (1981).

waratah ('wɒrətə) *n. Austral.* a shrub having dark green leaves and large clusters of crimson flowers. [from Abor.]

Warbeck ('wɔːbɛk) *n.* **Perkin** ('pɜːkɪn). ?1474–99, Flemish impostor, pretender to the English throne. Professing to be Richard, Duke of York, he led an unsuccessful rising against Henry VII (1497) and was later executed.

warble¹ ('wɔːbəl) *vb.* **1.** to sing (words, songs, etc.) with trills, runs, and other embellishments. **2.** (*tr.*) to utter in a song. ~*n.* **3.** the act or an instance of warbling. [C14: via OF *werbler*, of Gmc origin]

warble² ('wɔːbəl) *n. Vet. science.* **1.** a small lumpy abscess under the skin of cattle caused by the larvae of the warble fly. **2.** a hard lump of tissue on a horse's back, caused by prolonged friction of a saddle. [C16: from ?]

warble fly *n.* any of a genus of hairy beelike dipterous flies, the larvae of which produce warbles in cattle.

warbler ('wɔːblə) *n.* **1.** a person or thing that warbles. **2.** a small active passerine songbird of the Old World having a cryptic plumage and slender bill, that is an arboreal insectivore. **3.** a small bird of an American family, similar to the Old World songbird but often brightly coloured.

war correspondent *n.* a journalist who reports on a war from the scene of action.

war crime *n.* a crime committed in wartime in violation of the accepted customs, such as ill-treatment of prisoners, etc. —**war criminal** *n.*

war cry *n.* **1.** a rallying cry used by combatants in battle. **2.** a cry, slogan, etc., used to rally support for a cause.

ward (wɔːd) *n.* **1.** (in many countries) one of the districts into which a city, town, parish, or other area is divided for administration, election of representatives, etc. **2. a.** a room in a hospital, esp. one for patients requiring similar

kinds of care: *a maternity ward.* **b.** (*as modifier*): *ward maid.* **3.** one of the divisions of a prison. **4.** an open space enclosed within the walls of a castle. **5.** *Law.* Also called: **ward of court.** a person, esp. a minor or one legally incapable of managing his own affairs, placed under the control or protection of a guardian or of a court. **6.** the state of being under guard or in custody. **7.** a means of protection. **8. a.** an internal ridge or bar in a lock that prevents an incorrectly cut key from turning. **b.** a corresponding groove cut in a key. ~*vb.* **9.** (*tr.*) *Arch.* to guard or protect. ~See also **ward off.** [OE *weard* protector] —'**wardless** *adj.*

Ward (wɔːd) *n.* **1.** Mrs **Humphry,** married name of *Mary Augusta Arnold.* 1851–1920, English novelist. Her novels include *Robert Elsmere* (1888) and *The Case of Richard Meynell* (1911). **2.** Sir **Joseph George.** 1856–1930, New Zealand statesman; prime minister of New Zealand (1906–12; 1928–30).

-ward *suffix.* **1.** (*forming adjectives*) indicating direction towards: *a backward step.* **2.** (*forming adverbs*) a variant and the usual U.S. and Canad. form of **-wards.** [OE *-weard* towards]

war dance *n.* a ceremonial dance performed before going to battle or after victory, esp. by certain North American Indian peoples.

warden ('wɔːdən) *n.* **1.** a person who has the charge or care of something, esp. a building, or someone. **2.** a public official, esp. one responsible for the enforcement of certain regulations: *traffic warden.* **3.** a person employed to patrol a national park or a safari park. **4.** *Chiefly U.S. & Canad.* the chief officer in charge of a prison. **5.** *Brit.* the principal of any of various universities or colleges. **6.** See **churchwarden** (sense 1). [C13: from OF *wardein,* from *warder* to guard, of Gmc origin]

warder ('wɔːdə) *or* (*fem.*) **wardress** *n.* **1.** *Chiefly Brit.* an officer in charge of prisoners in a jail. **2.** a person who guards or has charge of something. [C14: from Anglo-F *wardere,* from OF *warder* to guard, of Gmc origin]

ward heeler *n. U.S. politics, disparaging.* a party worker who canvasses votes and performs chores for a political boss. Also called: **heeler.**

ward off *vb.* (*tr., adv.*) to turn aside or repel.

Wardour Street ('wɔːdə) *n.* a street in Soho where many film companies have their London offices: formerly noted for shops selling antiques and mock antiques.

wardrobe ('wɔːdrəʊb) *n.* **1.** a tall closet or cupboard, with a rail or hooks on which to hang clothes. **2.** the total collection of articles of clothing belonging to one person. **3. a.** the collection of costumes belonging to a theatre or theatrical company. **b.** (*as modifier*): *wardrobe mistress.* [C14: from OF *warderobe,* from *warder* to guard + *robe* ROBE]

wardrobe trunk *n.* a large upright rectangular travelling case, usually opening longitudinally, with one side having a hanging rail, the other having drawers or compartments.

wardroom ('wɔːd,ruːm, -,rʊm) *n.* **1.** the quarters assigned to the officers (except the captain) of a warship. **2.** the officers of a warship collectively, excepting the captain.

-wards *or* **-ward** *suffix forming adverbs.* indicating direction towards: *a step backwards.* Cf. **-ward.** [OE *-weardes* towards]

wardship ('wɔːdʃɪp) *n.* the state of being a ward.

ware¹ (wɛə) *n.* (*often in combination*) **1.** (*functioning as sing.*) articles of the same kind or material: *silverware.* **2.** porcelain or pottery of a specified type: *jasper ware.* ~See also **wares.** [OE *waru*]

ware² (wɛə) *vb. Arch.* another word for **beware.** [OE *wær.* See AWARE, BEWARE]

warehouse *n.* ('wɛə,haʊs). **1.** a place where goods are stored prior to their use, distribution, or sale. **2.** See **bonded warehouse. 3.** *Chiefly Brit.* a large commercial, esp. wholesale, establishment. ~*vb.* ('wɛə,haʊz, -,haʊs). **4.** (*tr.*) to store or place in a warehouse, esp. a bonded warehouse. —'**ware,houseman** *n.*

warehousing ('wɛə,haʊzɪŋ) *n. Business.* an attempt to maintain the price of a company's shares or to gain a significant stake in a company without revealing the identity of the purchaser.

wares (wɛəz) *pl. n.* **1.** articles of manufacture considered as being for sale. **2.** any talent or asset regarded as a saleable commodity.

warfare ('wɔː,fɛə) n. **1.** the act, process, or an instance of waging war. **2.** conflict or strife.

warfarin ('wɔːfərɪn) n. a crystalline insoluble compound, used to kill rodents and, in the form of its sodium salt, as a medical anticoagulant. [C20: from the patent owners *W(isconsin) A(lumni) R(esearch) F(oundation)* + (COU-M)ARIN]

war game n. **1.** a notional tactical exercise for training military commanders, in which no military units are actually deployed. **2.** a game in which model soldiers are used to create battles, esp. past battles, in order to study tactics.

warhead ('wɔː,hɛd) n. the part of the fore end of a missile or projectile that contains explosives.

Warhol ('wɔːhəʊl) n. **Andy,** real name *Andrew Warhola.* ?1926–87, U.S. artist and film maker; one of the foremost exponents of pop art.

warhorse ('wɔː,hɔːs) n. **1.** a horse used in battle. **2.** *Inf.* a veteran soldier or politician.

Warley ('wɔːlɪ) n. an industrial town in W central England, in the West Midlands: formed in 1966 by the amalgamation of Smethwick, Oldbury, and Rowley Regis. Pop.: 152 455 (1981).

warlike ('wɔː,laɪk) adj. **1.** of, relating to, or used in war. **2.** hostile or belligerent. **3.** fit or ready for war.

warlock ('wɔː,lɒk) n. a man who practises black magic. [OE *wǣrloga* oath breaker, from *wǣr* oath + *-loga* liar, from *lēogan* to lie]

warlord ('wɔː,lɔːd) n. a military leader of a nation or part of a nation: *the Chinese warlords.*

warm (wɔːm) adj. **1.** characterized by or having a moderate degree of heat. **2.** maintaining or imparting heat: *a warm coat.* **3.** having or showing ready affection, kindliness, etc.: *a warm personality.* **4.** lively or passionate: *a warm debate.* **5.** cordial or enthusiastic: *warm support.* **6.** quickly or easily aroused: *a warm temper.* **7.** (of colours) predominantly red or yellow in tone. **8.** (of a scent, trail, etc.) recently made. **9.** near to finding a hidden object or guessing facts, as in children's games. **10.** *Inf.* uncomfortable or disagreeable, esp. because of the proximity of danger. ~vb. **11.** (sometimes foll. by *up*) to make or become warm or warmer. **12.** (when *intr.,* often foll. by *to*) to make or become excited, enthusiastic, etc. (about): *he warmed to the idea of buying a new car.* **13.** (*intr.;* often foll. by *to*) to feel affection, kindness, etc. (for someone): *I warmed to her mother from the start.* ~n. *Inf.* **14.** a warm place or area: *come into the warm.* **15.** the act or an instance of warming or being warmed. ~See also **warm up.** [OE *wearm*] —'**warmer** n. —'**warmish** adj. —'**warmly** adv. —'**warmness** n.

warm-blooded adj. **1.** ardent, impetuous, or passionate. **2.** *Zool.* the nontechnical term for **homoiothermic.** —,**warm-'bloodedness** n.

war memorial n. a monument, usually an obelisk or cross, to those who die in a war, esp. those from a particular locality.

warm front n. *Meteorol.* the boundary between a warm air mass and the cold air above.

warm-hearted adj. kindly, generous, or readily sympathetic. —,**warm-'heartedly** adv. —,**warm-'heartedness** n.

warming pan n. a pan, often of copper and having a long handle, filled with hot coals and formerly drawn over the sheets to warm a bed.

warmonger ('wɔː,mʌŋɡə) n. a person who fosters warlike ideas or advocates war. —'**war,mongering** n.

warmth (wɔːmθ) n. **1.** the state, quality, or sensation of being warm. **2.** intensity of emotion: *he denied the accusation with some warmth.* **3.** affection or cordiality.

warm up vb. (adv.) **1.** to make or become warm or warmer. **2.** (*intr.*) to exercise immediately before a game, contest, or more vigorous exercise. **3.** (*intr.*) to get ready for something important; prepare. **4.** to run (an engine, etc.) until the working temperature is attained, or (of an engine, etc.) to undergo this process. **5.** to make or become more animated: *the party warmed up when Tom came.* **6.** to reheat (already cooked food) or (of such food) to be reheated. ~n. **warm-up. 7.** the act or an instance of warming up. **8.** a preparatory exercise routine.

warn (wɔːn) vb. **1.** to notify or make (someone) aware of danger, harm, etc. **2.** (*tr.; often takes a negative and an infinitive*) to advise or admonish (someone) as to action, conduct, etc.: *I warn you not to do that again.* **3.** (*takes a clause as object or an infinitive*) to inform (someone) in advance: *he warned them that he would arrive late.* **4.** (*tr.;* usually foll. by *away, off,* etc.) to give notice to go away, be off, etc. [OE *wearnian*] —'**warner** n.

warning ('wɔːnɪŋ) n. **1.** a hint, intimation, threat, etc., of harm or danger. **2.** advice to beware or desist. **3.** an archaic word for **notice** (sense 6). ~adj. **4.** (*prenominal*) intended or serving to warn: *a warning look.* —'**warningly** adv.

warp (wɔːp) vb. **1.** to twist or cause to twist out of shape, as from heat, damp, etc. **2.** to turn or cause to turn from a true, correct, or proper course. **3.** *Naut.* to move (a vessel) by hauling on a rope fixed to a stationary object ashore or (of a vessel) to be moved thus. **4.** (*tr.*) to flood (land) with water from which alluvial matter is deposited. ~n. **5.** the state or condition of being twisted out of shape. **6.** a twist, distortion, or bias. **7.** a mental or moral deviation. **8.** the yarns arranged lengthways on a loom, forming the threads through which the weft yarns are woven. **9.** *Naut.* a rope used for warping a vessel. **10.** alluvial sediment deposited by water. [OE *wearp* a throw] —'**warpage** n. —**warped** adj. —'**warper** n.

war paint n. **1.** painted decoration of the face and body applied by certain North American Indians before battle. **2.** *Inf.* finery or regalia. **3.** *Inf.* cosmetics.

warpath ('wɔː,pɑːθ) n. **1.** the route taken by North American Indians on a warlike expedition. **2. on the warpath. a.** preparing to engage in battle. **b.** *Inf.* in a state of anger.

warplane ('wɔː,pleɪn) n. any aircraft designed for and used in warfare.

warrant ('wɒrənt) n. **1.** anything that gives authority for an action or decision; authorization. **2.** a document that certifies or guarantees, such as a receipt, licence, or commission. **3.** *Law.* an authorization issued by a magistrate allowing a constable or other officer to search or seize property, arrest a person, or perform some other specified act. **4.** (in certain armed services) the official authority for the appointment of warrant officers. ~vb. (*tr.*) **5.** to guarantee the quality, condition, etc., of (something). **6.** to give authority or power to. **7.** to attest to the character, worthiness, etc., of. **8.** to guarantee (a purchaser of merchandise) against loss of, damage to, or misrepresentation concerning the merchandise. **9.** *Law.* to guarantee (the title to an estate or other property). **10.** to declare confidently. [C13: from Anglo-F, var. of OF *guarant,* from *guarantir* to guarantee, of Gmc origin] —'**warrantable** adj. —,**warranta'bility** n. —'**warrantably** adv. —'**warranter** n.

warrantee (,wɒrən'tiː) n. a person to whom a warranty is given.

warrant officer n. an officer in certain armed services who holds a rank between those of commissioned and noncommissioned officers. In the British army the rank has two classes: regimental sergeant major and company sergeant major.

Warrant of Fitness n. *N.Z.* a six-monthly certificate required for motor vehicles certifying mechanical soundness.

warrantor ('wɒrən,tɔː) n. an individual or company that provides a warranty.

warranty ('wɒrəntɪ) n., pl. -**ties. 1.** *Property law.* a covenant, express or implied, by which the vendor of real property vouches for the security of the title conveyed. **2.** *Contract law.* an express or implied term in a contract collateral to the main purpose, such as an undertaking that goods contracted to be sold shall meet specified requirements as to quality, etc. **3.** *Insurance law.* an undertaking by the party insured that the facts given regarding the risk are as stated. [C14: from Anglo-F *warantie,* from *warantir* to warrant, var. of OF *guarantir;* see WARRANT]

warren ('wɒrən) n. **1.** a series of interconnected underground tunnels in which rabbits live. **2.** a colony of rabbits. **3.** an overcrowded area or dwelling. **4.** *Chiefly Brit.* an enclosed place where small game animals or birds are kept, esp. for breeding. [C14: from Anglo-F *warenne,* of Gmc origin]

Warren[1] ('wɒrən) n. a city in SE Michigan, northeast of Detroit. Pop.: 161 134 (1981).

Warren[2] ('wɒrən) n. **Earl.** 1891–1974, U.S. lawyer; chief justice of the U.S. (1953–69). He chaired the commission that investigated the murder of President Kennedy.

warrigal ('wɒrɪgæl) *Austral.* ~*n.* **1.** a dingo. **2.** a wild horse or other wild creature. ~*adj.* **3.** untamed or wild. [C19: from Abor.]

Warrington ('wɒrɪŋtən) *n.* an industrial town in NW England, in N Cheshire on the River Mersey: dates from Roman times. Pop.: 173 000 (1985 est.).

warrior ('wɒrɪə) *n.* **a.** a person engaged in, experienced in, or devoted to war. **b.** (*as modifier*): *a warrior nation.* [C13: from OF *werreieor*, from *werre* WAR]

Warsaw ('wɔ:sɔ:) *n.* the capital of Poland, in the E central part on the River Vistula: became capital at the end of the 16th century; almost completely destroyed in World War II as the main centre of the Polish resistance movement; rebuilt within about six years; university (1818); situated at the junction of important trans-European routes. Pop.: 1 649 000 (1985). Polish name: **Warszawa** (var'ʃava).

Warsaw Pact *n.* a military treaty and association of E European countries, formed in 1955.

warship ('wɔ:,ʃɪp) *n.* a vessel armed, armoured, and otherwise equipped for naval warfare.

Wars of the Roses *pl. n.* the struggle for the throne in England (1455-85) between the House of York (symbolized by the white rose) and the House of Lancaster (symbolized by the red rose).

wart (wɔ:t) *n.* **1.** *Pathol.* any firm abnormal elevation of the skin caused by a virus. **2.** *Bot.* a small rounded outgrowth. **3. warts and all.** with all blemishes evident. [OE *weart(e)*] —**'warty** *adj.*

Warta (*Polish* 'varta) *n.* a river in Poland, flowing generally north and west across the whole W Polish Plain to the River Oder. Length: 808 km (502 miles).

Wartburg (*German* 'vartburk) *n.* a medieval castle in East Germany, in Thuringia southwest of Eisenach: residence of Luther (1521–22) when he began his German translation of the New Testament.

wart hog *n.* a wild pig of S and E Africa, having heavy tusks, wartlike protuberances on the face, and a mane of coarse hair.

wartime ('wɔ:,taɪm) *n.* **a.** a period or time of war. **b.** (*as modifier*): *wartime conditions.*

war whoop *n.* the yell or howl uttered, esp. by North American Indians, while making an attack.

Warwick[1] ('wɒrɪk) *n.* a town in central England, administrative centre of Warwickshire, on the River Avon: university (1965). Pop.: 21 936 (1981).

Warwick[2] ('wɒrɪk) *n.* **Earl of,** title of *Richard Neville,* known as *the Kingmaker.* 1428–71, English statesman. During the Wars of the Roses, he fought first for the Yorkists, securing the throne (1461) for Edward IV, and then for the Lancastrians, restoring Henry VI (1470). He was killed at Barnet by Edward IV.

Warwickshire ('wɒrɪk,ʃɪə, -ʃə) *n.* a county of central England: until 1974, when the West Midlands metropolitan county was created, it contained one of the most highly industrialized regions in the world, centred on Birmingham. Administrative centre: Warwick. Pop.: 480 700 (1986 est.). Area: 1981 sq. km (765 sq. miles).

wary ('wɛərɪ) *adj.* **warier, wariest. 1.** watchful, cautious, or alert. **2.** characterized by caution or watchfulness. [C16: from WARE[2] + -Y[1]] —**'warily** *adv.* —**'wariness** *n.*

was (wɒz; *unstressed* wəz) *vb.* (used with *I, he, she, it,* and with singular nouns) **1.** the past tense (indicative mood) of **be. 2.** *Not standard.* a form of the subjunctive mood used in place of *were,* esp. in conditional sentences: *if the film was to be with you, would you be able to process it?* [OE *wæs,* from *wesan* to be]

Wasatch Range ('wɔ:sætʃ) *n.* a mountain range in the W central U.S., in N Utah and SE Idaho. Highest peak: Mount Timpanogos, 3581 m (11 750 ft.).

wash (wɒʃ) *vb.* **1.** to apply water or other liquid, usually with soap, to (oneself, clothes, etc.) in order to cleanse. **2.** (*tr.*; often foll. by *away, from, off,* etc.) to remove by the application of water or other liquid and usually soap: *she washed the dirt from her clothes.* **3.** (*intr.*) to be capable of being washed without damage or loss of colour. **4.** (of an animal such as a cat) to cleanse (itself or another animal) by licking. **5.** (*tr.*) to cleanse from pollution or defilement. **6.** (*tr.*) to make wet or moist. **7.** (often foll. by *away,* etc.) to move or be moved by water: *the flood washed away the bridge.* **8.** (esp. of waves) to flow or sweep against or over (a surface or object), often with a lapping sound. **9.** to form by erosion or be eroded: *the*

stream washed a ravine in the hill. **10.** (*tr.*) to apply a thin coating of paint, metal, etc., to. **11.** (*tr.*) to separate (ore, etc.) from (gravel, etc.) by immersion in water. **12.** (*intr.*; *usually used with a negative*) *Inf., chiefly Brit.* to admit of testing or proof: *your excuses won't wash.* ~*n.* **13.** the act or process of washing. **14.** a quantity of articles washed together. **15.** a preparation or thin liquid used as a coating or in washing: *a thin wash of paint.* **16.** *Med.* **a.** any medicinal lotion for application to a part of the body. **b.** (*in combination*): *an eyewash.* **17. a.** the technique of making wash drawings. **b.** See **wash drawing. 18.** the erosion of soil by the action of flowing water. **19.** a mass of alluvial material transported and deposited by flowing water. **20.** land that is habitually washed by tidal or river waters. **21.** the disturbance in the air or water produced at the rear of an aircraft, boat, or other moving object. **22.** gravel, earth, etc., from which valuable minerals may be washed. **23.** waste liquid matter or liquid refuse, esp. as fed to pigs. **24.** an alcoholic liquid resembling strong beer, resulting from the fermentation of wort in the production of whisky. **25. come out in the wash.** *Inf.* to become known or apparent in the course of time. ~See also **wash down, wash out, wash up.** [OE *wæscan, waxan*]

Wash (wɒʃ) *n.* **the.** a shallow inlet of the North Sea on the E coast of England, between Lincolnshire and Norfolk.

washable ('wɒʃəbəl) *adj.* (esp. of fabrics or clothes) capable of being washed without deteriorating. —,**washa'bility** *n.*

wash-and-wear *adj.* (of fabrics, garments, etc.) requiring only light washing, short drying time, and little or no ironing.

washbasin ('wɒʃ,beɪsən) *n.* **1.** Also called: **washbowl.** a basin or bowl for washing the face and hands. **2.** Also called: **wash-hand basin.** a bathroom fixture with taps, used for washing the face and hands.

washboard ('wɒʃ,bɔːd) *n.* **1.** a board having a surface, usually of corrugated metal, on which, esp. formerly, clothes were scrubbed. **2.** such a board used as a rhythm instrument played with the fingers in skiffle, country-and-western music, etc. **3.** *Naut.* a vertical planklike shield fastened to the gunwales of a boat to prevent water from splashing over the side.

washcloth ('wɒʃ,klɒθ) *n.* **1.** another term for **dishcloth. 2.** the U.S. and Canad. word for **face cloth.**

washday ('wɒʃ,deɪ) *n.* a day on which clothes and linen are washed.

wash down *vb.* (*tr., adv.*) **1.** to wash completely, esp. from top to bottom. **2.** to take drink with or after (food or another drink).

wash drawing *n.* a pen-and-ink drawing that has been lightly brushed over with water to soften the lines.

washed out *adj.* (**washed-out** *when prenominal*). **1.** faded or colourless. **2.** exhausted, esp. when being pale in appearance.

washed up *adj.* (**washed-up** *when prenominal*). *Inf., chiefly U.S., Canad., & N.Z.* no longer hopeful, etc.: *our hopes for the new deal are all washed up.*

washer ('wɒʃə) *n.* **1.** a person or thing that washes. **2.** a flat ring or drilled disc of metal used under the head of a bolt or nut. **3.** any flat ring of rubber, felt, metal, etc., used to provide a seal under a nut or in a tap or valve seat. **4.** See **washing machine. 5.** *Austral.* a face cloth; flannel.

washerwoman ('wɒʃə,wumən) *or* (*masc.*) **washerman** *n., pl.* **-women** *or* **-men.** a person who washes clothes for a living.

washery ('wɒʃərɪ) *n., pl.* **-eries.** a plant at a mine where water or other liquid is used to remove dirt from a mineral, esp. coal.

wash-hand basin *n.* another name for **washbasin** (sense 2).

wash house *n.* (formerly) an outbuilding in which clothes were washed.

washing ('wɒʃɪŋ) *n.* **1.** articles that have been or are to be washed together on a single occasion. **2.** something, such as gold dust, that has been obtained by washing. **3.** a thin coat of something applied in liquid form.

washing machine *n.* a mechanical apparatus, usually powered by electricity, for washing clothing, linens, etc.

washing powder *n.* powdered detergent for washing fabrics.

washing soda *n.* crystalline sodium carbonate, esp. when used as a cleansing agent.

Washington[1] ('wɒʃɪŋtən) *n.* **1.** a state of the northwestern U.S., on the Pacific: consists of the Coast Range and the Olympic Mountains in the west and the Columbia Plateau in the east. Capital: Olympia. Pop.: 4 409 000 (1985 est.). Area: 172 416 sq. km (66 570 sq. miles). Abbrevs.: **Wash.** or (with zip code) **WA 2.** Also called: **Washington DC** the capital of the U.S., coextensive with the District of Columbia and situated near the E coast on the Potomac River: site chosen by President Washington in 1790; contains the White House and the Capitol; a major educational and administrative centre. Pop.: 626 000 (1986 est.). **3.** a town in Tyne and Wear: designated a new town in 1964; coal-mining. Pop.: 56 000 (1985 est.). **4. Mount.** a mountain in N New Hampshire, in the White Mountains: the highest peak in the northeast U.S.; noted for extreme weather conditions. Height: 1917 m (6288 ft.). **5. Lake.** a lake in W Washington, forming the E boundary of the city of Seattle: linked by canal with Puget Sound. Length: about 32 km (20 miles). Width: 6 km (4 miles). —**Washingtonian** (,wɒʃɪŋ'təʊnɪən) *adj., n.*

Washington[2] ('wɒʃɪŋtən) *n.* **1. Booker T(aliaferro).** 1856–1915, U.S. Black educationalist and writer. **2. George.** 1732–99, U.S. general and statesman; first president of the U.S. (1789–97). He was appointed commander in chief of the Continental Army (1775) at the outbreak of the War of American Independence, which ended with his defeat of Cornwallis at Yorktown (1781). He presided over the convention at Philadelphia (1787) that formulated the constitution of the U.S. and elected him president.

washing-up *n. Brit.* **1.** the washing of dishes, cutlery, etc., after a meal. **2.** dishes and cutlery waiting to be washed up. **3.** (*as modifier*): *a washing-up machine.*

wash out *vb.* (*adv.*) **1.** (*tr.*) to wash (the inside of something) so as to remove (dirt). **2.** Also: **wash off.** to remove or be removed by washing: *grass stains don't wash out easily.* ~*n.* **washout. 3.** *Geol.* **a.** erosion of the earth's surface by the action of running water. **b.** a narrow channel produced by this. **4.** *Inf.* **a.** a total failure or disaster. **b.** an incompetent person.

washroom ('wɒʃ,ruːm, -,rʊm) *n. U.S. & Canad.* a euphemism for **lavatory.**

washstand ('wɒʃ,stænd) *n.* a piece of furniture designed to hold a basin, etc., for washing the face and hands.

washtub ('wɒʃ,tʌb) *n.* a tub or large container used for washing anything, esp. clothes.

wash up *vb.* (*adv.*) **1.** *Chiefly Brit.* to wash (dishes, cutlery, etc.) after a meal. **2.** (*intr.*) *U.S.* to wash one's face and hands. ~*n.* **washup. 3.** *Austral.* the end, outcome of a process: *in the washup, three were elected.*

washy ('wɒʃɪ) *adj.* **washier, washiest. 1.** over-diluted, watery, or weak. **2.** lacking intensity or strength. —'**washiness** *n.*

wasn't ('wɒzᵊnt) *contraction of* was not.

wasp (wɒsp) *n.* **1.** a social hymenopterous insect, such as the **common wasp,** having a black-and-yellow body and an ovipositor specialized for stinging. **2.** any of various solitary hymenopterans, such as the digger wasp and gall wasp. [OE *wæsp*] —'**wasp,like** *adj.* —'**waspy** *adj.* —'**waspily** *adv.* —'**waspiness** *n.*

Wasp *or* **WASP** (wɒsp) *n. U.S. & Canad., usually derog.* a person descended from N European, usually Protestant, stock, forming a group often considered the most dominant, privileged, and influential in American society. [C20: W(*hite*) A(*nglo-*)S(*axon*) P(*rotestant*)]

waspish ('wɒspɪʃ) *adj.* **1.** relating to or suggestive of a wasp. **2.** easily annoyed or angered. —'**waspishly** *adv.*

wasp waist *n.* a very slender waist, esp. one that is tightly corseted. —'**wasp-,waisted** *adj.*

wassail ('wɒseɪl) *n.* **1.** (formerly) a toast or salutation made to a person at festivities. **2.** a festivity when much drinking takes place. **3.** alcoholic drink drunk at such a festivity, esp. spiced beer or mulled wine. ~*vb.* **4.** to drink the health of (a person) at a wassail. **5.** (*intr.*) to go from house to house singing carols at Christmas. [C13: from ON *ves heill* be in good health] —'**wassailer** *n.*

Wassermann test *or* **reaction** ('wæsəmən) *n. Med.* a diagnostic test for syphilis. [C20: after August von *Wassermann* (1866–1925), G bacteriologist]

wast (wɒst; *unstressed* wəst) *vb. Arch. or dialect.* (used with the pronoun *thou* or its relative equivalent) a singular form of the past tense (indicative mood) of **be.**

wastage ('weɪstɪdʒ) *n.* **1.** anything lost by wear or waste. **2.** the process of wasting. **3.** reduction in size of a workforce by retirement, etc. (esp. in **natural wastage**).

waste (weɪst) *vb.* **1.** (*tr.*) to use, consume, or expend thoughtlessly, carelessly, or to no avail. **2.** (*tr.*) to fail to take advantage of: *to waste an opportunity.* **3.** (when *intr.*, often foll. by *away*) to lose or cause to lose bodily strength, health, etc. **4.** to exhaust or become exhausted. **5.** (*tr.*) to ravage. **6.** (*tr.*) *Sl.* to murder or kill. ~*n.* **7.** the act of wasting or state of being wasted. **8.** a failure to take advantage of something. **9.** anything unused or not used to full advantage. **10.** anything or anyone rejected as useless, worthless, or in excess of what is required. **11.** garbage, rubbish, or trash. **12.** a land or region that is devastated or ruined. **13.** a land or region that is wild or uncultivated. **14.** *Physiol.* **a.** the useless products of metabolism. **b.** indigestible food residue. **15.** *Law.* reduction in the value of an estate caused by act or neglect, esp. by a life tenant. ~*adj.* **16.** rejected as useless, unwanted, or worthless. **17.** produced in excess of what is required. **18.** not cultivated, inhabited, or productive: *waste land.* **19. a.** of or denoting the useless products of metabolism. **b.** of or denoting indigestible food residue. **20.** destroyed, devastated, or ruined. **21. lay waste.** to devastate or destroy. [C13: from Anglo-F, from L *vastāre* to lay waste, from *vastus* empty]

wasted ('weɪstɪd) *adj.* **1.** not taken advantage of: *a wasted opportunity.* **2.** unprofitable: *wasted effort.* **3.** enfeebled and emaciated: *a thin wasted figure.* **4.** *Sl.* showing signs of habitual drug abuse.

wasteful ('weɪstfʊl) *adj.* **1.** tending to waste or squander. **2.** causing waste or devastation. —'**wastefully** *adv.* —'**wastefulness** *n.*

wasteland ('weɪst,lænd) *n.* **1.** a barren or desolate area of land. **2.** a region, period in history, etc., that is considered spiritually, intellectually, or aesthetically barren or desolate.

wastepaper ('weɪst,peɪpə) *n.* paper discarded after use.

wastepaper basket *or* **bin** *n.* an open receptacle for paper and other dry litter. Usual U.S. and Canad. word: **wastebasket.**

waste pipe *n.* a pipe to take excess or used water away, as from a sink to a drain.

waster ('weɪstə) *n.* **1.** a person or thing that wastes. **2.** a ne'er-do-well; wastrel.

wasting ('weɪstɪŋ) *adj.* (*prenominal*) reducing the vitality, strength, or robustness of the body: *a wasting disease.* —'**wastingly** *adv.*

wasting asset *n.* an unreplaceable business asset of limited life, such as an oil well.

wastrel ('weɪstrəl) *n.* **1.** a wasteful person; spendthrift; prodigal. **2.** an idler or vagabond.

Wast Water (wɒst) *n.* a lake in NW England, in Cumbria in the Lake District. Length: 5 km (3 miles).

wat (wɑːt) *n.* a Thai Buddhist monastery or temple. [Thai, from Sansk. *vāta* enclosure]

watap (wæ'tɑːp, wɑː-) *n.* a stringy thread made by North American Indians from the roots of various conifers and used for weaving and sewing. [C18: from Canad. F, from Cree *watapiy*]

watch (wɒtʃ) *vb.* **1.** to look at or observe closely or attentively. **2.** (*intr.;* foll. by *for*) to wait attentively. **3.** to guard or tend (something) closely or carefully. **4.** (*intr.*) to keep vigil. **5.** (*tr.*) to maintain an interest in: *to watch the progress of a child at school.* **6. watch it!** be careful! ~*n.* **7. a.** a small portable timepiece, usually worn strapped to the wrist (a **wristwatch**) or in a waistcoat pocket. **b.** (*as modifier*): *a watch spring.* **8.** a watching. **9.** a period of vigil, esp. during the night. **10.** (formerly) one of a set of periods into which the night was divided. **11.** *Naut.* **a.** any of the periods, usually of four hours, during which part of a ship's crew are on duty. **b.** those officers and crew on duty during a specified watch. **12.** the period during which a guard is on duty. **13.** (formerly) a watchman or band of watchmen. **14. on the watch.** on the lookout. ~See also **watch out.** [OE *wæccan* (vb.), *wæcce* (n.)] —'**watcher** *n.*

-watch *suffix of nouns.* indicating a regular television programme or newspaper feature on the topic specified: *Crimewatch.*

watchcase ('wɒtʃ,keɪs) *n.* a protective case for a watch, generally of metal such as gold or silver.

watch chain *n.* a chain used for fastening a pocket watch to the clothing. See also **fob**[1].

Watch Committee *n. Brit. history.* a local government committee responsible for the efficiency of the local police force.

watchdog ('wɒtʃ,dɒg) *n.* **1.** a dog kept to guard property. **2. a.** a person or group that acts as a protector against inefficiency, etc. **b.** (*as modifier*): *a watchdog committee.*

watch fire *n.* a fire kept burning at night as a signal or for warmth and light by a person keeping watch.

watchful ('wɒtʃfʊl) *adj.* **1.** vigilant or alert. **2.** *Arch.* not sleeping. — **'watchfully** *adv.* — **'watchfulness** *n.*

watch-glass *n.* **1.** a curved glass disc that covers the dial of a watch. **2.** a similarly shaped piece of glass used in laboratories for evaporating small samples of a solution, etc.

watchmaker ('wɒtʃ,meɪkə) *n.* a person who makes or mends watches. — **'watch,making** *n.*

watchman ('wɒtʃmən) *n., pl.* **-men.** **1.** a person employed to guard buildings or property. **2.** (formerly) a man employed to patrol or guard the streets at night.

watch night *n.* **1.** (in Protestant churches) the night of December 31, during which a service is held to mark the passing of the old year. **2.** the service held on this night.

watch out *vb.* (*intr., adv.*) to be careful or on one's guard.

watchstrap ('wɒtʃ,stræp) *n.* a strap of leather, cloth, etc., attached to a watch for fastening it around the wrist. Also called (U.S. and Canad.): **watchband.**

watchtower ('wɒtʃ,taʊə) *n.* a tower on which a sentry keeps watch.

watchword ('wɒtʃ,wɜːd) *n.* **1.** another word for **password.** **2.** a rallying cry or slogan.

water ('wɔːtə) *n.* **1.** a clear colourless tasteless odourless liquid that is essential for plant and animal life and constitutes, in impure form, rain, oceans, rivers, lakes, etc. Formula: H_2O. Related adj.: **aqueous.** **2. a.** any body or area of this liquid, such as a sea, lake, river, etc. **b.** (*as modifier*): *water sports; a water plant.* Related adj.: **aquatic.** **3.** the surface of a body or area: *fish swam below the water.* **4.** any form or variety of this liquid, such as rain. **5.** See **high water, low water.** **6.** any of various solutions of chemical substances in water: *ammonia water.* **7.** *Physiol.* **a.** any fluid secreted from the body, such as sweat, urine, or tears. **b.** (*usually pl.*) the amniotic fluid surrounding a fetus in the womb. **8.** a wavy lustrous finish on some fabrics, esp. silk. **9.** *Arch.* the degree of brilliance in a diamond. **10.** excellence, quality, or degree (in **of the first water**). **11.** *Finance.* capital stock issued without a corresponding increase in paid-up capital. **12.** (*modifier*) *Astrol.* of or relating to the three signs of the zodiac Cancer, Scorpio, and Pisces. **13. hold water.** to prove credible, logical, or consistent: *the alibi did not hold water.* **14. make water. a.** to urinate. **b.** (of a boat, etc.) to let in water. **15. pass water.** to urinate. **16. water under the bridge.** events that are past and done with. ~*vb.* **17.** (*tr.*) to sprinkle, moisten, or soak with water. **18.** (*tr.;* often foll. by *down*) to weaken by the addition of water. **19.** (*intr.*) (of the eyes) to fill with tears. **20.** (*intr.*) (of the mouth) to salivate, esp. in anticipation of food (esp. in **make one's mouth water**). **21.** (*tr.*) to irrigate or provide with water: *to water the land.* **22.** (*intr.*) to drink water. **23.** (*intr.*) (of a ship, etc.) to take in a supply of water. **24.** (*tr.*) *Finance.* to raise the par value of (issued capital stock) without a corresponding increase in the real value of assets. **25.** (*tr.*) to produce a wavy lustrous finish on (fabrics, esp. silk). ~See also **water down.** [OE *wæter*] — **'waterer** *n.* — **'waterless** *adj.*

water bag *n.* a bag, sometimes made of skin, leather, etc., but in Australia always canvas, for carrying water.

water bailiff *n.* an official responsible for enforcing laws on shipping and fishing.

water bear *n.* another name for a **tardigrade.**

water bed *n.* a waterproof mattress filled with water.

water beetle *n.* any of various beetles that live most of the time in freshwater ponds, rivers, etc.

water bird *n.* any aquatic bird, including the wading and swimming birds.

water biscuit *n.* a thin crisp plain biscuit, usually served with butter or cheese.

water blister *n.* a blister containing watery or serous fluid, without any blood or pus.

water boatman *n.* any of various aquatic bugs having a flattened body and oarlike hind legs, adapted for swimming.

waterborne ('wɔːtə,bɔːn) *adj.* **1.** floating or travelling on water. **2.** (of a disease, etc.) transported or transmitted by water.

waterbuck ('wɔːtə,bʌk) *n.* any of a genus of antelopes of swampy areas of Africa, having long curved ridged horns.

water buffalo *or* **ox** *n.* a member of the cattle tribe of swampy regions of S Asia, having widely spreading backcurving horns. Domesticated forms are used as draught animals.

water bug *n.* any of various heteropterous insects adapted to living in the water or on its surface, esp. any of the **giant water bugs** of North America, India, and southern Africa, which have flattened hairy legs.

water butt *n.* a barrel for collecting rainwater, esp. from a drainpipe.

water cannon *n.* an apparatus for pumping water through a nozzle at high pressure, used in quelling riots.

Water Carrier *or* **Bearer** *n.* **the.** the constellation Aquarius, the 11th sign of the zodiac.

water chestnut *n.* **1.** a floating aquatic plant of Asia, having four-pronged edible nutlike fruits. **2. Chinese water chestnut.** a Chinese plant with an edible succulent corm. **3.** the corm of the Chinese water chestnut, used in Oriental cookery.

water clock *or* **glass** *n.* any of various devices for measuring time that use the escape of water as the motive force.

water closet *n.* **1.** a lavatory flushed by water. **2.** a small room that has a lavatory. ~Usually abbreviated to **WC.**

watercolour *or U.S.* **watercolor** ('wɔːtə,kʌlə) *n.* **1.** water-soluble pigment, applied in transparent washes and without the admixture of white pigment in the lighter tones. **2. a.** a painting done in watercolours. **b.** (*as modifier*): *a watercolour masterpiece.* **3.** the art or technique of painting with such pigments. — **'water,colourist** *or U.S.* **'water,colorist** *n.*

water-cool *vb.* (*tr.*) to cool (an engine, etc.) by a flow of water circulating in an enclosed jacket. — **'water-,cooled** *adj.*

water cooler *n.* a device for cooling and dispensing drinking water.

watercourse ('wɔːtə,kɔːs) *n.* **1.** a stream, river, or canal. **2.** the channel, bed, or route along which this flows.

watercraft ('wɔːtə,krɑːft) *n.* **1.** a boat or ship or such vessels collectively. **2.** skill in handling boats or in water sports.

watercress ('wɔːtə,krɛs) *n.* an Old World cruciferous plant of clear ponds and streams, having pungent leaves that are used in salads and as a garnish.

water cure *n. Med.* a nontechnical name for **hydropathy** or **hydrotherapy.**

water cycle *n.* the circulation of the earth's water, in which water evaporates from the sea into the atmosphere, where it condenses and falls as rain or snow, returning to the sea by rivers.

water diviner *n. Brit.* a person able to locate the presence of water, esp. underground, with a divining rod.

water down *vb.* (*tr., adv.*) **1.** to dilute or weaken with water. **2.** to modify, esp. so as to omit anything unpleasant or offensive: *to water down the truth.* — **,watered-'down** *adj.*

waterfall ('wɔːtə,fɔːl) *n.* a cascade of falling water where there is a vertical or almost vertical step in a river.

water flea *n.* any of numerous minute freshwater crustaceans which swim by means of hairy branched antennae. See also **daphnia.**

Waterford ('wɔːtəfəd) *n.* **1.** a county of S Ireland, in Munster province on the Atlantic: mountainous in the centre and in the northwest. County town: Waterford. Pop.: 91 098 (1986). Area: 1838 sq. km (710 sq. miles). **2.** a port in S Ireland, county town of Co. Waterford: famous glass industry; fishing. Pop.: 39 516 (1986).

waterfowl ('wɔːtə,faʊl) *n.* **1.** any aquatic freshwater bird, esp. any species of the family Anatidae (ducks, geese, and swans). **2.** such birds collectively.

waterfront ('wɔːtə,frʌnt) *n.* the area of a town or city alongside a body of water, such as a harbour or dockyard.

water gap *n.* a deep valley in a ridge, containing a stream.

water gas *n.* a mixture of hydrogen and carbon monoxide produced by passing steam over hot carbon, used as a fuel and raw material.

water gate *n.* **1.** a gate in a canal, etc., that can be opened or closed to control the flow of water. **2.** a gate through which access may be gained to a body of water.

Watergate ('wɔːtə,geɪt) *n.* **1.** an incident during the 1972 U.S. presidential campaign, when agents employed by the re-election organization of President Richard Nixon were caught breaking into the Democratic Party headquarters in the Watergate building, Washington, DC. The political scandal was exacerbated by attempts to conceal the fact that White House officials had approved the burglary, and eventually forced the resignation of President Nixon. **2.** any similar public scandal, esp. involving politicians or a possible cover-up.

water gauge *n.* an instrument that indicates the presence or the quantity of water in a tank, reservoir, or boiler feed. Also called: **water glass**.

water glass *n.* **1.** a viscous syrupy solution of sodium silicate in water: used as a protective coating for cement and a preservative, esp. for eggs. **2.** another name for **water gauge**.

water gum *n.* any of several Australian gum trees that grow in swampy ground and beside creeks and rivers.

water hammer *n.* a sharp concussion produced when the flow of water in a pipe is suddenly blocked.

water hen *n.* another name for **gallinule**.

water hole *n.* **1.** a depression, such as a pond or pool, containing water, esp. one used by animals as a drinking place. **2.** a source of drinking water in a desert.

Waterhouse ('wɔːtə,haʊs) *n.* **George Marsden.** 1824–1906, New Zealand statesman, born in England: prime minister of New Zealand (1872–73).

water hyacinth *n.* a floating aquatic plant of tropical America, having showy bluish-purple flowers and swollen leafstalks. It forms dense masses in rivers, ponds, etc.

water ice *n.* an ice cream made from a frozen sugar syrup flavoured with fruit juice or purée.

watering can *n.* a container with a handle and a spout with a perforated nozzle used to sprinkle water over plants.

watering hole *n.* **1.** a pool where animals drink; water hole. **2.** *Facetious sl.* a pub.

watering place *n.* **1.** a place where drinking water for people or animals may be obtained. **2.** *Brit.* a spa. **3.** *Brit.* a seaside resort.

water jacket *n.* a water-filled envelope surrounding a machine or part for cooling purposes, esp. the casing around the cylinder block of a pump or internal-combustion engine.

water jump *n.* a ditch or brook over which athletes or horses must jump in a steeplechase or similar contest.

water level *n.* **1.** the level reached by the surface of a body of water. **2.** the water line of a boat or ship.

water lily *n.* any of various aquatic plants of temperate and tropical regions, having large leaves and showy flowers that float on the surface of the water.

water line *n.* **1.** a line marked at the level around a vessel's hull to which the vessel will be immersed when afloat. **2.** a line marking the level reached by a body of water.

waterlogged ('wɔːtə,lɒgd) *adj.* **1.** saturated with water. **2.** (of a vessel still afloat) having taken in so much water as to be unmanageable.

Waterloo (,wɔːtə'luː) *n.* **1.** a small town in central Belgium, in Brabant province south of Brussels: battle (1815) fought nearby in which British and Prussian forces under the Duke of Wellington and Blücher routed the French under Napoleon. Pop.: 17 764 (1970). **2.** a total or crushing defeat (esp. in **meet one's Waterloo**).

water main *n.* a principal supply pipe in an arrangement of pipes for distributing water.

waterman ('wɔːtəmən) *n.*, *pl.* **-men.** a skilled boatman. —'**waterman,ship** *n.*

watermark ('wɔːtə,mɑːk) *n.* **1.** a mark impressed on paper during manufacture, visible when the paper is held up to the light. **2.** another word for **water line**. ~*vb.* (*tr.*) **3.** to mark (paper) with a watermark.

water meadow *n.* a meadow that remains fertile by being periodically flooded by a stream.

watermelon ('wɔːtə,mɛlən) *n.* **1.** an African melon widely cultivated for its large edible fruit. **2.** the fruit of this plant, which has a hard green rind and sweet watery reddish flesh.

water meter *n.* a device for measuring the quantity or rate of water flowing through a pipe.

water milfoil *n.* any of various pond plants having feathery underwater leaves and small inconspicuous flowers.

water mill *n.* a mill operated by a water wheel.

water moccasin *n.* a large dark grey venomous snake of swamps in the southern U.S. Also called: **cottonmouth**.

water nymph *n.* any fabled nymph of the water, such as the Naiad, Nereid, or Oceanid of Greek mythology.

water of crystallization *n.* water present in the crystals of certain compounds. It is chemically combined in a specific amount but can often be easily expelled.

water ouzel *n.* another name for **dipper** (the bird).

water pipe *n.* **1.** a pipe for water. **2.** another name for **hookah**.

water pistol *n.* a toy pistol that squirts a stream of water or other liquid.

water plantain *n.* any of a genus of marsh plants of N temperate regions and Australia, having clusters of small white or pinkish flowers and broad pointed leaves.

water polo *n.* a game played in water by two teams of seven swimmers in which each side tries to throw or propel an inflated ball into the opponents' goal.

water power *n.* **1.** the power latent in a dynamic or static head of water as used to drive machinery, esp. for generating electricity. **2.** a source of such power, such as a drop in the level of a river, etc.

waterproof ('wɔːtə,pruːf) *adj.* **1.** not penetrable by water. Cf. **water-repellent, water-resistant**. ~*n.* **2.** *Chiefly Brit.* a waterproof garment, esp. a raincoat. ~*vb.* (*tr.*) **3.** to make (a fabric, etc.) waterproof.

water purslane *n.* a marsh plant of temperate and warm regions, having reddish stems and small reddish flowers.

water rail *n.* a large Eurasian rail of swamps, ponds, etc., having a long red bill.

water rat *n.* **1.** any of several small amphibious rodents, esp. the water vole or the muskrat. **2.** any of various amphibious rats of New Guinea, the Philippines, and Australia.

water rate *n.* a charge made for the public supply of water.

water-repellent *adj.* (of fabrics, garments, etc.) having a finish that resists the absorption of water.

water-resistant *adj.* (esp. of fabrics) designed to resist but not entirely prevent the penetration of water.

Waters ('wɔːtəz) *n.* **Muddy**, real name *McKinley Morganfield*. 1915–83, U.S. blues guitarist, singer, and songwriter. His songs include "Rollin' Stone" (1948) and "Got my Mojo Working" (1954).

water scorpion *n.* a long-legged aquatic insect that breathes by means of a long spinelike tube that projects from the rear of the body and penetrates the surface of the water.

watershed ('wɔːtə,ʃɛd) *n.* **1.** the dividing line between two adjacent river systems, such as a ridge. **2.** an important period or factor that serves as a dividing line.

waterside ('wɔːtə,saɪd) *n.* **a.** the area of land beside a body of water. **b.** (*as modifier*): *waterside houses*.

watersider ('wɔːtə,saɪdə) *n.* *Austral. & N.Z.* a dock labourer.

water-ski *n.* **1.** a type of ski used for planing or gliding over water. ~*vb.* **-skiing, -skied** *or* **-ski'd**. **2.** (*intr.*) to ride over water on water-skis while holding a rope towed by a speedboat. —'**water-,skier** *n.* —'**water-,skiing** *n.*

water snake *n.* any of various snakes that live in or near water, esp. any of a genus of harmless North American snakes.

water softener *n.* **1.** any substance that lessens the hardness of water, usually by precipitating calcium and magnesium ions. **2.** an apparatus that is used to remove chemicals that cause hardness.

water spaniel *n.* either of two large curly-coated breeds of spaniel (the Irish and the American), which are used for hunting waterfowl.

water splash *n.* a place where a stream runs over a road.

water sports *pl. n.* sports, such as swimming or windsurfing, that take place in or on water.

waterspout ('wɔːtə,spaʊt) *n.* **1.** *Meteorol.* **a.** a tornado occurring over water that forms a column of water and mist. **b.** a sudden downpour of heavy rain. **2.** a pipe or channel through which water is discharged.

water table *n.* **1.** the level below which the ground is saturated with water. **2.** a string course that has a moulding designed to throw rainwater clear of the wall below.

water thrush *n.* either of two North American warblers having brownish backs and striped underparts and occurring near water.

watertight ('wɔːtə,taɪt) *adj.* **1.** not permitting the passage of water either in or out: *a watertight boat.* **2.** without loopholes: *a watertight argument.* **3.** kept separate from other subjects or influences.

water tower ('tauə) *n.* a reservoir or storage tank mounted on a tower-like structure so that water can be distributed at a uniform pressure.

water vapour *n.* water in the gaseous state, esp. when due to evaporation at a temperature below the boiling point.

water vole *n.* a large amphibious vole of Eurasian river banks. Also called: **water rat.**

water wagtail *n.* another name for **pied wagtail.**

waterway ('wɔːtə,weɪ) *n.* a river, canal, or other navigable channel used as a means of travel or transport.

waterweed ('wɔːtə,wiːd) *n.* any of various weedy aquatic plants.

water wheel *n.* **1.** a simple water-driven turbine consisting of a wheel having vanes set axially across its rim, used to drive machinery. **2.** a wheel with buckets attached to its rim for raising water from a stream, pond, etc.

water wings *pl. n.* an inflatable rubber device shaped like a pair of wings, which is placed under the arms of a person learning to swim.

waterworks ('wɔːtə,wɜːks) *n.* **1.** *(functioning as sing.)* an establishment for storing, purifying, and distributing water for community supply. **2.** *(functioning as pl.)* a display of water in movement, as in fountains. **3.** *(functioning as pl.) Brit. inf., euphemistic.* the urinary system. **4.** *(functioning as pl.) Inf.* crying; tears.

waterworn ('wɔːtə,wɔːn) *adj.* worn smooth by the action or passage of water.

watery ('wɔːtərɪ) *adj.* **1.** relating to, containing, or resembling water. **2.** discharging or secreting water or a water-like fluid. **3.** tearful; weepy. **4.** insipid, thin, or weak.

Watford ('wɒtfəd) *n.* a town in SE England, in SW Hertfordshire: printing. Pop.: 76 500 (1986).

Watling Island ('wɒtlɪŋ) *n.* another name for **San Salvador Island.**

Watson ('wɒtsən) *n.* **1. James Dewey.** born 1928, U.S. biologist, whose contribution to the discovery of the helical structure of DNA won him a Nobel prize for physiology or medicine shared with Francis Crick and Maurice Wilkins in 1962. **2. John Broadus.** 1878–1958, U.S. psychologist; a leading exponent of behaviourism. **3. John Christian.** 1867–1941, Australian statesman, born in Chile: prime minister of Australia (1904).

Watson-Watt ('wɒtsən'wɒt) *n.* Sir **Robert Alexander.** 1892–1973, Scottish physicist, who played a leading role in the development of radar.

watt (wɒt) *n.* the derived SI unit of power, equal to 1 joule per second; the power dissipated by a current of 1 ampere flowing across a potential difference of 1 volt. Symbol: W [C19: after J. WATT]

Watt (wɒt) *n.* **James.** 1736–1819, Scottish engineer and inventor. His fundamental improvements to the steam engine led to the widespread use of steam power in industry.

wattage ('wɒtɪdʒ) *n.* **1.** power, esp. electric power, measured in watts. **2.** the power rating, measured in watts, of an electrical appliance.

Watteau ('wɒtəu; *French* vato) *n.* **Jean Antoine** (ʒɑ̃ ɑ̃twan). 1684–1721, French painter, esp. of *fêtes champêtres.*

Wattenscheid (*German* 'vatənʃaɪt) *n.* an industrial town in NW West Germany, in North Rhine-Westphalia east of Essen. Pop.: 81 200 (1970).

watt-hour *n.* a unit of energy equal to a power of one watt operating for one hour.

wattle ('wɒtəl) *n.* **1.** a frame of rods or stakes interwoven with twigs, branches, etc., esp. when used to make fences. **2.** the material used in such a construction. **3.** a loose fold of skin, often brightly coloured, hanging from the neck or throat of certain birds, lizards, etc. **4.** any of various chiefly Australian acacia trees having spikes of small

brightly coloured flowers and flexible branches. ~*vb.* (*tr.*) **5.** to construct from wattle. **6.** to bind or frame with wattle. **7.** to weave or twist (branches, twigs, etc.) into a frame. ~*adj.* **8.** made of, formed by, or covered with wattle. [OE *watol*] —**'wattled** *adj.*

wattle and daub *n.* a form of wall construction consisting of interwoven twigs plastered with a mixture of clay, water, and sometimes chopped straw.

wattmeter ('wɒt,miːtə) *n.* a meter for measuring electric power in watts.

Watts (wɒts) *n.* **1. George Frederick.** 1817–1904, English painter and sculptor, noted esp. for his painting *Hope* (1886) and his sculpture *Physical Energy* (1904) in Kensington Gardens, London. **2. Isaac.** 1674–1748, English hymn-writer.

Waugh (wɔː) *n.* **Evelyn** (**Arthur St. John**) ('iːvlɪn). 1903–66, English novelist. His early satirical novels include *Decline and Fall* (1928), *Vile Bodies* (1930), *A Handful of Dust* (1934), and *Scoop* (1938). His later novels include the more sombre *Brideshead Revisited* (1945) and the trilogy of World War II *Men at Arms* (1952), *Officers and Gentlemen* (1955), and *Unconditional Surrender* (1961).

waul *or* **wawl** (wɔːl) *vb.* (*intr.*) to cry or wail plaintively like a cat. [C16: imit.]

wave (weɪv) *vb.* **1.** to move or cause to move freely to and fro: *the banner waved in the wind.* **2.** (*intr.*) to move the hand to and fro as a greeting. **3.** to signal or signify by or as if by waving something. **4.** (*tr.*) to direct to move by or as if by waving something: *he waved me on.* **5.** to form or be formed into curves, undulations, etc. **6.** (*tr.*) to set waves in (the hair). ~*n.* **7.** one of a sequence of ridges or undulations that moves across the surface of a body of a liquid, esp. the sea. **8. the waves.** the sea. **9.** any undulation on or at the edge of a surface reminiscent of a wave in the sea: *a wave across the field of corn.* **10.** anything that suggests the movement of a wave, as by a sudden rise: *a crime wave.* **11.** a widespread movement that advances in a body: *a wave of settlers.* **12.** the act or an instance of waving. **13.** *Physics.* an energy-carrying disturbance propagated through a medium or space by a progressive local displacement of the medium or a change in its physical properties, but without any overall movement of matter. **14.** *Physics.* a graphical representation of a wave obtained by plotting the magnitude of the disturbance against time at a particular point in the medium or space. **15.** a prolonged spell of some particular type of weather: *a heat wave.* **16.** an undulating curve or series of curves or loose curls in the hair. **17. make waves.** to cause trouble; disturb the status quo. [OE *wafian* (vb.); C16 (n.) meaning from earlier *wāwe,* prob. from OE *wǣg* motion] —**'waveless** *adj.* —**'wave,like** *adj.*

waveband ('weɪv,bænd) *n.* a range of wavelengths or frequencies used for a particular type of radio transmission.

wave-cut platform *n.* a flat surface at the base of a cliff formed by erosion by waves.

wave down *vb.* (*tr., adv.*) to signal with a wave to (a driver or vehicle) to stop.

wave equation *n. Physics.* a partial differential equation describing wave motion.

waveform ('weɪv,fɔːm) *n. Physics.* the shape of the graph of a wave or oscillation obtained by plotting the value of some changing quantity against time.

wave front *n. Physics.* a surface associated with a propagating wave and passing through all points in the wave that have the same phase.

wave function *n. Physics.* a mathematical function of position and sometimes time, used in wave mechanics to describe the state of a physical system. Symbol: ψ

waveguide ('weɪv,gaɪd) *n. Electronics.* a solid rod of dielectric or a hollow metal tube, usually of rectangular cross section, used as a path to guide microwaves.

wavelength ('weɪv,lɛŋθ) *n.* **1.** the distance, measured in the direction of propagation, between two points of the same phase in consecutive cycles of a wave. Symbol: λ **2.** the wavelength of the carrier wave used by a particular broadcasting station. **3. on someone's** (*or* **the same**) **wavelength.** *Inf.* having similar views, feelings, or thoughts (as someone else).

wavelet ('weɪvlɪt) *n.* a small wave.

Wavell ('weɪvəl) *n.* **Archibald** (**Percival**), 1st Earl. 1883–1950, British field marshal. During World War II he was commander in chief in the Middle East (1939–41), defeating the Italians in N Africa. He was commander in chief in India (1941–43) and viceroy of India (1943–47).

wave mechanics n. (functioning as sing.) Physics. the formulation of quantum mechanics in which the behaviour of systems, such as atoms, is described in terms of their wave functions.

wave number n. Physics. the reciprocal of the wavelength of a wave.

waver ('weɪvə) vb. (intr.) **1.** to be irresolute; hesitate between two possibilities. **2.** to become unsteady. **3.** to fluctuate. **4.** to move back and forth or one way and another. **5.** (of light) to flicker or flash. ~n. **6.** the act or an instance of wavering. [C14: from ON vafra to flicker] —'waverer n. —'wavering adj. —'waveringly adv.

wave theory n. **1.** the theory proposed by Huygens that light is transmitted by waves. **2.** any theory that light or other radiation is transmitted as waves. ~Cf. **corpuscular theory.**

wavey ('weɪvɪ) n. Canad. a snow goose or other wild goose. Also called: **wawa.** [via Canad. F from Algonquian (Cree wehwew)]

wavy ('weɪvɪ) adj. **wavier, waviest. 1.** abounding in or full of waves. **2.** moving or proceeding in waves. **3.** (of hair) set in or having waves. —'wavily adv. —'waviness n.

wax[1] (wæks) n. **1.** any of various viscous or solid materials of natural origin: characteristically lustrous, insoluble in water, and sensitive to heat, they consist largely of esters of fatty acids. **2.** any of various similar substances, such as paraffin wax, that have a mineral origin and consist largely of hydrocarbons. **3.** short for **beeswax** or **sealing wax. 4.** Physiol. another name for **cerumen. 5.** a resinous preparation used by shoemakers to rub on thread. **6.** any substance or object that is pliable or easily moulded: he was wax in their hands. **7.** (modifier) made of or resembling wax: a wax figure. **8. put on wax.** to make a gramophone record of. ~vb. **9.** (tr.) to coat, polish, etc., with wax. **10.** (tr.) Inf. to make a gramophone record of. [OE weax] —'waxer n.

wax[2] (wæks) vb. (intr.) **1.** to become larger, more powerful, etc. **2.** (of the moon) to show a gradually increasing portion of illuminated surface, between new moon and full moon. **3.** to become: to wax eloquent. [OE weaxan]

wax[3] (wæks) n. Inf., chiefly Brit. a fit of rage or temper: he's in a wax today. [from ?]

waxberry ('wæksbərɪ) n., pl. -ries. the waxy fruit of the wax myrtle or the snowberry.

waxbill ('wæks,bɪl) n. any of various chiefly African finchlike weaverbirds having a brightly coloured bill and plumage.

wax cloth n. **1.** another name for **oilcloth. 2.** (formerly) another name for **linoleum.**

waxen ('wæksən) adj. **1.** made of, treated with, or covered with wax. **2.** resembling wax in colour or texture.

waxeye ('wæks,aɪ) n. a small New Zealand bird with a white circle around its eye. Also called: **silver-eye, blighty.**

wax flower n. Austral. any of a genus of shrubs having waxy pink-white five-petalled flowers.

wax light n. a candle or taper of wax.

wax myrtle n. a shrub of SE North America, having evergreen leaves and a small berry-like fruit with a waxy coating. Also called: **bayberry, candleberry, waxberry.**

wax palm n. **1.** a tall Andean palm tree having pinnate leaves that yield a resinous wax used in making candles. **2.** another name for **carnauba** (sense 1).

wax paper n. paper treated or coated with wax or paraffin to make it waterproof.

waxplant ('wæks,plɑːnt) n. a climbing shrub of E Asia and Australia, having fleshy leaves and clusters of small waxy white pink-centred flowers.

waxwing ('wæks,wɪŋ) n. any of a genus of gregarious passerine songbirds having red waxy wing tips and crested heads.

waxwork ('wæks,wɜːk) n. **1.** an object reproduced in wax, esp. as an ornament. **2.** a life-size lifelike figure, esp. of a famous person, reproduced in wax. **3.** (pl.; functioning as sing. or pl.) a museum or exhibition of wax figures.

waxy[1] ('wæksɪ) adj. **waxier, waxiest. 1.** resembling wax in colour, appearance, or texture. **2.** made of, covered with, or abounding in wax. —'waxily adv. —'waxiness n.

waxy[2] ('wæksɪ) adj. **waxier, waxiest.** Brit. sl. bad-tempered or irritable; angry.

way (weɪ) n. **1.** a manner, method, or means: a way of life. **2.** a route or direction: the way home. **3. a.** a means or line of passage, such as a path or track. **b.** (in combination): waterway. **4.** space or room for movement or activity (esp. in **make way, in the way, out of the way**). **5.** distance, usually distance in general: you've come a long way. **6.** a passage or journey: on the way. **7.** characteristic style or manner: I did it my way. **8.** (often pl.) habit: he has some offensive ways. **9.** an aspect of something; particular: in many ways he was right. **10. a.** a street in or leading out of a town. **b.** (cap. when part of a street name): Icknield Way. **11.** something that one wants in a determined manner (esp. in **get** or **have one's (own) way). 12.** the experience or sphere in which one comes into contact with things (esp. in **come one's way**). **13.** Inf. a state or condition, usually financial or concerning health (esp. in **in a good** (or **bad) way**). **14.** Inf. the area or direction of one's home: drop in if you're ever over my way. **15.** movement of a ship or other vessel. **16.** a guide along which something can be moved, such as the surface of a lathe along which the tailstock slides. **17.** (pl.) the wooden or metal tracks down which a ship slides to be launched. **18.** a course of life including experiences, conduct, etc.: the way of sin. **19. by the way.** incidentally. **20. by way of. a.** via. **b.** serving as: by way of introduction. **c.** in the state or condition of: by way of being an artist. **21. each way.** (of a bet) laid on a horse, dog, etc., to win or gain a place. **22. give way. a.** to collapse or break down. **b.** to yield. **23. give way to. a.** to step aside for or stop for. **b.** to give full rein to (emotions, etc.). **24. go out of one's way.** to take considerable trouble or inconvenience oneself. **25. have a way with.** to have such a manner or skill as to handle successfully. **26. have it both ways.** to enjoy two things that would normally be mutually exclusive. **27. in a way.** in some respects. **28. in no way.** not at all. **29. lead the way. a.** to go first. **b.** to set an example. **30. make one's way. a.** to proceed or advance. **b.** to achieve success in life. **31. on the way out.** Inf. **a.** becoming unfashionable, etc. **b.** dying. **32. out of the way. a.** removed or dealt with so as to be no longer a hindrance. **b.** remote. **c.** unusual and sometimes improper. **33. see one's way (clear).** to find it possible and be willing (to do something). **34. under way.** having started moving or making progress. ~adv. **35.** Inf. **a.** at a considerable distance or extent: way over yonder. **b.** very far: they're way up the mountain. [OE weg]

▷ **Usage.** The use of the way for as in sentences such as he does not write the way his father did is well established in the U.S. and is common in British informal usage. Careful writers, however, prefer as in formal contexts.

waybill ('weɪ,bɪl) n. a document attached to goods in transit specifying their nature, point of origin, and destination as well as the route to be taken and the rate to be charged.

wayfarer ('weɪ,fɛərə) n. a person who goes on a journey. —'way,faring n., adj.

wayfaring tree n. a shrub of Europe and W Asia, having white flowers and berries that turn from red to black.

Wayland or **Wayland Smith** ('weɪlənd) n. a smith, artificer, and king of the elves in European folklore. Scandinavian name: **Völund.** German name: **Wieland.**

waylay (weɪ'leɪ) vb. **-laying, -laid.** (tr.) **1.** to lie in wait for and attack. **2.** to await and intercept unexpectedly. —'way,layer n.

wayleave ('weɪ,liːv) n. access to property granted by a landowner for payment, for example to allow a contractor access to a building site.

waymark ('weɪ,mɑːk) n. a symbol or signpost marking the route of a footpath. —'way,marked adj.

Wayne (weɪn) n. **John,** real name Marion Michael Morrison. 1907–79, U.S. film actor, noted esp. for his many Westerns, which include Stagecoach (1939), The Alamo (1960), and True Grit (1969), for which he won an Oscar.

way-out adj. Inf. **1.** extremely unconventional or experimental. **2.** excellent or amazing.

-ways suffix forming adverbs. indicating direction or manner: sideways. [OE weges, lit.: of the way, from weg way]

ways and means pl. n. **1.** the revenues and methods of raising the revenues needed for the functioning of a state or other political unit. **2.** the methods and resources for accomplishing some purpose.

wayside ('wei,said) n. **1. a.** the side or edge of a road. **b.** (modifier) situated by the wayside: a wayside inn. **2. fall by the wayside.** to cease or fail to continue doing something: of the nine starters, three fell by the wayside.

wayward ('weiwəd) adj. **1.** wanting to have one's own way regardless of others. **2.** capricious, erratic, or unpredictable. [C14: changed from awayward turned or turning away] —'**waywardly** adv. —'**waywardness** n.

wayworn ('wei,wɔːn) adj. Rare. worn or tired by travel.

Waziristan (wə,zıərı'stɑːn) n. a mountainous region of N Pakistan, on the border with Afghanistan.

wb abbrev. for: **1.** water ballast. **2.** Also: **W/B, WB.** waybill. **3.** westbound.

Wb Physics. symbol for weber.

WBA abbrev. for World Boxing Association.

WBC abbrev. for World Boxing Council.

WC abbrev. for: **1.** Also: **wc.** water closet. **2.** (in London postal code) West Central.

WD abbrev. for: **1.** War Department. **2.** Works Department.

we (wiː) pron. (subjective) **1.** refers to the speaker or writer and another person or other people: we should go now. **2.** refers to all people or people in general: the planet on which we live. **3.** a formal word for **I** used by editors or other writers, and formerly by monarchs. **4.** Inf. used instead of you with a tone of condescension or sarcasm: how are we today? [OE wē]

WEA (in Britain) abbrev. for Workers' Educational Association.

weak (wiːk) adj. **1.** lacking in physical or mental strength or force. **2.** liable to yield, break, or give way: a weak link in a chain. **3.** lacking in resolution or firmness of character. **4.** lacking strength, power, or intensity: a weak voice. **5.** lacking strength in a particular part: a team weak in defence. **6. a.** not functioning as well as is normal: weak eyes. **b.** easily upset: a weak stomach. **7.** lacking in conviction, persuasiveness, etc.: a weak argument. **8.** lacking in political or strategic strength: a weak state. **9.** lacking the usual, full, or desirable strength of flavour: weak tea. **10.** Grammar. **a.** denoting or belonging to a class of verbs, in Germanic languages, whose conjugation relies on inflectional endings rather than internal vowel gradation, as look, looks, looking, looked. **b.** belonging to any part-of-speech class, in any of various languages, whose inflections follow the more regular of two possible patterns. **11.** (of a syllable) not accented or stressed. **12.** (of an industry, market, securities, etc.) falling in price or characterized by falling prices. [OE wāc soft, miserable] —'**weakish** adj.

weaken ('wiːkən) vb. to become or cause to become weak or weaker. —'**weakener** n.

weak interaction n. Physics. an interaction between elementary particles that is responsible for certain decay processes, operates at distances less than about 10^{-15} metres, and is 10^{12} times weaker than the strong interaction.

weak-kneed adj. Inf. yielding readily to force, intimidation, etc. —,**weak-'kneedly** adv.

weakling ('wiːklıŋ) n. a person or animal that is lacking in strength or weak in constitution or character.

weakly ('wiːklı) adj. **-lier, -liest. 1.** sickly; feeble. ~adv. **2.** in a weak or feeble manner.

weak-minded adj. **1.** lacking in stability of mind or character. **2.** another word for **feeble-minded.** —,**weak-'mindedly** adv. —,**weak-'mindedness** n.

weakness ('wiːknıs) n. **1.** a being weak. **2.** a failing, as in a person's character. **3.** a self-indulgent liking: a weakness for chocolates.

weal[1] (wiːl) n. a raised mark on the skin produced by a blow. [C19: var. of WALE, infl. in form by WHEAL]

weal[2] (wiːl) n. Arch. prosperity or wellbeing (now esp. in **the public weal, the common weal**). [OE wela]

weald (wiːld) n. Brit. arch. open or forested country. [OE]

Weald (wiːld) n. **the.** a region of SE England, in Kent, Surrey, and Sussex between the North Downs and the South Downs: formerly forested.

wealth (wɛlθ) n. **1.** a large amount of money and valuable material possessions. **2.** the state of being rich. **3.** a great profusion: a wealth of gifts. **4.** Econ. all goods and services with monetary or productive value. [C13 welthe, from WEAL[2]]

wealth tax n. a'tax on personal property.

wealthy ('wɛlθı) adj. **wealthier, wealthiest. 1.** possessing wealth; rich. **2.** of or relating to wealth. **3.** abounding: wealthy in friends. —'**wealthily** adv. —'**wealthiness** n.

wean[1] (wiːn) vb. (tr.) **1.** to cause (a child or young mammal) to replace mother's milk by other nourishment. **2.** (usually foll. by from) to cause to desert former habits, pursuits, etc. [OE wenian to accustom]

wean[2] (wein) n. Scot. & N English dialect. a child. [? short form of WEANLING, or a contraction of wee ane]

weaner ('wiːnə) n. **1.** a person or thing that weans. **2.** a pig that has just been weaned and weighs less than 40 kg. **3.** Austral. & N.Z. a lamb, pig, or calf in the year in which it is weaned.

weanling ('wiːnlıŋ) n. a child or young animal recently weaned. [C16: from WEAN[1] + -LING[1]]

weapon ('wɛpən) n. **1.** an object or instrument used in fighting. **2.** anything that serves to get the better of an opponent: his power of speech was his best weapon. **3.** any part of an animal that is used to defend itself, to attack prey, etc., such as claws or a sting. [OE wǣpen] —'**weaponed** adj. —'**weaponless** adj.

weaponry ('wɛpənrı) n. weapons regarded collectively.

wear[1] (wɛə) vb. **wearing, wore, worn. 1.** (tr.) to carry or have (a garment, etc.) on one's person as clothing, ornament, etc. **2.** (tr.) to carry or have on one's person habitually: she wears a lot of red. **3.** (tr.) to have in one's aspect: to wear a smile. **4.** (tr.) to display, show, or fly: a ship wears its colours. **5.** to deteriorate or cause to deteriorate by constant use or action. **6.** to produce or be produced by constant rubbing, scraping, etc.: to wear a hole in one's trousers. **7.** to bring or be brought to a specified condition by constant use or action: to wear a tyre to shreds. **8.** (intr.) to submit to constant use or action in a specified way: his suit wears well. **9.** (tr.) to harass or weaken. **10.** (when intr., often foll. by on) (of time) to pass or be passed slowly. **11.** (tr.) Brit. inf. to accept: Larry won't wear that argument. ~n. **12.** the act of wearing or state of being worn. **13. a.** anything designed to be worn: leisure wear. **b.** (in combination): nightwear. **14.** deterioration from constant or normal use. **15.** the quality of resisting the effects of constant use. ~See also **wear down, wear off, wear out.** [OE werian] —'**wearer** n.

wear[2] (wɛə) vb. **wearing, wore, worn.** Naut. to tack by gybing instead of by going through stays. [C17: from earlier weare, from ?]

Wear (wıə) n. a river in NE England, rising in NW Durham and flowing southeast then northeast to the North Sea at Sunderland. Length: 105 km (65 miles).

wearable ('wɛərəb²l) adj. suitable for wear or able to be worn. —,**weara'bility** n.

wear and tear n. damage, depreciation, or loss resulting from ordinary use.

wear down vb. (adv.) **1.** to consume or be consumed by long or constant wearing, rubbing, etc. **2.** to overcome or be overcome gradually by persistent effort.

wearing ('wɛərıŋ) adj. causing fatigue or exhaustion; tiring. —'**wearingly** adv.

wearisome ('wıərısəm) adj. causing fatigue or annoyance; tedious. —'**wearisomely** adv.

wear off vb. (adv.) **1.** (intr.) to decrease in intensity gradually: the pain will wear off in an hour. **2.** to disappear or cause to disappear gradually through exposure, use, etc.

wear out vb. (adv.) **1.** to make or become unfit or useless through wear. **2.** (tr.) to exhaust or tire.

weary ('wıərı) adj. **-rier, -riest. 1.** tired or exhausted. **2.** causing fatigue or exhaustion. **3.** caused by or suggestive of weariness: a weary laugh. **4.** (postpositive; often foll. by of or with) discontented or bored. ~vb. **-rying, -ried. 5.** to make or become weary. **6.** to make or become discontented or impatient. [OE wērig] —'**weariless** adj. —'**wearily** adv. —'**weariness** n. —'**wearying** adj. —'**wearyingly** adv.

weasand ('wiːzənd) n. a former name for the **trachea.** [OE wǣsend, wāsend]

weasel ('wiːz²l) n., pl. **-sel** or **-sels. 1.** any of various small predatory mammals, such as the **European weasel,** having reddish-brown fur, an elongated body and neck, and short legs. **2.** Inf. a sly or treacherous person. [OE weosule, wesle] —'**weaselly** adj.

weasel out *vb.* **-selling, -selled** *or U.S.* **-seling, -seled.** (*intr., adv.*) *Inf., chiefly U.S. & Canad.* **1.** to go back on a commitment. **2.** to evade a responsibility, esp. in a despicable manner.

weasel words *pl. n. Inf.* intentionally evasive or misleading speech; equivocation. [C20: from the weasel's supposed ability to suck an egg out of its shell without seeming to break the shell]

weather ('wɛðə) *n.* **1. a.** the day-to-day meteorological conditions, esp. temperature, cloudiness, and rainfall, affecting a specific place. **b.** (*modifier*) relating to the forecasting of weather: *a weather ship.* **2. make heavy weather. a.** *Naut.* to roll and pitch in heavy seas. **b.** (foll. by *of*) *Inf.* to carry out with great difficulty or unnecessarily great effort. **3. under the weather.** *Inf.* not in good health. ~*adj.* **4.** (*prenominal*) on or at the side or part towards the wind: *the weather anchor.* Cf. **lee** (sense 2). ~*vb.* **5.** to expose or be exposed to the action of the weather. **6.** to undergo or cause to undergo changes, such as discoloration, due to the action of the weather. **7.** (*intr.*) to withstand the action of the weather. **8.** (when *intr.*, foll. by *through*) to endure (a crisis, danger, etc.). **9.** (*tr.*) to slope (a surface, such as a roof) so as to throw rainwater clear. **10.** (*tr.*) to sail to the windward of: *to weather a point.* [OE *weder*] — 'weatherer *n.*

weather-beaten *adj.* **1.** showing signs of exposure to the weather. **2.** tanned or hardened by exposure to the weather.

weatherboard ('wɛðə,bɔːd) *n.* a timber board, with a groove (rabbet) along the front of its top edge and along the back of its lower edge, that is fixed horizontally with others to form an exterior covering on a wall or roof. — 'weather,boarding *n.*

weather-bound *adj.* (of a vessel, aircraft, etc.) delayed by bad weather.

weathercock ('wɛðə,kɒk) *n.* **1.** a weather vane in the form of a cock. **2.** a person who is fickle or changeable.

weathered ('wɛðəd) *adj.* **1.** affected by exposure to the action of the weather. **2.** (of rocks and rock formations) eroded, decomposed, or otherwise altered by the action of wind, frost, etc. **3.** (of a sill, roof, etc.) having a sloped surface so as to allow rainwater to run off.

weather eye *n.* **1.** the vision of a person trained to observe changes in the weather. **2.** *Inf.* an alert or observant gaze. **3. keep one's weather eye open.** to stay on the alert.

weatherglass ('wɛðə,glɑːs) *n.* any of various instruments, esp. a barometer, that measure atmospheric conditions.

weather house *n.* a model house, usually with two human figures, one that comes out to foretell bad weather and one that comes out to foretell good weather.

weathering ('wɛðərɪŋ) *n.* the mechanical and chemical breakdown of rocks by the action of rain, snow, cold, etc.

weatherly ('wɛðəlɪ) *adj.* (of a sailing vessel) making very little leeway when close-hauled, even in a stiff breeze. — 'weatherliness *n.*

weatherman ('wɛðə,mæn) *n., pl.* **-men.** *Inf.* a person who forecasts the weather, esp. one who works in a meteorological office.

weather map *or* **chart** *n.* a chart showing weather conditions, compiled from simultaneous observations taken at various weather stations.

weatherproof ('wɛðə,pruːf) *adj.* **1.** designed or able to withstand exposure to weather without deterioration. ~*vb.* **2.** (*tr.*) to render (something) weatherproof.

weather station *n.* one of a network of meteorological observation posts where weather data is recorded.

weather strip *n.* a thin strip of compressible material, such as spring metal, felt, etc., that is fitted between the frame of a door or window and the opening part to exclude wind and rain. Also called: **weatherstripping.**

weather vane *n.* a vane designed to indicate the direction in which the wind is blowing.

weather window *n.* a limited interval when weather conditions can be expected to be suitable for a particular project.

weather-wise *adj.* **1.** skilful in predicting weather conditions. **2.** skilful in predicting trends in opinion, reactions, etc.

weatherworn ('wɛðə,wɔːn) *adj.* another word for **weather-beaten.**

weave (wiːv) *vb.* **weaving, wove** *or* **weaved; woven** *or* **weaved. 1.** to form (a fabric) by interlacing (yarn, etc.), esp. on a loom. **2.** (*tr.*) to make or construct by such a process: *to weave a shawl.* **3.** to construct by interlacing (cane, twigs, etc.). **4.** (of a spider) to make (a web). **5.** (*tr.*) to construct by combining separate elements into a whole. **6.** (*tr.*; often foll. by *in, into, through*, etc.) to introduce: *to weave factual details into a fiction.* **7.** to create (a way, etc.) by moving from side to side: *to weave through a crowd.* **8. get weaving.** *Inf.* to hurry. ~*n.* **9.** the method or pattern of weaving or the structure of a woven fabric: *an open weave.* [OE *wefan*]

weaver ('wiːvə) *n.* **1.** a person who weaves, esp. as a means of livelihood. **2.** short for **weaverbird.**

weaverbird ('wiːvə,bɜːd) *or* **weaver** *n.* any of a family of small Old World passerine songbirds, having a short thick bill and a dull plumage and building covered nests: includes the house sparrow and whydahs.

web (wɛb) *n.* **1.** any structure, fabric, etc., formed by or as if by weaving or interweaving. **2.** a mesh of fine tough threads built by a spider from a liquid secreted from its spinnerets and used to trap insects. **3.** a similar network of threads spun by certain insect larvae, such as the silkworm. **4.** a fabric, esp. one in the process of being woven. **5.** a membrane connecting the toes of some aquatic birds or the digits of such aquatic mammals as the otter. **6.** the vane of a bird's feather. **7.** a thin piece of metal, esp. one connecting two thicker parts as in an H-beam or an I-beam. **8. a.** a continuous strip of paper as formed on a paper machine or fed from a reel into some printing presses. **b.** (*as modifier*): *web offset.* **9.** any structure, construction, etc., that is intricately formed or complex: *a web of intrigue.* ~*vb.* **webbing, webbed. 10.** (*tr.*) to cover with or as if with a web. **11.** (*tr.*) to entangle or ensnare. **12.** (*intr.*) to construct a web. [OE *webb*] — 'webless *adj.*

Webb (wɛb) *n.* **Sidney (James),** Baron Passfield. 1859–1947, English economist, social historian, and Fabian socialist. He and his wife (**Martha**) **Beatrice** (née *Potter*), 1858–1943, English writer on social and economic problems, collaborated in *The History of Trade Unionism* (1894) and *English Local Government* (1906–29), helped found the London School of Economics (1895), and started the *New Statesman* (1913).

webbed (wɛbd) *adj.* **1.** (of the feet of certain animals) having the digits connected by a thin fold of skin. **2.** having or resembling a web.

webbing ('wɛbɪŋ) *n.* **1.** a strong fabric of hemp, cotton, jute, etc., woven in strips and used under springs in upholstery or for straps, etc. **2.** the skin that unites the digits of a webbed foot.

webby ('wɛbɪ) *adj.* **-bier, -biest.** of, relating to, resembling, or consisting of a web.

weber ('veibə) *n.* the derived SI unit of magnetic flux; the flux that, when linking a circuit of one turn, produces in it an emf of 1 volt as it is reduced to zero at a uniform rate in one second. Symbol: Wb [C20: after W. E. WEBER]

Weber (*German* 'veːbər) *n.* **1.** Baron **Carl Maria Friedrich Ernst von** (karl maˈriːa ˈɛrnst fɔn). 1786–1826, German composer and conductor. His three romantic operas are *Der Freischütz* (1821), *Euryanthe* (1823), and *Oberon* (1826). **2. Ernst Heinrich** (ɛrnst ˈhainrɪç). 1795–1878, German physiologist and anatomist. He introduced the psychological concept of the just noticeable difference between stimuli. **3. Max** (maks). 1864–1920, German economist and sociologist, best known for *The Protestant Ethic and the Spirit of Capitalism* (1904–05). **4. Wilhelm Eduard** ('vɪlhɛlm 'eːduart), brother of Ernst Heinrich Weber. 1804–91, German physicist, who conducted research into electricity and magnetism.

Webern (*German* 'veːbərn) *n.* **Anton von** ('antoːn fɔn). 1883–1945, Austrian composer; pupil of Schoenberg, whose twelve-tone technique he adopted. His works include those for chamber ensemble, such as *Five Pieces for Orchestra* (1911–13).

webfoot ('wɛb,fʊt) *n.* **1.** *Zool.* a foot having the toes connected by folds of skin. **2.** *Anat.* a foot having an abnormal membrane connecting adjacent toes.

web-footed *or* **web-toed** *adj.* (of certain animals) having webbed feet that facilitate swimming.

Webster ('wɛbstə) *n.* **1. Daniel.** 1782–1852, U.S. politician and orator. **2. John.** ?1580–?1625, English dramatist, noted for his revenge tragedies *The White Devil*

(?1612) and *The Duchess of Malfi* (?1613). **3. Noah.** 1758–1843, U.S. lexicographer, famous for his *American Dictionary of the English Language* (1828).

webwheel ('wɛb,wiːl) *n.* **1.** a wheel containing a plate or web instead of spokes. **2.** a wheel of which the rim, spokes, and centre are in one piece.

wed (wɛd) *vb.* **wedding, wedded** or **wed. 1.** to take (a person of the opposite sex) as a husband or wife; marry. **2.** (*tr.*) to join (two people) in matrimony. **3.** (*tr.*) to unite closely. [OE *weddian*] —**'wedded** *adj.*

we'd (wiːd; *unstressed* wɪd) *contraction of* we had *or* we would.

Wed. *abbrev. for* Wednesday.

Weddell Sea ('wɛdəl) *n.* an arm of the S Atlantic in Antarctica.

wedding ('wɛdɪŋ) *n.* **1. a.** the act of marrying or the celebration of a marriage. **b.** (*as modifier*): *wedding day.* **2.** the anniversary of a marriage (in such combinations as **silver wedding** or **diamond wedding**).

wedding breakfast *n.* the meal usually served after a wedding ceremony or just before the bride and bridegroom leave for their honeymoon.

wedding cake *n.* a rich fruit cake, with one, two, or more tiers, covered with almond paste and decorated with royal icing, which is served at a wedding reception.

wedding ring *n.* a band ring with parallel sides, typically of precious metal, worn to indicate married status.

Wedekind (*German* 'veːdəkɪnt) *n.* **Frank.** 1864–1918, German dramatist, whose plays, such as *The Awakening of Spring* (1891) and *Pandora's Box* (1904), bitterly satirize the sexual repressiveness of society.

wedge (wɛdʒ) *n.* **1.** a block of solid material, esp. wood or metal, that is shaped like a narrow V in cross section and can be pushed or driven between two objects or parts of an object in order to split or secure them. **2.** any formation, structure, or substance in the shape of a wedge: *a wedge of cheese.* **3.** something such as an idea, action, etc., that tends to cause division. **4.** a shoe with a wedge heel. **5.** *Golf.* a club, a No. 10 iron with a face angle of more than 50°, used for bunker or pitch shots. **6.** (formerly) a body of troops formed in a V-shape. **7. thin end of the wedge.** anything unimportant in itself that implies the start of something much larger. ~*vb.* **8.** (*tr.*) to secure with or as if with a wedge. **9.** to squeeze or be squeezed like a wedge into a narrow space. **10.** (*tr.*) to force apart or divide with or as if with a wedge. [OE *wecg*] —**'wedge,like** *adj.* —**'wedgy** *adj.*

wedge heel *n.* a raised shoe heel with the heel and sole forming a solid block.

wedge-tailed eagle *n.* a large brown Australian eagle having a wedge-shaped tail. Also called: **eaglehawk,** (*Inf.*) **wedgie.**

Wedgwood ('wɛdʒwʊd) *Trademark.* ~*n.* **1. a.** pottery produced at the Wedgwood factory, near Stoke-on-Trent. **b.** such pottery having applied decoration in white on a coloured ground. ~*adj.* **2. a.** relating to pottery made at the Wedgwood factory. **b.** characteristic of such pottery: *Wedgwood blue.* [C18: after Josiah *Wedgwood* (1730–95), E potter]

wedlock ('wɛdlɒk) *n.* **1.** the state of being married. **2. born** or **conceived out of wedlock.** born or conceived when one's parents are not legally married. [OE *wedlāc,* from *wedd* pledge + -*lāc,* suffix denoting activity, ?from *lāc* game]

Wednesday ('wɛnzdɪ) *n.* the fourth day of the week; third day of the working week. [OE *Wōdnes dæg* Woden's day, translation of L *mercurii dies* Mercury's day]

wee[1] (wiː) *adj.* very small; tiny; minute. [C13: from OE *wǣg* weight]

wee[2] (wiː) *Inf., chiefly Brit.* ~*n.* **1. a.** the act or an instance of urinating. **b.** urine. ~*vb.* **2.** (*intr.*) to urinate. ~Also: **wee-wee.** [from ?]

weed (wiːd) *n.* **1.** any plant that grows wild and profusely, esp. one that grows among cultivated plants, depriving them of space, food, etc. **2.** *Sl.* **a. the weed.** tobacco. **b.** marijuana. **3.** *Inf.* a thin or unprepossessing person. **4.** an inferior horse, esp. one showing signs of weakness. ~*vb.* **5.** to remove (useless or troublesome plants) from (a garden, etc.). [OE *weod*] —**'weeder** *n.* —**'weedless** *adj.*

weedkiller ('wiːd,kɪlə) *n.* a substance, usually a chemical or hormone, used for killing weeds.

weed out *vb.* (*tr., adv.*) to separate out, remove, or eliminate (anything unwanted): *to weed out troublesome students.*

weeds (wiːdz) *pl. n.* a widow's black mourning clothes. Also called: **widow's weeds.** [C16: pl. of *weed* (OE *wǣd, wēd*) a band worn in mourning]

weedy ('wiːdɪ) *adj.* **weedier, weediest. 1.** full of or containing weeds: *weedy land.* **2.** (of a plant) resembling a weed in straggling growth. **3.** *Inf.* thin or weakly in appearance.

week (wiːk) *n.* **1.** a period of seven consecutive days, esp. one beginning with Sunday. Related adj.: **hebdomadal. 2.** a period of seven consecutive days beginning from or including a specified day: *a week from Wednesday.* **3.** the period of time within a week devoted to work. ~*adv.* **4.** *Chiefly Brit.* seven days before or after a specified day: *I'll visit you Wednesday week.* [OE *wice, wicu*]

weekday ('wiːk,deɪ) *n.* any day of the week other than Sunday and, often, Saturday.

weekend *n.* (,wiːk'ɛnd). **1. a.** the end of the week, esp. the period from Friday night until the end of Sunday. **b.** (*as modifier*): *a weekend party.* ~*vb.* ('wiːk,ɛnd). **2.** (*intr.*) *Inf.* to spend or pass a weekend.

weekends (,wiːk'ɛndz) *adv. Inf.* at the weekend, esp. regularly or during every weekend.

weekly ('wiːklɪ) *adj.* **1.** happening or taking place once a week or every week. **2.** determined or calculated by the week. ~*adv.* **3.** once a week or every week. ~*n., pl.* -**lies. 4.** a newspaper or magazine issued every week.

weeknight ('wiːk,naɪt) *n.* the evening or night of a weekday.

Weelkes (wiːlks) *n.* **Thomas.** ?1575–1623, English composer of madrigals.

ween (wiːn) *vb. Arch.* to think or imagine (something). [OE *wēnan*]

weeny ('wiːnɪ) *adj.* -**nier, -niest.** *Inf.* very small; tiny. [C18: from WEE[1] with the ending -*ny* as in TINY]

weeny-bopper *n. Inf.* a child of 8 to 12 years who is a keen follower of pop music. [C20: formed on the model of TEENYBOPPER, from WEENY]

weep (wiːp) *vb.* **weeping, wept. 1.** to shed (tears). **2.** (*tr.;* foll. by *out*) to utter, shedding tears. **3.** (when *intr.,* foll. by *for*) to lament (for something). **4.** to exude (drops of liquid). **5.** (*intr.*) (of a wound, etc.) to exude a watery fluid. ~*n.* **6.** a spell of weeping. [OE *wēpan*]

weeper ('wiːpə) *n.* **1.** a person who weeps, esp. a hired mourner. **2.** something worn as a sign of mourning.

weeping ('wiːpɪŋ) *adj.* (of plants) having slender hanging branches. —**'weepingly** *adv.*

weeping willow *n.* a Chinese willow tree having long hanging branches.

weepy ('wiːpɪ) *Inf.* ~*adj.* **weepier, weepiest. 1.** liable or tending to weep. ~*n., pl.* **weepies. 2.** a sentimental film or book. —**'weepily** *adv.* —**'weepiness** *n.*

weever ('wiːvə) *n.* a small marine fish having venomous spines around the gills and the dorsal fin. [C17: from OF *wivre* viper, ult. from L *vipera* VIPER]

weevil ('wiːvɪl) *n.* any of numerous beetles, many having elongated snouts, that are pests, feeding on plants and plant products. [OE *wifel*] —**'weevily** *adj.*

wee-wee *n., vb.* a variant of **wee**[2].

w.e.f. *abbrev. for* with effect from.

weft (wɛft) *n.* the yarn woven across the width of the fabric through the lengthways warp yarn. Also called: **filling, woof.** [OE]

Wegener (*German* 'veːgənər) *n.* **Alfred** ('alfreːt). 1880–1930, German meteorologist: regarded as the originator of the theory of continental drift.

Weichsel ('vaɪksəl) *n.* the German name for the **Vistula** (sense 1).

weigela (waɪ'giːlə, -'dʒiː-) *n.* a shrub of an Asian genus having clusters of showy bell-shaped flowers. [C19: from NL, after C. E. *Weigel* (1748–1831), G physician]

weigh[1] (weɪ) *vb.* **1.** (*tr.*) to measure the weight of. **2.** (*intr.*) to have weight: *she weighs more than her sister.* **3.** (*tr.;* often foll. by *out*) to apportion according to weight. **4.** (*tr.*) to consider carefully: *to weigh the facts of a case.* **5.** (*intr.*) to be influential: *his words weighed little with the jury.* **6.** (*intr.;* often foll. by *on*) to be oppressive (to). **7. weigh anchor.** to raise a vessel's anchor or (of a vessel) to have its anchor raised preparatory to departure. ~See also **weigh down, weigh in,** etc. [OE *wegan*] —**'weighable** *adj.* —**'weigher** *n.*

weigh[2] (weɪ) n. **under weigh.** a variant spelling of **under way.** [C18: var. due to the infl. of phrases such as *to weigh anchor*]

weighbridge ('weɪ,brɪdʒ) n. a machine for weighing vehicles, etc., by means of a metal plate set into a road.

weigh down vb. (adv.) to press (a person, etc.) down by or as if by weight: *his troubles weighed him down.*

weigh in vb. (intr., adv.) **1. a.** (of a boxer or wrestler) to be weighed before a bout. **b.** (of a jockey) to be weighed after, or sometimes before, a race. **2.** *Inf.* to contribute, as in a discussion, etc.: *he weighed in with a few sharp comments.* ~n. **weigh-in. 3.** the act of checking a competitor's weight, as in boxing, racing, etc.

weight (weɪt) n. **1.** a measure of the heaviness of an object; the amount anything weighs. **2.** *Physics.* the vertical force experienced by a mass as a result of gravitation. **3.** a system of units used to express weight: *troy weight.* **4.** a unit used to measure weight: *the kilogram is the weight used in SI units.* **5.** any mass or heavy object used to exert pressure or weigh down. **6.** an oppressive force: *the weight of cares.* **7.** any heavy load: *the bag was such a weight.* **8.** the main force; preponderance: *the weight of evidence.* **9.** importance; influence: *his opinion carries weight.* **10.** *Statistics.* one of a set of coefficients assigned to items of a frequency distribution that are analysed in order to represent the relative importance of the different items. **11.** *Printing.* the apparent blackness of a printed typeface. **12. pull one's weight.** *Inf.* to do one's full or proper share of a task. **13. throw one's weight around.** *Inf.* to act in an overauthoritarian manner. ~vb. (tr.) **14.** to add weight to. **15.** to burden or oppress. **16.** to add importance, value, etc., to (one side rather than another). **17.** *Statistics.* to attach a weight or weights to. [OE *wiht*] —'weighter n.

weighted average n. *Statistics.* a result produced by a technique designed to give recognition to the importance of certain factors when compiling the average of a group of values.

weighting ('weɪtɪŋ) n. **1.** a factor by which some quantity is multiplied in order to make it comparable with others. **2.** an allowance paid to compensate for higher living costs: *a London weighting.*

weightlessness ('weɪtlɪsnɪs) n. the condition of a person or apparatus in a spacecraft subject to no force except gravity. In this state the body is free from the stress normally experienced on earth where gravity is opposed by supporting forces acting on the surface of the body. —'weightless adj.

weightlifting ('weɪt,lɪftɪŋ) n. the sport of lifting barbells of specified weights in a prescribed manner. —'weight-,lifter n.

weight training n. physical exercise involving lifting weights, either heavy or light weights, as a way of improving muscle performance.

weight watcher n. a person who tries to lose weight, esp. by dieting.

weighty ('weɪtɪ) adj. **weightier, weightiest. 1.** having great weight. **2.** important. **3.** causing worry. —'weightily adv. —'weightiness n.

weigh up vb. (tr., adv.) to make an assessment of (a person, situation, etc.); judge.

Weihai or **Wei-hai** ('weɪ'haɪ) n. a port in NE China, in NE Shandong on the Yellow Sea: leased to Britain as a naval base (1898–1930). Pop.: 25 000 (1975 est.). Also called: **Weihaiwei** (,weɪ'haɪ,weɪ).

Weil (*French* vaɪl) n. **Simone** (simɔn). 1909–43, French philosopher and mystic, whose works include *Waiting for God* (1951), *The Need for Roots* (1952), and *Notebooks* (1956).

Weill (vaɪl) n. **Kurt** (kurt). 1900–50, German composer, in the U.S. from 1935. He wrote the music for Brecht's *The Rise and Fall of the City of Mahagonny* (1927) and *The Threepenny Opera* (1928).

Weimar (*German* 'vaɪmar) n. a city in SW East Germany: a cultural centre in the 18th and early 19th century; scene of the adoption (1919) of the constitution of the Weimar Republic. Pop.: 63 900 (1983 est.).

Weimaraner ('vaɪmə,rɑːnə, 'waɪmə,rɑː-) n. a breed of hunting dog, having a sleek short grey coat and short tail. [C20: after WEIMAR, where the breed was developed]

weir (wɪə) n. **1.** a low dam that is built across a river to raise the water level, divert the water, or control its flow.

2. a series of traps or enclosures placed in a stream to catch fish. [OE *wer*]

weird (wɪəd) adj. **1.** suggestive of or relating to the supernatural; eerie. **2.** strange or bizarre. **3.** *Arch.* of or relating to fate or the Fates. ~n. **4.** *Arch., chiefly Scot.* **a.** fate or destiny. **b.** one of the Fates. [OE (ge)*wyrd* destiny] —'weirdly adv. —'weirdness n.

weirdo ('wɪədəʊ) or **weirdie** ('wɪədɪ) n., pl. **-dos** or **-dies.** *Inf.* a person who behaves in a bizarre or eccentric manner.

Weismannism ('vaɪsmən,ɪzəm) n. the theory that all inheritable characteristics are transmitted by the reproductive cells and that characteristics acquired during the lifetime of the organism are not inherited. [C19: after August *Weismann* (1834–1914), G biologist]

Weisshorn ('vaɪs,hɔːn) n. a mountain in S Switzerland, in the Pennine Alps. Height: 4505 m (14 781 ft.).

Weizmann ('waɪtsmən, 'waɪz-) n. **Chaim** ('xaɪɪm). 1874– 1952, Israeli statesman, born in Russia. As a leading Zionist, he was largely responsible for securing the Balfour Declaration (1917); first president of Israel (1949–52).

weka ('wɛkə) n. a nocturnal flightless bird of New Zealand. Also called: **Maori hen, wood hen.** [from Maori]

welch (wɛlʃ) vb. a variant spelling of **welsh.**

Welch (wɛlʃ) adj., n. an archaic spelling of **Welsh.**

welcome ('wɛlkəm) adj. **1.** gladly and cordially received or admitted: *a welcome guest.* **2.** bringing pleasure: *a welcome gift.* **3.** freely permitted or invited: *you are welcome to call.* **4.** under no obligation (only in such phrases as **you're welcome,** as conventional responses to thanks). ~*sentence substitute.* **5.** an expression of cordial greeting. ~n. **6.** the act of greeting or receiving a person or thing; reception: *the new theory had a cool welcome.* **7. wear out** or **overstay one's welcome.** to come more often or stay longer than is pleasing. ~vb. (tr.) **8.** to greet the arrival of (guests, etc.) cordially. **9.** to receive or accept, esp. gladly. [C12: changed (through infl. of WELL[1]) from OE *wilcuma* (agent n. referring to a welcome guest), *wilcume* (a greeting of welcome), from *wil* WILL[2] + *cuman* to come] —'welcomely adv. —'welcomer n.

weld[1] (wɛld) vb. **1.** (tr.) to unite (pieces of metal or plastic), as by softening with heat and hammering or by fusion. **2.** to bring or admit of being brought into close union. ~n. **3.** a joint formed by welding. [C16: altered from obs. *well* to melt, weld] —'weldable adj. —,weld-a'bility n. —'welder or 'weldor n.

weld[2] (wɛld), **wold,** or **woald** (wəʊld) n. a yellow dye obtained from the plant dyer's rocket. [C14: from Low G]

Weld (wɛld) n. **Sir Frederick Aloysius.** 1823–91, New Zealand statesman, born in England: prime minister of New Zealand (1864–65).

Weldon ('wɛldən) n. **Fay.** born 1931, British feminist novelist and dramatist. Her novels include *Female Friends* (1975) and *Leader of the Band* (1988).

welfare ('wɛl,fɛə) n. **1.** health, happiness, prosperity, and wellbeing in general. **2. a.** financial and other assistance given to people in need. **b.** (*as modifier*): *welfare services.* **3.** Also called: **welfare work.** plans or work to better the social or economic conditions of various underprivileged groups. **4. on welfare.** *Chiefly U.S. & Canad.* in receipt of financial aid from a government agency or other source. [C14: from *wel fare;* see WELL[1], FARE]

welfare state n. a system in which the government undertakes the chief responsibility for providing for the social and economic security of its population, usually through unemployment insurance, old age pensions, and other social-security measures.

welkin ('wɛlkɪn) n. *Arch.* the sky, heavens, or upper air. [OE *wolcen, welcen*]

Welkom ('wɛlkəm, 'vɛl-) n. a town in central South Africa, in the Orange Free State. Pop.: 228 000 (1984 est.).

well[1] (wɛl) adv. **better, best. 1.** (*often used in combination*) in a satisfactory manner: *the party went very well.* **2.** (*often used in combination*) in a skilful manner: *she plays the violin well; a well-chosen example.* **3.** in a correct or careful manner: *listen well to my words.* **4.** in a prosperous manner: *to live well.* **5.** (*usually used with auxiliaries*) suitably; fittingly: *you can't very well say that.* **6.** intimately: *I knew him well.* **7.** in a kind or favourable manner: *she speaks well of you.* **8.** fully: *to be well informed.* **9.** by a considerable margin: *let me know well in advance.* **10.** (preceded by *could, might,* or *may*) indeed: *you may well have to do it yourself.* **11. all very well.** used ironically to express discontent, dissent, etc. **12. as well. a.** in addition; too. **b.** (preceded by *may* or *might*) with equal effect: *you might as well come.* **13. as well as.** in addition to. **14. (just) as well.** preferable or advisable: *it would be just as well if you paid me now.* **15. leave well (enough) alone.** to refrain from interfering with something that is satisfactory. **16. well and good.** used to indicate calm acceptance, as of a decision. ~*adj.* (*usually postpositive*) **17.** (when *prenominal, usually used with a negative*) in good health: *I'm very well, thank you; he's not a well man.* **18.** satisfactory or pleasing. **19.** prudent; advisable: *it would be well to make no comment.* **20.** prosperous or comfortable. **21.** fortunate: *it is well that you agreed to go.* ~*interj.* **22. a.** an expression of surprise, indignation, or reproof. **b.** an expression of anticipation in waiting for an answer or remark. ~*sentence connector.* **23.** an expression used to preface a remark, gain time, etc.: *well, I don't think I will come.* [OE *wel*]

well² (wɛl) *n.* **1.** a hole or shaft bored into the earth to tap a supply of water, oil, gas, etc. **2.** a natural pool where ground water comes to the surface. **3. a.** a cavity, space, or vessel used to contain a liquid. **b.** (*in combination*): *an inkwell.* **4.** an open shaft through the floors of a building, such as one used for a staircase. **5.** a deep enclosed space in a building or between buildings that is open to the sky. **6.** a bulkheaded compartment built around a ship's pumps for protection and ease of access. **7.** (in England) the open space in the centre of a law court. **8.** an abundant source: *he is a well of knowledge.* ~*vb.* **9.** to flow or cause to flow upwards or outwards: *tears welled from her eyes.* [OE *wella*]

we'll (wiːl) *contraction of* we will *or* we shall.

well-advised *adj.* (**well advised** *when postpositive*). **1.** acting with deliberation or reason. **2.** well thought out: *a well-advised plan.*

well-affected *adj.* (**well affected** *when postpositive*). favourably disposed (towards); steadfast or loyal.

Welland Canal ('wɛlənd) *n.* a canal in S Canada, in Ontario, linking Lake Erie to Lake Ontario: part of the St Lawrence Seaway, with eight locks. Length: 44 km (28 miles). Also called: **Welland Ship Canal.**

well-appointed *adj.* (**well appointed** *when postpositive*). well equipped or furnished.

wellaway ('wɛlə'weɪ) *interj. Arch.* woe! alas! [OE, from *wei lā wei,* var. of *wā lā wā,* lit.: woe! lo woe]

well-balanced *adj.* (**well balanced** *when postpositive*). **1.** having good balance or proportions. **2.** sane or sensible.

wellbeing ('wɛl'biːɪŋ) *n.* the condition of being contented, healthy, or successful; welfare.

well-bred *adj.* (**well bred** *when postpositive*). **1.** Also: **well-born.** of respected or noble lineage. **2.** indicating good breeding: *well-bred manners.* **3.** of good thoroughbred stock: *a well-bred spaniel.*

well-chosen *adj.* (**well chosen** *when postpositive*). carefully selected to produce a desired effect; apt: *a few well-chosen words.*

well-connected *adj.* (**well connected** *when postpositive*). having influential or important relatives or friends.

well-disposed *adj.* (**well disposed** *when postpositive*). inclined to be sympathetic, kindly, or friendly.

well-done *adj.* (**well done** *when postpositive*). **1.** (of food, esp. meat) cooked thoroughly. **2.** made or accomplished satisfactorily.

well dressing *n.* the decoration of wells with flowers, etc.: a traditional annual ceremony of great antiquity in some parts of Britain, originally associated with the cult of water deities.

Welles (wɛlz) *n.* (**George**) **Orson** ('ɔːsᵊn). 1915–85, U.S. film director, actor, producer, and screenwriter. His *Citizen Kane* (1941) and *The Magnificent Ambersons* (1942) are regarded as film classics.

Wellesley ('wɛlzlɪ) *n.* **1. Arthur.** See (1st Duke of) **Wellington. 2.** his brother, **Richard Colley,** Marquis Wellesley. 1760–1842, British administrator. As governor general of Bengal (1797–1805) he consolidated British power in India.

Wellesz (*German* 'vɛlɛs) *n.* **Egon** ('eːgɔn). 1885–1974, British composer, born in Austria.

well-favoured *adj.* (**well favoured** *when postpositive*). good-looking.

well-formed formula *n. Logic.* a group of logical symbols that makes sense; a logical sentence.

well-found *adj.* (**well found** *when postpositive*). furnished or supplied with all or most necessary things.

well-founded *adj.* (**well founded** *when postpositive*). having good grounds: *well-founded rumours.*

well-groomed *adj.* (**well groomed** *when postpositive*). having a tidy pleasing appearance.

well-grounded *adj.* (**well grounded** *when postpositive*). **1.** well instructed in the basic elements of a subject. **2.** another term for **well-founded.**

wellhead ('wɛl,hɛd) *n.* **1.** the source of a well or stream. **2.** a source, fountainhead, or origin.

well-heeled *adj.* (**well heeled** *when postpositive*). *Inf.* rich; prosperous; wealthy.

wellies ('wɛlɪz) *pl. n. Brit. inf.* Wellington boots.

well-informed *adj.* (**well informed** *when postpositive*). **1.** having knowledge about a great variety of subjects: *he seems to be a well-informed person.* **2.** possessing reliable information on a particular subject.

Wellingborough ('wɛlɪŋbərə, -brə) *n.* a town in central England, in Northamptonshire. Pop.: 43 899 (1981).

Wellington¹ ('wɛlɪŋtən) *n.* **1.** an administrative district, formerly a province, of New Zealand, on SW North Island: major livestock producer in New Zealand. Capital: Wellington. Pop.: 585 800 (1983 est.). Area: 28 153 sq. km (10 870 sq. miles). **2.** the capital city of New Zealand. Its port, historically Port Nicholson, on Wellington Harbour has a rail-ferry link between the North and South Islands; university (1897). Pop.: 319 100 (1983 est.).

Wellington² ('wɛlɪŋtən) *n.* **1st Duke of,** title of *Arthur Wellesley.* 1769–1852, British soldier and statesman; prime minister (1828–30). He was given command of the British forces against the French in the Peninsular War (1808–14) and routed Napoleon at Waterloo (1815).

Wellington boots *pl. n.* Also called: **gumboots.** *Brit.* knee-length or calf-length rubber boots, worn esp. in wet conditions. Often shortened to **wellingtons, wellies. 2.** military leather boots covering the front of the knee but cut away at the back to allow easier bending of the knee. [C19: after the 1st Duke of WELLINGTON]

wellingtonia (,wɛlɪŋ'təʊnɪə) *n.* a giant Californian coniferous tree, often reaching 90 metres high. Also called: **big tree, sequoia.** [C19: after the 1st Duke of WELLINGTON]

'well-ac'customed *adj.*	'well-a'ware *adj.*	'well-'covered *adj.*	'well-e'quipped *adj.*
'well-ac'quainted *adj.*	'well-be'haved *adj.*	'well-'culti,vated *adj.*	'well-es'tablished *adj.*
'well-'acted *adj.*	'well-be'loved *adj., n.*	'well-de'fended *adj.*	'well-es'teemed *adj.*
'well-a'dapted *adj.*	'well-'blessed *adj.*	'well-de'fined *adj.*	'well-'fed *adj.*
'well-ad'justed *adj.*	'well-'built *adj.*	'well-'demon,strated *adj.*	'well-fi'nanced *adj.*
'well-ad'ministered *adj.*	'well-'calcu,lated *adj.*	'well-de'scribed *adj.*	'well-'finished *adj.*
'well-'adver,tised *adj.*	'well-'clothed *adj.*	'well-de'served *adj.*	'well-'fitted *adj.*
'well-'aimed *adj.*	'well-'coached *adj.*	'well-de'veloped *adj.*	'well-'formed *adj.*
'well-'aired *adj.*	'well-'compen,sated *adj.*	'well-de'vised *adj.*	'well-'fought *adj.*
'well-ap'plied *adj.*	'well-con'cealed *adj.*	'well-di'gested *adj.*	'well-'furnished *adj.*
'well-'argued *adj.*	'well-con'ditioned *adj.*	'well-'disciplined *adj.*	'well-'governed *adj.*
'well-'armed *adj.*	'well-con'ducted *adj.*	'well-'docu,mented *adj.*	'well-'guarded *adj.*
'well-ar'ranged *adj.*	'well-con'firmed *adj.*	'well-'dressed *adj.*	'well-'handled *adj.*
'well-as'sorted *adj.*	'well-con'sidered *adj.*	'well-'earned *adj.*	'well-'hidden *adj.*
'well-as'sured *adj.*	'well-con'structed *adj.*	'well-edu,cated *adj.*	'well-'housed *adj.*
'well-at'tended *adj.*	'well-con'tented *adj.*	'well-em'ployed *adj.*	'well-'illus,trated *adj.*
'well-at'tested *adj.*	'well-con'trolled *adj.*	'well-en'dowed *adj.*	'well-in'clined *adj.*
'well-au'thenti,cated *adj.*	'well-'cooked *adj.*		

well-intentioned *adj.* (**well intentioned** *when postpositive*). having benevolent intentions, usually with unfortunate results.

well-knit *adj.* (**well knit** *when postpositive*). strong, firm, or sturdy.

well-known *adj.* (**well known** *when postpositive*). **1.** widely known; famous; celebrated. **2.** known fully or clearly.

well-mannered *adj.* (**well mannered** *when postpositive*). having good manners; polite.

well-meaning *adj.* (**well meaning** *when postpositive*). having or indicating good intentions, usually with unfortunate results.

well-nigh *adv. Arch. or poetic.* nearly; almost: *it's well-nigh three o'clock.*

▷ **Usage.** In strict usage, *well-nigh* is an adverb meaning *nearly* or *almost* and not a preposition meaning *near: he well-nigh cried; he was near* (not *well-nigh) death.*

well-off *adj.* (**well off** *when postpositive*). **1.** in a comfortable or favourable position or state. **2.** financially well provided for; moderately rich.

well-oiled *adj.* (**well oiled** *when postpositive*). *Inf.* drunk.

well-preserved *adj.* (**well preserved** *when postpositive*). **1.** kept in a good condition. **2.** continuing to appear youthful: *she was a well-preserved old lady.*

well-read ('wɛl'rɛd) *adj.* (**well read** *when postpositive*). having read widely and intelligently; erudite.

well-rounded *adj.* (**well rounded** *when postpositive*). **1.** rounded in shape or well developed: *a well-rounded figure.* **2.** full, varied, and satisfying: *a well-rounded life.*

Wells[1] (wɛlz) *n.* a city in SW England, in Somerset: 12th-century cathedral. Pop.: 9000 (1985 est.).

Wells[2] (wɛlz) *n.* **H(erbert) G(eorge).** 1866–1946, English writer. His science-fiction stories include *The Time Machine* (1895), *War of the Worlds* (1898), and *The Shape of Things to Come* (1933). His novels on contemporary social questions, such as *Kipps* (1905), *Tono-Bungay* (1909), and *Ann Veronica* (1909), affected the opinions of his day. His nonfiction works include *The Outline of History* (1920).

well-spoken *adj.* (**well spoken** *when postpositive*). **1.** having a clear, articulate, and socially acceptable accent and way of speaking. **2.** spoken satisfactorily or pleasingly.

wellspring ('wɛl,sprɪŋ) *n.* **1.** the source of a spring or stream. **2.** a source of abundant supply.

well-stacked *adj.* (**well stacked** *when postpositive*). *Brit. sl.* (of a woman) of voluptuous proportions.

well sweep *n.* a device for raising buckets from and lowering them into a well, consisting of a long pivoted pole, the bucket being attached to one end by a long rope.

well-tempered *adj.* (**well tempered** *when postpositive*). (of a musical scale or instrument) conforming to the system of equal temperament. See **temperament** (sense 4).

well-thought-of *adj.* respected.

well-thumbed *adj.* (**well thumbed** *when postpositive*). (of a book) having the pages marked from frequent turning.

well-to-do *adj.* moderately wealthy.

well-turned *adj.* (**well turned** *when postpositive*). **1.** (of a phrase, etc.) apt and pleasing. **2.** having a pleasing shape: *a well-turned leg.*

well-upholstered *adj.* (**well upholstered** *when postpositive*). *Inf.* (of a person) fat.

well-wisher *n.* a person who shows benevolence or sympathy towards a person, cause, etc. —'**well-,wishing** *adj., n.*

well-woman *n., pl.* **-women.** *Social welfare.* **a.** a woman who attends a health-service clinic for preventive monitoring, health education, etc. **b.** (*as modifier*): *well-woman clinic.*

well-worn *adj.* (**well worn** *when postpositive*). **1.** so much used as to be affected by wear: *a well-worn coat.* **2.** hackneyed: *a well-worn phrase.*

Wels (*German* vɛls) *n.* an industrial city in N central Austria, in Upper Austria. Pop.: 51 060 (1987).

welsh *or* **welch** (wɛlʃ) *vb.* (*intr.; often foll. by on*) **1.** to fail to pay a gambling debt. **2.** to fail to fulfil an obligation. [C19: from ?] —'**welsher** *or* '**welcher** *n.*

Welsh (wɛlʃ) *adj.* **1.** of, relating to, or characteristic of Wales, its people, their language, or their dialect of English. ~*n.* **2.** a language of Wales, belonging to the S Celtic branch of the Indo-European family. **3. the Welsh.** (*functioning as pl.*) the natives or inhabitants of Wales. [OE *Wēlisc, Wǣlisc*]

Welsh corgi *n.* another name for **corgi.**

Welsh dresser *n.* a sideboard with drawers and cupboards below and open shelves above.

Welsh harp *n.* a type of harp in which the strings are arranged in three rows.

Welshman ('wɛlʃmən) *or* (*fem.*) **Welshwoman** *n., pl.* **-men** *or* **-women.** a native or inhabitant of Wales.

Welsh poppy *n.* a perennial W European plant with large yellow flowers.

Welsh rabbit *n.* a savoury dish consisting of melted cheese sometimes mixed with milk, seasonings, etc., on hot buttered toast. Also called: **Welsh rarebit, rarebit.** [C18: a fanciful coinage; *rarebit* is a later folk-etymological var.]

Welsh terrier *n.* a wire-haired breed of terrier with a black-and-tan coat.

welt (wɛlt) *n.* **1.** a raised or strengthened seam in a garment. **2.** another word for **weal**[1]. **3.** (in shoemaking) a strip of leather, etc., put in between the outer sole and the inner sole and upper. ~*vb.* (*tr.*) **4.** to put a welt in (a garment, etc.). **5.** to beat soundly. [C15: from ?]

welter ('wɛltə) *vb.* (*intr.*) **1.** to roll about, writhe, or wallow. **2.** (esp. of the sea) to surge, heave, or toss. **3.** to lie drenched in a liquid, esp. blood. ~*n.* **4.** a confused mass; jumble. [C13: from MLow G, MDu. *weltern*]

welterweight ('wɛltə,weɪt) *n.* **1. a.** a professional boxer weighing 140–147 pounds (63.5–66.5 kg). **b.** an amateur boxer weighing 63.5–67 kg (140–148 pounds). **2. a.** a professional wrestler weighing 155–165 pounds (71–75 kg). **b.** an amateur wrestler weighing 69–74 kg (151–161 pounds).

Welwyn Garden City ('wɛlɪn) *n.* a town in SE England, in Hertfordshire: established (1920) as a planned industrial and residential community. Pop.: 40 496 (1981).

Wembley ('wɛmblɪ) *n.* part of the Greater London borough of Brent: site of the English national soccer stadium.

wen[1] (wɛn) *n.* **1.** *Pathol.* a sebaceous cyst, esp. one occurring on the scalp. **2.** a large overcrowded city (esp. London, **the great wen**). [OE *wenn*]

wen[2] (wɛn) *n.* a rune having the sound of Modern English *w.* [OE *wen, wyn*]

Wenceslaus *or* **Wenceslas** ('wɛnsɪsləs) *n.* **1.** 1361–1419, Holy Roman Emperor (1378–1400) and, as **Wenceslaus IV**, king of Bohemia (1378–1419). **2. Saint,** known as *Good King Wenceslas.* ?907–929, duke of Bohemia

'well-'judged *adj.*	'well-'paid *adj.*	'well-,recom'mended *adj.*	'well-'spent *adj.*
'well-'justi,fied *adj.*	'well-'phrased *adj.*	'well-re'garded *adj.*	'well-'stocked *adj.*
'well-'kept *adj.*	'well-'placed *adj.*	'well-'regu,lated *adj.*	'well-'suited *adj.*
'well-'liked *adj.*	'well-'planned *adj.*	'well-re'hearsed *adj.*	'well-sup'plied *adj.*
'well-'loved *adj.*	'well-'played *adj.*	'well-re'membered *adj.*	'well-sup'ported *adj.*
'well-'made *adj.*	'well-'pleased *adj.*	'well-,repre'sented *adj.*	'well-'taught *adj.*
'well-'managed *adj.*	'well-'practised *adj.*	'well-re'spected *adj.*	'well-'timed *adj.*
'well-'marked *adj.*	'well-pre'pared *adj.*	'well-re'viewed *adj.*	'well-'trained *adj.*
'well-'matched *adj.*	'well-pro'portioned *adj.*	'well-'ripened *adj.*	'well-'travelled *adj.*
'well-'merited *adj.*	'well-pro'tected *adj.*	'well-'satis,fied *adj.*	'well-'treated *adj.*
'well-'mixed *adj.*	'well-pro'vided *adj.*	'well-'schooled *adj.*	'well-'tried *adj.*
'well-'moti,vated *adj.*	'well-'quali,fied *adj.*	'well-'seasoned *adj.*	'well-'trodden *adj.*
'well-'noted *adj.*	'well-'reasoned *adj.*	'well-se'cured *adj.*	'well-under'stood *adj.*
'well-'ordered *adj.*	'well-re'ceived *adj.*	'well-'shaped *adj.*	'well-'used *adj.*
'well-'organ,ized *or* -,ised *adj.*	'well-'recog,nized *or* -,nised *adj.*	'well-'situ,ated *adj.*	'well-'written *adj.*

(?925–29); patron saint of Czechoslovakia. Feast day: Sept. 28.

wench (wɛntʃ) *n.* **1.** a girl or young woman: now used facetiously. **2.** *Arch.* a female servant. **3.** *Arch.* a prostitute. ~*vb.* (*intr.*) **4.** *Arch.* to frequent the company of prostitutes. [OE *wencel* child, from *wancol* weak] —'wencher *n.*

wend (wɛnd) *vb.* to direct (one's course or way); travel. [OE *wendan*]

Wend (wɛnd) *n.* (esp. in medieval European history) a member of the Slavonic people who inhabited the area between the Rivers Saale and Oder, in central Europe, in the early Middle Ages. Also called: **Sorb**.

wendigo ('wɛndɪ,gəʊ) *n. Canad.* **1.** (*pl.* **-gos**) (among Algonquian Indians) an evil spirit or cannibal. **2.** (*pl.* **-go** or **-gos**) another name for **splake**. [from Algonquian: evil spirit or cannibal]

Wendy house ('wɛndɪ) *n.* a small model house for children to play in. It is big enough for children, but not adults, to enter and use in comfort. [C20: after the house built for *Wendy*, the girl in J. M. Barrie's play *Peter Pan* (1904)]

wensleydale ('wɛnzlɪ,deɪl) *n.* **1.** a type of white cheese with a flaky texture. **2.** a breed of sheep with long woolly fleece. [after *Wensleydale*, North Yorkshire]

went (wɛnt) *vb.* the past tense of **go**.

wentletrap ('wɛntˀl,træp) *n.* a marine gastropod mollusc having a long pointed pale-coloured longitudinally ridged shell. [C18: from Du. *winteltrap* spiral shell, from *wintel*, earlier *windel*, from *wenden* to wind + *trap* a step]

Wentworth ('wɛntwəθ) *n.* **1. Thomas.** See (Earl of) **Strafford. 2. William Charles.** 1790–1872, Australian explorer and statesman who was a member of the exploring party that first crossed the Blue Mountains in 1813 and was later a leader in the movement for self-government in New South Wales.

wept (wɛpt) *vb.* the past tense and past participle of **weep**.

were (wɜ:; *unstressed* wə) *vb.* the plural form of the past tense (indicative mood) of **be** and the singular form used with *you*. It is also used as a subjunctive, esp. in conditional sentences. [OE *wērun*, *wǣron* p.t. pl. of *wesan* to be]

▷ **Usage.** *Were*, as a remnant of the past subjunctive in English, is used in formal contexts in clauses expressing hypotheses (*if he were to die, she would inherit everything*), suppositions contrary to fact (*if I were you, I would be careful*), and desire (*I wish he were there now*). In informal speech, however, *was* is often used instead.

we're (wɪə) *contraction of* we are.

weren't (wɜ:nt) *contraction of* were not.

werewolf ('wɪə,wʊlf, 'wɛə-) *n., pl.* **-wolves.** a person fabled in folklore and superstition to have been changed into a wolf by being bewitched or said to be able to assume wolf form at will. [OE *werewulf*, from *wer* man + *wulf* wolf]

wergild, weregild ('wɜ:,gɪld, 'wɛə-), *or* **wergeld** ('wɜ:,gɛld, 'wɛə-) *n.* the price set on a man's life in Anglo-Saxon and Germanic law codes, to be paid as compensation by his slayer. [OE *wergeld*, from *wer* man + *gield* tribute]

Werner (*German* 'vɛrnə) *n.* **1. Abraham Gottlob** ('a:brəham 'gɔtlo:p). 1749–1817, German geologist. He emphasized the importance of field and laboratory observation for understanding the earth. **2. Alfred** ('alfre:t). 1866–1919, Swiss chemist, born in Germany. He developed a coordination theory of the valency of inorganic complexes: Nobel prize for chemistry 1913.

wert (wɜ:t; *unstressed* wət) *vb. Arch. or dialect.* (used with the pronoun *thou* or its relative equivalent) a singular form of the past tense (indicative mood) of **be**.

Weser (*German* 've:zər) *n.* a river in N West Germany: flows northwest to the North Sea at Bremerhaven and is linked by the Mittelland Canal to the Ems, Rhine, and Elbe waterways. Length: 477 km (196 miles).

Wesermünde (*German* ve:zər'myndə) *n.* the former name (until 1947) of **Bremerhaven**.

Wesker ('wɛskə) *n.* **Arnold.** born 1932, English dramatist, noted for his socialist plays, such as *Roots* (1959), *Chips With Everything* (1962), and *The Merchant* (1978).

weskit ('wɛskɪt) *n.* an informal name for **waistcoat**.

Wesley ('wɛzlɪ) *n.* **1. Charles.** 1707–88, English Methodist preacher and writer of hymns. **2.** his brother, **John.** 1703–91, English preacher, who founded Methodism.

Wesleyan ('wɛzlɪən) *adj.* **1.** of or deriving from John Wesley. **2.** of or characterizing Methodism, esp. in its original form. ~*n.* **3.** a follower of John Wesley. **4.** a member of the Methodist Church. —'**Wesleyan,ism** *n.*

Wessex ('wɛsɪks) *n.* **1.** an Anglo-Saxon kingdom in S and SW England that became the most powerful English kingdom by the 10th century A.D. **2. a.** (in Thomas Hardy's works) the southwestern counties of England, esp. Dorset. **b.** (*as modifier*): *Wessex Poems*.

west (wɛst) *n.* **1.** the direction along a parallel towards the sunset, at 270° clockwise from north. **2. the west.** (*often cap.*) any area lying in or towards the west. Related adjs.: **Hesperian, Occidental. 3.** (*usually cap.*) *Cards.* the player or position at the table corresponding to west on the compass. ~*adj.* **4.** situated in, moving towards, or facing the west. **5.** (esp. of the wind) from the west. ~*adv.* **6.** in, to, or towards the west. **7. go west.** *Inf.* **a.** to be lost or destroyed. **b.** to die. [OE]

West[1] (wɛst) *n.* **the. 1.** the western part of the world contrasted historically and culturally with the East or Orient. **2.** the non-Communist countries of Europe and America contrasted with the Communist states of the East. **3.** (in the U.S.) that part of the U.S. lying approximately to the west of the Mississippi. **4.** (in the ancient and medieval world) the Western Roman Empire and, later, the Holy Roman Empire. ~*adj.* **5.** of or denoting the western part of a specified country, area, etc.

West[2] (wɛst) *n.* **1. Benjamin.** 1738–1820, U.S. painter, in England from 1763. **2. Mae.** 1892–1980, U.S. film actress. **3.** Dame **Rebecca**, real name *Mrs Cicily Isabel Andrews* (née *Fairfield*). 1892–1983, English novelist and critic.

West Atlantic *n.* the W part of the Atlantic Ocean, esp. the N Atlantic around North America.

West Bank *n.* **the.** a territory in the Middle East on the W bank of the River Jordan, comprising the hills of Judaea and Samaria and part of Jerusalem: formerly part of Palestine: became part of Jordan after the ceasefire of 1949: occupied by Israel since the 1967 Arab-Israeli War. The provision of the Camp David Agreement that the West Bank should be granted a degree of Palestinian autonomy has not been carried out. Pop.: 1 250 000 (1985 est.). Area: about 6000 sq. km (2320 sq. miles).

West Bengal *n.* a state of E India, on the Bay of Bengal: formed in 1947 from the Hindu area of Bengal; additional territories added in 1950 (Cooch Behar), 1954 (Chandernagor), and 1956 (part of Bihar); mostly low-lying and crossed by the Hooghly River. Capital: Calcutta. Pop.: 54 485 560 (1981). Area: 87 617 sq. km (33 829 sq. miles).

West Berlin *n.* the part of Berlin under U.S., British, and French control. —**West Berliner** *n., adj.*

westbound ('wɛst,baʊnd) *adj.* going or leading towards the west.

West Bromwich ('brɒmɪdʒ, -ɪtʃ) *n.* a town in central England, in the West Midlands: coal-mining and industrial centre. Pop.: 154 930 (1981).

west by north *n.* one point on the compass north of west.

west by south *n.* one point on the compass south of west.

West Country *n.* **the.** the southwest of England, esp. Cornwall, Devon, and Somerset.

West End *n.* **the.** a part of W central London containing the main shopping and entertainment areas.

westering ('wɛstərɪŋ) *adj. Poetic.* moving towards the west: *the westering star*.

Westerlies ('wɛstəlɪz) *pl. n. Meteorol.* the prevailing winds blowing from the west on the poleward sides of the horse latitudes, often bringing depressions and anticyclones.

westerly ('wɛstəlɪ) *adj.* **1.** of, relating to, or situated in the west. ~*adv., adj.* **2.** towards or in the direction of the west. **3.** (esp. of the wind) from the west. ~*n., pl.* **-lies. 4.** a wind blowing from the west. —'**westerliness** *n.*

western ('wɛstən) *adj.* **1.** situated in or facing the west. **2.** going or directed to or towards the west. **3.** (of a wind, etc.) coming from the west. **4.** native to the west. **5.** *Music.* See **country-and-western**. —'**western,most** *adj.*

Western ('wɛstən) *adj.* **1.** of or characteristic of the Americas and the parts of Europe not under Communist rule. **2.** of or characteristic of the West as opposed to the

Orient. **3.** of or characteristic of the western states of the U.S. ~*n.* **4.** (*often not cap.*) a film, book, etc., concerned with life in the western states of the U.S., esp. during the era of exploration.

Western Australia *n.* a state of W Australia: mostly an arid undulating plateau, with the Great Sandy Desert, Gibson Desert, and Great Victoria Desert in the interior; settlement concentrated in the southwest; rich mineral resources. Capital: Perth. Pop.: 1 440 607 (1986). Area: 2 527 636 sq. km (975 920 sq. miles).

Western Church *n.* **1.** the part of Christendom that derives its liturgy, discipline, and traditions principally from the patriarchate of Rome. **2.** the Roman Catholic Church, sometimes together with the Anglican Communion of Churches.

westerner ('wɛstənə) *n.* (*sometimes cap.*) a native or inhabitant of the west of any specific region.

Western Ghats *pl. n.* a mountain range in W peninsular India, parallel to the Malabar coast of the Arabian Sea. Highest peak: Anai Mudi, 2695 m (8841 ft.).

western hemisphere *n.* (*often caps.*) **1.** that half of the globe containing the Americas, lying to the west of the Greenwich or another meridian. **2.** the lands contained in this, esp. the Americas.

Western Isles *n.* (*functioning as sing. or pl.*) **1.** an island authority in W Scotland, consisting of the Outer Hebrides; created in 1975. Administrative centre: Stornoway. Pop.: 31 494 (1986 est.). Area: 2900 sq. km (1120 sq. miles). **2.** Also called: **Western Islands.** another name for the **Hebrides.**

westernize *or* **-ise** ('wɛstə,naɪz) *vb.* (*tr.*) to influence or make familiar with the customs, practices, etc., of the West. —**westerni'zation** *or* **-i'sation** *n.*

Western Ocean *n.* (formerly) another name for the **Atlantic Ocean.**

Western Roman Empire *n.* the westernmost of the two empires created by the division of the later Roman Empire, esp. after its final severance from the Eastern Roman Empire (395 A.D.). Also called: **Western Empire.**

Western Sahara *n.* a disputed region of NW Africa, on the Atlantic: mainly desert; rich phosphate deposits; a Spanish overseas province from 1958 to 1975; partitioned in 1976 between Morocco and Mauritania who faced growing resistance from the Polisario Front, an organization aiming for the independence of the region as the Democratic Saharan Arab Republic. Mauritania renounced its claim in 1979 and it was taken over by Morocco. Pop.: 180 000 (1986 est.). Area: 266 000 sq. km (102 680 sq. miles). Former name (until 1975): **Spanish Sahara.**

Western Samoa *n.* an independent state occupying four inhabited islands and five uninhabited islands in the S Pacific archipelago of the Samoa Islands: established as a League of Nations mandate under New Zealand administration in 1920 and a UN trusteeship in 1946; gained independence in 1962 as the first fully independent Polynesian state; a member of the Commonwealth. Languages: Samoan and English. Religion: Christian. Currency: tala. Capital: Apia. Pop.: 163 000 (1986). Area: 2841 sq. km (1097 sq. miles). —**Western Samoan** *adj., n.*

Western Wall *n. Judaism.* another name for **Wailing Wall.**

Westfalen (vɛst'faːlən) *n.* the German name for **Westphalia.**

West Flanders *n.* a province of W Belgium: the country's chief agricultural province. Capital: Bruges. Pop.: 1 081 913 (1981 est.). Area: 3132 sq. km (1209 sq. miles).

West Germany *n.* a republic in N central Europe, on the North Sea: established in 1949 from the zones of Germany occupied by the British, Americans, and French after the defeat of Nazi Germany; a member of the Common Market. It consists of a low-lying plain in the north, with plateaus and uplands (including the Black Forest and the Bavarian Alps) in the centre and south. Language: German. Religion: Christian, with a slight Protestant majority. Currency: mark. Capital: Bonn. Pop.: 61 140 000 (1986). Area: 248 574 sq. km (95 975 sq. miles). Official name: **Federal Republic of Germany.** See also **Germany.** —**West German** *adj., n.*

West Glamorgan *n.* a county in S Wales, formed in 1974 from part of Glamorgan and the county borough of Swansea. Administrative centre: Swansea. Pop.: 363 400 (1986 est.). Area: 817 sq. km (315 sq. miles).

West Hartlepool ('haːtlɪ,puːl) *n.* a former town in NE England, in Cleveland: part of Hartlepool since 1967.

West Indies ('ɪndɪz) *pl. n.* an archipelago off Central America, extending over 2400 km (1500 miles) in an arc from the peninsula of Florida to Venezuela, separating the Caribbean from the Atlantic: consists of the Greater Antilles, the Lesser Antilles, and the Bahamas; largest island is Cuba. Area: over 235 000 sq. km (91 000 sq. miles).

westing ('wɛstɪŋ) *n. Navigation.* movement, deviation, or distance covered in a westerly direction, esp. as expressed in the resulting difference in longitude.

West Irian *n.* the English name for **Irian Jaya.**

West Lothian *n.* (until 1975) a county of central Scotland, now part of Lothian region.

Westmeath (,wɛst'miːð) *n.* a county of N central Ireland, in Leinster province: mostly low-lying, with many lakes and bogs. County town: Mullingar. Pop.: 63 306 (1986). Area: 1764 sq. km (681 sq. miles).

West Midlands *n.* (*functioning as sing. or pl.*) (1974–86) a metropolitan county of central England, comprising the districts of Wolverhampton, Walsall, Dudley, Sandwell, Birmingham, Solihull, and Coventry. Administrative centre: Birmingham. Pop.: 2 632 300 (1986 est.). Area: 899 sq. km (347 sq. miles).

Westminster ('wɛst,mɪnstə) *n.* **1.** Also called: **City of Westminster.** a borough of Greater London, on the River Thames: contains the Houses of Parliament, Westminster Abbey, and Buckingham Palace. Pop.: 176 100 (1986 est.). **2.** the Houses of Parliament at Westminster.

Westminster Abbey *n.* a Gothic church in London: site of a Benedictine monastery (1050–65); scene of the coronations of almost all English monarchs since William I.

Westmorland ('wɛstmələnd, 'wɛsmə-) *n.* (until 1974) a county of NW England, now part of Cumbria.

west-northwest *n.* **1.** the point on the compass or the direction midway between west and northwest, 292° 30′ clockwise from north. ~*adj., adv.* **2.** in, from, or towards this direction.

Weston standard cell ('wɛstən) *n.* a primary cell used as a standard of emf: consists of a mercury anode and a cadmium amalgam cathode in an electrolyte of saturated cadmium sulphate. [C20: from a trademark]

Weston-super-Mare ('wɛstən,suːpə'mɛə, -,sjuː-) *n.* a town and resort in SW England, in SW Avon on the Bristol Channel. Pop.: 57 980 (1981).

West Pakistan *n.* the former name (until the end of 1971) of **Pakistan.**

Westphalia (wɛst'feɪlɪə) *n.* a former province of NW Prussia: incorporated into the West German state of North Rhine-Westphalia in 1946. German name: **Westfalen.** —**West'phalian** *adj., n.*

West Prussia *n.* a former province of NE Prussia, on the Baltic: assigned to Poland in 1945. German name: **Westpreussen** ('vɛstprɔysən).

West Riding *n.* (until 1974) an administrative division of Yorkshire, now contained in West Yorkshire.

west-southwest *n.* **1.** the point on the compass or the direction midway between southwest and west, 247° 30′ clockwise from north. ~*adj., adv.* **2.** in, from, or towards this direction.

West Sussex *n.* a county of SE England, comprising part of the former county of Sussex. Administrative centre: Chichester. Pop.: 694 700 (1986 est.). Area: 1989 sq. km (768 sq. miles).

West Virginia *n.* a state of the eastern U.S.: part of Virginia until the outbreak of the American Civil War (1861); consists chiefly of the Allegheny Plateau; bounded on the west by the Ohio River; coal-mining. Capital: Charleston. Pop.: 1 936 000 (1985 est.). Area: 62 341 sq. km (24 070 sq. miles). Abbrevs.: **W. Va.** or (with zip code) **WV** —**West Virginian** *adj., n.*

westward ('wɛstwəd) *adj.* **1.** moving, facing, or situated in the west. ~*adv.* **2.** Also: **westwards.** towards the west. ~*n.* **3.** the westward part, direction, etc. —'**westwardly** *adj., adv.*

West Yorkshire *n.* (1974–86) a metropolitan county of N England, comprising the districts of Bradford, Leeds, Calderdale, Kirklees, and Wakefield. Administrative centre: Wakefield. Pop.: 2 053 100 (1986 est.). Area: 2039 sq. km (787 sq. miles).

wet (wɛt) *adj.* **wetter, wettest. 1.** moistened, covered, saturated, etc., with water or some other liquid. **2.** not yet dry or solid: *wet varnish*. **3.** rainy: *wet weather*. **4.** employing a liquid, usually water: *a wet method of chemical analysis*. **5.** *Chiefly U.S. & Canad.* permitting the free sale of alcoholic beverages: *a wet state*. **6.** *Brit. inf.* feeble or foolish. **7. wet behind the ears.** *Inf.* immature or inexperienced. ~*n.* **8.** wetness or moisture. **9.** rainy weather. **10.** *Brit. inf.* a feeble or foolish person. **11.** (*often cap.*) *Brit. inf.* a Conservative politician who is not a hardliner. **12.** *Chiefly U.S. & Canad.* a person who advocates free sale of alcoholic beverages. **13. the wet.** *Austral.* (in northern and central Australia) the rainy season. ~*vb.* **wetting, wet** *or* **wetted**. **14.** to make or become wet. **15.** to urinate on (something). [OE *wǣt*] —'**wetly** *adv.* —'**wetness** *n.* —'**wettable** *adj.* —'**wetter** *n.* —'**wettish** *adj.*

wet-and-dry-bulb thermometer *n.* another name for **psychrometer.**

wet blanket *n. Inf.* a person whose low spirits or lack of enthusiasm have a depressing effect on others.

wet cell *n.* a primary cell in which the electrolyte is a liquid.

wet dream *n.* an erotic dream accompanied by an emission of semen.

wet fly *n. Angling.* an artificial fly designed to float or ride below the water surface.

wether ('wɛðə) *n.* a male sheep, esp. a castrated one. [OE *hwæther*]

wetland ('wɛtlənd) *n.* (*sometimes pl.*) **a.** an area of marshy land, esp. considered as part of an ecological system. **b.** (*as modifier*): *wetland species*.

wet look *n.* a shiny finish such as that given to certain clothing and footwear materials.

wet nurse *n.* **1.** a woman hired to suckle the child of another. ~*vb.* **wet-nurse.** (*tr.*) **2.** to act as a wet nurse to (a child). **3.** *Inf.* to attend with great devotion.

wet pack *n. Med.* a hot or cold damp sheet or blanket for wrapping around a patient.

wet rot *n.* **1.** a state of decay in timber caused by various fungi. The hyphal strands of the fungus are seldom visible, and affected timber turns dark brown. **2.** any of the fungi causing this decay.

wet suit *n.* a close-fitting rubber suit used by skin-divers, yachtsmen, etc., to retain body heat.

Wetterhorn (*German* 'vɛtər,hɔrn) *n.* a mountain in S Switzerland, in the Bernese Alps. Height: 3701 m (12 143 ft.).

wetting agent *n. Chem.* any substance added to a liquid to lower its surface tension and thus increase its ability to spread across or penetrate a solid.

we've (wiːv) *contraction of* we have.

Wexford ('wɛksfəd) *n.* **1.** a county of SE Ireland, in Leinster province on the Irish Sea: the first Irish county to be colonized from England; mostly low-lying and fertile. County town: Wexford. Pop.: 102 456 (1986). Area: 2352 sq. km (908 sq. miles). **2.** a port in SE Ireland, county town of Co. Wexford: sacked by Oliver Cromwell in 1649. Pop.: 11 417 (1981).

Weymouth ('weɪməθ) *n.* a port and resort in S England, in Dorset on the English Channel: administratively part of the borough of **Weymouth and Melcombe Regis.** Pop. (with Melcombe Regis): 57 400 (1985 est.).

wf *Printing. abbrev. for* wrong fount.

WFF *Logic. abbrev. for* well-formed formula.

WFTU *abbrev. for* World Federation of Trade Unions.

W. Glam. *abbrev. for* West Glamorgan.

whack (wæk) *vb.* (*tr.*) **1.** to strike with a sharp resounding blow. **2.** (*usually passive*) *Brit. inf.* to exhaust completely. ~*n.* **3.** a sharp resounding blow or the noise made by such a blow. **4.** *Inf.* a share or portion. **5.** *Inf.* a try or attempt (esp. in **have a whack at**). [C18: ? var. of THWACK, ult. imit.] —'**whacker** *n.*

whacking ('wækɪŋ) *Inf., chiefly Brit.* ~*adj.* **1.** enormous. ~*adv.* **2.** (intensifier): *a whacking big lie.*

whacky ('wækɪ) *adj.* **whackier, whackiest.** *U.S. sl.* a variant spelling of **wacky.**

whale[1] (weɪl) *n., pl.* **whales** *or* **whale.** **1.** any of the larger cetacean mammals, excluding dolphins, porpoises, and narwhals. They have flippers, a streamlined body, and a horizontally flattened tail and breathe through a blowhole on the top of the head. **2. a whale of a.** *Inf.* an exceptionally large, fine, etc., example of a (person or thing). [OE *hwæl*]

whale[2] (weɪl) *vb.* (*tr.*) to beat or thrash soundly. [C18: var. of WALE]

whaleboat ('weɪl,bəʊt) *n.* a narrow boat from 20 to 30 feet long having a sharp prow and stern, formerly used in whaling. Also called: **whaler.**

whalebone ('weɪl,bəʊn) *n.* **1.** Also called: **baleen.** a horny elastic material forming numerous thin plates that hang from the upper jaw in the toothless (whalebone) whales and strain plankton from water entering the mouth. **2.** a thin strip of this substance, used in stiffening corsets, bodices, etc.

whalebone whale *n.* any whale belonging to a cetacean suborder having a double blowhole and strips of whalebone between the jaws instead of teeth: includes the rorquals, right whales, and the blue whale.

whale oil *n.* oil obtained either from the blubber of whales (train oil) or the head of the sperm whale (sperm oil).

whaler ('weɪlə) *n.* **1.** Also called (U.S.): **whaleman.** a person employed in whaling. **2.** a vessel engaged in whaling. **3.** *Austral. obs. sl.* a tramp or sundowner. **4.** an aggressive shark of Australian coastal waters.

whale shark *n.* a large spotted whalelike shark of warm seas, that feeds on plankton and small animals.

whaling ('weɪlɪŋ) *n.* the work or industry of hunting and processing whales for food, oil, etc.

wham (wæm) *n.* **1.** a forceful blow or impact or the sound produced by it. ~*vb.* **whamming, whammed.** **2.** to strike or cause to strike with great force. [C20: imit.]

whang (wæŋ) *vb.* **1.** to strike or be struck so as to cause a resounding noise. ~*n.* **2.** the resounding noise produced by a heavy blow. **3.** a heavy blow. [C19: imit.]

Whangarei (,wɑːŋɑːˈreɪ) *n.* a port in New Zealand, the northernmost city of North Island: oil refinery. Pop.: 43 600 (1987).

whangee (wæŋˈiː) *n.* **1.** a tall woody grass of an Asian genus, grown for its stems. **2.** a cane or walking stick made from the stem this plant. [C19: prob. from Chinese (Mandarin) *huangli*, from *huang* yellow + *li* bamboo cane]

whare ('wɔːrɪ; *Maori* 'fɔrɛ) *n. N.Z.* **1.** a Maori hut or dwelling place. **2.** any simple dwelling place. [from Maori]

wharepuni ('fɔrɛ,pʊnɪ) *n. N.Z.* in a Maori community, a lofty carved building that is used as a guesthouse. [from Maori *whare* house + *puni* company]

wharf (wɔːf) *n., pl.* **wharves** (wɔːvz) *or* **wharfs.** **1.** a platform built parallel to the waterfront at a harbour or navigable river for the docking, loading, and unloading of ships. ~*vb.* (*tr.*) **2.** to moor or dock at a wharf. **3.** to store or unload on a wharf. [OE *hwearf* heap]

wharfage ('wɔːfɪdʒ) *n.* **1.** accommodation for ships at wharves. **2.** a charge for use of a wharf. **3.** wharves collectively.

wharfie ('wɔːfɪ) *n. Austral. & N.Z.* a wharf labourer; docker.

wharfinger ('wɔːfɪndʒə) *n.* an owner or manager of a wharf. [C16: prob. alteration of *wharfager*]

wharve (wɔːv) *n.* a wooden disc or wheel on a shaft serving as a flywheel or pulley. [OE *hweorfa*, from *hweorfan* to revolve]

what (wɒt; *unstressed* wət) *determiner.* **1. a.** used with a noun in requesting further information about the identity or categorization of something: *what job does he do?* **b.** (*as pron.*): *what is her address?* **c.** (*used in indirect questions*): *tell me what he said.* **2. a.** the (person, thing, persons, or things) that: *we photographed what animals we could see.* **b.** (*as pron.*): *bring me what you've written.* **3.** (*intensifier*; used in exclamations): *what a good book!* ~*adv.* **4.** in what respect? to what degree?: *what do you care?* **5. what about.** what do you think, know, etc., concerning? **6. what for. a.** for what purpose? why? **b.** *Inf.* a punishment or reprimand (esp. in **give (a person) what for**). **7. what have you.** someone or something unknown or unspecified: *cars, motorcycles, or what have you.* **8. what if. a.** what would happen if? **b.** what difference would it make if? **9. what matter.** what does it matter? **10. what's what.** *Inf.* the true state of affairs. [OE *hwæt*]

▷ **Usage.** In good usage, *what* is never used for *which*, as in *he gave me the letter what he had written. What* is used, however, for the things which and that or those which: *he saw what (that which) he had done.*

whatever (wɒt'ɛvə, wət-) *pron.* **1.** everything or anything that: *do whatever he asks you to.* **2.** no matter what: *whatever he does, he is forgiven.* **3.** *Inf.* an unknown or unspecified thing or things: *take a hammer, chisel, or whatever.* **4.** an intensive form of *what*, used in questions: *whatever can he have said to upset her so much?* ~*determiner.* **5.** an intensive form of *what: use whatever tools you can get hold of.* ~*adj.* **6.** (*postpositive*) absolutely; whatsoever: *I saw no point whatever in continuing.*

whatnot ('wɒt,nɒt) *n.* **1.** Also called: **what-d'you-call-it.** *Inf.* a person or thing the name of which is unknown or forgotten. **2.** *Inf.* unspecified assorted material. **3.** a portable stand with shelves for displaying ornaments, etc.

whatsit ('wɒtsɪt), **whatsitsname,** (*masc.*) **whatshisname,** *or* (*fem.*) **whatshername** *n.* *Inf.* a person or thing the name of which is unknown or forgotten.

whatsoever (,wɒtsəʊ'ɛvə) *adj.* **1.** (*postpositive*) at all: used as an intensifier with indefinite pronouns and determiners such as *none, anybody,* etc. ~*pron.* **2.** an archaic word for **whatever.**

whaup (hwɔːp) *n.* *Chiefly Scot.* a popular name for the **curlew.** [C16: rel. to OE *huilpe,* ult. imit. of the bird's cry]

wheal (wiːl) *n.* a variant spelling of **weal**[1].

wheat (wiːt) *n.* **1.** any of a genus of grasses, native to the Mediterranean region and W Asia but widely cultivated, having erect flower spikes and light brown grains. **2.** the grain of any of these grasses, used in making flour, pasta, etc. ~See also **durum.** [OE *hwæte*]

wheatbelt ('wiːt,bɛlt) *n.* an area in which wheat is the chief agricultural product.

wheatear ('wiːt,ɪə) *n.* a small northern songbird having a pale grey back, black wings and tail, white rump, and pale brown underparts. [C16: back formation from *wheatears* (wrongly taken as pl.), prob. from WHITE + ARSE]

wheaten ('wiːt'n) *adj.* **1.** made of the grain or flour of wheat. **2.** of a pale yellow colour.

wheat germ *n.* the vitamin-rich embryo of the wheat kernel.

wheatmeal ('wiːt,miːl) *n.* **a.** a brown flour intermediate between white flour and wholemeal flour. **b.** (*as modifier*): *a wheatmeal loaf.*

Wheatstone bridge ('wiːtstən) *n.* a device for determining the value of an unknown resistance by comparison with a known standard resistance. [C19: after Sir Charles *Wheatstone* (1802–75), E physicist and inventor]

whee (wiː) *interj.* an exclamation of joy, etc.

wheedle ('wiːd'l) *vb.* **1.** to persuade or try to persuade (someone) by coaxing words, flattery, etc. **2.** (*tr.*) to obtain thus: *she wheedled some money out of her father.* [C17: ?from G *wedeln* to wag one's tail, from OHG *wedil, wadil* tail] —'**wheedler** *n.* —'**wheedling** *adj.* —'**wheedlingly** *adv.*

wheel (wiːl) *n.* **1.** a solid disc, or a circular rim joined to a hub by spokes, that is mounted on a shaft about which it can turn, as in vehicles. **2.** anything like a wheel in shape or function. **3.** a device consisting of or resembling a wheel: *a steering wheel; a water wheel.* **4.** (usually preceded by *the*) a medieval torture in which the victim was tied to a wheel and then had his limbs struck and broken by an iron bar. **5.** short for **wheel of fortune** or **potter's wheel. 6.** the act of turning. **7.** a pivoting movement of troops, ships, etc. **8.** a type of firework coiled to make it rotate when let off. **9.** a set of short rhyming lines forming the concluding part of a stanza. **10.** *U.S. & Canad.* an informal word for **bicycle. 11.** *Inf., chiefly U.S. & Canad.* a person of great influence (esp. in **big wheel**). **12. at the wheel. a.** driving or steering a vehicle or vessel. **b.** in charge. ~*vb.* **13.** to turn or cause to turn on or as if on an axis. **14.** (when *intr.,* sometimes foll. by *about* or *around*) to move or cause to move on or as if on wheels; roll. **15.** (*tr.*) to perform with or in a circular movement. **16.** (*tr.*) to provide with a wheel or wheels. **17.** (*intr.; often foll. by *about*) to change direction. **18. wheel and deal.** *Inf.* to operate free of restraint, esp. to advance one's own interests. ~See also **wheels.** [OE *hweol, hweowol*]

wheel and axle *n.* a simple machine for raising weights in which a rope unwinding from a wheel is wound onto a cylindrical drum or shaft coaxial with or joined to the wheel to provide mechanical advantage.

wheel animalcule *n.* another name for **rotifer.**

wheelbarrow ('wiːl,bærəʊ) *n.* a simple vehicle for carrying small loads, typically being an open container supported by a wheel at the front and two legs behind.

wheelbase ('wiːl,beɪs) *n.* the distance between the front and back axles of a motor vehicle.

wheelchair ('wiːl,tʃɛə) *n.* special chair on large wheels, for use by invalids or others for whom walking is impossible or inadvisable.

wheel clamp *n.* a device fixed onto one wheel of an illegally parked car in order to immobilize it. The driver has to pay to have it removed.

wheeled (wiːld) *adj.* **a.** having a wheel or wheels. **b.** (*in combination*): *four-wheeled.*

wheeler ('wiːlə) *n.* **1.** Also called: **wheel horse.** a horse or other draught animal nearest the wheel. **2.** (*in combination*) something equipped with a specified sort or number of wheels: *a three-wheeler.* **3.** a person or thing that wheels.

Wheeler ('wiːlə) *n.* Sir (**Robert Eric**) **Mortimer.** 1890–1976, Scottish archaeologist, who did much to increase public interest in archaeology. He is noted esp. for his excavations at Mohenjo-Daro and Harappa in the Indus Valley and at Maiden Castle in Dorset.

wheeler-dealer *n.* *Inf.* a person who wheels and deals.

wheel horse *n.* **1.** another word for **wheeler** (sense 1). **2.** *U.S. & Canad.* a person who works steadily or hard.

wheelhouse ('wiːl,haʊs) *n.* another term for **pilot house.**

wheelie ('wiːlɪ) *n.* a manoeuvre on a bicycle or motorbike in which the front wheel is raised off the ground.

wheel lock *n.* **1.** a gunlock formerly in use in which the firing mechanism was activated by sparks produced by friction between a small steel wheel and a flint. **2.** a gun having such a lock.

wheel of fortune *n.* (in mythology and literature) a revolving device spun by a deity selecting random changes in the affairs of man.

wheels (wiːlz) *pl. n.* **1.** the main directing force behind an organization, movement, etc.: *the wheels of government.* **2.** an informal word for **car. 3. wheels within wheels.** a series of intricately connected events, plots, etc.

wheel window *n.* another name for **rose window.**

wheelwright ('wiːl,raɪt) *n.* a person who makes or mends wheels as a trade.

wheeze (wiːz) *vb.* **1.** to breathe or utter (something) with a rasping or whistling sound. **2.** (*intr.*) to make or move with a noise suggestive of wheezy breathing. ~*n.* **3.** a husky, rasping, or whistling sound or breathing. **4.** *Brit. sl.* a trick, idea, or plan. **5.** *Inf.* a hackneyed joke or anecdote. [C15: prob. from ON *hvæsa* to hiss] —'**wheezer** *n.* —'**wheezy** *adj.* —'**wheezily** *adv.* —'**wheeziness** *n.*

whelk[1] (wɛlk) *n.* a marine gastropod mollusc of coastal waters and intertidal regions, having a strong snail-like shell. [OE *weoloc*]

whelk[2] (wɛlk) *n.* a raised lesion on the skin; wheal. [OE *hwylca,* from ?] —'**whelky** *adj.*

whelm (wɛlm) *vb.* (*tr.*) *Arch.* to engulf entirely; overwhelm. [C13 *whelmen* to turn over, from ?]

whelp (wɛlp) *n.* **1.** a young offspring of certain animals, esp. of a wolf or dog. **2.** *Disparaging.* a youth. **3.** *Jocular.* a young child. **4.** *Naut.* any of the ridges, parallel to the axis, on the drum of a capstan to keep a rope, etc., from slipping. ~*vb.* **5.** (of an animal or, disparagingly, a woman) to give birth to (young). [OE *hwelp(a)*]

when (wɛn) *adv.* **1. a.** at what time? over what period?: *when is he due?* **b.** (*used in indirect questions*): *ask him when he's due.* **2. say when.** to state when an action is to be stopped or begun, as when someone is pouring a drink. ~*conj.* **3.** (*subordinating*) at a time at which; just as; after: *I found it easy when I tried.* **4.** although: *he drives when he might walk.* **5.** considering the fact that: *how did you pass the exam when you hadn't worked for it?* ~*pron.* **6.** at which (time); over which (period): *an age when men were men.* ~*n.* **7.** a question as to the time of some occurrence. [OE *hwanne, hwænne*]

▷ **Usage.** Care should be taken so that *when* and *where* refer explicitly to time or place, and are not used loosely to substitute for *in which* after the verb *to be: paralysis is a condition in which* (not *when* or *where*) *parts of the body cannot be moved.*

whenas (wɛn'æz) *conj.* *Arch.* **1. a.** when; whenever. **b.** inasmuch as; while. **2.** although.

whence (wɛns) *Arch. or formal.* ~*adv.* **1.** from what place, cause, or origin? ~*pron.* **2.** (*subordinating*) from what place, cause, or origin. [C13 *whannes*, adv. genitive of OE *hwanon*]

▷ **Usage.** Careful users of English avoid the expression *from whence*, since *whence* already means from which place: *the tradition whence* (not *from whence*) *such ideas flow.*

whencesoever (ˌwɛnssəʊˈɛvə) *conj.* (*subordinating*), *adv. Arch.* from whatever place, cause, or origin.

whenever (wɛnˈɛvə) *conj.* **1.** (*subordinating*) at every or any time that; when: *I laugh whenever I see that.* ~*adv.* also **when ever.** **2.** no matter when: *it'll be here, whenever you decide to come for it.* **3.** *Inf.* at an unknown or unspecified time: *I'll take it if it comes today, tomorrow, or whenever.* **4.** an intensive form of *when*, used in questions: *whenever did he escape?*

whensoever (ˌwɛnsəʊˈɛvə) *conj., adv. Rare.* an intensive form of **whenever.**

where (wɛə) *adv.* **1. a.** in, at, or to what place, point, or position?: *where are you going?* **b.** (*used in indirect questions*): *I don't know where they are.* ~*pron.* **2.** in, at, or to which (place): *the hotel where we spent our honeymoon.* ~*conj.* **3.** (*subordinating*) in the place at which: *where we live it's always raining.* ~*n.* **4.** a question as to the position, direction, or destination of something. [OE *hwǣr, hwār(a)*]

▷ **Usage.** See at **when.**

whereabouts (ˈwɛərəˌbaʊts) *adv.* **1.** at what approximate place; where: *whereabouts are you?* ~*n.* **2.** (*functioning as sing. or pl.*) the place, esp. the approximate place, where a person or thing is.

whereas (wɛərˈæz) *conj.* **1.** (*coordinating*) but on the other hand: *I like to go swimming whereas Sheila likes to sail.* ~*sentence connector.* **2.** (in formal documents) it being the case that; since.

whereat (wɛərˈæt) *Arch.* ~*adv.* **1.** at or to which place. ~*sentence connector.* **2.** upon which occasion.

whereby (wɛəˈbaɪ) *pron.* by or because of which: *the means whereby he took his life.*

wherefore (ˈwɛəˌfɔː) *n.* **1.** (*usually pl.*) an explanation or reason (esp. in the **whys and wherefores**). ~*adv.* **2.** *Arch.* why? ~*sentence connector.* **3.** *Arch. or formal.* for which reason: used in legal preambles.

wherefrom (wɛəˈfrɒm) *Arch.* ~*adv.* **1.** from what or where? whence? ~*pron.* **2.** from which place; whence.

wherein (wɛərˈɪn) *Arch. or formal.* ~*adv.* **1.** in what place or respect? ~*pron.* **2.** in which place, thing, etc.

whereof (wɛərˈɒv) *Arch. or formal.* ~*adv.* **1.** of what or which person or thing? ~*pron.* **2.** of which (person or thing): *the man whereof I speak is no longer alive.*

whereon (wɛərˈɒn) *Arch. or formal.* ~*adv.* **1.** on what thing or place? ~*pron.* **2.** on which thing, place, etc.

wheresoever (ˌwɛəsəʊˈɛvə) *conj.* (*subordinating*), *adv., pron. Rare.* an intensive form of **wherever.**

whereto (wɛəˈtuː) *Arch. or formal.* ~*adv.* **1.** towards what (place, end, etc.)? ~*pron.* **2.** to which. ~*Also* (archaic): **whereunto.**

whereupon (ˌwɛərəˈpɒn) *sentence connector.* at which; at which point; upon which.

wherever (wɛərˈɛvə) *pron.* **1.** at, in, or to every place or point which; where: *wherever she went, he would be there.* ~*conj.* **2.** (*subordinating*) in, to, or at whatever place: *wherever we go the weather is always bad.* ~*adv.* also **where ever.** **3.** no matter where: *I'll find you, wherever you are.* **4.** *Inf.* at, in, or to an unknown or unspecified place: *I'll go anywhere to escape: London, Paris, or wherever.* **5.** an intensive form of *where*, used in questions: *wherever can they be?*

wherewith (wɛəˈwɪθ, -ˈwɪð) *Arch. or formal.* ~*pron.* **1.** (*often foll. by an infinitive*) with or by which: *the pen wherewith I write.* **2.** something with which: *I have not wherewith to buy my bread.* ~*adv.* **3.** with what? ~*sentence connector.* **4.** with or after that; whereupon.

wherewithal *n.* (ˈwɛəwɪðˌɔːl). **1. the wherewithal.** necessary funds, resources, or equipment: *these people lack the wherewithal for a decent existence.* ~*pron.* (ˌwɛəwɪðˈɔːl). **2.** a less common word for **wherewith.**

wherry (ˈwɛrɪ) *n., pl.* **-ries. 1.** any of certain kinds of half-decked commercial boats. **2.** a light rowing boat. [C15: from ?] —**ˈwherryman** *n.*

whet (wɛt) *vb.* **whetting, whetted.** (*tr.*) **1.** to sharpen, as by grinding or friction. **2.** to increase (the appetite, desire, etc.); stimulate. ~*n.* **3.** the act of whetting. **4.** a person or thing that whets. [OE *hwettan*] —**ˈwhetter** *n.*

whether (ˈwɛðə) *conj.* **1.** (*subordinating*) used to introduce an indirect question or a clause after a verb expressing or implying doubt or choice: *he doesn't know whether she's in Britain or whether she's gone to France.* **2.** (*coordinating*) either: *any man, whether liberal or conservative, would agree with me.* **3.** **whether or no.** in any case: *he will be here tomorrow, whether or no.* **4. whether . . . or** (**whether**). if on the one hand . . . or even if on the other hand: *you'll eat that, whether you like it or not.* [OE *hwæther, hwether*]

whetstone (ˈwɛtˌstəʊn) *n.* **1.** a stone used for sharpening edged tools, knives, etc. **2.** something that sharpens.

whew (hwjuː) *interj.* an exclamation or sharply exhaled breath expressing relief, delight, etc.

whey (weɪ) *n.* the watery liquid that separates from the curd when milk is clotted, as in making cheese. [OE *hwæg*]

wheyface (ˈweɪˌfeɪs) *n.* **1.** a pale bloodless face. **2.** a person with such a face. —**ˈwheyˌfaced** *adj.*

which (wɪtʃ) *determiner.* **1. a.** used with a noun in requesting that its referent be further specified, identified, or distinguished: *which house did you want to buy?* **b.** (*as pron.*): *which did you find?* **c.** (*used in indirect questions*): *I wondered which apples were cheaper.* **2. a.** whatever of a class; whichever: *bring which car you want.* **b.** (*as pron.*): *choose which of the cars suits you.* ~*pron.* **3.** used in relative clauses with inanimate antecedents: *the house, which is old, is in poor repair.* **4.** as; and that: used in relative clauses with verb phrases or sentences as their antecedents: *he died of cancer, which is what I predicted.* **5. the which.** an archaic form of **which** often used as a sentence connector. [OE *hwelc, hwilc*]

▷ **Usage.** See at **that.**

whichever (wɪtʃˈɛvə) *determiner.* **1. a.** any (one, two, etc., out of several): *take whichever car you like.* **b.** (*as pron.*): *choose whichever appeals to you.* **2. a.** no matter which (one or ones): *whichever card you pick you'll still be making a mistake.* **b.** (*as pron.*): *it won't make any difference, whichever comes first.*

whichsoever (ˌwɪtʃsəʊˈɛvə) *pron.* an archaic or formal word for **whichever.**

whicker (ˈwɪkə) *vb.* (*intr.*) (of a horse) to whinny or neigh; nicker. [C17: imit.]

whidah (ˈwɪdə) *n.* a variant spelling of **whydah.**

whiff (wɪf) *n.* **1.** a passing odour. **2.** a brief gentle gust of air. **3.** a single inhalation or exhalation from the mouth or nose. ~*vb.* **4.** to puff or waft. **5.** (*tr.*) to sniff or smell. **6.** (*intr.*) *Brit. sl.* to stink. [C16: imit.]

whiffle (ˈwɪfᵊl) *vb.* **1.** (*intr.*) to think or behave in an erratic or unpredictable way. **2.** to blow or be blown fitfully or in gusts. **3.** (*intr.*) to whistle softly. [C16: frequentative of WHIFF]

whiffletree (ˈwɪfᵊlˌtriː) *n. Chiefly U.S.* another word for **swingletree.** [C19: var. of WHIPPLETREE]

Whig (wɪg) *n.* **1.** a member of the English political party that opposed the succession to the throne of James, Duke of York (1679–80), on the grounds that he was a Catholic. Standing for a limited monarchy, the Whigs later represented the desires of industrialists and Dissenters for political and social reform, and provided the core of the Liberal Party. **2.** (in the U.S.) a supporter of the War of American Independence. Cf. **Tory.** **3.** a member of the American political party that opposed the Democrats from about 1834 to 1855 and represented propertied and professional interests. **4.** *History.* a 17th-century Scottish Presbyterian, esp. one in rebellion against the Crown. ~*adj.* **5.** of, characteristic of, or relating to Whigs. [C17: prob. from *whiggamore*, one of a group of 17th-cent. Scottish rebels who joined in an attack on Edinburgh known as *the whiggamore raid*; prob. from Scot. *whig* to drive (from ?) + *more* horse] —**ˈWhiggery** *or* **ˈWhiggism** *n.* —**ˈWhiggish** *adj.*

while (waɪl) *conj. also* **whilst. 1.** (*subordinating*) at the same time that: *please light the fire while I'm cooking.* **2.** (*subordinating*) all the time that: *I stay inside while it's raining.* **3.** (*subordinating*) in spite of the fact that: *while I agree about his brilliance I still think he's rude.* **4.** (*coordinating*) whereas; and in contrast: *houses are expensive, while flats are cheap.* ~*prep., conj.* **5.** *Scot. & N*

English dialect. another word for **until**: *you'll have to wait while Monday.* ~*n.* **6.** (*usually used in adverbial phrases*) a period or interval of time: *once in a long while.* **7.** trouble or time (esp. in **worth one's while**): *it's hardly worth your while to begin work today.* [OE *hwīl*]

▷ **Usage.** The main sense of *while* is *during the time that.* However, many careful users of English would now accept as established the use of *while* to mean *although*: *while he disliked working, he was obliged to do so.* In careful usage, *while* is not used to mean *whereas* or *and*: *he thought that they were in Paris, whereas* (not *while*) *they had gone on to Rome; his friends went to Paris for their holiday, his brother to Rome, and* (not *while*) *his parents went to Berlin.* Careful writers try to avoid any ambiguity that may result from the possibility of two interpretations of *while* in context: *while* (*although* or *during the time that*) *his brother worked in the park, he refused to do any gardening at home.*

while away *vb.* (*tr., adv.*) to pass (time) idly and usually pleasantly.

whiles (waɪlz) *Arch. or dialect.* ~*adv.* **1.** at times; occasionally. ~*conj.* **2.** while; whilst.

whilom (ˈwaɪləm) *Arch.* ~*adv.* **1.** formerly; once. ~*adj.* **2.** (*prenominal*) one-time; former. [OE *hwīlum*, dative pl. of *hwīl* while]

whilst (waɪlst) *conj. Chiefly Brit.* another word for **while** (senses 1–4). [C13: from WHILES + -*t* as in *amidst*]

whim (wɪm) *n.* **1.** a sudden, passing, and often fanciful idea; impulsive or irrational thought. **2.** a horse-drawn winch formerly used in mining to lift ore or water. [C17: from C16 *whim-wham*, from ?]

whimbrel (ˈwɪmbrəl) *n.* a small European curlew with a striped head. [C16: from dialect *whimp* or from WHIMPER, from its cry]

whimper (ˈwɪmpə) *vb.* **1.** (*intr.*) to cry, sob, or whine softly or intermittently. **2.** to complain or say (something) in a whining plaintive way. ~*n.* **3.** a soft plaintive whine. [C16: from dialect *whimp*, imit.] —ˈwhimperer *n.* —ˈwhimpering *n., adj.* —ˈwhimperingly *adv.*

whimsical (ˈwɪmzɪkᵊl) *adj.* **1.** spontaneously fanciful or playful. **2.** given to whims; capricious. **3.** quaint, unusual, or fantastic. —**whimsicality** (ˌwɪmzɪˈkælɪtɪ) *n.* —ˈwhimsically *adv.*

whimsy *or* **whimsey** (ˈwɪmzɪ) *n., pl.* **-sies** *or* **-seys.** **1.** a capricious idea or notion. **2.** light or fanciful humour. **3.** something quaint or unusual. ~*adj.* **-sier, -siest.** **4.** quaint, comical, or unusual, often in a tasteless way. [C17: from WHIM]

whin[1] (wɪn) *n.* another name for **gorse.** [C11: from ON]

whin[2] (wɪn) *n.* short for **whinstone.** [C14 *quin*, from ?]

whinchat (ˈwɪnˌtʃæt) *n.* an Old World songbird having a mottled brown-and-white plumage with pale cream underparts. [C17: from WHIN[1] + CHAT]

whine (waɪn) *n.* **1.** a long high-pitched plaintive cry or moan. **2.** a continuous high-pitched sound. **3.** a peevish complaint, esp. one repeated. ~*vb.* **4.** to make a whine or utter in a whine. [OE *hwīnan*] —ˈwhiner *n.* —ˈwhining *or* ˈwhiny *adj.* —ˈwhiningly *adv.*

whinge (wɪndʒ) *vb.* (*intr.*) **1.** to cry in a fretful way. **2.** to complain. ~*n.* **3.** a complaint. [from Northern var. of OE *hwinsian* to whine] —ˈwhingeing *n., adj.*

whinny (ˈwɪnɪ) *vb.* **-nying, -nied.** (*intr.*) **1.** (of a horse) to neigh softly or gently. **2.** to make a sound resembling a neigh, such as a laugh. ~*n., pl.* **-nies. 3.** a gentle or low-pitched neigh. [C16: imit.]

whinstone (ˈwɪnˌstəun) *n.* any dark hard fine-grained rock, such as basalt. [C16: from WHIN[2] + STONE]

whip (wɪp) *vb.* **whipping, whipped. 1.** to strike (a person or thing) with several strokes of a strap, rod, etc. **2.** (*tr.*) to punish by striking in this manner. **3.** (*tr.*; foll. by *out, away,* etc.) to pull, remove, etc., with sudden rapid motion: *to whip out a gun.* **4.** (*intr.*; foll. by *down, into, out of,* etc.) *Inf.* to come, go, etc., in a rapid sudden manner: *they whipped into the bar for a drink.* **5.** to strike or be struck as if by whipping: *the tempest whipped the surface of the sea.* **6.** (*tr.*) to bring, train, etc., forcefully into a desired condition. **7.** (*tr.*) *Inf.* to overcome or outdo. **8.** (*tr.*; often foll. by *on, out,* or *off*) to drive, urge, compel, etc., by or as if by whipping. **9.** (*tr.*) to wrap or wind (a cord, thread, etc.) around (a rope, cable, etc.) to prevent chafing or fraying. **10.** (*tr.*) (in fly-fishing) to cast the fly repeatedly onto (the water) in a whipping motion. **11.** (*tr.*) (in sewing) to join, finish, or gather with whipstitch.

12. to beat (eggs, cream, etc.) with a whisk or similar utensil to incorporate air. **13.** (*tr.*) to spin (a top). **14.** (*tr.*) *Inf.* to steal: *he whipped her purse.* ~*n.* **15.** a device consisting of a lash or flexible rod attached at one end to a stiff handle and used for driving animals, inflicting corporal punishment, etc. **16.** a whipping stroke or motion. **17.** a person adept at handling a whip, as a coachman, etc. **18.** (in a legislative body) **a.** a member of a party chosen to organize and discipline the members of his faction. **b.** a call issued to members of a party, insisting with varying degrees of urgency upon their presence or loyal voting behaviour. **c.** (in the Brit. Parliament) a schedule of business sent to members of a party each week. Each item on it is underlined to indicate its importance: three lines means that the item is very important and every member must attend and vote according to the party line. **19.** an apparatus for hoisting, consisting of a rope, pulley, and snatch block. **20.** any of a variety of desserts made from egg whites or cream beaten stiff. **21.** See **whipper-in.** **22.** flexibility, as in the shaft of a golf club, etc. ~See also **whip-round, whip up, whips.** [C13: ?from MDu. *wippen* to swing] —ˈwhipˌlike *adj.* —ˈwhipper *n.*

whip bird *n. Austral.* any of several birds having a whistle ending in a note sounding like the crack of a whip.

whipcord (ˈwɪpˌkɔːd) *n.* **1.** a strong worsted or cotton fabric with a diagonally ribbed surface. **2.** a closely twisted hard cord used for the lashes of whips, etc.

whip graft *n. Horticulture.* a graft made by inserting a tongue cut on the sloping base of the scion into a slit on the sloping top of the stock.

whip hand *n.* (usually preceded by *the*) **1.** (in driving horses) the hand holding the whip. **2.** advantage or dominating position.

whiplash (ˈwɪpˌlæʃ) *n.* a quick lash or stroke of a whip or like that of a whip.

whiplash injury *n. Med. inf.* any injury to the neck resulting from a sudden thrusting forwards and snapping back of the unsupported head. Technical name: **hyperextension-hyperflexion injury.**

whipper-in *n., pl.* **whippers-in.** a person employed to assist the huntsman managing the hounds.

whippersnapper (ˈwɪpəˌsnæpə) *n.* an insignificant but pretentious or cheeky person, often a young one. Also called: **whipster.** [C17: prob. from *whipsnapper* a person who snaps whips, infl. by earlier *snippersnapper,* from ?]

whippet (ˈwɪpɪt) *n.* a small slender breed of dog similar to a greyhound. [C16: from ?; ? based on *whip it!* move quickly!]

whipping (ˈwɪpɪŋ) *n.* **1.** a thrashing or beating with a whip or similar implement. **2.** cord or twine used for binding or lashing. **3.** the binding formed by wrapping a rope, etc., with cord or twine.

whipping boy *n.* a person of little importance who is blamed for the errors, incompetence, etc., of others, esp. his superiors; scapegoat. [C17: orig. referring to a boy who was educated with a prince and who received punishment for any faults committed by the prince]

whippletree (ˈwɪpᵊlˌtriː) *n.* another name for **swingletree.** [C18: apparently from WHIP]

whippoorwill (ˈwɪpʊˌwɪl) *n.* a nightjar of North and Central America, having a dark plumage with white patches on the tail. [C18: imit. of its cry]

whip-round *Inf., chiefly Brit.* ~*n.* **1.** an impromptu collection of money. ~*vb.* **whip round. 2.** (*intr., adv.*) to make such a collection.

whips (wɪps) *pl. n.* (often foll. by *of*) *Austral. inf.* a large quantity: *I've got whips of cash at the moment.*

whipsaw (ˈwɪpˌsɔː) *n.* **1.** any saw with a flexible blade, such as a bandsaw. ~*vb.* **-sawing, -sawed, -sawed** *or* **-sawn.** (*tr.*) **2.** to saw with a whipsaw. **3.** *U.S.* to defeat in two ways at once.

whip scorpion *n.* any of an order of nonvenomous arachnids, typically resembling a scorpion but lacking a sting.

whip snake *n.* any of several long slender fast-moving nonvenomous snakes.

whipstitch (ˈwɪpˌstɪtʃ) *n.* a sewing stitch passing over an edge.

whipstock (ˈwɪpˌstɒk) *n.* a whip handle.

whip up *vb.* (*tr., adv.*) **1.** to excite; arouse: *to whip up a mob; to whip up discontent.* **2.** *Inf.* to prepare quickly: *to whip up a meal.*

whir *or* **whirr** (wɜː) *n.* **1.** a prolonged soft swish or buzz, as of a motor working or wings flapping. **2.** a bustle or rush. ~*vb.* **whirring, whirred. 3.** to make or cause to make a whir. [C14: prob. from ON; see WHIRL]

whirl (wɜːl) *vb.* **1.** to spin, turn, or revolve or cause to spin, turn, or revolve. **2.** (*intr.*) to turn around or away rapidly. **3.** (*intr.*) to have a spinning sensation, as from dizziness, etc. **4.** to move or drive or be moved or driven at high speed. ~*n.* **5.** the act or an instance of whirling; swift rotation or a rapid whirling movement. **6.** a condition of confusion or giddiness: *her accident left me in a whirl.* **7.** a swift round, as of events, meetings, etc. **8.** a tumult; stir. **9.** *Inf.* a brief trip, dance, etc. **10. give** (**something**) **a whirl.** *Inf.* to attempt or give a trial to (something). [C13: from ON *hvirfla* to turn about] — **'whirler** *n.* — **'whirling** *adj.* — **'whirlingly** *adv.*

whirligig ('wɜːlɪˌɡɪɡ) *n.* **1.** any spinning toy, such as a top. **2.** another name for **merry-go-round. 3.** anything that whirls about, spins, or moves in a circular or giddy way: *the whirligig of social life.* [C15 *whirlegigge*, from WHIRL + GIG[1]]

whirlpool ('wɜːlˌpuːl) *n.* **1.** a powerful circular current or vortex of water. **2.** something resembling a whirlpool in motion or the power to attract into its vortex.

whirlwind ('wɜːlˌwɪnd) *n.* **1.** a column of air whirling around and towards a more or less vertical axis of low pressure, which moves along the land or ocean surface. **2. a.** a motion or course resembling this, esp. in rapidity. **b.** (*as modifier*): *a whirlwind romance.* **3.** an impetuously active person.

whirlybird ('wɜːlɪˌbɜːd) *n.* an informal word for **helicopter.**

whish (wɪʃ) *n.*, *vb.* a less common word for **swish.**

whisht (hwɪʃt) *or* **whist** (hwɪst) *Arch. or dialect, esp. Scot.* ~*interj.* **1.** hush! be quiet! ~*adj.* **2.** silent or still. [C14: cf. HIST]

whisk (wɪsk) *vb.* **1.** (*tr.*; often foll. by *away* or *off*) to brush, sweep, or wipe off lightly. **2.** (*tr.*) to move, carry, etc., with a light or rapid sweeping motion: *the taxi whisked us to the airport.* **3.** (*intr.*) to move, go, etc., quickly and nimbly: *to whisk downstairs for a drink.* **4.** (*tr.*) to whip (eggs, etc.) to a froth. ~*n.* **5.** the act of whisking. **6.** a light rapid sweeping movement. **7.** a utensil for whipping eggs, etc. **8.** a small brush or broom. **9.** a small bunch or bundle, as of grass, straw, etc. [C14: from ON *visk* wisp]

whisker ('wɪskə) *n.* **1.** any of the stiff sensory hairs growing on the face of a cat, rat, or other mammal. Technical name: **vibrissa. 2.** any of the hairs growing on a man's face, esp. on the cheeks or chin. **3.** (*pl.*) a beard or that part of it growing on the sides of the face. **4.** (*pl.*) *Inf.* a moustache. **5.** *Chem.* a very fine filamentary crystal having greater strength than the bulk material. **6.** a person or thing that whisks. **7.** a narrow margin or small distance: *he escaped death by a whisker.* —**'whiskered** *or* **'whiskery** *adj.*

whiskey ('wɪskɪ) *n.* the usual Irish and U.S. spelling of **whisky.**

whiskey sour *n.* *U.S.* a mixed drink of whisky and lime or lemon juice, sometimes sweetened.

whisky ('wɪskɪ) *n.*, *pl.* **-kies.** a spirit made by distilling fermented cereals, which is matured and often blended. [C18: shortened from *whiskybae*, from Scot. Gaelic *uisge beatha*, lit.: water of life; see USQUEBAUGH]

whisky-jack *n.* *Canad.* another name for **Canada jay.**

whisky mac *n. Brit.* a drink consisting of whisky and ginger wine.

whisper ('wɪspə) *vb.* **1.** to speak or utter (something) in a soft hushed tone, esp. without vibration of the vocal cords. **2.** (*intr.*) to speak secretly or furtively, as in promoting intrigue, gossip, etc. **3.** (*intr.*) (of leaves, trees, etc.) to make a low soft rustling sound. **4.** (*tr.*) to utter or suggest secretly or privately: *to whisper treason.* ~*n.* **5.** a low soft voice: *to speak in a whisper.* **6.** something uttered in such a voice. **7.** a low soft rustling sound. **8.** a trace or suspicion. **9.** *Inf.* a rumour. [OE *hwisprian*] —**'whisperer** *n.*

whispering campaign *n.* the organized diffusion of defamatory rumours designed to discredit a person, group, etc.

whispering gallery *n.* a gallery or dome with acoustic characteristics such that a sound made at one point is audible at distant points.

whist (wɪst) *n.* a card game for four in which the two sides try to win the balance of the 13 tricks: forerunner of

bridge. [C17: ? changed from WHISK, referring to the sweeping up or whisking up of the tricks]

whist drive *n.* a social gathering where whist is played: the winners of each hand move to different tables to play the losers of the previous hand.

whistle ('wɪsᵊl) *vb.* **1.** to produce (shrill or flutelike sounds), as by passing breath through a narrow constriction most easily formed by the pursed lips. **2.** (*tr.*) to signal or command by whistling or blowing a whistle: *the referee whistled the end of the game.* **3.** (of a kettle, train, etc.) to produce (a shrill sound) caused by the emission of steam through a small aperture. **4.** (*intr.*) to move with a whistling sound caused by rapid passage through the air. **5.** (of animals, esp. birds) to emit (a shrill sound) resembling human whistling. **6. whistle in the dark.** to try to keep up one's confidence in spite of fear. ~*n.* **7.** a device for making a shrill high-pitched sound by means of air or steam under pressure. **8.** a shrill sound effected by whistling or blowing a whistle. **9.** a whistling sound, as of a bird, bullet, the wind, etc. **10.** a signal, etc., transmitted by or as if by a whistle. **11.** the act of whistling. **12.** an instrument, usually made of metal, that is blown down into end to produce a tune, signal, etc. **13. blow the whistle.** (usually foll. by *on*) *Inf.* **a.** to inform (on). **b.** to bring a stop (to). **14. clean as a whistle.** perfectly clean or clear. **15. wet one's whistle.** *Inf.* to take an alcoholic drink. ~See also **whistle for, whistle up.** [OE *hwistlian*]

whistle-blower *n. Inf.* a person who informs on someone or puts a stop to something.

whistle for *vb.* (*intr., prep.*) *Inf.* to seek or expect in vain.

whistler ('wɪslə) *n.* **1.** a person or thing that whistles. **2.** *Radio.* an atmospheric disturbance picked up by radio receivers, caused by the electromagnetic radiation produced by lightning. **3.** any of various birds having a whistling call, such as certain Australian flycatchers. **4.** any of various North American marmots.

Whistler ('wɪslə) *n.* **James Abbott McNeill.** 1834–1903, U.S. painter and etcher, living in Europe. He is best known for his sequence of nocturnes and his portraits.

whistle stop *n.* **1.** *U.S. & Canad.* **a.** a minor railway station where trains stop only on signal. **b.** a small town having such a station. **2. a.** a brief appearance in a town, esp. by a political candidate. **b.** (*as modifier*): *a whistle-stop tour.*

whistle up *vb.* (*tr., adv.*) to call or summon (a person or animal) by whistling.

whit (wɪt) *n.* (*usually used with a negative*) the smallest particle; iota; jot: *he has changed not a whit.* [C15: prob. var. of WIGHT]

Whit (wɪt) *n.* **1.** See **Whitsuntide.** ~*adj.* **2.** of or relating to Whitsuntide.

Whitaker ('wɪtəkə) *n.* Sir **Frederick.** 1812–91, New Zealand statesman, born in England: prime minister of New Zealand (1863–64; 1882–83).

Whitby ('wɪtbɪ) *n.* a fishing port and resort in NE England, in E North Yorkshire at the mouth of the River Esk: an important ecclesiastical centre in Anglo-Saxon times; site of an abbey founded in 656. See also **Synod of Whitby.** Pop.: 13 763 (1981).

white (waɪt) *adj.* **1.** having no hue, owing to the reflection of all or almost all incident light. **2.** (of light, such as sunlight) consisting of all the colours of the spectrum or produced by certain mixtures of primary colours, as red, green, and blue. **3.** comparatively white or whitish-grey or having parts of this colour: *white clover.* **4.** (of an animal) having pale-coloured or white skin, fur, or feathers. **5.** bloodless or pale, as from pain, emotion, etc. **6.** (of hair, etc.) grey, usually from age. **7.** benevolent or without malicious intent: *white magic.* **8.** colourless or transparent: *white glass.* **9.** capped with or accompanied by snow: *a white Christmas.* **10.** blank, as an unprinted area of a page. **11.** (of coffee or tea) with milk or cream. **12.** denoting flour, or bread made from flour, that has had part of the grain removed. **13.** *Physics.* having or characterized by a continuous distribution of energy, wavelength, or frequency: *white noise.* **14.** *Inf.* honourable or generous. **15.** *Poetic or arch.* having a fair complexion; blond. **16. bleed white.** to deprive slowly of resources. ~*n.* **17.** a white colour. **18.** the condition of being white; whiteness. **19.** the white or lightly coloured part of something. **20.** (usually preceded by *the*) the viscous fluid that surrounds the yolk of a bird's egg, esp. a hen's egg; albumen. **21.** *Anat.* the white part (sclera) of the eyeball. **22.**

any of various butterflies having white wings with scanty black markings. **23.** *Chess, draughts.* **a.** a white or light-coloured piece or square. **b.** the player playing with such pieces. **24.** anything that has or is characterized by a white colour, such as a white paint or white clothing. **25.** short for **white wine. 26.** *Archery.* the outer ring of the target, having the lowest score. ~*vb.* **27.** *Obs.* to make or become white. ~See also **white out, whites.** [OE *hwīt*] — ˈwhitely *adv.* — ˈwhiteness *n.* — ˈwhitish *adj.*

White[1] (waɪt) *n.* **1.** a member of the Caucasoid race. **2.** a person of European ancestry. ~*adj.* **3.** denoting or relating to a White or Whites.

White[2] (waɪt) *n.* **1. Gilbert.** 1720–93, English clergyman and naturalist, noted for his *Natural History and Antiquities of Selborne* (1789). **2. Jimmy.** born 1962, British snooker player. **3. Patrick (Victor Martindale).** born 1912, Australian novelist: his works include *Voss* (1957), *The Eye of the Storm* (1973), and *A Fringe of Leaves* (1976): Nobel prize for literature 1973.

white admiral *n.* a butterfly of Eurasia having brown wings with white markings.

white ant *n.* another name for **termite.**

whitebait (ˈwaɪtˌbeɪt) *n.* **1.** the young of herrings, sprats, etc., cooked and eaten whole as a delicacy. **2.** any of various small silvery fishes. [C18: from its formerly having been used as bait]

whitebeam (ˈwaɪtˌbiːm) *n.* a N temperate tree having leaves that are densely hairy on the undersurface and hard timber.

white blood cell *n.* a nontechnical name for **leucocyte.**

whitecap (ˈwaɪtˌkæp) *n.* a wave with a white broken crest.

white cedar *n.* either of two coniferous trees of North America, having scalelike leaves.

white clover *n.* a Eurasian clover plant with rounded white flower heads: cultivated as a forage plant.

white coal *n.* water, esp. when flowing and providing a potential source of usable power.

white-collar *adj.* of or designating nonmanual and usually salaried workers employed in professional and clerical occupations.

white currant *n.* a cultivated N temperate shrub having small rounded white edible berries.

whitedamp (ˈwaɪtˌdæmp) *n.* a mixture of poisonous gases, mainly carbon monoxide, occurring in coal mines.

whited sepulchre *n.* a hypocrite. [allusion to Matthew 23:27]

white dwarf *n.* one of a large class of small faint stars of enormous density, thought to mark the final stage in a star's evolution.

white elephant *n.* **1.** a rare albino variety of the Indian elephant, regarded as sacred in parts of S Asia. **2.** a possession that is unwanted by its owner. **3.** a rare or valuable possession the upkeep of which is very expensive.

White Ensign *n.* the ensign of the Royal Navy and the Royal Yacht Squadron, having a red cross on a white background with the Union Jack at the upper corner of the vertical edge alongside the hoist.

white-eye *n.* a songbird of Africa, Australia, New Zealand, and Asia, having a greenish plumage with a white ring around each eye.

white feather *n.* **1.** a symbol or mark of cowardice. **2. show the white feather.** to act in a cowardly manner. [from the belief that a white feather in a gamecock's tail was a sign of a poor fighter]

Whitefield (ˈwaɪtˌfiːld) *n.* **George.** 1714–70, English Methodist preacher, who separated from the Wesleys (?1741) because of his Calvinistic views.

whitefish (ˈwaɪtˌfɪʃ) *n., pl.* **-fish** or **-fishes.** a food fish typically of deep cold lakes of the N hemisphere, having large silvery scales and a small head.

white fish *n.* (in the Brit. fishing industry) any edible marine fish or invertebrate excluding herrings but including trout, salmon, and all shellfish.

white flag *n.* a white flag or a piece of white cloth hoisted to signify surrender or request a truce.

white flour *n.* flour that consists substantially of the starchy endosperm of wheat, most of the bran and the germ having been removed by the milling process.

whitefly (ˈwaɪtˌflaɪ) *n., pl.* **-flies.** any of a family of insects typically having a body covered with powdery wax. Many are pests of greenhouse crops.

white friar *n.* a Carmelite friar, so called because of the white cloak that forms part of the habit of this order.

white gold *n.* any of various white lustrous hard-wearing alloys containing gold together with platinum and palladium and sometimes smaller amounts of silver, nickel, or copper.

white goods *pl. n.* **1.** household linen such as sheets, towels, tablecloths, etc. **2.** large household appliances, such as refrigerators or cookers.

Whitehall (ˌwaɪtˈhɔːl) *n.* **1.** a street in London stretching from Trafalgar Square to the Houses of Parliament: site of the main government offices. **2.** the British Government.

Whitehead (ˈwaɪtˌhɛd) *n.* **Alfred North.** 1861–1947, English mathematician and philosopher, who collaborated with Bertrand Russell in writing *Principia Mathematica* (1910–13), and developed a holistic philosophy of science, chiefly in *Process and Reality* (1929).

white heat *n.* **1.** intense heat characterized by emission of white light. **2.** *Inf.* a state of intense excitement or activity.

white hope *n.* *Inf.* a person who is expected to bring honour or glory to his group, team, etc.

white horse *n.* **1.** the outline of a horse carved into the side of a chalk hill, usually dating to the Neolithic, Bronze, or Iron Ages. **2.** (*usually pl.*) a wave with a white broken crest.

Whitehorse (ˈwaɪtˌhɔːs) *n.* a town in NW Canada: capital of the Yukon Territory. Pop.: 18 385 (1986 est.).

white-hot *adj.* **1.** at such a high temperature that white light is emitted. **2.** *Inf.* in a state of intense emotion.

White House *n.* **the. 1.** the official Washington residence of the president of the U.S. **2.** the U.S. presidency.

white lead (lɛd) *n.* **1.** a white solid usually regarded as a mixture of lead carbonate and lead hydroxide; basic lead carbonate: used in paint and in making putty and ointments for the treatment of burns. **2.** either of two similar white pigments based on lead sulphate or lead silicate.

white leg *n.* another name for **milk leg.**

white lie *n.* a minor or unimportant lie, esp. one uttered in the interests of tact or politeness.

white light *n.* light that contains all the wavelengths of visible light at approximately equal intensities, as in sunlight.

white-livered *adj.* **1.** lacking in spirit or courage. **2.** pallid and unhealthy in appearance.

White man's burden *n.* the supposed duty of the White race to bring education and Western culture to the non-White inhabitants of their colonies.

white matter *n.* the whitish tissue of the brain and spinal cord, consisting mainly of nerve fibres covered with a protective white fatlike substance.

white meat *n.* any meat that is light in colour, such as veal or the breast of turkey.

white metal *n.* any of various alloys, such as Babbitt metal, used for bearings.

white meter *n.* *Brit.* an electricity meter used to record the consumption of off-peak electricity.

White Mountains *pl. n.* **1.** a mountain range chiefly in N New Hampshire: part of the Appalachians. Highest peak: Mount Washington, 1917 m (6288 ft.). **2.** a mountain range in E California and SW Nevada. Highest peak: White Mountain, 4342 m (14 246 ft.).

whiten (ˈwaɪt⁰n) *vb.* to make or become white or whiter; bleach. — ˈwhitener *n.* — ˈwhitening *n.*

White Nile *n.* See **Nile.**

white noise *n.* sound or electrical noise that has a relatively wide continuous range of frequencies of uniform intensity.

white oak *n.* a large oak tree of E North America, having pale bark, leaves with rounded lobes, and heavy light-coloured wood.

white out *vb.* (*adv.*) **1.** (*intr.*) to lose or lack daylight visibility owing to snow or fog. **2.** (*tr.*) to create or leave white spaces in (printed or other matter). ~*n.* **whiteout. 3.** a polar atmospheric condition consisting of lack of visibility and sense of distance and direction due to a uniform whiteness of a heavy cloud cover and snow-covered ground, which reflects almost all the light it receives.

white paper *n.* (*often caps.*) an official government report in any of a number of countries, which sets out the government's policy on a matter that is or will come before Parliament.

white pepper *n.* a condiment, less pungent than black pepper, made from the husked dried beans of the pepper plant.

white pine *n.* a North American coniferous tree having blue-green needle-like leaves, hanging brown cones, and rough bark.

white poplar *n.* **1.** Also called: **abele.** a Eurasian tree having leaves covered with dense silvery-white hairs. **2.** another name for **tulipwood** (sense 1).

white rose *n. English history.* an emblem of the House of York.

White Russia *n.* another name for the **Byelorussian Soviet Socialist Republic. —White Russian** *adj., n.*

whites (waɪts) *pl. n.* **1.** household linen or cotton goods, such as sheets. **2.** white or off-white clothing, such as that worn for playing cricket.

white sale *n.* a sale of household linens at reduced prices.

white sauce *n.* a thick sauce made from flour, butter, seasonings, and milk or stock.

White Sea *n.* an almost landlocked inlet of the Barents Sea on the coast of the NW Soviet Union. Area: 90 000 sq. km (34 700 sq. miles).

white settler *n.* a well-off incomer to a district who takes advantage of what it has to offer without regard to the local inhabitants. [C20: from earlier colonial sense]

white slave *n.* a girl or woman forced or sold into prostitution. **—white slavery** *n.* **—white-slaver** *n.*

white spirit *n.* a colourless liquid obtained from petroleum and used as a substitute for turpentine.

white spruce *n.* a N North American spruce tree with grey bark.

white squall *n.* a violent highly localized weather disturbance at sea, in which the surface of the water is whipped to a white spray by the winds.

whitethorn (ˈwaɪtˌθɔːn) *n.* another name for **hawthorn.**

whitethroat (ˈwaɪtˌθrəʊt) *n.* either of two Old World warblers having a greyish-brown plumage with a white throat and underparts.

white tie *n.* **1.** a white bow tie worn as part of a man's formal evening dress. **2. a.** formal evening dress for men. **b.** (*as modifier*): *a white-tie occasion.*

White Volta *n.* a river in W Africa, rising in N Burkina-Faso flowing southwest and south to join the Black Volta in central Ghana and form the Volta River. Length: about 885 km (550 miles).

whitewall (ˈwaɪtˌwɔːl) *n.* a pneumatic tyre having white sidewalls.

whitewash (ˈwaɪtˌwɒʃ) *n.* **1.** a substance used for whitening walls and other surfaces, consisting of a suspension of lime or whiting in water. **2.** *Inf.* deceptive or specious words or actions intended to conceal defects, gloss over failings, etc. **3.** *Inf.* a game in which the loser fails to score. *~vb.* (*tr.*) **4.** to cover with whitewash. **5.** *Inf.* to conceal, gloss over, or suppress. **6.** *Inf.* to defeat (someone) in a game by preventing him from scoring. **—ˈwhiteˌwasher** *n.*

white water *n.* **1.** a stretch of water with a broken foamy surface, as in rapids. **2.** light-coloured sea water, esp. over shoals or shallows.

white whale *n.* a small white toothed whale of northern waters. Also called: **beluga.**

white wine *n.* wine made from pale grapes or from black grapes separated from their skins.

whitewood (ˈwaɪtˌwʊd) *n.* **1.** any of various trees with light-coloured wood, such as the tulip tree, basswood, and cottonwood. **2.** the wood of any of these trees.

whitey *or* **whity** (ˈwaɪtɪ) *n., pl.* **whities.** *Chiefly U.S.* (used contemptuously by Black people) a White man or White men collectively.

whither (ˈwɪðə) *Arch. or poetic.* *~adv.* **1.** to what place? **2.** to what end or purpose? *~conj.* **3.** to whatever place, purpose, etc. [OE *hwider, hwæder;* Mod. E form infl. by HITHER]

whithersoever (ˌwɪðəsəʊˈɛvə) *adv., conj. Arch. or poetic.* to whichever place.

whiting[1] (ˈwaɪtɪŋ) *n.* **1.** an important gadoid food fish of European seas, having a dark back with silvery sides and underparts. **2.** any of various similar fishes. [C15: ?from OE *hwītling*]

whiting[2] (ˈwaɪtɪŋ) *n.* white chalk that has been ground and washed, used in making whitewash, metal polish, etc. Also called: **whitening.**

Whitlam (ˈwɪtləm) *n.* (**Edward**) **Gough** (gɒf). born 1916, Australian Labor statesman: prime minister (1972–75).

Whitley Bay (ˈwɪtlɪ) *n.* a resort in NE England, in Tyne and Wear on the North Sea. Pop.: 37 079 (1981).

whitlow (ˈwɪtləʊ) *n.* any pussy inflammation of the end of a finger or toe. [C14: changed from *whitflaw,* from WHITE + FLAW[1]]

Whitman (ˈwɪtmən) *n.* **Walt(er).** 1819–92, U.S. poet, whose life's work is collected in *Leaves of Grass* (1855 and subsequent enlarged editions). His poems celebrate existence and the multiple elements that make up a democratic society.

Whitney[1] (ˈwɪtnɪ) *n.* **Mount.** a mountain in E California: the highest peak in the Sierra Nevada Mountains and in continental U.S. (excluding Alaska). Height: 4418 m (14 495 ft.).

Whitney[2] (ˈwɪtnɪ) *n.* **1. Eli.** 1765–1825, U.S. inventor of a mechanical cotton gin (1793) and pioneer manufacturer of interchangeable parts. **2. William Dwight.** 1827–94, U.S. philologist, noted esp. for his *Sanskrit Grammar* (1879).

Whitsun (ˈwɪtsən) *n.* **1.** short for **Whitsuntide.** *~adj.* **2.** of or relating to Whit Sunday or Whitsuntide.

Whitsunday (ˌhwɪtˈsʌndɪ, ˌwɪt-) *n.* (in Scotland) May 15, one of the four quarter days.

Whit Sunday *n.* the seventh Sunday after Easter, observed as a feast in commemoration of the descent of the Holy Spirit on the apostles. Also called: **Pentecost.** [OE *hwīta sunnandæg* white Sunday, prob. after the ancient custom of wearing white robes at or after baptism]

Whitsuntide (ˈwɪtsənˌtaɪd) *n.* the week that begins with Whit Sunday, esp. the first three days.

Whittington (ˈwɪtɪŋtən) *n.* **Richard,** known as *Dick.* died 1423, English merchant, three times mayor of London. According to legend, he walked to London at the age of 13 with his cat and was prevented from leaving again only by the call of the church bells.

whittle (ˈwɪt²l) *vb.* **1.** to cut or shave strips or pieces from (wood, a stick, etc.), esp. with a knife. **2.** (*tr.*) to make or shape by paring or shaving. **3.** (*tr.; often foll. by away, down,* etc.) to reduce, destroy, or wear away gradually. [C16: var. of C15 *thwittle* large knife, ult. from OE *thwītan* to cut]

Whittle (ˈwɪt²l) *n.* Sir **Frank.** born 1907, English engineer, who invented the jet engine for aircraft (1941).

whity (ˈwaɪtɪ) *n., pl.* **whities.** **1.** *Inf.* a variant spelling of **whitey.** *~adj.* **2. a.** whitish in colour. **b.** (*in combination*): *whity-brown.*

whiz *or* **whizz** (wɪz) *vb.* **whizzing, whizzed. 1.** to make or cause to make a loud humming or buzzing sound. **2.** to move or cause to move with such a sound. **3.** (*intr.*) *Inf.* to move or go rapidly. *~n., pl.* **whizzes. 4.** a loud humming or buzzing sound. **5.** *Inf.* a person who is extremely skilful at some activity. [C16: imit.]

whiz-bang *or* **whizz-bang** *n* **1.** a World War I shell that travelled at such high velocity that the sound of its flight was heard only an instant before the sound of its explosion. **2.** a type of firework that jumps around emitting a whizzing sound and occasional bangs.

whiz kid, whizz kid, *or* **wiz kid** *n. Inf.* a person who is pushing, enthusiastic, and outstandingly successful for his or her age. [C20: from WHIZ, ? infl. by WIZARD]

who (huː) *pron.* **1.** which person? what person? used in direct and indirect questions: *he can't remember who did it; who met you?* **2.** used to introduce relative clauses with antecedents referring to human beings: *the people who lived here have left.* **3.** the one or ones who; whoever: *bring who you want.* [OE *hwā*]

▷ **Usage.** See at **whom.**

WHO *abbrev. for* World Health Organization.

whoa (wəʊ) *interj.* a command used esp. to horses to stop or slow down. [C19: var. of HO]

who-does-what *adj.* (of a dispute, strike, etc.) relating to the separation of kinds of work performed by different trade unions.

whodunit *or* **whodunnit** (huːˈdʌnɪt) *n. Inf.* a novel, play, etc., concerned with a crime, usually murder.

whoever (huːˈɛvə) *pron.* **1.** any person who: *whoever wants it can have it.* **2.** no matter who: *I'll come round tomorrow, whoever may be here.* **3.** an intensive form of *who,* used in questions: *whoever could have thought that?* **4.** *Inf.* an unspecified person: *give those to Cathy or whoever.*

whole (həʊl) *adj.* **1.** containing all the component parts necessary to form a total; complete: *a whole apple.* **2.** constituting the full quantity, extent, etc. **3.** uninjured or undamaged. **4.** healthy. **5.** having no fractional or decimal part; integral: *a whole number.* **6.** designating a relationship by descent from the same parents; full: *whole brothers.* **7. out of whole cloth.** *U.S. & Canad. inf.* entirely without a factual basis. ~*adv.* **8.** in an undivided or unbroken piece: *to swallow a plum whole.* ~*n.* **9.** all the parts, elements, etc., of a thing. **10.** an assemblage of parts viewed together as a unit. **11.** a thing complete in itself. **12. as a whole.** considered altogether; completely. **13. on the whole. a.** taking all things into consideration. **b.** in general. [OE *hāl, hǣl*] —'**wholeness** *n.*

whole blood *n.* blood for transfusion from which none of the elements has been removed.

wholefood ('həʊl,fuːd) *n.* (*sometimes pl.*) **a.** food that has been refined or processed as little as possible and is eaten in its natural state, such as brown rice, wholemeal flour, etc. **b.** (*as modifier*): *a wholefood restaurant.*

wholehearted (,həʊl'hɑːtɪd) *adj.* done, acted, given, etc., with total sincerity, enthusiasm, or commitment. —,**whole'heartedly** *adv.*

whole hog *n. Sl.* the whole or total extent (esp. in **go the whole hog**).

wholemeal ('həʊl,miːl) *adj. Brit.* (of flour, bread, etc.) made from the entire wheat kernel. Also called (esp. U.S. and Canad.): **whole-wheat.**

whole milk *n.* milk from which no constituent has been removed.

whole note *n.* the usual U.S. and Canad. name for **semibreve.**

whole number *n.* **1.** an integer. **2.** a natural number.

wholesale ('həʊl,seɪl) *n.* **1.** the business of selling goods to retailers in larger quantities than they are sold to final consumers but in smaller quantities than they are purchased from manufacturers. Cf. **retail** (sense 1). ~*adj.* **2.** of or engaged in such business. **3.** made, done, etc., on a large scale or without discrimination. ~*adv.* **4.** on a large scale or without discrimination. ~*vb.* **5.** to sell (goods) at wholesale. —'**whole,saler** *n.*

wholesale price index *n.* an indicator of price changes in the wholesale market.

wholesome ('həʊlsəm) *adj.* **1.** conducive to health or physical wellbeing. **2.** conducive to moral wellbeing. **3.** characteristic or suggestive of health or wellbeing, esp. in appearance. [C12: from WHOLE (healthy) + -SOME[1]] —'**wholesomely** *adv.* —'**wholesomeness** *n.*

whole tone *or U.S. & Canad.* **whole step** *n.* an interval of two semitones. Often shortened to **tone.**

whole-tone scale *n.* either of two scales produced by commencing on one of any two notes a chromatic semitone apart and proceeding upwards or downwards in whole tones for an octave.

whole-wheat *adj.* another term (esp. U.S. and Canad.) for **wholemeal.**

who'll (huːl) *contraction of* who will *or* who shall.

wholly ('həʊllɪ) *adv.* **1.** completely, totally, or entirely. **2.** without exception; exclusively.

whom (huːm) *pron.* the objective form of *who*, used when *who* is not the subject of its own clause: *whom did you say you had seen? he can't remember whom he saw.* [OE *hwām*, dative of *hwā* who]

▷**Usage.** In formal English, careful writers always use *whom* when the objective form of *who* is required. In informal contexts, however, many careful speakers consider *whom* to be unnatural, esp. at the beginning of a sentence: *who were you looking for?* Careful speakers usually prefer *whom* where it closely follows a preposition: *to whom did you give it?* as contrasted with *who did you give it to?*

whomever (huːm'evə) *pron.* the objective form of *whoever: I'll hire whomever I can find.*

whoop (wuːp) *vb.* **1.** to utter (speech) with loud cries, as of excitement. **2.** (huːp). *Med.* to cough convulsively with a crowing sound. **3.** (of certain birds) to utter (a hooting cry). **4.** (*tr.*) to urge on or call with or as if with whoops. **5.** (wʊp, wuːp). **whoop it up.** *Inf.* **a.** to indulge in a noisy celebration. **b.** *Chiefly U.S.* to arouse enthusiasm. ~*n.* **6.** a loud cry, esp. one expressing excitement. **7.** (huːp). *Med.* the convulsive crowing sound made during whooping cough. [C14: imit.]

whoopee *Inf.* ~*interj.* (wʊ'piː). **1.** an exclamation of joy, excitement, etc. ~*n.* ('wʊpiː). **2. make whoopee. a.** to engage in noisy merrymaking. **b.** to make love.

whoopee cushion *n.* a joke cushion that emits a sound like the breaking of wind when someone sits on it.

whooper *or* **whooper swan** ('wuːpə) *n.* a large Old World swan having a black bill with a yellow base and a noisy whooping cry.

whooping cough ('huːpɪŋ) *n.* an acute infectious disease characterized by coughing spasms that end with a shrill crowing sound on inspiration. Technical name: **pertussis.**

whoops (wʊps) *interj.* an exclamation of surprise or of apology.

whoosh *or* **woosh** (wʊʃ) *n.* **1.** a hissing or rushing sound. ~*vb.* **2.** (*intr.*) to make or move with such a sound.

whop (wɒp) *Inf.* ~*vb.* **whopping, whopped. 1.** (*tr.*) to strike, beat, or thrash. **2.** (*tr.*) to defeat utterly. **3.** (*intr.*) to drop or fall. ~*n.* **4.** a heavy blow or the sound made by such a blow. [C14: var. of *wap*, ? imit.]

whopper ('wɒpə) *n. Inf.* **1.** anything uncommonly large of its kind. **2.** a big lie. [C18: from WHOP]

whopping ('wɒpɪŋ) *adj. Inf.* uncommonly large.

whore (hɔː) *n.* **1.** a prostitute or promiscuous woman: often a term of abuse. ~*vb.* (*intr.*) **2.** to be or act as a prostitute. **3.** (of a man) to have promiscuous sexual relations, esp. with prostitutes. **4.** (often foll. by *after*) to seek that which is immoral, idolatrous, etc. [OE *hōre*] —'**whoredom** *n.* —'**whorish** *adj.*

whorehouse ('hɔː,haʊs) *n.* another word for **brothel.**

whoremonger ('hɔː,mʌŋɡə) *n.* a person who consorts with whores; lecher. Also called: **whoremaster.** —'**whore,mongery** *n.*

whoreson ('hɔːsən) *Arch.* ~*n.* **1.** a bastard. **2.** a scoundrel; wretch. ~*adj.* **3.** vile or hateful.

Whorf (wɔːf) *n.* **Benjamin Lee.** (1897–1943), U.S. linguist, who argued that human language determines perception.

whorl (wɜːl) *n.* **1.** *Bot.* a radial arrangement of petals, stamens, leaves, etc., around a stem. **2.** *Zool.* a single turn in a spiral shell. **3.** anything shaped like a coil. [C15: prob. var. of *wherville* whirl, infl. by Du. *worvel*] —**whorled** *adj.*

whortleberry ('wɜːtəl,berɪ) *n., pl.* -**ries. 1.** Also called: **bilberry, blaeberry, huckleberry.** a small Eurasian ericaceous shrub with greenish-pink flowers and edible sweet blackish berries. **2.** the fruit of this shrub. **3. bog whortleberry.** a related plant of mountain regions, having pink flowers and black fruits. [C16: SW English dialect var. of *hurtleberry*, from ?]

who's (huːz) *contraction of* who is *or* who has.

whose (huːz) *determiner.* **1. a.** of who? belonging to who? used in direct and indirect questions: *I told him whose fault it was; whose car is this?* **b.** (*as pron.*): *whose is that?* **2.** of who; of which: used as a relative pronoun: *a house whose windows are broken; a man whose reputation has suffered.* [OE *hwǣs*, genitive of *hwā* who & *hwæt* what]

▷**Usage.** Since *whose* is the possessive of both *who* and *which*, it is quite acceptable to use *whose* of things as well as of people in careful usage: *these are the houses whose foundations are unsteady; this is the man whose leg was broken.*

whoso ('huːsəʊ) *pron.* an archaic word for **whoever.**

whosoever (,huːsəʊ'evə) *pron.* an archaic or formal word for **whoever.**

who's who *n.* a book or list containing the names and short biographies of famous people.

why (waɪ) *adv.* **1. a.** for what reason?: *why are you here?* **b.** (*used in indirect questions*): *tell me why you're here.* ~*pron.* **2.** for or because of which: *there is no reason why he shouldn't come.* ~*n., pl.* **whys. 3.** (*usually pl.*) the cause of something (esp. in **the whys and wherefores**). ~*interj.* **4.** an introductory expression of surprise, indignation, etc.: *why, don't be silly!* [OE *hwī*]

Whyalla (waɪ'ælə) *n.* a port in S South Australia, on Spencer Gulf: iron and steel and shipbuilding industries. Pop.: 27 109 (1986).

whydah *or* **whidah** ('wɪdə) *n.* any of various predominantly black African weaverbirds, the males of which grow very long tail feathers in the breeding season. Also called: **whydah bird, whidah bird, widow bird.** [C18: after a town in Benin in W Africa]

WI *abbrev. for:* **1.** West Indian. **2.** West Indies. **3.** Wisconsin. **4.** (in Britain) Women's Institute.

Wicca *or* **wicca** ('wɪkə) *n.* the cult or practice of witchcraft. [C20 revival of OE *wicca* witch]

Wichita ('wɪtʃɪˌtɔː) *n.* a city in S Kansas, on the Arkansas River: the largest city in the state; two universities. Pop.: 288 070 (1986 est.).

wick[1] (wɪk) *n.* **1.** a cord or band of loosely twisted or woven fibres, as in a candle, that supplies fuel to a flame by capillary action. **2. get on (someone's) wick.** *Brit. sl.* to cause irritation to (someone). [OE *weoce*]

wick[2] (wɪk) *n. Arch.* a village or hamlet. [OE *wīc*; rel. to -*wich* in place names]

Wick (wɪk) *n.* a town in N Scotland, in the Highland region, at the head of **Wick Bay** (an inlet of the North Sea). Pop.: 7933 (1981).

wicked ('wɪkɪd) *adj.* **1. a.** morally bad. **b.** (*as collective n.*; preceded by *the*): *the wicked.* **2.** mischievous or roguish in a playful way: *a wicked grin.* **3.** causing injury or harm. **4.** troublesome, unpleasant, or offensive. **5.** *Sl.* very good. [C13: from dialect *wick*, from OE *wicca* sorcerer, *wicce* witch] — **'wickedly** *adv.* — **'wickedness** *n.*

wicker ('wɪkə) *n.* **1.** a slender flexible twig or shoot, esp. of willow. **2.** short for **wickerwork.** ~*adj.* **3.** made of, consisting of, or constructed from wicker. [C14: from ON]

wickerwork ('wɪkə,wɜːk) *n.* **a.** a material consisting of woven wicker. **b.** (*as modifier*): *a wickerwork chair.*

wicket ('wɪkɪt) *n.* **1.** a small door or gate, esp. one that is near to or part of a larger one. **2.** *Chiefly U.S.* a small window or opening in a door, esp. one fitted with a grating or glass pane. **3.** a small sluicegate. **4. a.** *Cricket.* either of two constructions, 22 yards apart, consisting of three stumps stuck in the ground with two wooden bails resting on top, at which the batsman stands. **b.** the strip of ground between these. **c.** a batsman's turn at batting or the period during which two batsmen bat: *a third-wicket partnership.* **d.** the act or instance of a batsman being got out: *the bowler took six wickets.* **5. keep wicket.** to act as a wicketkeeper. **6. on a good, sticky,** etc., **wicket.** *Inf.* in an advantageous, awkward, etc., situation. [C18: from OF *wiket*]

wicketkeeper ('wɪkɪt,kiːpə) *n. Cricket.* the player on the fielding side positioned directly behind the wicket.

wickiup, wikiup, *or* **wickyup** ('wɪki,ʌp) *n. U.S. & Canad.* a crude shelter made of brushwood or grass and having an oval frame, esp. of a kind used by nomadic Indians now in the Oklahoma area. [C19: of Amerind origin]

Wickliffe *or* **Wiclif** ('wɪklɪf) *n.* variant spellings of (John) **Wycliffe.**

Wicklow ('wɪkləʊ) *n.* **1.** a county of E Ireland, in Leinster province on the Irish Sea: consists of a coastal strip rising inland to the **Wicklow Mountains**; mainly agricultural, with several resorts. County town: Wicklow. Pop.: 94 482 (1986). Area: 2025 sq. km (782 sq. miles). **2.** a port in E Ireland, county town of Co. Wicklow. Pop.: 5178 (1981).

widdershins ('wɪdə,ʃɪnz) *adv. Chiefly Scot.* a variant spelling of **withershins.**

wide (waɪd) *adj.* **1.** having a great extent from side to side. **2.** spacious or extensive. **3. a.** (*postpositive*) having a specified extent, esp. from side to side: *two yards wide.* **b.** (*in combination*): extending throughout: *nationwide.* **4.** remote from the desired point, mark, etc.: *your guess is wide of the mark.* **5.** (of eyes) opened fully. **6.** loose, full, or roomy: *wide trousers.* **7.** exhibiting a considerable spread: *a wide variation.* **8.** *Phonetics.* another word for **lax** (sense 4) or **open** (sense 32). **9.** *Brit. sl.* unscrupulous and astute: *a wide boy.* ~*adv.* **10.** over an extensive area: *to travel far and wide.* **11.** to the full extent: *he opened the door wide.* **12.** far from the desired point, mark, etc. ~*n.* **13.** (in cricket) a bowled ball that is outside the batsman's reach and scores a run for the batting side. [OE *wīd*] — **'widely** *adv.* — **'wideness** *n.* — **'widish** *adj.*

wide-angle lens *n.* a lens system on a camera that has a small focal length and therefore can cover an angle of view of 60° or more.

wide-awake *adj.* (**wide awake** *when postpositive*). **1.** fully awake. **2.** keen, alert, or observant. ~*n.* **3.** Also called: **wide-awake hat.** a hat with a low crown and very wide brim.

wide-body *adj.* (of an aircraft) having a wide fuselage, esp. wide enough to contain three rows of seats abreast.

wide-eyed *adj.* innocent or credulous.

widen ('waɪdᵊn) *vb.* to make or become wide or wider. — **'widener** *n.*

wide-open *adj.* (**wide open** *when postpositive*). **1.** open to the full extent. **2.** (*postpositive*) exposed to attack; vulnerable. **3.** uncertain as to outcome. **4.** *U.S. inf.* (of a town or city) lax in the enforcement of certain laws, esp. those relating to the sale of alcohol, gambling, etc.

widespread ('waɪd,sprɛd) *adj.* **1.** extending over a wide area. **2.** accepted by or occurring among many people.

widgeon ('wɪdʒən) *n.* a variant spelling of **wigeon.**

widget ('wɪdʒɪt) *n. Inf.* any small mechanism or device, the name of which is unknown or temporarily forgotten. [C20: changed from GADGET]

Widnes ('wɪdnɪs) *n.* a town in NW England, in N Cheshire on the River Mersey: chemical industry. Pop.: 54 900 (1983 est.).

widow ('wɪdəʊ) *n.* **1.** a woman whose husband has died, esp. one who has not remarried. **2.** (*with a modifier*) *Inf.* a woman whose husband frequently leaves her alone while he indulges in a sport, etc.: *a golf widow.* **3.** *Printing.* a short line at the end of a paragraph, esp. one that occurs as the top line of a page or column. **4.** (in some card games) an additional hand or set of cards exposed on the table. ~*vb.* (*tr.; usually passive*) **5.** to cause to become a widow. **6.** to deprive of something valued. [OE *widuwe*] — **'widowhood** *n.*

widow bird *n.* another name for **whydah.**

widower ('wɪdəʊə) *n.* a man whose wife has died and who has not remarried.

widow's cruse *n.* an endless or unfailing source of supply. [allusion to I Kings 17:16]

widow's mite *n.* a small contribution by a person who has very little. [allusion to Mark 12:43]

widow's peak *n.* a V-shaped point in the hairline in the middle of the forehead. [from the belief that it presaged early widowhood]

width (wɪdθ) *n.* **1.** the linear extent or measurement of something from side to side. **2.** the state or fact of being wide. **3.** a piece or section of something at its full extent from side to side: *a width of cloth.* **4.** the distance across a rectangular swimming bath, as opposed to its length. [C17: from WIDE + -TH[1], analogous to BREADTH]

Wieland[1] ('viːlant) *n.* the German name for **Wayland.**

Wieland[2] (*German* 'viːlant) *n.* **Christoph Martin** ('krɪstɔf 'martiːn). 1733–1813, German writer, noted esp. for his verse epic *Oberon* (1780).

wield (wiːld) *vb.* (*tr.*) **1.** to handle or use (a weapon, tool, etc.). **2.** to exert or maintain (power or authority). [OE *wieldan, wealdan*] — **'wieldable** *adj.* — **'wielder** *n.*

wieldy ('wiːldɪ) *adj.* **wieldier, wieldiest.** easily handled, used, or managed.

Wien[1] (viːn) *n.* the German name for **Vienna.**

Wien[2] (*German* viːn) *n.* **Wilhelm** ('vɪlhɛlm). 1864–1928, German physicist, who studied black-body radiation: Nobel prize for physics 1911.

wiener ('wiːnə) *or* **wienerwurst** ('wiːnə,wɜːst) *n. U.S. & Canad.* a kind of smoked sausage, similar to a frankfurter. [C20: shortened from G *Wiener Wurst* Viennese sausage]

Wiener ('wiːnə) *n.* **Norbert** ('nɔːbət). 1894–1964, U.S. mathematician, who developed the concept of cybernetics.

Wiener Neustadt (*German* 'viːnər 'nɔyʃtat) *n.* a city in E Austria, in Lower Austria. Pop.: 35 050 (1981).

Wiener schnitzel ('viːnə 'ʃnɪtsəl) *n.* a thin escalope of veal, fried in breadcrumbs. [G: Viennese cutlet]

Wiesbaden (*German* 'viːsbaːdən) *n.* a city in W West Germany, capital of Hesse state: a spa resort since Roman times. Pop.: 266 700 (1986). Latin name: **Aquae Mattiacorum** ('ækwiː ,mætjə'kɔʊrəm).

Wiesel ('viːzəl) *n.* **Elie.** born 1928, U.S. human rights campaigner: noted esp. for his documentaries of wartime atrocities against the Jews; Nobel peace prize 1986.

wife (waɪf) *n., pl.* **wives. 1.** a man's partner in marriage; a married woman. Related adj.: **uxorial. 2.** an archaic or dialect word for **woman. 3. take to wife.** to marry (a woman). [OE *wīf*] — **'wifehood** *n.* — **'wifely** *adj.*

wig (wɪg) *n.* **1.** an artificial head of hair, either human or synthetic, worn to disguise baldness, as part of a theatrical or ceremonial dress, as a disguise, or for adornment.

~*vb.* **wigging, wigged.** (*tr.*) **2.** *Brit. sl.* to berate severely. [C17: shortened from PERIWIG] —**wigged** *adj.* —'**wigless** *adj.*

Wigan ('wɪɡən) *n.* an industrial town in NW England, in Greater Manchester: coal-mining centre since the 14th century. Pop.: 79 535 (1981).

wigeon *or* **widgeon** ('wɪdʒən) *n.* **1.** a Eurasian duck of marshes, swamps, etc., the male of which has a reddish-brown head and chest and grey-and-white back and wings. **2. American wigeon.** Also called: **baldpate.** a similar bird of North America, the male of which has a white crown. [C16: from ?]

wigging ('wɪɡɪŋ) *n. Brit. sl.* a reprimand.

wiggle ('wɪɡəl) *vb.* **1.** to move or cause to move with jerky movements, esp. from side to side. ~*n.* **2.** the act of wiggling. [C13: from MLow G, MDu. *wiggelen*] —'**wiggler** *n.* —'**wiggly** *adj.*

wight (waɪt) *n. Arch.* a human being. [OE *wiht*; rel. to OFrisian *āwet* something]

Wight (waɪt) *n.* **Isle of.** an island and county of S England in the English Channel. Administrative centre: Newport. Pop.: 124 600 (1986 est.). Area: 380 sq. km (147 sq. miles).

Wigner ('wɪɡnə) *n.* **Eugene Paul.** born 1902, U.S. physicist, born in Hungary. He is noted for his contributions to nuclear physics: shared the Nobel prize for physics 1963.

Wigtownshire ('wɪɡtən,ʃɪə, -ʃə) *n.* (until 1975) a county of SW Scotland, now part of Dumfries and Galloway region.

wigwag ('wɪɡ,wæɡ) *vb.* **-wagging, -wagged. 1.** to move (something) back and forth. **2.** to communicate with (someone) by means of a flag semaphore. ~*n.* **3. a.** a system of communication by flag semaphore. **b.** the message signalled. [C16: from obs. *wig*, prob. short for WIGGLE + WAG[1]] —'**wig,wagger** *n.*

wigwam ('wɪɡ,wæm) *n.* **1.** any dwelling of the North American Indians, esp. one made of bark, rushes, or skins spread over a set of arched poles lashed together. **2.** a similar structure for children. [from *wĭkwām* (of Amerind origin), lit.: their abode]

Wilberforce ('wɪlbə,fɔːs) *n.* **William.** 1759–1833, English politician and philanthropist, whose efforts secured the abolition of the slave trade (1807) and of slavery (1833) in the British Empire.

wilco ('wɪlkəʊ) *interj.* an expression in signalling, telecommunications, etc., indicating that a message just received will be complied with. [C20: abbrev. for *I will comply*]

wild (waɪld) *adj.* **1.** (of animals) living independently of man; not domesticated or tame. **2.** (of plants) growing in a natural state; not cultivated. **3.** uninhabited; desolate: *a wild stretch of land.* **4.** living in a savage or uncivilized way: *wild tribes.* **5.** lacking restraint or control: *wild merriment.* **6.** of great violence: *a wild storm.* **7.** disorderly or chaotic: *wild talk.* **8.** dishevelled; untidy: *wild hair.* **9.** in a state of extreme emotional intensity: *wild with anger.* **10.** reckless: *wild speculations.* **11.** random: *a wild guess.* **12.** (*postpositive*; foll. by *about*) *Inf.* intensely enthusiastic: *I'm wild about my new boyfriend.* **13.** (of a card, such as a joker in some games) able to be given any value the holder pleases. **14. wild and woolly. a.** rough; barbarous. **b.** (of theories, plans, etc.) not fully thought out. ~*adv.* **15.** in a wild manner. **16. run wild. a.** to grow without cultivation or care: *the garden has run wild.* **b.** to behave without restraint: *he has let his children run wild.* ~*n.* **17.** (*often pl.*) a desolate or uninhabited region. **18. the wild. a.** a free natural state of living. **b.** the wilderness. [OE *wilde*] —'**wildish** *adj.* —'**wildly** *adv.* —'**wildness** *n.*

wild boar *n.* a wild pig of parts of Europe and central Asia, having a pale grey to black coat and prominent tusks.

wild brier *n.* another name for **wild rose.**

wild carrot *n.* an umbelliferous plant of temperate regions, having clusters of white flowers and hooked fruits. Also called: **Queen Anne's lace.**

wildcat ('waɪld,kæt) *n., pl.* **-cats** *or* **-cat. 1.** a wild European cat that resembles the domestic tabby but is larger and has a bushy tail. **2.** any of various other felines, such as the lynx and the caracal. **3.** *U.S. & Canad.* another name for **bobcat. 4.** *Inf.* a savage or aggressive person. **5.** *Chiefly U.S. & Canad.* an exploratory drilling for petroleum or natural gas. **6.** (*modifier*) *Chiefly U.S.* involving risk, esp. financially or commercially unsound: *a wildcat project.* ~*vb.* **-catting, -catted. 7.** (*intr.*) *Chiefly U.S. &*

Canad. to drill for petroleum or natural gas in an area having no known reserves. —'**wild,catter** *n.* —'**wild-,catting** *n., adj.*

wildcat strike *n.* a strike begun by workers spontaneously or without union approval.

wild cherry *n.* another name for **gean.**

wild dog *n.* another name for **dingo.**

Wilde (waɪld) *n.* **Oscar (Fingal O'Flahertie Wills).** 1854–1900, Irish writer and wit, famous for such plays as *Lady Windermere's Fan* (1892) and *The Importance of being Earnest* (1895). *The Picture of Dorian Grey* (1891) is a macabre novel about a hedonist and *The Ballad of Reading Gaol* (1898) relates to his experiences in prison while serving a two-year sentence for homosexuality.

wildebeest ('wɪldɪ,biːst, 'vɪl-) *n., pl.* **-beests** *or* **-beest.** another name for **gnu.** [C19: from Afrik., lit.: wild beast]

wilder ('wɪldə) *vb. Arch.* **1.** to lead or be led astray. **2.** to bewilder or become bewildered. [C17: from ?]

Wilder ('waɪldə) *n.* **1. Billy,** real name *Samuel Wilder.* born 1906, U.S. film director and screenwriter, born in Austria. His films include *Double Indemnity* (1944), *The Lost Weekend* (1945), *Sunset Boulevard* (1950), *The Seven Year Itch* (1955), *Some Like it Hot* (1959), and *The Apartment* (1960). **2. Thornton.** 1897–1975 U.S. novelist and dramatist. His works include the novel *The Bridge of San Luis Rey* (1927) and the play *The Skin of Our Teeth* (1942).

wilderness ('wɪldənɪs) *n.* **1.** a wild uninhabited uncultivated region. **2.** any desolate area. **3.** a confused mass or collection. **4. a voice (crying) in the wilderness.** a person, group, etc., making a suggestion or plea that is ignored. [OE *wildēornes*, from *wildēor* wild beast + -NESS]

Wilderness ('wɪldənɪs) *n.* **the.** the barren regions to the south and east of Palestine, esp. those in which the Israelites wandered before entering the Promised Land and in which Christ fasted for 40 days and nights.

wild-eyed *adj.* glaring in an angry, distracted, or wild manner.

wildfire ('waɪld,faɪə) *n.* **1.** a highly flammable material, such as Greek fire, formerly used in warfare. **2. a.** a raging and uncontrollable fire. **b.** anything that is disseminated quickly (esp. in **spread like wildfire**). **3.** another name for **will-o'-the-wisp.**

wild flower *n.* **1.** any flowering plant that grows in an uncultivated state. **2.** the flower of such a plant.

wildfowl ('waɪld,faʊl) *n.* **1.** any bird that is hunted by man, esp. any duck or similar aquatic bird. **2.** such birds collectively. —'**wild,fowler** *n.* —'**wild,fowling** *adj., n.*

wild-goose chase *n.* an absurd or hopeless pursuit, as of something unattainable.

wilding ('waɪldɪŋ) *n.* **1.** an uncultivated plant or a cultivated plant that has become wild. **2.** a wild animal. ~Also called: **wildling.**

wildlife ('waɪld,laɪf) *n.* wild animals and plants collectively: a term used esp. of fauna.

wild pansy *n.* a Eurasian plant of the violet family having purple, yellow, and pale mauve spurred flowers. Also called: **heartsease, love-in-idleness.**

wild parsley *n.* any of various uncultivated umbelliferous plants that resemble parsley.

wild rice *n.* an aquatic North American grass with dark-coloured edible grain.

wild rose *n.* any of numerous roses, such as the dogrose and sweetbrier, that grow wild and have flowers with only one whorl of petals.

wild rubber *n.* rubber obtained from uncultivated rubber trees.

wild silk *n.* **1.** silk produced by wild silkworms. **2.** a fabric made from this, or from short fibres of silk designed to imitate it.

wild type *n. Biol.* the typical form of a species of organism resulting from breeding under natural conditions.

Wild West *n.* the western U.S. during its settlement, esp. with reference to its frontier lawlessness.

wildwood ('waɪld,wʊd) *n. Arch.* a wood or forest growing in a natural uncultivated state.

wile (waɪl) *n.* **1.** trickery, cunning, or craftiness. **2.** (*usually pl.*) an artful or seductive trick or ploy. ~*vb.* **3.** (*tr.*) to lure, beguile, or entice. [C12: from ON *vel* craft]

wilful *or U.S.* **willful** ('wɪlfʊl) *adj.* **1.** intent on having one's own way; headstrong or obstinate. **2.** intentional: *wilful murder.* —'**wilfully** *or U.S.* '**willfully** *adv.* —'**wilfulness** *or U.S.* '**willfulness** *n.*

Wilhelm I ('vɪlhɛlm) *n*. the German name of **William I** (sense 3).

Wilhelm II *n*. the German name of **William II** (sense 2).

Wilhelmina I (ˌwɪləˈmiːnə; *Dutch* wɪlhɛlˈmiːnaː) *n*. 1880–1962, queen of the Netherlands from 1890 until her abdication (1948) in favour of her daughter Juliana.

Wilhelmshaven (*German* vɪlhɛlmsˈhaːfən) *n*. a port and resort in N West Germany, in Lower Saxony: founded in 1853; was the chief German North Sea naval base until 1945; a major oil port. Pop.: 98 200 (1984 est.).

Wilhelmstrasse (*German* ˈvɪlhɛlmʃtraːsə) *n*. **1.** a street in the centre of Berlin, where the German foreign office and other government buildings were situated until 1945. **2.** Germany's ministry of foreign affairs until 1945.

Wilkes (wɪlks) *n*. **1. Charles.** 1798–1877, U.S. explorer of Antarctica. **2. John.** 1727–97, English politician, who was expelled from the House of Commons and outlawed for writing scurrilous articles about the government. He became a champion of parliamentary reform.

Wilkes Land *n*. a region in Antarctica south of Australia, on the Indian Ocean.

Wilkins ('wɪlkɪnz) *n*. **1.** Sir **George Hubert.** 1888–1958, Australian polar explorer and aviator. **2. Maurice Hugh Frederick.** born 1916, British biochemist, born in New Zealand. With Crick and Watson, he shared the Nobel prize 1962 for his work on the structure of DNA.

will[1] (wɪl) *vb. past* **would.** (takes an infinitive without *to* or an implied infinitive) used as an auxiliary. **1.** (esp. with *you, he, she, it, they,* or a noun as subject) to make the future tense. Cf. **shall** (sense 1). **2.** to express resolution on the part of the speaker: *I will buy that radio if it's the last thing I do.* **3.** to indicate willingness or desire: *will you help me with this problem?* **4.** to express commands: *you will report your findings to me tomorrow.* **5.** to express ability: *this rope will support a load.* **6.** to express probability or expectation: *that will be Jim telephoning.* **7.** to express customary practice or inevitability: *boys will be boys.* **8.** (*with the infinitive always implied*) to express desire: usually in polite requests: *stay if you will.* **9. what you will.** whatever you like. [OE *willan*]

▷ **Usage.** See at **shall.**

will[2] (wɪl) *n*. **1.** the faculty of conscious and deliberate choice of action. Related adj.: **voluntary. 2.** the act or an instance of asserting a choice. **3. a.** the declaration of a person's wishes regarding the disposal of his property after his death. **b.** a document in which such wishes are expressed. **4.** desire; wish. **5.** determined intention: *where there's a will there's a way.* **6.** disposition towards others: *he bears you no ill will.* **7. at will.** at one's own desire or choice. **8. with a will.** heartily; energetically. **9. with the best will in the world.** even with the best of intentions. ~*vb.* (*mainly tr.; often takes a clause as object or an infinitive*) **10.** (*also intr.*) to exercise the faculty of volition in an attempt to accomplish (something): *he willed his wife's recovery from her illness.* **11.** to give (property) by will to a person, society, etc.: *he willed his art collection to the nation.* **12.** (*also intr.*) to order or decree: *the king wills that you shall die.* **13.** to choose or prefer: *wander where you will.* [OE *willa*] —'**willer** *n*.

willed (wɪld) *adj*. (*in combination*) having a will as specified: *weak-willed.*

Willemstad (*Dutch* ˈwɪləmstat) *n*. the capital of the Netherlands Antilles, a port on the SW coast of Curaçao: important for refining Venezuelan oil. Pop.: 50 000 (1981).

willet ('wɪlɪt) *n*. a large American shore bird having a grey plumage with black-and-white wings. [C19: imit. of its call]

willful ('wɪlfʊl) *adj*. the U.S. spelling of **wilful.**

William ('wɪljəm) *n*. known as *William the Lion.* ?1143–1214, king of Scotland (1165–1214).

William I *n*. **1.** known as *William the Conqueror.* ?1027–1087, duke of Normandy (1035–87) and king of England (1066–87). He claimed to have been promised the English crown by Edward the Confessor, after whose death he disputed the succession of Harold II, invading England in 1066 and defeating Harold at Hastings. The conquest of England resulted in the introduction to England of many Norman customs, esp. feudalism. In 1085 he ordered the Domesday Book to be compiled. **2.** known as *William the Silent.* 1533–84, prince of Orange and count of Nassau: led the revolt of the Netherlands against Spain (1568–

76) and became first stadholder of the United Provinces of the Netherlands (1579–84); assassinated. **3.** German name *Wilhelm I.* 1797–1888, king of Prussia (1861–88) and first emperor of Germany (1871–88).

William II *n*. **1.** known as *William Rufus.* ?1056–1100, king of England (1087–1100); the son of William the Conqueror. He was killed by an arrow while hunting in the New Forest. **2.** German name *Kaiser Wilhelm.* 1859–1941, German emperor and king of Prussia (1888–1918): asserted Germany's claim to world leadership; forced to abdicate at the end of World War I.

William III *n*. known as *William of Orange.* 1650–1702, stadholder of the Netherlands (1672–1702) and king of Great Britain and Ireland (1689–1702). He was invited by opponents of James II to accept the British throne (1688) and ruled jointly with his wife Mary II (James' daughter) until her death in 1694.

William IV *n*. known as the *Sailor King.* 1765–1837, king of the United Kingdom (1830–37), succeeding his brother George IV; the third son of George III.

William of Malmesbury ('maːmzbəri, -brɪ) *n*. ?1090–?1143, English monk and chronicler, whose *Gesta regum Anglorum* and *Historia novella* are valuable sources for English history to 1142.

Williams ('wɪljəmz) *n*. **1. Hank,** real name *Hiram Williams.* 1923–53, U.S. country singer and songwriter. His songs (all 1948–52) include "Jambalaya", "Your Cheatin' Heart", and "Why Don't you Love me (like you Used to Do?)". **2. John.** born 1941, English classical guitarist. **3. J(ohn) P(eter) R(hys).** born 1949, Welsh Rugby Union player. A fullback, he played for Wales (1969–79; 1980–81) and the British Lions (1971–77). **4. Ralph Vaughan.** See (Ralph) **Vaughan Williams. 5. Tennessee.** real name *Thomas Lanier Williams.* 1912–83, U.S. dramatist. His plays include *The Glass Menagerie* (1944), *A Streetcar Named Desire* (1947), *Cat on a Hot Tin Roof* (1955), and *Night of the Iguana* (1961). **6. William Carlos** ('kaːləs). 1883–1963, U.S. poet, who formulated the poetic concept "no ideas but in things". His works include *Paterson* (1946–58), which explores the daily life of a man living in a modern city, and the prose work *In the American Grain* (1925).

Williamsburg ('wɪljəmzˌbɜːg) *n*. a city in SE Virginia: the capital of Virginia (1693–1779); the restoration of large sections of the colonial city was begun in 1926. Pop.: 9870 (1980).

Williamson ('wɪljəmsən) *n*. **Malcolm.** born 1931, Australian composer, living in Britain: Master of the Queen's Music since 1975. His works include operas and music for children.

William the Conqueror *n*. See **William I** (sense 1).

willie *or* **willy** ('wɪlɪ) *n*. *Brit. inf.* a childish or jocular term for **penis.**

willies ('wɪlɪz) *pl. n.* **the.** *Sl.* nervousness, jitters, or fright (esp. in **give** (*or* **get**) **the willies**). [C20: from ?]

willing ('wɪlɪŋ) *adj*. **1.** favourably disposed or inclined; ready. **2.** cheerfully compliant. **3.** done, given, accepted, etc., freely or voluntarily. —'**willingly** *adv*. —'**willingness** *n*.

Willis ('wɪlɪs) *n*. **Ted.** Baron Willis of Chislehurst. born 1918, British author. His works include the play *Hot Summer Night* (1959) and the novel *Death May Surprise Us* (1974).

williwaw ('wɪlɪˌwɔː) *n*. *U.S. & Canad.* **1.** a sudden strong gust of cold wind blowing offshore from a mountainous coast, as in the Strait of Magellan. **2.** a state of great turmoil. [C19: from ?]

will-o'-the-wisp (ˌwɪlədə'wɪsp) *n*. **1.** Also called: **friar's lantern, ignis fatuus, jack-o'-lantern.** a pale flame or phosphorescence sometimes seen over marshy ground at night. It is believed to be due to the spontaneous combustion of methane originating from decomposing organic matter. **2.** a person or thing that is elusive or allures and misleads. [C17: from *Will,* short for *William* + *wisp,* in former sense of a twist of hay burning as a torch]

willow ('wɪləʊ) *n*. **1.** any of a large genus of trees and shrubs, such as the weeping willow and osiers of N temperate regions, which have graceful flexible branches and flowers in catkins. **2.** the whitish wood of certain of these trees. **3.** something made of willow wood, such as a cricket bat. [OE *welig*]

willowherb ('wɪləu,hɜːb) *n.* **1.** any of various temperate and arctic plants having narrow leaves and terminal clusters of pink, purplish, or white flowers. **2.** short for **rosebay willowherb** (see **rosebay**).

willow pattern *n.* **a.** a pattern incorporating a willow tree, river, bridge, and figures, typically in blue on a white ground, used on porcelain, etc. **b.** (*as modifier*): *a willow-pattern plate*.

Willow South *n.* a city in S Alaska, about 113 km (70 miles) northwest of Anchorage: chosen as the site of the projected new state capital in 1976.

willowy ('wɪləuɪ) *adj.* **1.** slender and graceful. **2.** flexible or pliant. **3.** covered or shaded with willows.

willpower ('wɪl,pauə) *n.* **1.** the ability to control oneself and determine one's actions. **2.** firmness of will.

Wills (wɪlz) *n.* **1. Helen**, married name *Helen Moody*. born 1905, U.S. tennis player. She was Wimbledon singles champion a record eight times between 1927 and 1938. She also won the U.S. title seven times and the French title four times. **2. William John.** 1834–61, English explorer: Robert Burke's deputy in an expedition on which both men died after crossing Australia from north to south for the first time.

willy[1] ('wɪlɪ) *n., pl.* -**lies.** *Brit. inf.* a variant spelling of **willie**.

willy[2] ('wɪlɪ) *n. Austral. sl.* a sudden loss of temper; fit: *to throw a willy.*

willy-nilly ('wɪlɪ'nɪlɪ) *adv.* **1.** whether desired or not. ~*adj.* **2.** occurring or taking place whether desired or not. [OE *wile hē, nyle hē,* lit.: will he or will he not]

willy wagtail *n.* a black-and-white flycatcher found in Australasia and parts of Asia, having white feathers over the brows.

willy-willy ('wɪlɪ,wɪlɪ) *n., pl.* -**willies.** *Austral.* a small sometimes violent upward-spiralling cyclone or dust storm. [from Abor.]

Wilmington ('wɪlmɪŋtən) *n.* a port in N Delaware, on the Delaware River: industrial centre. Pop.: 70 195 (1980).

Wilno ('viːlnɔ) *n.* the Polish name for **Vilnius**.

Wilson ('wɪlsən) *n.* **1. Alexander.** 1766–1813, Scottish ornithologist in the U.S. **2. Sir Angus (Frank Johnstone).** born 1913, English writer, whose works include the collection of short stories *The Wrong Set* (1949) and the novels *Anglo-Saxon Attitudes* (1956) and *No Laughing Matter* (1967). **3. Charles Thomson Rees.** 1869–1959, Scottish physicist, who invented the cloud chamber: shared the Nobel prize for physics 1927. **4. Edmund.** 1895–1972, U.S. critic, noted esp. for *Axel's Castle* (1931), a study of the symbolist movement. **5. (James) Harold,** Baron of Rievaulx. born 1916, British Labour statesman; prime minister (1964–70; 1974–76). **6. Richard.** 1714–82, Welsh landscape painter. **7. (Thomas) Woodrow** ('wudrəu). 1856–1924, U.S. Democratic statesman; 28th president of the U.S. (1913–21). He led the U.S. into World War I in 1917 and proposed the Fourteen Points (1918) as a basis for peace. Although he secured the formation of the League of Nations the U.S. Senate refused to support it: Nobel peace prize 1919. —**Wilsonian** (wɪl'səunɪən) *adj.*

wilt[1] (wɪlt) *vb.* **1.** to become or cause to become limp or drooping: *insufficient water makes plants wilt.* **2.** to lose or cause to lose courage, strength, etc. ~*n.* **3.** the act of wilting or state of becoming wilted. **4.** any of various plant diseases characterized by permanent wilting. [C17: ? var. of *wilk* to wither, from MDu. *welken*]

wilt[2] (wɪlt) *vb. Arch. or dialect.* (used with the pronoun *thou* or its relative equivalent) a singular form of the present tense (indicative mood) of **will**[1].

Wilton ('wɪltən) *n.* a kind of carpet with a close velvet pile of cut loops. [after *Wilton,* town in Wiltshire, where first made]

Wilts. (wɪlts) *abbrev. for* Wiltshire.

Wiltshire ('wɪltʃə, -,ʃɪə) *n.* a county of S England, consisting mainly of chalk uplands, with Salisbury Plain in the south and the Marlborough Downs in the north; prehistoric remains (at Stonehenge and Avebury). Administrative centre: Trowbridge. Pop.: 545 200 (1986 est.). Area: 3481 sq. km (1344 sq. miles).

wily ('waɪlɪ) *adj.* **wilier, wiliest.** sly or crafty. —'**wiliness** *n.*

wimble ('wɪmbəl) *n.* **1.** any of a number of hand tools used for boring holes. ~*vb.* **2.** to bore (a hole) with a wimble. [C13: from MDu. *wimmel* auger]

Wimbledon ('wɪmbəldən) *n.* part of the Greater London borough of Merton: headquarters of the All England Lawn Tennis Club since 1877 and the site of the annual international tennis championships.

wimp (wɪmp) *n. Inf.* a feeble ineffective person. [C20: from ?] —'**wimpish** *or* '**wimpy** *adj.*

wimple ('wɪmpəl) *n.* **1.** a piece of cloth draped around the head to frame the face, worn by women in the Middle Ages and still worn by some nuns. ~*vb. Arch.* **2.** (*tr.*) to cover with or put a wimple on. **3.** (esp. of a veil) to lie or cause to lie in folds or pleats. [OE *wimpel*]

Wimpy ('wɪmpɪ) *n., pl.* -**pies.** *Trademark.* a hamburger served in a soft bread roll.

win (wɪn) *vb.* **winning, won. 1.** (*intr.*) to achieve first place in a competition. **2.** (*tr.*) to gain (a prize, first place, etc.) in a competition. **3.** (*tr.*) to succeed in or gain (something) with an effort: *we won recognition.* **4.** to gain victory or triumph in (a battle, argument, etc.). **5.** (*tr.*) to earn (a living, etc.) by work. **6.** (*tr.*) to capture: *the Germans never won Leningrad.* **7.** (when *intr.*, foll. by *out, through,* etc.) to reach with difficulty (a desired position) or become free, loose, etc., with effort: *the boat won the shore.* **8.** (*tr.*) to gain (the sympathy, loyalty, etc.) of someone. **9.** (*tr.*) to persuade (a woman, etc.) to marry one. **10.** (*tr.*) to extract (ore, coal, etc.) from a mine or (metal or other minerals) from ore. **11. you can't win.** *Inf.* an expression of resignation after an unsuccessful attempt to overcome difficulties. ~*n.* **12.** *Inf.* a success, victory, or triumph. **13.** profit; winnings. ~See also **win over.** [OE *winnan*] —'**winnable** *adj.*

▷ *Usage. Win* has become common in informal English as a noun meaning gain or victory. It is, however, regarded by careful users of English as inappropriate in formal contexts.

wince[1] (wɪns) *vb.* **1.** (*intr.*) to start slightly, as with sudden pain; flinch. ~*n.* **2.** the act of wincing. [C18 (earlier (C13) meaning: to kick): via OF *wencier, guenchir* to avoid, of Gmc origin] —'**wincer** *n.* —'**wincingly** *adv.*

wince[2] (wɪns) *n.* a roller for transferring pieces of cloth between dyeing vats. [C17: var. of WINCH[1]]

winceyette (,wɪnsɪ'ɛt) *n. Brit.* a plain-weave cotton fabric with slightly raised two-sided nap. [from Scot. *wincey,* prob. altered from *woolsey* in *linsey-woolsey,* a fabric made of linen & wool]

winch[1] (wɪntʃ) *n.* **1.** a windlass driven by a hand-or power-operated crank. **2.** a hand- or power-operated crank by which a machine is driven. ~*vb.* **3.** (*tr.;* often foll. by *up* or *in*) to pull or lift using a winch. [OE *wince* pulley]

winch[2] (wɪntʃ) *vb.* (*intr.*) an obsolete word for **wince**[1].

Winchester ('wɪntʃɪstə) *n.* a city in S England, administrative centre of Hampshire: a Romano-British town; Saxon capital of Wessex; site of **Winchester College** (1382), the oldest English public school. Pop.: 30 642 (1981).

Winchester rifle ('wɪntʃɪstə) *n. Trademark.* a breech-loading slide-action repeating rifle. Often shortened to **Winchester.** [C19: after O. F. *Winchester* (1810–80), U.S. manufacturer]

Winckelmann (*German* 'vɪŋkəlman) *n.* **Johann Joachim** (jo'han 'jo:axɪm). 1717–68, German archaeologist and art historian; one of the founders of neoclassicism.

wind[1] (wɪnd) *n.* **1.** a current of air, sometimes of considerable force, moving generally horizontally from areas of high pressure to areas of low pressure. **2.** *Chiefly poetic.* the direction from which a wind blows, usually a cardinal point of the compass. **3.** air artificially moved, as by a fan, pump, etc. **4.** a trend, tendency, or force: *the winds of revolution.* **5.** *Inf.* a hint; suggestion: *we got wind that you were coming.* **6.** something deemed insubstantial: *his talk was all wind.* **7.** breath, as used in respiration or talk: *you're just wasting your wind.* **8.** (often used in sports) the power to breathe normally: *his wind is weak.* **9.** *Music.* **a.** a wind instrument or wind instruments considered collectively. **b.** (*often pl.*) the musicians who play wind instruments in an orchestra. **c.** (*modifier*) of or composed of wind instruments: *a wind ensemble.* **10.** an informal name for **flatus. 11.** the air on which the scent of an animal is carried to hounds or on which the scent of a hunter is carried to his quarry. **12. between wind and water. a.** the part of a vessel's hull below the water line that is exposed by rolling or by wave action. **b.** any particularly susceptible point. **13. break wind.** to release intestinal gas through the anus. **14. get** *or* **have the wind up.** *Inf.* to become frightened. **15. how** *or* **which way the wind blows** *or* **lies.** what appears probable. **16. in the teeth** (*or* **eye**) **of the wind.** directly into the wind. **17. in the wind.** about to happen. **18. into the wind.** against the wind or upwind. **19. off the wind.** *Naut.* away from the direction from which the wind is blowing. **20. on the wind.** *Naut.* as near as possible to the direction from which the wind is blowing. **21. put the wind up.** *Inf.* to frighten or alarm. **22. raise the wind.** *Brit. inf.* to obtain the necessary funds. **23. sail close** *or* **near to the wind.** to come near the limits of danger or indecency. **24. take the wind out of someone's sails.** to disconcert or deflate someone. ~*vb.* (*tr.*) **25.** to cause (someone) to be short of breath: *the blow winded him.* **26. a.** to detect the scent of. **b.** to pursue (quarry) by following its scent. **27.** to cause (a baby) to bring up wind after feeding. **28.** to expose to air, as in drying, etc. [OE] — '**windless** *adj.*

wind² (waɪnd) *vb.* **winding, wound. 1.** (often foll. by *around, about,* or *upon*) to turn or coil (string, cotton, etc.) around some object or point or (of string, etc.) to be turned, etc., around some object or point: *he wound a scarf around his head.* **2.** (*tr.*) to cover or wreathe by or as if by coiling, wrapping, etc.: *we wound the body in a shroud.* **3.** (*tr.;* often foll. by *up*) to tighten the spring of (a clockwork mechanism). **4.** (*tr.;* foll. by *off*) to remove by uncoiling or unwinding. **5.** (*usually intr.*) to move or cause to move in a sinuous, spiral, or circular course: *the river winds through the hills.* **6.** (*tr.*) to introduce indirectly or deviously: *he is winding his own opinions into the report.* **7.** (*tr.*) to cause to twist or revolve: *he wound the handle.* **8.** (*tr.;* usually foll. by *up* or *down*) to move by cranking: *please wind up the window.* ~*n.* **9.** the act of winding or state of being wound. **10.** a single turn, bend, etc.: *a wind in the river.* ~See also **wind down, wind up.** [OE *windan*] — '**windable** *adj.*

wind³ (waɪnd) *vb.* **winding, winded** *or* **wound.** (*tr.*) *Poetic.* to blow (a note or signal) on (a horn, bugle, etc.). [C16: special use of WIND¹]

windage ('wɪndɪdʒ) *n.* **1. a.** a deflection of a projectile as a result of the effect of the wind. **b.** the degree of such deflection. **2.** the difference between a firearm's bore and the diameter of its projectile. **3.** *Naut.* the exposed part of the hull of a vessel responsible for wind resistance.

windbag ('wɪnd,bæg) *n.* **1.** *Sl.* a voluble person who has little of interest to communicate. **2.** the bag in a set of bagpipes, which provides a continuous flow of air to the pipes.

windblown ('wɪnd,bləʊn) *adj.* **1.** blown by the wind. **2.** (of trees, shrubs, etc.) growing in a shape determined by the prevailing winds.

wind-borne *adj.* (esp. of plant seeds or pollen) transported by wind.

windbound ('wɪnd,baʊnd) *adj.* (of a sailing vessel) prevented from sailing by an unfavourable wind.

windbreak ('wɪnd,breɪk) *n.* a fence, line of trees, etc., serving as a protection from the wind by breaking its force.

windburn ('wɪnd,bɜːn) *n.* irritation and redness of the skin caused by prolonged exposure to winds of high velocity.

windcheater ('wɪnd,tʃiːtə) *n.* a warm jacket, usually with a close-fitting knitted neck, cuffs, and waistband.

wind chest (wɪnd) *n.* a box in an organ in which air from the bellows is stored under pressure before being supplied to the pipes or reeds.

wind-chill ('wɪnd-) *n.* **a.** the serious chilling effect of wind and low temperature: measured on a scale that runs from hot to fatal to life. **b.** (*as modifier*): *wind-chill factor.*

wind cone (wɪnd) *n.* another name for **windsock.**

wind down (waɪnd) *vb.* (*adv.*) **1.** (*tr.*) to lower or move down by cranking. **2.** (*intr.*) (of a clock spring) to become slack. **3.** (*intr.*) to diminish gradually in force or power; relax.

winded ('wɪndɪd) *adj.* **1.** out of breath, as from strenuous exercise. **2.** (*in combination*) having breath or wind as specified: *broken-winded; short-winded.*

winder ('waɪndə) *n.* **1.** a person or device that winds. **2.** an object, such as a bobbin, around which something is wound. **3.** a knob or key used to wind up a clock, watch, or similar mechanism. **4.** any plant that twists itself around a support. **5.** a step of a spiral staircase.

Windermere ('wɪndə,mɪə) *n.* **Lake.** a lake in NW England, in Cumbria in the SE part of the Lake District: the largest lake in England. Length: 17 km (10.5 miles).

windfall ('wɪnd,fɔːl) *n.* **1.** a piece of unexpected good fortune, esp. financial gain. **2.** something blown down by the wind, esp. a piece of fruit.

windflower ('wɪnd,flaʊə) *n.* any of various anemone plants, such as the wood anemone.

wind gauge (wɪnd) *n.* **1.** another name for **anemometer. 2.** a scale on a gun sight indicating the amount of deflection necessary to allow for windage. **3.** *Music.* a device for measuring the wind pressure in the bellows of an organ.

wind harp (wɪnd) *n.* a less common name for **aeolian harp.**

Windhoek ('wɪnt,hʊk, 'vɪnt-) *n.* the capital of Namibia, in the centre, at an altitude of 1654 m (5428 ft.): formerly the capital of German South West Africa. Pop.: 105 100 (1983).

windhover ('wɪnd,hɒvə) *n. Brit.* a dialect name for a **kestrel.**

winding ('waɪndɪŋ) *n.* **1.** a curving or sinuous course or movement. **2.** anything that has been wound or wrapped around something. **3.** a particular manner or style in which something has been wound. **4.** a curve, bend, or complete turn in wound material, a road, etc. **5.** (*often pl.*) devious thoughts or behaviour: *the tortuous windings of political argumentation.* **6.** one or more turns of wire forming a continuous coil through which an electric current can pass, as used in transformers, generators, etc. ~*adj.* **7.** curving; sinuous: *a winding road.* — '**windingly** *adv.*

winding sheet *n.* a sheet in which a corpse is wrapped for burial; shroud.

winding-up *n.* the process of finishing or closing something, esp. the process of closing down a business.

wind instrument (wɪnd) *n.* any musical instrument sounded by the breath, such as the woodwinds and brass instruments of an orchestra.

windjammer ('wɪnd,dʒæmə) *n.* a large merchant sailing ship.

windlass ('wɪndləs) *n.* **1.** a machine for raising weights by winding a rope or chain upon a barrel or drum driven by a crank, motor, etc. ~*vb.* **2.** (*tr.*) to raise or haul (a weight, etc.) by means of a windlass. [C14: from ON *vindáss,* from *vinda* to WIND² + *ass* pole]

windlestraw ('wɪndᵊl,strɔː) *n. Irish, Scot.,* & *English dialect.* the dried stalk of any of various grasses. [OE *windel-strēaw,* from *windel* basket, from *windan* to wind + *strēaw* straw]

wind machine (wɪnd) *n.* a machine used, esp. in the theatre, to produce a wind or the sound of wind.

windmill ('wɪnd,mɪl, 'wɪn,mɪl) *n.* **1.** a machine for grinding or pumping driven by a set of adjustable vanes or sails that are caused to turn by the force of the wind. **2.** the set of vanes or sails that drives such a mill. **3.** Also called: **whirligig.** *Brit.* a toy consisting of plastic or paper vanes attached to a stick in such a manner that they revolve like the sails of a windmill. **4.** an imaginary opponent or evil (esp. in **tilt at** *or* **fight windmills**). ~*vb.* **5.** to move or cause to move like the arms of a windmill.

window ('wɪndəʊ) *n.* **1.** a light framework, made of timber, metal, or plastic, that contains glass or glazed opening frames and is placed in a wall or roof to let in light or air or to see through. Related adj.: **fenestral. 2.** an opening in the wall or roof of a building that is provided to let in light or air or to see through. **3.** short for **windowpane. 4.** the area behind a glass window in a shop used for display. **5.** any opening or structure resembling a window in function or appearance, such as the transparent area of an envelope revealing an address within. **6.** an opportunity to see or understand something usually unseen: *a window on the workings of Parliament.* **7.** short for **launch window** or **weather window. 8.** *Physics.* a region of the spectrum in which a medium transmits electromagnetic radiation. **9.** (*modifier*) of or relating to a window or windows: *a window ledge.* ~*vb.* **10.** (*tr.*) to furnish with or as if with windows. [C13: from ON *vindauga,* from *vindr* WIND¹ + *auga* eye]

window box *n.* a long narrow box, placed on or outside a windowsill, in which plants are grown.

window-dresser *n.* a person employed to design and build up a display in a shop window.

window-dressing n. **1.** the ornamentation of shop windows, designed to attract customers. **2.** the pleasant aspect of an idea, etc., which is stressed to conceal the real nature.

windowpane ('wɪndəʊ,peɪn) n. a sheet of glass in a window.

window sash n. a glazed window frame, esp. one that opens.

window seat n. **1.** a seat below a window, esp. in a bay window. **2.** a seat beside a window in a bus, train, etc.

window-shop vb. **-shopping, -shopped.** (intr.) to look at goods in shop windows without intending to buy. —'**window-,shopper** n. —'**window-,shopping** n.

windowsill ('wɪndəʊ,sɪl) n. a sill below a window.

windpipe ('wɪnd,paɪp) n. a nontechnical name for **trachea** (sense 1).

Wind River Range (wɪnd) n. a mountain range in W Wyoming: one of the highest ranges of the central Rockies. Highest peak: Gannet Peak, 4202 m (13 785 ft.).

wind rose (wɪnd) n. a diagram with radiating lines showing the frequency and strength of winds from each direction affecting a specific place.

windrow ('wɪnd,rəʊ, 'wɪn,rəʊ) n. **1.** a long low ridge or line of hay or a similar crop, designed to achieve the best conditions for drying or curing. **2.** a line of leaves, snow, dust, etc., swept together by the wind.

Windscale ('wɪnd,skeɪl) n. the former name of **Sellafield.**

windscreen ('wɪnd,skriːn) n. Brit. the sheet of flat or curved glass that forms a window of a motor vehicle, esp. the front window. U.S. and Canad. name: **windshield.**

windscreen wiper n. Brit. an electrically operated blade with a rubber edge that wipes a windscreen clear of rain, snow, etc. U.S. and Canad. name: **windshield wiper.**

windshield ('wɪnd,ʃiːld) n. the U.S. and Canad. name for **windscreen.**

windsock ('wɪnd,sɒk) n. a truncated cone of textile mounted on a mast so that it is free to rotate about a vertical axis: used, esp. at airports, to indicate the local wind direction. Also called: **air sock, drogue, wind sleeve, wind cone.**

Windsor[1] ('wɪnzə) n. **1.** a town in S England, in Berkshire on the River Thames, linked by bridge with Eton: site of **Windsor Castle,** residence of English monarchs since its founding by William the Conqueror; **Old Windsor,** royal residence in the time of Edward the Confessor, is 3 km (2 miles) southeast. Pop.: 27 886 (1983 est.). Official name: **New Windsor. 2.** a city in SE Canada, in S Ontario on the Detroit River opposite Detroit: motor-vehicle manufacturing; university (1963). Pop.: 193 111 (1986).

Windsor[2] n. **1.** the official name of the British royal family from 1917. **2. Duke of.** the title of **Edward VIII** from 1937.

Windsor chair n. a simple wooden chair, popular in England and America from the 18th century, usually having a shaped seat, splayed legs, and a back of many spindles.

Windsor knot n. a wide triangular knot, produced by making extra turns in tying a tie.

windstorm ('wɪnd,stɔːm) n. a storm consisting of violent winds.

wind-sucking n. a harmful habit of horses in which the animal arches its neck and swallows a gulp of air. —'**wind,sucker** n.

windsurfing ('wɪnd,sɜːfɪŋ) n. the sport of riding on water using a surfboard steered and propelled by an attached sail.

windswept ('wɪnd,swɛpt) adj. open to or swept by the wind.

wind tunnel (wɪnd) n. a chamber for testing the aerodynamic properties of aircraft, aerofoils, etc., in which a current of air can be maintained at a constant velocity.

wind up (waɪnd) vb. (adv.) **1.** to bring to or reach a conclusion: he wound up the proceedings. **2.** (tr.) to tighten the spring of (a clockwork mechanism). **3.** (tr.; usually passive) Inf. to make nervous, tense, etc.: he was all wound up before the big fight. **4.** (tr.) to roll (thread, etc.) into a ball. **5.** an informal word for **liquidate** (sense 2). **6.** (intr.) Inf. to end up (in a specified state): you'll wind up without any teeth. **7.** (tr.) Brit. sl. to tease (someone). ~n. **wind-up. 8.** the act of concluding. **9.** the end.

windward ('wɪndwəd) Chiefly naut. ~adj. **1.** of, in, or moving to the quarter from which the wind blows. ~n. **2.**

the windward point. **3.** the side towards the wind. ~adv. **4.** towards the wind. ~Cf. **leeward.**

Windward Islands pl. n. a group of islands in the SE West Indies, in the Lesser Antilles: consists of the French Overseas Department of Martinique and the independent states of Grenada, St Lucia, and St Vincent and the Grenadines. French name: **Îles du Vent.**

Windward Passage n. a strait in the West Indies, between E Cuba and NW Haiti. Width: 80 km (50 miles).

windy ('wɪndɪ) adj. **windier, windiest. 1.** of, resembling, or relating to wind; stormy. **2.** swept by or open to powerful winds. **3.** marked by or given to prolonged and often boastful speech: windy orations. **4.** void of substance. **5.** an informal word for **flatulent. 6.** Sl. frightened. —'**windily** adv. —'**windiness** n.

wine (waɪn) n. **1. a.** an alcoholic drink produced by the fermenting of grapes with water and sugar. **b.** (as modifier): the wine harvest. **c.** an alcoholic drink produced in this way from other fruits, flowers, etc.: elderberry wine. **2. a.** a dark red colour, sometimes with a purplish tinge. **b.** (as adj.): wine-coloured. **3.** anything resembling wine in its intoxicating or invigorating effect. **4. new wine in old bottles.** something new added to or imposed upon an old or established order. ~vb. **5.** (intr.) to drink wine. **6. wine and dine.** to entertain or be entertained with wine and fine food. [OE win, from L vinum] —'**wineless** adj.

wine bar n. a bar in a restaurant, etc., or an establishment that specializes in serving wine and usually food.

winebibber ('waɪn,bɪbə) n. a person who drinks a great deal of wine. —'**wine,bibbing** n.

wine box n. wine sold in a cubic carton with a tap for dispensing.

wine cellar n. **1.** a place, such as a dark cool cellar, where wine is stored. **2.** the stock of wines stored there.

wine cooler n. **1.** a bucket-like vessel containing ice in which a bottle of wine is placed to be cooled. **2.** the full name for **cooler** (sense 3).

wine gallon n. Brit. a former unit of capacity equal to 231 cubic inches.

wineglass ('waɪn,glɑːs) n. **1.** a glass drinking vessel, typically having a small bowl on a stem, with a flared foot. **2.** Also called: **wineglassful.** the amount that such a glass will hold.

wine grower n. a person engaged in cultivating vines in order to make wine. —**wine growing** n.

wine palm n. any of various palm trees, the sap of which is used, esp. when fermented, as a drink. Also called: **toddy palm.**

winepress ('waɪn,prɛs) n. any equipment used for squeezing the juice from grapes in order to make wine.

winery ('waɪnərɪ) n., pl. **-eries.** Chiefly U.S. & Canad. a place where wine is made.

wineskin ('waɪn,skɪn) n. the skin of a sheep or goat sewn up and used as a holder for wine.

wing (wɪŋ) n. **1.** either of the modified forelimbs of a bird that are covered with large feathers and specialized for flight in most species. **2.** one of the organs of flight of an insect, consisting of a membranous outgrowth from the thorax containing a network of veins. **3.** either of the organs of flight in certain other animals, esp. the forelimb of a bat. **4. a.** a half of the main supporting surface on an aircraft, confined to one side of it. **b.** the full span of the main supporting surface on both sides of an aircraft. **5.** an organ, structure, or apparatus resembling a wing. **6.** anything suggesting a wing in form, function, or position, such as a sail of a windmill or a ship. **7.** Bot. **a.** either of the lateral petals of a sweetpea or related flower. **b.** any of various outgrowths of a plant part, esp. the process on a wind-dispersed fruit or seed. **8.** a means or cause of flight or rapid motion; flight: fear gave wings to his feet. **9.** Brit. the part of a car body that surrounds the wheels. U.S. and Canad. name: **fender. 10.** Soccer, hockey, etc. **a.** either of the two sides of the pitch near the touchline. **b.** a player stationed in such a position; winger. **11.** a faction or group within a political party or other organization. See also **left wing, right wing. 12.** a part of a building that is subordinate to the main part. **13.** the space offstage to the right or left of the acting area in a theatre. **14. in** or **on the wings.** ready to step in when needed. **15.** either of the two pieces that project forwards from the sides of some chair backs. **16.** (pl.) an insignia in the form of stylized wings worn by a qualified aircraft pilot. **17.** a tactical formation in some air forces, consisting of two or more squadrons. **18.** any of various flattened organs or extensions in lower animals, esp. when used in locomotion. **19. clip (someone's) wings. a.** to restrict (someone's) freedom. **b.** to thwart (someone's) ambitions. **20. on the wing. a.** flying. **b.** travelling. **21. on wings.** flying or as if flying. **22. spread** or **stretch one's wings.** to make full use of one's abilities. **23. take wing. a.** to lift off or fly away. **b.** to depart in haste. **c.** to become joyful. **24. under one's wing.** in one's care. ~*vb.* *(mainly tr.)* **25.** *(also intr.)* to make (one's way) swiftly on or as if on wings. **26.** to shoot or wound (a bird, person, etc.) superficially, in the wing or arm, etc. **27.** to cause to fly or move swiftly: *to wing an arrow.* **28.** to provide with wings. [C12: from ON] —**winged** *adj.* —'**wingless** *adj.* —'**wing,like** *adj.*

Wingate ('wɪn,geɪt) *n.* **Orde Charles** (ɔːd). 1903–44, British soldier. During World War II he organized the Chindits in Burma to disrupt Japanese communications. He died in an air crash.

wing beat or **wing-beat** *n.* a complete cycle of moving the wing by a bird when flying.

wing-case *n.* the nontechnical name for **elytron.**

wing chair *n.* an easy chair having wings on each side of the back.

wing collar *n.* a stiff turned-up shirt collar worn with the points turned down over the tie.

wing commander *n.* an officer holding commissioned rank in certain air forces, such as the Royal Air Force: junior to a group captain and senior to a squadron leader.

wing covert *n.* any of the covert feathers of the wing of a bird, occurring in distinct rows.

wingding ('wɪŋ,dɪŋ) *n.* *Sl., chiefly U.S. & Canad.* **1.** a noisy lively party or festivity. **2.** a real or pretended fit or seizure. [C20: from ?]

winge (wɪndʒ) *vb., n.* *Austral.* a variant spelling of **whinge.**

winger ('wɪŋə) *n.* *Soccer, hockey, etc.* a player stationed on the wing.

wing loading *n.* the total weight of an aircraft divided by its wing area.

wingman ('wɪŋmæn) *n.* *pl.* -**men.** a player in the wing position in Australian Rules.

wing nut *n.* a threaded nut tightened by hand by means of two flat lugs or wings projecting from the central body. Also called: **butterfly nut.**

wingspan ('wɪŋ,spæn) or **wingspread** ('wɪŋ,sprɛd) *n.* the distance between the wing tips of an aircraft, bird, etc.

wing tip *n.* the outermost edge of a wing.

wink (wɪŋk) *vb.* **1.** *(intr.)* to close and open one eye quickly, deliberately, or in an exaggerated fashion to convey friendliness, etc. **2.** to close and open (an eye or the eyes) momentarily. **3.** *(tr.;* foll. by *away, back,* etc.) to force away (tears, etc.) by winking. **4.** *(tr.)* to signal with a wink. **5.** *(intr.)* (of a light) to gleam or flash intermittently. ~*n.* **6.** a winking movement, esp. one conveying a signal, etc., or such a signal. **7.** an interrupted flashing of light. **8.** a brief moment of time. **9.** *Inf.* the smallest amount, esp. of sleep. **10. tip the wink.** *Brit. inf.* to give a hint. [OE *wincian*]

wink at *vb.* *(intr., prep.)* to connive at; disregard: *the authorities winked at corruption.*

Winkelried (German 'vɪŋkəlriːt) *n.* **Arnold von** ('arnɔlt fɔn). died ?1386, Swiss hero of the battle of Sempach (1386) against the Austrians.

winker ('wɪŋkə) *n.* **1.** a person or thing that winks. **2.** *Dialect or U.S. & Canad. sl.* an eye. **3.** another name for **blinker** (sense 1).

winkle ('wɪŋkᵊl) *n.* **1.** See **periwinkle**[1]. ~*vb.* **2.** *(tr.;* usually foll. by *out, out of,* etc.) *Inf., chiefly Brit.* to extract or prise out. [C16: shortened from PERIWINKLE[1]]

winkle-pickers *pl. n.* shoes or boots with very pointed narrow toes.

Winnebago (,wɪnɪ'beɪgəʊ) *n.* **Lake.** a lake in E Wisconsin, fed and drained by the Fox river: the largest lake in the state. Area: 557 sq. km (215 sq. miles).

winner ('wɪnə) *n.* **1.** a person or thing that wins. **2.** *Inf.* a person or thing that seems sure to win or succeed.

winning ('wɪnɪŋ) *adj.* **1.** (of a person, character, etc.) charming, engaging, or attractive: *a winning smile.* **2.** gaining victory: *the winning goal.* ~*n.* **3.** a shaft or seam of coal. **4.** *(pl.)* money, prizes, or valuables won, esp. in gambling. —'**winningly** *adv.* —'**winningness** *n.*

winning gallery *n.* *Real Tennis.* the gallery farthest from the net on either side of the court, into which any shot played wins a point.

winning opening *n.* *Real Tennis.* the grille or winning gallery, into which any shot played wins a point.

winning post *n.* the post marking the finishing line on a racecourse.

Winnipeg ('wɪnɪ,pɛg) *n.* **1.** a city in S Canada, capital of Manitoba at the confluence of the Assiniboine and Red Rivers: University of Manitoba (1877) and University of Winnipeg (1871). Pop.: 594 551 (1986). **2. Lake.** a lake in S Canada, in Manitoba: drains through the Nelson River into Hudson Bay. Area: 23 553 sq. km (9094 sq. miles). —'**Winni,pegger** *n.*

Winnipeg couch *n.* *Canad.* a couch with no arms or back, opening out into a double bed.

Winnipegosis (,wɪnɪpə'gəʊsɪs) *n.* **Lake.** a lake in S Canada, in W Manitoba. Area: 5400 sq. km (2086 sq. miles).

winnow ('wɪnəʊ) *vb.* **1.** to separate (grain) from (chaff) by means of a wind or current of air. **2.** *(tr.)* to examine in order to select the desirable elements. **3.** *(tr.) Rare.* to blow upon; fan. ~*n.* **4. a.** a device for winnowing. **b.** the act or process of winnowing. [OE *windwian*] —'**winnower** *n.*

wino ('waɪnəʊ) *n., pl.* **winos.** *Inf.* a down-and-out who habitually drinks cheap wine.

win over *vb.* *(tr., adv.)* to gain the support or consent of (someone). Also: **win round.**

winsome ('wɪnsəm) *adj.* charming; winning; engaging: *a winsome smile.* [OE *wynsum,* from *wynn* joy + -*sum* -SOME[1]] —'**winsomely** *adv.*

Winston-Salem ('wɪnstən'seɪləm) *n.* a city in N central North Carolina: formed in 1913 by the uniting of Salem and Winston; a major tobacco manufacturing centre. Pop.: 148 080 (1986 est.).

winter ('wɪntə) *n.* **1. a.** *(sometimes cap.)* the coldest season of the year, between autumn and spring, astronomically from the December solstice to the March equinox in the N hemisphere and at the opposite time of year in the S hemisphere. **b.** *(as modifier): winter pasture.* **2.** the period of cold weather associated with the winter. **3.** a time of decline, decay, etc. **4.** *Chiefly poetic.* a year represented by this season: *a man of 72 winters.* ~Related adj.: **hibernal.** ~*vb.* **5.** *(intr.)* to spend the winter in a specified place. **6.** to keep or feed (farm animals, etc.) during the winter or (of farm animals) to be kept or fed during the winter. [OE] —'**winterer** *n.* —'**winterless** *adj.*

winter aconite *n.* a small Old World herbaceous plant cultivated for its yellow flowers, which appear early in spring.

winter cherry *n.* **1.** a Eurasian plant cultivated for its ornamental inflated papery orange-red calyx. **2.** the calyx of this plant. ~See also **Chinese lantern.**

winter garden *n.* **1.** a garden of evergreen plants. **2.** a conservatory in which flowers are grown in winter.

wintergreen ('wɪntə,griːn) *n.* **1.** any of a genus of evergreen ericaceous shrubs, esp. a subshrub of E North America, which has white bell-shaped flowers and edible red berries. **2. oil of wintergreen.** an aromatic compound, formerly made from this and various other plants but now synthesized: used medicinally and for flavouring. **3.** any of a genus of plants, such as **common wintergreen,** of temperate and arctic regions, having rounded leaves and small pink globose flowers. **4. chickweed wintergreen.** a plant of N Europe and N Asia belonging to the primrose family, having white flowers and leaves arranged in a whorl. [C16: from Du. *wintergroen* or G *Wintergrün*]

winterize or **-rise** ('wɪntə,raɪz) *vb.* *(tr.) U.S. & Canad.* to prepare (a house, car, etc.) to withstand winter conditions. —,**winteri'zation** or **-ri'sation** *n.*

winter jasmine *n.* a jasmine shrub widely cultivated for its winter-blooming yellow flowers.

winter solstice *n.* the time at which the sun is at its southernmost point in the sky (northernmost point in the S hemisphere) appearing at noon at its lowest altitude above the horizon. It occurs about December 22 (June 21 in the S hemisphere).

winter sports *pl. n.* sports held in the open air on snow or ice, esp. skiing.

Winterthur (*German* 'vɪntərtuːr) *n.* an industrial town in NE central Switzerland, in Zürich canton: has the largest technical college in the country. Pop.: 84 400 (1985).

wintertime ('wɪntə,taɪm) *n.* the winter season. Also (archaic): **wintertide.**

winterweight ('wɪntə,weɪt) *adj.* (of clothes) suitably heavy and warm for wear in the winter.

winter wheat *n.* a type of wheat that is planted in the autumn and is harvested the following summer.

wintry ('wɪntrɪ) *or* **wintery** ('wɪntərɪ) *adj.* **-trier, -triest. 1.** (esp. of weather) of or characteristic of winter. **2.** lacking cheer or warmth; bleak. — **'wintrily** *adv.* — **'wintriness** *or* **'winteriness** *n.*

winy ('waɪnɪ) *adj.* **winier, winiest.** having the taste or qualities of wine; heady.

wipe (waɪp) *vb.* (*tr.*) **1.** to rub (a surface or object) lightly, esp., with a cloth, hand, etc., as in removing dust, water, etc. **2.** (usually foll. by *off*, *away*, *from*, *up*, etc.) to remove by or as if by rubbing lightly: *he wiped the dirt from his hands.* **3.** to eradicate or cancel (a thought, memory, etc.). **4.** to erase (a recording) from (a tape). **5.** to apply (oil, etc.) by wiping. **6.** *Austral. inf.* to abandon or reject (a person). **7. wipe the floor with** (**someone**). *Inf.* to defeat (someone) decisively. ~*n.* **8.** the act or an instance of wiping. **9.** *Dialect.* a sweeping blow. [OE *wipian*]

wipe out *vb.* (*adv.*) **1.** (*tr.*) to destroy completely. **2.** (*tr.*) *Inf.* to kill. **3.** (*intr.*) to fall off a surfboard. ~*n.* **wipeout. 4.** an act or instance of wiping out. **5.** the interference of one radio signal by another so that reception is impossible.

wiper ('waɪpə) *n.* **1.** any piece of cloth, such as a handkerchief, etc., used for wiping. **2.** a cam rotated to allow a part to fall under its own weight, as used in stamping machines, etc. **3.** See **windscreen wiper. 4.** *Electrical engineering.* a movable conducting arm that makes contact with a row or ring of contacts.

wire ('waɪə) *n.* **1.** a slender flexible strand or rod of metal. **2.** a cable consisting of several metal strands twisted together. **3.** a flexible metallic conductor, esp. one made of copper, usually insulated, and used to carry electric current in a circuit. **4.** (*modifier*) of, relating to, or made of wire: *a wire fence.* **5.** anything made of wire, such as wire netting. **6.** a long continuous wire or cable connecting points in a telephone or telegraph system. **7.** *Old-fashioned.* an informal name for **telegram** or **telegraph. 8.** *U.S. & Canad. horse racing.* the finishing line on a racecourse. **9.** a snare made of wire for rabbits and similar animals. **10. get in under the wire.** *Inf., chiefly U.S. & Canad.* to accomplish something with little time to spare. **11. get one's wires crossed.** *Inf.* to misunderstand. **12. pull wires.** *Chiefly U.S. & Canad.* to exert influence behind the scenes; pull strings. ~*vb.* (*mainly tr.*) **13.** (*also intr.*) to send a telegram to (a person or place). **14.** to send (news, a message, etc.) by telegraph. **15.** to equip (an electrical system, circuit, or component) with wires. **16.** to fasten or furnish with wire. **17.** to snare with wire. **18. wire in.** *Inf.* to set about (something, esp. food) with enthusiasm. [OE *wir*] — **'wire,like** *adj.*

wire brush *n.* a brush having wire bristles, used for cleaning metal, esp. for removing rust, or for brushing against cymbals.

wire cloth *n.* a mesh or netting woven from fine wire, used in window screens, strainers, etc.

wiredraw ('waɪə,drɔː) *vb.* **-drawing, -drew, -drawn.** to convert (metal) into wire by drawing through successively smaller dies.

wire-gauge *n.* **1.** a flat plate with slots in which standard wire sizes can be measured. **2.** a standard system of sizes for measuring the diameters of wires.

wire gauze *n.* a stiff meshed fabric woven of fine wires.

wire grass *n.* any of various grasses that have tough wiry roots or rhizomes.

wire-guided *adj.* (of a missile) able to be controlled in mid-flight by signals passed along a wire connecting the missile to the firer's control device.

wire-haired *adj.* (of an animal) having a rough wiry coat.

wireless ('waɪəlɪs) *n.*, *vb. Chiefly Brit.* another word for **radio.**

wireless telegraphy *n.* another name for **radiotelegraphy.**

wireless telephone *n.* another name for **radiotelephone.** — **wireless telephony** *n.*

wire netting *n.* a net made of wire, often galvanized, that is used for fencing, etc.

wirepuller ('waɪə,pʊlə) *n. Chiefly U.S. & Canad.* a person who uses private or secret influence for his own ends. — **'wire,pulling** *n.*

wire recorder *n.* an early type of magnetic recorder in which sounds were recorded on a thin steel wire magnetized by an electromagnet. — **wire recording** *n.*

wire service *n. Chiefly U.S. & Canad.* an agency supplying news, etc., to newspapers, radio, and television stations, etc.

wiretap ('waɪə,tæp) *vb.* **-tapping, -tapped. 1.** (*intr.*) to make a connection to a telegraph or telephone wire in order to obtain information secretly. **2.** (*tr.*) to tap (a telephone) or the telephone of (a person). — **'wire,tapper** *n.*

wire wheel *n.* a wheel in which the rim is held to the hub by wire spokes, esp. one used on a sports car.

wire wool *n.* a mass of fine wire, used esp. to clean kitchen articles.

wirework ('waɪə,wɜːk) *n.* **1.** functional or decorative work made of wire. **2.** objects made of wire, esp. netting.

wireworks ('waɪə,wɜːks) *n.* (*functioning as sing. or pl.*) a factory where wire or articles of wire are made.

wireworm ('waɪə,wɜːm) *n.* the wormlike larva of various beetles, which feeds on the roots of many plants and is a serious pest.

wiring ('waɪərɪŋ) *n.* **1.** the network of wires used in an electrical system, device, or circuit. ~*adj.* **2.** used in wiring.

Wirral ('wɪrəl) *n.* **the.** a peninsula in NW England between the estuaries of the Rivers Mersey and Dee.

wiry ('waɪərɪ) *adj.* **wirier, wiriest. 1.** (of people or animals) slender but strong in constitution. **2.** made of or resembling wire, esp. in stiffness: *wiry hair.* **3.** (of a sound) produced by or as if by a vibrating wire. — **'wirily** *adv.* — **'wiriness** *n.*

wis (wɪs) *vb. Arch.* to know or suppose (something). [C17: a form derived from *iwis*, (from OE *gewiss* certain), mistakenly interpreted as *I wis* I know, as if from OE *witan* to know]

Wisconsin (wɪs'kɒnsɪn) *n.* **1.** a state of the N central U.S., on Lake Superior and Lake Michigan: consists of an undulating plain, with uplands in the north and west; over 168 m (550 ft.) above sea level along the shore of Lake Michigan. Capital: Madison. Pop.: 4 794 792 (1987 est.). Area: 141 061 sq. km (54 464 sq. miles). Abbrevs.: **Wis.** or (with zip code) **WI 2.** a river in central and SW Wisconsin, flowing south and west to the Mississippi. Length: 692 km (430 miles). — **Wis'consin,ite** *n.*

Wisden ('wɪzdən) *n.* **John.** 1826–84, English cricketer; publisher of *Wisden Cricketers' Almanack*, which first appeared in 1864.

wisdom ('wɪzdəm) *n.* **1.** the ability or result of an ability to think and act utilizing knowledge, experience, understanding, common sense, and insight. **2.** accumulated knowledge or enlightenment. **3.** *Arch.* a wise saying or wise sayings. ~Related adj.: **sagacious.** [OE *wisdōm*]

wisdom tooth *n.* **1.** any of the four molar teeth, one at the back of each side of the jaw, that are the last of the permanent teeth to erupt. Technical name: **third molar. 2. cut one's wisdom teeth.** to arrive at the age of discretion.

wise¹ (waɪz) *adj.* **1.** possessing, showing, or prompted by wisdom or discernment. **2.** prudent; sensible. **3.** shrewd; crafty: *a wise plan.* **4.** well-informed; erudite. **5.** informed or knowing (esp. in **none the wiser**). **6.** (*postpositive; often foll. by to*) *Sl.* in the know, esp. possessing inside information (about). **7.** *Arch.* possessing powers of magic. **8. be** *or* **get wise.** (often foll. by *to*) *Inf.* to be or become aware or informed (of something). **9. put wise.** (often foll. by *to*) *Sl.* to inform or warn (of). ~*vb.* **10.** See **wise up.** [OE *wīs*] — **'wisely** *adv.* — **'wiseness** *n.*

wise² (waɪz) *n. Arch.* way, manner, fashion, or respect (esp. in **any wise, in no wise**). [OE *wīse* manner]

-wise *adv. combining form.* **1.** indicating direction or manner: *clockwise; likewise.* **2.** with reference to: *businesswise.* [OE *-wīsan;* see WISE²]

▷ *Usage.* The addition of *-wise* to a noun as a replacement for a lengthier phrase (such as *as far as . . . is concerned*) is considered unacceptable by most careful speakers and writers: *talentwise, he's a little weak* (he's a little weak as regards talent).

wiseacre ('waɪz,eɪkə) *n.* **1.** a person who wishes to seem wise. **2.** a wise person: often used facetiously or contemptuously. [C16: from MDu. *wijsseggher* soothsayer. See WISE[1], SAY]

wisecrack ('waɪz,kræk) *Inf.* ~*n.* **1.** a flippant jibe or sardonic remark. ~*vb.* (*intr.*) **2.** to make a wisecrack. —'**wise,cracker** *n.*

wise guy *n. Inf.* a person who is given to making conceited, sardonic, or insolent comments.

Wiseman ('waɪzmən) *n.* **Nicholas Patrick Stephen.** 1802–65, British cardinal; first Roman Catholic archbishop of Westminster (1850–65).

wisent ('wiːzᵊnt) *n.* another name for **European bison.** See **bison** (sense 2). [G, from OHG *wisunt* BISON]

wise up *vb.* (*adv.*) *Sl., chiefly U.S. & Canad.* (often foll. by *to*) to become or cause to become aware or informed (of).

wish (wɪʃ) *vb.* **1.** (when *tr.*, *takes a clause as object or an infinitive;* when *intr.*, often foll. by *for*) to want or desire (something, often that which cannot be or is not the case): *I wish I lived in Italy.* **2.** (*tr.*) to feel or express a desire or hope concerning the future or fortune of: *I wish you well.* **3.** (*tr.*) to desire or prefer to be as specified. **4.** (*tr.*) to greet as specified: *he wished us good afternoon.* ~*n.* **5.** the expression of some desire or mental inclination: *to make a wish.* **6.** something desired or wished for: *he got his wish.* **7.** (*usually pl.*) expressed hopes or desire, esp. for someone's welfare, health, etc. **8.** (*often pl.*) *Formal.* a polite order or request. ~See also **wish on.** [OE *wȳscan*] —'**wisher** *n.*

wishbone ('wɪʃ,bəʊn) *n.* the V-shaped bone above the breastbone in most birds consisting of the fused clavicles. [C17: from the custom of two people breaking apart the bone after eating: the person with the longer part makes a wish]

wishful ('wɪʃfʊl) *adj.* having wishes or characterized by wishing. —'**wishfully** *adv.* —'**wishfulness** *n.*

wish fulfilment *n.* (in Freudian psychology) any successful attempt to fulfil a wish stemming from the unconscious mind, whether in fact, in fantasy, or by disguised means.

wishful thinking *n.* the erroneous belief that one's wishes are in accordance with reality. —**wishful thinker** *n.*

wish on *vb.* (*tr., prep.*) to hope that (someone or something) should be imposed (on someone); foist: *I wouldn't wish my cold on anyone.*

wishy-washy ('wɪʃɪ,wɒʃɪ) *adj. Inf.* **1.** lacking in substance, force, colour, etc. **2.** watery; thin.

Wisla ('viswa) *n.* the Polish name for **Vistula** (sense 1).

Wislany Zalew (*Polish* viʃˈlaːni ˈzaːlɛf) *n.* the Polish name for the **Vistula** (sense 2).

Wismar (*German* 'vɪsmar) *n.* a port in N East Germany, on an inlet of the Baltic: shipbuilding industries. Pop.: 57 800 (1981 est.).

wisp (wɪsp) *n.* **1.** a thin, light, delicate, or fibrous piece or strand, such as a streak of smoke or a lock of hair. **2.** a small bundle, as of hay or straw. **3.** anything slender and delicate: *a wisp of a girl.* **4.** a mere suggestion or hint. **5.** a flock of birds, esp. snipe. [C14: var. of *wips*, from ?] —'**wisp,like** *adj.* —'**wispy** *adj.*

wist (wɪst) *vb. Arch.* the past tense and past participle of **wit**[2].

wisteria (wɪ'stɪərɪə) *n.* any twining woody climbing plant of the genus *Wisteria*, of E Asia and North America, having blue, purple, or white flowers in large drooping clusters. [C19: from NL, after Caspar *Wistar* (1761–1818), U.S. anatomist]

wistful ('wɪstfʊl) *adj.* sadly pensive, esp. about something yearned for. —'**wistfully** *adv.* —'**wistfulness** *n.*

wit[1] (wɪt) *n.* **1.** the talent or quality of using unexpected associations between contrasting or disparate words or ideas to make a clever humorous effect. **2.** speech or writing showing this quality. **3.** a person possessing, showing, or noted for such an ability. **4.** practical intelligence (esp. in **have the wit to**). **5.** *Arch.* mental capacity or a person possessing it. ~See also **wits.** [OE *witt*]

wit[2] (wɪt) *vb.* **wot, wist. 1.** *Arch.* to be or become aware of (something). **2. to wit.** that is to say; namely (used to introduce statements, as in legal documents). [OE *witan*]

witan ('wɪtᵊn) *n.* (in Anglo-Saxon England) **1.** an assembly of higher ecclesiastics and important laymen that met

to counsel the king on matters such as judicial problems. **2.** the members of this assembly. ~Also called: **witenagemot.** [OE *witan*, pl. of *wita* wise man]

witblitz ('vɪt,blɪts) *n. S. African.* alcoholic drink illegally distilled. [from Afrik. *wit* white + *blits* lightning]

witch[1] (wɪtʃ) *n.* **1.** a person, usually female, who practises or professes to practise magic or sorcery, esp. black magic, or is believed to have dealings with the devil. **2.** an ugly or wicked old woman. **3.** a fascinating or enchanting woman. ~*vb.* (*tr.*) **4.** a less common word for **bewitch.** [OE *wicca*] —'**witch,like** *adj.*

witch[2] (wɪtʃ) *n.* a flatfish of N Atlantic coastal waters, having a narrow greyish-brown body marked with tiny black spots: related to the plaice, flounder, etc. [C19: ?from WITCH[1], from the appearance of the fish]

witchcraft ('wɪtʃ,krɑːft) *n.* **1.** the art or power of bringing magical or preternatural power to bear or the act or practice of attempting to do so. **2.** the influence of magic or sorcery. **3.** fascinating or bewitching influence or charm.

witch doctor *n.* a man in certain societies, esp. preliterate ones, who appears to possess magical powers, used esp. to cure sickness but also to harm people. Also called: **shaman, medicine man.**

witch-elm *n.* a variant spelling of **wych-elm.**

witchery ('wɪtʃərɪ) *n., pl.* **-eries. 1.** the practice of witchcraft. **2.** magical or bewitching influence or charm.

witches'-broom *n.* a dense abnormal growth of shoots on a tree or other woody plant, usually caused by parasitic fungi.

witchetty grub ('wɪtʃɪtɪ) *n.* the wood-boring edible caterpillar of an Australian moth. Also: **witchetty, witchety.** [C19 *witchetty*, from Abor.]

witch hazel *or* **wych-hazel** *n.* **1.** any of a genus of trees and shrubs of North America, having ornamental yellow flowers and medicinal properties. **2.** an astringent medicinal solution containing an extract of the bark and leaves of one of these shrubs, applied to treat bruises, inflammation, etc.

witch-hunt *n.* a rigorous campaign to expose dissenters on the pretext of safeguarding the public welfare. —'**witch-,hunting** *n., adj.*

witching ('wɪtʃɪŋ) *adj.* **1.** relating to or appropriate for witchcraft. **2.** *Now rare.* bewitching. —'**witchingly** *adv.*

witching hour *n.* **the.** the hour at which witches are supposed to appear, usually midnight.

witenagemot (,wɪtɪnəgɪ'məʊt) *n.* another word for **witan.** [OE *witena*, genitive pl. of *wita* councillor + *gemōt* meeting]

with (wɪð, wɪθ) *prep.* **1.** using; by means of: *he killed her with an axe.* **2.** accompanying; in the company of: *the lady you were with.* **3.** possessing; having: *a man with a red moustache.* **4.** concerning or regarding: *be patient with her.* **5.** in spite of: *with all his talents, he was still humble.* **6.** used to indicate a time or distance by which something is away from something else: *with three miles to go, he collapsed.* **7.** in a manner characterized by: *writing with abandon.* **8.** caused or prompted by: *shaking with rage.* **9.** often used with a verb indicating a reciprocal action or relation between the subject and the preposition's object: *agreeing with me.* **10. with it.** *Inf.* **a.** fashionable; in style. **b.** comprehending what is happening or being said. **11. with that.** after that. [OE]

withal (wɪ'ðɔːl) *adv.* **1.** *Literary.* as well. **2.** *Arch.* therewith. ~*prep.* **3.** (*postpositive*) an archaic word for **with.** [C12: from WITH + ALL]

withdraw (wɪð'drɔː) *vb.* **-drawing, -drew, -drawn. 1.** (*tr.*) to take or draw back or away; remove. **2.** (*tr.*) to remove from deposit or investment in a bank, etc. **3.** (*tr.*) to retract or recall (a promise, etc.). **4.** (*intr.*) to retire or retreat: *the troops withdrew.* **5.** (*intr.;* often foll. by *from*) to depart (from): *he withdrew from public life.* **6.** (*intr.*) to detach oneself socially, emotionally, or mentally. [C13: from WITH (in the sense: away from) + DRAW] —**with'drawer** *n.*

withdrawal (wɪð'drɔːəl) *n.* **1.** an act or process of withdrawing. **2.** the period a drug addict goes through following abrupt termination in the use of narcotics, usually characterized by physical and mental symptoms (**withdrawal symptoms**). **3.** Also called: **withdrawal method, coitus interruptus.** the deliberate withdrawing of the penis from the vagina before ejaculation, as a method of contraception.

withdrawing room n. an archaic term for **drawing room.**

withdrawn (wɪð'drɔ:n) vb. **1.** the past participle of **withdraw.** ~adj. **2.** unusually reserved or shy. **3.** secluded or remote.

withe (wɪθ, wɪð, waɪð) n. **1.** a strong flexible twig, esp. of willow, suitable for binding things together; withy. **2.** a band or rope of twisted twigs or stems. ~vb. **3.** (tr.) to bind with withes. [OE withthe]

wither ('wɪðə) vb. **1.** (intr.) (esp. of a plant) to droop, wilt, or shrivel up. **2.** (intr.; often foll. by away) to fade or waste: all hope withered away. **3.** (intr.) to decay or disintegrate. **4.** (tr.) to cause to wilt or lose vitality. **5.** (tr.) to abash, esp. with a scornful look. [C14: ? var. of WEATHER (vb.)] —'witherer n. —'withering adj. —'witheringly adv.

withers ('wɪðəz) pl. n. the highest part of the back of a horse, behind the neck between the shoulders. [C16: short for widersones, from wider with + -sones, ? var. of SINEW]

withershins ('wɪðə,ʃɪnz) or **widdershins** adv. Chiefly Scot. in the direction contrary to the apparent course of the sun; anticlockwise. [C16: from MLow G weddersinnes, from MHG, lit.: opposite course, from wider against + sinnes, genitive of sin course]

withhold (wɪð'həʊld) vb. **-holding, -held. 1.** (tr.) to keep back: he withheld his permission. **2.** (tr.) to hold back; restrain. **3.** (intr.; usually foll. by from) to refrain or forbear. —**with'holder** n.

within (wɪ'ðɪn) prep. **1.** in; inside; enclosed or encased by. **2.** before (a period of time) has elapsed: within a week. **3.** not differing by more than (a specified amount) from: live within your means. ~adv. **4.** Formal. inside; internally.

without (wɪ'ðaʊt) prep. **1.** not having: a traveller without much money. **2.** not accompanied by: he came without his wife. **3.** not making use of: it is not easy to undo screws without a screwdriver. **4.** (foll. by a present participle) not, while not, or after not: she can sing for two minutes without drawing breath. **5.** Arch. on the outside of: without the city walls. ~adv. **6.** Formal. outside.

withstand (wɪð'stænd) vb. **-standing, -stood. 1.** (tr.) to resist. **2.** (intr.) to remain firm in endurance or opposition. —**with'stander** n.

withy ('wɪðɪ) n., pl. **withies.** a variant spelling of **withe** (senses 1, 2). [OE widig(e)]

witless ('wɪtlɪs) adj. lacking wit, intelligence, or sense. —'witlessly adv. —'witlessness n.

witling ('wɪtlɪŋ) n. Arch. a person who thinks himself witty.

witness ('wɪtnɪs) n. **1.** a person who has seen or can give first-hand evidence of some event. **2.** a person or thing giving or serving as evidence. **3.** a person who testifies, esp. in a court of law, to events or facts within his own knowledge. **4.** a person who attests to the genuineness of a document, signature, etc., by adding his own signature. **5. bear witness to. a.** to give written or oral testimony to. **b.** to be evidence or proof of. ~Related adj.: **testimonial.** ~vb. **6.** (tr.) to see, be present at, or know at first hand. **7.** (tr.) to give evidence of. **8.** (tr.) to be the scene or setting of: this field has witnessed a battle. **9.** (intr.) to testify, esp. in a court of law, to events within a person's own knowledge. **10.** (tr.) to attest to the genuineness of (a document, etc.) by adding one's own signature. [OE witnes, from witan to know + -NESS] —'witnesser n.

witness box or esp. U.S. **witness stand** n. the place in a court of law in which witnesses stand to give evidence.

wits (wɪts) pl. n. **1.** (sometimes sing.) the ability to reason and act, esp. quickly (esp. in **have one's wits about one**). **2.** (sometimes sing.) right mind, sanity (esp. in **out of one's wits**). **3. at one's wits' end.** at a loss to know how to proceed. **4. live by one's wits.** to gain a livelihood by craftiness rather than by hard work.

-witted adj. (in combination) having wits or intelligence as specified: slow-witted; dim-witted.

Wittenberg (German 'vɪtənbɛrk; English 'wɪt²n,bɜ:g) n. a city in central East Germany, on the River Elbe: Martin Luther, as a philosophy teacher at Wittenberg university, began the Reformation here in 1517 by nailing his 95 theses to the doors of a church. Pop.: 54 043 (1983 est.).

witter ('wɪtə) vb. (intr.; often foll. by on) Inf. to chatter or babble pointlessly or at unnecessary length. [C20: ?from obs. whitter to warble, twitter]

Wittgenstein ('vɪtgən,ʃtaɪn, -,staɪn) n. **Ludwig Josef Johann** ('lu:tvɪç 'jo:zɛf jo'han). 1889–1951, British philosopher, born in Austria. After studying with Bertrand Russell, he wrote the Tractatus Logico-Philosophicus (1921), which explores the relationship of language to the world. He was a major influence on logical positivism but later repudiated this, and in Philosophical Investigations (1953) he argues that philosophical problems arise from insufficient attention to the variety of natural language use. —'Wittgen,steinian adj.

witticism ('wɪtɪ,sɪzəm) n. a clever or witty remark. [C17: from WITTY; coined by Dryden (1677) by analogy with criticism]

witting ('wɪtɪŋ) adj. Rare. **1.** deliberate; intentional. **2.** aware. —'wittingly adv.

witty ('wɪtɪ) adj. **-tier, -tiest. 1.** characterized by clever humour or wit. **2.** Arch. or dialect. intelligent. —'wittily adv. —'wittiness n.

Witwatersrand (wɪt'wɔ:təz,rænd; Afrikaans vət'vɑ:tərs'rant) n. a rocky ridge in NE South Africa, in S Transvaal: contains the richest gold deposits in the world, also coal and manganese; chief industrial centre is Johannesburg. Height: 1500–1800 m (5000–6000 ft.). Also called: **the Rand, the Reef.**

wive (waɪv) vb. Arch. **1.** to marry (a woman). **2.** (tr.) to supply with a wife. [OE gewīfian, from wīf wife]

wivern ('waɪvən) n. a less common spelling of **wyvern.**

wives (waɪvz) n. **1.** the plural of **wife. 2. old wives' tale.** a superstitious tradition, occasionally one that contains an element of truth.

wiz (wɪz) n., pl. **wizzes.** Inf. a variant spelling of **whiz** (sense 5).

wizard ('wɪzəd) n. **1.** a male witch or a man who practises or professes to practise magic or sorcery. **2.** a person who is outstandingly clever in some specified field. ~adj. **3.** Inf., chiefly Brit. superb; outstanding. **4.** of or relating to a wizard or wizardry. [C15: var. of wissard, from WISE¹ + -ARD] —'wizardly adj.

wizardry ('wɪzədrɪ) n. the art, skills, and practices of a wizard, sorcerer, or magician.

wizen ('wɪz²n) vb. **1.** to make or become shrivelled. ~adj. **2.** a variant of **wizened.** [OE wisnian]

wizened ('wɪz²nd) or **wizen** adj. shrivelled, wrinkled, or dried up, esp. with age.

wk abbrev. for: **1.** (pl. **wks**) week. **2.** work.

wkly abbrev. for weekly.

w.l. or **WL** abbrev. for water line.

WMO abbrev. for World Meteorological Organization.

WNW symbol for west-northwest.

WO abbrev. for: **1.** War Office. **2.** Warrant Officer. **3.** wireless operator.

woad (wəʊd) n. **1.** a European cruciferous plant, formerly cultivated for its leaves, which yield a blue dye. **2.** the dye obtained from this plant, used esp. by the ancient Britons as a body dye. [OE wād]

wobbegong ('wɒbɪ,gɒŋ) n. any of various sharks of Australian waters, having a richly patterned brown-and-white skin. [from Abor.]

wobble ('wɒb²l) vb. **1.** (intr.) to move or sway unsteadily. **2.** (intr.) to shake: her voice wobbled with emotion. **3.** (intr.) to vacillate with indecision. **4.** (tr.) to cause to wobble. ~n. **5.** a wobbling movement or sound. [C17: var. of wabble, from Low G wabbeln] —'wobbler n.

wobble board n. Austral. a piece of fibreboard used as a rhythmical musical instrument, producing a characteristic sound when flexed.

wobbly ('wɒblɪ) adj. **-blier, -bliest. 1.** shaky, unstable, or unsteady. ~n. **2. throw a wobbly.** Sl. to become suddenly very agitated or angry. —'wobbliness n.

Wodehouse ('wʊd,haʊs) n. Sir **P(elham) G(renville).** 1881–1975, U.S. author, born in England. His humorous novels of upper-class life in England include the Psmith and Jeeves series.

Woden or **Wodan** ('wəʊd²n) n. the foremost Anglo-Saxon god. Norse counterpart: **Odin.** [OE Wōden; related to ON Othinn, OHG Wuotan, G Wotan; see WEDNESDAY]

wodge (wɒdʒ) n. Brit. inf. a thick lump or chunk cut or broken off something. [C20: alteration of WEDGE]

woe (wəu) *n.* **1.** *Literary.* intense grief. **2.** (*often pl.*) affliction or misfortune. **3. woe betide (someone).** misfortune will befall (someone): *woe betide you if you arrive late.* ~*interj.* **4.** Also: **woe is me.** *Arch.* an exclamation of sorrow or distress. [OE *wā, wǣ*]

woebegone ('wəubɪˌɡɒn) *adj.* sorrowful or sad in appearance. [C14: from a phrase such as *me is wo begon* woe has beset me]

woeful ('wəufʊl) *adj.* **1.** expressing or characterized by sorrow. **2.** bringing or causing woe. **3.** pitiful; miserable: *a woeful standard of work.* —'**woefully** *adv.* —'**woefulness** *n.*

WOF (in New Zealand) *abbrev. for* Warrant of Fitness.

wog[1] (wɒɡ) *n. Brit. sl., derog.* a person who is not White. [prob. from GOLLIWOG]

wog[2] (wɒɡ) *n. Austral. sl.* any ailment or disease, such as influenza, a virus infection, etc. [C20: from ?]

woggle ('wɒɡ²l) *n.* the ring of leather through which a Scout neckerchief is threaded. [C20: from ?]

wok (wɒk) *n.* a large metal Chinese cooking pot having a curved base like a bowl: used esp. for stir-frying. [from Chinese (Cantonese)]

woke (wəuk) *vb.* the past tense of **wake**[1].

woken ('wəukən) *vb.* the past participle of **wake**[1].

Woking ('wəukɪŋ) *n.* a town in S England, in central Surrey: mainly residential. Pop.: 81 358 (1981).

wold[1] (wəuld) *n. Chiefly literary.* a tract of open rolling country, esp. upland. [OE *weald* bush]

wold[2] (wəuld) *n.* a variant of **weld**[2].

Wolds (wəuldz) *pl. n.* **the.** a range of chalk hills in NE England: consists of the **Yorkshire Wolds** to the north, separated from the **Lincolnshire Wolds** by the Humber estuary.

wolf (wulf) *n., pl.* **wolves. 1.** a predatory canine mammal which hunts in packs and was formerly widespread in North America and Eurasia but is now less common. Related adj.: **lupine. 2.** any of several similar and related canines, such as the red wolf and the coyote (**prairie wolf**). **3.** the fur of any such animal. **4.** a voracious or fiercely cruel person or thing. **5.** *Inf.* a man who habitually tries to seduce women. **6.** Also called: **wolf note.** *Music.* **a.** an unpleasant sound produced in some notes played on the violin, etc., owing to resonant vibrations of the belly. **b.** an out-of-tune effect produced on keyboard instruments accommodated esp. to the system of meantone temperament. **7. cry wolf.** to give a false alarm. **8. have** *or* **hold a wolf by the ears.** to be in a desperate situation. **9. keep the wolf from the door.** to ward off starvation or privation. **10. lone wolf.** a person or animal who prefers to be alone. **11. wolf in sheep's clothing.** a malicious person in a harmless or benevolent disguise. ~*vb.* **12.** (*tr.*; often foll. by *down*) to gulp (down). **13.** (*intr.*) to hunt wolves. [OE *wulf*] —'**wolfish** *adj.* —'**wolf,like** *adj.*

Wolf (German vɔlf) *n.* **1. Friedrich August** ('fri:drɪç 'august). 1759–1824, German classical scholar, who suggested that the Homeric poems, esp. the *Iliad*, are products of an oral tradition. **2. Hugo** ('hu:ɡo). 1860–1903, Austrian composer, esp. of songs, including the *Italienisches Liederbuch* and the *Spanisches Liederbuch*. **3.** (wulf). **Howlin'.** See **Howlin' Wolf**.

Wolf Cub *n. Brit.* the former name for **Cub Scout**.

Wolfe (wulf) *n.* **1. James.** 1727–59, English soldier, who commanded the British capture of Quebec, in which he was killed. **2. Thomas** (**Clayton**). 1900–38, U.S. novelist, noted for his autobiographical fiction, esp. *Look Homeward, Angel* (1929).

Wolf-Ferrari (*Italian* 'vɔlffer'ra:ri) *n.* **Ermanno** (er'manno). 1867–1948, Italian composer born of a German father, in Germany from 1909. His works, mainly in a lyrical style, include operas, such as *The Jewels of the Madonna* (1911) and *Susanna's Secret* (1909).

wolffish ('wulf,fɪʃ) *n., pl.* **-fish** *or* **-fishes.** a large northern deep-sea fish. It has large sharp teeth and no pelvic fins and is used as a food fish. Also called: **catfish.**

wolfhound ('wulf,haund) *n.* the largest breed of dog, used formerly to hunt wolves.

Wolfit ('wulfɪt) *n.* Sir **Donald.** 1902–68, English stage actor and manager.

wolfram ('wulfrəm) *n.* another name for **tungsten.** [C18: from G, orig. ?from the proper name *Wolfram*, used pejoratively of tungsten because it was thought inferior to tin]

wolframite ('wulfrə,maɪt) *n.* a black to reddish-brown mineral, a compound of tungsten, iron, and manganese: it is the chief ore of tungsten.

Wolfram von Eschenbach (*German* 'vɔlfram fɔn 'ɛʃənbax) *n.* died ?1220, German poet: author of the epic *Parzival*, incorporating the story of the Grail.

wolfsbane ('wulfs,beɪn) *or* **wolf's bane** *n.* any of several poisonous N temperate plants of the ranunculaceous genus *Aconitum* having hoodlike flowers.

Wolfsburg (*German* 'vɔlfsburk) *n.* a city in NE West Germany, in Lower Saxony: founded in 1938; motor-vehicle industry. Pop.: 122 000 (1986).

wolf spider *n.* a spider which chases its prey to catch it. Also called: **hunting spider.**

wolf whistle *n.* **1.** a whistle made by a man to express admiration of a woman's appearance. ~*vb.* **wolf-whistle. 2.** (when *intr.*, sometimes foll. by *at*) to make such a whistle (at someone).

Wollongong ('wulən,ɡɒŋ) *n.* a city in E Australia, in E New South Wales on the Pacific: an early centre of dairy farming; now a coal-mining and heavy industrial centre. Pop.: 237 600 (1985 est.).

Wollstonecraft ('wulstən,krɑːft) *n.* See (Mary Wollstonecraft) **Godwin.**

Wolof ('wɒlɒf) *n.* **1.** (*pl.* **-of** *or* **-ofs**) a member of a Negroid people of W Africa living chiefly in Senegal. **2.** the language of this people, belonging to the Niger-Congo family.

Wolsey ('wulzɪ) *n.* **Thomas.** ?1475–1530, English cardinal and statesman; archbishop of York (1514–30); lord chancellor (1515–29). He dominated Henry VIII's foreign and domestic policies but his failure to obtain papal consent for the king's divorce from Catherine of Aragon led to his arrest for high treason (1530); he died on the journey to face trial.

Wolverhampton (,wulvə'hæmptən) *n.* a town in W central England, in the West Midlands: iron and steel foundries. Pop.: 254 000 (1984).

wolverine ('wulvə,ri:n) *n.* a large musteline mammal of northern forests of Eurasia and North America having dark very thick water-resistant fur. Also called: **glutton.** [C16 *wolvering*, from WOLF + -ING[3] (later altered to *-ine*)]

wolves (wulvz) *n.* the plural of **wolf.**

woman ('wumən) *n., pl.* **women. 1.** an adult female human being. **2.** (*modifier*) female or feminine: *a woman politician.* **3.** women collectively. **4.** (usually preceded by *the*) feminine nature or feelings: *babies bring out the woman in him.* **5.** a female servant or domestic help. **6.** a man considered as having female characteristics, such as meekness. **7.** *Inf.* a wife or girlfriend. **8. the little woman.** *Brit. inf., old-fashioned.* one's wife. **9. woman of the streets.** a prostitute. ~*vb.* (*tr.*) **10.** *Obs.* to make effeminate. [OE *wīfmann, wimman*] —'**womanless** *adj.* —'**woman-,like** *adj.*

womanhood ('wumən,hud) *n.* **1.** the state or quality of being a woman or being womanly. **2.** women collectively.

womanish ('wumənɪʃ) *adj.* **1.** having qualities regarded as unsuitable to a man. **2.** characteristic of or suitable for a woman. —'**womanishly** *adv.* —'**womanishness** *n.*

womanize *or* **-ise** ('wumə,naɪz) *vb.* **1.** (*intr.*) (of a man) to indulge in casual affairs with women. **2.** (*tr.*) to make effeminate. —'**woman,izer** *or* **-,iser** *n.*

womankind ('wumən,kaɪnd) *n.* the female members of the human race; women collectively.

womanly ('wumənlɪ) *adj.* **1.** possessing qualities, such as warmth, attractiveness, etc., generally regarded as typical of a woman. **2.** characteristic of or belonging to a woman.

womb (wu:m) *n.* **1.** the nontechnical name for **uterus. 2.** a hollow space enclosing something. **3.** a place where something is conceived: *the Near East is the womb of western civilization.* **4.** *Obs.* the belly. [OE *wamb*] —**wombed** *adj.* —'**womb,like** *adj.*

wombat ('wɒmbæt) *n.* a burrowing herbivorous Australian marsupial having short limbs, a heavy body, and coarse dense fur. [C18: from Abor.]

women ('wɪmɪn) *n.* the plural of **woman.**

womenfolk ('wɪmɪn,fəuk) *pl. n.* **1.** women collectively. **2.** a group of women, esp. the female members of one's family.

Women's Institute *n.* (in Britain and Commonwealth countries) a society for women interested in engaging in craft and cultural activities.

Women's Liberation *n.* a movement directed towards the removal of attitudes and practices that preserve inequalities based upon the assumption that men are superior to women. Also called: **women's lib.**

Women's Movement *n.* a grass-roots movement of women concerned with women's liberation. See **Women's Liberation.**

won (wʌn) *vb.* the past tense and past participle of **win.**

wonder ('wʌndə) *n.* **1.** the feeling excited by something strange; a mixture of surprise, curiosity, and sometimes awe. **2.** something that causes such a feeling, such as a miracle. **3.** (*modifier*) exciting wonder by virtue of spectacular results achieved, feats performed, etc.: *a wonder drug.* **4. do** *or* **work wonders.** to achieve spectacularly fine results. **5. nine days' wonder.** a subject that arouses general surprise or public interest for a short time. **6. no wonder.** (*sentence connector*) (I am) not surprised at all (that): *no wonder he couldn't come.* **7. small wonder.** (*sentence connector*) (I am) hardly surprised (that): *small wonder he couldn't make it tonight.* ~*vb.* (when *tr.*, may take a clause as object) **8.** (when *intr.*, often foll. by *about*) to indulge in speculative inquiry: *I wondered about what she said.* **9.** (when *intr.*, often foll. by *at*) to be amazed (at something): *I wonder at your impudence.* [OE *wundor*] —'**wonderer** *n.*

Wonder ('wʌndə) *n.* **Stevie.** real name *Steveland Judkins Morris.* born 1950, U.S. Motown singer, songwriter, and multi-instrumentalist. His recordings include *Up-Tight* (1966), "Superstition" (1972), *Innervisions* (1973), and *Songs in the Key of Life* (1976).

wonderful ('wʌndəfʊl) *adj.* **1.** exciting a feeling of wonder. **2.** extremely fine; excellent. —'**wonderfully** *adv.*

wonderland ('wʌndə,lænd) *n.* **1.** an imaginary land of marvels or wonders. **2.** an actual place or scene of great or strange beauty or wonder.

wonderment ('wʌndəmənt) *n.* **1.** rapt surprise; awe. **2.** puzzled interest. **3.** something that excites wonder.

wonderwork ('wʌndə,wɜːk) *n.* something done or made that excites wonder. —'**wonder-,worker** *n.* —'**wonder-,working** *n., adj.*

wondrous ('wʌndrəs) *Arch. or literary.* ~*adj.* **1.** exciting wonder; marvellous. ~*adv.* **2.** (intensifier): *it is wondrous cold.* —'**wondrously** *adv.* —'**wondrousness** *n.*

wonky ('wɒŋkɪ) *adj.* **-kier, -kiest.** *Brit. sl.* **1.** unsteady. **2.** askew. **3.** liable to break down. [C20: var. of dialect *wanky,* from OE *wancol*]

Wŏnsan (wɒn'sæn) *n.* a port in SE North Korea, on the Sea of Japan: oil refineries. Pop.: 398 000 (1981).

wont (wəʊnt) *adj.* **1.** (*postpositive*) accustomed (to doing something): *he was wont to come early.* ~*n.* **2.** a manner or action habitually employed by or associated with someone (often in **as is my wont, as is his wont,** etc.). ~*vb.* **3.** (when *tr.*, usually passive) to become or cause to become accustomed. [OE *gewunod,* p.p. of *wunian* to be accustomed to]

won't (wəʊnt) *contraction of* will not.

wonted ('wəʊntɪd) *adj.* **1.** (*postpositive*) accustomed (to doing something). **2.** (*prenominal*) usual: *she is in her wonted place.*

woo (wuː) *vb.* **wooing, wooed. 1.** to seek the affection, favour, or love of (a woman) with a view to marriage. **2.** (*tr.*) to seek after zealously: *to woo fame.* **3.** (*tr.*) to beg or importune (someone). [OE *wōgian,* from ?] —'**wooer** *n.* —'**wooing** *n.*

wood (wʊd) *n.* **1.** the hard fibrous substance consisting of xylem tissue that occurs beneath the bark in trees, shrubs, and similar plants. **2.** the trunks of trees that have been cut and prepared for use as a building material. **3.** a collection of trees, shrubs, grasses, etc., usually dominated by one or a few species of tree: usually smaller than a forest: *an oak wood.* Related adj.: **sylvan. 4.** fuel; firewood. **5.** *Golf.* **a.** a long-shafted club with a wooden head, used for driving. **b.** (*as modifier*): *a wood shot.* **6.** *Tennis, etc.* the frame of a racket: *he hit a winning shot off the wood.* **7.** one of the biased wooden bowls used in the game of bowls. **8.** *Music.* short for **woodwind. 9. from the wood.** (of a beverage) from a wooden container rather than a metal or glass one. **10. out of the wood** *or* **woods.** clear of or safe from dangers or doubts: *we're not out of the wood yet.* **11. see the wood for the trees.** (*used with a negative*) to obtain a general view of a situation without allowing details to cloud one's analysis: *he can't see the wood for the trees.* **12.** (*modifier*) made of,

employing, or handling wood: *a wood fire.* **13.** (*modifier*) dwelling in or situated in a wood: *a wood nymph.* ~*vb.* **14.** (*tr.*) to plant a wood upon. **15.** to supply or be supplied with firewood. ~See also **woods.** [OE *widu, wudu*]

Wood (wʊd) *n.* Sir **Henry (Joseph).** 1869–1944, English conductor, who founded the Promenade Concerts in London.

wood alcohol *n.* another name for **methanol.**

wood anemone *n.* any of several woodland anemone plants having finely divided leaves and solitary white flowers. Also called: **windflower.**

wood avens *n.* another name for **herb bennet.**

woodbine ('wuːd,baɪn) *n.* **1.** a honeysuckle of Europe, SW Asia, and N Africa, having fragrant yellow flowers. **2.** *U.S.* another name for **Virginia creeper. 3.** *Austral. sl.* an Englishman.

wood block *n.* a small rectangular flat block of wood that is laid with others as a floor surface.

woodcarving ('wʊd,kɑːvɪŋ) *n.* **1.** the act of carving wood. **2.** a work of art produced by carving wood. —'**wood,carver** *n.*

woodchuck ('wʊd,tʃʌk) *n.* a North American marmot having coarse reddish-brown fur. Also called: **groundhog.** [C17: by folk etymology from Cree *otcheck* fisher, marten]

woodcock ('wʊd,kɒk) *n.* an Old World game bird resembling the snipe but larger and having shorter legs and neck.

woodcraft ('wʊd,krɑːft) *n.* *Chiefly U.S. & Canad.* **1.** ability and experience in matters concerned with living in a wood or forest. **2.** ability or skill at woodwork, carving, etc.

woodcut ('wʊd,kʌt) *n.* **1.** a block of wood with a design, illustration, etc., from which prints are made. **2.** a print from a woodcut.

woodcutter ('wʊd,kʌtə) *n.* **1.** a person who fells trees or chops wood. **2.** a person who makes woodcuts. —'**wood,cutting** *n.*

wooded ('wʊdɪd) *adj.* **a.** covered with or abounding in woods or trees. **b.** (*in combination*): *a soft-wooded tree.*

wooden ('wʊdⁿn) *adj.* **1.** made from or consisting of wood. **2.** awkward or clumsy. **3.** bereft of spirit or animation: *a wooden expression.* **4.** obstinately unyielding: *a wooden attitude.* **5.** mentally slow or dull. **6.** not highly resonant: *a wooden thud.* —'**woodenly** *adv.*

wood engraving *n.* **1.** the art of engraving pictures or designs on wood by incising them with a burin. **2.** a block of wood so engraved or a print taken from it. —**wood engraver** *n.*

woodenhead ('wʊdⁿn,hɛd) *n.* *Inf.* a dull, foolish, or unintelligent person. —,**wooden'headed** *adj.* —,**wooden-'headedness** *n.*

Wooden Horse *n.* another name for the **Trojan Horse** (sense 1).

wooden spoon *n.* a booby prize, esp. in sporting contests.

woodgrouse ('wʊd,graʊs) *n.* another name for **capercaillie.**

woodland ('wʊdlənd) *n.* **a.** land that is mostly covered with woods or dense growths of trees and shrubs. **b.** (*as modifier*): *woodland fauna.* —'**woodlander** *n.*

woodlark ('wʊd,lɑːk) *n.* an Old World lark similar to but slightly smaller than the skylark.

woodlouse ('wʊd,laʊs) *n., pl.* **-lice** (-,laɪs). any of various small terrestrial isopod crustaceans having a flattened segmented body and occurring in damp habitats.

woodman ('wʊdmən) *n., pl.* **-men. 1.** a person who looks after and fells trees used for timber. **2.** another word for **woodsman.**

woodnote ('wʊd,nəʊt) *n.* a natural musical note or song, like that of a wild bird.

wood nymph *n.* one of a class of nymphs fabled to inhabit the woods, such as a dryad.

woodpecker ('wʊd,pɛkə) *n.* a climbing bird, such as the **green woodpecker,** having a brightly coloured plumage and strong chisel-like bill with which it bores into trees for insects.

wood pigeon *n.* a large Eurasian pigeon having white patches on the wings and neck. Also called: **ringdove, cushat.**

woodpile ('wʊd,paɪl) *n.* a pile or heap of firewood.

wood pulp *n.* **1.** wood that has been ground to a fine pulp for use in making newsprint and other cheap forms of paper. **2.** finely pulped wood that has been digested by a chemical, such as caustic soda: used in making paper.

woodruff ('wodrʌf) n. any of several plants, esp. the sweet woodruff of Eurasia, which has small sweet-scented white flowers and whorls of narrow fragrant leaves used to flavour wine and liqueurs and in perfumery. [OE *wudurofe*, from WOOD + *rōfe*]

woods (wodz) pl. n. **1.** closely packed trees forming a forest or wood, esp. a specific one. **2.** another word for **backwoods** (sense 2). **3.** the woodwind instruments in an orchestra.

Woods n. **Lake of the.** See **Lake of the Woods.**

woodscrew ('wod,skru:) n. a metal screw that tapers to a point so that it can be driven into wood by a screwdriver.

woodshed ('wod,ʃɛd) n. a small outbuilding where firewood, garden tools, etc., are stored.

woodsman ('wodzmən) n., pl. **-men.** a person who lives in a wood or who is skilled in woodcraft. Also called: **woodman.**

wood sorrel n. a Eurasian plant having trifoliate leaves, an underground creeping stem, and white purple-veined flowers.

wood spirit n. Chem. another name for **methanol.**

wood tar n. any tar produced by the destructive distillation of wood.

wood warbler n. **1.** a European woodland warbler with a dull yellow plumage. **2.** another name for the **American warbler.** See **warbler** (sense 3).

woodwind ('wod,wɪnd) Music. ~adj. **1.** of, relating to, or denoting a type of wind instrument, formerly made of wood but now often made of metal, such as the flute. ~n. **2.** (functioning as pl.) woodwind instruments collectively.

woodwork ('wod,wɜːk) n. **1.** the art or craft of making things in wood. **2.** components made of wood, such as doors, staircases, etc.

woodworking ('wod,wɜːkɪŋ) n. **1.** the process of working wood. ~adj. **2.** of, relating to, or used in woodworking. —'**wood,worker** n.

woodworm ('wod,wɜːm) n. **1.** any of various insect larvae that bore into wooden furniture, beams, etc., esp. the larvae of the furniture beetle and the deathwatch beetle. **2.** the condition caused in wood by any of these larvae.

woody ('wodɪ) adj. **woodier, woodiest. 1.** abounding in or covered with forest or wood. **2.** connected with, belonging to, or situated in a wood. **3.** consisting of or containing wood or lignin: *woody tissue; woody stems.* **4.** resembling wood in hardness or texture. —'**woodiness** n.

woodyard ('wod,jɑːd) n. a place where timber is cut and stored.

woody nightshade n. a scrambling woody Eurasian plant, having purple flowers and producing poisonous red berry-like fruits. Also called: **bittersweet.**

woof[1] (wu:f) n. **1.** the crosswise yarns that fill the warp yarns in weaving; weft. **2.** a woven fabric or its texture. [OE *ōwef*, from *ō-*, ?from ON, + *wef* web (see WEAVE); modern form infl. by WARP]

woof[2] (wuf) interj. **1.** an imitation of the bark or growl of a dog. ~vb. **2.** (intr.) (of dogs) to bark.

woofer ('wu:fə) n. a loudspeaker used in high-fidelity systems for the reproduction of low audio frequencies.

wool (wol) n. **1.** the outer coat of sheep, yaks, etc., which consists of short curly hairs. **2.** yarn spun from the coat of sheep, etc., used in weaving, knitting, etc. **3. a.** cloth or a garment made from this yarn. **b.** (as modifier): *a wool dress.* **4.** any of certain fibrous materials: *glass wool; steel wool.* **5.** Inf. short thick curly hair. **6.** a tangled mass of soft fine hairs that occurs in certain plants. **7. keep one's wool on.** Brit. inf. to keep one's temper. **8. pull the wool over someone's eyes.** to deceive or delude someone. [OE *wull*] —'**wool,like** adj.

wool clip n. the total amount of wool shorn from a particular flock in one year.

Woolf (wolf) n. **1. Leonard Sidney.** 1880–1969, English publisher and political writer. **2.** his wife, **Virginia.** 1882–1941, English novelist and critic. Her novels, which include *Mrs. Dalloway* (1925), *To the Lighthouse* (1927), *The Waves* (1931), and *Between the Acts* (1941), employ such techniques as the interior monologue and stream of consciousness.

wool fat or **grease** n. another name for **lanolin.**

woolfell ('wol,fɛl) n. Obs. the skin of a sheep or similar animal with the fleece still attached.

woolgathering ('wol,gæðərɪŋ) n. idle or absent-minded daydreaming.

woolgrower ('wol,grəʊə) n. a person who keeps sheep for their wool. —'**wool,growing** n.

Woollcott ('wolkɒt) n. **Alexander.** 1887–1943, U.S. writer and critic. His collected essays include *Shouts and Murmurs* (1922).

woollen or U.S. **woolen** ('wolən) adj. **1.** relating to or consisting partly or wholly of wool. ~n. **2.** (often pl.) a garment or piece of cloth made wholly or partly of wool, esp. a knitted one.

Woolley ('wolɪ) n. Sir **(Charles) Leonard.** 1880–1960, English archaeologist, noted for his excavations at Ur in Mesopotamia (1922–34).

woolly or U.S. (often) **wooly** ('wolɪ) adj. **-lier, -liest. 1.** consisting of, resembling, or having the nature of wool. **2.** covered or clothed in wool or something resembling it. **3.** lacking clarity or substance: *woolly thinking.* **4.** Bot. covered with long soft whitish hairs: *woolly stems.* ~n., pl. **-lies. 5.** (often pl.) a garment, such as a sweater, made of wool or something similar. —'**woollily** adv. —'**woolliness** n.

woolly bear n. the caterpillar of any of various tiger moths, having a dense covering of soft hairs.

woolpack ('wol,pæk) n. **1.** the cloth wrapping used to pack a bale of wool. **2.** a bale of wool.

woolsack ('wol,sæk) n. **1.** a sack containing or intended to contain wool. **2.** (in Britain) the seat of the Lord Chancellor in the House of Lords, formerly made of a large square sack of wool.

woolshed ('wol,ʃɛd) n. Austral. & N.Z. a large building in which sheepshearing takes place.

wool stapler n. a person who sorts wool into different grades or classifications.

Woolworth ('wolwəθ) n. **Frank Winfield** ('wɪn,fi:ld). 1852–1919, U.S. merchant; founder of an international chain of department stores selling inexpensive goods.

woomera or **womera** ('woumərə) n. Austral. a type of notched stick used by Australian Aborigines to increase leverage and propulsion in the throwing of a spear. [from Abor.]

Woomera ('woumərə) n. a town in South Australia: site of the Long Range Weapons Establishment. Pop.: 1658 (1981).

Woop Woop ('wu:p ,wu:p) n. Austral. Sl. a jocular name for any backward or remote town or district.

Wootton ('wot²n) n. **Barbara (Frances)**, Baroness of Abinger. 1897–1988, English economist, educationalist, social scientist, and criminologist.

woozy ('wu:zɪ) adj. **woozier, wooziest.** Inf. **1.** dazed or confused. **2.** experiencing dizziness, nausea, etc. [C19: ? a blend of *woolly* + *muzzy* or *dizzy*] —'**woozily** adv. —'**wooziness** n.

wop (wɒp) n. Sl., derog. a member of a Latin people, esp. an Italian. [C20: prob. from It. dialect *guappo* dandy, from Sp. *guapo*]

Worcester ('wostə) n. **1.** a cathedral city in W central England, the administrative centre of Hereford and Worcester on the River Severn: scene of the battle (1651) in which Charles II was defeated by Cromwell. Pop.: 76 000 (1985 est.). **2.** an industrial city in central Massachusetts: Clark University (1887). Pop.: 157 770 (1986 est.). **3.** a town in S South Africa, in SW Cape Province. Pop.: 50 851 (1983 est.).

Worcester sauce ('wostə) or **Worcestershire sauce** n. a commercially prepared piquant sauce, made from a basis of soy sauce, with vinegar, spices, etc.

Worcestershire ('wostə,ʃɪə, -ʃə) n. a former county of W central England, since 1974 part of Hereford and Worcester.

Worcs. abbrev. for Worcestershire.

word (wɜːd) n. **1.** one of the units of speech or writing that is the smallest isolable meaningful element of the language, although many linguists would analyse these further into morphemes. **2.** an instance of vocal intercourse; chat, talk, or discussion: *to have a word with someone.* **3.** an utterance or expression, esp. a brief one: *a word of greeting.* **4.** news or information: *he sent word that he would be late.* **5.** a verbal signal for action; command: *when I give the word, fire!* **6.** an undertaking or promise: *he kept* *his word.* **7.** an autocratic decree; order: *his word must be obeyed.* **8.** a watchword or slogan, as of a political party: *the word now is "freedom".* **9.** *Computers.* a set of bits used to store, transmit, or operate upon an item of information in a computer. **10. as good as one's word.** doing what one has undertaken to do. **11. at a word.** at once. **12. by word of mouth.** orally rather than by written means. **13. in a word.** briefly or in short. **14. my word! a.** an exclamation of surprise, annoyance, etc. **b.** *Austral.* an exclamation of agreement. **15. of one's word.** given to or noted for keeping one's promises: *I am a man of my word.* **16. put in a word or good word for.** to make favourable mention of (someone); recommend. **17. take someone at his or her word.** to assume that someone means, or will do, what he or she says: *when he told her to go, she took him at his word and left.* **18. take someone's word for it.** to accept or believe what someone says. **19. the last word. a.** the closing remark of a conversation or argument, esp. a remark that supposedly settles an issue. **b.** the latest or most fashionable design, make, or model: *the last word in bikinis.* **c.** the finest example (of some quality, condition, etc.): *the last word in luxury.* **20. the word.** the proper or most fitting expression: *cold is not the word for it, it's freezing!* **21. upon my word! a.** *Arch.* on my honour. **b.** an exclamation of surprise, annoyance, etc. **22. word for word.** (of a report, etc.) using exactly the same words as those employed in the situation being reported; verbatim. **23. word of honour.** a promise; oath. **24.** *(modifier)* of, relating to, or consisting of words: *a word list.* ~*vb.* **25.** *(tr.)* to state in words, usually specially selected ones; phrase. ~See also **words.** [OE] —'**wordless** *adj.* —'**wordlessly** *adv.*

Word (wɜːd) *n.* **the.** **1.** *Christianity.* the 2nd person of the Trinity. **2.** Scripture, the Bible, or the Gospels as embodying or representing divine revelation. Often called: **the Word of God.** [translation of Gk *logos,* as in John 1:1]

wordage ('wɜːdɪdʒ) *n.* words considered collectively, esp. a quantity of words.

word association *n.* an early method of psychoanalysis in which the patient thinks of the first word that comes into consciousness on hearing a given word. In this way it was claimed that aspects of the unconscious could be revealed before defence mechanisms intervene.

word blindness *n.* the nontechnical name for **alexia** and **dyslexia.** —'**word-,blind** *adj.*

wordbook ('wɜːd,bʊk) *n.* a book containing words, usually with their meanings.

word deafness *n.* loss of ability to understand spoken words, esp. as the result of a cerebral lesion. Also called: **auditory aphasia.**

word game *n.* any game involving the formation, discovery, or alteration of a word or words.

wording ('wɜːdɪŋ) *n.* **1.** the way in which words are used to express a statement, report, etc., esp. a written one. **2.** the words themselves.

word order *n.* the arrangement of words in a phrase, clause, or sentence.

word-perfect or *U.S.* **letter-perfect** *adj.* **1.** correct in every detail. **2.** (of a speaker, actor, etc.) knowing one's speech, role, etc., perfectly.

wordplay ('wɜːd,pleɪ) *n.* verbal wit based on the meanings of words; puns, repartee, etc.

word processing *n.* the storage and organization of written text by electronic means, esp. for business purposes.

word processor *n.* an installation for word processing, typically consisting of a keyboard and a VDU incorporating a microprocessor, with storage and processing capabilities.

words (wɜːdz) *pl. n.* **1.** the text of a part of an actor, etc. **2.** the text of a song, as opposed to the music. **3.** angry speech (esp. in **have words with someone**). **4. eat or swallow one's words.** to retract a statement. **5. for words.** (preceded by *too* and an adj. or adv.) indescribably; extremely: *the play was too funny for words.* **6. have no words for.** to be incapable of describing. **7. in other words.** expressing the same idea but differently. **8. in so many words.** explicitly or precisely. **9. of many (or few) words.** (not) talkative. **10. put into words.** to express in speech or writing. **11. say a few words.** to give a brief speech. **12. take the words out of someone's mouth.** to say exactly what someone else was

about to say. **13. words fail me.** I am too happy, sad, amazed, etc., to express my thoughts.

word square *n.* a puzzle in which the player must fill a square grid with words that read the same across as down.

Wordsworth ('wɜːdz,wəθ) *n.* **1. Dorothy.** 1771–1855, English writer, whose *Journals* are noted esp. for their descriptions of nature. **2.** her brother, **William.** 1770–1850, English poet, whose work, celebrating nature, was greatly inspired by the Lake District, in which he spent most of his life. *Lyrical Ballads* (1798), to which Coleridge contributed, is often taken as the first example of English romantic poetry and includes his *Lines Written above Tintern Abbey.* Among his other works are *The Prelude* (completed in 1805; revised thereafter and published posthumously) and *Poems in Two Volumes* (1807), which includes *The Solitary Reaper* and *Intimations of Immortality.* —**Wordsworthian** (,wɜːdz'wɜːðɪən) *adj., n.*

word wrapping *n. Computers.* the automatic shifting of a word at the end of a line to a new line in order to keep within preset margins.

wordy ('wɜːdɪ) *adj.* **wordier, wordiest.** using or containing an excess of words: *a wordy document.* —'**wordily** *adv.* —'**wordiness** *n.*

wore (wɔː) *vb.* the past tense of **wear**[1] and **wear**[2].

work (wɜːk) *n.* **1.** physical or mental effort directed towards doing or making something. **2.** paid employment at a job or a trade, occupation, or profession. **3.** a duty, task, or undertaking. **4.** something done, made, etc., as a result of effort or exertion: *a work of art.* **5.** another word for **workmanship** (sense 3). **6.** the place, office, etc., where a person is employed. **7. a.** decoration, esp. of a specified kind. **b.** *(in combination)*: *wirework.* **8.** an engineering structure such as a bridge, building, etc. **9.** *Physics.* the transfer of energy expressed as the product of a force and the distance through which its point of application moves in the direction of the force. **10.** a structure, wall, etc., built or used as part of a fortification system. **11. at work. a.** at one's job or place of employment. **b.** in action; operating. **12. make short work of.** *Inf.* to dispose of very quickly. **13.** *(modifier)* of, relating to, or used for work: *work clothes; a work permit; a work song.* ~*vb.* **14.** *(intr.)* to exert effort in order to do, make, or perform something. **15.** *(intr.)* to be employed. **16.** *(tr.)* to carry on operations, activity, etc., in (a place or area): *that salesman works Yorkshire.* **17.** *(tr.)* to cause to labour or toil: *he works his men hard.* **18.** to operate or cause to operate, esp. properly or effectively: *to work a lathe; that clock doesn't work.* **19.** *(tr.)* to till or cultivate (land). **20.** to handle or manipulate or be handled or manipulated: *to work dough.* **21.** to shape or process or be shaped or processed: *to work copper.* **22.** to reach or cause to reach a specific condition, esp. gradually: *the rope worked loose.* **23.** *(intr.)* to move in agitation: *his face worked with anger.* **24.** *(tr.; often foll. by up)* to provoke or arouse: *to work someone into a frenzy.* **25.** *(tr.)* to effect or accomplish: *to work one's revenge.* **26.** to make (one's way) with effort: *he worked his way through the crowd.* **27.** *(tr.)* to make or decorate by hand in embroidery, tapestry, etc.: *she was working a sampler.* **28.** *(intr.)* (of liquids) to ferment, as in brewing. **29.** *(tr.) Inf.* to manipulate or exploit to one's own advantage. ~See also **work in, work off,** etc., **works.** [OE *weorc* (n.), *wircan, wyrcan* (vb.)] —'**workless** *adj.*

workable ('wɜːkəb[ə]l) *adj.* **1.** practicable or feasible. **2.** able to be worked. —,**worka'bility** or '**workableness** *n.*

workaday ('wɜːkə,deɪ) *adj.* *(usually prenominal)* **1.** being a part of general human experience; ordinary. **2.** suitable for working days; everyday or practical.

workaholic (,wɜːkə'hɒlɪk) *n.* a person obsessively addicted to work. [C20: from WORK + -HOLIC, coined in 1971 by U.S. author Wayne Oates]

workbag ('wɜːk,bæg) *n.* a container for implements, tools, or materials, esp. sewing equipment. Also called: **work basket, workbox.**

workbench ('wɜːk,bɛntʃ) *n.* a heavy table at which work is done by a carpenter, mechanic, toolmaker, etc.

workbook ('wɜːk,bʊk) *n.* **1.** an exercise book used for study, esp. with spaces for answers. **2.** a book of instructions for some process. **3.** a book in which is recorded all work done or planned.

work camp n. a camp set up for young people who voluntarily do manual work on a worthwhile project.

workday ('wɜːk,deɪ) n. **1.** the usual U.S. and Canad. term for **working day**. ~adj. **2.** another word for **workaday**.

worked (wɜːkt) adj. made or decorated with evidence of workmanship; wrought, as with embroidery or tracery.

worked up adj. excited or agitated.

worker ('wɜːkə) n. **1.** a person or thing that works, usually at a specific job: a research worker. **2.** an employee, as opposed to an employer or manager. **3.** a manual labourer working in a manufacturing industry. **4.** any other member of the working class. **5.** a sterile female member of a colony of bees, ants, or wasps that forages for food, cares for the larvae, etc.

worker director n. (in certain British companies) an employee of a company chosen by his or her fellow workers to represent their interests on the board of directors. Also called: **employee director**.

worker-priest n. a Roman Catholic priest who has employment in a secular job to be more in touch with the problems of the laity.

work ethic n. a belief in the moral value of work.

workforce ('wɜːk,fɔːs) n. **1.** the total number of workers employed by a company on a specific job, project, etc. **2.** the total number of people who could be employed: the country's workforce is growing.

work function n. Physics. the minimum energy required to transfer an electron from a point within a solid to a point just outside its surface. Symbol: φ or Φ

work-harden vb. (tr.) to increase the strength or hardness of (a metal) by a mechanical process, such as tension, compression, or torsion.

workhorse ('wɜːk,hɔːs) n. **1.** a horse used for nonrecreational activities. **2.** Inf. a person who takes on the greatest amount of work in a project.

workhouse ('wɜːk,haʊs) n. **1.** (formerly in England) an institution maintained at public expense where able-bodied paupers did unpaid work in return for food and accommodation. **2.** (in the U.S.) a prison for petty offenders serving short sentences at manual labour.

work in vb. (adv.) **1.** to insert or become inserted: she worked the patch in carefully. **2.** (tr.) to find space for: I'll work this job in during the day. ~n. **work-in**. **3.** a form of industrial action in which a factory that is to be closed down is occupied and run by its workers.

working ('wɜːkɪŋ) n. **1.** the operation or mode of operation of something. **2.** the act or process of moulding something pliable. **3.** a convulsive or jerking motion, as from excitement. **4.** (often pl.) a part of a mine or quarry that is being or has been worked. **5.** a record of the steps by which the solution of a problem, calculation, etc., is obtained: all working is to be submitted to the examiners. ~adj. (prenominal) **6.** relating to or concerned with a person or thing that works: a working man. **7.** concerned with, used in, or suitable for work: working clothes. **8.** (of a meal or occasion) during which business discussions are carried on: a working lunch. **9.** capable of being operated or used: a working model; in working order. **10.** adequate for normal purposes: a working majority; a working knowledge of German. **11.** (of a theory, etc.) providing a basis, usually a temporary one, on which operations or procedures may be carried out.

working bee n. N.Z. a voluntary group doing a job for charity.

working capital n. **1.** Accounting. current assets minus current liabilities. **2.** current or liquid assets. **3.** that part of the capital of a business enterprise available for operations.

working class n. **1.** Also called: **proletariat**. the social stratum, usually of low status, that consists of those who earn wages, esp. as manual workers. ~adj. **working-class**. **2.** of, relating to, or characteristic of the working class.

working day or esp. U.S. & Canad. **workday** n. **1.** a day on which work is done, esp. for an agreed or stipulated number of hours in return for a salary or wage. **2.** the part of the day allotted to work.

working drawing n. a scale drawing of a part that provides a guide for manufacture.

working party n. **1.** a committee established to investigate a problem, question, etc. **2.** a group of soldiers or prisoners assigned to perform some manual task or duty.

working week or esp. U.S. & Canad. **workweek** n. the number of hours or days in a week allocated to work.

work-in-progress n. Book-keeping. the value of work begun but not completed, as shown in a profit-and-loss account.

workload ('wɜːk,ləʊd) n. the amount of work to be done, esp. in a specified period.

workman ('wɜːkmən) n., pl. **-men**. **1.** a man who is employed in manual labour or who works an industrial machine. **2.** a craftsman of skill as specified: a bad workman.

workmanlike ('wɜːkmən,laɪk) or (less commonly) **workmanly** adj. appropriate to or befitting a good workman.

workmanship ('wɜːkmənʃɪp) n. **1.** the art or skill of a workman. **2.** the art or skill with which something is made or executed. **3.** the degree of art or skill exhibited in the finished product. **4.** the piece of work so produced.

workmate ('wɜːk,meɪt) n. a person who works with another; fellow worker.

work of art n. **1.** a piece of fine art, such as a painting or sculpture. **2.** something that may be likened to a piece of fine art, esp. in beauty, intricacy, etc.

work off vb. (tr., adv.) **1.** to get rid of or dissipate, as by effort: he worked off some of his energy by digging the garden. **2.** to discharge (a debt) by labour rather than payment.

work on vb. (intr., prep.) to persuade or influence or attempt to persuade or influence.

work out vb. (adv.) **1.** (tr.) to achieve or accomplish by effort. **2.** (tr.) to solve or find out by reasoning or calculation: to work out an answer; to work out a sum. **3.** (tr.) to devise or formulate: to work out a plan. **4.** (intr.) to prove satisfactory: did your plan work out? **5.** (intr.) to happen as specified: it all worked out well. **6.** (intr.) to take part in physical exercise, as in training. **7.** (tr.) to remove all the mineral in (a mine, etc.) that can be profitably exploited. **8.** (intr.; often foll. by to or at) to reach a total: your bill works out at a pound. ~n. **workout**. **9.** a session of physical exercise, esp. for training or to keep oneself fit.

work over vb. **1.** (tr., adv.) to do again; repeat. **2.** (intr., prep.) to examine closely and thoroughly. **3.** (tr., adv.) Sl. to assault or thrash.

workpeople ('wɜːk,piːpəl) pl. n. the working members of a population.

workroom ('wɜːk,ruːm, -,rʊm) n. **1.** a room in which work, usually manual labour, is done. **2.** a room in a house set aside for a hobby.

works (wɜːks) pl. n. **1.** (often functioning as sing.) a place where a number of people are employed, such as a factory. **2.** the sum total of a writer's or artist's achievements, esp. when considered together: the works of Shakespeare. **3.** the deeds of a person, esp. virtuous or moral deeds: works of charity. **4.** the interior parts of the mechanism of a machine, etc.: the works of a clock. **5. the works**. Sl. **a.** full or extreme treatment. **b.** a very violent physical beating: to give someone the works.

works council n. Chiefly Brit. **1.** a council composed of both employer and employees convened to discuss matters of common interest concerning a factory, plant, business policy, etc. **2.** a body representing the workers of a plant, factory, etc., elected to negotiate with the management about working conditions, wages, etc. ~Also called: **works committee**.

work sheet n. **1.** a sheet of paper used for the rough draft of a problem, design, etc. **2.** a piece of paper recording work in progress.

workshop ('wɜːk,ʃɒp) n. **1.** a room or building in which manufacturing or other forms of manual work are carried on. **2.** a room in a private dwelling, school, etc., set aside for crafts. **3.** a group of people engaged in study or work on a creative project or subject: a music workshop.

workshy ('wɜːk,ʃaɪ) adj. not inclined to work.

Worksop ('wɜːksɒp) n. a mining town in N central England, in W Nottinghamshire. Pop.: 36 893 (1981).

work station n. an area in an office where one person works.

work-study n. an examination of ways of finding the most efficient method of doing a job.

worktable ('wɜːk,teɪbəl) n. **a.** any table at which writing, sewing, or other work may be done. **b.** (in English cabinetwork) a small elegant table fitted with sewing accessories.

worktop ('wɜːk,tɒp) *n.* a surface in a kitchen, often of heat-resistant plastic, used for food preparation.

work-to-rule *n.* **1.** a form of industrial action in which employees adhere strictly to all the working rules laid down by their employers, with the deliberate intention of reducing the rate of working. ~*vb.* **work to rule.** **2.** (*intr.*) to decrease the rate of working by this means.

work up *vb.* **1.** (*tr., adv.*) to arouse the feelings of; excite. **2.** (*tr., adv.*) to cause to grow or develop: *to work up a hunger.* **3.** to move or cause to move gradually upwards. **4.** (*tr., adv.*) to manipulate or mix into a specified object or shape. **5.** (*tr., adv.*) to gain skill at (a subject). **6.** (*adv.*) (foll. by *to*) to develop gradually or progress (towards): *working up to a climax.*

world (wɜːld) *n.* **1.** the earth as a planet, esp. including its inhabitants. **2.** mankind; the human race. **3.** people generally; the public: *in the eyes of the world.* **4.** social or public life: *to go out into the world.* **5.** the universe or cosmos; everything in existence. **6.** a complex united whole regarded as resembling the universe. **7.** any star or planet, esp. one that might be inhabited. **8.** (*often cap.*) a division or section of the earth, its history, or its inhabitants: *the Ancient World; the Third World.* **9.** an area, sphere, or realm considered as a complete environment: *the animal world.* **10.** any field of human activity or way of life or those involved in it: *the world of television.* **11.** a period or state of existence: *the next world.* **12.** the total circumstances and experience of an individual that make up his life: *you have shattered my world.* **13.** a large amount, number, or distance: *worlds apart.* **14.** worldly or secular life, ways, or people. **15. bring into the world. a.** (of a midwife, doctor, etc.) to deliver (a baby). **b.** to give birth to. **16. come into the world.** to be born. **17. for all the world.** in every way; exactly. **18. for the world.** (*used with a negative*) for any inducement, however great. **19. in the world.** (intensifier): *usually used with a negative*): *no-one in the world can change things.* **20. man** (*or* **woman**) **of the world.** a man (or woman) experienced in social or public life. **21. not long for this world.** nearing death. **22. on top of the world.** *Inf.* elated or very happy. **23. out of this world.** *Inf.* wonderful; excellent. **24. set the world on fire.** to be exceptionally or sensationally successful. **25. the best of both worlds.** the benefits from two different ways of life, philosophies, etc. **26. think the world of.** to be extremely fond of or hold in very high esteem. **27. world of one's own.** a state of mental detachment from other people. **28. world without end.** for ever. **29.** (*modifier*) of or concerning most or all countries; worldwide: *world politics; a world record.* **30.** (*in combination*) throughout the world: *world-famous.* [OE *w(e)orold,* from *wer* man + *ald* age, life]

World Bank *n.* an international cooperative organization established in 1945 to assist economic development, esp. of backward nations, by the advance of loans guaranteed by member governments. Officially called: **International Bank for Reconstruction and Development.**

world-beater *n.* a person or thing that surpasses all others in its category; champion.

world-class *adj.* of or denoting someone with a skill or attribute that puts him or her in the highest class in the world: *a world-class swimmer.*

World Court *n.* another name for **International Court of Justice.**

World Cup *n.* an international association football championship competition held every four years between national teams selected through preliminary tournaments.

worldling ('wɜːldlɪŋ) *n.* a person who is primarily concerned with worldly matters.

worldly ('wɜːldlɪ) *adj.* **-lier, -liest. 1.** not spiritual; mundane or temporal. **2.** Also: **worldly-minded.** absorbed in or concerned with material things. **3.** Also: **worldly-wise.** versed in the ways of the world; sophisticated. —'**worldliness** *n.*

world music *n.* popular music of various ethnic origin and styles.

world power *n.* a state that possesses sufficient power to influence events throughout the world.

world-shaking *adj.* of enormous significance; momentous.

World War I *n.* the war (1914–18), fought mainly in Europe and the Middle East, in which the Allies (principally France, Russia, Britain, Italy after 1915, and the U.S. after 1917) defeated the Central Powers (principally Germany, Austria-Hungary, and Turkey). Also called: **First World War, Great War.**

World War II *n.* the war (1939–45) in which the Allies (Britain and France) declared war on Germany (Sept. 3, 1939) as a result of the German invasion of Poland (Sept. 1, 1939). Italy entered the war on the side of Germany (forming the Axis) on June 10, 1940. On June 22, 1941 the Axis powers attacked the Soviet Union and on Dec. 7, 1941 the Japanese attacked the U.S. at Pearl Harbor. On Sept. 8, 1943 Italy surrendered, the war in Europe ending on May 7, 1945 with the unconditional surrender of the Germans. The Japanese capitulated on Aug. 14, 1945. Also called: **Second World War.**

world-weary *adj.* no longer finding pleasure in living. —'**world-,weariness** *n.*

worldwide ('wɜːld'waɪd) *adj.* applying or extending throughout the world; universal.

worm (wɜːm) *n.* **1.** any of various invertebrates, esp. the annelids (earthworms, etc.), nematodes (roundworms), and flatworms, having a slender elongated body. **2.** any of various insect larvae having an elongated body, such as the silkworm and wireworm. **3.** any of various unrelated animals that resemble annelids, nematodes, etc., such as the glow-worm and shipworm. **4.** a gnawing or insinuating force or agent that torments or slowly eats away. **5.** a wretched or spineless person. **6.** anything that resembles a worm in appearance or movement. **7.** a shaft on which a helical groove has been cut, as in a gear arrangement in which such a shaft meshes with a toothed wheel. **8.** a spiral pipe cooled by air or flowing water, used as a condenser in a still. ~*vb.* **9.** to move, act, or cause to move or act with the slow sinuous movement of a worm. **10.** (foll. by *in, into, out of,* etc.) to make (one's way) slowly and stealthily; insinuate (oneself). **11.** (*tr.;* often foll. by *out of or from*) to extract (information, etc.) from by persistent questioning. **12.** (*tr.*) to free from or purge of worms. ~See also **worms.** [OE *wyrm*] —'**wormer** *n.* —'**worm-,like** *adj.*

WORM (wɜːm) *n. Computers. acronym for* write once read many times: an optical disk which enables users to store their own data.

wormcast ('wɜːm,kɑːst) *n.* a coil of earth or sand that has been excreted by a burrowing earthworm or lugworm.

worm-eaten *adj.* **1.** eaten into by worms: *a worm-eaten table.* **2.** decayed; rotten. **3.** old-fashioned; antiquated.

worm gear *n.* **1.** a device consisting of a threaded shaft (**worm**) that mates with a gear-wheel (**worm wheel**) so that rotary motion can be transferred between two shafts at right angles to each other. **2.** Also called: **worm wheel.** a gear-wheel driven by a threaded shaft or worm.

wormhole ('wɜːm,həʊl) *n.* a hole made by a worm in timber, plants, etc. —'**worm,holed** *adj.*

worms (wɜːmz) *n.* (*functioning as sing.*) any disease or disorder, usually of the intestine, characterized by infestation with parasitic worms.

Worms (wɜːmz; *German* vɔrms) *n.* a city in S West Germany, in Rhineland-Palatinate on the Rhine: famous as the seat of imperial diets, notably that of 1521, before which Luther defended his doctrines in the presence of Charles V; river port and manufacturing centre with a large wine trade. Pop.: 73 000 (1984).

worm's eye view *n.* a view seen from below or from a more lowly or humble point.

wormwood ('wɜːm,wʊd) *n.* **1.** Also called: **absinthe.** any of various plants of a chiefly N temperate genus, esp. a European plant yielding a bitter extract used in making absinthe. **2.** something that embitters, such as a painful experience. [C15: changed (through infl. of WORM & WOOD) from OE *wormōd, wermōd*]

wormy ('wɜːmɪ) *adj.* **wormier, wormiest. 1.** worm-infested or worm-eaten. **2.** resembling a worm in appearance, ways, or condition. **3.** (of wood) having irregular small tunnels bored into it and tracked over its surface, made by worms. **4.** low or grovelling. —'**worminess** *n.*

worn (wɔːn) *vb.* **1.** the past participle of **wear**[1] and **wear**[2]. ~*adj.* **2.** affected, esp. adversely, by long use or action: *a worn suit.* **3.** haggard; drawn. **4.** exhausted; spent. —'**wornness** *n.*

worn-out *adj.* (**worn out** *when postpositive*). **1.** worn or used until threadbare, valueless, or useless. **2.** exhausted; very weary.

worriment ('wʌrɪmənt) *n. Inf., chiefly U.S.* anxiety or the trouble that causes it; worry.

worrisome ('wʌrɪsəm) *adj.* **1.** causing worry; vexing. **2.** tending to worry. —'**worrisomely** *adv.*

worrit ('wʌrɪt) *vb.* (*tr.*) *Dialect.* to tease or worry. [prob. var. of WORRY]

worry ('wʌrɪ) *vb.* **-rying, -ried. 1.** to be or cause to be anxious or uneasy, esp. about something uncertain or potentially dangerous. **2.** (*tr.*) to disturb the peace of mind of; bother: *don't worry me with trivialities.* **3.** (*intr.*; often foll. by *along* or *through*) to proceed despite difficulties. **4.** (*intr.*; often foll. by *away*) to struggle or work: *to worry away at a problem.* **5.** (*tr.*) (of a dog, wolf, etc.) to lacerate or kill by biting, shaking, etc. **6.** (when *intr.*, foll. by *at*) to bite, tear, or gnaw (at) with the teeth: *a dog worrying a bone.* **7.** (*tr.*) to touch or poke repeatedly and idly. **8. not to worry.** *Inf.* you need not worry. ~*n.*, *pl.* **-ries. 9.** a state or feeling of anxiety. **10.** a person or thing that causes anxiety. **11.** an act of worrying. [OE *wyrgan*] —'**worried** *adj.* —'**worriedly** *adv.* —'**worrying** *adj.* —'**worryingly** *adv.*

worry beads *pl. n.* a string of beads that when fingered or played with supposedly relieves nervous tension.

worryguts ('wʌrɪ,gʌts) *n.* (*functioning as sing.*) *Inf.* a person who tends to worry, esp. about insignificant matters.

worse (wɜːs) *adj.* **1.** the comparative of **bad¹. 2. none the worse for.** not harmed by (adverse events or circumstances). **3. the worse for wear. a.** shabby or worn. **b.** a slang term for **drunk. 4. worse luck!** *Inf.* unhappily; unfortunately. **5. worse off.** (*postpositive*) in a worse, esp. a worse financial, condition. ~*n.* **6.** something that is worse. **7. for the worse.** into a less desirable or inferior state or condition: *a change for the worse.* ~*adv.* **8.** in a more severe or unpleasant manner. **9.** in a less effective or successful manner. [OE *wiersa*]

worsen ('wɜːsᵊn) *vb.* to grow or cause to grow worse.

worship ('wɜːʃɪp) *vb.* **-shipping, -shipped** or *U.S.* **-shiping, -shiped. 1.** (*tr.*) to show profound religious devotion and respect to; adore or venerate (God or any person or thing considered divine). **2.** (*tr.*) to be devoted to and full of admiration for. **3.** (*intr.*) to have or express feelings of profound adoration. **4.** (*intr.*) to attend services for worship. ~*n.* **5.** religious adoration or devotion. **6.** the formal expression of religious adoration; rites, prayers, etc. **7.** admiring love or devotion. [OE *weorthscipe*] —'**worshipper** *n.*

Worship ('wɜːʃɪp) *n. Chiefly Brit.* (preceded by *Your*, *His*, or *Her*) a title used to address or refer to a mayor, magistrate, etc.

worshipful ('wɜːʃɪpfʊl) *adj.* **1.** feeling or showing reverence or adoration. **2.** (*often cap.*) *Chiefly Brit.* a title used to address or refer to various people or bodies of distinguished rank. —'**worshipfully** *adv.* —'**worshipfulness** *n.*

Worsley ('wɜːzlɪ) *n.* a town in NW England, in Greater Manchester. Pop.: 49 021 (1981).

worst (wɜːst) *adj.* **1.** the superlative of **bad¹.** ~*adv.* **2.** in the most extreme or bad manner or degree. **3.** least well, suitably, or acceptably. **4.** (*in combination*) in or to the smallest degree or extent; least: *worst-loved.* ~*n.* **5. the worst.** the least good or most inferior person, thing, or part in a group, narrative, etc. **6.** (often preceded by *at*) the most poor, unpleasant, or unskilled quality or condition: *television is at its worst these days.* **7.** the greatest amount of damage or wickedness of which a person or group is capable: *the invaders came and did their worst.* **8.** the weakest effort or poorest achievement that a person or group is capable of making: *the applicant did his worst at the test because he did not want the job.* **9. at worst. a.** in the least favourable interpretation or view. **b.** under the least favourable conditions. **10. come off worst** *or* **get the worst of it.** to enjoy the least benefit from an issue or be defeated in it. **11. if the worst comes to the worst.** if all the more desirable alternatives become impossible or if the worst possible thing happens. ~*vb.* **12.** (*tr.*) to get the advantage over; defeat or beat. [OE *wierrest*]

worsted ('wʊstɪd) *n.* **1.** a closely twisted yarn or thread made from combed long-staple wool. **2.** a fabric made from this, with a hard smooth close-textured surface and no nap. **3.** (*modifier*) made of this yarn or fabric: *a worsted suit.* [C13: after *Worstead*, a district in Norfolk]

wort (wɜːt) *n.* **1.** (*in combination*) any of various unrelated plants, esp. ones formerly used to cure diseases: *liverwort.* **2.** the sweet liquid from the soaked mixture of warm water and ground malt, used to make a malt liquor. [OE *wyrt* root]

worth (wɜːθ) *adj.* (governing a noun with prepositional force) **1.** worthy of; meriting or justifying: *it's not worth discussing.* **2.** having a value of: *the book is worth £30.* **3. for all one is worth.** to the utmost. **4. worth one's weight in gold.** extremely helpful, kind, etc. ~*n.* **5.** high quality; excellence. **6.** value; price. **7.** the amount of something of a specified value: *five pounds' worth of petrol.* [OE *weorth*]

Worth (wɜːθ; *French* vɔrt) *n.* **Charles Frederick.** 1825–95, English couturier, who founded Parisian *haute couture.*

Worthing ('wɜːðɪŋ) *n.* a resort in S England, in West Sussex on the English Channel. Pop.: 93 400 (1985 est.).

worthless ('wɜːθlɪs) *adj.* **1.** without value or usefulness. **2.** without merit; good-for-nothing. —'**worthlessly** *adv.* —'**worthlessness** *n.*

worthwhile ('wɜːθ'waɪl) *adj.* sufficiently important, rewarding, or valuable to justify time or effort spent.

worthy ('wɜːðɪ) *adj.* **-thier, -thiest. 1.** (*postpositive*; often foll. by *of* or an infinitive) having sufficient merit or value (for something or someone specified); deserving. **2.** having worth, value, or merit. ~*n.*, *pl.* **-thies. 3.** *Often facetious.* a person of merit or importance. —'**worthily** *adv.* —'**worthiness** *n.*

wot (wɒt) *vb. Arch. or dialect.* (used with *I*, *she*, *he*, *it*, or a singular noun) a form of the present tense (indicative mood) of **wit²**.

Wotan ('vəʊtɑːn, 'vɔː-) *n.* the supreme god in Germanic mythology. Norse counterpart: **Odin.**

Wotton ('wɒtᵊn, 'wʊtᵊn) *n.* **Henry.** 1568–1639, English poet.

would (wʊd; *unstressed* wəd) *vb.* (takes an infinitive without *to* or an implied infinitive) used as an auxiliary: **1.** to form the past tense or subjunctive mood of **will¹. 2.** (with *you*, *he*, *she*, *it*, *they*, or a noun as subject) to indicate willingness or desire in a polite manner: *would you help me, please?* **3.** to describe a past action as being accustomed or habitual: *every day we would go for walks.* **4.** I wish: *would that he were here.*

▷ **Usage.** See at **should.**

would-be *adj.* (*prenominal*) **1.** *Usually derog.* wanting or professing to be: *a would-be politician.* **2.** intended to be: *would-be generosity.*

wouldn't ('wʊdᵊnt) *contraction of* would not.

wouldst (wʊdst) *vb. Arch. or dialect.* (used with the pronoun *thou* or its relative equivalent) a singular form of the past tense of **will¹.**

Woulfe bottle (wʊlf) *n. Chem.* a bottle with more than one neck, used for passing gases through liquids. [C18: after Peter *Woulfe* (?1727–1803), E chemist]

wound¹ (wuːnd) *n.* **1.** any break in the skin or an organ or part as the result of violence or a surgical incision. **2.** any injury or slight to the feelings or reputation. ~*vb.* **3.** to inflict a wound or wounds upon (someone or something). [OE *wund*] —'**wounding** *adj.* —'**woundingly** *adv.*

wound² (waʊnd) *vb.* the past tense and past participle of **wind²** and **wind³.**

wounded ('wuːndɪd) *adj.* **1. a.** suffering from wounds; injured, esp. in a battle or fight. **b.** (*as collective n.*; preceded by *the*): *the wounded.* **2.** (of feelings) damaged or hurt.

woundwort ('wuːnd,wɜːt) *n.* **1.** any of various plants, such as field woundwort, having purple, scarlet, yellow, or white flowers and formerly used for dressing wounds. **2.** any of various other plants used in this way.

wove (wəʊv) *vb.* a past tense of **weave.**

woven ('wəʊvᵊn) *vb.* a past participle of **weave.**

wove paper *n.* paper with a very faint mesh impressed on it by the paper-making machine.

wow¹ (waʊ) *interj.* **1.** an exclamation of admiration, amazement, etc. ~*n.* **2.** *Sl.* a person or thing that is amazingly successful, attractive, etc. ~*vb.* **3.** (*tr.*) *Sl.* to arouse great enthusiasm in. [C16: orig. Scot.]

wow² (waʊ, wəʊ) *n.* a slow variation or distortion in pitch that occurs at very low audio frequencies in sound-reproducing systems. See also **flutter** (sense 12). [C20: imit.]

wowser ('waʊzə) n. Austral. & N.Z. sl. **1.** a fanatically puritanical person. **2.** a teetotaller. [C20: from E dialect wow to complain]

wp abbrev. for word processor.

wpb abbrev. for wastepaper basket.

WPC (in Britain) abbrev. for woman police constable.

wpm abbrev. for words per minute.

WRAAC abbrev. for Women's Royal Australian Army Corps.

WRAAF abbrev. for Women's Royal Australian Air Force.

WRAC (in Britain) abbrev. for Women's Royal Army Corps.

wrack[1] or **rack** (ræk) n. **1.** collapse or destruction (esp. in **wrack and ruin**). **2.** something destroyed or a remnant of such. [OE wræc persecution, misery]

wrack[2] (ræk) n. **1.** seaweed or other marine vegetation that is floating in the sea or has been cast ashore. **2.** any of various seaweeds, such as serrated wrack. [C14 (in the sense: a wrecked ship, hence later applied to marine vegetation washed ashore): ?from MDu. wrak wreckage; the term corresponds to OE wræc WRACK[1]]

WRAF (in Britain) abbrev. for Women's Royal Air Force.

wraith (reɪθ) n. **1.** the apparition of a person living or thought to be alive, supposed to appear around the time of his death. **2.** a ghost or any apparition. [C16: Scot., from ?] —'**wraith**,**like** adj.

Wran (ræn) n. a member of the Women's Royal Australian Naval Service.

Wrangel Island ('ræŋgəl) n. an island in the Arctic Ocean, off the coast of the extreme NE Soviet Union: administratively part of the Soviet Union; mountainous and mostly tundra. Area: about 7300 sq. km (2800 sq. miles).

Wrangell ('ræŋgəl) n. **Mount.** a mountain in S Alaska, in the W Wrangell Mountains. Height: 4269 m (14 005 ft.).

Wrangell Mountains pl. n. a mountain range in SE Alaska, extending into the Yukon, Canada. Highest peak: Mount Blackburn, 5037 m (16 523 ft.).

wrangle ('ræŋgəl) vb. **1.** (intr.) to argue, esp. noisily or angrily. **2.** (tr.) to encourage, persuade, or obtain by argument. **3.** (tr.) Western U.S. & Canad. to herd (cattle or horses). ~n. **4.** a noisy or angry argument. [C14: from Low G wrangeln]

wrangler ('ræŋglə) n. **1.** one who wrangles. **2.** Western U.S. & Canad. a herder; cowboy. **3.** Brit. (at Cambridge University) a candidate who has obtained first-class honours in part II of the mathematics tripos. Formerly, the wrangler with the highest marks was called the **senior wrangler**.

WRANS abbrev. for Women's Royal Australian Naval Service. See also **Wran.**

wrap (ræp) vb. **wrapping, wrapped.** (mainly tr.) **1.** to fold or wind (paper, cloth, etc.) around (a person or thing) so as to cover. **2.** (often foll. by up) to fold paper, etc., around to fasten securely. **3.** to surround or conceal by surrounding. **4.** to enclose, immerse, or absorb: wrapped in sorrow. **5.** to fold, wind, or roll up. **6.** (intr.; often foll. by about, around, etc.) to be or become wound or extended. **7.** (often foll. by up) Also: **rap.** Austral. inf. to praise (someone). ~n. **8.** a garment worn wrapped around the body, esp. the shoulders, such as a shawl or cloak. **9.** Chiefly U.S. wrapping or a wrapper. **10. keep under wraps.** to keep secret. **11. take the wraps off.** to reveal. **12.** Also: **rap.** Austral. inf. a commendation. [C14: from ?]

wrapover ('ræp,əʊvə) or **wrapround** adj. **1.** (of a garment, esp. a skirt) not sewn up at one side, but worn wrapped round the body and fastened so that the open edges overlap. ~n. **2.** such a garment.

wrapped (ræpt) vb. **1.** the past participle of **wrap. 2. wrapped up in.** Inf. **a.** completely absorbed or engrossed in. **b.** implicated or involved in. ~adj. **3.** Also: **rapt.** Austral. inf. very pleased; delighted.

wrapper ('ræpə) n. **1.** the cover, usually of paper or cellophane, in which something is wrapped. **2.** a dust jacket of a book. **3.** the ripe firm tobacco leaf forming the outermost portion of a cigar. **4.** a loose negligee or dressing gown.

wrapping ('ræpɪŋ) n. the material used to wrap something.

wrapround ('ræp,raʊnd) or **wraparound** adj. **1.** made so as to be wrapped round something: a wraparound skirt. **2.** surrounding, curving round, or overlapping. **3.** curving round in one continuous piece: a wraparound windscreen.

~n. **4.** Printing. a flexible plate of plastic, metal, or rubber that is made flat but used wrapped round the plate cylinder of a rotary press. **5.** another name for **wrapover.**

wrap up vb. (adv.) **1.** (tr.) to fold paper around. **2.** to put warm clothes on. **3.** (intr.; usually imperative) Sl. to be silent. **4.** (tr.) Inf. **a.** to settle the final details of. **b.** to make a summary of.

wrasse (ræs) n. a marine fish of tropical and temperate seas, having thick lips, strong teeth, and usually a bright coloration: many are used as food fishes. [C17: from Cornish wrach]

wrath (rɒθ) n. **1.** angry, violent, or stern indignation. **2.** divine vengeance or retribution. **3.** Arch. a fit of anger or an act resulting from anger. [OE wræththu]

Wrath (rɒθ, rɔːθ) n. **Cape.** a promontory at the NW extremity of the Scottish mainland.

wrathful ('rɒθfʊl) adj. **1.** full of wrath; raging or furious. **2.** resulting from or expressing wrath. —'**wrathfully** adv. —'**wrathfulness** n.

wreak (riːk) vb. (tr.) **1.** to inflict (vengeance, etc.) or to cause (chaos, etc.): to wreak havoc on the enemy. **2.** to express or gratify (anger, hatred, etc.). **3.** Arch. to take vengeance for. [OE wrecan] —'**wreaker** n.

wreath (riːθ) n., pl. **wreaths** (riːðz, riːθs). **1.** a band of flowers or foliage intertwined into a ring, usually placed on a grave as a memorial or worn on the head as a garland or a mark of honour. **2.** any circular or spiral band or formation. **3.** (loosely) any floral design placed on a grave as a memorial. [OE wrǣth, wrǣd] —'**wreath**,**like** adj.

wreathe (riːð) vb. **1.** to form into or take the form of a wreath by intertwining or twisting together. **2.** (tr.) to decorate, crown, or encircle with wreaths. **3.** to move or cause to move in a twisting way: smoke wreathed up to the ceiling. [C16: ? back formation from wrēthen, from OE writhen, p.p. of wrīthan to writhe]

wreck (rɛk) vb. **1.** to involve in or suffer disaster or destruction. **2.** (tr.) to cause the wreck of (a ship). ~n. **3. a.** the accidental destruction of a ship at sea. **b.** the ship so destroyed. **4.** Maritime law. goods cast ashore from a wrecked vessel. **5.** a person or thing that has suffered ruin or dilapidation. **6.** Also called: **wreckage.** the remains of something that has been destroyed. **7.** Also called: **wreckage.** the act of wrecking or the state of being wrecked. [C13: from ON] —'**wrecking** n., adj.

wrecked (rɛkt) adj. Sl. in a state of intoxication, stupor, or euphoria, induced by drugs or alcohol.

wrecker ('rɛkə) n. **1.** a person or thing that ruins or destroys. **2.** Chiefly U.S. & Canad. a person whose job is to demolish buildings or dismantle cars. **3.** (formerly) a person who lures ships to destruction to plunder the wreckage. **4.** a U.S. and Canad. name for a breakdown van.

wrecking bar n. a short crowbar, forked at one end and slightly angled at the other to make a fulcrum.

Wrekin ('riːkɪn) n. **the.** an isolated hill in the English Midlands in Shropshire. Height: 400 m (1335 ft.).

wren (rɛn) n. **1.** any small brown passerine songbird of a chiefly American family (in Britain **wren**, in the U.S. and Canada **winter wren**). They have a slender bill and feed on insects. **2.** any of various similar birds, such as the Australian warblers, New Zealand wrens, etc. [OE wrenna, werna]

Wren[1] (rɛn) n. Inf. (in Britain and certain other nations) a member of the Women's Royal Naval Service. [C20: from the abbrev. WRNS]

Wren[2] (rɛn) n. Sir **Christopher.** 1632–1723, English architect. He designed St. Paul's Cathedral and over 50 other London churches after the Great Fire as well as many secular buildings.

wrench (rɛntʃ) vb. **1.** to give (something) a sudden or violent twist or pull, esp. so as to remove (something) from that to which it is attached: to wrench a door off its hinges. **2.** (tr.) to twist suddenly so as to sprain (a limb): to wrench one's ankle. **3.** (tr.) to give pain to. **4.** (tr.) to twist from the original meaning or purpose. **5.** (intr.) to make a sudden twisting motion. ~n. **6.** a forceful twist or pull. **7.** an injury to a limb, caused by twisting. **8.** sudden pain caused esp. by parting. **9.** a parting that is difficult or painful to make. **10.** a distorting of the original meaning or purpose. **11.** a spanner, esp. one with adjustable jaws. See also **torque wrench.** [OE wrencan]

wrest (rɛst) *vb.* (*tr.*) **1.** to take or force away by violent pulling or twisting. **2.** to seize forcibly by violent or unlawful means. **3.** to obtain by laborious effort. **4.** to distort in meaning, purpose, etc. ~*n.* **5.** the act or an instance of wresting. **6.** *Arch.* a small key used to tune a piano or harp. [OE *wræstan*] —'**wrester** *n.*

wrestle ('rɛsəl) *vb.* **1.** to fight (another person) by holding, throwing, etc., without punching with the closed fist. **2.** (*intr.*) to participate in wrestling. **3.** (when *intr.*, foll. by *with* or *against*) to fight with (a person, problem, or thing): *wrestle with one's conscience.* **4.** (*tr.*) to move laboriously, as with wrestling movements. ~*n.* **5.** the act of wrestling. **6.** a struggle or tussle. [OE *wræstlian*] —'**wrestler** *n.*

wrestling ('rɛslɪŋ) *n.* any of certain sports in which the contestants fight each other according to various rules governing holds and usually forbidding blows with the closed fist. The principal object is to overcome the opponent either by throwing or pinning him to the ground or by causing him to submit.

wrest pin *n.* (on a piano, harp, etc.) a pin, embedded in the **wrest plank,** around which one end of a string is wound: it may be turned by means of a tuning key to alter the tension of the string.

wretch (rɛtʃ) *n.* **1.** a despicable person. **2.** a person pitied for his misfortune. [OE *wrecca*]

wretched ('rɛtʃɪd) *adj.* **1.** in poor or pitiful circumstances. **2.** characterized by or causing misery. **3.** despicable; base. **4.** poor, inferior, or paltry. **5.** (*prenominal*) (intensifier qualifying something undesirable): *a wretched nuisance.* —'**wretchedly** *adv.* —'**wretchedness** *n.*

Wrexham ('rɛksəm) *n.* a town in N Wales, in SE Clwyd: seat of the Roman Catholic bishopric of Wales (except Glamorganshire); coal-mining. Pop.: 40 357 (1983 est.).

wrick (rɪk) *n.* **1.** a sprain or strain. ~*vb.* **2.** (*tr.*) to sprain or strain.

wrier *or* **wryer** ('raɪə) *adj.* the comparative of **wry**.

wriest *or* **wryest** ('raɪɪst) *adj.* the superlative of **wry**.

wriggle ('rɪgəl) *vb.* **1.** to make or cause to make twisting movements. **2.** (*intr.*) to progress by twisting and turning. **3.** (*intr.*; foll. by *into* or *out of*) to manoeuvre oneself by clever or devious means: *wriggle out of an embarrassing situation.* ~*n.* **4.** a wriggling movement or action. **5.** a sinuous marking or course. [C15: from MLow G] —'**wriggler** *n.* —'**wriggly** *adj.*

wright (raɪt) *n.* (*now chiefly in combination*) a person who creates, builds, or repairs something specified: *a playwright; a shipwright.* [OE *wryhta, wyrhta*]

Wright (raɪt) *n.* **1. Frank Lloyd.** 1869–1959, U.S. architect, whose designs include the Imperial Hotel, Tokyo (1916), the Guggenheim Museum, New York (1943), and many private houses. His "organic architecture" sought a close relationship between buildings and their natural surroundings. **2. Joseph.** 1855–1930, English philologist; editor of *The English Dialect Dictionary* (1898–1905). **3. Judith.** born 1915, Australian poet, critic, and conservationist. Her writings include *The Moving Image* (1946), *Woman to Man* (1949), and *The Generations of Man* (1959). **4. Wilbur** (1867–1912) and his brother, **Orville** (1871–1948), U.S. aviation pioneers, who designed and flew the first powered aircraft (1903).

wring (rɪŋ) *vb.* **wringing, wrung. 1.** (often foll. by *out*) to twist and compress to squeeze (a liquid) from (cloth, etc.). **2.** (*tr.*) to twist forcibly: *wring its neck.* **3.** (*tr.*) to clasp and twist (one's hands), esp. in anguish. **4.** (*tr.*) to distress: *wring one's heart.* **5.** (*tr.*) to grip (someone's hand) vigorously in greeting. **6.** (*tr.*) to obtain as by forceful means: *wring information out of.* **7. wringing wet.** soaking; drenched. ~*n.* **8.** an act or the process of wringing. [OE *wringan*]

wringer ('rɪŋə) *n.* another name for **mangle**² (sense 1).

wrinkle¹ ('rɪŋkəl) *n.* **1.** a slight ridge in the smoothness of a surface, such as a crease in the skin as a result of age. ~*vb.* **2.** to make or become wrinkled, as by crumpling, creasing, or puckering. [C15: back formation from *wrinkled*, from OE *gewrinclod*, p.p. of *wrinclian* to wind around] —'**wrinkly** *adj.*

wrinkle² ('rɪŋkəl) *n. Inf.* a clever or useful trick, hint, or dodge. [OE *wrenc* trick]

wrinklies ('rɪŋklɪz) *pl. n. Inf., derog.* old people.

wrist (rɪst) *n.* **1.** *Anat.* the joint between the forearm and the hand. Technical name: **carpus**. **2.** the part of a sleeve or glove that covers the wrist. **3.** *Machinery.* **a.** See

wrist pin. b. a joint in which a wrist pin forms the pivot. [OE]

wristband ('rɪst,bænd) *n.* **1.** a band around the wrist, esp. one attached to a watch or forming part of a long sleeve. **2.** a sweatband around the wrist.

wristlet ('rɪstlɪt) *n.* a band or bracelet worn around the wrist.

wrist pin *n.* **1.** a cylindrical boss or pin attached to the side of a wheel parallel with the axis, esp. one forming a bearing for a crank. **2.** the U.S. and Canad. name for **gudgeon pin.**

wristwatch ('rɪst,wɒtʃ) *n.* a watch worn strapped around the wrist.

wristy ('rɪstɪ) *adj.* (of a player's style of hitting the ball in cricket, tennis, etc.) characterized by considerable movement of the wrist.

writ (rɪt) *n.* **1.** a document under seal, issued in the name of the Crown or a court, commanding the person to whom it is addressed to do or refrain from doing some specified act. **2.** *Arch.* a piece or body of writing: *Holy Writ.* [OE]

write (raɪt) *vb.* **writing, wrote, written. 1.** to draw or mark (symbols, words, etc.) on a surface, usually paper, with a pen, pencil, or other instrument. **2.** to describe or record (ideas, experiences, etc.) in writing. **3.** to compose (a letter) or correspond regularly with (a person, organization, etc.). **4.** (*tr.; may take a clause as object*) to say or communicate by letter: *he wrote that he was on his way.* **5.** (*tr.*) *Inf., chiefly U.S. & Canad.* to send a letter to (a person, etc.). **6.** to write (words) in cursive as opposed to printed style. **7.** (*tr.*) to be sufficiently familiar with (a specified style, language, etc.) to use it in writing. **8.** to be the author or composer of (books, music, etc.). **9.** (*tr.*) to fill in the details for (a document, form, etc.). **10.** (*tr.*) to draw up or draft. **11.** (*tr.*) to produce by writing: *he wrote ten pages.* **12.** (*tr.*) to show clearly: *envy was written all over his face.* **13.** (*tr.*) to spell, inscribe, or entitle. **14.** (*tr.*) to ordain or prophesy: *it is written.* **15.** (*intr.*) to produce writing as specified. **16.** *Computers.* to record (data) in a location in a storage device. **17.** (*tr.*) See **underwrite** (sense 3a). ~See also **write down, write in,** etc. [OE *writan* (orig.: to scratch runes into bark)] —'**writable** *adj.*

▷ **Usage.** Careful writers and speakers avoid the omission of *to* after the verb *write* in clauses without a direct object: *I'll write to you* (not *I'll write you*). This omission of *to* is very common in informal English in the U.S., but is nevertheless not accepted as good formal usage.

write down *vb.* (*adv.*) **1.** (*tr.*) to set down in writing. **2.** (*tr.*) to harm or belittle by writing about (a person) in derogatory terms. **3.** (*intr.*; foll. by *to* or *for*) to write in a simplified way (to a supposedly less cultured readership). **4.** (*tr.*) *Accounting.* to decrease the book value of (an asset). ~*n.* **write-down. 5.** *Accounting.* a reduction made in the book value of an asset.

write in *vb.* (*tr.*) **1.** to insert in (a document, form, etc.) in writing. **2.** (*adv.*) to write a letter to a company, institution, etc. **3.** (*adv.*) *U.S.* to vote for (a person not on a ballot) by inserting his name.

write off *vb.* (*tr., adv.*) **1.** *Accounting.* **a.** to cancel (a bad debt or obsolete asset) from the accounts. **b.** to consider (a transaction, etc.) as a loss or set off (a loss) against revenues. **c.** to depreciate (an asset) by periodic charges. **d.** to charge (a specified amount) against gross profits as depreciation of an asset. **2.** to cause or acknowledge the complete loss of. **3.** to dismiss from consideration. **4.** to send a written order (for something): *she wrote off for a brochure.* **5.** *Inf.* to damage (something, esp. a car) beyond repair. ~*n.* **write-off. 6.** *Accounting.* **a.** the act of cancelling a bad debt or obsolete asset from the accounts. **b.** the bad debt or obsolete asset cancelled. **c.** the amount cancelled against gross profits, corresponding to the book value of the bad debt or obsolete asset. **7.** *Inf.* something damaged beyond repair, esp. a car.

write out *vb.* (*tr., adv.*) **1.** to put into writing or reproduce in full form in writing. **2.** to exhaust (oneself or one's creativity) by excessive writing. **3.** to remove (a character) from a television or radio series.

writer ('raɪtə) *n.* **1.** a person who writes books, articles, etc., esp. as an occupation. **2.** the person who has written something specified. **3.** a person who is able to write or write well. **4.** a scribe or clerk. **5.** a composer of music. **6. Writer to the Signet.** (in Scotland) a member of an ancient society of solicitors, now having the exclusive privilege of preparing crown writs.

writer's cramp *n.* a muscular spasm or temporary paralysis of the muscles of the thumb and first two fingers caused by prolonged writing.

write up *vb.* (*tr., adv.*) **1.** to describe fully, complete, or bring up to date in writing: *write up a diary.* **2.** to praise or bring to public notice in writing. **3.** *Accounting.* **a.** to place an excessively high value on (an asset). **b.** to increase the book value of (an asset) in order to reflect more accurately its current worth in the market. ~*n.* **write-up. 4.** a published account of something, such as a review in a newspaper or magazine.

writhe (raɪð) *vb.* **1.** to twist or squirm in or as if in pain. **2.** (*intr.*) to move with such motions. **3.** (*intr.*) to suffer acutely from embarrassment, revulsion, etc. ~*n.* **3.** the act or an instance of writhing. [OE *wrīthan*] —'**writher** *n.*

writing ('raɪtɪŋ) *n.* **1.** a group of letters or symbols written or marked on a surface as a means of communicating. **2.** short for **handwriting. 3.** anything expressed in letters, esp. a literary composition. **4.** the work of a writer. **5.** literary style, art, or practice. **6.** written form: *give it to me in writing.* **7.** (*modifier*) related to or used in writing: *writing ink.* **8. writing on the wall.** a sign or signs of approaching disaster. [sense 8: allusion to Daniel 5:5]

writing desk *n.* a piece of furniture with a writing surface and drawers and compartments for papers, writing materials, etc.

writing paper *n.* paper sized to take writing ink and used for letters and other manuscripts.

writ of execution *n. Law.* a writ ordering that a judgment be enforced.

written ('rɪtᵊn) *vb.* **1.** the past participle of **write.** ~*adj.* **2.** taken down in writing; transcribed: *written evidence; the written word.*

WRNS *abbrev. for* Women's Royal Naval Service. See also **Wren.**

Wroclaw (*Polish* 'vrɒtswaf) *n.* an industrial city in SW Poland, on the River Oder: passed to Austria (1527) and to Prussia (1741); returned to Poland in 1945. Pop.: 636 000 (1985). German name: **Breslau.**

wrong (rɒŋ) *adj.* **1.** not correct or truthful: *the wrong answer.* **2.** acting or judging in error: *you are wrong to think that.* **3.** (*postpositive*) immoral; bad: *it is wrong to cheat.* **4.** deviating from or unacceptable to correct or conventional laws, usage, etc. **5.** not intended or wanted: *the wrong road.* **6.** (*postpositive*) not working properly; amiss: *something is wrong with the engine.* **7.** (of a side, esp. of a fabric) intended to face the inside so as not to be seen. **8. get on the wrong side of.** *Inf.* to come into disfavour with. **9. go down the wrong way.** (of food) to pass into the windpipe instead of the gullet. ~*adv.* **10.** in the wrong direction or manner. **11. get wrong. a.** to fail to understand properly. **b.** to fail to provide the correct answer to. **12. go wrong. a.** to turn out other than intended. **b.** to make a mistake. **c.** (of a machine, etc.) to cease to function properly. **d.** to go astray morally. ~*n.* **13.** a bad, immoral, or unjust thing or action. **14.** *Law.* **a.** an infringement of another person's rights, rendering the offender liable to a civil action: *a private wrong.* **b.** a violation of public rights and duties, affecting the community as a whole and actionable at the instance of the Crown: *a public wrong.* **15. in the wrong.** mistaken or guilty. ~*vb.* (*tr.*) **16.** to treat unjustly. **17.** to discredit, malign, or misrepresent. [OE *wrang* injustice] —'**wronger** *n.* —'**wrongly** *adv.* —'**wrongness** *n.*

wrongdoer ('rɒŋ,duːə) *n.* a person who acts immorally or illegally. —'**wrong,doing** *n.*

wrong-foot *vb.* (*tr.*) **1.** *Tennis, etc.* to play a shot in such a way as to cause (one's opponent) to be off balance. **2.** to take by surprise so as to place in an embarrassing or disadvantageous situation.

wrongful ('rɒŋfʊl) *adj.* unjust or illegal. —'**wrongfully** *adv.* —'**wrongfulness** *n.*

wrong-headed *adj.* **1.** constantly wrong in judgment. **2.** foolishly stubborn; obstinate. —,**wrong-'headedly** *adv.* —,**wrong-'headedness** *n.*

wrong number *n.* a telephone number wrongly connected or dialled in error, or the person so contacted.

wrote (rəʊt) *vb.* the past tense of **write.**

wroth (rəʊθ, rɒθ) *adj. Arch. or literary.* angry; irate. [OE *wrāth*]

wrought (rɔːt) *vb.* **1.** *Arch.* a past tense and past participle of **work.** ~*adj.* **2.** *Metallurgy.* shaped by hammering or beating. **3.** (*often in combination*) formed, fashioned, or worked as specified: *well-wrought.* **4.** decorated or made with delicate care. [C16: var. of *worht,* from OE *geworht,* p.p. of (*ge*)*wyrcan* to work]

wrought iron *n.* **a.** a pure form of iron having a low carbon content: often used for decorative work. **b.** (*as modifier*): *wrought-iron gates.*

wrought-up *adj.* agitated or excited.

wrung (rʌŋ) *vb.* the past tense and past participle of **wring.**

WRVS *abbrev. for* Women's Royal Voluntary Service.

wry (raɪ) *adj.* **wrier, wriest** *or* **wryer, wryest. 1.** twisted, contorted, or askew. **2.** (of a facial expression) produced or characterized by contorting of the features. **3.** dryly humorous; sardonic. **4.** warped, misdirected, or perverse. ~*vb.* **wrying, wried. 5.** (*tr.*) to twist or contort. [C16: from dialect *wry* to twist, from OE *wrīgian* to turn] —'**wryly** *adv.* —'**wryness** *n.*

wrybill ('raɪ,bɪl) *n.* a New Zealand plover, having its bill deflected to one side enabling it to search for food beneath stones.

wryneck ('raɪ,nɛk) *n.* **1.** either of two cryptically coloured Old World woodpeckers, which do not drum on trees. **2.** another name for **torticollis. 3.** *Inf.* a person who has a twisted neck.

WSW *symbol for* west-southwest.

wt. *abbrev. for* weight.

Wuchang *or* **Wu-ch'ang** ('wuː'tʃæŋ) *n.* a former city of E central China: now a part of Wuhan.

Wuhan ('wuː'hæn) *n.* a city in SE China, in Hubei province, at the confluence of the Han and Yangtze Rivers: formed in 1950 by the union of the cities of Hanyang, Hankou, and Wuchang (the Han Cities); river port and industrial centre; university (1913). Pop.: 3 400 000 (1986 est.).

Wuhsien ('wuː'ʃjɛn) *n.* another name for **Suzhou.**

Wuhu ('wuː'huː) *n.* a port in E China, in E Anhui province on the Yangtze River. Pop.: 385 800 (1985 est.).

Wulfila ('wʊlfɪlə) *n.* a variant of **Ulfilas.**

Wu-lu-mu-ch'i ('wuː'luː'muː'tʃiː) *n.* a variant of **Urumqi.**

wunderkind ('wʌndə,kɪnd; *German* wʊndər,kɪnt) *n., pl.* -**kinds** *or* -**kinder** (*German* -,kɪndər). **1.** a child prodigy. **2.** a person who is exceptionally successful in his field while still young. [C20: from G *Wunderkind,* lit.: wonder child]

Wundt (*German* vʊnt) *n.* **Wilhelm Max** ('vɪlhɛlm maks). 1832–1920, German experimental psychologist.

Wuppertal (*German* 'vʊpərtaːl) *n.* a city in W West Germany, in North Rhine-Westphalia state on the **Wupper River** (a Rhine tributary): formed in 1919 from the amalgamation of the towns of Barmen and Elberfeld and other smaller towns; textile centre. Pop.: 373 300 (1986).

wurst (wɜːst, wʊəst, vʊəst) *n.* a large sausage, esp. of a type made in Germany, Austria, etc. [from G *Wurst,* lit.: something rolled]

Württemberg ('vɜːtəm,bɜːg; *German* 'vyrtəmbɛrk) *n.* a former state of S Germany: made part of the West German state of Baden-Württemberg after World War II.

Würzburg ('vɜːts,bɜːg; *German* 'vyrtsbʊrk) *n.* a city in S West Germany, in NW Bavaria on the River Main: university (1582). Pop.: 127 500 (1986).

wuthering ('wʌðərɪŋ) *adj. N English dialect.* **1.** (of a wind) blowing strongly with a roaring sound. **2.** (of a place) characterized by such a sound. [var. of *whitherin,* from *whither* blow, from ON *hvithra*]

Wutsin ('wuː'tsɪn) *n.* the former name (until 1949) of **Changzhou.**

Wuxi, Wusih, *or* **Wu-hsi** ('wuː'ʃiː, -'siː) *n.* a city in E China, in S Jiangsu province on the Grand Canal: textile industry. Pop.: 696 300 (1987 est.).

Wyatt ('waɪət) *n.* **1. James.** 1746–1813, English architect; a pioneer of neo-Gothic. **2.** Sir **Thomas.** ?1503–42, English poet at the court of Henry VIII.

wych-elm *or* **witch-elm** ('wɪtʃ,ɛlm) *n.* **1.** a Eurasian elm tree, having a rounded shape, longish pointed leaves, clusters of small flowers, and winged fruits. **2.** the wood of this tree. [C17: from OE *wice*]

Wycherley ('wɪtʃəlɪ) *n.* **William.** ?1640–1716, English dramatist. His Restoration comedies include *The Country Wife* (1675) and *The Plain Dealer* (1676).

Wycliffe *or* **Wyclif** ('wɪklɪf) *n.* **John.** ?1330–84, English religious reformer. A precursor of the Reformation, whose writings were condemned as heretical, he attacked the doctrines and abuses of the Church. He instigated the first complete translation of the Bible into English. His followers were called Lollards. Also: **'Wiclif, 'Wickliffe.** —'**Wycliffism** *or* '**Wyclifism** *n.* —'**Wyclif,fite** *or* '**Wyclif,ite** *n., adj.*

Wye (waɪ) *n.* a river in E Wales and W England, rising in Powys and flowing southeast into England, then south to the Severn estuary. Length: 210 km (130 miles).

Wykeham ('wɪkəm) *n.* **William of.** 1324–1404, English prelate and statesman, who founded New College, Oxford, and Winchester College: chancellor of England (1367–71; 1389–91); bishop of Winchester (1367–1404).

wynd (waɪnd) *n. Scot.* a narrow lane or alley. [C15: from the stem of WIND²]

Wyoming (waɪ'əʊmɪŋ) *n.* a state of the western U.S.: consists largely of ranges of the Rockies in the west and north, with part of the Great Plains in the east and several regions of hot springs. Capital: Cheyenne. Pop.: 485 111 (1986 est.). Area: 253 597 sq. km (97 914 sq. miles). Abbrevs.: **Wyo., Wy.,** or (with zip code) **WY** —**Wy'oming,ite** *n.*

WYSIWYG ('wɪzɪ,wɪg) *n., adj. Computers.* acronym for what you see is what you get: referring to what is displayed on the screen being the same as what will be printed out.

wyvern *or* **wivern** ('waɪvən) *n.* a heraldic beast having a serpent's tail and a dragon's head and a body with wings and two legs. [C17: var. of earlier *wyver*, from OF, from L *vīpera* VIPER]

X

x *or* **X** (ɛks) *n., pl.* **x's, X's,** *or* **Xs. 1.** the 24th letter of the English alphabet. **2.** a speech sound sequence represented by this letter, pronounced as *ks* or *gz* or, in initial position, *z*, as in *xylophone.*

x *symbol for:* **1.** *Commerce, finance, etc.* ex. **2.** *Maths.* the *x*-axis or a coordinate measured along the *x*-axis in a Cartesian coordinate system. **3.** *Maths.* an algebraic variable. **4.** multiplication.

X *symbol:* **1. a.** (formerly) indicating a film that may not be publicly shown to anyone under 18. Since 1982 replaced by symbol 18. **b.** (*as modifier*): *an X film.* **2.** denoting any unknown, unspecified, or variable factor, number, person, or thing. **3.** (on letters, cards, etc.) denoting a kiss. **4.** (on ballot papers, etc.) indicating choice. **5.** (on examination papers, etc.) indicating error. **6.** for Christ; Christian. [from the Gk letter khi (X), first letter of *Khristos* Christ] ~**7.** *the Roman numeral for* ten. See **Roman numerals.**

xanthein ('zænθɪɪn) *n.* the soluble part of the yellow pigment that is found in the cell sap of some flowers.

xanthene ('zænθiːn) *n.* a yellowish crystalline compound used as a fungicide.

xanthic ('zænθɪk) *adj.* **1.** of, containing, or derived from xanthic acid. **2.** *Bot., rare.* having a yellow colour.

xanthic acid *n.* any of a class of sulphur-containing acids.

xanthine ('zænθiːn, -θaɪn) *n.* **1.** a crystalline compound found in urine, blood, certain plants, and certain animal tissues. Formula: $C_5H_4N_4O_2$. **2.** any of three substituted derivatives of xanthine, which act as stimulants and diuretics.

Xanthippe (zæn'θɪpɪ) *or* **Xantippe** (zæn'tɪpɪ) *n.* **1.** the wife of Socrates, proverbial as a scolding and quarrelsome woman. **2.** any nagging, peevish, or irritable woman.

xantho- *or before a vowel* **xanth-** *combining form.* indicating yellow: *xanthophyll.* [from Gk *xanthos* yellow]

xanthochroism (zæn'θɒkrəʊ.ɪzəm) *n.* a condition in certain animals, esp. aquarium goldfish, in which all skin pigments other than yellow and orange disappear. [C19: from Gk *xanthokhro(os)* yellow-skinned + -ISM]

xanthoma (zæn'θəʊmə) *n. Pathol.* the presence in the skin of fatty yellow or brownish plaques or nodules, esp. on the eyelids, caused by a disorder of lipid metabolism.

xanthophyll *or esp. U.S.* **xanthophyl** ('zænθəʊfɪl) *n.* any of a group of yellow carotenoid pigments occurring in plant and animal tissue. — ˌxantho'phyllous *adj.*

xanthous ('zænθəs) *adj.* of, relating to, or designating races with yellowish hair and a light complexion.

Xanthus ('zænθəs) *n.* the chief city of ancient Lycia in SW Asia Minor: source of some important antiquities. — 'Xanthian *adj.*

Xavier ('zeɪvɪə, 'zæv-; *Spanish* xa'βjɛr) *n.* **Saint Francis,** known as the *Apostle of the Indies.* 1506–52, Spanish missionary, who was a founding member of the Jesuit society (1534) and later preached in Goa, Ceylon, the East Indies, and Japan. Feast day: Dec. 3.

x-axis *n.* a reference axis, usually horizontal, of a graph or two- or three-dimensional Cartesian coordinate system along which the *x*-coordinate is measured.

X-chromosome *n.* the sex chromosome that occurs in pairs in the diploid cells of the females of many animals, including humans, and as one of a pair with the Y-chromosome in those of males. Cf. **Y-chromosome.**

Xe *the chemical symbol for* xenon.

xebec, zebec, *or* **zebeck** ('ziːbɛk) *n.* a small three-masted Mediterranean vessel with both square and lateen sails, formerly used by Algerian pirates and later used for commerce. [C18: earlier *chebec* from F, ult. from Ar. *shabbāk*; present spelling infl. by Catalan *xabec*, Sp. *xabeque* (now *jabeque*)]

Xenakis (zɛ'nɑːkɪs; *Greek* ksɛ'nakis) *n.* **Yannis** ('janis). born 1922, Greek composer and musical theorist, born in Romania. He is noted for his use of electronic computers in composition: his works include *ST/10-1, 080262* (1962).

xeno- *or before a vowel* **xen-** *combining form.* indicating something strange, different, or foreign: *xenogamy.* [from Gk *xenos* strange]

Xenocrates (zɛ'nɒkrə.tiːz) *n.* ?396–314 B.C., Greek Platonic philosopher. — **Xenocratic** (ˌzɛnə'krætɪk) *adj.*

xenogamy (zɛ'nɒgəmɪ) *n. Bot.* another name for **cross-fertilization.** — **xe'nogamous** *adj.*

xenoglossia (ˌzɛnə'glɒsɪə) *n.* an ability claimed by some mediums, clairvoyants, etc., to speak a language with which they are unfamiliar. [C20: from Gk, from XENO- + *glossa* language]

xenolith ('zɛnəlɪθ) *n.* a fragment of rock differing in origin, composition, structure, etc., from the igneous rock enclosing it. — ˌxeno'lithic *adj.*

xenon ('zɛnɒn) *n.* a colourless odourless gaseous element occurring in trace amounts in air; formerly considered inert, it is now known to form compounds and is used in radio valves, stroboscopic and bactericidal lamps, and bubble chambers. Symbol: Xe; atomic no.: 54; atomic wt.: 131.30. [C19: from Gk: something strange]

Xenophanes (zɛ'nɒfə.niːz) *n.* ?570–?480 B.C., Greek philosopher and poet, noted for his monotheism.

xenophile ('zɛnə.faɪl) *n.* a person who likes foreigners or things foreign. [C19: from Gk, from XENO- + -PHILE]

xenophobia (ˌzɛnə'fəʊbɪə) *n.* hatred or fear of foreigners or strangers or of their politics or culture. [C20: from Gk, from XENO- + -PHOBIA] — 'xeno,phobe *n.* — ˌxeno'phobic *adj.*

Xenophon ('zɛnəfən) *n.* 431–?355 B.C., Greek general and historian; a disciple of Socrates. He accompanied Cyrus the Younger against Artaxerxes II and, after Cyrus' death at Cunaxa (401), he led his army of 10 000 Greek soldiers to the Black Sea, an expedition described in his *Anabasis.* His other works include *Hellenica,* a history of Greece, and the *Memorabilia, Apology,* and *Symposium,* which contain recollections of Socrates.

Xeres (*Spanish* 'xɛrɛθ) *n.* the former name of **Jerez.**

xeric ('zɪərɪk) *adj. Ecology.* of, relating to, or growing in dry conditions. — 'xerically *adv.*

xero- *or before a vowel* **xer-** *combining form.* indicating dryness: *xeroderma.* [from Gk *xēros* dry]

xeroderma (ˌzɪərəʊ'dɜːmə) *or* **xerodermia** (ˌzɪərəʊ'dɜːmɪə) *n. Pathol.* **1.** any abnormal dryness of the skin as the result of diminished secretions from the sweat or sebaceous glands. **2.** another name for **ichthyosis.** — **xerodermatic** (ˌzɪərəʊdə'mætɪk) *or* ˌxero-'dermatous *adj.*

xerography (zɪ'rɒgrəfɪ) *n.* a photocopying process in which an electrostatic image is formed on a selenium plate or cylinder. The plate or cylinder is dusted with a resinous powder, which adheres to the charged regions, and the image is then transferred to a sheet of paper on which it is fixed by heating. — **xe'rographer** *n.* — **xerographic** (ˌzɪərəʊ'græfɪk) *adj.* — ˌxero'graphically *adv.*

xerophilous (zɪ'rɒfɪləs) *adj.* (of plants or animals) adapted for growing or living in dry surroundings. — **xerophile** ('zɪərə.faɪl) *n.* — **xe'rophily** *n.*

xerophthalmia (ˌzɪərɒf'θælmɪə) *n. Pathol.* excessive dryness of the cornea and conjunctiva, caused by a deficiency of vitamin A. Also called: **xeroma** (zɪ'rəʊmə). — ˌxeroph'thalmic *adj.*

xerophyte ('zɪərə.faɪt) *n.* a xerophilous plant, such as a cactus. — **xerophytic** (ˌzɪərə'fɪtɪk) *adj.* — ˌxero'phytically *adv.* — 'xero,phytism *n.*

Xerox ('zɪərɒks) *n.* **1.** *Trademark.* **a.** a xerographic copying process. **b.** a machine employing this process. **c.** a copy produced by this process. ~*vb.* **2.** to produce a copy of (a document, illustration, etc.) by this process.

Xerxes I ('zɜːksiːz) *n.* ?519–465 B.C., king of Persia (485–465), who led a vast army against Greece. His forces were victorious at Thermopylae but his fleet was defeated at Salamis (480) and his army at Plataea (479).

Xhosa ('kɔːsə) *n.* **1.** (*pl.* **-sa** *or* **-sas**) a member of a cattle-rearing Negroid people of southern Africa, living chiefly in Cape Province of the Republic of South Africa. **2.** the language of this people, belonging to the Bantu group and characterized by several clicks in its sound system. —'**Xhosan** *adj.*

xi (zaɪ, saɪ, ksaɪ, ksiː) *n.*, *pl.* **xis**. the 14th letter in the Greek alphabet (Ξ, ξ).

Xi, Hsi, *or* **Si** (ʃiː) *n.* a river in S China, rising in Yünnan province and flowing east to the Canton delta on the South China Sea: the main river system of S China. Length: about 1900 km (1200 miles).

Xi An, Hsian, *or* **Sian** (ʃjɑːn) *n.* an industrial city in central China, capital of Shaanxi province: capital of China for 970 years at various times between the 3rd century B.C. and the 10th century A.D.; seat of the Northwestern University (1937). Pop.: 2 330 000 (1986). Former name: **Siking.**

Xiang, Hsiang, *or* **Siang** (ʃjɑːŋ) *n.* **1.** a river in SE central China, rising in NE Guangxi Zhuang and flowing northeast and north to Dongting Lake. Length: about 1150 km (715 miles). **2.** a river in S China, rising in SE Yünnan and flowing generally east to the Hongxiu (the upper course of the Xi River). Length: about 800 km (500 miles).

Xiangtan *or* **Siangtan** ('ʃjɑːŋ'tɑːn) *n.* a city in S central China, in NE Hunan on the Xiang River: centre of a region noted for tea production. Pop.: 337 100 (1987 est.).

Ximenes *or* **Ximenez** (*Spanish* xi'menes; *English* 'zɪmɪ,niːz) *n.* See (Francisco) **Jiménez de Cisneros.**

Xingú (*Portuguese* ʃiŋ'gu) *n.* a river in central Brazil, rising on the Mato Grosso plateau and flowing north to the Amazon delta, with over 650 km (400 miles) of rapids in its middle course. Length: 1932 km (1200 miles).

Xining, Hsining, *or* **Sining** ('ʃiː'nɪŋ) *n.* a city in W China, capital of Qinghai province, at an altitude of 2300 m (7500 ft.). Pop.: 473 000 (1987 est.).

Xinjiang Uygur ('ʃɪn'dʒjæŋ 'wiːɡʊə) *or* **Sinkiang-Uighur Autonomous Region** *n.* an administrative division of NW China: established in 1955 for the Uygur ethnic minority, with autonomous subdivisions for other small minorities; produces over half China's wool and contains valuable mineral resources. Capital: Urumqi. Pop.: 13 440 000 (1985). Area: 1 646 799 sq. km (635 829 sq. miles).

xiphisternum (,zɪfɪ'stɜːnəm) *n.*, *pl.* **-na** (-nə) *Anat.*, *zool.* the cartilaginous process forming the lowermost part of the breastbone (sternum). Also called: **xiphoid, xiphoid process.** [C19: from Gk *xiphos* sword + STERNUM]

xiphoid ('zɪfɔɪd) *adj.* **1.** *Biol.* shaped like a sword. **2.** of or relating to the xiphisternum. ~*n.* **3.** Also called: **xiphoid process.** another name for **xiphisternum.** [C18: from NL, from Gk, from *xiphos* sword + *eidos* form]

Xizang Autonomous Region ('ʃiː'zæŋ) *n.* the Pinyin transliteration of the Chinese name for **Tibet.**

Xmas ('ɛksməs, 'krɪsməs) *n.* *Inf.* short for **Christmas.** [C18: from symbol X for Christ + -MAS]

x-ray *or* **X-ray** *n.* **1. a.** electromagnetic radiation emitted when matter is bombarded with fast electrons. X-rays have wavelengths shorter than that of ultraviolet radiation, that is less than about 1×10^{-8} metres. Below about 1×10^{-11} metres they are often called gamma radiation or bremsstrahlung. **b.** (*as modifier*): *x-ray astronomy.* **2.** a picture produced by exposing photographic film to x-rays: used in medicine as a diagnostic aid as parts of the body, such as bones, absorb x-rays and so appear as opaque areas on the picture. ~*vb.* (*tr.*) **3.** to photograph (part of the body, etc.) using x-rays. **4.** to treat or examine by means of x-rays. [C19: partial translation of G *X-Strahlen* (from *Strahl* ray), coined by W. K. ROENTGEN in 1895]

x-ray astronomy *n.* the branch of astronomy concerned with the detection and measurement of x-rays emitted by certain celestial bodies, such as x-ray stars.

x-ray crystallography *n.* the study and practice of determining the structure of a crystal by passing a beam of x-rays through it and observing and analysing the diffraction pattern produced.

x-ray star *n.* a star that emits x-rays, as well as other types of radiation. The x-rays are detected and measured by instruments carried in satellites and space probes.

x-ray tube *n.* an evacuated tube containing a metal target onto which is directed a beam of electrons at high energy for the generation of x-rays.

Xuan-tong ('ʃwɑːn'tʊŋ) *n.* the Pinyin transliteration of the title as emperor of China of (Henry) **Pu-yi.**

Xuthus ('zuːθəs) *n.* *Greek myth.* a son of Hellen, regarded as an ancestor of the Ionian Greeks through his son Ion.

Xuzhou ('ʃuː'dʒəʊ), **Hsü-chou,** *or* **Süchow** *n.* a city in N central China, in NW Jiangsu province: scene of a decisive battle (1949) in which the Communists defeated the Nationalists. Pop.: 773 000 (1982).

xylem ('zaɪləm, -lɛm) *n.* a plant tissue that conducts water and mineral salts from the roots to all other parts, provides mechanical support, and forms the wood of trees and shrubs. [C19: from Gk *xulon* wood]

xylene ('zaɪliːn) *n.* an aromatic hydrocarbon existing in three isomeric forms, all three being colourless flammable volatile liquids used as solvents and in the manufacture of synthetic resins, dyes, and insecticides. Formula: $(CH_3)_2C_6H_4$. Systematic name: **dimethyl benzene.**

xylo- *or before a vowel* **xyl-** *combining form.* **1.** indicating wood: *xylophone.* **2.** indicating xylene: *xylidine.* [from Gk *xulon* wood]

xylocarp ('zaɪlə,kɑːp) *n.* *Bot.* a fruit, such as a coconut, having a hard woody pericarp. —,**xylo'carpous** *adj.*

xylograph ('zaɪlə,grɑːf) *n.* **1.** an engraving in wood. **2.** a print taken from a wood block. ~*vb.* **3.** (*tr.*) to print (a design, illustration, etc.) from a wood engraving. —**xylography** (zaɪ'lɒgrəfɪ) *n.*

Xylonite ('zaɪlənaɪt) *n.* *Trademark.* a thermoplastic of the cellulose nitrate type.

xylophagous (zaɪ'lɒfəgəs) *adj.* (of certain insects, crustaceans, etc.) feeding on or living within wood.

xylophone ('zaɪlə,fəʊn) *n.* *Music.* a percussion instrument consisting of a set of wooden bars of graduated length. It is played with hard-headed hammers. —**xylophonic** (,zaɪlə'fɒnɪk) *adj.* —**xylophonist** (zaɪ'lɒfənɪst) *n.*

xylose ('zaɪləʊz, -ləʊs) *n.* a white crystalline sugar found in wood and straw. It is extracted by hydrolysis with acids and used in dyeing, tanning, and in foods for diabetics.

xyster ('zɪstə) *n.* a surgical instrument for scraping bone; surgical rasp or file. [C17: via NL from Gk: tool for scraping, from *xuein* to scrape]

Y

y *or* **Y** (waɪ) *n., pl.* **y's, Y's,** *or* **Ys. 1.** the 25th letter of the English alphabet. **2.** a speech sound represented by this letter, usually a semivowel, as in *yawn*, or a vowel, as in *symbol* or *shy*. **3.** something shaped like a Y.

y *Maths. symbol for:* **1.** the *y*-axis or a coordinate measured along the *y*-axis in a Cartesian coordinate system. **2.** an algebraic variable.

Y *symbol for:* **1.** any unknown or variable factor, number, or thing. **2.** *Chem.* yttrium.

y. *abbrev. for* year.

-y¹ *or* **-ey** *suffix forming adjectives.* **1.** (*from nouns*) characterized by; consisting of; filled with; resembling: *sunny; sandy; smoky; classy.* **2.** (*from verbs*) tending to; acting or existing as specified: *leaky; shiny.* [from OE *-ig*, *-æg*]

-y², **-ie**, *or* **-ey** *suffix of nouns. Inf.* **1.** denoting smallness and expressing affection and familiarity: *a doggy; Jamie.* **2.** a person or thing concerned with or characterized by being: *a groupie; a goalie; a fatty.* [C14: from Scot. *-ie*, *-y*, familiar suffix orig. in names]

-y³ *suffix forming nouns.* **1.** (*from verbs*) indicating the act of doing what is indicated by the verbal element: *inquiry.* **2.** (*esp. with combining forms of Greek, Latin, or French origin*) indicating state, condition, or quality: *geography; jealousy.* [from OF *-ie*, from L *-ia*]

yabby *or* **yabbie** ('jæbɪ) *Austral. ~n., pl.* **-bies. 1.** a small edible freshwater crayfish. **2.** a saltwater prawn used as bait; nipper. *~vb.* **-bying, -bied. 3.** (*intr.*) to go out to catch yabbies. [from Abor.]

Yablonovy Mountains (*Russian* 'jablənəvɪj) *pl. n.* a mountain range in the SE Soviet Union, in Siberia. Highest peak: 1680 m (5512 ft.). Also called: **Yablonoi Mountains** ('jɑːblə,nɔɪ).

yacht (jɒt) *n.* **1.** a vessel propelled by sail or power, used esp. for pleasure cruising, racing, etc. *~vb.* **2.** (*intr.*) to sail or cruise in a yacht. [C16: from obs. Du. *jaghte*, short for *jahtschip*, from *jagen* to chase + *schip* ship] **—'yachting** *n., adj.*

yachtie ('jɒtɪ) *n. Austral. & N.Z. inf.* a yachtsman; sailing enthusiast.

yachtsman ('jɒtsmən) *or* (*fem.*) **yachtswoman** *n., pl.* **-men** *or* **-women.** a person who sails a yacht or yachts. **— 'yachtsmanship** *n.*

yack (jæk) *n., vb.* a variant spelling of **yak².**

yackety-yak ('jækɪtɪ'jæk) *n. Sl.* noisy, continuous, and trivial talk or conversation. [imit.]

yaffle ('jæfəl) *n.* another name for **green woodpecker** (see **woodpecker**). [C18: imit. of its cry]

Yafo ('jɑːfɔː) *n.* transliteration of the Hebrew name for **Jaffa** (sense 1).

Yagi aerial ('jɑːgɪ, 'jæɡɪ) *n.* a directional aerial, used esp. in television and radio astronomy, consisting of three or more elements lying parallel to each other, the principal direction of radiation being along the line of the centres. [C20: after Hidetsugu *Yagi* (1886–1976), Japanese engineer]

yah (jɑː, jɛə) *sentence substitute.* **1.** an informal word for **yes.** *~interj.* **2.** an exclamation of derision or disgust.

Yahata ('jɑːhɑː,tɑː) *n.* a variant of **Yawata.**

yahoo (jə'huː) *n., pl.* **-hoos.** a crude, brutish, or obscenely coarse person. [C18: from a race of brutish creatures resembling men in Jonathan Swift's *Gulliver's Travels* (1726)] **— ya'hooism** *n.*

Yahweh ('jɑːweɪ) *or* **Yahveh** ('jɑːveɪ) *n. Old Testament.* a vocalization of the Tetragrammaton. [from Heb., from YHVH, with conjectural vowels; see also JEHOVAH]

Yahwism ('jɑːwɪzəm) *or* **Yahvism** ('jɑːvɪzəm) *n.* the use of the name Yahweh, esp. in parts of the Old Testament, as the personal name of God.

Yahwist ('jɑːwɪst) *or* **Yahvist** ('jɑːvɪst) *n. Bible.* **the.** the conjectured author or authors of the earliest sources of the Pentateuch in which God is called *Yahweh* throughout. **—Yah'wistic** *or* **Yah'vistic** *adj.*

yak¹ (jæk) *n.* an ox of Tibet having long shaggy hair. [C19: from Tibetan *gyag*]

yak² (jæk) *Sl. ~n.* **1.** noisy, continuous, and trivial talk. *~vb.* **yakking, yakked. 2.** (*intr.*) to chatter or talk in this way. [C20: imit.]

yakka, yakker, *or* **yacker** ('jækə) *n. Austral. & N.Z. inf.* work. [C19: from Abor.]

Yakut Autonomous Soviet Socialist Republic (jæ'kʊt) *n.* an administrative division of the E Soviet Union, in NE Siberia on the Arctic Ocean: the coldest inhabited region of the world. Capital: Yakutsk. Pop.: 1 009 000 (1986). Area: 3 103 000 sq. km (1 197 760 sq. miles).

Yakutsk (*Russian* jɪ'kutsk) *n.* a port in the E Soviet Union, capital of the Yakut ASSR, on the Lena River. Pop.: 184 000 (1986).

Yale lock (jeɪl) *n. Trademark.* a type of cylinder lock using a flat serrated key. [C19: after L. *Yale* (1821–68), U.S. inventor]

Yalta (*Russian* 'jaltə) *n.* a port and resort in the SW Soviet Union, in the S Ukrainian SSR, in the Crimea on the Black Sea: scene of a conference (1945) between Churchill, Roosevelt, and Stalin, who met to plan the final defeat and occupation of Nazi Germany. Pop.: 84 000 (1983 est.).

Yalu ('jɑː,luː) *n.* a river in E Asia, rising in N North Korea and flowing southwest to Korea Bay, forming a large part of the border between North Korea and NE China. Length: 806 km (501 miles).

yam (jæm) *n.* **1.** any of various twining plants of tropical and subtropical regions, cultivated for their edible tubers. **2.** the starchy tuber of any of these plants, eaten as a vegetable. **3.** *Southern U.S.* the sweet potato. [C17: from Port. *inhame*, ult. of W African origin]

Yamagata (jæmə'gɑːtə) *n.* Prince **Aritomo** (,ærɪ'təʊməʊ). 1838–1922, Japanese soldier and politician. As war minister (1873) and chief of staff (1878), he modernized Japan's military system. He was premier of Japan (1889–93; 1898).

Yamani (jə'mɑːnɪ) *n.* Sheikh **Ahmed Zaki** ('ɑːmɛd 'zɑːkɪ). born 1930, Saudi Arabian politician; minister of petroleum and natural resources (1962–86).

Yamasaki (jæmə'sɑːkɪ) *n.* **Minoru.** 1912–86, U.S. architect. His buildings include St Louis Airport, Missouri (1953–55) and the World Trade Center, New York (1970–77).

Yamashita (jæmə'ʃiːtə) *n.* **Tomoyuki** (,təʊməʊ'juːkɪ). 1885–1946, Japanese general. He commanded Japanese forces in the Malayan campaign in World War II and took Singapore (1942); captured (1945) and hanged.

yammer ('jæmə) *Inf. ~vb.* **1.** to utter or whine in a complaining manner. **2.** to make (a complaint) loudly or persistently. *~n.* **3.** a yammering sound. **4.** nonsense; jabber. [OE *geōmrian* to grumble] **— 'yammerer** *n.*

Yamoussoukro (,jæmʊ'suːkrəʊ) *n.* the capital of the Côte d'Ivoire, situated in the S centre of the country. It replaced Abidjan as capital in 1983. Pop.: 70 000 (1983 est.).

Yanan ('jæn'æn) *or* **Yenan** *n.* a city in NE China, in N Shaanxi province: political and military capital of the Chinese Communists (1935–49). Pop.: 254 100 (1984 est.). Also called: **Fushih.**

Yang¹ (jæŋ) *n.* See **Yin and Yang.**

Yang² (jæŋ) *n.* **Chen Ning** ('tʃɛn 'nɪŋ). born 1922, US physicist, born in China: with Tsung-Dao Lee, he disproved the physical principle known as the conservation of parity and shared the Nobel prize for physics (1957).

Yangtze ('jæŋksɪ, 'jæŋktsɪ) *n.* the longest river in China, rising in SE Qinghai province and flowing east to the East China Sea near Shanghai: a major commercial waterway in one of the most densely populated areas of the world. Length: 5528 km (3434 miles). Also called: **Yangtze Jiang, Chang Jiang, Chang.**

Yanina ('jɑːnɪnə) *n.* a variant spelling of **Ioánnina.**

yank (jæŋk) *vb.* **1.** to pull with a sharp movement; tug. *~n.* **2.** a jerk. [C19: from ?]

Yank (jæŋk) *n.* **1.** a slang word for an **American. 2.** *U.S. inf.* short for **Yankee.**

Yankee ('jæŋkı) *or* (*inf.*) **Yank** *n.* **1.** *Often disparaging.* a native or inhabitant of the U.S.; American. **2.** a native or inhabitant of New England. **3.** a native or inhabitant of the Northern U.S., esp. a Northern soldier in the Civil War. ~*adj.* **4.** of, relating to, or characteristic of Yankees. [C18: ?from Du. *Jan Kees* John Cheese, nickname used derisively by Du. settlers for English colonists in Connecticut]

Yankee Doodle *n.* **1.** an American song, popularly regarded as a characteristically national melody. **2.** another name for **Yankee.**

Yantai ('jæn'taı), **Yentai,** *or* **Yen-t'ai** *n.* a port in E China, in NE Shandong. Pop.: 347 000 (1980 est.). Also called: **Chefoo.**

Yaoundé *or* **Yaunde** (*French* jaundе) *n.* the capital of Cameroon, in the southwest: University of Cameroon (1962). Pop.: 583 500 (1985 est.).

yap (jæp) *vb.* **yapping, yapped.** (*intr.*) **1.** (of a dog) to bark in quick sharp bursts; yelp. **2.** *Inf.* to talk at length in an annoying or stupid way; jabber. ~*n.* **3.** a high-pitched or sharp bark; yelp. **4.** *Sl.* annoying or stupid speech; jabber. **5.** *Sl., chiefly U.S.* a derogatory word for **mouth.** [C17: imit.] —'**yapper** *n.* —'**yappy** *adj.*

Yap (jɑːp, jæp) *n.* a group of four main islands in the W Pacific, in the W Caroline Islands: administratively a district of the U.S. Trust Territory of the Pacific Islands from 1947; became self-governing in 1979 as part of the Federated States of Micronesia; important Japanese naval base in World War II. Pop.: 8172 (1980). Area: 101 sq. km (39 sq. miles).

yapok (jə'pɒk) *n.* an amphibious nocturnal opossum of Central and South America. Also called: **water opossum.** [C19: after *Oyapok*, a river flowing between French Guiana & Brazil]

Yapurá (japu'ra) *n.* the Spanish name for **Japurá.**

Yaqui (*Spanish* 'jaki) *n.* a river in NW Mexico, rising near the border with the U.S. and flowing south to the Gulf of California. Length: about 676 km (420 miles).

yarborough ('jɑːbərə, -brə) *n. Bridge, whist.* a hand of 13 cards in which no card is higher than nine. [C19: supposedly after the second Earl of *Yarborough* (d. 1897), said to have bet a thousand to one against its occurrence]

yard[1] (jɑːd) *n.* **1.** a unit of length equal to 3 feet and defined in 1963 as exactly 0.9144 metre. **2.** a cylindrical wooden or hollow metal spar, slung from a mast of a vessel, and used for suspending a sail. [OE *gierd* rod, twig]

yard[2] (jɑːd) *n.* **1.** a piece of enclosed ground, often adjoining or surrounded by a building or buildings. **2. a.** an enclosed or open area used for some commercial activity, for storage, etc.: *a builder's yard.* **b.** (*in combination*): *a shipyard.* **3.** a U.S. and Canad. word for **garden** (sense 1). **4.** an area having a network of railway tracks and sidings, used for storing rolling stock, making up trains, etc. **5.** *U.S. & Canad.* the winter pasture of deer, moose, and similar animals. **6.** *N.Z.* short for **stockyard.** [OE *geard*]

Yard (jɑːd) *n.* **the. *Brit. inf.* short for **Scotland Yard.**

yardage[1] ('jɑːdıdʒ) *n.* a length measured in yards.

yardage[2] ('jɑːdıdʒ) *n.* **1.** the use of a railway yard for cattle. **2.** the charge for this.

yardarm ('jɑːd,ɑːm) *n. Naut.* the outer end of a yard, outside the sheave holes.

yard grass *n.* an Old World perennial grass with prostrate leaves, growing as a troublesome weed on open ground, yards, etc.

Yardie ('jɑːdı) *n.* a member of a Black criminal syndicate originally based in Jamaica. [origin unknown]

yard of ale *n.* **1.** the beer or ale contained in a narrow horn-shaped drinking glass. **2.** such a drinking glass itself.

yardstick ('jɑːd,stık) *n.* **1.** a measure or standard used for comparison. **2.** a graduated stick, one yard long, used for measurement.

Yarkand (jɑː'kænd) *n.* another name for **Shache.**

Yarmouth ('jɑːməθ) *n.* short for **Great Yarmouth.**

yarmulke ('jɑːməlkə) *n. Judaism.* a skullcap worn by Orthodox male Jews at all times and by others during prayer. [from Yiddish, from Ukrainian & Polish *yarmulka* cap, prob. from Turkish *yağmurluk* raincoat, from *yağmur* rain]

yarn (jɑːn) *n.* **1.** a continuous twisted strand of natural or synthetic fibres, used in weaving, knitting, etc. **2.** *Inf.* a long and often involved story, usually of incredible or fantastic events. **3. spin a yarn.** *Inf.* **a.** to tell such a story. **b.** to make up a series of excuses. ~*vb.* **4.** (*intr.*) to tell such a story or stories. [OE *gearn*]

yarn-dyed *adj.* (of fabric) dyed while still in yarn form, before being woven.

Yaroslavl (*Russian* jıra'slavlj) *n.* a city in the W central Soviet Union, on the River Volga: a major trading centre since early times and one of the first industrial centres in Russia; textile industries. Pop.: 634 000 (1987).

yarran ('jærən) *n.* a small hardy tree of inland Australia: useful as fodder and for firewood. [from Abor.]

Yarra River ('jærə) *n.* a river in SE Australia, rising in the Great Dividing Range and flowing west and southwest through Melbourne to Port Phillip Bay. Length: 250 km (155 miles).

yarrow ('jærəʊ) *n.* any of several plants of the composite family of Eurasia, having finely dissected leaves and flat clusters of white flower heads. Also called: **milfoil.** [OE *gearwe*]

yashmak *or* **yashmac** ('jæʃmæk) *n.* the face veil worn by Muslim women when in public. [C19: from Ar.]

yataghan ('jætəgən) *n.* a Turkish sword with a curved blade. [C19: from Turkish *yatağan*]

Yaunde (*French* jaunde) *n.* a variant spelling of **Yaoundé.**

yaup (jɔːp) *vb., n.* a variant spelling of **yawp.** —'**yauper** *n.*

Yavarí (jaβa'ri) *n.* the Spanish name for **Javari.**

yaw (jɔː) *vb.* **1.** (*intr.*) (of an aircraft, etc.) to turn about its vertical axis. **2.** (*intr.*) (of a ship, etc.) to deviate temporarily from a course. **3.** (*tr.*) to cause (an aircraft, ship, etc.) to yaw. ~*n.* **4.** the movement of an aircraft, etc., about its vertical axis. **5.** the deviation of a vessel from a straight course. [C16: from ?]

Yawata ('ja:wɑː,tɑː) *or* **Yahata** *n.* a former city in Japan, on N Kyushu: merged with Moji, Kokura, Tobata, and Wakamatsu in 1963 to form **Kitakyushu.**

yawl (jɔːl) *n.* **1.** a two-masted sailing vessel with a small mizzenmast aft of the rudderpost. **2.** a ship's small boat, usually rowed by four or six oars. [C17: from Du. *jol* or MLow G *jolle*, from ?]

yawn (jɔːn) *vb.* **1.** (*intr.*) to open the mouth wide and take in air deeply, often as in involuntary reaction to sleepiness or boredom. **2.** (*tr.*) to express or utter while yawning. **3.** (*intr.*) to be open wide as if threatening to engulf (someone or something): *the mine shaft yawned below.* ~*n.* **4.** the act or an instance of yawning. [OE *gionian*] —'**yawner** *n.* —'**yawning** *adj.* —'**yawningly** *adv.*

yawp (jɔːp) *Dialect U.S. & Canad. inf.* ~*vb.* (*intr.*) **1.** to yawn, esp. audibly. **2.** to shout, cry, or talk noisily. **3.** to bark or yowl. ~*n.* **4.** a shout, bark, or cry. **5.** a noisy, foolish, or raucous utterance. [C15 *yolpen,* prob. imit.] —'**yawper** *n.*

yaws (jɔːz) *n.* (*usually functioning as sing.*) an infectious disease of tropical climates characterized by red skin eruptions. [C17: of Carib origin]

y-axis *n.* a reference axis of a graph or two- or three-dimensional Cartesian coordinate system along which the *y*-coordinate is measured.

Yazd (jɑːzd) *or* **Yezd** *n.* a city in central Iran: a major centre of silk weaving. Pop.: 234 003 (1986).

Yb *the chemical symbol for* ytterbium.

Y-chromosome *n.* the sex chromosome that occurs as one of a pair with the X-chromosome in the diploid cells of the males of many animals, including humans. Cf. **X-chromosome.**

yclept (ı'klɛpt) *adj. Obs.* having the name of; called. [OE *gecleopod*, p.p. of *cleopian* to call]

Y connection *n. Electrical engineering.* a three-phase star connection.

yd *or* **yd.** *abbrev. for* yard (measure).

YDT (in Canada) *abbrev. for* Yukon Daylight Time.

ye[1] (jiː, *unstressed* jı) *pron.* **1.** *Arch.* or *dialect.* refers to more than one person including the person addressed. **2.** Also: **ee** (iː). *Dialect.* refers to one person addressed: *I tell ye.* [OE *gē*]

ye[2] (ðiː, *spelling pron.* jiː) *determiner.* a form of **the**[1], used as a supposed archaism: *ye olde oake.* [from a misinterpretation of *the* as written in some ME texts. The runic letter thorn (þ, representing *th*) was incorrectly transcribed as *y* because of a resemblance in their shapes]

yea (jeɪ) *sentence substitute.* **1.** a less common word for **aye** (yes). *~adv.* **2.** (*sentence modifier*) *Arch. or literary.* indeed; truly: *yea, though they spurn me, I shall prevail.* [OE *gēa*]

yeah (jɛə) *sentence substitute.* an informal word for **yes.**

yean (jiːn) *vb.* (of a sheep or goat) to give birth to (offspring). [OE *geēanian*]

yeanling ('jiːnlɪŋ) *n.* the young of a goat or sheep.

year (jɪə) *n.* **1.** the period of time, the **calendar year**, containing 365 days or in a **leap year** 366 days. It is divided into 12 calendar months, and reckoned from January 1 to December 31. **2.** a period of twelve months from any specified date. **3.** a specific period of time, usually occupying a definite part or parts of a twelve-month period, used for some particular activity: *a school year.* **4.** Also called: **astronomical year, tropical year, equinoctial year.** the period of time, the **solar year**, during which the earth makes one revolution around the sun, measured between two successive vernal equinoxes: equal to 365.242 19 days. **5.** the period of time, the **sidereal year**, during which the earth makes one revolution around the sun, measured between two successive conjunctions of a particular star: equal to 365.256 36 days. **6.** the period of time, the **lunar year**, containing 12 lunar months and equal to 354.3671 days. **7.** the period of time taken by a specified planet to complete one revolution around the sun. **8.** (*pl.*) age, esp. old age: *a man of his years should be more careful.* **9.** (*pl.*) time: *in years to come.* **10.** a group of pupils or students, who are taught or study together. **11. the year dot.** *Inf.* as long ago as can be remembered. **12. year in, year out.** regularly or monotonously, over a long period. *~Related adj.:* **annual.** [OE *gear*]

▷ **Usage.** In writing spans of years, it is important to choose a style that avoids ambiguity. The practice adopted in this dictionary is, in four-figure dates, to specify the last two digits of the second date if it falls within the same century as the first: *1801–08; 1850–51; 1899–1901.* In writing three-figure B.C. dates, it is advisable to give both dates in full: *159–156* B.C., not *159–56* B.C. unless of course the span referred to consists of 103 years rather than three years. It is also advisable to specify B.C. or A.D. in years under 1000 unless the context makes this self-evident.

yearbook ('jɪəˌbʊk) *n.* an almanac or other reference book published annually and containing details of events of the previous year.

yearling ('jɪəlɪŋ) *n.* **1.** the young of any of various animals, including the antelope and buffalo, between one and two years of age. **2.** a thoroughbred racehorse counted as being one year old until the second January 1 following its birth. **3. a.** a bond that is intended to mature after one year. **b.** (*as modifier*): *yearling bonds. ~adj.* **4.** being a year old.

yearlong ('jɪə'lɒŋ) *adj.* throughout a whole year.

yearly ('jɪəlɪ) *adj.* **1.** occurring, done, appearing, etc., once a year or every year; annual. **2.** lasting or valid for a year; annual: *a yearly subscription. ~adv.* **3.** once a year; annually.

yearn (jɜːn) *vb.* (*intr.*) **1.** (usually foll. by *for* or *after* or an infinitive) to have an intense desire or longing (for). **2.** to feel tenderness or affection. [OE *giernan*] — '**yearner** *n.* — '**yearning** *n., adj.* — '**yearningly** *adv.*

year of grace *n.* any year of the Christian era, as from the presumed date of Christ's birth.

year-round *adj.* open, in use, operating, etc., throughout the year.

yeast (jiːst) *n.* **1.** any of various single-celled fungi which reproduce by budding and are able to ferment sugars: a rich source of vitamins of the B complex. **2.** a commercial preparation containing yeast cells and inert material such as meal, used in raising dough for bread or for fermenting beer, whisky, etc. **3.** a preparation containing yeast cells, used to treat diseases caused by vitamin B deficiency. **4.** froth or foam, esp. on beer. *~vb.* **5.** (*intr.*) to froth or foam. [OE *giest*] — '**yeastless** *adj.* — '**yeast͵like** *adj.*

yeasty ('jiːstɪ) *adj.* **yeastier, yeastiest.** **1.** of, resembling, or containing yeast. **2.** fermenting or causing fermentation. **3.** tasting of or like yeast. **4.** insubstantial or frivolous. **5.** restless, agitated, or unsettled. **6.** covered with or containing froth or foam. — '**yeastily** *adv.* — '**yeastiness** *n.*

Yeats (jeɪts) *n.* **1. Jack Butler.** 1871–1957, Irish painter. **2.** his brother **W(illiam) B(utler).** 1865–1939, Irish poet and dramatist. His collections of verse include *Responsibilities* (1914), *The Tower* (1928), and *The Winding Stair* (1929). Among his plays are *The Countess Cathleen* (1892; 1912) and *Cathleen ni Houlihan* (1902); he was a founder of the Irish National Theatre Company at the Abbey Theatre in Dublin. He was awarded the Nobel prize for literature 1923.

yegg (jɛg) *n. Sl., chiefly U.S.* a burglar or safe-breaker. [C20: ?from the surname of a burglar]

Yeisk, Yeysk, or **Eisk** (*Russian* jejsk) *n.* a port and resort in the SW Soviet Union, on the Sea of Azov. Pop.: 64 418 (1970).

Yekaterinburg or **Ekaterinburg** (*Russian* jɪkətɪrim'burk) *n.* the former name (until 1924) of **Sverdlovsk.**

Yekaterinodar or **Ekaterinodar** (*Russian* jɪkətɪrina'dar) *n.* the former name (until 1920) of **Krasnodar.**

Yekaterinoslav or **Ekaterinoslav** (*Russian* jɪkətɪrina'slaf) *n.* the former name (1787–96, 1802–1926) of **Dnepropetrovsk.**

Yelisavetgrad or **Elisavetgrad** (*Russian* jɪliza'vjɛtgrət) *n.* the former name (until 1924) of **Kirovograd.**

Yelisavetpol or **Elisavetpol** (*Russian* jɪliza'vjɛtpəlj) *n.* the former name (until 1920) of **Kirovabad.**

Yelizaveta Petrovna (*Russian* jɪliza'vjɛtəpɪ'trɔvnə) *n.* See **Elizabeth**[2] (sense 3).

yell (jɛl) *vb.* **1.** to shout, scream, cheer, or utter in a loud or piercing way. *~n.* **2.** a loud piercing inarticulate cry, as of pain, anger, or fear. **3.** *U.S. & Canad.* a rhythmic cry, used in cheering in unison. [OE *giellan*] — '**yeller** *n.*

yellow ('jɛləʊ) *n.* **1.** any of a group of colours such as that of a lemon or of gold, which vary in saturation but have the same hue. Yellow is the complementary colour of blue. Related adj.: **xanthous. 2.** a pigment or dye of or producing these colours. **3.** yellow cloth or clothing: *dressed in yellow.* **4.** the yolk of an egg. **5.** a yellow ball in snooker, etc. *~adj.* **6.** of the colour yellow. **7.** yellowish in colour or having parts or marks that are yellowish. **8.** having a yellowish skin; Mongoloid. **9.** *Inf.* cowardly or afraid. **10.** offensively sensational, as a cheap newspaper (esp. in **yellow press**). *~vb.* **11.** to make or become yellow. *~See also* **yellows.** [OE *geolu*] — '**yellowish** *adj.* — '**yellowly** *adv.* — '**yellowness** *n.* — '**yellowy** *adj.*

yellow belly *n. Austral.* any of several freshwater food fishes with yellow underparts.

yellow-belly *n., pl.* **-lies.** a slang word for **coward.** — '**yellow-͵bellied** *adj.*

yellow bile *n. Arch.* one of the four bodily humours, choler.

yellow card *n. Soccer.* a card of a yellow colour displayed by a referee to indicate that a player has been officially cautioned for some offence.

yellow fever *n.* an acute infectious disease of tropical and subtropical climates, characterized by fever, haemorrhages, vomiting, and jaundice: caused by a virus transmitted by the bite of a certain mosquito. Also called: **yellow jack.**

yellowhammer ('jɛləʊˌhæmə) *n.* a European bunting, having a yellowish head and body and brown-streaked wings and tail. [C16: from ?]

yellow jack *n.* **1.** *Pathol.* another name for **yellow fever.** **2.** another name for **quarantine flag. 3.** any of certain large yellowish food fishes of warm and tropical Atlantic waters.

yellow jersey *n.* (in the Tour de France) a yellow jersey awarded as a trophy to the cyclist with the fastest time in each stage of the race.

yellow journalism *n.* the type of journalism that relies on sensationalism to attract readers. [C19: ? shortened from *Yellow Kid journalism*, referring to the *Yellow Kid*, a cartoon (1895) in the *New York World*, a newspaper having a reputation for sensationalism]

Yellowknife ('jɛləʊˌnaɪf) *n.* a city in N Canada, capital of the Northwest Territories on Great Slave Lake. Pop.: 11 077 (1985).

yellow line *n. Brit.* a yellow line painted along the edge of a road indicating vehicle waiting restrictions.

yellow metal *n.* **1.** a type of brass having about 60 per cent copper and 40 per cent zinc. **2.** another name for **gold.**

yellow pages *pl. n.* a classified telephone directory or section of a directory that lists subscribers by the business or service provided.

yellow peril *n.* the power or alleged power of Asiatic peoples, esp. the Chinese, to threaten or destroy White or Western civilization.

Yellow River *n.* the second longest river in China, rising in SE Qinghai and flowing east, south, and east again to the Gulf of Bohai south of Tianjin; it has changed its course several times in recorded history. Length: about 4350 km (2700 miles). Chinese name: **Hwang Ho.**

yellows ('jɛləʊz) *n. (functioning as sing.)* **1.** any of various fungal or viral diseases of plants, characterized by yellowish discoloration and stunting. **2.** *Vet. science.* another name for **jaundice.**

Yellow Sea *n.* a shallow arm of the Pacific between Korea and NE China. Area: about 466 200 sq. km (180 000 sq. miles). Chinese name: **Hwang Hai.**

yellow spot *n. Anat.* another name for **macula lutea.**

Yellowstone ('jɛləʊ,stəʊn) *n.* a river rising in N Wyoming and flowing north through Yellowstone National Park, then east to the Missouri. Length: 1080 km (671 miles).

Yellowstone Falls *pl. n.* a waterfall in NW Wyoming, in Yellowstone National Park on the Yellowstone River.

Yellowstone National Park *n.* a national park in the NW central U.S., mostly in NW Wyoming: the oldest and largest national park in the U.S., containing unusual geological formations and geysers. Area: 8956 sq. km (3458 sq. miles).

yellow streak *n. Inf.* a cowardly or weak trait.

yellow underwing *n.* any of several species of noctuid moths, the hind wings of which are yellow with a black bar.

yellowwood ('jɛləʊ,wʊd) *n.* **1.** any of several leguminous trees of the southeastern U.S., having clusters of white flowers and yellow wood yielding a yellow dye. **2.** Also called: **West Indian satinwood.** a rutaceous tree of the West Indies, with smooth hard wood. **3.** any of several other trees with yellow wood, esp. a conifer of southern Africa the wood of which is used for furniture and building. **4.** the wood of any of these trees.

yelp (jɛlp) *vb. (intr.)* **1.** (esp. of a dog) to utter a sharp or high-pitched cry or bark, often indicating pain. ~*n.* **2.** a sharp or high-pitched cry or bark. [OE *gielpan* to boast] — '**yelper** *n.*

Yemen ('jɛmən) *n.* **1.** a republic in SW Arabia, on the Red Sea: declared a republic in 1962; consists of part of the Red Sea rift valley, with arid coastal lowlands, rising to fertile upland valleys and mountains, and the Great Sandy Desert in the east. Language: Arabic. Religion: Muslim. Currency: riyal. Capital: San'a. Pop.: 6 533 265 (1987 est.). Area: 195 000 sq. km (75 290 sq. miles). Official name: **Yemen Arab Republic.** Also called: **North Yemen. 2.** See **South Yemen.** — '**Yemeni** *adj., n.*

yen[1] (jɛn) *n., pl.* **yen.** the standard monetary unit of Japan. [C19: from Japanese *en*, from Chinese *yüan* dollar]

yen[2] (jɛn) *Inf.* ~*n.* **1.** a longing or desire. ~*vb.* **yenning, yenned. 2.** *(intr.)* to yearn. [?from Chinese *yán* a craving]

Yenan ('jɛn'æn) *n.* a variant transliteration of the Chinese name for **Yanan.**

Yenisei *or* **Yenisey** (jɛnɪ'seɪ; *Russian* jɪni'sjej) *n.* a river in the central Soviet Union, in central Siberia, formed by the confluence of two headstreams in the Tuva ASSR: flows west and north to the Arctic Ocean; the largest river in volume in the Soviet Union. Length: 4129 km (2566 miles).

Yentai *or* **Yen-t'ai** ('jɛn'taɪ) *n.* a variant transliteration of the Chinese name for **Yantai.**

yeoman ('jəʊmən) *n., pl.* -**men. 1.** *History.* **a.** a member of a class of small freeholders who cultivated their own land. **b.** an attendant or lesser official in a royal or noble household. **2.** (in Britain) another name for **yeoman of the guard. 3.** *(modifier)* characteristic of or relating to a yeoman. **4.** a petty officer or noncommissioned officer in the Royal Navy or Marines in charge of signals. [C15: ?from *yongman* young man]

yeomanly ('jəʊmənlɪ) *adj.* **1.** of, relating to, or like a yeoman. **2.** having the virtues attributed to yeomen, such as staunchness, loyalty, and courage. ~*adv.* **3.** in a yeomanly manner.

yeoman of the guard *n.* a member of the ceremonial bodyguard (**Yeomen of the Guard**) of the British monarch.

yeomanry ('jəʊmənrɪ) *n.* **1.** yeomen collectively. **2.** (in Britain) a volunteer cavalry force, organized in 1761 for home defence: merged into the Territorial Army in 1907.

yep (jɛp) *sentence substitute.* an informal word for **yes.**

yerba *or* **yerba maté** ('jɜːbə) *n.* another name for **maté.** [from Sp. *yerba maté* herb maté]

Yerevan (*Russian* jɪrɪ'van) *n.* an industrial city in the SW Soviet Union, capital of the Armenian SSR: founded in the 8th century B.C.; a main focus of trade routes since ancient times; university. Pop.: 1 168 000 (1987). Also called: **Erevan** or **Erivan.**

Yerwa-Maiduguri ('jɜːwə,maɪdʊ'gʊrɪ) *n.* another name for **Maiduguri.**

yes (jɛs) *sentence substitute.* **1.** used to express affirmation, consent, agreement, or approval or to answer when one is addressed. **2.** used to signal someone to speak or keep speaking, enter a room, or do something. ~*n.* **3.** an answer or vote of yes. **4.** *(often pl.)* a person who votes in the affirmative. [OE *gēse*, from *iā sīe* may it be]

yeshiva (jə'ʃiːvə; *Hebrew* jə'ʃiːva) *n., pl.* -**vahs** *or* -**voth** (*Hebrew* -vɔt). **1.** a traditional Jewish school devoted chiefly to the study of the Talmud. **2.** a school run by Orthodox Jews for children of elementary school age, providing both religious and secular instruction. [from Heb. *yĕshîbhāh* a seat, hence, an academy]

Yeşil Irmak (jɛ'ʃiː lɪə'maːk) *n.* a river in N Turkey, flowing northwest to the Black Sea. Length: 418 km (260 miles). Ancient name: **Iris.**

Yeşilköy (jɛ'ʃil,kœi) *n.* the Turkish name for **San Stefano.**

yes man *n.* a servile, submissive, or acquiescent subordinate, assistant, or associate.

yester ('jɛstə) *adj. Arch.* of or relating to yesterday: *yester sun.* [OE *geostror*]

yester- *prefix.* indicating a period of time before the present one: *yesteryear.* [OE *geostran*]

yesterday ('jɛstədɪ, -,deɪ) *n.* **1.** the day immediately preceding today. **2.** *(often pl.)* the recent past. ~*adv.* **3.** on or during the day before today. **4.** in the recent past.

yesteryear ('jɛstə,jɪə) *Formal or literary.* ~*n.* **1.** last year or the past in general. ~*adv.* **2.** during last year or the past in general.

yestreen (jɛ'striːn) *adv. Scot.* yesterday evening. [C14: from YEST(E)R- + E(V)EN[2]]

yet (jɛt) *sentence connector.* **1.** nevertheless; still; in spite of that: *I want to and yet I haven't the courage.* ~*adv.* **2.** *(usually used with a negative or interrogative)* so far; up until then or now: *they're not home yet; is it teatime yet?* **3.** *(often preceded by just; usually used with a negative)* now (as contrasted with later): *we can't stop yet.* **4.** *(often used with a comparative)* even; still: *yet more potatoes for sale.* **5.** eventually in spite of everything: *we'll convince him yet.* **6. as yet.** so far; up until then or now. [OE *gēta*]

yeti ('jɛtɪ) *n.* another term for **abominable snowman.** [C20: from Tibetan]

Yevtushenko (jɛvtuː'ʃɛŋkəʊ; *Russian* jɪftu'ʃɛnkə) *n.* **Yevgeny Aleksandrovich** (jɪv'gjenij alɪk'sandrəvitʃ). born 1933, Soviet poet. His often outspoken poetry includes *Babi Yar* (1962) and *Bratsk Station* (1966).

yew (juː) *n.* **1.** any coniferous tree of the Old World and North America having flattened needle-like leaves, fine-grained elastic wood, and cuplike red waxy cones resembling berries. **2.** the wood of any of these trees, used to make bows for archery. **3.** *Archery.* a bow made of yew. [OE *īw*]

Yeysk (*Russian* jejsk) *n.* a variant spelling of **Yeisk.**

Yezd (jɛzd) *n.* a variant of **Yazd.**

Y-fronts *pl. n. Trademark.* boys' or men's underpants having a front opening within an inverted Y shape.

Ygerne (iː'gɛən) *n.* a variant of **Igraine.**

Yggdrasil *or* **Ygdrasil** ('ɪgdrəsɪl) *n. Norse myth.* the ash tree that was thought to bind together earth, heaven, and hell with its roots and branches. [ON prob. meaning: Uggr's horse, from *Uggr* a name of Odin, from *yggr, uggr* frightful + *drasill* horse, from ?]

YHA (in Britain) *abbrev. for* Youth Hostels Association.

YHVH *or* **YHWH** *Bible.* the letters of the **Tetragrammaton.**

Yichang (ˌjiːˈtʃæŋ), **Ichang,** or **I-ch'ang** n. a port in S central China, in Hubei province on the Yangtze River 1600 km (1000 miles) from the East China Sea: head of navigation of the Yangtze.

yid (jɪd) n. Sl. a derogatory word for a **Jew**. [C20: prob. from *Yiddish*, from MHG *Jude* JEW]

Yiddish (ˈjɪdɪʃ) n. **1.** a language spoken as a vernacular by Jews in Europe and elsewhere by Jewish emigrants, usually written in the Hebrew alphabet. It is a dialect of High German with an admixture of words of Hebrew, Romance, and Slavonic origin. ~adj. **2.** in or relating to this language. [C19: from G *jüdisch*, from *Jude* JEW]

Yiddisher (ˈjɪdɪʃə) adj. **1.** in or relating to Yiddish. **2.** Jewish. ~n. **3.** a speaker of Yiddish; Jew.

yield (jiːld) vb. **1.** to give forth or supply (a product, result, etc.), esp. by cultivation, labour, etc.; produce or bear. **2.** (tr.) to furnish as a return: *the shares yielded three per cent.* **3.** (tr.; often foll. by *up*) to surrender or relinquish, esp. as a result of force, persuasion, etc. **4.** (intr.; sometimes foll. by *to*) to give way, submit, or surrender, as through force or persuasion: *she yielded to his superior knowledge.* **5.** (intr.; often foll. by *to*) to agree; comply; assent: *he eventually yielded to their request for money.* **6.** (tr.) to grant or allow; concede: *to yield right of way.* ~n. **7.** the result, product, or amount yielded. **8.** the profit or return, as from an investment or tax. **9.** the annual income provided by an investment. **10.** the energy released by the explosion of a nuclear weapon expressed in terms of the amount of TNT necessary to produce the same energy. **11.** Chem. the quantity of a specified product obtained in a reaction or series of reactions. [OE *gieldan*] —**ˈyieldable** adj. —**ˈyielder** n.

yielding (ˈjiːldɪŋ) adj. **1.** compliant, submissive, or flexible. **2.** pliable or soft: *a yielding material.*

yield point n. the stress at which an elastic material under increasing stress ceases to behave elastically; the elongation becomes greater than the increase in stress.

Yin and Yang (jɪn) n. two complementary principles of Chinese philosophy: Yin is negative, dark, and feminine, Yang is positive, bright, and masculine. [from Chinese *yin* dark + *yang* bright]

Yinchuan, Yin-ch'uan, or **Yinchwan** (ˈjɪnˈtʃwɑːn) n. a city in N central China, capital of the Ningxia Hui AR, on the Yellow River. Pop.: 383 300 (1984 est.).

Yingkou or **Yingkow** (ˈjɪŋˈkaʊ) n. a port in NE China, in SW Liaoning province: a major shipping centre for Manchuria. Pop.: 410 400 (1980 est.).

yippee (jɪˈpiː) interj. an exclamation of joy, pleasure, anticipation, etc.

yips (jɪps) pl. n. **the.** Inf. (in sport) nervous twitching or tension that destroys concentration. [C20: from ?]

-yl suffix forming nouns. (in chemistry) indicating a group or radical: *methyl*. [from Gk *hulē* wood]

ylang-ylang (ˈiːlæŋˈiːlæŋ) n. **1.** an aromatic Asian tree with fragrant greenish-yellow flowers yielding a volatile oil. **2.** the oil obtained from this tree, used in perfumery. [C19: from Tagalog *ilang-ilang*]

ylem (ˈaɪləm) n. the original matter from which the basic elements are said to have been formed following the explosion postulated in the big-bang theory of cosmology. [ME, from OF *ilem*, from L *hȳlē* matter, from Gk *hulē* wood]

YMCA abbrev. for Young Men's Christian Association.

Ymir (ˈiːmɪə) or **Ymer** (ˈiːmə) n. Norse myth. the first being and forefather of the giants. He was slain by Odin and his brothers, who made the earth from his flesh, the water from his blood, and the sky from his skull.

-yne suffix forming nouns. denoting an organic chemical containing a triple bond: *alkyne*. [alteration of -INE[2]]

yob (jɒb) or **yobbo** (ˈjɒbəʊ) n., pl. **yobs** or **yobbos.** Brit. sl. an aggressive and surly youth, esp. a teenager. [C19: ? back sl. for BOY] —**ˈyobbery** n. —**ˈyobbish** adj.

yodel (ˈjəʊdəl) n. **1.** an effect produced in singing by an abrupt change of register from the chest voice to falsetto, esp. in folk songs of the Swiss Alps. ~vb. **-delling, -delled** or U.S. **-deling, -deled. 1.** to sing (a song) in which a yodel is used. [C19: from G *jodeln*, imit.] —**ˈyodeller** n.

yoga (ˈjəʊgə) n. (often cap.) **1.** a Hindu system of philosophy aiming at the mystical union of the self with the Supreme Being in a state of complete awareness and tranquillity through certain physical and mental exercises. **2.** any method by which such awareness and tranquillity are attained, esp. a course of related exercises and postures.

[C19: from Sansk.: a yoking, from *yunakti* he yokes] —**yogic** (ˈjəʊgɪk) adj.

yogh (jɒɡ) n. **1.** a character (ȝ) used in Old and Middle English to represent a palatal fricative very close to the semivowel sound of Modern English *y*. **2.** this same character as used in Middle English for both the voiced and voiceless palatal fricatives; when final or in a closed syllable in medial position the sound approached that of German *ch* in *ich*, as in *knyȝt* (knight). [C14: ?from *yok* yoke, from the letter's shape]

yoghurt, yogurt, or **yoghourt** (ˈjəʊgət, jɒg-) n. a thick custard-like food prepared from milk curdled by bacteria, often sweetened and flavoured with fruit. [C19: from Turkish *yoğurt*]

yogi (ˈjəʊgɪ) n., pl. **-gis** or **-gin** (-gɪn). a person who is a master of yoga.

Yogyakarta (ˌjəʊgjɑːˈkɑːtɑː, -jɒg-), **Jogjakarta, Jokjakarta,** or **Djokjakarta** n. a city in S Indonesia, in central Java: seat of government of Indonesia (1946–49); university (1949). Pop.: 398 727 (1980).

yo-heave-ho (ˌjəʊhiːvˈhəʊ) interj. a cry formerly used by sailors while pulling or lifting together in rhythm.

yohimbine (jəʊˈhɪmbiːn) n. an alkaloid found in the bark of a West African tree and used in medicine. [C19: from Bantu *yohimbé* a tropical African tree + -INE[1]]

yo-ho-ho interj. **1.** an exclamation to call attention. **2.** another word for **yo-heave-ho.**

yoicks (haɪk; spelling pron. jɔɪks) interj. a cry used by fox-hunters to urge on the hounds.

yoke (jəʊk) n., pl. **yokes** or **yoke. 1.** a wooden frame, usually consisting of a bar with an oxbow at either end, for attaching to the necks of a pair of draught animals, esp. oxen, so that they can be worked as a team. **2.** something resembling a yoke in form or function, such as a frame fitting over a person's shoulders for carrying buckets. **3.** a fitted part of a garment, esp. around the neck, shoulders, and chest or around the hips, to which a gathered, pleated, flared, or unfitted part is attached. **4.** an oppressive force or burden: *under the yoke of a tyrant.* **5.** a pair of oxen or other draught animals joined by a yoke. **6.** a part that secures two or more components so that they move together. **7.** (in the ancient world) a symbolic yoke, consisting of two upright spears with a third lashed across them, under which conquered enemies were compelled to march, esp. in Rome. **8.** a mark, token, or symbol of slavery, subjection, or suffering. **9.** Now rare. a link, tie, or bond: *the yoke of love.* ~vb. **10.** (tr.) to secure or harness (a draught animal) to (a plough, vehicle, etc.) by means of a yoke. **11.** to join or be joined by means of a yoke; couple, unite, or link. [OE *geoc*]

yokel (ˈjəʊkəl) n. Disparaging. (used chiefly by townspeople) a person who lives in the country, esp. one who is simple and old-fashioned. [C19: ?from dialect *yokel* green woodpecker]

Yokohama (ˌjəʊkəʊˈhɑːmə) n. a port in central Japan, on SE Honshu on Tokyo Bay: a major port and the country's third largest city situated in the largest and most populous industrial region of Japan. Pop.: 2 993 000 (1985).

Yola (ˈjəʊlə) n. a market town in E Nigeria, capital of Gongola state. Pop.: 8573 (1963).

yolk (jəʊk) n. **1.** the substance in an animal ovum that nourishes the developing embryo. **2.** a greasy substance in the fleece of sheep. [OE *geoloca*, from *geolu* yellow] —**ˈyolky** adj.

yolk sac n. Zool. the membranous sac that is attached to the surface of the embryos of birds, reptiles, and some fishes, and contains yolk.

Yom Kippur (jɒm ˈkɪpə; Hebrew jɔm kiˈpur) n. an annual Jewish holiday celebrated as a day of fasting, on which prayers of penitence are recited in the synagogue. Also called: **Day of Atonement.** [from Heb., from *yōm* day + *kippūr* atonement]

yomp (jɒmp) vb. (intr.) to walk or trek laboriously, esp. over difficult terrain. [C20: mil. sl., from ?]

yon (jɒn) determiner. **1.** Chiefly Scot. & N English. **a.** an archaic or dialect word for **that:** *yon man.* **b.** (as pronoun): *yon's a fool.* **2.** a variant of **yonder.** [OE *geon*]

yond (jɒnd) Obs. or dialect. ~adj. **1.** the farther, more distant. ~determiner. **2.** a variant of **yon.**

yonder (ˈjɒndə) adv. **1.** at, in, or to that relatively distant place; over there. ~determiner. **2.** being at a distance, either within view or as if within view: *yonder valleys.* [C13: from OE *geond* yond]

yoni ('jəʊnɪ) *n. Hinduism.* **1.** the female genitalia, regarded as a divine symbol of sexual pleasure and matrix of generation. **2.** an image of these as an object of worship. [C18: from Sansk., lit.: vulva]

Yonkers ('jɒŋkəz) *n.* a city in SE New York State, near New York City on the Hudson River. Pop.: 186 080 (1986 est.).

yonks (jɒŋks) *pl. n. Inf.* a very long time; ages: *I haven't seen him for yonks.* [C20: from ?]

Yonne (*French* jɔn) *n.* **1.** a department of N central France, in Burgundy region. Capital: Auxerre. Pop.: 311 019 (1982). Area: 7461 sq. km (2910 sq. miles). **2.** a river in N France, flowing generally northwest to the Seine at Montereau. Length: 290 km (180 miles).

yoo-hoo ('juː,huː) *interj.* a call to attract a person's attention.

YOP (jɒp) *n.* (formerly, in Britain) **a.** *acronym for* Youth Opportunities Programme. **b.** (*as modifier*): *a YOP scheme.*

yore (jɔː) *n.* **1.** time long past (now only in **of yore**). ~*adv.* **2.** *Obs.* in the past; long ago. [OE *geāra,* genitive pl. of *gēar* year]

york (jɔːk) *vb.* (*tr.*) *Cricket.* to bowl (a batsman) by pitching the ball under or just beyond the bat. [C19: back formation from YORKER]

York[1] (jɔːk) *n.* **1.** a walled city in NE England, in North Yorkshire, on the River Ouse: the military capital of Roman Britain; capital of the N archiepiscopal province of Britain since 625, with a cathedral (the Minster) begun in 1154; noted for its cycle of medieval mystery plays; university (1963). Pop.: 99 787 (1981). Latin name: **Eboracum. 2. Cape.** a cape in NE Australia, in Queensland at the N tip of Cape York Peninsula, extending into Torres Strait: the northernmost point of Australia.

York[2] (jɔːk) *n.* **1.** the English royal house, a branch of the Plantagenet line, that reigned from 1461 to 1485. **2. Alvin C(ullum).** 1887–1964, U.S. soldier and hero of World War I. **3. Prince Andrew, Duke of.** born 1960, second son of Elizabeth II of Great Britain and Northern Ireland. He married (1986) Miss Sarah Ferguson; their daughter, Princess Beatrice of York, was born in 1988.

Yorke Peninsula (jɔːk) *n.* a peninsula in South Australia, between Spencer Gulf and St Vincent Gulf: mainly agricultural with several coastal resorts.

yorker ('jɔːkə) *n. Cricket.* a ball bowled so as to pitch just under or just beyond the bat. [C19: prob. after the *Yorkshire* County Cricket Club]

yorkie ('jɔːkɪ) *n.* short for **Yorkshire terrier.**

Yorkist ('jɔːkɪst) *English history.* ~*n.* **1.** a member of or adherent of the royal House of York, esp. during the Wars of the Roses. ~*adj.* **2.** of, belonging to, or relating to the supporters or members of the House of York.

Yorks. (jɔːks) *abbrev. for* Yorkshire.

Yorkshire (jɔːk,ʃɪə, -ʃə) *n.* a former county of N England: it was the largest English county, divided administratively into East, West, and North Ridings. In 1974 it was much reduced in size and divided into the new counties of North, West, and South Yorkshire.

Yorkshire Dales *pl. n.* the valleys of the rivers flowing from the Pennines in W Yorkshire: chiefly Airedale, Ribbledale, Teesdale, Swaledale, Nidderdale, Wharfedale, and Wensleydale; tourist area. Also called: **the Dales.**

Yorkshire pudding ('jɔːkʃɪŋ) *n. Chiefly Brit.* a light puffy baked pudding made from a batter of flour, eggs, and milk, traditionally served with roast beef.

Yorkshire terrier *n.* a very small breed of terrier with a long straight glossy coat of steel-blue and tan. Also called: **yorkie.**

Yorktown ('jɔːk,taʊn) *n.* a village in SE Virginia: scene of the surrender (1781) of the British under Cornwallis to the Americans under Washington at the end of the War of American Independence.

Yoruba ('jɒrʊbə) *n.* **1.** (*pl.* **-bas** *or* **-ba**) a member of a Negroid people of W Africa, living chiefly in the coastal regions of SW Nigeria. **2.** the language of this people. — **'Yoruban** *adj.*

Yosemite Falls (jəʊ'sɛmɪtɪ) *pl. n.* a series of waterfalls in central California, in the Yosemite National Park, with a total drop of 770 m (2525 ft.): includes the **Upper Yosemite Falls,** 436 m (1430 ft.) high, and the **Lower Yosemite Falls,** 98 m (320 ft.) high.

Yosemite National Park *n.* a national park in central California, in the Sierra Nevada Mountains: contains the

Yosemite Valley, at an altitude of about 1200 m (4000 ft.), with sheer walls rising about another 1200 m (4000 ft.). Area: 3061 sq. km (1182 sq. miles).

Yoshihito (jɒʃɪ'hiːtəʊ) *n.* See **Taisho.**

Yoshkar-Ola (*Russian* jaʃ'kara'la) *n.* a city in the W Soviet Union, capital of the Mari ASSR. Pop.: 243 000 (1987).

you (juː; *unstressed* jʊ) *pron.* (*subjective or objective*) **1.** refers to the person addressed or to more than one person including the person or persons addressed: *you know better; the culprit is among you.* **2.** refers to an unspecified person or people in general: *you can't tell the boys from the girls.* ~*n.* **3.** *Inf.* the personality of the person being addressed: *that hat isn't really you.* **4. you know what** *or* **who.** a thing or person that the speaker does not want to specify. [OE *ēow,* dative & accusative of *gē* ye]
▷ **Usage.** See at **me.**

you'd (juːd; *unstressed* jʊd) *contraction of* you had *or* you would.

you'll (juːl; *unstressed* jʊl) *contraction of* you will *or* you shall.

young (jʌŋ) *adj.* **younger** ('jʌŋgə), **youngest** ('jʌŋgɪst). **1. a.** having lived, existed, or been made or known for a relatively short time: *a young man; a young movement; a young country.* **b.** (*as collective n.;* preceded by *the*): *the young.* **2.** youthful or having qualities associated with youth; vigorous or lively. **3.** of or relating to youth: *in my young days.* **4.** having been established or introduced for a relatively short time: *a young member.* **5.** in an early stage of progress or development; not far advanced: *the day was young.* **6.** (*often cap.*) of or relating to a rejuvenated group or movement or one claiming to represent the younger members of the population: *Young Socialists.* ~*n.* **7.** (*functioning as pl.*) offspring, esp. young animals: *a rabbit with her young.* **8. with young.** (of animals) pregnant. [OE *geong*] — **'youngish** *adj.*

Young (jʌŋ) *n.* **1. Brigham** ('brɪgəm). 1801–77, U.S. Mormon leader, who led the Mormon migration to Utah and founded Salt Lake City (1847). **2. Edward.** 1683–1765, English poet and dramatist, noted for his *Night Thoughts on Life, Death, and Immortality* (1742–45). **3. Lester.** 1909–59, U.S. saxophonist and clarinetist. He was a leading early exponent of the tenor saxophone in jazz. **4. Neil.** born 1945, Canadian rock guitarist, singer, and songwriter; noted for his eclecticism, high-pitched plaintive voice, and powerful guitar sound. His albums include *Rust Never Sleeps* (1979). **5. Thomas.** 1773–1829, English physicist, physician, and Egyptologist. He helped to establish the wave theory of light by his experiments on optical interference and assisted in the decipherment of the Rosetta Stone.

young blood *n.* young, fresh, or vigorous new people, ideas, attitudes, etc.

Young Fogey *n.* a young person who adopts the conservative values of an older generation.

young lady *n.* a girlfriend; sweetheart.

youngling ('jʌŋlɪŋ) *n. Literary.* **a.** a young person, animal, or plant. **b.** (*as modifier*): *a youngling brood.* [OE *geongling*]

young man *n.* a boyfriend; sweetheart.

Young Pretender *n.* See (Charles Edward) **Stuart.**

Young's modulus (jʌŋz) *n.* a modulus of elasticity, applicable to the stretching of a wire, etc., equal to the ratio of the applied load per unit area of cross section to the increase in length per unit length. [after Thomas YOUNG]

youngster ('jʌŋstə) *n.* **1.** a young person; child or youth. **2.** a young animal, esp. a horse.

Youngstown ('jʌŋz,taʊn) *n.* a city in NE Ohio: a major centre of steel production: university (1908). Pop.: 104 690 (1986 est.).

Young Turk *n.* **1.** a progressive, revolutionary, or rebellious member of an organization, political party, etc. **2.** a member of an abortive reform movement in the Ottoman Empire.

younker ('jʌŋkə) *n.* **1.** *Arch. or literary.* a young man; lad. **2.** *Obs.* a young gentleman or knight. [C16: from Du. *jonker,* from MDu. *jonc* young]

your (jɔː, jʊə; *unstressed* jə) *determiner.* **1.** of, belonging to, or associated with you: *your nose; your house.* **2.** belonging to or associated with an unspecified person or people in general: *the path is on your left heading north.* **3.** *Inf.* used to indicate all things or people of a certain type: *your part-time worker is a problem.* [OE *eower,* genitive of *gē* ye]

you're (jɔː; *unstressed* jə) *contraction of* you are.

yours (jɔːz, juəz) *pron.* **1.** something or someone belonging to or associated with you. **2.** your family: *greetings to you and yours.* **3.** used in conventional closing phrases at the end of a letter: *yours sincerely; yours faithfully.* **4. of yours.** belonging to or associated with you.

yourself (jɔːˈsɛlf, juə-) *pron.*, *pl.* **-selves. 1. a.** the reflexive form of *you.* **b.** (intensifier): *you yourself control your destiny.* **2.** (*preceded by a copula*) your usual self: *you're not yourself.*
▷ **Usage.** See at **myself.**

yours truly *pron.* an informal term for *I* or *me.* [from the closing phrase of letters]

youth (juːθ) *n.*, *pl.* **youths** (juːðz). **1.** the quality or condition of being young, immature, or inexperienced: *his youth told against him in the contest.* **2.** the period between childhood and maturity. **3.** the freshness, vigour, or vitality characteristic of young people. **4.** any period of early development. **5.** a young person, esp. a young man or boy. **6.** young people collectively: *youth everywhere is rising in revolt.* [OE *geogoth*]

Youth (juːθ) *n.* **Isle of.** an island in the NW Caribbean, south of Cuba: administratively part of Cuba from 1925. Chief town: Nueva Gerona. Pop.: 68 700 (1987 est.). Area: 3061 sq. km (1182 sq. miles). Former name: **Isle of Pines.** Spanish name: **Isla de la Juventud** ('izla ðe la xuβen'tuð).

youth club *n.* a centre providing leisure activities for young people.

youthful ('juːθfʊl) *adj.* **1.** of, relating to, possessing, or characteristic of youth. **2.** fresh, vigorous, or active: *he's surprisingly youthful for his age.* **3.** in an early stage of development: *a youthful culture.* **4.** Also: **young.** (of a river, valley, or land surface) in the early stage of the cycle of erosion, characterized by steep slopes, lack of flood plains, and V-shaped valleys. —**'youthfully** *adv.* —**'youthfulness** *n.*

youth hostel *n.* one of an organization of inexpensive lodging places for young people travelling cheaply. Often shortened to **hostel.**

you've (juːv; *unstressed* jʊv) *contraction of* you have.

yowl (jaʊl) *vb.* **1.** to express with or produce a loud mournful wail or cry; howl. ~*n.* **2.** a wail or howl. [C13: from ON *gaula*] —**'yowler** *n.*

yo-yo ('jəʊjəʊ) *n.*, *pl.* **-yos. 1.** a toy consisting of a spool attached to a string, the end of which is held while it is repeatedly spun out and reeled in. ~*vb.* **yo-yoing, yo-yoed.** (*intr.*) **2.** to change repeatedly from one position to another; fluctuate. [C20: orig. a trademark for this type of toy]

Ypres (*French* iprə) *n.* a town in W Belgium, in W Flanders province near the border with France: scene of many sieges and battles, esp. in World War I, when it was completely destroyed. Pop.: 35 000 (1985 est.). Flemish name: **Ieper.**

Ypsilanti (ˌɪpsɪˈlæntɪ), **Hypsilantis,** or **Hypsilantes** *n.* **1. Alexander** (ˌalekˈsander). 1792–1828, Greek patriot, who led an unsuccessful revolt against the Turks (1821). **2.** his brother, **Demetrios** (ðimitriˈɔs). 1793–1832, Greek revolutionary leader; commander in chief of Greek forces (1828–30) during the war of independence.

yr *abbrev. for:* **1.** (*pl.* **yrs**) year. **2.** younger. **3.** your.

yrs *abbrev. for:* **1.** years. **2.** yours.

Yser (*French* izɛr) *n.* a river in NW central Europe, rising in N France and flowing through SW Belgium to the North Sea: scene of battles in World War I. Length: 77 km (48 miles).

Yseult (ɪˈsuːlt) *n.* a variant spelling of **Iseult.**

Yssel ('aɪsəl) *n.* a variant spelling of **IJssel.**

YST (in Canada) *abbrev. for* Yukon Standard Time.

YT *abbrev. for* Yukon Territory.

YTS (in Britain) *abbrev. for* Youth Training Scheme.

ytterbia (ɪˈtɜːbɪə) *n.* another name for **ytterbium oxide.** [C19: NL; see YTTERBIUM]

ytterbium (ɪˈtɜːbɪəm) *n.* a soft malleable silvery element of the lanthanide series of metals that is used to improve the mechanical properties of steel. Symbol: Yb; atomic no.: 70; atomic wt.: 173.04. [C19: NL, after *Ytterby*, Swedish quarry where discovered]

ytterbium oxide *n.* a weakly basic hygroscopic substance used in certain alloys and ceramics.

yttria ('ɪtrɪə) *n.* another name for **yttrium oxide.** [C19: NL; see YTTERBIUM]

yttrium ('ɪtrɪəm) *n.* a silvery metallic element used in various alloys, in lasers, and as a catalyst. Symbol: Y; atomic no.: 39; atomic wt.: 88.90. [C19: NL; see YTTERBIUM]

yttrium metal *n. Chem.* any one of a group of elements including yttrium and the related lanthanides.

yttrium oxide *n.* a colourless or white insoluble solid used in incandescent mantles.

yuan ('juːˈæn) *n.*, *pl.* **-an.** the standard monetary unit of the People's Republic of China. [from Chinese *yüan* round object; see YEN[1]]

Yüan[1] ('juːˈæn) *n.* the imperial dynasty of China from 1279 to 1368.

Yüan[2] ('juːˈæn) or **Yüen** ('juːˈɛn) *n.* a river in SE central China, rising in central Guizhou province and flowing northeast to Lake Tungting. Length: about 800 km (500 miles).

Yucatán (ˌjuːkəˈtɑːn; *Spanish* juka'tan) *n.* **1.** a state of SE Mexico, occupying the N part of the Yucatán peninsula. Capital: Mérida. Pop.: 1 182 180 (1983 est.). Area: 39 340 sq. km (15 186 sq. miles). **2.** a peninsula of Central America between the Gulf of Mexico and the Caribbean, including the Mexican states of Campeche, Yucatán, and Quintana Roo, and part of Belize: a centre of Mayan civilization from about 100 B.C. to the 18th century. Area: about 181 300 sq. km (70 000 sq. miles).

Yucatán Channel *n.* a channel between W Cuba and the Yucatán peninsula.

yucca ('jʌkə) *n.* any of a genus of liliaceous plants of tropical and subtropical America, having stiff lancelike leaves and spikes of white flowers. [C16: from American Sp. *yuca*, ult. from Amerind]

yuck or **yuk** (jʌk) *interj. Sl.* an exclamation indicating contempt, dislike, or disgust.

yucky or **yukky** ('jʌkɪ) *adj.* **yuckier, yuckiest** or **yukkier, yukkiest.** *Sl.* disgusting; nasty.

Yugoslav or **Jugoslav** ('juːgəʊˌslɑːv) *n.* **1.** a native or inhabitant of Yugoslavia, a federal republic in SE Europe, on the Adriatic. **2.** (not in technical use) another name for **Serbo-Croatian** (the language). ~*adj.* **3.** of, relating to, or characteristic of Yugoslavia or its people.

Yugoslavia or **Jugoslavia** (ˌjuːgəʊˈslɑːvɪə) *n.* a federal republic in SE Europe, on the Adriatic: established in 1918 from the independent states of Serbia and Montenegro, and regions that until World War I had belonged to Austria-Hungary (Croatia, Slovenia, and Bosnia and Herzegovina); the name was changed from Kingdom of Serbs, Croats, and Slovenes to Yugoslavia in 1929; German invasion of 1941–44 was resisted chiefly by a Communist group led by Tito, who declared a people's republic in 1945; a socialist federal republic was declared in 1963. It is mainly mountainous and rugged, rising over 2700 m (9000 ft.) in the Julian Alps, with the fertile Danube-Sava Basin in the northeast. Languages: Serbo-Croatian, Slovene, and Macedonian. Currency: dinar. Capital: Belgrade. Pop.: 23 433 000 (1987). Area: 255 804 sq. km (98 766 sq. miles). —, **Yugo'slavian** or **Jugo'slavian** *adj.*, *n.*

Yukawa (juːˈkɑːwə) *n.* **Hideki** ('hiːdɛkɪ). 1907–81, Japanese nuclear physicist, who predicted (1935) the existence of mesons: Nobel prize for physics 1949.

Yukon ('juːkɒn) *n.* **the.** a territory of NW Canada, on the Beaufort Sea, between the Northwest Territories and Alaska: arctic and mountainous, reaching 6050 m (19 850 ft.) at Mount Logan, Canada's highest peak; mineral resources. Capital: Whitehorse. Pop.: 26 166 (1986 est.). Area: 536 327 sq. km (207 076 sq. miles). Abbrev.: **YT.** —'**Yukoner** *n.*

Yukon River *n.* a river in NW North America, rising in NW Canada on the border between the Yukon Territory and British Columbia: flows northwest into Alaska, U.S., and then southwest to the Bering Sea; navigable for about 2850 km (1775 miles) to Whitehorse. Length: 3185 km (1979 miles).

yulan ('juːlæn) *n.* a Chinese magnolia that is often cultivated for its showy white flowers. [C19: from Chinese, from *yu* a gem + *lan* plant]

yule (juːl) *n.* (*sometimes cap.*) *Literary, arch.,* or *dialect.* **a.** Christmas or the Christmas season. **b.** (*in combination*): *yuletide.* [OE *gēola,* orig. a pagan feast lasting 12 days]

yule log *n.* a large log of wood traditionally used as the foundation of a fire at Christmas.

yummy ('jʌmɪ) *Sl.* ~*interj.* **1.** Also: **yum-yum.** an exclamation indicating pleasure or delight, as in anticipation of delicious food. ~*adj.* **-mier, -miest. 2.** delicious, delightful, or attractive. [C20: from *yum-yum*, imit.]

Yünnan (juː'næn) *n.* a province of SW China: consists mainly of a plateau broken in the southeast by the Red and Black Rivers, with mountains in the west, rising over 5500 m (18 000 ft.); large deposits of tin, lead, zinc, and coal. Capital: Kunming. Pop.: 33 620 000 (1985). Area: 436 200 sq. km (168 400 sq. miles).

Yuppie ('jʌpɪ) (*sometimes not cap.*) ~*n.* **1.** *acronym for* young urban (*or* upwardly mobile) professional. ~*adj.* **2.** designed for or appealing to Yuppies.

Yurev (*Russian* 'jurjɪf) *n.* the former name (11th century until 1918) of **Tartu**.

yurt (juət) *n.* a circular tent consisting of a framework of poles covered with felt or skins, used by Mongolian and Turkic nomads of E and central Asia. [from Russian *yurta*, of Turkic origin]

Yuzovka (*Russian* 'juzəfkə) *n.* a former name (1872 until after the Revolution) of **Donetsk**.

Yvelines (*French* ivlin) *n.* a department of N France, in Île de France region. Capital: Versailles. Pop.: 1 196 111 (1982). Area: 2271 sq. km (886 sq. miles).

YWCA *abbrev. for* Young Women's Christian Association.

Z

z or **Z** (zɛd; *U.S.* ziː) *n., pl.* **z's, Z's,** or **Zs. 1.** the 26th and last letter of the English alphabet. **2.** a speech sound represented by this letter. **3. a.** something shaped like a Z. **b.** (*in combination*): *a Z-bend in a road.*

z *Maths. symbol for:* **1.** the *z*-axis or a coordinate measured along the *z*-axis in a Cartesian or cylindrical coordinate system. **2.** an algebraic variable.

Z *symbol for:* **1.** any unknown, variable, or unspecified factor, number, person, or thing. **2.** *Chem.* atomic number. **3.** *Physics.* impedance. **4.** zone.

z. *abbrev. for:* **1.** zero. **2.** zone.

Zaandam (*Dutch* zaːnˈdɑm) *n.* a former town in the W Netherlands, in North Holland: an important shipbuilding centre in the 17th century. It became part of Zaanstad in 1974.

Zaanstad (*Dutch* zaːnˈʃtat) *n.* a port in the W Netherlands, in North Holland: formed (1974) from Zaandam, Koog a/d Zaan, Zaandijk, Wormerveer, Krommenie, Westzaan, and Assendelft; food and machinery industries. Pop.: 128 248 (1986 est.).

zabaglione (ˌzæbəˈljəʊnɪ) *n.* a light foamy dessert made of egg yolks, sugar, and marsala, whipped together and served warm in a glass. [It.]

Zabrze (*Polish* ˈzabʒɛ) *n.* a city in SW Poland: a Prussian and German town from 1742 until 1945, when it passed to Poland; industrial centre in a coal-mining region. Pop.: 198 000 (1985). German name: **Hindenburg.**

Zacatecas (*Spanish* θakaˈtekas) *n.* **1.** a state of N central Mexico, on the central plateau: rich mineral resources. Capital: Zacatecas. Pop.: 1 209 951 (1983 est.). Area: 75 040 sq. km (28 973 sq. miles). **2.** a city in N central Mexico, capital of Zacatecas state: silver mines. Pop.: 120 000 (1980 est.).

Zacharias (ˌzækəˈraɪəs), **Zachariah** (ˌzækəˈraɪə), or **Zachary** (ˈzækərɪ) *n. New Testament.* John the Baptist's father, who underwent a temporary period of dumbness for his lack of faith (Luke 1).

Zacynthus (zəˈsɪnθəs, -ˈkɪn-) *n.* the Latin name for **Zante.**

zaffer or **zaffre** (ˈzæfə) *n.* impure cobalt oxide, used to impart a blue colour to enamels. [C17: from It. *zaffera*]

Zagazig (ˈzægəˌzɪg) or **Zaqaziq** (ˈzægəˌzɪg) *n.* a city in NE Egypt, in the Nile Delta: major cotton market. Pop.: 266 800 (1985).

Zagreb (ˈzɑːgrɛb) *n.* a city in NW Yugoslavia, capital of the republic of Croatia; university (1874); industrial centre. Pop.: 1 174 512 (1981). German name: **Agram.**

Zagreus (ˈzæɡrɪəs) *n. Greek myth.* a young god whose cult came from Crete to Greece, where he was identified with Dionysus. The son of Zeus by either Demeter or Persephone, he was killed by the Titans at the behest of Hera.

Zagros Mountains (ˈzæɡrɒs) *pl. n.* a mountain range in S Iran: has Iran's main oilfields in its W central foothills. Highest peak: Zard Kuh, 4548 m (14 920 ft.).

zaibatsu (ˈzaɪbætˈsuː) *n.* (*functioning as sing. or pl.*) the group or combine comprising a few wealthy families that controls industry, business, and finance in Japan. [from Japanese, from *zai* wealth + *batsu* family, person of influence]

Zaïre (zɑːˈɪə) *n.* **1.** a republic in S central Africa, with a narrow strip of land along the Congo estuary leading to the Atlantic in the west: Congo Free State established in 1885, with Leopold II of Belgium as absolute monarch; became the Belgian Congo colony in 1908; gained independence in 1960, followed by civil war and the secession of Katanga (until 1963). It consists chiefly of the Congo basin, with large areas of dense tropical forest and marshes, and the Mitumba highlands reaching over 5000 m (16 000 ft.) in the east. Official language: French. Religion: Christian and animist. Currency: zaïre. Capital: Kinshasa. Pop.: 31 780 000 (1987 est.). Area: 2 344 116 sq. km (905 063 sq. miles). Former names: **Congo Free State** (1885–1908), **Belgian Congo** (1908–60), (**Democratic Republic of the**) **Congo** (1960–71), **Congo-Kinshasa. 2.** the Zaïrese name (since 1971) for the (River) **Congo.** —**Zaïr'ese** *adj., n.*

Zákinthos (ˈzakɪnˌθɒs) *n.* transliteration of the Modern Greek name for **Zante.**

zakuski or **zakouski** (zæˈkʊskɪ) *pl. n., sing.* **-ka** (-kə). *Russian cookery.* hors d'oeuvres, consisting of tiny open sandwiches spread with caviar, smoked sausage, etc., or a cold dish such as radishes in sour cream, all usually served with vodka. [Russian, from *zakusit'* to have a snack]

Zama (ˈzɑːmə) *n.* the name of several ancient cities in N Africa, including the one near the site of Scipio's decisive defeat of Hannibal (202 B.C.).

Zambezi or **Zambese** (zæmˈbiːzɪ) *n.* a river in S central and E Africa, rising in NW Zambia and flowing across E Angola back into Zambia, continuing south to the Caprivi Strip of Namibia, then east forming the Zambia–Zimbabwe border, and finally crossing Mozambique to the Indian Ocean: the fourth longest river in Africa. Length: 2740 km (1700 miles). —**Zam'bezian** *adj.*

Zambia (ˈzæmbɪə) *n.* a republic in southern Africa: an early site of human settlement; controlled by the British South Africa Company by 1900 and unified as Northern Rhodesia in 1911; made a British protectorate in 1924; part of the Federation of Rhodesia and Nyasaland (1953–63), gaining independence within the Commonwealth in 1964; important mineral exports, esp. copper. Official language: English. Religion: mostly animist. Currency: kwacha. Capital: Lusaka. Pop.: 7 120 000 (1987 est.). Area: 752 617 sq. km (290 587 sq. miles). Former name (until 1964): **Northern Rhodesia.** —**'Zambian** *adj., n.*

Zamboanga (ˌzæmbəʊˈæŋɡə) *n.* a port in the Philippines, on SW Mindanao on Basilan Strait: founded by the Spanish in 1635; tourist centre, with fisheries. Pop.: 379 194 (1984 est.).

zambuck or **zambuk** (ˈzæmbʌk) *n. Austral. & N.Z. inf.* a first-aid attendant at a sports event. [from name of a proprietary ointment]

Zamenhof (*Polish* ˈzamɛnxɔf) *n.* **Lazarus Ludwig** (laˈzarus ˈludvik). 1859–1917, Polish oculist; invented Esperanto.

Zamora (*Spanish* θaˈmora) *n.* a city in NW central Spain, on the Douro River. Pop.: 58 560 (1980).

Zante (ˈzæntɪ) *n.* an island in the Ionian Sea, off the W coast of Greece: southernmost of the Ionian Islands; traditionally belonged to Ulysses, king of Ithaca. Pop.: 30 014 (1981). Area: 402 sq. km (155 sq. miles). Latin name: **Zacynthus.** Ancient Greek name: **Zakynthos** (zəˈkuːnθɒs). Modern Greek name: **Zákinthos.**

ZANU (ˈzɑːnuː) *n. acronym for* Zimbabwe African National Union.

zany (ˈzeɪnɪ) *adj.* **zanier, zaniest. 1.** comical in an endearing way; imaginatively funny or comical, esp. in behaviour. ~*n., pl.* **-nies. 2.** a clown or buffoon, esp. one in old comedies who imitated other performers with ludicrous effect. **3.** a ludicrous or foolish person. [C16: from It. *zanni,* from dialect *Zanni,* nickname for *Giovanni* John; one of the traditional names for a clown] —**'zanily** *adv.* —**'zaniness** *n.*

Zanzibar (ˌzænzɪˈbɑː) *n.* an island in the Indian Ocean, off the E coast of Africa: settled by Persians and Arabs from the 7th century onwards; became a flourishing trading centre for ivory, slaves, and cloves; made a British protectorate in 1890, becoming independent within the Commonwealth in 1963 and a republic in 1964; joined with Tanganyika in 1964 to form the United Republic of Tanzania. Pop.: 571 000 (1985 est.). —**Zanzi'bari** *adj., n.*

zap (zæp) *Sl.* ~*vb.* **zapping, zapped. 1.** (*tr.*) to attack, kill, or destroy, as with a sudden bombardment. **2.** (*intr.*) to move quickly. **3.** (*tr.*) *Computers.* **a.** to clear from the screen. **b.** to erase. **4.** (*intr.*) *Television.* to change channels rapidly by remote control. ~*n.* **5.** energy, vigour, or pep. ~*interj.* **6.** an exclamation used to express sudden or swift action. [imit.]

Zapata (zəˈpɑːtə; *Spanish* θaˈpata) *n.* **Emiliano** (emiˈljano). ?1877–1919, Mexican guerrilla leader.

zapateado *Spanish.* (ˌθapateˈaðo) *n., pl.* **-dos** (-ðos). a Spanish dance with stamping and very fast footwork. [from *zapatear* to tap with the shoe, from *zapato* shoe]

Zaporozhye (*Russian* zəpɑ'rɔʒjɛ) *n.* a city in the SW Soviet Union, in the Ukrainian SSR on the Dnieper River: developed as a major industrial centre after the construction (1932) of the Dnieper hydroelectric station. Pop.: 875 000 (1987). Former name (until 1921): **Aleksandrovsk.**

Zappa ('zæpə) *n.* **Frank.** born 1940, U.S. rock musician, songwriter, and producer: founder and only permanent member of the Mothers of Invention. His recordings include *Freak Out* (1966), *Hot Rats* (1969), and *Sheik Yerbouti* (1979).

zappy ('zæpɪ) *adj.* **-pier, -piest.** *Sl.* full of energy; zippy.

ZAPU ('zæpuː) *n. acronym for* Zimbabwe African People's Union.

Zaqaziq ('zækə,zɪk) *n.* a variant of **Zagazig.**

Zaragoza (*Spanish* θarɑ'ɣoθa) *n.* a city in NE Spain, on the River Ebro: Roman colony established 25 B.C.; under Moorish rule (714–1118); capital of Aragon (12th–15th centuries); twice besieged by the French during the Peninsular War and captured (1809); university (1474). Pop.: 571 855 (1981). Pre-Roman name: **Salduba.** Latin name: **Caesaraugusta.** English name: **Saragossa.**

Zarathustra (,zærə'θuːstrə) *n.* the Avestan name of **Zoroaster.** —,**Zara'thustrian** *or* ,**Zara'thustric** *adj., n.*

zareba *or* **zareeba** (zə'riːbə) *n.* (in northern E Africa, esp. formerly) **1.** a stockade or enclosure of thorn bushes around a village or camp site. **2.** the area so protected or enclosed. [C19: from Ar. *zarībah* cattlepen, from *zarb* sheepfold]

zarf (zɑːf) *n.* (esp. in the Middle East) a holder, usually ornamental, for a hot coffee cup. [from Ar.: container]

Zaria ('zɑːrɪə) *n.* a city in N central Nigeria: former capital of a Hausa state; agricultural trading centre; university (1962). Pop.: 274 000 (1983 est.).

Zarqa ('zɑːkə) *n.* the second largest town in Jordan, northeast of Amman. Pop.: 265 700 (1984 est.).

zarzuela (zɑː'zweɪlə) *n.* **1.** a type of Spanish vaudeville or operetta, usually satirical in nature. **2.** a seafood stew. [from Sp., after *La Zarzuela*, the palace near Madrid where such vaudeville was first performed (1629)]

Zátopek (*Czech* 'zɑːtɔpɛk) *n.* **Emil** ('emil). born 1922, Czech runner; winner of the 5000 and 10 000 metres and the marathon at the 1952 Olympic Games in Helsinki.

z-axis *n.* a reference axis of a three-dimensional Cartesian coordinate system along which the *z*-coordinate is measured.

ZB station *n.* (in New Zealand) a radio station of a commercial network.

Z chart *n. Statistics.* a chart often used in industry and constructed by plotting on it three series: monthly, weekly, or daily data, the moving annual total, and the cumulative total dating from the beginning of the current year.

Zea ('tsɛːa) *n.* the Italian name for **Keos.**

zeal (ziːl) *n.* fervent or enthusiastic devotion, often extreme or fanatical in nature, as to a religious movement, political cause, ideal, or aspiration. [C14: from LL *zēlus*, from Gk *zēlos*]

Zealand ('ziːlənd) *n.* the English name for **Sjælland.**

zealot ('zɛlət) *n.* an immoderate, fanatical, or extremely zealous adherent to a cause, esp. a religious one. [C16: from LL *zēlōtēs*, from Gk, from *zēloun* to be zealous, from *zēlos* zeal] —'**zealotry** *n.*

Zealot ('zɛlət) *n.* any of the members of an extreme Jewish sect or political party that resisted all aspects of Roman rule in Palestine in the 1st century A.D.

zealous ('zɛləs) *adj.* filled with or inspired by intense enthusiasm or zeal; ardent; fervent. —'**zealously** *adv.* —'**zealousness** *n.*

Zeami *or* **Seami** (siː'ɑːmɪ) *n.* **Motokiyo** (,mɔʊtəʊ'kiːəʊ). 1363–1443, Japanese dramatist, regarded as the greatest figure in the history of No drama.

zebec *or* **zebeck** ('ziːbɛk) *n.* variant spellings of **xebec.**

Zebedee ('zɛbɪ,diː) *n. New Testament.* the father of the apostles James and John (Matthew 4:21).

zebra ('ziːbrə, 'zɛbrə) *n., pl.* **-ras** *or* **-ra.** any of several mammals of the horse family, such as the common zebra of southern and eastern Africa, having distinctive black-and-white striped hides. [C16: via It. from OSp.: wild ass, prob. from Vulgar L *eciferus* (unattested) wild horse, from L *equiferus*, from *equus* horse + *ferus* wild] —**zebrine** ('ziːbraɪn, 'zɛb-) *or* '**zebroid** *adj.*

zebra crossing *n. Brit.* a pedestrian crossing marked on a road by broad alternate black and white stripes. Once on the crossing the pedestrian has right of way.

zebra finch *n.* any of various Australasian songbirds with zebra-like markings.

zebrawood ('zɛbrə,wʊd, 'ziː-) *n.* **1.** a tree of tropical America, Asia, and Africa, yielding striped hardwood used in cabinetwork. **2.** any of various other trees or shrubs having striped wood. **3.** the wood of any of these trees.

zebu ('ziːbuː) *n.* a domesticated ox having a humped back, long horns, and a large dewlap: used in India and E Asia as a draught animal. [C18: from F *zébu*, ? of Tibetan origin]

Zebulun ('zɛbjʊlən, zə'bjuː-) *n. Old Testament.* **1.** the sixth son whom Leah bore to Jacob: one of the 12 patriarchs of Israel (Genesis 30:20). **2.** the tribe descended from him. **3.** the territory of this tribe, lying in lower Galilee to the north of Mount Carmel and to the east of the coastal plain. Douay spelling: **Zabulon** ('zæbjʊlən, zə'bjuː-).

Zech. *Bible. abbrev. for* Zechariah.

Zechariah (,zɛkə'raɪə) *n.* **1.** *Old Testament.* **a.** a Hebrew prophet of the late 6th century B.C. **b.** the book containing his oracles, which are chiefly concerned with the renewal of Israel after the exile as a national, religious, and messianic community with the restored Temple and rebuilt Jerusalem as its centre. Douay spelling: **Zacharias.** **2.** a variant spelling of **Zachariah.** See **Zacharias.**

zed (zɛd) *n.* the British spoken form of the letter *z.* [C15: from OF *zede*, via LL from Gk *zēta*]

Zedekiah (,zɛdə'kaɪə) *n. Old Testament.* the last king of Judah, who died in captivity at Babylon. Douay spelling: **Sedecias** (,sɛdə'kaɪəs).

zedoary ('zɛdəʊərɪ) *n.* the dried rhizome of a tropical Asian plant, used as a stimulant and a condiment. [C15: from Med. L *zedoaria*, from Ar. *zadwār*, of Persian origin]

zee (ziː) *n.* the U.S. word for **zed** (letter *z*).

Zeebrugge (*Flemish* 'zeːbryxə; *English* 'ziː,brʊgə) *n.* a port in NW Belgium, in W Flanders on the North Sea: linked by canal with Bruges; German submarine base in World War I.

Zeeland (*Dutch* 'zeːlɑnt; *English* 'ziːlənd) *n.* a province of the SW Netherlands: consists of a small area on the mainland together with a number of islands in the Scheldt estuary; mostly below sea level. Capital: Middelburg. Pop.: 335 434 (1987). Area: 1787 sq. km (690 sq. miles). —'**Zeelander** *n.*

Zeeman effect ('ziːmən) *n.* the splitting of a spectral line of a substance into several closely spaced lines when the substance is placed in a magnetic field. [C20: after Pieter *Zeeman* (1865–1943), Du. physicist]

Zeffirelli (*Italian* dzeffi'rɛlli) *n.* **Franco** ('fraŋko). born 1923, Italian stage and film director and designer, noted esp. for his work in opera.

zein ('ziːɪn) *n.* a protein occurring in maize and used in the manufacture of plastics, paper coatings, adhesives, etc. [C19: from NL *zēa* maize, from L: a kind of grain, from Gk *zeia* barley]

Zeist (zaɪst; *Dutch* zɛjst) *n.* a city in the central Netherlands, near Utrecht. Pop.: 59 873 (1987).

Zeitgeist *German.* ('tsaɪt,gaɪst) *n.* the spirit, attitude, or general outlook of a specific time or period, esp. as it is reflected in literature, philosophy, etc. [G, lit.: time spirit]

Zen (zɛn) *Buddhism. n.* **1.** a Japanese school, of 12th-century Chinese origin, teaching that contemplation of one's essential nature to the exclusion of all else is the only way of achieving pure enlightenment. **2.** (*modifier*) of or relating to this school: *Zen Buddhism.* [from Japanese: from Chinese *ch'an* religious meditation, from Pali *jhāna*, from Sansk. *dhyāna*] —'**Zenic** *adj.* —'**Zenist** *n.*

zenana (zɛ'nɑːnə) *n.* (in the East, esp. in Muslim and Hindu homes) part of a house reserved for the women and girls of a household. [C18: from Hindi *zanāna*, from Persian, from *zan* woman]

Zend (zɛnd) *n.* **1.** a former name for **Avestan. 2.** short for **Zend-Avesta. 3.** an exposition of the Avesta in the Middle Persian language (Pahlavi). [C18: from Persian *zand* commentary, exposition; used specifically of the MPersian commentary on the Avesta, hence of the language of the Avesta itself] —'**Zendic** *adj.*

Zend-Avesta (,zɛndə'vɛstə) *n.* the Avesta together with the traditional interpretive commentary known as the Zend, esp. as preserved in the Avestan language among the Parsees. [from Avestan, representing *Avesta'-va-zend* Avesta with interpretation]

Zener diode ('zi:nə) *n.* a semiconductor diode that exhibits a sharp increase in reverse current at a well-defined reverse voltage: used as a voltage regulator. [C20: after C. M. *Zener* (b. 1905), U.S. physicist]

zenith ('zɛnɪθ) *n.* **1.** *Astron.* the point on the celestial sphere vertically above an observer. **2.** the highest point; peak; acme: *the zenith of someone's achievements.* [C17: from F *cenith*, from Med. L, from OSp. *zenit*, based on Ar. *samt*, as in *samt arrās* path over one's head] — **'zenithal** *adj.*

zenithal projection *n.* a type of map projection in which part of the earth's surface is projected onto a plane tangential to it, either at one of the poles (**polar zenithal**), at the equator (**equatorial zenithal**), or between (**oblique zenithal**).

Zenobia (zɪ'nəubɪə) *n.* 3rd century A.D., queen of Palmyra (?267–272), who was captured by the Roman emperor Aurelian.

Zeno of Citium ('zi:nəu əv 'sɪtɪəm) *n.* ?336–?264 B.C., Greek philosopher, who founded the Stoic school in Athens.

Zeno of Elea *n.* ?490–?430 B.C., Greek Eleatic philosopher; disciple of Parmenides. He defended the belief that motion and change are illusions in a series of paradoxical arguments, of which the best known is that of Achilles and the tortoise.

zeolite ('zi:ə,laɪt) *n.* **1.** any of a large group of glassy secondary minerals consisting of hydrated aluminium silicates of calcium, sodium, or potassium: formed in cavities in lava flows and plutonic rocks. **2.** any of a class of similar synthetic materials used in ion exchange and as selective absorbents. [C18: *zeo-*, from Gk *zein* to boil + -LITE; from the swelling up that occurs under the blowpipe] — **zeolitic** (,zi:ə'lɪtɪk) *adj.*

Zeph. *Bible. abbrev. for* Zephaniah.

Zephaniah (,zɛfə'naɪə) *n. Old Testament.* **1.** a Hebrew prophet of the late 7th century B.C. **2.** the book containing his oracles, which are chiefly concerned with the approaching judgment by God upon the sinners of Judah. Douay spelling: **Sophonias** (,sɒfə'naɪəs).

zephyr ('zɛfə) *n.* **1.** a soft or gentle breeze. **2.** any of several delicate soft yarns, fabrics, or garments, usually of wool. [C16: from L *zephyrus*, from Gk *zephuros* the west wind]

Zephyrus ('zɛfərəs) *n. Greek myth.* the god of the west wind.

zeppelin ('zɛpəlɪn) *n.* (*sometimes cap.*) a large cylindrical rigid airship built from 1900 to carry passengers and used in World War I for bombing and reconnaissance. [C20: after Count von ZEPPELIN]

Zeppelin (*German* 'tsɛpəli:n) *n.* Count **Ferdinand von** ('fɛrdɪnant fɔn). 1838–1917, German aeronautical pioneer, who designed and manufactured airships (zeppelins).

Zermatt (*German* tsɛr'mat) *n.* a village and resort in S Switzerland, in Valais canton at the foot of the Matterhorn: not accessible by car. Pop.: 3700 (1985 est.).

zero ('zɪərəʊ) *n., pl.* -ros *or* -roes. **1.** the symbol 0, indicating an absence of quantity or magnitude; nought. Former name: **cipher.** **2.** the integer denoted by the symbol 0; nought. **3.** the ordinal number between +1 and −1. **4.** nothing; nil. **5.** a person or thing of no significance; nonentity. **6.** the lowest point or degree: *his prospects were put at zero.* **7.** the line or point on a scale of measurement from which the graduations commence. **8. a.** the temperature, pressure, etc., that registers a reading of zero on a scale. **b.** the value of a variable, such as temperature, obtained under specified conditions. **9.** *Maths.* **a.** the cardinal number of a set with no members. **b.** the identity element of addition. ~*adj.* **10.** having no measurable quantity, magnitude, etc. **11.** *Meteorol.* **a.** (of a cloud ceiling) limiting visibility to 15 metres (50 feet) or less. **b.** (of horizontal visibility) limited to 50 metres (165 feet) or less. ~*vb.* **-roing, -roed.** **12.** (*tr.*) to adjust (an instrument, apparatus, etc.) so as to read zero or a position taken as zero. ~*determiner.* **13.** *Inf., chiefly U.S.* no (thing) at all: *this job has zero interest.* ~See also **zero in.** [C17: from It., from Med. L *zephirum*, from Ar. *sifr* empty]

zero gravity *n.* the state or condition of weightlessness.

zero hour *n.* **1.** *Mil.* the time set for the start of an attack or the initial stage of an operation. **2.** *Inf.* a critical time, esp. at the commencement of an action.

zero in *vb.* (*adv.*) **1.** (often foll. by *on*) to bring (a weapon) to bear (on a target), as while firing repeatedly. **2.** (*intr.;* foll. by *on*) *Inf.* to bring one's attention to bear (on a problem, etc.). **3.** (*intr.;* foll. by *on*) *Inf.* to converge (upon): *the police zeroed in on the site of the crime.*

zero option *n.* (in international nuclear arms negotiations) an offer to remove all shorter-range nuclear missiles or, in the case of the **zero-zero option** all intermediate-range nuclear missiles, if the other side will do the same.

zero-rated *adj.* denoting goods on which the buyer pays no value-added tax although the seller can claim back any tax he has paid.

zero stage *n.* a solid-propellant rocket attached to a liquid-propellant rocket to provide greater thrust at liftoff.

zeroth ('zɪərəʊθ) *adj.* denoting a term in a series that precedes the term otherwise regarded as the first term. [C20: from ZERO + -TH²]

zest (zɛst) *n.* **1.** invigorating or keen excitement or enjoyment: *a zest for living.* **2.** added interest, flavour, or charm; piquancy: *her presence gave zest to the occasion.* **3.** something added to give flavour or relish. **4.** the peel or skin of an orange or lemon, used as flavouring in drinks, etc. ~*vb.* **5.** (*tr.*) to give flavour, interest, or piquancy to. [C17: from F *zeste* peel of citrus fruits used as flavouring, from ?] — **'zestful** *adj.* — **'zestfully** *adv.* — **'zestfulness** *n.* — **'zesty** *adj.*

zeta ('zi:tə) *n.* the sixth letter in the Greek alphabet (Z, ζ). [from Gk]

ZETA ('zi:tə) *n.* a torus-shaped apparatus used for research on controlled thermonuclear reactions and plasma physics. [C20: from *z(ero-)e(nergy) t(hermonuclear) a(pparatus)*]

Zetland ('zɛtlənd) *n.* the official name (until 1974) of **Shetland.**

zeugma ('zju:gmə) *n.* a figure of speech in which a word is used to modify or govern two or more words although appropriate to only one of them or making a different sense with each, as in *Mr Pickwick took his hat and his leave* (Charles Dickens). [C16: via L from Gk: a yoking, from *zeugnunai* to yoke] — **zeugmatic** (zju:g'mætɪk) *adj.*

Zeus (zju:s) *n.* the supreme god of the ancient Greeks, who became ruler of gods and men after he dethroned his father Cronus and defeated the Titans. He was the husband of his sister Hera and father by her and others of many gods, demigods, and mortals. He wielded thunderbolts and ruled the heavens, while his brothers Poseidon and Hades ruled the sea and underworld respectively. Roman counterpart: **Jupiter.**

Zeuxis ('zju:ksɪs) *n.* late 5th century B.C., Greek painter, noted for the verisimilitude of his works.

Zhangjiakou ('dʒæŋ'dʒjækəʊ), **Changchiakow,** *or* **Changchiak'ou** *n.* a city in NE China, in NW Hebei province: a military centre, controlling the route to Mongolia, under the Ming and Manchu dynasties. Pop.: 1 094 000 (1980 est.). Former names: **Wanchüan, Kalgan.**

Zhangzhou ('dʒæŋ'dʒəʊ), **Changchow,** *or* **Ch'ang-chou** *n.* **1.** a city in E China, in S Jiangsu province, on the Grand Canal: also known as **Wutsin** until 1949, when the 7th-century name was officially readopted. Pop.: 300 000 (1958 est.). **2.** a city in SE China, in S Fujian province on the Saikoe River. Pop.: 100 000 (1970 est.). Former name: **Lungki.**

Zhao Ziyang (tʃaʊ zi:'jɑ:ŋ) *n.* born 1919, Chinese statesman; prime minister of China (1980–87).

Zhdanov (*Russian* 'ʒdanəf) *n.* a port in the SW Soviet Union, in the SE Ukrainian SSR near the Sea of Azov: industrial centre. Pop.: 529 000 (1987). Former name (until 1948): **Mariupol.**

Zhejiang ('dʒɛ'dʒjæŋ) *or* **Chekiang** *n.* a province of E China: mountainous and densely populated. Capital: Hangzhou. Pop.: 39 930 000 (1985). Area: 102 000 sq. km (39 780 sq. miles).

Zhengzhou ('dʒʌŋ'dʒəʊ), **Chengchow,** *or* **Cheng-chou** *n.* a city in E central China, capital of Henan province. Pop.: 1 590 000 (1986).

Zhitomir (*Russian* ʒɪ'tɔmɪr) *n.* a city in the SW Soviet Union, in the central Ukrainian SSR. Pop.: 287 000 (1987).

Zhivkov (*Bulgarian* 'ʒifkɒf) *n.* **Todor**. ('tɔdor). born 1911, Bulgarian statesman and party leader; prime minister (1962–71); president from 1971.

zho (zəʊ) *n.* a variant spelling of **zo**.

Zhou (dʒəʊ) *n.* the Pinyin transliteration of the Chinese name for **Chou**.

Zhou En Lai (ɛn laɪ) *n.* the Pinyin transliteration of the Chinese name for **Chou En-lai**.

Zhu De ('dʒu: 'deɪ) *n.* the Pinyin transliteration of the Chinese name for **Chu Teh**.

Zhu Jiang ('dʒu: 'dʒjæŋ), **Chu Chiang**, *or* **Chu Kiang** *n.* a river in SE China, in S Guangdong province, flowing southeast from Canton to the South China Sea. Length: about 177 km (110 miles). Also called: **Canton River**, **Pearl River**.

Zhukov (*Russian* 'ʒukəf) *n.* **Georgi Konstantinovich** (gɪ'ɔrgjɪ kɒnstan'tinəvɪtʃ). 1896–1974, Soviet marshal. In World War II, he led the offensives that broke the sieges of Stalingrad and Leningrad (1942–43) and later captured Warsaw and Berlin; minister of defence (1955–57).

Zia ul Haq ('zɪə ʊl 'hak) *n.* **Mohammed** (məʊ'hæmɪd). 1924–88, Pakistani general; president of Pakistan (1978–88), following the overthrow (1977) of Z. A. Bhutto by a military coup. He was killed in an air crash, possibly through sabotage.

zibeline ('zɪbə,laɪn, -lɪn) *n.* **1.** a sable or the fur of this animal. **2.** a thick cloth made of wool or other animal hair, having a long nap and a dull sheen. ~*adj.* **3.** of, relating to, or resembling a sable. [C16: from F, from OIt. *zibellino*, ult. of Slavonic origin]

zibet ('zɪbɪt) *n.* a large civet of S and SE Asia, having tawny fur marked with black spots and stripes. [C16: from Med. L *zibethum*, from Ar. *zabād* civet]

Zibo ('zi:'bɔ:), **Tzu-po**, *or* **Tzepo** *n.* a city in NE China, in Shandong province. Pop.: 2 300 000 (1986).

Ziegfeld ('zi:g,fɛld) *n.* **Florenz** ('flɒrənz). 1869–1932, U.S. theatrical producer, noted for his series of extravagant revues (1907–31), known as the Ziegfeld Follies.

ziff (zɪf) *n. Austral. inf.* a beard. [C20: from ?]

ziggurat ('zɪgʊ,ræt) *n.* a type of rectangular temple tower or tiered mound erected by the Sumerians, Akkadians, and Babylonians in Mesopotamia. [C19: from Assyrian *ziqqurati* summit]

Zigong ('zi:'gʊŋ), **Tzekung**, *or* **Tzu-kung** *n.* an industrial city in W central China, in Sichuan. Pop.: 600 000 (1975 est.).

zigzag ('zɪg,zæg) *n.* **1.** a line or course characterized by sharp turns in alternating directions. **2.** one of the series of such turns. **3.** something having the form of a zigzag. ~*adj.* **4.** (*usually prenominal*) formed in or proceeding in a zigzag. **5.** (of a sewing machine) capable of producing stitches in a zigzag. ~*adv.* **6.** in a zigzag manner. ~*vb.* **-zagging, -zagged. 7.** to proceed or cause to proceed in a zigzag. **8.** (*tr.*) to form into a zigzag. [C18: from F, from G *zickzack*, from *Zacke* point]

zigzagger ('zɪg,zægə) *n.* **1.** a person or thing that zigzags. **2.** an attachment on a sewing machine for sewing zigzag stitches, as for joining two pieces of material.

zilch (zɪltʃ) *n. Sl., chiefly U.S. & Canad.* nothing. [C20: from ?]

zillion ('zɪljən) *Inf.* ~*n.*, *pl.* **-lions** *or* **-lion. 1.** (*often pl.*) an extremely large but unspecified number, quantity, or amount: *zillions of flies in this camp.* ~*determiner.* **2.** amounting to a zillion: *a zillion different problems.* [C20: coinage after MILLION]

Zilpah ('zɪlpə) *n. Old Testament.* Leah's maidservant, who bore Gad and Asher to Jacob (Genesis 30:10–13).

Zimbabwe (zɪm'bɑ:bwɪ, -weɪ) *n.* **1.** a country in SE Africa, formerly a self-governing British colony founded in 1890 by the British South Africa Company, which administered the country until a self-governing colony was established in 1923; joined with Northern Rhodesia (now Zambia) and Nyasaland (now Malawi) as the Federation of Rhodesia and Nyasaland from 1953 to 1963; made a unilateral declaration of independence under the leadership of Ian Smith in 1965 on the basis of white minority rule; proclaimed a republic in 1970; in 1976 the principle of black majority rule was accepted and in 1978 a transitional government was set up, strongly opposed by some black nationalist organizations; gained independence in 1980 following the Lancaster House Conference (1979–80); a member of the Commonwealth. Official language:

English. Capital: Harare. Pop: 8 640 000 (1987 est.). Area: 390 624 sq. km (150 820 sq. miles). Former names: **Southern Rhodesia** (until 1964), **Rhodesia** (1964–79). **2.** a ruined fortified settlement in Zimbabwe, which at its height, in the 15th century, was probably the capital of an empire covering SE Africa. —**Zim'babwean** *n., adj.*

Zimmer ('zɪmə) *n. Trademark.* Also: **Zimmer aid.** another name for **walker** (sense 3).

zinc (zɪŋk) *n.* **1.** a brittle bluish-white metallic element that is a constituent of several alloys, esp. brass and nickel-silver, and is used in die-casting, galvanizing metals, and in battery electrodes. Symbol: Zn; atomic no.: 30; atomic wt.: 65.37. **2.** *Inf.* corrugated galvanized iron. [C17: from G *Zink*, ?from *Zinke* prong, from its jagged appearance in the furnace] —**'zincic** *adj.* —**'zincky, 'zincy,** *or* **'zinky** *adj.*

zinc blende *n.* another name for **sphalerite**.

zinc chloride *n.* a white soluble poisonous granular solid used in manufacturing parchment paper and vulcanized fibre and in preserving wood. It is also a soldering flux, embalming agent, and medical astringent and antiseptic.

zincite ('zɪŋkaɪt) *n.* a red or yellow mineral consisting of zinc oxide in hexagonal crystalline form. It occurs in metamorphosed limestone.

zincography (zɪŋ'kɒgrəfɪ) *n.* the art or process of etching on zinc to form a printing plate. —**zincograph** ('zɪŋkə,grɑ:f) *n.* —**zin'cographer** *n.*

zinc ointment *n.* a medicinal ointment consisting of zinc oxide, petrolatum, and paraffin.

zinc oxide *n.* a white insoluble powder used as a pigment in paints (**zinc white** or **Chinese white**), cosmetics, glass, and printing inks. It is an antiseptic and astringent and is used in making zinc ointment. Formula: ZnO. Also called: **flowers of zinc**.

zinc sulphate *n.* a colourless soluble crystalline substance used as a mordant, in preserving wood and skins, and in the electrodeposition of zinc.

zing (zɪŋ) *n. Inf.* **1.** a short high-pitched buzzing sound, as of a bullet or vibrating string. **2.** vitality; zest. ~*vb.* **3.** (*intr.*) to make or move with or as if with a high-pitched buzzing sound. [C20: imit.] —**'zingy** *adj.*

zinjanthropus (zɪn'dʒænθrəpəs) *n.* a type of australopithecine, remains of which were discovered in the Olduvai Gorge in Tanzania in 1959. [C20: NL, from Ar. *Zinj* East Africa + Gk *anthrōpos* man]

zinnia ('zɪnɪə) *n.* any of a genus of annual or perennial plants of the composite family, of tropical and subtropical America, having solitary heads of brightly coloured flowers. [C18: after J. G. *Zinn* (d. 1759), G botanist]

Zinovievsk (*Russian* zi'nɔvjifsk) *n.* a former name (1924–36) for **Kirovograd**.

Zinzendorf (*German* 'tsɪntsəndɔrf) *n.* Count **Nikolaus Ludwig von** ('ni:kolaus 'lu:tvɪç fɔn). 1700–60, German religious reformer, who organized the Moravian Church.

Zion ('zaɪən) *or* **Sion** *n.* **1.** the hill on which the city of Jerusalem stands. **2.** *Judaism.* **a.** the ancient Israelites of the Bible. **b.** the modern Jewish nation. **c.** Israel as the national home of the Jewish people. **3.** *Christianity.* heaven regarded as the city of God and the final abode of his elect.

Zionism ('zaɪə,nɪzəm) *n.* **1.** a political movement for the establishment and support of a national homeland for Jews in Palestine, now concerned chiefly with the development of the modern state of Israel. **2.** a policy or movement for Jews to return to Palestine from the Diaspora. —**'Zionist** *n., adj.* —**,Zion'istic** *adj.*

zip (zɪp) *n.* **1. a.** Also called: **zip fastener.** a fastening device operating by means of two parallel rows of metal or plastic teeth on either side of a closure that are interlocked by a sliding tab. U.S. and Canad. term: **zipper. b.** (*modifier*) having such a device: *a zip bag.* **2.** a short sharp whizzing sound, as of a passing bullet. **3.** *Inf.* energy; vigour; vitality. ~*vb.* **zipping, zipped. 4.** (*tr.;* often foll. by *up*) to fasten (clothing, etc.) with a zip. **5.** (*intr.*) to move with a zip: *the bullet zipped past.* **6.** (*intr.;* often foll. by *along, through*, etc.) to hurry; rush. [C19: imit.]

Zipangu (zɪ'pæŋgu:) *n.* Marco Polo's name for **Cipango**.

zip code *n.* the U.S. equivalent of **postcode**. [C20: from *z(one) i(mprovement) p(lan)*]

zip gun *n. U.S. & Canad. sl.* a crude home-made pistol, esp. one powered by a spring or rubber band.

zipper ('zɪpə) *n.* the U.S. & Canad. word for **zip** (sense 1a).

zippy ('zɪpɪ) *adj.* **-pier, -piest.** *Inf.* full of energy; lively.

zircalloy (zɜːk'ælɔɪ) *n.* an alloy of zirconium containing small amounts of tin, chromium, and nickel. It is used in pressurized-water reactors.

zircon ('zɜːkɒn) *n.* a reddish-brown, grey, green, blue, or colourless hard mineral consisting of zirconium silicate: it is used as a gemstone and a refractory. [C18: from G *Zirkon*, from F *jargon*, via It. & Ar., from Persian *zargun* golden]

zirconium (zɜː'kəʊnɪəm) *n.* a greyish-white metallic element, occurring chiefly in zircon, that is exceptionally corrosion-resistant and has low neutron absorption. It is used as a coating in nuclear and chemical plants, as a deoxidizer in steel, and alloyed with niobium in superconductive magnets. Symbol: Zr; atomic no.: 40; atomic wt.: 91.22. [C19: from NL; see ZIRCON] —**zirconic** (zɜː'kɒnɪk) *adj.*

zirconium oxide *n.* a white amorphous powder that is insoluble in water and highly refractory, used as a pigment for paints, a catalyst, and an abrasive.

Ziska ('zɪskə) *or* **Žižka** (*Czech* 'ʒɪʃka) *n.* **Jan** (jan). ?1370–1424, Bohemian soldier, who successfully led the Hussite rebellion (1420–24) against emperor Sigismund.

zit (zɪt) *n.* *U.S. sl.* a pimple. [from ?]

zither ('zɪðə) *n.* a plucked musical instrument consisting of numerous strings stretched over a resonating box, a few of which may be stopped on a fretted fingerboard. [C19: from G, from L *cithara*, from Gk *kithara*] —**zitherist** *n.*

Zlatoust (*Russian* zlətaˈust) *n.* a town in the central Soviet Union, on the Ay river: one of the chief metallurgical centres of the Urals. Pop.: 206 000 (1987).

zloty ('zlɒtɪ) *n., pl.* **-tys** *or* **-ty.** the standard monetary unit of Poland. [from Polish: golden, from *zlyoto* gold]

Zn *the chemical symbol for zinc.*

zo, zho, *or* **dzo** (zəʊ) *n., pl.* **zos, zhos, dzos** *or* **zo, zho, dzo.** a Tibetan breed of cattle, developed by crossing the yak with common cattle. [C20: from Tibetan]

zo- *combining form.* a variant of **zoo-** before a vowel.

-zoa *suffix forming plural proper nouns.* indicating groups of animal organisms: *Protozoa.* [from NL, from Gk *zóia*, pl. of *zóion* animal]

Zoan ('zəʊæn) *n.* the Biblical name for **Tanis.**

zodiac ('zəʊdɪˌæk) *n.* **1.** an imaginary belt extending 8° either side of the ecliptic, which contains the 12 **zodiacal constellations** and within which the moon and planets appear to move. It is divided into 12 equal areas, called **signs of the zodiac,** each named after the constellation which once lay in it. **2.** *Astrol.* a diagram, usually circular, representing this belt and showing the symbols, illustrations, etc., associated with each of the 12 signs of the zodiac, used to predict the future. [C14: from OF *zodiaque*, from L *zodiacus*, from Gk *zóidiakos* (*kuklos*) (circle) of signs, from *zóidion* animal sign, from *zóion* animal] —**zodiacal** (zəʊ'daɪəkəl) *adj.*

zodiacal constellation *n.* any of the 12 constellations after which the signs of the zodiac are named: Aries, Taurus, Gemini, Cancer, Leo, Virgo, Libra, Scorpio, Sagittarius, Capricorn, Aquarius, or Pisces.

zodiacal light *n.* a very faint cone of light in the sky, visible in the east just before sunrise and in the west just after sunset.

Zoffany ('zɒfənɪ) *n.* **John** *or* **Johann** ?1733–1810, British painter, esp. of portraits; born in Germany.

zoic ('zəʊɪk) *adj.* **1.** relating to or having animal life. **2.** *Geol.* (of rocks, etc.) containing fossilized animals. [C19: from NL, from Gk *zóion* animal]

-zoic *adj. and n. combining form.* indicating a geological era: *Palaeozoic.* [from Gk *zóē* life + -IC]

Zola ('zəʊlə; *French* zɔla) *n.* **Émile** (emil). 1840–1902, French novelist and critic; chief exponent of naturalism. In *Les Rougon-Macquart* (1871–93), a cycle of 20 novels, he explains the behaviour of his characters in terms of their heredity: it includes *L'Assommoir* (1877), *Nana* (1880), *Germinal* (1885), and *La Terre* (1887). He is also noted for his defence of Dreyfus in his pamphlet *J'accuse* (1898).

Zollverein *German.* ('tsɔlfɛrˌaɪn) *n.* the customs union of German states organized in the early 1830s under Prussian auspices. [C19: from *Zoll* tax + *Verein* union]

Zomba ('zɒmbə) *n.* a city in S Malawi: the capital of Malawi until 1971. Pop.: 53 000 (1985 est.).

zombie *or* **zombi** ('zɒmbɪ) *n., pl.* **-bies** *or* **-bis. 1.** a person who is or appears to be lifeless, apathetic, or totally lacking in independent judgment; automaton. **2.** a supernatural spirit that reanimates a dead body. **3.** a corpse brought to life in this manner. [from W African *zumbi* good-luck fetish]

zonation (zəʊ'neɪʃən) *n.* arrangement in zones.

zone (zəʊn) *n.* **1.** a region, area, or section characterized by some distinctive feature or quality. **2.** an area subject to a particular political, military, or government function, use, or jurisdiction: *a demilitarized zone.* **3.** (*often cap.*) *Geog.* one of the divisions of the earth's surface, esp. divided into latitudinal belts according to temperature. See **Torrid Zone, Frigid Zone, Temperate Zone. 4.** *Geol.* a distinctive layer or region of rock, characterized by particular fossils, etc. **5.** *Ecology.* an area, esp. a belt of land, having a particular flora and fauna determined by the prevailing environmental conditions. **6.** *Maths.* a portion of a sphere between two parallel planes intersecting the sphere. **7.** *Arch. or literary.* a girdle or belt. **8.** *N.Z.* a section on a transport route; fare stage. **9.** *N.Z.* a catchment area for a specific school. ~*vb.* (*tr.*) **10.** to divide into zones, as for different use, jurisdiction, activities, etc. **11.** to designate as a zone. **12.** to mark with or divide into zones. [C15: from L *zōna* girdle, climatic zone, from Gk *zónē*] —**zonal** *adj.* —**zonated** *adj.* —**zoning** *n.*

zone refining *n.* a technique for producing solids of extreme purity, esp. for use in semiconductors. The material, in the form of a bar, is melted in one small region that is passed along the solid. Impurities concentrate in the melt and are moved to the end of the bar.

zonetime ('zəʊnˌtaɪm) *n.* the standard time of the time zone in which a ship is located at sea, each zone extending $7\frac{1}{2}°$ to each side of a meridian.

zonked (zɒŋkt) *adj. Sl.* **1.** highly intoxicated from drugs or alcohol. **2.** exhausted. [C20: imit.]

zoo (zuː) *n., pl.* **zoos.** a place where live animals are kept, studied, bred, and exhibited to the public. Formal term: **zoological garden.** [C19: shortened from *zoological gardens* (orig. those in London)]

zoo- *or before a vowel* **zo-** *combining form.* indicating animals: *zooplankton.* [from Gk *zóion* animal]

zoogeography (ˌzəʊədʒɪˈɒɡrəfɪ) *n.* the branch of zoology concerned with the geographical distribution of animals. —**ˌzoogeˈographer** *n.* —**zoogeographic** (ˌzəʊəˌdʒɪə'ɡræfɪk) *or* **ˌzoo.geoˈgraphical** *adj.* —**ˌzoo.geoˈgraphically** *adv.*

zoography (zəʊ'ɒɡrəfɪ) *n.* the branch of zoology concerned with the description of animals. —**zo'ographer** *n.* —**zoographic** (ˌzəʊə'ɡræfɪk) *or* **ˌzoo'graphical** *adj.*

zooid ('zəʊɔɪd) *n.* **1.** any independent animal body, such as an individual of a coelenterate colony. **2.** a motile cell or body, such as a gamete, produced by an organism. —**zo'oidal** *adj.*

zool. *abbrev. for:* **1.** zoological. **2.** zoology.

zoolatry (zəʊ'ɒlətrɪ) *n.* **1.** (esp. in ancient or primitive religions) the worship of animals as the incarnations of certain deities, etc. **2.** extreme or excessive devotion to animals, particularly domestic pets. —**zo'olatrous** *adj.*

zoological garden *n.* the formal term for **zoo.**

zoology (zəʊ'ɒlədʒɪ, zuː-) *n., pl.* **-gies. 1.** the study of animals, including their classification, structure, physiology, and history. **2.** the biological characteristics of a particular animal or animal group. **3.** the fauna characteristic of a particular region. —**zoological** (ˌzəʊə'lɒdʒɪkəl, ˌzuːə-) *adj.* —**zo'ologist** *n.*

zoom (zuːm) *vb.* **1.** to make or cause to make a continuous buzzing or humming sound. **2.** to move or cause to move with such a sound. **3.** (*intr.*) to move very rapidly; rush: *we zoomed through town.* **4.** to cause (an aircraft) to climb briefly at an unusually steep angle, or (of an aircraft) to climb in this way. **5.** (*intr.*) (of prices) to rise rapidly. ~*n.* **6.** the sound or act of zooming. **7.** See **zoom lens.** [C19: imit.]

zoom in *or* **out** *vb.* (*intr., adv.*) *Photog., films, television.* to increase or decrease rapidly the magnification of the image of a distant object by means of a zoom lens.

zoom lens *n.* a lens system that allows the focal length of a camera lens to be varied continuously without altering the sharpness of the image.

zoomorphism (ˌzəʊə'mɔːfɪzəm) *n.* **1.** the conception or representation of deities in the form of animals. **2.** the use of animal forms or symbols in art, etc. —**zoo'morphic** adj.

-zoon n. combining form. indicating an individual animal or an independently moving entity derived from an animal: spermatozoon. [from Gk zōion animal]

zoophilism (zəʊ'ɒfɪ,lɪzəm) n. the tendency to be emotionally attached to animals. —**zoophile** ('zəʊə,faɪl) n.

zoophobia (,zəʊə'fəʊbɪə) n. an unusual or morbid dread of animals. —**zoophobous** (zəʊ'ɒfəbəs) adj.

zoophyte ('zəʊə,faɪt) n. any animal resembling a plant, such as a sea anemone. —**zoophytic** (,zəʊə'fɪtɪk) or ,**zoo'phytical** adj.

zooplankton (,zəʊə'plæŋktən) n. the animal constituent of plankton, which consists mainly of small crustaceans and fish larvae.

zoospore ('zəʊə,spɔː) n. an asexual spore of some algae and fungi that moves by means of flagella. —,**zoo'sporic** or **zoosporous** (,zəʊ'ɒspərəs, ,zəʊə'spɔːrəs) adj.

zoosterol (zəʊ'ɒstə,rɒl) n. any of a group of animal sterols, such as cholesterol.

zootechnics (,zəʊə'tɛknɪks) n. (functioning as sing.) the science concerned with the domestication and breeding of animals.

zootomy (zəʊ'ɒtəmɪ) n. the branch of zoology concerned with the dissection and anatomy of animals. —**zootomic** (,zəʊə'tɒmɪk) or ,**zoo'tomical** adj. —,**zoo'tomically** adv. —**zo'otomist** n.

zootoxin (,zəʊə'tɒksɪn) n. a toxin, such as snake venom, that is produced by an animal.

zoot suit (zuːt) n. Sl. a man's suit consisting of baggy tapered trousers and a long jacket with wide padded shoulders, popular esp. in the 1940s. [C20: from ?]

zoril or **zorille** (zə'rɪl) n. a skunk-like African mammal, having a long black-and-white coat. [C18: from F, from Sp. zorrillo a little fox, from zorro fox]

Zorn (Swedish sɔːrn) n. **Anders Leonhard** ('andərs 'leːɔnard). 1860–1920, Swedish painter and etcher, esp. of impressionist portraits and landscapes.

Zoroaster (,zɒrəʊ'æstə) n. Avestan name **Zarathustra**. ?628–?551 B.C., Persian prophet; founder of Zoroastrianism.

Zoroastrian (,zɒrəʊ'æstrɪən) adj. **1.** of or relating to Zoroastrianism. ~n. **2.** an adherent of Zoroastrianism.

Zoroastrianism (,zɒrəʊ'æstrɪən,ɪzəm) or **Zoroastrism** n. the dualistic religion founded by the Persian prophet Zoroaster in the late 7th or early 6th century B.C. and set forth in the sacred writings of the Zend-Avesta. It is based on the concept of a continuous struggle between Ormazd (or Ahura Mazda), the god of creation, light, and goodness, and his archenemy, Ahriman, the spirit of evil and darkness.

Zorrilla y Moral (Spanish θɔ'rriʎa i mo'ral) n. **José** (xo'se). 1817–93, Spanish poet and dramatist, noted for his romantic plays based on national legends, esp. Don Juan Tenorio (1844).

zoster ('zɒstə) n. Pathol. short for **herpes zoster**. [C18: from L: shingles, from Gk zōstēr girdle]

Zouave (zuː'ɑːv, zwɑːv) n. **1.** (formerly) a member of a body of French infantry composed of Algerian recruits noted for their dash, hardiness, and colourful uniforms. **2.** a member of any body of soldiers wearing a similar uniform, esp. a volunteer in such a unit of the Union Army in the American Civil War. [C19: from F, from Zwāwa, tribal name in Algeria]

Zoug (zug) n. the French name for **Zug**.

zounds (zaʊndz) or **swounds** (zwaʊndz, zaʊndz) interj. Arch. a mild oath indicating surprise, indignation, etc. [C16: euphemistic shortening of God's wounds]

Zr the chemical symbol for zirconium.

Zsigmondy (German 'ʃɪgmɔndi) n. **Richard Adolf** ('rɪçart 'aːdɔlf). 1865–1929, German chemist, born in Austria, noted for his work on colloidal particles and, with H. Siedentopf, his introduction (1903) of the ultramicroscope: Nobel prize for chemistry 1925.

zucchetto (tsuː'kɛtəʊ, suː-, zuː-) n., pl. **-tos**. R.C. Church. a small round skullcap worn by certain ecclesiastics and varying in colour according to the rank of the wearer, the Pope wearing white, cardinals red, bishops violet, and others black. [C19: from It., from zucca a gourd, from LL cucutia, prob. from L cucurbita]

zucchini (tsuː'kiːnɪ, zuː-) n., pl. **-ni** or **-nis**. Chiefly U.S., Canad., & Austral. another name for **courgette**. [It., pl.

of zucchino a little gourd, from zucca gourd; see ZUCCHETTO]

Zug (German tsuːk) n. **1.** a canton of N central Switzerland: the smallest Swiss canton; mainly German-speaking and Roman Catholic; joined the Swiss Confederation in 1352. Capital: Zug. Pop.: 81 600 (1986 est.). Area: 239 sq. km (92 sq. miles). **2.** a town in N central Switzerland, the capital of Zug canton, on Lake Zug. Pop.: 21 609 (1980). **3. Lake.** a lake in N central Switzerland, in Zug and Schwyz cantons. Area: 39 sq. km (15 sq. miles). French name: **Zoug.**

Zugspitze ('tsʊg,ʃpɪtsə) n. a mountain peak in S West Germany in the Bavarian Alps, on the Austrian border; the highest peak in West Germany. Height: 2963 m (9721 ft.).

zugzwang (German 'tsuːktsvaŋ) Chess. ~n. **1.** a position in which one player can move only with loss or severe disadvantage. ~vb. **2.** (tr.) to manoeuvre (one's opponent) into a zugzwang. [from G, from Zug a pull + Zwang force]

Zuider Zee or **Zuyder Zee** ('zaɪdə 'ziː; Dutch 'zœidər 'zeː) n. a former inlet of the North Sea in the N coast of the Netherlands: sealed off from the sea by a dam in 1932, dividing it into the Waddenzee and the freshwater IJsselmeer, with several large areas under reclamation.

Zuidholland (zœit'hɔlɑnt) n. the Dutch name for **South Holland.**

Zulu ('zuːluː, -luː) n. **1.** (pl. **-lus** or **-lu**) a member of a tall Negroid people of SE Africa, living chiefly in N Natal, who became dominant during the 19th century due to a warrior-clan system organized by the powerful leader, Shaka. **2.** the language of this people.

Zululand ('zuːluː,lænd, 'zuːluː-) n. a region of South Africa, in NE Natal on the Indian Ocean; partly corresponds to Kwazulu Bantustan. Chief town: Eshowe. Pop.: 3 422 140 (1983). Area: 26 838 sq. km (10 362 sq. miles).

Zungaria (zʊŋ'gɛərɪə) n. a variant transliteration of **Junggar Pendi.**

Zuñi ('zuːnjɪ, 'suː-) n. **1.** (pl. **-ñis** or **-ñi**) a member of a North American Indian people of W New Mexico. **2.** the language of this people. —'**Zuñian** adj., n.

Zurbarán (Spanish θurβa'ran) n. **Francisco de** (fran'θisko de). 1598–1664, Spanish Baroque painter, esp. of religious subjects.

Zürich ('zjʊərɪk; German 'tsyːrɪç) n. **1.** a canton of NE Switzerland: mainly Protestant and German-speaking. Capital: Zürich. Pop.: 1 131 600 (1986 est.). Area: 1729 sq. km (668 sq. miles). **2.** a city in NE Switzerland, the capital of Zürich canton, on Lake Zürich: the largest city and industrial centre in Switzerland; centre of the Swiss Reformation; financial centre. Pop.: 351 500 (1985). **3. Lake.** a lake in N Switzerland, mostly in Zürich canton. Area: 89 sq. km (34 sq. miles).

Zuyder Zee ('zaɪdə 'ziː; Dutch 'zœidər 'zeː) n. a variant spelling of **Zuider Zee.**

Zweig (German tsvaik) n. **1. Arnold** ('arnɔlt). 1887–1968, German novelist, famous for his realistic war novel The Case of Sergeant Grischa (1927). **2. Stefan** ('ʃtɛfan). 1881–1942, Austrian novelist, dramatist, essayist, and poet.

Zwickau (German 'tsvɪkau) n. a city in S East Germany: Anabaptist movement founded here (1521); coal-mining and industrial centre. Pop.: 120 573 (1986).

zwieback ('zwiː,bæk; German 'tsviːbak) n. a small type of rusk, which has been baked first as a loaf, then sliced and toasted. [G: twice-baked]

Zwingli (German 'tsvɪŋli) n. **Ulrich** ('ʊlrɪç) or **Huldreich** ('hʊltraiç). 1484–1531, Swiss leader of the Reformation, based in Zurich. He denied the Eucharistic presence, holding that the Communion was merely a commemoration of Christ's death.

Zwinglian ('zwɪŋlɪən, 'tsvɪŋ-) n. **1.** an upholder of the religious doctrines or movement of Zwingli. ~adj. **2.** of or relating to Zwingli, his religious movement, or his doctrines.

zwitterion ('tsvɪtər,aɪən) n. Chem. an ion that carries both a positive and a negative charge. [C20: from G Zwitter bisexual + ION]

Zwolle (Dutch 'zwɔlə) n. a town in the central Netherlands, capital of Overijssel province. Pop.: 89 348 (1987).

Zworykin ('zwɔːrɪkɪn) n. **Vladimir Kosma** ('vlædɪmɪə'kɒsmə). 1889–1982, U.S. physicist and television pioneer, born in Russia. He developed the first practical television camera.

zygapophysis (ˌzɪgə'pɒfɪsɪs, ˌzaɪgə-) *n.*, *pl.* **-ses** (-ˌsiːz). *Anat.*, *zool.* one of several processes on a vertebra that articulates with the corresponding process on an adjacent vertebra. [from Gk ZYG- + *apophusis* a sideshoot]

zygo- *or before a vowel* **zyg-** *combining form.* indicating a pair or a union: *zygodactyl; zygospore.* [from Gk *zugon* yoke]

zygodactyl (ˌzaɪgəʊ'dæktɪl, ˌzɪgə-) *adj. also* **zygodactylous.** **1.** (of the feet of certain birds) having the first and fourth toes directed backwards and the second and third forwards. ~*n.* **2.** a zygodactyl bird.

zygoma (zaɪ'gəʊmə, zɪ-) *n.*, *pl.* **-mata** (-mətə). another name for **zygomatic arch.** [C17: via NL from Gk, from *zugon* yoke] —**zygomatic** (ˌzaɪgəʊ'mætɪk, ˌzɪg-) *adj.*

zygomatic arch *n.* the slender arch of bone that forms a bridge between the cheekbone and the temporal bone on each side of the skull of mammals. Also called: **zygoma.**

zygomatic bone *n.* either of two bones, one on each side of the skull, that form part of the side wall of the eye socket and part of the zygomatic arch; cheekbone.

zygomorphic (ˌzaɪgəʊ'mɔːfɪk, ˌzɪg-) *or* **zygomorphous** *adj.* (of a flower) capable of being cut in only one plane so that the two halves are mirror images.

zygophyte ('zaɪgəʊˌfaɪt, 'zɪg-) *n.* a plant, such as an alga, that reproduces by means of zygospores.

zygospore ('zaɪgəʊˌspɔː, 'zɪg-) *n.* a thick-walled sexual spore formed from the zygote of some fungi and algae. —ˌzygo'sporic *adj.*

zygote ('zaɪgəʊt, 'zɪg-) *n.* **1.** the cell resulting from the union of an ovum and a spermatozoon. **2.** the organism that develops from such a cell. [C19: from Gk *zugótos* yoked, from *zugoun* to yoke] —**zygotic** (zaɪ'gɒtɪk, zɪ-) *adj.* —**zy'gotically** *adv.*

zymase ('zaɪmeɪs) *n.* a mixture of enzymes that is obtained as an extract from yeast and ferments sugars.

zymo- *or before a vowel* **zym-** *combining form.* indicating fermentation: *zymology.* [from Gk *zumē* leaven]

zymogen ('zaɪməʊˌdʒɛn) *n. Biochem.* any of a group of compounds that are inactive precursors of enzymes.

zymology (zaɪ'mɒlədʒɪ) *n.* the chemistry of fermentation. —**zymologic** (ˌzaɪməʊ'lɒdʒɪk) *or* ˌzymo'logical *adj.* —**zy'mologist** *n.*

zymolysis (zaɪ'mɒlɪsɪs) *n.* the process of fermentation. Also called: **zymosis.**

zymosis (zaɪ'məʊsɪs) *n.*, *pl.* **-ses** (-siːz). **1.** *Med.* **a.** any infectious disease. **b.** the developmental process or spread of such a disease. **2.** another name for **zymolysis.**

zymotic (zaɪ'mɒtɪk) *adj.* **1.** of, relating to, or causing fermentation. **2.** relating to or caused by infection; denoting or relating to an infectious disease. —**zy'motically** *adv.*

zymurgy ('zaɪmɜːdʒɪ) *n.* the branch of chemistry concerned with fermentation processes in brewing, etc.

SUPPLEMENTS

LANGUAGES AND ALPHABETS

A simplified tree of Indo-European languages

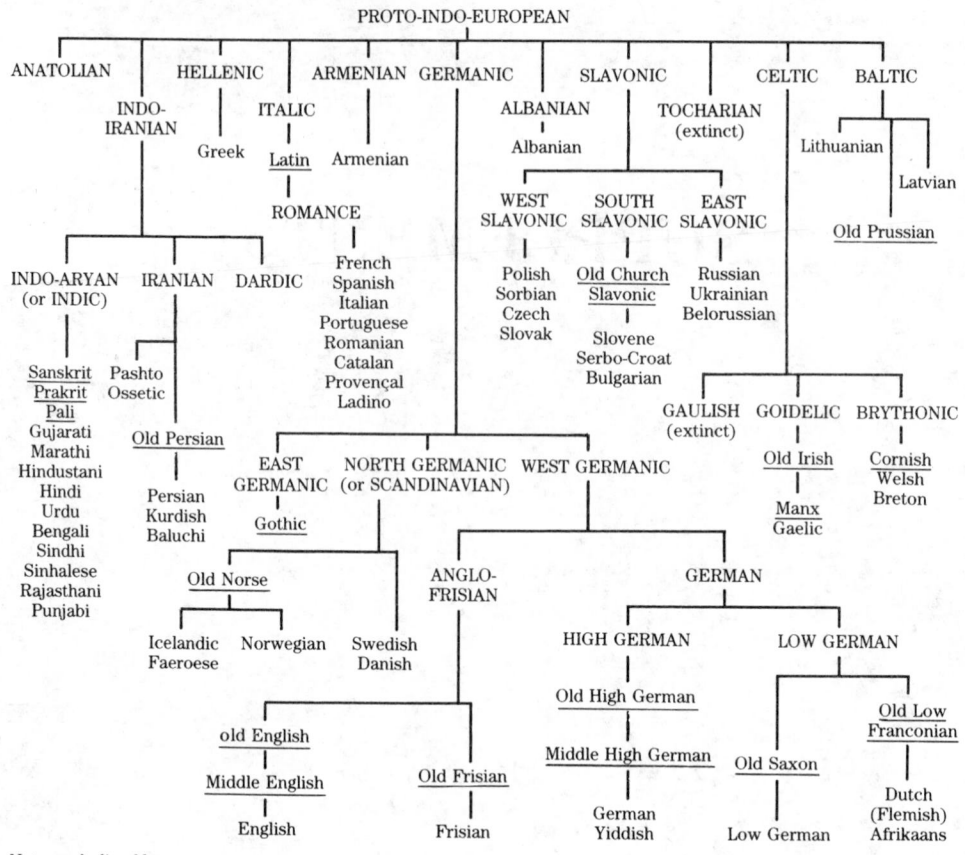

Note: underlined languages
are no longer spoken

The development of the modern Roman alphabet

Phoenician	⋖	ϡ	𐤋	◁	∃	Y	˥	目	2	2	↓	↳	↯	↯	O	⌐	φ	˥	W	✝	Y	Y	⊞	≖	王	工
Early Hebrew	⋖	9	∧	◁	∃	Y	˥	目	↗	↗	✓	↙	坊	坊	O	⌐	9	◁	W	X	Y	Y	⊞	≛	王	工
Early Aramaic	✦	ϡ	∧	∧	◢	4	4	目	⅂	⅂	✓	𝘭	𝔐	ヶ	O	⌐	⌐	◁	W	X	4	4	✦	≨	𝟤	⅃
Early Greek	A	ϱ	1	Δ	∃	˥	˥	B	2	2	⅄	1	⋈	坊	O	⌐	⌐	φ	◁	ϟ	X	Y	Y	Y	⊞	I
Classical Greek	A	B	Γ	Δ	E			Γ	H	I	I	K	Λ	M	N	O	Π		P	Σ	T	Y	Y	Y	Ξ	Z
Etruscan	A	ϱ	𝟕	𝟕	◁	𝘢	⅂	T	B	I	I	⅄	⅃	𝔐	И	⅄	O	⌐	⌐	◁	↑	T	Y	Y	◁	X	⅃
Early Latin	A	B	<	D	ℰ	F	<	H	I		I	K	⅄	M	N	O	⌐		Q	R	Ϸ	T	V	V	V	X	Y	Z
Classical Latin	A	B	C	D	E	F	G	H	I		I	K	L	M	N	O	P	Q	R	S	T	V	V	V	X	Y	Z
Russian-Cyrillic	А	Б	Г	Д	Е	Ф	Г	Н	I		К	Л	М	Н	О	П		Р	С	Т	У					З
Modern Roman	A	B	C	D	E	F	G	H	I	J	K	L	M	N	O	P	Q	R	S	T	U	V	W	X	Y	Z

1534

SYMBOLS USED IN MATHEMATICS, LOGIC, AND ELECTRONICS

Operation	Symbol	Operation	Symbol
AND operation, conjunction	$\wedge$.	equivalence	$\leftrightarrow \equiv$
OR operation, disjunction	$\vee$ +	biconditional	$\leftrightarrow \equiv$
NOT operation, negation	$' \underline{\ } \sim$	conditional	$\rightarrow \Rightarrow$
NAND operation	$\mid \Delta$	general binary operation	$\circ$
NOR operation	$\uparrow \nabla$	universal quantifier	$\forall$
EXOR operation	$\veebar$	existential quantifier	$\exists$

For set S and/or set T:

x is a member of S	$x \in S$	union of S and T	$S \cup T$
x is not a member of S	$x \notin S$	intersection of S and T	$S \cap T$
S is a subset of T	$S \subseteq T$	Cartesian product of	$S \times T$
S is a proper subset of T	$S \subset T$	S and T	
complement of S	$S' \sim S\ \bar{S}$	set of all x for which	$\{x \mid p(x)\}$
		$p(x)$ is true	
relation	R		
function of x	$f(x)$	greater than	$>$
function f from set X	$f : X \rightarrow Y$	greater than or equal to	$\geq$
to set Y		less than	$<$
inverse function	f^{-1}	less than or equal to	$\leq$
inverse relation	R^{-1}	approx. equal to	$\approx$
sum, with limits	$\displaystyle\sum_{i=1}^{n}$	not equal to	$\neq$
		infinity	∞
integral, with limits	$\displaystyle\int_{b}^{a} dx$		
elements of vector v	v_1		
elements of matrix A	a_{ij}		
transpose of matrix A	A^{T}		
inverse of matrix A	A^{-1}		

Greek alphabet

alpha	α, A	iota	ι, I	rho	ρ, P		
beta	β, B	kappa	κ, K	sigma	σ, Σ		
gamma	γ, Γ	lambda	λ, Λ	tau	τ, T		
delta	δ, Δ	mu	μ, M	upsilon	υ, Y		
epsilon	ϵ, E	nu	ν, N	phi	ϕ, Φ		
zeta	ζ, Z	xi	ξ, Ξ	chi	χ, X		
eta	η, H	omikron	o, O	psi	ψ, Ψ		
theta	θ, Θ	pi	π, Π	omega	ω, Ω		

Electronics

AC		heater		resistor	
AND gate		inductor		sawtooth wave	
capacitor		lamp		sine wave	
cathode		meter		square wave	
connector terminals		meter *or* motor		switch	
crystal		negative pulse		transformer	
DC		neon bulb		transistor (NPN)	
diode		NOT gate (inverter)		triangle wave	
earth		operational amplifier		tunnel diode	
electrolytic capacitor		OR gate		XOR gate	
flip-flop		positive pulse		Zener diode	

SYMBOLS FOR PHYSICAL QUANTITIES

Quantity	Symbol	Quantity	Symbol
absorptance	α	magnetic field strength	H
acceleration	a	magnetic flux	Φ
activity	A	magnetic flux density	B
admittance	Y	magnetic moment	m
amount of substance	n	magnetic susceptibility	χ
ampere turn	At	magnetomotive force	F
angular acceleration	a	magnification	m
angular displacement	θ	mass	m
angular frequency	ω	mean free path	λ
angular magnification	M	mean life	τ
angular momentum	L	molar heat capacity	C_m
angular velocity	ω	moment of force	M
atomic number, proton number	Z	moment of inertia	I
		momentum, linear	p
Bragg angle	θ		
Brewster angle	i	Néel temperature	θ_N
bulk modulus	K	neutron number	N
		nucleon number	A
capacitance	C		
centripetal acceleration	a	optical path	d
centripetal force	F	osmotic pressure	Π
characteristic temperature	θ		
charge	Q	parity	P
charge density	ρ	period	T
coefficient of friction	μ	permeability	μ
concentration	c	permittivity	ϵ
conductance	G	potential difference	V
conductivity, electrical	σ	potential energy	V
conductivity, thermal	λ	power	P
cubic expansion coefficient	γ	pressure	p
current	i	proton number, atomic number	Z
current density	j		
		radiance	L_e
decay constant	λ	radiant flux	Φ_e
declination	c	radiant intensity	I_e
degeneracy of an energy level	g	radius	r
density	ρ	radius of curvature	r
diameter	d	radius of gyration	k
diffusion coefficient	D	reactance	X
displacement	s	reflectance	ρ
		refractive constant	n
efficiency	η	relative atomic mass	A_r
electric displacement	D	relative density	d
electric field strength	E	relative molecular mass	M_r
electric flux	ψ	reluctance	R
electric potential	V	resistance	R
electrochemical equivalent	Z	resistivity	ρ
electromotive force	E	restitution, coefficient of	e
emessivity	ϵ	rest mass	m_0
energy	W, E		
enthalpy	H	shear modulus	G
entropy	S	solid angle	Ω
exitance	M	specific heat capacity	c
		specific rotary power	a_m
force	F	speed	u
frequency	f, v	surface tension	γ
		susceptance	B
half-life	$T_{1/2}$	susceptibility	χ
heat	Q, H		
heat capacity	C	temperature	T, t
horizontal intensity	B	thermodynamic temperature	T
		time	t
illumination, illuminance	E	torque	T
impedance	Z		
inclination	δ	velocity	v
internal energy	U, E	viscosity	η
ionization potential	I	voltage	V
irradiance	E	volume	V
		wavelength	λ
kinematic viscosity	ν	wave number	σ
kinetic energy	T, E_K, K	weight	W
		work	W
linear expansion coefficient	α	work function	Φ
luminance	L		
luminous flux	ϕ	Young modulus	E
luminous intensity	I		

CHEMISTRY AND PHYSICS

Periodic table of the elements

1A	2A	3B	4B	5B	6B	7B		8		1B	2B	3A	4A	5A	6A	7A	0
1 H																	2 He
3 Li	4 Be											5 B	6 C	7 N	8 O	9 F	10 Ne
11 Na	12 Mg	←			transition elements						→	13 Al	14 Si	15 P	16 S	17 Cl	18 Ar
19 K	20 Ca	21 Sc	22 Ti	23 V	24 Cr	25 Mn	26 Fe	27 Co	28 Ni	29 Cu	30 Zn	31 Ga	32 Ge	33 As	34 Se	35 Br	36 Kr
37 Rb	38 Sr	39 Y	40 Zr	41 Nb	42 Mo	43 Tc	44 Ru	45 Rh	46 Pd	47 Ag	48 Cd	49 In	50 Sn	51 Sb	52 Te	53 I	54 Xe
55 Cs	56 Ba	57* La	72 Hf	73 Ta	74 W	75 Re	76 Os	77 Ir	78 Pt	79 Au	80 Hg	81 Tl	82 Pb	83 Bi	84 Po	85 At	86 Rn
87 Fr	88 Ra	89† Ac															

*Lanthanides		57 La	58 Ce	59 Pr	60 Nd	61 Pm	62 Sm	63 Eu	64 Gd	65 Tb	66 Dy	67 Ho	68 Er	69 Tm	70 Yb	71 Lu
†Actinides		89 Ac	90 Th	91 Pa	92 U	93 Np	94 Pu	95 Am	96 Cm	97 Bk	98 Cf	99 Es	100 Fm	101 Md	102 No	103 Lr

Fundamental constants

Constant	Symbol	Value in SI units
acceleration of free fall	g	$9.806\,65$ m s^{-2}
Avogrado constant	L, N_A	$6.022\,52 \times 10^{23}$ mol^{-1}
electric constant	ϵ_0	8.854×10^{-12} F m^{-1}
electronic charge	e	$1.602\,10 \times 10^{-19}$ C
electronic rest mass	m_e	$9.109\,08 \times 10^{-31}$ kg
gas constant	R_0	$8.314\,34$ J K^{-1} mol^{-1}
gravitational constant	G	6.672×10^{-11} N m^2 kg^{-2}
magnetic constant	μ_0	$4\pi \times 10^{-7}$ H m^{-1}
neutron rest mass	m_n	$1.674\,82 \times 10^{-27}$ kg
Planck constant	h	$6.625\,59 \times 10^{-34}$ J s
proton rest mass	m_p	$1.672\,52 \times 10^{-27}$ kg
speed of light	c	$2.997\,924\,58 \times 10^8$ m s^{-1}

SI UNITS

Base and supplementary SI units

Physical quantity	SI unit	Symbol
length	metre	m
mass	kilogram	kg
time	second	s
electric current	ampere	A
thermodynamic temperature	kelvin	K
luminous intensity	candela	cd
amount of substance	mole	mol
plane angle (supplementary unit)	radian	rad
solid angle (supplementary unit)	steradian	sr

Derived SI units with special names

Physical quantity	SI unit	Symbol
frequency	hertz	Hz
energy	joule	J
force	newton	N
power	watt	W
pressure	pascal	Pa
electric charge	coulomb	C
electric potential difference	volt	V
electric resistance	ohm	Ω
electric conductance	siemens	S
electric capacitance	farad	F
magnetic flux	weber	Wb
inductance	henry	H
magnetic flux density (magnetic induction)	tesla	T
luminous flux	lumen	lm
illuminance	lux	lx
absorbed dose	gray	Gy
activity	becquerel	Bq
dose equivalent	sievert	Sv

Decimal multiples and submultiples used with SI units

Submultiple	Prefix	Symbol	Multiple	Prefix	Symbol
10^{-1}	deci–	d	10	deca–	da
10^{-2}	cent–	c	10^2	hecto–	h
10^{-3}	milli–	μ	10^3	kilo–	k
10^{-6}	micro–	a	10^6	mega–	M
10^{-9}	nano–	n	10^9	giga–	G
10^{-12}	pico–	p	10^{12}	tera–	T
10^{-15}	femto–	f	10^{15}	peta–	P
10^{-18}	atto–	a	10^{18}	exa–	E

Length

	metre	centimetre	inch	foot	yard
1 metre	1	100	39.3701	3.28084	1.09361
1 centimetre	0.01	1	0.393701	0.0328084	0.0109361
1 inch	0.0254	2.54	1	0.0833333	0.0277778
1 foot	0.3048	30.48	12	1	0.333333
1 yard	0.9144	91.44	36	3	1

	kilometre	mile	nautical mile
1 kilometre	1	0.621371	0.539957
1 mile	1.60934	1	0.868976
1 nautical mile	1.85200	1.15078	1

Area

	m^2	cm^2	in^2	ft^2
1 square metre	1	10^4	1550	10.7639
1 square centimetre	10^{-4}	1	0.155	1.07639×10^{-3}
1 square inch	6.4516×10^{-4}	6.4516	1	6.94444×10^{-3}
1 square foot	9.2903×10^{-2}	929.03	144	1

	m^2	km^2	yd^2	mi^2	acre
1 square metre	1	10^{-6}	1.19599	3.86019×10^{-7}	2.47105×10^{-4}
1 square kilometre	10^6	1	1.19599×10^6	0.386019	247.105
1 square yard	0.836127	8.36127×10^{-7}	1	3.22831×10^{-7}	2.06612×10^{-4}
1 square mile	2.58999×10^6	2.58999	3.0976×10^6	1	640
1 acre	4.04686×10^3	4.04686×10^{-3}	4840	1.5625×10^{-3}	1

Volume

	m^3	cm^3	in^3	ft^3	gallons
1 cubic metre	1	10^6	6.10236×10^4	35.3146	219.969
1 cubic centimetre	10^{-6}	1	0.0610236	3.53146×10^{-5}	2.19969×10^{-4}
1 cubic inch	1.63871×10^{-5}	16.3871	1	5.78704×10^{-4}	3.60464×10^{-3}
1 cubic foot	0.0283168	28316.8	1728	1	6.22882
1 gallon (UK)	4.54609×10^{-3}	4546.09	277.42	0.160544	1

Speed

	m/sec	km/hr	mi/hr	ft/sec
1 metre per second	1	3.6	2.23694	3.28084
1 kilometre per hour	0.277778	1	0.621371	0.911346
1 mile per hour	0.44704	1.609344	1	1.46667
1 foot per second	0.3048	1.09728	0.681817	1

Mass

	kg	g	lb
1 kilogram	1	1000	2.20462
1 gram	10^{-3}	1	2.20462×10^{-3}
1 pound	0.453592	453.592	1

Density

	kg/m^3	g/m^3	lb/ft^3
1 kilogram per cubic metre	1	10^{-3}	0.062428
1 gram per cubic centimetre	1000	1	62.428
1 pound per cubic foot	16.0185	0.0160185	1

Force

	N	kg	dyne	poundal	lb
1 newton	1	0.101972	10^5	7.23300	0.224809
1 kilogram force	9.80665	1	9.80665×10^5	70.9316	2.20462
1 dyne	10^{-5}	1.01972×10^{-6}	1	7.23300×10^{-5}	2.4809×10^{-6}
1 poundal	0.138255	1.40981×10^{-2}	1.38255×10^4	1	0.031081
1 pound force	4.44822	0.453592	4.44823×10^5	32.174	1

Pressure

	N/m^2(Pa)	kg/cm^2	lb/in^2	atmos
1 newton per square metre (pascal)	1	1.01972×10^{-5}	1.45038×10^{-4}	9.86923×10^{-6}
1 kilogram per square centimetre	980.665×10^2	1	14.2234	0.967841
1 pound per square inch	6.89476×10^3	0.0703068	1	0.068046
1 atmosphere	1.01325×10^5	1.03323	14.6959	1

Work and Energy

	J	cal_{IT}	kWhr	btu_{IT}
1 joule	1	0.238846	2.77778×10^{-7}	9.47813×10^{-4}
1 calorie (IT)	4.1868	1	1.16300×10^{-6}	3.96831×10^{-3}
1 kilowatt hour	3.6×10^6	8.59845×10^5	1	3412.14
1 British Thermal Unit (IT)	1055.06	251.997	2.93071×10^{-4}	1

GEOLOGICAL TIME SCALE

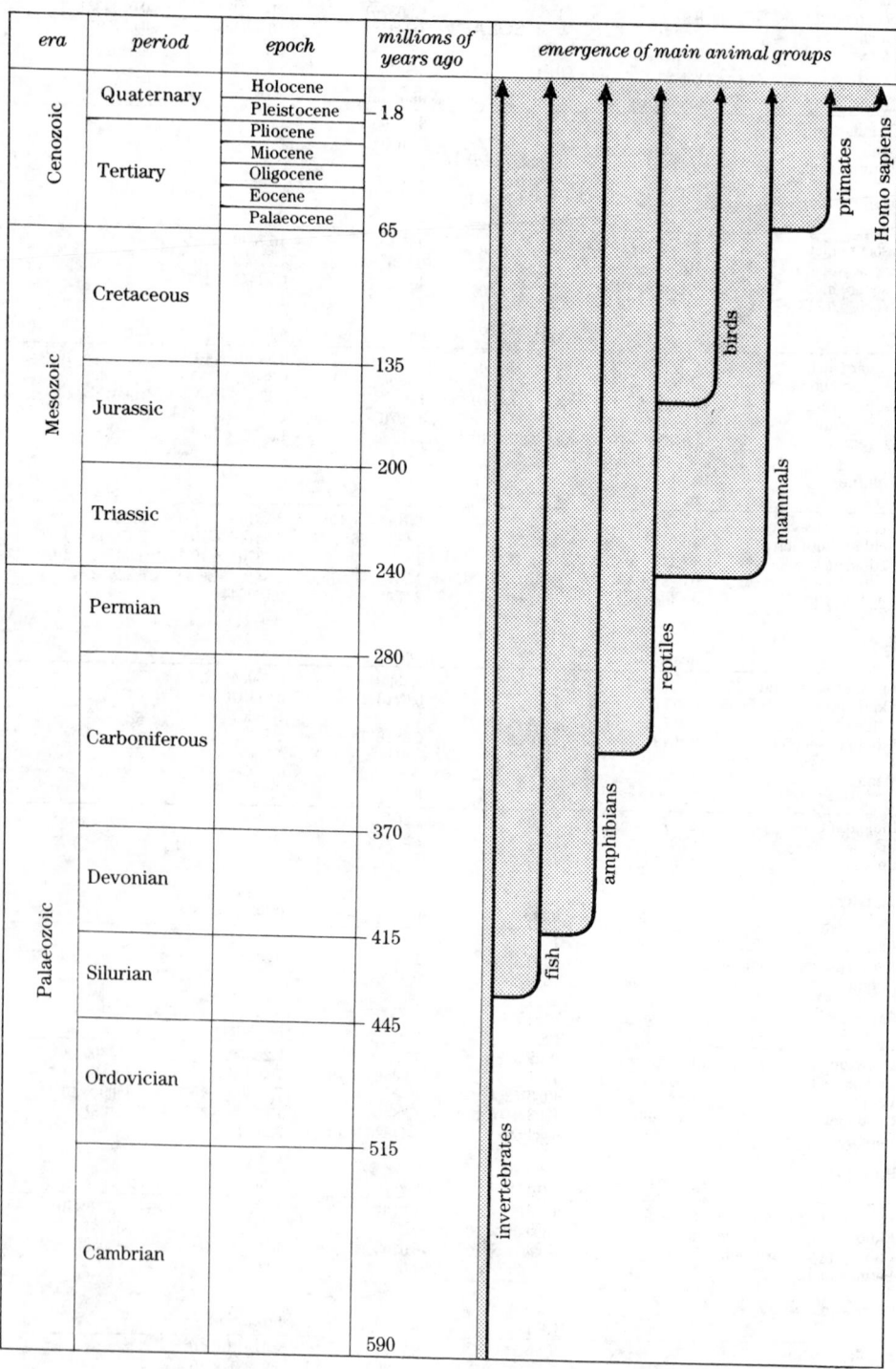

THE SOLAR SYSTEM

The Planets

Planet	*Equatorial diameter (kilometres)*	*Mass (earth masses = 5.974 × 10^{24} kg)*	*Mean distance from sun (millions of kilometres)*	*Sidereal period*
Mercury	4878	0.06	57.91	87.97 days
Venus	12 104	0.82	108.21	224.70 days
Earth	12 756	1.000	149.60	365.26 days
Mars	6787	0.11	227.94	686.980 days
Jupiter	142 800	317.83	778.34	11.86 years
Saturn	120 000	95.17	1427.01	29.46 years
Uranus	50 800	14.50	2869.6	84.01 years
Neptune	48 600	17.20	4496.7	164.79 years
Pluto	3000?	0.002	5907	247.70 years

Planetary Satellites

Planet & satellite	*Diameter (km)*	*Distance from primary (1000km)*	*Year of discovery*
EARTH			
Moon	3476	384.40	–
MARS			
Phobos	27	9.38	1877
Deimos	15	23.46	1877
JUPITER			
Metis	40	128	1979
Adrastea	24	128	1979
Amalthea	270	181	1892
Thebe	100	222	1979
Io	3630	422	1610
Europa	3100	671	1610
Ganymede	5260	1070	1610
Callisto	4800	1883	1610
Leda	20	11 110	1974
Himalia	180	11 480	1904
Lysithea	40	11 720	1938
Elara	80	11 740	1905
Ananke	30	21 200	1951
Carme	40	22 600	1938
Pasiphae	50	23 500	1908
Sinope	40	23 700	1914
SATURN			
1980 S28	40	138	1980
1980 S27	100	139	1980
1980 S26	100	142	1980
1980 S3	90	151	1978
1980 S1	100	151	1978
Mimas c-o	390	186	1982
Mimas	390	186	1789
Enceladus	500	238	1789
Tethys	1050	295	1684
1980 S25	35	295	1980
1980 S13	35	295	1980
Tethys c-o	15	295	1982
–	15	350	1982
Dione	1120	377	1684
1980 S6	160	378	1980
Dione c-o	15	378	1982
–	–	470	1982
Rhea	1530	527	1672
Titan	5150	1222	1655
Hyperion	400	1481	1848
Iapetus	1440	3560	1671
Phoebe	160	12 950	1898
URANUS			
Miranda	400	130	1948
Ariel	1300	191	1851
Umbriel	1100	266	1851
Titania	1600	436	1787
Oberon	1600	583	1787
NEPTUNE			
Triton	3800	355	1846
Nereid	300	5510	1949
PLUTO			
Charon	1000	20 000	1978

c-o = co-orbital

THE PLANT KINGDOM

A simplified classification

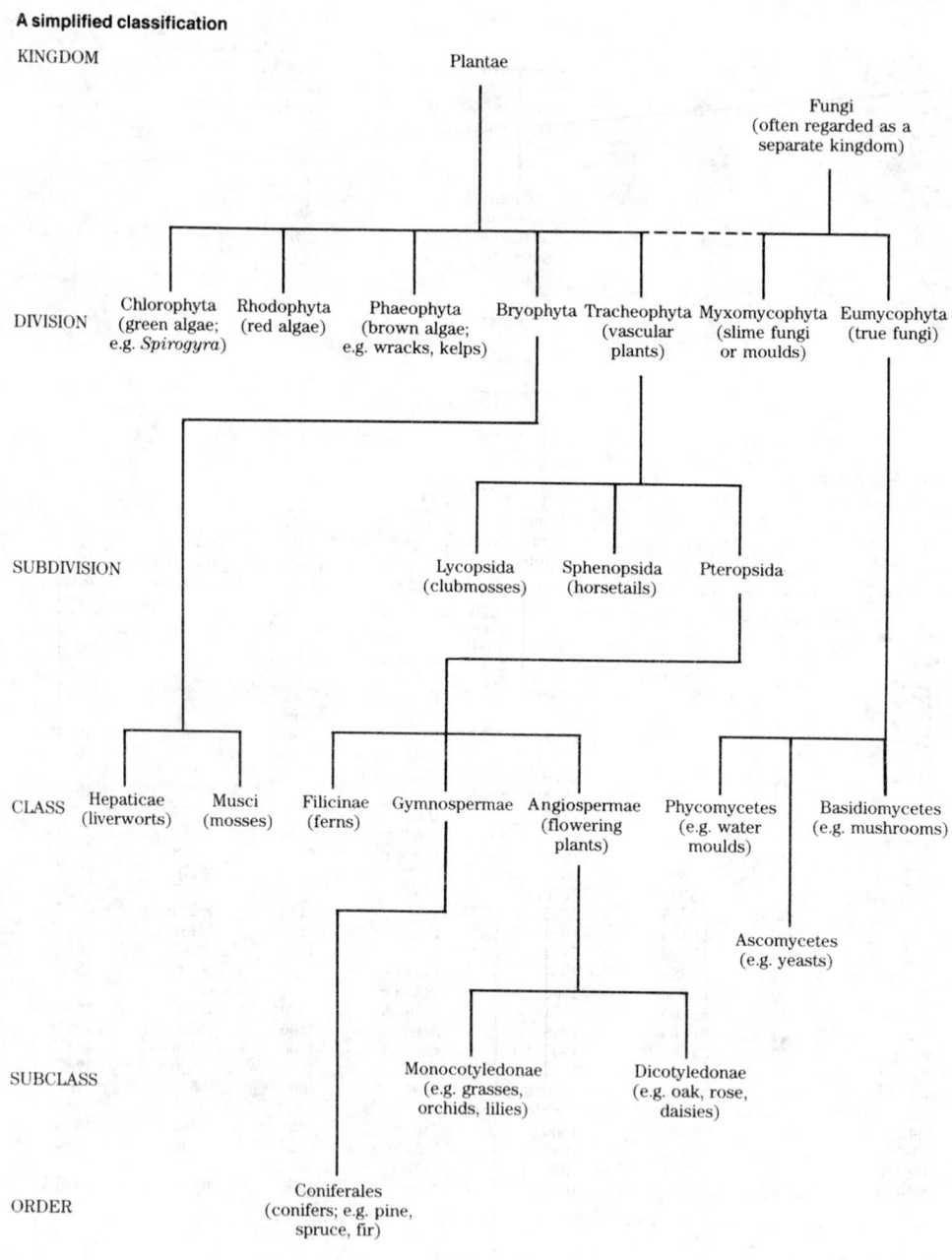

THE ANIMAL KINGDOM

A simplified classification

KINGDOM — Animalia

PHYLUM

Protozoa (e.g. *Amoeba*, *Plasmodium*)
Coelenterata (e.g. jellyfish, sea anemones, corals)
Nematoda (roundworms)
Annelida (segmented worms; e.g. earthworms, lugworms, leeches)
Echinodermata (e.g. starfish, sea urchins, brittlestars)
Porifera (sponges)
Platyhelminthes (flatworms; e.g. flukes, tapeworms)
Mollusca
Arthropoda
Chordata

SUBPHYLUM — Vertebrata

CLASS

Lamellibranchia (e.g. oysters mussels, clams)
Insecta
Agnatha (jawless fish; e.g. lampreys, hagfish)
Osteichthyes (bony fish)
Aves (birds)
Cephalopoda (e.g. squids, octopuses)
Crustacea (e.g. shrimps, crabs, lobsters)
Amphibia (e.g. frogs, toads)
Mammalia
Gastropoda (e.g. snails, slugs)
Arachnida (e.g. spiders, scorpions, mites)
Myriapoda (centipedes and millipedes)
Elasmobranchii (cartilaginous fish; e.g. sharks, rays)
Reptilia (e.g. crocodiles, snakes, lizards)

SUBCLASS

Dipnoi (lungfish)
Teleostei (e.g. salmon, plaice, eel)
Prototheria (monotremes; e.g. duckbilled platypus)
Metatheria (marsupial mammals; e.g. kangaroo, wombat)
Eutheria (placental mammals)

ORDER

Hemiptera (bugs)
Lepidoptera (butterflies and moths)
Coleoptera (beetles)
Primates (monkeys, apes, man, etc.)
Rodentia (rats, mice, squirrels, porcupines, etc.)
Perissodactyla (horses, rhinos, etc.)
Diptera (flies)
Hymenoptera (ants, bees, wasps)
Chiroptera (bats)
Cetacea (whales)
Carnivora (cats, dogs, bears, weasels, badgers, etc.)
Artiodactyla (pigs, hippos, deer, antelopes, cattle, etc.)

THE HUMAN BODY

A section of the backbone and spinal cord

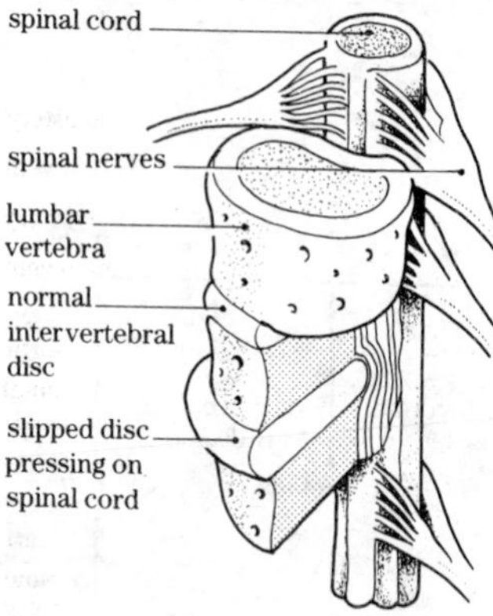

spinal cord

spinal nerves

lumbar vertebra

normal intervertebral disc

slipped disc pressing on spinal cord

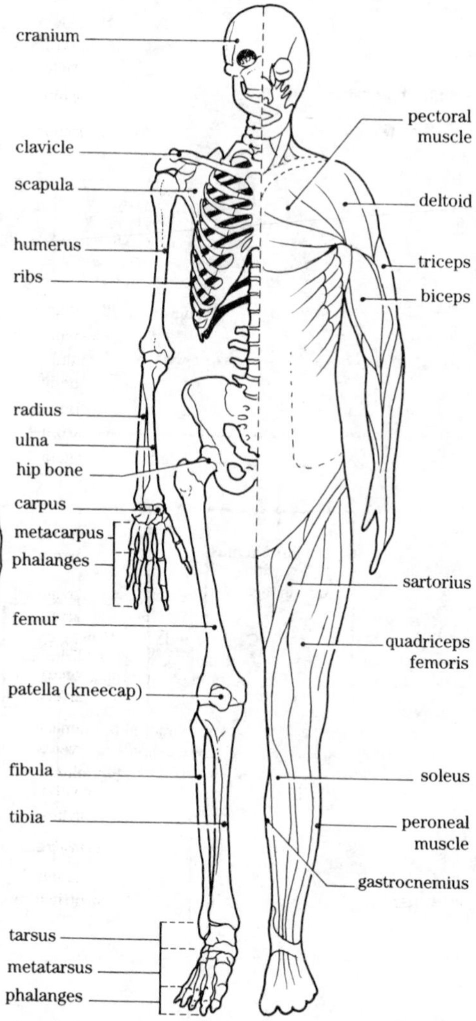

Muscles and bones of the arm

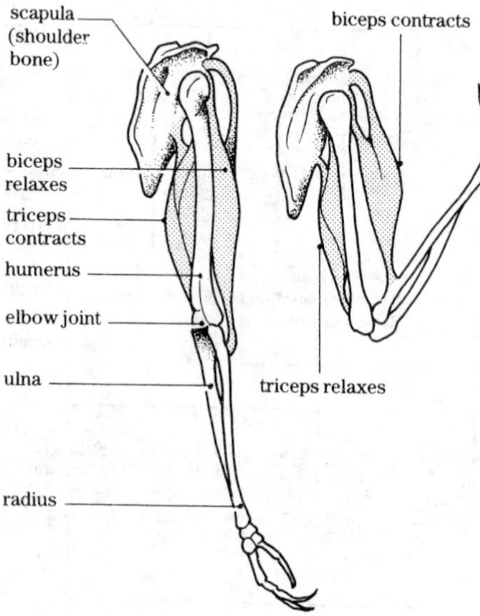

scapula (shoulder bone)

biceps contracts

biceps relaxes

triceps contracts

humerus

elbow joint

ulna

triceps relaxes

radius

Skeleton (left) and muscular system (right)

cranium

clavicle

scapula

humerus

ribs

pectoral muscle

deltoid

triceps

biceps

radius

ulna

hip bone

carpus

metacarpus

phalanges

femur

patella (kneecap)

fibula

tibia

sartorius

quadriceps femoris

soleus

peroneal muscle

gastrocnemius

tarsus

metatarsus

phalanges

Male reproductive system

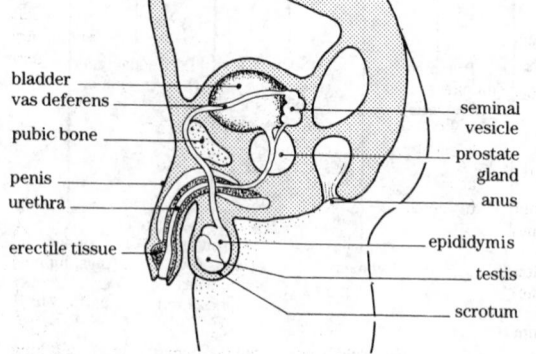

bladder

vas deferens

pubic bone

penis

urethra

erectile tissue

seminal vesicle

prostate gland

anus

epididymis

testis

scrotum

Female reproductive system

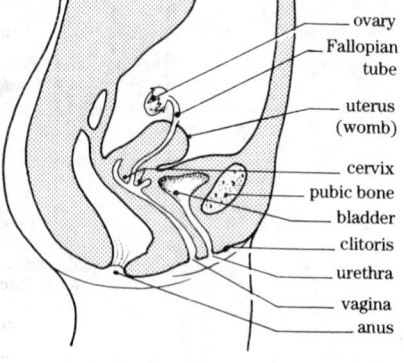

ovary

Fallopian tube

uterus (womb)

cervix

pubic bone

bladder

clitoris

urethra

vagina

anus

THE HUMAN BODY

Brain

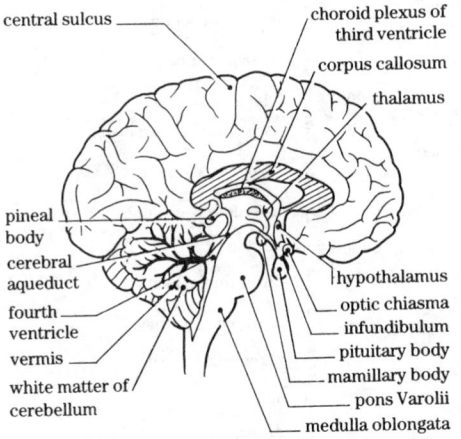

central sulcus

choroid plexus of third ventricle

corpus callosum

thalamus

pineal body

cerebral aqueduct

fourth ventricle

vermis

white matter of cerebellum

hypothalamus

optic chiasma

infundibulum

pituitary body

mamillary body

pons Varolii

medulla oblongata

Heart

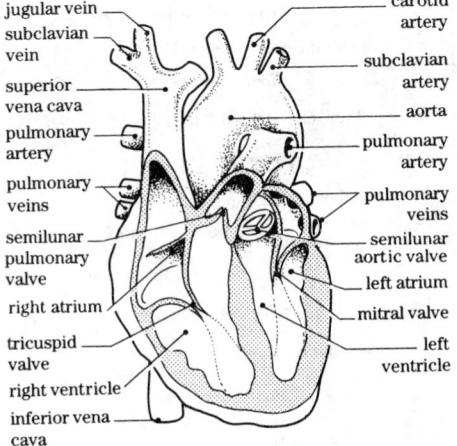

jugular vein

subclavian vein

superior vena cava

pulmonary artery

pulmonary veins

semilunar pulmonary valve

right atrium

tricuspid valve

right ventricle

inferior vena cava

carotid artery

subclavian artery

aorta

pulmonary artery

pulmonary veins

semilunar aortic valve

left atrium

mitral valve

left ventricle

Nervous system (left) and circulatory system (right)

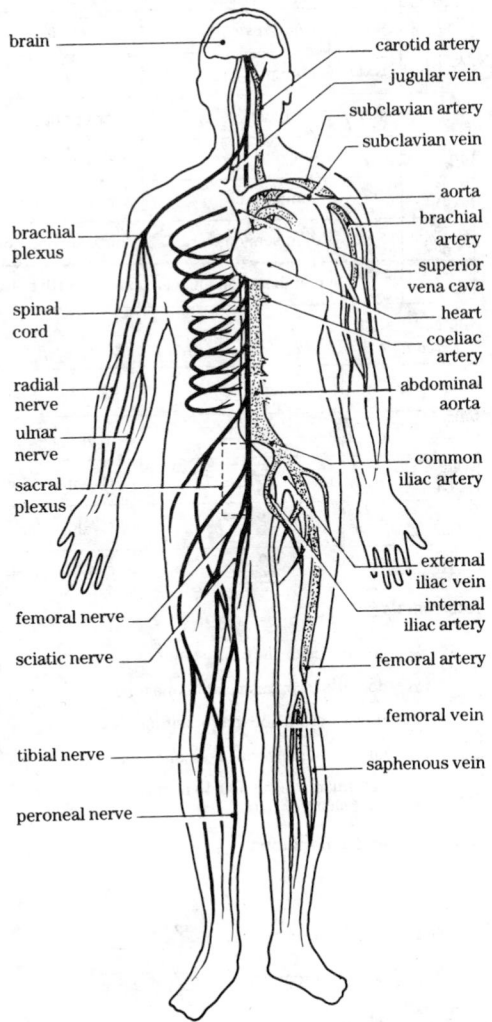

brain

brachial plexus

spinal cord

radial nerve

ulnar nerve

sacral plexus

femoral nerve

sciatic nerve

tibial nerve

peroneal nerve

carotid artery

jugular vein

subclavian artery

subclavian vein

aorta

brachial artery

superior vena cava

heart

coeliac artery

abdominal aorta

common iliac artery

external iliac vein

internal iliac artery

femoral artery

femoral vein

saphenous vein

Alimentary canal

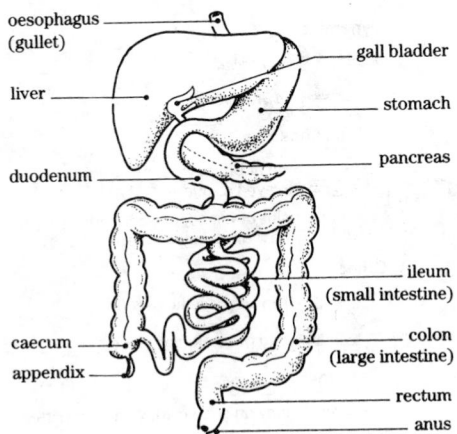

oesophagus (gullet)

liver

duodenum

caecum

appendix

gall bladder

stomach

pancreas

ileum (small intestine)

colon (large intestine)

rectum

anus

Lungs

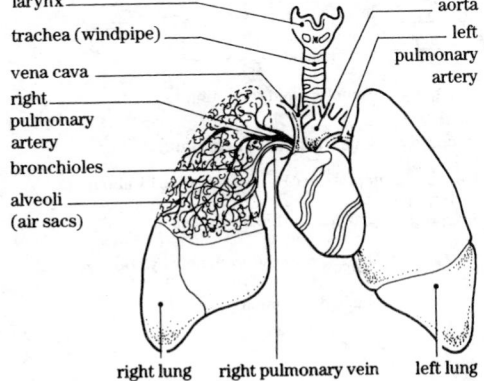

larynx

trachea (windpipe)

vena cava

right pulmonary artery

bronchioles

alveoli (air sacs)

aorta

left pulmonary artery

right lung   right pulmonary vein   left lung

MUSIC SYMBOLS, ETC.

Notes and rests

Note	Rest	British	American
𝅄	▬	breve	double-whole note
𝅝	▬	semibreve	whole note
𝅗𝅥	▬	minim	half note
𝅘𝅥	𝄽 or 𝄾	crotchet	quarter note
𝅘𝅥𝅮	𝄿	quaver	eighth note
𝅘𝅥𝅯	𝅀	semiquaver	sixteenth note
𝅘𝅥𝅰	𝅁	demisemiquaver	thirty-second note
𝅘𝅥𝅱	𝅂	hemidemisemiquaver	sixty-fourth note

Clefs

Fixed note	Position of middle C	Clef
𝄞	𝄞	G or treble clef
𝄢	𝄢	F or bass clef
𝄡	𝄡	C (soprano) clef
𝄡	𝄡	C (alto) clef
𝄡	𝄡	C (tenor) clef

Accidentals

♯   sharp; raising note one semitone

𝄪   double sharp; raising note one tone

♭   flat; lowering note one semitone

♭♭   double flat; lowering note one tone

♮   natural; restoring note to normal pitch after sharp or flat

Ornaments and decorations

acciaccatura

upper mordent; played

lower mordent; played

appoggiatura

turn; played

inverted turn; played

trill or shake

tremolo; rapid repetition

Staccato marks and signs of accentuation

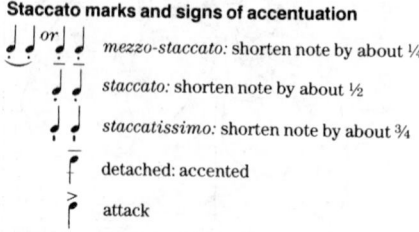

mezzo-staccato: shorten note by about ¼

staccato: shorten note by about ½

staccatissimo: shorten note by about ¾

detached: accented

attack

Time signatures

Simple duple:

$\frac{2}{2}$ or ¢   two minim beats

$\frac{2}{4}$ two crotchet beats

$\frac{2}{8}$ two quaver beats

Compound duple:

$\frac{6}{4}$ two dotted minim beats

$\frac{6}{8}$ two dotted crotchet beats

$\frac{6}{16}$ two dotted quaver beats

Simple triple:

$\frac{3}{2}$ three minim beats

$\frac{3}{4}$ three crotchet beats

$\frac{3}{8}$ three quaver beats

Compound triple:

$\frac{9}{4}$ three dotted minim beats

$\frac{9}{8}$ three dotted crotchet beats

$\frac{9}{16}$ three dotted quaver beats

Simple quadruple:

$\frac{4}{2}$ four minim beats

$\frac{4}{4}$ or C   four crotchet beats

$\frac{4}{8}$ four quaver beats

Compound quadruple:

$\frac{12}{4}$ four dotted minim beats

$\frac{12}{8}$ four dotted crotchet beats

$\frac{12}{16}$ four dotted quaver beats

Irregular rhythms

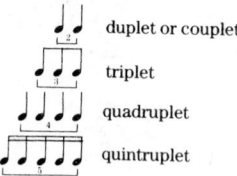

duplet or couplet

triplet

quadruplet

quintruplet

Dynamics

crescendo

diminuendo

Curved lines

tie or bind; two notes played as one

slur or legato; play smoothly (in one bow on stringed instrument)

Other

repeat preceding section

end of section or piece

⌢   pause

8^e play an octave above notes written

Range of some musical instruments

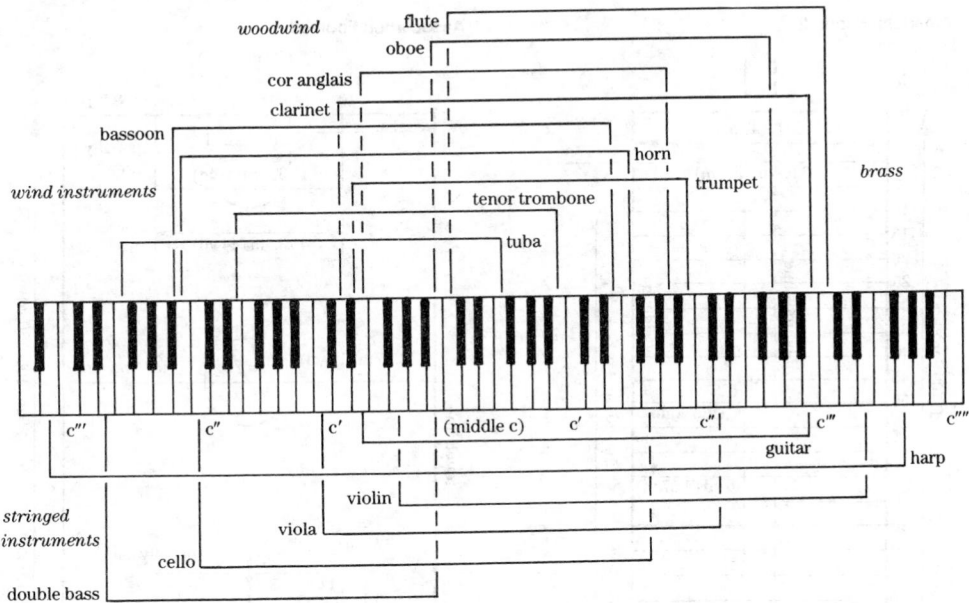

Keys and key signatures

Major key	Relative minor key	Key signature (sharp keys)	Key signature (flat keys)
C	A		
G	E		
D	B		
A	F♯		
E	C♯		
B = C♭	G♯		
F♯ = G♭	E♭		
C♯ = D♭	B♭		
A♭	F		
E♭	C		
B♭	G		
F	D		

SPORTS PITCHES (Football)

American Football

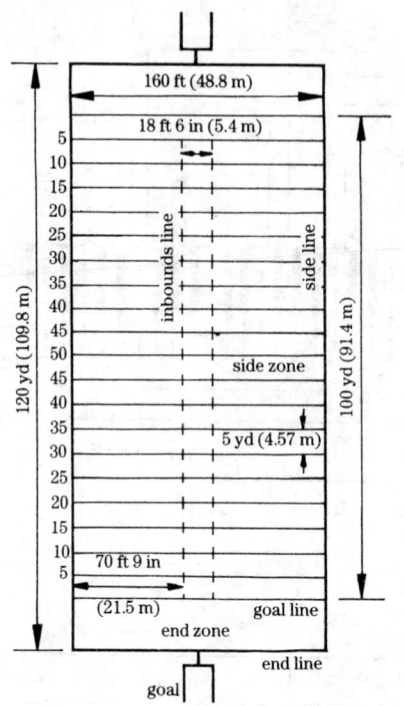

Association Football

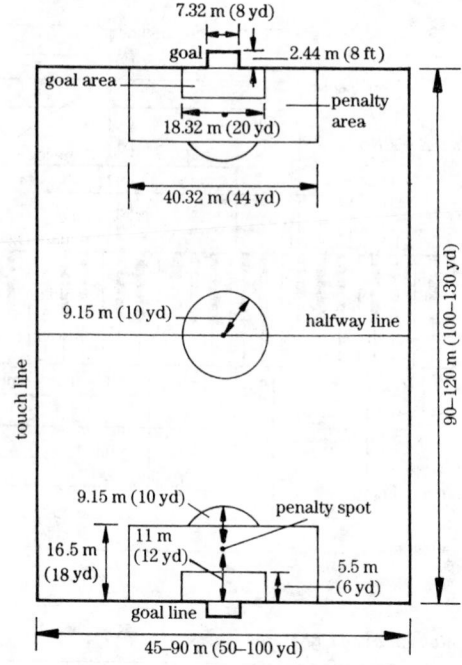

Rugby Union

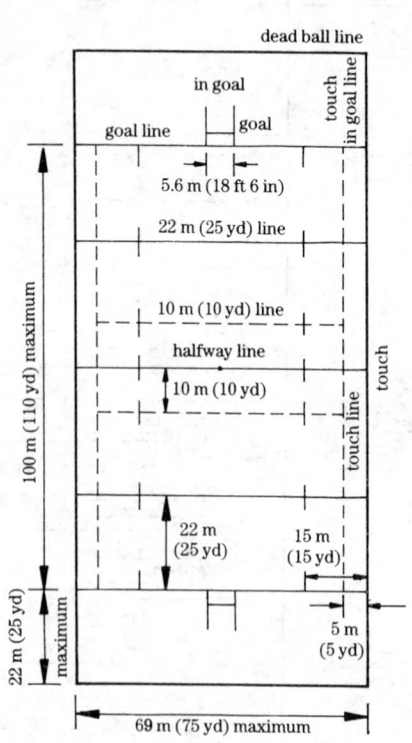

Australian Rules

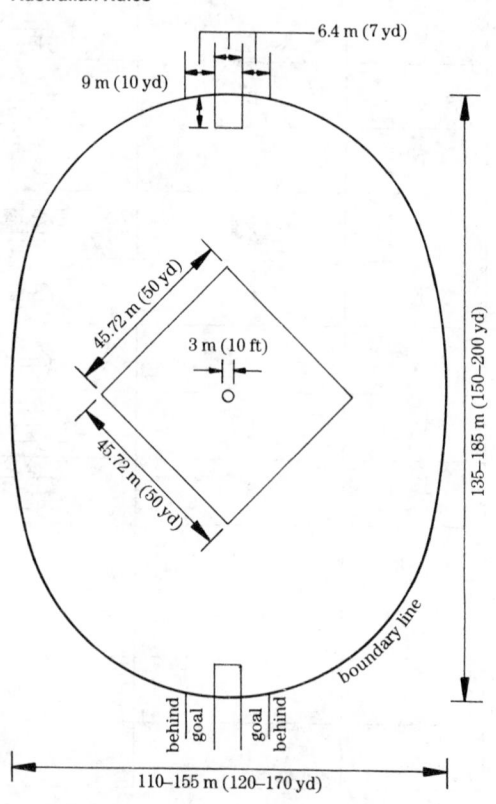

SPORTS PITCHES

Cricket; fielding positions (right-handed batsman)

Tennis

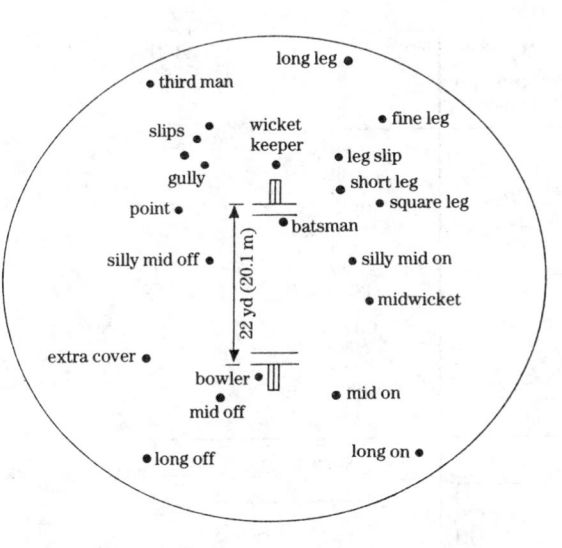

Hockey

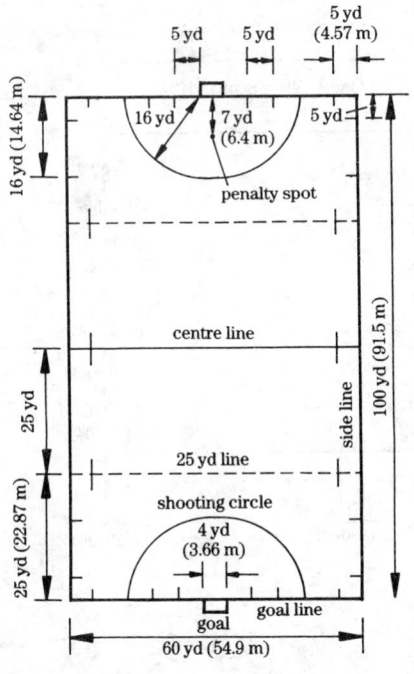

Basketball

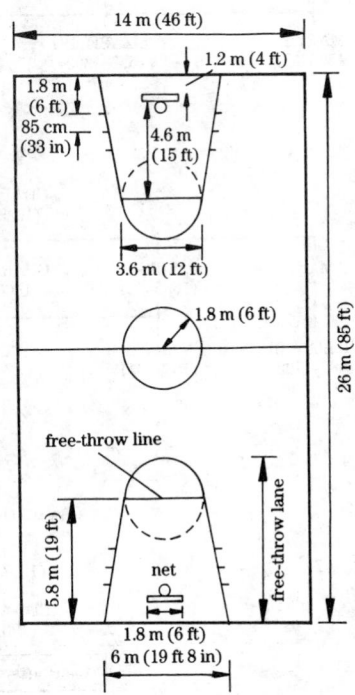

THE BRITISH MONARCHY

Kings and Queens of England

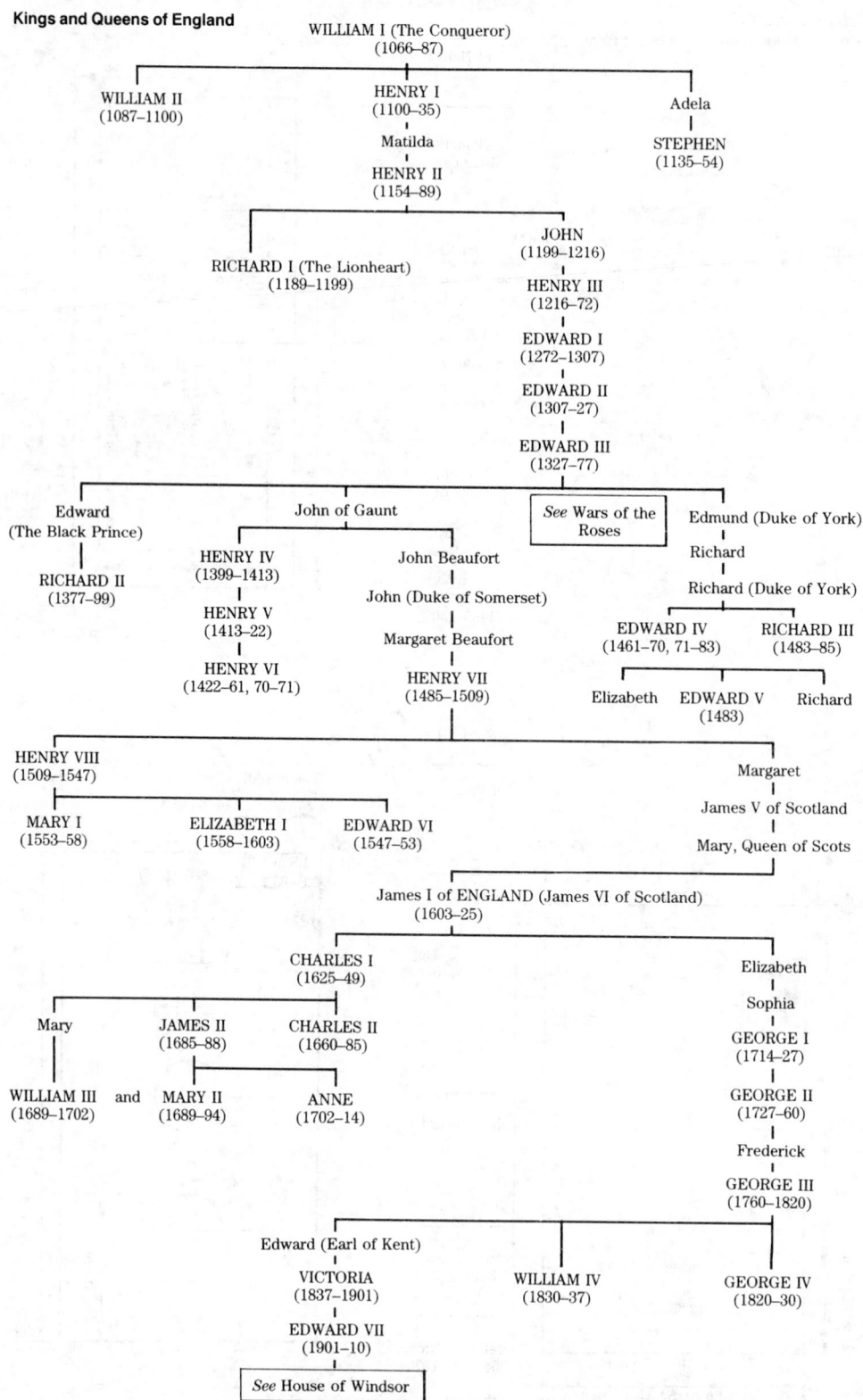

THE BRITISH MONARCHY

Wars of the Roses

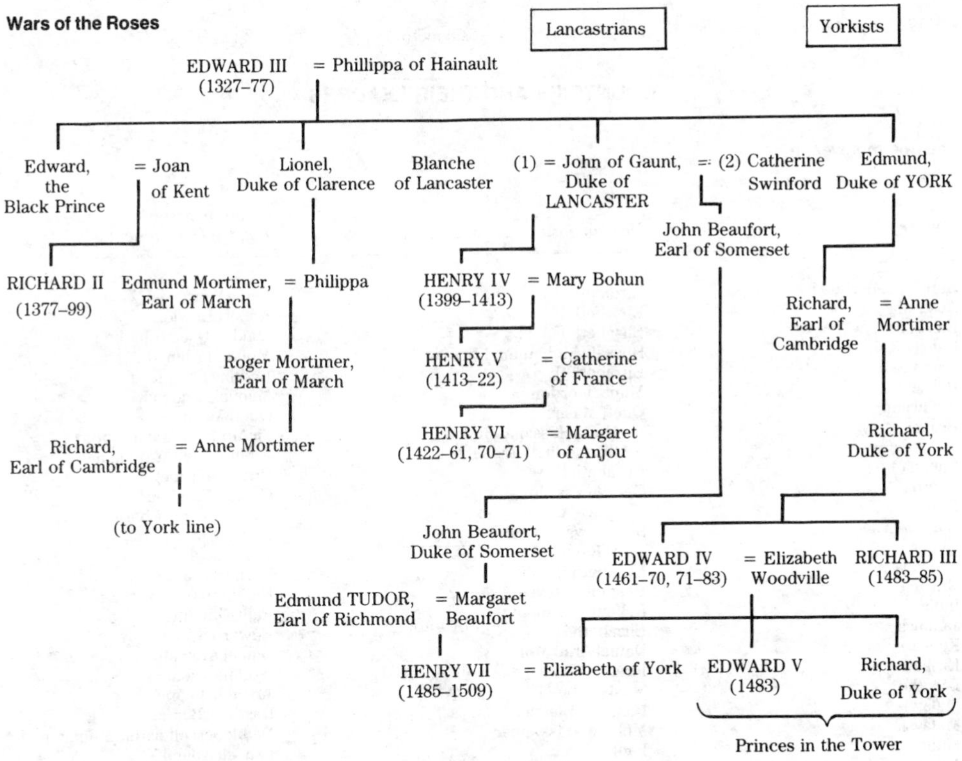

Lancastrians	Yorkists

EDWARD III = Phillippa of Hainault
(1327–77)

Edward, = Joan   Lionel,   Blanche   (1) = John of Gaunt,   = (2) Catherine   Edmund,
the   of Kent   Duke of Clarence   of Lancaster   Duke of   Swinford   Duke of YORK
Black Prince   LANCASTER
                                     John Beaufort,
                                   Earl of Somerset

RICHARD II   Edmund Mortimer, = Philippa   HENRY IV = Mary Bohun
(1377–99)   Earl of March   (1399–1413)   Richard, = Anne
                                           Earl of   Mortimer
          Roger Mortimer,   HENRY V = Catherine   Cambridge
          Earl of March   (1413–22)   of France

Richard, = Anne Mortimer   HENRY VI = Margaret   Richard,
Earl of Cambridge   (1422–61, 70–71)   of Anjou   Duke of York

(to York line)

John Beaufort,
Duke of Somerset   EDWARD IV = Elizabeth   RICHARD III
                    (1461–70, 71–83)   Woodville   (1483–85)
Edmund TUDOR, = Margaret
Earl of Richmond   Beaufort

HENRY VII = Elizabeth of York   EDWARD V   Richard,
(1485–1509)   (1483)   Duke of York

Princes in the Tower

House of Windsor

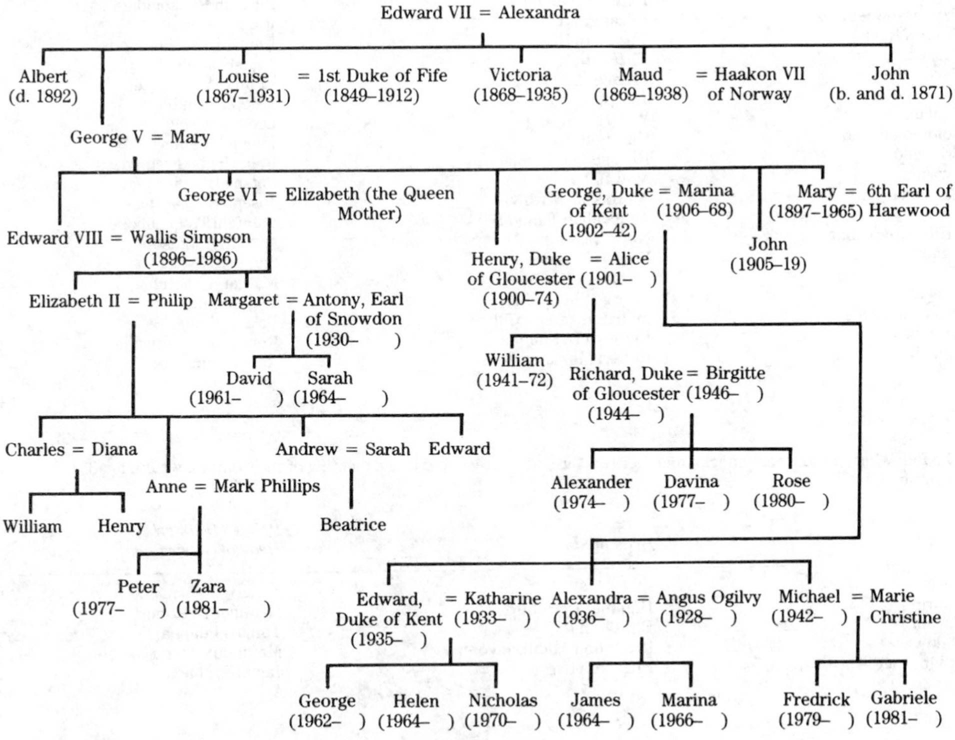

Edward VII = Alexandra

Albert   Louise = 1st Duke of Fife   Victoria   Maud = Haakon VII   John
(d. 1892)   (1867–1931)   (1849–1912)   (1868–1935)   (1869–1938)   of Norway   (b. and d. 1871)

George V = Mary

George VI = Elizabeth (the Queen   George, Duke = Marina   Mary = 6th Earl of
                 Mother)   of Kent   (1906–68)   (1897–1965) Harewood
Edward VIII = Wallis Simpson   (1902–42)
(1896–1986)   Henry, Duke = Alice   John
                     of Gloucester (1901–)   (1905–19)
Elizabeth II = Philip   Margaret = Antony, Earl   (1900–74)
                          of Snowdon
                         (1930–)
                David   Sarah   William   Richard, Duke = Birgitte
             (1961–) (1964–)   (1941–72)   of Gloucester (1946–)
Charles = Diana   Andrew = Sarah   Edward   (1944–)

               Anne = Mark Phillips
William   Henry   Beatrice   Alexander   Davina   Rose
                                                 (1974–)   (1977–)   (1980–)
         Peter   Zara
        (1977–) (1981–)   Edward,   = Katharine   Alexandra = Angus Ogilvy   Michael = Marie
                            Duke of Kent (1933–)   (1936–)   (1928–)   (1942–)   Christine
                            (1935–)

            George   Helen   Nicholas   James   Marina   Fredrick   Gabriele
           (1962–) (1964–) (1970–) (1964–) (1966–)   (1979–) (1981–)

n.b. Dates are given for those who are not entries in the text.

COUNTRIES AND THEIR LEADERS

The Commonwealth

Country	Head of State	Prime Minister/ Head of Government
Antigua & Barbuda	Elizabeth II	Vere C. Bird
Australia	Elizabeth II	Robert Hawke
Bahamas, The	Elizabeth II	Lynden Oscar Pindling
Bangladesh	Hussain Mohammed Ershad	Moudud Ahmed
Barbados	Elizabeth II	Erskine Sandiford
Belize	Minita Gordon	Manuel Esquivel
Botswana	Quett Masire	Quett Masire
Brunei	Sir Muda Hassanal Bolkia Mu'izuddin Waddaulah	Sir Muda Hassanal Bolkia Mu'izuddin Waddaulah
Canada	Elizabeth II	Brian Mulroney
Cyprus	George Vassilou	George Vassilou
Dominica	Calrence A. Seignoret	Mary Eugenia Charles
Gambia, The	Sir Dadwa Jawara	Sir Dawda Jawara
Ghana	Jerry Rawlings	Jerry Rawlings
Grenada	Elizabeth II	Herbert Blaize
Guyana	Desmond Hoyte	Hamilton Green
India	R. Venkataraman	Rajiv Gandhi
Jamaica	Elizabeth II	Edward Seaga
Kenya	Daniel Arap Moi	Daniel Arap Moi
Kiribati	Ieremia Tabai	Ieremia Tabai
Lesotho	Moshoeshoe II	Justin Lekhanya
Malawi	Hastings Banda	Hastings Banda
Malaysia	Mohmood Iskandar	Datuk Seri Mahathir Muhammed
Malta	Paul Xuerub	Fenech Adami
Mauritius	Elizabeth II	Sir Anerood Jugnauth
New Zealand	Elizabeth II	David Lange
Nigeria	Ibrahim Babangida	Ibrahim Babangida
Papua New Guinea	Elizabeth II	Rabbie Namaliu
St Kitts-Nevis	Elizabeth II	Kennedy A. Simmonds
St Lucia	Elizabeth II	John Compton
Seychelles	France -Albert Rene	France-Albert Rene
Sierra Leone	Joseph Momoh	Joseph Momoh
Singapore	Wee Kim Wee	Lee Kuan Yew
Solomon Islands	Elizabeth II	Ezekiel Alebua
Sri Lanka	Ranasinghe Premadasa	Ranasinghe Premadasa
Swaziland	Mswati III	Sotsha Dlamini
Tanzania	Ali Hassan Mwinyi	Joseph S. Warioba
Tonga	Taufa'ahan Tupou IV	Fatafehi Tu'ipelehake
Trinidad & Tobago	Noor Hassanali	A. N. R. Robinson
Uganda	Yoweri Museveni	Samson Kisekka
UK	Elizabeth II	Margaret Thatcher
Vanuatu	George Sokomanu	Walter Lini
Western Samoa	Malietoa Tanumafili	Va'ai Kolone
Zambia	Kenneth D. Kaunda	Kebby Musokotwane
Zimbabwe	Robert Mugabe	Robert Mugabe

The following countries are special members and are not represented at the meeting of the Commonwealth heads of government:

Country	Head of State	Prime Minister/ Head of Government
Nauru	Hammer DeRoburt	Hammer DeRoburt
Tuvalu	Elizabeth II	Tomasi Puapua
Maldives	Maumoon Abdul Gayoon	Maumoon Abdul Gayoon
St Vincent & The Grenadines	Elizabeth II	James Mitchell

COUNTRIES AND THEIR LEADERS

The EEC

Country	Head of State	Prime Minister/ Head of Government
Belgium	King Baudouin	Wilfried Martens
Denmark	Margrethe II	Poul Schluter
France	Francois M. Mitterrand	Michel Rocard
West Germany	Richard Von Weizsacher	Helmut Kohl
Greece	Christos Sartzetaxis	Andreas Papandreou
Ireland (Republic of)	Patrick Hillery	Charles J. Haughey
Italy	Francesco Cossiga	Ciriaco De Mita
Luxembourg	Grand Duke Jean	Jacques Santer
Netherlands	Queen Beatrix	Ruud Lubbers
Portugal	Mario Soares	Anibal Cavaco Silva
Spain	Juan Carlos I	Felipe Gonzalez Marquez
UK	Elizabeth II	Margaret Thatcher

Presidents of the United States of America

1. George Washington (F)	1789–97	
2. John Adams (F)	1797–1801	
3. Thomas Jefferson (D-R)	1801–09	
4. James Madison (D-R)	1809–17	
5. James Monroe (D-R)	1817–25	
6. John Quincy Adams (D-R)	1825–29	
7. Andrew Jackson (D)	1829–37	
8. Martin Van Buren (D)	1837–41	
9. William Henry Harrison (W)	1841	
10. John Tyler (W)	1841–45	
11. James K. Polk (D)	1845–49	
12. Zachary Taylor (W)	1849–50	
13. Millard Fillmore (W)	1850–53	
14. Franklin Pierce (D)	1853–57	
15. James Buchanan (D)	1857–61	
16. Abraham Lincoln (R)	1861–65	
17. Andrew Johnson (R)	1865–69	
18. Ulysses S. Grant (R)	1869–77	
19. Rutherford B. Hayes (R)	1877–81	
20. James A. Garfield (R)	1881	
21. Chester A. Arthur (R)	1881–85	

22. Grover Cleveland (D)	1885–89
23. Benjamin Harrison (R)	1889–93
24. Grover Cleveland (D)	1893–97
25. William McKinley (R)	1897–1901
26. Theodore Roosevelt (R)	1901–09
27. William Howard Taft (R)	1909–13
28. Woodrow Wilson (D)	1913–21
29. Warren G. Harding (R)	1921–23
30. Calvin Coolidge (R)	1923–29
31. Herbert C. Hoover (R)	1929–33
32. Franklin D. Roosevelt (D)	1933–45
33. Harry S. Trueman (D)	1945–53
34. Dwight D. Eisenhower (R)	1953–61
35. John F. Kennedy (D)	1961–63
36. Lyndon B. Johnson (D)	1963–69
37. Richard M. Nixon (R)	1969–74
38. Gerald R. Ford (R)	1974–77
39. James E. Carter, Jr. (D)	1977–81
40. Ronald W. Reagan (R)	1981–88
41. George H. W. Bush (R)	1988–

(D) Democratic; (D-R) Democratic Republican; (F) Federalist; (R) Republican; (W) Whig.

Soviet Leaders since World War II

Head of the Communist Party (1940s–1966: Title alternated between 'First Secretary' and 'General Secretary' – 1966: 'General Secretary')

Josef Stalin	Mar 1922 – Mar 1953
Georgiy Malenkov	Mar 1953
Nikita Khrushchev	Mar 1953 – Oct 1964
Leonid Brezhnev	Oct 1964 – Nov 1982
Yuri Andropov	Nov 1982 – Feb 1984
Konstantin Chernenko	Feb 1984 – Mar 1985
Mikhail Gorbachev	Mar 1985 –

Prime Minister (Chairman of the Supreme Soviet's Council of Ministers)

Josef Stalin	May 1941 – Mar 1953
Georgiy Malenkov	Mar 1953 – Feb 1955
Nikolai Bulganin	Feb 1955 – June 1958
Nikita Khrushchev	June 1958 – Oct 1964
Alexei Kosygin	Oct 1964 – Oct 1980
Nikolai Tikhonov	Oct 1980 – Sept 1985
Nikolai Ryzhkov	Sept 1985 –

(in 1930s and 1940s: 'Council of Peoples' Commissars')

POLITICAL BRITAIN
1945–1987

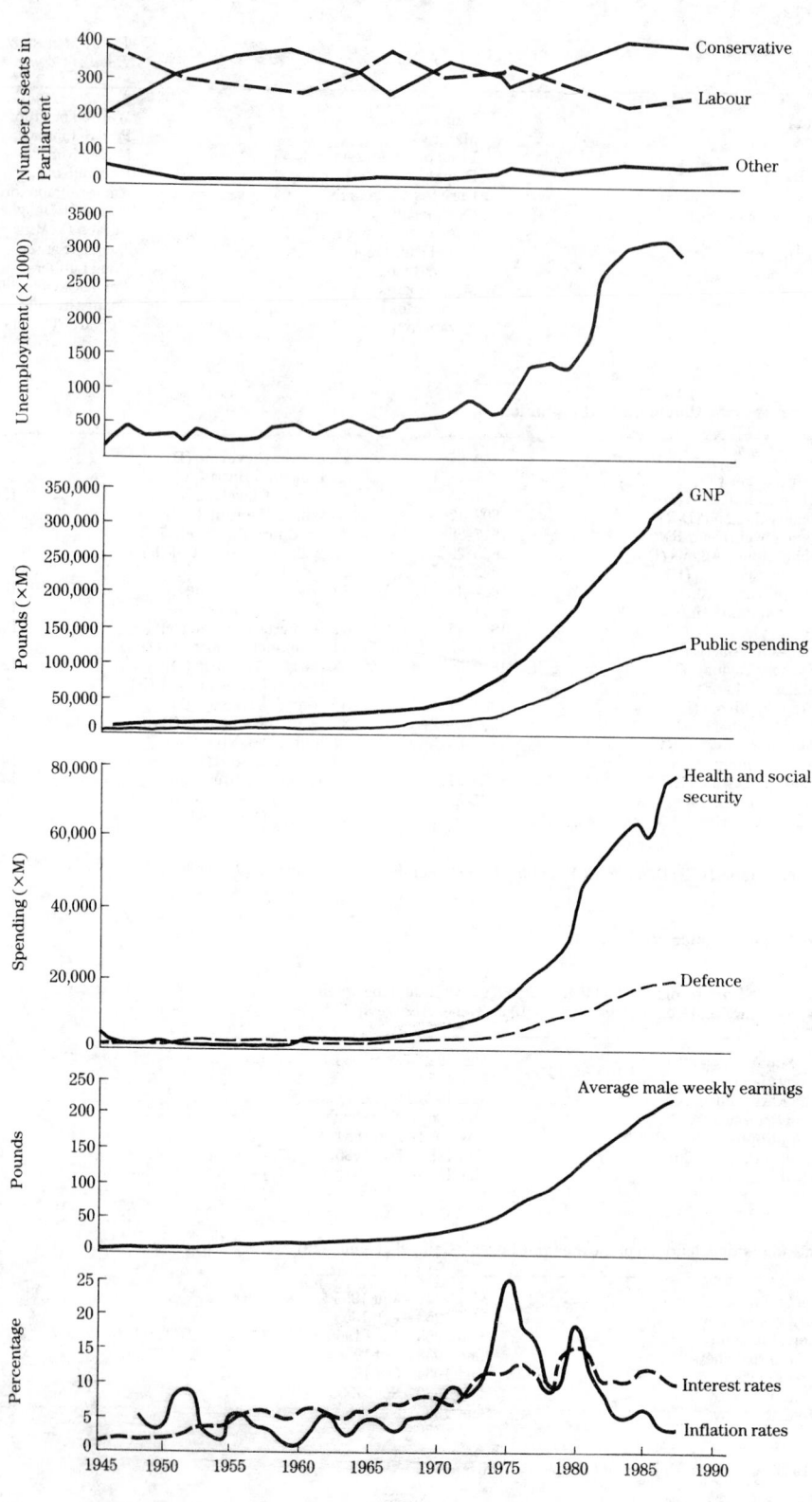

CAUSES OF DEATH IN BRITAIN
1945–1987

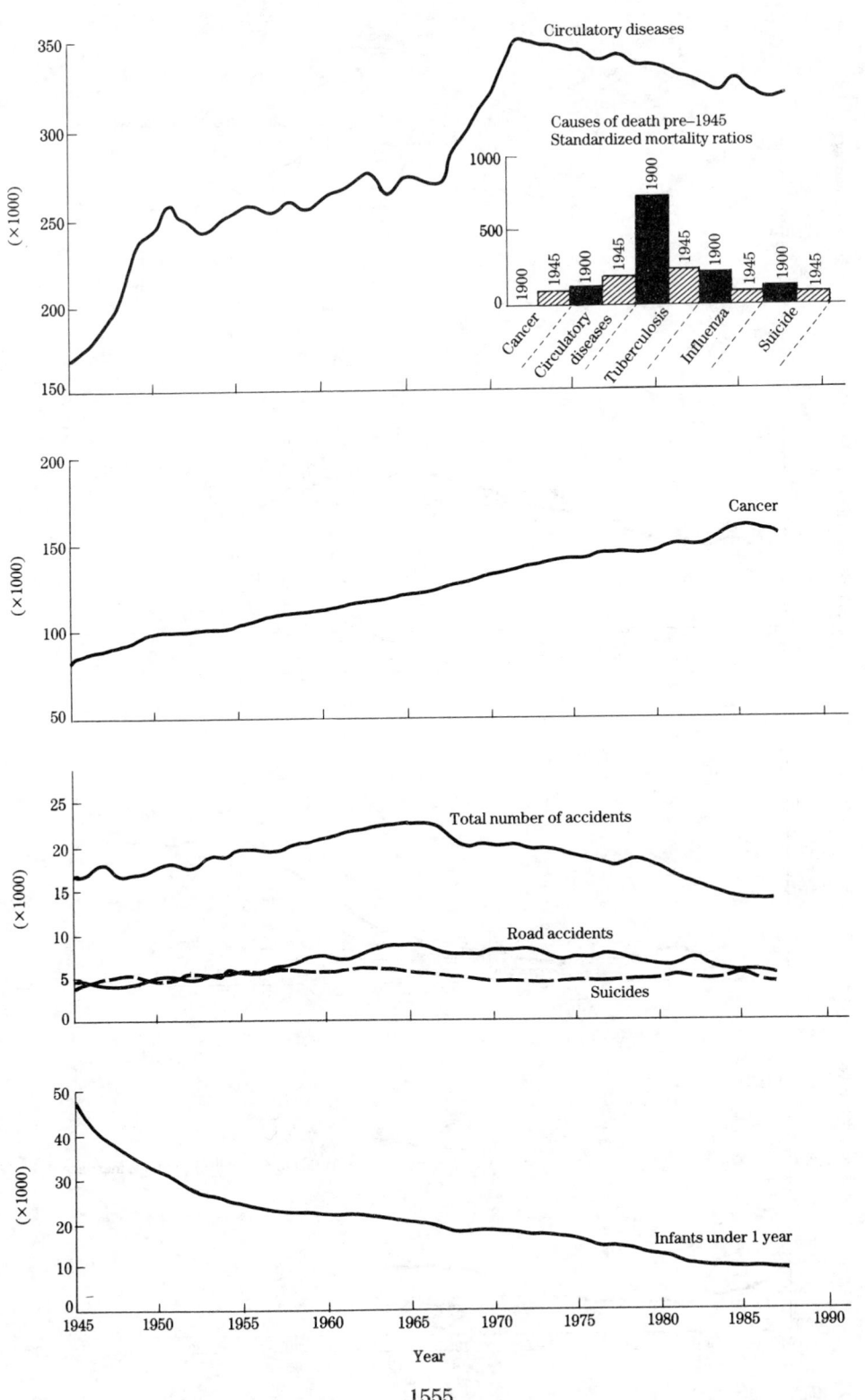

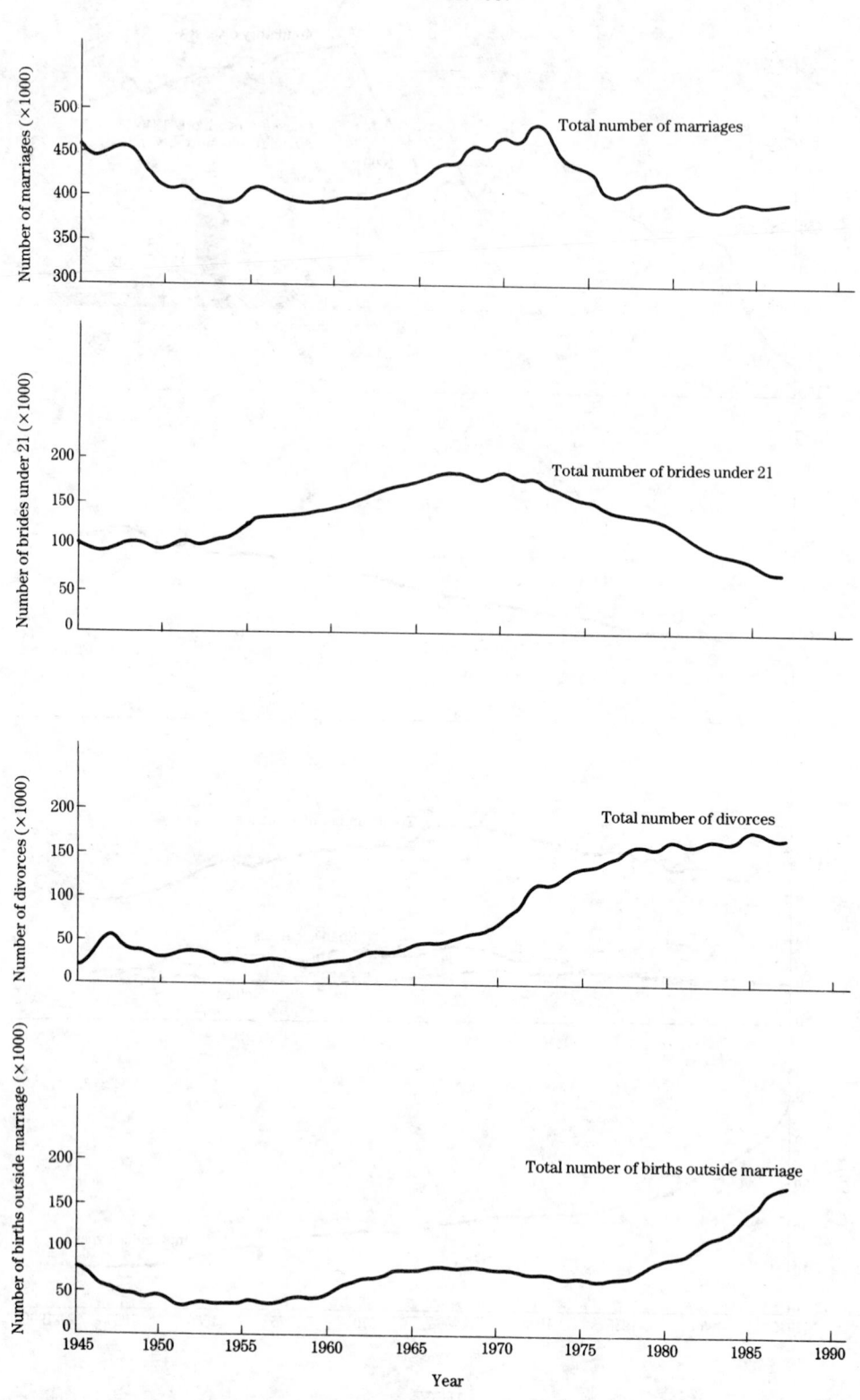

THE BRITISH FAMILY
1945–1987

Total number of marriages

Total number of brides under 21

Total number of divorces

Total number of births outside marriage

Year

THE FOUR NATIONS

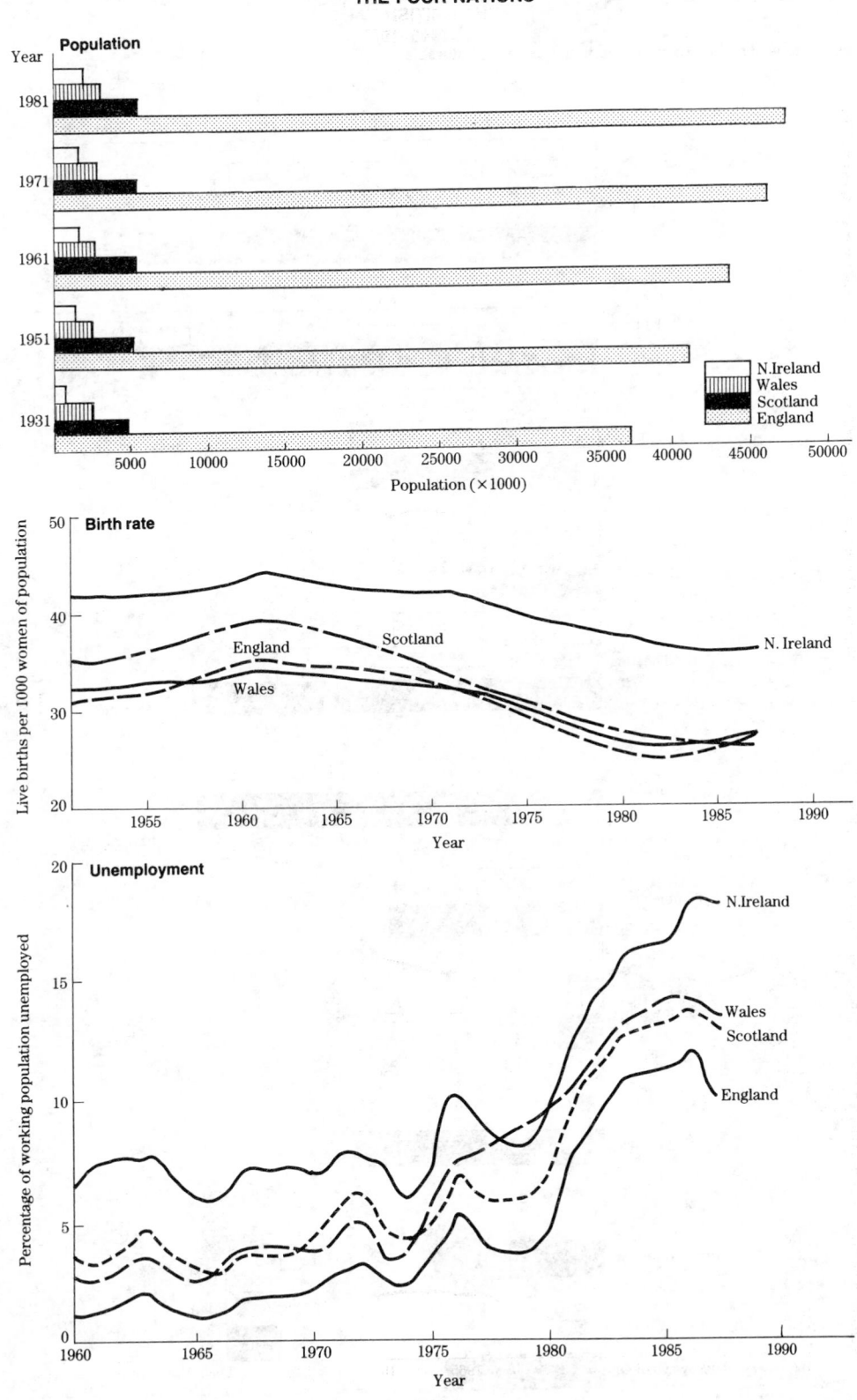

CONSUMER DURABLES

Percentage of households with particular consumer durables

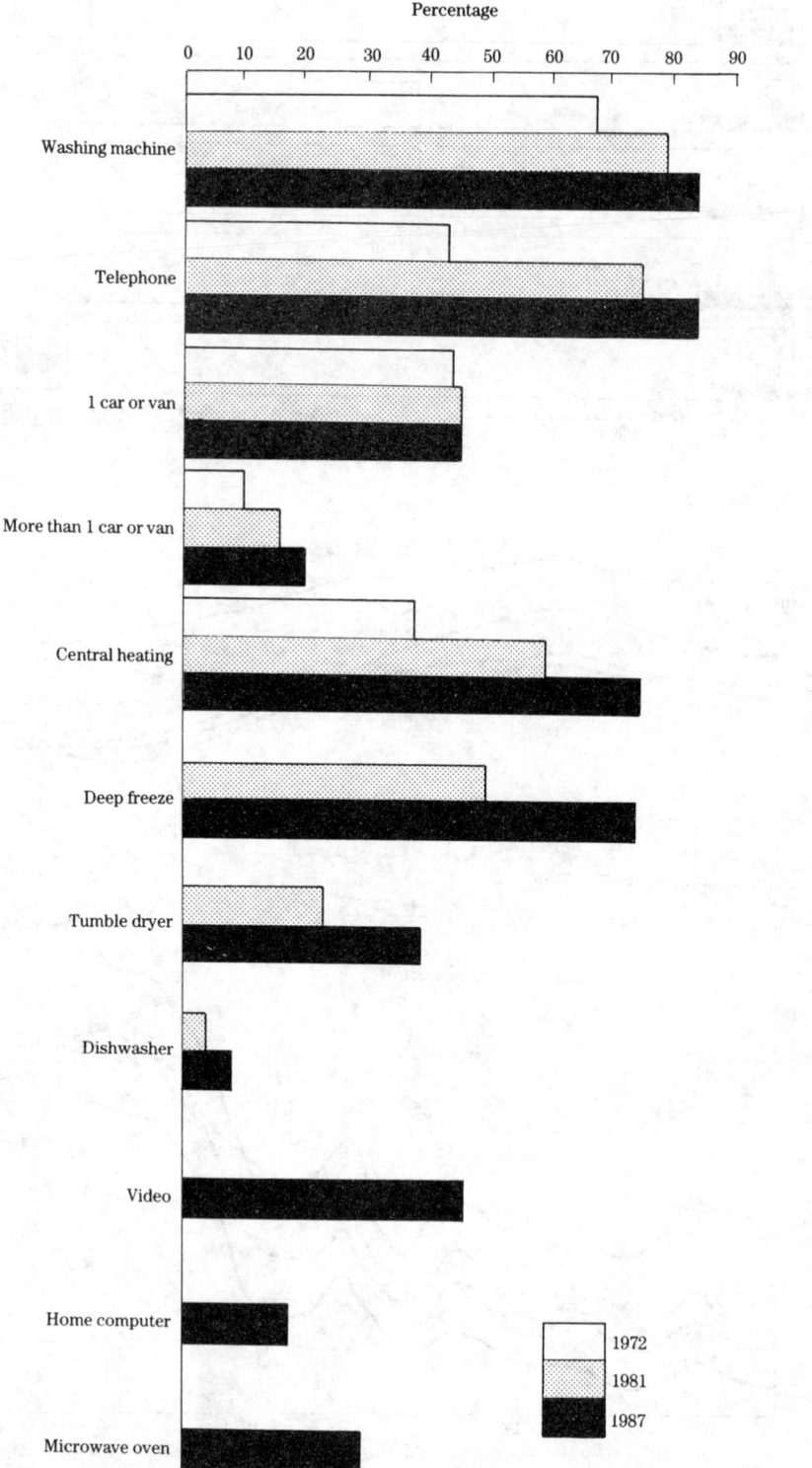

AUSTRALIA

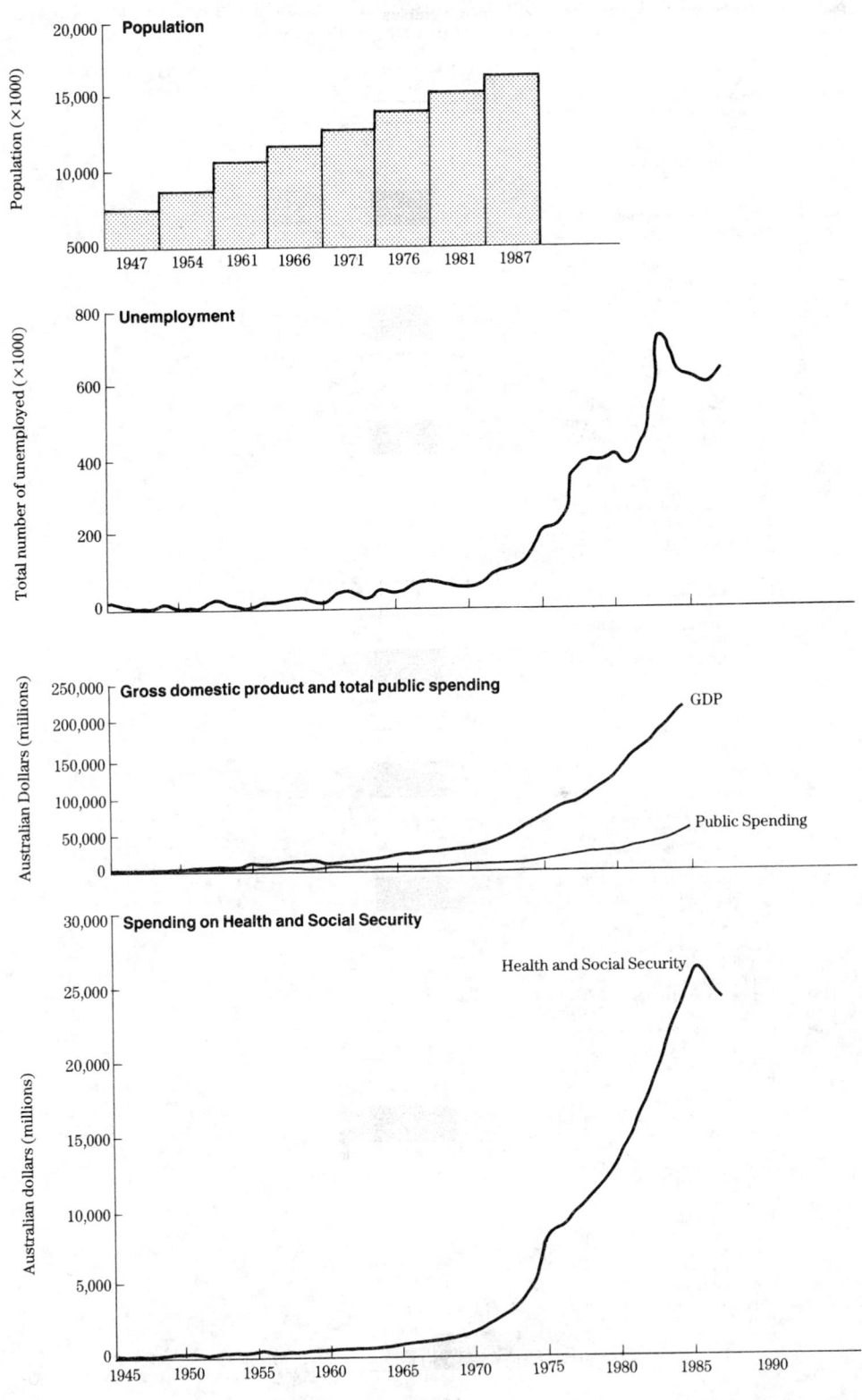

A Chronology of Events in England, Wales, Scotland, and Ireland from the Norman Conquest of England to the Present Day

	History	Arts and Learning	Science, Technology, and Exploration
1066	William, Duke of Normandy, defeated and killed Harold II of England at the battle of Hastings. **Accession of William I (the Conqueror)**		
		Norman architecture came to Britain.	
1067	First English rebellion against William I.		
1070		Work began on York Cathedral.	
1071	William I defeated Hereward the Wake; end of English resistance.		
1072	William I invaded Scotland.		
1078		Work began on the Tower of London.	
1079		Winchester Cathedral (Norman) started.	
c. 1080		Bayeux Tapestry begun.	
1086	Domesday Book compiled.		
1087	**Accession of William II (Rufus)**		
1093	Donald III (Bane) became king of Scots.		
1097	Edgar became king of Scots.		
1100	**Accession of Henry I** Henry I married Matilda, of the former Saxon royal family.		
1107	Alexander I became king of Scots.		
1114		Chichester cathedral founded.	
1120	Henry I's heir, William, drowned at sea.		
1124	David I became king of Scots.		
1127	Henry I's daughter, Matilda, recognized by the barons as heiress to the throne.		
1128		Holyrood Abbey founded.	
1132		Fountains Abbey founded.	
1135	**Accession of Stephen**		
1138	Civil war began in England; David I of Scotland defeated at the Battle of the Standard.		
1139	Matilda landed in England.		
1141	Matilda and Robert of Gloucester defeated and captured Stephen at Lincoln; Matilda defeated and Robert captured at Winchester; Robert exchanged for Stephen.		
1148	Matilda left England.		
1153	Malcolm IV became king of Scots. Treaty of Winchester established Henry of Anjou as Stephen's heir.		
1154	**Accession of Henry II**		
c. 1160		Winchester Bible begun.	
1162	Thomas à Becket became Archbishop of Canterbury.		
1165	William I (the Lion) became king of Scots.		
1166	Assize of Clarendon systematized the use of juries in royal courts.		
c. 1167		Oxford University founded.	
1170	Richard de Clare (Strongbow) landed in Ireland. Thomas à Becket murdered.		
1173	Henry II's sons rebelled.		
1174	Henry II suppressed his sons' rebellion.		
1177	Henry II's youngest son, John, appointed Lord of Ireland. Conquest of Ulster begun by John de Courcy.		

History	Arts and Learning	Science, Technology, and Exploration
1189 **Accession of Richard I (Lionheart)**		
1190 Richard I departed on the Third Crusade.		
1192 Richard I held prisoner in Germany; John attempted to seize the throne.		
1194 Richard I released.		
1199 **Accession of John**		
1204 Normandy, Maine, and Anjou conquered by France.		
1206 Stephen Langton became Archbishop of Canterbury.		
1208 Interdict imposed on England by the pope.		
1209	Cambridge University founded.	
1212 John excommunicated.		
1213 Settlement with the pope; interdict lifted.		
1214 Alexander II became king of Scots.		
1215 Barons forced John to accept Magna Carta at Runnymede; Magna Carta quashed by the pope; First Barons' War began.		
1216 **Accession of Henry III** (aged 9) Magna Carta reissued by the king.		
1217 Treaty of Kingston-upon-Thames ended the First Barons' War; Magna Carta reissued; Charter of the Forest issued.		
1220	Construction of Salisbury Cathedral began.	
1225 Magna Carta and the Charter of the Forest reissued, in their final forms.		
1227 Henry III declared himself of age.		
1242 Henry III defeated by the French at the battle of Saintes.		
1249 Alexander III became king of the Scots.		
c. 1250	Evesham Psalter produced.	
1258 Henry III forced to accept the Provisions of Oxford, which limited royal power.		
1259 Provisions of Westminster issued. Treaty of Paris recognized French possession of Normandy, Maine, Anjou, and Poitou.		
1264 Outbreak of the Second Barons' War; Simon de Montfort defeated Henry III at the battle of Lewes and became effective ruler. A parliament that included knights summoned by de Montfort.		
1265 Henry III's son, Edward, killed de Montfort at the battle of Evesham; re-establishment of royal power.		
1266 Dictum of Kenilworth offered conciliation to the rebel barons.		
1267 End of the Second Barons' War; Statute of Marlborough introduced reforms.		
1272 **Accession of Edward I**		
1274 Quo warranto inquiries began.		
1277 Edward I began the conquest of Wales.	Roger Bacon imprisoned for heresy.	
1282 Llywelyn ap Gruffudd, Prince of Wales, killed.		
1283 Dafydd ap Gruffudd, brother of Llywelyn, executed.		
1284 Statute of Rhuddlan established English government over Wales.		
1286 Margaret became queen of Scots.		

History	Arts and Learning	Science, Technology, and Exploration
1290 Statutes Quia Emptores and Quo Warranto issued. Edward I expelled the Jews from England. Margaret of Scots died; Scots throne vacant.		
1291	Nave of York Minster erected.	
1292 John de Baliol became king of Scots by the adjudication of Edward I; English overlordship of Scotland confirmed.		
1294 War began between England and France over Gascony.		
1295 Model Parliament summoned.		
1296 Edward I declared John de Baliol deposed; Scots defeated by Edward I at Dunbar; Scots throne vacant.		
1297 Scots, led by William Wallace, defeated the English at Stirling Bridge. Political crisis in England; Magna Carta and the Charter of the Forest reissued.		
1298 Edward I defeated Wallace at Falkirk.		
1300 Magna Carta and the Charter of the Forest reissued.		
1303 Peace between England and France.		
1305 Wallace captured and executed.		
1306 Robert I (the Bruce) became king of Scots.		
1307 English defeated by Robert I at Loudun Hill.		
Accession of Edward II		
1310 Ordainers appointed.		
1311 The Ordinances limited royal power.		
1312 Piers Gaveston, Edward II's favourite, killed by barons.		
1314 Robert I defeated Edward II at Bannockburn.		
1315 Thomas, Earl of Lancaster, gained control of the English government.		
1316 Robert I's brother, Edward, became high king of Ireland.		
1318 Edward II regained power in England. Edward Bruce defeated in Ireland.		
1321 The Elder and Younger Despensers, Edward II's favourites, banished.		
1322 Thomas of Lancaster executed; Ordinances repealed and the Despensers recalled.		
1325 Queen Isabella went to France.		
1326 Isabella returned with Roger de Mortimer; the Despensers executed and Edward II imprisoned.		
1327 Edward II deposed. **Accession of Edward III** (aged 14) Edward II murdered; Isabella and de Mortimer assumed control.		
1328 England recognized the independence of Scotland by the Treaty of Edinburgh.		
1329 David II became king of Scots.		
1330 Edward III seized power; de Mortimer executed.		
1332 Edward de Baliol crowned king of Scots.		
1333 Edward III recognized Edward de Baliol as king of Scots.		
1334 David II exiled in France.		

	History	Arts and Learning	Science, Technology, and Exploration
1337	Hundred Years' War began between England and France.		
1340	English navy victorious over the French at Sluys.		
1341	David II returned to Scotland. Political crisis in England.		
1346	English defeated the French at Crécy. Scots defeated by the English at Neville's Cross; David II captured.		
1347	Calais captured by the English.		
1348	Order of the Garter founded.		
1349	England devastated by the Black Death.		
1351	Statutes of Labourers and Provisors issued.		
1352	Statute of Treasons issued.		
1353	First statute of Praemunire issued.		
1356	Edward de Baliol surrendered to Edward III his claim to the Scots throne. Edward, the Black Prince, defeated the French at Poitiers; John II of France captured.		
1357	David II released.		
1360	Peace between England and France by the Treaty of Brétigny.		
1362	Prince Edward became prince of Aquitaine. Commons gained full control of lay taxation.		
c. 1362		*Piers Plowman* written by William Langland.	
1369	Hundred Years' War resumed.		
1371	Robert II became the first Stuart Scottish king.		
1376	Good Parliament attacked royal maladministration; several of the king's associates impeached.		
1377	**Accession of Richard II**	First Papal condemnation of John Wycliffe.	
1381	Peasants' Revolt suppressed.		
1382		Wycliffites purged from Oxford University.	
1384		John Wycliffe died.	
1386	Parliament impeached the chancellor and restricted royal power for one year.		
1388	Merciless Parliament impeached the king's friends. Scots defeated the English at Otterburn.		
1390	Robert III became king of Scots.		
c. 1390		Chaucer finished writing *The Canterbury Tales*.	
1394	Richard II subdued the Irish lords.		
1396	Treaty of Paris established a truce between England and France.		
1397	Richard II began to destroy his enemies.		
1398	Henry Bolingbroke banished by Richard II.		
1399	Richard deposed by Bolingbroke, who became king. **Accession of Henry IV**		
1400	Richard II died in prison. Welsh uprising led by Owen Glendower began.	(c.) Wilton Diptych painted.	
1401	Statute De Heretico Comburendo enabled the burning of heretics.		
1402	English defeated by Glendower at Pilleth.		
1403	Henry IV defeated the rebel Percy family at Shrewsbury.		

History	Arts and Learning	Science, Technology, and Exploration
1404 Royal financial crisis in England. Glendower captured Harlech and Aberystwyth.		
1405 Second Percy rebellion defeated.		
1406 James I became king of Scots, shortly after being captured by the English; Duke of Albany became governor of Scotland. Royal financial crisis in England; parliament imposed reforms.		
1408 Percy incursion from Scotland defeated. Henry, Prince of Wales, recaptured Aberystwyth.		
1409 Prince Henry recaptured Harlech; effective end of Glendower's rebellion.	Archbishop Arundel began a campaign against Lollardy at Oxford University.	
1410 Prince Henry gained control of the royal council.		
1411 Breach between Henry IV and Prince Henry.		
1412 Campaign in France by Prince Thomas.	St Andrews University founded.	
1413 **Accession of Henry V**		
1414 Suppression of Sir John Oldcastle's Lollard uprising.		
1415 English victory over the French at Agincourt.		
1417 Henry V began the conquest of Normandy.		
1420 Treaty of Troyes made Henry V heir to the French throne.		
1422 **Accession of Henry VI** (in infancy) Government by the council, headed by John, Duke of Bedford, and Humphrey, Duke of Gloucester. Henry VI succeeded to the throne of France, on the death of Charles VI.		
1424 James I of Scots released.		
1437 James II became king of Scots. Henry VI declared of age.		
1445 Henry VI married Margaret of Anjou.		
1450 The Duke of Suffolk, Henry VI's favourite, impeached and murdered. Cade's rebellion suppressed. Richard, Duke of York, failed to secure the removal of Edmund, Duke of Somerset, and other courtiers.		
1451	Glasgow University founded.	
1452 Richard of York marched on London.		
1453 Hundred Years' War ended with the French victory over the English at Castillon.		
1454 Richard of York temporarily became protector, during Henry VI's insanity.		
1455 Outbreak of the Wars of the Roses; Richard of York defeated the royalists (Lancastrians) at St Albans, where Somerset was killed.		
1459 Yorkist victory at Blore Heath negated by the royalist victory at Ludford Bridge; Richard of York fled to Ireland.		
1460 James III became king of Scots. Richard of York captured Henry VI at the battle of Northampton; York claimed the throne; York defeated and killed at the battle of Wakefield.	Winchester cathedral completed.	

History	Arts and Learning	Science, Technology, and Exploration
1461 Henry VI freed by the Lancastrian victory at St Albans; following the Yorkist victory at Mortimer's Cross, Edward, Duke of York, deposed Henry VI and seized the throne. **Accession of Edward IV** Lancastrians routed at the battle of Towton; Henry VI and Queen Margaret fled to Scotland.		
1464 Yorkists defeated the Lancastrians at Hedgeley Moor and Hexham.		
1465 Henry VI imprisoned in the Tower of London.		
1470 Richard, Earl of Warwick, switched allegiance to the Lancastrians; Henry VI restored to the throne.		
1471 Edward IV defeated and killed the Earl of Warwick at the battle of Barnet; Lancastrians finally defeated at the battle of Tewkesbury; Henry VI killed.		
?1475	First book printed in English, by William Caxton in Bruges.	
?1477	Caxton established the first printing press in England, at Westminster.	
1478 Edward IV's brother George, Duke of Clarence, executed.		
1482 Duke of Albany recognized as king of Scots by the English.		
1483 **Accession of Edward V** (aged 12) Edward V's uncle Richard, Duke of Gloucester, became protector; Richard declared Edward V illegitimate and himself the rightful king. **Accession of Richard III** Edward V and his brother Richard, Duke of York, disappeared: presumed killed by order of Richard III. Albany's uprising crushed by James III of Scots.		
1485 Richard III defeated and killed by Henry Tudor, the Lancastrian claimant to the throne, at the battle of Bosworth; end of the Wars of the Roses. **Accession of Henry VII**		
1487 Lambert Simnel's rebellion defeated at the battle of Stoke.		
1488 James III of Scots killed by rebels led by his son, who became James IV of Scots.		
1491 Perkin Warbeck, impersonating Edward V's brother Richard, claimed the throne.		
1494 Poynings' law subordinated the Irish parliament to the English parliament.	King's College, Aberdeen, founded by Bishop Elphinstone.	
1497 Warbeck captured after an abortive invasion of southwest England.		John Cabot landed in North America.
1499 Warbeck executed.		
1501 Arthur, Prince of Wales, married Catherine of Aragon.		
1502 Prince Arthur died.		
1503	William Dunbar wrote *The Thrissil and the Rois.*	
1509 **Accession of Henry VIII** Henry VIII married Catherine of Aragon.		

	History	Arts and Learning	Science, Technology, and Exploration
1513	French defeated by Henry VIII at the battle of the Spurs. Scots invasion of England defeated at Flodden and James IV killed; James V became king of Scots.		
1514		Construction of Hampton Court Palace began.	
1515	Thomas Wolsey appointed chancellor. Duke of Albany became regent of Scotland.		
1516		Thomas More's *Utopia* published.	
1518			Royal College of Physicians founded by Thomas Linacre.
1525		William Tyndale, in Cologne, started his translation of the New Testament into English.	
1527		Hans Holbein became resident in England.	
1529	Wolsey failed to secure papal annulment of Henry VIII's marriage to Catherine of Aragon, and was replaced as chancellor by Sir Thomas More.		
1532	Sir Thomas More resigned as chancellor.		
1533	Henry VIII secretly married Anne Boleyn. Thomas Cranmer became Archbishop of Canterbury; Cranmer annulled Henry VIII's marriage to Catherine of Aragon.		
1534	First Act of Supremacy established Henry VIII, instead of the pope, as head of the Church of England.		
1535	Sir Thomas More executed.		
1536	Anne Boleyn executed; Henry VIII married Jane Seymour. Ten Articles issued; smaller monasteries dissolved. Act of Union between England and Wales passed. Pilgrimage of Grace began.		
1537	Jane Seymour died. Dissolution of the larger monasteries began. Pilgrimage of Grace suppressed.		
1538	Henry VIII excommunicated by the pope.		
1540	Henry VIII married and divorced Anne of Cleves; Henry VIII married Catherine Howard. Thomas Cromwell executed. Six Articles issued; English Bible placed in churches; dissolution of the monasteries completed.		United Company of Barber-Surgeons founded.
1542	Catherine Howard executed. Mary became Queen of Scots (in infancy); Earl of Arran became governor of Scotland.		
1543	Henry VIII married Catherine Parr.		
1547	**Accession of Edward VI** (aged 9) Edward Seymour, Duke of Somerset, became protector. John Knox exiled from Scotland.		
1548	Mary Queen of Scots sent to France.		
1549	Duke of Somerset imprisoned by the Earl of Warwick (later Duke of Northumberland). First Book of Common Prayer issued.		
1552	Duke of Somerset executed. Second Book of Common Prayer issued.		

	History	Arts and Learning	Science, Technology, and Exploration
1553	Forty-Two Articles issued. Lady Jane Grey proclaimed queen by the Duke of Northumberland on the death of Edward VI, but within nine days Princess Mary secured the throne. **Accession of Mary I** Duke of Northumberland executed. Reversal of the Reformation began.		
1554	Wyatt's rebellion suppressed. Lady Jane Grey executed. Church of England reconciled with Rome. Mary I married Philip of Spain (later Philip II). Mary of Guise became governor of Scotland.		
1555	Bishops Ridley and Latimer burnt at the stake.		
1556	Archbishop Cranmer burnt at the stake.		
1557	War between England and France began.		
1558	French captured Calais, England's last possession in France. **Accession of Elizabeth I** William Cecil became secretary of state.		
1559	Protestantism re-established in England. John Knox returned to Scotland.		
1560	Mary of Guise died; Treaty of Edinburgh led to the withdrawal of French and English forces from Scotland. Reformed Calvinist church adopted by the Scottish parliament.		
1561	Mary Queen of Scots returned to Scotland.		
1562			John Hawkins made his first voyage to the New World, initiating a trade in slaves between West Africa and the West Indies.
1563	Thirty-Nine Articles issued.		
1565	Mary Queen of Scots married Lord Darnley. Uprising led by the Earl of Moray suppressed.		
1566	Mary Queen of Scots's secretary, David Rizzio, murdered by Darnley.		
1567	Darnley murdered; Mary Queen of Scots married the Earl of Bothwell; Mary imprisoned and forced to abdicate; James VI became king of Scots; Earl of Moray became regent.		
1568	Mary Queen of Scots fled to England, where she was imprisoned by Elizabeth I. Protestant colonization of Ireland began.		
1569	The northern rebellion started.		
1570	Northern rebellion suppressed. Elizabeth I excommunicated by the pope. Earl of Lennox became regent of Scotland.		
1571	Ridolfi plot exposed. Earl of Mar became regent of Scotland.		
1572	William Cecil became lord treasurer. Earl of Morton became regent of Scotland.	Society of Antiquaries founded.	
1573	Sir Francis Walsingham became secretary of state.		

	History	Arts and Learning	Science, Technology, and Exploration
1576		Richard Burbage opened 'The Theatre' in Shoreditch.	Frobisher made the first attempt to discover the Northwest Passage.
1578		Holinshed's *Chronicle* published.	
1579	Desmond's revolt in Ireland began.	Spenser's *Shepheards Calender* published.	
1580	Jesuit mission sent to England.		Circumnavigation of the world by Drake.
1581	Edmund Campion, a Jesuit, executed.		Magnetic dip reported by Norman.
1582	James VI captured in the Ruthven raid.		
1583	James VI escaped.	Edinburgh University founded.	
1585	Spain started preparations for an invasion of England.		John Davis discovered the Davis Strait.
1586	Babington plot exposed.	Camden wrote *Britannia*.	
1587	Mary Queen of Scots executed. Drake attacked Cádiz.	Marlowe wrote *Tamburlaine the Great*.	
1588	Spanish Armada defeated.	Marlowe's *Doctor Faustus* published. Bible translated into Welsh by William Morgan. 'Psalms, Sonets and Songs of Sadnes and Pietie' written by William Byrd.	
1589			Richard Hakluyt's *The Principle Navigations and Discoveries of the English Nation* published.
1590		Trinity College, Dublin, founded. Books 1–3 of Spenser's *Faerie Queene* published.	
1592		Shakespeare's first great plays – *Henry VI, Parts I–III* and *Richard III* – completed. Dublin University founded.	
1593	Conventicle Act passed.		
1595	O'Neill's revolt in Ulster began.		
1596	Cádiz sacked by the English. Sir Robert Cecil became secretary of state.	Books 4–6 of Spenser's *Faerie Queene* published.	
1597		Francis Bacon published his first *Essays*.	Gerard's *Herball* published.
1599		Globe Theatre, London, constructed.	
1600		Shakespeare started work on the major tragedies.	East India Company founded.
1601	Earl of Essex's rebellion suppressed. Poor Law Act passed. Spanish force landed at Kinsale.		
1602		Bodleian Library founded in Oxford.	
1603	O'Neill revolt suppressed. **Accession of James I**		
1604	Hampton Court Conference rejected the Puritans' demands. Peace between England and Spain.		
1605	Gunpowder Plot exposed.	Bacon's *Advancement of Learning* published.	
1606		Jonson's *Volpone* published.	
1607	Plantation of Ulster began.	George Chapman's *Bussy d'Amboise* published.	Settlement of Virginia, by the Virginia Company.
1609			Henry Hudson sailed down the Hudson River.
1610	Great Contract proposed.		Henry Hudson discovered Hudson's Bay.
1611	Great Contract rejected. Authorized Version of the Bible issued.	Thomas Middleton's *The Roaring Girl* and Shakespeare's last play, *The Tempest*, published.	
1612		First set of 'Madrigals and Motets' by Orlando Gibbons.	
1614		Raleigh wrote *The History of the World*. Jonson's *Bartholomew Fayre* and Webster's *The Duchess of Malfi* published.	Napier introduced the concept of logarithms.

History	Arts and Learning	Science, Technology, and Exploration
1615 Overbury scandal exposed.	Chapman's translation of Homer's *Odyssey* completed.	
1616 Duke of Somerset, James I's favourite, imprisoned.	Thomas Middleton's *The Witch* published. Inigo Jones began work on Queen's House, Greenwich.	
1618 Sir Walter Raleigh executed.		
1619	Dulwich College founded. *Fitzwilliam Virginal Book* compiled. Work started on Inigo Jones' Banqueting House, Whitehall.	
1620		Pilgrim Fathers left Plymouth for North America. First Scottish settlement of Nova Scotia.
1622		Slide rule invented by Oughtred.
1625 **Accession of Charles I** Act of Revocation passed in Scotland.		
1626 Parliament refused to grant taxation; Charles I collected a forced loan. Duke of Buckingham, Charles I's favourite, impeached.		
1628 Duke of Buckingham assassinated.		Harvey's discovery of the circulation of blood published.
1629 Parliament dissolved: it did not reassemble for 11 years.	Van Dyck appointed court painter.	
1633 William Laud became Archbishop of Canterbury.	Posthumous publication of Donne's poems.	
1634 Charles I began to levy Ship Money.	Milton's *Comus* published.	
1637 Riot in Scotland against the new prayer book.		
1638 National Covenant drawn up in Scotland.		
1639 Peaceful settlement of First Bishops' War in Scotland.		
1640 Short Parliament summoned and dissolved; treaty of Ripon ended Second Bishops' War in Scotland; Long Parliament summoned.		
1641 Execution of the Earl of Strafford; Parliament attacked the royal prerogative and issued the Grand Remonstrance. Irish rebellion began.		
1642 Attempted arrest of five MPs by Charles I; Charles I raised his standard at Nottingham, marking the start of the Civil War; inconclusive battle of Edgehill.	Theatres closed by decree.	
1643 Royalist victories at Adwalton Moor and Roundway Down; inconclusive battle of Newbury; Solemn League and Covenant formed between the Long Parliament and the Scottish Covenanters. Excise tax introduced.		
1644 Parliamentary victory at Marston Moor; Royalist victory at Lostwithiel; inconclusive battle of Newbury.		
1645 New Model Army formed; Parliamentary victories at Naseby, Langport, and Philiphaugh; Laud executed; use of the Book of Common Prayer banned.		
1646 Charles I surrendered to the Scots.		

History	Arts and Learning	Science, Technology, and Exploration
1647 Scots handed Charles I over to the English; constitutional debate in England; Charles escaped and allied with the Scots.		
1648 Parliamentary victory over the Scots at Preston; Long Parliament purged, to form the Rump. George Fox founded the Quakers.		
1649 Charles I tried and executed; monarchy abolished and a Commonwealth declared. Oliver Cromwell ordered massacres in Ireland, at Drogheda and Wexford.		
1650 Cromwell defeated the Scots at Dunbar.		
1651 Charles II crowned at Scone, but defeated by Cromwell at Worcester; Charles II exiled on the Continent. Navigation Act passed.	Hobbes's *Leviathan* published.	
1653 Rump dismissed by Cromwell; Barebones Parliament summoned and dissolved; Instrument of Government established the Protectorate, with Cromwell as lord protector. Royalist uprising in Scotland began.	Izaak Walton's *Compleat Angler* published.	
1654 Royal rising in Scotland suppressed.		
1655 Penruddock's rising suppressed; rule by major generals imposed.		Wallis's *Arithmetica Infinitorum* published.
1656 End of rule by major generals.		
1657 Cromwell refused to become king.		
1658 Cromwell died; his son, Richard, became lord protector.		
1659 Rump Parliament recalled; Richard Cromwell dismissed; Commonwealth re-established.		
1660 Long Parliament restored; Charles II restored. **Accession of Charles II** Lord Hyde (later the Earl of Clarendon) became lord chancellor.	Samuel Pepys began his diary.	
1661 Clarendon Code introduced; Cavalier Parliament summoned.		Boyle's *The Sceptical Chymist* published. Royal Society received a charter.
1662 Book of Common Prayer published.		Boyle's law published.
1663	Theatre Royal, Drury Lane, opened.	
1664 Great Plague began.	Wren started construction of the Sheldonian Theatre, Oxford.	
1665 Great Plague ravaged London.		Hooke's *Micrographica* published. First English scientific journal established.
1666 Great Fire of London. Pentland rising in Scotland suppressed.		
1667 Dutch raided the Thames. Earl of Clarendon dismissed; the Cabal became prominent.	Milton's *Paradise Lost* published.	
1668		First reflecting telescope made by Newton.
1670 By the secret treaty of Dover with France, Charles II promised to declare himself a Catholic.	Dryden appointed poet laureate; Blow became organist at Westminster Abbey.	Formation of Hudson's Bay Company.
1671	Milton's *Paradise Regained* published.	
1672 Declaration of Indulgence issued by Charles II.		

History	Arts and Learning	Science, Technology, and Exploration
1673 Declaration of Indulgence withdrawn; Test Act passed. Fall of the Cabal; Earl of Danby became lord treasurer.		
1675	Wycherley's *Country Wife* published. Wren started St Paul's cathedral.	Greenwich Observatory founded. Newton published a theory of light.
1677 Princess Mary married William of Orange.		
1678 'Popish Plot' caused panic.	Bunyan's *The Pilgrim's Progress* published.	
1679 Cavalier Parliament dissolved; Earl of Danby impeached; first attempt to exclude James, Duke of York, from the succession to the throne because of his Catholicism. Habeas Corpus Act passed. Scots Covenanters defeated at Bothwell Bridge.	Ashmolean Museum, Oxford, founded.	Hooke's law of elasticity published.
1680 Second Exclusion Bill defeated in the House of Lords.		
1681 Parliament summoned to Oxford, but dissolved when the third Exclusion Bill was introduced. French subsidy enabled Charles II to rule henceforth without parliament.		
1682	Advocates' Library, Edinburgh, founded.	Halley observed the comet later named after him.
1683 Rye House Plot exposed.		
1685 **Accession of James II** Rebellion led by the Duke of Monmouth, Charles II's illegitimate son, defeated at Sedgemoor; Monmouth executed; Judge Jeffreys' Bloody Assizes punished the rebels.		
1686 Catholics readmitted to high office.		
1687 First Declaration of Indulgence issued by James II.		Newton's *Principia* published.
1688 Second Declaration of Indulgence issued; James II imprisoned seven bishops, who were acquitted; a son born to James II; the Glorious Revolution: William of Orange landed at Torbay, causing James II to flee abroad.		Meteorological map produced by Halley.
1689 **Accession of William III and Mary II** Toleration Act and Bill of Rights passed. Scottish Jacobites won the battle of Killiecrankie. Grand Alliance formed to resist French expansionism; war with France began.	Aphra Behn died. Purcell wrote *Dido and Aeneas.*	
1690 William III defeated James II at the battle of the Boyne. Presbyterianism established in Scotland.	Locke's *An Essay concerning Human Understanding* published.	
1691 Treaty of Limerick ended Irish Jacobite resistance to William III.		
1692 Glencoe massacre of 38 MacDonalds. National debt introduced.		
1694 Mary II died; Triennial Act passed. Bank of England founded.	Wren's Greenwich Hospital begun.	
1695 Bank of Scotland founded.	Purcell died. Congreve wrote *Love for Love.*	
1696 First Whig Junto gained control of the English government.		
1697 Peace with France; fall of the Whig Junto.	John Aubrey died.	
1698 Scots Darién colony established.	Society for Promoting Christian Knowledge founded.	First steam engine built by Savery.

	History	Arts and Learning	Science, Technology, and Exploration
1699			NW Australia explored by Dampier.
1700	Darién colony failed.	*Way of the World* written by Congreve. Dryden died.	
1701	Act of Settlement passed.		Tull invented the seed drill. Magnetic map produced by Halley.
1702	**Accession of Anne** War of the Spanish Succession against France and Spain began.	Clarendon's *History of the Rebellion* published.	
1703			Newton elected president of the Royal Society.
1704	Duke of Marlborough defeated the French at Blenheim.		
1706	Marlborough defeated the French at Ramillies.	John Evelyn died.	
1707	Act of Union between Scotland and England passed.	Farquhar published *The Beaux' Stratagem.*	
1708	Second Whig Junto gained control of the government. Marlborough defeated the French at Oudenarde.		
1709	Marlborough defeated the French at Malplaquet.	*The Tatler* founded.	
1710	Tories won control of the government.	Berkeley's *A Treatise Concerning the Principles of Human Knowledge* published.	
1711	Marlborough dismissed.	*The Spectator* founded.	South Sea Company founded.
1712	Last English execution for witchcraft.	Handel settled in England.	Newcomen constructed a piston-driven steam engine.
1713	Peace of Utrecht ended the War of the Spanish Succession.		
1714	**Accession of George I**		
1715	Jacobite rising ('The Fifteen') suppressed.		Taylor's calculus theorem published.
1716	Septennial Act passed.		
1717		First performance of Handel's *Water Music* (on the Thames).	
1719	Jacobite invasion failed.	Defoe's *Robinson Crusoe* published. Handel appointed director of the Royal Academy of Music.	
1720	South Sea Company collapsed, amid great scandal (the 'South Sea Bubble').	Construction of St George's, Bloomsbury, by Hawksmoor.	
1721	Robert Walpole became first lord of the treasury.		Reflecting telescope built by John Hadley.
1722	Atterbury's plot exposed.		Guy's Hospital founded.
1725			Flamsteed's *Historia coelestis Britannica* published.
1726	Irish famine began.	Swift's *Gulliver's Travels* published.	
1727	**Accession of George II**		
1728		Chambers' *Cyclopaedia* published. Gay's *Beggar's Opera* first staged.	Stephen Hales's *Vegetable staticks* published.
1729	Oxford Methodists organized by Charles Wesley. Irish famine ended.		Bradley calculated the constant of aberration of light.
1732		London's Covent Garden opera house opened.	
1733	Excise Bill withdrawn after a public outcry.		Hales' observations on blood pressure, etc., published in *Haemastaticks*. Kay's loom patented.
1735		*The Rake's Progress* painted by Hogarth.	George Hadley's observations on the trade winds published.
1736	Laws against witchcraft repealed.		
1737		Oxford's Radcliffe Camera, by Gibbs, begun.	
1738	John Wesley experienced a spiritual conversion.		
1739	War of Jenkins' Ear began. Dick Turpin died.	Hume's *Treatise of Human Nature* published.	

	History	Arts and Learning	Science, Technology, and Exploration
1740	Famine in Ireland began. War of the Austrian Succession against France and Austria began.	*Rule Britannia* composed by Arne.	
1741	Famine in Ireland ended.	London debut of Garrick. Hume's *Essays, Moral and Political* published.	
1742	Robert Walpole resigned.	First performance of Handel's *Messiah* (in Dublin).	
1744			Anson returned from a voyage around the world.
1745	Jacobite rising ('The Forty-Five') began in Scotland; Jacobite victory at Prestonpans; Jacobite army reached Derby.		
1746	Jacobites defeated at Culloden.		
1748	War of the Austrian Succession ended.	Hume's *An Enquiry concerning Human Understanding* published.	
1749		Fielding's *Tom Jones* published. Bolingbroke's *The Idea of a Patriot King* published.	
1751		Gray's *Elegy written in a Country Churchyard* published.	Whytt showed the importance of bodily reflexes.
1752	Gregorian calendar introduced.		
1753		British Museum founded.	
1754			Cure for scurvy proposed by Lind.
1755		Dr Johnson's *Dictionary* published.	
1756	Seven Years' War began; Pitt the Elder became first minister.		Black's *Experiments* marked the start of modern chemistry.
1757			Concept of latent heat introduced by Black.
1758		Harewood House designed by the Adam brothers.	Achromatic lens invented by Dolland. Construction of Bridgewater Canal began.
1760	Conquest of Canada completed.		Wedgwood's pottery works at Burslem founded.
	Accession of George III		
1761	Pitt the Elder resigned.		
1762	Earl of Bute became prime minister.	*Mares and Foals* painted by Stubbs.	
1763	George Grenville became prime minister. John Wilkes arrested. Seven Years' War ended.		
1764	John Wilkes expelled from the House of Commons and outlawed. Stamp Act passed.	Kenwood House designed by Robert Adam.	Hargreaves invented the spinning jenny. Watt began work on his steam engine.
1765	Marquess of Rockingham became prime minister. Stamp Act repealed.		Concept of specific heat introduced by Cavendish.
1766	Earl of Chatham (Pitt the Elder) became prime minister.	Goldsmith's *The Vicar of Wakefield* published.	Cavendish published his work on hydrogen and carbon dioxide.
1767		Sterne's *Tristram Shandy* completed.	
1768	Duke of Grafton became prime minister.	Royal Society of Arts founded.	Cook embarked on a voyage to the South Pacific.
1769	John Wilkes again expelled from the House of Commons; controversy over Middlesex elections.		Patents granted for Watt's steam engine and Arkwright's spinning machine.
1770	Lord North became prime minister. Boston Massacre.	*The Blue Boy* painted by Gainsborough. Burke's *Thoughts on the Cause of the Present Discontents* published.	Source of the Blue Nile discovered by Bruce.
1772			Cook's second voyage began.
1773	Boston Tea Party.	Goldsmith's *She Stoops to Conquer* published.	
1774	Wilkes re-elected to the House of Commons. Intolerable Acts passed.		Oxygen discovered by Priestley.
1775	War of American Independence began.	Sheridan's *The Rivals* published.	
1776	American Declaration of Independence issued.	Gibbon's *Decline and Fall of the Roman Empire* and Adam Smith's *Wealth of Nations* published.	

	History	Arts and Learning	Science, Technology, and Exploration
1777	Americans defeated the British at Saratoga.	John Howard's *The State of the Prisons* published. Sheridan wrote *School for Scandal*.	
1778	France allied with the Americans.		
1779			Darby constructed the first cast-iron bridge at Coalbrookdale. Cook murdered in Hawaii. Crompton invented the spinning mule.
1780	Anti-Catholic Gordon riots in London. First running of the Epsom Derby.	Raikes organized first Sunday schools.	First Sunday newspapers appeared – *The British Gazette* and *Sunday Monitor*.
1781	Americans forced a British army to surrender at Yorktown.		
1782	Marquess of Rockingham became prime minister; Earl of Shelburne became prime minister. Irish parliament gained legislative independence.	Royal Irish Academy founded in Dublin.	Goodricke proposed that the star Algol was an eclipsing binary. Watt invented the rotary drive for steam engines.
1783	Duke of Portland became prime minister in the Fox-North coalition. US independence recognized; peace with the USA and her allies. Pitt the Younger became prime minister. Bank of Ireland founded.		
1784	First India Act passed.	Reynolds painted *Mrs Siddons as the Tragic Muse*.	Cort patented the dry-puddling process for making wrought iron.
1785		The *Daily Universal Register* (later *The Times*) founded.	Cartwright patented his power loom.
1787			Charles discovered the volume-temperature relationship for gases (Charles's law). Hope discovered strontium.
1788	Impeachment of Warren Hastings began. George III suffered his first attack of insanity. New South Wales established as a penal colony.		Uniformitarian theory of Earth's structure published by Hutton.
1789		Blake's *Songs of Innocence* and Bentham's *Principles of Morals and Legislation* published.	Herschel discovered two of Saturn's satellites.
1790	Burke's *Reflections on the Revolution in France* published.		
1791		Boswell's *Life of Samuel Johnson* published. *The Observer* newspaper founded. Paine completed his *Rights of Man*.	
1792	The radical Corresponding Society founded.		
1793	War between Britain and revolutionary France began.		Board of Agriculture established.
1794	British naval victory over French – the Glorious First of June.	Blake's *Songs of Experience* published.	Accommodation of the eye described by Young; colour blindness reported by Dalton. Hutton's *Theory of the Earth* published. Park embarked on his first expedition up the River Niger.
1795	Warren Hastings acquitted. Seditious Meetings and Treasonable Practices Acts passed. The Irish nationalist, Wolf Tone, banished. Speenhamland system of poor relief introduced.		
1796		Burns died.	Cowpox vaccine first used by Jenner.
1797	Naval mutinies at Spithead and the Nore. Naval victories of Cape St Vincent (against the Spanish) and Camperdown (against the Dutch).	Coleridge wrote *Kubla Khan* (published 1816).	
1798	Irish rebellion suppressed.	*Lyrical Ballads* published by Wordsworth and Coleridge.	Malthus's *An Essay on the Principle of Population* published. Earth's density measured by Cavendish. Rumford explored the conversion of work into heat.

History	Arts and Learning	Science, Technology, and Exploration
1799 First Combination Act passed. Income tax introduced.		
1800 Second Combination Act and Census Act passed. Act of Union between Great Britain and Ireland passed (effective from 1 Jan 1801).		Royal College of Surgeons founded. Electrolysis discovered by Nicholson.
1801 Henry Addington became prime minister. Naval victory at Copenhagen.		Dalton presented his law of partial pressures. Columbium (now called niobium) discovered by Hatchett. Henry's law (for the solubility of gases) published.
1802 Peace with France by the Treaty of Amiens. Royal Military College opened.	*Political Register* founded by Cobbett.	First table of atomic weights published by Dalton. West India Docks, London, completed.
1803 July rebellion in Ireland suppressed. War between Britain and France resumed.		Dalton propounded his atomic theory. Iridium and osmium discovered by Tennant. Young's experiments suggested the wave theory of light. Caledonian Canal begun.
1804 Pitt the Younger became prime minister.		Element palladium discovered by Wollaston.
1805 Nelson killed at the battle of Trafalgar.		Second expedition to the Niger River by Mungo Park. Rhodium discovered by Wollaston.
1806 Pitt the Younger died; Charles James Fox died.		Wind-speed scale proposed by Beaufort. East India Docks, London, completed.
1807 Slave trade abolished. Duke of Portland became prime minister.	Charles and Mary Lamb's *Tales from Shakespeare* published.	
1809 Spencer Perceval became prime minister.		
1810 George III became permanently insane.		Davy determined chlorine to be an element.
1811 George, Prince of Wales, became Prince Regent. *Hansard's Parliamentary Debates* first published. First outbreak of organized Luddite activity.	Austen's *Sense and Sensibility* published. Nash began work on Regent Street, London.	Functional differentiation of spinal nerve roots discovered by Bell.
1812 Spencer Perceval assassinated; Earl of Liverpool became prime minister. Anglo-American war began.	Byron's *Childe Harold's Pilgrimage* published.	Appendicitis described by Parkinson.
1813	Austen's *Pride and Prejudice* published.	Discovery of Brewster's law.
1814 Anglo-American war ended.	Scott's *Waverley* and Austen's *Mansfield Park* published.	
1815 First Corn Law passed. Napoleon finally defeated by Wellington, at Waterloo; peace with France.	Remodelling of Brighton Pavilion by Nash.	Prout proposed his hypothesis for the atomic weight of atoms.
1816 Spa Fields riots; Habeas Corpus suspended. Income tax abolished.		Davy introduced his miner's safety lamp.
1817 March of the Blanketeers. Gold sovereigns issued.	Ricardo's *Principles of Political Economy and Taxation* published.	Parkinson's disease described by Parkinson.
1818	Byron's *Don Juan* and Keats' *Endymion* published.	
1819 First Factory Act passed. Peterloo massacre of demonstrators in Manchester; Six Acts passed to combat radical agitation.		Naphthalene derived from coal tar by Kidd and Garden.
1820 **Accession of George IV** Cato Street conspiracy exposed. George IV unsuccessfully attempted to divorce Queen Caroline.	Keats' *Ode to a Nightingale* and Shelley's *Prometheus Unbound* published.	
1821 Queen Caroline excluded from George IV's coronation.	Scott's *Kenilworth* and de Quincy's *Confessions of an English Opium Eater* published. Constable painted the *Hay Wain*. Mill's *Elements of Political Economy* published. *Manchester Guardian* founded.	Faraday discovered the principle of the electric motor.

History	Arts and Learning	Science, Technology, and Exploration
1822	Lord Castlereagh, the foreign secretary, committed suicide; Robert Peel became home secretary.	Royal Academy of Music founded. *Sunday Times* founded.	
1823	Peel initiated reform of prisons and the criminal law; move towards free trade began. Catholic Association founded by O'Connell.		Babbage constructed a mechanical computer. Waterproof fabric invented by Macintosh.
1824	Combination Acts repealed.	Byron died. National Gallery opened (in Pall Mall).	Royal Society for the Prevention of Cruelty to Animals founded. Stockton-Darlington railway opened; Menai rail bridge by Telford completed. Benzene isolated by Faraday. Brown described Brownian motion.
1825		Hazlitt's *Spirit of the Age* published. Nash's Buckingham Palace begun.	
1827	George Canning became prime minister; Viscount Goderich became prime minister.	Blake died. Carlton House Terrace, Westminster, designed by Nash.	
1828	Wellington became prime minister. Test and Corporation Acts repealed, allowing Catholics and Nonconformists to hold public office. Daniel O'Connell elected to parliament in the Clare by-election.	University of London opened.	First electromagnet made by Sturgeon. Nicol invented the Nicol prism.
1829	Full Catholic emancipation conceded. Metropolitan Police formed.		Graham described his law governing the diffusion of gases. Stephenson's locomotive *The Rocket* won the Rainhill trials.
1830	Earl Grey became prime minister.	Cobbett's *Rural Rides* published.	Lyell's *Principles of Geology* published.
1831	Rejection of parliamentary reform by the House of Lords provoked rioting.	Law Society founded.	Faraday's first series of *Experimental Researches in Electricity* published.
1832	Great Reform Act extended the franchise and redistributed seats in the House of Commons.		Experiments on electromagnetic induction performed by Faraday. Hodgkin described Hodgkin's disease. Parallax of Alpha Centauri measured by Henderson.
1833	Factory Act limited children's working week. Slavery abolished within the British empire. Oxford Movement within the Church of England launched.	First of Turner's Venetian paintings exhibited.	
1834	Viscount Melbourne became prime minister; Sir Robert Peel became prime minister. Houses of Parliament destroyed by fire. Tolpuddle martyrs transported; Robert Owen founded the Grand National Consolidated Trades Union, which quickly collapsed.	Construction of Wilkins's National Gallery, Trafalgar Square, began.	
1835	Lord Melbourne became prime minister. Municipal Corporations Act passed.	Constable painted *The Valley Farm*.	
1836			Sturgeon invented the commutator for electric motors. Daniell introduced his electric cell. Gossage improved alkali manufacturing process.
1837	**Accession of Victoria**		Telegraph system invented by Wheatstone and Cooke.
1838	The People's Charter drawn up by the Chartists.		
1839	Bedchamber crisis. Parliament rejected the first Chartist petition; Newport rising suppressed.	Dickens's *Oliver Twist* published.	Darwin's *Voyage of the Beagle* published. Steam hammer designed by Nasmyth. Fox Talbot presented his photographic plates.
1840	Victoria married Prince Albert. Penny post introduced. New Zealand annexed.	Browning's *Sordello* published. Barry's Houses of Parliament begun.	
1841	Canadian parliament established. Sir Robert Peel became prime minister.		

	History	**Arts and Learning**	**Science, Technology, and Exploration**
1842	Income tax reintroduced. Second Chartist petition rejected. Mines Act prohibited women and young children from working underground. Chadwick's report revealed the insanitary conditions of the poor. Rebecca riots in Wales.		Bowman revealed the fine structures of kidney. Therapeutic uses of hypnosis proposed by Braid.
1843	Disruption of the Church of Scotland; Free Church of Scotland formed.	Tennyson's *Morte d'Arthur* published. Wordsworth appointed poet laureate.	Brunel's *Great Britain* launched.
1844	Bank Charter Act passed. Rochdale Pioneers opened a cooperative shop.	Elizabeth Barrett Browning's *Poems* published. Turner painted *Rain, Steam and Speed*.	
1845	Famine in Ireland began.	Disraeli's *Sybil* published.	Effect of magnetism on polarized light discovered by Faraday. Position of Neptune determined by J. C. Adams.
1846	Corn Laws repealed; Conservative Party split; Lord John Russell became prime minister.	Lear's *Book of Nonsense* published.	
1847		Charlotte Brontë's *Jane Eyre*, Emily Brontë's *Wuthering Heights*, and Thackeray's *Vanity Fair* published.	Use of chloroform as an anaesthetic introduced by Simpson.
1848	Third Chartist petition rejected. Public Health Act passed. Cholera epidemic.	J. S. Mill's *Principles of Political Economy* published. Pre-Raphaelite Brotherhood founded.	Joule published his work on the kinetics of gas molecules. Absolute temperature scale proposed by Kelvin.
1849		Dickens's *David Copperfield* published.	Joule's *On The Mechanical Equivalent of Heat* published. Addison's disease described by Addison.
1850		Elizabeth Barrett Browning's *Sonnets from the Portuguese* published. Tennyson appointed poet laureate. Paxton's Crystal Palace built.	
1851		J. M. W. Turner died.	Great Exhibition held in the Crystal Palace. The Royal School of Mines founded.
1852	Earl of Derby became prime minister; Earl of Aberdeen became prime minister.	Millais painted *Ophelia*; Holman Hunt painted *The Light of the World*.	Kelvin stated the law of conservation of energy and began his collaboration with Joule that led to discovery of the Joule-Kelvin effect. Theory of chemical valency constructed by Frankland.
1853		Mrs Gaskell's *Cranford* and Charlotte Brontë's *Villette* published.	Quaternions in algebra discovered by Hamilton. First manned glider built by Cayley.
1854	Crimean War began; charge of the Light Brigade, at the battle of Balaclava.	Kingsley's *Westward Ho!* and Tennyson's *Charge of the Light Brigade* published.	Boole's *The Laws of Thought* published.
1855	Viscount Palmerston became prime minister. Civil Service Commission established.		
1856	Crimean War ended. Department of Education established.		Bessemer's steel-making process introduced. First synthetic dye discovered by Perkin.
1857	Indian Mutiny began.	Borrow's *Romany Rye* and Trollope's *Barchester Towers* published. National Portrait Gallery, London, opened.	
1858	Earl of Derby became prime minister. Lionel de Rothschild, the first Jewish MP (elected in 1847), allowed to take his seat. Fenian Society formed. Indian mutiny suppressed; government of India transferred from the East India Company to the Crown.		Joint presentation by Darwin and Wallace on the evolution of species by natural selection. Discovery of Lake Tanganyika by Burton and Speke.

	History	Arts and Learning	Science, Technology, and Exploration
1859	Viscount Palmerston became prime minister.	J. S. Mill's *On Liberty*, Dickens's *Tale of Two Cities*, and George Eliot's *Adam Bede* published.	Darwin published the summation of his theory – *On The Origin of Species by Means of Natural Selection*. Tyndall discovered the Tyndall effect in colloidal suspensions.
1860	Gladstone's budget completed free trade.	George Eliot's *The Mill on the Floss* and Wilkie Collins's *The Woman in White* published.	T. H. Huxley defended Darwin's theory of evolution at Oxford. Maxwell's *Illustrations of Dynamical Theory of Gases* published. Graham made fundamental discoveries in colloid science.
1861	Prince Albert died.	George Eliot's *Silas Marner* and Spencer's *Education: Moral, Intellectual, Physical* published.	Batesian mimicry described by H. W. Bates. Crookes discovered thallium.
1862		Spencer's *First Principles* published.	Hooker and Bentham began work on their world flora: *Genera Plantarum*.
1863		*Little White Girl* painted by Whistler.	Huggins confirmed that stars are composed of known elements. Modern weather mapping introduced by Galton.
1864		Albert Memorial erected in Hyde Park.	Maxwell published his mathematical description of electromagnetic wave propagation. Newlands's law of octaves foreshadowed the periodic table. Gaseous nature of nebulae discovered by Huggins.
1865	Earl Russell (Lord John Russell) became prime minister.	Carroll's *Alice's Adventures in Wonderland* published.	Atlantic cable laid. Lister introduced the use of antiseptics in surgery.
1866	Earl of Derby became prime minister.		Short clinical thermometer invented by Allbutt.
1867	Second Reform Act extended the franchise. Fenian rising in Ireland failed. Canada became the first dominion within the British Empire.	Bagehot's *The English Constitution* published. *Boyhood of Raleigh* painted by Millais.	Exploration of the Congo by Livingstone.
1868	Benjamin Disraeli became prime minister; William Gladstone became prime minister. Trades Union Congress formed. Flogging abolished in the army in peacetime.	Browning's *The Ring and the Book* and Wilkie Collins's *The Moonstone* published.	Red shift in the spectrum of Sirius reported by Huggins. Helium lines in the sun's spectrum discovered by Lockyer.
1869	Church of Ireland disestablished.	Blackmore's *Lorna Doone* and J. S. Mill's *On The Subjection of Women* published.	Discoveries on the liquefaction of gases published by T. Andrews.
1870	Education Act introduced universal elementary education. Competitive examinations introduced for entry to the civil service. First Irish Land Act and first Married Women's Property Act passed. Home Government Association (which became the Home Rule Association in 1873) formed. Army reforms begun.		
1871	Trades Union Act gave legal status to trades unions. Bank Holidays introduced in England and Wales.	George Eliot's *Middlemarch* and Carroll's *Through The Looking Glass* published.	Darwin's *The Descent of Man* published. Encounter at Ujiji between Stanley and Livingstone.
1872	Secret ballot introduced. Licensing Act and Coal Mines Act passed.	Hardy's *Under the Greenwood Tree* published.	Vacuum flask invented by Dewar.
1873	Court system reorganized by Judicature Act.		Blood platelets discovered by Osler.
1874	Benjamin Disraeli became prime minister.		
1875	Britain purchased Suez Canal shares from the Khedive of Egypt. Public Health Act and Artisans' Dwellings Act passed.		Webb became the first cross-Channel swimmer.
1876	Victoria became empress of India. Plimsoll line introduced.		Bell patented his telephone system.

History	Arts and Learning	Science, Technology, and Exploration
		Manson linked insects to the spread of certain diseases.
1877 British Natal annexed the Transvaal.		
1878 Salvation Army founded. Congress of Berlin.	Gilbert and Sullivan wrote *HMS Pinafore*. Hardy's *Return of the Native* and Swinburne's *Poems and Ballads* published.	Swan invented the carbon-filament light bulb.
1879 Michael Davitt formed the Irish Land League. Gladstone's Midlothian campaign.		
1880 William Gladstone became prime minister. Bradlaugh started his campaign against religious oaths.		Seismograph invented by Milne.
1881 Second Irish Land Act passed. First Boer War began. Mahdi proclaimed a holy war in the Sudan.	D'Oyly Carte built the Savoy Theatre, London.	Phenomenon of hysteresis discovered by Ewing.
1882 Kilmainham treaty with Parnell; Phoenix Park murders in Dublin. Second Married Women's Property Act passed. First Boer War ended with recognition of the Transvaal's independence. Britain occupied Egypt.		
1883	R. L. Stevenson's *Treasure Island* published. Royal College of Music founded.	Galton introduced the notion of 'eugenics'.
1884 Third Reform Act extended the franchise. Fabian Society founded. Berlin conference marked the beginning of the European partition of Africa.	Spencer's *The Man versus the State* published.	Poynting's vector discovered by Poynting. Synthesis of isoprene by Tilden. Multistage steam turbine invented by Parsons.
1885 Marquess of Salisbury became prime minister. Age of consent raised to sixteen. General Gordon killed at Khartoum.	Gilbert and Sullivan wrote *The Mikado*.	
1886 William Gladstone became prime minister, but resigned after the defeat of an Irish Home Rule Bill; Marquess of Salisbury became prime minister. Burma annexed to British India.	Stevenson's *Dr Jekyll and Mr Hyde* published. *Bubbles* painted by Millais.	
1887 Victoria's Golden Jubilee. Police dispersal of a meeting in Trafalgar Square dubbed 'Bloody Sunday'.	Conan Doyle's *A Study in Scarlet* published.	Electromagnetic wave propagation along conductors discovered by Lodge.
1888 Local Government Act established county councils. Murders of six women in London attributed to 'Jack the Ripper'.	Kipling's *Plain Tales from the Hills* published.	Pneumatic rubber tyre invented by Dunlop.
1889 British South Africa Company founded.	Stevenson's *Master of Ballantrae* and Jerome's *Three Men in a Boat* published.	Cordite explosive formulated by Abel and Dewar.
1890 Parnell resigned as leader of the Irish nationalist MPs.	Booth's *In Darkest England and the Way Out* highlighted the plight of the poor.	
1891 Fees for elementary schooling abolished.	Wilde's *The Picture of Dorian Grey* published. Serialization of Conan Doyle's *The Adventures of Sherlock Holmes* began in *Strand* magazine.	The term 'electron' introduced by Stoney. Poynting calculated the Earth's mean density.
1892 William Gladstone became prime minister.	Wilde's *Lady Windermere's Fan* published.	Viscose process of rayon manufacture patented by Bevan and Cross. Rules of benzene chemistry determined by Crum, Brown, and Gibson.
1893 House of Lords defeated the second Home Rule Bill. Independent Labour Party formed.		Gravitational constant calculated by Poynting. 'Maunder minimum' for sunspot activity detected by Maunder.
1894 Earl of Rosebery became prime minister. Death duties introduced.	Shaw's *Arms and the Man* and Kipling's *Jungle Book* published.	Manchester Ship Canal opened. Radio wave detector devised by Lodge. Argon discovered by Ramsay and Rayleigh.

History	Arts and Learning	Science, Technology, and Exploration
1895 Marquess of Salisbury became prime minister. Jameson raid on the Transvaal.	National Trust founded. Work started on Westminster Cathedral. H. G. Wells's *The Time Machine* published. London School of Economics and Political Science founded.	Causal agent of trypanosomiasis isolated by Bruce. Helium identified by Ramsay and Crookes.
1897 Victoria's Diamond Jubilee.	Wells's *The Invisible Man* published. Opening of the Tate Gallery, London.	Ross showed how mosquitoes are vectors of malaria parasites. Discovery of electron credited to J. J. Thomson.
1898 Kitchener defeated the Khalifa's forces at Omdurman.	Hardy's *Wessex Poems*, Wilde's *Ballad of Reading Gaol*, and Wells's *War of the Worlds* published.	Xenon, neon, and krypton discovered by Ramsay and Travers. Liquid hydrogen obtained by Dewar. Charge of the electron determined by Townsend.
1899 Second Boer War began.	Wilde's *The Importance of Being Earnest* published. Elgar composed *The Enigma Variations*.	Alpha and beta rays differentiated by Rutherford.
1900 Labour Party formed. British forces broke the sieges of Ladysmith and Mafeking.	Elgar's *Dream of Gerontius* performed. Conrad's *Lord Jim* published.	Rutherford discovered gamma radiation. Seismic waves characterized as primary or secondary by Oldham.
1901 **Accession of Edward VII** Taff Vale case made unions liable for damages in strikes. Concentration camps used in the Boer War. Australia became a dominion.	Kipling's *Kim* published.	Physiological effects of adrenal extract demonstrated by J. N. Langley. Tryptophan isolated by Hopkins. Law governing electron emission from hot surfaces proposed by O. W. Richardson.
1902 Arthur Balfour became prime minister. Education Act established local education authorities. Boer War ended; Transvaal and Orange Free State annexed.	Bennett's *Anna of the Five Towns* and Conan Doyle's *Hound of the Baskervilles* published.	Existence of atmospheric layer (Heaviside-Kennelly layer) proposed by Heaviside. The digestive hormone secretin described by Bayliss and Starling.
1903 Women's Social and Political Union founded by Emmeline Pankhurst.	Shaw's *Man and Superman* published. Liverpool's Anglican cathedral begun.	Transmutation of radioactive elements described by Rutherford and Soddy.
1904 Entente Cordiale between Britain and France established.	Workers' Educational Association founded. Barrie's *Peter Pan* and Conrad's *Nostromo* published. Abbey Theatre, Dublin, founded. Synge wrote *Riders to the Sea*.	Thermionic vacuum tube invented by J. A. Fleming. Fitzgerald suggested the Lorentz-Fitzgerald contraction. Radon (formerly niton) discovered by Ramsay and Whytlaw-Gray.
1905 Sir Henry Campbell-Bannerman became prime minister.	Forster's *Where Angels Fear To Tread*, Wells's *Kipps*, and Shaw's *Major Barbara* published. *A Mass of Life* composed by Delius.	Nuclear transformation theory proposed by Rutherford and Soddy. Regulation of breathing by carbon dioxide shown by Haldane and Priestley. All-or-none law of nervous impulse demonstrated by Lucas.
1906 Trade Disputes Act gave unions immunity against damages claims arising from strikes.	Galsworthy's *The Man of Property* published.	Hopkins postulated the existence of 'accessory' factors (later called vitamins). Sherrington's *The Integrative Action of the Nervous System* published.
1907 Anglo-Russian entente established. Boy Scout movement founded. New Zealand became a dominion.	Conrad's *The Secret Agent* published. *Brigg Fair* composed by Delius. Synge's *The Playboy of the Western World* performed in Dublin.	Lactic acid production in active muscle shown by Hopkins and Fletcher. Rolls-Royce introduced the Silver Ghost.
1908 Herbert Asquith became prime minister. Borstal system established.	Bennett's *The Old Wives' Tale*, Forster's *A Room with A View*, and Graham's *The Wind in the Willows* published.	Concept of genetic diseases proposed by Garrod.
1909 House of Lords rejected Lloyd George's budget, causing a constitutional crisis. Old age pensions introduced.	*Fantasia on a Theme of Tallis* composed by Vaughan Williams.	
1910 **Accession of George V**		

	History	Arts and Learning	Science, Technology, and Exploration
	Two general elections fought over the House of Lords' powers. Edward Carson became leader of the Ulster Unionists. Union of South Africa formed, as a dominion.	Elgar's *Violin Concerto* and Vaughan Williams's *Sea Symphony* published; Bennett's *Clayhanger* and Forster's *Howards End* published.	Russell and Whithead's *Principia Mathematica* published.
1911	National Insurance Act introduced unemployment and sickness insurance. Parliament Act limited the powers of the House of Lords.	Brooke's *Poems*, Beerbohm's *Zuleika Dobson*, and Lawrence's *The White Peacock* published.	Nuclear model of the atom proposed by Rutherford. Cloud chamber constructed by C. T. R. Wilson.
1912	Ulster Volunteer Force formed; Irish Home Rule Bill approved by the House of Commons but defeated by the Lords. *Titanic* sank.	*On Hearing the First Cuckoo in Spring* composed by Delius.	Piltdown skull found by Woodward and Dawson. Bragg proposed Bragg's law for x-ray diffraction. Scott's expedition reached the South Pole.
1913	Trade Union Act legalized the political levy. Cat and Mouse Act allowed temporary release of suffragette hunger strikers from prison.	Lawrence's *Sons and Lovers* published.	Existence of isotopes suggested by Soddy. Moseley's law for x-ray spectral lines proposed by Moseley. First geological time scale constructed by A. Holmes.
1914	Curragh mutiny; Irish Home Rule Act passed, but suspended for the duration of World War I. World War I began; British Expeditionary Force sent to France; stalemate on the western front following the battles of Mons, Marne, and Ypres.	Joyce's *Dubliners* and Russell's *Our Knowledge of the External World* published.	Barcroft's *Respiratory Function of the Blood* published. Acetylcholine isolated from ergot by Ewins and Dale.
1915	Coalition government formed under Asquith. Gallipoli campaign failed; Battles of Ypres and Loos; *Lusitania* sunk by German submarines; zeppelin bombing raids on British cities began.	Buchan's *The Thirty-Nine Steps*, Lawrence's *The Rainbow*, and Somerset Maugham's *Of Human Bondage* published.	X-ray spectrometer constructed by Bragg.
1916	Lloyd George became prime minister of a coalition government. Easter Rising in Dublin suppressed. Battle of the Somme involved the first use of tanks; naval battle of Jutland; conscription introduced; British force captured at Kut-al-Almara.	Joyce's *Portrait of the Artist as a Young Man* and Brighouse's *Hobson's Choice* published.	Gaskell's *The Involuntary Nervous System* published posthumously.
1917	USA entered World War I; battles of Arras, Vimy Ridge, and Passchendaele; British captured Baghdad. 'Balfour declaration', on a Jewish homeland in Palestine, issued.		Thermal diffusion of gases predicted by Chapman.
1918	RAF formed; German cities bombed; German advance halted at the second battle of the Marne; Allied victory at Megiddo; World War I ended. School-leaving age raised to 14; men aged 21 and over and women aged 30 and over enfranchised. Dáil Eireann proclaimed by Sinn Féin MPs.	Wilfred Owen killed on the western front. Hopkins's *Poems* published posthumously.	Statistical treatment of inheritance of continuous variation by Fisher. Marie Stopes's *Married Love* published.
1919	Nancy Astor became the first woman MP. Irish Republican Army formed. Treaty of Versailles concluded.	Hardy's *Collected Poems* and Keynes's *The Economic Consequences of the Peace* published. Cenotaph, Whitehall, designed by Lutyens. Elgar's *Cello Concerto* performed.	Eddington's observations of a solar eclipse verified the general theory of relativity. Mass spectrograph produced by Aston. Artificial transmutation of the nucleus discovered by Rutherford.
1920	Ireland partitioned. British Communist Party formed. Welsh Anglican Church disestablished.	Holst's *The Planets* performed. *Christ Carrying the Cross* painted by Spencer. Galsworthy's *The Skin Game* published.	
1921	Southern Ireland became a dominion, as the Irish Free State.	Russell's *The Analysis of Mind* published.	

History	Arts and Learning	Science, Technology, and Exploration
1922 Andrew Bonar Law became prime minister. Labour replaced the Liberals as the main opposition party.	Joyce's *Ulysses*, T. S. Eliot's *The Waste Land*, and Housman's *Last Poems* published. T. S. Eliot founded *The Criterion*.	The enzyme lysozyme discovered by Fleming. Hopkins identified glutathione. Mathematical techniques of weather forecasting proposed by Richardson. BBC broadcasts began.
1923 Stanley Baldwin became prime minister.	Wodehouse's *The Inimitable Jeeves* published. Spencer painted *The Resurrection*.	
1924 James Ramsay MacDonald became prime minister of the first Labour government. Zinoviev letter published. Stanley Baldwin became prime minister.	Forster's *A Passage To India*, Shaw's *St Joan*, and O'Casey's *Juno and the Paycock* published.	Jeffrey's *The Earth* published. Heaviside-Kennelly layer confirmed by Appleton. Mass-luminosity relationship for stars discovered by Eddington. Method of nervous signalling discovered by Adrian.
1925 Old-age pension extended to low-income groups. Gold standard adopted.	Coward's *Hay Fever* performed in London.	
1926 General Strike by the TUC failed.	Walton composed 'Façade'. O'Casey's *The Plough and the Stars* performed. Milne's *Winnie the Pooh* and Trevelyan's *History of England* published. Woolf's *To The Lighthouse* and Yeats' *The Tower* published.	Eddington's *The Internal Constitution of the Stars* published. Baird demonstrated his picture-transmitting equipment. Sidgwick's *Electron Theory of Valency* published. Wave property of electrons shown by G. P. Thomson. Stokes provided evidence for the nature of yellow fever agent.
1927 Trade Disputes Act restricted trade unions.		
1928 Women aged 21 and over enfranchised. Revised prayer book rejected by the House of Commons.	Huxley's *Point Counterpoint* and Lawrence's *Lady Chatterley's Lover* published. E. Scott's Shakespeare Memorial Theatre, Stratford, begun.	Transformation of bacteria discovered by Griffiths. Fleming discovered penicillin.
1929 James Ramsay MacDonald became prime minister. Great depression began.	Graves' *Goodbye To All That* and Priestley's *The Good Companions* published. Epstein sculpted *Night and Day* (London Transport Building). Walton composed his *Violin Concerto*. Auden's *Poems* and Waugh's *Vile Bodies* published. Coward's *Private Lives* performed. Hitchcock directed *Murder*. BBC Symphony Orchestra formed. Epstein sculpted *Genesis*. Walton composed *Belshazzar's Feast*.	Ring form of sugar molecules proposed by Haworth. Theory of continental drift suggested by A. Holmes.
1930 Coal Mines Act set underground working day at 7½ hours.		Wallis employed geodetic construction for airframes. Jet engine patented by Whittle.
1931 MacDonald formed a coalition ('National') government and was expelled from the Labour Party. Invergordon mutiny over naval pay. Gold standard abandoned.		
1932 British Union of Fascists founded by Sir Oswald Mosley.	Gill's *Prospero and Ariel* unveiled on Broadcasting House. London Philharmonic Orchestra founded.	Neutron discovered by Chadwick. First artificial nuclear transformation performed by Cockcroft and Walton. Vitamin C synthesized by Haworth and Hirst. Cloud-chamber tracks of positrons obtained by Blackett and Occhialini.
1933 Oxford Union carried a pacifist motion.	Orwell's *Down and Out in Paris and London* and Woolf's *Flush* published.	
1934	Graves's *I, Claudius* and *Claudius the God* published. Korda directed *The Private Life of Henry VIII*. John Piper painted *Rye Harbour*. Glyndebourne festival founded.	Nuclear photoelectric effect demonstrated by Chadwick and Goldhaber. Tritium produced by Oliphant and Harteck.
1935 Stanley Baldwin became prime minister of the National government. Government of India Act gave greater self-government.	T. S. Eliot's *Murder in the Cathedral* and Compton-Burnett's *A House and Its Head* published. Auden and Isherwood wrote *The Dog Beneath the Skin*. Hitchcock directed *The 39 Steps*.	Jeffreys and Bullen's *Seismological Tables* published.
1936 **Accession of Edward VIII** Edward VIII abdicated in order to marry Mrs Wallis Simpson, a divorcee.	Auden's *On The Island*, Huxley's *Eyeless in Gaza*, Thomas's *Twenty-Five Poems*, and Ayer's *Language, Truth and Logic* published.	Acetylcholine shown by Dale to be the neuromuscular transmitter in voluntary muscles. Regular television broadcasts by the BBC began.

	History	Arts and Learning	Science, Technology, and Exploration
	Accession of George VI		
1937	Neville Chamberlain became prime minister of the National government.	Orwell's *The Road to Wigan Pier* published.	Tricarboxylic acid cycle (Krebs cycle) described by Krebs. Bawden and Pirie showed the tobacco mosaic virus to contain RNA. Inheritance of histocompatibility antigens demonstrated by Gorer.
1938	Munich agreement with Hitler over Czechoslovakia.	Greene's *Brighton Rock* and Isherwood's *Goodbye to Berlin* published. Hitchcock directed *The Lady Vanishes*.	
1939	World War II began; conscription introduced.	Joyce's *Finnegans Wake* published. Sutherland painted *Entrance to a Lane*. Epstein sculpted *Adam*; Moore unveiled his *Reclining Figure*.	Sulphapyridine developed by Ewins. Extract of penicillin obtained by Florey and Chain.
1940	Winston Churchill became prime minister of a coalition government; British Expeditionary Force evacuated from Dunkirk; RAF repulsed the Luftwaffe in the Battle of Britain; rationing introduced.	Greene's *The Power and the Glory* published. Piper painted *St Mary le Port, Bristol*.	
1941	USA instituted lend-lease with the Allies; Germany invaded the Soviet Union; treaty signed between Britain and Soviet Union; *Bismarck* sunk; U-boats disrupted Allied convoys in the Atlantic; Japan attacked Pearl Harbor; USA entered World War II.	Coward's *Blithe Spirit* performed. Moore produced drawings of life in air-raid shelters. Reed directed *Kipps*.	Maiden flight of an aircraft powered by Whittle's jet engine. Partition chromatography designed by Martin and Synge.
1942	Malaya, Hong Kong, and Singapore conquered by Japan; Montgomery defeated Rommel at El Alamein; Anglo-US landing near Algiers. Beveridge Report published.	Trevelyan's *English Social History* and C. S. Lewis's *The Screwtape Letters* published.	
1943	Soviet victory at Stalingrad; Allies invaded Italy; Allies captured Bizerta and Tunis; Germans surrendered in North Africa.	Moore sculpted *Madonna and Child*.	
1944	Allies invaded Normandy (D-Day) and advanced across France; Butler's Education Act introduced universal secondary education.	T. S. Eliot's *Four Quartets* published. Olivier directed *Henry V*.	Holmes's *Principles of Physical Geology* published.
1945	Germany surrendered. Clement Attlee became prime minister. Family Allowances Act passed. Japan surrendered after the atomic bombing of Hiroshima and Nagasaki.	Orwell's *Animal Farm* and Waugh's *Brideshead Revisited* published. Lean directed *Brief Encounter* and Asquith *The Way to the Stars*. Britten's *Peter Grimes* performed.	
1946	Comprehensive social security system introduced by the National Insurance Act; National Health Service established; coal mines and Bank of England nationalized; Trade Disputes Act repealed.	Thomas's *Deaths and Entrances* and Rattigan's *The Winslow Boy* published. Britten's *The Rape of Lucretia* and Ashton's *Symphonic Variations* (music by Franck) performed.	
1947	Fuel crisis; austere economic measures introduced. India and Pakistan became independent.	Britten's *Albert Herring* performed. Priestley's *The Linden Tree* and Mackenzie's *Whisky Galore* published.	Occhialini and Powell discovered evidence for the existence of the pion. ADP and ATP synthesized by Todd.
1948	Railways, canals, and road transport nationalized. Economic recovery helped by the Marshall plan. Britain's mandate over Palestine ended.	Greene's *The Heart of the Matter* published. Lean directed *Oliver Twist* and Reed *The Fallen Idol*.	Gold and Bondi's *The Steady-State Theory of the Expanding Universe* published.
1949	Parliament Act reduced the delaying powers of the House of Lords. Gas and iron and steel nationalized. NATO established. Irish Free State became the Republic of Ireland and left the Commonwealth.	Orwell's *Nineteen Eighty-Four*, T. S. Eliot's *The Cocktail Party*, and Ryle's *The Concept of Mind* published. Reed directed *The Third Man*.	Flash photolysis developed by G. Porter and Norrish.

	History	Arts and Learning	Science, Technology, and Exploration
1950		C. P. Snow's *The Masters* and Fry's *Venus Observed* published.	Hypothalamic control of pituitary hormones demonstrated by Harris. Parasexual cycle in fungi discovered by Pontecorvo and Roper. Hoyle's *The Nature of the Universe* published. First radio map of an external galaxy plotted by R. H. Brown.
1951	Winston Churchill became prime minister. Festival of Britain took place.	Fry's *A Sleep of Prisoners* and Greene's *The End of the Affair* published. Britten's *Billy Budd* and Vaughan Williams' *The Pilgrim's Progress* performed. Royal Festival Hall built.	Tinbergen's *The Study of Instinct* published.
1952	**Accession of Elizabeth II** First test of Britain's atomic bomb.	Thomas's *Collected Poems* and Waugh's *Men at Arms* published. Agatha Christie's *The Mousetrap* opened. Beckett wrote *En attendant Godot* (trans. 1954 as *Waiting for Godot*). Epstein sculpted *Madonna and Child*.	X-ray diffraction studies of DNA by Wilkins and Franklin suggested helical structure. Cameron's *Pathology of the Cell* published. The Comet, the world's first jet airliner, went into service.
1953	Iron and steel and road transport denationalized.	Fleming's *Casino Royale* published. Churchill won the Nobel Prize for Literature.	Hillary and Tenzing climbed Everest. Watson and Crick proposed a double-helical structure for DNA. Sliding filament theory of muscle contraction proposed by H. E. Huxley and Hanson. Medawar demonstrated acquisition of immunological tolerance by embryos. Industrial melanism described by Kettlewell.
1954		Rattigan's *Separate Tables*, Golding's *Lord of The Flies*, Amis's *Lucky Jim*, and Thomas's *Under Milk Wood* published. Britten's *The Turn of The Screw* and Walton's *Troilus and Cressida* performed.	
1955	Sir Anthony Eden became prime minister.	Greene's *The Quiet American* published. Olivier directed *Richard III*. Tippett's *The Midsummer Madness* performed.	Amino-acid sequence of insulin determined by Sanger.
1956	Egypt nationalized the Suez Canal; Anglo-French force attacked Egypt, but withdrew following international condemnation. Homosexuality legalized.	Wilson's *Anglo-Saxon Attitudes* published. Osborne's *Look Back In Anger* performed. Hepworth sculpted *Orpheus*.	Structure of vitamin B_{12} discovered by Hodgkin.
1957	Harold Macmillan became prime minister. The Gold Coast was the first British colony in Africa to become independent (as Ghana).	Braine's *Room at the Top*, Osborne's *The Entertainer*, Murdoch's *The Sandcastle*, and Hoggart's *The Uses of Literacy* published. Lean directed *Bridge on the River Kwai*.	250-foot radio telescope opened at Jodrell Bank. Theory concerning formation of elements in stars published by Hoyle and others. Interferon discovered by Isaacs and Lindemann. First three-dimensional structure of a protein (myoglobin) discovered by Kendrew.
1958	Life peerages introduced.	Durrell's *Balthazar*, Pinter's *The Birthday Party*, and Behan's *The Hostage* published.	Darlington's *Evolution of Genetic Systems* published.
1959	Oil discovered in the North Sea. European Free Trade Association (EFTA) established.	Wesker's *Roots*, Spark's *Memento Mori*, and V. S. Naipaul's *Miguel Street* published.	First hovercraft built by Cockerell. Issigonis's Mini introduced.
1960		Bolt's *A Man For All Seasons*, Pinter's *The Caretaker*, Durrell's *Clea*, and Sillitoe's *The Loneliness of the Long-Distance Runner* published. Britten's *A Midsummer Night's Dream* performed.	Skull of *Homo erectus* discovered by Louis Leakey.

	History	Arts and Learning	Science, Technology, and Exploration
1961		Fry's *Curtmantle*, Greene's *A Burnt-Out Case*, Murdoch's *A Severed Head*, and Spark's *The Prime of Miss Jean Brodie* published.	Crick and Brenner showed the molecular basis of genetic code.
1962	Commonwealth immigration to the UK restricted. National Economic Development Council created.	Lean directed *Lawrence of Arabia*. Wesker's *Chips with Everything* published.	British scientific satellite (Ariel I) launched by the USA. Properties of superconductor junctions (Josephson effects) proposed by Josephson. First experimental fast-breeder reactor built at Dounreay.
1963	Sir Alec Douglas-Home became prime minister. Cuts in the rail network inaugurated by Beeching. Soviet Union, Britain, and USA signed the Nuclear Test-Ban Treaty. Britain's entry to the EEC vetoed by de Gaulle.	Le Carré's *The Spy Who Came in from the Cold* published. Hitchcock directed *The Birds*.	
1964	Harold Wilson became prime minister.	Shaffer's *The Royal Hunt of the Sun*, Golding's *The Spire*, and C. P. Snow's *Corridors of Power* published. The Beatles achieved worldwide fame.	A. L. Hodgkin's *Conduction of the Nervous Impulse* and W. D. Hamilton's *Genetical Theory of Social Behaviour* published.
1965	Unilateral declaration of independence by Southern Rhodesia; economic sanctions imposed by Britain. First Race Relations Act passed.	Pinter's *The Homecoming* published. Lean directed *Dr Zhivago*.	Hoyle and Fowler's *Nucleosynthesis in Massive Stars and Supernovae* published.
1966		Greene's *The Comedians* and Shaffer's *Black Comedy* published. Stoppard's *Rosencrantz and Guildenstern are Dead* performed.	
1967	De Gaulle again vetoed Britain's entry to the EEC.	Swinging London embodied in Antonioni's *Blow-Up*.	First pulsar discovered by Bell and Hewish.
1968	Second Race Relations Act passed; Commonwealth immigration to Britain further restricted. Abortion legalized in some circumstances. Bus transport nationalized.	Orton's *Loot* and Nichols's *Joe Egg* published.	
1969	Open University founded. Outbreak of violence ('The Troubles') in Ulster; British army deployed in Ulster. The Post Office became a public corporation.	Orton's *What the Butler Saw* published. Schlesinger directed *Midnight Cowboy*, Anderson *If*, Attenborough *Oh! What a Lovely War*, and Russell *Women in Love*.	
1970	Edward Heath became prime minister. Major oil fields located in the North Sea.	Mercer's *Flint* and Bolt's *Vivat! Vivat! Regina* published.	
1971	Internment without trial introduced in Ulster. Decimal currency introduced. Industrial Relations Act passed.	Forster's *Maurice* published.	
1972	State of emergency declared to combat a miners' strike. Direct rule of Ulster from London imposed. Local Government Act, which reorganized the counties, passed. Expelled Ugandan Asians arrived in Britain.	Lloyd Webber and Rice's *Jesus Christ Superstar* opened.	Hominid skull, thought to be the 'missing link', discovered by R. Leakey.
1973	IRA bombs exploded in central London. Britain became a member of the EEC; Value Added Tax introduced. Energy Crisis and miners' strike caused a state of emergency and three-day working week.	Greene's *The Honorary Consul* and Schumacher's *Small is Beautiful* published.	Hawking and Ellis's *Large Scale Structure of Space and Time* published. Introduction of CT body scanners developed by Hounsfield.
1974	Harold Wilson became prime minister; three-day week ended. Industrial Relations Act repealed. Bombing campaign by the IRA in England.		Particle emissions from black holes postulated by Hawking.

History	Arts and Learning	Science, Technology, and Exploration
1975	EEC membership endorsed by a referendum. Sex Discrimination Act and Equal Pay Act passed.	Final part of Powell's *A Dance to the Music of Time*, Bradbury's *The History Man*, and Lodge's *Changing Places* published.	
1976	James Callaghan became prime minister. Britain sought a loan from the International Monetary Fund. Third Race Relations Act passed.	National Theatre opened.	First commercial flights of the Anglo-French supersonic airliner Concorde.
1977	Aerospace and shipbuilding industries nationalized.		
1978		Lloyd Webber and Rice's *Evita* opened.	Edwards and Steptoe achieved the birth of the first test-tube baby.
1979	Widespread strikes caused the 'Winter of Discontent'. Margaret Thatcher became prime minister. Lancaster House agreement ended the illegal independence of Rhodesia.	Shaffer's *Amadeus* performed.	
1980	Housing Act passed. Alternative Service Book introduced.	Burgess's *Earthly Powers*, Golding's *Rites of Passage,* and Greene's *Dr Fischer of Geneva* published.	
1981	Social Democratic Party founded. Riots in Brixton, Toxteth, and elsewhere. Liberal-SDP Alliance agreed. British Nationality Act passed. British Aerospace privatized.	Lloyd Webber's *Cats* opened.	
1982	War between Britain and Argentina over the Falkland Islands. Britoil and road haulage privatized.		
1983		Attenborough's *Gandhi* won 8 Oscars.	
1984	Miners' strike began. IRA bomb attack on the cabinet in Brighton. British Telecom privatized.		Thames barrier completed.
1985	Miners' strike ended. First women deacons ordained. Anglo-Irish Agreement concluded.		Genetic fingerprinting introduced.
1986	Campaign against AIDS began. London Stock Exchange reformed. Unemployment peaked at $3\frac{1}{4}$ million. Trustee Savings Bank, bus transport, and British Gas privatized.	Kingsley Amis's *The Old Devils* published.	
1987	British Airways and British Petroleum privatized.	Martin Amis's *Einstein's Monsters* published.	
1988	Social and Liberal Democratic Party formed. British Steel privatized.	Lloyd Webber's *The Phantom of the Opera* opened. Stoppard's *Hapgood* performed. Peter Carey's *Oscar and Lucinda* and Salman Rushdie's *The Satanic Verses* published.	Hawking's *A Brief History of Time* published.